READER'S DIGEST

UNIVERSAL
DICTIONARY

UNIVERSAL DICTIONARY
A Reader's Digest book adapted
and developed from the lexical databases of the
Houghton Mifflin Company of Boston, Massachusetts,
and from the Reader's Digest GREAT ILLUSTRATED DICTIONARY

Lexical Databases, Copyright © 1986
Houghton Mifflin Company of Boston

Reader's Digest UNIVERSAL DICTIONARY
First edition, Copyright © 1987
The Reader's Digest Association Limited
11 Westferry Circus, Canary Wharf,
London E14 4HE

Reprinted with amendments 1998

Copyright © 1987
The Reader's Digest Association Far East Limited
Philippines Copyright 1987
The Reader's Digest Association Far East Limited

TYPESETTING: Lehigh ROCAPPI, Pennsauken, New Jersey
TYPESETTING AMENDMENTS: Elite Typesetting Techniques, Eastleigh, Hampshire, UK
MAP REVISIONS: Map Creation Ltd, Maidenhead, UK
PRINTING AND BINDING: Brepols Fabrieken NV, Turnhout, Belgium

Printed in Belgium
ISBN 0 276 42419 0

READER'S DIGEST
UNIVERSAL
DICTIONARY

Published by The Reader's Digest Association Limited

LONDON · NEW YORK · SYDNEY · CAPE TOWN · MONTREAL

PREFACE

Open the pages of the Reader's Digest UNIVERSAL DICTIONARY and you are entering an Aladdin's cave of language. Here are old words and new words (what does HAZCHEM mean on a warning sign?), difficult words and everyday words, soothing words and threatening words, persuading words, and entreating words – words for all purposes and all occasions.

With more than 180,000 definitions and references, this work is outstanding among single-volume dictionaries of the English language. The definitions are given in words that are understandable and free of jargon. The pronunciations are set out for the most part in ordinary letters of the alphabet, rather than symbols which not everyone may understand.

The primary purpose of a dictionary is to show how to spell a word and to explain what it means. The UNIVERSAL DICTIONARY does this and more. It contains hundreds of examples of how particular words are used. It contains special usage notes to distinguish between words that can be confused (what is the difference between *deny* and *refute*?) and to give guidance on controversial or perplexing points (can something be *almost unique*?). Lists of synonyms remind you of the resources of our language and offer a range of possibilities to choose from.

There is information, too, about the origins of words, tracing their long journey from the Classical world, from Scandinavia, France, Germany, Spain, the Arab world, Africa, India, the Caribbean – from almost every segment of our planet, for English is the great borrower among languages, enriching its own resources by fossicking among other tongues. Words like *pagoda*, *bazaar* and *naive* still have an exotic ring to them – still speak English with a foreign accent, as it were. Less obviously borrowed, but still in their day new to the language, are such words as *coach* (from Hungarian), *horde* (from Turkish), *cotton* (from Arabic), and *cockroach* (from Spanish).

As well as offering a wealth of information about words, the UNIVERSAL DICTIONARY contains a world of information about things – about people, places, and events. Here are poets and painters, statesmen and writers, sportsmen and sportswomen, key facts about the nations, cities, principal rivers and mountain ranges of the world, and more than 100 maps. In short, it is an encyclopedic dictionary.

A work of this scale and scope could not be constructed without a firm foundation. Our foundation is one of the largest and most successful dictionaries of the English-speaking world, the Reader's Digest GREAT ILLUSTRATED DICTIONARY. We have monitored the language continuously to keep the data base for that vast reference work accurate and contemporary, just as we have taken account of the questions and suggestions of readers.

THE EDITORS

A GUIDE TO THE DICTIONARY

HOW THE ENTRIES ARE STRUCTURED

All the entries in this dictionary are listed in strict alphabetical order, letter by letter. This applies equally to hyphenated entries, or entries that consist of two or more words:

> **run·ny** (rúnni) *adj.*
> **Run·ny·mede** (rúnni-meed).
> **run off** *intr.*
> **run-off** (rún-off, -awf) *n.*
> **run-of-the-mill** (rún-əv-thə-mil) *adj.*

Single letters, word parts, and abbreviations are also listed in alphabetical order:

> **a, A** (ay) *n., pl.* **a's** or *rare* **as, As** or **A's.**
> **a** (ə; *strong form* ay). Indefinite article.
> **a-¹** prefix.
> **Å** Angstrom.
> **AAA** Amateur Athletics Association.

When an entry word contains a number, it is listed (in numerical order, where necessary) before a word that has a letter in the same position:

> **u·ra·ni·um** (yoo-rayni-əm, yŏo-) *n.*
> **uranium-235** *n.*
> **uranium-238** *n.*
> **uranium dioxide** *n.*

However, when an entry begins with a number, it is listed as though it were spelled out in full:

> **two-fold** (tŏo-fōld, -fóld) *adj.* **1.** Having two components.
> **2,4,5-T** (tŏo-fór-fív-tee) *n.* **Trichlorophenoxyacetic acid** *(see).*
> **two-hand·ed** (tŏo-hándid) *adj.* **1.** Requiring the use of two hands at once.

Words that have the same spelling but a different etymology are listed separately and distinguished by raised numbers:

> **sal·low¹** (sá-lō) *adj.* **-lower, lowest.** A pale sickly hue or complexion. [Middle English *salowe*, Old English *salo*, dusky, from Germanic.]
> **sallow²** *n.* Any of several of the broader-leaved European willows . . . [Middle English *salwe*, Old English *sealh*, from Germanic.]

Proper names
Mac- and **Mc-** entries are also listed in strict alphabetical order – that is, **Mc** is not listed as if it were spelled **Mac.**

> **Mac·Adam** (mə-kaddəm), **John**
> **Mba·ba·ne** (m-baa-ba'ani)
> **McKin·ley, Mount**

Towns and cities named after saints are entered under **Saint** or **St.,** following conventional spelling. Biographies of saints appear at the name of the saint: for Saint Paul, see **Paul.**

Proper names of people and places are alphabetised up to the comma, with the surname first:

> **Salis·bur·y¹** (sáwlz-bri, -bəri). Also **New Sarum.**
> **Salisbury².** See **Harare.**
> **Salisbury, Robert Arthur**
> **Salisbury Plain**

Fictional and legendary characters are entered with the forename or title first, if this is how they are best known:

> **Don Qui·xo·te**
> **Rob·in Hood**

Fixed phrases
Fixed phrases of two or more words whose meaning cannot be worked out from the literal sense of the individual words are entered under the key word (usually the first noun). For example, **blow the gaff** will be listed under **gaff; hand in glove** is listed under **hand.** The only exceptions to this rule are phrases that function as nouns, such as **green fingers** or **cold feet.** These are listed in their alphabetical place.

Fixed verb phrases with a special meaning, such as **put down** (to rebuke) or **come across** (to meet), will either be listed under the verb or, if they can be used in several ways – as adjectives or nouns, for example – will be entered separately.

Inflections
Inflections are grammatically different forms of a word, such as the plural of a noun, the past tense of a verb, or the comparative degree of an adjective. Inflections are shown in shortened form, unless the entry has only one syllable or the first syllable is a vowel standing alone:

> **ear·ly** (érli) *adj.* **-lier, -liest.**
> **o·bey** (ō-báy) *v.* **obeyed, obeying, obeys.**

Plurals
Plural forms of nouns are shown when these are irregular (that is, the plural is not formed simply by adding -s or -es) and when more than one plural is possible:

> **ra·di·us** (ráydi-əss) *n., pl.* **-dii** (-ī) or **-uses.**
> **car·go** (kár-go) *n., pl.* **-goes** or **-gos.**

In cases where it is difficult to tell whether a word takes a singular or a plural verb, the dictionary indicates what construction to use:

> **ge·net·ics** (jə-néttiks) *n.* **1.** *Used with a singular verb.* The biology of heredity. . . . **2.** *Used with a singular or plural verb.* The genetic constitution of an individual, group, or class.

Verbs
The principal parts of all verbs, whether regular or irregular, are shown following the base form, in the order past tense, past participle (if different), present participle, 3rd person singular present tense:

> **al·ter** (awl-tər) *v.* **-tered, -tering, -ters.**

Adjectives and adverbs
The comparative and superlative forms of adjectives and adverbs are shown following the base form, in the order comparative, superlative:

> **air·y** (air-i) *adj.* **-ier, -iest.**

Alternative forms of entry words
The first form given is always the preferred one. When a word has an alternative but still acceptable written form, this is shown after the entry word in one of two positions.

When an alternative form of a word is so close to the preferred spelling that it shares the same pronunciation, it is shown immediately after the entry word and before the pronunciation:

> **me·di·e·val, me·di·ae·val** (méddi-éev'l, med-, meédi-) *adj.*

Alternative American spellings of common words are shown like this:

> **co·lour,** *U.S.* **co·lor** (kúllər) *n.*

When an alternative form of a word is different enough in spelling to require a pronunciation of its own, this is shown after the part of speech:

> **po·et·ic** (po-éttik) *adj.* Also **poet·i·cal** (-'l).

Alternative forms that need qualifying, for example because they are found in more than one variety of English, or apply only to specific senses of a word, are also shown in this way:

> **jail** (jayl) *n.* Also *chiefly British* **gaol.**
> **di•van** (di-ván) *n.* Also **di•wan** (for senses 2, 5).

Alternative forms that fall more than ten places away from their preferred form in the alphabetical list are entered as follows:

> **fetus.** Variant of **foetus.**

Definitions
When an entry word has several meanings, these are listed with the central meaning shown first:

> **fell**[1] (fel) *tr.v.* **felled, felling, fells.** **1.** To cause to fall; cut or knock down: *fell a tree; fell an opponent.* **2.** To sew or finish (a seam) with the raw edges flattened, turned under, and stitched down.

The different meanings of a word are indicated by numbers, or, in the case of closely related meanings, by lower-case letters. Any italic label, such as *Plural* or *Slang*, that comes before the first definition number of a word applies to all the numbered meanings of that word. However, if it follows a letter or number, it applies to the definition(s) covered by that letter or number:

> **ef•flo•resce** . . . **2.** *Chemistry.* **a.** To become a powder by losing water of crystallisation. **b.** To become covered with a powdery deposit, as by evaporation.
> **ear•ful** (éerfŏŏl) *n. Informal.* **1.** A quantity of information or gossip. **2.** A severe reprimand.

In the example at **effloresce**, the label *Chemistry* applies to senses **2a** and **2b**. In the example at **earful**, the label *Informal* applies to senses **1** and **2**.

> **fi•du•ci•ar•y** . . . *adj.* **1.** Of, pertaining to, or involving one who holds something in trust for another . . . **2. a.** Of, pertaining to, or designating a trustee or trusteeship. **b.** Held in trust.

GUIDANCE ON THE USE OF WORDS

Some words or uses of a word are associated with a particular context – for example a geographical area, or a special style of speech or writing. Such specialised uses are marked by a range of italic labels.

Words no longer in current usage
Archaic indicates that a word is no longer in common use and will be found only in certain contexts, such as poetry or legal texts. Occasionally a modern author might use such words to give an old-fashioned "feel" to a piece of writing. *Obsolete* indicates that there is no evidence of a word or meaning being used since 1714, other than for literary effect.

Words used in specific geographical areas
Words, spellings or meanings that occur in specific areas of the English-speaking world are labelled accordingly:

> **flat** . . . *v.* **flatted, flatting, flats.** —*intr. Australian & N.Z.* To live in a flat.

Chiefly U.S. indicates that a word or meaning is mainly limited to American usage, but can be found in other parts of the English-speaking world, such as Britain, Australia, or South Africa.
Chiefly British indicates that a word or meaning is mainly found in British usage, but can also be found in other English-speaking areas. *Regional* indicates that a word or meaning is in widespread dialectal use in more than one English-speaking country. However, where it can be limited to a particular country or region this is shown.

> **fub•sy** (fubzi) *adj.* **-sier, -siest.** *British Regional.*

Informal indicates that a word or meaning is typically used by speakers addressing one another directly on relatively familar terms, as in a casual conversation. Informal terms are often mildly humorous or euphemistic in tone, for example, *creepy-crawly* or *funny bone*.
Slang indicates a closer degree of familiarity between speakers, or between reader and author, than *Informal*. Slang words are often associated with "in-groups" within the community, such as servicemen. They also tend to be associated with disreputable topics, such as drink or crime.
Nonstandard indicates that a word or meaning is in widespread use but is regarded as incorrect by most educated speakers of English. For example, the use of *disinterested* to mean "uninterested" is labelled *Nonstandard.* Controversial uses and those on which guidance may be helpful are dealt with more fully in usage notes.
Short notes describing a particular attitude on the part of the user will be found after some words or meanings. "Used derogatorily", for example, indicates that the speaker wishes to show contempt or disapproval. "Considered offensive" indicates that a word or meaning might cause offence, even when the speaker intends none.

Usage problems
Often, a single label is not enough. Frequently, a word, a pronunciation, or a grammatical construction is not used with total consistency by all members of society. Some prefer word A to refer to an object, others prefer word B. Is it *alright* or *all right? toilet* or *loo?* For such cases, usage notes have been employed to provide guidance.
These are placed after the main entry, whenever an important issue needs to be tackled. A usage note identifies areas of controversy over the meaning, pronunciations, or grammatical use of a word, so that the reader can see what the linguistic "state of play" is, in contemporary English. And, if he wishes to use the word himself, he can make a confident decision as to its appropriateness for his purpose. The usage notes never tell a reader what he should do, or how he should react. They simply present the alternatives, and allow him to make up his own mind. It is enough to know in what circumstances a usage is preferred, or avoided – for example, in formal writing, or in very informal speech. What was frowned upon a generation ago may be widely accepted today; but the reader who understands what the norms are will at least know when he is disregarding them.

Cross-references
Cross-references, usually shown in **bold face** print, direct you to another entry word in the dictionary where further information will be found.

GUIDE TO PRONUNCIATION

The pronunciation guide in this dictionary is based on a simple respelling system that uses for the most part familiar combinations of letters of the alphabet. The only symbol taken from outside the alphabet is (ə) which conveys the sound represented by the er in matter or the a in approve. The symbols used are as follows:

a, á	as in **trap** (trap), **backhand** (bák-hand)
aa, aá	as in **calm** (kaam), **father** (faáthər)
air, áir	as in **scarce** (skairss), **parent** (paír-ənt)
ar, ár, aar, aár	as in **cart** (kart), **party** (párti), **carnation** (kaar-náysh'n), **sari** (saári)
aw, áw	as in **thought** (thawt), **daughter** (dáwtər)
awr, áwr	see **or, ór**
ay, áy	as in **face** (fayss), **native** (náytiv)
b, bb	as in **stab** (stab), **rubber** (rúbbər)
ch	as in **church** (church), **nature** (náychər)
ck	see **k**
d, dd	as in **dead** (ded), **ladder** (láddər)
e, é	as in **ten** (ten), **ready** (réddi)
ee, eé	as in **meat** (meet), **machine** (mə-sheén)
eer, eér	as in **fierce** (feerss), **serious** (seér-i-əss)
er, ér, ur	as in **term** (term), **defer** (di-fér), **turn** (turn)
ew, éw	as in **few** (few), **music** (méwzik)
ewr, éwr	as in **pure** (pewr), **curious** (kéwr-i-əss)
ə	as in **about** (ə-bówt), **cannon** (kánnən)
ər	as in **persist** (pər-síst), **celery** (sélləri)
f, ff	such as in **sofa** (sófə), **suffer** (súffər)
g, gg	as in **giggle** (gígg'l), **stag** (stag)
h	as in **hat** (hat), **ahead** (ə-héd)
i, í	as in **grid** (grid), **ticket** (tíckit)
ī, ī́	as in **price** (prīss), **mighty** (mī́ti)
īr, ī́r	as in **fire** (fīr), **tyrant** (tī́r-ənt)
j	as in **judge** (juj), **age** (ayj)
k, ck	as in **kick** (kik), **pocket** (póckit), **six** (siks), **quite** (kwīt)
l, ll	as in **fill** (fil), **colour** (kúllər)
'l	as in **needle** (néed'l), **channel** (chánn'l)
m, mm	as in **man** (man), **summer** (súmmər)
'm	as in **rhythm** (ríth'm), **blossom** (blóss'm)
n, nn	as in **fan** (fan), **honour** (ónnər)
'n	as in **sudden** (súdd'n), **cotton** (kótt'n)
ng	as in **tank** (tangk), **finger** (fing-gər)
o, ó	as in **rod** (rod), **stockpot** (stók-pot)
ō, ó́	as in **goat** (gōt), **dodo** (dó̄-dō̄)
o͞o, o͝o	as in **would** (wo͝od), **pusher** (po͝oshər)
o͞o o͞o	as in **shoe** (sho͞o), **prudent** (pro͞od'nt)
oo	used in certain positions instead of o͝o or o͞o, as in **influence** (in-floo-ənss)
oor, oór	as in **poor** (poor), **surely** (sho͝orli)
or, ór, awr, áwr	as in **north** (north), **portion** (pór-sh'n), **swarm** (swawrm), **warden** (wáwrd'n)
ow, ów	as in **stout** (stowt), **powder** (pówdər)
owr, ówr	as in **sour** (sowr), **dowry** (dówr-i)
oy, óy	as in **boy** (boy), **poison** (póyz'n)
p, pp	as in **pepper** (peppər), **crop** (krop)
r, rr	as in **red** (red), **terror** (térrər)
s, ss	as in **sauce** (sawss), **fussy** (fússi), **list** (list), **box** (boks)
sh	as in **ship** (ship), **pressure** (préshər)
t, tt	as in **state** (stayt), **totter** (tóttər)
th	as in **thick** (thik), **author** (áwthər)
th	as in **this** (thiss), **mother** (múthər)
u, ú	as in **cut** (kut), **money** (múnni)
v, vv	as in **valve** (valv), **cover** (kúvvər)
w	as in **wet** (wet), **away** (ə-wáy)
y	as in **yes** (yess), **beyond** (bi-yónd)
z, zz	as in **zoo** (zo͞o), **scissors** (sizzərz)
zh	as in **vision** (vizh'n), **pleasure** (plezhər)

All pronunciations are shown in brackets following the entry word, or any alternative form of it. If part of an entry has already appeared separately elsewhere in the dictionary, its pronunciation is not repeated. Similarly, entry words followed by raised numbers, indicating that they have the same spelling but a different origin, are assumed to have the same pronunciation, unless otherwise indicated:

> **heel**[1] (heel) n. . . . [Middle English heel, he(e)le, Old English héla, from Germanic.]
> **heel**[2] v. **heeled, heeling, heels** . . . [Probably from obsolete heeld, to incline, Middle English he(e)lden, Old English hieldan, from Germanic.]
> **heel ball** n.

Alternative pronunciations
Most words in the dictionary have only a single pronunciation shown. If more than one is given, the first is always the one that the dictionary prefers. However, any other pronunciations shown are considered correct, unless otherwise marked, and are included to show the range of pronunciations acceptable in standard English.

To save space, where alternative pronunciations are given, only that part of the word which varies from the standard form is repeated:

> **gly·cer·ine** (glíssə-rin, -reen) n.

The meaning of ‖
Unlike most British dictionaries, this one recognises that there are other acceptable standard accents of English apart from "Received Pronunciation" (upper and upper-middle class speech that has no regional characteristics). The sign ‖ introduces alternative pronunciations which do not belong to Received Pronunciation but which are considered standard in a particular region or regions.

> **laugh** (laaf ‖ laf) v.

Some of the many regional variations shown in this dictionary are:

> ō̆, ó̆r, as in the regional pronunciation of **hoarse** (hōrss) and **pork** (pōrk), when they are distinguished from **horse** (horss) and **fork** (fork).
> r, rr as in those accents, such as Scottish, which pronounce the sound (r) when it is followed by a consonant or a pause. The dictionary shows (r) in pronunciations whenever it occurs in such accents or is used in the spelling of a word; for example, **river** (rivvər) and **farmer** (fármər).
> ur, úr and er, ér stand for the same sound in "Received Pronunciation" and some other accents. However, the dictionary shows (ur) in some pronunciations and (er) in others to take account of the distinction still made by most Scottish and Irish people, who pronounce **urn** and **earn** as (urn) and (ern) respectively.

In many cases a label is included to indicate the country or region where a particular alternative pronunciation is the one in standard use:

> **to·ma·to** (tə-maátō ‖ chiefly U.S. -máytō) n., pl. **-toes.**

In a label of this kind, also indicates that pronunciation in the area mentioned is split between the various possibilities shown:

> **one** (wun ‖ Northern England also won) adj.

Foreign pronunciations
Words and names from other languages are shown with an English-style pronunciation, if they have one. Otherwise, an approximation to the foreign-language pronunciation is shown wherever possible. The symbols used are as follows:

> **hl** as in Welsh Llanelli.
> **kh** as in Scottish loch, Arabic Khaled, and German Achtung.
> **N** indicates that the preceding vowel has been nasalised, as in the French pronunciation of **restaurant** (restə-rón), **vingt-et-un** (vaNt-ay-ö̈N), and **pension** (pónss-yóN). Note that (oN) corresponds to two different vowels in French which are not usually distinguished by English speakers.
> **ñ** indicates (n) and (y) pronounced together, as in the French pronunciation of **Dordogne**.
> ō̈, ó̈ as in French bœuf, German schön.
> ṻ, ú̈ as in French lune, German Führer.

Stress
Stress in words of more than one syllable is shown by the mark over the stressed vowel symbol.

> **hap·py** (háppi) adj.

The dictionary does not show secondary stresses that occur before or after the main stress in a word. However, if a word has more than one potentially stressed syllable, these are marked:

> **sev·en·teen** (sévv'n-teén) n.

When such a word is pronounced in isolation, the main stress goes on the *last* stressed syllable. In context, however, this stress may vary because of the rhythm of the sentence. For example, in the phrases, "a seventeen-year-old girl", and "she's seventeen", the stress falls on the first and last syllables respectively.

Pronunciations for derived words are shown at the end of entries only when they have a different stress from that of the entry word:

> **ger•i•at•rics** (jérri-áttrikss ‖ je'eri-) *n.* . . . —
> **ger•i•a•tri•cian** (ə-trish'n) *n.*

Syllabification

All entry words of more than one syllable, as well as their alternative and derived forms, are divided into syllables by centred dots which show where the word can be hyphenated, and can also be used as a spelling aid. No syllable dots are shown for words that have already appeared as separate entries.

> **as•cot** (áss-kət ‖ -kot) *n. U.S.* A kind of scarf. . . .
> **Ascot**[1]. A village in Berkshire, in southern
> England. . . .

THE ORIGINS OF WORDS

The text in square brackets at the end of the entry gives the etymology, or historical derivation, of the entry word, except in the instances mentioned below. If a word is native to the language, the etymology normally traces its history back to the earlier stages of English – Old English (AD 700–1150) and Middle English (1150–1500). If the word is derived from a foreign language, the etymology usually traces it back to its earliest written form in the language of its origin:

> **ef•fi•gy** (éffiji) . . . [Middle English *effigie*, from
> Latin *effigiēs*, likeness, image, from *effingere*, to
> form, portray: *ex-*, out of + *fingere*, fashion,
> shape.]

The etymologies are intended to be easily readable and therefore no special abbreviations have been used. The languages mentioned in the derivations (Old French, Old High German, Old Norse, for example), which are frequently earlier forms of modern languages, are all defined in the body of the dictionary. So too are technical terms such as "back-formation", "unattested", "akin", and "folk etymology".

Source words are usually printed in *italics*. They are omitted altogether, however, if identical to the entry word or to the source word listed just before. Where the source word is itself an entry in the dictionary, it is usually printed in SMALL CAPITALS; this alerts the reader to the fact that there is further information at that entry (either in its definition or in its etymology):

> **frank•in•cense** . . . [Middle English *frank encens*,
> from Old French *franc encens* : *franc*, free,
> superior, FRANK + *encens*, INCENSE.]

A cross-reference in **bold** type indicates that the reader should consult the etymology of this word where more information will be found:

> **dis•crete** . . . [Middle English, from Latin
> *discrētus*, separate. See **discreet**.]

Many words are combinations of other words or word-parts. This is shown in a number of ways, as in the example of **frankincense** above, or in simpler cases.

> **pul•sar** . . . [*puls*ating *star*.]
> **mel•a•no•sis** . . . [MELAN(o)- + -OSIS.]

In the case of some words, the combination is so obvious that the etymology can be omitted entirely – for example, at **evergreen** (EVER + GREEN) or **eventuality** (EVENTUAL + ITY). (The only other class of words usually not given an etymology is that of proper nouns, including trademarks.)

Certain other words, by contrast, have uncertain origins. If evidence is lacking or highly unreliable, the etymology will be limited to the simple explanation "origin obscure", often preceded by a century date to indicate when the word first appeared in written form in English:

> **flunk** . . . [19th century : origin obscure.]

In the case of a source word which is in turn of unknown origin, the obelisk or dagger symbol † is printed after it:

> **Men•sa** . . . [Latin *mensa*†, table.]

A special effort has been made to include in the etymologies information which explains the origin and changes in meaning of certain words and phrases. Such etymologies may trace a word or phrase back to a Biblical allusion, a name of a person or place, or a historical incident, for example:

> **mav•er•ick** . . . [After Samuel A. *Maverick* (1803–
> 1870), Texas cattleman who did not brand his
> calves.]
> **quark** . . . [From a line in James Joyce's *Finnegans
> Wake*, "three quarks for Muster Mark".]

The examples numbered below are a guide to the symbols and terms used in creating the entries in UNIVERSAL DICTIONARY. They summarise and illustrate the information given on the preceding pages and act as a quick source of reference for the reader. Each example is printed in blue to make it stand out from the surrounding text and given a number that keys in to the explanatory notes alongside.

---

fan heater n. A **convector heater** (see) in which a fan blowing air over heated wires causes heat to be transferred by forced convection.

fan·kle (fáng-k'l) tr.v. **fan·kled, -kling, kles.** Scottish. To entangle. ~ n. Scottish. A muddle.

fan·light (fán-līt) n. **1.** Architecture. A half-circle window, often with sash bars arranged like the ribs of a fan. Also called "fan window". **2.** A rectangular window over a door, often serving to admit light to a passage or hall. In this sense, also U.S. "transom".

fan mail n. Letters, usually of praise, to a public figure from his devotees or admirers.

fan·on (fánnən) n. Ecclesiastical. **1.** A capelike garment formerly worn only by a pope when celebrating Solemn High Mass. **2.** Formerly, any of various embroidered cloths, such as a maniple, a piece of silk attached to a bishop's crosier, or a cover for the offerings brought by worshippers. [Middle English fanoun, from Old French fanon, from Frankish fanon (unattested).]

fan palm n. Any palm tree having leaves with a short axis and consequently fanlike. Compare **feather palm.**

fan·tail (fán-tayl) n. **1.** Any of a breed of domestic pigeons having a rounded, fan-shaped tail. **2.** Any of several birds of the genus Rhipidura, of eastern Asia and Australia, having a long, fan-shaped tail. **3.** A tail, end, or part having a fanlike shape. **4.** The stern overhang of a ship. **5.** Something shaped like a fantail; for example, a flat jet of flame in certain types of burners. —**fan·tailed** adj.

fan·tan (fán-tan) n. **1.** A Chinese betting game in which the players lay wagers on the number of beans, coins, or other counters that will remain when a hidden pile of them has been divided by four. **2.** A card game in which sevens and their equivalent are played in sequence and the first to discard all his cards is the winner. [Cantonese fan t'an, "repeated division" : fan, times, division + t'an, distribution, division.]

fan·ta·sia (fan-táy-zi-ə, fán-tə-zeé-ə ‖ fan-táy-zhə, -zhi-ə) n. Music. **1.** An improvised composition, structured according to the composer's fancy. **2.** A medley of familiar themes, with variations and interludes. [Italian, fantasy, from Latin phantasia, FANTASY.]

fan·ta·sise, fan·ta·size (fántə-sīz) v. **-sised, -sising, -sises.** —tr. To portray in the mind; imagine; picture; fancy. —intr. To indulge in fantasies.

fan·tast (fán-tast) n. A visionary; a dreamer. [German Fantast, Phantast, from Medieval Latin phantasta, from Greek phantastēs, a boaster, one who is ostentatious, from phantazein, to make visible. See **fantasy.**]

fan·tas·tic (fan-táss-tik, fən-) adj. Also **fan·tas·ti·cal** (-tik'l) (for senses 1, 2, 3, 4). **1.** Bizarre in form, conception, or appearance; strange, wondrous; fanciful. **2. a.** Unbelievable; preposterous. **b.** Existing in fancy; unreal; illusory. **3.** Unrestrainedly fanciful; extravagant: fantastic hopes. **4.** Capricious or fitful. Said of a person or mood. **5.** Informal. **a.** Wonderful or remarkable. **b.** Very large; great. ~ n. Archaic. A person who is unrestrainedly fanciful or eccentric in behaviour or appearance. [Middle English fantastik, from Old French fantastique, from Medieval Latin fantasticus, from Late Latin phantasticus, imaginary, from Greek phantastikos, able to produce the appearance of, from phantazein, to make visible. See **fantasy.**] —**fan·tas·ti·cal·i·ty** (-ti-kál-əti), **fan·tas·ti·cal·ness** n. —**fan·tas·ti·cal·ly** adv.

Synonyms: fantastic, bizarre, grotesque, fanciful, exotic.

fan·ta·sy, phan·ta·sy (fántə-si, -zi) n., pl. **-sies. 1.** The realm of vivid imagination, reverie, depiction, illusion, and the like; the natural conjurings of mental invention and association; the visionary world; make-believe. **2.** A mental image, especially a disordered and weird image; an illusion; a phantasm. **3.** A capricious or whimsical idea or notion; a conceit. **4. a.** Literary or dramatic fiction characterised by highly fanciful or supernatural elements. **b.** An example of such fiction. **5.** Psychology. An imagined event or condition fulfilling a wish. Also used adjectivally: a fantasy world. **6.** Music. A fantasia. **7.** A coin, such as a commemorative coin, that is not issued as legal tender. ~ tr.v. **fantasied, -sying, -sies.** To imagine; visualise. [Middle English fantasie, fancy, fantasy, from Old French, from Latin phantasia, from Greek, appearance, perception, faculty of imagination, from phantazein, to make visible, from phainein, to show.]

Fan·tin-La·tour (foN-taN-la-tŏŏr), **(Ignace) Henri (Joseph Théodore)** (1836 – 1904). French painter, noted for his meticulous still-life paintings of flowers and portrait groups.

fan·toc·ci·ni (fántə-cheéni ‖ faántə-) pl.n. **1.** Puppets animated by moving wires; marionettes. **2.** Plays with marionettes; puppet shows. [Italian, plural of fantoccino, diminutive of fantoccio, puppet, doll, augmentative of fante, child, servant, short for infante, from Latin infans (stem infant-), INFANT.]

FAO Food and Agricultural Organisation.

FAQ fair average quality.

far (far) adv. **farther** (fárthər) or **further** (fúrthər), **farthest** (fárthist) or **furthest** (fúrthist). **1.** To, from, or at considerable distance, time, degree, or position. **2.** To or at a specific distance, time, degree, or position: Just how far are you taking this argument? **3.** To a considerable degree; much. Used chiefly in comparisons: "It is a far, far better thing I do" (Charles Dickens). —**as far as.** To the distance, extent, or degree that: as far as I know. —**by far.** To a considerable or evident degree. —**far and away.** By a considerable margin: He's far and away the better skier. —**far and wide.** All over; everywhere. —**far be it from me.** May I never; I neither hope nor dare: Far be it from me to insult you. —**far from.** Not at all; by no means: Far from being annoyed about it, she was very glad. —**far gone. 1.** In a very poor state: much deteriorated. **2.** So advanced as to be irreversible. **3.** Drunk. Used humorously. —**from far.** From a great distance. —**go far. 1.** To be successful; accomplish a great deal: That boy will go far. **2.** To provide for much or many; last a long time. —**so far. 1.** Up to the present moment. **2.** To a limited extent: You can only go so far on 25 pence. —**so far as.** To the extent that: so far as I can tell. —**so far so good.** Used to express satisfaction with current progress, while anticipating further difficulties. ~ adj. **farther** or **further, farthest** or **furthest. 1.** At a considerable distance: a far country. **2.** More distant; opposite: the far corner. **3.** Extensive or lengthy; a far trek. **4.** Politically extreme: the far right. —See Synonyms at **distant.** [Middle English fer, Old English feor(r), far, distant, remote.]

fa·rad (fárrəd, fá-rad). n. Abbr. **F** A unit of capacitance, equal to the capacitance of a capacitor having a charge of 1 coulomb on each plate and a potential difference of 1 volt between the plates. [After Michael FARADAY.]

far·a·day (fárrə-day) n. The quantity of electricity that is equivalent to unit amount of substance of electrons and has the value 9.6487 × 10⁴ coulombs per mole. [After Michael FARADAY.]

Far·a·day (fárrə-day, -di), **Michael** (1791 – 1867). British chemist and physicist, discoverer of electromagnetism. In 1831 he discovered the connection between electricity and magnetism, producing

---

KEY

1 Entry word.

2 Words made up of **two or more elements** are entered separately.

3 Brackets enclose **pronunciation.**

4 **Alternative spelling** with same meaning and pronunciation as entry word.

5 **Main forms** of verb.

6 **Alternative form** of entry word with same meaning and slightly different spelling.

7 Square brackets enclose **etymology** giving origin and history of entry word.

8 **Synonyms list** gives words with closely related meanings.

9 **Subject labels** precede specialised meanings.

10 **Syllable dots** divide up entry word into syllables for ease of spelling and hyphenation.

11 **Cross-reference** to etymology of another entry word.

12 **Abbreviations** included within dictionary text.

13 **Comparative** form of adverb.

14 **Superlative** form of adverb.

15 **Fixed phrases** shown at key entry word.

16 **Comparative** form of adjective.

17 **Superlative** form of adjective.

18 **Biographical** entry.

Abbr.	abbreviation	**s.a.e.; F.O.**	*N.Z.*	New Zealand (English)	
adj.	adjective	**lovable; red.**	*pl.n.*	plural noun	**environs; cattle.**
adv.	adverb	**merrily; moreover.**	*prep.*	preposition	**with; in spite of.**
comb.form.	combining form	**magneto-; Euro-.**	*pron.*	pronoun	**she; myself**
conj.	conjunction	**and; inasmuch as.**	*tr.v.*	transitive verb	**hinder; repatriate.**
interj.	interjection	**Hi! Ouch!**	*U.S.*	American (English)	
intr.	intransitive verb	**emigrate; subside.**	*v.*	verb (transitive and intransitive)	**grow; advertise.**
n.	noun	**marble; lawn tennis.**			

an electric current by rotating a copper disc between the poles of a magnet. He also investigated the process of electrolysis.

fa·rad·ic (fə-ráddik, fa-) *adj.* Also **far·a·da·ic** (fárrə-dáy-ik). Of, pertaining to, or using an intermittent asymmetric alternating electric current produced by an induction coil. [After Michael FARADAY.]

far·a·di·sa·tion (fárrə-dī-záysh'n ‖ *U.S.* -di-) *n.* Also **far·a·dism** (fárrə-diz'm). Medical therapy by application of faradic currents to stimulate nerve and muscle activity.

far·a·dise, far·a·dize (fárrə-dīz) *tr.v.* **-dised, -dising, -dises.** *Medicine.* To treat (an organ or part) with faradic currents.

far·an·dole (fárrən-dōl) *n.* **1.** A spirited circle dance of Provençal derivation. **2.** The music for this dance. [French, from Provençal ⑲ *farandoulo†*.]

far·a·way (faár-ə-way) *adj.* **1.** Very distant; beyond immediate contact; remote; *faraway lands.* **2.** Bemused or abstracted; dreamy: *a* ⑳ *faraway smile.* —See Synonyms at **distant.**

farce (farss) *n.* **1.** A theatrical composition in which broad improbabilities of plot and characterisation are used for humorous effect. ㉑ **2.** Something ludicrous; an empty show; a mockery: *"childish family portraits, with their farce of sentiment and smiling lies"* (Thackeray).

~ *tr.v.* **farced, farcing, farces.** *Archaic.* **1.** To intersperse or fill out ㉒ (one's speech or a play) with jokes or witticisms. **2.** *Obsolete.* To stuff (a bird, for example) for roasting. [Middle English *farse,* stuffing, from Old French *farce,* stuffing, farce, from *farcir,* from Latin *farcīre,* to stuff, hence to pad out with interludes.]

far·ceur (faar-súr, -sōr) *n.* Also **farc·er** (fár-sər). **1.** An actor in a ㉘ farce. **2.** A writer of farces. **3.** A comic; a joker. [French, from Old ㉘ French, author or actor of farce, from *farce,* FARCE.]

far·ci (faar-seé) *adj.* Stuffed. Said of food. [French, past participle of *farcir.*]

far·ci·cal (fár-sik'l) *adj.* **1.** Pertaining to farce. **2.** Resembling farce; ㉓ ludicrous; absurd. —**far·ci·cal·i·ty** (-si-kál-əti), **far·ci·cal·ness** *n.* —**far·ci·cal·ly** *adv.*

far·cy (fár-si) *n. Veterinary Medicine.* Chronic, cutaneous **glanders** ㉙ (*see*). [Middle English *farsi(n),* from Old French *farcin,* from Late Latin *farcīmen,* farcy, from Latin, sausage, from *farcīre,* to stuff. See **farce.**]

farcy bud *n. Veterinary Medicine.* A crater-like ulcer characteristic of farcy.

fard·ed (fárdid) *adj.* Painted with cosmetics. [Past participle of obsolete *fard,* from Old French *farder,* to paint (the face) with cosmetics, from Germanic.]

far·del (fárd'l) *n. Archaic.* A pack; a load; a burden. [Middle English, ㉔ from Old French, diminutive of *farde,* package; from Vulgar Latin *fardum* (unattested), from Arabic *fardah,* load.]

fare (fair) *intr.v.* **fared, faring, fares. 1.** To get along; *How did he fare* ㉕ *with his project?* **2.** To turn out; go. Used impersonally: *How does it fare with you?* **3.** *Rare.* To be entertained with food and drink. **4.** *Archaic.* To travel; wander.

fare·well (faír-wél) *interj.* May you fare well; Godspeed; good-bye.

㉖ ~ *n.* **1.** An acknowledgment at parting; a good-bye. **2.** A leavetaking; a departure.

㉖ ~ *adj.* (faír-wel). Pertaining to parting or leave-taking: *a farewell party.* [Middle English *fare well!* : *fare,* go, fare, imperative of *faren,* to FARE + WELL.]

far-fetched (fár-fécht) *adj.* Strained or improbable in nature or relevance: *a far-fetched alibi.*

far-flung (fár-flúng) *adj.* **1.** Widely distributed; wide-ranging: *far-flung reporters.* **2.** Remote; distant.

fa·ri·na (fə-reénə) *n.* **1.** Fine meal prepared from cereal grain and various other plant products, and often used as a cooked cereal or in puddings. **2.** Starch, especially that prepared from potato flour. [Latin *farīna,* ground corn, meal, from *far,* a kind of grain.]

far·i·na·ceous (fárri-náyshəss) *adj.* **1.** Made from, rich in, or consisting of starch. **2.** Having a mealy or powdery texture. **3.** Made from or with pasta. [Late Latin *farīnāceus,* mealy : Latin *farīna,* ㉗ FARINA + -ACEOUS.]

farm (farm) *n.* **1.** A tract of agricultural land on which livestock or crops are raised. **2.** Any land or water area devoted to the raising, breeding, or production of a specified type of animal or vegetable life : *a trout farm.* **3.** A place where something is stored or treated: *a sewage farm.* **4.** In West Africa, a garden, especially a vegetable garden. **5.** *Obsolete.* **a.** The system of leasing out the rights of collecting and retaining taxes in a certain district. **b.** A district so leased. **c.** A rent, tax, or toll so collected.

~ *v.* **farmed, farming, farms.** —*tr.* **1. a.** To cultivate or produce a ㉘ crop or raise livestock on (land). **b.** To cultivate or produce (a ㉘ crop). **c.** To breed (livestock). **2.** To have the right to operate or supervise and retain profits from (a business or tax district, for example).

farm·er·gen·er·al (fármər-jénrəl, -jénnərəl) *n., pl.* **farmers-general.** One who farmed certain taxes in prerevolutionary France.

farmer's lung *n.* An occupational lung disease characterised by chronic breathlessness and caused by an allergic reaction to fungal spores in hay that has not been properly dried.

farm hand *n.* A farm labourer. ㉙

farm·house (fárm-howss) *n., pl.* **-houses** (-howziz). **1.** The farmer's dwelling on a farm. **2.** A type of large white loaf.

farm·stead (fárm-sted) *n.* **1.** A farm including its land and buildings. **2.** That part of a farm including and surrounding the farm- ㉚ house. Compare **homestead.**

㉛ **Farn·bor·ough** (fárn-bərə, -brə ‖ -burrə, -burrō). Town in Hampshire, England, site of the Royal Aircraft Establishment.

㉜ **Farn·ham** (fárnəm). Market town of Surrey, southeast England. Situated on the river Wey, it is the seat of the 12th-century Farnham Castle, once the palace of the Bishops of Winchester.

far·o (faír-ō) *n.* A card game in which the players lay bets on the top card of the dealer's pack.

Fa·ro (faár-ō). Atlantic port and southernmost town of Portugal, and capital of the Algarve.

㉝ **Faroe.** See **Faeroe Islands.**

KEY	㉕ **Example sentence** shows entry word used in context.	㉜ **Geographical** entry.	㊵ **Cross-reference** to more common term with same meaning.
⑲ **Dagger** in etymology indicates obscure origin.	㉖ **Wavy dash** introduces new part of speech.	㉝ **Cross-reference** to preferred form of geographical entry.	㊶ Label indicates the **style** or **variety** of **English** to which the entry word belongs.
⑳ **Cross-reference** to entry word with synonym list.	㉗ **Cross-reference** to further etymological information.	㉞ **Irregular plural** of entry word.	㊷ **Scientific names** of plants and animals given.
㉑ **Quotation** from well-known author shows entry word used in context.	㉘ Brackets enclose **object** of verb.	㉟ Numbers distinguish entry words with the **same spelling but different origins.**	㊸ **Alternative term** for a particular meaning of an entry word.
㉒ Label indicates meaning of entry word was current in English only **before 1714.**	㉙ **Part of speech** is indicated.	㊱ **Cross-reference** to related entry word.	㊹ Note indicates **subject** of verb.
㉓ **Derived words** made up of the entry word and a word part that is entered elsewhere.	㉚ **Cross-reference** to entry word with closely related meaning.	㊲ **Usage note** comments on problems of spelling, grammar, style or meaning.	㊺ Dashes introduce **transitive and intransitive uses of verb.**
㉔ Label indicates meaning of entry word is **no longer current.**	㉛ **Parallel vertical lines** introduce standard regional pronunciations.	㊳ **Cross-reference** to entry word with usage note.	
		㊴ **Abbreviations** of entry word.	

far-off (faár-óff, -áwf) *adj.* Remote in space or time; distant; faraway. See Synonyms at **distant.**

fa·rouche (fa-roósh, fə-) *adj. French.* **1.** Sullenly shy. **2.** Wild. [Old French *faroche,* from Medieval Latin *forasticus,* from Latin *foras,* out of doors.]

Fa·rouk I (fə-roók) (1920–65). The last king of Egypt (1936–52). The defeat of the Egyptian army in the first Arab-Israeli war (1948–49) and Farouk's extravagant lifestyle alienated the people. In July 1952, his administration was overthrown by the Free Officers led by General Muhammad Neguib and a junior officer, Gamal Abdul Nasser. Farouk was forced to abdicate.

far-out (fár-ówt) *adj. Slang.* **1.** Extremely unconventional. **2.** Excellent; marvellous.

far point *n.* The farthest point at which an object can be seen distinctly by the eye at rest.

far·ra·go (fə-raá-gō, -ráy-) *n., pl.* **-gos.** A medley; a conglomeration; a mixture: *"This is a farrago of absurdity"* (Virginia Woolf). [Latin *farrāgo,* mixed fodder for cattle, from *far* (stem *farr-*), a grain.] **—far·rag·i·nous** (-rájinəss) *adj.*

far-reach·ing (fár-reéching) *adj.* Having a wide range, influence, or effect; extending far.

far·row[1] (fárrō) *n.* **1.** A litter of pigs. **2.** The act of giving birth to a litter of pigs.
~ *v.* **farrowed, -rowing, -rows.** —*tr.* To give birth to (a litter of pigs). —*intr.* To produce a farrow. [Perhaps Middle English *faren* (plural), Old English *fearh,* little pig.]

far·row[2] (fárrō) *adj.* Not pregnant; barren. Said of a cow. [Middle English (Scottish dialect) *fer(r)ow,* from Middle Dutch *verwe-* (unattested), cow past the age of bearing.]

far-sight·ed (fár-sītid) *adj.* **1. a.** Able to see objects better from a distance than from short range; long-sighted. **b.** Hyperopic. See **hyperopia. 2.** Planning prudently for the future; foresighted. **—far·sight·ed·ly** *adv.* **—far·sight·ed·ness** *n.*

far·ther (fárthər) *adv.* **1.** To or at a more distant or more remote point in space or time. **2.** *Archaic.* In addition.
~ *adj.* **1.** Remoter; more distant. **2.** *Archaic.* Additional. [Middle English, *ferther,* variant of *further,* FURTHER.]

Usage: Does a man travel *further* than he intended or *farther?* When it is a question of literal distance or direction, *farther* is preferred in careful usage: *It's farther away than I thought. Further* is commoner, however, in the expression of figurative distance: *We are now further from the truth. Farther* in such a sentence seems somewhat old-fashioned. In superlative forms, *farther* is still used figuratively: *Of all possible interpretations, this one is farthest from the truth.* In the general sense of "additional", whether referring to time, quantity, or manner, *further* is standard: *further reasons.*

far·ther·most (fárthər-mōst) *adj.* Farthest.

far·thest (fárthist) *adj.* Most remote or distant. See Usage note at **farther.**
~ *adv.* To or at the most distant or remote point in space or time. See Usage note at **farther.** [Middle English *ferthest,* from *ferther,* FARTHER.]

far·thing (fárthing) *n. Abbr.* f. **1.** A former British bronze coin worth one quarter of an old penny. If was abolished as legal tender in 1961. **2.** The sum of one quarter of an old penny. **3.** Something of little value. [Old English *fēorthing : fēortha,* FOURTH + -ING.]

far·thin·gale (fárthing-gayl) *n.* **1.** A hoop or series of hoops extending horizontally from the waist, worn beneath a woman's skirts in the 16th and 17th centuries. **2.** The skirt worn over this device. [Variant of Old French *verdugale, vertugalle,* from Spanish *verdugado,* from *verdugo,* rod, stick, shoot of a tree, from *verde,* green, from Latin *viridis,* from *virere,* to be green.]

fa·ta mor·ga·na (faátə mawr-gaánə ‖ -gánnə) *n.* A mirage *(see).* [Italian, Morgan le Fay (the mirage was attributed to her witchcraft).]

fat cat *n. Chiefly U.S. Slang.* A wealthy and highly privileged person; especially, a heavy contributor to a political party.

fat hen *n.* A common plant, *Chenopodium album,* with clusters of small green flowers and dark green leaves covered by thick white hairs. Also *U.S.* "pigweed". See **goosefoot.**

fa·tigue (fə-teég) *n.* **1.** Physical or mental weariness or exhaustion resulting from exertion. **2.** Tiring effort or activity; labour. **3.** *Physiology.* The decreased capacity or complete inability of an organism, organ, or part to function normally because of excessive stimulation or prolonged exertion. **4.** Weakness in metal, wood, or other material resulting from prolonged stress. **5.** *Military.* Manual or menial labour, such as barracks cleaning assigned to soldiers, often as a punishment: *a weekend on fatigue.* Also called "fatigue duty". **6.** *Plural.* **a.** *Military.* Clothing worn for manual or menial work. **b.** Military-style, fashionable clothing.
~ *v.* **fatigued, -tiguing, -tigues.** —*tr.* **1.** To tire out; exhaust. **2.** To weaken (a metal, for example) by prolonged stress. —*intr.* **1.** To be or become exhausted or tired out. **2.** To become weakened as a result of stress. Used of metals and other materials. [French, from Old French, from *fatiguer,* to fatigue, from Latin *fatīgāre†.*]

fat·ten (fátt'n) *v.* **-tened, -tening, -tens.** —*tr.* **1.** To make plump or fat. Often used with *up.* **2.** To fertilise (land). **3.** To increase the amount or substance of; swell. —*intr.* To grow fat or fatter. **—fat·ten·er** *n.*

fat·tish (fáttish) *adj.* Somewhat fat; chubby. **—fat·tish·ness** *n.*

fat·ty (fátti) *adj.* **-tier, -tiest. 1. a.** Containing fat. **b.** Containing excessive amounts of fat. **2.** Characteristic of fat; especially, greasy.

11

CONTRIBUTORS

CONSULTANT EDITOR

Dr. Robert Ilson
Honorary Research Fellow,
University College London

USAGE EDITOR

Professor David Crystal
Honorary Professor of Linguistics,
University College of North Wales

PRONUNCIATION EDITOR

Professor J.C. Wells
Professor of Phonetics,
University College London

ETYMOLOGY EDITOR

Dr. Thomas Hill Long

CHIEF LEXICOGRAPHER

Faye Carney

LEXICOGRAPHERS

Edwin Carpenter Elizabeth Collingwood
Emily Driver James Harpur
John Kahn Anna Lumley
Sarah Mitchell Sarah Overton
Michael Rundell Michael Scherk

The publishers wish to thank Market House Books Ltd
for assistance in compiling scientific entries, and the
following for help in verifying these entries: Jeremy
Bartlett, Mary Bickley, David Ellesmere, Anne Heysom,
Bruce Ingram, Michael Malone, Veronique Mott,
Christopher Townshend, and Linda Young. The publishers
also wish to thank Graham Pointon of the BBC
Pronunciation Unit for his advice.

For the 1998 reprint, the publishers would also like to
thank Geographical Research Associates, Michael Janes,
Stephanie Pickering and Ken Vickery.

a, A (ay) *n., pl.* **a's** or *rare* **as, As** or **A's. 1.** The first letter of the modern English alphabet. **2.** Any of the speech sounds represented by this letter. **3.** Anything shaped like the letter **A**.

a, A, a., A. *Note:* As an abbreviation or symbol, *a* may be a small or a capital letter, with or without a full stop. Established forms or those generally preferred precede the definition. When no form is given, all four forms are in general use in that sense. **1. a.** about. **2. A.** academician; academy. **3. a.** acceleration. **4. A., A.** acre. **5. a.** acreage. **6. a.** acting. **7. a.** adjective. **8. a.** afternoon. **9. A.** alto. **10. a., A.** amateur. **11. A.** America; American. **12. A** ammeter. **13. A** ampere. **14. a.** anonymous. **15. a., A.** answer. **16. a.** anterior. **17. a, a.** are (measurement). **18. A** area. **19. a** *Physics.* atto-. **20. a.** before [Latin *ante*]. **21 A** *Physics.* Helmholtz function. **22. a.** in the year [Latin *annō*]. **23. a.** year [Latin *annus*]. **24. A** A human blood type of the ABO group. See ABO. **25.** The first in a series.

a¹ (ə; *strong form* ay). Indefinite article functioning as an adjective. **1.** Used before nouns and noun phrases that denote a single, but unspecified, person or thing: *a region; a man.* **2.** Used before plural nouns modified by *few, good many,* or *great many*: *a few donations.* **3.** One kind of: *birds of a feather.* **4.** Any: *a broken leg soon mends; not a drop to drink.* **5.** Used before mass nouns to indicate: **a.** A particular type of: *a good education.* **b.** A unit of: *a beer.* **6.** Used before nouns that indicate a state or action, to denote a single instance: *had a long wait; cut prices at a stroke.* **7.** One like: *a Casanova.* **8.** A certain: *A Mrs. Brown just called.* **9.** A type of: *Chianti is a wine.* **10.** A work of art by: *It's a Picasso.* See **an**. [Middle English *a(n)*, from Old English, *an, ān,* one.]

Usage: The general rule of thumb is that *a* is used before words beginning with a consonant, and *an* before those beginning with a vowel, but difficulties may arise over abbreviations and words beginning with *u* and *h*. In all such cases it is the *sound* of the letters that determines which form is used, so it is an *M.B.E.*, *a union, an umbrella, a hair, an heir.*

In a few cases, *a* or *an* are used almost interchangeably. When *h* is in an unstressed syllable at the beginning of a word, *an* is sometimes used (*an hotel*) but it sounds old-fashioned. In rapid speech, however, the *h* may be so reduced in strength that the use of *an* sounds quite natural, so that variation occurs between *a habitual worry* and *an habitual worry.*

a² (ə). Indefinite article functioning as a preposition. In every; to each; per: *once a month; 30 pence a pound.* [Middle English *a, o,* reduced forms of *an, on,* in, at, ON.]

a³ (ə). *Regional.* Have: *He'd a come if he could.* [Middle English *a, ha,* reduced forms of *haven, habben,* to HAVE.]

A (ay) *n., pl.* **As** or **A's. 1.** The best or highest in quality, class, or rank, as: **a.** The highest mark awarded for academic work. **b.** In the United Kingdom, a first-class road. **c.** The highest socioeconomic class. **2. a.** The sixth note in the scale of C major. **b.** The key or a scale in which A is the tonic. **c.** A written or printed note representing A. **d.** A string, key, or pipe tuned to the pitch of A. **3.** A former film rating in Britain. See **P.G.**

a-¹ *prefix.* Indicates without, not, or opposite to; for example, **amoral, acotyledon.** [Greek *a-, an-,* not.]

a-² *prefix.* Indicates: **1.** On or in; for example, **aboard, abed. 2.** In the act of; for example, *a-fishing, a-going.* **3.** In a specified state or manner; for example, **aloud, asleep. 4.** In the direction of, situated at or towards; for example, **astern.** [Middle English *a-,* Old English *a-,* from *an, on,* in, at, ON.]

Å Angstrom.

A–1 (áy-wún ‖ -wón) *adj.* **1.** *Informal.* Excellent; splendid. **2.** Having a hull and equipment in top condition. Said of a ship. [The symbol used by Lloyd's Register to describe ships in first-class condition.]

A4 *n.* A standard British paper size (210 × 297 millimetres), one of a series ranging from A0 to A7 each of which is half the previous size.

AA 1. Alcoholics Anonymous. **2.** antiaircraft. **3.** Automobile Association.

AAA Amateur Athletic Association.

Aa·chen (áʹakh'n, áʹakən). *French* **Aix-la-Cha·pelle** (éks-la-sha-pél). City in North Rhine-Westphalia, Germany, near the Dutch and Belgian borders. Charlemagne made it the northern capital of his empire, and from 936 to 1531 many Holy Roman Emperors were crowned in its cathedral. It is now an important industrial and manufacturing centre.

Aalborg. See **Ålborg.**

Aalesund. See **Ålesund.**

Aal·to (áaltō), **(Hugo Henrik) Alvar** (1898–1976). Finnish architect whose work is noted for the use of contrasting materials, such as pine boarding and rough concrete. One of his finest buildings is the Paimio Tuberculosis Sanatorium, Finland (1929–33).

A. & M. (áy-ənd-ém, -ən-) Ancient and modern.

A. & R. (áy-ənd-ár, -ən-) Artists and repertory (or repertoire).

aard·vark (árdvaark) *n.* A burrowing mammal, *Orycteropus afer,* of southern Africa, having a stocky, hairy body, large ears, a long, tubular snout, and powerful digging claws for excavating ant and termite nests. Also called "ant bear". [Obsolete Afrikaans, "earth-pig" : *aarde,* earth, from Dutch, from Middle Dutch *aerde* + *vark,* pig, from Middle Dutch *varken,* little pig; akin to FARROW (litter of pigs).]

aard·wolf (árd-woolf) *n., pl.* **-wolves** (-woolvz). A hyena-like mammal, *Proteles cristatus,* of southern and eastern Africa, having grey fur with black stripes, and feeding mainly on termites and insect larvae. [Afrikaans, "earth-wolf" : *aarde,* earth (see **aardvark**) + *wolf,* WOLF.]

Aarhus. See **Århus.**

Aar·on (áir-ən ‖ *U.S. also* árrən). The original high priest of the Hebrew nation, the elder brother of Moses. Exodus 28:1–4; 40:12–13.

Aaron's beard *n.* The **rose of Sharon** (*see*).

Aaron's rod *n.* **1.** A common Eurasian plant, *Verbascum thapsus,* with whitish downy leaves and erect clusters of yellow flowers. Also called "common mullein". See **mullein. 2.** *Architecture.* A rod-shaped moulding decorated with a design of leaves, scrolls, or a twined serpent. [After the rod of the high priest Aaron which blossomed and produced almonds (Numbers 17:8).]

Ab. Variant of **Av.**

ab-¹ *prefix.* Indicates a position or quality off, outside of, opposite to or removed from another specified position or quality; for example, **abomasum, aboral, abnormal.** [Latin, from *ab,* away from. In Latin compounds, *ab-* becomes *a-* before *m, p,* and *v; au-* before *f;* and *abs-* before *t.*]

ab-² *prefix.* Indicates a centimetre-gram-second electromagnetic unit of measurement; for example, **abcoulomb.** [Short for ABSOLUTE.]

AB A human blood type of the ABO group. See **ABO.**

a.b. A.B. able-bodied seaman.

a·ba (ə-báa) *n.* **1.** A light fabric woven from the hair of camels or goats. **2.** A loose-fitting sleeveless garment of this fabric worn by Arabs. [Arabic *'abāʾ.*]

A.B.A. Amateur Boxing Association.

ab·a·ca (ábbə-kaʹa) *n.* A Philippine plant, *Musa textilis,* related to the banana. Its leafstalks are the source of **Manila hemp** (*see*). [Spanish *abacá,* from Tagalog *abaká.*]

a·back (ə-bák) *adv.* **1.** *Nautical.* Facing into a headwind in such a way that the sails are pressed against the mast. **2.** *Archaic.* Back; backwards. [Middle English *abak,* Old English *on bæc* : ON + *bæc,* BACK.]

ab·a·cus (ábbə-kəss) *n., pl.* **-cuses** or **-ci** (-sī). **1.** A manual calculating device consisting of a frame holding parallel rods strung with movable counters. **2.** A slab on the top of the capital of a column. [Latin *abacus,* from Greek *abax* (stem *abak-*), slab, mathematical table, originally a drawing board covered with dust, from Hebrew *'ābhāq,* dust.]

Ab·a·dan (ábbə-daʹan). City in southwest Iran, on Abadan Island in the Shatt al Arab. A major oil-refining and oil-exporting centre, it was severely damaged in the 1980–88 war with Iraq.

a·baft (ə-báaft ‖ ə-báft) *adv. Nautical.* Towards the stern.
~*prep. Nautical.* Behind: *abaft the mainmast.* [Middle English *o(n) baft* : ON + *baft,* from Old English *beæftan,* behind : *be,* at, BY + *æftan,* behind.]

ab·a·lo·ne (ábbə-lóni) *n.* Any of the various large, edible marine gastropod molluscs of the genus *Haliotis,* having an ear-shaped shell with a row of holes and a colourful, pearly interior often used for making ornaments. [American Spanish *abulón†.*]

ab·amp (ábbamp) *n.* An abampere.

ab·am·pere (ab-ámpeer) *n.* A centimetre-gram-second electromagnetic unit of current, equal to the current that produces a force of two dynes per centimetre of length on each of two infinitely long straight parallel wires one centimetre apart. It is equal to ten amperes. [AB- (absolute) + AMPERE.]

a·ban·don (ə-bándən) *tr.v.* **-doned, -doning, -dons. 1.** To forsake; desert: *abandon one's child.* **2.** To leave or leave behind; withdraw from: *abandon ship.* **3.** To surrender one's claim or right to. **4.** To give up completely and irrevocably; relinquish: *abandon hope.* **5.** To end prematurely: *abandon play because of rain.* **6.** To yield (oneself) completely and without restraint, as to emotion. **7.** To relinquish (property) to an insurer in order to make a full claim in case of damage or partial loss.
~*n.* A complete surrender of inhibitions. [Middle English *abandounen,* from Old French *abandoner,* from (*metre*) *a bandon,* "(to put) in one's power" : *a,* to, at, from Latin *ad,* to + *bandon,* power, from *ban,* jurisdiction, power, from Frankish *ban* (unattested); akin to Old English *gebann,* proclamation, BANNS.] —**a·ban·don·ment** *n.*

a·ban·doned (ə-bándənd) *adj.* **1.** Forsaken; deserted. **2.** Completely uninhibited. **3.** Shameless; immoral.

a·base (ə-báyss) *tr.v.* **abased, abasing, abases.** To lower in rank, prestige, or esteem; humble; humiliate. See Synonyms at **degrade.** [Middle English *abassen,* from Old French *abaissier,* from Vulgar Latin *abbassiāre* (unattested) : *ad-,* to + *bassiāre* (unattested), to lower, from Late Latin *bassus,* low.] —**a·base·ment** *n.*

a·bash (ə-básh) *tr.v.* **abashed, abashing, abashes.** To make ashamed or uneasy; embarrass. [Middle English *abaisen, abashen,* to gape with surprise, be dumbfounded, from Anglo-French *abaiss-,* variant of Old French *e(s)bass-,* present stem of *e(s)bahir : es-,* from Latin *ex-,* out of + *baer,* to gape, from Latin *batāre* (unattested), to yawn, gape.] —**a·bash·ment** *n.*

a·bate (ə-báyt) *v.* **abated, abating, abates.** —*tr.* **1.** To reduce in amount, degree, or intensity; lessen. **2.** To deduct from an amount; subtract. **3.** *Law.* **a.** To put an end to: *abate a nuisance.* **b.** To make void: *abate a writ.* —*intr.* **1.** To subside: *the storm abated.* **2.** *Law.* To become void. —See Synonyms at **decrease.** [Middle English *abaten,* from Old French *abatre,* to beat down, from Vulgar Latin *abbattuere* (unattested) : *ad-,* at, to (used here to express completed action) + *battuere†,* to beat.]

a·bate·ment (ə-báytmənt) *n.* **1.** Diminution in degree or intensity; moderation. **2.** The amount abated; reduction. **3.** *Law.* The act of abating; elimination or annulment.

ab·a·tis (ábbətis, ábbətee) *n., pl.* **-tis** or **-tises.** A defensive barricade of felled trees [18th century : French, from *abattre,* to fell. See **abate.**]

ab·at·toir (ábbətwaar) *n.* A slaughterhouse. [19th century : French, from *abattre,* to fell. See **abate.**]

ab·ax·i·al (ab-áksi-əl, áb-) *adj.* Facing away from the axis. Said of the lower surface of leaves. Compare **adaxial.**

abba. Variant of **aba.**

Ab·ba (ábbə) *n.* **1.** In the New Testament, God. Mark 14:36. **2.** *Small* **a.** Father. Used as a title of honour in several Eastern churches. [Middle English, from Late Latin, from Greek, from Aramaic *abbā,* father.]

ab·ba·cy (ábbə-si) *n., pl.* **-cies.** The office, term, or jurisdiction of an abbot. [Middle English *abbatie,* from Late Latin *abbātia,* from *abbās* (stem *abbāt-*), ABBOT.]

Ab·bas·sids (ə-bássidz, ábbəsidz). Arabic dynasty (750–1258) that expanded the Muslim Empire to cover much of Asia Minor, North Africa, and parts of Spain. It took its name from Al-Abbas (566–652), uncle of the prophet Muhammad, and its authority was based chiefly on the religious prestige enjoyed by the prophet's descendants. —**Ab·bas·sid** *adj. & n.*

ab·ba·tial (ə-báysh'l) *adj.* Of or pertaining to an abbey, abbot, or abbess. [Middle English *abbacyal,* from Late Latin *abbātiālis,* from *abbās* (stem *abbāt-*), ABBOT.]

ab·bé (ábbay) *n., pl.* **abbés.** In France, originally the superior of an abbey, now any priest. Used especially as a title. [French, from Old French, from Late Latin *abbās,* ABBOT.]

ab·bess (ább-ess, -iss) *n., pl.* **-besses.** The female superior of a convent of nuns. [Middle English *abbesse,* from Old French, from Late Latin *abbātissa,* from *abbās* (stem *abbāt-*), ABBOT.]

Ab·be·vil·li·an (ab-vílli-ən ‖ *U.S.* ábbə-) *adj.* Of or designating the earliest Palaeolithic archaeological sites in Europe, characterised by bifacial stone hand axes. Formerly called "Chellian". [After *Abbeville,* France, site of the archaeological finds.]

ab·bey (ábbi) *n., pl.* **-beys. 1.** A monastery or convent. **2.** A church that is or once was part of an abbey. [Middle English, from Old French *abaie,* from Late Latin *abbātia,* from *abbās,* ABBOT.]

ab·bot (ábbət) *n.* The superior of a monastery. [Middle English *abbod,* Old English *abbod, abbad,* from Late Latin *abbās* (stem *abbāt-*), from Late Greek *abbās,* from Aramaic *abbā,* father, ABBA.]

abbr., abbrev. abbreviation.

ab·bre·vi·ate (ə-bréevi-ayt) *tr.v.* **-ated, -ating, -ates. 1.** To make shorter by removing or leaving out parts. **2.** To reduce (a word or phrase) to a shorter form intended to represent the full form. [Middle English *abbreviaten,* from Late Latin *abbreviāre,* to shorten : *ab-, off,* or *ad-,* towards + *brevis,* short.] —**ab·bre·vi·a·tor** (-aytər) *n.*

ab·bre·vi·a·tion (ə-bréevi-áysh'n) *n. Abbr.* **abbr., abbrev. 1.** The act or product of abbreviating. **2.** A shortened form of a word or phrase used chiefly in writing to represent the complete form; for example, *U.K.* for *United Kingdom.* Compare **contraction.**

ABC¹ (áy-bée-sée) *n.* Also *U.S.* **ABCs** (for senses 1, 2). **1.** The alphabet. **2.** The rudiments of reading and writing. **3.** An alphabetical guidebook or instruction manual.

ABC² 1. American Broadcasting Company. **2.** atomic, biological, and chemical. **3.** Australian Broadcasting Commission.

ab·cou·lomb (ab-kóolom ‖ *U.S.* ábkōō-lóm) *n.* A centimetre-gram-second electromagnetic unit of charge, equal to the charge passing in one second through any cross-section of a conductor carrying a steady current of one abampere. It is equal to ten coulombs. [AB- (absolute) + COULOMB.]

ab·di·cate (ábdi-kayt) *v.* **-cated, -cating, -cates.** —*tr.* To relinquish (power or responsibility) formally. —*intr.* To relinquish formally high office or responsibility. Used especially of a monarch. [Latin *abdicāre,* to disclaim : *ab-,* away from + *dicāre,* to proclaim.] —**ab·di·ca·ble** (-kəb'l) *adj.* —**ab·di·ca·tion** (-káysh'n) *n.* —**ab·di·ca·tor** (-kaytər) *n.*

ab·do·men (áb-də-mən, -dó-, -men, -min) *n.* **1.** The part of the body in vertebrates that lies between the thorax and the pelvis, and that encloses the viscera; the belly. **2.** In arthropods, the major posterior

part of the body. [16th century : Latin *abdōmen†,* belly.] —**ab·do·mi·nal** (-dómmin'l) *adj.* —**ab·dom·i·nal·ly** *adv.*

ab·du·cens nerve (ab-déw-senz ‖ -dóō-) *n.* Either of the sixth pair of cranial nerves supplying the lateral rectus eye muscle. [Latin *abdūcens,* "leading away", present participle of *abdūcere,* to ABDUCT.]

ab·duct (ab-dúkt, əb-) *tr.v.* **-ducted, -ducting, -ducts. 1.** To carry off (a person) by force; kidnap. **2.** *Physiology.* To draw away from the median line of a bone or muscle or from an adjacent part or limb. [Latin *abdūcere* (past participle *abdūctus*) : *ab-,* away + *dūcere,* to lead.] —**ab·duc·tion** *n.* —**ab·duc·tor** (-dúktər) *n.*

Ab·dul Rah·man (ábdōōl raákhmən), **Tunku** (1903–73). Malaysian statesman who negotiated the independence of Malaya from Britain in 1957 and helped to establish the Federation of Malaysia in 1963. He was the first prime minister of Malaya (1957–63) and of Malaysia (1963–70).

a·beam (ə-béem) *adv.* At right angles to the keel of a ship or length of an aircraft or directly opposite the middle of its side. [A- (in the direction of) + BEAM (keel).]

a·be·ce·dar·i·an (áybeesee-daír-i-ən) *n.* Also **a·be·ce·da·ry** (áybee-séedəri). **1.** One who teaches or studies the alphabet. **2.** One who is just learning; a novice.

~*adj.* Arranged alphabetically. [Middle English, from Medieval Latin *abecedārium,* alphabet, from Late Latin *abecedārius,* pertaining to the alphabet, from the first four letters.]

a·bed (ə-béd) *adv. Archaic.* In bed.

A·bed·ne·go (ábbed-neégō, ə-bédnigō). One of the three young men, the others being Meshach and Shadrach, who came unharmed out of the fiery furnace in Babylon. Daniel 3:12–30.

A·bel (áyb'l). The second son of Adam and Eve, slain by his elder brother, Cain. Genesis 4:2. [Middle English, from Late Latin, from Greek, from Hebrew *Hebhel,* akin to Assyrian *ablu,* son.]

Ab·e·lard (ábbilard, *French* a-be-lár), **Peter,** *French* Pierre Abélard (1079–1142). French philosopher and theologian whose application of the principles of ancient Greek logic to the doctrines of the medieval Catholic Church led him into great controversy and charges of heresy. In Paris he secretly married one of his pupils, Héloïse, after she bore him a child. Héloïse's family had Abelard castrated; she became a nun and he became a monk.

a·bele (ə-béel, áyb'l) *n.* A tree, the **white poplar** *(see).* [16th century: Dutch *abeel,* from Old French *abel, aubel,* from Medieval Latin *albellus,* diminutive of Latin *albus,* white.]

a·be·li·a (ə-béeli-ə) *n.* Any of various shrubs of the genus *Abelia,* having tubular red, pink, or white flowers and widely grown as garden ornamentals.

A·be·li·an (ə-béeli-ən). *adj. Algebra.* **Commutative 2** *(see).* [After Niels Henrik *Abel* (1802–29), Norwegian mathematician.]

a·bel·mosk (áyb'lmosk) *n.* A hairy plant, *Hibiscus abelmoschus,* of tropical Asia, having large yellow flowers and musk-scented seeds that are used in perfumery. Also called "musk mallow". [New Latin *Abelmoschus,* from Arabic *ḥabb-al-musk* (vulgar pronunciation *ḥabb-el-mosk*), "grain of musk" : *ḥabb,* grain + *mosk,* MUSK.]

Ab·er·deen (ábbər-déen). City and port in northeast Scotland, on the North Sea coast at the mouth of the river Dee. Became a new Unitary Authority area in 1996. Granted a royal charter in 1176, it has a 14th-century cathedral and a university formed by the amalgamation in 1860 of its two ancient colleges, King's College (founded 1494) and Marischal College (founded 1593). It is known as the "Granite City" as the local stone is used in many of its buildings. Aberdeen is the third largest fishing port in Britain and the main town servicing the North Sea oil industry.

Aberdeen, George Hamilton-Gordon, 4th Earl (1784–1860). British statesman. He was Foreign Secretary under Wellington (1828–30) and Peel (1841–46) and became prime minister in 1852. He was held responsible for the disasters and mismanagement of the Crimean War and resigned in 1855.

Aberdeen An·gus (áng-gəss) *n.* Any of a breed of black, hornless beef cattle that originated in Scotland.

Ab·er·deen·shire (ábbər-déen-shər, -sheer; *Scottish* -shír). Former county of northeast Scotland. Part of Grampian Region from 1975, it became a new Unitary Authority area in 1996.

Aberdeen terrier *n.* The **Scottish terrier** *(see).*

Ab·er·do·ni·an (ábbər-dóni-ən) *n.* A native or inhabitant of Aberdeen. —**Ab·er·do·ni·an** *adj.*

Ab·er·fan (ábbər-ván). Coal-mining village in Merthyr Tydfil, South Wales, on the river Taff. In 1966 mining waste (slurry) from a giant tip overlooking the village engulfed part of it, killing 144 people including 116 schoolchildren.

ab·er·rant (ab-érrənt, əb-) *adj.* **1.** Deviating from the proper or expected course. **2.** Deviating from what is normal; untrue to type. —**ab·er·rance, ab·er·ran·cy** *n.*

ab·er·ra·tion (ábbə-ráysh'n) *n.* **1.** A deviation from the proper or expected course. **2.** A departure from the normal or typical. **3.** An abnormal alteration in one's mental state; a lapse in mental capacities. **4.** *Optics.* **a.** A defect of focus, such as blurring or distortion, in an image. **b.** A physical defect in an optical element, as in a mirror or lens, that causes such an imperfection. See **chromatic aberration, spherical aberration, astigmatism, coma. 5.** The apparent displacement of the position of a celestial body in the direction of motion of an observer on Earth, caused by the motion of the Earth. [Latin *aberrātiō,* diversion, from *aberrāre,* to go astray : *ab-,* from + *errāre,* to stray.]

Ab·e·ryst·wyth (ábbə-rist-with, *Welsh* -rúst-). Town in Ceredigion,

West Wales, on Cardigan Bay. It is a seaside resort, port, and university town, and contains the National Library of Wales.

a·bet (ə-bét) *tr.v.* **abetted, abetting, abets.** To encourage and assist; especially, to incite to a criminal act. [Middle English *abetten,* from Old French *abeter,* to entice : *a-,* from Latin *ad-,* to + *beter,* to bait, from Germanic).] **—a·bet·ment** *n.* **—a·bet·ter, a·bet·tor** *n.*

ab ex·tra (áb ékstrə) *adv. Latin.* From without.

a·bey·ance (ə-báy-ənss) *n.* **1.** The condition of being temporarily set aside or suspended. **2.** *Law.* A condition of undetermined rights or ownership, as of an estate that has not yet been assigned. [Anglo-French *abeiance,* variant of Old French *abeance,* desire, from *abaer,* "to gape at", yearn for : *a-,* from Latin *ad-,* to + *baer,* to gape (see **abash**).] **—a·bey·ant** *adj.*

ab·far·ad (ab-fárrəd, -fárrad ‖ *U.S. also* -fáarəd) *n.* A centimetre-gram-second electromagnetic unit of capacitance, equal to the capacitance of a capacitor having a charge of one abcoulomb and a potential difference of one abvolt. It is equal to 10^9 farads. [AB-(absolute) + FARAD.]

ab·hen·ry (ab-hénri) *n., pl.* **-ries.** A centimetre-gram-second electromagnetic unit of inductance, equal to the inductance resulting from a current variation of one abampere per second that produces an induced electromotive force of one abvolt. It is equal to 10^{-9} henry. [AB- (absolute) + HENRY.]

ab·hor (əb-hór, ə-bór) *tr.v.* **-horred, -horring, -hors.** **1.** To regard with horror or loathing; abominate. **2.** To reject vehemently; shun. [Middle English *abhorren,* from Latin *abhorrēre,* to shrink from : *ab-,* from + *horrēre,* to shudder, bristle.] **—ab·hor·rence** (-hórrənss ‖ *U.S. also* -háwrənss) *n.* **—ab·hor·rer** *n.*

ab·hor·rent (əb-hórrənt, ə-bórrənt ‖ *U.S. also* -háwrənt) *adj.* **1.** Disgusting; loathsome; repellent. **2.** In opposition; completely contrary: *Carelessness was abhorrent to his nature.* **—ab·hor·rent·ly** *adv.*

A·bib (áybib, áabib ‖ *U.S.* aavéev) *n.* In the ancient Hebrew calendar, an earlier name for the month of **Nisan** *(see).* [Hebrew *'ābhībh,* "(month of) fresh barley", "spring".]

a·bide (ə-bíd) *v.* **abode** (ə-bód) *or* **abided, abiding, abides.** *—tr.* **1.** To put up with; tolerate: *can't abide hypocrisy.* **2.** To withstand; persevere under: *abide the horrors of war.* **3.** *Archaic.* To wait patiently for: *"I will abide the coming of my Lord"* (Tennyson). *—intr.* **1.** To remain in one place or state. **2.** To continue; endure. **3.** *Archaic.* To dwell or sojourn. **—abide by.** **1.** To conform to; comply with. **2.** To accept the consequences of; rest satisfied with. [Middle English *abiden,* Old English *ābīdan :* *a-* (intensive) + *bīdan,* to remain, await.] **—a·bid·ance** *n.* **—a·bid·er** *n.*

a·bid·ing (ə-bíding) *adj.* Lasting; enduring: *an abiding devotion.* **—a·bi·ding·ly** *adv.*

Ab·i·djan (ábbi-jáan). City of the Ivory Coast, on the Gulf of Guinea. It lies on an enclosed lagoon and, since the completion of the Vridi Canal in 1950 linking Abidjan with the sea, is now the country's leading port and industrial centre.

ab·i·et·ic acid (ábbi-éttik) *n.* A yellowish resinous powder, $C_{19}H_{29}COOH$, occurring naturally in rosin and used in lacquers, varnishes, and soaps. [19th century : from Latin *abiēs†* (stem *abiēt-*), fir (the acid occurs in its resin).]

Ab·i·gail (ábbigayl) *n. Archaic.* A lady's maid. [From the name of a serving maid in *The Scornful Lady* (*c.*1613), play by Beaumont and Fletcher.]

Ab·i·gail (ábbigayl). The wife of David. I Samuel 25:14–44. [Hebrew *Abhīgayil,* "my father is joy".]

a·bil·i·ty (ə-billəti) *n., pl.* **-ties.** **1.** The quality of being able to do something; the fact of having the requisite means, skill, strength, mental capacity, or legal power. **2.** A natural or acquired skill or talent. [Middle English *abilite,* from Old French *habilite,* from Latin *habilitās,* from *habilis,* ABLE.]

Synonyms: ability, capacity, talent, skill, competence, aptitude.

–ability, –ibility *n. suffix.* Indicates: **1.** Ability to undergo the specified action or process: for example, **wearability. 2.** Possession of a specified quality; for example, **variability.** [-ABLE + -ITY or -IBLE + -ITY.]

ab in·i·ti·o (áb iníshi-ō) *adv. Latin.* From the beginning.

ab in·tra (áb íntrə) *adv. Latin.* From within.

a·bi·o·gen·e·sis (áy-bī-ō-jénnəsis ‖ ábbi-ō-) *n.* The hypothetical development of living organisms from nonliving matter as is assumed to have occurred in the origin of life on earth. Also called "autogenesis". See **primordial soup, spontaneous generation.** [A- (without) + BIO- + -GENESIS.] **—a·bi·o·ge·net·ic** (-ji-néttik) *adj.*

a·bi·ot·ic (áy-bī-óttik) *adj.* Devoid of life; inanimate. Said especially of environments or environmental factors.

ab·ject (ábjekt ‖ *U.S. also* ab-jékt) *adj.* **1.** Of the most contemptible kind: *an abject liar.* **2.** Of the most miserable kind; wretched: *abject poverty.* **3.** Humble and often ingratiating in manner. **—See Synonyms at mean** (base). [Middle English, "rejected", from Latin *abjectus,* cast away, from the past participle of *abjicere,* to cast away : *ab-,* away from + *jacere,* to throw.] **—ab·jec·tion** (ab-jéksh'n) *n.* **—ab·ject·ly** *adv.*

ab·jure (əb-joor, ab-) *tr.v.* **-jured, -juring, -jures.** **1. a.** To repudiate or recant solemnly. **b.** To renounce under oath; forswear. **2.** To abstain from; give up. [Middle English *abjuren,* from Old French *abjurer,* from Latin *abjūrāre :* *ab-,* away + *jūrāre,* to swear.] **—ab·ju·ra·tion** (ábjoor-áysh'n) *n.* **—ab·jur·er** *n.*

abl. ablative.

ab·late (áb-láyt, ab-) *tr.v.* **-lated, -lating, -lates.** To remove by ablation. [Back-formation from ABLATION.]

ab·la·tion (ab-láysh'n, əb-) *n.* **1.** Surgical excision or amputation of any part of the body. **2.** The totality of erosive processes by which a glacier or ice sheet is reduced. **3.** *Aerospace.* The dissipation of heat generated by atmospheric friction, especially in the atmospheric re-entry of a spacecraft or missile, by means of a melting **heat shield** *(see).* [Late Latin *ablātiō,* from *ablātus,* removed (past participle of *auferre,* to carry away) : *ab-,* away from + *-lātus,* carried.]

ab·la·tive (áblətiv) *n.* **1.** The grammatical case in certain Indo-European languages, such as Latin, that denotes separation, direction away from, and sometimes manner or agency. **2.** A form or construction in this case. [Middle English, from Old French *ablatif,* from Latin *ablātīvus,* "expressing removal", from *ablātus,* removed. See **ablation.**] **—ab·la·tive** *adj.*

ablative absolute *n.* In Latin grammar, an adverbial phrase syntactically independent from the rest of the sentence and containing two main constituents both in the ablative case. It is usually used to express cause, circumstance, or time; for example, in the sentence *Regibus expulsis, leges respublica condit (The kings having been expelled, the republic sets up laws),* the phrase *Regibus expulsis* is the ablative absolute.

ab·la·tor (ab-láytər) *n.* A **heat shield** *(see).* [ABLAT(ION) + -OR.]

ab·laut (áblowt) *n. Linguistics.* A patterned change in root vowels of verb forms, characteristic of Indo-European languages, indicating alteration of tense, aspect, or function; for example, *ring, rang, rung.* Also called "gradation", "vowel gradation". Compare **umlaut.** [German *Ablaut,* "off sound" : *ab,* off, away from, from Old High German *aba* + *Laut,* sound, from Middle High German *lūt,* from Old High German *hlūt.*]

a·blaze (ə-bláyz) *adj.* **1.** On fire. **2.** Radiant; aglow.

a·ble (áyb'l) *adj.* **abler, ablest. 1.** Having sufficient ability or resources. **2. a.** Capable; competent: *an able administrator.* **b.** Talented; gifted. **3.** Legally qualified: *able to inherit.* [Middle English, from Old French, from Latin *habilis,* manageable, apt, expert, from *habēre,* to hold, handle.]

–able, –ible *adj. suffix.* Indicates: **1.** Able to undergo the specified action; for example, **debatable, drinkable, collapsible. 2.** Having or sharing a specified quality; for example, **knowledgeable, comfortable, fashionable. 3.** Causing or deserving; for example, **honourable, objectionable.** [Middle English, from Old French, from Latin *-ābilis, -ībilis,* forms (with different vowel stems) of the passive adjectival suffix *-bilis.*]

a·ble-bod·ied (áyb'l-bóddid) *adj.* Physically strong and healthy.

able-bodied seaman *n. Abbr.* **a.b., A.B.** A merchant seaman certified for all seaman's duties. Also called "able seaman".

a·bloom (ə-bloom) *adj.* In bloom; flowering.

ab·lu·tion (ə-bloosh'n) *n.* **1.** A washing or cleansing of the body, especially as part of a religious ceremony. **2.** The liquid used in such cleansing. **3.** *Plural.* The act of washing oneself. Usually used humorously. **4.** *Plural. British.* Communal washing facilities and latrines, as in a military camp. [Middle English, from Latin *ablūtiō,* from *abluere,* to wash away : *ab-,* away from + *luere,* to wash, from *lavere,* variant of *lavāre,* to wash.] **—ab·lu·tion·ar·y** *adj.*

a·bly (áybli) *adv.* In an able manner; capably.

ABM antiballistic missile.

ab·ne·gate (ábnigayt) *tr.v.* **-gated, -gating, -gates.** To deny to oneself; give up; renounce. [Latin *abnegāre,* to refuse, reject : *ab-,* away from + *negāre,* to deny.]

ab·ne·ga·tion (ábni-gáysh'n) *n.* **1.** Renunciation. **2.** Self-denial or self-sacrifice; self-abnegation.

ab·nor·mal (ab-nórm'l, áb-, əb-) *adj.* **1.** Not normal; untypical; irregular. **2.** Peculiar; deviant. [Latin *abnormis,* departing from normal : *ab-,* away from + *norma,* rule, norm.] **—ab·nor·mal·ly** *adv.*

ab·nor·mal·i·ty (áb-nawr-mál-əti) *n., pl.* **-ties. 1.** The state or condition of not being normal. **2.** An abnormal phenomenon; an irregularity. **3.** A physical defect or deformity.

abnormal psychology *n.* The study of behavioural abnormalities and mental disorders in human beings.

A·bo (ábbō) *n., pl.* **Abos.** *Australian Informal.* An Australian Aborigine. Usually considered offensive. **—A·bo** *adj.*

Å·bo. See Turku.

ABO *n.* A classification of human blood types according to their compatibility in transfusion, which depends on the presence or absence of either of two antigens, A and B. Blood types are classified as A, B, AB, or O.

a·board (ə-bórd ‖ -bórd) *adv.* On or onto a ship, train, aeroplane, or other passenger vehicle.

~prep. On, in, onto, or into (a ship, train, or the like). [Middle English : A- (on) + BOARD.]

a·bode (ə-bód). Past tense and past participle of **abide.**

~n. A dwelling place or home. [Middle English *abod,* from *abiden,* ABIDE.]

ab·ohm (ab-óm) *n.* A centimetre-gram-second electromagnetic unit of resistance equal to 10^{-9} ohm. [AB- (absolute) + OHM.]

a·bol·ish (ə-bóllish) *tr.v.* **-ished, -ishing, -ishes.** To do away with (an institution or practice, for example); put an end to. [Middle English *abolysshen,* from Old French *abolire* (present stem *aboliss-*), from Latin *abolēre,* to destroy.] **—a·bol·ish·a·ble** *adj.* **—a·bol·ish·er** *n.* **—a·bol·ish·ment** *n.*

Synonyms: abolish, extirpate, eradicate.

a·bo·li·tion (ábbə-lísh'n) *n.* **1.** An act of abolishing or state of being abolished; annulment; extinction. **2.** *Sometimes capital* **A.** The ending of slavery and the slave trade in British territories, and later in the United States. [Latin *abolitiō*, from *abolitus*, past participle of *abolēre*, ABOLISH.] —**ab·o·li·tion·ar·y** *adj.*

ab·o·li·tion·ist (ábbə-lísh'n-ist) *n.* **1.** One who wishes to abolish a law, institution, or the like. **2.a.** *Sometimes capital* **A.** A supporter of the abolition of slavery in Britain and the United States. **b.** A supporter of the abolition of the transportation of convicts to Australia. —**ab·o·li·tion·ism** *n.*

ab·o·ma·sum (ábbō-máys'm, ábbə-) *n., pl.* **-sa** (-sə). The fourth division of the stomach in ruminant animals, in which true digestion takes place. [New Latin : AB- (away from) + OMASUM.] —**ab·o·ma·sal** *adj.*

A-bomb (áy-bom) *n.* A **nuclear bomb** (see).

a·bom·i·na·ble (ə-bómminəb'l) *adj.* **1.** Detestable; loathsome. **2.** *Informal.* **a.** Thoroughly unpleasant. **b.** Of extremely poor quality. [Middle English, from Old French, from Latin *abōminābilis*, from *abōminārī*, to ABOMINATE.] —**a·bom·i·na·bly** *adv.*

abominable snowman *n.* A legendary manlike animal reportedly inhabiting the high Himalayas. Also called "yeti". [Translation of Tibetan *metohkangmi* : *metoh*, abominable + *kangmi*, snowman.]

a·bom·i·nate (ə-bómminayt) *tr.v.* **-nated, -nating, -nates.** To detest; abhor. [Latin *abōminārī*, "to shun as a bad omen" : *ab-*, away from + *ōmen* (stem *ōmin-*), omen.] —**a·bom·i·na·tor** (-naytər) *n.*

a·bom·i·na·tion (ə-bómmi-náysh'n) *n.* **1.** Something or someone that causes great revulsion or abhorrence. **2.** An intense dislike or loathing for someone or something.

ab·o·ral (ab-áwrəl || -óral) *adj. Biology.* Opposite to or away from the mouth. [AB- (away from) + ORAL.] —**ab·o·ral·ly** *adv.*

ab·o·rig·i·nal (ábbə-ríjin'l) *adj.* **1.** Native; indigenous. **2.** Of or pertaining to aborigines.

~*n.* **1.** An aborigine. **2.** *Capital* **A.** An Australian Aborigine. —**ab·o·rig·i·nal·ly** *adv.*

ab·o·rig·i·ne (ábbə-ríjini) *n.* **1.** An indigenous inhabitant of a region. **2.** *Capital* **A.** A member of the indigenous dark-skinned people of Australia. **3.** *Capital* **A.** Any of the languages of this people. **4.** *Plural.* The plants and animals native to a geographical area. [Latin *Aborīginēs*, pre-Roman tribes inhabiting Latium, probably an alteration of some tribal name, reshaped by folk etymology as if derived from *ab orīgine*, "from the beginning".]

a·born·ing (ə-bór-ning || -bŏr-) *adv. U.S.* While coming into being or getting under way: *the project almost died aborning.* [A- (in the act of) + BORN + -ING.]

a·bort (ə-bórt) *v.* **aborted, aborting, aborts.** —*intr.* **1. a.** To miscarry. Used of a pregnant mammal. **b.** To be expelled prematurely from the womb. Used of a foetus. **2.** To cease organic growth before full development or maturation. **3.** To end prematurely; especially, to terminate an operation involving a missile or a space vehicle before completion. —*tr.* **1. a.** To cause the abortion of (a foetus). **b.** To terminate prematurely the pregnancy of. **2. a.** To interfere with the development of. **b.** To abandon or conclude prematurely. [Latin *abortāre*, frequentative of *aborīrī* (past participle *abortus*), to die, disappear, miscarry : *ab*, off, away, hence, badly + *orīrī*, to arise, appear, be born.]

a·bor·ti·cide *n.* **1.** The destruction of a foetus within the womb. **2.** An abortifacient drug. [ABORT + -CIDE.]

a·bor·ti·fa·cient (ə-bórti-fáysh'nt) *adj.* Causing abortion.

~*n.* Anything used to induce abortion. [ABORTION + -FACIENT.]

a·bor·tion (ə-bórsh'n) *n.* **1.** The premature expulsion of a foetus from the womb, which may be either spontaneous (a miscarriage) or induced. Compare **stillbirth.** **2.** An operation to remove a foetus from the womb. **3.** Cessation of normal growth, especially of an organ, prior to full development or maturation. **4.** An aborted organism. **5.** Anything malformed or incompletely developed. **6.** An action or plan that has not been carried to a successful conclusion.

a·bor·tion·ist (ə-bórsh'n-ist) *n.* One who performs abortions, especially illegal abortions.

a·bor·tive (ə-bórtiv) *adj.* **1.** Failing to accomplish an intended objective; fruitless. **2.** Partially or imperfectly developed. **3.** Causing abortion; abortifacient. —**a·bor·tive·ly** *adv.*

aboulia. Variant of **abulia.**

a·bound (ə-bównd || *West Indies also* ə-bungd) *intr.v.* **abounded, abounding, abounds. 1.** To be present in great numbers or large amount. **2.** To have a large number or amount; teem. Used with *in* or *with.* [Middle English *abounden*, from Old French *abonder*, from Latin *abundāre*, to overflow : *ab-*, away from + *undāre*, to flow, from *unda*, wave.]

a·bout (ə-bówt) *adv. Abbr.* **a. 1.** Approximately; roughly. **2.** Nearly; almost. **3.** To a reversed position or direction: *She turned about and retraced her steps.* **4.** In no particular direction; with no particular destination: *wandering about.* **5. a.** All around; on every side. **b.** In various places; here and there: *scattered about; lying about.* **6.** In the area or vicinity. **7.** In succession; one after another: *Turn about is fair play.* **8.** Prevailing; current: *There's a lot of flu about.* **9.** *Informal.* In an extreme degree. Used ironically as an understatement: *About time.* **10.** Into existence; so as to occur: *How did it come about? bring it about.*

~*prep.* **1.** On all sides of; surrounding. **2.** In the vicinity of; around: *somewhere about 110°.* **3.** In and around; here and there in; through. **4.** Almost the same as; close to; near. **5.** In reference to; relating to. **6.** On, attached to, or in the possession or character of: *He has his wits about him; an air of caution about her.* **7.** On the verge of doing something. Used with an infinitive: *The chorus is about to sing.* **8.** Willing or prepared. Used in the negative and with an infinitive to indicate determination: *I'm not about to give up now.*

9. Involved with or engaged in: *going about his work cheerfully; make me a cup while you're about it.*

~*adj.* Out of bed, after sleep or illness: *up and about.* [Middle English *about*, Old English *abūtan, onbūtan* : ON + *būtan,* outside.]

Usage: In the senses concerned with movement and location, *around/round,* and *about* are often interchangeable, but British English prefers *about* and American English *around. Round about* is used informally for extra indefiniteness of either quantity or location (*We stopped for a drink round about one/Birmingham*). See also **around.**

a·bout-turn (ə-bówt-túrn) *n.* **1.** A reversal of orientation, accomplished by a pivotal movement from a stationary position; a movement resulting in the body facing the opposite direction. Also *chiefly U.S.* "about-face". **2.** A total change of attitude or standpoint. Also called "about-face".

~*intr.v.* **about-turned, -turning, -turns.** Also *U.S.* **about-face. 1.** To make an about-turn. Used especially to give a military command. **2.** To reverse direction.

a·bove (ə-búv) *adv.* **1.** Overhead; on high: *the clouds above.* **2.** In heaven; heavenwards. **3.** Upstairs: *a table in the dining room above.* **4.** In a higher place. **5.** On the top or upper side. **6.** Beyond a given amount or figure: *designed for children of 12 and above.* **7.** Upstream: *the weir above.* **8.** In an earlier part of the text: *figures quoted above.* Also used in combination: *the above-mentioned figures.* **9.** In or to a higher rank or position: *promoted to the grade above.*

~*prep.* **1.** Over; higher than: *situated above the treeline.* **2. a.** Superior to; of more importance than: *placed his country above his family ties.* **b.** Of higher rank or status than. **3. a.** Beyond the level or reach of: *above suspicion.* **b.** Beyond the grasp or understanding of: *The political discussion was above me.* **4.** In preference to. **5.** Too honourable to bend to: *above petty misdeeds.* **6.** Greater than, in weight, price, age, temperature, or pitch: *above the age of 65; a shot heard above the music.* **7.** North of: *Limerick is directly above Cork.* **8.** Upstream from. —**above all.** Most of all. —**above and beyond.** In addition to. —**above (oneself).** Conceited: *He's been getting above himself lately.*

~*n.* Something that is above: *as the above should make clear.*

~*adj.* Appearing earlier in the same text: *flaws in the above interpretation.* [Middle English *aboven, abuven,* Old English *abufan* : A- (on) + *bufan,* above.]

Usage: *The above, cf. above,* and other such uses, are common in business and legal writing, but they are often considered awkward or stilted and are usually avoided in popular writing.

a·bove-board (ə-búv-bórd || -bŏrd) *adv.* Also **above board.** Without deceit or trickery.

~*adj.* Also **a·bove·board.** Honest; not concealed. [Originally a gambling term, "above the gambling table, not changing cards under the table".]

ab o·vo (áb ŏvō) *adv. Latin.* From the start. [Literally, "from the egg".]

abp., Abp. archbishop.

abr. abridged; abridgment.

ab·ra·ca·dab·ra (ábbrəkə-dábbrə) *n.* **1.** A word held to possess supernatural powers to ward off disease or disaster. **2.** A formula spoken by conjurors when performing a trick. **3.** Jargon; mumbo jumbo; gibberish. [Late Latin, from Late Greek *abrasadabra,* a magic word used by a Gnostic sect, probably derived from *Abraxas,* name of a Gnostic deity.]

a·brade (ə-bráyd) *tr.v.* **abraded, abrading, abrades. 1.** To rub off or wear away by or as if by friction. **2.** *Geology.* To wear away as a result of corrosion. [Latin *abrādere,* to scrape off : *ab-,* off + *rādere,* to scrape.] —**a·bra·dant** (-'nt) *adj. & n.* —**a·brad·er** *n.*

A·bra·ham (áyb-rə-ham, -həm, áab-). The first patriarch and progenitor of the Hebrew people; father of Isaac. Genesis 11–25. [Middle English, from Late Latin, from Late Greek, from Hebrew *Abhrāhām,* "father of a multitude", altered from *Abram,* "high father".]

Abraham, Plains of. A plateau near Quebec, east Canada, where the British under General Wolfe defeated the French under General Montcalm in 1759 and effectively won Canada for Britain.

a·bran·chi·ate (ə-bráng-ki-ayt, ay-, -ət, -it) *adj. Zoology.* Having no gills. [A- (without) + Greek *brankhia,* gills. See **branchia.**]

ab·ra·sion (ə-bráyzh'n) *n.* **1.** The process of wearing down or rubbing away by means of friction. **2.** A scraped or worn area; a graze. [Medieval Latin *abrāsiō,* from Latin *abrādere,* to ABRADE.]

a·bra·sive (ə-bráy-siv || -ziv) *adj.* **1.** Causing abrasion; harsh; rough. **2.** Harsh in manner; brusque.

~*n.* A substance that abrades, especially emery, pumice, or similar material, used to clean or smooth surfaces..

ab·re·act (áb-ri-ákt) *tr.v.* **-acted, -acting, -acts.** *Psychology.* To release repressed emotions by abreaction. [Translation of German *abreagieren* : AB- (away from) + *reagieren,* to react.]

ab·re·ac·tion (áb-ri-áksh'n) *n. Psychology.* The release of the tension resulting from conflict or from repressed emotion, achieved either unconsciously or through conscious examination and the acting out, in imagination, words, or action, of the situation causing the conflict.

a·breast (ə-brést) *adv.* **1.** Side by side. **2.** Up to date; aware: *abreast of the news.* [Middle English *abrest* : A- (on) + BREAST.]

a·bridge (ə-brij) *tr.v.* **abridged, abridging, abridges. 1.** To reduce the length of (a written text); condense. **2.** To cut short. **3.** To limit or curtail (freedom or rights). [Middle English *abregen,* from Old

French *abregier*, from Late Latin *abbreviāre*, to ABBREVIATE.] —**a·bridg·er** *n.*

a·bridg·ment, a·bridge·ment (ə-bríjmənt) *n. Abbr.* **abr. 1. a.** The action of abridging. **b.** The state of being abridged. **2.** A condensation of a book, play, or the like; an abridged version.

a·broad (ə-bráwd) *adv.* **1.** Out of one's own country. **2.** In a foreign country or countries. **3.** Away from one's place of residence; out-of-doors. **4.** On the move; at large; circulating. **5.** Broadly; widely. **6.** *Archaic.* Not on target; astray; in error.
~*n.* A foreign country; foreign countries collectively: *a student from abroad.* [Middle English *abro(o)d*, "broadly, widely scattered" : A- (on, in) + *brood*, BROAD.]

ab·ro·gate (áb-rə-gayt, -rō-) *tr.v.* **-gated, -gating, -gates.** To abolish or annul by authority. See Synonyms at **nullify.** [Latin *abrogāre* : *ab-*, away + *rogāre*, to ask, propose.] —**ab·ro·ga·tion** (-gáysh'n) *n.* —**ab·ro·ga·tor** *n.*

a·brupt (ə-brúpt) *adj.* **1.** Unexpectedly sudden. **2.** Curt; brusque. **3.** Touching on one subject after another with sudden transitions: *abrupt, nervous prose.* **4.** Steeply inclined. **5.** *Biology.* Appearing to be cut or broken off short; truncate. [Latin *abruptus,* past participle of *abrumpere,* to break off : *ab-,* off + *rumpere,* to break.] —**a·brupt·ly** *adv.* —**a·brupt·ness** *n.*

A·bruz·zi (a-broot-si). Also **A·bruz·zo** (-sō). Region of central Italy, bordering on the Adriatic in the east. It is mountainous, containing the highest peak in the Apennines, Monte Corno (2 914 metres; 9,560 feet), and fairly poor, with small-scale agriculture and industry. Capital, L'Aquila.

abs. 1. absence; absent. **2.** absolute; absolutely. **3.** abstract.

Ab·sa·lom (áb-sələm). In the Old Testament, David's favourite son, killed when rebelling against his father. II Samuel 13–39.

ab·scess (áb-sess, -siss) *n.* A localised collection of pus in any part of the body, surrounded by an inflamed area and often caused by bacterial infection.
~*intr.v.* **abscessed, -scessing, -scesses.** To form an abscess. [Latin *abscēssus,* "a going away (of bad humours)", hence, collection of pus, from *abscēdere,* to go away : *abs-, ab-,* away from + *cēdere,* to go.]

ab·scise (ab-síz) *v.* **-scised, -scising, -scises.** —*tr.* To remove; cut off. —*intr.* To be shed by abscission. [Latin *abscidere* (past participle *abscissus*) : *abs-, ab-,* away + *scindere,* to cut.]

ab·scis·sa (ab-síssə, əb-) *n., pl.* **-sas** or **-scissae** (-síssee). *Mathematics.* The coordinate representing the distance of a point from the *y*-axis in a plane Cartesian coordinate system, measured along a line parallel to the *x*-axis. Compare **ordinate.** [New Latin *(linea) abscissa,* "cut-off (line)", from Latin *abscissus,* past participle of *abscindere,* to cut off, ABSCISE.]

ab·scis·sion (ab-sízh'n, -sísh'n) *n.* **1.** The act of cutting off. **2.** The process by which plant parts, such as leaves and flowers, are shed. A layer of cells forms at the base of the plant part then disintegrates, causing the part to become separated.

ab·scond (əb-skónd, ab-) *intr.v.* **-sconded, -sconding, -sconds.** To leave quickly and secretly and hide oneself, especially in order to escape imprisonment, arrest, or prosecution. [Latin *abscondere* : *abs-, ab-,* away + *condere,* to hide.] —**ab·scond·er** *n.*

ab·seil (áb-sayl) *intr.v.* **-seiled, -seiling, -seils. 1.** In mountaineering and caving, to descend a steep or vertical rock-face using a rope attached above and secured round the body. **2.** To descend from a helicopter by means of a rope.
~*n.* An instance of abseiling. [German *abseilen,* to descend by means of a rope : *ab-,* down + *Seil,* rope.]

ab·sence (ábs'nss) *n. Abbr.* **abs. 1.** The state of being away. **2.** The time during which one is away. **3.** Lack: *in the absence of corroborating evidence.* **4.** Inattention; abstraction: *absence of mind.*

ab·sent (ábs'nt) *adj. Abbr.* **abs. 1.** Missing or not present. **2.** Not existent; lacking. **3.** Inattentive.
~*prep. U.S.* In the absence of; without : *Absent corroborating evidence, we lost.*
~*tr.v.* (əb-sént, ab-) **absented, -senting, -sents. 1.** To keep (oneself) away. **2.** To withdraw (oneself). [Middle English, from Old French, from Latin *absēns,* present participle of *abesse,* to be away : *abs-, ab-,* away from + *esse,* to be.] —**ab·sent·ly** *adv.*

ab·sen·tee (ábs'n-tée) *n.* One who is absent.
~*adj.* **1.** Habitually absent or not in residence: *absentee landlords.* **2.** Of or pertaining to one that is absent: *an absentee vote.*

ab·sen·tee·ism (ábs'n-tée-iz'm) *n.* Habitual failure to appear, especially for work.

ab·sent-mind·ed (ábs'nt-míndid) *adj.* Heedless of one's immediate surroundings or activity, especially because of preoccupation with unrelated matters; inattentive and forgetful. —See Synonyms at **forgetful.** —**ab·sent-mind·ed·ly** *adv.* —**ab·sent-mind·ed·ness** *n.*

ab·sinthe, ab·sinth (áb-sinth, -sánth) *n.* **1.** A pale green liqueur that has a high alcohol content, is flavoured with aniseed and wormwood, and becomes cloudy when water is added to it. Owing to the harmful effects of wormwood, substitutes are instead used. **2.** A plant, **wormwood** *(see).* [French, from Latin *absinthium,* wormwood, from Greek *apsinthion,* of Mediterranean origin.]

ab·so·lute (ábsə-loot, -loot) *adj. Abbr.* **abs. 1.** Perfect in quality or nature; complete: *absolute nonsense.* **2.** Not mixed; pure; unadulterated: *absolute alcohol.* **3. a.** Not limited by restrictions or exceptions; unconditional: *an absolute choice.* **b.** Unqualified in extent or degree; total: *an absolute pardon.* **4.** Not limited by constitutional provisions or other restraints: *an absolute monarch.* **5.** Unrelated to and independent of anything else: *an absolute value.* **6.** Not to be

doubted or questioned; positive; certain: *absolute truth.* **7.** *Grammar.* **a.** Designating a construction in a sentence that is syntactically independent of the main clause. For example, in *Their ship having sailed, we went home,* the construction *Their ship having sailed* is an absolute phrase. **b.** Pertaining to or characterising a transitive verb when its object is implied but not stated; for example, *inspires* in *We have a teacher who inspires.* **c.** Pertaining to or characterising an adjective or pronoun that stands alone, the noun it modifies being implied but not stated; for example, *Theirs* and *best* in *Theirs were the best.* **8.** *Physics.* **a.** Pertaining to measurements or units of measurement derived from fundamental relationships of space, mass, and time. **b.** Pertaining to absolute temperature. **c.** Indicating a pressure measurement that is not relative to atmospheric pressure. Compare **gauge. 9.** *Law.* Complete and unconditional; having no encumbrances; final.
~*n.* Something that is absolute. —**the Absolute.** *Philosophy.* **1.** Something regarded as the ultimate basis of all thought and being. **2.** Something regarded as independent of and unrelated to anything else. **3.** In the philosphy of Hegel, the ultimate condition towards which everything is moving. [Middle English *absolut,* from Latin *absolūtus,* completed, unfettered, unconditional, from the past participle of *absolvere,* to free from, complete : *ab-,* away from + *solvere,* to loose.] —**ab·so·lute·ness** *n.*

absolute alcohol *n.* Ethanol containing no more than one per cent of water by weight.

absolute ceiling *n.* The maximum altitude above sea level at which an aircraft or missile can maintain horizontal flight under standard atmospheric conditions.

absolute humidity *n.* The humidity of a gas, especially air, expressed as the mass of water in grams per cubic metre of gas. Compare **relative humidity.**

ab·so·lute·ly (ábsə-lootli, -léwtli) *adv. Abbr.* **abs. 1.** Definitely and completely; positively; unquestionably. **2.** *Grammar.* In an absolute manner: *He used that transitive verb absolutely.*
~*interj.* Used to express complete agreement.

absolute magnitude *n. Astronomy.* A measure of the brightness of a star or other astronomical body equal to the apparent magnitude it would have if it were 10 parsecs or 32.6 light-years from the Earth.

absolute majority *n.* A majority that is over 50 per cent of all votes cast; a total, as of votes or seats obtained, that is higher than the combined total obtained by all one's opponents. Compare **relative majority.**

absolute music *n.* Instrumental music designed not to represent images or actions but to have an intellectual and emotional content that depends solely on its rhythmic, melodic, and contrapuntal structures. Compare **programme music.**

absolute permeability *n.* The **magnetic constant** *(see).*

absolute permittivity *n.* See **permittivity.**

absolute pitch *n.* **1.** The precise pitch of an isolated note, as established by its rate of vibration measured on a standard scale. **2.** The ability to identify the pitch of any note heard, or to reproduce a note without reference to another previously sounded. Also called "perfect pitch". Compare **relative pitch.**

absolute scale *n.* A scale of temperature with absolute zero as the minimum and scale units equal in magnitude to centigrade degrees. It is equivalent to the **thermodynamic scale** *(see).*

absolute temperature *n.* Temperature measured or calculated on the absolute scale.

absolute value *n. Mathematics.* **1.** The numerical value or magnitude of a quantity, as of a vector or of a negative integer, without regard to its sign. **2.** The modulus of a complex number, equal to the square root of the sum of the squares of the real and imaginary parts of the number.

absolute zero *n. Physics.* The temperature at which substances possess minimal energy, equal to 0 Kelvin, −273.15°C, or −459.67°F.

ab·so·lu·tion (ábsə-lóosh'n, -léwsh'n) *n.* **1.** Forgiveness; release from obligation or punishment. **2.** *Roman Catholic Church.* **a.** The formal remission of sin imparted by a priest as part of the sacrament of penance. **b.** The specific words spoken by a priest in granting this remission.

ab·so·lut·ism (ábsə-lootiz'm, -lewtiz'm) *n.* **1.** A system of government in which all power is vested in a monarch or dictator. **2.** The political theory reflecting this system. —**ab·so·lut·ist** *n. & adj.*

ab·solve (əb-zólv ‖ ab-, -sólv) *tr.v.* **-solved, -solving, -solves. 1.** To pronounce free of blame or guilt. **2.** To relieve of a requirement or obligation. **3. a.** To grant a remission of sin to. **b.** To pardon or remit (a sin). [Middle English *absolven,* from Latin *absolvere,* to free from : *ab-,* away from + *solvere,* to loose, free.] —**ab·solv·a·ble** *adj.* —**ab·solv·er** *n.*

ab·sorb (əb-sórb, -zórb ‖ ab-) *v.* **-sorbed, -sorbing, -sorbs.** —*tr.* **1.** To take in through or as if through pores or interstices; soak in or up. **2.** To occupy the full attention, interest, or time of; engross. **3. a.** To take in so as to make part of an existing whole; incorporate. **b.** To take into the mind; assimilate. **4.** To receive (the impact of a projectile) without recoil. **5.** To defray (costs). **6.** To take in and use up (marketable goods): *The market could not absorb the increased sugar production.* **7.** *Physiology.* **a.** To assimilate (the products of digestion). **b.** To take up (gases and fluids) through surface tissues. **8.** *Chemistry.* To take in (a gas or liquid) and hold by means of physical forces. Compare **adsorb. 9.** *Physics.* To receive (electromagnetic radiation, for example) and retain fully, without reflection or transmission. —*intr.* To undergo absorption. [Old French *ab-*

sorber, from Latin *absorbēre : ab-,* away from + *sorbēre,* to suck.] —**ab·sorb·a·bil·i·ty** (-ə-bílləti) *n.* —**ab·sorb·a·ble** *adj.* —**ab·sorb·er** *n.*

ab·sorbed (əb-sórbd, -zórbd ‖ ab-) *adj.* Engrossed. —**ab·sorb·ed·ly** (əb-sórbid-li ‖ ab-) *adv.*

absorbed dose *n. Physics.* A **dose** (*see*).

ab·sor·be·fa·cient (əb-sórbi-fáysh'nt, -zórbi- ‖ ab-) *adj.* Inducing or causing absorption.

~*n.* A medicine that induces absorption. [ABSORB + -FACIENT.]

ab·sorb·ent (əb-sórbənt, -zórbənt ‖ ab-) *adj.* Capable of absorbing something.

~*n.* A substance having this capability. —**ab·sorb·en·cy** *n.*

absorbent cotton *n. U.S.* Cotton wool (*see*).

ab·sorb·ing (əb-sórb-ing, -zórb- ‖ ab-) *adj.* Fully occupying one's time or attention; engrossing. —**ab·sorb·ing·ly** *adv.*

ab·sorp·tance (əb-sórp-təns, -zórb- ‖ ab-) *n.* The ratio of the absorbed flux of incident radiation to the incident flux for a given body or surface. Compare **reflectance, transmittance.** [ABSORP-T(ION) + -ANCE.]

ab·sorp·tion (əb-sórp-sh'n, -zórp- ‖ ab-) *n.* **1.** The act or process of absorbing, or the state of being absorbed. **2.** A state of mental concentration. [Latin *absorptiō,* from *absorbēre,* to ABSORB.] —**ab·sorp·tive** *adj.*

absorption nebula *n. Astronomy.* A dark **nebula** (*see*).

absorption spectrum. *n. Physics.* The spectrum of dark lines or bands observed when radiation traverses an absorbing medium. Compare **emission spectrum.**

ab·sorp·tiv·i·ty (áb-sorp-tívvəti, -zorp-) *n.* The absorptance of a body per unit of radiation path length, measured under conditions in which the surfaces of the sample do not influence the amount of absorption.

ab·stain (əb-stáyn, ab-) *intr.v.* **-stained, -staining, -stains.** **1.** To do without or refrain by one's own choice: *abstain from alcohol.* **2.** To withhold one's vote. [Middle English *absteinen, abstenen,* from Old French *abstenir,* from Latin *abstinēre,* to hold (oneself) back : *abs-, ab-,* away from + *tenēre,* to hold.] —**ab·stain·er** *n.*

ab·ste·mi·ous (əb-stéemi-əss, ab-) *adj.* **1.** Sparing or restrained, especially in one's consumption of food and alcohol. **2.** Restricted to bare necessities; marked by moderation; sparing. [Latin *abstēmius : abs-, ab-,* away from + *-tēmus,* from *tēmētum†,* alcoholic drink, mead, wine.] —**ab·ste·mi·ous·ly** *adv.* —**ab·ste·mi·ous·ness** *n.*

ab·sten·tion (əb-sténsh'n, ab-) *n.* **1.** The act or habit of abstaining. **2. a.** A deliberate act of abstaining from voting. **b.** One who abstains from voting. [Late Latin *abstentiō* (stem *abstentiōn-*), from Latin *abstinēre,* to ABSTAIN.]

ab·ster·gent (əb-stérjənt, ab-) *adj.* Scouring or cleansing.

~*n.* A scouring agent.

ab·sti·nence (ábstinənss) *n.* **1. a.** Denial of the appetites; abstention. **b.** Abstention from alcoholic drinks. **2.** *Roman Catholic Church.* Abstention from specific foods, especially meat, on days of penitential observance. [Middle English, from Old French, from Latin *abstinentia,* from *abstinēns,* present participle of *abstinēre,* to ABSTAIN.] —**ab·sti·nent** *adj.* —**ab·sti·nent·ly** *adv.*

Synonyms: abstinence, self-denial, temperance, continence.

ab·stract (ábstrakt ‖ *U.S. also* abstrákt) *adj.* **abs., abstr.** **1.** Considered apart from concrete existence or specific objects and actions. **2.** Theoretical; not applied or practical. **3.** Not easily understood; abstruse. **4.** Thought of or stated without reference to a specific instance. **5.** Designating a genre of art that does not represent scenes or objects naturalistically, but in which the intellectual and emotional content depends solely on intrinsic form.

~*n.* (ábstrakt). *Abbr.* **abs., abstr.** **1.** A statement summarising the important points of a given text. **2.** The concentrated essence of a larger whole. **3.** Something abstract, such as a term. **4.** An abstract work of art. —**in the abstract.** Apart from actual substance or experience; in theory rather than in reality.

~*tr.v.* (ab-strákt, əb-; *also* ábstrakt *for sense 5*) **abstracted, -stracting, -stracts.** **1.** To take away; remove. **2.** To remove without permission; steal. **3.** To consider theoretically; think of (a quality or attribute) without reference to a particular example or object. **4.** To detach or disengage (thoughts or the attention). **5.** To summarise. [Middle English, from Latin *abstractus,* "removed from (concrete reality)", past participle of *abstrahere,* to pull away, remove : *abs-, ab-,* away from + *trahere,* to pull.] —**ab·stract·or, ab·stract·er** *n.* —**ab·stract·ly** *adv.* —**ab·stract·ness** *n.*

ab·stract·ed (ab-stráktid, əb-) *adj.* **1.** Removed or separated from something; apart. **2.** Lost or deep in thought; preoccupied; meditative. —See Synonyms at **forgetful.** —**ab·stract·ed·ly** *adv.* —**ab·stract·ed·ness** *n.*

abstract expressionism *n.* A school of painting that flourished after World War II until the early 1960s, characterised by the active and free application of the paint, as by splattering, and its nonrepresentational design. See **action painting; tachisme.**

ab·strac·tion (ab-stráksh'n, əb-) *n.* **1.** The act or process of abstracting. **2. a.** The act or process of separating the inherent qualities or properties from the actual physical object or concept to which they belong. **b.** A product of this process; a general idea or word representing a physical object or concept. **3.** Preoccupation. **4.** An abstract work of art.

ab·strac·tion·ism (ab-stráksh'n-iz'm, əb-) *n.* The theory and practice of abstract art. —**ab·strac·tion·ist** *n.* & *adj.*

abstract noun *n.* A noun that refers to a quality rather than a thing

or to an abstract idea as opposed to a material object. Compare **concrete noun.**

abstract of title *n. Law.* A statement of the history of an unregistered piece of land, for the purpose of establishing ownership.

ab·struse (ab-stróoss, əb-) *adj.* Difficult to understand because intellectually complicated or somewhat obscure. [Latin *abstrūsus,* past participle of *abstrūdere,* to hide : *abs-, ab-,* away + *trūdere,* to push.] —**ab·struse·ly** *adv.* —**ab·struse·ness** *n.*

ab·surd (əb-súrd ‖ -zúrd, ab-) *adj.* **1.** Ridiculous; foolishly incongruous or unreasonable. **2.** *Often capital* **A.** Reflecting or dealing with the Absurd. —See Synonyms at **foolish.**

~*n.* *Usually capital* **A.** A 20th-century philosophical concept, embodied in many modern novels and plays, emphasising the cruelty, ludicrousness, and ultimate futility of human life. Usually preceded by *the.* [French *absurde,* from Latin *absurdus.*] —**ab·surd·ism** *n.* —**ab·surd·ist** *n.* & *adj.* —**ab·surd·i·ty, ab·surd·ness** *n.* —**ab·surd·ly** *adv.*

A·bu-Bekr (ábboo-béckər, ə-bŏŏ-) (573-634). First Caliph of the Muslim Empire, who ruled from 632. He made Islam a political and military force throughout Arabia after the death of his son-in-law, the prophet Muhammad.

A·bū Dha·bi (ábbōō dáabi, dábbi). Sheikdom and town in eastern Arabia on the Gulf. The town is the capital of the **United Arab Emirates** *(see).* With enormous oil revenues, the sheikdom is one of the richest states in the world, in terms of income per head. — **A·bū Dha·bi·an** *adj.* & *n.*

A·bu·ja (abōō-jə). New city some 480 kilometres (300 miles) northeast of Lagos, which in 1991 replaced Lagos as Nigeria's federal capital and seat of government.

a·bu·li·a, a·bou·li·a (ə-bŏŏli-ə) *n. Psychology.* Loss or impairment of the ability to decide or act independently. [New Latin, from Greek *aboulia,* irresolution : *a-,* without + *boulē,* will.] —**a·bu·lic** *adj.*

a·bun·dance (ə-búndənss) *n.* Also **a·bun·dan·cy** (ə-búndənsi). **1.** A great quantity; a plentiful amount. **2.** Fullness to overflowing: *"My thoughts . . . are from the abundance of my heart."* (Thomas De Quincey). **3.** Affluence; wealth. **4.** *Chemistry.* The relative amount of a substance in a particular environment, especially the proportion of a particular element or mineral in the earth's crust, usually expressed in parts per million or as a percentage. **5.** *Physics.* The ratio of the number of atoms of a given isotope to the total number of atoms of the element in a given sample, especially the proportion in a naturally occurring sample.

a·bun·dant (ə-búndənt) *adj.* **1.** In plentiful supply; more than sufficient; ample. **2.** Amply supplied; abounding. Used with *in.* [Middle English *abundaunt,* from Old French *abundant,* from Latin *abundāns* (stem *abundant-*), present participle of *abundāre,* to ABOUND.] —**a·bun·dant·ly** *adv.*

ab ur·be con·di·ta (áb úrbi kóndi-tə, -táa). *Abbr.* **A.U.C.** *Latin.* From the founding of the city. Used to indicate the date in ancient Rome, the base year being 753 B.C.

a·buse (ə-béwz) *tr.v.* **abused, abusing, abuses. 1.** To use wrongly or improperly; misuse. **2.** To hurt or injure by maltreatment. **3.** To speak to in a contemptuous, coarse, or insulting way; revile. **4.** To masturbate. Used reflexively.

~ *n.* (ə-béwss). **1.** Misuse. **2.** A corrupt practice or custom. **3.** Maltreatment: *child abuse; substance abuse.* **4.** Insulting or coarse language. [Middle English *abusen,* from Old French *abuser,* from *abus,* improper use, from Latin *abūsus,* a using up, past participle of *abūtī,* to use up, make (improper) use of : *ab-,* away + *ūtī,* to USE.] —**a·bus·er** *n.*

Synonyms: abuse, misuse, mistreat, ill-treat, maltreat.

A·bu Sim·bel (ábbōō símb'l, símbel). Village in southern Egypt on the river Nile and the site of the massive temples constructed by Ramses II in about 1250 B.C. The temples were raised over 60 metres (200 feet) in order to escape the rising waters of Lake Nasser, caused by the building of the Aswan High Dam in 1966.

a·bu·sive (ə-béw-siv ‖ -ziv) *adj.* **1.** Of, pertaining to, or characterised by abuse. **2.** Marked by or using insulting or contemptuous language. —**a·bu·sive·ly** *adv.* —**a·bu·sive·ness** *n.*

a·but (ə-bút) *v.* **abutted, abutting, abuts.** —*intr.* To touch at one end or side; lie adjacent. Used with *on, upon,* or *against.* —*tr.* To border upon; be next to. [Middle English *abutten,* from Old French *abuter,* to buttress, put an end to : *a,* to + *buter,* to strike, finish, from Romance *bottāre* (unattested), to strike, push, from Germanic.]

a·bu·ti·lon (ə-béwti-lən, -lon) *n.* Any of various shrubs or plants of the genus *Abutilon;* especially, the **flowering maple** *(see).* [New Latin, from Arabic *aubūṭīlūn.*]

a·but·ment (ə-bútmənt) *n.* **1.** The act or process of abutting. **2. a.** That on which something abuts. **b.** The point of contact of two abutting objects or parts. **3.** *Architecture.* That element which shares a common boundary or surface with its neighbour. **4.** *Engineering.* **a.** A structure that supports an arch or the end of a bridge. **b.** A structure that anchors the cables of a suspension bridge.

a·but·tal (ə-bútt'l) *n.* **1.** An abutment. **2.** *Plural. Law.* The parts, especially of a piece of land, that abut against other property; boundaries.

ab·volt (áb-vōlt, -vŏlt ‖ -volt, -vólt) *n. Abbr.* **abv.** A centimetre-gram-second electromagnetic unit of potential difference or electromotive force, equal to the potential difference between two points such that one erg of work must be performed to move a one-abcoulomb charge from one of the points to the other. It is equal to 10^{-8} volt. [AB- (absolute) + VOLT.]

ab·watt (áb-wot, -wót) *n.* A centimetre-gram-second electromagnetic unit of power, equal to the power dissipated by a current of one abampere flowing between two points with a potential difference of one abvolt. It is equal to 10^{-7} watt. [AB (absolute) + WATT.]

a·bysm (ə-bízz'm) *n. Archaic & Poetic.* An abyss. [Middle English *abi(s)me*, from Old French, from Late Latin *abyssus*, ABYSS.]

a·bys·mal (ə-bízm'l) *adj.* **1.** Unfathomable; very great: *abysmal ignorance.* **2.** Of or resembling an abyss. **3.** *Informal.* Extremely poor in quality. —**a·bys·mal·ly** *adv.*

a·byss (ə-bíss) *n.* **1. a.** A very steep gorge or deep crack in a mountain or on the earth. **b.** An unfathomable chasm; a yawning gulf. **2.** Any immeasurably great depth or void. **3. a.** Primeval chaos. **b.** The bottomless pit; hell. [Late Latin *abyssus*, from Greek *abussos (limnē)*, "bottomless (lake)" : *a-*, not + *bussos*, bottom.]

a·byss·al (ə-bíss'l) *adj.* **1.** Abysmal. **2.** Of or pertaining to the depths of the oceans, usually below 1,000 fathoms: *abyssal plain.*

Ab·ys·sin·i·a (ábbi-sín-yə). See **Ethiopia.** —**Ab·ys·sin·i·an** *n. & adj.*

Abyssinian cat *n.* Any of a Near Eastern breed of cat, with short hair, long body, and reddish-brown coat tipped with small black markings.

Ac The symbol for the element actinium.

AC alternating current.

a.c. *Medicine.* before meals [New Latin *ante cibum*].

A.C. **1.** Air Corps. **2.** aircraftman. **3.** alternating current. **4.** appellation controlée. **5.** athletic club. **6.** before Christ [New Latin *ante Christum*]. **7.** Companion of the Order of Australia.

a/c, A/C account; account current.

a·ca·cia (ə-káyshə) *n.* **1.** Any of various chiefly tropical trees of the genus *Acacia*, having compound leaves and small yellow or white flowers. Some species yield gums having a wide variety of uses. **2.** A tree, the **false acacia** *(see).* **3.** A substance, **gum arabic** *(see).* [Latin, from Greek *akakia*, probably from Egyptian.]

acad. academic; academy.

ac·a·deme (áckədeem, -déem) *n.* **1.** *Sometimes capital* **A.** *Formal.* The world of scholarship and higher education; scholarly or academic life or its associated environment. **2.** *Archaic.* A place of learning; a university. **3.** *Archaic.* A scholar, teacher, or pedant. [Pseudo-Greek form of Greek *Akadēmia*, ACADEMY.]

ac·a·de·mi·a (áckə-déemi-ə) *n.* The academic world; academe. [New Latin, from Latin *Acadēmia*, ACADEMY.]

ac·a·dem·ic (áckə-démmik) *adj. Abbr.* **acad.** **1.** Of, pertaining to, or characteristic of a university, college, or other institution of learning. **2.** Scholarly to the point of being impractical or unaware of the outside world. **3.** Pertaining to or based on formal education, as in the humanities or sciences, rather than on practical or vocational training: *an education geared to children with academic ability.* **4.** Formalistic; conventional: *academic painters.* **5.** Merely theoretical; speculative: *a purely academic interest in violence.* **6.** *Capital* **A.** Of or pertaining to the Academy and philosophy of Plato. ~*n.* A member of a university or college; especially, a university teacher. —**ac·a·dem·i·cal·ly** *adv.*

academic freedom *n.* Liberty to pursue, discuss, and teach knowledge without hindrance or censorship.

ac·a·de·mi·cian (ə-káddə-mísh'n || *U.S. also* áckədə-) *n. Abbr.* **A.** A member of an academy or society of the arts or sciences.

ac·a·dem·i·cism (áckə-démmi-siz'm) *n.* Also **a·cad·e·mism** (ə-káddə-miz'm). Traditional formalism; conventionalism, especially in art.

A·ca·dé·mie Fran·çaise (ə-káddəmi frón-sáyz, -séz) *n. French.* An association of 40 French intellectuals, scholars, and writers founded by Cardinal Richelieu in 1635, whose official role is to produce and revise a dictionary of standard French.

a·cad·e·my (ə-káddəmi) *n., pl.* **-mies.** *Abbr.* **A., acad.** **1.** An association of artists or scholars. **2.** A school for special instruction: *a naval academy.* **3. a.** A secondary school, especially a private one. **b.** In Scotland, a grammar school. **4.** *Capital* **A. a.** The grove near Athens where Plato taught. **b.** The philosophy of Plato. **c.** The disciples of Plato. [Latin *Acadēmia*, from Greek *Akadēmia*, the Platonic school of philosophy, from *Akadēmia, Akadēmeia*, name of the place in Athens where Plato taught, after *Akadēmos*, legendary Attic hero.]

Academy Award *n.* Any of the golden statuettes awarded annually by the Academy of Motion Picture Arts and Sciences in the United States, given in recognition of achievement in cinema films. Also called "Oscar".

A·ca·di·a (əkáy-di-ə). *French* **A·ca·die** (áckadée). Region and former French colony in east Canada, encompassing Nova Scotia, Cape Breton Island, Prince Edward Island, New Brunswick, and part of Maine. Nova Scotia was ceded to Britain in 1713 and many of its inhabitants migrated or were deported (1755) to the southern colonies, including Louisiana, where their descendants came to be called Cajuns (from "Acadians"). The rest of Acadia, excluding Maine, came under British rule in 1763.

A·ca·di·an (ə-káydi-ən) *adj.* Of or pertaining to Acadia or its inhabitants. ~*n.* Any of the early French settlers of Acadia or their descendants. See **Cajun.**

a·ca·jou (áckə-zhoō || *U.S.* -zhoō) *n.* Mahogany. [French, cashew, from Portuguese *(a)caju*, from Tupi, mahogany, probably by confusion with Tupi *agapú*.]

acanthø-, acanth- *comb. form.* Indicates thorns; for example, **acanthocephalan.** [New Latin, from Greek *akanthos*, thorn plant, from *akantha*, thorn : *ak-*, sharp + *antha*, of Mediterranean origin.]

a·can·tho·ceph·a·lan (ə-kánthō-séffə-lən) *n.* Any of various parasitic worms of the phylum Acanthocephala, having a proboscis armed with hooked spines. [New Latin *Acanthocephala*, "thornheads" (from the spiky proboscis) : ACANTHO- + *-cephala*, neuter plural of *-cephalus*, -CEPHALOUS.]

a·can·thoid (ə-kánthoyd) *adj.* Resembling a thorn or spine. [ACANTH(O)- + -OID.]

ac·an·thop·ter·yg·i·an (áckən-thóptə-ríji-ən) *n.* Any fish of the superorder Acanthopterygii, which includes fishes having spiny fins, such as bass, perch, and mackerel. Compare **malacopterygian.** [New Latin *Acanthopterygii* : ACANTHO- + Greek *pterugion*, diminutive of *pterux*, wing, fin, from *pteron*, feather, wing.] —**ac·an·thop·ter·yg·i·an** *adj.*

a·can·thus (ə-kán-thəss) *n., pl.* **-thuses** or **-thi** (-thī). **1.** Any of various plants of the genus *Acanthus*, native to the Mediterranean region, having large, segmented, thistle-like leaves. **2.** An architectural ornament patterned after the leaves of the acanthus, used especially on capitals of Corinthian columns. [New Latin, from Greek *akanthos*, thorn plant, from *akantha*, thorn. See **acantho-.**] —**a·can·thine** *adj.*

a cap·pel·la (áa kə-péllə) *adv. or adj. Music.* Without instrumental accompaniment. [Italian, "in the manner of the chapel (or choir)".]

a ca·pric·cio (áa kə-prichi-ō) *adv. or adj. Music.* At whatever tempo and with whatever expression the performer or conductor desires. Used as a direction. [Italian, "capriciously".]

ac·a·ri·a·sis (áckə-rí-ə-siss) *n.* Infestation with mites or ticks. [New Latin : ACAR(ID) + -IASIS.]

ac·a·ri·cide (ə-kárri-sīd) *n.* A substance lethal to ticks and mites; a miticide. [ACARI(D) + -CIDE.] —**a·car·i·ci·dal** (-sīd'l) *adj.*

ac·a·rid (áckərid) *n.* Any arachnid of the order Acarina, which includes the mites and ticks. [New Latin *Acaridae* (family), from *Acarus* (genus), from Greek *akarit*, a kind of mite.] —**ac·a·rid** *adj.*

ac·a·roid gum (áckə-royd) *n.* A gum obtained from various Australian grass trees, and used in varnishes, lacquers, and paper. Also called "acaroid resin", "gum accroides". [New Latin *acaroides*, from Greek *akarit*, a kind of mite that bred in wax or resin. See **acarid.**]

a·car·pous (ay-kárpəss, áy-) *adj. Botany.* Producing no fruit; sterile. [A- (not) + -CARPOUS.]

ac·a·rus (áckə-rəss) *n., pl.* **-ri** (-rī). A mite, especially one of the genus *Acarus.* [New Latin *Acarus.* See **acarid.**]

ACAS (áykass). Advisory Conciliation and Arbitration Service.

ac·a·ta·lec·tic (áy-kátta-léktik, a-) *adj.* Designating a line of verse having the required number of syllables in the last foot. ~*n.* An acatalectic line. [Late Latin *acatalēcticus*, from Greek *akatalēktikos* : *a-*, not + *katalēktikos*, CATALECTIC.]

a·cau·date (ay-káwdayt, áy-) *adj. Zoology.* Having no tail. [A- (not) + CAUDATE.]

a·cau·les·cent (áckaw-léss'nt) *adj. Botany.* Stemless, or nearly so. [A- (not) + CAULESCENT.]

acc. 1. acceptance. **2.** accompanied. **3.** according to. **4.** account; accountant. **5.** accusative.

Accad. See **Akkad.**

ac·cede (ək-séed, ak-) *intr.v.* **-ceded, -ceding, -cedes. 1.** To give one's assent; agree. Often used with *to.* **2.** To take up or come into an office or high-ranking position. Used with *to: accede to the throne.* **3.** To become a party, as to an agreement. Used with *to: accede to a treaty.* —See Synonyms at **assent.** [Middle English *acceden*, from Latin *accēdere*, to go near, agree : *ad-*, to + *cēdere*, to go.] —**ac·ced·ence** (-séed'nss) *n.* —**ac·ced·er** *n.*

ac·cel·er·an·do (ək-séllə-rándō, ak-, əchéllə-, -ráandō) *adj. Music.* Gradually accelerating or quickening in time. Used as a direction. [Italian, from Latin *accelerandum*, gerund of *accelerāre*, to ACCELERATE.] —**ac·cel·er·an·do** *n. & adv.*

ac·cel·er·ate (ək-séllərayt, ak-) *v.* **-ated, -ating, -ates.** —*tr.* **1.** To increase the speed of. **2.** To cause to occur sooner than expected or usual: *accelerated promotion.* **3.** *Physics.* To cause a change of velocity in. —*intr.* **1.** To move or act faster. **2.** *Physics.* To change in velocity. —See Synonyms at **speed.** [Latin *accelerāre* : *ad-* (intensive) + *celerāre*, to hasten, from *celer*, swift] —**ac·cel·er·a·tive** (-rətiv, -raytiv) *adj.*

ac·cel·er·a·tion (ək-séllə-ráysh'n, ak-) *n.* **1. a.** The act of accelerating. **b.** The state of being accelerated. **2. a.** *Physics. Symbol* **a** The rate of change of velocity with respect to time. **b.** Broadly, the ability to increase speed: *a car with good acceleration.*

acceleration of free fall *n. Symbol* **g** The acceleration of freely falling bodies under the influence of terrestrial gravity in a vacuum. The standard value is 9.80665 metres per second per second (approximately 32 feet per second per second) at sea level. Also called "acceleration due to gravity" or "acceleration of gravity".

ac·cel·er·a·tor (ək-séllə-raytər, ak-) *n.* **1.** A device that controls the speed of a motor vehicle, especially by means of a pedal regulating the fuel intake to the engine. **2.** A substance that increases the speed of a chemical reaction. **3.** *Physics.* Any device, such as a cyclotron or linear accelerator, that accelerates charged subatomic particles or nuclei to energies useful for research. In this sense, also called "particle accelerator", "atom smasher".

ac·cel·er·om·e·ter (ək-séllə-rómmitər, ak-) *n.* Any of various devices used to measure acceleration. [ACCELER(ATION) + -O- + -METER.]

ac·cent (áks'nt, áksent) *n.* **1.** *Linguistics.* The relative prominence of a particular syllable of a word by greater intensity *(stress accent),* or by variation or modulation of pitch or tone *(pitch accent).* **2.** Vocal prominence or emphasis given to a particular syllable, word, or phrase. **3.** A characteristic pronunciation, especially: **a.** One that is typical of a particular regional or social group. **b.** One determined by the phonetic habits of the speaker's native language carried over to his use of another language. **4.** A mark or symbol used in printing and writing for any of various purposes, as: **a.** A mark used in certain languages to indicate the vocal quality to be given to a particular letter: *an acute accent.* **b.** A mark used to indicate the stressed syllables of a spoken word. **c.** A mark used to indicate an unusual or unexpected stress pattern, especially in poetry; for example, *venturèd, Délilàh.* **5.** Rhythmically significant stress in a line of verse. **6.** *Music.* **a.** Special stress given to a musical note within a phrase. **b.** A mark representing this stress. **c.** The rhythmical pattern of a piece of music based on the primary beat in each bar. **7.** *Mathematics.* **a.** A mark, or one of several marks, used as a superscript to distinguish variables represented by the same symbol; for example, x', x''. **b.** A mark used as a superscript to indicate the first derivative of a variable. **c.** Any of various marks used as a superscript to indicate a unit. See **prime. 8.** A distinctive character or quality: *a modern building but with a classical accent.* **9.** A strongly contrasting detail. **10.** Particular emphasis: *a sandwich course with the accent on practical experience.*

~*tr.v.* (ək-sént, ak- || *U.S. also* áksent) **accented, -centing, -cents. 1.** To stress or emphasise the pronunciation of. **2.** To mark with a written or printed accent. **3.** To emphasise or draw attention to; accentuate. [Middle English, from Old French, from Latin *accentus,* accentuation, originally "song added to (speech)" (translation of Greek *prosōidia,* PROSODY) : *ad-,* to + *cantus,* song, from the past participle of *canere,* to sing.]

ac·cen·tor (ə-séntər, ak-) *n.* Any of various sparrow-like songbirds of the family Prunellidae, most of which frequent mountainous regions. [Late Latin, "one who sings with another" : Latin *ad-,* to + *cantor,* singer, from *cantus,* song (see **accent**).]

ac·cen·tu·al (ək-séntew-əl, ak-, -sénchoo-) *adj.* **1.** Of or pertaining to accent. **2.** Designating verse rhythm based on stress accents rather than on the number of syllables. **—ac·cen·tu·al·ly** *adv.*

ac·cen·tu·ate (ək-séntew-ayt, ak-, sénchoo-) *tr.v.* **-ated, -ating, -ates. 1.** To give greater prominence or emphasis to; heighten or emphasise. **2.** To mark or pronounce with a stress or accent. [Medieval Latin *accentuāre,* from Latin *accentus,* ACCENT.] **—ac·cen·tu·a·tion** (-áysh'n) *n.*

ac·cept (ək-sépt, ak-) *v.* **-cepted, -cepting, -cepts.** —*tr.* **1.** To take or receive (something offered) willingly. **2.** To receive as adequate, satisfactory, or admissible: *accepted his excuse.* **3.** To admit, as to a group or place: *accepted in the best circles.* **4.** To regard with favour or approval. **5. a.** To regard as usual, proper, or right. **b.** To regard as true; believe in: *accept a person's views.* **6. a.** To bear up under resignedly or patiently: *accept one's fate.* **b.** To submit to without argument. **7. a.** To respond to affirmatively: *accept an invitation.* **b.** To take upon oneself (a duty or responsibilty, for example); undertake. **8.** To be able to hold (something applied or inserted): *This wood will not accept oil paints.* **9.** *Commerce.* To consent to pay (a bill, for example), as by a signed agreement. —*intr.* To receive something willingly. —See Synonyms at **assent.** [Middle English *accepten,* from Old French *accepter,* from Latin *acceptāre,* frequentative of *accipere* (past participle *acceptus*), to receive, "take to oneself" : *ad-,* to + *capere,* to take.] **—ac·cept·er** *n.*

ac·cept·a·ble (ək-séptəb'l, ak-) *adj.* **1.** Satisfactory; adequate. **2.** Welcome; gratifying: *a most acceptable gift.* **3.** Tolerable. **—ac·cept·a·bil·i·ty, ac·cept·a·ble·ness** *n.* **—ac·cept·a·bly** *adv.*

ac·cep·tance (ək-séptənss, ak-) *n. Abbr.* **acc., acpt. 1.** The act or process of accepting. **2.** The state or condition of being accepted or acceptable. **3.** Favourable reception; approval. **4.** Belief in something; agreement; assent. **5.** *Commerce.* **a.** A formal indication by a party of willingness to pay a bill of exchange when it falls due, as by writing the word *accepted* and affixing his signature across the face of the document. **b.** The bill itself when so endorsed. **6.** *Law.* Assent by one party, through conduct or the spoken word, to the terms and conditions of offer of another so that a contract becomes legally binding between them. **—ac·cep·tant** *adj.*

ac·cep·ta·tion (áksep-táysh'n) *n.* **1.** The usual or accepted meaning, as of a word or expression. **2.** *Archaic.* **a.** Favourable reception. **b.** Belief or assent.

ac·cept·ed (ək-séptid, ak-) *adj.* Generally approved, believed, or recognised.

ac·cept·or (ək-séptər, ak-) *n.* **1.** *Commerce.* One who formally accepts a bill of exchange. **2.** *Physics.* An impurity that accepts electrons in a semiconductor, thus increasing the p-type semiconductivity. **3.** *Chemistry.* An atom, molecule, or group that can accept a pair of electrons in forming a coordinate bond. Compare **donor. 4.** *Electronics.* A resonant circuit with the inductance and capacitance in series, which produces a large current at a particular frequency. Compare **rejector.**

ac·cess (áksess) *n.* **1.** A means of approaching or entering; a passage or entrance. **2.** The right or ability to enter, approach, or make use of. **3.** The state or quality of being approachable or reachable: *easy of access.* **4.** A sudden onset or outburst: *an access of rage.*

~*tr.v.* **accessed, -cessing, -cesses. 1.** To retrieve from a computer's storage files: *to access data.* **2.** To gain access to or use of.

~*adj. Chiefly British.* Of or pertaining to the release of broadcasting facilities by a radio or television station to an independent group or member of the public. [Middle English, from Old French *acces,* arrival, from Latin *accessus,* from the past participle of *accēdere,* to arrive : *ad-,* to + *cēdere,* to come.]

ac·ces·si·ble (ək-séssə-b'l, ak-) *adj.* **1.** Easily reached or entered. **2.** Easily obtained. **3.** Easily understood or appreciated: *a very accessible writer.* **4.** Susceptible; open: *accessible to flattery.* **—ac·ces·si·bil·i·ty, ac·ces·si·ble·ness** *n.* **—ac·ces·si·bly** *adv.*

ac·ces·sion (ək-sésh'n, ak-) *n.* **1.** The attainment of rank or high office. **2. a.** Increase by means of something added. **b.** An addition or acquisition; especially, a library book added to an existing collection. **3.** *Law.* **a.** The addition to or increase in value of property by means of improvements or natural growth. **b.** The right of a proprietor to ownership of such addition or increase. **4.** Agreement; assent. **5.** The act of formally accepting or becoming a party to a treaty or agreement: *Britain's accession to the Treaty of Rome.* **6.** Access; admittance. **7.** A sudden outburst; an access.

~*tr.v.* **accessioned, -sioning, -sions.** To record as acquired. **—ac·ces·sion·al** *adj.*

ac·ces·so·rise, ac·ces·so·rize (ək-séssə-rīz, ak-) *tr.v.* **-rised, -rising, -rises.** *Chiefly U.S.* To provide with accessories.

ac·ces·so·ry (ək-séssəri, ak-) *n., pl.* **-ries.** Also **ac·ces·sa·ry** (for sense 2). **1.** Something supplementary; an adjunct, as: **a.** A small decorative item of women's clothing, such as a belt or scarf. **b.** A minor or additional part, device, or attachment, as for a motor vehicle. **2. a.** One who incites or aids another in the commission of a crime, but is not present at the time of the crime. Used in the phrase *accessory before the fact.* **b.** One who aids a criminal after the commission of a crime, but was not present at the time of the crime. Used in the phrase *accessory after the fact.* —See Synonyms at **appendage.**

~*adj.* Also **accessary** (for sense 2). **1.** Having a secondary, supplementary, or subordinate function. **2.** Serving to aid or abet a criminal either before or after the commission of his crime, without being present at the time the crime was committed. [Middle English *accessorie,* from Medieval Latin *accessōrius,* from *accessor,* helper, accessory, subordinate, from Latin *accessus,* ACCESS.] **—ac·ces·so·ri·al** (áksess-áwr-i-əl, áksəss- || -ōr-) *adj.* **—ac·ces·so·ri·ly** *adv.* **—ac·ces·so·ri·ness** *n.*

accessory fruit *n.* A **pseudocarp** *(see).*

accessory nerve *n.* Either of the 11th pair of cranial nerves, which supply certain muscles in the neck and, with the vagus nerve, supply the internal laryngeal muscles.

ac·ciac·ca·tu·ra (ə-chåckə-to͝or-ə || *U.S.* aa-cháakə-) *n., pl.* **-ture** (-to͝or-ay) or **-turas** (-to͝or-əz). *Music.* A short grace note, usually immediately below a principal note, sounded immediately before or at the same time in order to add sustained dissonance. Compare **appoggiatura.** [Italian *acciaccatura,* "crushing sound", from *acciaccare*†, to crush.]

ac·ci·dence (áksi-d'nss || -denss) *n.* The part of grammar that deals with the inflections of words. [Latin *accidentia,* accidental or supplementary things, hence, inflections, from *accidere,* to happen (see **accident**).]

ac·ci·dent (áksi-d'nt || -dent) *n.* **1.** An unexpected and undesirable event, especially one resulting in damage, injury, or death; a mishap. **2.** Anything that occurs unexpectedly or unintentionally, such as an unplanned pregnancy. **3.** A property or attribute that is not essential to our conception of the nature of something. **4.** Any incidental or non-essential feature; an adjunct or accessory. **5.** Fortune; chance: *rich by accident of birth.* **6.** *Geology.* An irregular or unusual natural formation. [Middle English, from Old French, from Latin *(rēs) accidēns* (stem *accident-*), "(a thing) happening", from *accidere,* to fall upon, happen : *ad-,* to + *cadere,* to fall.]

ac·ci·den·tal (áksi-dént'l) *adj.* **1.** Occurring unexpectedly and unintentionally; *a verdict of accidental death.* **2.** Of or characterising a non-essential property or attribute; supplementary; incidental. **3.** *Music.* Of or designating a sharp, flat, or natural not indicated in the key signature.

~*n.* **1.** A factor or attribute that is not essential. **2.** *Music.* An accidental note or the symbol indicating this. **—ac·ci·den·tal·ly** *adv.*

Synonyms: *accidental, fortuitous, contingent, incidental, adventitious.*

accident insurance *n.* Insurance against injury or death because of accident.

ac·ci·dent-prone (áksi-d'nt-prōn || -dent-) *adj.* Especially liable to suffer an accident or injury.

ac·ci·die (áksidi) *n.* Also **a·ce·di·a** (ə-séedi-ə). Spiritual torpor; apathy. [Late Latin, from Greek *akēdia, akēdeia,* indifference, apathy : *a-,* not + *kēdos,* care.]

ac·cip·i·ter (ak-síppi-tər) *n.* Any hawk of the genus *Accipiter,* characterised by short wings and a long tail. [Latin, hawk.] **—ac·cip·i·trine** (-trīn, -trin, -treen) *adj.*

ac·claim (ə-kláym) *v.* **-claimed, -claiming, -claims.** —*tr.* **1.** To greet, especially publicly, with enthusiastic praise or approval. **2.** To acknowledge or declare with enthusiastic and unanimous approval: *acclaimed as the best play showing in town.* —See Synonyms at **praise.**

~*n.* Enthusiastic applause or approval. [Latin *acclāmāre,* to shout at : *ad-,* to + *clāmāre,* to shout.] **—ac·claim·er** *n.*

ac·cla·ma·tion (ácklə-máysh'n) *n.* **1.** The act of acclaiming or being acclaimed. **2.** A public expression of enthusiastic approval or praise. **3.** An expression of overwhelming or unanimous assent, as by cheers or shouts, taken as a vote of approval without a formal ballot. Used especially in the phrase *by acclamation.* **—ac·clam·a·to·ry** (ə-klámmə-tri, -təri) *adj.*

ac·cli·ma·tion (ácklī-máysh'n, ákli-) *n.* **1.** Acclimatisation. **2.** The adaptation of an organism to its immediate natural climatic environment. Compare **acclimatisation.**

ac·cli·ma·ti·sa·tion (ə-klīmət-īzáysh'n || *U.S.*-izáysh'n) *n.* **1.** The process of acclimatising or the state of being acclimatised. **2.** The climatic adaptation over several generations of an organism that has been moved to a new environment. Compare **acclimation.**

ac·cli·ma·tise, ac·cli·ma·tize (ə-klīmət-īz) *v.* **-tised, -tising, -tises.** Also *chiefly U.S.* **ac·cli·mate** (a-klīmat, áckli-mayt), **-mated, -mating, -mates.** —*tr.* To accustom to a new climate, environment, or situation; adapt. —*intr.* To become acclimatised. [French *acclimater* : *ac-*, from Latin *ad-*, to + *climat,* CLIMATE.] **—ac·cli·ma·tis·a·ble** *adj.* **—ac·cli·ma·tis·er** *n.*

ac·cliv·i·ty (ə-klívvəti) *n., pl.* **-ties.** An upward slope. Compare **declivity.** [Latin *acclīvitās,* from *acclīvis,* uphill : *ad-*, to + *clīvus,* slope.]

ac·co·lade (áckə-layd, -láyd) *n.* **1.** An expression of praise or approval: *critics' accolades.* **2.** An award or honour: *the highest accolade of the literary world.* **3.** The ceremonial bestowal of knighthood, as by a tap on the shoulder with the flat of a sword or, formerly, by an embrace. [French, from Provençal *acolada,* an embrace, from *acolar,* to embrace, from Vulgar Latin *accollāre* (unattested), to hug around the neck : *ad-*, to + *collum,* neck.]

ac·com·mo·date (ə-kómmə-dayt) *v.* **-dated, -dating, -dates.** —*tr.* **1.** To do a favour or service for; oblige. **2.** To furnish or supply with something needed; especially, to provide with lodging or housing. **3. a.** To contain comfortably or have space for. **b.** To admit the inclusion of: *The party accommodates a wide range of moderate views.* **4.** To adapt, adjust, or make fit. Often used with *to.* **5.** To bring into harmony or agreement; settle; reconcile. —*intr.* To become adjusted, as the eye to focusing on objects at a distance. —See Synonyms at **contain.** [Latin *accommodāre,* to make fit : *ad-*, to + *commodus,* fit, "conforming with the (right) measure" : *con-*, with + *modus,* measure.] **—ac·com·mo·da·tive** (-daytiv) *adj.*

ac·com·mo·dat·ing (ə-kómmə-dayting) *adj.* Helpful and obliging. **—ac·com·mo·dat·ing·ly** *adv.*

ac·com·mo·da·tion (ə-kómmə-dáysh'n) *n.* **1.** The act of accommodating or the state of being accommodated; adaptation, adjustment, or reconciliation. **2.** Anything that meets a need; a convenience. **3. a.** Space or premises for living or staying; especially, lodgings. **b.** *Plural. U.S.* Lodgings, or a seat or space in a public vehicle. **4.** An arrangement by which opposing views are settled; a compromise. **5.** *Physiology.* Adaptation or adjustment in an organism, organ, or part, as takes place in the lens of the eye to permit retinal focus of images of objects at different distances. **6.** *Commerce.* A loan or other financial favour.

accommodation address *n.* A postal address of a person or business which is different from the actual address.

accommodation bill *n.* A bill of exchange endorsed by a guarantor to ensure the credit of the drawer.

accommodation ladder *n. Nautical.* A portable ladder or stairway hung from the side of a ship.

ac·com·pa·ni·ment (ə-kúmp-əni-mənt, -ni- || -kómp-) *n.* **1.** Something that accompanies; a concomitant. **2.** Something added for embellishment, completeness, or symmetry; a complement. **3.** *Music.* A vocal or instrumental part that supports a solo part.

ac·com·pa·nist (ə-kúmp-ənist -nist || -kómp-) *n. Music.* A performer, such as a pianist, who plays an accompaniment.

ac·com·pa·ny (ə-kúmp-əni, -ni || -kómp-) *v.* **-nied, -nying, -nies.** —*tr.* **1.** To go along with; join in company. **2.** To supplement; add to: *the captions accompanying an illustration.* **3.** To coexist or occur with. **4.** To perform a musical accompaniment to or for. —*intr.* To play a musical accompaniment. [Middle English *accompanien,* from Old French *accompagner* : *ac-*, from Latin *ad-*, to + *compain(g),* companion, from Late Latin *compāniō,* COMPANION.]

Synonyms: *accompany, conduct, escort, chaperone.*

ac·com·plice (ə-kúmplis, -kómplis) *n.* One who aids or abets another in wrongdoing, especially in a criminal act. —See Synonyms at **partner.** [Middle English, from *a complice,* a COMPLICE (influenced by ACCOMPLISH).]

ac·com·plish (ə-kúmplish, -kómplish) *tr.v.* **-plished, -plishing, -plishes. 1.** To succeed in doing; achieve. **2.** To reach the end of; complete; finish. —See Synonyms at **perform, reach.** [Middle English *accomplissen,* from Old French *accomplir* (present stem *accompliss-*), to complete : *ac-*, from Latin *ad-*, to + *complir,* to complete, from Latin *complēre,* "to fill up", to finish : *com-* (intensive) + *plēre,* to fill.] **—ac·com·plish·a·ble** *adj.* **—ac·com·plish·er** *n.*

ac·com·plished (ə-kúmplisht, -kómplisht) *adj.* **1.** Skilled; proficient, especially through training and practice. **2.** Sophisticated; having many social accomplishments.

ac·com·plish·ment (ə-kúmplish-mənt, -kómplish-) *n.* **1.** The act of accomplishing or the state of being accomplished; completion. **2.** Something completed successfully; an achievement. **3.** A quality or faculty that contributes to a person's social poise; a social skill. **4.** Any talent or skill.

ac·cord (ə-kórd) *v.* **-corded, -cording, -cords.** —*tr.* **1.** To cause to conform or agree; bring into harmony. **2.** To grant or bestow: *I accord you my blessing.* —*intr.* To be consistent, in agreement, or in harmony. Often used with *with.*
~*n.* **1.** Agreement, harmony, or conformity. Used especially in the phrase *in accord with.* **2.** A settlement or compromise between conflicting opinions; especially, a settlement of points at issue between nations; a treaty. **—of (one's) own accord.** Voluntarily. **—with one accord.** Unanimously. [Middle English *acorden,* from Old French *acorder,* from Vulgar Latin *accordāre* (unattested), "to be heart-to-heart with" : Latin *ad-*, to + *cor* (stem *cord-*), heart.]

ac·cord·ance (ə-kórd'nss) *n.* **1.** Agreement; conformity. Used especially in the phrase *in accordance with.* **2.** The act of granting.

ac·cord·ant (ə-kórd'nt) *adj.* In agreement or harmony; corresponding; consonant. Usually used with *with.* **—ac·cord·ant·ly** *adv.*

ac·cord·ing as (ə-kórding) *conj.* **1.** Consistently with the way in which; to the extent that. **2.** Depending on whether.

ac·cord·ing·ly (ə-kórdingli) *adv.* **1.** In a way that corresponds or accords with what the circumstances imply or demand; appropriately. **2.** Consequently.

according to *prep. Abbr.* **acc. 1.** In accordance with. **2.** In proportion to. **3.** In the report of; as stated or shown by.

ac·cor·di·on (ə-kórdi-ən) *n.* A portable musical instrument with a small keyboard and free metal reeds that sound when air is forced past them by pleated bellows operated by the player. See **piano-accordion.** [German *Akkordion,* from *Akkord,* agreement, "harmony", from French *accord,* from Old French *acorder,* to ACCORD.] **—ac·cor·di·on·ist** *n.*

ac·cost (ə-kóst || -káwst) *tr.v.* **-costed, -costing, -costs. 1.** To approach and speak to, especially boldly or accusingly. **2.** To solicit sexually. [Old French *accoster,* from Vulgar Latin *accostāre* (unattested), to come alongside someone : Latin *ad-*, near + *costa,* side, rib.]

ac·couche·ment (ə-kóōshmon) *n.* A confinement; childbirth.

ac·cou·cheur (ákōō-shér || -shóor) *n. Feminine* **ac·cou·cheuse** (-shérz, -shōz || -shōōz). A midwife or obstetrician. [French, "one attending at the bedside" : *ac-*, at + *coucheur,* from *couche,* bed.]

ac·count (ə-kównt || *West Indian* -kúngt) *n.* **1.** A written or oral narration or description: *an eyewitness account of the accident.* **2.** An explanatory statement or report; especially, a statement explaining and justifying one's conduct: *called to give an account of his year in office.* **3.** A demonstration or exposition, as of one's qualities or abilities: *gave a good account of herself at the interview.* **4.** A particular version, report, or stated opinion: *by all accounts a formidable character.* **5.** Worth, standing, or importance: *a man of some account.* **6.** Consideration; notice: *taking into account the level of inflation.* **7.** Profit; advantage: *turned her talents to good account.* **8.** A precise list or enumeration of monetary transactions. **9.** *Abbr.* **a/c, A/C, acct., acc.** *Finance.* **a.** A business relationship involving the exchange of money or credit: *a bank account.* **b.** The client or customer involved in such a relationship. **c.** A specific section of a business involved in such a relationship: *the agency handling our advertising account.* **d.** The amount of money held by a depositor in a bank. **e.** A statement recording all transactions relating to an account during a particular period and showing the current balance of money held or due. **10.** *Often capital* **A.** On the London stock exchange, any of the consecutive two- or three-week periods during which credit is allowed on transactions made. Preceded by *the.* **—call to account. 1.** To hold answerable. **2.** To reprimand. **—on account. 1.** On credit. **2.** In part payment. **—on account of. 1.** Because of. **2.** For the sake of: *Don't wait on my account.* **3.** *Nonstandard.* Because. **—on no account.** Under no circumstances. **—on (one's) own account. 1.** On one's own behalf. **2.** At one's own risk. **3.** *Chiefly U.S.* On one's own.
~*tr.v.* **accounted, -counting, -counts.** To consider or esteem: "*Your honour is accounted a merciful man.*" (Shakespeare). **—account for. 1.** To provide a reckoning, as of (funds received and paid out), or of (people or things): *Six survivors have been accounted for.* **2.** To provide an explanation or justification for. **3.** To be the explanation or cause of. **4.** To kill, capture, or disable. [Middle English, from Old French *acont, acompt,* from *acunter, acompter,* "to count up to", reckon : *ac-*, from Latin *ad-*, to + *cunter, compter,* to COUNT (compute).]

ac·count·a·ble (ə-kówntəb'l) *adj.* **1.** Liable to be called to account for one's conduct; answerable. Used with *to* and/or *for.* **2.** Capable of being explained. **—ac·count·a·bil·i·ty, —ac·count·a·ble·ness** *n.* **—ac·count·a·bly** *adv.*

ac·count·an·cy (ə-kównt-ənsi) *n.* The practice, profession, or business of an accountant.

ac·count·ant (ə-kównt-ənt) *n. Abbr.* **acc.** One who keeps, audits, and inspects the financial records of individuals or business concerns and prepares financial reports and tax returns. See **chartered accountant.**

ac·count·ing (ə-kównt-ing) *n.* The principles and methods involved in keeping a financial record of business transactions and in preparing statements concerning the assets, liabilities, and operating results of a business.

ac·cou·tre (ə-kóōtər) *tr.v.* **-tred, -tring, -tres.** Also *U.S.* **ac·cou·ter.** To equip or attire, especially with a particular type of outfit or uniform. Usually used in the passive. [French *accoutrer,* from Old French *acoustrer,* from Vulgar Latin *acconsūtūrāre* (unattested), to equip (with clothes) : Latin *ad-*, to + *consūtūra* (unattested), sewing, clothes, from Latin *consuere,* to sew together : *con-*, together + *suere,* to sew.]

ac·cou·tre·ment, *U.S.* **ac·cou·ter·ment** (ə-kóōtrəmənt || ə-kóōtərmənt) *n.* **1.** The act of accoutring. **2.** *Plural.* Equipment, adornments, or accessories; especially, the equipment other than arms and uniform issued to a soldier. **3.** *Plural.* The outward forms whereby a thing may be recognised; trappings.

Ac·cra (ə-kraá, a-). The capital of Ghana, located on the Gulf of Guinea. It was originally the capital of an ancient Ga Kingdom, and became the capital of the Gold Coast, a British colony, in 1876.

It developed into the country's economic centre after the completion, in 1923, of a railway to the mining and agricultural regions inland.

ac·cred·it (ə-kréddit) *tr.v.* **-ited, -iting, -its. 1. a.** To ascribe or attribute to someone. **b.** To credit (someone) with something. **2. a.** To supply with credentials or authority; authorise. **b.** To appoint as an ambassador or envoy. **3.** To recognise or certify as of a prescribed standard. [French *accréditer,* from *(mettre) á crédit,* "(to put) to CREDIT".] **—ac·cred·i·ta·tion** (-áysh'n) *n.* **—ac·cred·it·ed** *adj.*

ac·crete (ə-kréet) *v.* **-creted, -creting, -cretes.** *—tr.* To attract or attach (additional elements) so as to cause increased growth. *—intr.* **1.** To grow together; fuse. **2.** To become attached, so as to cause increased growth. Used with *to.* [Back-formation from ACCRETION.]

ac·cre·tion (ə-kréesh'n) *n.* **1.** Growth or increase in size by the gradual addition, fusion, or inclusion of external elements; specifically, the process by which an astronomical body increases in size or mass as a result of gravitationally attracting less dense material surrounding or adjoining it. **2.** Something added externally to promote such growth or increase. **3.** *Biology.* **a.** Any growing together of plant or animal tissues that are normally separate. **b.** A build-up of foreign matter in a cavity. **4.** *Geology.* A slow build-up of material, such as deposition of a water-borne sediment. **5.** *Law.* **a.** An increase of land through a process of natural growth, as by alluvial deposit. **b.** An increase in the share of a property when a joint owner or beneficiary dies or fails to take up his share. [Latin *accrēscere* (past participle *accrētus*), to ACCRUE.] **—ac·cre·tion·ar·y, ac·cre·tive** *adj.*

accretion theory *n.* The theory that the continents have increased in size during geological time as continental drift has moved the landmasses about the globe, building up new mountain ranges.

ac·crue (ə-kro͞o) *intr.v.* **-crued, -cruing, -crues. 1.** To come to someone or something as a gain or addition. **2.** To increase or accumulate, as by natural growth or as interest on capital. **3.** *Law.* To become enforceable or permanent. Used of a right. [Middle English *acrewen,* probably from Old French *accreue,* growth, from the past participle of *accreistre,* to increase, from Latin *accrēscere* : *ad-,* in addition + *crēscere,* to grow.] **—ac·cru·al, ac·crue·ment** *n.*

acct. account.

ac·cul·tur·ate (ə-kúlchərayt) *v.* **-ated, -ating, -ates.** *—tr.* To cause to change by the process of acculturation. *—intr.* To change or be modified by acculturation.

ac·cul·tur·a·tion (ə-kúlchə-ráysh'n) *n.* The modification of the culture of an individual or group through prolonged contact with a different culture; especially, the modification of a primitive culture through contact with an advanced culture. [AD- (towards) + CULTUR(E) + -ATION.]

ac·cum·bent (ə-kúmbənt) *adj. Botany.* Resting against another part. Said especially of cotyledons. [Latin *accumbēns* (stem *accumbent-*), present participle of *accumbere,* to recline : *ad-,* near to + *cumbere,* to recline.] **—ac·cum·ben·cy** *n.*

ac·cu·mu·late (ə-kéwmewlayt) *v.* **-lated, -lating, -lates.** *—tr.* To amass or gather; pile up; collect. *—intr.* To grow or increase; mount up. —See Synonyms at **gather.** [Latin *accumulāre* : *ad-,* in addition + *cumulāre,* to pile up, from *cumulus,* a heap.] **—ac·cu·mu·la·ble** (ə-kéwmewləb'l) *adj.* **—ac·cu·mu·la·tive** (ə-kéwmew-lətiv, -laytiv) *adj.* **—ac·cu·mu·la·tive·ly** *adv.* **—ac·cu·mu·la·tive·ness** *n.*

ac·cu·mu·la·tion (ə-kéwmew-láysh'n) *n.* **1.** The act or process of accumulating; amassing or growing, as into a heap or large amount. **2.** A mass or quantity that has accumulated or been accumulated. **3.** The growth of capital by retention of interest or profit.

ac·cu·mu·la·tor (ə-kéwmewlaytər) *n.* **1.** Someone or something that accumulates. **2.** A register or electrical circuit in a calculator or computer that stores figures for computation. **3.** A **storage battery** *(see),* especially one used in a road vehicle. **4.** *British.* A single compound bet on several successive horse or dog races, in which the total winnings on each race become the stake of the next race and accumulate, provided that a win is recorded at each stage of the bet.

ac·cu·ra·cy (áckew-rəsi) *n.* Exactness; correctness; accurateness.

ac·cu·rate (áckew-rət, -rit) *adj.* **1. a.** Having no errors; correct. **b.** Marked by or showing careful attention to what is true or correct. **2.** Deviating only slightly or within acceptable limits from a standard. [Latin *accūrātus,* done with care, past participle of *accūrāre,* to attend to carefully : *ad-,* to + *cūrāre,* to care for, attend to, from *cūra,* care.] **—ac·cu·rate·ly** *adv.* **—ac·cu·rate·ness** *n.*

ac·curs·ed (ə-kúrssid || ə-kúrst) *adj.* Also **ac·curst** (ə-kúrst). **1.** Under a curse; doomed. **2.** Abominable; hateful. [Middle English *acursed,* from *acursen,* to curse, Old English *ācursian* : *ā-* (intensive) + *cursian,* to curse, from *curs,* CURSE.] **—ac·curs·ed·ly** *adv.* **—ac·curs·ed·ness** *n.*

ac·cu·sal (ə-kéwz'l) *n.* An accusation.

ac·cu·sa·tion (áckew-záysh'n) *n.* **1.** The act of accusing or the fact of being accused. **2.** An allegation. **3.** *Law.* A formal charge brought before a court against a person, stating that he is guilty of some punishable offence.

ac·cu·sa·tive (ə-kéwzətiv) *adj. Abbr.* **acc.** Of, pertaining to, or designating the case of a noun, pronoun, adjective, or participle that is the direct object of a verb or the object of certain prepositions. *~n.* **1.** The accusative case. **2.** A form or construction in this case. [Middle English, from Latin *(casus) accūsātīvus,* "(case) indicating accusation" (mistranslation of Greek *aitiatikos ptōsis,* "case of causation"), from *accūsāre,* to ACCUSE.] **—ac·cu·sa·tive·ly** *adv.*

ac·cu·sa·to·ri·al (əkéwzə-táwri-əl || -tōri-) *adj.* Of or designating a procedure of criminal justice in which the judge assesses the validity of an accusation as argued by a prosecutor. Compare **inquisitorial.**

ac·cu·sa·to·ry (ə-kéwzə-tri, -təri) *adj.* Containing or implying an accusation.

ac·cuse (ə-kéwz) *tr.v.* **-cused, -cusing, -cuses.** *—tr.* **1.** To charge with a shortcoming or error; blame. **2.** To bring charges against (someone) for a crime or offence. Used with *of.* [Middle English *acusen,* from Old French *acuser,* from Latin *accūsāre,* to accuse, "call to account" : *ad-,* to + *causa,* CAUSE.] **—ac·cus·er** *n.* **—ac·cus·ing·ly** *adv.*

ac·cused (ə-kéwzd) *n., pl.* **accused.** *Law.* The defendant in a criminal case. Preceded by *the.*

ac·cus·tom (ə-kústəm) *tr.v.* **-tomed, -toming, -toms.** To familiarise, as by constant practice, use, or habit. Often used reflexively. [Middle English *accustomen,* from Old French *aco(u)stumer* : *a-,* from Latin *ad-,* to + *costume,* CUSTOM.]

ac·cus·tomed (ə-kústəmd) *adj.* **1.** Usual, characteristic, or normal: *sitting in her accustomed place.* **2.** In the habit of; used to. Used with *to*: *accustomed to sleeping late.* —See Synonyms at **usual.**

AC/DC (áy-see-dée-see) *adj. Slang.* Bisexual. [Humorous allusion to *alternating* and *direct current* and an electrical appliance adaptable to either.]

ace (ayss) *n.* **1. a.** A single pip or spot on a playing card, dice, or domino. **b.** A playing card, dice, or domino having one spot or pip. **2.** In tennis: Any serve that one's opponent is unable to reach or return. **3.** A military aircraft pilot who has destroyed several enemy aircraft: *an air ace.* **4.** *Informal.* A person with great skill in a particular activity. **—hold all the aces.** To be in a position of advantage or control. **—within an ace of.** Very close to: *within an ace of victory.* *~adj. Informal.* **1.** Highly skilled; expert. **2.** Of the highest quality; really good.
~tr.v. **aced, acing, aces.** In tennis, to serve an ace against. [Middle English *aas,* from Old French *as,* from Latin *ās,* unit. See **as** (Roman coin).]

-acean *n & adj. suffix.* Indicates an animal belonging to a taxonomic class or order; for example, **cetacean.** [New Latin *-acea* and *-aceae,* neuter and feminine plural of *-aceus,* -ACEOUS.]

acedia. Variant of **accidie.**

A·cel·da·ma[1] (ə-kél-dəmə, -sél-, áckel-daámə). The potter's field near Jerusalem purchased by the priests as a burying ground for strangers with the reward which Judas had received for betraying Jesus and which he had returned to them. Matthew 27:7. [Greek *Akeldama,* from Aramaic *ḥăqēl dĕmā,* "field of blood".]

Aceldama[2] *n.* Any place with dreadful associations.

a·cel·lu·lar (áy-séllewlər) *adj. Biology.* Containing no cells; not made up of cells.

a·cen·tric (áy-séntrik) *adj.* **1.** Having no centre. **2.** Not centred; placed off-centre. [A- (not) + CENTRIC.]

-aceous *adj. suffix.* Indicates: **1.** Of or pertaining to; for example, **sebaceous. 2.** Resembling or of the nature of; for example, **farinaceous. 3.** Belonging to a taxonomic category, especially a botanical family; for example, **orchidaceous.** [New Latin *-aceus,* from Latin *-āceus,* "of a specific kind or group", originally an extension of an adjectival suffix *-āx,* (stem *-āc-*).]

a·ceph·a·lous (áy-séff'l-əss) *adj.* **1.** *Zoology.* Headless or lacking a clearly defined head. **2.** Having no leader: *an acephalous tribe.* [Medieval Latin *acephalus,* headless, from Greek *akephalos* : *a-* (not) + -CEPHALOUS.]

ac·e·rate (ássə-rayt) *adj.* Also **ac·e·rat·ed** (-raytid). *Biology.* Pointed at one end; needle-shaped. [Latin *ācer,* sharp.]

ac·er·bate (ássərbayt) *tr.v.* **-bated, -bating, -bates.** *Rare.* To vex; annoy. [Latin *acerbāre,* to make sour, from *acerbus,* ACERBIC.]

a·cerb·ic (ə-sérbik) *adj.* **1.** Sour; bitter; astringent. **2.** Harsh in manner or speech; cutting. [Latin *acerbus,* sharp, bitter.]

a·cer·bi·ty (ə-sérbəti) *n., pl.* **-ties. 1.** Sourness of taste. **2.** Acrimony; sharpness of speech of manner. **3.** An instance of this.

ac·e·rose (ássə-rōss, -rōz) *adj. Botany.* Slender and sharp-pointed, as a pine needle. [Incorrect use (by Linnaeus as if from Latin *ācer,* sharp, ACERATE) of Latin *acerōsus,* from *acus* (stem *acer-*), chaff.]

acet. acetone.

acet. a. acetic acid.

ac·e·tab·u·lum (ássi-tábbew-ləm) *n., pl.* **-la** (-lə). **1.** *Anatomy.* The cup-shaped cavity in the hipbone into which the head of the thighbone fits. **2.** *Zoology.* A sucker, such as that of an octopus or cuttlefish. [Latin *acētābulum,* vinegar cup, from *acētum,* vinegar; akin to *ācer,* sharp.] **—ac·e·tab·u·lar** (-lər) *adj.*

ac·e·tal (ássi-tal) *n.* **1.** A colourless, flammable, volatile liquid, $CH_3CH(OC_2H_5)_2$, used in cosmetics and as a solvent. **2.** Any of the class of compounds formed from aldehydes combined with alcohols. [German *Azetal* : ACET(O)- + AL(COHOL).]

ac·et·al·de·hyde (ásit-ál-di-hīd) *n.* A colourless, flammable liquid, CH_3CHO, used to manufacture acetic acid, perfumes, and drugs. Also called "ethanal". [ACET(O)- + ALDEHYDE.]

a·cet·a·mide (ə-séttəmīd, ássit-ámmīd) *n.* Also **a·cet·a·mid** (ə-séttəmid, ássit-ámmid). The crystalline amide of acetic acid, CH_3CONH_2, used as a wetting agent and in lacquers and explosives. Also called "ethanamide". [German *Azetamid* : ACET(O)- + AMIDE.]

ac·et·an·i·lide (ássit-ánn'l-īd) *n.* Also **ac·et·an·i·lid** (-id). A white crystalline compound, $C_6H_5NH(COCH_3)$, used medicinally to relieve pain and reduce fever. [ACET(O)- + ANIL(INE) + -IDE.]

ac·e·tate (ássitayt) *n.* **1.** A salt or ester of acetic acid. **2.** Cellulose acetate or any of various products, especially fibres and fabrics, derived from it. [ACET(O)- + -ATE.] —**ac·e·tat·ed** adj.

a·ce·tic (ə-séetik, ə-séttik) adj. Of, pertaining to, or containing acetic acid or vinegar. [Latin acētum, vinegar, akin to ācer, sharp.]

acetic acid CH₃CO. n. Abbr. **acet. a.** A clear, colourless organic acid, CH₃COOH, with a distinctive pungent odour, widely used as a solvent and in industry. It is the characteristic ingredient of vinegar. Also called "ethanoic acid" and, when at least 99.8 per cent pure, "glacial acetic acid".

acetic anhydride n. An organic liquid, (CH₃CO)₂O, with a pungent odour, combining with water to produce acetic acid and used as an acetylating agent.

a·cet·i·fy (ə-sétti-fī) v. **-fied, -fying, -fies.** —tr. To convert (a neutral liquid) to acetic acid or vinegar. —intr. To become acetic; turn into acetic acid or vinegar. [ACET(O)- + -FY.] —**a·cet·i·fi·ca·tion** (-fi-káysh'n) n. —**a·cet·i·fi·er** n.

aceto-, acet- comb. form. Indicates the presence of acetic acid or the acetyl radical; for example, **acetophenetidin, acetify.** [Latin acētum, vinegar.]

ac·e·to·a·ce·tic acid (ə-séetō-ə-séetik, ássitō-) n. A syrupy, colourless acid, CH₃COCH₂COOH, excreted in the urine and found in abnormal quantities in the urine of diabetics.

ac·e·tone (ássi-tōn) n. Abbr. **acet.** A colourless, volatile, extremely flammable liquid, CH₃COCH₃, widely used as an organic solvent and, in especially pure grades, to clean and dry electronic component materials. Also called "propanone". [German Azeton : ACET(O)- + -ONE.] —**ac·e·ton·ic** (-tónnik) adj.

acetone body n. Biochemistry. A **ketone body** (see).

ac·e·to·phe·net·i·din (ə-séetō-fə-nétti-din, ássitō-) n. A white powder or crystalline solid, CH₃CONHC₆H₄OC₂H₅, used in medicine to reduce fever and relieve pain. Also called "phenacetin". [ACETO- + PHEN(O)- + ET(HYL) + -ID(E) + -IN.]

ac·e·tous (ássitəs, ə-séetəss) adj. Also **ac·e·tose** (ássi-tōss). 1. Of, pertaining to, or producing acetic acid or vinegar. 2. Having an acetic taste; sour-tasting. [Late Latin acētōsus, vinegary, from acētum, vinegar.]

a·ce·tum (ə-séetəm) n. An acetic acid solution of a drug. [Latin acētum, akin to ācer, sharp.]

ac·e·tyl (ássitīl, ə-séetīl ‖ U.S. ássətil, ə-séet'l) n. The acetic acid radical CH₃CO. [ACET(O)- + -YL.] —**ac·e·tyl·ic** (ássi-tíllik) adj.

a·cet·y·late (ə-sétti-layt) v. **-lated, -lating, -lates.** —tr. To introduce an acetyl group into (an organic molecule), using a reagent such as acetic anhydride. —intr. To undergo introduction of an acetyl group. —**a·cet·y·la·tion** (-láysh'n) n.

ac·e·tyl·cho·line (ássitīl-kō̄-leen, əséetīl-, -lin ‖ U.S. ássatil-, əséet'l-) n. A white crystalline compound, C₇H₁₇NO₃, released at some nerve endings when a nerve impulse is transmitted from one nerve fibre to another. [ACETYL + CHOLINE.]

ac·e·tyl·cho·lin·es·ter·ase (ássitīl-kō̄leen-éstər-ayss, -kólleen-, -ayz) n. An enzyme, **cholinesterase** (see).

a·cet·y·lene (ə-séttil-een, -sétt'l- ‖ U.S. also -ən) n. A colourless, highly flammable or explosive gas, C₂H₂, used for metal welding and cutting and as an illuminant. Also called "ethyne". [ACETYL + -ENE.] —**a·cet·y·len·ic** adj.

acetylene series n. A series of unsaturated aliphatic hydrocarbons, each containing a triple carbon bond, having chemical properties resembling acetylene and having the general formula CₙH₂ₙ₋₂, with acetylene being the simplest member. Also called "alkyne series".

a·ce·tyl·sali·cyl·ic acid (ássitīl-sál-i-sillik, ə-séetīl- ‖ U.S. ássətil-, ə-séet'l-) n. A common drug, **aspirin** (see).

ace·y·deuc·y (áyssi-déwssi ‖ -dōossi) n. A variation of backgammon. [ACE + DEUCE.]

ach. Chiefly South African. Variant of **agh.**

A·chae·a (ə-kée-ə). Also **A·chai·a** (ə-kī́-ə). A region of ancient Greece occupying the north part of the Peloponnese on the Gulf of Corinth. The cities of the region banded together in the early third century B.C. to form the Achaean league, which defeated Sparta but was eventually beaten by the Romans. Rome annexed Achaea in 146 B.C. and later gave the name to a Roman province comprising all of Greece south of Thessaly. The name Achaea (Greek: Akhaïa) is now used for a modern prefecture in the northern Peloponnese, whose capital is Patras.

A·chae·an (ə-kée-ən) n. Also **A·cha·ian** (ə-kī́-ən). 1. A native or inhabitant of Achaea. 2. In epics about the Mycenaean period, any Greek. —**A·chae·an** adj.

A·chae·me·nid (ə-kéemə-nid, -kémmə-) n. A member of the ruling dynasty of Persia from the time of Cyrus the Great to the death of Darius III (559–330 B.C.). [Greek Akhaimenidēs, from Akhaimenēs, founder of the dynasty.] —**A·chae·me·nid** adj.

ache (ayk) intr.v. **ached, aching, aches.** 1. To suffer, or cause one to suffer, a dull, sustained pain. 2. Informal. To yearn painfully. —n. A dull, steady pain. [Middle English aken, Old English acan.]

A·che·be (ə-chébbay), **Chinua**, pen name of Albert Chinualumogo (1930–), Nigerian Ibo novelist and poet, whose writings deal with the conflict arising when traditional African society faces Western culture. His works include the novels Things Fall Apart (1958) and Deadly Voyage (1996).

a·chene (ə-kéen, ay-) n. Botany. A dry, thin-walled, one-seeded fruit, such as that of the buttercup and dandelion, that does not split open when ripe. [New Latin achēnium, "one that does not yawn or split open" : A- (not) + Greek khainein, to yawn.] —**a·che·ni·al** (-kéeni-əl) adj.

A·cher·nar (áykər-naar) n. A star in the constellation Eridanus that is one of the brightest stars in the sky and is 114 light-years from Earth. [Arabic ākhīr al-nahr, "the end of the river" (referring to the star's position in ERIDANUS).

Ach·e·ron (áckə-rən, -ron) n. Greek Mythology. 1. The river of woe over which Charon ferried the souls of the dead to Hades. 2. The underworld; Hades.

Ach·e·son (áchiss'n), **Dean Gooderham** (1893–1971). U.S. lawyer and statesman. He was Secretary of State under President Truman and later became a presidential adviser. He promoted the Marshall Plan and helped to establish NATO.

A·cheu·li·an, A·cheu·le·an (ə-shōoli-ən) adj. Archaeology. Of or designating a stage of culture of the European Lower Palaeolithic Age, about 250,000 years ago, characterised by symmetrical stone hand axes. [French acheuléen, after St. Acheul, village in northern France and site of the archaeological finds from which the culture was classified.]

à che·val (ásho-vál ‖ U.S. ásho-vaál) adv. Positioned so as to straddle a line on a gambling table between two numbers or cards. Used especially in roulette. [French, "on horseback".]

a·chieve (ə-chéev) v. **achieved, achieving, achieves.** —tr. 1. To accomplish; succeed in doing. 2. To attain or get as a result of one's efforts, skill, or perseverance. —intr. To attain a satisfactory standard: schoolchildren who fail to achieve. See **underachieve.** —See Synonyms at **perform, reach.** [Middle English acheven, from Old French achever, "to bring to a head", from a chef, "to a head" : a, to, from Latin ad- + chef, head, from Latin caput.] —**a·chiev·a·ble** adj. —**a·chiev·er** n.

a·chieve·ment (ə-chéevmənt) n. 1. The act of accomplishing, attaining, or finishing something. 2. Something that has been accomplished successfully, especially by means of skill, practice, or perseverance. 3. Heraldry. A coat of arms.

A·chil·les (ə-kílleez). In Greek legend, the greatest of the Greek warriors at the siege of Troy, who killed the Trojan Hector and was himself later killed by Paris. He was the son of Peleus and the sea nymph Thetis.

Achilles' heel n. A small but significant weakness; a vulnerable point. [From the myth that Achilles was invulnerable except in the heel.]

Achilles' tendon n. The large tendon running from the heel bone to the calf muscle of the leg.

Ach·ill Island (áckil). A rugged and mountainous island in the Republic of Ireland off the west coast of County Mayo. With an area of 148 square kilometres (57 square miles), it is the largest offshore Irish island.

Achitophel. Variant of **Ahithophel.**

ach·la·myd·e·ous (áckla-míddi-əss, áyklə-) adj. Botany. Having no floral envelope; without calyx or corolla. [A- (not) + CHLAMY-DEOUS.]

a·chon·drite (áy-kóndrīt) n. A stony meteorite that contains no chondrules (see). [A- (not) + CHONDRITE.]

a·chon·dro·pla·si·a (áy-kóndrō-pláyzi-ə ‖ U.S. -pláyzhə) n. Abnormal development of cartilage at the ends of the long bones, resulting in congenital dwarfism. [A- (not) + CHONDRO- + -PLASIA.] —**a·chon·dro·plas·tic** (-plástik, -pláastik) adj.

ach·ro·mat·ic (áckrō-máttik, áykrō-) adj. 1. Free from colour; having no hue. Said of neutral colours like grey, black, and white. 2. Optics. Refracting light without spectral colour separation. 3. Biology. Not readily absorbing colour from standard dyes. 4. Music. Having only the diatonic notes of the scale. [Greek akhrōmatos, colourless : a-, not, without + khrōma, colour.] —**ach·ro·mat·i·cal·ly** adv. —**a·chro·ma·tism** (ə-krōmə-tiz'm, áy-), **a·chro·ma·tic·i·ty** (-tíssəti) n.

achromatic lens n. A combination of lenses to produce images free of chromatic aberrations. Also called "achromat".

a·chro·ma·tise, a·chro·ma·tize (áy-krōmətīz, ə-) tr.v. **-tised, -tising, -tises.** To make achromatic; rid of colour.

a·chro·ma·tous (áy-krōmətəss, ə-) adj. 1. Without colour. 2. With less colour than is usual or needed. [Greek akhrōmatos, ACHRO-MATIC.]

a·chro·mic (áy-krṓ-mik, ə-) adj. Also **a·chro·mous** (-məss). Colourless. [A- (not) + CHROMIC.]

a·cic·u·la (ə-síckew-lə) n., pl. **-lae** (-lee). A needle-like object or part, such as a bristle, spine, or crystal. [New Latin, from Latin acicula, hairpin, diminutive of acus, needle.] —**a·cic·u·lar, a·cic·u·late** (-lət, -lit, -layt), **a·cic·u·lat·ed** (laytid) adj.

ac·id (ássid) n. 1. Chemistry. **a.** Any of a large class of substances whose aqueous solutions are capable of turning litmus indicators red, of reacting with and dissolving certain metals to form salts, of reacting with bases or alkalis to form salts, or of having a sour taste. **b.** A substance that ionises in solution to give the positive ion of the solvent. **c.** A substance capable of giving up a proton. **d.** Any molecule or ion that can combine with another by forming a covalent bond with two electrons of the other. In this sense, also called "Lewis acid". 2. A substance with a sour taste. 3. Slang. A hallucinogen, **LSD** (see). 4. Acid House or acid rock. —adj. 1. Chemistry. **a.** Of or pertaining to an acid. **b.** Having a high concentration of acid. 2. Having a sour taste. 3. Having or indicative of a biting, sharp, or unkind nature; caustic: an acid wit. 4. Geology. Designating an igneous rock containing more than 66 per cent of silica. 5. Designating soil having a pH value below 7.2. [Latin acidus, sharp, sour, from acēre, to be sour, akin to ācer, sharp.] —**ac·id·ly** adv. —**ac·id·ness** n.

ac·id-fast (ássid-faast ‖ -fast) adj. Not readily decolorised by acid. Said of stained tissues and microorganisms. —**ac·id-fast·ness** n.

a·cid-head (ássid-hed) *n. Slang.* A person who habitually uses the drug LSD.
Acid House *n.* Pop music identical or similar to House, often using catchwords at key moments and the repetition of musical phrases, and typically experienced at a venue where mood-altering drugs are consumed. [Probably from ACID (ROCK) + HOUSE.]
a·cid·ic (ə-síddik) *adj.* **1.** Acid. **2.** Tending to form an acid.
a·cid·i·fy (ə-síddi-fī) *v.* **-fied, -fying, -fies.** *—tr.* To make acid. *—intr.* To become acid. **—a·cid·i·fi·a·ble** *adj.* **—a·cid·i·fi·ca·tion** (-fikáysh'n) *n.* **—a·cid·i·fi·er** *n.*
ac·i·dim·e·ter (ássi-dímmitər) *n.* A hydrometer used to determine the relative density of acid solutions. Also called "acidometer". **—ac·i·di·met·ric** (-di-méttrik) *adj.* **—ac·i·dim·e·try** *n.*
a·cid·i·ty (ə-síddəti) *n.* **1.** The state, quality or degree of being acid; acidness. **2.** *Medicine.* Excessive acidity, **hyperacidity** *(see).*
ac·i·do·phil·ic (ássi-dō-fíllik) *adj. Microbiology.* **1.** Growing well in an acid medium. **2.** Easily stained with acid dyes. [ACID + -O- + -PHILIC.] **—a·cid·o·phil** (ássidō-fil, ə-síddō-), **a·cid·o·phile** (-fil) *n.*
ac·i·do·sis (ássi-dṓ-siss) *n.* A condition of pathologically high acidity of the blood and body tissues. **—ac·i·dot·ic** (-dóttik) *adj.*
acid precipitation *n.* Precipitation having an abnormally high sulphuric and nitric acid content caused by industrial pollution.
acid rain *n.* Acid precipitation falling as rain.
acid rock *n.* A type of rock music supposedly inspired by the drug LSD, characterised by free improvised instrumental passages.
acid salt *n.* A salt of a polyprotic acid in which one or more acid hydrogen atoms have not been replaced by positive ions, as in sodium bicarbonate ($NaHCO_3$).
acid test *n.* A rigorous or decisive test of worth or quality. [From the test of gold in nitric acid.]
a·cid·u·late (ə-síddew-layt) *tr.v.* **-lated, -lating, -lates.** To make slightly acid. [ACIDUL(OUS) + -ATE.] **—a·cid·u·la·tion** (-láysh'n) *n.*
a·cid·u·lous (ə-síddew-ləss) *adj.* **1.** Rather sour in taste. **2.** Sour in feeling or manner; biting; caustic. [Latin *acidulus,* sourish, diminutive of *acidus,* sour, ACID.]
acid value *n.* The amount of free acid in a fat, oil, or the like, expressed as the number of milligrams of potassium hydroxide necessary to neutralise the free acid in one gram of the substance.
ac·i·er·ate (ássi-ərayt) *tr. v.* **-ated, -ating, -ates.** To convert (iron) into steel. [French *acier,* steel, from Latin *aciēs,* sharpness, from *ācer,* sharp + -ATE.] **—ac·i·er·a·tion** (-əráysh'n) *n.*
ac·i·nac·i·form (ássi-nássi-fawrm) *adj. Botany.* Resembling a scimitar in shape: *acinaciform leaves.* [Latin *acinācēs,* short sabre, from Greek *akinakēs,* from Iranian + -FORM.]
ac·i·nar (ássinər) *adj. Anatomy.* Of or pertaining to an acinus.
a·cin·i·form (ə-sínnifawrm) *adj.* Having the shape of a cluster of grapes or of a berry such as the raspberry. [ACIN(US) + -FORM.]
ac·i·nus (ássi-nəss) *n., pl.* **-ni** (-nī). **1.** *Botany.* Any of the small divisions or drupelets of an aggregate fruit such as the raspberry. **2.** The stone or seed of a grape or berry. **3.** *Anatomy.* Any of the small saclike dilations composing a compound gland. [New Latin, from Latin *acinus,* berry (especially a grape), probably of Mediterranean origin.] **—a·cin·ic** (ə-sínnik) *adj.* **—a·ci·nous** *adj.*
-acious *adj. suffix.* Indicates a tendency towards or abundance of something; for example, **fallacious.** [French *-acieux,* from Latin *-ācius* and *āx* (stem *-āc-*), adjectival suffixes.]
-acity *n. suffix.* Indicates a quality or state of being; for example, **tenacity.** [French *-acité,* from Latin *-ācitās,* from *-āx* (stem *-āc-*), -ACIOUS.]
ack-ack (áck-áck, -ak) *n. Military Slang.* **1.** An antiaircraft gun. **2.** Antiaircraft fire. Also used adjectivally: *an ack-ack gun.* [British telephonic code for *AA,* abbreviation for ANTIAIRCRAFT.]
ackee. Variant of **akee.**
ac·knowl·edge (ək-nóllij, ak-) *tr.v.* **-edged, -edging, -edges. 1.** To admit or accept the existence, reality, or fact of: *acknowledge one's mistakes.* **2.** To accept as valid or as having authority. **3. a.** To express recognition of. **b.** To express thanks or gratitude for. **4.** To report the receipt of. **5.** *Law.* To accept or certify as legally binding: *acknowledge a deed.* [Middle English, blend of *acknowen* (to recognise, acknowledge, Old English *oncnāwan* : *on,* ON + *cnāwan,* to KNOW) and KNOWLEDGE.] **—ac·knowl·edge·a·ble** *adj.*
Synonyms: *acknowledge, admit, own, avow, confess, concede.*
ac·knowl·edg·ment, ac·knowl·edge·ment (ək-nóllijmənt, ak-) *n.* **1.** The act of admitting, or accepting responsibility for, something. **2.** Recognition of someone's or something's existence, validity, authority, or right. **3.** An answer or response in return for something done. **4. a.** An expression or token of appreciation or thanks. **b.** *Plural.* An author's expression of thanks, at the beginning or end of a work, to those who have helped him. **5.** A formal declaration made to authoritative witnesses to ensure legal validity.
a·clin·ic (áy-klínnik) *adj. Geology.* Having no inclination or dip. [Greek *aklinēs,* not inclining to either side : *a-,* not + *klinein,* to lean.]
aclinic line *n.* The **magnetic equator** *(see).*
ac·me (ákmi) *n.* The highest point of attainment; the peak. See Synonyms at **summit.** [Greek *akmē,* point, summit.]
ac·ne (ákni) *n.* An inflammatory disease of the sebaceous glands, characterised by pimples on the face, neck, and upper torso, that is common in adolescents. [New Latin, misreading of Greek *akmē,* eruption on the face, point, ACME.]
ac·node (ák-nōd) *n. Mathematics.* A point whose coordinates satisfy the equation of a curve but does not lie on the curve. Also called "isolated point". [Latin *acus,* needle + NODE (comparing the isolated point to a needle prick).]
a·cock (ə-kóck) *adj.* In a cocked position. **—a·cock** *adv.*
ac·o·lyte (áckəlīt) *n.* **1.** One who assists a priest in the performance of a religious service of ceremony; especially, in the Roman Catholic Church, an altar server who carries a candle. **2.** An attendant or follower. [Middle English *acolite,* from Old French, from Medieval Latin *acolytus,* variant of *acoluthus,* from Greek *akolouthos,* follower, following. See **anacoluthon.**]
A·con·ca·gua, Mount (áckən-kággew-ə, -kággwə, -kōn-). A mountain in the Andes in western Argentina, near the Chilean border. It rises to 6 960 metres (22,835 feet), and is the highest peak in the Western Hemisphere. Claims that Ojos del Salado, also in the Andes, is higher have been proven to be false.
ac·o·nite (áckənīt) *n.* **1.** Any plant of the genus *Aconitum,* such as **monkshood** or **wolfsbane** *(both of which see).* **2.** The dried, poisonous root of monkshood, *A. napellus,* sometimes used in medicine to relieve pain or to reduce fever. [Latin *aconītum,* from Greek *akoniton,* possibly from *akonitos,* "dustless", unconquerable (with reference to the deadly properties of the plant) : *a-,* without + *-konitos,* "dusty", from *koniein,* to raise dust, struggle, from *konis,* dust]
Açôres. See **Azores.**
a·corn (áy-korn || -kərn) *n.* The fruit of the oak tree, consisting of a thick-walled nut usually set in a woody, cuplike base. [Middle English, variant of *akern,* from Old English *æcern.*]
acorn barnacle *n.* A barnacle, such as *Balanus balanoides,* that lives attached to rocks and has a conical shell.
acorn valve *n.* A small, acorn-shaped valve used in very high frequency devices. Also *U.S.* "acorn tube".
acorn worm *n.* Any of the wormlike marine animals with an acorn-shaped proboscis that belong to the genus *Balanoglossus* or related genera.
a·cot·y·le·don (áy-kótti-léed'n, a-, ákoti-) *n. Botany.* A plant having no cotyledons, or seed leaves, such as a moss or fern. **—a·cot·y·le·don·ous** (-léed'n-əss) *adj.*
a·cous·tic (ə-kóoss-tik) *adj.* Also **a·cous·ti·cal** (-tik'l). **1.** Of or pertaining to sound, the sense of hearing, or the science of sound. **2. a.** Designed to carry, absorb, or control sound: *an acoustic delay line.* **b.** Designating a device that is operated by sound waves: *an acoustic mine.* **c.** Designating a device that is designed to assist hearing: *an acoustic aid.* **3.** Not using electronic amplification. Said of a musical instrument, especially a guitar. [Greek *akoustikos,* pertaining to hearing, from *akouein,* to hear.] **—a·cous·ti·cal·ly** *adv.*
ac·ous·ti·cian (áckoo-stísh'n) *n.* A specialist in acoustics.
acoustic nerve *n.* Either of the eighth pair of cranial nerves, each consisting of a *cochlear nerve,* which conducts acoustic stimuli to the brain, and a *vestibular nerve,* which conducts stimuli related to bodily equilibrium to the brain. Also called "auditory nerve", "vestibulocochlear nerve".
a·cous·tics (ə-kóostiks) *n.* **1.** *Used with a singular verb.* The scientific study of sound, especially of its production, perception, and interaction with materials and other forms of radiation. **2.** Also **a·cous·tic.** The quality and fidelity of the sound experienced in a particular room, auditorium, or other enclosed space: *a hall with poor acoustics, a poor acoustic.*
ACP state *n.* Any one of the less developed countries of Africa, the Caribbean, and the Pacific, which, by the Lomé Conventions, have a special trading association with the European Union.
ac·quaint (ə-kwáynt) *tr.v.* **-quainted, -quainting, -quaints. 1.** To make familiar. Used reflexively and with *with*: *acquaint oneself with the rules of the game.* **2.** To inform. Used with *with*: *acquaint someone with one's plans.* **3.** To cause to know personally. Used in the passive and with *with*: *I see you're already acquainted with each other.* [Middle English *aqueynten, acointen,* from Old French *acointer,* from Medieval Latin *accognitāre,* from Latin *accognitus,* past participle of *accognōscere,* to know perfectly : *ad-* (intensive) + *cognōscere,* to know : *co-, com-,* completely + *gnōscere,* to know.]
ac·quain·tance (ə-kwáyntənss) *n.* **1.** Knowledge of or information about someone or something, especially when based on direct experience. **2.** Knowledge of a person acquired by a relationship less intimate than friendship. **3.** A person whom one knows, but who is not a close friend. **—ac·quain·tance·ship** *n.*
ac·qui·esce (áckwi-éss) *intr.v.* **-esced, -escing, -esces.** To accept, consent, or comply passively or without protest. Often used with *in*: *acquiesce in a ruling.* See Synonyms at **assent.** [Latin *acquiēscere,* to remain at rest, agree tacitly : *ad-,* at, to + *quiēscere,* to rest, from *quiēs,* rest, QUIET.]
ac·qui·es·cence (áckwi-éss'nss) *n.* **1.** Passive assent or agreement without protest. **2.** The state of acquiescing or a tendency to acquiesce. **3.** *Law.* Failure to object to something such as an infringement of a right, taken as signifying acceptance or consent. **—ac·qui·es·cent** *adj.* **—ac·qui·es·cent·ly** *adv.*
ac·quire (ə-kwír) *tr.v.* **-quired, -quiring, -quires. 1.** To gain possession of. **2.** To get, especially by one's own efforts or qualities: *acquire a reputation for honesty.* **3.** To locate (an object in the atmosphere or in space) for the purpose of tracking: *acquire a target.* **4.** To steal. Used humorously or euphemistically. [Middle English *acqueren,* from Old French *acquerre,* from Latin *acquīrere,* to add to, get : *ad-,* in addition to + *quaerere,* to seek, obtain.]
ac·quired characteristic (ə-kwírd) *n.* A nonhereditary change in an organ caused by use or disuse or by environmental factors.
acquired taste *n.* Something which initially seems unpleasant, but for which one develops a liking.

ac·quire·ment (ə-kwírmənt) *n. Formal.* **1.** The act of acquiring. **2.** An attainment, such as a skill or social accomplishment.

ac·qui·si·tion (áckwi-zísh'n) *n.* **1.** The act of acquiring. **2.** Something or someone acquired, especially as an addition to an established category or group. **3.** *Aerospace.* The process of locating a satellite, guided missile, or moving target so that its track or orbit can be determined. [Middle English *acquisicioun*, from Latin *acquīsītiō* (stem *acquīsītiōn-*), from *acquírere*, to ACQUIRE.]

ac·quis·i·tive (ə-kwízzitiv) *adj.* **1.** Eager to acquire material possessions. **2.** Tending to acquire and retain ideas or information: *an acquisitive mind.* —**ac·quis·i·tive·ly** *adv.* —**ac·quis·i·tive·ness** *n.*

ac·quit (ə-kwít) *tr.v.* **-quitted, -quitting, -quits. 1.** To clear of a criminal charge; declare to be not guilty. **2.** To release or discharge from duty or obligation. **3.** To conduct (oneself) in the specified way: *acquitted herself well.* [Middle English *acquiten*, from Old French *aquiter*, from Vulgar Latin *acquītāre* (unattested), "to bring to rest", set free : *ad-*, to + *quitāre, quiētāre* (unattested), to put to rest, set free, from *quiēs*, QUIET.] —**ac·quit·ter** *n.*

ac·quit·tal (ə-kwítt'l) *n.* The judgment of a jury or judge that a person is not guilty of a crime as charged.

ac·quit·tance (ə-kwítt'nss) *n.* A written release from an obligation or debt; quittance.

a·cre (áykər) *n.* **1.** *Abbr.* **A, a., A.** A unit of area used in land measurement and equal to 4840 square yards or 4046.86 square metres or 0.4047 hectares. **2.** *Plural.* Property in the form of land. **3.** *Usually plural. Informal.* A wide expanse of space: *acres of room.* [Middle English *acre*, Old English *æcer*, field, acre; akin to Latin *ager*, field.]

A·cre (áykər, áakər). *Hebrew* 'Akko; *Arabic*, 'Akka. Town and port in northern Israel on the Bay of Haifa. During the Crusades it changed hands many times between Christians and Arabs. It finally fell to the Saracens in 1291, and became part of the Ottoman Empire in the 16th century. During World War I it was won by the British and became part of the Palestinian protectorate. Acre was ceded to the Arabs in the UN partition of Palestine (1948), but was captured by Israel shortly afterwards.

a·cre·age (áykərij, áykrij) *n.* Area of land in acres.

a·cred (áykərd) *adj.* Comprising or possessing many acres of land. Used chiefly in combination: *a many-acred estate.*

ac·rid (áckrid) *adj.* **1.** Harsh and irritating to the taste or smell. **2.** Bitterly caustic in language or tone. [From Latin *ācer* (stem *ācr-*), sharp, bitter (probably influenced by ACID).] —**a·crid·i·ty** (ə-kríddəti), **ac·rid·ness** *n.* —**ac·rid·ly** *adv.*

ac·ri·dine (áckrideen) *n.* A coal tar derivative, $C_{13}H_9N$, that has a strongly irritating odour and is used in the manufacture of dyes and synthetics.

ac·ri·fla·vine (áckri-fláyveen) *n.* A brown or orange powder, $C_{14}H_{14}N_3Cl$, derived from acridine and used as an antiseptic. [ACRI(DINE) + FLAVIN.]

ac·ri·mo·ni·ous (áckri-mṓni-əss) *adj.* Bitter and caustic in speech, tone, or manner; rancorous. —**ac·ri·mo·ni·ous·ly** *adv.* —**ac·ri·mo·ni·ous·ness** *n.*

ac·ri·mo·ny (áckri-məni ‖ *U.S.* -mōni) *n.* Bitterness or ill-natured animosity, especially in speech or manner. [Latin *ācrimōnia*, sharpness, from *ācer*, sharp.]

acro- *comb. form.* Indicates: **1.** A height or summit; for example, **acrophobia. 2.** An outer end, tip, or point; for example, **acrogen. 3.** An extremity of the body; for example, **acromegaly.** [Greek *akros*, topmost, extreme.]

ac·ro·bat (áckrə-bat) *n.* **1.** A performer, as in a circus, who is skilled in feats of agility and balance. **2.** One adept at quick changes of position, political stance, or the like. [French *acrobate*, from Greek *akrobatēs*, "one who walks on tiptoe", from *akrobatein*, to walk on tiptoe : ACRO- + *bat-*, stem of *bainein*, to walk.] —**ac·ro·bat·ic** (-báttik) *adj.* —**ac·ro·bat·i·cal·ly** *adv.*

ac·ro·bat·ics (áckrə-báttiks) *n.* **1.** *Used with a singular verb.* The art of an acrobat. **2.** *Used with a plural verb.* The feats performed by an acrobat. **3.** *Used with a plural verb.* Any manifestation of spectacular mental or physical agility.

ac·ro·car·pous (áckrō-kárpəss) *adj. Botany.* Having the spore-bearing capsule at the end or top of a leafy stem or stalk, as in many mosses. [New Latin *acrocarpus*, from Greek *akrokarpos*, bearing fruit at the top : ACRO- + -CARPOUS.]

ac·ro·cy·a·no·sis (áckrō-sī-ə-nṓsiss) *n.* Slow circulation of the blood through the small vessels in the skin, resulting in bluish-purple discoloration of the hands and feet.

ac·ro·dont (áckrədont) *adj. Zoology.* Having or designating teeth that lack roots and are fused to the bony ridge of the jaw, as in certain reptiles. [ACRO(O)- + -ODONT.]

a·crod·ro·mous (ə-króddrəməss) *adj.* Also **ac·ro·drome** (áckrə-drōm). Designating a pattern of leaf venation in which there are two or more main veins, each terminating at the leaf tip. [ACRO- + -DROMOUS.]

ac·ro·gen (áckrəjən) *n.* A flowerless plant, such as a fern or moss, in which all growth proceeds from the tip. [ACRO- + -GEN.] —**ac·ro·gen·ic** (áckrə-jénnik), **a·crog·e·nous** (ə-krójənəss) *adj.* —**a·crog·e·nous·ly** *adv.*

a·cro·le·in (ə-krṓli-in) *n.* A colourless, flammable, poisonous liquid, CH_2:CHCHO, having an acrid odour and vapours dangerous to the eyes. Also called "propenal". [ACR(ID) + OLEIN.]

ac·ro·meg·a·ly (áckrō-méggəli) *n.* Pathological enlargement of the bones of the hands, feet, and face, resulting from excess production of growth hormone by the pituitary gland. [French *acromégalie*,

"enlargement of extremities" : ACRO- + Greek *megal-*, stem of *megas*, big.] —**ac·ro·me·gal·ic** (áckrō-mi-gál-ik) *n. & adj.*

ac·ro·nym (áckrə-nim) *n.* A word formed from the initial parts of a name, such as *NATO*, from *N*orth *A*tlantic *T*reaty *O*rganisation, or *Comintern*, from *C*ommunist *Intern*ational. [ACR(O)- + -ONYM.] —**ac·ro·nym·ic** (-nímmik), **a·cron·y·mous** (ə-krónniməss) *adj.*

a·crop·e·tal (ə-króppit'l) *adj. Botany.* Developing upwards towards the apex from the base, as certain forms of inflorescence do. [ACRO- + -PETAL.] —**a·crop·e·tal·ly** *adv.*

ac·ro·pho·bi·a (áckrə-fṓbi-ə) *n.* Abnormally intense fear of being in high places. [ACRO- + -PHOBIA.] —**ac·ro·pho·bic** *adj.*

a·crop·o·lis (ə-króppʹl-iss) *n.* **1.** The fortified citadel of an ancient Greek city. **2.** *Capital* **A.** The citadel of Athens, which is the site of the Parthenon. [Greek *akropolis*, "upper city", citadel : ACRO- + *polis*, city.]

ac·ro·some (áckrə-sōm) *n.* A structure in the head of a sperm that contains enzymes to break down the egg wall and allow fertilisation. [ACRO- + SOME (body).]

ac·ro·spire (áckrə-spīr) *n. Botany.* The first sprout from a germinating grain seed. [Variant (influenced by ACRO-) of dialectal *akerspire*, "ear-sprout" : *aker*, ear of grain, ultimately from Old English *æhher, ēar* + Middle English *spire*, Old English *spīr*.]

a·cross (ə-króss ‖ ə-kráwss) *prep.* **1.** On or at the other side of: *across the road.* **2.** So as to cross; over; through: *draw lines across the paper.* **3.** From one side of to the other: *a bridge across a river.* **4.** Extending throughout: *across all social classes.*
~*adv.* **1.** From one side to the other: *The bridge swayed when he ran across.* **2.** On or to the opposite side: *We came across by ferry.* [Middle English *acros, on croice*, from Old French *a croix, en croix*, "in the form of a CROSS", hence "transversely".]

a·cross-the-board (ə-króss-thə-bórd ‖ -kráwss-, -bórd) *adj.* **1.** Affecting all categories or members, especially in an occupation or industry: *an across-the-board wage increase.* **2.** *U.S.* Each-way. Said of a bet in horse-racing.

a·cros·tic (ə-króstik ‖ ə-kráwstik) *n.* A poem or series of lines in which certain letters, usually the first in each line, form a name, motto, or message when read in sequence. [French *acrostiche*, from Old French, from Greek *akrostikhis*, "end-line" : ACRO- + *stikhos*, line of verse.] —**a·cros·tic** *adj.* —**a·cros·ti·cal·ly** *adv.*

ac·ry·late resin (áckrilayt) *n.* Any of a class of acrylic resins used in emulsion paints, adhesives, plastics, and textile and paper finishes. Also called "acrylate".

a·cryl·ic (ə-kríllik) *adj.* Based on or relating to acrylic acid.
~*n.* **1.** Acrylic fibre. **2.** Acrylic resin. **3.** Acrylic paint. [ACR(OLEIN) + -YL + -IC.]

acrylic acid *n.* An easily polymerised, colourless, corrosive liquid, H_2C:CHCOOH, used as a monomer for acrylate resins. Also called "propenoic acid".

acrylic fibre *n.* Any of numerous synthetic fibres polymerised from acrylonitrile.

acrylic paint *n.* A paint based on acrylic resin, which dries quickly to give a semigloss finish.

acrylic resin *n.* Any of numerous thermoplastic or thermosetting polymers or copolymers of acrylic acid, methacrylic acid, esters of these acids, or acrylonitrile. They are used to produce synthetic rubbers, exceptionally clear, lightweight plastics resistant to weather and corrosion, and other resin forms for many manufactured products including aircraft canopies and windows, contact lenses, refrigerator parts, protective coatings, and lubricant additives. Also called "acrylic".

ac·ry·lo·ni·trile (áckrilō-nítrīl ‖ *U.S.*-nītrəl) *n.* A colourless, liquid organic compound, H_2C:CHCN, used in the manufacture of acrylic rubber and fibres. [ACRYL(IC RESIN) + NITRILE.]

act (akt) *n.* **1.** The process of doing or performing something: *caught in the act of stealing.* **2. a.** Something that is done or performed; a deed: *a charitable act.* **b.** A deed indicative or symptomatic of a particular condition: *an act of faith; an act of lunacy.* **3.** An enactment, edict, or decree, as of a judicial or legislative body. **4.** *Usually plural.* A formal written record of proceedings or transactions. **5.** One of the major divisions or sections of a play, drama, or opera. **6. a.** A performance that forms part of a longer presentation, as in a variety show or circus: *a juggling act.* **b.** The artistes giving such a performance. **7.** *Informal.* A display of insincere behaviour; a pose: *put on an act.* **8.** *Australian & N.Z. Informal.* A display of bad temper.
~*v.* **acted, acting, acts.** —*tr.* **1.** To play the part of; assume the dramatic role of. **2.** To perform on the stage: *act a drama.* **3.** To behave like or pose as; impersonate: *act the fool.* **4.** To behave in a manner appropriate to: *Act your age!* **5.** *Archaic.* To activate; animate. —*intr.* **1.** To behave or conduct oneself: *He acts as if he owns the place.* **2. a.** To perform in a dramatic role or roles; be an actor. **b.** To be suitable for theatrical performance: *This scene acts well.* **3.** To behave affectedly or unnaturally; pretend; pose. **4.** To take action; do something: *promised to act on my suggestion.* **5.** To operate or function in a specified way: *His mind acts quickly.* **6.** To function in a particular capacity; serve: *This valve acts as an additional safeguard.* **7.** To perform actions or duties as a substitute for someone or something else. **8.** To produce a desired or characteristic effect: *The drug will act in an hour.* —**act out. 1.** To express by acting or mime. **2.** To enact. —**act up.** *Informal.* To misbehave, malfunction, or give trouble.. [Middle English *acte*, from Latin *āctus*, the process of action, and *āctum*, a thing done, both from

āctus, past participle of *agere,* to drive, to do.] —**ac·ta·bil·i·ty** (-ə-bīlləti) *n.* —**act·a·ble** *adj.*

Usage: *Act* followed by an adjective is generally felt to be nonstandard in Britain, though it is more acceptable in American English: *He's acting crazy; Don't act stupid.* The English standard equivalent uses a following adverb: *Don't act stupidly.*

A.C.T. Australian Capital Territory.

Ac·tae·on (ak-tée-ən). *Greek Mythology.* A young hunter who, having inadvertently observed Artemis while she was bathing, was turned by her into a stag and killed by his own dogs.

ACTH *n. Adrenocorticotropic hormone:* a pituitary hormone synthesised or extracted from mammalian pituitaries for use in stimulating secretion of cortisone and other adrenal cortex hormones. Also called "corticotropin".

ac·tin (áktin) *n.* A muscle protein, active with myosin in muscular contraction. [Latin *āctus,* an ACT + -IN.]

ac·ti·nal (áktin'l, ak-tín'l) *adj. Zoology.* Of or designating the part of a sea anemone or similar animal from which the tentacles or rays radiate. [ACTIN(O)- + -AL.] —**ac·ti·nal·ly** *adv.*

act·ing (ákting) *adj.* 1. *Abbr.***a.** Temporarily assuming the duties or authority of another: *acting chairman.* 2. Containing directions for use in a dramatic performance: *an acting text.*
~*n.* The art or occupation of an actor.

ac·tin·i·a (ak-tín-i-ə) *n., pl.* -**iae** (-i-ee). Also **ac·tin·i·an** (-i-ən). A sea anemone, or a related animal. [New Latin *actinia,* "the radially-structured ones", from Greek *aktis* (stem *aktin-*), ray.]

ac·tin·ic (ak-tínnik) *adj.* Of, pertaining to, or designating electromagnetic radiation, such as ultraviolet radiation, that can produce chemical change. [ACTIN(O)- + -IC.] —**ac·tin·i·cal·ly** *adv.*

ac·ti·nide (áktinīd) *n.* Any of a series of chemically similar, mostly synthetic, radioactive elements with atomic numbers ranging from 89 (actinium) to 103 (lawrencium). Also called "actinoid". [ACTIN(O)- + -IDE.]

ac·ti·nism (áktiniz'm) *n.* The intrinsic property in radiation that produces photochemical activity. [ACTIN(O)- + -ISM.]

ac·tin·i·um (ak-tínni-əm) *n. Symbol* **Ac** A radioactive element found in uranium ores and used, in equilibrium with its decay products, as a source of alpha rays. Its longest lived isotope is Ac 227 with a half-life of 21.7 years. Atomic number 89, melting point 1,050°C, boiling point (estimated) 3,200°C, relative density (calculated) 10.07, valency 3. [New Latin : ACTIN(O)- + -IUM.]

actino-, actin- *comb. form.* Indicates: 1. Radial or tentacled structure; for example, **actinoid.** 2. Radiation or radioactivity; for example, **actinometer.** [New Latin, from Greek *aktis,* ray.]

ac·ti·noid (áktinoyd) *adj.* Having a radial form, as a starfish.
~*n. Chemistry.* An actinide. [ACTIN(O)- + -OID.]

ac·tin·o·lite (ak-tínnəlīt) *n. Mineralogy.* A greenish variety of **amphibole** *(see).* [ACTINO- (from its radiated forms) + -LITE.]

ac·ti·nom·e·ter (áktin-ómmitər) *n.* Any of several instruments for measuring the intensity of radiation. [ACTINO- + -METER.] —**ac·ti·no·met·ric** (áktinō-méttrik) *adj.* —**ac·ti·nom·e·try** *n.*

ac·ti·no·mor·phic (áktinō-mórfik) *adj.* Also **ac·ti·no·mor·phous** (-mórfəss). *Biology.* Having radial symmetry; divisible vertically through two or more planes into similar halves. Compare **zygomorphic.** [ACTINO- + -MORPHIC.]

ac·ti·no·my·cete (áktinō-mǐseet, -mǐséet) *n.* Any of numerous generally filamentous and often pathogenic microorganisms of the order Actinomycetales, resembling both bacteria and fungi. [ACTINO- + -MYCETE.]

ac·ti·no·my·cin (áktinō-mǐsin) *n.* Any of various often toxic antibiotic substances found in soil bacteria and used to treat some forms of cancer. [New Latin *Actinomyces,* a genus of soil bacteria : ACTINO- + Greek *mukēs,* fungus (see –mycin).]

ac·ti·no·my·co·sis (áktinō-mī-kố-siss). *n.* An inflammatory infection of cattle, pigs, and sometimes man, caused by microorganisms of the genus *Actinomyces,* and characterised by lumpy tumours of the neck, chest, and abdomen. Also called "lumpy jaw". [ACTINO- + MYCOSIS.] —**ac·ti·no·my·cot·ic** (-mī-kóttik) *adj.*

ac·ti·non (áktinon) *n. Symbol* **An** A radioactive inert gaseous isotope of radon, with a half-life of 3.92 seconds. [ACTIN(O)- + -ON.]

ac·ti·no·u·ra·ni·um (áktinō-yoor-áyni-əm) *n.* The isotope of uranium with mass number 235; uranium-235.

ac·ti·no·zo·an (áktinō-zố-ən) *n. Zoology.* An **anthozoan** *(see).* [New Latin *actinozoa,* "the radiated life-forms" : ACTINO- + -ZOA.]

ac·tion (áksh'n) *n.* 1. The state or process of acting, functioning, or doing; the condition of exerting energy or being in operation: *sprang into action; temporarily out of action.* 2. Something done; an act or deed: *Actions speak louder than words.* 3. Movement, posture, or gesture. 4. Style or manner of movement: *a horse with good action.* 5. Activity; initiative; especially, organised activity in support of a cause of group: *T.U.C. day of action.* 6. The exertion or transmission of energy, force, or influence: *the action of water on a stone.* 7. **a.** The operating parts of a mechanism: *the action of a gun.* **b.** The way in which a mechanism works. 8. The series of events and episodes that form the plot of a story or play. 9. A judicial process; a lawsuit, especially one undertaken to obtain redress or enforce a claim. 10. **a.** Armed combat: *troops sent into action.* **b.** A military engagement. 11. **a.** *Slang.* The point of greatest activity or interest: *go where the action is.* **b.** The activity emanating from such a point, or its results: *wanted a piece of the action.*

ac·tion·a·ble (ákshʼnəbʼl) *adj.* Giving just cause for legal action. —**ac·tion·a·bly** *adv.*

action painting *n.* A predominantly U.S. school of abstract expressionism that exploits the random effects of spontaneous techniques such as dribbling and splattering paint into the canvas. See **tachisme.** —**action painter** *n.*

action potential *n.* The voltage change occurring across the membrane of a nerve or muscle cell during transmission of a nerve impulse.

action replay *n. British.* An immediate playback, often in slow motion, of a brief extract from a videotape recording of a televised event, especially a sporting event. Also *U.S.* "instant replay".

action stations *pl.n.* The positions taken up by members of a military force prior to going into action.
~*interj.* Used as a signal to warn troops to take up positions ready to go into action.

Ac·ti·um (ákti-əm). A promontory in ancient Greece, opposite modern Preveza. In 31 B.C. it was the scene of a sea and land battle, in which the forces of Octavian (later the emperor Augustus) under Agrippa decisively defeated Mark Antony and Cleopatra.

ac·ti·vate (áktiv-ayt) *tr.v.* -**vated,** -**vating,** -**vates.** 1. To set in motion or action; make active. 2. To purify (sewage) by aeration. 3. *Chemistry.* To accelerate a reaction in, as by heat. 4. *Physics.* To make radioactive. 5. *U.S.* To set up or organise (a military unit or post, for example). —**ac·ti·va·tion** (-áysh'n) *n.* —**ac·ti·va·tor** (-aytər) *n.*

ac·ti·vat·ed alumina (ákti-vaytid) *n.* Highly adsorbent aluminium oxide in granular form, used to filter oil, dry gases, or catalyse a reaction.

activated carbon *n.* Highly adsorbent carbon obtained by heating granulated charcoal to exhaust contained gases, used in gas absorption, solvent recovery, or deodorisation, and as an antidote to certain poisons. Also called "activated charcoal".

activated sludge *n.* A mass of sewage through which compressed air has been blown or which has been aerated by mechanical agitation. It is added to untreated sewage to increase the rate of bacterial decomposition.

ac·tive (áktiv) *adj.* 1. In a state of action, motion, or operation. 2. Given to or characterised by action or activity; lively; vigorous: *an active mind; over eighty, but still active.* 3. Producing action or change; especially, producing a particular or characteristic effect: *an active ingredient.* 4. Marked by or engaging in effective or productive activity; contributing; participating: *an active member of a club; gave active encouragement to the conspirators.* 5. Capable of action or effective operation; not passive or dormant: *an active volcano.* 6. Characterised by energetic action or activity; busy. 7. **a.** Designating a verb inflection or voice indicating that the subject of the sentence is performing or causing the action expressed by the verb. In the sentence *John bought a book, bought* is in the active voice. Compare **passive. b.** Expressing action rather than a state of being. Said of verbs such as *run, speak, move.* 8. Producing profit, interest, or dividends: *active accounts.* 9. Marked by or engaging in full military status: *on active service; active troops.*
~*n.* 1. The active voice. 2. A construction or form in the active voice. [Middle English, from Old French *actif,* from Latin *āctīvus,* from *āctus,* ACT.] —**ac·tive·ly** *adv.* —**ac·tive·ness** *n.*

Synonyms: active, energetic, dynamic, vigorous, lively.

ac·tiv·ist (áktiv-ist) *n.* One who favours the use of vigorous and direct action, especially in support of a political cause. —**ac·tiv·ism** *n.*

ac·tiv·i·ty (ak-tívvəti) *n., pl.* -**ties.** 1. The state or condition of being active. 2. Energetic action or movement. 3. A pursuit or occupation, especially when recreational. 4. The intensity of a radioactive source.

act of God *n. Law.* An unforeseeable or inevitable occurrence, such as a tornado, caused by nature and not by man.

ac·to·my·o·sin (áktō-mī-ə-sin) *n.* A system of actin and myosin that with other substances constitutes muscle fibre and is responsible for muscular contraction. [ACT(IN) + MYOSIN.]

Ac·ton (áktən), **John Emerich Edward Dalberg, 1st Baron** (1834–1902). British historian. A Liberal M.P. and friend of **Gladstone,** Acton was an influential Roman Catholic and led opposition to the doctrine of papal infallibility (declared in 1870). He became professor of modern history at Cambridge in 1895.

ac·tor (áktər) *n.* 1. A performer in a play, film, or broadcast. 2. One who takes part; a participant.

ac·tress (ák-triss, -trəss, -tress) *n.* A female actor.

Acts of the Apostles *n. Used with a singular verb.* The fifth book of the New Testament. Also called "Acts".

A.C.T.U. Australian Council of Trade Unions.

ac·tu·al (áktew-əl, ákchoo-əl) *adj.* 1. Existing in fact, rather than in theory or imagination; real: *The actual cost far exceeded the original estimate.* 2. Being, existing, or acting at the present moment. —See Synonyms at **real.** [Middle English *actuel,* from Old French, from Late Latin *āctuālis,* "pertaining to acts", from Latin *āctus,* an ACT.]

ac·tu·al·ise, also **ac·tu·al·ize** (áktew-ə-līz, ákchoo-) *tr.v.* -**ised,** -**ising,** -**ises.** 1. To make actual; realise in action. 2. To describe or portray realistically. —**ac·tu·al·i·sa·tion** (-lī-záysh'n ‖ *U.S.* -li-) *n.*

ac·tu·al·i·ty (áktew-ál-əti, ákchoo-) *n., pl.* -**ties.** 1. The state or fact of being actual; reality. 2. *Plural.* Actual conditions or facts.

ac·tu·al·ly (ákchə-li, ákchoo-, áktew-əli) *adv.* 1. In fact; in reality. 2. Believe it or not: *I not only gambled, I actually won.*

ac·tu·ar·y (áktew-əri, ákchew- ‖ -erri) *n., pl.* -**ies.** A statistician who calculates insurance risks and premiums. [Latin *āctuārius,* secretary of accounts, from *āctus,* public employment, state business, the process of action, ACT.] —**actu·ar·i·al** (-áiriəl) *adj.*

ac·tu·ate (áktew-ayt, ákchoo-) *tr.v.* -**ated,** -**ating,** -**ates.** 1. To put into action or motion; activate: *actuate a mechanism.* **2.** To move to action; impel: *actuated by greed.* [Medieval Latin *āctuāre,* from Latin *āctus,* an ACT.] —**ac·tu·a·tion** (-áysh'n) *n.* —**ac·tu·a·tor** (-aytər) *n.*

a·cu·i·ty (ə-kéw-əti) *n.* Keenness, sharpness, or acuteness, especially of the senses or the mind: *visual acuity.* [Middle English *acuitie,* from Medieval Latin *acuitās,* from Latin *acuere,* to sharpen, from *acus,* needle.]

a·cu·le·ate (ə-kéwli-ayt, -it) *adj.* **1.** Having a sting, as a bee does. **2.** Having prickles or thorns. [Latin *aculeātus,* from *aculeus,* diminutive of *acus,* needle, sting. See **acuity.**]

a·cu·men (áckew-mən, -men, ə-kéw-) *n.* The ability to make quick, shrewd, and accurate judgments; keenness of insight. [Latin *acūmen,* (mental) sharpness, from *acuere,* to sharpen, from *acus,* needle.]

a·cu·mi·nate (ə-kéwmin-ayt, -ət, -it) *adj. Biology.* Tapering to a sharp point: *acuminate leaves.* [Latin *acūminātus,* past participle of *acūmināre,* to sharpen, from *acūmen,* sharpness, ACUMEN.] —**a·cu·mi·na·tion** (-áysh'n) *n.*

ac·u·punc·ture (áckew-pungkchər) *n.* A traditional Chinese therapeutic technique whereby fine needles are inserted into the skin at particular points. This may stimulate nerves, causing the release of painkilling endorphins. Also called "stylostixis". [Latin *acū,* with a needle, from *acus,* needle + PUNCTURE.]

a·cut·ance (ə-kéwt'nss) *n.* The sharpness of outline in a photograph.

a·cute (ə-kéwt) *adj.* **1.** Having a sharp point or tip; not blunt. **2.** Keenly perceptive or discerning; shrewd; penetrating. **3.** Reacting readily to impressions; sensitive: *an acute sense of smell.* **4.** Serious enough to cause concern; critical; severe: *acute shortages.* **5.** Having a powerful, usually unpleasant, effect; keen; intense: *acute pain.* **6.** *Medicine.* Reaching a crisis rapidly. Said of a disease. Compare **chronic. 7.** *Music.* High in pitch; shrill. **8.** *Geometry.* **a.** Designating an angle less than 90°. **b.** Designating a triangle with all three interior angles less than 90°. —See Synonyms at **critical, sharp.** [Latin *acūtus,* sharp, from *acuere,* to sharpen, from *acus,* needle.] —**a·cute·ly** *adv.* —**a·cute·ness** *n.*

acute accent *n.* A mark (´) indicating: **1.** A raised pitch or rising tone, in certain languages such as Chinese and Ancient Greek. **2.** Primary stress of a spoken sound or syllable. **3.** Metrical stress in poetry. **4.** A particular sound quality or vowel length in certain languages such as French.

A.C.V. air-cushion vehicle (hovercraft).

A.C.W. aircraftwoman.

a·cy·clic (áy-síklik, áy-sícklik) *adj.* **1.** *Botany.* Not having or forming whorls; not cyclic. **2.** *Chemistry.* Having an open-chain molecular structure rather than a ring-shaped structure.

ac·yl (áyssīl ‖ *U.S.* áss'l) *n. Chemistry.* Any radical having the general formula RCO-, derived from an organic acid. [AC(ID) + -YL.]

ad (ad) *n. Informal.* An advertisement.

ad- *prefix.* Indicates motion towards; for example, adhere. [Latin, from *ad,* to, towards, at. In borrowed Latin compounds *ad-* indicates: **1.** Motion towards, as in **advent. 2.** Proximity, as in **adjacent. 3.** Addition, increase, as in **accrue. 4.** Relationship, dependence, as in **adjunct. 5.** Intensified action, as in **accelerate.** Before *c, f, g, l, n, q, r, s,* and *t, ad-* is assimilated to *ac-, af-, ag-, al-, an-, acq-, ar-, as-,* and *at-;* before *sc, sp, st,* and *gn,* it is reduced to *a-.*]

-ad *adv. suffix. Biology.* Indicates direction towards a specified anatomical part; for example, **dorsad.** [Coined from Latin *ad,* towards.]

A.D. anno Domini (usually small capitals : A.D.).

Usage: In formal usage, A.D. precedes the date when it is a specific year rather than a century: *He died in A.D. 961* (the *in* being generally omitted in American English). Informally, it is often used like B.C., which always follows the date.

a·dac·ty·lous (áy-dáktiləss) *adj.* Having no fingers or toes.

ad·age (áddij) *n.* A short maxim or proverb. [French, from Old French, from Latin *adagium,* proverb.]

a·da·gi·o (ə-dáa-ji-ō) *adj. Music.* Slowly. Used as a direction.
~*n., pl.* **adagios. 1.** *Music.* A composition or movement played in this tempo. **2.** In ballet, a section of a pas de deux in which the ballerina and her partner perform steps requiring lyricism and great skill in lifting, balancing, and turning. [Italian *adagio,* "at ease" : *ad-,* at, from Latin *at,* towards + *agio,* ease, from Old Provençal *aize,* from Vulgar Latin *adjacēs* (unattested), variant of Latin *adjacēns,* convenient, ADJACENT.] —**a·da·gi·o** *adj.*

Ad·am¹ (áddəm). **1.** The first man and progenitor of mankind, according to the Bible. Genesis 2:7. **2.** The unregenerate side of human nature: *the old Adam.* —**not know (someone) from Adam.** To be completely ignorant of the identity of. [Late Latin, from Hebrew *ādām,* "man", from *adāmāh,* earth.] —**A·dam·ic** (ə-dámmik) *adj.*

Adam² *adj.* In, pertaining to, or characteristic of the neoclassical style of furniture and architecture originated by Robert and James Adam: *an Adam fireplace.*

Adam, Robert (1728-92). British architect. Adam built in a delicate classical style, a development of the Palladian tradition, and was equally outstanding as an interior designer.

ad·a·mant (áddə-mənt ‖ -mant) *n.* **1.** A stone of uncertain identity formerly believed to be unbreakable. **2.** Any substance of exceptional hardness and resilience.
~*adj.* **1.** Unshakably firm in purpose or opinion; unyielding. **2.** Adamantine. —See Synonyms at **inflexible.** [Middle English *adama(u)nt,* diamond, magnet, from Old French *adamaunt,* from Latin *adamās* (stem *adamant-*), from Greek *adamas,* hard metal,

steel, diamond, possibly, "unbreakable" : *a-* not + *daman,* to tame, break down.] —**ad·a·mant·ly** *adv.*

ad·a·man·tine (áddə-mánt-īn ‖ -een, -in) *adj.* **1.** Made of or resembling adamant. **2.** Having the hardness or lustre of a diamond. **3.** Unyielding; inflexible.

Ad·am·ite (áddəmīt) *n. Archaic.* A descendant of Adam; a human being.

Ad·ams (áddəmz), **Ansel Easton** (1902-84). American photographer. A pioneer in the development of photography as an art, he specialised in photographs of American scenery.

Adams, Gerald, known as **Gerry Adams** (1948-). Northern Irish politician. He became a member of Sinn Fein and was elected vice-president in 1978 and president in 1983. Twice elected M.P. to the Westminster parliament (1983-92, 1997-) he has declined to take up his seat. He attended the 1996-98 peace talks chaired by U.S. senator George Mitchell (1933-) which have worked towards ending sectarian violence in Northern Ireland.

Adams, John (1735-1826). First vice-president (1789-97) and second president (1797-1801) of the United States. Adams played a leading part in the American Revolution, shaping the U.S. constitution, and helping to draft the Declaration of Independence.

Adams, John Quincy (1767-1848). Sixth president of the United States (1825-29) and son of John Adams. As Secretary of State (1817-25) he helped to formulate the **Monroe Doctrine.** He later became an active campaigner against slavery.

Adam's apple *n.* The projection of the largest laryngeal cartilage at the front of the throat, especially in men. [Translation of Hebrew *tappûah hāādām.*]

ad·ams·ite (áddəmzīt) *n. Symbol* **DM** A yellow crystalline compound, $(C_6H_4)_2(NH)AsCl$, used dispersed in air as a poison gas. [After Roger *Adams* (1889-1971), U.S. chemist.]

Adam's needle *n.* A plant, the **Spanish bayonet** *(see).* [From the spines on its leaves and with allusion to Genesis 3:7: " . . . they sewed fig leaves together, and made themselves aprons".]

a·dapt (ə-dápt) *v.* **adapted, adapting, adapts.** —*tr.* **1.** To adjust to a new environment or situation. **2.** To modify for a different use or purpose: *adapt a stage play for the radio.* —*intr.* To become adapted. [Latin *adaptāre,* to fit to : *ad-* to + *aptāre,* to fit, from *aptus,* APT.]

a·dapt·a·ble (ə-dápt-əb'l) *adj.* Capable of adapting or of being adapted. See Synonyms at **flexible.** —**a·dapt·a·bil·i·ty** (-ə-billəti), **a·dapt·a·ble·ness** *n.*

ad·ap·ta·tion (áddap-táysh'n) *n.* **1. a.** The act or process of adapting. **b.** The state of being adapted. **2.** Something that has adapted or been adapted so as to suit a new or special use or situation: *a new adaptation for radio.* **3.** An adjustment or process of adjustment, often hereditary, by which a species or individual improves its condition in relationship to its environment. **4.** The responsive alteration of a sense organ to repeated stimuli of a particular type. —**ad·ap·ta·tion·al** *adj.* —**ad·ap·ta·tion·al·ly** *adv.*

a·dapt·er, a·dapt·or (ə-dáptər) *n.* **1.** One that adapts. **2.** A device used to connect an electrical plug of one type into a supply point having a different fitting. **3.** A device that enables several electrical plugs to be fitted into one supply point. **4.** Any device that enables one part of an apparatus or machine to be fitted into another part having a different size or fitting.

a·dap·tive (ə-dáptiv) *adj.* Tending towards, fit for, or having a capacity for adaptation. —**a·dap·tive·ly** *adv.* —**a·dap·tive·ness** *n.*

adaptive radiation *n.* The evolution of one relatively unspecialised species into several related species characterised by different specialisations that fit them for life in various environments.

A·dar (ə-dáar) *n.* The sixth month of the year in the Hebrew calendar. [Hebrew *Adhār,* from Akkadian *ad(d)aru,* "the dark or cloudy month", from *adāru,* to be dark.]

Adar She·ni (shay-née) *n.* A Hebrew month, **Veadar** *(see).* [Hebrew *Adhār shēnī,* "second Adar".]

ad·ax·i·al (ad-áksi-əl, ád-) *adj.* Facing towards the axis. Said of the upper surface of leaves. Compare **abaxial.**

ADC, a.d.c., A.D.C. aide-de-camp.

add (ad) *v.* **added, adding, adds.** —*tr.* **1.** To join or unite so as to increase in size, quantity, or scope. **2.** To combine (a column of figures, for example) to form a total. Often used with *up.* **3.** To say or write further. **4.** To provide as an additional feature or quality; impart: *The arrival of Terry added a comical note to the proceedings.* —*intr.* **1.** To create or constitute an addition. Used with *to.* **2.** To find a sum in arithmetic. —**add up.** *Informal.* **1.** To come to a correct or desired total: *His figures don't add up.* **2.** To be reasonable, plausible, or consistent; make sense. —**add up to.** *Informal.* To mean; amount to. [Middle English *adden,* from Latin *addere,* to add, "to put to" : *ad-,* to + *-dere,* to put, from *dare,* to give.] —**add·a·ble, add·i·ble** *adj.*

ad·dax (áddaks) *n.* An antelope, *Addax nasomaculatus,* of northern Africa having long, spirally twisted horns. [Latin *addāx†.*]

add·ed value (áddid) *n. Economics.* The increase in the value of goods occurring in the process of production. It is measured as the difference between the producer's total revenue and the cost to him of raw materials. Compare **value-added tax.**

ad·dend (áddend, ə-dénd) *n.* Any of a set of numbers to be added. [Shortened from ADDENDUM.]

ad·den·dum (ə-dén-dəm) *n., pl.* **-da** (-də). Something added or to be added, especially as or in a supplement, appendix, or list of matter wrongly omitted from a publication. [Latin, neuter of *addendus,* gerundive of *addere,* to ADD.]

ad·der (áddər) *n.* **1.** Any of various venomous snakes of the family

Viperidae, especially the common viper, *Vipera berus,* of Eurasia. 2. Any of several similar snakes, such as the puff adder. [Middle English *addre,* from *an addre,* mistaken from *a naddre,* Old English *nædre,* snake.]

ad·der's-tongue (áddərz-tung ‖ *North of England also* -tong) *n.* 1. Any of several ferns of the genus *Ophioglossum;* especially, *O. vulgatum,* of the Northern Hemisphere, having a single sterile, leaf-like frond, and a spore-bearing stalk. 2. Any of various plants of the genus *Erythronium,* such as the **dogtooth violet** (*see*). [From the spike sticking out from the base of the frond of the fern, suggesting a snake's tongue.]

ad·dict (ə-díkt) *tr.v.* **-dicted, -dicting, -dicts.** 1. To cause to become physiologically or psychologically dependent, especially on a drug. Usually used in the passive and with *to.* 2. To devote (oneself) excessively or compulsively.
~*n.* (áddikt). 1. One who is addicted, especially to a drug. 2. *Informal.* A devotee: *a T.V. addict.* [Latin *addíctus,* "given over", one awarded to another as a slave, past participle of *addícere,* to award to : *ad-,* to + *dícere,* to say, pronounce, adjudge.] —**ad·dic·tion** *n.* —**ad·dic·tive** *adj.*

Ad·dis Ab·a·ba (áddiss ábbəbə). Capital and largest city of Ethiopia, situated in the centre of the country on a plateau more than 2 440 metres (8,000 feet) above sea level. It was made the capital in 1889 by Menelik II. Captured by the Italians in 1936 and made capital of Italian East Africa, it was liberated by the Allies in 1941 and returned to Ethiopia. It is also the headquarters of the Organisation of African Unity.

Ad·di·son (áddiss'n), **Joseph** (1672–1719). British essayist, poet, and Whig politician. He is best known for his witty, elegant essays, which were mainly contributed to two periodicals: Richard Steele's *Tatler,* and the *Spectator,* founded in 1711 by Steele and Addison.

Addison's disease *n.* A disease caused by failure of the adrenal cortex to function and marked by a bronzelike skin pigmentation, anaemia, and prostration. [After Thomas *Addison* (1793–1860), British physician who discovered it.]

ad·di·tion (ə-dísh'n) *n.* 1. The act or process of adding. 2. **a.** The result of adding. **b.** Something or someone added. 3. The process of combining numbers so as to find their sum. 4. *Chiefly U.S.* A part added to a building; an extension. —See Synonyms at **appendage.** —**in addition.** Besides; also. —**in addition to.** Over and above; as well as. See Usage note at **together.**

ad·di·tion·al (ə-dísh'n'l) *adj.* In addition; added; extra.

ad·di·tion·al·ly (ə-dísh'n-əli) *adv.* Furthermore; in addition. See Synonyms at **also.**

ad·di·tive (áddətiv) *adj.* 1. Marked by, produced by, or involving addition. 2. Designating any of certain colours of wavelengths that may be mixed with one another to produce other colours. Compare **subtractive.** See **primary colour.**
~*n.* A substance added in small amounts to something else, especially a food or drink, to improve, strengthen, or otherwise alter it.

ad·dle (ádd'l) *v.* **-dled, -dling, -dles.** —*tr.* 1. To muddle; confuse: *His brain is addled by too much drink.* —*intr.* 1. To become rotten. Used of an egg. 2. To become confused.
~*adj.* Mixed-up; confused. Usually used in combination: *addle-brained.* [Middle English *adel,* rotten, putrid, Old English *adela,* filth, urine; akin to Middle Low German *adelet.*]

ad·dress (ə-dréss) *tr.v.* **-dressed, -dressing, -dresses.** 1. To speak to; especially, to use a set form of address to. 2. To make a formal speech to. 3. To direct (a spoken or written comment) to the attention of. Used with *to: Please address your remarks to the chairman.* 4. To mark (a letter, parcel, or the like) with the name of the person and place to which it is to be delivered. 5. **a.** To direct (oneself) in speech. Used with *to.* **b.** To direct the efforts or attention of (oneself): *address oneself to a task.* **c.** To direct one's efforts or attention to (a problem, for example). 6. To consign (a ship or its cargo) to an agent or factor. 7. To adjust and aim a golf club or billiard cue when preparing to strike (a ball).
~*n.* (ə-dréss ‖ *U.S. also* áddress *for senses* 2,3,6). 1. A formal speech. 2. The location at which a particular organisation or person may be found or reached. 3. Information giving details of this, written on a letter, parcel, or the like. 4. Skilfulness, adroitness, or tact in handling a situation. 5. The act of consigning a ship or its cargo, as to an agent or factor. 6. *Computing.* A number used in information storage or retrieval that is assigned to a specific memory location. 7. *Usually plural. Archaic.* Courteous attention; wooing. Used chiefly in the phrase *pay one's addresses.* 8. *Archaic.* Manner or bearing of a person, especially in conversation. [Middle English *addressen,* from Old French *adresser,* from Vulgar Latin *addrictiâre* (unattested), to straighten, direct oneself towards : *ad-,* + *directiâre* (unattested), to straighten, from Latin *dírectus,* DIRECT.] —**ad·dress·er, ad·dress·or** *n.*

ad·dress·a·ble (ə-dréssəb'l) *adj.* Accessible through an address, as in a computer memory.

ad·dress·ee (áddress-ée) *n.* One to whom something, such as a letter, is addressed.

Ad·dress·o·graph (ə-dréssō-graaf, -graf) *n.* A trademark for a machine that prints addresses on letters.

ad·duce (ə-déwss, a- ‖ -dōoss) *tr.v.* **-duced, -ducing, -duces.** To cite as an example, explanation, or means of proof; bring forward for consideration. [Latin *addúcere,* to bring to (someone) : *ad-,* towards + *dúcere,* to lead.] —**ad·duce·a·ble, ad·duc·i·ble** *adj.*

ad·du·cent (ə-déwss'nt, a- ‖ -dōoss'nt) *adj. Physiology.* Drawing towards or together; adducting. Said of a muscle.

ad·duct (ə-dúkt, a-) *tr.v.* **-ducted, -ducting, -ducts.** To pull or draw (a limb) towards the main axis. Used of a muscle. [Back-formation from ADDUCTOR.] —**ad·duc·tion** *n.* —**ad·duc·tive** *adj.*

ad·duc·tor (ə-dúktər, a-) *n.* A muscle that adducts. [Latin *adductor,* "a bringer towards", from *addúcere,* to ADDUCE.]

-ade *n. comb. form.* Indicates a sweetened drink of; for example, **lemonade.** [French *-ade,* from Provençal, Portuguese, and Spanish *-ada* and Italian *-ata,* all from Latin *-āta,* feminine of *-ātus,* "furnished with", past participial ending of verbs in *-āre.*]

Ad·e·laide (áddilayd, ádd'l-ayd). Capital of South Australia, on the river Torrens in the southeast of the state. The products of its manufacturing industries include textiles, cars, and electronic devices, and it exports agricultural goods.

A·dé·lie Land (ə-dáyli). *French* **Terre Adélie.** Region of Antarctica on the coast of Wilkes Land, claimed by the French. Also called "Adélie Coast".

Adélie penguin *n.* A common Antarctic penguin, *Pygoscelis adeliae,* of medium size, with white underparts and black back and head. It lives and breeds in large exposed rookeries.

-adelphous *adj. comb. form. Botany.* Indicates stamens united by their filaments to form a specified number of groups; for example, **diadelphous.** [New Latin *-adelphus,* "having the stamens grouped together (in a 'brotherhood')", from Greek *adelphos,* brother.]

a·demp·tion (ə-démpsh'n) *n. Law.* The invalidation of a bequest, especially as a result of some action by the testator during his lifetime, such as the disposal of the property in question. [Latin *ademptiō,* a taking away, from *adimere* (past participle *ademptus*), to take to (oneself), take away : *ad-,* towards + *emere,* to buy, "take".]

A·den (áyd'n). Chief port of Yemen on the Gulf of Aden. It has always been one of the chief ports of southern Arabia. It was annexed by Britain in 1839, and became a major trading and refuelling station after the opening of the Suez Canal in 1869. Aden is the country's industrial and commercial centre.

A·den·au·er (ádd'n-ow-ər; *German* áad'n-), **Konrad** (1876–1967). German statesman and first Chancellor of the Federal Republic of Germany (1949–63). In 1946 Adenauer, a former Rhineland politician who had been twice imprisoned by the Nazis, became leader of the Christian Democratic Union (CDU), which won the first West German elections in 1949. Under Adenauer, West Germany embarked on a programme of economic reconstruction, and gained membership of NATO and the European Economic Community.

ad·en·ec·to·my (áddin-éktəmi) *n., pl.* **-mies.** Surgical excision of a gland. [ADEN(O)- + -ECTOMY.]

ad·e·nine (áddin-in, -een, -īn) *n. Biochemistry.* A purine derivative, $C_5H_5N_5$, that is a constituent of nucleic acid in the pancreas, spleen, and other organs. [ADEN(O)- + -INE.]

ad·e·ni·tis (áddin-ítiss) *n.* Inflammation of a lymph node or gland. [ADEN(O)- + -ITIS.]

adeno-, aden- *comb. form.* Indicates a gland or glands; for example, **adenocarcinoma.** [New Latin, from Greek *adēn,* gland.]

ad·e·no·car·ci·no·ma (áddinō-kársi-nṓ-mə) *n., pl.* **-mata** (-mə-tə) or **-mas.** A malignant tumour originating in glandular tissue. —**ad·e·no·car·ci·nom·a·tous** (-nōmətəss) *adj.*

ad·e·no·hy·poph·y·sis (áddinō-hī-póffi-siss, ə-dénnō-) *n.* The front section of the pituitary gland. Compare **neurohypophysis.**

ad·e·noid (áddin-oyd) *adj.* Also **ad·e·noi·dal** (áddi-nóyd'l). 1. Glandlike; glandular. 2. Of or pertaining to the adenoids.

ad·e·noi·dal (áddi-nóyd'l) *adj.* 1. Variant of **adenoid.** 2. **a.** Having a nasal or constricted tone: *an adenoidal singer.* **b.** Breathing through the mouth; open-mouthed.

ad·e·noids (áddin-oydz) *pl.n.* Lymphoid tissue growths in the nose above the throat that when swollen may obstruct nasal breathing, induce postnasal discharge, and make speech difficult. [Greek *adenoeidēs* : ADEN(O)- + -OID.]

ad·e·no·ma (áddi-nō-mə) *n., pl.* **-mata** (-mə-tə) or **-mas.** An epithelial tumour of glandular origin and structure that is usually benign or of low-grade malignancy. [ADEN(O)- + -OMA.] —**ad·e·nom·a·tous** (-nōmətəss, -nómətəss) *adj.*

a·den·o·sine (a-dénnə-seen, ə-, áddi-nō̄-) *n.* An organic compound, $C_{10}H_{13}N_5O_4$, that is a structural component of nucleic acids. [Blend of ADENINE and RIBOSE.]

adenosine diphosphate *n.* **ADP** (*see*).

adenosine monophosphate *n.* **AMP** (*see*).

adenosine triphosphate *n.* **ATP** (*see*).

ad·en·o·vir·us (áddinō-vír-əss, ə-dénnō-) *n.* Any of a group of viruses that cause respiratory infections producing symptoms like those of the common cold.

Aden Protectorate. See **Yemen.**

a·dept (ə-dépt, áddept) *adj.* Highly skilled; expert. See Synonyms at **proficient.**
~*n.* (áddept). One who is thoroughly proficient or highly skilled; an expert. [Latin *adeptus,* "having attained (knowledge or skill)", past participle of *adipíscī,* to attain : *ad-,* towards + *apíscī,* to reach for.] —**a·dept·ly** *adv.* —**a·dept·ness** *n.*

ad·e·quate (áddi-kwət, -kwit) *adj.* 1. **a.** Sufficient for a particular purpose or need. **b.** Able to satisfy a requirement or standard; suitable. **c.** Having the necessary qualities to meet the demands of a situation: *proved adequate to the task.* 2. Barely satisfactory or sufficient. —See Synonyms at **sufficient.** [Latin *adaequatus,* past participle of *adaequāre,* to make equal to : *ad-,* towards + *aequāre,* to make equal, from *aequus,* EQUAL.] —**ad·e·qua·cy** (-kwə-si), **ad·e·quate·ness** *n.* —**ad·e·quate·ly** *adv.*

Usage: The prepositions *to* and *for* following this word are becoming interchangeable. *To* is generally recommended in contexts such as *adequate to his needs, adequate to the task*; but *for* is increasingly common (*There was adequate food for our purposes*).

ad·here (əd-héer, ad-) *intr.v.* **-hered, -hering, -heres. 1.** To stick fast or together by or as if by grasping, suction, or being glued. Often used with *to.* **2.** To be devoted as a follower or supporter. Used with *to.* **3.** To follow closely or strictly. Used with *to*: *adhere to a plan.* [Latin *adhaerēre,* to stick to : *ad,* towards + *haerēre,* to stick.]

ad·her·ence (əd-héer-ənss, ad-) *n.* **1.** The act or state of adhering; adhesion. **2.** Fidelity or attachment, as to a party, cause, or set of rules.

ad·her·ent (əd-héer-ənt, ad-) *adj.* **1.** Sticking or holding fast; attached. **2.** *Botany.* Growing or fused together; adnate.
~n. A supporter, as of a cause, idea, or individual. **—ad·her·ent·ly** *adv.*

ad·he·sion (əd-héezh'n, ad-) *n.* **1. a.** The act or state of sticking together. **b.** Firm physical contact between surfaces; grip: *the tyre's adhesion to the road.* **2.** Loyalty or attachment; adherence. **3.** Assent or agreement, especially to join or associate oneself. **4.** The physical attraction or joining together of two substances; especially, the molecular attraction of dissimilar substances. Compare **cohesion. 2.** *Biology & Medicine.* An abnormal joining together of two organic parts. [Latin *adhaesiō,* from *adhaerēre,* to ADHERE.]

ad·he·sive (əd-héessiv, ad-, || -héeziv) *adj.* **1.** Tending to adhere; sticky. **2.** Gummed so as to adhere.
~n. An adhesive substance, such as paste or glue. **—ad·he·sive·ly** *adv.* **—ad·he·sive·ness** *n.*

ad hoc (ád hók) *adj.* For a specific purpose, case, or situation: *an ad hoc committee.* [Latin, "towards this".] **—ad hoc** *adv.*

ad ho·mi·nem (ád hómminem) *adj. Latin.* **1.** Appealing to personal interests, prejudices, or emotions rather than to reason: *an argument ad hominem.* **2.** Personally abusive: *an ad hominem attack.* [Literally, "to the man."] **—ad ho·mi·nem** *adv.*

ad·i·a·bat·ic (áy-dī-ə-báttik, áddi-ə-) *adj. Physics.* Of, pertaining to, or designating a reversible thermodynamic process executed at constant entropy; loosely, occurring without gain or loss of heat. [Greek *adiabatos,* "impassable (to heat)" : *a-,* not + *diabatos,* passable, from *diabainein,* to go through : *dia,* through + *bainein,* to go.] **—ad·i·a·bat·i·cal·ly** *adv.*

a·dieu (ə-déw || ə-dóō) *interj.* Goodbye; farewell.
~n., pl. **adieus** or **adieux** (-z). A farewell. [Middle English, from Old French, from *a dieu,* "(I commend you) to God" : *a,* to, from Latin *ad* + *dieu,* God, from Latin *deus,* god.]

ad in·fi·ni·tum (ád ínfi-nītəm) *adv. Abbr.* **ad inf.** To infinity; endlessly. [Latin.]

ad in·ter·im (ád íntərim) *adv. Abbr.* **ad int.** *Latin.* In the meantime; meanwhile. **—ad in·ter·im** *adj.*

a·di·os (áddi-óss, aádi-óss || -ōss) *interj.* Goodbye; farewell. [Spanish, perhaps translation of French *adieu,* ADIEU.]

ad·i·pose (áddi-pōss, -pōz) *adj.* Of or related to animal fat; fatty.
~n. The fat found in adipose tissue. [New Latin *adiposus,* from Latin *adeps*† (stem *adip-*), fat.] **—ad·i·pose·ness, ad·i·pos·i·ty** (-póssəti) *n.*

adipose fin *n.* An additional dorsal fin in certain fishes, such as the salmon, consisting mostly of fatty tissue and usually without supporting rays.

adipose tissue *n.* Connective tissue in the body that contains stored cellular fat.

Ad·i·ron·dack Mountains (addi-róndak). Also **Ad·i·ron·dacks** (addi-róndaks). Group of mountains in eastern New York state, United States. The highest peak is Mt. Marcy (1 628 metres; 5,344 feet). The region's lakes and forests attract many tourists, and there are also numerous winter sports resorts, including Lake Placid, venue of the Winter Olympic Games of 1932 and 1980.

ad·it (áddit) *n.* A horizontal, or near horizontal, passage cut in a hill slope for mining or drainage purposes. [Latin *aditus,* access, from the past participle of *adīre,* to approach : *ad-,* towards + *īre,* to go.]

A·di·va·si (aádi-vaa-si) *n., pl.* **Adivasis** or collectively **Adivasi.** A member of any of the aboriginal peoples of India.

adj. 1. adjective. **2.** adjourned. **3.** adjutant.

ad·ja·cent (ə-jáyss'nt) *adj.* **1.** Lying or being close in space or time. **2.** Having a common border; contiguous or adjoining. [Middle English, from Latin *adjacēns* (stem *adjacent-*), present participle of *adjacēre,* to lie near : *ad-,* near to + *jacēre,* to lie, "be thrown down", intransitive of *jacere,* to lay, throw.] **—ad·ja·cen·cy** *n.* **—ad·ja·cent·ly** *adv.*

adjacent angle *n.* Either of two angles having a common side and a common vertex and lying on opposite sides of the common side.

ad·jec·tive (ájik-tiv, ájek-) *n. Abbr.* **adj., a. 1.** A part of speech comprising a class of words that characterise a noun or other substantive by limiting, qualifying, or specifying. **2.** A word belonging to this class, such as *nice* in *a nice house.* **3.** A word used like an adjective, such as *brick* in *a brick house.*
~adj. **1.** Pertaining to or functioning as an adjective. **2.** Dependent; subordinate. **3.** *Law.* Concerned with court procedure as opposed to legal principles. Compare **substantive. 4.** Requiring the use of a mordant to make permanent: *adjective dyes.* [Middle English, from Old French *adjectif,* from Latin *adjectīvus,* "attributive", from *adjectus,* "attributed", added, from *adjicere,* to throw to, add : *ad-,* to + *jacere,* to throw.] **—ad·jec·ti·val** (-tīv'l) *adj.* **—ad·jec·ti·val·ly** *adv.*

ad·join (ə-jóyn) *v.* **-joined, -joining, -joins.** *—tr.* **1.** To be next to; be contiguous to. **2.** To attach; append. Used with *to.* *—intr.* To be nearby or contiguous: *in the adjoining room.* [Middle English *adjoinen,* from Old French *ajoindre,* from Latin *adjungere,* to join to : *ad-,* to + *jungere,* to join.]

ad·journ (ə-júrn) *v.* **-journed, -journing, -journs.** *—tr.* To break off (especially a meeting or court session) until a later time. *—intr.* **1.** To suspend proceedings or transfer to another time or place. **2.** To move from one place to another. Often used humorously: *We adjourned to the living room.* [Middle English *ajournen,* from Old French *ajourner,* "to put off to an appointed day" : *a-,* to, from Latin *ad-* + *jour,* day, from Late Latin *diurnum,* day, from *diurnus,* daily, from *diēs,* day] **—ad·journ·ment** *n.*

adjt. adjutant.

ad·judge (ə-júj) *tr.v.* **-judged, -judging, -judges. 1.** To determine or settle by judicial procedure; adjudicate. **2.** To order or pronounce judicially; rule. **3.** To award (costs or damages, for example) by law. **4.** To consider or pronounce to be; deem; judge. [Middle English *ajugen,* from Old French *ajuger,* from Latin *adjūdicāre,* to ADJUDICATE.]

ad·ju·di·cate (ə-jóōdi-kayt) *v.* **-cated, -cating, -cates.** *—tr.* **1.** To hear and settle (a case) by judicial procedure. **2.** To pronounce judicially; adjudge: *was adjudicated a bankrupt.* *—intr.* To act as a judge. Usually used with *on* or *upon.* [Latin *adjūdicāre,* to award to (judicially) : *ad-,* to + *jūdicāre,* to be a judge, from *jūdex,* a judge] **—ad·ju·di·ca·tion** (-káysh'n) *n.* **—ad·ju·di·ca·tive** (-kaytiv, -kətiv) *adj.* **—ad·ju·di·ca·tor** (-kaytər) *n.*

ad·junct (ájungkt) *n.* **1.** Something attached to another thing but in a subordinate or incidental relation. **2.** A person associated with another in a subordinate or auxiliary capacity; a helper; an assistant. **3.** A word or words added to clarify or modify other words in a sentence, but not grammatically essential to the sentence. **4.** *Logic.* A nonessential attribute of a thing. —See Synonyms at **appendage.**
~adj. Added or connected in a subordinate, auxiliary, or temporary capacity: *an adjunct clause; an adjunct professor.* [Latin *adjunctum,* from *adjunctus,* past participle of *adjungere,* to ADJOIN.] **—ad·junc·tion** (ə-júngksh'n) *n.* **—ad·junc·tive** (ə-júngktiv) *adj.*

ad·ju·ra·tion (ájoo-ráysh'n) *n.* An earnest or solemn appeal. **—ad·jur·a·to·ry** (əjóor-ə-tri, -təri, ájoo-ráytəri) *adj.*

ad·jure (ə-jóor) *tr.v.* **-jured, -juring, -jures. 1.** To command or enjoin solemnly, as under oath or penalty. **2.** To appeal to or entreat earnestly. [Middle English *adjuren,* from Latin *adjūrāre,* to swear to : *ad-,* to + *jūrāre,* to swear.] **—ad·jur·er, ad·ju·ror** (ə-jóor-ər) *n.*

ad·just (ə-júst) *v.* **-justed, -justing, -justs.** *—tr.* **1.** To change so as to match or fit; cause to correspond. **2.** To adapt; change so as to harmonise with new conditions. **3.** To regulate so as to make accurate or efficient. **4.** To decide how much is to be paid on (an insurance claim). *—intr.* To adapt oneself, as to changed conditions; become suited or fit. [Obsolete French *adjuster,* from Old French *ajoster,* from Vulgar Latin *adjuxtāre* (unattested), to put close to : Latin *ad-,* near to + *juxtā,* close by, near.] **—ad·just·a·ble** *adj.* **—ad·just·a·bly** *adv.* **—ad·just·er, ad·jus·tor** (-ər) *n.* **—ad·jus·tive** *adj.*

ad·just·ment (ə-jústmənt) *n.* **1.** The act of adjusting or state of being adjusted. **2.** A slight alteration or modification. **3.** A means for adjusting. **4.** The settlement of a debt or claim.

ad·ju·tant (ájoo-tənt, ájə-) *n.* **1.** *Abbr.* **adj., adjt.** *Military.* A staff officer who helps a commanding officer with and is responsible for administrative work. **2.** An assistant. **3.** A stork, the **marabou** *(see).* [Latin *adjūtāns* (stem *adjūtant-*), present participle of *adjūtāre,* to assist, AID.] **—ad·ju·tan·cy, ad·ju·tant·ship** *n.*

adjutant general *n., pl.* **adjutants general.** *Abbr.* **AG, A.G.** *Military.* **1.** In Britain, a high-ranking staff officer with administrative responsibilities. **2.** In the United States: **a.** *Capital* **A,** *capital* **G.** The chief administrative officer of the U.S. Army. Preceded by *the.* **b.** An adjutant of a unit that has a general staff. **c.** A high-ranking officer in the National Guard.

adjutant stork *n.* The **marabou** *(see).* [Referring to the military style of its movements when walking.

ad·ju·vant (ájoo-vənt, ájə-) *adj.* Helping or contributing.
~n. One that aids; specifically an ingredient that increases the effectiveness of a medicine.

Ad·ler (áddlər, aádlər), **Alfred** (1870–1937). Austrian physician and psychiatrist. Originally a follower of Sigmund Freud, Adler broke away in 1911. He rejected Freud's emphasis on sexuality and held that much behaviour arises from subconscious efforts to compensate for feelings of inferiority, and that neurosis results from overcompensation. **—Ad·le·ri·an** (ad-léer-i-ən) *adj. & n.*

Ad·ler (áddlər), **Larry,** born Lawrence Cecil Adler (1914–). U.S. harmonica player. Adler extended the conventional harmonica repertoire by playing works by classical composers such as Ravel.

ad lib (ád líb) *adv.* **1.** Without preparation; spontaneously. **2.** Without limit; freely. See Synonyms at **extemporaneous.**

ad-lib (ad-líb) *v.* **-libbed, -libbing, -libs.** *Informal.* *—tr.* To improvise and deliver without rehearsal (words, music, or the like). *—intr.* To improvise a speech, lines, or the like; extemporise.
~n. Words, music, or actions ad-libbed.
~adj. Spoken or performed spontaneously; impromptu. [Shortened from AD LIBITUM.] **—ad-lib·ber** *n.*

ad lib·i·tum (ád líbbitəm) *adv. Abbr.* **ad lib., ad libit.** *Music.* Without limit or restriction; performed as desired. Used as a direction. Compare **obbligato.** [Latin, "to the desire".]

ad li·tem (ád lī́-tem) *adv. Law.* For a lawsuit or action. Said of a guardian appointed for such a purpose.
ad loc (ád lók) *adv.* To (or at) the place already mentioned. [Latin *ad locum.*]
Adm. admiral; admiralty.
ad·man (ád-man) *n., pl.* **-men** (-men). *Informal.* A man employed in the advertising business.
ad·mass (ád-mass) *n. Chiefly British.* The mass of society perceived as being readily influenced by high-pressure advertising.
ad·meas·ure (ad-mézhər, əd-) *tr.v.* **-ured, -uring, -ures.** To divide and distribute proportionally; apportion. [Middle English *amesuren,* from Old French *amesurer,* to measure out to.] **—ad·meas·ure·ment** *n.* **—ad·meas·ur·er** *n.*
ad·min (ád-min) *n. Informal.* Administration.
ad·min·is·ter (əd-mínniss-tər || ad-) *v.* **-tered, -tering, -ters.** *—tr.* **1.** To have charge of; direct; manage; administrate (the affairs of a person, business, government, or the like). **2. a.** To give or perform in a formal or ritualistic way: *administer the last rites.* **b.** To apply or give as a remedy: *administer a sedative.* **3.** To dispense; put into operation: *administer justice.* **4.** To manage or dispose of (trusts and estates) under a will or an official appointment. **5.** To impose, offer, or tender (an oath, for example). *—intr.* **1.** To act as an administrator. **2.** To attend to the needs of others; minister. Used with *to: administering to their pleasure.* [Middle English *administren,* from Old French *administrer,* from Latin *administrāre,* to be an aid to : *ad-,* to + *ministrāre,* to serve, from *minister,* servant.] **—ad· min·is·tra·ble** (-trəb'l) *adj.* **—ad·min·is·trant** (-trənt) *adj.* & *n.*
ad·min·is·trate (əd-mínniss-trayt || ad-) *tr.v.* **-trated, -trating, -trates.** To administer; be in charge of the affairs of.
ad·min·is·tra·tion (əd-mínniss-tráysh'n || ad-) *n. Abbr.* **admin. 1.** The management of affairs, especially in government or business. **2.** The people who make up the managing body of any institution, public or private. **3.** The government, its executive branch, or its term of office: *a member of the Blair administration.* **4.** *Law.* The management and disposal of a trust or estate. **5.** The dispensing, applying, or tendering of something, such as an oath, sacrament, or medicine. **—ad·min·is·tra·tive** (-trətiv, -traytiv) *adj.* **—ad·min·is·tra·tive·ly** *adv.*
ad·min·is·tra·tor (əd-mínniss-traytər || ad-) *n. Abbr.* **admin. 1.** One who administers, especially public or business affairs. **2.** *Law.* A person appointed to administer an estate. **3.** *Capital* **A.** The chief executive official in any of the provinces of South Africa.
ad·mi·ra·ble (ádmərəb'l) *adj.* Deserving admiration; excellent. **—ad·mi·ra·ble·ness** *n.* **—ad·mir·a·bly** *adv.*
ad·mi·ral (ádmərəl) *n.* **1.** The commander in chief of a navy or fleet. **2.** *Abbr.* **Adm.** In the British or U.S. Navy: **a.** An officer holding the next-to-highest rank, who commands a whole fleet. **b.** Any officer of the highest grade; **Admiral of the Fleet, rear-admiral,** or **vice-admiral** *(all of which see).* **3.** The ship carrying an admiral; a flagship. **4.** Any of various brightly coloured butterflies of the genera *Limenitis* and *Vanessa.* [Middle English *a(d)miral,* from Medieval Latin *a(d)mīrālis* (reshaped as if from *admīrārī,* to admire), from Old French *amiral,* from Arabic *'amīr-al-,* "commander of" : *'amīr,* commander, EMIR + *al,* the.]
Admiral of the Fleet *n.* In the British or U.S. navy, the officer holding the highest rank, equivalent to field marshal or general of the army. Also *U.S.* "Fleet Admiral".
ad·mi·ral·ty (ádmərəlti) *n., pl.* **-ties.** *Abbr.* **Adm. 1.** *Capital* **A.** In Britain: **a.** The government department that controls naval affairs. **b.** The building in which this department is housed. **2. a.** A court exercising jurisdiction over all maritime causes. **b.** Maritime law.
Admiralty Islands. Group of 40 volcanic islands in the southwest Pacific Ocean. The islands lie in the Bismarck Archipelago, and are part of Papua New Guinea.
ad·mi·ra·tion (ádmə-ráysh'n) *n.* **1. a.** A feeling of pleasure and approval. **b.** A feeling of disinterested and pleased respect. **2.** An object of wonder; a marvel: *His success made him the admiration of all his friends.* **3.** *Archaic.* Wonder. —See Synonyms at **regard.**
ad·mire (əd-mī́r || ad-) *tr.v.* **-mired, -miring, -mires. 1.** To look at with pleasure and approval: *stood in front of the mirror admiring himself.* **2.** To have a high opinion of; regard with respect. **3.** *Archaic.* To marvel or wonder at. **4.** To express admiration for : *She thanked me for admiring her dress.* [Latin *admīrārī,* to wonder at : *ad-,* to, at + *mīrārī,* to wonder, from *mīrus,* wonderful.] **—ad·mir·ing** *adj.* **—ad·mir·ing·ly** *adv.*
ad·mir·er (əd-mī́r-ər || ad-) *n.* One who admires; especially, a man who is attracted to a particular woman.
ad·mis·si·ble (əd-míssə-b'l || ad-) *adj.* **1.** Capable of being accepted; allowable. Said especially of evidence in a court case. **2.** Qualified or permitted to enter. **—ad·mis·si·bil·i·ty** (-bílləti), **ad·mis·si·ble·ness** *n.* **—ad·mis·si·bly** *adv.*
ad·mis·sion (əd-mísh'n || ad-) *n.* **1. a.** The act of admitting or allowing to enter. **b.** The state of being allowed to enter. **2.** The right to enter; access. **3.** The cost of entering; entrance fee. **4.** The act or process of acceptance and entry into a position or situation; appointment. **5.** A confession of crime or wrongdoing. **6.** A voluntary acknowledgment that something is true. [Middle English *admissioun,* from Latin *admissiō* (stem *admissiōn-*), from *admittere* (past participle *admissus*), to ADMIT.] **—ad·mis·sive** (əd-míssiv || ad-) *adj.*

Usage: In the sense "permission to enter" (a building, country, club, and so on), *admission* is the normal term. *Admittance* is a more formal or official term: *No admittance, except on business.*

ad·mit (əd-mít || ad-) *v.* **-mitted, -mitting, -mits.** *—tr.* **1.** To permit to enter. **2.** To serve as an authorisation of entrance: *This ticket admits the whole group.* **3.** To permit to join or exercise certain rights, functions, or privileges. **4.** To have room for; be able to accommodate. **5.** To allow the possibility of; permit. **6.** To acknowledge; confess: *admit the truth.* **7.** To grant as true or valid, as for the sake of argument; concede. **8.** To acknowledge as being lawful or valid. *—intr.* **1.** To allow the possibility; permit. Used with *of.* **2.** To allow entrance; afford access. Used with *to: This door admits to the main hall.* —See Synonyms at **acknowledge.** [Middle English *admitten,* from Latin *admittere,* to send in to : *ad-,* to + *mittere,* to send.]
ad·mit·tance (əd-mítt'nss || ad-) *n.* **1.** The act of admitting or entering. **2.** Permission to enter; the power or right of entrance. See Usage note at **admission. 3.** *Electricity.* The reciprocal of impedance. It is the ratio of a current to a voltage, is measured in siemens, and may be expressed as a complex quantity, the real part of which is conductance and the imaginary part susceptance.
ad·mit·ted·ly (əd-míttidli || ad-) *adv.* By general admission; granted that: *admittedly the quality is poor.*
ad·mix·ture (ad-míks-chər, əd-) *n.* **1. a.** The act of mingling or mixing. **b.** The state of being mingled or mixed. **2.** That which is mingled or mixed; a mixture. **3.** Anything added in mixing; an ingredient. [From Latin *admixtus,* past participle of *admiscēre,* to mix into : *ad,* to + *miscēre,* to mix.]
ad·mon·ish (əd-mónnish || ad-) *tr.v.* **-ished, -ishing, -ishes. 1.** To reprove mildly or kindly, but firmly. **2.** To counsel against something; caution; warn. **3.** To remind or advise about something forgotten or disregarded, by means of a warning, reproof, or exhortation. —See Synonyms at **warn.** [Middle English *admonissen,* back-formation from *admonesten* (the stem *admonest-* was mistaken for a past participle), from Old French *admonester,* from Vulgar Latin *admonestāre* (unattested), variant of Latin *admonēre,* to bring to (someone's) mind : *ad-,* to + *monēre,* to remind, advise.] **—ad·mon·ish·er** *n.* **—ad·mon·ish·ing·ly** *adv.* **—ad·mon·ish·ment** *n.*

Synonyms: *admonish, reprove, rebuke, reprimand, reproach.*

ad·mo·ni·tion (ádmə-nísh'n) *n.* **1.** A mild rebuke or warning. **2.** Cautionary advice. [Middle English *admonicioun,* from Old French *amonition,* from Latin *admonitiō* (stem *admonitiōn-*), from *admonēre,* to ADMONISH.]
ad·mon·i·to·ry (əd-mónni-tri, -təri || ad-) *adj. Formal.* Cautionary.
ad·nate (ád-nayt) *adj. Biology.* Joined to or fused with another part or organ. Said of parts not usually united. [Latin *adnātus,* past participle of *adnāscī, agnāscī,* to be born in addition to. See **agnate.**] **—ad·na·tion** (ad-náysh'n) *n.*
ad nau·se·am (ád náwssi-am, náwzi-, -əm) *adv. Latin.* To a sickening or tedious degree.
ad·noun (ád-nown) *n. Grammar.* An adjective used as a noun, as in *the bold and the brave.* [AD- (additional) + NOUN (by analogy with ADVERB).] **—ad·nom·i·nal** (ad-nómmin'l) *adj.* **—ad·nom·i·nal·ly** *adv.*
a·do (ə-dṓō) *n.* Bustle; fuss; trouble; bother. [Middle English, from the phrase *at do,* "to do" : *at,* from Old Norse *at* (used with infinitive), to + *don,* to DO.]
a·do·be (ə-dṓbi) *n.* **1. a.** Clay or loess, probably wind-blown in origin, found in the deserts of the southwestern United States and Mexico. **b.** A sun-dried brick made from this or a similar material. **2.** A structure built with such bricks. [Spanish *adobe,* from Arabic *aṭṭōba, al-ṭōba,* "the brick".] **—a·do·be** *adj.*
ad·o·les·cence (ádd'l-éss'nss, áddōl-) *n.* **1.** The period of physical and psychological development from the onset of puberty to maturity. **2.** The state or condition of a person during that period.
ad·o·les·cent (ádd'l-éss'nt, áddōl-) *adj.* **1.** Of, pertaining to, or undergoing adolescence. **2.** Immature in attitude or behaviour; puerile. See Synonyms at **young.**
~n. An adolescent person. [Middle English, from Old French, from Latin *adolēscēns* (stem *adolēscent-*), present participle of *adolēscere,* to grow up : *ad-,* towards + *alēscere,* to grow, "be nourished", inceptive of *alere,* to nourish.]
Ad·o·nai (áddō-nī́, -ni-ī́ || -nóy). *Hebrew.* Lord. Used in Judaism as a spoken substitute for the name of God. See **Tetragrammaton.** [Hebrew *adōnāi,* "my lord(s)", from Phoenician *adōn,* lord.]
A·do·nic (ə-dṓnik || *U.S. also* -dónnik) *adj.* **1.** Of or designating a verse measure consisting of a dactyl followed by a spondee or trochee. **2.** Of or pertaining to Adonis.
~n. An Adonic verse. [This meter was said to have been first used in verses lamenting Adonis' death.]
A·don·is[1] (ə-dṓniss || *U.S. also* -dónniss). *Mythology.* A youth loved by Aphrodite/Venus for his striking beauty. [Greek *Adōnis,* from Phoenician *adōn,* lord. See also **Adonal.**]
Adonis[2] *n.* A young man of great physical beauty.
a·dopt (ə-dópt) *tr.v.* **adopted, adopting, adopts. 1.** To take into one's family through legal means and bring up as one's own child. **2.** To select and bring into a new relationship, as a friend, heir, or citizen, for example. **3.** To take and follow (a course of action, for example) by choice or assent: *adopt a new technique.* **4.** To take up and use (an idea or word, for example) as one's own. **5.** To take on or assume: *adopt the ambitions of a despot.* **6.** To vote to accept: *adopt a resolution.* **7.** *British.* To take over the responsibility of maintaining (a road, for example). Used of a local authority. [Latin *adoptāre,* to choose for oneself : *ad-,* to + *optāre,* to choose, desire.] **—a·dopt·a·ble** *adj.* **—a·dopt·er** *n.* **—a·dop·tion** *n.*
a·dopt·ed (ə-dóptid) *adj.* Related by adoption: *an adopted child.*
a·dop·tive (ə-dóptiv) *adj.* **1.** Related by adoption: *an adoptive parent.* **2.** Tending to adopt. **—a·dop·tive·ly** *adv.*

a·dor·a·ble (ə-dáwr-əb'l ‖ -dór-) *adj*. **1.** Delightful; lovable; charming. **2.** *Archaic*. Worthy of or eliciting worship. —**a·dor·a·bil·i·ty** (-əbíllɔti), **a·dor·a·ble·ness** *n*. —**a·dor·a·bly** *adv*.

ad·o·ra·tion (áddə-ráysh'n) *n*. **1.** The act of worship. **2.** Profound love or regard.

a·dore (ə-dáwr ‖ ə-dór) *tr.v*. **adored, adoring, adores**. **1.** To worship with divine honours. **2.** To love deeply. **3.** *Informal*. To like very much: *He adores being tickled*. —See Synonyms at **revere**. [Middle English *adoren*, from Old French *adorer*, from Latin *adōrāre*, to pray to : *ad-*, to + *ōrāre*, to speak, pray.] —**a·dor·er** *n*. —**a·dor·ing·ly** *adv*.

a·dorn (ə-dórn) *tr.v*. **adorned, adorning, adorns**. **1.** To be a decoration to; lend beauty to: *"the pale mimosas that adorned the favourite promenade"* (Ronald Firbank). **2.** To decorate; furnish with ornaments. **3.** To add lustre or distinction to. [Middle English *adornen*, from Old French *adorner*, from Latin *adornāre*, to put ornaments on : *ad-*, to + *ornāre*, to furnish, deck.] —**a·dorn·er** *n*. —**a·dorn·ment** *n*.

ADP *n*. *A*denosine *d*iphosphate: an organic compound, $C_{10}H_{15}N_5O_{10}P_2$, that is formed when ATP undergoes hydrolysis of the terminal phosphate bond and releases its energy.

A.D.P. automatic data processing.

ad rem (ád rém) *adj*. *Latin*. To the point; pertinent. —**ad rem** *adv*.

ad·re·nal (ə-dréen'l) *adj*. **1.** At, near, or on the kidneys. **2.** Of or pertaining to the adrenal glands or their secretions.
~*n*. An adrenal gland. [AD- (towards, near) + RENAL.]

adrenal cortex *n*. The three-zoned centre of the adrenal glands.

adrenal gland *n*. Either of two small dissimilarly shaped endocrine glands, one located above each kidney, consisting of the cortex, which secretes corticosteroid hormones, and the medulla, which secretes adrenaline. Also called "suprarenal gland".

ad·ren·a·line (ə-drénnə-lin, -leen) *n*. Also **ad·ren·a·lin** (especially for sense 2). **1.** A secretion of the adrenal glands causing acceleration of the heart, constriction of small blood vessels, dilation of the pupils, and an increase in metabolic rate. Also *U.S*. "epinephrine". **2.** Broadly, a substance that is supposed to cause heightened emotion and a sudden increase in physical strength, as during fear or anger. [ADRENAL + -INE.]

ad·ren·er·gic (ádrə-nérjik) *adj*. Of, pertaining to, or having chemical activity like that of adrenaline. Said of certain nerve fibres. [ADREN(ALINE) + Greek *ergon*, work, action.]

ad·re·no·cor·ti·co·trop·ic (ə-dréenō-kórtikō-tróppik, -trópik) *adj*. Also **ad·re·no·cor·ti·co·troph·ic** (-tróffik, -trófik). Stimulating or otherwise acting upon the cortex of the adrenal gland. [ADREN(AL) + CORTICO- + -TROPIC.]

adrenocorticotropic hormone *n*. See **ACTH**.

A·dri·an (áydri-ən), **Edgar Douglas, 1st Baron** (1889–1977). British physiologist. His research on nerve cells led to major advances in the understanding of the nervous and muscular systems. He won the 1932 Nobel prize for physiology and medicine (sharing it with Sir Charles Sherrington).

Adrian IV, born Nicholas Breakspear; also known as Hadrian IV (*c*. 1100–1159). Pope (1154–59); the only English pope.

Adrianople. See **Edirne**.

A·dri·at·ic (áydri-áttik) *adj*. Of or pertaining to the Adriatic Sea or to the peoples inhabiting its islands and coasts: *by the Adriatic*.

Adriatic Sea. A northern arm of the Mediterranean, between Italy and the Balkan peninsula. It is about 800 kilometres (500 miles) long, from the Gulf of Venice in the north to the Strait of Otranto.

a·drift (ə-dríft) *adv*. **1.** Without anchor or steering; drifting. **2.** Purposelessly; aimlessly. **3.** *Informal*. **a.** Wrong; not according to plan: *His schemes went badly adrift*. **b.** Unfastened or unattached: *Your shoelace has come adrift*. —**a·drift** *adj*.

a·droit (ə-dróyt) *adj*. **1.** Dexterous; deft. **2.** Resourceful and quick-thinking under pressure. —See Synonyms at **dexterous**. [French, from *à droit*, "rightly" : *à*, to, at, from Latin *ad-* + *droit*, right, from Latin *dīrectus*, DIRECT.] —**a·droit·ly** *adv*. —**a·droit·ness** *n*.

ad·sci·ti·tious (ád-si-tíshəss) *adj*. Not inherent or external; added as a supplementary part; adventitious. [From Latin *adscītus*, derived, assumed, past participle of *adscīscere*, to approve, arrogate to oneself : *ad-*, to + *scīscere*, to seek to know, assume, inceptive of *scīre*, to know.]

ad·sorb (ad-sórb, əd- ‖ -zórb) *tr.v*. **-sorbed, -sorbing, -sorbs**. To take up by adsorption. Compare **absorb**. [AD- + Latin *sorbēre*, to drink in, suck.]

ad·sor·bate (ad-sórb-ayt, əd-, -it ‖ -zórb-) *n*. An adsorbed substance.

ad·sor·bent (ad-sór-bənt, əd- ‖ -zórb-) *adj*. Capable of adsorption.
~*n*. An adsorbent material, such as activated carbon.

ad·sorp·tion (ad-sórp-sh'n, əd- ‖ -zórp-) *n*. The assimilation of gas, vapour, or dissolved matter by the surface of a solid. [ADSORB + -TION.] —**ad·sorp·tive** *adj*.

adsuki bean. Variant of **adzuki bean**.

ad·u·lar·i·a (áddew-laír-i-ə) *n*. *Mineralogy*. A variety of **orthoclase** (*see*). [Italian, from French *adulaire*, after *Adula*, mountain group in Switzerland.]

ad·u·late (áddew-layt) *tr.v*. **-lated, -lating, -lates**. To praise excessively or fawningly. [Back-formation from ADULATION.] —**ad·u·la·tor** (-laytər) *n*. —**ad·u·la·to·ry** (-láytəri, -lətri, -lətəri) *adj*.

ad·u·la·tion (áddew-láysh'n) *n*. Excessive praise or flattery. [Middle English *adulacioun*, from Old French *adulation*, from Latin *adulātiō*, from *adulārī*†, to flatter.]

a·dult (áddult, ə-dúlt ‖ ádd'lt) *n*. **1.** One who has attained maturity

or legal age. **2.** A fully grown, mature organism, such as an insect that has completed its final stage of metamorphosis.
~*adj*. **1.** Fully developed and mature. **2. a.** Pertaining to, befitting, or intended for mature persons: *adult education*. **b.** Sexually explicit; pornographic. Used euphemistically: *adult films*. [Latin *adultus*, past participle of *adolescēre*, to grow up. See **adolescent**.] —**a·dult·hood** *n*.

a·dul·ter·ant (ə-dúltərənt) *n*. A substance that adulterates.
~*adj*. Adulterating.

a·dul·ter·ate (ə-dúltər-ayt) *tr.v*. **-ated, -ating, -ates**. To make impure, spurious, or inferior by adding extraneous or improper ingredients.
~*adj*. **1.** Spurious; adulterated; corrupt. **2.** Adulterous. [Latin *adulterāre*, to pollute, commit adultery.] —**a·dul·ter·a·tion** (-áysh'n) *n*. —**a·dul·ter·a·tor** (-áytər) *n*.

a·dul·ter·er (ə-dúltərər ‖ -dúltrər) *n*. A person, especially a man, who commits adultery.

a·dul·ter·ess (ə-dúltər-iss, -ess, ‖ -dúltr-) *n*. A woman who commits adultery.

a·dul·ter·ine (ə-dúltər-īn, -in ‖ -een) *adj*. **1.** Characterised by adulteration; spurious; fake. **2.** Unauthorised by law; illegal. **3.** Born of adultery: *adulterine offspring*. [Latin *adulterīnus* from *adulterāre*, to commit adultery, ADULTERATE.]

a·dul·ter·ous (ə-dúltər-əss, -dúltr-) *adj*. Characterised by, inclined to, or having committed adultery. —**a·dul·ter·ous·ly** *adv*.

a·dul·ter·y (ə-dúltər-i ‖ -dúltr-) *n., pl*. **-ries**. Voluntary sexual intercourse between a married person and a partner other than the lawful husband or wife. Compare **fornication**. [Middle English *adulterie, a(d)vouterie*, from Old French *avoutrie, avoutire*, from Latin *adulterium*, from *adulter*, adulterer, from *adulterāre*, to ADULTERATE.]

ad·um·bral (ad-úmbrəl) *adj*. *Poetic*. In shadow. [AD- (in) + Latin *umbra*, shadow.]

ad·um·brate (áddəm-brayt, áddum-) *tr.v*. **-brated, -brating, -brates**. **1.** To give a sketchy outline of. **2.** To prefigure indistinctly; foreshadow. **3.** To disclose partially or guardedly. **4.** To overshadow; obscure. [Latin *adumbrāre*, to overshadow : *ad-*, to + *umbra*, shadow.] —**ad·um·bra·tion** (-bráysh'n) *n*. —**ad·um·bra·tive** (-braytiv, ad-úmbrətiv) *adj*. —**ad·um·bra·tive·ly** *adv*.

a·dust (ə-dúst) *adj*. *Archaic*. **1.** Burnt; scorched. **2.** Melancholy; gloomy. [Middle English, from Latin *adūstus*, from the past participle of *adūrere*, to set fire to : *ad-*, to + *ūrere*, to burn.]

adv. adverb; adverbial.

ad va·lo·rem (ád və-láwr-em, va-, -əm ‖ -ór-) *adj*. *Latin*. *Abbr*. **a.v.**, **ad val.** In proportion to the value: *ad valorem duties on imported goods*. —**ad va·lo·rem** *adv*.

ad·vance (əd-vaʹanss ‖ ad-, -vánss) *v*. **-vanced, -vancing, -vances**.
—*tr*. **1.** To move or bring forward in position. **2.** To put forward; propose; suggest. **3.** To aid the growth or progress of; further. **4.** To raise in rank; promote. **5.** To cause to occur sooner; hasten. **6.** To raise in amount or rate; increase. **7.** To pay (money or interest) before legally due. **8.** To supply or lend, especially on credit.
—*intr*. **1.** To go or move forward or onwards. **2.** To make progress; improve; grow. **3.** To rise in rank, position, or value.
~*n*. **1.** The act or process of moving or going forward. **2.** Improvement; progress. **3.** A rise or increase of price or value. **4.** *Plural*. Personal approaches made to secure acquaintance, favour, or an agreement; overtures. **5. a.** The furnishing of funds or goods on credit. **b.** The funds or goods so furnished; a loan. **6.** A payment of money before legally or normally due. —**in advance**. **1.** In front. **2.** Ahead of time; beforehand; early. Often used with *of*.
~*adj*. **1.** Made or given ahead of time; prior. **2.** Going before; in front; forward. [Middle English *advancen*, from Old French *avancier*, from Vulgar Latin *abantiāre* (unattested), from Latin *abante*, "from before" : *ab-*, away from + *ante*, before.] —**ad·vance·ment** *n*. —**ad·vanc·er** *n*.

Synonyms: advance, promote, forward, further.

ad·vanced (ad-vaʹanst ‖ ad-, -vánst) *adj*. **1. a.** Far on in development or progress: *The child is very advanced for her age*. **b.** Far on in life: *advanced in years*. **2.** Ahead of contemporary thought or practice: *advanced ideas*. **3.** At a high level of difficulty: *advanced mathematics*.

advanced gas-cooled reactor *n*. *Abbr*. **A.G.R.** A type of nuclear reactor in which the coolant is gaseous carbon dioxide, the moderator is graphite, and the fuel is ceramic uranium dioxide in a stainless-steel casing.

Advanced level *n*. See **A level**.

Advanced Passenger Train *n*. *Abbr*. **APT** A British prototype fast passenger train that negotiates curves in the track at high speeds.

advance guard *n*. *Military*. A detachment of troops sent ahead of the main force to reconnoitre and provide protection.

ad·van·tage (ad-vaʹant-ij ‖ ad-, -vánt-. *In sense 4 sometimes* -ayj) *n*. **1.** A factor favourable or conducive to success. **2.** Benefit or profit; gain. **3.** A position of relative superiority: *has the advantage*. **4.** In racket games, the first point scored after deuce, or the resulting score. In this sense, also called "vantage". —**take advantage of**. **1.** To put to good use; avail oneself of. **2.** To profit selfishly by; exploit. **3.** To seduce. Used euphemistically. —**to advantage**. So as to produce a good or favourable effect: *She uses her husky voice to advantage*.
~*tr.v*. **advantaged, -taging, -tages**. To afford profit or gain to; benefit. [Middle English *avantage*, from Old French, "the condition

of being ahead", from *avant,* before, from Latin *abante,* (from) before. See **advance.**]

ad·van·ta·geous (ád-vaan-táyjəss, -vən- ‖ -van-) *adj.* Affording benefit or gain; profitable; useful. —**ad·van·ta·geous·ly** *adv.* —**ad·van·ta·geous·ness** *n.*

ad·vec·tion (ad-vék·sh'n) *n. Meteorology.* The transfer of heat or water vapour by horizontally moving air. [Latin *advectiō* (stem *advectiōn-*), conveyance, from *advehere* (past participle *advectus*), to carry to : *ad-,* to + *vehere,* to carry.]

ad·vent (ád-vənt, -vent) *n.* The coming or arrival, especially of something expected or momentous. [Middle English, from Latin *adventus,* from the past participle of *advenīre,* to come to.]

Advent *n.* **1.** The birth of Christ. **2.** See **Second Coming. 3.** The period including four Sundays before Christmas, the first of which is called Advent Sunday.

Ad·vent·ist (ád-vən-tist, -ven-, ad-véntist) *n.* A member of any of several Christian denominations that believe Christ's second coming and the end of the world are near at hand. See **Seventh-Day Adventist.** —**Ad·vent·ism** *n.*

ad·ven·ti·ti·a (ád-vən-tíshə, -ven-, -tíshi-ə) *n.* The outermost covering of an organ, especially of a blood vessel. [New Latin, from Latin *adventicius,* ADVENTITIOUS.]

ad·ven·ti·tious (ád-vən-tíshəss, -ven-) *adj.* **1.** Acquired by accident; added by chance; not inherent. **2.** *Biology.* Appearing in an unusual place or in an irregular or sporadic manner: *adventitious shoots.* —See Synonyms at **accidental.** [Latin *adventicius,* "arriving (from outside)", from *adventus,* arrival, ADVENT.] —**ad·ven·ti·tious·ly** *adv.* —**ad·ven·ti·tious·ness** *n.*

ad·ven·tive (ad-véntiv, ad-) *adj. Biology.* Not native to, and not fully established in, a new habitat or environment; locally or temporarily naturalised: *an adventive weed.*
~n. Biology. An adventive organism. [Latin *adventus,* arrival, ADVENT.] —**ad·ven·tive·ly** *adv.*

Advent Sunday *n.* The first of the four Sundays of Advent; the Sunday nearest to the last day of November.

ad·ven·ture (əd-vénchər ‖ ad-) *n.* **1.** An undertaking of a hazardous nature; a risky enterprise. **2.** An unusual experience or course of events marked by excitement and suspense. **3.** Participation in hazardous or exciting experiences. **4.** A financial speculation or business venture.
~v. **adventured, -turing, -tures.** —*tr. Archaic.* To venture upon; risk; dare. —*intr.* **1.** To take risks; engage in hazardous activities. **2.** To dare to enter or embark. Used with *on* or *upon.* [Middle English *aventure,* from Old French, from Vulgar Latin *(rēs) adventūra* (unattested), "(a thing) that will happen", from Latin *adventūrus,* future participle of *advenīre,* to arrive. See **advent.**]

adventure playground *n. Chiefly British.* A play area in which the creative and adventurous side of children is exercised through the provision of building materials, logs, old tyres, or the like rather than manufactured play equipment such as swings and slides.

ad·ven·tur·er (əd-vénchərər ‖ ad-) *n.* **1.** One who adventures. **2.** A mercenary soldier. **3.** A heavy speculator. **4.** One who seeks wealth and social position by unscrupulous means.

ad·ven·tur·ess (əd-vénchər-iss, -ess ‖ ad-) *n.* A woman who seeks social and financial advancement by dubious means.

ad·ven·tur·ism (əd-vénchəriz'm ‖ ad-) *n.* Recklessness in political or financial activities. —**ad·ven·tur·ist** *n. & adj.*

ad·ven·tur·ous (əd-vénchər-əss ‖ ad-) *adj.* Also **ad·ven·ture·some** (-səm) (for sense 1). **1.** Inclined to undertake new and daring enterprises or activities; bold; daring. **2.** Hazardous; risky. —See Synonyms at **reckless.** —**ad·ven·tur·ous·ly** *adv.* —**ad·ven·tur·ous·ness** *n.*

ad·verb (ád-verb) *n. Abbr.* **adv. 1.** A part of speech comprising a class of words that modify a verb, adjective, whole sentence, or other adverb. **2.** A word belonging to this class, such as *rapidly* in *He runs rapidly.* [Middle English, from Old French *adverbe,* from Latin *adverbium* (translation of Greek *epirrhēma,* "added word") : *ad-,* additional + *verbum,* word.]

ad·ver·bi·al (əd-vérbi-əl, ad-) *n.* **1.** An adverb. **2.** A word, phrase, or clause functioning like an adverb: *"Nicely" and "in a nice way" can both be adverbials.* —**ad·ver·bi·al** *adj.* —**ad·ver·bi·al·ly** *adv.*

ad ver·bum (ád vérbəm) *adv. Latin.* Word for word; verbatim.

ad·ver·sar·i·al (ád-vər-saír-i-əl, -ver-) *adj.* Involving, or considered to involve, adversaries or strongly opposed interests.

ad·ver·sar·y (ádvər-səri, -sri ‖ -serri) *n., pl.* **-ies.** An opponent; an enemy. —**the Adversary.** The Devil. [Middle English *adversarie,* from Latin *adversārius,* opponent, from *adversus,* ADVERSE.]

ad·ver·sa·tive (əd-vérss-ətiv, ad-) *adj. Grammar.* Expressing antithesis or opposition. Said of words and clauses.
~n. An adversative word, such as *however* or *but.* [Latin *adversātivus,* from *adversāri,* to be opposed to, from *adversus,* ADVERSE.] —**ad·ver·sa·tive·ly** *adv.*

ad·verse (ad-vérss, ád-vérss) *adj.* **1.** Antagonistic in design or effect; hostile; opposed: *adverse criticism.* **2.** Contrary to one's interests or welfare; unfavourable; unpropitious: *adverse circumstances.* **3.** In an opposite or opposing direction or position: *adverse winds.* **4.** *Botany.* Facing the axis or main stem. —See Synonyms at **contrary.** [Middle English, from Old French *advers,* from Latin *adversus,* past participle of *advertere,* to turn towards (with hostility).] —**ad·verse·ly** *adv.* —**ad·verse·ness** *n.*

adverse possession *n. Law.* Occupation of a property in a way that threatens the rights of the owner.

ad·ver·si·ty (əd-vérssəti ‖ ad-) *n., pl.* **-ties. 1.** A state of hardship,

suffering, or affliction; misfortune. **2.** A calamitous event. —See Synonyms at **misfortune.**

ad·vert[1] (əd-vért, ad-) *intr.v.* **-verted, -verting, -verts.** *Formal.* To call attention; refer: *advert to a problem.* [Middle English *a(d)verten,* from Old French *a(d)vertir,* from Vulgar Latin *advertīre* (unattested), from Latin *advertere,* to turn towards. See **adverse.**] —**ad·vert·ence, ad·vert·en·cy** *n.* —**ad·vert·ent** *adj.* —**ad·vert·ent·ly** *adv.*

ad·vert[2] (ád-vert) *n. Chiefly British Informal.* An advertisement.

ad·ver·tise (ádvər-tīz ‖ -tíz) *v.* **-tised, -tising, -tises.** —*tr.* **1. a.** To make public announcement of: *advertise a vacancy.* **b.** To cause to be generally or publicly known. **2.** To proclaim publicly the qualities or advantages of (a product or service, for example) so as to increase sales. **3.** *Archaic.* To warn or notify. —*intr.* **1.** To call the attention of the public to a product, service, or the like. **2.** To ask in a public notice, as in a newspaper; make a public request. Often used with *for: advertise for a flat.* [Middle English *a(d)vertisen,* from Old French *a(d)vertir* (present participle *advertissant*), to ADVERT.] —**ad·ver·tis·er** *n.*

ad·ver·tise·ment (əd-vért-iss-mənt, -iz- ‖ ádvər-tízmənt) *n. Abbr.* **advt.** Any public notice, such as a poster, newspaper display short television film, or radio announcement, designed to sell a product, publicise a vacancy or service, influence opinion, or the like.

ad·ver·tis·ing (ádvər-tīz-ing ‖ -tíz-) *n.* **1.** The action of attracting public attention, as to a product or business. **2.** The business of preparing and distributing advertisements for publication or broadcast. **3.** Printed or broadcast advertisements collectively.

ad·vice (əd-víss ‖ ad-) *n.* **1.** Opinion from one not immediately concerned as to what could or should be done in a given situation; counsel. **2. a.** *Sometimes plural.* Information or a report, especially when communicated from a distance: *advices from an ambassador.* **b.** Formal notice regarding a financial transction: *wages advice.* [Middle English *a(d)vise,* from Old French *a(d)vis,* opinion, from Vulgar Latin *advīsum* (unattested), opinion, probably from some such phrase as *ad (meum) vīsum,* "according to (my) view" : *ad,* to + *vīsum,* view, from the neuter past participle of *vidēre,* to see.]

ad·vis·a·ble (əd-víza-b'l ‖ ad-) *adj.* Worthy of being recommended or suggested; prudent; expedient. —**ad·vis·a·bil·i·ty** (-bílləti), **ad·vis·a·ble·ness** *n.* —**ad·vis·a·bly** *adv.*

ad·vise (əd-víz ‖ ad-) *v.* **-vised, -vising, -vises.** —*tr.* **1.** To offer advice to; counsel. **2.** To recommend by way of advice; suggest. **3.** To inform; notify: *advise a person of a decision.* —*intr.* **1.** To offer or be able to give advice. **2.** *Chiefly U.S.* To consult; take counsel. Used with *with: advise with one's associates.* [Middle English *a(d)visen,* from Old French *a(d)viser,* from Vulgar Latin *advīsāre* (unattested), to observe (influenced by Latin *advīsum,* ADVICE) : Latin *ad-,* to, at + *vīsere,* desiderative of *vidēre* (past participle *vīsus*), to see.] —**ad·vi·so·ry** *adj.*
Usage: In the sense of "inform" or "notify", the use of *advise* is usually restricted to business correspondence.

ad·vised (əd-vízd ‖ ad-) *adj.* Considered; thought out. Used chiefly in the combinations *well-advised* and *ill-advised.* —**ad·vis·ed·ly** (əd-vízid-li ‖ ad-) *adv.*

ad·vise·ment (əd-vízmənt ‖ ad-) *n.* **1.** Careful consideration. **2.** Consultation.

ad·vis·er, ad·vi·sor (əd-vízər ‖ ad-) *n.* A person who offers advice, especially in an official or professional capacity.

ad·vo·caat, ad·vo·kaat (ádvō-kaa, ádvə-, -kaat) *n.* A sweet, thick, yellow Dutch liqueur made of raw egg yolks and brandy. Compare **eggnog.** [Dutch, shortened from *advocaatenborrel,* from *advocaat,* ADVOCATE (noun) + *borrel,* drink.]

ad·vo·ca·cy (ádvəkə-si) *n.* Active support, as of a cause.

ad·vo·cate (ádvə-kayt) *tr.v.* **-cated, -cating, -cates.** To speak in favour of; recommend. See Synonyms at **support.**
~n. (-kət, -kit, -kayt). **1.** A person who argues for a cause or idea; a supporter or defender. **2.** A person who pleads on another's behalf; an intercessor. **3.** *Law.* In Scotland and South Africa, a **barrister** *(see).* —See Usage note at **lawyer.** [Middle English *a(d)vocat,* a lawyer, from Old French, from Latin *advocātus,* "one summoned (to give evidence)", from *advocāre,* to call or summon to : *ad,* to + *vocāre,* to call.] —**ad·vo·ca·to·ry** (-káytəri, -kətri) *adj.*

ad·vo·cate-de·pute (ádvə-kət-déppewt) *n., pl.* advocates-depute. In Scotland, a member of the bar appointed by the Lord Advocate as a public prosecutor.

ad·vow·son (əd-vówz'n ‖ ad-) *n.* In English ecclesiastical law, the right to nominate the successor to a vacant benefice. [Middle English *avoweson, advounson,* from Anglo-French *a(d)voeson,* variant of Old French *avoueson,* from Medieval Latin *advocātiō,* presentation, summoning, from Latin *advocāre,* to summon, ADVOCATE.]

advt. advertisement.

ad·y·na·mi·a (áydī-námmi-ə, áddī-náymi-ə, áddi-) *n.* Loss of energy or strength, especially after illness; feebleness or debility. [A- (not) + Greek *dunamis,* power, from *dunasthai,* to be able.] —**ad·y·nam·ic** (-námmik) *adj.*

ad·y·tum (áddi-təm) *n., pl.* **-ta** (-tə). The sanctum in an ancient temple. [Latin, from Greek *aduton,* neuter of *adutos,* not to be entered : *a-,* not + *duein†,* to enter, sink.]

adze, *U.S.* **adz** (adz) *n.* An axelike tool with an arched blade at right angles to the handle, used for dressing wood. [Middle English *adse,* Old English *adesa†.*]

ad·zu·ki bean (ad-zóoki) *n.* Also **ad·su·ki bean** (ad-sóoki, -zóoki). A plant, *Phaseolus angularis,* with yellow flowers and pods bearing edible seeds, widely cultivated as a food crop in the Orient. [Japanese *azuki*, "red bean".]

A.E.A. Atomic Energy Authority (in Britain).

A.E. and P. Ambassador Extraordinary and Plenipotentiary.

AEC, A.E.C. Atomic Energy Commission (in the United States).

ae·cid·i·o·spore (ee-síddi-ō-spawr ‖ -spōr). Also **ae·ci·o·spore** (éessi-ō-spawr ‖ -spōr) *n. Botany.* A rust spore, formed in a chainlike series in an aecidium. [*Aecium* + *spore*.]

ae·cid·i·um (ee-síddi-əm) *n., pl.* **-cidia** (-síddi-ə). Also **ae·ci·um** (éessi-əm ‖ *U.S. also* éeshi-əm) *pl.* **-cia**. *Botany.* A cuplike structure in rust fungi, containing chains of aecidiospores. [New Latin, from Greek *aikia*, injury (rust fungi are destructive), from *aikēs*, unseemly.] **—ae·ci·al** (éessi-əl ‖ *U.S. also* éeshi-əl) *adj.*

a·e·des (ay-éedeez) *n., pl.* **aedes.** Any mosquito of the genus *Aedes*, such as *A. aegypti*, which transmits yellow fever and dengue. [New Latin *Aedes*, from Greek *aēdēs*, unpleasant : *a-*, not + *ēdos*, pleasant.]

ae·dile (éedīl) *n.* In ancient Rome, an elected official who was responsible for public works and games and for the supervision of markets, the grain supply, and the water supply. [Latin *aedīlis*, "(one) concerned with buildings", from *aedēs*, house.]

Ae·ge·an (ee-jée-ən, i-) *adj.* **1.** Of or pertaining to the Aegean Sea. **2.** Of, pertaining to, or designating the prehistoric civilisation that flourished in the Aegean area in the Bronze Age.

Aegean Sea. A northeastern arm of the Mediterranean between Greece and Turkey. It is roughly 630 kilometres (380 miles) long and 300 kilometres (186 miles) wide, and contains numerous, mainly Greek islands. These Aegean Islands include the Cyclades, the Dodecanese, and the Sporades.

Ae·gi·na (ee-jínə, i-). *Greek* **Ai·gi·na** (áyg-inə, áy-). Greek town and island in the Aegean, near Athens. It was a prosperous and important city-state in the fifth century B.C., but declined in importance after defeat by the Athenians, who expelled its inhabitants.

Ae·gir (ággər). *Norse Mythology.* The god of the sea.

ae·gis (éejiss) *n.* **1.** Protection or sponsorship: *a conference held under the aegis of the World Health Organisation.* **2.** *Greek Mythology.* An attribute of Zeus, usually represented in art as a goatskin shield. Compare **auspices.** [Latin, from Greek *aigis* (often depicted as a goatskin, and associated by folk etymology with *aix* (stem *aig-*), goat).]

Ae·gis·thus (ee-jís-thəss). In Greek legend, the son of Thyestes and lover of Clytemnestra.

ae·gro·tat (ī-grə-tat, ee-, -grō-) *n.* In some universities: **1.** A certificate showing that a student is unable to attend part of an examination because of illness. **2.** A degree or examination pass awarded in such a case of illness. [Latin, "he is ill".]

Ael·fric (ál-frik), also called Grammaticus (*c.* 955-*c.* 1020). English abbot and writer. He is considered the greatest prose writer of Anglo-Saxon times. His prolific output included *Homilies,* the first Christian texts written in English, *Lives of the Saints,* a Latin Grammar, and translations of Latin religious literature.

-aemia, -haemia, *U.S.* **-emia, -hemia** *n. comb. form.* Indicates blood; for example, **leukaemia, polycythaemia.**

Ae·ne·as (ee-née-əss, i-, -ass). In classical legend, a Trojan prince, the son of Anchises and Aphrodite, who, as recounted in the Aeneid, escaped the sack of Troy and after an arduous sea voyage settled in Italy, where his descendants eventually founded Rome.

Ae·ne·id (ee-née-id, i-) *n.* An epic poem in Latin by Virgil, telling of the adventures of Aeneas after the destruction of Troy.

Ae·o·li·an (ee-óli-ən) *adj.* **1.** Of or pertaining to Aeolus, god of the winds. **2.** *Music.* Of or designating a mode represented by the white notes of the scale of A on the piano keyboard. **3.** *Small* **a.** Of or caused by the action of the wind. Said of erosion.
~*n.* **1.** A member of one of the major Greek tribes that settled in central Greece and on the west coast of Asia Minor. **2.** Aeolic.

Aeolian harp *n.* A musical instrument consisting of an open box with strings stretched across it that sound when wind passes over them. Also called "wind harp".

Aeolian Islands. See **Lipari Islands.**

Ae·ol·ic (ee-óllik) *n.* One of the four main dialects of ancient Greek, spoken in Thessaly, Boeotia, and in the coastal region of Asia Minor north of Ionia. Compare **Arcado-Cyprian, Attic-Ionic, Doric.**

ae·ol·i·pile (ee-ólli-pīl) *n.* A prototype steam turbine invented about A.D. 100, consisting of a hollow sphere fitted with projecting angled exhaust jets and mounted to permit free rotation about the steam inlet axis. [Latin *aeolipila*, from Greek *aiolipulē*, "wind-vent" : *Aiolos,* AEOLUS + *pulē,* gate.]

Ae·o·lus (ée-ələss). *Greek Mythology.* The god of the winds. [Latin, from Greek *Aiolos,* from *aiolos†,* quick-moving.]

ae·on (ée-ən, -on) *n.* Also *chiefly U.S.* **e·on. 1.** An indefinitely long period of time; an eternity. **2.** *Geology.* A very long period of geological time; specifically, a period of 1,000,000,000 years. [Late Latin *aeōn,* age, from Greek *aiōn.*]

aer·ate (áir-ayt, áy-ər-) *tr.v.* **-ated, -ating, -ates. 1.** To charge (liquid) with a gas. **2.** To expose to the circulation of air for purification. **3.** To supply (blood) with oxygen. [AER(O)- + -ATE.] **—aer·a·tion** (-áysh'n) *n.*

aer·a·tor (áir-aytər, áy-ər-) *n.* A device for aerating liquids.

aer·i·al (áir-i-əl ‖ ay-éer-) *adj.* **1.** Existing or functioning in the air: *an aerial telephone cable.* **2.** *Literary.* Reaching high into the air; lofty. **3.** Light and airy; insubstantial; imaginary. **4.** Of, by, or from aircraft: *an aerial photograph.* **5.** *Botany.* Borne in the air rather than underground or under water: *aerial roots.*

~*n.* (áiri-əl). *Electronics.* The part of a radio, television, or radar system by means of which electromagnetic waves of radio frequencies are transmitted or received. Also *chiefly U.S.* "antenna". [Latin *āerius,* from Greek *āerios,* from *aēr,* air.]

aer·i·al·ist (áiri-əl-ist) *n.* An acrobat who performs on a tightrope, trapeze, or similar apparatus.

aerie. *Chiefly U.S.* Variant of **eyrie.**

aero-, aer- *comb. form.* Indicates: **1.** Air, gas, or the atmosphere; for example, **aeromechanics, aerosphere. 2.** Aircraft; for example, **aerodrome.** [Middle English, from Old French, from Latin, from Greek, from *aēr,* air.]

aer·o·bal·lis·tics (áir-ō-bə-lístiks) *n. Used with a singular verb.* The ballistics of missiles and other projectiles in the atmosphere.

aer·o·bat·ics (áir-ō-báttiks) *n. Used with a singular or plural verb.* The performance of stunts, such as rolls and loops, in an aeroplane or glider. [AERO- + (ACRO)BATICS.]

aer·obe (áir-ōb) *n.* An organism, such as a bacterium, requiring molecular oxygen or air to live. [French *aérobie,* "air-life" : AERO- + Greek *bios,* life.]

aer·o·bic (air-ōbik) *adj.* **1.** Of or indicating a process, such as respiration, dependent on molecular oxygen or air. **2.** Of or pertaining to aerobes. **3.** Of or pertaining to aerobics. **—aer·o·bic·al·ly** *adv.*

aer·o·bics (air-ōbiks) *n. Used with a singular verb.* A system of rigorous physical exercises designed to speed up the breathing and stimulate blood circulation. [AERO- + Greek *bios,* life + -ICS.]

aer·o·bi·ol·o·gy (áir-ō-bī-ólləji) *n.* The study of airborne microorganisms, pollen, spores, and the like, especially those causing disease.

aer·o·bi·o·sis (áir-ō-bī-ōssiss) *n.* Life in the presence of molecular oxygen or air. [AERO- + -BIOSIS.]

aer·o·drome (áirə-drōm) *n.* An **airfield** (*see*).

aer·o·dy·nam·ic (áir-o-dī-námmik) *adj.* **1.** Of or pertaining to aerodynamics. **2.** Embodying aerodynamic principles; streamlined: *the car's sleek aerodynamic lines.*

aer·o·dy·nam·ics (áir-ō-dī-námmiks) *n. Used with a singular verb.* The dynamics of gases, especially of atmospheric interactions with moving objects.

aer·o·dyne (áir-ō-dīn, -ə-) *n.* Any heavier-than-air aircraft that derives its lift chiefly from motion. Compare **aerostat.** [AERO- + -*dyne,* from Greek *dunamis,* power, from *dunasthai,* to be able.]

aer·o·em·bo·lism (áir-ō-émbəliz'm) *n.* The presence of nitrogen bubbles in the blood and tissues caused by a sudden reduction in atmospheric pressure, as occurs in decompression sickness.

aero engine (áir-ō) *n.* An engine used to power an aircraft.

aer·o·foil (áir-ə-foyl, -ō-) *n.* A part or surface of an aircraft, such as a wing, propeller blade, or rudder, whose shape and orientation control stability, direction, lift, thrust, or propulsion.

aer·o·gramme, aer·o·gram (áir-ə-gram, -ō-) *n.* An airmail letter written on a standard, lightweight form that folds into the shape of an envelope and can be sent at a low postage rate. Also *chiefly British* "air letter". [AERO- + -*gramme,* variant of -GRAM.]

aer·o·lite (áir-ō-līt, -ə-) *n.* A chiefly silicious meteorite. [AERO- + -LITE.] **—aer·o·lit·ic** (-littik) *adj.*

aer·ol·o·gy (air-ólləji) *n.* Total atmospheric meteorology as opposed to surface-based study; climatology. [AERO- + -LOGY.] **—aer·o·log·ic** (áir-ə-lójik), **aer·o·log·i·cal** *adj.* **—aer·ol·o·gist** (-ólləjist) *n.*

aer·o·me·chan·ics (áir-ō-mi-kánniks) *n. Used with a singular verb.* The science of the motion and equilibrium of air and other gases, comprising aerodynamics and aerostatics. **—aer·o·me·chan·i·cal** *adj.* **—aer·o·me·chan·i·cal·ly** *adv.*

aer·o·med·i·cine (áir-ō-méd-ss'n, -sin, -méddi-) *n.* The medical study and treatment of disturbances, disorders, and diseases resulting from or associated with atmospheric flight. Also called "aviation medicine". **—aer·o·med·i·cal** *adj.*

aer·o·me·te·or·o·graph (áir-ō-méeti-ərə-graaf, -graf ‖ -awrə-, -orrə-) *n.* An aircraft instrument for simultaneously recording temperature, atmospheric pressure, and humidity.

aer·om·e·ter (áir-ómmitər) *n.* A device for determining the weight and density of air or other gas.

aer·o·naut (áir-ə-nawt) *n.* A pilot or navigator of a balloon or lighter-than-air craft. [French *aéronaute* : AERO- (air) + Greek *nautēs,* sailor. See **nautical.**]

aer·o·nau·tics (áir-ə-náwtiks) *n. Used with a singular verb.* **1.** The science of aircraft design and construction. **2.** The theory and practice of aircraft navigation. **—aer·o·nau·tic, aer·o·nau·ti·cal** *adj.*

aer·on·o·my (áir-ónnəmi) *n.* The study of the upper atmosphere, especially of regions of ionised gas. [AERO- + -NOMY.]

aer·o·pause (áir-ō-pawz) *n.* The region of the atmosphere above which aircraft cannot fly. [AERO- + -PAUSE.]

aer·o·phyte (áir-ə-fīt) *n. Botany.* An **epiphyte** (*see*).

aer·o·plane (áir-ə-playn) *n.* A winged flying vehicle that is heavier than air and powered by jet engines or propellers. Also *U.S.* "airplane".

aer·o·sol (áir-ō-sol, -ə- ‖ sōl) *n.* **1.** A gaseous suspension of fine solid or liquid particles. **2. a.** A substance, such as a detergent, insecticide, or paint, packaged under pressure with a gaseous propellant for release as an aerosol. **b.** A usually hand-held metal container from which an aerosol is released. [AERO- + SOL(UTION).]

aer·o·space (áir-ō-spayss, -ə-) *adj.* **1.** Of or designating the Earth's atmosphere and the space beyond. **2.** Of or pertaining to the science or technology of flight. **—aer·o·space** *n.*

aerospace vehicle *n.* A vehicle capable of flight both within and outside the Earth's atmosphere.

aer·o·sphere (áir-ō-sfeer, -ə-) *n.* The lower portion of the atmosphere in which both unmanned and manned flight is possible; the troposphere and stratosphere.
aer·o·stat (áir-ō-stat, -ə-) *n.* An aircraft, especially a balloon or dirigible, deriving its lift from the buoyancy of surrounding air rather than from aerodynamic motion. Compare **aerodyne.** [French *aérostat*: AERO- + -STAT.]—**aer·o·stat·ic** (-státtik), **aer·o·stat·i·cal** *adj.*
aer·o·stat·ics (áir-ō-státtiks, -ə-) *n.* *Used with a singular verb.* The science of gases in equilibrium and of the equilibrium of balloons or aircraft under changing atmospheric flight conditions.
aer·o·ther·mo·dy·nam·ics (áir-ō-thérmō-dī-námmiks) *n.* *Used with a singular verb.* The study of the thermodynamics of gases, especially at high relative velocities.
ae·ru·go (i-rōōgō) *n.* **Verdigris** *(see).* [Latin *aerūgō,* from *aes* (stem *aer-*), copper, bronze.]
aer·y (áir-i, áy-əri) *adj. Poetic.* Ethereal; insubstantial.
Aes·chy·lus (éeski-ləss || *U.S. also* éskə-) (*c.* 525–456 B.C.). Greek dramatist. He wrote about 60 plays, of which seven complete tragedies survive. His best-known work is the trilogy of the *Oresteia* (458 B.C.): *Agamemnon, Choephori,* and *Eumenides.* His plays are concerned with the justice of the gods and are based on tales from mythology and history.
Aes·cu·la·pi·an (éeskew-láypi-ən || *U.S.* éskew-) *adj.* Of or pertaining to the healing art; medical: *the Aesculapian art.*
Aes·cu·la·pi·us (éeskew-láypi-əss || *U.S.* éskew-). The Roman god of medicine and healing; identified with the Greek god Asclepius.
Ae·sir (áy-seer) *pl.n.* The gods of Norse mythology. [Old Norse, plural of *āss,* a god.]
Ae·sop (ée-sop || *U.S. also* -səp) (6th century B.C.). Supposed author of *Aesop's Fables.* Nothing is known for certain about his life, but he is said to have been Greek and born a slave and to have been deformed. The fables are moral tales, originating in folklore, with animal protagonists. Among the best-known are "The Tortoise and the Hare" and "The Fox and the Grapes".
Ae·so·pi·an (ee-sṓpi-ən) *adj.* Also **Ae·sop·ic** (ee-sóppik). **1.** In the manner of Aesop's animal fables. **2.** Expressed allegorically or obliquely so as to elude political censorship.
aes·thete (éess-theet || *U.S.* éss-) *n.* A person who has, or affects to have, a sensitive appreciation of the beautiful, especially in art. [Back-formation from AESTHETIC.]
aes·thet·ic (eess-théttik, iss-, ess-) *adj.* **1.** Of or pertaining to aesthetics. **2.** Of or concerning the criticism of taste or the appreciation of the beautiful. **3.** Having or showing a well-developed sense of beauty. [French *esthétique,* from German *ästhetisch,* from New Latin *aestheticus,* from Greek *aisthētikos,* pertaining to sense perception, from *aisthēta,* perceptible things, from *aisthenasthai,* to perceive.] —**aes·thet·i·cal·ly** *adv.*
aes·the·ti·cian (éess-thə-tísh'n || *U.S.* éss-) *n.* A specialist in aesthetics or the theory of beauty.
aes·thet·i·cism (eess-thétti-siz'm, iss-, ess-) *n.* **1.** The pursuit of the sensuously beautiful; devotion to beauty and refined taste. Sometimes used derogatorily to characterise an excessive or affected appreciation of beauty. **2. a.** The belief that beauty is the basic principle from which all other principles, especially moral principles, are derived. **b.** The belief that art and artists should be judged according to aesthetic considerations alone.
aes·thet·ics (eess-théttiks, iss-, ess-) *n.* *Used with a singular verb.* The branch of philosophy dealing with the nature and perception of the beautiful.
aes·ti·val (eess-tī́v'l, ess- || *U.S. also* ésstiv'l) *adj. Formal.* Of or appearing in summer. [Middle English *estival,* from Old French, from Latin *aestivālis,* from *aestīvus,* from *aestās,* summer.]
aes·ti·vate (éesti-vayt, ésti-) *intr.v.* **-vated, -vating, -vates.** To pass the summer, especially in a state of dormancy, as lungfish and some other animals do. Compare **hibernate.** [Latin *aestīvāre,* from *aestīvus,* AESTIVAL.]
aes·ti·va·tion (éesti-váysh'n, ésti-) *n.* **1.** *Zoology.* A state of dormancy or torpor during the summer or periods of drought. Compare **hibernation. 2.** *Botany.* The arrangement of petals, sepals, and other floral organs in the unopened bud.
ae·ta·tis su·ae (ī-taátiss sṓō-ī, ee-táytiss séw-ee). *Abbr.* **aetat., aet.** *Latin.* Of his (or her) age.
ae·ther (éethər) *n.* **1.** *Capital* **A.** *Greek Mythology.* The poetic personification of the clear upper air breathed by the Olympians. **2.** Variant of **ether** (sense 3).
aethereal. Variant of **ethereal.**
ae·ti·ol·o·gy, *U.S.* **e·ti·ol·o·gy** (éeti-óllәji) *n.* **1.** The study of origins, causes, or reasons; especially, the branch of medicine dealing with the causes of diseases. **2.** A cause or origin, especially of a disease or disorder. —**ae·ti·o·log·i·cal** (-ə-lójik'l), **ae·ti·o·log·ic** *adj.* —**ae·ti·o·log·i·cal·ly** *adv.* —**ae·ti·ol·o·gist** *n.*
A.E.U. Amalgamated Engineering Union.
Af (aff) *n. South African.* A black African. Used by white speakers.
AF, A.F. 1. air force. **2.** Anglo-French. **3.** also **a.f.** audio frequency.
a·far (ə-fár) *adv. Literary.* At or to a distance; far away. [Middle English *afer,* from *on fer,* at a distance, and *of fer,* from a distance, from *fer,* FAR.]
Afars and Issas, French Territory of the. See **Djibouti.**
A.F.C. Australian Film Commission.
a·feard, a·feared (ə-féerd) *adj. Regional & Archaic.* Afraid; frightened. [Middle English *afered,* Old English *āfǣred,* past participle of *āfǣran,* to frighten : *ā-,* intensive prefix + *fǣran,* to frighten, from *fǣr,* fear.]

af·fa·ble (áffə-b'l) *adj.* Easy to speak to; approachable. —See Synonyms at **amiable.** [Old French, from Latin *affābilis,* from *affārī,* to speak to : *ad-,* to + *fārī,* to speak.] —**af·fa·bil·i·ty** (-bílləti) *n.* —**af·fa·bly** *adv.*
af·fair (ə-fáir) *n.* **1.** Anything that has been done or is to be done or dealt with. **2.** *Plural.* **a.** Personal or business concerns in general: *a man of affairs.* **b.** Matters or events of public interest: *affairs of state.* **3.** Any object or contrivance: *Our first car was a ramshackle affair.* **4.** A private matter; a personal concern. **5.** A matter causing scandal and controversy: *the Dreyfus affair.* **6.** A sexual relationship, usually of limited duration, between two people who are not married to one another; love affair or liaison. [Middle English *afere,* from Old French *afaire,* from the phrase *a faire,* "to do": *a,* to, from Latin *ad-* + *faire,* to do, from Latin *facere.*]
af·faire (ə-fáir) *n. French.* An affair (senses 5, 6).
af·faire d'hon·neur (ə-fáir donér, aa-, -nṓr) *n. French.* A matter in which honour is at stake; a duel.
af·fect¹ (ə-fékt) *tr.v.* **-fected, -fecting, -fects. 1.** To have an effect on; bring about a change in. **2.** To touch or move the emotions of. **3.** To have an adverse effect on; especially, to attack or infect. Used of disease, pain, or the like. **4.** *Archaic & Literary.* To allot or assign. Used only in the passive.
—*n.* (áffekt). *Psychology.* **1.** A feeling or emotion as distinguished from cognition, thought, or action. **2.** A strong feeling having active consequences. [Latin *afficere* (past participle *affectus*), to do something to, exert influence on : *ad-,* to + *facere,* to do.]
Synonyms: *affect, influence, impress, touch, move, strike.*
Usage: Because of their similarities in pronunciation, and their close relationship of meaning, *affect* and *effect* are often confused in their written form. Both may be used as verbs and as nouns, but *affect* is more commonly used as a verb, and *effect* as a noun. The usual meaning of *affect¹* is "influence": *His words affected me greatly.* The noun use of *affect* is rare, being restricted to psychological contexts in the sense of "strong feeling, emotion": *the study of affect*; the adjectival use is similar: *the study of affective behaviour in man.* The usual meaning of *effect,* as a verb, is "cause": *How shall we effect some economies?,* though this is relatively formal and uncommon. The everyday use of *effect* is as a noun, where it means "result": *The effect of passing his exams was remarkable*; or "influence": *He had a great effect on me.* The most common confusion is with this last use, where the corresponding verb would be *affect¹*. *He affected me.*
af·fect² (ə-fékt) *tr. v.* **-fected, -fecting, -fects. 1.** To simulate in order to make some desired impression; pretend to feel: *affect indifference.* **2.** To imitate; **assume**: *affect an American accent.* **3. a.** To display a preference for. **b.** *Archaic.* To fancy; love. **c.** To tend to by nature; tend to assume: *affect crystalline form.* [Middle English *affecter,* from Latin *affectāre,* to strive after, frequentative of *afficere* (past participle *affectus*), to AFFECT¹.] —**af·fect·er** *n.*
af·fec·ta·tion (áffek-táysh'n) *n.* **1.** A pretence or false display. **2.** Any artificial behaviour or mannerism adopted to impress others. [Latin *affectātiō* (stem *affectātiōn-*), from *affectāre,* to strive after, to AFFECT².]
af·fect·ed¹ (ə-féktid) *adj.* Emotionally stirred or moved.
affected² *adj.* **1.** Assumed or simulated to impress others. **2.** Speaking or behaving in an artificial or insincere way to make a particular impression. **3.** Disposed or inclined. Used with *to* or *towards*: *was well affected to their cause.* **4.** Fancied; taken up: *a book much affected by experts in the subject.* —**af·fect·ed·ly** *adv.* —**af·fect·ed·ness** *n.*
af·fect·ing (ə-fékting) *adj.* Full of pathos; touching; moving: *an affecting sight.* See Synonyms at **moving.** —**af·fect·ing·ly** *adv.*
af·fec·tion (ə-féksh'n) *n.* **1.** A fond or tender feeling towards another. **2.** *Often plural.* Feeling or emotion. **3.** Any pathological condition of the mind or body. **4.** The act of affecting or state of being affected. **5.** Mental disposition or tendency. —See Synonyms at **love.** [Middle English *affecioun,* from Old French *affection,* from Latin *affectiō* (stem *affectiōn-*), (friendly) disposition, from *afficere,* to AFFECT¹.] —**af·fec·tion·al** *adj.* —**af·fec·tion·al·ly** *adv.*
af·fec·tion·ate (ə-féksh'n-ət, -it) *adj.* **1.** Having or showing fond feelings or affection; loving; tender. **2.** *Archaic.* Strongly or favourably disposed. Used with *to.* —**af·fec·tion·ate·ly** *adv.* —**af·fec·tion·ate·ness** *n.*
af·fec·tive (ə-féktiv, a-) *adj.* **1.** *Psychology.* Pertaining to or resulting from emotions or feelings rather than from thought. **2.** Pertaining to or arousing affection or emotion; emotional. —**af·fec·tiv·i·ty** (áf-fek-tívvəti) *n.*
af·fen·pin·scher (áff'n-pinshər, -pinchər) *n.* Any of a breed of small dogs of European origin, having dark, wiry, shaggy hair and a tufted muzzle. [German *Affenpinscher,* "monkey-terrier" (so called because its face resembles a monkey's) : *Affe,* monkey, APE + *Pinscher,* terrier (see **Doberman pinscher**).]
af·fer·ent (áffərənt) *adj.* Directed towards a central organ or section, as are nerves that conduct impulses from the periphery of the body inwards to the brain or spinal cord. Compare **efferent.** [Latin *afferēns* (stem *afferent-*), present participle of *afferre,* to bring towards : *ad-,* towards + *ferre,* to bring.]
af·fet·tu·o·so (ə-féttew-ṓzō, -féchoo, -ṓssō) *adv. Music.* With tender or passionate feeling. [Italian.] —**af·fet·tu·o·so** *adj.*
af·fi·ance (ə-fī́-ənss) *tr. v.* **-anced, -ancing, -ances.** To promise (oneself or another) in marriage; betroth. [Middle English *affiaunce,* from Old French *affiance,* "trust", from *affier,* to trust to, from Medieval Latin *affīdāre* : Latin *ad-,* to + *fīdāre,* variant of Latin

fīdere, to trust.]

af·fi·ant (ə-fī-ənt) *n. Law. U.S.* One who makes an affidavit. [Old French, present participle of *affier,* to trust to. See **affiance.**]

af·fi·da·vit (áffi-dáyvit) *n. Law.* A written declaration made under oath before a commissioner for oaths or other authorised officer. [Medieval Latin *affīdāvit,* "he has pledged", from *affīdāre,* to trust to. See **affiance.**]

af·fil·i·ate (ə-fílli-ayt) *v.* **-ated, -ating, -ates.** *—tr.* **1.** To adopt as an associate or subsidiary member or branch of a group or larger organisation: *an affiliated member; a union affiliated to the T.U.C.* **2.** To associate (oneself) as a subordinate or subsidiary. Used with *with.* **3.** *Law.* To impute the paternity of (an illegitimate child). Used with *upon* or *to.* *—intr.* To associate or connect oneself: *We decided to affiliate.*

~n. (-ət, -ayt, -it). A person or organisation associated with another in a subordinate relationship. [Medieval Latin *affīliāre,* "to take to oneself as a son" : *ad-,* to + *fīlius,* son.] **—af·fil·i·a·tion** (-áysh'n) *n.*

affiliation order *n. Law.* In Britain, a court order requiring that a man who has been adjudged to be the father of an illegitimate child should make regular payments towards the child's maintenance.

af·fine (áffīn, ə-fīn) *adj.* **1.** Of or pertaining to a mathematical transformation of coordinates that is equivalent to a translation, contraction, or expansion with respect to a fixed origin and fixed coordinate system. **2.** Of or pertaining to the geometry of affine transformations. [Old French *affin,* AFFINED.]

af·fined (ə-fīnd) *adj.* Joined by kinship or affinity. [French *affiné,* from Old French *affin,* closely related, from Latin *affīnis,* neighbouring, allied by marriage : *ad-,* near to + *fīnis,* border.]

af·fin·i·ty (ə-fínnəti) *n., pl.* **-ties.** **1.** A natural personal attraction or liking. **2.** Relationship by marriage or adoption rather than by blood. **3.** An inherent similarity between organisms or things: *The language has some affinities with Russian.* **4.** A chemical or physical attraction or attractive force. —See Synonyms at **likeness.** [Middle English *affinite,* from Old French *afinite,* from Latin *affīnitās,* from *affīnis,* AFFINED.]

af·firm (ə-fúrm) *v.* **-firmed, -firming, -firms.** *—tr.* **1.** To declare positively or firmly; maintain the truth or existence of, especially in response to a question or doubt. **2.** To ratify or confirm. *—intr. Law.* To declare solemnly and formally to tell the truth, but without taking an oath. —See Synonyms at **assert.** [Middle English *affermen,* from Old French *afermer,* from Latin *affirmāre,* "to give firmness to", strengthen, assert : *ad-,* to + *firmāre,* to make firm, from *firmus,* firm.] **—af·firm·a·ble** *adj.* **—af·firm·a·bly** *adv.* **—af·firm·ant** *adj. & n.* **—af·firm·er** *n.*

af·fir·ma·tion (áffər-máysh'n) *n.* **1.** The act of affirming or state of being affirmed. **2.** *Law.* A solemn and formal declaration to tell the truth, as made by a person who conscientiously objects to taking an oath. **3.** Any formal or solemn declaration.

af·firm·a·tive (ə-fúrmətiv) *adj.* **1.** Responding with the word yes or any other expression of agreement or consent: *an affirmative reply.* **2.** Asserting that something is true as represented; confirming. **3.** *Logic.* Designating a proposition in which the predicate states something to be true about the subject; for example, *Apples have seeds.*

~n. **1.** A word or phrase showing agreement or assent: *My request was answered in the affirmative.* **2.** *Chiefly U.S.* The side in a debate that upholds a proposition.

~interj. Chiefly U.S. Used, especially in a military context, to express confirmation or consent. Compare **negative.** **—af·firm·a·tive·ly** *adv.*

affirmative action *n. Chiefly U.S.* Action taken to provide equal opportunity, as in job appointments, for members of previously disadvantaged groups, such as ethnic minorities. Also used adjectivally: *an affirmative-action employer.*

af·fix (ə-fíks) *tr.v.* **-fixed, -fixing, -fixes.** **1.** To secure (an object) to another; attach: *affix a label to a parcel.* **2.** To impute; attribute: *affix blame for the error to him.* **3.** To place at the end; append: *affix a postscript.*

~n. (áffiks). **1.** Something that is attached, joined, or added. **2.** *Grammar.* A word element, such as a prefix or suffix, that is always attached to a base, stem, or root. [Medieval Latin *affīxāre* : Latin *ad-,* to + *fīxāre,* to fix, frequentative of *fīgere* (past participle *fīxus*), to fasten.] **—af·fix·er** *n.*

af·fla·tus (ə-fláytəss) *n.* A creative impulse; an inspiration. Used chiefly in the phrase *divine afflatus.* [Latin *afflātus,* inspiration, past participle of *afflāre,* to breathe on : *ad-,* towards + *flāre,* to blow.]

af·flict (ə-flíkt) *tr.v.* **-flicted, -flicting, -flicts.** To inflict physical or mental suffering upon; cause great distress to. [Middle English *afflicten,* from Latin *affligere* (past participle *afflīctus*), to dash against : *ad-,* to + *flīgere,* to strike.] **—af·flict·er** *n.* **—af·flic·tive** *adj.* **—af·flic·tive·ly** *adv.*

af·flic·tion (ə-flíksh'n) *n.* A condition or cause of pain, suffering, or distress, such as disease or grief.

af·flu·ence (áffloo-ənss) *n.* **1.** A plentiful supply of material goods; the state of being affluent; wealth. **2.** *Archaic.* An abundance.

af·flu·ent (áffloo-ənt) *adj.* **1.** Wealthy; amply supplied with material goods and comforts: *the affluent society.* **2.** Copious; abundant. **3.** Flowing freely.

~n. A stream or river that flows into another or other body of water; a tributary. [Middle English, from Old French, from Latin *affluēns* (stem *affluent-*), present participle of *affluere,* to flow to : *ad-,* towards + *fluere,* to flow.] **—af·flu·ent·ly** *adv.*

af·flux (áffluks) *n.* A flowing towards a particular area: *an afflux of blood to the head.* [Medieval Latin *affluxus,* from Latin, past participle of *affluere,* to flow to. See **affluent.**]

af·ford (ə-fórd || -fōrd) *tr.v.* **-forded, -fording, -fords.** **1.** To have the financial means for; be able to meet the expense of. Preceded by *can* or *be able.* **2.** To be able to spare or give up. Preceded by *can* or *be able to.* **3.** To be able to do or bear (something) without incurring serious loss, difficulty, or criticism. Preceded by *can* or *be able to* and often used with an infinitive or clause: *He can afford to take a tolerant attitude.* **4.** To provide or give. [Middle English *aforthen,* Old English *geforthian,* to further, achieve, carry out, from *forthian,* to promote, from *forth,* forward.] **—af·ford·a·ble** *adj.*

af·for·est (a-fórrist, ə-) *tr.v.* **-ested, -esting, -ests.** To convert (open land) into forest. [Medieval Latin *afforestāre* : *ad-,* to + *forestāre,* from Late Latin *forestis,* FOREST.] **—af·for·es·ta·tion** (-áysh'n) *n.*

af·fran·chise (ə-fránchīz, a-) *tr.v.* **-chised, -chising, -chises.** To free from servitude; liberate from obligation or liabilities. [15th century : alteration of Old French *affranchir* (stem *affranchiss-*), to free, from *franchir,* to free.] **—af·fran·chise·ment** *n.*

af·fray (ə-fráy) *n. Law.* A public quarrel or brawl noisy enough to disturb those not involved. See Synonyms at **conflict.**

~tr.v. **affrayed, -fraying, -frays.** *Archaic.* To frighten. [Middle English, from Old French *effray, esfrei,* from *affreer, esfreer,* to fight in public, from Vulgar Latin *exfridāre* (unattested), "to break the peace" : Latin *ex,* out of + Frankish *frithuz* (unattested), peace.]

af·fri·cate (áffri-kət, -kit) *n. Phonetics.* A speech sound produced when the breath stream is completely stopped and then released at articulation; for example, the *t* plus *sh* sound in *churn* or *clutch* or the *j* sound in *judge.* Also called "affricative". [Latin *(vox) affricāta,* "rubbed" (sound), feminine past participle of *affricāre,* to rub against : *ad-,* to + *fricāre,* to rub.] **—af·fri·cate** (-kayt) *v.* **—af·fri·ca·tion** (-káysh'n) *n.* **—af·fric·a·tive** *adj. & n.*

af·fright (ə-frīt) *tr.v.* **-frighted, -frighting, -frights.** *Archaic.* To frighten; terrify.

~n. Archaic. **1.** Terror. **2.** A cause of terror. **—af·fright·ment** *n.*

af·front (ə-frúnt) *tr.v.* **-fronted, -fronting, -fronts.** **1.** To slight or insult openly; cause offence to. **2.** *Archaic.* To meet face to face defiantly; confront. —See Synonyms at **offend.**

~n. **1.** An open or intentional slight or insult. **2.** Anything that causes offence. [Middle English *affronten,* from Old French *afronter,* from Vulgar Latin *affrontāre* (unattested) : Latin *ad-,* to + *frōns* (stem *front-*), forehead, FRONT.]

af·fu·sion (ə-féwzh'n) *n.* A pouring on of water, especially as in baptism. [Latin *affūsiō* (stem *affūsiōn-*), from *affūsus,* past participle of *affundere,* to pour on : *ad-,* to + *fundere,* to pour.]

Af·ghan (áf-gan, -gən, -gaan) *n.* **1.** A native or inhabitant of Afghanistan or a person of Afghan descent. **2.** A major language of Afghanistan, **Pashto** *(see).* **3.** *Small* **a.** A wool coverlet knitted or crocheted in colourful geometric designs. **4.** *Small* **a.** A sheepskin or goatskin coat, usually embroidered. **—Af·ghan** *adj.*

Afghan hound *n.* A large, slender dog of an ancient breed, having long, thick hair, a pointed muzzle, and drooping ears.

af·ghan·i (af-gaáni, -gánni) *n.* The basic monetary unit of Afghanistan, equal to 100 puls.

Af·ghan·i·stan, Islamic State of (af-gánni-staan, -stan, -staán, -stán). Arid, landlocked state of west central Asia, dominated by mountains radiating from the Hindu Kush. Only 10 per cent is cultivable, yet normally 85 per cent of workers are in farming, mostly at subsistence level. The country is rich in minerals, but only gas and coal are exploited to any extent. Dried fruit, gas, skins, cotton, and wool are the main exports, and the country is famed for its carpets. Afghanistan lies astride ancient invasion routes, and is ethnically diverse as a result. Most people are Muslim, and less than 8 per cent are literate. The area was part of the Persian empire, and was later conquered by Alexander the Great. It fell to the Arabs, who introduced Islam (8th century), and later to Genghis Khan (1220), and Tamerlane (14th century). The country was part of the Mogul empire (16th century), until an Afghan chief revolted and founded the present state (1747). This buffer state between Russia and British India survived to win complete independence (1919), and was proclaimed a republic (1973). A military coup (1978) led to an unpopular regime dependent on the U.S.S.R., and to Soviet occupation of the country (1979), resistance to which grew in the 1980s. By early 1989 Soviet troops had withdrawn, and in 1992 the regime was overthrown. In 1994 a newly formed militant extremist Islamic group, the Taliban, progressively defeated government forces and mujahideen (resistance groups), capturing Kabul in 1996 and thereafter controlling all but the far north of the country. Area, 652 225 square kilometres (251,773 square miles). Population, 20,880,000. Capital, Kabul. See map, next page.

a·fi·ci·o·na·do (ə-fish-yə-naádō, -fiss- || *U.S. also* -féess-ee-ə-) *n., pl.* **-dos.** **1.** An enthusiastic admirer or follower; a devotee. **2.** A devotee of bullfighting. [Spanish, from the past participle of *aficionar,* to incite affection, from *afición,* from Latin *affectiō,* AFFECTION.]

a·field (ə-féeld) *adv.* Off the usual or desired track; away from one's home or usual environment. Used chiefly in the phrase *far afield.*

a·fire (ə-fīr) *adj.* **1.** On fire. **2.** Intensely interested and involved: *He was afire with enthusiasm about the new project.* **—a·fire** *adv.*

a·flame (ə-fláym) *adj.* **1.** On fire; flaming. **2.** Keenly excited and interested: *aflame with a desire to learn.* **—a·flame** *adv.*

af·la·tox·in (áfflə-tóksin) *n.* A poison, produced by the fungus *Aspergillus flavus,* growing on peanuts and cereals, that is thought to cause certain cancers. [*A(spergillus) fla(vus)* + TOXIN.]

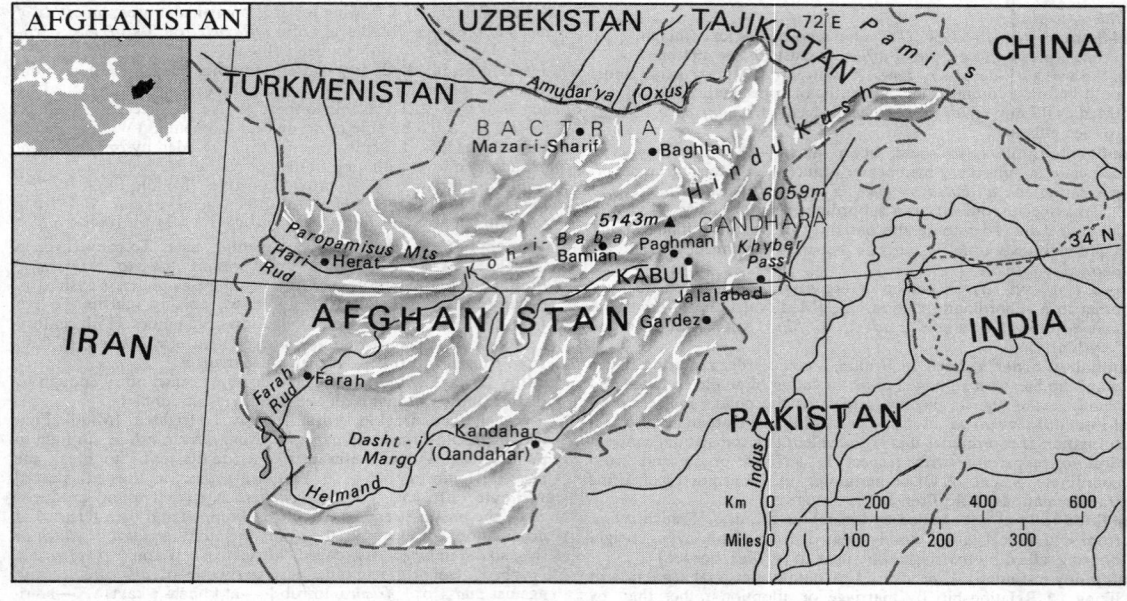

AFL-CIO, A.F.L.-C.I.O. The American Federation of Labor and Congress of Industrial Organizations.

a·float (ə-flōt) *adj.* **1.** Floating. **2.** On a boat or ship away from the shore; at sea. **3.** In circulation; being spread about. Said of rumours and gossip. **4.** Awash; flooded. **5.** Drifting about; moving without guidance. **6.** Out of debt: *trying to keep the company afloat.* —**a·float** *adv.*

a·flut·ter (ə-flúttər) *adj.* In a flutter; nervous and excited.

A.F.M. Air Force Medal.

a·foot (ə-fŏŏt) *adj.* **1.** Being prepared or carried out; astir: *some nasty business afoot.* **2.** *Archaic.* Walking; on foot. —**a·foot** *adv.*

a·fore (ə-fór ‖ ə-fōr) *adv.* **1.** *Archaic & Regional.* Before. **2.** *Nautical.* In front.
~*prep.* **1.** *Archaic & Regional.* Before. **2.** *Nautical.* In front of.
~*conj. Archaic & Regional.* Before. [Middle English afor(e)n, Old English onforan : ON + foran, dative of for, FORE.]

a·fore·men·tioned (ə-fór-ménsh'nd, -mensh'nd ‖ -fōr-) *adj.* Especially in legal documents, mentioned previously or before.
~*n., pl.* **aforementioned.** The person mentioned already. Preceded by *the.*

a·fore·said (ə-fór-sed ‖ -fōr-) *adj.* Especially in legal contexts, spoken of or referred to earlier.
~*n., pl.* **aforesaid.** The person, thing, or fact already stated or referred to. Preceded by *the.*

a·fore·thought (ə-fór-thawt ‖ -fōr-) *adj.* Planned or intended beforehand; premeditated. Used chiefly in the legal phrase *malice aforethought.*

a·fore·time (ə-fór-tīm ‖ -fōr-) *adv. Archaic.* At a former or past time; previously. —**a·fore·time** *adj.*

a for·ti·o·ri (áy fór-ti-áwrī, -shi-, áa fór-ti-áwree ‖ -fōr-) *adv.* With greater reason; all the more: *If there are to be cuts in the education budget, then a fortiori there should be cuts in the defence budget.*

a·foul (ə-fówl) *adv.* In or into a condition of entanglement, conflict, or collision. —**run** or **fall afoul of.** To become entangled with; come into collision with. —**a·foul** *adj.*

a·fraid (ə-fráyd) *adj.* **1.** Filled with fear; frightened or apprehensive: *afraid of snakes.* **2.** Disinclined; averse: *not afraid of work.* **3.** Filled with regret. Used especially as a polite way of lessening the force of an unpleasant statement: *I'm afraid that I disagree with you.* [Middle English af(f)raied, past participle of affraien, to frighten, from Old French affreer, to AFFRAY.]

af·reet, af·rit (áffreet, ə-fréet) *n. Arabic Mythology.* A powerful evil spirit or gigantic and monstrous demon. [Arabic *'ifrīt,* probably from Persian *āfrīda,* "a created being," from *āfrīdan,* to create.]

a·fresh (ə-frésh) *adv.* Anew; again; from the beginning: *start afresh.*

Af·ri·ca (áffrikə). The second largest continent after Asia, consisting mostly of high, monotonous plateaus, which drop dramatically to narrow coastal plains. It has a very short coastline for its area and has few inlets with deep harbours. Africa has few fold mountains: only the Atlas ranges in the northeast, part of the great Alpine-Himalayan system, and the older, smoother Cape ranges in the far south. Some ranges, such as the rugged Drakensberg and Ruwenzori, are the edges of tilted plateaus, while the others are generally of volcanic origin. The East African or Great Rift Valley slashes through the continent from the mouth of the Zambezi to Djibouti, and continues in the Red Sea. The valley encloses lakes Malawi and Turkana, while lakes Tanganyika and Albert lie in an arm to the west. Africa's largest lake, Victoria, lies in a shallow depression between the two arms of the valley. Africa's longest rivers, the Nile, Congo, and Niger, are among the ten longest in the world. Many rivers leave the plateaus by spectacular falls, such as those on the river Tugela in South Africa, and these provide great potential for hydroelectric schemes. There are also vast areas of inland drainage, with no outlet to the sea, the Chad and Makgadikgadi depressions being two of them. Two thirds of the continent lies within the Tropics, and though temperatures are much modified by altitude, Africa is the hottest continent. It is also one of the driest: one third of it has less than 250 millimetres (10 inches) of rain a year. The Sahara, covering 25 per cent of the total area, and the Namib and Kalahari deserts are among the world's harshest. Savannas, increasingly dry as they near the deserts, cover another 40 per cent of the land. Soils in Africa are often poor, but rich chernozems (black earths) cover much of the East African highlands, and the alluvium of the great river valleys provides good soils. Soil erosion, frequently the result of overgrazing by livestock, is a problem in many countries. Arable land covers less than 7.5 per cent of the continent, yet farming provides a living for some 75 per cent of its people, the highest proportion of any continent. Africa's great strength lies in its vast and varied mineral reserves. It has 30 per cent of the Western world's known mineral resources apart from oil, and already produces more than 10 per cent of the world's oil. Many African countries, especially those with fewer natural resources, are finding tourism an increasingly valuable source of foreign exchange. The continent's sunny climate, warm seas, sandy beaches, and scenery are a good base for development, while another asset is its remarkably varied wildlife, in many places preserved in national parks and game reserves. Area, 30 334 562 square kilometres (11,712,252 square miles).

Af·ri·can (áffrikən) *adj. Abbr.* **Afr.** Of or pertaining to Africa, or any of its peoples, languages, fauna, or the like.
~ *n.* **1.** A native or inhabitant of Africa. **2.** A member of any of the indigenous peoples of Africa. **3.** *South African.* A black person.

Af·ri·can-A·mer·i·can (áffrikən-ə-mérrikən) *adj. & n.* **Afro-American** (*see*).

Af·ri·can·der, Af·ri·kan·der (áffri-kándər) *n.* **1.** Any of a breed of cattle with a humped back and large, spreading horns, originally developed in South Africa. **2.** Any of a breed of fat-tailed South African sheep. **3.** *Obsolete.* An Afrikaner. [Afrikaans *Afrikaander,* alteration (influenced by *Hollander*) of Dutch *Afrikaner.*] —**Af·ri·can·der, Af·ri·kan·der** *adj.*

Af·ri·can·ise, Af·ri·can·ize (áffrikən-īz) *tr.v.* **-ised, -ising, -ises.** To make African; especially, to transfer to African control or give a specifically African character to. —**Af·ri·can·i·sa·tion** (-ī-záysh'n) *n.*

Af·ri·can·ism (áffrikən-iz'm) *n.* A characteristically African feature; especially, a word or expression from an African language when used in a non-African language.

Af·ri·can·ist (áffrikən-ist) *n.* A specialist in African affairs, culture, or languages.

African lily *n.* A plant, *Agapanthus africanus,* native to southern Africa, having rounded clusters of blue, violet, or white flowers.

African mahogany *n.* **1.** Any of several African trees of the genus *Khaya;* especially, *K. ivorensis,* having wood similar to that of true mahogany. **2.** The wood of this tree, used for furniture, musical instruments, and boat interiors. **3.** Any of various other African woods resembling true mahogany.

African marigold *n.* A widely cultivated plant, *Tagetes erecta,* native to Mexico, having finely divided foliage and showy, rounded, orange or yellow flowers.

African National Congress *n. Abbr.* **A.N.C.** Formerly, a banned South African movement favouring majority rule. After the 1994 elections, it formed the largest party in Parliament.

African trypanosomiasis *n.* Sleeping sickness (*see*).

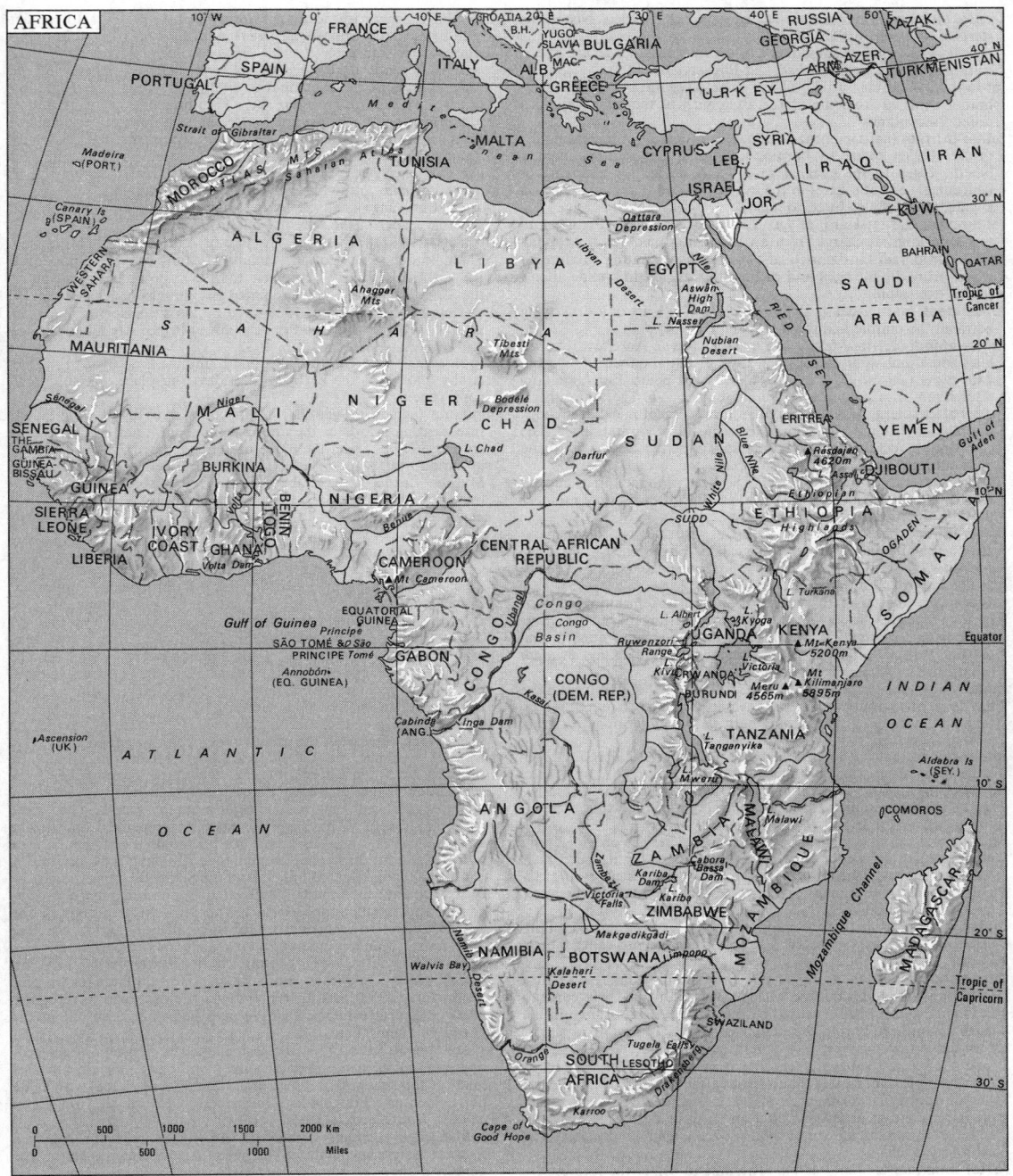

AFRICA

African violet *n.* Any of several plants of the genus *Saintpaulia*, native to tropical East Africa and widely cultivated as house plants. Also called "saintpaulia".

Af·ri·kaans (áffri-kaánss ‖ -kaánz) *n.* A language developed from 17th-century Dutch among the Afrikaners. It shares with English official-language status in the Republic of South Africa. Also called "Taal", formerly "Cape Dutch". —Af·ri·kaans *adj.*

Af·ri·kan·er (áffri-kaánər) *n.* An Afrikaans-speaking descendant of the Dutch settlers of South Africa. —Af·ri·kan·er *adj.*

Af·ri·kan·er·dom (áffri-kaánər-dəm) *n.* The sense of solidarity among Afrikaners; loyalty to and pride in the cultural and political values of the Afrikaner people and their pioneer origins.

Af·ro (áffrō) *n., pl.* -ros. A hairstyle in which the hair is shaped into a round frizzy mass. [Noun use of AFRO-.]

Afro- *comb. form.* Indicates Africa or African or African and; for example, Afro-American. [Latin *Āfr-*, stem of *Āfer*, an African.]

Af·ro·A·mer·i·can (áffrō-ə-mérrikən) *adj.* Of or pertaining to black Americans of African ancestry, their history, or their culture. ~ *n.* A black American of African ancestry.

Af·ro·A·si·at·ic (áffrō-áyshi-áttik, -áyssi-, -áyzhi-) *n.* A family of languages of southwestern Asia and northern Africa. Also called "Hamito-Semitic", "Semito-Hamitic". —Af·ro·A·si·at·ic *adj.*

Af·ro·Car·ib·be·an (áffrō-kárri-beé-ən) *n. Chiefly British.* A black person of African or, especially, Caribbean descent. —Af·ro·Car·ib·be·an *adj.*

af·ror·mo·si·a (áffrawr-mōzi-ə, -mózhə) *n.* 1. Any of several North and West African trees of the genus *Pericopsis*. 2. The hard teaklike wood of this tree. [AFRO- + *Ormosia* (genus name), from Greek *hormos*, necklace, alluding to the use of its berries in necklaces.]

aft (aaft ‖ aft) *adv.* At, in, towards, or close to the stern of a vessel or the back of an aeroplane. [Probably shortening of ABAFT.] —aft *adj.*

af·ter (aáftər ‖ áftər) *prep.* 1. Following in place or order: *D comes after C.* 2. Following in time; subsequent to: *Come after dinner.* 3. Following continually: *week after week of cold weather.* 4. In quest or pursuit of: *The police are after her.* 5. a. Considering; bearing in mind: *After the way he treated her, I'm not surprised she left.* b. In spite of: *After all my work, the job still wasn't finished on time.* 6. Concerning: *He asked after you.* 7. Next to or lower than in order or importance: *Football is his favourite sport after cricket.* 8. In the style of; in imitation of: *a painting after the style of Picasso.* 9. With the same name as; in honour or memory of: *named after her mother.* 10. *U.S.* Past the hour of; past: *It's ten after three.* —after all. 1. When everything is considered. 2. Eventually; ultimately. ~ *adv.* 1. Behind; in the rear. 2. At a later time; afterwards. ~ *adj.* 1. Subsequent in time or place; later; following: *in after*

37

years. Often used in combination: *afterglow.* **2.** *Nautical.* Nearer the stern of a vessel; further aft.
~*conj.* Following or subsequent to the time that: *I saw her after I arrived.* [Middle English *after,* Old English *æfter.*]

af·ter·birth (a̋af-tər-burth || áf-) *n.* The placenta and foetal membranes expelled from the uterus after birth of the offspring. Also called "secundines".

af·ter·burn·er (a̋af-tər-burnər || áf-) *n.* **1.** A device for increasing the thrust of a jet engine by burning additional fuel with the uncombined oxygen in the exhaust gases. **2.** A device for removing or neutralising harmful gases in the exhaust of an internal-combustion engine, especially as fitted to a car.

af·ter·care (a̋af-tər-kair || áf-) *n.* Treatment or special care given to someone after discharge from an institution, such as a hospital.

af·ter·damp (a̋af-tər-damp || áf-) *n.* An asphyxiating mixture of gases, primarily nitrogen and carbon dioxide, left in a mine after a fire or explosion.

af·ter·deck (a̋af-tər-dek || áf-) *n. Nautical.* The part of a deck lying between the middle and stern of a ship.

af·ter·ef·fect (a̋af-tər-i-fekt || áf-) *n. Often plural.* An effect that follows some time after its cause or after an initial effect.

af·ter·glow (a̋af-tər-glō || áf-) *n.* **1.** The light emitted or remaining after removal of a source of illumination, as: **a.** The atmospheric glow after sunset. **b.** The glow of an incandescent metal as it cools. **c.** Emission from a phosphor after removal of excitation. **2.** The comfortable feeling following a pleasant experience. **3.** A lingering pleasant impression, as of past happiness or success.

af·ter·heat (a̋af-tər-heet || áf-) *n.* The heat produced in a nuclear reactor after it has been shut down, as a result of residual radioactivity in the fuel elements.

af·ter·im·age (a̋af-tər-immij || áf-) *n.* A visual image that persists after a visual stimulus ceases. Also called "photogene".

af·ter·life (a̋af-tər-līf || áf-) *n.* **1.** A life believed to follow death. **2.** The later part of one's life.

af·ter·math (a̋af-tər-math, -maath || áf-) *n.* **1.** A resulting state or period, especially following a disaster or misfortune: *in the aftermath of the explosion.* **2.** A second growth or crop of grass in one season. [AFTER + obsolete *math,* mowing, Middle English *math* (unattested), Old English *mǣth.*]

af·ter·noon (a̋af-tər-no͞on || áf-) *n.* **1.** *Abbr.* **a., aft. a.** The part of the day from noon until evening. **b.** The part of the day between lunchtime and evening. **2.** The closing part: *in the afternoon of one's life.* **—af·ter·noon** *adj.*

af·ter·noons (a̋af-tər-no͞onz || áf-) *adv. Chiefly U.S. Informal.* Regularly in the afternoon; on any afternoon.

af·ter·pains (a̋af-tər-paynz || áf-) *pl.n.* The cramps or pains following childbirth, resulting from the contraction of the womb.

af·ters (a̋af-tərz || áf-) *n. British Informal.* Dessert.

af·ter-sales service (a̋af-tər-sáylz || áf-) *n.* A service provided by a manufacturer or vendor to maintain a product for its purchaser.

af·ter·sen·sa·tion (a̋af-tər-sen-saysh'n || áf-) *n.* A sensory impression, such as an afterimage or aftertaste, that persists or recurs after removal of a stimulus.

af·ter·shave lotion (a̋af-tər-sháyv || áf-) *n.* An astringent lotion, usually scented, applied to the face after shaving. Also called "aftershave".

af·ter·shock (a̋af-tər-shok || áf-) *n.* A relatively small earthquake following a large-magnitude earthquake, occurring fairly close to the focus, and probably caused by mechanical readjustment in the earth's mantle following the release of energy by the main shock.

af·ter·taste (a̋af-tər-tayst || áf-) *n.* **1.** A taste that remains in the mouth after the substance causing it is no longer present. **2.** A usually unpleasant feeling that remains after an event or experience.

af·ter·thought (a̋af-tər-thawt || áf-) *n.* **1.** An idea, response, or explanation that occurs to one after an event or decision. **2.** A later addition to something completed: *Their youngest child was a bit of an afterthought.*

af·ter·time (a̋af-tər-tīm || áf-) *n.* The time to come; the future.

af·ter·wards (a̋af-tər-wərdz || áf-) *adv.* Also *U.S.* **af·ter·ward.** At a later time; subsequently.

af·ter·word (a̋af-tər-wurd || áf-) *n.* Something added to the end of a literary work, such as an epilogue.

Ag The symbol for the element silver. [Latin *argentum.*]

A.G. **1.** adjutant general. **2.** attorney general.

a·ga, a·gha (a̋agə) *n.* A high-ranking official of the Ottoman Empire. [Turkish *ağa,* "lord".]

A·ga (a̋agə) *n.* A trademark for a domestic heating apparatus incorporating ovens, hobs, and a water-heating boiler.

A·ga·dir (ággə-dée̋r). Port in southwest Morocco. In 1911 it was the scene of an international crisis known as the Agadir Incident, when Britain forcibly protested at Germany's sending a gunboat there. War was averted through French arbitration. In 1960 earthquakes virtually destroyed the town, killing over 10,000 inhabitants.

a·gain (ə-gén, ə-gáyn || ə-gín) *adv.* **1.** Once more; another time; anew. **2.** Back to a previous place, position, or state: *He left home, but went back again.* **3.** Furthermore; moreover. **4.** On the other hand: *He might go, and again he might not.* **—again and again.** Repeatedly; frequently. **—as much again.** The same amount again. [Middle English *again, ayen,* Old English *ongēan,* in return, towards, against, from Germanic : ON + *gagin* (unattested), straight.]

a·gainst (ə-génst, ə-gáynst || ə-gínst) *prep.* **1.** In a direction or course opposite to: *row against the current.* **2.** So as to come into forcible contact with: *waves dashing against the shore.* **3.** In contact with so as to rest or press on: *He leant against the tree.* **4.** In opposition or resistance to: *the war against crime; 10 votes for and 12 against.* **5.** Contrary to: *against my better judgment; against all the odds.* **6.** In contrast or comparison with the setting or background of: *dark colours against a fair skin.* **7.** In preparation for; in anticipation of: *food stored against winter.* **8.** As a defence or safeguard from, or from the effects of: *protection against the cold; insurance against fire and theft.* **9.** Unfavourable or disadvantageous to: *Her age is against her.* [Middle English *against, ayenst,* alteration of *ayenes, againes,* from *again, ayen,* against. See **again.**]

A·ga Khan (a̋agə ka̋an) *n.* A hereditary title of the religious and spiritual leader of the sect of Ismaili Muslims.

Aga Khan III (1877–1957). The title of Aga Sultan Sir Mahomed Shah, leader (*imam*) of the Ismaili Muslim sect. He represented India at the League of Nations in the 1930s, becoming president of the League in 1937. He appointed his grandson, Aga Khan IV (formerly Prince Karim; 1936–) to be his successor as imam, in preference to his son (the Prince's father) Prince Aly Khan. Prince Karim became 49th imam in 1957.

a·gal (ə-ga̋al) *n.* A cord worn wound round the head by many desert Arabs that keeps the kaffiyeh (headdress) in place. [Arabic *'igal,* cord, rope.]

ag·a·ma (ággəmə, ə-gámmə) *n.* Any of various small, long-tailed, insect-eating lizards of the family Agamidae, found in Old World tropics. [Carib. (from the name of another lizard).]

Ag·a·mem·non (ággə-mém-nən, -non) In Greek legend, the king of Mycenae, leader of the Greeks against Troy, husband of Clytemnestra, and father of Orestes, Electra, and Iphigenia.

a·ga·mete (áy-gámmeet, ə-) *n. Biology.* A single-celled organism that reproduces asexually.

a·gam·ic (áy-gámmik, ə-) *adj.* Also **ag·a·mous** (ággəməss). *Biology.* Occurring or reproducing without the union of male and female cells; asexual or parthenogenetic. [Late Latin *agamus,* unmarried, from Greek *agamos* : *a-,* not + -GAMOUS.] **—a·gam·i·cal·ly** *adv.*

ag·a·mo·gen·e·sis (áy-gámmō-jénnəsiss, ə-, ággəmō-) *n. Biology.* Asexual reproduction, as by budding, cell division, or parthenogenesis. [AGAM(IC) + GENESIS.] **—ag·a·mo·ge·net·ic** (-jə-néttik) *adj.*

ag·a·pan·thus (ággə-pánthəss) *n.* Any plant of the genus *Agapanthus,* which includes the **African lily** *(see).* [New Latin : Greek *agapē,* love, AGAPE + *anthos,* flower.]

a·gape[1] (ə-gáyp || *U.S. also* ə-gáp) *adv.* In a state of wonder or amazement, often with the mouth wide open. **—a·gape** *adj.*

a·ga·pe[2] (ággə-pee, -pay) *n., pl.* **-pae** (-pee). **1.** Christian love. **2.** In the early Christian Church, the **love feast** *(see)* accompanied by a celebration of the Eucharist. [Greek *agapē*†, love.]

a·gar (áy-gaar, -gər || a̋a-) *n.* Also **a·gar-a·gar** (áy-gaar-áy-gaar, -gər-, -gər || a̋a-, -a̋a-). A mucilaginous material prepared from certain marine algae and used as a base for bacterial culture media, as a laxative, and for thickening certain foods. [Malay, "jelly, gelatine".]

ag·a·ric (ággərik, ə-gárrik) *n.* **1.** Any fungus of the family Agaricaceae, including the common cultivated mushroom, *Agaricus campestris,* and the **fly agaric** *(see).* **2.** The dried fruiting body of the fungus *Fomes laricis,* formerly used in medicine. [Latin *agaricum,* from Greek *agarikon,* perhaps after *Agaria,* city in Sarmatia.]

Ag·as·siz (ággə-sée̋, -see), **(Jean) Louis (Rodolphe)** (1807–73). Swiss-born U.S. naturalist and geologist. He won fame for his pioneering studies of fossil fishes, and was the first man to recognise from geological evidence that ice ages had once occurred in the Northern Hemisphere.

ag·ate (ágg-ət, -it) *n.* **1.** A fine-grained quartz, a variety of chalcedony, with colour banding or irregular clouding. **2.** A child's marble made of this material or a glass imitation of it. **3.** A tool with agate parts, such as a bookbinder's burnisher. [Old French, from Latin *achātēs,* from Greek *akhātēs*†.]

a·ga·ve (ə-gáyvi, ággayv || -ga̋avi) *n.* Any of numerous fleshy-leaved tropical American plants of the genus *Agave,* which includes the **century plant** *(see).* Some species yield valuable fibres. [New Latin, "noble (plant)" (probably so named because of its height), from Greek *agauē,* feminine of *agauos*†, noble.]

age (ayj) *n.* **1.** The period or amount of time during which someone or something has existed. **2.** An advanced stage of life or existence; the state of being old. **3.** That time in life when a person becomes eligible or entitled to do something, such as being qualified to assume certain civil and personal rights and responsibilities. Used chiefly in the phrases *of age* and *under age.* **4.** Any of the various stages of life: *at an awkward age.* **5.** *Sometimes capital* **A.** Any period in history or geology designated by a specified characteristic: *the atomic age; the Stone Age.* **6.** A generation: *future ages.* **7.** *Often plural. Informal.* A very long time: *We waited an age. They left ages ago.* **8.** *Psychology.* See **mental age.** **—come of age.** **1.** To reach the age (currently 18 in Britain) at which one is considered an adult in law. **2.** To reach a state of maturity.
~*v.* **aged, ageing** or **aging, ages.** —*tr.* To cause to grow or seem older or more mature. —*intr.* **1.** To become old. **2.** To show signs of old age. **3.** To mature with age. Used especially of alcoholic drinks. [Middle English, from Old French *age, aage,* from Vulgar Latin *aetāticum* (unattested), from Latin *aetās* (stem *aetāt-*), age.] **—ag·er** *n.*

-age *n. suffix.* Indicates: **1.** Collectively; for example, **acreage, baggage.** **2.** Relation to or connection with; for example, **parentage.** **3.** Result, action, or process; for example, **passage, spillage.** **4.** Condition or position; for example, **vagabondage, marriage.**

5. Charge or fee; for example, **postage, cartage. 6.** Residence or place; for example, **vicarage, orphanage. 7.** Rate; for example, **mileage.** [Middle English, from Old French, from Late Latin *-āticum,* from the neuter of *-āticus* : Latin *-ātus,* -ATE + -IC.]

a·ged (áyjid *for senses 1, 4;* ayjd *for senses 2, 3, and occasionally for other senses*) *adj.* **1.** Old; advanced in years. **2.** Of the age of: *aged three.* **3.** Having undergone the process of ageing; matured. **4.** *Geology.* Near the base level of erosion. —See Synonyms at **old.** —**a·ged·ness** *n.*

A·gee (áyjee), **James** (1909–55). U.S. writer. His most influential work, done in collaboration with the photographer Walker Evans, was *Let Us Now Praise Famous Men* (1941), a harrowing documentary account of the lives of Alabama sharecroppers during the Depression.

age group *n.* All the people of a particular age or between two particular ages, considered as a group.

age·ing, ag·ing (áyjing) *n.* **1.** The process of becoming old or mature. **2.** Any artificial process for imparting the characteristics of age.
~*adj.* **1.** Making one look older than one is: *Her hairstyle is rather ageing.* **2.** Growing old in a way that seems incongruous or inappropriate: *an ageing playboy.*

age·ism (áyj-iz'm) *n.* Unfair discrimination based on age, especially against middle-aged and elderly people. —**age·ist** *adj. & n.*

age·less (áyj-ləss, -liss) *adj.* **1.** Never seeming to grow old. **2.** Existing forever; eternal. —**age·less·ly** *adv.* —**age·less·ness** *n.*

a·gen·cy (áyjən-si) *n., pl.* **-cies. 1.** Action; operation; power: *Rust occurs through the agency of moisture in the air.* **2. a.** A business or service authorised to act for others: *an employment agency.* **b.** The office or premises from which such a business operates. **3.** An organisation set up by a government department or international body. [Latin *agentia,* from *agēns,* acting, AGENT.]

a·gen·da (ə-jéndə) *n.* A list of things to be done, especially the programme for a meeting. [Latin, plural of *agendum,* neuter gerundive of *agere,* to do.]

a·gen·e·sis (áy-jénnə-siss) *n.* Also **ag·e·ne·si·a** (áyjə-néezi-ə). *Biology.* Failure of an organism, organ, or part to develop.

a·gent (áyjənt) *n.* **1.** One that acts or has the power or authority to act. **2. a.** One who acts for or as the representative of another: *an actor's agent.* **b.** A sales representative: *an insurance agent.* **3.** A means by which something is done or caused; an instrument. **4.** A force or substance that causes changes: *a chemical agent.* [Middle English, from Latin *agēns* (stem *agent-*), present participle of *agere,* to act, drive, do.] —**a·gen·tial** (ay-jénsh'l) *adj.*

a·gent-gen·er·al (áyjənt-jénrəl, -jénnərəl) *n., pl.* **agents-general.** The London representative of an Australian state or a Canadian province.

Agent Orange *n.* A powerful toxic herbicide containing the chemical 2,4,5-T, used as a defoliant. [After the colour of the identifying stripe on the barrels containing the herbicide.]

a·gent pro·vo·ca·teur (ázhon-prə-vóckə-tér, -tör) *n., pl.* **agents provocateurs** (*pronounced as singular*). A person employed to associate with individuals or groups suspected of seditious or other criminal activities, and to incite them to commit illegal acts so as to incur punishment. [French, "provocative agent".]

age of consent *n. Law.* The age at which a person may choose to have sexual intercourse.

Age of Reason *n.* The period of the **Enlightenment** *(see),* especially in Britain, France, and the United States. Preceded by *the.*

age-old (áyj-ṓld, -ōld) *adj.* Very old or of long standing.

ag·e·ra·tum (ájə-ráytəm) *n.* **1.** Any of various plants of the genus *Ageratum*; especially, *A. houstonianum,* a commonly cultivated species having clusters of usually violet-blue flowers. **2.** Loosely, any of several other plants having similar flower clusters. [New Latin *Ageratum,* from Latin *agēraton,* from Greek, neuter of *agēratos,* ageless : *a-,* not + *-gēratos,* from *gēras,* old age.]

ag·gior·na·men·to (ad-jórnə-mén-tō, ajórnə- || *U.S.* aad-) *n., pl.* **-ti** (-tee). *Italian.* The process or an instance of modernising an institution or organisation.

ag·glom·er·ate (ə-glómmə-rayt) *v.* **-ated, -ating, -ates.** —*tr.* To form or collect into a rounded mass. —*intr.* To take the shape of a rounded mass.
~*adj.* (-rət, -rit). Gathered into a rounded mass.
~*n.* (-rət, -rit, -rayt). **1.** A confused or jumbled mass of things clustered together; a heap. **2.** A volcanic rock consisting of angular fragments more than 2 millimetres (1/12 inch) in diameter fused together. [Latin *agglomerāre* : *ad-,* to + *glomerāre,* to wind into a ball, from *glomus* (stem *glomer-*), ball.] —**ag·glom·er·a·tive** (-rətiv, -raytiv) *adj.* —**ag·glom·er·a·tor** (-raytər) *n.*

ag·glom·er·a·tion (ə-glómmə-ráysh'n) *n.* **1.** The action of agglomerating or the state of being agglomerated. **2.** A confused or jumbled mass; an agglomerate.

ag·glu·ti·nate (ə-glóoti-nayt) *v.* **-nated, -nating, -nates.** —*tr.* **1.** To join together by causing adhesion, as with glue. **2.** *Linguistics.* To form (words) by combining words, or words and word elements. **3.** *Physiology.* To cause (red blood cells or microorganisms) to clump together. —*intr.* **1.** To join together into a group or mass. **2.** *Linguistics.* To form words by agglutination. **3.** To undergo agglutination. [Latin *agglūtināre* : *ad-,* to + *glūtināre,* to glue, from *glūten,* glue.] —**ag·glu·ti·nant** *adj. & n.*

ag·glu·ti·na·tion (ə-glóoti-náysh'n) *n.* **1.** The process of agglutinating; adhesion of distinct parts. **2.** A mass formed in this manner. **3.** *Linguistics.* The process of forming words by combining component units that retain their original forms and meanings with little change, as in the formation of *houseboat* from *house* and *boat.*

ag·glu·ti·na·tive (ə-glóoti-nətiv, -naytiv) *adj.* **1.** Tending towards, concerning, or characteristic of agglutination. **2.** *Linguistics.* Designating a language, such as Turkish, in which words are formed primarily by means of agglutination.

ag·glu·ti·nin (ə-glóotinin) *n.* An antibody that induces agglutination in blood cells or microorganisms. [AGGLUTIN(ATION) + -IN.]

ag·grade (ə-gráyd) *tr.v.* **-graded, -grading, -grades.** To fill and raise the level of (the bed of a stream or a beach, for example) by depositing sediment. [AD- (towards) + GRADE.] —**ag·gra·da·tion** (ággrə-dáysh'n) *n.* —**ag·gra·da·tion·al** *adj.*

ag·gran·dise, ag·gran·dize (ə-gránd-īz, ággrənd-) *tr.v.* **-dised, -dising, -dises. 1.** To increase the scope of; enlarge; extend. **2.** To make greater in power, influence, stature, or reputation. **3.** To make (something) seem greater; exaggerate. [French *aggrandir* (present stem *aggrandiss-*) : *a,* to, from Latin *ad-* + *grandir,* to grow larger, from Latin *grandīre,* from *grandis,* great, GRAND.] —**ag·gran·dise·ment** (-iz-, -īz-) *n.* —**ag·gran·dis·er** *n.*

ag·gra·vate (ággrəvayt) *tr.v.* **-vated, -vating, -vates. 1.** To make worse or more serious. **2.** *Informal.* To annoy or exasperate; provoke; irritate. —See Synonyms at **annoy.** [Latin *aggravāre,* to make heavier : *ad-,* in addition to + *gravāre,* to burden, from *gravis,* heavy.] —**ag·gra·vat·ing** *adj.* —**ag·gra·va·tor** (-ər) *n.*

Usage: Purists disapprove of the use of *aggravate* in the sense of "annoy" *(Don't aggravate him any further!).* This use is, however, extremely common in informal speech, and increasingly in use elsewhere.

ag·gra·va·tion (ággrə-váysh'n) *n.* **1.** The action of aggravating. **2.** The state of being aggravated. **3.** A thing that irritates or makes worse or more troublesome. **4.** *Informal.* Exasperation; bother. **5.** *British Slang.* Aggressive or unruly behaviour; aggro: *a spot of aggravation between two gangs of youths.*

ag·gre·gate (ággri-gət, -git, -gayt) *adj.* **1.** Gathered together so as to make a whole; total. **2.** *Botany.* Crowded or massed into a dense cluster. **3.** *Geology* Consisting of a mixture of mineral or rock fragments separable by mechanical means. Said of rock.
~*n.* **1.** Any total or whole considered with reference to its constituent parts; a group of distinct particulars massed together; a gross amount: *"an empire is the aggregate of many states under one common head"* (Edmund Burke). **2.** The mineral materials, such as sand or stone, used in making concrete. —**in the aggregate.** Considered collectively or as a whole.
~*tr.v.* (ággri-gayt) **aggregated, -gating, -gates. 1.** To gather into a mass, sum, or whole. **2.** To total; add up to. [Middle English *aggregat,* from Latin *aggregātus,* past participle of *aggregāre,* to add to (the flock), attach to : *ad-,* to + *gregāre,* to herd, from *grex* (stem *greg-*), flock.] —**ag·gre·gate·ly** *adv.* —**ag·gre·ga·tion** (-gáysh'n) *n.* —**ag·gre·ga·tive** (-gətiv, -gaytiv) *adj.* —**ag·gre·ga·tor** (-gaytər) *n.*

aggregate fruit *n.* A fruit, such as a raspberry or blackberry, consisting of a cluster of drupelets formed from the ovaries of a single flower.

ag·gress (ə-gréss) *v.* **-gressed, -gressing, -gresses.** —*intr.* To start an attack or a quarrel. —*tr.* To commit an act of aggression against. [Latin *aggredī* (past participle *aggressus*), to approach (with hostility), attack : *ad-,* towards + *gradī,* to step, go.]

ag·gres·sion (ə-grésh'n) *n.* **1.** The act or an instance of commencing an attack, invasion, or quarrel; an assault. **2.** The habit or practice of launching attacks. **3.** *Psychology.* Hostile action or behaviour.

ag·gres·sive (ə-gréssiv) *adj.* **1.** Inclined to provoke argument or hostility; belligerent. **2.** Assertive; bold; forceful: *an aggressive salesman.* —**ag·gres·sive·ly** *adv.* —**ag·gres·sive·ness** *n.*

ag·grieve (ə-gréev) *tr.v.* **-grieved, -grieving, -grieves. 1.** To distress or afflict. **2.** To injure unjustly; give reason for just complaint. [Middle English *agreven,* from Old French *agrever,* from Latin *aggravāre,* to make heavier, AGGRAVATE.]

ag·grieved (ə-gréevd) *adj.* **1.** Hurt or offended, especially because of wrongful or unfair treatment. **2.** *Law.* Treated unjustly by a decision of the court or other legal authority. —**ag·griev·ed·ly** (ə-gréevidli) *adv.* —**ag·griev·ed·ness** *n.*

ag·gro (ággrō) *n. British Slang.* Aggressive or disruptive conduct. [Shortened from AGGRAVATION.]

agh (aakh) *interj.* Also *Chiefly South African* **ach.** Used to express feelings of impatience, disgust, or sympathy.

agha. Variant of **aga.**

a·ghast (ə-gáast || ə-gást) *adj.* Shocked, as by something horrible; appalled: *stood aghast at the sight.* [Middle English *agast,* past participle of *agasten,* to frighten : *a-* (intensive) + *gasten,* to frighten, Old English *gæstan,* from *gāst,* ghost.]

ag·ile (áj-īl || *U.S.* -əl) *adj.* **1.** Able to move in a quick and easy fashion; active. **2.** Mentally alert. —See Synonyms at **nimble.** [Middle English, from Old French, from Latin *agilis,* easily moved, light, nimble, from *agere,* to drive.] —**ag·ile·ly** *adv.* —**ag·ile·ness, a·gil·i·ty** (ə-jílləti) *n.*

a·gin (ə-gín) *prep. Regional.* Against.

A·gin·court (ájin-kawr, ázhin-, -kort || -kōr, -kōrt). *French* **A·zin·court** (azhankóor). Village in northern France, scene of a decisive battle that took place in 1415 when an English army led by Henry V defeated a much larger French force. The victory, largely due to the superiority of the English archers, left nearly 6,000 French dead while the English losses were few.

ag·i·o (áji-ō) *n., pl.* **-os.** *Finance.* **1.** A premium paid for changing one kind of money into another. **2.** An allowance or premium for the difference in value between two currencies being exchanged. 3. Agiotage. [Italian *ag(g)io,* alteration of dialectal *lajjē,* from Medieval Greek *allagion,* exchange, from *allagē,* change, from *allos,* other.]

ag·i·o·tage (ájə-tij, áji-ə-) *n. Finance.* **1.** The business of brokerage; speculation in stocks and shares. **2.** Exchange transactions, especially of currencies. [French, from *agioter,* to practise stockjobbing, from *agio,* stockbrokering, from Italian *aggio,* AGIO.]

a·gist (ə-jist) *tr.v.* **agisted, agisting, agists.** *Law.* To feed and take care of (cattle or horses) in return for payment. [Middle English *agisten,* to pasture, from Old French *agister,* "to provide lodging for" : *a-,* from Latin *ad,* to + *gister,* to lodge, from Vulgar Latin *jacitāre* (unattested), to make lie down, frequentative of Latin *jacēre,* to lie, intransitive of *jacere,* to throw.] **—a·gist·ment** *n.*

ag·i·tate (áji-tayt) *v.* **-tated, -tating, -tates.** *—tr.* **1.** To move with violence or sudden forcefulness: *a storm agitating the ocean.* **2.** To excite or trouble; disturb. **3.** To arouse interest in (a cause, for example) by the written or spoken word; discuss; debate. **4.** *Archaic.* To ponder over; consider. *—intr.* To stir up public interest in a cause: *agitate for better working conditions.* [Latin *agitāre,* frequentative of *agere,* to do, drive.] **—ag·i·tat·ed·ly** (-taytidli) *adv.*

ag·i·ta·tion (áji-táysh'n) *n.* **1.** The act of agitating. **2.** The state of being agitated; disturbance; commotion. **3.** Extreme emotional disturbance. **4.** The stirring up of public interest, especially in favour of political or social change. **—ag·i·ta·tion·al** *adj.*

a·gi·ta·to (áji-taáatō || *U.S.* aáji-) *adv. Music.* Agitated; fast and stirring. Used as a direction. [Italian, from Latin *agitātus,* past participle of *agitāre,* to AGITATE.] **—a·gi·ta·to** *adj.*

ag·i·ta·tor (áji-taytər) *n.* **1.** A person who agitates, especially one who engages in political agitation. **2.** A machine for stirring or shaking. **—ag·i·ta·to·ri·al** (-tə-táwri-əl, -tōri-) *adj.*

a·git·prop (ájit-prop) *n.* Political agitation and propaganda, especially in aid of left-wing or radical causes. [Shortened from Russian *Agitpropbyuro,* a Communist Party propaganda department, from *agitatsya-propaganda* agitation-propaganda.] **—a·git·prop** *adj.*

A·gla·ia (a-glī-ə, ə- || *U.S. also* -gláy-). *Greek Mythology.* One of the three **Graces** *(see).* [Greek, personification of *aglaia,* splendour, from *aglaos,* bright, splendid.]

a·gleam (ə-gleém) *adj.* Brightly shining. **—a·gleam** *adv.*

ag·let, ai·glet (ágglit) *n.* **1.** A tag or metal sheath on the end of a lace, cord, or ribbon to facilitate its passing through eyelet holes. **2.** A similar device used as an ornament. [Middle English, from Old French *aguillette,* diminutive of *aguille,* needle, from Late Latin *acūcula,* pin, pine needle, diminutive of Latin *acus,* needle.]

a·gley (ə-gláy || ə-glī). Also **a·glee** (ə-gleé) *adv. Scottish.* Off in the wrong direction; awry: *"The best laid schemes o'mice an' men/Gang aft agley"* (Robert Burns). [Scottish, "squintingly" : *a-,* on + *gley,* to squint, from Middle English (Scottish dialect) *gleyen*†.]

a·glim·mer (ə-glímmər) *adj.* Lighting up faintly; glimmering. **—a·glim·mer** *adv.*

a·glit·ter (ə-glíttər) *adj.* Glittering; sparkling. **—a·glit·ter** *adv.*

a·glow (ə-glṓ) *adj.* Glowing; in a glow. **—a·glow** *adv.*

A.G.M. Annual general meeting.

ag·ma (ág-mə, áng-mə) *n.* A phonetic symbol, **eng** *(see).* [Greek, "fragment".]

ag·mi·nate (ágmi-nayt, -nət, -nit) *adj.* Also **ag·mi·nat·ed** (-naytid). Gathered in clusters. [Latin *agmen* (stem *agmin-*), moving multitude, troop.]

ag·nail (ág-nayl) *n.* **1.** A hangnail. **2.** A painful sore or swelling around a fingernail or toenail; a whitlow. [Middle English *agnail,* Old English *angnægl,* "painful prick in the flesh" : *ang-,* painful + *nægl,* (iron) nail.]

ag·nate (ág-nayt) *adj.* **1.** Related on or descended from the father's or male side. **2.** From a common source; akin.
~n. A relative on the male or father's side only. [Middle English, from Latin *agnātus,* "born in addition", past participle of *agnāscī,* to be born in addition to : *ad-,* in addition + *nāscī, gnāscī,* to be born.] **—ag·nat·ic** (ag-náttik) *adj.* **—ag·nat·i·cal·ly** *adv.* **—ag·na·tion** *n.*

Ag·ni (úg-ni). *Hinduism.* The Vedic god of fire and guardian of man. [Sanskrit *agniḥ,* fire.]

ag·no·men (ag-nṓ-men, -mən) *n., pl.* **-nomina** (-nómminə). **1.** An additional cognomen given to a citizen of ancient Rome, often in honour of military victories, as Publius Cornelius Scipio *Africanus.* **2.** A nickname. [Latin *agnōmen* : *ad-,* additional + *(g)nōmen,* name.]

Ag·non (ag-nón), **Shmuel Yosef,** born Samuel Czaczkes (1888–1970). Israeli novelist. Born in Galicia (then in Austria), he moved to Palestine in 1907. His dramatic and influential novels, written in Hebrew, include *A Guest for the Night* (1938) and *The Day Before Yesterday* (1945). He was awarded the Nobel prize for literature in 1966 (sharing it with Nelly Sachs).

ag·nos·tic (ag-nóstik) *n.* One who professes agnosticism.
~adj. **1.** Pertaining to agnostics. **2.** Uncertain or uncommitted on any particular question at issue. [19th century : A- (not) + GNOSTIC (coined by T.H. Huxley as a description of his own views, as opposed to those of Victorian "gnostics", who believed that there were immaterial or spiritual phenomena).] **—ag·nos·ti·cal·ly** *adv.*

ag·nos·ti·cism (ag-nósti-siz'm) *n.* The philosophical view that it is impossible to know whether or not God exists.

Ag·nus De·i (ág-nŏŏss dáy-ee, aág-, -nəss, aán-yəss, -deé-ī) *n.* **1.** The Lamb of God, an emblem of Christ, derived from John 1:29 and Isaiah 53:7. **2.** A representation of this. **3.** A wax disc stamped with this emblem and blessed by the pope. **4. a.** A threefold prayer said or sung shortly after the Eucharistic Prayer in the Mass. **b.** A musical setting of the Latin text of this prayer. [Latin.]

a·go (ə-gṓ) *adv.* In the past: *It happened long ago.* [Middle English *ago(n),* past participle of *agon,* to go away, be past, Old English *āgān* : *ā-* (intensive) + *gān,* to go.]

a·gog (ə-góg) *adv.* In a state of keen anticipation; highly excited: *The court was all agog to hear the verdict.* [Middle English, from Old French *en gogues,* "in merriments", from *gogue,* merriment, probably imitative of hubbub.] **—a·gog** *adj.*

à go·go, à-go-go (ə gṓgō || *U.S.* aa-) *adj. Informal.* Unlimited; galore: *champagne à gogo.* [French, "in a joyful manner", from *gogo,* probably reduplication of the first syllable of *gogue,* merriment, from Old French. See **agog.**] **—à go·go** *adv.*

-agogue, *U.S.* **-agog** *n. comb. form.* Indicates: **1.** A leader or inciter of; for example, **demagogue. 2.** *Medicine.* Something that stimulates the flow of; for example, **emmenagogue.** [Late Latin *-agōgus,* from Greek *-agōgos,* from *agōgos,* leading, drawing forth, from *agein,* to lead.] **—-a·gog·ic** *adj. comb. form.* **—-a·go·gy** *n. comb. form.*

a·gone (ə-gón || -gáwn, -gaán) *adj. Archaic.* Gone; gone by; past. [Middle English *agon,* AGO.] **—a·gone** *adv.*

a·gon·ic (ay-gónnik, ə-) *adj.* Having no angle. [Greek *agōnos* : *a-,* not + *gōnia,* angle.]

agonic line *n.* An imaginary line on the earth's surface connecting points where the magnetic declination is zero.

ag·o·nise, ag·o·nize (ággə-nīz) *v.* **-nised, -nising, -nises.** *—intr.* **1.** To be in extreme pain or suffer great anguish. **2.** To make a prolonged or intense mental effort: *agonise over a problem. —tr.* To cause great pain or anguish to. [Old French *agoniser,* from Late Latin *agōnizāre,* from Greek *agōnizesthai,* to contend for a prize, to struggle, from *agōnia,* contest, AGONY.] **—ag·o·nis·ing·ly** *adv.*

ag·o·nist (ággə-nist) *n. Physiology.* A muscle whose contraction effects movement of a part of the body. It is opposed by contraction in another muscle, the **antagonist** *(see).* [Back-formation from ANTAGONIST.]

ag·o·nis·tic (ággə-nístik) *adj.* **1.** Striving to overcome in argument; competitive; combative. **2.** Straining to achieve effect. **3.** Of or pertaining to contests, originally those of the ancient Greeks. [Late Latin *agōnisticus,* from Greek *agōnistikos,* from *agōnistēs,* contestant, from *agōn,* contest.] **—ag·o·nis·ti·cal·ly** *adv.*

ag·o·ny (ággəni) *n., pl.* **-nies. 1.** The suffering of intense physical or mental pain. **2.** A sudden or intense emotion of a particular sort: *an agony of doubt.* **3.** A violent or intense struggle. **—last agony** or **agonies.** The struggle that precedes death. **—put** or **pile on the agony.** *Informal.* To overdramatise one's sufferings to create an effect or gain sympathy; pile it on. [Middle English *agonie,* from Old French, from Late Latin *agōnia,* from Greek, contest, anguish, from *agōn,* contest, from *agein,* to drive.]

agony aunt *n.* A person who advises readers in an agony column.

agony column *n. Informal. British.* A newspaper or magazine feature containing readers' letters on personal problems together with the columnist's replies and advice.

ag·o·ra¹ (ággə-rə) *n., pl.* **-rae** (-ree, -rī) or **-ras.** *Often capital* **A. 1.** A marketplace in ancient Greece, customarily used for holding meetings of the people's assembly. **2.** The assembly itself. [Greek *agora,* from *ageirein,* to assemble.]

a·go·ra² (ággə-raá) *n., pl.* **-rot** or **-roth** (-rót || *U.S.* -rṓt). A former Israeli monetary unit equal to $^{1}/_{100}$ of the pound of Israel. [Hebrew *'agōrāh,* from *āgōr,* to collect.]

ag·o·ra·pho·bi·a (ággərə-fṓbi-ə) *n.* Abnormal fear of open spaces or of going out in public. [New Latin : Greek *agora,* open space, AGORA + -PHOBIA.] **—ag·o·ra·pho·bic** (-fṓbik || -fóbbik) *adj. & n.*

A·gos·ti·ni (ággoss-teéni || *U.S.* aágoss-), **Giacomo** (1944–). Italian racing motorcyclist. He won the 350cc world championship 7 times (1968–74) and the 500cc world championship 8 times (1966–72 and 1975), thus winning a record number of 15 titles.

a·gou·ti (ə-gŏŏti) *n., pl.* **-tis** or **-ties.** Any of several burrowing rodents of the genus *Dasyprocta,* of tropical America, having grizzled brownish or dark grey fur. [French, from Spanish *agutí,* from Guarani *acutí.*]

agr. agricultural; agriculture.

A.G.R. advanced gas-cooled reactor.

A·gra (aágrə). City in north central India in Uttar Pradesh on the river Jumna. It was a capital of the Mogul Empire in the 16th and 17th centuries. The **Taj Mahal** was built there (1630–48) by Shah Jahan. Modern Agra is an important commercial city whose products include carpets and glassware.

a·graffe (ə-gráf) *n.* **1.** A hook-and-loop clasp on armour and clothing. **2.** In stonemasonry, a cramp iron for holding stones together. [French *agrafe,* from Old French *agrafer,* to hook on to : *a-,* to, from Latin *ad-* + *grafer,* to hook, from *grafe,* hook, from Old High German *krāpfo.*]

a·gran·u·lo·cy·to·sis (ə-grànnewlō-sī-tṓ-siss, ay-) *n.* A drug-induced disease marked by high fever, lesions of the mucous membranes, and a marked decrease in granular white blood corpuscles. [New Latin : A- (not) + GRANUL(E) + -O- + -CYT(E) + -OSIS.]

a·gra·pha (ággrəfə) *pl.n. Often capital* **A.** The sayings of Jesus not recorded in the Gospels. [Greek, "things unwritten", neuter plural of *agraphos,* unwritten : *a-,* not + *graphein,* to write.]

a·graph·i·a (áy-gráffi-ə, ə-) *n. Pathology.* Acquired inability to write, caused by disease of the parietal lobe of the brain. [New Latin : A- (not) + Greek *graphein,* to write.] **—a·graph·ic** *adj.*

a·grar·i·an (ə-gráiri-ən) *adj.* **1.** Relating to or concerning the land and its ownership, cultivation, and tenure. **2.** Pertaining to agricultural or rural matters.
~*n.* A person who favours equitable distribution of land. [From Latin *agrārius,* from *ager* (stem *agri*-), land, field.]
a·grar·i·an·ism (ə-gráiri-ən-iz′m) *n.* A movement for equitable distribution of land and for agrarian reform.
a·gree (ə-grée) *v.* **agreed, agreeing, agrees.** —*intr.* **1.** To grant consent; be willing. Used with the infinitive: *He agreed to accompany us.* **2.** To correspond; be in accord: *The copy agrees with the original.* **3.** Often used with *with.* **a.** To be of one opinion: *They agreed with us; we agreed.* **b.** *Informal.* To approve of a practice or policy: *He didn't agree with capital punishment.* **4.** To come to an understanding or to terms. Used with *about, upon,* or *on: Is it possible to agree on such great problems?* **5.** To be beneficial to the constitution or health. Used with *with: Spicy food does not agree with him.* **6.** *Grammar.* To correspond in gender, number, case, or person. —*tr.* **1.** To grant or concede: *He agreed that we should go.* **2.** *Chiefly British.* To come to an understanding or settlement regarding: *agree terms.* [Middle English *agreen,* from Old French *agreer,* from Vulgar Latin *aggrātāre* (unattested), to be pleasing to: *ad*-, to + *grātus,* pleasing, beloved, agreeable.]
Synonyms: agree, conform, harmonise, accord, correspond, coincide.
a·gree·a·ble (ə-grée-əb′l) *adj.* **1.** Pleasing; pleasant; to one's liking. **2.** Ready to consent or submit. —See Synonyms at **amiable.** —**a·gree·a·bil·i·ty** (ə-bílləti), **a·gree·a·ble·ness** *n.* —**a·gree·a·bly** *adv.*
a·greed (ə-gréed) *adj.* **1.** Determined by common consent: *the agreed meeting place.* **2.** Of one opinion: *Both parties were agreed.* **3.** Allowed; granted. Used as an interjection.
a·greed-val·ue policy (ə-gréed-vál-yoo) *n.* An insurance policy requiring the insurer to pay the insured the full face value of the policy in the event of total loss, regardless of the actual value of the property lost. Also called "valued policy".
a·gree·ment (ə-gréemənt) *n.* **1.** The act of agreeing. **2.** The state of being agreed; concord; harmony. **3.** An arrangement between parties regarding a course of action; a covenant; a treaty. **4.** *Law.* **a.** A properly executed and legally binding contract. **b.** The writing or document embodying this. **5.** *Grammar.* Correspondence in gender, number, case, or person between words.
a·gres·tal (ə-gréss-t'l) *adj. Botany.* Growing wild, especially in cultivated areas. [From Latin *agrestis,* rural, from *ager* (stem *agr*-), field, land.]
a·gres·tic (ə-gréss-tik) *adj.* Also **a·gres·ti·cal** (-tik'l). **1.** Rural; rustic. **2.** Unpolished; crude.
ag·ri·busi·ness (ággri-biznəss, -bizniss) *n.* Farming engaged in as a business, including the production, processing, and distribution of farm products and the manufacture of farm machinery, equipment, and supplies. [AGRI(CULTURE) + BUSINESS.]
A·gric·o·la (ə-grickələ), **Georgius,** born Georg Bauer (1494–1555). German mineralogist. In his book *De re metallica* (On Metals), published in 1556, he dealt with mineralogy, geology, and mining, and produced the first systematic and scientific description of minerals and ores.
Agricola, Gnaeus Julius (*c.*A.D. 40–93). Roman general and conqueror of Britain. A consul in *c.*A.D. 71, he was governor of Britain (*c.*A.D. 78–84). An enlightened ruler, he circumnavigated the mainland and pacified most of the island, subduing north Wales and advancing far into Scotland.
ag·ri·cul·ture (ággri-kulchər ‖ -kúlchər) *n. Abbr.* **agr., agric.** The science or occupation of cultivating the soil, producing crops, and raising livestock; farming. [Latin *agricultūra,* originally *agrī cultūra,* "cultivation of land" : *agrī,* genitive of *ager,* land + *cultūra,* cultivation, CULTURE.] —**ag·ri·cul·tur·al** (-kúlchərəl) *adj.* —**ag·ri·cul·tur·al·ly** *adv.* —**ag·ri·cul·tur·ist** (-kúlchərist), **ag·ri·cul·tur·al·ist** *n.*
ag·ri·mo·ny (ággri-məni ‖ *U.S.* -mōni) *n., pl.* **-nies. 1.** Any of various plants of the genus *Agrimonia,* having compound leaves, long clusters of small yellow flowers, and bristly fruits. **2.** Any of several other plants, such as the **hemp agrimony** *(see).* [Middle English *agrimonie,* from Old French *aigremoine,* from Latin *agrimōnia,* alteration of *argemōnia,* from Greek *argemōnē, argemōnia,* poppy, perhaps from Hebrew *'argāmān,* red-purple.]
ag·ri·ol·o·gy (ággri-ólləji) *n.* The study of primitive cultures. [Greek *agrios,* wild, from *agros,* open field + -LOGY.] —**ag·ri·o·lo·gi·cal** (-ə-lójik'l) *adj.*
A·grip·pa (ə-gríppə), **Marcus Vipsanius** (63 B.C.–12 B.C.). Roman general and statesman, the adviser of the emperor Augustus, whose daughter, Julia, he married. He was in command of the fleet that defeated the forces of Mark Antony and Cleopatra at Actium.
Ag·rip·pi·na (ággri-péenə), known as the Elder (*c.*13 B.C.–A.D. 33). Roman matron, daughter of Agrippa, granddaughter of Augustus, and mother of the emperor Caligula. She accompanied her husband, Germanicus Caesar, on all his campaigns and was famous for her courage. After Germanicus' death Tiberius banished her to the island of Pandataria, where she died of starvation.
Agrippina, known as the Younger (*c.* A.D. 15–59). Roman empress, daughter of Agrippina the Elder, and mother of the emperor Nero. She was known for her ambition and ruthlessness, and it is thought that she murdered her third husband, her uncle the emperor Claudius. She managed to place Nero on the throne and exerted considerable power through her son. Eventually they quarrelled and Nero had her murdered.
agro– *comb. form.* Indicates field, earth, or soil; for example, **agro**-

biology, agronomy. [Greek *agros,* open field.]
ag·ro·bi·ol·o·gy (ággrō-bī-ólləji) *n.* The science of plant and animal growth and nutrition as related to soil variation and crop yield. —**ag·ro·bi·o·lo·gic** (-bī-ə-lójik), **ag·ro·bi·o·lo·gi·cal** *adj.* —**ag·ro·bi·o·lo·gi·cal·ly** *adv.* —**ag·ro·bi·ol·o·gist** (-bī-ólləjist) *n.*
a·grol·o·gy (ə-grólləji) *n.* The applied science of soils in relation to crops. Compare **pedology.** [AGRO- + -LOGY.] —**ag·ro·log·ic** (ággrə-lójik), **ag·ro·log·i·cal** *adj.* —**ag·ro·log·i·cal·ly** *adv.* —**a·grol·o·gist** (ə-gróllǝjist) *n.*
a·gron·o·my (ə-grónnəmi) *n.* The application of the various soil and plant sciences to soil management and the raising of crops; scientific agriculture. Also "agronomics". [French *agronomie* : AGRO- + -NOMY.] —**agro·nom·ic** (ággrə-nómik), **agro·nom·i·cal** *adj.* —**a·gron·o·mist** (ə-grónnəmist) *n.*
ag·ros·tol·o·gy (ággrə-stólləji) *n.* The botanical study of grasses. [Greek *agrōstis,* a kind of wild grass, from *agros,* field + -LOGY.]
a·ground (ə-grównd) *adv.* On the ground or bottom; stranded, as in shallow water: *The ship ran aground.* —**a·ground** *adj.*
a·gue (áygew) *n.* **1.** An attack of malarial fever, with alternate fever and chills. **2.** A recurrent chill or fit of shivering. [Middle English, from Old French *ague,* from Medieval Latin *(fēbris) acūta,* "sharp (fever)", feminine of *acūtus,* sharp, past participle of *acuere,* to sharpen, from *acus,* needle.] —**a·gu·ish** (áygew-ish) *adj.* —**a·gu·ish·ly** *adv.* —**a·gu·ish·ness** *n.*
A·gul·has, Cape (ə-gúlləss). Headland in South Africa, the most southerly point of Africa. Its meridian (longitude 20°E) marks the divide between the Atlantic and Indian Oceans.
ah (aa) *interj.* Used to express various emotions, such as surprise, delight, pain, satisfaction, or regret. See **ooh.** [Middle English *a(h),* from Old French.]
A.H. in the year of the Hegira [Latin *anno Hegirae*]. Used to indicate the date in the Muslim world, the base year being A.D. 622.
a·ha (aa-háa, ə-háa) *interj.* Used to express surprise, triumph, or pleasure. [Middle English : AH + HA.]
A·hab (áy-hab). A king of Israel of the ninth century B.C., husband of Jezebel. I Kings 16:29.
A·has·u·e·rus (ə-házzew-éer-əs, ay-). A king of ancient Persia, usually identified with Xerxes, the husband of Esther. Esther 1:1.
a·head (ə-héd) *adv.* **1.** At or to the front or leading position. **2.** Before in space or in time. **3.** Onwards; forwards. —**ahead of.** Before: **a.** In front of. **b.** Prior to; an anticipation of: *reached an agreement ahead of the conference.* —**get ahead.** To attain success. —**a·head** *adj.*
a·hem (ə-hém) *interj.* Used to attract attention or to express doubt or warning. [Imitative. See **hem²**.]
a·him·sa (ə-him-saa) *n.* An Indian doctrine of nonviolence, expressing belief in the sacredness of all living creatures and the possibility of reincarnation, strictly practised by the Jains and subscribed to by Buddhists and Hindus. [Sanskrit *ahiṁsā,* non-injury : *a*-, without + *hiṁsā,* injury, from *hiṁsati,* he injures.]
a·his·tor·i·cal (áy-histórrik'l) *adj.* Also **a·his·tor·i·c.** Not historical; unrelated to history.
A·hith·o·phel, A·chit·o·phel (ə-híthəfel). A counsellor of David, who became an adviser to Absalom in his rebellion and hanged himself when his advice was disregarded.
Ah·ma·da·bad, Ah·me·da·bad (áamədə-baad). Town in Gujarat state, India. Founded in 1412 as the capital of the former Gujarat kingdom, it is the largest town of Gujarat as well as being the state's cultural and commercial centre.
-aholic. Variant of **-oholic.**
a·hoy (ə-hóy) *interj. Nautical.* Used to hail a ship or person, or to attract attention. [AH + HOY (interjection).]
Ah·ri·man (áarimən) *n.* In Zoroastrianism, the spirit of evil, understood by some as the arch rival of Ormazd *(see).* [Persian *Ahrīman,* probably from Avestan *aṅra mainyu,* "the evil spirit" : *aṅra,* evil, hostile, probably from Iranian root *ans*-†, to hate + *mainyu,* spirit.]
A·hu·ra Maz·da (ə-hóor-ə mázdə). **Ormazd** *(see).*
Ah·ve·nan·maa (akve-náan-maa). Also **Å·land Islands** (áw-lənd, áa-). Province of Finland, comprising about 80 inhabited islands and 6,000 uninhabited islets lying in the Baltic Sea between Finland and Sweden, at the entrance to the Gulf of Bothnia. Ahvenanmaa (or Åland), the largest island, has the capital, Maarianhamina.
ai (áa-i, ī) *n., pl.* **ais.** A **three-toed sloth** *(see).* [Portuguese, from Tupi *ai, hai.*]
A.I. 1. artificial insemination. **2.** artificial intelligence.
ai·a (ī-ə) *n. South African.* **1.** A child's nursemaid or nanny, especially a coloured woman. **2.** *Informal.* An old coloured woman. [Portuguese, nurse. Compare **ayah.**]
aid (ayd) *v.* **aided, aiding, aids.** —*intr.* To help; assist. —*tr.* To give help or assistance to. —See Synonyms at **help.**
~*n.* **1.** The act or result of helping; assistance; cooperation. **2. a.** One that helps; an assistant or helper. **b.** A device that helps: *a hearing aid; a teaching aid.* **3. Foreign aid** *(see).* **4.** An aide-de-camp or aide. **5.** In medieval England: **a.** Any of several revenues or subsidies paid to the king. **b.** A money payment to a feudal lord by a vassal. —**in aid of. 1.** In support of: *a bazaar in aid of charity.* **2.** *British Informal.* For the purpose of: *What's all this in aid of?* [Middle English *eyden, aiden,* from Old French *aider,* from Latin *adjūtāre,* frequentative of *adjuvāre,* to give aid to, help : *ad,* to + *juvāre*†, to help.] —**aid·er** *n.*
A.I.D. 1. acute infectious disease. **2.** Agency for International Development. **3.** artificial insemination by donor.
Ai·dan (áyd'n), **Saint** (*c.* A.D. 600–651). Irish monk. From the mon-

astery at Iona he was sent as a missionary to Northumbria in 635. He founded a famous monastery at Lindisfarne (Holy Island) and became its first bishop.

aide (ayd) n. 1. An aide-de-camp. 2. An assistant; a helper: *a president's aide*. [French, from *aider*, to help, AID.]

aide-de-camp (áyd-də-kón ‖ -kámp) n., pl. **aides-de-camp** (áydz-də-). *Abbr.* **ADC, a.d.c., A.D.C.** A naval or military officer acting as secretary and confidential assistant to a superior officer of general or flag rank. [French, "camp assistant".]

aide-mé·moire (áyd-mem-wáar) n., pl. **aide-mé·moire.** A statement in summary form, usually of the terms of an agreement, used in drafting a formal document. [French, "help-memory".]

AIDS (aydz) n. *A*cquired *I*mmune *D*eficiency *S*yndrome: an abnormal condition of the body's immune system, in which the body's defences against disease are weakened.

aiglet. Variant of **aglet.**

ai·grette, ai·gret (áy-gret, ay-grét) n. 1. An ornamental tuft of upright plumes, especially the tail feathers of an egret. 2. An ornament or item of jewellery, such as a spray of gems, resembling such a tuft. [French. See **egret.**]

ai·guille (ay-gwéel) n. 1. A sharp, pointed mountain peak. 2. A needle-shaped drill for boring holes in rock or masonry. [French, "needle", from Old French, AGLET.]

ai·guil·lette (áygwi-lét) n. A plaited metallic cord or braid worn on the shoulder of a military uniform. [French, AGLET.]

A.I.H. artificial insemination by husband.

ai·ki·do (īkidō, īkéedō) n. A 20th-century Japanese martial art similar to judo.

ail (ayl) v. **ailed, ailing, ails.** —*intr.* 1. To feel ill or have pain; be unwell. 2. To be in a weak or unsound condition: *an ailing economy.* —*tr.* To cause pain; make ill or uneasy; trouble: *What ails you?* [Middle English *eilen,* Old English *eglan,* to trouble, from *egle,* troublesome.]

ai·lan·thus (ay-lánthəss) n. A deciduous tree, *Ailanthus altissima,* native to China and widely grown for ornament, especially in urban areas. It has compound leaves and clusters of small greenish flowers with an unpleasant odour. Also called "tree of heaven". [New Latin, from Amboinese (an Indonesian language) *ai lanto,* "tree (of) heaven"; Latin form influenced by Greek *anthos,* flower.]

ai·le·ron (áylə-ron) n. A movable control surface on the trailing edge of an aircraft wing. [French, diminutive of *aile,* wing, from Old French, from Latin *āla.*]

ail·ment (áylmənt) n. A physical or mental disorder; especially, a mild illness.

Ail·sa Craig (áylsə kráyg). A bleak, cone-shaped granite island in the Firth of Clyde, southwest Scotland. It is a prominent seamark roughly three kilometres (two miles) in circumference, and a bird sanctuary.

ai·lu·ro·phobe (ay-lóorə-fōb, -léwrə-) n. A person with an intense fear or dislike of cats. [Greek *ailouros,* cat + -PHOBE.]

aim (aym) v. **aimed, aiming, aims.** —*tr.* To direct (a weapon, remark, or blow, for example) at someone or something. —*intr.* 1. To direct a weapon. 2. **a.** To direct one's efforts towards something; strive: *aim at perfection.* **b.** To intend; propose; plan. Used with *for* or with an infinitive: *We are aiming for an early start. We aim to get to the bottom of this.*
~*n.* 1. The act of aiming or pointing. 2. The sighting or line of fire of something aimed: *take aim.* 3. A purpose; an intention; a plan. —See Synonyms at **intention.** [Middle English *aimen,* to guess, aim, from Old French *aesmer,* to guess at : *a-,* at, to, from Latin *ad-* + *esmer,* to guess, from Latin *aestimāre,* to ESTIMATE.]

aim·less (áym-ləss, -liss) adj. Without direction or purpose. —**aim·less·ly** adv. —**aim·less·ness** n.

ain¹ (ayn) adj. Scottish. Own.

ain². Variant of **ayin.**

ain't (aynt). *Nonstandard.* Contraction of *am not.* Also extended in use to mean *are not, is not, has not,* and *have not.*

Usage: Although widely used in colloquial speech, *ain't* is considered nonstandard by educated speakers. It should always be avoided in writing or formal speech, unless you are deliberately trying to create a humorous effect, or using a fixed phrase like *Things ain't what they used to be. Aren't I* (as in *aren't I coming too?*) has sometimes also been attacked on the grounds that it misleadingly suggests a corresponding form *I are.* But the full form, *am I not,* is so formal that in many contexts it may be considered ridiculously stilted, and *aren't I* is therefore quite acceptable usage in educated British English. The form *amn't I* has some currency in regional English, especially in Scotland and Ireland, but is considered nonstandard.

Ain·tree (áyn-tree). A racecourse nine kilometres (six miles) northeast of Liverpool, England. The Grand National, the most famous race of the steeplechase season, has been run here since 1839.

Ai·nu (ī-nōō) n., pl. **-nus.** 1. A member of an aboriginal Caucasian people inhabiting the northernmost islands of Japan. 2. The language of this people. [Ainu, "man".]

ai·o·li (ī-ṓli) n. Garlic-flavoured mayonnaise. [French, from *ail,* garlic.]

air (air) n. 1. **a.** A colourless, odourless, tasteless gaseous mixture, mainly nitrogen (approximately 78 per cent) and oxygen (approximately 21 per cent) with lesser amounts of argon, carbon dioxide, neon, helium, and other gases. **b.** This mixture with varying amounts of moisture, low-altitude pollutants, and particulate mat-

ter, enveloping the Earth; the atmosphere. **c.** The air or atmosphere in an enclosed space: *The air in the conference room is invariably half cigar smoke.* **d.** In ancient thought, one of the four **elements** (see). **2. a.** The sky; the firmament. **b.** The space above the ground: *leapt into the air.* **3.** An atmospheric movement; a breeze; a wind. **4.** The sky as a medium of transport or conveyance: *sent it by air.* **5.** Utterance; public expression: *give air to one's grievances.* **6.** A peculiar or characteristic impression; an appearance or aura: *an air of excitement.* **7.** Personal bearing, appearance, or manner; mien: *He has an air of gentility.* **8.** *Plural.* Affectations; haughty manner: *She gives herself airs.* **9.** *Music.* A melody or tune, especially: **a.** The soprano or treble part in a harmonised composition. **b.** A solo for voice or instrument, with or without accompaniment. **10.** *Archaic.* Breath. —**clear the air.** To dispel emotional differences and tensions. —**in the air. 1.** In circulation; prevalent. **2.** Uncertain; not settled; being thought out or formulated. —**on (the) air.** Broadcast, or being broadcast, on radio or television. —**take the air.** To go outdoors for fresh air; take a short walk or ride. —**up in the air.** Not decided; uncertain. —**walk on air.** To feel elated or extremely happy.
~ v. **aired, airing, airs** —*tr.* **1.** To expose (a room or laundry, for example) to air or warmth, in order to dry, cool, or freshen; ventilate. **2.** To give public utterance to; circulate: *air one's grievances.* **3.** To broadcast; put on air: *air a programme.* —*intr. Chiefly U.S.* To be broadcast; go on air: *The programme airs tonight.* —See Synonyms at **vent.** [Blend of senses of several origins: 1. Atmosphere: Middle English *eir, ayr,* from Old French *air,* from Latin *āēr,* from Greek *aēr,* breath, atmospheric air; 2. Manner, appearance: French *air,* from Old French *aire,* nature, quality, originally "place of origin", from Latin *ager,* place, field, and Latin *ārea,* open space, threshing floor, AREA; 3. Melody: Italian *aria,* ARIA. In English these senses have interacted inextricably, with the first prevailing.]

AIR All India Radio.

air bag n. A safety device designed for use in cars, consisting of a large bag that inflates upon collision and prevents passengers from pitching forwards.

air base n. A base of operations for military aircraft.

air battery n. A rechargeable battery in which the current is produced as a result of oxidation of a metal.

air bearing n. A device that uses compressed air to separate working parts, for example of a dental drill, to reduce noise level.

air bed n. An inflatable mattress, especially one used for supporting patients with extensive burns.

air bladder n. *Biology.* **1.** An air-filled structure near the spinal column in many fishes, which functions to maintain buoyancy or, in some species, as an aid in respiration or hearing. Also called "swim bladder". **2.** Any air-filled saclike structure, such as one of the dilated parts of the thallus in certain seaweeds.

air·boat (áir-bōt) n. A swamp boat (see).

air·borne (áir-born ‖ -bōrn) adj. Abbr. **abn 1.** Carried by or through the air: *airborne pollen.* **2.** Transported in aircraft: *airborne troops.* **3.** Flying; in flight.

air brake n. A brake operated by compressed air.

air brick n. A brick with holes running through it, built into a wall as a means of ventilation.

air bridge n. A transport link by aircraft between two points.

air·brush (áir-brush) n. An atomiser using compressed air to spray paint or other liquids on a surface.
~*tr.v* **airbrushed, -brushing, -brushes.** To paint or coat (a surface) using an airbrush.

air·burst (áir-burst) n. An explosion of a bomb or shell in the atmosphere.

Air·bus (áir-buss) n. Proprietary name for a wide-bodied jet aircraft carrying a large number of passengers over relatively short distances.

air chamber n. **1.** Any enclosure filled with air for a special purpose. **2.** Such a compartment, especially in a hydraulic system, in which air elastically compresses and expands to regulate the flow of a fluid.

air chief marshal n. The second-highest officer in the Royal Air Force and certain other air forces, equivalent to a general in the army.

air commodore n. A high-ranking officer in the Royal Air Force and certain other air forces, equivalent to a brigadier in the army.

air-con·di·tion (áir-kən-dish'n, -dish'n ‖ -kon-) tr.v. **-tioned, -tioning, -tions.** To provide with or ventilate by air conditioning. —**air-con·di·tioned** adj.

air conditioning n. **1.** A system or apparatus for controlling, especially lowering, the temperature and humidity of a building or vehicle. **2.** The state or condition so produced. —**air conditioner** n.

air-cool (áir-kōol) tr.v. **-cooled, -cooling, -cools.** To cool (an engine, for example) by a flow of air.

air corridor n. An air route established by international agreement, along which aircraft are allowed to fly.

air cover n. **1.** Protection for ground operations provided by military aircraft. **2.** The aircraft so employed.

air·craft (áir-kraaft ‖ -kraft) n., pl. **aircraft.** Any machine or device, such as an aeroplane, helicopter, glider, or balloon, capable of flight in the air or, by means of buoyancy or aerodynamic forces.

aircraft carrier n. A large naval ship designed as a mobile air base at sea, having a long flat deck to serve as a landing strip.

air·craft·man (áir-kraaft-mən ‖ -kraft-, -mən) n., pl. **-men** (-mən,

-men). *Abbr.* **A.C.** A serviceman of the lowest rank in the Royal Air Force.

air·craft·wom·an (áir-kraaft-woŏmən ‖ -kraft-) *n., pl.* **-women** (-wimmin). *Abbr.* **A.C.W.** A servicewoman of the lowest rank in the Women's Royal Air Force.

air cushion *n.* **1.** An inflatable cushion. **2.** The downward flow of air that lifts and supports a hovercraft. **3.** An **air spring** (see).

air-cush·ion vehicle (áir-koŏsh'n) *n. Abbr.* **A.C.V.** A vehicle supported by a cushion of air, **a hovercraft** (see).

air door *n.* A strong current of warm air directed upwards and used instead of a conventional door, as to prevent heat loss from a building. Also called "air curtain".

air-drop (áir-drop) *n.* A delivery, as of supplies or troops, by parachute from aircraft in flight.

~*tr.v.* **airdropped, -dropping, -drops.** To drop (supplies or troops, for example) from an aircraft.

air-dry (áir-drī) *tr.v.* **-dried, -drying, -dries.** To dry by exposure to the air.

~*adj.* Sufficiently dry so that further exposure to air will not evaporate moisture.

Aire·dale (áir-dayl) *n.* A large terrier of a breed developed in England, having a wiry tan coat marked with black. Also called "Airedale terrier". [After *Airedale,* in Yorkshire Dales.]

air embolism *n. Pathology.* Obstruction of blood flow from the heart by the presence of air in the circulation, resulting from surgery, injury, or the like.

air·field (áir-feeld) *n.* An area with hard-surfaced runways where aircraft can take off and land, but usually smaller than an airport and without its facilities for travellers. Also called "aerodrome".

air·flow (áir-flō) *n.* The air currents caused by the motion of an object such as an aeroplane or motor vehicle.

air·foil (áir-foyl) *U.S.* An **aerofoil** (see).

air force *n. Abbr.* **AF, A.F.** The aviation branch of a country's armed forces, such as the Royal Air Force.

air·frame (áir-fraym) *n.* An aircraft body excluding its engine.

air freight *n.* **1.** A system of transporting freight by air. **2.** The amount charged for this service. **—air-freight** *tr.v.*

air gas *n.* A manufactured fuel gas, **producer gas** (see).

air·glow (áir-glō) *n.* A faint photochemical light in the upper atmosphere, observable in regions of low and middle latitude. Compare **aurora.**

air gun *n.* A gun discharged by compressed air.

air·head (áir-hed) *n. Chiefly U.S. Informal.* A silly fool.

air hole *n.* **1.** A hole or opening through which gas or air may pass. **2.** An opening in the frozen surface of a body of water. **3.** *Aeronautics.* An **air pocket** (see).

air hostess *n.* A stewardess on an aircraft.

air·i·ly (áir-əli, -ili) *adv.* **1.** In a light spirit; gaily; jauntily. **2.** In a light manner; delicately; gently.

air·i·ness (áir-i-nəss, -niss) *n.* **1.** The quality or state of being light or airy. **2.** Delicacy. **3.** Gaiety; jauntiness.

air·ing (áir-ing) *n.* **1.** Exposure to fresh or warm air for ventilation or drying. **2.** The circulation or public utterance of ideas, opinions, or the like: *to give the subject an airing.*

airing cupboard *n.* A heated cupboard in a house, used to make household linen or clothing completely dry and aired.

air jacket *n.* A container surrounding a piece of equipment or apparatus, filled with air to maintain the apparatus at a constant temperature.

air lane *n.* A regular route of travel for aircraft; an airway.

air layering *n.* A method of plant propagation in which a twig or shoot attached to the parent plant is wrapped in moist sphagnum moss or polythene so that it will form roots and can later be removed and replanted.

air·less (áir-ləss, -liss) *adj.* **1.** Without air. **2.** Lacking fresh air; stuffy. **3.** Without a breeze or wind; still. **—air·less·ness** *n.*

air letter *n.* An **aerogramme** (see).

air·lift (áir-lift) *n.* An operation by which passengers, troops, or supplies are transported by air when surface routes are blocked.

~ *tr.v.* **airlifted, -lifting, -lifts.** To transport by airlift.

air line *n.* A flexible pipe carrying compressed air, as used in garages to fill pneumatic tyres.

air·line (áir-līn) *n.* **1.** A system for the scheduled transport of passengers and freight by air. **2.** A business organisation providing such a system of air transport. **3.** An air route. **4.** *Chiefly U.S.* The shortest distance between two geographical points; a direct line; a beeline.

air·lin·er (áir-līnər) *n.* A large passenger aeroplane.

air lock *n.* **1.** An airtight chamber, usually located between two regions of unequal pressure, in which air pressure can be regulated so as to allow access or communication between the regions while maintaining their pressure difference. **2.** A bubble or pocket of air or vapour, as in a pipe, that stops the normal flow of fluid through the conducting panel.

air mail, air·mail (áir-mayl) *n.* **1.** The system of conveying mail by aircraft. **2.** Mail conveyed by aircraft. **—air-mail** *adj.*

air-mail *tr.v.* **-mailed, -mailing, -mails.** To send (a letter, for example) by air mail.

air·man (áir-mən ‖ -man) *n., pl.* **-men** (-mən, -men). A pilot, navigator, or member of any technical profession dealing primarily with aircraft, especially one serving in an air force.

air marshal *n.* **1.** A high-ranking officer in the Royal Air Force and certain other air forces, equivalent to a lieutenant-general in the

army. **2.** The highest-ranking officer in the Royal Australian Air Force.

air mass *n. Meteorology.* A large body of air with only small horizontal variations of temperature, pressure, and moisture content.

air mile *n.* A unit of distance in air navigation. See **nautical mile.**

air miss *n.* A near-collision between aircraft in flight. [AIR + (near) MISS.]

air piracy *n.* The hijacking of an aeroplane in flight. **—air pirate** *n.*

air·plane (áir-playn) *n. U.S.* An **aeroplane** (see).

air plant *n. Botany.* An **epiphyte** (see).

air pocket *n.* A downward air current that causes an aircraft to lose altitude abruptly. Also called "air hole".

air·port (áir-port ‖ -pōrt) *n.* A tract of levelled land where aircraft can take off and land, especially one equipped with hard-surfaced landing strips, a control tower, hangars, facilities for passengers and cargo, and usually a customs house.

air pump *n.* A piece of equipment for compressing, removing, or forcing a flow of air.

air raid *n.* An attack by hostile military aircraft, especially when armed with bombs. **—air-raid** (áir-rayd) *adj.*

air rifle *n.* A low-powered rifle using manually compressed air to fire small pellets.

air sac *n. Biology.* An air-filled space, such as one of the spaces in a bird's body that forms a connection between the lungs and the bone cavities, or a dilation in the trachea of many insects.

air scoop *n.* An air inlet on an aircraft, designed to take in air for ventilation or pressure.

air·screw (áir-skroō) *n. British.* The propeller of an aeroplane.

air-sea rescue (áir-see) *n.* A rescue at sea, carried out by aircraft.

air·ship (áir-ship) *n.* A self-propelled lighter-than-air craft with directional control surfaces; a dirigible.

air·sick·ness (áir-sik-nəss, -niss) *n.* Nausea resulting from nervous tension or changes in pressure or motion in an aircraft. **—air·sick** *adj.*

air sock *n.* A **windsock** (see).

air·space (áir-spayss) *n.* The portion of the atmosphere above a particular land area; especially, the air above a nation or other political subdivision that is considered to be under its jurisdiction.

air speed *n.* Speed, especially of an aircraft, relative to the air.

air spray *n.* **1.** A device for spraying liquids using compressed air; an aerosol. **2.** The liquid sprayed by such a device.

air spring *n.* An enclosed volume of air which, by its resilience, acts as a spring or shock absorber. Also called "air cushion".

air·stream (áir-streem) *n.* **1.** The current of air passing over a surface. **2.** A wind, especially at high altitude.

air·strip (áir-strip) *n.* A cleared area serving as an airfield.

airt (airt) *n. Scottish.* Any of the points on the compass; a direction, especially of the wind. [Middle English *art,* from Scottish Gaelic *aird,* probably from Old Irish *aird†.*]

air terminal *n.* See **terminal.**

air·tight (áir-tīt) *adj.* **1.** Impermeable to air or other gas. **2.** Having no weak points; sound: *an airtight excuse.*

air time *n.* **1.** The period of time during which a radio or television station broadcasts. **2.** An amount of broadcasting time allocated or available for a particular purpose.

air-to-air missile (áir-too-áir ‖ -tə-) *n.* A missile, usually guided, designed to be fired from aircraft at aircraft.

air-to-surface missile (áir-tə-súrfiss) *n.* A missile, usually guided, designed to be fired from aircraft at targets on the ground. Also called "air-to-ground missile".

air-traf·fic control (áir-tráffik) *n.* **1.** A system of directing aircraft movements in which the required speed, direction, and altitude of each aircraft in a given area is communicated by radio to its pilot. **2.** The people operating this system. **—air-traf·fic controller** *n.*

air vice-marshal *n.* **1.** A high-ranking officer in the Royal Air Force and certain other air forces, equivalent to a major-general in the army. **2.** An officer in the Royal Australian Air Force of the highest rank but one.

air·waves (áir-wayvz) *pl.n.* The medium used for the transmission of radio and television signals: *a new programme coming to you over the airwaves.*

air·way (áir-way) *n.* **1.** A passageway for a current of air, as to the lungs or to a mine. **2.** A designated route of passage for an aircraft; an air lane.

air·wom·an (áir-woŏmən) *n., pl.* **-women** (-wimmin). A female airman.

air·wor·thy (áir-wurthi) *adj.* Prepared and in fit condition to fly. Said of aircraft. **—air·wor·thi·ness** *n.*

air·y (áir-i) *adj.* **-ier, -iest.** **1.** Having the constitution or nature of air. **2.** High in the air; lofty; towering. **3. a.** Open to the air; breezy; full of fresh air. **b.** Spacious; uncluttered. **4.** Resembling air; immaterial: *an airy apparition.* **5.** Insubstantial; irrational; unrealistic: *airy political views.* **6.** Light as air; graceful or delicate: *an airy veil.* **7.** *Informal.* Nonchalant or breezy in manner.

air·y-fair·y (áir-i-fáir-i) *adj.* **1.** Extremely light and delicate; insubstantial. **2.** *Informal.* Unrealistic; fanciful: *airy-fairy notions.*

Aisha. See **Ayesha.**

aisle (īl) *n.* **1.** A part of a church divided laterally from the nave by a row of pillars or columns. **2.** A passageway between rows of seats, such as in a church or auditorium. *Informal.* **rolling in the aisles.** Overwhelmed by laughter. [Middle English *eile* (influenced by *ile, isle,* ISLE), from Old French *ele, aile,* wing of a building, from Latin *āla,* wing.]

ait. Variant of **eyot.**

aitch (aych) *n.* The letter *h.* [Obsolete *ache,* from French *hache,* probably from Vulgar Latin *hacca†* (unattested), of obscure origin.]

aitch·bone (áych-bōn) *n.* **1.** The rump bone in cattle. **2.** The cut of meat containing this bone. [Middle English *hachboon,* from phrase *an hach boon,* originally *a nachebon* : *nache, nage,* buttock, from Old French, from Late Latin *natica,* from Latin *natis,* buttock + *bon,* BONE.]

Aix-en-Pro·vence (éks-ON-pro-vónss, áyks-). City and spa in Bouches-du-Rhône département, southeast France. It has been the capital of Provence since the 12th century and is an important cultural centre.

Aix-la-Chapelle. See **Aachen.**

A·jan·ta (ə-júntə). Village in Maharashtra state, west central India. The famous Ajanta caves, cut into the side of a steep gorge, contain splendid examples of Buddhist sculptures and wall paintings dating from *c.* 200 B.C. to A.D. 650.

a·jar¹ (ə-jár) *adv.* Partially opened. Said of doors and windows. [Middle English *on char,* "in the act of turning" : ON + *char,* a turn, Old English *cierr* (see **char**).] —**a·jar** *adj.*

ajar² *adv.* Not harmonious; jarring: *ajar with the times.* [A- (on, in the act of) + JAR (discord).] —**a·jar** *adj.*

A·jax¹ (áyjaks). *Greek Mythology.* A Greek warrior of great stature and prowess who fought against Troy; son of Telamon of Salamis.

Ajax². *Greek Mythology.* A Greek warrior of small stature and arrogant character who fought against Troy; son of Ileus of Locris.

AK 47 *n.* A type of rifle, a **Kalashnikov** *(see).*

a.k.a. also known as.

Ak·bar (ák-baar, úk-, -bər), known as the Great (1542–1605). The greatest of India's Mogul emperors, who reigned from 1556. His conquests added most of northern India to the Mogul Empire.

ak·ee, ack·ee (ácki) *n.* **1.** A tropical tree, *Blighia sapida,* native to Africa and cultivated in the West Indies, having fragrant flowers and capsules containing black seeds. **2.** The edible aril surrounding these seeds, used in tropical cooking. [Native name in Liberia.]

A·ke·la (ə-káylə) *n. British.* The adult organiser of a pack of Cub Scouts. [After *Akela,* the leader of a wolf-pack in Kipling's *The Jungle Book* (1894–95).]

Akhaïa. See **Achaea.**

A·khe·na·ton (áckə-náa-t'n, -ton). Also **Ikh·na·ton** (died *c.* 1360 B.C.). King of Egypt, who reigned from *c.* 1379–*c.* 1360 B.C. Originally named Amenhotep IV, he changed his name on rejecting the old gods and initiating the worship of the sun-god, Aton. He built a new capital at Tell-el-Amarna. Married to Nefertiti.

Akh·ma·to·va (akh-mát-əvə, aakh-, -máat-), **Anna,** pen name of Anna Andreevna Gorenko (1889–1966). Russian poet. Her intense and lyrical poems, often dealing with tragic love, have established her as one of the foremost 20th-century Russian poets.

a·kim·bo (ə-kímbō) *adj.* With the hands on the hips and the elbows bowed outwards. Used chiefly in the phrase *with arms akimbo.* [Middle English *in kenebowe,* "in keen bow", "in a sharp curve", probably from Old Norse *i keng boginn* (unattested), "bent like a bow" : *keng,* accusative of *kengr†,* a curve, hook + *boginn,* accusative of *bogi,* a bow.] —**a·kim·bo** *adv.*

a·kin (ə-kín) *adj.* **1.** Of the same kin; related. **2.** Having a similar quality or character; analogous. Often used with *to.* **3.** *Linguistics.* Related in origin; cognate. Said of languages or of words in different languages derived from the same root. [A- (of) + KIN.]

Akka. See **Acre.**

Ak·kad or **Ac·cad** (áckad ‖ *U.S. also* áakaad). Ancient region of central Mesopotamia, now in Iraq. The Akkadian empire flourished from *c.* 2340 B.C. to *c.* 2240 B.C., especially under Sargon, who ruled from his capital of Agade (or Akkad).

Ak·ka·di·an, Ac·ca·di·an (ə-káddi-ən, -káydi-) *n.* **1.** A native or inhabitant of Akkad. **2.** The Semitic language spoken in ancient Akkad.
~*adj.* Of, pertaining to, or relating to the Akkadians or their Semitic language.

Akko. See **Acre.**

Ak·mo·la (áck-mōlə). See **Astana.**

Ak·ron (áckrən). City in northeastern Ohio. It became known as the rubber capital of the world in the early 20th century.

Ak·sum or **Ax·um** (áksōōm). Town in northern Ethiopia that was the centre of the North Ethiopian empire from the first to the eighth centuries A.D. Its kings were converted to Christianity in the fourth century. According to tradition, the Arc of the Covenant was brought there from Jerusalem and placed in the Church of St. Mary of Zion, where the emperors of Ethiopia were crowned.

-al¹ *adj. suffix.* Indicates a relation to or connection with; for example, **adjectival.** [Middle English *-al, -el,* from Old French, from Latin *-ālis.*]

-al² *n. suffix.* Indicates the act or process of doing or experiencing the action specified; for example, **denial, arrival.** [Middle English *-aille,* from Old French, from Latin *-ālia,* substantive neuter plural of *-ālis,* adjectival suffix.]

-al³ *n. & adj. suffix. Chemistry.* Indicates an aldehyde, an organic compound; for example, **ethanal, butanal.** [*Al*dehyde.]

Al The symbol for the element aluminium.

al. alcohol; alcoholic.

à la (áa-laa, á-, -lə) *prep.* Also **a la.** In the style or manner of; in accordance with: *mushrooms à la grecque; a poem à la Ogden Nash.* [French, short for *à la mode de,* "in the manner of".]

a·la (áylə) *n., pl.* **alae** (áylee). *Biology.* A winglike structure or part,

such as the flattened part of certain bones, the membranous border of some seeds, or one of the side petals of certain flowers, such as the sweet pea. [Latin *āla,* wing]

a.l.a. all letters answered.

Al·a·bam·a (ál-ə-bámmə). State in the southeastern United States. It was admitted as the 22nd state in 1819. Montgomery is the capital and Birmingham the largest city. Alabama is still a major cotton-growing state, but since World War II mining and manufacturing have expanded to account for the largest share of the state's income. Products include coal, oil, steel, chemicals, and textiles. Alabama was the centre of much of the black civil rights movement in the 1960s. —**Al·a·bam·an** (ál-ə-bámmən) *adj. & n.*

al·a·bas·ter (ál-ə-baass-tər, -bass-) *n.* **1.** A dense, translucent, white or tinted, fine-grained gypsum, often used in sculpture. **2.** A variety of hard calcite, translucent and sometimes banded. **3.** Pale yellowish pink to yellowish grey.
~*adj.* Also **al·a·bas·trine** (-trin, -treen). Of or similar to alabaster; smooth and white. [Middle English *alabastre,* from Old French, from Latin *alabaster,* from Greek *alabast(r)os,* perhaps of Egyptian origin.]

à la carte (áa-laa-kárt, á-, -lə) *adj.* Having a separate price for each item. Said of a menu or part of a menu. Compare **prix fixe, table d'hôte.** [French, "by the menu".] —**à la carte** *adv.*

a·lack (ə-lák) *interj.* Also **a·lack·a·day.** *Archaic.* Used to express sorrow, regret, or alarm. [Middle English *alacke,* "ah, (what) loss!" : probably *a, ah,* AH + LACK, by analogy with *alas.*]

a·lac·ri·ty (ə-láckrə-ti) *n.* **1.** Cheerful willingness; eagerness; eager promptness. **2.** Lively action; sprightliness. [Latin *alacritās,* from *alacer* (stem *alacr-*), lively, eager.] —**a·lac·ri·tous** (-təss) *adj.*

A·lad·din (ə-láddin ‖ ə-ládd'n). In the *Arabian Nights,* a boy who acquires a magic lamp and a magic ring with which he can summon two genies to fulfil any desire.

A·lain-Four·ni·er (a-laN-foorn-yáy), pen name of Henri-Alban Fournier (1886–1914). French novelist. He is principally remembered for his novel *Le Grand Meaulnes* (1913), translated into English as *The Lost Domain.* He was killed in battle in World War I.

à la king *adj.* Prepared in a cream sauce with green peppers and mushrooms: *chicken à la king.*

Alamannian, Alamannic. Variants of **Alemannic.**

Alamein. See **El Alamein.**

Al·a·mo (ál-ə-mō). A chapel built in 1744 as part of the Mission of San Antonio de Valero, at San Antonio, Texas. During the Texas Revolution against Mexican rule, some 182 revolutionaries were besieged there from February 24 to March 6, 1836, by General Santa Anna and an army of thousands. All the insurgents, including Davy Crockett, William B. Travis, and James Bowie, were killed.

à la mode *adj.* **1.** According to or in style or fashion; fashionable. **2. a.** *Chiefly U.S.* Served with ice cream. **b.** Braised with vegetables and served in a rich, brown sauce. [French, "in the fashion".]

a·la·mode (ál-ə-mōd, áalə-) *n.* A lustrous plain-weave silk fabric, used especially for head coverings and scarfs. [From À LA MODE.]

Al·a·mo·gor·do (ál-əmo-górdō). A town in southern New Mexico. The first atomic bomb was exploded at the White Sands Missile Range, 97 kilometres (60 miles) northwest of the city, in a test on July 16, 1945.

Al·an·brooke (ál-ən-brŏōk), **Alan Francis Brooke, 1st Viscount** (1883–1963). British field marshal. During World War II he was commander in chief of the home forces from 1940 to 1941 and chief of the Imperial General Staff from 1941 to 1946.

Åland Islands. See **Ahvenanmaa.**

al·a·nine (ál-ə-neen) *n.* An amino acid, $CH_3CH(NH_2)COOH$, a constituent of most protein. [German *Alanin* : AL(DEHYDE) + *-an-* (euphonic infix) + -IN(E).]

a·lar (áylər) *adj.* **1.** Of, pertaining to, or having wings or alae. **2.** Shaped like or resembling a wing. **3.** *Anatomy.* Pertaining to the armpit; axillary. [Latin *ālāris,* from *āla,* wing.]

Al·a·ric (ál-ərik) (*c.* 370–410). King of the Visigoths. In 395 he invaded and plundered Greece, and from 400 onwards he attacked Italy, capturing Rome in 410.

a·larm (ə-lárm) *n.* **1.** A sudden fear caused by an awareness of danger; fright. **2.** A warning of approaching or existing danger. **3.** An electrical or mechanical device that serves to warn of danger, fire, or the like by means of a sound or signal. **4. a.** The sounding mechanism of an alarm clock. **b.** An alarm clock. **5.** *Archaic.* A call to arms. **6.** In fencing, a stamp on the ground with the advancing foot. —See Synonyms at **fear.**
~*tr.v.* **alarmed, alarming, alarms. 1.** To fill with alarm or apprehension. **2.** To warn of approaching or existing danger. —See Synonyms at **frighten.** [Middle English *alarme,* from Old French, from Old Italian *allarme,* from *all'arme,* "to arms!" : *alla,* to, from Latin *ad illam,* to that, from *ille,* that + *arme,* arms, from Latin *arma.*] —**a·larm·a·ble** *adj.* —**a·larm·ing·ly** *adv.*

alarm bird *n.* Any of various Australian birds, such as the kookaburra, having a characteristic loud cry.

alarm clock *n.* A clock that can be set to sound a bell or buzzer at any desired hour, especially to wake a person up.

a·larm·ist (ə-lárm-ist) *n.* A person who needlessly alarms or attempts to alarm himself or others, as by inventing or spreading frightening rumours and prophesying political or social calamities. —**a·larm·ism** *n.* —**a·larm·ist** *adj.*

a·lar·um (aə-láar-əm, -laír-, -lárrəm) *n. Archaic.* **1.** An alarm, especially a call to arms. **2.** A clamorous confusion onstage, especially in Elizabethan drama. Used chiefly in the phrase *alarums and excursions*. [Middle English *alarom, alarme*, ALARM.]

a·la·ry (áyləri) *adj.* **1.** Of or pertaining to wings. **2.** Resembling a wing; wing-shaped. [Latin *ālārius*, from *āla*, wing.]

a·las (ə-láss, ə-láass) *interj.* An exclamation expressing regret, grief, compassion, or alarm. [Middle English, from Old French : *a*, AH + *las*, wretched, from Latin *lassus*, weary.]

A·las·ka (ə-láskə). Largest state in the United States, situated in the extreme northwest of North America, and separated from the rest of the country by Canada. It has a total area of 1 530 694 square kilometres (591,004 square miles), but is sparsely populated. It was admitted as the 49th state in 1959. Alaska is mostly mountainous, and much of it is frozen all the year. Gold was once mined extensively, but platinum and coal mining are now more important. Mining, together with oil and natural gas, are the most valuable industries. Fishing and timber are also important. —**A·las·kan** (ə-láskən) *adj. & n.*

Alaskan malamute *n.* A dog, the **malamute** *(see).*

a·las·tor (ə-lástawr) *n. Often capital* **A.** An avenging deity or spirit,

frequently evoked in the tragedies written for the classic Greek theatre; a masculine personification of Nemesis. [Greek *alastōr*, "unforgetting one", from *alastos*, unforgettable : *a*-, not + *lathein*, *lanthanesthai* (stem *las*-), to forget.]

a·late (áylayt) *adj.* Also **a·lat·ed** (áylaytid). *Biology.* Having thin, winglike extensions or parts; winged. [Latin *ālātus*, from *āla*, wing.]

Al-Ayzanyah. See **Bethany.**

alb (alb) *n.* A long white linen robe with tapered sleeves worn by a priest, especially during Mass. [Middle English *albe, aube*, Old English *albe*, from Medieval Latin *(vestis) alba*, "white (garment)", from Latin *albus*, white.]

Alb. Albania; Albanian.

Al·ba·ce·te (álbə-tháyti). Province of southeastern central Spain. The provincial capital, Albacete, was the site of battles between Moors and Christians in 1145 and 1146.

al·ba·core (álbə-kawr ‖ -kōr) *n., pl.* **-cores** or collectively **albacore**. A large marine fish, *Thunnus alalunga*, of warm seas, having edible flesh that is a major source of tinned tuna. [Portuguese *albacor*, from Arabic *al-bakrah* : *al*, the + *bakr*, young camel.]

Al·ban (áwl-bən ‖ ól-, ál-), **Saint** (*c.* 300). First Christian martyr in Britain. A soldier in the Roman army in Britain, he was executed for having given shelter to a Christian priest, who converted him to Christianity. In 793 an abbey was founded on the site of his martyrdom, and the town of St. Albans in Hertfordshire subsequently grew around it.

Al·ba·ni·a, Republic of (al-báyn-i-ə, awl-, -yə), *Albanian* **Shqi·pë·ri** (shkípə-rée). Country lying on the Adriatic Sea. Most of the country is either mountainous or swampy. It is fast developing its rich mineral resources, hydroelectric potential, and manufacturing, but farming remains the major occupation. After more than four centuries of Turkish rule, Albania proclaimed its independence in 1912, and that independence was guaranteed by the Allied powers after World War I. The country became a republic in 1925. In 1944 the Communist party gained control, and Albania became a satellite of the U.S.S.R. It declared itself the first atheist state, abolishing all public worship in 1967. In 1961 it broke with the Soviets and in 1968 withdrew from the Warsaw Pact after the Soviet intervention in Czechoslovakia. Between 1961 and 1976, its closest links were with China. In 1990 widespread pro-democracy demonstrations led to major reforms, and free elections, held in 1992, brought defeat for the Communists. Area, 28 748 square kilometres (11,097 square miles). Population, 3,670,000. Capital, Tirana.

Al·ba·ni·an (al-báyn-yən ‖ awl-) *adj. Abbr.* **Alb.** Of or pertaining to Albania, its inhabitants, or its language.

~ *n.* **1.** A native or inhabitant of Albania. **2.** The Indo-European language of Albania.

Al·ba·ny (áwl-bəni ‖ ól-). City in upper New York state that since 1797 has been the state capital.

al·ba·ta (al-báytə) *n.* A metallic alloy, **nickel silver** *(see).* [Latin *albata*, "clothed in white", from *albus*, white.]

al·ba·tross (álbə-tross ‖ -trawss) *n., pl.* **-trosses** or collectively **albatross**. **1.** Any of various large, web-footed birds of the family Diomedeidae, chiefly of the oceans of the Southern Hemisphere, having a hooked beak and long, narrow wings. The wandering albatross, *Diomedea irrorata*, has the largest wingspan of any bird. **2.** An obvious handicap, constant burden, or heavy cross to bear. **3.** In golf, a score at a hole of three strokes below par. [Alteration (influenced by Latin *albus*, white) of Portuguese *alcatraz*, pelican, from Arabic *al-ghaṭṭās* : *al*, the + *ghaṭṭās*, white-tailed sea eagle. Sense 2 is a reference to S.T. Coleridge's Ancient Mariner, who sinned by killing an albatross and who had to wear it around his neck in penance.]

al·be·do (al-béedō) *n., pl.* **-dos**. The fraction of incident electromagnetic radiation reflected by a surface. [Late Latin *albēdo*, whiteness, from Latin *albus*, white.]

Al·bee (ál-bee, áwl-), **Edward (Franklin)** (1928–). U.S. playwright. His *Who's Afraid of Virginia Woolf?* (1962) is a savage and comic play about a domestic power struggle. He won Pulitzer prizes for *A Delicate Balance* (1967), *Seascape* (1975), and *Three Tall Women* (1991).

al·be·it (awl-bée-it ‖ al-) *conj.* Although; even though; notwithstanding. [Middle English *al be it*, "let it be entirely (that)" : *al*, ALL + *be*, subjunctive of *been*, to BE + IT.]

Al·bé·niz (al-báynith), **Isaac Manuel Francisco** (1860–1909). Spanish composer and concert pianist. He used traditional folk songs, and is known for his piano music, especially *Iberia*.

Al·bert I (ál-bərt; *French* al-báir) (1875–1934). King of the Belgians (1909–34). During World War I he was commander in chief of the Belgian army and he led the Belgian and French forces that reconquered Belgium in 1918.

Albert, Lake. Shallow body of water 160 kilometres (100 miles) long and 30 kilometres (18 miles) wide, lying above sea level in the Great Rift Valley on the border between Uganda and the Democratic Republic of the Congo. Its high salinity is caused by rapid evaporation.

Albert, Prince (1819–1861). Prince Consort and husband of Queen Victoria. He was a strong influence on the queen and an active patron of the arts, sciences, and industry, sponsoring the Great Exhibition of 1851.

Al·ber·ta (al-bértə). Province in western Canada. The capital and largest city is Edmonton. Wheat and cattle-farming were the basis of the province's economy until the discovery of petroleum and natural gas in the early 1960s. —**Al·ber·tan** (-tən) *adj. & n.*

Al·ber·ti (al-báir-ti), **Leon Battista** (1404–72). Italian Renaissance architect. Among his buildings are the churches of Santa Maria Novella in Florence (built 1446–51) and Sant' Andrea in Mantua (1472–94).

al·bes·cent (al-béss'nt) *adj.* Becoming white or moderately white; whitish. [Latin *albescēns* (stem *albescent*-), from *albescere*, to become white, from *albus*, white.]

Al·bi (ál-bi, áwl-). Capital of the Tarn *département* in the Languedoc region of southern France, on the river Tarn. It was the centre of the Albigensian heresy in the 12th and 13th centuries.

Al·bi·gen·ses (álbi-jénsseez) *pl.n.* The members of a Catharist religious sect that flourished in southern France in the 12th and 13th centuries, and was eradicated by the Inquisition under Pope Innocent III, following the Albigensian Crusade. See **Catharism**. [Medieval Latin, inhabitants of *Albiga*, ALBI (where the sect was dominant).] —**Al·bi·gen·si·an** (-jénssi-ən, -jénsh'n) *adj.* —**Al·bi·gen·si·an·ism** *n.*

al·bin·ism (álbiniz'm) *n.* **1.** Absence of normal pigmentation in a person, animal, or plant. **2.** The state or condition of being an albino. [French *albinisme*, from German *Albinismus*, from ALBINO.] —**al·bin·ic** (al-bínnik), **al·bin·is·tic** (álbi-nístik) *adj.*

al·bi·no (al-béenō ‖ *U.S.* -bínō) *n., pl.* **-nos**. An organism lacking normal pigmentation; especially, a person having abnormally pale skin and very light hair, and lacking normal eye colouring, or an animal, such as a rabbit, having white hair or fur and red eyes. [Portuguese, from *albo,* white, from Latin *albus* (originally applied to black Africans having albinism).]

Al·bi·no·ni (albi-nōni), **Tomaso** (1671–1750). Italian violinist and composer, court musician to the Duke of Mantua. He wrote about 50 operas and was the first composer to write concertos for solo violin.

Al·bi·on (álbi-ən) *Archaic or Literary.* England or Great Britain. [Latin *Albiōn,* from Celtic *alb-* (unattested), high. See also **Alps.**]

al·bite (ál-bīt) *n.* A widely distributed white feldspar, $NaAlSi_3O_8$, one of the common rock-forming plagioclase group. [Swedish *albit,* from Latin *albus,* white.] **—al·bit·ic** (-bíttik), **al·bit·i·cal** (-bíttik'l) *adj.*

Al·borg, Aal·borg (áwl-bawrg). City and port in northern Jutland, Denmark, situated on the Lim Fjord.

al·bum (ál-bəm) *n.* **1.** A book or binder with blank pages for the insertion and preservation of stamps, photographs, keepsakes, autographs, or the like. **2. a.** A long-playing gramophone record, usually of popular music. **b.** A set of gramophone records stored together in sleeves in one booklike holder. **3.** A printed collection of miscellaneous musical compositions. **4.** A tall, handsomely printed book, especially popular in the 19th century, often having a profusion of illustrations and short, sentimental texts. [Latin, blank tablet, neuter of *albus,* white.]

al·bu·men (ál-bew-min, -men, -mən, al-béw-) *n.* **1.** The white of an egg, consisting of a mixture of proteins (albumins). **2.** The material stored in a plant seed; the endosperm. **3.** Variant of **albumin.** [Latin *albūmen,* from *albus,* white.]

al·bu·min, al·bu·men (ál-bew-min, al-béw-) *n.* Any of several simple, water-soluble proteins that are coagulated by heat and are found in egg white, blood serum, milk, various animal tissues, and many plant juices and tissues. [ALBUM(EN) + -IN.]

al·bu·mi·noid (al-béwmin-oyd) *adj.* Also **al·bu·mi·noi·dal** (-óyd'l) Resembling albumin.
~*n. Biochemistry.* **Scleroprotein** *(see).*

al·bu·mi·nous (al-béwminəss) *adj.* Of, like, or containing albumin.

al·bu·mi·nu·ri·a (al-béwmi-néwri-ə, álbewmi- || -noŏr-i-ə) *n.* The presence of albumin and other serum proteins in the urine, sometimes indicative of kidney disease. Also called "proteinuria". [ALBUMIN + -URIA.] **—al·bu·mi·nu·ric** *adj.*

al·bu·mose (álbew-mōss, -mōz) *n. U.S. Biochemistry.* **Proteose** *(see).* [French : *album(ine),* ALBUM(IN) + -OSE.]

Al·bu·quer·que (ál-bə-kerki). A town in the United States, on the upper Rio Grande. It is the largest city in New Mexico.

al·bur·num (al-búrnəm) *n. Botany.* **Sapwood** *(see).* [Latin, from *albus,* white.]

alc. alcohol; alcoholic.

Al·ca·ic (al-káy-ik) *adj.* Of or designating a verse form used in Greek and Latin poetry, consisting of strophes having four lines each containing four feet.
~*n. Often plural.* Verse composed in Alcaic strophes. [Late Latin *Alcaicus,* from Greek *Alkaïkos,* "of Alcaeus" *(fl.* 600 B.C.), Greek lyric poet.]

al·cai·de, al·cay·de (al-káyd, -kīdi) *n.* In former times, the commander or governor of a fortress in Spain, Portugal, or Latin America. [Spanish, from Arabic *al-qā'id,* the commander, from *qād,* to command.]

al·cal·de (al-kál-di, -kaál-) *n.* The mayor or chief judicial official of a Spanish or Latin-American town. [Spanish, from Arabic *al-qāḍī* : *al,* the + *qāḍī,* judge, from *qaḍā,* to judge.]

Al·ca·traz (ál-kə-traz). A rocky island in San Francisco Bay, California. The island served as a federal prison until 1963.

al·caz·ar (ál-kə-zár || *U.S. also* al-kázzər, -kázər) *n.* A Spanish palace or fortress, originally one built by the Moors. [Spanish *alcázar,* from Arabic *al-qaṣr* : *al,* the + *qaṣr,* castle, from Latin *castra,* fort, plural of *castrum,* camp.]

Al·cá·zar de San Juan (ál-kə-zár; *Spanish* al-káthaar). Town of Roman origin in the Ciudad Real province of Spain. It was the centre of the order of San Juan from the 14th to the 16th century.

Al·ces·tis (al-séstiss). In Greek legend, the wife of King Admetus of Thessaly. She agreed to die in place of her husband, and was later rescued from Hades by Hercules.

al·che·mise, al·che·mize (ál-kə-mīz) *tr.v.* **-mised, -mising, -mises.** To transform by or as if by alchemy; transmute.

al·che·mist (ál-kə-mist) *n.* A practitioner of alchemy. **—al·che·mis·tic** (-místik), **al·che·mis·ti·cal** (-místik'l) *adj.*

al·che·my (ál-kəmi) *n.* **1.** In medieval Europe, a philosophy and branch of science that sought to find a way of turning base metals into gold, a universal cure, and the elixir of life. **2.** Any seemingly magical power or process of transmuting. **—See Synonyms at magic.** [Middle English, from Old French *alquemie,* from Medieval Latin *alchymia,* from Arabic *al-kīmiyā',* "the art of transmutation" : *al,* the + *kīmiyā',* from Greek *khēm(e)ia,* "art of transmutation (of metals)".] **—al·chem·i·cal** (al-kémmik'l), **al·chem·ic** (al-kémmik) *adj.* **—al·chem·i·cal·ly** *adv.*

al·che·rin·ga (álchə-ríng-gə) *n.* Also **al·che·ra** (-rə). In Australian Aboriginal mythology, the **Dreamtime** *(see).* [Native Australian.]

Al·ci·bi·a·des (ál-si-bí-ədeez) *(c.* 450–404 B.C.). Athenian general and politician. He was brought up by his uncle, Pericles, and became a protégé of Socrates. His brilliant political career foundered during the Peloponnesian War against Sparta (431–404 B.C.), when he commanded a disastrous military attack on Syracuse in 415.

Alc·me·ne (alk-méeni). *Greek Mythology.* Amphitryon's wife, who gave birth to Hercules after being seduced by Zeus.

Al·cock (áwl-kok, ál-, ól-), **Sir John William** (1892–1919). British aviator. On June 14, 1919, together with (Sir) Arthur Whitten Brown (1886–1948), he made the first nonstop flight across the Atlantic Ocean. They flew from Newfoundland to Ireland in a Vickers-Vimy bomber, taking 16 hours 27 minutes.

al·co·hol (ál-kə-hol || -hōl) *n.* **1.** *Abbr.* **al., alc.** A colourless volatile flammable liquid, C_2H_5OH, synthesised or obtained by fermentation of sugars and starches, and widely used, either pure or denatured, as a solvent or in drugs, cleaning solutions, explosives, and intoxicating beverages. Also called "ethanol", "ethyl alcohol", "grain alcohol". **2.** Intoxicating drink containing alcohol. **3.** Any of a series of compounds that contain a hydroxyl group bound to a hydrocarbon group. Simple examples are methanol (CH_3OH) and butanol (C_4H_9OH). [New Latin *alcohol (vini),* spirit of (wine), from Medieval Latin *alcohol,* fine powder of antimony used to tint the eyelids, any powder obtained by sublimation, quintessence, from Arabic *al-koḥl, al-kuḥl* : *al,* the + *koḥl, kuḥl,* KOHL.]

al·co·hol·ic (ál-kə-hóllik) *adj. Abbr.* **al., alc. 1.** Of, pertaining to, or resulting from alcohol. **2.** Containing or preserved in alcohol. **3.** Suffering from alcoholism.
~*n.* A person who drinks habitually and to excess, and is unable to stop doing so; a sufferer from alcoholism.

al·co·hol·ic·i·ty (ál-kə-hol-íssəti) *n.* Alcoholic content.

Alcoholics Anonymous *n. Abbr.* **A.A.** A society for alcoholics who wish to cure themselves of alcoholism.

al·co·hol·ise, al·co·hol·ize (ál-kə-hol-īz) *tr.v.* **-ised, -ising, -ises.** To make alcoholic; saturate, mix, or treat with alcohol. **—al·co·hol·i·sa·tion** (-ī-záysh'n || *U.S.* -i-) *n.*

al·co·hol·ism (ál-kə-hol-iz'm) *n.* **1.** Habitual excessive consumption of alcohol. **2.** A chronic pathological condition resulting from this, chiefly affecting the nervous and gastroenteric systems and characterised by mental disturbance, muscular incoordination, and eventually cirrhosis of the liver.

al·co·hol·om·e·ter (ál-kə-hol-ómmitər) *n.* A hydrometer for determining the percentage of alcohol in liquids.

alcohol thermometer *n.* A simple glass thermometer containing alcohol coloured with a red dye, used instead of a mercury thermometer for measuring lower temperatures.

Al·co·ran, Al·ko·ran (ál-ko-ráan || -kaw-, -rán) *n.* The sacred book of the Muslims, the **Koran** *(see).*

Al·cott (áwl-kott || ól-), **Louisa May** (1832–88). U.S. novelist. Her most famous work, *Little Women* (1868–69), was a largely autobiographical account of herself and her family.

al·cove (ál-kōv) *n.* **1. a.** A recessed partly enclosed area connected to or forming part of a room. **b.** Any arched niche or recess, as in a wall. **2.** A secluded bower or similar enclosed structure in a garden. [French *alcôve,* from Spanish *alcoba,* from Arabic *al-qubbah,* "the vault".]

Al·cuin (ál-kwin), *Anglo-Saxon* Ealhwine; also known as Albinus (735–804). English scholar and theologian. In 781 he became an adviser to Charlemagne, whose court became the centre of the revival of learning and the arts that came to be known as the Carolingian Renaissance.

Al·cy·o·ne (al-sí-əni) *n.* **1.** *Astronomy.* The brightest star in the Pleiades, in the constellation Taurus. **2.** *Greek Mythology.* One of the **Pleiades** *(see).*

Ald. Alderman.

Al·dab·ra (al-dábrə). Group of four coral islands in the Indian Ocean north of Madagascar, famous for its giant tortoises and other wildlife. Formerly British, it joined the Seychelles in 1976.

Al·deb·a·ran (al-débbərən) *n.* A double star in the constellation Taurus, one of the brightest stars in the sky, 68 light-years from Earth. [Middle English, from Medieval Latin *Aldebaran,* from Arabic *al-dabarān,* "the follower (of the Pleiades)" : *al,* the + *dabarān,* following, from *dabar,* to follow.]

Alde·burgh (áwl-bərə, áwld- || ól-, óld-). Seaside town in Suffolk, eastern England. It is the site of an annual summer music festival, established by Benjamin Britten.

al·de·hyde (ál-di-hīd) *n.* **1.** Any of a class of highly reactive organic chemical compounds obtained by oxidation of primary alcohols, characterised by the common group CHO (the *aldehyde group*), and used in the manufacture of resins, dyes, and organic acids. Examples are formaldehyde (HCHO) and butanal (C_3H_7CHO). **2.** Such a compound, **acetaldehyde** *(see).* [German *Aldehyd,* from New Latin, abbreviation of *al(cohol) dehyd(rogenatum),* "dehydrogenised alcohol".]

al den·te (al dénti) *adj.* Cooked so as to be still slightly firm. Said of pasta. [Italian, "to the tooth".]

al·der (áwl-dər || ól-) *n.* **1.** Any of various deciduous shrubs or trees of the genus *Alnus,* growing in cool, moist places, and having toothed rounded leaves, woody cones, and reddish wood used in underwater construction and turnery. **2.** Any of several similar shrubs or trees. [Middle English *alder,* Old English *aler, alor;* akin to Old Norse *ölr,* Latin *alnus.*]

alder fly *n.* Any insect of the group Sialoidea, related to the lacewings, found near water and having large wings.

al·der·man (áwl-dər-mən) *n., pl.* **-men** (-mən). **1.** *Abbr.* **Ald., Aldm.** In England and Wales before 1974, a member of the higher branch of a municipal or borough council, elected by the councillors themselves. **2.** *Abbr.* **Ald., Aldm.** In many U.S. town and city governments, a member of the municipal legislative body. **3.** In Anglo-Saxon England: **a.** A high-ranking noble. **b.** The chief officer of a shire. [Middle English *alderman*, guild official, Old English *(e)aldorman*, viceroy : *(e)aldor*, chief, "elder", from *(e)ald*, old + MAN.] —**al·der·man·cy** (-si) *n.* —**al·der·man·ic** (-mánnik) *adj.*

Al·der·mas·ton (áwl-dər-maass-tən ‖ ól-, -mass-). Village near Reading, England. To the south is the United Kingdom Atomic Energy Research Establishment. The first protest march between London and Aldermaston led by the Campaign for Nuclear Disarmament took place in 1958.

Al·der·ney¹ (áwl-dərni ‖ ól-). Northernmost island of the larger Channel Islands. It was part of the domain of Normandy from the 11th century, but is today included in the bailiwick of Guernsey, although it is self-governing.

Alderney² *n., pl.* **-neys.** One of a breed of small dairy cattle originally bred in the Channel Islands.

Al·der·shot (áwl-dər-shot ‖ ól-). A small town in Hampshire, in southern England. Since 1854 it has been the site of the largest army training centre in Britain.

Al·dine (áwl-dīn, -deen ‖ ól-) *adj.* Of, pertaining to, or published by the press of Aldus **Manutius** *(see)* and his family.

Aldm. alderman.

aldo- *comb. form.* Indicates the presence of an aldehyde group; for example, **aldohexose, aldopentose.** [From ALDEHYDE.]

al·do·hex·ose (ál-dō-héks-ōss, -ōz) *n.* An aldose sugar that has six carbon atoms in its molecules.

al·dol (ál-dol ‖ -dōl) *n.* **1.** A thick colourless to pale yellow liquid, $CH_3CH(OH)CH_2CHO$, obtained from acetaldehyde and used to make perfumes and in ore flotation. **2.** Any of a class of organic chemical compounds that have a hydroxyl group and an aldehyde group in their molecules on adjacent carbon atoms.

al·do·pent·ose (ál-dō-pént-ōss, -ōz) *n.* An aldose sugar that has five carbon atoms in its molecules.

al·dose (ál-dōss, -dōz) *n. Chemistry.* Any of a class of monosaccharide sugars containing an aldehyde group. Also called "aldose sugar". Compare **ketose.**

al·dos·te·rone (al-dóstə-rōn) *n.* A steroid hormone, secreted by the adrenal cortex, that regulates salt and water balance by its action on the kidneys.

al·dox·ime (al-dókseem) *n.* A chemical compound formed by reaction of an aldehyde with hydroxylamine and having the characteristic group ·CHNON or :CNOH in its molecules.

al·drin (áwl-drin ‖ ól-) *n.* A brownish-white crystalline pesticide. [After Kurt *Alder* (1902–58), German chemist.]

Aldus Manutius. See **Manutius.**

ale (ayl) *n.* **1.** A fermented alcoholic drink containing malt and formerly made without hops, similar to but often heavier than beer. **2.** *British Informal.* Beer. Used humorously. [Middle English *ale*, Old English *alu, ealu.*]

a·le·a·to·ry (áyli-ə-təri, -tri) *adj.* **1.** Dependent upon chance or luck. **2.** Using or consisting of elements chosen at random or arrived at by chance. Said of musical or other artistic compositions. [Latin *āleātōrius*, from *āleātor*, gambler, from *ālea†*, dice.]

A·lec·to (ə-léktō). *Greek Mythology.* One of the **Furies** *(see).*

a·lee (ə-lée) *adv. Nautical.* At, on, or to the leeward side. Compare **aweather.**

al·e·gar (áyli-gər, ál-i-) *n.* Vinegar produced by the fermentation of ale; malt vinegar. [Middle English ALE + (VINE)GAR.]

ale·house (áyl-howss) *n.* **1.** In former times, a place where ale was sold and drunk. **2.** *British Informal.* A pub. Used humorously.

Aleichem, Sholem. See **Sholem Aleichem.**

A·le·khine (ál-i-keen; *Russian* al-yékhin) **Alexander** (1892–1946). Russian-born French chess master. In 1927 he defeated Capablanca and gained the World Championship. He lost it in 1935, but regained it in 1937 and held it until his death.

Al·e·man·ni (ál-i-mánni, -maʾanī) *pl.n.* A group of Germanic tribes that settled in Alsace and nearby areas during the fourth century A.D. [Latin, from Germanic *Alamanniz* (unattested); akin to Gothic *alamannam* (dative plural), mankind : probably ALL + MAN.]

Al·e·man·nic, Al·a·man·nic (ál-i-mánnik) *n.* The High German dialect of the Alemanni, forms of which are now spoken in Alsace and parts of southern Germany and Switzerland.
~*adj.* Also **Al·e·man·ni·an, Al·a·man·ni·an** (-mánni-ən). Of or pertaining to the Alemanni or their language.

a·lem·bic (ə-lémbik) *n.* **1.** An apparatus formerly used for distilling. **2.** Something that purifies or transforms by a process comparable to distillation. [Middle English, from Old French *alambic*, from Medieval Latin *alambicum*, from Arabic *al-anbīq* : *al*, the + *anbīg*, still, from Greek *ambix†* (stem *ambik*-), cup.]

Al·en·çon (ál-ON-SON). Capital of the Orne département, in Normandy, northwestern France. It is famous for the lace called "point d'Alençon".

a·leph, a·lef (ál-ef, aál-, -if) *n.* The first letter of the Hebrew alphabet. [Hebrew *āleph*, "ox"; akin to ALPHA.]

a·leph-null (ál-ef-núl, aál-, -if-) *n. Mathematics.* The first **transfinite number** *(see).* Also called "aleph-zero". [ALEPH (symbol for transfinite number) + NULL (smallest possible entity).]

A·lep·po (ə-léppō). *Arabic* **Ha·leb** (haa-léb). City in northwest Syria, which was probably first settled as long ago as 6000 B.C. It was once a major station on the caravan route across Syria to Baghdad, and was a centre of Christianity in the Middle East.

a·lert (ə-lért) *adj.* **1.** Vigilantly attentive; watchful: *alert to danger.* **2.** Mentally responsive and perceptive; quick. **3.** Brisk; lively.

~*n.* **1.** A warning signal of attack or danger; especially, a siren warning of an air raid. **2.** The period of time during which such a warning is in effect. —**on the alert.** Watchful and prepared for danger or emergency.
~*tr.v.* **alerted, alerting, alerts.** To notify or cause to be aware of approaching or potential danger; warn: *a campaign alerting people to the dangers of smoking.* [French *alerte*, from Italian *all'erta*, "on the watch" : *alla*, at the, from Latin *ad illam*, from *ille*, that + *erta*, watch, from *(torre) erta*, watchtower, "high (tower)", from Latin *ērectus*, raised, ERECT.]

Å·le·sund, Aa·le·sund (áwlə-soon). Fishing port and town in Norway, dating from the ninth century. It is the headquarters of cod and halibut trawling and of the Arctic sealing fleet.

Al·etsch Glacier (ál-ech, aʾal-). Glacier in the Bernese Alps. It occupies 171 square kilometres (66 square miles) and is the largest glacier in Europe.

a·leu·rone (ə-loor-ōn, -lewr- ‖ *U.S. also* al-yər-) *n.* Also **a·leu·ron** (-on). A protein consisting of minute granules, forming the outermost layer of the endosperm in cereal grains. [German *Aleuron*, from Greek *aleuron*, flour.] —**al·eu·ron·ic** (-ónnik) *adj.*

Al·e·ut (ál-yōot, ál-i-ōot) *n., pl.* **Aleuts** or collectively **Aleut.** Also **A·leu·tian** (for sense 1). **1.** A member of a people inhabiting the Aleutian Islands. **2.** A subfamily of the Eskimo-Aleut family of languages, spoken in the Aleutian Islands. [Russian *aleút*, probably from Chukchi *aliuit*, "beyond the shore".]

A·leu·tian (ə-lóosh'n, -léwsh-) *adj.* Of or pertaining to the Aleuts, their language, or their culture.
~*n.* **1.** Variant of **Aleut** (sense 1). **2.** *Plural.* The Aleutian Islands.

Aleutian Islands. Also **Aleutians.** Archipelago of volcanic islands extending westwards for nearly 2 000 kilometres (1,250 miles) from the tip of the Alaska Peninsula, United States. There are radar stations (part of the U.S. Distant Early Warning Line) and military bases on the islands, which have been of vital strategic importance because of their proximity to Russia.

A level *n. British.* **1.** Advanced level; the higher of the two standards of examination for the **GCE** *(see),* taken, usually two years after O level or GCSE, as a prerequisite for university entrance. **2. a.** An examination at this level. **b.** A certificate awarded for passing such an examination. Compare **O level.**

ale·wife¹ (áyl-wif) *n., pl.* **-wives** (-wīvz). A fish, *Alosa* (or *Pomolobus*) *pseudoharengus*, closely related to the herrings, of North American Atlantic waters and some inland lakes. Also called "oldwife". [Alteration (by association with ALEWIFE, alehouse keeper, "pot-bellied woman") of obsolete *allowes* (plural), probably from French *alose*, shad, from Gaulish Latin *alōsa†*.]

alewife² *n., pl.* **-wives.** Formerly, a woman who kept an alehouse.

Al·ex·an·der I (ál-ig-zaándər ‖ -ik-, -zándər; *Russian* -iksándr) (1777–1825). Tsar of Russia. He came to the throne in 1801 when his father, Paul I, was murdered. His plans to liberalise his country's government were delayed by prolonged wars with Napoleon, until eventually he was converted to rigid conservatism.

Alexander II (1818–81). Tsar of Russia. Considered the ablest and most liberal of the Romanov dynasty, he came to the throne in 1855 and immediately began a programme of political, educational, and military reforms. In 1861 he emancipated Russia's ten million male serfs and their families, an act that won him the title of "tsar liberator". He was assassinated by a member of a revolutionary party.

Alexander III (1845–94). Tsar of Russia. He came to the throne after the assassination of his father, the liberal Alexander II, and immediately abandoned all reforms, reaffirming his "faith in the principle of autocracy". He pursued extreme reactionary policies, persecuted Jews and reformers, increased repressive police powers, and let the education system decline.

Alexander VI, born Rodrigo **Borgia** (c.1431–1503). Pope (1492–1503). On achieving the papacy (through bribery) he is said to have commented "God has given us the papacy. Let us enjoy it". He used papal wealth and power for the advancement of his illegitimate children, and together with his son, Cesare **Borgia**, he embarked on the conquest of central Italy for the benefit of his family and himself. He was also a great patron of the arts.

Alexander Nev·sky (név-ski, néf-) (1220-63). Russian hero and saint, Prince of Novgorod (1236) and Grand Duke of Kiev and Novgorod (1246) and Vladimir (1252). He is famous for defeating the Swedes in 1240, in a great battle near the river Neva (thus acquiring the name Nevsky). In 1242 he won a victory against the Teutonic Knights on the frozen waters of Lake Peipus.

Alexander of Tunis, Sir Harold Rupert Leofric George Alexander, 1st Earl (1891–1969). British field marshal. In World War II he oversaw the evacuation of the British forces from Dunkirk and Burma. He directed the campaign that led to the Allied victory in North Africa (1943), and then led the successful invasions of Sicily and Italy (1944–45), ending the war as Allied supreme commander in the Mediterranean. Governor general of Canada (1946–52), and British Minister of Defence (1952–54).

al·ex·an·ders (ál-ig-zaán-dərz ‖ -ik-, -zán-) *pl.n.* An umbelliferous plant, *Smyrnium olusatrum*, native to southern Europe, whose stems were formerly eaten like celery. [Middle English, from Old French from Medieval Latin *alexandrum*, perhaps alteration (through association with *Alexander* the Great) of Latin *holus atrum*, "black vegetable" : *holus*, vegetable + *atrum*, neuter of *ater*, black.]

Alexander the Great (356–323 B.C.). King of Macedonia and conqueror of an empire that covered much of Asia. He was the son of the founder of the Macedonian Empire, Philip II, and the pupil of

Aristotle, and ascended the throne after the murder of his father in 336 B.C. He forcibly united the warring Greek states and in 334 invaded the Persian Empire with some 35,000 men, defeating its king, Darius III, at Issus. Within four years Alexander had conquered Asia Minor, Syria, Egypt (where he founded Alexandria), Babylonia, and Persia itself. He then invaded northern India and defeated the Indian king, Porus, in 326. A mutiny in his army prevented his advancing to the Ganges and he returned reluctantly to Babylon where he died of a fever.

Al·ex·an·dra¹ (ál-ig-zaán-drə || -ik-, -zán-) (1844–1925). Queen consort of Edward VII. She founded the Queen Alexandra's Royal Army Nursing Corps and the Alexandra Rose Day.

Alexandra² (1872–1918). Last tsaritsa of Russia. A German princess, the granddaughter of Queen Victoria, she married Nicholas II in 1894. During World War I she was in charge of the government and, influenced by the monk Rasputin, ruled disastrously. After the 1917 Revolution she and her family were imprisoned and later shot.

Al·ex·an·dri·a (ál-ig-zaán-dri-ə || -ik-, -zán-). Egypt's leading port, standing at the western tip of the Nile Delta on the Mediterranean Sea. It was founded by Alexander the Great in 332 B.C. and became a repository of Jewish, Arab, and Hellenistic culture, famous for its two royal libraries. Its pharos (lighthouse) was one of the Seven Wonders of the Ancient World. Early Christianity flourished there, and Alexandria remains the seat of the patriarch of the Eastern Orthodox Church. It was captured by the Arabs in 642 and soon after was replaced by Cairo as the capital of Egypt.

Al·ex·an·dri·an (ál-ig-zaándri-ən || -ik-, -zándri-) *adj.* **1.** Of or pertaining to Alexander the Great. **2.** Of or pertaining to Alexandria in Egypt. **3.** Of, characteristic of, or designating the learned school of Hellenistic literature, science, and philosophy that flourished in Alexandria in the last three centuries B.C. **4.** Characterised by the careful study or imitation of earlier forms and masterpieces, rather than by originality. Said of writers and literary works. **5.** Of or designating the school of early Christian philosophy and theology of Alexandria.
~*n.* **1.** A native or inhabitant of Alexandria, Egypt, especially of Hellenistic times. **2.** A scholar, writer, or theologian of the Alexandrian school.

al·ex·an·drine (ál-ig-zán-drīn, -ik-, -zaán-, -drin) *n. Often capital* **A. 1.** The commonest French verse form, consisting of a line of twelve syllables with a caesura usually falling after the sixth syllable. **2.** A line of English verse composed in iambic hexameter, usually with a caesura after the third foot. [French *alexandrin,* from Old French, from *Alexandre,* title of a romance about Alexander the Great, written in this metre.] —**al·ex·an·drine, Al·ex·an·drine** *adj.*

al·ex·an·drite (ál-ig-zán-drīt, -ik-, -zaán-) *n.* A greenish mineral that appears red in artificial light, used as a gemstone. It is a form of chrysoberyl. [German *Alexandrit,* named in honour of Tsar ALEXANDER I.]

a·lex·i·a (ə-léksi-ə) *n.* A disorder in which cerebral lesions cause loss of the ability to read. Also called "word blindness". Compare **dyslexia.** [New Latin : A- (without) + Greek *lexis,* speech, from *legein,* to speak.]

a·lex·in (ə-léksin) *n.* Also **a·lex·ine** (ə-lékseen). A blood component, **complement** (see). [German *Alexin,* "protection (from bacteria)", from Greek *alexein,* to protect, ward off.]

a·lex·i·phar·mic (ə-léksi-fármik) *adj.* Preventing or resisting effects of poison or infection; antidotal; prophylactic.
~*n.* An antidote. [Obsolete *alexipharmac,* from French *alexipharmaque,* from Greek *alexipharmakos : alexein,* to ward off + *pharmakon,* poison (see **pharmaco-**).]

Alf (álf) *n. Australian Informal.* A stereotype of an uncultivated hard-drinking and aggressively male-chauvinist man. Compare **ocker, Roy.** [From the name *Alf.*]

al·fal·fa (al-fál-fə) *n.* A plant, *Medicago sativa,* native to Eurasia, having compound leaves with three leaflets, and clusters of small purple flowers. It is widely cultivated for forage and is used as a commercial source of chlorophyll. Also called "lucerne". [Spanish, from Arabic *al-fasfaṣah,* best fodder.]

Al Fatah *n.* See **Fatah, Al.**

al·fil·a·ri·a, al·fil·e·ri·a (álfi-laír-i-ə, al-fíllə-rée-ə) *n.* A plant, *Erodium cicutarium,* native to Europe but widely naturalised in North America, having finely divided leaves and small pink or purplish flowers. Also called "pin clover". [American Spanish *alfilerillo,* from Spanish, diminutive of *alfiler,* a pin, from Arabic *al-khilāl,* thorn, pin.]

Al·fon·sín (ál-fon-seén), **Raúl** (1926–). Argentine lawyer and politician. President of Argentina (1983–89).

Al·fred the Great (ál-frid || frəd) (849–99). King of Wessex. He became ruler of Wessex in 871 and conducted several wars against the Danes, driving them from Wessex. Alfred built Britain's first navy, reorganised Wessex's army, and set up a whole complex of fortified earthworks, called *burghs.* He was also an able administrator, drew up a legal code, and encouraged scholarship.

al·fres·co (al-fréskō) *adv.* In the fresh air; outdoors: *let's eat alfresco.*
~*adj.* Taking place outdoors; outdoor: *an alfresco meal.* [Italian, "in the fresh (air)" : *a il,* in the + *fresco,* fresh, FRESCO.]

Al Furāt. See **Euphrates.**

Alf·vén wave (alf-váyn) *n. Physics.* A transverse wave propagated through a plasma, such as the matter in a star, under the influence of magnetohydrodynamic forces. [After Hannes Olof Gösta *Alfvén* (1908–), Swedish astrophysicist.]

al·gae (ál-jee) *pl.n. Singular* **-ga** (-gə). Primitive, chiefly aquatic, one-celled or multicellular plants that lack true stems, roots, and leaves but contain chlorophyll. Included among the algae are kelps and other seaweeds, and the diatoms. [Latin *algae,* plural of *alga†,* seaweed.] —**al·gal** (ál-gəl) *adj.*

al·gar·ro·ba (ál-gə-rōbə) *n.* **1.** A tree, the **mesquite** *(see).* **2.** A tree, the **carob** *(see).* **3.** The edible pod of either of these trees. [Spanish, from Arabic *al-kharrūbah : al,* the + *kharrūbah,* CAROB.]

Al·garve (al-gárv). Former kingdom and province of southernmost Portugal, now the district of Faro. Farming, fishing, and tourism are the main industries, and it is also noted for cork.

al·ge·bra (ál-jibrə) *n.* **1.** A generalisation of arithmetic in which symbols, usually letters of the alphabet, represent numbers and are related by operations that hold for all numbers in the set or sets thereof. **2.** A set of entities (such as matrices, propositions, or vectors) together with operations for combining these entities to give other members of the set. See **algebraic structure.** [Medieval Latin, from Arabic *aljebr, al-jabr,* "the (science of) reuniting" (referring to the solving of algebraic equations) : *al,* the + *jabr,* reunification, bone-setting.] —**al·ge·bra·ist** (ál-ji-bráy-ist) *n.*

al·ge·bra·ic (ál-ji-bráy-ik) *adj.* **1.** Of, pertaining to, or involving algebra. **2.** Designating an expression, equation, or function in which only numbers, letters, and arithmetical operations are contained or used. **3.** Indicating or restricted to a finite number of algebraic operations. —**al·ge·bra·i·cal·ly** *adv.*

algebraic logic *n.* A method of presenting a problem for a calculator or computer with the operations entered in the order in which they would be written out.

algebraic number *n.* **1.** Any positive or negative number. **2.** A number that is a root of a polynomial equation with rational coefficients.

algebraic operation *n.* Addition, subtraction, multiplication, division, exponentiation, root extraction, or any finite combination of these operations.

algebraic structure *n.* The general set of operations and relationships in an algebra, considered independently of the particular mathematical entities used.

algebraic sum *n.* The sum of algebraic quantities produced by arithmetic addition, in which negative quantities are added by the subtraction of corresponding positive quantities. For example, the algebraic sum of 6 and −2 is 4.

Al·ge·ci·ras (ál-ji-séer-əss, -je-, -théer-). Port and tourist centre in southern Spain, situated across the bay from Gibraltar.

Al·ger (al-zháy). *English* **Al·giers** (al-jéerz). Capital of Algeria, and an ancient Mediterranean port. It was taken by the French (1830), and during World War II was the seat of the French government in exile and headquarters of the Allied forces in North Africa.

Al·ge·ri·a, Democratic and Popular Republic of (al-jéeri-ə). *French* **Al·gé·rie** (alzhay-rée). Country in northwest Africa bordering the Mediterranean Sea, the second-largest country in Africa, after Sudan. Arab armies conquered Algeria in the seventh century, and the north fell to the Ottoman Turks in 1519. The French invaded the country in 1830, and in 1871 the north became three départements of metropolitan France. Algeria gained its independence, after a long terrorist and guerrilla campaign, in 1962. In the early 1990s the rise of violent Islamic fundamentalism created instability, general elections were cancelled in 1992, and since then more than 60,000 have died in the conflict between government and fundamentalists. The country has two distinct regions: the northern cultivated region of the Mediterranean littoral and the Atlas mountains (about 15 per cent of the country), and the arid wastes of the Sahara in the south. Algeria has extensive deposits of oil and natural gas, which account for 90 per cent of its exports. Area, 2 381 741 square kilometres (919,352 square miles). Population, 29,170,000. Capital, Alger (Algiers). —**Al·ge·ri·an** (al-jéeri-ən) *adj. & n.*

–algia *n. comb. form.* Indicates pain or a painful condition; for example, **neuralgia.** [Greek, from *algos†,* pain.]

al·gi·cide (ál-ji-sīd) *n.* A chemical used to kill algae in water.

al·gid (ál-jid) *adj.* Chilly; clammy. Said especially of the skin of patients with malaria. [Latin *algidus,* from *algēre†,* to be cold.] —**al·gid·i·ty** *n.*

Algiers. See **Alger.**

al·gin (ál-jin) *n.* A gelatinous substance consisting of alginic acid or its salts or esters, obtained from certain algae, especially the giant kelp, and used as an emulsifier, a thickener for foods, and a fabric dressing. [ALG(AE) + -IN.]

al·gi·nate (ál-ji-nayt) *n.* A salt or ester of alginic acid.

al·gin·ic acid (al-jínnik) *n.* A gelatinous substance obtained from certain seaweeds. See **algin.**

algo– *comb. form.* Indicates pain; for example, **algolagnia.** [Greek, from *algos†,* pain.]

al·goid (ál-goyd) *adj.* Of or resembling algae.

Al·gol (ál-gol) *n.* A double, eclipsing, variable star in the constellation Perseus, almost as bright as Polaris. [Arabic *al ghūl,* "the ghoul" : *al,* the + *ghūl,* GHOUL.]

AL·GOL (ál-gol) *n.* An arithmetical language by which numerical procedures may be precisely presented to a computer in a standard form. [*Algorithmic Oriented Language.*]

al·go·lag·ni·a (ál-gō-lágni-ə) *n.* Sexual gratification derived from inflicting or experiencing pain. See **masochism, sadism.** [New

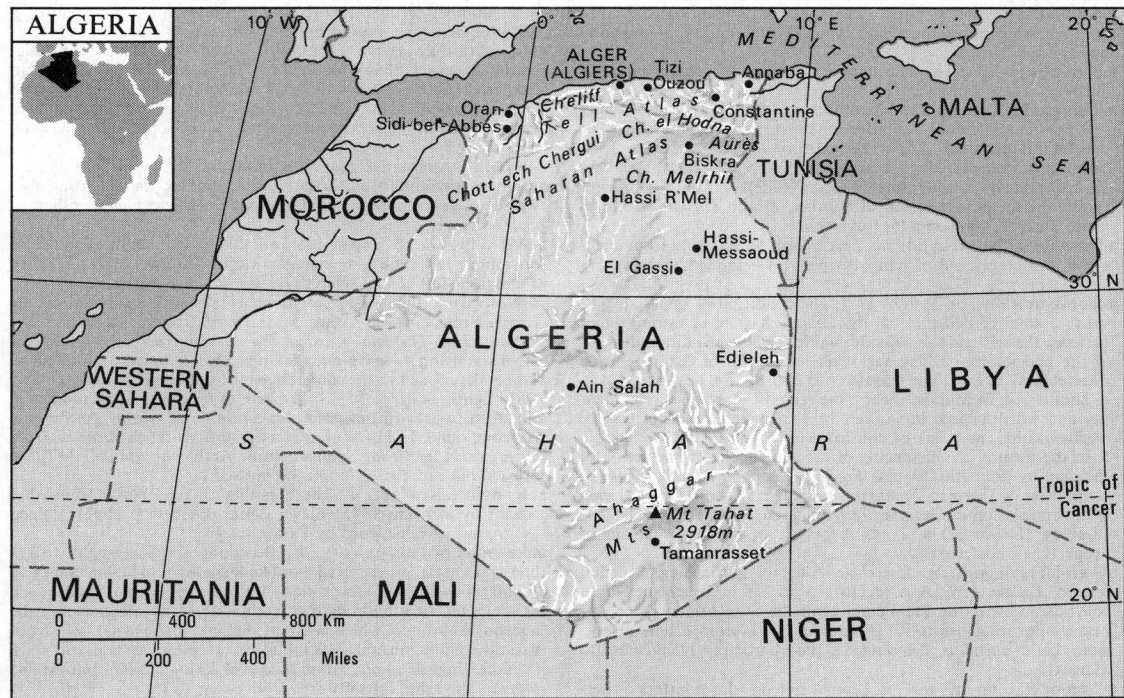

ALGERIA

ALGER (ALGIERS) · Tizi Ouzou · Annaba · MALTA
Oran · Cheliff · Atlas · Constantine
Sidi-bel-Abbès · Tell · Ch. el Hodna
Chott ech Chergui · Aurès
Saharan Atlas · Biskra
Ch. Melrhir
Hassi R'Mel
MOROCCO
Hassi-Messaoud
El Gassi
ALGERIA
Ain Salah · Edjeleh · LIBYA
WESTERN SAHARA
S A H A R A
Ahaggar Mts · Mt Tahat 2918m · Tamanrasset
Tropic of Cancer
MAURITANIA · MALI
NIGER

0 — 400 — 800 Km
0 — 200 — 400 Miles

Latin : ALGO- + Greek *lagneia,* lust, from *lagnos,* lustful.] —**al·go·lag·ni·ac** (-ak) *n. & adj.*

al·gol·o·gy (al-góllǝji) *n.* The study of algae. [ALG(AE) + -LOGY.] —**al·go·log·i·cal** (ál-gǝ-lójik'l) *adj.* —**al·gol·o·gist** (al-góllǝjist) *n.*

al·gom·e·ter (al-gómmitǝr) *n.* An apparatus for determining sensitivity to pain caused by pressure. [ALGO- + -METER.] —**al·go·met·ric** (ál-gǝ-méttrik), **al·go·met·ri·cal** *adj.* —**al·gom·e·try** (al-gómmǝtri) *n.*

Al·gon·ki·an (al-góngki-ǝn) *n., pl.* **-ans** or collectively **Algonkian** (for sense 2). **1.** *Geology.* In Canada, the late **Proterozoic** *(see).* **2.** Variant of **Algonquian.** [After the rock formations in the Great Lakes District of North America, homeland of the Algonquin.]

Al·gon·qui·an (al-góng-ki-ǝn, -kwi-) *n., pl.* **-ans** or collectively **Algonquian** (for sense 2). Also **Algonkian. 1.** A principal family of about 50 North American Indian languages spoken in an area stretching from the Atlantic to the Rocky Mountains, and from Labrador in the north to North Carolina and Tennessee in the south, and used by such tribes as the Ojibwa, Delaware, Cree, Fox, Blackfoot, Illinois, and Shawnee. **2.** A member of a tribe using a language of this family. [From ALGONQUIN.] —**Al·gon·gui·an, Al·gon·ki·an** *adj.*

Al·gon·quin (al-góng-kin, -kwin) *n., pl.* **-quins** or collectively **Algonquin.** Also **Al·gon·kin** (-kin). **1.** A member of any of several Algonquian-speaking North American Indian tribes formerly inhabiting the region along the Ottawa river and near the northern tributaries of the St. Lawrence river. See **Ottawa¹. 2.** The Algonquian language of these tribes. [Canadian French¹, from earlier *Algoumequins*† (plural).]

al·go·pho·bi·a (ál-gǝ-fóbi-ǝ, -gō-) *n.* Abnormal fear of pain. [New Latin : ALGO- + -PHOBIA.]

al·go·rism (ál-gǝ-riz'm) *n.* **1.** The Arabic system of numbers; the decimal system. **2.** Variant of **algorithm.** [Middle English *algorisme,* from Old French, from Medieval Latin *algorismus,* after Muhammad ibn-Musa AL-KHWARIZMI.]

al·go·rithm (ál-gǝ-rith'm) *n.* Also **algorism.** *Mathematics.* A mechanical or recursive computation procedure. [Variant (influenced by ARITHMETIC) of ALGORISM.] —**al·go·rith·mic** (-rithmik) *adj.*

algorithmic language *n.* An arithmetical language presenting numerical procedures to a computer in a standard form.

Al·ham·bra, the (al-hámbrǝ, ǝ-lámbrǝ) Citadel and palace overlooking Granada in southern Spain. It was built by the Moorish kings in the 13th and 14th centuries and is the best example of Moorish architecture in Spain.

A·li (ál-i, aáli), surnamed "The Lion of God" (*c.* A.D. 600–661). Fourth Caliph of Islam (656–661). He was the cousin and son-in-law (by his marriage to Fatimah) of the prophet **Muhammad** and one of the first converts to Islam. His reign was marred by conflict between his supporters and rivals, and after his assassination Islam came to be divided into Sunnis and Shiites, the Shiites holding that Ali and his descendants had the only valid claim to the Caliphate.

A·li (aáli, aa-lée), **Muhammad,** originally Cassius Marcellus Clay (1942–). U.S. boxer. He won the world heavyweight championship in 1964. He became a Black Muslim, changed his name, and refused military service in 1967. For this last action he was stripped of his title and his licence to box was withdrawn for three years. He re-gained the championship by defeating George Foreman in 1974, losing it briefly in 1978 and regaining it again that year. He was defeated by Larry Holmes in 1980.

a·li·as (áyli-ǝss) *n., pl.* **-ases.** An assumed name.
~ *adv.* Otherwise named or known as; a.k.a.: *Johnson, alias Rogers.* [Latin *aliās,* otherwise, from *alius,* other.]

A·li Ba·ba (ál-i báa-bǝ, -baa ‖ aáli). In the *Arabian Nights,* a poor woodcutter who gains entrance to the treasure cave of the forty thieves by saying the magic words "Open, Sesame!"

al·i·bi (ál-i-bī) *n., pl.* **-bis. 1.** *Law.* **a.** A form of defence whereby an accused person attempts to prove that he was elsewhere when an act (such as a crime) was committed. **b.** The evidence supporting this. **2.** *Informal.* An excuse.
~ *tr.v.* **alibied, -biing, -bis.** *Informal.* To provide an excuse or alibi for. [Latin *alibī,* elsewhere : *alius,* other + *ubī,* where.]

A·li·can·te (ál-i-kánti). Mediterranean port and tourist resort in the Valencia region of southeastern Spain. It is the capital of Alicante province.

Al·ice-band (állis-band) *n.* A firm, U-shaped headband worn over the crown and tucked behind the ears. [After the headband worn by Alice in Tenniel's illustrations of *Through the Looking-Glass.*]

Al·ice-in-Won·der·land (ál-iss-in-wúndǝr-land) *adj.* Absurd; fantastic; surreal. [After the fantastic logic and events of Wonderland in Lewis Carroll's book.]

Al·ice Springs (ál-iss ‖ *locally* -ǝss). Town in Nothern Territory, Australia, lying almost at the midpoint of the continent, formerly called Stuart. It is a centre for tourism and transport, and is the headquarters of the regional Flying Doctor Service.

al·i·cy·clic (ál-i-sīklik, -siklik) *adj.* Of, pertaining to, or designating chemical compounds having both aliphatic and cyclic characteristics or structures. Examples of alicyclic compounds include cyclohexane and sucrose. [German *alicyclisch* : ALI(PHATIC) + CYCLIC.]

al·i·dade (ál-i-dayd) *n.* Also **al·i·dad** (-dad). **1.** A surveying instrument consisting of a rule with sights at each end, used on a plane table to draw lines of sight onto distant objects. Also called "sight rule". **2.** A similar rule with a telescope mounted parallel to it. **3.** The index of a graduated surveying instrument such as an astrolabe. [French, from Medieval Latin *allidada,* from Arabic *al-'iḍāda,* "the revolving radius of a circle", from *'aḍud,* humerus.]

a·li·en (áyli-ǝn) *adj.* **1.** Owing political allegiance to a country other than the one in which one is resident; foreign: *a large alien population.* **2. a.** Belonging to, characteristic of, or derived from another place, society, or person; not one's own; unfamiliar; strange: *the problems of adjusting to an alien culture.* **b.** Belonging or pertaining to another planet or world; extraterrestrial: *an alien spaceship.* **3.** Inconsistent or incompatible; repugnant. Used with *to: Lying is alien to his nature.* —See Synonyms at **extrinsic.**
~ *n.* **1.** A foreign resident of a country who has not been naturalised. **2.** A member of another family, people, region, or the like; especially, a being from another planet or world; an extraterrestrial. **3.** A person who is excluded from some group; an outsider. **4.** *Ecology.* A plant native to one region but naturalised in another.
~ *tr.v.* **aliened, -ening, -ens.** *Law. Rare.* To alienate (property). [Middle English, from Old French, from Latin *aliēnus,* belonging to another, from *alius,* other.]

a·li·en·a·ble (áyli-ən-əb'l) *adj. Law.* Capable of being transferred to the ownership of another. Said typically of property. **—a·li·en·a·bil·i·ty** (-ə-billəti) *n.*

a·li·en·age (áyli-ənij) *n.* The state or condition of being alien or an alien.

a·li·en·ate (áyli-ən-ayt) *tr.v.* **-ated, -ating, -ates. 1.** To cause (someone previously friendly or affectionate) to become unfriendly or indifferent; estrange. **2.** To dissociate or isolate (oneself). **3.** To cause to be transferred; turn away: *"he succeeded . . . in alienating the affections of my only ward"* (Oscar Wilde). **4.** *Law.* To transfer (property) to the ownership of another. [Latin *aliēnāre,* from *aliēnus,* ALIEN.] **—a·li·en·a·tor** (-aytər) *n.*

a·li·en·at·ed (áyli-ən-aytid) *adj. Psychology.* **1.** Suffering from alienation. **2.** Loosely, out of sympathy with one's immediate social environment.

a·li·en·a·tion (áyli-ən-áysh'n) *n.* **1.** The condition of being an outsider; a state of isolation. **2.** *Psychology.* A state of estrangement between the self and the objective world, or between different parts of the personality. **3.** The act of alienating, as: **a.** Estrangement; disaffection. **b.** *Law.* The transference of property, or the title to it, to another. **4.** In Marxist theory, the sense of loss of personal identity and worth caused in workers by the fragmentation of labour, mechanisation, and lack of control over the means of production. **5.** In the theatre, the distancing of the audience from the action of the play by dramatic devices: *Brecht's alienation effects.* [Sense 4: translation of German *Entäusserung.* Sense 5: short for *alienation effect,* translation of German *Verfremdungseffekt.*]

a·li·en·ee (áyli-ən-ée) *n. Law.* A person to whom ownership of property is transferred.

a·li·en·ist (áyli-ən-ist) *n.* **1.** *Archaic.* A doctor specialising in mental illness. **2.** *Law. U.S.* A psychiatrist who has been accepted by a court as an expert on the mental competence of principals or witnesses appearing before it. [French *aliéniste,* from *aliéné,* insane, from Latin *aliēnātus,* "estranged", past participle of *aliēnāre,* to ALIENATE.]

a·li·en·or (áyli-ən-ór, -ənər) *n. Law.* A person who transfers ownership of property to another.

a·lif (ál-if, aálif) *n.* The first letter of the Arabic alphabet. [Arabic.]

a·li·form (áyli-form, ál-i-) *adj.* Shaped like a wing; alar. [Latin *āl(a),* wing + -I- + -FORM.]

a·light¹ (ə-lít) *intr.v.* **alighted** or **alit** (ə-lít), **alighting, alights. 1.** To come down and settle, as after flight. Used with *on* or *upon*: *a bird alighting on a branch.* **2. a.** To get out (of a vehicle, for example). **b.** To dismount. Used with *from.* **3.** To come upon by chance. Used with *on* or *upon*: *His gaze alighted on an old vase.* [Middle English *ali(g)hten,* Old English *ālīhtan* : *ā-* (intensive) + *līhtan,* to dismount, lighten, from *līht,* LIGHT (adjective).]

a·light² *adj.* **1.** Burning. **2.** Lighted; lit up. Used after the noun. [Middle English *alight,* Old English *ālīht,* past participle of *ālīhtan,* to light up : A- + *līhtan,* to light, from *līht,* LIGHT.] **—a·light** *adv.*

a·lign (ə-lín) *v.* **aligned, aligning, aligns.** *—tr.* **1.** To arrange in a line. **2.** To ally (oneself, for example) with one side of an argument, cause, policy, or the like. **3.** To bring (two or more parts of a machine, for example) into correct relation with one another. *—intr.* To fall into line or position. [French *aligner,* from Old French : *a-,* from Latin *ad-,* to + *ligne,* LINE.] **—a·lign·er** *n.*

a·lign·ment (ə-línmənt) *n.* **1.** Arrangement or position in a straight line. **2.** A ground plan, as of a railway. **3.** The act of aligning or the condition of being aligned: *an alignment of left-wing parties.* **4.** The correct or proper adjustment or positioning of related parts, as of a machine.

alignment chart *n. Mathematics.* A **nomogram** *(see).*

a·like (ə-lík) *adj.* Having a close resemblance; similar. Usually used after the noun: *His sons are alike.*

~*adv.* In the same way or manner, or to the same degree: *They dress and walk alike.* [Middle English *ilik,* Old English *gelīc* : *ge-* (collective prefix) + *līc,* form.] **—a·like·ness** *n.*

al·i·ment (ál-i-mənt) *n. Formal.* **1.** Food; nourishment. **2.** Something that supports or sustains. **3.** In Scots law, alimony or maintenance.

~*tr.v.* (-ment) **alimented, -menting, -ments.** *Formal.* To supply with food or other sustenance. [Middle English, from Latin *alimentum,* from *alere,* to nourish.] **—al·i·men·tal** (-mént'l) *adj.* **—al·i·men·tal·ly** *adv.*

al·i·men·ta·ry (ál-i-mént-əri, -ri) *adj.* **1.** Of or pertaining to food or nutrition. **2.** Providing nourishment.

alimentary canal *n.* The mucous-membrane-lined tube of the digestive system, extending from the mouth to the anus and including the oesophagus, stomach, and intestines.

al·i·men·ta·tion (ál-i-men-táysh'n) *n.* **1.** The act or process of giving or receiving nourishment. **2.** Support; sustenance.

al·i·mo·ny (ál-i-məni || *U.S.* -mōni) *n., pl.* **-nies. 1.** *Law.* **a.** Formerly in Britain, **maintenance** *(see),* as paid by a husband to his former wife, or wife pending a divorce. **b.** *U.S.* **Maintenance** *(see).* **2.** Sustenance; support. [Latin *alimōnia,* nutriment, support, from *alere,* to nourish.]

al·i·phat·ic (ál-i-fáttik) *adj.* Of, pertaining to, or designating organic chemical compounds with reactions characteristic of compounds with open chains of carbon atoms rather than the closed cyclic chains of **aromatic** *(see)* compounds. See **alicyclic.** [From Greek *aleiphar* (stem *aleiphat-*), oil, from *aleiphein,* to anoint.]

al·i·quant (ál-i-kwənt, -kwont) *adj.* Of, pertaining to, or designating a number or quantity that is not an exact factor or divisor of some other number or quantity. [New Latin *aliquantus,* from Latin, "a certain quantity" : *alius,* some + *quantus,* how much.]

al·i·quot (ál-i-kwot) *adj.* **1.** *Mathematics.* Of, pertaining to, or designating an exact divisor or factor of a quantity, especially of an integer. **2.** Contained exactly or an exact number of times. [French *(partie) aliquote,* aliquot (part), from Medieval Latin *(pars) aliquotae,* from Latin *aliquot,* some, several : *alius,* some, other + *quot,* how many.]

a·lit (ə-lít). Alternative past tense of **alight.**

a·li·un·de (áyli-úndi) *adv. Law.* From another source; from elsewhere: *evidence aliunde.* [Latin, from elsewhere : *alius,* other + *unde,* whence.]

a·live (ə-lív) *adj.* **1.** Having life; in a living state. **2.** In existence or operation; not extinct or inactive: *keep love alive.* **3.** In a state of animation; full of life; lively: *Her performance was spendidly alive.* **4.** Now living. Used as an intensive, usually with a superlative: *the strongest man alive.* **5.** Aware; sensitive: *alive to the moods of others.* **6.** Swarming: *The square was alive with happy people.* —See Synonyms at **living. —alive and kicking.** Lively; active. **—look alive.** To be alert. Used in the imperative. [Middle English *alive, on live,* Old English *on līfe* : ON + *līfe,* dative of *līf,* LIFE.] **—a·live·ness** *n.*

a·liz·a·rin (ə-lízzə-rin) *n.* Also **a·liz·a·rine** (-rin, -reen). An orange-red compound, $C_{14}H_8O_4$, used as a dyestuff. [French *alizarine,* from *alizari,* madder, from Spanish, from Arabic *al-'aṣārah,* the juice pressed out : *al,* the + *'aṣara,* he pressed.]

al·ka·hest (ál-kə-hest) *n.* The hypothetical universal solvent once sought by alchemists. [Medieval Latin *alchahest,* probably coined as a pseudo-Arabic word by Paracelsus.]

al·ka·les·cent (álkə-léss'nt) *adj.* Becoming alkaline; slightly alkaline. [ALKAL(I) + -ESCENT.] **—al·ka·les·cence, al·ka·les·cen·cy** *n.*

al·ka·li (ál-kə-lī) *n., pl.* **-lis** or **-lies. 1.** *Chemistry.* A soluble base such as ammonia or a hydroxide or carbonate of an alkali metal, the aqueous solution of which is bitter, slippery, and caustic. **2.** Any of various soluble mineral salts found in natural water and arid soils. [Middle English *alcaly,* from Medieval Latin *alcali,* from Arabic *al-qalīy,* the ashes (of saltwort), from *qalay,* to fry.]

al·ka·li·fy (ál-kəli-fī, al-kál-ifī) *v.* **-fied, -fying, -fies.** *—tr.* To make alkaline; alkalise. *—intr.* To become alkaline.

alkali metal *n.* Any of a group of soft, white, low-density, low-melting, highly reactive metallic elements, comprising lithium, sodium, potassium, rubidium, caesium, and francium. The alkali metals constitute Group I of the periodic table of the elements.

al·ka·lim·e·ter (ál-kə-límmitər) *n.* **1.** An apparatus for measuring alkalinity. **2.** An apparatus for measuring the amount of carbon dioxide evolved from a solid. **—al·ka·lim·e·try** (-límmitri) *n.*

al·ka·line (ál-kə-līn || *U.S. also* -lin) *adj.* **1.** Of, relating to, containing, or having the nature of an alkali. **2.** Designating a soil having a pH greater than 7.

alkaline earth *n.* **1.** An oxide of an alkaline-earth metal. **2.** Loosely, an alkaline-earth metal. **—al·ka·line-earth** (ál-kə-līn-erth) *adj.*

alkaline-earth metal *n.* Any of a group of silvery, fairly reactive metallic elements, comprising beryllium, magnesium, calcium, strontium, barium, and radium. The alkaline-earth metals constitute Group II of the periodic table of the elements. Sometimes, especially in the United States, the term is restricted to calcium, strontium, and barium.

al·ka·lin·i·ty (ál-kə-línnəti) *n.* The alkali concentration or alkaline quality of an alkali-containing substance or solution.

al·ka·lise, al·ka·lize (ál-kə-līz) *v.* **-lised, -lising, -lises.** Also **al·ka·lin·ise** (-linīz). *—tr.* To make alkaline. *—intr.* To become an alkali. **—al·ka·li·sa·tion** (-lī-záysh'n || *U.S.* -li-) *n.*

al·ka·loid (ál-kə-loyd) *n.* Any of various physiologically active nitrogen-containing organic bases derived from plants, including nicotine, quinine, cocaine, atropine, and morphine. [German : ALKAL(I) + -OID.] **—al·ka·loi·dal** (-lóyd'l) *adj.*

al·ka·lo·sis (ál-kə-lṓ-siss) *n.* Pathologically high alkali content in the blood and tissues. [New Latin : ALKAL(I) + -OSIS.]

al·kane (ál-kayn) *n. Chemistry.* Any of a class of saturated hydrocarbons found in natural gas and petroleum. The hydrocarbons form a series (the *alkane series*) with the general formula C_nH_{2n+2}. The first four members are methane (CH_4), ethane (C_2H_6), propane (C_3H_8), and butane (C_4H_{10}). Also called "paraffin". [ALK(YL) + -ANE.]

al·ka·net (ál-kənet) *n.* **1. a.** A European plant, *Alkanna tinctoria,* the roots of which yield a red dye. **b.** The root of this plant, or a dye prepared from it. **2.** Any of several hairy plants of the genus *Anchusa,* native to the Old World, having clusters of blue flowers. Also called "bugloss". [Middle English, from Spanish *alcaneta,* diminutive of *alcana,* henna, from Medieval Latin *alchanna,* from Arabic *al-hinnā',* the HENNA.]

al-Kartum, Al Khartum. See **Khartoum.**

al·kene (ál-keen) *n.* Any of a class of unsaturated aliphatic hydrocarbons that contain at least one double carbon-carbon bond in their molecules. The simplest alkenes have only one double bond and form a series (the *alkene series*) with the general formula C_nH_{2n}. The first members of the series are ethene ($CH_2{:}CH_2$), propene ($CH_3CH{:}CH_2$), and butene ($C_2H_5CH{:}CH_2$). Also called "olefine", "olefin". [ALK(YL) + -ENE.]

Al Khalil. See **Hebron.**

al-Khwa·riz·mi (ál-kwaa-rízmi), **Muhammad ibn-Musa** (*c.* 780–*c.* 850). Arab mathematician. His work introduced the Hindu system of notation into Arabic mathematics, and a tenth-century Latin

translation of it introduced this system, now known as "Arabic numerals", to western mathematics. The word "algebra" comes from the title of al-Khwarizmi's treatise on it (called *al-jebr*), and the word for the calculating procedure he discussed, "algorism" (algorithm), is derived from his name.
al·kie, al·ky (ál-ki) *n., pl.* **-kies.** *Slang.* An alcoholic.
Alkoran. Variant of **Alcoran,** the **Koran** *(see).*
al·kox·ide (al-kóks-īd) *n. Chemistry.* Any of a class of chemical compounds that are salts formed by removing a hydrogen atom from the hydroxyl group of an alcohol. Sodium methoxide, $NaOCH_3$, is a simple example. [ALK(YL) + OX(Y)- + -IDE.]
Al Kut (al-kŏŏt). Also **Kut-al-A·mar·a** (kŏŏt-al-ə-máarə). Agricultural trading centre, situated on the river Tigris in southern Iraq.
al·kyd resin (ál-kid) *n.* A widely used durable synthetic resin derived from glycerol and phthalic anhydride. Also called "alkyd". [Blend of ALKYL and ACID.]
al·kyl (ál-kil) *n. Chemistry.* A monovalent radical, such as ethyl or propyl, having the general formula C_nH_{2n+1}. [German : ALC(OHOL) + -YL.]
al·kyl·a·tion (ál-ki-láysh'n) *n. Chemistry.* Any process in which an alkyl group is added to or substituted in a molecule, as in the reaction of alkenes with alkanes to make high-octane fuels.
al·kyl·ben·zene (ál-kil-bén-zeen) *n. Chemistry.* Any of a class of hydrocarbons with molecules that have an alkyl group joined to a benzene ring. Toluene ($C_6H_5{\cdot}CH_3$) is the simplest example.
alkyl halide *n.* A type of organic compound, a **haloalkane** *(see).*
al·kyne (ál-kīn) *n.* Any of a class of unsaturated aliphatic hydrocarbons that contain at least one carbon-carbon triple bond in their molecules. The simplest alkynes have only one triple bond and form a series (the *alkyne series*) with the general formula C_nH_{2n-2}. The first members of the series are acetylene ($CH{\equiv}CH$), propyne ($CH_3CH{\equiv}CH$), and butyne ($C_2H_5CH{\equiv}CH$). Also called "acetylene". [ALKY(L) + -(I)NE.]
all (awl) *adj.* **1.** The total entity or extent of: *all Europe.* **2.** The entire or total number, amount, or quantity of: *all animals.* Often used after a pronoun: *I like them all.* **3.** Every one of a group or class: *all the staff.* **4.** The greatest possible: *in all honesty.* **5. a.** Many: *all sorts of books.* **b.** Every. Used in the phrase *all manner of.* **6.** Any whatsoever: *beyond all doubt.* **7.** Nothing but; only: *He was all skin and bones.*
~*pron.* **1.** Each and every one: *Education for all.* **2. a.** Each and every thing: *Ten ships sailed and all have now docked.* **b.** Everything collectively: *He remembered all he saw.*
~*n.* Everything one has: *She gave her all.* **—all and sundry.** Everyone without restriction. **—all in all. 1.** With everything being taken into account. **2.** Of the highest importance. **—at all. 1. a.** To some or any extent: *He can't walk at all.* **b.** Whatever: *He did no work at all.* Used as an intensive in negative sentences. **2. a.** Ever: *Do you see him at all now?* **b.** To any extent; in any way: *Does he feel better at all?* Used in questions to suggest some doubt in the speaker's mind: *Have you a religion at all?* **—for all.** To the limited extent that: *for all I care.* **—in all.** Including everyone or everything: *five desks in all.*
~*adv.* **1.** Wholly; entirely; completely: *This is all wrong.* **2.** *Informal.* Very; thoroughly: *The coat was all dirty.* **3.** Each; apiece: *a score of five all.* **4.** Exclusively: *The cake is all for you.* **5. a.** To a great extent or degree: *happens all too often.* **b.** To such an extent: *all the more reason not to trust him.* **6.** Used as an intensive in combination with various often vulgar words to indicate a total lack: *It's got damn all to do with you.* **—all about.** Mainly or exclusively concerned with: *Winning, that's what it's all about.* **—all along.** Over a period of time; consistently: *I hoped all along that he'd come.* **—all but.** Nearly; almost: *He all but fainted.* **—all in. 1.** *Informal.* Tired; exhausted. **2.** Inclusive of all incidental charges. *£30 all in.* **—all of.** Not less than: *It's all of ten miles.* **—all that.** Particularly. Used in the negative: *It wasn't all that difficult.* **—all there.** *Informal.* Mentally alert; not lacking in intelligence. **—all the same. 1.** Nevertheless. **2.** Of little importance: *It's all the same to me.* [Middle English *al(le),* Old English *all, eall.*]
Usage: *All* can occur with either a singular or plural verb, according to whether an uncountable or a countable noun respectively is present or understood. *All is not lost, all human life is there, all (members) were present,* are equally correct. The use of *of* before the definite article in such phrases is optional: *all (of) the members*; it is often preferred in American English, and omitted in British English, especially in writing. See also **all right.**
all-[1] *comb. form.* Indicates: **1.** Wholly; entirely; throughout; for example, **all-night, all-wool. 2.** Extremely; very; for example, **all-important. 3.** Representing the whole of; for example, *an all-England team.* **4.** Every kind of; for example, *an all-weather coat.*
all-[2]**.** Variant of **allo-.**
al·la bre·ve (ál-ə bráyvi || *U.S.* áalə brévvay, brév). *adv. Music.* In duple or quadruple time with the minim being the unit of time. [Italian, "according to the breve".] **—al·la bre·ve** *adj.*
Al·lah (ál-ə, -aa || *U.S. also* áal-) *n.* The supreme being in the Muslim religion. [Arabic *Allāh* : *al,* the + *Ilāh,* god.]
Al·la·ha·bad (ál-əhə-bád, -baád). City in Uttar Pradesh, India, at the confluence of the Ganges and Jumna rivers. It was an important centre of the movement for Indian national independence.
al·la·man·da, al·la·man·de (ál-ə-mándə) *n.* Any of several woody vines of the genus *Allamanda,* native to tropical America, having showy, funnel-shaped yellow flowers. [After Jean N.S. *Allamand* (1713–87), Swiss scientist.]
al·lan·ite (ál-ən-īt) *n.* A rare brown mineral found in certain igneous rocks, consisting of an aluminosilicate of calcium, iron, and several lanthanoid elements. [After T. *Allan* (1777–1833), British mineralogist.]
al·lan·toid (ə-lántoyd) *adj.* Also **al·lan·toi·dal** (ál-ən-tóyd'l). **1.** Of or having an allantois. **2.** *Botany.* Shaped like a sausage.
~*n.* The **allantois** *(see).* [French *allantoïde,* from Old French, from Greek *allantoeidēs (humēn),* "the sausage-shaped (membrane)": *allantos*†, sausage + -OID.]
al·lan·to·is (ál-ən-tō-iss, ə-lán-toyss, -tō-iss) *n., pl.* **-toides** (-tō-i-deez). A membranous sac that develops from the hindgut in the embryos of mammals, birds, and reptiles. In mammals it takes part in the formation of the umbilical cord and the placenta. [New Latin, from Greek *allantoeidēs,* ALLANTOID.] **—al·lan·to·ic** (ál-ən-tō-ik) *adj.*
al·lar·gan·do (ál-ar-gándō, áa-lar-) *adv. Music.* To be performed more slowly. Used as a direction. [Italian, from *allargare,* to make slow, widen, ultimately from Latin *largus,* abundant, LARGE.]
al·lay (ə-láy) *tr.v.* **-layed, -laying, -lays. 1.** To lessen or relieve (pain or grief, for example); reduce the intensity of. **2.** To calm or pacify (fear, for example); set at rest. —See Synonyms at **relieve.** [Middle English *alaien,* Old English *ālecgan* : *ā-,* away, aside + *lecgan,* to lay.] **—al·lay·er** *n.*
All-Black (áwl-blak) *n.* A member of New Zealand's international Rugby Union team. **—All-Black** *adj.*
all clear *n.* **1.** A signal, usually by siren, that an air raid is over. **2.** An indication of the absence of immediate obstacles or impending danger. **3.** Official approval to proceed: *We need the all clear from the boss.*
al·le·ga·tion (ál-i-gáysh'n) *n.* **1.** The act of alleging. **2.** A statement offered without proof, especially regarding the wrongdoings of another; a mere assertion. **3.** *Law.* A statement, charge, or claim put forward by a party to be proved or supported with evidence. [Middle English, from Latin *allēgātiō* (stem *allēgātiōn-*), from *allēgāre,* to dispatch, adduce: *ad-,* towards + *lēgāre,* to charge.]
al·lege (ə-léj) *tr.v.* **-leged, -leging, -leges. 1.** To assert to be true; affirm; declare. **2.** To assert without proof. **3.** To bring forward (a plea or excuse, for example) in support or denial of a claim or accusation. **4.** *Archaic.* To cite or quote, as in confirmation. —See Synonyms at **assert.** [Middle English *alleg(g)en,* from Anglo-French *alegier,* Old French *esligier,* from Vulgar Latin *exlītigare* (unattested), to clear of charges in a lawsuit: *ex-,* out of + *lītigāre,* to LITIGATE.] **—al·leg·er** *n.*
al·leged (ə-léjd, *rarely* ə-léjid) *adj.* Claimed to exist or to be as described but without proof; merely supposed: *the alleged theft.* **—al·leg·ed·ly** (ə-léjidli) *adv.*
Al·le·ghe·ny Mountains (ál-i-gáyni, -génni). Also **Al·le·ghe·nies** (-gáyniz, -génniz). Mountain range forming the western part of the Appalachian Mountains in the eastern United States. It stretches some 800 kilometres (500 miles) through Pennsylvania, Maryland, Virginia, and West Virginia, and rises to 1 480 metres (4,860 feet) at Spruce Knob in West Virginia.
al·le·giance (ə-leéjənss) *n.* **1.** Loyalty, or the obligation of loyalty, as to a nation, sovereign, or cause. **2.** The obligations of a vassal to his overlord. —See Synonyms at **fidelity.** [Middle English *allegeaunce,* from Old French *ligeance,* from *li(e)ge,* LIEGE.] **—al·le·giant** *adj.*
al·le·gor·i·cal (ál-i-górrik'l) *adj.* Also **al·le·gor·ic** (ál-i-górrik). Pertaining to, characteristic of, or having the nature of allegory. **—al·le·gor·i·cal·ly** *adv.*
al·le·go·rise, al·le·go·rize (ál-i-gər-īz || -gawr-) *v.* **-rised, -rising, -rises.** —*tr.* **1.** To express as, or in the form of, an allegory. **2.** To interpret allegorically. —*intr.* To use or make allegory. **—al·le·go·ri·sa·tion** (-ī-záysh'n || *U.S.* -i-) *n.* **—al·le·go·ris·er** *n.*
al·le·go·ry (ál-i-gəri || *U.S.* -gawri, -gōri) *n., pl.* **-ries. 1.** The representation of a subject in a story, play, or picture, using the people or events portrayed to illustrate deeper or more general truths. **2.** An instance of such representation: *The story of the Holy Grail is an allegory of man's spiritual quest.* **3.** Any symbolic representation. [Middle English *allegorie,* from Old French, from Latin *allēgoria,* from Greek from *allēgorein,* to speak figuratively, "speak in other terms": *allos,* other + *agoreuein,* to speak (in public), from *agora,* an assembly.] **—al·le·go·rist** *n.*
al·le·gret·to (ál-i-gréttō || *U.S. also* áal-) *adv. Music.* In quick tempo; slower than allegro but faster than andante. Used as a direction.
~*n., pl.* **allegrettos.** *Music.* A movement or passage in this tempo. [Italian, diminutive of ALLEGRO.] **—al·le·gret·to** *adj.*
al·le·gro (ə-láygrō, ə-léggrō) *adv. Music.* In rapid tempo; faster than allegretto but slower than presto. Used as a direction.
~*n., pl.* **allegros.** *Music.* A movement or passage in this tempo. [Italian, "lively", from Latin *alacer,* brisk.] **—al·le·gro** *adj.*
al·lele (ə-leél) *n.* Any of the alternative forms of a gene, which occupy the same relative position on homologous chromosomes. Also called "allelomorph". [German *Allel,* short for ALLELOMORPH.] **—al·le·lic** (ə-leélik, ə-léllik) *adj.*
al·le·lo·morph (ə-leélə-mawrf, -léllə-) *n.* An allele. [Greek *allēlōn,* reciprocally, from *allos,* another + -MORPH.] **—al·le·lo·mor·phic** (-mórfik) *adj.* **—al·le·lo·mor·phism** (-mórfiz'm) *n.*
al·le·lu·ia (ál-i-lŏŏ-yə || -léw-) *interj.* Used as a Christian expression of praise to God or of thanksgiving.
~*n., pl.* **alleluias. 1.** A part of the Catholic Mass beginning and ending with this word. **2.** A musical setting of this. [Middle Eng-

lish, from Medieval Latin *allēlūja,* from Late Greek *allēlouia,* from Hebrew *hallelūyāh,* HALLELUJAH.]

al·le·mande (ál-i-mánd, ál-mand ‖ *U.S.* ál-ə-mand, -mən) *n.* **1. a.** A lively, late 18th-century dance in ³/₄ time. **b.** A movement in square dancing and country dancing. **2.** *Music.* The first movement of a 17th- or 18th-century classical suite. [French, feminine of *allemand,* German, from Latin *Alemannus,* singular of ALEMANNI.]

Al·len (ál-ən), **Bog of.** Group of peat bogs in the east central part of the Republic of Ireland. Covering about 958 square kilometres (370 square miles), they provide fuel for local power stations.

Allen, Woody, born Allen Stewart Konigsberg (1935–). U.S. film director, comic actor, and writer. His films include *Bananas* (1971), *Sleeper* (1973), *Annie Hall* (1977, three oscars), and *Hannah and her Sisters* (1986, Oscar).

Al·len·de (aa-yèn-di, -day), **Salvador** (1908–73). Chilean statesman, president of Chile (1970-1973) and the first democratically elected Marxist head of government. He attempted to achieve socialism by gradual peaceful change, including land reform and nationalisation, but many measures, especially the nationalisation of foreign investments, were controversial, and financial credit was withdrawn from the Chilean economy. Right-wing opposition to Allende in Chile was encouraged by U.S. intervention, and his government was overthrown by a military coup in 1973, in which he was killed.

al·ler·gen (ál-ər-jen, -jən) *n.* A substance that causes an allergy. [German *Allergen* : *Allergie,* ALLER(GY) + -GEN.] —**al·ler·gen·ic** (-jénnik) *adj.*

al·ler·gic (ə-lérjik) *adj.* **1.** Characteristic of or concerning allergy. **2.** Having an allergy. **3.** *Informal.* Having a dislike; averse. Used with *to: allergic to work.*

al·ler·gist (ál-ərjist) *n.* A doctor specialising in allergies.

al·ler·gy (ál-ərji) *n., pl.* **-gies. 1.** Excessive sensitivity to some environmental factor or substance, such as pollens, particular foods, dust, or microorganisms, causing an adverse physical reaction. **2.** *Informal.* A dislike; an aversion. [German *Allergie,* "altered reaction" : ALL(O)- + Greek *ergon,* work, effect.]

al·le·thrin (a-léthrin, ə-) *n.* A synthetic amber liquid insecticide, similar to pyrethrin. [*Allyl* *pyrethrin.*]

al·le·vi·ate (ə-léevi-ayt) *tr.v.* **-ated, -ating, -ates.** To make more bearable; reduce (pain or grief, for example). —See Synonyms at **relieve.** [Late Latin *alleviāre,* to lighten : Latin *ad-,* towards + *levis,* light.] —**al·le·vi·a·tion** (-áysh'n) *n.* —**al·le·vi·a·tor** *n.*

al·le·vi·a·tive (ə-léevi-aytiv, -ətiv) *adj.* Also **al·le·vi·a·to·ry** (-ətri, -ətəri). Promoting alleviation.

al·ley¹ (ál-i) *n., pl.* **-leys. 1.** A narrow street or passageway between or behind buildings. **2.** A path between flowerbeds or trees in a garden or park. **3.** A **bowling alley** *(see).* **4.** *U.S.* In tennis, the **tramlines** *(see).* —**up (someone's) alley.** *Chiefly U.S. Informal.* Compatible with one's interests or qualifications; up someone's street. [Middle English *aley,* from Old French *alee,* from the feminine past participle of *aler,* to go, from Latin *ambulāre,* to walk.]

al·ley² *n., pl.* **-leys.** Also **al·ly** *pl.* **-lies.** A large playing marble. [Short for ALABASTER.]

Al·leyn (ál-in), **Edward** (1566–1626). English actor, one of the finest of the Elizabethan stage. Alleyn created the leading roles in Marlowe's *Tamburlaine* and *Doctor Faustus.* In 1613 he founded and endowed Dulwich College.

al·ley·way (ál-i-way) *n.* A narrow passage between buildings.

All Fools' Day *n.* April 1, **April Fools' Day** *(see).*

all found *adv.* Including board and lodging. Said chiefly of prices or wages.

all fours *pl.n.* **1.** All four limbs of an animal or person: *A baby crawls on all fours.* **2.** *Used with a singular verb.* A card game, usually for two players, in which seven points, acquired in any of four ways, have to be acquired for a winning score. Also called "pitch". *Chiefly U.S.* "seven-up".

all hail *interj. Archaic.* All health. Used as a greeting.

All·hal·low·mas (áwl-hál-ō-məss, -mass) *n.* Also **All·hal·lows** (áwl-hál-ōz). *Archaic.* **All Saints' Day** *(see).*

all-heal (áwl-heel) *n.* Any of several plants reputed to have healing powers, such as **valerian** and **self-heal** *(both of which see).*

al·li·a·ceous (ál-i-áyshəss) *adj. Botany.* **1.** Belonging to the same genus (*Allium*) as onions and garlic. **2.** Tasting or smelling of onions or garlic. [Latin *allium†,* garlic + -ACEOUS.]

al·li·ance (ə-lī-ənss) *n.* **1. a.** A formal pact of union joining nations or parties in a common cause. **b.** The nations or parties so conjoined. **2.** The act of allying or the state of being allied. **3.** Any union or relationship based on kinship, marriage, or common interest. **4.** A sharing or affinity of qualities or characteristics. **5.** *Botany.* A subclass of related plant families. [Middle English *alliaunce,* from Old French *aliance,* from *alier,* to ALLY.]

al·lied (ál-īd, , ə-līd) *adj.* **1.** Joined, especially in a pact; united. **2.** Of a similar nature; related: *allied studies.* **3.** *Capital* **A.** Of or pertaining to the Allies.

Al·lies (ál-īz, *rarely* ə-līz) *pl.n.* **1.** In World War I, the nations allied against the Central Powers of Europe. They were France, Great Britain, and initially Russia, and later many others, including the United States. **2.** In World War II, the nations, primarily the United Kingdom, the U.S.S.R., and the United States, allied against the Axis powers.

al·li·ga·tor (ál-i-gaytər) *n.* **1.** Either of two large, amphibious reptiles, *Alligator mississipiensis,* of the southeastern United States, or *A. sinensis,* of China, having sharp teeth and powerful jaws, and

differing from crocodiles in having a broader, shorter snout. **2.** Loosely, any crocodilian reptile. **3.** Leather made from the hide of an alligator. **4.** A tool or machine having movable, adjustable toothed jaws for gripping or crushing. [Obsolete *alagarto,* from Spanish *el lagarto* : *el,* the, from Latin *ille,* that + *lagarto,* lizard, from Latin *lacertus,* LIZARD.]

alligator pear *n.* A tree, the **avocado** *(see),* or its fruit. [Folk etymology, variant of AVOCADO (the trees are said to grow in places infested by alligators).]

all-im·por·tant (áwl-impórtənt) *adj.* Of vital importance.

all-in-clu·sive (áwl-in-klōō-siv ‖ -kléw-, -ziv) *adj.* Including all incidental charges.

Al·ling·ham (ál-ing-əm), **Margery (Louise)** (1904–66). British detective-story writer. She created a popular fictional detective in the deceptively mild Albert Campion, and wrote a number of ingenious and later serious thrillers including *The Crime at Black Dudley* (1928). *Flowers for the Judge* (1936), *Tiger in the Smoke* (1952), and *The China Governess* (1963).

all-in wrestling (áwl-in) *n.* Professional wrestling with few restrictions on holds. —**all-in wrestler** *n.*

al·lit·er·ate (ə-líttərayt) *v.* **-ated, -ating, -ates.** —*intr.* **1.** To use alliteration in speech or writing. **2.** To have or contain alliteration. —*tr.* To form or arrange with alliteration. [Back-formation from ALLITERATION] —**al·lit·er·a·tor** *n.*

al·lit·er·a·tion (ə-littə-ráysh'n) *n.* The occurrence in a phrase or line of speech or writing of two or more words having the same initial sound; for example, *wailing in the winter wind.* [New Latin *alliterātiō* (stem *alliterātiōn-*) : Latin *ad-,* to + *littera,* LETTER.]

al·lit·er·a·tive (ə-líttə-rətiv, -raytiv) *adj.* Of, manifesting, or characterised by alliteration. —**al·lit·er·a·tive·ly** *adv.* —**al·lit·er·a·tive·ness** *n.*

al·li·um (ál-i-əm) *n.* Any of various plants of the genus *Allium,* characterised by their pungent odour, and including the onion, leek, chive, garlic, and shallot. [New Latin *Allium,* from Latin *allium,* *ālium†,* garlic.]

all-night (áwl-nīt) *adj.* Open or continuing throughout the night. —**all-night·er** *n.*

allo-, all- *comb. form.* Indicates divergence, opposition, or difference; for example, **allopathy** *(see).* [Greek, other, altered, from *allos,* other.]

Al·lo·a (ál-ō-ə). Burgh in central Scotland, on the river Forth. It is noted for its whisky, glass, and worsted yarns.

al·lo·bar (ál-ə-baar) *n. Physics.* A mixture of isotopes differing in composition from the natural isotopic composition of the element. [ALLO- + Greek *baros,* weight]

al·lo·cate (ál-ə-kayt, -ō-) *tr.v.* **-cated, -cating, -cates. 1.** To designate for a special purpose; set apart. **2.** To distribute as a share; apportion; allot. **3.** *Rare.* To determine the location; locate. —See Synonyms at **assign.** [Medieval Latin *allocāre,* to place to : Latin *ad-,* towards + *locāre,* to place, from *locus,* place, LOCUS.] —**al·lo·ca·ble** (-k'əb'l) *adj.*

al·lo·ca·tion (ál-ə-káysh'n) *n.* **1.** The act of allocating or the state of being allocated. **2.** A portion or share that has been allocated.

al·lo·chem (ál-ə-kem) *n. Geology.* A discrete particle, such as a fossil, oolite, or intraclast, found in a limestone. [ALLO- + CHEM (ICAL), referring to rocks, such as limestones, deposited from solution]

al·lo·cu·tion (ál-ə-kéwsh'n) *n.* A formal and authoritative speech or address, especially one that advises or informs. [Latin *allocūtiō,* from *alloqui* (past participle *allocūtus*), to speak to : *ad-,* to + *loquī,* to speak.]

al·lo·di·um, a·lo·di·um (ə-lṓ-di-əm) *n., pl.* **-dia** (-di-ə). Land held in absolute ownership, and without obligation or service to any feudal overlord. [Medieval Latin *allodium,* from Frankish *al-ōd* (unattested), "complete property": *al-,* ALL + *-ōd* (unattested), property.] —**al·lo·di·al** *adj.* —**al·lo·di·al·ly** *adv.*

al·log·a·my (ə-lóggəmi) *n. Botany.* **Cross-fertilisation** *(see).* [ALLO- + -GAMY.] —**al·log·a·mous** *adj.*

al·lo·graph (ál-ə-graf, -graaf) *n.* **1.** Writing, especially a signature, made by one person on behalf of another. **2.** Any of several ways of representing a sound in writing, or of writing a letter of the alphabet. [ALLO- + -GRAPH.]

al·lom·er·ism (ə-lómməriz'm) *n.* Similarity in crystalline form in substances that have different chemical compositions. [ALLO- + Greek *meros,* part.] —**al·lom·er·ous** *adj.*

al·lom·e·try (ə-lómmətri) *n. Biology.* The study of the change in proportion of various parts of an organism as a consequence of growth. [ALLO- + -METRY.] —**al·lo·met·ric** (ál-ə-métrik) *adj.*

al·lo·morph (ál-ə-mawrf) *n.* **1.** In mineralogy, a **paramorph** *(see).* **2.** *Linguistics.* Any of the variant forms of a morpheme; for example, the phonetic *s* of *cats, z* of *dogs,* and *iz* of *horses* are allomorphs of the English morpheme *s.* [ALLO- + -MORPH.] —**al·lo·mor·phic** (-mórfik) *adj.* —**al·lo·mor·phism** *n.*

al·lo·path (ál-ə-path). Also **al·lop·a·thist** (ə-lóppəthist) *n.* A person who practises allopathy.

al·lop·a·thy (ə-lóppəthi) *n.* Medical treatment by orthodox means, using drugs that alleviate the symptoms of the disease. Compare **homeopathy.** [German *Allopathie* : ALLO- + -PATHY.] —**al·lo·path·ic** (ál-ə-páthik) *adj.* —**al·lo·path·i·cal·ly** *adv.*

al·lo·pat·ric (ál-ə-pátrik) *adj. Ecology.* Occurring in separate, widely differing geographical areas. Compare **sympatric.** [From ALLO- + Greek *patra,* fatherland, from *patēr,* father.] —**al·lo·pat·ri·cal·ly** *adv.*

al·lo·phane (ál-ə-fayn) *n.* An amorphous clay mineral, essentially hydrous aluminium silicate. [Greek *allophanēs*, "appearing otherwise" : ALLO- + -PHANE.]

al·lo·phone (ál-ə-fōn) *n. Linguistics.* Any of the variant forms of a phoneme; for example, the aspirated *p* of *pit* and the unaspirated *p* of *spit* are allophones of the English phoneme *p.* [ALLO- + -PHONE.] —**al·lo·phon·ic** (-fónnik) *adj.*

al·lo·pu·ri·nol (ál-ō-péwr-in-ol ‖ -ōl) *n.* A drug, $C_5H_4N_4O$, used in the treatment of gout, that acts by reducing the amount of uric acid in the blood and tissues. [ALLO- + PURIN(E) + -OL.]

all-or-none (áwl-awr-nún ‖ -ər-) *adj.* Designating a physiological response, especially a nerve impulse, that will occur only if the stimulus that elicits it is above a certain threshold value. Above this threshold the response is maximal.

all-or-noth·ing (áwl-awr-núthing ‖ -ər-) *adj.* Depending upon or prepared to accept only complete success: *He had an all-or-nothing approach to the venture.*

al·lot (ə-lót) *tr.v.* **-lotted, -lotting, -lots.** 1. To distribute; apportion. 2. To give or assign; allocate: *allot three weeks to a project.* —See Synonyms at **assign.** [Middle English *alotten,* from Old French *aloter* : *a-,* from Latin *ad-,* to + *lot,* a portion, lot, from Frankish *lot* (unattested).] —**al·lot·tee** *n.* —**al·lot·ter** *n.*

al·lot·ment (ə-lótmənt) *n.* 1. The act of allotting. 2. That which is allotted. 3. In Britain, a piece of ground, generally rented from a local authority, for cultivation, especially for growing vegetables.

al·lo·trope (ál-ə-trōp) *n.* Any of the different crystalline or molecular forms of an element that displays allotropy. [Back-formation from ALLOTROPY.]

al·lot·ro·py (ə-lóttrəpi) *n.* The existence of two or more crystalline or molecular structural forms of an element. Diamond and graphite, for example, are allotropic forms of carbon. [ALLO- + -TROPY.] —**al·lo·trop·ic** (ál-ə-tróppik) *adj.* **al·lo·trop·i·cal** *adj.* —**al·lo·trop·i·cal·ly** *adv.*

all' ot·ta·va (ál ə-táavə ‖ U.S. also áal ō-) *adv. Music.* Symbol **8va** To be played an octave higher or lower than written. [Italian, "at the octave".] —**all' ot·ta·va** *adj.*

all out *adv.* With maximum effort, determination, or strength: *She went all out to win the contest.*

all-out (áwl-owt) *adj.* Complete; without reservation; out-and-out: *an all-out effort.*

all over *adv.* 1. In every possible place; everywhere. 2. *Informal.* Typically; in every respect: *He refused to back down—that's him all over.*

all-o·ver (áwl-ōvər) *adj.* Covering an entire surface.

al·low (ə-lów) *v.* **-lowed, -lowing, -lows.** *tr.* 1. To raise or constitute no objection, restraint, or bar to; let happen or be done; permit: *Do the rules allow a recount?* 2. To acknowledge or admit; concede: *allow the legality of a claim.* 3. To permit to have. 4. To make provision for: *allow time for a coffee break.* 5. To permit the presence of: *No pets allowed.* 6. To treat (an expense) as an amount that may be deducted from one's taxable income in assessing one's tax liability. 7. To provide (the needed amount): *allow funds in case of emergency.* —*intr.* 1. To make an allowance or provision. Used with *for: allow for bad weather.* 2. To permit or accommodate; be susceptible. Used with *of: a clause allowing of several interpretations.* [Middle English *allowen,* from Old French *al(l)ouer,* to permit, approve, a blend of: (a) Medieval Latin *allocāre,* to assign, ALLOCATE, and (b) Latin *allaudāre,* to give praise to : *ad-,* to + *laudāre,* to praise, LAUD.]

al·low·a·ble *adj.* 1. That may be allowed; permissible. 2. Tax-deductible: *allowable expenses.*

al·low·ance (ə-lów-ənss) *n.* 1. The act of allowing. 2. A regular provision of money, food, or the like, as to a dependant. 3. Money provided for a particular purpose: *a clothing allowance.* 4. A price reduction granted as in exchange for used merchandise; a discount. 5. An amount of income which a taxpayer may earn without incurring any tax liability. 6. *Often plural.* A consideration of modifying factors or extenuating circumstances: *make allowances for his age.* —*tr.v.* **allowanced, -ancing, -ances.** 1. To restrict to an allowance. 2. To put on an allowance.

Al·lo·way (ál-ə-way). Village in Scotland, three kilometres (two miles) south of Ayr, on the river Doon. It was the birthplace of the poet Robert Burns.

al·low·ed·ly (ə-lów-idli) *adv.* By general admission; admittedly.

al·loy (ál-oy, ə-lóy) *n.* 1. A macroscopically homogeneous mixture or solid solution of two or more metals or of a metal with an element such as carbon, with the atoms of one replacing or occupying interstitial positions between atoms of the other. 2. Anything added that lowers value or purity. —*tr.v.* (ə-lóy, ál-oy) **alloyed, -loying, -loys.** 1. To combine (metals) to form an alloy. 2. To lower the purity or value of (a metal) by mixing with an inferior metal. 3. To debase or reduce in purity by the addition of an inferior element. [Old French *aloi,* from *aloier, aleier,* to alloy, to bind, from Latin *alligāre,* to bind to, ALLY.]

al·loyed junction (ə-lóyd, ál-oyd) *n. Electronics.* A semiconductor junction formed by alloying a metal contact with a wafer of semiconducting material.

alloy steel *n.* Any of various types of steel that contain large amounts of other metals, such as chromium, vanadium, or tungsten, used for special purposes. Compare **carbon steel.**

all-pur·pose (áwl-púrpəss) *adj.* Fulfilling many different functions; capable of being used in various ways: *an all-purpose vehicle.*

all right, al·right (áwl-rıt) *adj.* 1. Satisfactory; as desired; average. 2. Correct. 3. Not injured or sick. 4. Permissible: *Is it all right to leave now?* 5. *Chiefly U.S. Informal.* a. Excellent. b. Honest; dependable. —*adv.* 1. To one's satisfaction. 2. Safely. 3. Very well; yes. Used to express agreement or concession. 4. Without a doubt: *He's a fool, all right!*

Usage: It used to be said that *it is not all right to write alright.* Formal written English still prefers two words, *all right,* but *alright* is increasingly common, presumably on analogy with *altogether, already,* and *almost.*

all-round (áwl-równd) *adj.* 1. Comprehensive in extent or depth: *all-round vocational training.* 2. Able to do many or all things well; generally excellent; versatile: *an all-round athlete.*

all-round·er (áwl-równdər) *n.* A person who has many talents or abilities, especially in sport.

All Saints' Day *n.* November 1, a church festival in honour of all saints.

all-seed (áwl-seed) *n. Botany.* Any of several plants having many seeds, such as **knotgrass** (see).

All Souls' Day *n.* November 2, observed by the Roman Catholic Church as a day of prayer for souls in purgatory.

all-spice (áwl-spíss) *n.* 1. A tropical American tree, *Pimenta officinalis,* having small white flowers and aromatic berries. 2. The dried berries of this tree, used whole or ground as a spice. Also called "pimento". [ALL + SPICE, after its supposed flavour of nutmeg, cloves, and cinnamon.]

all-star (áwl-staar) *adj.* Made up wholly of star performers: *a play with an all-star cast.*

all-time (áwl-tím) *adj. Informal.* Of all time: *one of the all-time greats of football.*

all told *adv.* In all; altogether; with everything or everyone considered: *over 50 deaths all told..*

al·lude (ə-lōōd, ə-léwd) *intr.v.* **-luded, -luding, -ludes.** To make an indirect reference; refer, without identifying specifically. Used with *to.* [Latin *allūdere,* to play with, jest at : *ad-,* to + *lūdere,* to play, from *lūdus,* game.]

all-up (áwl-úp) *n. Australian Slang.* A bet in which the stake and winnings from a previous event are put on a subsequent one.

al·lure (ə-léwr, ə-lóor) *tr. v.* **-lured, -luring, -lures.** To entice with something desirable; tempt; exercise fascination over. —*n.* The power to entice or tempt; fascination; strong attraction. [Middle English *aluren,* from Old French *aleurrer* : *a-,* to + *leurrer,* to lure, from *loirre, leurre,* LURE.] —**al·lure·ment** *n.* —**al·lur·er** *n.*

al·lur·ing (ə-léwr-ing, -lóor-) *adj.* Tempting, enticing, or fascinating. —**al·lur·ing·ly** *adv.*

al·lu·sion (ə-lōōzh'n, ə-léwzh'n) *n.* 1. The act of alluding 2. An indirect, but pointed or meaningful, reference. [Late Latin *allūsiō* (stem *allūsiōn-*), a playing with, from Latin *allūdere* (past participle *allūsus*), to play with, ALLUDE.]

al·lu·sive (ə-lōō-siv, -léw- ‖ -ziv) *adj.* Containing or making allusions; suggestive. —**al·lu·sive·ly** *adv.* —**al·lu·sive·ness** *n.*

al·lu·vi·al (ə-lōōvi-əl, -léwvi-) *adj.* 1. Of, pertaining to, or composed of alluvium. 2. *Australian.* Containing gold deposits. Said of soil.

alluvial fan *n.* A fan-shaped accumulation of alluvium deposited at the mouth of a ravine. Also called "alluvial cone".

alluvial plain *n.* A plain resulting from the deposit of alluvium.

al·lu·vi·on (ə-lōōvi-ən, -léwvi-) *n.* 1. Alluvium. 2. The flow of water against a shore or bank. 3. Inundation by water; flooding. 4. *Law.* The formation of new land, especially along a river bed, by deposited alluvium. Compare **avulsion.** [Latin *alluviō* (stem *alluviōn-*), from *alluere,* to wash against : *ad-,* to + *lavere,* to wash.]

al·lu·vi·um (ə-lōō-vi-əm, -léw-) *n., pl.* **-viums** or **-via** (-vi-ə). Any sediment deposited by flowing water, as in a river bed, flood plain, or delta. Also called "alluvion". [Latin, from the neuter of *alluvius,* alluvial, from *alluere,* to wash against. See **alluvion.**]

all-weath·er (áwl-wéthər) *adj.* Suitable for or usable in any kind of weather: *all-weather garments.*

al·ly¹ (ə-lí, ál-ī) *v.* **-lied, -lying, -lies.** —*tr.* 1. To unite or connect in a formal relationship or bond, as by treaty, marriage, or other arrangement. Used with *to* or *with: The United States allies itself with Great Britain.* 2. To connect or associate. Used chiefly in the passive. —*intr.* To enter into an alliance. —*n.* (ál-ī ‖ ə-lí) *pl.* **allies.** 1. One that is united with another in some formal or personal relationship. See **Allies.** 2. A close associate or supporter. 3. *Biology.* A plant or animal species or other group that is related to another such group. —See Synonyms at **partner.** [Middle English *al(l)ien,* from Old French *alier,* from Latin *alligāre,* to bind to : *ad-,* to + *ligāre,* to bind.]

ally² Variant of **alley** (a marble).

al·lyl (ál-il) *n.* The univalent organic radical $CH_2{:}CHCH_2$. [Latin *allium†,* garlic + -YL (so called because it was first obtained from garlic).] —**al·lyl·ic** (ə-líllik, a-) *adj.*

allyl alcohol *n.* A colourless, poisonous, flammable liquid, $CH_2{:}CHCH_2OH$, used in poison gas, resins, plastics, and herbicides.

allyl resin *n.* Any of a class of synthetic resins derived from allyl alcohol esters and dibasic acids, and used as laminating adhesives and in varnishes and moulding compounds.

all you *pron. West Indian Informal.* You, and people like you.

almacantar. Variant of **almucantar.**

Al Madinah. See **Medina.**

Al·ma·gest (ál-məjest) *n.* 1. A comprehensive work on astronomy and geography compiled by Ptolemy about A.D. 150. **2.** *Sometimes small* **a.** In medieval science, any similar work concerned with astronomy or alchemy. [Middle English *almageste*, from Old French, from Arabic *al-majisti* : *al*, the + Greek *megistē (suntaxis)*, greatest (collection), feminine of *megistos*, superlative of *megas*, great.]

al·ma ma·ter, Al·ma Ma·ter (ál-mə máytər, maátər ‖ *U.S. also* aál-) *n.* **1.** The school, college, or university that one has attended. **2.** *U.S.* The song of an institution of higher learning. [Latin, "cherishing or fostering mother".]

al·ma·nac (áwl-mənak ‖ ál-, ól-) *n.* **1.** An annual publication including calendars with weather records, astronomical information, tide tables, and other related tabular information. **2.** An annual publication composed of various lists, charts, and tables of useful information in many unrelated fields. [Middle English *almenak*, from Medieval Latin (Roger Bacon) *almanac(h)†*.]

Al Manamah. See Manama.

al·man·dine (ál-mən-din, -dīn ‖ *U.S.* -deen) *n.* Also **al·man·dite** (-dīt). A deep violet-red garnet, essentially $Fe_3Al_2(SiO_4)_3$, found in metamorphic rocks and used as a gemstone. [Variant of earlier *alabandine*, from Middle English *alabandina*, from Late Latin *(gemma) alabandīna*, "(gem) of *Alabanda*", town in Caria, ancient district of Asia Minor, famous for jewellery.]

Al·ma-Tad·e·ma (ál-mə táddimə), **Sir Lawrence** (1836-1912). Dutch-born British painter. He is famous for his grand romantic paintings set in classical Greece and Rome and ancient Egypt.

al·me·mar (al-méemaar) *n. Judaism.* A kind of pulpit, a **bema** *(see).* [Hebrew *almēmār*, from Arabic *al-minbar*, the pulpit.]

Al·me·ría (ál-me-rée-ə, -mə-). Seaport on the Gulf of Almería in the Mediterranean and the capital of Almería province in the Andalusia region of Spain.

al·might·y (awl-mīti) *adj.* **1.** All-powerful; omnipotent: *almighty God.* **2.** *Informal.* Great. Used as an intensive: *an almighty din.* —**the Almighty.** God.
~*adv. Chiefly U.S. Slang.* Extremely: *almighty scared.* [Middle English *almighty*, Old English *ealmihtig* : *eall*, ALL + *mihtig*, from *miht*, MIGHT.] —**al·might·i·ly** *adv.*

al·mond (áa-mənd ‖ aál-, ál-, *U.S. also* á-) *n.* **1.** A small tree, *Prunus amygdalus,* native to the Mediterranean region, having pink flowers and fruit containing an edible nut. **2.** The nut itself, ellipsoid in shape, and having a yellowish-brown shell. **3.** Something having the oval, pointed shape of an almond. **4.** Light yellowish-brown. [Middle English *almande*, from Old French, from Late Latin *amandula*, corruption of Latin *amygdala*, from Greek *amugdalē†*.] —**almond** *adj.*

al·mon·er (áa-mənər ‖ ál-) *n.* **1.** One who distributes alms, as for a church or royal family. **2.** *British.* Formerly, a **medical social worker** *(see).* [Middle English *a(u)moner*, from Anglo-French, from Old French *aumosnier*, from *amosne*, alms, from Vulgar Latin *alemosina* (unattested), from Late Latin *eleēmosyna*, ALMS.]

al·mon·ry (áa-mənri ‖ ál-) *n., pl.* **-ries.** The house of an almoner; a place at which alms are distributed.

Al·mo·ra·vides, Al·mo·ra·vids (al-máwrə-vīdz, -vidz ‖ -mõrə-) *pl.n.* A Berber dynasty and Muslim sect, based in the western Sahara, that conquered northwestern Africa and much of Spain in the 11th and 12th centuries. [Arabic *al-murābitūn*, "holy ones", from *murābit*, holy man.]

al·most (áwl-mōst ‖ ól-, -məst, -mŏst) *adv.* Slightly short of; not quite; all but; very nearly. [Middle English *almost*, Old English *(e)almēst*, completely, for the most part : *eall*, ALL + *mæst*, MOST.]

alms (aamz ‖ aalmz) *pl.n.* Money or goods given to the poor as charity. [Middle English *almes, almesse*, from Old English *ælmesse*, from Germanic *alemosina* (unattested), alteration (through influence of Latin *alimōnia;* see **alimony**) of Late Latin *eleēmosyna*, from Greek *eleēmosunē*, pity, from *eleēmōn*, pitiful, from *eleos†*, pity.]

alms·house (áamz-howss ‖ áalmz-) *n.* **1.** *British.* A house founded and supported by a charity to provide accommodation for the poor and elderly. **2.** A poorhouse.

alms·man (áamz-mən ‖ áalmz-) *n., pl.* **-men** (-mən). One dependent on alms for his support.

al·mu·can·tar, al·ma·can·tar (ál-mə-kántər) *n. Astronomy.* **1.** A circle on the celestial sphere that is parallel to the horizontal plane. **2.** An instrument for measuring azimuth and altitude. [Middle English, from Medieval Latin *almucantarath*, from Arabic *almukantarāt*, the sundial.]

al·ni·co (ál-ni-kō) *n.* Any of a class of hard, strong alloys of aluminium, cobalt, copper, iron, nickel, and sometimes niobium or tantalum, used to make strong permanent magnets. [*Al*uminium *ni*ckel *co*balt.]

alodium. Variant of **allodium.**

al·oe (ál-ō) *n.* Any of various plants of the genus *Aloe,* mostly native to southern Africa, having fleshy, spiny-toothed leaves and red or yellow flowers. [Middle English *aloe*, Old English *aluwe*, from Latin *aloē,* from Greek, probably of Oriental origin.] —**al·o·et·ic** (ál-ō-éttik) *adj.*

al·oes (ál-ōz) *n. Used with a singular verb.* **1.** A cathartic drug derived from the aloe, **bitter aloes** *(see).* **2.** The fragrant wood of a tree, *Aquilaria agallocha,* of tropical Asia. In this sense, also called "aloes wood", "eaglewood". [See **aloe.**] —**al·o·et·ic** (ál-ō-éttik) *adj.*

a·loft (ə-lóft ‖ ə-láwft) *adv.* **1.** In or into a high place; high or higher up. **2.** *Nautical.* In or towards the upper rigging. [Middle English, from Old Norse *ā lopt* : *ā,* on, in + *lopt,* air, sky]

a·lo·ha (ə-ló-ə, aa-lô-haa) *interj.* Used in Hawaii to express greeting or farewell. [Hawaiian, "love".]

al·o·in (ál-ō-in) *n.* A bitter crystalline compound obtained from the aloe and used as a laxative. [ALO(E) + -IN.]

a·lone (ə-lón) *adj.* **1.** Apart from others; single; solitary. **2. a.** Excluding anything or anyone else; with nothing further; only: *Man cannot live by bread alone.* **b.** Taking no one or nothing else into account: *The price alone should have made you suspicious.* **3.** Unique or by oneself in a particular position, belief, or ability: *I wasn't alone in opposing his plan.* —**go it alone.** *Informal.* To take action independently of others. —**leave alone.** *Informal.* To refrain from tampering or interfering with. —**let alone.** Not to speak of or think of; even less: *I haven't a minute to spare, let alone an hour.* [Middle English, from *al one* : ALL + ONE.] —**a·lone** *adv.* —**a·lone·ness** *n.*

a·long (ə-lóng ‖ *U.S.* ə-láwng) *adv.* **1.** With a progressive onward motion; forwards: *walking along at a brisk pace.* **2.** In association; together. Usually used with *with.* See Usage note at **together.** **3.** As company; as a companion: *Bring your son along.* **4.** In a line; from one to another: *Read the note, and pass it along.* —**be along.** *Informal.* To come; arrive at a place: *Our guests should be along soon.* ~*prep.* **1.** Over or through the length of: *running along the road.* **2.** In a line with; following the length or path of: *trees growing along the river.* [Middle English *along*, Old English *andlang*, "extending opposite" : *and-*, against, facing + *lang*, extending, LONG.]

a·long·shore (ə-lóng-shawr ‖ -shōr, *U.S.* -láwng-) *adv.* Along, near, or by the shore, either on land or in the water.

a·long·side (ə-lóng-sīd ‖ *U.S.* -lawng-) *adv.* Along, near, at, or to the side of something, especially a ship.
~*prep.* By the side of; side by side with.

a·loo (ál-ōō, ə-lóō) *n.* Potato. Used in Indian cuisine. [Indic.]

a·loof (ə-lōōf) *adj.* Distant, especially in one's relations with other people; reserved.
~*adv.* At a distance, but within view; apart; withdrawn. [From obsolete *aloufe!* (nautical use), "(steer the ship) up into the wind!" : A- (to) + *loufe*, LUFF.] —**a·loof·ly** *adv.* —**a·loof·ness** *n.*

al·o·pe·ci·a (ál-ə-péesh-ə, -péessi-, -péeshi-) *n.* Loss of hair; baldness. [Latin *alopēcia*, mange of fox, baldness, from Greek *alōpekia*, from *alōpēx*, fox.] —**al·o·pe·cic** (-péessik) *adj.*

a·loud (ə-lówd) *adv.* **1.** Louder than a whisper; audibly: *afraid to say it aloud.* **2.** With the voice; not silently: *Read aloud.*

Al·o·y·sius (ál-ō-íshəss), **Saint**, born Luigi Gonzaga (1568–91). Italian Jesuit, patron saint of youth, canonised in 1726.

alp (alp) *n.* **1.** A shoulder high on a mountain side; especially, the gentle, grassy slope above a U-shaped glaciated valley, often used as summer pasture. **2.** A high mountain peak, especially one of the **Alps** *(see).*

A.L.P. Australian Labor Party.

al·pac·a (al-páckə) *n.* **1.** A domesticated South American mammal, *Lama pacos,* related to the llama, and having fine, long wool. **2. a.** The silky wool of this animal. **b.** Cloth made from this wool. **3.** A glossy cotton or rayon-and-wool fabric, usually black. [Spanish, from Aymara *alpaco*, from *packo*, reddish brown.]

al·pen·glow (ál-pən-glō) *n.* A rosy glow appearing round snow-covered mountain peaks at sunrise or dusk on a clear day. [Partial translation of German *Alpenglühen* : *Alpen,* ALPS + *glühen,* to glow.]

al·pen·horn (ál-pən-hawrn) *n.* Also **alp·horn** (álp-hawrn). A curved wooden horn, sometimes as long as 6 metres (20 feet), used, especially formerly, by herdsmen in the Alps to call cows to pasture. [German *Alpenhorn* : *Alpen,* ALPS + *Horn,* HORN.]

al·pen·stock (ál-pən-stok) *n.* A long staff with an iron point, used by mountain climbers. [German *Alpenstock* : *Alpen,* ALPS + *Stock,* a staff, from Old High German *stoc.*]

al·pes·trine (al-péstrin) *adj. Botany.* Growing at high altitudes; alpine or subalpine. [Medieval Latin *alpestris,* mountainous, from *Alpes,* the ALPS.]

al·pha (ál-fə) *n.* **1.** The first letter in the Greek alphabet, written A, α. Transliterated in English as *A, a.* **2.** A first-class mark for an examination, essay, or the like. **3.** *Astronomy.* The brightest or main star in a constellation. **4.** *Physics* **a.** An alpha particle. **b** An alpha ray.
~*adj. Chemistry.* Closest to the functional group of atoms in a molecule. [Middle English, from Latin, from Greek, from a Phoenician word akin to Hebrew *āleph,* ALEPH.]

alpha and omega *n.* **1.** The first and the last: "*I am Alpha and Omega, the beginning and the ending, saith the Lord*" (Revelation 1:8). **2.** The most important part of something.

Alpha A·quil·ae (ə-kwíllee) *n.* A star, Altair *(see).*

al·pha·bet (ál-fə-bet, -bit) *n.* **1.** The set of letters in which a language or group of languages is written, arranged in the order fixed by custom. **2.** Any system of characters or symbols representing sounds, words, or things: *the semaphore alphabet.* **3.** The basic or elementary principles of anything; rudiments; ABC. [Latin *alphabē-tum,* from Greek *alphabētos* : ALPHA + BETA.]

al·pha·bet·i·cal (ál-fə-béttik'l) *adj.* Also **al·pha·bet·ic** (-béttik). **1.** Arranged in the customary order of the letters of an alphabet. **2.** Of, pertaining to, or expressed by an alphabet. —**al·pha·bet·i·cal·ly** *adv.*

al·pha·bet·ise, al·pha·bet·ize (ál-fə-bet-īz, -bət-) *tr.v.* **-ised, -ising, -ises.** **1.** To arrange in or put into alphabetical order. **2.** To express by or supply with an alphabet. —**al·pha·bet·i·sa·tion** (-ī-záysh'n ‖ *U.S.* -i-) *n.* —**al·pha·bet·is·er** *n.*

Alpha Cen·tau·ri (sen-táwr-ī, -i) *n.* A double star in Centaurus, the brightest in the constellation, 4.4 light-years from Earth. Also called "Rigil Kent".

Alpha Cru·cis (krōo-siss) *n.* A double star in the constellation Crux, approximately 230 light-years from Earth. Also called "Acrux".

alpha decay *n. Physics.* A form of radioactive decay in which an unstable nucleus emits an alpha particle, transforming into a lighter nucleus.

al·pha·foe·to·pro·tein (ál-fə-feetō-prō-teen, -tee-in) *n.* A protein formed in the foetus and present in the amniotic fluid surrounding it in the womb. Its presence in high levels is used as a prenatal diagnostic test for such abnormal conditions as spina bifida. See **amniocentesis.**

alpha iron *n.* An allotropic form of iron, **ferrite** *(see).*

Alpha Le·o·nis (lee-ōniss) *n.* A star, **Regulus** *(see).*

al·pha·nu·mer·ic (ál-fə-new-mérrik || ál-fə-mér·ic (ál-fə-mérrik). **1. a.** Consisting of both alphabetical and numerical symbols. **b.** Consisting of such symbols and also of punctuation marks, mathematical symbols, and other conventional symbols used in computer work. **2.** Of, pertaining to, or employing an alphanumeric code or system.

alpha particle *n. Symbol* α A positively charged particle consisting of two protons and two neutrons; a helium-atom nucleus.

alpha privative *n.* The Greek negative prefix *a-* *(an-* before vowels). See **a-** (negative prefix).

alpha ray *n.* A narrow stream of alpha particles.

alpha rhythm *n.* One of the electroencephalographic waveforms found in recordings of the electrical activity of the adult brain, characteristically 8 to 12 smooth, regular oscillations per second in subjects at rest. Also called "alpha wave". Compare **beta rhythm.**

al·pho·sis (al-fō-siss) *n. Pathology.* Lack of skin pigment, as in albinism. [New Latin : Greek *alphos,* kind of leprosy + *-osis.*]

al·pine (ál-pīn) *adj.* **1.** Of or pertaining to high mountains. **2. a.** *Biology.* Living or growing on mountains above the treeline. **b.** *Botany.* Small enough to be suitable for growing in a rock garden. **3.** Intended for or concerned with mountaineering. **4.** *Capital* **A. a.** Of, pertaining to, or characteristic of the Alps or their inhabitants. **b.** *Geology.* Of, pertaining to, or designating the last great mountain-building period. It began in mid-Tertiary times and resulted in the main fold-mountain ranges of Europe and Asia, including the Alps. **c.** Of or pertaining to a subdivision of the Caucasian race predominant around the Alps. **d.** Of or designating downhill and slalom skiing events. Compare **Nordic.** ~*n. Botany.* An alpine plant. [Latin *Alpīnus,* of the ALPS.]

alpine azalea *n.* A low-growing, shrubby plant, *Loiseleuria procumbens,* of northern regions, having small evergreen leaves and clusters of small pink or white flowers.

al·pin·ist (ál-pin-ist) *n. Sometimes capital* **A.** A mountain climber. —**al·pin·ism** *n.*

Alps (alps). A major mountain system consisting of a great arc of fold mountains, which runs for about 800 kilometres (500 miles) from the north shore of the Ligurian Sea through southeast France, northern Italy, Switzerland, Germany, and Austria, into Slovenia. The highest peak, Mont Blanc, in Haute-Savoie, France, rises to 4 807 metres (15,771 feet).

al·read·y (awl-réddi, áwl- || ol-) *adv.* **1.** By a specified or implied time: *already dead when they found him.* **2.** As early or soon as this: *Is he back already?* **3.** Before; previously: *I've already asked her and don't feel like asking again.* **4.** *U.S. Slang.* For goodness' sake! Used as an intensive of irritation: *That's enough already!* [Middle English *al redy :* ALL + READY.]

Usage: The use of *already* with the simple past tense is common in informal American speech, and is becoming so in colloquial British English: *I already got it; he already went.* In formal English, however, only the *have* form of the verb is acceptable: *He has already gone.*

alright. Variant of **all right.** See Usage note at **all right.**

Al·sace (al-sáss, ál-). *German* **El·sass** (él-zass). Region of eastern France, lying on the border with Germany. Annexed by Germany, along with Lorraine, after the Franco-Prussian War of 1870, it was returned to France by the Treaty of Versailles (1919).

Al·sa·tian (al-sáysh'n) *adj.* Of or pertaining to Alsace, its inhabitants, or their culture. ~*n.* **1.** A native or inhabitant of Alsace. **2.** A dog, a **German shepherd** *(see).*

al·sike clover (ál-sik, áwl-, -sīk) *n.* A plant, *Trifolium hybridum,* native to Eurasia and widely cultivated for forage, having compound leaves and pink or whitish flowers. [After *Alsike,* town in Sweden, where it was first found.]

al·so (áwl-sō || ól-) *adv.* Besides; in addition; too. [Middle English *also,* from Old English *(e)alswā,* even so, altogether thus : *(e)al-,* all + *swā,* so.]

Synonyms: also, too, besides, moreover, furthermore.

Usage: The use of *also* as a connective word, in the sense of "and", should be avoided in formal written English. *He studied French and German, also Russian and Greek* is a poorly constructed sentence, which would be better in the form *He studied French and German, and also Russian and Greek.*

al·so-ran (áwl-sō-ran) *n.* **1.** A horse or dog that fails to finish in the first three, or sometimes four, places in a race. **2.** *Informal.* One that is defeated in a race, election, or other competition; a loser or failure.

alt (alt) *n. Music.* The first octave above the treble staff. Used chiefly in the phrase *in alt.* [Latin *altus,* high, deep.]

alt. altitude.

Al·tai Mountains (al-táy-ī, -tī, ál-tī). Central Asian mountain range. It lies mostly in Russia, but spreads into Xinjiang (China) and Mongolia. Belukha, the highest peak in Russia, rises to 4 506 metres (14,783 feet).

Al·ta·ic (al-táy-ik) *n.* A language family of Europe and Asia, including Turkic, Tungus, Mongolian, and possibly Korean. [After the ALTAI MOUNTAINS, where the languages originated.] —**Al·ta·ic** *adj.*

Al·tair (ál-tair, al-taír || *U.S. also* -tír) *n.* A very bright, double, variable star in the constellation Aquila, approximately 15.7 light-years from Earth. Also called "Alpha Aquilae". [Arabic *al-tā'ir,* "the star".]

Al·ta·mi·ra (ál-tə-méer-ə). Caves lying 21 kilometres (13 miles) southwest of Santander in north Spain, containing magnificent Stone Age wall paintings discovered in 1879.

al·tar (áwl-tər || ól-) *n.* **1.** Any elevated place or structure upon which sacrifices may be offered or incense burnt, or before which religious ceremonies may be enacted. **2.** In Christian churches, a table or similar structure upon which the Eucharist is celebrated. —**lead to the altar.** To marry. [Middle English *altar,* Old English *altar,* from Late Latin *altāre,* "high place", from Latin *altus,* high.]

altar boy *n.* Especially in the Roman Catholic Church, an attendant who assists a priest in the performance of a religious service; an acolyte.

al·tar·piece (áwl-tər-peess || ól-) *n.* A painting, carving, or the like placed above and behind an altar.

alt·az·i·muth (alt-ázzimoth) *n.* A mounting for astronomical telescopes that permits both horizontal (azimuth) rotation and vertical (altitude) rotation. [ALT(ITUDE) + AZIMUTH.]

Alt·dorf or **Al·torf** (ált-dawrf). Town in central Switzerland, the capital of Uri canton, home of the legendary hero William Tell. A bronze statue erected in 1895 marks the spot where Tell is supposed to have shot an apple, with his crossbow, off the head of his son.

Alt·dor·fer (ált-dawrfər), **Albrecht** (c. 1480–1538). German painter. He is often regarded as the first true landscape painter as many of his scenes contain no figures, or only insignificant ones.

al·ter (áwl-tər || ól-) *v.* **-tered, -tering, -ters.** —*tr.* **1.** To modify or make different, usually without changing the fundamental nature of. **2.** To adjust or remake (a garment) for a better fit. **3.** *Chiefly U.S. & Australian.* To castrate or spay. —*intr.* To change or become different. —See Synonyms at **change.** [Middle English *alteren,* from Old French *alterer,* from Medieval Latin *alterāre,* from Latin *alter,* other.] **al·ter·a·bil·i·ty** (-ə-bílləti), **al·ter·a·ble·ness** *n.* —**al·ter·a·ble** *adj.* —**al·ter·a·bly** *adv.*

al·ter·a·tion (áwl-tə-ráysh'n || ól-) *n.* **1.** The act or procedure of altering. **2.** The condition resulting from altering; a modification; a change.

al·ter·a·tive (áwl-tə-rətiv, -raytiv || ól-) *adj.* **1.** Tending to alter or produce alteration. **2.** *Medicine.* Tending to restore normal health. ~*n.* Also **al·ter·ant** (-tərənt). An alterative treatment or medicine.

al·ter·cate (áwl-tər-kayt || ól-) *intr.v.* **-cated, -cating, -cates.** To argue or dispute vehemently. [Latin *altercārī,* to have differences with another, from *alter,* another.]

al·ter·ca·tion (áwl-tər-káysh'n || ól-) *n.* A heated and noisy quarrel.

al·ter e·go *n.* (ál-tər éegō, éggō || áwl-, ól-) *n.* **1.** Another side of oneself; a second self. **2.** An intimate or inseparable friend; a constant companion. [Latin, "other I".]

al·ter·nate (áwl-tər-nayt || ól-, *rarely* ál-) *v.* **-nated, -nating, -nates.** —*intr.* **1.** To occur in successive turns. Usually used with *with:* *The rainy season alternates with the dry season.* **2.** To pass from one state, action, or place to a second, back to the first, and so on indefinitely. Usually used with *between: alternate between optimism and pessimism.* **3.** To change direction regularly. Used of an electric current or voltage. —*tr.* **1.** To do or perform by turns. **2.** To cause to follow in turns; interchange regularly. ~*adj.* (awl-térn-ət, -it || ol-, *U.S.* áwl-tər-nət, ál-). **1.** Happening or following in turns; succeeding each other continuously: *alternate rain and sunshine.* **2.** Every other one of a series: *on alternate days.* **3.** *U.S.* In place of another; substitute: *an alternate plan.* **4.** *Botany.* **a.** Growing at alternating intervals on either side of a stem. Said especially of leaves. Compare **opposite.** **b.** Arranged alternately between other parts, as stamens are between petals. —See Usage note at **alternative.** ~*n.* (*U.S.* áwl-tər-nət, ál-). *Chiefly U.S.* A person acting in the place of another; a substitute. [Latin *alternāre,* from *alternus,* by turns, interchangeable, from *alter,* other.] —**al·ter·nate·ness** *n.*

alternate angle *n. Geometry.* An angle on one side of a **transversal** *(see)* that cuts two lines, equal to one of the intersected lines as a side.

al·ter·nate·ly (awl-térn-ət-li, -it- || ol-, *U.S.* áwl-tərn-, ál-) *adv.* In alternate order or place; by turns. —See Usage note at **alternative.**

al·ter·nat·ing current (áwl-tər-nayting || ól-) *n. Abbr.* **ac, A.C.** An electric current that reverses direction in a circuit at regular intervals, especially one that varies sinusoidally.

al·ter·na·tion (áwl-tər-náysh'n || ól-, ál-) *n.* Successive changes from one state to another and back again.

alternation of generations *n.* The occurrence within the life cycle of many plants and certain animals of alternating sexual and asexual reproductive stages. Also called "digenesis", "heterogenesis", "metagenesis", "xenogenesis".

al·ter·na·tive (awl-térnətiv || ol-, al-) *n.* **1.** The possibility or necessity of choosing only one of two or more things, courses of action,

or the like: *You have the alternative of paying a fine or going to prison.* **2.** Either or any of the things from which one is to be chosen: *Is there any alternative to taking the train?* —See Synonyms at **choice.**
~adj. **1.** Offering or necessitating a choice between two or more things or courses; constituting an alternative. **2.** *Grammar.* Indicating that the words or phrases connected are alternatives: *an alternative conjunction.* **3.** Different from or opposed to conventional and established types: *alternative medicine; the alternative press.* —**al·ter·na·tive·ly** *adv.*
Usage: The traditional attitude in grammar books has been to restrict this word to contexts where a choice between only two items is involved, but the use of the word to refer to more than two is increasingly widespread, especially when an unspecified quantity is expressed: *There were several alternatives.* There is a tendency, especially in American English, to use *alternate* and *alternately* as substitutes for *alternative* and *alternatively.* This should be avoided: *alternate* and *alternately* should keep the sense of following by turns, whereas *alternative* and *alternatively* should always carry the sense of a choice between possibilities.

Alternative Service Book *n. Abbr.* **A.S.B.** A prayer book for use in the Church of England, containing forms of services, in contemporary language, which may be used instead of those in the Book of Common Prayer.

al·ter·na·tor (áwl-tər-naytər || ól-, ál-) *n.* An electric generator that produces alternating current.

al·thae·a, *U.S.* **al·the·a** (al-thée-ə) *n.* **1.** Any plant of the genus *Althaea,* which includes the hollyhock. **2.** A shrub, the **rose of Sharon** *(see).* [Latin, marsh mallows, from Greek *althaia,* "healer", from *althein,* to heal.]

Al·thing (ál-thing, áwl-) *n.* The Icelandic parliament. [Icelandic, from Old Norse *althingi,* assembly of all. See **all, thing.**]

alt·horn (ált-hawrn) *n.* A brass instrument that sometimes replaces the French horn. Also called "alto horn". [German *Althorn* : *alt,* alto, from Italian *alto,* ALTO + *Horn,* HORN.]

al·though (awl-thō̆ || ol-, *Scottish* -thô̆) *conj.* Regardless of the fact that; even though. [Middle English : *al,* ALL + THOUGH.]
Usage: Although and *though* are often interchangeable: *I came to work, (al)though I was ill; (Al)though I was ill, I came to work. Though* is more colloquial, and tends to occur when the clause it introduces is in second position in the sentence. *Although* is preferred with clauses in first position. Note that *though* has a certain mobility in some constructions *(Angry though I was. . .),* which does not extend to *although.*

al·tim·e·ter (ál-ti-meetər, al-tímmitər || áwl-, ól-) *n.* An instrument for determining altitude, used especially in aircraft and commonly based on sensing of pressure changes with altitude or on determination of the frequency delay in a radio signal reflected from the ground. [Latin *altus,* high + -METER.] —**al·tim·e·try** (al-tímmitri || awl-, ol-) *n.*

al·ti·plan·a·tion (álti-plə-náysh'n) *n. Geology.* The process in which terraces are formed in rock on a hillside by weathering. [*alti-,* from Latin *altus,* high + PLANATION.]

al·tis·si·mo (al-tíssimō̆) *adj. Music.* **1.** Of the highest pitch. **2.** Of or in the octave G to F, two octaves above the treble staff. [Italian, "highest", superlative of *alto,* high, from Latin *altus,* high.] —**al·tis·si·mo** *n. & adv.*

al·ti·tude (ál-ti-tewd || áwl- ól-, -tōōd) *n. Abbr.* **alt. 1.** The height of a thing above a particular level, especially above sea level or above the earth's surface. Also called "elevation". **2.** *Often plural.* A high location or area: *the difficulty of breathing at high altitudes.* **3.** *Astronomy.* The angular distance of a celestial object above the horizon. **4.** *Geometry.* The perpendicular distance from the base of a geometric figure or solid to the opposite vertex, parallel side, or parallel surface. **5.** A high position or rank. [Middle English, from Latin *altitūdō,* from *altus,* high.] —**al·ti·tud·i·nal** (-téwd-in'l || *U.S. also* -tōōd-) *adj.*

altitude sickness *n.* Illness with symptoms such as nausea, breathlessness, and exhaustion, caused by oxygen deficiency, as encountered at high altitudes. Also called "mountain sickness".

al·to (ál-tō̆ || áwl-, ól-) *n., pl.* **-tos.** *Abbr.* **A.** *Music.* **1.** A low female singing voice; a contralto. **2.** A high male singing voice; a counter-tenor. **3.** The range between soprano and tenor. **4.** A singer whose voice lies within this range. **5.** An instrument that plays notes within this range, such as an alto saxophone. **6.** A vocal or instrumental part written for such a voice or instrument.
~adj. Pertaining to or playing notes within this range. [Italian, "high", from Latin *altus,* high.]

alto clef *n.* The C clef that places middle C on the third line of the staff.

al·to·cu·mu·lus (ál-tō̆-kéwmewləss) *n.* A cloud formation of rounded, fleecy, white or grey masses arranged in bands or waves, occurring at 2 000 to 6 100 metres (6,000 to 20,000 feet). [Latin *altus,* high + CUMULUS.]

al·to·geth·er (áwl-tə-géthər, -tōō- || ól-) *adv.* **1.** Entirely; completely; utterly. **2.** With all included or counted; in all; all told: *Altogether 100 people were there.* **3.** On the whole; with everything considered: *Altogether, I'm sorry it happened.* —**in the altogether** *Informal.* Naked; nude. [Middle English *al togeder* : *al,* ALL + TOGETHER.]
Usage: A clear distinction is made in standard English writing between this form and *all together. All together* means that several people or things have been physically or metaphorically brought

together: *prisoners herded all together, nations standing all together.*

al·to-re·lie·vo (ál-tō̆-ri-léevō̆) *n., pl.* **-vos.** Also *Italian* **al·to-ri·lie·vo** (ál-tō̆-rili-áy-vō̆, áal-) *pl.* **-vi** (-vee). **High relief** *(see).* [Italian *alto rilievo,* "high relief".]

al·to·stra·tus (ál-tō̆-stráytəss, -stráatəss || *U.S. also* -stráttəss) *n.* An extended cloud formation of bluish or grey sheets or layers occurring at 2 000 to 6 100 metres (6,000 to 20,000 feet). [Latin *altus,* high + STRATUS.]

al·tri·cial (al-trísh'l) *adj.* Of or characterising birds that are helpless and naked when hatched, such as young pigeons. Compare **precocial.** [Latin *altricēs,* plural of *altrix,* feminine of *altōr,* nourisher, from *alere,* to nourish.]

al·tru·ism (ál-troo-iz'm) *n.* **1.** Concern for the welfare of others, as opposed to egoism; selflessness. **2.** *Zoology.* Instinctive cooperative behaviour by an animal that apparently protects or benefits other members of its species, and its species in general, rather than itself. [Italian *altrui,* others, from Latin *alteri,* plural of *alter,* other.] —**al·tru·ist** *n.* —**al·tru·is·tic** (-ístik) *adj.* —**al·tru·is·ti·cal·ly** *adv.*

al·u·del (ál-yōō-del || -yə-) *n. Chemistry.* A pear-shaped glass apparatus, open at both ends, formerly used to collect condensed mercury and other liquids. [Middle English *alutel,* from Old French *aludel,* from Spanish, from Arabic *al-'uthāl,* the vessel.]

al·u·la (ál-yōō-lə || -yə-) *n., pl.* **-lae** (-lee). **1.** The feathers attached to the part of a bird's wing corresponding to the thumb. Also called "bastard wing". **2.** A small lobe near the base of the wing in certain insects. [New Latin, diminutive of Latin *āla,* wing.] —**al·u·lar** (-lər) *adj.*

al·um (ál-əm) *n.* Any of various double sulphates of a trivalent metal such as aluminium, chromium, or iron, and a univalent metal or radical such as potassium, sodium, or ammonium; especially, potassium aluminium sulphate (*potash alum,* $K_2SO_4.Al_2(SO_4)_3.12H_2O$) which is widely used as a mordant and size for paper and, medicinally, as an astringent and styptic. See **chrome alum.** [Middle English, from Old French, from Latin *alūmen†.*]

a·lu·mi·na (ə-léwm-inə, -lōōm-) *n.* Any of several forms of aluminium oxide, Al_2O_3, occurring naturally as corundum, in a hydrated form in bauxite, and with various impurities as ruby, sapphire, and emery. It is used in aluminium production, in abrasives, refractories, ceramics, and electrical insulation, and as an absorbent material. [New Latin, from Latin *alūmen* (stem *alūmin-*), ALUM.]

a·lu·mi·nate (ə-léwm-i-nayt, -lōōm-, -nət) *n.* A chemical compound containing the negative ion AlO_2^-.

a·lu·mi·nif·er·ous (ə-léwm-i-níffərəss, -lōōm-) *adj.* Containing or yielding aluminium, alumina, or alum. [Latin *alūmen* (stem *alūmin-*), ALUM + -FEROUS.]

a·lu·min·ise, a·lu·min·ize (ə-léwm-i-nīz, -lōōm-) *tr.v.* **-ised, -ising, -ises.** To coat or cover with aluminium or aluminium paint.

a·lu·min·i·um (ə-léwm-ínni-əm, -ōō-, -lōōm-) *n.* Also *U.S.* **a·lu·mi·num** (ə-lōōmənəm). *Symbol* Al A silvery-white, ductile metallic element, the most abundant in the earth's crust, but found only in combination, chiefly in bauxite. It is used to form many hard, light, corrosion-resistant alloys. Atomic number 13, atomic weight 26.98, melting point 660.2°C, boiling point 2,467°C, relative density 2.69, valency 3. [New Latin, earlier *aluminum* : ALUMINA + -IUM.]

aluminium foil *n.* Aluminium in the form of a very thin sheet, used chiefly as a protective wrapping for foodstuffs. Also called "foil".

aluminium oxide *n.* A white crystalline compound, Al_2O_3, occurring naturally as alumina.

aluminium sulphate *n.* A white crystalline compound, $Al_2(SO_4)_3$, used chiefly in papermaking, water purification, sanitation, and tanning.

a·lu·min·o·sil·i·cate (ə-léwm-inō̆-síllikayt, -lōōm-) *n.* Any of a large number of complex inorganic crystalline substances or glasses, consisting of silicate compounds in which some of the silicon atoms have been replaced by aluminium atoms. Many are found naturally in rocks and minerals. [ALUMIN(IUM) + SILICATE.]

a·lu·mi·no·ther·my (ə-léwm-inō̆-thérmi,-lōōm-) *n. Chemistry.* The reduction of metal oxides to metals using aluminium powder, the **thermite process** *(see).*

a·lu·mi·nous (ə-léwm-inəss, -lōōm-) *adj.* Of, pertaining to, or containing aluminium or alum.

a·lum·nus (ə-lúm-nəss) *n., pl.* **-ni** (-nī). *Feminine* **a·lum·na** (ə-lúm-nə) *pl.* **-nae** (-nee). *Chiefly U.S.* A graduate or former student of a school, college, or university. [Latin *alumnus,* a pupil, foster son, from *alere,* to nourish.]

al·um·root (ál-əm-rōōt || -róōt) *n.* **1.** Any of various North American plants of the genus *Heuchera,* having clusters of small white, reddish, or green flowers and astringent roots.

A·lun·dum (ə-lúndəm) *n.* A trademark for a hard, artificial abrasive of fused alumina, used in making oilstones and grinding wheels.

al·u·nite (ál-yōō-nīt || -yə-, -ə-) *n.* A grey mineral, chiefly $KAl_3(SO_4)_2(OH)_6$, used in making alum and fertiliser. Also called "alumstone". [French, from *alun,* ALUM.]

al·ve·o·lar (ál-vi-ə̆lər, al-vée-ələr) *adj.* **1.** Of or pertaining to an alveolus. **2.** *Anatomy.* **a.** Pertaining to the section of the jaw containing the tooth sockets. **b.** Pertaining to the alveoli of the lungs. **3.** *Phonetics.* Formed with the tip of the tongue touching or near the hard ridge behind the upper teeth, as the English *t, d,* and *s* are.
~ n. Phonetics. An alveolar consonant or sound. [French *avéolaire,* from *alvéole,* ALVEOLUS.]

al·ve·o·late (al-vée-ə-láyt, -lit) *adj.* Having alveoli; deeply pitted; honeycombed. [Latin *alveolātus,* hollowed, from ALVEOLUS.] —**al·ve·o·la·tion** (-láysh'n) *n.*

al·ve·o·lus (al-vée-ə-ləss, ál-vi-ō̆-) *n., pl.* **-li** (-lī). **1.** A small cavity or pit, such as a honeycomb cell. **2.** A tooth socket in the jawbone. **3.** An air sac of the lungs, at the end of a bronchiole, through which exchange of respiratory gases takes place. [Latin, small cavity, diminutive of *alveus*, a cavity, hollow, from *alvus*, a hollow, belly.]

al·ways (áwl-wiz, -wayz, -wəz ‖ ól-) *adv.* **1.** On every occasion; every time: *always leaves at six.* **2.** Ceaselessly; forever: *friends always.* **3.** Continually; repeatedly: *He's always fiddling with his car.* **4.** In every instance: *Cats always have whiskers.* **5.** As a possibility; as a last resort: *You could always just refuse.* [Middle English *always*, adverbial genitive of *alwei*, Old English *ealne weg*, "(along) all the way" : *ealne*, accusative of *eall*, ALL + *weg*, WAY.]

al·ys·sum (ál-issəm, ə-líssəm) *n.* **1.** Any of various plants of the genus *Alyssum*, having dense clusters of yellow or white flowers. Also called "madwort". **2.** See **sweet alyssum**. [New Latin, from Greek *alusson*, madwort (believed to cure rabies), from neuter of *alussos*, curing rabies : *a-*, not + *lussa*, rabies, madness.]

Alz·heim·er's disease (álts-hīmərz, álz-) *n.* A degenerative disease of the brain, often occurring in middle age, causing progressive loss of mental faculties. Also called "presenile dementia". [After Alois Alzheimer (1864–1915), German doctor.]

am (am, *weak form* əm). The first person singular, present indicative of **be**.

am, AM amplitude modulation.

Am The symbol for the element americium.

Am. America; American.

a.m. ante meridiem

A.M. **1.** Albert medal. **2.** ante meridiem. **3.** in the year of the world [Latin *anno mundi*].

a·mah, a·ma (áa-mə ‖ -maa) *n.* In the Orient, a maidservant who looks after children; especially, a wet nurse. [Portuguese *ama*, wet nurse, from Medieval Latin *amma*, from Latin *amma* (unattested), mother.]

a·main (ə-máyn) *adv. Archaic & Poetic.* **1.** With strength and intensity. **2.** With speed or haste. **3.** Greatly; exceedingly. [A- (on, by) + MAIN (strength).]

Am·a·lek·ite (ə-mál-ə-kīt ‖ U.S. *also* ámmələkīt) *n.* A member of an ancient nomadic tribe reputedly descended from Esau's grandson Amalek and hostile to the Israelites. Genesis 36:12–16. Exodus 17:13. I Samuel 15:7. [Hebrew *'Amālēqī*, after *'Amālēq*, Amalek.]

a·mal·gam (ə-mál-gəm) *n.* **1.** Any of various alloys of mercury with other metals, such as tin or silver: *dental amalgam*. **2.** Any combination or mixture of diverse elements. [Middle English *amalgame*, from Old French, from Medieval Latin *amalgama*†.]

a·mal·ga·mate (ə-mál-gə-mayt) *v.* **-mated, -mating, -mates.** *—tr.* **1.** To mix so as to make a unified whole; blend; unite; combine. **2.** To mix or alloy (a metal) with mercury. *—intr.* **1.** To combine, unite, or consolidate. **2.** To form an amalgam with mercury. Used of metals. —See Synonyms at **mix.** —**a·mal·ga·ma·tive** (-mətiv, -maytiv) *adj.* —**a·mal·ga·ma·tor** *n.*

a·mal·ga·ma·tion (ə-mál-gə-máysh'n) *n.* **1.** The act of or condition resulting from amalgamating. **2.** A merger, as of several companies. **3.** *Chemistry.* The dissolving of a metal in mercury to form an alloy.

a·mand·la (ə-máandlə) *interj. South African.* Power. Used as a slogan by supporters of black power. [Zulu.]

am·a·ni·ta (ámmə-níta, -néetə) *n.* Any of various mushrooms of the genus *Amanita*, most of which are extremely poisonous. See **death cap, fly agaric**. [From Greek *amanitai*† (plural), a type of fungus.]

a·man·ta·dine (ə-mántə-deen) *n.* An antiviral drug, $C_{10}H_{17}NHCl$, used in the treatment of influenza and Parkinson's disease. [Alteration (through influence of *amine*) of *adamantane*, an organic compound, from ADAMANT.]

a·man·u·en·sis (ə-mánnew-én-siss) *n., pl.* **-ses** (-seez). **1.** One employed to take dictation or to copy manuscript. **2.** A personal assistant to a writer. [Latin *āmanuensis*, from *(servus) ā manū*, "(slave) at hand(writing)" : *ab-*, by + *manus*, hand.]

am·a·ranth (ámməranth) *n.* **1.** Any of various plants of the genus *Amaranthus*, having clusters of small greenish, red, or purplish flowers. See **pigweed, tumbleweed, love-lies-bleeding.** **2.** *Poetic.* An imaginary flower that never fades. **3.** Deep reddish purple. [New Latin *amaranthus*, variant (influenced by *-anthus*, flower) of Latin *amarantus*, from Greek *amarantos*, unfading : *a-*, not + *marainein*, to waste, wither.]

am·a·ran·thine (ámmə-rán-thīn ‖ U.S. *also* -thin) *adj.* **1.** Of, pertaining to, or resembling the amaranth. **2.** Eternally beautiful; unfading; everlasting. **3.** Deep purple in colour.

am·a·relle (ámmə-rél) *n.* A variety of sour cherry having pale red fruit. [German *Amarelle*, from Medieval Latin *amarellum*, from Latin *amārus*, bitter.]

am·a·ret·to (ámmə-réttō) *n.* An almond-flavoured Italian liqueur. [Italian, "bitter", from *amaro*, bitter; referring to bitter almonds, on which the liqueur is based.]

am·a·ryl·lis (ámmə-rílliss) *n.* **1.** A bulbous plant, *Amaryllis belladonna*, native to southern Africa, having large, lily-like reddish or white flowers. Also called "belladonna lily". **2.** Any of several related or similar plants. [After AMARYLLIS.]

Am·a·ryl·lis. A shepherdess who appears in the pastoral poetry of Virgil and other classical writers. [Latin girl's name, from Greek *Amarullis.*]

a·mass (ə-máss) *tr.v.* **amassed, amassing, amasses. 1.** To pile or gather up in a mass. **2.** To collect for oneself; accumulate, especially for one's own pleasure or profit. See Synonyms at **gather.** [Old French *amasser* : *a-*, to, from Latin *ad-* + *masser*, to gather together, from *masse*, a MASS.] —**a·mass·a·ble** *adj.* —**a·mass·er** *n.* —**a·mass·ment** *n.*

am·a·teur (ámmə-tər, -chər, -tewr, -tér) *n.* **1.** A person who engages in any art, science, study, or sporting activity as a pastime rather than as a profession. Compare **dilettante. 2.** *Abbr.* **a., A.** A sportsman or sportswoman who has never participated in competition for money or a livelihood. **3.** One lacking professional skill or judgment in a certain area, as in art.
~*adj.* **1.** *Abbr.* **a., A.** Pertaining to or performed by an amateur or amateurs. **2.** *Abbr.* **a., A.** Made up of amateurs: *an amateur orchestra.* **3.** Not professional; unskilful. [French, from Latin *amātōr*, a lover, from *amāre*, to love.] —**am·a·teur·ism** *n.*

am·a·teur·ish (ámmə-tər-ish, -chər-, tewr-, -tér-) *adj.* Characteristic of an amateur; not professional; unskilful. —**am·a·teur·ish·ly** *adv.* —**am·a·teur·ish·ness** *n.*

A·ma·ti¹ (ə-máati). A family of violin makers in Cremona, Italy, in the 16th and 17th centuries. They include **Andrea Amati** (c. 1505–75) who established the early design for the modern violin. His grandson **Nicolò Amati** (1596–1684) was the most famous craftsman and was also the teacher of Stradivari and Guarneri.

Amati² *n.* A violin, cello, or similar instrument made by Nicolò Amati or any of the members of his family.

am·a·tive (ámmətiv) *adj. Rare.* Amorous. [Medieval Latin *amātīvus*, from Latin *amāre*, to love.] —**am·a·tive·ness** *n.*

am·a·tol (ámmə-tol ‖ -tōl) *n.* A highly explosive mixture of ammonium nitrate and trinitrotoluene. [*Ammonium* + trinitro*toluene*.]

am·a·to·ry (ámmə-təri, -tri) *adj.* Also **am·a·to·ri·al** (ámmə-táwri-əl ‖ -tóri-). Of, pertaining to, or expressive of love, especially sexual love. [Latin *amātōrius*, from *amātōr*, a lover, from *amāre*, to love.]

am·au·ro·sis (ámmaw-rō̆-siss) *n.* Partial or complete blindness, especially when not associated with disease of the eye. Compare **amblyopia.** [Greek *amaurōsis*, from *amauroun*, to darken, from *(a)maurost*, dark.] —**am·au·rot·ic** (-róttik) *adj.*

a·maze (ə-máyz) *tr.v.* **amazed, amazing, amazes. 1.** To affect with surprise or great wonder; astonish. **2.** *Obsolete.* To bewilder. —See Synonyms at **surprise.**
~*n. Archaic & Poetic.* Amazement; wonder. [Middle English *amasen*, Old English *āmasian†*, to bewilder. See **maze.**] —**a·maz·ed·ly** (-idli) *adv.*

a·maze·ment (ə-máyzmənt) *n.* **1.** A state of extreme surprise or wonder; astonishment. **2.** *Obsolete.* Bewilderment; perplexity.

a·maz·ing (ə-máyzing) *adj.* Causing amazement; greatly surprising; wonderful. —**a·maz·ing·ly** *adv.*

Am·a·zon¹ (ámmə-z'n ‖ U.S. *also* -zon) *n.* **1.** *Greek Mythology.* A member of a nation of female warriors reputed to have lived in Scythia, near the Black Sea. **2.** *Often small* **a.** Any tall, vigorous, athletic woman. [Middle English, from Latin *Amāzon*, from Greek. Probably of non-Indo-European origin but interpreted by the Greeks as *a-*, without + *mazos*, breast (from the belief that the Amazons removed their right breasts in order to make it easier to use their bows).] —**Am·a·zo·ni·an** (-zṓni-ən) *adj.*

Amazon². *Portuguese* **Rio Amazonas.** River formed by the confluence of the Ucayali and Marañón rivers, it flows 6 570 kilometres (4,082 miles) from northern Peru across northern Brazil into the Atlantic Ocean. It carries so great a volume of water (more than any other river) that fresh water is to be found in the ocean some 320 kilometres (200 miles) from its mouth. Its vast basin covers an area of more than 6 475 000 square kilometres (2,500,000 square miles). It is the second-longest river in the world, after the Nile. —**Am·a·zo·ni·an** *adj.*

Amazon ant *n.* Any of several small red ants of the genus *Polyergus*, that take over and enslave the young ants of other species. [After the legend that the Amazons raised captured children.]

am·a·zon·ite (ámmə'n-īt) *n.* A blue-green variety of microcline, often used as a semiprecious stone. Also called "amazon stone". [After the river AMAZON, near which it is found.]

amb., Amb. ambassador.

am·bas·sa·dor (am-bássə-dər ‖ əm-, U.S. *also* -dawr) *n. Abbr.* **amb., Amb. 1.** A diplomatic official of the highest rank appointed and accredited as representative in residence by one government to another. Called in full "ambassador extraordinary and plenipotentiary". **2.** Any of various diplomatic officials of the highest rank. **3.** A diplomatic official heading his country's permanent mission to certain international organisations, such as the United Nations. **4.** Any authorised messenger or representative. **5.** One who stands for or represents a particular belief, set of values, or culture: *an ambassador for change.* [Middle English *ambassadour*, from Old French *ambassadeur*, from Old Italian *ambasciator*, from Vulgar Latin *ambactiātor* (unattested), from Medieval Latin *ambactia*, mission, from Germanic *ambakhtaz* (unattested), from Latin *ambactus*, vassal, probably from Celtic.] —**am·bas·sa·do·ri·al** (-dáwri-əl, -dóri-) *adj.* —**am·bas·sa·dor·ship** *n.*

am·bas·sa·dress (am-bássə-driss, -dress) *n.* **1.** The wife of an ambassador. **2.** A female ambassador or representative.

am·ber (ámbər) *n.* **1.** A hard, translucent, brownish-yellow fossil resin, found chiefly along the shores of the Baltic Sea, and used for making jewellery and other ornamental objects. **2.** Medium to dark or deep orange yellow. **3.** The yellow stage of a traffic light's sequence, signalling 'prepare for red or green'. **4.** An amber-toned stage light used to simulate sunlight. [Middle English *ambre*, from Old French, from Medieval Latin *ambra, ambar*, from Arabic *'anbar*, ambergris, amber.] —**am·ber** *adj.*

am·ber·gris (ámbər-greess, -griss) *n.* A waxy, greyish substance, mainly cholesterol, formed in the intestines of sperm whales and found floating at sea or washed ashore. It is used as a fixative in perfumes. [Middle English *ambregris*, from Old French *ambre gris* : AMBER + *gris*, grey, from Frankish *gris* (unattested).]

am·ber·oid (ámbəroyd) *n*. Also **am·broid** (ámbroyd). A synthetic form of amber made by melting together small pieces of amber and other resins under pressure.

ambi– *comb. form.* Indicates both; for example, **ambiversion**. [Latin, round, on both sides.]

am·bi·ance, am·bi·ence (ámbi-ənss, -ONss) *n*. 1. The atmosphere or character of a place: *a strange ambiance.* 2. A pleasant or congenial atmosphere or environment: *a restaurant lacking in ambiance.* [French, from *ambiant*, surrounding, from Latin *ambiēns*, AMBIENT.]

am·bi·dex·trous (ámbi-dékstrəss) *adj.* 1. Able to use both hands with equal facility. 2. Unusually dexterous or adroit, especially in more than one activity; versatile. 3. Deceptive; hypocritical [Late Latin *ambidexter* : Latin *ambi-*, AMBI- + *dexter*, right-handed.] **—am·bi·dex·ter** (-dékstər) *n. & adj.* **—am·bi·dex·ter·i·ty** (-dek-stér-rəti) *n*. **—am·bi·dex·trous·ly** *adv.*

am·bi·ent (ámbi-ənt) *adj.* Surrounding; designating or pertaining to the immediate environment: *the ambient temperature.* [Latin *ambiēns* (stem *ambient-*), present participle of *ambīre*, to go round : *ambi-*, round + *īre*, to go).]

am·bi·gu·i·ty (ámbi-géw-əti) *n., pl.* **-ties.** 1. The state of being ambiguous. 2. Something ambiguous.

am·big·u·ous (am-bígew-əss) *adj.* 1. Open to more than one interpretation. 2. Doubtful or uncertain. [Latin *ambiguus*, uncertain, "going about", from *ambigere*, to wander about : *ambi-*, around + *agere*, to drive, lead).] **—am·big·u·ous·ly** *adv.* **—am·big·u·ous·ness** *n*.

am·bit (ámbit) *n*. 1. The external boundary of something; a circuit. 2. The sphere or scope of something. [Middle English, from Latin *ambitus*, a going round, from *ambīre* (past participle *ambitus*), to go round. See **ambient**.]

am·bi·tion (am-bish'n) *n*. 1. An eager or strong desire to achieve success, distinction, fortune, or the like; will to succeed. 2. A strong desire to achieve a particular end. 3. The object or goal desired. [Middle English *ambicioun*, from Old French *ambition*, from Latin *ambitiō* (stem *ambitiōn-*), a going round (for votes), from *ambīre*, to go round. See **ambient**.]

am·bi·tious (am-bíshəss) *adj.* 1. Full of, characterised by, or motivated by ambition. 2. Greatly desirous; eager. Used with *of* or an infinitive: *"I am not ambitious of ridicule"* (Edmund Burke). 3. Showing or requiring much skill, ambition, or effort; challenging: *an ambitious plan.* **—am·bi·tious·ly** *adv.* **—am·bi·tious·ness** *n*.

am·biv·a·lence (am-bívvə-lənss, ámbi-váy-lənss) *n*. Also **am·biv·a·len·cy** (-i). The simultaneous existence in a person's mind of mutually conflicting feelings or thoughts towards or about something or someone. [German *Ambivalenz* (coined by Freud).] **—am·biv·a·lent** *adj.* **—am·biv·a·lent·ly** *adv.*

am·bi·ver·sion (ámbi-vér-sh'n, -zh'n) *n*. *Psychology.* A personality showing both introversion and extroversion. [AMBI- + (INTRO)VERSION or (EXTRO)VERSION.] **—am·bi·vert** (-vert) *n*.

am·ble (ámb'l) *intr.v.* **-bled, -bling, -bles.** 1. To move along smoothly by lifting first both legs on one side and then both on the other. Used of horses and other animals. 2. To walk slowly; move with a leisurely gait. 3. To ride an ambling horse. *~n.* 1. An ambling gait, especially that of a horse. 2. An unhurried or easy pace. 3. A leisurely walk. [Middle English *amblen*, from Old French *ambler*, from Latin *ambulāre*, to AMBULATE.] **—am·bler** *n*.

Am·bler (ámblər), **Eric** (1909–86). British novelist. He wrote many successful thrillers, including *The Mask of Dimitrios* (1939), *A Passage of Arms* (1959), and *Send No More Roses* (1977).

am·blyg·o·nite (am-blíggənīt) *n*. A white or creamy white mineral with composition $(Li,Na)Al(PO_4)(F,OH)$. It is an important source of lithium. [German *Amblygonit*, "the stone with obtuse angles (in its crystals)" : Greek *amblugōnios*, having obtuse angles : *amblus*, blunt + *gōnia*, angle + -ITE.]

am·bly·o·pi·a (ámbli-ṓpi-ə) *n*. Dimness of vision without apparent physical defect or disease of the eye. Compare **amaurosis.** [New Latin, from Greek *ambluōpia* : *amblus*, blunt, dim + -OPIA.] **—am·bly·op·ic** (-ópik, -óppik) *adj.*

am·bo (ámbṓ) *n., pl.* **-bos** or **ambones** (am-bṓneez). Either of the two pulpits or raised stands in early Christian churches from which parts of the service were chanted or read. [Medieval Latin, from Greek *ambōn*†, pulpit, a raised edge or rim.]

am·boy·na, am·boi·na (am-bóynə) *n*. The reddish-brown, curly-grained wood of a tree, *Pterocarpus indicus*, of southeastern Asia, used for decorative cabinetwork. [After *Amboina* in the Moluccas, Indonesia.]

ambroid. Variant of **amberoid.**

Am·brose (ámbrōz), **Saint** (*c.* 340–397). Bishop of Milan and leader of the early Christian Church. He was influential in imposing orthodoxy on the early Church, and strengthened the power of the Church against the state. **—Am·bro·si·an** *adj.*

am·bro·si·a (am-brōzi-ə, -brōzhi- ‖ -brōzhə) *n*. 1. *Greek & Roman Mythology.* The food of the gods, thought to impart immortality. Compare **nectar.** 2. Anything with an especially delicious flavour or fragrance. 3. **Beebread** (*see*). [Latin, from Greek, "immortality", from *ambrotos*, immortal : *a-*, not + *mbrotos*, archaic form of *brotos*, mortal.] **—am·bro·si·al, am·bro·si·an** *adj.*

ambrosia beetle *n*. Any of various small bark beetles that tunnel

into solid wood and feed on fungi. [After *ambrosia fungus*, on which the beetles feed.]

Am·bro·si·an chant (am-brōzi-ən) *n*. A type of liturgical chant, supposedly introduced by St. Ambrose and used to the present day in the Cathedral of Milan.

am·bro·type (ámbro-tīp) *n*. In early photography, a positive picture produced by backing a glass negative with black paper or paint. [Greek *ambro(tos)*, immortal (see **ambrosia**) + -TYPE.]

am·bry (ámbri) *n., pl.* **-bries.** Also **au·mbry** (áwmbri). 1. In churches, a niche near the altar for keeping sacred vessels and vestments. 2. *Archaic.* A small storeroom or cupboard. [Middle English *aumbry*, from Old French *armarie, aumaire*, from Medieval Latin *almārium*, store, from Latin *armārium*, from *arma*, tools, ARMS.]

ambs·ace (áymz-ayss) *n*. 1. Double aces, the lowest throw at dice. 2. Misfortune; bad luck. 3. The smallest amount or most worthless thing possible. [Middle English *ambes as*, from Old French, from Latin *ambās ās*, "both aces" : *ambās*, feminine accusative of *ambō*, both + *ās*, a unit (see **ace**).]

am·bu·la·crum (ámbew-láy-krəm) *n., pl.* **-cra** (-krə). *Zoology.* Any of the five radial areas on the undersurface of the starfish and similar echinoderms, on which the tube feet are borne. [New Latin, from Latin *ambulācrum*, avenue (hence the row of pores for protrusion of the tube feet), from *ambulāre*, to AMBULATE.] **—am·bu·la·cral** *adj.*

am·bu·lance (ámbewlənss) *n*. 1. A vehicle specially equipped to transport the sick or injured. 2. *British.* A vehicle equipped to carry those who cannot walk easily, such as the elderly or disabled. [French, from *(hôpital) ambulant*, itinerant (hospital), from Latin *ambulāns* (stem *ambulant-*), present participle of *ambulāre*, to AMBULATE.]

am·bu·lant (ámbewlənt) *adj.* Moving or walking about; shifting from place to place. [French. See **ambulance**.]

am·bu·late (ámbew-layt) *intr.v.* **-lated, -lating, -lates.** To walk from place to place; move about. [Latin *ambulāre*, to go about, walk : *ambi-*, around, about + *-ul-*, *-el-* (unattested), to go).] **—am·bu·la·tion** (-láysh'n) *n*.

am·bu·la·to·ry (ámbew-lətri, -láytəri) *adj.* 1. Of, pertaining to, or adapted for walking. 2. Capable of walking; not bedridden. 3. Moving about; not stationary. 4. *Law.* Capable of being changed or revoked, as a will is during the life of the testator. *~n., pl.* **ambulatories.** 1. An aisle around the east end of a church. 2. A covered place for walking, as in a cloister.

am·bus·cade (ámbəss-káyd) *n*. *Archaic.* An ambush. *~tr.v.* **ambuscaded, -cading, -cades.** *Archaic.* To ambush. [Old French *embuscade*, from Old Italian *imboscata*, feminine past participle of *imboscare*, to ambush, from Vulgar Latin *imboscāre* (unattested), to AMBUSH.] **—am·bus·cad·er** *n*.

am·bush (ám-bŏŏsh) *n*. 1. A lying in wait to attack by surprise. 2. A surprise attack made from a concealed position. 3. **a.** Those in hiding to make such an attack. **b.** Their hiding place. 4. Any hidden peril or trap. *~tr.v.* **ambushed, -bushing, -bushes.** To attack from a concealed position. [Middle English *embushen*, to ambush, from Old French *embuschier*, from Vulgar Latin *imboscāre* (unattested), "to hide in the bushes" : *in*, in + *boscus* (unattested), bush, from Germanic.] **—am·bush·er** *n*.

A.M.D.G. To the greater glory of God [Latin *ad majorem Dei gloriam*]. Used as the motto of the Jesuits.

ameba. *U.S.* Variant of **amoeba.**

ameer. Variant of **emir.**

a·me·li·o·rate (ə-méel-i-ə-rayt, -yə-) *v.* **-rated, -rating, -rates.** *—tr.* To make better; improve. *—intr.* To become better. [French *améliorer*, to improve, from Old French *ameillorer* : *a-*, to, from Latin *ad-* + *meillor*, better, from Latin *melior*, better.] **—a·me·li·o·ra·ble** (-rəb'l) *adj.* **—a·me·li·o·ra·tive** *adj.* **—a·me·li·o·ra·tor** (-raytər) *n*.

a·me·li·o·ra·tion (ə-méel-i-ə-ráysh'n, -yə-) *n*. 1. The act of ameliorating or the state of being ameliorated. 2. Something resulting from amelioration; an improvement. 3. *Linguistics.* A change in the meaning of a word to a more favourable sense; for example, the word *shrewd* has undergone amelioration from its earlier senses of "mischievous" and "dangerous". Also called "elevation", "melioration". Compare **deterioration.**

a·men (áa-mén, áy-) *interj.* Used at the end of a prayer or a statement to express concurrence, ratification, or approval. *~n.* 1. An utterance of this interjection. 2. Any expression of conviction or assent. [Middle English *amen*, Old English *amen*, from Late Latin *amēn*, from Greek, from Hebrew *āmēn*, certainly, verily.]

A·men, A·mon (áamən, ámmən). *Egyptian Mythology.* The god of life and reproduction, represented as a man with a ram's head. Sometimes identified with **Amen-Ra.**

a·me·na·ble (ə-méen-əb'l, -mén-) *adj.* 1. Willing to follow advice or suggestion; tractable. 2. Responsible to authority; accountable. 3. Open or liable to testing, criticism, or judgment. *—See* Synonyms at **obedient, responsible.** [Anglo-French (legal use), from French *amener*, to lead, bring, from Old French : *a-*, to, from Latin *ad-* + *mener*, to lead, from Latin *mināre*, to drive (cattle), from *minārī*, "to shout at", threaten, from *minae*, threats.] **—a·me·na·bil·i·ty** (-ə-billəti), **a·me·na·ble·ness** *n*. **—a·me·na·bly** *adv.*

a·mend (ə-ménd) *v.* **amended, amending, amends.** *—tr.* 1. To remove the faults or errors of; correct; rectify. 2. To improve; better. 3. To alter formally (a legislative measure, for example) by adding, deleting, or rephrasing. *—intr.* To improve one's conduct; reform. **—See** Synonyms at **correct.** [Middle English *amenden*, from Old

French *amender,* alteration of Latin *ēmendāre,* to free from faults : *ex-,* removal, out of + *menda, mendum,* defect, fault.] —**a·mend·a·ble** *adj.* —**a·mend·er** *n.*

a·mend·a·to·ry (ə-méndə-tri, -təri) *adj. Chiefly U.S.* Serving or tending to amend; constituting an amendment.

a·mend·ment (ə-méndmənt) *n.* **1.** The act or process of amending. **2.** A correction, alteration, or improvement. **3.** An alteration formally proposed for or made in a legislative measure, document, or the like: *to move an amendment to a bill.*

a·mends (ə-méndz) *pl.n.* Reparation or compensation made as satisfaction for insult or injury. Used chiefly in *make amends.* —See Synonyms at **reparation.** [Middle English *amendes,* from Old French, plural of *amende,* reparation, from *amender,* to AMEND.]

Amenhotep IV. See **Akhenaton.**

a·men·i·ty (ə-méen-əti, -mén-) *n., pl.* **-ties. 1.** Pleasantness; agreeableness. **2.** A feature or facility that increases physical or material comfort: *recreational amenities.* **3.** *Plural.* Social courtesies; pleasantries; civilities. [Middle English *amenite,* from Old French, from Latin *amoenitās,* from *amoenus†,* pleasant, delightful.]

a·men·or·rhoe·a (áy-menə-rée-ə, a-ménnə-) *n.* Also *chiefly U.S.* **a·men·or·rhe·a.** Abnormal suppression or absence of menstruation. [New Latin : A- (not) + Greek *mēn,* month + -RRHOEA.]

Amen-Ra (áamən-ráa). The chief national god of ancient Egypt during the period of Theban domination, regarded as the sun-god.

am·ent¹ (ámmənt, áymənt) *n. Botany.* A catkin *(see).* [New Latin *amentum,* from Latin *ammentum,* a thong, strap.] —**am·en·ta·ceous** (ámmən-táyshəss, áymən-) *adj.* —**am·en·tif·er·ous** (-tíffərəss) *adj.*

a·ment² (áy-ment, -mənt, ámmənt) *n. Psychology.* A mentally deficient or feeble-minded person. [Latin *āmēns* (stem *āment-)* : *ā-,* out of, away from + *mēns,* mind.]

a·men·tia (áy-ménshə, ə-) *n. Psychology.* Subnormal mental development; feeble-mindedness. [Latin *āmentia,* from *āmēns,* AMENT.]

Amer. America; American.

A·mer·a·sian (ámmər-áysh'n, -áyzh'n) *n.* A person of mixed American and Asian descent. —**A·mer·a·sian** *adj.*

a·merce (ə-mérss) *tr.v.* **amerced, amercing, amerces. 1.** Formerly, to punish by a fine imposed arbitrarily at the discretion of the court. **2.** To punish by imposing any arbitrary penalty. [Middle English *amercien,* from Anglo-French *amercier,* from *a merci,* at the mercy of : *a-,* to, from Latin *ad-* + *merci,* mercy, from Latin *mercēs,* wages.] —**a·merce·ment** *n.* —**a·merc·er** *n.*

A·mer·i·ca (ə-mérrikə) *Abbr.* **A., Am., Amer. 1.** The United States of America. **2.** North America, Central America, and South America together. In this sense, also called "the Americas". [After *Americus* Vespucius (Latinised form of Amerigo VESPUCCI).]

A·mer·i·can (ə-mérrikən) *adj. Abbr.* **A., Am., Amer. 1.** Of, relating to, belonging to, or characteristic of the United States of America, its language, people, culture, government, or history. **2.** Of or pertaining to the Americas. **3.** Of or pertaining to the American Indians. **4.** Indigenous to the Americas. Often used with plant and animal names: *American elm; American elk.*
—*n. Abbr.* **A., Am., Amer. 1.** A native or inhabitant of America. **2.** A citizen of the United States.

A·mer·i·ca·na (ə-mérri-káanə ‖ *U.S. also* -kannə, -káynə) *pl.n.* **1.** Objects relating to American history, folklore, or geography. **2.** A collection of such objects. [AMERIC(A) + -ANA.]

American dream *n.* **1.** The democratic and egalitarian ideals on which the United States was founded and towards which it claims to be constantly striving. **2.** The material affluence that the United States is traditionally supposed to offer its inhabitants.

American eagle *n.* The bald eagle *(see),* especially as it appears on the Great Seal of the United States.

American English *n.* The English language as used in the United States. Also called "American".

American Federation of Labor *n. Abbr.* **AFL, A.F.L., A.F.** of **L.** A federation of U.S. trade unions organised in 1886, and merged with the Congress of Industrial Organisations in 1955.

American football *n.* A U.S. game similar to Rugby football with 11 players in each team, characterised by forward passing and the bulky protective equipment worn by the players.

American Independence *n.* The independence from European rule of countries of the Americas; especially, the independence from British rule of 13 British colonies in North America. See **Declaration of Independence.**

American Indian *n.* A member of any of the aboriginal peoples of North America (except the Eskimos), South America, and Central America, considered to belong to the Mongoloid ethnic division of the human species. —**American Indian** *adj.*

A·mer·i·can·ise, A·mer·i·can·ize (ə-mérrikən-īz) *v.* **-ised, -ising, -ises.** —*tr.* To cause to become American in character, spirit, or form. —*intr.* To become American in character, spirit, or form. —**A·mer·i·can·i·sa·tion** (-ī-záysh'n ‖ *U.S.* -i-) *n.*

A·mer·i·can·ism (ə-mérrikən-iz'm) *n.* **1.** A custom, trait, or tradition originating in or peculiar to the United States. **2.** A usage of language characteristic of American English. **3.** Allegiance to the United States and its values and institutions.

A·mer·i·can·ist (ə-mérrikən-ist) *n.* **1.** A specialist in some facet of America, such as its history or geology. **2.** An anthropologist specialising in the study of American aboriginal culture.

American plan *n. U.S.* A system of hotel tariffs in which a guest pays a fixed daily rate for room, meals, and service. Compare **European plan.**

American Revolution *n. U.S.* The **War of American Independence** *(see).*

American robin *n.* See **robin.**

American sable *n.* See **sable.**

American Samoa. Also **Eastern Samoa.** An unincorporated territory of the United States comprising the seven easternmost islands of the Samoan archipelago, lying in the south Pacific Ocean about 1 000 kilometres (620 miles) northeast of Fiji. The islands are administered by the U.S. Department of the Interior. The capital is Pago Pago on Tutuila, the main island. See **Samoa.**

American Spanish *n.* The variety of Spanish spoken in the Americas.

American Standard Version *n. Abbr.* **ASV, ARV** A revised version of the Authorised Version of the Bible published in the United States in 1901. Also called "American Revised Version".

Americas, the. The landmasses and islands between the main bodies of the Atlantic and Pacific Oceans, also known as the New World or Western Hemisphere. With some 28 per cent of the world's land, the Americas approach Asia in size, but have only just over a quarter of Asia's population. They stretch through more degrees of latitude than any other continent, through more than 15 300 kilometres (about 9,500 miles). Two areas with roughly the same north-south extent result from a division at the Panama isthmus: North America (Panama and all lands and islands to the north) and South America. These in turn can be divided into North America (Mexico and lands to the north); South America (as above); and Central America. Another, cultural, division can be made into North America (or Anglo-America), and Latin America (all lands south of the United States); virtually all of Latin America was for 300 years part of either the Spanish or Portuguese empire. The region of Pre-Columbian civilisation of Central America (southern Mexico, Belize, Guatemala, western Honduras, and El Salvador) is sometimes called Middle America.

America's Cup *n.* An international yachting trophy awarded to the winner of a yacht race between a selected challenger and a selected American yacht. It was first won by the yacht *America* in 1851.

am·er·ic·i·um (ámmə-ríssi-əm ‖ *U.S. also* -ríshi-) *n. Symbol* **Am** A white metallic transuranic element of the actinide series, having isotopes with mass numbers from 237 to 246 and half-lives from 25 minutes to 7,950 years. Its longest-lived isotopes, Am-241 and Am-243, are alpha-ray emitters used as radiation sources in research. Atomic number 95, relative density 13.67, valencies 3, 4, 5, 6. [New Latin, from AMERICA (where it was first produced).]

Amerigo Vespucci. See **Vespucci.**

Am·er·in·di·an (ámmər-índi-ən) *n.* Also **Am·er·ind** (ámmərind). An American Indian or an Eskimo. [AMER(ICAN) + INDIAN.] —**Am·er·in·di·an, Am·er·ind·ic** *adj.*

am·e·thyst (ámmithist) *n.* **1.** A purple or violet form of transparent quartz used as a gemstone. **2.** A purple variety of corundum, used as a gemstone. Also called "oriental amethyst". **3.** Moderate to reddish purple. [Middle English *ametist,* from Old French *ametiste,* from Latin *amethystus,* from Greek *amethystos,* amethyst, "antiintoxicant" (amethyst was thought to be a remedy for intoxication) : *a-,* not + *methuskein,* to intoxicate, from *methuein,* to be drunk, from *methu,* wine.] —**am·e·thys·tine** (-thíst-īn ‖ *U.S.* -in) *adj.*

amethystine python *n.* The largest Australian python, *Liasis amethystinus.* Also called "rock python".

am·e·tro·pi·a (ámmi-trṓpi-ə) *n.* Any eye abnormality, such as shortsightedness, long-sightedness, or astigmatism, resulting from faulty refraction. [New Latin : Greek *ametros,* beyond measure, disproportionate : *a-,* without + *metron,* measure + -OPIA.]

Am·har·ic (am-hárrik ‖ *U.S. also* aam-háarik) *n.* A southern Semitic language, the official language in Ethiopia. —**Am·har·ic** *adj.*

a·mi·a·ble (áymi-ə-b'l, áym-yə-b'l) *adj.* **1.** Friendly and likable; good-natured; agreeable. **2.** Cordial; congenial. [Middle English, from Old French, from Late Latin *amīcābilis,* AMICABLE.] —**a·mi·a·bil·i·ty** (-billəti), **ami·a·ble·ness** *n.* —**a·mi·a·bly** *adv.*

  Synonyms : *amiable, affable, good-natured, obliging, agreeable, pleasant.*

am·i·an·thus (ámmi-ánth-əss) *n.* Also **am·i·an·tus** (-ánt-). An asbestos with fine, silky fibres. [Latin *amiantus,* from Greek *amiantos (lithos),* "unpolluted (stone)" : *a-,* not + *miainein,* to pollute, defile.]

am·i·ca·ble (ámmikə-b'l) *adj.* Characterised by or showing friendliness; especially, made in a spirit of good will and without rancour: *an amicable settlement of their dispute.* [Middle English, from Late Latin *amīcābilis,* from Latin *amīcus,* friend.] —**am·i·ca·bil·i·ty** (-bílləti), **am·i·ca·ble·ness** *n.* —**am·i·ca·bly** *adv.*

am·ice (ámmiss) *n.* In Christian churches, a liturgical vestment consisting of an oblong piece of white linen worn round the neck and shoulders and partly under the alb. [Middle English *amyse,* perhaps from Old French *amis,* plural of *amit,* amice, from Latin *amictus,* mantle, "(a garment) thrown round one", from *amicīre,* to throw round : *ambi-,* round + *jacere,* to throw.]

A.M.I.C.E. Associate Member of the Institution of Civil Engineers.

A.M.I. Chem. E. Associate Member of the Institution of Chemical Engineers.

A·mi·ci (a-méechi), **Giovanni Battista** (1786–1863). Italian astronomer. He is noted for his improvements in designing scientific instruments, especially telescopes and microscopes, and particularly for his development of the **achromatic lens** *(see).*

a·mi·cus cu·ri·ae (ə-mík-əss kéwr-i-ee, -méek-, -ī) *n.,pl.* **amici curiae** (ə-mí-sī, ə-méekee). *Law.* A person invited to advise a court on a matter of law in a case to which he is not a party. [Latin, "friend of the court".]

a·mid (ə-mid) *prep.* Also **a·midst** (ə-midst). Surrounded by, in the middle of, or in the course of. —See Synonyms at **among**. [Middle English *amidde*, Old English *onmiddan* : ON + *middan*, dative singular of *midd(e)*, middle.]

am·ide (ámmid ‖ *U.S. also* ámmid) *n.* **1.** An organic compound, such as acetamide, containing the CONH₂ group. **2.** A compound with a metal replacing hydrogen in ammonia, such as sodium amide, NaNH₂. [AM(MONIA) + -IDE.] —**a·mid·ic** (ə-míddik) *adj.*

am·i·dol (ámmi-dol ‖ -dōl) *n.* A colourless crystalline compound (NH₂)₂C₆H₃OH·2HCl, used as a photographic developer. [German *Amidol* (trademark) : *amide* + phenol.]

a·mid·ships (ə-mid-ships) *adv.* Nautical. To, near to, or in the middle of a ship —**a·mid·ships** *adj.*

A.M.I.E.E. Associate Member of the Institution of Electrical Engineers.

A·mi·ens (ámmi-ənz, -AN, -ON). City in northern France dating from pre-Roman times. Situated in the Somme valley north of Paris, it is the principal city and capital of the Somme département. It has been a centre of textile manufacturing since the Middle Ages, and its fine Gothic cathedral is the largest church in France.

a·mi·go (ə-meégō) *n., pl.* **-gos.** A friend. [Spanish, from Latin *amicus*, friend.]

A.M.I. Mech. E. Associate Member of the Institution of Mechanical Engineers.

A·min (aa-meén) **(Dada), Idi** (*c.* 1925–). President of Uganda from 1971 to 1979. He became commander in chief of the Ugandan army in 1966, and in 1971 led the military coup that overthrew President Obote. In 1972 he ordered the expulsion of Uganda's 80,000-strong Asian community. Thereafter his rule became increasingly brutal and repressive, and in 1979 he fled the country after being deposed in a Tanzanian-backed coup.

Amindivi Islands. See **Lakshadweep.**

a·mine (ə-meén, ámmin) *n.* Any of a group of organic compounds of nitrogen, such as ethylamine, C₂H₅NH₂, that may be considered ammonia derivatives in which one or more hydrogen atoms have been replaced by a hydrocarbon radical. [AM(MONIUM) + -INE.]

–amine *n. comb. form.* Indicates an amine; for example, **methylamine.**

a·mi·no (ə-mīnō, ə-meénō ‖ *U.S. also* ámminō) *adj.* Pertaining to or consisting of an amine or other chemical compound containing NH₂ combined with a nonacid organic radical. [Independent use of AMINO-.]

amino– *comb. form.* Indicates replacement of one of the hydrogen atoms in ammonia by a nonacid organic radical; for example, **aminophenol.** [From AMINE.]

amino acid *n.* **1.** Any organic compound containing both an amino group (NH₂) and a carboxyl group (COOH). Amino acids are essential components of proteins.

a·mi·no·ben·zo·ic acid (ə-mīnō-ben-zō-ik, -meénō- ‖ *U.S. also* ámminō-) *n.* Any of three benzoic acid derivatives, NH₂C₆H₄COOH, especially the yellowish para form, which is part of the vitamin B complex.

a·mi·no·phe·nol (ə-mīnō-feén-ol, meénō- ‖ ōl, *U.S. also* ámminō-) *n.* Any of three organic compounds with composition C₆H₄NH₂OH, used as photographic developers and dye intermediates.

a·mi·no·py·rine (ə-mīnō-pír-een, -meénō- ‖ *U.S. also* ámminō-) *n.* A colourless crystalline compound, C₁₃H₁₇N₃O, used to reduce fever and relieve pain. [AMINO- + (ANTI)PYRINE.]

amir. Variant of **emir.**

A·mis (áy-miss), **Sir Kingsley** (1922–95). British novelist, poet, and critic. His first novel, *Lucky Jim* (1954), a satire on provincial university life, became an immediate popular success. His other works include *Jake's Thing* (1978), *The Green Man* (1969), *The Riverside Villas Murder* (1973), and *The Old Devils* (1986). His son, Martin (Louis) Amis (1949–) is also a novelist. His first success, *The Rachel Papers* (1973), was followed by several other novels, including *The Information* (1995), *Night Train* (1997).

A·mish (aámish, ámmish) *pl.n.* An orthodox U.S. Anabaptist sect that separated from the Mennonites in the late 17th century. [German *amisch*, after Jacob Amman, 17th-century Swiss Mennonite bishop.] —**A·mish** *adj.*

a·miss (ə-míss) *adj.* Out of proper order, wrong, or out of place in the circumstances: *What is amiss?*
~*adv.* In an improper, erroneous, or defective way. —**take amiss.** To misunderstand; feel offended by. [Middle English *a mis* : A- (on, at) + *mis*, a mistake, from *missen*, to MISS.]

a·mi·to·sis (áy-mī-tō-siss, ámmi-) *n.* Biology. Cell division characterised by simple nuclear cleavage without the formation of chromosomes. [New Latin : A- (not) + MITOSIS.] —**a·mi·tot·ic** (-tóttik) *adj.* —**a·mi·tot·i·cal·ly** *adv.*

am·i·ty (ámməti) *n., pl.* **-ties.** Peaceful and cordial relations, especially between nations; friendship. Compare **comity.** [Middle English *amite*, from Old French *amitie*, from Medieval Latin *amīcitās*, from Latin *amīcus*, friend.]

Am·man (ə-maán, a-, -mán). The capital and by far the largest and most modern city of Jordan, situated on the Jabbok river in the north of the country. Since 1948 remains from the Chalcolithic period (*c.* 4000 B.C.–*c.*3000 B.C.) have been unearthed on the site.

am·me·ter (ámmitər, ám-meetər) *n. Abbr.* **A** An instrument that measures electric current. [AM(PERE) + -METER.]

am·mine (ámmeen, ə-meén) *n.* Any of a class of chemical compounds, such as aniline, derived from replacement of hydrogen atoms in ammonia by univalent hydrocarbon radicals. [AMM(ONIA) + -INE.] —**am·mi·no** (ə-mīnō, ə-meénō ‖ *U.S. also* ámminō) *adj.*

am·mo (ámmō) *n. Informal.* Ammunition.

am·mo·coete (ámmə-seet) *n.* The blind, wormlike larva of the lamprey. [New Latin *Ammocoetes* (former genus name), "ones that lie in sand" : Greek *ammos*, sand + *koitē*, bed, from *keisthei*, to lie.]

am·mo·ni·a (ə-mōni-ə, ə-mōn-yə) *n.* **1.** A colourless, pungent gas, NH₃, extensively used to manufacture fertilisers and a wide variety of nitrogen-containing organic and inorganic chemicals. **2.** A solution of ammonia in water, **ammonium hydroxide** (see). [New Latin, from Latin *(sal) ammōniācus*, "(salt) of Amen", from Greek *ammōniakos*, from *Ammōn*, AMEN (it was originally obtained from a region near the temple of Amen, in Libya).]

am·mo·ni·ac¹ (ə-mōni-ak) *adj.* Also **am·mo·ni·a·cal** (ámmə-nī-ək'l). Of, containing, or similar to ammonia.

ammoniac² *n.* A strong-smelling gum resin from the stems of a plant, *Dorema ammoniacum*, of northern Asia, formerly used in medicine as an expectorant and stimulant. Also called "gum ammoniac". [Middle English *ammonyak*, from Latin *ammōniacum*, from Greek *ammōniakon*, neuter of *ammōniakos*, of Amen. See **ammonia.**]

am·mo·ni·ate (ə-mōni-ayt) *tr.v.* **-ated, -ating, -ates.** To treat or combine with ammonia.
~*n.* A compound that contains ammonia. —**am·mo·ni·a·tion** (-áysh'n) *n.*

ammonia water *n. Chemistry.* Ammonium hydroxide.

am·mon·i·fi·ca·tion (ə-mŏni-fi-káysh'n, -mónni-) *n.* **1.** Impregnation with ammonia or an ammonium compound. **2.** The generation of ammonia or ammonium compounds by the action of bacteria on nitrogenous organic matter in soil.

am·mon·i·fy (ə-mŏni-fī, -mónni-) *v.* **-fied, -fying, -fies.** —*tr.* To subject to ammonification. —*intr.* To undergo ammonification. [AM-MONI(A) + -FY.] —**am·mo·ni·fi·er** *n.*

am·mon·ite¹ (ámmən-īt) *n.* **1.** The coiled, flat, chambered shell of any of various extinct cephalopod molluscs of the subclass Ammonoidea, found as fossils in Mesozoic formations. **2.** Any mollusc of the subclass Ammonoidea. [New Latin *Ammonītēs*, from Latin *(cornus) Ammōnis*, "(horn) of Amen" (because it resembles the horns of Amen), from *Ammōnis*, genitive of *Ammōn*, AMEN.]

ammonite² *n.* **1.** An explosive mixture of ammonium nitrate and a small quantity of TNT or a similar substance. **2.** A nitrogenous fertiliser made from animal wastes. [*Ammonium* + *nitrate.*]

Ammonite *n.* A member of a Semitic people living east of the river Jordan, mentioned frequently in the Old Testament. [Late Latin *Ammonītēs*, the Ammonites, from Hebrew '*Ammōn*, city or people of Amman, from Canaanite *'am-*, "folk".]

am·mo·ni·um (ə-mōni-əm, ə-mōn-yəm) *n.* The chemical ion NH₄⁺. [New Latin : AMMON(IA) + -IUM.]

ammonium carbonate *n.* A white powder with composition (NH₄)HCO₃·(NH₄)CO₂NH₂ used in baking powders, smelling salts, and fire-extinguishing compounds. Also called "sal volatile".

ammonium chloride *n.* A slightly hygroscopic white crystalline compound, NH₄Cl, used in dry cells, as a soldering flux, as an expectorant, and in various industrial applications. Also called "sal ammoniac".

ammonium hydroxide *n.* A colourless basic aqueous solution of ammonia, NH₄OH, used as a household cleanser and to manufacture many products including textiles, rayon, rubber, fertilisers, and plastics. Also called "ammonia water", "ammonia".

ammonium nitrate *n.* A colourless crystalline salt, NH₄NO₃, used in fertilisers, explosives, and solid rocket propellants.

ammonium sulphate *n.* A brownish-grey to white crystalline salt, (NH₄)₂SO₄, used in fertilisers and water purification.

am·mu·ni·tion (ámmew-nish'n) *n.* **1. a.** Bullets, shells, or the like, along with their fuses and primers, that can be fired from guns or otherwise propelled. **b.** Any nuclear, biological, chemical, or explosive material used in warfare. **2.** Any means of attack or defence, such as facts that can be used in an argument. [Obsolete French *amunition*, from phrase *l'amunition*, misinterpretation of *la munition*, the MUNITION.]

am·ne·si·a (am-neézi-ə, -neéz-yə, -neezhə) *n.* Partial or total loss of memory, especially through shock, psychological disturbance, brain damage, or illness. [New Latin, from Greek *amnēsia* : *a-*, not + *mnasthai*, to remember.] —**am·ne·si·ac** (am-neézi-ak, -neezhi-) *n.* & *adj.* —**am·nes·tic** (am-néstik) *adj.*

am·nes·ty (ámnəsti) *n., pl.* **-ties.** **1.** A general pardon granted by a government, especially to people guilty of political offences. **2.** A period during which this is in force. **3.** A period of immunity during which penalties for past infringements are waived.
~*tr.v.* **amnestied, -tying, -ties.** To grant an amnesty to. [Greek *amnēstia*, "forgetfulness", from *amnēstos*, forgotten : *a-*, not + *mnasthai*, to remember.]

Amnesty International *n.* An organisation that investigates violations of human rights and campaigns for the release of prisoners of conscience and the humane treatment of political prisoners.

am·ni·o·cen·te·sis (ám-ni-ō-sen-teé-siss) *n., pl.* **-teses.** The withdrawal of a sample of amniotic fluid from a pregnant woman, usually for the diagnosis of genetic or developmental disorders in the foetus. [AMNION + Greek *kentesis*, a puncturing, from *kentein*, to prick.]

am·ni·o·gra·phy (ám-ni-óggrəfi) *n.* Radiography of the amnion in order to examine the placenta and umbilical cord. [AMNIO(N) + -GRAPHY.]

am·ni·on (ám-ni-ən, -on) n., pl. **-ons** or **-nia** (-ni-ə). A thin, tough, membranous sac that contains a watery fluid (amniotic fluid) in which the embryo of a mammal, bird, or reptile is suspended. It is the inner one of two embryonic membranes. Compare **chorion**. [New Latin, from Greek amnion, caul, diminutive of amnos, lamb.] —**am·ni·ot·ic** (ám-ni-óttik), **am·ni·on·ic** (ám-ni-ónnik) adj.

am·ni·os·co·py (ám-ni-óskəpi) n. Examination of the interior of the amniotic sac by means of an instrument (amnioscope) passed through the wall of the abdomen. [AMNIO(N) + -SCOPY.]

am·n't (ámm'nt). Chiefly Scottish & Irish. Contraction of am not. See Usage note at **ain't**.

a·moe·ba, U.S. **a·me·ba** (ə-mée-bə) n., pl. **-bas** or **-bae** (-bee). Any of various protozoans of the genus Amoeba and related genera, occurring in water and soil, and as internal animal parasites, characteristically having an indefinite, changeable form and moving by means of pseudopodia. [New Latin, from Greek amoibē, change, from ameibein, to change.] —**a·moe·bic** (-bik) adj.

am·oe·bi·a·sis (ámmi-bī-ə-siss) n., pl. **-ses** (-seez). Any infection caused by amoebas, especially by Entamoeba histolytica. [New Latin : AMOEB(A) + -IASIS.]

amoebic dysentery n. An infectious, inflammatory dysentery of the colon, caused by Entamoeba histolytica and resulting in severe pain and diarrhoea.

a·moe·bo·cyte (ə-méebə-sīt) n. Any cell, such as a leucocyte, having amoebic form. [AMOEB(A) + -CYTE.]

a·moe·boid (ə-mée-boyd) adj. Of or resembling an amoeba, especially in changeable form and means of locomotion.

a·mok (ə-mók, áamó) adv. Also **a·muck** (ə-múk). 1. In a frenzy to do violence or kill. 2. In a wild, frantic, or uncontrollable manner. Used in the phrase *run amok*. [Malay.]

Amon. Variant of **Amen**.

a·mong (ə-múng ‖ Northern England also ə-móng) prep. Also **a·mongst** (-st). 1. In the midst of; surrounded by. 2. In the group, number, or class of: *among the fastest runners in the country; among other things*. 3. In the company of; in association with: *travelling among a group of tourists*. 4. With or by many or most of: *a custom popular among the Greeks*. 5. By the joint action of: *Among us, we will get the job done*. 6. With portions to each of: *Distribute this among you*. 7. Each with the other; between one another in a group: *Don't fight among yourselves*. [Middle English among, Old English on gemang : on, ON + gemang, a crowd.]

Synonyms: among, amid, between.

Usage: The English grammatical tradition has tried to maintain a clear distinction between the use of among and between. Between is supposed to be used when only two items are to be distinguished: *Look at the difference between John and Alec*; for more than two, among is to be preferred. However, actual usage is somewhat different. Between is used when any number of items are distinguished—provided that they are named separately: *Look at the differences between John and Alec and Paul. Switzerland lies between Austria, Germany, France, Italy, and Liechtenstein*. Even when items are not named separately, between can still be used if the number of the items is specified: *The prize was divided equally between the seven of us*. But here among could replace between, and if the number of prizewinners were not specified, only among could be used: *The prize was divided among all the workers*.

a·mon·til·la·do (ə-mónti-laádo; Spanish -yaathṓ) n., pl. **-dos**. A fairly pale medium-dry sherry. [Spanish (vino) amontillado, "(wine) made in Montilla" : a-, to, from Latin ad- + Montilla, Spanish town.]

a·mor·al (ay-mórrəl, a-) adj. 1. Not admitting of moral distinctions or judgments; outside the sphere of morality; non-moral. 2. Lacking moral judgment or sensibility; unable to distinguish between right and wrong. [A- (not) + MORAL.] —**a·mo·ral·i·ty** (áy-mo-rál-əti, á-, -mə-, -maw-), **a·mor·al·ism** n. —**a·mor·al·ly** adv.

am·o·ret·to (ámmə-réttó ‖ U.S. also áamə-) n., pl. **-retti** (-réttee) or **-tos**. A cupid. [Italian, diminutive of Amore, Cupid, from Latin Amor, from amor, love, from amāre, to love.]

am·o·rist (ámmərist) n. One who is dedicated to or writes about love. [From Latin amor, love.]

Am·o·rite (ámmərīt) n. A member of a people inhabiting Canaan before the Israelites, mentioned frequently in the Old Testament. [Hebrew Emōrī.]

am·o·ro·so¹ (ammə-rṓ-sō) adv. Music. In a loving manner; tenderly. Used as a direction. [Italian, "amorous".] —**am·o·ro·so** adj.

amoroso² n. A rich, dark Spanish sherry. [Spanish, "amorous".]

am·o·rous (ámmərəss) adj. 1. Strongly attracted to love, especially sexual love. 2. Indicative of love: *an amorous glance*. 3. Of or concerned with love: *an amorous poem*. 4. In love; enamoured. Sometimes used with of. [Middle English, from Old French, from Medieval Latin amōrōsus, from Latin amor, love.] —**am·o·rous·ly** adv. —**am·o·rous·ness** n.

a·mor·phism (ə-mórfiz'm) n. The state or quality of being amorphous, especially with respect to lack of crystalline structure.

a·mor·phous (ə-mórfəs) adj. 1. Without definite form; lacking a specific shape. 2. Of no particular type or character; formless; indeterminate. 3. Lacking distinct crystalline structure. [Greek amorphos : A-, + -MORPHOUS.] —**a·mor·phous·ly** adv. —**a·mor·phous·ness** n.

am·or·ti·sa·tion (ə-mór-tī-záysh'n, ámmawr-, ámmər-, -ti-) n. 1. The

act or process of amortising or the condition of being amortised. 2. The money set aside for this purpose.

am·or·tise, am·or·tize (ə-mór-tīz, rarely -tiz ‖ U.S. also ámmərtīz) tr.v. **-tised, -tising, -tises**. 1. Finance. To liquidate (a debt) by instalment payments or payment into a sinking fund. 2. Accounting. a. To reduce gradually the book value of (an asset) over a period equal to its projected useful life. b. To provide for the cost of replacing (an asset) by periodic payments into a sinking fund. 3. Law. To transfer (property) in mortmain. [Middle English amortisen, from Old French amortir (present stem amortiss-), from Vulgar Latin admortīre (unattested), to deaden : ad-, to + mortus (unattested), dead, from Latin mors (stem mort-), death.] —**am·or·tis·a·ble** adj.

A·mos¹ (áy-moss ‖ U.S. -məss). A Hebrew prophet of the eighth century B.C.

Amos² n. A book of the Old Testament containing the prophecies of Amos.

a·mount (ə-mównt) n. Abbr. **amt.** 1. The total figure or quantity; a sum or aggregate: *could only raise half the amount needed*. 2. A quantity or supply: *attracted a tremendous amount of interest*. 3. A principal plus its interest, as in a loan. 4. The overall effect or meaning; import.
~intr.v. **amounted, amounting, amounts**. 1. To add up in number or quantity: *The total purchase amounts to ten pounds*. 2. To be equivalent or tantamount: *accusations amounting to an indictment*. [Middle English amounten, to rise, from Old French amonter, from amont, upwards, "to the mountain" : a-, to, from Latin ad- + mont, mountain, from Latin mōns (stem mont-).]

a·mour (ə-móor) n. A love affair, especially an illicit one: *His latest amours were in all the gossip columns*. [Middle English, from Old French, from Old Provençal amor, from Latin amor, love, from amāre, to love.]

a·mour-pro·pre (ámmoor-própr, -próppər) n. Self-esteem. [French, "self-love".]

Amoy. See **Xiamen**.

amp (amp) n. 1. An ampere. 2. Informal. An amplifier.

AMP n. Adenosine monophosphate: a mononucleotide, $C_{10}H_{14}N_5O_7P$, found in cells, that is reversibly convertible to ADP and ATP.

am·pe·lop·sis (ámpi-lópsiss) n. Any of several woody vines of the genus Ampelopsis, having small greenish or yellowish flowers and occurring in warm regions of Asia and America. [New Latin Ampelopsis : Greek ampelos, grapevine, + -OPSIS.]

am·per·age (ámpər-ij, ámpeer-) n. The strength of an electric current expressed in amperes.

am·pere (ám-peer, -pair) n. Abbr. **A** 1. The SI unit of electric current. It is the steady current that when flowing in straight parallel wires of infinite length and negligible cross-section, separated by a distance of one metre in free space, produces a force between the wires of 2×10^{-7} newton per metre of length. 1 ampere is equal to 1 coulomb per second. 2. A former unit of electric current, the international ampere, equal to 0.999835 ampere. Also shortened to "amp". [After André-Marie AMPÈRE.]

Am·père (ám-pair; French aaN-páir), **André-Marie** (1775–1836). French physicist and mathematician. He formulated Ampère's law, which is a mathematical description of the magnetic field produced by a current-carrying conductor. The SI unit of electric current is named after him.

am·pere-hour (ámpeer-ówr) n. The electric charge transferred past a specific circuit point by a current of one ampere in one hour.

am·pere-turn (ámpeer-túrn) n. A unit of magnetomotive force equal to the magnetomotive force around a path linking one turn of a conducting loop carrying a current of one ampere.

am·per·sand (ámpər-sand) n. The character or sign (&) representing and. [From & per se and, "& by itself (equals) and", phrase formerly used to explain the character.]

am·phet·a·mine (am-féttə-min, -meen) n. 1. A colourless volatile liquid, $C_9H_{13}N$, used primarily as a central-nervous-system stimulant. Prolonged use may lead to dependence. 2. A phosphate or sulphate of amphetamine, similarly used. [Alpha methyl phenyl ethyl amine.]

amphi– prefix. Indicates: 1. On both sides; on both ends; of both kinds; both; for example, **amphibious**. 2. Around; on all sides; for example, **amphithecium**. [Latin, from Greek, from amphi, around, on both sides, on all sides.]

am·phi·ar·thro·sis (ámfi-aar-thró-siss) n., pl. **-ses** (-seez). A relatively immobile joint between bony surfaces connected by ligaments or elastic cartilage.

am·phib·i·an (am-fíbbi-ən) n. 1. Any of various cold-blooded, smooth-skinned vertebrate organisms of the class Amphibia, such as a frog, toad, or salamander, characteristically hatching as aquatic larvae that breathe by means of gills and metamorphosing to an adult form having air-breathing lungs. 2. Any amphibious organism. 3. An aircraft that can take off and land either on land or on water. 4. A vehicle that can move over land and on water.
~adj. Of or pertaining to an amphibian, especially one of the Amphibia. [New Latin Amphibia, plural of amphibium, an amphibian, from Greek amphibion, neuter of amphibios, AMPHIBIOUS.]

am·phi·bi·ot·ic (ámfi-bī-óttik) adj. Living in water during a stage of development and on land during the adult stage.

am·phib·i·ous (am-fíbbi-əss) adj. 1. Living or able to live on land and in water. 2. a. Able or trained to operate on land and in water: *amphibious vehicles; amphibious troops*. b. In

tions on both land and water: *an amphibious invasion.* **3.** Of a mixed or twofold nature. [Greek *amphibios,* "living a double life" : AMPHI- + *bios,* life.] —**am·phib·i·ous·ly** *adv.* —**am·phib·i·ous·ness** *n.*

am·phi·bole (ámfi-bōl) *n.* Any of a large group of structurally similar hydrated double silicate minerals including hornblende and several types of asbestos, containing various combinations of sodium, calcium, magnesium, iron, and aluminium. [French, from Late Latin *amphibolus,* ambiguous (from its many varieties), from Greek *amphibolos,* doubtful, from *amphiballein,* to throw around, doubt : AMPHI- + *ballein,* to throw.] —**am·phi·bol·ic** (-bóllik) *adj.*

am·phib·o·lite (am-fíbbəlīt) *n.* A metamorphic rock composed chiefly of amphibole with some plagioclase and quartz. [AMPHIBOL(E) + -ITE.]

am·phi·bol·o·gy (ámfi-bólləji) *n., pl.* **-gies.** Also **am·phib·o·ly** (am-fíbbəli) *pl.* **-lies. 1.** Ambiguity arising from a grammatical construction that can be understood in more than one way. **2.** A statement containing such ambiguity; for example, *Flying planes can be dangerous.* [Middle English *amphilbologie,* from Late Latin *amphibologia,* from *amphibolia,* from Greek *amphibolia,* from *amphibolos,* ambiguous. See **amphibole.**] —**am·phib·o·log·i·cal** (am-fíbbə-ló-jik'l, ámfi-bə-) *adj.* —**am·phib·o·log·i·cal·ly** *adv.*

am·phi·coe·lous (ámfi-séeləss) *adj.* Concave on both ends or sides, as the vertebrae of most fishes are. [Late Greek *amphikoilos* : AMPHI- + *koilos,* hollow.]

am·phic·ty·o·ny (am-fíkti-əni) *n., pl.* **-nies.** In ancient Greece, a group of neighbouring states associated for a common religious or political purpose; especially, such a group formed to protect and maintain a common religious centre or shrine, such as the one at Delphi. [Greek *amphiktuonia,* from *amphiktuones,* neighbours : AMPHI- + *ktizein,* to found.] —**am·phic·ty·on·ic** (-ónnik) *adj.*

am·phi·mix·is (ámfi-míksiss) *n.* True sexual reproduction, with fusion of sperm and egg nuclei. Compare **apomixis.** [New Latin : AMPHI- + Greek *mixis,* a mingling, from *mignunai,* to mingle.] —**am·phi·mic·tic** (-míktik) *adj.*

am·phi·ox·us (ámfi-óksəss) *n.* A primitive chordate organism, the **lancelet** (*see*). [New Latin, "sharp at both ends" : AMPHI- + Greek *oxus,* sharp.]

am·phi·pod (ámfi-pod) *n.* Any of numerous small crustaceans of the order Amphipoda, which includes the sand hoppers. [New Latin *Amphipoda,* "having feet on both sides" : AMPHI- + -POD.]

am·phip·ro·style (am-fíprə-stīl, ámfi-prô-stīl) *adj.* Amphistylar with a prostyle at each end, but none along the sides. Said especially of an ancient temple. [Latin *amphiprostylos,* from Greek *amphiprostulos,* "with pillars in front and behind" : AMPHI- + *prostulos,* with pillars in front (see **prostyle**).] —**am·phi·pro·style** *n.*

am·phis·bae·na (ámfiss-béenə, ámfiz-) *n.* **1.** A mythological serpent having a head at each end of its body. **2.** A wormlike burrowing lizard of the genus *Amphisbaena.* [Latin, from Greek *amphisbaina,* "one that goes in both directions" : *amphis,* both ways, + *bainein,* to go.] —**am·phis·bae·nic** *adj.*

am·phi·sty·lar (ámfi-stílar) *adj. Architecture.* Having columns at both front and back or on each side. [AMPHI- + Greek *stulos,* a pillar.]

am·phi·the·a·tre (ámfi-thee-ətər ‖ *South of England also* -éttər) *n.* **1.** An oval or round structure having tiers of seats rising gradually outwards from an open space or arena at the centre. **2.** Any public place where contests are held; an arena. **3.** A level area surrounded by upward sloping ground. **4.** A rising, semicircular gallery in a theatre. [Latin *amphitheatrum,* from Greek *amphitheatron* : AMPHI- + THEATRE.] —**am·phi·the·at·ric** (-thee-átrik), **am·phi·the·at·ri·cal** *adj.* —**am·phi·the·at·ri·cal·ly** *adv.*

am·phi·the·ci·um (ámfi-thee-si-əm ‖ -shi-) *n., pl.* **-cia** (-si-ə ‖ -shi-ə). *Botany.* The outer layer of cells of the spore-capsule of a moss. [New Latin : AMPHI- + Greek *thēkion,* diminutive of *thēkē,* a case.]

am·phit·ri·chous (am-fítri-kəss) *adj.* Having a flagellum or flagella at both ends, as certain microorganisms do. [AMPHI- + -TRICHOUS.]

Am·phi·tri·te (ámfi-tríti). *Greek Mythology.* The goddess of the sea, wife of Poseidon, and one of the Nereids.

am·phit·ro·pous (am-fítrəpəss) *adj. Botany.* Partly inverted, so that the point of attachment is near the middle. Said of an ovule. [AMPHI- + -TROPOUS.]

am·pho·ra (ámfə-rə) *n., pl.* **-rae** (-ree) *or* **-ras.** A large two-handled jar with a narrow neck, used by the ancient Greeks and Romans to carry wine or oil. [Latin *amphora,* from Greek *amphoreus, amphiphoreus* : AMPHI- + *phoreus,* a bearer, from *pherein,* to bear.] —**am·pho·ral** (-rəl) *adj.*

am·pho·ter·ic (ámfə-térrik) *adj. Chemistry.* Capable of reacting either as an acid or as a base. [Greek *amphoteros,* either of two, from *amphō,* both.]

am·pi·cil·lin (ámpi-sillin) *n.* An antibiotic given orally or by injection to treat a variety of infections of the urinary, respiratory, and intestinal tracts. [AM(INO-) P(EN)ICILLIN.]

am·ple (ámp'l) *adj.* **-pler, -plest. 1.** Large in extent or capacity; spacious: *an ample living room.* **2.** Large in degree, scope, or amount: *a family of ample means.* **3.** Rather stout; portly. Used euphemistically: *an ample figure.* **4.** Enough or more than enough for a particular need or purpose. [Middle English, from Old French, from Latin *amplus†,* wide, ample.] —**am·ple·ness** *n.*

am·plex·i·caul (am-pléksi-kawl) *adj. Botany.* Having a base that clasps or encircles the stem, as some leaves do. [New Latin *amplexicaulis,* embracing stem : Latin *amplexus,* past participle of *amplectī,* to wind around : AM(BI)- + *plectere,* to plait + *caulis,* stem.]

am·pli·fi·ca·tion (ámplifi-káysh'n) *n.* **1.** The act or result of amplifying; especially, the process of expanding a statement, narrative, or the like, as for clarification or rhetorical effect. **2. a.** Material used to amplify a statement. **b.** A statement so amplified. **3.** *Physics.* **a.** The process of increasing the magnitude of a variable quantity, especially of a voltage or current, without altering any other quality. **b.** The result of such a process.

am·pli·fi·er (ámplifi-ər) *n.* **1.** One that amplifies, enlarges, or extends. **2.** Any of various electronic devices or circuits that increase the current or voltage of a signal fed into them; for example, an audio-frequency amplifier that feeds the loudspeakers in a radio, record-player, or the like.

am·pli·fy (ámpli-fī) *v.* **-fied, -fying, -fies.** —*tr.* **1.** To enlarge (a statement or idea, for example) by adding material that clarifies, illustrates, or otherwise expands. **2.** To extend, enhance, or increase, as in scope or importance. **3.** *Physics.* To produce amplification of. —*intr.* To write or discourse at greater length on what has been written or said. [Middle English *amplifien,* from Old French *amplifier,* from Latin *amplificāre* : *amplus,* AMPLE + *facere,* to make.] —**am·pli·fi·ca·to·ry** (ámplifi-káytəri) *adj.*

am·pli·tude (ámpli-tewd ‖ -tōōd) *n.* **1.** Greatness of size or extent; magnitude. **2.** Fullness of scope; breadth or range, as of mind. **3.** *Astronomy.* The angular distance along the horizon from true east or west to the intersection of the vertical circle of a celestial body with the horizon. **4.** *Physics.* The maximum value of a periodically varying quantity. **5.** *Mathematics.* **a.** The maximum ordinate value of a periodic curve. **b.** The angle made with the positive horizontal axis by the vector representation of a complex number. In this sense, also called "argument". [Latin *amplitūdō,* from *amplus,* AMPLE.]

amplitude modulation *n. Abbr.* **AM, am** The encoding of a carrier wave by variation of its amplitude in accordance with an input signal. Compare **frequency modulation.**

am·ply (ámpli) *adv.* In an ample manner; largely; liberally; sufficiently.

am·poule, am·pule (ám-pōōl ‖ -pewl) *n.* A small glass tube, sealed after filling and used chiefly as a container for a hypodermic injection solution. [French, from Old French, from Latin *ampulla,* AMPULLA.]

am·pul·la (am-pōōl-ə, -púl-) *n., pl.* **-lae** (-ee). **1.** A nearly round bottle with two handles used by the ancient Romans for wine, oil, or perfume. **2. a.** A container used for wine or water at the Eucharist. **b.** A vessel for consecrated wine or holy oil. **3.** *Anatomy.* A small dilation in a canal or duct, especially in the semicircular canal of the ear. [Latin, diminutive of *amp(h)ora,* AMPHORA.] —**am·pul·lar** (-ər) *adj.*

am·pul·la·ceous (ámpōō-láyshəss) *adj.* Resembling an ampulla; bladder-shaped. [Latin *ampullāceus* : AMPULL(A) + -ACEOUS.]

am·pu·tate (ámpew-tayt) *tr.v.* **-tated, -tating, -tates.** To cut off (a part of the body, usually a limb), especially by surgery. [Latin *amputāre,* to cut around : AM(BI)- + *putāre,* to cut.] —**am·pu·ta·tion** (-táysh'n) *n.* —**am·pu·ta·tor** (-taytər) *n.*

am·pu·tee (ámpew-tée) *n.* A person who has had one or more limbs removed by amputation.

am·ri·ta, am·ree·ta (am-réetə, um-) *n. Hindu Mythology.* **1.** The ambrosia, prepared by the gods, that bestows immortality. **2.** The immortality achieved by drinking this ambrosia. [Sanskrit *amṛta,* "deathless" : *a-,* without + *mṛta,* death.]

Am·rit·sar (am-rítsər, um-). The administrative centre and one of the largest cities of the Punjab, northwestern India, on the border with Pakistan. Founded in 1577 by the fourth guru of the Sikhs, Ram Das, it has remained the centre of the Sikh faith. In 1919 it was the scene of a massacre in which hundreds of Indian nationalists were killed by British-led troops.

Am·ster·dam (ámstər-dám, -dam) The official capital and largest city of the Netherlands, in North Holland province. It lies on the IJ, an arm of the Ijsselmeer, and is linked to the North Sea by a ship canal. It has an important stock exchange and is a centre of the diamond-cutting industry. Among its many museums, the Rijksmuseum, with a large collection of Dutch paintings, is outstanding. —**Am·ster·dam·mer** *n.*

amt. amount.

amu *Physics.* atomic mass unit.

amuck. Variant of **amok.**

A·mu·dar'ya (a-mōō-dáari-ə). Ancient name **Ox·us** (óksəss). A river that rises in the Pamir mountains of central Asia and flows about 2 580 kilometres (1,600 miles) northwest to the Aral Sea.

am·u·let (ámmew-lət, -lit) *n.* An object worn, especially around the neck, as a charm against evil or injury. [Latin *amulētum†.*]

A·mund·sen (aámənd-sən, ámmənd-), **Roald (Engelbreth Gravning)** (1872–1928). Norwegian explorer. He was the first to navigate the Northwest Passage (1903–06), and he fixed the position of the North Magnetic Pole. He became the first person to reach the South Pole, in 1911, 34 days ahead of Robert Falcon Scott. With the Italian explorer Umberto Nobile he was the first to make a flight over the North Pole. Amundsen died on a flight to the Arctic to search for Nobile, whose airship had crashed.

A·mur (ə-moór, a-). *Chinese* **Heilong Jiang.** One of the principal waterways of Asia. It is formed by the confluence of the rivers Shilka and Argun on the northern border of Manchuria and flows some 2 900 kilometres (1,800 miles) to the Sea of Japan. For more than 1 600 kilometres (1,000 miles) it serves as the border between China and Russia.

a·muse (ə-méwz) *tr.v.* **amused, amusing, amuses. 1.** To occupy in an agreeable, pleasing, or entertaining fashion. **2.** To cause to laugh or smile by giving pleasure. [Old French *amuser,* "to cause to idle away time" : *a,* to, from Latin *ad-* + *muser,* to idle, MUSE.] —**a·mus·er** *n.*

a·muse·ment (ə-méwzmənt) *n.* **1.** The pleasurable occupation of time or the attention; diversion; entertainment: *sang for the amusement of the theatre queues.* **2.** The state of being amused, entertained, or pleased. **2.** Something that amuses.

amusement arcade *n.* An enclosed area housing coin-operated games and gambling machines.

amusement park *n.* An open-air fairground.

a·mus·ing (ə-méwzing) *adj.* **1.** Entertaining or pleasing. **2.** Arousing laughter. —**a·mus·ing·ly** *adv.* —**a·mus·ing·ness** *n.*

a·myg·dale (ə-mígdayl) *n.* An amygdule. [Greek *amugdalē,* ALMOND.]

a·myg·da·loid (ə-mígdə-loyd) *n.* A volcanic rock containing many amygdules.

~*adj.* Also **a·myg·da·loi·dal** (-lóyd'l) (for sense 2). **1.** Almond-shaped. **2.** *Geology.* Resembling amygdaloid. [Latin *amygdala,* ALMOND + -OID.]

a·myg·dule (ə-mígdewl) *n.* A cavity in a lava that has been filled with a mineral subsequent to the formation of the lava. [Latin *amygdala,* ALMOND (from its almond-like shape) + (NOD)ULE.]

am·yl (ámmil) *n.* Any univalent organic radical with the formula C_5H_{11}. See **pentyl.** [Latin *amylum,* starch, AMYLUM.]

am·y·la·ceous (ámmi-láyshəss) *adj.* Of, pertaining to, or resembling starch; starchy. [AMYL(O)- + -ACEOUS.]

amyl acetate *n.* An organic compound, $CH_3COOC_5H_{11}$, used commercially in isomeric mixtures as a flavouring agent, as a paint and lacquer solvent, and in the preparation of penicillin. Also called "banana oil", "pear oil".

amyl alcohol *n.* Any of eight isomers of the composition $C_5H_{11}OH$, one of which, $CH_3CH_2CH(CH_3)CH_2OH$, is the principal constituent of fusel oil.

am·y·lase (ámmi-layz, -layss) *n.* Any of various enzymes that convert starch or glycogen to sugar. [AMYL(O)- + -ASE.]

am·yl·ene (ámmi-leen) *n. Chemistry.* **Pentene** (see).

amyl nitrite *n.* The nitrous acid ester of isoamyl alcohol, $(CH_3)_2CHCH_2CH_2NO_2$, used in medicine as a vasodilator, mainly in the treatment of angina pectoris. Compare **popper** 3.

amylo-, amyl- *comb. form.* Indicates starch; for example, **amylolysis, amylase.** [Latin *amylum,* starch, AMYLUM.]

am·y·loid (ámmiloyd) *n.* **1.** A starchlike substance. **2.** *Pathology.* A hard starchlike protein deposited in tissues in certain degenerative diseases. [AMYL(O)- + -OID.] —**am·y·loid** *adj.*

am·y·lol·y·sis (ámmi-lóllə-siss) *n.* The enzymatic conversion of starch to sugars. [AMYLO- + -LYSIS.] —**am·y·lo·lyt·ic** (-lō-líttik) *adj.*

am·y·lo·pec·tin (ámmilō-péktin) *n.* The major and insoluble portion of starch. Compare **amylose.**

am·y·lop·sin (ámmi-lópsin) *n.* The starch-digesting amylase produced by the pancreas. [AMYLO- + (TRY)PSIN.]

am·y·lose (ámmi-lōss, -lōz) *n.* The relatively soluble portion of starch. Compare **amylopectin.** [AMYL(O)- + -OSE.]

am·y·lum (ámmiləm) *n.* Starch. [Latin, from Greek *amulon,* starch, the finest flour, from neuter of *amulos,* "not ground in a mill": A-(not) + *mulē,* mill.]

a·my·o·to·ni·a (áy-mī-ə-tóni-ə) *n.* Lack of muscle tone. [New Latin : A- (without) + MYO- + -TONIA.]

an¹ (an, *weak form* ən). **1.** The indefinite article, a form of *a* used before words beginning with a vowel or with an unpronounced *h*: *an elephant; an hour.* See Usage note at **a. 2.** Indefinite article functioning as a preposition. In every; to each; per: *30 pence an hour.* [Middle English *an,* Old English *ān,* one.]

an², an' (an, *weak form* ən) *conj. Archaic.* And if; if. [Middle English *an,* Old English *an,* short for AND.]

An *Physics.* actinon.

an- *prefix.* Indicates not or without; for example, **anaerobe, anosmia.** Compare **a-** (not). [Greek *an-,* not, without, lacking.]

-an¹, -ian, -ean *adj. suffix.* Indicates: **1.** Pertaining to, belonging to, or resembling; for example, **cetacean, Mexican. 2.** Believing in or adhering to; for example, **Anglican.** [Latin *-ānus,* adjectival suffix.]

-an², -ian, -ean *n. suffix.* Indicates: **1. a.** A person belonging to or coming from; for example, **American, Liverpudlian. b.** A believer in or follower of; for example, **Darwinian, Lutheran. 2.** An expert or specialist in; for example, **historian, mathematician. 3.** *Chemistry.* **a.** A heterocyclic compound; for example, **furan. b.** An anhydride of a carbohydrate; for example, **dextran.** [Latin *-ānus,* adjectival suffix.]

an. 1. before [Latin *ante*]. **2.** in the year [Latin *annō*].

an·a¹ (a'anə ‖ *U.S. also* ánnə) *n., pl.* **ana** or **anas. 1.** A collection of a person's memorable sayings. **2.** A collection of anecdotes and other information relating to or illustrating the character of a person or place. [Independent use of -ANA.]

an·a² (áynə, áanə, ánnə) *adv. Abbr.* **aa** *Pharmacology.* Both in the same quantity; of each. Used to refer to ingredients in prescriptions. [Middle English, from Medieval Latin, from Greek, to the amount of, literally "up".]

ana- *prefix.* Indicates: **1.** Upward progression; for example, **anabolism, anaphase. 2.** Reversion; for example, **anaplasia. 3.** Renewal or intensification; for example, **anaphylaxis.** [In borrowed Greek compounds, *ana-* indicates: 1. Upwards, as in **anaba-**

sis. 2. According to, as in **analogy. 3.** Back, as in **anabiosis. 4.** Backwards, reversed, as in **anachronism. 5.** Again, anew, as in **anaphora.** Greek, from *ana,* up, throughout, according to.]

-ana, -iana *pl.n. suffix.* Indicates a collection of assorted material, such as, facts, anecdotes, objects, and pictures, relating to or illustrating the character of a specified place, person, topic, or period; for example, **Victoriana** [New Latin, from Latin *-āna,* "the things pertaining to", neuter plural of *-ānus,* -AN.]

an·a·bae·na (ánnə-béenə) *n.* Any of various freshwater algae of the genus *Anabaena,* sometimes occurring in drinking water and causing a bad taste and odour. [New Latin *Anabaena,* from Greek *anabainein,* to go up (from their periodic rise to the surface) : *ana-,* up + *bainein,* to go.]

an·a·ban·tid (ánnə-bántid) *n.* Any of various tropical freshwater fishes of the family Anabantidae, which includes the **Siamese fighting fish** and the **climbing perch** (*both of which see*). [New Latin *Anabantidae* : *Anabas* (stem *Anabant-*), type genus, from Greek *anabas,* aorist participle of *anabainein,* to go up + -IDAE.]

An·a·bap·tist (ánnə-báptist) *n.* A member of one of the radical movements of the Reformation, which insisted that only adult baptism was valid and held that true Christians should not bear arms, use force, or hold government office. [New Latin *anabaptista,* "one who is rebaptised", from Late Greek *anabaptizein,* to baptise again: Greek *ana-,* again + *baptizein,* to baptise, from *baptein,* to dip.] —**An·a·bap·tism** *n.* —**An·a·bap·tist** *adj.*

an·a·bas (ánnə-bass) *n.* Any member of the genus *Anabas,* which includes freshwater fishes of Africa and Asia resembling perch. [New Latin *Anabas.* See **anabantid.**]

a·nab·a·sis (ə-nábbə-siss) *n., pl.* **-ses** (-seez). A large-scale military advance; specifically, the expedition across Asia Minor (401 B.C.) made by Greek mercenaries led by Cyrus the Younger of Persia, as described by Xenophon. [Greek, a going up or forward, from *anabainein,* to go up. See **anabaena.**]

an·a·bat·ic (ánnə-báttik) *adj.* Of, pertaining to, or designating rising wind currents. Compare **katabatic.** [Late Greek *anabatikos,* from Greek, rising, from *anabainein,* to go up. See **anabaena.**]

an·a·bi·o·sis (ánnə-bī-ō-siss) *n.* A restoring to life from a deathlike condition; resuscitation. [New Latin, from Greek *anabiōsis,* from *anabioun,* to come back to life : *ana-,* back + *bioun,* to live, from *bios,* life.]

an·a·bi·ot·ic (ánnə-bī-óttik) *adj.* In a state resembling death, but capable of resuscitation.

an·a·bol·ic steroid (ánnə-bóllik) *n.* Any of a group of synthetic male sex hormones used to increase muscle and bone growth in debilitated underweight patients and in athletes.

a·nab·o·lism (ə-nábbəliz'm) *n.* The metabolic process by which simple substances are synthesised into the complex materials of living tissue; constructive metabolism. Compare **catabolism.** [ANA- + (META)BOLISM.] —**an·a·bol·ic** (ánnə-bóllik) *adj.*

a·nab·o·lite (ə-nábbə-līt) *n.* A product of anabolism. —**a·nab·o·lit·ic** (-líttik) *adj.*

a·nach·ro·nism (ə-náckrə-niz'm) *n.* **1.** The representation of something as existing or happening at other than its proper or historical time. **2. a.** Anything out of its proper time. **b.** Someone or something no longer appropriate to or in harmony with the time. [French *anachronisme,* from Greek *anakhronismos,* from *anakhronizein,* to be an anachronism : *ana-,* backwards, reversed + *khronizein,* to belong to a particular time, from *khronos,* time (see **chronic**).] —**a·nach·ro·nis·tic** (-nístik), **a·nach·ro·nous** (-nəss) *adj.* —**a·nach·ro·nis·ti·cal·ly, a·nach·ro·nous·ly** *adv.*

an·a·cli·nal (ánnə-klīn'l) *adj.* Designating valleys and similar formations that progress in an opposite direction to the dip of surrounding rock strata. [ANA- + -CLINAL.]

an·a·cli·sis (ánnə-klī-siss) *n.* Psychological dependence on others. [New Latin, from Greek *anaklisis,* a leaning back, from *anaklinein,* to lean on.] —**an·a·clit·ic** (-klíttik) *adj.*

an·a·co·lu·thon (ánnəkə-lóo-thon, -léw-, -thən) *n., pl.* **-thons** or **-tha** (-thə). A statement characterised by an abrupt change to a second grammatical construction inconsistent with the first, sometimes used for rhetorical effect; for example, *I warned him that if he continues to drink, what will become of him?* [Late Latin, from Greek *anakolouthon,* inconsistent, from *anakolouthos,* inconsistent : *an-,* not + *akolouthos,* following : *a-,* together + *keleuthos†,* path.] —**an·a·co·lu·thic** *adj.*

an·a·con·da (ánnə-kóndə) *n.* **1.** A large, nonvenomous, arboreal snake, *Eunectes murinus,* of South America, that constricts its prey. **2.** Any of several similar or related snakes. [Unexplained alteration of Sinhalese *henakandayā,* whip snake (originally applied to a snake of Sri Lanka) : *hena,* lightning + *kanda,* stem.]

an·a·cous·tic (ánnə-kōostik) *adj.* Designating a medium or structure that is unable to support the propagation of sound. [AN- + ACOUSTIC]

A·nac·re·on (ə-náckri-ən, -on) (c.572-c.488 B.C.). Greek poet, noted for his songs praising love and wine.

A·nac·re·on·tic (ə-náckri-óntik) *adj.* Characteristic of or in the style of the poems of Anacreon; specifically, convivial or amatory.

an·a·cru·sis (ánnə-krōo-siss) *n.* One or more unstressed syllables at the beginning of a line of verse, before the reckoning of the normal metre begins. [New Latin, from Greek *anakrousis,* the beginning of a tune, from *anakrouein,* to strike up: ANA- + *krouein,* to strike.]

an·a·dem (ánnədem) *n. Poetic.* A wreath or garland for the head. Compare **diadem.** [Latin *anadēma,* from Greek, from *anadein,* to bind up : ANA- + *dein,* to bind.]

an·a·di·plo·sis (ánnədi-plṓ-siss) n. Rhetorical repetition at the beginning of a phrase of the word or words with which the previous phrase ended; for example, *ruined his reputation—his reputation that had taken so long to establish.* [Latin *anadiplōsis*, from Greek, from *anadiploun,* to reduplicate.]

a·nad·ro·mous (ə-nádrəməss) adj. Migrating up rivers from the sea to breed in fresh water, as salmon do. Compare catadromous. [Greek *anadromos,* a running up : ANA- + *dromos,* a running.]

a·nae·mi·a, U.S. a·ne·mi·a (ə-néemi-ə, ə-néem-yə) n. A pathological deficiency in the oxygen-carrying pigment haemoglobin in the blood or in the number of red blood cells. Symptoms include pallor, tiredness and lack of energy, and breathlessness. [New Latin, from Greek *anaimia,* deficiency of blood. See an-, -aemia.]

a·nae·mic (ə-néemik) adj. 1. Of, relating to, or suffering from anaemia. 2. Listless and weak; pallid. 3. Lacking in vigour: *an anaemic performance.*

an·aer·obe (ánnə-rōb, an-áïr-ōb) n. A microorganism, such as a bacterium, able to live in the absence of free oxygen.

an·aer·o·bic (án-ə-rṓbik, -aïr-) adj. 1. Of or designating a process, such as respiration, that does not require free oxygen. 2. Of or pertaining to anaerobes. —an·aer·o·bi·cal·ly adv.

an·es·the·si·a, U.S. an·es·the·si·a (ánnəss-theézi-ə, ánniss-, -theézhə, -theézh-yə) n. 1. Total or partial loss of sensation, especially tactile sensibility, induced by disease of or injury to a nerve. 2. Loss of sensation induced by anaesthetics to enable painless surgery to be performed. It may be total unconsciousness (*general anaesthesia*) or loss of sensation in a particular part of the body (*local anaesthesia*). [New Latin, from Greek *anaisthēsia,* lack of sensation : AN- + *aisthēsis,* feeling.]

an·aes·the·si·ol·ogy (ánnəss-theézi-óllə̵ji, ánniss-) n. The medical study and application of anaesthetics. —an·aes·the·si·olo·gist n.

an·aes·thet·ic (ánnəss-théttik, ánniss-) adj. 1. Relating to or resembling anaesthesia. 2. Causing anaesthesia. 3. Insensitive.
~ n. Any agent that causes unconsciousness or insensitivity to pain. See general anaesthetic, local anaesthetic.

an·aes·the·tise, an·aes·the·tize (ə-néess-thə-tīz || U.S. -néss-) tr.v. -tised, -tising, -tises. To induce anaesthesia in, especially by means of drugs. —an·aes·the·ti·sa·tion (-tī-záysh'n || U.S. -ti-) n.

an·aes·the·tist (ə-néess-thət-ist || U.S. -néss-). 1. British. A qualified medical practitioner who specialises in administering anaesthetics. Also *Chiefly U.S.* anaesthesiologist. 2. U.S. A doctor or nurse trained to administer anaesthetics.

an·a·glyph (ánnə-glif) n. 1. An ornament carved in low relief. 2. A photographic process whereby two superimposed images of an object, usually in red and green, produce a three-dimensional effect when viewed through red and green lenses. [Greek *anagluphos,* wrought in low relief, from *anagluphein,* to carve in relief : ana-, up + *gluphein,* to carve.] —an·a·glyph·ic (-gliffik)

an·a·glyp·ta (ánnə-gliptə) n. A thick embossed wallpaper, used especially to cover uneven walls. [Formerly a trademark.]

an·a·go·ge, an·a·go·gy (ánnə-goji, -gōji, -goggi) n. A mystical interpretation of a word, passage, or text; specifically, scriptural exegesis that detects hidden spiritual allusions or meanings. [Late Latin *anagōgē,* from Late Greek, spiritual uplift, from *anagein,* to uplift, lead up : ANA-, + *agein,* to lead.] —an·a·gog·ic (-gójik), an·a·gog·i·cal adj. —an·a·gog·i·cal·ly adv.

an·a·gram (ánnə-gram) n. A word or phrase formed by reordering the letters of another word or phrase: *"pear" is an anagram of "reap".* [French *anagramme,* from New Latin *anagramma* : ANA- + -GRAM.] —an·a·gram·mat·ic (-grə-máttik) adj. —an·a·gram·mat·i·cal·ly adv. —an·a·gram·ma·tise (-grámmətīz) tr.v.

a·nal (áyn'l) adj. 1. Of, pertaining to, or near the anus. 2. In psychoanalysis, of, pertaining to, or designating: a. The stage of psychosexual development of the infant in which gratification is derived from anal sensations. b. Personality traits originating during toilet training; especially, anal-retentive *(see)* ones. Compare genital, oral. [New Latin *analis,* from Latin *ānus,* ANUS.]

anal. 1. analogous; analogy. 2. analysis; analytic.

a·nal·cime (ə-nál-sim, a-, -seem, -sīm) n. Also a·nal·cite (-sīt, -sit). *Mineralogy.* A white or colourless zeolite, found in some dolerites and basalts. [French, from Greek *analkimos,* weak (from its weak electric power) : AN- (not) + *alkimos,* strong, from *alkē,* strength.]

an·a·lects (ánnə-lekts) pl.n. Also an·a·lec·ta (-léktə). Selections or parts of a literary work or group of works. [Latin *analecta,* from Greek *analekta,* neuter plural of *analektos,* select, from *analegein,* to gather : ana-, up + *legein,* to gather.] —an·a·lec·tic (-léktik) adj.

an·a·lem·ma (ánnə-lémmə) n. A graduated scale, in the shape of a figure of eight, indicating the sun's declination and the equation of time for every day of the year, usually found on sundials and globes. [Latin, a sundial, from Greek *analēmma,* a support, from *analambanein,* to take up, restore. See analeptic.]

an·a·lep·tic (ánnə-léptik) adj. Restorative or stimulating; tonic.
~ n. A restorative, stimulant, or tonic. [Greek *analēptikos,* from *analambanein,* to take up, restore : ana-, up + *lambanein,* to take.]

a·nal-ex·pul·sive (áyn'l-ik-spúl-siv, -ek-) adj. *Psychoanalysis.* Of, designating, or exhibiting personality traits such as conceit, suspicion, ambition, and generosity, originating in habits, attitudes, or values associated with infantile pleasure in the expulsion of faeces.

anal fin n. An unpaired fin in fishes, located on the ventral median line between the tail and the anus.

an·al·ge·si·a (ánn'l-jéez-i-ə, -jéess-, -jéezhə) n. *Medicine.* Insensibility to pain without loss of consciousness. [New Latin, from Greek *analgēsia,* want of feeling : AN- (not) + *algēsia,* sense of pain, from

algein, to feel pain, from *algos,* pain.]

an·al·ge·sic (ánn'l-jée-zik, -sik) n. A drug or other substance that reduces or eliminates pain; a pain-killer.
~ adj. Of or causing analgesia; pain-killing.

an·a·log, an·a·logue (ánnə-log || -lawg) adj. 1. Designating a watch or clock in which the time is indicated by means of hands moving round a dial in the traditional manner. 2. Designating a means of recording sound in which the changes to the recording medium are continuous and analogous to the changes in the wave form of the sound. Compare digital.

analog computer n. A computer in which numerical data are represented by analogous physical magnitudes or electrical signals. Compare digital computer.

an·a·log-dig·i·tal converter (ánnə-log-dijit'l || U.S. also -lawg-) n. A device that converts the output of an analog computer into a form that can be read by a digital computer.

an·a·log·i·cal (ánnə-lójik'l) adj. Of, consisting of, or based upon an analogy. —an·a·log·i·cal·ly adv.

a·nal·o·gise, a·nal·o·gize (ə-nállə̵jīz) v. -gised, -gising, -gises. —tr. To make an analogy to. —intr. To employ analogy.

a·nal·o·gous (ə-nállə̵gəs. *Note: The pronunciation* ə-nállə̵jəs *is also heard. It is modelled on* analogy.*) adj. Abbr.* anal. 1. Similar or alike in a way that permits the drawing of an analogy; comparable in certain respects. 2. *Biology.* Similar in function but not in evolutionary origin, like the gills of a fish and the lungs of a mammal. Compare homologous. [Latin *analogus,* from Greek *analogos,* proportionate, resembling : ana-, according to + *logos,* proportion, word, from *legein,* to speak.] —a·nal·o·gous·ly adv. —a·nal·o·gous·ness n.

an·a·logue (ánnə-log || U.S. also -lawg) n. Also *Chiefly U.S.* a·na·log 1. Something that bears an analogy to something else. 2. *Biology.* An organ or structure that is similar in function to one in another kind of organism, but is of dissimilar evolutionary origin. 3. *Chemistry.* A structural derivative of a parent compound. [French, from Greek *analogos,* ANALOGOUS.]

a·nal·o·gy (ə-nál-ə̵ji) n., pl. -gies. *Abbr.* anal. 1. a. Correspondence in some respects between things otherwise dissimilar. b. A statement illustrating such correspondence: *to draw an analogy.* 2. A form of logical inference, or an instance of it, based on the assumption that if two things are known to be alike in some respects, then they will be alike in other respects. 3. *Biology.* Correspondence in function or position but not in evolutionary origin. 4. *Linguistics.* The creation of new forms on the model of known ones: *A child might say "teached" instead of "taught" by analogy with "reached".* —See Synonyms at likeness. [Latin *analogia,* from Greek, from *analogos,* ANALOGOUS.]

a·nal-re·ten·tive (áyn'l-ri-téntiv) adj. *Psychoanalysis.* Of, designating, or exhibiting personality traits such as meticulousness, avarice, and obstinacy, originating in habits, attitudes, or values associated with infantile pleasure in the retention of faeces.

a·nal·y·sand (ə-nálə̵-sand) n. A person who is being psychoanalysed. [From ANALYSE (by analogy with MULTIPLICAND).]

an·a·lyse, U.S. an·a·lyze (ánnə-līz) tr.v. -lysed, -lysing, -lyses. 1. To separate into constituent elements or basic principles so as to elucidate the interrelation of the parts and the nature or significance of the whole; examine methodically. 2. To make a chemical or mathematical analysis of. 3. To psychoanalyse. [French *analyser,* from *analyse,* ANALYSIS.] —an·a·lys·a·ble adj. —an·a·lys·er n.

a·nal·y·sis (ə-nál-ə̵-siss) n., pl. -ses (seez). *Abbr.* anal. 1. The breaking down of a complex intellectual or substantial whole, for example, an argument or a set of statistics, into its constituent elements in order to examine their nature, significance, and interrelationships. Compare synthesis. 2. A statement of the results of such a study. 3. *Chemistry.* a. Separation of a substance into constituents or the determination of its composition. b. The stated findings of such separation or determination. 4. *Mathematics.* a. Methodology principally involving algebra and calculus as opposed to synthetic geometry, group theory, and number theory. b. The method of proof in which a known truth is sought as a consequence of reasoning from the thing to be proved. 5. *Psychoanalysis.* —in the last or final analysis. When everything has been taken into account; in the end. [Medieval Latin, from Greek *analusis,* a loosening, from *analuein,* to undo : ana-, back + *luein,* to loosen, free.]

analysis si·tus (sī-tewss, -təss) n. Formerly, topology *(see).* [New Latin, "analysis of region".]

an·a·lyst (ánnəlist) n. 1. One who analyses. 2. A psychoanalyst. 3. A systems analyst.

an·a·lyt·ic (ánnə-líttik) adj. Also an·a·lyt·i·cal (-líttik'l). *Abbr.* anal. 1. Of, pertaining to, or based on analysis: *adopted an analytic approach to the problem.* 2. Showing an ability to analyse and reason from a perception of the parts and interrelations of a subject; skilled in analysis: *an analytic mind.* 3. *Linguistics.* Characteristically expressing grammatical distinctions by using two or more words instead of an inflected form: *English is analytic in its use of the comparative "more beautiful" instead of "beautifuler".* 4. *Philosophy.* Designating a statement or proposition whose truth depends entirely on the meaning of the words from which it is composed, rather than any fact about the world. In this sense, compare synthetic. —an·a·lyt·i·cal·ly adv.

analytical geometry n. The analysis of geometrical structures and properties principally by algebraic operations on variables defined in terms of position coordinates. Also called "coordinate geometry".

analytical reagent *n.* A chemical of high purity containing known amounts of contaminants and therefore suitable for use in a quantitative analysis.

an·a·lyt·ics (ánnə-líttiks) *n. Used with a singular verb.* The branch of logic dealing with analysis.

an·am·ne·sis (ánnam-née-siss) *n., pl.* **-ses** (-seez). **1.** *Psychology.* Recalling to memory; recollection. **2.** *Medicine.* The complete case history of a patient. **3.** That part of the Eucharist which recalls Christ's passion. [New Latin, from Greek *anamnēsis*, from *anamimnēskein*, to recall to memory : *ana-*, back + *mimnēskein*, to call to mind.] **—an·am·nes·tic** (-néstik) *adj.* **—an·am·nes·ti·cal·ly** *adv.*

an·a·mor·phic (ánnə-mórfik) *adj.* Having, producing, or designating different optical magnification along mutually perpendicular radii: *an anamorphic lens.* [ANA- + -MORPHIC.]

an·a·mor·pho·sis (ánnə-mawr-fṓ-siss, -mórfə-) *n., pl.* **-ses** (-seez). *Optics.* An image distorted so that it can be viewed without distortion only from a special angle or with a special instrument. [Medieval Greek *anamorphōsis*, "a forming anew", from Late Greek *anamorphoun*, to transform : *ana-*, again + *morphoun*, to form, from *morphē*, form.]

Anancy (ə-nán-si, a-, -naán-) *n. West Indian.* **1.** A spider. **2.** A spider who is the hero of West Indian folk tales, renowned for his cunning. [Twi *anànse*, spider, from *Anànse* the spider god.]

A·nan·da (ə-nándə, aánəndə). The Buddha's cousin, personal attendant, and official reciter of his sutras. Noted for great compassion.

an·an·drous (an-ándrəss) *adj. Botany.* Having no stamens. [Greek *anandros*, "without a man" : AN- + *anēr* (stem *andr-*), man.]

an·an·thous (an-ánthəss) *adj. Botany.* Lacking flowers. Said of some angiosperms. [AN- + -ANTHOUS.]

an·a·paest, an·a·pest (ánnə-peest ‖ *U.S.* -pest) *n.* **1.** A metrical foot composed of two short syllables followed by one long one, written (ˇˇ¯). **2.** A line of verse in this metre: *" 'Twas the night before Christmas and all through the house"* (Clement Moore). [Latin *anapaestus*, from Greek *anapaistos*, "struck back" (an anapaest being a dactyl reversed) : *ana-*, back + *paiein*, to strike.] **—an·a·paest·ic** (-péestik, -péstik) *adj.*

an·a·phase (ánnə-fayz) *n. Biology.* The stage of mitosis in which the chromatids move towards the poles of the nuclear spindle. [ANA- + PHASE.]

a·naph·o·ra (ə-náffərə) *n.* **1.** The deliberate repetition in rhetoric of a word or phrase at the beginning of several successive verses, clauses, or paragraphs. **2.** *Linguistics.* Reference to something previously mentioned, as by the use of a pronoun. [Late Latin, from Greek *anaphora*, repetition, from *anapherein*, to repeat : *ana-*, again + *pherein*, to carry] **—an·a·phor·ic** (-fórrik) *adj.*

an·aph·ro·dis·i·a (án-afrə-dízzi-ə ‖ *U.S.* an-áffrə-) *n.* Absence or decline of sexual desire. [AN- + Greek *aphrodisia*, sexual desire (see **aphrodisiac**).] **—an·aph·ro·dis·i·ac** (-dízzi-ak) *adj. & n.*

an·a·phy·lac·toid (ánnə-fi-láktoyd) *adj. Pathology.* **1.** Of or pertaining to an anaphylactic reaction that occurs without causing antibodies. **2.** Of or pertaining to a toxic reaction caused in an unsensitised person by an excessive dose of a substance that causes anaphylaxis in a sensitised person.

an·a·phy·lax·is (ánnə-fi-láksiss) *n.* Hypersensitivity to a foreign substance, induced by a small preliminary or sensitising injection of the substance. [New Latin : ANA- + (PRO)PHYLAXIS.] **—an·a·phy·lac·tic** (-láktik) *adj.* **—an·a·phy·lac·ti·cal·ly** *adv.*

an·a·pla·si·a (ánnə-pláyzi-ə ‖ *U.S.* -pláyzhə) *n. Biology.* Reversion of cells to a more primitive or less differentiated form. [ANA- + -PLASIA.]

an·a·plas·tic (ánnə-plástik, -plaástik) *adj.* **1.** Pertaining to or involving the restoration of a lost or absent part, as by plastic surgery. **2.** Of or pertaining to anaplasia of cells.

an·a·plas·ty (ánnə-plasti, -plaásti) *n.* Plastic surgery. [French *anaplastie*, from Greek *anaplasis*, remodelling, from *anaplassein*, to form anew : ANA- + *plassein*, to mould.]

an·arch (ánnark) *n. Literary.* A leader or advocate of anarchy.

an·ar·chic (an-ár-kik, ən-) *adj.* Also **an·ar·chi·cal** (-kik'l). **1.** Of, like, or promoting anarchy. **2.** Lacking order or control; chaotic. **—an·ar·chi·cal·ly** *adv.*

an·ar·chism (ánnər-kiz'm, *rarely* ánnaar-) *n.* **1.** The theory that all forms of government are oppressive and undesirable, and should be abolished and replaced by voluntary cooperation. **2.** Rejection of all forms of coercive control and authority. **—an·ar·chis·tic** (-kístik) *adj.*

an·ar·chist (ánnər-kist, ánnaar-) *n.* **1.** An advocate of anarchism. **2.** One who actively promotes anarchism or anarchy, as by the use of terrorism to destabilise the existing order.

anarcho- *comb. form.* Indicates anarchistic tendencies or anarchism; for example, *anarcho-syndicalism.* [Medieval Latin, from Greek *anarkhos*, without a ruler. See **anarchy.**]

an·ar·chy (ánnər-ki, ánnaar-) *n., pl.* **-chies.** **1.** Absence of any form of political authority. **2.** Political disorder and confusion. **3.** Any state of disorder or confusion, especially when caused by absence of a recognised authority or cohesive principle: *classroom anarchy.* [Greek *anarkhia*, from *anarkhos*, without a ruler : AN- + *arkhos*, ruler, -ARCH.]

an·ar·thri·a (an-ár-thri-ə) *n.* Loss of the ability to speak. Compare **aphasia, dysphasia.** [New Latin, from Greek *anarthros*, not articulated. See **anarthrous.**] **—an·arth·ric** (-thrik) *adj.*

an·ar·throus (an-árthrəss) *adj. Zoology.* Lacking joints; unjointed.

[Greek *anarthros*, not articulated : AN- (without) + *arthron*, joint, article.]

an·a·sar·ca (ánnə-sárkə) *n.* A general accumulation of serum in the subcutaneous connective tissue, resulting in swelling of the trunk and legs. [New Latin, from Greek *ana sarka*, "throughout the body" : *ana*, throughout + *sarka*, accusative of *sarx*, flesh.] **—an·a·sar·cous** (-sárkəss) *adj.*

An·a·sta·si·a (ánnə-staáz-i-ə, -stáyz-, -stáyzhə), **Grand Duchess** (1901–19?). Youngest daughter of the last Tsar of Russia, Nicholas II. She is thought to have been killed with the rest of her family after the Russian Revolution, but several women have since claimed to be her without conclusive proof, most notably (from 1920) a woman known as Anna Anderson.

an·as·tig·mat (an-ástigmat, ən-, ánnə-stígmat) *n.* A compound lens corrected for astigmatism and for at least one off-axis zone in the image plane. [AN- (not) + ASTIGMAT(IC).]

an·as·tig·mat·ic (ánnə-stig-máttik) *adj.* **1.** Not astigmatic. Said of a lens that forms an accurate point image of a point object. **2.** Of or designating a compound lens in which the separate components compensate for the astigmatism of each. [AN- + ASTIGMATIC.]

a·nas·to·mose (ə-nástə-mōz, -mōss) *v.* **-mosed, -mosing, -moses.** *—tr.* To join by anastomosis. *—intr.* To become connected by anastomosis. [Back-formation from ANASTOMOSIS.]

a·nas·to·mo·sis (ánnástə-mṓ-siss, ə-nástə-) *n., pl.* **-ses** (-seez). **1.** The union or connection of branches, as of rivers, veins of leaves, or blood vessels. **2.** A surgical connection of separate or severed hollow organs to form a continuous channel. [New Latin, from Greek *anastomōsis*, an outlet, opening, from *anastomoun*, to furnish with a mouth : *ana-*, up + *stoma*, a mouth, opening.] **—a·nas·to·mot·ic** (-móttik) *adj.*

a·nas·tro·phe (ə-nástrəfi) *n.* Inversion, as for rhetorical effect, of the normal syntactic order of words; for example, *to market went she.* [Greek *anastrophē*, a turning upside down, from *anastrephein*, to turn upside down : *ana-*, back + *strephein*, to turn.]

anat. anatomical; anatomy.

an·a·tase (ánnə-tayz, -tayss) *n.* A rare blue or light yellow to black mineral consisting of titanium dioxide in tetragonal form. Formerly called "octahedrite". [French, from Greek *anatasis*, extension (from its long crystals), from *anateinein*, to extend, stretch up : *ana-*, up + *teinein*, to stretch.]

a·nath·e·ma (ə-náthəmə) *n., pl.* **-mas. 1.** Someone or something cursed, reviled, or detested: *Fascism was anathema to her.* **2.** A formal ecclesiastical pronouncement of damnation; a denunciation or excommunication. **3.** Any vehement denunciation; an imprecation; a curse. [Late Latin, a curse, a person cursed, an offering, from Greek *anathēma*, votive offering, from *anatithenai*, to dedicate : *ana-*, up + *tithenai*, to put.]

a·nath·e·ma·tise, a·nath·e·ma·tize (ə-náthəmə-tīz) *tr.v.* **-tised, -tising, -tises.** To proclaim an anathema on; denounce or curse. **—a·nath·e·ma·ti·sa·tion** (-tī-záysh'n ‖ *U.S.* -ti-) *n.*

An·a·to·li·a (ánnə-tṓl-i-ə, -yə). Also **Asia Minor.** The Asian part of Turkey. In ancient times it was the great meeting-place of Oriental and Occidental commerce. The region was slowly conquered by the Ottoman Turks in the 14th and 15th centuries and remained part of the Ottoman Empire until the republic of Turkey was established.

An·a·to·li·an (ánnə-tṓl-i-ən, -yən) *n.* **1.** A native or inhabitant of Anatolia. **2.** Any of a family of extinct Indo-European languages of ancient Anatolia. **—An·a·to·li·an** *adj.*

Anatolian Ka·ra·bash (kárrə-básh, -bash) *n.* A dog of an ancient, powerfully built breed, having a short, dense coat and labrador-like head.

a·nat·o·mise, a·nat·o·mize (ə-náttə-mīz) *tr.v.* **-mised, -mising, -mises. 1.** To dissect. **2.** To analyse in minute detail. **—a·nat·o·mi·sa·tion** (-mī-záysh'n ‖ *U.S.* -mi-) *n.*

a·nat·o·mist (ə-náttəmist) *n.* An expert in or student of anatomy.

a·nat·o·my (ə-náttəmi) *n., pl.* **-mies.** *Abbr.* **anat. 1.** The structure of a plant or animal, or of any of its parts. **2.** The science of the shape and structure of organisms and their parts. **3.** A treatise on this science. **4.** The dissection of a plant or animal to disclose its various parts and their positions, structure, and interrelation. **5.** Any detailed examination or analysis. **6.** The human body. Used humorously. [Middle English *anatomie*, from Old French, from Late Latin *anatomia*, from Greek *anatomē*, dissection, from *anatemnein*, to dissect : *ana-* + *temnein*, to cut.] **—an·a·tom·i·cal** (ánnə-tómmik'l) *adj.* **—an·a·tom·i·cal·ly** *adv.*

a·nat·ro·pous (ə-náttrəpəss) *adj. Botany.* Inverted so that the micropyle is next to the hilum, and the embryonic root is at the other end. Said of an ovule. [ANA- + -TROPOUS.]

anatto. Variant of **annatto.**

An·ax·ag·o·ras (ánnak-sággər-ass, -əss) (*c.*500–*c.*428 B.C.). Greek philosopher. Born in Clazomenae, Asia Minor (now in Turkey), he moved to Athens where he gained the friendship of Pericles. He taught that the universe was composed of an infinite number of elements and gave the true explanation of solar eclipses.

A·nax·i·man·der (ə-náksi-mándər, a-) (*c.*611–*c.*547 B.C.). Greek philosopher and astronomer from Miletus, Asia Minor (now in Turkey). One of the earliest thinkers to speculate on the origin of the universe, he held that it arose out of the separation of opposite qualities from one primordial substance, and that animal life had evolved from the sea.

An·ax·im·e·nes (ánnak-símmɔneez) (*c.*570–*c.*500 B.C.). Greek philosopher from Miletus, Asia Minor (now in Turkey). He held that the fundamental matter of the universe was air or vapour, and that all other substances were derived from it by condensation, compression, or rarefaction.

an·bur·y (án-bəri ‖ *U.S.* -berri) *n.* **1.** A soft tumour afflicting horses and oxen. **2.** A disease of root crops, such as turnips and swedes, in which the roots are clubbed. [16th century : perhaps from *ang-,* "painful" (as in Old English *angnægl,* AGNAIL), + *-bury,* BERRY (referring to the reddish tumour).]

anc. ancient.

A.N.C. African National Congress.

–ance, –ancy *n. suffix.* Indicates an action, quality, or condition; for example, **riddance, compliancy.** [Middle English *-ance, -aunce,* from Old French *-ance,* from Latin *-antia,* abstract noun suffix of *-ant-,* stem of *-āns,* present participle ending, -ANT.]

an·ces·tor (ánsestər) *n.* **1.** Any person from whom one is descended, especially if more remote than a grandparent; a forebear. **2.** An early or original type of a later person or thing; a precursor. **3.** *Biology.* The actual or hypothetical organism or stock from which later kinds have evolved. [Middle English *ancestre, ancessour,* from Old French *ancestre, ancessor,* from Latin *antecessor,* "one that goes before", from *antecessus,* part participle of *antecēdere,* to go before : ANTE + *cēdere,* to go.]

an·ces·tral (an-séstrəl) *adj.* Pertaining to, evolved from, or inherited from an ancestor or ancestors. **—an·ces·tral·ly** *adv.*

an·ces·try (ánsestri) *n., pl.* **-tries. 1.** Ancestral descent or lineage. **2.** Ancestors collectively. [Middle English *ancestrie,* from Old French *ancesserie,* from *ancessour,* ANCESTOR.]

An·chi·e·ta (ánchi-áytə), **José de** (1534–97). Portuguese scholar, author, and Jesuit missionary, who spent most of his life in Brazil. He arrived in Brazil in 1558 and played a leading part in converting the native Indians to Christianity. His best-known work is *De beata virgine dei matre Maria* ("The Blessed Virgin Mary"). He also wrote the first grammar of the Tupi language.

An·chi·ses (ang-kī-seez, an-). In Greek and Roman legend, the father of Aeneas, rescued by his son from the ruins of Troy.

an·chor (áng-kər) *n.* **1.** A heavy, usually metal, object attached to a vessel by a cable and cast overboard to keep the vessel in place, usually by flukes which grip the seabed. **2.** Anything used to keep an object firmly in position. **3.** Someone or something providing psychological stability. **4.** *Radio & Television. Chiefly U.S.* An anchorman or anchorwoman. **—at anchor.** Anchored. **~v. anchored, -choring, -chors.** *—tr.* **1.** To hold fast by or as if by an anchor. **2.** *U.S.* To act as the anchor of (a news broadcast, for example). *—intr.* To drop anchor or lie at anchor. Used of a ship. [Middle English *anker,* Old English *ancer, ancor,* from Latin *anc(h)ora,* from Greek *ankura.*]

an·chor·age (áng-kərij) *n.* **1.** A place for anchoring. **2.** A fee charged for the privilege of anchoring. **3. a.** The act of anchoring. **b.** The condition of being at anchor. **4.** Something that provides stability or support.

Anchorage. Chief port and largest city of Alaska. It is situated on Cook Inlet in the southern part of the state, and was founded in 1915 as the headquarters for the building of the Alaska railway.

an·cho·ress (áng-kə-riss, -ress) *n.* A female anchorite.

an·cho·rite (áng-kə-rīt) *n.* Also **an·cho·ret** (-ret). A person who has retired into seclusion, usually for religious reasons; a hermit; a recluse. [Middle English, from Medieval Latin *anchorīta,* variant of Late Latin *anchorēta,* from Late Greek *anakhōrētēs,* "one who withdraws (from the world)", from *anakhōrein,* to withdraw : Greek *ana-,* back + *khōrein,* to make room.] **—an·cho·rit·ic** (-ríttik) *adj.*

an·chor·man (áng-kər-man) *n., pl.* **-men** (-men). One who plays a crucial part in providing strength, stability, or cohesion, especially: **1.** The runner, usually the strongest in a team, who performs in the last stage of a relay race. **2.** In cricket, a batsman who plays a long, defensive innings. **3.** The presenter or coordinator of a broadcast involving several different contributors or correspondents.

anchor ring *n. Mathematics.* A torus *(see).*

an·chor·wom·an (áng-kər-wŏomən) *n., pl.* **-women** (-wimmin). *Radio & Television.* A female anchorman.

an·cho·vy (án-chəvi ‖ -chŏvi, -chŏvi) *n., pl.* **-vies** or collectively **anchovy.** Any of various small, herring-like marine fishes of the family Engraulidae. Several species, especially *Engraulis encrasicholus,* are widely used as food fish. [Spanish *anchova, anchoa,* perhaps from Basque *anchu.*]

anchovy pear *n.* A West Indian tree, *Grias cauliflora,* that bears edible fruit similar in taste to the mango. [The fruit is so called after its use, like anchovies, as a first course or hors d'oeuvre.]

an·chu·sa (ang-kéwssə) *n.* Any plant of the genus *Anchusa.* See **bugloss.** [New Latin *Anchusa,* from Latin *anchūsa,* a plant used as a cosmetic, from Greek *ankhousa†,* alkanet.]

anchylose. Variant of **ankylose.**

anchylosis. Variant of **ankylosis** *n.*

anchylostomiasis. Variant of **ancylostomiasis.**

an·cien ré·gime (ON-si-áN re-zhéem, ray-) *n.* **1.** The political and social system existing in France before the Revolution of 1789. **2.** Any system or regime that has been superseded. [French, "old regime".]

an·cient[1] (áynsh'nt) *adj. Abbr.* **anc. 1.** Having lived or existed for a long time; very old. **2.** Of, existing in, or occurring in times long past; especially, belonging to the historical period prior to the fall of the Western Roman Empire (A.D. 476). **—See Synonyms at old.** **~n. 1.** A person who lived in ancient times, especially one belonging to any of the classical civilisations of antiquity. **2.** *Plural.* The ancient Greek and Roman authors. **3.** *Archaic.* A very old person. [Middle English *ancien,* from Old French, from Vulgar Latin *anteā-*

nus (unattested), "going before", from Latin *ante,* before.] **—an·cient·ness** *n.*

ancient[2] *n. Archaic.* **1.** An ensign; a flag. **2.** A flag-bearer or person holding the rank of ensign. [Variant of ENSIGN.]

Ancient Greek *n.* The Greek language of historical antiquity, from its first documentation in the 14th century B.C. until the time of the late Roman Empire, divided into two principal dialect areas, **East Greek** and **West Greek** *(both of which see).*

ancient lights *n. Used with a singular verb.* In English law, windows whose light has long been enjoyed and may not be obstructed by an adjacent owner.

an·cient·ly (áynsh'ntli) *adv.* In ancient times.

Ancient Mariner *n.* **1.** A person who seems to bring suffering or bad luck. **2.** A person who insists on recounting his adventures, usually at great length; a compulsive and usually boring raconteur. [After the aged storyteller in S.T. Coleridge's poem *The Rime of the Ancient Mariner.* He had killed an albatross and thereby brought down a curse on his ship, his fellow sailors, and himself.]

ancient monument *n.* In Britain, a site or building of archaeological or historical interest, especially one maintained by the Department of the Environment or a local authority.

an·cil·lar·y (an-sílləri ‖ *U.S.* ánsə-lerri. *Note: the pronunciation* ansilli-əri *is not considered correct.*) *adj.* **1.** Subordinate: *"For Degas, sculpture was never more than ancillary to his painting"* (Herbert Read). **2.** Helping; auxiliary: *ancillary staff in a hospital.* **~n., pl. ancillaries.** One who works in a subordinate or auxiliary capacity. [Latin *ancillāris,* servile, from *ancilla,* maidservant, feminine diminutive of *anculus,* servant.]

an·cip·i·tal (an-síppit'l) *adj.* Flattened and two-edged, as certain plant stems are. [From Latin *anceps* (stem *ancipit-*), two-headed : AMBI- + *caput,* head.]

an·con (áng-kon) *n., pl.* **–cones** (ang-kōneez). A projecting bracket used in classical architecture to carry the upper elements of a cornice; a console. [Latin *ancōn,* from Greek *ankōn,* elbow, bend of the arm.] **—an·co·nal** (ang-kōn'l, áng-kən'l) *adj.*

An·co·na (ang-kōnə). Adriatic port and capital of the province of the same name in central Italy.

–ancy. Variant of **-ance.**

an·cy·lo·sto·mi·a·sis, an·ky·lo·sto·mi·a·sis, an·chy·lo·sto·mi·a·sis (ánsi-lóstə-mī-ə-siss, áng-ki-, -lóstə-, -lō-stō-) *n.* A disease caused by hookworm infestation of the human intestine and marked by progressive anaemia. Also called "hookworm disease". [New Latin : *Ancylostoma,* hookworm (genus), "hook-mouth" : Greek *ankulos,* crooked + *stoma,* mouth + -IASIS.]

Ancyra. See **Ankara.**

and (and, *weak forms* ənd, ən) *conj.* **1.** Together with or along with; also; in addition; as well as. Used to connect words, phrases, or clauses, especially those having the same grammatical function: *trials and tribulations; a long and happy life.* **2. a.** Added to; plus: *Two and two makes four.* **b.** Prepared, served, eaten, or drunk with as a unit: *bread and butter; gin and tonic.* **3.** As a result. Used to express an actual or likely consequence: *She felt tired and went to bed. One more remark like that and I'll knock your block off.* **4.** Next in time; then: *paid the bill and left.* **5.** Used instead of *to* after verbs such as *go, come,* or *try: try and find it; come and see.* **6.** Used, especially in news broadcasting, to initiate discussion of an announced topic: *The Middle East—and Egypt has announced . . .* **7.** Used as a connection between identical words to express repetition, continuation, or progression: *rolled over and over; waited and waited; getting hotter and hotter.* **8.** Used to express a contrast in quality between things of the same basic type: *There are cameras and cameras.* **9.** Used, especially after *good* and *nice,* to give adverbial force to the words preceding it: *nice and warm.* **10.** Used to introduce a comment or parenthetic remark: *Here's our meal—and not before time! After that—and this is the funny bit— he fell into the pool.* **11.** *Archaic.* If: *and it please you.* [Middle English *and,* Old English *and, ond.*]

Usage: And is not generally used at the beginning of a sentence in formal writing—except for special literary effect. Where *and* is used within a sentence to connect words or clauses it is not preceded by a comma unless the subject of the clause changes: *John and Anna and I; I went and came back on the same day; I went, and she met me at the station.*

An·da·lu·si·a (ándə-lŏoz-i-ə, -lŏozh-, -lŏoss-). Spanish **An·da·lu·cí·a** (-lŏo-thée-a). The largest region in Spain, covering much of the south of the country. It was the last part of Spain to be reconquered from the Moors, in the 15th century, and contains some magnificent Moorish architecture, including the historic towns of Seville, Granada, and Córdoba. **—An·da·lu·si·an** (-ən) *n. & adj.*

an·da·lu·site (ándə-lŏo-sīt) *n.* A mineral consisting of aluminium silicate, Al_2SiO_5, usually found in prisms of various colours. [French *andalusite,* discovered in ANDALUSIA.]

An·da·man and Nic·o·bar Islands (ándə-mən; ník-ə-baar). Indian possessions in the Bay of Bengal. The Andamans comprise more than 200 small islands, the Nicobars 19. Port Blair on South Andaman Island is the capital.

An·da·man·ese (ándəmən-éez, -éess) *n., pl.* **Andamanese. 1.** A member of a Negrito people native to the Andaman Islands. **2.** The agglutinative language of this people, not known to be connected with any other language family. **—An·da·man·ese** *adj.*

an·dan·te (an-dánti ‖ *U.S. also* aan-dáant-ay, -i) *adv. Music.* In a moderate tempo; faster than adagio, but slower than allegretto. Used as a direction: *performed andante.* **~n. Music.** A movement or passage in a moderate tempo. [Italian, "walking", present participle of *andare,* to walk, from Vulgar Latin *ambitāre* (unattested), from Latin *ambulāre,* to AMBULATE.] —**an·dan·te** *adj.*

an·dan·ti·no (ándan-téenō ‖ *U.S. also* áandaan-) *adv. Music.* In a tempo slightly faster than andante. Used as a direction.
~*n., pl.* **andantinos.** *Music.* A movement or passage in this tempo. [Italian, diminutive of ANDANTE.] —**an·dan·ti·no** *adj.*

An·de·an (an-deé-ən, -ándi-ən) *adj.* Of, pertaining to, or resembling the Andes or their inhabitants. —**An·de·an** *n.*

An·der·sen (ándərss'n), **Hans Christian** (1805–75). Danish writer, famous chiefly for his fairy tales. The son of a poor shoemaker, he made his reputation with the publication in 1835 of his first collection of fairy tales, *Eventyr* ("Tales Told for Children").

An·der·son (ándərss'n), **Carl David** (1905–91). U.S. physicist. In 1936 he was awarded the Nobel prize for his discovery of the positively charged particle, the positron.

Anderson, Elizabeth Garrett (1836–1917). British doctor and campaigner for women's right to enter the medical profession as doctors. Unable to gain admission to a medical school, she studied privately, and in 1865 was licensed to practise by the Society of Apothecaries. In 1866 she was appointed a general medical assistant at St. Mary's Dispensary, London, which was renamed the Elizabeth Garrett Anderson Hospital in 1918. She was the sister of the feminist Millicent **Fawcett.**

Anderson, Marian (1902–93). U.S. contralto. She was most famous for her interpretation of Negro spirituals and was the first black singer to perform at the Metropolitan Opera in New York (1955).

An·des (ándeez). Mountain system running along the Pacific coast of South America for 8 000 kilometres (5,000 miles), loftier than any other mountain range in the world except the Himalayas. Its maximum width is 480 kilometres (300 miles), and its highest peak, Aconcagua on the Chile-Argentina border (6 960 metres; 22,835 feet), is the highest mountain in the Western Hemisphere.

an·de·site (ándizīt) *n.* A fine-grained volcanic rock containing plagioclase feldspar. [German *Andesit,* from the ANDES.]

AND gate *n. Computing.* A logic circuit with two or more input wires that emits a signal only if all input wires receive coincident signals. See **OR gate.** [So called because the emission of the signal is comparable to the use of the conjunction *and* in logic.]

An·dhra Pra·desh (ándrə prə-désh, -dáysh). State in southeastern India, bordering on the Bay of Bengal. It was created in 1956 from the Telegu-speaking regions of Madras and Hyderabad. The capital is Hyderabad.

and·i·ron (ánd-ī-ərn) *n.* Either of a pair of metal supports for holding up logs in a fireplace. Also called "firedog". [Middle English *aundiren,* variant of Old French *andier,* firedog, from Gaulish *andero-* (unattested), young bull (andirons were often decorated with heads of animals at the top).]

and/or *conj.* Used to indicate that either *and* or *or* may be used to connect words, phrases, or clauses, depending upon what meaning is intended.
Usage: And/or is mainly used in legal, commercial, and technical contexts, where it is a succinct way of setting forth three distinct and exclusive possibilities: either of two things considered separately, or the two in combination. Thus, *an offence punishable by a fine and/or imprisonment* means "by a fine, or by imprisonment, or by both".

An·dor·ra (an-dáwrə, -dórrə). Tiny independent state high in the eastern Pyrenees on the Franco-Spanish border. Officially called the Principality of Andorra, it is an ancient coprincipality whose nominal heads of state are the "princes" - the president of France and the Spanish bishop of Urgel. Area, 453 square kilometres (175 square miles). Population, 71,000. Capital, Andorra la Vella. See map at **France. An·dor·ran** *adj. & n.*

an·dra·dite (ándrə-dīt, an-dráa-) *n.* A green to brown or black calcium-iron garnet, Ca$_3$Fe$_2$(SiO$_4$)$_3$ used as a gem. [After José B. de *Andrada* e Silva (1765–1838), Brazilian geologist.]

An·dre·a del Sar·to (an-dráy-ə del sártō), born Andrea d'Agnolo (1486–1531). Florentine painter. He painted chiefly religious subjects in the classical manner of Raphael and is best known for the fresco cycle of the life of John the Baptist, in the Chiostro dello Scalzo, Florence.

An·drew (ándrō). One of the Apostles, the brother of Simon called Peter. [Middle English, from Latin *Andreas,* from Greek, probably from *andreios,* manly, from *anēr* (stem *andr-*), man.]

andro-, andr- *comb. form.* Indicates: 1. The male sex or masculine; for example, **androgen.** 2. *Botany.* Stamen or anther; for example, **androecium.** [Greek, from *anēr* (stem *andr-*), man.]

an·droe·ci·um (an-dréesi-əm ‖ -shi-, -sh-) *n., pl.* **-cia** (-shi-ə, -shə). The stamens of a flower considered collectively. [New Latin : ANDR(O)- + Greek *oikion,* residence, diminutive of *oikos,* house.] —**an·droe·ci·al** (-əl) *adj.*

an·dro·gen (ándrə-jən) *n.* Any of the steroid hormones (like testosterone) that develop and maintain male sex organs and secondary masculine characteristics such as deepening of the voice and growth of facial hair. Compare **oestrogen.** [ANDRO- + -GEN.] —**an·dro·gen·ic** (-jénnik) *adj.*

an·drog·y·nous (an-dróji-nəss) *adj.* 1. Having both female and male characteristics. 2. *Botany.* Composed of staminate and pistillate flowers. Said of the flower spikes of plantain and similar plants. [Latin *androgynus,* from Greek *androgunos* : ANDRO- + -GYNOUS.] —**an·drog·y·ny** (-ni) *n.*

an·droid (ándroyd) *adj.* Possessing human features.
~*n.* In science fiction, a synthetic human created from biological materials, as distinguished from a robot. Also called "humanoid". [Late Greek *androeidēs,* manlike : ANDR(O)- + -OID.]

An·drom·a·che (an-drómməki). In Greek legend, the faithful wife of Hector, captured by the Greeks at the fall of Troy.

An·drom·e·da[1] (an-drómmidə). In Greek legend, the daughter of Cepheus and Cassiopeia, who married Perseus after he had rescued her from a sea monster.

Andromeda[2] *n.* A constellation in the Northern Hemisphere near Lacerta and Perseus.

An·dro·pov (an-drópoff; *Russian* ən-dráwpəff), **Yuri Vladimirovich** (1914–84). General Secretary of the Communist Party of the U.S.S.R (1982), after the death of L.I. Brezhnev; President (1983). Andropov was the Soviet Ambassador to Hungary in 1956 when that country was invaded by the U.S.S.R. From 1967 until May of 1982 he was chairman of the K.G.B., the Soviet security police, leaving that post just six months before achieving the country's most important political appointment.

an·dros·ter·one (an-dróstərōn) *n.* An androgen formed from the metabolism of testosterone, excreted in male urine, and synthetically produced from cholesterol. [ANDRO- + STER(OL) + -ONE.]

-androus *adj. comb. form. Botany.* Indicates a specified number or type of stamens; for example, **monandrous.** [New Latin *-andrus,* from Greek *-andros,* "having men", from *anēr* (stem *andr-*), man.]

-andry *n. comb. form.* Indicates the state or custom of having a specified number of husbands; for example, **monandry.** [Greek *anēr* (stem *andr-*), man.]

-ane *n. suffix. Chemistry.* Indicates a saturated hydrocarbon; for example, **hexane, propane.** [Variant of -ENE, -INE, or -ONE.]

a·near (ə-néer) *adv. Archaic.* 1. Near. 2. Nearly; almost.
~*tr.v.* **aneared, anearing, anears.** *Archaic.* To approach: *"The castle tonight . . . anears its fall."* (Elizabeth Barrett Browning). —**a·near** *prep.*

an·ec·dot·age (ánnik-dōtij, ánnek-) *n.* 1. Anecdotes collectively. 2. Garrulous old age or senility. Used humorously. [Sense 2 is a blend of ANECDOTE and DOTAGE.]

an·ec·do·tal (ánnik-dōt'l, ánnek-) *adj.* Characterised by, containing, or given to telling anecdotes : *only anecdotal evidence.*

an·ec·dote (ánnik-dōt, ánnek-) *n.* 1. A short account of some interesting or humorous incident. 2. *Plural.* Secret or hitherto undivulged particulars of history or biography. [French, from Greek *anekdota,* "things unpublished", from *anekdotos,* unpublished : AN- (not) + *ekdotos,* given out, from *ekdidonai,* to give out : *ek-,* out + *didonai,* to give.] —**an·ec·dot·ic** (ánnik-dóttik) *adj.* —**an·ec·dot·ist** (-dótist), **an·ec·dot·al·ist** (-dōt'list) *n.*

an·e·cho·ic (án-i-kŏ-ik, -e-) *adj.* Neither having nor producing echoes: *an anechoic chamber.* [AN- (not) + ECHOIC.]

A·nei·rin, A·neu·rin (ə-nīr-in, a-). Welsh poet of the late sixth century. He is believed to have written the 13th-century *Book of Aneirin,* with the epic *Gododin.*

anemia *U.S.* Variant of **anaemia.**

anemo- *comb. form.* Indicates wind; for example, **anemology.** [Greek *anemos,* wind.]

a·nem·o·chore (ə-néemō-kawr, -némmə-) *n.* A plant, such as the dandelion, having seeds, spores, or similar reproductive parts that are dispersed by the wind. [ANEMO- + -CHORE.]

a·nem·o·graph (ə-némmə-graf, -graaf) *n.* A recording anemometer. [ANEMO- + -GRAPH.] —**a·nem·o·graph·ic** (-gráffik) *adj.*

an·e·mog·ra·phy (ánni-mógrəfi) *n.* The science of recording wind direction and force. [ANEMO- + -GRAPHY.]

an·e·mol·o·gy (ánni-mólləji) *n.* The scientific study of winds. [ANEMO- + -LOGY.]

an·e·mom·e·ter (ánni-mómmitər) *n.* 1. An instrument for measuring wind force and speed. 2. Any instrument for measuring the rate of flow of a fluid. [ANEMO- + -METER.] —**an·e·mo·met·ric** (-mə-méttrik), **an·e·mo·met·ri·cal** *adj.*

an·e·mom·e·try (ánni-mómmətri) *n.* The determination of the force, speed, and direction of wind. [ANEMO- + -METRY.]

a·nem·o·ne (ə-némmɐni) *n.* 1. Any of various plants of the genus *Anemone,* of the North Temperate Zone, having white, yellow, purple, or red cup-shaped flowers. Some species are also called "windflower". See **pasque flower, wood anemone.** 2. A marine invertebrate, the **sea anemone** *(see).* [Latin *anemōnē,* from Greek, perhaps from Semitic.]

anemone fish *n.* Any of various small, brightly coloured marine damselfishes of the genus *Amphiprion,* found near sea anemones.

an·e·moph·i·lous (ánni-móffi-ləss) *adj.* Pollinated by wind-dispersed pollen. [ANEMO- + -PHILOUS.] —**an·e·moph·i·ly** *n.*

an·en·ceph·al·y (ánnen-séffəli) *n.* Partial or complete congenital absence of the cerebral hemispheres of the brain, which is often associated with spina bifida and similar conditions. [AN- + -*cephaly* : ENCEPHAL(O)- + -Y (state or condition).] —**an·en·ceph·al·ic** (-si-fál-ik) *adj.*

a·nent (ə-nént) *prep. Archaic & Scottish.* Regarding; concerning. [Middle English *anent, onevent,* Old English *onemn, on efen,* alongside, together : ON + *efen,* EVEN.]

an·er·oid (ándəroyd) *adj.* Not using fluid. [French *anéroïde* : A- (not) + Greek *nēron,* water.]

aneroid barometer *n.* A barometer in which variations of atmospheric pressure are measured by the relative bulges of a thin elastic metal disc covering a partially evacuated chamber, the movements being magnified by a train of levers to move a needle over a calibrated scale.

anesthesia. *U.S.* Variant of **anaesthesia.**

an·e·thole (ánni-thōl) *n.* A white, crystalline substance, CH₃CH:CHC₆H₄OCH₃, with the odour of liquorice, used as flavouring and in colour photography as a sensitiser. [Latin *anēthum*, anise, dill, from Greek *anēthon*, variant of *anison*, ANISE + -OLE.]

Aneto, Pico de. See **Pico de Aneto.**

an·eu·ploi·dy (ánnew-ploydi) *n.* A condition in which one or more chromosomes are either added to or missing from the normal chromosome complement. [AN- + EUPLOIDY.] —**an·eu·ploid** *adj.*

an·eu·rysm, an·eu·rism (ánnewr-iz'm, án-yə-rizz'm) *n.* A blood-filled sac caused by pathological dilation of the wall of a weakened blood vessel. [Greek *aneurusma*, from *aneurunein*, to dilate : *ana-*, "throughout" + *eurunein*, to dilate, widen, from *eurus*, wide.] —**an·eu·rys·mal** (-rízm'l) *adj.*

a·new (ə-néw ‖ ə-nóō) *adv.* **1.** Again. **2.** In a new and different way, form, or manner; afresh. [Middle English *anewe, of newe*, Old English *of nīwe* : OF + *nīwe*, NEW.]

an·frac·tu·os·i·ty (ánfrak-tew-óssəti ‖ *U.S.* an-frákchoo-) *n., pl.* **-ties. 1.** The state or quality of being anfractuous. **2.** Something anfractuous, such as a winding passage or a complicated process.

an·frac·tu·ous (an-frák-tew-əss) *adj.* Full of twists and turns; winding; tortuous. [French *anfractueux*, from Late Latin *anfractuōsus*, from Latin *anfractus*, a winding : *an-*, from AMBI- + *fractus*, past participle of *frangere*, to break.]

an·ga·ry (áng-gəri) *n. International Law.* The right of a belligerent state to seize, use, or destroy the property of a neutral, provided that full compensation is made. [Late Latin *angaria*, enforced service to a lord, from Greek *angareia*, impressment for public service, from *angaros*, mounted courier, perhaps of Persian origin.]

an·gel (áynjəl) *n.* **1.** *Theology.* **a.** An immortal spiritual being attendant upon God, conventionally represented as a winged being of human form. **b.** In medieval angelology, one of nine orders of spiritual beings (listed from highest to lowest in rank): seraphim, cherubim, thrones, dominations or dominions, virtues, powers, principalities, archangels, and angels. **2.** A guardian spirit or guiding influence. **3.** A sweet-tempered or kind person, especially a child or a woman. **4.** *Informal.* A financial backer of an enterprise, especially a dramatic production. [Middle English, from Old French *angele*, from Late Latin *angelus*, from Greek *angelos* (translation of Hebrew *mal'ākh*), messenger, perhaps of Persian origin.]

angel cake *n.* A white, almond-flavoured sponge cake made from egg whites, sugar, and flour. Also *U.S.* "angel food cake". [From its pure white colour.]

Angel Fall. *Spanish* **Salto Angel.** The highest waterfall in the world, with a drop of 980 metres (3,215 feet). Set among the dense forests of southeastern Venezuela, it was discovered in 1935 and named after James Angel, a U.S. pilot who crashed nearby in 1937.

an·gel·fish (áynjəl-fish) *n., pl.* **-fishes** or collectively **angelfish. 1.** Any of several brightly coloured fishes of the family Chaetodontidae, of warm seas, having laterally compressed bodies. **2.** A freshwater fish, *Pterophyllum scalare*, native to rivers of South America, having a laterally compressed, usually striped body. It is a popular aquarium fish. Also called "scalare". **3.** A shark, the **monkfish** *(see).* [After its fancied resemblance to the brilliance of an angel and, in some species, alluding to its fins as an angel's wings.]

an·gel·ic (an-jéllik) *adj.* Also **an·gel·i·cal** (-jéllik'l). **1.** Of or consisting of angels: *angelic hosts.* **2.** Suggestive of or resembling an angel, as in innocence, kindness, or beauty. —**an·gel·i·cal·ly** *adv.*

an·gel·i·ca (an-jéllikə) *n.* **1.** Any of various plants of the genus *Angelica*, having compound leaves and clusters of small white or greenish flowers; especially, *A. archangelica* (garden angelica) whose aromatic seeds, leaves, stems, and roots are used in medicine and as flavouring. **2.** The candied stem of this plant, used especially for decorating cakes and sweet dishes. [New Latin, from Medieval Latin *(herba) angelica*, "angelic (herb)", from Late Latin, feminine of *angelicus*, from Greek *angelikos*, from *angelos*, messenger. See **angel.**]

An·gel·i·co (an-jélliko ‖ aan-), **Fra** (*c.* 1387–1455). Florentine painter, famous for his frescos of religious subjects. His real name was Guido di Pietro, which he changed when he became a Dominican monk. His best known work is the cycle of 35 paintings that decorates the sanctuary of the Church of SS. Annunziata.

an·gel·ol·o·gy (áynjəl-óllƏji) *n.* The branch of theology having to do with angels. See **angel.** [ANGEL + -LOGY.]

angel shark *n.* A raylike shark, the **monkfish** *(see).* [From its winglike pectoral fins.]

an·gels-on-horse-back (áynjəlz-on-hórssbak) *n.* Oysters wrapped in bacon and served on toast as a savoury. Compare **devils-on-horseback.**

An·ge·lus (án-ji-ləss, -jə-) *n. Roman Catholic Church.* **1.** A devotional prayer at morning, noon, and night to commemorate the Annunciation. **2.** A bell rung as a summons to recite this prayer. In this sense, also called "Angelus bell". [Medieval Latin, "*Angelus (Domini . . .),*" "The Angel (of the Lord)" (the beginning of the liturgy commemorating the Incarnation), from *angelus*, ANGEL.]

an·ger (áng-gər) *n.* A feeling of extreme displeasure, hostility, indignation, or exasperation towards someone or something.
   —*tr.v.* **angered, -gering, -gers.** To make angry; enrage or provoke. [Middle English, from Old Norse *angr*, grief.]

   Synonyms: anger, rage, fury, ire, wrath, resentment, indignation.

An·gers (ON-zháy). Town of pre-Roman origin, the capital of the

Maine-et-Loire département in western France. Formerly the capital of Anjou, it boasts a rich heritage of medieval architecture.

An·ge·vin (ánjivin) *adj.* **1.** Of or pertaining to Anjou. **2.** Of or pertaining to the ruling house of Anjou, especially as represented by the Plantagenet kings of England, from Henry II, the son of Geoffrey, Count of Anjou, to Richard II (1154–1399). [French, from Old French, from Medieval Latin *Andegavīnus*, from *Andegavia*, ANJOU.] —**An·ge·vin** *n.*

an·gi·na (an-jīnə) *n.* **1.** Any disease, such as croup or diphtheria, in which intermittent and painful suffocation or spasms occur. **2.** Angina pectoris. [Latin, quinsy, from Greek *ankhonē*, a strangling.]

angina pec·to·ris (péktəriss) *n.* Severe paroxysmal pain in the chest characterised by feelings of suffocation and apprehension, caused by a momentary lack of adequate blood supply to the heart. [New Latin, "angina of the chest".]

angio-, angi- *comb. form.* Indicates: **1.** Blood or lymph vessel; for example, **angiography. 2.** Seed vessel; for example, **angiosperm.** [Greek *angeion*, vessel, diminutive of *angos†*, vessel.]

an·gi·o·graph·y (ánji-óggrəfi) *n.* The X-ray examination of blood vessels after injecting a radiopaque dye into them. Compare **arteriography.** —**an·gi·o·gra·phic** (-ə-gráffik) *adj.*

an·gi·ol·o·gy (ánji-óllƏji) *n.* The study of blood and lymph vessels.

an·gi·o·ma (ánji-ō-mə) *n., pl.* **-mas** or **-mata** (-mətə). A tumour composed of lymph vessels or blood vessels. [ANGIO- + -OMA.] —**an·gi·o·ma·tous** (-ōmətəss ‖ *U.S. also* -ómmətəss) *adj.*

an·gi·o·sperm (ánji-ō-sperm, -ə-) *n. Botany.* Any plant of the class Angiospermae, characterised by having seeds enclosed in an ovary; a flowering plant. —**an·gi·o·sper·mous** (-spérməss) *adj.*

an·gi·o·ten·sin (ánji-ō-tén-sin, -ə-) *n.* A protein in the blood that causes constriction of blood vessels and stimulates secretion of the hormone aldosterone from the adrenal cortex. [ANGIO- + TENS(ION) + -IN.]

Ang·kor (áng-kawr). Major archaeological site in northwest Cambodia, the capital of the Khmer empire from the 9th to the 15th century. The ruins include two major Hindu temple complexes, Angkor Wat (12th century) and Angkor Thom (13th century).

Angl. Anglican.

an·gle¹ (áng-g'l) *intr.v.* **-gled, -gling, -gles. 1.** To fish with a hook and line. **2.** To try to get something by deceitful or indirect means. Used with *for: angle for an invitation.* [Middle English *anglen*, from *angel*, a fishhook, Old English *angul, ongul*.]

angle² *n.* **1.** *Geometry.* **a.** The figure formed by two lines diverging from a common point. **b.** The figure formed by two planes diverging from a common line. **c.** The rotation required to superimpose either of two such lines or planes on the other. **d.** The space between such lines or surfaces. **e.** A solid angle *(see).* **2.** An angular or projecting corner, as of a building. **3. a.** The place, position, or direction from which an object is presented to view. **b.** *Informal.* A particular aspect of a complex whole, viewed separately: *he deals with the advertising angle.* **c.** *Informal.* A particular viewpoint: *From his angle, it's a disaster.* **4.** *Slang.* A scheme; a devious method.
   —*v.* **angled, -gling, -gles.** —*tr.* **1.** To move or turn at an angle. **2.** To aim or hit (a ball, for example) at an angle. **3.** *Informal.* To impart a particular bias or point of view to (a story or report, for example). —*intr.* To move or proceed by angles: *The path angled through the woods.* [Middle English, from Old French, from Latin *angulus*, angle, corner.]

An·gle (áng-g'l) *n.* A member of a Germanic people that migrated to England from southern Denmark in the fifth century A.D., founded the kingdoms of Northumbria, East Anglia, and Mercia, and together with the Jutes and Saxons formed the Anglo-Saxon peoples. [Latin *Anglī, Anglii* (plural), from Germanic; related to Old English *angul*, fishook; perhaps alluding to the shape of the original homeland, the Angul district of Schleswig.]

angle bracket *n.* Either of the punctuation marks < >, used to enclose written or printed material, or to indicate an integral in quantum mechanics.

angle iron *n.* A length of steel or iron having an L-shaped cross-section, used as part of a structural framework.

angle of attack *n.* **1.** The acute angle between the chord of an aerofoil and a line representing the undisturbed relative airflow. **2.** Any other acute angle between two reference lines designating the cant of an aerofoil relative to the oncoming air.

angle of bank *n.* The angle between an aircraft's lateral axis in flight and the horizontal.

angle of deviation *n.* The angle between the refracted ray and the incident ray when a light ray passes from one medium to another.

angle of dip *n.* See **magnetic dip.**

angle of incidence *n.* **1.** *Physics.* The angle formed by the path of a body or of radiation incident on a surface and a perpendicular to the surface at the point of impact. **2.** *Aviation.* The angle of attack.

angle of reflection *n.* The acute angle formed by the path of a reflected body or reflected radiation with a perpendicular to the surface at the point of reflection.

angle of refraction *n.* The acute angle formed by the path of refracted radiation with a perpendicular to the refracting surface at the point of refraction.

angle of repose *n.* The maximum angle to the horizontal that a pile of rocks, soil, or the like can sustain without sliding.

angle of view *n.* The angle included by two lines drawn from opposite extreme corners of an image to the centre of a lens.

angle of yaw *n.* The angle between an aircraft's longitudinal axis and its line of travel, as seen from above.

angle plate *n.* **1.** A right-angled metal bracket, used on the face plate of a lathe to hold pieces being worked. **2.** A flat steel plate in the shape of a right-angled triangle, used to strengthen frameworks, connect structural members, and the like.

an·gler (áng-glər) *n.* **1.** One who fishes with a hook and line. **2.** Any of various marine fishes of the order Lophiiformes (or Pediculati), having a long dorsal fin ray that is suspended over the mouth and serves to attract prey. In this sense, also called "anglerfish".

An·gle·sey (áng-g'l-si ‖ -see). *Welsh* **Môn** (mōn) or **Yn·ys Môn** (únniss mōn). Island separated from the northwestern mainland of Wales by the Menai Strait. Formerly a separate county, then from 1974 part of the county of Gwynedd. In 1996 it became a new Unitary Authority area of Wales.

angle shades *n. Used with a singular verb.* A common moth, *Phlogophora meticulosa*, that resembles a withered leaf when the wings are folded. [From the angular markings of the wings.]

an·gle·site (áng-g'l-sīt, -glə-) *n.* A lead sulphate mineral, occurring in white or tinted crystals. [After ANGLESEY, where it was first found.]

an·gle·worm (áng-g'l-wurm) *n.* A worm, such as an earthworm, used as bait in fishing.

An·gli·a (áng-gli-ə). The medieval Latin name for England. [Latin, from *Anglī*, the ANGLE(S).]

An·gli·an (áng-gli-ən) *n.* **1.** An Angle. **2.** The Old English dialects of Northumbrian and Mercian. —**An·gli·an** *adj.*

An·gli·can (áng-glikən) *adj. Abbr.* **Angl.** Of, or characteristic of the Church of England, or any other of the churches related to it in origin and communion, such as the Protestant Episcopal Church. ~*n.* A member of the Church of England or of any of the churches related to it. [Medieval Latin *Anglicānus*, from *Anglicus*, English, from *Anglī*, ANGLE(S).] —**An·gli·can·ism** *n.*

Anglican Communion *n.* The Church of England and those episcopal churches, chiefly in English-speaking countries, that are in agreement with it as to doctrine and are in communion with the Archbishop of Canterbury. Also called "Anglican Church".

An·gli·ce Often small **a** (áng-glissi) *adv.* In the English form: *Firenze, Anglice Florence.* [Medieval Latin *Anglicē*, adverb of *Anglicus*, English, from Latin *Anglī*, the ANGLE(S).]

An·gli·cise, An·gli·cize (áng-gli-sīz) *v.* **-cised, -cising, -cises.** *Often small* **a.** —*tr.* To make English in form, idiom, style, or character. —*intr.* To become Anglicised. —**An·gli·ci·sa·tion** (-sī-záysh'n ‖ *U.S.* -si-) *n.*

An·gli·cism (áng-gli-siz'm) *n. Often small* **a.** **1.** A word, phrase, or idiom peculiar to the English language. **2.** Attachment to or admiration of English customs or values.

an·gling (áng-gling) *n.* The act, process, or art of fishing with a hook and line and usually a rod.

An·glo (áng-glō) *n., pl.* **-glos.** *U.S. Informal.* **1.** An Anglo-American. **2.** Any white resident of the United States not of Latin descent. [Short for ANGLO-AMERICAN.] —**An·glo** *adj.*

Anglo- *comb. form.* Indicates: **1.** English or England; for example, **Anglophone. 2.** Involving the English or British and; for example, *Anglo-Scottish; Anglo-Israeli relations.* [New Latin, from Medieval Latin *Anglī*, the English people, from Latin, the ANGLE(S).]

An·glo-A·mer·i·can (áng-glō-ə-mérrikən) *n.* A resident of the United States whose language, ancestry, and culture are English. —**An·glo-A·mer·i·can** *adj.*

An·glo-Bo·er War (áng-glō-bō-ər, -boor) *n. South African.* The **Boer War** *(see).*

An·glo-Cath·o·lic (áng-glō-káth-lik, -káthə-, *rarely* -ka'ath-) *n.* A member of the Anglican Communion who inclines towards the Roman Catholic Church in matters of ritual and worship. —**An·glo-Cath·o·lic** *adj.* —**An·glo-Ca·thol·i·cism** (-kə-thólli-siz'm) *n.*

An·glo-French (áng-glō-frénch) *n.* The dialect of Old French used in medieval England. See **Norman French.** Also called "Anglo-Norman". —**An·glo-French** *adj.*

An·glo-In·di·an (áng-glō-índi-ən, -índ-yən) *n.* **1.** A person of British and Indian descent. **2.** A person of British origin living in India during British rule. **3.** The dialect of English used in India. —**An·glo-In·di·an** *adj.*

An·glo-I·rish (áng-glō-ír-irish) *pl.n.* Inhabitants of Ireland of English origin. Preceded by *the.* —**An·glo-Ir·ish** *adj.*

An·glo-Nor·man (áng-glō-nórmən) *n.* **1.** Any of the Norman people who settled in England after 1066, or a descendant of these settlers. **2.** The Anglo-French language spoken by these people. —**An·glo-Nor·man** *adj.*

An·glo·phile (áng-glō-fīl, -glə-) *n.* An admirer of England and English customs or manners. —**An·glo·phile** *adj.* —**An·glo·phil·i·a** (-fílli-ə) *n.*

An·glo·phobe (áng-glə-fōb, -glə-) *n.* One who has an aversion to England and English customs or manners. —**An·glo·phobe** *adj.* —**An·glo·pho·bi·a** (-fóbi-ə) *n.*

An·glo·phone (áng-glə-fōn, -glō-) *adj.* **1.** English-speaking: *Anglophone Africa.* **2.** Of or for English-speakers; especially, being in English. Compare **Francophone.** —**An·glo·phone** *n.*

An·glo-Sax·on (áng-glō-sáksən) *n. Abbr.* **AS, A.S., AS. 1.** A member of one of the Germanic peoples (Angles, Saxons, and Jutes) who settled in Britain in the fifth and sixth centuries A.D. **2.** Any of the descendants of these peoples who were dominant in England until the Norman Conquest of 1066. **3. a. Old English** *(see).* **b.** Plain, unadorned English, especially if with four-letter words. **4.** Any person of English ancestry. —**An·glo-Sax·on** *adj.*

An·go·la, The Republic of (ang-gôlə). Country in southwest Africa. Formerly Portuguese West Africa, it gained its independence in 1975 after a long guerrilla war. A civil war then ensued between the National Front for the Liberation of Angola (FNLA), the National Union for the Total Independence of Angola (UNITA), and the People's Movement for the Liberation of Angola (MPLA). The Cuban-backed MPLA gained recognition, but UNITA with South African backing forced concessions. In 1991 Cuban troops withdrew and elections were held, but civil war continued. A peace agreement signed in 1994 was supported by the UN, but the conflict between government and UNITA continued. The country has great hydroelectric potential, and considerable mineral resources. Coffee, oil, diamonds, and iron ore are the chief exports. Area 1 246 700 square kilometres (481,226 square miles). Population, 11,190,000. Capital, Luanda. —**An·go·lan** *n. & adj.*

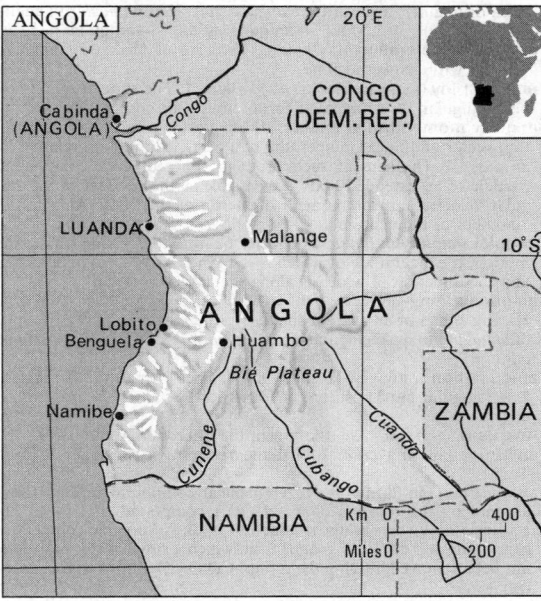

An·go·ra¹ (ang-gáwrə ‖ -gôrə) *n. Often small* **a. 1. a.** The hair of the Angora goat, **mohair** *(see).* **b.** The fine, light hair of the Angora rabbit, sometimes blended with wool in fabrics. **2.** A yarn or fabric made from either of these fibres.

Angora². See **Ankara.**

Angora cat *n.* A long-haired domestic cat similar to the Persian cat.

Angora goat *n.* Any of a breed of domestic goats having long, silky hair.

Angora rabbit *n.* Any of a breed of domestic rabbits having long, soft, usually white hair.

an·gos·tu·ra bark (áng-gə-stéwr-ə ‖ -stoor-) *n.* The bitter, aromatic bark of either of two Brazilian trees, *Galipea officinalis* or *Cusparia felorifuga*, used as a tonic in Angostura bitters. Also called "angostura". [From *Angostura*, former name of Ciudad Bolívar.]

Angostura bitters *pl.n.* A trademark for a tonic used to flavour alcoholic drinks. [After ANGOSTURA BARK.]

an·gry (áng-gri) *adj.* **-grier, -griest. 1.** Feeling or showing anger; incensed or enraged. **2.** Indicative of or resulting from anger: *an angry silence.* **3.** Having a menacing aspect; seeming to threaten: *angry clouds.* **4.** Inflamed: *an angry sore.* [Middle English, from ANGER.] —**an·gri·ly** (-grəli) *adv.* —**an·gri·ness** *n.*

angry young man *n.* **1.** Any of a group of British writers of the 1950s whose works are characterised by vigorous social protest. **2.** Any young man with strongly felt radical or anti-Establishment views. [Perhaps from *Angry Young Man* (1951), an autobiography by L. A. Paul (1901–), British journalist.]

angst (angst ‖ *U.S.* aangst) *n.* A strong but ill-defined feeling of anxiety. [German *Angst*, from Middle High German *angest*.]

ang·strom, Ång·ström (áng-strəm, -strum) *n. Symbol* **Å** A unit of length equal to one hundred-millionth (10^{-8}) of a centimetre, used to specify radiation wavelengths but now largely replaced by the nanometre (1Å = 0.1nm). Also called "angstrom unit". [After Anders Jonas ÅNGSTRÖM.]

Ang·ström (áng-strəm; *Swedish* åwng-strom), **Anders Jonas** (1814–74). Swedish physicist. He was a founder of the science of spectroscopy, and laid the foundations of modern spectral analysis. He discovered by investigating the solar spectrum that there is hydrogen in the Sun's atmosphere.

An·guil·la (ang-gwíllə). One of the Leeward Islands in the Caribbean Sea, discovered by Columbus in 1493. A British colony ruled from St. Kitts since the 17th century, it was linked with St. Kitts-Nevis as a British associated state in 1962. The *Anguillans* sought independence from Britain and St. Kitts in 1967, and again in 1969.

when British troops and London police quelled their revolt. The island finally became a separate self-governing dependency in 1980.

an·guil·li·form (ang-gwilli-fawrm) *adj.* Having the elongated shape of an eel. [New Latin *anguilla*, from Latin, eel, diminutive of *anguis*, snake + -ı- + -FORM.]

an·guine (áng-gwin) *adj.* Of, pertaining to, or resembling a snake; snakelike. [Latin *anguīnus*, from *anguis*, snake.]

an·guish (áng-gwish) *n.* Extreme pain, especially mental pain; torment; torture.
~*v.* **anguished, -guishing, -guishes.** —*tr.* To cause to suffer or feel anguish. —*intr.* To suffer or feel anguish. [Middle English *anguisshe*, from Old French *anguisse*, from Latin *angustia*, straightness, narrowness, from *angustus*, narrow.]

an·guished (áng-gwisht) *adj.* Filled with or expressing anguish: *an anguished cry.*

an·gu·lar (áng-gew-lər) *adj.* 1. Having, forming, or consisting of an angle or angles. 2. Measured by an angle or degrees of an arc. 3. Bony and lean; gaunt. 4. Lacking grace or smoothness in movement or manner; awkward: *an angular gait.* [Latin *angulāris* : angulus, ANGLE + -āris, -AR.] —**an·gu·lar·ly** *adv.* —**an·gu·lar·ness** *n.*

angular acceleration *n. Physics.* The rate of change of angular velocity with respect to time.

an·gu·lar·i·ty (áng-gew-lárrəti) *n., pl.* **-ties.** 1. The state or quality of being angular. 2. An angular form, outline, or corner.

angular momentum *n. Physics.* 1. The vector product of the position vector and linear momentum of a particle in motion relative to an axis. 2. The sum of such products, one for each component particle of an extended body, expressible as the product of the angular velocity and the moment of inertia of the body. Also called "moment of momentum".

angular velocity *n. Physics.* A vector quantity describing rotational motion, the magnitude of which is the time rate of change of angle, and the direction of which is along the axis of rotation.

an·gu·late (áng-gew-layt, -lət, -lit) *adj.* Also **an·gu·lat·ed** (-laytid). Having angles or an angular shape. [Latin *angulātus*, past participle of *angulāre*, to make angular, from *angulus*, ANGLE.] —**an·gu·late·ly** *adv.*

an·gu·la·tion (áng-gew-láysh'n) *n.* 1. The formation of angles. 2. An angular part, position, or formation. 3. The measurement of angles.

An·gus (áng-gəs) *n.* A cattle breed, the **Aberdeen Angus** *(see).*

an·hin·ga (an-híng-gə) *n.* A bird, the *darter (see).* [Portuguese, from Tupi.]

an·hy·dride (an-hídrīd) *n.* 1. A chemical compound formed from another by the removal of water. 2. A compound that forms an acid or a base when water is added to it. 3. An organic compound containing two carboxyl groups from which a single water molecule has been removed, leaving the group -CO.O.CO-. [ANHYDR(OUS) + -IDE.]

an·hy·drite (an-hídrīt) *n.* A white to greyish or reddish mineral, anhydrous orthorhombic calcium sulphate, $CaSO_4$, occurring as layers in gypsum deposits. [ANHYDR(OUS) + -ITE.]

an·hy·drous (an-hídrəss) *adj.* Without water, especially water of crystallisation. [Greek *anudros*, waterless : *an-*, without + *hudōr*, water.]

an·i·con·ic (án-ī-kónnik) *adj.* Not in human or animal form. Said of mythical symbols, portrayals of gods, or the like. [AN- (not) + ICONIC.]

an·il (ánnil) *n.* An indigo plant, *Indigofera suffruticosa,* or the blue dye obtained from it. [French, from Portuguese, from Arabic *an-nīl,* the indigo plant, from Persian *nīl,* indigo.]

an·ile (áynīl, ánnīl) *adj.* Feeble and frail like a old woman; senile. [Latin *anīlis,* from *anus,* old woman.] —**an·il·i·ty** (ay-nílləti, a-).

an·i·line (ánni-lin, -leen) *n.* Also **an·il·i·ty** (-lin). A colourless, oily, poisonous benzene derivative, $C_6H_5NH_2$, used in the manufacture of rubber, dyes, resins, pharmaceuticals, and varnishes. [German *Anilin* : ANIL + -INE.] —**an·i·line, an·i·lin** *adj.*

aniline dye *n.* Any of numerous synthetic dyes, originally those derived from aniline.

an·i·ma (ánnimə) *n.* 1. The soul. 2. In the psychology of Carl Jung: **a.** The soul, or true inner self. Compare **persona.** **b.** The feminine inner personality, as present in the unconscious of the male. Compare **animus.** [Latin, feminine of *animus,* mind, ANIMUS.]

an·i·mad·ver·sion (ánnimad-vérsh'n, -vérzh'n) *n.* 1. Hostile criticism. 2. A considered remark, usually censorious or critical. Used with *on* or *upon.* [Latin *animadversiō,* from *animadvertere,* to ANIMADVERT.] —**an·i·mad·ver·sive** (-vér-siv ‖ -ziv) *adj.*

an·i·mad·vert (ánnimad-vért) *intr.v.* **-verted, -verting, -verts.** *Formal.* To remark or comment critically, usually with strong disapproval or censure. Used with *on* or *upon.* [Latin *animadvertere,* to direct the mind to, censure : *animus,* mind + *advertere,* to turn towards : *ad-,* to + *vertere,* to turn.]

an·i·mal (ánnimal) *n.* 1. Any organism of the kingdom Animalia, distinguished from plants by certain typical characteristics, such as the power of locomotion, fixed structure and limited growth, nonrigid cell walls, specialised sense organs and rapid response to stimuli, and nonphotosynthetic metabolism. 2. Any such organism other than a human being; especially, a mammal. 3. A person of inhuman character or behaviour; someone who is bestial or brutish. 4. A person considered in terms of a characteristic quality: *John's quite a domestic animal in his way.* 5. Animality. Preceded by the: *Drinking releases the animal in him.*
~*adj.* 1. Of, pertaining to, or characteristic of animals. 2. Pro-

duced by or derived from animals: *animal fat.* 3. Pertaining to the sensual or physical as distinct from the spiritual nature of human beings. [Latin, an animal, from *animālis,* living, from *anima,* feminine of *animus,* breath, soul.]

an·i·mal·cule (ánni-mál-kewl) *n.* Also **an·i·mal·cu·lum** (-kew-ləm) *pl.* **-la** (-lə). 1. A microscopic or minute organism usually regarded as an animal, such as an amoeba or paramecium. 2. *Archaic & Poetic.* A tiny animal, such as a mosquito. [New Latin *animalculum,* diminutive of ANIMAL.] —**an·i·mal·cu·lar** (-lər) *adj.*

animal husbandry *n.* The care and breeding of domestic animals such as cattle, pigs, sheep, and horses.

an·i·mal·ise, an·i·mal·ize (ánniməl-īz) *tr.v.* **-ised, -ising, -ises.** 1. To make coarse and brutal. 2. To endow (a deity) with the attributes, especially the form, of an animal. Compare **anthropomorphise.** —**an·i·mal·i·sa·tion** *n.* (-ī-záysh'n ‖ U.S. -i-).

an·i·mal·ism (ánniməl-iz'm) *n.* 1. A state of sound health resulting from the full satisfaction of physical drives. 2. A state of brutish indifference to all but the physical appetites. 3. The doctrine that human beings are purely animal with no spiritual nature. —**an·i·mal·ist** *n.* —**an·i·mal·is·tic** (-istik) *adj.*

an·i·mal·i·ty (ánni-mál-əti) *n.* 1. The characteristics or nature of an animal. 2. Animals collectively; the animal kingdom. 3. The animal as distinct from the spiritual nature of mankind.

animal kingdom *n.* The category of living organisms that includes all animals. Compare **mineral kingdom, plant kingdom.**

animal magnetism *n.* 1. Magnetic personal presence. 2. Sensuality. 3. *Archaic.* Hypnotism or mesmerism.

animal starch *n.* A polysaccharide, **glycogen** *(see).*

an·i·mate (ánni-mayt) *tr.v.* **-mated, -mating, -mates.** 1. To give life to; fill with life. 2. To impart interest or zest to; enliven. 3. To fill with spirit, courage, or resolution; encourage. 4. To impart motion or activity to. 5. To make, design, or produce (a film, for example) by means of animation.
~*adj.* (-mət, -mit ‖ -mayt). 1. Possessing life; living. 2. Lively; vivacious. [Latin *animāre,* to fill with breath, from *anima,* breath, soul. See **animal.**]

an·i·mat·ed (ánnimaytid) *adj.* 1. Filled with life, activity, vigour, or spirit; enlivened: *an animated discussion.* 2. Made or designed so as to seem alive and moving: *an animated doll.* 3. Involving or using animation: *an animated film.* —**an·i·mat·ed·ly** *adv.*

animated cartoon. *n.* A cinematic film involving the animation of cartoon figures. Also called "cartoon".

animated oat *n.* A grass, *Avena sterilis,* of the Mediterranean region, having seeds that move or twist in response to changes in moisture.

an·i·ma·tion (ánni-máysh'n) *n.* 1. The act, process, or result of animating. 2. The condition or quality of being animate; liveliness; spirit; vitality. 3. **a.** An optical illusion of continuous movement achieved by the rapid succession of separate still, but gradually varying drawings, utilised for entertainment in animated cartoons, for example. **b.** The act or process of achieving this illusion.

an·i·ma·tism (ánnimə-tiz'm) *n.* 1. In social anthropology, the cultural belief that all animate and inanimate objects are infused with a single common life force. Compare **animism.** 2. *Psychology.* The ascribing of consciousness to animate and inanimate objects. —**an·i·ma·tist** *n. & adj.* —**an·i·ma·tis·tic** (-tístik) *adj.*

a·ni·ma·to (ánni-maátò ‖ U.S. a'ani-) *adv. Music.* In an animated or lively manner. Used as a direction. [Italian, from Latin *animātus,* past participle of *animāre,* to ANIMATE.] —**a·ni·ma·to** *adj.*

an·i·ma·tor, an·i·mat·er (ánnimaytər) *n.* 1. One that animates. 2. An artist or technician who produces an animated cartoon.

an·i·mism (ánni-miz'm) *n.* 1. Any of various cultural beliefs whereby natural phenomena and things animate and inanimate are held to possess individual innate souls. Compare **animatism.** 2. Any belief in spiritual beings or spiritual forces. 3. The hypothesis, first advanced by Pythagoras and Plato, of an immaterial force animating the universe. 4. An 18th-century doctrine that viewed the soul as the vital principle and source of both the normal and the abnormal phenomena of life. [German *Animismus,* from Latin *anima,* breath, soul. See **animal.**] —**an·i·mist** *n.* —**an·i·mis·tic** (-místik) *adj.*

an·i·mos·i·ty (ánni-móssəti) *n., pl.* **-ties.** Active hostility or open enmity. [Middle English *animosite,* from Old French, from Late Latin *animōsitās,* vehemence, spirit, from Latin *animōsus,* bold, spirited, from *animus,* soul, mind.]

an·i·mus (ánnimǝss) *n.* 1. An animating motive; an intention or purpose. 2. A feeling of animosity; bitter hostility or hatred. 3. In the psychology of Carl Jung, the masculine inner personality, as present in the unconscious of the female. Compare **anima.** [Latin, mind, soul.]

an·i·on (án-ī-ən) *n.* A negatively charged ion that migrates to an anode, as in electrolysis. Compare **cation.** [Greek, "that which goes up" (i.e., towards the anode), neuter present participle of *anienai,* to go up : *an(a)-,* up + *ienai,* to go.] —**an·i·on·ic** (-ónnik) *adj.*

an·ise (ánniss) *n.* A plant, *Pimpinella anisum,* native to the Mediterranean region, having clusters of small yellowish-white flowers and liquorice-flavoured seeds. See **aniseed.** [Middle English *anis,* from Old French, from Latin *anīsum,* from Greek *anison†.*]

an·i·seed (ánni-seed) *n.* The liquorice-flavoured seed of the anise plant, used in medicine and as flavouring. [Middle English *anis seed* : ANISE + SEED.]

an·i·sei·ko·ni·a (ánnī-sī-kǒni-ə ‖ U.S. an-ī-) *n.* An ocular defect in which the perception of image, shape, and size differ in each eye.

[New Latin : ANIS(O)- + Greek *eikōn,* image.] —**an·i·sei·kon·ic** (-kónnik) *adj.*

an·i·sette (ánni-zét, -sét) *n.* An aniseed-flavoured liqueur. [French, diminutive of *anis,* ANISE.]

aniso– *comb. form.* Indicates not equal or alike; for example, **anisomerous.** [New Latin, from Greek *anisos,* unequal : AN-, not + *isos,* equal (see ISO-).]

an·i·sog·a·my (ánni-sóggəmi) *n. Biology.* A union between markedly different gametes. [ANISO- + -GAMY.] —**an·i·sog·a·mous** (-sóggəməss) *adj.*

an·i·sole (ánni-sōl) *n.* A colourless liquid, $C_6H_5OCH_3$, used as a solvent, vermicide, and flavouring. [ANIS(E) + -OLE.]

an·i·som·er·ous (ánnī-sómmərəss) *adj. Botany.* Having or designating floral whorls that have unequal numbers of parts. [ANISO- + -MEROUS.]

an·i·so·met·ric (ánnī-sō-métrik, -sə- || *U.S.* an-ī-) *adj.* **1.** Not isometric. **2.** Denoting a crystal that has unequal axes. [French *anisométrique* : AN- (not) + ISOMETRIC.]

an·i·so·me·tro·pi·a (ánnī-sōmi-trōpi-ə || *U.S.* an-ī-səmə-) *n. Pathology.* Difference in the refractive power of the eyes. [New Latin : Greek *anisometros* : AN- (not) + *isometros,* ISOMETR(IC) + -OPIA.]

an·i·so·trop·ic (ánnī-sō-tróppik, -sə- || *U.S.* an-ī-) *adj.* **1.** Not isotropic. **2.** *Physics.* Having properties that differ according to the direction of measurement. [AN- (not) + ISOTROPIC.] —**an·i·so·trop·ic·al·ly** *adv.* —**an·i·sot·ro·pism** (-sóttrəpiz'm), **an·i·sot·ro·py** (-sóttrəpi) *n.*

An·jou (ON-zhoō). Ancient region of western France, ruled by the powerful counts of Anjou in the early Middle Ages. From their line came Geoffrey Plantagenet (1131–51), Count of Anjou and the father of the English king Henry II. See Angevin.

An·ka·ra (ángkərə). In ancient times, known as **An·cy·ra** (an-sīr-ə), later **An·go·ra** (ang-gáw-rə || -gō-). The capital and second-largest city of Turkey, lying 900 metres (3,000 feet) above sea level in the west central part of the country.

ankh (angk) *n.* An ansate cross (see). [Egyptian *ānkh,* soul, life.]

an·kle (ángk'l) *n.* **1.** The joint, consisting of the talus bone and related structures, that connects the foot with the leg. **2.** The slender section of the leg immediately above the foot. [Middle English *ankel* and *anclowe,* respectively from Old Norse *ankula* (unattested) and Old English *anclēow.*]

an·kle·bone (ángk'l-bōn) *n. Anatomy.* The **talus** (see).

ankle sock *n.* A sock that reaches just above the ankle.

an·klet (ángklit) *n.* **1.** An ornament worn around the ankle. **2.** *U.S.* An ankle sock. [ANKL(E) + -LET.]

an·ky·lose, an·chy·lose (ángki-lōz, -lōss) *v.* -losed, -losing, -loses. —*tr.* To join or consolidate by ankylosis. —*intr.* To become joined or consolidated by ankylosis. [Back-formation from ANKYLOSIS.]

an·ky·lo·sis, an·chy·lo·sis (ángki-lō-siss) *n. Pathology.* The stiffening of a joint as the result of abnormal bone fusion, surgery, or growth of fibrous tissue within the joint. [New Latin, from Greek *ankulōsis,* stiffening of the joints, from *ankuloun,* to bend, from *ankulos,* bent, curved, crooked.] —**an·ky·lo·tic** (-lóttik) *adj.*

ankylostomiasis. Variant of **ancylostomiasis.**

an·lace, an·e·lace (ánliss, ánnilayss) *n.* A two-edged medieval dagger. [Middle English *anlas, anelas*†.]

an·la·ge (án-laa-gə || *U.S.* aán-) *n., pl.* -gen (-gən) or -ges. **1.** *Embryology.* The initial cell structure from which an embryonic part or organ develops; a primordium. **2.** A fundamental principle; a foundation. [German *Anlage,* from Middle High German *anlāge,* a request, a laying on : *ane-,* on, from Old High German *ana* + *lāge,* act of laying, from Old High German *āga.*]

ann. 1. annals. **2.** annual. **3.** annuity.

an·na (ánnə) *n.* **1.** A former monetary unit of India, Burma, and Pakistan, equal to ¹/₁₆ of a rupee, and still used unofficially. **2.** A copper coin worth one anna. [Hindi *ānā,* from Sanskrit *aṇu-*†, small.]

an·na·berg·ite (ánnə-berg-īt) *n.* A rare mineral consisting of hydrated nickel arsenate, $Ni_3(AsO_4)_2 \cdot 8H_2O$. Also called "nickel bloom". [After *Annaberg,* Saxony, where it was discovered.]

An·na Com·ne·na (ánnə kom-néenə) (1083–*c.*1148). Byzantine princess and historian, daughter of the emperor Alexis I Comnenus. She wrote the *Alexiad,* a history of her father's reign, one of the great works of medieval historical literature.

an·nal·ist (ánnə-list) *n.* One who writes annals; a historian. [French *annaliste,* from Old French, from *annales,* annals, from Latin *annālēs,* ANNALS.] —**an·nal·is·tic** (-lístik) *adj.*

an·nals (ánn'lz) *pl.n. Abbr.* **ann. 1.** A chronological record of the events of successive years. **2.** Any descriptive account or record; a history. **3.** A periodical journal compiling the records and reports of a particular learned field, society, or the like. [Latin *(librī) annālēs,* "yearly (books)", from *annālis,* yearly, from *annus,* year.]

An·nam, A·nam (a-nám, ánnam). Region in central Vietnam and a former kingdom. Originally centred on the Red River valley, it was ruled by China from 111 B.C. until A.D. 939, and came under French influence in the 19th century. Its capital was Hué.

An·na·mese (ánnə-meéz || -meéss) *n., pl.* Annamese (for sense 1). Also **An·na·mite. 1.** A native or inhabitant of Annam. **2.** Formerly, the Vietnamese language. —**An·na·mese** *adj.*

An·nan (ánnan), **Kofi** (1938–). Ghanaian international civil servant. He worked for the World Health Organisation (1962–71) and then for the United Nations, including as special envoy to the former Yugoslavia (1995–96). He was appointed secretary-general of the U.N. in January 1997.

An·nap·o·lis (ə-náppə-liss). Capital of the state of Maryland, on the Atlantic seaboard of the United States. Site of the Annapolis Convention of 1786, which led to the U.S. Constitution, and of the U.S. Naval Academy.

An·na·pur·na (ánnə-púr-nə, -poór-). Himalayan mountain in north central Nepal. Annapurna I, one of the world's highest peaks, rises to 8 078 metres (26,503 feet), and was scaled by French mountaineers in 1950.

an·nates (ánnayts, ánnəts) *pl.n. Roman Catholic Church.* A full year's revenue formerly paid to the pope by a bishop or other ecclesiastic on first being appointed. [French, plural of *annate,* from Medieval Latin *annāta,* a year's revenue, from Latin *annus,* year, + *-āta,* "product of" (past participial ending forming nouns).]

an·nat·to, a·nat·to (ə-náttō || *U.S.* ə-naátō) *n., pl.* -tos. Also **ar·nat·to** (aar-). **1.** A small tropical American tree, *Bixa orellana,* having red or pinkish flowers and seeds used as a colouring in cooking. **2.** A yellowish-red dye obtained from the seed coat of the annatto. [Carib (the name of the tree).]

Anne (an), **(Elizabeth Alice Louise)** (1950–). British princess royal, second child and only daughter of Elizabeth II. She has represented Great Britain in equestrian events at the Olympic Games.

Anne, Queen (1665–1714). Queen of England, Scotland, and Ireland from 1702, the last monarch of the Stuart line. She was the second daughter of James II, and came to the throne on the death of William III. She was the last English monarch to exercise the royal veto over legislation, in 1707.

an·neal (ə-néel) *tr.v.* -nealed, -nealing, -neals. **1.** To subject (glass or metal) to a process of heating and slow cooling in order to toughen and reduce brittleness. **2.** To temper. **3.** To strengthen (the will or determination). ~*n.* An act of or treatment by annealing. [Middle English *anelen,* Old English *onǣlan* : ON + *ǣlan,* to set fire to, from *āl,* fire.]

an·ne·lid (ánnəlid) *adj.* Also **an·nel·i·dan** (ə-néllidən). Of or belonging to the phylum Annelida, which includes the earthworms, leeches, and other worms having cylindrical segmented bodies. ~*n.* Also **an·nel·i·dan.** An annelid worm. [New Latin *Annelida,* from French *annélide* : *annelés,* ringed, from *anneler,* to encircle, from Old French *annel,* ring, from Latin *annellus,* diminutive of *ānulus,* small ring + -IDE.]

Anne of Cleves (kleevz) (1515–57). Fourth wife of Henry VIII of England, sister of the German Protestant prince William, Duke of Cleves. She married Henry in January 1540, but the marriage was never consummated and they were divorced in July 1540.

an·nex (ə-néks, a- || ánneks) *tr.v.* -nexed, -nexing, -nexes. **1.** To add or join; append or attach, especially to something larger or more significant. **2.** To incorporate (territory) into an existing state or empire. **3.** To add or attach, as an attribute, condition, or consequence. **4.** To take possession of without permission. ~*n.* (ánneks, ánniks). *U.S.* An annexe. [Middle English *annexen,* from Old French *annexer,* from Latin *annectere* (past participle *annexus*), to bind to : *ad-,* to + *nectere,* to tie.] —**an·nex·a·ble** *adj.*

an·nex·a·tion (ánnek-sáysh'n) *n.* **1.** The act or process of annexing. **2.** The condition of being annexed. **3.** Something that has been annexed. —**an·nex·a·tion·al** *adj.* —**an·nex·a·tion·ism** (-iz'm) *n.* —**an·nex·a·tion·ist** *n. & adj.*

an·nexe, *U.S.* **an·nex** (ánneks || ánniks) *n.* **1.** An auxiliary building added on to, or situated near, a larger one. **2.** An addition to a record or document; an appendix or addendum. [French *annexe,* from Latin *annexum,* "something added", from *annectere* (past participle *annexus*), to bind to. See **annex.**]

an·ni·hi·late (ə-nī-ə-layt || -nī-hi-) *v.* -lated, -lating, -lates. —*tr.* **1.** To destroy completely; wipe out; reduce to nonexistence. **2.** To nullify or render void; abolish. **3.** *Informal.* To overwhelm completely; render helpless or ineffective. —*intr.* To participate in annihilation, as do an electron and a positron. [Late Latin *annihilāre,* to reduce to nothing : Latin *ad-,* to + *nihil,* nothing.] —**an·ni·hi·la·tive** (-laytiv, -lətiv), **an·ni·hi·la·to·ry** *adj.* —**an·ni·hi·la·tor** (-laytər) *n.*

an·ni·hi·la·tion (ə-nī-ə-láysh'n || -nī-hi-) *n.* **1.** The act or process of annihilating. **2.** The condition or result of having been annihilated; utter destruction. **3.** *Theology.* The destruction of the soul at the death of the body. **4.** *Physics.* The phenomenon in which a particle and an antiparticle, such as an electron and a positron, collide with a resultant release of energy (*annihilation radiation*) approximately equivalent to the sum of their masses.

an·ni·hi·la·tion·ism (ə-nī-ə-láysh'n-iz'm || -nī-hi-) *n. Theology.* The doctrine that the souls of the wicked are destroyed at death.

an·ni mi·ra·bi·les. Plural of **annus mirabilis.**

an·ni·ver·sa·ry (ánni-vér-səri) *n., pl.* -ries. **1.** The annual recurrence of the date on which a notable event took place in some preceding year: *a wedding anniversary.* **2.** A commemorative celebration on this date. [Middle English *anniversarie,* from Medieval Latin *(diēs) anniversāria,* "anniversary (day)", from Latin *anniversārius,* "returning yearly" : *annus,* year + *versus,* past participle of *vertere,* to turn.] —**an·ni·ver·sa·ry** *adj.*

an·no Dom·i·ni (ánnō dómmi-nī || -nee) *adv. Abbr.* A.D. (usually small capitals). In a specified year of the Christian era. [Latin, "in the year of the Lord".]

an·no·tate (ánnə-tayt, ánnō-) *v.* -tated, -tating, -tates. —*tr.* To provide (a literary work) with a critical commentary or explanatory notes; gloss. —*intr.* To gloss a text. [Latin *annotāre,* to note down

: *ad-*, to + *notāre*, to mark, from *nota*, a mark, note.] —**an·no·ta·tive** *adj.* —**an·no·ta·tor** *n.*

an·no·ta·tion (ánnə-táysh'n, ánnō-) *n.* **1.** The act or process of annotating. **2.** A critical or explanatory note; a commentary.

an·nounce (ə-nównss ‖ *West Indian also* -núngss) *v.* **-nounced, -nouncing, -nounces.** —*tr.* **1.** To bring to public notice; declare or proclaim officially or formally. **2.** To proclaim the presence, readiness, or arrival of: *announce a visitor.* **3.** To make known in advance; serve to indicate: *The footsteps announced the presence of an unexpected visitor.* —*intr. Chiefly U.S.* To serve as a broadcasting announcer. [Middle English *announcen,* from Old French *annoncer,* from Latin *annuntiāre : ad-,* to + *nuntiāre,* to announce, from *nuntius,* messenger.]

an·nounce·ment (ə-nównss-mənt) *n.* **1.** The act of announcing. **2.** Something that has been announced. **3.** A printed or published statement or notice, as in a newspaper.

an·nounc·er (ə-nównss-ər) *n.* **1.** Someone who announces. **2.** One who provides programme continuity and delivers news bulletins on television or radio.

an·noy (ə-nóy) *v.* **-noyed, -noying, -noys.** —*tr.* **1.** To bother or irritate; anger slightly. **2.** To injure or harm; molest. —*intr.* To behave in an annoying manner.
~*n. Archaic & Poetic.* Something that annoys. [Middle English *anoien,* from Old French *anoier, enuier,* from Late Latin *inodiāre,* to make odious, from Latin *in odiō,* "in hatred", odious : *in,* in + *odiō,* ablative of *odium,* hatred.] —**an·noy·er** *n.* —**an·noy·ing·ly** *adv.*
Synonyms: annoy, irritate, bother, irk, vex, provoke.

an·noy·ance (ə-nóy-ənss) *n.* **1.** Something that annoys; a nuisance. **2.** The act of annoying. **3.** Vexation; irritation.

an·nu·al (ánnew-əl ‖ ánnewl, án-yəl) *adj. Abbr.* **ann. 1.** Recurring, done, or performed every year; yearly. **2.** Of or pertaining to the year; determined by a year's time: *an annual income.* **3.** *Botany.* Living and growing for only one year or season. Compare **perennial, biennial.**
~*n.* **1. a.** A periodical published yearly; a yearbook. **b.** A special issue, as of a children's comic, published yearly. **2.** A plant that lives and grows for only one year or season. [Middle English *annuel,* from Old French, from Late Latin *annuālis,* from Latin *annus,* year.] —**an·nu·al·ly** *adv.*

annual parallax *n. Astronomy.* **Parallax** *(see)* in a celestial body caused by motion of the Earth around the Sun, defined by the angle subtended at the celestial body by the Earth's radius. Also called "heliocentric parallax".

annual ring *n.* Any of the concentric layers of wood, especially in a tree trunk, indicating a year's growth in temperate climates and seasonal growth in regions of wet and dry seasons. Also called "growth ring".

an·nu·i·tant (ə-néw-i-tənt, -ə- ‖ -nōō-) *n.* A person who receives or is qualified to receive an annuity.

an·nu·i·ty (ə-néw-əti, -iti ‖ -nōō-) *n., pl.* **-ties.** *Abbr.* **ann. 1. a.** The annual payment of an allowance or income. **b.** The sum of money involved in such a payment. **2.** The right to receive or the obligation to make an annuity. **3. a.** The interest or dividends paid annually on an investment of money. **b.** The investment made. [Middle English *annuite,* from Old French, from Medieval Latin *annuitās,* yearly payment, from Latin *annuus,* yearly, from *annus,* year.]

an·nul (ə-núl) *tr.v.* **-nulled, -nulling, -nuls. 1.** To make or declare void or invalid; nullify or cancel (a marriage or a law, for example). **2.** To obliterate the existence or effect of; annihilate. —See Synonyms at **nullify.** [Middle English *annullen,* from Old French *annuler,* from Late Latin *annullāre,* to make into nothing : Latin *ad-,* to + *nullus,* none, null.] —**an·nul·la·ble** *adj.*

an·nu·lar (ánnewlər) *adj.* Forming or shaped like a ring. [Old French *annulaire,* from Latin *annulāris, ānulāris,* from *annulus, ānulus,* ring.] —**an·nu·lar·i·ty** *n.* —**an·nu·lar·ly** *adv.*

annular eclipse *n.* A solar eclipse in which the moon covers all but a bright ring around the circumference of the sun.

annular ligament *n.* A ligament or fibrous band that encircles a part of the body, such as the ankle or wrist.

an·nu·late (ánnew-layt, -lət, -lit) *adj. Also* **an·nu·lat·ed** (-laytid). Having or consisting of rings or ringlike segments. [Latin *annulātus, ānulātus,* from *annulus, ānulus,* ring. See **annulet.**] —**an·nu·late·ly** *adv.*

an·nu·la·tion (ánnew-láysh'n) *n.* **1.** The act or process of forming rings. **2.** A ringlike structure or segment.

an·nu·let (ánnew-lit, -let) *n.* **1.** *Architecture.* A ringlike moulding around the capital of a pillar. **2.** *Heraldry.* A ring shape. **3.** A small ring. [Diminutive formation from Latin *annulus, ānulus,* ring.]

an·nul·ment (ə-núlmənt) *n.* **1.** The act of annulling. **2.** A retrospective as well as prospective invalidation, especially of an unconsummated marriage.

an·nu·lus (ánnew-ləss) *n., pl.* **-luses** or **-li** (-lī). **1.** A ringlike figure, part, structure, or marking. **2.** *Geometry.* The figure bounded by and containing the area between two concentric circles. [Latin *annulus, ānulus,* ring.]

an·nun·ci·ate (ə-nún-si-ayt, -shi-) *tr.v.* **-ated, -ating, -ates.** *Rare.* To announce; proclaim. [Latin *annuntiāre,* to **ANNOUNCE.**] —**an·nun·ci·a·tion** (-áysh'n) *n.* —**an·nun·ci·a·tive, an·nun·ci·a·to·ry** (-ətri, -ətəri) *adj.*

Annunciation *n.* **1.** The angel Gabriel's announcement of the Incarnation to the Virgin Mary. Luke 1:26–38. **2.** The festival, Lady Day (March 25), in celebration of this event.

Annunciation lily *n.* The **Madonna lily** *(see).* [From its frequent depiction in paintings of the Annunciation.]

an·nun·ci·a·tor (ə-nún-si-aytər, -shi-) *n.* **1.** An electrical signalling device used in hotels or offices to indicate the source of calls on a switchboard. **2.** A signalling device indicating the position of a train.

an·nus mi·rab·i·lis (án-əss mi-ráabi-liss, -ōōss ‖ -rábbi-) *n., pl.* **anni mirabiles** (ánnee, -layz) **1.** A remarkable or fateful year. **2.** The year 1666, memorable for the Great Fire of London and the English victory over the Dutch. [New Latin, "wondrous year", originally designating the year 1588 in a forecast of its disasters.]

a·no·a (ə-nō-ə) *n.* A small buffalo, *Anoa depressicornis,* of Celebes and the Philippines, having short, pointed horns. [Native name in Celebes.]

an·ode (án-ōd) *n.* **1.** Any positively charged electrode, as of an electrolytic cell or electron tube. **2.** The negatively charged terminal of a primary cell or of an accumulator that is supplying current. [Greek *anodos,* a way up (i.e., from the positive pole into the electrolyte) : *ana-,* up + *hodos,* road, way.] —**an·od·al** (-ōd'l), **an·od·ic** (-óddik) *adj.*

anode ray *n.* A positive ray *(see).*

an·o·dise (án-ə-dīz, -ō-) *tr.v.* **-dised, -dising, -dises.** To coat (a metallic surface) electrolytically with a protective oxide. [ANOD(E) + -ISE.] —**an·o·di·sa·tion** *n.*

an·o·dyne (án-ə-dīn, -ō-) *adj.* **1.** Able to soothe or relieve pain. **2.** Relaxing; soothing. **3.** Watered-down; insipid; innocuous: *anodyne references to progress and freedom.*
~*n.* **1.** A medicine that relieves pain. **2.** Anything that soothes or comforts. [Latin *anōdynus,* from Greek *anōdunos,* free from pain : AN- (without) + *odunē,* pain.] —**an·o·dyn·ic** *adj.*

an·o·e·sis (ánnō-ée-siss) *n. Psychology.* A state of consciousness involving sensation but not thought. [A- (without) + Greek *noēsis,* thought, understanding.] —**an·o·et·ic** (-éttik) *adj.*

an·oes·trus (an-éess-trəss ‖ *U.S.* -éss-) *n. Zoology.* In many mammals, an interval of sexual inactivity between two periods of oestrus. [New Latin : AN- (without) + OESTRUS.] —**an·oes·trous** *adj.*

a·noint (ə-nóynt) *tr.v.* **anointed, anointing, anoints. 1.** To apply oil, ointment, or a similar substance to. **2.** To put oil on as a sign of sanctification or consecration in a religious ceremony. [Middle English *anointen,* from Old French *enoindre* (past participle *enoint*), from Latin *inunguere : in-,* upon + *unguere,* to smear, anoint.] —**a·noint·er** *n.* —**a·noint·ment** *n.*

a·no·le (ə-nōl, ə-nōli) *n.* Any of various chiefly tropical New World lizards of the genus *Anolis,* characterised by a distensible throat flap and the ability to change colour. Also called "American chameleon". [New Latin *Anolis,* from French *anolis,* anole, from Carib *anoli.*]

anomalistic month *n.* A month measured as the interval between two successive passages of the moon through perigee and equal to 27.55455 mean solar days.

anomalistic year *n.* A year measured as the interval between two successive passages of the earth through perihelion and equal to 365.25964 mean solar days.

a·nom·a·lous (ə-nómmələss) *adj.* Deviating from the normal or common order, form, or rule; abnormal; irregular. [Late Latin *anōmalos,* from Greek, uneven, irregular : AN- (not) + *homalos,* even, from *homos,* same.] —**a·nom·a·lous·ly** *adv.* —**a·nom·a·lous·ness** *n.*

a·nom·a·ly (ə-nómmə-li) *n., pl.* **-lies. 1.** Deviation from the normal or common order, form, or rule; abnormality. **2.** Anything anomalous, irregular, or abnormal. **3.** *Astronomy.* **a.** The angular deviation, as observed from the Sun, of a planet from its perihelion. **b.** The angular deviation of a satellite from its perigree. [Latin *anōmalia,* from Greek *anōmalia.* See **anomalous.**] —**a·nom·a·lis·tic** (-lístik) *adj.* —**a·nom·a·lis·ti·cal·ly** *adv.*

an·o·mie, an·o·my (án-ō-mi, -ə-) *n.* **1.** The absence of the social consensus necessary for governing a society. **2.** The state of alienation experienced by an individual or class in such a situation. **3.** Disorientation of the personality resulting in unsocial behaviour. [Greek *anomia,* lawlessness, from *anomos,* without law : A- (without) + *nomos,* law + French *-ie* (state, condition; see **-y**[2]); popularised by Durkheim as *anomie.*] —**an·om·ic** *adj.*

a·non (ə-nón) *adv. Archaic & Literary.* **1.** In a short time; soon. **2.** Once again. **3.** At once; immediately. —**ever and anon.** every now and again. [Middle English *anon, onon,* from Old English *on ān,* "in one", at once : *on,* in, ON + *ān,* one.]

anon. anonymous.

an·o·nym (ánnənim) *n.* **1.** An anonymous publication or person. **2.** A pseudonym. [French *anonyme,* noun use of adjective, ANONYMOUS.]

a·non·y·mous (ə-nónniməss) *adj. Abbr.* **a., anon. 1.** Having an unknown name. **2.** Of unknown or undeclared authorship, origin, or agency: *an anonymous donation.* **3.** Inconspicuous; lacking in individuality. [Late Latin *anōnymus,* from Greek *anōnumos,* nameless : AN- (without) + *onoma,* name.] —**a·no·nym·i·ty** (ánnə-nímməti), **a·non·y·mous·ness** *n.* —**a·non·y·mous·ly** *adv.*

a·noph·e·les (ə-nóffə-leez) *n.* Any of various mosquitoes of the genus *Anopheles,* many of which carry the malaria parasite and transmit the disease to humans by their bite. [New Latin *Anopheles,* "the hurtful ones", from Greek *anophelēs,* useless, hurtful : AN- (without) + *ophelos,* advantage.] —**a·noph·e·line** (-līn) *adj.*

an·o·rak (ánnərak) *n.* A padded waterproof and windproof jacket with a hood; parka. [Eskimo (Greenland) *ánorâq.*]

an·o·rex·i·a (ánnə-réksi-ə) *n.* **1.** Loss of appetite. **2.** Anorexia nervosa. [Late Latin *anorexia,* from Greek : AN- (without) + *orexis,* a longing, from *oregein,* to reach out for.] —**an·o·rec·tic** *adj.*

an·o·rex·ic (ánno-réksik) *adj.* **1.** Of, pertaining to, or suffering from anorexia nervosa; anorectic. **2.** Emaciated in appearance. — **an·o·rex·ic** *n.*

an·or·thite (an-órthīt) *n.* A plagioclase feldspar with high calcium oxide content, occurring in igneous rocks. [French : AN- (not) + Greek *orthos,* straight (from its oblique crystals) + -ITE.] —**an·or·thit·ic** (ánnawr-thíttik) *adj.*

an·or·tho·site (an-órtha-sīt) *n.* A plutonic rock, chiefly plagioclase. [French *anorthose* (see **anorthite**) + -ITE.]

an·os·mi·a (an-ózmi-ə) *n.* Loss of the sense of smell. [New Latin : AN- (without) + Greek *osmē,* smell + -IA.] —**an·os·mic** *adj.*

an·oth·er (ə-núthər) *adj.* **1.** Distinctly different from the first: *That's another matter.* **2.** Some other; any other: *in another country; Come again another day.* **3. a.** Additional; one more: *Take another cake.* **b.** Reminiscent of the specified phenomenon: *another Hitler; another Babylon.*
~*pron.* **1.** A different one. **2.** One of the same kind. **3.** An additional one. [Middle English *an other.*]

A.N. Other *n. Chiefly British.* A person still to be named or selected. [From *another* (spelt as if the initials and surname of the unnamed person).]

A·nouilh (ánnoo-ee, a-nōō-i), **Jean (Marie Lucien Pierre)** (1910–87). French dramatist. Many of his plays written during the Nazi occupation of France were derived from classical tradition, for example, *Antigone* (1946). Two of the best-received of his postwar plays were *Ring Around the Moon* (1948), and *Becket* (1959).

an·ov·u·lant (an-óvvewlənt) *n.* A drug that prevents ovulation. [AN- (not) + OVUL(ATION) + -ANT.] —**an·ov·u·lant** *adj.*

an·ov·u·lar (án-óvvew-lər, an-) *adj.* Also **an·ov·u·lat·o·ry** (-lətri, -láytəri). Pertaining to or characterised by the failure or suppression of ovulation. [AN-, without + OVUL(ATION) + -AR.]

an·ox·ae·mi·a (ánnoks-eémi-ə) *n.* An abnormally low concentration of oxygen in the blood. [New Latin : AN- (without) + OX(Y)- + -AEMIA.] —**an·ox·ae·mic** *adj.*

an·ox·i·a (an-óksi-ə) *n.* **1.** Absence or lack of oxygen. **2.** The condition resulting from a deficiency in the supply of oxygen to the tissues; especially, **hypoxia** (*see*). [AN- (without) + OX(Y)- + -IA.] —**an·ox·ic** *adj.*

ans. answer.

an·sate (an-sayt) *adj.* Also **an·sat·ed** (-id). Having a handle or a part resembling a handle. [Latin *ānsātus,* from *ānsa,* handle.]

ansate cross *n.* A cross shaped like a T with a loop at the top used, especially in Egyptian art, as a symbol of life. Also called "ankh", "crux ansata".

An·schluss (án-shlŏŏss ‖ *U.S.* áan-) *n. Sometimes small* **a.** A union; specifically, the political union of Nazi Germany and Austria in 1938. [German, from *anschließen,* to join: *an-* to, up + *schließen,* to close.]

An·selm (án-selm), **Saint** (*c.*1033–1109). Italian theologian and philosopher, and Archbishop of Canterbury from 1093 until his death. In his *Proslogium* the argument for the existence of God marks him as one of the founders of **Scholasticism.**

an·ser·ine (án-sə-rīn) *adj.* Also **an·ser·ous** (-rəss) (for sense 3). **1.** Of, belonging to, or pertaining to the subfamily Anserinae, which includes geese, swans, and certain ducks. **2.** Resembling a goose; gooselike. **3.** Stupid; silly; foolish. [New Latin *Anserinae,* from Latin *ānserīnus,* gooselike: *ānser,* goose : + -īnus, -INE.]

an·swer (áan-sər ‖ án-) *n. Abbr.* **ans., a., A. 1.** A spoken or written result, as of a question, request, statement, accusation, or letter. **2. a.** A solution, as to a problem. **b.** The correct response or solution. **3.** An act in response or retaliation. **4.** *Law.* A defendant's defence against charges filed against him. **5.** *Music.* A phrase similar to one just played but in a different pitch. **6.** A counterpart; an equivalent: *America's answer to the royal family.*
~*v.* **answered, -swering, -swers.** —*intr.* **1.** To respond in words or action. Used with *to.* **2. a.** To be liable or accountable. Used with *for.* **b.** To atone; make amends. Used with *for.* **3.** To serve the purpose; suffice; do: *use three words where one would answer.* **4.** To correspond; match. Used with *to: answering to the description.* —*tr.* **1. a.** To reply to. **b.** To say in reply. **2.** To respond correctly to; solve. **3.** To fulfil the demands of; serve: *"my fortune has answered my desires"* (Izaak Walton). **4.** To conform or correspond to. **5.** To be responsible for; meet; discharge (a claim or debt, for example). **6.** To offer an explanation or justification for (an accusation, charge, or the like). **7.** To attend to a signal or summons from: *answer the phone.* —**answer back.** To give a rude or defiant reply instead of showing politeness or deference. [Middle English *answer(e),* Old English *andswaru.*] —**an·swer·er** *n.*

Synonyms: answer, respond, reply, retort.

an·swer·a·ble (áan-sərə-b'l ‖ án-) *adj.* **1.** Responsible; accountable; liable. Used with *for* or *to.* **2.** Able to be answered. **3.** Corresponding; suitable. Used with *to.* —See Synonyms at **responsible.** — **an·swer·a·bil·i·ty** (-bílləti), **an·swer·a·ble·ness** *n.* —**an·swer·a·bly** *adv.*

an·swer·ing machine (áan-səring ‖ án-), **an·swer·phone** (áan-sər-fōn) *n.* A machine that can be plugged into a telephone in the subscriber's absence to record any message a caller may wish to leave.

answering service *n.* A commercial service that deals with tele-

phone calls and telephone messages for its clients.

ant (ant) *n.* Any of various social insects of the family Formicidae, characteristically having wings only in the males and fertile females, and living in colonies that have a complex social organisation. [Middle English *ante, amete,* Old English *æmette.*]

ant-. Variant of **anti-.**

-ant *n. & adj. suffix.* Indicates performing, promoting, or causing a specified state or action; for example, **deodorant, codant.** [Middle English, from Old French, from Latin *-āns* (stem *-ant-*), present participial ending of first conjugation verbs.]

ant. 1. antenna. **2.** antonym.

an·ta (án-tə) *n., pl.* **-tae** (-tee). *Architecture.* **1.** A thickening of the projecting end of the lateral wall of a Greek temple. **2.** A pier that constitutes one boundary of the porch. [Latin *antae* (plural), door jamb.]

ant·ac·id (ant-ássid) *adj.* Correcting acidity; neutralising acids.
~*n.* A substance that neutralises acid, especially in the stomach as a medicinal remedy. [ANT(I)- + ACID.]

an·tag·o·nise, an·tag·o·nize (an-tággəniz) *tr.v.* **-nised, -nising, -nises. 1.** To incur or provoke the dislike or hostility of. **2.** To counteract. [Greek *antagōnizesthai,* to struggle against : *anti-,* against + *agōnizesthai,* to struggle, from *agōn,* contest (see **agony**).]

an·tag·o·nism (an-tággəniz'm) *n.* **1.** Active, and often mutual, resistance, opposition, or hostility. **2.** The condition of being an opposing principle, force, or factor. **3.** The opposing action of two muscles such that the contraction of one is accompanied by the relaxation of the other. **4.** The interaction of two substances, such as drugs or hormones, such that one partly or wholly inhibits the action of the other. [French *antagonisme.* See ANTAGONIST, -ISM.]

an·tag·o·nist (an-tággə-nist) *n.* **1.** One who opposes and actively competes with another; an adversary. **2.** *Anatomy.* A muscle whose action opposes that of another muscle. Compare **agonist. 3.** *Pharmacology.* A drug that counteracts or neutralises another drug. Compare **agonist.** [French *antagoniste,* from Late Latin *antagōnista,* from Greek *antagōnistēs : antagōnizesthai,* to struggle against (see **antagonise**) + *-istes,* -IST.] —See Synonyms at **opponent.** —**an·tag·o·nis·tic** (-nístik) *adj.* —**an·tag·o·nis·ti·cal·ly** *adv.*

Antakya. See **Antioch.**

An·ta·nan·a·ri·vo (ántə-nánnə-réevō). Formerly **Ta·nan·a·rive** (ta-nánnə-reev). The capital and largest city of Madagascar. It was founded in the early 17th century as a walled citadel.

Ant·arc·tic (ánt-árktik ‖ -ártik) *n.* Antarctica and its surrounding waters. Preceded by *the.* [Middle English *Antartik,* from Medieval Latin *Antarticus,* from Latin *antarcticus,* southern, from Greek *antarktikos : anti-,* opposite + ARCTIC.] —**Ant·arc·tic** *adj.*

Ant·arc·ti·ca (ánt-árktikə, -ártikə). The coldest, stormiest, and driest continent, lying over the South Pole. It has nine per cent of the world's land, about 13 338 500 square kilometres (8,336,600 square miles), 95 per cent of it covered by an ice sheet more than 3 kilometres (1.9 miles) thick in places, making up 90 per cent of the world's permanent ice and snow. Temperatures average –50°C (–58°F) at the pole, and the world's lowest recorded temperature, –88.2°C (–126.9°F), occurred near the Russian base, Vostok. Antarctica's rocks are believed to contain coal, gas, metal ore, and oil deposits, but their extraction through the constantly moving ice sheet would be extremely difficult. The surrounding seas are a potentially rich source of food. There is no permanent population in Antarctica; and the Antarctic Treaty of 1959 forbids any military use of the area. See map, next page.

Antarctic Circle *n.* A parallel of latitude 66°32′ south, along which the Sun does not set on one day of the year, around December 22.

An·tar·es (an-taír-eez) *n.* A double and variable star, the brightest in the southern sky, about 424 light-years from Earth in the constellation Scorpius. [Greek *antarēs,* "opposing Mars" (that is, rivalling Mars in colour) : ANTI- + ARES.]

ant bear *n.* **1.** An anteater. **2.** An aardvark (*see*).

ant cow *n.* An aphid that yields a honey-like substance on which ants feed.

an·te (ánti) *n.* **1.** In poker, the stake that each player must put into the pool before receiving his hand, or before receiving new cards. **2.** An amount paid or required in advance, as for a financial venture.
~*tr.v.* **anted** or **-teed, -teing, -tes.** In poker, to put (one's stake) into the pool. Often used with *up.* [Latin *ante,* before.]

ante– *prefix.* Indicates: **1.** In front of; for example, **anteroom. 2.** Previous to; for example, **antenatal.** [Latin, from *ante,* before, in front of; previous to.]

ant·eat·er (ánt-eetər) *n.* **1.** Any of several tropical American mammals of the family Myrmecophagidae, that lack teeth and feed on ants and termites; especially, *Myrmecophaga tridactyla,* having a long, narrow snout, a long, sticky tongue, and a long, shaggy-haired tail. This species is also called "giant anteater" and sometimes "ant bear". **2.** Any of several other animals that feed on ants, such as the echidna, the pangolin, and the aardvark.

an·te·bel·lum, an·te·bel·lum (ánti-béllǝm) *adj.* Belonging to the period prior to a war, especially the American Civil War. [Latin *ante bellum,* before the war.]

an·te·cede (ánti-séed) *tr.v.* **-ceded, -ceding, -cedes.** To go before in rank, place, or time; precede. [Latin *antecēdere :* ANTE- + *cēdere,* to go.]

an·te·ce·dence (ánti-séed'nss) *n.* Precedence.

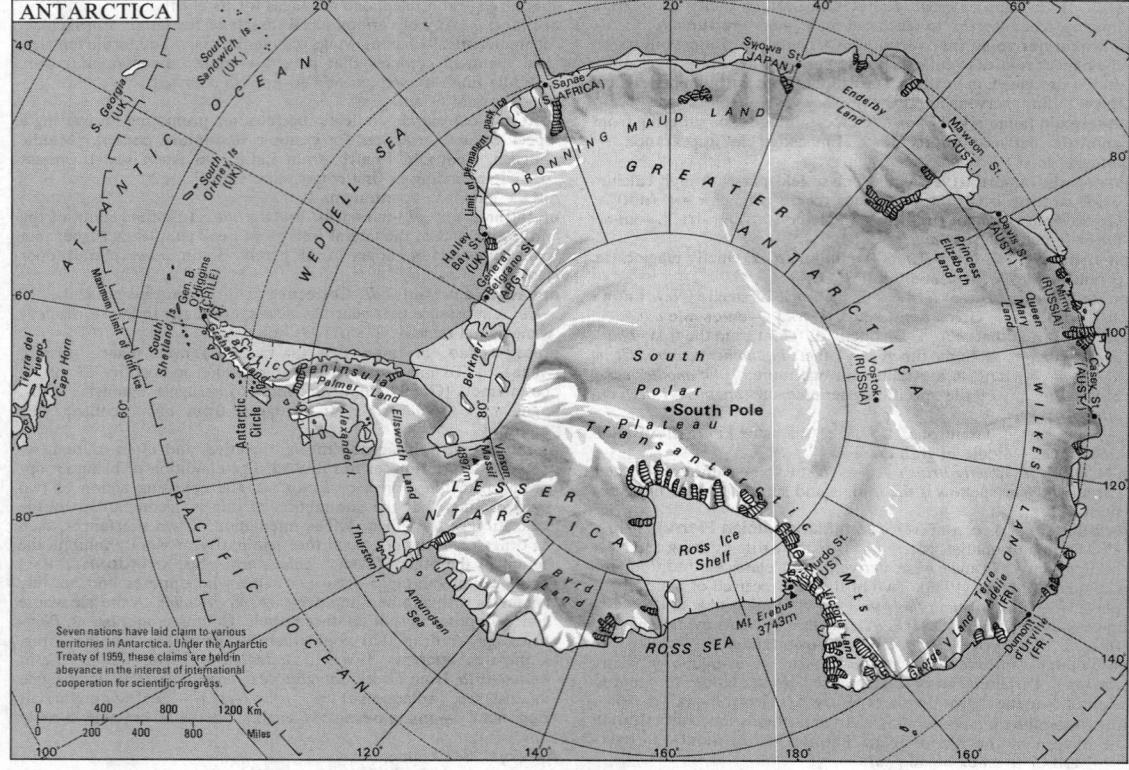

ANTARCTICA

Seven nations have laid claim to various
territories in Antarctica. Under the Antarctic
Treaty of 1959, these claims are held in
abeyance in the interest of international
cooperation for scientific progress.

an·te·ce·dent (ánti-séed'nt) *adj.* Going before; preceding; prior.
~*n.* **1.** An occurrence or circumstance that precedes another, often having a causal relationship with what follows. **2.** *Plural.* One's ancestors, ancestry, or past life. **3.** *Grammar.* The word, phrase, or clause to which a pronoun refers. **4.** *Mathematics.* The first term of a ratio. **5.** *Logic.* The first proposition or premise within a conditional proposition. —**an·te·ce·dent·ly** *adv.*

antecedent drainage *n.* A river pattern which survives subsequent uplift and folding during earth movements.

an·te·cham·ber (ánti-chaymbər) *n.* A smaller room serving as an entrance into a larger room; an anteroom. [French *antichambre : anti-,* before + *chambre,* room, CHAMBER.]

an·te·cha·pel (ánti-chapp'l) *n.* An inner porch or vestibule at the western end of a chapel.

an·te·date (ánti-dáyt ‖ *U.S.* -dayt) *tr.v.* **-dated, -dating, -dates.**
1. To be of an earlier date than; precede in time. **2.** To give a date earlier than the actual date to (a document, manuscript, or the like), especially in order to deceive: *antedate a cheque.* **3.** To assign a date to (a historical period or event) that is earlier than previously thought. **4.** *Archaic.* To bring about sooner than expected.
~*n.* A date earlier than one previously suggested.

an·te·di·lu·vi·an (ánti-di-lóov-iən, -dī-, -léwv-) *adj.* **1.** Occurring or belonging to the era before the Flood. Genesis 7, 8. **2. a.** Very old; antiquated. **b.** Old-fashioned; extremely conservative.
~*n.* **1.** A person or thing existing before the Flood. **2.** A very old person. [From ANTE- + Latin *diluvium,* flood (see **diluvial**).]

an·te·fix (ánti-fiks) *n., pl.* **-fixes** or **-fixa** (-fiksə). *Architecture.* An upright ornament along the eaves of a tiled roof to conceal the joints between the rows of tiles. [Latin *antefīxus,* "fastened before" (the joints) : *ante-,* before + *fīxus,* past participle of *fīgere,* to fasten.] —**an·te·fix·al** (-fiksəl) *adj.*

an·te·lope (ántilōp) *n., pl.* **-lopes** or collectively **antelope. 1.** Any of various slender, swift-running, long-horned ruminants of the family Bovidae, of Africa and Asia; especially, any member of the subfamily Antilopinae. **2.** An animal that resembles a true antelope, such as the **pronghorn** *(see).* **3.** Leather made from the hide of an antelope. [Middle English, from Old French *antelop,* a fabulous oriental beast, from Medieval Latin *anthalopus,* from Late Greek *antholops†.*]

an·te·me·rid·i·an (ántimə-ríddi-ən) *adj.* Of, pertaining to, or taking place in the morning. [Latin *antemerīdiānus : ante-,* before + *merīdiānus,* MERIDIAN.]

an·te me·rid·i·em (ánti məriddi-əm) *adv. Abbr.* **a.m., A.M.** Before noon. Used chiefly in the abbreviated form to specify the hour: *10.30 a.m.* [Latin : *ante-,* before + *merīdiēs,* midday, noon (see **meridian**).]

an·te mor·tem (ánti mór-təm, -tem) *adv. Latin.* Before death. —**an·te-mor·tem, an·te·mor·tem** *adj.*

an·te·na·tal (ánti-náyt'l) *adj.* **1.** Before birth; prenatal. **2.** Pertaining to or occurring during the period of pregnancy: *an antenatal clinic.*
~*n. Informal.* A medical examination of a pregnant woman.

an·ten·na (an-ténnə) *n., pl.* **-tennae** (-ténnee) (for sense 1) or **-nas** (for sense 2). **1.** One of the paired, flexible, jointed sensory appendages on the head of an insect, myriapod, or crustacean. **2.** *Abbr.* **ant.** An **aerial** *(see).* [Medieval Latin, from Latin *antemna,* *antenna†,* sail yard.] —**an·ten·nal** *adj.*

an·ten·nule (an-ténnewl) *n. Zoology.* A small antenna, especially either of the first pair in crustaceans. [French, diminutive of *antenne,* ANTENNA.]

an·te·pen·di·um (ánti-pén-di-əm) *n., pl.* **-dia** (-di-ə). **1.** A hanging for the front of an altar. **2.** A pulpit cloth. [Medieval Latin : Latin *ante-,* in front of + *pendēre,* to hang.]

an·te·pe·nult (ánti-pin-últ, -pen- ‖ *U.S. also* -péenult) *n.* The third syllable from the end in a word; for example, *te* is the antepenult of the word *antepenult.* [Late Latin *antepaenultima,* feminine of *antepaenultimus,* ANTEPENULTIMATE.]

an·te·pe·nul·ti·mate (ánti-pin-últimət, -pen-) *adj.* Third from the end in a series.
~*n.* An antepenult. [Late Latin *antepaenultimus :* Latin ANTE- + *paenultimus,* PENULT.]

an·te·post (ánti-pōst) *adj.* **1.** Made before the runners' numbers are posted on the board. Said of a racing bet. **2.** Occurring in or pertaining to the period before a horse race.

an·te·ri·or (an-téer-i-ər) *adj.* **1.** Placed in front; located forward. **2.** Prior in time; earlier. **3.** *Zoology.* **a.** Of or pertaining to the head end in lower animals. **b.** Of or pertaining to the front of the body in higher animals and man; ventral. **c.** Located on or near the front of the body or of an organ. **4.** *Botany.* In front of and facing away from the axis or stem. Said of part of a flower or leaf. Compare **posterior.** [Latin, comparative of *ante,* before.] —**an·te·ri·or·i·ty** (-órrəti) *n.* —**an·te·ri·or·ly** *adv.*

an·te·room (ánti-róom, -rŏŏm) *n.* A small room, leading into a larger room, that is often used as a waiting room; antechamber.

ant·he·li·on (an-thée-li-ən ‖ ant-hée-) *n., pl.* **-lia** (-li-ə) or **-ons.** A luminous, white, halo-like area occasionally seen in the sky opposite the Sun on the **parhelic circle** *(see).* [Greek *anthēlion,* from *anthēlios,* opposite the Sun : *ant(i)-,* opposite + *hēlios,* Sun.]

an·thel·min·tic (án-thel-mín-tik ‖ ánt-hel-) *adj.* Also **an·thel·min·thic** (-thik). Acting to expel or destroy intestinal worms.
~*n.* An anthelmintic remedy; a vermifuge. [ANT(I)- + Greek *helmins* (stem *helminth-),* worm.]

an·them (án-thəm, -them) *n.* **1.** A song of praise or loyalty, as to a nation. **2.** A choral composition, often set to words from the Bible. **3.** A religious chant sung in alternation as part of a church service. [Middle English *antem, antefn,* Old English *antefn,* antiphonal song, from Medieval Latin *antiphōna,* from Late Greek, "sung responses", neuter plural of *antiphōnos,* singing in response : *anti-,* opposite + *phōnē,* voice.]

an·the·mi·on (an-thée-mi-ən) *n., pl.* **-mia** (-mi-ə). A pattern of honeysuckle, lotus, or palm leaves in a radiating cluster, used especially as a motif in ancient Greek art and architecture. [Greek, diminutive of *anthemon,* name of a plant, from *anthos,* flower.]

an·ther (ánthər) *n. Botany.* The organ that forms the upper end of a stamen, and that produces and discharges pollen. [New Latin *an-*

thera, from Medieval Latin *anthēra,* pollen, from Latin, medicine composed of flowers, from Greek *anthēros,* flowery, from *anthos,* flower.] **—an·ther·al** *adj.*

an·ther·id·i·um (ánthə-ríd-i-əm) *n., pl.* **-ia** (-i-ə). *Botany.* An organ that produces male gametes in the algae, fungi, mosses, and ferns. Compare **archegonium.** [New Latin : *anthera,* ANTHER + -IDIUM.] **—an·ther·id·i·al** *adj.*

an·ther·o·zo·id (ánthərə-zṓ-id, -zoyd) *n. Botany.* A male gamete, usually produced by an antheridium. [ANTHER + ZO(O)ID.]

an·the·sis (an-thée-siss) *n. Botany.* The blooming or time of full bloom of a plant. [New Latin, from Greek *anthēsis,* from *anthein,* to bloom, from *anthos,* flower.]

ant hill *n.* **1.** A mound formed by ants or termites in digging or building a nest. **2.** Anything suggestive of this, such as a teeming city or an overcrowded building. Also called "ant heap".

antho– *comb. form. Botany.* Indicates a plant or flower; for example, **anthocyanin.** [Greek *anthos,* blossom, flower.]

an·tho·cy·a·nin (ánthō-sī́-ənin) *n.* Any of a class of water-soluble pigments, found in the sap of certain plants, that impart red, purple, or blue colouring to flowers, fruits, and autumn leaves. [ANTHO- + CYANIN(E).]

an·tho·di·um (an-thṓ-di-əm) *n., pl.* **-dia** (-di-ə). *Botany.* A **capitulum** (*see*). [New Latin, from Greek *anthōdēs,* flower-like : ANTHO- + -OID.]

an·thol·ogise, an·thol·o·gize (an-thóllə-jīz) *intr. & tr.v.* **-gised, -gising, -gises.** To compile or include in an anthology.

an·thol·o·gy (an-thóllə-ji) *n., pl.* **-gies. 1.** A collection of literary pieces, such as poems, short stories, or plays, usually suggesting a common theme. **2.** Any collection of works of art, such as paintings, based on a specific period, theme, or subject. [New Latin *anthologia,* from Medieval Greek, from Greek, "flower gathering", a collection : ANTHO- + -LOGY.] **—an·tho·lo·gi·cal** (ánthə-lójik'l) *adj.* **—an·tho·lo·gist** *n.*

An·tho·ny (ántəni ‖ ánthəni), **Saint** (*c.* 251–356). Egyptian hermit and monk, known as St. Anthony of Egypt and St. Anthony the Abbot. He forswore a wealthy inheritance and went into the desert to become a hermit. Although he wrote no rule and founded no order he is considered to be the founder of Christian monasticism.

Anthony of Padua, Saint (1195–1231). Portuguese friar. The most celebrated follower of St. Francis of Assisi. He gained a reputation as a miracle worker before his death in Padua.

Anthony, Susan Brownell (1820–1906). U.S. feminist leader and suffragette. She played a major part in getting the first legislation passed giving married women legal rights over their children, property, and wages. In 1869, with Elizabeth Stanton, she founded the National American Woman Suffrage Association.

-anthous *adj. comb. form.* Indicates a flower; for example, **ananthous.** [New Latin *-anthus,* from Greek *anthos,* flower.]

an·tho·zo·an (ánthə-zṓ-ən) *n.* Any of various marine organisms of the class Anthozoa, growing singly or in colonies, and including the corals and sea anemones. Also called "actinozoan". [New Latin *Anthozoa,* "flower-like organisms" : ANTHO- + -ZOA.] **—an·tho·zo·an, an·tho·zo·ic** *adj.*

an·thra·cene (ánthrə-seen) *n.* A crystalline tricyclic hydrocarbon, $C_6H_4(CH)_2C_6H_4$, extracted from coal tar and used in the manufacture of dyes and organic chemicals. [Greek *anthrax* (stem *anthrak-*), ANTHRAX + -ENE.]

an·thra·cite (ánthrə-sīt) *n.* A hard coal containing more than 85 per cent of carbon and little volatile matter, that burns with a clean flame. Also called "hard coal". [Greek *anthrakitēs,* a kind of coal, from ANTHRAX.] **—an·thra·cit·ic** (-síttik) *adj.*

an·thrac·nose (an-thrák-nōss) *n.* Any of several diseases of plants caused by fungi and characterised by black spots on the leaves, twigs, or fruit. [French : Greek *anthrax,* charcoal, carbuncle, ANTHRAX + Greek *nosos,* disease.]

an·thrax (án-thraks) *n., pl.* **-thraces** (-thrə-seez). **1.** *Pathology.* An infectious, often fatal disease of warm-blooded animals, especially of cattle and sheep, caused by the bacterium *Bacillus anthracis.* It is transmissible to man, capable of affecting various organs, and especially characterised by malignant ulcers. **2.** A lesion caused by this disease. [Latin, virulent ulcer, from Greek *anthrax†,* charcoal, carbuncle, pustule.]

anthrop. anthropological; anthropology.

an·throp·ic (an-thróppik) *adj.* Of or pertaining to humans or the era of human life. [Greek *anthrōpikos,* from *anthrōpos,* human being.]

anthropo–, anthrop– *comb. form.* Indicates man or human; for example, **anthropoid, anthroposophy.** [From Greek *anthrōpos,* human being.]

an·thro·po·cen·tric (ánthrə-pō-séntrik, -pə-) *adj.* **1.** Regarding the human race as the central fact of the universe. **2.** Interpreting reality exclusively in terms of human values and experience. **—an·thro·po·cen·tri·ci·ty** (-sen-tríssəti), **an·thro·po·cen·trism** (-séntriz'm) *n.*

an·thro·po·gen·e·sis (ánthrə-pō-jénnə-siss, -pə-) *n.* The scientific study of the origin of man. [New Latin : ANTHROPO- + -GENESIS.] **—an·thro·po·ge·ne·tic** (-jə-néttik) *adj.*

an·thro·po·gen·ic (ánthrə-pō-jénnik, -pə-). **1.** Anthropogenetic. **2.** Originating as a result of human activity. [ANTHROPO- + -GENIC.]

an·thro·po·ge·og·ra·phy (ánthrə-pō-jee-óggrəfi) *n.* **1.** The science of the geographical distribution of human communities. **3. Human geography** (*see*).

an·thro·poid (ánthrə-poyd) *adj.* **1.** Resembling man. Said of the tailless semi-erect apes of the family Pongidae, which includes gorillas, chimpanzees, orang-utans, and gibbons. **2.** Resembling or characteristic of an ape; apelike. **3.** Shaped like a human being: *an anthropoid sarcophagus.*

~*n.* **1.** Any member of the family Pongidae. Also called "anthropoid ape", "pongid". **2.** A person resembling an ape in appearance, behaviour, or intelligence. [Greek *anthrōpoeidēs* : ANTHROP(O)- + -OID.] **—an·thro·poi·dal** (-póyd'l) *adj.*

an·thro·pol·o·gy (ánthrə-póllǝji) *n. Abbr.* **anthrop., anthropol.** The scientific study of the origin and of the physical, social, and cultural development and behaviour of mankind. [New Latin *anthropologia* : ANTHROPO- + -LOGY.] **—an·thro·po·log·ic** (-pǝ-lójik), **an·thro·po·log·i·cal** (-pǝ-lóji-k'l) *adj.* **—an·thro·po·log·i·cal·ly** *adv.* **—an·thro·pol·o·gist** (-póllǝjist) *n.*

an·thro·pom·e·try (ánthrə-pómmətri) *n.* The study of or technique for measuring the various sizes and proportions of the human body, for use in anthropological classification and comparison. [ANTHROPO- + -METRY.] **—an·thro·po·met·ric** (-pō-métrik, -pə-), **an·thro·po·met·ri·cal** *adj.* **—an·thro·po·met·ri·cal·ly** *adv.*

an·thro·po·mor·phism (ánthrə-pō-mórfiz'm, -pə-) *n.* The attribution of human form, motivation, characteristics, or behaviour to inanimate objects, animals, gods, or natural phenomena. **—an·thro·po·mor·phic** *adj.* **—an·thro·po·mor·phise** *tr.v.*

an·thro·po·mor·phous (ánthrə-pō-mórfəss, -pə-) *adj.* **1.** Having or suggesting human form and appearance. **2.** Of or pertaining to anthropomorphism. [Greek *anthrōpomorphos* : ANTHROPO- + -MORPHOUS.] **—an·thro·po·mor·phous·ly** *adv.*

an·thro·pop·a·thism (ánthrə-póppə-thiz'm) *n.* The attribution of human feelings to nonhuman beings, such as gods, animals, inanimate objects, or natural phenomena. [From Greek *anthrōpopathēs,* with human feelings : ANTHROPO- + *pathos,* feeling (see **-pathy**).] **—an·thro·po·pa·thic** (-pō-páthik, -pə-) *adj.*

an·thro·poph·a·gi (ánthrə-póffə-jī, -gī) *pl.n. Singular* **-gus** (-gəss). Eaters of human flesh; cannibals. [Latin *anthrōpophagī,* plural of *anthrōpophagus,* from Greek *anthrōpophagos,* man-eating : ANTHROPO- + -PHAGOUS.] **—an·thro·po·phag·ic** (-pō-fájik, -pə-), **an·thro·poph·a·gous** (-póffəgəss) *adj.* **—an·thro·poph·a·gy** (-póffəji) *n.*

an·thro·pos·o·phy (ánthrə-póssəfi) *n.* A 20th-century religious system of thought derived from theosophy by Rudolph Steiner, which centres on human beings rather than God and concentrates on the development of all the human faculties. [ANTHROPO- + -SOPHY.] **—an·thro·po·soph·ic** (-pō-sóffik, -pə-) *adj.* **—an·thro·pos·o·phist** (-póssəfist) *n.*

-anthropus *n. comb. form.* Indicates man; for example, **Meganthropus.** [New Latin, from Greek *anthrōpos,* human being.]

an·thur·i·um (an-théwr-i-əm ‖ -thoór-) *n.* Any of various tropical American plants of the genus *Anthurium,* many of which are cultivated as potted plants for their showy foliage. [New Latin *Anthurium,* "flower-tail" : ANTH(O)- + Greek *oura,* tail.]

an·ti (ánti ‖ *U.S. also* ántī) *n., pl.* **-tis.** *Informal.* A person who is opposed to a party, policy, proposal, or the like. [Noun use of ANTI-.] **—an·ti** *adj.*

anti– (ánti- ‖ *U.S. also* ántī) **ant–** (ant-) *prefix.* Indicates: **1. a.** Opposition to; for example, **antismoking, antiabortion. b.** Hostility towards; for example, **anti-Semitic, antiwoman. 2.** Opposite to, especially in character; for example, **anticlimax, antihero. 3.** Reciprocal correspondence to; for example, **antilogarithm. 4.** Converse operation to; for example, **anticyclone, anticlockwise. 5.** Action against, prevention of; for example, **antifreeze, antidepressant.** *Note:* Many compounds other than those entered here may be formed with *anti-.* In forming compounds, *anti-* is normally joined to the following element without a space or hyphen: *antibody.* However, if the second element begins with a capital letter, it is separated with a hyphen: *anti-British.* It is also preferable to use the hyphen if the second element begins with i: *anti-intellectual.* The hyphen may always be used to aid clarity, as in nonce coinages: *anti-antivivisection,* or when the compound brings together three or more vowels: *anti-aesthetic.* [In borrowed Greek compounds *anti-* indicates : **1.** Over against, opposite, as in **antichrist. 2.** Against, opposite, as in **antipathy. 3.** Responding to, as in **antiphon. 4.** Instead of, as in **antonomasia. 5.** Mirroring, counterfeiting, as in **antirrhinum.** Greek, from *anti,* opposite, against.]

an·ti·air·craft (ánti-aír-kraaft ‖ -kraft) *adj. Abbr.* **A.A.** Defensive, especially from a surface position, against aircraft or missile attack. ~*n.* An antiaircraft weapon.

an·ti·bal·lis·tic missile (ánti-bə-lístik) *n. Abbr.* **ABM** A defensive missile designed to intercept and destroy a ballistic missile in flight.

an·ti·bar·y·on (ánti-baír-i-on) *n.* The antiparticle of the **baryon** (*see*).

An·tibes (oN-téeb). Fashionable resort on the French Riviera, lying across the Bay of Angels from Nice. It is the centre of one of Europe's largest flower-producing regions and is noted for the collection of Picasso paintings in the Grimaldi Museum.

an·ti·bi·o·sis (ánti-bī́-ō-siss) *n.* An association between two or more organisms, particularly microorganisms, that is injurious to one of them, due to the production of an antibiotic by the others. Compare **symbiosis.** [New Latin : ANTI- + -BIOSIS.]

an·ti·bi·ot·ic (ánti-bī-óttik) *n.* Any of various substances, such as penicillin and streptomycin, produced by certain fungi, bacteria, and similar organisms, that are effective in inhibiting the growth of or destroying microorganisms, and are widely used in the prevention and treatment of diseases.

~*adj.* **1.** Of or pertaining to antibiotics. **2.** Of or pertaining to antibiosis. [New Latin *antibioticus* : ANTI- + BIOTIC.] —**an·ti·bi·ot·ic·al·ly** *adv.*

an·ti·bod·y (ánti-bodi) *n., pl.* -**ies.** 1. Any of various proteins in the blood that are generated in reaction to antigens, which they neutralise, thus producing immunity against infections. 2. An object composed of antimatter. [20th century : translation of German *Antikörper* : ANTI- + *Körper*, body.]

an·tic (ántik) *n.* 1. *Often plural.* A ludicrous or extravagant act or gesture; a caper; a prank. 2. *Archaic.* A clown; a jester. —*adj. Archaic.* Ludicrous; odd; fantastic. [Italian *antico,* "grotesque", "ancient" (originally with reference to fantastic sculptures found in ancient Roman ruins, hence, anything fantastic or grotesque), from Latin *antiquus,* ANTIQUE.]

an·ti·cat·a·lyst (ánti-káttəlist) *n. Chemistry.* An inhibitor (see).

an·ti·cath·ode (ánti-káthōd) *n.* An electrode that is the target in a cathode-ray tube, especially in an X-ray tube.

an·ti·chlor (ánti-klawr || -klōr) *n.* A substance, such as sodium thiosulphate, used to neutralise the excess chlorine or hypochlorite left after bleaching textiles, fibre, or paper pulp. [ANTI- + CHLOR(INE).] —**anti·chlo·ristic** (-ístik) *adj.*

an·ti·cho·lin·er·gic (ánti-kóllin-érjik || -kōlən-) *adj.* Opposing or antagonistic to the physiological action of parasympathetic or other cholinergic nerve fibres. —*n.* A drug that blocks nerve impulses.

an·ti·cho·lin·es·ter·ase (ánti-kóllin-éstər-ayz || -ayss) *n.* Any substance that inhibits the activity of cholinesterase (see).

an·ti·christ (ánti-krīst) *n.* 1. An enemy of Christ or Christianity. 2. *Capital* A. The great antagonist who was expected by the early Church to take over the world but to be conquered for ever by Christ at the Second Coming. 3. A false Christ. [Middle English *Antecrist,* from Old French, from Late Latin *Antichrīstus,* from Greek *Antikhristos* (I John 2:18) : ANTI- + *Khristos,* CHRIST.]

an·tic·i·pant (an-tíssipənt) *adj.* 1. Coming or acting in advance. 2. Expectant.

an·tic·i·pate (an-tíssi-payt) *tr.v.* -**pated,** -**pating,** -**pates.** 1. To sense or realise beforehand; foresee. 2. To look forward to as likely or certain; expect. 3. To act in advance so as to prevent or counter; forestall. 4. To foresee and fulfil or satisfy in advance. 5. To cause to happen in advance; accelerate; precipitate. 6. To consider prematurely; bring up before the proper time. 7. To use in advance, as income not yet available. 8. To pay (a debt) before it is due. —See Synonyms at **expect.** [Latin *anticipāre,* to take before : *ante-,* before + *capere,* to take.] —**an·tic·i·pator** (-paytər) *n.* —**an·tic·i·pa·tory** (-pətri, -paytəri || -páytəri), **an·tic·i·pa·tive** (-paytiv, -pətiv) *adj.* —**an·tic·i·pa·tive·ly** *adv.*

Usage: There is no problem over the use of *anticipate* in the senses "forestall" and "consider prematurely", but difficulties do arise with the general senses of "expect" or "look forward to". It is one thing, for example, to look forward to marriage; quite another to anticipate it.

an·tic·i·pa·tion (an-tíssi-páysh'n) *n.* 1. The act of anticipating. 2. The act or state of looking forward to something. 3. Foreknowledge; intuition; premonition. 4. *Law.* The use or assignment of funds from a trust fund before legitimately available for use. 5. *Music.* The introduction of a note or notes before the chord to which they belong.

an·ti·cler·i·cal (ánti-klérrik'l) *adj.* Opposed to the influence and power of the clergy, especially in political affairs. —**an·ti·cler·i·cal** *n.* —**an·ti·cler·i·cal·ism** *n.*

an·ti·cli·max (ánti-klímaks) *n.* 1. A decline viewed in disappointing contrast with a previous rise: *the anticlimax of a brilliant career.* 2. Something trivial or commonplace coming to conclude a series of significant events. 3. *Rhetoric.* a. A sudden descent from the impressive or significant to the ludicrous or inconsequential; bathos. b. An instance of this; for example, *For God, for country, and for my dog.* —**an·ti·cli·mac·tic** (-klī-máktik) *adj.* —**an·ti·cli·mac·ti·cal·ly** *adv.*

an·ti·cli·nal (ánti-klín'l) *adj.* Sloping downwards in opposite directions, as an anticline does. [ANTI- + -CLINAL.]

an·ti·cline (ánti-klīn) *n. Geology.* A fold with strata sloping downwards on both sides from a common crest. [ANTI- + -CLINE.]

an·ti·clock·wise (ánti-klók-wīz) *adv. British.* In a direction opposite to that of the hands of a clock. Also *U.S.* "counterclockwise". —**an·ti·clock·wise** *adj.*

an·ti·co·ag·u·lant (ánti-kō-ággwələnt) *n.* Any substance that suppresses or counteracts coagulation, especially of the blood. —*adj.* Acting as an anticoagulant.

an·ti·co·in·ci·dence gate (ánti-kō-ínssidənss) *n.* An electronic circuit that produces an output signal if one but not both of its input wires receives a signal within a specific interval of time.

an·ti·col·our (ánti-kullər) *n. Physics.* The colour (see) of an antiparticle in quantum chromodynamics.

an·ti·con·vul·sant (ánti-kən-vúlss'nt || -kon-) *n.* Any drug that reduces or prevents fits suffered in various forms of epilepsy. —*adj.* Also **an·ti·con·vul·sive** (-iv). Acting as an anticonvulsant.

an·ti·cy·clone (ánti-síklōn) *n.* An extensive system of winds spiralling outwards from a high-pressure centre, and circling clockwise in the Northern Hemisphere and anticlockwise in the Southern Hemisphere. —**an·ti·cy·clonic** (-sī-klónnik) *adj.*

an·ti·de·pres·sant (ánti-di-préss'nt) *n.* Any drug that relieves the symptoms of depression. —**an·ti·de·pres·sant, an·ti·de·pres·sive** *adj.*

an·ti·di·ur·et·ic hormone (ánti-dī-yoor-éttik) *n.* **Abbr. ADH** A hormone, **vasopressin** (see).

an·ti·dote (ánti-dōt) *n.* 1. A remedy or other agent to counteract or neutralise the effects of a poison. 2. Anything that relieves or counteracts an unwanted condition. [Latin *antidotum,* from Greek *antidoton,* from *antididonai,* to give as a remedy against : ANTI- + *didonai,* to give.] —**an·ti·do·tal** (-dōt'l) *adj.* —**an·ti·do·tal·ly** *adv.*

an·ti·e·lec·tron (ánti-i-léktron) *n.* A positron (see).

an·ti·en·zyme (ánti-én-zīm) *n.* A substance that neutralises or counteracts an enzyme. —**an·ti·en·zy·matic** (-zī-máttik, -zi-), **an·ti·en·zy·mic** (-zímik) *adj.*

an·ti·feb·rile (ánti-féeb-rīl, -féb- || *U.S. also* -rəl) *adj.* Able to reduce fever; antipyretic. —*n.* An antifebrile drug or agent; an antipyretic.

an·ti·fer·ro·mag·ne·tism (ánti-férrō-mágnit-iz'm) *n. Physics.* The property of certain substances that have relative permeabilities as of paramagnetic substances but behave as ferromagnetic substances when their temperature is changed.

an·ti·foul·ing (ánti-fówling) *adj.* Designating an agent designed to prevent build-up on surfaces, clogging of valves, and the like.

antifouling paint *n.* A paint applied to ships' bottoms to prevent the growth of barnacles and other marine organisms.

an·ti·freeze (ánti-freez) *n.* A substance, often a liquid such as ethylene glycol or alcohol, mixed with another liquid to lower the freezing point of the latter; especially, the liquid added to the cooling water of an internal-combustion engine to prevent freezing.

an·ti·g (ánti-jée) *adj.* Tending to counteract or protect against gravity: *an anti-g suit.* —*n.* Antigravity.

an·ti·gen (ánti-jən) *n.* Any substance that, when introduced into the body, stimulates the production of an antibody. [ANTI- + -GEN.] —**an·ti·gen·ic** (-jénnik) *adj.* —**an·ti·gen·i·cal·ly** *adv.* —**an·ti·ge·nic·i·ty** (-jə-níssəti) *n.*

An·tig·o·ne (an-tíggəni) *Greek Mythology.* The daughter of Oedipus and Jocasta, who performed funeral rites over the body of her brother Polynices in defiance of her uncle Creon.

an·ti·grav·i·ty (ánti-grávvəti) *n.* A supposed effect involving the neutralisation of a gravitational field so as to produce weightlessness. Also called "anti-g".

An·ti·gua and Barbuda (an-téegə. *Note: spelling pronunciations, such as* an-tíggewə *or* an-téegwə *are not used by those familiar with the island.*) Island state in the Leeward Islands of the Caribbean. Discovered by Columbus (1493), it became a British colony (1667), and was a British associated state from 1967 until independence in 1981. The islands of Redonda (uninhabited) and Barbuda (population 1500) are included in its territory. Antigua is a communications and business centre for the Caribbean area. Formerly dependent on sugar, it now relies on tourism and cotton. Area, 442 square kilometres (171 square miles). Population, 70,000. Capital, St. John's. —See map at **Latin America.** —**An·ti·guan** (an-téegən) *adj. & n.*

an·ti·ha·la·tion backing (ánti-hə-láysh'n) *n.* A backing applied to a photographic film, consisting of a dye or pigment that absorbs light, to prevent halation that would otherwise occur as a result of light being reflected back into the emulsion.

an·ti·he·ro (ánti-heer-ō) *n.* A main character in a dramatic or literary work who is characterised by a lack of traditional heroic qualities.

an·ti·his·ta·mine (ánti-hístə-meen, -min) *n.* Any of various drugs used to reduce physiological effects associated with histamine production in allergies and colds. —**an·ti·his·ta·min·ic** (-mínnik) *adj.*

an·ti·knock (ánti-nók) *n.* A substance, such as tetraethyl lead, added to petrol to reduce engine knock.

An·ti·Leb·a·non Mountains (ánti-lébbə-nən || -non). Range of mountains on the Lebanon-Syria border. The highest peak, Mount Hermon, rises to 2 814 metres (9,232 feet).

an·ti·lep·ton (ánti-lépton) *n. Physics.* The antiparticle of any **lepton** (see).

An·til·les (an-tílleez). Two groups of islands in the West Indies. The Greater Antilles include Cuba, Haiti, the Dominican Republic, Jamaica, and Puerto Rico; the Lesser Antilles include the Leeward Islands, the Windward Islands, the Netherlands Antilles, Trinidad and Tobago, and Barbados.

an·ti·log·a·rithm (ánti-lóggə-rith'm) *n.* The number for which a given logarithm stands; for example, where log *x* equals *y, x* is the antilogarithm of *y.* Also called "antilog". See **logarithm.** —**an·ti·log·a·rith·mic** (-ríthmik) *adj.*

an·ti·ma·cas·sar (ánti-mə-kássər) *n.* A protective or decorative covering for the backs of chairs and sofas where the head normally rests. [ANTI- + MACASSAR (OIL).]

an·ti·mag·net·ic (ánti-mag-néttik) *adj.* Impervious to the effect of a magnetic field; magnetisation-resistant. Said especially of watch movements.

an·ti·ma·lar·i·al (ánti-mə-laír-i-əl) *adj.* Effective against malaria. —*n.* An antimalarial drug.

an·ti·mat·ter (ánti-mattər) *n.* A hypothetical form of matter consisting of antiparticles and having positron-surrounded nuclei composed of antiprotons and antineutrons. See **antiparticle.**

an·ti·mere (ánti-meer) *n. Biology.* A part or division corresponding to an opposite or similar part in an organism characterised by bilateral or radial symmetry. Also called "actinomere". [ANTI- + -MERE.] —**an·ti·mer·ic** (-mérrik) *adj.*

an·ti·mi·cro·bi·al (ánti-mī-krōbi-əl) *adj.* Capable of destroying or suppressing the growth of microorganisms. —*n.* An antimicrobial agent.

an·ti·mis·sile (ánti-miss-īl, -míss- || *U.S.* -əl) *n.* A missile designed to intercept and destroy another missile in flight.

an·ti·mo·ni·al (ánti-mṓni-əl) *adj.* Of or containing antimony.
~*n.* A medicine with antimony as an ingredient.

an·ti·mo·ny (ánti-məni || *U.S.* -mṓni) *n. Symbol* **Sb** A metallic element having four allotropic forms the most common of which is a hard, extremely brittle, lustrous, silver-white, crystalline material. It is used in a wide variety of alloys, especially with lead in battery plates, and in the manufacture of flame-proofing compounds, paints, semiconductor devices, and ceramic products. Atomic number 51, atomic weight 121.75, melting point 630.5°C, boiling point 1,380°C, relative density 6.684, valencies 3, 5. [Middle English, from Medieval Latin *antimonium†.*]

antimony glance *n.* An antimony ore, **stibnite** *(see).*

an·ti·ne·o·plas·tic (ánti-nee-ō-plástik) *adj.* Inhibiting the growth or spread of malignant tumours.

an·ti·neu·tri·no (ánti-new-treenō || -nṓo-) *n., pl.* **-nos.** *Physics.* The **antiparticle** *(see)* of the neutrino.

an·ti·neu·tron (ánti-néw-tron || -nṓo-) *n. Symbol* **n̄** *Physics.* The **antiparticle** *(see)* of the neutron.

ant·ing (ánting) *n.* The putting or rubbing by some birds of ants into their plumage, possibly to repel parasites.

an·ti·node (ánti-nōd) *n. Physics.* The region or point of maximum amplitude between adjacent **nodes** *(see).*

an·ti·no·mi·an (ánti-nṓmi-ən) *n. Theology.* A member of any Christian sect holding that faith alone is sufficient for salvation and that it is not necessary to obey any moral law.
~*adj.* 1. Of or pertaining to such a sect or doctrine. 2. Opposed to universal applicability of moral laws. [From Medieval Latin *antinomus,* from Greek : ANTI- + *nomos,* law.] **—an·ti·no·mi·an·ism** *n.*

an·tin·o·my (an-tínnəmi) *n., pl.* **-mies.** 1. Opposition or contradiction, especially between two laws or rules. 2. Contradiction between propositions that seem equally necessary and reasonable; a paradox. [Latin *antinomia,* from Greek : ANTI- + *nomos,* law.]

an·ti·nu·cle·on (ánti-néw-kli-on || -nṓo-) *n. Physics.* An antiproton or an antineutron.

An·ti·och (ánti-ok). Turkish **An·ta·kya** (an-taák-yə). Ancient city in southeastern Turkey, lying on the river Orontes near its mouth on the Mediterranean. St. Paul preached there and followers of Christ first adopted the name "Christian" there.

an·ti·ox·i·dant (ánti-óksidənt) *n.* A chemical compound or substance that inhibits oxidation. **—an·ti·ox·i·dant** *adj.*

an·ti·par·al·lel (ánti-parrə-lel) *adj.* 1. *Physics.* Parallel but rotating or pointing in opposite directions: *antiparallel spin.* 2. *Mathematics.* **a.** Designating two parallel lines that cut another pair of parallel lines in such a way that the interior opposite angles of the quadrilateral so formed are supplementary. **b.** Having the same magnitude but opposite senses. Said of vectors. Compare **parallel.**

an·ti·par·ti·cle (ánti-paartik'l, -pártik'l) *n.* A subatomic particle, such as a positron, antiproton, or antineutron, having the same mass, average lifetime, spin, magnitude of magnetic moment, and magnitude of electric charge as the particle to which it corresponds, but having the opposite sign of electric charge, opposite intrinsic parity, and opposite direction of magnetic moment. See **annihilation.**

an·ti·pas·to (ánti-páss-tō, -paáss- || *U.S.* aánti-) *n., pl.* **-tos** or **-ti** (-tee, -ti). *Italian.* An appetiser; an hors d'oeuvre. [Italian : *anti-* (from Latin ANTE- before) + *pasto,* food, from Latin *pastus,* past participle of *pascere,* to feed.]

An·tip·a·ter (an-típpətər) (c.397-c.319 B.C.). Macedonian general and ruler. He acted as regent of Macedonia from 334 B.C. to 323, during Alexander the Great's Asian campaign, and again from 321 to 319 for the mentally deficient Philip III and the infant Alexander IV. After his death the centralised unity of the Macedonian empire quickly disintegrated.

an·ti·pa·thet·ic (ánti-pə-théttik) *adj.* Also **an·ti·pa·thet·i·cal** (-thét-tik'l) 1. Having an inherent feeling of aversion, repugnance, or opposition. Often used with *to: antipathetic to new ideas.* 2. Causing a feeling of antipathy. **—an·ti·pa·thet·i·cal·ly** *adv.*

an·tip·a·thy (an-típpəthi) *n., pl.* **-thies.** 1. A strong feeling of aversion or opposition. 2. The object of this feeling. [Latin *antipathia,* from Greek *antipatheia,* from *antipathēs,* of opposite feelings : ANTI- (opposite) + *pathos,* feeling (see **-pathy**).]

an·ti·pe·ri·od·ic (ánti-péer-i-óddik) *adj.* Preventing regular recurrence of disease or fever.
~*n.* An antiperiodic drug.

an·ti·per·i·stal·sis (ánti-perri-stál-siss) *n. Physiology.* Contractions of the alimentary canal that push food back towards the mouth. Compare **peristalsis.**

an·ti·per·son·nel (ánti-pérssə-nél) *adj. Abbr.* **AP** *Military.* Designed to inflict casualties on the military personnel or civilian population of an enemy country rather than on equipment or arms.

an·ti·per·spi·rant (ánti-pérsspərənt) *n.* A preparation applied to the skin to reduce or prevent perspiration.

an·ti·phlo·gis·tic (ánti-flə-jístik, -flō-) *adj.* Reducing inflammation. **—an·ti·phlo·gis·tic** *n.*

an·ti·phon (ánti-fən, -fon) *n.* 1. A plainsong setting of words, usually from the Bible, sung as a response as part of a liturgy. 2. A plainsong setting of a short liturgical text chanted or sung as a response before or after a psalm, psalm verse, or canticle. 3. A response; an answer: *a resounding antiphon of dissent.* [Late Latin *antiphona,* from Greek *antiphōna,* sung responses, ANTHEM.]

an·tiph·o·nal (an-tíff'n-əl) *adj.* 1. Pertaining to or resembling an an-

tiphon. 2. Sung or played as a response or in alternation (as in antiphony).
~*n.* Variant of **antiphonary.** **—an·tiph·o·nal·ly** *adv.*

an·tiph·o·nar·y (an-tíff'n-əri || *U.S.* -erri) *n., pl.* **-ies.** Also **an·tiph·o·nal** (-'l). A bound collection of antiphons, especially of the responsive choral parts of the divine office.

an·tiph·o·ny (an-tíff'n-i) *n., pl.* **-nies.** 1. Responsive or antiphonal singing or chanting. 2. A composition that is sung in alternation or responsively; an antiphon. 3. A musical or other sound effect that answers or echoes another.

an·tiph·ra·sis (an-tíffrə-siss) *n.* The use of a word in a sense contrary to its normal or accepted meaning for ironic or humorous effect; for example, *He is just a mere baby of thirty years.* [Late Latin, from Greek, from *antiphrazein,* "to speak by using the opposite sense": *anti-,* opposite + *phrazein,* to speak.]

an·tip·o·dal (an-típpəd'l) *adj.* 1. Of, pertaining to, or situated on the opposite side or opposite sides of the Earth or Moon. 2. Diametrically opposed; exactly opposite.

an·ti·pode (ánti-pōd) *n.* Also **an·tip·o·des** (an-típpə-deez). A direct or exact opposite or contrary. [Back-formation from ANTIPODES.]

an·tip·o·des (an-típpə-deez) *pl.n.* 1. Any two places or regions that are on opposite sides of the Earth. 2. *Often capital* **A.** Australia and New Zealand. Usually preceded by *the.* 3. *Sometimes used with a singular verb.* Variant of **antipode.** [Middle English, from Latin, from Greek, plural of *antipous* (stem *antipod-*), with the feet opposite : ANTI- + *pous,* foot.] **—an·tip·o·de·an** (-dée-ən) *n. & adj.*

an·ti·pope (ánti-pōp) *n.* A person claiming to be or elected pope in opposition to the one considered to have been chosen by church law. [Middle English, from Old French *antipape,* from Medieval Latin *antipāpa* : ANTI- + *pāpa,* POPE.]

an·ti·pro·ton (ánti-prṓton) *n. Physics.* The **antiparticle** *(see)* of the proton.

an·ti·py·ret·ic (ánti-pīr-éttik) *adj.* Reducing or tending to reduce fever; antifebrile.
~*n.* Medication that reduces fever. **—an·ti·py·re·sis** (-ée-siss) *n.*

an·ti·py·rine (ánti-pír-een) *n.* A white powder, $C_{11}H_{12}N_2O$, used to reduce fever and relieve pain. [German *Antipyrin* (trademark) : ANTI- + PYR(O)- + -INE.]

antiq. 1. antiquarian; antiquary. 2. antiquities; antiquity.

an·ti·quar·i·an (ánti-kwáir-i-ən) *adj. Abbr.* **antiq.** 1. Of or pertaining to antiquaries or the study of antiquities. 2. Dealing in or having to do with old rare books.
~*n.* Variant of **antiquary.** **—an·ti·quar·i·an·ism** *n.*

an·ti·quar·y (ánti-kwəri || -kwerri) *n., pl.* **-ies.** *Abbr.* **antiq.** Also **an·ti·quar·i·an.** A student or collector of or dealer in antiquities or antiques. [Latin *antīquārius,* from adjective, of antiquity, from *antīquus,* ANTIQUE.]

an·ti·quate (ánti-kwayt) *tr.v.* **-quated, -quating, -quates.** 1. To make obsolete or old-fashioned. 2. To antique. [Latin *antiquāre,* to leave in its ancient state, from *antīquus,* ANTIQUE.] **—an·ti·qua·tion** (-kwáysh'n) *n.*

an·ti·quat·ed (ánti-kwaytid) *adj.* 1. So old as to be no longer useful or applicable; outmoded; obsolete: *antiquated laws.* 2. Very old; aged. **—an·ti·quat·ed·ness** *n.*

an·tique (an-téek, án-) *adj.* 1. Belonging to, made in, or typical of an earlier period. 2. Of or belonging to ancient times; especially, of, from, or characteristic of ancient Greece or Rome. 3. Of or dealing in antiques. 4. Old-fashioned. **—See Synonyms at old.**
~*n.* 1. An object having special value because of its age; especially, a piece of furniture or other work of art valued for its workmanship, beauty, and age. 2. The style or manner of ancient times, especially that of ancient Greek or Roman art. Preceded by *the: an admirer of the antique.*
~*tr.v.* **antiqued, -tiquing, -tiques.** To give the appearance of an antique to. [French, from Latin *antīquus,* ancient, former.] **—antique·ly** *adv.* **—an·tique·ness** *n.* **—an·ti·quer** *n.*

an·tiq·ui·ty (an-tíkwəti) *n., pl.* **-ties.** *Abbr.* **antiq.** 1. *Sometimes capital* **A.** Ancient times, especially the times preceding the Middle Ages. 2. The people of ancient times. 3. The quality of being old or ancient; considerable age: *a carving of great antiquity.* 4. *Plural.* Things belonging to or dating from a time long past.

an·ti·ra·chit·ic (ánti-rə-kíttik) *adj.* Curing or preventing rickets.
~*n.* An antirachitic drug or food.

an·tir·rhi·num (ánti-rínəm) *n.* Any plant of the genus *Antirrhinum,* such as a **snapdragon** *(see).* [New Latin, from Greek *antirrhinon,* "plant having snoutlike flowers" : *anti-,* counterfeiting + *rhis†* (stem *rhin-*), nose (see **rhino-**).]

an·ti·scor·bu·tic (ánti-skawr-béwtik) *adj.* Curing or preventing scurvy.
~*n.* A food or drug that cures or prevents scurvy.

an·ti·Sem·ite (ánti-séemit, -sémmīt) *n.* A person who is hostile towards or prejudiced against Jews. **—an·ti·Se·mit·ic** (-si-míttik) *adj.* **—an·ti·Se·mi·tism** (-sémmitiz'm) *n.*

an·ti·sep·sis (ánti-sépsiss) *n.* The destruction of microorganisms that cause disease, fermentation, or putrefaction. Compare **asepsis.**

an·ti·sep·tic (ánti-séptik) *adj.* 1. Of, pertaining to, or designating antisepsis. 2. Capable of producing antisepsis. 3. Thoroughly clean. 4. *Informal.* Devoid of enlivening or enriching qualities; austere; clinical.
~*n.* An antiseptic drug or agent. **—an·ti·sep·ti·cal·ly** *adj.*

an·ti·se·rum (ánti-seer-əm) *n., pl.* **-rums** or **-ra** (-ə). Human or animal serum containing antibodies against at least one antigen, used to treat or provide immunity to an infection.

an·ti·slav·er·y (ánti-sláyvəri) *adj.* Opposed to or against slavery.

an·ti·so·cial (ánti-sósh'l) *adj.* **1.** Shunning the society of others; unsociable. **2.** Upsetting or offensive to other people: *antisocial behaviour.* **3.** Opposed to or interfering with the social order or general welfare of society. **—an·ti·so·cial·ly** *adv.*

an·ti·spas·mod·ic (ánti-spaz-móddik) *adj.* Easing or preventing spasms.
~*n.* An antispasmodic drug.

an·ti·stat·ic (ánti-státtik) *adj.* Of or designating a material or substance that has been treated in such a way that the effects of static electricity are avoided.

an·tis·tro·phe (an-tístrəfi) *n.* **1.** In ancient Greek choral poetry or drama, the movement following and in the same metre as the strophe, sung while the chorus moves in the opposite direction from that of the strophe. **2.** The second stanza, and those like it, in a poem consisting of alternating stanzas in contrasting metric form. [Late Latin, from Greek *antistrophē* : ANTI- + STROPHE.] **—an·ti·stro·phic** (ánti-stróffik) *adj.* **—an·ti·stro·phi·cal·ly** *adv.*

an·ti·sub·ma·rine (ánti-súbmə-réen ‖ -reen) *adj. Abbr.* **AS** Directed against enemy submarines.

an·ti·tank (ánti-tángk) *adj. Abbr.* **AT** Designed or used for combat against tanks or other armoured vehicles.

an·tith·e·sis (an-títhə-siss) *n., pl.* **-ses** (-seez). **1.** Direct contrast; opposition. **2.** The direct or exact opposite: *Despair is the antithesis of hope.* **3. a.** The juxtaposition of sharply contrasting ideas in balanced or parallel words, phrases, or grammatical structures; for example, *They died that we might live.* **b.** The second and contrasting part of such a juxtaposition. **4.** In Hegelian philosophy, the second stage of the **dialectic** process. [Late Latin, from Greek, opposition, from *antitithenai,* to oppose : ANTI- + *tithenai,* to set, place.]

an·ti·thet·i·cal (ánti-théttik'l) *adj.* Also **an·ti·thet·ic** (-théttik). **1.** Pertaining to, of the nature of, or including antithesis. **2.** Directly opposed in every respect. **—See Synonyms at opposite.** [Late Latin *antitheticus,* from Greek *antithetikos,* from *antitithenai,* to oppose. See **antithesis.**] **—an·ti·thet·i·cal·ly** *adv.*

an·ti·tox·ic (ánti-tóksik) *adj.* **1.** Counteracting a toxin or poison. **2.** Of, pertaining to, or constituting an antitoxin.

an·ti·tox·in (ánti-tóksin) *n.* **1.** An antibody formed in response to, and capable of neutralising, a poison of biological origin. **2.** An animal serum containing such antibodies.

an·ti·trades (ánti-traydz) *pl.n.* The westerly winds above the trade winds of the tropics, which become the westerly winds of the middle latitudes.

an·ti·trust (ánti-trúst) *adj. U.S.* Opposing or concerned with the regulation of trusts, cartels, or similar business monopolies.

an·ti·tus·sive (ánti-tússiv) *adj.* Capable of relieving coughing.
~*n.* An antitussive drug.

an·ti·type (ánti-tīp) *n.* One that is foreshadowed or represented by a symbol or earlier type, such as a figure in the New Testament who has a counterpart in the Old Testament. [Medieval Latin *antitypus,* from Greek *antitupos,* "opposite to the die" (hence, anything resembling the impression made by a die or stamp) : *anti-,* opposite + *tupos,* die (see **type**).] **—an·ti·typ·i·cal** (-típpik'l) *adj.*

an·ti·ven·in (ánti-vén-in) *n.* Also **an·ti·ven·ene** (-een), **an·ti·ven·om** (-əm). **1.** An antitoxin active against a particular venom. **2.** An antiserum containing such an antitoxin. [ANTI- + VEN(OM) + -IN.]

ant·ler (ánt-lər) *n.* Either of a pair of hard, bony, deciduous growths, usually elongated and branched, that characteristically grow on the heads of male deer and related animals. [Middle English *aunteler,* from Old French *antoillier,* from Vulgar Latin *anteoculāris* (unattested), "before the eyes" : ANTE- + Latin *oculus,* eye.] **—ant·lered** (-lərd) *adj.*

Ant·li·a (ántli-ə) *n.* A constellation in the Southern Hemisphere near Hydra and Vela. [Latin *antlia,* pump, from Greek *antlia, antlos,* bucket.]

ant lion *n.* Any insect of the family Myrmeleontidae, of which the adults resemble dragonflies; especially, the larva of such an insect, which digs holes to trap ants and other insects for food. Also *U.S.* "doodlebug". [Translation of Greek *murmēko-leōn,* with reference to its large jaws and its prey.]

An·to·nes·cu (ántə-néskōō), **Ion** (1882–1946). Romanian marshal and prime minister. He was chief of staff of the Romanian army, and was appointed prime minister with unlimited powers on September 5, 1940 by King Carol II. For the rest of World War II Antonescu acted as Hitler's puppet and connived at violent pogroms against the Jews. He was executed for his war crimes in 1946.

An·to·nine Wall (ántə-nīn). A defensive Roman frontier in Scotland, which stretched for about 58 kilometres (36 miles) between the Clyde and the Firth of Forth. It was built in A.D. 142 on the orders of the emperor Antoninus Pius. Small traces of the wall remain.

An·to·ni·o·ni (ántō-ni-ṓni), **Michelangelo** (1912–). Italian film director. He developed a highly visual style in which realism was subordinated to a metaphorical treatment of subject. Among his films are *L'Avventura* (1959), *The Red Desert* (1964), *Blow-up* (1966), *Zabriskie Point* (1969), and *Beyond the Clouds* (1995).

Antonius, Marcus. See **Mark Antony.**

an·to·no·ma·si·a (ántə-nə-máyzi-ə, -nō- ‖ *U.S.* -máyzhə) *n.* **1.** The substitution of a title or epithet for a proper name, as in calling a king "His Majesty". **2.** The substitution of a personal name for a common noun to designate a member of a group or class, as in calling a libertine "a Don Juan". [Latin, from Greek, from *antono-*

mazein, to name instead : *ant(i)-,* instead of + *onomazein,* to name, from *onoma,* name.] **—an·to·no·mas·tic** *adj.* **—an·to·no·mas·ti·cal·ly** *adv.*

an·to·nym (ántənim) *n. Abbr.* **ant.** A word having a sense opposite to a sense of another word; for example, *light* is an antonym of *dark.* Compare **synonym.** [ANT(I)- + -ONYM.] **—an·ton·y·mous** (an-tónniməss) *adj.* **—an·ton·y·my** (an-tónnimi) *n.*

an·tre (ántər) *n. Chiefly Poetic.* A cavern or cave. [French, from Latin *antrum,* cave. See **antrum.**]

An·trim (ántrim). A predominantly agricultural county in northeastern Northern Ireland, whose county town is Belfast.

an·trorse (an-tróss ‖ *U.S.* án-trawrss) *adj. Biology.* Directed forwards and upwards. [New Latin *antrorsus* : perhaps blend of ANTERIOR and DEXTRORSE.] **—an·trorse·ly** *adv.*

an·trum (án-trəm) *n., pl.* **-tra** (-trə). A cavity, usually in bone; especially, either of the sinuses in the jaw opening into the nose. [Late Latin, cavity in the body, from Latin, cave, from Greek *antron.*]

Ant·werp (ántwerp). *Flemish* **Ant·wer·pen** (ántwerpə) *French* **An·vers** (ON-váir, *locally also* -váirss). One of Europe's busiest ports, lying on the river Scheldt in north Belgium. It was a trading centre as early as the eighth century, and the world's first stock exchange was founded there in 1460. It has been one of the leading centres of the diamond industry since the 15th century.

A·nu·bis (ə-néw-biss ‖ -nōō-). *Egyptian Mythology.* A jackal-headed god, son of Osiris, who conducted the dead to judgment.

A·nu·ra·dha·pur·a (ə-nóor-ədə-póor-ə, únnōō-ráadə-). Market town in northern Sri Lanka, and the capital of North-Central Province. It was founded in the fifth century B.C. and became the capital of the Sinhalese kingdom, and a major centre of Buddhism.

a·nu·ran (ə-néwr-ən ‖ -noor-) *adj.* Of or belonging to the Anura, an order of amphibians that contains the frogs and the toads; salientian.
~*n.* A frog or toad. Also called "salientian". [New Latin *Anura* : AN- (without) + Greek *oura,* tail.]

an·u·re·sis (ánnewr-ee-siss) *n.* Inability to urinate. Compare **diuresis.** [AN- (without) + Greek *ouresis,* urination, from *ourein,* to urinate, from *ouran,* urine.] **—an·u·retic** (-éttik) *adj.*

a·nu·ri·a (ə-néwr-i-ə, a- ‖ -noor-) *n.* The pathological condition characterised by failure of the kidneys to produce urine. [New Latin : AN- (not) + -URIA.] **—a·nu·ric** *adj.*

a·nu·rous (ə-néwr-əss, ə- ‖ -noor-) *adj.* Having no tail; tailless. [AN- + -UROUS.]

a·nus (áynəss) *n., pl.* **anuses.** The excretory opening at the end of the alimentary canal. [Latin *ānus,* ring.]

an·vil (ánvil) *n.* **1.** A heavy block of iron or steel, with a smooth, flat top on which metals are shaped by hammering. **2.** A part of a tool or device that resembles an anvil in shape or function, such as: **a.** The lower part of a telegraph key. **b.** The flat jaw of a pair of secateurs, against which the cutting jaw acts. **c.** The fixed jaw in a set of calipers, against which the object to be measured is placed. **3.** *Anatomy.* A bone, the **incus** (*see*). [Middle English *anvil(t), anvelt,* Old English *anfealt, anfilt* : *an,* ON + *-fealt,* "beaten".]

anx·i·e·ty (ang-zī́-əti) *n., pl.* **-ties.** **1.** A state of uneasiness and distress about future uncertainties; apprehension; worry; angst. **2.** A cause of such uneasiness; a worry. **3.** *Psychiatry.* Intense fear or dread lacking specific cause. **4.** Eagerness: *his anxiety to go home.* [Latin *anxietās* (stem *anxietāt-*), from *anxius,* ANXIOUS.]
Synonyms: anxiety, worry, concern, solicitude.

anx·ious (ángk-shəss, áng-) *adj.* **1.** Worried and tense about some uncertain event or matter; uneasy. **2.** Attended with, showing, or causing such worry; full of anxieties: *this is an anxious time for her.* **3.** Eagerly or earnestly desirous. Used with *to*: *anxious to leave.* **—See Synonyms at eager.** [Latin *anxius,* from *angere,* to torment, choke.] **—anx·ious·ly** *adv.* **—anx·ious·ness** *n.*

an·y (énni ‖ *Ireland also* ánni) *adj.* **1 a.** One or some, taken at random from three or more; a, an, or some: *Any book will do.* Pick any four numbers. **b.** Each and every: *Any child knows that.* **c.** All: *Any profit is taxed.* **2. a.** Some, regardless of quantity, number, or extent: *Did you buy any butter?* **b.** Even the smallest amount or quantity: *Don't make any noise!* **c.** Unlimited in extent, amount, or number: *any amount of luck; any number of books.* **3.** Of an ordinary or indeterminate kind. Used in negative statements, often with *just*: *Edwin can't wear just any tie.* **4.** No matter how large or small: *not at any price.*
~*pron.* **1.** Any one or ones among three or more. **2.** Any quantity or part; some. **3.** Anybody; any person.
~*adv.* **1.** To any degree or extent. Used with comparative forms: *Is he any better now?* **2.** *U.S. Informal.* At all: *The medicine didn't help any.* [Middle English *any, eny,* Old English *ænig.*]
Usage: *Any* may be used with either a singular or a plural verb: *Any of these books would be suitable* implies "any one of . . ."; *Are any available?* implies "some". In negative constructions, *any* is the accepted usage. *I haven't any money* does not have a corresponding form *I haven't some money.* There is, however, a more formal alternative, *I have no money.* See also **any more, some.**

An·yang (án-yáng, áan-yaáang). Agricultural trading centre in Henan province, northeast China. It was the capital of the Shang dynasty *c.* 1711 B.C.–*c.* 1066 B.C.

an·y·bod·y (énni-bodi, -bədi ‖ *Ireland also* ánni-) *pron.* Any person, no matter who; anyone.
~*n., pl.* **anybodies.** A person of some consequence: *everybody who is anybody.*

an·y·how (énni-how ‖ *Ireland also* ánni-) *adv.* **1.** In any case; at any rate. **2.** Carelessly; neglectfully.

any more, an·y·more (énni-mór ‖ -mór; *Ireland also* anni-) *adv.* Any longer; from now on. Used in negative and interrogative constructions.

an·y·one (énni-wun, *rarely* -wən ‖ *Ireland also* ánni-; *Northern England also* -won) *pron.* Any person, no matter who; anybody.
   Usage: A controversy arises over the appropriate pronoun to use in certain types of sentence where *anyone* is the subject: *Anyone can do what — wants.* The use of the traditionally neutral pronoun *he* in this context may be misleading if females are involved, and in recent years has attracted criticism as being sexist. *She* is equally misleading if males may be involved, and *he or she* is extremely awkward. For such reasons, the use of *they, their,* or the like, long-attested but widely condemned, has taken on a new respectability as an idiomatic solution to the problem. The traditional grammarian, however, would wish the singular sense of *anyone* to be matched by a singular pronoun and verb, and this principle is still the safest one to follow in formal speech or writing.

an·y·place (énni-playss) *adv. U.S.* Anywhere.

an·y·road (énni-rōd) *adv.* British Regional. Anyway.

an·y·thing (énni-thing ‖ *Ireland also* ánni-) *pron.* Any object, act, occurrence, or matter whatever.
   ~ *adv.* To any degree or extent; at all. **—anything but.** By no means; not at all. **—like anything.** *Informal.* Used as an intensive: *She screamed like anything.* **—or anything.** *Informal.* Something similar: *Did he argue or anything?*

an·y·time (énni-tīm ‖ *Ireland also* ánni-) *adv.* At any time.

an·y·way (énni-way ‖ *Ireland also* ánni-) *adv.* **1.** Nevertheless; at any rate; in any case. **2.** In any manner or by any means whatever. **3.** Carelessly; neglectfully.

an·y·where (énni-wair, -hwair ‖ *Ireland also* ánni-) *adv.* **1.** To, in, or at any place. **2.** To any extent or degree; at all: *We aren't anywhere near being finished.* **—anywhere from** or **between.** Any quantity, degree, time, or the like between given bounds: *It could last anywhere from 20 minutes to an hour.* **—get anywhere.** To succeed to any degree.

an·y·wise (énni-wīz ‖ *Ireland also* ánni-) *adv.* In any way or manner. [Old English *on ænige wīsan,* in any wise.]

An·zac (án-zak) *n.* **1.** A soldier in the Australian and New Zealand Army Corps formed in World War I. **2.** Any soldier from New Zealand or Australia. **—An·zac** *adj.*

Anzac Day *n.* In Australia and New Zealand, April 25 observed each year in commemoration of the landing at Gallipoli in 1915.

Anzus, ANZUS (ánzəss) *n.* An alliance of Australia, New Zealand, and the United States, formed in 1951 to provide mutual aid in the Pacific.

a.o.b., A.O.B. Any other business.

A-OK (áy-ō-káy) *adj. Chiefly U.S.* Functioning perfectly; excellent; fine; A-1. [From the phrase *all systems o.k.*] **—A-OK** *adv.*

AONB Area of Outstanding Natural Beauty.

AOR adult oriented rock.

Aorangi. See Mount **Cook.**

a·o·rist (áir-ist, áy-ər-ist) *n.* A verb tense originally used in classical Greek. It usually denotes past action without indicating completion, continuation, or repetition of this action. [Greek *(khronos) aoristos,* "the indefinite (tense)" : A- (not) + *horistos,* definable, from *horizein,* to delimit, from *horos†,* boundary, limit.] **—a·o·rist, a·o·ris·tic** *adj.* (-ístik) **—a·o·ris·ti·cal·ly** *adv.*

a·or·ta (ay-ór-tə) *n., pl.* **-tas** or **-tae** (-tee). *Anatomy.* The main trunk of the systemic arteries, carrying oxygenated blood from the left side of the heart to the arteries of all limbs and organs except the lungs. [New Latin, from Greek *aortē,* aorta, "appendices (of the heart)", from *aeirein,* to raise up.] **—a·or·tic, a·or·tal** *adj.*

aortic arch *n.* The section of the aorta that passes over the top of the heart and back down to the fourth thoracic vertebra.

A·o·te·a·ro·a (á'a-ō-tée-a-rō-ə). The Maori name for **New Zealand.** [Maori, "land of the long white cloud".]

a·ou·dad (á'a-ōō-dad, ówdad) *n.* A wild sheep, *Ammotragus lervia,* of northern Africa, having long, curved horns and a beardlike growth of hair on the neck and chest. Also called "Barbary sheep". [French, from Berber *audad.*]

ap. apothecary.

a.p. **1.** additional premium. **2.** author's proof.

A.P. Associated Press.

a·pace (ə-páyss) *adv.* At a rapid pace; rapidly; swiftly. [Middle English *apas, apace,* step by step, from Old French *a pas : a,* to, from Latin *ad + pas,* step, PACE.]

a·pache (ə-pásh, ə-pá'ash) *n., pl.* **apaches** (*pronounced as singular*). A member of the Parisian underworld. [French, from (English) APACHE (alluding to the tribe's warlike or violent character).]

A·pach·e (ə-páchi) *n., pl.* **-es** or collectively **Apache. 1.** A member of a formerly nomadic tribe of North American Indians inhabiting the southwestern United States and northern Mexico. **2.** The Athapascan language of this tribe. [Spanish, probably from Zuñi *Apachu,* enemy.]

apanage. Variant of **appanage.**

a·part (ə-párt) *adv.* **1. a.** In pieces. **b.** To pieces. **2. a.** Separately or at a distance in time, place, or position: *Over the years, they grew apart.* **b.** To one side; aside. **3.** One from another: *It's easy to confuse the two pictures if you see them apart.* **4.** Independently or separately in consideration or thought. **5.** Out of consideration or set aside; aside: *These few problems apart, it's all going well.* **—apart**

from. 1. With the exception of. **2.** Besides: *Apart from me, there are four others.*
   ~ *adj.* Having individualising features or characteristics. Used after the noun: *a race apart.* [Middle English, from Old French *a part,* to the side : *a,* to + PART.]

a·part·heid (ə-párt-hayt, -hīt) *n.* **1.** An official policy of racial segregation formerly practised in the Republic of South Africa with a view to promoting and maintaining white ascendancy. **2. a.** Any policy of separating groups. **b.** A condition of separateness among groups. [Afrikaans, "apartness" : *apart,* separate, from French *á part,* APART + *-heid,* -HOOD.]

a·part·ment (ə-pártmənt) *n. Abbr.* **apt. 1.** *Plural.* A suite of rooms within a larger building set aside for a particular purpose or person: *state apartments.* **2.** *Chiefly U.S.* A flat. **3.** A room. [French *appartement,* from Italian *appartemento,* from *appartare,* to separate, from *a parte,* APART.]

apartment house *n. Chiefly U.S.* A block of flats. Also called "apartment building".

a·part·ners (ə-pártnərz) *pl. n. Informal.* Sexual partners with separate residences. [Blend of APART + PARTNERS.]

ap·as·tron (áp-ástrən) *n. Astronomy.* The point in an orbit around a star that is farthest from the star; especially, this point in the orbit of one star around another in a binary system. Compare **periastron.** [New Latin, from Greek : *ap(o)-,* away from + *astron,* star.]

ap·a·tet·ic (áppə-téttik) *adj. Zoology.* Pertaining to or designating coloration serving as natural camouflage to an animal. [Greek *apatētikos,* deceptive, from *apateuein,* to cheat, from *apatē†,* deceit, fraud.]

ap·a·thet·ic (áppə-théttik) *adj.* **1.** Feeling or showing little or no emotion. **2.** Uninterested; indifferent; listless. **—See Synonyms at indifferent.** [Blend of APATHY and PATHETIC.] **—ap·a·thet·i·cal·ly** *adv.*

ap·a·thy (áppəthi) *n.* **1.** Lack of emotion or feeling. **2.** Lack of interest or absence of response, especially to what is generally found exciting, interesting, or moving; indifference. [Greek *apatheia,* from *apathēs,* without feeling : a- (without) + *pathos,* feeling.]

ap·a·tite (áppə-tīt) *n.* A natural, variously coloured form of calcium fluoride phosphate, $Ca_5F(PO_4)_3$, with chlorine, hydroxyl, or carbonate sometimes replacing the fluoride. It is a source of phosphorus compounds and is used in the manufacture of fertilisers. [German *Apatit,* "the deceptive stone" (often mistaken for other minerals), from Greek *apatē,* deceit. See **apatetic.**]

ape (ayp) *n.* **1.** Any of various large, tailless Old World primates of the family Pongidae, including the chimpanzee, gorilla, gibbon, and orang-utan. **2.** Broadly, any monkey. **3.** A mimic or imitator. **4.** *Informal.* A large, clumsy, coarse person. **—go ape.** *Informal.* To go wild : *go ape about a film.*
   ~ *tr.v.* **aped, aping, apes.** To mimic. See Synonyms at **imitate.** [Middle English *ape,* Old English *apa,* from Germanic *apan-* (unattested).]

a·peak (ə-péek) *adv. Nautical.* In a vertical or almost vertical position or direction. [Earlier *apike* : A- + PIKE (peak).]

ape-man (áyp-man) *n., pl.* **-men** (-men). Loosely, any of several extinct primates considered intermediate between apes and modern man; missing link.

Ap·en·nines (áppi-nīnz, áppe-). Mountain system running about 1 350 kilometres (840 miles) along the length of peninsular Italy. It has two active volcanoes, Vesuvius and Etna. The highest peak, at 2 914 metres (9,560 feet), is Mt. Corno.

a·per·çu (ápper-séw, -sōō) *n., pl.* **-çus.** *French.* **1.** A perceptive insight; especially, one expressed succinctly. **2.** An outline; a synopsis; a summary. [Past participle of *apercevoir,* to PERCEIVE.]

a·pe·ri·ent (ə-péer-i-ənt) *adj.* Gently purgative; laxative.
   ~ *n.* A mild laxative. [Latin *aperiēns* (stem *aperient-*), present participle of *aperīre,* to uncover, open.]

a·pe·ri·od·ic (áy-peer-i-óddik) *adj.* **1.** Not occurring at regular intervals; irregular. **2.** *Electronics.* Of or designating a circuit that is not capable of resonance at the frequency used. **—a·pe·ri·od·i·cal·ly** *adv.* **—a·pe·ri·o·dic·i·ty** (-ə-dissəti) *n.*

a·pé·ri·tif (ə-pérri-téef) *n.* An alcoholic drink taken to stimulate the appetite before a meal. [French, from Old French *aperitif,* from Medieval Latin *aperitīvus,* from Latin *aperīre,* to open.]

ap·er·ture (áppər-tewr, -chewr, -chər) *n.* **1.** A hole, gap, slit, or other opening; an orifice. **2.** *Optics.* **a.** An adjustable opening in an optical instrument that limits the amount of light passing through a lens or onto a mirror. **b.** The effective diameter of a lens or mirror divided by its focal length. See **f-number. 3.** The diameter of a radio telescope. [Latin *apertūra,* from *apertus,* open, from the past participle of *aperīre,* to open.] **—a·per·tur·al** (-téwrəl) *adj.*

aperture synthesis *n.* A technique in radio astronomy in which two or more small separate movable antennas are used in conjunction to build up a radio map of the source.

a·pet·al·ous (ay-pétt'l-əss) *adj. Botany.* Having no petals. **—a·pet·al·y** (ay-pétt'l-i) *n.*

a·pex (áypeks) *n., pl.* **apexes** or **apices** (áypi-seez, áppi-). **1.** The highest point of something; the vertex. **2.** The culmination. **3.** The pointed end of something; the tip. **3.** *Astronomy.* A point on the celestial sphere towards which the solar system moves relative to neighbouring stars. Also called "solar apex". **—See Synonyms at summit.** [Latin *apex,* point, summit, top.]

APEX¹ Association of Professional, Executive, Clerical, and Computer staff.

A·PEX², A·pex *n. Advance Purchase Excursion:* a system of discount air fares available on bookings paid for in advance of a minimum stipulated period.

a·phaer·e·sis, *U.S.* **a·pher·e·sis** (ə-féer-ə-siss ‖ *U.S.* -férrə-) *n.* The loss of one or more letters or sounds from the beginning of a word, as in *round* for *around*, *gainst* for *against*, or *most* for *almost*. [Late Latin, from Greek *aphairesis*, a taking away, from *aphairein*, to take away from : *ap(o)-*, away from + *hairein*†, to take.] —**a·phae·ret·ic** (áffə-réttik) *adj.*

a·pha·gi·a (ə-fáy-ji-ə, -jə) *n.* Inability or refusal to swallow. [New Latin : A- (not) + -PHAGIA.]

aph·a·nite (áffə-nīt) *n.* Any igneous rock with constituents so fine that they cannot be seen by the naked eye. [French : Greek *aphanēs*, unseen : A- (not) + *phainesthai*, to be seen, from *phainein*, to see + -ITE.] —**aph·a·nit·ic** (-níttik) *adj.* —**aph·a·nit·ism** (-nitiz'm) *n.*

a·pha·si·a (ə-fáy-zi-ə, á-, áy-, -fáyzhi-ə, -fáyzhə) *n.* Partial or total loss of the ability to generate and understand speech, that is the consequence of brain damage. Compare **dysphasia**. [New Latin, from Greek : A- (without) + -PHASIA.] —**a·pha·si·ac** (-fáy-zi-ak) *n.* —**a·pha·sic** (-fáyzik) *adj. & n.*

ap·he·li·on (ap-héel-i-ən, ə-féel-) *n.*, *pl.* **-lia** (-i-ə). The point in an orbit round the Sun that is farthest from the Sun. Compare **perihelion**. [New Latin, variant of *aphelium* : Greek *ap(o)-*, away from + *hēlios*, Sun.]

ap·he·li·o·trop·ic (ap-héeli-ə-tróppik, a-féeli-, ə-féeli-) *adj. Biology.* Turning away from the sun, as roots do. [AP(O)- (away from) + HELIOTROPIC.] —**a·phe·li·o·trop·i·cal·ly** *adv.* —**a·phe·li·ot·ro·pism** (-óttrəpiz'm) *n.*

aph·e·sis (áffi-siss) *n.* Aphaeresis of a short unstressed vowel from the beginning of a word; for example, *squire* for *esquire*. [New Latin, from Greek *aphesis*, a letting go, from *aphienai*, to let go : *ap(o)-*, away + *hienai*, to send.] —**a·phet·ic** (ə-féttik, a-) *adj.* —**a·phet·i·cal·ly** *adv.*

a·phid (áyfid ‖ *U.S. also* áffid) *n.* Any of various small, soft-bodied insects of the family Aphididae, such as greenflies and blackflies, that feed by sucking sap from plants. Also called "plant louse". [From New Latin *aphis* (stem *aphid-*), APHIS.] —**a·phid·i·an** (ə-fíddi-ən) *adj. & n.*

aphid lion *n.* The larva of any of several insects of the family Chrysopidae, such as the lacewing, that feed on aphids.

a·phis (áyfiss ‖ *U.S. also* áffiss) *n.*, *pl.* **aphides** (áyfi-deez ‖ *U.S. also* áffə-). An aphid, especially one of the genus *Aphis*. [New Latin *Aphis* (coined by Linnaeus), of obscure origin but perhaps due to a misreading of Greek *koris*, bug.]

a·pho·ni·a (ay-fṓn-i-ə, a-, ə-, -yə) *n.* Loss of speech, or voicelessness, as a result of disease or injury to the organs of speech. Compare **dysphonia**. [New Latin, from Greek *aphōnia*, voicelessness, from *aphōnos*, voiceless : A- (without) + *phōnē*, voice.]

a·phon·ic (ay-fónnik, ə-) *adj.* **1.** *Pathology.* Affected with or having aphonia. **2.** *Phonetics.* Voiceless.

aph·o·rism (áffə-riz'm) *n.* A pithy statement of a truth or opinion; a maxim; an adage. See Synonyms at **saying**. [Old French *aphorisme*, from Greek *aphorismos*, a delimitation, from *aphorizein*, to mark off by boundaries : *ap(o)-*, off, away from + *horizein*, to limit, from *horos*†, boundary, limit.] —**aph·o·ris·tic** (-rístik) *adj.* —**aph·o·rist** *n.* —**aph·o·ris·ti·cal·ly** *adv.*

a·pho·tic (ə-fóttik, ay-, -fṓtik) *adj.* **1.** Without light. **2.** Of or designating the ocean zone below the level at which photosynthesis can occur (about 200 metres or 656 feet). [A- (not) + PHOTIC.]

aph·ro·dis·i·ac (áffrə-dízzi-ak) *adj.* Stimulating or intensifying sexual desire.

~n. Anything having aphrodisiac properties, such as a drug or food. [Greek *aphrodisiakos*, from *aphrodisia*, aphrodisiac pleasures, from *aphrodisios*, of Aphrodite.]

Aph·ro·di·te (áffrə-dī́ti) *Greek Mythology.* The goddess of love and beauty, identified with the Roman goddess Venus. Also called "Cytherea".

a·phyl·lous (ə-fílləss, ay-) *adj. Botany.* Having or bearing no leaves. [Greek *aphullos* : A- (not) + -PHYLLOUS.] —**a·phyl·ly** (-filli) *n.*

A·pi·a (aa-pée-aa, ə-pée-ə). Capital and only port of Samoa, on the northern coast of Upolu Island. Vailima, the former home of Robert Louis Stevenson, is the residence of the head of state.

a·pi·an (áypi-ən) *adj.* Of or pertaining to bees. [Latin *apiānus*, from *apis*†, bee.]

a·pi·ar·i·an (áypi-áir-i-ən) *adj.* Pertaining to the breeding and care of bees.

a·pi·a·rist (áyp-yə-rist, -i-ə- ‖ *U.S. also* -i-errist) *n.* A beekeeper.

a·pi·a·ry (áyp-yəri, -i-əri ‖ *U.S.* -i-erri) *n.*, *pl.* **-ies**. A place containing a number of beehives, in which bees are kept, raised, and exploited, usually for their honey. [Latin *apiārium*, beehive, from *apis*†, bee.]

ap·i·cal (áppik'l, áypik'l) *adj.* **1.** Of, pertaining to, located at, or constituting the apex. **2.** *Phonetics.* Of or designating consonants articulated with the tip of the tongue, such as *t*, *d*, and *s*. [New Latin *apicalis*, from Latin *apex* (stem *apic-*), APEX.]

a·pi·ces. Alternative plural of **apex.**

a·pic·u·late (ə-pickew-lət, -lit, -layt) *adj. Botany.* Ending with a sharp, abrupt tip: *an apiculate leaf.* [From New Latin *apiculus*, a sharp point, diminutive of Latin *apex* (stem *apic-*), APEX.]

a·pi·cul·ture (áypi-kulchər ‖ -kúlchər) *n.* The breeding and care of bees. [Latin *apis*†, bee + CULTURE.] —**a·pi·cul·tur·al** (-kúlchərəl) *adj.* —**a·pi·cul·tur·ist** (-kúlchərist) *n.*

a·piece (ə-péess) *adv.* To or for each one; each: *Give them an apple apiece.* [Middle English *a pece* : A + PIECE.]

A·pis (áypiss) *n.* A sacred bull of the ancient Egyptians.

ap·ish (áypish) *adj.* **1.** Slavishly or foolishly imitative. **2.** Silly; foolish. [AP(E) + -ISH.] —**ap·ish·ly** *adv.* —**ap·ish·ness** *n.*

a·piv·o·rous (ay-pívvərəss) *adj.* Feeding on bees. [Latin *apis*†, bee + -VOROUS.]

APL *n.* A computer programming language designed for use at remote terminals. [*A Programming Language.*]

a·pla·cen·tal (áy-plə-sént'l, ápplə-) *adj.* Having no placenta. Said of marsupials and monotremes. [A- (not) + PLACENT(A) + -AL.]

ap·la·nat·ic (ápplə-náttik) *adj.* Of, pertaining to, or designating optical systems that correct for spherical aberration and coma. [Greek *aplanētos*, unable to go astray : A- (not) + *planētos*, *planēs*, wandering, from *planasthai*, to wander.]

a·pla·no·spore (ə-pláynō-spawr ‖ -spōr) *n.* A nonmotile, asexual spore characteristic of the green algae and pin moulds. [A- (not) + Greek *planos*, wandering + SPORE.]

a·pla·si·a (ə-pláyz-yə, -i-ə ‖ -pláyzhə) *n* Defective development or congenital absence of tissue, of an organ, or of an organ part. [New Latin : A- (not) + -PLASIA.]

a·plas·tic (ay-plástik, -pláastik) *adj.* **1.** Lacking form. **2.** *Pathology.* Of, relating to, or characterised by aplasia: *aplastic anaemia.* [A- (not) + -PLASTIC.]

a·plen·ty (ə-plénti) *adj.* In abundance. Used after the noun: *goods aplenty.* —**a·plen·ty** *adv.*

ap·lite (ápplīt) *n.* Also **hap·lite** (hápplīt). A fine-grained, light-coloured granitic rock consisting primarily of orthoclase and quartz. [German *Aplit* : Greek *haplous*, single, simple (see **haploid**) + -ITE.] —**ap·lit·ic** (a-plíttik) *adj.*

a·plomb (ə-plóm, *rarely* ápplon ‖ *U.S. also* ə-plúm) *n.* Self-confidence; poise; assurance. [French, uprightness, from Old French *a plomb*, perpendicularly, according to the plummet : *a*, to + plomb, plummet, lead weight, from Latin *plumbum*, lead.]

ap·noe·a, *U.S.* **ap·ne·a** (ap-née-ə ‖ *U.S. also* ápni-ə) *n.* Temporary suspension of respiration. [New Latin, from Greek *apnoia*, absence of respiration : A- (without) + *pnoē*, breathing, from *pnein*, to breathe.] —**ap·noe·ic** *adj.*

apo-, **ap-** *prefix.* Indicates: **1.** Being away from; for example, **aphelion**. **2.** Lack of; for example, **apogamy**. **3.** Separation of; for example, **apocarpous**. **4.** *Geology.* Derived from; for example, **apophysis**. **5.** *Chemistry.* Derived from; for example **apomorphine**. [In borrowed Greek compounds, *apo-* indicates: **1.** Away from, as in **apogee**. **2.** Away, off, as in **apothecary**. **3.** Return, as in **apodosis**. **4.** Intensive action, as in **aposiopesis**. **5.** Keeping off, defence, as in **apology**. **6.** Change from an existing state, as in **apotheosis**. **7.** Reversal, as in **Apocalypse**. Greek *apo-*, from *apo*, away from, off.]

Apoc. **1.** Apocalypse. **2.** Apocrypha; Apocryphal.

A·poc·a·lypse (ə-póckə-lips) *n.* **1.** *Abbr.* **Apoc.** The last book of the New Testament, **Revelation** *(see).* **2.** *Small* **a.** A prophetic disclosure or revelation; especially, a vision of the end of the world. **3.** *Small* **a.** An event marked by violent destruction and upheaval. [Middle English *Apocalipse*, from Late Latin *Apocalypsis*, from Greek *apokalupsis*, revelation, from *apokaluptein*, to uncover : *apo-*, reversal + *kaluptein*, to cover.]

a·poc·a·lyp·tic (ə-póckə-líptik) *adj.* Also **a·poc·a·lyp·ti·cal** (-'l). **1.** Of or pertaining to a prophetic disclosure or revelation. **2.** Making violent and doom-laden predictions. **3.** Suggesting the end of the world: *an apocalyptic spectacle.* —**a·poc·a·lyp·ti·cal·ly** *adv.*

ap·o·carp (áppə-kaarp) *n. Botany.* An apocarpous gynoecium or fruit. [Back-formation from APOCARPOUS.]

ap·o·car·pous (áppə-kárpəss) *adj. Botany.* Having distinctly separated carpels. [APO- + -CARPOUS.] —**ap·o·car·py** (-kaarpi) *n.*

ap·o·ca·tas·ta·sis (áppō-kə-tástə-siss) *n. Theology.* The doctrine of **Universalism** *(see).* [Latin, from Greek, restoration, from *apokathistanai*, to re-establish, "set back down" : *apo-*, back + *kata-*, down + *histanai*, (cause to) stand.]

ap·o·chro·mat·ic (áppə-krō-máttik, -krə-) *adj. Optics.* Corrected for both chromatic and spherical aberration. —**a·po·chro·mat·ism** (-krṓmətiz'm) *n.*

a·poc·o·pe (ə-póckəpi) *n.* A cutting off or omitting of the last sound or syllable of a word; for example, *goin'* for *going*. [Latin *apocopē*, from Greek *apokopē*, from *apokoptein*, to cut off : *apo-*, off + *koptein*, to cut.]

ap·o·crine (áppə-krin, -krīn ‖ -kreen) *adj.* Of, pertaining to, or designating a type of glandular secretion in which the gland loses part of its cytoplasm when secreting. Compare **holocrine**, **merocrine**. [APO- + Greek *krinein*, to separate.]

A·poc·ry·pha (ə-póckrifə) *n. Used with a singular or plural verb. Abbr.* **Apoc.** **1.** The 14 books of the Septuagint included in the Vulgate but considered uncanonical by Protestants. Eleven of these books are accepted in the Roman Catholic canon, and appear in the Douay Bible. **2.** Various early Christian writings proposed as additions to the New Testament, but rejected by the major canons. **3.** *Small* **a.** Any writings of questionable authorship or authenticity. [Middle English *Apocripha*, from Medieval Latin *scripta apocrypha*, hidden writings (that is, hidden and excluded from the canon because spurious); from Late Latin *apocryphus*, hidden, from Greek *apokruphos*, from *apokruptein*, to hide away : *apo-*, away + *kruptein*, to hide.]

a·poc·ry·phal (ə-póckrif'l) *adj.* **1.** Of questionable authorship or authenticity. **2.** False; counterfeit. **3.** *Capital* **A.** *Abbr.* **Apoc.** Of or pertaining to the Apocrypha. —**a·poc·ry·phal·ly** *adv.*

a·po·cyn·thi·on (áppə-sínthi-ən, áppō-) *n.* See **apolune.**

ap·o·dal (áppəd'l) *adj. Zoology.* Having no limbs, feet, or footlike appendages. [From Greek *apous* (stem *apod-*) : A- (without) + *pous,* foot.]

ap·o·dic·tic (áppə-díktik) *adj.* Also **ap·o·deic·tic** (-díktik). Clearly proven or demonstrated; incontestable. [Latin *apodicticus,* from Greek *apodeiktikos,* from *apodeiknunai,* to point out or away from : *apo-,* away from + *deiknunai,* to show.]

a·pod·o·sis (ə-póddə-siss) *n., pl.* **-ses** (-seez). *Grammar.* The clause stating the conclusion or consequence of a conditional sentence. Compare **protasis.** [New Latin, from Greek, response (to the protasis), "a giving back", from *apodidonai,* give up or back : *apo-,* back + *didonai,* to give.]

ap·o·en·zyme (áppō-énzīm) *n.* An inactive enzyme that needs to be combined with a **coenzyme** *(see)* to become functional.

a·pog·a·my (ə-póggəmi) *n. Botany.* In ferns, the production of the sporophyte directly from a cell of the gametophyte, without the formation of gametes. Compare **apospory.** [APO- (away from) + -GAMY.] —**ap·o·gam·ic** (áppə-gámmik), **a·pog·a·mous** (ə-póggəməss) *adj.*

ap·o·gee (áppə-jee, áppō-) *n.* 1. The point in an orbit round the Earth that is most distant from the Earth. Compare **perigee.** 2. The farthest or highest point; the apex. [French *apogée,* from New Latin *apogaeum,* from Greek *apogaion,* neuter of *apogaios,* "away from the earth" : *apo-,* away from + *gaia, gē,* earth.] —**ap·o·ge·an** (-jée-ən) *adj.*

a·po·lit·i·cal (áy-pə-líttik'l) *adj.* Having no association with or interest in politics. —**a·po·lit·i·cal·ly** *adv.*

A·pol·li·naire (ə-pólli-naír, a-), **Guillaume,** born Wilhelm Apollinaris de Kostrowitzky (1880–1918). French poet, early surrealist, and leading figure in avant-garde literary and painting circles.

A·pol·lo¹ (ə-póllō). *Greek & Roman Mythology.* The god of the sun, prophecy, music, medicine, and poetry.

Apollo² *n., pl.* **Apollos.** A young man of great physical beauty. [After APOLLO (the god).]

Apollo³ *n.* Any of a series of 17 U.S. spacecraft designed to land people on the moon. The first 10 Apollo craft were used to test various aspects of the programme, the first moon landing (July 1969) being achieved by Apollo 11. The remaining members of the series also made manned moon landings, except Apollo 13, which was safely aborted. [After APOLLO (the god).] —**Apollo** *adj.*

Ap·ol·lo·ni·an (áppə-lōn-yən, -i-ən) *adj.* 1. *Capital* **A.** Of or pertaining to Apollo or his cult. 2. *Sometimes small* **a.** In the philosophy of Nietzsche, characteristic of or embodying the theoretical, rational, calm, harmonious qualities of human nature. Compare **Dionysian.** 3. Noble; dignified; serene. —**Ap·ol·lo·ni·an** *n.*

Ap·ol·lo·ni·us of Per·ga (áppə-lṓni-əss əv pérgə) (*c.* 262 B.C.–*c.* 190 B.C.). Greek mathematician. He was the first to define, in his work on conic sections, the curves called the *parabola, hyperbola,* and *ellipse.*

a·pol·o·get·ic (ə-póllə-jéttik) *adj.* 1. Making an apology or excuse. 2. Conveying self-recrimination and regret: *an apologetic smile.* 3. Explaining or defending in speech or writing. ~*n.* A formal defence or apology. —**a·pol·o·get·i·cal·ly** *adv.*

a·pol·o·get·ics (ə-póllə-jéttiks) *n. Used with a singular verb.* The branch of theology that deals with the defence and proof of Christianity.

ap·o·lo·gi·a (áppə-lṓji-ə || -lṓjə) *n.* A formal defence or justification. [Latin, APOLOGY.]

a·pol·o·gise, a·pol·o·gize (ə-póllə-jīz) *intr.v.* **-gised, -gising, -gises.** 1. To make excuse for or regretful acknowledgment of a fault or offence. 2. To make a formal defence or justification in speech or writing. —**a·pol·o·gis·er** *n.*

a·pol·o·gist (ə-pólləjist) *n.* A person who argues in defence or justification of another person or cause.

ap·o·logue (áppə-log) *n.* A moral fable. [French *apologue,* from Latin *apologus,* from Greek *apologos,* fable : *apo-,* away, off + *logos,* discourse.]

a·pol·o·gy (ə-pólləji) *n., pl.* **-gies.** 1. A statement, either written or spoken, expressing regret or asking pardon for a fault or offence. 2. A formal justification or defence. 3. An inferior substitute: *a poor apology for a dinner.* [French *apologie,* from Late Latin *apologia,* from Latin *apologiā,* speech in defence : *apo-,* defence + *logos,* discourse, speech.]

a·po·lune (áppə-lṓōn, áppō-, -lewn) *n.* The point in an orbit round the Moon that is farthest from the Moon. Also called "apocynthion", "aposelene", "aposelenium". Compare **perilune.** [APO- (away from) + *lune,* from Latin *lūna,* Moon.]

ap·o·mict (áppə-mikt, áppō-) *n. Biology.* An organism, especially a plant, that is the result of apomixis. [APO- + Greek *miktos,* mixed, from *mignugnai,* to mix.]

ap·o·mix·is (áppə-míksiss, áppō-) *n.* An asexual reproductive process in which a new individual is produced from a female cell or cells other than the egg cell, often in a manner that mimics sexual reproduction. [New Latin : APO- + Greek *mixis,* a mingling, from *mignugnai,* to mix.]

ap·o·mor·phine (áppə-mór-feen) *n.* A poisonous white crystalline alkaloid, $C_{17}H_{17}NO_2$, derived from morphine and used medicinally as an emetic, expectorant, and hypnotic.

a·po·neu·ro·sis (áppə-newr-rṓ-siss, áppō- || -noo-) *n., pl.* **-ses** (-seez). A sheetlike membrane, resembling a flattened tendon, that forms the end of certain muscles and connects them to bones. [New Latin, from Greek *aponeurōsis,* from *aponeurousthai,* to become a

nerve : *apo-* (change) + *neuron,* nerve.] —**ap·o·neu·rot·ic** (-róttik) *adj.*

ap·o·phthegm, *U.S.* **ap·o·thegm** (áppə-them, áppō-) *n.* A terse and witty instructive saying; a maxim; a proverb. [Greek *apophthegma,* a pointed saying, from *apophthengesthai,* to speak out plainly : *apo-,* away from + *phthengesthai,* to speak; akin to *phthongos,* sound (see **diphthong**).] —**ap·o·phtheg·mat·ic** (-theg-máttik), **ap·o·phtheg·mat·i·cal** *adj.* —**ap·o·phtheg·mat·i·cal·ly** *adv.*

a·poph·y·ge (ə-póffiji) *n. Architecture.* The curvature at the top and bottom of the shaft of a column. [Greek *apophugē,* "escape" : *apo-,* away + *phugē,* flight.]

a·poph·y·sis (ə-póffi-siss) *n., pl.* **-ses** (-seez). 1. *Biology.* A swelling, projection, or outgrowth of an organ or part. 2. *Geology.* A branch from a dyke or vein. [New Latin from Greek *apophusis,* side-shoot : *apo-,* off, away + *phusis,* growth, from *phuein,* to grow.] —**a·poph·y·sate, a·poph·y·se·al** (-sée-əl) *adj.*

ap·o·plec·tic (áppə-pléktik) *adj.* 1. Of, resembling, or causing apoplexy. 2. Having or exhibiting symptoms of apoplexy. 3. *Informal.* Extremely annoyed. —**ap·o·plec·ti·cal·ly** *adv.*

ap·o·plex·y (áppə-pleksi) *n.* Sudden loss of muscular control, with diminution or loss of sensation and consciousness, resulting from rupture or blocking of a blood vessel in the brain; a stroke. [Middle English *apoplexie,* from Old French, from Late Latin *apoplēxia,* from Greek, from *apoplēssein,* to cripple by a stroke : *apo-* (intensive) + *plēssein,* to strike.]

a·port (ə-pórt || ə-pṓrt) *adv. Nautical.* On or towards the port, or left, side.

a·po·se·le·ne (áppō-sə-léeni) *n.* Also **a·po·se·le·ni·um** (-léeni-əm). An **apolune** *(see).* [APO- (away from) + Greek *selēnē,* Moon.]

ap·o·se·mat·ic coloration (áppə-si-máttik, áppō-) *n.* **Warning coloration** *(see).* [APO- (away from) + SEMATIC.]

ap·o·si·o·pe·sis (áppō-sī-ə-pée-siss, áppə-) *n., pl.* **-ses** (-seez). A sudden and dramatic breaking off in the middle of a sentence, as though the speaker were unwilling or unable to continue, done for rhetorical effect. [Late Latin *aposiōpēsis,* from Greek, a becoming silent, from *aposiōpān,* to maintain silence : *apo-* (intensifier) + *siōpān,* to be silent, from *siōpē,* silence.] —**ap·o·si·o·pet·ic** (-péttik) *adj.*

a·po·spor·y (áppə-spáwri, áppō- || -spṓri) *n. Botany.* In mosses and ferns, the development of the gametophyte directly from a cell of the sporophyte, without spore formation. Compare **apogamy.** [APO- (away from) + SPOR(E) + -Y (state).]

a·pos·ta·sy (ə-póstəssi) *n., pl.* **-sies.** An abandonment of one's religious faith, or any cause or principle to which one was attached. [Middle English *apostasie,* from Late Latin *apostasia,* from Greek, desertion, revolt, from *apostanai,* "to stand away from", rebel : *apo-,* away from + *stanai,* to stand.]

a·pos·tate (ə-póst-ayt, -ət, -it) *n.* One who is guilty of apostasy. [Middle English, from Late Latin *apostata,* from Greek *apostatēs,* deserter, rebel, from *apostanai,* to rebel. See **apostasy.**] —**a·pos·tate** *adj.*

a·pos·ta·tise, a·pos·ta·tize (ə-póstə-tīz) *intr.v.* **-tised, -tising, -tises.** To give up or abandon one's faith, political party, or cause.

a pos·te·ri·o·ri (áy-pos-térr-i-áwr-ī, áa-, -téeri-, -ee || -ṓr-) *adj. Logic.* Of, pertaining to, or designating arguments, propositions, or knowledge derived from reasoning from facts or particulars to general principles, or from effects to causes; inductive; empirical. Compare **a priori.** [Latin, "from the subsequent".] —**a pos·te·ri·o·ri** *adv.*

a·pos·tle (ə-póss'l) *n.* 1. *Usually capital* **A.** Any of the twelve disciples chosen by Christ to preach his gospel. Luke 6:13–16. 2. A missionary of the early Christian Church. 3. A leader of the first Christian mission to a country or region. 4. Any of the twelve members of the Mormon administrative council. 5. One who leads or advocates a new cause. [Middle English *apostel, apostle,* Old English *apostol,* from Late Latin *apostolus,* from Greek *apostolos,* messenger, envoy, from *apostellein,* to send away from : *apo-,* away from + *stellein,* to place.]

Apostles' Creed *n.* A Christian creed traditionally ascribed to the Twelve Apostles.

Apostle spoon, apostle spoon *n.* A spoon, usually of silver, with a knop in the image of a robed man, representing an Apostle.

ap·os·tol·ic (áppə-stóllik, ápposs-) *adj.* 1. Of, pertaining to, or contemporary with the Apostles. 2. Of, pertaining to, or conforming to the faith, teaching, or practice of the Apostles. 3. Of or pertaining to the pope as successor to Saint Peter.

apostolic delegate *n. Roman Catholic Church.* A representative of the pope in a country that does not have formal diplomatic relations with the Vatican state. Compare **nuncio.**

Apostolic Fathers *pl.n.* Church Fathers, including Clement of Rome, Ignatius of Antioch, and Polycarp of Smyrna, who had received personal instruction from the Apostles themselves or from their disciples.

apostolic see *n.* 1. A bishopric founded, according to tradition, by one of the Apostles. 2. *Capital* **A,** *capital* **S.** The See of Rome founded, according to tradition, by the Apostle Peter.

apostolic succession *n.* The doctrine that authority in the Christian Church is derived from the Apostles through an unbroken succession of bishops.

a·pos·tro·phe¹ (ə-póstrəfi) *n.* The superscript sign (') used in punctuation to indicate the omission of a letter or letters from a word, the omission of a number or numbers, as from a date, the possessive case, and certain plurals, especially those of numbers and letters. [French, from Old French, from Late Latin *apostrophus,* from

apostrophe² / append

Greek *(prosŏidia) apostrophos*, "(accent of) turning away", sign of elision, from *apostrephein*, to turn away : *apo-*, away + *strephein*, to turn.] —**ap·os·troph·ic** (ăppə-strŏffĭk) *adj.*

apostrophe² *n.* A digression in discourse; especially, a device by which a speaker or writer breaks off to address an absent or imaginary person. [Latin *apostrophē*, from Greek, from *apostrephein*, to turn away. See **apostrophe** (sign).] —**ap·os·troph·ic** (ăppə-strŏffĭk) *adj.*

a·pos·tro·phise, a·pos·tro·phize (ə-pŏstrə-fīz) *v.* **-phised, -phising, -phises.** —*tr.* To address by apostrophe. —*intr.* To speak or write in apostrophe.

apothecaries' measure *n.* A system of liquid volume measure formerly used in pharmacy.

apothecaries' weight *n.* A system of weights formerly used in pharmacy and based on an ounce equal to 480 grains and a pound equal to 12 ounces.

a·poth·e·car·y (ə-pŏthi-kri, -kəri ‖ -kerri) *n., pl.* **-ries.** *Abbr.* **ap.** *Archaic.* One who prepares and sells drugs and medicines; a pharmacist. [Middle English, from Medieval Latin *apothecārius*, from Late Latin, from Greek *apothēca*, storehouse, from Greek *apothēkē*, from *apotithenai*, to put away : *apo-*, away + *tithenai*, to put.]

ap·o·the·ci·um (ăppə-thée-si-əm ‖ -shi-) *n., pl.* **-cia** (-si-ə ‖ -shi-ə). An open disc-shaped or cup-shaped fruiting body in ascomycete fungi, lined with a layer bearing the spores. [New Latin, from Latin *apothēca*, storehouse (see **apothecary**).] —**ap·o·the·cial** (-thée-si-əl, -shəl) *adj.*

apothegm. *U.S.* Variant of **apophthegm.**

ap·o·them (ăppə-them, ăppō-) *n. Geometry.* In a regular polygon, the perpendicular distance from the centre to any of the sides. [APO-, away from + Greek *thema*, position, THEME.]

a·poth·e·o·sis (ə-pŏthi-ō-siss ‖ ăppəthi-) *n., pl.* **-ses** (-seez). 1. Exaltation to divine rank or stature; deification. 2. An exalted or glorified ideal. 3. The culmination or highest development; the quintessence. [Late Latin *apotheōsis*, from Greek *apotheōsis*, from *apotheoun*, to deify : *apo-* (change) + *theos*, god.]

a·po·the·o·sise, a·po·the·o·size (ə-pŏthi-ə-sīz, -ō- ‖ ăppə-thée-) *tr.v.* **-sised, -sising, -sises.** To glorify, exalt, or deify.

a·po·tro·pa·ic (ăppətrə-páyik) *adj.* Having the power or purpose of averting evil: *an apotropaic ritual.* [Greek *apotropaios*, from *apotrepein*, to turn away : *apo-* away + *trepein*, to turn.] —**a·po·tro·pa·ic·al·ly** *adv.*

app. 1. apparatus. 2. appendix. 3. applied. 4. appoint; appointed.

ap·pal, *U.S.* **ap·pall** (ə-pắwl) *tr.v.* **-palled, -palling, -pals** or *U.S.* **-palls.** To fill with consternation, dismay, or horror. [Middle English *ap(p)allen*, from Old French *apalir*, to grow pale : *a-*, to, from Latin *ad-*, to + *palir*, from Latin *pallescere*, from *pallēre*, to be pale.]

Appalachian (ăppə-láych-ən, -láychi-, -lách-) **Mountains.** Also **Appalachians.** Mountain range in eastern North America, stretching from Newfoundland to Alabama. It includes the Alleghenies, Blue Ridge, and Cumberland mountains. The highest peak, Mount Mitchell (2 037 metres; 6,684 feet), lies in North Carolina. —**Ap·pa·la·chi·an** *adj.*

ap·pal·ling (ə-pắwling) *adj.* 1. Causing dismay; frightful; horrifying. 2. *Informal.* Very bad; terrible. —**ap·pal·ling·ly** *adv.*

ap·pa·loo·sa (ăppə-lōōssə) *n.* A horse of a breed developed in northwestern North America, characteristically having a spotted rump. [Perhaps after *Palouse*, a river in Idaho.]

ap·pa·nage, ap·a·nage (ăppənij) *n.* 1. Land or some other source of revenue given by a king for the maintenance of a member of the ruling family. 2. A perquisite. 3. A natural or rightful attribute or adjunct. [French *apanage*, from Old French, from *apaner*, to make provisions for, from Medieval Latin *appānāre* : Latin *ad-*, to + *pānis*, bread.]

ap·pa·rat (ăppə-ráat, -rat ‖ *U.S. also* áapə-) *n.* The organisation and administrative apparatus of a political party, in former times especially that of the Communist party in the U.S.S.R. and some other Communist countries. [Russian, from German, APPARATUS.]

ap·pa·rat·chik (ăppə-rát-chik, -ráat-) *n., pl.* **-chiks** or **-chiki** (-chickee). 1. One who belongs to an apparat. 2. A bureaucrat. Used humorously. [Russian : APPARAT + -*chik*, suffix indicating agent, adherent, member.]

ap·pa·ra·tus (ăppə-ráytəs, -ráatəss ‖ -ráttəss) *n., pl.* **apparatus** or **-tuses.** *Abbr.* **app.** 1. The totality of things provided or necessary for the accomplishment of a particular task or purpose. 2. A machine, instrument, or other piece of equipment with a specific function. 3. *Physiology.* A group of organs having a collective function: *the respiratory apparatus.* 4. A political, bureaucratic, or other organisational system. 5. A set of principles or standards, as for judging or testing. [Latin *apparātus*, from the past participle of *apparāre*, to prepare : *ad-*, to + *parāre*, to make ready.]

apparatus cri·ti·cus (kríttikəss) *n.* 1. Reference materials used in literary research. 2. Special appendixes, notes, or glossaries in an edition of a text. Also called "critical apparatus". [New Latin, "critical apparatus".]

ap·par·el (ə-párrəl) *n. Formal.* 1. Clothing, especially outer garments; attire. 2. Anything that covers or adorns. 3. The equipment of a vessel, especially a sailing ship.

~ *tr.v.* **apparelled** or *U.S.* **appareled, -elling** or *U.S.* **-eling, -els.** 1. *Archaic.* To clothe; dress. 2. *Poetic.* To adorn; embellish. [Middle English *appareil*, from Old French *apareil*, preparation, furnishings, from *apareillier*, to prepare, from Vulgar Latin *apparīculāre* (unattested), from Latin *apparāre* : *ad-*, to + *parāre*, to make

ready.]

ap·par·ent (ə-párrənt, *rarely* ə-páir-ənt) *adj.* 1. Readily seen; open to view; visible. 2. Readily understood or perceived; plain or obvious. 3. Seeming; as seen but not necessarily real. 4. See **heir apparent.** —See Synonyms at **evident.** [Middle English, from Old French *aparent*, present participle of *aparoir*, to APPEAR.] —**ap·par·ent·ness** *n.*

ap·par·ent·ly (ə-párrənt-li) *adv.* 1. So far as one can tell; evidently. 2. According to the information one has: *Apparently they're going to cut the interest rate.* 3. Seemingly but perhaps not actually.

apparent magnitude *n. Astronomy.* **Magnitude** *(see).*

apparent time *n.* Local time *(see).*

ap·pa·ri·tion (ăppə-rísh'n) *n.* 1. A ghostly figure; a spectre. 2. A sudden or unusual sight. 3. An appearance. [Middle English *apparicioun*, from Old French *apparition*, from Late Latin *apparitiō* (stem *apparitiōn-*), appearance, epiphany (translation of Greek *epiphaneia*), from Latin *apparēre*, to APPEAR.] —**ap·pa·ri·tion·al** *adj.*

ap·pa·ri·tor (ə-párri-tər, -tawr) *n.* An official sent to carry out the orders of an ecclesiastical or, formerly, civil court. [Latin, from *apparēre*, to serve, APPEAR (as a servant).]

ap·pas·sio·na·to (ə-páss-yə-naátō ‖ *U.S.* -paà-si-ə-) *adv. Music.* In an impassioned manner. Used as a direction. [Italian, "impassioned", past participle of *appasionare*, to inspire with passion : *ap-* (intensive) + *passionare*, from *passione*, from Late Latin *passiō*, PASSION.] —**ap·pas·sio·na·to** *adj.*

ap·peal (ə-péel) *n.* 1. An earnest or urgent request, entreaty, or supplication. 2. A resort or application to some higher authority, as for sanction, corroboration, or a decision: *an appeal to reason.* 3. The power of attracting or of arousing interest. 4. *Law.* **a.** The transfer of a case from a lower to a higher court for a new hearing. **b.** A request for a new hearing. **c.** A case so transferred. 5. In cricket, a request made to an umpire by one or several members of the fielding side that a batsman be declared out. 6. A campaign to raise funds or resources, usually for a charitable cause: *launched an appeal on behalf of the refugees.*

~ *v.* **appealed, -pealing, -peals.** —*intr.* 1. To make an earnest or urgent request, as for help or sympathy. 2. To resort or have recourse to some higher authority, as for sanction, corroboration, or review : *appeal against a decision.* 3. To be attractive or interesting. 4. *Law.* To make or apply for an appeal. 5. In cricket, to request an umpire to declare a batsman out. —*tr.* 1. *Law.* To transfer or apply to transfer (a case) to a higher court for rehearing. 2. To make an appeal against : *appeal a decision.* [Middle English *appelen, apelen,* from Old French *apeler,* from Latin *appellāre,* to apply to, entreat, address.] —**ap·peal·a·ble** *adj.* —**ap·peal·er** *n.* —**ap·peal·ing·ly** *adv.*

ap·pear (ə-péer) *intr.v.* **-peared, -pearing, -pears.** 1. To come into view; become visible. 2. To come into existence. 3. To seem or look. 4. To seem likely. 5. To come before the public; be presented or published. 6. To present oneself formally; especially, in law, to present oneself before a court as defendant, plaintiff, or counsel. [Middle English *apperen, aperen,* from Old French *aparoir,* from Latin *apparēre* : *ad-*, towards + *parēre†*, to show.]

ap·pear·ance (ə-péer-ənss) *n.* 1. The act or an instance of appearing. 2. An act or instance of being present: *put in an appearance.* 3. The outward aspect of something. 4. Something that appears; a phenomenon. 5. An apparition. 6. A pretence or semblance; a false show. 7. *Plural.* Outward indications: *Appearances can be deceptive.*

ap·pease (ə-péez) *tr.v.* **-peased, -peasing, -peases.** 1. To bring peace to; soothe. 2. To placate or conciliate by yielding to the demands of. 3. To satisfy or relieve: *appease thirst.* —See Synonyms at **pacify.** [Middle English *appesen, apesen,* from Old French *apaisier* : *ap-*, to + *pais,* peace, from Latin *pāx.*] —**ap·peas·a·ble** *adj.* —**ap·peas·a·bly** *adv.* —**ap·peas·er** *n.*

ap·pease·ment (ə-péezmənt) *n.* 1. **a.** The act of appeasing. **b.** The condition of being appeased. 2. The policy of granting concessions to potential enemies with the aim of maintaining peace.

ap·pel (ə-pél) *n. Fencing.* 1. A quick stamp of the foot used as a feint to produce an opening. 2. A blow with a weapon to produce an opening. [French, a call, challenge, from *appeler,* to call, from Old French *apeler,* to APPEAL.]

ap·pel·lant (ə-péllənt) *adj. Law.* Appellate.
~*n.* One who appeals against a court decision.

ap·pel·late (ə-pél-ət, -ayt, -it) *adj.* Having the power to hear appeals and to reverse court decisions: *an appellate court.* [Latin *appellātus,* past participle of *appellāre,* to APPEAL.]

ap·pel·la·tion (ăppə-láysh'n) *n.* 1. A name, title, or epithet. 2. The act of naming. [Middle English *appellacioun,* from Latin *appellātiō* (stem *appellātiōn-*), from *appellāre,* to APPEAL.]

ap·pel·la·tion con·trô·lée (ăppel-áss-yoN koN-trō-láy, -trō-lay) *n. French. Abbr.* **A.C.** 1. A designation or certification awarded to a wine, officially testifying to its quality and its origin in any of several specific regions. 2. A wine thus endorsed. ["Certified name".]

ap·pel·la·tive (ə-péllətiv) *adj.* 1. Of or relating to the assignment of names. 2. *Grammar.* Used to designate a class; common: *appellative nouns.*
~*n.* A name or descriptive epithet. [Middle English, from Late Latin *appellātivus,* from *appellāre,* to call by name, APPEAL.] —**ap·pel·la·tive·ly** *adv.*

ap·pel·lee (ăppel-ée ‖ ăppə-lée) *n. Law.* One who is accused or has an appeal made against him. [Old French *apele,* from *apeler,* to APPEAL.]

ap·pend (ə-pénd) *tr.v.* **-pended, -pending, -pends.** 1. To add as a supplement. **2.** To attach; fix. Used with *to.* [Latin *appendere* : *ad-*, to + *pendere*, to hang.]

ap·pend·age (ə-péndij) *n.* **1.** Something appended, especially something of lesser importance. **2.** *Biology.* Any part or organ that is joined to an axis or trunk, such as an arthropod limb.
Synonyms: appendage, adjunct, accessory, addition, attachment.

ap·pen·dant (ə-péndənt) *adj.* **1.** Hanging attached; suspended. **2.** Accompanying; attendant: *faith and its appendant hope.* **3.** *Law.* Belonging as a subsidiary right.
~*n.* **1.** Something attached or added. **2.** *Law.* A subsidiary right.

ap·pen·dic·ec·to·my (ə-péndiss-éktəmi) *n., pl.* **-mies.** Also **ap·pen·dec·to·my** (áppən-déktəmi, áppen-). The surgical removal of the vermiform appendix. [Latin *appendix* (stem *appendic-*) + -EC-TOMY.]

ap·pen·di·ci·tis (ə-péndi-sítiss) *n.* Inflammation of the vermiform appendix. [APPENDIX + -ITIS.]

ap·pen·dic·u·lar (áppen-díckew-lər, áppən-) *adj.* **1.** Of, pertaining to, or consisting of an appendage or appendages. **2.** Of or pertaining to the vermiform appendix. **3.** *Biology.* Of or pertaining to limbs: *appendicular skeleton.* [Latin *appendicula*, diminutive of *appendix* (stem *appendic-*), APPENDIX.]

ap·pen·dix (ə-pén-diks) *n., pl.* **-dixes** or **-dices** (-di-seez). *Abbr.* **app. 1. a.** An appendage. **b.** A collection of supplementary material at the end of a book. **2.** The **vermiform appendix** (*see*). [Latin *appendix*, appendage, from *appendere*, to APPEND.]
Usage: In its medical sense, the plural is *appendixes.* In the sense of "supplementary material at the end of a book", formal usage still prefers *appendices.*

ap·per·ceive (áppər-seév) *tr.v.* **-ceived, -ceiving, -ceives. 1.** To be conscious of perceiving. **2.** *Psychology.* To perceive in terms of past perceptions. [Middle English *apperceiven, aperceiven*, from Old French *aperceivre* : *a-*, towards + *perceivre*, to PERCEIVE.]

ap·per·cep·tion (áppər-sépsh'n) *n.* **1.** Conscious perception with full awareness. **2.** *Psychology.* The process of understanding by which newly observed qualities of something are related to past experience. —**ap·per·cep·tive** (-séptiv) *adj.*

ap·per·tain (áppər-táyn) *intr.v.* **-tained, -taining, -tains.** To belong as a function or part; pertain properly. Used with *to.* [Middle English *apperteinen*, from Old French *apartenir*, from Vulgar Latin *appartenere*, variant of Late Latin *appertinēre*, to PERTAIN.]

ap·pe·stat (áppi-stat) *n.* The mechanism in the hypothalamus of the brain that controls appetite. [APPE(TITE) + -STAT.]

ap·pe·tence (áppi-tənss) *n.* Also **ap·pe·ten·cy** (-tənssi) *pl.* **-cies. 1.** A strong craving or desire. **2.** A tendency or proclivity; a propensity. [Latin *appetentia*, from *appetēns* (stem *appetent-*), present participle of *appetere*, to strive after, desire eagerly. See **appetite.**]

ap·pe·tis·er, ap·pe·tiz·er (áppi-tīzər) *n.* **1.** A food or drink served before a meal, or before the main course of a meal, to stimulate the appetite. **2.** Something that stimulates the senses or arouses expectations.

ap·pe·tis·ing (áppi-tīzing) *adj.* Stimulating the appetite.

ap·pe·tite (áppi-tīt) *n.* **1.** A desire for food or drink. **2.** Any physical craving or desire. **3.** A strong wish or urge to partake of something. [Middle English *appetit, apetit*, from Old French *apetit*, from Latin *appetītus*, from *appetere*, to strive after, desire eagerly : *ad-*, towards + *petere*, to seek.] —**ap·pe·ti·tive** (ə-péttitiv, áppi-tītiv) *adj.*

Ap·pi·an Way (áppi-ən). Roman road connecting Rome and Brundisium (Brindisi) some 589 kilometres (366 miles) long. It was inaugurated in 312 B.C. by the statesman Appius Claudius Caecus.

ap·plaud (ə-pláwd) *v.* **-plauded, -plauding, -plauds.** —*intr.* To express approval, especially by clapping the hands. —*tr.* **1.** To express approval of by clapping the hands. **2.** To praise; approve. [Latin *applaudere*, to clap at : *ad-*, to + *plaudere†*, to clap.] —**ap·plaud·er** *n.*

ap·plause (ə-pláwz) *n.* Publicly expressed approval, especially when shown by the clapping of hands. [Medieval Latin *applausus*, from Latin, past participle of *applaudere*, to APPLAUD.]

ap·ple (áp'l) *n.* **1.** A tree, *Malus pumila* (or *Pyrus malus*), of temperate regions, having fragrant pink or white flowers and edible fruit. **2.** The firm, rounded fruit of this tree, having skin that is red, yellow, or green. Also used adjectively: *apple pie.* **3. a.** Any of several trees or plants having fruit resembling the apple, such as the **custard apple** or the **crab apple** (*both of which see*). **b.** The fruit of any of these trees or plants. See **oak apple, thorn apple. 4.** The hard wood of an apple tree. **5.** *Informal.* An enthusiast for and operator of citizens' band radio. —**apple of (someone's) eye.** A precious or much-loved person or thing. —**she's apples.** *Australian Informal.* Everything is fine. [Middle English *appel*, Old English *æppel.*]

ap·ple·cart (áp'l-kaart) *n.* A cart loaded with apples. —**upset the applecart.** To spoil a plan or scheme.

apple green *n.* Moderate to vivid yellowish green. —**ap·ple-green** *adj.*

Apple Islander *n.* A Tasmanian.

Apple Isle. Tasmania.

ap·ple·jack (áp'l-jak) *n.* *U.S.* Brandy distilled from cider. [APPLE + JACK (fellow, chap).]

ap·ple-pie bed (áp'l-pī, -pí) *n.* A bed which has been made with one of the sheets folded double as a joke, so that one cannot lie down. [Perhaps alteration of French *nappe pliée*, folded sheet.]

apple-pie order *n. Informal.* Very good condition.

ap·ple-pol·ish (áp'l-pollish) *intr.v.* **-ished, -ishing, -ishes.** *U.S. Informal.* To seek favour by toadying. —**ap·ple-pol·ish·er.**

apples and pears *pl.n. British Informal.* Stairs. [Rhyming slang.]

apple sauce *n.* **1.** Apples stewed to a pulp, sweetened, and sometimes spiced. **2.** *U.S. Slang.* Foolishness; nonsense.

Ap·ple·ton layer (áp'l-tən) *n.* The **F** layer (*see*) of the ionosphere. [After Sir Edward *Appleton* (1892–1965), British physicist.]

ap·pli·ance (ə-plī-ənss) *n.* **1.** A device or instrument; especially, one operated by electricity and designed for household use, such as a refrigerator or vacuum cleaner. **2.** An attachment or accessory; especially, one that adapts a tool for a different use. **3.** A fire engine. —See Synonyms at **tool.** [From APPLY.]

ap·pli·ca·ble (ápplika-b'l, ə-plícka-b'l) *adj.* **1.** Capable of being applied; appropriate. **2.** In force; effective: *New rates are applicable from Monday.* —**ap·pli·ca·bil·i·ty** (-billəti) *n.* —**ap·pli·ca·bly** *adv.*

ap·pli·cant (ápplikənt) *n.* One who applies, as for a job. [Latin *applicāns* (stem *applicant-*), present participle of *applicāre*, to APPLY.]

ap·pli·ca·tion (áppli-káysh'n) *n.* **1.** The act of applying or putting something on. **2.** Anything that is applied, such as a cosmetic or curative agent. **3.** The act of putting something to a special use or purpose. **4. a.** A method of applying or using; a specific use: *industrial applications.* **b.** The capacity of being usable; relevance: *The theory has no application in this case.* **5.** Attention, diligence, or effort. **6. a.** A formal request, as for employment or admission. **b.** A written statement making such a request. **c.** The printed form upon which such a statement is often made: *fill in an application.* ~*adj.* Also **ap·pli·ca·tions.** *Computing.* Pertaining to or designating software designed for specific applications. Used before the noun: *applications software ; applications programs.* [Middle English *applicacioun*, from Latin *applicātiō* (stem *applicātiōn-*), from *applicāre*, to APPLY.]

ap·pli·ca·tive (ə-plíckətiv, áppli-kaytiv) *adj.* **1.** Characterised by actual application to something. **2.** Of practical use; applicatory. —**ap·pli·ca·tive·ly** *adv.*

ap·pli·ca·tor (áppli-kaytər) *n.* An instrument for applying something, such as a medicament or glue.

ap·pli·ca·to·ry (áppli-kətri, -kaytəri, -káytəri, ə-plíckətri ‖ *U.S.* ápplikə-tawri, ə-plícka-, -tōri) *adj.* Of practical value; useful.

ap·plied (ə-plíd) *adj. Abbr.* **app., appl.** Intended to have practical consequences; capable of being put to practical use: *applied physics.* Compare **theoretical.**

ap·pli·qué (ə-pléekay, a- ‖ *U.S.* áppli-káy) *n.* A decoration or ornament made by cutting pieces of one material and applying them to the surface of another.
~*tr.v.* **appliquéd, -quéing, -qués.** To decorate with appliqué work. [French, past participle of *appliquer*, to put on, apply, from Latin *applicāre*, to APPLY.] —**ap·pli·qué** *adj.*

ap·ply (ə-plí) *v.* **-plied, -plying, -plies.** —*tr.* **1.** To bring near to or into contact with something; put on or onto: *apply the glue to both surfaces.* **2.** To put to or adapt for a special use: *This principle is applied in glass manufacture.* **3.** To use (an epithet, for example) with reference to a particular person or thing. Used with *to.* **4.** To devote (oneself or one's efforts) to something. **5.** To bring into operation: *applied the brakes.* —*intr.* **1.** To be pertinent or relevant. **2.** To request or seek employment, acceptance, or admission. Used with *for* or *to.* [Middle English *applien, aplien*, from Old French *aplier*, from Latin *applicāre*, to join to, apply to : *ad-*, to + *plicāre*, to fold together.]

ap·pog·gia·tu·ra (ə-pójə-toór-ə, -póji-ə-, -téwr-) *n., pl.* **-re** (-ay) or **-ras** (-əz). *Music.* A grace note of varying length, usually one step above the note it precedes. Compare **acciaccatura.** [Italian, "a supporting", from *appoggiare*, to lean on, from Vulgar Latin *appodiāre* (unattested) : Latin *ad-*, to + *podium*, balcony, from Greek *podion*, small foot, base, diminutive of *pous* (stem *pod-*), foot.]

ap·point (ə-póynt) *v.* **-pointed, -pointing, -points.** —*tr.* **1.** To select or designate to fill an office or position. **2.** To fix or set by authority or by mutual agreement. **3.** To order, require, or enjoin with authority; prescribe. **4.** To furnish; equip. Used chiefly in the passive and in combination: *a well-appointed flat.* —*intr. Law.* To dispose of property under the legal power of appointment. [Middle English *appointen, apointen*, from Old French *apointier*, to arrange, from *(rendre) à point*, "(to bring) to a point" : *a-*, to + POINT.] —**ap·point·ee** (ə-póyn-tée, áppoyn-) *n.*

ap·point·ive (ə-póyntiv) *adj. Chiefly U.S.* Pertaining to or filled by appointment: *appointive office.*

ap·point·ment (ə-póyntmənt) *n.* **1.** The act of appointing or state of being appointed, as to an office or position. **2.** The office or position to which a person has been appointed. **3.** An arrangement to do something or meet someone at a particular time and place. **4.** *Usually plural.* Fittings or equipment. **5.** *Law.* The act of directing the disposal of property by virtue of a power granted under a preceding deed.

ap·poin·tor (ə-póynt-ər, -ór) *n. Law.* One who executes a power of appointment of property.

Ap·po·mat·tox (áppə-máttəks). Town in central Virginia, in the United States, where the American Civil War came virtually to a close. The Confederate general Robert E. Lee surrendered to the Union general Ulysses S. Grant there on April 9, 1865.

ap·port (ə-pórt) *n.* **1.** In spiritualism, the act of conjuring up or transporting a material object. **2.** The object so transported. [French *apporter*, to bring, from Latin *apportāre* : *ad-* near to + *portāre*, to carry.]

ap·por·tion (ə-pór-sh'n ‖ -pór-) *tr.v.* **-tioned, -tioning, -tions.** To divide and assign according to some plan or proportion; allot; par-

tition. See Synonyms at **assign**. [French *apportionner* : *a-*, to + *portionner*, to divide into portions, from PORTION.]
ap·por·tion·ment (ə-pór-sh'n-mənt || -pṓr-) *n.* **1. a.** The act of apportioning or the condition of being apportioned. **b.** An amount apportioned. **2.** In the United States, the proportional distribution of the number of members of the House of Representatives on the basis of the population of each state.
ap·pose (appṓz, ə-pṓz) *tr.v.* **-posed, -posing, -poses. 1.** To put or apply (one thing) to another. **2.** To arrange (things) near to each other or side by side. [Back-formation from APPOSITION (by analogy with COMPOSE, COMPOSITION).]
ap·po·site (áppə-zit || -zīt) *adj.* Fitting; suitable; appropriate. See Synonyms at **relevant.** [Latin *appositus*, "situated near", past participle of *appōnere*, to place near to, apply to. See **apposition.**] **—ap·po·site·ly** *adv.* **—ap·po·site·ness** *n.*
ap·po·si·tion (áppə-zísh'n) *n.* **1.** *Grammar.* **a.** A construction in which one noun or noun phrase is placed after another to explain it, and has the same function in the sentence. In the sentence *Gladstone, the famous statesman, was born in Liverpool, Gladstone* and *the famous statesman* are in apposition. **b.** The relationship between such nouns or noun phrases. **2.** A placing side by side or next to each other. **3.** *Biology.* The growth in thickness of a cell wall by deposition of successive layers of material. [Middle English *apposicioun*, from Medieval Latin *appositiō*, from Latin *appōnere* (past participle *appositus*), to place near to, apply to : *ad-*, near to + *pōnere*, to put.] **—ap·po·si·tion·al** *adj.* **—ap·po·si·tion·al·ly** *adv.*
ap·pos·i·tive (ə-pózzətiv, a-) *adj.* In or pertaining to apposition. *~n.* A word or phrase that is in apposition. [From APPOSITION.] **—ap·pos·i·tive·ly** *adv.*
ap·prais·al (ə-práyz'l) *n.* **1.** The act of appraising. **2.** An account or evaluation of the merits and defects of someone or something. **3.** An expert or official valuation of something, as for taxation.
ap·praise (ə-práyz) *tr.v.* **-praised, -praising, -praises. 1.** To evaluate, especially in an official capacity. **2.** To estimate the quality, amount, size, and other features of; judge. —See Synonyms at **estimate.** [Middle English *appreisen*, partly from *preise*, value, PRAISE, partly from Old French *aprisier*, from Late Latin *appretiāre*, to set a value on : *ad-*, to + *pretiāre*, to value, from Latin *pretium*, price.] **—ap·prais·a·ble** *adj.* **—ap·praise·ment** *n.* **—ap·prais·er** *n.*
ap·pre·cia·ble (ə-preésh-əb'l, -i-əb'l) *adj.* Capable of being noticed, estimated, or measured; noticeable. See Synonyms at **perceptible. —ap·pre·cia·bly** *adv.*
ap·pre·ci·ate (ə-preéshi-ayt, -preéssi-) *v.* **-ated, -ating, -ates.** *—tr.* **1.** To be fully aware of or sensitive to; realise: *He doesn't appreciate the difficulties involved.* **2.** To be thankful or show gratitude for. **3.** To value greatly; enjoy with appreciation: *appreciate a fine wine.* **4.** To raise in value or price. *—intr.* To go up in value or price. [Late Latin *appretiāre*, to set a value on : *ad-*, to + *pretiāre*, to value, from *pretium*, price.] **—ap·pre·ci·a·tor** (-aytər) *n.*
Synonyms: *appreciate, value, prize, esteem, treasure, cherish.*
ap·pre·ci·a·tion (ə-preéshi-áysh'n, -preéssi-) *n.* **1.** Gratefulness; gratitude. **2.** Awareness or delicate perception, especially of aesthetic qualities or values: *an appreciation of Manet's brushwork.* **3.** An assessment of the true nature of someone or something: *a fair appreciation of the economic situation.* **4.** A generally favourable expression of criticism. **5.** A rise in value or price.
ap·pre·cia·tive (ə-preésh-yətiv, -ətiv || -i-aytiv) *adj.* Capable of or showing appreciation. **—ap·pre·cia·tive·ly** *adv.*
ap·pre·hend (áppri-hend) *v.* **-hended, -hending, -hends.** *—tr.* **1.** To take into custody; arrest. **2.** To grasp mentally; understand. **3.** *Formal.* To anticipate with anxiety. *—intr.* To understand. [Middle English *apprehenden*, from Latin *apprehendere*, to lay hold on, seize : *ad-*, to + *prehendere*, to seize.]
Synonyms: *apprehend, comprehend, grasp, understand.*
ap·pre·hen·si·ble (áppri-hénssib'l) *adj.* Capable of being apprehended or understood. **—ap·pre·hen·si·bly** *adv.*
ap·pre·hen·sion (áppri-hénsh'n) *n.* **1.** A fearful or uneasy anticipation of the future. **2.** A seizing or capturing; an arrest. **3.** The ability to apprehend or understand; understanding. **4.** *Formal.* An opinion or estimate. [Middle English *apprehensioun*, from Late Latin *apprehensiō* (stem *apprehensiōn-*), from *apprehendere* (past participle *apprehensus*), APPREHEND.]
Synonyms: *apprehension, foreboding, presentiment, misgiving.*
ap·pre·hen·sive (áppri-hénssiv) *adj.* **1.** Anxious or fearful about the future; uneasy. **2.** *Formal.* Capable of understanding; quick to apprehend. **3.** *Archaic.* Aware; conscious. **—ap·pre·hen·sive·ly** *adv.* **—ap·pre·hen·sive·ness** *n.*
ap·pren·tice (ə-préntiss) *n.* **1.** One bound by legal agreement to work for another for a given length of time in return for instruction in a trade, art, or business. Often used adjectivally: *an apprentice engineer.* **2.** Any beginner; a learner.
~tr.v. **apprenticed, -ticing, -tices.** To place or take on as an apprentice; bind by indenture. [Middle English *aprentis*, from Old French, from *aprendre*, to learn, from Latin *appre(he)ndere*, to APPREHEND.] **—ap·pren·tice·ship** *n.*
ap·pressed (ə-prést, a-) *adj.* Lying flat or pressed closely against something, as leaves on a stem are. [Latin *appressus*, past participle of *apprimere*, to press to : *ad-*, to + *premere*, to press.]
ap·prise (ə-prīz) *tr.v.* **-prised, -prising, -prises.** To cause to know; make aware; inform. Used with *of.* [French *apprendre* (past participle *appris*), to cause to learn, inform, from Old French *aprendre*, to learn, from Latin *appre(he)ndere*, to APPREHEND.]
ap·pro (ápprō) *n.* *Chiefly British Informal.* Approval: *I buy mail-order goods on appro.*
ap·proach (ə-prṓch) *v.* **-proached, -proaching, -proaches.** *—intr.* To come or draw nearer or nearer in space, time, or magnitude. *—tr.* **1.** To come near or nearer to. **2.** To come close to in appearance, quality, condition, or other characteristics; approximate to: *Her talent approaches genius.* **3.** To make a proposal to; make overtures to. **4.** To begin to deal with or work on. **5.** *Archaic.* To bring or draw closer.
~n. **1.** The act of coming or drawing near. **2.** A fairly close resemblance; an approximation. **3.** A way or means of reaching someone or a destination; an access: *All approaches to the town are blocked.* **4.** The method used in dealing with or accomplishing something. **5.** *Often plural.* An advance or overture made by one person to another. **6.** In golf, the stroke following the drive from the tee, with which the player tries to get the ball onto the putting green. Also called "approach shot". **7.** *Aeronautics.* The last stage in an aircraft's flight before it lands: *We are now commencing the approach to Heathrow.* Often used adjectivally: *the approach path.* **8.** *Plural. Military.* Works such as trenches or bulwarks for the protection of troops besieging a fortified position. [Middle English *aprochen*, from Old French *aprochier*, from Late Latin *appropiāre*, to go nearer to : *ad-*, to + *propius*, nearer, from *prope*, near.]
ap·proach·a·ble (ə-prṓch-əb'l) *adj.* **1.** Capable of being approached or reached; accessible. **2.** Easily approached; receptive to overtures; friendly. **—ap·proach·a·bil·i·ty** (-ə-bíllәti) *n.*
ap·pro·bate (ápprə-bayt, ápprō-) *tr.v.* **-bated, -bating, -bates. 1.** In Scots law, to accept as valid. **2.** *U.S.* To sanction; authorise. **—approbate and reprobate.** In Scots law, to accept some parts of a deed as valid but not others. [Middle English *approbaten*, from Latin *approbāre*, to APPROVE.] **—ap·pro·ba·tive** (-baytiv), **ap·pro·ba·to·ry** (ápprə-báytəri, ápprō- || *U.S.* ə-prṓbə-tawri, -tōri) *adj.*
ap·pro·ba·tion (ápprə-báysh'n, ápprō-) *n.* **1.** Praise; commendation. **2.** Official approval. —See Synonyms at **regard.**
ap·pro·pri·a·ble (ə-prṓpri-əb'l) *adj.* Capable of being appropriated.
ap·pro·pri·ate (ə-prṓpri-ət, -it) *adj.* Suitable for a particular person, condition, occasion, or place; proper; fitting. See Synonyms at **fit.**
~tr.v. (ə-prṓpri-ayt) **appropriated, -ating, -ates. 1.** To set apart for a specific use. **2.** To take possession of or make use of exclusively for oneself, often without permission. [Middle English *appropriaten*, from Late Latin *appropriāre* (past participle *appropriātus*), to make one's own : Latin *ad-* to + *proprius*, own.] **—ap·pro·pri·ate·ly** *adv.* **—ap·pro·pri·ate·ness** *n.* **—ap·pro·pri·a·tive** (-ətiv, -aytiv) *adj.* **—ap·pro·pri·ator** (-aytər) *n.*
appropriate technology *n.* Technology suited to local conditions in certain developing countries, characterised by the use of relatively simple tools, machines, and methods, as opposed to advanced labour-saving machinery.
ap·pro·pri·a·tion (ə-prṓpri-áysh'n) *n.* **1.** The act of appropriating for a specific use or purpose. **2.** The act of appropriating to oneself. **3.** Public funds set aside for a specific purpose.
ap·prov·al (ə-proóv'l) *n.* **1.** The act or an instance of approving. **2.** Commendation; favourable regard; good opinion. **—on approval.** For examination or trial by a potential customer without the obligation to buy.
ap·prove (ə-proóv) *v.* **-proved, -proving, -proves.** *—tr.* **1.** To confirm or consent to officially; sanction; ratify: *approve the proposals.* **2.** To view with approval; commend. **3.** *Archaic.* To prove or demonstrate: *"the letter he spoke of which approves him an intelligent party"* (Shakespeare). *—intr.* To feel, voice, or demonstrate approval. Usually used with *of*: *approve of capital punishment.* [Middle English *approven*, from Old French *aprover*, from Latin *approbāre*, to make good, admit as good : *ad-*, to + *probus*, good.] **—ap·prov·a·ble** *adj.* **—ap·prov·ing·ly** *adv.*
Synonyms: *approve, endorse, sanction, certify, ratify.*
approved school *n.* Formerly, a school for young offenders in Britain. Compare **community home.**
approx. approximate; approximately.
ap·prox·i·mate (ə-próksi-mət, -mit) *adj. Abbr.* **approx. 1.** Almost exact, correct, complete, or perfect. **2.** *Rare.* Very similar; closely resembling. **3.** Close together; near.
~v. (-mayt) **approximated, -mating, -mates.** *—tr.* **1.** To come close to; be nearly the same as. **2.** To cause to approach; bring near. *—intr.* To come near or close in degree, nature, quality, or other characteristics. [Late Latin *approximātus*, past participle of *approximāre*, to come near to : Latin *ad-*, to + *proximāre*, to come near, from *proximus*, nearest.]
ap·prox·i·mate·ly (ə-próksi-mət-li, -mit-) *adv.* **1.** Almost; about: *approximately two o'clock.* **2.** Imperfectly; not exactly.
ap·prox·i·ma·tion (ə-próksi-máysh'n) *n.* **1.** An approximate assessment. **2.** A partially accurate account: *an approximation of the facts.* **3.** *Mathematics.* An inexact result or relationship, adequate for a given purpose. **—ap·prox·i·ma·tive** (-mətiv || -maytiv) *adj.* **—ap·prox·i·ma·tive·ly** *adv.*
appt. appoint; appointed.
ap·pulse (ə-púlss, a-, ápulss) *n.* An apparent close approach of two celestial bodies in which no occultation or eclipse occurs. [Latin *appulsus*, approach, from past participle of *appellere*, to drive towards : *ad-*, towards + *pellere*, to drive.]
ap·pur·te·nance (ə-púrt-inənss || -nənss) *n.* **1.** Something added to another more important thing; an appendage; an accessory. **2.** *Plural.* Any equipment or apparatus used for a specific purpose or task; gear. **3.** *Law.* A right, privilege, or minor property that is regarded as accompanying the principal property for purposes

such as passage of title, conveyance, or inheritance. [Middle English *appurtenaunce,* from Anglo-French *apurtenance,* variant of Old French *apertenance,* from Vulgar Latin *appertinentia* (unattested), from Late Latin *appertinēre,* to APPERTAIN.]

ap·pur·te·nant (ə-púrt-inənt ‖ -nənt) *adj.* **1.** *Law.* Constituting an appurtenance. **2.** Belonging, accessory, or relating.

Apr. April.

APR. Annual Percentage Rate.

a·prax·i·a (ay-práksi-ə, ə-) *n.* The inability to perform coordinated movements as a result of lesions in the cerebral cortex. [New Latin, from Greek, inaction : *a-,* without + Greek *praxis,* action, from *prassein,* to do.] —**a·prac·tic** (-práktik) *adj.*

a·près- (áppray) *comb. form.* Indicates a time following a specified period or activity; for example, *après-forty, après-swim.*

a·près-ski (áppray-skée) *n.* Social activities in the evening at a ski resort. —**a·près-ski** *adj.*

a·pri·cot (áypri-kot ‖ áppri-) *n.* **1.** A tree, *Prunus armeniaca,* native to western Asia and Africa, widely cultivated for its edible fruit. **2.** The juicy, yellow-orange, peachlike fruit of this tree. **3.** Moderate, light, or strong orange to orange yellow. [Earlier *abrecock,* perhaps from obsolete Catalan *abercoc,* from Arabic *al-birqūq,* "the apricot", from Late Greek *praikokion,* from Latin *(prūnum) praecoquum,* "early-ripening (plum)", from *praecoquere,* to ripen early : *prae-,* before + *coquere,* to ripen, cook.] —**a·pri·cot** *adj.*

A·pril (áypril, áyprəl) *n. Abbr.* **Apr.** The fourth month of the year according to the Gregorian calendar. April has 30 days. [Middle English, from Latin *aprīlis,* perhaps "month of Venus", from Etruscan *apru,* from Greek *Aphrŏ,* short form of *Aphroditē,* APHRODITE.]

April fool *n.* The victim of a trick played on April Fools' Day.

April Fools' Day *n.* April 1, marked as a day for playing practical jokes before noon. Also called "All Fools' Day".

a pri·o·ri (áy-prī-áwrī, áʹa-pree-áwree) *adj.* **1.** *Logic.* Pertaining to or proceeding from a known or assumed cause or general principle to a necessarily related effect or conclusion; deductive. **2. a.** Based on reason alone; not provable empirically. **b.** Based on a hypothesis or convention rather than on experiment or experience. **3.** Claimed as true without examination; not supported by factual study. Compare **a posteriori.** [Latin, "from the previous (causes or hypotheses)".] —**a pri·or·i·ty** (-órrəti) *n.*

a·pron (áypron ‖ áypərn) *n.* **1.** A garment worn over all or part of the front of the body to protect one's clothes or as a decorative part of a costume. **2.** Anything resembling an apron in appearance or function. **3.** The hard-surfaced area in front of and around airport hangars and terminal buildings. **4.** The part of a stage in a theatre extending in front of the curtain. **5. a.** A platform of planking or other material at the entrance to a dock. **b.** A covering or structure along the shoreline of a body of water for protection against erosion. **c.** A platform serving a similar purpose below a dam or in a sluiceway. **6.** A continuous conveyor belt. **7.** *Geology.* An area covered by sand and gravel deposited at the front of a glacial moraine. **8.** A panel, board, or the like, placed between a window and a skirting board. **9.** A metal plate that protects a machine operator, gunner, or the like, from the pieces of flying debris. —**tied to (someone's) apron strings.** Controlled by or dependent on. ~*tr.v.* **aproned, aproning, aprons.** To cover, protect, or provide with an apron; put an apron or aprons on. [Middle English *(an) apron,* originally *(a) napron,* from Old French *naperon,* diminutive of *nape,* tablecloth, from Latin *mappa,* napkin.]

apron stage *n.* A stage, usually without a curtain, which extends into the area occupied by the audience.

ap·ro·pos (áprə-pŏ, -pō) *adj.* Appropriate; pertinent; opportune. ~*adv.* **1.** Pertinently; relevantly; opportunely. **2.** By the way; incidentally. Used to introduce a remark. ~*prep.* Also **apropos of.** Speaking of; with reference to. [French *à propos,* "to the purpose".]

a·pro·tic (áy-prōtik) *adj. Chemistry.* Having no protons; not producing or accepting hydrogen ions. Used of substances or solutions that are not hydrogen acids or hydroxide bases. [A- (without) + PROT(ON) + -IC.]

apse (aps) *n.* **1.** *Architecture.* A semicircular or polygonal, usually domed, projection of a building, especially at the altar or east end of a church. Also called "apsis". **2.** *Astronomy.* An orbital position, the apsis. [Medieval Latin *apsis, absis.* See apsis.] —**ap·si·dal** (áp-sidəl, ap-sīdʹl) *adj.*

ap·sis (áp-siss) *n., pl.* **-sides** (-sideez). **1.** *Astronomy.* The point of greatest or least distance of a celestial body from a centre of attraction. Also called "apse". **2.** *Architecture.* An apse. [Medieval Latin *apsis,* architectural apse, from Latin, arch, vault, orbit, from Greek *apsis, hapsis,* "a fastening together", from *haptein†,* to fasten.]

apt (apt) *adj.* **1.** Exactly suitable; appropriate. **2.** Likely: *The handle is apt to break off.* **3.** Inclined; given: *He is apt to stammer when he is excited.* **4.** Quick to learn or understand. —See Synonyms at fit, relevant. [Middle English, from Latin *aptus,* fit, suited, from the past participle of *apere,* to fasten.] —**apt·ly** *adv.* —**apt·ness** *n.*

APT[1] Advanced Passenger Train.

APT[2] *n.* A computer programming language designed for use with computer-controlled machine tools. [*Automatically Programmed Tool.*]

apt. apartment.

ap·ter·al (áptərəl) *adj. Architecture.* Having no columns along the sides. [Greek *apteros,* wingless, APTEROUS.]

ap·ter·ous (áptərəss) *adj.* **1.** *Zoology.* Having no wings: *an apterous insect.* **2.** *Botany.* Having no winglike parts or extensions. [Greek

apteros, wingless : *a-,* without + -PTEROUS.]

ap·te·ryg·i·al (áp-tə-ríji-əl, -te-) *adj. Zoology.* Without wings or fins. [A- (without) + Greek *pterux* (stem *pterug-*), wing, fin.]

ap·ter·yx (áptəriks) *n.* A bird, the **kiwi** *(see).* [New Latin : A- (without) + Greek *pterux,* wing, from *pteron,* feather, wing.]

ap·ti·tude (ápti-tewd ‖ -tōd) *n.* **1.** A natural talent, skill, or ability. Used with *for* or *in: an aptitude for sculpture.* **2.** Quickness in learning and understanding. **3.** The state or quality of being fitting; aptness. —See Synonyms at ability. [Middle English, from Late Latin *aptitūdō,* fitness, from *aptus,* APT.]

aptitude test *n.* A standardised test designed to measure the ability of an individual to develop skills or acquire knowledge.

A·pu·lei·us (áppew-lée-əss), **Lucius,** also known as Apuleius of Madaura *(c.* A.D. 125–*c.* A.D. 180). Roman philosopher and satirist, born in Algeria. His most famous work, *The Golden Ass,* or *Metamorphoses,* is the story of a man who is changed into an ass.

A·pu·li·a (ə-péwl-yə, -i-ə). *Italian* **Pu·glia** (pōōl-ya). A farming region, chiefly low-lying, in southeast Italy. Its southern portion forms the heel of the Italian "boot". Bari is the chief city. —**A·pu·li·an** *adj. & n.*

A·pus (áypəss) *n.* A constellation in the Southern Hemisphere near Musca and Pavo. [New Latin, from Latin *apus,* the swallow, from Greek *apous,* the swift, "footless" (probably because the swift is seldom seen perching) : *a-,* without + *pous,* foot.]

a·py·re·tic (áppīr-éttik) *adj.* Without fever. [A- (without) + Greek *puretos,* fever.]

aq. aqueous.

A·qa·ba, A·ka·ba (áckə-bə ‖ aʹakə-baa). Jordan's only seaport, situated at the head of the Gulf of Aqaba.

aq·ua (ákwə ‖ *U.S. also* áʹakwə) *n., pl.* **-uas** or **aquae** (ákwee, ákwī ‖ *U.S. also* áʹakwī) **1.** *Pharmacology.* Liquid; solution, especially in water. **2.** A colour, aquamarine. [Latin, water.] —**aq·ua** *adj.*

aqua- *comb. form.* Indicates water; for example, **aquarium, aqualung.** [Latin.]

aq·ua·cul·ture (ákwə-kulchər) *n.* The farming of sea organisms for human use.

Aq·ua·dag (ákwə-dag ‖ *U.S. also* áʹakwə-) *n.* A trademark for a colloidal suspension of graphite in water, used as a lubricant and conducting coating.

aqua fortis *n. Chemistry.* **Nitric acid** *(see).* [New Latin, "strong water".]

aq·ua·lung (ákwə-lung ‖ *U.S. also* áʹakwə-) *n.* An underwater breathing apparatus consisting of a cylinder of compressed air attached to a face mask by a tube.

aq·ua·ma·rine (ákwə-mə-réen ‖ *U.S. also* áʹakwə-) *n.* **1.** A transparent blue-green variety of beryl, used as a gemstone. **2.** Pale blue to light greenish blue. [New Latin *aqua marina,* from Latin, sea water: *aqua,* AQUA- + *marinus,* of the sea, MARINE.] —**aq·ua·ma·rine** *adj.*

aq·ua·naut (ákwə-nawt ‖ *U.S. also* áʹakwə-) *n.* A person trained to live in underwater installations and conduct or assist in scientific research. [AQUA- + Greek *nautēs,* sailor.]

aq·ua·plane (ákwə-playn ‖ *U.S. also* áʹakwə-) *n.* A board on which one rides in a standing position while it is pulled over the water by a motorboat. ~*intr.v.* **aquaplaned, -planing, -planes. 1.** To ride on an aquaplane. **2.** To skid uncontrollably on a wet road surface. Used of a motor vehicle. [AQUA- + PLANE (surface).]

aqua re·gi·a (réeji-ə) *n.* A corrosive, fuming mixture of concentrated hydrochloric and nitric acids, used for testing metals and dissolving platinum and gold. Also called "nitrohydrochloric acid". [New Latin, "royal water" (because it dissolves gold and platinum, which were known as the "noble metals").]

aq·ua·relle (ákwə-rél ‖ *U.S. also* áʹakwə-) *n.* A drawing done in transparent watercolours. [French, from obsolete Italian *acquarella,* watercolor, from *acqua,* water, from Latin *aqua.*] —**aq·ua·rel·list** *n.*

a·quar·ist (ákwərist ‖ ə-kwáir-ist) *n.* One who keeps an aquarium.

a·quar·i·um (ə-kwáir-i-əm) *n., pl.* **-ums** or **aquaria** (-i-ə). **1.** A tank, bowl, or other water-filled enclosure in which living aquatic animals and plants are kept. **2.** A place for the public exhibition of such animals and plants. [19th century : noun use of Latin *aquārius,* of water, from *aqua,* water, formed by analogy with *vivarium.*]

A·quar·i·us (ə-kwáir-i-əss) *n.* **1.** A constellation in the equatorial region of the Southern Hemisphere near Pisces and Aquila. **2. a.** The 11th sign of the **zodiac** *(see).* Also called "the Water Carrier". **b.** One born under this sign. [Latin *aquārius,* from *aqua,* water.] —**A·quar·i·an** *n. & adj.*

a·quat·ic (ə-kwáttik ‖ ə-kwóttik) *adj.* **1.** Living or growing in or on the water. **2.** Taking place in or on the water. ~*n.* **1.** An aquatic organism. **2.** *Plural.* Aquatic sports. [Old French *aquatique,* from Latin *aquāticus,* from *aqua,* water.]

aq·ua·tint (ákwə-tint ‖ *U.S. also* áʹakwə-) *n.* **1.** A process of etching capable of producing several tones by varying the etching time of different areas of a copper plate so that the resulting print resembles the flat tints of an ink or wash drawing. **2.** An etching made in this way. ~*tr.v.* **aquatinted, -tinting, -tints.** To etch in aquatint. [French *aquatinte,* from Italian *acqua tinta,* "tinted water", watercolour, hence aquatint (which imitates watercolour) : *acqua,* water + *tinta,* tinted, from Latin *tincta,* feminine of *tinctus,* dyed (see tint).]

aq·ua·vit (ákwə-vit, -veet ‖ *U.S. also* áʹakwə-) *n.* A strong, clear Scandinavian alcoholic spirit, distilled from potato or grain mash and flavoured with caraway seed. [Swedish, Danish, and Norwegian *akvavit,* from Medieval Latin *aqua vītae,* "water of life".]

aqua vi·tae (vítee, véetī) n. 1. Whisky, brandy, or other strong spirits. 2. *Archaic.* Alcohol. [Middle English *aquavite,* from Medieval Latin *aqua vītae,* "water of life", originally an alchemist's term for alcohol or spirits.]

aq·ue·duct (ák-wi-dukt, -wə-) n. 1. A man-made channel designed to transport water over long distances, usually by gravity. 2. An elevated structure supporting a channel or canal passing over a river or low ground. 3. *Anatomy.* A channel or passage carrying fluid in the body. [Latin *aquae ductus* : *aquae,* genitive of *aqua,* water + DUCT.]

a·que·ous (áykwi-əss, ákwi-) adj. 1. Pertaining to, similar to, containing, or dissolved in water; watery. 2. *Geology.* Formed from matter deposited by water, as are certain sedimentary rocks. [Medieval Latin *aqueus,* from Latin *aqua,* water.]

aqueous humour n. A clear, lymphlike fluid in the chamber of the eye between the cornea and the lens. Compare **vitreous humour.**

aqui– comb. form. Indicates water; for example, **aquiculture.** [Latin, from *aqua,* water.]

aq·ui·cul·ture (ákwi-kulchər ‖ *U.S. also* áakwi-) n. A method of cultivation, hydroponics *(see).* —**aq·ui·cul·tur·al** (-kúlchərəl) adj.

aq·ui·fer (ákwi-fər ‖ *U.S. also* áakwi-) n. A water-bearing rock, rock formation, or group of formations. [AQUI- + -FER.] —**a·quif·er·ous** (əkwíffərəss, a-) adj.

Aq·ui·la (ákwilə) n. A constellation in the Northern Hemisphere and the Milky Way. [Latin *aquila,* EAGLE.]

aq·ui·le·gi·a (ákwi-lée-jə, -ji-ə) n. A plant, the **columbine** *(see).* [New Latin, from Medieval Latin *aquilēgia, aquilēja*†, columbine.]

aq·ui·line (ákwi-līn ‖ -lin) adj. 1. Of or similar to an eagle. 2. Curved or hooked like an eagle's beak: *an aquiline nose.* [Latin *aquilīnus,* from *aquila,* eagle. See **eagle.**]

A·qui·nas (ə-kwīn-əss, a-, -ass), **Saint Thomas** (1225–74). Italian Doctor of the Church, theologian, and philosopher, the outstanding representative of the medieval system of thought known as **Scholasticism** *(see).* By far the most influential example of Aquinas' application of Aristotelian methods to Christian theology is *Summa Theologiae* (1267–73).

A·qui·no (ə-kée-nō), **(Maria Corazon) "Cory"** (1933–). Filipino politician. After the murder of her husband, Benigno Aquino, in 1983 she became leader of the opposition to President Marcos. In 1986 she succeeded Marcos as President of the Philippines. Retired (1992); Fulbright prize for international peace (1996).

Aq·ui·taine (áckwi-táyn, akee-tén). Region of southwest France, stretching north from the Pyrenees to the river Garonne. It formed the Roman province of Aquitania, and was subsequently part of the Visigothic and Frankish kingdoms.

aq·uo ion (ákwō) n. *Chemistry.* A complex ion in which a metal ion is coordinated to water molecules, as is the hexaquocopperII ion [Cu(H₂O)₆]²⁺. [*Aquo,* from Latin *aqua,* water.]

–ar¹ adj. suffix. Indicates like, pertaining to, or of the nature of; for example, **titular, polar, spectacular.** [Middle English *-ar, -er,* from Old French *-er,* from Latin *-āris,* dissimulated alteration (after bases ending in *l*) of *-ālis,* -AL.]

–ar² n. suffix. Indicates someone performing or involved with a specified occupation; for example, **pedlar, bursar, burglar.** [Middle English variant of -er¹.]

Ar 1. The symbol for the element argon. 2. The symbol for an aromatic group in an organic compound.

A·ra (aára) n. A constellation in the Southern Hemisphere near the constellations Norma and Telescopium. [Latin *āra,* altar.]

Ar·ab (árrəb) n. 1. A native or inhabitant of Arabia. 2. A member of a Semitic people originally from Arabia, but later widely scattered throughout the Middle East, North Africa, and the Arabian Peninsula. 3. A horse of a swift, graceful breed native to Arabia, used mainly for riding. 4. A waif; a **street Arab** *(see).*
~adj. Of or pertaining to the Arabs or Arabia. [Middle English, from Latin *Arabs,* from Greek *Arabs, Araps,* from Arabic *'arab.*]

ar·a·besque (árrə-bésk) n. 1. A complex and ornate design with intertwined flowers, leaves, and geometrical figures. 2. A ballet position in which the dancer stands on one leg, with the other leg extended backwards and the arms stretched out. 3. A short, elaborately constructed piece of music.
~adj. Pertaining to, resembling, or formed as an arabesque. [French, from Italian *arabesco,* "made or done in Arabic fashion".]

A·ra·bi·a (ə-ráybi-ə). Peninsula in southwest Asia, including Saudi Arabia and its adjoining states to the south and east. It is estimated to have about a third of the world's petroleum reserves.

A·ra·bi·an (ə-ráyb-yən, -i-ən) adj. *Abbr.* **Ar., Arab.** Of or pertaining to Arabia or the Arabs; Arab.
~n. 1. A native or inhabitant of Arabia. 2. A horse of a breed native to Arabia; an Arab.

Arabian camel n. A one-humped domesticated camel, *Camelus dromedarius,* used as a beast of burden in desert regions of north Africa and southwest Asia. Compare **Bactrian camel.** See **dromedary.**

Arabian Gulf. Also **Arab Gulf.** See **Gulf, The.**

Arabian Nights n. A collection of oriental stories of love and adventure dating from the tenth century A.D. and including the stories of Aladdin and Sinbad. Also called the "Thousand and One Nights".
~adj. Sumptuous and exotic: *an Arabian Nights confection.*

Ar·a·bic (árrəbik) adj. Of or pertaining to Arabia, the Arabs, their language, or their culture.
~n. *Abbr.* **Ar., Arab.** 1. The southwest Semitic language of the Arabs, which is now (in a variety of dialects) the prevailing language of the Arabian peninsula and most of the Middle East and

North Africa. 2. The literary language of the Koran, as employed in formal usage in Arabic-speaking countries; classical Arabic.

Arabic numerals pl.n. The numerical symbols 1, 2, 3, 4, 5, 6, 7, 8, 9, and 0. Compare **Roman numerals.**

a·rab·i·nose (ə-rábbi-nōss, -nōz) n. A pentose sugar, C₅H₁₀O₅, found in plant gums, pectins, and mucilages, especially of certain conifers. It is used in bacteriology as a constituent of culture media. [*Arabin,* from (GUM) ARAB(IC) + -IN + -OSE.]

Ar·ab·ist (árrəbist) n. 1. A specialist in the Arabic language or culture, or in the politics of the Arab world. 2. A supporter of Arab interests.

ar·a·ble (árrəb'l) adj. Fit for the cultivation of crops.
~n. Arable land. [Middle English, from Old French, from Latin *arābilis,* from *arāre,* to plough.]

Arab League n. An association of independent Arab nations formed in 1945 by Iraq, Jordan, Lebanon, Saudi Arabia, Egypt, Syria, and Yemen. There are now 22 members, including Palestinian-administered territories.

Ar·a·by (árrəbi). *Poetic.* Arabia.

a·ra·ceous (ə-ráyshəss, a-) adj. *Botany.* Aroid. [New Latin *Araceae* (family), from Latin *arum,* ARUM.]

A·rach·ne (ə-rák-ni). *Greek Mythology.* A maiden who was transformed into a spider by Athena for beating her in a weaving contest. [Latin *Arachnē,* from Greek *Arakhnē,* from *arakhnē*†, spider.]

a·rach·nid (ə-rák-nid) n. Any of various arthropods of the class Arachnida, such as a spider, scorpion, tick, or harvestman, characteristically having four pairs of legs, simple eyes, and no antennae. Also called "arachnoid". [New Latin *Arachnida,* from Greek *arakhnē,* spider, ARACHNE.] —**a·rach·ni·dan** (-nid'n) adj. & n.

a·rach·noid (ə-rák-noyd) n. 1. The middle of the three delicate membranes covering the spinal cord and brain, lying between the pia mater and dura mater. Also called "arachnoid mater". 2. An arachnid.
~adj. 1. Of or pertaining to the arachnoid membrane. 2. Of or pertaining to the arachnids. 3. *Botany.* Covered with or consisting of thin, soft, entangled hairs like the threads of a cobweb. [New Latin *arachnoides,* from Greek *arakhnoeidēs,* cobweb-like : *arakhnē,* spider, ARACHNE + -OID.]

Ar·a·fat (árrə-fat), **Yasser,** born Muhammad Abed Ar'uf Arafat (1929–). Palestinian resistance leader, born in Jerusalem. In 1956 he helped to found the Al Fatah organisation, and with its backing became leader of the PLO in the late 1960s. Considered a moderate, he negotiated a peace agreement with Israel (1993), shared with Shimon Peres and Yitzhak Rabin the Nobel peace prize (1994), and was elected president of the Palestinian National Council (1996).

Ar·a·gon (árrəgən). Region of northeast Spain containing the provinces of Huesca, Teruel, and Zaragoza. It became an independent kingdom (1035), and united with Castile (1479) to form the nucleus of modern Spain. —**Ar·a·go·nese** (-éez ‖ -éess) adj. & n.

a·rag·o·nite (ə-rággə-nīt, árrəgə-) n. An orthorhombic mineral form of calcium carbonate, dimorphous with calcite. [After ARAGON, where it was first found.]

Ar·al·dite (árrəl-dīt) n. A trademark for a strong epoxy-resin adhesive.

A·ral Sea (árrəl; *Russian* a-rál). The sixth largest inland body of water in the world, covering some 36 260 square kilometres (14,000 square miles) in Kazakhstan and Uzbekistan.

Ar·am (áir-əm). A Biblical name for ancient Syria.

Aram, Eugene (1704–59). English philologist. Largely self-taught, Aram was the first man to demonstrate that the Celtic languages belong to the Indo-European group. In 1759 he was executed for the murder, fourteen years earlier, of his friend Daniel Clark.

Ar·a·mae·an, Ar·a·me·an (árrə-mée-ən) adj. Of or pertaining to Aram, its inhabitants, language, or culture.
~n. 1. A native or inhabitant of Aram. 2. The Aramaic language.

Ar·a·ma·ic (árrə-máy-ik) n. A Northwest Semitic language used as the commercial lingua franca for nearly all of southwest Asia after about 300 B.C., and still spoken in parts of Syria and Lebanon. Compare **Biblical Aramaic.** —**Ar·a·ma·ic** adj.

Ar·an (árrən) adj. Knitted from undyed wool in an elaborate cable-stitch pattern which originated in the Aran Islands off the west coast of Ireland: *an Aran sweater.*

ar·a·pai·ma (árrə-pímə) n. A large South American freshwater food fish, *Arapaima gigas,* sometimes attaining a length of 4½ metres (15 feet). Also called "pirarucu". [Spanish and Portuguese, from Tupi.]

Ar·a·rat, Mount (árrə-rat). *Turkish* **Agri Dagi.** Massif in eastern Turkey. Great Ararat (5 165 metres; 16,945 feet) is its highest peak, and it is traditionally regarded as the resting place of Noah's ark.

ar·a·ro·ba (árrə-rōbə) n. 1. A Brazilian tree, *Andira araroba,* having yellowish wood from which a medicinal powder is obtained. 2. The powder itself, found in cavities in the wood. In this sense, also called "Goa powder". See **chrysarobin.** [Portuguese, probably from Tupi : *arara,* parrot + *yba,* tree.]

Ar·au·ca·ni·an (árraw-káyn-yən, -i-ən) n. Also **A·rau·can** (ə-ráwkən). 1. A South American Indian language family spoken in Chile and the western pampas of Argentina. 2. A member of any of the Araucanian-speaking peoples. —**Ar·au·ca·ni·an** adj.

ar·au·car·i·a (árraw-káir-i-ə) n. Any of several evergreen trees of the coniferous genus *Araucaria.* See **bunya, monkey puzzle.** [New Latin *Araucaria,* from Spanish *Araucano,* (tree) of *Araucania,* region of Chile.]

Ar·a·wak (árrə-wak ‖ *U.S.* -waak) n., pl. **-waks** or collectively **Ara-**

wak. 1. A member of an American Indian people living chiefly in the northeast corner of South America. 2. The language of this people, of the Arawakan family of languages.

Ar·a·wa·kan (árrə-wáckən ‖ U.S. -waákən) n., pl. **-kans** or collectively **Arawakan.** 1. A South American Indian language family spoken in a wide area of the Amazon basin. 2. A member of any of the Arawakan-speaking peoples. —**Ar·a·wa·kan** adj.

ar·ba·lest (árbə-lest, -list) n. Also **ar·be·list** (-list). A medieval weapon designed on the crossbow principle and used for firing arrows, stones, balls, and other missiles. [Middle English arbelast, arblast, from Old French arbaleste, from Late Latin arcuballista: Latin arcus, bow + BALLISTA.] —**ar·ba·lest·er** (-lestər) n.

ar·bi·ter (árbitər) n. 1. One chosen or appointed to judge or decide a disputed issue; an arbitrator. 2. One who has the power to judge or ordain at will. 3. One who has the authority to make influential judgments: an arbiter of taste. —See Synonyms at **judge.** [Middle English arbitre, from Old French, from Latin arbiter†, judge.]

ar·bi·tra·ble (árbitrəb'l) adj. Subject to arbitration; capable of being referred to an arbitrator.

ar·bi·trage (árbi-traazh, -tráazh, -trij) n. 1. The purchase of securities, commodities, or the like, on one market for immediate resale on another in order to profit from a price discrepancy. 2. Loosely, stagging, especially in order to profit from a successful takeover bid. [French, arbitration, from arbitrer, to ARBITRATE.]

ar·bi·trag·eur (-úr, -ốr) n. Chiefly U.S. A speculator who specialises in buying up the shares of companies threatened by takeover bids, with the object of reselling them at a profit if the bid succeeds.

ar·bit·ra·ment (aar-bíttrəmənt) n. 1. The act of arbitrating. 2. The judgment or award made by an arbitrator. [Middle English, from Old French arbitrement, from arbitrer, to ARBITRATE.]

ar·bi·trar·y (árbi-trəri, -tri ‖ -trerri) adj. 1. Determined by chance or caprice; random. 2. Based on or subject to individual judgment or prejudice. 3. Established by a court or judge, rather than by a specific law or statute; discretionary. 4. Not limited by law; absolute; despotic: the arbitrary power of a dictator. —See Synonyms at **dictatorial.** [Middle English, from Latin arbitrārius, from arbiter, ARBITER.] —**ar·bi·trar·i·ly** (-trərili ‖ -tráir-əli) adv. —**ar·bi·trar·i·ness** n.

ar·bi·trate (árbitrayt) v. **-trated, -trating, -trates.** —tr. 1. To judge or decide as or in the manner of an arbitrator. 2. To submit to settlement or judgment by arbitration. —intr. 1. To serve as an arbitrator or arbiter. 2. To refer a dispute to arbitration. [Latin arbitrārī (past participial stem arbitrāt-), from arbiter, ARBITER.]

ar·bi·tra·tion (árbi-tráysh'n) n. The process by which the parties to a dispute submit their differences to the judgment of an impartial party appointed by mutual consent or statutory provision. See Synonyms at **mediation.**

Arbitration Court n. In Australia, the court that deals with industrial disputes over wage claims, working conditions, or the like.

ar·bi·tra·tor (árbi-traytər) n. 1. A person chosen to settle the issue between parties engaged in a dispute or controversy. 2. One having the ability or power to make authoritative decisions; an arbiter. —See Synonyms at **judge.**

arbor¹. U.S. Variant of **arbour.**

ar·bor² (árbər) n. 1. A rotating shaft in a machine tool or power tool to which a grinding wheel or milling cutter is fitted. 2. A rotating shaft fitted with a device for holding a workpiece while it is being machined. 3. A spindle of a wheel, as in watches and clocks. 4. Archaic. A tree. [French arbre (in a Latinised respelling), axle, axis, tree, from Latin arbor†, tree.]

Arbor Day n. In the United States, Canada, Australia, and New Zealand, a day set apart annually for community tree planting.

ar·bo·re·al (aar-báwri-əl ‖ -bóri-) adj. 1. Pertaining to or resembling a tree. 2. Living in trees. —**ar·bo·re·al·ly** adv.

ar·bo·re·ous (aar-báwri-əss ‖ -bóri-) adj. 1. Having many trees; wooded. 2. Resembling or characteristic of a tree; treelike.

ar·bo·res·cent (árbə-réss'nt) adj. Having the form or characteristics of a tree; treelike. [Latin arborēscēns (stem arborēscent-), present participle of arborēscere, to grow to be a tree, from arbor†, tree.] —**ar·bo·res·cence** n.

ar·bo·re·tum (árbə-rée-təm) n., pl. **-tums** or **-ta** (-tə). A place where many different species and varieties of tree are grown for scientific study and public exhibition. [New Latin, from Latin arborētum, a place where trees are grown, from arbor†, tree. See **arbor** (shaft).]

ar·bo·ri·cul·ture (árbəri-kulchər ‖ aar-bórri-, báwri-, bóri-) n. The cultivation of trees for ornament or for the production of timber. [Latin arbor†, tree + -i- + culture, by analogy with agriculture.] —**ar·bo·ri·cul·tur·al** (-kúlchərəl) adj. —**ar·bo·ri·cul·tur·ist** n.

ar·bor·i·sa·tion, ar·bor·i·za·tion (árbər-ī-záysh'n ‖ U.S. -i-) n. 1. A treelike shape or arrangement, as in certain minerals or fossils. See **dendrites.** 2. The formation of such a shape or arrangement.

ar·bor·vi·tae, arbor vi·tae (árbər-vítee, -víti, -véetī) n. 1. A coniferous tree, the **thuja** (see). 2. Anatomy. The white matter of the cerebellum seen in cross-section, having the appearance of a tree. [New Latin arbor vitae, "tree of life", referring to the tree's remaining green all year.]

ar·bour, U.S. **ar·bor** (árbər) n. A shady garden shelter or bower, often made of latticework, covered with climbing plants. [Middle English erber, garden, bower (altered through the influence of Latin arbor, tree) from old French erbier, herbage, plot of grass, from erbe, herbe, from Latin herba, HERB.]

ar·bo·vi·rus (ár-bō-vír-əss, -bə-) n. Any of various viruses that are transmitted by arthropods, especially insects, and cause such diseases as encephalitis and yellow fever. [Arthropod-borne virus.]

Ar·broath (aar-brốth). A Scottish fishing port on the North Sea coast. The Declaration of Arbroath, asserting Scotland's independence from England, was issued by the Scottish parliament in 1320.

Ar·buth·not, (aar-búth-nət, -not), **John** (1667–1735). Scottish physician and essayist. His five anti-Whig pamphlets, published as The History of John Bull (1712), were satirical pieces which introduced the character of John Bull to English tradition.

ar·bu·tus (ar-béwtəss) n. 1. Any of several broad-leaved, evergreen, temperate trees of the genus Arbutus, having clusters of white or pinkish flowers, especially the **strawberry tree** (see). 2. A plant, **trailing arbutus** (see). [New Latin Arbutus, from Latin arbūtus†, strawberry tree, referring to the appearance of its berries.]

arc (ark) n. 1. Anything shaped like a bow, curve, or arch. 2. In geometry, a segment of a curve. 3. Electricity. A luminous discharge of electric current crossing a gap between two electrodes.
~adj. Mathematics. Designating an inverse trigonometric function: the arc sine of a quantity.
~intr.v. **arced** (arkt) or **arcked, arcing** (árking) or **arcking, arcs.** To form an arc. [Middle English ark, Old English arc, from Latin arcus, bow, arc.]

ar·cade (aar-káyd) n. 1. Architecture. a. A series of arches supported by columns, piers, or pillars. b. An arched, roofed building or part of a building. 2. A roofed passageway or lane, especially one with shops on either side. [French, from Italian arcata, from arco, arch, from Vulgar Latin arca (unattested). See **arch.**] —**ar·cad·ed** (-káydid) adj.

Ar·ca·di·a¹ (aar-káyd-i-ə, -yə). Mountainous central region of the Peloponnese in ancient Greece. Its people, isolated from the rest of the world, lived a simple, pastoral life.

Arcadia² n. Any place or region thought to epitomise rustic contentment and simplicity.

Ar·ca·di·an (aar-káyd-i-ən, -yən) adj. 1. Of, pertaining to, or characteristic of Arcadia. 2. Sometimes small a. Rustic, peaceful, and simple; pastoral. —See Synonyms at **rural.**
~n. 1. A native of Arcadia. 2. A person who leads or prefers a simple, rural life. 3. The Ancient Greek dialect of Arcadia, belonging to Arcado-Cyprian.

Ar·ca·do·Cyp·ri·an (aar-káydō-síppri-ən) n. One of the four main dialects of ancient Greek, comprising Arcadian, Pamphylian, and Cypriot. Compare **Aeolic, Attic-Ionic, Doric.** —**Ar·ca·do·Cyp·ri·an** adj.

Ar·ca·dy (árkədi). Poetic. Arcadia.

ar·ca·na (aar-káynə, -kaánə) pl.n. Either of the divisions of the **tarot** (see) cards, the major arcana (the 22 trump cards) or the minor arcana (the 56 ordinary cards). [Latin, plural of ARCANUM.]

ar·cane (aar-káyn) adj. Known or understood only by those having special, secret knowledge; esoteric. [Latin arcānus, closed, secret, from arcēre, to close up, shut, from arca, chest.]

ar·ca·num (aar-káy-nəm) n., pl. **-na** (-nə). 1. A profound secret; a mystery. 2. The reputed great secret of nature that alchemists sought to find. 3. An elixir. [Latin arcānum, a mystery, secret, from the neuter of arcānus, closed, secret, ARCANE.]

arc-bou·tant (ár-bōō-tón) n., pl. **arcs-boutants** (pronounced as singular). French. A flying buttress (see).

arch¹ (arch) n. 1. A curved structure, especially of masonry, forming the upper edge of an opening or a support, as in a bridge or doorway. 2. Any similar structure, such as a monument. 3. Anything curved like an arch. 4. Anatomy. Any of various arch-shaped structures, especially the structure in the foot formed by the tarsal and metatarsal bones. 5. One of the three basic patterns by which fingerprints are classified, consisting of numerous curved ridges one above the other. Compare **loop, whorl.**
~v. **arched, arching, arches.** —tr. 1. To supply with an arch. 2. To cause to form an arch or similar curve: arch one's eyebrows. 3. To span: a bridge arching the river. —intr. To form an arch or archlike curve. [Middle English arche, from Old French, from Vulgar Latin arca (unattested), plural noun from Latin arcus, bow, ARC.]

arch² adj. 1. Chief; principal. Used before the noun: an arch supporter of government policy. 2. Mischievous; roguish: an arch glance. [From ARCH-.] —**arch·ly** adv. —**arch·ness** n.

arch- comb. form. Indicates: 1. Highest rank or chief status; for example, **archduke, archbishop.** 2. Ultimate of a kind; for example, **archfiend.** [Middle English arche-, arch-, from Old English ærce-, arce-, erce-, and Old French arch(e)-, both from Latin arch(i)-, from Greek arkh(i)-, from arkhos, chief, ruler, from arkheint, to begin, rule.]

-arch n.comb. form. Indicates a ruler or leader; for example, **monarch, matriarch.** [Middle English -arche, from Old French, from Late Latin -archa, from Greek -arkhēs, from arkhos, ruler, from arkheint, to rule.]

arch. 1. archaic; archaism. 2. archery. 3. archipelago. 4. architect; architectural; architecture.

Arch. archbishop.

Ar·chae·an, Ar·che·an (aar-kée-ən) adj. Geology. Of, pertaining to, or designating the oldest rocks of the Precambrian era, predominantly highly metamorphosed sedimentary and volcanic rocks.

archaeo-, archeo- comb. form. Indicates ancient times or an early condition; for example, **archaeology, archaeopteryx.** [New Latin, from Greek arkhaio-, from arkhaios, ancient, from arkhē, beginning, from arkheint, to begin.]

ar·chae·o·as·tron·o·my (árki-ō-əstrónnəmi) n. The study of megalithic sites and other ancient structures with a view to showing that they were built to align with or predict astronomical observations.

ar·chae·ol·o·gy, ar·che·ol·o·gy (árki-óllǝji) *n.* The scientific study of the material remains of past ages as evidence of man's life, culture, and history in former times. [French *archéologie,* from Late Latin *archaeologia,* "the study of antiquity", from Greek *arkhaiologia* : ARCHAEO- + -LOGY.] —**ar·chae·o·log·i·cal** (-ǝ-lójik'l), **chae·o·log·ic** *adj.* —**ar·chae·olo·gist** (-óllǝjist) *n.*

ar·chae·o·mag·net·ism (árki-ō-mágnit-iz'm) *n.* A technique used in archaeology for dating clay objects by measuring the extent to which they have been magnetised by the earth's magnetic field.

ar·chae·op·ter·yx (árki-óptǝriks) *n.* An extinct primitive bird of the genus *Archaeopteryx,* of the Jurassic period, having wings, feathers, teeth, and a long tail, and representing a transitional form between reptiles and birds. [New Latin, "ancient bird" : ARCHAEO- + Greek *pterux,* bird, wing, from *pteron,* feather, wing.]

ar·chae·o·zo·ol·o·gy (árki-ō-zō-óllǝji, -zōō-) *n.* The scientific study of ancient animal remains, especially fossilised bones, as evidence of early domestication, the hunting habits of a given culture, climatic changes, and the like.

ar·cha·ic (aar-káy-ik) *adj. Abbr.* **arch.** 1. Belonging to a much earlier time; ancient: *archaic sculpture.* 2. No longer current or applicable; antiquated: *archaic laws.* 3. Formerly common, but now used chiefly to suggest an earlier style or period. Said of words and language. —See Synonyms at **old.** [French *archaïque,* from Greek *arkhaikos,* from *arkhaios,* ancient, from *arkhē,* beginning, from *arkheint,* to begin.] —**ar·cha·i·cal·ly** *adv.*

archaic smile *n.* A representation of the human mouth with slightly upturned corners, characteristic of early Greek sculpture.

ar·cha·ise, ar·cha·ize (ár-kay-īz, -ki-) *v.* **-ised, -ising, -ises.** —*tr.* To impart an archaic quality or character to; make archaic. —*intr.* To use archaisms. [Greek *arkhaïzein,* from *arkhaios,* ancient, ARCHAIC.] —**ar·cha·is·er** *n.*

ar·cha·ism (ár-kay-iz'm, -ki-) *n. Abbr.* **arch.** 1. An archaic word or expression. 2. An archaic style or quality. 3. The imitation of archaic styles, as in literature or art. [New Latin *archaeismus,* from Greek *arkhaïsmos,* from *arkhaios,* ancient, ARCHAIC.] —**ar·cha·ist** *n.* —**ar·cha·is·tic** (-ístik) *adj.*

arch·an·gel (árk-áynj'l, -aynj'l) *n.* In medieval angelology, a celestial being next in rank above an angel. See **angel.** [Middle English, from Anglo-French *archangele,* from Late Latin *archangelus,* from Greek *arkhangelos* : ARCH- + ANGEL.] —**arch·an·gel·ic** (-an-jéllik) *adj.*

Archangel. See **Arkhangelsk.**

arch·bish·op (árch-bíshǝp) *n. Abbr.* **abp., Abp., Arch., Archbp.** A bishop of the highest rank, heading an archdiocese or province. [Middle English *erchebishop, archebishop,* Old English *ǽrcebiscop, arcebiscop,* from Late Latin *archiepiscopus,* from Late Greek *arkhiepiskopos* : ARCH- + *episkopos,* BISHOP.]

arch·bish·op·ric (árch-bíshǝprik) *n.* 1. The rank, office, or term of an archbishop. 2. The area over which an archbishop has jurisdiction; an archdiocese.

arch·dea·con (árch-déekǝn) *n.* A clergyman, chiefly in the Anglican Church, in charge of temporal and other affairs in a diocese, with powers delegated from the bishop. [Middle English *archedeken,* Old English *ǽrcediakon,* from Late Latin *archidiāconus,* from Late Greek *arkhidiakonos* : ARCH- + DEACON.]

arch·dea·con·ry (árch-déekǝnri) *n., pl.* **-ries.** 1. The rank, office, or jurisdiction of an archdeacon. Also called "archdeaconate", "archdeaconship". 2. The residence or district of an archdeacon.

arch·di·o·cese (árch-dī-ǝ-siss || -seess, -seez) *n.* A diocese under an archbishop's jurisdiction. —**arch·di·oc·e·san** (-óssi-zǝn, -sǝn) *adj.*

arch·du·cal (árch-déwk'l || -dóōk'l) *adj.* Of or pertaining to an archduke or an archduchy.

arch·duch·ess (árch-dúchiss) *n.* 1. The wife or widow of an archduke. 2. A woman having a rank equivalent to that of an archduke; especially, an Austrian princess.

arch·duch·y (árch-dúchi) *n., pl.* **-ies.** The territory over which an archduke or an archduchess has authority.

arch·duke (árch-déwk || -dóōk) *n.* In certain royal families, especially that of imperial Austria, a nobleman having a rank equivalent to that of a sovereign prince.

Archean. Variant of **Archaean.**

arched (archt) *adj.* 1. Forming an arch or a curve like that of an arch. 2. Provided, made, or covered with an arch or arches.

ar·che·go·ni·um (árki-gō-ni-ǝm) *n., pl.* **-nia** (-ni-ǝ). *Botany.* A multicellular female sex organ of mosses, ferns, and conifers, which produces a single gamete. Compare **antheridium.** [New Latin, diminutive of Greek *arkhegonos,* primal parent : ARCH- (chief) + -*gonos,* race.] —**ar·che·go·ni·al** *adj.* —**ar·che·go·ni·ate** (-ni-ayt, -ǝt, -it) *adj.*

arch·en·e·my (árch-énnǝmi) *n., pl.* **-mies.** 1. A chief or principal enemy. 2. *Often capital* **A.** The devil; Satan. Preceded by *the.*

ar·chen·ter·on (aar-kéntǝ-ron, -rǝn) *n.* The embryonic digestive tract, essentially a cavity in the gastrula. [New Latin : ARCH- + ENTERON.] —**ar·chen·ter·ic** (árken-térrik) *adj.*

archeo-. Variant of **archaeo-.**

archeology. Variant of **archaeology.**

arch·er (árchǝr) *n.* 1. One who shoots with a bow and arrow. 2. *Capital* **A.** The constellation and sign of the zodiac, **Sagittarius** (*see*). [Middle English, from Old French *archier,* from Late Latin *arcārius,* alteration of *arcuārius,* "of a bow", from Latin *arcus,* bow, ARC.]

Archer, Frederick Scott (1813–57). British photographer. He invented the "wet collodion process", by which more than one photograph could be printed from a glass negative.

Archer, Thomas (*c.* 1668–1743). English baroque architect. Among the churches he designed are St. John, Smith Square, London, and St. Paul's, Deptford.

arch·er·fish (árchǝr-fish) *n., pl.* **-fishes** or collectively **archerfish.** Any of several small freshwater Indo-Australian fishes of the family Toxotidae, capable of capturing insects by squirting water at them.

arch·er·y (árchǝri) *n.* 1. The art, sport, or skill of shooting with a bow and arrows. 2. The equipment of an archer. 3. A troop or body of archers.

ar·che·spore (árki-spawr || -spōr) *n.* Also **ar·che·spo·ri·um** (-spáwri-ǝm || -spōri-) *pl.* **-sporia** (-spáwri-ǝ || -spōri-ǝ). *Botany.* A cell or mass of cells producing spores in a sporangium. [New Latin *archesporium* : ARCH- + *spora,* SPORE.] —**ar·che·spo·ri·al** *adj.*

ar·che·type (árki-tīp) *n.* 1. An original model or type after which other similar things are patterned; a prototype. 2. A perfect or typical example. 3. In the psychology of C. G. Jung, an inherited idea in the individual unconscious that is thought to derive from the collective experience of mankind as a whole. —See Synonyms at **ideal.** [Latin *archetypum,* from Greek *arkhetupon,* neuter of *arkhetupos,* "first-moulded" : ARCH- + *tupos,* mould, stamp, TYPE.] —**ar·che·typ·al** (-tīp'l), **ar·che·typ·i·cal** *adj.* —**ar·che·typ·i·cal·ly** *adv.*

arch·fiend (árch-féend) *n.* 1. A chief or foremost fiend. 2. *Often capital* **A.** Satan; the devil. Usually preceded by *the.*

ar·chi·di·ac·o·nal (árki-dī-áckǝn'l) *adj.* Of or pertaining to an archdeacon, his duties, or his office. [From Late Latin *archidiāconus,* ARCHDEACON.]

ar·chi·di·ac·o·nate (árki-dī-áckǝ-nǝt, -nit, -nayt) *n.* The office or order of archdeacons. [Medieval Latin *archidiāconātus,* from Late Latin *archidiāconus,* ARCHDEACON.]

ar·chi·e·pis·co·pal (árki-i-pískǝ-p'l) *adj.* Of or pertaining to an archbishop or an archbishopric. [Medieval Latin *archiepiscopālis,* from Late Latin *archiepiscopus,* ARCHBISHOP.] —**ar·chi·e·pis·co·pal·i·ty** (-pál-ǝti) *n.* —**ar·chi·e·pis·co·pal·ly** *adv.*

ar·chi·e·pis·co·pate (árki-i-pískǝp-ǝt, -it, -ayt) *n.* The rank, office, or term of an archbishop. [Medieval Latin *archiepiscopātus,* from Late Latin *archiepiscopus,* ARCHBISHOP.]

ar·chil. Variant of **orchil.**

Ar·chi·lo·chi·an (árki-lóki-ǝn) *adj.* Of, pertaining to, or characteristic of Archilochus, Greek satiric poet of the early seventh century B.C., or of the verse form invented by him.

ar·chi·mage (árki-mayj) *n.* A great magician or chief wizard. [Late Greek *arkhimagos* : ARCH- + *magos,* magician. See **magi.**]

ar·chi·man·drite (árki-mándrīt) *n.* In the Eastern Orthodox Church: 1. A cleric ranking below a bishop. 2. The head of a monastery or group of monasteries. [Late Latin *archimandrītēs, archimandrīta,* from Late Greek *arkhimandritēs* : ARCH- + *mandrat,* monastery, from Greek, enclosure, cattle pen.]

Archimedean screw *n.* An ancient apparatus for raising water, consisting of either a spiral tube around an inclined axis or an inclined tube containing a tight-fitting, broad-threaded screw. Also called "Archimedes' screw".

Ar·chi·me·des (árki-méedeez) (*c.* 287 B.C.–212 B.C.). Greek mathematician and inventor from Syracuse. He is considered, with K. F. **Gauss** and Isaac **Newton,** one of the three greatest mathematicians of all time. He discovered and analysed the principle of the lever, and invented the Archimedean screw for raising water. His most famous discovery, the principle of buoyancy, is said to have come to him when he observed the amount of water his body displaced in his bath. In his excitement he ran naked through the streets shouting "Eureka!" ("I have found it"). When Syracuse fell to the Romans he was killed, it is said, while drawing geometric figures in the sand. —**Ar·chi·me·de·an** (-méed-yǝn, -i-ǝn, -mi-dée-ǝn) *adj.*

Archimedes' principle *n.* The principle that the apparent loss in the weight of a body immersed in a fluid is equal to the weight of the fluid displaced.

ar·chine, ar·shin (aar-shéen) *n.* A Russian unit of linear measure equivalent to about 71 centimetres (28 inches). [Russian *arshin,* of Turkic origin; akin to Turkish and Kazan Tatar *aršyn,* an ell.]

ar·chi·pel·a·go (árki-péllǝgō) *n., pl.* **-goes** or **-gos.** 1. *Abbr.* **arch.** A large group of islands. 2. A sea containing many groups of islands, such as the Aegean. [From *Archipelago,* the Aegean Sea, from Italian *Arcipelago,* "the Chief Sea" (a misinterpretation of Greek *Aigaion pelagos,* the Aegean Sea) : ARCH- + Greek *pelagos,* sea.] —**ar·chi·pe·lag·ic** (-pi-lájik, -pe-) *adj.*

archit. architecture.

ar·chi·tect (árkitekt) *n. Abbr.* **arch.** 1. One who designs and supervises the construction of buildings or other large structures, such as ships. 2. Any planner or deviser: *the architect of European unity.* [French *architecte,* from Latin *architectus,* from Greek *arkhitektōn,* master builder : ARCH- + *tektōn,* builder, craftsman.]

ar·chi·tec·ton·ic (árki-tek-tónnik) *adj.* 1. Of or pertaining to architecture or design. 2. Having qualities characteristic of architecture; designed and structured. 3. *Philosophy.* Of or pertaining to the scientific systematisation of knowledge. [Latin *architectōnicus,* architectural, from Greek *arkhitektōnikos,* from *arkhitektōn,* ARCHITECT.] —**ar·chi·tec·ton·i·cal·ly** *adv.*

ar·chi·tec·ton·ics (árki-tek-tónniks) *n. Used with a singular verb.* 1. The science of architecture. 2. Structural design, as in a musical work. 3. *Philosophy.* The scientific systematisation of knowledge.

ar·chi·tec·ture (árki-tekchǝr) *n. Abbr.* **arch., archit.** 1. The art and science of designing and erecting buildings. **2.** A structure, or structures collectively. **3.** A particular style and method of design and construction: *Byzantine architecture.* **4.** The planning or design evidenced in any structure or arrangement: *the architecture of nature.* [French, from Latin *architectūra,* from *architectus,* ARCHITECT.] —**ar·chi·tec·tur·al** (-tékchərəl) *adj.* —**ar·chi·tec·tur·al·ly** *adv.*

ar·chi·trave (árki-trayv) *n. Architecture.* **1.** The lowermost part of an entablature, resting directly on top of a column as in classical architecture. Also called "epistyle". **2.** The moulding around a door or window. [Old French, from Old Italian, "chief beam" : ARCH- + *trave,* beam, from Latin *trabs.*]

ar·chi·val (aar-kív'l) *adj.* Of, pertaining to, or kept in archives.

ar·chives (ár-kīvz) *pl.n.* **1.** An organised body of records pertaining to an organisation, institution, or the like. **2.** A place in which such records are preserved. **3.** Any repository of evidence or information: *the archives of the mind.* [French, originally singular *archive,* from Late Latin *archī(v)um,* from Greek *arkheion,* public office (plural *arkheia,* public records, archives), from *arkhē,* beginning, hence first place, government, from *arkhein†,* to begin.]

ar·chi·vist (ár-kiv-ist ‖ -kīv-) *n.* One who is in charge of archives.

ar·chi·volt (árki-vōlt ‖ -volt) *n. Architecture.* **1.** Decorative moulding carried round an arched wall opening. **2.** The underside of an arch. [Italian *archivolto* : *arco,* arch, from Latin *arcus,* ARC + -I- + *volta,* VAULT.]

ar·chon (ár-kən, -kon) *n.* **1.** Any of the nine principal governing officials of ancient Athens. **2.** Any of various officials of the Byzantine Empire. **3.** *Sometimes capital* **A.** In certain Gnostic systems, any of several powers believed to be superior to the angels. [Latin *archōn,* from Greek *arkhōn,* "ruler", from the present participle of *arkhein†,* to rule.] —**ar·chon·ship** *n.*

arch·priest (árch-préest) *n.* Formerly, a priest holding first rank among the members of a cathedral chapter, acting as chief assistant to a bishop. Now used only as a title of honour. [Middle English *archeprest,* from Old French *archeprestre,* from Late Latin *archi-presbyter* : ARCH + -I- + *presbyter,* PRIEST.] —**arch·priest·hood, arch·priest·ship** *n.*

arch·way (árchway) *n.* **1.** A passageway under an arch. **2.** An arch covering or enclosing an entrance or passageway.

-archy *n. comb. form.* Indicates rule or government; for example, **oligarchy.** [Middle English *-archie,* from Old French, from Latin *-archia,* from Greek *-arkhia,* from *-arkhēs,* -ARCH]

ar·ci·form (árssi-fawrm) *adj.* Formed like an arc. [Latin *arci-,* from *arcus,* bow, ARC + -I- + -FORM.]

arcked. Alternative past tense and past participle of **arc.**

arcking. Alternative present participle of **arc.**

arc lamp *n.* A lamp in which the light is produced by an electric arc between two closely spaced electrodes. Often carbon electrodes are used to produce an intense white light.

A.R.C.M. Associate of the Royal College of Music.

A.R.C.O. Associate of the Royal College of Organists.

arc·tic (árktik ‖ ártik. *Note. In England the pronunciation* ártik *is considered incorrect. It is more readily accepted elsewhere*). *adj.* **1.** *Usually capital* **A.** Of, pertaining to, or characteristic of a geographical area extending from the North Pole to the northern timberline. Compare **Antarctic.** **2. a.** Characteristic of the North Pole or polar regions; extremely cold. **b.** Suitable for very cold conditions: *arctic clothing.* [Middle English *artik,* from Latin *ar(c)ticus,* from Greek *arktikos,* from *arktos,* bear, hence the northern constellation Ursa Major, the Great Bear, hence "north".] —**arc·ti·cal·ly** *adv.*

Arctic Circle *n.* A parallel of latitude, 66° 32′ north, along which the sun does not set on one day in the year, around June 21.

Arctic Current. See **Labrador Current.**

arctic fox *n.* A fox, *Alopex lagopus,* inhabiting arctic regions, having fur that is white or light-grey in winter and brown or blue-grey in summer. Also called "blue fox".

Arctic Ocean. The world's smallest ocean, covering some 14 000 000 square kilometres (5,500,000 square miles) over the North Pole. It is covered by pack ice throughout the year, and its main outlet is the East Greenland Current, which takes icebergs far into the Atlantic Ocean. See map, next page.

arctic tern *n.* A tern, *Sterna paradisaea,* that breeds in the Arctic and migrates to the Antarctic.

Arc·to·gae·a (árk-tō-jée-ə, -tə-) *n.* The zoogeographical region that incudes the Palaearctic, Nearctic, Ethiopian, and Oriental regions. Compare **Notogaea.** [New Latin, "north earth", from Greek *arktos,* bear, Ursa Major, north + *gaia,* earth.] —**Arc·to·gae·an** *adj.*

Arc·tu·rus (aark-téwr-əss ‖ -tóor-) *n.* The brightest star in the constellation Boötes, approximately 36 light-years from earth. [Middle English *Artur, Arcturus,* from Latin *Arcturus,* from Greek *Arktouros,* "guardian of the Bear" (from its position behind the tail of Ursa Major) : *arktos,* bear + *ouros,* a guard.] —**Arc·tu·ri·an** *adj.*

ar·cu·ate (árkew-ayt, -ət, -it) *adj.* Also **ar·cu·at·ed** (-aytid). Having the form of a bow; curved; arched: *arcuate veins in a leaf; arcuate horns.* [Latin *arcuātus,* past participle of *arcuāre,* to bend like a bow, from *arcus,* bow.] —**ar·cu·ate·ly** *adv.*

ar·cu·a·tion (árkew-áysh'n) *n. Architecture.* The use of arches or vaults in building.

ar·cus se·ni·lis (árkəss si-ní-liss) *n.* A narrow, opaque circle around the cornea of the eye, often seen in old people. [Latin, "senile bow".]

arc-weld (árk-wéld) *tr.v.* **-welded, -welding, -welded.** To weld by heat produced by an electric arc between an electrode and the

workpiece.

~*n.* (-weld). A weld produced by this technique. —**arc-weld·ing** *n.*

ard (ard) *n.* A primitive plough, used in prehistoric times and now in some less developed countries. [Middle English, from Old Norse *arthr,* plough, from Latin *arātrum.*]

-ard, -art *n. suffix* Indicates: **1.** One who does something to excess; for example, **drunkard, braggart. 2.** One who is characterised by a particular, especially undesirable, quality; for example, **slug-gard.** [Middle English, from Old French from Germanic *-hart, -hard,* "bold, hardy", often in proper names such as *Raynard, Gerhart.*]

ar·deb (árdeb) *n.* A unit of dry measure in several countries of the Near East, usually equal to 0.195 cubic metres (5½ bushels), but with variations in different localities. [Colloquial Arabic *ardabb,* from Greek *artabē,* probably from Egyptian.]

Ar·den (ár'd'n), **John** (1930–). British writer, with plays like *Sergeant Musgrave's Dance* (1959) and *Armstrong's Last Goodnight* (1964), and novels like *Jack Juggler and the Emperor's Whore* (1995).

Ar·dennes (ár-dén, aar-, -dénz). Wooded plateau of southeast Belgium, extending into France and Luxembourg.

ar·dent (ár'nt) *adj.* **1. a.** Expressing or characterised by warmth of passion or desire. **b.** Displaying or characterised by strong enthusiasm or devotion; fervent; zealous: *"an impassioned age, so ardent and serious in its pursuit of art"* (Walter Pater). **2.** Glowing; flashing; fierce: *ardent eyes.* **3.** *Archaic.* Hot as fire; burning: *an ardent sun.* [Middle English *ardaunt,* from Old French *ardant,* from Latin *ardēns* (stem *ardent-*), present participle of *ardēre,* to burn.] —**ar·dent·ly** *adv.* —**ar·den·cy** *n.*

ardent spirits *pl.n.* Strong alcoholic drinks, such as whisky or gin.

ar·dour, *U.S.* **ar·dor** (árdər) *n.* **1. a.** Great warmth or intensity, as of emotion, passion, or desire. **b.** Fervent enthusiasm or devotion; zeal. **2.** Intense heat, as of fire. [Middle English *ardour,* from Old French, from Latin *ardor,* from *ardēre,* to burn.]

ar·du·ous (árdew-əss) *adj.* **1.** Demanding great care, effort, or exertion; strenuous. **2.** Testing severely the powers of endurance; full of hardships: *a long, arduous journey.* **3.** Hard to climb or surmount; steep: *an arduous path.* —See Synonyms at **burdensome, hard.** [Latin *arduus,* high, steep, difficult.] —**ar·du·ous·ly** *adv.* —**ar·du·ous·ness** *n.*

are[1] (ar; *weak form* ər). Present tense, indicative plural, and second person singular of **be.**

are[2] (ar, air) *n. Abbr.* **a, a.** A metric unit of area equal to 100 square metres (119.559 square yards). [French, from Latin *ārea,* AREA.]

ar·e·a (áir-i-ə) *n.* **1.** A flat, open, or unoccupied piece of ground. **2.** A part of the earth's surface; a region. **3.** A distinct spatial extent; a part, section, or locality having a particular function or characteristic quality: *a residential area; a room with a living area and a dining area.* **4.** A field of study or activity: *the whole area of finance.* **5.** *Abbr.* **A** The measure of a planar region or of the surface of a solid. **6.** *Computing.* That part of a computer memory which stores data of a particular type. [Latin *ārea†,* open field.] —**ar·e·al** *adj.*

Synonyms: area, region, zone, district, locality.

area of special scientific interest *n.* See **site of special scientific interest.**

ar·e·ca (árrikə, ə-réekə) *n.* Any of various tall palms of the genus *Areca,* of southeast Asia, having white flowers and red or orange egg-shaped nuts; for example, the betel palm. [New Latin *Areca,* from Portuguese *areca,* from Malayalam *atekka, atakka.*]

a·re·na (ə-réenə) *n.* **1.** The area in the centre of an ancient Roman amphitheatre where contests and other spectacles were held. **2.** Any similar place: *a boxing arena.* **3.** A sphere or field of conflict, interest, or activity: *the political arena.* [Latin *(h)arēna,* sand, arena covered with sand, perhaps from Etruscan.]

ar·e·na·ceous (árri-náyshəss) *adj.* **1.** Sandlike in appearance or qualities: *arenaceous limestone.* **2.** Growing in sandy areas. [Latin *(h)arēnaceus* : *(h)arēna,* sand, ARENA + -ACEOUS.]

arena theatre *n.* A theatre-in-the-round (*see*).

a·rene (árreen) *n. Chemistry.* An aromatic hydrocarbon or a derivative of an aromatic hydrocarbon. [AR(OMATIC) + -ENE.]

ar·e·nic·o·lous (árri-níckələss) *adj.* Growing or living in sand. [Latin *(h)arēna,* sand, ARENA + -COLOUS.]

aren't (arnt ‖ áarənt). Contraction of *are not.*

a·re·o·la (ə-rée-ə-lə, -ō-) *n., pl.* **-lae** (-lee) or **-las.** Also **ar·e·ole** (-ōl). **1.** *Biology.* A small space or interstice, such as an area bounded by small veins in a leaf or an insect's wing. **2.** *Anatomy.* A small, dark-coloured area around a centre portion, as about a nipple or part of the iris of the eye. [New Latin, from Latin *āreola,* diminutive of *ārea,* open place, AREA.] —**a·re·o·lar, a·re·o·late** *adj.*

Ar·e·op·a·gus (árri-óppə-gəss) *n.* The highest council of ancient Athens. [Greek *Areios pagos,* Ares' hill.] —**Ar·e·op·a·gite** (-gīt) *n.* —**Ar·e·op·ag·it·ic** (-gíttik) *adj.*

Ar·es (áir-eez). *Greek Mythology.* The god of war, identified with the Roman god Mars. [Greek *Arēs†,* god of war, the planet Mars.]

a·rête (a-ráyt, ə-, -rét) *n.* **1.** A sharp, narrow mountain ridge or spur. **2.** A ridge between two adjacent cirques. [French *arête,* fishbone, spiny ridge, from Old French *areste,* from Latin *arista†,* fishbone, spine, beard of grain.]

Ar·e·thu·sa (árri-théw-zə, árre-, -thōo- ‖ -sə). *Greek mythology.* A nymph who was turned into a spring so as to avoid the attentions of the river god Alpheus.

A·re·ti·no (árri-téenō), **Pietro** (1492–1556). Italian writer and satirist. He wrote five comedies, but was best known for his satirical

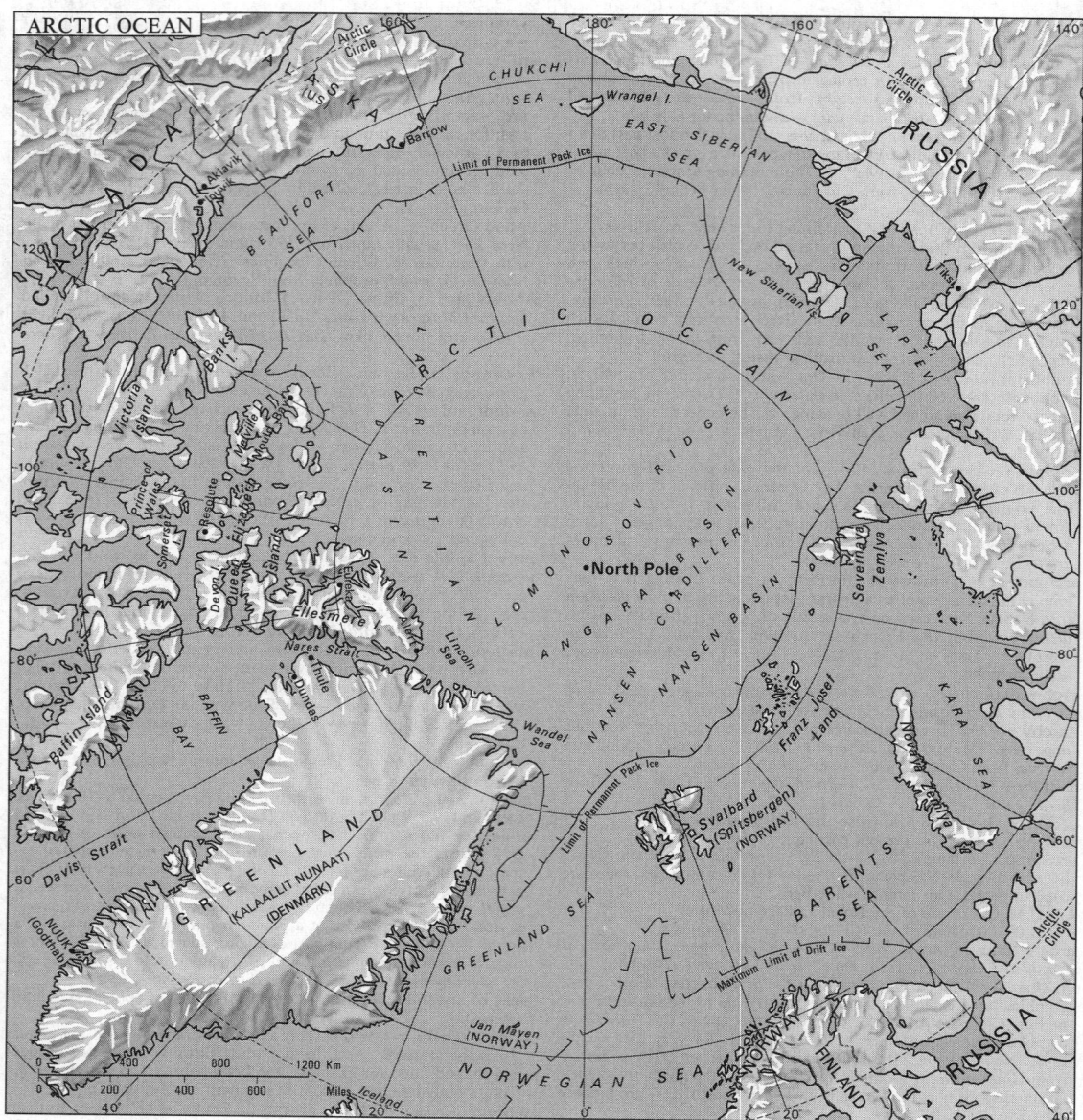

ARCTIC OCEAN

attacks on the wealthy and powerful, which, together with a collection of lewd poems, *Sonnetti lussuriosi* (1524), compelled him to flee Rome in 1527. For the rest of his life he lived in Venice, amassing wealth by writing satires or by being paid not to write them.

arg. argent.

argal[1]. Variant of **argol**.

argal[2]. Variant of **argali**.

ar·ga·li (árgəli) *n., pl.* **-lis** or collectively **argali**. Also **ar·gal** (árg'l). A large wild sheep, *Ovis ammon*, of semiarid regions of central and northern Asia, having massive, spirally curved horns in the male. [Mongolian *argali*, mountain goat.]

Ar·gand diagram (ár-gand, -gənd) *n. Mathematics.* A diagram in which complex numbers are represented in a coordinate system with two perpendicular axes determining the real and imaginary parts of the number. The number $x + iy$ is the point (x, y) or the directed line segment from the origin to the point (x,y). [After Jean-Robert *Argand* (1768–1822), Swiss mathematician.]

ar·gent (árjənt) *n.* **1.** *Poetic.* Silver or anything resembling it. **2.** *Abbr.* **arg.** *Heraldry.* The metal silver, represented by the colour white. [Middle English, from Old French, from Latin *argentum.*] —**ar·gent** *adj.*

ar·gen·tic (aar-jéntik) *adj.* Of or containing silver. Said especially of chemical compounds containing silver having a valency of 2 or 3. [Latin *argentum*, silver + -IC.]

ar·gen·tif·er·ous (árjən-tiffərəss) *adj.* Bearing or producing silver. [ARGENT + -I- + FEROUS.]

Ar·gen·ti·na (ár-jən-téenə, -jen-). Also **The Ar·gen·tine** (-teen, -tīn). *Spanish* **Republica Argentina.** Country of South America. It was a Spanish colony from 1620 until independence was proclaimed in 1816. Since 1929 the military have intervened in the government several times, notably in 1943, which paved the way for the rise of Colonel Juan Perón (president 1946-55; 1973-74). He was succeeded by his third wife Isabel, who was deposed by the military (1976). In 1982 Argentinian forces occupied South Georgia and the Falkland Islands, which the country claims, but were expelled by a British task force. Democratic elections in 1983 returned a civilian government. Argentina is among the most developed Latin American countries. The fertile pampas and sheep ranches of Patagonia provide exports: meat, cereals, hides and skins, wool, and linseed oil. Industry is now the chief export earner. There are oil and gas reserves, and much hydro-electric power. Area, 2 766 889 square kilometres (1,068,302 square miles). Population, 35,220,000. Capital, Buenos Aires. [Spanish *(Tierra) Argentina*, "silvery (land)" (with reference to the rivers and lakes), from Latin, feminine of *argentīnus*, silvery, ARGENTINE.] —**Ar·gen·tine** (-teen, -tīn), **Ar·gen·tin·ian** (-tinni-ən) *n. & adj.*

ar·gen·tine (árjən-tīn ‖ -teen) *adj.* Silvery. ~*n.* **1.** Any of various silvery metals. **2.** Any of several small, silvery marine fishes of the family Argentinidae. [French *argentin*, from Latin *argentīnus*, from *argentum*, silver, ARGENT.]

ar·gen·tite (árjən-tīt) *n.* A valuable silver ore, Ag_2S, with a lustrous, lead-grey colour. [Latin *argentum*, silver, ARGENT + -ITE.]

ar·gen·tous (aar-jéntəss) *adj.* Of or containing silver. Said especially of chemical compounds containing silver with a valency of 1. [Latin *argentum*, silver + -OUS.]

ar·gil (árjil) *n.* Clay, especially that used by potters. [Middle English *argil, argilla*, from Latin *argilla*, from Greek *argillos*.]

ar·gil·la·ceous (árji-láyshəss) *adj.* Containing, made of, or resembling clay; clayey. [Latin *argillāceus : argilla*, ARGIL + -ACEOUS.]

ar·gil·lite (árji-līt) *n.* A metamorphic rock, intermediate between shale and slate, that does not possess true slaty cleavage. [Latin *argilla*, ARGIL + -ITE.] —**ar·gil·lit·ic** (-líttik) *adj.*

ar·gi·nine (árji-nīn, -neen) *n.* An essential amino acid, $C_6H_{14}N_4O_2$, obtained from plant and animal protein or the digestive action of

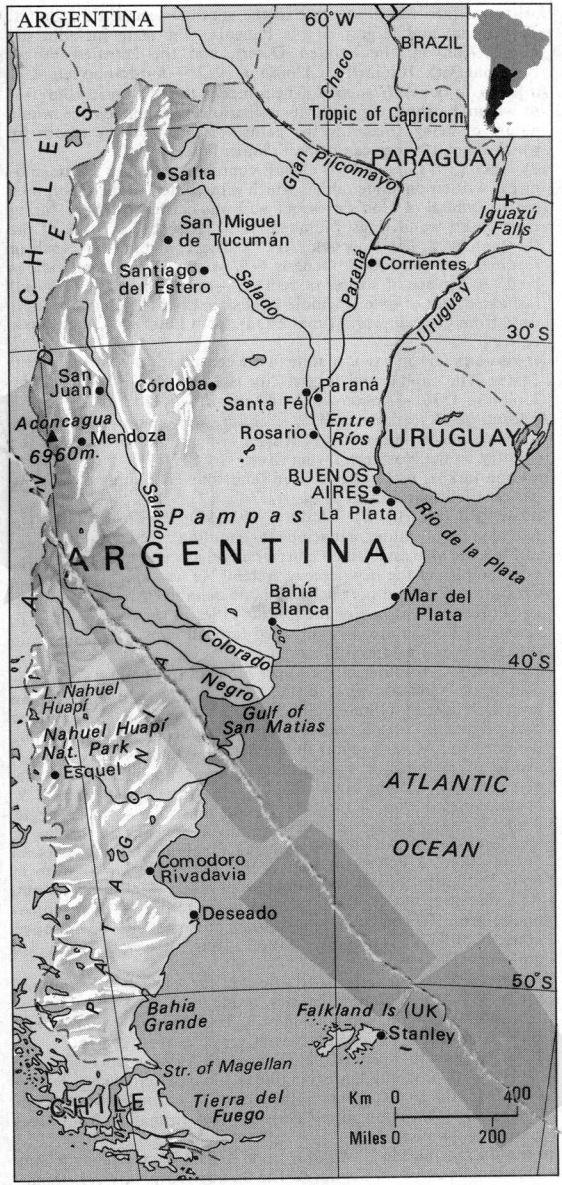

ARGENTINA

bacteria. [German *Arginin* : perhaps Greek *arginoeis,* bright, white + -INE.]

Ar·give (ár-gīv, -jīv) *adj.* **1.** Of or pertaining to Argos, an ancient Greek city-state. **2.** *Literary.* Greek.
~*n.* A Greek, especially an inhabitant of Argos.

argle-bargle. Variant of **argy-bargy.**

Ar·go[1] (árgō). *Greek Mythology.* The ship in which Jason sailed in search of the Golden Fleece.

Argo[2] *n.* A constellation in the Southern Hemisphere, now known by the names of its four smaller parts, **Carina, Puppis, Pyxis,** and **Vela** *(all of which see).* [After the ship ARGO.]

ar·gol, ar·gal (árg'l) *n.* Crude tartar deposited on casks as a by-product of winemaking. [Middle English *argoile,* from Anglo-French *argoil*†.]

ar·gon (ár-gon, -gən) *n. Symbol* **Ar** A colourless, odourless, inert gaseous element constituting approximately one per cent of the earth's atmosphere, from which it is commercially obtained by fractionation of liquid air for use in electric lamps, fluorescent tubes, and electronic valves, and as an inert-gas shield in arc-welding. Atomic number 18, atomic weight 39.94, melting point −189.4°C, boiling point −185.9°C. [Greek, neuter of *argos,* inert, idle, "not working": *a-,* without + *ergon,* work.]

ar·go·naut (árgə-nawt) *n.* A mollusc, the **paper nautilus** *(see).* [New Latin *Argonauta* (genus name), from Latin, ARGONAUT.]

Ar·go·naut (árgə-nawt) *n. Greek Mythology.* One who sailed with Jason on the *Argo* in search of the Golden Fleece. [Latin *Argonauta,* from Greek *Argonautēs* : *Argō,* name of Jason's ship + *nautēs,* sailor, from *naus,* ship.] —**Ar·go·naut·ic** (-náwtik) *adj.*

Ar·gonne (aar-gón). Wooded, hilly region of east France, forming a natural barrier between the districts of Champagne and Lorraine. It was a major battleground throughout World War I.

ar·go·non (árgə-non) *n.* An inert gas *(see).* [ARGON + -ON (inert gas).]

ar·go·sy (árgəssi) *n., pl.* **-sies. 1.** A large merchant ship. **2.** A fleet of such ships. [Earlier *argose, ragusye,* from Italian *ragusea,* vessel of *Ragusa,* former name of the port of Dubrovnik, Croatia.]

ar·got (ár-gō ‖ -gət) *n.* A specialised vocabulary or set of idioms used by a particular class or group; especially, formerly, the jargon of the underworld; cant [French *argot*†.] —**ar·got·ic** (-góttik) *adj.*

ar·gu·a·ble (árgew-əb'l) *adj.* **1.** Open to argument; questionable. **2.** That can be supported by argument. —See Synonyms at **doubtful.** —**ar·gu·a·bly** *adv.*

ar·gue (árgew) *v.* **-gued, -guing, -gues.** —*tr.* **1.** To put forward reasons for or against; debate. **2.** To prove or attempt to prove by reasoning; maintain in argument; contend. **3.** To give evidence of; indicate. **4.** To persuade or influence, as by presenting reasons: *He argued me into going.* —*intr.* **1.** To put forward reasons for or against an opinion, procedure, proposal, or the like. **2.** To quarrel; engage in a dispute. —See Synonyms at **discuss.** [Middle English *arguen,* from Old French *arguer,* to blame, argue against, from Latin *arguere,* to make clear, assert, prove.] —**ar·gu·er** *n.*
Synonyms: argue, quarrel, wrangle, squabble, haggle, bicker.

ar·gu·fy (árgew-fī) *v.* **-fied, -fying, -fies.** *Informal.* —*tr.* To argue excessively over. —*intr.* To argue stubbornly; wrangle. —**ar·gu·fi·er** *n.*

ar·gu·ment (árgwmənt) *n.* **1. a.** A discussion in which reasons are put forward in support of or against an opinion, procedure, proposal, or the like; a debate. **b.** A quarrel; a contention. **2. a.** A course of reasoning aimed at demonstrating the truth or falsehood of something. **b.** A fact or statement advanced in support of or against a plan of action, suggestion, proposal, or the like. **3.** A summary or short statement of the plot or subject of a literary work. **4.** *Logic.* The minor premise in a syllogism. **5.** *Mathematics.* **a.** The independent variable of a function. **b.** The **amplitude** *(see)* of a complex number. [Middle English, from Old French, from Latin *argūmentum,* from *arguere,* to ARGUE.]
Synonyms: argument, dispute, controversy, wrangling.

ar·gu·men·ta·tion (árgew-men-táysh'n, -mən-) *n.* **1.** The act or process of presenting and elaborating an argument. **2.** Deductive reasoning in debate. **3.** A debate.

ar·gu·men·ta·tive (árgew-méntətiv) *adj.* **1.** Given to excessive arguing; disputatious. **2.** Of or characterised by argument; controversial: *an argumentative discourse.* —**ar·gu·men·ta·tive·ly** *adv.* —**ar·gu·men·ta·tive·ness** *n.*

ar·gu·men·tum (árgew-mén-təm) *n., pl.* **-ta** (-tə). *Logic.* An argument, proof, or appeal to reason in support or refutation of a proposition. [Latin, "argument."]

Ar·gus (árgəss). *Greek Mythology.* A giant with a hundred eyes who was made guardian of Io and later slain by Hermes.

Ar·gus-eyed (árgəss-īd) *adj.* Extremely observant; vigilant.

argus pheasant *n.* Either of two birds, the great argus, *Argusianus argus,* or the crested argus, *Reinardia orellata,* both having long tails with eyelike markings in the male. [After the eyelike markings, imagined to resemble the numerous eyes of Argus.]

ar·gy-bar·gy (árji-bárji, *rarely* árgi-bárgi) *n.* Also **ar·gle-bar·gle** (árg'l-bárg'l). *Chiefly British Informal.* Quarrelling; bickering. [19th century : Scottish, variant of *argle-bargle,* reduplication of *argue,* altered through confusion with or perhaps through influence of *haggle.*] —**ar·gy-bar·gy** *intr.v.*

ar·gyle (aar-gīl ‖ ár-gīl) *n. Often capital* **A.** A geometric knitting pattern of varicoloured, diamond-shaped areas on a solid colour background. [After Campbell of *Argyle* (Argyll), the clan whose tartan was adapted for this pattern.]

Ar·gyll (aar-gīl). Also **Ar·gyll·shire** (-shər, -sheer ‖ *Scottish* -shīr). Former county in west central Scotland; from 1975 divided between Highland and Strathclyde Regions; from 1996 part of Argyll and Bute Unitary Authority area.

Ar·hat (ár-hət) *n.* In Buddhism, one who has reached Nirvana. [Sanskrit, "(one) deserving respect", from *arhati* "he deserves".]

År·hus (ór-hōoss). Commercial and industrial city, situated on Århus Bay, in Jutland, Denmark. It is Denmark's second-largest city, and one of its oldest. Until 1948 its name was spelt "Aarhus".

a·ri·a (áari-ə) *n. Music.* **1.** A solo vocal piece with instrumental accompaniment, as in an opera or oratorio. **2.** An air; a melody. [Italian *aria,* melody, "(atmospheric) air", from Latin *āera,* accusative of *āēr,* air, from Greek *āēr.*]

Ar·i·ad·ne (árri-ádni). *Greek Mythology.* The daughter of Minos and Pasiphae who gave Theseus the thread with which to find his way out of the Minotaur's Labyrinth.

Ar·i·an[1] (áir-i-ən) *adj.* Of or pertaining to Arius, Arianism, or Aries. ~*n.* **1.** A believer in Arianism. **2.** An Aries.

Arian[2]. Variant of **Aryan.**

-arian *adj. & n. suffix.* Indicates: **1.** Sect; for example, **Unitarian. 2.** Belief, advocacy; for example, **authoritarian, vegetarian.** [Latin *-ārius,* -ARY + -AN.]

Ar·i·an·ism (áir-i-ən-iz'm) *n. Theology.* The doctrines of Arius, denying that Jesus was of the same substance as God and holding instead that he was only the highest of created beings.

ar·id (árrid) *adj.* **1.** Very dry; lacking sufficient rainfall to support agriculture; parched. **2.** Lacking interest or feeling; lifeless; dull. [French *aride,* from Latin *āridus,* from *ārēre,* to be dry or parched.] —**a·rid·i·ty** (ə-ríddəti, a-), **ar·id·ness** *n.* —**ar·id·ly** *adv.*

ar·i·el (áir-i-əl) *n.* A gazelle, *Gazella arabica* (or *dama*), native to Arabia. [Arabic *'aryal,* stag.]

Ar·ies (áir-eez, árri-) *n.* **1.** A constellation in the Northern Hemisphere near Taurus and Pisces. **2. a.** The first sign of the **zodiac** *(see)*. Also called the "Ram". **b.** One born under this sign. [Latin, *ariĕs*, ram].

a·ri·et·ta (árri-éttə || áari-) *n.* Also **a·ri·ette** (-ét). A short aria. [Italian, diminutive of ARIA.]

a·right (ə-rī́t) *adv.* Properly; correctly. [Middle English *aright*, Old English *ariht*, *on riht* : A- (on) + *riht*, RIGHT (noun).]

ar·il (árril) *n. Botany.* An outer covering or appendage of some seeds, arising at or near the hilum. It is often fleshy or brightly coloured, as in the yew. [New Latin *arillus*, from Medieval Latin *arillus*†, raisin, grape seed.] **—ar·il·late** (-ayt) *adj.*

ar·il·lode (árril-ōd) *n. Botany.* An appendage or covering that resembles an aril but arises from the micropyle rather than the hilum. [New Latin *arillus*, ARIL + -ODE (like).]

a·ri·o·so (áari-ṓzō, árri- || -ṓ-so) *adv. Music.* In the style of an aria. Used as a direction.

~n., pl. **ariosos.** A piece of recitative sung in this style, rather than the usual declamatory style. [Italian, from ARIA.] **—a·ri·o·so** *adj.*

A·ri·os·to, (árri-óstō) **Ludovico** (1474–1533). Italian poet and dramatist. He is chiefly remembered for his epic comic masterpiece, *Orlando Furioso*, published in its final form in 1532.

a·rise (ə-rī́z) *intr.v.* **arose** (ə-rṓz), **arisen** (ə-rízz'n), **arising, arises. 1.** To get up, as from a sitting or prone position. **2.** To move upwards; ascend. **3.** To come into being; originate. **4.** To result, issue, or proceed. Used with *from*. **5.** To come to notice; become apparent. [Middle English *arisen*, Old English *ārīsan* : A- (up) + *rīsan*, RISE.]

a·ris·ta (ə-ríss-tə) *n., pl.* **-tae** (-tee). A bristle-like part, such as the awns of grasses or the antennae of certain insects. [New Latin, from Latin *arista*†, beard of grain, spine.] **—a·ris·tate** (-tayt) *adj.*

Ar·is·tar·chus (árri-stárkəss) **of Samos** (*fl. c.* 270 B.C.). Greek astronomer of the Alexandrian school. He was one of the first men to propose that the Sun was the centre of the universe and that the earth moves round it.

ar·is·toc·ra·cy (árriss-tóckrəssi) *n., pl.* **-cies. 1.** A hereditary privileged ruling class or nobility. **2.** Government by the nobility or by a privileged minority or upper class. **3.** A state or country having this form of government. **4.** *Rare.* **a.** Government by the best citizens. **b.** A state having such government. **5.** Any group or class considered to be superior. [Old French *aristocratie*, from Late Latin *aristocratia*, from Greek *aristokratia*, "rule by the best (citizens)" : *aristos*, best + -CRACY.]

a·ris·to·crat (árristə-krat || ə-rístə-) *n.* **1.** A member of the nobility or aristocracy. **2.** A person having the tastes, opinions, manners, and other characteristics of an upper class. **3.** A person who advocates government by an aristocracy. **4.** *Informal.* One that is superior in a specified field: *a tennis aristocrat*. [French *aristocrate*, from *aristocratie*, ARISTOCRACY.] **—a·ris·to·crat·ic** (-kráttik), **a·ris·to·crat·i·cal** (-kráttik'l) *adj.* **—a·ris·to·crat·i·cal·ly** *adv.*

Ar·is·toph·a·nes (árri-stóffəneez) (*c.* 448 –*c.* 387 B.C.). Greek comic poet and dramatist, considered the greatest of ancient writers of satirical comedy. Among his surviving plays are *The Clouds* (423), *Lysistrata* (411), and *The Frogs* (405).

Aristotelian logic *n.* Aristotle's deductive method of logic and the logical system based on this, especially the theory of the syllogism.

Ar·is·tot·le (árri-stott'l) (384 B.C.–322 B.C.). Greek ethical, metaphysical, and political philosopher, who wrote on most branches of learning, including physics and biology, and whose influence extended for more than a thousand years. From 367 B.C. to 347 he studied under Plato; from 342 to *c.* 339 he was tutor to Alexander the Great. He returned to Athens and opened a school, the Lyceum, in 335. The most important of his surviving works are the six-volume treatise on logic, *Organum*, the *Physics*, the *Nicomachean Ethics*, and the *Politics*. The fundamental propositions of Aristotle's system of thought were that theory should follow upon the empirical observation of nature and things, and that logic, based upon the syllogism, was the essential method of all rational inquiry. **—Ar·is·to·te·li·an** (árris-tə-téel-yən, -i-ən) *n. & adj.* **—Ar·is·to·te·li·an·ism** *n.*

a·rith·me·tic (ə-ríthmətik) *n.* **1.** The mathematics of integers under simple operations such as addition, subtraction, multiplication, division, involution, and evolution. **2.** Counting or problem-solving involving arithmetic operations.

~adj. **ar·ith·met·ic** (árrith-méttik). Also **ar·ith·met·i·cal** (-méttik'l). Of or pertaining to arithmetic. [Middle English *ar(i)smet(r)yk*, *arithmet(r)ik*, from Old French *ar(i)smetique*, from Latin *arithmētica*, from Greek *arithmētikē (tekhnē)*, "(the art) of counting", from the feminine of *arithmētikos*, of counting, from *arithmein*, to count, from *arithmos*, number.] **—ar·ith·met·i·cal·ly** *adv.*

a·rith·me·ti·cian (ə-ríth-mə-tísh'n, árrith-) *n.* An arithmetic expert.

ar·ith·met·ic mean (árrith-méttik) *n.* The number obtained by dividing the sum of a set of quantities by the number of quantities in the set. Also called "average", "mean".

ar·ith·met·ic progression (árrith-méttik) *n.* Also **arithmetical progression.** A sequence, such as the odd integers 1, 3, 5, 7, . . ., in which each term after the first is formed by adding a constant to each preceding term.

ar·ith·met·ic series (árrith-méttik) *n. Mathematics.* A series in which the terms form an arithmetic progression, as in 1 + 3 + 5, etc.

-arium *n. suffix.* Indicates a place or housing for; for example, **planetarium, terrarium.** [Latin, from the neuter of *-ārius*, -ARY.]

Ar·i·us (áir-i-əss || *chiefly U.S.* ə-rī́-əss) (*c.* 250-336). Christian priest of Alexandria, whose teaching gave rise to the heresy *Arianism*.

A·ri·zo·na (árri-zṓnə). A state in the southwestern United States. The capital and largest city is Phoenix. The state includes the Grand Canyon, the Painted Desert, and the Petrified Forest National Park. It joined the Union in 1912. **—A·ri·zo·nan** *adj. & n.*

Ar·ju·na (árjŏŏnə). *Hinduism.* The prince in the **Bhagavad-Gita** *(see)* to whom Krishna, disguised as a charioteer, expounds the whole nature of being, including the nature of God and the means by which human beings can come to know him.

ark (ark) *n.* **1.** *Capital* **A.** The chest containing the Ten Commandments written on stone tablets which represented to the Hebrews a sacred symbol of God's presence and was carried by them during their desert wanderings. Numbers 10:35. Also called "Ark of the Covenant". **2.** The **Holy ark** *(see)*. **3.** The boat built by Noah in readiness for the Flood. Genesis 6–9. **4.** Any large, commodious boat. **5.** A place of shelter or refuge. **—out of the ark.** Very old-fashioned; out-of-date. [Middle English *ark*, Old English *arc*, *aerc*, *earc*, from Germanic *ark-* (unattested), from Latin *arca*, chest, box, coffer.]

Ar·kan·sas (árkən-saw). A state in the central southwestern United States. The capital and largest city is Little Rock. It joined the Union in 1836. **—Ar·kan·san** (aar-kánzən) *adj. & n.*

Ar·khan·gelsk (arkhən-gyélsk). *English* **Arch·an·gel** (árk-aynjəl). City and major timber port of Russia, lying in the northwest of the country on the Northern Dvina river.

ar·kose (árkōz) *n.* Coarse-grained sandstone containing at least 25 per cent feldspar as well as quartz.

Ark·wright (árk-rīt), **Sir Richard** (1732-92). British inventor. He patented his invention, a machine for spinning called a water frame, in 1769. He also established cotton mills that were among the earliest examples of the new factory system. He was knighted in 1786.

Arles (arl). City and port on the Rhône delta in Provence in southern France. It was one of the leading cities in the western Roman empire (a Roman arena is still used for bullfights and plays), and the capital of a medieval kingdom.

arm¹ (arm) *n.* **1.** Either of the upper limbs of the human body connecting the hand and wrist to the shoulder. **2.** A part similar to an arm, such as the forelimb of an animal, a branch of a tree, or a long part projecting from a central support in a machine. **3.** Anything designed to cover or support the human arm, such as a sleeve on an article of clothing or a projecting support on a chair or sofa. **4.** Anything branching out from a large mass: *an arm of the sea.* **5.** *Mathematics.* Either of the two straight lines that form an angle. **6.** *Physics.* Any of the resistors forming a Wheatstone bridge or similar circuit. **7.** An administrative or functional branch, as of an organisation. **8.** Power; authority: *the arm of the law.* **—arm in arm.** With arms linked one through the other. **—at arm's length.** At a distance; not on friendly or intimate terms. **—twist (someone's) arm.** To coerce or put pressure on someone. **—with open arms.** Cordially; hospitably. [Middle English *arm*, Old English *arm*, *earm*.]

arm² *n.* **1.** A weapon, especially a firearm. **2.** A branch of a military force, such as the infantry, cavalry, or air force.

~v. **armed, arming, arms.** *—intr.* **1.** To supply or equip oneself with weapons. **2.** To prepare oneself for or as if for warfare. *—tr.* **1.** To equip with weapons. **2.** To prepare for war; fortify. **3.** To provide with anything that strengthens, increases efficiency, or prepares. **4.** *Military.* To prepare (a bomb, for example) for detonation, as by releasing a safety device. [Back-formation from ARMS (plural).] **—arm·er** *n.*

ar·ma·da (aar-máadə || -máydə) *n.* **1.** A fleet of warships. **2.** Any large mobile force. **3.** *Capital* **A.** The **Spanish Armada** *(see)*. [Spanish, from Medieval Latin *armāta*, army, fleet, from Latin *armātus*, past participle of *armāre*, to arm, from *arma*, arms.]

ar·ma·dil·lo (ármə-dillō) *n., pl.* **-los.** Any of several omnivorous burrowing mammals of the family Dasypodidae, of southern North America and Central and South America, having a covering of armour-like, jointed, bony plates. [Spanish, diminutive of *armado*, armour-plated, past participle of *armar*, to arm, from Latin *armāre*, from *arma*, arms.]

Ar·ma·ged·don (ármə-gédd'n) *n.* **1.** The scene of a final battle between the forces of good and evil, prophesied in the Bible to occur at the end of the world. Revelation 16:16. **2.** Any great conflict causing widespread destruction. [Late Latin *Armagedōn*, from Greek, from Hebrew *har megiddōn*, the mountain region of *Megiddo*, site of several great battles in the Old Testament.]

Ar·magh (aar-maá). A market town in the county of Armagh, in the south of Northern Ireland. It is the seat of both the Roman Catholic and the Protestant primates of Ireland.

Ar·ma·gnac (ármən-yak) *n.* A dry brandy of superior quality made in the département of Gers in southwest France. [After *Armagnac*, former name of the region.]

ar·ma·ment (ármәmənt) *n.* **1.** The weapons and supplies of war with which a military unit is equipped. **2.** *Often plural.* All the military forces and war equipment of a country. **3.** A military force equipped for war. **4.** The process of arming for war. [Late Latin *armāmentum* (singular), from Latin *armāmenta* (plural), implements, equipment, from *arma*, tools, ARMS.]

ar·ma·men·tar·i·um (ármə-men-táir-i-əm) *n., pl.* **-ums** or **-ia** (-i-ə). **1.** The complete equipment of a doctor or medical institution, including books, supplies, and instruments. **2. arsenal** 2. [Latin, "store of weapons". See **armament, -arium.**]

ar·ma·ture (ármə-tewr, -choor, -chər) *n.* **1.** *Electricity.* **a.** The rotating part of a dynamo consisting essentially of copper wire wound around an iron core. **b.** The moving part of an electromagnetic device such as a relay, buzzer, or loud-speaker. **c.** A piece of soft iron connecting the poles of a magnet; a keeper. **2.** *Biology.* The protective covering or structure of an animal or plant. **3.** A framework serving as a supporting core for clay sculpture. **4.** *Archaic.* Armour. [Latin *armātūra,* equipment, from *armāre,* to arm, from *arma,* weapons, tools.]

arm·band (árm-band) *n.* A strip of material worn around the upper arm for identification or as a sign of mourning.

arm·chair (árm-cháir, -chair) *n.* A chair, usually upholstered, with supports at the sides for the arms or elbows. —*adj.* Remote from active involvement; purely theoretical: *an armchair revolutionary.*

armed (armd) *adj.* **1.** Equipped with weapons. **2.** Having or characterised by an arm or arms of a specified kind or number. Usually used in combination: *strong-armed.* **3.** Ready to face adversity.

armed forces *pl.n.* The military forces of a country or countries. Also called "armed services".

Ar·me·ni·a (aar-méen-ya). Ancient Asian kingdom centred on Mount Ararat, and now divided between Turkey, Iran, and the Republic of Armenia. Established in the eighth century B.C., it became the world's first country to make Christianity the state religion (A.D. 303). It was partitioned between Persia and the Eastern Roman Empire (A.D. 387), and thereafter endured many conquerors. Between 1894 and 1915 the Turks massacred most of their Armenians.

Armenia, Republic of. Formerly a constituent republic of the U.S.S.R., on the southern flanks of the Caucasus Mts., independent since 1991. In 1988 an earthquake killed about 25,000 people. Conflict with Azerbaijan over Armenia's claim to the Nagorno-Karabakh enclave has persisted throughout the 1990s. Area, 29 800 square kilometres (11,506 square miles). Population, 3,760,000. Capital, Yerevan. See map at **Caucasus.**

Ar·me·ni·an (aar-méen-yan, -i-ən) *n.* **1. a.** A native or inhabitant of Armenia or the Republic of Armenia. **b.** A descendant of Armenians. **2.** The Indo-European language of the Armenians. —**Ar·me·ni·an** *adj.*

Armenian Church *n.* The independent church of the Armenians, founded in about A.D. 300 and similar to the Eastern Orthodox Church in its practices and doctrines.

ar·met (ár-met) *n.* A medieval light helmet with a neck guard and movable visor. [Old French *armet,* partly from *arme,* singular of *armes,* ARMS, and partly from Old Spanish *almete,* from Old French *helmet,* HELMET.]

arm·ful (árm-fool) *n., -pl. -fuls.* The amount one arm can hold.

arm·hole (árm-hōl) *n.* An opening which is for the arm in a garment and to which the sleeve is attached if the garment has sleeves.

ar·mi·ger (ármijər) *n.* **1.** An armourbearer for a knight; a squire. **2.** A person entitled to heraldic arms. [Latin *armiger : arma,* ARMS + *gerere,* to carry.] —**ar·mig·e·rous** *adj.*

ar·mil·lar·y sphere (ármi-ləri, aar-míllari ‖ -lerri) *n.* An astronomical model with solid rings, all circles of a single sphere, used to display relationships among the principal circles on the celestial sphere. [Old French *armillaire,* from Medieval Latin *armilla,* ring, from Latin *arm* ring, from *armus,* arm.]

Ar·min·i·an·ism (aar-mínni-ən-iz'm) *n.* The doctrine of Jacobus Arminius and his followers, opposing the Calvinist doctrine of absolute predestination and holding that salvation is possible for all. It was the basis of the Methodist position of John and Charles Wesley. —**Ar·min·i·an** *adj. & n.*

Ar·min·i·us (aar-mínni-əss), **Jacobus** (1560–1609). Theologian of the Dutch Reformed Church. His opposition to the strict predestinarianism of John Calvin became known as Arminianism and had a wide influence throughout Europe.

ar·mi·stice (ármistiss ‖ aar-místiss) *n.* A temporary cessation or suspension of hostilities by mutual consent; a truce. [French, from New Latin *armistitium : Latin arma,* ARMS + *-stitium,* "stoppage".]

Armistice Day *n.* November 11, celebrated as the anniversary of the armistice of World War I in 1918, now observed on Remembrance Sunday. See **Veterans Day.**

arm·let (árm-lət, -lit) *n.* **1.** A band or bracelet worn on the arm for ornament or identification. **2.** A small inlet, as of the sea.

ar·moire (aarm-waar, ármər) *n.* A large, ornate cabinet or wardrobe. [Old French, variant of *armaire,* from Latin *armārium,* closet, from *arma,* weapons, tools.]

ar·mo·ri·al (aar-máwri-əl ‖ -móri-) *adj.* Of or pertaining to heraldry or heraldic arms. —*n.* A book containing coats of arms. [From *armory,* a rare word for heraldry + -AL.]

Ar·mor·i·ca (aar-mórri-kə). A literary name for Brittany.

Ar·mor·i·can (aar-mórri-kən) *adj.* Also **Ar·mor·ic** (aar-mórrik). **1.** Of or pertaining to Armorica or the people or language of Armorica. **2.** *Geology.* Hercynian. —*n.* Also **Ar·mor·ic.** **1.** A native or inhabitant of Armorica. **2.** The language of Armorica; Breton.

ar·mour, *U.S.* **ar·mor** (ármər) *n.* **1.** A defensive covering, such as chain mail, leather, or metal plates, worn as protection against weapons. **2.** Any tough, protective covering, such as the bony scales or plates covering certain animals, or metal plates on tanks or warships. **3.** Anything serving as a safeguard or protection. **4.** The armoured vehicles of an army collectively. —*tr.v.* **armoured, -mouring, -mours.** To cover with armour. [Mid-

dle English *armure,* from Old French, from Latin *armātūra,* equipment, from *armāre,* to arm, from *arma,* ARMS.]

ar·mour·bear·er (ármər-bair-ər) *n.* One who carries the arms or armour of a warrior.

ar·mour·clad (ármər-klád, -klad) *adj.* Wearing or covered with armour.

ar·moured (ármərd) *adj.* **1.** Clad with armour or a protective covering, such as scales. **2.** Equipped with armoured vehicles, like a military unit. **3.** Strengthened or reinforced. Said of glass.

armoured car *n.* **1.** A light, armoured, military vehicle usually having a mounted machine gun and used especially for reconnaissance. **2.** A light armoured van used for transporting money or valuables.

ar·mour·er (ármərər) *n.* **1.** One who makes or repairs armour. **2.** A manufacturer of weapons. **3.** *Military.* A serviceman in charge of maintenance and repair of the small arms of a unit.

armour plate *n.* Hard steel plate used to cover warships, vehicles, and fortifications. —**ar·mour-plat·ed** (ármər-pláytid) *adj.*

ar·mour·y (árməri) *n., pl.* **-ies. 1. a.** A storehouse for arms; an arsenal. **b. arsenal** 2. **2. a.** A building for storing arms and military equipment. **b.** *U.S.* An armoury serving as a headquarters for military reserve personnel. **3.** *Chiefly U.S.* An arms factory. [Middle English *armourie,* from *armure,* ARMOUR.]

arm·pit (árm-pit) *n.* The hollow under the arm at the shoulder.

arm·rest (árm-rest) *n.* A support for the arm, as on a piece of furniture or the inner surface of the door of a vehicle.

arms (armz) *pl.n.* **1.** Weapons. **2.** Warfare. **3.** Heraldic bearings. **4.** Insignia, as of a state, official, family, or organisation. —**bear arms against.** To attack with arms; wage war on. —**in** or **under arms.** Armed. —**lay down (one's) arms.** *Military.* To surrender. —**order arms.** *Military.* To bring a rifle vertically against the right side of the body with the butt touching the ground. —**shoulder arms.** *Military.* To hold a rifle in a sloping position with the barrel over the shoulder and the butt in the hand. —**up in arms.** Angry; ready to protest. [Middle English *armes,* from Old French, from Latin *arma,* weapons, tools.]

arms race *n.* The continuous increasing or building up of weapons and forces by two or more nations, in order to maintain equality or superiority of military power.

Arm·strong (árm-strong ‖ *U.S. also* -strawng), **Louis** (1900–71). American jazz musician, popularly known as "Satchmo". He was born in New Orleans. In 1922 he joined King Oliver's band in Chicago and thereupon quickly rose to national fame, as both a trumpeter and a singer.

ar·my (ármi) *n., pl.* **-mies. 1.** A large body of people organised and trained for warfare on land. **2.** The entire military land forces of a country. **3.** A tactical and administrative military unit consisting of a headquarters, two or more army corps, and auxiliary forces. **4.** Any large group of people organised for a specific cause. **5.** A large multitude, as of people or animals. —See Synonyms at **multitude.** [Middle English *armee,* from Old French, from Medieval Latin *armāta,* army, fleet, from Latin *armātus,* past participle of *armāre,* to arm, from *arma,* arms.]

army ant *n.* Any of various chiefly tropical New World ants of the subfamily Dorylinae, forming large colonies that move from place to place. Also called "legionary ant".

ar·my·worm (ármi-wurm) *n.* Any of various insect larvae that travel in large groups, destroying crops; especially, the caterpillar of a New World moth, *Leucania* (or *Pseudaletia*) *unipuncta.*

Arne (arn), **Thomas (Augustine)** (1710–78). British composer. Largely self-taught, he wrote songs, oratorios, and operas. The song "Rule, Britannia" comes from his opera, *Alfred* (1740).

Arn·hem (árnəm). Industrial town and port on the Lower Rhine river, in the eastern Netherlands. It was the site of a major defeat inflicted upon British airborne troops in September 1944.

Arnhem Land. Northernmost part of Northern Territory in Australia, containing the largest of the country's 17 Aboriginal reservations.

ar·ni·ca (árnikə) *n.* **1.** Any of various Alpine or Arctic plants of the genus *Arnica,* having bright-yellow, rayed flowers. **2.** A tincture of the dried flower heads of *A. montana,* used for sprains and bruises. [18th century : New Latin *Arnica†.*]

Ar·no (árnō). River of central Italy. It rises in the Apennines and flows some 240 kilometres (150 miles) to the Ligurian Sea. In 1966 it flooded, causing severe damage to art treasures in Florence.

Ar·nold (árn'ld), **Sir Malcolm (Henry)** (1921–). British composer of eight symphonies, two operas, *The Dancing Master* (1951) and *The Open Window* (1956), and more than eighty film scores, including the music for *The Bridge on the River Kwai* (Oscar, 1957).

Arnold, Matthew (1822–88). British poet, critic, and essayist, the son of Thomas Arnold. His famous poem, "Dover Beach" (1867), expressed his personal moral and religious doubts. He is most widely known for his classic study *Culture and Anarchy* (1869), a trenchant polemic against the materialism of Victorian society.

Arnold, Thomas (1795–1842). English schoolmaster and historian, the father of Matthew Arnold. From 1828 to 1842 Arnold was headmaster of Rugby School, where, by his insistence on Christian conduct and his introduction of a modern curriculum, he did much to reform and raise the status of English public schools.

ar·oid (árroyd, áir-oyd) *adj.* Also **a·ra·ceous** (ə-ráyshəss, a-). Of or belonging to the Araceae, a family of plants that includes the arums and callas. —*n.* Any of various plants of the family Araceae.

a·ro·ma (ə-rōmə) *n.* **1.** A pleasant characteristic odour, as of a plant, spice, or food. **2.** A distinctive, intangible quality; an aura. —See Synonyms at **smell.** [Latin *arōma,* from Greek *arōma*†, aromatic herb or spice.]

a·ro·ma·ther·a·py (ərṓmə-thérrəpi) *n.* A form of therapy in which disorders are treated by body massage using aromatic oils.

ar·o·mat·ic (árrə-máttik, árrō-) *adj.* **1.** Having an aroma; fragrant, sweet-smelling, or spicy. **2.** *Chemistry.* Of, pertaining to, or containing the six-carbon-atom ring characteristic of the benzene series and related organic groups. Compare **aliphatic.**
—*n.* An aromatic plant or substance. [Middle English, from Old French *aromatique,* from Late Latin *arōmaticus,* from Greek *arōmatikos* : AROMA (stem *arōmat-*) + -IC.] **—ar·o·mat·i·cal·ly** *adv.*

ar·o·ma·tic·i·ty (ə-rṓmə-tíssəti || árrəmə-) *n.* **1.** Aromatic quality or character. **2.** The characteristic structure or properties of the aromatic chemical compounds.

a·ro·ma·tise, a·ro·ma·tize (ə-rṓmə-tīz) *v.* **-tised, -tising, -tises.** *—tr.* **1.** To make aromatic or fragrant. **2.** *Chemistry.* To change (a compound) into an aromatic compound. *—intr.* To become aromatic. Used of chemical compounds. **—a·ro·ma·ti·sa·tion** (-tī-záysh'n || *U.S.* -ti-) *n.*

arose. Past tense of **arise.**

a·round (ə-równd || *West Indies also* -rúngd) *adv.* **1.** In all directions from a specific point: *famous for miles around.* **2.** *Chiefly U.S.* On or to all sides or in all directions; about: *looked around in vain.* **3.** *U.S.* In a circle or circular motion. **4.** *U.S.* In or towards the opposite direction, position, or attitude; round: *swung around at the noise.* **5.** *Chiefly U.S.* From one place to another; here and there; about: *wander around.* **6.** *Chiefly U.S. Informal.* Close at hand; round: *He waited around all day.* **7.** *U.S.* In circular measurement; round: *a waist three feet around.* **8.** *Chiefly U.S.* In existence; about: *There is one around somewhere.* **—get around.** *Informal.* **1.** To circumvent; get round. **2.** To have wide knowledge of worldly matters; get about. **—get around to.** *Informal.* To find time or occasion to give one's attention to; get round to.
—*prep.* **1.** On all sides of. **2.** So as to enclose, surround, or envelop. **3.** About the circumference or periphery of; encircling. **4.** *U.S.* About the central point of: *the Earth's motion around the Sun.* **5.** In or to a place or places within or near: *driving around the countryside.* **6.** *U.S.* On or to the other side of: *the house around the corner.* **7.** *Chiefly U.S.* Approximately; about: *around 20 guests.* **8.** *Chiefly U.S.* So as to get past or avoid: *a way around the problem.* [Middle English : A- (on) + ROUND (noun).]

Usage: In both adverbial and prepositional senses, *around* is, in most cases, the preferred form in American English, whereas *round* is the preferred form in British English. In its sense of "approximately, about", *around* is a usual U.S. term, but now has some currency in British English. See also **about.**

a·rous·al (ə-rówz'l) *n.* The act of arousing or state of being aroused.

a·rouse (ə-rówz) *tr.v.* **aroused, arousing, arouses. 1.** To awaken from or as if from sleep. **2.** To excite or stimulate. —See Synonyms at **provoke.** [16th century : A- (intensive) + ROUSE, by analogy with *rise, arise, wake, awake,* and the like.] **—a·rous·er** *n.*

Arp (arp), **Jean** or **Hans** (1887–1966). French sculptor and painter. Arp was an experimental artist who produced abstract works in a variety of forms, including collages, full rounded sculptures, painted wood reliefs, and painted cutouts.

ar·peg·gi·o (aar-péji-ō || *U.S. also* -péj-) *n., pl.* **-os.** *Music.* **1.** The playing of the notes of a chord in rapid succession rather than simultaneously. **2.** A chord played or sung in this manner. [Italian *arpeggio,* "chord played as on a harp", from *arpeggiare,* to play the harp, from *arpa,* harp, from Germanic *harpon-* (unattested), HARP.] **—ar·peg·gi·oed** *adj.*

ar·pent (árpənt, aar-póN) *n.* An old French unit of land measurement approximately equivalent to an acre. [French, from Old French, from Vulgar Latin *arependis* (unattested), variant of Latin *arepennis,* half acre, of Gaulish origin; related to Old Irish *airchenn* (a land measure).]

arquebus. Variant of **harquebus.**

arr. 1. arrival; arrive; arrived. **2.** arranged (by).

ar·rack, a·rak (árrək || ə-rák) *n.* A strong, alcoholic drink of the Middle and Far East, usually distilled from rice or molasses. [Arabic *'araq,* sweet juice, liquor, as in *'araq at-tamr,* fermented juice of the date.]

ar·raign (ə-ráyn) *tr.v.* **-raigned, -raigning, -raigns. 1.** *Law.* To call before a court to answer an indictment. **2.** To call to account; charge; accuse. [Middle English *arreinen,* from Old French *araisnier,* from Vulgar Latin *adrationāre* (unattested), "to call to account" : *ad-,* to + Latin *ratiō,* reason, from *rērī* (past participle *ratus*), to think, reckon.] **—ar·raign·er** *n.*

ar·raign·ment (ə-ráynmənt) *n.* The act or procedure of arraigning or being arraigned; especially, the formal summoning of a prisoner in a law court to answer an indictment.

Ar·ran (árrən). A granite island at the mouth of the Firth of Clyde in west Scotland.

ar·range (ə-ráynj) *v.* **-ranged, -ranging, -ranges.** *—tr.* **1.** To put into a deliberate order or relation; dispose. **2.** To plan or prepare for: *arrange a picnic.* **3.** To agree about; settle: *arrange the date of the marriage.* **4.** *Music.* To adapt (music) for other instruments or voices, or for another style of performance or play. **5.** To adapt (a play or book) for broadcasting on radio or television. *—intr.* **1.** To come to an agreement. Often used with *with.* **2.** To make preparations; plan. Often used with *for.* [Middle English *arangen, arengen,* from Old French *arangier, arengier* : *a-,* from *ad,* to + *rengier,* to put in a line, from *renc, reng,* line, row, from Frankish *hring* (unattested), circle, ring.] **—ar·rang·er** *n.*

ar·range·ment (ə-ráynjmənt) *n.* **1.** The act or process of arranging. **2.** The condition, manner, or result of being arranged; disposal; order. **3.** Something that has been arranged. **4.** A collection or set of things that have been arranged. **5.** *Often plural.* A provision or plan made in preparation for some undertaking. **6.** An agreement; a settlement; a disposition. **7.** *Music.* **a.** An adaptation of a composition for other voices or instruments, or to another style or level of difficulty. **b.** A composition so arranged.

ar·rant (árrənt) *adj.* Out-and-out, unmitigated; thoroughgoing: *an arrant knave.* [14th century : variant of ERRANT, wandering; pejorative sense developed through use in phrases such as *arrant* (i.e. vagabond) *thief,* hence, "out-and-out thief".] **—ar·rant·ly** adv.

ar·ras (árrəss) *n.* **1.** A tapestry. **2.** A wall hanging, especially of tapestry. [Middle English, from Anglo-French *(drap de) Arras,* (cloth of) ARRAS.]

Ar·ras (árrəss). Administrative centre of the Pas-de-Calais département, lying on the Scarpe river of northern France. It was a famous woollen and tapestry centre in the Middle Ages.

Ar·rau (a-rów), **Claudio** (1903–91). Chilean pianist. He made his first European tour in 1918. He gained a special reputation for his interpretation of Beethoven.

ar·ray (ə-ráy) *tr.v.* **-rayed, -raying, -rays. 1.** To arrange or draw up (troops, for example) in battle order. **2.** To deck in finery; adorn.
—*n.* **1.** An orderly arrangement, especially of troops. **2.** An impressive display of numerous persons or objects. **3.** Splendid attire; finery. **4.** *Mathematics.* **a.** A rectangular arrangement of quantities in rows and columns, as in a matrix or determinant. **b.** Numerical data linearly ordered by magnitude. **5.** *Law.* The list of jurors empanelled to try a case. **6.** *Electronics.* A regular arrangement of aerials used for radar or radio astronomy. —See Synonyms at **multitude.** [Middle English *arayen, arrayen,* from Old French *areer, arayer,* from Vulgar Latin *arrēdāre* (unattested), to arrange : *ad,* towards + *rēdāre* (unattested), to provide, from Germanic.]

ar·ray·al (ə-ráy-əl) *n.* **1.** The act or process of arraying. **2.** Something arrayed; an array.

ar·rear (ə-réer) *n.* **1.** *Usually plural.* An unpaid and overdue debt, or an unfulfilled obligation. **2.** *Usually plural.* The state of being behind in fulfilling contractual obligations or payments. Used with *in*: *with the rent in arrears.* [Middle English *ar(r)ere,* behind, from Old French *arriere, arrere,* from Late Latin *ad retrō,* backward : *ad-,* towards + *retrō,* backward, behind.]

ar·rear·age (ə-réer-ij) *n.* **1.** The state of being in arrears. **2.** An amount owed in payment. **3.** *Rare.* Something held in reserve.

ar·rest (ə-rést) *tr.v.* **-rested, -resting, -rests. 1.** To prevent the motion, progress, growth, or spread of; stop or check. **2.** To seize and hold under authority of the law. **3.** To capture and hold briefly (the attention, for example); engage.
—*n.* **1. a.** The act of arresting. **b.** The state of being arrested. **2.** A device for arresting motion, especially of a moving part. **—under arrest.** Detained in legal custody. [Middle English *aresten,* from Old French *arester,* from Vulgar Latin *arrestāre* (unattested), to cause to stop : Latin *ad-,* to + *restāre,* to stop, stay behind : *re-,* back + *stāre,* to stand.] **—ar·rest·er** *n.* **—ar·rest·ment** *n.*

ar·rest·able (ə-réstəb'l) *adj.* Liable to incur or lead to arrest if committed: *an arrestable offence.*

ar·rest·ing (ə-résting) *adj.* **1.** Attracting and holding the attention; striking. **2.** Making an arrest. **—ar·rest·ing·ly** *adv.*

arrest of judgment *n. Law.* **1.** A request by the accused before being sentenced that judgment be postponed owing to some irregularity. **2.** The suspension of judgment by a court if an indictment does not disclose an offence known to law.

Ar·rhe·ni·us (ə-ráyni-əss), **Svante August** (1859–1927). Swedish chemist, a pioneer of modern physical chemistry. His research into the aqueous solutions of bases and acids led to the discovery, called the Arrhenius theory, of electrolytes for which he was awarded the Nobel prize in chemistry in 1903.

ar·rhyth·mi·a (ə-ríth-mi-ə, a-) *n.* Any irregularity in the force or rhythm of the heartbeat. [New Latin, from Greek, from *arrhuthmos,* unrhythmical : *a-,* not + *rhuthmos,* RHYTHM.]

ar·rhyth·mic (ə-ríth-mik, a-) *adj.* Also **ar·rhyth·mi·cal** (-mik'l). **1.** Lacking rhythm or regularity of rhythm. **2.** *Pathology.* Characterised by arrhythmia. **—ar·rhyth·mi·cal·ly** *adv.*

ar·ri·ère-ban (árri-air-bán || -baán) *n.* **1.** In medieval France, a royal proclamation by which vassals were summoned to military service. **2.** The vassals so summoned. [French, from Old French *arriereban,* alteration of *arban, herban,* from Old High German *heriban* : *heri,* army + *ban,* proclamation.]

ar·rière-pen·sée (árri-air-póN-say, -poN-sáy) *n.* An intention or a thought which is not disclosed, often because of an ulterior motive. [French, "behind thought".]

Ar Rimal. See **Rub al Khali.**

ar·ris (árris) *n., pl.* **arris** or **-rises.** *Architecture.* The sharp edge or ridge formed by two surfaces meeting at an angle, as in a moulding. [Old French *areste* (modified), ridge, ARÊTE.]

ar·ri·val (ə-rīv'l) *n. Abbr.* **arr. 1.** The act of arriving. **2.** One that arrives or has arrived. Also used adjectivally: *the arrival lounge at the airport.* **3.** The reaching of a goal or objective as a result of some process or effort.

ar·rive (ə-rīv) *intr.v.* **-rived, -riving, -rives. 1.** To reach a destination; come to a particular place. **2.** To reach a goal or object through some process or effort. Usually used with *at*: *arrive at a decision.*

3. To come at length; take place: *The day of crisis has arrived.* **4.** *Informal.* To achieve success or recognition. **5.** *Informal.* To be born. [Middle English *ariven,* from Old French *ariver,* from Vulgar Latin *arripāre* (unattested), to land, come to shore : Latin *ad-,* to + *rīpa,* shore.] **—ar·riv·er** *n.*

ar·ri·ve·der·ci (ə-reévə-dérchi, a-, dáirchi) *interj. Italian.* Until we meet again; goodbye.

ar·ri·viste (árree-veést) *n., pl.* **-vistes** (-veést(s)). A social climber or opportunist; an upstart. [French, from *arriver,* to ARRIVE.] **— ar·ri·visme** (-veéz'm, -veézmə) *n.*

ar·ro·ba (ə-rōbə) *n.* **1.** A unit of weight in Spanish-speaking countries equal to about 11 kilograms (25 pounds). **2.** A unit of weight in Portuguese-speaking countries equal to about 15 kilograms (32 pounds). **3.** A liquid measure used in Spanish-speaking countries, having varying value, but approximately equal to 16 litres (17 quarts) when used to measure wine. [Spanish and Portuguese, from Arabic *ar-rub',* the quarter (of a quintal).]

ar·ro·gant (árrəgənt) *adj.* **1.** Excessively convinced of one's own importance; haughty. **2.** Characterised by or arising from haughty self-importance. —See Synonyms at **proud.** [Middle English, from Latin *arrogāns* (stem *arrogant-*), present participle of *arrogāre,* ARROGATE.] **—ar·ro·gance** *n.* **—ar·ro·gant·ly** *adv.*

ar·ro·gate (árrə-gayt) *tr.v.* **-gated, -gating, -gates. 1.** To appropriate presumptuously; claim or assume without right. **2.** To attribute to another without justification. [Latin *arrogāre,* to claim for oneself : *ad-,* to + *rogāre,* to ask.] **—ar·ro·ga·tion** (-gáysh'n) *n.* **—ar·ro·ga·tive** (-gaytiv, ə-róggətiv) *adj.* **—ar·ro·ga·tor** (-gaytər) *n.*

ar·ron·disse·ment (arróN-deess-móN) *n. French.* **1.** The chief administrative subdivision of a département in France. **2.** A municipal subdivision of some large French cities. [French, from *arrondir,* to make round, round out, from *rond,* ROUND.]

ar·row (árrō) *n.* **1.** A straight, thin shaft, shot from a bow and usually made of light wood with a pointed head at one end and flight-stabilising feathers at the other. **2.** Anything similar in form, function, or speed, such as a sign or symbol used to indicate direction. [Middle English *arewe, arwe,* Old English *arwe, earh.*]

ar·row·head (árrō-hed) *n.* **1.** The pointed, removable striking tip of an arrow. **2.** Something shaped like an arrowhead, such as a mark indicating a limit on a drawing. **3.** Any aquatic or marsh plant of the genus *Sagittaria,* especially *S. sagittifolia,* having arrowhead-shaped leaves and purple-spotted white flowers.

ar·row·root (árrō-rōot ‖ -rōot) *n.* **1.** A tropical American plant, *Maranta arundinacea,* having roots that yield an edible starch. **2.** The edible starch from this plant and from certain plants of the genera *Manihot, Curcuma,* and *Tacca.* [After the use of the root by the American Indians to absorb poison from arrow wounds.]

arrow worm *n.* Any of various small, transparent marine wormlike animals of the phylum Chaetognatha, having prehensile bristles on each side of the mouth.

ar·roy·o (ə-róy-ō) *n., pl.* **-os.** In the southwest United States: **1.** A deep gully cut by a stream; a dry ravine. **2.** A brook or creek. [Spanish, from Vulgar Latin *arrugium* (unattested), variant of Latin *arrugia*†, mineshaft.]

arse (arss, aass) *n.* Also *U.S.* **ass** (ass). **1.** *Vulgar.* The buttocks. **2.** *Vulgar.* The anus. **3.** *Vulgar Slang.* A foolish person. **—arse about** or **around.** *Vulgar Slang.* To behave in a foolish or irritating manner. [Middle English *ars, ers,* Old English *ærs,* from Germanic; akin to Old Norse *ars,* German *Arsch.*]

ar·se·nal (árss'n'l) *n.* **1.** An establishment for the storing, manufacturing, or repairing of arms, ammunition, and other war material. **2.** A stock of weapons or things that may be used as weapons: *an arsenal of debating points.* [Italian *arsenale, arzanale,* originally, naval dockyard, from Arabic *dār-aṣ-ṣinā'ah* : *dār,* house + *aṣ-,* variant of *al-,* the + *ṣinā'ah,* manufacture, from *ṣana'a,* he made.]

ar·se·nate (árss'n-ayt, -ət, -it) *n.* A salt or ester of arsenic acid.

ar·se·nic (árssnik, árss'n-ik) *n.* **1.** *Symbol* **As** A highly poisonous metallic element having three allotropic forms, yellow, black, or grey, of which the brittle, crystalline grey form is the most common. Arsenic and its compounds are used in insecticides, weed killers, solid-state doping agents, and various alloys. Atomic number 33, atomic weight 74.922, valency 3 or 5. Grey arsenic melts at 817°C (at 28 atm. pressure), sublimes at 613°C, and has a relative density of 5.73. **2.** Arsenic trioxide.

~adj. (*also, especially in reference to a valency of 5,* aar-sénnik). Of or containing arsenic. Used especially of chemical compounds containing arsenic with a valency of 5. [Middle English, from Old French, from Latin *arsenicum, arrenicum,* from Greek *arsenikon, arrhenikon,* yellow orpiment, alteration (influenced by *arsenikos, arrhenikos,* male, virile) of Syriac *zarnīkā,* from Iranian; akin to Avestan *zarniya,* gold.]

ar·sen·ic acid (aar-sénnik) *n.* A poisonous, white, translucent, crystalline compound, H_3AsO_4, used to manufacture arsenates.

ar·sen·i·cal (aar-sénnik'l) *adj.* Of or containing arsenic.

~n. A drug or preparation containing arsenic.

arsenical nickel *n.* A nickel ore, **niccolite** *(see).*

ar·se·nic trioxide *n.* (árssnik, árss'n-ik). A poisonous, white powder, As_2O_3, used in insecticides, rat poison, and weed killers.

ar·se·nide (árss'n-īd) *n.* A compound of arsenic with a more electropositive element. [ARSEN(IC) + -IDE.]

ar·se·ni·ous (aar-seén-yəss, -i-əss) *adj.* Of or containing arsenic. Used especially of chemical compounds containing arsenic with a valency of 3.

ar·se·no·py·rite (árss'n-ō-pír-īt, aar-sénnō-) *n.* A silver-white to grey arsenic ore, essentially SFeAs. Also called "mispickel". [ARSEN(IC) + -O- + PYRITE.]

arshin. Variant of **archine.**

ar·sine (ár-seen ‖ *U.S. also* -seén) *n.* A colourless, flammable, very poisonous gas, AsH_3, used as a military poison gas, as a solid-state doping agent, and in organic synthesis. [ARS(ENIC) + -INE.]

ar·sis (ár-siss) *n., pl.* **-ses** (-seez). **1.** Originally, the unaccented or shorter part of a foot of verse. **2.** In modern usage, the accented or longer part of a foot of verse. **3.** *Music.* The upbeat, or unaccented part, of a measure. Compare **thesis.** [Late Latin, accented syllable, "raising of the voice", from Greek, unaccented syllable, "raising of the foot in beating time", from *aeirein,* to lift.]

A.R.S.M. Associate of the Royal School of Mines.

ar·son (árss'n) *n.* The crime of maliciously burning property belonging to someone else, or of burning one's own property for some illegal purpose; for example, to collect insurance. [Anglo-French (legal use), from Old French, from Medieval Latin *arsiō* (stem *arsion-*), act of burning, from Latin *ardēre* (past participle *arsus*), to burn.] **—ar·son·ist** *n.*

ars·phen·a·mine (aarss-fénnə-meen, -min) *n.* A yellow hygroscopic arsenical powder, $C_{12}H_{12}N_2O_2As{\cdot}2HCl{\cdot}2H_2O$, formerly used to treat syphilis. A trademark is "Salvarsan". [ARS(ENIC) + PHEN(YL) + AMINE.]

art¹ (art) *n.* **1.** Human effort to imitate, supplement, alter, or counteract the work of nature. **2.** The conscious production or arrangement of sounds, colours, forms, words, movements, or other elements in a manner that affects the sense of beauty; especially, the production of the beautiful in a graphic or plastic medium, for example, painting and sculpture. **3.** The product of these activities; human works of beauty, collectively. Also used adjectivally: *an art exhibition.* **4.** High quality of conception or execution, as found in works of beauty; aesthetic value. **5.** Any field or category of art, such as music, ballet, or literature. **6.** *Plural.* Nonscientific branches of learning, for example, languages or philosophy. **7. a.** A system of principles and methods employed in the performance of a set of activities: *the art of building.* **b.** A trade or craft that applies such a system of principles and methods: *pursuing the baker's art.* **8.** Any skill or faculty, whether acquired by study and practice or based on intuition: *the art of conversation.* **9. a.** *Usually plural.* Artful devices; stratagems; tricks. **b.** Artfulness; contrivance; cunning. **10.** *Printing.* Illustrative material as distinguished from text. **—get (something) down to a fine art.** To become skilled at doing something through constant repetition or practice. [Middle English, from Old French, from Latin *ars* (stem *art-*).]

art² (art; *occasional weak form* ərt). *Archaic.* Second person singular, present indicative of **be.** Used with *thou.*

-art. Variant of **-ard.**

art. 1. article. **2.** artificial. **3.** artillery.

Art De·co (déckō) *n. Sometimes small* **a,** *small* **d.** A style of decoration and architecture popular in the 1920s and 1930s, characterised by bold geometrical and rectilinear shapes and the use of man-made materials, such as plastic and steel. [Shortened from French *arts décoratifs,* decorative arts.]

Ar·taud (ártō, aar-tō), **Antonin** (1896–1948). French dramatist, director, and theoretician. His view that the theatre ought to harrow and disquiet the audience was put forward in two treatises, *Manifesto of the Theatre of Cruelty* (1932) and *The Theatre and its Double* (1938). His own plays were unsuccessful but his theories had a great influence on the generation of dramatists of the Absurd.

ar·te·fact, *U.S.* **ar·ti·fact** (árti-fakt) *n.* **1.** An object produced or shaped by human workmanship; especially, a simple tool, weapon, or ornament of archaeological or historical interest. **2.** A phenomenon or thing not normally present, but produced by some external agency or action; for example, a structure seen in a microscopical specimen after fixation that is not present in the living tissue. [Latin *arte,* "by skill", ablative of *ars,* ART + *factum,* something made, from past participle of *facere,* to make.]

ar·tel (aar-tél) *n.* Formerly, a cooperative enterprise of industrial or agricultural workers in the U.S.S.R. [Russian *artel',* from Italian *artieri,* plural of *artiere,* artisan, from *arte,* art, work, from Latin *ars* (stem *art-*).]

Ar·te·mis (ártimiss). *Greek Mythology.* The virgin goddess of the hunt and the moon, and twin sister of Apollo. Identified with the Roman goddess Diana.

ar·te·mis·i·a (árti-mízzi-ə ‖ -mízhə, -mízhi-ə) *n.* Any of various plants of the genus *Artemisia,* which includes sagebrush and wormwood. [Middle English, from Latin, from Greek, "plant sacred to Artemis", from ARTEMIS.]

ar·te·ri·al (aar-teér-i-əl) *adj.* **1.** Of, like, or in an artery or arteries. **2.** Of or designating the blood in the arteries that has absorbed oxygen in the lungs and is bright red. **3.** Of or designating a route in a transport or communications system carrying a main flow and having many branches. **—ar·te·ri·al·ly** *adv.*

ar·te·ri·a·lise, ar·te·ri·al·ize (aar-teér-i-əl-īz) *tr.v.* **-ised, -ising, -ises.** To convert (venous blood) into arterial blood by absorption of oxygen in the lungs. **—ar·te·ri·al·i·sa·tion** (-ī-záysh'n ‖ *U.S.* -i-) *n.*

arterio-, arter- *comb. form.* Indicates an artery or the arteries; for example, **arteriosclerosis.** [Greek *artērio-,* from *artēria,* ARTERY.]

ar·te·ri·o·gra·phy (aar-teér-i-óggrəfi) *n.* The X-ray examination of an artery that has been injected with a radiopaque substance. **—ar·te·ri·o·gram** (-əgram) *n.* **—ar·te·ri·o·graph·ic** (ə-gráffik) *adj.*

ar·te·ri·ole (aar-teér-i-ōl) *n. Anatomy.* One of the small thin-walled branches of an artery, which subdivides into capillaries. [New Latin *arteriola,* diminutive of Latin *artēria,* ARTERY.] **—ar·te·ri·o·lar** (-ələr, -ōlər) *adj.*

ar·te·ri·o·scle·ro·sis (aar-tẽer-i-ō-skleer-ṓ-siss, -sklər-) *n.* Any chronic disease in which thickening and hardening of arterial walls interferes with blood circulation. Also called "hardening of the arteries". [ARTERIO- + SCLEROSIS.] **—ar·te·ri·o·scle·rot·ic** (-óttik) *adj.*

ar·te·ri·o·ve·nous (aar-tẽer-i-ō-vẽenəss) *adj.* Of, pertaining to, or connecting both arteries and veins.

ar·te·ri·tis (ártə-rītiss) *n.* Inflammation of an artery. [ARTER(IO)- + -ITIS.]

ar·ter·y (ártəri) *n., pl.* **-ies.** **1.** *Anatomy.* Any of a branching system of muscular tubes that carry blood away from the heart. **2.** A major route in a transport or communications system, which local routes join. [Middle English *arterie,* from Latin *artēria,* from Greek; probably related to *airein,* to raise.]

ar·te·sian (aar-tẽez-yən, -tẽezh-, -i-ən) **well** *n.* A well drilled through impermeable strata to reach water capable of rising to the surface by internal hydrostatic pressure. [French *(puits) artésien,* (well) of *Artois* (former French province), where such wells were first drilled.]

art form *n.* Any activity that can be considered a medium of artistic expression.

artful (ártf'l) *adj.* **1.** Deceitful or tricky; cunning; crafty. **2.** Having or showing skill, especially in finding the means to an end; clever; ingenious. **3.** Exhibiting art or technical skill. **4.** *Archaic.* Artificial. —See Synonyms at **sly.** **—art·ful·ly** *adv.* **—art·ful·ness** *n.*

Artful Dodger *n.* A person who manages to escape from difficulties, usually in an ingenious and engaging way. [After the young pickpocket in Dickens's novel *Oliver Twist* (1838).]

ar·thral·gia (aar-thrál-jə || -ji-ə) *n.* Pain in a joint. [ARTHR(O)- + -ALGIA.] **—ar·thral·gic** (-jik) *adj.*

ar·thri·tis (aar-thrītiss || *Note. The pronunciation* árthər-ītiss *is considered incorrect*) *n.* Inflammation of a joint or joints, producing pain and stiffness. See **osteoarthritis, rheumatoid arthritis.** [Latin, from Greek : ARTHR(O)- + -ITIS.] **—ar·thrit·ic** (-thríttik) *adj. & n.*

arthro–, arthr– *comb. form.* Indicates joint; for example, **arthropod, arthritis.** [Greek *arthron.*]

ar·thro·mere (árthrə-meer, árthrō-) *n.* One of the body segments of an arthropod. [ARTHRO- + -MERE.] **—ar·thro·mer·ic** (-mérrik, -mẽer-ik) *adj.*

ar·throp·a·thy (aar-thróppəthi) *n.* Any disease of a joint. [ARTHRO- + -PATHY.]

ar·thro·pod (árthrə-pod, árthrō-) *n.* Any of numerous invertebrate organisms of the phylum Arthropoda, which includes the insects, crustaceans, arachnids, millipedes, and centipedes, having a horny, segmented external covering and jointed limbs. [New Latin *Arthropoda* : ARTHRO- + -POD.] **—ar·throp·o·dous** (aar-thróppədəss), **ar·throp·o·dal** (-dəl) *adj.*

ar·thro·spore (árthrə-spawr, árthrō- || -spōr) *n. Botany.* A sporelike cell characteristic of segmented filamentous fungi or certain algae. [ARTHRO- + SPORE.] **—ar·thro·spor·ic, ar·thro·spor·ous** *adj.*

Ar·thur (árthər). Legendary British king of the sixth century A.D., whose court was at Camelot.

Ar·thu·ri·an (aar-théwr-i-ən || -thóor-) *adj.* Of or pertaining to King Arthur and his Knights of the Round Table: *Arthurian legends.*

ar·tic (aar-tík) *n. Informal.* An articulated lorry.

ar·ti·choke (árti-chōk) *n.* **1.** A thistle-like plant, *Cynara scolymus,* having a large flower head with numerous fleshy, scalelike bracts. **2.** The unopened flower head of this plant, cooked and eaten as a vegetable. Also called "globe artichoke". **3.** The **Jerusalem artichoke** *(see).* [Italian (northern dialect) *articiocco, arciciocco,* alteration of *arcicioffo,* from Old Spanish *alcarchofa,* from Arabic *al-kharshūf,* the artichoke.]

ar·ti·cle (ártik'l) *n. Abbr.* **art.** **1.** An individual thing belonging to a class; an item: *an article of clothing.* **2.** A piece of material goods or property. **3.** A particular section or item of a series in a document, such as a contract, constitution, or creed: *the Thirty-nine Articles of the Church of England.* **4.** A nonfictional literary composition that forms an independent part of a publication, such as a newspaper, magazine, or reference work. **5.** *Grammar.* Any of a class of words used to signal nouns and to specify their application. In English, the articles are *a* and *an* (indefinite articles) and *the* (definite article). **6.** A specific part or detail; a particular.
~tr.v. **articled, -cling, -cles.** **1.** To bind, as for a period of training or apprenticeship, by articles set forth in a contract: *an articled clerk.* **2.** *Archaic.* To make specific or formal charges against; accuse. [Middle English, from Old French, from Latin *articulus,* small joint, division, part, diminutive of *artus,* joint.]

article of faith *n.* **1.** A belief which is an essential part of a church's creed. **2.** Any deeply-held conviction.

articles of association *pl.n.* **1.** The set of rules by which a registered company is administered. **2.** The document in which these rules are set down, which must by law be open to public inspection.

Articles of Confederation *pl.n.* The first constitution of the United States, adopted by the original 13 states in 1781 and lasting until 1788, when the present Constitution was ratified.

ar·tic·u·lar (aar-tíckew-lər) *adj.* Of or pertaining to a joint or joints. [Middle English *articuler,* from Latin *articulāris,* from *articulus,* small joint, ARTICLE.] **—ar·ticu·lar·ly** *adv.*

ar·tic·u·late (aar-tíckew-lət, -lit) *adj.* **1.** Capable of, speaking in, or characterised by clear, expressive language. **2.** Spoken in or divided into clear and distinct words or syllables. **3.** Endowed with the power of speech. **4.** *Biology.* Having joints or segments.
~ v. (aar-tíckew-layt), **articulated, -lating, -lates.** *—tr.* **1.** To utter (a speech sound or sounds) by moving the necessary organs of speech. **2.** To pronounce distinctly and carefully; enunciate. **3.** To express in coherent verbal form; give words to (an emotion, for example). **4.** To unite by means of a joint or joints. *—intr.* **1.** To utter a speech sound or sounds. **2.** To speak clearly and distinctly. **3.** To form a joint; be jointed. [Latin *articulātus,* jointed, distinct, past participle of *articulāre,* to divide into joints, utter distinctly, from *articulus,* small joint, ARTICLE.] **—ar·tic·u·late·ly** *adv.* **—ar·tic·u·late·ness** *n.*

articulated lorry *n.* A lorry consisting of a tractor and a detachable trailer that can pivot at a sharp angle for greater manoeuvrability. Also informally called "artic".

ar·tic·u·la·tion (aar-tíckew-láysh'n) *n.* **1.** The act or process of speaking. **2.** *Phonetics.* **a.** The movements of speech organs employed in producing a particular speech sound. **b.** Any speech sound, especially a consonant. **3. a.** A jointing together or an instance of being jointed together. **b.** The method or manner of jointing. **4.** *Zoology.* **a.** A joint between bones, or between movable parts of an outside shell. **b.** The manner in which jointed parts are connected. **5.** *Botany.* **a.** A joint between two separable parts, such as a leaf and a stem. **b.** A node, or a space on a stem between two nodes. —See Synonyms at **diction.** **—ar·tic·u·la·tive** (-lətiv, -laytiv), **ar·tic·u·la·to·ry** (-lətri, -lətəri, -láytəri) *adj.*

ar·tic·u·la·tor (aar-tíckew-laytər) *n.* **1.** A person who or thing that articulates. **2.** *Phonetics.* An organ used in producing speech sounds, such as the tongue, lips, hard palate, or glottis.

artifact. *U.S.* Variant of **artefact.**

ar·ti·fice (ártifiss) *n.* **1.** A crafty expedient; an artful device or stratagem. **2.** Subtle but base deception; trickery. **3.** Ingenuity; cleverness; skill. [French, from Old French, craftsmanship, from Latin *artificium,* from *artifex,* craftsman : *ars* (stem *art-*), ART + *-fex,* -maker, from *facere,* to make.]
Synonyms: *artifice, trick, ruse, wile, feint, stratagem, manoeuvre, dodge, guile, finesse, subterfuge.*

ar·tif·i·cer (aar-tíffissər) *n.* **1.** A skilled worker; a craftsman. **2.** One that contrives, devises, or effects something. **3.** A skilled mechanic in one of the armed forces, especially the Royal Navy.

ar·ti·fi·cial (árti-físh'l) *adj. Abbr.* **art.** **1.** Made by man, rather than occurring in nature. **2.** Made in imitation of something natural. **3.** Feigned; pretended. **4.** Affected; forced. [Middle English, from Old French, from Latin *artificiālis,* from *artificium,* ARTIFICE.] **—ar·ti·fi·ci·al·i·ty** (-físhi-ál-əti) *n.* **—ar·ti·fi·cial·ly** *adv.*
Synonyms: *artificial, synthetic, ersatz, simulated, counterfeit.*

artificial cinnabar *n. Chemistry.* **Mercuric sulphide** *(see).*

artificial horizon *n.* **1.** A gyroscopic instrument displaying a line on a flight indicator which lies within the horizontal plane, and about which the pitching and banking movements of an aeroplane are shown. **2.** A level reflecting surface, such as a dish of mercury, used with a sextant on land to establish a horizontal reference in a navigational or astronomical instrument.

artificial insemination *n. Abbr.* **A.I.** The introduction of semen into the female reproductive organs by means other than sexual contact. See **A.I.D., A.I.H.**

artificial intelligence *n. Abbr.* **A.I.** **1.** The branch of computer science concerned with programming and designing computers to simulate human intelligence. **2.** Such intelligence.

artificial kidney *n.* A **kidney machine** *(see).*

artificial respiration *n.* Any of various methods of restoring or initiating normal breathing in an asphyxiated but living person, usually by rhythmic forcing of air into and out of the lungs by mouth-to-mouth breathing or manual pressure on the chest.

artificial satellite *n. Aerospace.* A man-made **satellite** *(see).*

artificial silk *n.* **Rayon** *(see).*

ar·til·ler·ist (aar-tíllərist) *n.* An artilleryman; a gunner.

ar·til·ler·y (aar-tílləri) *n. Abbr.* **art., arty.** **1.** Large-calibre firing weapons, such as howitzers, cannons, and missile launchers on suitable mounts, which are served by crews. **2.** Troops armed with such guns. **3.** The branch of an armed force that specialises in the use of large mounted guns. **4.** The science of the use of guns; gunnery. **5.** Catapults, crossbows, slings, and similar devices for discharging missiles. [Middle English *artil(le)rie,* from Old French *artillerie,* from *artillier,* alteration (influenced by *art,* ART) of *atillier,* to fortify, arm, from Latin *apticulāre* (unattested), from *aptāre,* to fit, adapt, from *aptus,* fitting, APT.]

ar·til·ler·y·man (aar-tilləri-mən, -man) *n., pl.* **-men** (-mən, -men). A soldier in the artillery.

ar·ti·o·dac·tyl (árti-ō-dáktil) *n.* Any of various hoofed mammals of the order Artiodactyla, which includes cattle, deer, camels, hippopotamuses, and others, having an even number of toes, either two or four, on each foot. [New Latin *Artiodactyla,* "the even-toed ones" : Greek *artios,* even, matching + DACTYL.] **—ar·ti·o·dac·tyl, ar·ti·o·dac·ty·lous** *adj.*

ar·ti·san (árti-zán, -zan || *U.S.* -zən, -sən) *n.* A skilled manual worker; a craftsman. [Old French, from Italian *artigiano,* from Vulgar Latin *artitiānus* (unattested), a skilled labourer, from Latin *artītus,* skilled in arts, from *artīre,* to instruct in the arts, from *ars* (stem *art-*), ART.]

art·ist (ártist) *n.* **1.** One who creates works of art; especially, a painter or sculptor. **2.** Anyone whose work shows skill, imagination, or other artistic qualities. **3.** An artiste. **4.** *Chiefly U.S. & Australian Slang.* One who is adept at, or keen on, a particular activity: *a booze artist.* See **piss-artist.** [Old French *artiste,* from Italian *ar-*

tista, one skilled in the arts, from *arte,* ART.]

ar·tiste (aar-te'est) *n.* A public performer or entertainer, especially a singer or dancer. [French, from Old French, ARTIST.]

ar·tis·tic (aar-tístik) *adj.* **1.** Of, relating to, or befitting art or artists. **2.** Appreciative of or sensitive to art or beauty. **—ar·tis·ti·cal·ly** *adv.*

art·ist·ry (ártistri) *n.* Artistic ability, quality, or workmanship.

art·less (árt-ləss, -liss) *adj.* **1.** Without guile, cunning, or deceit; ingenuous; naive. **2.** Free of artificiality; natural; simple. **3.** Lacking art or skill; crude. **4.** Uncultured; ignorant. **—art·less·ly** *adv.* **—art·less·ness** *n.*

Art Nou·veau (ár nōō-vṓ || árt) *n. Sometimes small* **a,** *small* **n.** A style of decoration and architecture first current in the 1890s, characterised particularly by depiction of leaves and flowers in sinuous, flowing lines. Also used adjectivally. [French, "new art".]

art·work (árt-wurk) *n.* **1.** Work in the graphic or plastic arts; especially, small handmade decorative or artistic objects. **2.** *Printing.* The illustrative and decorative matter in a publication, as opposed to the text.

art·y (árti) *adj.* **-ier, -iest.** *Informal.* Ostentatious or affected in trying to appear artistic. **—art·i·ly** *adv.* **—art·i·ness** *n.*

art·y-craft·y (árti-kraáfti || -kráfti) *adj.* Also *U.S.* **art·sy-craft·sy** (árt-si-kráftsi) *Informal.* **1.** Decorative rather than useful or comfortable: *arty-crafty furniture.* **2.** Pretentiously or self-consciously artistic.

ar·um (áir-əm) *n.* **1.** Any of various plants of the genus *Arum,* having arrow-shaped leaves and small flowers on a spadix surrounded by or enclosed within a spathe. See also **lords and ladies, cuckoopint. 2.** Any of several similar or related plants, such as the **calla** *(see).* In this sense, also called "arum lily". [New Latin *Arum,* from Latin *arum,* cuckoopint, from Greek *aron*†.]

a·run·di·na·ceous (ə-rúndi-náyshəss) *adj.* Of, pertaining to, or resembling a reed; reedlike. [Latin *arundināceus,* from *(h)arundō*†, reed.]

aruspex. Variant of **haruspex.**

ar·vo (árvō) *n.* Also *South African* **ar·vey, ar·vie** (árvee). *Australian Informal.* Afternoon. [AFTERNOON (shortened and altered).]

-ary *adj. suffix.* Indicates: of, engaged in, or connected with; for example, **functionary, parliamentary, reactionary.** [Middle English *-arie,* from Old French *-arie, -aire,* from Latin *-ārius, -āria, -ārium,* noun suffixes, from *-ārius,* adjective suffix.] **—-ary** *n. suffix.*

Ar·y·an, Ar·i·an (áir-i-ən; *rarely* aár-) *n.* **1.** A member of the prehistoric people that spoke Proto-Indo-European. **2.** A member of any of the peoples descended from this people; especially, any speaker of an Indic or Iranian language. **3.** Proto-Indo-European, or a language or language group descended from it, especially Indo-Aryan. **4.** In Nazi ideology, a Caucasian Gentile, especially of Nordic type. [Sanskrit *ārya* (adjective and noun), noble, Aryan.] **—Ar·y·an, Ar·i·an** *adj.*

ar·yl (árril) *n. Chemistry.* **1.** A radical or group derived from an aromatic hydrocarbon by removal of a hydrogen atom, for example, the phenyl group C_6H_5. **2.** An organometallic compound in which a metal atom is directly bound to an aryl group. [AR(OMATIC) + -YL.]

ar·y·te·noid (árri-te'enoyd || *U.S. also* ə-ritt'n-oyd) *adj. Anatomy.* **1.** Of, pertaining to, or designating either of two small cartilages attached to the back of the larynx and to the vocal cords. **2.** Of, pertaining to, or designating any of three small muscles of the larynx.

~n. An arytenoid cartilage or muscle. [New Latin *arytaenoides,* from Greek *(khondros) arutainoeidēs,* "the ladle-shaped (cartilage)" : *arutaina,* ladle, from *aruein*†, to draw water + -OID.] **—ar·y·te·noi·dal** (-tee) *adj.*

as¹ (az; *weak form* əz) *adv.* **1.** To the same extent or degree; equally. **2.** For instance: *large carnivores, as the bear or lion.* **3.** Considered in the specified way: *workers as distinct from management.*

~conj. **1.** To the same degree or extent that. Often used as the consequent in correlative constructions: *(as) sweet as sugar; not so bad as you suggest.* **2.** In the same manner or way that: *Think as I think; treat him as a friend.* **3.** At the same time that; while. **4.** Since; because. **5.** Though: *Unaccustomed as I am to public speaking.* **6.** *Nonstandard.* That: *I don't know as I can.* **—as for** or **to.** With regard to; concerning. **—as from** or **of.** Starting from a specified time. **—as if** or **though.** In the same way that it would be if. **—as is.** *Informal.* Just the way it is; without making changes.

~pron. **1.** A fact that: *The sun is hot, as everyone knows.* **2.** Which also; so too: *Jean comes from Glasgow, as does her husband.* **3.** *Regional.* Who or which: *Those as want to can come with me.*

~prep. In the role, capacity, or function of: *acting as a mediator.* [Middle English *as* (adverb and conjunction), reduced form of Old English *alswā, ealswā, aelswā,* just as, likewise, ALSO.]

Usage: In positive comparisons, the double use of *as* is required: *He's as tall as I am.* In negative comparisons, traditional grammar prescribes *so . . . as (He's not so tall as I am),* but *as . . . as* is still widely used. Several *as* constructions are potentially ambiguous. A sentence such as *He came as I was leaving* could be interpreted to mean either "He came at the same time as I left" or "He came because I was leaving". In consequence, many speakers prefer *because* to *as* in such contexts. A similar ambiguous case is *He likes her as much as Jim,* which could mean "as much as he likes Jim" or "as much as Jim likes her". This prompts some speakers to use *I* in place of *me* in such sentences as: *He likes her as much as I (do), He likes her as much as (he likes) me.* See also **like, than.**

as² (ass) *n., pl.* **asses** (áss-iz, -eez). **1.** An ancient Roman copper coin of low value, a quarter of a **sesterce** *(see).* **2.** A unit of weight in ancient Rome equal to about one troy pound. [Latin *ās,* a whole, unit, copper coin, perhaps from Etruscan.]

As The symbol for the element arsenic.

AS 1. Anglo-Saxon. **2.** antisubmarine.

As. Asia; Asian.

AS., A.S. Anglo-Saxon.

ASA, A.S.A. 1. Amateur Swimming Association. **2.** American Standards Association (used in photography preceded by a number, as a measurement of film speed).

as·a·fet·i·da, as·a·foet·i·da (ássə-fétti-də, -féeti-) *n.* A yellow-brown, bitter, unpleasantly pungent resinous material obtained from the roots of several plants of the genus *Ferula,* used as a spice in oriental cuisine, and formerly used in medicine. [Middle English *asa-fetida,* from Medieval Latin *asafoetida* : *asa,* gum, from Persian *azā*†, mastic + Latin *foetida,* feminine of *foetidus,* FETID.]

A·san·te·he·ne (ashánti-he'eni) *n.* The paramount chief of the Ashanti people. [Ashanti, "Ashanti chief".]

a.s.a.p., asap *adv.* As soon as possible.

as·a·ra·bac·ca (ássərə-báckə, ə-saárə-) *n.* A creeping, perennial plant, *Asarum europaeum,* with shiny, kidney-shaped leaves and dull, purple flowers. [Alteration of obsolete *asarabacara,* from Spanish *asarabácara* : *ásaro,* ASARUM + *bácara,* clary, from Latin *baccaris,* plant with aromatic roots, from Greek *bakkaris.*]

as·a·rum (ássərəm) *n.* The dried, strong-scented roots of the wild ginger, formerly used in medicine and as a flavouring agent. [New Latin, from Latin, wild spikenard, from Greek *asaron*†.]

as·bes·tos (ass-béss-toss, az-, -təss) *n. Abbr.* **asb.** Any of the fibrous varieties of four distinct incombustible, chemical-resistant silicate minerals, used for fireproofing electrical insulation, building materials, brake linings, and chemical filters. See **chrysotile, crocidolite.**

~adj. **1.** Of, made of, or containing asbestos. **2.** *Informal.* Tough and resilient: *an asbestos stomach.* [17th century : Middle English *asbeston,* a mythical stone with unquenchable heat, from Old French, from Latin, from Greek, from *asbestos,* inextinguishable : A- (not) + *sbennunai,* to extinguish.] **—as·bes·tine** (-tin, -teen), **as·bes·tic** *adj.*

as·bes·to·sis (áss-bess-tṓ-siss, áz-) *n.* A chronic lung disease caused by prolonged inhalation of asbestos particles, characterised by breathlessness. [New Latin : ASBEST(OS) + -OSIS.]

as·ca·ri·a·sis (áskə-rī́-əsiss) *n.* Infestation with nematode worms of the species *Ascaris lumbricoides,* usually in the intestines, but also in the liver, lungs, or stomach. [New Latin : Late Latin *ascaris,* ASCARID + -IASIS.]

as·ca·rid (áskarid) *n.* Any of various nematode worms of the family Ascaridae, such as the common intestinal parasite *Ascaris lumbricoides.* [Late Latin *ascaris* (stem *ascarid-*), intestinal worm, from Greek *askaris*†.]

as·cend (ə-sénd) *v.* **-cended, -cending, -cends.** *—intr.* **1.** To go or move upwards; rise. **2.** To rise gradually. **3.** To slope upwards. *—tr.* **1.** To move upwards upon or along; climb. **2.** To succeed to. Used in the phrase *ascend the throne.* —See Synonyms at **rise.** [Middle English *ascenden,* from Latin *ascendere* : *ad-,* towards + *scandere,* to climb .] **—as·cend·a·ble, as·cend·i·ble** *adj.*

as·cen·dan·cy, as·cen·den·cy (ə-sén-dən-si) *n.* Also **as·cen·dance, as·cen·dence** (-dəns). The state of being in the ascendant; superiority or decisive advantage.

as·cen·dant, as·cen·dent (ə-sén-dənt) *adj.* **1.** Inclining or moving upwards; ascending; rising. **2.** Dominant in position or influence; superior.

~n. **1.** The position or state of being dominant or in a position of decisive advantage: *in the ascendant.* **2.** *Astrology.* The section of the zodiac that rises in the east at the time of a particular event, such as a person's birth. Compare **descendant. 3.** *Rare.* An ancestor.

as·cend·er (ə-séndər) *n.* **1.** One that ascends. **2.** *Printing.* **a.** The part of certain lower-case letters that extends above most other lower-case letters. **b.** Any letter containing such a part, as *d, f,* or *k.*

as·cen·sion (ə-sénsh'n) *n.* **1.** The act or process of ascending; ascent. **2.** *Astronomy.* The rising of a star above the horizon. **—the Ascension.** The ascent of Christ into heaven, celebrated on *Ascension Day,* the 40th day after Easter. Acts 1:9. [Middle English *ascencion,* from Latin *ascensiō* (stem *ascension-*), from *ascendere,* ASCEND.] **—as·cen·sion·al** *adj.*

Ascension. Island in the South Atlantic Ocean, 1 130 kilometres (700 miles) northwest of St. Helena. Britain made it a dependency of St. Helena in 1922. Rocky and barren, it has a B.B.C. relay station, an airstrip, and a U.S. tracking station.

as·cent (ə-sént) *n.* **1.** The act or process of ascending. **2.** An advancement, especially in social status. **3.** An upward slope or incline. **4.** A going back in time or genealogical succession. [17th century (Shakespeare and the King James Bible); from ASCEND (by analogy with DESCEND, DESCENT).]

as·cer·tain (ássər-táyn) *tr.v.* **-tained, -taining, -tains. 1.** To discover through examination or experimentation; find out. **2.** *Archaic.* To make certain and definite. [Middle English *ascertainen,* from Old French *acertainer, acertener* : *a-,* from Latin *ad-,* to + *certain,* CERTAIN.] **—as·cer·tain·a·ble** *adj.* **—as·cer·tain·a·ble·ness** *n.* **—as·cer·tain·a·bly** *adv.* **—as·cer·tain·ment** *n.*

as·cet·ic (ə-séttik, a-) *n.* A person who renounces material comforts and leads a life of austere self-discipline, especially as an act of religious devotion.

~adj. Also **as·cet·i·cal** (-séttik'l). Pertaining to or characteristic of an ascetic; self-denying; austere. —See Synonyms at **severe.**

[Greek *askētikos*, from *askētēs*, hermit, "one who exercises (self-discipline)", from *askein†*, to exercise.] —**as·cet·i·cal·ly** *adv.*

as·cet·i·cism (ə-sétti-siz'm) *n.* **1.** Ascetic practice or discipline. **2.** A doctrine or theory supporting this practice, such as the belief that the ascetic life releases the soul from bondage to the body and permits union with the divine.

Asch (ash ‖ *U.S. also* aash), **Sholem** or **Shalom** (1880–1957). Polish writer who wrote in modern Yiddish. A prolific novelist, his most controversial works were those in which he sought to reconcile Judaism and Christianity: *The Nazarene* (1939), *The Apostle* (1943), *Mary* (1949), and *The Prophet* (1955). He lived in the United States from 1909 until 1956, then in Israel until his death.

As·cham (ásh'm), **Roger** (1515–1568). English humanist scholar. Latin secretary to Edward VI, Mary I, and Elizabeth I, his historical importance rests largely on his advocacy of the use of the vernacular in literature.

as·cid·i·an (ə-síddi-ən, a-) *n.* Any of various saclike marine animals of the class Ascidiacea, which includes the sea squirts. —*adj.* Of or belonging to the Ascidiacea. [New Latin *Ascidia* (genus name), from Greek *askidion*, little wineskin, from *askos†*, wineskin. See **ascus**.]

as·cid·i·um (ə-sid-i-əm) *n., pl.* **-ia** (-i-ə). *Botany.* A sac-shaped or bottle-shaped part or organ, such as a leaf of a pitcher plant. [New Latin, from Greek *askidion*, little wineskin, from *askos†*, wineskin. See **ascus**.]

as·ci·tes (ə-síteez) *n.* An abnormal accumulation of serous fluid in the peritoneal cavity. [Middle English *aschytes*, from Late Latin *ascītēs*, from Greek *askītēs*, from *askos†*, bag, belly. See **ascus**.] —**as·cit·ic** (ə-síttik), **as·cit·i·cal** *adj.*

As·cle·pi·us (a-skléepi-əs). *Greek Mythology.* Apollo's son, the god of medicine, identified with the Roman god Aesculapius.

asco- *comb. form.* Indicates a saclike or bladder-like part; for example, **ascospore.** [New Latin, from Greek *askos†*, bag, bladder. See **ascus**.]

as·co·carp (áskə-kaarp, áskō-) *n. Botany.* A globular structure containing the spore sacs of ascomycetous fungi. [ASCO- + -CARP.] —**as·co·car·pous** *adj.*

as·co·my·cete (áskə-mī-séet, áskō-, -mí-seet) *n. Botany.* Any of numerous fungi that produce spores in a saclike structure, or ascus. [New Latin *Ascomycetes* : ASCO- + -MYCETE.] —**as·co·my·cet·ous** (-séetəss) *adj.*

a·scor·bic acid (ə-skórbik) *n.* A white, crystalline vitamin, $C_6H_8O_6$, found in citrus fruits, tomatoes, potatoes, and leafy green vegetables. It is used to prevent scurvy. Also called "vitamin C". [A- (not) + SCORB(UT)IC.]

as·co·spore (áskə-spawr, áskō- ‖ -spōr) *n. Botany.* A sexual spore formed in an ascus. —**as·co·spo·rous** (-əss, ass-kóspərəss), **as·co·spo·ric** (-spórrik, -spáwrik) *adj.*

as·cot (áss-kət ‖ -kot) *n. U.S.* A kind of scarf or tie, knotted so that its broad ends are laid flat upon each other. [After *Ascot,* where it was popularly first worn.]

Ascot¹. A village near Windsor, in southern England. The Royal Ascot meeting, a week of horse races on the flat, was begun by Queen Anne in 1711.

Ascot² *n.* A trademark for a type of gas-operated geyser, used to heat domestic water.

as·cribe (ə-skríb) *tr.v.* **-cribed, -cribing, -cribes.** **1.** To attribute to a specified cause, source, or origin: *a work ascribed to Homer.* **2.** To assign as an attribute. —See Synonyms at **attribute.** [Middle English *ascriben,* from Latin *ascrībere,* to add to in writing : *ad-,* in addition + *scrībere,* to write.] —**as·crib·a·ble** *adj.*

as·crip·tion (ə-skrípsh'n) *n.* **1.** The act of ascribing. **2.** A statement that ascribes. [Latin *ascrīptiō,* from *ascrībere,* ASCRIBE.]

as·cus (áskəss) *n., pl.* **asci** (ássī, áskī). *Botany.* A saclike structure in certain fungi, containing ascospores. [New Latin, from Greek *askos†,* wineskin, bag, bladder, belly.]

as·dic (ázdik) *n.* A sonar device used in antisubmarine warfare. [Allied Submarine Detection Investigation Committee.]

-ase. *n. comb. form. Chemistry.* Indicates an enzyme; for example, *amylase.* [Diast*ase.*]

a·sea (ə-sée) *adv.* Towards or on the sea; at sea.

ASEAN Association of Southeast Asian Nations.

a·seis·mic (ay-sízmik) *adj.* Designating a region, such as Britain, where earthquakes are rare or slight.

a·sep·sis (ay-sépsiss, ə-, a-) *n.* The state of being free of pathogenic organisms. Compare **antisepsis.** [A- (without) + SEPSIS.]

a·sep·tic (ay-séptik, ə-, a-) *adj.* **1.** Of or pertaining to asepsis. **2.** Lacking animation or emotion: *aseptic smile.* [A- (not) + SEPTIC.]

a·sex·u·al (ay-sék-sew-əl, ə-, a-, -shoo-) *adj.* **1.** Having no evident sex or sex organs; sexless. **2.** Pertaining to or characterising reproduction involving a single individual, and without male or female gametes, as in binary fission or budding. **3.** Having no apparent interest in or desire for sex. [A- (not) + SEXUAL.] —**a·sex·u·al·i·ty** (-al-əti, áy-) *n.* —**a·sex·u·al·ly** *adv.*

As·gard (áss-gaard, áz-). Also **As·garth** (-gaarth), **As·gar·dhr** (-gaarthrə). *Norse Mythology.* The heavenly residence of the gods and slain heroes of war. Compare **Valhalla.**

ash¹ (ash) *n.* **1.** The soft, powdery, greyish-white to black residue left over when something is burnt. **2.** *Geology.* Pulverised particulate matter ejected by volcanic eruption. **3.** *Plural.* Ruins: *bombs reduced the town to ashes.* **4.** *Plural.* Human remains, especially after cremation. [Middle English *asshe,* Old English *asce, æsce.*]

ash² *n.* **1.** Any of various trees of the genus *Fraxinus;* especially, *F. excelsior,* having compound leaves, clusters of small greenish flowers, and winged seeds. **2.** The durable, close-grained, elastic wood of any of these trees. Compare **mountain ash.** [Middle English *asshe,* Old English *æsc.*]

ash³ *n.* The alphabetical digraph (æ) used especially in Old English. [Old English *æsc,* the name of the letter in the runic alphabet.]

a·shamed (ə-sháymd) *adj.* **1.** Feeling shame or guilt. **2.** Reluctant through fear of resulting humiliation or shame. **3.** Feeling inferior, inadequate, or embarrassed on account of someone or something. [Middle English, Old English *āscamod,* past participle of *āscamian,* to feel shame : *ā-,* intensive + *scamian,* to be ashamed.] —**a·sham·ed·ly** (ə-sháymidli) *adv.* —**a·shamed·ness** *n.*

A·shan·ti¹ (ə-shánti). An ancient powerful kingdom of the Ashanti people of Africa. It was annexed to the British Gold Coast Colony in 1901, and is now an administrative region of Ghana, with Kumasi as the capital.

Ashanti² *n., pl.* **-tis** or collectively **Ashanti. 1.** An inhabitant of Ashanti. **2.** A dialect of **Twi** (*see*), spoken by the Ashantis.

ash blonde *adj.* Very fair or pale blonde.

Ash·croft (ásh-kroft ‖ -krawft). **Dame Peggy (Edith Margaret Emily)** (1907—91). English actress. Her performance as Juliet in Gielgud's production of *Romeo and Juliet* in 1935 established her reputation. As well as classical theatre, her roles included plays by modern dramatists, such as Harold Pinter. She was awarded the D.B.E. in 1956.

Ash·down (ásh-down), **Jeremy John Durham,** known as Paddy (1941–). British politician. He was elected leader of the Social and Liberal Democrats in 1988. He has been a Liberal MP for Yeovil since 1983.

Ashe (ash), **Arthur Robert** (1943–93). American lawn tennis player. He was the first black to win the United States championship (1968) and the Wimbledon championship (1975). He also won the Australian championship (1970).

ash·en¹ (ásh'n) *adj.* **1.** Consisting of or resembling ashes. **2.** Very pale.

ashen² *adj.* Pertaining to or made from the wood of the ash tree.

Ash·er¹ (áshər). A son of Jacob. Genesis 49:20.

Asher² *n.* The tribe of Israel descended from Asher.

Ash·es (áshiz) *pl.n.* A trophy, consisting of the ashes of a cremated cricket stump in an urn, for which England and Australia compete in cricket. Preceded by *the.*

ash·et (áshit) *n. Scottish.* A large plate or serving dish. [French *assiette,* a seating of guests at dinner; hence: course, dish, from Old French, from Vulgar Latin *assedita* (unattested), a sitting, seating, from Latin *assiditus,* past particle of *assidēre,* to sit by, from *ad-* and by + *sedēre,* to sit.]

Ash·ga·bat (áshkə-bat ‖ -baat). The capital of Turkmenistan, situated in a fertile oasis. After an earthquake in 1948 the city had to be almost entirely rebuilt.

Ash·ke·lon, Ash·qe·lon (áshkə-lən, -lon). Site of an ancient city in southwestern Israel. Herod greatly enlarged the city and built fine public buildings, many of which have been excavated in the 20th century. It was destroyed by Saladin in 1270. The modern coastal resort, Ashquelon, is nearby.

Ash·ke·na·zi (áshkə-náazi ‖ *U.S.* aashkə-) *n., pl.* **-nazim** (-náazim). A central or eastern European Jew, generally Yiddish-speaking, or the descendant of such a person. Compare **Sephardi.** —**Ash·ke·na·zic** *adj.*

Ash·ke·na·zy (ásh-kə-náazi ‖ aash-), **Vladimir Davidovich** (1937–). Russian-born pianist and conductor. He is noted especially for his interpretations of the 19th-century masters. He took Icelandic nationality in 1972.

ash-key (ásh-kee) *n.* The winged seed of the ash tree. [After its keylike shape.]

Ashkhabad. See **Ashgabat.**

ash·lar, ash·ler (áshlər) *n.* **1.** A squared block of building stone. **2.** Masonry of such stones. **3.** A thin, dressed rectangle of stone for facing walls. In this sense, also called "ashlar veneer". [Middle English *asheler,* from Old French *aisselier,* beam, from Latin *axilla,* diminutive of *axis,* board, plank, probably variant of *assis,* akin to *assert†,* beam.]

ash-leaved maple (ásh-leevd). A tree, the **box-elder** (*see*).

Ash·ley (ásh-li), **Laura** (1925–85). British designer of clothes, furniture fabrics, curtains, and wallpaper, who based her ideas on flowing lines and Victorian floral prints.

a·shore (ə-shór ‖ ə-shōr) *adv.* **1.** Towards or on the shore. **2.** On land; aground.

ash-plant (ásh-plaant ‖ -plant) *n.* A horse-whip or walking stick made from an ash sapling.

ash·ram (ásh-ram, áash-) *n.* **1.** A Hindu religious retreat or hermitage. **2.** Loosely, the meeting-place of any eastern religious community. [Sanskrit *āsrama,* from *ā,* towards + *srama,* religious training.]

Ash·ton (áshtən), **Sir Frederick William Mallandaine** (1904–88). British dancer and choreographer. He joined the Vic-Wells Ballet in 1933 and made his name as a mime and character dancer. His ballets include *The Dream* (1964) and *A Month in the Country* (1976). He was director of the Royal Ballet from 1963 to 1970.

Ash·to·reth (ásh-to-reth, -to-). The ancient Syrian and Phoenician goddess of sexual love and fertility. Identified with Astarte.

ash-tray (ásh-tray) *n.* A receptacle for tobacco ash.

A·shur¹ (áshoor). Town on the banks of the Tigris river, in northern

Iraq. It was the religious capital of Assyria in ancient times, when it was known as Qal'at Shargat. The town was destroyed by the Babylonians in 614 B.C.

A·shur². Also **As·shur, As·sur, A·sur.** *Assyrian Mythology.* The principal deity and god of war and empire.

Ash Wednesday *n.* The seventh Wednesday before Easter and the first day of Lent, on which Roman Catholics customarily have ashes placed on the forehead as a sign of penitence.

ash·y (áshi) *adj.* **-i·er, -i·est. 1.** Pertaining to, resembling, or covered with ashes. **2.** Ashen; pale.

A·sia (áy-shə, áyzhə). The largest of the continents, making up about 33 per cent of the earth's land area. It has an even greater proportion of the world's people: roughly three out of every five humans live in Asia. This great landmass both physically and culturally falls into five broad subcontinents: North Asia comprises most of the former U.S.S.R., that part of it east of the Ural Mountains. East Asia or the **Far East** is made up of the temperate and subtropical parts in the east, where most people are of Mongoloid origin. The hot, dry lands of the west, whose inhabitants are largely of Semitic stock, many of whom are Muslims, comprise West Asia or the **Middle East.** The generally humid tropical lands of the south can be divided into two: **Middle South Asia** is the subcontinent of India (including Pakistan, Bangladesh, and Sri Lanka), with largely Dravidian and Indo-Aryan people. **Southeast Asia,** the remainder of the continent, has great ethnic and cultural diversity, many of its peoples having come from other parts of Asia in historic times.

Asia Minor. See **Anatolia.**

A·sian (áysh'n, áyzh'n) *adj. Abbr.* **As.** Of or pertaining to Asia or its people; especially, *British,* to Middle South Asia.
~*n.* **1.** A native or inhabitant of Asia. **2.** *British.* A person of Indian, Pakistani, Bangladeshi, or Sri Lankan extraction.

A·si·at·ic (áyshi-áttik, -áyzhi-) *n.* A person of Asian origin. —**A·si·at·ic** *adj.*

a·side (ə-síd) *adv.* **1.** On or to one side. **2.** Out of one's thoughts or mind; away from consideration: *Put doubts aside.* **3.** In reserve: *put a little money aside.* **4.** Apart; dispensed with: *all joking aside.* —**aside from.** Excluding; excepting; apart from.
~*n.* **1.** A piece of dialogue that other actors on stage are supposed by dramatic convention not to hear. **2.** A remark made in an undertone, not intended to be heard by anyone present. **3.** A parenthetical departure; a digression.

as·i·nine (ássi-nīn) *adj.* **1.** Like an ass. **2.** Utterly stupid: *an asinine remark.* [Latin *asinīnus,* from *asinus,* ass.] —**as·i·nine·ly** *adv.* —**as·i·nin·i·ty** (-nínnəti) *n.*

A.S.I.O. Australian Security Intelligence Organisation.

Asiut. See **Asyut.**

ask (aask ‖ ask *Note: the pronunciations* aaks, aks *are considered incorrect.*) *v.* **asked, asking, asks.** —*tr.* **1.** To put a question to. **2.** To seek information about; enquire about. **3.** To make a request of or for: *asked her forgiveness.* **4. a.** To require or call for. **b.** To expect or demand: *ask too much of a child; How much are they asking for their house?* **5.** To invite. —*intr.* **1.** To enquire. Used with *about.* —**ask after.** To enquire about the health or well-being of. —**ask for.** *Informal.* To act in a manner that provokes (trouble, punishment, or the like): *He's really asking for it.* **2.** To make a request. Often used with *for.* [Middle English *asken, axen,* Old English *āscian, ācsian.*] —**ask·er** *n.*
Synonyms: ask, question, enquire, query, interrogate, quiz, examine.

a·skance (ə-skáanss, ə-skánss) *adv.* Also **a·skant** (ə-skánt). **1.** With a sideways or oblique glance. **2.** With disapproval, suspicion, or distrust. [Earlier *a scanche, a sca(u)nce, a sconce†,* obliquely.]

a·ska·ri (ə-skáari, a-) *n.* In parts of Africa, a native soldier or watchman, formerly one in the service of colonial authorities. [Arabic *'askarī,* soldier.]

a·skew (ə-skéw) *adj.* Crooked; oblique.
~*adv.* To one side; obliquely; awry. [16th century : A- (on) + SKEW.]

a·slant (ə-slaánt ‖ ə-slánt) *adj.* Oblique; slanting.
~*adv.* At a slant; obliquely.
~*prep.* Obliquely over or across; athwart. [A- (on) + SLANT.]

ASLEF (áz-lef). Associated Society of Locomotive Engineers and Firemen.

a·sleep (ə-sléep) *adj.* **1.** Sleeping. **2.** Inactive; dormant. **3.** Numb: *My leg is asleep.* **4.** Dead. Used euphemistically.
~*adv.* Into a condition of sleep. [A- (on) + SLEEP, replacing Middle English *o slepe,* from Old English *on slæpe.*]

a·slope (ə-slōp) *adv.* At a slope or slant.
~*adj.* Sloping.

As·ma·ra (ass-maárə, az-). The capital of Eritrea.

As·mo·de·us (ass-mōd-yəss, az-, -i-əss, -mə-dée-əss). In Jewish demonology, king of the demons. [Latin *Asmodaeus,* from Greek *Asmodaios,* from Middle Hebrew *Ashmədāy,* from Avestan

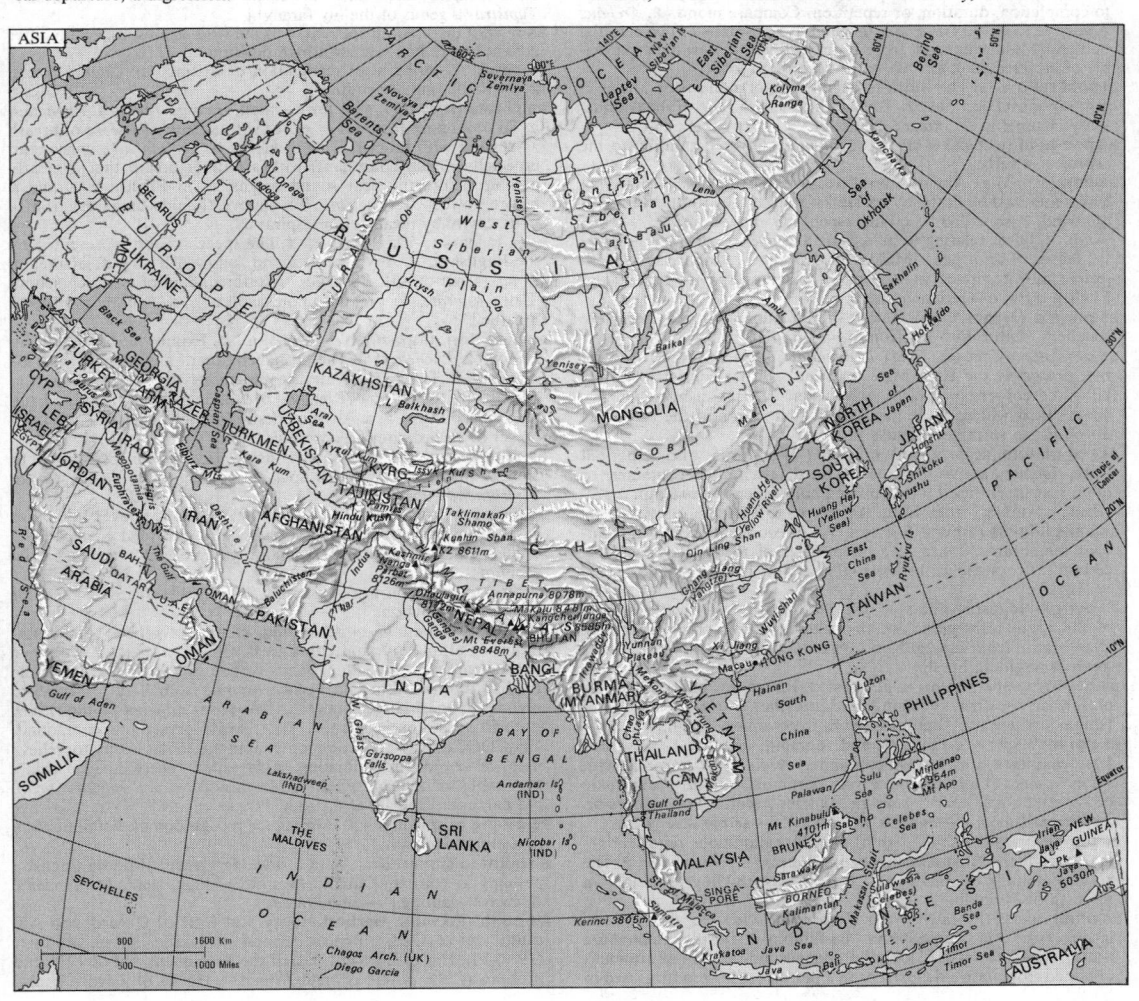

Aĕsma-daĕva, "spirit of anger" : aĕsma, anger + daĕva, demon.]

A·so, Mount (aä-sō). Also A·so·san (aä-sō-saan). A volcanic mountain in central Kyushu in Japan. It has one of the largest craters in the world, containing five volcanic cones. The highest peak is Ta-ka-dake (1 593 metres; 5,225 feet). One peak, Naka-dake, is active.

a·so·cial (ay-sōsh'l) adj. 1. Avoiding the society of others; not gregarious. 2. Inconsiderate of others; self-centred.

asp¹ (asp; rarely aasp) n. 1. A viper, Vipera aspis, of southern Europe, with a brown skin marked with black stripes. 2. The venomous snake that killed Cleopatra, probably the Egyptian cobra, Naja haje. 3. The horned viper (see). [Middle English aspis, from Latin, from Greek aspis†.]

asp² (asp) n. Rare. A tree, the aspen. [See aspen.]

Aspadana. See Isfahan.

as·par·a·gine (ə-spárrə-jeen, -jin) n. A non-essential amino acid, $C_4H_8N_2O_3$, found mainly in asparagus, potatoes, and beetroot. [AS-PARAG(US) + -INE.]

as·par·a·gus (ə-spárrəgəss) n. Any of several plants of the genus Asparagus, native to Eurasia, having small scales or needle-like branchlets rather than true leaves; especially, the widely cultivated species A. officinalis, the young shoots of which are eaten as a vegetable. [Latin, from Greek asparagos, aspharagos†.]

asparagus beetle n. A small spotted beetle, Crioceris asparagi, that infests and damages asparagus plants.

asparagus fern n. An ornamental asparagus plant, Asparagus plumosus, native to southern Africa, having fernlike foliage.

as·par·tic acid (ə-spártik). n. Also as·pa·rag·ic acid (áspə-rájik). A non-essential amino acid, $C_4H_7NO_4$, found especially in young sugar cane and sugar beet. [Aspartic, irregularly from ASPARAGUS (because it is obtained by hydrolysis of a crystalline amino acid found in asparagus) + ACID.]

as·pect (áspekt) n. 1. Appearance to the eye, especially when seen from a specific view. 2. a. An angle or viewpoint on an idea or problem: study the case from every possible aspect. b. A particular feature or element of a problem or idea: a different aspect of the same problem. 3. A particular facial expression, mien, or air: a matron of grim aspect. 4. A position facing or commanding a given direction; an exposure. 5. A side or surface facing in a particular direction: the ventral aspect of the body. 6. Astrology. The configuration of the stars or planets in relation to one another or to the subject. 7. Grammar. A category of the verb denoting primarily the relation of the action to the passage of time, especially in reference to completion, duration, or repetition. Compare mood. 8. Archaic. A gaze; a look. 9. Astronomy. The relative positions of two celestial bodies. [Middle English, from Latin aspectus, a view, past participle of aspicere, look at : ad-, at + specere, to look.]

aspect ratio n. 1. The width-to-height ratio of a television image. It is 4:3 in most countries. 2. The width-to-length ratio of the conductivity channel in an integrated circuit.

a·spec·tu·al (a-spéktew-əl) adj. Grammar. Of or pertaining to the aspect of a verb.

as·pen (áspən) n. Any of several trees of the genus Populus, having leaves attached by flattened leafstalks, so that they flutter readily in the wind. Also called "quaking aspen". Compare poplar.
~adj. 1. Of or relating to an aspen. 2. Shivering or trembling like the leaves of an aspen. [Middle English aspen, "of an aspen" (adjective misinterpreted as a noun), replacing aspe, an aspen, Old English æspe, of Germanic origin.]

as·per·ate (áspərayt) tr.v. -ated, -ating, -ates. To make uneven; roughen. [Latin asperāre, from asper†, rough.]

as·per·ges (ə-spér-jez, -jeez) n. Roman Catholic Church. A short rite, preceding the High Mass on Sundays, that consists of sprinkling the congregation with holy water. [Latin asperges me, Domine, "thou wilt sprinkle me, Lord", first words of the rite, from aspergere, to sprinkle, ASPERSE.]

as·per·gil·lum (áspər-jíl-əm) n., pl. -la (-ə) or -lums. Also as·per·gill (-jil). Roman Catholic Church. A brush, perforated container, or other instrument used for sprinkling holy water. [New Latin aspergillum, sprinkler, from Latin aspergere, to sprinkle on, ASPERSE.]

as·per·gil·lo·sis (áspərjil-ó-siss) n. An infectious disease of the mucous membranes, lungs, and other parts of the body, caused by certain fungi of the genus Aspergillus. [New Latin : ASPERGILL(US) + -OSIS.]

as·per·gil·lus (áspər-jílləss) n., pl. -gilli (-jíllī). Any of various fungi of the genus Aspergillus, which includes many common moulds. [New Latin, from aspergillum, ASPERGILLUM, from its resemblance to an aspergillum brush.]

as·per·i·ty (a-spérrəti, ə-) n. pl. -ties. 1. Roughness or harshness, as of surface, weather, or sound: the asperities of the climate. 2. Ill temper; irritability. [Latin asperitās, from asper†, rough.]

as·perse (ə-spérss, a-) tr.v. -persed, -persing, -perses. 1. To spread false charges against; defame; slander. 2. Rare. To sprinkle with water or dust. [Latin aspergere (past participle aspersus), to sprinkle on, spatter : ad-, to + spargere, to strew, scatter.] —as·pers·er, as·pers·or (-ər) n. —as·per·sive (-iv) adj. —as·per·sive·ly adv.

as·per·sion (ə-spér-sh'n || -zh'n) n. 1. A calumnious report or remark; slander. Often used in the phrase cast aspersions on. 2. The act of defaming or slandering. 3. Rare. A sprinkling; especially, a baptism by sprinkling.

as·phalt (áss-falt || -fawlt. Note: the pronunciation ásh- is considered incorrect). n. Also as·phal·tum (ass-fált-əm || -fáwlt-), as·phal·tus (-təss). 1. A brownish-black solid or semisolid mixture of bitumens obtained from native deposits or as a petroleum by-product, used in

paving, roofing, and waterproofing. Also called "mineral pitch". 2. Mixed asphalt and crushed stone gravel or sand, used for paving or roofing.
~tr.v. asphalted, -phalting, -phalts. To pave or coat with asphalt. [Middle English, asp(h)alt, aspaltoun, from Late Latin asphaltus, from Greek asphaltos, asphalton†, bitumen, pitch.] —as·phal·tic (ass-fál-tik) adj.

a·spher·ic (ay-sférrik || -sféer-ik) adj. Also a·spher·i·cal (-'l). Not spherical. Said of lenses and mirrors designed with parabaloidal or other surfaces in order to reduce aberrations.

as·pho·del (ás-fə-del) n. 1. An unidentified flower of classical legend, said to resemble the narcissus and to cover the Elysian Fields. 2. Any of several plants of the genus Asphodeline or the genus Asphodelus, of the Mediterranean region, having clusters of white or yellow flowers. See bog asphodel. [Latin asphodelus, from Greek asphodelos†.]

as·phyx·i·a (ass-fíksi-ə, əss-) n. Unconsciousness or death occurring when oxygen is prevented from reaching the tissues; suffocation. [New Latin, from Greek asphuxia, stopping of the pulse : a-, not + sphuxis, heartbeat, pulsation, from sphuzein†, to throb.] —as·phyx·i·al adj.

as·phyx·i·ant (ass-fíksi-ənt, əss-) adj. Inducing or tending to induce asphyxia.
~n. A substance or condition that causes asphyxia.

as·phyx·i·ate (ass-fíksi-ayt, əss-) v. -ated, -ating, -ates. —tr. To cause asphyxia in; smother. —intr. To undergo asphyxia; suffocate. —as·phyx·i·a·tion (-áysh'n) n. —as·phyx·i·a·tor (-aytər) n.

as·pic¹ (áspik) n. A clear jelly made of stock and gelatine and used as a mould or garnish in cookery. [French (sauce) or (ragoût) à l'aspic, from aspic, ASPIC (snake), from the fancied resemblance of the different colours of the jelly to those of the snake.]

aspic² n. Poetic & Archaic. The asp, a poisonous snake. [Old French, from aspe, from Latin aspis, ASP (snake).]

aspic³ n. A species of lavender, Lavandula spica, that yields a fragrant oil used in perfumery. [French, from Old French, from Old Provençal espic, spike (of a grain such as barley), from Latin spīca, spike.]

as·pi·dis·tra (áspi-dístrə) n. Any of several Asian plants of the genus Aspidistra; especially, A. lurida, having long, tough, evergreen leaves and small brownish flowers. This species is widely cultivated as a house plant. [New Latin Aspidistra : Greek aspis† (stem aspid-), shield (referring to the shape of the leaves) + -istra, after Tupistra (a genus of the lily family).]

as·pi·rant (áspirənt, ə-spír-ənt) n. One who aspires, especially after advancement, honours, or a high position.
~adj. 1. Aspiring after recognition or distinction: aspirant poets. 2. Poetic. Rising; ascending.

as·pi·rate (áspə-rayt, áspi-) tr.v. -rated, -rating, -rates. 1. Phonetics. a. To pronounce (a vowel or word) with the initial release of breath associated with English h, as in hurry. b. To follow (a consonant, especially a stop consonant) with a puff of breath that is clearly audible before the next sound begins, as in English p, t, and k before vowels. 2. Medicine. To remove (liquids or gases) from a body cavity by means of an aspirator.
~n. (áspər-ət, -it). Phonetics. 1. The speech sound represented by the English h. 2. Any speech sound followed by a puff of breath.
~adj. (áspər-ət, -it). Phonetics. Aspirated. Said of a speech sound. [Latin aspīrāre, to breathe upon, aspirate : ad-, to + spīrāre, to breathe.]

as·pi·ra·tion (áspə-ráysh'n, áspi-) n. 1. Expulsion of breath in speech. 2. Phonetics. a. The pronunciation of a consonant with aspiration. b. The puff of air accompanying the release of a stop consonant. 3. Medicine. Removal of liquids or gases from the body with an aspirator. 4. a. A strong desire for high achievement. b. An object of such desire; an ambition.

as·pi·ra·tion·al (áspə-ráyshənəl, áspi-) adj. Of or pertaining to aspiration, and especially to upward social mobility: better wine at aspirational pubs.

as·pi·ra·tor (áspə-raytər) n. 1. Any device that removes liquids or gases from a space by suction, especially one used medically to evacuate a bodily cavity. 2. A suction pump used to create a partial vacuum.

as·pir·a·to·ry (ə-spír-ə-tri, -tēri) adj. Of, concerning, or suited for breathing or suction.

as·pire (ə-spír) intr.v. -pired, -piring, -pires. 1. To have a great ambition or ultimate desire. Often used with to or after. 2. To strive towards an end; aim. 3. Archaic. To rise upwards; soar. [Middle English aspiren, from Old French aspirer, from Latin aspīrāre, to breathe upon, desire, ASPIRATE.] —as·pir·er n. —as·pir·ing·ly adv.

as·pi·rin (áss-prin, -pərin) n. 1. A white crystalline compound, $CH_3COOC_6H_4COOH$, commonly used in tablet form to relieve pain, fever, and inflammation. Also called "acetylsalicylic acid". 2. A tablet of aspirin. [German, from AC(ETYL) + spir(aeic acid), old name for salicylic acid, from SPIRAEA + -IN.]

as·pir·ing (ə-spír-ing) adj. Aiming for recognition or distinction: an aspiring young lawyer.

a·squint (ə-skwint) adv. With a sidelong glance. [Middle English : perhaps A- (on) + Dutch schuinte†, a slope, slant, from schuin, sideways, slanting.] —a·squint adj.

Asquith (áskwith), Herbert Henry, 1st Earl of Oxford and Asquith (1852-1928). British Liberal politician, prime minister (1908-16). His government passed the Parliament Act of 1911 and took away the power of veto from the House of Lords. It also introduced unemployment insurance and old-age pensions. In 1915 he formed a coalition government with the Conservatives and a year later was forced to resign in favour of Lloyd George. He remained leader of the Liberal Party until 1926.

ass¹ (ass; *also, for sense 2,* aass) *n., pl.* **asses** (-iz). **1.** Any of several hoofed mammals of the genus *Equus*; especially, *E. asinus* of Africa and *E. hemionus* of Asia, resembling and closely related to the horses and zebras but having longer ears. See **donkey, onager. 2.** A stupid person, especially one who is vain and self-important. [Middle English *asse,* Old English *assa,* from Old Celtic *as(s)in* (unattested), from Latin *asinus.*]

ass² (ass) *n., pl.* **asses** (-iz). *Vulgar.* **1.** *U.S.* Variant of **arse. 2.** *Chiefly U.S. Vulgar Slang.* Sexual intercourse. **3.** *U.S. Vulgar Slang.* Women collectively, considered as sexual objects.

assagai Variant of **assegai.**

as·sai¹ (a-sī || *U.S.* aa-) *n.* **1.** Any of several palm trees of the genus *Euterpe,* of tropical South America, having edible, fleshy purple fruit. **2.** A beverage made from this fruit. [Brazilian Portuguese *assaí,* from Tupi *assahi.*]

assai² *adv. Music.* Very. Used in directions: *allegro assai.* [Italian "enough", from Vulgar Latin *ad satis* (unattested), "to the point of sufficiency". See **assets.**]

as·sail (ə-sáyl) *tr.v.* **-sailed, -sailing, -sails. 1.** To attack with or as if with violent blows; assault. **2.** To attack verbally, as with ridicule or censure. **3.** To trouble: *She was assailed by doubts.* —See Synonyms at **attack.** [Middle English *asailen,* from Old French *asaillir,* from Medieval Latin *assalīre* from Latin *assilīre,* to jump on : *ad-,* to + *salīre,* to leap.] **—as·sail·a·ble** *adj.* **—as·sail·a·ble·ness** *n.* **—as·sail·ant, as·sail·er** *n.* **—as·sail·ment** *n.*

As·sam (a-sám, ə-). A state in the far northeast of India, almost isolated from the rest of the country by Bangladesh. The capital is Dispur. It is a tea-growing region, but also has important oil reserves and refineries.

As·sa·mese (ássə-méez || -méess) *adj.* Of or pertaining to Assam, its people, or their language.
~*n., pl.* **Assamese. 1.** A native or inhabitant of Assam. **2.** The Indo-European Indic language of the Assamese.

as·sas·sin (ə-sássin) *n.* **1.** A murderer, especially one who carries out a plot to kill a prominent public figure. **2.** Capital **A.** A member of a secret order of Muslim fanatics who terrorised and killed Christian Crusaders. [French, from Medieval Latin *assassīnus,* from Arabic *ḥashshāshīn,* plural of *ḥashshāsh,* "hashish eater" (originally referring to members of an Ismaili sect who took the drug before attacking their enemies), from *ḥashīsh,* HASHISH.]

as·sas·si·nate (ə-sássi-nayt) *tr.v.* **-nated, -nating, -nates. 1.** To murder (a prominent person). **2.** To injure treacherously by slander. **—as·sas·si·na·tive** (-nətiv, -naytiv) *adj.* **—as·sas·si·na·tor** (-naytər) *n.*

as·sas·si·na·tion (ə-sássi-náysh'n) *n.* **1.** Murder, especially of a prominent person. **2.** Malicious injury, especially of a person's good reputation: *character assassination.*

assassin bug *n.* Any of various predatory insects of the large family Reduviidae, having short, curved, powerful beaks adapted for sucking blood and capable of inflicting a painful bite on humans. Some species transmit disease. See **kissing bug.**

as·sault (ə-sáwlt || ə-sólt) *n.* **1.** A violent attack, either physical or verbal. **2.** *Military.* **a.** An attack upon a fortified area or place. **b.** The concluding stage of an attack in which there is close combat with the enemy. **3.** *Law.* An unlawful attempt or threat to injure another physically. **4.** Rape.
~*tr.v.* **assaulted, -saulting, -saults.** To make an assault on. —See Synonyms at **attack.** [Middle English *assaut,* from Old French *asaut, assaut,* from Vulgar Latin *assaltus* (unattested), variant of Latin *assultus,* past participle of *assilīre,* ASSAIL.] **—as·sault·er** *n.*

assault and battery *n. Law.* The threat to make a physical attack on someone and the carrying out of the threat.

assault course *n.* **1.** A military exercise in which troops are made to go over a course of physical obstacles. **2.** Any procedure presenting a series of difficulties.

as·say (ə-sáy, a-, ássay) *n.* **1. a.** The qualitative or quantitative analysis of a substance, especially of a precious metal or drug. **b.** A substance to be so analysed. **c.** The result of such an analysis. **2.** Any analysis or examination. **3.** *Obsolete.* An attempt; an essay.
~*v.* (ə-sáy, a-) **assayed, -saying, -says.** —*tr.* **1.** To subject to chemical analysis; make an assay of. **2.** To examine by trial or experiment; put to a test: *assay one's ability.* **3.** To evaluate; assess. **4.** To attempt; try. —*intr.* To be shown by analysis as having a certain proportion, usually of a precious metal. —See Synonyms at **estimate.** [Middle English, from Old French *assai, essai,* trial, ESSAY.] **—as·say·a·ble** *adj.* **—as·say·er** *n.*

assay office *n.* In Britain, an office which tests the purity of the metal in gold and silver objects, and hallmarks them.

as·se·gai, as·sa·gai (ássi-gī) *n.* **1.** A light spear or javelin used by southern African tribesmen. **2.** A tree, *Curtisia faginea,* of southern Africa, the wood of which is used for making spears.

as·sem·blage (ə-sémblij) *n.* **1. a.** The act of assembling. **b.** The state of being assembled. **2.** A collection of people or things. **3.** A fitting together of parts, as of a machine. **4.** A sculpture consisting of an arrangement of miscellaneous objects, such as scraps of metal, cloth, or string.

as·sem·ble (ə-sémb'l) *v.* **-bled, -bling, -bles.** —*tr.* **1.** To bring or gather together into a group or whole. **2.** To fit or join together the parts of. **3.** *Computing.* To run an assembler program on (data). —*intr.* **1.** To gather together; congregate. **2.** To be capable of undergoing assembly: *The kit assembles into a bookcase.* —See Synonyms at **gather.** [Middle English *assemblen,* from Old French *assembler,* from Vulgar Latin *assimulāre* (unattested), to bring together : Latin *ad-,* to + *simul,* together, at the same time.] **—as·sem·bler** *n.*

as·sem·bler (ə-sémblər) *n.* **1.** A person or device that assembles something. **2.** *Computing.* A program that converts input data into machine code. Compare **compiler.**

as·sem·bly (ə-sémbli) *n., pl.* **-blies.** *Abbr.* **assy. 1. a.** The act of assembling. **b.** The state of being assembled. **2 a.** A group of persons gathered together for a common purpose. **b.** In schools, a morning meeting of the pupils and staff for worship and/or announcements. **3. a.** A legislative council. **b.** *Capital* **A.** In certain U.S. states, the lower house of the legislature. **4. a.** The putting together of manufactured parts to make a completed product, such as a machine or electronic circuit. **b.** A set of parts so assembled. **5.** *Military.* The signal calling troops to form ranks.

assembly language *n. Computing.* A programming language that is a close approximation to machine code.

assembly line *n.* A line of factory workers and equipment on which the product being assembled passes consecutively from operation to operation until completed. Also called "production line". **—as·sem·bly-line** *adj.*

as·sem·bly·man (ə-sémbli-mən) *n., pl.* **-men** (-mən). In the United States, a member of a legislative assembly.

as·sent (ə-sént) *intr.v.* **-sented, -senting, -sents.** To express agreement; concur. Used with *to*: *assent to his plan.*
~*n.* **1.** Agreement, as to a proposal; compliance. **2.** Acquiescence; consent. [Middle English *assenten,* from Old French *assenter,* from Latin *assentārī,* frequentative of *assentīre,* "to join in feeling", agree with : *ad-,* towards + *sentīre,* to feel, think.] **—as·sent·er, as·sent·or** (ə-séntər) *n.* **—as·sent·ing·ly** *adv.* **—as·sent·ive** *adj.* **—as·sent·ive·ness** *n.*

Synonyms: *assent, agree, accede, acquiesce, accept, consent, concur, subscribe.*

as·sen·ta·tion (ássen-táysh'n) *n. Formal.* Ill-considered or servile agreement with another's opinions.

as·sert (ə-sért) *tr.v.* **-serted, -serting, -serts. 1.** To state or express positively; affirm. **2.** To defend or maintain (one's rights, for example). **3.** To put (oneself) forward forcefully or boldly. [Latin *asserere,* "to join to oneself", maintain, claim : *ad-,* to + *serere,* to join.] **—as·sert·a·ble, as·sert·i·ble** *adj.* **—as·sert·er, as·sert·or** (ə-sértər) *n.*

Synonyms: *assert, asseverate, declare, affirm, aver, avow, allege.*

as·ser·tion (ə-sérsh'n) *n.* **1.** The act of asserting or declaring. **2.** A declaration stated positively but with no support or attempt at proof. **—as·ser·tion·al** *adj.*

as·ser·tive (ə-sértiv) *adj.* **1.** Inclined to bold or confident assertion: aggressive. **2.** Self-assertive. **—as·ser·tive·ly** *adv.* **—as·ser·tive·ness** *n.*

as·ser·to·ry (ə-sértəri) *adj.* Asserting or affirming.

as·ses¹. Plural of **as** (Roman coin).

ass·es². Plural of **ass.**

as·sess (ə-séss) *tr.v.* **-sessed, -sessing, -sesses. 1.** To estimate the value of (property) for taxation. **2.** To set or determine the amount of (a tax, fine, or other payment). **3.** To charge (a person or property) with a tax, fine, or other special payment. **4.** To evaluate; appraise. —See Synonyms at **estimate.** [Middle English *assessen,* from Old French *assesser,* from Latin *assidere* (past participle *assessus*), "to sit beside", be an assistant judge (hence in Medieval Latin, to tax): *ad-,* near to + *sedēre,* to sit.] **—as·sess·a·ble** *adj.*

as·sess·ment (ə-séssmənt) *n.* **1.** The act of assessing. **2.** An account of an act of assessing. **3.** An amount assessed as for taxation or costing purposes. **4.** An evaluation; an appraisal.

assessment centre *n.* A centre for young offenders where they stay pending a decision about their future.

as·ses·sor (ə-séssər) *n.* **1.** An official who makes assessments, as for taxation. **2.** An assistant to a judge, selected for his special knowledge of a particular area. **3.** Any adviser or assistant. **—as·ses·so·ri·al** (áss-e-sáwri-əl || -sōri-) *adj.*

as·set (ásset) *n.* **1.** A useful or valuable quality, person, or thing. **2.** A valuable item that is owned. [Back-formation from ASSETS.]

as·sets (ássets) *pl.n.* **1.** *Accounting.* The entries on a balance sheet showing all of a person's or enterprise's properties and claims against others that may be applied, directly or indirectly, to cover liabilities. Assets include the value of tangible things, such as cash and stock, and that of intangibles, such as a trademark or goodwill. **2.** The entire property owned by a person, especially a dead person or a bankrupt, which can be used to settle debts. [Anglo-French *asetz,* (legal use), from Old French *asez,* "enough (to satisfy creditors)", from Vulgar Latin *ad satis* (unattested), "to the point of sufficiency", enough : Latin *ad-,* to + *satis,* sufficient.]

Synonyms: *assets, possessions, belongings, effects, property.*

as·set-strip·ping (ásset-stripping) *n. Chiefly British.* In business, the practice of taking over a company, often one that is in difficulties, and immediately selling off its assets to finance another enterprise. **—as·set-strip·ping** *adj.*

as·sev·er·ate (ə-sévvə-rayt) *tr.v.* **-ated, -ating, -ates.** To declare seriously or positively; affirm. See Synonyms at **assert.** [Latin *asseverāre,* to assert earnestly : *ad-,* to + *sevērus,* earnest, serious.] **—as·sev·er·a·tion** (-ráysh'n) *n.*

as·sib·i·late (ə-síbbi-layt) *tr.v.* **-lated, -lating, -lates.** *Phonetics.* To make sibilant; pronounce with a hissing sound. [AD- (in addition to) + SIBILATE.] **—as·sib·i·la·tion** (-láysh'n) *n.*

as·si·du·i·ty (ássi-déw-əti || -dōō-) *n., pl.* **-ties.** **1.** Close and constant application; unflagging effort; diligence. **2.** *Plural.* Constant personal attentions; solicitude.

as·sid·u·ous (ə-síddew-əss) *adj.* **1.** Constant in application or attention; diligent; devoted: *an assiduous churchgoer.* **2.** Unceasing; persistent. —See Synonyms at **busy.** [Latin *assiduus,* from *assidēre,* to sit beside, attend to : *ad-,* near to + *sedēre,* to sit.] **—as·sid·u·ous·ly** *adv.* **—as·sid·u·ous·ness** *n.*

as·sign (ə-sín) *tr.v.* **-signed, -signing, -signs.** **1.** To set apart or fix for a particular purpose; designate. **2.** To select for a duty or office; appoint. **3.** To give out as a task; allot. **4.** To ascribe; attribute. **5.** *Law.* To transfer (property, rights, or interests). **6.** *Military.* To place (a unit or personnel) integrally into a particular organisation. Compare **attach.** —See Synonyms at **attribute, commit.**

~*n. Law.* An assignee. [Middle English *assignen,* from Old French *assigner,* from Latin *assignāre,* to mark out : *ad-,* to + *signāre,* to mark, from *signum,* sign.] **—as·sign·a·bil·i·ty** *n.* **—as·sign·a·ble** *adj.* **—as·sign·a·bly** *adv.* **—as·sign·er** *n.*

Synonyms: *assign, allot, apportion, allocate.*

as·sig·nat (ássin-yaá, ássig-nat) *n.* Any of the notes of the paper currency issued in France (1789–96) by the revolutionary government backed by the security of confiscated lands. [French, from Latin *assignātum,* "something assigned", past participle of *assignāre,* ASSIGN.]

as·sig·na·tion (ássig-náysh'n) *n.* **1.** The act of assigning. **2.** *Law.* In Scotland, an assignment. **3.** *Formal.* An appointment for a meeting between lovers; a tryst.

as·sign·ee (ássī-neé, ássi-, ə-sī-) *n. Law.* **1.** A person to whom a transfer of property, rights, or interest is made. **2.** One appointed to act for another; a deputy; an agent.

as·sign·ment (ə-sínmənt) *n.* **1.** The act of assigning. **2.** Something assigned, such as a task. **3.** A position or post of duty to which one is assigned. **4.** *Law.* **a.** The transfer of a claim, right, interest, or property. **b.** The document or deed by which this transfer is made. **c.** That which is transferred. —See Synonyms at **task.**

as·sign·or (ássī-nór, ássi-, ə-sí-, ə-sínər) *n. Law.* A person who makes an assignment.

as·sim·i·la·ble (ə-símmilə-b'l) *adj.* Capable of being assimilated. **—as·sim·i·la·bil·i·ty** (-bílləti) *n.*

as·sim·i·late (ə-símmi-layt) *v.* **-lated, -lating, -lates.** —*tr.* **1.** *Physiology.* **a.** To consume and incorporate into the body; digest. **b.** To transform (digested food) into living tissue; metabolise constructively. **2.** To absorb and incorporate (knowledge, for example). **3.** To cause to belong or become integrated: *Can the community assimilate these newcomers?* **4.** To make similar; cause to assume a resemblance. **5.** *Linguistics.* To alter (a sound) by assimilation. —*intr.* To become assimilated. [Middle English *assimilaten,* from Latin *assimilāre, assimulāre,* to make similar to : *ad-,* to + *simulāre, similāre,* to simulate, from *similis,* similar.] **—as·sim·i·la·tor** (-laytər) *n.*

as·sim·i·la·tion (ə-símmi-láysh'n) *n.* **1. a.** The act or process of assimilating. **b.** The condition or process of being assimilated. **2.** *Biology.* The process by which the molecules of digested food are incorporated into living tissue; constructive metabolism. **3.** *Linguistics.* The process by which a sound is modified to make it resemble an adjacent sound. For example, the prefix *in-* in *intolerable* becomes *im-* in *impossible* by assimilation. **4.** The process whereby a group, especially a minority or immigrant group, gradually adopts the characteristics of another culture.

as·sim·i·la·tive (ə-símmi-lətiv, -laytiv) *adj.* Also **as·sim·i·la·to·ry** (-lətri, -lətəri, -láytəri). Marked by or causing assimilation.

As·si·si (ə-seé-si, a-, -zi). Town in the Umbrian region of central Italy, lying on the slopes of the Apennines. St. Francis of Assisi was born here in 1182 and the convent built immediately after his canonisation in 1228 still stands.

as·sist (ə-síst) *v.* **-sisted, -sisting, -sists.** —*tr.* **1.** To aid; help. **2.** To aid in a professional capacity: *assist a surgeon in an operation.* —*intr.* **1.** To give aid or support. **2.** *Rare.* To be present; attend. Usually used with *at.* —See Synonyms at **help.**

~*n.* **1.** *Chiefly U.S.* An act of giving aid; help. **2. a.** In baseball, a handling of the ball that enables a runner to be put out. **b.** In ice hockey, a pass of the puck to the teammate scoring a goal. [Middle English *assisten,* from Old French *assister,* from Latin *assistere,* to stand beside, help : *ad-,* near to + *sistere,* to stand.] **—as·sist·er** *n.*

as·sis·tance (ə-sístənss) *n.* **1.** The act of assisting. **2.** Aid.

as·sis·tant (ə-sístənt) *n. Abbr.* **asst.** **1.** One that assists; a helper; especially, a professional aide. **2.** A person serving customers in a shop.

~*adj. Abbr.* **asst.** **1.** Holding an auxiliary position; subordinate. **2.** Giving aid; auxiliary.

Assistant Secretary *n.* An administrative officer in the British government service between an Under Secretary and a Principal.

Assiut. See **Asyut.**

as·size (ə-síz) *n.* **1.** In English History: **a.** A session of a legislative or judicial body or court. **b.** A decree, verdict, or edict rendered at such a session. **2.** *Plural.* **a.** Any of the periodic court sessions formerly held in each of the counties of England and Wales for the trial of civil or criminal cases. Its functions are now carried out by the High Court and the Crown Court. **b.** The time or place of such sessions. [Middle English *assise,* from Old French, feminine of *assis,* past participle of *as(s)eeir,* to seat, from Vulgar Latin *assedēre* (unattested), from Latin *assidēre,* to sit beside, be an assistant judge. See **assiduous.**]

assn. association.

assoc. associate; association.

as·so·ci·a·ble (ə-sóss-yəb'l, -sósh-, -i-əb'l) *adj.* Capable of being associated. **—as·so·ci·a·bil·i·ty, as·so·ci·a·ble·ness** *n.*

as·so·ci·ate (ə-só-si-ayt, -shi-) *v.* **-ated, -ating, -ates.** —*tr.* **1.** To bring into company with another; join in a relationship. **2.** To connect or join together; combine; link. **3.** To connect in the mind or imagination: *I always associate the Lake District with Wordsworth.* —*intr.* **1.** To join in or form a league, union, or association. **2.** To keep company. —See Synonyms at **join.**

~*n.* (-si-ət, -shi-, -it, -ayt). *Abbr.* **assoc.** **1.** A person united with another or others in some action, enterprise, or business; a partner; a colleague. **2.** A companion; a comrade. **3.** Anything that habitually accompanies or is associated with another; an attendant circumstance. **4.** A member of an institution or society who is granted only partial status or privileges. —See Synonyms at **partner.**

~*adj.* (-si-ət, -shi-, -it, -ayt). *Abbr.* **assoc.** **1.** Joined with another or others and having equal or nearly equal status: *an associate editor.* **2.** Having partial status or privileges: *an associate member of the club.* **3.** Following or accompanying; concomitant. [Middle English *associaten,* from Latin *associāre,* to join to : *ad-,* to + *sociāre,* to join, from *socius,* companion.]

Associated Statehood *n.* A constitutional status of a type once enjoyed by several former British colonies in the Caribbean, involving internal self-government and the option to take full independence at any time. The *Associated States* (which, apart from Anguilla, are now independent) were Dominica, St. Christopher-Nevis-Anguilla, and St. Lucia.

as·so·ci·a·tion (ə-só-si-áysh'n, -shi-) *n.* **1.** The act of associating. **2.** The state of being associated. **3.** *Abbr.* **assn., assoc.** An organised body of people who have some interest, activity, or purpose in common; a society. **4.** A mental connection or relation between thoughts, feelings, ideas, or sensations. **5.** *Chemistry.* Any of various processes of chemical combination, such as hydration, solvation, or complex-ion formation, depending on relatively weak chemical bonding. **6.** *Ecology.* A large community of plants in a specific area with one or two dominant species. **—as·so·ci·a·tion·al** *adj.*

association football *n. Chiefly British.* The official name for **soccer** *(see).*

as·so·ci·a·tion·ism (ə-só-si-áysh'n-iz'm, -shi-) *n.* The psychological theory that association is the basic principle of all mental activity. **—as·so·ci·a·tion·ist** *n. & adj.*

Association of Southeast Asian Nations *n. Abbr.* **ASEAN** An alliance formed in 1967 to stimulate economic growth in Southeast Asia. Its members in 1998 were Brunei, Burma, Indonesia, Laos, Malaysia, Philippines, Singapore, Thailand, and Vietnam.

as·so·ci·a·tive (ə-sóss-yətiv, -sósh-, -i-ətiv, -i-aytiv) *adj.* **1.** Of, characterised by, resulting from, or causing association. **2.** *Mathematics.* Independent of the grouping of elements. Said of mathematical operations: *If* $a + (b + c) = (a + b) + c$, *the operation indicated by* $+$ *is associative.* **—as·so·ci·a·tive·ly** *adv.*

as·soil (ə-sóyl) *tr.v.* **-soiled, -soiling, -soils.** *Rare.* **1.** To absolve or pardon. **2.** To atone for. [Middle English *assoilen,* from Anglo-French *as(s)oilier,* from Old French *assoldre* (stem *assoil-*), from Latin *absolvere,* to set free from : *ab-,* away from + *solvere,* to loosen, set free.]

as·so·nance (ássənənss) *n.* **1.** Resemblance in sound, especially in the vowel sounds of words. **2.** A partial rhyme in which the accented vowel sounds correspond but the consonants differ, as in *brave* and *vain.* **3.** Rough similarity; approximate agreement. [French, from Latin *assonāns,* present participle of *assonāre,* to sound in response to : *ad-,* to + *sonāre,* to sound.] **—as·so·nant** *adj. & n.*

as·sort (ə-sórt) *v.* **-sorted, -sorting, -sorts.** —*tr.* **1.** To separate into groups according to kinds; classify. **2.** *Archaic.* To supply with a variety of goods. —*intr.* **1.** To fall into a class; match. Often used with *with.* **2.** *Rare.* To associate; consort. Used with *with.* [Old French *assorter* : *a-,* from Latin *ad-,* to + *sorte,* kind, from Vulgar Latin *sorta* (unattested), kind, from Latin *sors* (stem *sort-*), chance, fortune, lot.] **—as·sort·a·tive** (-ətiv) *adj.* **—as·sort·er** *n.*

as·sort·ed (ə-sórtid) *adj.* **1.** Consisting of a number of different kinds; various. **2.** Placed in classes; classified. **3.** Suited or matched. Often used in combination: *well-assorted; ill-assorted.* —See Synonyms at **miscellaneous.**

as·sort·ment (ə-sórtmənt) *n.* **1.** The act of assorting; separation into classes. **2.** A collection of various things; a variety.

Assouan, Assuan. See **Aswân.**

A.S.S.R. Autonomous Soviet Socialist Republic, part of the former USSR.

asst. assistant.

as·suage (ə-swáyj) *tr.v.* **-suaged, -suaging, -suages.** **1.** To make less severe or burdensome; ease: *assuage her grief.* **2.** To satisfy; appease, as thirst. **3.** To pacify or calm. —See Synonyms at **relieve.** [Middle English *aswagen,* from Old French *assouagier,* from Vulgar Latin *assuāviāre* (unattested), to sweeten : *ad-,* to + *suāvis,* sweet.] **—as·suage·ment** *n.* **—as·suag·er** *n.*

as·sua·sive (ə-swáy-siv || -ziv) *adj.* Soothing. [AD- + *-suasive,* as in PERSUASIVE but influenced by ASSUAGE).]

as·sume (ə-séwm, ə-sōōm) *tr.v.* **-sumed, -suming, -sumes.** **1.** To take for granted; suppose. **2.** To undertake: *assume responsibility.* **3. a.** To appropriate or usurp. **b.** To invest oneself formally with: *assume the presidency.* **4.** To take on; adopt: "*the god assumes a human form*"

(John Ruskin). **5.** To put on; don (a garment, for example). **6.** To feign; affect. **7.** *Theology.* To receive, as into heaven. —See Synonyms at **presume.** [Middle English *assumen,* from Latin *assūmere,* to take to oneself, adopt : *ad-,* to + *sūmere,* to take.] **—as·sum·a·ble** *adj.* **—as·sum·a·bly** *adv.* **—as·sum·er** *n.*

as·sumed (ə-séwmd, ə-sōōmd ‖ ə-shōōmd) *adj.* **1.** Pretended; adopted; fictitious: *an assumed name.* **2.** Taken for granted. **—as·sum·ed·ly** (ə-séwm-idli, -sōōm- ‖ -shōōm-) *adv.*

as·sum·ing (ə-séwm-ing, -sōōm-) *adj.* Presumptuous or arrogant. *~conj.* Accepting as provisionally true, for the sake of argument; supposing: *Assuming you miss the train, how will you get there?* **—as·sum·ing·ly** *adv.*

as·sump·sit (ə-súmpsit) *n. Law. Rare.* **1.** An agreement or promise not under seal; a contract. **2.** A legal action to enforce or recover damages for a breach of such an agreement. [New Latin, "he undertook", from *assūmere,* to undertake, ASSUME.]

as·sump·tion (ə-súmpsh'n) *n.* **1.** The act of assuming. **2.** A statement accepted or supposed to be true without proof or demonstration. **3.** Presumption or arrogance. **4.** *Logic.* A minor premise. **5.** *Capital* **A. a.** *Theology.* The bodily taking up of the Virgin Mary into heaven. **b.** A church feast on August 15 celebrating this event. [Middle English, from Latin *assumptiō* (stem *assumptiōn-*); a taking up, adoption, from *assūmere,* ASSUME.]

as·sump·tive (ə-súmptiv) *adj.* **1.** Of or characterised by assumption: *assumptive facts.* **2.** Taken for granted. **3.** Presumptuous; assuming. **—as·sump·tive·ly** *adv.*

as·sur·ance (ə-shōōr-ənss, -sháwr- ‖ -shéwr-) *n.* **1. a.** The act of assuring. **b.** The state of being assured. **2.** A statement or indication that inspires confidence. **3. a.** Freedom from doubt; certainty. **b.** Self-confidence. **4.** Boldness; audacity. **5.** *Chiefly British.* Insurance making provision for events that are certain rather than probable, especially death. —See Synonyms at **certainty, confidence.**

as·sure (ə-shōōr, ə-sháwr ‖ ə-shéwr) *tr.v.* **-sured, -suring, -sures.** **1.** To inform confidently, with a view to removing doubt. **2.** To cause to feel sure; convince. **3.** To give confidence to; reassure. **4.** To make certain; ensure: *This will assure the success of our enterprise.* **5.** To make safe or secure. **6.** To insure, as against death. **7.** *Law.* To transfer (ownership); convey. [Middle English *assuren,* from Old French *assurer,* from Medieval Latin *assēcūrāre,* to make sure : Latin *ad-,* to + *sēcūrus,* SECURE.] **—as·sur·a·ble** *adj.* **—as·sur·er** *n.*

as·sured (ə-shōórd, ə-sháwrd ‖ ə-shéwrd) *adj.* **1.** Undoubted; guaranteed; made certain. **2.** Confident; bold. **3.** Insured, especially against death. —See Synonyms at **sure.** *~ n., pl.* **assured. 1.** A person whose life is insured. **2.** A person who stands to benefit from a life-insurance policy. **—as·sur·ed·ly** (ə-shōōr-idli, -sháwr- ‖ -shéwr-) *adv.* **—as·sur·ed·ness** *n.*

as·sur·gent (ə-súrjənt) *adj.* **1.** Rising or tending to rise. **2.** *Botany.* Slanting or curving upwards; ascending. [Latin *assurgēns* (stem, *assurgent-*), present participle of *assurgere,* to rise up to : *ad-,* to + *surgere,* to SURGE.] **—as·sur·gen·cy** *n.*

assy. assembly.

Assyr. Assyrian.

As·syr·i·a (ə-sírri-ə). An ancient civilisation of western Asia, which began to develop at the beginning of the third millennium B.C. around the city of Ashur, on the upper Tigris river. The zenith of the Assyrian empire was reached between the ninth and seventh centuries B.C., when it extended from the Mediterranean across Arabia and Armenia. Its capital Nineveh fell in 612 B.C. to the Medes and Babylonians.

As·syr·i·an (ə-sírri-ən) *adj.* Of or pertaining to Assyria, its people, their language, or their culture. *~ n.* **1.** A native or inhabitant of Assyria. **2.** *Abbr.* **Assyr.** The Semitic language of Assyria.

As·syr·i·ol·o·gy (ə-sirri-óllə ji) *n.* The study of the ancient civilisation of Assyria. **—As·syr·i·ol·o·gist** *n.*

a·sta·ble (áy-stáyb'l) *adj.* **1.** Not stable. **2.** *Electronics.* Designating or pertaining to a component or circuit that can exist in two distinct states.

As·taire (ə-stáir), **Fred,** (born Frederick Austerlitz (1899–1987). U.S. dancer and actor. His first film with Ginger Rogers, *Flying Down to Rio* (1933), marked the start of one of Hollywood's most famous partnerships. Among his other films are *Top Hat* (1935), *Easter Parade* (1948), and *Daddy Long Legs* (1955). In 1949, he was awarded a special Academy Award.

Astana (ə-stárn-ə). Capital of Kazakstan.

As·tar·te (ə-stárti, ə-). *Phoenician Mythology.* The goddess of love and fertility. [Latin *Astartē,* from Greek, from Phoenician *'strt,* akin to Hebrew *'Ashtoreth.*]

a·sta·sia (ə-stáyz-yə, ay-, -stáyzh-, -) *n.* Inability to stand because of poor muscular coordination. [New Latin, from Greek instability, from *astatos,* unstable : *a-,* not + *statos,* standing.]

a·stat·ic (ay-státtik, a-) *adj.* **1.** Unsteady; unstable. **2.** Stable in all positions or orientations. **3.** *Physics.* Pertaining to or designating a device having two magnetic coils to compensate for the earth's magnetic field: *an astatic galvanometer.* **—a·stat·i·cal·ly** *adv.* **—a·stat·i·cism** (-státti-siz'm) *n.*

as·ta·tine (ásta-teen) *n. Symbol* **At** A highly unstable radioactive element that resembles iodine in solution and accumulates in the thyroid gland. Its longest-lived isotope is At 210, having a half-life of 8.3 hours, and used in medicine as a radioactive tracer. Atomic number 85, valencies probably 1, 3, 5, and 7. [Greek *astatos,*

unstable : *a-,* not + *statos,* standing + -INE.]

as·ter (ástər) *n.* **1.** Any of various tall, perennial plants of the genus *Aster,* having rayed, daisy-like flowers ranging in colour from white to bluish purple or pink. See **Michaelmas daisy. 2.** The **China aster** *(see).* **3.** *Biology.* A star-shaped structure appearing in the cytoplasm of the cell and associated with the centrosome during mitosis. [New Latin, from Latin *astēr,* star, from Greek.]

–aster *n. suffix.* Indicates inferiority or fraudulence; for example, **poetaster.** [Middle English, from Latin, suffix denoting either smallness or partial resemblance (often pejorative).]

as·te·ri·at·ed (a-stéer-i-aytid) *adj.* In mineralogy, exhibiting asterism. [Greek *asterios,* starry, from *astēr,* star.]

as·ter·isk (ástərisk) *n.* **1.** A star-shaped figure (*) used in printing to indicate an omission or a reference to a footnote. **2.** *Linguistics.* This sign used to indicate an unattested or incorrect form or entity. *~ tr.v.* **asterisked, -isking, -isks.** To indicate by means of an asterisk; mark with an asterisk. [Late Latin *asteriscus,* from Greek *asteriskos,* little star, asterisk, diminutive of *astēr,* star.]

as·ter·ism (ástər-iz'm) *n.* **1.** Three asterisks in triangular form used to call attention to a following passage. **2.** *Astronomy.* **a.** A cluster of stars. **b.** A constellation. **3.** In mineralogy, a six-rayed starlike figure observed in some crystal structures by using reflected or transmitted light. [Greek *asterismos,* from *asterizein,* to arrange in constellations, from *astēr,* star.] **—as·ter·is·mal** (-ízm'l) *adj.*

a·stern (ə-stérn) *adv. Nautical.* **1.** Behind a vessel. **2.** Towards the rear of a vessel. **3.** To the rear; backwards. [17th century : A- (towards) + STERN, formed by analogy with *ahead.*] **—a·stern** *adj.*

a·ster·nal (ay-stérn'l) *adj. Anatomy.* **1.** Not connected to the sternum. **2.** Lacking a sternum.

as·ter·oid (ástər-oyd) *n.* **1.** *Astronomy.* Any of numerous celestial bodies with characteristic diameters between one and several hundred miles and orbits lying in a zone, the *asteroid belt,* chiefly between Mars and Jupiter. Also called "minor planet", "planetoid". **2.** *Zoology.* A starfish. *~ adj.* Also **as·ter·oi·dal** (-óyd'l). Star-shaped. [Greek *asteroeidēs,* like a star : *astēr,* star + -OID.]

Asterope. Variant of **Sterope.**

as·the·ni·a (ass-théen-yə, -i-ə) *n.* Also **as·the·ny** (ásthəni). *Pathology.* Loss or lack of strength; weakness. [New Latin, from Greek *astheneia,* from *asthenēs,* weak : *a-,* without + *sthenos†,* strength.]

as·then·ic (ass-thénnik) *adj.* **1.** Of or having a slender, long-limbed physique. **2.** Of or having asthenia. *~ n.* A slender, long-limbed person. **—as·then·i·cal** *adv.*

as·the·no·pi·a (áss-thi-nōpi-ə) *n.* Eyestrain, especially with headache and dimming of the vision. [New Latin : ASTHEN(IA) + -OPIA.] **—as·the·nop·ic** (-nóppik) *adj.*

as·then·o·sphere (əss-thénnə-sfeer, ass-, -thénnə-) *n.* A deformable zone in the earth's mantle lying between the lithosphere and the mesosphere (a depth of between 50 and 240 kilometres; 30 and 150 miles). [Greek *asthenēs,* weak (see **asthenia**) + SPHERE.]

asth·ma (áss-mə, ásth- ‖ *U.S.* áz-) *n.* A chronic respiratory disease, often arising from allergies, and accompanied by laboured breathing, chest constriction, and coughing. [Middle English *asma,* from Medieval Latin, from Greek *asthma†.*] **—asth·mat·ic** (-máttik) *adj. & n.* **—asth·mat·i·cal·ly** *adv.*

As·ti (ásti). Town in the Piedmont region of northwest Italy, famous for its sparkling white wine, Asti Spumante.

as·tig·mat·ic (ástig-máttik) *adj.* **1.** Of or having astigmatism. **2.** Correcting astigmatism. **—as·tig·mat·i·cal·ly** *adv.*

a·stig·ma·tism (ə-stígmətiz'm, a-) *n.* **1.** A refractive defect of a lens that prevents focusing of sharp distinct images. It occurs when the lens has different curvatures in two different directions. **2.** Faulty vision caused by such defects in the lens of the eye. [A- (without) + Greek *stigma* (stem *stigmat-*), spot, (tattoo) mark, "focus", from *stizein,* to tattoo.]

a·stil·be (ə-stílbi) *n.* Any plant of the genus *Astilbe,* cultivated as garden plants for their ornamental pink or white plumelike flower clusters. [New Latin : A- (not) + Greek *stilbē,* from *stilbos,* glittering, with reference to the small, inconspicuous individual flowers.]

a·stir (ə-stúr) *adj.* **1.** Moving about. **2.** Out of bed; awake. [Scottish *asteer* : A- (on) + *steer,* variant of STIR (noun).]

A.S.T.M.S. (*also* ástimz). Association of Scientific, Technical, and Managerial Staffs.

a·stom·a·tous (ay-stómmə-təss, a-, -stōmə-) *adj.* Also **as·tom·ous** (ástəməss), **a·stom·a·tal** (ay-stómmət'l, -stōmət'l). *Biology.* Having no mouth or stomata.

As·ton (ástən), **Francis William** (1877-1945). British physicist and chemist. In 1922 he was awarded the Nobel prize in chemistry for the development of the mass spectograph, which led to the discovery of a number of isotopes of nonradioactive elements and the accurate determination of atomic weights of elements.

a·ston·ied (ə-stónnid) *adj. Archaic.* Bewildered; dazed. [Middle English *aston(y)ed,* past participle of *astonen,* ASTONISH.]

a·ston·ish (ə-stónnish) *tr.v.* **-ished, -ishing, -ishes.** To fill with sudden wonder or amazement; surprise greatly. —See Synonyms at **surprise.** [Extension (with verbal suffix *-ish,* as in ABOLISH, FINISH) of obsolete *astony,* Middle English *astonen, astonien,* from Old French *estoner,* from Vulgar Latin *extonāre* (unattested), to strike with thunder, stun : Latin *ex-,* out of + *tonāre,* to thunder.] **—a·ston·ish·ing** *adj.* **—a·ston·ish·ing·ly** *adv.*

a·ston·ish·ment (ə-stónnishmənt) *n.* **1.** Great surprise or amazement. **2.** A cause of amazement; a marvel.

As·tor (ástər), **John Jacob** (1763-1848). U.S. fur-trader and land investor. He founded the fortune of the Astors, one of the United States' wealthiest families.

Astor, Nancy (Witcher Langhorne), Viscountess (1879-1964). British Conservative politician, born in the United States. Her second husband was Waldorf Astor, the great-great-grandson of John Jacob Astor. When he succeeded to his peerage in 1919 she was elected to his old seat of Plymouth and thus became the first woman to sit in the House of Commons. She held the seat until 1945.

a·stound (ə-stównd) *tr.v.* **astounded, astounding, astounds.** To strike with sudden wonder. See Synonyms at **surprise.** [Originally the past participle of obsolete *astone,* to amaze, from Middle English *astonen,* ASTONISH.] **—a·stound·ing·ly** *adv.*

a·strad·dle (ə-strádd'l) *adv.* In a straddling position; astride. *~prep.* So as to straddle; astride.

As·trae·a (astrée-ə). *Greek Mythology.* The goddess of justice. [New Latin, from Greek *astraios,* starry, from *astēr,* star.]

as·tra·gal (ástrəg'l) *n. Architecture.* A narrow, convex moulding, often having the form of beading. [Latin *astragalus,* from Greek *astragalos,* ankle-bone (from the shape of the moulding).]

as·trag·a·lus (a-strággə-ləss, ə-) *n., pl.* **-li** (-lī). A bone, the **talus** (see). [New Latin, from Greek *astragalos.*] **—as·trag·a·lar** (-lər) *adj.*

as·tra·khan, as·tra·chan (ástra-kán, -ka'an ‖ -kən) *n.* **1.** The curly or wavy fur made from the wool of young lambs from the region of Astrakhan. **2.** A fabric with a curly, looped pile, made to resemble this fur.

As·tra·khan (ástrə-ka'an, -kán; *Russian* -khən). City on the delta islands of the Volga, in southeastern Russia. The city was taken from the Tatars by Ivan the Terrible in 1556.

as·tral (ástrəl) *adj.* **1.** Of, pertaining to, consisting of, emanating from, or resembling the stars. **2.** *Biology.* Pertaining to or shaped like an aster; star-shaped. **3.** In theosophy, consisting of or pertaining to a substance from which a higher, non-physical body is made; mystical. [Late Latin *astrālis,* from Latin *astrum,* star, from Greek *astron.*] **—as·tral·ly** *adv.*

as·tra·pho·bi·a (ástrə-fṓb-yə, -i-ə) *n.* Fear of lightning and thunder. [New Latin : Greek *astrapē,* lightning + -PHOBIA.]

a·stray (ə-stráy) *adv.* **1.** Away from the correct path or direction. **2.** Away from the right or good; towards evil or wrong ways. **3.** Missing: *My glasses have gone astray.* [Middle English *astray, astraie,* from Old French *estraie,* past participle of *estraier,* to STRAY.] **—a·stray** *adj.*

as·trict (ə-strikt) *tr.v.* **-tricted, -tricting, -tricts.** To bind, especially by moral or legal obligations. [Latin *astrictus,* past participle of *astringere,* to bind fast, ASTRINGE.] **—as·tric·tion** *n.*

as·tric·tive (ə-stríktiv) *adj.* Astringent. *~n.* An astringent. **—as·tric·tive·ly** *adv.* **—as·tric·tive·ness** *n.*

a·stride (ə-strīd) *adv.* **1.** With the legs separated so that one is on each side of something. **2.** With the legs wide apart. *~prep.* **1.** Upon or over and with a leg on each side of. **2.** With a part on each side of; spanning or bridging.

as·tringe (ə-strínj) *tr.v.* **-tringed, -tringing, -tringes.** To draw together; constrict. [Latin *astringere,* to bind together : *ad-,* to + *stringere,* to bind.]

as·trin·gent (ə-strínjənt) *adj.* **1.** *Medicine.* Tending to draw together or constrict tissue; contracting; styptic. **2.** Harsh; severe. **3.** Sharp-tasting; acidic. *~n.* **1.** An astringent substance or drug, such as alum, used to harden the skin or reduce bleeding. **2.** An astringent cosmetic preparation; especially, a lotion for toning up the complexion. **—as·trin·gen·cy** *n.* **—as·trin·gent·ly** *adv.*

as·tri·on·ics (ástri-ónniks) *n. Used with a singular verb.* Electronics used in astronautics. [Irregularly from ASTRO(NAUTICS) + (ELECTR)ONICS.]

astro-, astr– *comb. form.* Indicates: **1.** Star or star-shaped; for example, **astrocyte. 2.** Outer space; for example, **astronautics.** [Middle English, from Old French, from Latin, from Greek *astron,* star.]

as·tro·bi·ol·o·gy (ástrō-bī-ólləji) *n.* **Exobiology** (see).

as·tro·bleme (ástrō-bleem) *n.* An ancient crater on the earth's surface formed by the impact of a meteorite. [ASTRO- + Greek *blēma,* a shot, wound.]

as·tro·chem·is·try (ástrō-kémmistri) *n.* The study of the composition and reactions of substances present in celestial objects and interstellar matter.

as·tro·com·pass (ástrō-kúmpəss, -kumpəss) *n.* A navigational instrument for determining direction relative to a fixed star.

as·tro·cyte (ástrō-sīt, ástrə-) *n. Biology.* A star-shaped cell, especially a neuroglial cell. [ASTRO- + -CYTE.]

as·tro·cy·to·ma (ástrō-sī-tṓ-mə) *n., pl.* **-mas** or **-mata** (-mətə). A malignant brain tumour composed of astrocytes. [ASTROCYT(E) + -OMA.]

as·tro·dome (ástrə-dōm) *n.* **1.** A transparent dome on the top of an aircraft, through which celestial observations are made for navigation. **2.** *Capital* **A.** In the United States, an enclosed stadium, used mainly for sports events, with a translucent dome.

as·tro·dy·nam·ics (ástrō-dī-námmiks) *n. Used with a singular verb.* The dynamics of celestial bodies.

as·tro·ge·ol·o·gy (ástrō-jee-ólləji) *n.* The study of the structure, composition, and formation of rocks and minerals on other planets.

as·troid (ástroyd) *n. Geometry.* A type of plane curve; a hypocycloid that has four cusps. [ASTRO- + -OID (referring to its starlike shape).]

astrol. astrologer; astrological; astrology.

as·tro·labe (ástrō-layb, ástrə-) *n.* A medieval instrument consisting of a graduated vertical circle with a movable arm, used to determine the altitude of the sun or other celestial bodies for astronomical or navigational purposes. [Middle English, from Old French, from Medieval Latin *astrolabium,* from Greek *(organon) astrolabon,* "(instrument) for taking the stars" : ASTRO- + *lambanein,* to take.]

as·trol·o·gy (ə-strólləji ‖ a-) *n. Abbr.* **astrol.** The study of the positions and aspects of heavenly bodies with a view to assessing or predicting their supposed influence on human characteristics and the course of human affairs. [Middle English *astrologie,* from Old French, from Latin *astrologia,* from Greek, from *astrologos,* astronomer, (later) astrologer : ASTRO- + -LOGY.] **—as·trol·o·ger, as·trol·o·gist** *n.* **—as·tro·log·ic** (ástrə-lójik), **as·tro·log·i·cal** *adj.* **—as·tro·log·i·cal·ly** *adv.*

as·trom·e·try (ə-strómmətri, a-) *n.* The scientific measurement of the positions and movements of celestial bodies. [ASTRO- + -METRY.] **—as·tro·met·ric** (ástrō-méttrik), **as·tro·met·ri·cal** *adj.*

astron. astronomer; astronomical; astronomy.

as·tro·naut (ástrə-nawt) *n.* A person trained to pilot, navigate, or otherwise participate in the flight of a spacecraft. Also called "cosmonaut". [ASTRO- + Greek *nautēs,* sailor, from *naus,* ship.]

as·tro·nau·tics (ástrə-náwtiks) *n. Used with a singular verb.* The science and technology of space flight. [ASTRO- + Latin *nautica,* neuter plural of *nauticus,* NAUTICAL.] **—as·tro·nau·tic, as·tro·nau·ti·cal** *adj.* **—as·tro·nau·ti·cal·ly** *adv.*

as·tro·nav·i·ga·tion (ástrō-návvi-gáysh'n) *n.* **1.** Navigation of outer space, as in spacecraft. **2. Celestial navigation** (see). **—as·tro·nav·i·ga·tor** (-gaytər) *n.*

as·tron·o·mer (ə-strónnəmər) *n. Abbr.* **astron.** A scientist specialising in astronomy. [Middle English, from Late Latin *astronomus,* from Greek *astronomos,* "star-arranger" : ASTRO- + -*nomos,* from *nemein,* to arrange (see **-nomy**).]

as·tro·nom·i·cal (ástrə-nómmik'l) *adj.* Also **as·tro·nom·ic** (-nómmik). **1.** *Abbr.* **astron.** Of or pertaining to astronomy. **2.** Inconceivably large; immense. **—as·tro·nom·i·cal·ly** *adv.*

astronomical telescope *n.* A reflecting or refracting telescope designed for astronomical observation. Compare **terrestrial telescope.**

astronomical unit *n. Abbr.* **A.U.** A unit of length used in measuring astronomical distances, equal to the distance of the earth from the sun, approximately 150 million kilometres (93 million miles).

astronomical year *n.* **A tropical year** (see).

as·tron·o·my (ə-strónnəmi) *n. Abbr.* **astron.** The scientific study of the universe beyond the earth, especially the observation, calculation, and theoretical interpretation of the positions, dimensions, distribution, motion, composition, and evolution of celestial bodies and phenomena. See **astrophysics, astrometry, celestial mechanics, cosmology.** [Middle English *astronomie,* from Old French, from Latin *astronomia,* from Greek, from *astronomos,* ASTRONOMER.]

as·tro·pho·tog·ra·phy (ástrō-fə-tóggrəfi) *n.* Astronomical photography. **—as·tro·pho·to·graph·ic** (-fōtə-gráffik) *adj.*

as·tro·phys·ics (ástrō-fizziks) *n. Used with a singular verb.* The branch of astronomy concerned with the theoretical physics of celestial bodies and phenomena. **—as·tro·phys·i·cal** *adj.* **—as·tro·phys·i·cist** (-fízzi-sist) *n.*

as·tro·sphere (ástrō-sfeer) *n. Biology.* **1.** The central portion of a cell aster; the centrosphere. **2.** The entire cell aster with the exception of the centrosome. [ASTRO- + -SPHERE.]

As·tro·Turf (ástrō-turf) *n.* A trademark for an artificial grasslike surfacing material made of nylon and vinyl, used especially on sports fields.

As·tu·ri·as (a-stṓor-i-ass, -stéwr-). Region and old kingdom (established in 718) in northern Spain, coinciding with the present-day province of Oviedo. The ninth-century shrine at Santiago de Compostela remains a spiritual centre of Christian Spain. **—As·tu·ri·an** *n. & adj.*

As·tu·ri·as, Miguel Ángel (1899–1974). Guatemalan novelist, poet, and diplomat. In 1923 he settled in Paris and came under the influence of André Breton. *Men of Corn* (1949) is usually considered to be his best novel. He received the Nobel prize for literature (1967).

as·tute (ə-stéwt ‖ ə-stṓot) *adj.* Keen in judgment. See Synonyms at **shrewd.** [Latin *astūtus,* from *astus,* craft.] **—as·tute·ly** *adv.* **—as·tute·ness** *n.*

As·ty·a·nax (ə-stí-ə-naks, a-). In Greek legend, the young son of Hector and Andromache, killed by the conquering Greeks.

a·sty·lar (ay-stílər, a-) *adj.* Not having columns or pilasters. [A- (without) + Greek *stulos,* pillar.]

A·sun·ci·ón (ə-sṓon-si-ón, -ṓn). Chief port, industrial centre, and capital of Paraguay, situated on the Paraguay river.

a·sun·der (ə-súndər) *adv.* **1.** Into separate parts or pieces. **2.** Apart from each other, either in position or direction. [Middle English *asonder,* Old English *onsundran, onsundrum* : *on,* on + *sundran, sundrum,* singly, separately, from *sunder,* apart, separate.] **—a·sun·der** *adj.*

Asur. Variant of **Ashur.**

A·swân, As·suan (áss-wa'an, -wán). City in southern Egypt, on the Nile river. It was an important station in the trade between ancient Egypt and the Sudan.

Aswan High Dam. Dam built on the Nile river about 11 kilometres (7 miles) south of Aswân, opened in 1971. The building costs were largely paid by the U.S.S.R. The dam is 114 metres (375 feet) high and 3 600 metres (11,800 feet) long. Its reservoir, Lake Nasser, is one of the largest artificial lakes in the world.

a·syl·lab·ic (áy-si-lábbik) *adj.* Not syllabic.

a·sy·lum (ə-sī-ləm) *n., pl.* **-lums** or **-la** (-lə). **1.** A place offering protection or safety. **2.** Formerly, a temple or church affording sanctuary for criminals or debtors. **3.** In international law, immunity from arrest or extradition granted to a refugee from another country: *political asylum.* **4.** Formerly, an institution for the care of the blind, the deaf, or especially the mentally ill. —See Synonyms at **shelter.** [Middle English *asilum,* from Latin *asylum,* from Greek *asulon,* sanctuary, from *asulos,* inviolable : *a-,* without + *sulon†,* right of seizure.]

a·sym·met·ric (ássi-métrik, áyssi-) *adj.* Also **a·sym·met·ri·cal** (-métrik'l). *Abbr.* **asym.** Not symmetrical. —**a·sym·met·ri·cal·ly** *adv.*

asymmetric atom *n. Chemistry.* An atom that is attached to four different groups in a molecule, so that the compound exhibits optical isomerism.

a·sym·me·try (á-símmətri, áy-) *n.* Lack of symmetry or balance. [Greek *asummetria* : *a-,* without + *summetria,* SYMMETRY.]

a·symp·to·mat·ic (ássimp-tə-máttik, áy-símp-) *adj.* Neither causing nor exhibiting symptoms. —**a·symp·to·mat·i·cal·ly** *adv.*

as·ymp·tote (ássimp-tōt, ássim-) *n. Mathematics.* A straight line that approaches a curve so that the perpendicular distance from a moving point on the curve to the line approaches zero as the point moves an infinite distance from the origin. **2.** A plane that approaches a curved surface at infinite distance from the origin. [New Latin *asymptota,* from Greek *(grammē) asumptōtos,* "(a line) not falling together" : *a-,* not + *sumptōtos,* from *sumpiptein,* to fall together : *sun-,* together + *piptein,* to fall.] —**as·ymp·tot·ic** (-tóttik), **as·ymp·tot·i·cal** *adj.* —**as·ymp·tot·i·cal·ly** *adv.*

a·syn·chro·nism (á-síng-krə-niz'm, áy) *n.* Lack of synchronism. —**a·syn·chro·nous** (-nəss) *adj.* —**a·syn·chro·nous·ly** *adv.*

asynchronous motor *n.* An electric motor that operates so that its speed is not related to the frequency of the alternating-current supply.

a·syn·de·ton (a-sínditən) *n.* The omission of conjunctions from constructions in which they would normally be used; for example: *He wrote, he drew, he painted.* Compare **parataxis.** [Late Latin, from Greek *asundeton,* from *asundetos,* "without conjunctions", unconnected : *ā-,* not + *sundetos,* bound together, from *sundein,* to bind together : *sun-,* together + *dein,* to bind.] —**as·yn·det·ic** (ássin-déttik) *adj.* —**as·yn·det·i·cal·ly** *adv.*

a·syn·tac·tic (áy-sin-táktik) *adj.* Not syntactic.

As·yut or **As·iut, Assiut** (asséwt). An industrial city in central Egypt, situated on the river Nile.

at¹ (at, *weak form* ət) *prep.* **1. a.** In the location of: *at the market.* **b.** In the position of: *at the centre of the page.* **2.** To or towards the direction of: *Look at him.* **3.** Present in; attending: *at the dance.* **4.** In the duration of; during: *at night.* **5.** In the state or condition of: *at peace with one's conscience.* **6.** In the manner of: *at a run.* **7.** In exchange for: *at thirty pence a pound.* **8.** On the exact or approximate moment of: *at three o'clock.* **9.** Because of: *rejoice at a victory.* **10.** Engaged in: *at war.* **11.** According to: *at one's discretion.* **12.** Dependent upon: *at the mercy of the court.* **13.** Maintaining or in accordance with a given rate, speed, or degree: *flying at 5 000 metres at 800 kilometres per hour.* [Middle English *at, atte,* Old English *æt.*]

at² (aat, at) *n., pl.* **at.** A monetary unit equal to $1/100$ of the kip of Laos. [Thai.]

aT *Physics.* attotesla.

At The symbol for the element astatine.

at. **1.** atomic. **2.** atmosphere (unit of pressure).

A.T. Administrative Trainee.

At·a·ca·ma Desert (áttə-ka'amə ‖ a'atə-). Arid region of northwest Chile. It is one of the world's driest areas, much of it having no recorded rainfall. It has some nitrate and copper reserves.

a·tac·tic (ay-táktik) *adj. Chemistry.* Of or pertaining to a polymer with a nonregular arrangement of groups along its chain. Compare **stereospecific.** [A- (not) + -TACTIC.]

ataghan. Variant of **yataghan.**

A·ta·huall·pa, A·ta·hual·pa (áttə-wál-pə, -wa'al-) Also **A·ta·ba·li·pa** (-ba'alipə) (*c.* 1502-33). The last Inca to rule Peru, captured and executed by the Spaniards.

At·a·lan·ta (áttə-lántə). *Greek Mythology.* A maiden who agreed to marry any man who could outrun her, and who was defeated by Hippomenes when he dropped three golden apples that she paused to pick up.

at·a·man (áttə-mən, -man) *n., pl.* **-mans.** A Cossack chief. [Russian, from Polish *hetman,* from German *Hauptmann,* captain, from Middle High German *houbetman,* from Old High German *houbitman* : *houbit,* head + *man,* man.]

at·a·rac·tic (áttə-ráktik) *adj.* Also **at·a·rax·ic** (-ráksik). Pertaining to or conducive to calmness and peace of mind. —*n.* A drug that reduces nervous tension; a tranquilliser. [Greek *ataraktos,* undisturbed : *a-,* not + *taraktos,* disturbed, from *tarattein,* to disturb.]

at·a·rax·i·a (áttə-ráksi-ə) *n.* Peace of mind; emotional tranquillity. [Greek *ataraxia,* from *ataraktos,* ATARACTIC.]

A·ta·türk (áttə-turk, -türk), **Kemal,** born Mustafa Kemal (1881-1938). Turkish national leader, the founder of modern Turkey. In 1919 he organised the Turkish Nationalist Party and set up a rival government to the Ottoman sultan at Ankara. In 1923, after a civil war, he was elected the first president of the Turkish repub-

lic, a position which he held until his death. His rule was marked by westernisation and internal reform. "Atatürk" means "Father of the Turks".

a·tav·ic (ə-távvik) *adj.* Of or concerning a remote ancestor.

at·a·vism (áttə-viz'm) *n.* **1.** The reappearance of a characteristic in an organism after several generations of absence, caused by a recessive gene or complementary genes. **2.** An individual or part displaying atavism. Also informally called "reversion", "throwback". **3.** Reversion to a primitive or earlier state of behaviour. [French *atavisme,* from Latin *atavus,* ancestor, great-great-great-grandfather: *atta,* father + *avus,* grandfather.] —**at·a·vist** *n.* —**at·a·vis·tic** -vistik) *adj.* —**at·a·vis·ti·cal·ly** *adv.*

a·tax·i·a (ə-táksi-ə, a-, ay-) *n.* Also **a·tax·y** (-táksi). Loss or lack of muscular coordination. [Greek *ataxia,* from *ataktos,* disorderly : *a-,* not + *taktos,* ordered, from *tattein,* to arrange.]

a·tax·ic (ə-táksik, a-, ay-) *adj.* Of or pertaining to ataxia. —*n.* An individual exhibiting symptoms of ataxia.

A.T.C. Air Traffic Control.

ate. Past tense of **eat.**

–ate¹ *adj. suffix.* Indicates: **1.** Possessing; for example, **nervate, affectionate. 2.** Shaped like; for example, **lyrate. 3.** Having the general characteristics of; for example, **Latinate.** [Middle English *-at,* from Old French, from Latin *-ātus,* ending of the past participle of verbs in *-āre* (first conjugation). It thus appears in: **1.** Participial adjectives; for example, **ornate. 2.** Nouns converted from adjectives, either in Latin or in English; for example, **associate. 3.** Verbs originally formed from the corresponding nouns and adjectives in *-ate;* for example, **aggregate, conjugate;** and subsequently, by analogy with these, adopted directly from Latin, taking participial form but infinitive sense; for example, **desiccate, eradicate.**]

-ate² *n. suffix.* Indicates: **1.** The product of a specified chemical or other process; for example, **distillate. 2.** *Chemistry.* **a.** The salt of an oxygen acid; for example, **nitrate, sulphate. b.** The ester of an oxygen acid or carboxylic acid; for example, **acetate, stearate.** [Special use of -ATE¹.]

-ate³ *n. suffix.* Indicates: **1.** Rank or status; for example, **magistrate. 2.** A group of people performing a specified function or holding a specified office; for example, **electorate.** [Latin *-ātus,* an abstract suffix made up of the *-āt-* of *-ātus,* participial ending (-ATE¹), and the feminine *-us* of fourth declension nouns. It originally designated the collective status of a group, as in **senate,** later the power of a specific type of ruler, as in **triumvirate.**]

-ate⁴ *v. suffix.* Indicates: **1.** To cause to become; for example, **activate. 2.** To supply or impregnate with; for example, **oxygenate.** [Abstracted from verbs of Latin origin ending in *-ate.* See -ate¹.]

at·el·ier (a-télli-ay, áttel-yay ‖ U.S. átt'l-yáy) *n.* A workshop or artist's studio. [French, from Old French *astelier,* woodpile, hence carpenter's shop, from *astele,* splinter, shaving, chip, from Late Latin *astella,* variant of Latin *astula, assula,* diminutive of *assis,* board, plank, probably variant of *axis.* See **ashlar.**]

a tem·po (aa témpō) *adv. Music.* In normal time; resuming the original tempo. Used as a direction. [Italian, "in time".]

a·tem·po·ral (ay-témpərəl) *adj.* Independent of time; timeless.

A·ten, A·ton (áatən). *Egyptian Mythology.* A sun god, regarded during the reign of Akhenaton as the only god.

Ath·a·bas·ka, Ath·a·bas·ca (áthə-báskə). River in northern Alberta in Canada, rising in the Rockies and flowing 1 230 kilometres (765 miles) northeast into Lake Athabaska.

Ath·a·na·sian (áthə-náyz-yən, -náyss-, -náyzh-, -náysh) *adj.* Of or pertaining to Athanasius. —*n.* A follower of Athanasius and his teachings.

Athanasian creed *n.* A Christian creed or profession of faith dating from about A.D. 425, expounding the doctrine of the Trinity. [After St. ATHANASIUS.]

Ath·a·na·si·us (áthə-náyz-i-əss, -náysh-, -náyss-, -yəss), **Saint** (*c.* 297-373). Doctor of the (Christian) Church and patriarch of Alexandria (328-373). He played an important part at the First Council of Nicaea in the debate against **Arianism** *(see).* He was formerly thought to be the author of the Athanasian creed.

Ath·a·pas·can (áthə-báskən) *n.* Also **A·tha·bas·can** (-báskən). **1.** A North American Indian language family including languages of Alaska, northwest Canada, and the coast of Oregon and California, and the Navaho and Apache languages of the southwest United States. **2.** A member of an Athapascan-speaking people. —*adj.* Of or designating this language family. [From the name of Lake *Athabaska* in western Canada, Northern Cree *athapaskaaw,* "there is scattered grass".]

a·the·ism (áy-thee-iz'm) *n.* **1.** Disbelief in or denial of the existence of God. Compare **agnosticism. 2.** The doctrine that there is no God or that the word "God" and statements about it or using it are meaningless. [Old French *atheisme,* from *athee,* atheist, from Greek *atheos,* godless : *a-,* without + *theos,* god.] —**a·the·ist** *n.*

a·the·is·tic (áy-thee-ístik) *adj.* Also **a·the·is·ti·cal** (-ístik'l). **1.** Pertaining to or characteristic of atheism or atheists. **2.** Inclined to atheism. —**a·the·is·ti·cal·ly** *adv.*

ath·e·ling (áthə-ling, áthə-) *n.* An Anglo-Saxon nobleman or prince. [Middle English *atheling.* Old English *ætheling,* prince : *æthel,* noble + *-ing,* descendant of.]

Ath·el·stan (áth'l-stən) (895-940). King of Mercia and Wessex, the first Saxon ruler to establish his authority over all England. He was elected king of Mercia in 924 and a year later was crowned king of the whole country.

a·the·mat·ic (áthi-mattik, áythee-) *adj.* **1.** *Music.* Not based on

105

themes. **2.** *Linguistics.* Designating a verb that has no vowel between the stem and the ending.

A·the·na (ə-theé-nə). Also **A·the·ne** (-ni). *Greek Mythology.* The goddess of wisdom and the arts. Identified with the Roman goddess Minerva. Also called "Pallas Athena", "Pallas Athene".

ath·e·nae·um, *U.S.* **ath·e·ne·um** (áthi-neé-əm) *n.* **1.** An institution, such as a literary club or scientific academy, for the promotion of learning. **2.** A library, reading room, or similar place. [Late Latin *Athēnaeum,* a Roman school of art, after Greek *Athēnaion,* the temple of Athena at Athens, where philosophy was taught, from *Athēnē,* ATHENA.]

Ath·ens (áthinz). *Greek* **A·thi·ne, A·thi·nai** (a-theé-ne). Capital and industrial centre of Greece, lying in the east of the country near the Saronic Gulf. At the time of the Persian Wars (500–499 B.C.) it was the most powerful Greek city state and the cradle of democracy. The zenith of its cultural achievements and imperial power was reached during the time of Pericles (443–429 B.C.), when Socrates, Sophocles, Aeschylus, and Euripides all flourished. It became the capital of modern Greece when the country won its independence from the Turks in 1834.

a·ther·man·cy (a-thérmən-si, ay-) *n. Physics.* The inability of substances to transmit infrared radiation. [Greek *athermantos,* not heated : A-(not) + *thermantos,* from *thermē,* heat.] **—a·ther·man·ous** (-əss) *adj.*

ath·er·o·ma (áthə-rṓ-mə) *n., pl.* **-mas** or **-mata** (-mətə). *Pathology.* **1.** A deposit or degenerative accumulation of pulpy, acellular, lipid-containing materials, especially in arterial walls. **2.** A form of arteriosclerosis induced and characterised by such deposits. [New Latin, from Latin, from Greek *athērōma,* a cyst full of gruel-like pus, from *athēra,* gruel, from *athēr*†, beard of grain.] **—ath·er·o·ma·to·sis** (-tṓ-siss) *n.* **—ath·er·om·a·tous** (-təss, -rómmətəss) *adj.*

ath·er·o·scle·ro·sis (átherō-skleer-ṓ-siss, -sklər-) *n. Pathology.* A disease in which fatty deposits form on the arteries and obstruct the blood flow; atheromatous arteriosclerosis; atheroma. [*atheroma* + *sclerosis.*] **—ath·er·o·scle·rot·ic** (-óttik) *adj.*

a·thirst (ə-thúrst) *adj.* **1.** Strongly desirous; eager. Usually used with *for*: *athirst for freedom* **2.** *Archaic.* Thirsty.

ath·lete (áth-leet || *West Indies also* áath-. *Note: the pronunciation* áthə- *is considered incorrect*) *n.* **1.** One who takes part in competitive sports, especially track and field events. **2.** A person possessing the natural prerequisites for sports competition, such as strength, speed, agility, and endurance. [Middle English, from Latin *athlēta,* from Greek *athlētēs,* contestant, from *athlein,* to contend for an award, from *athlon*†, award, prize.]

athlete's foot *n.* A contagious skin infection caused by parasitic fungi usually affecting the feet and causing itching, blisters and cracking. Also called "tinea pedis" and informally "foot rot".

ath·let·ic (ath-léttik || *West Indies also* aath-. *See note at* **athlete**). *adj.* **1.** Of, pertaining to, or befitting athletics or athletes. **2.** Physically strong; muscular. **3.** Physically active and agile. **—ath·let·i·cal·ly** *adv.* **—ath·let·i·cism** (-létti-siz'm) *n.*

ath·let·ics (ath-léttiks || *West Indian also* aath-. *See note at* **athlete**). *n.* **1. a.** *Used with a plural verb. U.S.* Physical activities, such as competitive sports or games. **b.** *Usually used with a singular verb.* Track and field sporting events. Also *U.S.* "track and field". **2.** *Used with a singular verb.* The principles or practice of athletic exercises and training.

athletic supporter *n. U.S.* A **jockstrap** *(see).*

ath·o·dyd (áthō-dīd, áthə-, -did) *n.* A simple jet engine. See **ramjet, pulsejet.** [*A*ero*th*ermo*dy*namic *d*uct.]

at-home (ət-hṓm) *n.* An informal reception at one's home.

-athon, -thon *n. comb. form.* Indicates a prolonged or strenuous event or activity, often involving financial sponsorship; for example, **telethon, talkathon.** [Abstracted from MARATHON.]

Ath·os, Mount (áthoss, áythoss). A mountain peak, rising to 2 030 metres (6,660 feet) at the southern tip of the Athos peninsula in northeast Greece. It is the site of the virtually independent group of 20 monasteries of the Order of St. Basil of the Eastern Orthodox Church. In 1927 Mount Athos was granted the status of a theocratic republic under the suzerainty of Greece.

a·thwart (ə-thwáwrt) *adv.* **1.** From side to side; crossways; transversely. **2.** So as to thwart or obstruct; perversely.
~prep. **1.** From one side to the other of; across. **2.** Contrary to; against. **3.** *Nautical.* Across the course, line, or length of. [Middle English : A- (on) + THWART (side).]

a·tilt (ə-tílt) *adv.* **1.** In a tilted position; inclined upwards. **2.** As if tilting with a lance: *"Break a lance, and run atilt at death"* (Shakespeare). **—a·tilt** *adj.*

-ation *n. suffix.* Indicates: **1.** Action or process of; for example, **strangulation, negotiation. 2.** State, condition, or quality of; for example, **isolation, moderation. 3.** Result or product of; for example, **dramatisation, civilisation.** [Middle English *-acioun,* from Old French *-ation,* from Latin *-ātiō* (stem *-ātiōn-*), abstract noun suffix, from *-ātus.* See **-ate**[1], **-ion.**]

-ative *adj. suffix.* Indicates relation, nature, or tendency; for example, **authoritative, illustrative, formative.** [Middle English, from Old French *-atif,* from Latin *-ātīvus,* from *-ātus.* See **-ate**[1], **-ive.**]

Atkins, Tommy. See **Tommy Atkins.**

At·lan·ta (ət-lántə, at-). The capital of Georgia, in the United States, situated in the northwest part of the state. It was founded in 1837, but had to be almost entirely rebuilt after being burnt to a shell on November 15, 1864, just before General Sherman began his famous march to the sea from the town. **—At·lan·tan** *adj. & n.*

At·lan·te·an (át-lan-teé-ən, ət-lánti-ən) *adj.* **1.** Of, pertaining to, or resembling Atlas. **2.** Of or pertaining to Atlantis. [Latin *Atlanteus* : *Atlas* (stem *Atlant-*), ATLAS + -AN.]

at·lan·tes. *Architecture.* Plural of **atlas.**

At·lan·tic (ət-lántik || at-) *adj.* **1.** *Abbr.* **Atl.** Of, in, near, upon, or pertaining to the Atlantic Ocean. **2.** Of or pertaining to Atlas or to the Atlas Mountains.
~n. The Atlantic Ocean. [Latin *(mare) Atlanticum,* from Greek *(pelagos) Atlantikos,* "(the sea) of Atlas" (the sea lying beyond the Atlas Mountains), from *Atlas* (stem *Atlant-*), ATLAS.]

Atlantic Charter *n.* A declaration of the aims of the Allied Nations concerning a postwar settlement in World War II, made jointly by Churchill and Roosevelt after a meeting at sea in August 1941.

Atlantic City. A resort and convention city on the Atlantic coast of New Jersey, in the United States. The city thrives almost exclusively on tourism and gambling.

Atlantic Ocean. The world's second largest ocean, with an area of 82 217 000 square kilometres (31,744,000 square miles). Its average depth is 3 660 metres (12,000 feet). It is divided into two great basins, the North Atlantic and the South Atlantic, the former with clockwise-flowing currents, the latter with anticlockwise. Down the centre of the ocean, running for 16 000 kilometres (10,000 miles) is the Mid-Atlantic Ridge.

Atlantic salmon *n.* A food fish, *Salmo salar,* of northern Atlantic waters. See **salmon.**

At·lan·tis (ət-lántiss, at-). Legendary island in the Atlantic west of Gibraltar, said by Plato to have sunk beneath the sea.

at·las (át-ləss) *n., pl.* **-lases** or **-lantes** (ət-lánteez, at-) (for sense 4). **1.** A bound collection of maps. **2.** Any volume of tables, charts, or plates that systematically illustrate a subject: *anatomical atlas.* **3.** A large size of drawing paper, measuring 66 by 84 or 86 centimetres (26 by 33 or 34 inches). **4.** *Usually plural. Architecture.* A figure of a man used as a masonry column on a building to support an entablature. **5.** *Anatomy.* The top or first cervical vertebra of the neck, which supports the skull. [From representations of the mythical Titan ATLAS upholding the heavens, common in 16th-century books of maps.]

Atlas. *Greek Mythology.* A giant, one of the Titans, who was condemned to support the heavens upon his shoulders for rebelling against the gods. [Latin, from Greek *Atlas* (stem *Atlant-*); the name was subsequently applied to the Atlas Mountains in northwest Africa and then to the sea nearby (Atlantis, Atlantic).]

Atlas Mountains. Series of fold mountain ranges extending from Morocco, through Algeria, into Tunisia. They form a climatic barrier between the Mediterranean lowlands and the Sahara. The highest peak is Jebel Toubkal (4 165 metres; 13,665 feet).

atm. atmosphere; atmospheric.

at·man (áat-mən) *n. Hinduism.* **1.** The individual soul; the principle of life. **2.** *Capital* **A.** The universal soul, from which all individual souls arise; Brahma. [Sanskrit *ātman,* breath, spirit, soul.]

atmo- *comb. form.* Indicates the presence of or relation to vapour; for example, **atmosphere.** [New Latin, from Greek *atmos,* vapour, breath.]

at·mol·y·sis (at-móllə-siss) *n., pl.* **-ses** (-seez). The separation of a mixture of gases, each with different diffusibility, by diffusion through a porous material. [ATMO- + -LYSIS.]

at·mom·e·ter (at-mómmitər) *n.* An instrument that measures the rate of water evaporation. [ATMO- + -METER.] **—at·mo·met·ric** (át-mō-méttrik, -mə-) *adj.* **—at·mom·e·try** (-mómmətri) *n.*

atmos. atmosphere; atmospheric.

at·mos·phere (átməss-feer) *n.* **1.** *Abbr.* **atm., atmos.** The gaseous mass or envelope surrounding a celestial body, especially that surrounding the earth, and retained by the body's gravitational field. **2.** The quality of the air or climate in a specific place: *a very smoky atmosphere.* **3.** *Abbr.* **atm** *Physics.* A unit of pressure equal to 1.01325×10^5 newtons per square metre. **4.** A psychological environment: *He grew up in an atmosphere of austerity.* **5.** The predominant tone or mood of a work of art. **6. a.** A pervading quality, effect, or mood, especially as associated with a particular place: *a depressing atmosphere.* **b.** A distinctively pleasant or exciting quality or mood: *a Greek restaurant with lots of atmosphere.* [New Latin *atmosphaera,* "sphere of vapour" : ATMO- + -SPHERE.]

at·mos·pher·ic (át-məss-férrik || *U.S. also* -feér-ik) *adj.* Also **at·mos·pher·i·cal** (-'l). *Abbr.* **atm., atmos. 1.** Of, pertaining to, or existing in the atmosphere. **2.** Produced by, dependent on, or coming from the atmosphere. **—at·mos·pher·i·cal·ly** *adv.*

atmospheric pressure *n.* The pressure exerted by the atmosphere. At sea level it has a mean value of one atmosphere per square metre (760 mmHg) but reduces with increasing altitude.

at·mos·pher·ics (át-məss-férriks || *U.S. also* -feér-iks) *n. Used with a singular verb.* **1.** Electromagnetic radiation produced by natural phenomena such as lightning. **2.** Radio interference produced by such radiation. Also called "sferics".

at·oll (áttol; *rarely* ə-tól || *U.S. also* áttawl) *n.* A ringlike coral reef that nearly or entirely encloses a lagoon. [Malayalam *atoḷu,* "reef", native name for the Maldive Islands.]

at·om (áttəm) *n.* **1.** Anything considered an irreducible constituent of a specified system. **2.** The irreducible, indestructible material unit of ancient **atomism** *(see).* **3.** *Physics & Chemistry.* A unit of matter, the smallest unit of an element, consisting of a dense, central, positively charged **nucleus** *(see)* surrounded by a system of electrons, equal in number to the number of nuclear protons, the entire structure having an approximate diameter of 10^{-8} centimetre

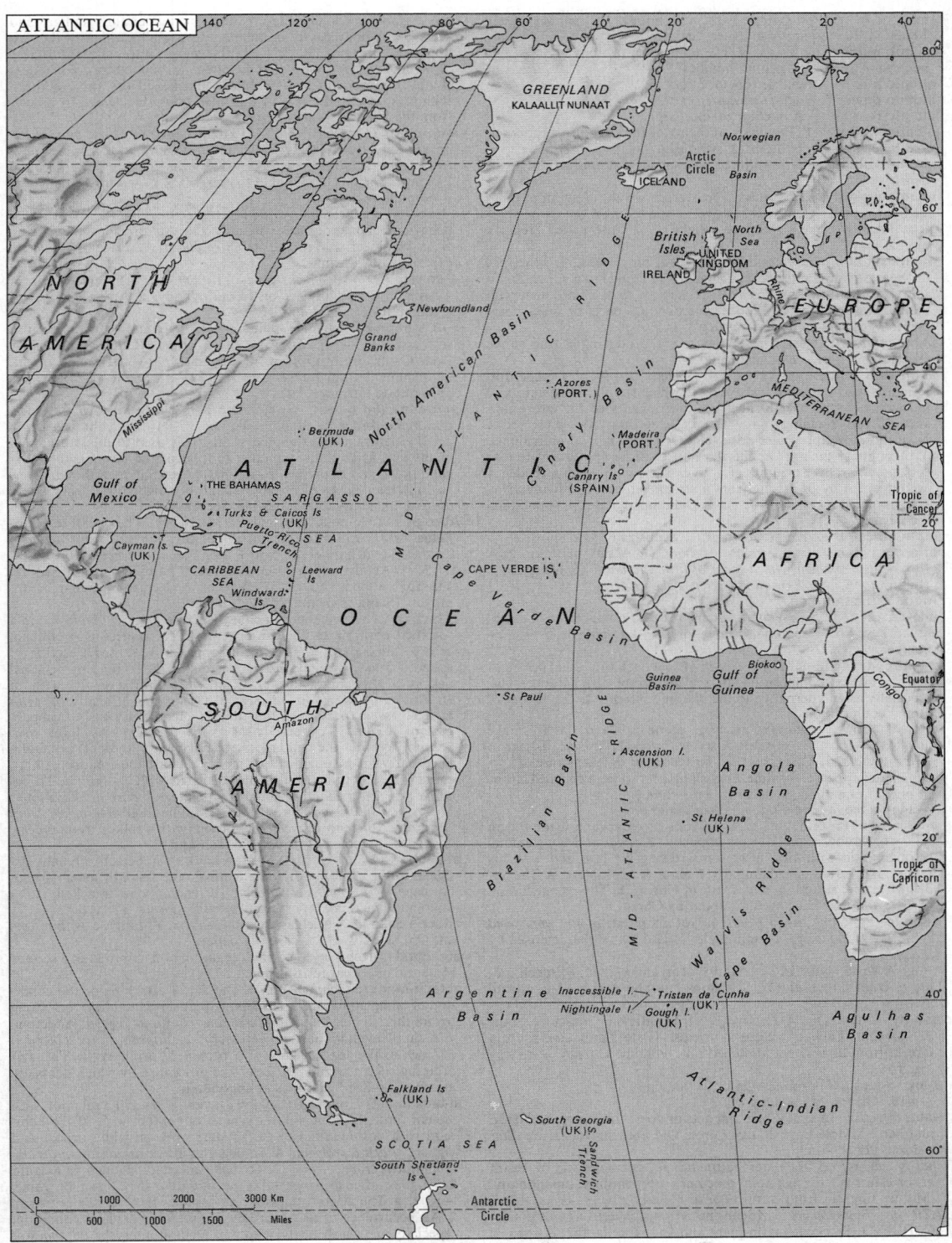

ATLANTIC OCEAN

GREENLAND
KALAALLIT NUNAAT

Norwegian
Arctic
Circle
ICELAND Basin

NORTH
AMERICA

British
Isles
UNITED
KINGDOM
IRELAND

North
Sea

EUROPE

MEDITERRANEAN
SEA

Newfoundland

Grand
Banks

North American Basin

Azores
(PORT.)

Canary Basin

40°

Mississippi

Bermuda
(UK)

Madeira
(PORT.)

ATLANTIC

Canary Is
(SPAIN)

Tropic of
Cancer

Gulf of
Mexico

THE BAHAMAS

SARGASSO

Turks & Caicos Is
(UK)

Puerto Rico
Trench

SEA

OCEAN

Cape Verde

CAPE VERDE IS.

AFRICA

Cayman Is.
(UK)

CARIBBEAN
SEA

Leeward
Is

Windward
Is

Basin

Guinea
Basin

Biokoo

Gulf of
Guinea

Congo

Equator

SOUTH

Amazon

AMERICA

St Paul

Ascension I.
(UK)

MID - ATLANTIC RIDGE

Angola
Basin

St Helena
(UK)

20°

Brazilian Basin

Walvis Ridge

Cape Basin

Tropic of
Capricorn

Argentine
Basin

Inaccessible I.

Nightingale I.

Tristan da Cunha
(UK)

Gough I.
(UK)

Agulhas
Basin

40°

Falkland Is
(UK)

South Georgia
(UK)

S. Sandwich
Trench

Atlantic-Indian
Ridge

60°

SCOTIA SEA

South Shetland
Is

Antarctic
Circle

| 0 | 1000 | 2000 | 3000 Km |
| 0 | 500 | 1000 | 1500 Miles |

and characteristically remaining undivided in chemical reactions except for limited removal, transfer, or exchange of outer electrons. **4.** This unit regarded as a source of nuclear energy. [Middle English *attome, attomus,* from Latin *atomus,* from Greek *atomos,* indivisible : *a-*, not + *temnein,* to cut. See **-tome, -tomy.**]

a·tom·ic (ə-tómmik) *adj.* **1.** Of or relating to an atom or atoms. **2.** Of or employing atomic energy: *an atomic submarine.* **3.** Very small; infinitesimal. **—a·tom·i·cal·ly** *adv.*

atomic age *n. Often capital* A, *capital* A. The current era as characterised by the discovery, technological applications, and sociopolitical consequences of atomic energy.

atomic bomb *n.* A **nuclear bomb** (see).

atomic clock *n.* An extremely precise timekeeping device regulated in correspondence with a characteristic invariant frequency of an atomic or molecular system.

atomic energy *n.* **Nuclear energy** *(see).*

Atomic Energy Authority *n.* A government body formed in Britain in 1954 to control research and development in nuclear energy.

Atomic Energy Commission *n. Abbr.* **AEC, A.E.C.** A five-member advisory board formed in the United States in 1946 for the domestic control of atomic energy.

atomic heat *n.* The product of an element's atomic weight and its specific heat capacity.

at·o·mic·i·ty (áttə-míssəti) *n.* **1.** The state of being composed of atoms. **2.** *Chemistry.* **a.** The number of atoms in a molecule. **b.** Valency.

atomic mass *n.* The mass of an atomic system or constituent, usually expressed in atomic mass units. See **relative atomic mass.**

atomic mass unit *n. Abbr.* **amu** A unit of mass equal to $1/12$ the mass of the carbon isotope with mass number 12, approximately 1.6604×10^{-24} gram. Also called "dalton".

atomic number *n. Symbol* **Z** The number of protons in an atomic nucleus. Also called "proton number".

atomic pile *n.* A **nuclear reactor** *(see).*

atomic power *n.* **Nuclear power** *(see).*

atomic reactor *n.* A **nuclear reactor** *(see).*

atomic theory *n.* **1.** The physical theory of the structure, properties, and behaviour of the atom. **2.** Atomism.

atomic volume *n.* The ratio of an element's atomic weight to its density.

atomic weight *n. Abbr.* **at wt** The average weight of an atom of an element, usually expressed relative to one atom of the carbon isotope taken to have a standard weight of 12. Also called "relative atomic mass".

at·om·ise, at·om·ize (áttəm-īz) *tr.v.* **-ised, ising, -ises. 1.** To reduce or separate into atoms. **2. a.** To reduce (a liquid) to a spray. **b.** To spray (a liquid) in this form. **3.** To subject to bombardment with atomic weapons. **4.** To reduce to individual parts or units; fragment. **—at·om·i·sa·tion** (-ī-záysh'n || *U.S.* -i-) *n.*

at·om·is·er (áttəm-īzər) *n.* A device for producing a fine spray, especially of perfume or medicine.

at·om·ism (áttəm-iz'm) *n.* **1.** The ancient theory of Democritus, Epicurus, and Lucretius, according to which simple, indivisible, and indestructible atoms are the basic components of the entire universe. **2.** In sociology, any theory according to which social institutions and processes arise solely from the acts of individuals. **3.** In political theory: **a.** The division or tendency to divide into subclasses, groups, or units of a given society. **b.** Such a tendency accompanied by or arising from a strong subjective individualism. **—at·om·ist** *n.* **—at·om·is·tic** (-ístik), **at·om·is·ti·cal** *adj.* **—at·om·is·ti·cal·ly** *adv.*

atom smasher *n.* An atomic particle **accelerator** *(see).*

at·o·my (áttəmi) *n., pl.* **-mies.** *Archaic.* **1.** A tiny particle. **2.** A tiny being: *"Drawn with a team of little atomies"* (Shakespeare). [Latin *atomī*, plural of *atomus*, ATOM.]

Aton. Variant of **Aten.**

a·to·nal (ay-tṓn'l, a-, ə-) *adj. Music.* Lacking a tonal centre or established key. Compare **serial, twelve-tone. —a·to·nal·ism** *n.* **—a·to·nal·ly** *adv.*

a·to·nal·i·ty (áy-tō-nál-əti) *n. Music.* **1.** The lack of a tonal centre or key in musical composition, or the deliberate disregarding of it, especially as an alternative to the diatonic system. **2.** The theory of atonal composition.

a·tone (ə-tṓn) *v.* **atoned, atoning, atones.** *—intr.* **1.** To make amends, as for a sin or fault. Used with *for.* **2.** *Archaic.* To agree. *—tr. Archaic.* **1.** To expiate. **2.** To reconcile or harmonise. **3.** To conciliate; appease. [Middle English *atonen*, to be reconciled, from *at one*, of one mind, in accord : AT + ONE.] **—a·ton·a·ble, a·tone·a·ble** *adj.* **—a·ton·er** *n.*

a·tone·ment (ə-tṓn-mənt) *n.* **1.** Amends or reparation made for an injury or wrong; expiation; recompense. **2.** *Judaism.* Man's annual reconciliation with God after transgressing his law, and with his fellow man after quarrelling. **3.** *Capital* **A.** *Theology.* **a.** The redemptive life, suffering, and death of Christ. **b.** The reconciliation of God and man thus brought about by Christ.

a·ton·ic (ay-tónnik, a-, ə-) *adj.* **1.** Not accented: *atonic words and syllables.* **2.** *Pathology.* Pertaining to, caused by, or characterised by atony.

~n. A word, syllable, or sound that is unaccented. [French *atonique*, from Greek *atonos.* See **atony.**] **—at·o·nic·i·ty** (áttə-níssəti, áytō-) *n.*

at·o·ny (áttəni) *n.* **1.** *Pathology.* **1.** Insufficient muscular tone. **2.** *Phonetics.* Lack of accent or stress. [Late Latin *atonia*, from Greek, from *atonos*, not stretched : *a-*, without + *tonos*, a stretching, TONE.]

a·top (ə-tóp) *adv. Archaic.* On or at the top.

~prep. On top of. **—a·top** *adj.*

-ator *n. suffix.* Indicates one that acts or does; for example, **aviator, radiator.** [Middle English *-atour*, from Old French, from Latin *-ātor* : *-ātus*, -ATE + -OR.]

-atory *adj. suffix.* Indicates pertinence to, characteristic of, result of, or effect of; for example, **placatory, perspiratory, amendatory.** [Middle English, from Latin *-ātōrius* : *-ātus*, -ATE + *-ōrius*, -ORY.]

ATP *n. Biochemistry.* *A*denosine *t*ri*p*hosphate: a nucleotide, $C_{10}H_{16}N_5O_{13}P_3$, occurring in plant and animal cells, that is a major energy source for vital processes. The energy is released when ATP is converted to ADP.

at·ra·bil·i·ous (áttrə-bíl-i-əss) *adj.* Also **at·ra·bil·i·ar** (-i-ər). *Formal.* **1.** Inclined to melancholy. **2.** Having a peevish disposition; surly. [Latin *ātra bīlis*, black bile (translation of Greek *melankhōlia*, MELANCHOLY) : *ātra*, feminine of *āter*, black + *bīlis*, BILE.] **—at·ra·bil·i·ous·ness** *n.*

A·treus (áy-tri-ōōss, -trōōss, -əss). *Greek Mythology.* A king of Mycenae, father of Agamemnon and Menelaus.

a·tri·o·ven·tric·u·lar (áytri-ō-ven-tríckew-lər) *adj. Anatomy.* Pertaining to the atria and the ventricles of the heart. [New Latin *atrio-*, heart chamber, ATRIUM + VENTRICULAR.]

a·trip (ə-tríp) *adj. Nautical.* Just clear of the bottom; aweigh. Said of an anchor. [A- (on) + TRIP (to raise an anchor).] **—a·trip** *adv.*

a·tri·um (áytri-əm) *n., pl.* **-ums** or **atria** (-ə) **1. a.** An open central court, especially in an ancient Roman house. **b.** A central courtyard in a multistorey building that serves as a lightwell, typically has a glazed roof, and often features such amenities as plants and seats. **2.** A body cavity or chamber; especially, either of the two upper chambers of the heart. In this sense, also called "auricle". **3.** A court in front of a church, often surrounded by colonnades. [Latin *ātrium;* akin to *āter*, black, blackened (by fire), perhaps with reference to the part of a Roman house blackened by smoke from the hearth.] **—a·tri·al** *adj.*

a·tro·cious (ə-trṓshəss) *adj.* **1.** Extremely evil or cruel; monstrous: *an atrocious crime.* **2.** *Informal.* Exceptionally bad; terrible: *atrocious decor; atrocious behaviour.* [Latin *ātrōx* (stem *ātrōc-*), "dark-looking", horrible, cruel; akin to *āter*, black.] **—a·tro·cious·ly** *adv.* **—a·tro·cious·ness** *n.*

a·troc·i·ty (ə-tróssəti) *n., pl.* **-ties. 1.** Atrocious condition, quality, or behaviour; monstrousness; vileness. **2. a.** An atrocious action, situation, or object; an outrage. **b.** *Often plural.* A savage or brutal act committed in wartime.

at·ro·phy (áttrə-fi) *n., pl.* **-phies. 1.** *Pathology.* The emaciation or wasting of tissues, organs, or the entire body. **2.** Any wasting away or diminution: *moral atrophy.*

~v. **atrophied, -phying, -phies.** *—tr.* To cause to wither; affect with atrophy. *—intr.* To waste away; wither. [Late Latin *atrophia*, from Greek, from *atrophos*, ill-nourished : *a-*, without + *trophē*, nourishment, from *trephein*, to feed.] **—a·troph·ic** (a-tróffik, ə-), **at·ro·phous** (áttrəfəss) *adj.*

at·ro·pine (áttrə-peen, -pin) *n.* Also **at·ro·pin** (-pin). An extremely poisonous, bitter, crystalline alkaloid, $C_{17}H_{23}NO_3$, obtained from deadly nightshade and related plants. It is used to dilate the pupil of the eye, as an antispasmodic, to treat peptic ulcers and similar conditions, and as premedication before general anaesthesia. [New Latin *Atropa*, genus of belladonna, deadly nightshade, from Greek *atropos*, unchangeable, inflexible. See **Atropos.**]

At·ro·pos (áttrə-poss, -pəss). *Greek Mythology.* The one of the three **Fates** *(see)* who cuts the thread of life. [Greek, from *atropos*, inexorable, inflexible : *a-*, not + *trop-*, stem of *trepein*, to turn.]

A.T.S. 1. Auxiliary Territorial Service. **2.** Army Transport Service.

at·ta·boy (áttəboy) *interj.* Used to express encouragement or approval. [Slang respelling of *that's a boy!*]

at·tach (ə-tách) *v.* **-tached, -taching, -taches.** *—tr.* **1.** To fasten in a specified position to; connect or join. **2.** To connect as an adjunct or associated part. **3.** To affix or append; add. **4.** To ascribe or assign: *I attach no significance to the threat.* **5.** To bind by personal ties, as of affection or loyalty. Usually used in the passive with *to*: *He's very attached to his mother.* **6.** To appoint officially. **7.** *Military.* To assign (personnel) to a unit on a temporary basis. Compare **assign. 8.** *Law.* To seize (persons or property) by legal writ. **9.** *Law.* To order the withholding of payment of (a debt) because a third party holds judgment for money against the creditor. **10.** To cause (oneself) to be part of or associated with. *—intr.* **1.** To become attached; adhere. **2.** To be an integral part of something: *Misery attaches to such a way of life.* [Middle English *attachen*, from Old French *attacher, estachier*, to fasten (with a stake), from *estache*, STAKE.] **—at·tach·a·ble** *adj.* **—at·tach·er** *n.*

at·ta·ché (ə-táshay, a- || *U.S.* áttə-sháy) *n.* A person officially assigned to the staff of a diplomatic mission to serve in some particular capacity: *a cultural attaché.* [French, "one attached (to a diplomatic mission)", past participle of *attacher*, ATTACH.]

attaché case *n.* A briefcase resembling a small suitcase, with hinges and flat sides, used for carrying papers.

at·tached (ə-tácht) *adj.* Married, engaged, or committed to a serious romantic or sexual relationship.

at·tach·ment (ə-táchmənt) *n.* **1.** The act of attaching or the condition of being attached. **2.** Something that serves to attach one thing to another; a tie, band, or fastening. **3.** Fond regard; affection. **4.** A supplementary part; an accessory: *an attachment for a blender.* **5.** *Law.* **a.** The legal seizure of a person or property. **b.** The writ ordering such a seizure. **6.** *Law.* The procedure by which debts are attached. —See Synonyms at **appendage.**

at·tack (ə-ták) *v.* **-tacked, -tacking, -tacks.** *—tr.* **1.** To set upon with violent force; begin hostilities against or conflict with. **2.** To bombard with hostile criticism. **3.** To start work on with purpose and vigour: *attack a problem.* **4.** To begin to affect harmfully: *a disease that attacks crops.* *—intr.* **1.** To make an attack; launch an assault. **2.** To play offensively or take the initiative in a sport or game.

~n. **1. a.** The act of attacking; an assault. **b.** A hostile criticism. **2.** An occurrence of or seizure by a disease or medical condition, especially one whose main symptoms recur at intervals: *an attack of asthma.* **3.** The act of setting to work on any task or undertaking. **4.** *Music.* **a.** The manner in which a passage or phrase is begun. **b.** Force and incisiveness in performing. **5.** *Sports.* The offensive players, or the positions taken up by them, in a game between two teams. [French *attaquer*, from Old French, from Old Italian *attaccare*, variant of *estaccare* (unattested), to attach, join (battle), from *stacca* (unattested), STAKE.] **—at·tack·er** *n.*

Synonyms: *attack, bombard, assail, storm, assault, beset.*

at·tain (ə-táyn) *v.* **-tained, -taining, -tains.** *—tr.* **1.** To gain, reach, or accomplish by mental or physical effort. **2.** To arrive at, as in time for example: *attain a ripe old age.* *—intr.* To succeed in gaining or reaching something; arrive at. Usually used with *to*: *He attained to the highest office in the land.* —See Synonyms at **reach.** [Middle English *atteignen*, from Anglo-French, from Old French *ataindre* (stem *ataign-*), to reach to, from Vulgar Latin *attangere* (unattested), from Latin *attingere* : *ad-*, to + *tangere*, to touch.] **—at·tain·a·ble** *adj.* **—at·tain·a·bil·i·ty** (-ə-bílləti), **at·tain·a·ble·ness** *n.*

at·tain·der (ə-táyndər) *n.* **1.** Formerly, the loss of a traitor's or felon's civil rights which followed a sentence of death or outlawry. See **bill of attainder. 2.** *Obsolete.* Dishonour. [Middle English *attendre,* conviction, from Anglo-French, noun use of *ateindre,* from Old French *ataindre,* to ATTAIN.]

at·tain·ment (ə-táynmənt) *n.* **1.** The act of attaining. **2.** Something that is attained; an accomplishment or acquisition.

at·taint (ə-táynt) *tr.v.* **-tainted, -tainting, -taints. 1.** *Law.* To condemn by a sentence of attainder. **2.** *Archaic.* To impart stigma to; disgrace. **3.** *Obsolete.* To accuse or prove guilty. Used with *of.*
~*n.* **1.** Attainder. **2.** *Archaic.* A disgrace; a stigma. [Middle English *attaynten,* from Old French *ataint,* past participle of *ataindre,* to convict, originally, to ATTAIN (sense influenced by TAINT).]

at·tar (áttər, *sometimes* áttaar) *n.* Also **ot·tar** (óttər), **ot·to** (óttō). A fragrant essential oil or perfume obtained from the petals of flowers, especially certain species of roses *(attar of roses).* [Persian *'atṭār,* perfumed, from *'iṭr,* perfume, from Arabic.]

at·tempt (ə-témpt) *tr.v.* **-tempted, -tempting, -tempts. 1.** To endeavour to do or achieve; try. **2.** To try to climb (a mountain). **3.** *Archaic.* To tempt. **4.** *Archaic.* To attack.
~*n.* **1. a.** An effort or try. **b.** A try at conquering or winning something: *an attempt on the world record.* **2.** An attack; an assault: *an attempt on one's life.* **3.** The result of an attempt, especially when unsuccessful. [Middle English *attempten,* from Old French *attempter,* from Latin *attemptāre* : *ad-,* to + *temptāre,* to try, TEMPT.] **—at·tempt·a·ble** *adj.* **—at·tempt·er** *n.*

at·tend (ə-ténd) *v.* **-tended, -tending, -tends.** *—tr.* **1.** To be present at: *attend school.* **2.** To accompany as a circumstance or follow as a result: *The speech was attended by wild applause.* **3.** To accompany as an attendant or servant; wait upon. **4.** To take care or charge of (a sick person, for example). **5.** *Archaic.* To listen to; heed. **6.** *Archaic.* To wait for; expect. *—intr.* **1.** To be present. **2.** To pay attention; heed. Used with *to.* **3.** To remain ready to serve; wait. Used with *on* or *upon*: *We attend upon your wishes.* **4.** To apply or direct oneself. Used with *to*: *Please attend to the matter at once.* **5.** To deal with the needs of; take care of. Used with *to*: *attend to a patient.* [Middle English *attenden,* from Old French *atendre,* from Latin *attendere,* to stretch towards, direct attention to : *ad-,* towards + *tendere,* to stretch.] **—at·tend·er** *n.*

at·ten·dance (ə-téndənss) *n.* **1.** The act of attending. **2.** The persons or number of persons who are present, as at a class.

attendance centre *n.* A place which young offenders in Britain are sentenced to attend regularly for supervision and guidance as an alternative to a custodial sentence.

at·ten·dant (ə-téndənt) *n.* **1.** One who attends; especially, one who waits on another. **2.** One who is present, as at a class. **3.** An accompanying thing or circumstance; a consequence or concomitant. **4.** One who is employed to provide a service, perform a particular function, or take care of something: *a lavatory attendant.*
~*adj.* Accompanying or consequent: *attendant circumstances.* **—at·tend·ant·ly** *adv.*

at·tend·ee (ə-tén-dée) *n. Informal.* An attender, as at a meeting.

at·ten·tion (ə-ténshən) *n. Abbr.* **attn. 1.** Concentration of the mental powers upon an object; a close or careful observing or listening. **2.** The ability or power to concentrate mentally. **3. a.** Observation; notice: *Your suggestion has come to our attention.* **b.** Consideration, especially with a view to deciding on a course of action. **4.** Consideration or courtesy. **5.** *Usually plural.* An act of courtesy, consideration, or gallantry indicating romantic interest. **6.** *Military.* **a.** A posture assumed by a soldier, with the body erect, eyes to the front, arms at the sides, and heels together. **b.** A command to assume this position. [Middle English *attencioun,* from Latin *attentiō* (stem *attentiōn-*), from *attendere,* ATTEND.] **—at·ten·tion·al** *adj.*

attention deficit disorder *n.* A syndrome in which a short attention span allegedly leads to hyperactivity and disruptive behaviour, as at school.

attention span *n.* The span of one's capacity for attention; how long one can concentrate uninterruptedly: "*people with the attention span of a flea*" (Michael Ignatieff).

at·ten·tive (ə-téntiv) *adj.* **1.** Paying attention; observant; listening. **2.** Courteous or devoted; considerate; thoughtful. **—at·ten·tive·ly** *adv.* **—at·ten·tive·ness** *n.*

at·ten·u·ate (ə-ténnew-ayt) *v.* **-ated, -ating, -ates.** *—tr.* **1.** To make slender, fine, or small. **2.** To reduce in strength, force, value, or amount; weaken. **3.** To lessen in density; dilute or rarefy (a liquid or gas). **4.** *Medicine.* To make (a pathogenic microorganism) less virulent, as by treating with heat or chemicals. *—intr.* To become thin, weak, fine, or reduced in power.
~*adj.* (-ət, -it, -ayt). **1.** Thinned; diluted; weakened. **2.** *Botany.* Gradually tapering to a point; slender and pointed. [Latin *attenuāre,* to make thin : *ad-,* to + *tenuāre,* to make thin, from *tenuis,* thin.] **—at·ten·u·a·ble** *adj.*

at·ten·u·a·tion (ə-ténnew-áysh'n) *n.* **1.** An act or instance of attenuating or the state of being attenuated. **2.** *Physics.* **a.** The loss in energy of radiation, sound, or the like as it passes through matter, primarily as a result of absorption or scattering. **b.** The power loss suffered by an electric current passing through a circuit.

at·ten·u·a·tor (ə-ténnew-aytər) *n.* Any device or object that causes attenuation; especially, a device that reduces the power of a wave, signal, or the like, without causing distortion.

at·test (ə-tést) *v.* **-tested, -testing, -tests.** *—tr.* **1.** To affirm to be correct, true, or genuine; corroborate. **2.** To certify by signature or oath; affirm officially. **3.** To supply evidence of: *His benevolent face attests his goodwill.* **4.** To constitute documentary or other material proof of the former existence of; authenticate. Used especially in archaeology and historical linguistics. **5.** To put under oath. *—intr.* To bear witness; give testimony. Used with *to* : *I attest to his good faith.*
~*n. Archaic.* An act of attesting. [French *attester,* from Old French, from Latin *attestārī* : *ad-,* to + *testārī,* to be a witness, from *testis,* witness.] **—at·test·ant** *n.* **—at·tes·ta·tion** (áttess-táysh'n) *n.* **—at·test·er, at·tes·tor** (-ər), **at·tes·ta·tor** (-aytər) *n.*

at·tic (áttik) *n.* **1.** A storey or room directly below the roof of a house. **2.** *Architecture.* A low wall or storey above the cornice of a classical façade. [French *attique,* "attic storey", a top storey above or enclosed by columns in an Attic style.]

Attic *adj.* **1.** Of, pertaining to, or characteristic of ancient Attica, Athens, or the Athenians. **2.** *Sometimes small* **a.** Characterised by classical purity and simplicity.
~*n.* The Ancient Greek dialect of Athens, in which the bulk of Classical Greek literature is written, belonging to Attic-Ionic.

At·ti·ca (áttikə). Region of ancient Greece, occupying the area around Athens. According to Greek legend there were four Attic tribes, unified into a single community by Theseus.

At·tic-I·on·ic (áttik-ī-ónnik) *n.* One of the four main dialects of ancient Greek, spoken in Attica and Ionia. Compare **Aeolic, Arcado-Cyprian, Doric.**

At·ti·cism (átti-siz'm) *n.* **1.** Something characteristic of the Attic Greek language. **2.** An expression or style of expression characterised by simplicity, conciseness, and elegance.

Attic salt *n.* Dry, delicate, pointed wit. Also called "Attic wit".

At·til·a (ə-tíllə, áttilə), also known as Attila the Hun (died 453). Leader of the Huns and the most notorious of the Barbarian invaders of the Roman Empire. From 441 he attacked the Empire repeatedly from the east, gaining much territory, but was checked at Constantinople (443), in Gaul (451), and in Italy (452).

at·tire (ə-tír) *tr.v.* **-tired, -tiring, -tires.** To dress, especially in elaborate or splendid garments; clothe.
~*n.* **1.** Clothing, especially of an elaborate or special kind: *formal attire.* **2.** *Heraldry.* The antlers of a deer. [Middle English *attiren,* from Old French *atirier,* to arrange into ranks, put in order : *a-,* from Latin *ad-,* to + *tire,* order, rank (see **tier**).]

at·ti·tude (átti-tewd || -tōōd) *n.* **1.** A position of the body or manner of carrying oneself, indicative of a mood or condition: *"men . . . sprawled alone or in heaps, in the careless attitudes of death"* (John Reed). **2.** A state of mind or feeling with regard to some matter. **3. a.** A disposition or way of behaving. **b.** *Slang.* Bad attitude; especially, a bloody-minded, bolshie attitude. **4.** *Aeronautics.* The orientation of an aircraft's axes relative to some reference line or plane, such as the horizon. **5.** *Aerospace.* The orientation of a spacecraft relative to its direction of motion. **6.** A ballet position in which a dancer stands on one leg with the other leg raised and bent backwards. [French, from Italian *attitudine,* disposition, from Late Latin *aptitūdō,* faculty, fitness, from Latin *aptus,* fit, APT.] **—at·ti·tu·di·nal** (-téw-din'l || -tōō-, -d'n'l) *adj.*

at·ti·tu·di·nise, at·ti·tu·di·nize (átti-téw-di-nīz || -tōō-, -d'n-īz) *intr.v.* **-nised, -nising, -nises.** To assume an affected attitude.

Att·lee (áttli), **Clement Richard Attlee, 1st Earl** (1883–1967). British politician. In 1935 he became leader of the Labour party. He was deputy prime minister (1942–45) in Churchill's wartime coalition government. As Labour prime minister from 1945 to 1951 he presided over the establishment of the National Health Service, the expansion of public ownership of industry, and the granting of independence to India. He received his peerage in 1955.

atto- *prefix. Symbol* **a** Indicates one trillionth (10^{-18}); for example, **attotesla.** [Danish or Norwegian *atten,* eighteen, from Old Norse *āttjān.*]

at·torn (ə-túrn) *intr.v.* **-torned, -torning, -torns.** *Law.* To acknowledge a new owner as landlord. [Middle English *attournen,* from Old French *atorner,* to turn to, assign to : *a-,* from Latin *ad-,* to + *torner,* to turn, from Latin *tornāre,* to TURN.] **—at·torn·ment** *n.*

at·tor·ney (ə-túrni) *n., pl.* **-neys.** *Abbr.* **atty. 1.** A person authorised by another to act on his behalf in legal and business matters. **2.** *U.S.* An attorney at law; a lawyer. —See Usage note at **lawyer.** [Middle English *attourney,* from Old French *atorne,* "one appointed", past participle of *atorner,* to appoint, ATTORN.] **—at·tor·ney·ship** *n.*

attorney at law *n.* In the United States, a lawyer qualified to perform the same functions as an English solicitor or barrister.

attorney general *n., pl.* **attorneys general** or **attorney generals. 1.** The chief law officer and legal counsel of the government of a state or country. **2.** In some states of the United States, a public prosecutor.

Attorney General *n., pl.* **Attorneys General** or **Attorney Generals.** *Abbr.* **A.G., Atty. Gen. 1.** In England and Wales, the Crown's chief legal adviser, who is usually also a Member of Parliament. **2.** In the United States, the chief law officer and legal adviser of the government, who is also a Cabinet member and head of the Department of Justice.

at·tract (ə-trákt) *v.* **-tracted, -tracting, -tracts.** *—tr.* **1.** To cause to draw near or adhere. **2.** To draw or direct to oneself by some quality or action: *attract attention.* **3.** To evoke interest or admiration in; allure. *—intr.* To possess or use the power of attraction; be magnetic or alluring. [Middle English *attracten,* from Latin *attrahere* (past participle *attractus*) : *ad-,* towards + *trahere,* to draw.] **—at·tract·a·ble** *adj.* **—at·trac·tor** (-ər), **at·tract·er** *n.*

at·tract·ant (ə-tráktənt) *n.* A substance that attracts, especially the chemical *(sex attractant)* produced by moths and other insects to attract opposite-sexed insects of the same species. See **pheromone**.

at·trac·tion (ə-tráksh'n) *n.* **1.** The act of attracting. **2.** The quality or power of attracting; allure; charm. **3.** A feature, characteristic, or factor that attracts. **4.** A public spectacle or entertainment. **5.** A force that causes one body to attract another body with which it is not in contact: *gravitational attraction; magnetic attraction*.

at·trac·tive (ə-tráktiv) *adj.* **1.** Having the power to attract. **2.** Pleasing to the eye or mind; appealing. **3.** Personally engaging; charming. —**at·trac·tive·ly** *adv.* —**at·trac·tive·ness** *n.*

at·trib·ute (ə-tríbbewt; *Note: there is also a commonly heard pronunciation* áttri-bewt, *regarded by purists as incorrect for the verb*) *tr.v.* **-uted, -uting, -utes.** To regard or assign as belonging to or resulting from someone or something; ascribe: *attribute a saying to Churchill.* ~*n.* (áttri-bewt). **1.** A quality or characteristic belonging to a person or thing; a distinctive feature. **2.** An object associated with and serving to identify a character, person, or office: *Lightning bolts are the attribute of Zeus.* **3.** *Grammar.* An adjective or a phrase used as an adjective. —See Synonyms at **quality**. [Latin *attribūtum*, "quality belonging to something", noun use of past participle of *attribuēre* : *ad-*, to + *tribuēre*, to allot, grant (see **tribute**).] —**at·trib·ut·a·ble** (ə-tríbbewtəb'l; *see note above*) *adj.* —**at·trib·ut·er, at·trib·u·tor** (ə-tríbbewtər; *see note above*) *n.*

Synonyms: attribute, ascribe, impute, credit, assign.

at·tri·bu·tion (áttri-béwsh'n) *n.* **1.** The act of attributing. **2.** Something that is ascribed; an attribute.

at·trib·u·tive (ə-tríbbewtiv) *adj.* **1.** Pertaining to or designating an adjective, or a word or phrase used adjectivally, that is directly attached to and usually in front of the noun it modifies, without being separated from it by a verb. For example, in the sentence *The young girl is ill, young* is an attributive adjective. Compare **predicative**. **2.** Of or having the nature of an attribution or attribute. **3.** Of an attributed origin: *an attributive Rubens.* ~*n. Grammar.* An attributive adjective or adjectival phrase. —**at·trib·u·tive·ly** *adv.* —**at·trib·u·tive·ness** *n.*

at·trit·ed (ə-trítid) *adj.* Worn down by attrition. [Latin *attrītus*, from past participle of *atterere*, to rub away. See **attrition**.]

at·tri·tion (ə-trísh'n) *n.* **1.** A rubbing away or wearing down by friction, especially of rock particles during transport by wind or water. **2.** The act or result of gradually wearing down and exhausting an opponent by constant stress and harassment; *a war of attrition.* **3.** *Chiefly U.S.* A gradual reduction in personnel, through retirement, resignation, or death; **natural wastage** *(see)*. **4.** *Theology.* Repentance for sin motivated by fear of punishment rather than by love of God. In this sense, compare **contrition**. ~*tr.v. U.S.* To reduce the number of (a work force) by not filling positions that have fallen vacant. [Middle English *attricioun*, from Medieval Latin *attrītiō* (stem *attrītiōn-*), "chastisement", from Latin, a rubbing against, from *atterere*, to rub against : *ad-*, against + *terere*, to rub.]

at·tune (ə-téwn ‖ ə-tŏŏn) *tr.v.* **-tuned, -tuning, -tunes. 1.** To bring into harmony. **2.** To accustom to a special perception. Usually used in the passive: *an ear attuned to dissonance.* **3.** To tune (an instrument). [16th century : AD- (to) + TUNE.]

atty. attorney.

Atty. Gen. attorney general.

a·twit·ter (ə-twittər) *adj.* In a state of nervous excitement.

At·wood (át-wŏŏd), **Margaret** (1939–). Canadian writer. Her works include a collection of poems, *The Circle Game* (1966), and the novels *The Handmaid's Tale* (1995) and *Alias Grace* (1996).

at wt atomic weight.

a·typ·i·cal (áy-típpik'l) *adj.* Also **a·typ·ic** (áy-típpik). Not typical; varying from the type. —**a·typ·i·cal·ly** *adv.*

Au The symbol for the element gold. [Latin *aurum*.]

A.U. astronomical unit.

au·bade (ō-báad) *n.* **1.** A musical composition intended to be played or sung at dawn or early in the morning. **2.** A poem appropriate to this time of day. [French, from Old French, from Old Provençal *auba, alba*, dawn, from Vulgar Latin *alba* (unattested), feminine of Latin *albus*, white.]

au·ber·gine (ōbər-zheen, -jeen) *n.* **1. a.** A tropical plant, *Solanum melongena*, cultivated for its edible fruit. **b.** The egg-shaped fruit of this plant, eaten as a vegetable and having a glossy, dark-purple skin. Also *chiefly U.S.* "eggplant". **2.** Blackish purple. [French, from Catalan *alberginia*, from Arabic *al-bādindjān*, from Persian *bādin-gān*, from Sanskrit *vātimgana*.]

Au·brey (áwbri), **John** (1626–97). English antiquarian and writer. His work, *Brief Lives* (published in the 19th century), contains brilliant sketches of his contemporaries.

Aubrey hole *n.* Any of the 56 holes that form the outer ring of the circle at Stonehenge. [After John AUBREY.]

au·brie·tia, au·bre·tia (aw-bréeshə) *n.* Any trailing plant of the genus *Aubrieta*, having purple or red flowers and widely cultivated in gardens. [New Latin, after Claude *Aubriet*, 18th-century French painter of animals and flowers, in whose honour it was named.]

au·burn (áwbərn) *n.* Reddish brown to brown. [Middle English *aborne*, blond, from Old French *auborne, alborne*, from Medieval Latin *alburnus*, whitish, from Latin *albus*, white.] —**au·burn** *adj.*

Au·bus·son (ō-bew-sóN, -bü-). Town in the Creuse département in central France. It has been famous for its manufacture of carpets and tapestries since the 16th century.

A.U.C. ab urbe condita.

Auck·land (áwklənd). The largest city and chief port of New Zealand, situated on an isthmus in the northern part of the North Island. It was the capital until 1865. —**Auck·land·er** *n.*

au cou·rant (ō-kōō-róN) *adj. French.* Informed on current affairs; up-to-date. [French, "in the current".]

auc·tion (áwk-sh'n ‖ ók-) *n.* **1.** A public sale in which property or items of merchandise are sold to the highest bidder. **2.** The bidding in the game of bridge. —**all over the auction.** *Australian Slang.* All over the place; everywhere. ~*tr.v.* **auctioned, -tioning, -tions.** To sell at or by an auction. Often used with *off.* [Latin *auctiō* (stem *auctiōn-*), (a sale by) increase (of bids), from *augēre*, to increase.]

auction bridge *n.* A variety of the game of bridge in which tricks made in excess of the contract are scored towards game. Compare **contract bridge**.

auc·tion·eer (áwk-sh'n-éer ‖ ók-) *n.* A person who conducts an auction and controls the bidding. ~*intr.v.* **auctioneered, -eering, -eers.** To act as an auctioneer.

auc·tion·eer·bird (áwk-sh'n-éer-burd ‖ ók-) *n.* A small Australian black-headed bird, *Orthonyx spaldingi*, that lives in mountain scrub and has a loud call. Also called "chowchilla".

auc·to·ri·al (awk-táwri-əl ‖ tór-) *adj.* Of or pertaining to an author; authorial. [Latin *auctor*, AUTHOR + -IAL.]

au·da·cious (aw-dáyshəss) *adj.* **1.** Fearlessly daring; bold. **2.** Lacking restraint or tact; arrogantly insolent. —See Synonyms at **brave, reckless**. [Latin *audāx* (stem *audāc-*), bold, from *audēre*, to dare, "be eager", from *avidus*, AVID.] —**au·da·cious·ly** *adv.* —**au·da·cious·ness** *n.*

au·dac·i·ty (aw-dássəti) *n., pl.* **-ties. 1.** Boldness; daring. **2.** Unrestrained impudence; presumption. **3.** An instance of boldness or presumption. —See Synonyms at **temerity**.

Au·den (áwd'n), **W(ystan) H(ugh)** (1907–73). British poet. In the 1930s he was a member of the literary circle that included Christopher Isherwood, with whom he wrote several verse dramas. From 1956 to 1961 he was Professor of Poetry at Oxford University.

au·di·bil·i·ty (áwdə-bílləti) *n.* The capacity to be heard.

au·di·ble (áwdəb'l) *adj.* Capable of being heard. [Late Latin *audībilis*, from *audīre*, to hear.] —**au·di·ble·ness** *n.* —**au·di·bly** *adv.*

au·di·ence (áwd-i-ənss, -yənss) *n.* **1.** A gathering of spectators or listeners, as at a concert, play or film. **2.** The readers, hearers, or viewers reached by a book, radio broadcast, or television programme. **3.** A formal meeting or conference, as with a king or pope. **4.** An opportunity to be heard or to express one's views. **5.** The act of hearing or attending. [Middle English, from Old French, from Latin *audientia*, from *audiēns* (stem *audient-*), present participle of *audīre*, to hear.]

au·di·ent (áwdi-ənt) *adj. Archaic.* Hearing; listening. [Latin *audiēns* (stem *audient-*), present participle of *audīre*, to hear.]

au·dile (áw-dīl) *adj. Psychology.* Capable of learning chiefly from auditory, rather than tactile or visual, stimuli. ~*n.* An audile person. [Latin *audīre*, to hear, by analogy with *tactile*]

au·di·o (áwdi-ō) *adj.* **1.** Of or pertaining to audible sound. **2. a.** Of or pertaining to the broadcasting of sound. **b.** Of or pertaining to the high-fidelity reproduction of sound. ~*n.* **1.** The audio part of television equipment. **2.** Audio broadcasting or reception. **3.** Audible sound. Compare **video**. [Independent use of AUDIO-.]

audio– *comb. form.* Indicates sound or hearing; for example, **audiometer**. [Latin *audīre*, to hear.]

audio frequency *n. Abbr.* **a.f., A.F., AF** A frequency in a range, usually between 15 and 20,000 hertz, characteristic of signals audible to the normal human ear.

au·di·o·lin·gual (áwdi-ō-líng-gwəl ‖ -gew-əl, -gewl) *adj.* Designating an approach to language-learning that involves speaking and listening rather than reading and writing.

au·di·ol·o·gy (áwdi-óllə ji) *n.* The scientific study of hearing; especially, the study and treatment of hearing defects. —**au·di·o·log·i·cal** (-ə-lójik'l) *adj.* —**au·di·ol·o·gist** (-óllə jist) *n.*

au·di·om·e·ter (áwdi-ómmitər) *n. Medicine.* An instrument for measuring hearing thresholds for pure tones of normally audible frequencies. —**au·di·o·met·ric** (-ə-méttrik, -ō-) *adj.* —**au·di·om·e·try** (-ómmətri) *n.*

au·di·o·phile (áwdi-ō-fīl) *n.* One who has a great interest in high-fidelity sound reproduction.

au·di·o·tape (áwdi-ō-tayp) *n.* A sound tape recording, as opposed to a videotape.

au·di·o·typ·ist (áwdi-ō-tīpist) *n.* One who types directly from tape recordings as opposed to written material. Compare **copy typist**. —**au·di·o·typ·ing** *n.*

au·di·o·vis·u·al (áwdi-ō-vízzew-əl, -vízhew-, -vizhoo- ‖ -vízzewl, -vízh'l) *adj. Abbr.* **A.V. 1.** Both audible and visible. **2.** Of or pertaining to educational materials, such as sound filmstrips, that present information in audible and visible form.

audiovisual aids *pl.n.* Also **audiovisuals.** Educational materials that present information in audible and visual form.

au·dit (áwdit) *n.* **1.** An examination of records or accounts to check their accuracy. **2.** An adjustment or correction of accounts. **3.** An examined and verified account. **4.** *Rare.* An audience or hearing. ~*v.* **audited, -diting, -dits.** —*tr.* **1.** To examine, verify, or correct (accounts, records, or claims). **2.** *U.S.* To register for and attend a college course without receiving academic credit. —*intr.* To examine accounts. [Middle English, from Latin *audītus*, a hearing, from the past participle of *audīre*, to hear.]

au·di·tion (aw-dĭsh'n) *n.* **1.** The act or sense of hearing. **2.** A presentation of something heard; a hearing. **3.** A performance given by an actor, musician, or other performer, as a test of his suitability for a particular job or role. —*v.* **auditioned, -tioning, -tions.** —*tr.* To give (a person) an audition. —*intr.* To perform or be tested in an audition. [Latin *audītiō* (stem *audītiōn-*), from *audīre*, to hear. See **audit.**]

au·di·tive (âwditiv) *adj.* Auditory.

au·di·tor (âwdĭtər) *n.* **1.** One who hears; a listener. **2.** One who audits accounts. **3.** *U.S.* One who audits a course of study. [Middle English *auditour*, from Old French *auditeur*, from Latin *audītor*, hearer (in Medieval Latin, also one who audits accounts), from *audīre*, to hear.]

au·di·to·ri·um (âwdi-tâwri-əm ‖ -tôri-) *n., pl.* **-ums** or **-toria** (-ə). **1.** The part of a theatre, concert hall, or similar building where the audience sits. **2.** A large building for public meetings or artistic performances. [Latin *audītōrium*, from *audīre*, to hear.]

au·di·to·ry (âwdi-tri, -təri) *adj.* Of or pertaining to the sense, the organs, or the experience of hearing. [Late Latin *audītōrius*, from Latin *audīre*, to hear.]

auditory nerve *n. Anatomy.* The **acoustic nerve** (see).

Au·du·bon (âwdə-bən, -bon), **John James** (1785–1851). American naturalist and painter, born in Haiti. He was the first ornithologist to ring birds so as to discover their migratory habits. His *Birds of America* (1827–38) is a classic of both naturalism and art.

A.U.E.W. Amalgamated Union of Engineering Workers.

au fait (ō fáy) *adj.* **1.** Skilled or knowledgeable; expert. **2.** Conversant or familiar. Often used with **with.** [French, "to the point".]

Auf·klä·rung (ówf-klair-ōong) *n. German.* The Enlightenment.

au fond (ō fôN) *adv. French.* Basically; essentially. [French, "at the bottom".]

auf Wie·der·seh·en (owf véedər-zayn, ówf) *interj. German.* Until we see one another again; farewell.

Aug. August.

Au·ge·an Stables (aw-jée-ən) *pl.n.* **1.** *Greek Mythology.* The stables of King Augeas, which had not been cleaned for 30 years and which Hercules had to clean as one of his 12 labours. **2.** A place or state of extreme filth or corruption. [After *Augeas*, king of Elis in Greek mythology.]

au·gend (âw-jend, -jénd) *n. Mathematics.* A quantity to which another quantity, the addend, is added. [Latin *augendum*, "the thing to be increased", gerundive of *augēre*, to increase.]

au·ger (âwgər) *n.* **1.** A tool with a corkscrew-shaped bit, for boring wood. **2.** A tool for boring into the earth. [Middle English *an auger*, originally *a nauger*, Old English *nafogār*, "tool for piercing wheel hubs".]

Au·ger effect (ówgər) *n. Physics.* The emission of an electron instead of a photon by an excited ion when a vacancy in an inner electron shell is filled. [After Pierre *Auger* (1899–1993), French physicist.]

aught[1], ought (awt; *also* owt *for sense 2*) *pron.* Also *regional* **owt** (owt, ōt). **1.** All: *For aught we know he may have changed his name.* **2.** *Archaic & British Regional.* Anything whatever; any least part. —*adv. Archaic.* At all; in any respect. [Middle English *aught, ought,* Old English *āuht, āwiht,* "ever a thing", anything.]

aught[2], ought (awt) *n. British Regional & U.S.* **1.** A cipher; the symbol 0; zero. **2.** *Archaic.* Nothing. [From *an aught,* originally *a* NAUGHT.]

au·gite (âw-gīt, -jīt) *n.* A dark green to black pyroxene mineral that contains aluminium, iron, and magnesium. [Latin *augītēs*, a precious stone, from Greek *augitēs*, from *augē*, ray, brightness.]

aug·ment (awg-mént, âwg-) *v.* **-mented, -menting, -ments.** —*tr.* **1.** To add to so as to make greater, as in size, extent, or quantity; enlarge; increase. **2.** *Music.* To increase (a perfect or major interval) by a semitone. Compare **diminish.** —*intr.* To become greater; enlarge. —See Synonyms at **increase.** —*n.* (âwg-ment). *Grammar.* A way of indicating the past tense in Greek and Sanskrit verbs, consisting of the prefixing of a vowel or the lengthening of the initial vowel. [Middle English *augmenten*, from Old French *augmenter*, from Late Latin *augmentāre*, from *augmentum*, increase, from Latin *augēre*, to increase.] —**aug·ment·a·ble** *adj.*

aug·men·ta·tion (âwg-men-táysh'n) *n.* **1. a.** The act or process of augmenting. **b.** The condition of being augmented. **2.** Something that enlarges or increases; an addition. **3.** *Music.* The repetition of a theme in notes of usually double the value of those originally assigned to it. Compare **diminution.**

aug·men·ta·tive (awg-méntətiv) *adj.* Also **aug·men·tive** (awg-méntiv). **1.** Having the tendency or ability to augment. **2.** *Grammar.* Designating a word or affix that produces an increase in size or intensity when added to another word, such as *super-* in *superstar.* Compare **diminutive.** —*n.* Also **aug·men·tive.** An augmentative word or affix.

aug·men·ted (awg-méntid, âwg-) *adj. Music.* Increased from the corresponding major or perfect interval by a semitone. Said of an interval.

au gra·tin (ō gráttaN ‖ aw grátt'n, *U.S. also* graát'n) *adj.* Covered with breadcrumbs and sometimes grated cheese, and browned in an oven or grilled: *cauliflower au gratin.* [French, "with the crust (of bread crumbs)".] —**au gra·tin** *adv.*

Augs·burg (ówgz-burg; *German* ówks-boork). Industrial city in Ba-

varia, Germany, lying on the river Lech. It was the home of the great banking families of Fugger and Welser.

au·gur (âwgər) *n.* **1.** One of a group of religious officials of ancient Rome who foretold events by observing and interpreting signs and omens. **2.** A seer or prophet; a soothsayer. —*v.* **augured, -guring, -gurs.** —*tr.* **1.** To predict or prognosticate, as from signs or omens. **2.** To serve as an omen of; betoken. —*intr.* **1.** To conjecture or foretell from signs or omens. **2.** To be a sign or omen. Used in the phrase *augur ill* or *well.* —See Synonyms at **foretell.** [Latin *augur, auger : au-,* perhaps from *avis*, bird + *gerere,* to do, perform (with reference to observing birds' flight or examining their viscera as a means of divination). See **auspice.**] —**au·gu·ral** (âwgew-rəl) *adj.*

au·gu·ry (âwgewri) *n., pl.* **-ries.** **1.** The art, ability, or practice of auguring; divination. **2.** The rite performed by an augur. **3.** A sign or omen; an indication. [Middle English *augurie*, from Old French, from Latin *augurium*, from *augur,* AUGUR.]

au·gust (aw-gúst ‖ âw-gust) *adj.* **1.** Inspiring awe or admiration; majestic. **2.** Venerable for reasons of age or high rank. —See Synonyms at **grand.** [Latin *augustus,* venerable, magnificent.] —**au·gust·ly** *adv.* —**au·gust·ness** *n.*

Au·gust (âwgəst) *n. Abbr.* **Aug.** The eighth month of the year according to the Gregorian calendar. August has 31 days. [Middle English *August,* Old English *August,* from Latin *(mensis) Augustus,* (month) of Augustus, after the emperor AUGUSTUS.]

Au·gus·tan (aw-gústən) *adj.* **1.** Pertaining to or characteristic of the emperor Augustus or his reign or times. **2.** Pertaining to or characteristic of any era resembling the reign of Augustus, as in classicism and refinement. —*n.* A writer in an Augustan age.

Augustan age *n.* **1.** The golden age of Latin literature during the reign of Augustus (27 B.C. to A.D. 14), to which Horace, Livy, and Ovid belonged. **2.** A similar period of great literary achievement, as during the 18th century in England.

Au·gus·tine of Canterbury (aw-gústin ‖ âwgəst-in, -een), **Saint** (died 605). Founder of the Christian Church in southern Britain and first Archbishop of Canterbury. A Benedictine prior, he was appointed by Pope Gregory I to lead an evangelising mission to Britain in 597. He was received by King Ethelbert of Kent, who gave him land at Canterbury. Ethelbert adopted the Christian faith and in 598 Augustine was ordained as bishop of the English at Arles.

Augustine of Hippo (híppō), **Saint** (354–430). Latin Father and Doctor of the Church. Raised as a Christian, he abandoned the faith for Manichaeism after studying in Carthage. He later came under the influence of Saint Ambrose, Bishop of Milan, and in 387 was baptised. In 391 he was chosen by the Christians of Hippo (in present-day Algeria) to be their priest. He remained in Hippo for the rest of his life, becoming bishop *c.* 395. His *Confessions* (*c.* 400) and *The City of God* (after 412), are eloquent and moving testaments of Christian piety and belief.

Au·gus·tin·i·an (âwgəss-tínni-ən) *adj.* **1.** Pertaining to Saint Augustine of Hippo or his doctrines. **2.** Designating or belonging to any order following or influenced by the rule of Saint Augustine. —*n.* **1.** A follower of the principles and doctrines of Saint Augustine of Hippo. **2.** A monk or friar belonging to any of the Augustinian orders. —**Au·gus·tin·i·an·ism, Au·gus·tin·ism** *n.*

Au·gus·tus (âw-gústəss) *n.* **1.** A title of the Roman emperors. **2.** After Hadrian, the title of the senior emperor as distinct from his junior colleague, the **Caesar** (see). [Latin *Augustus,* AUGUST, "Imperial Majesty", adopted by Octavian as a personal title when he acquired supreme power.]

Augustus, born Gaius Octavius, also known as Gaius Julius Caesar Octavian (63 B.C.–A.D. 14). First Roman emperor, the grandnephew of Julius Caesar. Named by Caesar as his heir, Octavian became leader of the faction against Mark Antony. In 43 B.C. he, Antony, and Lepidus formed the Second Triumvirate, whose armies defeated Brutus and Cassius at Philippi in 42. Antony's intrigues with Cleopatra led to the appointment of Octavian as general in 31. Following the defeat of Antony and Cleopatra at Actium in the same year, Octavian controlled all the lands of the Empire. In 29 the senate named him *imperator,* or emperor, and in 27 gave him the honorary title of Augustus. He subsequently devoted himself to consolidating Caesar's conquests, restoring civilian rule in Rome, building roads, and reforming the taxation system.

au jus (ō zhōō, zhü) *adj.* Served with the natural juices or gravy: *roast beef au jus.* [French, "with juice".]

auk (awk) *n., pl.* **auks** or collectively **auk.** Any of several sea birds of the family Alcidae, of northern regions, having a squat body, short wings, and black and white plumage, such as the **razorbill** (see). See **great auk, little auk.** [Norwegian *alk, alka,* from Old Norse *ālka.*]

auk·let (âwk-lət, -lit) *n.* Any of various small auks of the genus *Aethia* and related genera, of northern Pacific coasts and waters.

au lait (ō láy) *adj.* Cooked or served with milk. [French, "with milk".]

auld (awld) *adj. Scottish.* Old.

auld lang syne (áwld láng zīn, sīn) *n.* The good old days long past. [Scottish, "old long since" : AULD + LANGSYNE.]

au·lic (áwlik) *adj. Archaic.* Pertaining to a royal court; courtly. [French *aulique,* from Latin *aulicus,* from Greek *aulikos,* from *aulē,* court.]

Au·lic Council (áwlik) *n.* The emperor's privy council in the Holy

Roman Empire from 1498, when it was established by Maximilian I, until the dissolution of the Empire in 1806.

aumbry. Variant of **ambry.**

au na·tu·rel (ṓ náttŏō-rél, natü-) *adj.* **1.** In a natural state; nude. **2.** Cooked simply. Said of food. [French, "in the natural".]

aunt (aant ‖ ant) *n.* **1.** The sister of one's father or mother. **2.** The wife of one's uncle. [Middle English *aunte,* from Anglo-French, from Old French *ante,* from Latin *amita,* paternal aunt.]

aunt·ie, aunt·y (áanti ‖ ánti) *n.* **1.** Variant of **aunt.** Used as a familiar form of address. **2.** Any adult female friend of one's parents. Used by children. **3.** A familiar form of address used in some parts of Africa for any woman older than oneself.

Aunt·ie (áanti ‖ ánti) *n. British Informal.* The B.B.C., especially when thought of affectionately as a rather old-fashioned institution.

aunt Fanny *Interj.* Used, chiefly with *my,* to express scornful disbelief.

Aunt Sally *n., pl.* **Aunt Sallies.** *British.* **1.** A fairground game in which sticks or balls are thrown at a wooden dummy. **2. a.** Someone or something that is the object of insults or derision. **b.** Any easy target of criticism; a scapegoat. [After the fairground dummy, usually the head of an old woman smoking a clay pipe.]

au pair (ṓ páir) *n.* Also **au pair girl.** A foreign girl who lives with a family, doing housework and looking after the children in exchange for board and lodging.
~*intr.v.* **au paired, au pairing, au pairs.** To work as an au pair. [French, "on equal basis", by exchange of services rather than money.]

au·ra (áwrə) *n., pl.* **-ras** or **aurae** (áwree). **1.** An invisible breath or emanation. **2.** A distinctive air or quality that characterises a person or thing: *an aura of nobility.* **3.** A supposed emanation of light surrounding a person, and visible to people claiming psychic powers. **4.** A sensation, as of a cold breeze or flashes of light, preceding the onset of certain nervous disorders, especially epilepsy. [Middle English, from Latin, from Greek : breath, breeze, akin to *āēr,* AIR.]

au·ral¹ (áwrəl. *Note: to avoid confusion with oral some speakers have adopted the pronunciation* ṓw-rəl) *adj.* Of, pertaining to, or perceived by the ear.
~*n.* An aural examination in music. [Latin *auris,* ear + -AL.]

aural² (áwrəl) *adj.* Characterised by or pertaining to an aura.

au·re·ate (áwri-ət, -it, -ayt) *adj.* **1.** Of a golden colour; gilded. **2.** Speaking in or characterised by a florid and pompous style. [Middle English *aureat,* from Medieval Latin *aureātus,* from Latin *aureus,* golden, from *aurum,* gold.] —**au·re·ate·ly** *adv.* —**au·re·ate·ness** *n.*

Au·re·li·an (aw-réeli-ən), also known as Lucius Domitius Aurelianus. (A.D. *c.* 215–275). Roman emperor (270–275). In a series of victories he held the barbarians in check beyond the Rhine and regained Britain, Gaul, Spain, Syria, and Egypt for the Empire.

au·re·ole (áwri-ōl) *n.* Also **au·re·o·la** (aw-rée-ələ). **1.** A circle of light or radiance surrounding the head or body of a representation of a deity or holy person; a halo. **2.** A bright, circumferential region around a luminous celestial body, such as the sun or moon, especially when observed through a haze or fog. **3.** *Geology.* A zone around an intrusion which has been altered by the heat and chemicals generated during the intrusion of the magma. [Middle English *aureole, auriole,* from Old French *auriole,* from Medieval Latin *(corōna) aureola,* golden (crown), from Latin *aureolus,* golden, from *aurum,* gold.]

Au·re·o·my·cin (áwri-ō-mí-sin) *n.* A trademark for **chlortetracycline** (*see*).

au·re·us (áwri-əss) *n., pl.* **aurei** (-ī). A gold coin of the late Roman Republic and of the Roman Empire.

au re·voir (ṓ rə-vwár) *interj. French.* Until we meet again; goodbye.

au·ric¹ (áwrik) *adj.* Of, pertaining to, derived from, or containing gold, especially with valency 3. [Latin *aurum,* gold.]

auric² *adj.* Of or pertaining to an aura.

au·ri·cle (áwrik'l) *n.* Also **au·ric·u·la** (aw-rickew-lə) *pl.* **-lae** (-lee) or **-las.** **1.** *Anatomy.* **a.** The external part of the ear; the pinna. **b.** An atrium (*see*) of the heart. **2.** *Biology.* Any earlike part, process, or appendage, especially at the base of an organ. [Latin *auricula,* diminutive of *auris,* ear.] —**au·ri·cled** (áwrik'ld) *adj.*

au·ric·u·la (aw-rickew-lə) *n., pl.* **-las** or **-lae** (-lee). **1.** A species of primrose, *Primula auricula,* native to the Alps but widely cultivated, having clusters of variously coloured flowers. Also called "bear's-ear". **2.** Variant of **auricle.** [New Latin, "little ear" (from the shape of the leaves), from Latin, AURICLE.]

au·ric·u·lar (aw-rickew-lər) *adj.* **1.** Of or pertaining to the sense or organs of hearing. **2.** Perceived by or spoken into the ear: *an auricular confession.* **3.** Having the shape of an ear. **4.** Of or pertaining to an auricle of the heart.
~*n. Plural.* The feathers covering the opening of the ear in some birds, such as owls. [Late Latin *auriculāris,* from *auricula,* AURICLE.] —**au·ric·u·lar·ly** *adv.*

au·ric·u·late (aw-rickew-lət, -lit, -layt) *adj.* Also **au·ric·u·lat·ed** (-laytid). **1.** Having ears or earlike parts or extensions: *an auriculate leaf.* **2.** Having the shape of an ear. [Latin *auricula,* AURICLE.] —**au·ric·u·late·ly** *adv.*

au·rif·er·ous (aw-ríffərəss) *adj.* Containing gold; gold-bearing. Said of rocks or gravels. [Latin *aurifer : aurum,* gold + -FER.]

au·ri·form (áwri-fawrm) *adj.* Ear-shaped. [Latin *auris,* ear + -FORM.]

Au·ri·ga (aw-rígə) *n.* A constellation in the Northern Hemisphere near Lynx and Perseus. Also called the "Charioteer". [Latin *aurīga,* charioteer.]

Au·rig·na·cian (áwrig-náysh'n, áwreen-yásh'n) *adj. Sometimes small a. Archaeology.* Of or relating to the Upper Palaeolithic culture between Mousterian and Solutrean, associated with Cro-Magnon man, and characterised by artefacts such as figures of stone and bone, and the use of dress and adornment. [After *Aurignac,* commune in the French Pyrenees, near which such artefacts were found.]

au·rochs (áw-roks ‖ ów-) *n.* **1.** An extinct bovine mammal, *Bos taurus primigenius,* of northern Africa, Europe, and western Asia, believed to be the forerunner of domestic cattle. Also called "urus". **2.** Loosely, the European bison, or wisent. [German, from Old High German *ūrohso : ūro,* bison, from Germanic *ūrus* (unattested) + *ohso,* OX.]

au·ro·ra (aw-ráwrə, ə- ‖ -rṓrə) *n.* **1.** High-altitude, many-coloured, flashing luminosity, visible in night skies of polar and sometimes temperate zones, and thought to be caused by the capture of charged particles, especially ones of solar origin, by the earth's magnetic field. Compare **airglow.** **2.** *Poetic.* The dawn. **3.** *Rare.* An early part or stage; a beginning. [Latin *aurōra,* dawn.]

Au·ro·ra (aw-ráwrə ‖ -rṓrə). *Roman Mythology.* The goddess of the dawn, identified with the Greek goddess Eos.

aurora aus·tra·lis (o-stráyliss, aw-) *n.* Aurora occurring in southern regions. Also called "southern lights". [New Latin : AURORA + AUSTRAL.]

aurora bo·re·al·is (báwri-áyliss ‖ bṓri-) *n.* Aurora occurring in northern regions. Also called "northern lights". [New Latin : AURORA + BOREAL.]

au·ro·ral (aw-ráwrəl, ə- ‖ -rṓrəl) *adj.* Also *poetic* **au·ro·re·an** (aw-ráwri-ən ‖ -rṓri-) (for sense 1). **1.** Pertaining to or resembling the dawn. **2.** *Meteorology.* Pertaining to, caused by, or like an aurora. —**au·ro·ral·ly** *adv.*

au·rous (áwrəss) *adj.* Of or pertaining to gold, especially with valency 1. [Late Latin *aurōsus,* from Latin *aurum,* gold.]

au·rum (áwrəm) *n. Symbol* **Au** The element gold. [Latin, gold.]

Aus. **1.** Australia; Australian. **2.** Austria; Austrian.

Auschwitz. See **Oświęcim.**

aus·cul·tate (áwss-kəl-tayt, óss-, -kul-) *v.* **-tated, -tating, -tates.** *Medicine.* —*tr.* To examine (a person) by auscultation. —*intr.* To examine by auscultation. [Back-formation from AUSCULTATION.] —**aus·cul·ta·tive** (-taytiv, aw-skúltətiv) *adj.* —**aus·cul·ta·to·ry** (-taytəri, awskúltə-tri, -təri) *adj.*

aus·cul·ta·tion (áwss-kəl-táysh'n, óss-, -kul-) *n.* **1.** *Medicine.* Diagnostic monitoring, with a stethoscope or other instrument, of sounds within the body. **2.** The act of listening. [Latin *auscultātiō* (stem *auscultātiōn-*), from *auscultāre,* to listen to.]

aus·form (ówss-fawrm) *tr.v.* **-formed, -forming, -forms.** To subject a metal, especially steel, to deformation, quenching, and tempering while it is in the austenite temperature range, in order to improve its wear properties. [*Austenitic* de*form.*]

Aus·gleich (ówss-glīkh) *n., pl.* **-gleiche** (-ə). *German.* Compromise; agreement; specifically, the treaty between Hungary and Austria in 1867 organising their dual monarchy.

aus·pex (áwspeks) *n., pl.* **auspices** (áwspisseez). An augur of ancient Rome, especially one who interpreted omens taken from the actions of birds. [Latin. See **auspice.**]

aus·pi·cate (áwspikayt) *tr.v.* **-cated, -cating, -cates.** *Rare.* To begin or inaugurate with a ceremony designed to bring good luck. [Latin *auspicārī,* from *auspex,* bird augur. See **auspice.**]

aus·pice (áwspiss) *n., pl.* **auspices** (-iz ‖ -eez). **1.** *Usually plural.* Protection or support; patronage. Used in the phrase *under the auspices of.* Compare **aegis.** **2.** A portent, omen, or augury, especially when observed in the actions of birds. **3.** Observation of and divination from the actions of birds. [Latin *auspicium,* bird divination, from *auspex* (stem *auspic-*), a bird augur : *au-,* from *avis,* bird + *-spex,* from *specere,* to look.]

aus·pi·cious (aw-spíshəss) *adj.* **1.** Attended by favourable circumstances; promising. **2.** Marked by success; fortunate; prosperous. —See Synonyms at **favourable.** —**aus·pi·cious·ly** *adv.* —**aus·pi·cious·ness** *n.*

Aus·sie (ózzi) *n. Slang.* **1.** An Australian. **2.** Australia. —**Aus·sie** *adj.*

Aust. **1.** Austria; Austrian. **2.** Australia; Australian.

Aus·ten (óstin, áwstin), Jane (1775–1817). English novelist. Although her subject matter and personal experience may have been limited, her novels, which include *Sense and Sensibility* (1811), *Pride and Prejudice* (1813), *Mansfield Park* (1814), and *Emma* (1816), are notable for their incisive social satire, irony, and wit, and for their fine observation of manners and morality.

aus·ten·ite (óss-tin-īt, áwss-) *n.* **1.** A nonmagnetic solid solution of ferric carbide or carbon in iron, used in making corrosive-resistant steel. **2.** Any solid solution based on the gamma phase of iron, especially when stabilised by the addition of nickel. [After Sir William Roberts-*Austen* (1843–1902), British metallurgist.]

aus·ten·it·ic (óss-ti-níttik, áwss-) *adj.* Designating a form of steel that contains sufficient nickel, nickel and chromium, or manganese to maintain the structure of austenite: *austenitic stainless steel.*

Aus·ter (áwstər) *n. Poetic.* The south wind. [Latin *auster†,* south wind, the south.]

aus·tere (aw-stéer, o-) *adj.* **1.** Severe or stern in disposition or appearance; sombre; grave. **2.** Strict or severe in moral discipline; ascetic. **3.** Without adornment or ornamentation; simple; bare.

4. *Archaic.* Bitter or sour to the taste; astringent. —See Synonyms at **severe.** [Middle English, from Old French, from Latin *austērus,* from Greek *austēros,* harsh, rough, severe.] —**aus·tere·ly** *adv.*

aus·ter·i·ty (aw-stérrəti, o-) *n., pl.* **-ties. 1.** The quality of being austere. **2.** Severely simple living conditions, especially as an economic policy: *wartime austerity.* **3.** *Usually plural.* An ascetic habit or practice: *Hermits were renowned for their austerities.*

Aus·tin (óss-tin, áwss-) *adj.* Augustinian. Now used only in the phrase *Austin Friars.* [Shortening of *Augustine.*]

Austin. The capital of the state of Texas in the United States.

Austin, Herbert, 1st Baron (1866–1941). British industrialist, the founder of the Austin Motor Company.

Austin, John (1790–1859). English jurist. His influential lectures were published as *The Province of Jurisprudence* (1832) and *Lectures on Jurisprudence* (1863).

Austin, John Langshaw (1911–60). English philosopher, concerned with the analysis of philosophical concepts and problems through an examination of ordinary language. His best-known works are *Sense and Sensibilia* (1962) and *How to Do Things with Words* (1962).

aus·tral (áwstrəl, óstrəl) *adj.* **1.** Of, pertaining to, or coming from the south: *austral winds.* **2.** *Capital* **A.** Australian; Australasian. [Middle English, from Latin *austrālis,* from *auster†,* south, AUSTER.]

Aus·tral·a·sia (óss-trə-láy-zi-ə, áwss-, -zhə, -zhi-ə, -shə). An imprecise term referring to lands in the Pacific Ocean. The name is used in a broad sense to include the Malay Archipelago, Micronesia, Polynesia, and Melanesia in addition to New Zealand, the island of New Guinea, and Australia. It is used more commonly to refer simply to Australia and New Zealand and their dependencies (or former dependencies), such as Papua New Guinea. See also **Oceania.** —**Aus·tral·a·sian** *n. & adj.*

Aus·tral·i·a (oss-tráyl-yə, awss-, -i-ə). Official name **Commonwealth of Australia.** Island continent lying between the Indian and Pacific Oceans. Nearly half of it is desert or dry scrub. About 85 per cent of its people live in towns, and nearly 20 per cent of workers are in manufacturing, the chief products being, steel, aluminium, vehicles, textiles, and machinery. However, primary products, particularly minerals, wool, beef, and sugar are still the main exports. The population, about 75 per cent of British or Irish descent, includes some 140,000 Aboriginals. Dutch navigators were the first

Europeans to sight Australia (1606), and Captain Cook claimed the east coast for Britain (1770). The first colony, a penal settlement, was established at Sydney Cove (1788), and by 1850 there were colonies at what are now the other six state capitals. Discovery of gold in New South Wales and Victoria (1851) stimulated their growth, and in 1901 the Commonwealth of Australia, a federation of six former colonies (Tasmania, Victoria, South Australia, Western Australia, Queensland, and New South Wales), was born. Northern Territory came under federal control, and the Capital Territory was created in 1911. Australia became a dominion within the Commonwealth in 1931. Since 1945, traditional ties with Europe have weakened. Australia signed the ANZUS Pact (1952) and was a member of SEATO (1954–77); some Australians now favour a republican government. Area, 7 686 848 square kilometres (2,967,-123 square miles). Population, 18,290,000. Capital, Canberra.

Australia Day *n.* In Australia, the national holiday held on January 26 or the first Monday following it to commemorate the landing of the British in 1788.

Aus·tra·lian (oss-tráyl-i-ən, awss-) *n.* **1.** A native or citizen of the Commonwealth of Australia. **2.** An aborigine of Australia. **3.** Any of the languages of the Australian aborigines. **4.** English as it is spoken by Australians.

~*adj.* **1.** Of or pertaining to Australia or its inhabitants and their languages or cultures. **2.** *Ecology.* Of or designating the zoogeographic region that includes Australia and the islands adjacent to it, and New Guinea.

Australian Alps. A chain of mountain ranges forming a segment of the Great Dividing Range, or Eastern Highlands, occupying the southeastern corner of Australia.

Australian Antarctic Territory. A territory claimed by Australia, including all the islands and lands south of latitude 60° and between longitudes 160° and 45°E, except for Adélie Coast.

Australian Capital Territory. Formerly **Federal Capital Territory.** The name for the separate administrative unit enclosed by New South Wales in Australia, comprising the national capital, Canberra, and land around it. The territory has an area of 2 430 square kilometres (940 square miles).

Australian crawl *n.* A swimming stroke, a variation of the **crawl** *(see)* executed with an eight-beat flutter kick to each stroke.

Aus·tral·i·an·ise, Aus·tral·i·an·ize (oss-tráyl-yən-īz, awss-, -i-ən-) *v.*

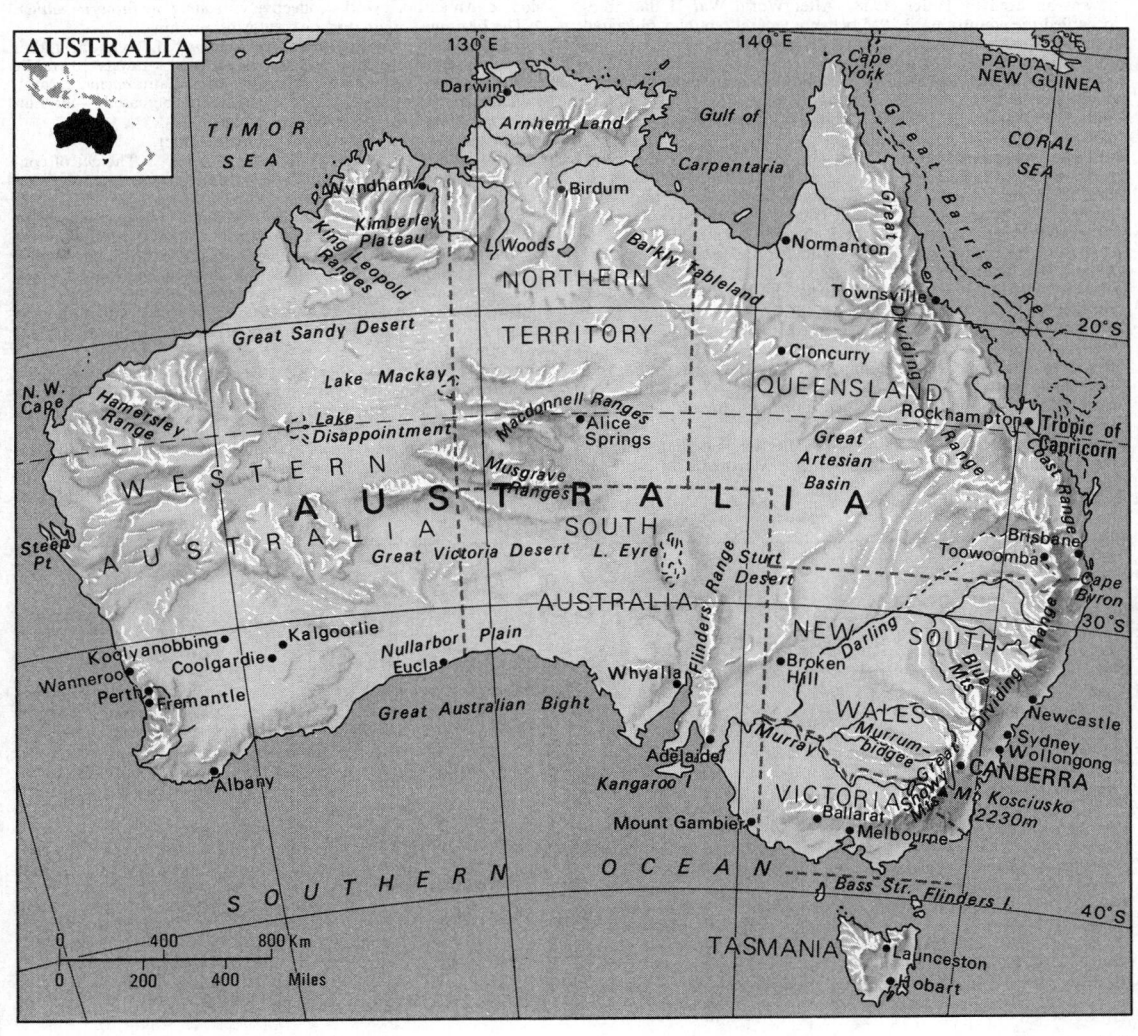

-ised, -ising, -ises. *—intr.* To become integrated into Australian culture and society. Said especially of new immigrants to Australia. *—tr.* **1.** To integrate into Australian culture and society. **2.** To make Australian in character or emphasis.

Aus·tral·i·an·ism (oss-tráyl-yən-iz'm, awss-, -i-ən-) *n.* **1.** A characteristically Australian feature; especially, a linguistic usage peculiar to Australia. **2.** Loyalty to Australia and Australian ideas.

Australian Rules *n. Used with a singular verb.* In Australia, a variety of football played on an oval pitch between teams of 18 players.

Australian salute *n.* A movement of the hand over the face, as when brushing off flies. Also called "Barcoo salute".

Australian terrier *n.* A small dog of a breed developed in Australia, having a coarse blackish coat with tan markings.

Aus·tra·loid (óstrə-loyd, áwstrə-) *adj.* Of or pertaining to an ethnic group including the Australian aborigines. [AUSTRAL(IAN) + -OID.] **—Aus·tra·loid** *n.*

aus·tra·lo·pith·e·cine (óstrə-lō-píthi-sīn, áwstrə-) *n.* Any of several extinct human-like primates of the genera *Australopithecus* and *Paranthropus* or *Zinjanthropus,* known chiefly from late Pliocene and Pleistocene fossil remains found in southern and eastern Africa. *—adj.* Of, pertaining to, or characteristic of the australopithecines. [New Latin *Australopithecus,* "southern ape" : AUSTRAL + New Latin *pithēcus,* ape, from Greek *pithēkos* (see **pithecanthropus**).]

Aus·tra·sia (oss-tráy-zhə, awss-, -shə). The eastern portion of the Frankish kingdom from the sixth to the eighth century, consisting of parts of eastern France, western Germany, and the Netherlands. It was eventually absorbed by the empire of the Carolingian kings. **—Aus·tra·sian** *adj.*

Aus·tri·a (óss-tri-ə, áwss-). *German* **Republik Österreich.** Landlocked Alpine republic in Central Europe. A former territory of Rome, and of Charlemagne's empire, it came under the Habsburgs (1246), who were also Holy Roman Emperors (1438–1806). Under the statesman Prince Metternich (1773–1859), the arbiter of Europe, they built a vast multinational empire, which was a bulwark against the Turks. However, discontent grew within the empire. The Hungarians forced the dual monarchy of Austria-Hungary on Franz Josef I (1867), and the assassination of the empire's heir, Archduke Franz Ferdinand, in Sarajevo (1914) unleashed World War I. In 1919 Austria was defeated, reduced to its German-speaking area, and became a republic. After suffering economic collapse, it was annexed by Hitler (1938). After World War II the Allies occupied the country until 1955, when a federal republic, obligated to remain neutral, was set up. Austria has reserves of oil, gas, lignite, and iron ore. It exports iron and steel, machinery, wooden goods, timber from its vast forests, and livestock products. Tourism is a major industry. Area, 83 858 square kilometres (32,378 square miles). Population, 8,110,000. Capital, Vienna. **—Aus·tri·an** *n. & adj.*

Aus·tri·a-Hun·ga·ry (óss-tri-ə-húng-gəri, áwss-). Two states ruled (1867–1918) by the Habsburgs, one as emperors of Austria (Austria, Bohemia, Moravia, Austrian Poland, Austrian Silesia, and Slovenia), the other as kings of Hungary (Hungary, Croatia, Transylvania, and lands along the Dalmatian coast).

Austro-[1] *comb. form.* Indicates southern; for example, **Austro-Asiatic.** [Latin *auster†,* the south, AUSTER.]

Austro-[2] *comb. form.* Indicates Austrian; for example, **Austro-Hungarian.**

Aus·tro-A·si·at·ic, Aus·tro·a·si·at·ic (óstrō-á-yshi-áttik, áwstrō-, -zhi-, -si-, -zi-) *n.* A family of languages of southeastern Asia, believed to have once been dominant in northeastern India and Indochina. **—Austro-Asiatic** *adj.*

Aus·tro-Hun·gar·i·an (óstrō-hung-gáir-i-ən, áwstrō-) *adj.* Of or pertaining to Austria-Hungary.

Aus·tro·ne·sia (óstrō-néez-yə, áwstrō-, -néeshə, -néezhə). The islands in the Pacific including Indonesia, Melanesia, Micronesia, and Polynesia.

Aus·tro·ne·sian (óstrō-néez-yən, áwstrō-, -néesh'n, -néezh'n) *adj.*

Of or pertaining to Austronesia, its peoples, or their languages. *—n.* A family of languages spoken in Austronesia, including the Indonesian, Melanesian, Micronesian, and Polynesian subfamilies. Also called "Malayo-Polynesian".

aut-. Variant of **auto-**[1].

au·ta·coid, au·to·coid (áwtə-koyd) *n.* Any organic substance, such as a hormone, formed in an organ and secreted into the blood or lymph, from which it acts on other parts of the organism. [AUT(O)- + Greek *akos,* cure.]

au·tar·chy (áwt-aarki) *n., pl.* **-chies. 1.** Absolute rule or power; autocracy. **2.** A country under such rule. **3.** Autarky. [Greek *autarkhia,* from *autarkhos,* self-governing : AUT(O)- + -ARCH.] **—au·tar·chic** (aw-tárkik), **au·tar·chi·cal** *adj.*

au·tar·ky (áwt-aarki) *n., pl.* **-kies. 1.** A policy of national self-sufficiency and nonreliance on imports or economic aid. **2.** A self-sufficient region or country. Also called "autarchy". [Greek *autarkeia,* self-sufficiency, from *autarkēs,* self-sufficient : AUT(O)- + *arkein,* to suffice.] **—au·tar·kic** (aw-tárkik), **au·tar·ki·cal** *adj.*

au·te·col·o·gy (áwti-kólləji) *n.* The ecology of a species or an individual organism. Compare **synecology**. [AUT(O)- + ECOLOGY.]

auth. 1. authentic. **2.** author. **3.** authorised. **4.** authority.

au·then·tic (aw-théntik) *adj. Abbr.* **auth. 1. a.** Worthy of trust, reliance, or belief: *authentic records.* **b.** Having an undisputed origin; genuine. **2.** *Law.* Executed with due process of law: *an authentic deed.* **3.** *Music.* **a.** Designating a medieval mode having a range from its final note to the octave above it. **b.** Designating a cadence with the dominant chord immediately preceding the tonic chord. Compare **plagal.** —See Synonyms at **real.** [Middle English *autentik,* from Old French *autentique,* from Late Latin *authenticus,* from Greek *authentikos,* genuine, authoritative, from *authentēs†,* perpetrator, author.] **—au·then·ti·cal·ly** *adj.*

au·then·ti·cate (aw-thénti-kayt) *tr.v.* **-cated, -cating, -cates. 1.** To establish as worthy of belief. **2.** To confirm as authentic; prove or verify (a painting, for example) as genuine. **3.** To invest (a deed, for example) with legal validity. —See Synonyms at **confirm. —au·then·ti·ca·tion** (-káysh'n) *n.* **—au·then·ti·ca·tor** (-kaytər) *n.*

au·then·tic·i·ty (áwthen-tíssəti) *n.* The condition or quality of being authentic, trustworthy, or genuine. See Synonyms at **truth.**

au·thor (áwthər) *n. 1. Abbr.* **auth. a.** The original writer of a book, essay, article, or the like. **b.** One who practises writing as a profession. **c.** An author's works collectively: *reading my favourite author.* **2.** The beginner, originator, or creator of anything. *—tr.v.* **authored, -thoring, -thors.** *Nonstandard.* **1.** To be the author of; write. **2.** To originate; create: *author a new fashion.* [Middle English *autour,* from Old French *autor,* from Latin *auctor,* creator, from *augēre* (past participle *auctus*), to create, increase.] **—au·thor·i·al** (aw-tháwri-əl ‖ -thóri-) *adj.*

au·thor·ess (áwthər-iss, -ess) *n.* A female author.

au·thor·i·sa·tion (áwthər-ī-záysh'n ‖ *U.S.* -i-) *n.* **1.** The act of conferring authority; permission. **2.** Written permission. **3.** Legal power, right, or sanction.

au·thor·ise, au·thor·ize (áwthərīz) *tr.v.* **-ised, -ising, -ises. 1.** To grant authority or power to. **2.** To approve or give permission for; sanction. **3.** To be sufficient grounds for; justify. [Middle English *autorisen,* from Old French *autoriser,* from Medieval Latin *auctorizāre,* from Latin *auctor,* AUTHOR.] **—au·thor·i·ser** *n.*

au·thor·ised (áwthərīzd) *adj. Abbr.* **auth. 1.** Invested with authority; authoritative. **2.** Having official permission. **3.** Sanctioned by law or command.

Authorised Version *n. Abbr.* **A.V.** An Anglican translation of the Bible from Hebrew and Greek into English, published in 1611 under the auspices of James I. Also called "King James Bible".

au·thor·i·tar·i·an (aw-thórri-táir-i-ən ‖ ə-) *adj.* **1.** Characterised by or favouring absolute obedience to authority, as against individual freedom. **2.** Favouring strong government powers.

—n. One who believes in or practises authoritarian policies or methods. **—au·thor·i·tar·i·an·ism** *n.*

au·thor·i·ta·tive (aw-thórri-tətiv, ə-, -taytiv) *adj.* **1.** Having or arising from proper authority; official: *authoritative sources.* **2.** Attempting to wield authority; commanding: *an authoritative voice.* **—au·thor·i·ta·tive·ly** *adv.* **—au·thor·i·ta·tive·ness** *n.*

au·thor·i·ty (aw-thórrə-ti, ə-) *n., pl.* **-ties.** *Abbr.* **auth. 1.** The right or power to act, command, enforce laws, exact obedience, determine, or judge. **2. a.** A person or group invested with this right or power. **b.** *Plural.* Government officials having this right or power. Preceded by *the.* **3.** Power delegated to others; authorisation: *You have my authority to decide.* **4.** *Often capital* **A.** A public agency or corporation with administrative powers limited to a specified field: *the British Tourist Authority.* **5. a.** An accepted source of expert information or advice, such as a book or person. **b.** A quotation or citation from such a source used in defence or support of one's actions, opinions, or the like. **6.** An expert in a given field: *an authority on plants.* **7.** Power to influence or persuade resulting from knowledge or experience: *write with authority.* **8.** A claim to be accepted or believed: *on the authority of the press.* **9.** An authoritative statement or decision that provides adequate grounds for a course of action or that may be taken as a precedent. [Middle English *autorite, auctorite,* from Old French *auctorite,* from Latin *auctōritās* (stem *auctōritāt-*), from *auctor,* AUTHOR.]

au·thor·ship (áwthər-ship) *n.* **1.** The profession or occupation of writing. **2.** A source or origin, as of a book or idea.

au·tism (áwtiz'm) *n.* **1.** Abnormal subjectivity; acceptance of fantasy rather than reality. **2.** A mental illness of children characterised by inability to communicate or to relate to other people and, often, mental subnormality. [New Latin *autismus* : AUT(O)- + -ISM.] **—au·tis·tic** (aw-tístik) *adj.*

au·to (áwtō) *n., pl.* **-tos.** *U.S. Informal.* A motor car.

auto-¹, aut- *comb. form.* Indicates: **1.** Acting or directed from within; for example, **autogenesis, autism. 2.** Self; same; for example, **autobiography.** [Greek, from *autos*†, self.]

auto-² *comb. form.* Indicates self-propelled; automotive; for example, **autogiro.** [From AUTOMOBILE.]

auto. 1. automatic. **2.** automotive.

au·to·an·ti·bod·y (áwtō-ánti-bodi) *n., pl.* **-ies.** An antibody that acts against cells of the organism in which it is formed. See **autoimmune.**

au·to·bahn (áwtō-baan, ówtō-) *n., pl.* **-bahns** or **-bahnen** (-ən). In Germany or Switzerland, a motorway. [German *Autobahn* : AUTO- (automobile) + *Bahn,* road, from Middle High German *ban, bane.*]

au·to·bi·og·ra·phy (áwtō-bī-óggrəfi) *n., pl.* **-phies. 1.** The written story of one's own life; memoirs. **2.** Such writings as a literary form. **—au·to·bi·og·ra·pher** *n.* **—au·to·bi·o·graph·ic** (-bī-ə-gráffik), **au·to·bi·o·graph·i·cal** *adj.* **—au·to·bi·o·graph·i·cal·ly** *adv.*

au·to·ca·tal·y·sis (áwtō-kə-tál-ə-siss) *n., pl.* **-ses** (-seez). Catalysis of a chemical reaction by one of the products of the reaction.

au·to·ceph·a·lous (áwtō-séffələss) *adj.* Independent of outside authority; having its own head. Said especially of Eastern Christian churches. [Late Greek *autokephalos* : *auto-,* self + *kephalē,* head.]

au·toch·thon (aw-tók-thən, -thon) *n., pl.* **-thons** or **-thones** (-eez). **1.** *Plural.* The earliest known or aboriginal inhabitants of a particular place. **2.** *Ecology.* Any indigenous plant or animal. [Greek *autokhthōn,* "one sprung from the land itself", indigenous : AUTO- + *khthōn,* earth.]

au·toch·tho·nous (aw-tók-thənəss) *adj.* Also **au·toch·tho·nal** (-thənəl), **au·toch·thon·ic** (áwtok-thónnik). Native to a particular place; aboriginal; indigenous. **—au·toch·thon·ism** (-thə-niz'm), **au·toch·tho·ny** (-thəni) *n.* **—au·toch·tho·nous·ly** *adv.*

au·to·clave (áwtō-klayv, áwtə-) *n.* A strong, pressurised, steam-heated vessel, used to establish special conditions for chemical reactions, for sterilisation, and for cooking.
~*tr.v.* **autoclaved, -claving, -claves.** To process in an autoclave. [French, "self-locking" : AUTO- + Latin *clāvis,* key.]

au·toc·ra·cy (aw-tóckrə-si) *n., pl.* **-cies. 1.** Government by a single person having unlimited power; despotism. **2.** A country or state having this form of government. [From AUTOCRAT.]

au·to·crat (áwtə-krat) *n.* **1.** A ruler having absolute or unrestricted power; a despot. **2.** Any arrogant and domineering person. [French *autocrate,* from Greek *autokratēs,* ruling by oneself : AUTO- + -CRAT.] **—au·to·crat·ic** (kráttik), **au·to·crat·i·cal** *adj.* **—au·to·crat·i·cal·ly** *adv.*

au·to·cross (áwtō-kross || -krawss). *n.* A form of motor racing, with races held on a rough grass track. Compare **motocross.**

Au·to·cue (áwtō-kew) *n.* A trademark for a device used in television that shows an actor or speaker an enlarged line-by-line reproduction of a script, unseen by the audience.

au·to-da-fé (áwtō-də-fáy, ówtō-, -daa-) *n., pl.* **au·tos-da-fé** (áwtōz-, ówtōz-). **1.** The public announcement of the sentences imposed on persons tried by the Inquisition. **2.** The public execution of these sentences by the secular authorities, especially the burning of heretics at the stake. [Portuguese *auto da fé,* "act of the faith" : *auto,* act, from Latin *āctus,* ACT + *da,* of the + *fé,* faith, from Latin *fidēs.*]

au·to·di·dact (áwtō-didakt, -dīdakt) *n.* A person who is self-taught. [Greek *autodidaktos,* self-taught : AUTO- + *didaktos,* taught (see **didactic**).] **—auto·di·dactic** (-di-dáktik, -dī-) *adj.*

au·toe·cious (aw-tééshəss) *adj. Biology.* Completing all stages of a life cycle on the same host. Said especially of certain rust fungi. Compare **heteroecious.** [AUT(O)- + *-oecious,* from Greek *oikos,* house.] **—au·toe·cism** (aw-téé-siz'm) *n.*

au·to·er·o·tism (áwtō-érrətiz'm) *n.* Also **au·to·e·rot·i·cism** (-i-rótti-siz'm). Self-arousal and self-satisfaction of sexual desire, as by masturbation. **—au·to·e·rot·ic** (-i-róttik) *adj.*

au·tog·a·my (aw-tóggə-mi) *n.* **1.** *Botany.* Fertilisation of a flower by its own pollen; self-fertilisation. **2.** *Biology.* The union of nuclei within and arising from a single cell, as in certain protozoans. [AUTO- + -GAMY.] **—au·tog·a·mous** (-məss) *adj.*

au·to·gen·e·sis (áwtō-jénnə-siss) *n. Biology.* **Abiogenesis** *(see).* **—au·to·ge·net·ic** (-jə-néttik) *adj.* **—au·to·ge·net·i·cal·ly** *adv.*

au·to·gen·ic (áw tə-jénnik) *adj.* **1.** Autogenous. **2.** Designating or relating to a system of training in self-induced relaxation using relaxation of posture, breathing techniques, the visualisation of appropriate responses to stressful situations, and verbalised autosuggestion. [AUTO- + -GENIC.] **—au·to·gen·ics** *n. Used with a singular verb.*

au·tog·e·nous (aw-tójənəss) *adj.* Also **au·to·gen·ic.** Self-generated; self-produced. [Greek *autogenēs,* self-producing : AUTO- + -GENOUS.] **—au·tog·e·nous·ly** *adv.*

au·to·gi·ro, au·to·gy·ro (áwtō-jī́r-ō) *n., pl.* **-ros.** An aircraft powered by a conventional propeller and supported in flight by a freewheeling horizontal rotor mounted above the fuselage, which provides lift by rotating. [AUTO- + Greek *guros,* circle.]

au·to·graft (áwtō-graaft, áwtə- || -graft) *n. Medicine.* A tissue graft obtained from the body of the recipient.

au·to·graph (áwtə-graaf, -graf) *n.* **1.** A person's own signature or handwriting. **2.** A holograph, in the author's own handwriting.
~*tr.v.* **autographed, -graphing, -graphs. 1.** To write one's name or signature on or in; sign. **2.** To write in one's own handwriting.
~*adj.* **1.** Written in a person's own handwriting. **2.** Containing signatures or autographs. [Latin *autographum,* from Greek *autographon,* autograph manuscript, from *autographos,* written by oneself : AUTO- + -GRAPH.] **—au·to·graph·ic** (-gráffik), **au·to·graph·i·cal** *adj.* **—au·to·graph·i·cal·ly** *adv.*

au·tog·ra·phy (aw-tóggrəfi) *n.* **1.** The writing of something in one's own handwriting. **2.** Autographs collectively.

au·to·hyp·no·sis (áwtō-hip-nō-siss) *n.* **1.** The act or process of hypnotising oneself. **2.** A self-induced hypnotic state. **—au·to·hyp·not·ic** (-nóttik) *adj.*

au·to·im·mune (áwtō-i-méwn) *adj.* Relating to or caused by the action of antibodies against the body's own tissues. **—au·to·im·mun·i·ty** *n.*

au·to·in·fec·tion (áwtō-in-féksh'n) *n.* Infection, as with recurrent boils, caused by germs or viruses persisting on or in the body.

au·to·in·oc·u·la·tion (áwtō-i-nóckew-láysh'n) *n.* Inoculation with a vaccine made from microorganisms derived from the recipient.

au·to·in·tox·i·ca·tion (áwtō-in-tóksi-káysh'n) *n.* Self-poisoning caused by endogenous microorganisms, metabolic wastes, or other toxins in the body. Also called "autotoxaemia".

au·to·i·on·i·sa·tion (áwtō-ī-ənī-záysh'n || *U.S.* -əni-) *n. Physics.* A process in which an excited atom or molecule emits an electron rather than a photon when it decays. See **Auger effect.**

au·to·load·ing (áwtō-lṓding) *adj.* Semiautomatic.

au·tol·y·sate (áw-tólli-zayt, -sayt) *n. Biochemistry.* An end product of autolysis.

au·tol·y·sin (áwtə-lī́-sin, aw-tóllə-sin) *n. Biochemistry.* A substance that causes autolysis. [AUTOLYS(IS) + -IN.]

au·tol·y·sis (aw-tóllə-siss) *n. Biochemistry.* The destruction of tissues or cells of an organism by autogenous enzymes. [AUTO- + -LYSIS.] **—au·to·lyt·ic** (áwtə-líttik) *adj.*

au·to·mat (áwtə-mat) *n.* **1.** *Chiefly U.S.* A restaurant in which the customers obtain food from closed compartments by inserting coins in a slot. **2.** A **vending machine** *(see).* [From trademark *Automat,* from AUTOMATIC.]

au·to·mate (áwtə-mayt) *v.* **-mated, -mating, -mates.** —*tr.* **1.** To convert (a process, factory, or machine) to automation. **2.** To control or operate by automation. —*intr.* To convert to or make use of automation. [Back-formation from AUTOMATIC.]

au·to·mat·ic (áwtə-máttik) *adj. Abbr.* **auto. 1. a.** Acting or operating in a manner essentially independent of external influence or control; self-moving. **b.** Self-regulating. **2.** Lacking volition, intention, or conscious planning; involuntary; reflex. **3.** Occurring as a matter of course or routine: *automatic weekly inspections.* **4.** Having automatic transmission. Said of a motor vehicle. **5.** Capable of firing continuously until ammunition is exhausted. Said of firearms. Compare **semiautomatic.** —See Synonyms at **spontaneous.**
~*n.* **1.** An automatic firearm, especially an automatic pistol. **2.** An automatic machine, vehicle, or device. [Greek *automatos,* acting by itself, spontaneous, acting of one's own will : AUTO- + *-matos,* willing.] **—au·to·mat·i·cal·ly** *adv.*

au·tom·a·tic·i·ty (áwtə-mə-tíssəti, -ma-) *n.* **1.** The state of being automatic. **2.** Automatic action.

automatic pilot *n.* An aircraft control mechanism that automatically maintains altitude, preset course, and steadiness. Also called "autopilot", "robot pilot". **2.** *Informal.* Automatic, mechanical, stereotyped behaviour: *He just went through the motions on automatic pilot.*

automatic pistol *n.* A pistol that can be fired automatically or semiautomatically.

automatic rifle *n.* A light machine gun that can be fired automatically or semiautomatically, normally the latter.

automatic transmission *n.* A device in a motor vehicle that enables gear changes to be operated mechanically according to car or engine speed, rather than manually.

au·to·ma·tion (áwtə-máysh'n) *n.* **1. a.** The automatic operation or control of a process, equipment, or a system. **b.** The act or process of conversion to such operation or control. **2.** The totality of mechanical and electronic techniques and equipment used to achieve such operation or control. **3.** The condition of being automatically controlled or operated. [AUTOM(ATIC) + -ATION.] **—au·tom·a·tise** (aw-tómmə-tīz) *tr.v.* **—au·to·ma·tive** *adj.*

au·tom·a·tism (aw-tómmə-tiz'm) *n.* **1. a.** The state or quality of being automatic. **b.** Automatic mechanical action. **2.** *Philosophy.* The theory that all living organisms are automatons. **3.** *Physiology.* **a.** The automatic operation of organs and cells, such as the beating of the heart. **b.** Performance of an act without conscious control, as in the operation of the reflexes. **4.** The effort at suspension of consciousness made by certain surrealist writers and artists in order to express subconscious ideas and feelings. [French *automatisme* : *automate,* AUTOMATON + *-isme,* -ISM.] **—au·tom·a·tist** *n.*

au·tom·a·ton (aw-tómmə-tən || -ton) *n., pl.* **-tons** or **-ta** (-tə). **1.** A **robot** *(see).* **2.** One that behaves in an automatic or mechanical fashion. [Latin, self-operating machine, from Greek *automaton,* neuter of *automatos,* AUTOMATIC.] **—au·tom·a·tous** *adj.*

au·to·mo·bile (áwtə-mə-beel || -beél, -mṓbeel) *n. Chiefly U.S.* A **car** *(see).* [French : AUTO- + MOBILE.] **—au·to·mo·bil·ist.**

au·to·mo·tive (áwtə-mṓtiv) *adj. Abbr.* **auto. 1.** Self-moving; self-propelling. **2.** Of or pertaining to self-propelled vehicles.

au·to·net·ics (áwtə-néttiks) *n. Used with a singular verb.* The study of automatic guidance and control systems. [AUTO- + *-netics,* as in CYBERNETICS.]

au·to·nom·ic (áwtə-nómmik) *adj.* Also **au·to·nom·i·cal** (-'l). **1.** Independent; autonomous. **2.** *Physiology.* Of or pertaining to the autonomic nervous system. **3.** Resulting from internal causes; self-generated; spontaneous. **—au·to·nom·i·cal·ly** *adv.*

autonomic nervous system *n.* The division of the vertebrate nervous system that regulates involuntary action, as of the intestines, heart, and glands, and comprises the **sympathetic nervous system** and the **parasympathetic nervous system.**

au·ton·o·mous (aw-tónnəməss) *adj.* **1. a.** Independent. **b.** Self-contained. **2. a.** Independent of the laws of another state or government; self-governing. **b.** Of or pertaining to an autonomy. **3.** Autonomic. [Greek *autonomos,* self-ruling : AUTO- + *nomos,* law.] **—au·ton·o·mous·ly** *adv.*

au·ton·o·my (aw-tónnəmi) *n., pl.* **-mies. 1.** The condition or quality of being self-governing. **2.** Self-government or the right of self-government; self-determination; independence. **3.** A self-governing state, community, or group. **4.** A condition of moral or personal independence. [Greek *autonomia,* from *autonomos,* AUTONOMOUS.] **—au·ton·o·mist** *n.*

au·to·phyte (áwtə-fīt) *n. Botany.* An autotrophic plant. [AUTO- + -PHYTE.] **—au·to·phyt·ic** (-fíttik) *adj.*

au·to·pil·er (áwtō-pīlər) *n. Computing.* A specific automatic compiler. [*auto*matic + com*piler.*]

au·to·pi·lot (áwtō-pīlət) *n.* An **automatic pilot** *(see).*

au·to·plas·ty (áwtō-plasti) *n. Medicine.* Surgical repair or replacement with tissue taken from the same body as that on which the surgery is performed. [AUTO- + -PLASTY.] **—au·to·plas·tic** (-plástik) *adj.* **—au·to·plas·ti·cal·ly** *adv.*

au·top·sy (áwt-opsi, -əpsi, aw-tópsi) *n., pl.* **-sies.** The examination and dissection of a dead body to determine the cause of death. Also called "necropsy", "post-mortem". [New Latin *autopsia,* from Greek, a seeing for oneself : AUT(O)- + Greek *opsis,* sight.] **—au·top·sic** (aw-tópsik), **au·top·si·cal** *adj.* **—au·top·sist** *n.*

au·to·ra·di·o·gra·phy (áwtō-ráydiyóggrəfi) *n.* A process of making a photographic record of the amount and distribution of radioactive material in an object, by the direct exposure of a photographic plate to radiation emitted by the object. Also called "radioautography". **—au·to·ra·di·o·graph** (-ō-graaf, -graf) *n.* **—au·to·ra·di·o·graph·ic** (-gráffik) *adj.*

au·to·ro·ta·tion (áwtō-rō-táysh'n) *n.* Rotation of the blades of a helicopter in free unpowered descent.

au·to·some (áwtə-sōm) *n.* Any chromosome that is not a sex chromosome. [AUTO- + (CHROMO)SOME.] **—au·to·som·al** (-sṓm'l) *adj.*

au·to·sug·ges·tion (áwtō-sə-jés-chən, -jésh- || *U.S.* -səg-) *n. Psychology.* The process by which a person induces self-acceptance of an opinion, belief, or plan of action. **—au·to·sug·gest·i·bil·i·ty** (-jéstəbilləti) *n.* **—au·to·sug·gest·i·ble** (-jéstəb'l) *adj.* **—au·to·sug·ges·tive** (-jéstiv) *adj.*

au·tot·o·mise, au·tot·o·mize (aw-tóttəmīz) *v.* **-mised, -mising, -mises.** *—tr.* To cause the autotomy of (a body part). *—intr.* To undergo autotomy.

au·tot·o·my (aw-tóttəmi) *n. Zoology.* The spontaneous casting off of a body part, such as the tail of certain lizards, for self-protection. [AUTO- + -TOMY.] **—au·to·tom·ic** (áwtə-tómmik) *adj.*

au·to·tox·ae·mi·a, *U.S.* **au·to·tox·e·mi·a** (áwtō-tok-seémi-ə) *n.* Also **au·to·tox·i·co·sis** (-tóksi-kṓ-siss). *Pathology.* **Autointoxication** *(see).*

au·to·tox·in (áwtō-tóksin, áwtə-) *n.* A poison that acts on the organism in which it is generated. **—au·to·tox·ic** *adj.*

au·to·trans·form·er (áwtō-transs-fórmər, -traanss-, tranz-) *n.* An electrical transformer in which the primary and secondary coils have some or all windings in common.

au·to·troph (áwtə-trof) *n. Biology.* An autotrophic organism, such as a green plant. [Back-formation from AUTOTROPHIC.]

au·to·troph·ic (áwtə-tróffik, -trṓfik) *adj. Biology.* Designating or characterising plants or certain microorganisms capable of manufacturing their own food from inorganic materials, as in photosynthesis. **—au·to·troph·i·cal·ly** *adv.* **—au·tot·ro·phy** (aw-tóttrəfi) *n.*

aut·ox·i·da·tion (áwt-óksi-dáysh'n) *n. Chemistry.* **1.** An oxidation reaction that involves atmospheric oxygen as the oxidising agent. **2.** An oxidation reaction that is induced by a second reaction taking place in the system.

au·tumn (áwtəm) *n.* **1.** The season of the year between summer and winter, strictly lasting from the autumnal equinox to the winter solstice and considered to be from September to November in the Northern Hemisphere and from March to May in the Southern. Also *U.S.* "fall". **2.** A time or period of maturity verging on decline. [Middle English *autumpne,* from Old French *autompne,* from Latin *autumnus,* perhaps of Etruscan origin.] **—au·tum·nal** (aw-túm-nəl) *adj.* **—au·tum·nal·ly** *adv.*

autumnal equinox *n.* **1.** The **equinox** *(see)* of September 22 or 23 in the Northern Hemisphere or March 21 or 22 in the Southern Hemisphere when the sun crosses the celestial equator going towards the equator, marking the start of autumn. **2.** *Astronomy.* The point in Virgo on the celestial sphere at which the celestial equator and the ecliptic intersect. Compare **vernal equinox.**

autumn crocus *n.* A plant, *Colchicum autumnale,* native to Europe and northern Africa, having pink or purplish flowers that bloom in the autumn. Also called "meadow saffron" "naked ladies".

au·tun·ite (áwtənīt, aw-túnnīt) *n.* A yellowish fluorescent minor ore of uranium with composition $Ca(UO_2)_2(PO_4)_2.10\text{-}12H_2O$. [After *Autun,* France, where it was discovered.]

Au·vergne (ō-vérn, -váirn). A mainly agricultural region, and former province of central France, around Clermont-Ferrand.

aux. auxiliary.

aux·e·sis (awg-zeé-siss, awk-seé-) *n. Biology.* An increase in the size of a cell or tissue without cell division. [Greek *auxēsis,* growth, from *auxanein,* to grow, increase.]

aux·il·ia·ry (awg-zíl-yəri, og-, awk-síl-, ok-) *adj. Abbr.* **aux. 1.** Giving assistance or support; aiding; helping. **2.** Subsidiary; supplementary; additional. **3.** Held in or used as a reserve: *auxiliary troops.* **4.** *Nautical.* Equipped with a motor to supplement the sails.
~*n., pl.* **auxiliaries. 1.** One that assists or helps; an assistant. **2.** *Plural.* Foreign troops serving a country in wartime. **3.** An auxiliary verb. **4.** *Nautical.* A sailing vessel equipped with a motor. **5.** *Naval.* A vessel for use in other than combat services, such as a supply ship. [Latin *auxiliārius,* from *auxilium,* help.]

auxiliary verb *n. Grammar.* A verb that accompanies particular forms of the main verb of a clause to form a phrasal unit expressing the tense, mood, voice, or aspect of the main verb. *Have, may, can, must,* and *will* are some auxiliary verbs, as in *He will come.*

aux·in (áwksin) *n.* Any of several plant hormones, or similar synthetic substances, that affect growth by increasing cell elongation. [Greek *auxein,* to grow + -IN] **—aux·in·ic** (awk-sínnik) *adj.*

aux·o·chrome (áwksə-krōm) *n.* A group of atoms that produces or intensifies the colour of a dye. [*auxo-* (increasing), from Greek *auxein,* to grow + -CHROME.]

Av (av, awv, aab) *n.* Also **Ab** (ab, aab, awv). The 11th month of the year in the Hebrew calendar, usually coinciding with August. [Hebrew *ābh,* from Akkadian *abu.*]

av. 1. avenue. **2.** average. **3.** avoirdupois.

Av. avenue.

a.v. ad valorem.

A.V. 1. audio-visual. **2.** Authorised Version.

a·vail (ə-váyl) *v.* **availed, availing, avails.** *—tr.* To be of use or advantage to; assist; help. *—intr.* To be of use, value, or advantage; serve. **—avail (oneself) of.** To make use of.
~*n.* Use, benefit, or advantage. Now used chiefly in the phrase *to* or *of no avail.* [Middle English *availen* : A- (intensive) + *vailen,* to avail, from Old French *valoir* (stem *vail-*), to be worth, from Latin *valēre,* to be strong, be worth.] **—a·vail·ing·ly** *adv.*

a·vail·a·ble (ə-váyl-əb'l) *adj.* **1.** Accessible for use or obtainable. **2.** At the disposal of an employer, visitor, or the like. **—a·vail·a·bil·i·ty** (-ə-bílləti), **a·vail·a·ble·ness** *n.* **—a·vail·a·bly** *adv.*

av·a·lanche (ávvə-laansh, -laanch || -lanch) *n.* **1.** A fall or slide of a large mass of snow, rock, or other material down a mountainside. **2.** Something resembling such an overwhelming fall or slide. **3.** *Physics.* A shower of ionising ions and electrons produced by a single ion moving through a medium, as in a Geiger counter.
~ *v.* **avalanched, -lanching, -lanches.** *—intr.* To fall, as does an avalanche. *—tr.* To overwhelm. [French, from Swiss French *avalantse,* altered (through influence of *avaler,* to descend) from Savoyard *lavantse,* from Vulgar Latin (unattested) *labanca*†.]

Av·a·lon (ávvə-lon). *Celtic Mythology.* An island paradise in the western seas where King Arthur and other heroes went at death.

a·vant-garde (ávvon-gárd || *U.S.* áavaant-) *n.* A group, as of writers and artists, regarded as pre-eminent in the invention and application of new styles and techniques in a given field.
~*adj.* **1.** Of or belonging to the avant-garde, as in the arts. **2.** Ahead of the times. [French, VANGUARD.]

av·a·rice (ávvəriss) *n.* An extreme desire to amass wealth; greed; cupidity. [Middle English, from Old French, from Latin *avāritia,* from *avārus,* greedy, from *avēre*†, to desire.] **—av·a·ri·cious** (ávvə-ríshəss) *adj.* **—av·a·ri·cious·ly** *adv.* **—av·a·ri·cious·ness** *n.*

a·vast (ə-vaást || ə-vást) *interj.* Used as a nautical command to stop: *Avast heaving there.* [Shortened from Dutch *houd vast,* "hold fast" : *houd,* imperative of *houden,* to hold + *vast,* fast.]

av·a·tar (ávvə-taar, -tár) *n.* **1. a.** One regarded as the incarnation or embodiment of some known model or category. **b.** An entity regarded as an extreme or notably complete manifestation of its kind; an exemplar; an archetype. **2.** In Hinduism, the descent to earth of a deity in human or animal form. Used as a generic term for the incarnations of Vishnu. [Sanskrit *avatāra,* descent, from *avatarati,* he descends : *ava,* down + *tarati,* he crosses.]

a·vaunt (ə-váwnt || ə-vaánt) *interj. Archaic.* Used as a command to be gone. [Middle English, from Old French *avant,* "forward", "go away!" See **vanguard.**]

avdp. avoirdupois.

A·ve (aávi, aávay) *n., pl.* **Aves.** The Ave Maria.

ave., Ave. avenue

Ave·bur·y (áyv-bri, -bəri || -berri). A village on the Marlborough Downs, Wiltshire, in southern England. It is situated on one of the most important prehistoric sites in Europe, lying within a Neolithic ring of upright stones older and larger than those at Stonehenge.

A·ve Ma·ri·a (aávay mə-reé-ə, aávi). *n.* **1.** A Roman Catholic prayer, based on the greetings of Gabriel and Elizabeth to the Virgin Mary. Luke 1:28, 42. Also called "Ave", "Hail Mary". **2. a.** A recitation of this prayer. **b.** The hour when it is customarily said. **3.** One of the small beads on a rosary used to count recitations of this prayer. [Middle English, from Medieval Latin, "Hail Mary!"]

a·venge (ə-vénj) *v.* **avenged, avenging, avenges.** *—tr.* **1.** To take revenge or exact satisfaction for (a wrong or injury). **2.** To take vengeance on behalf of. *—intr.* To take vengeance. [Middle English *avengen* : *a-,* from Latin *ad-,* to + *vengen,* to revenge, from Old French *vengier,* from Latin *vindicāre,* from *vindex* (stem *vindic-*), protector, avenger.] **—a·veng·er** *n.* **—a·veng·ing·ly** *adv.*

a·vens (áyvənz || *U.S.* ávvənz) *n., pl.* **avens** or **-enses. 1.** Any of various plants of the genus *Geum,* having irregularly shaped leaves, white, yellow, or reddish flowers, and plumed seed clusters. **2.** Any of several related plants of the genus *Dryas,* of mountainous and arctic regions. In this sense, also called "mountain avens". [Middle English *avence,* from Old French, from Medieval Latin *avencia*†.]

a·ven·tu·rine (ə-véntew-rin, -reen) *n.* Also **a·ven·tu·rin** (-rin). **1.** An opaque or semitranslucent brown glass flecked with small metallic particles, often of copper or chromic oxide. **2.** Any of several varieties of quartz or feldspar flecked with particles of mica, haematite, or other materials. Also called "sunstone". [French, from *aventure,* accident, ADVENTURE; so called because of its accidental discovery.] **—a·ven·tu·rine** *adj.*

av·e·nue (ávvi-new || -nōō) *n. Abbr.* **av., Av., ave., Ave. 1. a.** A wide street or thoroughfare. **b.** Any path resembling such a thoroughfare. **c.** A road, normally lined with trees. **2.** A drive or road, usually tree-lined, leading to a country house. **3.** An opening or means of approach to a given place, activity, or goal: *new avenues of trade.* [French, from Old French, approach, avenue, feminine past participle of *avenir,* to approach, arrive, from Latin *advenīre,* to come to : *ad-,* to + *venīre,* to come.]

a·ver (ə-vér) *tr.v.* **averred, averring, avers. 1.** To declare in a positive manner; affirm. **2.** *Law.* To assert formally as a fact; justify or prove (a plea). —See Synonyms at **assert.** [Middle English *averren,* from Old French *averer,* from Medieval Latin *adverāre,* to assert as true : *ad-,* to + *vērus,* true.] **—a·ver·ment** *n.* **—a·ver·ra·ble** *adj.*

av·er·age (ávvrij, ávvərij) *n. Abbr.* **av., avg. 1.** Something such as an amount, degree, or standard that is considered typical, normal, or representative. **2.** *Mathematics.* **a.** A number that typifies a set of numbers of which it is a function. **b.** The **arithmetic mean** *(see).* **3.** A ratio, relative proportion, or degree indicating position or achievement: *a goal average; batting averages.* **4.** *Law.* **a.** The incurrence of and loss due to damage at sea to a ship or cargo. **b.** The equitable distribution of such a loss among concerned parties. **c.** Any charges incurred through such a loss. **—on (the) average.** As a mean rate, amount, or the like.
~adj. **1.** Of, pertaining to, or constituting a mathematical average. **2.** Typical; usual; not out of the ordinary. **3.** *Informal.* Moderate to mediocre. **4.** *Law.* Assessed in compliance with the laws of average.
~v. **averaged, -aging, -ages.** *—tr.* **1.** To calculate the average of; especially, to calculate the arithmetic mean of (a set of numbers, quantities, or the like). **2.** To accomplish or obtain an average of: *average three hours work a day.* **3.** To distribute proportionately. *—intr.* **1.** To be or amount to an average. **2.** To buy or sell more goods or shares to obtain more than an average price. **—average out. 1.** *Informal.* To attain an average eventually. **2.** To work out so as to attain an average. [Alteration (by *-age,* as in *damage*) of obsolete *averie,* financial loss on damaged shipping, hence such loss shared equitably among investors, hence numerical average, from Old French *avarie,* damage to shipping, from Old Italian *avaria,* from Arabic *'awārīyah,* damaged goods, from *'awar,* fault, blemish.]
Synonyms: *average, medium, mediocre, fair, middling, indifferent, run-of-the-mill, so-so, tolerable.*

A·ver·ro·ës (ə-vérrō-eez), *Arabic* **Ibn Rushd** (1126–98). Spanish-Arab philosopher. He attempted to bring together the Islamic and Greek traditions of thought.

a·verse (ə-vérss) *adj.* **1.** Opposed; reluctant; disinclined. Usually used with *to.* **2.** *Botany.* Turned away from the central stem or axis: *averse leaves.* [Latin *āversus,* past participle of *āvertere,* AVERT.] **—a·verse·ly** *adv.* **—a·verse·ness** *n.*

a·ver·sion (ə-vérsh'n, ə-vérzh'n) *n.* **1.** Intense dislike. Used with *to.* **2.** A feeling of extreme repugnance. **3.** A greatly disliked person or thing: *a pet aversion.*

aversion therapy *n.* A form of therapy designed to overcome an addiction or a harmful habit by associating it, in the mind of the patient, with something unpleasant, such as vomiting.

a·vert (ə-vért) *tr.v.* **averted, averting, averts. 1.** To turn away: *avert one's eyes.* **2.** To ward off or prevent: *avert disaster.* [Middle English *averten,* from Old French *āvertir,* from Vulgar Latin *āvertīre* (unattested), variant of Latin *āvertere* : *ab-,* away from + *vertere,* to turn.] **—a·vert·ed·ly** (-idli) *adv.* **—a·vert·i·ble, a·vert·a·ble** *adj.*

Av·e·ry (áyvəri), **Oswald Theodore** (1877–1955). Canadian-born bacteriologist. In 1944 he isolated and identified DNA.

A·ves·ta (ə-véstə) *n.* The sacred writings of the Zoroastrian religion, the **Zend-Avesta** *(see).* [Middle Persian *apastāk*†, text.]

A·ves·tan (ə-véstən) *n.* Also **A·ves·tic** (ə-véstik). The dialect of Old Iranian in which the Avesta was written. Also called "Zend".
~adj. Of or pertaining to the Avesta or to the language in which it was written.

avg. average.

av·go·lem·o·no (ávgō-lémmənō) *n.* A Greek chicken soup or sauce made with eggs and lemons. [Modern Greek *avgolemono* : *avgon,* egg + *lemonion,* lemon.]

a·vi·an (áyv-yən, -i-ən) *adj. Zoology.* Of, pertaining to, or characteristic of birds. [Latin *avis,* bird.]

a·vi·ar·y (áyv-yəri, i-əri || *U.S.* -i-erri) *n., pl.* **-ies.** Any enclosure built to house live birds. [Latin *aviārium,* from *avis,* bird.] **—av·i·a·rist** *n.*

a·vi·a·tion (áyvi-áysh'n || *U.S. also* ávvi-) *n.* **1.** The art or science of operating aircraft. **2.** The production of aircraft; the aircraft industry. [French, from Latin *avis,* bird.] **—a·vi·ate** (-ayt) *v.*

aviation medicine *n.* The branch of medicine comprising **aeromedicine** and **space medicine** *(both of which see).*

a·vi·a·tor (áyvi-aytər || *U.S. also* ávvi-) *n.* One who operates an aeroplane; a pilot. [French *aviateur,* from *aviation,* AVIATION.]

a·vi·a·trix (áyvi-aytriks || *U.S. also* ávvi-) *n., pl.* **-trixes.** A female aviator.

Av·i·cen·na (ávvi-sénnə), *Arabic* **Ibn Sina** (980–1037). Persian philosopher and physician. His most famous work was the *Canon of Medicine.*

a·vi·cul·ture (áyvi-kulchər || *U.S. also* ávvi-) *n.* The raising or keeping of birds. [Latin *avis,* bird + CULTURE.] **—a·vi·cul·tur·ist** (-kúlchərist) *n.*

av·id (ávvid) *adj.* **1. a.** Eager. Often used with *of* or *for*: *avid for adventure.* **b.** Greedy. **2.** Enthusiastic; ardent: *an avid sportsman.* —See Synonyms at **eager.** [French *avide,* from Latin *avidus,* from *avēre,* to long for. See **avarice.**] **—av·id·ly** *adv.*

av·i·din (ávvidin) *n.* A protein in egg albumin, capable of inactivating biotin, consequently causing a deficiency of this vitamin in the consumer. [AVID + -IN, from its affinity for biotin.]

a·vid·i·ty (ə-víddəti, a-) *n.* **1. a.** Eagerness. **b.** Greed. **2.** *Chemistry.* **a.** The dissociation-dependent strength of an acid or base. **b.** Degree of **affinity** *(see).*

a·vi·fau·na (áyvi-fáwnə || *U.S. also* ávvi-) *n.* All the birds of a region. [New Latin : Latin *avis,* bird + FAUNA.] **—a·vi·fau·nal** *adj.*

A·vi·gnon (ávveen-YON). Industrial city in the Vaucluse département in southeastern France, lying on the river Rhône. It was the seat of several antipopes from 1377 to 1408, and still contains the papal palace, one of the greatest of medieval fortress-castles.

A·vi·la (ávvilə). Capital of the province of the same name, in central Spain, on the upper Adaja river.

a·vi·on·ics (áyvi-ónniks || *U.S. also* ávvi-) *n. Used with a singular verb.* The science and technology of electronics applied to aeronautics and astronautics. [*avi*ation + electr*onics.*] **—a·vi·on·ic** *adj.*

a·vir·u·lent (áy-vírrew-lənt, -vírrōō-) *adj. Medicine.* Not infectious or virulent.

a·vi·ta·min·o·sis (áy-víttə-min-ṓ-siss, -vítə-) *n.* Any disease caused by deficiency of vitamins. [A- (without) + VITAMIN + -OSIS.]

av·i·zan·dum (ávvi-zándəm) *n.* **1.** In Scots law, a judge's decision to delay giving judgment for a certain time. **2.** The period of this delay. [Medieval Latin, "a being considered", gerund of *avisare,* to consider. See **advise.**]

A.V.M. 1. air vice-marshal. **2.** automatic vending machine.

av·o·ca·do (ávvə-kaádō) *n., pl.* **-dos. 1.** A tropical American tree, *Persea americana,* cultivated for its edible fruit. **2.** The oval or pear-shaped fruit of this tree, having a large seed, and bland, greenish-yellow pulp. Also called "alligator pear", "avocado pear". **3.** A dull green. [Spanish, "advocate", alteration of *aguacate,* from Nahuatl *ahuacatl,* "testicle" (from the shape of the fruit).]

av·o·ca·tion (ávvō-káysh'n, ávvə-) *n.* **1.** An activity engaged in, usually for enjoyment, in addition to one's regular work or profession; a hobby. **2.** One's regular work or profession. Sometimes used humorously. [Latin *āvocātiō* (stem *āvocātiōn-*), a calling away, diversion, from *āvocāre,* to call away : *ab-,* away + *vocāre,* to call.]

av·o·cet (ávə-set) *n.* Any of several long-legged shore birds of the genus *Recurvirostra,* having a long, slender, upturned beak. *R. avosetta,* with a black and white plumage, is the common European species. [French *avocette,* from Italian *avosetta*†.]

a·vo·di·re (ávvədi-ráy) *n.* **1.** A tree, *Turreanthus africana,* of western Africa, having light-coloured wood with a clearly marked grain. **2.** The wood of this tree, used in cabinetwork. [French *avodiré*†.]

A·vo·ga·dro number (ávvə-gáddrō, -gaádrō || aávə-) *n.* Also **Avogadro's number.** *Symbol* $\mathbf{N_A}$ or **L** The number of molecules in one mole of a substance, approximately 6.0225×10^{23}. Also called "Avogadro constant". [After Amedeo *Avogadro* (1776–1856), Italian physicist.]

Avogadro's law *n.* The principle that equal volumes of different gases under identical conditions of pressure and temperature contain the same number of molecules. Also called "Avogadro's hypothesis". [After Amedeo *Avogadro.*]

a·void (ə-vóyd) *tr.v.* **avoided, avoiding, avoids. 1.** To keep away from; stay clear of; shun. **2.** To prevent from happening. **3.** *Law.*

To annul or make void (a contract or deed). —See Synonyms at **escape**. [Middle English *avoiden*, from Anglo French *avoider*, from Old French *esvuidier*, "to empty out", hence, to leave : *es-*, from Latin *ex-*, out + *vuidier*, to empty, from *vuide* VOID.] —a·**void·a·ble** *adj.* —a·**void·a·bly** *adv.* —a·**void·er** *n.*

a·**void·ance** (ə-vóyd'nss) *n.* **1. a.** The act of avoiding or shunning something. **b. Tax avoidance** (*see*). **2.** *Law.* A making void; an annulment. **3.** *Anthropology.* The custom, common among many primitive tribes, by which a member of a family may not meet or speak to another member.

av·**oir·du·pois** (ávvər-də-póyz, ávwaar-dew-pwaa) *n. Abbr.* **av.**, **avdp.**, **avoir.** **1.** Avoirdupois weight. **2.** *Informal.* Weight; heaviness. Said of a person. [Middle English *avoir de pois*, "commodities sold by weight", from Old French *aver de peis* : *aver*, property, from *aver*, *aveir*, to possess, have, from Latin *habēre*, to have + *de*, of, from Latin *dē* + *pois*, *peis*, weight, from *peser*, to weigh, POISE.]

avoirdupois weight *n.* A system of weights and measures, formerly used in most English-speaking countries, based on a pound containing 16 ounces or 7,000 grains and equal to 453.59 grams.

A·von[1] (áyv'n) Also **Upper Avon.** English river which rises near Naseby, Northamptonshire, and flows 155 kilometres (96 miles) through Stratford-upon-Avon to the river Severn near Tewkesbury, Gloucestershire.

Avon[2]. Also **Lower Avon.** English river which rises near Tetbury, Gloucestershire and flows some 121 kilometres (75 miles) through Bath and Bristol to the Severn estuary at Avonmouth.

Avon[3]. A county in southwest England, created in 1972 and comprising Bath, Bristol, and areas formerly in Somerset and Gloucestershire. Abolished in 1996 when new Unitary Authority areas were established.

a·**vouch** (ə-vówch) *tr.v. Archaic.* **avouched, avouching, avouches. 1.** To take responsibility for; guarantee. **2.** To assert positively; affirm. **3.** To acknowledge one's responsibility for; confess; avow. [Middle English *avouchen*, from Old French *avochier*, from Latin *advocāre*, to call on (as adviser) : *ad-*, to + *vocāre*, to call.]

a·**vow** (ə-vów) *tr.v.* **avowed, avowing, avows.** To acknowledge openly; confess: *avow guilt.* —See Synonyms at **acknowledge, assert.** [Middle English *avowen*, from Old French *avouer*, from Latin *advocāre*, to call on (as adviser), appeal to. See **avouch**.] —a·**vow·a·ble** *adj.* —a·**vow·a·bly** *adv.* —a·**vow·er** *n.*

a·**vow·al** (ə-vów-əl) *n.* An admission or acknowledgment.

a·**vowed** (ə-vówd) *adj.* Frankly acknowledged; confessed: *an avowed rebel.* —a·**vow·ed·ly** (ə-vów-idli) *adv.*

a·**vul·sion** (ə-vúlsh'n) *n.* **1.** A ripping off or forcible separation, as of a part of the body by injury. **2.** A part removed in this way. **3.** *Law.* The removal of soil from one property to another by the movement of floodwater, a shift in the course of a boundary stream, or encroachment by the sea. In this sense, compare **alluvion.**

a·**vun·cu·lar** (ə-vúngkewlər) *adj.* **1.** Of, pertaining to, or resembling an uncle, especially a benevolent uncle. **2.** Benevolent; kindly and friendly. [Latin *avunculus*, maternal uncle.]

a·**vun·cu·late** (ə-vúngkew-lət,-lit, -layt) *n.* Customs regulating relations between a maternal uncle and his nephew in certain societies and concerning various duties and rights, especially of inheritance. [Latin *avunculus*, maternal uncle + -ATE (group, rank).]

A·**WACS, A·wacs** (áy-waks) *n.* *Airborne Warning And Control System:* a defence system of aircraft equipped with radar used by the U.S. Air Force to detect enemy bombers.

a·**wait** (ə-wáyt) *v.* **awaited, awaiting, awaits.** —*tr.* **1.** To wait for. **2.** To be in store for. —*intr.* To wait. —See Synonyms at **expect.** [Middle English *awaiten*, from Anglo-French *awaitier*, watch for, wait for: *a-*, to + *waitier*, to watch, WAIT.]

a·**wake** (ə-wáyk) *v.* **awoke** (ə-wṓk) or *rare* **awaked, awoken** (ə-wṓkən) or **awaked, awaking, awakes.** —*tr.* **1.** To rouse from sleep; waken. **2.** To stir up or excite (memories or fears, for example). —*intr.* **1.** To wake up. **2.** To become alert. **3.** To become aware or cognisant. Often used with *to* : *They awoke to reality.* See **wake.** ~*adj.* **1.** Not asleep. **2.** Alert; vigilant; watchful. [Middle English *awaken*, *awakien*, Old English *awacan*, *awacian* : A- (intensive) + *wacan*, *wacian*, to be awake, WAKE.]

a·**wak·en** (ə-wáykən) *v.* **-ened, -ening, -ens.** —*tr.* To cause to wake up. —*intr.* To wake up; awake. See Usage note at **wake.** [Middle English *awak(e)nen*, Old English *āwæcnan*, *āwæcnian* : A- (on) + *wæcnan*, *woecnian*, to WAKE.]

a·**wak·en·ing** (ə-wáyk-ning, -əning) *adj.* **1.** Waking up. **2.** Rousing. ~*n.* **1.** The act of waking; an emergence from sleep. **2.** A stirring up; a rousing of attention, awareness, or interest.

a·**ward** (ə-wáwrd) *tr.v.* **awarded, awarding, awards. 1.** To grant as merited or due. **2.** To declare as legally due: *awarded damages.* **3.** To bestow for performance or quality: *award a prize.* ~*n.* **1.** A decision, especially one made by a judge or arbitrator. **2.** Something awarded, such as a medal or a sum of money. [Middle English *awarden*, from Anglo-French *awarder*, variant of Old North French *eswarder*, to judge after careful observation : *es-*, from Latin *ex-*, out + *warder*, to observe, keep, judge, from Germanic.] —a·**ward·ee** (ə-wáwr-dée) *n.* —a·**ward·a·ble** *adj.* —a·**ward·er** *n.*

a·**ware** (ə-wáir) *adj.* **1.** Conscious; cognisant. Often used with *of*: *aware of their limitations.* **2.** Well-informed; knowledgeable: *politically aware.* **3.** *Informal.* Sensitive and perceptive: *an aware person.* [Middle English *awar*, *iwar*, Old English *gewær*.] —a·**ware·ness** *n.*

a·**wash** (ə-wósh ‖ ə-wáwsh) *adj.* **1.** Level with or washed by waves. **2. a.** Flooded. **b.** As if flooded : *awash with money; awash with or in feeling.* **3.** Floating on waves.

a·**way** (ə-wáy) *adv.* **1. a.** From a particular place or position; off. **b.** To or at another place or position. **2.** At a distance. **3.** In a different direction; aside: *He glanced away.* **4.** Out of existence: *The music faded away.* **5.** From one's possession or notice: *He gave the money away.* **6.** Continuously; persistently: *He worked away at his job.* **7.** Immediately: *Fire away!* **8.** *Informal.* In a penal or mental institution: *put away for robbery.* **9.** So as to pass a period of time in a specified activity: *danced the night away.* **10.** At or on an opponent's pitch or ground: *playing away on Saturday.* —**away with. 1.** Take away. **2.** Go away: *Away with you!* ~*adj.* **1.** Absent. **2.** At a distance: *He is miles away.* **3. a.** Played on the pitch or ground of one's opponents. **b.** Of, pertaining to, or occurring at an away match or game: *six away goals.* ~*interj.* Used as an order of dismissal. [Middle English *away*, *on way*, from Old English *aweg*, *oweg*, *onweg*, "on the way (from)" : *a-*, *on*, on + *weg*, WAY.]

awe (aw) *n.* **1. a.** An emotion of mingled reverence, dread, and wonder inspired by something majestic or sublime. **b.** Respect, tinged with fear, for authority. **2.** *Archaic.* The power to inspire reverence or fear. —*tr.v.* **awed, aweing, awes.** To inspire with awe. [Middle English *awe*, *age*, *aghe*, from Old Norse *agi*.]

a·**wea·ry** (ə-wéer-i) *adj. Poetic.* Tired; weary.

a·**weath·er** (ə-wéthər) *adv. Nautical.* To windward. Compare **alee.**

a·**weigh** (ə-wáy) *adj. Nautical.* Hanging just clear of the bottom. Said of an anchor. [A- (on) + WEIGH.]

awe·in·spir·ing (áw-in-spīr-ing ‖ áwr-) *adj.* Causing great admiration or wonder; spell-binding.

awe·some (áw-səm) *adj.* **1.** Inspiring awe. **2.** Expressing or characterised by awe. **3. a.** Extraordinary; impressive: *awesome responsibilities.* **b.** *Slang.* Far-out: *totally awesome video games.* —**awe·some·ly** *adv.* —**awe·some·ness** *n.*

awe·strick·en (áw-strickən) *adj.* Also **awe·struck** (áw-struk). Full of awe.

aw·ful (áwf'l, áwfōol) *adj.* **1.** Extremely bad or unpleasant; terrible; horrible. **2.** *Rare.* Dreadful; appalling; fearsome. **3.** *Informal.* Used as an intensive: *an awful fool; an awful lot of people.* [Middle English *awful*, *aweful* : AWE + -FUL.] —**aw·ful·ness** *n.*

aw·ful·ly (*sense 1* áw-fōóli; *sense 2* áwfli) *adv.* **1.** In an extremely unpleasant manner; horribly. **2.** *Informal.* Used as an intensive: *He's awfully late.*

a·**while** (ə-wīl, ə-hwīl) *adv.* For a short time.

Usage: The following are standard English uses: *stay awhile, stay for a while, stay a while.* However, the version *stay for awhile,* where *awhile* is used after a preposition, is unacceptable.

awk·ward (áwkwərd) *adj.* **1.** Not graceful; ungainly. **2.** Not dexterous; clumsy; unskilful. **3.** Hard to handle; unwieldy: *an awkward bundle.* **4.** Difficult or dangerous: *an awkward climb.* **5.** Inconvenient; uncomfortable: *an awkward pose.* **6.** Causing embarrassment; trying: *an awkward predicament.* **7.** Embarrassed; ill-at-ease: *I felt awkward.* **8.** Difficult to cope with; contrary; perverse. [Middle English *awkeward*, "in the wrong direction", awry : *awke*, backhanded, perverse, wrong, from Old Norse *afugr*, turned backwards + -WARD.] —**awk·ward·ly** *adv.* —**awk·ward·ness** *n.*

Synonyms: awkward, clumsy, maladroit, inept, gauche, bungling, ungainly.

awkward age *n.* The period between childhood and adulthood; adolescence.

awl (awl) *n.* A pointed tool for making holes, as in wood. [Middle English *aule*, *al*, Old English *æl*, from Germanic (unattested).]

awl·wort (áwl-wurt ‖ -wawrt) *n.* A small aquatic plant, *Subularia aquatica*, of the Northern Hemisphere, having narrow, pointed leaves and minute white flowers. [From the shape of its leaves.]

awn (awn) *n. Botany.* A slender, bristle-like terminal part, such as are found on the spikelets of many grasses. [Middle English *awne*, *agene*, from Old Norse *ögn*; akin to Gothic *ahana*, chaff.]

awn·ing (áwning) *n.* A rooflike structure, as of canvas, stretched over a frame as a shelter from the weather. [17th century (nautical use) : origin obscure.]

a·**woke.** A past tense of **awake.**

a·**wok·en.** A past participle of **awake.**

A·**WOL, a·wol** (áy-wol) *adj. Military.* Absent without leave. —A·WOL *adv.*

a·**wry** (ə-rī) *adv.* **1.** Turned or twisted to one side; askew. **2.** Away from the correct course; amiss; wrong. [Middle English *awrie*, on *wry* : ON + *wry*, twisted, WRY.] —a·**wry** *adj.*

axe, *U.S.* **ax** (aks) *n.* **1.** A tool having an iron head with a sharp cutting edge mounted on a handle, used for felling, chopping, or splitting trees and wood. **2.** Any similar tool or weapon, such as a battle-axe. **3.** Anything that acts drastically to remove or reduce something: *The axe fell on the research programme.* —**have an axe to grind.** To pursue a private, selfish, or subjective aim. ~*tr.v.* **axed, axing, axes. 1.** To work on with an axe. **2. a.** To cancel (a project, for example). **b.** To reduce substantially (manpower or expenditure, for example). **c.** To dismiss from employment. [Middle English *ax*, *axe*, Old English *æx*, *aces*.]

ax·el (áks'l) *n.* In ice-skating, a jump involving one and a half twists in the air. [After *Axel Paulsen* (died 1938), Norwegian skater.]

axe·man (áks-mən, -man) *n.*, *pl.* **-men** (-mən, -men). A man who wields an axe.

a·**xen·ic** (áy-zéenik ‖ *U.S. also* -zénnik) *adj. Biology.* Free of symbionts or parasites; uncontaminated. Said of cultures or culture media. [A- (without) + XEN(O)- + -IC.]

ax·es. Plural of **axis.**

ax·i·al (áksi-əl) *adj.* **1.** Pertaining to or forming an axis. **2.** Located on, around, or in the direction of an axis. [AXI(S) + -AL.] **—ax·i·al·ly** *adv.*

ax·il (áksil) *n.* The angle between the upper surface of a leafstalk, flower stalk, branch, or similar part, and the stem or axis from which it arises. [Latin *axilla,* armpit.]

ax·il·la (ak-sil-ə) *n., pl.* **-lae** (-ee). The armpit, or an analogous part such as the underside of a bird's wing. [Latin *axilla,* armpit.]

ax·il·lar (ak-sillər || áksilər) *adj.* Axillary.
~*n.* Any of the feathers in the axilla of a bird's wing.

ax·il·lar·y (ak-sílləri || *U.S.* áksi-lerri) *adj.* **1.** *Anatomy.* Of, relating to, or near the armpit. **2.** *Botany.* Of, pertaining to, or located in an axil: *axillary buds.*
~*n., pl.* **axillaries.** An axillar.

ax·i·ol·o·gist (áksi-óləjist) *n.* An expert in or student of axiology.

ax·i·ol·o·gy (áksi-óllə̄ji) *n. Philosophy.* The study of the nature of values and value judgments. [Greek *axios,* worth + -LOGY.] **—ax·i·o·log·i·cal** (-ə-lójik'l) *adj.* **—ax·i·o·log·i·cal·ly** *adv.*

ax·i·om (áksi-əm) *n.* **1.** A self-evident or universally recognised truth; a maxim. **2.** An established rule, principle, or law. **3.** *Mathematics & Logic.* A statement or proposition requiring no proof, as: **a.** An undemonstrated proposition concerning an undefined set of elements, properties, functions, and relationships: a postulate. **b.** A self-evident, self-consistent, or accepted principle. [Latin *axiōma,* from Greek, "that which is thought fitting or worthy", from *axioun,* to think worthy, from *axios,* worthy.]

ax·i·o·mat·ic (áksi-ə-máttik) *adj.* Also **ax·i·o·mat·i·cal** (-'l). **1.** Of, pertaining to, or resembling an axiom; self-evident. **2.** Based on logical axioms: *axiomatic method; axiomatic set theory.* **3.** Containing axioms; aphoristic. **—ax·i·o·mat·i·cal·ly** *adv.*

ax·is (áksiss) *n., pl.* **axes** (ákseez). **1.** A straight line about which a body or geometrical object rotates or may be conceived to rotate. **2.** *Mathematics.* **a.** A line, half-line, or line segment serving to orient a space or object, especially a line about which the object is symmetrical. **b.** A reference line from which distances or angles are measured in a coordinate system. **3.** A centre line to which parts of a structure or body may be referred. **4.** In the visual arts, an imaginary line to which elements of the work are referred for measurement or symmetry. **5.** *Anatomy.* **a.** The second cervical vertebra, on which the head turns. **b.** Any of various central structures, such as the spinal column. **c.** An imaginary line through the centre of the body or one of its parts, used as a positional referent. **6.** *Botany.* The main stem or central part about which organs or plant parts such as branches are arranged. **—the Axis** or **the Axis powers.** The alliance of Germany and Italy (1936), later including Japan and other nations, that opposed the Allies in World War II. [Latin *axis,* hub, axis, axle.]

axis deer *n.* A deer, *Axis axis,* of central Asia, having a brown coat with white spots. Also called "chital". [Latin *axis†,* given by Pliny as the Indian name of an unidentified animal.]

ax·le (áks'l) *n.* **1.** A supporting shaft or bar upon which a wheel or wheels revolve. **2.** The spindle of an axletree. **3.** Either end of an axletree. [Middle English *axil, axel,* from Old Norse *öxull.*]

ax·le·tree (áks'l-tree) *n.* A crossbar or rod supporting a vehicle, such as a drawn cart, and having terminals on which wheels revolve.

Ax·min·ster (áksminstər) *n.* A kind of carpet with a long, soft cutwool pile, formerly handmade in Axminster, England.

ax·o·lotl (áksə-lótt'l || -lott'l) *n.* Any of several western North American and Mexican salamanders of the genus *Ambystoma,* especially *A. mexicanum.* [Nahuatl : *atl,* water + *xolotl,* servant, spirit.]

ax·on (ákson) *n.* Also **ax·one** (áksōn). The long unbranched process extending from the cell body of a nerve cell, which generally conducts impulses away from the nerve cell. Also called "neuraxon". [New Latin, from Greek *axōn,* axis.]

a·yah (ī-ə, áa-yə) *n.* A native maid or nurse in India. [Hindi *āyā, āya,* from Portuguese *aia,* nursemaid, from Latin *avia,* grandmother.]

a·ya·tol·lah (í-ə-tóllə || *U.S.* áa-yə-tólə) *n.* In the Shiite branch of Islam, a religious leader of the highest rank. [Arabic *āyatollāh,* sign of God.]

Ayck·bourn (áyck-born), **Sir Alan** (1939–). British playwright. A highly successful writer of domestic comedies, he has more than 30 plays to his credit, including *Relatively Speaking* (1965), *Absurd Person Singular* (1972), and *Woman in Mind* (1986).

aye¹, ay (ī) *n.* A vote or voter voting in favour of a proposal.
~*adv.* Yes; yea. [16th century : probably the same word as the pronoun *I,* used as an affirmative answer.]

aye², ay (ay) *adv. Regional & Poetic.* Always; ever. [Middle English *ay, ei,* from Old Norse *ei.*]

aye-aye (ī-ī) *n.* A small, nocturnal, arboreal mammal, *Daubentonia madagascariensis,* of Madagascar, related to the lemurs. [French, from Malagasay *aiay,* probably imitative of its cry.]

Ay·er (air), **Sir Alfred Jules** (1910–89). British philosopher. His book *Language, Truth and Logic* (1936) was the first, and most influential, exposition of **logical positivism** *(see)* in English.

A·yers Rock (áy-ərz). The largest monolith in the world, situated in the southwestern part of Northern Territory in Australia.

Ay·e·sha or **A·i·sha** (aa-éeshə, áa-ee-shaa) (614–678). The third and favourite wife of Muhammad, the founder of Islam. She led an unsuccessful revolt against Muhammad's successor, Ali.

a·yin, a·in (áa-yin, -īn) *n.* The 16th letter of the Hebrew alphabet. [Hebrew *'ayin.*]

Ay·ma·ra (ī-maár-ə, íma-ráa) *n., pl.* **-ras** or collectively **Aymara.** **1.** A member of an Indian people inhabiting Bolivia and Peru. **2.** A language family including that spoken by the Aymara people. **—Ay·ma·ran** *adj. & n.*

Ayr·shire¹ (áir-shər, -sheer || *Scottish* -shīr). Formerly, a county in southwest Scotland, then from 1975 part of Strathclyde Region. After 1996 divided into the new Unitary Authority areas of North, South, and East Ayrshire.

Ayrshire² *n.* Any of a breed of brown and white dairy cattle originating in Ayrshire in the late 18th century.

A·yur·ve·da (áa-yoor-vaydə, -veedə) *n.* The ancient Hindu system of medicine based on naturopathy and homeopathy. [Sanskrit : *āyur,* life + *veda,* knowledge.]

a·zal·e·a (ə-záyli-ə) *n.* Any of a group of deciduous or evergreen shrubs, part of the genus *Rhododendron,* of the North Temperate Zone, many of which are cultivated for their showy, variously coloured flowers. [New Latin, "the dry plant" (growing in dry soil), from Greek, feminine of *azaleos,* dry.]

a·zan (aa-zaán) *n.* The Muslim summons to prayer, called by the muezzin from a minaret of a mosque five times a day. [Arabic *adhān,* from *adhina,* to proclaim. See **muezzin.**]

A·za·ña (y Di·az) (a-thaán-yə (ee dée-ath)), **Manuel** (1880–1940). Spanish writer and politician. He was prime minister from 1931 to 1933 and again in 1936. In May 1936, he was elected president. He fled to France in 1939 after the Nationalist victory in the civil war.

A·za·ni·a (ə-záyn-yə, a-, -nī-ə) *n.* South Africa. Used by black African nationalists. [Latin *Azania,* Africa, probably from Arabic *Zanj,* a dark-skinned African.]

az·a·thi·o·prine (ázzə-thí-ə-preen) *n.* A drug that suppresses the body's immune response, used mainly to assist the survival of organ transplants. [*Aza-,* variant of AZO- + THIO- + P(U)RINE.]

A·za·zel (ə-záyz'l, ázzə-zel) **1.** In ancient Hebrew tradition, a demon or evil spirit to whom the scapegoat was sent on the day of atonement carrying the sins of the Jewish people. **2.** In Milton's *Paradise Lost,* one of the fallen angels in league with Satan. [Hebrew *'azāzēl,* "removal", hence scapegoat (ritually "sent" into the wilderness) : *'ez,* goat + *'azl,* to go.]

a·zed·a·rach (ə-zéddə-rak) *n.* **1.** A tree, the **chinaberry** *(see).* **2.** The astringent bark of this tree, formerly used as an emetic. [French *azedarac,* from Persian *āzād-dirakht : āzād,* free + *dirakht,* tree.]

a·ze·o·trope (ə-zée-ə-trōp) *n.* A mixture of two or more liquids that, at a given pressure and temperature, boils without change of composition (the composition of the vapour is the same as that of the boiling liquid). [A- (not, without) + Greek *zeō,* (infinitive *zein,* boil) + -TROPE.] **—a·ze·o·trop·ic** (-tróppik) *adj.*

A·zer·bai·jan, Republic of or **A·zer·bai·dzhan** (ázzər-bī-jaán). Former constituent republic of the U.S.S.R. situated in the southeastern Transcaucasus. It was formed from territory ceded by Persia to Russia in 1813 and 1828. Baku is a centre of oil oilfields. More than half the people are Turkic-speaking Azerbaijanis, who are Shiite Muslims. In 1988 ethnic violence against Christian Armenians erupted over Armenian claims to Nagorno-Karabakh, and in 1990 escalated into war with Armenia, the conflict continuing throughout the 1990s. Area, 86600 square kilometres (33,436 square miles). Population 7,550,000. Capital, Baku. See map at **Caucasus.**

A·zer·bai·ja·ni (ázzər-bī-jaáni) *n., pl.* **-nis** or collectively **Azerbaijani.** **1.** A native or inhabitant of Azerbaijan. **2.** The Turkic language of Azerbaijanis.

a·zide (áyzīd) *n. Chemistry.* **1.** An inorganic compound containing the negative ion N_3^-. **2.** An organic compound containing the group $-N_3$. **3.** The group or radical N_3. [AZO- + -IDE].

A·zil·ian (ə-zil-i-ən) *adj. Archaeology.* Of or denoting a western European culture following the Magdalenian era and preceding the Neolithic. [After le Mas d'*Azil,* village in the French Pyrenees, where artefacts of this culture were found.]

az·i·muth (ázziməth) *n.* **1.** The horizontal angular distance from a fixed reference direction to a position, object, or object referent, as to a to great circle intersecting a celestial body, usually measured clockwise in degrees along the horizon from a point due south. **2.** A horizontal bearing measured clockwise from a given direction. **3.** *Military.* The lateral deviation of a projectile or bomb. [Middle English, from Old French *azimut,* from Arabic *as-sumūt,* plural of *as-samt,* "the way", compass bearing, from Latin *semita†,* path.] **—az·i·muth·al** (-múth'l) *adj.* **—az·i·muth·al·ly** *adv.*

azimuthal projection *n.* A zenithal projection *(see).*

az·ine (áy-zeen, -zin || á-) *n.* A six-membered heterocyclic compound, such as pyridine, containing one or more atoms of nitrogen in the ring. [AZ(O)- + -INE.]

azine dye *n.* Any of various dyes derived from phenazine *(see).*

az·o (áyzō, ázzō) *adj. Chemistry.* Containing a nitrogen group. [From AZO-.]

azo-, az- *comb. form. Chemistry.* Indicates the presence of a nitrogen group, especially one attached at both ends in a covalent bond to other groups; for example, **azobenzene, azole.** [French *azote,* nitrogen, "lifeless" (unlike the life-sustaining oxygen) : A- (not) + Greek *zōē,* life.]

az·o·ben·zene (áyzō-bénzeen, -ben-zéen || ázzō-) *n.* A yellow or orange crystalline compound, $C_6H_5N_2C_6H_5$, used in the manufacture of dyes and as a fumigant.

azo dye *n.* Any of various red, brown, or yellow acidic or basic dyes containing the azo group.

azo group *n. Chemistry.* The group of atoms $-N:N-$.

a·zo·ic (ay-zṓ-ik, ə-) *adj.* Of or pertaining to geological periods that precede the appearance of life. [A- (not) + -ZOIC.]

a·zole (áyzōl, ə-zṓl ‖ ázzōl) *n.* **1.** Any organic compound having a five-membered heterocyclic ring. **2. Pyrrole** *(see).* [AZ(O)- (because it contains atoms of nitrogen) + -OLE.]

a·zon·ic (ay-zónnik) *adj.* Not restricted to any particular zone or region; not local. [A- (not) + ZONE + -IC.]

A·zores (ə-zórz ‖ ə-zṓrz). *Portuguese* **Açô·res** (ə-sáwrish). Group of nine volcanic islands in the Atlantic Ocean, forming an autonomous region of Portugal. Europe's most westerly land, lying some 1 190 kilometres (740 miles) from mainland Portugal, they were settled by the Portuguese in the mid-15th century. The islanders live by fishing, farming, and tourism. Ponta Delgada is the capital.

az·o·tae·mi·a (ázzə-téemi-ə) *n. Medicine.* **Uraemia** *(see).* [New Latin : French *azote,* nitrogen (see **azo-**) + NAEMIA.] —**az·o·tae·mic** (-mik) *adj.*

az·oth (áz-oth) *n.* In alchemy: **1.** Mercury. **2.** Paracelsus's universal remedy. [Arabic *az-zā'ūq,* the mercury.]

a·zo·to·bac·ter (ə-zṓtō-baktər, ay-) *n.* Any of various nitrogen-fixing bacteria of the family Azotobacteraceae. [New Latin : French *azote,* nitrogen (see **azo-**) + BACTER(IA).]

Az·ra·el (áz-ray-əl, -ri-, -el). The angel who separates the soul from the body at death in Muslim and Jewish legend. [Arabic *Azrā'īl,* from Hebrew *'Āzar'ēl,* "God has helped".]

AZT *n.* A drug, $C_{10}H_{13}N_5O_4$, used against retroviral diseases and especially to retard the development of the symptoms of AIDS. [From *Azidothymidine* (Azidothymidine).]

Az·tec (áztek) *n.* **1.** A member of an Indian people of Central Mexico who established a great empire that was overthrown by Cortés in the 16th century. **2.** The language of this people, Nahuatl. ~*adj.* Also **Az·tec·an** (áztekən). Of the Aztecs, their language, culture, or empire. [Spanish *Azteca,* from Nahuatl *Aztecatl* (plural *Azteca*) : *Azt(a)lan,* the supposed place of origin of the people, "near the crane"; *aztatl* (plural *azta*), crane + *tlan,* near + *-tecatl,* suffix denoting origin.]

az·u·lene (ázzew-leen, ázhōō-) *n.* A blue, oily, terpene compound present in camomile and wormwood. [Azul-, from Spanish *azul,* blue + -ENE.]

az·ure (ázh-ər, áyzh-, -yoor, ázzwr, ə-zéwr. *Note: the traditionally accepted pronunciation is* ázh-ər) *n.* **1. a.** Light purplish blue, like a summer sky. **b.** *Heraldry.* The colour blue. **2.** An azure pigment. **3.** *Poetic.* The blue sky. [Middle English, from Old French *azur* from Old Spanish *azul, azur,* from Arabic *allāzaward,* lapis lazuli, from Persian *lāzhuward,* LAPIS LAZULI.] —**az·ure** *adj.*

az·u·rite (ázhoor-īt, ázhər-, ázzewr-) *n.* An azure-blue vitreous mineral of basic copper carbonate, $Cu_3(CO_3)_2(OH)_2$, used as a copper ore and as a gemstone. [French : Old French *azur,* AZURE + -ITE.]

az·y·gous (ázzigəss, áy-zīgəss) *adj. Biology.* Occurring singly; unpaired. [New Latin *azygos,* from Greek *azugos,* unwedded, unpaired : *a-,* without + *zugon,* yoke.]

B

b, B (bee) *n., pl.* **b's** or *rare* **bs, Bs** or **B's. 1.** The second letter of the modern English alphabet. **2.** Any of the speech sounds represented by this letter.

b, B, b., B. *Note:* As an abbreviation or symbol, *b* may be a small or a capital letter, with or without a full stop. Established forms or those generally preferred precede the definition. When no form is given, all four forms are in general use in that sense. **1. B.** bachelor. **2. B.** bacillus. **3. b** *Physics.* barn. **4. B** baryon number. **5. b, B.** base. **6. b., B.** *Music.* basso. **7. B.** Baumé scale. **8. b., B.** bay. **9. B.** Bible. **10. B** *Chess.* bishop. **11. b., B.** bolivar. **12. b., B.** book. **13. b., B.** born. **14. B** The symbol for the element boron. **15. b** *Cricket.* bowled. **16. B.** breadth. **17. B.** British. **18. b., B.** brother. **19. B.** brotherhood. **20. B** A human blood type of the ABO group. See **ABO. 21.** The second in a series.

B *n., pl.* **Bs** or **B's. 1.** The second best or highest in quality, class, or rank, as: **a.** The second highest mark awarded for academic work that is good but not excellent. **b.** In the United Kingdom, a secondary road that is of a reasonable standard but may be narrow or winding. **c.** The second highest socioeconomic class. **2. a.** The seventh note in the scale of C major. **b.** The key or a scale in which B is the tonic. **c.** A written or printed note representing B. **d.** A string, key, or pipe tuned to the pitch of B. **3.** Something second-rate; especially, something that is the inferior or secondary item of a pair. Often used adjectivally: *a B film; the B side of a record.* **4.** A fairly soft pencil or pencil-lead. Often used adjectivally: *a B pencil.* **5.** *Physics.* A quantum number, **bottom** *(see).*

B- *U.S. Military.* bomber: *a B-52.*

Ba[1] The symbol for the element barium.

Ba[2] (baa) *n.* In ancient Egyptian religion, the soul or life after death represented as a bird with a human head. [Egyptian.]

B.A. 1. Bachelor of Arts. **2.** British Academy. **3.** British Airways. **4.** British Association (for the Advancement of Science).

baa (baa ‖ ba) *intr.v.* **baaed, baaing, baas.** To make a bleating sound, as a sheep does. ~*n.* The bleat of a sheep. [Imitative.]

B.A.A. British Airports Authority.

Baa·der-Mein·hof Gang (baádər-mín-hoff). A German revolutionary group, also known as the Red Army Faction, committed to the destruction of capitalism through acts of terrorism and violence. The group's original leading members, Andreas Baader (1943–1977) and Ulrike Meinhof (1934–1976), both died in prison.

Ba·al (báy-əl, baal) *n., pl.* **-alim** (-im). **1. a.** Any of various local fertility and nature gods of the ancient Semitic peoples, considered to be false idols by the Hebrews. **b.** The chief god of the Phoenicians and Canaanites. **2.** *Sometimes small* **b.** Any false god or idol. [Hebrew *bá'al,* owner, master, lord.] —**Ba·al·ism** *n.*

Ba'al·bek, Baal·bek (baál-bek). Village in east Lebanon, site of an ancient Phoenician city, probably devoted to Baal. It is now a tourist centre famous for its extensive Roman ruins.

Baal Shem Tov, Baal Shem Tob (baál shém tov, sháym, tōv), original name Israel ben Eliezer (c.1700–1760). Polish-born Jewish religious leader and mystic, and founder of **Chassidism.** His name means "Master of the Holy Name" and he is also known by the acronym "Besht".

baas (baass) *n., pl.* **baas.** *South African.* **1.** A master or boss. **2.** Sir; master. Used formerly as a term of address, chiefly by blacks to whites. [Afrikaans, from Dutch *baas,* master or captain.]

baas·skap (baáss-skaap) *n. South African.* The condition of mastery or overlordship; especially, the political supremacy of South African whites over blacks. [Afrikaans, from Dutch : *baas,* master + -skap, -SHIP.]

Bab (baab), **the,** title of Ali Muhammad of Shiraz (c. 1819–50). Persian founder of **Babism** *(see)* and one of the three central figures of the Bahai faith, who proclaimed himself as the Bab (or "Gateway") to the truth.

ba·ba (baá-baa, -bə) *n.* A sponge cake leavened with yeast, sometimes made with raisins and usually flavoured with rum. Also called "rum baba". [French, from Polish, "old woman".]

ba·bas·su (baába-sōō) *n.* A Brazilian palm tree, *Orbignya martiana* (or *O. speciosa*), bearing hard nuts that yield an oil similar to coconut oil. [Brazilian Portuguese *babaçú,* probably a native name.]

Bab·bage (bábbij), **Charles** (1791–1871). British mathematician and inventor. He designed a computer that was based on principles like those used in modern computers, and which had data fed in and stored on punched cards and a memory.

bab·bitt (bábbit) *tr.v.* **-bitted, -bitting, -bitts.** To line or face with Babbitt metal. ~*n. Capital* **B.** Babbitt metal.

Bab·bitt (bábbit) *n.* A member of the American middle class whose attachment to its ideals is such as to make him a model of narrow-mindedness and self-satisfaction. [After George F. *Babbitt,* main character in Sinclair Lewis' novel *Babbitt* (1922).] —**Bab·bitt·ry** *n.*

Babbitt metal *n.* **1.** A soft alloy composed of tin with small amounts of copper and antimony, used in bearings because of its low coefficient of friction. **2.** Any of various antifriction alloys based on lead. [After Isaac *Babbitt* (1799–1862), American inventor.]

bab·ble (bább'l) *v.* **-bled, -bling, -bles.** —*intr.* **1.** To utter an incoherent or meaningless confusion of words or sounds. **2.** To talk foolishly or idly; chatter. **3.** To make a continuous low, murmuring sound, as flowing water does. —*tr.* **1.** To utter in a rapid, indistinct voice. **2.** To blurt out impulsively; disclose without careful consideration. ~*n.* **1.** Inarticulate or meaningless talk or sounds. **2.** Idle or foolish talk; chatter; prattle. **3.** A continuous murmuring sound. **4.** Jargon, especially that characteristic of a particular field of interest or activity. Used in combination: *psychobabble; Eurobabble.* [Middle English *babelen,* of imitative origin.]

bab·bler[1] (bábblər) *n.* **1.** One who babbles. **2.** A small songbird of the Old World family Timaliidae, occurring especially in Southeast Asia and having a loud babbling cry.

babbler[2] *n. Australian Slang.* A camp or sheep station cook. [From *babbling brook,* rhyming slang for *cook.*]

babe (bayb) *n.* **1.** *Regional & Poetic.* A baby; an infant. **2.** *Slang.* An innocent or naive person. **3.** *Chiefly U.S. Slang.* A term of familiar address, usually used to a girl or young woman. [Middle English *babe,* imitative of a baby's sounds.]

ba·bel (báyb'l ‖ bább'l) *n. Often capital* **B. 1.** A confusion of sounds, voices, or languages: *"in the babel of two hundred voices he* *would forget himself"* (Joseph Conrad). **2.** A scene of noise and confusion. [After BABEL.]

Babel. A city (now thought to be Babylon) in Shinar where, according to Genesis 11:1-9, an attempt to construct a tower to reach heaven incurred the wrath of God, who interrupted the work by making the builders unable to understand one another's language. [Hebrew *Bābhél*, from Akkadian *Bāb-ilu*, "gate of God".]

Ba·bi (ba´abi) *n.* **1.** Babism. **2.** A follower of the Bab.

bab·i·rus·sa, bab·i·rous·sa (ba´abi-ro͞osˈsə, bábbi-) *n.* A hairless wild pig, *Babyrousa babyrussa*, of the East Indies, having four long, upward-curving tusks in the male. [Malay *bābīrūsa* : *bābī*, hog + *rūsa*, deer.]

Bab·ism (ba´abiz'm) *n.* The beliefs and practices of a 19th-century Persian religious sect, founded about 1844 by the Bab *(see)*, in which polygamy, concubinage, begging, trading in slaves, and the use of alcohol or drugs were forbidden. Also called "Babi".

ba·boon (bə-bo͞onˈ ‖ *U.S.* ba-) *n.* **1.** Any of several chiefly African omnivorous monkeys of the genus *Chaeropithecus* (or *Papio*) and related genera, having an elongated, doglike muzzle and large teeth. See **gelada, hamadryas. 2.** *Slang.* A large, clumsy, often coarse person. [Middle English *baboyne*, from Old French *babuin*, gaping figure, baboon.]

ba·bu, ba·boo (ba´abo͞o) *n.* **1.** A form of address in Hindi equivalent or similar to *Mister*, placed before a man's full name or after his first name. **2. a.** A Hindu clerk possessing a prerequisite degree of literacy in English. Considered offensive. **b.** A native of India who has acquired some superficial education in English. Used derogatorily. [Hindi *bābū*, "father".]

ba·bush·ka (bə-bo͞oshˈkə, -bo͞oshˈ-) *n.* A woman's headscarf, folded triangularly and tied under the chin. [Russian, "grandmother", diminutive of *baba*, old woman.]

ba·by (ba´abi) *n., pl.* **-bies. 1.** A newborn or very young boy or girl; an infant. **2.** The youngest member of a family or group. **3.** A newborn or very young animal. **4.** An adult or young person who acts like an infant. **5.** *Slang.* **a.** *Chiefly U.S.* A girlfriend or boyfriend. **b.** A term of familiar address, used to a female or a male. **6.** *Slang.* **a.** An object of personal concern: *The project was his baby.* **b.** *Chiefly U.S.* Any thing or person : *Put this baby back in the drawer.* ~ *adj.* **1.** Of or pertaining to a baby or babies. **2.** Infantile; childsih. **3.** Small in comparison with others of the same kind. ~ *tr.v.* **babied, -bying, -bies.** To treat oversolicitously; coddle. [Middle English *babie*, imitative. See **babe, -y.**] —**ba·by·hood** *n.*

baby blue *n.* Very light to very pale greenish or purplish blue. —**ba·by-blue** (ba´abi-blo͞oˈ) *adj.*

baby blues *pl.n. Informal.* Postnatal depression.

baby boomer *n.* A person born during the 1947-57 period of exceptionally high birth rate. [BABY¹ + BOOM³.]

Ba·by-bounc·er (ba´abi-bownˈsər) *n.* A trademark for a baby's seat that is suspended on springs and can be hung, for example, from a door frame.

Baby Buggy. 1. A trademark for a lightweight pushchair which, unlike the traditional flat-folding type, folds inwards when not in use. Also called "buggy", "stroller". **2.** *Small* **b.**, *small* **b.** *U.S. Informal.* A pram.

baby carriage *n. Chiefly U.S.* A pram.

baby face *n. Slang.* **1.** A plump, smooth face like a baby's. **2.** An adult having a baby face. —**ba·by-faced** (ba´abi-faystˈ) *adj.*

baby grand *n.* A small grand piano.

ba·by·ish (ba´abi-ish) *adj.* **1.** Like a baby; childlike. **2.** Childish; immature. —**ba·by·ish·ly** *adj.* —**ba·by·ish·ness** *n.*

Bab·y·lon¹ (bábbi-lən ‖ -lon) City in ancient Mesopotamia, some 88 kilometres (55 miles) south of modern Baghdad. Founded in the second millennium B.C., it flourished as Hammurabi's capital. It was virtually destroyed by the Assyrians under Sennacherib (*c.* 689 B.C.), but rose again, achieving vast wealth as the capital of the neo-Babylonian empire. Nebuchadnezzar II rebuilt the city, and his Hanging Gardens were one of the Seven Wonders of the World. Babylon fell to Cyrus the Great (538 B.C.) and became a minor centre of the Persian empire.

Babylon² *n.* **1.** A place of great luxury and corruption. **2.** A place of captivity or exile. **3.** In Rastafarian ideology, the corrupt and materialistic values of the West. See **Zion.** [After BABYLON.]

Bab·y·lo·ni·a (bábbi-lōnˈi-ə, -yə). Empire of ancient Mesopotamia. Created in the second millennium B.C., it rose to greatness under Hammurabi. It then fell to successive invaders, eventually to the Assyrians (*c.* 722 B.C.). A native king established the Chaldean or neo-Babylonian empire (*c.* 625 B.C.), and under Nebuchadnezzar II this expanded to include all Mesopotamia and Palestine. The empire declined after his death, and fell to the Persians (538 B.C.).

Bab·y·lo·ni·an (bábbi-lōnˈi-ən) *adj.* **1.** Of or pertaining to ancient Babylonia or Babylon, their people, culture, or language. **2.** Characterised by a luxurious, pleasure-seeking, and immoral way of life. ~ *n.* **1.** A native or inhabitant of ancient Babylon or Babylonia. **2.** The Semitic language of the Babylonians, a form of Akkadian.

Babylonian captivity *n.* **1.** The deportation of the Jews to Babylonia and their period of exile there, initiated by Nebuchadnezzar II in 597 B.C. and formally terminated by Cyrus in 538 B.C. Also called "Babylonian exile". **2.** The period (1309–78) when certain French popes resided at Avignon rather than Rome.

baby minder *n.* A child minder who looks after very young children or babies.

baby sitter *n.* A person who looks after one or more children while the parents are out, especially in the evening. —**ba·by-sit** *v.*

baby talk *n.* **1.** The early speech of a very young child. **2.** The infantile speech of an adult imitating a very young child.

ba·by-tears (ba´abi-teerzˈ) *n.* Also **ba·by's-tears** (ba´abiz-). *Used with a singular or plural verb.* A creeping plant, *Helxine soleirolii*, native to Corsica, having numerous very small leaves and minute green flowers.

baby tooth *n.* A milk tooth *(see).*

Ba·car·di (bə-kárdi) *n.* **1.** A trademark for a brand of rum originally distilled in Cuba. **2.** A cocktail made with this rum, containing lime or lemon juice and sugar or grenadine.

bac·ca·lau·re·ate (bácko-láwri-ət, -it) *n.* **1.** The university degree of **bachelor** *(see).* **2.** A secondary-school qualification: *an international baccalaureate.* [Medieval Latin *baccalaureātus*, from *baccalaureus*, variant (influenced by *bacca lauri*, "laurel berry") of *baccalaris* (unattested), BACHELOR.]

bac·ca·rat (bácko-raa, -raˈ ‖ *U.S. also* baˈaka-) *n.* A card game in which two or more players bet against a dealer and the winner is the player holding two or three cards totalling closest to nine. [French *baccarat*†.]

bac·cate (báckayt) *adj.* **1.** Bearing berries. **2.** Resembling a berry in texture or form. [Latin *baccatus*, "having berries", from *baca, bacca*, berry, perhaps akin to BACCHUS.]

Bac·chae (báckee) *pl.n.* The priestesses and female followers of Bacchus. [Latin, from Greek *Bakkhai*, plural of *Bakkhē*, priest of BACCHUS.]

bac·cha·nal (bácko-n'l, -nal ‖ -nál, -naˈal) *n.* **1.** A participant in the Bacchanalia. **2.** *Sometimes plural.* The Bacchanalia. **3.** Any drunken or riotous celebration. **4.** A reveller. ~ *adj.* Bacchanalian. [Latin *bacchānālis*, of BACCHUS.]

Bac·cha·na·li·a (bácko-náylˈi-ə) *n., pl.* **Bacchanalia. 1.** *Plural.* The ancient Roman festival in honour of Bacchus. **2.** *Small* **b.** A riotous or drunken festivity; a revel. [Latin *bacchānālia*, neuter plural of *bacchānālis*, BACCHANAL.]

bac·cha·na·li·an (bácko-náylˈi-ən) *adj.* **1.** Of or pertaining to Bacchanalia. **2.** Characterised by riotous, drunken revelry; orgiastic. ~ *n.* A drunken reveller; a bacchanal.

bac·chant (báckənt ‖ *U.S. also* bə-kánt, -kaˈant) *n., pl.* **-chants** or **-chantes** (-s, -eez). **1.** A priest or votary of Bacchus. **2.** A boisterous reveller. ~ *adj.* **1.** Wine-loving. **2.** Riotous; carousing. [Latin *bacchāns* (stem *bacchant-*), present participle of *bacchārī*, to celebrate the festival of Bacchus, from Greek *bakkhân*, from *Bakkhos*, BACCHUS.]

bac·chante (bə-kánti, -kánt ‖ *U.S. also* -kaˈanti, -kaˈant) *n.* **1.** A priestess or female votary of Bacchus. **2.** A female participant in a drunken or orgiastic revel. [French, from Latin *bacchāns*, BACCHANT.]

Bac·chic (báckik) *adj.* **1.** Of or pertaining to Bacchus. **2.** *Small* **b.** Drunken and carousing; bacchanalian.

Bac·chus (báckəss). The god of grape-growing, wine, and pleasure, often identified with Dionysus. [Latin, from Greek *Bakkhos*.]

bac·cif·er·ous (bak-sífférəss) *adj. Botany.* Bearing berries. [Latin *baccifer* : *bacca*, berry + -FEROUS.]

bac·ci·form (báksi-fawrm) *adj.* Having the shape of a berry. [Latin *bacca*, berry + -FORM.]

bac·cy (bácki) *n. Chiefly British Informal.* Tobacco.

bach¹ (baakh) *n. Welsh.* Little one. Used as a term of address.

bach² (bach) *intr.v.* **bached, baching, baches.** Also **batch.** *U.S., Australian, & N.Z. Informal.* To live alone and keep house for oneself, especially in a makeshift fashion. Used especially in the expression *bach it.* [Short for BACHELOR.]

bach³ (bach) *n. N.Z.* A small holiday- or beach-house. [Short for BACHELOR.]

Bach (baakh, bakh), **Johann Sebastian** (1685–1750). German composer and musician. Among his religious works are over 200 cantatas, the *St. Matthew Passion* (1729), and the *Mass in B minor* (1733–38). His many orchestral pieces include the six *Brandenburg Concertos* (1721), and he wrote numerous compositions for the keyboard including *The Well-Tempered Clavier* (1722, 1744) and the *Goldberg Variations* (1742). Of those of his 20 children who became musicians, two are especially renowned. **Carl Philipp Emanuel Bach** (1714–88) played an important part in the development of the symphony; **Johann Christian Bach** (1735–82) became music master to the British royal family and is sometimes known as the "English" or "London" Bach.

bach·e·lor (báchᵊlər, -lər) *n.* **1.** An unmarried man. **2.** In feudal times, a young knight in the service of another knight. Also called "bachelor-at-arms". See **knight bachelor. 3.** A person who holds a college or university degree signifying successful completion of an undergraduate course. **4.** A young male fur seal who is kept from the breeding territory by older males. Also called "bachelor seal". [Middle English *bacheler*, from Old French, squire, from Vulgar Latin *baccalaris*† (unattested), whence Medieval Latin *baccalaureus*, BACCALAUREATE.] —**bach·e·lor·dom** *n.* —**bach·e·lor·hood** *n.* —**bach·e·lor·ship** *n.*

bachelor girl *n. Chiefly U.S.* A young unmarried woman who is financially independent.

Bachelor of Arts *n. Abbr.* **B.A. 1.** An academic degree conferred by a college or university upon a person who has completed his or her undergraduate studies, usually in the arts or humanities. Compare **Master of Arts, Doctor of Philosophy. 2.** A person who has received this degree.

Bachelor of Science *n. Abbr.* **B.Sc. 1.** An academic degree conferred by a college or university upon a person who has completed his or her undergraduate studies in the sciences and some social sciences. Compare **Master of Science, Doctor of Philosophy.** **2.** A person who has received this degree.

bach·e·lor's-but·tons (bách-ələrz-bútt'nz, -lərz-) *n. Used with a singular or plural verb.* Any of various plants of the daisy family having button-like flower heads.

Bach trumpet (baakh) *n.* A small modern trumpet designed to simplify the playing of the high trumpet parts found in the works of J.S. Bach and similar composers.

ba·cil·lar·y (bə-sílləri || *U.S. also* báss'l-erri) *adj.* Also **ba·cil·lar** (bə-sillər || *U.S. also* báss'l-ər). **1.** Of, pertaining to, or caused by bacilli. **2.** Rod-shaped.

ba·cil·li·form (bə-síllifawrm) *adj.* Rod-shaped.

ba·cil·lus (bə-síl-əss) *n., pl.* **-li** (-ī). **1.** *Abbr.* **B.** Any rod-shaped bacterium. Compare **coccus, spirillum**. **2.** Any of various rod-shaped, aerobic bacteria of the genus *Bacillus,* often occurring in chainlike formations. See Usage note at **germ**. [New Latin, from Late Latin, diminutive of Latin *baculum,* rod, stick.]

bac·i·tra·cin (bássi-tráy-sin) *n.* An antibiotic obtained from the bacterium *Bacillus subtilis* and usually used externally to treat skin infections. [BACI(LLUS) + Margaret *Tracy,* an American child in whose blood it was first isolated in 1945 + -IN.]

back[1] (bak) *n.* **1. a.** The region of the vertebrate body located nearest the spine, in man consisting of the rear area from the neck to the pelvis. **b.** The analogous dorsal region in other animals, such as insects. **2. a.** The backbone or spine. **b.** The surface of the human body, or any part of it, or any part of the body of an animal, that is located on the side facing away from the front: *the back of the leg.* **3. a.** The part, area, or surface farthest from the front. **b.** The upper or convex side of something: *the back of one's hand.* **4.** The part opposite to or behind that adapted for use or view. **5.** The reverse or underside, as of a coin or sheet of paper. **6. a.** A part that supports or strengthens from the rear: *the back of a chair.* **b.** Something that covers the back; for example, that part of a garment that covers the back. **7. a.** The part of a book where the pages are stitched together into the binding. **b.** The binding itself. **8 a.** In ball games such as football or hockey, a player taking a position behind the forwards and concerned mainly with defending the goal. **b.** The position of such a player. **—at the back of (one's) mind.** In one's memory or subconscious. **—back to front.** The wrong way round; reversed. **—behind (someone's) back.** Without someone's knowledge or approval. **—get off (someone's) back.** *Informal.* To cease pestering or scolding someone. **—get or put (someone's) back up.** *Informal.* To annoy or antagonise. **—in back of.** *U.S.* At the rear of; behind. **—on (one's) back.** Incapacitated or helpless; bedridden. **—put (one's) back into.** To put great effort into. **—stab in the back.** To attack or betray (a friend or colleague). **—the back of beyond.** A very remote, insignificant, and inaccessible place. **—turn (one's) back on.** **1.** To ignore the plight of; forsake. **2.** To turn away from; renounce. **—with (one's) back to the wall.** In a desperate position from which one cannot retreat.

~*v.* **backed, backing, backs.** *—tr.* **1.** To cause to move backwards or in a reverse direction. **2.** To furnish or strengthen with a back, backing, or lining. **3. a.** To provide with support, assistance, or encouragement. **b.** To provide a musical backing for. **4.** To bring forward evidence in support of; substantiate. Often used with *up*: *backing up an argument with facts.* **5.** To bet on. **6.** To form the back or background of. **7.** To endorse by signing on the back of. *—intr.* **1.** To move backwards. **2.** To shift anticlockwise, in direction, as from south to southeast. Used of the wind. Compare **veer**. **3.** To have the back facing in a particular direction: *the house backs onto the park.* **—back and fill.** **1.** To manoeuvre a sailing vessel in a narrow channel by alternately filling and spilling the sails. **2.** To turn a vehicle round in a narrow space by making small turning movements alternately backwards and forwards. **—back down.** To withdraw from a position, opinion, or commitment; abandon a former stand. **—back off.** To retreat or draw away. **—back out.** To withdraw from an enterprise, commitment, or plan, especially before completion: *He announced he was backing out of the project.*

~*adj.* **1.** Located at the rear. **2.** Distant from a centre of activity; remote. **3.** Of a past date; not current. **4.** Owing or due from an earlier time; in arrears. **5.** Moving in a backward direction. **6.** *Phonetics.* Articulated with the tongue pulled to the rear of the mouth. **7.** *Physics.* Acting in opposition to a primary effect: *a back emf.*

~*adv.* **1.** At, to, or towards the rear or back; backwards. **2.** In, to, or towards a former location. **3.** In, to, or towards a former condition. **4.** In, to, or towards a past time. **5.** Away; at a distance: *Stand back!* **6.** In reserve or concealment. **7.** In check. **8.** In return. **9.** In retort. **—back and forth** from one place to another and back again; to and fro. **—go back on.** To fail to keep (a promise or commitment). [Middle English *bak,* Old English *bæc,* from Germanic *bakam* (unattested).]

back[2] *n.* A shallow vat or tub used chiefly by brewers. [Dutch *bak,* from French *bac,* from Old French, from Vulgar Latin *bacca* (unattested), a water vessel, perhaps from Celtic.]

back·ache (bák-ayk) *n.* A usually persistent ache or pain in the lower back.

back·bench·er (bák-bénchər) *n.* Any of the Members of Parliament who sit on the rear benches of the House of Commons and are not ministers or shadow ministers. Also called "bencher". See **front-bench, crossbencher.**

back·bite (bák-bīt) *v.* **-bit** (-bit), **-bitten** (bitt'n) or *informal* **-bit, -biting, -bites.** *—tr.* To slander the character or reputation of an absent person). *—intr.* To speak spitefully or slanderously of a person in his absence. **—back·bit·er** *n.*

back·blocks (bák-bloks) *pl.n. Australian.* A remote and sparsely populated area, especially in the interior of Australia. **—back·block·er** *n.*

back·board (bák-bawrd || -bōrd) *n.* **1.** A board that can be worn, or one that can be placed under the mattress of a bed, to support the back. **2.** *Basketball.* The board from which the basket projects.

back boiler *n.* A form of boiler incorporated into the back of a domestic fireplace to heat water. Also *chiefly U.S.* "water back".

back·bone (bák-bōn) *n.* **1.** The vertebrate spine or spinal column. **2.** Anything that resembles a backbone in appearance or position, such as the keel of a ship. **3.** A main support or major sustaining factor. **4.** Strength of character; fortitude; determination. **5.** The main ridge of a mountain range or the main range of mountains in a region. —See Synonyms at **courage.** **—back·boned** *adj.*

back·break·ing (bák-brayking) *adj.* Demanding great physical exertion; exhausting; arduous. **—back·break·er** *n.*

back calculate *v.* To extrapolate from the present to the past, as when calculating that a motorist who has passed a breath test some time after driving would have failed one immediately after driving. **—back calculation** *n.*

back·chat (bák-chat) *n.* Impertinent answering back or repartee.

back·cloth (bák-kloth || -klawth) *n.* **1.** A large, usually painted, cloth forming the background to a stage set. **2.** A setting or background.

back·comb (bák-kōm) *v.* **-combed, -combing, -combs.** *—tr.* To comb (the hair) from the ends towards the roots to give fullness. *—intr.* To backcomb the hair.

back country *n. Chiefly Australian & N. Z.* Remote, sparsely populated areas.

back·court (bák-kawrt || -kōrt) *n.* **1.** In tennis and other racket games, the part of a court between the service line and the base line. **2.** In other games, such as handball or basketball, the part of the playing area furthest from the goal or target wall.

back·cross (bák-kross || -krawss) *v.* **-crossed, -crossing, -crosses.** *Genetics. —tr.* To mate (a first-generation hybrid) with a parent or member of the parental stock. *—intr.* To cross in this way.

~*n. Genetics.* The act or result of backcrossing.

back·date (bák-dáyt) *tr.v.* **-dated, -dating, -dates.** To make retrospective in application: *The June pay rise was backdated to January.*

back door *n.* **1.** A door to a building other than the front or main door. **2.** An unfair, covert, or underhand method used to obtain a promotion, job, or the like: *He got into the company through the back door.*

back·door (bák-dawr || -dōr) *adj.* Done or formed secretly or surreptitiously; clandestine.

back·drop (bák-drop) *n.* **1.** A painted curtain or screen forming the background to a stage set. **2.** The setting, as of a historical event.

backed (bakt) *adj.* Having or furnished with a back or backing. Usually used in combination: *a low-backed chair.*

back·er (báckər) *n.* **1.** One who supports, gives aid to, or invests in a person, group, or enterprise. **2.** One who bets on a contestant.

back·field (bák-feeld) *n.* **1.** In American football, the players stationed behind the line of scrimmage. **2.** The area occupied by these players.

back·fill (bák-fil) *tr.v.* **-filled, -filling, -fills.** To refill (an excavated trench).

back·fire (bák-fīr) *n.* **1.** An explosion of prematurely ignited fuel or of unburnt exhaust gases in an internal-combustion engine. **2.** A fire started purposely in the path of an oncoming fire so that the latter will be extinguished on reaching an area that has already been burnt out. **3.** An explosion of ammunition in the breech of a gun.

~*intr.v.* **backfired, -firing, -fires.** **1.** To explode in or make the sound of a backfire. **2.** To start or employ a backfire. **3.** To produce an unexpected and undesired result: *His plot backfired on him.*

back-for·ma·tion (bák-fawr-maysh'n) *n. Linguistics.* **1.** A new word created by removing from an existing word what is mistakenly thought to be an affix; for example, *laze* (from lazy) or *edit* (from editor). **2.** The process of forming words in this way.

back·gam·mon (bak-gámmən, bák-gammən) *n.* A game for two persons, played on a specially marked board with pieces whose moves are determined by throws of dice. [BACK (referring to the movement of the pieces) + GAMMON (a type of victory in the game).]

back·ground (bák-grownd || *West Indies also* -grungd) *n.* **1.** The ground located behind closer areas. **2. a.** The space in pictorial representation, usually appearing as if in the distance, arranged to provide relief for the principal objects. **b.** The general scene or surface against or upon which designs, patterns, figures, or the like are seen or represented. **3.** An area or position of relative obscurity or unimportance. **4.** The underlying or supporting causes of or the contributory circumstances connected with an occurrence or development; the context in which something occurs. **5. a.** A person's experience, training, and education, often in a specified area. **b.** A person's social class, personal history, or family circumstances. **6. a.** Music or sounds heard as accompaniment to dialogue or action in a dramatic performance, film, or broadcast. **b.** Subdued music played in a public place, such as a restaurant or airport, to create atmosphere. **7.** Radiation at a constant low level at any specific location, usually due to traces of naturally occurring radioactive elements and cosmic rays. Also called "background radiation".

8. Noise or interference, usually at a constant level, that is picked up by electronic devices. —**back·ground** adj.

back·hand (bák-hand) n. **1.** In sports such as tennis and table-tennis, a stroke or motion, as of a racket, made with the back of the hand facing outwards and the arm typically held across the body. Compare **forehand. 2.** Handwriting characterised by letters that slant to the left.
~adj. Backhanded.
~adv. With a backhanded stroke or motion.
~tr.v. **backhanded, -handing, -hands.** To perform, hit, or catch backhand.

back·hand·ed (bák-hándid ‖ -handid) adj. **1.** Made with the back of the hand or with the back of the hand facing outwards and moving away from the body. **2.** Slanting towards the left. **3.** Containing a disguised insult or rebuke: a backhanded compliment. **4.** Twisted or formed in a direction opposite to the normal one: backhanded rope. —**back·hand·ed·ly** adv. —**back·hand·ed·ness** n.

back·hand·er (bák-handər, -hándər) n. **1.** Informal. A bribe. **2.** A backhanded stroke or hit. **3.** An indirect verbal attack.

back·ing (bácking) n. **1.** Material that provides support or strength from the back. **2.** Support or aid; endorsement. **3.** Those who provide aid or support. **4.** A musical accompaniment for a performer.

backing pump n. Any of the two or more pumps used in a modern vacuum pump system, which is connected directly to the atmosphere and is used to reduce the pressure to a value of between 100 and 0.1 pascal, prior to further evacuation by a second pump.

backing store n. A storage device in a computer, such as a tape or disk, outside the main memory. It usually has a larger capacity but longer access time than the main memory.

back·lash (bák-lash) n. **1.** A strongly adverse, usually delayed, reaction to some prior development that has been construed as a threat, as in the context of morality or social or race relations. **2.** A sudden or violent backward whipping motion. **3.** A snarl in the part of a fishing line wound round the reel. **4.** The play resulting from loose connections between gears or other mechanical elements, which is most evident on reversal of movement.

back·less (bák-ləss, -liss) adj. Having no back; especially, cut to the waist or very low at the back. Said of a dress.

back·list (bák-list) n. A publisher's list of older titles kept in print.

back·log (bák-log ‖ U.S. also -lawg) n. **1.** An accumulation, especially of unfinished work or unfilled orders. **2.** A reserve supply or source. **3.** Chiefly U.S. A large log placed at the back of a fire to support other logs and maintain heat.

back matter n. Printing. End matter (see).

back number n. **1.** An out-of-date periodical or newspaper. **2.** Informal. An out-of-date or old-fashioned person or thing.

back·pack (bák-pak) n. **1.** A piece of equipment, such as a set of oxygen cylinders, made to be carried on the back. **2.** Chiefly U.S. A rucksack.
~v. **back-packed, -packing, -packs.** —intr. To hike while carrying supplies in a backpack. —tr. To carry in a backpack. —**back·pack·er** n.

back passage n. The rectum (see). Used euphemistically.

back·ped·al (bák-péddʼl ‖ -peddʼl) intr.v. **-alled** or U.S. **-aled, -alling** or U.S. **-aling, -als. 1.** To turn the pedals backwards, as on a bicycle. **2.** To withdraw from or qualify a previous commitment, stance, opinion, or the like. **3.** In boxing, to go backwards.

back projection n. The projection of a film onto a screen from behind the screen, often used as a background for a scene being filmed from the front.

back·ra, buck·ra (búckrə ‖ bŏokra, báckrə) n. West Indian & U.S. A white person. Used by black people, often as a term of address equivalent to Sir or boss.
~adj. West Indian & U.S. Of very good quality; especially, characteristic of or used by a white person: backra house; backra rum. [Probably from Efik mbakara, master.]

back·rest (bák-rest) n. A support or rest for the back.

back·room (bák-rŏom, -rōom, -rŏom, -rōom) adj. Of or pertaining to a planning department or scientific laboratory in which confidential work, often governmental and military, is carried out and from which indirect influence is often exercised. —**back room** n.

back-room boy n. Informal. A person engaged in back-room work.

Backs (baks) pl.n. The gardens and grounds behind colleges of Cambridge University that border the river Cam. Preceded by the.

back·saw (bák-saw) n. A saw that is reinforced by a metal band along its back edge.

back·scat·ter (bák-skattər) n. The deflection of waves or particles through angles greater than 90° by electromagnetic or nuclear forces. Also called "backscattering".

back·scratch·er (bák-skrachər) n. **1.** A long-handled implement made of wood or plastic, used to scratch one's own back. **2.** Informal. One involved in the giving and receiving of favours for personal gain, often in an underhand way, as in politics or business. —**back·scratch·ing** n.

back seat n. **1.** A seat in the back, especially of a vehicle or an auditorium. **2.** Informal. A subordinate position. Used chiefly in the phrase take a back seat.

back-seat driver (bákseet) n. Informal. **1.** A passenger in a car who constantly advises, corrects, or nags the driver. **2.** Any person who persists in giving unsolicited advice.

backsheesh, backshish. Variants of **baksheesh.**

back·side (bák-sīd) n. Informal. The buttocks; rump.

back·sight (bák-sīt) n. **1.** The sight on a rifle nearer the stock. **2.** In surveying, a reading taken facing backwards to a previous position.

back·slap·ping (bák-slapping) adj. Excessively hearty. —**back·slap·ping** n.

back·slide (bák-slīd) intr.v. **-slid** (-slid), **-slid** or **-slidden** (-sliddʼn), **-sliding, -slides.** To revert to a bad habit, sin, wrongdoing, or the like. —**back·slid·er** n.

back·space (bák-spayss) intr.v. **-spaced, -spacing, -spaces.** To move the carriage of a typewriter back one or more spaces by striking the key used for this purpose.
~n. The key on a typewriter used for backspacing. Also called "backspacer".

back·spin (bák-spin) n. A spin that tends to retard, arrest, or reverse the linear motion of an object, especially of a ball.

back·stage (bák-stáyj) adv. **1.** In or towards the dressing rooms, wings, or other areas behind the performing area in a theatre. **2.** In or towards a place closed to public view; privately.
~adj. (bákstayj). **1.** Occurring or situated behind the performing area of a theatre. **2.** Not open or known to the public; private or concealed.

back·stairs (bák-staírz, -stairz) n. A secondary staircase at the back of a house; especially, one formerly used by servants.
~adj. Also **back·stair** (-staír). **1.** Furtive; clandestine. **2.** Scandalous.

back·stay (bák-stay) n. **1.** A rope or shroud extending from the top of the mast aft to the ship's side or stern to help support the mast. **2.** A support at or for the back of something.

back·stitch (bák-stich) n. A stitch made by inserting the needle at the midpoint of the preceding stitch, so that each stitch overlaps another by half its length. —**back·stitch** v.

back·stop (bák-stop) n. **1.** A device that prevents excessive backward movement, as of a machine part. **2.** Anything that serves, actually or figuratively, as a safeguard or restraint at the back.

back straight n. Chiefly British. The part of a racing circuit farthest from the spectators and opposite the home straight.

back·street (bák-street) n. A minor or side street, especially one away from a main thoroughfare.
~adj. **1.** Situated on or pertaining to a backstreet. **2.** Operating or performed illegally or secretly: a backstreet abortion.

back·stretch (bák-strech) n. Chiefly U.S. The back straight.

back·stroke (bák-strōk) n. **1.** A swimming stroke that resembles an inverted crawl. It is executed with the swimmer on his back, using a flutter kick, and moving his arms in backward circular strokes. **2.** Chiefly U.S. A backhanded stroke. **3.** A stroke or motion made in return or as a recoil.

back·swim·mer (bák-swimmər) n. Any of various water bugs of the family Notonectidae, that swim or float on their backs.

back·sword (bák-sawrd ‖ -sōrd) n. **1.** A sword with only one cutting edge. **2.** A stick used in fencing practice, a **singlestick** (see). **3.** One who fights with a backsword.

back talk n. U.S. Backchat.

back-to-back (bák-tə-bák) adj. **1.** Facing away from each other. **2.** British. Having the backs facing or adjoining. Said of rows of houses. **3.** Informal. In succession: two films back-to-back.
~n. British. A back-to-back house. —**back-to-back** adv.

back·track (bák-trak) intr.v. **-tracked, -tracking, -tracks. 1.** To go back over the course by which one has come. **2.** To reverse one's position or policy; retreat.

back up tr.v. **1.** To support or help, especially through reinforcement, confirmation, or safeguards. **2.** Printing. To print the reverse side of (a sheet). **3.** Computing. To provide a duplicate copy of (a data file). —intr.v. To accumulate.

back-up (bák-up) n. **1. a.** A reserve supply, as of provisions. **b.** One kept in reserve, as a safeguard or substitute, for example. **2.** Support or backing. **3.** Computing. A copy of a data file made and kept in case of computer failure. **4.** An overflow caused by clogged plumbing.
~adj. **1.** Kept in reserve; standby: a back-up pilot. **2.** Supporting; auxiliary.

back·veld (bák-felt, -velt) n. South African. A remote, rural, thinly populated area. [Afrikaans backvelt, "back field".] —**back·veld** adj. —**back·veld·er** (-feldər) n.

back·ward (bákwərd) adj. **1. a.** Directed or facing towards the back or rear. **b.** Directed towards the beginning or start. **c.** Directed towards the past; regressive. **2. a.** Done with the back leading or first: a backward somersault. **b.** Done or arranged in reverse or in a manner contrary to the usual. **3.** Unwilling to act; reluctant; shy. **4.** Behind others in progress or development; retarded.
~adv. Chiefly U.S. Variant of **backwards.** —**back·ward·ly** adv. —**back·ward·ness** n.

back·wards (bák-wərdz) adv. Also chiefly U.S. **backward. 1.** To or towards the back or rear. **2.** With the back leading. **3.** In a manner or order contrary to the usual or expected; in reverse. **4.** To, towards, or into the past.

back·wash (bák-wosh ‖ wawsh) n. **1.** Water moved backwards, as by the action of oars or a motor. **2.** A backward flow of air, as from the propeller of an aircraft. **3.** A flow of water back down a beach after a wave has broken. **4.** A condition resulting from some disturbing or irregular event; an aftermath.
~tr.v. **backwashed, -washing, -washes** To remove oil from (wool).

back·wa·ter (bák-wawtər ‖ U.S. also -wottər) n. **1.** Water held or pushed back by or as if by a dam or current; especially, a body of stagnant or still water thus formed. **2.** A place or situation regarded as stagnant or backward: a cultural backwater.

backwoods / baffle

back·woods (bák-wŏŏdz, -wŏŏdz) *pl.n.* **1.** *Chiefly U.S.* Heavily wooded, uncultivated, areas. **2.** Any remote, thinly populated, and backward area. **—back·woods** *adj.*

back·woods·man (bák-wŏŏdz-mən, -wŏŏdz-) *n., pl.* **-men** (-mən). **1.** One who lives or was brought up in a backwoods area, especially one who is unfamiliar with the customs of urban life; a rustic. **2.** *British.* A peer who rarely or never attends the House of Lords.

back yard, back·yard (bák-yárd) *n.* **1. a.** A yard at the rear of a house. **b.** *U.S.* A back garden. **2.** A region or sphere of special concern, especially one that is geographically close: *a war in America's back yard.*

baclava. Variant of **baklava.**

ba·con (báykən) *n.* The salted and often smoked meat from the back and sides of a pig. **—bring home the bacon.** *Informal.* **1.** To provide food and other necessities. **2.** To make good; succeed. **—save (one's) bacon.** To escape harm or loss. [Middle English *bacon, bakoun,* from Old French *bacon, bacun,* from Frankish *bako* (unattested), ham, from Germanic *bakkon* (unattested), perhaps akin to *bakam* (unattested), BACK.]

Ba·con (báykən), **Francis** (1909–92). Irish-born British painter. He is best known for his disturbing portraits in which subjects are distorted and invested with feelings of terror.

Bacon, Francis, 1st Baron Verulam, Viscount St. Albans (1561-1626). English philosopher, politician, and Lord Chancellor. His many influential writings include *The Advancement of Learning* (1605) and the *Novum organum* (1620), in which he put forward a new theory of scientific knowledge based on observation and experiment that came to be known as the inductive method.

Bacon, Roger (*c.* 1214–*c.* 1292). English scientist, encyclopedist, philosopher, alchemist, and Franciscan monk; for these diverse skills he was called *Doctor Mirabilis* ("Admirable Doctor").

Ba·co·ni·an (báy-kṓn-yən, bə-, -i-ən) *adj.* Of, pertaining to, or characteristic of the works or thought of Francis Bacon (1561–1626). **~n. 1.** A follower of the doctrines of Francis Bacon. **2.** One who believes that Francis Bacon wrote Shakespeare's plays.

bac·te·rae·mi·a (báktə-rēemi-ə) *n.* Also *Chiefly U.S.* **bac·te·re·mi·a.** The presence of viable bacteria in the blood. [New Latin : BACTER(IO)- + -AEMIA.] **—bac·te·rae·mic** *adj.* **—bac·te·rae·mi·cal·ly** *adv.*

bac·te·ri·a (bak-tếer-i-ə) *pl.n. Singular* **-rium** (-əm). *Abbr.* **bact.** Microorganisms, usually single-celled, constituting the class Schizomycetes, occurring in a wide variety of forms. Most bacteria are either free-living saprophytes, bringing about decomposition, or parasites, many of which cause disease. See Usage note at **germ.** [New Latin, plural of *bacterium,* from Greek *baktērion,* diminutive of *baktron,* rod.] **—bac·te·ri·al** *adj.* **—bac·te·ri·al·ly** *adv.*

bac·te·ri·cide (bak-tếeri-sīd) *n.* A substance that destroys bacteria. [BACTERI(O)- + -CIDE.] **—bac·te·ri·ci·dal** (-sī́d'l) *adj.*

bac·te·rin (báktərin) *n.* A vaccine prepared from dead bacteria. [BACTER(IO)- + -IN.]

bacterio-, bacteri-, bacter- *comb. form.* Indicates bacteria, bacterial activity, or relationship to bacteria; for example, **bacteriophage, bactericide, bacteroid.** [From BACTERIA.]

bac·te·ri·ol·o·gy (bak-tếer-i-óllaji) *n. Abbr.* **bacteriol.** The study of bacteria, especially in relation to medicine and agriculture. [BACTERIO- + -LOGY.] **bac·te·ri·o·log·i·cal** (-ə-lójik'l), **bac·te·ri·o·log·ic** *adj.* **—bac·te·ri·o·log·i·cal·ly** *adv.* **—bac·te·ri·ol·o·gist** (-óllajist) *n.*

bac·te·ri·ol·y·sis (bak-tếer-i-óllə-siss) *n.* The dissolution of bacteria, especially by the action of specific antibodies. [New Latin : BACTERIO- + -LYSIS.] **—bac·te·ri·o·lyt·ic** (-ə-líttik) *adj.*

bac·te·ri·o·phage (bak-tếer-i-ə-fayj) *n.* A virus that is parasitic on and destroys bacteria. Also called "phage". [BACTERIO- + -PHAGE.] **—bac·te·ri·o·phag·ic** (-fájik), **bac·te·ri·oph·a·gous** (-óffəgəss) *adj.* **—bac·te·ri·o·phag·i·cal·ly** *adv.*

bac·te·ri·o·sta·sis (bak-tếer-i-ō-stáy-siss, -stássiss) *n.* The arresting or inhibition of bacterial growth and reproduction, usually by the action of drugs. [New Latin : BACTERIO- + -STASIS.] **—bac·te·ri·o·stat·ic** (-státtik) *adj.* **—bac·te·ri·o·stat·i·cal·ly** *adv.*

bac·te·ri·um. Singular of **bacteria.**

bac·te·roid (báktə-royd) *adj.* Also **bac·te·roi·dal** (-róyd'l). Resembling bacteria in appearance or action. **~n.** Any of various irregularly shaped bacteria, such as those occurring on the roots of leguminous plants. [BACTER(IO)- + -OID.]

Bac·tri·an camel (báktri-ən) *n.* A two-humped camel, *Camelus bactrianus,* native to central and southwestern Asia and used as a beast of burden. Compare **Arabian camel.**

bac·u·li·form (bə-kéwli-fawrm, báckewli-) *adj.* Rod-shaped. [Latin *baculum,* stick, staff + -FORM.]

bad¹ (bad) *adj.* **worse** (wurss), **worst** (wurst). **1.** Inferior; poor in quality. **2.** Evil; wicked; sinful. **3.** Misbehaving; disobedient; naughty. **4.** Disagreeable; unpleasant; disturbing: *bad news.* **5.** Unfavourable: *bad reviews.* **6.** Rotten; spoiled; decomposed. **7.** Harmful in effect; detrimental: *bad habits.* **8.** Not able to be recovered or discharged: *a bad debt.* **9. a.** Faulty or incorrect: *bad grammar.* **b.** Incompetent: *bad at sums.* **10.** Not valid or genuine: *a bad cheque.* **11.** Severe; violent; intense: *a bad cold.* **12.** In poor health; in pain; ill. **13.** Sorry; regretful; unhappy: *Don't feel bad about it.* **14. bad·der, bad·dest.** *U.S. Slang.* Very good; excellent. **—in bad.** *Informal.* In trouble or disfavour. **~n.** Wickedness: *go to the bad.* **~adv.** *Chiefly U.S. Informal.* Badly. [Middle English *badde,* perhaps from Old English *bæddel,* effeminate man, hermaphrodite.] **—bad·ness** *n.*

bad². *Archaic.* A past tense of **bid.**

bad blood *n.* Bitterness; animosity.

bad·der·locks (báddər-loks) *n. Used with a singular or plural verb.* An edible seaweed, *Alaria esculenta,* having long, yellowish-green fronds. [18th century : origin obscure.]

bad·dy, bad·die (báddi) *n., pl.* **-dies.** *Informal.* A criminal or villain, especially as portrayed in a film, play, or book.

bade. A past tense of **bid.**

Ba·den¹ (baád'n) or **Baden bei Wien.** Spa town in Lower Austria, near Vienna, at the foot of the Wienerwald.

Baden². Health resort in Aargau canton, northern Switzerland, famous for its hot springs.

Baden³. Former state in southwest Germany. It is bounded by the rivers Main and Rhine. The region is now part of Baden-Württemberg.

Ba·den-Ba·den (baád'n-baád'n). Fashionable spa town in Baden-Württemberg, Germany. Its hot springs have been known since Roman times.

Ba·den-Pow·ell (báyd'n-pṓ-əl, *also* -pów-), **Robert Stephenson Smyth, 1st Baron** (1857–1941). British general, founder of the Scout movement. As a soldier he is famous for his heroic defence of **Mafeking** during the Boer War.

Ba·den-Würt·tem·berg (baád'n-véwrt-təm-berg, -vûr-). State of Germany. It was formed (1952) by the amalgamation of Baden, Württemberg-Baden, and Württemberg-Hohenzollern. Stuttgart is its capital.

bad faith *n.* A dishonest and deceiving attitude.

badge (baj) *n.* **1.** A small metal disc worn on clothing, bearing a design, slogan, or the like. **2.** A device or emblem worn as an insignia of rank, office, or membership of an organisation, or as an award or honour. **3.** Any characteristic mark or symbol. **—See Synonyms at sign.** [Middle English *bag(g)e†.*]

badg·er (bájər) *n.* **1.** Any of several large carnivorous, burrowing animals of the family Mustelidae, such as *Meles meles,* of Eurasia, typically having black and white stripes on the head, short legs, long claws on the front feet, and a heavy, silvery grizzled coat. **2.** The fur or hair of a badger. **3.** Any of several mammals related to or resembling the badger, such as the **honey badger** *(see),* or, in Australia, the wombat or the bandicoot. **~tr.v.** **badgered, -ering, -ers.** To harass persistently; pester. [16th century : perhaps BADGE (from the white mark on its forehead) + -ARD.]

Bad Godesberg. See **Bonn.**

bad·i·nage (báddi-naazh, -náazh) *n.* Light, playful banter; flippant repartee. [French, from *badin,* fool, joker, from Provençal, from *badar,* to gape, from Vulgar Latin *batāre* (unattested).]

bad·lands (bád-landz) *pl.n. Chiefly U.S.* An area of barren land characterised by roughly eroded ridges, peaks, and plateaus.

Badlands, The. A heavily eroded arid region of southwest South Dakota, United States, characterised by gullies and sharply indented ridges. It is now a National Monument.

bad·ly (bádli) *adv.* **worse, worst. 1.** In a bad manner. **2.** Very much; greatly.

badly off *adj.* **worse off, worst off.** In a state of poverty or need.

bad·min·ton (bád-mintən) *n.* **1.** A game played by volleying a shuttlecock back and forth over a high, narrow net by means of a light, long-handled racket. **2.** A drink usually made with claret, soda water, and sugar and served cold. [After BADMINTON.]

Badminton. A village in England, situated in the Cotswolds. Annual horse trials are held in the grounds of Badminton House (built 1682) the country seat of the Dukes of Beaufort, and the game of badminton is reputed to have originated there.

bad·mouth (bád-mowth, -mowth) *tr.v.* **-mouthed, -mouthing, -mouths.** *Chiefly U.S. Slang.* To criticise or disparage, often spitefully or unfairly; run down.

bad news *n. Used with a singular verb. Slang.* A troublesome or undesirable person, thing, or situation.

Baeda. See **Bede.**

Bae·de·ker (báydikər) *n.* **1.** Any of a series of guidebooks to Europe and the Middle East produced by the German publisher Karl Baedeker (1801–59) or his company. **2.** Any guidebook.

Baeke·land (báyk-land), **Leo Hendrick** (1863–1944). Belgian-born U.S. chemist and inventor. He invented the first plastic that hardens permanently on heating and that does not soften when reheated, which he called "Bakelite". He also invented the first commercially successful photographic printing paper.

Baer (bair), **Karl Ernst von** (1792–1876). Estonian-born German zoologist. He made pioneering researches in the mammalian reproductive system, discovering the mammalian egg, and he is considered to be one of the founders of the science of embryology.

Ba·ez (bǐ-ez, bī́-ez), **Joan** (1941–). U.S. folk singer and political activist.

Baf·fin Island (báffin). Formerly **Baffin Land.** The largest island in the Canadian Arctic Archipelago, and at 476,068 square kilometres (183,810 square miles) the fifth-largest island in the world.

baf·fle (baff'l) *tr.v.* **-fled, -fling, -fles. 1.** To foil; thwart; frustrate: *The police were baffled by the lack of clues.* **2.** To perplex to the point of helplessness; bewilder. **3.** To impede the force or movement of; interfere with. **—See Synonyms at puzzle.** **~n.** Any structure used to impede, regulate, or alter the flow of a fluid or to control the emission or distribution of sound. Also called "baffle board", "baffle plate". [Perhaps obscurely related to French *bafouer*, to hoodwink, deceive, from Old French *beffert*, ridicule.] —**baf·fle·ment** *n.* —**baf·fler** *n.*

baf·fling (báffling) *adj.* **1.** Of a nature that defies solution or understanding; bewildering. **2.** *Nautical.* Shifting in direction and tending to impede or interfere with progress. Said of winds.

bag (bag) *n.* **1.** A container in the form of a sack or pouch, made from a flexible material, such as paper, cloth, plastic, or leather. **2.** A woman's handbag. **3.** A suitcase, satchel, or other piece of hand luggage. **4.** An organic sac or pouch, such as the udder of a cow. **5.** Something resembling a bag or pouch. **6.** *Nautical.* The bulging part of a sail. **7. a.** The amount held in a bag; a bagful. **b.** *British.* Any of various units of dry measure. **8.** The amount of game killed or permitted to be killed in a single day during one shooting expedition, or by one member of a shoot. **9.** *Informal.* A collection of persons or things: *His friends were a mixed bag.* **10.** *Plural. Informal.* A great deal. **11.** *Plural. Informal.* Wide, loose-fitting trousers. **12.** *Slang.* An area of interest, activity or skill: *Cooking is not my bag.* **13.** *Slang.* An unpleasant or unattractive woman: *a disagreeable old bag.* **14.** A small amount of heroin, marijuana, or some other drug wrapped in paper. —**bag and baggage.** With all one's belongings; completely: *He moved out bag and baggage.* —**in the bag.** *Slang.* Assured of successful outcome; virtually accomplished or won.
~*v.* **bagged, bagging, bags.** —*tr.* **1.** To put into a bag. **2.** To cause to bulge like a bag. **3.** To capture or kill (game). **4. a.** *Informal.* To gain possession of; capture or steal. **b.** To reserve the right to do or have. **5.** *Australian Slang.* To disparage; belittle. —*intr.* **1.** To hang or bulge loosely. **2.** To swell out. [Middle English *bagge*, from Old Norse *baggit*.]

ba·gasse (bə-gáss) *n.* The dry pulp remaining from sugar cane or sugar beet after the juice has been extracted, used for making paper and as a fuel. [French, from Spanish *bagazo*, dregs, from *baga*, pod, husk, from Latin *bāca, bacca*, berry.]

bag·a·telle (bágga-tél) *n.* **1.** An unimportant or insignificant thing; a trifle. **2.** A short piece of light verse or music. **3.** A game similar to pinball, played on a sloping board with a metal ball, released by a hand-operated spring, that scores by becoming lodged in pins or holes. [French, from Italian *bagatella*, diminutive formation perhaps from Latin *bāca, bacca*, berry.]

Bage·hot (bájət), **Walter** (1826–77). British economist, journalist, political theorist, and literary critic. He wrote *The English Constitution* (1867), an analysis of the comparative powers of the British organs of government.

ba·gel (báyg'l), **bei·gel** (bíg'l) *n.* A ring-shaped roll with a tough, chewy texture, made from plain yeast dough that is dropped briefly into nearly boiling water and then baked. [Yiddish *beygel*, ultimately from Middle High German *bouc*, ring, bracelet, from Old High German *boug*.]

bag·ful (bág-fŏŏl) *n., pl.* **-fuls** or **bagsful.** The amount held by or contained in a bag.

bag·gage (bággij) *n.* **1. a.** Luggage carried while travelling by aeroplane or ship. **b.** *Chiefly U.S.* Luggage. **2.** The movable equipment and supplies of an army; impedimenta. **3.** *Informal.* A badly-behaved, impudent, or saucy girl or woman. **4.** A set of ideas, beliefs, theories, or the like, especially when out-of-date or redundant. [Middle English *bagage*, from Old French, from *baguet*, bundle, pack.]

bag·ging (bágging) *n.* Coarse material used for making bags.

bag·gy (bággi) *adj.* **-gier, -giest.** Bulging or hanging loosely: *baggy trousers.* —**bag·gi·ly** *adv.* —**bag·gi·ness** *n.*

Bagh·dad or **Bag·dad** (bág-dád). The capital of Iraq since 1921, reputed to be the fabled city of the "Thousand and One Nights". Situated on the river Tigris near the centre of the country, it was built by the Abbassid caliph, Al Mansur (8th century A.D.)-on the site of an old Babylonian town. Modern Baghdad is an important industrial, commercial, and cultural centre in the Arab world.

bag lady *n.* *Chiefly U.S.* A female down-and-out or vagrant, especially one who carries her belongings in plastic bags.

bag·man (bág-mən) *n., pl.* **-men** (-mən). **1.** *British.* A travelling salesman. **2.** *U.S. Slang.* A person who collects money for racketeers. **3.** *Australian.* A tramp; a swagman.

bagn·io (bán-yō, bàan-) *n., pl.* **-ios. 1.** A brothel. **2.** *Obsolete.* A prison for slaves in the Orient. **3.** *Obsolete.* A public bathhouse in Italy or Turkey. [Italian *bagno*, "bath", from Latin *balneum*, from Greek *balaneiont*.]

bag of bones *n.* *Informal.* A very thin person or animal.

bag·pipes (bág-pīpss) *pl. n.* A musical instrument having a flexible bag inflated either by being blown into through a tube with valves or by bellows, a double-reed melody pipe, and from one to four drone pipes. —**bag·pip·er** *n.*

bags (bagz) *interj.* Also **bags I.** *Informal.* Used, especially by children, to lay claim to an article or to reserve the right to do something.

ba·guette (ba-gét) *n.* Also **ba·guet** (for senses 1, 2, 3). **1.** A gem cut into the form of a narrow rectangle. **2.** The form of such a gem. **3.** *Architecture.* A narrow, convex moulding. **4.** A long, stick-shaped loaf of French bread. [French, "small rod", from Italian *bacchetta*, diminutive of *bacchio*, rod, from Latin *baculum*, stick, staff.]

bag·worm (bág-wurm) *n.* The larva of any of several moths of the family Psychidae, that encloses itself in a characteristic fibrous case, and that feeds upon and destroys tree foliage.

bah (baa ‖ ba) *interj.* Used to express impatient rejection or contempt. [Probably from French (imitative).]

ba·ha·dur (bə-háa-dər, -door ‖ *U.S. also* -háw-) *n.* A Hindu title of respect. Often used with the names of army officers. [Hindi *bahādur*, hero, from Persian *bahādurt*, brave.]

Ba·ha·i (bə-háa-i, baa-, -hī) *adj.* Of, pertaining to, or designating a religion founded in 1863 by the Iranian religious leader Bahaullah, developed from **Babism** *(see)*, and emphasising the spiritual unity of all mankind.
~*n.* A teacher of or believer in the Bahai faith. [Persian *bahā'ī*, "of glory", from *Bahā' u'llāh*, Bahaullah, "Glory of God".] —**Ba·ha·ism** (-háa-iz'm, -hī-) *n.* —**Ba·ha·ist** *adj. & n.*

Ba·ha·mas, Commonwealth of The (bə-háaməz). Island state in the Atlantic Ocean, comprising some 700 islands, and islets, and numerous cays. Columbus made his first landfall there in 1492. The islands became a British colony (1717), internally self-governing (1964), and independent within the Commonwealth (1973). Tourism, including gambling, provides more than 60 per cent of state revenues. Agriculture, fishing, and small industries are developing, but 80 per cent of food requirements are still imported. Some 80 per cent of the people are black descendants of slaves. Area, 13 935 square kilometres (5,379 square miles). Population 280,000. Capital, Nassau on New Providence Island. See map at **Cuba.** —**Ba·ha·mi·an** (bə-háymi-ən) *adj. & n.*

Ba·ha·sa Indonesia (bə-háa-sə, baa-) *n.* The Malay language that is the official language of the Republic of Indonesia.

Bahasa Malaysia *n.* Also **Bahasa Malay.** The Malay language that is the official language of Malaysia.

Ba·hi·a (bə-héə, baa-, -ée-). State of northeast Brazil. Its capital is Salvador (also called Bahia).

Bah·rain, State of (baa-ráyn, bàahə-). Arab country comprising a group of low, sandy islands off eastern Arabia. It was the first Arabian state to strike oil (1932), but this is now running out. However, oil revenues have created a welfare state and new industries, including oil refining (of imported and home-produced oil), and ship repairing. Bahrain is also a banking, communications, and tax-free entrepôt centre for the Gulf region. Area, 695 square kilometres (268 square miles). Population, 600,000. Capital, Manama on Bahrain Island. See map at **Gulf States.**

Bahr el Azraq. See Blue Nile.

Bahret Lut. See Dead Sea.

baht (baat) *n., pl.* **bahts** or **baht. 1.** The basic monetary unit of Thailand, equal to 100 satangs. **2.** A note worth one baht. [Thai *bāt*.]

ba·hu·vri·hi (bàahoo-vréehee) *adj.* Designating a word made up of two elements, the first of which describes a feature of the second; for example, *greybeard.* Compare **dvandva.** [Sanskrit "having much rice", a compound made in this way.] —**ba·hu·vri·hi** *n.*

Bai·kal, Lake (bī-kal, bī-kál, -kàal). The world's deepest lake, situated in Siberia in Russia. Its maximum depth is 1 742 metres (5,714 feet), and it covers 31 492 square kilometres (12,159 square miles).

bail¹ (bayl) *n.* **1.** Security, usually a sum of money, exchanged for the release of an arrested person, as a guarantee of his appearance for trial. **2.** Release from imprisonment provided by the payment of such security. **3.** The person who provides such security. —**jump bail.** To fail to appear in court when required after having been allowed bail. —**stand** or **go bail for.** To supply bail for; act as security for.
~*tr.v.* **bailed, bailing, bails. 1.** To secure the release of (a person) by providing bail. Often used with *out.* **2.** To release (a person) for whom bail has been paid. **3.** To deliver or transfer (property) to another for a special purpose, but without permanent transference of ownership. —**bail out.** *Informal.* To extricate (another) from a difficult situation. [Middle English *baile*, "custody", from Old French *bail*, from *baillier*, to take charge of, carry, from Latin *bājulāre*, from *bājulust*, carrier.] —**bail·er** *n.*

bail² *v.* **bailed, bailing, bails.** Also **bale.** —*tr.* **1.** To remove (water) from a boat by repeatedly filling a container and emptying it over the side. **2.** To empty (a boat) of water by this means. Usually used with *out.* —*intr.* To empty a boat of water by scooping or dipping. —**bail out.** *Chiefly U.S.* To bale out from an aircraft.
~*n.* A container used for bailing. [Middle English *baille*, bucket, from Old French, probably from Vulgar Latin *bājula* (unattested), "carrier (of water)", from Latin *bājulus*, carrier. See **bail** (security).] —**bail·er** *n.*

bail³, bale (bayl) *n.* **1.** The arched, hooplike handle of a pail, kettle, or similar container. **2.** An arch or hoop, such as those used to support the top of a covered wagon. **3.** *Australian & N.Z.* A frame used to secure the head of a cow while it is being milked. —**bail up.** *Australian & N.Z.* To secure (a cow) in a bail. [Middle English *baile*, handle, probably from Old Norse *beygla*, bow, from *beygja* to bend.]

bail⁴ *n.* **1.** *Cricket.* One of the two small bars of wood placed across the top of the stumps to form the wicket. **2.** A pole or bar used to separate horses in an open stable. **3.** The hinged bar on a typewriter holding the paper against the platen. —**bail up.** *Australian.* **1.** To hold up in order to rob. **2.** To accost in order to speak to. [Middle English, from Old French *bail(e)*, enclosed court, from *bailert* to enclose.]

bail·a·ble (báyləb'l) *adj.* **1.** Eligible for bail. **2.** Allowing or admitting of bail: *a bailable offence.*

Baile Átha Cliath. See Dublin.

bail·ee (báy-lée) *n.* A person to whom property is bailed.

bai·ley (báyli) *n., pl.* **-leys.** The outer wall of a castle or the space enclosed by it. [Middle English *bailly, baile,* variant of BAIL (cricket, etc.).]

Bailey bridge *n.* A temporary steel bridge that can be assembled rapidly from prefabricated parts. [Designed by Sir Donald *Bailey* (1901–85), British engineer.]

bail·ie (báyli) *n.* Formerly, a Scottish municipal magistrate, elected by town councillors. [Middle English *bailli,* from Old French, variant of *baillif,* BAILIFF.]

bail·iff (báyliff) *n.* **1.** *Chiefly British.* An agent who administers an estate on behalf of a landowner; a steward. **2.** An official who assists a sheriff and who has the power to execute writs, processes, and arrests. **3.** *Chiefly U.S.* A court attendant entrusted with a variety of duties, such as the custody of prisoners under arraignment. **4.** Formerly, a king's officer such as a sheriff or mayor, especially the chief officer of a hundred. **5.** The chief civil officer in Jersey and Guernsey. [Middle English *baillif,* from Old French, from Medieval Latin *bājulīvus,* from Latin *bājulus,* carrier, "person in charge". See **bail** (security).]

bail·i·wick (báyli-wik) *n.* **1.** The office or district of a bailiff. **2.** A person's specific area of interest, skill, or authority. Used humorously. [Middle English *bailliwik* : BAILIE + WICK.]

bail·ment (báylmənt) *n. Law.* **1.** The process of providing bail for an accused person. **2.** The act of delivering goods or personal property to another in trust.

bail·or (báyl-ər, -ôr) *n. Law.* A person who bails property to another.

bails·man (báylz-mən) *n., pl.* **-men.** (-mən). *Law. Archaic.* One who provides bail or security for another.

Bai·ly's beads (báyliz ‖ báyleez) *pl. n.* Bright spots of sunlight that appear briefly around the edge of the moon's disc immediately before and after the central phase in a solar eclipse, caused by the sun's shining through lunar valleys. [After Francis *Baily* (1774–1844), British astronomer.]

bain-ma·rie (bán-mə-rée) *n., pl.* **bains-ma·rie** (*pronounced as singular*). A device consisting of a large pan containing hot water in which smaller pans may be set to cook slowly or keep warm. [French, from Medieval Latin *balneum Mariae,* "bath of Mary" (mistranslation of Medieval Greek *kaminos Marias,* "furnace of Mary"), after *Mary,* sister of Moses and an alleged alchemist.]

Bai·ram (bī-rám, bī-ram) *n.* Either of two Muslim festivals occurring after Ramadan: *Lesser Bairam* occurs at the end of Ramadan and lasts for 3 days; *Greater Bairam* occurs 70 days later and lasts for 4 days. [Turkish *bayrām.*]

Baird (baird), **John Logie** (1888–1946). Scottish electrical engineer noted for his pioneering work in the field of television, and in the use of radar and fibre optics.

bairn (bairn) *n. Scottish & Northern English.* A child. [Middle English *barn,* Old English *bearn.*]

Bairns·fa·ther (baírnz-faathər), **(Charles) Bruce** (1888–1959). British cartoonist and author, famous for his World War I cartoon character, *Old Bill.*

bait¹ (bayt) *n.* **1.** Food or other lure placed on a hook or in a trap and used in the catching of fish, birds, or other animals. **2.** Any enticement; a temptation. **3. a.** *Chiefly British. Archaic.* A stop for food or rest during a journey or a break from work. **b.** The food or drink consumed during such a break.
~*v.* **baited, baiting, baits.** —*tr.* **1.** To place food or other lure in or on (a trap or fishing hook). **2.** To lure or entice, especially by trickery or strategy. **3.** To set dogs upon (a chained animal, for example) for sport. **4.** To attack or torment, especially with persistent insult, criticism, or ridicule. **5.** To tease. **6.** *Archaic.* To feed (an animal) on a journey. —*intr. Archaic.* To stop for food or rest during a journey. —See Synonyms at **harass.** [Middle English, partly from Old Norse *beita,* to hunt with dogs, harass, and partly from Old Norse *beita* (a separate word), pasture, food, fish bait.] —**bait·er** *n.*

bait². *Falconry.* Variant of **bate.**

baize (bayz) *n.* A cotton or woollen material resembling felt, often bright green in colour, and used chiefly as a cover for snooker and billiard tables. [French *baie* (plural *baies*), from *bai,* BAY (probably its original colour).]

Baja California. See **Lower California.**

Baj·an (báyjən) *adj. & n. Informal.* Barbadian. [From (Bar)*badian.*]

bake (bayk) *v.* **baked, baking, bakes.** —*tr.* **1. a.** To cook with continuous, even, dry heat, especially in an oven. **b.** To make by baking: *bake a cake; bake bread.* **2.** To harden, dry, or otherwise affect by subjecting to heat in or as if in an oven. —*intr.* **1.** To cook food, primarily bread, cakes, or pastry, by baking. **2.** To become cooked by baking. **3.** To become hard, dry, or otherwise affected by exposure to steady, dry heat. **4.** *Informal.* To feel very hot.
~*n.* **1.** The act or process of baking. **2.** *Chiefly U.S.* A social gathering at which food is baked and served. Sometimes used in combination: *a clambake.* [Middle English *baken,* Old English *bacan.*]

baked Alaska (baykt) *n.* A pudding consisting of ice cream covered with meringue, which is baked for a short time at a high temperature.

baked beans *pl. n.* Haricot beans baked and served in tomato sauce and usually tinned.

Ba·ke·lite (báykəlīt) *n.* A trademark for any of a group of thermosetting plastics having high chemical and electrical resistance and used in a variety of manufactured articles. [After Leo BAEKELAND.]

bak·er (báykər) *n.* **1.** One who bakes and sells bread, cakes, or the like. **2.** *U.S.* A portable oven.

Ba·ker (báykər), **Dame Janet Abbott** (1933–). British mezzo-soprano. She is particularly noted for her performances in early opera, but retired in 1982. She was made a Dame in 1976.

baker's dozen *n.* A group of 13; one dozen plus one. [After the former custom among bakers of adding an extra roll to every dozen purchased as a safeguard against the possibility that 12 rolls might be underweight.]

bak·er·y (báykəri) *n., pl.* **-ies.** **1.** A place where products such as bread, cake, and pastries are baked. Also called "bakehouse". **2.** A shop where baked goods are sold.

Bake·well tart (báyk-wel) *n.* A pastry tart filled with jam and topped by an almond-flavoured paste. [After *Bakewell,* Derbyshire.]

Bakh·ta·ran (bək-tá-rán). See **Ker·man·shah.**

Ba·kı. See **Baku.**

bak·ing (báyking) *adj. Informal.* Extremely hot.
~*adv.* Used as an intensive: *baking hot.*

baking powder *n.* Any of various powdered mixtures of sodium bicarbonate, starch, and at least one slightly acidic compound such as cream of tartar, used as a raising agent in baking.

baking soda *n.* A chemical compound, **sodium bicarbonate** *(see).*

bak·kie (bácki) *n. South African.* **1.** A light lorry or van with an open back. **2.** A bowl or similar container. [Afrikaans *bak,* container + *-ie,* diminutive suffix.]

ba·kla·va, ba·cla·va (báa-klə-vaa, báklə-) *n.* A dessert made of paper-thin layers of pastry, chopped nuts, and honey. [Turkish.]

bak·sheesh (bák-sheesh, -shéesh) *n.* Also **bak·shish, back·sheesh, back·shish.** In Turkey, Egypt, India, and other Eastern countries, a tip, gratuity, or charitable gift. [Persian *bakhshīsh,* from *bakhshīdan,* to give.]

Bakst (bakst ‖ baakst), **Léon** (1866-1924). Russian artist noted for his work in modernising theatre design. His best-known works were for ballets produced by Sergei **Diaghilev** in Paris.

Ba·ku (baa-kōō, -kōō). *Azeri* Baki (baáka). Capital and major port of Azerbaijan, on the Caspian Sea, and a centre of oil production.

Ba·ku·nin (bə-kōōnin), **Mikhail Aleksandrovich** (1814–76). Russian anarchist and political theorist. Imprisoned in Russia for his revolutionary activities and exiled to Siberia, he escaped to London (1861). After many arguments with Marx, his brand of anarchism took final shape as the antithesis of Marx's communism.

BAL *n.* British Anti-Lewisite: a colourless, oily, viscous liquid, $C_3H_5(SH)_2(OH)$, used as an antidote for poisoning caused by lewisite, organic arsenic compounds, and heavy metals including mercury and gold. Also called "dimercaprol".

bal. balance.

Bala, Lake (bál-ə). *Welsh* **Llyn Tegid.** The largest natural lake in Wales, situated in Gwynedd. Drained in the north by the river Dee, it is 6 kilometres (4 miles) long.

bal·a·cla·va (bál-ə-kláàvə) *n. Sometimes capital* **B.** **1.** A woollen hood almost completely covering the head and neck. **2.** A similar hood often covering the shoulders as well, worn by soldiers and sailors, and originally worn by soldiers fighting in the Crimean War. Also called "balaclava helmet". [After BALAKLAVA.]

Ba·la·kla·va (bál-ə-kláàvə). A small port in south Crimea in Ukraine, now part of Sevastopol. It is famous for the battle between Russian troops and Turkish and British troops (1854) in the Crimean War, during which the British Light Brigade made a hopeless charge against heavy Russian guns.

bal·a·lai·ka (bál-ə-líkə) *n.* A Russian musical instrument with a triangular body and three strings. [Russian.]

bal·ance (bál-ənss) *n. Abbr.* **bal.** **1. a.** A weighing device typically consisting of a rigid beam, horizontally suspended by a low-friction support at its centre, with identical weighing pans hung at either end, one of which holds an unknown weight while the effective weight in the other is changed by known amounts until the beam is level and motionless. Also called "beam balance". **b.** Any of various other weighing devices, such as a **spring balance** *(see).* **2.** A critical state in which the outcome is still to be determined: *lives hanging in the balance.* **3.** A stable state characterised by cancellation of all forces, weights, or the like by equal opposing ones. **4.** A state of bodily equilibrium. **5.** A stable mental or psychological state; emotional equilibrium. **6.** A harmonious or satisfying arrangement or proportion of parts or elements, as in a design or composition. **7. a.** An influence or force tending to produce equilibrium; a counterpoise. **b.** A control or mechanism for achieving balance; specifically, a control balancing the average sound level from a high-fidelity system. **8.** The difference in magnitude between opposing forces, weights, or influences, representing the excess held by one side over another: *The balance of control lies with the parents.* **9. a.** Equality of totals in the debit and credit sides of an account. **b.** The difference between such totals, either on the credit or the debit side of an account. **10.** *Informal.* Anything that remains or is left over. **11.** *Chemistry.* Equality of the number, kinds, and net electric charge of reacting atoms on each side of a chemical equation. **12.** *Mathematics.* Equality with respect to the net number of reduced symbolic quantities on each side of an equation. **13.** A balance wheel *(see).* **14.** A dance movement first towards and then away from one's partner. **15.** *Capital* **B.** *Astronomy.* A constellation and sign of the zodiac, **Libra** *(see).* —**on balance.** All things considered. —**strike a balance.** To achieve a state or position between extremes.
~*v.* **balanced, -ancing, -ances.** —*tr.* **1.** To weigh or poise in or as

if in a balance. **2.** To compare as if weighing in the mind. **3.** To bring into or maintain in a state of equilibrium. **4.** To act as an equalising weight or force to; offset; counterbalance. **5. a.** To calculate the difference between the debits and credits of (an account). **b.** To reconcile or equalise the sums of the debits and credits of (an account). **c.** To settle by paying what is owed. **6.** To bring into or keep in equal or satisfying proportion or harmony. **7.** *Mathematics.* To bring (an equation) into mathematical balance. **8.** *Chemistry.* To bring (a chemical equation) into chemical balance. **9.** To move towards and then away from (one's dance partner). —*intr.* **1.** To be in or come into equilibrium. **2.** To be equal or equivalent. **3.** To sway or waver as if losing or regaining equilibrium. **4.** To be in or come into a state of balance. Used of a chemical or mathematical equation. **5.** To move towards and then away from one's dance partner. [Middle English, from Old French, from Vulgar Latin *bilancia* (unattested), scales, from Late Latin *(lībra) bilanx* (stem *bilanc-*), (a balance) having two scales : Latin *bi-*, double + *lanx†*, scale, plate, pan.]

balance of nature *n.* The state of stability achieved by plant and animal communities in their natural environment by means of such interactions as adaptation and competition.

balance of payments *n.* A systematic recording of a nation's total payments to foreign countries and international institutions, including the price of imports and the outflow of capital and gold, and its total receipts from abroad, including the price of exports, invisible trade, and the inflow of capital and gold.

balance of power *n.* **1.** A distribution of power between nations, often by means of alliance and counteralliance, whereby no one nation is able to dominate or conquer the others. **2.** Any similar distribution of power.

balance of terror *n.* A balance of power between nations, especially the Eastern and Western blocs, maintained by an equivalent distribution of nuclear weapons.

balance of trade *n.* The difference in value between the total exports and imports of a nation. Also called "visible balance".

bal·anc·er (bál-ənssər) *n.* **1.** One that balances. **2.** A rudimentary insect wing, a **haltere** *(see).*

balance sheet *n.* A statement of the assets and liabilities of a business, association, or individual at a given date.

balance wheel *n.* A wheel that regulates rate of movement in machine parts; especially, a wheel that swings back and forth against a hair spring in a watch or small clock. Also called "balance".

Bal·an·chine (bál-ən-cheén, -cheen), **George.** born Georgy Melitonovich Balanchivadze (1904–83). Russian-born U.S. ballet dancer, choreographer, and director. In 1948 he was appointed artistic director of the New York City Ballet. He choreographed over 100 ballets including *Firebird*, in 1950, and *Don Quixote*, in 1965.

Ba·la·ra·ma (búllə-ráa-mə, -maa). *Hinduism.* See **Rama.**

bal·as (bál-əss) *n.* A rose-red to orange spinel, used as a semiprecious gem. [Middle English, from Old French *balais*, from Arabic *bálakhsh*, from Persian *Badhakhshān*, a region in northeastern Iran, where the gem is found.]

ba·la·ta (bə-láatə, bál-ətə) *n.* **1.** A tropical American tree, *Manilkara bidentata*, that yields a latex-like sap. **2.** A tough, non-elastic, gum obtained from this sap and used for golf-ball covers, industrial belting, and gaskets. [American Spanish, from Carib.]

Ba·la·ton, Lake (bál-ə-ton, ból-). The largest lake in Central Europe, situated in western Hungary. It has an area of 600 square kilometres (230 square miles), and many lakeside resorts.

bal·bo·a (bal-bṓ-ə) *n.* **1.** The basic monetary unit of Panama, equal to 100 centesimos. **2.** A coin worth one balboa. [After Vasco Núñez de BALBOA.]

Bal·bo·a, Vasco Núñez de (1475–1517). Spanish explorer and colonial governor, who discovered the Pacific Ocean (1513).

bal·brig·gan (bal-bríggən) *n.* **1.** A knitted unbleached cotton fabric, often used in the manufacture of underwear. **2.** *Usually plural.* Underwear made of this fabric. [After *Balbriggan*, Irish seaport where it was first manufactured.]

Bal·con (báwl-kən), **Sir Michael** (1896–1977). British film producer who as head of Ealing Studios from 1938–59 was responsible for such classics as *Kind Hearts and Coronets* (1949) and *The Lavender Hill Mob* (1951). He also produced *The Thirty-Nine Steps* (1935) and *Saturday Night and Sunday Morning* (1960).

bal·co·ny (bál-kəni) *n., pl.* **-nies. 1.** A platform that projects from the wall of a building and is surrounded by a railing, balustrade, or parapet. **2.** A gallery above the dress circle in a theatre or auditorium. **3.** *U.S.* The dress circle. [Italian *balcone*, from Germanic *balkon* (unattested).]

bald (bawld ‖ bold) *adj.* **balder, baldest. 1.** Having little or no hair on the top of the head. **2.** Lacking natural or usual covering: *a bald spot on the lawn.* **3.** Having the tread worn away through use. Said of a tyre. **4.** Having white feathers or markings on the head: *a bald eagle.* **5.** Lacking ornament; bare; unadorned. **6.** Undisguised; blunt: *a bald statement.* [Middle English *ballede*, perhaps Old English *bǽllede* (unattested), from *ball-* (unattested), "white patch".] —**bald·ly** *adv.* —**bald·ness** *n.*

bal·da·chin, bal·da·quin (báwl-də-kin ‖ bál-, ból-) *n.* Also **bal·da·chi·no** (-kéenō). **1.** A rich fabric of silk and gold brocade. **2.** A canopy of fabric carried in church processions or placed over an altar, throne, or dais. **3.** *Architecture.* A stone or marble structure built in the form of a canopy, especially over the altar of a church.

[Italian *baldacchino*, from Old Italian, from *Baldacco*, BAGHDAD, famous in the Middle Ages for its brocades.]

bald eagle *n.* A North American eagle, *Haliaeetus leucocephalus*, having a dark body and a white head and tail. It appears on the Great Seal of the United States. Also called "American eagle".

Bal·der (báwl-dər ‖ ból-). *Norse mythology.* The god of peace and light, son of Odin and Frigg, renowned for his goodness and beauty.

bal·der·dash (báwldər-dash ‖ bóldər-) *n.* Nonsense. [16th century ("froth", "mixture of drinks") : origin obscure.]

bald-faced (báwld-fayst ‖ bóld-) *adj.* **1.** Having a white face or face markings. **2.** *Chiefly U.S.* Brash; undisguised.

bald·head (báwld-hed ‖ ból-) *n.* **1.** A person whose head is bald. **2.** Any of several birds having white markings on the head.

bald-head·ed (báwld-héddid ‖ bóld-) *adj.* Having a bald head.

balding (báwlding ‖ bóld-) *adj.* Becoming bald.

bald·pate (báwld-payt ‖ bóld-) *n.* A baldheaded person.

bal·dric (báwl-drik ‖ ból-) *n.* A belt, usually of ornamented leather, worn over one shoulder and across the chest to support a sword or bugle. [Middle English *baud(e)rik*, from Old French *baldrei, baudrei†*.]

Bald·win (báwld-win), **James (Arthur)** (1924–87). U.S. black author and dramatist whose first novel *Go Tell it on the Mountain* (1953), was based on his early experiences of religion and deprivation in Harlem, New York City.

Baldwin, Stanley, 1st Earl Baldwin of Bewdley (1867–1947). British Conservative prime minister (1923–1929; 1935–1937). As prime minister, he responded to the General Strike of 1926 with an anti-union bill, the Trade Disputes Act of 1927, and was at the political centre of the events leading to Edward VIII's abdication.

bale¹ (bayl) *n.* A large bound package or bundle of raw or processed material.

~*tr.v.* **baled, baling, bales.** To wrap or form into bales. —**bale out. 1.** To parachute from an aircraft, especially in an emergency. **2.** To abandon a project or enterprise. [Middle English, probably from Old French, from Germanic.] —**bal·er** *n.*

bale² *n. Archaic & Poetic.* **1.** Evil influence. **2.** Mental suffering; anguish. [Middle English *bale*, Old English *bealu*, from Germanic.]

bale³. Variant of **bail** (to empty a boat).

bale⁴. Variant of **bail** (hoop or hooplike device).

Bâle. See **Basel.**

Bal·e·ar·ic Islands (bál-i-árrik). *Spanish* **Islas Baleares.** Archipelago in the Mediterranean, off the east coast of Spain. A Spanish province, it includes the islands of Mallorca (Majorca), Menorca (Minorca), Ibiza, and Formentera. Because of their mild climate, the principal local industry is tourism.

ba·leen (bə-léen, ba-) *n.* **Whalebone** *(see).* [Middle English *balene*, whale, baleen, from Old French *baleine*, from Latin *balaena*, whale.]

bale·fire (báyl-fīr) *n. Archaic.* **1.** A funeral pyre. **2.** A bonfire; a beacon. [Old English *bǽl* and Old Norse *bál*, "great fire, pyre" + FIRE.]

bale·ful (bayl-f′l) *adj.* **1.** Harmful or malignant in intent or effect. **2.** Portending evil; dire. —**bale·ful·ly** *adv.* —**bale·ful·ness** *n.*

Usage: Similarity in form leads to confusion between *baleful* and *baneful. Baleful* literally means something that exerts evil influence, or foreshadows evil; *baneful* means poisonous or deadly. Both are figuratively used with a less emphatic meaning. So, *she gave me a baleful look* generally means threatening or gloomy, rather than evil, and *the baneful effects of pollution* simply means harmful.

Ba·len·ci·a·ga (bál-en-si-áágə), **Cristóbal** (1895–1972). Spanish fashion designer. He settled in Paris in 1937 and became noted for his stark, elegant designs.

Bal·four (bál-fər, -fawr ‖ -fōr), **A(rthur) J(ames), 1st Earl** (1848–1930). British Conservative prime minister (1902–05). He served as Foreign Secretary in Lloyd George's Cabinet from 1916–19.

Balfour Declaration *n.* A statement by A.J. Balfour on 2 November 1917 that Britain would support the establishment of a national home for Jews in Palestine, on condition that the rights of existing non-Jewish communities there would be safeguarded.

Ba·li (baáli). Indonesian island east of Java. Mountainous and volcanic with a tropical climate and fertile soil, it is sometimes called the "Jewel of the East". The Balinese are renowned for the delicacy of their arts and crafts. Bali resisted the spread of Islam through Indonesia in the 16th and 17th centuries and has been Hindu since the seventh century A.D.

Ba·li·nese (baáli-neéz ‖ -neéss) *adj.* Of or pertaining to Bali, its people, culture, or language.

~*n.* **1.** A native or inhabitant of Bali. **2.** The Indonesian language spoken in Bali.

balk. Variant of **baulk.**

Bal·kan (báwl-kən ‖ ból-) *adj.* Of or pertaining to the Balkans or their inhabitants.

Bal·kan·ise, Bal·kan·ize (báwl-kə-nīz ‖ ból-) *tr.v.* **-ised, -ising, -ises.** *Sometimes small* **b.** To divide (a region or territory) into small, often mutually hostile, units. [From the division of the Balkan countries by the Great Powers in the early 20th century.] —**Bal·kan·i·sa·tion** (-nī-záysh'n ‖ *U.S.* -ni-) *n.*

Bal·kans (báwl-kənz ‖ ból-). Also **Balkan Peninsula.** Region of southeast Europe. Formerly part of the Roman and Byzantine empires, it broke into rival states, which, with the exception of Montenegro, fell to the Ottoman Turks by 1500. Nationalist movements arose, and by 1908, Greece, Romania, Bulgaria, Serbia, and Montenegro were independent, but Bosnia, Croatia, Dalmatia, and Hercegovina were part of Austria-Hungary, and Macedonia, Albania, and Thrace were still Turkish. The First Balkan War (1912-13) resulted in independence for Albania, and the division of Macedonia between Bulgaria, Greece, Montenegro, and Serbia. The Second Balkan War (1913), and World War I, largely the result of Austrian pressure on Serbia, led to the emergence of Yugoslavia, comprising Serbia, Montenegro, Bosnia, Dalmatia (Slovenia), Croatia. Herzegovina, and part of Macedonia. In 1991–2 all except Serbia and Montenegro broke away from Yugoslavia.

Bal·kis (bál-kiss). The name given in the Koran to the Queen of Sheba.

ball[1] (bawl) *n.* **1. a.** A spherical or almost spherical body. **b.** Anything approximately spherical: *a ball of flame.* **2. a.** Any of various rounded or ovoid objects used in sports and games. **b.** A game played with such an object. **c.** *U.S.* Baseball. **3. a.** *Sports.* A ball moving, thrown, hit, or kicked in a particular manner: *a low ball.* **b.** *Cricket.* One delivery of the ball by the bowler. **4. a.** A solid projectile of spherical or pointed shape, such as that shot from a cannon. **b.** Projectiles of this kind collectively. **5.** A rounded part or protuberance, especially of the body: *the ball of the foot.* **6.** *Vulgar.* A testicle. **7.** *Plural. Vulgar Slang.* **a.** Nonsense. **b.** Courage; nerve. **8.** *Mathematics.* A three-dimensional region formed by the set of points that are less than a fixed distance from a given point; the interior of a sphere. **—keep the ball rolling.** To make sure that a project, event, or the like continues. **—on the ball.** *Slang.* Alert, competent, or efficient. **—play ball.** *Informal.* To cooperate. **—set** or **start the ball rolling.** *Informal.* To get something under way.
~*v.* **balled, balling, balls.** —*tr.* **1.** To form into a ball. **2.** *Chiefly U.S. Vulgar.* To have sexual intercourse with. —*intr.* **1.** To become formed into a ball. **2.** *Chiefly U.S. Vulgar.* To have sexual intercourse. [Middle English *bal,* from Old Norse *böllr,* from Germanic *balluz* (unattested).]

ball[2] *n.* A formal gathering for social dancing. **—have a ball.** *Informal.* To have a very enjoyable time. [French *bal,* from Old French, from *baller,* to dance, from Late Latin *ballāre,* from Greek *ballizein.*]

Ball (bawl), **John** (died 1381). English priest and rebel leader. He was executed after the failure of the Peasants' Revolt (1381).

bal·lad (bál-əd) *n.* **1.** A narrative poem, often of folk origin and intended to be sung, consisting of simple stanzas and usually having a recurrent refrain. **2.** The music for such a poem. **3.** A popular song of a romantic or sentimental nature, in which the same melody is used for each stanza. [Middle English *balade,* from Old French *ballade,* from Provençal *balada,* piece to be accompanied by dancing, from *balar,* to dance, from Late Latin *ballāre.* See **ball** (dance).]

bal·lade (ba-laád, bə-) *n.* **1.** *Prosody.* A verse form usually consisting of three stanzas of eight or ten lines each, with the same concluding line in each stanza, and an envoy, or brief final stanza, ending with the same last line as that of the preceding stanzas. **2.** A musical composition, usually for the piano, having the romantic or dramatic quality of a ballad. [Earlier form of BALLAD.]

bal·lad·eer (bál-ə-deér) *n.* One who sings ballads.

bal·lad·mon·ger (bál-əd-mung-gər || -mong-) *n.* **1.** A seller or pedlar of popular ballads. **2.** An inferior poet.

ballad stanza *n.* A four-line stanza often used in ballads, rhyming in the second and fourth lines, and having four metrical feet in the first and third lines, and three in the second and fourth.

ball-and-sock·et joint (báwl-ənd-sókit, -ən-) *n.* **1.** A joint consisting of a spherical knob or knoblike part fitted into a socket so that some degree of motion is possible in nearly any direction. **2.** *Anatomy.* A freely movable joint, such as the hip or shoulder joint, in which the rounded head of a long bone fits into a rounded cavity.

bal·last (bál-əst) *n.* **1.** Any heavy material placed in the hold of a ship or the gondola of a balloon to enhance stability. **2.** Coarse gravel or crushed rock laid to form a bed for roads or railway tracks. **3.** That which gives stability, especially to character. **4.** *Electronics.* A circuit element, such as a resistor, used to stabilise or maintain the current in a circuit.
~*tr.v.* **ballasted, -lasting, -lasts. 1.** To stabilise or provide with ballast. **2.** To fill (a road or railway bed) with ballast. [Perhaps from Old Swedish or Old Danish *barlast,* "bare load" (cargo carried only for its weight) : *bar,* bare + *last,* load.]

ball bearing *n.* **1.** A friction-reducing bearing, consisting essentially of a ring-shaped track containing freely revolving hard metal balls against which a rotating shaft or other part turns, in direct contact either with the balls or with a second matched ring. **2.** A hard ball used in such a bearing.

ball boy *n.* In tennis, a person who collects the ball when it is out of play.

ball cock *n.* A self-regulating device controlling the supply of water in a tank or cistern by means of a floating hollow ball connected to a valve that opens or closes with a change in water level.

bal·le·ri·na (bál-ə-reénə) *n.* **1.** A principal female dancer in a corps de ballet. **2.** Any female ballet dancer. Compare **prima ballerina.** [Italian, from *ballare,* to dance. See **ball** (dance).]

Ba·lles·te·ros (baalyes-taíros), **Severiano** (1957–). Spanish golfer who has won the British Open three times and the US Masters twice, and captained the Europeans in the 1997 Ryder Cup.

bal·let (bál-ay, -i || *U.S. also* ba-láy) *n.* **1.** An artistic dance form characterised by grace and precision of movement and an elaborate formal technique. Sometimes preceded by *the.* **2.** A theatrical presentation of group or solo dancing to a muscial accompaniment usually in costume and with scenic effects, and conveying a story, theme, or atmosphere. **3.** A musical composition written or used for ballet. **4.** A company or group that performs ballet. [French, from Italian *balletto,* diminutive of *ballo,* a dance. See **ball** (dance).] **—bal·let·ic** (ba-léttik) *adj.*

bal·let·o·mane (bál-it-ō-mayn, -et-, -ə-, ba-lét-) *n.* An ardent admirer of the ballet. [BALLET + -o- + *mane* (from MANIA).] **—bal·let·o·ma·ni·a** (-máyn-yə, -i-ə) *n.*

ball·flow·er (báwl-flow-ər) *n. Architecture.* An ornament in the form of a ball cupped in the petals of a circular flower.

ball game *n.* **1.** A game played with a ball. **2.** *Informal.* A state of affairs; business: *This makes the election a whole new ball game.*

ball girl *n.* A female ball boy.

Bal·li·ol (báyl-yəl, báyli-əl), **John de** (*c.* 1250–1315). Scottish king. He rose against English domination (1295) but was defeated by the English at Dunbar (1296) and fled to France.

bal·lis·ta (bə-líss-tə) *n., pl.* **-tae** (-tee). A military engine used in ancient and medieval warfare to hurl heavy projectiles. [Latin, from Greek *ballein,* to throw.]

bal·lis·tic (bə-lístik) *adj.* **1.** Of or pertaining to ballistics. **2.** Of or pertaining to projectiles, their motion, or their effects. **3.** Of, pertaining to, or designating a measuring instrument that relies on a short impulse or current pulse to cause a movement the magnitude of which is related to the quantity to be measured: *a ballistic galvanometer.* **—go ballistic.** *Slang.* Go through the roof; go bananas. [From BALLISTA.] **—bal·list·i·cal·ly** *adv.*

ballistic missile *n.* A projectile that assumes a free-falling trajectory after an internally guided, self-powered ascent. Compare **guided missile.**

bal·lis·tics (bə-lístiks) *n. Used with a singular verb.* **1. a.** The study of the dynamics of projectiles. **b.** The study of the flight characteristics of projectiles. **2. a.** The study of the functioning of firearms. **b.** The study of the firing, flight, and effect of ammunition. **—bal·lis·ti·cian** (bál-istísh'n) *n.*

ball lightning *n.* A rare form of atmospheric lightning in which the electrical discharge occurs as a slow-moving, luminous ball. Also called "fireball".

ballocks. Variant of **bollocks.**

ball of fire *n. Informal.* A lively, dynamic person.

bal·lo·net (bál-ə-nét || *U.S.* -náy) *n.* One of several small auxiliary gasbags placed inside a balloon or a nonrigid airship that can be inflated or deflated during flight to control and maintain shape and buoyancy. [French *ballonnet,* diminutive of *ballon,* BALLOON.]

bal·lon sonde (bállon sond) *n.* A hydrogen-filled balloon carrying self-recording meteorological instruments, used to obtain data from the upper atmosphere. Also called "sounding balloon".

bal·loon (bə-lóón) *n.* **1.** A spherical or pear-shaped, flexible, nonporous bag inflated with a gas lighter than air, such as helium, that causes it to rise and float in the atmosphere; especially, such a bag with sufficient capacity to lift a suspended gondola. See **barrage balloon, hot-air balloon. 2.** A small, brightly coloured, inflatable rubber bag used as a toy or decoration. **3.** A rounded or irregularly shaped outline containing the words a character in a cartoon is represented as saying. **—when the balloon goes up.** *British Informal.* When the critical moment arrives.
~*v.* **ballooned, -looning, -loons.** —*intr.* **1.** To ascend or ride in a balloon. **2.** To expand or swell out like a balloon. —*tr.* **1.** To cause to expand by or as if by inflating. **2.** *British.* In games, to send (a ball) high into the air. [French *ballon,* from Italian *ballone,* augmentative of *balla,* BALL.] **—bal·loon·ist** *n.*

balloon sail *n.* A comparatively large foresail, used when going before the wind in races to supplement or replace a jib.

balloon tyre *n.* A pneumatic tyre with a wide tread, inflated to low pressure, and now used chiefly on heavy goods vehicles.

bal·lot (bál-ət) *n.* **1.** A written or printed paper or ticket used to cast or register a vote, especially a secret vote. Also called "ballot paper". **2.** The act, process, or system of voting, especially by the use of secret ballots or voting machines. **3.** The total of all votes cast in an election. **4.** The right to vote; the franchise. **5.** Formerly, a small ball used to register a vote.
~*v.* **balloted, -loting, -lots.** —*intr.* **1.** To cast a ballot; vote. **2.** To draw lots. —*tr.* To obtain a vote from: *The union balloted its membership.* [Italian *ballotta,* small ball or pebble used for voting, diminutive of *balla,* BALL.]

ballot box *n.* **1.** A box in which a voter places his completed ballot paper. **2.** The process or system of secret voting; the ballot: *The government's popularity will be tested at the ballot box.*

bal·lotte·ment (bə-lótmənt) *n.* A technique for detecting or examining a floating object in the body, as: **1.** The use of a finger to push sharply against the uterus and detect the presence or position of a foetus by its return impact. **2.** A test for a floating kidney in which the kidney is moved by alternating external digital pressures. [French, a tossing, from *ballotter,* to toss, from *ballotte,* diminutive of *balle,* BALL.]

ball·park (báwl-paark) *n. Chiefly U.S.* A ground or stadium in which baseball is played. **—in the ballpark.** *Informal.* Within the proper range; approximately right.
~*adj. Chiefly U.S. Informal.* Approximate: *a ballpark figure.*

ball-pein hammer (báwl-peen) *n.* Also *chiefly U.S.* **ball-peen hammer.** A hammer having one end of the head hemispherical.

ball-point pen (báwl-poynt) *n.* A pen having as its writing point a small ball bearing that transfers ink stored in a cartridge onto a writing surface. Also called "ball point". A trademark is "Biro".

ball·room (báwl-rōōm, -rŏŏm) *n.* A large room for dancing.

ballroom dancing *n.* Formal, social dancing to dances with conventional rhythms and steps, such as the waltz, quickstep and foxtrot.

balls up *tr.v. Vulgar Slang.* To make a mess of; botch.

balls-up (báwlz-up) *n.* Also *U.S.* **ball-up** (báwl-up). *Vulgar Slang.* A mess; an unsuccessful effort.

ball·sy (báwlzi) *adj. Slang.* Having courage or nerve.

ball valve *n.* A valve regulated by a free-floating ball that moves in response to pressure. It is often used as a one-way valve.

bal·ly (bál-i) *adv. British Informal.* Used euphemistically as an intensive. [From the pronunciation of *bl. . .y* ("bloody").] —**bal·ly** *adj.*

bal·ly·hoo (bál-i-hŏŏ ‖ -hŏŏ) *n., pl.* **-hoos.** *Informal.* **1.** Sensational or clamorous advertising. **2.** Noisy shouting or uproar.
~*tr.v.* **ballyhooed, -hooing, -hoos.** *Informal.* To advertise by sensational methods; publicise exaggeratedly. [20th century (U.S.) : origin obscure.]

balm (baam ‖ baalm) *n.* **1.** An aromatic, oily resin exuded by various chiefly tropical trees and shrubs, and used in medicine. **2.** Any tree or shrub yielding such a substance. **3.** Any aromatic ointment, oil, unguent, or similar substance. **4.** An aromatic herb, *Melissa officinalis,* native to Europe, having clusters of small, fragrant white flowers. Also called "lemon balm". **5.** Any of several similar aromatic plants. **6.** A pleasing, aromatic fragrance. **7.** Something that soothes, heals, or comforts. [Middle English *baume, basme,* from Old French *basme,* from Latin *balsamum,* BALSAM.]

bal·ma·caan (bál-mə-káan ‖ *U.S. also* -kán) *n.* A loose, full overcoat with raglan sleeves, originally made of rough, woollen cloth. [After *Balmacaan,* an estate near Inverness, Scotland.]

balm of Gilead *n.* **1.** An aromatic evergreen tree of the genus *Commiphora;* especially, *C. opobalsamum,* of Africa and Asia Minor. **2.** A fragrant resin obtained from this tree. **3.** A North American hybrid poplar tree, *Populus candicans,* having broad, heart-shaped leaves. **4.** A fragrant resin obtained from the **balsam fir** *(see).*

Bal·mor·al¹ (bal-mórrəl ‖ -máwrəl) *n.* **1.** A brimless Scottish cap with a flat, round top. **2.** *Sometimes small* **b.** A heavy, laced walking shoe. [After BALMORAL Castle.]

Balmoral². A castle close to the river Dee. It is the private residence of the British monarch in Scotland.

balm·y (báami ‖ báalmi) *adj.* **-ier, -iest. 1.** Having the quality or fragrance of balm. **2.** Mild and pleasant: *a balmy breeze.* —**balm·i·ly** *adv.* —**balm·i·ness** *n.*

bal·ne·al (bál-ni-əl) *adj.* Of or pertaining to baths or bathing. [From Latin *balneum,* bath, from Greek *balaneion†,* bath.]

bal·ne·ol·o·gy (bál-ni-óllə̆ji) *n.* The study of the therapeutic use of mineral baths. [Latin *balneum,* bath (see **balneal**) + -LOGY.]

ba·lo·ney, bo·lo·ney (bə-lóni) *n. Slang.* Nonsense. [Perhaps from BOLOGNA (sausage).]

B.A.L.P.A. (bálpə) British Airline Pilots' Association.

bal·sa (báwl-sə, ból-) *n.* **1.** A tree, *Ochroma lagopus,* of tropical America, having wood that is unusually light in weight. **2.** The wood of this tree. **3.** A raft consisting of a frame fastened to buoyant cylinders of wood or metal. [Spanish *balsa†,* raft.]

bal·sam (báwl-səm, ból-) *n.* **1.** An oily or gummy oleoresin, usually containing benzoic or cinnamic acids, obtained from the exudations of various trees and shrubs, and used as a base for cough syrups, other medications, and perfumes. See **balsam of Peru, Canada balsam. 2.** Any similar substance, especially a fragrant ointment used as medication. **3.** Any of various trees yielding an aromatic, resinous

substance; especially, the balsam fir. **4.** Any of several garden plants of the genus *Impatiens;* especially, *I. balsamina.* [Latin *balsamum,* from Greek *balsamon,* from Hebrew *bāsām,* "spice".]

balsam fir *n.* A small, evergreen tree, *Abies balsamea,* of northeastern North America. It yields Canada balsam. Also called "balsam", "Canada balsam".

bal·sam·ic (bawl-sámmik, bol-) *adj.* **1.** Of, pertaining to, or resembling balsam. **2.** Containing or yielding balsam.

bal·sam·if·er·ous (báwl-sə-míffərəss, ból-) *adj.* Yielding balsam.

balsam of Peru *n.* The aromatic resin of a tropical American tree, *Myroxylon pereirae,* used to make perfume and other products.

balsam poplar *n.* A North American tree, *Populus balsamifera,* having large, resin-coated buds. Also called "tacamahac".

Balt (bawlt ‖ bolt) *n.* A member of the Baltic-speaking people inhabiting the southeastern shores of the Baltic Sea.

Bal·tha·zar¹, Bal·tha·sar (bal-tházzər, bál-thə-zár, -thəzaar). One of the three **Magi** *(see)* who travelled to see the infant Jesus.

Balthazar² *n.* A wine bottle that holds as much as 16 standard bottles. [Probably after BALTHAZAR (the Magus).]

bal·ti (báwl-ti, baál-) *n.* **1. karahi** *(see).* **2.** A restaurant featuring baltis. [Perhaps from *Baltistan,* Himalayan valley in west Kashmir.]

Bal·ti (bul-tée, bal-) *n.* A Tibeto-Burmese language of the people of northern Kashmir.

Bal·tic (báwl-tik ‖ ból-) *adj.* **1.** Of or pertaining to the Baltic Sea, or to the Baltic States and their inhabitants or cultures. **2.** Of or designating a group of languages of the Indo-European family, consisting of Lithuanian, Lettish, and Old Prussian. See **Balto-Slavic.**
~*n.* The Baltic language group.

Baltic Sea. Arm of the Atlantic Ocean bounded by Denmark, Sweden, Finland, Russia, Latvia, Lithuania, Estonia, Poland, and Germany. It opens to the North Sea by channels between Denmark and Sweden, and via the Kiel and Göta canals. It is relatively shallow and unsalty, and freezes for up to five months each year.

Baltic States. Countries on the southeast coast of the Baltic Sea, comprising Latvia, Lithuania, and Estonia. They were subject to Russian rule from the 18th century until 1991, except for a brief period of independence between the two World Wars.

Bal·ti·more (báwl-ti-mawr ‖ ból-, -mŏr, -mər). Industrial city, seaport, and cultural centre in Maryland, in the United States. Situated at the mouth of the Patapsco River, it has been a busy port and shipbuilding centre since the 18th century.

Baltimore oriole *n.* An American songbird, *Icterus galbula,* of which the male has bright orange, black, and white plumage. [After Cecil Calvert, Lord *Baltimore* (1605–75) (the colours of the male are the same as those in Lord Baltimore's coat of arms).]

Bal·to-Sla·vic (báwltō-slaávik ‖ bóltō-, slávvik) *n.* A subfamily of the Indo-European language family, composed of the Baltic group and the Slavonic group.

Ba·lu·chi (bə-lŏŏchi) *n., pl.* **-chis** or collectively **Baluchi. 1.** A native or inhabitant of Baluchistan. **2.** The Iranian language of the Baluchis. —**Ba·lu·chi** *adj.*

Ba·lu·chi·stan (bə-lŏŏchi-staán, -staan, -stan). Province in Pakistan, bordering Iran and Afghanistan. An arid and mountainous region, its inhabitants are mostly Muslim Baluchi and Pathan nomads. Quetta is the capital.

ba·lu·chi·ther·i·um (bə-lŏŏchi-théer-i-əm) *n.* An extinct, rhinoceros-like mammal of the genus *Baluchitherium,* of the Oligocene and Miocene epochs, which was one of the largest land mammals ever to have lived. [New Latin.]

bal·un (bál-un) *n.* An electrical device for coupling an aerial to a transmission line. [*bal*anced + *un*balanced (impedance).]

bal·us·ter (bál-əstər) *n.* One of the posts or supports of a handrail, as on banisters. [French *balustre,* from Italian *balaustro,* from *balaustra,* flower of the pomegranate (from the shape of the post), from Latin *balaustium,* from Greek *balaustion†.*]

bal·us·trade (bál-ə-stráyd) *n.* A rail and the row of posts that support it, as along the edge of a staircase. [French, from Italian *balaustrata,* from *balaustro,* BALUSTER.]

Ba·ma·ko (bámmə-kŏ, baámə-). Port on the river Niger and the capital of Mali in West Africa.

Bam·ba·ra (bam-baárə, baam-) *n., pl.* **-ras** or collectively **Bambara. 1.** A member of a Negroid people of the upper Niger river valley. **2.** The Mande language of this people.

bam·bi·no (bam-bée-nŏ ‖ *U.S.* baam-) *n., pl.* **-nos** or **-ni** (-nee). **1.** Used as an affectionate term for a child or baby, especially an Italian one. **2.** A representation of the infant Jesus. [Italian, diminutive of *bambo,* child.]

bam·boo (bam-bŏŏ, bám-) *n., pl.* **-boos. 1.** Any of various mostly tropical grasses of the subfamily Bambusoideae, having hard-walled stems with ringed joints. **2.** The hollow woody stems of these plants, used in building, in making furniture and utensils, and in certain crafts. **3.** Any of various tall, bamboo-like grasses such as those of the genera *Arundinaria* and *Dendrocalamus.* [Earlier *bamboos* (misunderstood as plural), from Dutch *bamboes,* unexplained variant of Portuguese *mambu,* from Malay.] —**bam·boo** *adj.*

Bamboo Curtain *n.* A political barrier existing between the People's Republic of China and other major powers, such as the United States and the U.S.S.R., especially during the leadership of Mao Ze-dong. [Formed by analogy with IRON CURTAIN.]

bam·boo·zle (bam-bŏŏz'l) *tr.v.* **-zled, -zling, -zles.** *Informal.* **1.** To trick or deceive by elaborate misinformation; hoax. **2.** To mystify or confuse. —See Synonyms at **deceive.** [Probably a cant variant of *bumbazzle,* from *bombace,* padding, BOMBAST.] —**bam·boo·zle·**

BALTIC STATES

129

ment *n.*

ban¹ (ban) *tr.v.* **banned, banning, bans. 1.** To prohibit, especially by official decree. **2.** *Archaic.* To heap curses upon; execrate. **3.** Formerly, in South Africa, to deprive (a politically suspect person) of the right of free movement and association with others. —*n.* **1.** A prohibition, especially one imposed by law or official decree. **2.** *Archaic.* An excommunication or condemnation by church officials. **3.** In feudal times, a summons to arms. **4.** *Archaic.* Censure through public opinion. **5.** *Archaic.* A curse or imprecation. [Middle English *bannen,* to summon, banish, curse, partly from Old English *bannan,* to summon, proclaim, and partly from Old Norse *banna,* to prohibit, curse, both ultimately from Germanic *bannan* (unattested).]

ban² (ban ‖ *U.S.* baan) *n., pl.* **bani** (-ee). A coin equal to 1/100 of the leu of Romania. [Romanian, from Serbo-Croatian *bân,* lord, from Turkish; akin to *bayan,* rich.]

Banaba. See **Ocean Island.**

ba·nal (bə-nâal, báyn'l ‖ -nál) *adj.* Lacking originality, depth, and inspiration; trite and drearily predictable: *a banal love story.* See Synonyms at **trite.** [French, commonplace, from Old French, common to everyone, shared (as by tenants in a feudal jurisdiction), from *ban,* summons to military service, from Frankish *ban* (unattested).] —**ba·nal·i·ty** (bə-nál-əti ‖ bay-) *n.* —**ba·nal·ly** *adv.*

ba·nan·a (bə-náanə ‖ *U.S.* -nánnə) *n.* **1.** Any of several treelike tropical or subtropical plants of the genus *Musa;* especially, *M. sapientum,* having long, broad leaves and hanging clusters of edible fruit. **2.** The crescent-shaped fruit of any of these plants, having white, pulpy flesh and thick, easily removed yellow, green, or reddish skin. [Portuguese and Spanish, from a native name in Guinea.]

banana oil *n.* **1.** A liquid mixture of nitrocellulose and amyl acetate, or a similar solvent, having a banana-like odour. **2.** An organic compound, **amyl acetate** *(see).*

banana republic *n. Informal.* A small country, especially in Central America, often economically dependent on a single crop, such as bananas, and regarded as politically unstable.

ba·na·nas (bə-náanəz ‖ *U.S.* -nánnəz) *adj. Slang.* Mad; wild. Often used in the phrase *go bananas.* [20th century : origin obscure.]

banana split *n.* A dessert consisting of a banana cut lengthways and served with ice cream, syrup, fruit, and nuts.

ba·nau·sic (bə-náwzik) *adj.* Materialistic and practical, especially to the point of being dull or pedestrian. [Greek *banausikos,* suitable for artisans, from *baunos,* forge.]

Ban·bur·y (bán-bri, -bəri). Market town in Oxfordshire. It has been long famous for its pastry cakes, and its stone cross, destroyed by the Puritans (1602) but replaced in the 19th century.

ban·co (báng-kō ‖ *U.S.* baáng-) *n., pl.* **-cos.** A bet in certain gambling games for the entire amount the banker offers to accept. —*interj.* Used to announce a banco. [Italian *banco, banca,* BANK (financial establishment).]

band¹ (band) *n.* **1.** A thin strip of flexible material used to encircle and bind one object or to hold a number of objects together: *a rubber band.* **2.** A narrow strip of fabric used to trim, finish, or reinforce articles of clothing. Often used in combination: *a waistband.* **3.** Any strip or stripe that contrasts with its surroundings in colour, texture, or material. **4. a.** *Plural.* The two strips hanging from the front of a collar as part of the dress of certain clergymen, scholars, and lawyers. **b.** A high collar popular in the 16th and 17th centuries. **5.** A belt around wheels in machinery. **6.** A limited part of a range or series: *price bands.* **7.** *Architecture.* A flat string along a wall. **8.** *Biology.* Any chromatically or functionally differentiated strip or stripe in or on an organism. **9.** *Physics.* **a.** A range of some physical variable, as of radiation wavelength or frequency, between well-defined limits; especially, a range of emitted or absorbed wavelengths in a spectrum. **b.** A restricted range of very closely spaced electron energy levels in solids, the distribution and nature of which determine the electrical properties of a material. **10.** The cords across the back of a book, to which the quires or sheets are attached. **11.** A track on a gramophone record. **12.** *Computing.* The recording area on a magnetic disk or drum. **13.** *British.* A group of schoolchildren classified according to their ability. —*tr.v.* **banded, banding, bands. 1. a.** To tie, bind, or encircle with a band. **b.** To mark with a band or bands. **2.** *British.* To group (children) in schools according to the level of their ability. [Middle English, from Old French *bande,* bond, tie, link, from Germanic.]

band² *n.* **1.** A group of people, especially when joined together for a common purpose: *a band of robbers.* **2.** A group of musicians who play together, especially: **a.** One not including stringed instruments. **b.** One playing popular music, such as jazz or rock. **3.** *Anthropology.* A self-sufficient subdivision of a tribe. **4.** *Chiefly U.S.* A group of animals, as a flock or herd. —*v.* **banded, banding, bands.** —*tr.* To assemble or unite in a group. —*intr.* To form a group; unite. Often used with *together: to band together to fight.* [Middle English, from Old French *bande,* a troop, from Medieval Latin *banda,* from Germanic.]

band³ *n. Archaic.* **1.** *Usually plural.* A physical restraint; a manacle or fetter. **2.** A moral or legal restraint; a bond. [Middle English, from Old Norse.]

Ban·da (bándə), **Hastings Kamuzu** (c. 1906–97). President of Malawi 1964–94. African statesman. He practised medicine in the U.K. during World War II, and then in the United States. In 1958 he returned to Malawi (then called Nyasaland) to lead the fight for independence from the British, won in 1964. He was its president from 1964 to 1994.

band·age (bándij) *n.* A strip of fabric or other material used as a protective covering for a wound or other injury. —*tr.v.* **bandaged, -aging, -ages.** To apply a bandage to. [French, from *bande,* BAND (strip).] —**band·ag·er** *n.*

Band-Aid (bánd-ayd) *n.* A trademark for a small adhesive plaster with a gauze pad in the centre, used on minor wounds.

ban·dan·na, ban·dan·a (ban-dánnə, *rarely* -dáanə) *n.* A large handkerchief or scarf, usually brightly coloured. [Probably from Portuguese *bandana,* from Hindi *bāndhnū* tie- a dyeing process, from *bāndhnā,* to tie, from Sanskrit *bandhnāti.*]

Ban·da·ra·na·i·ke (bándərə-nî-ikə), **Sirimavo Ratwatte Dias** (1916–). Sri Lankan stateswoman, the world's first woman prime minister. She served 1960–65, 1970–77, 1994– .

Bandaranaike, Solomon W(est) R(idgeway) D(ias) (1899-1959). Sri Lankan statesman who was prime minister of what was then Ceylon (1956-59). He was assassinated by a Buddhist monk.

Ban·dar Se·ri Be·ga·wan (bán-daar sérri bə-gaá-wən, baán-). Formerly **Brunei Town.** Capital of Brunei.

b. & b. bed and breakfast.

band·box (bánd-boks) *n.* A lightweight, rounded box originally designed to hold collars but now used for any small articles of dress. —**as if (one) came out of a bandbox.** Extremely smart and neat.

ban·deau (bándō, ban-dṓ) *n., pl.* **-deaux** (-z) or **-deaus.** A narrow band for the hair; a fillet. [French, from Old French *bandel,* diminutive of *bande,* BAND (strip).]

ban·de·ril·la (bándə-réel-yə, -rée-) *n.* In bullfighting, a decorated barbed dart that is thrust into the bull's ɴeck or shoulder muscles by a banderillero. [Spanish, diminutive of *bandera,* banner, from Vulgar Latin *bandāria* (unattested), BANNER.]

ban·de·ril·le·ro (bándə-reel-yáir-ō, -ree-) *n., pl.* **-ros.** In bullfighting, one whose role is to implant the banderillas. [Spanish, from BANDE-RILLA.]

ban·de·role, ban·de·rol (bándə-rōl) *n.* Also **ban·ne·rol** (bánnə-). **1.** A narrow forked flag or streamer attached to a staff or lance or flown from a masthead. **2.** *Art & Architecture.* A representation of a ribbon or scroll bearing an inscription. [French, from Italian *banderuola,* diminutive of *bandiera,* BANNER.]

ban·di·coot (bándi-kōōt) *n.* **1.** Any of several ratlike marsupials of the family Peramelidae, of Australia and adjacent islands, having a long, tapering snout and long hind legs. **2.** Any of several large rats of the genera *Bandicota* and *Nesokia,* of southeastern Asia. In this sense, now usually called "bandicoot rat" and sometimes "mole-rat". [Telegu *pandikokku* : *pandi,* pig + *kokku,* rat.]

ban·dit (bándit) *n., pl.* **-dits** or **banditti** (ban-dítee). A robber; especially, an outlaw who belongs to a gang. [Italian *bandito,* from the past participle of *bandire,* to BAN.] —**ban·dit·ry** *n.*

band leader *n.* One who conducts a band, especially a large band that plays popular dance music.

band·mas·ter (bánd-maastər ‖ -mastər) *n.* One who conducts a band, especially a military or brass band.

ban·dog (bán-dog ‖ -dawg) *n.* A dog kept chained up, as a watchdog or because of its ferocious nature. [Middle English *band-dogge* : BAND (fetter) + DOG.]

ban·do·leer, ban·do·lier (bándə-leér) *n.* A belt fitted with small pockets or loops for carrying cartridges and worn across the chest by soldiers. [French *bandoulière,* from Spanish *bandolera,* from *banda,* sash, probably from Germanic.]

ban·dore (ban-dór, bán-dawr ‖ -dōr) *n.* A 16th-century stringed, bass musical instrument resembling the lute. Also called "pandore". [Portuguese *bandurra,* from Late Latin *pandūra,* a three-stringed lute, from Greek *pandoura.*]

band-pass filter (bánd-paass ‖ -pass) *n. Electronics.* A filter that blocks all signals but those within a selected frequency range.

band saw *n.* A power saw consisting essentially of a toothed metal band driven round the circumferences of two wheels.

band shell *n.* A bandstand equipped at the rear with a concave, almost hemispheric wall that serves as a sounding board.

bands·man (bándz-mən) *n., pl.* **-men** (-mən, -men). A musician in a band, especially a military or brass band.

band spectrum *n.* A spectrum in which a number of bands of closely spaced lines occur as a result of emission or absorption of radiation.

band·stand (bánd-stand) *n.* A platform for a band or orchestra, usually outdoors and having a roof.

Ban·dung (bán-dōong, baán-, -dōong). City in Indonesia, in west Java. The Bandung Conference (1955) was attended by representatives of 29 African and Asian countries opposed to colonialism.

band·wag·on (bánd-waggən) *n.* **1.** *U.S.* A decorated wagon used to transport musicians in a parade. **2.** *Informal.* A cause or party that attracts increasing support. —**climb** or **jump on the bandwagon.** *Informal.* To support or shift one's support to a party, cause, or enterprise that appears likely to win or succeed.

band·width (bánd-width, -wit-th) *n. Electronics.* **1.** The frequency range used by a transmitted signal on either side of the carrier frequency. **2.** The range of frequencies over which an amplifier gives a power amplification that falls within a stipulated fraction of the maximum value.

ban·dy¹ (bándi) *tr.v.* **bandied, bandying, bandies. 1.** To toss, throw, or strike back and forth: *"A sunrise breeze bandied the curtains."* (Truman Capote). **2.** To exchange (words or blows). **3.** To discuss in a casual or frivolous manner. **4.** To pass round or along indiscriminately. [Perhaps from French *bander,* to form sides (as for a game), oppose oneself against, from BAND (group).]

bandy² *adj.* Bowed or bent in an outward curve: *bandy legs.*
—knock (someone) bandy. *Australian Informal.* To amaze or outdo (someone).
~*n., pl.* **bandies. 1.** An early form of hockey. **2.** A stick, bent at one end, used in playing this game. [Adjective sense from noun (hockey stick), obscurely related to BANDY (toss, exchange, etc.).]
ban·dy-leg·ged (bándi-légd, -legd, *rarely* -legid) *adj.* Having **bow legs** (*see*); bow-legged. [From BANDY (curved stick).]
bane (bayn) *n.* **1.** Someone or something that is a nuisance or cause of distress: *the bane of one's life.* **2.** *Poetic.* Fatal injury or ruin. **3.** A cause of death, destruction, or ruin. **4.** A deadly poison. Used in combination: *henbane; wolf's-bane.* [Middle English *bane,* Old English *bana,* slayer, cause of death or destruction, ruin.]
bane·ber·ry (báyn-bəri ‖ -berri) *n., pl.* **-ries. 1.** Any plant of the genus *Actaea,* especially *A. spicata,* having clusters of white flowers and red or white poisonous berries. **2.** A berry of any of these plants.
bane·ful (báyn-fʼl, -fool) *adj.* **1.** Full of venom or harm. **2.** Destructive; pernicious: *"Criticism is really, in itself, a baneful and injurious employment."* (Matthew Arnold). —See Usage note at **baleful.**
Banff (bamf, banf). County town of the former county of Banffshire, now in Aberdeenshire Unitary Authority area, northeast Scotland, on the Moray Firth.
bang¹ (bang) *n.* **1.** The sudden loud noise of an explosion. **2.** A sudden loud impact or thump. **3.** *Vulgar Slang.* An act of sexual intercourse. **4.** *U.S. Slang.* A sense of excitement; a thrill. **5.** *Slang.* An injection of an addictive drug, such as heroin. **—with a bang.** With notable success.
~*v.* **banged, banging, bangs.** —*tr.* **1.** To hit noisily and repeatedly: *banging the table with his fist.* **2.** To close suddenly and loudly; slam. **3.** To handle noisily or violently: *bang the dishes in the sink.* **4.** To hit sharply: *I've banged my elbow.* **5.** *Vulgar Slang.* To have sexual intercourse with. **6.** *Slang.* To inject (an addictive drug). —*intr.* **1.** To make a sudden loud noise. **2.** To crash noisily against something. **3.** To strike with a sudden loud sound.
~*adv.* **1.** With a bang. **2.** Exactly; precisely: *bang on time.* **3.** Suddenly; completely: *If we make one mistake, bang go our hopes of winning.* **—bang on.** *Informal.* Exactly right: *That answer was bang on.* **—go bang.** To burst or explode. [16th century : perhaps from Scandinavian, akin to Old Norse *bang,* a hammering.]
bang² *n. Often plural.* Hair cut in a fringe straight across the forehead.
~*tr.v.* **banged, banging, bangs.** To cut (hair) straight across the forehead. [Perhaps ultimately from Old Norse *banga,* to cut off.]
Ban·ga·lore (báng-gə-lór ‖ -lór). Capital city of Karnataka in south India, 290 kilometres (180 miles) west of Madras.
bangalore torpedo *n.* A piece of metal pipe filled with an explosive, used primarily to clear a path through barbed wire or to detonate land mines. [After BANGALORE, where it was first used.]
bang·er (báng-ər) *n. Chiefly British.* **1.** A firework that explodes with a sudden loud noise. **2.** *Informal.* A sausage. **3.** *Informal.* An old car, especially one in a poor state of repair. [Sense 2: probably from the sputtering sound made in cooking.]
Bangkok. See **Krung Thep.**
Ban·gla·desh, People's Republic of (bang-glə-dèsh, -dáysh ‖

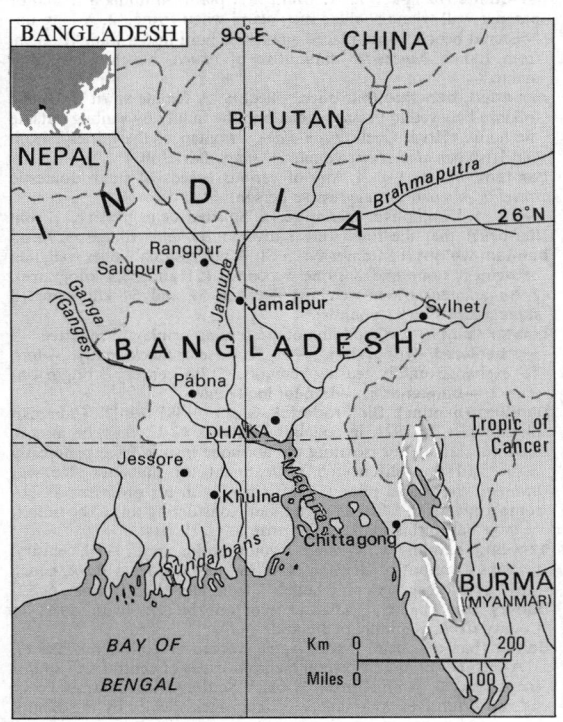

baáng-). Formerly **East Pakistan.** Muslim country of south Asia, lying mostly in the fertile Ganges-Brahmaputra delta. Formerly part of Bengal, it became East Pakistan on Indian independence (1947), but Calcutta, Bengal's chief port and industrial centre for its jute, became part of India. Disastrously weakened economically, East Pakistan was neglected by the government in West Pakistan. Unrest erupted into a savage civil war (1971), and independent Bangladesh was born. Sheikh Mujibur Rahman, the East Bengali leader, was released from prison in West Pakistan to form the country's first government (1972), but was killed in a military coup (1975). A countercoup installed another military regime, and General Ziaur Rahman took over the government the same year. He was elected president (1978), but was assassinated (1981). A bloodless military coup (1982) was led by General Hussein Ershad, who became president (1983). He was forced to resign in 1990 and democratic parliamentary elections followed. Despite some industrialisation, and advances that have made more than 75 per cent of the land cultivable, political instability, droughts, floods and cyclones have kept Bangladesh a poor country dependent on foreign aid. Area, 147 570 square kilometres (56,977 square miles). Population, 120,070,000. Capital, Dacca (Dhaka). **—Bang·la·desh·i** *adj. & n.*
ban·gle (báng-gʼl) *n.* **1.** A rigid bracelet or anklet, especially one with no clasp. **2.** An ornament hung from a bracelet, necklace, or the like. [Hindi *baṅgrī,* glass bracelet.]
Ban·gor¹ (báng-gər ‖ -gawr). City in north Wales, on the Menai Strait. Its cathedral of St. Demiol, founded in the 12th century, contains the tombs of the Welsh princes. In 1884, a college of the University of Wales was established here.
Ban·gor² (báng-gər). The largest town in County Down, Northern Ireland, lying on the south shore of Belfast Lough.
bang·tail (báng-tayl) *n.* **1.** An animal's tail that has been cut straight across and short. **2.** An animal, especially a horse, with such a tail. [Probably BANG (cut) + TAIL.]
Ban·gui (bón-gée). Capital of the Central African Republic. Situated on the Ubangi River, it is the chief port of the country and also handles goods for Chad.
bang up *tr.v. British Informal.* **1.** To lock (a prisoner) up in a cell. **2.** To raise; increase: *bang up a price.*
bang-up (báng-up) *adj. U.S. Slang.* Excellent: *a bang-up job.*
Bang·we·u·lu, Lake (báng-wi-óoloo). A shallow lake bordered by swamps, on a plateau in northeast Zambia. It was discovered by Dr. David Livingstone in 1868.
ba·ni. Plural of **ban** (coin).
ban·i·an (bánni-ən, bán-yən) *n.* **1.** A member of a Hindu merchant or trader caste, whose members eat no meat. **2.** A loose shirt, jacket, or gown worn in India. **3.** Variant of **banyan.** [Portuguese, from Gujarati *vāṇiyo,* from Sanskrit *vāṇija,* merchant.]
ban·ish (bánnish) *tr.v.* **-ished, -ishing, -ishes. 1.** To force to leave a country or place by official decree; exile. **2.** To drive away; expel: *He banished all doubts from his mind.* [Middle English *banishen,* from Old French *banir* (present stem *baniss-*), from Vulgar Latin *bannīre* (unattested), from Germanic *bannjan* (unattested), to BAN.]
—ban·ish·er *n.* **—ban·ish·ment** *n.*
ban·is·ter, ban·nis·ter (bánnister) *n.* **1.** *Usually plural.* The handrail or balustrade of a staircase. **2.** A baluster. [From earlier *barrister,* variant of BALUSTER.]
ban·jax (bánjaks) *tr. v.* **-jaxed, -jaxing, -jaxes.** *Slang.* **1.** To stun. **2.** To astound.
ban·jo (bán-jō, -jó) *n., pl.* **-jos** or **-joes.** A fretted stringed musical instrument, having a long narrow neck and a hollow circular body with a stretched diaphragm of vellum upon which the bridge rests. [Southern (U.S.) black pronunciation of BANDORE; compare Kimbundu *mbanza,* stringed instrument.] **—ban·jo·ist** *n.*
banjo clock *n.* A wall clock of a type made in the United States in the 19th century, so called because it resembles a banjo in shape.
Ban·jul (bán-jóol). Formerly **Bath·urst** (báth-urst, -ərst). Capital of The Gambia, in West Africa. Situated at the mouth of the river Gambia, it is a port, and the country's only sizeable town.
bank¹ (bangk) *n.* **1.** Any piled-up mass, as of snow or clouds; a mound; a ridge. **2.** A steep natural incline. **3.** An artificial embankment, especially one built on a bend in a road to help vehicles to corner safely. **4. a.** The slope of land adjoining a body of water, especially adjoining a lake, river, or sea. **b.** A part of a town situated on one side of a river flowing through it: *The Left Bank.* **5.** *Often plural.* A large elevated area of a sea floor. **6.** The cushion of a billiard or pool table. **7.** *Aviation.* The lateral tilt of an aircraft when turning. —See Usage note at **shoal¹.**
~*v.* **banked, banking, banks.** —*tr.* **1.** To border or protect with a ridge or embankment. Often used with *up.* **2.** To pile up; amass. Often used with *up: bank up earth along a wall.* **3.** To cover (a fire) with ashes or fresh fuel to ensure continued low burning. Often used with *up.* **4.** To construct with a slope rising to the outside edge. Often used with *up.* **5.** *Aviation.* To tilt (an aircraft) laterally in flight. **6.** In billiard games, to strike (a ball) so that it rebounds from the table's cushion. —*intr.* **1.** To take the form of or rise in a bank or banks. **2.** *Aviation.* To tilt an aircraft laterally when turning. **3.** To round a sloping embankment, especially at speed. [Middle English *banke,* probably from Old Danish *banke,* sandbank, from Germanic *bankon* (unattested).]
bank² *n. Abbr.* **bk. 1.** A business establishment or organisation authorised to perform one or more of the following services: receive and safeguard money and other valuables; lend money at interest; negotiate bills of exchange, such as cheques and drafts; purchase

and exchange foreign currency; issue currency. **2.** An office or building in which such an establishment, or a branch of such an organisation, is located. **3. a.** The funds owned by a gambling establishment. **b.** The funds held by a dealer or banker in some gambling games. **4. a.** The reserve stock, as of money, pieces, cards, or chips from which the players may draw, in games such as poker or dominoes. **b.** The player holding such a reserve stock. **5.** A supply or stock held in reserve: *a blood bank.* **6.** Any place of safekeeping or storage. **7.** *Obsolete.* A moneychanger's table or place of business.
~*v.* **banked, banking, banks.** —*tr.* To deposit (money) in a bank. —*intr.* **1.** To transact business with a bank; especially, to maintain a bank account. **2.** To operate a bank. **3.** To hold the bank in some gambling games. **4.** *Informal.* To depend or rely. Used with *on* or *upon.* —See Synonyms at **rely.** [French *banque*, from Italian *banca*, bench, moneychanger's table, from Germanic *bank* (unattested), BENCH.]

bank³ *n.* **1.** A set of similar or matched things arranged in a row: *a bank of desks.* **2.** A row of keys on a keyboard. **3.** *Nautical.* **a.** A bench for rowers in a galley. **b.** A row of oars in a galley. **4.** The lines of type under a newspaper headline. **5.** *Printing.* A slanting table on which type matter in galleys or sheets is stored or corrected before being made up in pages. **6.** A row of fixed electrical contacts forming part of an automatic switching unit in a telephone circuit.
~*tr.v.* **banked, banking, banks.** To arrange or set up in a row: *"Every street was banked with purple-blooming trees"* (Doris Lessing). [Middle English *bank*, from Old French *banc*, from Germanic *bank* (unattested), BENCH.]

bank·a·ble (bángkǝb'l) *adj.* **1.** Acceptable to or at a bank. **2.** *Informal.* So popular as to guarantee the financial success of a film, television series, or the like simply by appearing in it: *a bankable star.*

bank acceptance *n.* A draft or bill of exchange drawn upon and accepted by a bank. Also called "banker's acceptance".

bank account *n.* **1.** An agreement between a bank and a customer whereby money is deposited with the bank and can be added to or withdrawn. **2.** The amount the customer deposits with the bank.

bank annuities *pl. n. British.* **Consols** *(see).*

bank·book (bángk-bŏŏk || -bŏŏk) *n.* A passbook *(see)* held by a person having a deposit account at a bank.

bank discount *n.* The interest on a loan, calculated in advance, and deducted at the time the loan is made.

bank·er¹ (bángkǝr) *n.* **1.** A person who owns or manages a bank. **2.** The player in charge of the bank in games such as poker or dominoes.

banker² *n.* A forecast of a result that is repeated at each of several entries on a football-pools' coupon.

banker³ *n.* A workbench used by masons and sculptors.

banker's card *n.* A cheque card *(see).*

banker's order *n.* A standing order *(see).*

bank·et (bángkit) *n.* A gold-bearing conglomerate consisting of almond-shaped pebbles, found in South Africa. [Dutch, "banquet", a type of almond sweet (alluding to the shape of the pebbles).]

Bank·head (bángk-hed), **Tallulah** (1903–68). U.S. actress. Noted as much for her extravagant lifestyle as for her performances on stage and screen, she did, however, win acclaim for her appearances in plays such as *The Little Foxes* by Lillian Hellman (1939).

bank holiday *n.* **1.** In England and Wales, a public holiday on which banks are legally closed. **2.** In Scotland and elsewhere, a weekday on which banks are legally closed.

bank·ing (bángking) *n. Abbr.* **bkg.** The business of a bank or the occupation of a banker.

bank manager *n.* The person in charge of a local branch of a bank.

bank·note (bángk-nōt) *n.* A note issued by an authorised bank representing its promise to pay a specific sum to the bearer on demand and acceptable as money. Also *U.S.* "bank bill".

bank rate *n.* The rate of discount established by a country's central bank or banks. It has been discontinued in Britain. See **minimum lending rate.**

bank·roll (bángk-rōl) *n. Chiefly U.S.* **1.** A roll of paper money. **2.** *Informal.* A person's ready cash.
~*tr.v.* **bankrolled, -rolling, -rolls.** *Chiefly U.S. Informal.* To provide financial backing for (a business enterprise, for example).

bank·rupt (bángk-rupt, -rǝpt) *n. Abbr.* **bkpt.** **1.** *Law.* An individual or corporate debtor, who, after a petition to the court by himself or his creditors, is judged legally insolvent. His remaining property is then administered for his creditors or distributed among them in accordance with the law. **2.** Any person unable to pay his creditors in full. **3.** One who is or has become devoid of some resource or quality: *an intellectual bankrupt.*
~*adj.* **1.** Subject to legal procedure because of insolvency; legally declared a bankrupt. **2.** Financially ruined; impoverished. **3.** Completely lacking in some quality; destitute: *morally bankrupt.*
~*tr.v.* **bankrupted, -rupting, -rupts.** To cause to become bankrupt. [16th century : from Italian *banca rotta*, "broken bench", symbol of an insolvent moneychanger : *banca*, moneychanger's bench + *rotta*, past participle of *rompere*, to break (assimilated to Latin *rupta*).]
—**bank·rupt·cy** *n.*

Banks (bangks), **Sir Joseph** (1743–1820). British botanist and explorer. His most famous expedition was the circumnavigation of the world with Captain James Cook on the *Endeavour* (1768–71). He discovered and catalogued many species of animal and plant life, especially from Australia, and promoted the introduction of crop

plants from their native regions to other parts of the world.

bank·si·a (bángksi-ǝ) *n.* Any shrub or tree of the Australian genus *Banksia*, whose flowers are borne on densely packed spikes that form cylindrical heads.

bank statement *n.* A statement showing the transactions and current balance of a bank account, especially one that is sent regularly to the holder of the account.

ban·ner (bánnǝr) *n.* **1.** A strip of cloth, either hung overhead or carried between poles, bearing a message or slogan. **2.** A piece of cloth attached to a staff and used as a standard by a monarch, knight, or military commander. **3. a.** The flag of a nation, state, army, or sovereign. **b.** An ensign bearing a motto, emblem, or legend, as of a society or trade union. **4.** A headline spanning the width of a newspaper page. Also called "banner headline". **5.** A principle, ideal, or slogan: *campaigning under the banner of democracy.*
~*adj. U.S.* Outstanding; superior. [Middle English *banere*, from Anglo-French, from Old French *baniere*, from Vulgar Latin *bandāria* (unattested), from Late Latin *bandum*, standard, from Germanic.]

banner cloud *n.* A type of cloud that forms in clear skies on the side of a mountain peak sheltered from the wind, as air rising to pass over the peak cools.

ban·ner·et¹, ban·ner·ette (bánnǝ-rét) *n.* A small banner. [Middle English *baneret*, from Old French *banerete*, diminutive of *baniere*, BANNER.]

ban·ner·et² (bánnǝ-rit, -rǝt) *n.* **1.** A feudal knight entitled to lead men into battle under his own standard. **2.** The rank of such a knight, between knight bachelor and baron. Also called "knight banneret". [Middle English *baneret*, from Old French, "bannered", from *baniere*, BANNER.]

bannerol. Variant of **banderole.**

bannister. Variant of **banister.**

Ban·nis·ter (bánnistǝr), **Sir Roger (Gilbert)** (1929–). British middle-distance runner, the first man to break the four-minute-mile barrier (6 May 1954) with a time of 3 minutes 59.4 seconds. He won British and European championships. Master of Pembroke College, Oxford (1985–93).

ban·nock (bánnǝk). *n.* Also **bon·nock** (bonnǝk). *Regional.* A round, flat pancake, usually unleavened, made of oatmeal, barley, or wheat flour and sometimes containing dried fruit. [Middle English *bannok*, Old English *bannuc*, perhaps from Celtic.]

Ban·nock·burn (bánnǝk-burn). Small town in Scotland, on Bannock burn, a tributary of the river Forth. It is the site of the battle (1314) where the Scots, under Robert the Bruce, won a famous victory over the English, under Edward II.

banns, bans (banz) *pl.n.* A spoken or published announcement in a church of an intended marriage, usually read out on three successive Sundays. [Middle English *banes*, plural of *bane, ban*, proclamation, BAN.]

ban·quet (bángkwit) *n.* **1.** An elaborate and sumptuous meal. **2.** A ceremonial dinner honouring a particular guest or occasion.
~*v.* **banqueted, -queting, -quets.** —*tr.* To entertain at a banquet. —*intr.* To partake of a banquet; feast. [Old French, diminutive of *banc*, bench, from Germanic.] —**ban·quet·er** *n.*

ban·quette (bang-két) *n.* **1.** *Military.* A platform lining a trench or parapet wall where soldiers may stand when firing. **2.** A long upholstered bench, either placed against or built into a wall. [French, from Italian *banchetta*, diminutive of *banca*, bench, from Germanic.]

ban·shee, ban·shie (bán-shee, -shée) *n.* A female spirit in Gaelic folklore believed to presage a death in the family by wailing outside the house. [Irish Gaelic *bean sídhe*, "woman of the fairies", from Old Irish *ben síde* : *ben*, woman + *síde†*, fairy folk.]

ban·tam (bántǝm) *n.* **1.** Any of various breeds of small domestic fowl. **2.** A small but aggressive person.
~*adj.* **1.** Diminutive; miniature. **2.** Spirited or aggressive. [From the belief that the fowl were native to *Bantam*, village in Java.]

ban·tam·weight (bántǝm-wayt) *n.* **1.** A professional boxer weighing between 8 stone and 8 stone 6 pounds (51 and 53.5 kilograms). **2.** An amateur boxer weighing between 51 and 54 kilograms (8 stone and 8 stone 7 pounds).

ban·ter (bántǝr) *n.* Good-humoured teasing or playful repartee.
~*v.* **bantered, -tering, -ters.** —*tr.* To tease or mock gently. —*intr.* To exchange mildly teasing remarks. [17th century : origin obscure.] —**ban·ter·er** *n.* —**ban·ter·ing·ly** *adv.*

Ban·ting (bánting), **Sir Frederick Grant** (1891–1941). Canadian physiologist. In 1921, in collaboration with C. H. Best, he discovered a technique for isolating the hormone insulin from pancreatic tissue and thus discovered a treatment for diabetics. He was awarded the Nobel prize (1923) jointly with his professor at Toronto University, J.J.R. Macleod, but, considering this to be unfair, he gave half of his share of the prize to C. H. Best.

bant·ling (bántling) *n. Archaic.* A young child; a brat. [16th century: perhaps a variant of German *Bankling*, bastard, from *Bank*, bench (i.e., "a child begotten on a bench"), from Old High German *banc.*]

Ban·try Bay (bántri). Atlantic inlet on the southwest coast of County Cork, Republic of Ireland.

Ban·tu (bán-tōō, bàan-, -tōō) *n., pl.* **Bantus** or collectively **Bantu.** **1.** A member of any of several Negroid tribes of central and southern Africa. **2.** *South African.* A black South African. Usually considered offensive. **3.** A family of languages spoken by the Bantu, including Kongo, Luba, Kikuyu, Luganda, Nyanja, Swahili, and Zulu. —**Ban·tu** adj.

~adj. Of or pertaining to any of the Bantu peoples or their languages.

Ban·tu·stan (bán-tōō-staán, baán, -staan) n. In South Africa, a former **homeland** (see). Sometimes used derogatorily.

banx·ring (bánks-ring) n. A small squirrel-like animal from Java. [Javanese.]

ban·yan, ban·ian (bánni-ən, bán-yən, -yan) n. A tree, *Ficus benghalensis,* of tropical India and the East Indies, having large, oval leaves, reddish fruit, and many aerial roots that develop into additional trunks. Also called "bo". Compare **peepul**. [Originally name applied to one such tree near Bandar Abbas, Iran, beneath which banians had built a pagoda.]

ban·zai (bán-zí, baán-) n. A Japanese battle cry, patriotic cheer, or greeting. [Japanese, "(may you live) ten thousand years", from Chinese *wàn sùi : wàn,* ten thousand + *sùi,* year.]

banzai attack n. A desperate, suicidal attack, as practised by Japanese troops in World War II. Also called "banzai charge".

ba·o·bab (báy-ō-bab, -ə- ‖ U.S. also baá-) n. A tree, *Adansonia digitata,* of tropical Africa, having an extremely thick trunk, large, pendulous white flowers, and hard-shelled, fleshy fruit called monkey bread. [New Latin (16th century) : probably a native Central African name.]

bap (bap) n. British. A soft, round, flat bread roll. [16th century : origin obscure.]

bap., bapt. 1. baptised. 2. baptism.
Bap., Bapt. Baptist.

bap·tise, bap·tize (báp-tíz, bap- ‖ U.S. also báptíz) v. -tised, -tising, -tises. —tr. 1. To dip or immerse (a person) in water or to sprinkle water on (a person) during a baptismal ceremony. 2. a. To cleanse or purify. b. To initiate. 3. To give a first or Christian name to; christen. —intr. To administer baptism. [Middle English *baptizen,* from Old French *baptiser,* from Late Latin *baptizāre,* from Greek *baptizein,* from *baptein,* to dip.] —**bap·tis·er** n.

bap·tism (báp-tiz'm) n. Abbr. **bap., bapt.** 1. A Christian sacrament, symbolic of spiritual regeneration, in which, as a result of immersion or sprinkling with water, accompanied by the recital of a form of words, the recipient is considered cleansed of original sin, given a name, and admitted into Christianity or a specific Christian church. 2. Any ceremony, trial, or experience by which one is initiated, purified, or given a name. [Middle English *bapteme,* from Old French *bapteme, baptesme,* from Late Latin *baptisma,* from Greek, from *baptizein,* to BAPTISE.] —**bap·tis·mal** (-tízm'l) adj. —**bap·tis·mal·ly** adv.

baptism of fire n. 1. A soldier's first experience of actual combat conditions. 2. Any severe ordeal experienced for the first time.

Bap·tist (báptist) n. Abbr. **Bap., Bapt.** 1. A member of any of various Protestant denominations believing that the sacrament of baptism should be given only to adult members upon a profession of faith and usually by immersion. 2. Small **b.** One who baptises. —**the Baptist.** John the Baptist. —**Bap·tist** adj.

bap·tis·ter·y, bap·tis·try (báptistri) n., pl. -ies. 1. A part of a church, or a separate building, where baptisms take place. 2. A font used for baptism. 3. A tank for baptising by total immersion used in Baptist churches.

bar¹ (bar) n. 1. A relatively long, straight, rigid piece of any solid material used, for example, as a support, barrier, or structural or mechanical member, or to fasten something. 2. a. A solid oblong block of a substance, such as soap or chocolate. b. A rectangular block of a precious metal. c. A unit of quantity based on such a block. 3. Anything that impedes or prevents; an obstacle. 4. A ridge of mud, sand, or shingle parallel to the shore, extending across a river mouth or harbour, across a bay, or linking an island to the mainland. 5. A stripe or band, such as one formed by light or colour. 6. The heating element in an electric fire. 7. Heraldry. A pair of horizontal parallel lines drawn across a shield. 8. Law. a. The nullifying, defeating, or preventing of a claim or action. b. The process by which this is done. 9. The area in an English court of law that separates the area reserved for the judges, jury, and Queen's Counsel from that open to junior barristers and the general public. 10. Capital **B. a.** In Britain and many English-speaking countries, barristers or advocates collectively. Preceded by *the.* **b.** In the United States, the legal profession collectively. Preceded by *the.* 11. The place where an accused person stands during his trial in a court of law. 12. **a.** A particular court of law. **b.** Any tribunal or place of judgment. **c.** Anything referred to as an authority. 13. In the House of Commons and the House of Lords, the place where nonmembers stand to address the house. 14. Music. **a.** Any of a series of divisions of equal time value, into which a piece of music is divided by bar lines. Also chiefly U.S. "measure". **b.** A **bar line** (see). **c.** A **double bar** (see). 15. **a.** A counter at which alcoholic drinks and sometimes meals or snacks are served. **b.** An establishment or room containing such a counter. 16. **a.** A counter where goods or services of a specified kind are sold or provided: *a heel bar.* **b.** An establishment or room containing such a counter: *a snack bar.* 17. An insignia added to a military decoration indicating that it has been awarded a second time. 18. Variant of **barre**. —**be called to the Bar.** To be admitted as a barrister. —**be called within the Bar.** To be made a Queen's Counsel. —**behind bars.** In prison. —See Synonyms at **obstacle.** —See Usage note at **shoal¹.**

~tr.v. **barred, barring, bars.** 1. To fasten securely with a bar. 2. To keep in or out with or as if with bars. 3. To obstruct or impede; block. 4. To exclude. 5. To mark with bars or stripes. 6. Music. To indicate measures in (a piece of music) by using bars. 7. Law. To stop (an action or claim) by legal objection. —See Synonyms at **hinder¹.**

~prep. Excluding; except for: barring: *That was his best performance, bar none.* [Middle English *barre,* from Old French, from Vulgar Latin (unattested) *barra†.*]

bar² n. A unit of pressure equal to 10⁵ newtons per square metre or 0.98697 standard atmosphere. [German, from Greek *baros,* weight.]

bar. 1. barometer; barometric. 2. barrel. 3. barrister.

Ba·rab·bas (bə-rábbəss). A condemned thief whose release was demanded of Pilate by the multitude, instead of that of Jesus. Matthew 27:16–26.

ba·ra brith (baárə bréeth) n. A rich Welsh bread made with mixed fruit. [Welsh, "speckled bread" : *bara,* bread + *brith,* speckled (that is, studded with currants).]

bar·a·the·a (bárrə-thée-ə) n. A soft fabric of silk and cotton or silk and wool. [19th century : origin obscure.]

barb¹ (barb) n. 1. A sharp point projecting in reverse direction to the main point of a weapon or tool, as on an arrow, fishhook, or spear. 2. A cutting or biting remark. 3. Botany. A hooked bristle or hairlike projection. 4. Ornithology. Any of the many parallel filaments projecting from the main shaft of a feather. 5. Any of various Old World freshwater fishes of the genus *Barbus* (or *Puntius*) and related genera, many of which are popular in home aquariums. 6. Any of the small folds of mucous membrane below the tongue of horses and cattle. 7. A white linen covering for a woman's head, throat, and chin, worn in medieval times; nowadays worn by certain orders of nuns. 8. Obsolete. A beard.

~tr.v. **barbed, barbing, barbs.** To provide or furnish with a barb or barbs. [Middle English *barbe,* beard, beardlike appendage, from Old French, from Latin *barba,* beard.]

barb² n. 1. A hardy racehorse of a breed that originated in northern Africa. 2. Any of a breed of domestic pigeons having dark plumage. 3. Australian. A type of sheepdog, a black **kelpie** (see). [French *barbe,* Barbary horse, from Italian *barbero,* BARBARY.]

barb³ n. Chiefly U.S. Slang. A barbiturate.

Bar·ba·dos (baar-báy-doss, -dōz, -dəss). Prosperous West Indian island, the most easterly of the Antilles. It was probably first visited by the Portuguese, who named it Los Barbados (Bearded) because of its numerous bearded fig-trees. The British first landed in 1605 and began colonising it in 1627. The island was a British colony until 1966 when it became independent within the Commonwealth. The economy is based on sugar and tourism. It is densely populated, and over 80 per cent of the people are black descendants of African slaves. Area, 431 square kilometres (166 square miles). Population, 259,000. Capital, Bridgetown. See map at **Trinidad and Tobago.** —**Bar·ba·di·an** adj. & n.

bar·bar·i·an (baar-bair-i-ən) n. 1. One belonging to a people or tribe considered to have a primitive civilisation. 2. A fierce, brutal, or cruel person. 3. An insensitive, uncultured person; a boor. 4. Originally, a foreigner: especially, one not Greek or Roman and therefore regarded as uncivilised.

~adj. Characteristic of or resembling a barbarian; rough and uncivilised. [French *barbarien,* from Latin *barbaria,* foreign country, from *barbarus,* BARBAROUS.] —**bar·bar·i·an·ism** n.

bar·bar·ic (baar-bárrik) adj. 1. Of, pertaining to, or characteristic of a barbarian or barbarians. 2. Marked by crudeness or wildness of taste, style, or manner. 3. Extremely cruel and inhuman.

bar·ba·rise, bar·ba·rize (bárbəríz) v. -ised, -ising, -ises. —tr. To make crude or barbarous; corrupt. —intr. To become barbarous.

bar·ba·rism (bárbəriz'm) n. 1. An instance, act, trait, or custom characterised by brutality or coarseness. 2. a. The use of words or forms considered incorrect or nonstandard in a language. b. A specific word or form so used. 3. Anything that offends against accepted standards or taste of manners. [Old French *barbarisme,* from Latin *barbarismus,* from Greek *barbarismos,* foreign or incorrect speech, from *barbaros,* foreign, BARBAROUS.]

bar·bar·i·ty (baar-bárrəti) n., pl. -ties. 1. Harsh or cruel conduct. 2. An inhuman, brutal act. 3. Crudity; coarseness.

Bar·ba·ros·sa¹ (bárbə-róssə ‖ -ráwssə), born Khayr ad-Din (died 1546). Turkish pirate. He served under the Ottoman Sultan of Turkey in an alliance to protect his holdings on the Barbary coast of North Africa against the Spanish and the Portuguese. His military prowess extended to the capture of Algiers (1529) and Tunis (1534). His greatest achievement was in 1538, when he defeated the Emperor Charles V's fleet to give the Turks unopposed control of the Eastern Mediterranean.

Barbarossa². See Frederick I.

bar·ba·rous (bárbərəss) adj. 1. Primitive in culture and customs; uncivilised. 2. Characterised by savagery; cruel; brutal. 3. Lacking refinement or culture; coarse; boorish. 4. Of, pertaining to, or designating language that violates classical or accepted usage standards. —See Synonyms at **cruel.** [Latin *barbarus,* from Greek *barbaros,* non-Greek, foreign, rude.] —**bar·ba·rous·ly** adv. —**bar·ba·rous·ness** n.

Bar·ba·ry (bárbəri). A region of the North African coast from Egypt to the Atlantic Ocean. It takes its name from the Berbers, inhabitants of the area since the second millennium B.C. It fell to the Arabs (7th century A.D.), who introduced Islam. Between the 16th and 19th centuries, it was notorious for its pirates.

Barbary ape n. A tailless monkey, *Macaca sylvanus,* of Gibraltar

133

and northern Africa. A species of macaque, it is the only monkey found wild in Europe.

Barbary sheep *n.* The **aoudad** *(see).*

bar·bate (bárbayt) *adj. Biology.* Having a beard, or tufted hairs resembling a beard. [Latin *barbātus,* from *barba,* beard.]

bar·be·cue (bárbikew) *n.* **1. a.** A pit or outdoor fireplace for cooking meat or other food. **b.** A grill or similar apparatus used for cooking food out of doors. **2.** Meat or other food cooked over an open fire or on a spit. **3.** A social gathering, usually held outdoors, at which food is prepared on a barbecue.

~*tr.v.* **barbecued, -cuing, -cues.** To roast or grill over hot charcoal or an open fire. [American Spanish *barbacoa,* from Haitian Creole, framework of sticks set on posts, from Taino.]

barbed (barbd) *adj.* **1.** Having a barb or barbs. **2.** Piercing or stinging: *a barbed statement.*

barbed wire *n.* Twisted strands of fencing wire with barbs at regular intervals. Also *chiefly U.S.* "barbwire".

bar·bel (bárb'l) *n.* **1.** Any of the slender, whisker-like sensory organs on the head of certain fishes, such as catfish. **2.** Any of several Old World freshwater fish of the genus *Barbus,* resembling the carp but with a longer snout. [Middle English, from Old French, from Late Latin *barbellus,* diminutive of *barbus,* barbel (the fish), from Latin *barba,* beard (from its beardlike fleshy filaments).]

bar·bell (bár-bel) *n.* A bar with adjustable weights at each end, used in weightlifting.

bar·bel·late (bárbəlayt, baar-bél-ət, -it, -ayt) *adj.* Having minute, hooked bristles or hairs. [From New Latin *barbella,* short stiff hair, diminutive of Latin *barbula,* little beard, diminutive of *barba,* beard.]

bar·ber (bárbər) *n.* One whose business is to cut men's hair and to shave or trim beards.

~*tr.v.* **barbered, -bering, -bers. 1.** To cut the hair of. **2.** To shave or trim the beard of. [Middle English *barbour,* from Old French *barbeor,* from Medieval Latin *barbātor,* from *barba,* beard, from Latin.]

bar·ber·ry (bár-bəri || -berri) *n., pl.* **-ries.** A shrub of the genus *Berberis,* having small leaves, clusters of yellow flowers, and small orange or red berries. [Variant (influenced by BERRY) of Middle English *barbere,* from Old French *berberis†.]*

bar·ber·shop (bárbər-shop) *n. Chiefly U.S.* The place of business of a barber.

~*adj. Chiefly U.S.* Of or designating male voices singing sentimental songs in close, usually four-part, harmony: *a barbershop quartet.*

barber's itch *n.* Any of various infections of the skin beneath a beard, especially ringworm. Not in technical usage.

bar·bet (bárbit) *n.* Any of various tropical birds of the family Capitonidae, having a broad bill bristled at the base and brightly coloured plumage, and related to the toucans. [French, from Latin *barbātus,* BARBATE.]

bar·bette (baar-bét) *n.* **1.** A platform or mound within a fort high enough to permit firing of guns over the parapet. **2.** An armoured protective cylinder around a revolving turret on a warship. [French, diminutive of *barbe,* beard.]

bar·bi·can (bárbikən) *n.* A tower or other fortification on the approach to a castle or town, especially one at a gate or drawbridge. [Middle English, from Old French *barbacane†.]*

bar·bi·cel (bárbi-sel) *n. Ornithology.* Any of the minute projections that fringe the edges of the barbules of feathers and interlock with those on adjacent barbules. [New Latin *barbicella,* diminutive of Latin *barba,* beard.]

bar billiards *n.* A table game resembling billiards, popular in public houses and men's clubs, in which balls have to be struck past wooden pegs and pocketed into holes on the table.

Bar·bi·rol·li (bárbə-rólli), **Sir John** (1899–1970). British cellist and conductor, born of Franco-Italian parents. He was conductor of several major opera companies in Britain and in the United States. From 1943 he was principal conductor of the Hallé Orchestra which he developed into one of the world's leading orchestras.

bar·bi·tone (bárbitōn) *n.* A barbiturate drug, $C_8H_{12}N_2O_3$, used as a sedative or to induce sleep. Also *U.S.* "barbital". [BARBIT(URIC ACID) + -ONE.]

bar·bi·tu·rate (baar-bíttew-rət, -rit, -rayt || *U.S. also* bárbi-téw-, -tōō-) *n.* **1.** A salt or ester of barbituric acid. **2.** Any of a group of barbituric acid derivatives used as sedatives or to induce sleep. Prolonged use may lead to dependence. [BARBITUR(IC ACID) + -ATE.]

bar·bi·tu·ric acid (bárbi-téwr-ik || -tóor-) *n.* An organic acid, $C_4H_4N_2O_3$, used in the manufacture of barbiturates and some plastics. [Partial translation of German *Barbitursäure : Barbitur* perhaps from the name *Barbara* + UR(IC) + *Säure,* ACID.]

Bar·bi·zon school (bárbi-zon) *n.* A 19th-century group of landscape painters in France, including Corot, Daubigny, Millet, and Rousseau. [After *Barbizon,* a small village near Paris, where they worked.]

Bar·bu·da (bar-bōōdə). Small Caribbean island, now part of **Antigua and Barbuda** *(see).* Area, 161 square kilometres (62 square miles).

bar·bule (bárbewl) *n. Biology.* A small barb or pointed projection; especially, any of the small projections fringing the edges of the barbs of feathers. [Latin *barbula,* diminutive of *barba,* beard.]

Bar·busse (baar-büss), **Henri** (1873–1935). French novelist and journalist who came to fame with the publication of his novel *Under Fire* (1916), based on his experiences in World War I.

barb·wire (bárb-wîr) *n. Chiefly U.S.* **Barbed wire** *(see).*

Bar·ca (bárkə). The name of a prominent family of ancient Carthage, whose members included Hannibal and other Carthaginian generals.

bar·ca·role, bar·ca·rolle (bárkə-ról, -ṓl, -rol, -rōl) *n.* **1.** A Venetian gondolier's song, with a rhythm suggestive of rowing. **2.** A musical composition imitating this. [French, from Italian *barcaruola,* from *barcaruolo,* gondolier, from *barca,* barge, from Late Latin *barca,* BARK (ship).]

Bar·ce·lo·na (bársi-lṓnə, bárthe-). City in Catalonia, northeast Spain, on the Mediterranean coast. Founded by the Carthaginians, it prospered under the Romans and the Visigoths. It was captured by the Moors (713) and by Charlemagne (801). With the incorporation of Catalonia into Spain, the city grew as the centre of Catalan separatist, anarcho-syndicalist, and socialist movements. In the Civil War (1936–39) it was the seat of the Republican government. Barcelona is a major cultural centre and an enclave of Catalan art and literature. It is the largest port in Spain and a leading commercial and industrial centre. —**Bar·ce·lo·nan** *adj. & n.*

B.Arch. Bachelor of Architecture.

bar·chan, bar·chane, bar·khan (baar-kaán) *n.* A type of crescent-shaped sand dune, concave on the side sheltered from the prevailing wind. [Russian *barkhan,* from Kirghiz.]

bar chart *n.* A **bar graph** *(see).*

bar code *n.* A code in the form of vertical lines and numbers printed on a book or item of merchandise, for example, so that it can be identified by an optical scanner.

bar·code (bár-kōd) *tr. v.* **-coded, -coding, -codes.** To provide with a bar code.

Barcoo River. See **Coopers Creek.**

bard[1] (bard) *n.* **1.** Any of an ancient Celtic order of singing poets who composed and recited verses on the legends and history of their people. **2.** Any poet, especially: **a.** An exalted national poet. **b.** One honoured as an outstanding poet in an Eisteddfod. —**the Bard.** Shakespeare. —See Synonyms at **poet.** [Middle English, from Gaelic and Irish *bárd* and Welsh *bardd.*] —**bard·ic** *adj.*

bard[2], **barde** (bard) *n.* **1.** A piece of bacon or fat placed on or threaded into meat or game to prevent it from drying out during roasting. **2.** Any piece of armour used to protect or ornament a horse.

~*tr.v.* **barded, barding, bards. 1.** To place bards in or on (meat). **2.** To equip (a horse) with bards. [Old French *barde,* probably from Old Italian *barda,* from Arabic *barda'ah,* stuffed packsaddle.]

Bar·dot (baar-dṓ, bárdō), **Brigitte,** born Camille Javal (1934–). French actress and animal-welfare supporter. Amongst her best-known films is *And God Created Woman* (1956).

bard·ol·a·try (baar-dóllətri) *n.* Inordinate admiration of Shakespeare and his works. Usually used facetiously. [BARD (Shakespeare) + -LATRY.] —**bard·ol·a·ter** (-dóllətər) *n.*

Bard·sey (bárdzi). *Welsh* **Ynys Enlli** (únniss énhlee). Welsh island off the north point of Cardigan Bay in the Irish Sea.

bar·dy, bar·di (bárdi) *n., pl.* **-dies.** *Australian.* An edible wood-boring grub, *Bardistus cibarius,* or its larvae. —**starve the bardies.** *Australian Informal.* Used as an exclamation of surprise or disgust. [From a native Australian language.]

bare[1] (bair) *adj.* **barer, barest. 1.** Without the usual or appropriate covering or clothing; naked: *a bare chest.* **2.** Exposed to view; unconcealed. **3.** Lacking the usual furnishings, equipment, or decoration: *walls bare of pictures.* **4.** Without addition, adornment, or qualification; simple; plain: *the bare facts.* **5.** Just sufficient; mere: *the bare necessities of life.* **6.** Empty. **7.** *Obsolete.* Bareheaded. —See Synonyms at **empty.**

~*tr.v.* **bared, baring, bares. 1.** To make bare; strip of covering. **2.** To expose; reveal: *the dog bared its teeth.* —See Synonyms at **strip.** [Middle English *bare,* Old English *bær,* from Germanic *bazaz* (unattested).] —**bare·ness** *n.*

bare[2]. *Archaic.* Past tense of **bear.**

bare·back (báir-bak) *adj.* Also **bare·backed** (-bakt). On a horse or pony, with no saddle: *a bareback rider.* —**bare·back** *adv.*

bare·faced (báir-fayst, *rarely* -fáyst) *adj.* **1. a.** Having no covering over the face. **b.** Having no beard. **2.** Unconcealed; without disguise. **3.** Presumptuous and shameless; brazen: *a barefaced lie.* —See Synonyms at **shameless.** —**bare·fac·ed·ly** (-fáystli, -fáysidli) *adv.* —**bare·fac·ed·ness** *n.*

bare·foot (báir-fŏŏt) *adj.* Also **bare·foot·ed** (-fŏŏtid). Wearing nothing on the feet. —**bare·foot** *adv.*

barefoot doctor *n.* A medical worker, especially in rural areas of developing countries, who carries out such tasks as treating simple injuries and ailments, or assisting at childbirth.

ba·rege, ba·rège (bə-rézh, -ráyzh) *n.* A sheer fabric woven of silk or cotton and wool, used for women's clothes. [French *barège,* first made in *Barèges,* France.]

bare·hand·ed (báir-hándid) *adj.* **1.** Having no covering on the hands. **2.** With the hands alone; unaided by tools or weapons. —**bare·hand·ed** *adv.*

bare·head·ed (báir-héddid) *adj.* Having no head covering. —**bare·head·ed** *adv.*

bare·legged (báir-légd, -légid) *adj.* Having the legs uncovered. —**bare·leg·ged** *adv.*

bare·ly (báirli) *adv.* **1.** By a very little; hardly; only just. **2.** Meagrely; scantily. **3.** *Archaic.* Without disguise; openly. —See Synonyms at **hardly.**

Bar·en·boim (bárrən-boym), **Daniel** (1942–). Israeli pianist and conductor. He married the cellist Jacqueline Du Pré (1967), and has been musical director of the Orchestre de Paris (1975–89), the Chicago Symphony Orchestra (1991–), and the Deutsche Staatsoper, Berlin (1992–).

Bar·ents Sea (bárrants || chiefly U.S. báarants). Shallow section of the Arctic Ocean lying between Svalbard and Novaya Zemlya. The North Atlantic Current keeps its southern ports ice-free all the year. The sea floor is potentially rich in oil and gas and this, and the desire of the U.S.S.R. to command the shipping lanes to the strategic ice-free port of Murmansk, led to dispute over the Norwegian-Soviet border across the sea. It is named after the Dutch navigator Willem Barents (1550–1597).

bar·fly (bár-flī) n., pl. **-flies.** Chiefly U.S. Slang. One who frequents bars.

bar·gain (bár-gin || -gən) n. **1.** An agreement or deal made between parties, especially one involving the sale and purchase of goods or services. **2.** The terms or conditions of such an agreement: He met his part of the bargain by handing over the goods. **3.** The property acquired or services rendered as a result of such an agreement. **4.** Something offered or acquired at a price advantageous to the buyer. **—into the bargain.** Over and above what is expected. **—strike a bargain.** To agree on the terms of a transaction. ~v. bargained, -gaining, -gains. —intr. **1.** To negotiate the terms of a sale, exchange, or other agreement. **2.** To arrive at an agreement. —tr. To exchange or trade: He bargained his watch for a meal. **—bargain away.** To give up or lose (something of value, such as rights or freedom) without getting anything substantial in return. **—bargain for.** To expect; count on: got more then she'd bargained for. **—bargain on.** To rely on. [Middle English bargaynen, from Old French bargaignier, haggle in the market, probably from Germanic.] **—bar·gain·er** n.

bargaining counter. Also chiefly U.S. **bargaining chip.** Something used by one side in negotiations, to try to get concessions from the other side.

barge (barj) n. **1.** A long, large boat, usually flat-bottomed, used chiefly on inland waterways for transporting freight. It may have its own power or be towed by other craft. **2.** A large pleasure boat used for parties, pageants, or formal ceremonies. **3.** Slang. Any old or unwieldy boat or ship. **4.** In the navy, a power boat reserved for the use of a flag officer. ~v. barged, barging, barges. —tr. To carry by barge. —intr. Informal. **1.** To move about clumsily. **2.** To collide. Used with into. **3.** To enter or interrupt rudely and abruptly; intrude. Used with in or into. [Middle English, from Old French barge, perhaps from Medieval Latin barica (unattested), from Greek baris, BARK (ship).]

barge·board (bárj-bawrd || -bōrd) n. Architecture. A board, often ornately carved, attached along the projecting edge of a gable roof. [Barge, perhaps akin to Medieval Latin bargus, gallows.]

barge·gee (bár-jée) n. British. The master or a crew member of a barge.

barge·man (bárj-mən) n., pl. **-men** (-mən, -men). U.S. A bargee.

barge·pole (bárj-pōl) n. A stout pole used for guiding and pushing a barge. **—not touch with a bargepole.** To refuse or avoid any association or dealings with.

bar graph n. A graph consisting of parallel, usually vertical, bars or rectangles with lengths proportional to specific quantities in a set of data. Also called "bar chart".

Ba·ri (báari). Seaport in Italy, on the Adriatic Sea. Once the Roman colony of Barium, it was held successively by Goths, Lombards, Byzantines, Normans, and Venetians, and became part of the kingdom of Naples (1557).

ba·ril·la (bə-rílla || U.S. -réel-yə, -rée-) n. **1.** Either of two Old World plants, Salsola kali (or S. soda), or a similar plant, Halogeton soda, that were formerly burned to obtain a form of sodium carbonate. **2.** The sodium carbonate thus obtained. [Spanish barrilla†.]

bar·ite (baír-it) n. Chiefly U.S. **Barytes** (see).

bar·i·tone (bárri-tōn) n. **1.** A male singer or voice having a range higher than a bass and lower than a tenor. **2.** A part written for a baritone. **3.** A brass wind instrument with a similar range. ~adj. **1.** Of, pertaining to, or having the range of a baritone. **2.** Having the second-lowest range in a family of instruments: the baritone saxophone. [Italian baritono, from Greek barutonos, deep sounding : barus, heavy, + tonos, pitch, TONE.]

bar·i·um (baír-i-əm) n. Symbol **Ba** A soft, silvery-white, alkaline-earth metal, used to deoxidize copper, in various alloys, and in rat poison. Atomic number 56, atomic weight 137.34, melting point 725°C, boiling point 1 140°C, relative density 3.50, valency 2. [BA-R(YTA) + -IUM.] **—bar·ic** (baír-ik, bárrik) adj.

barium enema n. A preparation of barium sulphate infused into the rectum in order to reveal the large intestine by X-ray.

barium hydroxide n. A white, poisonous, crystalline compound, $Ba(OH)_2$, used in the extraction of beet sugar. Also called "baryta".

barium meal n. A preparation of barium sulphate swallowed before X-ray examination of the stomach and small intestine.

barium oxide n. A white soluble powder, BaO, used as a dehydrating agent and in the manufacture of certain types of glass. Also called "baryta".

barium sulphate n. A fine white powder, $BaSO_4$, used as a pigment, as a filler for textiles, rubbers, and plastics, and as an indicator in X-ray photography of the digestive tract.

barium yellow n. **1.** A pigment made of barium chromate, $BaCrO_4$. **2.** Light or moderate greenish yellow to brilliant yellow.

bark¹ (bark) n. **1.** The characteristic harsh, abrupt, usually gruff sound of a dog and certain other animals. **2.** Any similar sound, such as a gunshot or cough. ~v. barked, barking, barks. —intr. **1.** To emit a bark. **2.** Informal. To cough. **3.** To speak sharply; snap: He barked at his assistant. **4.** Chiefly U.S. Informal. To work as a barker. —tr. To utter sharply in a loud, harsh voice. [Middle English berken, to bark, Old English beorcan.]

bark² n. **1.** The protective outer covering of the woody stems, branches, and main trunks of trees and other woody plants, consisting of dead cells. **2.** A specific kind of bark used for a special purpose, as in tanning or medicine. ~tr.v. barked, barking, barks. **1.** To remove bark from (a tree or log). **2.** To rub off the skin of; graze. **3.** To tan, dye, or treat medically using bark. [Middle English barke, from Old Norse börkr, from North Germanic barkuz (unattested).]

bark³. Chiefly U.S. Variant of **barque**.

barkantine, barkentine. Chiefly U.S. Variants of **barquentine**.

bark beetle n. Any of various small beetles of the family Scolytidae that damage trees by boring along the surface of the wood beneath the bark.

bark·er¹ (bárkər) n. **1.** An animal or person making a barking sound. **2.** Informal. A person at a fairground stall or sideshow who attracts customers with loud, colourful sales talk.

barker² n. A person or machine that removes bark from trees or prepares it for tanning.

Barker (bárkər), **George** (1913–91). British poet and novelist. He wrote his first novel Alanna Autumnal at 20. This and his first volume of verse Thirty Preliminary Poems, were published in 1933. His books include The True Confessions of George Barker (1950), Collected Poems (1957), and Street Ballads (1992).

Barker, Harley Granville. See **Granville-Barker, Harley.**

Bark·hausen effect (bárk-howz'n) n. A phenomenon exhibited by ferromagnetic materials, in which the process of magnetisation and demagnetisation proceeds in discrete jumps. [First described by Heinrich Barkhausen (1881–1956), German physicist.]

Bar·king (bárking). Borough in the eastern part of Greater London, created in 1965 by the amalgamation of most of the municipal boroughs of Barking and Dagenham.

barking deer n. The **muntjac** (see).

bark·y (bárki) adj. **-ier, -iest.** Covered with, containing, or resembling bark.

bar·ley (bárli) n. **1.** A widely cultivated cereal grass of the genus Hordeum; especially, H. vulgare, bearing bearded flower spikes with edible seeds. **2.** The grain of this plant, used as food and in making beer, ale, and whisky. See **pearl barley.** [Middle English barrlig, originally "of barley", Old English bærlic, from bære, bere, barley.]

bar·ley·corn (bárli-kawrn) n. **1.** The seed or grain of barley. **2.** Formerly, a unit of measure equal to the length of a grain of barley, or approximately ⅓ inch.

barley sugar n. A clear, hard sweet made by boiling down sugar, formerly with an extract of barley added. ~adj. Also **bar·ley·su·gar.** Resembling the twisted strands of a stick of barley sugar: a table with barley-sugar legs.

barley water n. A drink prepared by boiling pearl barley in water, to which lemon juice is often added.

barley wine n. A very strong beer.

bar line n. Music. A vertical line dividing a staff into bars. Also called "bar".

barm (barm) n. The yeasty foam that rises to the surface of fermenting malt liquors. [Middle English berme, Old English beorma.]

bar·maid (bár-mayd) n. A woman who serves drinks in a bar.

bar·man (bár-mən, -man) n., pl. **-men** (-mən, -men). A man who serves drinks in a bar.

barm cake n. British Regional. A soft, flat bread roll.

Bar·me·ci·dal (bármi-síd'l) adj. Also **Bar·me·cide** (-sīd). Plentiful or abundant in appearance only; illusory: a Barmecide feast. [From Barmecide, name of an eighth-century noble Persian family, one of whom served a beggar an imaginary feast in the Arabian Nights.]

bar mitz·vah, bar miz·vah (baar míts-və). n. Judaism. **1.** A thirteen-year-old Jewish male, considered an adult and thenceforth responsible for his moral and religious duties. **2.** The ceremony conferring and celebrating this status. ~ tr.v. **bar mitzvahed, -vahing, -vahs.** To admit to the status of bar mitzvah. [Hebrew, "son of the commandment".]

barm·y (bármi) adj. **-ier, -iest. 1.** Full of barm; frothy; foamy. **2.** British Informal. Slightly mad; foolish.

barn (barn) n. **1.** A large farm building used for storing grain, hay, and other farm products, and sometimes also used for sheltering livestock. **2.** Any building that resembles a barn in being uncomfortably large and bare. **3.** U.S. A large shed for the housing of railway vehicles. **4.** Physics. Symbol **b** A unit of area equal to 10^{-28} square metre, used to express nuclear cross-sections. [Middle English bern, from Old English bern, berern : bere, BARLEY + ern, ærn, house, from Germanic razn- (unattested) (see **ransack**).]

bar·na·cle (bárnək'l) n. **1.** Any of various marine crustaceans of the order Cirripedia that, in the adult stage, form a hard shell from which feathery food-catching appendages protrude, and which remain attached to a submerged surface, thus fouling ship bottoms. See **acorn barnacle, goose barnacle. 2.** The barnacle goose. [Middle English bernak, bernacle, barnacle goose, from Medieval Latin bernaca, berneca†, barnacle, barnacle goose (from the belief that the geese were produced from the shellfish which supposedly clung to trees).] **—bar·na·cled** adj.

barnacle goose / barrator, barrater

barnacle goose *n.* A goose, *Branta leucopsis,* of northern Europe and Greenland, the adult birds having black, white, and grey plumage.

Bar·nard (bárnaard, bár-nút), **Christiaan (Neethling)** (1922-). South African surgeon noted for pioneering heart transplant operations. He performed the world's first heart transplant (3 December 1967) at the Groote Schuur Hospital, Cape Town. The recipient was Louis Washkansky, who died of pneumonia 18 days after the operation.

Bar·nard (bárn-ərd, -aard), **Edward Emerson** (1857–1923). U.S. astronomer. He is noted for his discovery of Jupiter's fifth satellite (1892), and for his discovery of Barnard's Star (1916).

Bar·nar·do (bər-nárdō, baar-), **Thomas John** (1845–1905). British doctor who devoted himself to the protection and education of orphans and destitute children. He founded the first of his famous homes at Stepney, in London (1867).

Barnard's star *n.* A star in the constellation Ophiuchus, 6 light-years from the Sun and the second-nearest star system to the Sun. It has an extremely large proper motion, which indicates the presence of an orbiting system of planets.

Bar·na·to (bər-náatō, baar-), **Barney,** born Barnett Isaacs (1852–97). South African mining magnate and politician.

barn dance *n.* **1.** *Chiefly British.* A kind of country dance. **2.** *U.S.* A social gathering, usually held in a barn, with music and square dancing.

barn door *n.* **1.** The door of a barn. **2.** A target so large that it is hard to miss.

Bar·net (bárnit). A mainly residential borough in northwest Greater London.

bar·ney (bárni) *n. Informal.* A noisy quarrel
~*intr.v.* **barneyed, -neying, -neys.** To quarrel noisily. [19th century : origin obscure.]

barn owl *n.* A long-legged owl, *Tyto alba,* having light-brown and white plumage and a heart-shaped face, and often frequenting barns and other buildings.

Barns·ley (bárnzli) Industrial town on the river Dearne, in South Yorkshire, England.

Barn·sta·ple (bárn-stəp'l, *locally also* -stəb'l). Town and holiday resort on the estuary of the river Taw, in north Devon, England.

barn·storm (bárn-stawrm) *v.* **-stormed, -storming, -storms.** *Chiefly U.S.* —*intr.* **1.** To travel about the countryside making political speeches, especially in an election campaign. **2.** To tour rural areas presenting theatrical performances, often in makeshift theatres. **3.** To tour rural area giving exhibitions of stunt flying, especially in the early days of aviation. —*tr.* To travel through in order to go barnstorming. —**barn·storm·er** *n.*

barn swallow *n. U.S.* The common **swallow** (see). [The bird often builds its nest in the eaves of barns.]

Bar·num (bárnəm), **P(hineas) T(aylor)** (1810–91). U.S. showman who first popularised "freak shows" in 1842. Among his exhibits were Chang and Eng, the original Siamese twins. His circus was established in 1871 and in 1881 merged with that of his great rival, J. A. Bailey.

barn·yard (bárn-yaard) *n.* The area of ground surrounding a barn, often enclosed by a fence; a farmyard.
~*adj.* **1.** Of or pertaining to a barnyard: *a barnyard fence.* **2.** Rustic; earthy: *barnyard humour.*

baro– *comb. form.* Indicates weight or pressure; for example, **barometer.** [From Greek *baros,* weight.]

Ba·ro·da (bə-rōdə). City in southeast Gujarat, India. Once the capital of the princely state of Baroda, it is distinguished by many fine public buildings, palaces, and Hindu temples.

bar·o·gram (bárrə-gram) *n.* A graphic record produced by a barograph. [BARO- + -GRAM.]

bar·o·graph (bárrə-graaf, -graf) *n.* A self-recording barometer. [BARO- + -GRAPH.] —**bar·o·graph·ic** (-gráffik) *adj.*

ba·rom·e·ter (bə-rómmitər) *n.* **1.** *Abbr.* **bar.** An instrument for measuring atmospheric pressure, used in weather forecasting and in determining altitude. The main types are the **aneroid barometer** and the **mercury barometer** (both of which see). **2.** Anything that gives notice of fluctuations; an indicator: *This by-election will be a barometer of the government's popularity.* [BARO- + -METER.] —**bar·o·met·ric** (bárrə-métrik), **bar·o·met·ri·cal** *adj.* —**bar·o·met·ri·cal·ly** *adv.* —**ba·rom·e·try** (bə-rómmətri) *n.*

bar·on (bárrən) *n.* **1.** Formerly: **a.** A feudal tenant holding his rights and title directly from the king or another feudal superior. **b.** A lord or nobleman; a peer. **2.** *Abbr.* **Bn., bn.** A member of the lowest rank of nobility in Great Britain, certain European countries, and Japan. **3.** The rank or title of such a nobleman. **4.** A man with great and coercive power in a specific sphere of activity; especially, a magnate. **5.** A cut of beef consisting of a double sirloin. Also called "baron of beef". [Middle English, from Anglo-French, from Old French, from Medieval Latin *barō†* (stem *barōn*-), man, warrior.]

bar·on·age (bárrənij) *n.* **1.** The rank, title, or dignity of a baron. **2.** A list of barons. **3.** All of the peers of a kingdom.

bar·on·ess (bárrən-iss, -ess) *n.* **1.** The wife or widow of a baron. **2.** A woman holding a barony in her own right.

bar·on·et (bárrə-nit, -net || *U.S. also* -nét) *n.* **1.** A British hereditary title of honour, ranking next below a baron, held by commoners. **2.** *Abbr.* **Bart., Bt.** The bearer of such a title. [Middle English, diminutive of BARON.]

bar·on·et·age (bárrə-nit-ij, -net-) *n.* **1.** The rank or dignity of a baronet. **2.** A list of baronets. **3.** Baronets collectively.

bar·on·et·cy (bárrə-nit-si, -net-) *n., pl.* **-cies.** The dignity or rank of a baronet.

ba·ro·ni·al (bə-rōn-yəl, -i-əl) *adj.* **1.** Of or pertaining to a baron or barony. **2.** Suited for or befitting a baron; stately; grand.

bar·o·ny (bárrəni) *n., pl.* **-nies.** **1.** The domain of a baron. **2.** The rank or dignity of a baron. **3.** In Ireland, a division of a county. **4.** In Scotland, a large estate.

ba·roque (bə-rók, -rōk) *adj.* **1.** *Often capital* **B. a.** Of, pertaining to, or designating a style in art and architecture developed in Europe from the late 16th to the early 18th centuries, typified by elaborate and ornate scrolls, curves, and other symmetrical ornamentation. **b.** Of, pertaining to, or designating music of the same period, characterised especially by elaborate ornamentation. **2.** Ornate or flamboyant in style; richly ornamented **3.** Irregular in shape: *baroque pearls.*
~*n.* **1.** *Often capital* **B.** The baroque style in art, architecture, and music. **2.** Any elaborate or ornate style. [French (originally used of pearls), from Portuguese *barroco†,* and Spanish *barrueco†* (in architecture), from Italian *barroco†.*]

bar·o·re·cep·tor (bárrō-ri-séptər, -rə- || -ree-) *n. Physiology.* A group of nerve endings, found in the walls of various blood vessels and the heart, that is sensitive to changes in blood pressure.

bar·o·scope (bárrə-skōp) *n.* Any instrument or device for estimating atmospheric pressure; especially, a manometer with one limb open to the atmosphere. [BARO- + -SCOPE.]

bar·o·stat (bárrə-stat, bárrō-) *n.* **1.** Any device for maintaining a constant pressure. **2.** A device used on gas turbines that regulates the input and output pressures of the fuel-metering equipment, in order to compensate for variations of atmospheric pressure. [BARO- + -STAT.]

Ba·rot·se·land (bə-rótsi-land). A former kingdom in central Africa, now Western Province, Zambia, inhabited by the Lozi people. Under their chief, Lewanika (died 1916), the kingdom became part of the protectorate of Northern Rhodesia, and when Zambia became independent (1964) Barotseland tried unsuccessfully to become a separate kingdom.

ba·rouche (bə-rŏosh) *n.* A four-wheeled carriage with a collapsible top, two double seats inside opposite each other, and a box seat outside in front for the driver. [German *Barutsche,* from Italian *baroccio,* earlier *biroccio* (unattested), from Late Latin *birotium,* two-wheeled, from Latin *birotus* : BI- + *rota,* wheel.]

barque (bark) *n.* Also *chiefly U.S.* **bark** **1.** A sailing ship with from three to five masts, all of them square-rigged except the after mast which is fore-and-aft rigged. Compare **barquentine.** **2.** *Poetic.* Any boat, especially a small sailing vessel.

bar·quen·tine (bárkən-teen) *n.* Also *chiefly U.S.* **bar·kan·tine, bar·ken·tine.** A sailing ship with from three to five masts, all of them fore-and-aft rigged except the foremast, which is square-rigged. Compare **barque.**

bar·rack¹ (bárrək) *tr.v.* **-racked, -racking, -racks.** To house in barracks.

bar·rack² *v.* **-racked, -racking, -racks.** —*intr.* **1.** To jeer or shout at a player, speaker, or team. **2.** *Australian.* To shout support for a team. Used with *for.* —*tr.* To shout against; jeer at. [From native Australian *borak,* banter, chaff.] —**bar·rack·er** *n.*

bar·racks (bárrəks) *n., pl.* **barracks.** *Used with a singular or plural verb.* **1. a.** *Abbr.* **bks.** A building or group of buildings used to house soldiers. **b.** A post or station of the Royal Canadian Mounted Police. **2.** Any large building used for temporary accommodation. **3.** Any unadorned or unattractive building. [From French *baraque,* from Italian *baracca,* soldier's tent, from Spanish *barraca,* mud hut, perhaps from Catalan *barraca†.*]

bar·ra·coon (bárrə-kŏon) *n.* Formerly, a barracks in which slaves and convicts were temporarily confined. [Spanish *barracón,* augmentative of *barraca,* hut. See **barracks.**]

bar·ra·cu·da (bárrə-kéwdə, -kŏodə) *n., pl.* **-das** or collectively **barracuda.** Any of various voracious, mostly tropical, marine fishes of the genus *Sphyraena;* especially, *S. barracuda,* having a long, narrow body and projecting jaws with fanglike teeth. [American Spanish *barracuda†.*]

bar·rage¹ (bárraazh, bárraaj || bárrij, *U.S.* báarij) *n.* An artificial obstruction in a watercourse, used especially to promote irrigation or prevent flooding. [French, from *barrer,* bar.]

bar·rage² (bárraazh, bárraaj || bárrij, bə-raázh) *n.* **1.** A heavy curtain of artillery fire often placed in front of friendly troops to screen and protect them. **2.** Any rapid, concentrated discharge of missiles, or heavy, blanket bombardment. **3.** An overwhelming concentrated outpouring, as of words or blows: *a barrage of questions.* **4.** A deciding bout in fencing.
~*tr.v.* **barraged, -raging, -rages.** To direct a barrage at. [French, from *(tir de) barrage,* barrier (fire), from BARRAGE (barrier).]

barrage balloon *n.* A balloon anchored singly or as one of a series, supporting cables or nets in order to hinder the passage of low-flying enemy aircraft.

bar·ra·mun·da (bárrə-múndə) *n., pl.* **-das** or collectively **barramunda.** Also **bar·ra·mun·di** (-múndi) *pl.* **-dis** or collectively **barramundi.** Any of several Australian food fishes, such as the river fish *Scleropages leichhardtii,* or the lungfish *Neoceratodus forsteri.* [From a native Australian name.]

Bar·ran·quil·la (bárrəng-kée-yə). A large seaport on the Rio Magdalena near its mouth on the Caribbean Sea, northern Colombia.

bar·ra·tor, bar·ra·ter (bárrətər) *n. Law.* One who commits barratry.

[Middle English, from Anglo-French *baratour*, from Old French *barateor*, swindler, from *barater*, to cheat, BARTER.]

bar·ra·try (bárrətri) *n., pl.* **-tries.** **1.** *Law.* Formerly, the offence of exciting or stirring up quarrels or groundless lawsuits. **2.** *Maritime Law.* An unlawful breach of duty on the part of a ship's master or crew that is to the prejudice or disadvantage of the ship's owner. **3.** The sale or purchase of positions in the church or state. [Middle English *barratrie*, the purchase of church offices, from Old French *baraterie*, deception, from *barater*, to cheat, BARTER.] —**bar·ra·trous** *adj.* —**bar·ra·trous·ly** *adv.*

Bar·rault (ba-rō), **Jean-Louis** (1910–94). French actor, director, and producer. He was producer-director with the Comédie Française (1940–46) and director of the Theâtre de France (1959–68). His film credits include *La Symphonie Fantastique* (1942) and *Les Enfants du Paradis* (1944).

barre (bar) *n.* A bar fixed to a wall in a studio to aid ballet dancers when practising. [French.]

bar·ré (bárray || *U.S.* bə-ráy, baa-) *n. Music.* A technique, used by guitar- and lute-players, of laying the forefinger over some or all of the strings and so changing the pitch. [French, "barred".]

bar·rel (bárrəl) *n.* **1.** A large, nearly cylindrical container, traditionally made of wooden staves bound together with hoops, and having a flat top and bottom of equal diameter and, usually, sides that bulge outwards in the middle. **2.** The quantity that a barrel with a given or standard capacity will hold. **3.** *Abbr.* **bar., bbl, bbl., bl.** Any of various units of volume or capacity; especially, a unit used to measure the volume of oil, equal to 35 Imperial gallons. **4.** The metal, cylindrical part of a firearm through which the bullet travels. **5.** A cylinder that contains a movable piston. **6.** The drum of a capstan. **7.** The cylinder within the mechanism of a timepiece that contains the mainspring. **8.** The cylindrical part or hollow shaft of any of various other instruments and mechanisms. **9.** The ink container of a fountain pen. **10.** The trunk of an animal, such as a cow or horse. **11.** *Informal.* A large quantity: *a barrel of fun.* —**over a barrel.** Helpless; defenceless. —**scrape the (bottom of the) barrel.** To use one's last and poorest resources.
~*v.* **barrelled** or *U.S.* **barreled, -relling** or *U.S.* **-reling, -rels.** —*tr.* To put or pack in a barrel or barrels. —*intr. U.S. Informal.* To move at high speed. Usually used with *along.* [Middle English *barel*, from Old French *baril*, probably from *barre*, BAR (rod).]

bar·rel-chest·ed (bárrəl-chéstid, -chestid) *adj.* Having a very large outward-curving chest.

bar·rel·house (bárrəl-howss) *n.* **1.** An early style of jazz characterised by free group improvisation and an accented two-beat rhythm. **2.** *U.S. Informal.* A disreputable, old-time saloon or brothel.

barrel organ *n.* A portable musical instrument operated by the action of a revolving barrel with pegs or pins which open air valves leading from a bellows to a series of pipes.

barrel roll *n.* A flight manoeuvre in which an aircraft makes a complete rotation on its longitudinal axis while approximately maintaining its original direction.

barrel vault *n. Architecture.* A simple vault with a continuous semicircular section.

bar·ren (bárrən) *adj.* **1. a.** Not producing offspring; childless or fruitless. **b.** Incapable of producing offspring; infertile; sterile. **2.** Lacking vegetation, especially useful vegetation; unproductive. **3.** Unproductive of results or gains; unprofitable. **4.** Devoid; lacking: *writing barren of insight.* **5.** Lacking in liveliness or interest. —See Synonyms at **empty, sterile.**
~*n. Usually plural. U.S.* A tract of unproductive land, often with a scrubby growth of trees: *the pine barrens of New Jersey.* [Middle English *barein(e)*, from Anglo-French, from Old French *baraigne*, *barhaine†.*] —**bar·ren·ly** *adv.* —**bar·ren·ness** *n.*

bar·ren·wort (bárrən-wurt) *n.* A European perennial herbaceous plant, *Epimedium alpinum*, with clusters of red and yellow flowers. [From the belief that it caused sterility.]

Bar·rett (bárrit), **Elizabeth.** See **Browning, Elizabeth Barrett.**

bar·rette (bə-rét, baa-) *n. U.S.* A hair-slide *(see).* [French, diminutive of *barre*, BAR.]

bar·ri·cade (bárri-káyd, -kayd) *n.* **1.** A structure set up across a road, as a means of defence or to obstruct passage. **2.** Anything acting to obstruct passage; a barrier. —See Synonyms at **bulwark.**
~*tr.v.* **barricaded, -cading, -cades.** **1.** To close off or block with a barricade. **2.** To keep in or out by means of a barricade. [French, from *barrique*, barrel (the earliest barricades were made of earth-filled barrels), from Spanish *barrica*, from *barril*, BARREL.] —**bar·ri·cad·er** *n.*

Bar·rie (bárri), **Sir J(ames) M(atthew)** (1860–1937). Scottish novelist and dramatist. His first novel, *The Little Minister* (1891), was an immediate success. With *The Little White Bird* (1902), he began the Peter Pan cycle, which was continued with the play, *Peter Pan* (1904), *Peter Pan in Kensington Gardens* (1906), and *Peter Pan and Wendy* (1908). His later plays include *What Every Woman Knows* and *Dear Brutus* (1917). He was made a baronet (1913).

bar·ri·er (bárri-ər) *n.* **1.** A fence, wall, or other structure built to prevent or control access or passage. **2.** Anything, material or immaterial, that acts to obstruct or prevent passage. **3.** A boundary or limit. **4.** Anything that separates or holds apart: *class barriers.* **5.** *Plural.* The palisades or fences enclosing the lists of a medieval tournament. **6.** *Geology.* An **ice barrier** *(see).* —See Synonyms at **obstacle.** [Middle English; from Anglo-French *barrere*, from Old French *barriere*, probably from *barre*, BAR.]

barrier beach *n.* A long, narrow bar of sand built up parallel to a coastline by wave action, and exposed at high tide. Also called "barrier island".

barrier cream *n.* A cream used to protect the hands from oil, solvents, or the like.

barrier reef *n.* A long, narrow coral reef or rock parallel to and relatively near a coastline, separated from the coastline by a lagoon too deep for coral growth.

bar·ring (báaring) *prep.* Excluding the occurrence of; excepting: *Barring strong headwinds, the plane will arrive on time.*

bar·ri·o (bárri-ō || *U.S.* báari-ō) *n., pl.* **-os.** **1.** An enclave, ward, or urban district in a Spanish-speaking country. **2.** A chiefly Spanish-speaking community or neighbourhood, especially in a U.S. city. [Spanish, from Arabic *barrī*, of an open area, from *barr*, open area.]

bar·ris·ter (bárristər) *n.* In England and Wales, a lawyer admitted to plead at the bar in the superior courts. Compare **advocate, solicitor.** See Usage note at **lawyer.** [16th century : from BAR + -*rister*, perhaps by analogy with *minister.*]

bar·room (bár-rŏŏm, -rŏŏm) *n. U.S.* A room or building in which alcoholic beverages are sold at a counter or bar.

bar·row¹ (bárrō) *n.* **1. a.** A cart, usually on wheels and with handles, often with a canvas roof, used by street traders. **b.** The load carried on such a cart. **2.** A **wheelbarrow** *(see).* [Middle English *bar(o)we*, Old English *bearwe*, basket, wheelbarrow.]

barrow² *n. Archaeology.* A large mound of earth or stones placed over a burial site. Also "mound, tumulus". [Middle English *borewe*, *burgh*, Old English *beorg*, from Germanic *bergaz* (unattested).]

barrow³ *n.* A pig that has been castrated before reaching sexual maturity. [Middle English *barow*, Old English *bearg*, *barg.*]

barrow boy *n. Chiefly British.* A boy or man who trades from a barrow in the street.

Bar·row-in-Fur·ness (bárrō-in-fúrniss). Seaport in southwest Cumbria on the Furness coast, in northwest England. Its shipyards produced the first British nuclear submarine (1960).

Bar·ry (bárri). Port in South Glamorgan, on the Bristol Channel, in South Wales. Barry Island, a popular holiday resort, is joined to the mainland south of Barry.

Barry, Sir Charles (1795–1860). British architect who designed the Houses of Parliament in London, after the fire of 1834. He was also responsible for the Travellers' Club (1829) and the Reform Club (1837), both among London's architectural landmarks.

bar sinister *n.* **1.** A heraldic bend or baton sinister held to signify bastardy. Not in technical usage. **2.** A hint or proof of illegitimate birth.

Bart (bart), **Lionel** (1930–). British composer, lyricist, and dramartist whose most famous musical, *Oliver* (1960), revolutionised the British musical.

Bart. baronet.

bar·tend·er (bár-tendər) *n. Chiefly U.S.* A barman.

bar·ter (bártər) *v.* **-tered, -tering, -ters.** —*intr.* **1.** To trade goods or services without the exchange of money. **2.** To haggle or bargain. —*tr.* To exchange (goods or services) without using money: *He bartered his watch for food.*
~*n.* **1.** The act or practice of bartering. **2.** Any exchange, as of agreements or concessions. **3.** Something that is bartered. [Middle English *barteren*, probably from Old French *barater*, to barter, cheat, perhaps from Vulgar Latin *prattāre* (unattested), cheat, do, from Greek *prattein*, to do, manage.] —**bar·ter·er** *n.*

Barth (bart), **Karl** (1886–1968). Swiss Protestant theologian, who advocated a return to the principles of the Reformation and the teachings of the Bible. In his books *Epistle to the Romans* (1919) and *Church Dogmatics*, which he started in 1936 and completed in 1962, he emphasises the sovereignty of God and the inherent sinfulness of mankind.

Bar·tho·lin's glands (bártholinz) *pl. n. Anatomy.* A pair of glands that secrete a lubricating substance at the external opening of the vagina during sexual stimulation. [Named in honour of his father, Thomas, by Caspar *Bartholin* (1655–1738), Danish anatomist.]

Bar·thol·o·mew (baar-thóllə-mew), **Saint.** Sometimes called Nathanael. One of the Twelve Apostles. Mark 3:18.

bar·ti·zan, bar·ti·san (bárti-zən, -zán) *n. Architecture.* A small, overhanging turret on a wall or tower. [Spurious architectural term (coined by Sir Walter Scott), from Scottish *bartisane*, corruption of *bratticing*, from BRATTICE.] —**bar·ti·zaned** *adj.*

Bart·lett (bárt-lit, -lət) *n.* A widely grown English variety of pear having large, juicy, yellow fruit. [Named after Enoch *Bartlett* (1779–1860), U.S. merchant who cultivated and popularised it.]

Bar·tók (bár-tok), **Béla** (1881–1945). Hungarian pianist and composer. In 1940, he took up residence in the United States, where he died in poverty. His compositions blend elements of East European folk music with dissonant harmonies. In addition to three piano concertos, he composed the music for the opera *Duke Bluebeard's Castle* (1911) and for the ballet *The Miraculous Mandarin* (1919). His most popular work is the *Concerto for Orchestra* (1943).

Bar·ton (bárt'n), **Sir Edmund** (1849–1920). Australian statesman who became Australia's first prime minister (1901–03). Under his leadership, the Federal Convention, a Bill that united the separate states in 1897, was drafted.

Bar·uch (baár-ŏŏk, baír-, -ək) *n.* A book of the Old Testament Apocrypha.

bar·y·cen·tre (bárri-sentər) *n. Physics.* **Centre of mass** *(see).* [Greek *barus*, heavy + CENTRE.]

bar·y·cen·tric coordinates (bárri-séntrik) *pl. n.* Mathematical coordinates defining the position of a given point in space in terms of four numbers, such that four masses proportional to these numbers placed at four reference points would have their centre of mass at the given point. In two dimensions, three numbers and reference points are used.

bar·ye (bárri) *n.* A unit of pressure in the centimetre-gram-second system, equal to a pressure of one dyne per square centimetre. [French, from Greek *barus,* heavy.]

bar·y·on (bárri-on) *n.* Any of a family of subatomic particles, including the nucleon and hyperon multiplets, that participate in strong interactions, have half-integral spins, and are generally more massive than mesons. [Greek *barus,* heavy + -ON.] **—bar·y·on·ic** (-ónnik) *adj.*

baryon number *n. Symbol* **B** A quantum number equal to the difference between the number of baryons and the number of antibaryons in a system of subatomic particles.

ba·ry·ta (bə-rītə) *n.* **1. Barium hydroxide** *(see).* **2. Barium oxide** *(see).* [From BARYTES + *-a,* as in *soda,* etc.]

ba·ry·tes (bə-rīteez) *n.* Also *chiefly U.S.* **ba·rite** (báir-īt). A colourless crystalline mineral consisting of barium sulphate, the chief source of barium chemicals. Also called "heavy spar". [From Greek *barus,* heavy + -*(y)tes,* by analogy to other minerals ending in *-ites.*]

bas·al (báyss'l ‖ *U.S.* báyz'l) *adj.* **1.** Pertaining to, located at, or forming a base. **2.** Of primary importance; basic. **—bas·al·ly** *adv.*

basal complex *n.* The part of the earth's crust that lies below any sedimentary rock or sediment and extends down to the Moho; it is usually Precambrian in age. Also called "basement complex".

basal ganglia *pl. n.* Several masses of grey matter situated deep within the brain that are concerned with the unconscious control of voluntary movements.

basal metabolism *n.* The least amount of energy required to maintain vital functions, such as respiration and digestion, in an organism at complete rest. **—basal metabolic** *adj.*

ba·salt (bássawlt, báss'lt, bə-sáwlt ‖ báy-sawlt, -solt) *n.* **1.** A hard, fine-grained, dense, dark volcanic rock composed chiefly of plagioclase, augite, and magnetite, and often having a glassy appearance. **2.** A kind of black, unglazed pottery. In this sense, also called "basaltware". [Earlier *basaltes,* from Latin *basaltēs,* manuscript error for *basanītēs (lapis),* from Greek *basanītēs,* from *basanos,* touchstone.] **—ba·sal·tic** (bə-sáwl-tik, -sól-) *adj.*

bas·cule (básskewl) *n.* **1.** A device counterbalanced so that when one end is lowered, the other is raised. **2.** A bridge that incorporates such a device. **3.** A road, forming part of a bridge, that can be raised and lowered. [French, seesaw, from earlier *basse cule,* variant (influenced by *basse,* low) of earlier *bacule* : *bat(t)re,* to beat, BATTER + *cul,* buttocks, from Latin *cūlus.*]

base¹ (bayss) *n. Abbr.* **b., B. 1. a.** The lowest or supporting part or layer; a foundation. **b.** An infrastructure: *the nation's industrial base.* **2.** The fundamental principle or underlying concept of a system or theory. **3.** The fundamental ingredient from which a mixture is prepared; a chief constituent: *a paint with an oil base.* **4.** The fact, observation, or premise from which a measurement, study, or reasoning process is begun. **5.** *Sports.* **a.** A goal, starting point, or safety area. **b.** In baseball, any of the four corners of the infield, which players must pass in order to score. **6.** A centre of organisation, supply, or activity; a headquarters. **7.** *Military.* **a.** A fortified centre of operations. **b.** A supply centre for a large force. **8.** *Architecture.* The lowest part of a structure, considered as a separate architectural unit: *the base of a column.* **9.** *Heraldry.* The lower part of a shield. **10.** *Linguistics.* **a.** A morpheme or morphemes regarded as a form to which affixes or other bases may be added; a root or stem. For example, in the words *filled* and *refill, fill* is the base. **b. Base component** *(see).* **11.** *Mathematics.* **a.** The side or face of a geometric figure or solid to which an altitude is drawn or is considered to be drawn. **b.** The number that is raised to various powers to generate the principal counting units of a number system. **c.** The number raised to the logarithm of a designated number in order to produce that designated number. **12.** A line used as a reference for measurement or calculations. **13.** *Chemistry.* **a.** Any of a large class of compounds, including the hydroxides and oxides of metals, that have a bitter taste and are slippery in solution, and have the ability to turn litmus blue and to react with acids to form salts. **b.** A molecular or ionic substance capable of combining with a proton to form a new substance. **c.** A substance that provides a pair of electrons for a coordinate bond with an acid. Also called "Lewis base". **14.** *Biology.* **a.** The region of a part or organ, such as a leaf, that is closest to its point of attachment. **b.** The point of attachment of such an organ. **15.** *Electronics.* **a.** The region in a transistor between the emitter and the collector. **b.** The electrode attached to this region.

~*adj.* **1.** Forming or serving as a base. **2.** Situated at or near the base or bottom.

~*tr.v.* **based, basing, bases. 1.** To provide with a base: *a mixture based on alcohol; a firm based in London.* **2.** To provide an intellectual basis for; establish. Used with *on* or *upon.* **3.** To provide the imaginative basis or central idea for: *The play was based on a novel by Dickens.* [Middle English, from Old French, from Latin *basis,* pedestal, base, from Greek.]

Synonyms: base, basis, foundation, grounds.

Usage: Base and *basis* both have the written plural *bases,* but the pronunciation differs. The plural form of *base* is (báysiz); the plural of *basis,* (báyseez). *Base* is mainly used literally and refers to

the lowest or supporting part or layer of something. It is occasionally used figuratively, as in *the industrial base of the economy. Basis* is nearly always used figuratively to mean foundation, as in *the basis of an argument.*

base² *adj.* **baser, basest. 1.** Having or proceeding from low moral standards; treacherous; contemptible. **2.** Inferior in quality or value; unrefined; shabby. **3.** Not precious; common: *a base metal.* **4.** Valueless, or greatly depreciated in value; debased: *base currency.* **5.** Corrupted by extraneous elements: *base Latin.* **6. a.** *Archaic.* Of low birth, rank, or position. **b.** Characteristic of a person of low station; servile; menial. **—See Synonyms at mean** (ignoble). [Middle English *bas,* low, inferior, from Old French, from Late Latin *bassus,* fat, low.] **—base·ly** *adv.* **—base·ness** *n.*

base·ball (báyss-bawl) *n.* **1.** A game played with a wooden bat and hard ball by two opposing teams of nine players, each team batting and fielding alternately, the players batting having to run a course of four bases laid out in a diamond pattern in order to score. It is the U.S. national game. **2.** The ball used in this game.

base·board (báyss-bawrd ‖ -bórd) *n.* **1.** Any board or plate that serves as a base of something. **2.** *U.S.* A **skirting board** *(see).*

base·born (báyss-bórn) *adj. Archaic.* **1.** Of humble birth. **2.** Born of unmarried parents; illegitimate. **3.** Ignoble; contemptible.

base component *n.* In transformational grammar, a set of rules specifying the deep structure of the language. Also called "base".

based (bayst) *adj.* Having as a base or located at a base, especially of the specified type. Used in combination: *land-based missiles; an oil-based economy.*

Ba·sel (báʼaz'l) or **Ba·sle** (báʼaz'l, baal). *French* **Bâle** (baal). City in Switzerland, the capital of Basel canton. It lies on the river Rhine, at the meeting point of the French, German, and Swiss borders. It is a major business and industrial centre, and the country's main river port.

basela. Variant of **bonsella.**

base·less (báyss-ləss, -liss) *adj.* Having no basis or foundation.

base level *n.* The lowest level to which a land surface can be reduced by the action of running water.

base·line (báyss-līn) *n.* **1.** A line or imaginary level used as a base for measurement or comparison, as in surveying. **2.** In tennis, a line bounding each end of a court, marking the limits of play. **3.** In baseball, a path between successive bases.

base·ment (báyss-mənt) *n.* **1.** The substructure or foundation of a building. **2.** The lowest habitable storey of a building, usually below ground level. Often used adjectively: *a basement flat.* [Probably from Dutch (obsolete), perhaps from Italian *basamento,* foundation (of a column), from *basare,* to BASE.]

basement complex *n.* A **basal complex** *(see).*

base metal *n.* Any relatively common, inexpensive metal, such as iron or copper, as distinguished from a precious metal, such as gold or silver.

ba·sen·ji (bə-sénji) *n., pl.* **-jis.** A small dog of a breed originally from Africa, having a short, smooth coat, and not uttering the barking sound characteristic of most dogs. [Bantu.]

base point *n. Heraldry.* The lowest point on a shield.

base rate *n. British.* The rate of interest offered by clearing banks, used as a basis for lending rates.

ba·ses¹. Plural of **basis.** —See Usage note at **base.**

bas·es². Plural of **base.** —See Usage note at **base.**

bash (bash) *tr.v.* **bashed, bashing, bashes.** *Informal.* **1.** To strike or smash with a heavy and crushing blow. Often used with *in.* **2.** To beat; thrash. Often used with *up.* **—bash into.** *Informal.* To crash into; collide with.

~*n.* **1.** *Informal.* A heavy, crushing blow. **2.** *British Informal.* An attempt; a try. **3.** *Slang.* A celebration; a party. [17th century : imitative, perhaps a blend of BANG + *-sh,* as in SMASH or CRASH].

ba·shaw (bə-sháw) *n. Archaic.* A **pasha** *(see).*

bash·ful (básh-f'l) *adj.* **1.** Inclined to shrink from notice through shyness; diffident; self-conscious. **2.** Characterised by, showing, or resulting from social shyness or self-consciousness. **—See Synonyms at shy.** [Middle English *baschen,* short for *abashen,* to ABASH + -FUL.] **—bash·ful·ly** *adv.* **—bash·ful·ness** *n.*

bash·i·ba·zouk (báshi-bə-zōōk) *n.* A member of the Turkish irregulars, a 19th-century cavalry troop noted for its brutality. [Turkish *başıbozuk,* irregular soldier : *baş,* head + *bozuk,* depraved, out of order.]

–bashing *n. comb. form. Informal.* Indicates: **1.** The beating up or maltreatment of; for example, *baby-bashing.* **2.** The continual criticising and maligning of; for example, *union-bashing.* **3.** Mindless, routine, or mundane activity; for example, *square-bashing.* **—basher** *n. comb. form.*

Bash·kir (básh-keer) *n., pl.* **-kirs** or collectively **Bashkir. 1.** A member of a Mongoloid people living in the Bashkortostan. **2.** The Turkic Language of this people.

Bashkir Autonomous Soviet Socialist Republic. Also **Bash·kir·i·a** (-keer-i-ə, -kírri-). Part of the former U.S.S.R. in the southwest Urals. See **Bashkortostan.**

Bashkortostan (bash-kórto-staan, -stan) Autonomous Russian republic, formerly Bashkir A.S.S.R. The region's main agricultural crops are grains. Oil and oil products are the most important industries. The capital and main administrative and industrial centre is Ufa.

basi-, baso- *comb. form.* Indicates: **1.** The base or lower part; for example, **basipetal 2.** A chemical base; for example, **basophil.** [Latin *basis,* BASIS.]

ba·sic (báyssik ‖ bássik) *adj.* **1. a.** Of, pertaining to, or constituting a basis; underlying; fundamental. **b.** Simple; unadorned; without extras: *a basic salary.* **2.** *Chemistry.* **a.** Producing, resulting from, or pertaining to a base. **b.** Containing a base, especially in excess of acid. **3.** *Metallurgy.* Of, designating, or produced by a steel-making process in which the furnace is lined with a basic material, such as magnesium oxide. The lining combines with acidic impurities in the ore to form basic slag.

BASIC *n.* *Computing.* *B*eginner's *A*ll-purpose *S*ymbolic *I*nstruction *C*ode: a simple high-level computer-programming language.

ba·si·cal·ly (báyss-ikli, -ikəli ‖ báss-) *adv.* Fundamentally; essentially.

Basic English *n.* A simplified, copyrighted form of English with a vocabulary of 850 English words and a short list of words in international use, intended to provide a basis for an auxiliary language and for the introductory teaching of English. [Coined by C.K. Ogden to represent *B*ritish *A*merican *S*cientific *I*nternational *C*ommercial.]

ba·sic·i·ty (bay-síssəti) *n.* *Chemistry.* The quality or degree of being a base.

basic process *n.* A method of steel production that uses a furnace lined with a basic refractory material.

basic rock *n.* A dark-coloured igneous rock containing less than 52 per cent silica bound up in its feldspar, and rich in iron and magnesium.

ba·sics (báyssiks) *pl. n.* Fundamental, traditional or rudimentary principles or practices; fundamentals; essentials: *back to basics.*

basic salt *n.* A salt formed from a base by replacement of only part of the hydroxide or oxide content, as in basic lead carbonate, $2PbCO_3.Pb(OH)_2$.

basic slag *n.* Furnace slag containing a sufficiently high proportion of calcium phosphate to make it useful as a fertiliser. It is produced during the course of basic-process steel making.

ba·sid·i·o·my·cete (bə-síddi-ō-mī-seét, -mí-seet) *n.* Any fungus of the class Basidiomycetes, which includes the mushrooms, puffballs, and other fungi that produce spores in a basidium. [New Latin *Basidiomycetes* : BASIDI(UM) + -MYCETE.] —**ba·sid·i·o·my·ce·tous** (-seétəss) *adj.*

ba·sid·i·o·spore (bə-síddi-ō-spawr ‖ -spōr) *n.* A spore formed in a basidium. [BASIDI(UM) + SPORE.]

ba·sid·i·um (bə-síddi-əm) *n., pl.* **-ia** (-ə). A club-shaped structure characteristic of basidiomycetous fungi, which produces sexual spores, usually four, at the tips. [New Latin, from Greek *basidion*, diminutive of BASIS.] —**ba·sid·i·al** *adj.*

Ba·sie (báyssi) **Count,** born William Basie (1904–84). U.S. jazz musician noted for his "big band" sound. One of the great jazz pianists, he was influenced by Harlem ragtime music.

ba·si·fy (báyssi-fī) *tr.v.* **-fied, -fying, -fies.** *Chemistry.* To make basic. [BAS(E) + -FY.] —**ba·si·fi·ca·tion** (-fi-káysh'n) *n.* —**ba·si·fi·er** *n.*

bas·il (bázz'l ‖ *U.S. also* báyz'l) *n.* **1.** A herb, *Ocimum basilicum*, native to the Old World, having spikes of small white flowers and aromatic leaves used as seasoning. Also called "sweet basil". **2.** A related plant, *Calamintha vulgaris*, native to Europe, having dense clusters of small pink or purplish flowers. This species is also called "wild basil". [Middle English *basile*, from Old French, from Medieval Latin *basilicum*, from Greek *basilikon*, "royal", from *basileus†*, king.]

bas·i·lar (bázzi-lər, bássi-) *adj.* Also **bas·i·lar·y** (-lri, -ləri ‖ -lerri). Pertaining to or located at or near the base, especially the base of the skull. [New Latin *basilaris*, from Latin *basis*, BASE (bottom).]

ba·sil·ic (bə-zíl-ik, -sil-) *adj.* Also **ba·sil·i·cal** (-ik'l), **ba·sil·i·can** (-ikən). Of or pertaining to a basilica.

ba·sil·i·ca (bə-zilli-kə, -silli-) *n.* **1.** Any of various oblong buildings of ancient Rome having two rows of columns dividing the interior into a nave and two side aisles, used as a court or place of assembly. **2.** A building of this kind or design used as a Christian church. **3.** *Roman Catholic Church.* **a.** Any of several ancient churches in Rome. **b.** A church or cathedral accorded certain special ceremonial rights. [Latin, from Greek *basilikē (stoa)*, "royal (portico, court)", from *basileus†*, king.]

bas·i·lisk (bázzi-lisk ‖ bássi-) *n.* **1.** A legendary serpent or dragon with lethal breath and glance. Compare **cockatrice. 2.** Any of various tropical American lizards of the genus *Basiliscus*, having an erectile crest at the back of the head. [Middle English, from Latin *basiliscus*, from Greek *basiliskos*, "princelet", diminutive of *basileus†* king; the serpent was believed to have a mark resembling a crown on its head.]

Bas·il the Great (bázz'l, bázzil) **Saint** (*c.* A.D. 330–379). Bishop of Caesarea in Cappadocia (from 370) who is credited with the authorship of the liturgy of St. Basil, which is still used on certain days in the Eastern Orthodox Church. He is often linked with his brother, St. Gregory of Nyssa and with St. Gregory of Nazianzus, known as the Cappadocian Fathers, who were the chief opponents of the heresy of Arianism.

ba·sin (báyss'n) *n.* **1.** An open, rounded container with sides that narrow towards the base, used especially for holding or mixing liquids. **2.** The amount such a container will hold. **3.** A washbasin; a sink. **4. a.** An artificially enclosed area of a river or harbour, so designed that the water level remains unaffected by tidal changes. **b.** A small enclosed or partly enclosed body of water. **5.** A region drained by a single river system. Also called "river basin". **6.** A vast depression on the earth's surface, filled by an ocean. Also called "ocean basin". **7.** *Geology.* **a.** A tract of land in which the rock strata are tilted towards a common centre. **b.** Any bowl-shaped depression in the surface of the land. [Middle English *ba(s)cin*, from Old French *bacin*, from Late Latin *bacchinus* (unattested), from Vulgar Latin *bacca* (unattested), water vessel, perhaps from Gaulish.]

bas·i·net (bássi-nit, -net) *n.* A light, round, close-fitting medieval helmet, often with a visor. [Middle English *bacinet*, from Old French, diminutive of *bacin*, BASIN.]

ba·sip·e·tal (bə-síppit'l) *adj.* *Botany.* Developing or growing in order from the top towards the base. Said of certain leaves and flowers. Compare **acropetal.** [BASI- + -PETAL.] —**ba·sip·e·tal·ly** *adv.*

ba·sis (báy-siss) *n., pl.* **-ses** (-seez). **1.** A foundation upon which something rests. **2.** The chief or most stable component of anything; a fundamental ingredient. **3.** A principle; a criterion. —See Synonyms and Usage note at **base.** [Latin, pedestal, foot, base, from Greek.]

bask (baask ‖ bask) *intr.v.* **basked, basking, basks. 1.** To lie in or enjoy the sensation of pleasant warmth. **2.** To thrive in the presence of a pleasant or advantageous influence. [Middle English *basken*, probably from Scandinavian; akin to Norwegian dialectal *baska* to splash in the water, and Old Norse *batha*, to BATHE.]

bas·ket (báaskit ‖ báskit) *n.* **1. a.** A container made of interwoven material, such as rushes, twigs, or strips of wood, usually having a handle. **b.** The amount a basket will hold. **2.** Something resembling such a container in shape or function, such as the container suspended from a hot-air balloon. **3.** In basketball: **a.** Either of the two goals, each consisting of a metal hoop from which an open-bottomed circular net is suspended. **b.** The score, normally worth two points, made by throwing the ball through the basket. [Middle English, from Anglo-French and Old French *basket†*.]

bas·ket·ball (báaskit-bawl ‖ báskit-) *n.* **1.** A game played between two teams of five men or six women players each, the object being to throw the ball through an elevated basket on the opponent's side of the rectangular court. **2.** The round, inflated ball used in this game.

basket chair *n.* A chair made of wickerwork or cane.

basket hilt *n.* A sword hilt with a basket-shaped guard serving to cover and protect the hand.

bas·ket·ry (báass-kitri ‖ báss-) *n.* **1.** The craft or process of making baskets. **2.** Baskets collectively.

basket star *n.* Any of various marine organisms of the genus *Gorgonocephalus* and class Ophiuroidea, related to the starfishes, and having slender, many-branched arms. Also called "basket fish".

basket weave *n.* A textile weave consisting of double threads interlaced to produce a chequered pattern similar to that of a woven basket.

bask·ing shark (báaski-ing, bassk-) *n.* A very large shark, *Cetorhinus maximus*, that feeds on plankton and often floats near the surface of the water. Also called "sailfish".

Basle. See Basel.

bas mitzvah, bas mizvah. Variants of **bat mitzvah.**

baso-. Variant of **basi-.**

ba·so·phil (báyssə-fil) *n.* A cell, especially a white blood cell, having granules that exhibit an affinity for basic dyes. [BASO- + -PHIL(E).] —**ba·so·phil·ic** (-fíllik), **ba·soph·i·lous** (bə-sóffiləss, bay-) *adj.*

Ba·so·tho (bə-sóotōo, baa-, -sōtō) *n, pl.* **-thos** or collectively **Ba·sotho.** A member of an African people, a *Mosotho* (*see*).

basque (bask, baask) *n.* A woman's close-fitting bodice. [French, variant (influenced by *basquine*, petticoat) of earlier *baste*, from Provençal *basta*, perhaps from Germanic.]

Basque (bask, baask) *n.* **1.** A member of a people of unknown origin inhabiting the western Pyrenees in France and Spain. **2.** The language of the Basques, of no known relationship to any other language. [French, from Latin *Vascō†* (stem *Vascōn-*), whence also GASCON.] —**Basque** *adj.*

Bas·ra (báz-rə). Iraq's only port, lying on the Shatt al Arab in the southeast of the country.

bas-re·lief (báa-ri-leéef, báss, -leef) *n.* In sculpture, relief that projects very little from the background. Also called "basso-relievo", "low relief". [French, from Italian *bassorilievo*, low relief : *basso*, low, BASE + *rilevo*, RELIEF.]

bass¹ (bass) *n., pl.* **basses** or collectively **bass. 1.** Any of various marine fishes of the family Serranidae having an elongated body and a spiny dorsal fin; especially, the game fish *Morone labrax* and the **stone bass** (*see*). **2.** Any of several North American freshwater fishes of the family Centrarchidae, such as the largemouth bass (*Micropterus salmoides*). See **rock bass, sea bass.** [Middle English, from dialect *barse*, from Old English *bærs*.]

bass² (bayss) *n.* **1.** A low-pitched tone. **2.** The notes in the lowest register of a musical instrument. **3.** The lowest part in vocal or instrumental part music. **4.** A male singing voice of the lowest range. **5.** A man who has such a singing voice. **6.** A musical instrument that produces notes in a low register; especially, a **double bass** (*see*) or a **bass guitar** (*see*). **7.** The response to the low-frequency notes of an audio-frequency amplifier, especially in a record player or tape recorder.
~*adj.* **1.** Having a deep tone; low in pitch. **2.** Being the largest and having lowest range of a family of instruments: *a bass recorder.*

bass³ (bass) *n.* A fibrous plant product, **bast** (*see*). [Variant of BAST.]

Bas·sa·no (bə-saánō) **Jacopo,** also known as Giacomo da Ponte (*c.* 1517–92). Italian painter of the Venetian school. He is one of the earliest known artists to depict rustic life in both secular and religious scenes.

bass clef (bayss) n. A musical clef that designates F below middle C as being on the fourth line above the bottom of the staff. Also called "F clef".

bass drum (bayss) n. A large drum having a cylindrical body and two drumheads, both of which can be struck to produce a low, resonant sound.

bas·set (bássit) n. A basset hound. [French, Old French, from *basset*, short and low, from *bas*, BASE.]

basset horn n. An alto clarinet in F, having a range of $3^1/_2$ octaves and sounding notes a fifth lower than they are written. [German *Bassetthorn*, part translation of French *cor de bassette*, from Italian *corno di bassetto* : *corno*, horn + *di*, of + *bassetto*, diminutive of *basso*, BASS.]

basset hound n. A short-haired dog of a breed originating in France, having a long body, short, bent forelegs, and long, drooping ears.

bass fiddle (bayss) n. *Informal.* A **double bass** (see).

bass guitar (bayss) n. An electric guitar that has the same pitch as a double bass. Also called "bass".

bas·si·net (bássi-nét) n. An oblong basket, often resting on legs, used as a cot for an infant. [French, small basin, from Old French *bacinet*, diminutive of *bacin*, BASIN.]

bass·ist (báyss-ist) n. 1. A person who plays a double bass. 2. A person who plays a bass guitar.

bas·so (bássō ‖ báassō) n., pl. **-sos** or **bassi** (bássee ‖ báassee). *Abbr.* **b., B.** A bass singer, especially an operatic bass. [Italian, from Late Latin *bassus*, fat, short, low.]

basso continuo n. **a continuo** (see). [Italian, "continuous bass".]

bas·soon (bə-sŏŏn ‖ U.S. *also* ba-) n. A low-pitched woodwind instrument with a double reed, having a long wooden body attached to a lateral tube that leads to the mouthpiece. [French *basson*, from Italian *bassone*, augmentative of *basso*, BASS.] —**bas·soon·ist** n.

basso os·ti·na·to (ósti-náatō) n. A **ground bass** (see). [Italian, "persistent bass".]

basso pro·fun·do (prə-fún-dō ‖ prō-fŏŏn-) n., pl. **basso profundos** or **bassi profundi** (-dee). *Music.* 1. A bass voice of the lowest range. 2. A singer having such a voice. [Italian, "deep bass".]

bas·so-re·lie·vo (bássō-ri-léevō ‖ báassō-) n., pl. **-vos**. Also Italian **bas·so-ri·lie·vo** (-ree-lyáy-vō) pl. **-vi** (-vee). In sculpture, **bas-relief** (see). [Italian, BAS-RELIEF.]

Bass Rock (bass). Islet at the entrance to the Firth of Forth in Scotland. It has a lighthouse and is a sanctuary for sea-birds.

bass saxophone (bayss) n. A large saxophone with a low range, usually supported on a stand while being played.

Bass Strait (bass). A channel separating mainland Australia from Tasmania. It is 240 kilometres (150 miles) at its widest point, and 290 kilometres (180 miles) long.

bass viol (bayss) n. *Music.* A **viola da gamba** (see).

bass·wood (báss-wŏŏd) n. 1. Any of several linden trees of eastern North America; especially, *Tilia americana*. 2. The soft, light-coloured wood of any of these trees.

bast (bast) n. *Botany.* 1. The fibrous or somewhat woody outer layer of the stems of certain plants, such as flax, hemp, and ramie used to make cordage and textiles. Also called "bass". 2. A plant tissue, phloem (see). [Middle English *baste*, Old English *bæst*, from Common Germanic *bastaz* (unattested).]

bas·tard (báass-tərd, báss-) n. 1. An illegitimate child. 2. *Slang.* a. An odious or obnoxious person. Used derogatorily. b. A person, especially a man. Used familiarly or humorously: *lucky bastard.* c. A tedious or difficult task or problem. 3. Any product of irregular, inferior, or dubious origin.
~*adj.* 1. Born of unmarried parents; illegitimate. 2. Not genuine; spurious. 3. Of inferior breed or kind. 4. Resembling a known kind or species, but not truly such: *bastard toadflax.* [Middle English, from Old French, perhaps (*fils de*) *bast*, "packsaddle (son)", from Medieval Latin *bastum*, packsaddle, perhaps from Vulgar Latin *bastāre* (unattested), to carry, from Greek *bastazein†*, to lift, bear.] —**bas·tard·ly** adj.

bas·tard·ise, bas·tard·ize (báass-tərd-īz, báss-) *tr.v.* **-ised, -ising, -ises.** To debase; corrupt. —**bas·tard·i·sa·tion** (-ī-záysh'n ‖ U.S. -i-) n.

bas·tard·ry (báass-tərdri, báss-) n. *Chiefly Australian.* Unforgivable or cruel behaviour.

bastard toadflax n. A perennial European plant, *Thesium humifusum*, with creeping stems and small greenish flowers.

bastard wing n. *Ornithology.* An **alula** (see).

bas·tard·y (báass-tərdi, báss-) n. The condition of being of illegitimate birth; illegitimacy.

baste¹ (bayst) *tr.v.* **basted, basting, bastes.** To sew loosely with large running stitches so as to hold together temporarily; tack. [Middle English *basten*, from Old French *bastir*, from Germanic *bastjan* (unattested), to sew with bast, from *bastaz* (unattested), BAST.]

baste² *tr.v.* **basted, basting, bastes.** To pour pan drippings or sauce over (roasting meat). [16th century : Origin obscure.]

baste³ *tr.v.* **basted, basting, bastes.** 1. To beat vigorously; thrash. 2. To berate. [Perhaps ultimately from Old Norse *beysta*, to thrash, strike.]

Bas·ti·a (báss-ti-ə, báass-). Port on the northeast coast of Corsica, France, and the largest city on the island.

bas·tille, bas·tile (ba-stéel) n. 1. A prison. 2. A fortress. [Middle English, from Old French, variant of *bastide*, from Provençal *bastida*, from the past participle of *bastir*, to build.]

Bas·tille (bastéel; *French* ba-stée-yə). A fortress in Paris used as a prison until captured on July 14, 1789, at the outset of the French Revolution.

bas·ti·na·do (básti-náydō, -náadō) n., pl. **-does.** Also **bas·ti·nade** (-náyd, -náad). 1. A beating with a stick or cudgel, especially on the soles of the feet. 2. A stick or cudgel.
~*tr.v.* **bastinadoed, -doing, -does.** Also **bas·ti·nade, -naded, -nading, -nades.** To subject to a beating, especially on the soles of the feet. [Spanish *bastonada*, from *baston*, stick, BATON.]

bast·ing (báysting) n. 1. The act of sewing together loosely. 2. The thread used to baste. 3. *Plural.* The loose stitches used to baste material; tacking.

bas·ti·on (báss-ti-ən ‖ -chən) n. 1. A projecting part of a rampart or other fortification. 2. Any well-fortified or defended position. 3. A person, place, or institution regarded as a defender or stronghold of a belief, cause, or the like. —See Synonyms at **bulwark.** [French, from earlier *bastillon*, from Old French *bastille*, BASTILLE.]

bast·naes·ite, bast·nas·ite (bást-nə-sīt) n. A yellowish to reddish-brown mineral, a fluorocarbonate of several lanthanide elements, used as a lanthanide and europium ore. [Swedish *bastnäsit*, after *Bastnäs*, Sweden, where it was discovered.]

Ba·su·to (bə-sŏŏ-tō) n., pl **-tos** or collectively **Basuto.** 1. A Mosotho (see). 2. The dialect of Sotho (see) spoken in Lesotho. In both senses, not in current usage.

Basutoland. See **Lesotho.**

bat¹ (bat) n. 1. A stout wooden stick or club; a cudgel. 2. A blow, as with a stick. 3. a. In cricket, a wooden club having a broad, flat-surfaced hitting end and a narrow handle. b. In baseball, a rounded wooden club, wider and heavier at the hitting end and tapering at the handle, used to strike the ball. c. The club or racket used in other games, such as table tennis. d. Either of a pair of sticks with flat round ends used to guide taxiing aircraft. 4. *Informal.* Pace or speed. 5. In cricket, a batsman. 6. *Slang.* A binge; a spree. —**carry (one's) bat.** In cricket, to reach the end of an innings without being got out. Used of a batsman. —**keep a straight bat.** *British Informal.* To behave honestly and honourably. —**off (one's) own bat.** *Informal.* Without aid or prompting.
~*v.* **batted, batting, bats.** —*tr.* 1. To hit with, or as if with, a club or bat. 2. *Chiefly U.S. Informal.* To discuss or consider at length. Usually used with *around.* —*intr.* 1. To have a turn at batting. Used of a player or a team. 2. *Informal.* To move, especially at speed. Used with *around* or *along.* [Middle English *bat*, late Old English *batt*, cudgel, club, probably from Old French *batte*, club from *battre*, to beat.]

bat² n. 1. Any of various nocturnal flying mammals of the order Chiroptera, having membranous wings that extend from the fore-limbs to the hind limbs or tail. The order is subdivided into the **fruit bats** and the **insectivorous bats** *(both of which see).* 2. *Slang.* A small-minded, nagging person, usually a woman. Used chiefly in the phrase *old bat.* —**have bats in the belfry.** *Slang.* To be eccentric; have foolish or crazy ideas. [16th-century variant of Middle English *bakke* from Scandinavian; akin to Middle Swedish *-bakka*, from Old Norse *-blaka* in *ledhrblaka*, "leather-flapper", bat.]

bat³ *tr.v.* **batted, batting, bats.** To wink or flutter: *to bat one's eyelashes.* —**not bat an eye** or **eyelid.** To evince no sign of surprise or emotion. [Probably a variant of BATE (flap).]

bat. battalion.

Ba·taan (bə-táan, -tán). A mountainous, jungle-covered peninsula in west Luzon, the Philippines. In World War II, it was the scene of defensive action by U.S. and Filipino troops who resisted the Japanese advance for three months (1942).

Batavia. See **Jakarta.**

batch¹ (bach) n. 1. The amount of loaves, cakes, or the like produced at one baking. 2. The quantity of something produced as the result of one operation: *a batch of cement.* 3. The quantity of material needed for one operation: *a batch of dough.* 4. Any group of persons or things treated or regarded as a set: *He was working on a second batch of enquiries.* [Middle English *bacche*, Old English *bæcce* (unattested), from *bacan*, to BAKE.]

batch². Variant of **bach.**

batch processing n. *Computing.* A system in which data are accumulated and processed together as a single unit. Compare **time sharing.**

bate¹ (bayt) *tr.v.* **bated, bating, bates.** 1. To lessen the force of; hold back: *with bated breath.* 2. To take away; subtract. [Middle English *baten*, variant of *abaten*, to ABATE.]

bate² *intr.v.* **bated, bating, bates.** Also **bait.** To flap the wings wildly, as if in impatience. Used of a hawk. [Middle English *baten*, from Old French *bat(t)re*, to beat, BATTER.]

bate³ n. *British Informal.* A temper; a rage: *in a bate.* [19th century: variant of BAIT (referring to the state of mind of a person being baited).]

ba·teau (ba-tō) n., pl. **-teaux** (-tōz). A light, flat-bottomed boat, used especially in Louisiana and Canada. [Canadian French, from French, from Old French *batel*, from Old English *bāt*, BOAT.]

Bates (bayts), **Henry Walter** (1825–92). British naturalist and explorer who gave his name to Batesian mimicry, a phenomenon he discovered in the Amazon valley.

Bates, H(erbert) E(rnest) (1905–74). British novelist and short-story writer. During World War II he served with the Royal Air

Force and, as "Flying Officer X", wrote many short stories based on his experiences. He also wrote war novels under his own name, the best known of which is *Fair Stood the Wind for France* (1944). His other novels include *The Darling Buds of May* (1958) and *A Moment in Time* (1964).

Bates·i·an mimicry (báyts-i-ən) *n.* A defence mechanism that confers a degree of protection against predators on an otherwise defenceless species of animal, in which the harmless species bears a strong resemblance to another species that is dangerous or unpalatable to its predators. Also called "protective colouring".

Bate·son (báyts'n), **William** (1861–1926). British biologist, one of the founders of the science of genetics.

bat·fish (bát-fish) *n., pl.* **-fishes** or collectively **batfish**. Any of various marine fishes of the family Ogcocephalidae, having a flattened body and fleshy pectoral and pelvic fins, and living on the sea floor.

bat·fowl (bát-fowl) *intr.v.* **-fowled, -fowling, -fowls**. To catch roosting birds at night by blinding them with a light. [BAT (club) + FOWL, later associated with BAT (animal) and the use of a blinding light.]

bath¹ (baath ‖ bath) *n., pl.* **baths** (baaᵺz ‖ baths, baaths, baᵺz). **1.** A large oblong container, usually made of enamelled metal or plastic, in which one sits to wash the body. Also chiefly *U.S.* "bathtub". **2.** The act of washing, dipping, or immersing the body in water. **3.** The water used for bathing. **4.** A liquid, or a liquid and its container, used to regulate the temperature of, soak, or otherwise act upon an immersed object. **5.** A bathroom. **6.** *Usually plural.* A public building with facilities for swimming and, sometimes, for washing. **7.** *Often plural.* A resort providing therapeutic baths; a spa.
~*v. British.* **bathed, bathing, baths.** —*tr.* To wash (a person or animal) in a bath. —*intr.* To wash oneself in a bath. [Middle English *bath*, Old English *bæth*.]
Usage: Both British and American English use *bathe* for going in the sea or applying liquid in a soothing way; but in American usage *bathe* also means taking a bath. In British English one *baths a* baby; in American English one *gives a bath to a* baby. Spelling is no guide as to which verb is being used. *Bathing* or *bathed* can be derived from *to bath* or *to bathe*. In speech, a distinction is made: *bath* produces (báathing) and (baatht), *bathe* produces (báything) and (báythd).

bath² (bath, baath) *n.* An ancient Hebrew unit of liquid measure, equal to approximately 8.3 Imperial gallons. [Hebrew.]

Bath (baath ‖ bath). City on the river Avon in southwest England. Its Roman baths are considered to be among the best of the Roman remains in Britain. It was a fashionable spa town in the 18th century and has many elegant Georgian buildings.

Bath brick *n.* Fine calcareous and siliceous silt pressed into blocks and used for scouring and polishing metal. [After BATH.]

Bath bun *n. British.* A sweet, sticky bun containing currants and spices. [After BATH, where it was first made.]

Bath chair *n. Sometimes small* **b**. A hooded wheelchair used by invalids, as at a spa. [After BATH, where it was first made.]

bathe (bayth) *v.* **bathed, bathing, bathes.** —*intr.* **1.** To go swimming; swim. **2.** *Chiefly U.S.* To take a bath; wash oneself. **3.** To become immersed in or as if in liquid. —*tr.* **1.** To immerse in liquid. **2.** To wash or wet. **3.** To apply a liquid to for soothing or healing purposes. **4.** To suffuse: *The garden was bathed in sunlight*. ~*n. Chiefly British.* An act of swimming. See Usage note at **bath**. [Middle English *bathen*, Old English *bathian*.] —**bath·er** *n.*

bath·ers (báythərz) *pl. n. Informal.* A swimming costume.

ba·thet·ic (bə-théttik) *adj.* Characterized by bathos.

bath·house (báath-howss ‖ báth-) *n.* **1.** A building equipped for bathing. **2.** A building with dressing rooms for swimmers.

bath·ing beauty (báything) *n.* An attractive young woman in a swimming costume, especially one who is a contestant in a beauty contest.

bathing machine (báything) *n.* In former times, a small hut on wheels which would be moved to the edge of the sea, and in which bathers changed their clothes.

bathing suit (báything) *n.* A garment worn for swimming; a swimming costume. Also called "bathing costume".

batho–. Variant of bathy–.

bath·o·lith (bátha-lith) *n.* Also **bath·o·lite** (-līt). A large irregularly shaped body of intrusive igneous rock, usually covering more than 100 square kilometres (40 square miles). [German : BATHO- + -LITH.] —**bath·o·lith·ic** (-líthik) *adj.*

ba·thom·e·ter (bə-thómmitər) *n.* An instrument used to measure the depth of water. [BATHO- + -METER.]

ba·thos (báythoss) *n.* **1. a.** A ludicrously abrupt transition from an elevated or inspired to a commonplace style. **b.** An anticlimax. **c.** The lowest point; a nadir. **2. a.** Insincere or grossly sentimental pathos. **b.** Extreme triteness or dullness. —See Usage note at **pathos**. [Greek, depth, from *bathus*, deep.]

bath·robe (báath-rōb ‖ báth-) *n. Chiefly U.S.* A loose-fitting robe worn before and after bathing and for lounging; a dressing gown.

bath·room (báath-rōom, -rŏom ‖ báth-) *n.* **1.** A room equipped for taking a bath or shower and usually also containing a washbasin and lavatory. **2.** *Chiefly U.S.* A lavatory. Used euphemistically.

bath salts *pl. n.* Crystals for scenting or softening bath water.

Bath·she·ba (bath-sheéba, báthshiba). The wife of Uriah and later of David and, by David, the mother of Solomon. II Samuel 11–12.

bath·tub (báath-tub, báth-) *n. Chiefly U.S.* An oblong tub for bathing; a bath.

Bath·urst¹ (báthərst). City in New South Wales, Australia, on the Macquarie River. It was the scene of a gold rush in 1851.

Bathurst². See Banjul.

bathy–, batho– *comb. form.* Indicates deepness or some relationship to depth; for example, **bathyscaph, bathometer**. [Greek *bathus*, deep, and *bathos*, depth.]

bath·y·al (báthi-əl) *adj.* Of, pertaining to, or designating a zone on the continental slope between 200 and 2 000 metres (650 and 6,550 feet) below sea level. [BATHY- + -AL.]

ba·thym·e·try (bə-thímmətri) *n.* The measurement of the depth of large bodies of water. [French *bathymétrie* : BATHY- + -METRY.] —**bath·y·met·ric** (báthi-méttrik), **bath·y·met·ri·cal** *adj.* —**bath·y·met·ri·cal·ly** *adv.*

bath·y·scaph (báthi-skaf) *n.* Also **bath·y·scaphe** (-skayf, -skaf.) A free-diving, self-contained, deep-sea research vessel, consisting essentially of a large flotation hull with a manned observation capsule fixed to its underside. [BATHY- + Greek *skaphē*, basin, light boat.]

bath·y·sphere (báthi-sfeer) *n.* A reinforced, spherical deep-diving chamber, manned, and lowered by cable.

ba·tik, bat·tik (báttik ‖ bə-teék) *n.* **1.** A method of dyeing print into a fabric in which the parts of the cloth not intended to be dyed are covered with removable wax. **2.** The print that is dyed into cloth by this method. **3.** The cloth so dyed. [Malay, from Javanese, "painted".] —**ba·tik** *adj.*

Ba·tis·ta (y Zal·dí·var) (bə-teésta) (ee zal-deévaar), **Fulgencio** (1901–73). Cuban president (1940–44; 1954–58). His repressive and authoritarian style of government proved unpopular, and, on New Year's Day, 1959, he was ousted by a revolutionary movement led by Dr. Fidel **Castro.**

ba·tiste (ba-teést, bə-) *n.* A fine, plain-woven fabric made from various fibres and used especially for clothing. [Earlier *baptist cloth* (translation of French *toile de Batiste*), first made by *Baptiste* of Cambrai (13th century).]

bat·man (bát-mən) *n., pl.* **-men** (-mən). In the British armed forces, a soldier who is an officer's personal servant. [Obsolete *bat*, from Old French *ba(s)t*, from Provençal, from Medieval Latin *bastum*, packsaddle + MAN.]

bat mitz·vah, bat miz·vah (baat míts-və) *n.* Also **bas mitz·vah** (baas), **bas miz·vah**. *Judaism.* **1.** A Jewish girl, usually between twelve and fourteen years old, considered an adult and thenceforth responsible for her religious and moral duties. **2.** In some congregations, the ceremony marking the arrival of a girl's religious commitment. See **bar mitzvah**. [Hebrew *bat mitzvāh*, "daughter of the commandment".]

ba·ton (bát'n, bátton, bátton ‖ *U.S. also* bə-tón) *n.* **1.** A short staff carried by some public and military officials as a symbol of office. **2.** A slender wooden stick or rod used by a conductor to direct an orchestra or band. **3.** The hollow metal rod with heavy rubber tips twirled by a drum major or majorette. **4.** *British.* A short thick stick used by the police as a weapon. **5.** *Heraldry.* A shortened narrow **bend** (diagonal line) *(see)* on a coat of arms, often signifying bastardy. [French *bâton*, from Old French *baston*, from Vulgar Latin *baston-* (unattested) from Late Latin *bastum*, stick.]

Bat·on Rouge (bátt'n rōozh). State capital of Louisiana, United States. Situated on the river Mississippi at the head of ocean-going navigation, it is also a major industrial and commercial centre.

ba·tra·chi·an (bə-tráyki-ən) *adj.* Of or pertaining to frogs and toads.
~*n.* A frog or toad. [New Latin *Batrachia* (former order name), from Greek *batrakhos†*, frog.]

bats (bats) *adj. Informal.* Eccentric; insane.

bats·man (báts-mən) *n., pl.* **-men** (-mən). **1.** In cricket, one who bats. **2.** *Aeronautics.* A ground official who signals to landing aircraft with a pair of bats.

batt (bat) *n.* A mass of cotton fibres, **batting** *(see)*.

bat·tal·i·on (bə-tál-yən) *n. Abbr.* **bat., batt., bn., Bn.** **1.** A tactical military unit, typically consisting of a headquarters company and four infantry companies, or a headquarters battery and four artillery batteries. **2.** An indefinite number of military troops in battle array. **3.** *Often plural.* A large group or number. [French *battaillon*, from Italian *battaglione*, augmentative of *battaglia*, troop, BATTLE.]

bat·ten¹ (bátt'n) *intr.v.* **-tened, -tening, -tens. 1. a.** To become fat. **b.** To feed gluttonously; gorge oneself. **2.** To thrive and prosper, especially at another's expense: *slum landlords who batten on the poor.* [Ultimately from Old Norse *batna*, to improve.]

batten² *n.* **1.** A strip of wood used in building to support tiles, slates, laths, or the like. **2.** A narrow strip of wood, used for flooring. **3.** Any of several flexible strips of wood placed in pockets at the outer edge of a sail to keep it flat.
~*tr.v.* **battened, -tening, -tens. 1.** To furnish with battens: *batten a sail.* **2.** To fasten or make secure with battens. Usually used with *up* or *down*: *batten down the hatches.* [French *bâton*, BATON.]

Bat·ten (bátt'n), **Jean** (1909–82). N.Z. aviator and the first woman to make a solo flight from England, across the south Atlantic ocean, to South America (1935).

Bat·ten·berg (bátt'n-burg) **1.** See **Mountbatten, Louis Alexander. 2.** See **Mountbatten of Burma, Louis, 1st Earl.**

Battenberg cake *n.* An oblong cake made of coloured sponge strips sandwiched together and encased in marzipan.

bat·ter¹ (báttər) *v.* **-tered, -tering, -ters.** —*tr.* **1. a.** To hit heavily and repeatedly with violent blows. **b.** To subject (a child or woman) to persistent violence or psychological cruelty. Used chiefly in the phrases *battered baby* and *battered wife*. **2.** To damage by heavy

wear. —*intr.* To pound repeatedly with heavy blows.
~*n. Printing.* 1. A damaged area on the face of type or on a plate.
2. The defect in print resulting from such damaged type. [Middle English *bateren*, from Anglo-French, from Old French *bat(t)re*, to beat, from Latin *battuere*.]

batter² *n.* A thick, beaten, liquid mixture, as of flour, milk, and eggs, used in cooking. [Middle English *bater*, from Anglo-French *batour*, from Old French *bateüre*, akin to BATTER (beat).]

batter³ *n.* A slope, as of the outer side of a wall, that recedes from bottom to top.
~*tr.v.* **battered, -tering, -ters.** To construct so as to slope thus. [Middle English *batter*†.]

batter⁴ *n.* In baseball, the player whose turn it is to bat.

bat·ter·ing-ram (báttring-ram, báttəring-) *n.* 1. A heavy beam used in ancient warfare to batter down walls and gates. 2. Any device resembling this or used for similar purposes.

Bat·ter·sea (báttər-si, -see). Part of the Greater London borough of Wandsworth, on the south bank of the river Thames. The river at Battersea is crossed by three of London's most famous bridges, the Albert (built 1873), the Battersea (1890) and the Chelsea (1937).

bat·ter·y (báttri, báttəri) *n., pl.* **-ies.** 1. A number of **primary cells** *(see)* connected together to provide a source of electric current. 2. One or more primary cells connected together in which the electrolyte is in the form of a paste. Also called "dry battery". 3. One or more **secondary cells** *(see)* connected together as a source of electric current; especially, the device used for this purpose in a motor vehicle. Also called "accumulator". 4. **a.** A beating or pounding. **b.** *Law.* The unlawful beating of another person. Compare **assault and battery.** 5. **a.** An emplacement for one or more pieces of artillery. **b.** A set of guns or other heavy artillery, as on a warship. **c.** *Abbr.* **btry.** The basic tactical artillery unit, corresponding to the company in the infantry. 6. An array or grouping of like things to be used together. 7. The pitcher and catcher on a baseball team. 8. The percussion section of an orchestra. 9. A system of keeping poultry confined in cages in order to produce high yields of eggs and cheaper meat. Often used adjectivally: *battery hens.* [French *batterie*, from *battre*, from Old French *bat(t)re*, to BATTER.]

battik. Variant of **batik.**

bat·ting (bátting) *n.* 1. The action of one who bats. 2. Cotton or wool fibre wadded together and used for stuffing furniture and mattresses. Also called "batt", "cotton batting". [Sense 2, from the beating of raw cotton or wool to clean it.]

batting average *n.* In cricket, the average number of runs per innings scored by a batsman, calculated for a season, a test series, or his career.

batting crease *n.* A **popping crease** *(see).*

bat·tle (bátt'l) *n.* 1. A large-scale combat between armed forces. 2. Armed fighting; combat. 3. Any intense competition; a struggle. ~*v.* **battled, -tling, -tles.** —*intr.* To engage in or as if in battle. —*tr.* To force; fight: *He battled his way through the crowd.* —**give battle.** To begin fighting. [Middle English *bataille*, from Old French, from Vulgar Latin *battālia* (unattested), from Late Latin *battuālia*, fighting and fencing exercises, from Latin *battuere*, to BATTER.]

Bat·tle (bátt'l). Town in East Sussex, England. The battle of Hastings was fought (1066) on a ridge, called Senlac, to the southeast. William the Conqueror built an abbey to commemorate his victory over the Saxon king, Harold II.

bat·tle-axe (bátt'l-aks) *n., pl.* **-axes.** 1. A heavy broad-headed axe, formerly used as a weapon. 2. *Slang.* An overbearing woman; a virago.

battle cruiser *n.* A warship with less heavy armour than a battleship, and with the speed of a cruiser.

battle cry *n.* 1. A shout uttered by troops in battle. 2. A slogan used by the proponents of a cause.

bat·tle·dore (bátt'l-dawr ‖ -dōr) *n.* 1. An early form of badminton played with a flat wooden racket and a shuttlecock. Also called "battledore and shuttlecock". 2. The racket used in this game. [Middle English *batildore*, perhaps from Old Provençal *batedor*, beater, from *bat(t)re*, to BATTER.]

battle fatigue *n.* **Combat fatigue** *(see).*

bat·tle·field (bátt'l-feeld) *n.* A field or area where an actual or figurative battle is fought. Also called "battleground".

bat·tle·ment (bátt'l-mənt) *n. Usually plural.* A parapet built on top of a wall, with indentations for defence or decoration. [Middle English *batelment*, from Old French *bataillier*, to provide with battlements, from *batailles*, battlements, plural of *bataille*, BATTLE.] —**bat·tle·ment·ed** (-mentid) *adj.*

battle royal *n., pl.* **battles royal.** 1. A battle in which numerous combatants participate. 2. A fight to the finish. 3. An intense altercation.

bat·tle·ship (bátt'l-ship) *n.* Any of a class of warships of the largest size, carrying the greatest number of guns and batteries and clad with the heaviest armour.

battleship grey *n.* Medium grey.

bat·tue (ba-tōō, -téw; *French* -tū) *n.* 1. The driving of wild game from cover by beaters towards waiting hunters. 2. A shoot employing this procedure. 3. Wholesale massacre, as of a defenceless crowd. [French, from the feminine past participle of *bat(t)re*, to beat, BATTER.]

bat·ty (bátti) *adj.* **-tier, -tiest.** *Informal.* Eccentric; crazy.

bau·ble (báwb'l) *n.* 1. A small, showy ornament or trinket, such as a Christmas tree decoration. 2. A baton surmounted by a gro-

tesquely carved head, carried by a court jester as a mock sceptre of his office. [Middle English *babel, babulle*, from Old French *babel, baubel*†, plaything.]

baud (bawd) *n.* A unit for the speed of telegraphic or telephonic transmission equal to a transmission speed of one unit element per second. [After J. M. E. *Baudot* (1845–1903), French engineer and inventor of a telegraph system.]

Baude·laire (bōd-lair, bōdə-, -laír), **Charles** (1821–67). French poet and literary, art, and music critic. He discovered Edgar Allan Poe, translated many of his works, and published an autobiographical novel *La Fanfarlo* (1847) and a single volume of poetry, *Les Fleurs du mal* (1857, revised 1861).

Bau·douin I (bō-dwaN, -dwáN) (1930–93). King of the Belgians. He ascended to the throne in 1951, succeeding his father, Leopold III. He married Fabiola de Mora y Aragon in 1960.

Bau·haus (bów-howss). An institute founded in 1919 by Walter Gropius in Weimar, Germany, for the study of art, design, and architecture and noted for its development of a style of functional architecture and its experimental use of building materials. It was closed by the Nazis in 1933. [German, "architecture house".]

bau·hin·i·a (baw-hínni-ə) *n.* Any plant of the leguminous genus *Bauhinia*, consisting of woody climbers with flattened stems and showy flowers, widely cultivated for ornament. [After Jean (1541–1613) and Gaspard (1560–1624) *Bauhin*, Swiss physicians and botanists.]

baulk, balk (bawk ‖ bawlk) *v.* **baulked, baulking, baulks.** —*intr.* 1. To stop short and refuse to go on. 2. To refuse obstinately or show great reluctance; shrink. Used with *at: He baulked at the very idea of compromise.* 3. *Sports.* To make an incomplete or misleading move, especially an illegal one. —*tr.* 1. To put obstacles in the way of; check or thwart. 2. *Archaic.* To allow to go by; miss: *baulk an opportunity.*
~*n.* 1. A hindrance, check, or defeat. 2. A blunder or failure. 3. **a.** In baseball, an illegal move; especially, a false move to throw the ball made by the pitcher when there are runners on base. **b.** In various other sports, an incomplete or misleading move. 4. **a.** An unploughed strip of land. **b.** A ridge between furrows. 5. **a.** A wooden beam or rafter. 6. On a billiard table, the space between the cushion and the baulk line. [Old English *balc*, ridge, hindrance, from Old Norse *bálkr*, partition, from Germanic *balkuz* (unattested).] —**baulk·er** *n.*

baulk line *n.* On a billiard table, a line drawn parallel to one end, from behind which a player makes his opening shot.

baulk·y, balk·y (báwki ‖ báwlki) *adj.* **-ier, -iest.** Given to stopping at obstacles, real or imagined. Said especially of horses.

Baum (bawm, baam), **L(yman) Frank** (1856–1919). U.S. novelist famous for writing *The Wonderful Wizard of Oz* (1900).

Bau·mé scale (bōmay, bō-máy) *n. Abbr.* **Bé, B.** A hydrometer scale in which 1 degree Baumé is equivalent to 145 $(1-v)$ for liquids heavier than water and $140v-130$ for liquids lighter than water, where *v* is the reciprocal of the relative density of the liquid at 60°F. [After Antoine *Baumé* (1728–1804), French pharmacist; inventor of a hydrometer.]

Baum·gar·ten (bówm-gaart'n), **Alexander Gottlieb** (1714–62). German philosopher noted for his work, *Aesthetica* (1750). A follower both of the philosopher Christian Wolff (1679–1754), and of **Leibniz,** he invented the term aesthetics.

baux·ite (báwksīt) *n.* The principal ore of aluminium. It is composed mainly of aluminium hydroxide, with some iron hydroxide, and forms as a result of leaching of the soil in tropical conditions. It is used as an abrasive and catalyst. Compare **laterite.** [French, first found at Les *Baux*, southern France.]

Ba·va·ri·a (bə-vaír-i-ə). *German* **Bay·ern** (bí-ərn). Large state in Germany, lying in the extreme south. The Bavarian Alps contain Germany's highest peak, the Zugspitze (2 963 metres; 9,721 feet). Beer, grain, salt, graphite, lignite, and iron ore are the region's chief products. The capital is Munich.

Ba·var·i·an (bə-vaír-i-ən) *n.* 1. A native or inhabitant of Bavaria. 2. The High German dialect spoken in Bavaria and Austria. —**Ba·var·i·an** *adj.*

baw·bee (báw-bée) *n. Scottish Informal.* A halfpenny. [After Alexander Orok of *Sillebawby*, 16th-century Scottish master of the mint.]

bawd (bawd) *n. Archaic.* 1. A woman who keeps a brothel; a madam. 2. A prostitute. [Middle English *bawde*, probably from Old French *baude, baud*, lively, bold, from Old High German *bald*, bold.]

bawd·ry (báwdri) *n.* Obscene or coarse language on the subject of sex. [Middle English *bawdery*, from BAWD.]

bawd·y (báwdi) *adj.* **-ier, -iest.** Humorously coarse; vulgar; lewd. —**bawd·i·ly** *adv.* —**bawd·i·ness** *n.*

bawd·y·house (báwdi-howss) *n. Archaic.* A brothel.

bawl (bawl) *v.* **bawled, bawling, bawls.** —*intr.* 1. To weep loudly, as from pain or annoyance; howl. 2. To cry out loudly and vehemently; shout. —*tr.* To utter in a loud, vehement voice. —**bawl out.** *Informal.* To reprimand or scold in a loud voice.
~*n.* A loud, extended outcry; a wail. [Middle English *baulen*, probably from Scandinavian, of imitative origin; akin to Icelandic *baula*, to low.] —**bawl·er** *n.*

bay¹ (bay) *n.* 1. *Abbr.* **b., B.** A body of water partly enclosed by land, but having a wide outlet to the sea. 2. A broad stretch of low land between hills. [Middle English *baye*, from Old French *baie*, from Old Spanish *bahia*, perhaps from Iberian.]

bay² *n.* **1.** *Architecture.* A part of a building or other structure marked off by vertical elements. **2. a.** A **bay window** *(see).* **b.** Any opening or recess in a wall. **3.** An extension of a building; a wing. **4.** A compartment in a barn, used for storing hay or grain. **5.** A ship's sick bay. **6.** A compartment in an aircraft: *the bomb bay.* **7.** *British.* A dead end in a railway station marking the termination of a line, with a platform surrounding it on three sides. [Middle English, from Old French *baee,* an opening, from *baer,* to gape, from Medieval Latin *batāre,* to yawn, gape.]

bay³ *adj.* Reddish-brown: *a bay colt.*
~*n.* **1.** A reddish-brown colour. **2.** An animal, especially a horse, of this colour. [Middle English, from Old French *bai,* from Latin *badius.*]

bay⁴ *n.* **1.** A deep, prolonged barking, especially of hounds closing in on prey. **2.** The position of one cornered by pursuers and forced to turn and fight at close quarters. **3.** The position of someone or something checked or kept at a safe distance.
~*v.* **bayed, baying, bays.** —*intr.* To utter a deep, prolonged bark or howl. —*tr.* **1.** To pursue or challenge with barking: *"I had rather be a dog, and bay the moon"* (Shakespeare). **2.** To express by barking. **3.** To bring to bay: *"too big for the dogs which tried to bay it"* (William Faulkner). [Middle English *baien,* short for *abaien,* from Old French *abaiier, abayer,* from Vulgar Latin *abbaiāre* (unattested).]

bay⁵ *n.* **1.** The true laurel, *Laurus nobilis,* native to the Mediterranean area, having stiff, glossy, aromatic leaves. See **bay leaf.** Also called "bay laurel," "bay tree," "laurel". **2.** Any of several similar trees or shrubs, such as the **sweet bay** *(see).* **3.** *Usually plural.* A crown or wreath made of the leaves and branches of the bay or similar plants, conferred or awarded in classical times as a sign of honour. **4.** *Plural. Archaic.* Renown; honour. [Middle English *baye,* laurel berry, from Old French *baie,* from Latin *bāca,* berry.]

ba·ya·dere (bī-ə-déer, -dáir) *n.* A fabric with vividly contrasting horizontal stripes. [French *bayadère,* Hindu dancing girl, from Portuguese *bailadeira,* from *bailar,* to dance.]

Ba·yard (báy-ərd, baa-yaàr), **Pierre du Terrail, Seigneur de** (*c.* 1476–1524). French soldier, popularly known, for his fearlessness and chivalry, as *"le chevalier sans peur et sans reproche".*

bay·ber·ry (báy-bəri, -beri || -berri) *n., pl.* **-ries.** **1.** Any of several aromatic shrubs or small trees of the genus *Myrica;* especially, *M. pensylvanica,* of eastern North America, bearing grey, waxy berries. **2.** A tropical American tree, *Pimenta acris,* yielding an oil used in making bay rum. Also called "bay rum tree". **3.** The fruit of any of these trees or shrubs.

Bayern. See **Bavaria.**

Bayes·i·an (báyz-i-ən) *adj.* Of or designating a method or theory for reassessing the probability of a proposition in the light of new relevant information. [After Thomas *Bayes* (1701–61), British mathematician.]

Ba·yeux (bī-ér, bay-, -yér || -yő; *French* baa-yő). Small town in northwestern France, in the Calvados département of Normandy. It was the first French town (June 8, 1944) to be liberated from Nazi occupation by the Allies in World War II.

Bayeux tapestry *n.* An 11th- or 12th-century tapestry, 50 centimetres (20 inches) wide by 70.5 metres (231 feet) long, embroidered with scenes depicting the Norman Conquest of England, and preserved in the town of Bayeux.

Bayle (bayl, bel), **Pierre** (1647–1706). French philosopher, a forerunner of the 18th-century Enlightenment. Although he was brought up as a Calvinist, he devoted his writings to the cause of religious tolerance and sceptical subversion of Christian belief. His most famous work was the *Dictionnaire historique et critique* (1697).

bay leaf *n.* The dried, aromatic leaf of the bay, *Laurus nobilis,* used as seasoning in cooking.

Bay·lis (báy-liss), **Lilian Mary** (1874–1937). English theatre manager. She founded the Old Vic, London (1912), as a theatre for the production of Shakespeare plays. In 1931 she assumed the management of the Sadler's Wells theatre and transformed it into a centre for opera and ballet. She became a Companion of Honour (1929).

Bay·liss (báy-liss), **Sir William Maddock** (1860–1924). British physiologist. Most of his research was devoted to investigating the action of the heart, the circulatory system, and the mechanics of digestion. With E. H. Starling, he discovered the hormone **secretin** *(see),* produced in the small intestine.

bay lynx *n.* The bobcat *(see).*

Bay of Pigs. *Spanish* **Ba·hí·a de Co·chin·os** (ba-hée-a day kochée-nős). Bay on the southern coast of Cuba, the site of the unsuccessful Bay of Pigs invasion of 17 April, 1961, when a force of about 1,500 U.S.-trained troops, rebels against the regime of Fidel Castro, landed there from Guatemala.

bay·o·net (báy-ə-nit, -net || -nét) *n.* A knife or spike adapted to fit the muzzle end of a rifle and used in close combat.
~*tr.v.* **bayoneted** or **bayonetted, -neting** or **-netting, -nets.** To stab or prod with a bayonet. [French *baïonnette,* first manufactured at BAYONNE.]

bayonet fitting *n.* A method of fastening two cylindrical parts together, similar to the original method of attaching a bayonet to a rifle. It is used in fitting light bulbs into holders, two pins on the bulb cap engaging with two L-shaped slots on the holder.

Ba·yonne (bī-ón, bay-, -yón). Port in the Pyrénées-Atlantique département of France, now joined with the resort of Biarritz. The town gave its name to the bayonet, which was first used by local Basques in the 17th century.

bay·ou (bī-ōō || *locally also* -ō, -ə) *n., pl.* **-ous.** In the southern United States, a marshy, sluggish body of water tributary to a lake or river. [Louisiana French, from Choctaw *bayuk.*]

Bay·reuth (bī-royt, -róyt). Industrial city of Bavaria, southeast Germany. Richard Wagner lived there from 1872 to 1883, and the Festival Theatre, devoted to the performance of his operas, was opened in 1876.

bay rum *n.* An aromatic liquid obtained by distilling the leaves of the bayberry tree, *Pimenta acris,* with rum, and now also synthesised from alcohol, water, and various oils.

bay rum tree *n.* A tree, the **bayberry** *(see).*

Bay Street *n.* The controlling financial interests of Canada. [After the main street of the financial district of Toronto.]

bay tree *n.* A tree, the **bay** *(see).*

bay window *n.* A large window or series of windows projecting from the wall of a building and forming a recess within. Also called "bay".

bay·wood (báy-wŏŏd) *n.* The wood of a tropical American mahogany, *Swietenia macrophylla.* [After the *Bay* of Campeche, Mexico.]

ba·zaar, ba·zar (bə-zár) *n.* **1.** An Oriental market, usually consisting of an area of streets lined with shops and stalls. **2.** A shop selling miscellaneous articles. **3.** A fair at which miscellaneous articles are sold, usually for charity. [Earlier *bazarro, bazar,* probably from Italian *bazarro,* from Turkish, from Persian *bāzār,* from Middle Persian *bāchār,* from Old Persian *abēcharish†.*]

ba·zoo·ka (bə-zōŏkə) *n.* A portable military weapon consisting of a long, metal, smoothbore tube for firing small, armour-piercing, explosive rockets at short range. [After the *bazooka,* a crude wind instrument made of pipes, invented by Bob Burns (1896–1956), U.S. comedian.]

BBC, B.B.C. British Broadcasting Corporation.

bbl, bbl. barrel (of oil).

B.C. 1. before Christ (unusually small capitals: B.C.). See Usage note at **A.D. 2.** British Columbia.

BCG Bacillus Calmette-Guérin (a strain of tuberculosis bacillus used in a vaccine against the disease).

B. Com. Bachelor of Commerce.

bd. 1. board. **2.** bond. **3.** bound.

B.D. 1. Bachelor of Divinity. **2.** bank draft. **3.** bills discounted.

bdel·li·um (délli-əm) *n.* **1.** An aromatic gum resin similar to myrrh, produced by various trees of the genus *Commiphora,* of western Asia and Africa. **2.** A substance mentioned in the Bible, variously interpreted to be carbuncle, rock crystal, pearl, or gum resin. Numbers 11:7. [Latin, from Greek *bdellion,* probably from Hebrew *bədōlaḥ.*]

bd. ft. board foot.

bds. bound in boards.

B.D.S. Bachelor of Dental Surgery.

be (bee; *weak form* bi)

	1st person	2nd person	3rd person
Present Tense			
singular	**am** (am; *w.f.* əm)	**are** (ar; *w.f.* ər)†	**is** (iz)
plural	**are**	**are**	**are**

†*Archaic 2nd person singular* **art** (art; *w.f.* ərt)

	1st person	2nd person	3rd person
Past Tense			
singular	**was** (woz; *w.f.* wəz ‖ *U.S.* wuz)	**were** (wer, wair; *w.f.* wər)‡	**was**
plural	**were**	**were**	**were**

‡*Archaic 2nd person singular* **wast** (wost; *w.f.* wəst) *or* **wert** (wert; *w.f.* wərt)

Present Participle: being (bé'e-ing) **Present Subjunctive: be**
Past Participle: been (been, bin) **Past Subjunctive: were**

v. Used as an auxiliary verb in certain constructions, as: **a.** With the past participle of a transitive verb to form the passive voice: *The competition is held annually; Our club may be disbanded for lack of funds.* **b.** With the present participle of a verb to express a continuing action: *We are working to improve housing conditions.* **c.** With the present participle or the infinitive of a verb, to express intention, obligation, or future action: *We're leaving tomorrow; All visitors are to leave by 10 p.m.* **d.** *Archaic.* With the past participle of certain intransitive verbs to form the perfect tense: *Christ is risen from the dead.* —*intr.* **1.** To exist in actuality; have reality or life: *I think, therefore I am.* **2.** To exist in a specified place; stay; reside: *"Oh, to be in England,/ Now that April's there"* (Robert Browning). **3.** To occupy a specified position: *The food is on the table.* **4.** To take place; occur: *Her party was last week.* **5.** To go. Used chiefly in the past and perfect tenses: *Have you ever been to Italy?* **6.** *Archaic.* To belong; befall. Used in the subjunctive: *Peace be unto you.* **7.** Used as a copula linking a subject and a predicate nominative, adjective, or pronoun, in such senses as: **a.** To equal in meaning or identity: *"To be a Christian was to be a Roman."* (James Bryce). **b.** To signify; indicate: *A is excellent, C is passable, F is a fail.* **c.** To belong to a specified class or group: *A human is a primate.* **d.** To have or show a specified essential quality or characteristic: *She is courageous. All men are mortal.* **e.** To have or show a specified quality or characteristic at a particular time: *I'm busy just now.* **f.** To represent or embody the essential character of; symbolise: *She is the Tory party.* [**1.** Be; been: Middle English *be(e)n; be(o)n,* Old English *bēon; bēon,* to come to be. **2.** Am; art; is; are (singular and plural): Middle English *am; art, eart; is; are* (singular), aren (plural); Old English *eam, eom; eart; is; (e)aron* (plural only), from Germanic *es-* (unattested) and *ar-* (unattested). 3. Was; were: Middle English *wes, was; ware, were* (singular), *weren, were* (plural); Old English *wæs; wære* (singular) *wæron* (plural), from Germanic *wes-* (unattested).]

Usage: In British English, the informal construction *been and* is used to express surprise: *He's been and got married!* The double use of *be,* in *be being* or *been being,* sounds inelegant but can be necessary, as in *Jane's the one who ought to be being questioned like this.* Here, *be being* emphasises the duration of the action. The use of *being as* or *being that* instead of *because* or *since* (*Being as you're tired, you might as well stay at home*) is considered nonstandard.

be– *v. prefix.* Indicates: 1. A complete or profuse covering or affecting; for example, **becloud, besmear.** 2. A thorough or excessive degree; for example, **bewilder.** 3. An action that causes a condition to exist; for example, **besot, befriend.** [Middle English, Old English, weak form of *bi-,* BY. In Middle English *be-* indicates: 1. Thoroughly, as in **beloved, betray.** 2. On all sides, as in **besiege.** 3. About, over, in relation to, as in **betroth, bequest.** Old English *be-, bi-* indicates: 1. About, over, as in **bethink.** 2. On all sides, as in **beset.** 3. Away, away from, as in **benumb.**]

Be The symbol for the element beryllium.

Bé Baumé scale.

B/E 1. bill of entry. 2. bill of exchange.

beach (beech) *n.* 1. The shore of a body of water. 2. The sand or pebbles on a shore. 3. The accumulation of shingle, sand, and rocks on the coast between the lowest level reached by spring tides and the highest point attained by storm waves. ~*tr.v.* **beached, beaching, beaches.** To haul or drive (a boat for example) ashore. [16th century : origin obscure.]

beach buggy *n.* A car usually open and fitted with balloon tyres, used for driving on beaches and sand.

beach·comb·er (beech-kōmər) *n.* 1. One who collects flotsam and jetsam from beaches and port areas; especially, a vagrant who makes a living in this way. 2. A long wave rolling in towards a beach. [Sense 2, from COMB, in the sense "to break with foam".]

beach flea *n.* A small crustacean, the **sand hopper** (see).

beach·head (beech-hed) *n.* 1. A position on an enemy shoreline captured by advance troops of an invading force. 2. A first achievement that opens the way for further development.

beach-la-mar (beech-lə-mar) *n.* A dialect, **bêche-de-mer** (see). [Alteration of Portuguese *bicho do mar.*]

beach sagewort *n.* A seacoast plant, *Artemisia stellerana,* originally native to Asia but now widespread, covered with dense, white down and having small yellow flowers. Also called "dusty miller".

bea·con (beekən) *n.* 1. a. A signal fire lit on a hill or other high place; especially, one used to warn of an enemy's approach. b. *Chiefly British.* A hill suitable for such a fire. 2. A lighthouse or other signalling or guiding device on a coast. 3. A radio transmitter that emits a characteristic signal as a warning or guide. 4. Anything that warns or guides. 5. A **belisha beacon** (see). ~*v.* **beaconed, -coning, -cons.** —*tr.* To provide a beacon for. —*intr.* To serve as a beacon. [Middle English *beken,* sign, standard, Old English *bēacen.*]

Beac·ons·field (beckənz-feeld, beekənz-), **1st Earl of.** See Disraeli.

bead (beed) *n.* 1. A small, ball-shaped piece of glass, metal, wood, or other material pierced for stringing or threading. 2. *Plural.* a. A necklace made of such pieces. b. A rosary. 3. Any small, round object, especially: a. A small drop of moisture. b. A bubble of gas in a liquid. c. A small knob of metal on the muzzle of a rifle or gun, used for sighting. 4. *Architecture.* A strip of stone or wood, with one moulded edge placed flush against a wall, door, or window frame. 5. *Chemistry.* A **borax bead** (see). 6. *Metallurgy.* A small blob of metal from a welding rod applied to the material to be welded in order to test the nature of the weld. —**count** or **say** or **tell** (**one's**) **beads.** To say the rosary. ~*v.* **beaded, beading, beads.** —*tr.* To ornament or cover with beads. —*intr.* To collect into beads. [Middle English *bede, bead,* prayer, prayer bead, bead, Old English *gebed,* prayer, from Germanic *bedh-* (unattested).]

bead·ing (beeding) *n.* 1. Beads or material used for beads. 2. Ornamentation with beads. 3. *Architecture.* A narrow, half-rounded moulding. 4. Any narrow strip of trimming. 5. A narrow piece of openwork lace through which ribbon may be run.

bea·dle (beed'l) *n.* 1. Formerly, a minor parish official in an English church, whose duties included keeping order and ushering during services. 2. An official at certain English universities who supervises and walks before processions. 3. *Judaism.* A **shammes** (see). [Middle English *bedele, bidel,* herald, messenger, beadle, from Old French *bedel* (of Germanic origin), replacing Old English *bydel.*]

bea·dle·dom (beed'l-dəm) *n.* Petty bureaucratic officiousness.

bead test *n. Chemistry.* A test to identify the component elements of a substance. See **borax bead.**

bead·work (beed-wurk) *n.* 1. Decorative work in beads. 2. *Architecture.* Beaded moulding.

bead·y (beedi) *adj.* **-ier, -iest.** 1. Small, round, and shiny: *beady eyes.* 2. Shrewd, piercing: *a beady look.* 3. Decorated or covered with beads.

bea·gle (beeg'l) *n.* Any of a breed of small hounds having short legs, drooping ears, and a smooth coat with white, black, and tan markings. [Middle English *begle,* perhaps from Old French *bee-gueule,* noisy person : probably *beer,* to gape, from (unattested)

Vulgar Latin *batāre* (see **bay,** opening) + *gueule,* throat, from Latin *gula.*]

beak (beek) *n.* 1. The horny, projecting structure forming the mandibles of a bird; a bill. 2. A part or organ resembling this, as in some turtles, insects, or fish. 3. Any hard, cone-shaped, or pointed structure or part. 4. *Informal.* A person's nose. 5. *British Slang.* a. A schoolmaster. b. A judge. [Middle English *bec, bek,* from Old French *bec,* from Latin *beccus,* from Gaulish.]

beak·er (beekər) *n.* 1. a. A large drinking cup with a wide mouth. b. The contents of such a cup. 2. An open glass cylinder with a pouring lip, used as a standard laboratory container or vessel for mixing and heating. [Middle English *biker, beker,* from Old Norse *bikarr,* probably from Vulgar Latin *bicārium* (unattested), perhaps from Greek *bikos,* drinking-jar.]

Beaker Folk *pl.n.* An ancient people inhabiting Britain in the Bronze Age, whose artefacts, especially clay beakers, have been found in their round burial barrows. Also called "Beaker People".

be-all and end-all (bee-awl, end-awl) *n.* The chief aim or consideration, to the exclusion of all others. [From Shakespeare's *Macbeth* (1605), Act I, scene 7, in which Macbeth considers the murder of Duncan: ". . .this blow/Might be the be-all and the end-all. . .".]

beam (beem) *n.* 1. A squared-off log or large oblong piece of timber, metal, or stone, used especially in construction. 2. *Nautical.* a. The breadth of a ship at the widest point. b. A transverse structural member of the framing of a vessel, used to support a deck and to brace the sides against stress. c. The shank of an anchor. 3. A steel tube or wooden roller with flanged ends on which the warp is wound in a loom. 4. An oscillating lever connected to an engine piston rod and used to transmit power to the crankshaft. 5. The bar of a balance, from which weighing pans are suspended. 6. Either of the main stems of a deer's antlers. 7. The main horizontal bar on a plough to which the share, coulter, and handles, if any, are attached. 8. a. A ray of light or other electromagnetic radiation. b. A group of particles travelling together in close parallel trajectories. 9. A **radio beam** (see). 10. A smile or happy expression. —**broad in the beam.** *Informal.* Wide-hipped; fat. —**off (the) beam.** 1. Not following the radio beam. Said of an aircraft. 2. *Informal.* Not on the right track; mistaken. ~*v.* **beamed, beaming, beams.** —*tr.* 1. To emit or transmit: *beaming the message.* 2. To express by means of a broad or radiant smile. —*intr.* 1. To radiate light; shine. 2. To smile expansively. [Middle English *beme, beem,* Old English *bēam,* tree, beam.]

beam compass *n.* A form of compass used for drawing large circles. It consists of a horizontal beam along which two vertical legs slide, one fitted with a pin to act as a centre and the other with a pen or pencil. Not in technical usage. Also called "trammel".

beam-ends (beem-endz, -endz) *pl.n.* The ends of a ship's beams. —**on her beam-ends.** Listing so far over that the beams are nearly vertical and there is danger of capsizing. —**on (one's) beam-ends.** *Informal.* Having no money at all.

beam hole *n.* A hole through a nuclear-reactor shield enabling a beam of radiation to be used for experimental purposes.

beam rider *n.* A guided missile that steers itself along the axis of a scanned beam of microwave radiation. —**beam riding** *n.*

beam·y (beemi) *adj.* **-ier, -iest.** 1. Broad at the beam. Said of a ship. 2. Emitting beams, as of light; radiant.

bean (been) *n.* 1. Any of several plants of the genus *Phaseolus,* having compound leaves, white or yellow flowers, and seed-bearing pods. See **French bean, lima bean, runner bean, string bean.** 2. The edible seed or pod of any of these plants. 3. Any of several related plants bearing similar pods and seeds. See **broad bean.** 4. Any of various other seeds or pods resembling beans, such as the coffee bean or the jojoba bean. 5. *Slang.* A small amount of money: *I haven't a bean.* 6. *British Slang.* A fellow; a chap: *old bean.* 7. *Chiefly U.S. Slang.* The head. —**full of beans.** *Informal.* Very lively; energetic. —**spill the beans.** *Informal.* To disclose what was not meant to be disclosed. [Middle English *ben(e),* Old English *bēan.*]

bean·bag (been-bag) *n.* A small bag filled with dried beans and used for throwing in games.

bean caper *n.* A plant of the genus *Zygophyllum;* especially, *Z. fabago,* a shrub of the Middle East, bearing edible buds used as capers.

bean curd *n.* A soft soya bean cheese of the Orient. Also called "tofu". [Translation of Chinese (Mandarin) *dòu fù : dòu,* bean + *fù,* curdled.]

bean·feast (been-feest) *n. British Informal.* 1. An annual dinner given by a firm to its employees. 2. A party or celebration. [19th century : beans and bacon were always served at such annual dinners.]

bean·o (beenō) *n. British Informal.* A party or celebration. [BEAN (FEAST) + -O.]

bean·pole (been-pōl) *n.* 1. A thin pole used to support bean plants. 2. *Slang.* A very tall, thin person.

bean sprout *n.* A young, tender shoot of certain beans, such as the soya bean or the mung bean, as used in Chinese cooking. Also called "beanshoot".

bean·stalk (been-stawk) *n.* The stem of a bean plant.

bean tree *n.* Any of various trees, such as the catalpa, that bear beanlike fruit.

bear¹ (bair) *v.* **bore** (bor ‖ bōr) or *archaic* **bare** (bair), **borne** (born ‖ bōrn) (for all senses) or **born** (born) (for sense 11 only), **bearing, bears.** —*tr.* 1. To support; hold up: *bore him on her shoulders.*

2. To carry on one's person; convey. **3.** To carry as if in the mind; maintain: *bearing love for others.* **4.** To transmit at large; bring: *bearing glad tidings.* **5.** To show; have as a visible characteristic: *bearing a scar on his right arm.* **6.** To have as a visible quality or form; exhibit: *"A thousand different shapes it bears"* (Abraham Cowley). **7.** To conduct or comport (oneself) in a particular way. **8.** To be accountable for; assume. **9.** To tolerate; endure: *couldn't bear her husband.* **10.** To be capable of undergoing; admit of: *doesn't bear thinking about.* **11.** To give birth to. **12.** To produce; yield. **13.** To offer; render: *bearing witness.* **14.** To move by steady pressure; push: *"boats against the current, borne back ceaselessly into the past."* (F. Scott Fitzgerald). *—intr.* **1.** To yield a product; produce. **2.** To withstand stress, difficulty, or attrition. Often used with *up.* **3.** To have relevance; apply. Used with *on.* **4.** To turn or proceed in a specified direction: *"I bore right, to avoid the Beduin"* (T.E. Lawrence). —See Usage at **borne**; Synonyms below and at **convey.** **—bear down.** To exert downward muscular pressure to aid childbirth. Used of a woman in labour. **—bear down on** or **upon. 1.** To come towards in an aggressive or threatening way. **2.** To exert pressure on; weight on. **—bear out.** To prove right or justified : confirm: *The results bear out her claims.* **—bear with.** To be patient or tolerant with. [Bear, bore, borne; Middle English *beren, bare, boren,* Old English *beran, bær, boren.*]

Synonyms: *bear, endure, stand, suffer, abide, tolerate.*

bear² *n.* **1.** Any of various usually omnivorous mammals of the family Ursidae, having a shaggy coat, strong claws, and a short tail, and walking with the entire lower surface of the foot touching the ground. See **black bear, brown bear, grizzly bear, polar bear. 2.** Any of various animals resembling a bear in some respect, such as the **koala** *(see).* **3.** A person who is awkward, clumsy, or ill-mannered. **4.** *Capital* **B.** *Astronomy.* Either of two constellations, the **Great Bear** or the **Little Bear** *(both of which see).* **5.** *Finance.* A person who sells stocks or shares on the stock market in anticipation of a fall in prices or who tries by speculative selling to effect such a fall, in order to buy later at a profit. Compare **bull.**

~v. **beared, bearing, bears.** *Finance. —tr.* To engage in speculative selling so as to lower the price of (stocks and shares) or prices in (a market). *—intr.* To fall in price. Compare **bull.**

~adj. Finance. Characterised by falling prices: *a bear market.* Compare **bull.** [Middle English *bere,* Old English *bera.* Sense 5 and adjective, 18th century : originally probably *bearskin jobber,* alluding to the proverb, *To sell the bear's skin before one has caught the bear.*]

bear·a·ble (báir-əbl) *adj.* Capable of being borne; endurable; tolerable. **—bear·a·bly** *adv.*

bear-bait·ing (báir-bayting) *n.* The former sport of setting dogs to attack or torment a chained bear.

bear·ber·ry (báir-bri, -bəri || -berri) *n., pl.* **-ries.** A trailing shrub, *Arctostaphylos uva-ursi,* of the Northern Hemisphere, having small evergreen leaves, white or pink flowers, and red berries.

beard (beerd) *n.* **1. a.** The hair on the chin, cheeks, and throat of a man: *three day's growth of beard.* **b.** This hair allowed to grow and cover the skin: *a foot-long beard.* **2.** Any similar hairy or hairlike growth such as that on or near the face of certain mammals. **3.** A tuft or group of bristles on certain plants, especially cereals; an awn. **4.** The barb or hook of a fishhook, arrow, or the like. **5.** The gills of an oyster. **6.** *Printing.* The part of a piece of type between the face and the shoulder; the neck.

~tr.v. **bearded, bearding, beards. 1.** To furnish with a beard. **2.** To grasp by the beard. **3.** To confront boldly: *beard the lion in his den.* [Middle English *berd,* Old English *beard.*]

beard·ed collie (béerdid) *n.* A dog of a breed recognised in 1944, having a brown, black, or grey coat with or without collie markings, and a long beard.

bearded iris (béerdid) *n.* Any of many varieties of iris having beardlike growths at the bases of the three lower, recurved petals.

bearded lizard *n.* A large Australian lizard, *Amphibolurus barbatus,* having a distensible pouch at the throat.

bearded reedling *n.* A small Eurasian marsh bird, *Panurus biarmicus,* having black, moustache-like markings in the male. Also called "bearded tit", "reedling".

bearded vulture *n.* A bird, the **lammergeier** *(see).*

beard·less (béerd-ləss, -liss) *adj.* **1. a.** Having no beard. **b.** Having the beard shaved off; clean-shaven. **2. a.** Not old enough to have a beard. **b.** Immature; inexperienced. **—beard·less·ness** *n.*

Beardsley (béerdzli), **Aubrey (Vincent)** (1872–98). British illustrator. His flowing designs, characteristic of the Art Nouveau style, are usually figurative ink drawings done in black and white, contrasting areas of elaborate intricacy with stark white spaces and dense black shadows. Works that he illustrated include Wilde's *Salome,* Pope's *Rape of the Lock,* and Ben Jonson's *Volpone.*

bear·er (báir-ər) *n.* **1.** One that carries or supports. **2. a.** A porter. **b.** A domestic or personal servant, especially in India during the British Raj. **3.** A person who presents for payment a cheque or other redeemable note. **4.** A **pallbearer** *(see).* **5.** Any fruit-bearing plant.

bear garden *n.* **1.** Formerly, a place where bears were confined and exhibited, as for bearbaiting. **2.** A place or scene of tumult.

bear hug *n.* A very tight, enveloping hug or embrace.

bear·ing (báir-ing) *n.* **1.** The manner in which a person carries or conducts himself; deportment. **2.** *Engineering.* **a.** Any part that supports another part or structure. **b.** A device that supports, guides, and reduces the friction of motion between fixed and moving machine parts. **3.** Anything that bears weight or acts as a support. **4.** The part of an architectural arch or beam that rests on a support. **5. a.** The act or period of producing fruit or offspring. **b.** The quantity produced; the yield. **6.** Direction, especially angular direction measured from one position to another using geographical or celestial reference lines. **7.** *Usually plural.* The position or situation of a person or object relative to the surroundings. **8.** Relevance; relationship; connection: *This has no bearing on the subject.* **9.** *Heraldry.* A charge or device on a field.

Synonyms: *bearing, carriage, manner, demeanour, air, mien, presence.*

bearing rein *n.* A short rein connected from a bit to a saddle, designed to keep a horse from lowering its head. Also *U.S.* "check-rein".

bear·ish (báir-ish) *adj.* **1.** Like a bear; clumsy, boorish, or surly. **2.** Causing, expecting, or characterised by falling stock-market prices. Compare **bullish. —bear·ish·ly** *adv.* **—bear·ish·ness** *n.*

bé·ar·naise sauce (báy-ər-náyz, -néz). *n.* A sauce made from butter, egg yolks, lemon juice, or vinegar, and flavoured with tarragon, shallots, and chervil. Also called "sauce béarnaise". [French *béarnaise,* feminine of *béarnais,* of Béarn, region in southwestern France.]

bear's breech *n.* Also **bear's breeches** (bríchiz). Either of two tall, widely cultivated perennial plants of the genus *Acanthus,* with purple-tinged whitish flowers. *A. mollis* has ovate leaves, while those of *A. longifolius* are deeply lobed.

bear's-ear (báirz-eer) *n.* A plant, the **auricula** *(see).*

bear·skin (báir-skin) *n.* **1.** Something, such as a rug, made from the skin of a bear. **2.** A tall military headdress made of black fur. **—bear·skin** *adj.*

beast (beest) *n.* **1.** Any animal except a human; especially, any large, four-footed animal. **2.** The qualities of an animal; animal nature. **3.** A brutal or odious person. [Middle English *beste,* from Old French, from Latin *bēstia*†.]

beast·ly (béestli) *adj.* **-lier, -liest. 1.** Of or like a beast; bestial. **2.** *Informal.* Disagreeable; nasty; abominable.

~adv. Harshly; bitterly: *It's beastly cold outside.* **—beast·li·ness** *n.*

beast of burden *n.* An animal used for transporting loads.

beast of prey *n.* An animal that kills and eats other animals.

beat (beet) *v.* **beat, beaten** (béet'n) or **beat, beating, beats.** *—tr.* **1. a.** To strike or hit repeatedly. **b.** To strike (a drum, for example) in order to produce a noise. **2.** To punish by hitting or whipping; flog. **3.** To pound or strike against repeatedly: *waves beating the shore.* **4.** To shape or break by repeated blows; forge. **5.** To make flat by pounding or trampling. **6.** To mix rapidly with an instrument to a frothy consistency: *beat two eggs in a bowl.* **7.** To flap (wings, for example). **8.** To sound (a signal), as on a drum. **9.** To mark or count (time or rhythm) with the hands or with a baton. **10.** To disturb (bushes, for example) in order to drive out game for shooting. **11.** To defeat or subdue. **12.** *Informal.* To excel or surpass. **13.** To evade or overcome (a problem, for example). **14.** To succeed or arrive in advance of; forestall: *They beat us to it.* **15.** *Slang.* To perplex or baffle. *—intr.* **1.** To inflict repeated blows. **2.** To throb or pulsate rhythmically. **3.** *Physics.* **a.** To cause beating by superposing waves of different frequencies. **b.** To undergo beating. Said of waves of alternating electrical signals. **4.** To emit sound when struck: *The gong beat thunderously.* **5.** To sound a signal, as on a drum. **6.** To admit of rapid whipping to a froth. **7.** To hunt through woods or undergrowth to drive out game. **8.** *Nautical.* To progress against the wind by tacking. —See Synonyms at **defeat, pulsate. —beat back.** To force to retreat or withdraw. **—beat down.** To force or persuade (a seller) to accept a lower price. **—beat it.** *Slang.* To get going; go away. Usually used in the imperative. **—beat off.** To drive away. **—beat up.** *Informal.* To give a thorough beating to; thrash.

~n. **1.** A stroke or blow, especially one that produces a sound or acts as a signal. **2.** A periodic pulsation or throb. **3.** *Physics.* An amplitude pulse produced by beating. **4.** *Music.* **a.** A regular and rhythmical unit of time. **b.** The pulse given to a piece of music by the recurrence of this unit. **c.** The gesture given by a conductor or the symbol representing this unit of time. **5.** The measured and rhythmical sound of verse; metre. **6.** The area regularly covered by a policeman, sentry, or newspaper reporter. **7.** A process of disturbing the undergrowth to drive out game when shooting. **8.** A member of the beat generation. **9.** *U.S. Slang.* A **scoop** *(see)* in journalism. —See Synonyms at **rhythm.**

~adj. Informal. Worn-out; exhausted: *She was dead beat.* [Beat, beat, beaten; Middle English *beten, bette, beten,* Old English *bēatan, bēot, bēaten.*]

beat·en (béet'n) *adj.* **1.** Defeated; completely baffled. **2.** Made thin or formed by hammering. **3.** Worn by many footsteps; much travelled: *a beaten path.* **4.** *Chiefly U.S.* Exhausted; worn out. **—off the beaten track** or **path. 1.** In a remote, out-of-the-way place. **2.** Not well-known; unusual.

beat·er (béetər) *n.* **1.** One that beats, especially an instrument for beating: *a carpet beater.* **2.** A person who drives wild game from under cover for a hunter.

beat generation *n.* In the 1950s, a group of young Americans, including Jack Kerouac, Allen Ginsberg, and William Burroughs, who expressed disillusionment with Western values and turned for inspiration to Eastern religion, trying experimental literary forms, and adopting a Bohemian lifestyle. [Perhaps from BEATEN (exhausted).]

be·a·tif·ic (bee-ə-tíffik) *adj.* **1.** Showing or producing exalted joy or blessedness: *a beatific smile.* **2.** *Theology.* Pertaining to the joys of heaven. [Late Latin *beātificus* : Latin *beātus*, blessed, from the past participle of *beāre*, to make happy + *facere*, to do.] —**be·a·tif·i·cal·ly** *adv.*

be·at·i·fy (bee-átti-fī) *tr.v.* **-fied, -fying, -fies. 1.** To make blessedly happy. **2.** *Roman Catholic Church.* To proclaim (a deceased person) to be one of the blessed and thus worthy of public religious honour, usually prior to canonisation. **3.** To exalt above all others. [Late Latin *beātificāre*, from *beātificus*, BEATIFIC.] —**be·at·i·fi·ca·tion** (-fi-káysh'n) *n.*

beat·ing (béeting) *n.* **1.** Punishment by whipping, flogging, or thrashing. **2.** A defeat. **3.** A throbbing or pulsation, as of the heart. **4.** *Physics.* The periodic alternation of amplitude maxima and minima produced by interference between two waves of different frequency.

be·at·i·tude (bee-átti-tewd, ‖ -tōōd) *n.* **1.** Supreme blessedness or happiness. **2.** *Capital* B. Any of the nine declarations of blessedness made by Jesus in the Sermon on the Mount. Matthew 5:3-11. [Latin *beātitūdo*, from *beātus*, blessed. See **beatific**.]

Beat·les (béet'lz), **The.** English pop group, comprising John Lennon (1940-80), Ringo Starr (1940-), Paul McCartney (1942-), and George Harrison (1943-). They were all born in Liverpool and began performing together in Liverpool clubs in 1960. They first gained international fame in 1962, with records such as "Love Me Do" and "Please Please Me". For the next eight years they were the most famous pop group in the world. The group disbanded in 1970.

beat·nik (béetnik) *n.* **1.** A member of the beat generation. **2.** Especially in the 1950s, a person whose dress and behaviour showed pointed, often exaggerated, disregard for conventional norms. [BEAT + -NIK.]

Bea·ton (béet'n), **Sir Cecil (Walter Hardy)** (1904-80). English photographer, internationally famous for his portraits of celebrities. He also designed many film and stage shows, including *My Fair Lady* (1964).

beau (bō) *n., pl.* **beaus** (bōz) or **beaux** (bōz). **1.** The sweetheart of a woman or girl. Now usually used humorously. **2.** A man excessively interested in fine clothes and social etiquette; a dandy. [French, fine, handsome, from Latin *bellus*, pretty, handsome, fine.]

Beau Brum·mell (bō brúmm'l) *n.* A dandy; a fop. [After George Bryan ("Beau") BRUMMELL (1778-1840), British dandy.]

Beauce (bōss). Flat limestone plain in northwestern France, lying between the rivers Seine and Loire and stretching from Paris south to the Orléans Forest. The central town of the region is Chartres. The plain is one of the principal regions of France for the cultivation of wheat and sugar-beet.

Beau·fort (bō-fərt, -fawrt), **Margaret, Countess of Richmond and Derby** (1443-1509). English noblewoman, known for her piety and good works. She was the mother of Henry VII, by the first of three husbands, Edmund Tudor, Earl of Richmond. She founded Christ's College, Cambridge (1505) and, by a testamentary endowment, St. John's College, Cambridge (1511).

Beaufort scale *n.* A scale on which successive ranges of wind velocities at 10 metres (32.8 feet) above the ground are assigned code numbers from 0 to 12, corresponding to names from *calm* to *hurricane.* [After Sir Francis *Beaufort* (1774-1857), British admiral.]

Beaufort Sea. Sea in the Arctic Ocean, lying between Point Barrow, Alaska, and the Canadian Arctic Archipelago. It is never free of pack ice.

beau geste *n.* (bō zhést) *pl.* **beaux gestes** (*pronounced as singular*) or **beau gestes** (zhésts). **1.** A gracious gesture. **2.** A gesture noble in form but meaningless in substance. [French, "beautiful gesture".]

Beau·har·nais (bō-aar-náy), **Alexandre, Vicomte de** (1760-94). French general, who fought on the side of the revolutionaries in the American War of Independence and then in France in the Revolutionary army. He was guillotined during the Reign of Terror.

beau i·de·al (bō éeday-ál ‖ ī-dée-əl) *n., pl.* **beaux ideals** (bōz). **1.** The concept of perfect beauty. **2.** An idealised type or model. [French *beau idéal*, "ideal beauty".]

Beau·jo·lais¹ (bōzhə-lay ‖ -láy). Hilly region of eastern central France, lying west of the river Saône between Mâcon and Lyon. It is one of the most famous wine districts in France.

Beau·jo·lais² (bōzhə-lay ‖ U.S. bōzhō-láy). *Often small* **b.** A light red or white wine from central France.

Beau·mar·chais (bō-maar-sháy), **Pierre Auguste Caron de** (1732-99). French dramatist. His two most famous plays, both rich with comic innuendo against feudal privileges, served as the basis for Rossini's *The Barber of Seville* (1775) and Mozart's *The Marriage of Figaro* (1784).

Beaune (bōn). Small town in Côte d'Or département in southeastern France. The centre of the Burgundy wine industry, its vineyards date from the period of Roman occupation.

beaut (bewt) *n. Slang.* Something outstanding of its kind. —*adj. Australian Slang.* Very fine. [Short for BEAUTY, BEAUTIFUL.]

beau·te·ous (béwt-yəss, -i-əss) *adj. Poetic.* Beautiful, especially to the sight. —**beau·te·ous·ly** *adv.* —**beau·te·ous·ness** *n.*

beau·ti·cian (bew-tish'n) *n.* One skilled in cosmetic treatment, especially one working in a beauty salon. [BEAUT(Y) + -ICIAN.]

beau·ti·ful (béwti-f'l, -fōōl) *adj.* **1.** Pleasing to the senses. **2.** Pleasing to the mind: *a beautiful irony.* **3.** Excellent. **4.** Desirable; of great worth: *Small is beautiful.* ~*n.* Beauty, as an aesthetic or philosophical principle. Preceded by *the.* —**beau·ti·ful·ly** (-fli, -fōōli) *adv.* —**beau·ti·ful·ness** *n.* **Synonyms:** *beautiful, lovely, pretty, handsome, comely, fair.*

beautiful people *pl.n.* **1.** That section of society which is young, fashionable, and affluent. **2.** Hippies collectively.

beau·ti·fy (béwti-fī) *v.* **-fied, -fying, -fies.** —*tr.* To make beautiful; adorn. —*intr.* To become beautiful. [BEAUT(Y) + -FY.] —**beau·ti·fi·ca·tion** (-fi-káysh'n) *n.* —**beau·ti·fi·er** *n.*

beau·ty (béwti) *n., pl.* **-ties. 1.** A quality which appeals to the senses or the mind through harmony of form or colour, excellence of artistry or craftsmanship, truthfulness, originality, or some other, often unspecifiable, property. **2.** Appearance or sound that arouses a strong, contemplative delight; loveliness: *a man who has preserved his youthful beauty.* **3.** A person or thing that arouses such delight; especially, a woman widely regarded as beautiful. **4.** A part, characteristic, or attribute that arouses such delight; a specific excellence or grace. **5.** The feature that is most effective, gratifying, or telling: *The beauty of the venture is that we stand to lose nothing.* **6.** *Informal.* An outstanding or conspicuous example. **7.** *Physics.* A quantum number, **bottom** *(see).* [Middle English *beau(l)te*, from Old French *bealte, beaute*, from Vulgar Latin *bellitās* (unattested), from Latin *bellus*, pretty, handsome, fine.]

beauty contest *n.* A competition in which a number of young women, often wearing swimming costumes, parade before a panel of judges that chooses a winner on the basis of looks.

beauty queen *n.* A young woman who has won a beauty contest or who enters such contests.

beauty salon *n.* An establishment providing women with services that include hair treatment, manicures, facials, and the like. Also called "beauty parlour", "beauty shop".

beauty sleep *n.* Sleep, especially in the hours before midnight, supposed to preserve a youthful appearance.

beauty spot *n.* **1.** Formerly, a small black mark glued on a woman's face or shoulders to accentuate the fairness of her skin. Also called "patch". **2.** A mole or freckle. **3.** A place of outstanding natural beauty.

Beau·vais (bō-váy). Town in the Oise département in northern France. Its world-famous tapestry works, established as a royal factory in the 17th century, was destroyed in World War II. The Cathedral of St. Pierre, intended to be the largest in Christendom, was never completed, but its Gothic choir remains the loftiest (48 metres; 157 feet) in the world.

Beau·voir (bō-vwaar, -vwár), **Simone de** (1908-86). French writer and feminist thinker. For many years the lover of Jean-Paul Sartre, she devoted much of her writing to the exploration of existentialist themes. Her best-known works are the feminist treatise, *The Second Sex* (1949-50), her autobiography, and the study of different cultures' treatment of old age, *The Coming of Age* (1970).

beaux. Alternative plural of **beau**.

beaux-arts (bō-zár) *pl.n. French.* The fine arts.

bea·ver¹ (béevər) *n.* **1.** A large, amphibious rodent, genus *Castor*, of Eurasia and North America, having thick brown fur, webbed hind feet, a paddle-like, hairless tail, and chisel-like front teeth adapted for gnawing bark and felling trees used to build dams. **2.** The fur of a beaver. **3.** *Rare.* **a.** A full beard. **b.** A bearded man. **4.** A top hat, originally made of the beaver's underfur. **5.** A napped wool fabric, similar to felt, used for outer garments. **6.** Greyish brown to light or dark greyish yellowish brown. ~*intr.v.* **beavered, -vering, -vers.** To work with determination. Used with *away*. [Middle English *bever*, Old English *be(o)for*.]

beaver². Variant of **bevor**.

bea·ver·board (béevər-bawrd ‖ -bōrd) *n.* A light semirigid building material of compressed wood pulp, used for walls and partitions. [From the former trademark *Beaverboard.*]

Bea·ver·brook (béevər-brook), **(William) Max(well) Aitken, 1st Baron** (1879-1964). British press baron, financier, and politician, born in Canada. He came to England in 1910, was elected to Parliament, and remained in the House of Commons until 1917, when he was given a peerage. He gained control of the *Daily Express* in 1916, and the *Evening Standard* in 1923. He was Minister of Aircraft Production (1940-41), of War Production (1942), and Lord Privy Seal (1943-45). His writings include *Politicians and the War, 1914-1916* (1928), and *Men and Power 1917-1918* (1956).

be·bop (béebop) *n.* A type of music, **bop** *(see).* [Imitative of a two-beat phrase in this music.]

be·calm (bi-kaám, bə- ‖ -kaálm) *tr.v.* **-calmed, -calming, -calms. 1.** To render (a ship) motionless for lack of wind. **2.** To make calm or still; soothe.

be·came. Past tense of **become**.

be·cause (bi-kóz, bə-, -káz ‖ bee-, -káwz, -kúz, -káwss) *conj.* **1.** For the reason that; since. **2.** *Nonstandard.* The fact that: *Because you're here doesn't mean that I'm ready.* —**because of.** By reason of; on account of. [Middle English *bi cause* : *bi*, BY + CAUSE.]

Usage: In clauses introduced by *The reason that. . .or The reason is. . .,* the use of *because* is common but superfluous. In a sentence like *The reason why you're tired is because you went to bed late* the notion of "cause" is expressed twice; it is sufficient to say *The reason you're tired is that you went to bed late*, or, more simply, *You're tired because you went to bed late.*

bec·ca·fi·co (béckə-féekō) *n., pl.* **-cos.** Any small songbird or warbler of various genera, eaten as a delicacy in Italy. [Italian, "figpecker" : *beccare*, to peck, from *becco*, BEAK + *fico*, FIG.]

bé·cha·mel sauce (bésha-mel, báyshə, -mél). *n.* A white sauce, made from butter, flour, milk or cream, and seasonings. Also called "sauce béchamel". [French *sauce béchamelle*, after Louis de *Béchamel*, former general of Louis XIV, who invented it.]

be·chance (bi-cháanss, bə- ‖ bee-, -chánss) *v.* **-chanced, -chancing, -chances.** *Rare.* —*intr.* To happen; chance. —*tr.* To befall; happen to.

bêche-de-mer (bésh-də-maír) *n., pl.* **bêches-de-mer** (*pronounced as singular*). **1.** A marine animal, the **trepang** (*see*), or a food prepared from it. **2.** A lingua franca that combines Malay and English, spoken in the southwest Pacific. In this sense, also called "beach-lamar". [French, from earlier *biche de mer*, from Portuguese *bicho do mar*, "sea worm" : *bicho*, worm, from Late Latin *bēstulus*, diminutive of Latin *bēstia*, BEAST + *mar*, sea, from Latin *mare*. The designation of the language is probably from the use of trepang as an important trade item in this area.]

Bech·stein (békstīn) *n.* A trademark for a fine make of piano.

Bech·u·a·na (béchoo-áanə, be-chwáanə; *also, wrongly,* béckew-) *n., pl.* **-nas** or collectively **Bechuana.** **1.** A former name for a member of a Bantu people inhabiting Botswana in south-central Africa. **2.** A language, **Tswana** (*see*).

Bech·u·a·na·land (bech-wá-nə-land, -oo-áa-) See **Botswana.**

beck[1] (bek) *n.* A gesture of beckoning or summons. —**at (someone's) beck and call.** Having to carry out someone's every wish. [Middle English, from *beckon*, to BECKON.]

beck[2] *n. Northern English.* A small brook. [Middle English, from Old Norse *bekkr.*]

Beck·er (béckər), **Boris** (1967-). German tennis player. He became the youngest ever Wimbledon men's singles champion in 1985 at the age of 17, and won the title again in 1986 and 1989. He won the U.S. title in 1989, the Australian title in 1991 and the Grand Slam Cup in 1996.

beck·et (béckit) *n. Nautical.* A device, such as a looped rope, hook and eye, strap, or grommet, for holding or fastening loose ropes, spars, or oars in position. [18th century : origin obscure.]

Beck·et (béckit), **Saint Thomas** (1118–70). English cleric, also known as Thomas à Becket. He entered the household of Theobald, Archbishop of Canterbury in *c.* 1142 and was appointed Archdeacon of Canterbury in 1154. In the same year Henry II made him his Chancellor. Appointed Archbishop of Canterbury in 1162, he fell into disfavour with Henry by becoming the spokesman for the Church. Charged in 1164 with misappropriating crown funds as Chancellor, Becket fled the country and remained in exile for six years. He returned in 1170 and immediately became embroiled in the controversy surrounding Henry's illegal appointment of his eldest son as Archbishop of York. At Henry's behest, four knights of the royal household murdered Becket in Canterbury cathedral on 29 December. He was canonised in 1173.

Beck·ett (béckit), **Samuel (Barclay)** (1906–89). Irish playwright, novelist, and critic. He settled in Paris in 1937, and many of his works were written in both French and English. His first novel, *Murphy* (1938), was followed by *Malone Dies* (1951) and *Molloy* (1951). He is known to a wider audience for his plays in the style of the Theatre of the Absurd, especially *Waiting for Godot* (1952), *Endgame* (1957), *Krapp's Last Tape* (1959), and *Happy Days* (1961). In 1969 he won the Nobel prize for literature.

Beck·mann (bék-man), **Max** (1884–1950). German painter and print-maker. Beckmann developed an Expressionist manner under the influence of **Munch**, and in the 1920s he came to his most lasting style, the painting of brutal, often grotesque, large figurative canvases.

Beck·mann thermometer (békmən) *n.* A mercury thermometer with a small adjustable range, used in scientific experiments for the accurate measurement of small temperature changes. [After Ernst *Beckmann* (died 1923), German chemist.]

beck·on (béckən) *v.* **-oned, -oning, -ons.** —*tr.* **1.** To signal or summon (another), as by nodding or waving. **2.** To attract as if with gestures; invite: *a sunny day that seemed to beckon them outside.* —*intr.* **1.** To make a summoning or signalling gesture. **2.** To be attractive or enticing.
~*n. Archaic.* A gesture or motion of summons. [Middle English *beknen*, Old English *bēcnan, bīecnan.*] —**beck·on·er** *n.* —**beck·on·ing·ly** *adv.*

be·cloud (bi-klówd, bə- ‖ bee-) *tr.v.* **-clouded, -clouding, -clouds.** **1.** To darken with clouds. **2.** To confuse; obscure.

be·come (bi-kúm, bə- ‖ bee-) *v.* **-came** (-káym), **-come, -coming, -comes.** —*intr.* To grow or come to be: *After two months together, their relationship was becoming predictable.* —*tr.* **1.** To be appropriate or suitable to: *"it would not become me … to interfere with parties"* (Jonathan Swift). **2.** To show to advantage; look good with or on. —**become of.** To be the fate or subsequent condition of; happen to. [Middle English *becomen*, Old English *becuman* : BE- + COME.]

be·com·ing (bi-kúmming, bə- ‖ bee-) *adj.* **1.** Appropriate; suitable; proper. **2.** Pleasing or attractive to the eye. —**be·com·ing·ly** *adv.*

bec·que·rel (bécka-rél, békwə-) *n.* A unit of activity of a radioactive material in the SI system, equal to an activity of one nuclear disintegration per second. [After Antoine Henri BECQUEREL.]

Bec·que·rel (bécka-rél), **Antoine Henri** (1852–1908). French physi-

cist, grandson of Antoine César (1788–1878), one of the first investigators of electrochemistry, and son of Alexandre Edmond (1820–91), the inventor of the phosphoroscope. Principally devoted to the study of the effect of the earth's magnetism on the atmosphere, he discovered radioactivity in uranium (1896) and shared the Nobel prize for physics with Marie and Pierre Curie (1903).

bed (bed) *n.* **1. a.** A piece of furniture for reclining and sleeping, typically consisting of a flat, rectangular frame, a mattress resting on springs, and bedclothes. **b.** A bedstead. **c.** A mattress or a mattress with bedclothes. **2. a.** Rest or sleep. **b.** Any place or surface upon which one may rest or sleep. **c.** A place where one may sleep for the night; a lodging. **3. a.** Sexual intercourse. **b.** A situation of sexual intimacy: *I give all my secrets away in bed.* **4.** A small plot of cultivated or planted land: *a flower bed.* **5.** The bottom of a watercourse or other body of water. **6.** Part of a river or sea bed used for cultivation, especially of oysters. **7.** A supporting, underlying, or securing part, especially: **a.** A layer of food on which another kind of food rests: *lobster on a bed of rice.* **b.** A foundation of crushed rock or a similar substance for a road or railway; a roadbed. **c.** A layer of mortar upon which stones or bricks are laid. **d.** The flat underside of something, as of a brick. **e.** The heavy table of a printing press in which the type forme is placed. **8.** *Geology.* **a.** A rock **stratum** (*see*). **b.** A deposit, as of ore or lava, parallel to the local stratification. Compare **mass, vein.** —**be brought to bed.** *Archaic.* To give birth. Used with *of* : *be brought to bed of a child.* —**go to bed with.** *Informal.* To have sexual intercourse with. —**put** or **go to bed.** In journalism, to send or go to press; have or be printed. ~*v.* **bedded, bedding, beds.** —*tr.* **1.** To provide with a bed or sleeping place. **2.** To put to bed. **3.** To embed. **4.** To make a bed for; spread litter for. Usually used with *down*: *She bedded down the sheep under a lean-to.* **5.** To plant in a prepared bed of soil. Usually used with *out.* **6.** To lay flat or arrange in layers. **7.** To have sexual intercourse with. —*intr.* **1.** To go to bed. Usually used with *down.* **2.** To form layers or strata. [Middle English *bed(e)*, Old English *bed(d)*, from Germanic *badhjam* (unattested).]

B.Ed. Bachelor of Education.

bed and board *n.* Sleeping accommodation and meals.

bed and breakfast *n. Abbr.* **b. & b.** *British.* **1.** Overnight accommodation and breakfast. **2.** A guest house or private house providing this. —**bed-and-breakfast** *adj.*

bed and breakfasting *n. Finance.* A method of tax avoidance whereby shares are sold one day and bought back the next day to avoid capital gains tax. [Referring to the temporary nature of the transaction, as if it were bed and breakfast accommodation.]

be·daub (bi-dáwb, bə- ‖ bee-) *tr.v.* **-daubed, -daubing, -daubs. 1.** To smear; soil. **2.** To ornament in a vulgar and showy fashion.

be·daz·zle (bi-dázz'l, bə- ‖ bee-) *tr.v.* **-zled, -zling, -zles.** To dazzle so completely as to confuse or blind. —**be·daz·zle·ment** *n.*

bed·bug, bed bug (béd-bug) *n.* A wingless, bloodsucking insect of the genus *Cimex*; especially, *C. lectularius*, that has a flat, reddish body and a disagreeable odour and that often infests dirty human dwellings.

bed·cham·ber (béd-chaymbər) *n. Archaic.* A bedroom.

bed·clothes (béd-klōthz, -klōz) *pl.n.* Coverings, such as sheets and blankets, used on a bed.

bed·da·ble (béddəb'l) *adj.* Sexually attractive; potentially satisfying as a sexual partner.

bed·der (béddər) *n.* At Cambridge University, a usually female employee of a college who makes students' beds and tidies their rooms. Compare **scout** (college servant).

bed·ding (bédding) *n.* **1.** Bedclothes. **2.** Straw or similar material for animals to sleep on. **3.** Something that forms a foundation or bottom layer. **4.** *Geology.* Stratification or layering of rocks.

bedding plant *n.* A young ornamental plant ready and suitable to be bedded out in the garden.

Bede (beed), **Saint** (*c.* 673–735). Anglo-Saxon Benedictine monk and scholar known as the "The Venerable Bede". His theological works gained him the title of Doctor of the Church, the only Englishman so honoured. He is best known for *Historia Ecclesiastica Gentis Anglorum (Ecclesiastical History of the English Nation)*, a record of the spread of Christianity and Anglo-Saxon culture in Britain. He was canonised in 1899.

be·deck (bi-dék, bə- ‖ bee-) *tr.v.* **-decked, -decking, -decks.** To deck out or adorn in a showy fashion; cover with decorations.

bedes·man (béedz-mən) *n., pl.* **-men** (-mən). Formerly, an almsman. [Variant of *beadsman*, an almsman who had promised to pray (or say the rosary) for his benefactor.]

be·dev·il (bi-devv'l, bə- ‖ bee-) *tr.v.* **-illed** or *U.S.* **-iled, -illing** or *U.S.* **-iling, -ils. 1.** To torment devilishly; plague; harass. **2.** To worry, annoy, or frustrate. **3.** To possess as with a devil; bewitch. **4.** To spoil; ruin. —**be·dev·il·ment** *n.*

be·dew (bi-déw, bə- ‖ bee-, -dŏŏ) *tr.v.* **-dewed, -dewing, -dews.** To wet with or as if with dew.

bed·fel·low (béd-fellō) *n.* **1.** A person with whom one shares a bed; a bedmate. **2.** A temporary associate, collaborator, or ally.

Bed·ford (bédfərd). Town in central England, lying on the river Ouse. The county town of Bedfordshire, it was the site of a British victory over the Saxons in 571, and is now an industrial centre.

Bedford cord *n.* A heavy cotton or woollen fabric in a ribbed weave with wide or narrow raised cords, similar to corduroy. [After BEDFORD, where it was made.]

Bed·ford·shire (bédfərd-shər, -sheer ‖ -shīr). County in central

England, most of it lying in the fertile valley of the river Ouse (the Great Ouse). Its county town is Bedford.

be·dight (bi-dít, ba- || bee-) *tr.v.* **-dight, -dight** or **-dighted, -dighting, -dights.** *Archaic.* To dress or adorn. [Middle English *bedighten* : *be-*, thoroughly + DIGHT.]

be·dim (bi-dím, ba- || bee-) *tr.v.* **-dimmed, -dimming, -dims.** To make dim.

be·di·zen (bi-dīz'n, ba-, -dízz'n || bee-) *tr.v.* **-zened, -zening, -zens.** To dress or ornament vulgarly or tastelessly. [BE- + DIZEN.] —**be·di·zen·ment** *n.*

bed jacket *n.* A woman's jacket worn when sitting up in bed.

bed·lam (béd·ləm) *n.* **1.** Any place or scene of noisy uproar and confusion. **2.** *Archaic.* A lunatic asylum; a madhouse. [Middle English *Bedlem, Bethlem,* Hospital of St. Mary of *Bethlehem,* in southeastern London, which was an asylum at one time.]

bed linen *n.* The sheets and pillowcases used on a bed.

Bed·ling·ton terrier (béd·lingtən) *n.* A dog of a breed developed in England, having long legs and a woolly greyish or brownish coat. [After *Bedlington,* Northumberland.]

bed·mate (béd-mayt) *n.* One with whom a bed is shared.

bed moulding *n. Architecture.* **1.** The moulding between the corona and frieze of an entablature. **2.** Any moulding below a projection.

bed of roses *n.* A state of idyllic comfort or luxury.

Bed·ou·in, Bed·u·in (béddoo-in) *n., pl.* **-ins** or collectively **Bedouin.** **1.** An Arab of any of the nomadic tribes of the deserts of North Africa, Arabia, Jordan, and Syria. **2.** Loosely, a wanderer. [Middle English *Bedoin,* from Old French *beduin,* from Arabic *badāwīn,* desert dwellers, plural of *badāwī,* from *badw,* desert.] —**Bed·ou·in** *adj.*

bed·pan (béd-pan) *n.* **1.** A metal, glass, or plastic receptacle for the excreta of people who are bedridden. **2.** A **warming pan** *(see).*

bed·plate (béd-playt) *n.* A metal plate, frame, or platform serving as a base or support for a machine.

bed·post (béd-pōst) *n.* Any of the four vertical posts at the corners of some beds.

be·drag·gled (bi-drágg'ld, ba- || bee-) *adj.* Wet, limp, and untidy. Said of the hair, clothes, or appearance.

bed·rid·den (béd-ridd'n) *adj.* Confined to one's bed because of illness or infirmity. [Middle English *bedreden, bedrede,* Old English *bedrida,* from noun, "one who is bedridden" : BED + *rīda,* a rider, from *rīdan,* to RIDE.]

bed·rock (béd-rok) *n.* **1.** The solid rock that underlies all soil, sand, clay, gravel, and loose material on the earth's surface. **2.** The lowest or bottom level. **3.** Fundamental principles.

bed·roll (béd-rōl) *n.* A portable roll of bedding used especially by campers and others who sleep outdoors. Compare **sleeping bag.**

bed·room (béd-rōōm, -rōōm) *n.* A room for sleeping in.

bed·set·tee (béd-se-tée, -sə-) *n.* A settee which can fold down to form a bed.

bed·side (béd-sīd) *n.* The space alongside a bed, especially the bed of a sick person.
~*adj.* Near a bed: *a bedside table.*

bedside manner *n.* The attitude and conduct of a doctor in the presence of a patient, intended to inspire confidence and allay fears.

bed·sit·ter (béd-síttər) *n.* A form of furnished accommodation, usually designed for a single person, consisting of a single room for both sleeping and daytime use. Also called "bedsit", "bed-sitting room".

bed·sore (béd-sawr || -sōr) *n.* A pressure-induced ulceration of the skin with necrosis and sometimes deep muscular infection, occurring during long confinement in bed. Also called "decubitus ulcer", "pressure sore".

bed·spread (béd-spred) *n.* A usually decorative bed covering.

bed·stead (béd-sted, -stid) *n.* The frame of a bed, which supports the mattress.

bed·straw (béd-straw) *n.* Any of various plants of the genus *Galium,* such as *G. verum* (lady's bedstraw), having whorled leaves, small white or yellow flowers, and prickly burrs. [After its former use as a mattress stuffing.]

bed·time (béd-tīm) *n.* The time when one goes or should go to bed.

Beduin. Variant of **Bedouin.**

bed·wet·ting (béd-wetting) *n.* Urinating in bed, especially when considered as a condition that may require medical or psychiatric treatment; nocturnal **enuresis** *(see).* —**bed·wet·ter** *n.*

bed table *n.* A small table which can be placed over a bed, especially for the use of sick persons.

bee¹ (bee) *n.* **1.** Any of various winged, hairy-bodied, usually stinging insects of the order Hymenoptera, including many solitary species, such as the **carpenter bee** and **leaf-cutting bee** *(both of which see),* as well as the social members of the family Apidae. They are characterised by structures for sucking nectar and gathering pollen from flowers. See **bumblebee, honeybee. 2.** *Chiefly U.S.* A social gathering where people combine work, competition, and amusement: *a spelling bee.* [Middle English *bee,* Old English *bēo.*]

bee² *n.* A bee block. [Middle English *bege,* a ring of metal, Old English *bēag.*]

Beeb (beeb) *n. Informal.* The British Broadcasting Corporation. Used as a nickname, preceded by *the.*

bee block *n. Nautical.* A piece of hardwood on either side of a bowsprit through which forestays are reeved. Also called "bee".

bee·bread (bée-bred) *n.* A brownish substance consisting of a mixture of pollen and nectar, fed by bees to their larvae. Also called "ambrosia".

beech (beech) *n.* **1.** Any tree of the genus *Fagus,* characterised by

smooth, light-coloured bark and edible nuts partly enclosed in a prickly husk, especially *F. sylvatica,* of Europe. **2.** Any tree of the genus *Nothofagus,* of the Southern Hemisphere, similar to the northern beeches but with evergreen leaves. **3.** The wood of any of these trees. [Middle English *beche,* Old English *bēce.*] —**beech** *adj.*

Bee·cham (béechəm), **Sir Thomas** (1879–1961). British symphony conductor. He founded the London Philharmonic (1932) and the Royal Philharmonic (1946) orchestras and did much to popularise the works of Delius.

beech marten *n.* A **stone marten** *(see).*

beech mast *n.* The nuts of the beech tree; beechnuts.

beech·nut (béech-nut) *n.* The small, triangular nut of the beech tree, which provides food for livestock.

beedi, beedie (bée·di) *n.* A hand-rolled cigarette, tied with thread, originating in India. [Hindi.]

bee-eat·er (bée-eetər) *n.* Any of various chiefly tropical Old World birds of the family Meropidae, having brightly coloured plumage and a downward-curving bill, and feeding chiefly on bees.

beef (beef) *n., pl.* **beeves** (beevz) or **beefs** (only form for sense 4). **1.** The flesh of a slaughtered full-grown bull, ox, or cow. **2.** A full-grown bull, ox, or cow, especially one intended for use as meat. **3.** *Informal.* Human muscle; brawn. **4.** *Slang.* A complaint. ~*intr.v.* **beefed, beefing, beefs.** *Slang.* To complain. —**beef up.** *Slang.* To reinforce; build up; fill out. [Middle English *boef, beef,* beef, ox, from Old French *boef,* from Latin *bōs* (stem *bov-*), ox.] —**beef** *adj.*

beef bour·gui·gnon *n.* (bóor-geen-yón) *n.* Also *French* **boeuf bour·gui·gnon** (bérf, bóf || bóof). Braised cubes of beef simmered in a seasoned sauce with red wine, mushrooms, carrots, and onions. [Partial translation of French *boeuf bourguignon,* beef Burgundy style, from *Bourgogne,* BURGUNDY.]

beef·burg·er (béef-burgər) *n.* A hamburger.

beef·cake (béef-kayk) *n. Slang.* **1.** A photograph, as in an advertisement, of a scantily clothed man showing his muscular physique. **2.** Such photographs collectively. **3.** Men who appear, or look as though they might appear, in such photographs. Compare **cheesecake.** [By analogy with CHEESECAKE.]

beef cattle *pl.n.* Cows, bulls, or oxen bred and raised for meat.

beef·eat·er (béef-eetər) *n. Informal.* A yeoman of the royal guard in England or a yeoman warder of the Tower of London, wearing a characteristic red and gold or red and black uniform. [17th century : popular term for a well-fed servant.]

bee fly *n.* Any of various flies of the family Bombyliidae, resembling bees and having larvae that are parasitic on the young of bees, wasps, and other insects.

beef·steak (béef-stayk) *n.* A thick slice of beef, as from the loin or the hindquarters, suitable for grilling or frying.

beef stro·ga·noff (strógga-nof || *U.S.* stróga-, stráwga-, -nawf) *n.* Thinly sliced beef fillet sautéed and served with mushrooms and sour cream. [After Count Paul *Stroganoff,* 19th-century Russian diplomat.]

beef tea *n.* Broth made from beef extract or by boiling pieces of lean beef, often used as a restorative and for invalids.

beef Wellington *n.* Roast fillet of beef, covered with pâté de foie gras and pastry, and baked. [After the 1st Duke of WELLINGTON.]

beef·wood (béef-wŏod) *n.* Any of various trees of the genus *Casuarina,* mostly native to Australia, having small, scalelike leaves and flowers and very hard wood. Also called "she-oak". [Perhaps from its reddish colour.]

beef·y (béefi) *adj.* **-ier, -iest. 1.** Resembling beef. **2.** Muscular in build; heavy; brawny. —**beef·i·ness** *n.*

bee·hive (bée-hīv) *n.* **1.** A hive, either natural or man-made, for bees. **2.** Any place teeming with activity. **3.** A hairstyle in which the hair is backcombed and piled on top of the head.

bee·hive shelf *n.* A small circular glass or porcelain shelf with a hole in the top, used in chemistry for collecting gases over water.

bee·keep·er (bée-keepər) *n.* One who keeps bees; an apiarist.

bee·line (bée-līn) *n.* A fast, direct course. Used chiefly in the phrase *make a beeline for.* [From the belief that a pollen-laden bee flies straight back to its hive.]

Be·el·ze·bub (bee-élzibub). **1.** The Devil. **2.** In Milton's *Paradise Lost,* the chief of the fallen angels, next to Satan in power. [Late Latin, from Greek *Beelzeboub,* from Hebrew *bá'al zəbūb,* "lord of flies", god of the Ekronites (II Kings 1:2) : *bá'al,* lord + *zəbūb,* fly.]

bee moth *n.* A pyralid moth, such as *Galleria mellonella* that lays its eggs in beehives, where the larvae feed on the honeycombs and the young bees. Also called "wax moth".

been. Past participle of **be.**

been-to, bin·tu (béen-tōō, bín-) *n. Informal.* An African or Asian who has lived in Britain for part of his life, especially one who has received his education there, and has since returned to his country of origin. Used in various African and Asian countries. [From *been to (Britain).*] —**been-to** *adj.*

bee orchid *n.* A European orchid, *Ophrys apifera,* having a flower that resembles a bumblebee.

beep (beep) *n.* A high-pitched sound such as that emitted by a car horn or some types of electrical apparatus.
~*intr.v.* **beeped, beeping, beeps.** To make a beep. [Imitative.]

beer (beer) *n.* **1.** A fermented alcoholic beverage brewed from malt and flavoured with hops. **2.** Any of various drinks made from extracts of roots and plants. **3.** A glass or mug of such a drink. [Middle English *ber(e),* Old English *bēor,* from a West Germanic word, from Late Latin *biber,* a drink, from Latin *bibere,* to drink.]

beer and skittles *n. Slang.* Easygoing existence.
Beer·bohm (béer-bōm), **Sir (Henry) Max(imilian)** (1872-1956). English caricaturist and writer, called by George Bernard Shaw "the incomparable Max". He was the half-brother of the actor-producer, Sir Herbert Beerbohm Tree. His first satirical essays, *The Works of Max Beerbohm,* and his first caricatures, *Caricatures of Twenty-five Gentlemen,* both appeared in 1896. His only novel, *Zuleika Dobson,* an Oxford fantasy, was published in 1911. After 1910, he lived, apart from the World War II years, in Rapallo, Italy. He was knighted in 1939.
beer gut *n.* A person's stomach that is excessively large from the regular consumption of beer or some other alcoholic beverage; a paunch. Also called "gut".
Beer·she·ba (beer-shéebə, béershibə). *Hebrew* **Be'·er She·va'** (bairshévvə). Town in southern Israel. It was famous in Biblical times as the abode of Isaac and Jacob, and as the place where Abraham covenanted with the Philistines. The city is still, as it has been for centuries, a watering place and market centre for the nomadic Bedouins of the Negev.
beer-up (béer-up) *n. Australian Informal.* A bout of drinking.
beer·y (béer-i) *adj.* **-ier, -iest.** 1. Smelling or tasting of beer. 2. Affected or produced by beer. 3. Prone to drinking beer.
bee's knees *n. Used with a singular verb. Informal.* A person or thing considered to be marvellous. Preceded by *the.*
beest·ings, *U.S.* **beast·ings** (béest-ingz) *n. Used with a singular or plural verb.* The first milk given by a cow or other mammal after parturition; colostrum. [Middle English *bestynge* (singular), Old English *bēsting* (unattested), from *bēost,* beestings; akin to Middle Dutch *biest,* Old High German *biost*†.]
bees·wax (béez-waks) *n.* 1. The yellowish to dark brown wax secreted by the honeybee for making honeycombs. 2. Commercial wax obtained by processing and purifying the crude wax of the honeybee, used in making candles, crayons, and polishes.
~*tr.v.* **beeswaxed, -waxing, -waxes.** To polish with this wax.
bees·wing (béez-wing) *n.* 1. A thin crust of tartar scales that sometimes forms on old port or other old wines. 2. Wine affected by this crust. [From *bee's wing.*]
beet (beet) *n.* Any of several widely cultivated plants of the genus *Beta;* especially, *B. vulgaris,* having leaves sometimes eaten as greens and a thickened, fleshy root. See **beetroot, sugar beet.** [Middle English *bete,* Old English *bēte,* from Latin *bēta*†.]
Beet·ho·ven (báyt-hōv'n, -ōv'n), **Ludwig van** (1770-1827). German composer. He was an outstanding representative of the transition from the classical to the romantic era of musical composition. In 1801 his hearing began to fail and by 1819 he was deaf. He was born in Bonn, but settled in Vienna (1792). He wrote music of all genres; e.g., 9 symphonies, 5 piano concertos, one violin concerto, 32 piano sonatas, 10 violin sonatas, 5 cello sonatas, two masses, and one opera, *Fidelio.*
bee·tle¹ (béet'l) *n.* 1. Any of numerous insects of the order Coleoptera, having biting mouth parts and front wings modified to form horny wing covers that overlie the membranous rear wings when at rest. 2. Loosely, any insect resembling a beetle.
~*intr.v.* **beetled, -tling, -tles.** To hurry off; scuttle. Usually used with *off.* [Middle English *bityl,* Old English *bitula, biter,* from *bītan,* to BITE.]
beetle² *adj.* Jutting; overhanging: *beetle brows.*
~*intr.v.* **beetled, -tling, -tles.** To overhang. [Middle English *bitel-(-brouwed),* origin obscure.]
beetle³ *n.* 1. A heavy mallet with a large wooden head. 2. A heavy wooden club used in stamping and finishing handmade linen. 3. A cloth-finishing machine that stamps cloth with revolving wooden hammers.
~*tr.v.* **beetled, -tling, -tles.** 1. To pound with a beetle. 2. To stamp and finish (cloth) with a beetle. [Middle English *betel,* Old English *bētel,* from Germanic *bautilaz* (unattested), from *bautan* (unattested), to BEAT.]
bee·tle-browed (béet'l-browd) *adj.* Having projecting and shaggy eyebrows.
beetle drive *n.* A dice game in which the players are required to draw or assemble a figure representing a beetle. It is often played in order to raise money for charity.
beet·root (béet-rōot ‖ -rōot) *n.* 1. A variety of the beet plant cultivated for its edible root. 2. The bulbous, dark red taproot of this plant, eaten in salads or pickled, for example. **—beet-root** *adj.*
beet sugar *n.* The sugar that is obtained from sugar beet.
beeves. A plural of **beef.**
B.E.F. British Expeditionary Force.
be·fall (bi-fáwl, bə- ‖ bee-) *v.* **-fell** (-fél), **-fallen** (-fáwlən), **-falling, -falls.** *—intr.* To come to pass; happen. *—tr.* To happen to: *"There shall no evil befall thee."* (Psalms 91:10). *—See Synonyms at* **happen.**
be·fit (bi-fít, bə- ‖ bee-) *tr.v.* **-fitted, -fitting, -fits.** To be suitable to or appropriate for.
be·fit·ting (bi-fítting, bə- ‖ bee-) *adj.* Appropriate; suitable; proper. **—be·fit·ting·ly** *adv.*
be·fog (bi-fóg, bə- ‖ bee-, -fáwg) *tr.v.* **-fogged, -fogging, -fogs.** 1. To cover or obscure with or as if with fog; make foggy. 2. To cause confusion in; muddle.
be·fool (bi-fōol, bə- ‖ bee-) *tr.v.* **-fooled, -fooling, -fools.** 1. To make a fool of; hoodwink; trick; deceive. 2. To treat as a fool.
be·fore (bi-fór, bə- ‖ bee-, -fōr) *adv.* 1. In front; ahead; in advance. 2. In the past; previously.

~*prep.* 1. In front of; ahead of. 2. Prior to. 3. Awaiting: *Your happiness lies before you.* 4. In or into the presence of: *She ordered the man to be brought before her.* 5. Under the consideration or jurisdiction of: *the case before the court.* 6. In preference to; sooner than. 7. In advance of, or in precedence to, as in rank, condition, or development: *The princess is before her brother in the line of succession.*
~*conj.* 1. In advance of the time when: *before he went.* 2. Rather than; sooner than: *She would die before she would betray her cause.* [Middle English *before(n),* Old English *beforan,* from Germanic : *bi-* (unattested), BY + *forana* (unattested), from the front.]
be·fore·hand (bi-fór-hand, bə- ‖ bee-, -fōr-) *adv.* In anticipation; in advance; early: *We arrived beforehand.* **—be·fore·hand** *adj.*
be·fore·time (bi-fór-tūm, bə- ‖ bee-, -fōr-) *adv. Rare.* Formerly.
be·foul (bi-fówl, bə- ‖ bee-) *tr.v.* **-fouled, -fouling, -fouls.** 1. To make dirty; soil. 2. To speak badly of; cast aspersions upon.
be·friend (bi-frénd, bə- ‖ bee-) *tr.v.* **-friended, -friending, -friends.** 1. To make friends with; initiate friendship with. 2. To act as a friend to; aid; assist.
be·fud·dle (bi-fúdd'l, bə- ‖ bee-) *tr.v.* **-dled, -dling, -dles.** 1. To confuse; perplex. 2. To stupefy with or as if with alcoholic drink.
beg¹ (beg) *v.* **begged, begging, begs.** *—tr.* 1. To ask for or as charity. 2. To ask earnestly for, or of; entreat. 3. To leave a (point) unresolved. *—intr.* 1. To solicit alms. 2. To make a humble or urgent plea. 3. To sit on the haunches with forepaws raised. Used of a dog. **—beg off.** To seek release from (a penalty or obligation). **—go begging.** To be unclaimed or unwanted. [Middle English *beggen*†.]
Synonyms: beg, crave, beseech, implore, entreat, importune.
beg² (beg, bayg) *n.* A governor or other official of the Ottoman Empire or Mogul Empire; a bey. [Ottoman Turkish, BEY.]
be·gan. Past tense of **begin.**
be·get (bi-gét, bə- ‖ bee-) *tr.v.* **-got** (-gót) or *archaic* **-gat** (-gát), **-gotten** (-gótt'n) or **-got, -getting, -gets.** 1. To father; sire. 2. To cause to exist. [Middle English *begeten,* to acquire, procreate, Old English *begietan.*] **—be·get·ter** *n.*
beg·gar (bégger) *n.* 1. One who solicits alms. 2. One who has no money; an impoverished person; a pauper. 3. *Chiefly British Informal.* A fellow; a chap: *lucky beggar.* **—beggars cannot be choosers.** People who have nothing must accept what is offered.
~*tr.v.* **beggared, -garing, -gars.** 1. To impoverish; make a beggar of. 2. To exhaust the resources of: *His beauty beggars all description.* [Middle English *begger(e), beggar(e),* from *beggen,* to BEG; sense 3, euphemistic alteration of BUGGER.]
beg·gar·ly (béggərli) *adj.* Of or pertaining to a beggar; very poor or meagre: *a beggarly pension.* **—beg·gar·li·ness** *n.*
beg·gar-my-neigh·bour (béggər-mə-náybər, -mi-, -mī-) *n.* A simple card game of chance in which, by means of court cards, one must capture all one's opponents' cards.
~*adj.* Helping oneself at the expense of others: *a beggar-my-neighbour policy.*
beg·gar's-lice (béggərz-līss) *pl.n. Used with a singular or plural verb.* Any of several plants bearing small, prickly fruit that cling readily to clothing or the fur of animals, such as the **stickseed** (see). 2. The seeds of such a plant.
beg·gar-ticks (béggər-tiks) *pl.n.* 1. *Used with a singular verb.* Any of several plants having seeds that cling to clothing, often by means of barbed bristles; especially, the **bur marigold** and the **tick trefoil** (both of which see). 2. The seeds of any of these plants.
beg·gar·y (béggəri) *n.* 1. Extreme poverty; penury. 2. The state or condition of being a beggar. 3. Beggars collectively.
be·gin (bi-gín, bə- ‖ bee-) *v.* **-gan** (-gán), **-gun** (-gún), **-ginning, -gins.** *—intr.* 1. To start; commence. 2. To come into being: *when life began.* *—tr.* 1. To start to do; commence. 2. To be the cause or origin of: *It was her obstinacy that began the quarrel.* 3. To show some likelihood of or capacity for: *doesn't begin to tackle the problem.* **—to begin with.** As a start; in the first place. [Begin, began, begun; Middle English *beginnen, bigan, begun,* Old English *beginnan, began, begunnen,* from West Germanic *bi-ginnan* (unattested) : *bi-,* BE- + *-ginnan* (unattested), origin obscure.]
Synonyms: begin, commence, start, initiate, inaugurate.
Usage: The preposition which follows determines the sense of *begin.* Begin on means to "start doing something" (*We begin on the new programme next week*). Begin with means "take first" (*I'll begin with the red paint and then use the green*).
Be·gin (béggin, báygin), **Menachem** (1913-92). Israeli politician, born in Brest in Russia. He was sent to a labour camp in Siberia in 1941 for Zionist activities. Released in 1942, he went to Palestine and joined the Zionist underground movement, Irgun, which was campaigning for an independent Jewish state, and became its leader (1943-48). He helped to found the Herut ("Freedom") party (1948), became its leader and was elected to the **Knesset.** He became joint-chairman of the newly founded Likud party (1973), led it to victory and became prime minister (1977-83). He shared the Nobel peace prize with Anwar Sadat (1978).
be·gin·ner (bi-gínnər, bə- ‖ bee-) *n.* 1. One who begins something. 2. One who is just starting to learn or do something; a novice.
be·gin·ning (bi-gínning, bə- ‖ bee-) *n.* 1. The act or process of bringing, or being brought, into being; a start; a commencement. 2. The time when something begins or is begun: *"In the beginning God created the heaven and the earth."* (Genesis 1:1). 3. The place where something begins or is begun: *at the beginning of the road.* 4. The source or origin of something: *"The fear of the Lord is the beginning of wisdom."* (Psalms 111:10). 5. The first part: *the beginning of the*

play. **6.** *Often plural.* The early or rudimentary phase: *the beginnings of history; the beginnings of an agreement.*

be·gird (bi-gúrd, bə- ‖ bee-) *tr.v.* **-girt** (-gúrt) or **-girded, -girt, -girding, -girds.** *Poetic.* To gird or encircle; surround.

be·gone (bi-gón, bə- ‖ bee-, -gáwn) *interj.* Used as an order of dismissal. [Middle English : BE (imperative) + GONE.]

be·go·nia (bi-gōn-yə, bə- ‖ bee-) *n.* Any of various plants of the genus *Begonia,* mostly native to the tropics but widely cultivated, having leaves that are often brightly coloured or veined and irregular, and waxy flowers of various colours. [New Latin, after Michel Bégon (1638–1710), French governor of Santo Domingo and patron of science.]

be·gor·ra (bi-górrə, bə-) *interj.* Used to express surprise, alarm, or the like. It is used only humorously, as a supposed characteristic of Irish speakers. [Euphemistic for *by God!*]

be·got. Past tense and alternative past participle of **beget.**

be·got·ten. Past participle of **beget.**

be·grime (bi-grím, bə- ‖ bee-) *tr.v.* **-grimed, -griming, -grimes.** To smear or soil with dirt or grime.

be·grudge (bi-grúj, bə- ‖ bee-) *tr.v.* **-grudged, -grudging, -grudges. 1. a.** To envy the possession or enjoyment of: *She begrudged his youth.* **b.** To envy for a possession: *She begrudged him his youth.* **2.** To give with reluctance.

be·guile (bi-gíl, bə- ‖ bee-) *tr.v.* **-guiled, -guiling, -guiles. 1.** To deceive by guile; delude: *"The serpent beguiled me and I did eat."* (Genesis 3:13). **2. a.** To take away from by guile; cheat. Used with *of* or *out of.* **b.** To divert; distract the attention of. **3.** To attract strongly; fascinate. **4.** To cause to vanish unnoticed or without pain: *"The history of a soldier's wound beguiles the pain of it."* (Lawrence Sterne). —See Synonyms at **deceive, lure.** —**be·guile·ment** *n.* —**be·guil·er** *n.*

be·guine (bi-géen, bə-) *n.* **1.** A ballroom dance in the rhythm of a bolero based on a dance originating in Martinique and St. Lucia. **2.** The music for this dance. [American French *béguine,* from French *béguin,* hood, flirtation (as in *avoir un béguin pour quelqu'un,* "to be sweet on someone"), probably from Old French *Beguine,* BEGUINE.]

Beg·uine (béggeen ‖ báy-geen) *n.* A member of any of several Roman Catholic lay sisterhoods existing in the Netherlands since the 12th century. [Old French *Beguine,* perhaps after Lambert le *Bègue* (Lambert the Stammerer), priest of Liège who founded the community.]

be·gum (béegəm) *n.* A Muslim lady of high rank. [Urdu *begam,* from Ottoman Turkish *begim,* possessive of *beg,* BEY.]

be·gun. Past participle of **begin.**

be·half (bi-haáf, bə- ‖ bee-, -háf) *n.* Interest, support, or benefit: *petitioned on behalf of her sister.* [Middle English *(on min) behalfe,* "on my side" : *be,* BY + *half,* side, HALF.]

Usage: American English can make a distinction between *on behalf of* and *in behalf of,* so that *I am here on behalf of Joan* means essentially "I shall do what Joan would do if she were here", whereas *I am here in behalf of Joan* means "I am here to further Joan's interest". Besides its standard meaning (exemplified at *behalf* n.), *on behalf of* has spawned two non standard senses. One is "on the part of", as in *Her life was saved by prompt action on behalf of the rescue team.* The other is "for the sake of", as in *Don't wait on my behalf.*

Be·han (bée-ən ‖ -hən), **Brendan** (1923–64). Irish writer. He joined the I.R.A. in 1937, was arrested in England in 1940 and sentenced to three years in a reform school. The years there were described in *Borstal Boy* (1958). In 1942 he was convicted, in Dublin, of attempted murder and sentenced to 14 years' imprisonment. He was released in 1946. His prison years provided the experience for his most famous play, *The Quare Fellow* (1954). His later works include the play *The Hostage* (1959), and the books *Brendan Behan's Island* (1962) and *Confessions of an Irish Rebel* (1965).

be·have (bi-háyv, bə- ‖ bee-) *v.* **-haved, -having, -haves.** —*intr.* **1.** To act, react, function, or perform in a particular way. **2. a.** To conduct oneself in a specified way. **b.** To conduct oneself in a proper way. —*tr.* **1.** To conduct (oneself) properly. **2.** To conduct (oneself) in a specified way. [Middle English *behaven,* to hold oneself in a certain way : *be-,* thoroughly + *haven,* to HAVE.]

be·hav·iour, *U.S.* **be·hav·ior** (bi-háyv-yər, bə- ‖ bee-) *n.* **1.** The manner in which one behaves; deportment; demeanour. **2.** The actions or reactions of persons or things under specified circumstances. —**be·hav·iour·al** *adj.* —**be·hav·iour·al·ly** *adv.*

Synonyms: behaviour, conduct, deportment.

behavioural science *n.* A science, such as sociology, psychology, or anthropology, that seeks to discover general truths about human behaviour. —**behavioural scientist** *n.*

be·hav·iour·ism (bi-háyv-yər-iz'm, bə- ‖ bee-) *n.* The psychological school holding that objectively observable organismic behaviour constitutes the only valid scientific basis for psychological data and investigation and stressing the role of environment as a determinant of human and animal behaviour. —**be·hav·iour·ist** *n.* —**be·hav·iour·is·tic** (-ístik) *adj.*

behaviour therapy *n. Psychology.* Any method of treating psychological disorders that involves the patient's learning new patterns of behaviour. It includes **aversion therapy** *(see).*

be·head (bi-héd, bə- ‖ bee-) *tr.v.* **-headed, -heading, -heads.** To separate the head from; decapitate.

be·he·moth (bi-hée-moth, bə-, -məth ‖ bee-, -mawth, bée-ə-) *n.* **1.** A huge animal, possibly the hippopotamus. Job 40:15–24. **2.** An enormous, or enormously powerful, person or thing. [Hebrew *bəhēmōth,* intensive plural ("great beast") of *bahēmāh,* beast.]

be·hest (bi-hést, bə- ‖ bee-) *n.* An order or authoritative command; a request or bidding. Used chiefly in the phrase *at the behest of.* [Middle English *behest,* promise, command, Old English *behǽs.*]

be·hind (bi-hínd, bə- ‖ bee-) *adv.* **1.** In, to, or towards the rear: *He walked behind.* **2.** In a place or condition that has been passed or left: *He left his gloves behind.* **3.** In arrears; late: *fell behind in her payments.* **4.** Below the standard level; in an inferior position: *fall behind in class.* **5.** Slow: *His watch is running behind.* **6.** *Rare.* In reserve; yet to come: *There is no more behind.*

~ *prep.* **1.** At the back of or in the rear of: *She sat behind him.* **2.** On the farther side of; beyond: *behind the door.* **3.** In a place or time that has been passed or left by: *Their worries are behind them.* **4.** After (a set time); later than: *The project was behind schedule.* **5.** Inferior to; less advanced than: *behind us in technology.* **6.** Hidden or concealed by: *behind the scenes.* **7.** Serving to support: *He had the army behind him.*

~ *n. Informal.* The buttocks. [Middle English *bihinden,* Old English *behindan, bihindan : bi-,* BY + *hindan,* from behind.]

be·hind·hand (bi-hínd-hand, bə- ‖ bee-) *adv.* **1.** In arrears. **2.** Behind time; slow. **3.** In a backward state. —**be·hind·hand** *adj.*

Behn (ben), **Aphra** (1640–89). English writer, the first English-woman to make a professional career in letters. Her poetry is largely forgotten, but *Oroonoko* (1688) retains its place in English literary history as one of the earliest English novels.

be·hold (bi-hōld, bə- ‖ bee-) *tr.v.* **-held** (-héld), **-holding, -holds.** *Archaic.* To gaze at; look upon. See Synonyms at **see.**
~ *interj. Archaic.* Used to express amazement or draw attention. [Middle English *beholden,* Old English *behealdan,* to possess, hold, observe.]

be·hold·en (bi-hōldən, bə- ‖ bee-) *adj.* Obliged; indebted. [Middle English *beholden,* bound by obligation, Old English *behealdan,* past participle of *behealdan,* to hold, BEHOLD.]

be·hoof (bi-hōof) *n. Rare.* Benefit; advantage; use. [Middle English *behove,* Old English *behōf.*]

be·hove (bi-hōv, bə- ‖ bee-) *tr. v.* **-hoved, -hoving, -hoves.** Also *chiefly U.S.* **be·hoove** (-hōōv). *Formal.* To be necessary or proper for. Used impersonally: *It behoves us to consider the question carefully.* [Middle English *behoven,* Old English *behōfian,* to require, be needful or fitting.]

Beh·ring (baír-ing), **Emil (Adolph) von** (1854–1917). German bacteriologist. He is most famous for his work in serum therapy, and for his demonstrations of serum immunisation against diphtheria and tetanus he received the Nobel prize in physiology and medicine in 1901. Behring coined the word "antitoxin".

Bei·der·becke (bídər-bek), **Bix,** born Leon Bismark Beiderbecke (1903–31). U.S. jazz musician. He was a self-taught pianist and cornet player, and was the first white jazz musician to be recognised as a luminary of the jazz world by black musicians.

beige (bayzh ‖ bayj) *n.* **1.** Light greyish brown, or yellowish brown to greyish yellow. **2.** A soft fabric of unbleached and originally undyed wool. [French, from Old French *beget.*] —**beige** *adj.*

Bei·jing (báy-jing). Also **Pe·king** (pée-king); (1928–49) **Pei·p'ing** (páy-píng). Capital and second largest city of the People's Republic of China. It is a major cultural, communications, and industrial centre. Founded by the Zhou as a frontier town on the North China Plain (c. 700 B.C.), the city was Kublai Khan's capital of Khanbalik (1264–67). The Ming made it their capital (1421), and it remained China's capital until 1912. Foreign troops occupied the city in 1860, and during the Boxer Rebellion (1900–01), and thereafter foreign garrisons were stationed in it. The city changed hands many times in the civil war following the setting up of the Chinese Republic (1911–12). The Communists took Beijing (1949), and made it China's capital once more. In it is preserved the Inner or Tatar City containing the Imperial or **Forbidden City.** In 1989 thousands of pro-democracy demonstrators were massacred in Tiananmen Square.

be·ing (bée-ing) *n.* **1. a.** Existence or a state of existence. **b.** A condition of particular existence. **2.** An object, idea, or symbol that exists, is thought to exist, or is represented as existing. **3.** A person: *"The artist after all is a solitary being."* (Virginia Woolf). **4.** One's basic or essential nature. **5.** *Philosophy.* **a.** That which can be conceived as existing. **b.** Absolute existence in its perfect and unqualified state; the essence of existence.

Bei·ra (bír-ə ‖ *chiefly U.S.* báy-rə). Port in Mozambique, at the mouth of the Pungoe river. It is a beach resort and railway terminal, handling trade for Zimbabwe and Malawi.

Bei·rut or **Bey·routh** (báy-rōōt, baír-). Capital and chief port of the Lebanon. Founded by the Phoenicians, it was an important Greek and Roman trade centre. It fell to the Arabs (635), and was much fought over during the Crusades. The Ottoman Turks took the city, and later allowed the Druses to control it. The French captured Beirut (1918), and it became Lebanon's capital (1920). The city prospered as the chief financial and trade centre of the Middle East, but from 1958 was severely damaged in the country's factional strife, in which the Syrians intervened (1976 and 1987). It became a stronghold of the PLO, and suffered at the hands of the Israelis until most of the PLO was evacuated (1982). Serious faction fighting resumed in 1983, but has declined since 1989.

Beit (bīt), **Alfred** (1853–1906). South African diamond buyer and mining magnate. Born in Hamburg, he went to Kimberley, South Africa, in the early days of the diamond rush, and gained immense wealth from diamond-mining and gold-mining.

Be·ja (béejə, báyjə) *n., pl.* **Beja. 1.** A member of a pastoral people living as nomads in the area between the Nile and the Red Sea. **2.** The Cushitic language of this people.

be·ja·bers (bi-jáybərz, bə-) *interj.* Used to express surprise, alarm, or the like. Used only humorously as a supposed characteristic of Irish speakers. [Euphemistic for *By Jesus!*]

Bé·jart (báy-zhaar, -zhár), **Maurice,** born Maurice-Jean de Berger (1927–). French dancer and choreographer. He is a leading member of the dance avant-garde. In 1954 he formed *Les Ballets de l'Etoile,* later renamed the *Ballet Théâtre de Paris.*

be·jew·elled (bi-jóo-əld, bə- ‖ bee-, -jóold) *adj.* Adorned with or as if with jewels.

bel (bel) *n.* A unit used for comparing two levels of power, voltage, current, or sound intensity, equal to the logarithm to the base 10 of the ratio of the two levels. See **decibel.** [After Alexander Graham BELL.]

Bel. *Babylonian Mythology.* The god of heaven and earth.

be·la·bour (bi-láybər, bə- ‖ bee-) *tr.v.* **-boured, -bouring, -bours. 1.** To beat, hit, or whip; attack with blows. **2.** To attack verbally. **3.** To go over repeatedly or for an absurd amount of time; harp upon: *to belabour a point.*

be·lah (béelə, bə-láə) *n.* Any of various types of Australian tree, especially the casuarina. [From a native Australian name.]

Be·la·rus (béllə-róoss, byéllə-), **Be·lo·rus·sia** (béllō-rushə), **Bye·lo·rus·sia** (byéllō). Independent country and former constituent republic of the U.S.S.R. bordering on Russia, Poland, Ukraine, Latvia, and Lithuania. The capital is Minsk. Peat is the region's most important natural resource. Western Belarus, awarded to Poland by the Treaty of Riga (1921), was overrun by Soviet troops (1939) and annexed to the U.S.S.R. The republic was popularly known as White Russia. Area, 207 600 square kilometres (80,155 square miles). Population, 10,250,000. Capital, Minsk. See map at **Commonwealth of Independent States.**

Be·la·rus·sian (béllə-róo-si-ən), **Bye·lo·rus·sian** (byéllə-, -rúsh'n) *adj.* Also **Be·lo·rus·sian.** Of or pertaining to Belarus, its people, or their language.

~ *n.* Also **Be·lo·rus·sian, Bye·lo·rus·sian. 1.** A native or inhabitant of Belarus. **2.** The Slavonic language of the Belarussians. Also called "White Russian".

be·lat·ed (bi-láytid, bə- ‖ bee-) *adj.* Tardy; after the appropriate time: *a belated birthday card.* [Past participle of obsolete *belate,* to delay : BE- + LATE.] —**be·lat·ed·ly** *adv.* —**be·lat·ed·ness** *n.*

Be·lau, Republic of (bə-lów). see **Pa·lau** (pə-lów).

be·lay (bi-láy, bə- ‖ bee-) *v.* **-layed, -laying, -lays.** —*tr.* **1.** *Nautical.* To secure or make fast (a rope) by winding on a cleat or pin. **2.** To secure (a mountain climber) at the end of a length of rope. —*intr.*

1. To secure a rope. **2.** *Nautical.* To stop. Used in the imperative. ~*n.* In mountain climbing, the securing of a rope on a rock or other projection. [Middle English *beleggen,* to beset, surround, Old English *belecgan,* to cover, surround. Current senses (from 16th century), from Dutch *beleggen.*]

be·lay·ing pin (bi-láy-ing, bə- ‖ bee-) *n. Nautical.* A short, removable wooden or metal pin, fitted in a hole in the rail of a boat, and used for securing running gear.

bel can·to (bél kántō ‖ U.S. ka'antō) *n.* A style of operatic singing characterised by rich tonal lyricism and brilliant display of vocal technique. [Italian, "beautiful singing".]

belch (belch) *v.* **belched, belching, belches.** —*intr.* **1.** To expel gas noisily from the stomach through the mouth; eruct. **2.** To expel contents violently; erupt: *The volcano belched with a roar.* **3.** To issue spasmodically; gush forth. —*tr.* **1.** To expel (gas) noisily from the stomach through the mouth; eruct. **2.** To eject violently from within: *The volcano belched hot lava.*

~*n.* A belching; an eructation. [Middle English *belchen,* perhaps Old English *bealcan* or *b(i)elcan* (unattested).] —**belch·er** *n.*

bel·dam, bel·dame (béldəm) *n. Archaic.* An old woman, especially one who is loathsome or ugly. [Middle English, grandmother : Old French *bel-,* prefix indicating respect, from BELLE + DAME.]

be·lea·guer (bi-léegər, bə- ‖ bee-) *tr.v.* **-guered, -guering, -guers. 1.** To besiege by surrounding with troops. **2.** To harass; plague; beset. [Dutch *belegeren* : *be-,* around + *leger,* camp, from Middle Dutch.] —**be·lea·guer·er** *n.* —**be·lea·guer·ment** *n.*

Be·lém (bə-lémm). Formerly **Pa·rá** (pə-ráa). Seaport on the river Pará in northern Brazil. It is a communications and market centre for much of the Amazon basin.

bel·em·nite (bélləm-nīt) *n.* A pointed, cigar-shaped fossil, the internal shell of any of various extinct cephalopods related to the cuttle-fish. Also called "thunderstone". [New Latin *belemnites,* from Greek *belemnon,* dart; from the superstitious belief that such fossils were thunderbolts.]

bel esprit (bél ess-prée) *n., pl.* **beaux esprits** (bōz ess-prée). *French.* A witty and intelligent person. ["Fine mind".]

Bel·fast (bél-fa'ast, -faast ‖ -fást, -fast). Capital and largest city of Northern Ireland. Because of its large natural harbour on Belfast Lough, it has enjoyed a substantial trade and was a flourishing shipbuilding centre. In the 19th century it was also one of the great linen centres of the world.

bel·fry (bélfri) *n., pl.* **-fries. 1.** A tower or steeple, sometimes separate from the main church, in which one or more bells are hung. **2.** The part of a tower or steeple in which the bells are hung. **3.** A tower used for breaching walls in medieval warfare. [Middle English *berfrey* (altered through influence of *bell*), portable siege tower, bell tower, from Old French *berfrei,* from Germanic, probably from

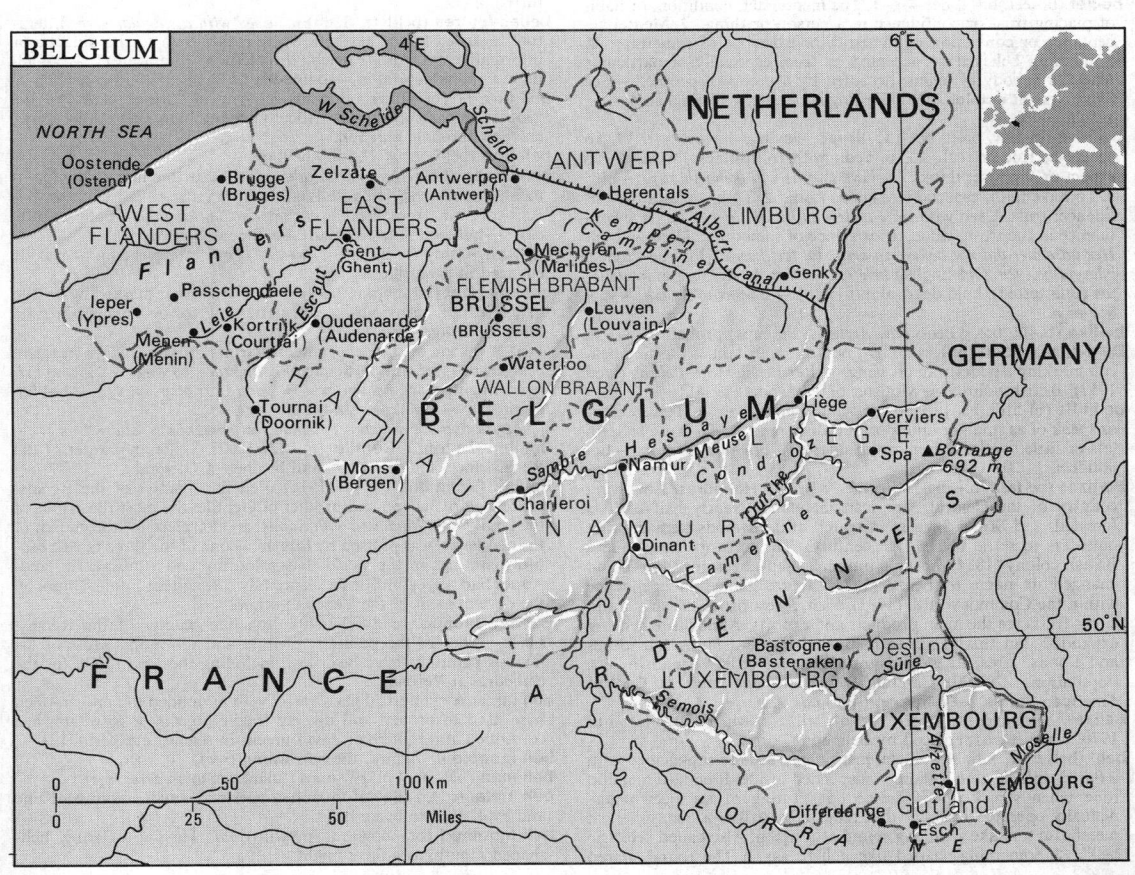

bergan (unattested), protect + *frithuz* (unattested), shelter.] —**bel·fried** *adj.*

Belg. Belgian; Belgium.

Bel·gae (bél-jee, -gī) *pl.n.* An ancient Gallic people who formerly inhabited what is now Belgium and northern France.

Bel·gian (béljən) *n. Abbr.* **Belg.** A native or inhabitant of Belgium. See **Fleming, Walloon.** —**Bel·gian** *adj.*

Belgian Congo. See **Congo, Democratic Republic of the**

Belgian hare *n.* A large, reddish-brown rabbit of a domestic breed developed in England from Belgian stock.

Bel·gic (béljik) *adj.* Of or pertaining to Belgium or the Belgians, to the Netherlands, or to the Belgae.

Bel·gium (béljəm). Kingdom of northwest Europe, whose strategic position made it the "cockpit of Europe". It was a Roman province, and later part of Charlemagne's empire. United under the dukes of Burgundy (14th century), it fell to the Habsburgs (1477), and passed to Spain. Napoleon occupied the country (1797), and after Waterloo, it became part of the United Netherlands. Belgium won its independence (1830), and its neutrality was guaranteed by the Great Powers (1839), but this was violated by Germany in both World Wars. Belgium joined the Benelux Union (1948), and was a founding member of the EEC. The country is culturally divided into Dutch-speaking Flanders to the north of Brussels, and French-speaking Wallonia to the south. Apart from coal, Belgium has few raw materials, yet it is one of the world's most industrialised countries, with over half its workers in manufacturing. Following land improvements, more than half its area is farmed intensively. Engineering goods, textiles, chemicals, glass, and foodstuffs are the main products. Area, 30 528 square kilometres (11,787 square miles). Population, 10,160,000. Capital, Brussels.

Bel·grade (bél-gráyd ‖ *chiefly U.S.* -grayd). *Serbo-Croatian* **Be·o·grad** (bé-o-graad). The capital and largest city of Serbia and capital of the Federal Republic of Yugoslavia, lying at the confluence of the Danube and Sava rivers. Founded as a Celtic fortress (third century B.C.), it became (12th century) the capital of Serbia, which fell to the Ottoman Turks (1521). A major Turkish stronghold, garrisoned until 1867, Belgrade was made the capital of independent Serbia (1882), and (1918) of the Kingdom of the Serbs, Croats, and Slovenes (which became Yugoslavia in 1929).

Be·li·al (béel-yəl, -i-əl). A satanic personification of wickedness and ungodliness alluded to in the New Testament. II Corinthians 6:15. [Hebrew *bəlīyya'al*, "uselessness" : *bəlīy*, without + *ya'al*, use.]

be·lie (bi-lī́, bə- ‖ bee-) *tr.v.* **-lied, -lying, -lies.** 1. To misrepresent or picture falsely; disguise: *"He spoke roughly in order to belie his air of gentility"* (James Joyce). 2. To show to be false: *Their laughter belied their grief.* 3. To disappoint or leave unfulfilled. 4. *Archaic.* To tell lies about; slander; defame. [Middle English *belien*, Old English *belēogan.*] —**be·li·er** *n.*

be·lief (bi-léef, bə- ‖ bee-) *n.* 1. The mental act, condition, or habit of placing trust or confidence in a person or thing. 2. Mental acceptance or conviction of the truth or existence of something. 3. Something believed or accepted as true; especially, a particular tenet, or a body of tenets, accepted by a group of people. —See Synonyms at **opinion**. [Middle English *beleve*, Old English *bileafe, gelēafa.*]

be·lieve (bi-léev, bə- ‖ bee-) *v.* **-lieved, -lieving, -lieves.** —*tr.* 1. To accept as true or real. 2. To credit with truthfulness; trust. 3. To expect or suppose; think: *I believe that he will come shortly.* —*intr.* 1. To have faith, especially religious faith. 2. To have faith or confidence; trust. Used with *in*: *I believe in his ability.* 3. To have confidence in the truth, value, or existence of something. Used with *in*: *Her gardener did not believe in artificial fertilisers.* [Middle English *bileven, beleven,* Old English *belēfan, gelēfan,* from Germanic *glaubjan* (unattested), hold dear; akin to **lief.**] —**be·liev·a·ble** *adj.* —**be·liev·er** *n.*

be·like (bi-lī́k, bə- ‖ bee-) *adv. Archaic.* Perhaps; probably.

Be·li·sha beacon (bi-léeshə, bə-, be-) *n.* In Britain, a flashing beacon marking a pedestrian crossing. [After Leslie Hore-*Belisha* (died 1957), British politician, Minister of Transport (1934).]

be·lit·tle (bí-litt'l, bə- ‖ bee-) *tr.v.* **-tled, -tling, -tles.** 1. To represent or speak of as small or unimportant; disparage. 2. To cause to seem less or little. —See Synonyms at **decry.** —**be·lit·tle·ment** *n.* —**be·lit·tler** *n.*

Be·lize[1] (be-léez, bi-, bə-). Formerly **British Honduras.** Low-lying country of the Central American mainland. Nearly half of it is forested, and British loggers in search of hardwoods were the first outsiders to settle there (17th century). The territory was made a British colony (1884), became internally self-governing (1964), and changed its name to Belize (1973). Belize gained independence within the Commonwealth (1981). Fish, forest products, sugar, and citrus fruits are the main products and exports. Agriculture is being expanded, but this has been hampered by devastating hurricanes and floods. Area, 22 965 square kilometres (8,867 square miles). Population, 220,000. Capital, Belmopan. See map at **Central American States.** —**Be·liz·e·an** (-iən) *adj. & n.*

Belize[2]. Port and the largest city of Belize. It was the capital until 1970, when it was replaced by Belmopan.

bell[1] (bel) *n.* 1. A hollow, metal instrument, usually cup-shaped with a flared opening and a clapper suspended inside. It emits a metallic tone when struck. 2. A device constituting of an electromagnetically operated hammer that repeatedly strikes a hemispherical metal disc to make a ringing sound as a signal. Also called "electric bell". 3. Something shaped like a bell, as: a. The round, flared

mouth of some musical wind instruments. b. The corolla of a flower. c. A hollow, usually inverted vessel, such as a diving bell. 4. *Nautical.* a. A stroke on a bell to mark the half-hour intervals. b. The time indicated by the striking of a bell, divided into half hours. 5. *British Slang.* A telephone call; a ring: *I'll give you a bell.* —**ring a bell.** To remind one of something previously known or experienced.

~*v.* **belled, belling, bells.** —*tr.* 1. To put a bell on. 2. To shape or cause to flare like a bell. —*intr.* To flare like a bell. [Middle English *belle,* Old English *belle,* perhaps akin to BELL².]

bell² *n.* The bellowing or baying cry of certain animals, such as a deer in rut or a beagle on the hunt.

~*intr.v.* **belled, belling, bells.** To bellow; bay. [Middle English *bellen,* to bay, Old English *bellan.*]

Bell (bel), **Alexander Graham** (1847–1922). U.S. inventor, born in Edinburgh. He went to Canada in 1870 and settled in New England shortly afterwards. He was the inventor of the telephone, the first electrical transmission of speech by his apparatus taking place in 1876. The Bell Telephone Company was founded in 1877. He also invented the audiometer, an early hearing aid, and flat and cylindrical wax recorders for phonographs.

bel·la·don·na (béllə-dónnə) *n.* A poisonous alkaloid derived from the leaves and roots of the deadly nightshade, from which the drugs **atropine** and **hyoscyamine** (*both of which see*) are obtained. [Italian, "fair lady" (supposedly from its use in cosmetics).]

belladonna lily *n.* A plant, the **amaryllis** (*see*).

Bel·la·trix (béllətriks, bi-láytriks, bə-) *n.* A giant star; the third brightest in the constellation Orion.

bell·bird (bél-burd) *n.* 1. Any of various tropical American birds of the genus *Procnias,* family Cotingidae, having a characteristic bell-like call. 2. A New Zealand honeyeater, *Anthornis melanura.*

bell, book, and candle *n.* 1. The three items used in the service of excommunication and other religious rites. 2. *Informal.* The ritual ratification of these rites.

bell-bot·toms (bél-bottəmz) *pl.n.* Trousers with legs that flare out at the bottom. —**bell-bot·tomed** *adj.*

bell·boy (bél-boy) *n. Chiefly U.S.* A boy or man employed by a hotel to carry luggage, run errands, and the like.

bell buoy *n.* A buoy fitted with a warning bell that is activated by the movement of the waves.

belle (bel) *n.* 1. An attractive and much-admired girl or woman. 2. The most attractive girl or woman at a specified place: *the belle of the ball.* [French, "beautiful", from Latin *bella,* feminine of *bellus,* handsome, pretty.]

belle é·poque (bél ay-pók) *n.* The period preceding World War I. [French, "fine period".]

Bel·ler·o·phon (bə-lérrə-fən, bi- ‖ -fon). *Greek Mythology.* The Corinthian hero who, with the aid of the winged horse Pegasus, slew the Chimera.

belles-let·tres (bél-létr, -létrə) *n. Used with a singular verb.* Literature regarded for its aesthetic value rather than for its didactic or informative content. [French, "fine letters" (literature).] —**bel·let·rism** *n.* —**bel·let·rist** *n.* —**bel·le·tris·tic** (bélli-trístik, bél-e-) *adj.*

bell-flow·er (bél-flowr, -flow-ər) *n.* Any of various plants of the genus *Campanula,* characteristically having blue, bell-shaped flowers. See **harebell, bluebell.**

bell·hop (bél-hop) *n. U.S.* A bellboy.

bel·li·cose (bélli-kōss, -kōz) *adj.* Warlike in manner or temperament; pugnacious. [Middle English, from Latin *bellicōsus,* from *bellicus,* of war, from *bellum,* earlier *duellum,* war.] —**bel·li·cose·ly** *adv.* —**bel·li·cos·i·ty** (-kóssəti), **bel·li·cose·ness** *n.*

bel·lig·er·en·cy (bi-líjərən-si, bə-) *n.* The state of being at war or engaged in a warlike conflict.

bel·lig·er·ent (bi-líijərənt, bə-) *adj.* 1. Given to or marked by hostile or aggressive behaviour. 2. Of, pertaining to, or engaged in warfare: *the belligerent powers.*

~*n.* A person or state engaging in warfare. [Latin *belligerāns* (stem *belligerant-*), present participle of *belligerāre,* to wage war, from *belliger,* waging war : *bellum,* war + *gerere,* to bear, carry.] —**bel·lig·er·ence** *n.* —**bel·lig·er·ent·ly** *adv.*

Synonyms: belligerent, pugnacious, contentious, quarrelsome.

Bel·li·ni (be-léeni), **Gentile** (*c.* 1429-1507). Venetian painter of the Renaissance, son of Jacopo and brother of Giovanni.

Bellini, Giovanni (*c.* 1430-1516). Venetian painter of the Renaissance, son of Jacopo and brother of Gentile, the most illustrious of the family. His *Madonna with Saints,* an altarpiece for the church of Frari, Venice, was praised by **Ruskin** as one of the three most beautiful paintings in the world. His colouring and atmospheric landscapes had a great influence, especially through his pupil, **Titian,** on the development of the Venetian school.

Bellini, Jacopo (*c.* 1400-1470). Venetian painter of the Renaissance, father of the painters, Gentile and Giovanni. Most of his famous paintings have been lost, including the *Crucifixion* for the cathedral at Verona.

bell jar *n.* A cylindrical glass vessel with a rounded top and an open base used to protect and display fragile objects or to establish a controlled atmosphere or environment in scientific experiments.

bell magpie *n.* A bird, the **currawong** (*see*).

bell·man (bél-mən) *n., pl.* **-men** (-mən). A **town crier** (*see*).

bell metal *n.* An alloy of tin and copper with small amounts of zinc and lead, used to make bells.

bell-mouthed (bél-mowthd, -mowtht) *adj.* Having a flaring, bell-shaped mouth, as a flask might.

Bel·loc (bél-ok), **(Joseph) Hilaire (Pierre)** (1870-1953). British writer and politician, born in France. He became a British citizen in 1902 and was a Liberal M.P. (1906–10). He is famous chiefly for his droll verse, especially *The Bad Child's Book of Beasts* (1896).

bel·low (béllō) *v.* -lowed, -lowing, -lows. —*intr.* **1.** To roar, as a bull does. **2.** To shout in a deep voice. —*tr.* To utter in a loud and powerful voice.
~*n.* **1.** The roar of a bull, elephant, or other large animal. **2.** A very loud utterance; a shout. **3.** The sound of artillery, thunder, or the like. [Middle English *belwen*, Old English *belgan* (unattested).] —**bel·low·er** *n.*

Bellow, Saul (1915–). U.S. novelist, born in Quebec, Canada, of Jewish Russian parents. His novels include *Dangling Man* (1944), *The Adventures of Augie March* (1953), and his most famous one, *Herzog* (1964). He won the Nobel prize in 1976.

bel·lows (bél-ōz || -əz) *n., pl.* **bellows.** **1.** An apparatus for producing a strong current of air, as for sounding a pipe organ or increasing the draught to a fire. It consists of a flexible, valved air chamber that is contracted and expanded by pumping to force the air through a nozzle. **2.** Something resembling a bellows, such as the pleated windbag of an accordion. [Middle English *belwes*, *belows*, plural or *belu*, *below*, probably from Old English *belga*, plural of *bel(i)g*, *bælig*, bag, bellows. See **belly.**]

bell pull *n.* A sash, cord, or handle that is pulled to ring a bell.

bell-ring·er (bél-ring-ər) *n.* **1.** One who rings church bells, especially on ceremonial occasions. **2.** One who plays musical handbells.

Bell Rock. Also **Inch·cape Rock** (inch-kayp). Sandstone reef, lying in the North Sea off the coast of Scotland, 19 kilometres (12 miles) southeast of Arbroath. It has a lighthouse.

bells of Ireland *n.* Used with a singular or plural verb. A plant, *Molucella laevis*, with clusters of white flowers surrounded by a green bell-shaped calyx, often grown in gardens.

bell tent *n.* A bell-shaped tent supported by a single tent-pole in the middle.

bell·weth·er (bél-wethər) *n.* **1.** A male sheep, usually castrated, with a bell hung from its neck, that leads a flock of sheep. **2.** One that is followed, such as a leader. **3.** One that acts as a standard.

bel·ly (bélli) *n., pl.* **-lies. 1.** The part of the body of mammals between the rib cage and the pelvis that contains the intestines; the abdomen. **2.** The underside of the body of certain other vertebrates, such as snakes, amphibians, and fish. **3. a.** The stomach. **b.** Appetite for food; gluttony. **4.** Any part that bulges or protrudes: *the belly of a sail*. **5.** The deep, hollow interior of something: *a ship's belly*. **6.** The bulging part of a muscle. **7.** The front part of the body of a stringed musical instrument. In this sense, also called "table". **8.** *Archaic.* The womb; the uterus.
~ *v.* **bellied, -lying, -lies.** —*intr.* To swell out; bulge: *"mud-coloured clouds bellied downwards from the sky"* (Thomas Hardy).
~ *tr.* To cause to bulge. [Middle English *bely*, *baly*, Old English *bel(i)g*, *bæl(i)g*, bag, purse, bellows.]

bel·ly·ache (bélli-ayk) *n.* *Informal.* An ache or pain in the stomach or abdomen.
~*intr.v.* **bellyached, -aching, -aches.** *Slang.* To grumble or complain, especially in a whining manner. —**bel·ly·ach·er** *n.*

bel·ly·band (bélli-band) *n.* **1.** A band passed around the belly of an animal to secure something, such as a saddle. **2.** An encircling cloth band for holding in the protruding navel of a baby.

bel·ly·but·ton (bélli-butt'n) *n.* *Informal.* The **navel** *(see)*.

belly dance *n.* A dance performed by women, originally in the Middle East, in which the hips and naked abdomen jerk and undulate. —**bel·ly-dance** (bélli-daánss) *intr.v.* —**belly dancer** *n.*

belly flop *n.* **1.** A dive in which the diver lands flat on the water rather than entering it headfirst. **2.** A belly landing.

bel·ly·ful (bélli-fŏŏl) *n.* *Informal.* An amount that satisfies or exceeds what one desires or can endure.

belly landing *n.* A landing of an aircraft onto the underside of its fuselage, without the use of its undercarriage. Also called "belly flop".

belly laugh *n.* A deep, unrestrained laugh.

Bel·mo·pan (bél-mə-pán,-mō-). Capital of Belize since 1970.

Be·lo Ho·ri·zon·te (béllō hórri-zónti || *chiefly U.S.* báylō, háwri-). City in eastern Brazil. An important manufacturing and marketing centre, it was the first of Brazil's planned cities, built 1895–97.

be·long (bi-lóng, bə- || bee-, *U.S.* -láwng) *intr.v.* **-longed, -longing, -longs. 1.** To be the property or concern of. Used with *to*: *"the earth belongs to the living"* (Thomas Jefferson). **2.** To be part of or in natural association with something. **3. a.** To be a native or inhabitant of. **b.** To be a member of an organisation. Used with *to*: *belong to a club*. **4.** To have a proper or suitable place: *Those clothes belong in the drawer*. **5.** *Informal.* To be socially acceptable: *made her feel belonged*. [Middle English *belongen* : *be-*, thoroughly + *longen*, to suit (see **long**, to yearn).]

be·long·ing (bi-lóng-ing, bə- || bee-, *U.S.* -láwng-) *n.* **1.** Plural. Personal possessions; effects. **2.** Close and secure relationship: *a sense of belonging*. —See Synonyms at **assets.**

Belorussia. See **Belarus.**

Belorussian. Variant of **Belarussian.**

be·lov·ed (bi-lúvvid, bə-, -lúvd || bee-) *adj.* Held in great affection.
~*n., pl.* **beloved.** One that is loved. [Middle English, past participle of *beloven*, to love thoroughly : *be-*, thoroughly + *loven*, to **LOVE.**]

be·low (bi-lṓ, bə- || bee-) *adv.* **1.** In or to a lower place; beneath. **2. a.** On or to a lower floor; downstairs. **b.** *Nautical.* On or to a lower deck. **3.** Farther down or on, as on a page. **4.** In or to hell or Hades. **5.** On earth. **6.** In a lower rank or class.
~*prep.* **1.** Lower than; beneath. **2.** Unworthy of or unsuitable to the rank or dignity of. **3.** Downstream of. **4.** South of. [Middle English *bilooghe* : *bi*, BY + *loogh*, *lowe*, LOW.]
Usage: below, under, beneath, underneath. Below, in its principal physical sense, denotes only position lower than a given point of reference. *Under* specifies position directly below, lower than the point of reference and in an approximately vertical line with it. *Below* is also used to indicate direction and distance in a horizontal plane : *a town on the Thames below Henley. Beneath* may have the basic sense of *below* or, more often, of *under. Underneath* combines the basic sense of *under* with that of at least partial concealment. Figuratively, *below* indicates deficiency or lesser status in a general way: *below normal; below one's rank. Under* indicates specific deficiency or explicitly subordinate relationship: *under legal age; serve under a captain. Beneath* applies to deficiency in moral or social senses: *beneath ordinary decency; beneath one's level.*

Bel·shaz·zar (bel-sházzər). The grandson of Nebuchadnezzar II and the regent of Babylon, who was warned of his downfall and death at Persian hands by the writing on the wall. Daniel 5.

belt (belt) *n.* **1.** A band of leather, cloth, or other flexible material, worn round the waist to support clothing, secure tools or weapons, or serve as decoration. **2.** *Sports.* A belt worn as a mark of distinction: *won a black belt in judo*. **3.** See **seat belt. 4.** A strip of armour surrounding a warship at the water line. **5.** A continuous band of a flexible material for transferring motion or power or conveying materials from one wheel or shaft to another. See **conveyor belt, fan belt. 6.** A geographical, sociological, or meteorological region, especially an elongated one, that is distinctive in some specific way. **7.** A narrow channel. **8.** *Slang.* A powerful blow; a punch. —**below the belt. 1.** *Boxing.* In the area below the waistline, where a blow is foul. **2.** *Informal.* Not according to the rules; unfair. —**tighten (one's) belt.** To become more thrifty and frugal.
~*v.* **belted, belting, belts.** —*tr.* **1.** To encircle; gird. **2.** To attach with or as if with a belt. **3.** To mark with or as if with a belt. **4.** To strike with a belt. **5.** *Slang.* To strike forcefully; punch. **6.** *Slang.* To sing in a loud and forceful manner. Often used with *out*: *belted out a note*. —*intr. Slang.* To run, ride, or drive very quickly. —**belt up. 1.** To fasten a seat belt. **2.** *Slang.* To stop talking; shut up. [Middle English *belt*, Old English *belt*, from Common Germanic *baltjaz* (unattested), from Latin *balteus*, probably from Etruscan.]

Bel·tane (bél-tayn, -tən) *n.* **1.** May Day in the old Scottish calendar. **2.** The ancient Celtic May Day celebration. [Middle English *beltane*, from Scottish Gaelic *bealltainn*, probably from Old Celtic *belo-te(p)nia* (unattested).]

belt drive *n.* A mechanism for transmitting power between drive shafts by means of a belt connecting pulleys on a shaft. Compare **direct drive.**

belt·ing (bélting) *n.* **1.** Belts collectively. **2.** The material used to make belts. **3.** *Informal.* A physical beating.

belt·way (bélt-way) *n.* *U.S.* A ring road *(see)*.

be·lu·ga (bə-lṓōgə, bi-) *n.* **1.** The **white whale** *(see)*. **2.** A sturgeon, *Huso huso*, of the Black and Caspian seas, whose roe is used for caviar. Also called "beluga sturgeon". [Russian *byeluga*, sturgeon, and *byelukha*, white whale : *byelii*, white + *-uga*, *-ukha*, augmentative suffix.]

bel·ve·dere (bél-və-deer, -vi-) *n.* A structure, such as a summerhouse or an open roofed gallery, situated so as to command a fine view. [Italian, "beautiful view".]

B.E.M. British Empire Medal.

be·ma (bee-mə) *n., pl.* **-mata** (-mətə). Also **bi·mah** (bee-mə) *pl.* **-mahs. 1.** *Judaism.* The platform from which services are conducted in a synagogue. Also called "almemar". **2.** *Eastern Orthodox Church.* The enclosed area about the altar; the sanctuary. [Late Latin *bēma*, from Greek, platform.]

Bem·ba (bémbə) *n. pl.* **-bas** or collectively **Bemba. 1.** A member of a south central African people, living mainly in Zambia. **2.** The language of this people.

be·mean (bi-méen, bə- || bee-) *tr.v.* **-meaned, -meaning, -means.** To lower in dignity or estimation; demean. [BE- + MEAN (base).]

be·mire (bi-mír, bə- || bee-) *tr.v.* **-mired, -miring, -mires. 1.** To soil with mud. **2.** To bog down in mud. Usually used in the passive.

be·moan (bi-mṓn, bə- || bee-) *v.* **-moaned, -moaning, -moans.** —*tr.* **1.** To lament; mourn over. **2.** To express pity or grief for. —*intr.* To mourn; lament.

be·muse (bi-méwz, bə- || bee-) *tr.v.* **-mused, -musing, -muses.** To confuse or stupefy.

be·mused (bi-méwzd, bə- || bee-) *adj.* **1.** Confused; bewildered. **2.** Deep in thought; engrossed.

ben[1] (ben) *n. Scottish.* The inner room or parlour of a house.
~*adv. Scottish.* Inside; within.
~*adj. Scottish.* Inner.
~*prep. Scottish.* Within. [Middle English *ben, binne(n)*, within, Old English *binnan* : *be*, BY + *innan*, within.]

ben[2] *n. Scottish & Irish.* A mountain peak. Used in names of mountains: *Ben Nevis.* [Scottish Gaelic *beann*, peak, height.]

ben[3] *n.* Any of several Asiatic trees of the genus *Moringa*, bearing winged seeds that yield an oil used in perfumes and cosmetics. [Dialectal Arabic *bēn*, from Arabic *bān*.]

Benares. See **Varanasi.**

Ben Bel·la (bén béllə), **Ahmed** (1918–). Algerian revolutionary leader and politician. He was the leader of the terrorist wing of the

Algerian nationalist movement against France after World War II and he helped to found the National Liberation Front (1954). When Algeria gained its independence (1962), he became its first prime minister, after serving six years in prison. He was elected Algeria's first president (1963), but was ousted by a coup (1965). House arrest (1965–79) and exile (1981–90) preceded his return to Algeria (1990).

bench (bench) *n.* **1.** A long seat, usually made of wood or stone and without a back, for two or more persons. **2.** A thwart in a boat. **3. a.** The seat for judges in a courtroom. **b.** The office or position of a judge. **4.** The judge or judges composing a court. **5. a.** A seat occupied by persons in some official capacity. **b.** The office of the persons occupying such a seat. **6.** A strong worktable, such as one used in carpentry. **7.** A platform on which animals, especially dogs, are exhibited. **8.** *Sports.* **a.** The place where the players on a team sit while they are not participating in the game. **b.** *U.S.* The reserve players on a team. **9.** *Geology.* **a.** A level, narrow stretch of land interrupting a slope. **b.** A level elevation of land along a shore or coast, especially one marking a former shoreline. **10.** The working platform in a quarry or a mine.
~*adj.* Used in work done at a bench: *a bench plane.*
~*tr.v.* **benched, benching, benches. 1.** To furnish with a bench or benches. **2.** To seat on a bench, especially in a judicial capacity. **3.** To show (dogs) in a bench show. [Middle English *bench,* Old English *benc.*]

bench·er (bénchər) *n.* **1.** *British.* A member of the inner or higher bar who acts as a governor of one of the Inns of Court. **2.** A **backbencher** *(see).*

Bench·ley (bénchli), **Robert (Charles)** (1889–1945). U.S. actor, film director, drama critic, and comic essayist. He is best remembered for his essays, represented in *The Benchley Roundup* (1954).

bench mark *n.* **1.** *Abbr.* **B.M.** A surveyor's mark made on some stationary object of previously determined position and elevation, and used as a reference point in tidal observations and surveys. **2.** A standard or reference point against which something is measured; a touchstone.

bench warrant *n. Law.* A warrant issued by a judge or court, ordering the arrest of an offender.

bend¹ (bend) *v.* **bent** (bent) or *rare* **bended, bending, bends.** —*tr.* **1.** To bring (a bow, for example) into tension by pulling or exerting pressure. **2. a.** To cause to assume a curved or angular shape. **b.** To force to assume a different shape or direction. **3.** To cause to swerve from a straight line; turn; deflect. **4.** To turn or direct (one's eyes or attention, for example): *"And to my cries . . . Thine ear with favour bend."* (Milton). **5.** To influence coercively; subdue. **6.** To decide; resolve. Used in the passive, with *on: He was bent on leaving.* **7.** To apply (the mind) closely; concentrate. **8.** *Nautical.* To fasten: *bend a mainsail onto the boom.* —*intr.* **1. a.** To turn or be altered from straightness or from an initial shape or position: *Wire bends easily.* **b.** To assume a curved, crooked, or angular form or direction: *The saplings bent in the wind.* **2.** To take a new direction; swerve. **3.** To incline the body; stoop. **4.** To bow in submission; yield. **5.** To apply oneself closely; concentrate. Used with *to.* —**bend over backwards.** *Informal.* To make a considerable effort. ~*n.* **1.** The act or fact of bending. **2.** The state of being bent. **3.** Something bent; a curve; a crook. **4.** *Nautical.* **a.** *Plural.* The thick planks in a ship's side; the wales. **b.** A knot that joins a rope to a rope or another object. —**round the bend.** *Chiefly British Informal.* Mad or eccentric; dotty. —**the bends.** Decompression sickness *(see).* [Bend, bent, bent; Middle English *benden, bente* and *bende, bente* and *bende,* Old English *bendan, bende, bended.*] —**bend·y** *adj.*

bend² *n. Heraldry.* A band passing diagonally down from the upper corner of a heraldic shield. [Middle English *bend,* Old English *bend,* ribbon, band.]

ben·day (bén-dáy) *n. Sometimes capital* **B.** *U.S.* **1.** A method of adding a tone to a printed image by imposing a transparent sheet of dots or other patterns on the image at some stage of a photographic reproduction process. **2.** A screen or pattern used in this process. [After Benjamin *Day* (1838–1916), New York printer.]

bend·er (béndər) *n.* **1.** One that bends. **2.** *Slang.* A drinking bout. **3.** *British Slang.* A male homosexual. **4.** *British.* An improvised igloo-shaped shelter made from plastic sheeting stretched over a framework of bent branches.

bend sinister *n. Heraldry.* A band passing diagonally down from the upper right corner of a heraldic shield. See **bar sinister.**

be·neath (bi-neeth, bə- ‖ bee-) *adv.* **1.** In a lower place; below. **2.** Underneath.
~*prep.* **1.** Below; under. **2.** Covered by: *The earth lay beneath a blanket of snow.* **3.** Under the power or influence of. **4.** Lower than in rank or station; inferior to: *An earl is beneath a duke.* **5.** Unworthy of; unbefitting: *It is beneath him to beg.* —See Usage note at **below.** [Middle English *benethe(n),* Old English *binithan* : *bi,* BY + *nithan, neothan,* from below, BELOW.]

Ben·e·dic·i·te (bénni-dí-səti ‖ *U.S.* -díssəti) *n.* **1.** A canticle, used in various Christian churches, beginning *"Benedicite, omnia opera Domini Domino"* ("All ye works of the Lord, bless the Lord"). **2.** *Small.* **b.** An invocation of a blessing, especially before meals. [Middle English, from Latin, imperative of *benedīcere,* to bless.]

ben·e·dict (bénni-dikt) *n. Also* **ben·e·dick** (-dik). A confirmed bachelor who has recently married. [After *Benedick,* a character in Shakespeare's *Much Ado About Nothing* (1598–99).]

Benedict, Saint (c. 480– c. 547). Italian monk, founder of the Benedictine order, known from his birthplace as Benedict of Nursia. After studying in Rome, he lived as a hermit in Subiaco, then moved to Monte Cassino, where he founded the first Benedictine monastery and established the principles of the order, and of western monasticism in general, in the book *The Rule of St. Benedict.*

Ben·e·dic·tine (bénni-dík-tin, -tīn) *adj.* Of or pertaining to St. Benedict of Nursia or his monastic order.
~*n.* (bénni-dík-tin, -tīn *for sense 1;* -teen *for sense 2).* **1.** A monk or nun belonging to the order founded by St. Benedict. **2.** A trademark for a liqueur made originally by Benedictine monks.

ben·e·dic·tion (bénni-díksh'n) *n.* **1.** A blessing or the act of blessing. **2.** An invocation of divine blessing, usually at the end of a service. **3.** *Roman Catholic Church. Usually capital* **B.** A short service consisting of prayers, the singing of a Eucharistic hymn, and the blessing of the congregation with the Host. Also called "Benediction of the Blessed Sacrament". **4.** The state of blessedness. [Middle English *benediccioun,* from Old French *benediction,* from Latin *benedictiō* (stem benedictiōn-), from *benedictus,* blessed, from *benedīcere,* to bless : *bene,* well + *dīcere,* to say.] —**ben·e·dic·tive, ben·e·dic·to·ry** (-díktəri) *adj.*

Benedict's solution *n.* A solution of potassium, sodium tartrates, copper sulphate, and sodium carbonate, used to detect the presence of reducing sugars, especially in urine. [After S. R. *Benedict* (1884–1936), U.S. chemist.]

Ben·e·dic·tus (bénni-diktəss) *n.* **1.** A short canticle that begins, *"Benedictus qui venit in nomine Domini"* ("Blessed is he that cometh in the name of the Lord"). Matthew 21:9. **2.** A canticle starting *"Benedictus Dominus Deus Israel"* ("Blessed be the Lord God of Israel"). Luke 1:68. **3.** A musical setting of either of these canticles. [Latin, "blessed". See **benediction.**]

ben·e·fac·tion (bénni-fáksh'n) *n.* **1.** The act of conferring help or a benefit. **2.** A charitable gift or deed. [Late Latin *benefactiō* (stem *benefactiōn-*), from *benefactus,* past participle of *beneficere,* to do well : Latin *bene,* well + *facere,* to do.]

ben·e·fac·tor (bénni-faktər ‖ -fáktər) *n.* One who gives financial or other aid. [Late Latin, from *benefactiō,* BENEFACTION.]

ben·e·fac·tress (bénni-fak-triss ‖ -fák-, -tress) *n.* A female benefactor.

be·nef·ic (bi-néffik, bə-) *adj. Rare.* Exerting a beneficent influence; beneficent. [Latin *beneficus.* See **beneficence.**]

ben·e·fice (bénnifiss) *n.* **1. a.** A church office, such as a rectory, endowed with fixed capital assets. **b.** The revenue from such assets. **2.** A piece of land granted in feudal tenure to a vassal.
~*tr.v.* **beneficed, -ficing, -fices.** To endow or provide with a benefice. [Middle English, from Old French, from Medieval Latin *beneficium,* from Latin, favour, benefit, from *beneficus,* beneficent. See **beneficence.**]

be·nef·i·cence (bi-néffi-sənss, bə-) *n.* **1.** The quality of charity or kindness: *nature's beneficence.* **2.** A charitable act or gift. [French, from Latin *beneficentia,* from *beneficus,* beneficent, generous : *bene,* well + *facere,* to do.]

be·nef·i·cent (bi-néffi-sənt, bə-) *adj.* **1.** Characterised by or performing acts of kindness or charity: *"even cruel savage brutes . . . have at times . . . beneficent impulses"* (W.H. Hudson). **2.** Conferring benefit; beneficial. —**be·nef·i·cent·ly** *adv.*

ben·e·fi·cial (bénni-físh'l) *adj.* **1.** Promoting a favourable result; enhancing well-being; advantageous. **2.** *Law.* Receiving or having the right to receive proceeds or other advantages: *a beneficial interest in sales.* [From BENEFICE, in the obsolete sense "benefit".] —**ben·e·fi·cial·ly** *adv.* —**ben·e·fi·cial·ness** *n.*

ben·e·fi·ci·ar·y (bénni-físh-əri, -i-əri ‖ *U.S.* -i-erri) *n., pl.* **-ies. 1.** One who receives a benefit. **2.** *Law.* The recipient of funds, property, or other benefits from an insurance policy, will, or similar settlement. **3.** The holder of an ecclesiastical benefice.
~*adj.* Pertaining to or holding a feudal benefice. [Latin *beneficiārius,* of a favour, from *beneficium,* favour, BENEFICE.]

ben·e·fit (bénnifit) *n.* **1.** Anything that promotes or enhances well-being; an advantage. **2.** A payment or series of payments made, for example by the government or by an insurance company, to one in need: *unemployment benefit.* **3.** A public entertainment, performance, or social event held to raise funds for a person or cause. **4.** *Archaic.* An act of charity; a kindly deed.
~*v.* **benefited, -fiting, -fits.** —*tr.* To be helpful or advantageous to. —*intr.* To gain advantage; profit. Used with *from.* [Middle English *benfet,* from Anglo-French, from Latin *benefactum,* benefit, good deed, from *bene facere,* to do well : *bene,* well + *facere,* to do.]

benefit of clergy *n.* **1.** The exemption from trial or punishment except by church court given to the clergy in the Middle Ages. **2.** The church's official approval. Used euphemistically: *cohabiting without benefit of clergy.*

benefit of the doubt *n.* A favourable judgment granted in the absence of full evidence.

benefit society *n.* A **friendly society** *(see).*

Be·ne·lux (bénni-luks). The economic union established (1948) by Belgium, the Netherlands, and Luxembourg. It came into effect (1960) as the world's first completely free international market for goods and labour.

Be·neš (bén-esh), **Eduard** (1884-1948). Czechoslovakian politician. He served under **Masaryk** as foreign minister (1918–35) and succeeded him as president. He resigned from the presidency after the Munich Agreement (1938). He was again elected president (1946), but after the imposition of a Soviet-style constitution, he once more resigned and died soon afterwards.

Be·nét (bə-náy), **Stephen Vincent** (1898-1943). U.S. poet and short-story writer. He is remembered chiefly for his long narrative of the American Civil War, *John Brown's Body*.

be·nev·o·lence (bi-névvələnss, bə-) *n.* **1.** An inclination or tendency to perform charitable acts; goodwill. **2.** A kindly act. **3.** In medieval England, a compulsory tax or payment exacted by some sovereigns without the consent of Parliament.

be·nev·o·lent (bi-névvələnt, bə-) *adj.* **1.** Characterised by benevolence; kindly. **2.** Of or concerned with charity: *a benevolent fund.* —See Synonyms at **kind.** [Middle English, from Latin *benevolēns* (stem *benevolent-*), "wishing well" : *bene,* well + *volēns,* present participle of *velle,* to wish.] —**be·nev·o·lent·ly** *adv.*

B. Eng. Bachelor of Engineering.

Ben·gal (béng-gáwl, bén-). Region of eastern India and Bangladesh, a state of India before the partition into India and Pakistan (1947). The western part became the Indian state of West Bengal, whose capital is Calcutta. The eastern part became East Pakistan (1947) and Bangladesh (1971).

Bengal, Bay of. Large bay in the Indian Ocean, bordered by Sri Lanka and India on the west, Bangladesh on the north, and Burma and Thailand on the east.

Ben·ga·li (beng-gáwli, ben-) *n.* **1.** An inhabitant of Bengal. **2.** The modern Indic language spoken in Bengal. It is the official language of Bangladesh and the main language of the Indian state of West Bengal.
~*adj.* Of or characteristic of Bengal, its inhabitants, or its language.

ben·ga·line (béng-gə-léen, -leen) *n.* A fabric having a crosswise ribbed effect, made of silk, wool, or synthetic fibres. [French, after its similarity to a fabric made in BENGAL.]

Bengal light *n.* A type of firework that burns with a brilliant, sustained blue light, formerly used for signalling. [First made in and exported from Bengal.]

Ben·gha·zi or **Ben·ga·si** (ben-gáazi). Town in northeastern Libya, on the Mediterranean coast. It is the second-largest town in the country and the most important port. From 1951 to 1972 the city shared the status of being the nation's capital with Tripoli.

Ben·Gur·i·on (ben-góor-i-ən, -on), **David,** born David Grün (1886-1973). Israeli politician, born in Poland. He settled in Palestine (1906) and became an active member of the Zionist campaign for an independent Jewish nation. He founded the Mapai party in 1930. After World War II he led the resistance movement against the British, and when Israel was created (1948), became prime minister. He held the office until 1953 and was again prime minister (1955-61, 1961-63).

Ben·guel·a (beng-gwélə). Seaport of Angola. It gives its name to the Benguela Current, a cold current flowing northwards along the west coast of southern Africa.

be·night·ed (bi-nítid, bə-) *adj.* **1.** In moral or intellectual darkness; unenlightened; ignorant. **2.** *Archaic.* Overtaken by darkness or night. —**be·night·ed·ly** *adv.* —**be·night·ed·ness** *n.*

be·nign (bi-nín, bə-) *adj.* **1.** Of a kind disposition. **2.** Manifesting gentleness and mildness. Often said of weather. **3.** Tending to promote well-being; beneficial. **4.** *Pathology.* Not malignant: *a benign tumour.* Compare **malignant.** —See Synonyms at **favourable, kind.** [Middle English *benigne,* from Old French, from Latin *benignus,* "well-born" : *bene,* well + -GENOUS.] —**be·nign·ly** *adv.*

be·nig·nant (bi-níg-nənt, bə-) *adj.* **1.** Favourable; beneficial. **2.** Kind and gracious. —**be·nig·nant·ly** *adv.*

be·nig·ni·ty (bi-níg-nəti, bə-) *n., pl.* **-ties.** Also **be·nig·nan·cy** (-nən-si). **1.** The quality or condition of being benign. **2.** A kindly or gracious act.

Be·nin[1], Republic of (be-neén, bi-, bə-, -nin). Formerly (until 1975) **Da·ho·mey** (də-hômi). Republic of western Africa. Formerly several ancient African kingdoms colonised by France, it gained its independence (1960). It is one of the smallest countries in Africa and, despite rich reserves of offshore petroleum, chromite, and iron ore, is one of the poorest and least industrially developed, largely because of political instability. The mainstays of the economy are palm products, cotton, and coffee. Area, 112 522 square kilometres (43,484 square miles). Population, 5,510,000. Capitals, Porto Novo (seat of government) and Cotonou. See map at **West African States.**

Be·nin[2] or **Benin City** (be-nín, bə-, bi-). Port in southeastern Nigeria, on the river Benin. It is the centre of Nigeria's rubber industry. From the 14th to the 17th century it was the capital of the African kingdom of Benin, noted for its bronze works of art.

ben·i·son (bénni-zən, -sən) *n. Archaic.* A blessing or benediction. [Middle English *benes(u)n,* from Old French *beneisson,* from Latin *benedictiō,* BENEDICTION.]

ben·ja·min (bénjəmin) *n.* A resin, **benzoin** *(see).* Also called "gum benjamin". [Variant (influenced by the name) of earlier *benjoin,* BENZOIN.]

Ben·ja·min[1] (bénjəmin). The youngest son of Jacob and Rachel, favourite son of Jacob. Genesis 35:18. [Hebrew, "son of the right hand" : *bēn,* son + *yāmīn,* right hand.]

Benjamin[2] *n.* The tribe of Israel descended from Benjamin. —**Ben·ja·mite** (bénjə-mīt) *adj. & n.*

benjamin bush *n.* The **spicebush** *(see).*

Benn (ben), **Anthony (Neil) Wedgwood,** known as Tony Benn (1925-). British politician. He was elected as a Labour M.P. (1950)

but succeeded to the peerage as Viscount Stansgate (1960). His struggle to renounce his title ended in victory—a constitutional landmark—with the Peerage Act (1963). He re-entered the House of Commons and served as Postmaster-General (1964-66), Minister of Technology (1966-70), and Secretary of State for industry (1974-75). In the 1970s he established himself as a leader of the Labour Party's left wing. The *Benn Diaries, 1940-90* were published in 1995.

ben·ne, ben·ni (bénni) *n.* A plant, the **sesame** *(see),* or its seeds or oil. [Of African origin, akin to Mandingo *bēne.*]

Ben·nett (bénnit), **(Enoch) Arnold** (1867-1931). English novelist and dramatist. Most of his novels are set in the "Five Towns" of the Midlands potteries district. Influenced by the French realist writers, Bennett specialised in a sympathetic depiction of everyday life among the lower middle classes. His novels include *The Old Wives' Tale* (1908) and the *Clayhanger* trilogy (1910-16).

Bennett, Richard Rodney (1936-). British composer and pianist. He is most widely known for his film scores, including *Far From the Madding Crowd* (1967) and *Murder on the Orient Express* (1974). He has written four full-length operas, the first and most popular being *The Mines of Sulphur* (1965). As a pianist he is best known for his jazz recitals. He has been visiting professor of composition at the Royal Academy of Music since 1995.

Ben Ne·vis (bén névvis). Highest mountain in Great Britain, rising to 1 343 metres (4,406 feet), in the Lochaber district of the Scottish Highlands.

ben·ny (bénni) *n., pl.* **-nies.** *Slang.* An amphetamine tablet. [From BENZEDRINE.]

bent[1] (bent). Past tense and past participle of **bend.**
~*adj.* **1.** Deviating from a straight line; crooked. **2.** On a fixed course of action; determined. Used with *on: "I perceived he was bent on refusing my mediation"* (Emily Brontë). **3.** *Slang.* **a.** Corrupt; dishonest. **b.** Homosexual. **4.** *Archaic.* Heading towards; on the way to.
~*n.* **1.** The state of being crooked. **2.** An individual tendency, disposition, or inclination: *"The natural bent of my mind was to science."* (Thomas Paine). **3.** The limit of endurance. Used chiefly in the phrase *to the top of one's bent.* **4.** A structural member or framework used for strengthening a bridge or trestle transversely.

bent[2] *n.* **1.** Any of several grasses of the genus *Agrostis,* some species of which are used in lawn mixtures and for hay. Also called "bent grass". **2.** The stiff stalk of various grasses. **3.** *Rare.* A moor; a heath. [Middle English *bent,* grassy plain, Old English *beonet-* (attested in place names), from West Germanic *binut-* (unattested).]

Ben·tham (bén-thəm), **Jeremy** (1748-1832). English political theorist and philosopher. He was one of the first Englishmen to systematically analyse law and legislation and he laid the foundations of the ethical system known as **utilitarianism.**

Ben·tham·ism (bénthəm-iz'm) *n.* The utilitarian philosophy of Jeremy Bentham. See **utilitarianism.** —**Ben·tham·ite** (-īt) *n. & adj.*

ben·thos (bén-thoss) *n.* **1.** The bottom of the sea or of a lake, especially at considerable depths. **2.** The organisms living on sea or lake bottoms. [Greek, depth of the sea.] —**ben·thic** (-thik), **ben·thal** (-thəl), **ben·thon·ic** (-thónnik) *adj.*

Ben·tinck[1] (béntingk), **Lord (William) George (Frederick Cavendish)** (1802-1848). English politician. He sat as an inactive Whig and then Conservative backbencher in the House of Commons for 20 years, and then emerged (1846) as the leader of those Conservatives who refused to support Peel's repeal of the Corn Laws.

Bentinck[2], William Henry Cavendish. See **Portland, 3rd Duke of.**

Bentinck[3], Lord William Henry Cavendish (1774-1839). English colonial statesman. As the first governor-general of all British India (1828-35) he suppressed *sati* (or *suttee*) (the burning of widows on their husband's pyres).

Bent·ley (béntli), **Edmund Clerihew** (1875-1956). British man of letters. His detective story, *Trent's Last Case* (1913), is a classic, but he is famous for inventing the short verse biography, the **clerihew.**

ben·ton·ite (béntə-nīt) *n.* Clay formed by the weathering of volcanic rock. It is used in cements, adhesives, fillers, and as a drilling mud in oil wells. [After Fort *Benton,* Montana.] —**ben·ton·it·ic** (-níttik) *adj.*

bent·wood (bént-wŏŏd) *n.* Wood that has been steamed until pliable and then bent into shape.
~*adj.* Of or designating a style of furniture made of wood so treated.

be·numb (bi-núm, bə- ‖ bee-) *tr.v.* **-numbed, -numbing, -numbs. 1.** To make numb, especially by cold. **2.** To make inactive; stupefy. [Middle English *benomen,* past participle of *benimen,* to take away, Old English *beniman* : *be-,* away + *niman,* to take.] —**be·numb·ment** *n.*

Benz (benz, *German* bents), **Karl Friedrich** (1844-1929). German engineer. He is credited with manufacturing the first car to be driven by an internal-combustion engine, patented in 1886. His company merged with Daimler (1926) to become Daimler-Benz, the makers of the famous Mercedes Benz, named after his wife.

benz·al·de·hyde (ben-zál-di-hīd) *n.* A colourless or yellowish, strongly reactive, volatile oil, C_6H_5CHO, used as a solvent, flavouring, and in perfumery. [German *Benzaldehyd* : *benzoin* + *aldehyde.*]

Ben·ze·drine (bénzidreen) *n.* A trademark for a brand of **amphetamine** *(see).*

ben·zene (bénzeen; *rarely* ben-zéen) *n.* A clear, colourless, highly refractive, flammable liquid, C_6H_6, derived from petroleum and used to manufacture a wide variety of chemical products including detergents, insecticides, and motor fuels. In nontechnical usage, also called "benzol". [BENZ(OIN) + -ENE.]

benzene hexachloride *n.* **Hexachlorocyclohexane** *(see).*

benzene ring *n.* The hexagonal ring structure in the benzene molecule and its substitutional derivatives, each vertex of which is occupied and distinguished by a carbon atom. Also called "benzene nucleus".

benzene series *n.* A series of chemically related aromatic hydrocarbons containing the benzene ring, the simplest member of which is benzene.

ben·zi·dine (bénzi-deen, -din) *n.* A yellowish, white, or reddish-grey crystalline powder, $C_{12}H_{12}N_2$, used in the manufacture of dyes and to detect bloodstains; biphenyl-4,4'-diamine.

benzine (bénzeen, ben-zéen) *n.* A mixture of hydrocarbons obtained by distillation of petroleum, boiling in the range 35–80°C. [German *Benzin* : BENZ(OIN) + -INE.]

ben·zo·ate (bénzō-ayt) *n.* A salt or ester of benzoic acid. Also called "benzenecarboxylate".

benzoate of soda *n. Chemistry.* **Sodium benzoate** *(see).*

ben·zo·ic acid (ben-zō-ik) *n.* A white crystalline acid, C_6H_5COOH, used to season tobacco and in perfumes, dentifrices, and germicides. Also called "benzenecarboxylic acid".

ben·zo·in (bén-zō-in, -zoyn) *n.* **1.** Any of several resins containing benzoic acid, obtained as a gum from various trees of the genus *Styrax* and used in ointments, perfumes, and medicine. Also called "benjamin", "gum benzoin". **2.** Any of various aromatic shrubs and trees of the genus *Lindera*, which includes the **spicebush** *(see).* **3.** A white or yellowish crystalline compound, $C_6H_5CHOH.CO.L_6H_5$, derived from benzaldehyde and used as an antiseptic; 2-hydroxy-1,2-diphenylethanone. [Earlier *benjoin*, from French, from New Latin *benzoe*, from Arabic *lubān jāwī*, "frankincense of Java".]

ben·zol (bén-zol ‖ -zōl) *n.* **Benzene** *(see).* Not in technical usage.

ben·zo·phe·none (bénzō-fi-nōn) *n.* A white crystalline compound, $(C_6H_5)_2CO$, used in perfumery and in medicine. Also called "diphenylmethanone".

ben·zo·yl (bénzō-il) *n.* The univalent radical C_6H_5CO—derived from benzoic acid. Also called "benzenecarbonyl".

benzoyl peroxide *n.* A flammable, white, granular solid, $(C_6H_5CO)_2O_2$, used as a bleaching agent for flour, fats, waxes, and oils, as a polymerisation catalyst, and in pharmaceuticals. Also called "di(benzoyl) peroxide", "di(benzenecarbonyl)peroxide".

Ben-Zvi (ben-tsvée), **Yishak**, born Isaac Shimshelevitz (1884–1963). Israeli politician, born in Russia. In 1952 he became president of Israel; he was re-elected (1958, 1962).

ben·zyl (bén-zil) *n.* The univalent radical $C_6H_5CH_2$—derived from toluene.

Beograd. See **Belgrade.**

Be·o·wulf (báy-ə-wōōlf). The hero of an anonymous Old English epic poem believed to have been composed in northern England in the early 8th century.

be·queath (bi-kwéeth, bə-, -kwéeth ‖ bee-) *tr.v.* **-queathed, -queathing, -queaths. 1.** *Law.* To give or leave (property) by will. **2.** To pass on or hand down: *His mother bequeathed to him a love of paintings.* [Middle English *bequethen*, Old English *becwethan*, to say, bequeath : *be-*, about, over + *cwethan*, to say, speak.] **—bequeath·al** (-əl) *n.* **—be·queath·ment** *n.* **—be·queath·ment** *n.*

be·quest (bi-kwést, bə- ‖ bee-) *n.* **1.** The act of bequeathing. **2.** That which is bequeathed; a legacy. [Middle English : *be-*, about + *-quiste*, a decree, Old English *-cwiss*.]

be·rate (bi-ráyt, bə- ‖ bee-) *tr.v.* **-rated, -rating, -rates.** To rebuke or scold harshly. See Synonyms at **scold.** [BE- + RATE (verb).]

Ber·ber (bérbər) *n.* **1.** A member of any of several Muslim tribes of North Africa. **2.** The branch of the Afro-Asiatic languages spoken by these tribes. **—Ber·ber** *adj.*

Ber·be·ra (bérbərə). Port on the Gulf of Aden in northern Somalia. The town was captured from the Egyptians by Britain (1884); from then until 1941 it was the capital of British Somaliland.

ber·ber·ine (bérbə-reen) *n.* A bitter-tasting yellow alkaloid, $C_{20}H_{19}NO_5$, obtained from the root of a North American plant, *Hydrastis canadensis*, from the barberry, and from other plants, and used in medicine as a tonic. [German *Berberin* : New Latin *Berberis* (genus), from Old French *berberis*, BARBERRY + -IN.]

ber·ber·is (bérbəriss) *n.* Any shrub of the genus *Berberis*, many species of which are grown in gardens for their ornamental foliage, flowers, or berries. See **barberry.** [19th century : Medieval Latin, origin obscure.]

ber·ceuse (bair-sérz, ber-, -sőz ‖ -sőoz) *n., pl.* **-ceuses** *(pronounced as singular).* **1.** A cradlesong or lullaby. **2.** A musical composition with a soothing accompaniment, usually in moderate $6/8$ time. [French, from *bercer*, to rock.]

Berch·tes·ga·den (bérkhtiz-gaad'n). Town in the Bavarian Alps of Germany. It lies in a deep valley, surrounded on three sides by Austrian territory. The chalets and air-raid shelters of Hitler, Goering, and other Nazi leaders are on the Obersalzberg peak overlooking the town.

be·reave (bi-réev, bə- ‖ bee-) *tr.v.* **-reaved** or **-reft** (-réft), **-reaving, -reaves. 1.** To deprive, as of life or hope: *"To a man bereft of the sense of purpose"* (G. Wilson Knight). **2.** To leave desolate, especially on the death of a loved one: *"cry aloud for the man who is dead, for the woman and children bereaved"* (Alan Paton). [Bereave, bereft; Middle English *bireven*, *birefte*, *bireft*, Old English *berēafian*, *berēafode*, *berēafod.*] **—be·reave·ment** *n.* **—be·reav·er** *n.*

Ber·en·son (bérrən-s'n), **Bernard** (1865–1959). U.S. art critic and historian, born in Lithuania. He is most famous for his writings on the Italian Renaissance, especially the comprehensive *Italian Painters of the Renaissance* (1894–1907).

be·ret (bérray, bérri ‖ U.S. bə-ráy) *n.* A flat cloth cap without a peak, worn originally by men in the Basque country. [French *béret*, from Old Gascon *barret*, cap, from Late Latin *birrus*†, hooded cape.]

beretta. Variant of **biretta.**

berg (berg) *n.* **1.** An **iceberg** *(see).* **2.** *South African.* A mountain.

Berg (berg, bairk), **Alban** (1885–1935). Austrian composer. A pupil of **Schoenberg,** he adopted his atonal manner and, with **Webern** and Schoenberg, formed the "Second Viennese School" of composers. He is best known for his two operas, *Wozzeck* (1925) and *Lulu* (1937), for the chamber *Lyric Suite* (1926), and his last completed work, the *Violin Concerto* (1935).

Ber·ga·mo (bérgomō). Industrial city in the Lombardy region of northern Italy, lying in the foothills of the Alps between the rivers Brembo and Serio.

ber·ga·mot (bérgə-mot) *n.* **1.** A small, spiny tree, *Citrus aurantium bergamia*, bearing sour, pear-shaped fruit, the rind of which yields an aromatic oil. Also called "bergamot orange". **2.** The oil itself, used in perfumery. Also called "bergamot oil". **3.** A Mediterranean plant, *Mentha citrata*, that produces a lemon-scented oil used in perfumery. Also called "bergamot mint". [French *bergamote*, from Italian *bergamotta*, probably from Turkish *beg-armûdī*, "bey's pear".]

Ber·gen[1] (ber-gən). Norway's second largest city, built on Bergen Fiord in the southwest of the country. Founded (*c.* 1070) by King Olaf III, it was the capital of Norway in the 12th and 13th centuries, and is now the centre of the country's oil industry.

Bergen[2]. See **Mons.**

Bergerac, Cyrano de. See **Cyrano de Bergerac.**

Ber·gius process (bérg-yəss) *n.* A process for the manufacture of diesel oil and petrol from coal by hydrogenation of finely powdered coal with a catalyst at high temperatures. [After Friedrich *Bergius* (1884–1949), German chemist.]

Berg·man (bérgmən, bair-yə-man), **(Ernst) Ingmar** (1918–). Swedish film director. *Smiles of a Summer Night* (1955) announced the main elements of his highly distinctive style: a slow pace, laconic dialogue, and the heavy use of symbolism to explore the psychological states of his characters. Most critics consider his finest achievement to be his studies of psychosis, such as *The Silence* (1963), and *Persona* (1966). Other films include *The Seventh Seal* (1957) and *Fanny and Alexander* (1982).

Bergman, Ingrid (1915–82). Swedish film and stage actress, who gained international fame in the Hollywood version of *Intermezzo* (1939). Thereafter she retained her place as one of the great international film stars. She won an Academy Award for best actress three times in *Gaslight* (1944), *Anastasia* (1956), and *Murder on the Orient Express* (1974). She was awarded an Emmy for her portrayal of Golda Meir in *A Woman Called Golda* (1982).

berg·schrund (bérg-shrōond; German báirg-shrōont) *n. Geology.* A crevasse at the head of a glacier which separates the moving ice from stationary ice adhering to the valley walls. [German *Bergschrund* : *Berg*, mountain + *Schrunde*, crack.]

Berg·son (bérg-s'n, bairk-són), **Henri** (1859–1941). French philosopher. The central item in Bergson's philosophy is the opposition between the life-force and the material world. He also assigned an important role to intuition, as opposed to the rational intelligence, in man's perception of reality. Among his best-known works are *Time and Free Will* (1889), *Creative Evolution* (1907), and *The Creative Mind* (1934). He won the Nobel prize for literature in 1927. **—Berg·so·ni·an** (-sóni-ən) *n. & adj.*

Berg·son·ism (bérg-sōniz'm) *n.* Bergson's philosophy, which asserts that the flow of time as personally experienced is free and unrestricted rather than measured as on a clock and contends that all living forms arise from a persisting natural force, the **élan vital** *(see).*

berg wind (berg) *n.* A hot wind that blows from the plateau in South Africa down to the coast. [Afrikaans, "hill wind".]

be·rhyme (bi-rím, bə- ‖ bee-) *tr.v.* **-rhymed, -rhyming, -rhymes. 1.** To celebrate in verse. **2.** To lampoon in verse.

Be·ri·a (báir-i-ə), **Lavrenti Pavlovich** (1899–1953). Soviet politician, born in Georgia. In 1938 he became Minister for Internal Affairs, and modernised the Soviet secret police and intelligence services. In July, 1953, he was arrested with six others, convicted of conspiracy and executed.

ber·i·ber·i (bérri-bérri, -berri) *n.* A thiamine (vitamin B₁) deficiency disease of the peripheral nervous system, endemic in South East Asia, and characterised by partial paralysis of the extremities, emaciation, and anaemia. [Singhalese, reduplication of *beri*, weakness.]

Ber·ing Sea (báir-ing, bérring). Part of the north Pacific Ocean, lying north of the Aleutian Islands, and connected to the Arctic Ocean by the Bering Strait.

Bering Strait. A narrow stretch of water (90 kilometres; 56 miles wide), separating Alaska from Siberia and connecting the Arctic Ocean and the Bering Sea. It is believed that in prehistoric times the strait formed a land bridge by which the original inhabitants of North America arrived from Asia. The strait, like the sea of the same name, was named after its discoverer, the Danish explorer, Vitus Bering, who traversed it (1728).

Ber·i·o (bérri-ō), **Luciano** (1925–). Italian composer, the most famous representative of the musical avant-garde in Italy after World

War II. An early experimenter in electronic and aleatoric music, he is best known for his compositions for solo voice.

berk, burk (berk) *n. British Slang.* A fool; an idiot. [Shortened from *Berkshire* (or *Berkeley*) *Hunt*, rhyming slang for *cunt.*]

Berke·le·ian·ism (bar·klée-əniz'm ‖ ber-, bárkli-, bérkli-) *n.* The philosophy of George Berkeley, holding that material objects have no existence independent of a mind perceiving them and that the uniform and continuous nature of the universe must be maintained by a divine mind always perceiving everything.

Berke·ley (bérkli), **Busby**, born William Berkeley Enos (1895-1976). U.S. dance director. His trademark, lavish dance routines with precisely synchronised chorus lines, first appeared in *The Gold Diggers* series (1933-37) and *Footlight Parade* (1933).

Berke·ley (bárkli), **George** (1685-1753). Irish philosopher and clergyman. His important treatises are the *Essay Towards a New Theory of Vision* (1709) and the *Treatise Concerning the Principles of Human Knowledge* (1710). The basic tenet of his philosophy, directed against the materialism of Hobbes, was that to be is to perceive or to be perceived. He was appointed bishop of Cloyne (1734). —**Berke·le·ian** *adj. & n.*

Berke·ley (bárkli), **Sir Lennox** (1903–89), British composer. A student of Nadia Boulanger, he wrote four operas and a ballet, but is best known for his chamber music, especially the *Trio* (1954) for horn, violin, and piano. He was knighted in 1979.

ber·ke·li·um (ber-kéeli-əm, bérkli-əm) *n. Symbol* **Bk** A transuranic element, atomic number 97, valencies 3, 4. The most stable isotope has mass number 247 and a half-life of 1400 years. [New Latin, after BERKELEY (California).]

Berk·shire[1] (bárk-shər, -sheer ‖ bérk-, -shīr). A chiefly agricultural county (but no longer with administrative status) in central southern England, lying in the Thames basin. The county town is Reading.

Berkshire[2] *n.* A pig of a domestic breed having a black body with white on the feet and face.

ber·ley, bur·ley (bér-li, búr-li) *n. Australian.* **1.** Ground bait for angling. **2.** *Slang.* Nonsense; codswallop.

ber·lin (bər-lín, ber-) *n.* Also **ber·line** (-léen) (for senses 2, 3). **1.** A light wool used in tapestry or for making clothing, especially gloves. Also called "Berlin wool". **2.** A four-wheeled covered carriage with a seat behind. **3.** A limousine with a glass window between the front and rear seats. [After BERLIN.]

Berlin (ber-lín, bér-). Capital city of Germany, and a German state, situated on the rivers Spree and Havel. It was the centre of the Prussian state, and from 1871 was the capital of the German Empire. After World War II the city fell within East German territory. East Berlin became the East German capital, but West Berlin formed part of West Germany. The city was a flashpoint for Cold War tensions, and the two parts were divided by the Berlin Wall, a wire and concrete barrier erected by the East German government in August 1961. Following demonstrations, dismantling of the Wall began in 1989. In 1991 Berlin was reinstated as capital of the reunified Germany.

Berlin (ber-lín), **Irving**, born Israel Baline (1888 – 1989). U.S. popular composer, born in Russia. Although he never learnt to read music or to play the piano, except in the key of F sharp, he became the most versatile and successful of 20th-century popular songwriters. He wrote more than 1,500 songs. His first major success was *Alexander's Ragtime Band* (1911). Among his most famous musical comedies were *Top Hat* (1935), and *Annie Get Your Gun* (1946).

Berlin, Sir Isaiah (1909 – 98). British historian and philosopher, born in Latvia. He was president of the British Academy (1974 – 78). Most of his career was spent at Oxford, where he was Chichele Professor of Social and Political Theory (1957 – 67) and master of Wolfson College (1966 – 75).

Ber·lin·guer (báir-ling-gwáir), **Enrico** (1922-84). Italian politician. He joined the Italian Communist party in 1944 and was elected to its central committee in the following year. He was a member of the Italian parliament from 1968, and secretary, or leader, of the Communist Party from 1958. He was a leading advocate of Eurocommunism.

Ber·li·oz (báir-li-ŏz, bér-), **(Louis) Hector** (1803-69). French composer, the leading representative of the Romantic movement in French music. His early work, the *Symphonie fantastique* (1830), is notable for its freedom from classical form and expansive scoring for a very large orchestra. His other most famous works are the symphonies *Harold in Italy* (first performed 1834) and *Romeo and Juliet* (1839), the operas *Benvenuto Cellini* (1838) and *The Trojans* (1855, 1858), the "concert opera" *The Damnation of Faust* (1846), and the oratorio *The Childhood of Christ* (1854).

berm, berme (berm) *n.* **1. a.** A narrow ledge or shelf, as along a slope. **b.** A shoulder of a road. **2.** A ledge between the parapet and the moat in a fortification. [French *berme*, from Dutch *berm*, slope, edge of a dyke or dam, from Middle Dutch *berme*, perhaps akin to Old Norse *barmr*, brim.]

Ber·mu·da (bər-méwdə). A self-governing British colony in the north Atlantic Ocean, comprising about 300 coral islands, some 20 of which are inhabited. The capital, Hamilton, is on the largest of the islands, called Bermuda or Great Bermuda. Bermuda has been a British colony since 1609, and relies on tourism.

Bermuda grass *n.* A grass, *Cynodon dactylon*, that has wiry, creeping rootstocks and is used for lawns and pasturage in warm regions. Also called "scutch grass", "wiregrass".

Bermuda lily *n.* A plant, the **Easter lily** *(see).*

Bermuda rig *n.* A fore-and-aft rig, distinguished by a tall triangular mainsail, widely used on cruising and racing vessels. Also called

"Marconi rig". —**Ber·mu·da-rigged** (bər-méwdə-rígd) *adj.*

Bermuda Triangle. Area of the north Atlantic Ocean remarkable for the number of ships and aeroplanes that have disappeared without explanation in its waters. The triangle lies approximately in the area between latitude 25° to 40°N and longitude 55° to 85°W, between Bermuda, Puerto Rico, and Florida.

Bermuda shorts *pl. n.* Shorts that end slightly above the knees. Also called "Bermudas".

Bern (bern, bairn). *French* **Berne.** The capital of Switzerland, situated on the river Aar in the west central part of the country. The city joined the Swiss Confederation (1353) and became its capital (1848). Bern is also the name of the canton that surrounds the city.

Ber·na·dette (bérnə-dét), **Saint,** born Marie-Bernarde Soubirous (1844-79). French girl whose visions of the Virgin Mary at a grotto near her birthplace, Lourdes, led to the establishment of a shrine there. She had her first visions when she was 14 (1858). She was canonised in 1933.

Bernadotte, Jean Baptiste Jules. See **Charles XIV, King of Sweden and Norway.**

Ber·nard (bérnərd ‖ *chiefly U.S.* bər-nárd) **of Clair·vaux** (klair-vŏ), **Saint.** (c. 1090–1153). French mystic and Doctor of the Church. He entered the Cistercian order (1112) and was sent to establish a monastery (1115) at Clairvaux, where he remained abbot for the rest of his life. He is sometimes called the second founder of the Cistercian brotherhood. His simple devotion to the Virgin Mary and the infant Christ make him a precursor of the movement known as the *devotio moderna.* His most influential writings, apart from his sermons (more than 300 of which survive), were *On the Steps of Humility and Pride* (c.1125) and *On the Love of God* (c.1127).

Ber·nard·ine (bérnərd-in, -een) *adj.* **1.** Of or pertaining to St. Bernard of Clairvaux. **2.** Of or pertaining to the Cistercians, the order of monks reformed by St. Bernard in 1115.
~*n.* A member of a Cistercian order.

Ber·nese O·ber·land (bér-neez ŏbər-land, báir-). The Alps of the canton of Bern in west central Switzerland, also called the Bernese Alps. Its highest peaks are the Finsteraarhorn (4 274 metres; 14,022 feet and Jungfrau (4 158 metres; 13,642 feet).

Bern·hardt (bérn-haart, bair-nár), **Sarah,** born Henriette Rosine Bernard (1844-1923). French actress, one of the most renowned in the history of the theatre. She made her debut at the *Comédie Française* (1862), but her great reputation did not begin until her appearance there as *Phèdre* (1874). In 1912 she appeared in two films, *La Dame aux camélias* and *Queen Elizabeth.* She continued acting all over the world even after her leg was amputated (1915).

Ber·ni·ni (bair-néeni), **Giovanni Lorenzo** or **Gianlorenzo** (1598-1680). Italian sculptor, painter, and architect, the outstanding representative of the Italian Baroque. He was appointed architect to St. Peter's in Rome (1629), and made the great ornate baldachino over the High Altar and the *Cathedra Petri* monument enshrining St. Peter's throne. He later decorated the apse of St. Peter's with a group of the Fathers of the Church, designed the colonnade around the piazza at the front of the church, and created the royal staircase in the Vatican.

Ber·noul·li (ber-nóoli), **Daniel** (1700-82). Swiss physician, mathematician, and physicist, son of Jean. He was one of the first natural philosophers who could properly be called a mathematical physicist. He anticipated the law of the conservation of energy and did important pioneering work in the molecular theory of gases; he also contributed to probability theory and the theory of differential equations. He is best known for his formulation of **Bernoulli's principle,** which appears in *Hydrodynamica* (1738).

Bernoulli, Jacques (1654-1705). Swiss mathematician, brother of Jean. He was professor of natural philosophy at Basel (1687-1705). He is one of the most important founders of the theory of ordinary calculus and the calculus of variations. He was the first user of the word "integral", in his solution to the problem of the isochronous curve.

Bernoulli, Jean (1667-1748). Swiss mathematician, brother of Jacques and father of Daniel. He succeeded his brother as professor of natural philosophy at the university at Basel. He is important for his development of integral and exponential calculus.

Bernoulli distribution *n. Statistics.* The **binomial distribution** *(see).* [After Jaques BERNOULLI.]

Bernoulli effect *n.* The phenomenon of internal pressure reduction with increased stream velocity in a fluid. [After Daniel BERNOULLI.]

Bernoulli's principle *n.* **1.** *Statistics.* The probability theorem stating that for a very large number of independent repeated Bernoulli trials the observed relative frequency of successes will approximate to the probability of success on each trial. Also called "law of large numbers". **2.** *Physics.* The relationship between internal fluid pressure and fluid velocity, essentially a statement of the conservation of energy, that has as a consequence the Bernoulli effect. Also called "Bernoulli's theorem". [Statistics principle, after Jacques BERNOULLI; physics principle, after Daniel BERNOULLI.]

Bernoulli trial *n. Statistics.* An experiment having just two possible results, usually denoted *success* and *failure,* with the property that the occurrence of one excludes the occurrence of the other in any given trial. [After Jacques BERNOULLI.]

Bern·stein (bérn-stīn, -steen), **Leonard** (1918–90). U.S. symphony conductor and composer. He was the permanent conductor of the New York Philharmonic (1958-70). He wrote a number of serious choral and symphonic works, but is best known for his musical comedies and dramas, including *On The Town* (1944) and *West Side Story* (1957).

berretta. Variant of **biretta.**

ber·ry (bérri) *n., pl.* **-ries. 1.** Any of various usually fleshy, edible fruits, such as the strawberry, blackberry, or raspberry. **2.** *Botany.* A fleshy fruit, such as the grape, date, or tomato, that usually has two or more seeds and does not split open when ripe. **3.** Any of various seeds or dried kernels, such as that of the coffee plant. **4.** The small, dark egg of certain crustaceans or fishes.
~*intr.v.* **berried, -rying, -ries. 1.** To hunt for or gather berries. **2.** To produce or bear berries. [Middle English *berye*, Old English *beri(g)e*.]

Berry, Chuck, born Charles Edward Anderson Berry (1926–   ). U.S. popular songwriter and singer. He was one of the first singers in the 1950s to evolve the rock-and-roll style.

ber·seem (ber-séem) *n.* A clover, *Trifolium alexandrinum,* native to northern Africa and southwestern Asia, and grown for soil improvement in dry regions of southwestern North America. Also called "Egyptian clover". [Arabic *barsīm, birsīm,* from Coptic *bersīm.*]

ber·serk (bər-zérk, ber-, -sérk) *adj.* **1.** Destructively or frenetically violent. Used chiefly in the phrase *go beserk.* **2.** Deranged.
~*n.* A berserker. —**ber·serk** *adv.*

ber·serk·er (bər-zérk-ər, ber-, -sérk-) *n.* A fierce Norse warrior who fought in battle with frenzied violence and fury. [Icelandic *berserkr,* "bear's skin" : *björn* (stem *ber-*), a bear + *serkr,* shirt, SARK.]

berth (berth) *n.* **1.** A usually built-in bed or bunk in a ship or train. **2.** *Nautical.* A space at a wharf for a ship to dock or anchor. **3.** *Nautical.* Enough space for a ship to manoeuvre; sea room. **4.** A position of employment, especially on a ship. —**give a wide berth to.** To stay at a substantial distance from; avoid.
~*v.* **berthed, berthing, berths.** —*tr.* **1.** To bring (a ship) to a berth. **2.** To provide (a ship) with a berth. **3.** To provide a bunk for, as on a ship or train. —*intr.* To come to a berth; dock. [Probably BEAR (verb, in nautical sense, "to sail in a certain direction") + -TH (noun suffix expressing result).]

ber·tha (bérthə) *n.* A wide, deep collar, often of lace, that covers the shoulders of a low-necked dress. [French *berthe,* Bertha (name).]

Ber·the·lot (baír-tə-lṓ, -lō̃), **Pierre-Eugène Marcelin** (1827–1907). French chemist and politician. He made seminal contributions to both the science of thermochemistry and the synthesis of organic compounds. He was Minister of Public Instruction (1886–87) and Minister for Foreign Affairs (1895–96).

Ber·til·lon system (bértilon; *French* bairti-yón) *n.* A former system for identifying persons, especially criminal, by means of a record of various body measurements, colouring, markings, and the like. [After Alphonse *Bertillon* (1853–1914), French criminologist.]

Ber·wick·shire (bérrik-shər, -sheer ‖ -shír). A former county of Scotland, since 1975 included in Borders Region, now in the Borders Unitary Authority area.

Ber·wick-up·on-Tweed (bérrik-əpon-tweéd). Market town and port in the county of Northumberland, at the mouth of the river Tweed, now in the Borders Unitary Authority area. A border town, it passed back and forth from Scottish to English control until finally becoming permanently English (1482).

ber·yl (bérril, bérrəl) *n.* A mineral, essentially aluminium beryllium silicate, $Be_3Al_2Si_6O_{18}$, occurring in hexagonal prisms. It is the chief source of beryllium and is used as a gem. [Middle English, from Old French, from Latin *bēryllus,* from Greek *bērullos,* perhaps of Dravidian origin.] —**beryl·line** (-in, -een) *adj.*

be·ryl·li·um (be-rílli-əm, bə-) *n. Symbol* **Be** A lightweight, corrosion-resistant, rigid, steel-grey metallic element used as an aerospace structural material, as a moderator and reflector in nuclear reactors, and in a copper alloy used for springs, electrical contacts, and nonsparking tools. Atomic number 4, atomic weight 9.0122, melting point 1 287°C, boiling point 2 500°C, relative density 1.848, valency 2. [New Latin, from BERYL.]

Ber·ze·li·us (bər-zeéli-əss, bair-sáyli-ōóss), **Jöns Jakob, Baron** (1779–1848). Swedish chemist, one of the most important founders of modern chemistry. He made enormous contributions to the development of the science in atomic weights (he published a table of these in 1828), electrochemical theory (by his experiments in electrolysis of various solutions), and the discovery of the elements selenium and thorium and the isolation of silicon. He coined the words "isomerism", "allotropy", and "protein". His most important publication was the *Theory of Chemical Proportions and the Chemical Action of Electricity* (1814).

Bes (bess). *Egyptian Mythology.* A god of music and revelry.

Be·san·çon (bə-zón-son, -són). Industrial city in eastern France, on the river Doubs. It is famous for watches and clocks.

Bes·ant (bézz'nt, bi-zánt), **Annie,** born Annie Wood (1847–1933). English free-thinker and theosophist. In 1889 she became a disciple of Helena **Blavatsky** and for the rest of her life devoted herself to theosophy. She later became the founder-president of the Indian Home Rule League (1916) and president of the Indian National Congress (1917).

be·seech (bi-seéch, bə- ‖ bee-) *tr.v.* **-sought** (-sáwt) or **-seeched, -seeching, -seeches. 1.** To address an earnest or urgent request to; implore. **2.** To request earnestly; beg for. —See Synonyms at **beg.** [Middle English *besechen,* to seek : *be-,* thoroughly + *sechen, seken,* to SEEK.] —**be·seech·er** *n.* —**be·seech·ing·ly** *adv.*

be·seem (bi-seém, bə- ‖ bee-) *tr.v.* **-seemed, -seeming, -seems.** Ar-

chaic. To be appropriate for; befit. [Middle English *besemen,* to seem, appear to do well : *be-,* thoroughly + *semen,* to SEEM.]

be·set (bi-sét, bə- ‖ bee-) *tr.v.* **-set, -setting, -sets. 1.** To attack from all sides. **2.** To trouble persistently; harass: *beset by doubts.* **3.** To surround; hem in. **4.** To stud, as with jewels. —See Synonyms at **attack.** [Middle English *besetten,* Old English *besettan* : *be-,* on all sides + SET (place).] —**be·set·ment** *n.*

be·set·ting (bi-sétting, bə- ‖ bee-) *adj.* Constantly troubling or attacking.

be·shrew (bi-shrṓo, bə- ‖ bee-) *tr.v.* **-shrewed, -shrewing, -shrews.** *Archaic.* To invoke evil upon; curse. [Middle English *beshrewen,* to corrupt, curse : *be-,* thoroughly + *shrewen,* to curse, from *shrewe,* SHREW.]

be·side (bi-síd, bə- ‖ bee-) *prep.* **1.** Next to; at or by the side of. **2.** In comparison with. **3.** *Rare.* Except for; besides. **4.** Wide of; unrelated to: *beside the point.* —**beside (oneself).** Out of one's senses with excitement, grief, rage or the like; extremely agitated.
~*adv.* In addition; besides. See Usage note at **besides.** [Middle English *biside,* Old English *be sīdan* : *be,* BY + *sīdan,* dative of *sīde,* SIDE.]

be·sides (bi-sídz, bə- ‖ bee-) *adv.* **1.** In addition; also; over and above. **2.** Moreover; furthermore. —See Synonyms at **also.**
~*prep.* **1.** In addition to. **2.** Except for. [Middle English *bisides,* adverbial genitive of *biside,* BESIDE.]

Usage: Besides is the usual form for "in addition to" or "except for", as in *Besides his books, there were lots of maps. Beside his books,* means "next to".

be·siege (bi-seéj, bə- ‖ bee-) *tr.v.* **-sieged, -sieging, -sieges. 1.** To surround with an armed force in order to compel surrender; lay siege to. **2.** To crowd round; hem in. **3.** To harass or importune, as with requests. —**be·siege·ment** *n.* —**be·sieg·er** *n.*

be·smear (bi-smeér, bə- ‖ bee-) *tr.v.* **-smeared, -smearing, -smears. 1.** To smear over. **2.** To tarnish; defile.

be·smirch (bi-smúrch, bə- ‖ bee-) *tr.v.* **-smirched, -smirching, -smirches. 1.** To soil; make dirty. **2.** To dim the purity or lustre of (someone's reputation, for example); tarnish; dishonour. —**be·smirch·er** *n.* —**be·smirch·ment** *n.*

be·som (beéz'm) *n.* **1.** A bundle of twigs attached to a handle and used as a broom. **2.** In curling, the broom used to sweep the ice from the path of a curling stone. **3.** *Rare.* The broom plant. **4.** *Northern British.* A sluttish or impudent woman.
~*tr. v.* **besomed, -soming, -soms.** To sweep using a besom. [Middle English *besem,* Old English *bes(e)ma,* from West Germanic *besmo-* (unattested).]

be·sot·ted (bi-sóttid, bə- ‖ bee-) *adj.* **1.** Muddled or stupefied, especially with drink. **2.** Infatuated.

be·sought. Past tense and past participle of **beseech.**

be·span·gle (bi-spáng-g'l, bə- ‖ bee-) *tr.v.* **-spangled, -spangling, -spangles.** To ornament or cover with spangles.

be·spat·ter (bi-spáttər, bə- ‖ bee-) *tr.v.* **-tered, -tering, -ters. 1.** To spatter or soil thoroughly, as with mud. **2.** To cast aspersions on; defame.

be·speak (bi-speék, bə- ‖ bee-) *tr.v.* **-spoke** (-spók) or *archaic* **-spake** (-spáyk), **-spoken** (-spókən) or **-spoke, -speaking, -speaks. 1.** To be or give a sign of; indicate; signify. **2.** *Poetic.* To speak to; address. **3.** To engage or claim in advance; reserve. **4.** To foretell; portend.

be·spec·ta·cled (bi-spéktək'ld, bə- ‖ bee-) *adj.* Wearing spectacles.

be·spoke (bi-spók, bə- ‖ bee-) *adj. Chiefly British.* **1.** Made-to-order. Usually said of clothing. **2.** Dealing in custom-made articles: *a bespoke tailor.*

be·spread (bi-spréd, bə- ‖ bee-) *tr.v.* **-spread, -spreading, -spreads.** To cover or spread over, usually thickly.

be·sprent (bi-sprént, bə-) *adj. Poetic.* Besprinkled. [Middle English *bespreynt,* past participle of *besprengen,* to besprinkle, Old English *besprengan* : *be-,* around, over + *sprengan,* to scatter, burst.]

be·sprin·kle (bi-spríngk'l, bə- ‖ bee-) *tr.v.* **-kled, -kling, -kles.** To sprinkle over, as with water. [Middle English *besprengeln,* frequentative of *besprengen,* to besprinkle. See **besprent.**]

Bes·sa·ra·bi·a (béssə-ráybi-ə). Historic region in southeastern Europe, now falling mainly within Ukraine and Moldova. Russia gained the area (1812), but it declared itself the independent republic of Moldavia (1918) and voted for union with Romania. Romania was forced formally to cede it to the U.S.S.R. (1940).

Bes·sel equation (béss'l) *n.* The differential equation, $x^2f''(x) + xf'(x) + (x^2-n^2)f(x) = 0$. [After F. W. *Bessel* (1784–1846), German astronomer.]

Bessel function *n.* Any of the solutions of the Bessel equation, having many applications in mathematical physics, including the representation of current density and magnetic field strength, and in problems of heat conduction.

Bes·se·mer (béssimər), **Sir Henry** (1813–98). British engineer and inventor. Over his lifetime he patented more than 100 inventions. He is most famous for inventing the **Bessemer process.** He was knighted in 1879.

Bessemer converter *n.* A large pear-shaped container in which molten pig iron is converted to steel by the Bessemer process. [After Sir Henry BESSEMER.]

Bessemer process *n.* A method for making steel by blasting compressed air through molten iron, burning out excess carbon and other impurities. [After Sir Henry BESSEMER.]

best (best) **1.** Superlative of **good. 2.** Superlative of **well.**

~*adj.* **1.** Surpassing all others in quality; most excellent. **2.** Most satisfactory, suitable, or useful; most desirable or attractive: *the best solution.* **3.** Greatest; largest: *It took the best part of a week.*
~*adv.* **1.** In the best way; most creditably, attractively, or advantageously. **2.** To the greatest degree or extent; most. —**had best.** Should; ought to; would be wisest to; had better.
~*n.* **1.** That which is best among several. Preceded by *the.* **2.** The best person or persons. Preceded by *the.* **3.** The best condition or quality: *look your best.* **4.** One's best clothing. **5.** The best effort one can make: *doing his best.* **6.** One's warmest wishes or regards: *Give them my best.* —**at best. 1.** When interpreted most favourably. **2.** Under the most favourable conditions. —**for the best.** For the ultimate good. —**make the best of.** To do as well as possible under unfavourable conditions.
~*tr.v.* **bested, besting, bests.** To prevail over; surpass; defeat: *"I'm a rough customer, I expect, but I know when I'm bested".* (Nathanael West). [Middle English *best,* Old English *bet(e)st.*]
  Usage: Strictly, *best* is used only when more than two are being compared, so one should say *the best of them all* and *the better of the two.* However, *The best of the two* is commonly heard.
Best, Charles Herbert (1899–1978). Canadian physician and physiologist, famous for collaborating with **Macleod** and **Banting** in the extraction of the hormone, insulin, from a dog's pancreas (1921) and the subsequent demonstration that it could be used to arrest the progress of diabetes mellitus, then a fatal disease.
be·stead (bi-stéd, bə- ‖ bee-) *tr.v.* **-steaded** or **-stead, -steading, -steads.** *Archaic.* To be of service to; avail; aid.
~*adj. Archaic.* Placed; located. [BE- + STEAD (to help).]
best end *n.* A cut of meat, usually lamb or veal, from between the neck and loins.
bes·tial (bést-yəl, -i-əl ‖ béss-chəl) *adj.* **1.** Of or pertaining to an animal. **2.** Having the qualities of, or behaving in the manner of, a brute; savage; depraved. **3.** Subhuman in intelligence. [Middle English, from Old French, from Late Latin *bēstiālis,* from Latin *bēstia,* BEAST.] —**bes·tial·ly** *adv.*
bes·tial·ise, bes·tial·ize (bést-yəl-īz, -i-əl- ‖ béss-chəl-) *tr.v.* **-ised, -ising, -ises.** To make bestial; brutalise.
bes·ti·al·i·ty (bésti-ál-əti ‖ béss-chi-) *n., pl.* **-ties. 1.** The quality of being bestial; animal nature. **2.** An action or conduct marked by repugnant carnality or brutality. **3.** Sexual relations between a human being and an animal.
bes·ti·ar·y (bést-i-əri, -yəri ‖ béss-chi-, *U.S.* -erri) *n., pl.* **-ies.** A medieval collection of allegorical fables about the habits and traits of animals, each fable followed by an interpretation of its moral significance. **2.** A modern version of such a collection. [Medieval Latin *bēstiārium,* from Latin *bēstia,* BEAST.]
be·stir (bi-stúr, bə- ‖ bee-) *tr.v.* **-stirred, -stirring, -stirs.** To cause to become active; rouse. Usually used reflexively: *She bestirred herself and went for a walk.*
best man *n.* The bridegroom's chief attendant at a wedding.
be·stow (bi-stó, bə- ‖ bee-) *tr.v.* **-stowed, -stowing, -stows. 1.** To present as a gift or honour; confer. Used with *on* or *upon.* **2.** To give in marriage. **3.** To apply; use: *"On Hester Prynne's story . . . I bestowed much thought."* (Nathaniel Hawthorne). **4.** *Archaic.* To store; house. [Middle English *bestowen :* be- (intensive) + STOW.] —**be·stow·able** *adj.* —**be·stow·al, be·stow·ment** *n.*
be·strew (bi-stróo, bə- ‖ bee-) *tr.v.* **-strewed, -strewing, -strews. 1.** To scatter or cast things profusely on (a surface). **2.** To lie scattered over or about.
be·stride (bi-stríd, bə- ‖ bee-) *tr.v* **-strode** (-stród), **-stridden** (-strídd'n), **-striding, -strides. 1.** To sit or stand on with the legs widely spread; straddle. **2.** To step over.
best seller *n.* A book or other product that is among those sold in the largest numbers. —**best-sell·ing** (bést-sélling) *adj.*
bet (bet) *n.* **1.** An agreement between two parties such that the one proved wrong about an uncertain outcome will forfeit a stipulated thing or sum to the other; a wager. **2.** The fact, event, or outcome on which a bet is made. **3.** The object or amount risked; the stake. **4. a.** A plan or course of action: *Your best bet is to leave now.* **b.** *Informal.* A view; opinion: *My bet is that she won't come.* —**hedge (one's) bets. 1.** To protect oneself from possible loss by betting on more than one outcome. **2.** To guard against risk; cover onself.
~*v.* **bet** or *rare* **betted, betting, bets.** —*tr.* **1.** To stake (an object or amount, for example) in a bet. **2.** To make a bet with. **3.** To predict confidently. —*intr.* To make or place a bet. —**you bet.** *Informal.* Surely. [16th century : perhaps short for ABET in the sense of "instigation".]
be·ta (béetə ‖ *U.S.* báytə) *n.* **1.** The second letter in the Greek alphabet, written B, β. Transliterated in English as *B, b,* and sometimes, for Modern Greek words, as *V, v.* **2.** A second-class mark for an examination, essay, or the like. **3.** *Physics.* **a.** A beta particle. **b.** A beta ray. [Greek *bēta,* from Hebrew *bēth,* BETH.]
beta blocker *n.* Any of a group of drugs that slow down the action of the heart by blocking the action of nerve endings called *beta receptors.* They are used to treat abnormal heart conditions and high blood pressure.
be·ta·ine (béetə-een, bi-táy-, -in) *n.* A sweet, crystalline alkaloid, $C_5H_{11}NO_2$, occurring in sugar beets and other plants and formerly used in treatment of muscular degeneration. [Latin *bēta,* BEET + -INE.]
be·take (bi-táyk, bə- ‖ bee-) *tr.v.* **-took** (-tóok), **-taken, -taking, -takes. 1.** To cause (oneself) to go or move. **2.** *Archaic.* To commit or apply (oneself) to something: *He betook himself to fasting.*

Be·tan·court (bét-an-kóor, -kóort), **Rómulo** (1908–81), Venezuelan politician. He founded the National Democratic party (1935), later renamed Democratic Action. He spent several years in exile but served twice as president.
beta particle *n.* A high-speed electron or positron, especially one emitted in radioactive decay.
beta ray *n.* A stream of beta particles, especially of electrons.
beta rhythm *n.* The waveform occurring in electroencephalograms of the adult brain, characteristically having a frequency from 18 to 30 cycles per second and associated with an alert waking state. Also called "beta wave". Compare **alpha rhythm.**
be·ta·tron (béeta-tron ‖ *U.S.* báytə-) *n.* A fixed-radius magnetic induction electron **accelerator** *(see)* capable of accelerating electrons to energies of a few million to a few hundred million electron volts. [BETA + -TRON.]
be·tel (béet'l) *n.* A climbing Asiatic plant, *Piper betle,* the leaves of which are chewed with the betel nut, especially in southeastern Asia, to induce both stimulating and narcotic effects. [Portuguese *betel, betle,* from Malayalam *veṭṭila.*]
Be·tel·geuse, Be·tel·geux (béet'l-zherz, -jōōz, -jérz) *n.* A bright red intrinsic-variable star, about 600 light years from Earth, in the constellation Orion. [French *Bételgeuse,* from Arabic *bīt al-jauzā',* "shoulder of the Giant (Orion)".]
betel nut *n.* Also **be·tel·nut** (béet'l-nut). The seed of the fruit of the betel palm, chewed, together with betel leaves and lime, by many peoples of southeastern Asia.
betel palm *n.* A palm tree, *Areca catechu,* of tropical Asia, having feather-like leaves and orange or scarlet fruit. See **betel nut.**
bête noire (báyt nwár) *n., pl.* **bêtes noires** (pronounced as singular). Someone or something that one especially dislikes or avoids. [French, "black beast".]
beth (bet) *n.* The second letter of the Hebrew alphabet. [Hebrew *bēth,* "house".]
Beth·a·ny (béthəni). *Arabic* **Al-'Ayzariyah.** Small village at the southeastern foot of the Mount of Olives, in the Israeli-occupied West Bank. The miracle of Lazarus's resurrection took place there (the Arabic name means "Lazarus").
Be·the (báytə), **Hans Albrecht** (1906–). American physicist, born in Germany. His chief work has been the study of nuclear reactions in stars, especially that by which hydrogen is converted to helium. He was awarded the Nobel prize in physics (1967).
beth·el (béth'l) *n.* **1.** A Nonconformist chapel. **2.** A chapel for seamen. [Hebrew *bēth 'Ēl,* "house of God".]
Bethel. A town of Biblical Palestine, about 18 kilometres (11 miles) north of Jerusalem. Genesis 28:19.
be·think (bi-thíngk, bə- ‖ bee-) *v.* **-thought** (-tháwt), **-thinking, -thinks.** *Archaic.* —*tr.* **1.** To reflect upon; think about; consider. **2.** To remind (oneself); remember. —*intr.* To meditate; ponder. [Middle English *bethinken,* Old English *bethencan :* be-, about + *thencan,* to THINK.]
Bethlehem (béth-li-hem, -əm). Small market town in the Judaean Hills, south of Jerusalem, in the Israeli-occupied West Bank. Traditionally held to be the birthplace of Christ, it was the home and probably the birthplace of **David,** who was annointed King of Israel by Samuel here.
be·tide (bi-tíd, bə- ‖ bee-) *v.* **-tided, -tiding, -tides.** —*tr.* To happen to: *Woe betide you if you harm her daughter.* —*intr. Archaic.* To take place; befall. —See Synonyms at **happen.** [Middle English *betiden :* be-, thoroughly + *tiden,* to happen, Old English *tīdan.*]
be·times (bi-tímz, bə- ‖ bee-) *adv. Archaic.* **1.** Early; in good time: *He awoke betimes.* **2.** Quickly; soon. [Middle English, adverbial genitive of *betime :* be, BY + TIME.]
bê·tise (be-téez) *n., pl.* **bêtises** (pronounced as singular). **1.** A foolish or gauche remark or action. **2.** Folly; ignorance. [French.]
Bet·je·man (béchəmən), **Sir John** (1906–84). British Poet Laureate 1972–84. He produced many collections of poems, including a verse autobiography, *Summoned by Bells* (1960), and wrote extensively on Victorian architecture.
be·to·ken (bi-tókən, bə- ‖ bee-) *tr.v.* **-kened, -kening, -kens.** To give a sign or portent of: *Those clouds betoken snow.* See Synonyms at **foretell.** [Middle English *betokenen,* Old English *bitācnian* (unattested).] —**be·to·ken·er** *n.*
bet·o·ny (béttəni) *n., pl.* **-nies.** Any of several plants of the genus *Stachys;* especially, *S. officinalis,* native to Eurasia, having a spike of reddish-purple flowers. [Middle English *betone,* from Old French *betoine,* from Latin *bētonica, vettonica,* probably after the *Vettones,* an ancient Iberian tribe.]
be·took. Past tense of **betake.**
be·tray (bi-tráy, bə- ‖ bee-) *tr.v.* **-trayed, -traying, -trays. 1.** To give aid or information to an enemy of; commit treason against or be a traitor to: *betray one's nation.* **2.** To be disloyal or faithless to. **3.** To divulge in a breach of confidence: *"A servant . . . betrayed their presence . . . to the Germans."* (William Styron). **4.** To make known unintentionally: *"Only the young have the right to betray their ignorance"* (Henry Adams). **5.** To show unintentionally; reveal; indicate: *His shaking hands betrayed his nervousness.* **6.** To deceive; lead astray. **7.** *Archaic.* To seduce and forsake (a woman). —See Synonyms at **reveal, deceive.** [Middle English *betrayen :* be-, thoroughly + *trayen,* to betray, from Old French *trair,* from Latin *trādere : trāns-,* over + *dare,* to give.] —**be·tray·al, be·tray·ment** *n.* —**be·tray·er** *n.*
be·troth (bi-tróth, bə-, -tróth ‖ bee-) *tr.v.* **-trothed, -trothing, -troths.** *Archaic.* **1.** To promise to give in marriage. **2.** To promise to marry.

be·troth·al (bi-tró̄th'l, bə- ‖ bee-, -tró̄th'l) *n.* Also **be·troth·ment** (-tró̄th-mənt ‖ -tró̄th-). **1.** The act of becoming betrothed or of betrothing. **2.** A mutual promise to marry; an engagement.

be·trothed (bi-tró̄thd, bə-, -tró̄tht) *adj.* Engaged to be married.
~*n., pl.* **betrothed.** A person who is engaged to be married.

bet·ter¹ (béttər) Comparative of **good. 2.** Comparative of **well.**
~*adj.* **1.** Greater in excellence or higher in quality. **2.** More useful, suitable, or desirable. **3.** Larger; greater: *the better part of a summer.* **4.** Healthier than before.
~*adv.* **1.** In a more useful, suitable, or desirable way. **2.** To a greater or higher extent or degree. —**go one better.** To outdo or improve upon (someone or something). —**had better.** Ought to; would be wise to; had best. —**think better of.** To change one's mind about (a course of action) after reconsideration.
~*n.* **1.** Something more useful, excellent, desirable, or suitable. Usually used with *the.* **2.** *Plural.* One's superiors, especially in social standing, competence, or intelligence —**all the better for.** Better as a result of. —**all the better to.** Better for the purpose of. —**for the better.** Resulting in or aiming for an improvement. —**for better (or) for worse.** Whatever happens subsequently; despite any future setbacks. —**get** or **have the better of. 1.** To overcome; defeat. **2.** To gain an advantage over.
~*v.* **bettered, -tering, -ters.** —*tr.* **1.** To improve. Often used reflexively. **2.** To surpass or exceed. —*intr.* To become better. —See Synonyms at **improve.** [Middle English *bettre,* Old English *betera.*]

bet·ter², bet·tor (bettər) *n.* One who bets.

better half *n.* A spouse. Used humorously.

bet·ter·ment (béttərmənt) *n.* **1.** An improvement. **2.** *Law.* Any improvement, excluding mere repairs, that adds to the value of real property.

better-off (bétter-óff). Comparative of **well-off**
~*adj.* **1.** In a better condition. **2.** Wealthier; more prosperous.

bet·ting shop (bétting) *n.* Licensed premises where bets may be placed; a bookmaker's shop.

be·tween (bi-twéen, bə- ‖ bee-) *prep.* **1.** Intermediate in the space separating two places or things. **2.** Intermediate to two times, quantities, or degrees: *between 11 o'clock and 12 o'clock.* **3.** At a point in relation to two specified points, such that a perpendicular from the first point can be dropped to the line joining the two other points. **4.** Connecting spatially: *a path between the house and the road.* **5.** Connecting in reciprocal action or effort: *an agreement between workers and management.* **6.** By the combined efforts of: *Between them, they succeeded.* **7.** In the combined possession of: *They had three pounds between them.* **8.** Either one or the other of: *choose between riding and walking.* —See Synonyms and Usage note at **among.** —**between ourselves** or **you and me.** In confidence.
~*adv.* In an intermediate space, position, or time; in the interim. —**in between.** In an intermediate position or situation. [Middle English *betwene,* Old English *betwēonum.*]

be·tween·times (bi-twéen-tīmz, bə- ‖ bee-) *adv.* In the interval; between other acts.

be·twixt (bi-twíkst, bə- ‖ bee-) *adv. Archaic & Poetic.* Between.
~*prep. Archaic & Poetic.* Between. —**betwixt and between.** In an intermediate or indecisive state; in a middle position; neither wholly one nor wholly the other. [Middle English *betwix(te),* Old English *betwēohs, betwihs.*]

Beu·lah (béwlə). **1.** In the Old Testament, the land of Israel. Isaiah 62:4. **2.** The land of peace described in Bunyan's *Pilgrim's Progress.*

BeV *Chiefly U.S.* A thousand million electron volts. The abbreviation GeV (gigaelectron volts) is preferred in standard international usage.

Be·van (bévv'n), **A·neu·rin** (ə-nír-in), known as Nye (1897–1960). British politician. A coal miner and trade unionist, he was a Labour member of Parliament (1929–60). As Minister of Health (1945–51) he was the chief architect of the National Health Service.

bev·el (bévv'l) *n.* **1.** The angle or inclination of a line or surface that meets another at any angle but 90 degrees. **2.** A rule with an adjustable arm, used to measure or draw angles or to fix a surface at an angle. In this sense, also called "bevel square".
~*adj.* Inclined at an angle; slanted.
~*v.* **bevelled** or *U.S.* **beveled, -elling** or *U.S.* **-eling, -els.** —*tr.* To cut at an inclination that forms an angle other than a right angle. —*intr.* To be inclined; slope. [Old French *bevel* (unattested), from *baif,* open-mouthed, from *bayer,* to gape. See **bay** (space).]

bevel gear *n.* Either of a pair of gears with teeth surfaces cut so that the gear shafts are not parallel.

bev·er·age (bévvərij) *n.* Any of various liquid refreshments, usually excluding water. [Middle English *beverege,* from Old French *beverage,* from Vulgar Latin *biberāticum* (unattested), from Latin *bibere,* to drink.]

Bev·e·ridge (bévvərij), **William Henry, 1st Baron** (1879–1963). British economist and politician. His report paved the way for the welfare-state legislation of **Attlee's** Labour government (1945–51).

Bev·er·ly Hills (bévvərli). City in California, completely encompassed by greater Los Angeles. It adjoins Hollywood and is famous as the residential area of wealthy stars of showbusiness.

Bev·in (bévvin), **Ernest** (1881–1951). British trade unionist and politician. Bevin became secretary of the dock workers' union (1911) which became the Transport and General Workers' Union (1921). He entered Parliament (1940) and joined Churchill's war cabinet as Minister of Labour and National Service. As Foreign Secretary (1945–51) he played an important part in the establishment of NATO.

be·vor, bea·ver (béevər) *n.* **1.** A moveable piece of medieval armour attached to a helmet or breastplate to protect the mouth and chin. **2.** The visor on a helmet. [Middle English *baviere,* from Old French, *bib,* from *baver,* to slaver, from *beve,* saliva, from (unattested) Vulgar Latin *baba* (imitative).]

bev·vy (bévvi) *n., pl.* **-vies.** *Regional.* **1.** A drink, usually alcoholic. **2.** A drinking spree. [Perhaps from Old French *bevee,* a drinking. See **beverage.**] —**bev·vied** *adj.*

bev·y (bévvi) *n., pl.* **-ies. 1.** A group of animals or birds, especially larks or quail. **2.** A group, especially of girls. [15th century : origin obscure.]

be·wail (bi-wáyl, bə- ‖ bee-) *v.* **-wailed, -wailing, -wails.** —*tr.* To express sorrow or regret over; cry or complain about. —*intr.* To wail or lament. —**be·wail·er** *n.* —**be·wail·ment** *n.*

be·ware (bi-waír, bə- ‖ bee-) *v.* **-wared, -waring, -wares.** —*tr.* To be on guard against; be cautious of. Used chiefly in the imperative or infinitive. —*intr.* To be wary or careful. Used chiefly in the imperative or infinitive, sometimes with *of.* [Middle English *be war :* BE (imperative) + *war(e),* WARY.]

Be·wick (béw-ik), **Thomas** (1753–1828). English illustrator and wood engraver, whose best-known work is his *History of British Birds* (1797–1804).

be·wil·der (bi-wíldər, bə- ‖ bee-) *tr.v.* **-dered, -dering, -ders. 1.** To confuse or befuddle, especially with numerous conflicting situations, objects, or statements. **2.** *Rare.* To cause to become lost. —See Synonyms at **puzzle.** [BE- + archaic *wilder,* to stray, probably from WILDERNESS.] —**be·wil·der·ing·ly** *adv.*

be·wil·der·ment (bi-wíldərmənt, bə- ‖ bee-) *n.* **1.** The condition of being bewildered. **2.** A situation of perplexity or confusion.

be·witch (bi-wích, bə- ‖ bee-) *tr.v.* **-witched, -witching, -witches. 1.** To place under one's power by magic; cast a spell over. **2.** To captivate completely; fascinate. [Middle English *bewicchen :* be-, thoroughly + *wicchen,* to bewitch, Old English *wiccian.*] —**be·witch·er** *n.* —**be·witch·ing·ly** *adv.* —**be·witch·ment** *n.*

be·wray (bi-ráy, bə- ‖ bee-) *tr.v.* **-wrayed, -wraying, -wrays.** *Archaic.* To disclose, especially inadvertently; betray. [Middle English *bewreien :* be-, thoroughly + *wreien,* to accuse, Old English *wrēgan,* from Germanic *wrōgian* (unattested).]

bey (bay) *n.* **1.** A provincial governor in the Ottoman Empire. **2.** A native ruler of the former kingdom of Tunis. **3. a.** A Turkish title of honour and respect. **b.** A Turkish form of address equivalent to *Mr.* [Turkish, prince, lord, gentleman, from Ottoman Turkish *beg.*]

be·yond (bi-yónd, -ónd ‖ bee-) *prep.* **1.** Farther away than; on the far side of. **2.** After (a specified time); later than. **3. a.** Past or outside the limits, reach, or scope of. **b.** Not comprehensible to: *It's beyond me.* **4.** Besides; other than.
~*adv.* Farther along; to the farther side.
~*n. Sometimes capital* **B.** That which is outside the scope of human experience; especially, life after death: *the great beyond.* [Middle English *beyonde,* Old English *begeondan : be,* BY + *geondan,* farther, from *geond,* YONDER.]

bez·ant, bez·zant (bézz'nt ‖ bi-zánt) *n.* Also **byz·ant** (bízz'nt ‖ bi-zánt). **1.** A gold coin issued in Byzantium; a solidus. **2.** *Architecture.* A flat disc, used as an ornament. **3.** *Heraldry.* A round gold mark. [Middle English *besant,* from Old French, from Latin *Bȳzantius,* of BYZANTIUM.]

bez·el, bez·il (bézz'l) *n.* **1.** A slanting surface or bevel on the edge of various cutting tools. **2.** The upper, faceted portion of a cut gem, above the girdle. **3.** A groove or flange designed to hold the bevelled edge of a watch crystal or a gem. [Probably from Old French *besel†* (unattested).]

be·zique (bi-zéek) *n.* **1.** A card game similar to whist for two players, played with two packs of cards with all of the cards from two to six removed. **2.** The highest-scoring combination in this game, that of queen of spades and knave of diamonds. [French *bésigue†.*]

be·zoar (bée-zawr ‖ -zōr) *n.* A hard gastric or intestinal mass, found chiefly in ruminants. Once considered an antidote to poison. [Middle English *bezear,* from Old French *bezar,* from Arabic *bāzahr,* from Persian *pād-zahr : pād,* protecting against, + *zahr,* poison.]

bf. boldface.

b.f. 1. boldface. **2.** *Accounting.* brought forward.

B/F *Accounting.* brought forward.

Bha·ga·vad-Gi·ta, bha·ga·vad-gi·ta (búggəvəd-géetə, bággəvəd-) *n.* A sacred Hindu text that is incorporated into the *Mahabharata,* an ancient Sanskrit epic. It takes the form of a philosophical dialogue in which Krishna, disguised as a charioteer, explains to the prince Arjuna the whole nature of being. [Sanskrit *Bhagavad-gītā,* "Song of the Blessed One" : *Bhágaḥ,* god of wealth, "the allotter", from *bhájati,* apportion, enjoy + *gītā,* a song.]

bha·ji·a (ba'aji-ə) *n.* Also **bha·gi** (ba'a-ji). An Indian savoury consisting of a vegetable deep-fried in gram flour batter. [Hindi.]

bhak·ti (búkti) *n. Hinduism.* The devotional way of achieving salvation, open to all irrespective of sex or caste. [Sanskrit, "portion", from *bhajati,* he allocates.]

bhang (bang) *n.* **1.** A plant, **hemp** (see). **2.** Any of several narcotics made from hemp. [Hindi *bhāng,* from Sanskrit *bhangā†,* hemp.]

bhang·ra (bangrə) *n.* Anglo-Asian danceable music that combines pop with Punjabi music. [Indic.]

Bharat. See **India, Union of.**

bha·ra·ta·na·tyam (búrrətə-naát-yəm) *n.* Also **bha·ra·ta na·tya** (-yə). A traditional Hindu dance, formerly performed as a religious ceremony, involving pantomime and song. [Sanskrit, "Bharata's dancing" : *Bharata,* supposed author of a classical treatise on dance and drama + *nátyam,* dancing, dramatic art.]

bhin·di (bíndi) *n.* Okra *(see)* as used in Indian dishes. [Hindi.]

Bho·pal (bō-pa'al). The capital city of Madhya Pradesh state in central India. A major railway junction and trade centre, it is the site of the 19th-century Táj-ul-Masjid, the largest mosque in India. In 1984 the city was the scene of disaster, when about 3,000 people were killed by a gas leakage from a chemical plant.

bhp, b.h.p. brake horsepower.

Bhu·tan, Kingdom of (bōō-ta'an, -tán). Isolated country in the eastern Himalayas. Although independent, its foreign affairs were directed by Great Britain (1910–49), and since then by India. The country's eight fertile valleys opening on to the plains of India support more than 95 per cent of its people. The main sources of foreign exchange are tourism and exports of timber, postage stamps, fruit, and handicrafts. Less than five per cent of the people are literate. Area, 46 500 square kilometres (17,954 square miles). Population, 1,810,000. Capital, Thimphu. See map at **India.**

Bhu·tan·ese (bōōtə-neéz ‖ -neéss) *n., pl.* **Bhutanese.** Also **Bhu·ta·ni** (bōō-ta'ani) *pl.* **-nis** or collectively **Bhutani.** 1. A native or inhabitant of Bhutan. 2. The Sino-Tibetan language spoken in Bhutan. Also called "Dzongkha". —*adj.* Of or characteristic of Bhutan, its people, or their language or culture.

Bhut·to (bōōtō) **Benazir** (1953–). Pakistani politician. Prime Minister of Pakistan (1988–90, 1993–97), and daughter of Z. A. Bhutto.

Bhutto, Zulfikar Ali (1928–79). Pakistani politician. In 1963 he was appointed foreign minister, quarrelled with the government over the peace terms with India (1965) and formed his own opposition party, the Pakistan People's Party (1967). In 1971 he became president of Pakistan and subsequently prime minister (1973). In 1977 he won a massive victory at the polls; but his opponents claimed that he had rigged the elections, and in July he was deposed by an army coup. Two years later he was executed for alleged crimes against the state.

bi (bī) *adj. Slang.* Bisexual. —*n. Slang.* A bisexual person.

bi-¹. Variant of **bio-.**

bi-², bin- *comb. form.* Indicates: 1. Two; for example, **binocular.** 2. **a.** Appearance or occurrence in intervals of two; for example, **bicentennial. b.** Appearance or occurrence twice during; for example, **biannual.** 3. Occurrence on both sides or directions; for example, **biconcave, bilateral.** 4. *Chemistry.* **a.** An acid salt, in which only part of the hydrogen of the acid has been replaced; for example, **sodium bicarbonate. b.** An organic compound containing a double radical; for example, **biphenyl.** [Latin *bi-, bin-,* from *bis,* twice.]

Bi The symbol for the element bismuth.

Bi·a·fra (bee-áffrə, bī-, -a'afrə). Former Eastern Region of Nigeria, chiefly peopled by the Ibo. It seceded as Biafra (1967–70), reverting only after a savage civil war. It now forms the federal states of Anambra, Imo, and Cross River. —**Bi·af·ran** *adj. & n.*

Biafra, Bight of. The eastern arm of the Gulf of Guinea on the west coast of Africa, stretching from the Niger delta to northern Gabon.

Bia·ly·stok (bya-wístok, -lístok, bee-ál-i-stok). Industrial and railway city in northeast Poland. Nearly half of the city's population was killed during the Nazi occupation (1941–44).

bi·an·nu·al (bī-ánnew-əl ‖ -ánnewl, -án-yəl) *adj.* Happening twice each year; semiannual. —**bi·an·nu·al·ly** *adv.*

Usage: There is confusion between this word and *biennial. Biannual* means "twice a year"; *biennial* means "once in two years" or "lasting for two years".

Biar·ritz (beér-ríts, -ríts). Seaside resort and spa in southwestern France, on the Bay of Biscay. It is a fashionable gambling resort.

bi·as (bī-əss) *n.* 1. **a.** Preference or inclination that inhibits impartial judgment; prejudice. **b.** A particular instance of this. 2. A line cutting diagonally across the grain of fabric: *cut cloth on the bias.* 3. **a.** A weight or irregularity in a ball that causes it to swerve, as in bowls. **b.** The tendency of such a ball to swerve. 4. The fixed voltage applied to an electrode in a valve, transistor, or electronic circuit. 5. *Statistics.* **a.** An influence that distorts the true expected value of a statistic. **b.** A distortion in findings from an oversight in investigation. —*adj.* Slanting or diagonal; oblique: *a bias fold.* —*adv.* Obliquely; aslant. —*tr.v.* **biased** or **biassed, biasing** or **biassing, biases** or **biasses.** 1. To cause to have a prejudiced view; prejudice or influence. 2. To apply a small voltage to (an electrode). [French, from Old French *biais,* oblique, from Old Provençal, perhaps from Greek *epikarsios*†, oblique.]

bias binding *n.* A strip of material cut across the grain of a fabric used to strengthen hems, finish edges, or the like.

bi·ath·lete (bī-áth-leet) *n.* One who takes part in a biathlon.

bi·ath·lon (bī-áth-lon, -lən) *n.* A cross-country skiing competition in which competitors must shoot at targets as they ski.

bi·au·ric·u·lar (bī-aw-ríckew-lər) *adj.* Also **bi·au·ric·u·late** (-lət, -lit). Possessing two auricles.

bi·ax·i·al (bī-áksi-əl) *adj.* Having two axes. Used especially of crystals that have two optic axes. —**bi·ax·i·al·i·ty** (-ál-əti) *n.* —**bi·ax·i·al·ly** *adv.*

bib (bib) *n.* 1. A piece of cloth or plastic worn under the chin by small children, to protect the clothing during meals. 2. The part of an apron, smock, or pair of overalls worn over the chest. 3. A

European food fish, *Gadus luscus,* related to the cod, with a barbel on its lower jaw. Also called "pout", "whiting pout". —*v.* **bibbed, bibbing, bibs.** *Archaic.* —*tr.* To drink; imbibe. —*intr.* To indulge in drinking; tipple. [Middle English *bibben,* to tipple, drink, perhaps from Latin *bibere.*]

Bib. Bible; Biblical.

bib and tucker *n. Informal.* Clothing; an outfit. Usually used in the phrase *one's best bib and tucker.*

bibb (bib) *n.* 1. A bracket on the mast of a ship to support the trestletrees. 2. A bibcock. [Variant of BIB (napkin).]

bib·ber (bíbbər) *n.* A tippler; a drinker: *a wine-bibber.* [From BIB (to drink).]

bib·cock (bíb-kok) *n.* A tap with a nozzle that is bent downwards. Also called "bibb". [BIB (napkin) + COCK.]

bi·be·lot (bíbblō) *n.* A trinket or small decorative curio. [French, from Old French *beubelet,* from a reduplication of *bel,* beautiful, from Latin *bellus,* handsome, fine.]

bibl., Bibl. Biblical.

Bi·ble (bī'b'l) *n. Abbr.* **B., Bib.** 1. The sacred book of Christianity, a collection of ancient writings including the books of both the Old Testament and the New Testament, and, in the Roman Catholic Bible, the deuterocanonical books. See **Old Testament, New Testament, Apocrypha, Authorised Version, Revised Version, Revised Standard Version, Douay Bible, Vulgate, New English Bible, Jerusalem Bible.** 2. The Old Testament, the sacred book of Judaism. See **Hebrew Scriptures.** 3. *Small* **b.** Any book or collection of writings constituting the guiding text of a religion, political movement, or individual lifestyle. 4. *Small* **b.** Any book considered authoritative in its field. [Middle English, from Old French, from Medieval Latin *biblia,* from Greek *(ta) biblia,* "(the) books", plural of *biblion,* book, originally a diminutive of *biblos, bublos,* papyrus, scroll, book, after *Bublos,* Phoenician port from which the Egyptian papyrus was exported to Greece.]

Bible Belt *n.* Those sections of the United States, especially in the South and Middle West, where Protestant fundamentalism prevails. [Coined by H.L. MENCKEN, about 1925.]

Bible paper *n.* A thin, strong, opaque printing paper used for Bibles and reference books. Also called "India paper".

Bible thumper *n. Informal.* A person who enthusiastically, dogmatically, and often aggressively expounds and refers to the Bible or religion. —**Bible-thumping** *n. & adj.*

Bib·li·cal (bíbblik'l) *adj. Sometimes small* **b.** *Abbr.* **Bib., Bibl., bibl.** 1. Of, pertaining to, or contained in the Bible. 2. In keeping with the nature of the Bible, especially: **a.** Suggestive of the personages or times depicted in the Bible. **b.** Suggestive of the prose or narrative style of the Authorised Version. [Obsolete *biblic,* probably from Medieval Latin *biblicus,* from *biblia,* BIBLE.] —**Bib·li·cal·ly** *adv.*

Biblical Aramaic *n.* A form of Aramaic that was the original language of the non-Hebrew portions of the Old Testament, such as certain passages in Ezra, Daniel, and Jeremiah. Also called "Chaldee". Compare **Aramaic.**

Bib·li·cist (bíbbli-sist) *n.* Also **Bib·list** (bíbblist). 1. An expert in the Bible. 2. A person who interprets the Bible literally. 3. One who emphasises the authority of the Bible rather than tradition. [From obsolete *biblic,* BIBLICAL.] —**Bib·li·cism** *n.*

biblio- *comb. form.* Indicates books; for example, **bibliomania.** [Greek *biblion,* book. See **Bible.**]

bib·li·o·film (bíbbli-ō-film) *n.* A type of microfilm used especially to photograph the pages of books.

bibliog. bibliographer; bibliography.

bib·li·og·ra·pher (bíbbli-óggrəfər) *n.* Also **bib·li·o·graph** (-əgraaf, -əgraf). *Abbr.* **bibliog.** 1. An expert in the description and cataloguing of printed matter. 2. One who compiles a bibliography.

bib·li·og·ra·phy (bíbbli-óggrəfi) *n., pl.* **-phies.** *Abbr.* **bibliog.** 1. **a.** A list of the works of a particular author or publisher, or of sources of information in print on a particular subject. **b.** A list of sources used as reference for the writing of a book, thesis, or the like. 2. **a.** The description and identification of the editions, dates of issue, authorship, and typography of books or other written material. **b.** A compilation of such information. [French *bibliographie,* from New Latin *bibliographia* : BIBLIO- + -GRAPHY.] —**bib·li·o·graph·ic** (-ə-gráffik), **bib·li·o·graph·i·cal** *adj.* —**bib·li·o·graph·i·cal·ly** *adv.*

bib·li·ol·a·try (bíbbli-óllətri) *n.* 1. Excessive adherence to a literal interpretation of the Bible. 2. Extreme devotion to or concern with books. [BIBLIO- + -LATRY.] —**bib·li·ol·a·ter** (-óllətər) *n.* —**bib·li·ol·a·trous** *adj.*

bib·li·o·man·cy (bíbbli-ō-manssi, -ə-) *n., pl.* **-cies.** Divination by interpretation of a passage chosen at random from a book, especially the Bible. [BIBLIO- + -MANCY.]

bib·li·o·ma·ni·a (bíbbli-ō-máyn-yə, -ə-, -i-ə) *n.* An exaggerated liking for acquiring and owning books. [BIBLIO- + -MANIA.] —**bib·li·o·ma·ni·ac** (-i-ak, -yak) *n. & adj.* —**bib·li·o·ma·ni·a·cal** (-mə-nī-ək'l) *adj.*

bib·li·o·phile (bíbbli-ə-fīl, -ō-) *n.* Also **bib·li·o·phil** (-fil), **bib·li·oph·i·list** (-óff'l-ist). 1. One who loves books. 2. A book collector. [French : BIBLIO- + -PHILE.] —**bib·li·o·phil·ic** (-fillik) *adj.* —**bib·li·oph·i·lism** (-óff'l-iz'm), **bib·li·oph·i·ly** (-óff'l-i) *n.* —**bibli·ophi·lis·tic** (-óff'l-ístik) *adj.*

bib·li·o·pole (bíbbli-ə-pōl, -ō-) *n.* Also **bib·li·op·o·list** (-ópp'l-ist). A person who deals in rare books. [Latin *bibliopōla,* from Greek *bibliopōlēs* : BIBLIO- + *pōlēs,* seller, from *pōlein,* to sell.] —**bib·li·o·pol·**

ic (-póllik) *adj.* —**bib·li·op·o·ly** (-ópp'l-i) *n.*

bib·li·o·the·ca (bíbbli-ə-théekə, -ō-) *n.* **1.** A book collection; a library. **2.** A catalogue of books. [Latin *bibliothēca,* from Greek *bibliothēkē,* "case for books" : BIBLIO- + *thēkē,* receptacle, case.] —**bib·li·o·the·cal** *adj.*

Biblist. Variant of **Biblicist.**

bib·u·lous (bíbbew-ləss) *adj.* Given to or marked by convivial drinking. [Latin *bibulus,* from *bibere,* to drink.] —**bib·u·lous·ly** *adv.* —**bib·u·lous·ness** *n.*

bi·cam·er·al (bī-kámmərəl, bī-) *adj.* Composed of two houses, chambers, or branches: *a bicameral legislature.* [BI- + Late Latin *camera,* room, CHAMBER.] —**bi·cam·er·al·ism** *n.*

bi·cap·su·lar (bī-kápsewlər, bī-) *adj. Botany.* **1.** Having two capsules. **2.** Having a capsule with two locules.

bi·carb (bī-kárb) *n. Informal.* **Sodium bicarbonate** *(see).*

bi·car·bon·ate (bī-kárbə-nit, bī-, -kárb-, -nət, -nayt) *n.* The group HCO_3 or ion $-HCO_3$ or a compound, such as sodium bicarbonate, containing this group or ion. Also called "hydrogen carbonate".

bicarbonate of soda *n.* **Sodium bicarbonate** *(see).*

bice blue (bīss) *n.* Moderate blue, the colour of azurite. [Partial translation of French *azur bis,* "dark blue" : AZURE + *bis,* brown, tawny, from Old French *bis†.*]

bice green *n.* Moderate yellow green, the colour of malachite. [See **bice blue.**]

bi·cen·ten·a·ry (bī-sen-téenəri ‖ *U.S. also* bī-séntə-nerri) *n., pl.* **-ries.** A 200th anniversary or its celebration. —**bi·cen·ten·a·ry** *adj.*

bi·cen·ten·ni·al (bī-sen-ténni-əl) *adj.* **1.** Happening once every 200 years. **2.** Lasting for 200 years. **3.** Pertaining to a 200th anniversary.

~*n. Chiefly U.S.* A bicentenary.

bi·cen·tric (bī-sén-trik) *adj.* Having two centres. —**bi·cen·tric·i·ty** (-tríssəti) *n.*

bi·ceph·a·lous (bī-séffə-ləss) *adj.* Two-headed.

bi·ceps (bī-seps) *n., pl.* **biceps** or **-cepses** (-sepsiz). Any muscle having two heads or points of origin, especially: **1.** The large muscle at the front of the upper arm that flexes the elbow joint. **2.** The large muscle at the back of the thigh that flexes the knee joint. [New Latin, from Latin, "two-headed" : BI- + *-ceps,* from *caput,* head.]

bi·chlo·ride (bī-kláwr-īd ‖ -klōr-) *n. Chemistry.* **Dichloride** *(see).*

bi·chro·mate (bī-krōmayt) *n.* A **dichromate** *(see).*

bi·cip·i·tal (bī-síppit'l) *adj.* Of or pertaining to the biceps. [New Latin *biceps* (stem *bicipit-*), BICEPS.]

bick·er (bíckər) *intr.v.* **-ered, -ering, -ers. 1.** To engage in a petty quarrel; squabble. **2.** *Poetic.* To flicker; glisten; quiver. —See Synonyms at **argue.**

~*n.* A petty quarrel; a tiff. [Middle English *bikeren†,* to attack.] —**bick·er·er** *n.*

bick·y, bik·ky (bícki) *n. British Informal.* A biscuit.

bi·col·our (bī-kullər) *adj.* Also **bi·col·oured** (bī-kullərd). Having two colours.

bi·con·cave (bī-kon-káyv, -kóngkayv) *adj.* Concave on both sides or surfaces. Said especially of a lens. —**bi·con·cav·i·ty** (-kávvəti) *n.*

bi·con·di·tion·al (bī-kən-dísh'n-əl ‖ -kon-) *n. Logic.* **1.** A statement containing two propositions related in such a way that one can be true only if the other is true, and false only if the other is false. **2.** The relation that exists between two such propositions. Compare **equivalence.** —**bi·con·di·tion·al** *adj.*

bi·con·vex (bī-kon-véks, -kónveks) *adj.* Convex on both sides or surfaces. Said especially of a lens. —**bi·con·vex·i·ty** (-véksəti) *n.*

bi·corn (bī-kawrn) *adj.* Also **bi·cor·nate** (-kórn-ayt, -ət, -it), **bi·cor·nu·ate** (bī-kórnew-ayt, -it). **1.** Having two horns or two horn-shaped parts. **2.** Shaped like a crescent. [Latin *bicornis* : BI- + *cornū,* HORN.]

bi·cor·po·ral (bī-kórpərəl) *adj.* Also **bi·cor·po·re·al** (bī-kawr-páwri-əl ‖ -pōri-). Having two distinct bodies or main parts.

bi·cul·tur·al·ism (bī-kúlchərəliz'm, bī-) *n.* The coexistence of two separate cultures in one community. —**bi·cul·tur·al** *adj.*

bi·cus·pid (bī-kúspid) *adj.* Also **bi·cus·pi·date** (-ayt). Having two points or cusps, as the crescent moon or the **mitral valve** *(see)* of the heart do.

~*n.* A bicuspid tooth, especially a **premolar** *(see).* [New Latin *bicuspis* (stem *bicuspid-*) : BI- + Latin *cuspis,* point, CUSP.]

bi·cy·cle (bī-sik'l) *n.* A vehicle, usually designed for one person, consisting of a metal frame mounted upon two wire-spoked wheels with narrow rubber tyres, one behind the other. It has a seat, handlebars for steering, brakes, and two pedals by which it is driven. ~*intr.v.* **bicycled, -cling, -cles.** To ride or travel on a bicycle. [French : BI- + Greek *kuklos,* circle, wheel.] —**bi·cy·clist** (bī-siklist) *n.*

bicycle clip *n.* Either of a pair of metal hoops that are worn over the ankles when cycling in order to keep the trouser legs out of the way of the bicycle chain.

bicycle kick *n.* In soccer, a kick in which a player meets an aerial pass and propels it by an acrobatic leap backwards.

bicycle pump *n.* A portable hand pump for inflating bicycle tyres.

bi·cy·clic (bī-síklik, bī-, -sícklik) *adj.* Also **bi·cy·cli·cal** (-síklik'l, -sícklik'l) **1.** Consisting of or having two cycles. **2.** *Botany.* Composed of or arranged in two distinct whorls, as are the petals or stamens of a flower. **3.** *Chemistry.* Consisting of or having molecules containing two rings.

bid (bid) *v.* For transitive senses 1, 2, 3: **bade** (bad, bayd) or *archaic* **bad** (bad), **bidden** (bídd'n) or **bid, bidding, bids.** For remaining senses: **bid, bid, bidding, bids.** —*tr.* **1. a.** To direct; command. **b.** To enjoin politely. **2.** To utter (a greeting or salutation). **3.** To invite to attend; summon. **4.** In card games, to state one's intention to take (tricks of a certain number or suit): *bid four hearts.* **5.** To offer or propose (an amount). —*intr.* **1.** To make an offer to pay or accept a specified price. **2.** To seek to win or attain something; strive: *bid for the contract.* —See Synonyms at **command.** —**bid fair.** To appear likely; seem. *Note:* In this phrase the past tense and past participle is **bid.**

~*n.* **1. a.** An offer or proposal of a price, as for an item at an auction or for a contract. **b.** The amount offered or proposed. **2.** In card games: **a.** The act of bidding. **b.** The number of tricks or points declared. **c.** The trump or no-trump declared. **d.** The turn of a player to bid. **3.** A serious attempt to gain something; a striving: *a bid for the party leadership.* [Bid, bade, bidden; from two verbs: 1. Middle English *bidden,* ask, beseech, demand, command, *bad, beden,* Old English *biddan, bæd* (plural *bǣdon*), *(ge)beden.* 2. Middle English *beden,* to offer, present, proclaim, command (last sense adopted from *bidden*), *bead, boden,* Old English *bēodan, bēad* (plural *budon*), *(ge)boden.*] —**bid·der** *n.*

bi·dar·ka (bī-dárkə) *n.* A hide-covered canoe used by Eskimos of Alaska. [Russian *baidarka,* diminutive of *baidara†.*]

bid·da·ble (bíddəb'l) *adj.* **1.** Worth bidding on. Said of a hand or suit in cards. **2.** Docile; tractable. —**bid·da·bil·i·ty** *n.*

bid·den. A past participle of **bid.**

bid·ding (bídding) *n.* **1.** A demand that something be done; a command. **2.** A request to appear; a summons. **3. a.** The act of making bids, as at an auction or in playing cards. **b.** The bids collectively. —**at (someone's) bidding.** At the service of; on the command of. —**do (someone's) bidding.** To follow the orders of.

bid·dy¹ (bíddi) *n., pl.* **-dies.** *Regional.* A hen; a fowl. [Perhaps imitative of a call used for hens.]

biddy² *n., pl.* **-dies.** *Informal.* A garrulous or interfering old woman. [Pet form of *Bridget,* a feminine name.]

bide (bīd) *intr. v.* **bided** or **bode** (bōd), **bided, biding, bides.** *Archaic & Scottish.* **1.** To remain in some place, condition, or state: *"England shall bide till Judgment Tide."* (Rudyard Kipling). **2.** To stay or tarry: *bide for a while.* See also **bide one's time** at **time.** [Bide, bode; Middle English *biden, bod* (past singular), Old English *bīdan, bād.*]

bi·den·tate (bī-déntayt) *adj.* **1.** *Biology.* Having two teeth or two toothlike projecting parts. **2.** *Chemistry.* Designating a ligand that can coordinate at two separate positions to the same atom or ion.

bi·det (beeday ‖ *U.S.* bee-dáy) *n.* A basin-like fixture designed to be straddled for washing the genitals and the posterior parts. [French, "small horse", possibly from Old French *bider†,* to trot.]

Bie·der·mei·er (beedər-mī-ər) *adj.* **1.** Of, pertaining to, or designating a type of German furniture of the first half of the 19th century, modelled after Empire styles. **2.** Staid and conventional; philistine. [After Gottlieb *Biedermeier,* the imaginary humdrum author of poems written by L. *Eichroth* (1827–92), German poet.]

Biel (beel). *French Bienne* (byen). Town in canton Bern in northwest Switzerland, renowned for its clocks.

Bie·le·feld (beelə-, -feld, -felt). Major industrial city in North Rhine-Westphalia in Germany, long famous as a linen centre.

bi·en·ni·al (bī-énni-əl) *adj.* **1.** Lasting or living for two years. **2.** Happening every second year. **3.** *Botany.* Having a normal life cycle of two years. Compare **annual, perennial.**

~*n.* **1.** An event that occurs once every two years. **2.** A plant that normally requires two years to reach maturity, producing leaves in the first year, blooming and producing fruit in its second year, and then dying. —See Usage note at **biannual.** [From BIENNIUM.] —**bi·en·ni·al·ly** *adv.*

bi·en·ni·um (bī-énni-əm) *n., pl.* **-ums** or **-ennia** (-énni-ə). A two-year period. [Latin : BI- + *annus,* year.]

bier (beer) *n.* A stand on which a corpse, or a coffin containing a corpse, is placed to lie in state or to be carried to the grave. [Middle English *bere,* Old English *bēr, bǣr.*]

bier·kel·ler (beer-kellər) *n.* A bar that is German in character and sells German beers. [German, "beer cellar".]

bi·fa·cial (bi-fáysh'l) *adj.* **1.** Having two faces, fronts, or façades. **2.** *Botany.* Having upper and lower surfaces that are distinct and dissimilar. Said of leaves. **3.** Having two opposing surfaces that are alike.

biff (bif) *tr.v.* **biffed, biffing, biffs.** *Slang.* To strike or punch. ~*n. Slang.* A blow or cuff. [Imitative.]

bi·fid (bífid) *adj. Biology.* Divided or cleft into two parts or lobes. [Latin *bifidus* : BI- + -FID.] —**bi·fid·i·ty** (bī-fíddəti) *n.* —**bi·fid·ly** *adv.*

bi·fi·lar (bī-fílər) *adj. Physics.* Fitted with or involving the use of two threads or wires, as in certain types of electrical measuring instruments or resistors. [BI- + FILAR.] —**bi·fi·lar·ly** *adv.*

bi·flag·el·late (bī-flájə-layt, -lət, -lit) *adj. Biology.* Having two flagella: *a biflagellate protozoan.*

bi·fo·cal (bī-fōk'l, bī-) *adj.* **1.** Having two different focal lengths. **2.** Correcting for both near and distant vision.

bi·fo·cals (bī-fōk'lz, bī-) *pl.n.* Spectacles with bifocal lenses, used for both near and distant vision.

bi·fo·li·ate (bī-fōli-ət, -it, -ayt) *adj.* Having two leaves.

bi·fo·li·o·late (bī-fōli-ə-layt, -lət, -lit) *adj.* Having two leaflets.

bi·fo·rate (bī-fō-rayt, -fáw- ‖ -fō-) *adj. Biology.* Having two openings or perforations. [BI- + Latin *forātus,* past participle of *forāre,* to pierce, bore.]

bi·forked (bī-fawrkt) *adj.* Divided into two branches; bifurcate.

bi·form (bī-fawrm) *adj.* Also **bi·formed** (-fawrmd). Having a combination of features or qualities of two distinct forms, as a sphinx does.

bi·fur·cate (bī-fər-kayt ‖ bī-fúr-) *v.* **-cated, -cating, -cates.** —*tr.* To divide or separate into two parts or branches. —*intr.* To separate into two parts; fork. ~*adj.* (-kayt, -kət, -kit). Also **bi·fur·cat·ed** (-kaytid). Forked or divided into two parts. [Medieval Latin *bifurcātus* (adjective), from Latin *bifurcus*, two-forked : BI- + *furca*, forked stake (see **fork**).] —**bi·fur·cate·ly** *adv.* —**bi·fur·ca·tion** (-káysh'n) *n.*

big (big) *adj.* **bigger, biggest. 1.** Of considerable size, number, quantity, magnitude, or extent; large or larger than average. **2.** Grown-up. **3.** Elder. **4.** *Literary.* Pregnant. Used with *with: big with child.* **5.** Filled up; brimming over. **6.** Having or exercising considerable authority, control, or influence. **7.** Conspicuous in position, wealth, or importance; prominent; influential. **8.** Of great significance; important; momentous. **9.** Loud and firm; resounding. **10.** *Informal.* Bountiful; generous; kindly. Often used ironically: *That's big of her.* **11.** *Informal.* **a.** Self-important; boastful; pompous. **b.** Ambitious: *big ideas.* —**big on.** *Informal.* Enthusiastic about: *big on women's rights.* ~*adv. Informal.* **1. a.** Pompously; pretentiously; boastfully: *"Toad talked big about all he was going to do in the days to come".* (Kenneth Grahame). **b.** Ambitiously: *think big.* **2.** With considerable success; in an outstanding manner: *His speech went down big at the conference.* [Middle English *big, byg,* strong, stout, full-grown, origin obscure.] —**big·gish** *adj.* —**big·ness** *n.*

big·a·mous (bíggəməss) *adj.* **1.** Involving bigamy. **2.** Guilty of bigamy. —**big·a·mous·ly** *adv.*

big·a·my (bíggəmi) *n., pl.* **-mies.** *Law.* The criminal offence of marrying one person while still legally married to another. [Middle English *bigamie,* from Old French, from *bigame,* bigamous, from Late Latin *bigamus* : BI- + -GAMOUS.] —**big·a·mist** *n.*

Big Apple *n.* New York. Used as a nickname, preceded by *the.*

big·ar·reau (bíggə-rō, -rō) *n.* Any of several varieties of sweet cherry with firm, often light-coloured flesh. [French, from *bigarrer,* to variegate : BI- + Old French *garre*†, variegated.]

big band *n.* A large dance or jazz band.

Big Bang *n. Informal.* A spectacular event (such as the deregulation of the London Stock Exchange) with significant repercussions. [Probably from the *big bang theory.*]

big bang theory *n.* A theory that the universe originated as a small, very dense mass that exploded, throwing out matter in all directions, from which galaxies and stars subsequently formed. The theory accounts for the **expanding universe** and the **microwave background** (*both of which see*). Also called "superdense theory". Compare **steady-state theory.**

Big Ben *n.* The bell in the clock tower of the Houses of Parliament in London. **2. a.** The clock itself. **b.** Loosely, the clock tower.

Big Bertha *n.* A large cannon used by the Germans in World War I. [Translation of German *dicke Bertha,* "fat Bertha", after *Bertha Krupp von Bohlen und Halbach* (1886–1957), proprietress of the Krupp Works, where the cannon was made.]

big brother *n.* **1.** An older brother, or someone with whom one has a similar protective relationship. **2.** *Capital B, capital B.* A vague, threatening figure representing the all-seeing, omnipresent power of an authoritarian government. [Sense 2, after *Big Brother,* a character in George Orwell's novel *1984* (1949).]

big business *n.* **1.** Commercial operations on a large scale, especially when regarded as powerful or manipulative. **2.** Any activity or undertaking regarded as commercially successful.

big deal *n. Informal.* An impressive achievement or proposition. ~*interj. Informal.* Used ironically to express contempt.

big dipper *n.* **1.** A roller coaster (*see*). **2.** *Capital B, capital D.* *Astronomy. U.S.* A constellation, the **Plough** (*see*).

bi·gem·i·nal (bī-jémmin'l) *adj.* Occurring in pairs; twinned. [Late Latin *bigeminus,* doubled : BI- + Latin *geminus,* paired, double, twin.]

big end *n. British.* **1.** The end of the connecting rod in an internal-combustion engine that is attached to the crankshaft. **2.** The bearing between this end of the connecting rod and the crankpin of the crankshaft.

big·eye (bíg-ī) *n.* Any of several tropical or subtropical marine fishes of the family Priacanthidae, having large eyes and reddish scales.

big game *n.* **1.** Large animals or fish hunted or caught for sport. **2.** *Slang.* An important objective. —**big-game** (bíg-gáym) *adj.*

big·gie (bíggi) *n. Informal.* A big version, organisation, or individual; a big one.

big gun *n. Slang.* An important person; a bigwig.

big·head (bíg-hed) *n.* **1.** *Informal.* A conceited person. **2.** Any of various diseases of animals characterised by swelling of the head, such as osteomalacia or (in sheep) *Clostridium* infection. —**big·head·ed** (-héddid) *adj.* —**big·head·ed·ness** *n.*

big·heart·ed (bíg-hártid) *adj.* Generous; charitable. —**big·heart·ed·ly** *adv.* —**big·heart·ed·ness** *n.*

bight (bīt) *n.* **1. a.** A loop in a rope. **b.** The middle or slack part of an extended rope. **2.** A bend or curve, especially in a shoreline. **3.** A wide bay formed by such a bend or curve. ~*tr.v.* **bighted, bighting, bights.** To tie or secure with a bight of a rope. [Middle English *byght,* bend, bay, armpit, Old English *byht,* bend, angle.]

big·mouth (bígmowth) *n. Slang.* A loud-mouthed or gossipy person. —**big-mouthed** (-mówthd, -mówtht) *adj.*

big noise *n. British Slang.* An important or well-known person.

big·no·ni·a (big-nṓni-ə) *n.* A tropical American plant of the genus *Bignonia*; especially, the **cross-vine** (*see*). Bignonias are cultivated for their ornamental trumpet-shaped flowers. [New Latin, after the Abbé Jean-Paul *Bignon* (1662–1743), librarian to Louis XV.]

big·ot (bíggət) *n.* A person of strong conviction or prejudice, especially in matters of religion, race, or politics, who is intolerant of those who differ with him. [French, from Old French *bigot*†, a pejorative term for the Normans.] —**big·ot·ed** *adj.* —**big·ot·ed·ly** *adv.* —**big·ot·ed·ness** *n.*

big·ot·ry (bíggətri) *n.* The attitude, state of mind, or behaviour characteristic of a bigot; intolerance.

big screen *n. Informal.* The cinema. Compare **small screen.**

big shot *n. Slang.* An important, powerful, or influential person. Often used derogatorily.

big smoke *n. Informal.* Any large city. Usually preceded by *the.* [From native Australian phrase for any large city.]

big stick *n. Informal.* A display or threat of force.

big time *n. Slang.* The most prestigious level of attainment in a field. —**big-time** *adj.* —**big-tim·er** *n.*

big top *n. Informal.* **1.** The main tent of a circus. **2.** The circus.

big tree *n.* The **giant sequoia** (*see*).

big wheel *n.* **1.** A huge vertically revolving wheel with suspended cars in which passengers ride, at a fairground. Also *chiefly U.S.* "Ferris Wheel". **2.** *Chiefly U.S. Slang.* A person of importance.

big·wig (bíg-wig) *n. Informal.* An important person; a dignitary.

Bi·har (bi-hár). State in east central India, crossed by the Ganges. Patna is the capital, but Ranchi is important as an administrative headquarters. Buddha passed his early years in Bihar, and the town of Buddh Gaya is a leading Buddhist centre.

Bi·ha·ri (bi-háari) *n.* **1.** A native or inhabitant of Bihar. **2.** The Indic language spoken in northeastern India. —**Bi·ha·ri** *adj.*

bi·jou (bée-zhōō) *n., pl.* **-jous** or **-joux** (-zhōōz). **1.** A small, exquisitely wrought trinket. **2.** Any charming, delicately made thing. ~*adj.* Small and charming. Often used humorously. [French, from Breton *bizou,* ring with a stone, from *biz*†, finger.]

bi·jou·te·rie (bee-zhōōtəri) *n.* **1.** Jewellery and trinkets. **2.** A collection of jewellery or trinkets. [French, from BIJOU.]

bike (bīk) *n. Informal.* **1.** A bicycle. **2.** A motorcycle. ~*intr.v.* **biked, biking, bikes.** *Informal.* To ride a bike. [Short for BICYCLE.]

bi·ker (bík-ər) *n.* Also *Australian & N.Z.* **bi·kie** (-i). A person who rides a motorcycle, especially a tough who dresses in black leather and belongs to a gang.

bi·ki·ni (bi-kéeni) *n.* A relatively brief two-piece bathing suit worn by women. [French, after BIKINI Atoll (referring to the "atomic" impact of the first bikinis).]

Bikini Atoll. Atoll in the west central Pacific Ocean, part of the Ralik, or western, chain of the Marshall Islands, now a commonwealth of the United States. The area was used by the U.S. government to test nuclear bombs (1946–58).

bikky. Variant of **bicky.**

Bi·ko (béekō), **Steve,** born Bantu Stephen Biko (1947–77). Black South African political leader, honorary president of the Black People's Convention. In 1969, he co-founded the radical "Black Consciousness" movement, the South African Students' Organisation. He was expelled from the University of Natal (1973) and joined the Black Community Programme to rally Black opposition to the Nationalist regime. He spent several periods in police detention and died in September, 1977, six days after being arrested.

bi·la·bi·al (bī-láyb-yəl, -i-əl) *adj.* **1.** *Phonetics.* Pronounced or articulated with both lips. Said of certain consonants, such as *p, b,* and *m.* **2.** Pertaining to or having a pair of lips. ~*n. Phonetics.* A bilabial sound or consonant. —**bi·la·bi·al·ly** *adv.*

bi·la·bi·ate (bī-láybi-ayt, -ət, -it) *adj. Botany.* Having two lips. Said of a flower or corolla.

bil·an·der (bíllandər) *n.* A small two-masted sailing vessel, used especially on canals in the Low Countries. [Dutch *bijlander,* "ship that sails by the land" : *bij,* by + *land,* land.]

bi·lat·er·al (bī-láttrəl, -láttərəl) *adj.* **1.** Of, pertaining to, or having two sides; two-sided. **2.** Having two symmetrical sides. **3.** Affecting or undertaken by two sides equally; binding on both parties. **4.** Occurring on one of two sides after affecting the other: *bilateral recurrence of breast cancer.* **5.** Pertaining to descent through both the paternal and maternal lines. Compare **unilateral.** —**bi·lat·er·al·ism, bi·lat·er·al·ness** *n.* —**bi·lat·er·al·ly** *adv.*

bilateral symmetry *n.* The arrangement of the parts of an organism or organ such that it can be divided into two halves that are mirror images of each other along only one plane. Compare **radial symmetry.**

Bil·ba·o (bil-bá-ō, -báy-, -bów). Major port of Spain, situated on the Nervión estuary near the Bay of Biscay. It is the largest city of the three Basque provinces and the centre of a heavily industrialised, iron-producing region.

bil·ber·ry (bíl-bri, -bəri ‖ *U.S.* -berri) *n., pl.* **-ries. 1.** Any of several shrubby or woody plants of the genus *Vaccinium,* having edible blue or blackish berries. The European species, *V. myrtillus,* is also called "whortleberry". **2.** The fruit of any of these plants. [Probably from Scandinavian, akin to Danish *böllebaer : bolle,* ball, round roll + *baer,* berry.]

bil·bo (bílbō) *n., pl.* **-bos** or **-boes.** A kind of well-tempered sword,

used in former times. [After BILBAO, famous for its ironworks.]
bil·boes (bílbōz) *pl.n.* An iron bar with sliding fetters, formerly used to shackle the feet of prisoners. [16th century : origin obscure.]
Bild·ungs·ro·man (bíldŏŏngz-rō-maán; *German* bíldŏŏngss-) *n.* A novel concerning the hero's early life and development. [German, "education novel".]
bile (bīl) *n.* **1.** *Physiology.* A bitter, alkaline, brownish-yellow or greenish-yellow liquid that is secreted by the liver, stored in the gall bladder, and discharged into the duodenum, where it aids in digestion, chiefly by emulsifying fats so that they can be more easily absorbed. Bile contains the pigments bilirubin and biliverdin. **2.** Bitterness of temper; irascibility; ill humour; spleen. **3.** In medieval medicine, either of two humours: *black bile,* thought to cause melancholy or *yellow bile,* thought to cause anger. [French, from Latin *bīlis,* from Old Latin *bis(t)lis* (unattested), perhaps from Celtic.]
bile duct *n.* Any of the ducts that drain bile from the liver. They join to form the *common bile duct,* which opens into the duodenum.
bilge (bilj) *n.* **1.** The lowest inner part of a ship's hull. **2.** Water that collects in this part. Also called "bilge water". **3.** The bulge of a barrel or cask. **4.** *Informal.* Stupid talk; nonsense.
~*v.* **bilged, bilging, bilges.** —*intr.* **1.** To spring a leak in the bilge. **2.** To bulge or swell. —*tr.* To break open the bilge of. [Probably variant of BULGE.] **—bilg·y** *adj.*
bilge keel *n.* Either of two beams or fins fastened lengthways along the outside of a ship's bilge to inhibit heavy rolling.
bil·har·zi·a·sis (bil-haar-tsī́-ə-siss, -zī́-) *n.* Also **bil·har·zi·a** (bil-hártsi-ə, -hárzi-). A disease, **schistosomiasis** *(see).* [New Latin : *Bilharzia,* schistosomes discovered by T. *Bilharz* (1825–62), German parasitologist + -IASIS.]
bil·i·ar·y (bíl-yəri, bílli-əri || *U.S.* -erri) *adj.* Of or pertaining to bile or to bile ducts: *biliary colic.*
~*n. South African.* A disease of livestock and pet animals, transmitted by ticks. Also called "biliary fever".
bi·lin·e·ar (bī-lín-yər, bī́-, -línni-ər) *adj. Mathematics.* Linear with respect to each of two variables or positions.
bi·lin·gual (bīlíng-gwəl, bī́- || -gew-əl, -gewl) *adj.* **1.** Able to speak two languages with equal skill. **2.** Written or expressed in two languages. **3.** In which two languages are used equally: *a bilingual city.*
~*n.* A bilingual person. [Latin *bilinguis* : BI- + *lingua,* tongue.] **—bi·lin·gual·ism** *n.* **—bi·lin·gual·ly** *adv.*
bil·i·ous (bíl-yəss, bílli-əss) *adj.* **1.** Of, pertaining to, or containing bile; biliary. **2.** Pertaining to, characterised by, or experiencing gastric distress, especially nausea and vomiting. **3.** Reminiscent of bile, especially in colour; sickly. **4.** Of a peevish disposition; sour-tempered; irascible. **—bil·i·ous·ly** *adv.* **—bil·i·ous·ness** *n.*
bil·i·ru·bin (bílli-rŏŏbin, bīli-) *n.* A reddish-yellow organic compound, $C_{33}H_{36}O_6N_4$, occurring in bile and derived from haemoglobin during normal and pathological destruction of erythrocytes. [Latin *bīlis,* BILE + *ruber,* red.]
-bility *n. suffix.* Indicates a potential state; for example, **visibility.** [Middle English *-bilite,* from Old French, from Latin *-bilitās,* from *-bilis,* adjective suffix. See **-able.**]
bil·i·ver·din (bílli-vérdin, bīli-) *n.* A green compound, $C_{33}H_{34}O_6N_4$, occurring in bile, sometimes formed by oxidation of bilirubin. [Swedish : *bili-,* from Latin *bīlis,* BILE + obsolete French *verd,* green, from Latin *viridis,* from *virēre,* to be green.]
bilk (bilk) *tr.v.* **bilked, bilking, bilks. 1.** To defraud, cheat, or swindle. Often used with *out of.* **2.** To evade payment of. **3.** To baulk or frustrate. **4.** To elude.
~*n.* **1.** One who cheats. **2.** A hoax or swindle. [Perhaps an alteration of BAULK (to refuse to go farther), originally used in cribbage, "to deprive opponent of his score".] **—bilk·er** *n.*
bill[1] (bil) *n.* **1.** An itemised statement of money owed for goods or services supplied. **2.** A statement or list of particulars, such as a playbill or menu. **3.** The entertainment offered by a theatre. **4.** An advertising poster or similar public notice. **5.** *Chiefly U.S.* A piece of legal paper money; a banknote. **6.** A **bill of exchange** *(see)* or a similar commercial note. **7.** A draft of a proposed law presented for approval to a legislative body. **8.** *Law.* A **bill of indictment** *(see).* **—fill** or **fit the bill.** *Informal.* To be quite satisfactory; meet all necessary requirements. **—foot the bill.** *Informal.* To pay the complete cost of.
~*tr.v.* **billed, billing, bills. 1.** To present a statement of costs or charges to. **2.** To enter on a statement of costs or a particularised list. **3.** To advertise, announce, or schedule, either by public notice or as part of a programme. [Middle English *bille,* from Anglo-French, from Medieval Latin *billa,* variant of *bulla,* seal affixed to a document, document, from Latin, bubble, ball, amulet.]
bill[2] *n.* **1.** The beak of a bird. **2.** A beaklike mouthpart, such as that of a turtle. **3.** A narrow promontory. **4.** The tip of the fluke of an anchor.
~*intr.v.* **billed, billing, bills.** To touch beaks together. **—bill and coo.** To kiss and murmur amorously. [Middle English *bile.*]
bill[3] *n.* **1.** A pruning implement, a **billhook** *(see).* **2.** A halberd or similar weapon with a hooked blade and a long handle. [Middle English *bil,* Old English *bil.*]
bil·la·bong (bílla-bong) *n. Australian.* **1.** A dead-end channel extending from the main stream of a river. **2.** A stream bed filled with water only in the rainy season. **3.** A stagnant pool or backwater. [Native Australian name : *billa,* river, water + *bong,* dead.]
bill·board (bíl-bawrd || -bōrd) *n. Chiefly U.S.* A **hoarding** *(see).*
bil·let[1] (bíllit) *n.* **1.** A lodging for troops in a nonmilitary building. **2.** A written order directing that such quarters be provided. **3.** Any assigned quarters. **4.** *Informal.* A position of employment; a job.
~*v.* **billeted, -leting, -lets.** —*tr.* **1.** To quarter (soldiers), especially in nonmilitary buildings. **2.** To serve (a person) with an order to provide such quarters. **3.** To assign lodging to. —*intr.* To be quartered; lodge. [Middle English *bylett,* from Old French *billette, bullette,* diminutives of *bulle,* document, from Medieval Latin *bulla,* document, BILL.] **—bil·let·tee** *n.* **—bil·let·er** *n.*
billet[2] *n.* **1.** A short, thick piece of firewood. **2.** *Architecture.* One of a series of square or log-shaped decorations forming part of a moulding. **3.** A bar of iron or steel in an intermediate stage of manufacture. [Middle English, from Old French *billette, billot,* diminutive of *bille,* log, block, tree trunk, from Medieval Latin *billus, billa,* branch, trunk, probably from Celtic; akin to Irish *bile*†, sacred tree, large tree.]
bil·let-doux (bílli-dŏŏ, bíllay-; *French* bee-yay-) *n., pl.* **billets-doux** (-dŏŏz). A love letter. Often used humorously. [French : *billet,* short note, from Old French *billette, bullette,* short note, BILLET[1] + *doux,* sweet.]
bill·fish (bíl-fish) *n., pl.* **-fishes** or collectively **billfish. 1.** Any of various fishes of the family Istiophoridae, such as a marlin or sailfish, having an elongated, swordlike or spearlike snout and upper jaw. **2.** Any of various other fishes having long, pointed jaws.
bill·fold (bíl-fōld) *n. U.S.* A wallet.
bill·head (bíl-hed) *n.* A sheet of paper with a business name and address printed at the top, used for making out bills.
bill·hook (bíl-hŏŏk) *n.* An implement with a curved blade attached to a handle, used especially for clearing brush and for rough pruning. Also called "bill".
bil·liard (bíl-yərd) *adj.* Of, pertaining to, or used in billiards.
bil·liards (bíl-yərdz) *n. Used with a singular verb.* **1.** A game played on a rectangular, cloth-covered table with raised, cushioned edges, in which a long, tapering cue is used to hit three small, hard balls against one another or the side cushions of the table. **2.** Any of several similar games, such as one played on a table with pockets. Compare **pool, snooker.** [French *billard,* bent stick, billiard cue, from Old French, from *bille,* log. See **billet** (stick).]
bill·ing (bílling) *n.* The relative importance of performers as indicated by the position and type size in which their names are listed on programmes, theatre hoardings, or advertisements.
bil·lings·gate (bíllingz-gayt, -git) *n.* Foul-mouthed abuse. [With allusion to scurrilous fishmongers at BILLINGSGATE.]
Billingsgate. Formerly, the oldest market in London, situated at the north end of London Bridge until it moved to West India Dock (1982). It had been principally a fish market since the 16th century.
bil·lion (bíl-yən) *n., pl.* **billion** (for senses 1 and 2), or **-lions** (for sense 3). **1.** The cardinal number represented by 1 followed by 12 zeros, usually written 10^{12}. Called in U.S. usage "trillion". **2.** In U.S. usage, and often in Britain, the cardinal number represented by 1 followed by 9 zeros, usually written 10^9. **3.** An indefinitely large number. [French : BI- + (M)ILLION.] **—bil·lion** *adj.*
Usage: The older British use means "a million million" (10^{12}). The U.S. use means "a thousand million" (10^9), and this is now in common international use. For example, to an economist, £1 billion usually means £1000 million.
bil·lion·aire (bíl-yə-naír) *n.* A person whose wealth amounts to at least a billion pounds, dollars, or comparable monetary units. [*billion* + million*aire.*]
bil·lionth (bíl-yənth) *n.* **1.** The ordinal number one billion in a series. **2.** One of a billion equal parts. **—bil·lionth** *adj. & adv.*
bill of attainder *n.* A former legislative act, last used in the 18th century, pronouncing a person guilty of a crime, usually treason, without trial and subjecting him to **attainder** *(see).*
bill of exchange *n. Abbr.* **B/E** A written order directing that a specified sum of money be paid to a specified person on a specified date. Also called "bill".
bill of fare *n.* A menu.
bill of health *n.* A certificate stating whether or not there is infectious disease aboard a ship or in its port of departure, and given to the ship's master for presentation at the next port of arrival. **—clean bill of health.** *Informal.* A statement that someone or something is in a satisfactory condition.
bill of indictment *n. Law* A written statement charging someone with a crime, formerly presented to a grand jury to be ratified. Also called "bill".
bill of lading *n. Abbr.* **B/L** A document listing and acknowledging receipt of goods for shipment.
bill of rights *n.* **1.** A formal summary of those rights and liberties considered essential to a people or group of people. **2.** *Capital* **B,** *capital* **R.** A declaration of rights restricting the power of the Crown, enacted by the English Parliament in 1689. **3.** *Capital* **B,** *capital* **R.** The first ten amendments to the Constitution of the United States.
bill of sale *n. Abbr.* **b.s.** A document that attests a transference of the ownership of personal property.
bil·lon (bíllən) *n.* **1.** An alloy of gold or silver with a greater proportion of another metal such as tin or copper, used in making coins. **2.** An alloy of silver with a high percentage of copper, used in making medals and tokens. [French, from Old French, ingot, from *bille,* log. See **billet** (stick).]
bil·low (bíllō) *n.* **1.** A large wave or ocean swell. **2.** A great swell or surge, as of smoke or sound.
~*v.* **billowed, -lowing, -lows.** —*intr.* **1.** To surge or roll in or as if in billows. **2.** To swell out: *billowing sails.* —*tr.* To cause to swell

or rise in billows. [Old Norse *bylgja*.] —**bil·low·i·ness** n. —**bil·low· y** *adj.*

bill·post·er (bíl-pōstər) n. One who posts up notices, posters, or advertisements. Also called "billsticker". —**bill·post·ing** n.

bil·ly (bílli) n., pl. **-lies.** A metal pot or kettle used in camp cooking. [Short for *billycan* : *billa*, a native Australian word for water + CAN (container).]

Billy Bun·ter (búntər) n. A fat and greedy schoolboy. [After a character in a series of boys' stories by Frank *Richards*.]

billy goat n. *Informal.* A male goat. Compare **nanny goat.**

bil·ly-o, bil·ly-oh (bílli-ō) n. *Informal.* Used as an intensive: *shouting like billy-o.* [19th century : origin obscure.]

bi·lo·bate (bī-lố-bayt, bī-) *adj.* Also **bi·lo·bat·ed** (-baytid), **bi·lobed** (bī-lốbd). Divided into or having two lobes.

bi·loc·u·lar (bī-lóckew-lər) *adj.* Also **bi·loc·u·late** (-lət, -lit, -layt). *Biology.* Divided into or containing two chambers, cavities, or cells. [BI- + LOCULUS.]

bil·sted (bílsted) n. A tree, the **sweet gum** *(see).* [Origin obscure.]

bil·tong (bíl-tong) n. *South African.* Narrow strips of meat, salted and dried in the sun. [Afrikaans : *bil*, buttock + *tong*, tongue.]

Bim (bim) n. *Informal.* A Barbadian. [19th century : origin obscure.]

bimah. Variant of **bema.**

bim·bo (bím-bó) n., pl. **-bos.** *Informal.* A young, attractive sex object, usually female. [Italian, baby.]

bi·mes·tri·al (bī-méstri-əl) *adj.* Bimonthly. [Latin *bimē(n)stris* : BI- + *mēnsis*, month.]

bi·me·tal·lic (bī-mi-tál-ik, -me-) *adj.* **1.** Consisting of two metals. **2.** Of, based on, or employing the principles of bimetallism.

bimetallic strip n. A strip consisting of two metals welded together, each metal having a different coefficient of expansion, so that a change of temperature causes the strip to buckle. Used in switches, thermostats, and the like.

bi·met·al·lism (bī-métt'l-iz'm) n. **1.** The use of gold and silver as the monetary standard of currency and value. **2.** The doctrine advocating such a standard. —**bi·met·al·list** n.

bi·mod·al (bī-mố'l, bī-) *adj.* Having two distinct statistical modes. —**bi·mo·dal·i·ty** (-mō-dál-əti) n.

bi·mo·lec·u·lar (bī-mə-léckew-lər) *adj.* Pertaining to, consisting of, or affecting two molecules.

bi·month·ly (bī-múnthli, bī-) *adj.* **1.** Happening every two months. **2.** Happening twice a month; semimonthly. ~*adv.* **1.** Once every two months. **2.** Twice a month; semimonthly. ~*n., pl.* **bimonthlies.** A publication issued bimonthly.

Usage: The terms *bimonthly* and *biweekly* are ambiguous—they can mean "once in two months/weeks" and "twice a month/week". The latter use is sometimes criticised, but unlike the case of *biannual* and *biennial*, there is no alternative word. There is some use of *semi-weekly, half-weekly,* to differentiate the two ideas, but these are not widely accepted terms.

bi·morph (bī-mawrf) n. Also **bimorph cell.** *Electronics.* A cell consisting of two piezoelectric crystals cemented together so that a voltage applied to the cell causes one crystal to expand and the other to contract, or so that a mechanical deformation of the cell causes a voltage to be generated. Used in microphones, vibration detectors, record player pickups, and the like.

bin (bin) n. **1.** A storage receptacle or container, as for coal, wool, or corn. **2.** A container for household refuse; a dustbin. **3.** *Slang.* A loony bin *(see).* **4.** A storage rack containing one kind of wine. ~*tr.v.* **binned, binning, bins.** To place or store in a bin. [Middle English *binne*, Old English *binn, binne,* basket, crib.]

bi·na·ry (bínəri) *adj.* **1.** Characterised by or composed of two different parts; twofold; double. **2.** *Chemistry.* Consisting of, or containing only molecules consisting of, just two kinds of atoms. **3.** Of, designating, or belonging to a number system that has 2 as its base. **4.** Of or pertaining to an alloy consisting of two components. **5.** *Music.* Having two subjects or themes. ~*n., pl.* **binaries.** An entity consisting of two distinct parts, especially a **binary star** *(see).* [Late Latin *bīnārius*, from *bīnī*, two by two.]

binary code n. *Computing.* A code consisting of a unique group of bits, each having two possible values, used to represent each of a set of numbers or letters.

binary coded decimal n. *Abbr.* **BCD** A number in binary code expressed in groups of four bits, each group representing one digit of the decimal number.

binary digit n. Either of the digits 0 or 1 used to express a number in the binary notation.

binary fission n. *Fission (see),* especially of a cell or of an atomic nucleus, that results in just two approximately equal products.

binary measure n. *Music.* A measure of two beats to the bar.

binary notation n. A number system having only two digits, 0 and 1. Any number can be expressed using combinations of these digits and the system is used in computers, as the digits 0 and 1 can be represented by an electrical system in the "off" and "on" states. Also called "binary system".

binary star n. A stellar system consisting of two stars orbiting about a common centre of mass and often appearing as a single visual or telescopic object. Also called "binary", "double star".

bi·nate (bínayt) *adj.* *Botany.* Consisting of two parts or divisions; growing in pairs: *a binate leaf.* [Latin *bīnī*, two by two.] —**bi·nate· ly** *adv.*

bin·au·ral (bīn-áwr-əl, bin-) *adj.* **1.** Having or related to two ears; hearing with both ears. **2.** Of or pertaining to sound transmission from two sources, which may vary acoustically, as in tone or pitch, relative to a listener. Compare **stereophonic.** ~*n.* Binaural sound recording or transmission. [BIN- + AURAL.]

bind (bīnd) v. **bound** (bownd), **binding, binds.** —*tr.* **1.** To tie or secure, as with a rope or cord. **2.** To fasten or wrap by encircling with a belt, girdle, or the like. **3.** To bandage. Often used with *up*: *bind up a wound.* **4.** To hold or restrain with or as if with bonds. **5.** To compel, oblige, or unite, as with a sense of moral duty. **6.** *Law.* To place under legal obligation by contract or oath. **7.** To make certain or irrevocable: *bind a bargain.* **8.** To hold or employ as an apprentice; indenture. Sometimes used with *out* or *over.* **9.** To cause to cohere or stick together in a mass. **10.** To enclose and fasten (a book) between covers. **11.** To furnish with an edge or border for reinforcement or ornamentation. **12.** To constipate. **13.** *Chemistry.* To cause to form a chemical bond. —*intr.* **1.** To tie up or fasten anything. **2.** To be tight and uncomfortable. **3.** To become stiff, compact, or solid; cohere; jam. **4.** To be obligatory or compulsory. **5.** *Chemistry.* To form a chemical bond. **6.** *Slang.* To complain. Used especially by servicemen. —**bind off.** *U.S.* In knitting, to cast off (stitches). —**bind over.** *Law.* To hold on bail or place under a legal obligation. ~*n.* **1. a.** Something that binds. **b.** The act of binding. **c.** The state of being bound. **2.** *Informal.* A difficult situation or dilemma; a nuisance. **3.** *Music.* A tie *(see).* **4.** In a coal mine, clay found between layers of coal. **5.** A bine *(see).* [Bind, bound, bound; Middle English *binden, bond, b(o)unden,* Old English *bindan, band* (plural *bundon), bunden.*]

bind·er (bíndər) n. **1.** One who binds books by trade; a bookbinder. **2.** Something used to tie or fasten, such as a cord, rope, or band. **3.** A firm cover with rings or clamps for holding sheets of paper. **4.** A material used to ensure uniform consistency, solidification, or adhesion to a surface, such as the gum in paint. **5. a.** An attachment on a reaping machine that ties grain in bundles. **b.** Formerly, a machine for reaping and tying grain. **6.** *Law.* A payment or written statement making an agreement legally binding until the completion of a formal contract, especially an insurance contract. **7.** A beam or steel girder supporting floor joists.

bind·er·y (bíndəri) n., pl. **-ies.** A place in which books are bound.

bindi-eye (bíndi-ī) n. Any small Australian perennial herb of the genus *Calotis* having burrlike fruit. [20th century : origin obscure.]

bind·ing (bínding) n. **1.** The action or process of one that binds. **2.** Something that binds or is used as a binder. **3.** The cover that holds together the pages of a book. **4.** A strip sewn or attached over or along the edge of something for protection or reinforcement. ~*adj.* **1.** Serving to bind. **2.** Uncomfortably tight and confining. **3.** Having the power to hold to an agreement or commitment; obligatory. —**bind·ing·ly** *adv.* —**bind·ing·ness** n.

binding energy n. *Symbol* E_B **1.** The net energy required to decompose a system, especially an atomic nucleus, into its constituent particles. Also called "mass defect". **2.** The net energy required to remove a particle from a system, especially to remove an electron from its orbit in an atom or molecule. See **ionisation potential.**

bind·weed (bínd-weed) n. **1.** Any of several trailing or twining plants of the genera *Convolvulus* and *Calystegia,* having pink or white trumpet-shaped flowers. **2.** Any of various similar trailing or twining plants.

bine (bīn) n. **1.** The flexible stem of any of various climbing and twining plants, such as the hop, woodbine, or bindweed. **2.** Any of these plants. [Variant of dialectal *bind,* clinging vine, Middle English *bynde,* from *binden,* to BIND.]

bin-end (bín-énd, -end) n. One of the last remaining bottles in a wine bin, sometimes sold at a discount.

Bi·net-Si·mon scale (béenay símən, bi-náy) n. A scale evaluating mental ability through a series of early psychological tests of childhood intelligence. Also called "Binet Scale", "Binet-Simon test". See **Stanford-Binet scale.** [After Alfred *Binet* (1857–1911) and Théodore *Simon* (1873–1961), French psychologists.]

binge (binj) n. *Slang.* **1.** A drunken spree or revel. **2.** A burst of self-indulgence in something, especially after a period of restraint. ~*intr.v.* **binged, binging, binges.** *Informal.* To indulge in a binge, especially by overeating: *binging and dieting.* [British dialectal *binge†,* to fill a boat with water, to drink heavily.]

bin·go (bíng-gō) n. A game of chance in which players have a card bearing a pattern of numbered squares, which they cross off as numbers are drawn and announced by a caller. The first player to cross off all the numbers on the card wins. ~*interj.* **1.** Used by a player to announce a win. **2.** Used to express pleasurable surprise or unexpected satisfaction. [Originally the winner's exclamation, from *bing,* ringing sound, sound expressing surprise (imitative).]

bin·man (bín-man) n., pl. **-men** (-men, -mən). *British.* A dustman.

bin·na·cle (bínnək'l) n. The nonmagnetic stand on which a ship's compass case is supported. [Earlier *bittacle,* from Middle English *bitakle,* from Spanish *bitácula* or Portuguese *bitácola,* from Latin *habitāculum,* little house, from *habitāre,* to dwell, abide, from *habēre,* to have.]

bin·oc·u·lar (bī-nóckew-lər, bi-) *adj.* Pertaining to, used by, or involving both eyes at the same time. ~*n.* Also *rare* **bin·o·cle** (bínnək'l). A binocular optical device, such as a microscope for use with both eyes. [BIN- + OCULAR.] —**bin·oc·u·lar·i·ty** (-lár-ərti) n. —**bin·oc·u·lar·ly** *adv.*

bin·oc·u·lars (bi-nockewlərz) pl.n. A portable optical device for looking at distant objects, designed for use by both eyes at once.

binocular vision *n.* The ability of both eyes to focus on the same object at the same time, possessed by primates (including man) and predators (such as owls).

bi·no·mi·al (bī-nṓm-yəl, -i-əl) *adj.* Consisting of or pertaining to two names or terms.

~*n.* **1.** *Mathematics.* An expression consisting of two terms connected by a plus or minus sign; a polynomial in two terms. **2.** A taxonomic name in **binomial nomenclature** *(see).* [New Latin *binōmium* : BI- + Greek *nomos,* portion, part.] —**bi·no·mi·al·ly** *adv.*

binomial distribution *n.* *Statistics.* The frequency distribution of the probability of a specified number of successes in an arbitrary number of repeated independent Bernoulli trials.

binomial nomenclature *n.* A system of naming plants and animals by a double name, the first of which is the name of the genus and the second that of the species within the genus; for example, *Odobenus rosmarus,* the walrus.

binomial theorem *n.* A mathematical theorem that specifies the expansion of a binomial to any power without requiring the explicit multiplication of the binomial terms. If *n* is a positive integer, $(x+a)^n = x^n + (n/1!) ax^{n-1} + [n(n-1)/2!]a^2x^{n-2} + \ldots a^n$

bint (bint) *n. Vulgar Slang.* A woman. Used derogatorily. [Arabic, daughter, girl.]

bin·tu·rong (bíntewr-ong, bin-téwr-ong) *n.* An arboreal mammal, *Arctictis binturong,* of Southeast Asia, closely related to the palm civets. It has shaggy hair and a prehensile tail. [Malay.]

bi·nu·cle·ate (bī-néwkli-ayt, -ət, -it ‖ -nṓokli-) *adj.* Also **bi·nu·cle·ar** (-ər), **bi·nu·cle·at·ed** (-aytid). Having two nuclei.

bio-, bi- *comb. form.* Indicates: **1.** Life or living organisms; for example, **biocide, bionics. 2.** Biology; for example, **biophysics.** [Greek, from *bios,* life, mode of life.]

bi·o·as·say, bi·o·as·say (bī-ō-ə-sáy, -ássay) *n.* Evaluation of the activity of a drug, hormone, or other substance by comparison of its effect with that of a standard on a test organism. —**bi·o·as·say** *tr.v.*

bi·o·cat·a·lyst (bī-ō-kátta-list) *n.* A substance, especially an enzyme, that initiates or modifies the rate of a biological process. —**bi·o·cat·a·lyt·ic** (-líttik) *adj.*

biochemical oxygen demand *n. Abbr.* **BOD** A measure of the organic pollution of water: the amount of oxygen used by microorganisms in a sample of water in a given period of time. Also called "biological oxygen demand".

bi·o·chem·is·try (bī-ō-kémmi-stri) *n.* The chemistry of biological substances and processes. —**bi·o·chem·i·cal** (-kəl) *adj.* —**bi·o·chem·i·cal·ly** *adv.* —**bi·o·chem·ist** *n.*

bi·o·cide (bī-ə-sīd, -ō-) *n.* A substance, such as a pesticide or an antibiotic, that is capable of destroying living organisms. [BIO- + -CIDE.] —**bi·o·ci·dal** (-sīd'l) *adj.*

bi·o·cli·ma·tol·o·gy (bī-ō-klīmə-tóllaji) *n.* The study of the effects of climatic conditions on organic life.

bi·o·de·grad·a·ble (bī-ōdi-gráydəb'l) *adj.* Capable of being decomposed by natural biological processes: *a biodegradable detergent.*

bi·o·en·er·get·ics (bī-ō-énnər-jéttiks) *n. Used with a singular verb.* **1.** The study of energy relationships between organisms, particularly the cycle of energy in a natural community. **2.** A therapeutic system alleged to free the flow of vital energy by using breathing techniques and various ways of working with the body to release physical and emotional blocks. It is based on certain ideas of Wilhelm Reich as developed by Alexander Lowen —**bi·o·en·er·get·ic** *adj.*

bi·o·en·gi·neer·ing (bī-ō-énji-néer-ing) *n.* **1.** The design and manufacture of aids or replacements for defective or missing organs, such as artificial limbs, heart pacemakers, and hearing aids. **2.** The design, manufacture, and use of equipment for industrial biosynthetic processes, such as fermentation.

bi·o·feed·back (bī-ō-féedbak) *n.* A technique whereby one seeks consciously to regulate a bodily function thought to be involuntary, such as heartbeat or blood pressure, by using an instrument to monitor the function and to signal changes in it.

bi·o·fla·vo·noid (bī-ō-fláyvənoyd) *n.* Any of a group of biologically active substances found widely in plants and functioning in the maintenance of the walls of small blood vessels. Also called "vitamin P". [BIO- + FLAVON(E) + -OID.]

bi·o·gen·e·sis (bī-ō-jénnə-siss) *n.* Also **bi·og·e·ny** (bī-ójəni). **1.** The doctrine that living organisms develop only from other living organisms and not from nonliving matter. Compare **abiogenesis. 2.** The generation of living organisms from other living organisms. —**bi·o·ge·net·ic** (-jə-néttik), **bi·o·ge·net·i·cal, bi·og·e·nous** (-ójənəss) *adj.* —**bi·o·ge·net·i·cal·ly** *adv.*

bi·o·ge·og·ra·phy (bī-ō-ji-óggrəfi) *n.* The biological study of the geographical distribution of plants and animals. —**bi·o·ge·o·graph·ic** (-jée-ə-gráffik), **bi·o·ge·o·graph·i·cal** *adj.*

bi·o·gen·ic (bī-ō-jénnik) *adj.* Developing or produced by living organisms. —**bi·o·gen·ic·al·ly** *adv.*

bi·og·ra·pher (bī-óggrəfər ‖ *U.S. also* bee-) *n. Abbr.* **biog.** One who writes a biography.

bi·o·graph·i·cal (bī-ə-gráffik'l) *adj.* Also **bi·o·graph·ic** (-gráffik) *Abbr.* **biog. 1.** Containing, consisting of, or pertaining to the facts or events in a person's life. **2.** Of or pertaining to biography as a literary form. —**bi·o·graph·i·cal·ly** *adv.*

bi·og·ra·phy (bī-óggrəfi ‖ *U.S. also* bee-) *n., pl.* **-phies.** *Abbr.* **biog. 1.** An account of a person's life written by another; a life history. **2.** Such writings as a literary form. [New Latin *biographia,* from Medieval Greek : BIO- + -GRAPHY.]

bi·o·log·i·cal (bī-ə-lójik'l) *adj.* Also **bi·o·log·ic** (-lójik). *Abbr.* **biol.** **1.** Of or pertaining to biology. **2.** Of, pertaining to, caused by, or affecting life or living organisms. **3.** Of or pertaining to detergents that contain enzymes, designed to remove certain types of stain, such as blood or sweat, from fabric.

~*n. Pharmacology.* A drug derived from a biological source. —**bi·o·log·i·cal·ly** *adv.*

biological clock *n.* An intrinsic biological mechanism responsible for the periodicity or other time-dependent aspects of certain classes of behaviour in living organisms.

biological control *n.* The control of pests using other organisms, usually their natural predators, parasites, or diseases.

biological warfare *n.* Warfare in which disease-producing microorganisms or organic biocides are used to destroy livestock, crops, or human life.

bi·ol·o·gy (bī-óllaji) *n. Abbr.* **biol. 1.** The science of life and life processes, including the study of structure, functioning, growth, origin, evolution, ecology, and distribution of living organisms. **2.** The life processes or characteristic phenomena of any group or category of living organisms. **3.** The plant and animal life of a specific region or place. [German *Biologie* : BIO- + -LOGY.] —**bi·ol·o·gist** *n.*

bi·o·lu·mi·nes·cence (bī-ō-lṓomi-néss'nss, -léwmi-) *n.* The emission of visible light by living organisms such as the firefly, various fish, fungi, bacteria, and other organisms. It is the result of the biochemical oxidation of the compound luciferin. Compare **fluorescence, phosphorescence.** —**bi·o·lu·mi·nes·cent** *adj.*

bi·ol·y·sis (bī-óllə-siss) *n.* Death caused or accompanied by lysis. [New Latin : BIO- + -LYSIS.] —**bi·o·lyt·ic** (bī-ə-líttik) *adj.*

bi·o·mass (bī-ō-mass) *n.* The weight of: **1.** All the living organisms in a given area. **2.** All the members of one species in that area. **3.** Vegetable matter used as fuel or as a source of energy.

bi·ome (bī-ōm) *n. Ecology.* A community of living organisms of a single major ecological region, such as a desert or tropical forest. [BI(O)- + -OME.]

bi·om·e·try (bī-ómmətri) *n.* Also **bi·o·met·rics** (bī-ə-méttriks, -ō-). *Used with a singular verb.* The statistical study of biological data. —**bi·o·met·ric, bi·o·met·ri·cal** *adj.* —**bi·o·met·ri·cal·ly** *adv.*

bi·o·morph (bī-ō-mawrf, -ə-) *n.* In art and sculpture, a form representing a living object. [BIO- + -MORPH.] —**bi·o·morph·ic** (-mórfik), **bi·o·morph·ic·al** *adj.*

bi·on·ic (bī-ónnik) *adj.* **1.** Of or pertaining to bionics. **2.** In science fiction, having certain functions carried out by electronic equipment instead of by the normal physiological processes.

bi·on·ics (bī-ónniks) *n. Used with a singular verb.* The application of biological principles to the study and design of engineering, especially electronic, systems. [BI(O)- + (ELECTR)ONICS.]

bi·o·nom·ics (bī-ə-nómmiks) *n. Used with a singular verb.* **Ecology** *(see).* [French *bionomique,* pertaining to ecology, from *bionomie,* ecology : BIO- + -NOMY.] —**bi·o·nom·ic, bi·o·nom·i·cal** *adj.* —**bi·o·nom·i·cal·ly** *adv.*

bi·o·phys·i·cist (bī-ō-fízzi-sist) *n.* A scientist whose speciality is biophysics.

bi·o·phys·ics (bī-ō-fízziks) *n. Used with a singular verb.* The physics of biological processes and the use of techniques of physics in studying biology. —**bi·o·phys·i·cal** *adj.* —**bi·o·phys·i·cal·ly** *adv.*

bi·o·pic (bī-ō-pik) *n. Informal.* A biographical film. [*Bio*graphical and *pic*ture.]

bi·o·plasm (bī-ō-plaz'm) *n.* Living protoplasm. [BIO- + -PLASM.]

bi·o·poi·e·sis (bī-ō-poy-ée-siss) *n.* The synthesis of living organisms from nonliving but self-replicated molecules, such as DNA. It is the basis of the origin and evolution of life. [BIO- + -POIESIS.]

bi·op·sy (bī-opsi) *n., pl.* **-sies.** The examination of tissues removed from the body as an aid to medical diagnosis. [French *biopsie* : BI(O)- + -OPSY.] —**bi·op·sic** (bī-ópsik) *adj.*

bi·o·rhythm (bī-ō-rith'm, -ə-) *n. Often plural.* A phenomenon found to a greater or lesser extent in most organisms whereby patterns of growth, behaviour, or the like, exhibit a natural periodic cycle in response to environmental changes or to various internal control mechanisms. —**bi·o·rhyth·mic** (-rithmik) *adj.*

bi·o·scope (bī-ə-skōp) *n.* **1.** An early film projector, used about 1900. **2.** *South African.* A cinema. [BIO- + -SCOPE.]

–biosis *n. comb. form.* Indicates a specific way of living; for example, **symbiosis.** [New Latin, from Greek *biōsis,* way of life, from *bioun,* to live, from *bios,* mode of life.]

bi·o·sen·sor (bī-ō-sen-sər, -sawr) *n.* A sensor whose active sensing agent is a biochemical, organic substance (such as a protein) rather than something inorganic (such as a photoelectric cell). *"The biosensor ... uses a biological system, such as an enzyme, to recognise chemical changes and express them electronically on a display or printout."* (*The Times*). [BIO- + SENSOR.]

bi·o·sphere (bī-ə-sfeer, -ō-) *n.* The totality of regions of the earth that support self-sustaining and self-regulating ecological systems. [BIO- + -SPHERE.]

bi·o·sta·tis·tics (bī-ō-stə-tístiks) *n. Used with a singular verb.* Statistical techniques used in studies of health and social welfare.

bi·o·syn·the·sis (bī-ō-sínthə-siss) *n., pl.* **-theses** (-seez). The production of complex substances from simple ones by or with living organisms. —**bi·o·syn·thet·ic** (-sin-théttik) *adj.* —**bi·o·syn·thet·i·cal·ly** *adv.*

bi·o·ta (bī-ōtə) *n.* The animal and plant life of a particular region considered as a total ecological entity. [New Latin, from Greek *biotē,* way of life, from *bios,* life.]

bi·o·tech·nol·o·gy (bī-ō-tek-nóllaji) *n.* **1.** The manipulation of the physiology, usually by genetic techniques, of microorganisms, especially bacteria, to produce useful chemicals on an industrial scale. See **genetic engineering**. 2. *U.S.* **Ergonomics** *(see)*.

bi·ot·ic (bī-óttik) *adj.* Pertaining to life or specific life conditions. [Greek *biōtikos*, from *bios*, mode of life.]

biotic potential *n.* 1. The likelihood of survival of a specific organism in a specific environment, especially in an unfavourable environment. 2. The growth rate of a population that maintains a stable age distribution.

bi·o·tin (bī-ə-tin) *n.* A colourless crystalline vitamin, $C_{10}H_{16}N_2O_3S$, part of the vitamin B complex found in large quantities in liver, egg yolk, milk, and yeast. [Greek *biotos*, life, from *bios*, life, mode of life + -IN.]

bi·o·tite (bī-ə-tīt) *n.* A dark-brown to black mica, $K(Mg, Fe)_3(Al-Si_3)O_{10}(OH,F)_2$, found in igneous and metamorphic rocks. [German *Biotit*, after J.B. *Biot* (1774–1862), French physicist.] —**bi·o·tit·ic** (-títtik) *adj.*

bi·o·tope (bī-ə-tōp) *n.* A limited ecological region or niche, such as a dung heap, in which the environment is suitable for certain forms of life. [BIO- + Greek *topos*, place (see **topic**).]

bi·o·type (bī-ə-tīp) *n.* 1. A group of organisms having identical genetic characteristics. 2. A group of organisms in a species that is identical in form but differs in physiology from other members of the species. —**bi·o·typ·ic** (-típpik) *adj.*

bip·a·rous (bíppərəss) *adj.* 1. *Biology.* Producing two offspring in a single birth. 2. *Botany.* Having two axes or branches. Said of certain flower clusters. [BI- + -PAROUS.]

bi·par·ti·san (bī-paarti-zán, -pártizan) *adj.* Consisting of or supported by members of two parties, especially two major political parties. —**bi·par·ti·san·ism** *n.* —**bi·par·ti·san·ship** *n.*

bi·par·tite (bī-pártīt, bī-) *adj.* Also **bi·part·ed** (-id). 1. Having or consisting of two parts. 2. Having two corresponding parts, one for each party: *a bipartite treaty.* 3. *Botany.* Divided into two, almost to the base. Said of certain leaves. [Latin *bipartītus*, past participle of *bipartīre*, to divide into two parts : BI- + *partīre*, to part, from *pars* (stem *part-*), a share, part.] —**bi·par·tite·ly** *adv.* —**bi·par·ti·tion** (bī-paar-tísh'n) *n.*

bi·ped (bī-ped) *n.* An animal with two feet. ~*adj.* Also **bi·ped·al** (-péed'l, -pédd'l). Having two feet; two-footed. [Latin *bipes*, "two-footed" : BI- + -PED.]

bi·pet·al·ous (bī-pétt'l-əss) *adj. Botany.* Having two petals; dipetalous.

bi·phen·yl (bī-fénn'l, bī-, -féen'l) *n.* A colourless crystalline compound, $C_6H_5C_6H_5$, used as a heat-transfer agent, in fungicides, and in organic synthesis. Also called "diphenyl".

bi·pin·nate (bī-pínnayt, bī-) *adj. Botany.* Having opposite leaflets that are subdivided into opposite leaflets. Said of compound leaves. —**bi·pin·nate·ly** *adv.*

bi·plane (bī-playn) *n.* An early aircraft distinguished by single or paired wings fixed at two different levels, especially one above and one below the fuselage. Compare **monoplane**.

bi·pod (bī-pod) *n.* A stand having two legs, as for the support of an instrument or a weapon. [BI- + -POD.]

bi·po·lar (bī-pṓlər, bī-) *adj.* 1. Pertaining to or having two poles. 2. Relating to or involving both of the Earth's poles. 3. Having or expressing two opposite or contradictory ideas or qualities. —**bi·po·lar·i·ty** (bī-pō-lárrəti, -pə-) *n.*

bi·pro·pel·lant (bī-prə-péllənt) *n.* A two-component rocket propellant, such as liquid hydrogen and liquid oxygen, combined as fuel and oxidiser. Also called "dipropellant".

bi·quad·rat·ic (bī-kwod-ráttik) *adj. Mathematics.* Quartic. ~*n. Mathematics.* A **quartic** *(see)*.

bi·quar·ter·ly (bī-kwór-tərli, bī-, -kór-) *adj.* Happening or appearing twice during each three-month period of a year.

bi·ra·cial (bī-ráysh'l, bī-) *adj.* Of, for, or consisting of members of two races. —**bi·ra·cial·ism** *n.*

bi·ra·di·al (bī-ráydi-əl, bī-) *adj. Biology.* Both bilaterally and radially symmetrical.

bi·ra·mous (bírrəməss, bī-ráyməss) *adj. Biology.* Divided into two parts. Said of the limbs of crustaceans.

birch (burch) *n.* 1. Any of several deciduous trees of the genus *Betula*, such as the **silver birch** *(see)*, common in the Northern Hemisphere, and having white, yellowish, or grey bark that can be separated from the wood in sheets. 2. The hard, close-grained wood of any of these trees. 3. A rod or bundle of twigs from a birch tree, used to administer a whipping. Used with *the.* ~*tr.v.* **birched, birching, birches.** To whip (someone) with or as if with birch twigs or a birch rod. [Middle English *birche*, Old English *birce, beorc(e)*.] —**birch**, *Archaic.* **birch·en** (búrchən) *adj.*

Birch·er (búrch-ər) *n.* Also **Birch·ite** (-īt), **Birch·ist** (-ist). 1. A member of the **John Birch Society** *(see)*. 2. A supporter of its doctrines and activities. —**Birch·ism** *n.*

bird (burd) *n.* 1. Any member of the class Aves, which includes warm-blooded, egg-laying feathered vertebrates with forelimbs modified to form wings. 2. A bird hunted as game. 3. *Slang.* A rocket or guided missile. 4. A target, a **clay pigeon** *(see)*. 5. *Slang.* One who is odd or remarkable. 6. *British Slang.* A young woman. 7. *Slang.* A sound of disapproval or derision. Used chiefly in the expressions *give (someone) the bird; get the bird.* 8. *Slang.* A prison sentence; imprisonment. Used chiefly in the phrase *do bird.* —**a bird in the hand.** A certainty; something achieved. —**for the birds.** *Slang.* Objectionable or worthless. —**like a bird.** Without difficulty. —**the birds and (the) bees.** Human reproduction and sexuality, as explained to children. Often used humorously. [Middle

English *byrd, bryd,* young bird, Old English *brid†.* Sense 8, short for *birdlime,* rhyming slang for *time.*]

bird-bath (búrd-baath ‖ -bath) *n.* A garden trough or basin filled with water in which birds may bathe.

bird-brain (búrd-brayn) *n. Slang.* A silly, frivolous person. —**bird-brained** (-braynd) *adj.*

bird-cage (búrd-kayj) *n.* A cage for birds.

bird-call (búrd-kawl) *n.* 1. The song of a bird. 2. **a.** An imitation of the song of a bird. **b.** A small device for producing this.

bird cherry *n.* A cherry tree, *Prunus padus,* native to Eurasia, having clusters of white flowers and small black fruit.

bird dog *n. Chiefly U.S.* A dog used to hunt game birds; a gun dog.

bird fancier *n.* A person who keeps, breeds, or deals with birds.

bird-house (búrd-howss) *n.* 1. An aviary. 2. A small box made as a nesting place for birds.

bird-ie (búrdi) *n.* 1. *Informal.* A small bird. 2. *Golf.* One stroke under par for any hole.

bird-lime (búrd-līm) *n.* 1. A sticky substance smeared on branches to capture small birds. 2. Something that captures and ensnares. ~*tr.v.* **birdlimed, -liming, -limes.** 1. To smear with birdlime. 2. To catch with birdlime.

bird louse *n.* A louse *(see)*.

bird-man (búrd-man) *n., pl.* **-men** (-men). 1. A person who is interested in birds; an ornithologist. 2. A person who tries to fly without assistance from an engine.

bird-nest·ing (búrd-nesting) *n.* Also **birds'-nest·ing** (búrdz-). The activity of looking for birds' nests, usually with the intention of taking the eggs.

bird of paradise *n.* Any of various birds of the family Paradisaeidae, native to New Guinea and adjacent areas, usually having brilliant plumage and long tail feathers in the male.

bird-of-par·a·dise flower *n.* (búrd əv párrədīss) *n.* A perennial plant, *Strelitzia reginae,* having purple bracts and large orange or yellow flowers with blue tongues. [After its stalks of colourful flowers resembling birds of paradise.]

bird of passage *n.* A migratory bird or a transient person.

bird of prey *n.* Any of various predatory carnivorous birds, such as the eagle or hawk, having powerful claws and a strong bill.

bird pepper *n.* 1. A tropical plant, *Capsicum frutescens,* that is the probable ancestor of the mild peppers and many of the hot peppers. 2. The narrow, extremely pungent fruit of this plant.

bird-seed (búrd-seed) *n.* A mixture of various kinds of seeds used for feeding birds, especially caged birds.

bird's-eye (búrdz-ī) *adj.* Dappled or patterned with spots thought to resemble birds' eyes: *bird's-eye maple.* ~*n.* 1. Any of various plants having small, brightly coloured flowers, such as the bird's-eye primrose. 2. **a.** A fabric woven with a pattern of small diamonds, each having a dot in the centre. **b.** The pattern of such a fabric.

bird's-eye primrose *n.* A plant, *Primula farinosa,* native to Eurasia, having clusters of small, purplish, yellow-throated flowers.

bird's-eye speedwell *n. U.S.* A plant, **germander speedwell** *(see)*.

bird's eye view *n.* A view from high above or from a position of superiority. Compare **worm's eye view**.

bird's-foot (búrdz-foot) *n., pl.* **bird's-foots.** 1. A European plant, *Ornithopus perpusillus,* with small whitish flowers and curved pods. 2. Any of various other plants that have flowers, leaves, or pods resembling a bird's foot or claw.

bird's-foot trefoil *n.* A sprawling plant, *Lotus corniculatus,* having yellow flowers and seed pods resembling the claws of a bird.

bird's-nest fungus *n.* Any of various fungi of the family Nidulariaceae, having a cuplike fruiting body containing several round, egglike structures that enclose the spores.

bird's-nest orchid *n.* A brown parasitic orchid, *Neottia nidus-avis,* that grows in woods in Europe and Asia and has thick intertwining roots.

bird's-nest soup *n.* A Chinese soup made from a gelatinous coating on the nests of certain swifts native to the Orient. [Translation of Chinese (Mandarin) *yàn wō tāng* : *yàn,* the swallow or swift + *wō,* nest + *tāng,* soup.]

birds of a feather *pl. n.* People who are alike in some way. Used chiefly in the saying *Birds of a feather flock together.*

bird-song (búrd-song) *n.* 1. The singing of birds. 2. A bird's cry or call.

bird spider *n.* Any spider of the tropical American family Avicula-iidae, which is large and hairy and preys on birds.

lrd strike *n.* A collision of a bird, or flock of birds, with an aircraft.

bird table *n.* A small raised platform, usually in a garden, on which food is placed for wild birds.

bird-watch·er (búrd-wochər) *n.* A person who observes and identifies birds in their natural surroundings. —**bird-watch·ing** *n.*

bi·re·frin·gence (bī-ri-frínjənss, -rə- ‖ -ree-) *n.* The resolution or splitting of a light wave into two waves, travelling at different speeds, by an optically anisotropic medium such as a crystal of calcite, topaz, or quartz. Also called "double refraction". —**bi·re·frin·gent** *adj.*

bi·reme (bī-reem) *n.* An ancient galley equipped with two tiers of oars on each side. [Latin *birēmis* : BI- + *rēmus,* oar.]

bi·ret·ta, ber·ret·ta (bə-réttə) *n.* A stiff square cap that is worn by Roman Catholic clergy and is black for a priest, purple for a bishop, and red for a cardinal. [Italian *berretta* or Spanish *birreta,* from Medieval Latin *birretum,* cap, from Late Latin *birrus,* hooded cloak. See **beret.**]

bi·ri·a·ni, bi·ry·a·ni (bírri-a'ani) *n.* Any of a number of Indian dishes made with highly flavoured meat, fish, or vegetables cooked on a bed of saffron'rice. [Urdu.]

Birk·beck (búr-bek, búrk-), **George** (1776–1841). British educational reformer. His lectures to working men in Glasgow (1800–04) led to the establishment of the first Mechanics' Institute in Britain (1823). He was one of the founders of London University (1827). Birkbeck College in London, is named after him.

Bir·ken·head (búrkən-héd, -hed). Industrial port in the Wirral in northwest England, on the Mersey estuary, opposite Liverpool.

Bir·ken·head, Frederick Edwin Smith, 1st Earl of (1872–1930). British lawyer and politician. He was Solicitor General (1915), Attorney General (1915–19), Lord Chancellor (1919–22) and Secretary of State for India (1924–28).

bir·kie (búrki) *adj. Scottish.* Cocky; cheeky and lively. [Perhaps from Scandinavian; compare Old Norse *berkja,* to bark, boast.]

birl¹ (burl) *v.* **birled, birling, birls.** *Scottish.* —*tr.* **1.** To spin round. **2.** To toss (a coin). —*intr.* To spin round. [Blend of BIRR and WHIRL.]

birl², birle (burl) *tr.v.* **birled, birling, birls.** *Scottish.* To pour out (drink). [Old English *byrelian;* akin to *byrele,* cup-bearer.]

birl³. Variant of **burl** (an attempt).

birl·ing (búrling) *n. U.S.* A game of skill, originating among lumberjacks, in which two competitors try to balance on a floating log while spinning it with their feet. Also called "logrolling". [From BIRL (spin round).]

Bir·ming·ham¹ (búrming-əm ‖ -həm). City in the West Midlands in England, the second largest city in the United Kingdom, and centre of the car industry. It owes its leading industrial position partly to the fact that it lies equidistant from London, Bristol, Manchester, and Liverpool and partly to its proximity to the coal deposits of the Black Country and iron deposits to the east.

Birmingham² (búrming-ham). The largest city in Alabama in the United States. It is the centre of a mining and industrial region.

Birmingham Wire Gauge *n. Abbr.* **BWG** A scale for describing the diameter of metal rod or wire from 0.34 inch (BWG 0) to 0.004 inch (BWG 36).

Bi·ro (bír-ō) *n., pl.* **-ros.** A British trademark for a ball-point pen.

Birobidzhan. See **Jewish Autonomous Region.**

birr¹ (bur) *n. Chiefly Scottish & U.S.* A whirring sound. *~intr.v.* **birred, birring, birrs.** To make this sound. [Middle English *bir(re), byrr,* strong wind, onrush, from Old Norse *byrr,* favourable wind.]

birr² *n.* The basic monetary unit of Ethiopia, equal to 100 cents. [Amharic.]

birth (burth) *n.* **1.** The beginning of existence; the fact of being born. **2.** Any beginning or origin. **3. a.** The act of bearing young; parturition. **b.** The passage of a child or other young mammal from the uterus. **4.** Ancestry; parentage: *a man of noble birth.* **5.** Origin; lineage: *a Cornishman by birth.* —**give birth to.** To bring forth. *~tr.v.* **birthed, birthing, births.** *Rare.* **1.** To deliver (a baby). **2.** To bear (a child). [Middle English *birth,* from Old Norse *byrth* : BEAR (verb) + -TH (noun suffix expressing result).]

birth canal *n.* The cavity of the uterus and the vagina traversed by the infant during birth.

birth certificate *n.* An official record of a person's name, sex, and parentage, and the date and place of birth.

birth control *n.* **1.** Voluntary limitation or control of conception, especially by planned use of contraceptive techniques. **2.** Contraceptive materials.

birth·day (búrth-day, -di) *n.* **1.** The day of one's birth. **2.** The anniversary of one's birth. Also used adjectivally: *birthday party.*

Birthday honours *pl.n. Chiefly British.* Decorations or titles conferred on the sovereign's official birthday.

birthday suit *n. Informal.* A state of complete nakedness. Used humorously.

birth·ing (búrthing) *adj.* Pertaining to or used during the act of giving birth: *a bad birthing position; a birthing pool for giving birth in water.* —**birth·ing** *n.*

birth·mark (búrth-maark) *n.* A mole, mark, or blemish present on the body from birth; especially, a naevus.

birth·place (búrth-playss) *n. Abbr.* **b.pl.** The place where someone is born or where something originates.

birth·rate (búrth-rayt) *n.* The number of live births in a specified population per unit time, especially per thousand of the population per year.

birth·right (búrth-rīt) *n.* **1.** Any privilege granted a person by virtue of birth or status. **2.** Any special privilege accorded the first-born.

birth·stone (búrth-stōn) *n.* A jewel associated with a specific month and thought to bring good luck to a person born in that month.

birth trauma *n.* **1.** An injury sustained by an infant during birth. **2.** An emotional shock sustained by an infant during birth.

birth·wort (búrth-wurt ‖ -wawrt) *n.* Any of several climbing plants of the genus *Aristolochia,* such as the European species *A. clematitis,* having reddish or brownish, usually unpleasantly scented flowers. [Formerly given to women in childbirth.]

biryani. Variant of **biriani.**

bis (biss) *adv.* Twice; again; encore. Used chiefly as a direction in music. [French, from Latin, twice.]

BIS, B.I.S. 1. Bank for International Settlements. **2.** British Information Service.

Bis·cay, Bay of (bíss-kay, -ki). The section of the Atlantic Ocean east of a line running roughly from Ushant Island, off Brittany, to Cape Ortegal in northwestern Spain.

bis·cuit (bískit) *n., pl.* **-cuits** or **biscuit. 1.** Any of various small, flat, usually unleavened cakes, dry, crisp, and hard in texture. See *U.S.* **cookie. 2.** Pale brown; beige. **3.** *Ceramics.* Pottery that has been fired once but not glazed. Also called "bisque". —**take the biscuit.** *Informal.* To be the most surprising or outstanding instance of something ever encountered. [Middle English *besquite,* from Old French *bescoit, bescuit,* from (unattested) Medieval Latin *biscoctus (panis),* "twice-cooked (bread)" : Latin *bis-,* BI- + *coctus,* past participle of *coquere,* to cook.]

bise (beez) *n.* A cold, dry, northerly wind that blows in Switzerland and the adjacent areas of France and Italy. [Middle English, from Old French, from Germanic; akin to Old Swedish *bisa,* whirlwind.]

bi·sect (bī-sékt, bī- ‖ *U.S. also* bī-sekt) *v.* **-sected, -secting, -sects.** —*tr.* To cut or divide into two equal parts. To split; fork: *The road bisects at the junction.* [BI- + -SECT.] —**bi·sec·tion** (-séksh'n) *n.* —**bi·sec·tion·al** *adj.* —**bi·sec·tion·al·ly** *adv.*

bi·sec·tor (bī-séktər) *n.* Anything that bisects, especially a straight line or plane that bisects an angle.

bi·ser·rate (bī-sérrayt, bī-, -sérrət, -sérrit) *adj. Biology.* **1.** Having serrations that are themselves serrated; doubly serrate: *biserrate leaves.* **2.** Serrated on both sides: *biserrate antennae.*

bi·sex·u·al (bī-séksew-əl, -sékshoo- ‖ -séksho͞ol) *adj.* **1.** Of or pertaining to both sexes. **2.** Having both male and female organs; hermaphroditic. Said of some plants and animals. **3.** Sexually attracted to members of both sexes. *~n.* **1.** A bisexual organism; a hermaphrodite. **2.** A person who is sexually attracted to members of both sexes. —**bi·sex·u·al·ism, bi·sex·u·al·i·ty** (-ál-əti) *n.* —**bi·sex·u·al·ly** *adv.*

bish (bish) *n. British Slang.* A blunder; a mistake. [20th century : origin obscure.]

bish·op (bíshəp) *n.* **1.** *Abbr.* **bp.** A high-ranking Christian clergyman, in modern churches usually in charge of a diocese and having the power to confirm and ordain, and in some churches regarded as having received the highest ordination in unbroken succession from the apostles. **2.** *Abbr.* **B** A mitre-shaped chesspiece that can move diagonally across any number of unoccupied spaces of the same colour linked in a straight line. **3.** Mulled port spiced with oranges, sugar, and cloves. [Middle English *bisshop,* Old English *biscop, bisceop,* from Vulgar Latin *biscopus* (unattested), variant of Late Latin *episcopus,* from Greek *episkopos,* guardian, overseer : *epi-,* on, over + *skopos,* one who watches.] —**bish·op·hood** (-hōod) *n.*

bish·op·bird (bíshəp-burd) *n.* Any of certain African weaverbirds of the genus *Euplectes* that have black, red, and yellow plumage in the male.

bish·op·ric (bíshəprik) *n.* **1.** The office or rank of a bishop. **2.** The diocese of a bishop. [Middle English *bishopriche, bisshoprike,* Old English *bisceoprīce* : BISHOP + *rīce,* realm.]

bishop's weed *n.* A plant, the **ground elder** (*see*).

Bis·marck (bíz-maark), **Prince Otto Eduard Leopold von** (1815–98). German politician, known as the "Iron Chancellor". In 1862 he became prime minister of Prussia and was largely responsible for the successful war against Austria (1866) and the creation of the North German Confederation, excluding Austria (1867). After the Franco-Prussian War (1870–71) he became chancellor of the new German empire. His chancellorship (1871–90) was notable for a complex series of foreign alliances and for his sweeping social reforms, introduced in the mid-1880s, by which he sought to stem the advance of German socialism.

Bismarck Archipelago. Group of volcanic islands in the south Pacific Ocean, now part of Papua New Guinea. The largest island is New Britain.

bis·muth (bízməth) *n. Symbol* **Bi** A white, crystalline, brittle, highly diamagnetic metallic element used in alloys to form sharp castings for objects sensitive to high temperatures and in various low-melting alloys for fire-safety devices. Atomic number 83, atomic weight 208.980, melting point 271.3°C, boiling point 1 560°C, relative density 9.747, valencies 3, 5. [New Latin *bisemutum,* Latinisation of German *Wismut*†.] —**bis·muth·al, bis·muth·ic** *adj.*

bis·muth·in·ite (biz-múthinīt) *n.* A grey, natural form of bismuth sulphide that occurs in veins associated with tin, copper, lead, and other ores, and is used as a source of bismuth. Also called "bismuth glance".

bi·son (bíss'n ‖ *U.S. also* bíz'n) *n., pl.* **bison. 1.** A hoofed mammal, *Bison bison,* of western North America, having a dark-brown coat, a shaggy mane, and short, curved horns. Also called "buffalo". **2.** A similar, somewhat smaller animal, *B. bonasus,* of Europe. In this sense, also called "wisent". [Latin *bisōn,* from Germanic.]

bisque¹ (beesk, bisk) *n.* A thick, rich soup usually made from shellfish, but sometimes from other fish or meat. [French *bisque*†.]

bisque² (beesk, bisk) *n.* **1.** *Ceramics.* Biscuit (*see*). **2.** Pale orange yellow to yellowish grey. [From BISCUIT.]

bisque³ (bisk) *n.* An advantage allowed an inferior player in certain games; especially, a free point taken when desired in a tennis set. [French *bisque*†.]

Bis·sau (bi-sów). Capital, largest city, and chief port of Guinea-Bissau in West Africa.

bis·sex·tile (bi-séks-tīl ‖ bī-, *U.S. also* -til) *adj.* Of or pertaining to a leap year. *~n.* A leap year. [Late Latin *bissextilis,* from Latin *bissextus,* intercalary day in the Julian calendar, which followed February 24, the sixth day before the calends of March : *bis*, twice, BI- + *sextus*, sixth.]

bis·ta·ble (bī-stáyb'l) *adj.* Having two stable states: *a bistable circuit.*

bis·tort (bístawrt) *n.* Any of several plants of the genus *Polygonum;* especially, a Eurasian plant, *P. bistorta*, having pointed clusters of small, pinkish flowers. Also called "snakeroot", "snakeweed". [Old French *bistorte*, "twice-twisted" : Latin *bis*, twice, BI- + *tortus*, past participle of Latin *torquēre*, to twist.]

bis·tou·ry (bíss-tōō-ri, -tə-) *n., pl.* **-ries.** A long, narrow surgical knife for minor incisions. [French *bistouri*, from Old French *bistorie, bistorit*, dagger, from Italian (northern dialect) *bistorino* (unattested), variant of *pistorino*, "of Pistoia", from *Pistoja*, Pistoia, Italy (where sharp knives were made).]

bis·tre, *U.S.* **bis·ter** (bístər) *n.* **1.** A water-soluble, yellowish-brown pigment made from soot obtained from beech or other wood. **2.** Greyish to yellowish brown. [French *bistre*†.] —**bis·tre, bis·tred** *adj.*

bis·tro (béestrō ‖ bísstrō) *n., pl.* **-tros.** A small bar, restaurant, or nightclub. [French *bistro*†.]

bi·sul·cate (bī-súlkayt, bī-) *adj.* Cleft or cloven, as a hoof. [BI- + SULCATE.]

bi·sul·phate (bī-súlfayt, bī-) *n. Chemistry.* The inorganic acid group HSO_4 or any compound containing it.

bi·sul·phide (bī-súlfīd, bī-) *n. Chemistry.* A **disulphide** (see).

bi·sul·phite (bī-súlfīt, bī-) *n. Chemistry.* The inorganic acid group HSO_3 or any compound containing it.

bit[1] (bit) *n.* **1.** A small piece, portion, or amount. **2.** A brief amount of time; a moment. **3.** A **bit part** (see). **4.** *Informal.* A melodramatic demonstration of character or feelings: *he did his intellectual bit.* **5.** *Informal.* Trivia; nonsense. *I don't believe in this fitness bit.* **6.** *British.* Formerly, a small coin: *a threepenny bit.* **7.** *U.S. Informal.* An amount equal to one eighth of a dollar. Used only in multiples of two. —**a bit.** Somewhat; to some extent. —**a bit of.** **1.** Some. **2.** In some way; to some degree: *a bit of a bore.* —**a bit of all right.** *Informal.* An attractive thing or person, especially a woman. —**a bit on the side.** *Informal.* Sexual intercourse, usually outside marriage. —**bit by bit.** Little by little; gradually. —**do (one's) bit.** To make one's contribution; do one's share. —**every bit as.** Quite as; to the same degree as. —**to bits. 1.** Into small pieces or fragments. **2.** To distraction: *thrilled to bits.* [Middle English *bit*, Old English *bita*, piece bitten off, morsel.]

bit[2] *n.* **1.** The sharp part of a tool, such as the blade of a knife, plane, or the like. **2.** A pointed and threaded tool for drilling and boring, that is secured in a brace, bitstock, or drill press. **3.** The part of a key that enters the lock and engages the bolt or tumblers. **4.** The metal mouthpiece of a bridle, serving to control, curb, and direct an animal. See **harness. 5.** Anything that controls, guides, or curbs. **6.** The gripping end of a pair of pincers. **7.** The copper end of a soldering iron. —**take the bit between (one's) teeth.** To start up and proceed uncontrollably.

~*tr.v.* **bitted, bitting, bits. 1.** To place a bit in the mouth of (a horse). **2.** To check or control, as if with a bit. [Middle English *bitt*, cutting edge, mouthpiece of a bridle, Old English *bite*, a sting, bite.]

bit[3] *n. Computing.* **1.** A single character of a language having just two characters, such as either of the binary digits 0 or 1. **2.** A unit of information equivalent to the choice of either of two equally likely states of an information-containing system. **3.** A unit of information storage capacity, as of a computer memory. [*binary digit.*]

bit[4]. Past tense and alternative past participle of **bite.**

bitch (bich) *n.* **1.** A female dog or other canine animal. **2.** *Slang.* A spiteful woman. Used derogatorily. **3.** *Slang.* A complaint. **4.** *Chiefly U.S. Slang.* A difficult or confounding problem.

~*intr.v.* **bitched, bitching, bitches.** *Slang.* **1.** To talk spitefully. **2.** To complain; grumble. **3.** *Chiefly U.S.* To botch; bungle. Used with *up*. [Middle English *bicche*, Old English *bicce*, female dog, from Germanic *bekjōn-* (unattested).]

bitch·y (bíchi) *adj.* **-ier, -iest.** *Slang.* Malicious, spiteful, or ill-tempered. —**bitch·i·ly** *adv.* —**bitch·i·ness** *n.*

bite (bīt) *v.* **bit** (bit), **bitten** (bítt'n), **biting, bites.** —*tr.* **1.** To cut, grip, or tear with or as if with the teeth. **2. a.** To pierce the skin of with the teeth, fangs, or sting. **b.** To nibble; gnaw: *bite one's nails.* **3.** To cut into with a sharp instrument, such as a knife or drilling bit. **4.** To grip, grab, or seize. **5.** To eat into; corrode. **6.** To cause to sting or smart. **7.** *Informal.* To irritate. —*intr.* **1. a.** To injure something with or as if with the teeth. **b.** To have a tendency to do this: *Does your dog bite?* **2.** To have a stinging effect or a sharp taste. **3.** To grip or cut into something. **4.** To have the desired, usually unpleasant, effect: *The new tax is really beginning to bite.* **5.** To take or swallow bait. —**bite back.** To restrain oneself from saying (something tactless, hurtful, or the like).

~*n.* **1.** The act of biting. **2.** A wound or injury resulting from biting. **3.** A stinging or smarting sensation. **4.** An incisive, penetrating quality. **5.** An amount of food taken into the mouth at one time; a mouthful. **6.** *Informal.* A light meal or snack. **7.** An attempt by a fish to take the bait on an angler's line. **8. a.** A secure grip or hold applied by a tool or machine upon a working surface. **b.** A surface, as on a file, applying such a grip. **9.** *Dentistry.* The angle at which the upper and lower teeth meet when they come into contact. **10.** The corrosive action of acid upon an etcher's metal plate. —**put the bite on.** *U.S. Slang.* To borrow money from. [Bite, bit, bitten; Middle English *biten, bot* (past plural *biten*), *biten*, Old English *bī-*

tan, bāt (past plural *biton*), *biten.*] —**bit·er** *n.*

Bi·thy·ni·a (bī-thínni-ə, bī-). An ancient country in Asia Minor, in the northwest of present-day Turkey. Originally inhabited by Thracians, by the end of the first century B.C. it had been absorbed into the Roman Empire.

bit·ing (bíting) *adj.* **1.** Causing a stinging sensation. **2.** Bitterly cold and penetrating. Said especially of the wind. **3.** Incisive; caustic. —See Synonyms at **incisive.** —**bit·ing·ly** *adv.*

bit part *n.* A small role in a play or film, having only a few spoken lines.

bit·stock (bít-stok) *n.* A brace or handle in which a drilling or boring bit is secured.

bitt (bit) *n.* Either of a pair of vertical posts set on the deck of a ship and used to secure cables.

~*tr.v.* **bitted, bitting, bitts.** To wind (a cable) around a bitt. [Middle English, probably of Low German origin, akin to Low German and Dutch *beting.*]

bit·ten. Past participle of **bite.**

bit·ter (bíttər) *adj.* **-terer, -terest. 1.** Having or being a taste that is sharp, acrid, and unpleasant. **2.** Causing sharp pain to the body or discomfort to the mind; harsh. **3.** Difficult or distasteful to accept or admit: *the bitter truth.* **4.** Exhibiting or proceeding from strong animosity: *bitter foes.* **5.** Marked by resentfulness or rancour: *a bitter old man.*

~*n. British.* A sharp-tasting beer made with hops.

~*v.* **bittered, -tering, -ters.** —*tr.* To make bitter. —*intr.* To become bitter. [Middle English *bitter*, Old English *biter.*] —**bit·ter·ly** *adv.* —**bit·ter·ness** *n.*

bitter almond *n.* A variety of the common almond, *Prunus amygdalus amara*, having bitter kernels that yield a highly poisonous oil, which is used for flavouring when the prussic acid in it has been removed.

bitter aloes *n. Used with a singular verb.* A cathartic drug derived from the juice of the fleshy leaves of a tropical plant, *Aloe barbadensis.* See **aloe.**

bitter apple *n.* A plant, the **colocynth** (see), or its fruit.

bitter end *n.* **1.** *Nautical.* The end of a rope or cable that is wound around a bitt. **2.** A final, painful or difficult conclusion; the absolute end.

bit·ter·ling (bíttərling) *n.* A small colourful freshwater fish, *Rhodeus sericeus*, related to the carp and often kept in aquaria. [German: BITTER + -LING.]

bit·tern[1] (bíttərn) *n.* Any of several wading birds of the genera *Botaurus* and *Ixobrychus*, having mottled, brownish plumage, and notable for its deep, resonant cry. [Middle English *botor, bitter*, from Old French *butor*, from Vulgar Latin *būtitaurus* (unattested), perhaps "bird (that bellows) like an ox" (after its booming call) : Latin *būtiō*, bittern + *taurus*, ox, bull.]

bittern[2] *n.* The solution of magnesium and calcium bromides and other salts remaining after sodium chloride has been crystallised out of sea water. [From BITTER.]

bitter orange *n.* The **Seville orange** (see).

bitter principle *n. Pharmacology.* Any of a large number of bitter substances, frequently of vegetable origin.

bit·ters (bíttərz) *pl.n.* A bitter, usually alcoholic liquid made with herbs or roots and used in cocktails or as a tonic.

bit·ter·sweet (bíttər-sweet) *n.* **1.** A sprawling vine, *Solanum dulcamara*, native to Eurasia, having purple flowers and poisonous scarlet berries. Also called "woody nightshade". **2.** A North American woody vine, *Celastrus scandens*, having orange or yellowish fruits that split open to expose seeds enclosed in fleshy scarlet arils.

~*adj.* **1.** Bitter and sweet at the same time. **2.** Producing a mixture of pain and pleasure.

bit·ter·weed (bíttər-weed) *n.* Any of various plants that yield or contain a bitter principle.

bit·ter·wood (bíttər-wŏŏd) *n.* **1.** The wood of the tree *Quassia amara.* See **quassia. 2.** Any of various other trees from whose bitter wood a substitute for quassia is obtained.

bit·ty (bítti) *adj.* **1.** Full of bits or flecks. **2.** Consisting of incoherent bits. —**bit·ti·ness** *n.*

bi·tu·men (bíttew-mən, -min, -men ‖ bi-téw-, -tōō-) *n.* **1.** Any of various mixtures of hydrocarbons, occurring naturally or obtained by distillation from coal or petroleum, found in asphalt and tar, and used for surfacing roads and for waterproofing. **2.** The part of coal that can be extracted by an organic solvent. [Middle English *bithumen*, from Latin *bitūmen*, from Gaulish *bet* (unattested).] —**bi·tu·mi·noid** (bi-téwmin-oyd ‖ -tōōmin-) *adj.*

bi·tu·mi·nise, bi·tu·mi·nize (bi-téwmin-īz ‖ -tōōmin-) *tr.v.* **-nised, -nising, -nises.** To treat with bitumen. —**bi·tu·mi·ni·sa·tion** (-ī-záysh'n ‖ *U.S.* -i-) *n.*

bi·tu·mi·nous (bi-téw-minəss ‖ -tōō, *U.S. also* bī-) *adj.* **1.** Like or containing bitumen. **2.** Of or pertaining to bituminous coal.

bituminous coal *n.* A mineral coal that burns with a smoky, yellow flame, yielding volatile bituminous constituents. Also called "soft coal".

bi·va·lent (bī-váylənt) *adj.* **1.** *Chemistry.* Having a valency of 2; divalent. **2.** *Genetics.* Composed of two homologous chromosomes. **3.** *Logic.* **a.** Having one of two truth values in a two-valued logical system. **b.** Either true or false.

~*n. Genetics.* A pair of homologous chromosomes associated together during meiosis. —**bi·va·lence, bi·va·len·cy** *n.*

bi·valve (bī-valv) *n.* Any mollusc of the class Bivalvia (or Pelecypoda), having a shell consisting of two dorsally hinged valves. Bivalves include oysters, cockles, clams, scallops, and mussels. Also called "lamellibranch", "pelecypod".

~*adj.* Also **bi·val·vate** (-vál-vayt), **bi·val·vu·lar** (-vál-vew-lər) (for sense 2). **1.** Having a two-valved shell. **2.** Consisting of two similar separable parts.

biv·ou·ac (bívvoo-ak, bív-wak) *n.* A temporary encampment using available materials to construct a shelter, instead of a tent.
~*intr.v.* **bivouacked, -acking, -acks** or **-acs.** To encamp in a bivouac. [French, earlier *biwacht,* probably from Swiss German *beiwacht,* "supplementary night watch", from German *Beiwache, Beiwacht : bei,* by, at + *Wache,* watch.]

biv·vy (bívvi) *n., pl.* **-vies.** A small tent; a bivouac. [Shortening of BIVOUAC.]

bi·week·ly (bī-wéekli) *adj.* **1.** Happening every two weeks. **2.** Happening twice a week; semiweekly. See Usage note at **bimonthly.**
~*n., pl.* **biweeklies.** A publication issued every two weeks.
~*adv.* **1.** Every two weeks. **2.** Twice a week; semiweekly.

bi·year·ly (bī-yéer-li, -yér-) *adj.* **1.** Biennial. **2.** Biannual. —**bi·year·ly** *adv.*

bi·zarre (bi-zár) *adj.* Strikingly unconventional and far-fetched in style or appearance; odd; grotesque. See Synonyms at **fantastic.** [French, originally "handsome", "brave", from Spanish *bizarro,* from Basque *bizar,* beard ("bearded", hence "spirited").] —**bi·zarre·ly** *adv.* —**bi·zarre·ness** *n.*

Bi·zet (bée-zay), **Georges** (1838–75). French composer. His reputation rests chiefly on the opera *Carmen* (1873–74), the Symphony in C Major, and the *Arlésienne* suite.

Bk The symbol for the element berkelium.
bk. 1. bank. **2.** book.
bkg. banking.
bkpg. bookkeeping.
bkpt. bankrupt.
bks. 1. barracks. **2.** books.
bl. 1. bale **2.** barrel. **3.** black. **4.** blue.
B.L. 1. Bachelor of Laws. **2.** Barrister-at-law. **3.** British Leyland. **4.** British Library.
B/L bill of lading.

blab (blab) *v.* **blabbed, blabbing, blabs.** —*tr.* To reveal (a secret), especially through indiscretion. —*intr.* **1.** To talk of secret matters. **2.** To chatter indiscreetly.
~*n.* **1.** A person who blabs. **2.** Lengthy chatter. [Middle English *blabben,* akin to *blabberen,* to BLABBER.] —**blab·by** *adj.*

blab·ber (blábbər) *intr.v.* **-bered, -bering, -bers.** To chatter.
~*n.* **1.** Idle chatter. **2.** One who blabs. [Middle English *blabberen,* from an imitative Germanic root *blab-* (unattested).]

blab·ber·mouth (blábbər-mowth) *n., pl.* **-mouths** (-mowthz). *Slang.* One who chatters indiscreetly and at length.

black (blak) *n. Abbr.* **bl., blk. 1.** An achromatic colour value of minimum lightness or maximum darkness; one extreme of the neutral grey series, the opposite being white. Although strictly a response to zero stimulation of the retina, the perception of black appears to depend on contrast with surrounding colour stimuli. **2.** Clothing of this colour, especially for mourning. **3.** *Also capital* **B. a.** Any member of a Negroid people; a Negro. **b.** Loosely, any member of a dark-skinned ethnic group. **4.** The black-coloured chess or draughts pieces, or the player using them. **5.** Any black area, quality, or thing. —**in the black.** In credit; prosperous.
~*adj.* **blacker, blackest.** *Abbr.* **bl., blk. 1.** Being of the darkest achromatic visual value; producing or reflecting comparatively little light and having no predominant hue. **2.** Having no light whatsoever: *a black cave.* **3.** *Also capital* **B. a.** Belonging to a Negroid group. **b.** Loosely, belonging to an ethnic group having dark skin. **4. a.** Dark in colour or having parts that are dark in colour. Used with animal and plant names: *black bass; blackthorn.* **b.** Reddish purple. Said of grapes, cherries, or currants. **5.** Soiled, as from soot. **6.** Evil; sinister: *black deeds; black-hearted.* **7.** Cheerless and depressing; gloomy. **8.** Angered; sullen; threatening: *a black look.* **9.** Attended with disaster; calamitous. **10.** Of or designating a form of humour dealing with the abnormal and grotesque aspects of life and society and evoking a sense of the comedy of human despair and failure. **11.** Indicating or incurring censure or dishonour: *a black record of environmental pollution.* **12.** Wearing black clothing: *the black knight.* **13.** Served without milk or cream. Said of tea or coffee. **14.** *British.* Boycotted or not approved by a trade union: *black labour.* **15.** Evading the attention of the tax authorities: *the black economy.* **16.** Purporting to originate from one's own side, when in fact being enemy propaganda: *black radio.*
~*tr.v.* **blacked, blacking, blacks. 1.** To make black or dirty; soil. **2.** To put black dye, paint, or polish on. **3.** To bruise (an eye) with a blow. **4.** *British.* To refuse to have anything to do with (a cargo, for example) because of trade union objections. [Middle English *blak,* Old English *blæc.*] —**black·ly** *adv.* —**black·ness** *n.*

Usage: Black as a noun or adjective is nowadays the preferred term to use when referring to a dark-skinned ethnic group. Terms such as *black organisation* and *black English* are common, and are used by the *black community.* However, the use of *black* in Britain may offend immigrants from India, Pakistan, Bangladesh, or Sri Lanka. Alternatives such as *Negro, non-white,* and *coloured,* have more specialised meanings. In South African English *coloured* means people of mixed white and non-white origin and is used mainly as an adjective. See also **ethnic.**

Black, Joseph (1728–99). Scottish chemist and physicist. He rediscovered what was then called "fixed air" (carbon dioxide) and for-

mulated the concepts of latent heat and specific heat.

black·a·moor (blácka-moor, -mawr) *n. Archaic.* Any dark-skinned person; especially, a North African. [Earlier *black More :* BLACK + MOOR.]

black-and-blue (blácken-blōō) *adj.* Discoloured from coagulation of blood below the surface of the skin.

black-and-tan (blácken-tán) *n.* An alcoholic drink that is a mixture of stout and bitter.

Black and Tans *pl.n.* Auxiliary members of the Royal Irish Constabulary, mostly British ex-servicemen, specially recruited to suppress the Sinn Fein rebellion of 1920–21. [After the colour of the uniform.]

black-and-tan terrier *n.* A **Manchester terrier** (see).

black and white *n.* **1. a.** Print or writing: *Be sure to get the agreement in black and white.* **b.** Explicit, unmistakable terms: *I told you then, in black and white.* **2.** Tones of black and white. **3.** A picture or photograph in tones of black and white.
~*adj.* Also **black-and-white** (blák-'n-wīt, -'nd-). **1.** Pertaining or restricted to film or photography in tones of black and white: *a black and white television set.* **2.** Presenting exaggeratedly simplistic ideas, usually polarised in moral terms.

black art *n.* Black magic *(see).*

black·ball (blák-bawl) *n.* A negative vote that blocks the admission of an applicant to an organisation.
~*tr.v.* **blackballed, -balling, -balls. 1.** To vote against; especially, to veto the admission of. **2.** To exclude from a social group; ostracise. [From the small black ball dropped into a ballot-box to represent an adverse vote.] —**black·ball·er** *n.*

black bass *n.* Any of several North American freshwater game fishes of the genus *Micropterus.*

black bear *n.* Either of two black or dark-brown bears, *Ursus* (or *Euarctos*) *americanus,* of North America, or *Selenarctos thibetanus,* of Asia. The Asian species has a pale V-shaped chest marking.

black beetle *n.* The common **cockroach** *(see).*

black belt *n.* **1. a.** The rank of expert in a system of self-defence such as judo or karate. **b.** The black-coloured sash that symbolises this rank. **c.** A person who holds this rank. **2.** *U.S.* An area with a predominantly black population.

black·ber·ry (blák-bri, -bəri ‖ *U.S.* -berri) *n., pl.* **-ries. 1.** Any of several woody plants of the genus *Rubus,* having thorny stems and black, glossy, edible fruits. Also called "bramble" See **dewberry, loganberry. 2.** The fruit of any of these plants.
~*intr.v.* **blackberried, -berrying, -berries.** To gather blackberries: *go blackberrying.*

black bile *n.* One of the four **humours** *(see)* of medieval physiology, supposed to cause melancholia.

black bindweed *n.* A vine, *Polygonum convolvulus,* native to Europe and having black seed pods.

black·bird (blák-burd) *n.* **1.** A common Eurasian bird, *Turdus merula,* of the thrush family, of which the male is black with a yellow bill and the female is brown. **2.** Any of various American birds of the family Icteridae, having black or predominantly black plumage in the male.

black·board (blák-bawrd ‖ -bōrd) *n.* A panel with a black or sometimes coloured surface for writing on with chalk, used especially in schools.

blackboard jungle *n.* **1.** A school with a reputation for violence by pupils. **2.** The phenomenon of aggression and violence in schools. [From the title of a book (1954) by Evan Hunter, popularised as a film.]

black body *n., pl.* **-ies.** *Physics.* A theoretically perfect absorber of all incident radiation. Also called "full radiator".

black body radiation *n.* The thermal radiation emitted by a black body at a given temperature. The total amount of radiation emitted is given by the **Stefan-Boltzmann law** and the spectral energy distribution by **Planck's formula** *(both of which see).*

black book *n.* A record of people liable to punishment. —**in (someone's) black books.** In disfavour with someone.

black box *n.* **1.** A device or theoretical construct, especially an electric circuit, with known or specified performance characteristics but unknown or unspecified constituents and means of operation. **2.** A **flight recorder** *(see).* **3.** Any device used for automatically recording the details of a journey. See **tachograph.**

black bread *n.* Coarse rye bread.

black bryony *n.* A climbing European plant, *Tamus communis,* having small, greenish flowers and poisonous red berries.

black buck, black·buck (blák-buk) *n.* An antelope, *Antilope cervicapra,* of India, of which the male has a dark back and spiral horns. Also called "sasin".

Black·burn (blák-burn). Industrial town in northwest England, in the central Lancashire coalfield. It stands on the Leeds-Liverpool canal.

black·cap (blák-kap) *n.* **1.** A small European bird, *Sylvia atricapilla,* of which the male is grey with a black crown. **2.** Any of various other black-crowned birds.

black·cock (blák-kok) *n.* The male of the **black grouse** *(see).*

Black Country *n.* A name for part of the industrial West Midlands in Britain. Preceded by *the.*

black·cur·rant (blak-kúrrənt, blák-) *n.* **1.** A widely cultivated Eurasian shrub, *Ribes nigrum,* producing clusters of small edible black berries. **2.** The fruit of this shrub.

black·damp (blák-damp) *n.* A gas composed of a mixture of carbon dioxide and nitrogen, found in mines after fires and explosions of combustible gases. Also called "chokedamp".

Black Death n. A form of plague that was pandemic throughout Europe and much of Asia during periods in the 14th century. [From the dark splotches it causes on the skin.]

black diamond n. **1.** A variety of diamond, **carbonado** (see). **2.** *Plural. Informal.* Coal.

black dog n. *British.* A melancholy state or mood; depression. Usually preceded by *the.*

black earth n. A type of soil, **chernozem** (see). **—black-earth** adj.

black-en (bláckən) v. **-ened, -ening, -ens.** *—tr.* **1.** To make black. **2.** To stain (someone's reputation, for example); defame. *—intr.* To become black or dark. **—black-en-er** n.

Blac-kett (bláckit), **Patrick Maynard Stuart, Baron** (1897–1974). British physicist. For his contributions to the study of cosmic radiation, he was awarded the Nobel prize for physics (1948).

black eye n. A bruised discoloration of the flesh surrounding the eye, resulting from a blow.

black-eyed pea (blák-īd) n. A plant, the **cowpea** (see).

black-eyed Susan n. **1.** A plant, the **rudbeckia** (see). **2.** A vine, *Thunbergia alata,* native to tropical Africa, having white or orange-yellow flowers with purple throats.

black-face (blák-fayss) n. A black-faced sheep.

black-fish (blák-fish) n., pl. **-fishes** or collectively **blackfish. 1.** An oceanic fish *Centrolophus niger,* of northern regions. **2.** The **pilot whale** (see). **3.** A female salmon that has recently spawned. Compare **redfish.**

black flag n. The flag used by pirates, the **Jolly Roger** (see). Usually preceded by *the.*

black-fly (blák-flī) n., pl. **-flies** or collectively **blackfly.** A black aphid, *Aphis fabae,* that feeds in large masses on bean plants, spinach, dock, and the like. Also called "bean aphid".

black fly n. Any of various small, dark-coloured, bloodsucking flies of the family Simuliidae. Also called "buffalo gnat".

Black-foot (blák-fŏŏt) n., pl. **-feet** or collectively **Blackfoot. 1.** A member of any of three peoples of North American Indians formerly inhabiting the regions of Montana, Alberta, and Saskatchewan. **2.** The Algonquian language spoken by these peoples. [Translation of Blackfoot *Siksika;* said to be so named because the soles of their moccasins were black from walking across burnt prairie.] **—Black-foot** adj.

black-footed ferret (blák-fŏŏtid) n. A weasel-like mammal, *Mustela nigripes,* of central North America, related to the polecat and having yellowish fur and dark feet. Also called "ferret".

Black Forest. See **Schwarzwald.**

Black Forest gateau n. A rich chocolate cake sandwiched with black cherries and cream. [After the *Black Forest* (Schwarzwald) in Germany, referring to its dark colour.]

Black Friar n. A Dominican friar. [After the black mantles worn by the Dominican friars.]

black frost n. A condition in which the air temperature falls below freezing point without frost forming, causing blackening and internal damage in vegetation.

black gold n. Crude oil.

black grouse n. A Eurasian game bird, *Lyrurus tetrix,* of which the black male is called "blackcock", the mottled female is called "greyhen", and the collective plural is "black game".

black-guard (blággaard, blággərd) n. **1.** A scoundrel. **2.** A scurrilous person.
~adj. Of or like a blackguard; foulmouthed.
~v. Rare. **blackguarded, -guarding, -guards.** *—tr.* To abuse or revile. *—intr.* To behave like a blackguard. [Originally, the kitchen workers and menials of a noble household or of an army.] **—black-guard-ism** n. **—black-guard-ly** adj. & adv.

Black Hand n. A secret society organised for acts of terrorism and blackmail, composed mainly of Sicilians active in the United States in the early 20th century. Compare **Mafia.**

black hat n. *Australian.* Especially formerly, a recent immigrant to Australia.

black-head (blák-hed) n. **1.** A plug of dried fatty matter capped with blackened dust and epithelial debris that clogs a pore of the skin. Also called "comedo". **2.** *Veterinary Medicine.* An infectious, often fatal, liver and intestinal disease of turkeys and some wildfowl. Also called "infectious enterohepatitis". **3.** Any of various birds with dark head markings.

black-heart (blák-haart) n. **1.** A disease of potatoes and other plants, in which the inner tissues darken. **2.** Abnormal blackening of the stems in woody plants, probably caused by extreme cold. **3.** A variety of dark-skinned purple-fleshed cherry.

black-heart-ed (blák-hártid) adj. Evil by nature; wicked.

Black-heath (blák-hēeth). District and former village in southeast Greater London, in the boroughs of Greenwich and Lewisham. Its common was used as a rallying-point by Wat Tyler and Jack Cade for attacks on London in the rebellions of 1381 and 1450.

black hole n. **1.** A region in space caused by a star collapsing under its own gravitational force to such an extent that its gravitational field prevents any matter, light, or other electromagnetic radiation leaving the region. See **singularity, white hole. 2.** *Informal.* A bottomless pit: *pour money endlessly into black holes.*

Black Hole of Calcutta n. **1.** A small dungeon in Calcutta in which 123 of the 146 British prisoners confined there on June 20, 1756, died of suffocation. **2.** *Small* **b,** *small* **h.** An uncomfortable confined space.

black horehound n. A strong-smelling plant, *Ballota nigra,* native to Europe, having clusters of purple flowers.

black humour n. The humour of the morbid and the absurd, especially as a literary genre.

black ice n. **Glaze ice** (see).

black-ing (blácking) n. **1. Lamp black** (see). **2.** A black paste or liquid used as shoe polish.

black-ish (bláckish) adj. Somewhat black. **—black-ish-ly** adv.

black-jack [1] (blákjak) n. *U.S.* A small leather-covered bludgeon used as a hand weapon.
~tr.v. **blackjacked, -jacking, -jacks.** To hit with a blackjack. [BLACK + JACK (tool).]

blackjack [2] n. A type of pontoon, played especially in casinos. [BLACK + JACK (knave in cards).]

blackjack [3] n. A tankard made of tarred or waxed leather. [BLACK + Middle English *jakke,* leather coat, container, from Old French *jacque* (see **jacket**).]

blackjack [4] n. Sphalerite or zinc sulphide ore. [BLACK + JACK (impertinent, worthless person); miners' term for this worthless mixture in lead ore.]

blackjack [5] n. *Australian Informal.* Treacle or syrup. [BLACK + JACK (fellow, thing, etc.).]

blackjack [6] n. *South African.* Any of the black, spiky seeds of the weed *Bidens pilosa,* which adhere to coats of animals or to clothing.

black lead n. **Graphite** (see).

black-leg (blák-leg) n. **1.** *Veterinary Medicine.* An infectious, usually fatal, gas gangrene affecting the heavily muscled upper parts of the legs of sheep and cattle. **2.** A bacterial or fungous plant disease that causes the stems of plants to turn black, such as a fungal disease of brassicas caused by *Phoma lingam.* **3.** One who cheats in gambling, especially a professional gambler; a cardsharp. **4.** *British.* A strikebreaker; a scab. *—intr.v.* **blacklegged, -legging, -legs.** To break a strike by continuing to work or taking over a striker's job.

black letter n. *Printing.* **1. Gothic** (see). **2.** Loosely, any heavy, black typeface. **—black-let-ter** adj.

black light n. Invisible ultraviolet or infrared radiation.

black lightning n. *Australian.* An Aboriginal fire used for cooking, signalling, or the like that is thought to be the cause of a bushfire.

black-list (blák-list) n. A list of persons or organisations to be disapproved of, boycotted, or suspected of disloyalty. *—tr.v.* **blacklisted, -listing, -lists.** To place (a name) on a blacklist.

black lung n. A disease suffered by coal miners involving chronic inflammation of the lungs as a result of inhaling coal dust.

black magic n. Magic as practised in league with the Devil; witchcraft. Also called "black art". See Synonyms at **magic.**

black-mail (blák-mayl) n. **1.** Extortion by the threat of exposure or criminal prosecution. **2.** Money extorted in this manner. **3.** The appealing to a person's feelings of guilt or emotional weaknesses in order to influence his behaviour: *emotional blackmail.*
~tr.v. **blackmailed, -mailing, -mails. 1.** To extort money or something of value from (a person) by means of blackmail. **2.** To coerce or influence the behaviour of by means of blackmail. [BLACK + *mail,* tribute, Middle English *maill, male,* Old English *māl,* agreement, from Old Norse *māl,* speech, agreement.] **—black-mail-er** n.

Black Maria n. A police van used especially for transporting offenders.

black mark n. A sign of disapprobation, discredit, or the like.

black market n. **1.** The illicit trade in goods or currencies in violation of price controls, rationing, or other restrictions. **2.** A place where such trade takes place. **—black marketeer** n.

black-mar-ket (blák-márkit) tr.v. **-keted, -keting, -kets.** To trade (goods) on a black market.

black mass n. A travesty of the Roman Catholic Mass practised by Satanists.

black measles n. A severe form of measles, characterised by a dark rash due to subcutaneous bleeding.

black medick n. A clover-like plant, *Medicago lupulina,* native to Europe, having compound leaves, small yellow flower heads, and black pods. Also called "nonesuch".

Black-more (blák-mawr ‖ -mōr), **Richard Doddridge** (1825–1900). British novelist and poet. He wrote several volumes of verse and published 15 novels, but he is remembered now only for his historical romance *Lorna Doone* (1869).

Black Muslim n. A supporter of the movement of the **Nation of Islam** (see).

black mustard n. A plant, *Brassica nigra,* native to Eurasia, having clusters of yellow flowers. Its pungent seeds, ground to a powder, are a source of the condiment mustard.

black-necked stork n. The **jabiru** (see).

black nightshade n. An annual plant, *Solanum nigrum,* having small white flowers and black berries. It is widespread as a weed.

black out tr.v. **1.** To cause or produce the blacking out of (a city, theatre, or radio station, for example). **2.** To suppress or delete for political reasons or by censorship.*—intr.* To undergo a blackout; especially, to suffer a temporary loss of consciousness, memory or vision.

black-out (blákowt) n. **1.** The extinguishing or concealing of lights that might be visible to enemy aircraft during an air raid at night. Compare **dim-out. 2.** A temporary loss of electric power. **3.** In the theatre, the sudden extinguishing of all stage lights to indicate passage of time, or to mark the end of an act or a scene. **4.** A temporary loss of consciousness or vision. **5.** A suppression or stoppage, as of news for political reasons. **6.** *Electronics.* A temporary loss of function, as in a valve, caused by a high transient current. **7.** A temporary loss or stoppage of radio or television communication or broadcasting caused by a technical fault, a strike, or the like.

Black Panther *n.* A member of a militant organisation of blacks in the United States who sought Black Power.

black pepper *n.* See **pepper.**

black poplar *n.* An ornamental poplar tree, *Populus nigra,* native to Eurasia, having spreading branches and pointed, triangular leaves. See **Lombardy poplar.**

Black Power *n.* A movement among blacks, especially American Negroes, to achieve social equality through political power gained by uniting the Negro community in specifically Negro political and cultural institutions, rather than by seeking integration into the white community.

Black Prince. See **Edward, Prince of Wales.**

black pudding *n.* A sausage prepared from cooked pig's blood, minced fat, herbs and spices. Also called "blood pudding", "blood sausage".

black rat *n.* A type of **rat** *(see).*

Black Rod *n.* An officer of the House of Lords in Britain, whose main duty as chief usher is to summon the Commons to the Lords at the opening and prorogation of Parliament.

black rot *n.* Any of various plant diseases, particularly affecting fruits and vegetables, caused by fungi or bacteria and resulting in darkening of the leaves and decay.

Black Sash *n.* A movement in South Africa of women against apartheid.

Black Sea. A sea lying between Europe and Asia. It is connected to the Mediterranean Sea by the Bosporus, the Sea of Marmara, and Dardanelles. The main Ukrainian Black Sea port of Odessa, frozen for three months, is kept open all year by ice breakers.

black sheep *n.* **1.** A sheep with black fleece. **2.** A person considered undesirable or disgraceful by his family or peer group.

Black Shirt *n.* A member of a fascist party organisation, especially Mussolini's Italian Fascist party. [After the black shirts of Italian Fascist uniforms.]

black·smith (blák-smith) *n.* **1.** One who forges and shapes iron with an anvil and hammer. **2.** One who makes, repairs, and fits horseshoes. [Middle English *blaksmith,* "a worker in black metal" (iron).] **—black·smith·ing** *n.*

black·snake (blák-snayk) *n.* **1.** Any of various venomous black snakes, such as the Australian species *Pseudechis porphyriacus.* **2.** Any of various dark-coloured, nonvenomous snakes, such as the black racer, *Coluber constrictor,* of North America. **3.** *Western U.S.* A long, tapering, braided rawhide or leather whip with a snapper on the end.

black spot *n.* **1.** Any of various plant diseases caused by fungi or bacteria and resulting in small black spots on the leaves. **2.** A part of a road where traffic accidents frequently occur.

Black·stone (blák-stən, -stŏn), **Sir William** (1723–80). British jurist. His enduring fame rests on his monumental four-volume *Commentaries on the Laws of England* (1765–69), the most comprehensive single treatment of the body of English law.

black stump *n. Australian & N. Z.* An imaginary last post at the edge of civilisation. Used chiefly in the phrases *this side of the black stump, beyond the black stump.*

black swan *n.* A large black Australian swan *Cygnus atratus,* with a red bill.

black tea *n.* A dark tea, the leaf of which is fully fermented or oxidised before drying. Compare **green tea, oolong.**

black·thorn (blák-thawrn) *n.* A thorny Eurasian shrub, *Prunus spinosa,* having clusters of white flowers and bluish-black, plumlike fruit. Also called "sloe".

black tie *n.* **1.** A black bow tie worn with a dinner jacket. **2.** Formal evening wear for men, typically consisting of a black dinner jacket, black trousers with a stripe down the side, and a black bow tie. Also *U.S.* "tuxedo". Compare **white tie. —black-tie** *adj.*

black·top (blák-top) *n. Chiefly U.S.* **1.** A bituminous material, such as asphalt, used to pave roads. **2.** A road so paved.

black velvet *n.* **1. a.** A drink consisting of stout and champagne. **b.** A drink consisting of stout and cider. **2.** *Australian Slang.* Dark-skinned woman.

black vomit *n.* **1.** A vomit consisting of bloody matter. **2.** Severe yellow fever with symptomatic regurgitation of such vomit.

black walnut *n.* **1.** A deciduous walnut tree, *Juglans nigra,* of eastern North America, having dark, hard wood and edible nuts. **2.** The grained wood of this tree, used for cabinetwork.

black-wa·ter fever (blák-wawtər ‖ *U.S. also* -wotter) *n.* A severe, frequently fatal malaria with symptomatic excretion of blood in the urine caused by destruction of red blood cells.

black widow *n.* A New World spider, *Latrodectus mactans,* of which the extremely venomous female is black with red markings. [From the fact that the female eats its mate.]

Black·wood (blák-wŏod) *n.* In bridge, a conventional bidding sequence of four and five no-trumps, used in order to find out the aces and kings of a partner's hand. [After E.F. *Blackwood,* 20th-century U.S. bridge-player.]

blad·der (bláddər) *n.* **1.** *Anatomy.* Any of various distensible membranous sacs found in most animals, especially the **urinary bladder** *(see).* **2.** Anything resembling such a sac: *the bladder of a football.* **3.** *Botany.* An inflated, hollow structure, such as the air sac in certain seaweeds. **4.** *Pathology.* A blister, pustule, or cyst filled with fluid or air. [Middle English *bladdre,* Old English *blǽdre.*] **—blad·-**

der·y *adj.*

bladder campion *n.* A plant, *Silene cucubalus,* native to Europe, having white flowers and an inflated calyx.

blad·der·nose (bláddər-nŏz) *n.* An aquatic mammal, the **hooded seal** *(see).*

blad·der·nut (bláddər-nut) *n.* Any of several shrubs or small trees of the genus *Staphylea,* of the North Temperate Zone, having small, whitish flowers and inflated seed pods.

blad·der·worm (bláddər-wurm) *n.* The bladder-like, encysted larva of the tapeworm.

blad·der·wort (bláddər-wurt ‖ -wawrt) *n.* Any of various aquatic plants of the genus *Utricularia,* having violet or yellow flowers, and, in most species, small bladders that trap minute aquatic animals.

blad·der·wrack (bláddər-rak) *n.* **1.** A rockweed, *Fucus vesiculosus,* having forked, brownish-green fronds with air-filled bladders. **2.** Any of several other seaweeds with bladders.

blade (blayd) *n.* **1.** The flat-edged cutting part of a sharpened tool or weapon. **2.** *Archaic & Poetic.* **a.** A sword. **b.** A swordsman. **3.** A light-headed, reckless young man. Not in current usage. **4.** Any flat, thin structural member or section, such as the flat part of an oar or propeller. **5.** *Anatomy.* The **scapula** *(see).* **6.** *Botany.* **a.** The leaf of a grass or similar plant. **b.** The expanded, usually green part of a leaf, as distinguished from the leafstalk. **7.** *Phonetics.* The upper surface of the tongue, just behind the tip. **8.** The runner attached to the sole of an ice skate. [Middle English *blade,* Old English *blæd,* leaf, blade.] **—blad·ed** *adj.*

blae·ber·ry (bláy-bri, -bəri ‖ -berri) *n. Scottish & Northern English.* A shrub, the **whortleberry** *(see).* [Middle English, *blae,* Scottish and Northern English dialect, from Old Norse *blár,* BLUE.]

blah (blaa) *n.* Also **blah blah.** *Slang.* Worthless nonsense; drivel. [Imitative.]

blain (blayn) *n.* A skin sore; a blister; a blotch. [Middle English *blein, blain,* an inflammatory swelling, Old English *blegen.*]

Blair (blair), **Tony,** born Anthony Charles Lynton Blair (1953–). British Labour prime minister (1997–). Trained as a barrister, he was elected to Parliament in 1983. He was elected leader of the Labour party (1994) on the death of John Smith (1938–94), becoming prime minister on Labour's landslide victory, after eighteen years in opposition, in the 1997 general election.

Blake (blayk), **Robert** (1599–1657). English admiral who was on the Parliamentarian side in the English Civil War. He pursued Prince Rupert to the Mediterranean (1650) and virtually destroyed the Royalist fleet there.

Blake, William (1757–1827). British poet and painter. He trained as an engraver and illustrated his own poems. Both his poems and his paintings have a mystical, visionary quality. His first important volumes of poetry were the childlike *Songs of Innocence* (1789) and *Songs of Experience* (1794). In these and his later, prophetic volumes, such as *The Marriage of Heaven and Hell* (*c.* 1790), Blake railed against both cruelty and injustice and made a plea for the freedom of the human spirit.

blame (blaym) *tr.v.* **blamed, blaming, blames. 1.** To hold responsible; accuse. **2.** To find fault with; censure. **3.** To place responsibility for (something) on a person or thing: *blamed the accident on the cyclist.* —See Synonyms at **criticise.** ~*n.* **1.** The responsibility for a fault or error. **2.** Censure; condemnation. **—be to blame.** To be guilty or responsible. Used with *for.* [Middle English *blamen,* from Old French *blamer,* earlier *blasmer,* from Vulgar Latin *blastēmāre* (unattested), alteration of Late Latin *blasphēmāre,* to reproach, BLASPHEME.] **—blame·a·ble, blam·a·ble** *adj.* **—blam·er** *n.*

blame·ful (bláym-f'l, -fŏŏl) *adj.* Deserving of blame; blameworthy. **—blame·ful·ly** *adv.* **—blame·ful·ness** *n.*

blame·less (bláym-ləss, -liss) *adj.* Free from blame or guilt; innocent. **—blame·less·ly** *adv.* **—blame·less·ness** *n.*

blame·wor·thy (bláym-wurthi) *adj.* Deserving of blame; reprehensible. **—blame·wor·thi·ness** *n.*

Blanc (blоN), **Louis** (1811–82). Spanish-born French politician and political theorist. His lasting importance rests on his writings, especially *The Organisation of Work* (1839), one of the most influential of early socialist treatises.

Blanc, Mont. See **Mont Blanc.**

blanc fixe (blángk fíks; *French* blоN féeks) *n.* Powdered barium sulphate used as a white base for water-colour pigments. [French, "fixed white".]

blanch (blaanch ‖ blanch) *v.* **blanched, blanching, blanches.** Also **blench** (blench). —*tr.* **1.** To take colour from; bleach. **2.** To whiten (a growing food plant, such as celery) by covering to cut off direct light. **3.** To whiten (a metal) by soaking in acid or by coating with tin. **4. a.** To loosen the skin of (almonds, for example) by scalding. **b.** To boil (food) briefly to remove strong or bitter flavours or to kill enzymes prior to freezing. **5.** To cause to turn pale. —*intr.* To turn white or become pale as through shock or illness. [Middle English *blaunchen,* from Old French *blanchir,* from *blanche,* feminine of *blanc,* white, from Vulgar Latin *blancus* (unattested), from Germanic.] **—blanch·er** *n.*

blanc·mange (blə-mónzh ‖ -mónj) *n.* A flavoured and sweetened milk pudding, thickened with cornflour and set with gelatine in a mould. [Middle English *blancmanger,* dish of chopped chicken or fish with rice, from Old French, "white food" : *blanc,* white (see **blanch**) + *manger,* food, from *mangier,* to eat (see **mange**).]

bland (bland) *adj.* **blander, blandest. 1.** Characterised by a moderate, undisturbing, or tranquil quality: **a.** Pleasant in manner; ingratiating. **b.** Free of irritation; soothing: *a bland diet.* **c.** Mild; balmy. **2.** Lacking a distinctive character; mediocre. [Latin *blandus,* caressing, flattering, "soft-spoken".] —**bland·ly** *adv.* —**bland·ness** *n.*

blan·dish (blándish) *tr.v.* **-dished, -dishing, -dishes.** To coax by flattery or wheedling; cajole. [Middle English *blandishen,* from Old French *blandir* (present stem *blandiss-*), from Latin *blandīrī,* from *blandus,* flattering, BLAND.] —**blan·dish·er** *n.*

blan·dish·ment (blándishmənt) *n. Usually plural.* Flattery or wheedling.

blank (blangk) *adj.* **blanker, blankest. 1.** Bearing no writing, print, or marking of any kind. **2.** Not finished or filled in: *a blank questionnaire.* **3.** Having no finishing grooves or cuts: *a blank key.* **4. a.** Expressing nothing; vacant. **b.** Vacuous; having no inspiration: *my mind was blank.* **c.** Confused, uncomprehending: *a blank look.* **5.** Devoid of activity or character; empty. **6.** Barren; fruitless: *blank efforts.* **7.** Utter; complete: *a blank refusal.* **8.** Having no openings or ornamentation: *a blank wall.* —See Synonyms at **empty.**

~*n.* **1.** An empty space; a void: *His memory was a complete blank.* **2. a.** An empty space on a document to be filled in. **b.** A document having one or more such spaces. **3.** An unfinished material, part, or article, such as a key form, that is prepared ready for eventual finishing. **4.** A gun cartridge with a charge of powder but no bullet. Also called "blank cartridge". **5.** A lottery ticket that wins no prize. **6.** A mark, usually a dash (—), indicating the omission of a word or letter. **7.** The centre white circle of a target; the bull's eye. **8.** Something used to seal an opening. **9.** *Archaic.* Any goal or target. —**draw a blank.** *Informal.* To fail utterly; achieve nothing.

~*tr.v.* **blanked, blanking, blanks. 1.** To remove from view; obliterate: *The strong glare of the sun blanked it from view.* **2.** To omit; delete; invalidate. Often used with *out.* **3.** *U.S.* To prevent (an opponent in a game or sport) from scoring. **4.** To punch or stamp (a piece of material), ready for further eventual punching or stamping. Often used with *out.* **5.** To seal or block (an opening or means of access). Often used with *off.* **6.** *British Slang.* To cut; snub. [Middle English *bla(u)nk,* white, not written on, from Old French *blanc.* See **blanch.**] —**blank·ly** *adv.* —**blank·ness** *n.*

blank cheque *n.* **1.** A cheque that has been signed, but which has not had the amount filled in. **2.** Unrestrained freedom of action or choice.

blan·ket (blángkit) *n.* **1.** A large piece of wool or other thick cloth used as a covering for warmth, especially on a bed. **2.** A thick layer that covers or encloses: *a blanket of snow.* **3.** *Physics.* A layer of fertile material surrounding the core of a breeder reactor.

~*adj.* **1.** Covering a wide range of conditions or requirements. **2.** Unrestricted; applying to everything: *a blanket generalisation.*

~*tr.v.* **blanketed, -keting, -kets. 1.** To cover with or as if with a blanket. **2.** To conceal or suppress as if with a blanket. **3.** *Nautical.* To cut off (a sailing boat) from the wind by passing close on the windward side. [Middle English, originally, a white woollen material, from Old French *blanquet, blanchet,* diminutive of *blanc,* white. See **blanch.**]

blanket stitch *n.* A stitch that forms loops and is used for reinforcing the edges of materials, especially the edges of blankets. —**blanket-stitch** (blángkit-stitch) *tr.v.*

blank verse *n.* Verse consisting of unrhymed lines, usually of iambic pentameter.

blan·quette de veau (blang-két də vố, blON-) *n.* A stew or fricassée of veal in a white sauce. [French, white dish of veal. See **blanket.**]

Blan·qui (blON-kée), **Louis Auguste** (1805–81). French revolutionary leader and political theorist. He fought for the deposition of Napoleon III, and proclamation of the Paris commune. His ideas, close to those of **Marx,** were expressed in his treatise, *Critique Sociale,* published four years after his death.

Blan·tyre (blán-tīr). Also **Blan·tyre-Lim·be** (-límbay). The oldest and largest town in Malawi, situated in the Shire Highlands. It was founded as a mission of the Church of Scotland by David **Livingstone** (1876) and named after the village where he was born.

blare (blair) *v.* **blared, blaring, blares.** —*intr.* To sound loudly and insistently. —*tr.* To utter or proclaim loudly.

~*n.* A loud, strident noise. [Middle English *bleren,* to bellow, from Middle Dutch.]

blar·ney (blárni) *n.* Smooth, flattering talk.

~*v.* **blarneyed, -neying, -neys.** —*tr.* To beguile with blarney. —*intr.* To flatter. [After the *Blarney Stone.*]

Blarney. A village in County Cork, Republic of Ireland. Blarney Castle (*c.* 1446) has on its southern wall the famous Blarney Stone, said to impart gifts of eloquence and flattery to those who kiss it.

Blas·co I·bá·ñez (bláss-kō ee-báan-yeth, bláass-), **Vicente** (1867–1928). Spanish politician and novelist. He founded the republican paper *El Pueblo* (1891), was elected to the Spanish parliament (1901), and spent more than 30 periods in prison for his antimonarchist views before settling in France (1923). His most famous novel is *The Four Horsemen of the Apocalypse* (1916).

bla·sé (bláazay ‖ *U.S.* blaa-záy) *adj.* **1.** Indifferent, unaffected, or lacking enthusiasm, especially as a result of habitual and excessive indulgence. **2.** Filled with ennui; weary. [French, past participle of *blaser,* to blunt, cloy, "to cause to be bloated with strong liquor", from Middle Dutch *blasen,* to blow up, cause to swell.]

blas·pheme (blass-féem, blaas-) *v.* **-phemed, -pheming, -phemes.** —*tr.* **1.** To speak of (God or something sacred) in an irreverent or impious manner. **2.** To revile; execrate: *"and every tongue/ Cursed and blasphemed him as he passed"* (P.B. Shelley). —*intr.* To utter

blasphemy. [Middle English *blasfemen, blasphemen,* from Old French *blasfemer,* from Late Latin *blasphēmāre,* to reproach, blaspheme, from Greek *blasphēmein,* from *blasphēmos,* evil-speaking, BLASPHEMOUS.] —**blas·phem·er** *n.*

blas·phe·mous (bláss-fəməss, bláass-) *adj.* Impiously irreverent. See Synonyms at **profane.** [Late Latin *blasphēmus,* from Greek *blasphēmos,* evil-speaking, impious.] —**blas·phe·mous·ly** *adv.* —**blas·phe·mous·ness** *n.*

blas·phe·my (bláss-fəmi, bláass-) *n., pl.* **-mies.** Any contemptuous or profane act, utterance, or writing concerning God or something considered sacred.

blast (blaast ‖ blast) *n.* **1. a.** A strong gust of wind. **b.** The battering effect of such a gust. **2.** A forcible stream of air or other gas from an opening, especially one in a blast furnace to aid combustion. **3. a.** The blowing of a whistle or wind instrument. **b.** The sound or noise produced by this. **4. a.** An explosion. **b.** A charge of explosive. **c.** The powerful, destructive rush of air resulting from an explosion. **5.** Any disease of plants that results in failure of flowers to open, or failure of fruit or seeds to mature. **6.** *Chiefly U.S.* A violent verbal assault or outburst. —See Synonyms at **wind.** —**(at) full blast.** At full speed, volume, or capacity.

~*v.* **blasted, blasting, blasts.** —*tr.* **1.** To tear to pieces by or as if by explosion; blow up. **2.** To cause to deteriorate; ruin; frustrate: *His dreams were all blasted by the news of his rejection.* **3.** To cause to shrivel, wither, or mature imperfectly by or as if by blast or blight. **4.** To make, dislodge, or open (something) by or as if by explosion: *blast a channel through the reefs.* **5.** *Slang.* To attack or criticise vigorously. **6.** *Slang.* To damn. Used euphemistically. —*intr.* **1.** To detonate explosives. **2.** To emit a sudden loud noise. **3.** *Slang.* To shoot. Sometimes used with *away.* **4.** *Electronics.* To distort sound recording or transmission by overloading a microphone or loud-speaker.

~*interj. Informal.* Used to express annoyance or frustration. [Middle English *blast,* Old English *blæst.*] —**blast·er** *n.*

-blast *n. comb. form.* **1.** Indicates a germ, sprout, or growth; for example, **erythroblast. 2.** Indicates embryonic tissue; for example, **epiblast.** [Greek *blastos,* shoot, bud.] —**-blast·ic** *adj. comb. form.*

blast·ed (blaastid ‖ blástid) *adj.* **1.** Blighted; withered; shrivelled. **2.** *Slang.* Damned.

blas·te·ma (blastée-mə) *n., pl.* **-mas** or **-mata** (-mətə). **1.** A segregated region of embryonic cells from which a specific organ develops. **2.** A mass of undifferentiated animal cells that develops into a new tissue or organ during regeneration of lost parts. [New Latin, from Greek *blastēma,* offspring, offshoot, from *blastos,* sprout, bud.] —**blas·te·mal** (-məl), **blas·te·mat·ic** (blásti-máttik), **blas·te·mic** (-mik) *adj.*

blast furnace *n.* Any furnace in which combustion is intensified by a blast of air, especially a furnace for smelting iron by blowing air through a hot mixture of ore, coke, and flux.

blasting gelatine *n.* A **dynamite** *(see)* containing nitrocellulose in addition to nitroglycerin.

blasto– *comb. form.* Indicates growth, budding, or germination; for example, **blastoderm.** [Greek *blastos.* See **-blast.**]

blas·to·coel, blas·to·coele (blást-ō-seel, -ə-) *n. Embryology.* The cavity of a **blastula** *(see).* Also called "segmentation cavity". [BLASTO- + *-coel,* variant of -CELE.] —**blas·to·coel·ic** (-séelik) *adj.*

blas·to·cyst (blást-ō-sist, -ə-) *n. Embryology.* **1.** The **blastula** *(see)* of mammals. **2.** The **germinal vesicle** *(see).* —**blas·to·cys·tic** (-sistik) *adj.*

blas·to·derm (blást-ō-derm, -ə-) *n.* **1.** The layer of cells surrounding the blastocoel. It gives rise to the **germinal disc** *(see)* from which the embryo develops in most placental vertebrates. **2.** The embryonic structure resulting from cleavage in heavily yolked eggs, such as those of birds. [BLASTO- + -DERM.] —**blas·to·der·mat·ic** (-der-máttik), **blas·to·derm·ic** (-dérmik) *adj.*

blas·to·disc (blást-ō-disk, -ə-) *n. Embryology.* The **germinal disc** *(see).*

blast off *intr.v.* To commence flight; take off. Used of rockets or space vehicles.

blast-off, blast-off (bláast-off, -awf ‖ blást-) *n.* The launching of a rocket or space vehicle.

blas·to·gen·e·sis (blást-ō-jénnə-siss, -ə-) *n. Biology.* **1.** The theory that inherited characteristics are transmitted from parent to offspring by germ plasm. **2.** Reproduction by budding or other asexual means. —**blas·to·ge·net·ic** (-ji-néttik), **blas·to·gen·ic** (-jénnik) *adj.*

blas·to·mere (blást-ō-meer, -ə-) *n.* A cell formed during the cleavage of a fertilised ovum. [BLASTO- + -MERE.] —**blas·to·mer·ic** (-mérrik) *adj.*

blas·to·pore (blást-ō-pawr, -ə- ‖ -pōr) *n.* The mouthlike opening into the primitive intestinal cavity of the gastrula. [BLASTO- + PORE (orifice).] —**blas·to·po·ral** (-páwr-əl ‖ -pōr-) *adj.*

blas·tu·la (bláss-tew-lə) *n., pl.* **-las** or **-lae** (-lee). An early embryo⟨ form, resulting from cleavage and consisting essentially of a ⟨ cellular sphere. Also called "blastosphere". [New L⟨ Greek *blastos,* bud, germ.] —**blas·tu·lar** (-lər) *adj.* ⟨ (-láysh'n) *n.*

bla·tant (bláyt'nt) *adj.* **1.** Offensively cons⟨ ous: *a blatant lie.* **2.** Unpleasantly lo⟨ Spenser (*"the blattant beast"*, a symb⟨ Latin *blatīre,* to blab, gossip.] —**bl⟨**

Usage: Blatant is often confused w⟨ offensiveness and obtrusiveness, especial⟨

haviour. *Flagrant* stresses a wrong or evil that is glaring or notorious. There are *blatant errors* or *remarks*, but *flagrant miscarriages of justice.*

blath·er (bláthər) *intr.v.* **-ered, -ering, -ers.** Also **bleth·er** (bléthər). To talk nonsense; babble.
~*n.* Also **bleth·er.** Absurd or foolish talk; nonsense. [Middle English *blether,* from Old Norse *bladhra,* to prattle, akin to *bladhra,* bladder.] —**blath·er·er** *n.*

blath·er·skite (bláthər-skīt) *n.* **1.** A babbling, foolish person. **2.** Absurd and foolish talk. [Earlier *bletherskate* : BLATHER + SKATE (fish).]

Bla·vat·sky (blə-vátski), **Helena Petrovna,** born Helena Petrovna Hahn (1831–91). Russian theosophist. She began the theosophist movement in Russia in the late 1850s, and founded the Theosophical Society in New York. Her demonstrations of supernatural phenomena were declared fraudulent by the London Society for Psychical Research (1885).

blaze[1] (blayz) *n.* **1.** A brilliant burst of fire; a flame. **2. a.** Any bright, hot, steady light or glare. **b.** Any bright, conspicuous display: *a blaze of colour; a blaze of publicity.* **3.** A destructive fire, especially one that spreads rapidly. **4.** A sudden outburst, as of emotion or activity. **5.** *Plural. Slang.* Hell. Used euphemistically especially in the phrase *go to blazes* and as an intensive: *gallop like blazes; What the blazes is going on here?*
~*v.* **blazed, blazing, blazes.** —*intr.* **1.** To burn with a bright flame. **2.** To shine brightly. **3.** To be deeply excited, as by emotion. **4.** To shoot rapidly and continuously. Used with *away.* —*tr.* To shine or be resplendent with: *Her eyes blazed fire.* [Middle English *blase,* Old English *blæse,* torch, bright fire.] —**blaz·ing·ly** *adv.*
Synonyms: blaze, flame, flare, flash, glare, incandescence, glow.

blaze[2] *n.* **1.** A white or light-coloured spot or stripe on the face of a horse or other animal. **2.** A mark cut on a tree to indicate a trail.
~*tr.v.* **blazed, blazing, blazes. 1.** To mark (a tree) by cutting the bark. **2.** To indicate (a trail) by marking trees in this manner. **3.** To make (a trail) into new, unexplained areas of knowledge or research. Used in the phrase *blaze the trail.* [Probably from Middle Low German *bles.*]

blaz·er (bláyzər) *n.* **1.** One that blazes. **2.** A lightweight, informal sports jacket, often striped or coloured and worn as part of a uniform for a school, club, college, or the like.

blaz·ing (bláyzing) *adj.* Very hot.
~*adv.* Used as an intensive: *blazing hot.*

bla·zon (bláyz'n; *in senses 1 and 2 also* blázz'n) *tr.v.* **-zoned, -zoning, -zons. 1.** To describe (heraldic bearings or a coat of arms) in proper heraldic terms. **2.** To paint or depict (heraldic bearings or a coat of arms) with accurate heraldic detail. **3.** To adorn or embellish with or as if with blazons. **4.** To announce publicly; proclaim loudly and widely. Often used with *abroad.*
~*n.* **1.** A heraldic charge or coat of arms. **2. a.** The heraldic description or representation of a heraldic charge or coat of arms. **b.** The heraldic terms used to describe coats of arms. **3.** An ostentatious or showy display. [Middle English *blasoun,* shield, coat of arms, from Old French *blason†.*] —**bla·zon·er** *n.* —**bla·zon·ment** *n.*

bla·zon·ry (bláyz'nri, blázz'nri) *n., pl.* **-ries. 1.** The art of properly and accurately describing or representing heraldic bearings. **2.** Coats of arms and heraldic bearings collectively. **3.** Any showy or brilliant display.

bld. boldface.

bldg. building.

bleach (bleech) *v.* **bleached, bleaching, bleaches.** —*tr.* **1.** To remove the colour from, as by means of sunlight or chemical agents. **2.** To make white or colourless. —*intr.* To become white or colourless.
~*n.* **1.** Any chemical agent used for bleaching. **2.** The degree of bleaching obtained. **3.** The act of bleaching. [Middle English *blechen,* Old English *blǽcan.*]

bleach·er (bléechər) *n.* **1.** One that bleaches. **2.** *Usually plural. U.S.* An unroofed outdoor grandstand for seating spectators. [Sense 2, from the bleaching effect of exposure to sun.]

bleaching powder *n.* A white powder, CaCl(OCl).4H$_2$O, made by the action of chlorine on lime and used as a bleach and strong disinfectant. Also called "chlorinated lime".

bleak[1] (bleek) *adj.* **bleaker, bleakest. 1.** Exposed to the elements; unsheltered; barren. **2.** Cold and cutting; harsh. **3.** Offering no hope or encouragement: *bleak prospects.* **4.** Gloomy and sombre; depressing; dreary. [Middle English *bleike,* pale, from Old Norse *bleikr,* shining, white.] —**bleak·ly** *adv.* —**bleak·ness** *n.*

bleak[2] *n.* A European freshwater fish of the genus *Alburnus,* related to the carp, having silvery scales used in the manufacture of artificial pearls. [Middle English *bleke,* probably from Old Norse *bleikja,* "white colour".]

blear (bleer) *tr.v.* **bleared, blearing, blears.** *Archaic.* **1.** To blur (the eyes) with or as if with tears. **2.** To blur; dim.
~*adj. Archaic.* Bleary. [Middle English *bleren,* probably of Low German origin, akin to Low German *blerr†* (in *blerr-oged,* bleary-eyed).]

blear·y (bléer-i) *adj.* **-ier, -iest. 1.** Blurred or dimmed as by tears or lack of sleep. Said of the eyes. **2.** Vague or indistinct; blurred.
—**blear·i·ly** *adv.* —**blear·i·ness** *n.*

blear·y-eyed (bléer-i-īd) *adj.* Also **blear-eyed** (bléer-íd). **1.** With eyes blurred by or as if by tears or lack of sleep. **2.** Dull of mind or perception.

bleat (bleet) *v.* **bleated, bleating, bleats.** —*intr.* **1.** To utter a bleat.

2. To utter any similar sound, especially a whine. —*tr.* To utter in a whining voice.
~*n.* **1.** The characteristic cry of a goat, sheep, or calf. **2.** Any similar sound, such as a whining cry. [Middle English *bleten,* Old English *blǽtan.*] —**bleat·er** *n.*

bleb (bleb) *n.* **1.** A small blister or pustule. Compare **bulla. 2.** An air bubble. [Variant of BLOB.] —**bleb·by** *adj.*

bleed (bleed) *v.* **bled** (bled), **bleeding, bleeds.** —*intr.* **1.** To lose or emit blood. **2.** To suffer injury or death, as in battle. **3.** To feel sympathetic grief or anguish. Often used ironically, especially in the expression: *My heart bleeds for you.* **4.** To exude sap or a similar fluid, as a bruised plant does. **5.** *Slang.* To pay out money, especially an exorbitant amount. **6.** To become mixed or run. Used of dyes in wet cloth or paper. **7.** To show through a layer of paint. Used of a stain or resin in wood. **8.** *Printing.* To be printed so as to go over the edge or edges of a page, either purposely or by trimming the margins too closely. Often used with *off.* —*tr.* **1. a.** To take blood from, either surgically or with leeches. **b.** To extract sap or juice from. **2.** To exude (blood or sap, for example). **3. a.** To draw liquid or gaseous contents from; especially, to remove air from a hydraulic brake system or from a radiator in a central-heating system. **b.** To draw off (liquid or gaseous matter) from a container. **4.** *Slang.* To obtain large amounts of money from, especially by improper means. **5.** *Printing.* **a.** To print (an illustration, for example) so that it will go over the edge or edges of a page. **b.** To trim (a page or sheet, for example) too closely so as to mutilate the printed or illustrative matter. **6.** To feed (continuous small amounts of fluid) into a system.
~*n. Printing.* **1.** Illustrative matter that purposely bleeds. **2.** A page trimmed so as to bleed. Also called "bleed page". **3.** The part thus trimmed off. **4.** The fine tube used for bleeding fluid into or out of a system. [Bleed, bled, bled; Middle English *bleden, bledde, bledde,* Old English *blēdan, blēdde, blēdd,* from Germanic *blōthjan* (unattested), from *blōtham* (unattested), BLOOD.]

bleed·er (bléedər) *n.* **1.** A **haemophiliac** (see). Not in technical usage. **2.** A bloodletter. **3.** *British Slang.* **a.** An annoying or contemptible person. **b.** A person. Used affectionately: *a lucky bleeder.*

bleeder resistor *n.* A resistor connected across a power-supply output to improve the voltage regulation.

bleed·ing (bléeding) *adj. British Slang.* Used as an intensive or to express annoyance, disgust, or the like: *I missed the bleeding bus.* [Derived from the slang sense of BLOODY.] —**bleed·ing** *adv.*

bleed·ing-heart (bléeding-hárt ‖ -haart) *n.* **1.** Any of several plants of the genus *Dicentra,* having nodding, pink flowers; especially, the widely cultivated species *D. spectabilis,* native to Japan. **2.** A person who is considered excessively sympathetic towards those who claim to be underprivileged or exploited.

bleep (bleep) *n.* **1.** A high-pitched noise of short duration produced electronically. **2.** A bleeper.
~*v.* **bleeped, bleeping, bleeps.** —*intr.* To make a bleep. —*tr.* To call by means of a bleeper. [Imitative.]

bleep·er (bléepər) *n.* A circuit or device that bleeps; especially, a small portable radio receiver used to call the wearer in a hospital, factory, or the like. Also called "bleep".

blem·ish (blémmish) *tr.v.* **-ished, -ishing, -ishes.** To impair or spoil by a flaw; mar.
~*n.* A flaw or defect; a stain; a disfigurement. [Middle English *blemisshen,* from Old French *blemir, blesmir* (present stem *blemiss-*), to make pale, from Germanic.] —**blem·ish·er** *n.*
Synonyms: blemish, imperfection, fault, defect, flaw.

blench[1] (blench) *intr.v.* **blenched, blenching, blenches.** To draw back or shy away, as in fear; quail; flinch. See Synonyms at **recoil.** [Middle English *blenchen,* to deceive, start aside, evade, Old English *blencan,* to deceive.] —**blench·er** *n.*

blench[2]. Variant of **blanch.**

blend (blend) *v.* **blended** or *poetic* **blent** (blent), **blending, blends.** —*tr.* **1.** To combine or mix so as to render the constituent parts indistinguishable from one another. **2.** To mix (different varieties or grades, as of coffee or tea, for example) so as to obtain a new mixture of some particular quality or consistency. —*intr.* **1.** To form a uniform mixture; intermingle. **2.** To become merged into one; unite. **3.** To pass imperceptibly into another or one another: *"standing motionless beside that door, as though trying to make myself blend with the dark wood."* (William Faulkner). **4.** To go together; harmonise: *The new carpet blends well with the curtains.* —See Synonyms at **mix.**
~*n.* **1.** That which is blended; a mixture. **2.** The act of blending. **3.** *Linguistics.* A word produced by combining parts of other words, such as *smog,* from *smoke* and *fog;* a portmanteau word. [Middle English *blenden,* from Old Norse *blanda* (stem *blend-*).]

blende (blend) *n.* **1.** Any of various shiny minerals composed chiefly of metallic sulphides. **2.** A mineral, **sphalerite** (see). [German *Blende,* short for *blendendes Erz,* "deceptive ore" (often mistaken, on account of its metallic gleam, for a lead ore), from *blenden,* to blind, deceive, from Old High German *blenten.*]

blended whisky *n.* A blend of malt whisky and grain whisky.

blend·er (bléndər) *n.* **1.** One that combines or blends. **2.** A mechanical device with rotating blades used for combining food ingredients, as to make pureés, soups, and the like. Also *chiefly British* "liquidiser".

Blen·heim Palace (blénnim). The country seat of the dukes of Marlborough, outside Woodstock in Oxfordshire. The palace, designed by Sir John **Vanbrugh,** is considered to be one of the finest examples of the baroque in English architecture.

blen·ny (blénni) *n., pl.* **-nies.** Any of numerous small, elongated marine fishes of the family Blenniidae, especially a fish of the genus *Blennius,* which has a long dorsal fin and long, rayed pelvic fins. [Latin *blennius, blendius,* from Greek *blennos,* "slime" (from the slimy coating on its scales).]

blent. *Poetic.* Alternative past tense and past participle of **blend.**

bleph·a·ri·tis (bléffə-rítiss) *n.* Inflammation of the eyelid. [New Latin : Greek *blepharon*†, eyelid + -ITIS.]

bleph·a·ro·spasm (bléffərō-spaz'm) *n.* Uncontrollable winking, caused by involuntary contraction of an eyelid muscle. [New Latin *blepharospasmus* : BLEPHAR(ITIS) + SPASM.]

Blé·ri·ot (blérri-ō, bleér-i-), **Louis** (1872–1936). French inventor and aviator. On July 25, 1909, he flew his 25-horsepower aeroplane over the English Channel from Calais to Dover, the first time that an aeroplane had flown across open sea.

bles·bok (bléss-bok) *n., pl.* **-boks** or collectively **blesbok.** Also **bles·buck** (-buk). An African antelope, *Damaliscus albifrons* (or *D. dorcasphillipsi*) having a reddish-brown coat, and a face marked with white. [Afrikaans : *bles,* white mark on animal's face + *bok,* buck.]

bless (bless) *tr.v.* **blessed** (blest) or **blest, blessing, blesses. 1.** To make holy by religious rite; sanctify. **2.** To make the sign of the cross over, so as to sanctify. **3.** To invoke divine favour upon. **4.** To preserve from evil. Used as an exclamation: *Bless my soul!* **5.** To honour as holy; glorify: *Bless the Lord.* **6.** To confer well-being or prosperity upon. **7.** To endow or favour. Usually used in the passive: *blessed with good health.* **—bless you.** Used conventionally as an interjection after a person has sneezed or coughed. [Middle English *blessen,* Old English *blētsian, blœdsian,* from Germanic *blōthisō jan* (unattested), "to hallow with blood", from *blōtham* (unattested), BLOOD.] **—bless·er** *n.*

bless·ed (bléssid) *adj.* Also **blest** (blest). **1.** Made sacred by a religious rite; consecrated. **2.** Worthy of profound respect or worship. **3.** *Roman Catholic Church.* Enjoying the eternal happiness of heaven. Used as a title for those who have been beatified. **4.** Enjoying happiness; fortunate. **5.** Bringing happiness or bliss. **6.** Damned. Used euphemistically or as an intensive. **—bless·ed·ly** *adv.* **—bless·ed·ness** *n.*

Bles·sed Sacrament (bléssid) *n. Roman Catholic Church.* The consecrated Host.

Bles·sed Virgin (bléssid) *n. Abbr.* **B.V.** The Virgin Mary.

bless·ing (bléssing) *n.* **1. a.** The act of one who blesses. **b.** The prescribed words or ceremony for such an act. **2.** An expression or utterance of good wishes. **3.** A special favour granted by God. **4.** Anything promoting or contributing to happiness, well-being, or prosperity; a boon: *a blessing in disguise.* **5.** Approval: *This plan has my blessing.* **6.** A short prayer before or after a meal.

blest. 1. Alternative past tense and past participle of **bless. 2.** Variant of **blessed.**

blet (blet) *n.* Internal softening or incipient decay of certain fruits. The medlar is edible only when it has reached this state. [French *blettir,* become overripe, from *blet(te),* overripe, from Old French, from Germanic.]

blether. Variant of **blather.**

blew. Past tense of **blow.**

blew·its (blōō-its ‖ bléw-) *n. Used with a singular verb.* An edible mushroom, *Tricholoma saevum,* having a bluish stalk and a pale brown cap. [Probably from BLUE.]

Bligh (blī), **William** (1754–1817). British admiral, known chiefly from the mutiny of his ship the *Bounty* (1789). He accompanied James **Cook** on the explorer's last expedition (1776–79) as sailing master and served as governor of New South Wales (1805–08).

blight (blīt) *n.* **1.** Any of several plant diseases that result in sudden dying of leaves, growing tips, or an entire plant. **2.** An environmental condition, such as air pollution, that injures or kills plants or animals. **3.** Something that withers hopes or ambitions, impairs growth, or halts prosperity. **4.** The state or result of being blighted; dilapidation; decay: *urban blight.*
~v. **blighted, blighting, blights.** *—tr.* **1.** To cause to decline or decay. **2.** To ruin; destroy. **3.** To frustrate: *a mishap that blighted his hopes. —intr.* To suffer blight. [17th century : origin obscure.]

blight·er *n. Chiefly British Slang.* **1.** An annoying or contemptible person. **2.** A person. Used affectionately: *You lucky blighter!*

blight·y (blīti) *n. Often capital* **B.** *British Slang.* England; home. Used especially by soldiers serving abroad. [Hindi *bilāyatī, wilāyatī,* "foreign", "English", from Arabic *wilāyat,* district, realm, from *waliya,* he rules.]

bli·mey (blīmi) *interj. British Slang.* Used to express surprise, irritation, or the like. [From *(God) blind me!*]

blimp[1] (blimp) *n.* A nonrigid, buoyant aircraft, such as a barrage balloon. [Probably (type) B + LIMP.]

blimp[2] *n. Chiefly British.* One whose views exhibit a blend of ultraconservative jingoism and misinformation. [After Colonel *Blimp,* a cartoon character invented by David Low.] **—blimp·ish** *adj.*

blind (blīnd) *adj.* **blinder, blindest. 1.** Without the sense of sight. **2.** Of or for sightless persons. **3.** Performed without the use of sight, relying wholly on instruments: *blind flying.* **4.** Performed without preparation, forethought, or knowledge: *a blind attempt.* **5.** Unable or unwilling to perceive or understand: *blind to all her faults.* **6.** Not based on reason or evidence: *blind faith.* **7.** *Informal.* Drunk. **8.** Acting without human control: *blind fate.* **9.** Hidden from sight: *a blind seam.* **10.** Affording poor visibility to an oncoming driver: *a blind corner.* **11.** Closed at one end: *a blind alley.* **12.** Having no opening: *a blind wall.* **13.** *Botany.* Failing to flower. Said of cultivated plants. **14.** *Informal.* Used as an intensive: *didn't take a blind bit of notice.* **15.** *U.S.* Illegibly or incompletely addressed: *blind mail.*
~n. **1. a.** Something that hinders vision or shuts out light: *a Venetian blind.* **b.** A piece of fabric, usually mounted on rollers, used to cover a window. Also *U.S.* "window shade". **2.** *Chiefly U.S.* A **hide** *(see),* as used in hunting. **3.** Any subterfuge or front. **4.** *British Slang.* A drinking bout. **5.** In poker, a bet made, before seeing one's cards.
~adv. **1.** Without being able to see; blindly: *fly blind.* **2.** *Informal.* Into a stupor: *They drank themselves blind.* Also used as an intensive, chiefly in the phrase *blind drunk.* **3.** Without a filling, or with a temporary filling of dried peas, beans, or the like inserted merely to retain shape during cooking: *bake a pastry shell blind.*
~tr.v. **blinded, blinding, blinds. 1.** To deprive of sight. **2.** To dazzle. **3.** To deprive (a person) of his powers of perception or judgment. [Middle English *blind,* Old English *blind,* blind, obscure.] **—blind·ly** *adv.* **—blind·ness** *n.*

blind alley *n.* **1.** A passageway open only at one end; a dead end. **2.** *Informal.* Any project or situation that offers no prospect of progress or development.

blind date *n. Informal.* **1.** A social engagement between two people, usually a man and a woman, who have not previously met. **2.** Either of the persons keeping such an engagement.

blind·er (blīndər) *n.* **1.** One that causes blinding. **2.** *British Slang.* Something unusually accomplished; especially, a brilliant piece of play in football or cricket. **3.** *British Slang.* A bout of drinking. Used chiefly in the phrase *go on a blinder.* **4.** *Plural. Chiefly U.S.* **Blinkers** *(see).*

blind·fish (blīnd-fish) *n., pl.* **-fishes** or collectively **blindfish.** Any of various fishes having rudimentary, nonfunctioning eyes; especially, the **cavefish** *(see).*

blind·fold (blīnd-fōld) *tr.v.* **-folded, -folding, -folds. 1.** To cover the eyes with or as if with a bandage. **2.** To hamper the sight or comprehension of; mislead; delude.
~n. A bandage over the eyes.
~adj. **1.** With eyes covered. **2.** Reckless. [Middle English *blindfolde, blindfelde,* past participle of *blindfellen,* to strike blind, from Old English *geblindfellian,* "to strike blind" : *ge-,* Y- + BLIND + *fellan,* to strike down, FELL.]

blind Freddy *n. Australian Informal.* An extremely stupid or unperceptive person. Used chiefly in the expression *even blind Freddy could see that!*

blind gut *n. Anatomy.* The **caecum** *(see).*

blind hinge *n.* A hinge so constructed that it allows the hinged piece to swing shut by its own weight unless held open.

blind·ing (blīnding) *adj.* **1.** Tending to make sightless. **2.** Dazzling; overpowering. **—blind·ing·ly** *adv.*

blind·man's buff (blīnd-manz búf) *n.* A game in which one person, blindfolded, tries to catch and identify one of the other players. [*Buff,* short for BUFFET (a blow).]

blind spot *n.* **1.** *Anatomy.* The small, optically insensitive region where the optic nerve enters the retina of the eye. **2.** Any part of an area that cannot be directly observed, especially that part of a motor-vehicle driver's surroundings that is not reflected in the vehicle's mirrors and cannot be seen without sharply turning the head. **3.** An area where radio reception is weak. **4.** A subject about which one is markedly ignorant or prejudiced.

blind staggers *n. Used with a singular verb.* A disease of horses, the **staggers** *(see).*

blind·sto·rey (blīnd-stawri ‖ -stōri) *n., pl.* **-eys.** *Architecture.* A storey having no windows.

blind trust *n.* A trust fund whose donors are kept unknown from its beneficiary, typically so that they cannot influence him.

blind·worm (blīnd-wurm) *n.* A lizard, the **slowworm** *(see).* [Perhaps so called because its eyes close after death.]

bli·ni (blínni, bleéni) *n., pl.* **blinis** or **blini.** A small buckwheat pancake served with caviar or sour cream. [Russian, plural of *blin,* pancake, from Old Russian *blinŭ, mlinŭ.*]

blink (blingk) *v.* **blinked, blinking, blinks.** *—intr.* **1.** To close and open one or both eyes rapidly. **2.** To look through half-closed eyes, as in a bright glare; squint. **3.** To shine with intermittent gleams; flash on and off. **4.** To pretend not to be aware of something, especially something unpleasant. Used with *at.* **5.** To become startled or dismayed. Usually used with *at. —tr.* **1.** To close and open (the eyes or an eye) rapidly. **2.** To ignore or refuse to acknowledge.
~n. **1.** The act or an instance of blinking; a brief closing of the eyes. **2.** A quick look or glimpse; a glance. **3.** The time it takes to blink. **4.** A flash of light; a gleam; a twinkle; a glimmer. **5.** An **iceblink** *(see).* **—on the blink.** *Informal.* Not in proper working condition; out of order. [Middle English *blinken,* partly a variant of *blenchen,* BLENCH (flinch), and perhaps partly from Middle Dutch *blinken,* to glitter.]

blink comparator *n.* An instrument used in astronomy to present rapidly alternating views of two photographs of the same region of sky. It allows the observer to identify the movement or appearance of celestial objects.

blink·er (blingkər) *n.* **1.** A light that blinks in order to convey a message or warning, as, for example, on a control panel. **2.** *Slang.* An eye. **3.** *Plural.* A pair of leather flaps attached to a horse's bridle to restrict side vision. Also *chiefly U.S.* "blinders". **4.** Loosely, anything that reduces ability to see or understand.

blink·ered (blingkərd) *adj.* **1.** Wearing blinkers. Said of a horse. **2.** Obtuse; showing unwillingness or inability to understand.

blink·ing (blíngking) *adj. British Slang.* Used as an intensive: *you blinking idiot!* —**blink·ing** *adv.*

blintz (blints) *n.* Also **blin·tze** (blíntsə). A thin, folded pancake filled with cream cheese, cottage cheese, fruit, or seasoned mashed potatoes, and often served with sour cream. [Yiddish *blintse,* from Russian *blinyets,* diminutive of *blin,* BLINI.]

blip (blip) *n.* **1.** A spot of light on a radar screen. **2.** A regularly repeated sound.
~*intr. v.* **blipped, blipping, blips.** To produce a blip. [Imitative.]

bliss (bliss) *n.* **1.** Serene happiness. **2.** The ecstasy of salvation; spiritual joy. —See Synonyms at **ecstasy.** [Middle English *blis(se),* Old English *bliss, blīths,* from Germanic *blīthsjo* (unattested), from *blīthiz†* (unattested), BLITHE.] —**bliss·ful** *adj.* —**bliss·ful·ly** *adv.* —**bliss·ful·ness** *n.*

Bliss (bliss), **Sir Arthur Edward Drummond** (1891–1975). British composer. His works were written in a romantic, melodic manner distinct from the avant-garde tendencies of his contemporaries in Europe. He was Master of the Queen's Musick (1953–75).

blis·ter (blístər) *n.* **1.** A thin, rounded swelling of the skin, containing watery serum, caused by burning or friction. **2.** A similar swelling on a plant. **3.** An air bubble on a painted surface or in a casting. **4.** A rounded, often transparent protuberance on certain aircraft, used for observation or as a gun position.
~*v.* **blistered, -tering, -ters.** —*tr.* To cause a blister or blisters to form upon. —*intr.* To break out in blisters. [Middle English *blester, blister,* possibly from Old French *blestre,* from Middle Dutch *bluyster,* "swelling".] —**blis·ter·y** *adj.*

blister beetle *n.* Any of various beetles of the family Meloidae, that secrete a substance capable of blistering the skin. Some species cause damage to crops. See **Spanish fly.**

blister copper *n.* An almost pure form of copper produced in an intermediate stage of copper refining. [From its blistered surface caused by release of gas in the refining process.]

blis·ter·ing (blístəring) *adj.* Scathing; harshly condemnatory: *a blistering attack on government policy.*

blister pack *n.* A type of packet for pills or tablets with plastic bubbles which are pushed in to eject the pill or tablet through the backing foil.

blister rust *n.* Any of several diseases of pine trees, caused by fungi, resulting in cankers and blisters on the bark.

B.Litt. Bachelor of Letters. [Latin *Baccalaureus Litterarum.*]

blithe (blīth ‖ blīth) *adj.* **1.** Filled with gaiety; cheerful. **2.** Frivolous; casual; carefree: *blithe optimism.* —See Synonyms at **jolly.** [Middle English *blithe,* Old English *blīthe,* from Germanic *blīthiz†* (unattested), gentle, mild.] —**blithe·ly** *adv.* —**blithe·ness** *n.*

blith·er·ing (blíthəring) *adj.* **1.** Talking senselessly; jabbering. **2.** *British Informal.* Stupid; silly. [From *blither,* variant of BLATHER.]

blithe·some (blíth-səm ‖ blíth-) *adj. Archaic or Poetic.* Cheerful; merry. —**blithe·some·ly** *adv.* —**blithe·some·ness** *n.*

blitz (blits) *n.* **1.** A blitzkrieg. **2.** An intensive air raid or series of air raids. **3.** Any intense campaign or effort: *I'm going to have a blitz on the spare room.* —**the Blitz.** The period in 1940–41 during which British cities and towns were subjected to continual night-time bombing by the German Luftwaffe.
~*tr.v.* **blitzed, blitzing, blitzes.** To subject to a blitz. [Short for BLITZKRIEG.]

blitz·krieg (blíts-kreeg) *n.* **1.** A swift, sudden military offensive, usually by combined air and land forces. **2.** Any swift, concerted effort. [German *Blitzkrieg,* "lightning war".]

bliz·zard (blízzərd) *n.* **1.** A violent windstorm accompanied by intense cold and driving, powdery snow or ice crystals. **2.** A very heavy snowstorm with high winds. [19th century : originally American, perhaps imitative.]

blk. **1.** black. **2.** block. **3.** bulk.

bloat (blōt) *v.* **bloated, bloating, bloats.** —*tr.* **1.** To cause to swell up or inflate, as with liquid or gas. **2. a.** To puff up, as with vanity. **b.** To puff up (the face or body), as from overeating. **3.** To cure (herring or other fish) by soaking in brine and half-drying in smoke. —*intr.* To become swollen or inflated.
~*n. Veterinary Medicine.* A swelling of the intestinal tract of a domestic animal, caused by the gases of fermentation of green forage. [From *bloat,* swollen, earlier *blowt,* soft, flabby, from Middle English *blout,* probably from Old Norse *blautr,* soft, wet, soaked.]

bloat·er (blōtər) *n.* A herring lightly smoked and salted.

blob (blob) *n.* **1.** A soft, amorphous mass. **2.** A shapeless splotch or daub of colour.
~*tr.v.* **blobbed, blobbing, blobs.** To splash or mark with blobs; splotch. [Middle English, bubble (imitative).]

bloc (blok) *n.* A group of persons, parties, or nations united for common action or by a common interest. [French, BLOCK.]

Bloch (blokh, blok), **Ernest** (1880–1959). Swiss-born U.S. composer. He is famous for his chamber music, such as the Piano Quintet (1923) and his five string quartets, and also for works with Jewish themes, such as the *Israel Symphony* (1916).

block (blok) *n.* **1.** A large, solid piece of wood, stone, or other hard substance having one or more flat sides. **2. a.** Such a piece used in construction work. **b.** A child's toy model of such a piece: *a set of building blocks.* **3.** A large solid piece of wood, especially: **a.** One on which chopping or cutting is done: *a butcher's block.* **b.** One on which people were formerly beheaded. Usually preceded by *the.* **c.** One from which a horse may be mounted. **4.** A piece of wood or metal engraved for use in printing. **5. a.** A pulley or a system of pulleys set in a casing. **b.** The casing holding the pulleys. See **block and tackle.** **6.** The casting containing the cylinders of an internal-combustion engine. **7.** A group acting or regarded as a unit; a bloc. **8.** A set or quantity of like items sold, handled, or regarded as a unit, such as theatre tickets, shares, or postage stamps. **9.** A large building divided into separate units, such as flats or offices. **10. a.** A rectangular section of a built-up area bounded on all sides by intersecting streets. **b.** *Chiefly U.S.* The distance between these streets: *The theatre is three blocks away.* **11. a.** *Australian & N.Z.* A large subdivision of land for housing or farming. **b.** An enclosed area of land offered to settlers by a government, especially as formerly in Australia. **12.** A length of railway track controlled by signals. See **block system.** **13.** Something that hinders; an obstacle. **14.** An act of obstructing or hindering; especially, in sports, an act of bodily obstruction. **15.** In athletics, a **starting block** *(see).* **16.** In cricket, a mark made on the pitch by a batsman to mark his position relative to his wicket. Also called "blockhole". **17.** *Medicine.* Interruption, especially obstruction, of a neural, digestive, or other physiological process. See **heart block, nerve block. 18.** *Psychology.* Sudden cessation of a thought or creative process without an immediate observable cause, sometimes considered to be a consequence of repression. **19.** A hardhearted, insensitive person. **20.** *Slang.* A person's head. Used chiefly in the phrase *knock (someone's) block off.* **21.** *Computing.* A group of words or numbers treated as a unit in a storage device. —**do (one's) block.** *Australian & N.Z. Informal.* To become very agitated or angry. —**off (one's) block.** *Australian & N.Z. Informal.* Mad; crazy. —**on the block.** *Chiefly U.S.* Up for auction. —See Synonyms at **obstacle.**
~*v.* **blocked, blocking, blocks.** —*tr.* **1.** To shape into a block or blocks. **2.** To support, strengthen, or retain in place by means of a block or blocks. **3.** To stop or impede the passage of or movement through; hinder or obstruct: *block traffic; block a piece of legislation.* **4.** *Sports.* To impede the movement of (one's opponent or the ball) by means of physical interference. **5.** In cricket, to play (a ball) defensively. **6.** *Medicine.* To interrupt the proper functioning of (a physiological process). **7.** To stamp or emboss a design or lettering on (the cover of a book), especially using gold or other foil. **8.** *Finance.* To restrict or prevent the use or conversion of (currency or assets). **9.** *Psychology.* To repress or fail to recognise (an area or subject that causes pain or anxiety). Often used with *out.* —*intr.* **1.** *Sports.* To obstruct the movement of an opponent. **2.** In cricket, to play a defensive stroke. —See Synonyms at **hinder.** —**block in.** *Sports.* To block. —**block out. 1.** To plan or project broadly without details; sketch out. **2.** To obscure from view. —**block up.** To fill with solid material: *block up the windows of an old house.* [Middle English *block(ke),* from Old French *bloc,* from Middle Dutch *blok,* trunk of a tree, from Germanic.] —**block** *adj.* —**block·er** *n.*

block·ade (blo-káyd) *n.* **1.** The closing off of a country, city, harbour, or other area to traffic and communication by hostile ships or forces. **2.** The forces employed to close such an area. —**run a blockade.** To succeed in getting through a blockade.
~*tr.v.* **blockaded, -ading, -ades.** To set up a blockade against. [From BLOCK (after AMBUSCADE).] —**block·ad·er** *n.*

block·age (blóckij) *n.* **1.** The act of blocking. **2.** An obstruction.

block and tackle *n.* An apparatus of pulley blocks and ropes or cables used for hauling and hoisting heavy objects.

block·board (blók-bawrd ‖ -bōrd) *n.* An inferior form of plywood made by bonding thick strips of wood together between two sheets of veneer.

block·bust·er (blók-bustər) *n. Informal.* **1.** A powerful bomb capable of destroying large areas. **2.** Anything of devastating effect. **3.** A film or play that attracts large audiences and earns large amounts of money.

block diagram *n.* **1.** A diagram of a system, such as a computer program or electrical circuit, in which the essential units are represented by rectangles or blocks, connected by lines showing the relationship between the units. **2.** A diagram giving a three-dimensional representation of a landform or section of country.

blocked (blokt) *adj. Slang.* Under the influence of a narcotic drug.

block-graze *tr. v.* **-grazed, -grazing, -grazes.** *Chiefly Australian.* To graze (livestock) on an area of land until it is bare before moving them to the next area.

block·head (blók-hed) *n.* A stupid person; a dolt.

block·house (blók-howss) *n.* **1.** A military fortification constructed of concrete or other sturdy material, with loopholes for defensive firing or for observation. **2.** *Aerospace.* A heavily reinforced building used for protecting personnel and equipment during launch operations of missiles, rockets, or the like.

blockie *n. Australian Informal.* A farmer with a small amount of land.

block·ish (blóckish) *adj.* **1.** Like or resembling a block. **2.** Dull; stupid. —**block·ish·ly** *adv.* —**block·ish·ness** *n.*

block lava *n.* Lava formed into sharp, angular blocks.

block letter *n.* **1.** A plain capital letter, often used when filling in forms. Also called "block capital". **2.** *Printing.* A sans-serif style of type. —**block-let·ter** *adj.*

block plane *n.* A small plane used by carpenters for cutting across the grain of wood.

block printing *n.* Printing from engraved or carved wooden or linoleum blocks.

block release *n.* A system whereby trainees and apprentices may leave work for a set period in order to study at a college. Compare **day release**.

block system *n.* A system for controlling and safeguarding the flow of railway trains, in which the track is divided into sections or blocks, each controlled by automatic signals.

block tin *n.* An impure commercial form of tin cast in blocks.

block vote *n.* A single vote cast by the representative of a large group, as at a union conference, for example, that is held to represent the votes of all the members of that group.

Bloem·fon·tein (blōōm-fən-tayn, -fon-). City in South Africa, capital of the (formerly Orange) Free State. Founded as a Boer fort (1846), it is unofficially called the judicial capital of South Africa, because the appellate division of the Supreme Court sits there.

Blois (blwaa). City in north central France, lying on the river Loire. Its historical importance dates from the sixth century when it became the seat of the powerful counts of Blois, the ancestors of the royal Capetian line.

bloke (blōk) *n. Chiefly British Slang.* A fellow; a man.

blonde (blond) *adj.* **blonder, blondest.** Also *masculine* **blond.** **1.** Having fair hair and skin and usually light eyes. **2.** Of a flaxen or golden colour or of any light shade of auburn or pale yellowish brown. Said of human hair. **3.** Pale yellowish brown. ~*n.* A woman or girl with fair hair. [Old French, probably from Germanic.] —**blond·ish** *adj.* —**blond·ness** *n.*

Usage: The word derives from French, and is usually used in the feminine form (*blonde*). Both forms, however, can be used adjectivally: *She has blonde hair; he is blond, he has blond hair.*

Blon·din (blón-daN, -dáN), **Charles,** born Jean-François Gravelet (1824–97). French acrobat and stunt-performer whose speciality was tight-rope walking. He walked across Niagara Falls several times, the first time in 1859, in a variety of ways—with a man on his back, on stilts, and blindfolded.

blood (blud) *n.* **1.** The fluid circulated by the heart through the vertebrate vascular system, carrying oxygen and nutrients throughout the body and waste materials to excretory channels. It consists of **blood plasma** *(see)* in which are suspended red blood cells (erythrocytes), white cells (leucocytes), and platelets. **2.** A functionally similar fluid in an invertebrate. **3.** A fluid resembling blood, such as the juice of certain plants. **4.** Loosely, life; lifeblood. **5.** Bloodshed; murder. **6.** Temperament; temper; disposition. **7.** Descent from a common ancestor; parental lineage. **8.** Family relationship; kinship. **9.** Descent from noble or royal lineage. Preceded by *the: a princess of the blood.* **10.** Recorded descent from purebred stock. Said of animals. **11.** Racial or national ancestry. **12.** Members or personnel, especially ones providing fresh or new impetus: *new blood in the organisation.* **13.** *Archaic.* A dashing young man; a rake; a dandy. —**blood is thicker than water.** Family ties and loyalties are stronger than any others. —**in cold blood.** Dispassionately; deliberately; coldly. —**in (one's) blood.** Fundamental or inherent in one's character. —**make (one's) blood boil.** To make extremely angry. —**make (one's) blood run cold.** To terrify. ~*tr.v.* **blooded, blooding, bloods. 1. a.** To give (a hound or hunting dog) its first taste of blood. **b.** To initiate (a novice in fox-hunting) by marking his face with the blood of the fox. **2.** To initiate (a new member or recruit) into an organisation. ~ *adj.* Purebred: *a blood mare.* [Middle English *blood,* Old English *blōd,* from Germanic *blōtham* (unattested).]

blood-and-thunder (blúd-'n-thúndər) *adj.* Designating or pertaining to a melodramatic, action-packed book or film.

blood bath *n.* A savage and indiscriminate killing; a massacre.

blood brother *n.* **1.** One's brother by birth. **2.** A boy or man who swears to treat another as his brother, often at a ceremony where the blood of the two is mingled.

blood count *n.* **1.** The number of red and white blood cells in a specific volume of blood. **2.** The determination of this number.

blood·cur·dling (blúd-kurdling) *adj.* Causing great horror; terrifying. —**blood·cur·dling·ly** *adv.*

blood donor *n.* A person who gives blood for transfusion.

blood·ed (blúddid) *adj.* **1.** Having blood or a temperament of a specified kind. Used in combination: *a cold-blooded reptile; a hot-blooded person.* **2.** Thoroughbred.

blood feud *n.* A long-lasting dispute, usually between families or tribes, involving killing on both sides.

blood fluke *n.* A trematode worm, such as a **schistosome** *(see),* that lives in the blood vessels of its host.

blood group *n.* Any of several immunologically distinct, genetically determined classes of human blood, clinically identified by characteristic agglutination reactions based on the presence or absence of certain antigens. Also called "blood type".

blood·guilt (blúd-gilt) *n.* Guilt owing to murder or bloodshed.

blood heat *n.* The usual temperature of human blood: 37°C; 98.4°F (Britain); 98.6°F (U.S.A.).

blood·hound (blúd-hownd) *n.* **1.** One of a breed of hounds with a smooth coat, drooping ears, sagging jowls, and a keen sense of smell. **2.** *Informal.* Any relentless pursuer.

blood·less (blúd-ləss, -liss) *adj.* **1.** Having no blood. **2.** Pale and anaemic in colour. **3.** Achieved without bloodshed. **4.** Lacking spirit or emotion. —**blood·less·ly** *adv.* —**blood·less·ness** *n.*

Bloodless Revolution *n.* The **Glorious Revolution** *(see).*

blood·let·ting (blúd-letting) *n.* **1.** The bleeding of a vein as a supposedly therapeutic measure; bleeding; venesection. **2.** A draining away, as of lifeblood. **3.** Bloodshed. —**blood·let·ter** *n.*

blood·line (blúd-līn) *n.* Direct line of descent; strain; pedigree.

blood money *n.* **1.** Money paid as compensation to the next of kin of a murder victim. **2.** Money paid to a hired killer. **3.** Money gained at the cost of another's life or livelihood.

blood orange *n.* A variety of orange in which the pulp is streaked with red.

blood plasma *n.* The pale-yellow or grey-yellow, protein-containing fluid portion of the blood in which the blood cells are normally suspended. Also called "plasma".

blood platelet *n.* A constituent of blood, a **platelet** *(see).*

blood poisoning *n.* Any condition in which the blood contains poisons or the bacteria that produce them; **septicaemia** or **toxaemia** *(both of which see).*

blood pressure *n.* The pressure of the blood against the walls of the arteries, primarily maintained by contraction of the left ventricle.

blood pudding *n.* **Black pudding** *(see).*

blood rain *n.* Rain in which the raindrops are coloured by fine, reddish dust particles brought from desert regions by the wind.

blood red *n.* Moderate to vivid red. —**blood-red** (blúd-rédd) *adj.*

blood relation *n.* A person who is related by birth rather than by marriage. Also called "blood relative". —**blood relationship** *n.*

blood·root (blúd-rōōt) *n.* See **sanguinaria.**

blood sausage *n.* **Black pudding** *(see).*

blood serum *n.* A fluid, **serum** *(see).*

blood·shed (blúd-shed) *n.* **1.** The shedding of blood. **2.** Carnage. —**blood·shed·der** *n.*

blood·shot (blúd-shot) *adj.* Red and inflamed: *bloodshot eyes.*

blood sports *n.* Sports, such as fox-hunting, that involve the killing of animals.

blood·stain (blúd-stayn) *n.* A stain caused by blood. —**blood·stained** *adj.*

blood·stock (blúd-stok) *n.* Thoroughbred horses, especially racehorses.

blood·stone (blúd-stōn) *n.* A variety of deep-green chalcedony flecked with red. Also called "heliotrope".

blood·stream (blúdstreem) *n.* The stream of blood flowing through the circulatory system of a living body.

blood·suck·er (blúd-suckər) *n.* **1.** Any animal that sucks blood, such as a leech. **2.** One who clings to or preys upon another; a parasite. —**blood·suck·ing** *adj. & n.*

blood test *n.* Examination of a blood sample in order to determine the level of alcohol or drugs, the presence of bacteria, the blood group, or the like.

blood·thirst·y (blúd-thursti) *adj.* **1. a.** Keen and ready for bloodshed; murderous; cruel. **b.** Keen and ready for violence. **2.** Displaying or pandering to such feelings: *a bloodthirsty film.* —**blood·thirst·i·ly** *adv.* —**blood·thirst·i·ness** *n.*

blood type *n.* **Blood group** *(see).*

blood vessel *n.* Any elastic, tubular canal, such as an artery, vein, or capillary, through which blood circulates.

blood·worm (blúd-wurm) *n.* The red aquatic larva of the midge *Chironomus plumosus* found in stagnant pools.

blood·y (blúddi) *adj.* **-ier, -iest. 1.** Stained with blood. **2.** Of, characteristic of, or containing blood. **3.** Accompanied by or giving rise to bloodshed: *a bloody fight.* **4.** Bloodthirsty; cruel. **5.** Suggesting the colour of blood; blood-red. **6.** *Chiefly British Slang.* Used as an intensive: *bloody fool.* ~*adv. Chiefly British Slang.* Used as an intensive: *a bloody good film.* ~*tr.v.* **bloodied, -ying, -ies.** To stain, spot, or colour with or as if with blood. —**blood·i·ly** *adv.* —**blood·i·ness** *n.*

Bloody Mary *n.* A drink made with vodka, tomato juice, and seasonings.

Bloody Mary. See **Mary I.**

blood·y-mind·ed (blúddi-míndid) *adj. British Informal.* Obstinate; deliberately unhelpful or obstructive.

bloom[1] (blōōm) *n.* **1.** The flower or blossoms of a plant. **2. a.** The condition or time of being in flower: *a rose in bloom.* **b.** A condition or time of vigour, freshness, and beauty; prime: *the bloom of girlhood.* **3.** A fresh, rosy complexion. **4.** *Botany.* A delicate, powdery coating, such as that found on some fruits, such as the plum, or on some leaves and stems. **5.** A similar coating, as on newly minted coins. **6.** A cloudy appearance on old paint or varnish. ~*v.* **bloomed, blooming, blooms.** —*intr.* **1.** To bear flowers. **2.** To shine with health and vigour; glow. **3.** To grow or flourish. —*tr.* To coat the outer surface of (a lens) with a thin transparent layer so as to minimise reflection. [Middle English *blom, blome,* from Old Norse *blōm, blōmi.*] —**bloom·y** *adj.*

bloom[2] *n.* **1.** A large bar of steel prepared for rolling. **2.** A mass of wrought iron ready for further working. ~*tr. v.* **bloomed, blooming, blooms.** To form (metal) into a bar or ingot. [Middle English *blome,* lump of metal, Old English *blōma.*]

bloom·er (blōōmər) *n.* **1.** A plant that blooms. **2.** *Slang.* A blunder. **3.** *British.* A type of loaf having notches cut in the top.

bloom·ers (blōōmərz) *pl. n.* **1.** A costume formerly worn by women and girls that was composed of loose trousers gathered about the ankles and sometimes worn under a short skirt. **2.** Women's long, and usually loose underpants. [After Amelia *Bloomer* (1818–1894), U.S. reformer who advocated this type of undergarment.]

bloom·ing (blōōming) *adj.* **1.** Flowering; blossoming. **2.** Flourishing; growing. **3.** *Slang.* Utter; thorough. Used as an intensive: *a blooming idiot.* [Sense 3, probably a euphemism for BLOODY.] —**bloom·ing·ly** *adv.* —**bloom·ing·ness** *n.*

Blooms·bur·y Group (blo͝omz-bri, -bəri) *n.* A group of writers, artists, and intellectuals who met for discussion in homes in the Bloomsbury district of London in the 1910s and 1920s, the principal figures of which included Virginia Woolf and Lytton Strachey.

bloop·er (blo͞opər) *n. Chiefly U.S. Informal.* A clumsy mistake, especially one made in public; a faux pas. [From *bloop* (imitative).]

blos·som (blóss'm) *n.* **1.** A flower or mass of flowers, especially on a plant that yields edible fruit. **2.** The condition or time of flowering: *peach trees in blossom.*
~intr.v. **blossomed, -soming, -soms. 1.** To come into flower; bloom. **2.** To develop; flourish: *She blossomed into a beauty.* [Middle English *blosme,* Old English *blōstm, blōstma.*] **—blos·som·y** *adj.*

blot¹ (blot) *n.* **1.** A spot; a stain: *a blot of ink.* **2.** A stain on one's reputation or character; a disgrace. **3.** Something that detracts from beauty or excellence: *That factory is a blot on the landscape.*
~v. **blotted, blotting, blots.** *—tr.* **1.** To spot or stain. **2.** To bring moral disgrace to. **3.** To obliterate; cancel. Used with *out*: *"Whosoever hath sinned against me, him will I blot out of my book."* (Exodus 32:33). **4.** To make obscure; darken; hide. Usually used with *out*: *clouds blotting out the moon.* **5.** To destroy utterly; annihilate. Used with *out.* **6.** To dry or soak up with absorbent material. *—intr.* **1.** To spill or spread in a blot or blots. **2.** To become blotted; absorb or soak up: *a paper that blots easily.* —See Synonyms at **erase.** [Middle English *blot, blotte,* perhaps from Old French *blotte, blostre,* clod of earth, probably from Germanic.]

blot² *n.* **1.** An exposed piece in backgammon. **2.** *Archaic.* A weak point. [Probably from Dutch *bloot,* "naked", from Middle Dutch, naked, poor.]

blotch (bloch) *n.* **1.** A spot or blot; a splotch. **2.** A discoloration on the skin; a blemish. [Probably a blend of BLOT and BOTCH.] **—blotched** *adj.* **—blotch·i·ness** *n.* **—blotch·y** *adj.*

blot·ter (blóttər) *n.* **1.** A piece or pad of blotting paper, especially one with a firm backing. **2.** *Chiefly U.S.* A book containing daily records of occurrences or transactions: *a police blotter.*

blotting paper *n.* Absorbent paper used to soak up excess ink.

blot·to (blóttō) *adj. Informal.* Very drunk. [Perhaps from BLOT.]

blouse (blowz ‖ blowss) *n.* **1.** A woman's or child's loosely fitting shirt-like garment extending from the neck to the waist or slightly below the waist. **2.** A loosely fitting garment resembling a long shirt, sometimes belted at the waist, often worn by European peasants. **3.** A jacket or tunic worn as part of a uniform.
~v. **bloused, blousing, blouses.** *—intr.* To hang loosely. *—tr.* To make full and loose. [French *blouse*†.]

blou·son (blo͞ozon ‖ *U.S. also* blówss-on) *n.* A short, loose jacket similar in style to a blouse and fitting tightly at the waist and often at the wrists. [French *blouson*†.]

blow¹ (blō) *v.* **blew** (blo͞o ‖ blew), **blown** (blōn), **blowing, blows.** *—intr.* **1.** To be in a state of motion. Used of the wind. **2. a.** To move along or be carried by or as if by the wind: *Her hat blew away.* **b.** To be brought into a specified state by the action of the wind: *The door blew open; the chimney blew down.* **3.** To expel a current of air, as from the mouth or from a bellows. **4.** To produce a sound by expelling a current of air, as in sounding a musical wind instrument. **5.** To breathe hard; pant. **6.** To storm: *It blew all night.* **7.** To spout water and air. Used of a whale. **8.** *Chiefly Australian & U.S. Slang.* To boast. Used with *off.* **9.** *Slang.* To go away; depart. **10.** To break down as a result of excess current. Used of fuses or electronic components. *—tr.* **1.** To cause to move by means of a current of air. **2.** To bring into a specified state by means of a current of air: *The wind blew the door shut.* **3.** To clear out or make free of obstruction by forcing air through: *to blow one's nose.* **4. a.** To shape or form (glass, for example) by forcing air or gas through the material when molten. **b.** To shape or form by forcing air through the mouth: *blow a smoke-ring.* **5.** To cause (a wind instrument) to sound: *The guard blew a whistle.* **6.** To cause (a horse) to be out of breath. **7.** To cause to explode or bring into a specified state by means of an explosion. Used with *up, down, apart,* or other adverbs: *The bomb blew both his legs off.* **8.** To lay or deposit eggs in. Used of a fly. **9.** To burn out or destroy (a fuse or other component) by excess current. **10.** *Slang.* To spend (money) freely. **11.** *Slang.* To handle ineptly; bungle: *blew his only chance.* **12.** *Informal.* To curse; damn. Used euphemistically: *I'm blowed if I'll do it!* **13.** *Vulgar Slang.* To fellate (somebody). **—blow hot and cold.** To vacillate between favour and opposition. **—blow over. 1.** To subside; wane: *The storm blew over quickly.* **2.** To be forgotten: *The scandal will soon blow over.* **—blow through.** *Australian & N.Z. Informal.* To leave.
~n. **1. a.** A blast of air or wind. **b.** A storm. **2.** The act of blowing. **3.** A sound produced by blowing. [Blow, blew, blown; Middle English *blowen, blew, blowen,* Old English *blāwan, blēow, blāwen.*]

blow² *n.* **1.** A sudden hard stroke or hit, as with the fist or an instrument. **2.** A setback or unexpected shock. **—come to blows.** To begin to fight. [Middle English (northern dialect) *blaw,* perhaps from Germanic *bleuwan* (unattested), to strike.]

blow³ *n.* A mass of blossoms. Used chiefly in the phrase *in full blow.* *—intr. v.* **blew** (blo͞o ‖ blew), **blown** (blōn), **blowing, blows.** *Poetic.* To bloom. [Middle English *blowen,* to blossom, Old English *blōwan.*]

blow-by-blow (blṓ-bī-blṓ) *adj.* Described exactly and in a detailed way: *a blow-by-blow account of the accident.*

blow-dry (blṓ-drī, -drī) *n.* A method of styling the hair by drying it with a hair-drier and shaping it with a brush at the same time. Also called "blow-wave". **—blow-dri·er** *n.* **—blow-dry** *tr.v.*

blow·er (blṓ-ər) *n.* **1.** One that blows, especially a mechanical device, such as a fan. **2.** *Informal.* A telephone. **3.** A source of fire damp in a mine.

blow·fish (blṓ-fish) *n., pl.* **-fishes** or collectively **blowfish.** The **puffer** *(see).*

blow·fly (blṓ-flī) *n., pl.* **-flies.** Any of several flies of the family Calliphoridae, that deposit their eggs in carcasses or carrion or in open sores and wounds. See **bluebottle.**

blow·hard (blṓ-haard) *n. Chiefly U.S. Slang.* A boaster; a braggart.

blow·hole (blṓ-hōl) *n.* **1.** A nostril at the highest point on the head of whales and other cetaceans. **2.** A hole in ice through which whales, dolphins, seals, and other aquatic mammals come up for air. **3.** A vent to permit the escape of air or other gas. **4.** A virtually vertical vent that reaches from the roof of a sea cave to the cliff top.

blow·ie (blṓ-i) *n. Australian Informal.* A blowfly.

blow in (blṓ-in) *intr.v. Informal.* To arrive casually or without warning.

blow-in (blṓ-in) *n. Australian Informal.* A stranger or newcomer, especially one who is unwelcome.

blow·lamp (blṓ-lamp) *n.* A portable hand burner fuelled by paraffin or bottled gas and used by plumbers for soldering and by painters for removing old paint. Also *chiefly U.S.* "blowtorch".

blown (blōn) *adj.* Completely expanded or opened. Often used in combination: *a full-blown flower.*

blow off *tr. v.* To release or let off (steam from a boiler, for example). *—intr.v.* **1.** To be released or let off. Used of gas or liquid under pressure. **2.** *Informal.* To expel air from the anus. **3.** *Informal.* To give vent to pent-up emotions.

blow·off (blṓ-off, -awf) *n.* **1.** Something blown off, such as a gas. **2.** A device or channel for blowing off something.

blow out *intr. v.* **1.** To be extinguised by a current of air. Used of a candle or other flame. **2.** To burst suddenly. Used of a tyre. **3.** To burn out or melt. Used of a fuse or other electrical device. **4.** To eject gas or oil in an uncontrolled flow. Used of a gas or oil well. *—tr. v.* To extinguish (a candle, for example) by blowing.

blow·out (blṓ-owt) *n.* **1. a.** A sudden rupture or bursting, as of a car tyre. **b.** The hole made in this way. **2.** A sudden escape of a confined gas. **3.** The burning out of a fuse. **4.** An uncontrolled flow from a gas or oil well. **5.** A basin-shaped or trough-shaped depression formed by wind eddying in a sand dune or sand deposit. **6.** *Slang.* A very large and lavish meal.

blow·pipe (blṓ-pīp) *n.* **1.** A metal tube in which a flow of gas is mixed with a controlled flow of air to concentrate the heat of a flame. **2.** A long narrow pipe through which darts or pellets may be blown. **3.** A long narrow iron pipe used to gather, work, and blow molten glass.

blow·torch (blṓ-tawrch) *n.* **1.** A portable burner for mixing gas and oxygen to produce a very hot flame for welding, flame cutting, glass blowing, or the like. **2.** *Chiefly U.S.* A blowlamp.

blow up *intr. v.* **1.** To come into being: *A storm blew up off the coast.* **2.** To explode. **3.** To lose one's temper. *—tr. v.* **1.** To cause to explode. **2.** To enlarge the size of (a photographic print). **3.** To increase the importance of. **4.** To fill with air.

blow·up (blṓ-up) *n.* **1.** An explosion. **2.** A violent outburst of temper. **3.** A photographic enlargement.

blow-wave (blṓ-wayv) *n.* A **blow-dry** *(see).* **—blow-wave** *tr.v.*

blow·y (blṓ-i) *adj.* **-ier, -iest.** Windy; breezy.

blow·zy, blow·sy (blówzi) *adj.* **-zier** or **-sier, -ziest** or **-siest. 1.** Having a coarsely ruddy and bloated appearance. **2.** Dishevelled; frowzy; unkempt: *blowzy hair.* —See Synonyms at **sloppy.** [From obsolete *blowse,* beggar wench, slattern, perhaps from *blowzy,* windy, from BLOW.]

blub (blub) *intr. v.* **blubbed, blubbing, blubs.** *British.* To blubber.

blub·ber¹ (blúbbər) *v.* **-bered, -bering, -bers.** *—intr.* To weep and sob in a noisy manner. *—tr.* To utter while crying and sobbing: *The child blubbered his name.* —See Synonyms at **cry.**
~n. A loud weeping and sobbing. [Middle English *bloberen, blubren,* to bubble, foam, from *blober, bluber,* foam, bubble (imitative).] **—blub·ber·er** *n.* **—blub·ber·ing·ly** *adv.*

blubber² *n.* **1.** The thick layer of fat between the skin and the muscle layers of whales and other marine mammals. **2.** Excessive body fat.
~adj. Swollen and protruding. Usually used in combination: *blubber-mouthed.* [Middle English *blober, bluber,* foam, bubble, entrails, fish or whale oil. See **blubber** (verb).] **—blub·ber·y** *adj.*

Blü·cher (blo͞okər; *German* blü̇khər), **Gebhard Leberecht von, Prince of Wahlstatt** (1742–1819). Prussian field marshal. His astute leadership of the Prussian army played a crucial part in the campaigns against Napoleon culminating in 1815 when he arrived at Waterloo in time to secure Wellington's famous victory.

bludge (bluj) *v.* **bludged, bludging, bludges.** *Australian & N.Z. Slang.* *—tr.* To scrounge; cadge: *bludge a cigarette.* *—intr.* To scrounge. Sometimes used with *on*: *bludging on his friends.* [Perhaps from CADGE.] **—blud·ger** *n.*

bludg·eon (blújən) *n.* A short, heavy club, usually of wood, that has one end loaded or thicker than the other.
~tr.v. **bludgeoned, -eoning, -eons. 1.** To hit with or as if with a bludgeon. **2.** To threaten or bully. [18th century : origin obscure.] **—bludg·eon·er, bludg·eon·eer** (-éer) *n.*

blue (blo͞o ‖ blew) *n.* **1.** *Abbr.* **bl.** Any of a group of colours that may vary in lightness and saturation, whose hue is that of a clear sky; the hue of that portion of the spectrum lying between green and violet; one of the additive or light primaries; one of the psycholog-

ical primary hues, evoked in the normal observer by radiant energy of wavelength approximately 475 nanometres. **2. a.** Any pigment or dye imparting this colour. **b. Blueing** *(see).* **3. a.** Any object of this colour. **b.** Blue dress or uniform: *the girls in blue.* **4.** A butterfly belonging to any of eleven groups of British butterfly of the subfamily *Lycaenidae,* such as the Common Blue and the Chalk-hill Blue, in which the males are normally blue and the females brown. **5. a.** A person who represents or has represented Oxford or Cambridge University in a sport. **b.** The honour that this confers. **6.** *British Informal.* A member of the Conservative Party or loosely, a politically conservative person. Used chiefly in the phrase *a true blue.* **7.** *Australian Slang.* A row; an argument. **8.** *Often capital* **B.** *Australian Slang.* A name for a person with red hair. Also called "bluey". **9.** *Australian Informal.* A loyal friend or a person to whom one is grateful: *you're a true blue mate!* **10.** *Australian & N.Z. Informal.* A blunder; an embarrassing mistake. **11.** *Australian Informal.* A summons or traffic ticket. **12.** *Slang.* An amphetamine. **—cop the blue.** *Australian Informal.* To be held responsible; take the blame. **—into the blue.** At a far distance or into the unknown. **—out of the blue. 1.** From an unexpected, unforeseen, or unknown source. **2.** At a completely unexpected time.
~*adj.* **bluer, bluest. 1.** *Abbr.* **bl.** Of the colour blue. **2.** Bluish, or having parts that are blue or bluish. Used with plant and animal names: *blue spruce, blue whale.* **3.** Having a grey or purplish colour, as from cold or contusion. **4.** Wearing blue. **5. a.** Gloomy; depressed. **b.** Dismal; dreary: *a blue day.* **c.** *Music.* Of or pertaining to the blues. **6.** *Physics.* Designating one of the three quark colours, the others being green and red. **7.** *Rare.* Aristocratic; patrician. **8. a.** Indecent; risqué: *a blue joke.* **b.** Pornographic: *blue films.* **9.** *Australian Slang.* Drunk. **—true blue.** *Informal.* **1.** Loyal and sincere. **2.** Genuine or real. Compare **true-blue** *n.*
~ *v.* **blued, blueing** or **bluing, blues.** —*tr.* To make blue. **2.** To use blueing on. **3.** *Slang.* To squander; waste. —*intr.* To become blue. [Middle English *bleu, blewe,* from Old French *bleu,* from Romance *blāvus* (unattested), from Germanic.] **—blue-ly** *adv.* **—blue-ness** *n.*

blue asbestos *n.* A variety of commercial asbestos, **crocidolite** *(see).*

blue baby *n.* An infant born with bluish skin caused by inadequate oxygenation of the blood, a symptom of a congenital malformation of the heart.

blue-beard (blo͞o-beerd ‖ bléw-) *n. Often capital* **B.** Any man thought to be a wife-slayer or a killer of women. [French *Barbe-bleue,* character in fairy tale (by Perrault) who murdered a number of wives in succession.]

blue-beat (blo͞o-beet) *n.* A type of rhythmic West Indian popular music in ¹²/₈ time with the accent on the third beat in every group of three beats.

blue-bell (blo͞o-bel ‖ bléw-) *n.* **1.** A European plant, *Endymion non-scriptus,* having a one-sided cluster of fragrant, blue-violet flowers. **2.** The **harebell** *(see),* which is the bluebell of Scotland. **3.** Any of various other plants with blue, bell-shaped flowers.

blue-ber-ry (blo͞o-bri, -bəri ‖ bléw-, -berri) *n., pl.* **-ries. 1.** Any of several North American shrubs of the genus *Vaccinium,* having small, urn-shaped flowers and edible berries. **2.** The juicy, blue, purplish, or blackish berry of any of these shrubs. Also used adjectivally: *blueberry pie.*

blue-bird (blo͞o-burd ‖ bléw-) *n.* Any of several North American birds of the genus *Sialia,* having blue plumage and, in the male of most species, a rust-coloured breast.

blue blood *n.* Noble or aristocratic descent. [Translation of Spanish *sangre azul;* probably from the blue colour of the veins of fair-complexioned aristocrats.] **—blue-blood-ed** (blo͞o-blúddid ‖ bléw-) *adj.*

blue-bon-net (blo͞o-bonnit ‖ bléw-) *n.* A broad, blue woollen cap, worn in Scotland.

blue-book (blo͞o-bo͞ok ‖ bléw-, -bo͞ok) *n.* **1.** An official publication of the British government, so named from its blue covers. **2.** *Chiefly U.S. Informal.* A book listing socially prominent people.

blue-bot-tle (blo͞o-bott'l ‖ bléw-) *n.* **1.** Any of several blowflies of the genus *Calliphora,* having a bright metallic-blue body and breeding in decaying organic matter. **2.** A plant, the **cornflower** *(see).* **3.** *British Informal.* A policeman.

blue cheese *n.* Any of various cheeses having a greenish-blue mould and a sharp flavour.

blue chip *n.* **1.** *Finance.* A stock that sells at a high price because of public confidence in its long record of steady earnings. Also called "blue-chip stock". **2.** A valuable asset held in reserve. **3.** A blue-coloured gambling chip of high value.
~*adj.* Of the highest quality or prestige.

blue-col-lar (blo͞o-kollər ‖ bléw-) *adj.* Of or pertaining to wage earners in jobs performed in clothing such as overalls and often involving manual labour, especially when regarded as a social class. Compare **white-collar.**

blued (blo͞od) *adj. Australian Informal.* Drunk.

blue devils *pl. n.* **1.** *Slang.* Delirium tremens. **2.** *Informal.* A feeling of depression or despondency.

blue-eyed boy (blo͞o-īd ‖ bléw-) *n. Chiefly British Informal.* The male favourite of a person or group.

blue-eyed Mary *n.* A European plant, *Omphalodes verna,* with bright blue flowers, often cultivated in gardens.

blue-fish (blo͞o-fish ‖ bléw-) *n., pl.* **-fishes** or collectively **bluefish. 1.** A voracious bluish-coloured food and game fish, *Pomatomus sal-*

tatrix, of temperate and tropical waters of the Atlantic and Indian oceans. **2.** Broadly, any of various other fishes that are predominantly blue in colour.

Blue-fields (blo͞o-feeldz). A port in southeast Nicaragua, the most important of the country's Caribbean ports. British and Dutch pirate ships used it as a harbour in the 16th and 17th centuries and it was named after a Dutch corsair, Bleufeldt.

blue flier *n.* The full-grown female red kangaroo.

blue fox *n.* **1.** The arctic fox *(see)* during its summer colour phase, when its pelt is bluish grey. **2.** The fur of such a fox.

blue funk *n. British Informal.* A state of panic.

blue-grass (blo͞o-graass ‖ bléw-, -grass) *n.* **1.** Any of several grasses of the genus *Poa;* especially, *P. pratensis,* native to Eurasia but naturalised throughout North America. This species is also called "Kentucky bluegrass". **2.** A type of folk music that originated in the southern United States, characterised by rapid tempos, jazzlike improvisation, and emphasis on nonelectrified stringed instruments, such as banjos and guitars.

blue-green algae (blo͞o-green ‖ bléw-) *n.* Algae of the division Cyanophyta, considered to be among the simplest forms of plants.

blue-gum (blo͞o-gum) *n.* Also **blue gum.** A tall timber tree, *Eucalyptus globulus,* native to Australia, having aromatic leaves that yield a medicinal oil and outer bark that peels off in shreds.

blue-ing, blu-ing (blo͞o-ing ‖ bléw-) *n.* **1.** A blue dye used in washing white fabrics to give a faint blue colour, thereby counteracting yellowing of the fabric; formerly added separately to the wash, now generally mixed in with the washing powder. Also called "blue". **2.** A dye used to give a blue tint to grey hair. **3.** The process in which a thin layer of blue oxide forms on an iron or steel surface.

blueish. Variant of **bluish.**

blue-jack-et (blo͞o-jackit ‖ bléw-) *n.* A sailor in the British or U.S. navy. [From the blue jacket of the Navy.]

blue jay *n.* A common North American bird, *Cyanocitta cristata,* having a crested head and predominantly blue plumage.

blue jeans *pl. n.* A pair of blue denim jeans.

blue john *n.* A purple or blue form of fluorspar found in Derbyshire in England, used in ornaments and vases.

blue mould *n.* Any of several fungi of the genus *Penicillium,* forming a bluish growth on food and other surfaces.

Blue Mountains[1]. A section of the Great Dividing Range chain of mountains in New South Wales, eastern Australia. The region is a popular holiday and tourist district.

Blue Mountains[2]. A range of mountains in the northwest United States, part of the Columbia Plateau. It extends from central Oregon into Washington state.

blue-pen-cil (blo͞o-pénss'l ‖ bléw-) *tr.v.* **-cilled** or *U.S.* **-ciled, -cilling** or *U.S.* **-ciling, -cils.** To edit, revise, or correct with or as if with a blue pencil; especially, to censor.

blue peter *n. Nautical.* A blue flag with a white square in the centre, flown to signal that a ship is ready to sail. [Probably from the Christian name *Peter.*]

blue pointer *n.* A large shark with a pointed snout that inhabits Australian waters.

blue-print (blo͞o-print ‖ bléw-) *n.* **1.** A photographic reproduction, as of architectural plans or technical drawings, rendered as white lines on a blue background. Also called "cyanotype". **2.** Any carefully designed plan or model.
~*tr.v.* **blueprinted, -printing, -prints. 1.** To make a blueprint of. **2.** *Chiefly U.S.* To plan for.

blue riband *n.* **1.** The first prize; the highest distinction or honour. **2.** The record for the fastest crossing of the Atlantic, awarded to passenger vessels.

blue ribbon *n.* **1.** A badge of honour worn especially by members of the Order of the Garter. **2.** *Chiefly U.S.* A blue riband. **3.** *U.S.* The badge of various temperance societies.

blues (blo͞oz ‖ blewz) *n. Sometimes used with a singular verb.* **1.** A state of depression or melancholy. **2.** A style of jazz evolved from black southern American secular songs and usually distinguished by slow tempo and flattened thirds and sevenths.

blue shift *n.* A shift of spectral lines towards shorter wavelengths, observed in the spectra of stars that are approaching the solar system. Compare **red shift.**

blue-shift (blo͞o-shift ‖ bléw-) *v.* **-shifted, -shifting, -shifts.** —*intr.* To undergo a blue shift. Used of a star or stellar spectrum. —*tr.* To cause a blue shift in (a spectrum).

blue-stock-ing (blo͞o-stocking ‖ bléw-) *n.* A serious intellectual or scholarly woman. [After the *Blue Stocking Society,* name given derisively to a group of 18th-century intellectuals that met in the London houses of several prominent women. Some of the male members wore ordinary blue stockings instead of formal black silk.] **—blue-stock-ing** *adj.*

blue-stone (blo͞o-stōn ‖ bléw-) *n.* **1.** A bluish-grey sandstone used for paving and building. **2.** Any similar stone. **3.** A mineral form of blue hydrated copper sulphate.

blu-et (blo͞o-it ‖ bléw-) *n.* A slender, low-growing plant, *Houstonia caerulea,* of eastern North America, having small, light-blue flowers with yellow centres. [French *bleuet, bluet,* diminutives of *bleu,* **BLUE.**]

blue-throat (blo͞o-thrōt ‖ bléw-) *n.* A small European songbird, *Cyanosylvia svecica,* with a brown plumage, pale underparts, and in the male a blue throat patch.

blue-tit (blo͞o-tit ‖ bléw-) *n.* A common European songbird, *Parus* *caeruleus,* with a blue crown and wings, a yellow breast, and a white face.

blue-tongue (blōō-túng) *n.* **1.** Any of various fat-bodied, Australian skinks of the genus *Tiliqua* that have large blue tongues which they poke out when disturbed. **2.** *Australian.* A handyman.

blue vitriol *n. Chemistry.* The blue hydrated crystalline form of **copper sulphate** *(see).*

blue water sailing *n. Australian & N. Z.* Ocean sailing, as opposed to sailing on inland waters.

blue·weed (blōō-weed ‖ bléw-) *n. U.S.* A plant, **viper's bugloss** *(see).*

blue whale *n.* The largest whale, *Sibbaldus musculus,* having a bluish-grey back and longitudinal grooves along the throat and belly. Also called "sulphur-bottom", "Sibbald's rorqual".

blu·ey (blōō-i) *n.* **1.** *Australian Informal.* A bushman's bundle; a swag. **2.** Used as a name for a red-headed person; blue.

bluff¹ (bluf) *v.* **bluffed, bluffing, bluffs.** —*tr.* **1.** To mislead, deceive, or hoodwink. **2.** To impress, deter, or intimidate by a display of confidence greater than the facts support. **3.** To try to mislead (opponents) in poker by heavy betting on a poor hand or by little or no betting on a good one. —*intr.* To feign strength when in a state of weakness, or to feign weakness when strong. —*n.* **1.** The act or practice of bluffing. **2.** *U.S.* One who bluffs. —**call (someone's) bluff.** To challenge or expose someone's bluff. [19th century (as poker term) : Dutch *bluffen,* to boast, from Middle Dutch, to swell up.] —**bluff·a·ble** *adj.* —**bluff·er** *n.*

bluff² *n.* A steep headland, promontory, river bank, or cliff. —*adj.* **bluffer, bluffest. 1.** Presenting a broad, steep front. **2.** Having a rough, blunt but not unkind manner. —See Synonyms at **gruff.** [17th century (nautical use) : origin obscure.] —**bluff·ly** *adv.* —**bluff·ness** *n.*

bluing. Variant of **blueing.**

blu·ish, blue·ish (blōō-ish ‖ bléw-) *adj.* Somewhat or slightly blue. —**blu·ish·ness** *n.*

Blum (blōōm), **Léon** (1872–1950). French statesman, cofounder of the French Socialist party (1905), becoming its leader in 1920. He was prime minister of the first Popular Front Communist-Socialist coalition government (1936–37), and again in 1938 and 1946–47.

Blun·den (blúndən), **Edmund (Charles)** (1896–1974). British writer. He is best known for *Undertones of War* (1928), a collection of prose and poetry derived from his experience of World War I.

blun·der (blúndər) *n.* A stupid, clumsy, or foolish act or remark. —See Synonyms at **error.** —*v.* **blundered, -dering, -ders.** —*intr.* **1.** To move awkwardly or clumsily, as if blind; stumble. **2.** To get into an unpleasant position through carelessness or ineptitude: *The country blundered into full-scale war.* **3.** To make a stupid mistake because of ignorance or confusion. —*tr. Rare.* **1.** To botch or bungle. **2.** To say stupidly or thoughtlessly. [Middle English *blund(e)ren, blond(e)ren,* to proceed blindly, bungle, probably from Old Norse *blunda,* to shut the eyes.] —**blun·der·er** *n.* —**blun·der·ing·ly** *adv.*

blun·der·buss (blúndər-buss) *n.* **1.** A short musket with a wide bore and flaring muzzle, formerly used to scatter shot at close range. **2.** *Informal.* A stupid, clumsy person. [Alteration (influenced by BLUNDER) of Dutch *donderbus* : *donder,* thunder + *bus,* gun, from Middle Dutch *busse,* box, tube, from Late Latin *buxis,* BOX.]

blunge (blunj) *tr. v.* **blunged, blunging, blunges.** To mix (clay, for example) with water for use in making ceramics, usually by means of a machine. [Blend of BLEND + PLUNGE.]

blung·er (blúngər) *n.* A large vat in which water and clay or a similar substance are mixed. [From BLUNGE.]

blunt (blunt) *adj.* **blunter, bluntest. 1.** Having a thick, dull edge or end; not sharp or pointed. **2. a.** Having an abrupt and frank manner; brusque. **b.** Direct; straightforward: *a blunt refusal.* **3.** Slow to understand or perceive; dull. —See Synonyms at **gruff.** —*v.* **blunted, blunting, blunts.** —*tr.* **1.** To make blunt. **2.** To make less sensitive or alert: *senses blunted by too much drinking.* **3.** To lessen the force or destructiveness of: *blunt the enemy's attack.* —*intr.* To become blunt. [Middle English *blont, blunt†,* dull, blunt, stupid.] —**blunt·ly** *adv.* —**blunt·ness** *n.*

Blunt (blunt), **Anthony (Frederick)** (1907–83). British art critic and historian. He was Surveyor of the King's and Queen's Pictures (1945–72). In 1979 it was revealed that he had been a Soviet spy during the 1940s and he was stripped of his 1956 knighthood.

blur (blur) *v.* **blurred, blurring, blurs.** —*tr.* **1.** To make indistinct and hazy in outline or appearance; obscure. **2.** To smear or stain; smudge. **3.** To lessen the perception of; dim. —*intr.* To become indistinct or smudged. —*n.* **1.** A blot or smudge. **2.** A hazy and indistinct visual or mental image. [16th century : perhaps akin to BLEAR.] —**blur·ry** *adj.*

blurb (blurb) *n.* A brief commendatory publicity notice, as on a book jacket. [Coined in 1907 by Gelett *Burgess* (1866–1951), American humorist and illustrator.]

blurt (blurt) *tr. v.* **blurted, blurting, blurts.** To utter suddenly and impulsively. Often used with *out.* [Probably imitative.]

blush (blush) *v.* **blushed, blushing, blushes.** —*intr.* **1.** To become suddenly red in the face from modesty, embarrassment, or shame; flush. **2.** To become red or rosy. **3.** To feel ashamed or regretful about something. Usually used with *at* or *for.* —*tr.* To give a reddish hue to. —*n.* **1.** A sudden reddening of the face from modesty, embarrassment, or shame. **2.** A red or rosy colour. —**at** or **on first blush.** At first sight or glance.

—*adj.* Having the rosy colour of a blush. [Middle English *blusshen, blisshen,* Old English *blyscan.*] —**blush·ful** *adj.* —**blush·ing·ly** *adv.*

blush·er (blúshər) *n.* **1.** One that blushes. **2.** A cosmetic used to give colour to the cheeks. **3.** A common brownish mushroom, *Amanita rubescens,* related to the death cap, found during summer and autumn in woodland areas.

blus·ter (blústər) *v.* **-tered, -tering, -ters.** —*intr.* **1.** To blow in loud, violent gusts, as wind does in a storm. **2.** To speak noisily and boastfully. **3.** To threaten ineffectually. —*tr.* To force or bully (one's way) with swaggering threats. —*n.* **1.** A violent, gusty wind. **2.** Turbulence or confusion. **3.** Swaggering talk. [Middle English *blusteren,* porbably akin to Low German *blüstern.*] —**blus·ter·er** *n.* —**blus·ter·y, blus·ter·ous** *adj.*

blvd. boulevard.

b.m. board measure.

B.M. 1. Bachelor of Medicine. **2.** bench mark. **3.** British Museum.

B.M.A. British Medical Association.

B.M.J. British Medical Journal.

BMR basal metabolic rate.

B.Mus. Bachelor of Music.

bn., Bn. 1. baron. **2.** battalion.

B'nai B'rith (bə-náy bə-réeth, brith) *n.* A Jewish international fraternal society. [Hebrew *bonē bərîth,* "sons of the covenant".]

bo (bō) *n., pl.* **bos.** *U.S. Slang.* A fellow; a pal. Often used as a form of address. [Probably short for HOBO or BOZO.]

b.o. 1. branch office. **2.** buyer's option.

B.O. *n. Informal.* Body odour; an unpleasant bodily smell.

bo·a (bō-ə; *rarely* baw) *n.* **1.** Any of various large, nonvenomous, chiefly tropical snakes of the family Boidae, which includes the pythons, anacondas, boa constrictors, and other snakes that coil around and crush their prey. **2.** A long, fluffy scarf made of fur, feathers, or other soft material. [New Latin *Boa* (genus), from Latin *boa†,* a large water snake.]

boa constrictor *n.* A large, nonvenomous snake, *Constrictor constrictor,* of tropical America, having brown markings, which kills its prey by constriction.

Bo·a·ner·ges¹ (bō-ə-nérjeez). The name given by Jesus to the Apostles John and James. Mark 3:17. [Hebrew *bonē reghesh,* "sons of thunder".]

Boanerges² *n., pl.* **Boanerges.** A vociferous, loud-voiced preacher or orator.

boar (bor ‖ bōr) *n., pl.* **boars** or (for sense 2) collectively **boar. 1.** An uncastrated male pig. **2.** A **wild boar** *(see).* [Middle English *bor,* Old English *bār,* from West Germanic *bairoz* (unattested).]

board (bord ‖ bōrd) *n. Abbr.* **bd. 1.** A long, flat slab of sawn timber; a plank. **2.** A flat piece of wood or similarly rigid material, adapted for a special use: *a diving board; a notice board.* **3.** A flat, usually specially marked surface on which a game is played. **4.** The hard pasteboard cover of a book. **5.** *Plural.* **a.** The stage of a theatre. **b.** The acting profession. In both senses, preceded by *the.* **6. a.** A table, especially one set for serving food. **b.** Food or meals collectively: *board and lodging.* **7.** A table at which official meetings are held; a conference table. **8.** *Used with a singular or plural verb.* **a.** The directors of a company. Also used adjectively: *a board meeting.* **b.** Any committee, body of administrators, or the like: *a board of trustees.* **9.** A panel, usually plastic, on which an electrical circuit is mounted, especially one serving as a base for a printed circuit: *a printed circuit board.* **10.** *Nautical.* **a.** The side of a ship. **b.** A lee-board. **c.** A centreboard. **11.** *Australian & N.Z.* A shearing shed, its floor, or the shearers employed there. —**across the board.** *Informal.* Affecting all members or divisions equally. —**by the board.** Overboard. —**go by the board.** To be ignored, neglected, or discarded. —**on board.** Aboard —**sweep the board.** To win every possible prize, event, or the like. —**take on board.** *Informal.* To realise and face up to: *Britain is now a multiracial country and this must be taken on board.* —*v.* **boarded, boarding, boards.** —*tr.* **1.** To cover or close with boards. Used with *up: board up a door.* **2.** To furnish with meals in return for payment. **3.** To arrange for (a person) to be fed and housed elsewhere. Often used with *out.* **4.** To enter or go aboard (a ship or public vehicle). **5.** To come alongside (a ship), especially in order to force one's way aboard. **6.** In ice hockey, to block (an opposing player) into the boards surrounding the rink. —*intr.* **1.** To receive meals, or meals and lodging, in return for payment. **2.** To be a boarder at a school. [Middle English *bord,* Old English *bord,* plank, table, border, ship's side.]

board·er (bórd-ər ‖ bōrd-) *n.* **1.** One who pays a stipulated sum to stay in someone else's house and receive regular meals; a lodger. **2.** A pupil who lives at a boarding school during the school term. **3.** A person who is detailed to go aboard an enemy ship.

board foot *n., pl.* **board feet.** *Abbr.* **bd. ft.** A unit of timber measurement equal to the volume of a piece of wood one foot square by one inch thick.

board·ing house (bórding) *n.* A private home that takes in paying guests and provides meals and lodging.

boarding school *n.* A school where pupils are provided with meals and lodging. Compare **day school.**

board measure *n. Abbr.* **b.m.** Measurement of timber in board feet.

Board of Customs and Excise. See **excise.**

board of trade *n.* **1.** *Capital* B, *capital* T. A British government committee dealing with problems of trade and commerce. **2.** *U.S.* An association of bankers and businessmen formed to promote common commercial interests; a **chamber of commerce** *(see).*

board rule *n.* A measuring stick for determining the volume of timber in board feet.

board·walk (bórd-wawk ‖ bórd-) *n. U.S.* **1.** A path made of wooden planks. **2.** A promenade, especially of planks, along a beach or waterfront.

boar·fish (bór-fish ‖ bór-) *n., pl.* **-fishes** or collectively **boarfish.** Any of several marine fishes of the genus *Antigonia,* having a deep, flattened body, bright red colouring, and spiny fins.

boar·hound (bór-hownd ‖ bór-) *n.* A large dog, such as the Great Dane, used for hunting wild boar.

boart. Variant of **bort.**

Bo·as (bő-az, -ass), **Franz** (1858–1942). German-born U.S. anthropologist. Boas laid special emphasis on the systematic analysis of language structures and culture, and is considered one of the founders of American anthropology.

boast¹ (bőst) *v.* **boasted, boasting, boasts.** —*intr.* To speak with excessive pride about one's own accomplishments, talents, or possessions. Often used with *of* or *about.* —*tr.* **1.** To brag about with excessive pride. **2.** To take pride in, or be enhanced by, the possession of: *The school boasts excellent sporting facilities.* ~*n.* **1.** An instance of excessive self-praise. **2.** Something that one is proud of. [Middle English *bosten,* from *bost,* bragging, threat, perhaps from Germanic, akin to German dialectal *bauste(r)n,* to swell.] —**boast·er** *n.* —**boast·ing·ly** *adv.*
   Synonyms: boast, brag, crow, vaunt.

boast² *tr.v.* **boasted, boasting, boasts.** To shape or form (stone) roughly with a broad chisel. [Origin obscure.]

boast·ful (bőst-f'l, -fŏŏl) *adj.* Tending to boast or brag. —**boast·ful·ly** *adv.* —**boast·ful·ness** *n.*

boat (bőt) *n.* **1.** A relatively small, usually open craft of a size that might be carried on a ship. **2.** A ship. Not in nautical usage. **3.** A dish shaped somewhat like a boat: *a gravy boat.* —**burn (one's) boats.** To commit oneself irrevocably to a course of action. —**in the same boat.** In the same predicament. —**miss the boat.** *Informal.* To lose an opportunity by failing to act at the right moment. —**push the boat out.** *Informal.* To celebrate, especially in an extravagant way. —**rock the boat.** To upset the existing state of affairs; behave disruptively. ~*v.* **boated, boating, boats.** —*intr.* To travel by boat. —*tr.* **1.** To transport by boat. [Middle English *bo(o)t,* from Old English *bāt* and Old Norse *bātr.*]

boat·bill (bőt-bil) *n.* A nocturnal tropical American wading bird, *Cochlearius cochlearius,* having a large bill shaped like an inverted boat. Also called "boat-billed heron".

boat·er (bőtər) *n.* A stiff straw hat with a flat crown.

boat hook *n.* A pole with a metal point and hook at one end, used to manoeuvre boats and other floating objects.

boat·house (bőt-howss) *n.* A shed built at the water's edge or over the water, in which boats are kept.

boat·load (bőt-lőd) *n.* The number of passengers or quantity of cargo that a boat carries or can safely carry.

boat·man (bőt-mən) *n., pl.* **-men** (-mən). One who works on, deals with, or operates boats. —**boat·man·ship** *n.*

boat people *pl.n.* Refugees, especially those from Vietnam or other parts of Southeast Asia, who have made their escape in small boats.

boat race *n.* A rowing competition; especially, a race between boats representing the universities of Oxford and Cambridge, held annually on the river Thames between Putney and Mortlake.

boat·swain, bo's'n, bo·sun (bőss'n) *n.* A warrant officer or petty officer in charge of a ship's deck crew, rigging, anchors, and cables, who has a whistle as his badge of office. [Middle English *botswein,* Old English *bātswān* : BOAT + SWAIN.]

boatswain's chair *n.* A short board secured by ropes and used as a seat by sailors when working aloft or over a ship's side.

boat train *n.* A train scheduled to take passengers to catch or meet a particular ship.

Bo·az (bő-az). The husband of Ruth. Ruth 2:4.

bob¹ (bob) *n.* **1. a.** A quick jerking movement of the head or body. **b.** A quick bow or curtsy. **2.** A short line at the end of a stanza of verse. **3. a.** Any small knoblike dangling object: *a plumb bob.* **b.** *Plural.* Small, unimportant objects: *bits and bobs.* **4.** A fishing float or cork. **5.** A small lock or curl of hair. **6.** A short haircut on a woman or child, in which the hair is cut to the same length all round the back and sides of the head. **7.** The docked tail of a horse. **8.** A polishing disc rotated by a spindle and impregnated with an abrasive. **9.** In bell-ringing, one of several types of change. **10.** *Archaic.* A tap or a light blow. ~*v.* **bobbed, bobbing, bobs.** —*intr.* **1.** To move up and down: *The cork bobbed on the water.* **2.** To curtsy or bow. **3.** To grab at floating or hanging objects with the teeth. Usually used with *for: He bobbed for apples.* **4.** To fish with a bob. —*tr.* **1.** To move (especially the head) up and down. **2.** To cut short: *She bobbed her hair.* **3.** *Archaic.* To hit lightly and quickly; tap. —**bob up.** To appear suddenly, as a cork emerging from under water. [As "a pendent object", Middle English *bobbet,* cluster of flowers or fruit. As verb "to move up and down", Middle English *bobben* (probably imitative).] —**bob·ber** *n.*

bob² *n., pl.* **bob.** *British.* Especially formerly, a shilling [19th century : origin obscure.]

bob·bin (bóbbin) *n.* **1.** A spool or reel that holds thread or yarn for spinning, weaving, knitting, sewing, or making lace. **2.** Narrow braid used as trimming. **3.** A spool wound with insulated wire that

forms part of an electromagnetic device, such as an electric bell. [French *bobine* (expressive).]

bob·bi·net (bóbbi-nét) *n.* A machine-woven net fabric with hexagonal meshes. [*bobbin* + *net.*]

bobbin lace *n.* An intricate handmade lace made by interlacing thread around small notched pins or bobbins stuck into a pillow according to a certain pattern. Also called "pillow lace".

bob·ble (bóbb'l) *intr. v.* **-bled, -bling, -bles.** To bob up and down. ~*n.* An ornamental woolly ball, as on a knitted hat. [Frequentative of BOB (verb).]

bob·by (bóbbi) *n., pl.* **-bies.** *British Informal.* A policeman. [After Sir Robert PEEL, who was Home Secretary of England when the Metropolitan Police Force was created (1828).]

bob·by-daz·zler (bóbbi-dázzlər) *n. British Informal.* A striking or exceptional person or thing. [19th century : expanded from *dazzler,* something striking.]

bobby pin *n.* A **kirby-grip** *(see).* [From BOB (lock of hair).]

bobby socks, bobby sox *pl. n. U.S. Informal.* Ankle socks worn by girls or women. [From the name *Bobby,* pet form for the name *Robert* (influenced by BOBBY PIN).]

bob·by-sox·er (bóbbi-soksər) *n. U.S. Informal.* A teenage girl of the 1940s who followed current fads. [From the BOBBY SOCKS worn by the teen-age girls.]

bob·cat (bób-kat) *n.* A wild cat, *Lynx rufus,* of North America, having reddish-brown fur with dark markings, tufted ears, and a short tail. Also called "bay lynx". [From its bobbed tail.]

bob·o·link (bóbbə-lingk) *n.* An American migratory songbird, *Dolichonyx oryzivorus,* of which the male has black, white, and yellowish plumage in the breeding season. [Originally *bobolincon*; imitative of its call.]

bob·sleigh (bób-slay) *n.* **1.** A long racing sledge with a steering mechanism controlling the front runners. **2. a.** A long sledge made of two shorter sledges joined in tandem. **b.** Either of these two smaller sledges. Also *chiefly U.S.* "bobsled". ~*intr.v.* **bobsleighed, -sleighing, -sleighs.** To ride or race in a bobsleigh. [From BOB (to cut short).]

bob·stay (bób-stay) *n. Nautical.* A rope or chain used to steady the bowsprit. [From BOB (up-and-down motion).]

bob·sy-die (bóbzi-dī) *n. N.Z. Informal.* A fuss. Used chiefly in the phrase *kick up bobsy-die.* [Alteration of 19th-century *Bob's a-dying,* a fuss.]

bob·tail (bób-tayl) *n.* **1.** A short or shortened tail. **2.** A horse or other animal having such a tail. ~*adj.* **1.** Having the tail short or cut short: *a bobtail nag.* **2.** Cut short; abbreviated; curtailed. ~*tr.v.* **bobtailed, -tailing, -tails.** **1.** To cut the tail of (a horse or other animal); dock. **2.** To cut short; abbreviate.

bo·cage (bo-ka'azh) *n.* The representation of woodland scenes in ceramics. [French, from Old French, BOSCAGE.]

Boc·cac·cio (bo-ka'ach-ő, bə-, -ka'achi-, ka'chi-), **Giovanni** (1313–75). French-born Italian poet and writer. His reputation rests chiefly on *The Decameron* (1348–53), a collection of 100 tales exposing the nature of man, set against the melancholy background of the Black Death.

Boc·cher·i·ni (bóckə-reéni), **(Ridolfo) Luigi** (1743–1805). Italian cellist and composer. He made his name as a composer, especially as a developer and prolific composer of chamber music.

Boche (bosh) *n., pl.* **Boches.** *Slang.* A German, especially a German soldier. Used derogatorily. [French, short for *alboche* : probably *al-,* from *allemand,* German (see **allemande**) + *caboche,* pate, hard skull, from Old French *caboce,* head (see **cabbage**).]

bock beer (bok) *n.* A strong dark beer, the first that is drawn from the vats in springtime. Also called "bock". [German *Bockbier,* short for *Eimbockbier* : *Eimbock, Einbeck* (town in Germany) + *Bier,* BEER.]

boco. *Chiefly Australian.* Variant of **boko.**

bod (bod) *n. British Informal.* A person; a fellow. [Shortened from BODY.]

BOD 1. biochemical oxygen demand. **2.** biological oxygen demand.

bode¹ (bőd) *tr.v.* **boded, boding, bodes. 1.** To be an omen of: *His ill will bodes no good.* **2.** *Obsolete.* To predict; foretell. —*intr.* To be a sign or omen: *The fine weather bodes well for the game.* —See Synonyms at **foretell.** [Middle English *boden,* Old English *bodian,* to announce, proclaim, from *boda,* messenger.]

bode². Alternative past tense of **bide.**

bo·de·ga (bő-deé-gə ‖ -dáy-) *n.* **1.** A wineshop, sometimes combined with a grocery, especially in a Spanish-speaking country. **2.** A warehouse for wine storage. [Spanish, from Latin *apothēca,* from Greek *apothēkē,* storehouse, from *apotithenai,* to put away : *apo-,* away + *tithenai,* to put, place.]

Bodensee. See **Constance, Lake.**

bodge¹ (boj) *tr.v.* **bodged, bodging, bodges.** To spoil through clumsiness; make a mess of; botch. ~*n.* A carelessly-done piece of work. [Variant of BOTCH.]

bodge² *intr.v.* **bodged, bodging, bodges.** To make chairs out of beechwood.

bod·ger (bójər) *adj.* Also **bod·gie** (bóji). *Australian Informal.* **1.** Worthless; inferior. **2.** False or assumed. Said especially of names. [From BODGE.]

bod·gie (bóji) *n. Australian & N.Z.* **1.** An unruly and unconventionally dressed young man, especially in the 1950s. **2.** Any worthless or uncouth person. ~*adj.* Variant of **bodger.**

~*tr.v.* **bodgied, -gling, -gies.** *Australian & N.Z. Informal.* To patch (something) up, especially temporarily. Used with *up*.

bo·dhi·satt·va (bṓdi-sát-və, bóddi-, sút-, -wə) *n. Mahayana Buddhism.* One who, out of compassion, forgoes nirvana in order to save others. [Sanskrit, "one whose essence is enlightenment" : *bodhi,* enlightenment, from *bodhati,* he awakes + *sattva,* essence, from *sat, sant,* existing.]

bod·ice (bóddiss) *n.* **1.** The fitted part of a dress that extends from the waist to the shoulder. **2.** A woman's laced outer garment, worn like a waistcoat over a blouse. **3.** A woman or child's vest that buttons up the front. [Originally *bodies,* plural of BODY (originally referring to the two sides of a whalebone corset).]

bodice ripper *n. Informal.* A work of fiction featuring scenes of unbridled heterosexual lust.

–bod·ied (bóddid ‖ bóddeed) *adj. comb. form.* Indicates a specified kind of body: *strong-bodied; full-bodied wine.*

bod·i·less (bóddi-ləss, -liss) *adj.* Having no body, form, or substance; incorporeal. **—bod·i·less·ness** *n.*

bod·i·ly (bóddili, bódd'l-i) *adj.* **1.** Of, pertaining to, within, or exhibited by the body. **2.** Physical as opposed to mental or spiritual. ~*adv.* **1.** In the flesh; in person. **2.** As a complete physical entity: *He carried her bodily from the room.*

bod·ing (bṓding) *n.* An omen or foreboding, especially of evil.

bod·kin (bódkin) *n.* **1.** A small, sharply pointed instrument for making holes in fabric or leather. **2.** A blunt needle for pulling tape or ribbon through a series of loops or a hem. **3.** A long hairpin, usually with an ornamental head. **4.** *Printing.* A pointed tool for extracting letters from set type when correcting. [Middle English *boidekyn*†.]

Bod·lei·an (bód-lée-ən). The library of the University of Oxford. It is one of the five libraries that automatically receive a free copy of every book published in the United Kingdom, in accordance with the copyright laws. [After Sir Thomas *Bodley* (1545–1613), English diplomat who re-founded it (1603).]

bod·y (bóddi) *n., pl.* **-ies. 1. a.** The entire material structure and substance of an organism, especially of a human being or an animal. **b.** A corpse or carcass. **2. a.** The trunk or torso of a human being or animal. **b.** The part of a garment covering the torso. **3.** *Informal.* A person. **4. a.** *Law.* A group of individuals regarded as an entity; a corporation. **b.** A number of persons, concepts, or things regarded collectively; a group: *We walked out in a body; a legislative body.* **5.** The main or central part of something, as: **a.** The nave of a church or the auditorium of a theatre. **b.** The central content of a book or document as opposed to the prefatory matter, codicils, indexes, and the like. **c.** The passenger- and cargo-carrying part of an aircraft, ship, or vehicle. **d.** The sound box of a musical instrument. **e.** The majority: *The body of party opinion favoured the reform.* **6. a.** Any bounded mass of matter: *a body of water.* **b.** Any perceptible three-dimensional piece of matter: *a foreign body in one's ear; heavenly bodies.* **7.** Consistency of substance, as in paint, textiles, wine, and the like: *a sauce with body.* **8.** *Printing.* The part of a block of type underlying the impression surface.

~*tr.v.* **bodied, -ying, -ies.** *Rare.* To give form or shape to. Usually followed by *forth:* "*Imagination bodies forth the form of things unknown.*" (Shakespeare). [Middle English *body,* Old English *bodig,* from Germanic *bot-* (unattested), container.]

body blow *n.* **1.** In boxing, a blow delivered to the front of the body above the waist. **2.** A serious setback; a major disappointment.

body building *n.* The strengthening of the body by means of physical exercises, especially in a way that makes the muscles prominent. **—body builder** *n.*

body carpet *n. Chiefly Australian.* Carpet that is wall-to-wall.

body cavity *n.* The internal cavity of all multicellular animals except sponges, which contains the heart, digestive tract, and many other organs.

body-centred (bóddi-sentərd) *adj.* Having a lattice point at the centre of the body as well as at the corners. Said of a crystal. Compare **face-centred.**

body corporate *n. Law.* A **corporation** *(see).*

body count *n.* The total number of persons killed in a battle or war.

body double *n.* A person who doubles for an actor when scenes are filmed where the actor's body or some part thereof is the centre of interest.

bod·y·guard (bóddigaard) *n.* **1.** A person or group of persons, usually armed, responsible for the physical safety of one or more specific persons. **2.** An escort or retinue.

body image *n.* A person's concept of the identity, shape, and relative positions of the different parts of his body.

body language *n.* Unspoken communication through conscious and unconscious gestures and positioning of the body.

bod·y·line bowling (bóddi-līn) *n.* An intimidatory style of fast bowling in cricket in which the ball is aimed repeatedly at the batsman's leg stump, in a manner that threatens his body.

body paint *n.* Paint that is applied to the body for decoration.

body politic *n.* The people, collectively, of a politically organised nation or state.

body pop·ping (pópping) *n.* A type of dancing characterised by convulsive body movements and mimed robotic gestures, popular in the 1980s. It is often combined with **breakdancing** *(see).* [20th century : origin obscure.]

body snatcher *n.* In former times, a person who stole corpses from graves for dissection.

bod·y·shoot (bóddi-shōōt) *tr.v.* **-shot, -shooting, -shoots.** *Austra-*

lian. To surf (a wave) without a board.

body stocking *n.* A tight one-piece undergarment for the torso, sometimes also with sleeves and legs, worn by women.

body surfing *n.* A form of surfing without a board in which one swims with a wave and allows it to carry one towards the shore. **—bod·y-surf** (bóddi-surf) *intr.v.*

body wall *n.* The part of an animal's body that encloses the body cavity, made up of ectoderm and mesoderm.

bod·y·work (bóddi-wurk) *n.* **1.** The external, usually metal, structure of a motor vehicle. **2.** Therapeutic manipulation or massage, as in osteopathy or rolfing.

boehm·ite (bérm-īt ‖ *U.S.* báym-, bŏm-) *n.* A natural, white, hydrated aluminium hydroxide, AlO(OH), that occurs as orthorhombic crystals in some bauxites. [German *Böhmit,* after J. *Böhm,* 20th-century German scientist.]

Boe·o·tia (bee-ṓsh-ə, -yə). Region of ancient Greece, lying north of Attica and the Gulf of Corinth. In the seventh century B.C., the cities of the region formed the Boeotian League, although they never succeeding in escaping from the dominance of Thebes.

Boe·o·tian (bee-ṓsh'n) *adj.* **1.** Of or pertaining to Boeotia or its inhabitants. **2.** *Archaic.* Stupid; boorish. ~*n.* **1.** An inhabitant of Boeotia. **2.** *Archaic.* A stupid, boorish person.

Boer (bṓ-ər, boor, bor ‖ bṓr) *n.* A Dutch colonist or a descendant of a Dutch colonist in South Africa. [Dutch, "peasant", "farmer", from Middle Dutch *gheboer.*] **—Boer** *adj.*

boer·e·wors (bṓor-ə-vawrss) *n.* A spiced South African sausage, usually of beef and pork. [Afrikaans, *boere,* farmers, country-style + *wors,* sausage.]

Boer War. A war (1899–1902) in which Great Britain defeated the Boers of the Orange Free State and the Transvaal Republic in South Africa. Also called "Anglo-Boer War".

Bo·e·thi·us (bṓ-éethi-əss), **Anicius Manlius Severinus** (*c.*480–524). Also **Bo·e·ti·us** (-éeshəss) or **Bo·ece** (bṓ-eess). Roman philosopher. His famous work, *De consolatione philosophiae* (On the Consolation of Philosophy), written in prison in the weeks before his execution without trial by Theodoric the Ostrogoth, became one of the most influential accounts of classical thought.

bof·fin (bóffin) *n. British Informal.* A scientist or technical expert, originally one carrying out work for the Royal Air Force. [20th century : origin obscure.]

Bo·fors gun (bṓ-fərz ‖ bṓo-, -fawrz) *n.* A double-barrelled, automatic antiaircraft gun. [First made at the munitions works in *Bofors,* Sweden.]

bog (bog ‖ *U.S. also* bawg) *n.* **1.** A permanently water-logged ground, with a surface layer of decaying vegetation, particularly *Sphagnum* mosses, which forms highly acid peat. **2.** An area of such ground; a marsh; a swamp. **3.** *British Slang.* A lavatory. ~*v.* **bogged, bogging, bogs.** —*tr.* To hinder; slow; impede. Usually used with *down.* —*intr.* To be hindered and slowed. Usually used with *down: bogged down in work.* [Scottish and Irish Gaelic *bogach,* from *bog,* soft.] **—bog·gish** *adj.* **—bog·gish·ness** *n.*

Bo·garde (bṓ-gaard), **Sir Dirk,** born Derek Niven van den Bogaerde (1921–). British actor and writer, knighted in 1991. Among his films are *The Servant* (1963) and *Death in Venice* (1971). He has published novels and seven volumes of autobiography.

Bo·gart (bṓ-gaart), **Humphrey DeForest** (1899–1957). U.S. actor. In the 1930s, 1940s, and 1950s he appeared in numerous roles as a reticent, tough hero with a soft heart, in films such as *Casablanca* (1942) and *The African Queen* (1951), and, with the actress Lauren Bacall (whom he married in 1945), in *To Have and Have Not* (1944) and *The Big Sleep* (1946).

bog asphodel *n.* Either of two related bog plants, *Narthecium ossifragum,* of Europe, or *N. americanum,* of the southeastern United States, having a spike of yellow flowers and iris-like leaves.

bog·bean (bóg-been ‖ *U.S. also* báwg-) *n.* An aquatic or creeping plant, *Menyanthes trifoliata,* with pink or white flowers in spikes, and three-lobed leaves held conspicuously above the surface. Also called "buckbean".

bo·gey (bṓgi) *n., pl.* **-geys. 1.** In golf: **a.** An estimated standard score. **b.** One stroke over par on a hole. **2.** *Military Slang.* Any unidentified flying aircraft. **3.** *Slang.* A bit of mucus from the nose. **4.** Variant of **bogy**[1].

bo·gey·man, bo·gy·man (bṓgi-man) *n., pl.* **-men** (-men). Also *chiefly U.S.* **boo·gie·man** (bṓogi-). **1.** A mischievous spirit, bogy, or hobgoblin. **2.** An imaginary spirit invented to frighten children. **3.** *Chiefly British.* A person who is regarded as threatening or malicious. Used humorously.

bog·gle (bogg'l) *intr.v.* **-gled, -gling, -gles. 1.** To hesitate or evade as if in fear or doubt. Usually used with *at.* **2.** To shy away from; start with surprise: *the mind boggles.* ~*n.* The act of boggling. [Probably from *boggle,* Northern dialectal variant of BOGLE.] **—bog·gler** *n.*

bog·gy (bógi ‖ *U.S. also* báwgi) *adj.* **-gier, -giest. 1.** Like a bog; swampy. **2.** Full of bogs. **—bog·gi·ness** *n.*

bo·gie[1]**, bo·gy** (bṓgi) *n., pl.* **bogies. 1.** A railway coach or locomotive undercarriage with two, four, or six wheels that swivel so that curves may be negotiated. **2.** One of several wheels or supporting and aligning rollers inside the track of a tractor or tank. In this sense, also called "bogie wheel".

bogie[2]**.** Variant of **bogy** (hobgoblin).

bo·gle (bṓg'l) *n.* A hobgoblin, a **bogy** *(see).* [Scottish *bogill;* akin to Welsh *bwg,* ghost, *bwgwl,* menace.]

bog moss *n.* **Peat moss** *(see).*

bog myrtle *n.* A fragrant shrub, *Myrica gale,* with narrow, oval leaves, and orange male catkins or reddish female catkins on separate plants. Also called "gale", "sweet gale".

Bog·nor Re·gis (bóg-nər réejiss). Resort town on the coast of West Sussex, in southern England. It gained the title "Regis" after George V convalesced there in 1929.

bo·gong (bŏ-gong) *n.* Also **bu·gong** (boō-). An edible nocturnal Australian moth, regarded as a delicacy by Aborigines. [From a native Australian language.]

bog orchid *n.* An orchid, *Malaxis* (or *Hammarkya*) *paludosa,* growing in bogs, with yellow-green flowers and oval leaves that usually have small bulbils on their edges.

Bo·go·tá (Santa Fé de) bógga-taá ‖ *Chiefly U.S.* bŏga-). Largest city and capital of Colombia, on a high plateau in the Andes mountains where several rivers meet to form the Bogotá River.

bog rosemary *n.* A low-growing evergreen shrub, *Andromeda polifolia,* growing in wet ground, and having small pink bell-like flowers. Also called "marsh andromeda", "moorwort".

bog rush *n.* A densely tufted plant, *Schoenus nigricans,* with narrow, wiry leaves and stems carrying black, pointed spikes.

bog·trot·ter (bóg-tróttə ‖ *U.S. also* báwg-) *n. Slang.* An Irishman. Used derogatorily.

bo·gus (bógəss) *adj.* Counterfeit; fake. [19th century (U.S.) : perhaps of African origin; compare Hausa *boko,* deceit, fraud.]

bog·wood (bóg-woŏd ‖ *U.S. also* báwg-) *n.* Wood that has been preserved in a peat bog. Also called "bog oak".

bo·gy¹, bo·gie, bo·gey (bógi) *n., pl.* **-gies.** 1. An evil or mischievous spirit; a hobgoblin. Also called "bogle". 2. Something that causes annoyance or harassment. [Originally used as proper name; compare BOGLE, BUGBEAR.] —**bo·gy·ism** *n.*

bogy². Variant of **bogie¹**.

bogyman. Variant of **bogeyman**.

bo·hea (bō-hée) *n.* A black Chinese tea. The name originally referred to the choicest grade but later was applied to an inferior variety. [Chinese (Fujian dialect) *bu-i,* corresponding to Mandarin *wŭ-yí,* after *Wu-yi Shan,* a range of hills in northern Fujian Province, where the black tea is grown.]

Bo·he·mi·a¹ (bō-héemi-ə). *Czech* **Če·chy** (chékhi). A historic region of the present-day Czech Republic, and a former kingdom. The Czechs, a west Slav people, settled in the area between the first and the fifth centuries A.D. They maintained the independence of Bohemia until the 15th century, when the crown passed to Hungary and then to the Habsburgs. Nationalist efforts by the Czechs in the 19th century failed to re-establish an independent Bohemia and it became a province of the new republic of Czechoslovakia (1918), losing its provincial status in an administrative reorganisation (1948).

Bohemia² *n. Often small* **b.** 1. A community of persons with artistic or literary tastes whose manners and moral standards are unconventional. 2. The district in which they live.

Bo·he·mi·an (bō-héem-yən, -i-ən) *n.* 1. A native or inhabitant of Bohemia. 2. *Archaic.* The language of the Czechs. 3. *Often small* **b.** A person with artistic or literary interests who disregards conventional standards of behaviour. —**Bo·he·mi·an** *adj.* —**Bo·he·mi·an·ism** *n.*

Bohemian Brethren *pl.n.* A Protestant religious society organised in the 15th century by the Hussites.

Böhm (berm ‖ bŏm; *German* bŏm), **Karl** (1894–1981). Austrian conductor. He was conductor of the Vienna State Opera (1943–45 and 1954–56), and, throughout his career, was closely associated with the Vienna Philharmonic.

Böhm, Theobald (1794–1881). German flautist and flute-maker. In 1828 he founded a factory at Munich and by 1832 had produced the first *Böhm flute,* in which the fingerholes were covered by keys, the prototype of the modern flute.

Bohr (bor ‖ bōr), **Niels (Henrik David)** (1885–1962). Danish physicist. His pioneering theoretical work used quantum theory to explain and develop the nuclear model of the atom put forward by Ernest Rutherford. He was awarded the Nobel prize in physics (1922).

Bohr-Som·mer·feld theory (bór-zómmər-felt) *n.* A modification of the Bohr theory, allowing for elliptical as well as circular orbits. [After Arnold *Sommerfeld* (1868–1951), German physicist who produced the modification.]

Bohr theory *n.* A model of atomic structure, in which electrons travel around the nucleus in certain orbits representing specific energy states determined by quantum theory, a jump from one orbit to another being accompanied by the emission or absorption of a quantum of energy. The model explains the spectrum of the hydrogen atom. [After Niels BOHR.]

bo·hunk (bō-hungk) *n. U.S. Slang.* A person from east-central Europe, especially a labourer. Used derogatorily. [Bohemian + Hungarian.]

boil¹ (boyl) *v.* **boiled, boiling, boils.** —*intr.* 1. To vaporise a liquid by the application of heat. 2. To reach **boiling point** *(see).* 3. To undergo the action of boiling; especially, to cook by boiling. 4. To be in a state of agitation, as boiling water; seethe. 5. To be greatly excited, as with rage or passion. —*tr.* 1. To heat to boiling point. 2. To cook or clean by boiling. 3. To separate by evaporation as a result of boiling. —**boil away.** To evaporate by boiling. —**boil down.** 1. To reduce in bulk or size by boiling. 2. To condense or summarise. —**boil down to.** To be in essence; amount to. —**boil over.** 1. To overflow while boiling. 2. To explode in rage or passion. —**boil up.** *Australian & N.Z.* To make tea.

~*n.* The state, condition, or act of boiling. [Middle English *boillen,* from Old French *bo(u)illir,* from Latin *bullīre,* to bubble, boil.]

boil² *n.* A painful swelling of the skin and subcutaneous tissue with a hard pus-filled centre, caused by bacterial infection, usually occurring at a hair follicle. Also called "furuncle". Compare **carbuncle.** [Middle English *bile, bule, boyl,* Old English *bȳl, bȳle.*]

Boi·leau or **Boi·leau-Des·pré·aux** (bwaa-lō; -day-práy-ō, -pray-ó), **Nicolas** (1636–1711). French poet and critic. His most celebrated work, *The Art of Poetry* (1674), a treatise in verse, was a comprehensive summation of classical rules and conventions in French literature.

boiled sweet (boyld) *n.* A hard sweet made of boiled sugar.

boil·er (bóylər) *n.* 1. An enclosed vessel in which water is heated and circulated, either as hot water or as steam, for heating or power. 2. A container for boiling liquids, such as a double boiler. 3. A large metal tub for boiling laundry. 4. A hen, usually old and tough, to be cooked by boiling. Also called "boiling fowl". 5. *Australian Informal.* A nagging old woman; an old hag.

boil·er·mak·er (bóylər-maykər) *n.* Metalworker who works in heavy industry, for example shipbuilding, especially a welder. —**boil·er·mak·ing** *n.*

boil·er·plate (bóylər-playt) *n.* A steel plate used in making the shells of steam boilers.

boiler suit *n.* 1. A hard-wearing workman's suit combining shirt and overalls in one piece. 2. A fashionable garment resembling this, worn especially by women.

boil·ing (bóyling) *adj. Informal.* Very hot.
~*adv.* Used as an intensive: *boiling hot.*

boiling point *n.* 1. *Abbr.* **bp, b.p.** The temperature at which a liquid boils, especially under standard atmospheric conditions. 2. *Informal.* The point at which a person loses his temper.

boil·ing-wa·ter reactor (bóyling-wawtər) *n. Abbr.* **BWR** A type of nuclear reactor in which boiling water is used as both moderator and coolant.

boil off *tr.v.* To remove (impurities) from a liquid mixture by boiling. —*intr.v.* To be removed by boiling. Used of impurities, fractions, and the like in liquid mixtures.

boil-off (bóyl-off, -awf) *n.* The vaporisation of a liquid, such as a rocket fuel.

Bois de Bou·logne (bwaä də bŏ-lóyn, boō-). A large park in west Paris that includes the race courses of Auteuil and Longchamps.

bois de rose (bwaä də rōz) *n.* Dusty deep pink. [French, "rosewood".]

Boi·se (bóy-si, -zi). Capital and largest city of the state of Idaho in the western United States, situated on the Boise river.

bois·ter·ous (bóystrəss, bóystərəss) *adj.* 1. Rough and stormy; violent and turbulent. 2. Loud, noisy, and unrestrained. [Middle English *boistres,* variant of *boist(e)ous†,* rude, fierce, stout.] —**bois·ter·ous·ly** *adv.* —**bois·ter·ous·ness** *n.*

Bok·mål (bŏŏk-mawl, bóōk-) *n.* One of the two officially recognised and mutually intelligible forms of Norwegian. It is the language in which newspapers and most literature are written. Also called "Dano-Norwegian", formerly "Riksmål". Compare **Nynorsk.** [Norwegian, "book language".]

Bokhara. See Bukhara.

bo·ko, bo·co (bŏkō) *n. Chiefly Australian.* An animal that has lost one eye.

bo·la (bóla) *n., pl.* **bolas** or *rare* **bolases.** Also **bo·las** (bólass). A rope with weights attached, used in South America to catch cattle or game by entangling the legs. [American Spanish *bolas,* plural of Spanish *bola,* ball, from Latin *bulla,* bubble, round object.]

bold (bōld) *adj.* **bolder, boldest.** 1. Fearless and daring; courageous. 2. Requiring or exhibiting courage and bravery. 3. Unduly forward and brazen in manner. 4. Clear and distinct to the eye; standing out prominently: *bold handwriting.* 5. Steep, as a cliff. 6. *Printing.* Designating thick, heavy type; bold-face. See Synonyms at **brave, shameless.** —**make bold.** *Archaic.* To take the liberty; dare. [Middle English *bold,* Old English *bald, beald.*] —**bold·ly** *adv.* —**bold·ness** *n.*

bold face *n. Abbr.* **bf, bf., b.f., bld.** *Printing.* Type that has thick, heavy lines so as to give a conspicuous black impression. Compare **light face.** —**bold-face** (bóld-fayss) *adj.*

bold-faced (bóld-fayst) *adj.* 1. Impudent; brazen. 2. **a.** Printed or set in bold face. **b.** Marked for printing in bold face.

bole¹ (bōl) *n.* The trunk of a tree. [Middle English, from Old Norse *bolr.*]

bole² *n.* 1. Any of various fine soft clays; especially, a reddish-brown variety used as a pigment. 2. Moderate reddish brown. [Middle English, a red clay, from Medieval Latin *bōlus,* clod of earth, BOLUS.]

bo·lec·tion (bō-léksh'n) *n. Architecture.* A moulding that projects from the surface of a panel. [18th century : origin obscure.]

bo·le·ro (bə-laír-ō-; *also, in sense 1 only,* bóllarō) *n., pl.* **-ros.** 1. A short jacket or waistcoat, often with no front fastening, usually worn by women. 2. A Spanish dance in triple time. 3. The music for this dance. [Spanish, apparently from *bola,* ball. See **bola.**]

bo·le·tus (bə-léet-əss, bō-) *n., pl.* **-tuses** or **-ti** (-ee). Any fungus of the genus *Boletus,* having an umbrella-shaped cap with spore-bearing tubules on the underside. Some species are poisonous and others edible. [New Latin *Boletus,* from Latin *bōlētus†,* fungus.]

Bo·leyn (bə-lín) or **Bul·len** (bŏŏllin), **Anne** (c.1507–36). Second wife of Henry VIII and mother of Elizabeth I. In order to marry her

Henry VIII divorced his first wife, Catherine of Aragon, thus breaking with the Roman Catholic Church and providing the occasion for the official Reformation in England. Henry and Anne were secretly married (January 1533). She produced no male heir, and was convicted of adultery and beheaded (1536).

bo·lide (bṓlĭd) *n.* A meteoric fireball. [French, from Latin *bolis,* from Greek *bolis†,* missile.]

bol·i·var (bóllǐ-vaar ‖ -vər) *n., pl.* **-vars** or Spanish **bolivares**. *Abbr.* **b., B.** 1. The basic monetary unit of Venezuela, equal to 100 centimos. 2. A coin worth one bolivar. [After Simón Bolívar.]

Bo·lí·var (bo-lée-vaar, bólli-, -vər), **Simón** (1783–1830). Venezuelan revolutionary hero, known as "The Liberator". He defeated the Spanish forces at Boyaca (1819) and was made president of Greater Colombia (now Colombia, Venezuela, and Ecuador). He helped to liberate Peru and present-day Bolivia (named after him) and became the most powerful man on the continent.

Bo·liv·i·a (bə-lívvi-ə). A landlocked republic in central western South America. The largest and most important city is La Paz. The country was named after Simón Bolívar who helped win its independence from Spain (1825). The western half of the country is dominated by the Andes mountains and includes the high, populated plateau of the Altiplano, 3 900 metres (13,000 feet) high, containing Lake Titicaca; the east is a lowland region of forests and plains. Most of the population is concentrated in the southern Andes plateau. Area, 1 098 581 square kilometres (424,165 square miles). Population, 7,590,000. Capital, Sucre. —**Bo·liv·i·an** *adj. & n.*

boll (bōl) *n.* The rounded seed pod of certain plants, such as flax or cotton. [Middle English *bolle,* from Middle Dutch.]

Böll (berl ‖ bŏl; *German* bŏl), **Heinrich** (1917–85). German writer. His novels include *Tomorrow and Yesterday* (1957), *The Clown* (1963), and *The Lost Honour of Katharina Blum* (1975). He was awarded the Nobel prize for literature in 1972.

bol·lard (bóllaard, bóllərd) *n.* 1. A small marker post on a traffic island. 2. A post placed on a pavement, path, or street to prevent traffic from driving or parking there. 3. A thick post on a ship or wharf, used for securing ropes and hawsers. [Middle English : probably BOLE (tree trunk) + -ARD.]

bol·loc·king (bólləking) *n. Slang.* A telling-off; a severe reprimand.

bol·locks, bal·locks, bol·lix (bólləks) *pl.n.* 1. *Vulgar.* The testicles. 2. *Vulgar Slang.* Nonsense.

~*interj. Vulgar Slang.* Used to express annoyance or disbelief.

~ *tr.v.* **bollock(s)ed, -lock(s)ing, -locks(es).** *Vulgar Slang.* 1. To bungle or botch. Usually used with *up.* 2. To give a severe reprimand to. [Old English *beallucas,* diminutive (plural) or *beallu* (unattested), BALL. See **-ock**.]

boll weevil *n.* A small, greyish, long-snouted beetle, *Anthonomus grandis,* of Mexico and the southern United States, having destructive larvae that hatch in and damage cotton bolls.

boll·worm (bṓl-wurm) *n.* The larval stage of various moths, such as *Pectinophora gossypiella,* that feeds on and destroys cotton bolls.

Bo·lo·gna¹ (bə-lṓn-yə, -lṓn-). An industrial town in the Emilia-Romagna region of northern central Italy. It has one of the world's oldest universities, established in the 11th century.

Bologna² (bə-lṓni) *n.* **Polony** *(see).* [After Bologna, where it was originally made.]

bo·lom·e·ter (bō-lómmitər, bə-) *n.* An instrument that measures radiant heat by detecting the change in electrical resistance produced in prepared metal foil strips by the heating effect of the incident radiation. [Greek *bolē,* beam, ray + -METER.] —**bo·lo·met·ric** (bṓ-lə-méttrik, -lō-) *adj.*

Bol·she·vik (ból-shə-vik, -shi-, -she- ‖ bŏl-) *n., pl.* **-viks** or **viki** (-véeki). 1. **a.** A member of the Communist Party of the Soviet Union. **b.** A member of the left-wing majority group of the Russian Social Democratic Party adopting Lenin's theses on party organisation (1903). Compare **Menshevik.** 2. *Loosely,* a Communist. 3. *Often small* **b.** Any extreme radical : *a literary bolshevik.* Used derogatorily. [Russian *Bol'shevik,* "one of the majority" : *bol'shii,* greater, from *bol'shoi,* large + noun suffix *-vik.*] —**Bol·she·vik** *adj.*

Bol·she·vism (ból-shə-viz'm, -shi-, -she- ‖ bŏl-) *n.* 1. The strategy developed by the Bolsheviks between 1903 and 1917 with a view to seizing state power and establishing the dictatorship of the proletariat. 2. Soviet Communism. 3. *Often small* **b.** Loosely, extreme radicalism in politics, art, or the like.

Bol·she·vist (ból-shə-vist, -shi-, -she- ‖ bŏl-) *n.* A Bolshevik. —**Bol·she·vist, Bol·she·vis·tic** (-vístik) *adj.*

bol·shie, bol·shy (ból-shi ‖ bŏl-) *adj. Informal.* 1. Uncooperative; difficult. 2. Bolshevist.

~*n., pl.* **-shies.** A Bolshevik. Used derogatorily. [Shortened from Bolshevik.]

bol·ster (bṓl-stər ‖ bŏl-) *n.* 1. A long, narrow pillow or cushion, typically hard and stiff. 2. A structural support, such as a horizontal bar across the top of a post or column.

~*tr.v.* **bolstered, -stering, -sters.** 1. To support or prop up, as with a pillow. 2. To support or strengthen: *bolster one's confidence.* 3. To apply padding to. [Middle English *bolster,* Old English *bolster,* cushion.] —**bol·ster·er** *n.*

bolt¹ (bōlt ‖ bolt) *n.* 1. A bar made of wood or metal that slides into a socket and is used to fasten doors and gates. 2. A metal bar or rod in the mechanism of a lock, thrown or withdrawn by turning the key. 3. A fastener consisting of an externally threaded cylindrical piece, formed from a pin, rod, or wire and having a head at one end. It is designed to be inserted through holes in assembled parts and secured by a mating nut that is tightened by application of torque. 4. **a.** A sliding metal bar that positions the cartridge in breech-loading rifles, closes the breech, and ejects the spent cartridge. **b.** A similar device in any breech mechanism. 5. A short, heavy arrow with a thick head, used especially with a crossbow. 6. A flash of lightning or a thunderbolt. 7. A sudden movement towards or away from something. 8. A large roll of cloth of a definite length, especially as it comes from the loom. —**bolt from the blue.** A sudden, usually shocking, surprise. —**shoot (one's) bolt.** To do all that one can; exhaust one's resources.

~*v.* **bolted, bolting, bolts.** —*tr.* 1. To secure or lock with or as if with a bolt or bolts. 2. To arrange or roll (lengths of cloth, for example) on a bolt. 3. To eat hurriedly and with little chewing; gulp. 4. *Archaic.* To shoot or discharge (an arrow or other missile). —*intr.* 1. To move or spring suddenly towards or from something. 2. To break from the rider's control and run away. Used of a horse. 3. To make off suddenly; run away. 4. *Horticulture.* To flower and produce seeds prematurely.

~*adv.* Rigidly straight. Used in the phrase *bolt upright.* [Middle English *bolt,* Old English *bolt,* heavy arrow.] —**bolt·er** *n.*

bolt², **boult** *tr.v.* **bolted, bolting, bolts.** To pass through a sieve; sift. [Middle English *bulten, bolten,* from Old French *buleter,* from Middle Dutch *biutelen.*] —**bolt·er** *n.*

Bolt (bōlt), **Robert (Oxton)** (1924–95). British playwright. His most popular successes were *A Man for All Seasons* (1960) and *Vivat! Vivat Regina!* (1970). He also wrote numerous screenplays and won Academy Awards for *Dr. Zhivago* (1965) and *A Man for All Seasons* (1966).

bolt hole *n.* A way or means of escape.

Bol·ton (bṓltən). Industrial town and Unitary Authority area northwest of Manchester, in northwest England. It was the centre of the woollen trade from the 14th to the 18th century, when its economy shifted to cotton-spinning.

bolt-on (bṓlt-on) *adj.* 1. Capable of being attached by bolts. 2. Additional; supplementary: *a bolt-on clause to the contract.*

bolt·rope (bōlt-rōp) *n.* A rope sewn into the outer edge of a sail to prevent the sail from tearing.

Boltz·mann (bólts-man, bŏlts-, -mən), **Ludwig** (1844–1906). Austrian physicist, one of the founders of modern physics, whose chief contribution was in the kinetic theory of gases. He developed the law known as the **Stefan-Boltzmann law.**

Boltzmann constant *n. Physics. Symbol* **k** The ratio of the universal gas constant to the Avogadro constant. It has the value $1.380\ 622 \times 10^{-23}$ joule per kelvin. [After Ludwig Boltzmann.]

bo·lus (bṓləss) *n., pl.* **-luses.** 1. A soft, small, round mass, particularly of chewed food. 2. *Pharmacology.* A large pill or tablet. [Medieval Latin *bōlus,* from Greek *bōlos†,* lump, clod.]

bo·ma (bómmə, báwmə) *n.* In Central and East Africa: 1. A protective enclosure for domestic animals; a camp; a stockade. 2. A military or police post. 3. A magistrate's office. [Swahili.]

Bo·ma (bṓmə). A port and railway terminus on the river Congo in southwest Congo. It was an important slave market up to the 19th century and was the capital of the Congo Free State (the Belgian Congo after 1908) from 1886 to 1926.

bomb (bom ‖ *rarely* bum) *n.* 1. An explosive weapon detonated by impact, proximity to an object, a timing mechanism, or other predetermined means. 2. Any of various weapons detonated to release smoke, gas, pellets, poisons, or other destructive materials. 3. A

container for a radioactive substance used in radiotherapy: *a cobalt bomb*. **4.** A spherical mass of molten rock ejected into the air during a volcanic eruption. **5.** *Slang*. A lot of money: *it cost a bomb*. **6.** *Australian & N.Z. Slang*. An old car. **7.** A jump made into the water, with the knees tucked under the chin and encircled by the arms, causing a large splash. **8.** *U.S. Slang*. A dismal failure or complete fiasco. **—like a bomb.** *Informal*. **1.** Very fast. **2.** Very successfully. **—the bomb.** Often capital **B. 1.** The atom or hydrogen bomb. **2.** Nuclear weapons collectively.
~v. **bombed, bombing, bombs.** *—tr.* To attack, damage, or destroy with a bomb or bombs. *—intr.* **1.** To drop a bomb or bombs. **2.** *Slang*. To go, especially to drive, quickly. Often used with *along*. **3.** *U.S. Slang*. To fail miserably. Usually used with *out*. **—bomb out.** To render homeless by dropping a bomb on. [French *bombe*, from Italian *bomba*, probably from Latin *bombus*, booming, humming, from Greek *bombos*.]

bom·bard (bóm-baard) *n.* An early form of cannon that fired stone balls.
~tr.v. (bom-bárd) **bombarded, -barding, -bards. 1.** To attack with bombs, explosive shells, or missiles. **2.** To attack persistently with arguments, criticism, or the like. **3.** *Physics.* To subject (an atom, nucleus, or the like) to a stream of high energy particles. **4.** *Archaic.* To attack with a bombard. **—See Synonyms at attack.** [Middle English *bombarde*, cannon, from Old French, from Medieval Latin *bombarda*, probably from Latin *bombus*, booming. See **bomb.**] **—bom·bard·er** *n.* **—bom·bard·ment** *n.*

bom·bar·dier (bóm-bər-deér) *n.* **1.** *Military.* The member of an aircraft crew who operates the bombing equipment. **2.** *British.* A corporal in the artillery. **3.** Formerly, a soldier who operated a bombard. [French, from Old French *bombarde*, BOMBARD.]

bombardier beetle *n.* Any of various beetles of the genus *Brachinus* and related genera, that expel an acrid secretion from the posterior end of the abdomen.

bom·bar·don (bom-bárd'n, bóm-bər-dən) *n.* **1.** A brass musical instrument resembling a tuba but with a lower pitch; a bass or contrabass tuba. **2.** A 16-foot reed stop on the organ. [French, from Italian *bombardone*, augmentative of *bombardo*, from *bombarda*, bombard, from Medieval Latin. See **bombard.**]

bom·bast (bóm-bast) *n.* **1.** Grandiloquent and pompous speech or writing. **2.** Formerly, a soft material used for padding. [Earlier *bombace*, cotton padding, from Old French, from Late Latin *bombax*, cotton, silk, alteration of Latin *bombyx*, silkworm, silk, from Greek *bombux*, of Oriental origin, akin to Turkish *pambuk*, cotton.] **—bom·bast·er** *n.*

bom·bas·tic (bom-bástik) *adj.* Characterised by bombast; pompous; grandiloquent. **—bom·bas·ti·cal·ly** *adv.*

bom·bax (bóm-baks) *n.* Any of various trees of the genus *Bombax*, especially the cotton tree. [New Latin, from Late Latin. See **bombast.**]

bombax cotton *n.* The silky, cotton-like fibre produced by various trees of the genus *Bombax*.

Bom·bay (bóm-báy). An industrial city and port on the northwest coast of India, built on the islands of Bombay and Salsette. It is the capital of Maharashtra state, where it is officially known as Mumbai, and India's main seaport and commercial centre.

Bombay bloomers *pl.n. Australian Informal.* Loose-fitting shorts worn for playing sport.

Bombay duck *n.* **1.** A food fish, *Harpodon nehereus*, of India. **2.** The dried flesh of this fish eaten as a savoury.

bom·ba·zine (bóm-bə-zeen, -zéen) *n.* Also **bom·ba·sine** (-seen, -séen). A fine twilled fabric of silk and worsted or cotton, often dyed black and used for mourning clothes. [French *bombasin*, from Late Latin *bombacīnum*, variant of *bombȳcīnum*, from Latin, neuter of *bombȳcīnus*, silken, from *bombyx*, silk. See **bombast.**]

bomb bay *n.* The compartment in the fuselage of a military aircraft from which bombs are dropped.

bomb calorimeter *n.* A device used to measure the calorific value of fuels, foods, and the like by burning them in oxygen at high pressure and noting the rise in temperature of the calorimeter and its contents.

bomb disposal *n.* The rendering harmless, removal, or safe detonation of unexploded bombs.

bombe (bomb ‖ bom) *n.* A frozen dessert consisting of a mould or melon containing two or more layers of ice cream of different flavours or textures. [French, "bomb" (from its shape).]

bombed (bomd) *adj. Slang.* Drunk or under the influence of drugs.

bomb·er (bómmər) *n.* **1.** A military aircraft designed to carry and drop bombs. **2.** One who plants or drops bombs.

bom·bo·ra, bom·boo·ra (bom-báwrə) *n. Australian.* A dangerous stretch of water above a submerged reef. [From a native Australian language.]

bomb·proof (bóm-proof ‖ -proof) *adj.* Designed and constructed to resist destruction by bombs.

bomb rack *n.* A framework or mechanical holder for bombs on a military aircraft.

bomb·shell (bóm-shel) *n.* **1.** A bomb. **2.** A shocking surprise. **3.** A stunningly attractive woman.

bomb shelter *n.* A shelter, often below ground, built to withstand attacks by bombs.

bomb·sight (bóm-sīt) *n.* A device in aircraft for aiming bombs.

bomb·site (bóm-sīt) *n.* Also **bomb site.** A derelict area, often an open space, where the buildings have been destroyed by bombing.

bom·by·cid (bómbi-sid) *n.* Any moth of the family Bombycidae,

which now includes only the silkworm moths.
~adj. Of, pertaining to, or belonging to the Bombycidae. [New Latin *Bombycidae*, from Latin *bombyx*, silkworm. See **bombast.**]

Bon (bōn, bawn) *n.* A Japanese Buddhist festival held in July to honour ancestral spirits. Also called "Feast of Lanterns". [Japanese *bon*, basin, sacrificial vessel (later used as a festive lantern), from Chinese (Mandarin) *pén*.]

bo·na fi·de (bóna fídi ‖ bónnə, *U.S. chiefly* fíd) *adj.* **1.** Done or made in good faith; sincere: *a bona fide offer*. **2.** Authentic; genuine: *a bona fide Rembrandt*. [Latin, "in good faith".]

bona fi·des (fídeez) *n. Law.* Honest intention; good faith. [Latin, "good faith".]

Usage: Bona fides is a singular Latin noun that takes a singular verb: *His bona fides is not in question.* Use of a plural verb is incorrect, and arises from confusion over the adjectival form *bona fide*, as in *a bona fide traveller*.

bo·nan·za (bə-nánzə) *n.* **1.** Any source of great wealth or prosperity. **2.** *U.S.* A rich mine, vein, or pocket of ore. [Spanish, fair weather, prosperity, from Vulgar Latin *bonacia* (unattested), from Latin *bonus*, good (after Latin *malacia*, calm at sea, taken as if from *malus*, bad).]

Bo·na·parte (bóna-paart), **Jérôme** (1784–1860). Napoleon's youngest brother, king of Westphalia (1807–13). He lost the Westphalian crown when Germany was liberated from Napoleon (1813). He then took part in the French army's campaigns and fought at Waterloo. He became marshal of France (1850) and president of the senate under **Napoleon III.**

Bonaparte, Joseph (1768–1844). Napoleon's eldest brother, king of Naples (1805–08) and of Spain (1808–13).

Bonaparte, Louis (1778–1846). Brother of Napoleon and king of Holland (1806–10). He served with Napoleon in the Italian campaign (1796–97) and was his aide-de-camp in Egypt (1798–99). He was the father of **Napoleon III.**

Bonaparte, Lucien (1775–1840). Brother of Napoleon. He played an important part in Napoleon's coup of 18 Brumaire (1799) but, disillusioned with his brother's policies, he went to Italy. He was reconciled with Napoleon during his brief exile at Elba.

Bonaparte, Napoleon. See **Napoleon I.**

Bo·na·part·ist (bóna-paartist) *n.* A follower or supporter of Napoleon Bonaparte, his policies and dynastic claims, or of the Bonaparte family. **—Bo·na·part·ism** *n.*

bon ap·pe·tit (bón appe-tée) *interj.* Used to wish someone a good appetite and a pleasant meal. [French.]

bo·na va·can·ti·a (bónə və-kánti-ə) *pl.n. Law.* Unclaimed goods. [Latin, goods without an owner.]

bon·bon (bón-bon) *n.* A sweet, usually having a centre of fondant, fruit, or nuts, and coated with chocolate or fondant. [French, baby-talk reduplication of *bon*, good, from Latin *bonus*.]

bonce (bonss) *n. British Slang.* The head. [19th century : origin obscure.]

bond (bond) *n.* **1.** Anything that binds, ties, or fastens together, as: **a.** A shackle; a fetter. **b.** A cord, rope, or band. **2.** *Usually plural.* Captivity; confinement. **3.** *Often plural.* A uniting force or tie; a link. **4.** A binding agreement; a covenant. **5.** The duty, promise, or obligation by which one is bound: "*To trust a man on his oath or bond*" (Shakespeare). **6. a.** A substance or an agent that causes two or more objects or parts to cohere. **b.** Such a union or cohesion. **7.** *Chemistry.* A chemical bond (*see*). **8.** *Law.* **a.** Any written and sealed obligation, especially one requiring payment of a stipulated amount of money on or before a given day. **b.** A sum of money paid as bail or surety. **9.** *Finance.* **a.** A certificate of debt issued by a government or corporation, guaranteeing payment of the original investment plus interest by a specified future date. **b.** *South African.* A company loan or mortgage on a house or property. **10.** See **premium bond. 11.** The state or condition of storing taxable goods in a warehouse until the taxes or duties due on them are paid. Used chiefly in the phrase *in bond*. **12.** Any overlapping arrangement of bricks or other masonry components in a wall. **13.** Bond paper.
~v. **bonded, bonding, bonds.** *—tr.* **1.** To mortgage or place a guaranteed bond on. **2.** To furnish a bond or surety for. **3.** To join securely, as with glue or cement. **4.** To lay (bricks or other building materials) in an overlapping pattern for solidity. *—intr.* To secure or hold something together with or as if with a cord, rope, adhesive substance, or the like. [Middle English *bond, band,* from Old Norse *band*.] **—bond·a·ble** *adj.* **—bond·er** *n.*

Bond, Edward (1934–). British playwright. His plays include *Saved* (1965), *Lear* (1972), *The Women* (1978), *Restoration* (1981) and *In the Company of Men* (1990). He also wrote the libretto for the German composer Hans Werner Henze's opera, *We Come to the River* (1976).

bond·age (bóndij) *n.* **1.** The condition of a slave or serf; serfdom; servitude. **2.** A state of subjection to any force, power, or influence. **3.** In early English law, **villeinage** (*see*). **4.** The condition or practice of deriving sexual pleasure from being tied or chained up or tying or chaining up another. **—See Synonyms at servitude.**
~adj. Designating aggressive-looking clothing, usually of black leather, that is covered in studs, straps, or chains. [Middle English, from Anglo-Latin *bondāgium*, from Middle English *bonde*, serf, peasant, Old English *bōnda*, householder, from Old Norse *bóndi*, *būandi*, "tiller of the soil", husbandman, from the present participle of *búa*, to live, dwell.]

bonded warehouse *n.* A warehouse in which dutiable goods are stored pending payment of duty, or until they are exported.

bond·hold·er (bónd-hōldər) *n.* The owner of a bond or bonds.

bond·ing (bónding) *n. Anthropology.* The forming of close, specialised human relationships, such as those that link parent and child, husband and wife, or friend and friend.

bond·maid (bónd-mayd) *n.* A female bondservant.

bond paper *n.* A superior grade of strong white paper made wholly or in part from rag pulp. Also called "bond".

bond·ser·vant (bónd-servənt) *n.* **1.** A person obligated to service without wages. **2.** A slave or serf. Also called "bondslave". [*Bond-*, from Middle English *bonde*, serf. See **bondage**.]

bonds·man (bóndz-mən) *n., pl.* **-men** (-mən, -men). **1.** A male bondservant. **2.** A person who provides bond or surety for another.

bone (bōn) *n.* **1. a.** The dense, semirigid, porous, calcified connective tissue of the skeleton of most vertebrates. **b.** Any of numerous anatomically distinct skeletal structures made of this material. **c.** A piece of this material. **2.** *Plural.* **a.** The skeleton. **b.** The body. **3.** An animal structure or material, such as ivory, resembling bone. **4.** Something made of bone or of material resembling bone, especially: **a.** A piece of whalebone or similar material used as a corset stay. **b.** *Plural. Informal.* Dice. **5.** *Plural.* Essentials; basic principles. Used chiefly in the phrase *the bare bones.* **—feel in (one's) bones.** To have an intuition of. **—have a bone to pick with.** To have grounds for a dispute with. **—make no bones about.** To be frank and candid about. **—point the bone.** *Australian.* **1.** To cast a spell intended to cause someone's death. **2.** To curse or bring misfortune upon. Used with *at.*
~adv. Used as an intensive: *bone dry; bone idle.*
~tr.v. **boned, boning, bones. 1.** To remove the bones from. **2.** To stiffen (a corset or piece of clothing) with whalebone or similar material. **3.** To fertilise with bone meal. **—bone up.** *Informal.* To study intensively, usually at the last minute. Often used with *on.* [Middle English *bon, ban,* from Old English *bān,* from Germanic *bainam* (unattested).]

bone ash *n.* The white, powdery calcium phosphate ash of burnt bones, used as a fertiliser, in making ceramics, and in cleaning and polishing compounds.

bone-black (bón-blak) *n.* Also **bone black.** A black pigment containing about ten per cent charcoal, made by roasting bones in an airtight container, and used in polishes, as a filtering medium, and in decolorising sugar.

bone china *n.* Porcelain made of clay mixed with bone ash.

bone·fish (bón-fish) *n., pl.* **-fishes** or collectively **bonefish.** A marine game fish, *Albula vulpes,* of warm, shallow waters, having silvery scales. [From its many small bones.]

bone·head (bón-hed) *n. Slang.* A stupid or dense person. **—bone·head·ed** (-héddid, -heddid) *adj.* **—bone·head·ed·ness** *n.*

bone marrow *n.* The tissue contained in the bone cavities that in early life forms the blood cells and platelets.

bone meal *n.* Bones crushed and ground to a coarse powder, used as plant fertiliser and animal feed.

bone of contention *n.* Grounds or cause for dispute or disagreement; the subject of a dispute.

bone-pointer *n. Australian.* An Aboriginal regarded as having magical powers.

bon·er (bónər) *n. Slang.* A blunder. [BON(E) + -ER.]

bone·set·ter (bón-settər) *n.* A person with no medical qualifications who tends to broken bones or dislocated limbs.

bone shaker *n.* **1.** Formerly, a bicycle with solid tyres. **2.** An old car or other vehicle with poor suspension.

bone·yard (bón-yaard) *n. Informal.* A cemetery.

bon·fire (bón-fīr) *n.* A large outdoor fire. [Middle English *banefyre,* a fire in which bones were burned : BON(E) + FIRE.]

bonfire night *n.* **Guy Fawkes Night** (*see*).

bong (bong ‖ *Chiefly U.S. also* bawng) *n. U.S.* A deep ringing sound, as of a bell.
~v. **bonged, bonging, bongs.** *Chiefly U.S.* *—tr.* To announce or proclaim with or as if with a deep ringing sound: *bong the hour.* *—intr.* To ring. [Imitative.]

bon·go (bóng-gō) *n., pl.* **-gos.** An antelope, *Boocercus eurycerus,* of central Africa, having a reddish-brown coat with narrow, vertical, white stripes and spirally twisted horns. [Native African name.]

bongo drums *pl.n.* A pair of connected drums having parchment heads that can be tuned, played by beating with the hands. Also called "bongos", "bongoes". [American Spanish *bongó* (probably imitative).]

Bon·hoef·fer (bón-höffər), **Dietrich** (1906–45). German Protestant theologian and philosopher. In 1933 he denounced Hitler in a radio broadcast and two years later was forbidden to teach and banned from Berlin. He then worked for the anti-Nazi underground movement. In 1945, after spending two years in prison, during which time he wrote *Letters and Papers from Prison,* he was executed for alleged participation in a plot to assassinate Hitler. His most important philosophical work was his *Ethics,* compiled from his notes and published posthumously (1949).

bon·ho·mie (bónnə-mi, -mee ‖ -mée) *n.* An outgoing affable disposition; good nature; geniality. [French, from *bonhomme,* good-natured man.]

bon·i·face (bónni-fayss) *n.* An innkeeper. [After *Boniface,* an innkeeper in the *Beaux Stratagem,* by George FARQUHAR.]

Bon·i·face (bónni-fayss, -fass), **Saint** (c. 675–754). English monk, known as the Apostle of Germany. He was born in Devonshire and named Winfrid or Wynfrith. Pope Gregory II gave him the name of Boniface (718) and encouraged his missionary work in Germany. He was killed by pagans in Friesland. His feast day is June 5.

Bon·ing·ton (bónning-tən), **Sir Chris(tian John Storey)** (1934–). English mountain climber who took part in the first ascents of many peaks and was in the British expedition that made the first ascent of the southwest face of Mount Everest (1975). President, British Mountaineering Council (1988–91); knighted 1996.

bo·ni·to (bə-néetō) *n., pl.* **-tos** or collectively **bonito. 1.** Any of several marine food and game fishes of the genus *Sarda,* related to and resembling the tuna. **2.** Any of several similar fishes. [Spanish, "beautiful" (from its appearance), from Latin *bonus,* good.]

bonk (bongk) *v.* **bonked, bonking, bonks.** *—tr.* **1.** *Informal.* To hit; strike. **2.** *Slang.* To have sexual intercourse with. *—intr.* **1.** *Informal.* To make a hollow thudding or knocking sound. **2.** *Slang.* To have sexual intercourse.
~n. Informal. A blow; knock: *a bonk on the head.*
~interj. Informal. Used to imitate the sound of a blow. [Perhaps imitative.]

bon·kers (bóngkərz) *adj. British Informal.* Mad; eccentric. [20th century : origin obscure.]

bon mot (bón mō) *n., pl.* **bons mots** (mōz). A clever saying, usually a terse and apt witticism. [French, "good word".]

Bonn (bon). German city on the river Rhine in the western part of the country. It was founded as a Roman garrison (first century AD). Its baroque architectural character goes back to its rebuilding after being destroyed in 1685. Capital of West Germany from 1949, now seat of government until Berlin takes over by the year 2000.

bonne bouche (bón bōosh) *n., pl.* **bonnes bouches** (*pronounced as singular*). **1.** Something small and tasty, often eaten at the end of a meal. **2.** A short pleasing item, such as a musical encore. [French, "good mouth".]

bonne femme (fam ‖ fem) *adj.* Designating dishes cooked in a simple, homemade style. [French (*à la*) *bonne femme,* "(in the manner of) a good housewife".]

bon·net (bónnit) *n.* **1. a.** A cloth, head-covering, often with a brim, that is held in place by ribbons tied under the chin, and worn by babies, and formerly by women and girls. **b.** A hat shaped like a bonnet usually with a large brim at the front. **2.** *Scottish.* A cap with a small peak worn by men. **3.** *U.S.* A feather headdress worn by some American Indians. **4.** A removable metal plate over a valve or other machinery part. **5.** *British.* A hinged metal lid forming part of the body of a motor vehicle and providing access to the engine. Also *U.S.* "hood". **6.** A cowl on a chimney. **7.** *Nautical.* A strip of canvas laced to a fore-and-aft sail to increase sail area. [Middle English *bonet,* from Old French, from Medieval Latin *abonnis†,* cap.] **—bon·net·ed** *adj.*

bonnet monkey *n.* A macaque, *Macaca radiata,* having a thatch of hair on the head resembling a bonnet.

Bon·ne·ville Salt Flats (bónni-vil). A very flat region of the Great Salt Lake Desert, in northwest Utah, U.S.A., regularly used in attempts to set land speed records.

Bonnie Prince Charlie. See **Stuart, Charles Edward.**

bonnock. Variant of **bannock.**

bon·ny (bónni) *adj.* **-nier, -niest.** *Chiefly Northern British.* **1.** Pleasing or attractive to the eye; pretty; fair. **2.** Healthy; robust. **3.** Cheerful; pleasant. [Perhaps from Old French *bon,* good, from Latin *bonus.*] **—bon·ni·ly** *adv.* **—bon·ni·ness** *n.*

Bonny, Bight of. See **Biafra, Bight of.**

bon·ny·clab·ber (bónni-klabbər) *n. Regional & Archaic.* Sour clotted milk. [Probably from Irish *bainne clabair,* "milk of the churn-dasher" : *bainne,* milk, from Middle Irish *banne,* milk, drop + *clabair,* genitive of *clabaire†,* dasher (part of a churn).]

bo·no·bo (bə-nōbō) *n.* The **pygmy chimpanzee** (*see*).

bon·sai (bón-sī ‖ *U.S. also* -sī) *n., pl.* **bonsai. 1.** The art of producing dwarfed trees or shrubs by growing them from normal seed in small, shallow pots and restricting root and shoot growth by pruning. **2.** A tree or shrub grown by this method. [Japanese, "potted plant" : *bon,* basin, pot + *sai,* to plant.]

bon·sel·la, bon·se·la (bon-séllə) *n.* Also **ba·se·la** (baa-), **pa·se·la** (paa-). *South African.* A small gift or gratuity. [From a Bantu language.]

bon·spiel (bón-speel) *n. Scottish.* A curling match. [Probably from Dutch *bon(d)spel* (unattested), "league game" : *bond,* league, from Middle Dutch + *spel,* game, from Middle Dutch from Germanic *spillōn* (unattested), to play (see **spiel**).]

bon ton (bón tón) *n. Archaic.* **1.** Sophisticated manners; style. **2.** Stylish or fashionable society. [French, "good tone".]

bo·nus (bónəss) *n., pl.* **-nuses. 1.** Something given or paid in addition to the usual or expected, especially an extra payment to employees at Christmas or for higher productivity. **2.** An extra dividend paid to shareholders from profits. **3.** A dividend paid to policy-holders by an insurance company, and generally reinvested. **4.** An incidental, extra, or unexpected benefit. **5.** A premium paid for a loan. [Latin *bonus,* good.]

Synonyms: bonus, bounty, subsidy, grant, dividend, premium, reward, gratuity.

bonus issue *n.* A **scrip issue** (*see*).

bon vi·vant (bón vee-vón) *n., pl.* **bons vivants** (*pronounced as singular*). Also *English* or *pseudo-French* **bon vi·veur** (bón vee-vér ‖ -vóor) *pl.* **bons viveurs** (*pronounced as singular*). A person who enjoys good food and drink and lives luxuriously.

bon voy·age (bón vwaa-yaázh) *interj.* Used to wish a departing traveller a pleasant journey. [French, "good journey".]

bon·y (bŏni) *adj.* **-ier, -iest. 1.** Of, pertaining to, resembling, or made of bone. **2.** Having an internal skeleton of bones rather than cartilage. Said of fish. **3.** Having many bones. **4.** Having protruding or prominent bones; lean; gaunt. **—bon·i·ness** *n.*

bonze (bonz) *n.* A Mahayana Buddhist monk, especially of China, Japan, and adjacent countries. [French *bonze* or Portuguese *bonzo,* from Japanese *bonsō,* from Chinese *fàn sēng* : *fàn,* Buddhist, from Sanskrit *brahmanas* + *sēng* monk.]

bon·zer (bónzər) *adj. Australian Slang.* Excellent; very good. [Perhaps from BONANZA.]

boo (bōō) *n., pl.* **boos.** A vocal sound uttered to show contempt, scorn, or disapproval.
~interj. Used to frighten or surprise, or to express disapproval or derision.
~v. **booed, booing, boos.** *—intr.* To utter "boo." *—tr.* To say "boo" to; jeer at. [Imitative.]

boob (bōōb) *n. Slang.* **1.** A foolish and embarrassing mistake. **2.** A woman's breast. **3.** A stupid or foolish person; a simpleton. [Short for BOOBY; sense 2, probably from BUB (breast).]

boo-boo (bōō-bōō) *n., pl.* **-boos.** *Slang.* A stupid or thoughtless mistake; a blunder. [From BOOB (mistake).]

boob tube *n.* **1.** A strapless elasticated bodice worn as a top by women. **2.** *U.S. Slang.* A television set.

boo·by (bōōbi) *n., pl.* **-bies. 1.** *Informal.* A stupid or childish person. **2.** *Vulgar Slang.* A woman's breast. **3.** Any of several tropical sea birds of the genus *Sula,* typically with brightly coloured bills and feet, resembling and related to the gannets. [Spanish *bobo,* from Latin *balbus,* stammering.]

booby hatch *n.* **1.** *Nautical.* A raised covering over a small hatchway. **2.** *U.S. Slang.* A mental hospital. [Sense 1, from BOOBY (bird), since these birds commonly light there at sea. Sense 2, from BOOBY (stupid person).]

booby prize *n.* An insignificant or comical prize given to the person who receives the lowest score in a game or contest.

booby trap *n.* **1.** A concealed or camouflaged explosive device designed to be detonated by some unsuspecting action of the intended victim. **2.** A practical joke in the form of a concealed device designed to catch the intended victim unawares. **3.** Any device or situation that catches a person off guard.

boo·by-trap (bōōbi-trap) *tr.v.* **-trapped, -trapping, -traps.** To fit with a booby trap.

boo·dle (bōōd'l) *n. Slang.* **1.** Money, especially money accepted as a bribe. **2.** *U.S.* A crowd or mob; a caboodle.
~v. **boodled, -dling, -dles.** *Chiefly U.S. Slang. —intr.* To accept a bribe. *—tr.* To bribe or swindle. [Dutch *boedel,* estate, effects, from Middle Dutch *bōdel,* riches, property.] **—boo·dler** *n.*

boo·gie (bōōgi ‖ *U.S.* bŏōgi) *n.* A fast type of rock'n'roll dance.
~intr.v. **boogied, -gieing, -gies.** To perform such a dance. [Shortened from BOOGIE-WOOGIE.]

boogieman. *Chiefly U.S.* Variant of **bogeyman.**

boog·ie-woog·ie (bōōgi-wōōgi ‖ *U.S.* bŏōgi-wŏōgi) *n.* A style of jazz piano-playing characterised by a repeated rhythmic and melodic pattern in the bass. [20th century : probably of African origin; compare Hausa *buga,* to beat (drums), West African English (Sierra Leone), *bogi(bogi),* to dance.] **—boog·ie-woog·ie** *adj.*

boo-hoo (bōō-hōō) *intr.v.* **-hooed, -hooing, -hoos.** To weep or pretend to weep noisily.
~n., pl. **boohoos.** Noisy or pretended weeping. [Imitative.]

book (bŏōk ‖ bŏōk) *n. Abbr.* **b., B., bk. 1.** A volume made up of written or printed pages fastened along one side, and having cardboard, leather, or paper protective covers. **2. a.** Any written or printed literary work. **b.** *Nonstandard.* A magazine or comic. **3.** A bound volume of blank or ruled pages. **4. a.** Any of the volumes in which financial transactions are recorded. **b.** *Plural.* Such records collectively. **5.** A main division of a larger written or printed work: *a book of the Old Testament.* **6.** The script of a play. **7.** *Capital* B. The Bible. Often preceded by *the.* **8.** A telephone directory. Preceded by *the: I'm in the book.* **9.** *Plural. Informal.* Studies; lessons: *at his books.* **10.** Something regarded as a source of knowledge. **11.** A number of similar items bound together between covers or in a small packet: *a cheque-book; a book of matches.* **12.** A record of bets placed on a race. **13.** In card games, the number of tricks needed before any tricks can have scoring value, as the first six tricks taken by the declaring side in bridge. **—bring to book. 1.** To compel (someone) to explain or account for his conduct. **2.** To reprimand. **—by** or **according to the book.** Strictly according to established rules. **—close the books.** In bookkeeping, to make no further entries in and to draw up statements from the records as they stand. **—cook the books.** To falsify accounts so as to conceal financial irregularities. **—in (one's) books.** In one's opinion. **—in (someone's) good** or **bad books.** In favour (or disfavour) with someone. **—keep books.** To keep financial records. **—like a book.** Thoroughly; completely: *She knows him like a book.* **—on the books. 1.** Recorded or registered. **2.** Registered as a member, employee or the like. **—run a book.** To accept bets on the outcome of a race, competition, or the like. **—throw the book at.** *Slang.* **1.** To make all possible charges against (an offender or lawbreaker, for example). **2.** To reprimand or punish severely.
~tr.v. **booked, booking, books. 1.** To list or register in or as if in a book. **2.** To record a person's name and address with a view to charging him with an offence. **3.** To take the name of (a football player) after he has committed an offence. **4.** To arrange for in

advance; reserve (tickets, for example). **5.** To hire (entertainers; for example). **—book in. 1.** To register, as at a hotel. **2.** To reserve a room for. **—book out.** To pay one's bill and leave a hotel; check out. [Middle English *bok,* Old English *bōc,* written document, composition.]

book·bind·er·y (bŏōk-bīndəri ‖ bŏōk-) *n., pl.* **-ies.** A business establishment where books are bound.

book·bind·ing (bŏōk-bīnding ‖ bŏōk-) *n.* The art, trade, or profession of binding books. **—book·bind·er** *n.*

book·case (bŏōk-kayss ‖ bŏōk-) *n.* A piece of furniture with shelves for holding books.

book club *n.* An organisation that sells books, usually at a discount, to members who have agreed to buy a minimum number.

book end *n.* A prop placed at the end of a row of books to keep them upright.

book·ie (bŏōki ‖ bŏōki) *n. Informal.* A bookmaker.

book·ing (bŏōking ‖ bŏōking) *n.* **1.** An engagement, as for a performance by an entertainer. **2.** A reservation, as of tickets or a hotel room. **3.** The recording of a person's name by a police officer or referee after an offence.

book·ish (bŏōkish ‖ bŏōkish) *adj.* **1.** Of, relating to, or resembling a book. **2.** Fond of books; studious. **3.** Relying on book learning rather than practical experience. Often used derogatorily. **—book·ish·ly** *adv.* **—book·ish·ness** *n.*

book jacket *n.* A dust jacket *(see).*

book·keep·ing (bŏōk-keeping ‖ bŏōk-) *n. Abbr.* **bkpg.** The art or practice of recording the accounts and transactions of a business. **—book·keep·er** *n.*

book learning *n.* Knowledge gained from books rather than from practical experience. Also called "booklore". **—book·learn·ed** (bŏōk-lernid, -lernd ‖ bŏōk-) *adj.*

book·let (bŏōk-lət, -lit ‖ bŏōk-) *n.* A small bound book or pamphlet, usually with paper covers.

book·louse (bŏōk-lowss ‖ bŏōk-) *n., pl.* **-lice** (-līss). Any of various small, often wingless insects of the order Psocoptera (or Corrodentia), some species of which damage books.

book·mak·er (bŏōk-maykər ‖ bŏōk-) *n.* **1.** Someone who accepts bets, as on a horse race, and pays out on winning bets. Also called "turf accountant", informally "bookie". **2.** *Rare.* One who edits, prints, publishes, or binds books.

book·man (bŏōk-mən ‖ bŏōk-) *n., pl.* **-men** (-mən). Anyone who belongs to the literary world, such as a writer, critic, publisher, or bookseller.

book·mark (bŏōk-maark ‖ bŏōk-) *n.* A marker, such as a ribbon, a strip of leather or a piece of paper, placed between the pages of a book.

book·mo·bile (bŏōk-mō-beel) *n. Chiefly U.S.* A small van equipped to serve as a mobile lending library.

Book of Common Prayer *n.* The book of services and prayers used in the Church of England and, with certain modifications, in the other churches of the Anglican Communion.

Book of Kells. See **Kells.**

Book of Mormon *n.* See **Mormon**[1,2].

book·plate (bŏōk-playt ‖ bŏōk-) *n.* A label pasted on the inside cover of a book and bearing the owner's name or other identification.

book·rest (bŏōk-rest ‖ bŏōk-) *n.* A frame for supporting an open book. Also called "bookstand".

book·sel·ler (bŏōk-sellər ‖ bŏōk-) *n.* A person who sells books.

book·shop (bŏōk-shop ‖ bŏōk-) *n. Also U.S.* **book·store.** A shop that primarily sells books.

book·stall (bŏōk-stawl ‖ bŏōk-) *n.* A stall or stand where newspapers, magazines, or books are sold.

book·stand (bŏōk-stand ‖ bŏōk-) *n.* **1.** A small counter or stall where newspapers, magazines, or books are sold. **2.** A bookrest.

book token *n.* A voucher, usually given as a gift, which can be exchanged for books at a bookshop.

book value *n.* The value of a company's assets as set down in its financial records.

book·worm (bŏōk-wurm ‖ bŏōk-) *n.* **1.** Any of various insects, especially booklice and silverfish, that infest books and feed on the paste in the bindings. **2.** One who spends much time reading or studying.

Boole (bŏōl), **George** (1815–64). British mathematician and logician. He developed a calculus of symbolic logic, which was one of the first systems to show the use of symbolic mathematics as a tool in logical inference. It became one of the foundations of computer technology.

Bool·e·an algebra (bŏōli-ən) *n.* Any of various algebraic systems based on mathematical forms and relationships borrowed from the symbolic logic of George Boole.

boom¹ (bōōm) *v.* **boomed, booming, booms.** *—intr.* **1.** To make a deep, resonant, usually sustained sound: *His voice boomed down the corridor.* **2.** To flourish or progress usually with sudden rapid growth: *Business boomed.* *—tr.* To give forth or utter with a deep, resonant sound. Often used with *out.*
~n. **1.** A booming sound, as of an explosion. **2.** A time of general prosperity and economic growth. **3.** A sudden increase, as in numbers, growth, wealth, or popularity: *an investment boom, a baby boom.*
~adj. Of or resulting from a boom: *the boom years.* [Middle English *bomben, bummen* (imitative).]

boom² *n.* **1.** *Nautical.* A long spar extending from a mast to hold or

extend the foot of a sail. **2.** A long pole extending upwards at an angle from the mast of a derrick to support or guide objects lifted or suspended. **3. a.** A barrier composed of a chain of floating logs enclosing other free-floating logs. **b.** The area enclosed by such a barrier. **4.** A floating barrier serving to obstruct navigation or protect the entrance to a waterway. **5.** A long, movable arm used to support an overhead microphone.
~*tr.v.* **boomed, booming, booms.** *Nautical.* To extend (a sail) on a boom. Used with *out.* [Dutch, tree, pole, from Middle Dutch.]

boom·er (bōōmər) *n.* **1.** A large male kangaroo. **2.** *Australian & N.Z. Informal.* Anything large, successful, or exciting.

boo·mer·ang (bōōmərang) *n.* **1.** A flat, curved wooden missile, some types of which can be hurled so that they return to the thrower. It is used as a weapon by Australian aborigines. **2.** A statement or course of action that rebounds to the disadvantage of its originator.
~*intr.v.* **boomeranged, -anging, -angs.** To result in adverse effect upon the originator; backfire. [Native Australian word, variously recorded as *wo-mur-rāng, būmarin.*]

boom·slang (bōōm-slang, bōōrm-, -slung) *n.* A large venomous green snake, *Dispholidus typus,* occurring in the African savannah, especially southern Africa. [Afrikaans, *boom,* tree + *slang,* snake.]

boom town *n.* A town which expands rapidly from sudden prosperity, often through the discovery of local mineral resources.

boon¹ (bōōn) *n.* **1.** Something granted to benefit or please; a blessing: *Those phrase books are a boon to travellers.* **2.** *Archaic.* A favour or request. [Middle English *bone,* prayer, thing prayed for, hence favour, from Old Norse *bōn,* prayer, request.]

boon² *adj.* Jolly; convivial. Used chiefly in the phrase *boon companion.* [Middle English *bone,* "good", from Old French *bon,* from Latin *bonus.*]

boon·docks (bōōn-doks) *pl.n. U.S. Slang.* **1.** Wild and dense brush; jungle. Preceded by *the.* **2.** Back country; hinterland. Preceded by *the.* [Tagalog *bundok,* mountain.]

boon·dog·gle (bōōn-dogg'l ‖ *U.S. also* -dawg'l) *intr.v.* **-gled, -gling, -gles.** *U.S. Informal.* To waste time on unnecessary work.
~*n. U.S.* Pointless, unnecessary, and time-wasting work. [20th century : origin obscure.] **—boon·dog·gler** *n.*

Boone (bōōn), **Daniel** (1734–1820). U.S. frontiersman and folk hero. He undertook the colonisation of Kentucky, founding Boonesborough on the Kentucky river (1775), after leading settlers across the Appalachian mountains.

boong (bōōng) *n. Australian & N.Z.* A coloured person. Used derogatorily. [Perhaps from a native Australian language.]

boor (boor, bor) *n.* A person with rude, clumsy manners and little respect for the feelings of others. [Dutch *boer,* farmer, peasant, from Middle Dutch *gheboer.*]

boor·ish (boor-ish, bôr-) *adj.* Like a boor; rude; ill-mannered. **—boor·ish·ly** *adv.* **—boor·ish·ness** *n.*

boost (bōōst) *tr.v.* **boosted, boosting, boosts. 1.** To raise or lift by or as if by pushing up from behind or below. **2.** To increase; raise: *to boost production.* **3.** To encourage; help to improve: *to boost someone's reputation.* **4.** *Chiefly U.S.* To promote or publicise; advocate actively. **—See Synonyms at lift.**
~*n.* **1.** A lift or help. **2.** An increase: *a boost in salary.* **3.** Anything that encourages or improves.

boost·er (bōōstər) *n.* **1.** Any device for increasing power or effectiveness. **2.** A person, thing, or event that is a source of encouragement or progress. **3.** *Electronics.* A radio-frequency amplifier. **4. a.** A rocket that assists the main propulsive system of an aircraft or spacecraft. **b.** A rocket used to launch a missile or space vehicle. In this sense, also called "booster rocket", "launch vehicle". **5.** A supplementary dose of a vaccine injected to maintain immunity. **6.** A **supercharger** *(see).*

boot¹ (bōōt) *n.* **1.** A piece of footwear, usually of leather or rubber, that covers the foot and ankle, and may extend as far as the knee. **2.** A protective sheath for a horse's leg. **3.** An instrument of torture formerly used to crush the foot and leg. **4.** Any protective covering or sheath, especially a rubber sheath fitted over a coupling between two shafts. **5.** An enclosed compartment in a car in which luggage and the like can be carried. Also *U.S.* "trunk". **6.** *Informal.* A kick. **7.** *Slang.* A very ugly person. **—bet your boots.** To be certain. **—give (someone) the boot.** *Informal.* To dismiss someone from a job. **—lick (someone's) boots.** To be obsequious towards. **—put the boot in.** To attack or harass someone when he is already in a difficult position. **—too big for (one's) boots.** Arrogant.
~*tr.v.* **booted, booting, boots. 1.** To put boots on. **2.** *Informal.* To kick. **3.** *Informal.* To discharge; dismiss. Usually used with *out.* [Middle English *bote,* from Old French *bote†.*]

boot² *intr.v.* **booted, booting, boots.** *Archaic.* To be of help or advantage; avail.
~*n. Archaic.* Advantage; avail. **—to boot.** In addition; besides. [Middle English *bote,* Old English *bōt,* advantage, addition, recompense.]

boot·black (bōōt-blak) *n.* A person who cleans and polishes shoes for a living. Also called "shoeblack".

boot camp *n.* **1.** *U.S.* A training camp for military recruits. **2.** An establishment for the rehabilitation of offenders through a rigorous programme of military-style discipline. [Perhaps so called because the recruits wear boots.]

boot·ed (bōōtid) *adj.* **1.** Wearing boots. **2.** *Zoology.* In birds, having a horny sheath (in poultry, feathers) covering the lower part of the legs.

boo·tee (bōō-tée, -tee) *n.* **1.** A soft, usually knitted, shoe for a baby. **2.** A short boot covering the ankle, worn, especially formerly, by women and children. [Diminutive of BOOT (shoe).]

Bo·ö·tes (bō-ōteez) *n.* A constellation in the Northern Hemisphere near Virgo and Canes Venatici which contains the star Arcturus. [Latin *Boōtēs,* from Greek, "ploughman", from *boōtein,* to plough, from *bous,* ox.]

booth (bōōth ‖ bōōth) *n., pl.* **booths** (bōōthz ‖ bōōths). **1.** A small enclosed compartment, usually accommodating only one person and providing privacy: *a telephone booth.* **2.** A small enclosed seating area in a restaurant, public house, or the like. **3.** A small stall or stand for the display and sale of goods, as at a fairground. [Middle English *both, b(o)uth,* from Old Danish *bōth,* dwelling, stall.]

Booth (bōōth), **Charles** (1840–1916). British social scientist. His 17-volume work, *Life and Labour of the People in London* (1891–1903), was one of the great early contributions to the modern study of social science.

Booth (bōōth ‖ bōōth), **William** (1829–1912). British religious leader, the founder of the Salvation Army. He became a minister in the Methodist New Connection church (1852). In 1861 he left the church to devote himself to independent evangelical work, establishing the East London Revival Society, later known as the Christian Mission (1865). In 1878 this organisation became the Salvation Army, with Booth as its first general.

boot·jack (bōōt-jak) *n.* A forked device for holding a boot secure while the foot is being withdrawn.

boot·lace (bōōt-layss) *n.* A strong lace for tying boots or shoes.

bootlace fungus *n.* The **honey fungus** *(see).*

bootlace worm *n.* A dark brown ribbon worm, *Lineus longissimus,* found in shallow waters. They grow up to 6 metres (20 feet) in length, and are the longest worms in existence.

boot·leg (bōōt-leg) *v.* **-legged, -legging, -legs.** —*tr.* To make, sell, or transport (alcohol, for example) for sale illegally, especially as during the period of **Prohibition** *(see)* in the United States. —*intr.* To engage in bootlegging.
~*n.* Goods smuggled or illicitly produced or sold.
~*adj.* Produced, sold, or transported for sale illegally: *bootleg gin.* [From smugglers' practice of carrying liquor in the legs of tall boots.] **—boot·leg·ger** *n.*

boot·less (bōōt-ləss, -liss) *adj.* Having no advantage or benefit; useless; unavailing; fruitless: *a bootless effort.* **—boot·less·ly** *adv.* **—boot·less·ness** *n.*

boot·lick (bōōt-lik) *v.* **-licked, -licking, -licks.** —*tr.* To be servile towards. —*intr.* To behave in a servile manner. **—boot·lick·er** *n.*

boots (bōōts) *n., pl.* **boots.** *British.* A servant in a hotel who cleans and shines shoes.

boot·strap (bōōt-strap) *n.* A leather or cloth loop sewn at each side or the top rear of a boot to help in pulling it on. **—by (one's) bootstraps.** By one's own efforts. Used chiefly in the phrase *pull oneself up by one's bootstraps.*
~*adj.* **1.** Designating a technique or device for loading the first few programs into a computer so that the remaining programs can be introduced by way of an input device: *a bootstrap loader.* **2.** Denoting an electronic device, such as an amplifier, that uses the output voltage to bias the input. **3.** Denoting a self-consistent theory of nuclear interactions.

boot tree *n.* A shoetree for a boot.

boo·ty (bōōti) *n., pl.* **-ties. 1.** Plunder taken from an enemy in time of war. **2.** Any seized or stolen goods. **3.** Any valuable prize, award, or gain. [Middle English *bottyne,* from Old French *butin,* from Middle Low German *būte,* exchange, from Germanic *būti-ōn* (unattested).]

booze (bōōz) *n. Informal.* Alcoholic drink.
~*intr.v.* **boozed, boozing, boozes.** *Informal.* To drink alcoholic beverages excessively or chronically. [Middle English *bousen,* to carouse, from Middle Dutch *būsen†.*] **—booz·y** *adj.*

booz·er (bōōzər) *n. Informal.* **1.** A person who drinks alcohol, especially to excess. **2.** *Chiefly British & Australian.* A pub.

booze-up (bōōz-up) *n. Chiefly British & Australian Informal.* A bout of drinking.

bop¹ (bop) *tr.v.* **bopped, bopping, bops.** *Informal.* To hit or strike.
~*n.* A blow; a punch. [Imitative.]

bop² *n.* **1.** A style of jazz with a fast driving rhythm, very complex harmonies, and demanding virtuoso skills and techniques. Also called "bebop". **2.** *Informal.* A dance or a session of dancing to disco or pop music.
~*intr.v.* **bopped, bopping, bops.** *Informal.* To dance to disco or pop music. [Short for BEBOP.]

bo·peep (bō-péep) *n.* **1.** A game, **peep-bo** *(see).* **2.** *Australian Informal.* A peep; a look. Used chiefly in the phrase *have a bo-peep.*

Bo·phu·tha·tswa·na (bō-pōōtət-swaanə) *n.* Formerly one of the segregated areas known as Bantu homelands in South Africa.

bop·per (bóppər) *n.* **1.** *Informal.* One who bops or plays bop. **2.** A **teenybopper** *(see).*

bor. borough.

bo·ra¹ (báwrə ‖ bórə) *n.* A violent cold wind from the northeast blowing on the Dalmatian coast of Yugoslavia in winter. [Italian (Venetian dialect), from Latin *Boreās,* BOREAS.]

bora² *n. Australian.* An Aboriginal initiation ceremony for boys going into manhood. [From a native Australian language.]

bo·rac·ic (bə-rássik, bo-) *adj.* Containing boron: *boracic lint.* [Medieval Latin *borax* (stem *borac-*), BORAX + -IC.]

bo·rac·ite (báwr-ə-sīt ‖ bór-) *n.* A white mineral consisting of borate and magnesium chloride, $Mg_6Cl_2B_{14}O_{26}$, found in some gypsum beds.

bor·age (bórrij, *rarely* búrrij ‖ *U.S. also* báwrij) *n.* A plant, *Borago officinalis,* native to southern Europe and northern Africa, having hairy leaves and star-shaped blue flowers. The young, cucumber-flavoured leaves are sometimes used as seasoning. [Middle English, from Old French *bourrache,* from Medieval Latin *borrāgō,* probably from Arabic *abū 'āraq,* "father of sweat" (from its use medicinally as a sudorific).]

bo·rak, bo·rax (báwrak, -s) *n. Australian & N.Z. Informal.* Banter or nonsense. **—poke borak at.** *Australian & N.Z. Informal.* To make fun of; ridicule. [From a native Australian language.]

bo·rane (báwr-ayn ‖ bór-) *n.* Any of a series of boron-hydrogen compounds.

bora ring *n. Australian.* A circle inside which an Aboriginal bora takes place.

bo·rate (báwr-ayt, -ət, -it ‖ bór-) *n.* A salt or ester of boric acid.

bo·rax (báwr-aks ‖ bór-, -aks) *n.* **1.** A hydrated **sodium borate** *(see).* **2.** An anhydrous sodium borate used in the manufacture of glass and various ceramics. [Middle English *boras, borax,* from Old French *boras,* from Medieval Latin *borax,* from Arabic *būraq,* from Persian *būrah†.*]

borax bead *n.* A bead made of fused borax supported on a platinum wire, used in qualitative chemical analysis. When a substance of unknown composition is fused with the bead in a flame, the bead may change colour depending on the presence of certain elements in the substance.

bo·ra·zon (báwr-ə-zon, -z'n ‖ bór-) *n.* An extremely hard boron nitride formed at very high pressures and temperatures. [BOR(ON) + AZ(O)- + -ON.]

bor·bo·ryg·mus (bórbə-rígməss) *n.* Rumbling in the abdomen due to movement of fluid and gases in the intestines. [New Latin, from Greek (imitative).]

Bor·deaux¹ (bawr-dó, bór-). A port in southwestern France, lying at the mouth of the river Garonne. Although it is an industrial town, its economy rests chiefly on the trade in Bordeaux wines.

Bordeaux² *n., pl.* Bordeaux (-dóz). Any of the red or white wines produced in the regions around Bordeaux.

Bordeaux mixture *n.* A mixture of copper sulphate, lime, and water, used as a fungicide. [Translation of French *bouillie bordelaise.*]

bor·de·laise sauce (bórdə-láyz, -léz) *n.* A brown sauce made with Bordeaux wine and often with mushrooms. Also called "sauce bordelaise".

bor·del·lo (bawr-délló) *n., pl* **-los.** Also *archaic* **bor·del** (bórd'l). A brothel. [Middle English, from Old French *bordel,* smallholding, small farm, diminutive of *borde,* from Frankish; akin to BOARD.]

Bor·den, (bórd'n), **Sir Robert Laird** (1854–1937). Canadian politician. Elected leader of the opposition Progressive Conservative party (1901), he became prime minister (1911–20).

bor·der (bórdər) *n.* **1.** A margin, rim, or edge around or along something. **2.** A design or a decorative strip on the edge or rim of something such as a plate. **3.** A strip of ground, around a lawn or along the side of a path for example, in which flowers or shrubs are planted. **4.** The line or frontier area separating political divisions or geographical regions; a boundary. **—the Borders.** The boundary and adjacent areas between England and Scotland. —See Synonyms below and at **boundary.**
~ *adj.* Of, pertaining to, forming, or located on a border.
~ *tr.v.* **bordered, -dering, -ders. 1.** To put a border, rim, or edging on. **2.** To lie along or adjacent to the border of. **—border on** or **upon. 1.** To adjoin. **2.** To be almost like; approach in character: *an act that borders on heroism.* [Middle English *bordure,* from Old French, from *border,* to border, from *bord,* side of a vessel, border, from Frankish *bord* (unattested), board, plank.]

Synonyms: border, margin, edge, verge, brink, brow, rim, brim.

Border, Allan (Robert) (1955-). Australian cricketer. In 1993 he became the first man to score more than 10,000 runs in Test cricket. He holds the records for most Test matches and most one-day internationals played. Retired 1995 from Test cricket.

bor·der·er (bórdər-ər) *n.* A person who lives on or near a border, especially the border between Scotland and England.

bor·der·land (bórdər-land) *n.* **1.** Land located on or near a border or frontier. **2.** An uncertain or indeterminate area, situation, or condition: *the borderland between merry and rolling drunk.*

bor·der·line (bórdər-līn) *n.* **1.** A line that establishes or marks a border; a demarcation. **2.** An indefinite division between two qualities or conditions: *the borderline between genius and madness.*
~ *adj.* **1.** Verging on a given quality or condition; indeterminate; dubious: *a borderline case of paranoia.* **2.** Not quite or only just measuring up to an accepted standard: *a borderline result.*

border terrier *n.* A small, hardy, rough-coated breed of terrier, bred to hunt foxes in the border country of Scotland and England.

Bor·det (bórday ‖ bawr-dáy), **Jules** (1870-1961). Belgian medical researcher. His work led to the **Wassermann test** for syphilis. In 1906 he discovered the bacillus of whooping cough. Nobel prize (1919).

bor·dure (bór-dewr ‖ -jər) *n. Heraldry.* A border around a shield. [Middle English, BORDER.]

bore¹ (bor ‖ bōr) *v.* **bored, boring, bores.** —*tr.* **1.** To make a hole in or through, as with a drill or lathe. **2.** To make (a tunnel or well, for example) by drilling, digging, or burrowing. **3.** To make (one's way) with difficulty. —*intr.* **1.** To make a hole in or through something by or as if by drilling. **2.** To advance steadily or laboriously.
~ *n* **1.** A hole made by or as if by drilling, especially in order to

find water or minerals; specifically, in Australia, an artesian well. Also called "borehole". **2. a.** The hollow part of a hole, tube, or cylinder. **b.** The interior diameter of this. **3.** The calibre of a firearm. Often used in combination: *12-bore.* **4.** A drilling tool. [Middle English *boren,* Old English *borian.*]

bore² *tr.v.* **bored, boring, bores.** To tire or weary with dullness, repetition, or tediousness.
~ *n.* **1.** A tiresome or tedious person or activity. **2.** A nuisance; a bother. [18th century : origin obscure.]

bore³ *n.* A high wave travelling upstream in the tidal reaches of certain rivers, caused by the surge of a flood tide upstream in a narrowing estuary or by colliding tidal currents. Also called "eagre". [Middle English *bare,* from Old Norse *bāra,* wave, billow.]

bore⁴. Past tense of **bear.**

bo·re·al (báwri-əl, bórri- ‖ bóri-) *adj.* **1.** Pertaining to the north; northern. **2.** Of or concerning the north wind. **3.** *Capital* **B.** Of or pertaining to the coniferous forest areas of the North Temperate Zone and Arctic region. **4.** *Capital* **B.** Of or designating a climatic zone with short summers and hard winters. **5.** *Capital* **B.** Of or designating a climatic period of cold winters and warm summers (7500 B.C. to 5500 B.C.). [Middle English *boriall,* from Late Latin *boreālis,* from BOREAS.]

Bo·re·as (bórri-ass, báwri-, -əss ‖ bóri-). **1.** The north wind. **2.** The god personifying the north wind in Greek mythology. [Middle English, from Latin *Boreās,* from Greek *Boreas.*]

bore·cole (bór-kōl ‖ bór-) *n.* A vegetable, **kale** *(see).* [Dutch *boerenkool,* "peasants' cabbage" : *boer,* BOOR (peasant) + *kool,* cabbage, from Latin *caulis,* stalk (see **cole**).]

bore·dom (bór-dəm ‖ bór-) *n.* The condition of being bored.

bore·hole (bór-hōl ‖ bór-) *n.* A bore, as for water or minerals; specifically, in South Africa, a narrow well drilled through to an underground source of water, which is usually pumped to the surface by means of a windmill.

bor·er (báwrər ‖ bórər) *n.* **1.** A tool used for boring or drilling. **2.** One who works with such a tool. **3.** An insect or insect larva, such as the **corn borer** *(see),* that bores into plant material. **4.** Any of various molluscs that bore into soft rock or plant material.

Borg (borg), **Björn** (1956-). Swedish tennis player. He won his first major title in 1974 and from 1976 until 1980 won the Wimbledon men's singles championships five consecutive times, a record for the 20th century. He retired from world tennis from 1983 to 1992.

Bor·ges (bór-khess), **Jorge Luis** (1899–1986). Argentinian writer. He was a poet, essayist, and literary critic, but is best known for the metaphysical fantasy of his short stories, as in *Ficciones* (1945).

Bor·gia (bór-ji-ə, -jə), **Cesare** (1476–1507). Italian soldier and politician, illegitimate son of Pope **Alexander VI.** The Pope made him Archbishop of Valenzia and then a cardinal.

Borgia, Lucrezia (1480–1519). Italian noblewoman, daughter of Pope **Alexander VI** and sister of Cesare. Her three successive marriages helped to increase the political power of the Borgia family. Later, her court at Ferrara became a cultural centre of the Italian Renaissance.

Borgia, Rodrigo. See **Alexander VI.**

bo·ric (báwrik, bórrik ‖ bórik) *adj.* Of, pertaining to, derived from, or containing boron or boric acid.

boric acid *n.* A white or colourless crystalline compound, H_3BO_3, used as an antiseptic, preservative, and fireproofing agent. Also called "orthoboric acid".

boric oxide *n.* A hard, colourless, transparent glass, B_2O_3, used in heat-resistant glassware, as a fire-resistant paint additive, and in the production of boron.

bo·ride (báwrīd ‖ bórīd) *n.* A binary compound of boron with a more electropositive element or radical.

bor·ing¹ (báwr-ing ‖ bór-) *n.* **1.** The making of a hole by or as if by drilling. **2.** A hole made in this way. **3.** *Plural.* The material, chips, or dust produced by such drilling.

boring² *adj.* Uninteresting and tiresome; dull.

Synonyms: boring, monotonous, tedious, irksome, tiresome, humdrum, dreary.

Bor·mann (bór-mən, -man), **Martin Ludwig.** (1900– *c.* 1945). German Nazi leader. In 1942 he became Hitler's private secretary. He disappeared after Hitler's suicide in 1945 and was sentenced to death in his absence at the Nuremberg trials (1946). It is now thought that he committed suicide in May 1945.

born (born). A past participle of **bear.** See Usage note at **borne.**
~ *adj.* **1.** *Abbr.* **b., B.** Brought into life or being. **2.** Having or appearing to have a specified innate quality or talent: *a born artist.*

Born, Max (1882-1970). British theoretical physicist, born in Germany. He helped to develop quantum and wave mechanics and was awarded the Nobel prize for physics (1954).

born-a·gain (bórn-ə-gén, -gáyn) *adj.* **1. a.** Characteristic of or being a person who has undergone a personal, and usually very emotional, conversion or reconversion to Christianity, often through revelation or a similar experience; evangelical. **b.** Having or showing zeal like that of a born-again Christian : *a born-again vegetarian; born-again vegetarianism.* **2.** Feeling, appearing, or behaving as if having been reborn or turned into a new person.

borne¹ (born ‖ bōrn). A past participle of **bear. —borne in on** or **upon.** Brought to the notice of; realised by: *the extent of our dilemma was gradually borne in on us.*

Usage: In the sense of "give birth to", the use of *borne* and *born* as the past participles of *bear* sometimes causes confusion. *Borne* is used in the active voice, as in *Mary has borne three sons,* and in the passive when followed by *by: Three sons were borne by Mary.* When *by* does not follow in the passive, *born* is used: *A child is born, Three sons were born to Mary.*

borne² *adj.* Carried or supported in a specified way. Often used in combination: *windborne; seaborne.*

Bor·ne·o (bórni-ō). The largest island of the Malay Archipelago, lying north of Java and southwest of the Philippines. It is the third-largest island in the world. Kalimantan state, which occupies 70 per cent of the island, belongs to Indonesia; the states of Sarawak in the west and Sabah in the north belong to Malaysia, and Brunei, in the northwest, is independent. The interior of the island consists of dense jungle and mountains; the coastal regions, of mangrove swamp. The island is thinly populated and the most numerous people are **Dyaks.**

bor·ne·ol (bórni-ol || -ōl) *n.* A solid terpene alcohol, $C_{10}H_{17}OH$, from the tree *Dryobalanops camphora* : used in perfumery and the manufacture of celluloid, and as an antiseptic. [BORNEO + -OL.]

born·ite (bórnīt) *n.* A brownish-bronze copper ore with composition Cu_5FeS_4. [After Ignaz von *Born* (1742–91), Austrian mineralogist.]

Bo·ro·bu·dur (bórrō-bōōdər). One of the greatest of Buddhist shrines, in central Java in Indonesia. The monument was built in A.D. *c.*800 and, although badly weathered, still stands.

Bo·ro·din (bórrə-din; *Russian* -déen), **Alexander Porfirevich** (1833–87). Russian composer. His output was small, since he was primarily a chemist, but he is remembered for his opera, *Prince Igor* (unfinished at his death), and his two string quartets.

bo·ron (báwr-on, -ən || bôr-) *n. Symbol* **B** A nonmetallic element, extracted chiefly from kernite and borax, and used in flares, propellant mixtures, nuclear-reactor control elements, abrasives, and hard metallic alloys. It exists in two allotropic forms: a soft, brown, amorphous variety and a hard crystalline form. Atomic number 5, atomic weight 10.811, melting point 2 300°C, sublimation 2 550°C, relative density (crystal) 2.34, valency 3. [*borax* + carbon.]

boron carbide *n.* An extremely hard, black, crystalline compound, B_4C, used as an abrasive, in control rods for nuclear reactors, and as a reinforcing filament in composite structural materials.

boron chamber *n. Physics.* A type of particle detector that detects and counts slow neutrons by their effect on boron atoms.

boron nitride *n.* An inert white solid, BN, used as a lubricant, heat shield, and insulator at high temperatures. It has two crystalline forms: one similar to graphite and the other, **borazon** *(see),* similar to diamond.

bo·ro·sil·i·cate glass (báwrō-sílli-kət, -kayt, -kit || bôrō-) *n.* A strong heat-resistant glass that contains a proportion of boron atoms in place of silicon atoms (up to five per cent boric oxide).

bor·ough (búrrə || *U.S.* búrrō) *n. Abbr.* **bor. 1.** *British.* **a.** A town that was originally incorporated by royal charter and had a municipal corporation and certain rights, such as self-government. Compare **burgh. b.** A town that makes up the constituency of a member of Parliament. **c.** Any of the 32 divisions that make up Greater London. **d.** Any of a number of divisions of the metropolitan counties in England. **2.** A self-governing incorporated town in certain U.S. states. **3.** Any of the five administrative units of New York City. **4.** In New Zealand, a town or village that is a municipality with a council. [Middle English *burgh, borugh,* Old English *burg, burh,* fortress, fortified town.]

bor·ough-Eng·lish (búrrə-íng-glish, búrrər- || *U.S.* búrrō-) *n.* An old custom in certain boroughs of England whereby the right to inherit an estate went to the youngest son or, in default of issue, to the youngest brother. [Middle English, from Anglo-French *(tenure en) Burgh Engloys,* (tenure in) English borough.]

BOSNIA AND HERZEGOVINA

bor·row (bórrō || *U.S. also* báwrō) *v.* **-rowed, -rowing, -rows.** —*tr.* **1.** To obtain or receive on loan with the promise or understanding of returning it or its equivalent. **2.** To adopt or use as one's own: *They borrowed his ideas.* **3.** In subtraction, to increase a figure in the minuend by ten and make up for it by decreasing the next, larger denomination by one. **4.** *Nonstandard.* To lend. —*intr.* **1.** To take or receive a loan; obtain or receive something. **2.** *Golf.* To play a ball, especially when putting, so as to allow for the slope or wind. [Middle English *borwen,* Old English *borgian.*] —**bor·row·er** *n.*

borscht, borsht (borsht) *n.* Also **borsch** (borsh). A Russian soup made from beetroot and sometimes cabbage, served hot or cold, often with sour cream. [Russian *borshch,* "cow parsnip" (the original base of the soup).]

bor·stal (bórst'l) *n.* Formerly, a disciplinary institution for offenders aged 15 to 21. [After *Borstal* near Rochester, Kent, where the Borstal Institution for young offenders was established in 1901.]

bort, boart (bort) *n.* Also **bortz** (borts). **1.** Poor-quality diamonds used for industrial cutting and abrasion. **2.** An impure diamond, a **carbonado** *(see).* [Perhaps from Dutch *boort,* perhaps from Old French *bourt,* bastard, from Latin *burdus,* hinny.] —**bort·y** *adj.*

bor·zoi (bórzoy) *n.* A rather large, slenderly built dog of a breed originating in Russia, having a narrow, pointed head and a silky, predominantly white coat. Also called "Russian wolfhound". [Russian *borzoi*†, "swift".]

bos·cage, bos·kage (bóskij) *n. Literary.* A mass of trees or shrubs; a thicket. [Middle English *boskage,* from Old French *boscage,* from *bosc,* forest, from Germanic.]

Bosch (bosh), **Karl** (1874–1940). German industrialist and chemist. He developed the **Bosch process,** but was more famous for his contribution to developing methods for the high-pressure synthesis of gases, especially ammonia. For this latter work he shared the Nobel prize in chemistry with Friedrich Bergius (1931).

Bosch (bosh, boss), **Hieronymus** (*c.* 1450–1516). Flemish painter. He was strikingly original, producing wildly grotesque and allegorical canvases, which have nothing in common with the prevailing Flemish style of the period, but seem to prefigure **Surrealism.**

Bosch process (bosh) *n.* A method of making hydrogen by the action of carbon monoxide on steam over a hot catalyst. [After K. BOSCH.]

Bose (bōss), **Satyenda Nath** (1894–1974). Indian physicist. In 1924 he devised a radiation law for black bodies. His work led to the **Bose-Einstein statistics.**

Bose, Sir Jagadis Chandra (1858–1937). Indian physicist and plant physiologist. He invented an instrument known as the crescograph for measuring the growth of plants.

Bose-Ein·stein statistics (bōss-ín-shtīn, -stīn) *pl.n.* Quantum statistics concerning a system of identical bosons for which there can be any number of particles in the same quantum state simultaneously. [After S.N. BOSE and A. EINSTEIN.]

bosh (bosh) *n. Informal.* Meaningless talk or opinions; nonsense. [Turkish *boş,* empty, useless.]

bos·ky (bóski) *adj. Literary.* **1.** Covered with bushes, shrubs, or trees. **2.** Shaded by trees or bushes. [Middle English *bosk,* wooded, from *bosk, bush,* bush, from Old Norse *buskr.*] —**bos·ki·ness** *n.*

Bos·man (bóss-mən, báwss-mən), **Herman Charles** (1905–51). South African author and journalist. He is best remembered for a collection of short stories, *Mafeking Road.*

bo's'n. Variant of **boatswain.**

Bos·nia and Her·ze·go·vi·na (bózni-ə; hérts-ə-gō-véenə, hairts-, -i-, -gə-, góvvinə). An independent republic, formerly historical Balkan provinces which formed one of the constituent republics of the former Yugoslavia. The republic, situated in the Dinaric Alps, is an ethnic mixture. As a result civil war broke out in 1992. Peace is maintained by means of a strong United Nations presence. Area, 51 129 square kilometres (19,741 square miles). Population: 4,510,000. Capital, Sarajevo.

Bos·ni·an (bózni-ən) *adj.* Also **Bos·ni·ac** (-ak). Of or pertaining to Bosnia.

~*n.* Also **Bos·ni·ac. 1.** A native of Bosnia. **2.** The Serbo-Croatian language of this people.

bos·om (bŏozz'm || bŏoz'm) *n.* **1. a.** The chest of a human being; especially, the female breasts. **b.** Either of the two female breasts. **2.** The part of a garment covering the chest. **3.** The midst or heart: *"Deep in the bosom of the hills."* (George Eliot). **4.** A close enveloping relationship: *in the bosom of her family* **5.** The chest considered as the seat of feelings, hopes, and desires.

~*adj.* Beloved; intimate: *a bosom friend.* [Middle English *bosom,* Old English *bōsm.*]

bos·om·y (bŏozz'm-i || bŏoz'm-i) *adj.* Having large breasts; busty.

bos·on (bō-zon, -son) *n.* A particle, such as a photon, pion, or alpha particle, having zero or integral spin and obeying Bose-Einstein statistics. Compare **fermion.** [S.N. BOSE + -ON.]

Bos·po·rus (bóspərəss). The strait joining the Black Sea and the Sea of Marmara. Istanbul lies on its northern shore, Üsküdar on the southern. Opposing currents make the waters extremely turbulent.

boss¹ (boss || bawss) *n.* **1. a.** An employer or supervisor of workers; a manager; a foreman. **b.** A person who makes decisions or exercises authority. **2.** *U.S.* A professional politician who controls a party or political machine often by underhand or shady means. —**boss of the board.** *Australian Informal.* The person in charge of a group of shearers, such as the owner.

~*v.* **bossed, bossing, bosses.** —*tr.* **1.** To supervise or control.

2. To command in an arrogant or domineering manner. Often used with *about* or *around*. —*intr.* To be or act as a boss.
~*adj.* *U.S. Slang.* First-rate; topnotch. [Dutch *baas*, master, from Middle Dutch *baes*, from Germanic *basa-* (unattested).]

boss² *n.* **1.** A circular or knoblike protuberance, as on a shield. **2.** A raised area used as ornamentation. **3.** *Architecture.* A raised ornament, as at the intersection of the ribs in vaulted roofs. **4.** *Machinery.* **a.** An enlarged part of a shaft to which another shaft is coupled or to which a wheel or gear is keyed. **b.** A hub, especially of a propeller. **5.** A metal ornament used for protecting the corners or centres of books. **6.** *Geology.* An intrusive mound of igneous rock. ~*tr.v.* **bossed, bossing, bosses. 1.** To decorate with bosses. **2.** To emboss. [Middle English *boce*, from Old French, from Vulgar Latin *bottia†* (unattested).]

BOSS *n.* Bureau for State Security: formerly, the South African intelligence and state security organisation.

bossa nova (bóssə nóvə) *n.* **1.** A rhythmic dance similar to the samba, originating in Brazil. **2. a.** A complex dance rhythm extending over two bars. **b.** A musical composition using this rhythm, as one written for the dance. [Portuguese, "new voice".]

boss boy *n.* *South African.* A black or coloured foreman.

boss cocky *n.* *Australian.* A person in charge; especially, a farmer.

boss-eyed (bóss-īd ‖ báwss-) *adj.* *Chiefly British Informal.* Having the eyes going in different directions; cross-eyed. [See **boss shot**.]

bos·sism (bóss-iz'm ‖ báwss-) *n.* *U.S.* The domination of a political organisation by a political boss.

boss·y¹ (bóssi ‖ báwssi) *adj.* **-ier, -iest.** Commanding, domineering, or overbearing. —**boss·i·ly** *adv.* —**boss·i·ness** *n.*

bossy² *adj.* Decorated with studs or similar raised ornaments.

boss-y-boots (bóssi-bōots ‖ báwssi-) *n.* *British Informal.* A bossy person.

Bos·ton¹ (bóss-tən ‖ báwss-). City in eastern Massachusetts, on the Atlantic seaboard of the United States. It played a prominent role in the developing opposition to colonial rule which led to the American War of Independence. In the 19th century it was one of the centres in the movement to abolish Negro slavery in the south.

Boston². Port in the Parts of Holland district of Lincolnshire in England. Puritans sailed from Boston to Massachusetts Bay (1630) and gave the American settlement its name. The town itself got its name from St. Botolph (Botulph's tun, or town), who founded a monastery there in the seventh century.

Boston Tea Party *n.* A protest staged by American colonists in Boston (December 16, 1773) against the British tax on imported tea. The colonists, disguised as Indians, boarded British ships in Boston Harbour and threw chests of tea overboard.

Boston terrier *n.* A small dog of a breed that originated in New England as a cross between a bull terrier and a bulldog.

bosun. Variant of **boatswain.**

Bos·well (bóz-wəl, -wel) *n.* An assiduous and devoted admirer, student, and recorder of another's words and deeds. [After James BOSWELL.] —**Bos·wel·li·an** *adj.*

Boswell, James (1740–95). Scottish lawyer and author. He wrote the famous biography *The Life of Samuel Johnson, LL.D* (1791).

Bos·worth Field (bóz-wərth, -wurth). Site of the final battle in the Wars of the Roses, near Leicester, where Richard III, the last Plantagenet king, was defeated on August 22, 1485, by Henry Tudor.

bot¹, bott (bot) *n.* The parasitic larva of a botfly. [Middle English, probably of Low German origin; akin to Dutch *bot†*.]

bot² *n.* *Australian & N.Z. Informal.* A persistent borrower; a scrounger; a parasite. —**have the bot.** *N.Z.* To be ill or moody. ~*intr. v.* **botted, botting, bots.** *Australian & N.Z. Informal.* To borrow money; scrounge. Often used with *on*: *He is always botting on his employees for a cigarette.* [Perhaps shortened from BOTFLY, referring to its bite.]

bot. 1. botanical; botanist; botany. **2.** bottle.

bo·tan·i·cal (bə-tánnik'l, bo-) *adj.* Also **bo·tan·ic** (-tánnik). *Abbr.* **bot.** Of or pertaining to plants, plant life, or the science of botany. ~*n.* A drug, medicinal preparation, or similar substance obtained from a plant or plants. [French *botanique*, from Late Latin *botanicus*, from Greek *botanikos*, from *botanē†*, pasture, herb, plant.] —**bo·tan·i·cal·ly** *adv.*

botanical garden *n.* A place where plants are grown for scientific study and public exhibition, and at which herbaria and libraries are maintained.

bot·a·nist (bóttənist) *n.* *Abbr.* **bot.** One who studies plants.

bot·a·nise, bot·a·nize (bóttənīz) *v.* **-nised, -nising, -nises.** —*intr.* **1.** To secure plants for botanical study. **2.** To examine plants scientifically. —*tr.* To investigate (an area) for botanical study. —**bot·a·nis·er** *n.*

bot·a·ny (bóttəni) *n., pl.* **-nies.** *Abbr.* **bot. 1.** The study of plants, covering their classification, form, function, ecology, and economic importance. **2.** The plant life of a particular area or period. **3.** The characteristics of a plant group: *the botany of grasses.* **4.** A particular system of botany: *the botany of Linnaeus.* [From BOTANICAL.]

Botany Bay. Inlet of the Tasman Sea, just south of Sydney in Australia. It was visited by Captain Cook (1770) and given its name by Sir Joseph Banks, the botanist in Cook's crew, for the variety of new flora which he found on its shores.

Botany wool *n.* The wool of the merino sheep. [After BOTANY BAY.]

bo·tar·go (bə-tárgō) *n.* A relish made from the roe of tuna or mullet. [From Italian *bottarga* (obsolete), from Egyptian Arabic *batārikh*, roe, from Coptic.]

botch (boch) *tr.v.* **botched, botching, botches. 1.** To ruin through clumsiness. Often used with *up.* **2.** To make or perform clumsily; bungle. **3.** To repair or mend clumsily. ~*n.* A ruined or defective piece of work: *"I have made a miserable botch of this description."* (Nathaniel Hawthorne). [Middle English *bocchen†*, to patch up, mend.] —**botch·er** *n.*

botch·y (bóchi) *adj.* **-ier, -iest.** Carelessly or clumsily done or made; imperfect. —**botch·i·ly** *adv.*

bo·tel, boat·el (bō-tél) *n.* **1.** A quayside hotel catering for boat-owners. **2.** A boat which is used as a hotel. [BOAT + HOTEL.]

bot·fly (bót-flī) *n., pl.* **-flies.** Also **bot fly.** Any of various winged insects, chiefly of the families Gasterophilidae, Oestridae, and Cuterebridae, having larvae that are parasitic on man, livestock, rodents, and other animals. See **bots.**

both (bōth) *adj.* One and the other; two in conjunction: *Both boys arrived.* ~*pron.* The one and the other: *Both are patriots.* ~*conj.* Used with *and* to show that each of two coordinated words or things in coordinated phrases or clauses is included: *both Keats and Shelley.* [Middle English *bothe, bathe*, from Old Norse *bāthir.*]

Usage: Both is redundant when more than two things or items are expressed, as in *Poor in both content, taste, and style,* and in such phrases as *both together, both the man as well as the woman.* Strict usage also prefers *each* in cases where people or things are being considered separately, as in *Each pointed to the other* or *We each got a letter.*

Bot·ha (bóortə, bótə), **Louis** (1862–1919). South African general in the Second Anglo-Boer War, and first prime minister of the Union of South Africa after its establishment in 1910.

Botha, P(ieter) W(illem) (1916–). Prime minister of the Republic of South Africa from 1978 to 1989, and President 1984–9.

Bo·tham (bóthəm), **Ian Terence** (1955–). English cricketer. With hard-hitting batting and attacking pace bowling, he became a great Test all-rounder. In 102 Test matches, 1977–92, he scored 5200 runs, took 383 wickets, and made 120 catches.

both·er (bóthər) *v.* **-ered, -ering, -ers.** —*tr.* **1.** To irritate, particularly by small annoyances; pester; harass. **2. a.** To make agitated or nervous; fluster. **b.** To make confused or perplexed; bewilder; puzzle. **3.** To disturb, as by asking questions or by intrusion. **4.** To give trouble to: *a back complaint that bothers him constantly.* —*intr.* To trouble or concern oneself. —See Synonyms at **annoy.** ~*n.* **1.** A cause or state of disturbance or confusion. **2.** A person or thing that causes annoyance or disturbance. **3.** *British Slang.* Aggressive behaviour or disturbance. ~*interj.* *Chiefly British.* Used to express mild irritation. [18th century : Anglo-Irish, perhaps akin to POTHER.]

both·er·a·tion (bóthə-ráysh'n) *n.* Irritation; vexation; bother. ~*interj.* Used to express irritation.

both·er·some (bóthər-səm) *adj.* Causing vexation or irritation; troublesome.

Both·ni·a (bóth-ni-ə), **Gulf of.** The northernmost arm of the Baltic Sea, lying between Sweden and Finland, and separated from the Baltic by the Åland Islands. The gulf is 725 kilometres (450 miles) long and is ice-covered for five months of the year.

Both·well (bóth-wəl, bóth-, -wel), **James Hepburn, 4th Earl of** (c. 1536–78). Scottish courtier, the third husband of Mary, Queen of Scots. He helped to suppress the rebellion led by the Earl of Moray (1565) and became the adviser and confidant of the Queen. In 1567 he was acquitted of the murder of her husband, Lord **Darnley.** He was forced to flee to Denmark soon after his own marriage to Mary.

both·y (bóthi) *n., pl.* **bothies.** *Scottish.* A hut or other shelter, used by people, especially shepherds, working outdoors. [18th century : perhaps akin to BOOTH.]

bo tree (bō) *n.* An Asiatic tree, the **peepul** *(see)*. According to Buddhist tradition, the Buddha attained enlightenment under it. [Sinhalese *bo*, from Pali *bodhi(taru)*, "(tree of) wisdom", from Sanskrit *bodhi*, wisdom, enlightenment, from *bodhati*, he awakes.]

bot·ry·oi·dal (bóttri-óyd'l) *adj.* Also **bot·ry·oid** (-oyd). Formed like a bunch of grapes. Said especially of minerals. [Greek *botruoeidēs* : *botrus†*, bunch of grapes + -OID.] —**bot·ry·oi·dal·ly** *adv.*

bots (bots) *n.* Used with a singular verb. A disease of horses and cattle caused by infestation of the intestines with botfly larvae.

Bo·tswa·na (bot-swáanə, bóot-, bŏoch-waánə). Republic in southern Africa, lying between Namibia and Zimbabwe, north of South Africa. It was known as Bechuanaland until it gained independence (1966). It is a high tableland, mostly covered by arid desert sands. Cattle-breeding is the chief economic activity, but important reserves of nickel, copper, diamonds, and coal were discovered in the 1960s. Area 581 730 square kilometres (224,607 square miles). Population, 1,490,000. Capital, Gaborone. See map, next page.

bott. Variant of **bot.**

botte (bot) *n.* In fencing, a hit with the sword. [French, "hit".]

Bot·ti·cel·li (bótti-chélli), **Alessandro di Mariano di Vanni Filipepi,** known as Sandro (1445–1510). Italian painter of the Florentine Renaissance. His flowing draughtmanship is seen to advantage in his two best-known paintings, *Primavera* and the *Birth of Venus.*

bot·tle (bótt'l) *n. Abbr.* **bot., btl. 1.** A receptacle, usually glass, having a narrow neck and mouth that can be plugged, corked, or capped. **2.** The quantity a bottle contains. In the case of wine bottles, this is usually between 70 and 75 centilitres. **3. a.** A bottle used for feeding milk to a baby. **b.** The milk fed to a baby from this. **4.** *British Slang.* Courage; nerve. **5.** *Physics.* A configuration of magnetic fields used to confine a plasma in a fusion reactor.

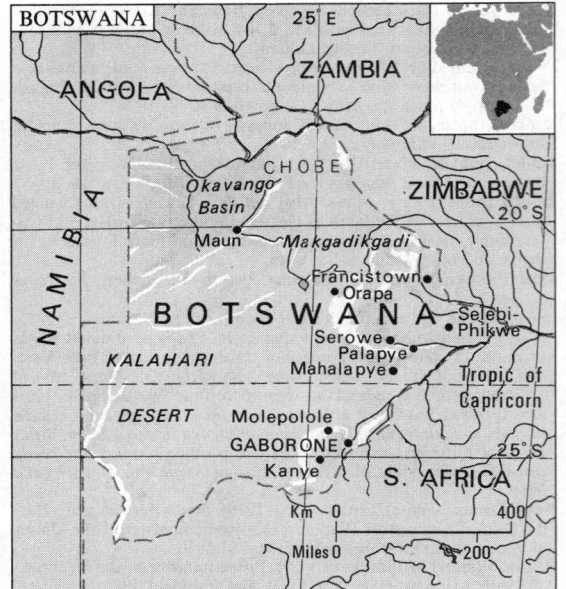

BOTSWANA

---hit the bottle. *Slang.* To drink alcohol to excess. ---the bottle.
1. Intoxicating drink: *addicted to the bottle.* 2. Milk or another similar preparation fed to a baby from a bottle.
~*tr.v.* bottled, -tling, -tles. 1. To place in a bottle or bottles. 2. To preserve (fruit) in a jar. 3. To confine as if in a bottle. Used with *up: bottle up one's emotions.* 4. To hit with a bottle, especially a broken one. ---bottle out. *British Slang.* To lose courage; chicken out. [Middle English *botel*, from Old French *botele, botaille*, from Medieval Latin *butticula*, diminutive of Late Latin *buttis*, cask, BUTT; sense 4 of noun, from rhyming slang *bottle and glass*, CLASS.] ---bot·tler *n.*
bottle bank *n.* A skip to which empty bottles may be returned so that the glass may be recycled.
bot·tle·brush (bótt'l-brush) *n.* 1. A brush used for cleaning out bottles. 2. Any of various shrubs or trees of the genera *Callistemon* and *Melaleuca*, native to Australia. They have dense spikes of red flowers with protruding stamens that suggest a brush used to clean bottles. 3. Any of various similar plants of the genus *Greyia*, native to southern Africa. 4. Any of various similar shrubs or trees.
bottle-feed (bótt'l-feed) *tr.v.* -fed (-fed), -feeding, -feeds. To feed a baby) from a bottle rather than from the breast.
bottled gas *n.* Gas, such as butane or propane, stored under pressure in portable tanks.
bottle gourd *n.* 1. An Old World vine, *Lagenaria siceraria*, cultivated for its gourd-like and ornamental hard-shelled fruits. Also called "calabash". 2. The fruit of this plant. Also called "calabash".
bottle green *n.* Dark bluish green. ---bot·tle-green *adj.*
bot·tle·neck (bótt'l-nek) *n.* 1. The narrow part of a bottle near the top. 2. a. A point on a road where traffic is held up because of an obstruction or narrow section. b. The hold-up so caused. 3. a. Part of a process which is slower than other parts and causes delay. b. The delay caused. 4. *Music.* A style of playing the guitar, especially in blues and country-and-western music, with a hollow metal cylinder which is held around the finger and slid along the strings.
~*tr.v.* bottlenecked, -necking, -necks. To impede or slow down by creating a bottleneck.
bot·tle-nosed dolphin (bótt'l-nōzd) *n.* Any of several marine mammals of the genus *Tursiops*, having a short, protruding beak. Also called "bottlenose".
bottle party *n.* A party to which guests are expected to bring drink.
bottle store *n. Chiefly N.Z. & South African.* A shop in which bottles of alcoholic drinks are sold; an off-licence.
bottle tree *n.* Any of several trees of the genus *Brachychiton*, native to Australia, characterised by a bottle-like swelling of the trunk.
bot·tom (bóttəm) *n.* 1. a. The lowest or deepest part of anything. b. The far end of something. c. The last place, as on a list. d. The worst or least favourable point: *started life at the bottom.* 2. The underside. 3. The supporting part of something; a foundation; a base. 4. The basic underlying cause or origin: *to find out what's at the bottom of the dispute.* 5. The land below a body of water: *a river bottom.* 6. a. *Nautical.* The part of a ship's hull below the water line. b. A ship: *"English merchants did much of their overseas trade in foreign bottoms"* (G.M. Trevelyan). 7. *Plural.* The trousers of pyjamas. 8. *Informal.* The buttocks. 9. The seat of a chair. 10. *British Informal.* Weight or authority. 11. *Chiefly U.S. Often plural.* Low-lying alluvial land adjacent to a river. 12. The lowest part of a mine. 13. *Physics.* A quantum number, a property of certain types of elementary particle, originally postulated to account for the long lifetime of the upsilon particle. Also called "beauty", "b". ---at bottom. Basically; actually. ---get to the bottom of. To find out the truth about.

~*adj.* 1. Lowest; undermost; fundamental. 2. *Physics.* a. Designating a type of quark with unit quantum number bottom. b. Pertaining to an elementary particle that contains one or more bottom quarks and no bottom antiquarks.
~*v.* bottomed, -toming, -toms. ---*tr.* 1. To provide with an underside or foundation. 2. To provide (a chair) with a bottom. 3. To establish on a foundation or basis; ground; found. Used with *on* or *upon: The theory is bottomed on questionable assumptions.* 4. To grasp the meaning of; fathom: *bottom a mystery.* ---*intr.* 1. To rest on or touch the bottom: *The submarine bottomed on the ocean floor.*
---bottom out. To descend to the lowest point possible, after which only a rise may occur: *Coffee bottomed out in the market.* [Middle English *botme*, Old English *botm*, from Germanic.]
bottom drawer *n.* 1. A drawer formerly used by young women to store household goods such as linen or silverware before marriage. Also *U.S.* "hope chest", *Australian & N.Z.* "glory box". 2. *British.* The contents of this drawer.
bottom dollar *n. Chiefly U.S. Slang.* The last of one's money. Used chiefly in the phrase *bet one's bottom dollar.*
bot·tom·less (bóttəm-ləss, -liss) *adj.* 1. Having no bottom. 2. Unfathomable; limitless.
bottomless pit *n.* An unending drain on resources.
bottom line *n. Chiefly U.S.* 1. The lowest line in a financial statement, showing net income or loss. 2. *Informal.* The end result or basic implications or purpose.
bot·tom·most (bóttəm-mōst) *adj.* Deepest, most profound.
bot·tom·ry (bóttəmri) *n.* A contract by which a shipowner borrows money to finance a voyage, pledging the vessel as security. [BOTTOM (a ship) + -RY, by analogy with Dutch *bodemerij*.]
bot·u·lin (bóttle-lin) *n.* Any of several nerve toxins produced by the bacterium *Clostridium botulinum* and found in improperly tinned or improperly smoked foods. [New Latin *botulinus*, from Latin *botulus*, sausage.]
bot·u·lism (bóttew-liz'm) *n.* An often fatal food poisoning caused by botulin and characterised by vomiting, abdominal pain, coughing, muscular weakness, and visual disturbance. [German *Botulismus*, "sausage-poisoning", from Latin *botulus*, sausage.]
Bot·vin·nik (bót-vinnik), **Mikhail Moiseiyvich** (1911---95). Soviet chess grandmaster and world champion. He first won the Soviet championship in 1931. He was world champion three times (1948---57, 1958---60, and 1961---63).
bou·chée (boōshay, boō-sháy) *n.* A puff pastry case, usually filled with savoury foods. [French, "mouthful".]
Bou·cher (boōshay, boō-sháy), **François** (1703---70). French painter. He was an outstanding representative of the rococo style of the 18th century, noted for his tapestries.
bou·clé (boō-klay ‖ *U.S.* boō-kláy) *n.* 1. A type of yarn, usually three-ply and having one thread looser than the others, which produces a rough-textured cloth. 2. Fabric woven or knitted from this yarn. [French, "curled".]
Bou·dic·ca (boōdicka, boō-dícka). Also **Bo·a·di·ce·a** (bō-ə-di-sée-ə) (died A.D. 60). Queen of the Iceni people of eastern Britain. When her husband, King Prasutagus, died in A.D. 59 or 60, she led the Iceni of what is now Norfolk and Suffolk in a fierce and temporarily successful onslaught against the Romans, who had seized all of her late husband's kingdom.
bou·doir (boō-dwaar ‖ -dwawr) *n.* A woman's private sitting room, dressing room, or bedroom. Often humorous. [French, "place for pouting", from Old French *bouder*, to pout, sulk (imitative).]
bouf·fant (boōfoN ‖ *U.S.* boō-faánt) *adj.* Puffed-out; full: *a bouffant hairstyle.* [French, present participle of *bouffer*, to swell, puff up (the cheeks), from Old French (imitative).]
bouffe (boōf) *n.* Comic opera. See *opera buffa.*
Bou·gain·ville (boōgən-vil). Volcanic island in the south Pacific Ocean, the largest of the Solomon Islands. It forms part of Papua New Guinea.
Bou·gain·ville (boōgən-vil, -véel), **Louis (Antoine) de** (1729---1811). French navigator and explorer. In *c.* 1764 he established a short-lived French colony on the Falkland Islands and (1766---69) made a voyage round the world with a crew that included astronomers and naturalists.
bou·gain·vil·le·a, bou·gain·vil·lae·a (boōgən-víl-i-ə, -yə) *n.* Any of several woody tropical American vines of the genus *Bougainvillea*, having inconspicuous flowers surrounded by showy red, purple, or orange bracts. [After Louis Antoine de BOUGAINVILLE.]
bough (bow) *n.* A large branch of a tree. [Middle English *bow, bough*, Old English *bōg, bōh*, from Germanic.]
bought. Past tense and past participle of **buy.**
bought·en. *Regional.* Alternative past participle of **buy.**
bou·gie (boō-zhee, boō-zhée ‖ -jee) *n. Medicine.* A slender, pliable implement inserted into a bodily canal, such as the urethra or rectum, to dilate the passageway. [French, from Old French, a fine wax imported from *Bougie* (Arabic *Bujiya*), town in Algeria.]
bouil·la·baisse (boō-yə-béss, -báyss, -bess, -bayss) *n.* A highly seasoned fish stew made with several kinds of fish and shellfish. [French, earlier *bouille-abaisse*, from Provençal *bouiabaisso*, "boil (and) settle" (jocular command to the pot, because the fish is rapidly cooked).]
bouil·lon (boō-yoN ‖ *U.S. also* boōl-yon, -yən) *n.* The stock, often served as a broth, made from the liquid in which beef or chicken is simmered. [French, from Old French, from *boulir*, to boil, from Latin *bullīre*.]
boul. boulevard.

Bou·lan·ger (boͦo-loN-zhay, -zháy), **Georges-Ernest-Jean-Marie** (1837–91). French general and politician. After the Franco-Prussian war, he rallied the extreme right wing in France against Germany for the loss of Alsace-Lorraine. For a time he was the most popular French politician, but was dismissed from the government and the army (1887) by republicans who viewed him as a potential military dictator.

Boulanger, Nadia (1887–1979). French teacher of musical composition. She taught and influenced several generations of modern composers, including Milhaud, Copland, Elliott Carter, and Lennox Berkeley.

boul·der (bōldər) n. A large, rounded, stone block lying on the surface of the ground, or sometimes embedded in the soil, and generally different in composition from other rocks in the immediate vicinity. [Middle English *bulder (ston),* from Scandinavian, akin to dialectal Swedish *bullersten,* stone in a stream : *buller-,* "rounded object".]

boulder clay n. An unstratified clay deposited by glaciers and ice sheets. Also called "till".

Boulder Dam. See **Hoover Dam.**

bou·le[1] (boͦo-lee, -lay) n. **1. a. Capital B.** The senate of 400 members founded in ancient Athens by Solon. **b.** A legislative assembly in any of the states of ancient Greece. **2. Capital B.** The lower house of the modern Greek legislature. [Greek *boulē,* "will", "council".]

boule[2] (boͦol) n. A pear-shaped synthetic sapphire, ruby, or other alumina-based gem, produced by fusing and tinting alumina. [French, "ball", from Latin *bulla,* bubble, ball.]

boule[3]. Variant of **buhl.**

boules (boͦol) n. *Used with a singular verb.* A ball game akin to bowls, played in France with metal balls on a hard surface. [French, "bowls".]

boul·e·vard (boͦol-vaar, boͦolə-, -vaard ‖ *U.S. also* boͦolə-) n. *Abbr.* **blvd., boul.** A broad city street, often tree-lined and landscaped. [French, from Old French *boloart, belouart,* rampart, promenade converted from an old rampart, from Middle Dutch *bolwerc,* from Middle High German, **BULWARK.**]

bou·le·var·dier (boͦol-várd-yay, boͦolə- ‖ *U.S. also* boͦolə-vaar-déer) n. A man-about-town. [French, a man who frequents boulevards, from **BOULEVARD.**]

Bou·lez (boͦo-lezz ‖ boͦo-lézz), **Pierre** (1925–). French composer and conductor. He is a leading exponent of the French avant garde, in particular as an adherent of 12-tone atonality. His best-known works are *Le Marteau sans Maître* (1955) and *Pli selon pli* (1960).

boulle. Variant of **buhl.**

Bou·logne-sur-Mer (boͦo-lóyn-sewr-maír, bə-, -soor- ‖ *Chiefly U.S.* -lón-). Also **Boulogne.** Port and resort in the Pas-de-Calais département in northwest France, on the English Channel. It has grown from its Celtic origins to be the leading fishing port in France.

boult. Variant of **bolt** (to sift).

Boult (bōlt), **Sir Adrian Cedric** (1889–1983). British orchestral conductor. In 1930 he became conductor of the new BBC Symphony Orchestra, with whom he stayed until 1950, when he became musical director of the London Philharmonic.

Bou·mé·di·enne (boͦo-may-di-én), **Houari** (1928–78). Algerian independence leader and politician. He studied in Cairo in the early 1950s, then returned secretly to Algeria in 1955 to take part in guerrilla action against the French. He was head of the National Liberation Army operating from Tunisia (1960–67) and when Algeria gained its independence he served under **Ben Bella** as Minister of Defence. He directed an army coup that overthrew Ben Bella (1965) and assumed the presidency of Algeria.

bounce (bownss ‖ *West Indies* bungss) v. **bounced, bouncing, bounces.** —*intr.* **1. a.** To rebound elastically from an impact, as a rubber ball. **b.** To collide and rebound elastically several times in succession. **2.** To walk or move in a springy or excited way: *The child bounced into the room.* **3.** *Informal.* To be sent back by a bank as valueless: *The cheque bounced.* **4.** *Informal.* To recover after a setback. Used with *back.* —*tr.* **1.** To cause (a body, such as a ball) to collide and rebound. **2.** To cause to rebound repeatedly. **3.** *Slang.* To expel by force. **4.** *Informal.* To send back (a worthless cheque). **5.** *British.* To induce to do or believe something by unfair pressure or bluff. **6.** *U.S. Slang.* To dismiss from employment. —*n.* **1.** A bound or rebound. **2.** A sudden spring or leap. **3. a.** A loud or heavy blow or thump. **b.** *Archaic.* The sound of an explosion: *"He speaks plain cannon fire, and smoke and bounce."* (Shakespeare). **4.** Capacity to bounce; spring: *A ball with bounce.* **5.** Spirit; liveliness. **6.** *U.S. Slang.* Expulsion; dismissal. **7.** *British.* An instance of impudent bluff: *"The whole story is a bounce of his own."* (Thomas De Quincey). [Middle English *bunsen, bonchen,* to beat, thrust, stamp (probably imitative).]

bounc·er (bówn-sər ‖ *West Indies also* búng-) n. **1.** One that bounces. **2.** A person employed to expel disorderly people from a public place. **3.** In cricket, an intimidatory ball which bounces up high, towards the upper half of the batsman's body. Also called "bumper".

bounc·ing (bówn-sing ‖ *West Indies also* búng-) adj. Vigorous; healthy: *a bouncing baby.*

bouncing Bet n. A plant, the **soapwort** (*see*). [*Bet,* pet form of *Elizabeth* (from its flower clusters, suggesting bouncing girls).]

bounc·y (bówn-si ‖ *West Indies also* búng-) adj. **-ier, -iest. 1. a.** Characterised by a capacity to bound or spring. **b.** Elastic; springy. **2.** Having vigour and buoyancy; lively. —**bounc·i·ly** adv.

bound[1] (bownd ‖ *West Indies also* bungd) *intr.v.* **bounded, bounding, bounds. 1.** To leap forward or upwards; spring. **2.** To progress quickly by bounds. —*n.* **1.** A leap; a jump. **2.** A bounce. [French *bondir,* to bounce, originally "to rebound", from Old French, to resound, from Vulgar Latin *bombitīre* (unattested), to hum, buzz, from Latin *bombīre,* to buzz, from *bombus,* a deep hollow sound, buzz, from Greek *bombos.*]

bound[2] n. **1.** *Usually plural.* Boundary; limit: *His joy knew no bounds.* **2.** *Plural.* The territory on, within, or near limiting lines: *the bounds of the kingdom.* —See Synonyms at **boundary.** —**out of bounds. 1.** In an area outside official boundaries. **2.** Transgressing moral or conventional limits. —*v.* **bounded, bounding, bounds.** —*tr.* **1.** To set a limit to. **2.** To constitute the boundary or limit of. **3.** To identify and set the boundaries of; demarcate. —*intr.* To border on another country, state, or place; adjoin. —See Synonyms at **limit.** [Middle English *bounde,* from Old French *bunde,* from Medieval Latin *bodina,* from Gaulish *bodina†* (unattested).]

bound[3]. Past tense and past participle of **bind.** —*adj.* **1. a.** Confined by bonds; tied. **b.** Restricted; obstructed. Often used in combination: *snowbound.* **2.** Under legal or moral obligation; under contract: *bound by his promise.* **3.** Indentured: *a bound apprentice.* **4.** *Abbr.* **bd.** Encased in a cover or binding: *bound volumes.* **5.** Predetermined; certain: *We are bound to be late.* **6.** *Rare.* Constipated. —**bound up in.** Wholly dedicated to: *She is bound up in her career.* —**bound up with.** Inseparably connected with or dependent on. —**I'll be bound.** *Informal.* **1.** I am sure: *It's about to rain, I'll be bound.* **2.** I am amazed: *Well, I'll be bound!*

bound[4] adj. **1.** Heading (for); going (towards): *bound for Sydney.* Often used after an expression of direction: *outward bound; homeward bound.* **2.** Intended (for); on one's way (to): *bound for a career in medicine.* [Middle English *boun,* prepared, ready to go, from Old Norse *būinn,* past participle of *būa,* to dwell, prepare.]

bound·a·ry (bówn-dri, -dəri ‖ *West Indies also* búng-) n., *pl.* **-ries. 1.** Something that indicates a border or limit. **2.** The border or limit so indicated. **3.** In cricket: **a.** The edge of the field. **b.** A ball hit by the batsman over the edge of the field. **c.** The runs scored from this ball. [From dialect *bounder,* from **BOUND** (limit).]

Synonyms: boundary, border, frontier, limit, bound, end, confine.

boundary layer n. *Physics.* The nearly motionless fluid layer found immediately adjacent to the surface of a solid, past which the fluid flows.

boundary rider n. *Australian.* A person employed to ride round the boundary of a sheep or cattle station and maintain the fences.

bound·en (bówn-dən ‖ *West Indies also* búng-) adj. **1.** Obligatory. Used only in the phrase *his bounden duty.* **2.** *Archaic.* Under obligation; obliged. [From *bounden,* obsolete past participle of **BIND.**]

bound·er (bówn-dər ‖ *West Indies also* búng-) n. **1.** One that bounds. **2.** *Chiefly British Informal.* A man who fails to behave like a gentleman. Used humorously.

bound form n. A linguistic element that always occurs as part of another word, as *-ly* in *lovely.* Compare **free form.**

bound·less (bównd-ləss, -liss ‖ *West Indies also* búngd-) adj. Without limit; infinite. See Synonyms at **infinite.** —**bound·less·ly** adv. —**bound·less·ness** n.

boun·te·ous (bówn-ti-əss ‖ *West Indies also* búng-) adj. **1.** Giving generously and kindly. **2.** Copious; plentiful. [Middle English *bountevous, bounteuous,* from Old French *bontif, bontive,* benevolent, from *bonte,* **BOUNTY.**] —**boun·te·ous·ly** adv. —**boun·te·ous·ness** n.

boun·ti·ful (bówn-ti-f'l ‖ *West Indies also* búng-) adj. **1.** Generous. **2.** Abundant; plentiful. —**boun·ti·ful·ly** adv. —**boun·ti·ful·ness** n.

boun·ty (bównti ‖ *West Indies also* búngti) n., *pl.* **-ties. 1.** Liberality in giving. **2.** Something that is given liberally. **3.** A reward, inducement, or payment, especially one given by a government for acts beneficial to the state, such as killing predatory animals or enlisting for military service. —See Synonyms at **bonus.** [Middle English *bounte,* from Old French *bonté,* from Latin *bonitās* (stem *bonitāt-*), goodness, from *bonus,* good.]

bounty hunter n. One who hunts predatory animals or criminals and outlaws for a bounty.

bou·quet (boͦo-káy, bō-, boͦo- ‖ bố-kay, boͦo-) n. **1.** A cluster of flowers; a nosegay. **2.** The fragrance typical of a wine or a liqueur. **3.** A compliment; praise. —See Synonyms at **smell.** [French, from Old North French *bosquet,* clump, diminutive of Old French *bosc,* forest, from Germanic.]

bou·quet gar·ni (gaar-née) n. *pl.* **bouquets garnis** (*pronounced as singular, or* -káyz). A bunch of herbs tied together or wrapped in cheesecloth, immersed in a soup, stew, or the like as seasoning. [French, "garnished bouquet".]

Bour·ba·ki (boͦor-ba-kée), **Nicolas.** Collective pseudonym for a group of mathematicians, most of them French. Since the late 1930s the group, in a series of articles, has been writing a comprehensive review of the study of mathematics, marked by its own language and terminology, which are occasionally at variance with orthodox terms. The group includes André Weil, Henri Cartan, Samuel Eilenberg, and Claude Chevalley.

bour·bon (búr-bən, boͦor-, -bon) n. An American whiskey distilled from a fermented mash containing not less than 51 per cent maize. [After *Bourbon* County, Kentucky.]

Bour·bons (boͦor-bənz, -bonz; *French* -bón). Members of the French royal line descending from Louis I, Duke of Bourbon (*c.* 1270–1342). They make up one of the most powerful ruling houses in modern European history. The first Bourbon king of France was Henry IV, and the line occupied the French throne until 1793 (when the French monarchy was abolished); it was briefly restored in 1814 and ruled again until the overthrow of Charles X in the July revolution of 1830. The Bourbons have been kings of Spain since 1700 and another branch of the family ruled in Naples and Sicily from 1734 until 1860.

bour·don (boórd'n) *n.* **1.** The monotonic drone bass of a bagpipe. **2.** An organ stop, commonly of the 16-foot pipes. [Middle English *burdoun*, from Old French *bourdon*, drone, from Vulgar Latin *burdō* (stem *burdon-*) (unattested), of imitative origin.]

Bourdon gauge *n.* A type of pressure gauge having a narrow spiral tube attached to a pointer and closed at one end, which tends to uncoil as the pressure in the tube increases. [After Eugène *Bourdon* (1808–84), French inventor.]

bourg (boórg; *French* boor) *n.* **1.** A French medieval village, especially one situated near a castle. **2.** A French market town. [Middle English, fortified town, from Old French, from Late Latin *burgus.*]

bour·geois¹ (boór-zhwaa, bór- ‖ *U.S. also* -zhwaá) *n., pl.* **bourgeois.** **1.** One belonging to the bourgeoisie. **2.** *Plural.* The middle classes; the bourgeoisie. **3.** One whose attitudes and behaviour are marked by conformity to the standards and conventions of the middle class. **4.** In Marxist theory, a member of the property-owning class; a capitalist, as opposed to a member of the proletariat. ~*adj.* **1.** Of or typical of the middle class. Often used derogatorily to suggest such qualities as mediocrity or a preoccupation with respectability and material values. **2.** In Marxist theory, of, pertaining to, or dominated by the property-owning class. [French, from Old French *burgeis,* from *bourg,* fortified town, BOURG.]

bour·geois² (bur-jóyss) *n. Printing.* A size of type, approximately 9-point. [French, "middle class", perhaps from its middling size between long primer and brevier.]

bour·geoise (boór-zhwaaz, bór-, -zhwaáz) *n., pl.* **-geoises** (-iz). A female member of the bourgeoisie. —**bour·geoise** *adj.*

bour·geoi·sie (boór-zhwaa-zée, bór-) *n.* **1.** The middle classes. **2.** In Marxist theory, the social group opposed to the proletariat in the class struggle; the capitalist class. [French.]

bour·geoi·si·fy (boor-zhwáazi-fī, bawr-) *tr. v.* **-fied, -fying, fies.** To turn (a member of the working class) into a member of the bourgeoisie; impart bourgeois values to. —**bour·geoi·si·fi·ca·tion** (-fi-káysh'n) *n.*

Bour·gui·ba (boor-geéba), **Habib** (1903–). Tunisian politician. His political career began in the 1930s, when he formed a nationalist party opposed to French rule, the **Néo-Destour** party, and was several times imprisoned. He was released (1954) to take part in the pre-independence negotiations and was elected prime minister of independent Tunisia (1956). He became president (1957) and was voted president for life (1975). He was ousted in 1987.

bourn¹, bourne (boorn, born ‖ bórn) *n.* A stream or small brook. [Middle English *burne,* variant of *burn,* BURN (brook).]

bourn², bourne *n. Archaic.* **1.** The terminal point of a journey or course of action; a goal. **2.** A boundary, as between properties. [French *borne,* from Old French, BOUND (limit).]

Bourne·mouth (bórn-məth; *rarely* boórn-, -mowth). Resort town on England's southern coast, at the eastern border of Dorset.

bour·rée (boórray, boór-ay ‖ *U.S.* boo-ráy, boó-) *n.* **1.** An old French dance resembling the gavotte, and usually in quick duple time beginning with an upbeat. **2.** The music for this dance. [French, "faggot" (probably from its rude movements), from *bourrer,* to stuff, from Old French *bourre,* stuffing, fluff, from Late Latin *burra,* shaggy garment.]

Bourse (boorss) *n.* The stock exchange of a city of continental Europe, especially Paris. [French, "purse", from Late Latin *bursa,* from Greek.]

bouse (bowz) *v.* **boused, bousing, bouses.** Also **bowse.** *Nautical.* —*tr.* To hoist or pull up with a tackle. —*intr.* To hoist. [16th century : origin obscure.]

bour·sin (boórsan, bóorsaN) *n.* A soft, creamy French cheese, flavoured with herbs and garlic or peppercorns.

bou·stro·phe·don (boō-strə-feé-d'n, bów-, -don) *adj. & adv.* An ancient method of writing in which the lines are inscribed alternately from right to left and from left to right. [Greek *boustrophēdon,* turning like an ox (while ploughing): *bous,* ox + *strephein,* to turn.] —**bou·stroph·e·don·ic** (-dónnik) *adj.*

bout (bowt) *n.* **1.** A contest between antagonists; a match: *a wrestling bout.* **2.** A period of time spent in a particular way or state; a spell: *bouts of depression and drinking.* [Earlier *bought,* a turn (as in ploughing), Middle English *bought,* bend, turn.]

bou·tique (boō-teék) *n.* A small retail shop that specialises in gifts, fashionable clothes, or accessories. [French, from Old Provençal *botica,* from Greek *apothēkē,* storeroom, from *apotithenai,* to put away : *apo-,* away + *tithenai,* to put, place.]

bou·ton·niere, bou·ton·nière (booton-yáir, -i-áir ‖ *U.S.* boōt-ə-neér, -ən-yáir) *n. Chiefly U.S.* A flower **buttonhole** (*see*). [French.]

Bout·ros-Ghal·i (boōt-ros gaáli), **Boutros** (1922–). Egyptian diplomat. Minister for foreign affairs (1977–91). He was the first Arab and the first African to become Secretary-General of the United Nations (1992–96).

Bou·vier des Flan·dres (boōv-yay day flaán-dərz ‖ flán-, *U.S.* boōv-yáy) *pl.* **Bouviers des Flandres** (*pronounced as singular*). A rough-coated dog of a breed originally used in Belgium for herding and guarding cattle. [French, "cowherd of Flanders".]

bou·zou·ki (boō-zoóki, boō-, bə-) *n.* A Greek fretted string instrument, similar to the mandolin in sound. [Modern Greek *mpouzouki,* perhaps from Turkish *büyük,* large.]

Bo·vet (bóvay ‖ bō-váy), **Daniel** (1907–92). Italian pharmacologist, born in Switzerland. For his discovery of gallamine and development of antihistamines, sulpha drugs, and other muscle relaxants used in surgery, he was awarded the Nobel prize for medicine (1957).

bo·vid (bōvid) *adj.* Of or belonging to the family Bovidae, which includes hoofed, hollow-horned ruminants such as cattle, sheep, goats, buffaloes, and antelopes. ~*n.* A member of the Bovidae. [New Latin *Bovidae,* from Latin *bōs* (stem *bov-*), ox, cow.]

bo·vine (bōv-īn ‖ *U.S. also* -een) *adj.* **1.** Of, pertaining to, or resembling an ox, cow, or other ruminant animal of the genus *Bos.* **2.** Sluggish; dull; stolid. ~*n.* A bovine animal. [Late Latin *bovīnus,* from Latin *bōs* (stem *bov-*), ox, cow.]

bovine spongiform encephalopathy *n. Abbr.* **BSE.** A slowly progressive, invariably fatal, and so far untreatable disease of cattle, affecting chiefly the brain and causing it to assume a spongy appearance. BSE may be related to scrapie and CJD. Also called "mad cow disease".

Bov·ril (bóvril) *n.* A trademark for a beef extract, used for making drinks or flavouring foods.

bov·ver (bóvvər) *n. British Slang.* Violence or disorderly behaviour especially by gangs of youths. [From pronunciation of BOTHER.]

bovver boots *pl.n.* In Britain, heavy boots worn as part of the characteristic clothing of certain gangs of youths.

bovver boy *n.* In Britain, a youth belonging to a gang, usually wearing heavy boots and trousers with braces, and having closely cropped hair, commonly thought of as disorderly and aggressive.

bow¹ (bow) *n.* **1.** The front section of a ship or boat. **2.** The oar or oarsman closest to the bow of a boat. ~*adj.* Of or close to the bow. [Middle English, from Middle Low German *boog.*]

bow² (bow) *v.* **bowed, bowing, bows.** —*intr.* **1.** To bend or curve downwards; stoop. **2.** To incline the body or head or bend the knee in greeting, consent, courtesy, acknowledgment, submission, or veneration. **3.** To yield or comply; defer: *I bow to your superior knowledge.* —*tr.* **1.** To bend (the head, knee, or body) in order to express greeting, consent, courtesy, submission, or veneration. **2.** To convey (greeting or consent, for example) by bowing. **3.** To escort deferentially and with bows: *He bowed us into the restaurant.* **4.** To cause to acquiesce or submit. **5.** To oppress; overburden. Often used with *down: Grief bowed him down.* —See Synonyms at **yield.** —**bow and scrape.** To behave in an obsequious manner. —**bow out.** To remove oneself from a situation or agreement. ~*n.* An inclination of the head or body, as in greeting, consent, courtesy, acknowledgment, submission, or veneration. —**make (one's) bow.** To enter or retire formally. —**take a bow.** To recognise and accept applause or an introduction. [Middle English *bowen,* Old English *būgan.*]

bow³ (bō) *n.* **1. a.** Something that is bent, curved, or arched: *a bow in a wall; a rainbow.* **2.** A weapon consisting of a curved rod of a resilient material, usually wood, held tightly in an arch by a taut bowstring strung from end to end and used to propel arrows. **3.** An archer, or archers collectively. **4.** A rod having horsehair drawn tightly between its two raised ends, used in playing instruments such as the violin, cello, or viola. **5. a.** A knot usually having two loops and two ends; a bowknot. **b.** This knot made with ribbon or braid and used to decorate the hair, clothing, or the like. **6.** The loop forming the handle of a pair of scissors or large key. ~*v.* **bowed, bowing, bows.** —*tr.* **1.** To bend (something) into the shape of a bow. **2.** To play (a stringed instrument) with a bow. —*intr.* **1.** To bend into a curve or bow. **2.** To play a stringed instrument with a bow. [Middle English *bowe,* Old English *boga,* bow, arch.]

bow compass (bō) *n.* A drawing compass with legs that are connected by an adjustable metal spring band. Also called "bow-spring compass".

Bowd·ler (bówdlər), **Thomas** (1754–1825). British editor, famous for his expurgated editions of classic literary works, especially his *Family Shakespeare* (1818).

bowd·ler·ise, bowd·ler·ize (bówd-lər-īz ‖ *U.S.* bód-) *tr.v.* **-ised, -ising, -ises.** To expurgate prudishly. [After Thomas BOWDLER.] —**bowd·ler·ism** *n.* —**bowd·ler·i·sa·tion** (-ī-záysh'n ‖ *U.S.* -i-) *n.*

bow·el (bów-əl) *n.* **1.** An intestine, especially in humans. **2.** *Usually plural.* The digestive tract below the stomach. **3.** *Plural.* The inner depths of anything: *in the bowels of the ship.* **4.** *Plural. Archaic.* The seat of pity or the gentler emotions. [Middle English *b(o)uel,* from Old French *bo(u)el, boiel,* from Latin *botellus,* diminutive of *botulus,* sausage.]

bowel movement *n.* **1.** The discharge of waste matter from the body; defecation. **2.** The matter discharged; faeces.

Bow·en (bō-in), **Elizabeth (Dorothea Cole)** (1899–1973). British novelist and short-story writer, born in Ireland. Her first collection of short stories, *Encounters,* appeared in 1923; her first novel, *The Hotel,* in 1927. Her most popular novels were *The House in Paris* (1935) and *The Heat of the Day* (1949).

bow·er¹ (bowr, bów-ər) *n.* **1.** A shaded, leafy recess; an arbour. **2.** *Poetic.* A private chamber; a boudoir. **3.** *Poetic.* A rustic cottage; a country retreat. ~*tr.v.* **bowered, -ering, -ers.** *Poetic.* To enclose in or as if in a bower; embower. [Middle English *bour,* dwelling, inner apartment,

bower² *n.* In the game of euchre, either of the two highest cards, the jack of trumps *(right bower)* or the jack of the same colour as the trump *(left bower)*. [German *Bauer*, "farmer", "peasant", jack (in cards), from Middle High German *būre, gebūre,* from Old High German *gibūro.*]

bower³ *n.* The heaviest of a ship's anchors, carried at the bow. Also called "bower anchor".

bow·er·bird (bówr-burd, bów-ər-) *n.* **1.** Any of various songbirds of the family Ptilonorhynchidae, of Australia and New Guinea. The males of many species build bowers of grasses, twigs, and coloured materials to attract females. **2.** *Australian Informal.* A person who collects trivia.

Bow·er·y, the (bówr-i, bów-əri). A street and section of lower Manhattan in New York City, frequented by derelicts and alcoholics.

bow·fin (bṓ-fin) *n.* A primitive, bony, freshwater fish, *Amia calva,* of central and eastern North America. Also "dogfish", "mudfish".

bow·front (bṓ-frunt) *adj.* Having an outward-curving front: *a bow-front bureau.*

bow·head (bṓ-hed) *n.* A whale, *Balaena mysticetus,* of Arctic seas, having a large head. [From the curved top of its head.]

bow·ie knife (bṓ-i, bōō-i) *n.* A single-edged, steel hunting knife, about 38 centimetres (15 inches) in length, having a hilt and a crosspiece. [After Colonel James *Bowie* (1790–1836), U.S. Texas colonist (probably designed by his brother, Rezin P. Bowie).]

bow·knot (bṓ-not) *n.* A knot with large, decorative loops.

bowl¹ (bōl) *n.* **1. a.** A hemispherical container, wider than deep, for food or fluids. **b.** The contents of such a vessel. **2.** A bowl-shaped part of something, such as a spoon or pipe. **3.** *Chiefly U.S.* A bowl-shaped building such as an amphitheatre or a football stadium. **4.** A bowl-shaped topographical depression. **5.** *Archaic.* A drinking goblet. [Middle English *bolle,* Old English *bolla.*]

bowl² *n.* **1. a.** In the game of bowls, a large, wooden ball weighted or slightly flattened so as to roll with a bias. **b.** In the game of tenpin bowling, a large heavy ball with holes for the fingers. **2.** A roll or throw of the ball, as in bowls. **3.** *Machinery.* A revolving cylinder or drum.
~*v.* **bowled, bowling, bowls.** —*intr.* **1.** To participate in a game of bowling. **2.** To throw or roll a ball in bowls or tenpin bowling. **3.** To move smoothly and rapidly. Usually used with *along.* **4.** In cricket, to deliver the ball from one end of the pitch towards the batsman at the other, keeping the arm straight throughout. —*tr.* **1.** To throw or roll (a ball) in bowls or tenpin bowling. **2.** To make or achieve by bowling. **3.** In cricket, to get (a batsman) out with a bowled ball that knocks the bails off the wicket. Used with *out.* —**bowl over. 1.** To knock over (a person or thing); cause to fall. **2.** *Informal.* To take by surprise; astound. [Middle English *boule, bowle,* originally "ball", from Old French *boule,* from Latin *bulla.*]

bow legs (bō) *pl.n.* Legs having an abnormal outward curvature that leaves a wide gap at the knees. Also called "bandy legs".

bow·leg·ged (bṓ-lēgid, -légd, -legid, -legd) *adj.* Having bow legs; bandy-legged.

bowl·er¹ (bṓl-ər) *n.* One that bowls, especially in cricket.

bowler² *n. Chiefly British.* A stiff felt hat with a round crown and a narrow, curved brim. Also *U.S.* "derby". [After John *Bowler,* 19th-century London hatmaker.]

bow·line (bṓ-lin ‖ -līn) *n.* **1.** *Nautical.* A rope leading from the weather edge of a square sail to the bow to hold it forward when sailing close-hauled. **2.** A knot forming a loop that does not slip. In this sense, also called "bowline knot". —**on a bowline.** *Nautical.* Close-hauled. [Middle English *bouline,* probably from Middle Low German *bōlīne* : *boog,* BOW (of a ship) + *līne,* line.]

bowl·ing (bṓl-ing) *n.* **1. Tenpin bowling** *(see).* **2.** Any of various similar games, such as skittles or ninepins. **3.** The game of bowls.

bowling alley *n.* **1.** A smooth, level, wooden alley used in bowling. **2.** A building or room containing such alleys.

bowling average *n.* The number of runs scored off a bowler in a cricket season divided by the number of batsmen he has got out.

bowling crease *n.* In cricket, a line marked at the bowler's end of the wicket beyond which he must not go when delivering a ball.

bowling green *n.* A level, grassy area for lawn bowls.

bowls (bōlz) *n. Used with a singular verb.* A game played on a bowling green between two people or two opposing sides in which large balls are bowled at a small white ball called the jack, the object being to approach it as closely as possible.

bow·man¹ (bṓ-mən) *n., pl.* **-men** (-mən). *Archaic.* An archer.

bow·man² (bów-mən) *n., pl.* **-men** (-mən). An oarsman stationed at the bow of a boat.

Bow·man's capsule (bṓmənz) *n. Anatomy.* In vertebrates, the cup-shaped end of a kidney tubule that surrounds a knot of blood capillaries and with them forms the Malpighian body. [After Sir William *Bowman* (1816–92), English surgeon.]

bow pen (bō) *n.* A bow compass with a pen at the end of one leg.

bow saw (bō) *n.* A type of saw with a narrow blade held in a large frame, used for cutting curves.

bowse. *Nautical.* Variant of **bouse.**

bow·ser (bówzər) *n.* **1.** A petrol tanker used especially for refuelling aircraft. **2.** *Australian.* A petrol pump. [From a trademark.]

bow·shot (bṓ-shot) *n.* The distance an arrow can be shot.

bow·sprit (bṓ-sprit ‖ bów-) *n.* A spar extending forward from the stem of a ship. [Middle English *bouspret,* from Middle Low German *bōchsprēt, bugsprēt.*]

Bow Street runner (bō) *n.* A member of the first organised police force in London, set up in 1748 by Bow Street magistrate's court.

bow·string (bṓ-string) *n.* The string of a bow.

bowstring hemp *n.* **1.** The fibre from the leaves of any plant of the genus *Sansevieria,* used for cordage and in packing. **2.** The **sansevieria** *(see).*

bow tie (bō) *n.* A man's small tie tied in the shape of a bow.

bow window (bō) *n.* A bay window built in a curve.

bow-wow (bów-wów; *in sense 2,* bów-wow) *n.* **1.** An imitation or representation of the bark of a dog. **2.** A dog. Used by or to children. [Imitative.]

bow·yang (bṓ-yang) *n. Australian & N.Z.* Either of a pair of ties worn below the knee, especially by sheep shearers, to prevent trouser legs from getting in the way. [From English dialect *bowy-yangs,* leggings.]

bow·yer (bṓ-yər) *n.* **1.** *Archaic.* An archer. **2.** One who makes bows.

box¹ (boks) *n.* **1. a.** A rigid, usually rectangular container, typically having a lid or cover. **2.** The amount or quantity such a container can hold. **3.** A separate compartment in a public place, such as a theatre, for the accommodation of a small group. **4. a.** A small structure serving as a shelter or used for a particular purpose: *a sentry box; a telephone box.* **b.** Any of various containers used for a particular purpose: *a money box.* **5.** *British.* A small country house: *a shooting box.* **6.** A separate compartment or partitioned area for a horse, especially in a stable. See **loose box. 7.** The raised seat for a driver of a coach or carriage. **8.** A stand or area in a courtroom reserved for specific people: *the witness box.* **9.** Either of the two marked areas around the goals on a soccer pitch where penalties may be incurred. **10.** In baseball, any of various designated areas for certain players, especially the batter. **11.** A protective rigid casing worn by sportsmen, especially cricketers, to protect the genitals. **12.** Featured printed matter, enclosed by lines, a border, or white space and placed within or between text columns. **13.** A pigeonhole, receptacle, or file used by a post office, newspaper office, or mail agency for sorting subscribers' or advertisers' mail. **14.** An insulating, enclosing, or protective casing or part in a machine, such as a steering box. Often used in combination: *a gearbox.* **15.** *Australian.* A mixing up, usually accidental, of flocks of sheep. **16.** *U.S., Australian & N.Z. Slang.* The vagina. —**box of birds.** *Australian & N.Z. Informal.* A happy, lively person. —**one out of the box.** *Australian & N.Z. Informal.* An outstanding or wonderful person or thing. —**the box.** *Chiefly British Informal.* Television.
~*tr.v.* **boxed, boxing, boxes. 1.** To pack or put in a box. **2.** To confine in or as if in a box. Often used with *in* or *up.* **3.** *Nautical.* To boxhaul. **4.** *Australian.* To mix up (flocks of sheep). [Middle English *box,* Old English *box,* from Late Latin *buxis,* variant of Latin *pyxis,* box (made of boxwood), from Greek *puxis,* from *puxos,* box tree.]

box² *n.* A blow or slap with the hand: *a box on the ear.*
~*v.* **boxed, boxing, boxes.** —*tr.* **1.** To hit with the hand or fist. **2.** To take part in a boxing match with. —*intr.* To fight with the fists; spar. [Middle English *box†.*]

box³ *n., pl.* **box** or **boxes. 1.** Any evergreen tree or shrub of the genus *Buxus;* especially, *B. sempervirens,* used for hedges, borders, and garden mazes. Also called "boxwood". **2.** The wood of this tree, **boxwood** *(see).* **3.** Any of several trees whose timber or foliage resembles that of box. [Middle English *box,* Old English *box,* from Latin *buxus,* from Greek *puxos.*]

Box and Cox *n. Sometimes small* **b,** *small* **c. 1.** Two people who live in the same house but never see each other. **2.** Two people who take turns to perform the same role, function, or position. [After a stage play by J. Maddison Morton (1811–91) in which two characters share a room in this way.] —**Box and Cox** *v.*

box calf *n.* Calfskin treated with chromium salts and having square markings on the grain. [After Joseph *Box,* 19th-century London bootmaker.]

box camera *n.* A camera shaped like a box with a simple lens and viewfinder.

box·car (bóks-kaar) *n. U.S.* An enclosed railway freight car.

box coat *n.* **1.** A heavy overcoat formerly worn by coachmen. **2.** A coat designed to hang loose from the shoulders. [From BOX (seat for coach driver).]

box·el·der (bóks-éldər) *n.* A widely cultivated maple tree, *Acer negundo,* of North America, having compound leaves with lobed leaflets. Also called "ash-leaved maple".

box·er¹ (bóksər) *n.* One who boxes; specifically, one whose profession is boxing.

boxer² *n.* A short-haired dog of a breed developed in Germany, having a brownish coat and a short, square-jawed muzzle. [German *Boxer,* from English BOXER, from its pugnacious nature.]

Boxer *n.* A member of a secret society in China that attempted in 1900 to drive foreigners from the country by violence and to force Chinese Christians to renounce their religion. [Rough translation of Mandarin Chinese *yì hé quán,* "righteous harmonious fists", altered from *yì hé tuán,* "Righteous Harmonious Brigade" (name of the society) : *yì,* righteousness + *hé,* harmony + *tuán,* brigade.]

boxer shorts *pl. n.* Loose-fitting underpants for men or boys. [From their resemblance to the shorts worn by boxers in the ring.]

box·fish (bóks-fish) *n., pl.* **-fishes** or collectively **boxfish.** A fish, the **trunkfish** *(see).*

box girder *n.* A hollow girder with a square or rectangular section.

box·haul (bóks-hawl) *tr.v.* **-hauled, -hauling, -hauls.** To turn (a square-rigged ship) about on its heel by bracing the foresails against the wind and steering round.

box·ing (bóksing) n. The sport or profession of fighting with the fists; especially, the modern sport of fighting with gloved hands, inside a raised ring.

Boxing Day n. The first weekday after Christmas, observed as a holiday in Britain and other Commonwealth countries, when Christmas boxes were traditionally given to household employees and other service workers.

boxing glove n. A heavily padded leather glove worn in boxing.

box jellyfish n. A highly venomous jellyfish, *Chironex fleckeri*, common in Australian waters.

box junction n. In Britain, an area of road painted with criss-cross yellow stripes that a vehicle is not allowed to enter until its exit from the area is clear.

box kite n. A tailless kite consisting of a rectangular, box-shaped frame, encircled with cloth or paper bands.

box lacrosse n. *Chiefly Canadian*. A form of lacrosse played in an enclosure by teams of seven players. Also informally called "boxla".

box office n. 1. An office that sells tickets, makes bookings, or gives information for a theatre, cinema, or the like. 2. The drawing power of a theatrical entertainment or of a performer; popular appeal. —**box-of·fice** adj.

box pleat n. A double pleat formed by two facing folds.

box-room (bóks-rōōm, -rōōm) n. A small room in which trunks, boxes, suitcases, or the like are stored.

box seat n. 1. A seat in a theatre or concert hall box. 2. *Australian & N.Z.* The most sought-after or advantageous position.

box set n. A stage set with a ceiling and three walls.

box spanner n. A type of spanner with a socket that fits over the nut.

box spring n. Any of a set of coiled springs enclosed in a frame and used as a base for a mattress, chair, or the like.

box-wood (bóks-wōōd) n. 1. The hard, light-yellow wood of the box tree, used to make musical instruments, rulers, inlays, and engraving blocks. 2. A shrub or tree, **box** (*see*).

boy (boy) n. 1. A male child or youth. 2. **a.** *Informal*. Any grown man; a fellow. Often used in the plural to imply a spirit of camaraderie amongst a group of men. **b.** An immature or inexperienced man. 3. A native manservant, especially formerly in British colonies and South Africa. 4. Used to address or call a domestic animal.
~*interj. Chiefly U.S.* Used as a mild exclamation. [Middle English *boye, bay, bye*, originally "male servant", "knave", possibly from Norman French *abuié, embuié* (unattested), "fettered", from Old French *embuier*, to fetter, from Vulgar Latin *imboiāre* (unattested) : *in-*, in + *boiae*, collar for the neck, fetters, from Greek *boeiai (dorai)*, ox(hides), hence thongs made from oxhide, from *bous*, ox.] —**boy·hood** n.

bo·yar (bóy-ər, -aar, bṓ-yaar) n. Also **bo·yard** (-ard). 1. A member of a former Russian aristocratic order abolished by Peter I. 2. A member of a former aristocratic class of Romania. [Earlier *boiaren*, from Russian *boyarin*, from Old Russian, "of the highest rank", from Old Slavic *boljarinŭ*, from Old Turkic *boila*, a title.]

boy·cott (bóykot) tr.v. **-cotted, -cotting, -cotts.** To abstain from using, buying, or dealing with, as a protest or means of coercion. ~*n.* The act or an instance of boycotting. [After Charles C. *Boycott* (1832–97), land agent for the Earl of Erne, in County Mayo, Ireland, who was ostracised by the tenants for refusing to lower the rents.] —**boy·cott·er** n.

boy·friend (bóy-frend) n. A favoured male sexual or romantic partner; a sweetheart or lover.

boy·ish (bóy-ish) adj. Characteristic of, befitting, or having the youthful, attractive appearance of a boy: *a boyish prank*. —**boy·ish·ly** adv. —**boy·ish·ness** n.

boy·la (bóyla) n. *Australian*. An Aboriginal witch doctor. [From a native Australian language.]

Boyle (boyl), **Robert** (1627–91). Irish physicist and chemist, sometimes called the father of chemistry, since his precision in defining chemical elements and chemical reactions was a major step in separating the science of chemistry from alchemy.

Boyle's law n. The principle that at a fixed temperature the pressure of a gas varies inversely with its volume. The law is obeyed only by a hypothetical ideal gas. Real gases approximately obey Boyle's law at high temperatures and low pressures. [After R. BOYLE.]

Boys' Brigade n. An organisation for boys, founded in Britain (1883) to develop self-discipline and team spirit.

Boy Scout n. Sometimes small **b**, small **s**. 1. Formerly, a **scout** (*see*). 2. *Informal*. One thought to have a naive idealism or sense of duty. Usually considered offensive.

boy·sen·ber·ry (bóyz'n-bri, -bəri || -berri) n., pl. **-ries.** 1. A prickly bramble hybridised from the loganberry and various blackberries and raspberries. 2. The large, wine-red, edible berry borne by this plant. [After Rudolph *Boysen*, 20th-century U.S. horticulturist.]

Boz. Pen name of Charles **Dickens**.

bp, b.pt. boiling point.

bp. bishop.

B.P. 1. British Petroleum. 2. British Pharmacopoeia.

B/P bills payable.

B.P.C. British Pharmaceutical Codex.

bpd, b.p.d. barrels per day.

B. Pharm. Bachelor of Pharmacy.

B. Phil. Bachelor of Philosophy.

b.pl. birthplace.

bpi, b.p.i. bits per inch.

Br The symbol for the element bromine.

br. 1. branch. 2. bridge. 3. *Law*. brief. 4. brother. 5. brown.

Br. 1. Breton. 2. Britain; British. 3. Brother (religious).

B.R. British Rail; British Railways.

B/R bills receivable.

bra (braa) n. A brassiere. —**bra·less** adj.

braai (brī) v. **braaied, braaiing, braais.** *South African.* —*tr.* To grill (food, especially meat) over a fire; barbecue. —*intr.* To cook in this way.
~*n. South African.* 1. A braaivleis. 2. Any item of equipment, such as an outdoor fireplace or a portable barbecue stove, in which a fire is made for braaiing meat. [Afrikaans, to roast, grill.]

braai·vleis (brī́-flayss) n. *South African.* A barbecue. [Afrikaans, *braai*, to grill + *vleis*, meat.]

braa·ta (bráwtə) n. *West Indian.* A small amount added to something, as to food that one is buying. [Spanish *barata*, cheap, a bargain.]

Bra·bant (brə-bánt) n. Former industrial and agricultural province of central Belgium. It is now split into two densely populated provinces: Dutch speaking Flemish Brabant to the north, and French speaking Walloon Brabant to the south.

Brab·ham (brábbəm), **Sir John Arthur,** known as **Jack** (1926–). Australian motor racing driver. He won the Formula One world championship in 1959 and 1960. In 1966 he was the first driver to win the world championship in a car of his own construction.

bra-burn·ing (braá-burning) n. Militant feminist protest or public demonstration. Used derogatorily. —**bra-burn·ing** adj. —**bra-burn·er** n.

brace (brayss) n., pl. **braces** or **brace** (for sense 13 only). 1. A device that holds or fastens two or more parts together or in place; a clamp. 2. Any device that steadies or holds something erect, such as a supporting beam in a building. 3. *Plural. Chiefly British.* A pair of straps, often elasticated, worn over the shoulders to hold a pair of trousers up. Also *U.S.* "suspenders". 4. *Medicine*. An appliance used to support a bodily part. 5. *Often plural. Dentistry.* An arrangement of adjustable bands and wires fixed to the teeth to correct irregular alignment. 6. *Nautical*. A rope by which a yard is controlled and secured on a square-rigged ship. 7. *Archery*. A protective pad strapped to the bow arm. 8. *Music*. A leather loop that slides to change the tension on the cords of a drum. 9. *Music*. **a.** A symbol connecting two or more staves. **b.** A set of connected staves. 10. A cranklike handle with an adjustable aperture at one end for securing and turning a bit. See **brace and bit**. 11. *Printing*. Either of two symbols { }, used to connect written or printed lines that should be considered together or are related in some way. 12. *Mathematics*. Either of a pair of symbols, { }, used to indicate aggregation or to clarify the grouping of quantities when parentheses and square brackets have already been used. Also informally called "bracket". 13. A pair of like things: *a brace of partridges*. —See Synonyms at **couple**.
~*tr. v.* **braced, bracing, braces.** 1. To provide or strengthen with a brace or braces. 2. To support or hold steady with or as if with a brace or braces. 3. To prepare or position so as to be ready for an impact or danger. 4. To invigorate; stimulate. 5. *Nautical*. To turn (the yards of a ship) by the braces. —**brace up**. To summon one's strength or endurance. [Middle English, arm guard, support, from Old French *brace*, the two arms, from Latin *bracchia*, plural of *bracchium*, arm, from Greek *brakhiōn*.]

brace and bit n. A hand tool for boring holes, consisting of a drilling bit rotated by a handle.

brace·let (bráyss-lət, -lit) n. 1. An ornamental band or chain encircling the wrist. 2. *Plural. Chiefly U.S. Slang.* Handcuffs. [Middle English, from Old French *bracelet*, diminutive of *bracel*, "little arm", armlet, from Latin *bracchiāle*, from *bracchium*, arm.]

brac·er¹ (bráyssər) n. 1. Something or someone that braces. 2. *Informal*. A stimulating drink, especially an alcoholic one; a tonic.

bracer² n. An arm or wrist guard worn by archers and fencers. [Middle English, arm guard, from Old French *brasseure*, from *bras*, arm, from Latin *bracchium*.]

bra·chi·al (bráyk-yəl, -i-əl || brák-) adj. Of, pertaining to, or resembling the arm or a similar or homologous part. [Latin *bracchialis*, from *bracchium*, arm, BRACHIUM.]

bra·chi·ate (bráyki-ayt, -ət, -it || brácki-) adj. *Botany*. Having widely spreading branches arranged in pairs.
~*intr.v.* (-ayt) **brachiated, -ating, -ates.** To swing by the arms from branch to branch, as certain apes do. [Latin *bracchiātus*, from *bracchium*, arm, BRACHIUM.] —**bra·chi·a·tion** (-áysh'n) n.

brach·i·o·pod (bráyki-ə-pod, brácki-) n. Any of various marine invertebrates of the phylum Brachiopoda, having dorsal and ventral shells and tentacled structures on either side of the mouth, used for feeding. Also called "lamp shell". [BRACHI(UM) + -POD.] —**brach·i·o·pod** adj.

bra·chi·o·saur·us (bráyki-ə-sáwrəss, brácki-, -ō-) n. A dinosaur belonging to the genus *Brachiosaurus*, which grew up to 50 tonnes in weight and was the heaviest known dinosaur. [BRACHI(UM) + -SAURUS.]

bra·chis·to·chrone (brə-kístə-krōn) n. *Mathematics*. A curve that is the path of an object falling freely between two points in the shortest possible time. [Greek *brakhistos*, shortest, superlative of *brakhus*, short + *khronos*, time.]

bra·chi·um (bráyki-əm || brácki-) n., pl. **brachia** (-ə). An arm or a homologous anatomical structure, such as a flipper or wing. [Latin *bracchium,* arm, forearm, from Greek *brakhiōn.*]

brachy– *comb. form.* Indicates shortness; for example, **brachyuran.** [Greek *brakhus,* short.]

brach·y·ce·phal·ic (brácki-si-fál-ik, -ke-) *adj.* Also **brach·y·ceph·a·lous** (-séffələss). Having a short, almost round head, the width of which is at least 80 per cent as great as the length. Compare **dolichocephalic, mesocephalic.** See **cephalic index.** [BRACHY- + -CEPHALIC.] —**brach·y·ceph·a·ly** (-séffəli), **brach·y·ceph·a·lism** (-séffəliz'm) *n.*

brach·y·dac·tyl·ic (brácki-dak-tíllik) *adj.* Also **brach·y·dac·ty·lous** (-dáktiləss). Having abnormally short fingers or toes. [BRACHY- + -DACTYLIC.] —**brach·y·dac·tyl·i·a** (-dak-tílli-ə), **brach·y·dac·ty·ly** (-dáktili) *n.*

bra·chyl·o·gy (bra-kílləji) *n., pl.* **-gies. 1.** Brief, concise speech. **2.** A shortened or condensed phrase or expression. [Late Latin *brachylogia,* from Greek *brakhulogia* : BRACHY- + -LOGY.]

bra·chyp·ter·ous (bra-kíptər-əss) *adj.* Having short wings. Said of certain insects. [Greek *brakhupteros* : BRACHY- + -PTEROUS.] —**bra·chyp·ter·ism** (-iz'm) *n.*

brach·y·u·ran (brácki-yóor-ən) *adj.* Also **brach·y·u·ral** (-əl), **brach·y·u·rous** (-əss). Of or belonging to the Brachyura, a group of crustaceans characterised by a short abdomen concealed under the cephalothorax, and including the true crabs. —*n.* A member of the Brachyura. [New Latin *Brachyura,* "short-tailed ones" : BRACHY- + *-ura,* plural of *-urus,* -UROUS.]

brac·ing (bráyssing) *adj.* Invigorating; strengthening. —*n.* **1.** A brace. **2.** Braces collectively; a system of braces. —**brac·ing·ly** *adv.* —**brac·ing·ness** *n.*

brack·en (bráckən) *n.* **1.** A fern, *Pteridium aquilinum,* having tough stems and branching, finely divided fronds. Also called "brake". **2.** An area overgrown with this fern. **3.** Any large, coarse fern. [Middle English (northern dialect) *braken,* from Old Norse *brakni* (unattested).]

brack·et (bráckit) *n.* **1.** A simple rigid structure in the shape of an L, one arm of which is fixed to a vertical surface, with the other projecting horizontally to support a shelf or other weight. **2.** Any of various functionally similar fixtures adapted to support loads. **3.** A small shelf or shelves supported by brackets. **4. a.** *Informal.* A parenthesis *(see).* **b.** Either of a pair of symbols, [ ], used to enclose written or printed material or to indicate a mathematical expression considered in some sense a single quantity. Also called "square bracket". **c.** An angle bracket *(see).* **d.** *Informal.* A brace *(see).* **5.** A section or group within a classification, especially one of taxpayers according to income. **6.** *Military.* The space between two rounds of artillery, the first aimed beyond a target and the second aimed short of it, used to determine range. —*tr.v.* **bracketed, -eting, -ets. 1.** To support or hold with a bracket or brackets. **2. a.** To place (qualifying, explanatory, or unrelated material) within brackets. Often used with *off.* **b.** *Mathematics.* To put within brackets, especially angle brackets, to indicate a specified relationship. **c.** To enclose in brackets. Often used with *together.* **3.** To classify or group together. **4.** *Military.* To fire beyond and short of (a target) in order to determine range. [Earlier *bragget,* from Old French *braguette,* codpiece, diminutive of *brague,* mortise, breeches (in plural), from Old Provençal *braga,* from Latin *brāca.*]

bracket fungus *n.* Any of various fungi that form shelflike growths on tree trunks and wood.

brack·ish (bráckish) *adj.* **1.** Containing some salt; briny. Usually said of water. **2.** Distasteful; unpalatable. [From obsolete *brack,* briny, brine, from Dutch *brak,* salty, from Middle Dutch *bract.*] —**brack·ish·ness** *n.*

bract (brakt) *n.* A leaflike plant part, usually small but sometimes showy and brightly coloured, located below a flower or an inflorescence. [New Latin *bractea,* from Latin *bractea,* properly *brattea†,* metal plate or leaf.] —**brac·te·al** (brákti-əl) *adj.*

brac·te·ate (brákti-ayt, -ət, -it) *adj. Botany.* Bearing bracts. [New Latin *bracteatus,* from *bractea,* BRACT.]

brac·te·o·late (brákti-ə-layt, -ō-, -lət, -lit) *adj. Botany.* Bearing small bracts, or bracteoles.

brac·te·ole (brákt-i-ōl) *n.* Also **bract·let** (brákt-lət, -lit). *Botany.* A small or secondary bract. [New Latin *bracteola,* from Latin, diminutive of *bractea,* metal plate or leaf. See **bract.**]

brad (brad) *n.* A tapered nail with a small head or a slight side projection instead of a head. [Middle English *brad, brod,* from Old Norse *broddr,* spike.]

brad·awl (brád-awl) *n.* A small awl with a chisel edge, used to make holes in wood for brads or screws.

Brad·bury (brád-bri, -bəri || -berri), **Ray** (1920–). U.S. science fiction writer. Most of his works are a combination of social criticism and technological fantasy. His novels include *Fahrenheit 451* (1953), *Something Wicked This Way Comes* (1962), *The Halloween Tree* (1972), and *A Graveyard for Lunatics* (1990).

Brad·ford (brád-fərd || *locally* brát-). Textile manufacturing town and Unitary Authority area in northern England, situated about 15 kilometres (9 miles) west of Leeds on the eastern slopes of the Pennines. It has been an important wool centre since the 14th century, and since the 18th the most important worsted centre in the country, both for its spinning mills and for its wool exchange.

Brad·laugh (brád-law), **Charles** (1833–91). British secularist and politician. In the 1860s and 1870s he campaigned for a number of unpopular causes, such as birth control, national education, and votes for women. In 1880 he was elected to the House of Commons for Northampton, but was refused permission to take his seat when

he insisted on the right to affirm, rather than swear on the Bible. Eventually, after being re-elected by Northampton twice, he won the right for an atheist to sit in Parliament (1886).

Brad·ley (brádli), **Omar (Nelson)** (1893–1981). U.S. general. He played a major part in the Allied victory in World War II. He was appointed chief of staff to the US army (1948) and was promoted to general (1950). He retired from the army in 1953.

Brad·man (brádman), **Sir Donald (George)** (1908–). Australian cricketer, known as "the Don". During his career (1927–49) he scored 117 first-class centuries, and established a number of remarkable records in Test matches, including: 29 centuries (all but 10 against England), most runs in a Test series (974 against England in 1930), 300 runs scored in a day, and the highest Test average (99.94). In addition, he has never lost a Test series as Australia's captain. He was knighted (1949).

brady– *comb. form.* Indicates slowness; for example, **bradycardia.** [New Latin, from Greek *bradus†,* slow.]

Bra·dy (bráydi), **Mathew** (*c.* 1823–96). U.S. photographer. He learned the daguerrotype process from Samuel Morse and opened his own studio in New York in 1844. He was famous for his portraits and was appointed official Union photographer of the Civil War (1861).

brad·y·car·di·a (bráddi-kárd-i-ə, -yə) *n.* Abnormally slow heartbeat, as less than 50 beats per minute. [New Latin : BRADY- + Greek *kardia,* heart (see **cardia**).] —**brad·y·car·dic** *adj.*

brad·y·kin·in (bráddi-kînin, bráydi-) *n.* A protein, $C_{50}H_{73}N_{15}O_{11}$, found in blood plasma that causes contraction of smooth muscle and dilates blood vessels. [BRADY- + Greek *kin(ēsis),* motion + -IN.]

brae (bray) *n. Scottish.* A hillside; a slope. [Middle English (Scottish and northern dialects) *bra,* from Old Norse *brā,* eyelash.]

Brae·mar (bráy-már). Scottish village, officially called the Castleton of Braemar, on Clunie Water, northeast Scotland. It is the site of the royal residence of Balmoral and of the annual highland games, the Braemar Royal Highland Gathering, held each September.

brag (brag) *v.* **bragged, bragging, brags.** —*intr.* To talk boastfully about oneself, one's possessions, or the like. Often used with *about.* —*tr.* To assert boastfully: *He used to brag he'd become prime minister.* —See Synonyms at **boast.** —*n.* **1.** Arrogant or boastful speech or behaviour. **2.** A braggart; a boaster. **3.** A card game using three cards, similar to poker. [Middle English *braggen,* probably from *brag†,* "spirited", "mettlesome", hence boastful.] —**brag·ger** *n.*

Bra·gan·ça or **Bra·gan·za** (brə-gán-sə, -zə). Town in northeast Portugal, capital of the province of the same name. It lies in the Sierra de la Culebra, almost on the border with Spain. Its 12th-century castle was the seat of the Bragança family which ruled Portugal from 1640 to 1910 and Brazil from 1822 to 1889.

Bragg (brag), **Sir William Henry** (1862–1942). British physicist. He shared the Nobel prize in physics (1915) with his son, Sir William Lawrence Bragg (1890–1971), for their analysis of X-ray spectra and the structure of crystals. He was knighted in 1920.

brag·ga·do·ci·o (brággə-dōchi-ō || -dōshi-ō) *n., pl.* **-os. 1.** A braggart. **2. a.** Empty or pretentious bragging. **b.** Swaggering manner; cockiness. [After *Braggadocchio,* name coined by Spenser for his personification of boasting : *braggad-,* alteration of BRAGGART + *-occio,* Italian augmentative suffix.]

Bragg angle *n.* The angle between an incident X-ray beam and a set of crystal planes for which the reflected or transmitted radiation displays maximum intensity as a result of constructive interference. [After William Lawrence *Bragg,* British physicist.]

brag·gart (brág-ərt, -aart) *n.* One given to loud, empty boasting; a bragger. [French *bragard,* from *braguer,* to brag, obscurely related to Middle English *braggen,* BRAG.] —**brag·gart** *adj.*

Bragg's law *n.* The fundamental law of X-ray crystallography, $n\lambda = 2d\sin\theta,$ where n is an integer, λ is the wavelength of a beam of X-rays incident on a crystal with lattice planes separated by distance $d,$ and θ is the Bragg angle.

Bra·gi (bráagi). Also **Bra·ge** (bráagə). *Norse Mythology.* The son of Odin, husband of Ithunn, and god of poetry.

Bra·he (braa, bráa-ə, -hi), **Tycho** (1546–1601). Danish astronomer. His precise fixing of the planets and the stars, by far the most accurate positioning achieved until then, formed the foundation for **Kepler's** laws of planetary motion. He also made detailed study of a supernova (first observed 1572), now known as Tycho's star.

Brah·ma¹ (bráamə) *n. Hinduism.* **1.** The personification of divine reality in its creative aspect as a member of the Hindu triad. See **Vishnu, Shiva. 2.** Variant of **Brahman.** [Sanskrit *bráhman,* prayer, the universal soul, the Absolute, akin to *brahmán-,* priest. See **Brahman.**]

Brah·ma² (bráamə, bráymə) *n. Sometimes small* **b.** A large domestic fowl of a breed originating in Asia, and having feathered legs. [Short for *Brahmaputra;* first brought from Lakhimpur, India, on the Brahmaputra river.]

Brah·man (bráa-mən) *n., pl.* **-mans** (for sense 2). Also **Brah·ma** (-mə) (for sense 1), **Brah·min** (-min) (for sense 2). *Hinduism.* **1.** The essential divine reality of the universe; the eternal spirit from which all being originates and to which all returns. **2.** A member of the highest caste, originally composed only of priests. [Sanskrit *brāhmaṇas,* member of the Brahman caste, from *brahmán-,* priest.] —**Brah·man·ic** (-mánnik), **Brah·man·i·cal** *adj.*

Brah·man·ism (bráa-mən-iz'm) *n.* Also **Brah·min·ism** (-min-).

1. The religious practices and beliefs of ancient India as reflected in the Vedas, the earliest religious texts. 2. The social and religious system of the Brahmans and orthodox Hindus of India, characterised by a caste system and various forms of pantheism. —**Brahman·ist** n.

Brah·min (bráa-min) n. 1. Variant of **Brahman** (sense 2). 2. Chiefly U.S. A highly cultured and socially exclusive person. —**Brahmin·ic** (-mínnik), **Brah·min·i·cal** adj.

Brah·min·ism (bráamin-iz'm) n. 1. Variant of **Brahmanism**. 2. Chiefly U.S. The attitude or conduct typical of a social or cultural elite.

Brahms (braamz), **Johannes** (1833–97). German composer. His work was a blend of classical tradition with the new Romantic impulse. He wrote a relatively small number of large-scale works including the four symphonies (1876–85), the German Requiem (1868), two piano concertos (1881), and the violin concerto (1878), and numerous chamber works.

Brahms and Liszt adj. British Slang. Drunk. [Rhyming slang.]

braid (brayd) tr.v. **braided, braiding, braids**. 1. To interweave three or more strands of; plait. 2. To decorate or edge with an ornamental trim. 3. To produce by interweaving: braid a rug. 4. To fasten or entwine (hair) with a band or ribbon. ~n. 1. A narrow length of fabric, hair, or other material that has been braided or plaited. 2. A thin, flat, woven strip of cloth with a regular diagonal pattern, used for binding or decorating fabrics; an ornamental trim. 3. A ribbon or band entwined in or used to fasten the hair. [Middle English breyden, to move quickly, pull, twist, braid, Old English bregdan.] —**braid·er** n.

braid·ing (bráyding) n. 1. A length of braid. 2. Braided work.

Braille (brayl) n. Sometimes small b. A system of writing and printing for the blind, in which varied arrangements of raised dots representing letters and numerals can be identified by touch. [After Louis BRAILLE.]

Braille (brayl, brī), **Louis** (1809–52). French inventor of the Braille system. He was blinded himself at the age of three.

brain (brayn) n. 1. The portion of the central nervous system in the vertebrate cranium that is responsible for the interpretation of sensory impulses, the coordination and control of bodily activities, and the exercise of emotion, memory, and thought. 2. A functionally similar portion of the invertebrate nervous system. 3. a. Intellectual capacity or potential; mind: She has a good brain. b. Often plural. Intelligence; intellectual ability. 4. A highly intelligent or intellectual person. 5. Often plural. The planner or organiser of an enterprise or undertaking. 6. Plural. The brain of a calf, pig, or sheep used as food. —See Synonyms at **mind**. —**on the brain**. Obsessively in the mind or thoughts. —**pick (someone's) brains**. To elicit and use the ideas, knowledge, or thoughts of. —**rack (one's) brains**. To make a great mental effort. ~tr.v. **brained, braining, brains**. 1. To smash in the skull of. 2. Slang. To hit on the head. [Middle English brain, Old English b4regen.]

brain·child (bráyn-chĭld) n. Informal. An original idea, plan, or the like, attributed to a specific person or group.

brain coral n. Any of several corals of the genus Meandrina, forming rounded colonies that resemble the surface of the human brain.

brain drain n. The emigration of highly skilled or trained people, such as scientists or doctors, to another country, especially for higher salaries.

brain death n. Cessation of respiration and other vital reflexes due to irreversible brain damage, although the heart may continue beating with the aid of life-support systems. —**brain dead** adj.

brain fever n. Pathology. Any of several diseases of the brain, such as **encephalitis** or **meningitis** (both of which see).

brain·less (bráyn-ləss, -liss) adj. 1. Devoid of intelligence; stupid. 2. Lacking a brain. —**brain·less·ly** adv. —**brain·less·ness** n.

brain·pan (bráyn-pan) n. The part of the skull that contains the brain; the cranium.

brain scanner n. A CAT scanner (see) used to X-ray the brain.

brain·sick (bráyn-sik) adj. Chiefly U.S. Of, pertaining to, or induced by insanity; mad. —**brain·sick·ly** adv. —**brain·sick·ness** n.

brain stem n. The part of the brain consisting of the medulla oblongata, pons, midbrain, and part of the forebrain, connecting the spinal cord to the forebrain and cerebrum.

brain·storm (bráyn-stawrm) n. 1. A sudden and violent disturbance in the brain. 2. Informal. A sudden mental aberration. 3. Chiefly U.S. A clever idea; a brainwave.

brain·storm·ing (bráyn-stawrming) n. Chiefly U.S. A method of attacking problems or creating original ideas by intense discussion and spontaneous idea-swapping within a group.

brain·teas·er (bráyn-teezər) n. Informal. A difficult or puzzling problem. Also called "brain-twister".

brains trust n. Also U.S. **brain trust**. A group of experts assembled together, as for a broadcast, to give their views on a series of topics.

brain·wash (bráyn-wosh ‖ -wawsh) tr.v. **-washed, -washing, -washes**. To subject to brainwashing. [Back-formation from BRAINWASHING.]

brain·wash·ing (bráyn-woshing ‖ -wawshing) n. Intensive indoctrination, usually political, aimed at changing a person's basic convictions and attitudes and replacing them with a fixed and unquestioned set of beliefs.

brain·wave (bráyn-wayv) n. 1. A fluctuation of electric potential between parts of the brain, as seen on an electroencephalogram. 2. Informal. A sudden inspiration or brilliant idea.

brain·y (bráyni) adj. **-ier, -iest**. Informal. Intelligent; acute; clever. —**brain·i·ly** adv. —**brain·i·ness** n.

braise (brayz) tr.v. **braised, braising, braises**. To cook (meat or vegetables) by browning in fat, then simmering in a small quantity of liquid in a covered container. [French braiser, from braise, hot charcoal, from Old French brese, from Germanic.]

brake[1] (brayk) n. 1. A device for slowing or stopping motion, as of a vehicle or machine, especially by contact friction. 2. Often plural. Anything serving to slow or stop action or movement. 3. A device for separating the fibres of flax or hemp by crushing or beating. 4. A heavy harrow for breaking clods of earth. 5. A handle on a pump or other machine. 6. A **shooting brake** (see). ~v. **braked, braking, brakes**. —tr. 1. To reduce the speed of with or as if with a brake. 2. To crush (flax or hemp) in a brake. 3. To break up (clods of earth) with a harrow. —intr. To operate or apply a brake or brakes. [Middle English brake, crushing instrument, pestle, flax brake, from Middle Dutch braeke.]

brake[2] n. Any of several ferns, especially **bracken** (see). [Middle English, variant of BRACKEN.]

brake[3] n. An area overgrown with dense brushwood, briars, and undergrowth; thicket. [Middle English (ferne)-brake, Old English (fearn)braca, bed of fern : FERN + bracu (unattested), dense growth.]

brake[4]. Variant of **break** (carriage).

brake[5]. Archaic. Past tense of **break**.

brake·age (bráykij) n. The action or capacity of a brake.

brake band n. A flexible belt that is tightened around a brake drum to arrest the motion of a wheel or shaft.

brake drum n. A metal cylinder to which pressure is applied in order to arrest rotation of a wheel or shaft attached to the cylinder.

brake fluid n. The liquid used in a hydraulic brake cylinder.

brake horsepower n. Abbr. **bhp., b.hp.** The useful horsepower of an engine, usually determined from the force exerted on a dynamometer connected to the engine's drive shaft.

brake light n. A red light on the back of a vehicle which lights up when the brakes are applied. Also chiefly U.S. "stoplight".

brake lining n. A renewable thin strip on the outside of a brake shoe to minimise wear.

brake·man (bráyk-mən) n., pl. **-men** (-mən, -men). Also chiefly U.S. **brakesman** (bráyks-) (for sense 2). 1. A person in a coalmine who operates the winch at the pithead. 2. A guard on a train.

brake shoe n. A curved metal block that presses against and thereby arrests the rotation of a wheel or brake drum.

brake van n. British. A railway carriage from which the brakes can be applied; the guard's van.

brak·ing rocket (bráyking) n. Aerospace. A retrorocket (see).

bram·ble (brámb'l) n. 1. Any prickly plant or shrub of the genus Rubus, especially the blackberry. 2. Any similar prickly shrub or bush such as the dog rose. [Middle English brembel, Old English brǽmbel, brēmel.] —**bram·bly** adj.

bram·bling (brámbling) n. A finch, Fringilla montifringilla, of northern Eurasia, having black, white, and rust-brown plumage. [BRAMB(LE) + -LING.]

Bram·ley (brámli) n. A variety of cooking apple with firm juicy flesh. Also called "Bramley's seedling". [After Matthew Bramley, 19th-century English butcher, who may first have grown it.]

bran (bran) n. 1. The seed husk or outer coating of cereals such as wheat, rye, and oats, separated from the flour by sifting. 2. Cereal by-products used as a food. [Middle English bran, bren, from Old French bran, perhaps from Gaulish brenno-† (unattested).]

branch (braanch ‖ branch) n. Abbr. **br.** 1. A secondary woody stem or limb growing from the trunk or main stem of a tree, bush, or shrub, or from another secondary limb. 2. Any part resembling or suggestive of a branch. 3. A limited part of a larger or more complex body, such as: a. An academic or vocational field of specialisation. b. A local unit of a business, enterprise, bank, or the like. c. A division of a family, tribe, or other group believed to stem from a common ancestor. 4. Linguistics. A subdivision of a family of languages. 5. a. A tributary of a river. b. U.S. Any small stream, creek, or brook. 6. Geometry. A part of a curve that is separated, as by discontinuities or extreme points. 7. Computing. A change from a main program sequence into a subroutine. Also called "jump". ~v. **branched, branching, branches**. —intr. 1. To put forth or spread out in branches. 2. To separate into subdivisions; diverge. —tr. 1. To separate (something) into or as if into branches. 2. Archaic. To embroider with a design of flowers or foliage. —**branch off**. 1. To divide into branches; fork. 2. To separate from the main part or course; diverge. —**branch out**. To enlarge the scope of one's interest, business, or activities. [Middle English braunche, from Old French branche, from Late Latin branca, foot, paw.]

-branch n. comb. form. Zoology. Indicates gills; for example, **elasmobranch**. [New Latin -branchia, from Latin branchia, BRANCHIA.]

branched chain (braanchd ‖ brancht) n. Chemistry. A chain of atoms in a molecule with one or more side chains attached.

bran·chi·a (bránki-ə) n., pl. **-chiae** (-ki-ee). Zoology. A gill or similar breathing organ. [Latin, from Greek brankhia†, gills.] —**bran·chi·al** adj.

bran·chi·ate (bránki-ayt, -ət, -it) adj. Having branchiae or gills.

bran·chi·o·pod (bránki-ə-pod) n. Any of various crustaceans of the subclass Branchiopoda, characteristically having a segmented body and flattened, limblike appendages. The group includes the water fleas. [New Latin Branchiopoda : BRANCHIA + -POD.]

branch line n. A minor railway line that branches off from a main line.

Bran·cu·si (brang-kōōzi, brəng-, -kōōsh), **Constantin** (1876–1957). Romanian sculptor, who settled in Paris in 1904. He broke sharply with the realist tradition in sculpture, making abstract sculptures of great geometric simplicity, chiefly in metal and stone.

brand (brand) *n.* **1. a.** A trademark or distinctive name identifying a product or a manufacturer. **b.** The make of a product thus marked: *a popular brand of soap.* **2.** A particular type: *a strange brand of humour.* **3.** A mark indicating identity or ownership, burned on the hide of an animal with a hot iron. **4.** A mark formerly burnt into the flesh of criminals or slaves. **5.** Any mark of disgrace or notoriety; a stigma. **6.** An iron that is heated and used for branding. **7.** A piece of burning or charred wood. **8.** *Archaic.* A sword: *"So flash'd and fell the brand Excalibur."* (Tennyson). **9.** A disease of plants caused by the rust fungus *Puccinia arenariae* in which brown spots appear on the leaves.
~*tr.v.* **branded, branding, brands. 1.** To mark with or as if with a brand. **2.** To mark with disgrace or infamy; stigmatise. [Middle English *brand,* fire, torch, sword.]

Bran·den·burg¹ (brándən-burg, *German* -boork). A former principality in Prussia, now lying in Poland and eastern Germany. Its centre was Berlin. In 1701 Elector Frederick III took the title King of Prussia, and thereafter the history of Brandenburg is the history of Prussia.

Brandenburg². A state of Germany, created from former East German counties.

Brandenburg³. An industrial town in eastern Germany, standing on the river Havel. It was the headquarters of the ruling Hohenzollern family of Brandenburg (15th–early 18th century).

brand·ing iron (bránding) *n.* A metal rod heated and used for branding.

bran·dish (brándish) *tr.v.* **-dished, -dishing, -dishes. 1.** To wave or flourish (a weapon, for example) menacingly. **2.** To display ostentatiously.
~*n.* A menacing or defiant wave or flourish. [Middle English *braundisshen,* from Old French *brandir* (present stem *brandiss-*), from *brand,* sword, blade, from Germanic.] —**bran·dish·er** *n.*

brand·ling (brándling) *n.* A common reddish-brown earthworm, *Eisenia foetida,* often used as bait by fishermen. [BRAND (because of its red markings) + -LING.]

brand-new, brand new (bránd-néw ‖ -nóō) *adj.* In fresh and unused condition; completely new.

Bran·do (brándō), **Marlon** (1924–). U.S. actor. His films include *A Streetcar Named Desire* (1951), *On the Waterfront* (1954), and *The Godfather* (1972), for which he refused an Oscar in protest at how the film industry treated American Indians.

Brandt (brant), **Bill** (1905–83). British photographer. Before World War II he concentrated chiefly on photographs of everyday life, in both London and the coal-mining regions of the north. After the war, he turned more to landscape subjects and nude portraiture.

Brandt, Willy, born Herbert Ernst Karl Frahm (1913–92). German politician. He was elected as a Social Democrat to the West German Bundestag (1949) and became mayor of West Berlin (1957). He was Chancellor (1969–74) until the revelation that one of his close aides was an East German spy. He was awarded the Nobel peace prize (1971) for his efforts to reduce tension between East and West.

bran·dy (brándi) *n., pl.* **-dies.** A strong alcoholic drink distilled from wine or from fermented fruit juice.
~*tr.v.* **brandied, -dying, -dies.** To mix, flavour, or preserve with brandy. [Earlier *brandy wine,* from Dutch *brandewijn, brantwijn* : *brant,* past participle of *branden,* to burn, distil + WINE.]

brandy bottle *n.* A plant, the **yellow water lily** *(see).*

brandy butter *n.* A rich sauce of butter, sugar, and brandy, traditionally eaten with Christmas pudding and mince pies.

brandy snap *n.* A sweet, crisp wafer in the shape of a hollow tube, flavoured with ginger and sometimes filled with cream.

branks (brangks) *n. Used with a singular or plural verb.* A metal bridle with a bit to restrain the tongue, formerly used to punish scolds. [Perhaps an alteration of earlier *bernaks,* plural of Middle English *bernak,* bridle, from Anglo-French *bernac*†.]

Bran·son (brán-s'n), **Richard (Charles Nicholas)** (1950–). British businessman and hot-air balloonist. His Virgin mail-order company expanded into a successful chain of record stores, followed by airline, cinema, radio and railway companies. He received the blue riband for the fastest sea-crossing of the Atlantic in 1986 and was the first to cross the Atlantic (1987) and the Pacific (1991) by hot air balloon.

brant. *Chiefly U.S.* Variant of **brent.**

Braque (braak, brak), **Georges** (1882–1963). French painter, a leading member of the School of Paris and cofounder of the cubist movement. It was his landscapes of 1908, influenced by Picasso, that gave rise to the term "cubism". He later abandoned the cubist manner, painting still lifes with a flat perspective, large interior scenes, and in the 1950s the large black birds against a blue sky that dominate his last period.

brash¹ (brash) *adj.* **brasher, brashest. 1.** Hasty and unthinking; rash. **2.** Self-assertive; cocky; impudent. **3.** Vulgar; flashy: *a brash colour scheme.* **4.** Brittle. Said of wood or timber. —See Synonyms at **shameless.** [Perhaps imitative, influenced by BREAK and RASH.] —**brash·ly** *adv.* —**brash·ness** *n.*

brash² *n.* A mass or pile of rubble or fragments. [Perhaps from French *brèche,* breach, from Old French, from Old High German *brehha,* fracture, from *brehhan,* to break.]

bra·sil (brə-zíl) *n.* Brazilwood *(see).*

Bra·sil·i·a or **Bra·síl·i·a** (brə-zíl-yə, -i-ə). Capital of Brazil, a new town built in the central highlands of the country, 970 kilometres (603 miles) northwest of Rio de Janeiro. The city was laid out by the architect Lucio Costa in the shape of an aeroplane; the civic buildings were almost all designed by Oscar **Niemeyer.**

brasilin. Variant of **brazilin.**

brass (braass ‖ brass) *n.* **1.** An alloy of copper (more than 50 per cent) and zinc with other metals in varying lesser amounts. **2. a.** Ornaments, objects, or utensils made of brass. **b.** An ornament made of brass, especially a horse-brass. **3.** *Music.* The family of wind instruments, such as the French horn and trombone, made of brass. **b.** *Sometimes used with a plural verb.* The section of an orchestra made up of these instruments. **4.** A memorial plaque made of brass, often inscribed with a representation of a dead person. See **brass rubbing. 5.** *Engineering.* A bushing sleeve or similar lining for a bearing, made from a copper alloy. **6.** *Informal.* Blatant self-assurance; effrontery; nerve. **7.** *Slang. Used with a plural verb.* High-ranking military officers or other high officials: *the top brass.* **8.** *Northern English Informal.* Money. [Middle English *bras,* Old English, *bræs.*†] —**brass** *adj.*

bras·sard (brássaard, bra-sárd ‖ brə-) *n.* Also **bras·sart** (brássərt ‖ brə-sárt). **1.** A cloth badge worn round the upper arm. **2.** A piece of armour for the arm. [French, from *bras,* arm, from Latin *brachium,* from Greek *brakhíōn.*]

brass·bound (bráass-bownd ‖ brass-, *West Indies also* -bungd) *adj.* Strengthened or ornamented with brass: *a brassbound wooden box.*

brassed off (braast ‖ brast) *adj. British Slang.* Fed up; irritated.

bras·se·rie (brássə-ri, -rée) *n.* **1.** A bar in which food may be served. **2.** A French-style restaurant. [French, "brewery".]

brass hat *n. Slang.* **1.** A high-ranking military officer. **2.** Any high-ranking official. [Because of the gold braid on his cap.]

bras·si·ca (brássikə) *n.* Any plant of the genus *Brassica,* indigenous to the Mediterranean region but widely cultivated as vegetables, such as cabbages, Brussels sprouts, and swedes. [Latin, "cabbage".]

brass·ie, brass·y (brássi, bráassi) *n., pl.* **-ies.** A wooden golf club with a brass-plated sole, used for long low shots.

bras·siere, bras·sière (brázzi-ər, brássi-, -air ‖ *U.S.* brə-zéer) *n.* A woman's undergarment worn to support and give contour to the breasts. Also called "bra". [French *brassière,* from Old French *braciere,* armour for the arm, arm guard, from *bras,* arm, from Latin *brachium,* from Greek *brakhíōn.*]

brass-mon·key weather (bráass-múngki ‖ brass-) *n. British Slang.* Exceptionally cold weather. [A brass monkey, in the days of sailing ships, was the tray on which cannon balls were piled. In very cold weather, the brass tray contracted much more rapidly than the iron cannonballs and so the pyramid of balls collapsed.]

brass rubbing *n.* **1.** The process of reproducing on paper the design on a memorial brass by rubbing with graphite or the like. **2.** The impression produced in this way.

brass tacks *pl. n. Informal.* Essential facts or details.

brass·y (bráassi ‖ brássi) *adj.* **-ier, -iest. 1.** Of or decorated with brass. **2.** Resembling brass in colour. **3.** Resembling or characterised by the sound of brass instruments; strident. **4.** Cheap and showy; flashy. **5.** *Informal.* Brazen; insolent; impudent. —**brass·i·ly** *adv.* —**brass·i·ness** *n.*

brat (brat) *n.* A child, especially an ill-mannered one. [Perhaps from dialectal *brat,* coarse garment, Middle English *brat,* Old English *bratt,* cloak, from Old Irish *bratt*†.] —**brat·tish, brat·ty** *adj.*

Bra·ti·sla·va (brátti-sláavə). Capital of Slovakia, an industrial city lying on the river Danube near the Austrian and Hungarian borders. From 1541 to 1784 it was the capital of Hungary.

brat·tice (bráttiss) *n.* A partition, especially one erected in a mine for ventilation.
~*tr.v.* **bratticed, -ticing, -tices.** To equip with a brattice. [Middle English *bretais,* defensive structure, from Anglo-French *breteske,* variants of Old French *bretesque,* from Medieval Latin *(turris) brittisca,* perhaps "British (tower)", parapet (this type of fortification originated in Britain), probably from Latin *Britto,* BRITON.]

brat·wurst (bráat-voorst, -wurst ‖ brát-) *n.* A sausage made with finely chopped, seasoned fresh pork. [German *Bratwurst,* from Old High German *brātwurst* : *brāt(o),* meat + *wurst,* sausage, WURST.]

Braun (brown), **Eva** (1912–45). German salesgirl, mistress and wife of Adolf Hitler. She went to live with him in 1936 but the liaison was kept secret and she was never seen in public with him. They married only a few hours before committing suicide on April 30, 1945.

Braun, Wernher von (1912–77). U.S. aeronautical physicist, born in Germany. He worked on weapons and rocket research in Germany (1932–45), including the V-2 rockets which were used to bombard London (1944–45). After surrendering to Allied troops, he went to New Mexico to join the U.S. Army Ordnance Corps research and testing station at White Sands. He was the director of the army team that put the first American satellite, Explorer I, into space (January 1958). He retired in 1972.

bra·va·do (brə-váadō) *n., pl.* **-does** or **-dos. 1.** Defiant or swaggering show of courage; false bravery. **2.** *Rare.* An instance of such behaviour. [Spanish *bravada, bravata,* from *bravo,* BRAVE.]

Bra·vais lattice (brávvay, brə-váy) *n. Physics.* A **space lattice** *(see).* [After Auguste *Bravais* (died 1863), French physicist.]

brave (brayv) *adj.* **braver, bravest. 1.** Possessing or displaying courage; valiant. **2.** Making a fine display; splendid. **3.** *Archaic.* Excellent.
~*n.* **1.** A North American Indian warrior. **2.** *Archaic.* A boast or challenge. **3.** *Archaic.* A bully.

~*tr. v.* **braved, braving, braves. 1.** To undergo or face courageously. **2.** To defy; challenge. [Old French *brave*, courageous, noble, from Italian and Spanish *bravo*, from Vulgar Latin *brabus* (unattested), wild, savage, altered from Latin *barbarus*, foreign, barbarous, from Greek *barbaros*.] —**brave·ly** *adv.* —**brave·ness** *n.*

Synonyms: *brave, courageous, fearless, intrepid, bold, daring, audacious, gallant, valiant, valorous, doughty, game, gritty, mettlesome, plucky, dauntless, undaunted.*

brave new world *n.* A future that holds out a promise of social progress and human contentment. Often used ironically. [After the title of a novel (1932) by Aldous Huxley, which was itself taken from Shakespeare's *The Tempest* (c. 1611).]

brav·er·y (bráyv-əri, -ri) *n., pl.* **-ies. 1.** The state or quality of being brave; courage. **2.** Splendour, as of attire; show. —See Synonyms at **courage.**

bra·vo¹ (bráa-vó ‖ -vō) *interj.* Used to express approval.
~*n., pl.* **bravos.** A shout or cry of "bravo". [Italian, fine, BRAVE.]
bra·vo² (bráavō) *n., pl.* **-voes** or **-vos.** A hired assassin; a killer. [Italian, "brave".]

bra·vu·ra (brə-véwr-ə, -vóor-) *n.* **1.** *Music.* **a.** Brilliant technique or style in performance. **b.** A piece of music requiring this. **2.** A bold or showy manner. [Italian, "bravery", spirit, from *bravo*, BRAVE.] —**bra·vu·ra** *adj.*

braw (braw) *adj.* **brawer, brawest.** *Scottish.* Fine or splendid. [Earlier *brawf*, Scottish variant of BRAVE.]

brawl (brawl) *n.* A noisy quarrel or fight.
~*intr.v.* **brawled, brawling, brawls. 1.** To fight or quarrel noisily. **2.** To flow noisily: *a brawling stream.* [Middle English *brawlen, brallen*, probably related to Dutch and Low German *brallen* (imitative).] —**brawl·er** *n.* —**brawl·ing·ly** *adv.*

brawn (brawn) *n.* **1.** Solid and well-developed muscles. **2.** Muscular strength and power. **3.** *British.* A pickled or preserved preparation, made from meat of the head or feet of a pig. [Middle English, from Anglo-French *braun*, variant of Old French *braon*, flesh, muscle.]
brawn·y (bráwni) *adj.* **-ier, -iest.** Strong and muscular. —**brawn·i·ly** *adv.* —**brawn·i·ness** *n.*

bray¹ (bray) *v.* **brayed, braying, brays.** —*intr.* **1.** To utter the loud, harsh cry of a donkey. **2.** To sound loudly and harshly. —*tr.* To utter loudly and harshly.

~*n.* **1.** A loud, harsh cry, as of a donkey. **2.** Any sound resembling this. [Middle English *brayen*, to make noise, roar, from Old French *braire*, probably from Celtic.] —**bray·er** *n.*

bray² *tr.v.* **brayed, braying, brays. 1.** To crush and pound in or as if in a mortar. **2.** To spread (printing ink) thinly over type. [Middle English *brayen*, from Old French *breier*, to break, from Germanic.]
bray·er (bráy-ər) *n. Printing.* A small hand roller used to spread ink thinly and evenly over type.

Braz. Brazil; Brazilian.

braze¹ (brayz) *tr.v.* **brazed, brazing, brazes.** *Archaic.* To make hard like brass; inure. [Middle English *brasen*, Old English *brasian*, from *bræs*, BRASS.]

braze² *tr.v.* **brazed, brazing, brazes.** To solder (two pieces of metal) together using a hard solder with a high melting point. [Probably from French *braser*, from Old French, to burn, from *brese*, burning coals, from Germanic.] —**braz·er** *n.*

bra·zen (bráyz'n) *adj.* **1.** Made of brass. **2.** Resembling brass in colour, quality, or hardness. **3.** Having a loud, resonant sound like that of a brass trumpet. **4.** Impudent; bold. —See Synonyms at **shameless.**
~*tr.v.* **brazened, -zening, -zens.** To face or undergo with bold or brash self-assurance. Usually used with *out*. [Middle English *brasen*, Old English *bræsen*, from *bræs*, BRASS.] —**bra·zen·ly** *adv.* —**bra·zen·ness** *n.*

bra·zen-faced (bráyz'n-fayst) *adj.* Impudent and shameless.

bra·zi·er¹ (bráyzi-ər, bráyzhər) *n.* One who works in brass. [Middle English *brasier*, from *bras*, BRASS.]

brazier² *n.* A metal stand for holding burning coals or charcoal, usually used outdoors. [French *brasier*, from *braise*, burning coals, from Old French *brese*, from Germanic.]

Bra·zil (brə-zíl). *Portuguese* **Brasil.** Republic in eastern South America and largest Latin American country, occupying nearly half of the South American continent. The capital is Brasilia. Northern and western Brazil consists of the densely forested lowlands of the Amazon basin and is sparsely inhabited by South American Indian tribes. The more temperate southern part of the country produces three-quarters of the national agricultural and industrial ouput. Brazil contains huge deposits of iron ore, perhaps a quarter of the world's total. It produces a quarter of the world's coffee. The coun-

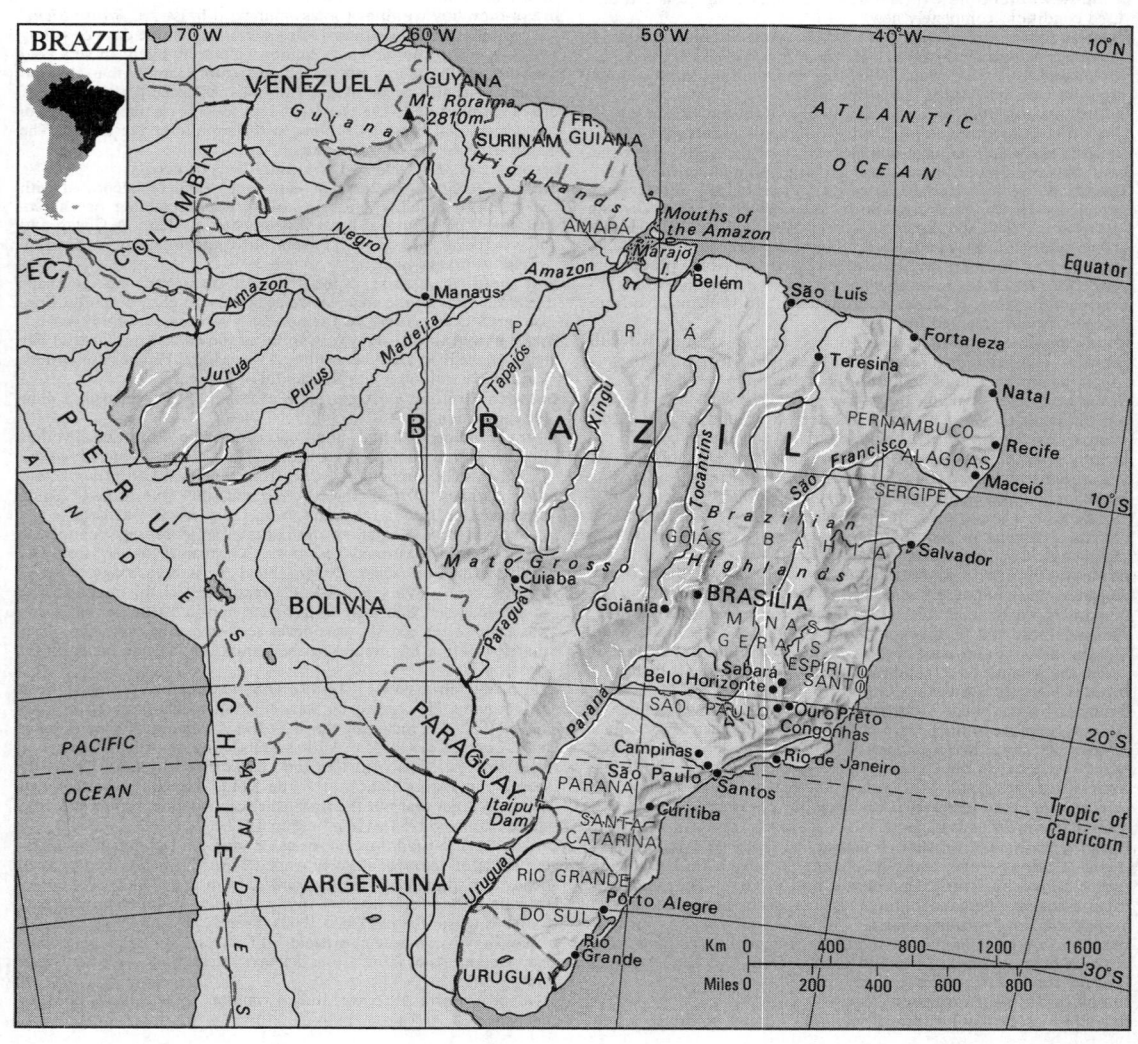

try was ruled by Portugal from 1500 until 1822. It became a republic (1889) when Emperor Pedro II was forced to abdicate. Area, 8 511 966 square kilometres (3,286,500 square miles). Population, 157,870,000. **—Bra·zil·i·an** adj. & n.

braz·i·lin, bras·i·lin (brázzilin, brə-zíllin) n. A crystalline compound, $C_{16}H_{14}O_5$, obtained from brazilwood and used as a dye. [French brésiline, from brésil, brazilwood.]

brazil nut n. 1. A tree, *Bertholletia excelsa*, of tropical South America, bearing hard, round, woody pods that contain the nuts. 2. The edible nut of this tree. Also called "brazil". [After BRAZIL.]

bra·zil·wood (brə-zíl-wŏod) n. The red wood of any of several tropical trees of the genus *Caesalpinia*, used especially for cabinetwork and as the source of a red or purple dye, brazilin. Also called "brazil", "brasil". [Middle English *brasil*, from Old French *bresil*, "reddye wood", probably from *brese*, burning coals, from Germanic.]

Braz·za·ville (brázzə-vil, -veel). Capital and largest city of the Republic of the Congo. It lies on the Congo river and is an important port, receiving rubber, wood, and agricultural products and sending them on to the coast for export. The city was founded by the French explorer, Savorgnan de Brazza (1880), and was the capital of French Equatorial Africa (1910-58).

B.R.C.S. British Red Cross Society.

breach (breech) n. 1. A violation or infraction, as of a law, obligation, contract, or promise. 2. A gap or rift, especially in a solid structure such as a dyke or fortification. 3. A breaking up or disruption of friendly relations; an estrangement. 4. The leaping of a whale from the water. 5. The breaking of waves or surf. ~v. **breached, breaching, breaches.** —tr. To make a hole or gap in; break through. —intr. To leap from the water. Used of a whale. [Middle English *breche, brek*, partly from Old French *breche*, from Old High German *brehha*, from *brehhan*, to break, and partly from Old English *bræc, brēc*, from *brecan*, to break.]

Synonyms: breach, infraction, violation, transgression, trespass, encroachment, infringement.

breach of promise n. Law. Formerly, the failure to fulfil a promise, especially a promise to marry someone.

breach of the peace n. Law. A disturbance of public order caused, for example, by fighting or rioting.

bread (bred) n. 1. A staple food made from flour or meal mixed with a liquid, usually combined with a leavening agent, and kneaded, shaped into loaves, and baked. 2. Food in general, regarded as necessary for sustaining life. 3. a. The necessities of life; livelihood: *earn one's bread.* b. Slang. Money. ~tr.v. **breaded, breading, breads.** To coat with breadcrumbs, as before cooking. [Middle English *bread, bred*, Old English *brēad.*]

bread and butter n. Informal. 1. A means of support; a livelihood. 2. A staple, but not exclusive, source of income.

bread-and-but·ter (brédd'n-búttər) adj. 1. Providing a basic income: *a bread-and-butter job.* 2. Basic; of fundamental concern: *an election campaign fought on bread-and-butter issues.* 3. Expressing gratitude for hospitality: *a bread-and-butter note.*

bread·bas·ket (bréd-baaskit ‖ -baskit) n. 1. An important cereal-producing region. 2. Slang. The stomach.

bread·board (bréd-bawrd ‖ -bōrd) n. 1. A board on which bread is sliced. 2. An experimental model, especially of an electronic circuit; a prototype.

bread·crumb (bréd-krum) n. 1. A crumb of bread. 2. The soft inner part of a loaf of bread. ~tr. v. **breadcrumbed, -crumbing, -crumbs.** To coat with breadcrumbs prior to cooking.

bread·fruit (bréd-frōot ‖ -frewt) n., pl. **-fruit** or **-fruits.** 1. A tree, *Artocarpus communis*, of Polynesia, having deeply lobed leaves and round, usually seedless fruit. 2. The edible fruit of this tree, having a texture like that of bread when baked or roasted.

bread·line (bréd-līn) n. Chiefly U.S. A queue of persons waiting to be given free food, either from a relief agency or as charity. **—on the breadline.** Living at subsistence level; destitute.

bread mould n. A fungus, *Rhizopus nigricans*, that forms a dense, cottony growth on bread and other foods.

bread·nut (bréd-nut) n. 1. A tree, *Brosimum alicastrum*, of Central America and the West Indies, bearing round, nutlike fruit. 2. The fruit of this tree, ground to produce a substitute for wheat flour.

bread sauce n. A sauce made from milk and breadcrumbs and flavoured with onion and spices, traditionally served with poultry.

breadth (bredth, bret-th ‖ breth) n. 1. Abbr. **b., B.** The measure or dimension from side to side of something, as distinguished from length or thickness; width. 2. An extent or piece of something, usually comforming to a standard width: *swam a breadth of the pool.* 3. Wide extent or scope. 4. Freedom from narrowness, as of views or interests. [Middle English *brede*, Old English *brædu*, from Germanic *braidjōn* (unattested), from *braithaz* (unattested), BROAD.]

breadth·ways (brédth-wayz, bret-th- ‖ bréth-wayz) adv. Also chiefly U.S. **breadth·wise** (-wīz). In the direction of the breadth.

bread·win·ner (bréd-winnər) n. One who supports a family or household by his or her earnings.

break (brayk) v. **broke** (brōk) or archaic **brake** (brayk), **broken** (brōkən), **breaking, breaks.** —tr. 1. To separate or reduce to pieces with sudden or violent force; smash. 2. To crack without actually separating into pieces. 3. To render unusable or inoperative. 4. To part or pierce the surface of. 5. To cause to burst. 6. To fracture a bone of. 7. To force or make a way through; penetrate: *break the sound barrier.* 8. To force one's way out of; escape from. 9. To put an end to by force or strong opposition: *break a strike.* 10. To fail

to conform to; act contrary to; violate. 11. a. To bring abruptly to an end: *A scream broke the silence.* b. To discontinue temporarily; interrupt; suspend: *break a journey.* 12. To cause to give up a habit. Used with of. 13. To train to obey; tame; especially, to accustom (a horse) to the saddle. 14. To disrupt or destroy the order or regularity of: *break ranks.* 15. To destroy the completeness of: *break a set of books.* 16. To lessen in force or effect: *break a fall.* 17. To weaken or destroy, as in spirit or health: *"For a hero loves the world till it breaks him"* (W. B. Yeats). 18. To overwhelm with grief or sorrow: *break one's heart.* 19. To cause to be without money or to go into bankruptcy. 20. Military. To reduce in rank; demote. 21. To reduce to or exchange for smaller monetary units: *break a ten-pound note.* 22. To surpass or outdo: *break a record.* 23. To make known (news, for example). 24. To find the solution or key to; decipher. 25. Tennis. To win a game against (the service of an opponent). 26. Electricity. To open: *break a circuit.* 27. In cricket, to knock one or both bails off (a wicket). 28. Australian. To clear (an area of land) for farming. Often used with in. 29. Chiefly Canadian. To open up, clear, or make (a path, track, or other way) through heavy snow, usually in front of a vehicle. —intr. 1. To become separated into pieces or fragments; come apart. 2. To become unusable or inoperative. 3. To give way; collapse. 4. To diminish or discontinue abruptly: *His fever broke.* 5. To rise to or emerge from the surface of the water. Used of fish. 6. To move away or escape suddenly. 7. To weaken in spirit, resolve, or self-control: *He broke under torture.* 8. a. To come into being or public notice, especially suddenly: *The story broke at 12 o'clock.* b. To dawn. 9. To come to an end after a long time: *The cold spell finally broke.* 10. To be overwhelmed with sorrow. Used of the heart. 11. To begin abruptly to utter, express, or do something: *Her face broke into a smile. The horse broke into a gallop.* 12. To interrupt or discontinue an activity. Often used with up: *The meeting broke up at four o'clock.* 13. Linguistics. To undergo breaking. Used of a vowel. 14. To collapse or crash into surf or spray. Used of waves. 15. a. To change from one tone quality to another, as from emotion. Used of the voice. b. To change from one musical register to another. 16. In cricket, to change direction after bouncing. Used of a ball. 17. In boxing and wrestling, to disengage from one's opponent after a clinch. **—break even.** To operate economically making neither a profit nor a loss. **—break in** or **upon.** To interrupt or intrude on. **—break into.** 1. To enter forcibly, suddenly, or illegally. 2. To interrupt. 3. To begin to draw on (a reserve): *break into one's savings.* 4. To become employed or established in a profession or sphere of activity: *trying to break into publishing.* **—break off.** 1. To stop suddenly, as in speaking. 2. To discontinue (a relationship). **—break with.** 1. To discontinue a relationship with. 2. To depart from (a tradition or precedent, for example).

~n. Also **brake** (for sense 19). 1. The act of breaking; a separating into parts. 2. The result of breaking; a fracture or crack. 3. a. A beginning; a coming into being: *the break of day.* b. An opening; a clearing. 4. A dash, especially to escape: *made a break for it.* 5. An interruption or disruption of continuity or regularity. 6. A brief rest or holiday, as from work. 7. A sudden or marked change. 8. Informal. A chance occurrence; especially, an unexpected opportunity. 9. A severing of ties. 10. Chiefly British. A short mid-morning interval for recreation between school classes. 11. Prosody. A pause in a line; a caesura. 12. In tennis, an instance of winning a game against an opponent's service. 13. Electricity. Interruption of a flow of current. 14. Music. a. The point at which a register or a tonal quality changes to another register or tonal quality. b. The change itself. c. In jazz, an improvised solo cadenza played during the pause between the regular phrases or choruses of a melody. 15. In cricket, the swerving of a ball from a straight path as it bounces. 16. In billiards and snooker: a. The opening shot. b. A run or unbroken series of successful shots. 18. A short interruption in a radio or television programme, during which advertisements are broadcast. 19. A high, open, horse-drawn carriage with four wheels. [Break, broke, broken; Middle English *breken, brok* (or *brak*), *broken*, Old English *brecan, bræc* (plural *brǣcon*), *brocen*, from Germanic *brekan* (unattested).]

Synonyms: break, crack, fracture, rupture, burst, split, splinter, shatter, shiver, smash, crush.

break·a·ble (bráykəb'l) adj. Capable of being broken. See Synonyms at **fragile.** ~n. Plural. Articles capable of being broken easily.

break·age (bráykij) n. 1. The act or result of breaking. 2. A quantity or article broken. 3. a. Loss or damage as a result of breaking. b. An allowance in compensation for such a loss or damage.

break·a·way (bráykəway) adj. Withdrawing, or favouring withdrawal, from a main group: *a breakaway political faction.* ~n. 1. One that breaks away. 2. Australian. A sudden mad rush, as of cattle, for example; a stampede.

break·bone fever (bráyk-bōn) n. A viral disease, **dengue** (see).

break·danc·ing (bráyk-danss-ing) n. A type of dance incorporating gymnastics such as handsprings, popular in the 1980s. It may accompany **body popping** (see). [20th century : origin obscure.]

break down intr.v. 1. To fail to function; cease to be useful or operable. 2. To have a physical or mental collapse. 3. To become seriously distressed or upset. 4. To discontinue prematurely or inconclusively: *Peace talks have broken down.* 5. To undergo chemical decomposition. —tr.v. 1. To distress; upset. 2. To overcome (opposition, for example). 3. To consider in parts; analyse. 4. To effect chemical decomposition in. 5. To demolish; destroy. **—break**

it down. *Australian Informal.* Stop it! Cut it out!
break·down (bráyk-down || *West Indies also* -dung) *n.* **1. a.** The act or an instance of failing to function or ceasing to be effective. **b.** The condition resulting from this. **2.** *Electricity.* The failure of an insulator or insulating medium to prevent discharge or current flow. **3.** A collapse in physical or mental health. **4.** An analysis, outline, or summary consisting of itemised data or essentials. **5.** Disintegration or decomposition into parts or elements. **6.** An electrical discharge between electrodes that occurs at a certain voltage in a gas discharge tube.
breakdown van *n.* A van with a small crane, used for towing away cars that have broken down.
break·er[1] (bráykər) *n.* **1.** One that breaks. **2.** A machine or plant for breaking up some hard substance, such as rock or coal. **3.** *Electricity.* A **circuit breaker** *(see).* **4.** A wave that crests or breaks into foam, especially against a shoreline. **5.** A person who crushes or scraps old cars. **6.** *Slang.* **a.** A citizens' band radio enthusiast. **b.** One who interrupts a conversation on citizens' band radio. **7.** A machine for processing material, such as rags in paper-making.
breaker[2] *n.* A small water cask for use on a ship's lifeboat. [Spanish *bareca, barrica,* BARREL.]
break-e·ven point (bráyk-éev'n) *n.* The stage at which a business, project, or speculator can operate economically without making a loss, but not yet making a profit.
break·fast (brék-fəst || bráyk-) *n.* **1.** The first meal of the day. **2.** A formal meal: *a wedding breakfast.* [Middle English *brekfast, brekefast,* from *breken faste,* to break (one's) fasting.] **—break·fast** *intr.v.* **—break·fast·er** *n.*
break·front (bráyk-frunt) *n.* A high, wide cabinet or bookcase having a central section projecting beyond the end sections.
break in *tr.v.* **1.** To train (a horse, for example) to obey; tame. **2.** To accustom to duties. **3.** To wear or use until comfortable or suited to one's requirements. *—intr. v.* **1.** To break into premises, usually to steal. **2.** To interrupt a speaker.
break-in (bráyk-in) *n.* An act of forcible entry, as into a building, dwelling, or office, for an illegal purpose such as theft.
break·ing (bráyking) *n. Linguistics.* The change of a simple vowel to a diphthong, often caused by the influence of neighbouring consonants. Also called "vowel fracture".
breaking and entering *n. Law.* Formerly, the gaining of unauthorised access, as by forcing a lock, to another's premises for the purpose of committing a crime.
breaking point *n.* **1.** The point at which the stress on a material is sufficient to cause it to break. Also called "breaking load". **2.** The stage at which a person is no longer able to bear psychological stress.
break·neck (bráyk-nek) *adj.* Dangerous: *breakneck speed.*
break out *intr. v.* **1.** To begin or arise suddenly. **2.** To escape, as from prison. **3.** To become affected with eruptions or with a rash. Used of the skin, or of a skin-disease sufferer.
break-out (bráyk-owt) *n.* An escape, as from prison.
break through *intr. v.* **1.** To penetrate an obstacle or defence. **2.** To overcome a difficulty and be able to make progress.
break·through (bráyk-throō) *n.* **1.** An act of breaking through an obstacle or restriction. **2.** A military offensive that penetrates an enemy's lines of defence. **3.** A major achievement or success that permits further progress, as in scientific research.
break up *tr. v.* **1.** To disband or disrupt. **2. a.** To take apart; separate. **b.** To fragment, as by cutting or digging. **3.** To put a stop to; discontinue. *—intr. v.* **1. a.** To end. Used of a relationship. **b.** To part. Used of partners, especially in or as in a marriage. **2.** *British.* To begin the holiday period at the end of a school term. **3.** *Chiefly Canadian.* To melt in the spring thaw. Used of ice on a frozen river or lake. **4.** *Slang.* To be overcome by laughter or emotion.
break·up (bráyk-up) *n.* **1.** The act of breaking up; a separation or dispersal. **2.** A collapse; dissolution.
break·wa·ter (bráyk-wawtər || *U.S. also* -wottər) *n.* A structure that protects a harbour or shore from the full impact of waves.
bream (breem) *n., pl.* **bream. 1.** Any of several European freshwater fishes of the genus *Abramis,* having a deep, flattened body and silvery scales. **2.** Any of several similar or related fishes. [Middle English *breme,* from Old French *breme, bresme,* from Germanic.]
Bream (breem), **Julian (Alexander)** (1933–). British guitarist and lutenist. He has made a major contribution to the revival of interest in Renaissance music, especially music for the lute.
breast (brest) *n.* **1. a.** Either of two fleshy milk-secreting organs on a woman's chest; the human mammary gland. **b.** A homologous organ in other mammals. **2.** A source of nourishment. **3. a.** The front of the body, extending from the neck to the abdomen. **b.** A homologous part in other animals. **4.** This part of the human body regarded as the seat of affection or emotion. **5.** The section of a garment that covers this part of the body. **6.** Anything likened to this part of the body: *the breast of a hill.* **7.** A coal face. **—make a clean breast of.** To make a full confession of.
~tr.v. **breasted, breasting, breasts. 1.** To meet with the breast: *She breasted the tape just ahead of the others.* **2.** To encounter or face bravely. **3.** To come to the breast of: *The figure breasted the hill.* [Middle English *brest,* Old English *brēost.*]
breast·bone (brést-bōn) *n. Anatomy.* The **sternum** *(see).*
breast·feed (brést-feed) *v.* **-fed** (-fed), **-feeding, -feeds.** *—tr.* To feed (a baby) mother's milk from the breast; suckle. *—intr.* To feed a baby in this way.
breast·plate (brést-playt) *n.* **1.** A piece of armour that covers the breast. **2.** A square cloth set with 12 precious stones representing the 12 tribes of Israel, worn by a Jewish high priest. **3.** The plastron of a turtle's or tortoise's shell.
breast stroke *n.* A swimming stroke in which one lies face down in the water and extends the arms in front of the head, then sweeps them both back laterally under the surface of the water while performing a frog kick.
breast·work (brést-wurk) *n.* A temporary, quickly constructed fortification, usually breast-high. See Synonyms at **bulwark.**
breath (breth) *n.* **1.** The air inhaled and exhaled in respiration. **2.** The act or process of breathing; respiration. **3.** The capacity to breathe, especially as evidence of life. **4.** A single respiration. **5.** Exhaled air, as evidenced by vapour, odour, or heat. **6.** A momentary pause or rest. **7. a.** A momentary stirring of air. **b.** A slight gust of fragrant air. **8.** A trace or suggestion: *a breath of scandal.* **9.** A soft-spoken sound; a whisper. **10.** *Phonetics.* Exhalation of air without vibrating the vocal cords, as in the articulation of *p* and *s.* Compare **voice. —catch (one's) breath. 1.** To pause until one's normal breathing is regained. **2.** To be left breathless for a moment, as in admiration. **—in the same breath.** At the same time. **—out of breath.** Breathless, as from exertion. **—save (one's) breath.** Not to waste time in pointless excuses, pleading, or the like. **—take (someone's) breath away.** To leave one as if breathless from awe or surprise. **—under** or **below (one's) breath.** In a whisper or muted voice. [Middle English *breth,* vapour, air from the lungs, Old English *brǣth,* odour, exhalation.]
breath·a·lyse (bréthə-līz) *tr.v.* **-lysed, -lysing, -lyses.** To test (a driver) for excessive consumption of alcohol, using a Breathalyser.
Breath·a·lys·er (bréthə-līzər) *n.* A trademark for a device used to test whether a driver has consumed an excessive amount of alcohol, consisting of crystals which react to the presence of alcohol in the driver's breath by changing colour. [BREATH + (AN)ALYSE + -ER.]
breathe (breeth) *v.* **breathed, breathing, breathes.** *—intr.* **1.** To inhale and exhale. **2.** To be alive; live. **3.** To move or stir gently, as air does. **4.** To take in oxygen for combustion. Used of machinery. **5.** To come into contact with, or allow the passage of, air: *open the wine and let it breathe.* *—tr.* **1.** To inhale and exhale during respiration. **2.** To impart (a quality) as if by breathing; instil: *breathe life into a portrait.* **3.** To exhale; emit. **4.** To utter, especially quietly; whisper: *Don't breathe a word of this.* **5.** To express; evince; manifest. **6.** To allow (a person or animal) to rest or regain breath. **7.** *Phonetics.* To utter with a voiceless exhalation of air. [Middle English *brethen,* from *breth,* BREATH.] **—breath·a·ble** *adj.*
breath·er (bréethər) *n.* **1.** One who breathes in a specified manner. **2.** *Informal.* A short rest period. **3.** An opening for ventilation
breath·ing (bréething) *n.* Either of two marks used in writing Greek, indicating aspiration of an initial sound (ʽ) *rough breathing,* or the absence of such aspiration (ʼ) *smooth breathing.*
breathing space *n.* **1.** Sufficient space to permit ease of breathing or movement. **2.** Time allowing an opportunity to rest or solve a problem.
breath·less (bréth-ləss, -liss) *adj.* **1.** Out-of-breath. **2.** Holding the breath from excitement or suspense. **3.** Inspiring or marked by sudden excitement that takes the breath away: *a breathless flight.* **4.** Having no air or breeze; still. **5.** *Formal.* Without breath; not breathing; dead. **—breath·less·ly** *adv.* **—breath·less·ness** *n.*
breath·tak·ing (bréth-tayking) *adj.* Inspiring awe; deeply impressive or exciting; taking one's breath away. **—breath·tak·ing·ly** *adv.*
breath test *n.* A test using a Breathalyser which indicates whether a driver has drunk more than the permissible quantity of alcohol.
breath·y (bréthi) *adj.* **-ier, -iest.** Marked by audible or noisy breathing: *a breathy voice.*
brec·ci·a (bréchi-ə) *n.* Rock composed of angular fragments greater than 2 millimetres in diameter, cemented in a fine matrix. [Italian, from Old High German *brehha,* breaking, fragment, from *brehhan,* to break.] **—brec·ci·at·ed** (-aytid) *adj.*
Brecht (brekht), **Bertolt** (1898–1956). German playwright. His most popular work, *The Threepenny Opera,* with music by Kurt Weill, was produced in 1928. In 1933 he fled to Denmark to escape the Nazis and in 1941 went to the United States, where he wrote *The Caucasian Chalk Circle* (1948). He settled in East Berlin (1949) and was awarded the Stalin Peace Prize (1954). **—Brecht·i·an** *adj. & n.*
bred. Past tense and past participle of **breed.**
Bre·da (breédə, bráydə). Industrial town in the southern Netherlands, standing at the confluence of the rivers Merk and Aa. Charles II of England lived there during much of his exile and issued the Declaration of Breda (1660), announcing the conditions for his return to the English throne.
breech (breech) *n.* **1.** The lower rear portion of the human trunk; the buttocks. **2.** The lower part of a pulley. **3.** The part of a firearm to the rear of the barrel or, in a cannon, to the rear of the bore. [Middle English *breech,* Old English *brēc,* breeches, plural of *brōc,* leg covering.]
breech·block (breéch-blok) *n.* The metal part that closes the breech end of the barrel of a breechloading gun and that is removed to insert a cartridge and replaced before firing.
breech delivery *n.* Delivery of a baby with the buttocks or feet appearing first. Also called "breech birth".
breech·es (bríchiz) *pl.n.* **1.** Trousers extending to or just below the knee. **2.** *Informal & Regional.* Any trousers. [Plural of BREECH.]
breeches buoy *n.* An apparatus used for rescues at sea, consisting of sturdy canvas breeches for the rescued person's legs, attached at the waist to a ring buoy that is suspended from a pulley running

along a rope from ship to shore or from ship to ship.

breech·ing (bríching ‖ bréeching) *n.* **1.** The strap of a harness that passes behind a draught animal's haunches. **2.** The parts of a gun that make up the breech. **3.** Formerly, a rope securing the breech of a cannon to the side of a ship to control the recoil.

breech·load·er (bréech-lōdər) *n.* Any gun or firearm loaded at the breech. **—breech·load·ing** *adj.*

breech presentation *n.* The position of a foetus during labour in which the buttocks or feet appear first in the cervix.

breed (breed) *v.* **bred** (bred), **breeding, breeds.** —*tr.* **1.** To produce (offspring); give birth to or hatch. **2.** To bring about; engender. **3. a.** To cause to reproduce; raise. **b.** To develop new or improved strains in (animals or plants) by selection, hybridisation, and similar methods. —*intr.* **1.** To produce offspring. **2.** To be engendered; arise: *Panic bred in this atmosphere.*

~*n.* **1.** A genetic strain or type of organism, usually a domestic animal, having consistent and recognisable inherited characteristics; especially, such a strain developed and maintained by man. **2.** A distinctively different kind or type: *a new breed of university student.* [Middle English *breden, bred,* Old English *brēdan, bredd* (unattested).]

breed·er (bréedər) *n.* **1.** A person who breeds animals or plants. **2.** An animal kept to produce offspring. **3.** One that breeds; a cause; a source. **4.** *Physics.* A breeder reactor.

breeder reactor *n.* A nuclear reactor that produces, as well as consumes, fissionable material; especially, one that produces more fissionable material than it consumes. Also called "breeder".

breed·ing (bréeding) *n.* **1.** One's line of descent: *a man of noble breeding.* **2.** Good upbringing or social background, as shown by effortless observance of social proprieties.

breeks (breeks) *pl.n. Chiefly Scottish.* Breeches; trousers. [Middle English (northern dialect) *breke,* variant of *brech,* BREECH.]

breeze¹ (breez) *n.* **1.** *Meteorology.* A wind; a gentle wind. **2.** *Meteorology.* A wind of from 6.5 to 50 kilometres (4 to 31 miles) per hour. **3.** *Chiefly British Informal.* A commotion or disturbance; an argument. **4.** *Informal.* An easily accomplished task. —See Synonyms at **wind.**

~*intr.v.* **breezed, breezing, breezes. 1.** To blow lightly. **2.** *Informal.* To move in a quick and usually nonchalant manner: *He breezed in.* **—breeze up.** *Nautical.* To blow more strongly. Used of wind. [Perhaps from Old Spanish *briza*†, northeast wind.]

breeze² *n. Archaic.* A gadfly or similar insect. [Middle English *brese,* Old English *brīosa*†.]

breeze³ *n. British.* The refuse left when coal, coke, or charcoal is burned, used in breeze blocks and as a concrete filler. [French *braise,* burning coals, from Old French *brese,* from Germanic.]

breeze block *n.* A form of building brick made from the ashes of coal, coke, or charcoal, bonded together by cement and used where a heavy load does not have to be borne.

breeze·way (bréez-way) *n.* A roofed, open-sided passageway connecting two structures, such as a house and a garage.

breez·y (bréezi) *adj.* **-ier, -iest. 1.** Exposed to breezes; windy. **2.** Fresh and animated; lively; sprightly. **3.** Casual; nonchalant. **—breez·i·ly** *adv.* **—breez·i·ness** *n.*

breg·ma (brég-mə) *n., pl.* **-mata** (-mətə). *Anatomy.* The junction of the sagittal and coronal sutures at the top of the skull. **—breg·mat·ic** (-máttik) *adj.*

Bre·men (bráymən). City in northern Germany, capital of the state of the same name, on the river Weser. It is Germany's second most important port after Hamburg, and in the Middle Ages was a leading member of the Hanseatic League.

Bre·mer·ha·ven (bráymər-haaf'n). Port in northern Germany, on the estuary of the river Weser. It has a deep natural harbour and is the largest fishing port in continental Europe.

brems·strah·lung (brémss-shtraalŏong) *n.* The electromagnetic radiation produced by an electrically charged subatomic particle, such as an electron, subjected to a change in velocity, as by deceleration in the electric field of an atomic nucleus. [German, "braking radiation" : *Bremse,* brake + *Strahlung,* radiation.]

Bren·dan (bréndən), **Saint** (*c.* 484–*c.* 577). Irish abbot, also known variously as Brenainn (in modern Irish), Brandanus (in Latin), and Brandon. He is the legendary hero of a number of sea voyages, including one to America, and almost certainly visited the Scottish isles.

Bren·del (brénd'l), **Alfred** (1931–). Austrian pianist. Although admired for his interpretation of the 19th-century masters generally, he has made his name as a performer of Schubert and Beethoven.

Bren gun (bren) *n.* A .303 calibre gas-operated, air-cooled light machine gun, adopted by the British Army in World War II. [BR(NO), Czech Republic, where it was first made + EN(FIELD), England, where it was later manufactured.]

Bren·ner Pass (brénnər). One of the lowest Alpine passes, connecting Innsbruck, Austria, with Bolzano, Italy. It has been the major northern entrance to Italy since Roman times, but a road was not constructed through it until 1772. A railway through the pass, requiring 30 tunnels and 60 large bridges, was completed in 1867.

brent (brent) *n., pl.* **brents** or collectively **brent.** Also *U.S.* **brant** (brant). Any of several wild geese of the genus *Branta* that breed in Arctic regions, especially *B. bernicla,* having a dark grey plumage and short neck. Also called "brent goose". [16th century : origin obscure.]

br'er (brair, brer ‖ brər) *n. Southern U.S. Informal.* Brother.

Bre·scia (bréshə, bráyshə). Industrial city in northern Italy, stand-

ing where the river Garza meets the Po plain. It is the capital of the province of the same name.

Brest¹ (brest). Port and naval station in northwest France, on the Brittany coast. Its large landlocked harbour was built by Cardinal Richelieu (1631) as a military base and arsenal, with a 24-kilometre- (14-mile-) long roadstead leading to open water.

Brest². Industrial city of Belarus, near the Polish border. It was formerly called Brest-Litovsk, and belonged to Lithuania, then Poland, before being ceded to Russia (1795). Germany and the U.S.S.R. signed the peace treaty of Brest-Litovsk, ending World War I on the eastern front (March 1918).

Bretagne. See **Brittany.**

breth·ren (bréth-rin, -rən). Plural of **brother.** Used chiefly in archaic, ceremonial, or ironic contexts.

Bret·on (brétt'n, bréttON) *n.* **1.** A native or inhabitant of Brittany. **2.** The Celtic language of Brittany. [French, from Old French, BRITON.] **—Bret·on** *adj.*

Bre·ton (bréttON ‖ brə-tón), **André** (1896–1966). French poet and literary theorist, founder of surrealism. He began to write after World War I, at first linking himself with dadaism, but breaking with that movement to write the first manifesto of surrealism (1924).

Breu·er (bróy-ər), **Josef** (1842–1925). Austrian physician and psychologist. He collaborated with Freud in writing *Studies in Hysteria* (1895). He was the first man to relieve hysteria by cathartic methods, and it was his therapy which provided the basis of Freud's development of the theory of psychoanalysis.

Breughel. See **Bruegel.**

breve (breev ‖ *U.S. also* brev) *n.* **1.** A symbol (˘) placed over a vowel to show that it has a short sound. Compare **macron.** **2.** *Prosody.* A similar symbol used to indicate that a syllable is short or unstressed. **3.** *Music.* A single note equivalent to two semibreves. **4.** *Archaic.* A letter of authority, especially one from a pope. [Middle English, variant of *bref,* BRIEF.]

bre·vet (brévvit ‖ *U.S.* brə-vét) *n. Abbr.* **brev., bvt.** A commission, often granted as an honour, promoting a military officer in rank without an increase in pay or authority.

~*tr.v.* **brevetted** or **-veted, -vetting** or **-veting, -vets.** To promote by brevet.

~*adj.* Held or awarded by brevet. [Middle English, from Old French *brevet,* diminutive of *bref,* letter, BRIEF.]

bre·vi·ar·y (brév-yəri, bréev- ‖ *U.S.* -i-erri) *n., pl.* **-ies.** A book containing the hymns, offices, and prayers said or sung by Roman Catholic clergy at the canonical hours. [Latin *breviārium,* summary, abridgment, from *breviāre,* to abridge, from *brevis,* short, BRIEF.]

bre·vier (brə-véer) *n. Printing.* Formerly, a size of type, 8-point. [Dutch, "type size for breviaries", from Latin *breviārium,* BREVIARY.]

brev·i·ty (brévvəti) *n.* **1.** Briefness; shortness. **2.** Concise expression; terseness. [Latin *brevitās,* from *brevis,* BRIEF.]

brew (broō ‖ brew) *v.* **brewed, brewing, brews.** —*tr.* **1.** To make (ale or beer) from malt and other ingredients by infusion, boiling, and fermentation. **2.** To make (a beverage) by boiling, steeping, or mixing various ingredients. **3.** To concoct; devise. —*intr.* **1.** To brew ale or beer. **2.** To be in the process of infusion. **3.** To be imminent; impend. Used of storms. **4.** To be in preparation. Used of plots, quarrels, or the like.

~*n.* **1.** A beverage made by brewing. **2.** The quality or quantity of beverage brewed at one time. **3.** A concoction. [Middle English *brewen,* Old English *brēowan,* from Germanic.] **—brew·er** *n.*

brew·age (broō-ij ‖ bréw-) *n.* **1.** Something prepared by brewing. **2.** The process of brewing.

brewer's yeast *n.* **1.** A yeast, *Saccharomyces cerevisiae,* used in brewing. **2.** The yeast obtained as a by-product of brewing.

brew·er·y (broō-əri ‖ bréw- *n., pl.* **-ies.** **1.** An establishment where beer, ale, or similar beverages are brewed. **2.** A company that manufactures and sells beer or a similar beverage.

brew·is (broō-iss ‖ bréw-, -z) *n. Regional.* **1.** A broth. **2.** Bread soaked in broth, gravy, milk, or the like. [Middle English *browis, brewes,* from Old French *broez, bro(u)ez,* from *breu,* broth.]

Brey·ten·bach (bráyt'n-bukh), **Breyten** (1939–). South African poet, a member of the so-called *Sestigers* (people of the sixties). After living in Paris for some years, he returned to South Africa in the 1970s, and was imprisoned for a time under the country's Terrorism Act.

Brezh·nev (bré<u>zh</u>-nef, *Russian* -nif), **Leonid Ilyich** (1906–82). Soviet politician and president. He joined the Komsomol (Communist Youth) in 1923 and the Party in 1931. For the next 20 years his career advanced as a protégé of Khrushchev in the Ukraine. In 1957 he was promoted to membership of the Presidium (now the Politburo) and became its chairman (1960). In 1964, when Khrushchev was dismissed, he replaced him as First Secretary of the party. He became president in 1977. In 1968, when Soviet troops entered Czechoslovakia, he enunciated the "Brezhnev doctrine", which asserts that the U.S.S.R. has the right to enter any Warsaw Pact country in which the authority of the Communist government is threatened.

Bri·an (brí-ən), **Havergal** (1876–1972). British composer. Of his many symphonies, operas, choral works, and songs, only a handful were performed in his lifetime. The best-known is the *Gothic Symphony* (1919).

Brian Bo·ru (bə-rōō) (*c.*926–1014). King of Ireland. Most of his life was spent fighting the Danes and their allies, the Norse of Ireland,

Iceland, the Hebrides, and the Orkneys. In 1014 his forces routed the Danish coalition at Clontarf, ending Norse power in Ireland. He was killed at the end of the battle.

Bri·and (brée-ON ‖ bree-óN), **Aristide** (1862–1932). French politician and lawyer who became prime minister for the first of 11 times in 1909. His greatest achievements were as Foreign Minister (1925–32), when he was the chief architect of the Locarno Pact, guaranteeing the borders of Belgium, France, and Germany, and the Briand-Kellogg Pact (a declaration against war signed by 62 countries). He shared the Nobel peace prize (1926) with Gustav Stresemann.

bri·ar¹, **bri·er** (brí-ər) n. Any of various thorny plants or bushes, especially a wild rose bush such as the **sweetbriar** (see). [Old English brēr, brǣr†.]

briar², **brier** 1. A shrub or small tree, Erica arborea, of southern Europe, having a hard, woody root used to make tobacco pipes. Also called "tree heath". 2. A pipe made from briar-root or from a similar wood. [French bruyère, heath, from Gallo-Roman brūcaria (unattested), from Gaulish brūko (unattested).]

bri·ar-root (brí-ər-rōōt ‖ -rōōt) n. The hard, woody root of the briar, Erica arborea.

bribe (brīb) n. 1. Anything, such as money, property, or a favour, offered or given to someone in a position of trust to induce him to act dishonestly. 2. Something offered or serving to influence or persuade. ~v. **bribed, bribing, bribes.** —tr. 1. To give, offer, or promise a bribe to. 2. To gain influence over or corrupt by bribery. —intr. To give, offer, or promise bribes. [Middle English briben, to purloin, steal, from Old French briber, brimbert†, to beg.] —**brib·a·ble** adj. —**brib·er** n.

brib·er·y (brībəri) n., pl. **-ies.** The act of giving, offering, or taking a bribe.

bric-a-brac (brickə-brak) n. Miscellaneous, usually small, objects displayed in a room as ornaments and valued for their antiquity, rarity, or curiosity value. [French, from obsolete à bric et à brac, at random, perhaps based on bric, piece.]

brick (brik) n. 1. A moulded, rectangular block of clay, baked by the sun or in a kiln until hard, and used as a building and paving material. 2. These blocks collectively. 3. Any object shaped like a brick. 4. A building block used by children. 5. Informal. A trustworthy or obliging person. 6. Informal. A tactless blunder. Used in the phrase drop a brick. ~tr.v. **bricked, bricking, bricks.** 1. To construct, line, or pave with brick. 2. To close or wall with brick. Usually used with up or in: He bricked up the windows of the old house. [Middle English brike, breke, probably from Middle Dutch bricke, akin to Middle Low German brikeʈ.] —**brick** adj. —**brick·y** adj.

brick·bat (brík-bat) n. 1. A piece of brick, especially one used as a weapon or missile. 2. A critical remark.

brick·ie (bricki) n. Informal. A bricklayer.

brick·lay·er (brík-lay-ər) n. A person employed at or skilled in building with bricks. —**brick·lay·ing** n.

brick red n. 1. Moderate reddish brown. 2. Moderate to strong brown. —**brick-red** (brík-réd) adj.

brick·work (brík-wurk) n. 1. A structure made of bricks. 2. Construction with bricks.

brick·yard (brík-yaard) n. A place where bricks are made.

bri·dal (brīd'l) adj. Of or pertaining to a bride or a marriage ceremony; nuptial. [Middle English bridale, wedding feast, Old English brȳdealu, "bride ale" : BRIDE + ALE.]

bridal wreath n. Any of various shrubs of the genus Spiraea, cultivated for their profuse white flowers.

bride¹ (brīd) n. A woman who has recently been married or is about to be married. [Middle English bride, Old English brȳd, from Germanic brūdhiz (unattested).]

bride² n. A loop, bar, or tie connecting pattern segments in lacework or needlework. [French, "bridle", from Middle High German brīdel, rein.]

Bride (brīd), **Saint.** Also **Brid·get** (bríjit) or **Brig·id** (bríjid, brée-id) (c.453–c.523). Irish holy woman, said to have been buried at Downpatrick with St. Patrick and St. Columba and, like them, a patron saint of Ireland. Her feast day is February 1.

bride-groom (brīd-grōōm, -grŏŏm) n. A man who has recently been married or is about to be married. [Alteration (influenced by GROOM) of Middle English bridegome, Old English brȳdguma : brȳd, BRIDE + guma, man .]

bride price n. In certain societies, money or goods given by a bridegroom's family to the bride's family. Also called "bride wealth".

brides·maid (brídz-mayd) n. A woman, usually young and unmarried, who attends the bride at a wedding. Compare **maid of honour, matron of honour.**

bride·well (bríd-wəl, -wel) n. Archaic. A prison for petty offenders. [After St. Bride's Well, London, site of such a prison (16th century).]

bridge¹ (brij) n. Abb. **br.** 1. A structure spanning and providing passage over a road, waterway, railway, or other obstacle. 2. a. Anything resembling such a structure in form. b. Anything which forms a connection: a bridge between peoples. 3. The upper bony ridge of the human nose. 4. The part of a pair of glasses that rests against this ridge. 5. Music. a. A thin, upright piece of wood in some stringed instruments that supports the strings above the soundboard. b. A transitional passage connecting two subjects or movements. 6. Dentistry. A fixed replacement for one or several,

but not all, of the natural teeth, anchored at each end to a natural tooth. Also called "bridgework". 7. Nautical. A crossways platform or area above the main deck of a ship from which the ship is controlled. 8. In games such as billiards, a notched piece of wood or a rest made with the hand on which to steady the cue. Also called "rest". 9. Electricity. Any of various circuits containing a branch that connects two points of equal potential and consequently carries no current when the circuit is suitably adjusted. 10. A platform above a theatre stage. —**burn (one's) bridges.** To eliminate the possibility of retreat. ~tr.v. **bridged, bridging, bridges.** 1. To build a bridge over. 2. To cross by a bridge. 3. To form a link across (a period of time, for example). [Middle English brigge, Old English brycg, from Germanic.] —**bridge·a·ble** adj.

bridge² n. Any of several card games derived from whist, played with one pack of cards divided equally among four people. [19th century : origin obscure.]

Bridge, Frank (1879–1941). British composer and conductor, remembered chiefly as the teacher of composition to Benjamin Britten, his only pupil. His only large-scale orchestral work to enter the British repertory was The Sea (1910–11).

bridge-board (brij-bawrd ‖ -bōrd) n. A notched board at either side of a staircase, that supports the treads and risers.

bridge-build·er (brij-bildər) n. One who works for better relations between opposing groups; a conciliator. —**bridge-build·ing** n.

bridge-head (brij-hed) n. 1. A military position established by advance troops on the enemy's side of a river or pass to afford protection for the main attacking force. 2. Any foothold established in hostile territory. [Translation of French tête de pont.]

Bridge of Sighs. Italian **Ponte dei Sospiri.** A stone bridge of the 16th century, in Venice, connecting the Doge's palace to the state prison, so named because prisoners were taken over the bridge from the hall in which they had been sentenced to the prison. The bridge over the river Cam, behind St. John's College, Cambridge, resembles the Venetian original and is often called by the same name.

Bridg·es (brijiz), **Robert (Seymour)** (1844–1930). British poet, who became poet laureate in 1913. His poems are admired for their metrical invention and lyrical simplicity. His long poetic disquisition on the growth of the human soul, The Testament of Beauty (1929), is considered his finest achievement.

Bridg·et of Sweden (brijit), **Saint** (1302–73). Swedish nun and patron saint of Sweden, who founded the Order of the Most Holy Saviour (Bridgettines) for nuns and monks. She settled in Rome (1350), founded a house where she sheltered the poor, campaigned for Church reform, and worked, unsuccessfully, to bring the papacy back to Rome from Avignon. Her feast day is October 8.

Bridge-town (brij-town ‖ West Indies also -tung). Capital and largest city of Barbados, in the West Indies. It is the country's only sea port.

Bridge-wa·ter Canal (brij-wawtər). An inland canal in northwestern England, connecting Worsley to Liverpool. It was one of the great engineering feats of the early Industrial Revolution, completed in 1761 for the Duke of Bridgewater by James Brindley. Brindley avoided the use of locks by designing the canal as an aqueduct on arches, allowing the water to flow by the natural force of gravity.

bridge-work (brij-wurk) n. Dentistry. 1. A bridge. 2. Prosthetics involving a bridge or bridges.

bridg·ing (brijing) n. Wooden braces between beams, as of a floor or roof, that provide reinforcement and distribution of stress.

bridging loan n. A short-term loan made by a bank to enable a house purchaser to buy a new house before the purchaser's previous house has been sold.

Bridg·man (brijmən), **Percy Williams** (1882–1961). U.S. physicist, who investigated the conduction of electricity in metals, the properties of crystals, and the behaviour of matter when subjected to high pressure. For his contributions to the last of those fields he was awarded the Nobel prize in physics (1946).

Bridg·wa·ter (brij-wawtər). Port and market town in Somerset, southwestern England, standing on the estuary of the river Parrett on the Bristol Channel. It was the site of medieval wool and wine fairs and now produces bricks and plastics.

brid·ie (brídi) n. Scottish. A semicircular pasty with a forcemeat filling. [Origin obscure.]

bri·dle (brīd'l) n. 1. The harness fitted around a horse's head, normally consisting of a headstall, bit, and reins, used to restrain or guide the animal. 2. Any device or condition that controls or restrains free movement; a curb or check. 3. Nautical. A span of chain, wire, or rope that can be secured at both ends to an object and slung from its centre point. 4. A bridling gesture. ~v. **bridled, -dling, -dles.** —tr. 1. To put a bridle on. 2. To control or restrain with or as if with a bridle. —intr. 1. To lift the head and draw in the chin as an expression of scorn or resentment. 2. To become scornful or angry; take offence. [Middle English bridel, Old English brídel, from Germanic.] —**bri·dler** n.

bridle hand n. The left hand, in which the reins are usually held, as by a cavalry soldier.

bridle-path (bríd'l-paath ‖ -path) n. A pathway suitable for horses. Also called "bridleway".

bri·doon (bri-dōōn ‖ U.S. brī-) n. A part of certain military bridles that consists of a rein and a bit resembling a snaffle, which may be reined independently of the curb bit. [French bridon, from bride, a bridle. See **bride** (loop).]

Brie¹ (bree). Agricultural region of northern France, lying east of Paris between the Seine and Marne valleys. It is a region of wheat and sugar-beet cultivation, but is famous more for its rose nurseries, and, above all, for Brie cheese.

Brie² n. A soft, white, mould-ripened, whole-milk cheese. [French, first made in BRIE.]

brief (breef) adj. **briefer, briefest. 1.** Short in time or duration. **2. a.** Short in length or extent. **b.** Scanty. **3.** Condensed in expression; succinct. **4.** Curt; abrupt. ~n. **1.** A short or condensed statement. **2.** A condensation or abstract of a large document or series of documents. **3.** Law. A document containing all facts and points of law pertinent to a specific case, prepared by a solicitor and given to a barrister. **4.** Roman Catholic Church. A papal letter pertaining to matters of discipline. **5.** A set of instructions; a briefing. **6.** Plural. Short, tight-fitting underpants. **7.** British Slang. A lawyer. —**hold a brief for. 1.** Law. To be the barrister in charge of (a case). **2.** To argue in favour of; defend: I hold no brief for disarmament. —**in brief.** In short; in a few words. ~tr.v. **briefed, briefing, briefs. 1.** To give concise preparatory instructions or advice to. **2.** To summarise. **3.** British. To send a legal brief to; instruct (a barrister). **4.** British. To authorise and retain (a barrister) as counsel. [As an adjective, Middle English bref, from Old French bref, from Latin brevis; as a noun, Middle English bref, letter of authority, from Old French bref, from Late Latin breve, summary, from Latin, neuter of brevis, short.] —**brief·ly** adv. —**brief·ness** n.

brief·case (breef-kayss) n. A portable rectangular case of leather or similar material, used for holding books and papers. [From BRIEF (document).]

brief·ing (bree-fing) n. **1.** The act or procedure of giving or receiving concise preparatory instructions, information, or advice. **2.** The information conveyed during this procedure.

brief·less (breef-ləss, -liss) adj. Having no brief, thus no clients. Said of a barrister.

brier. Variant of briar.

brig (brig) n. A two-masted sailing ship, developed from the brigantine and differing from it mainly by being square-rigged on both masts. [Short for BRIGANTINE.]

bri·gade (bri-gáyd) n. **1.** A body of troops consisting of a number of military units with supporting services, smaller than a division and normally commanded by a brigadier. **2.** A group of persons organised for a specific purpose: a fire brigade. **3.** A group of persons having some characteristic quality or supporting a particular cause: the law and order brigade. ~tr.v. **brigaded, -gading, -gades.** To form into a brigade. [French, from Old French, from Old Italian brigata, troop, company, from brigare, to form a troop, fight, from briga, strife, perhaps from Celtic.]

brig·a·dier (brigə-deér) n. **1.** An officer of the British and certain other armies ranking below a major general and above a colonel, equivalent in rank to a commodore in the navy and an air commodore in the air force, and usually commanding a brigade. **2.** A brigadier general. [French, from BRIGADE.]

brigadier general n., pl. **brigadier generals. 1.** An officer ranking above a colonel and below a major general in the U.S. Army, Air Force, and Marine Corps. Also called "brigadier". **2.** Formerly, a brigadier.

brig·and (brigənd) n. A robber, especially one of a gang of bandits. [Middle English brigaunt, foot soldier, bandit, from Old French brigand, from Italian brigante, from the past participle of brigare, to fight. See **brigade.**] —**brig·and·age** (-ij), **brig·and·ism** n.

brig·an·dine (brigən-deen) n. A protective jacket made of canvas or leather lined with overlapping scales or plates, worn in medieval times.

brig·an·tine (brigən-teen, -tīn) n. A two-masted sailing ship, square-rigged on the foremast and differing from a brig mainly by being fore-and-aft rigged with square topsails on the mainmast. Also called "hermaphrodite brig". [French, from Old French brigandin, from Italian brigantino, "pirate ship".]

bright (brīt) adj. **brighter, brightest. 1.** Emitting or reflecting light; shining. **2. a.** Vivid or brilliant in colour. **b.** Characterising a dye that produces a highly saturated colour. **3.** Glorious; splendid. **4.** Full of promise and hope; auspicious. **5.** Happy; cheerful. **6.** Clever; intelligent. —See Synonyms here and at **intelligent.** ~n. A thin, flat paintbrush used for highlighting. ~adv. In a bright manner. [Middle English bright, Old English beorht, from Germanic.] —**bright·ly** adv.

> **Synonyms:** bright, brilliant, radiant, lustrous, lambent, luminous, incandescent.

Bright, John (1811–89). British politician and one of the founders of the Anti-Corn Law League (1839). He was a leading campaigner in the movement that led to the Second Reform Act (1867) and the Third (1884). From 1858 he represented Birmingham in Parliament, serving in Gladstone's governments as president of the Board of Trade (1868–70) and Chancellor of the Duchy of Lancaster (1873–74 and 1880–82). He resigned from the Cabinet in 1882 in protest against the bombardment of Alexandria.

bright·en (brīt'n) v. **-ened, -ening, -ens.** —tr. To make bright or brighter. —intr. To become bright or brighter.

bright·ness (brīt-nəss, -niss) n. **1.** The state or quality of being bright. **2. a.** The effect or sensation by means of which an observer is able to distinguish differences in luminance. **b.** Physics. Lumi-

nance (see). No longer in technical usage. **3.** The dimension of a colour that represents its similarity to one of a series of achromatic colours ranging from very dim (dark) to very bright (dazzling).

Bright·on (brīt'n). Resort town on an old Saxon site on the East Sussex coast, merging in the west with Hove. Formerly known as Brighthelmstone, it became a fashionable resort after 1783, when the Prince of Wales, later Prince Regent and George IV, began to frequent it. The famous pavilion, designed by John Nash in a combination of Chinese and Indian styles, was built for George IV.

Bright's disease n. Chronic **nephritis** (see). [After Richard Bright (1789–1858), British physician who first described it.]

bright·work (brīt-wurk) n. Metal parts or fixtures, especially on a ship, made bright by polishing.

Brigid, Saint. See Saint **Bride.**

brill¹ (bril) n., pl. **brills** or collectively **brill.** An edible flatfish, Scophthalmus rhombus, of European waters. [15th century : origin obscure.]

brill² adj. British Informal. Brilliant; excellent. [Shortened from BRILLIANT.]

bril·li·ance (bril-yənss, -i-ənss) n. Also **bril·li·an·cy** (-i). **1.** Extreme brightness. **2.** Sharpness and clarity of musical tone. **3.** Splendour; magnificence. **4.** Exceptional clarity and agility of intellect or invention.

bril·li·ant (bril-yənt, -i-ənt) adj. **1.** Full of light; shining. **2. a.** Brightly vivid in colour. **b.** Designating a colour that has a combination of high lightness and strong saturation. **3.** Music. Sharp and clear in tone. **4.** Glorious; splendid; magnificent. **5.** Superb; excellent; wonderful. Used also as a general term of approval. **6.** Marked by extraordinary powers of intellect or invention. —See Synonyms at **bright, intelligent.** ~n. **1.** A cut for precious gems, especially diamonds, having 58 facets and shaped like two cones joined at their bases with the top one cut off close to the base. **2.** A precious stone having this cut. [French brillant, present participle of briller, to shine, from Italian brillare.†] —**bril·li·ant·ly** adv. —**bril·li·ant·ness** n.

bril·lian·tine (bril-yən-teen) n. An oily, perfumed preparation for the hair. [French brillantine, from brillant, BRILLIANT.]

brim (brim) n. **1.** The rim or uppermost edge of a cup or other vessel. **2.** A projecting rim or edge: the brim of a hat. **3.** A border or edge, especially one surrounding a body of water. ~v. **brimmed, brimming, brims.** —tr. To fill to the brim. —intr. To be full to the brim; be filled. Used with with. —**brim over.** To overflow: brim over with happiness. [Middle English brimme, from Germanic; akin to Middle High German brem.]

brim·ful, brim-full (brim-foόl) adj. Completely full.

brim·stone (brim-stōn) n. **1.** Obsolete. **Sulphur** (see). Now used chiefly in the phrase fire and brimstone. **2.** A bright yellow butterfly, Gonepteryx rhamni, common in northern temperate regions of Eurasia. **3.** A very common moth, Opisthographis luteolata, of Europe and temperate Asia. [Middle English brimston, Late Old English brynstān, probably "burning stone", from bryne, burning.] —**brim·ston·y** adj.

brin (brin) n. Any of the ribs of a fan. [French brin†.]

Brin·di·si (brindi-zi, -zee). Port in the Apulia region of southeastern Italy, on the Adriatic coast. In ancient times, as Brundisium, it was an important centre of trade with the eastern Mediterranean, and it was also the point of departure for crusades in the Middle Ages.

brin·dle (brind'l) adj. Brindled. ~n. **1.** A brindled colour. **2.** A brindled animal.

brin·dled (brind'ld) adj. Tawny or greyish with streaks or spots of a darker colour. [Variant of earlier brinded, brended, from Middle English brende, perhaps from Scandinavian; akin to Old Norse brandr, piece of burning wood.]

brine (brīn) n. **1.** Water saturated with or containing large amounts of a salt, especially of sodium chloride. **2. a.** The water of a sea or ocean. **b.** A large body of salt water. **3.** Salt water used for preserving and pickling foods. ~tr.v. **brined, brining, brines.** To immerse or pickle in brine. [Middle English brine, Old English brŷne†, from Germanic.]

Bri·nell hardness (bri-nél) n. The relative hardness of metals and alloys, determined by forcing a steel ball into a test piece under standard conditions and measuring the surface area of the resulting indentation to calculate the relevant Brinell number. [After Johann A. Brinell (1849–1925), Swedish engineer.]

Brinell number n. Abbr. Bhn. The numerical value assigned to the Brinell hardness of metals and alloys. It is calculated by dividing the load on the ball in kilograms by the area of the indentation in square millimetres.

brine shrimp n. Any of various small crustaceans of the genus Artemia. [So called because they have been observed living in highly saline water.]

bring (bring) tr.v. **brought** (brawt), **bringing, brings. 1.** To take with oneself to a place; convey or carry along: brought enough money with him. **2.** To carry as an attribute or contribution: brought years of experience to her new post. **3.** To lead or cause to come to a specified state, situation, or location: brought to ruin; brought tears to our eyes. **4.** To succeed in persuading; induce: His confession brought others to confess. **5.** To cause to occur as a consequence or concomitant: Floods brought death to the valley. **6.** To cause to become apparent to the mind; recall: bring back memories. **7.** Law. To advance or set forth (charges or evidence, for example) in a court. **8.** To sell for; fetch. —**bring about.** To cause to happen. —**bring forth. 1.** To give rise to; effect; produce. **2.** Archaic. To give birth to. **—bring forward. 1.** To present; cite in argument: *bring forward an opinion.* **2.** To cause to occur sooner; move to an earlier time. **3.** *Accounting.* To carry (a sum) from one page or column to another. **—bring in. 1.** To give or submit (a verdict). **2.** To produce or yield (profits or income). **3.** *N.Z.* To clear (land) for farming. **—bring off.** To accomplish successfully. **—bring on. 1.** To give rise to; cause. **2.** To cause to appear: *bring on the dessert.* **—bring out. 1.** To reveal or expose. **2.** To produce or publish. **3.** To encourage; especially, to encourage (a shy person) to speak out or participate. **4.** To cause (workers) to strike. **—bring over.** To win over. **—bring round. 1.** To cause to recover consciousness. **2.** To persuade to adopt an opinion or course of action. **—bring to. 1.** To cause to recover consciousness. **2.** To cause (a ship) to turn into the wind and lose headway. **—bring up. 1.** To take care of and educate (a child); rear. **2.** To introduce into discussion; mention. **3.** To vomit or cough up. [Bring, brought, brought; Middle English *bringen, broughte, brought,* Old English *bringan, brōhte, brōht,* from Germanic *brengen* (unattested).] **—bring·er** *n.*

Usage: In formal speech or writing, *bring* should be used where there is movement towards the speaker, *take* where movement is in the opposite direction. In casual speech the distinction is not generally observed, and *I'll bring it to you* is commonly used.

bring-and-buy sale (bring-ən-bī) *n. Chiefly British.* A charity bazaar or jumble sale to which people may bring items for sale and buy items brought by others.

bring down *tr.v.* **1.** To cause to fall, come down, or collapse. **2.** To reduce; lower. **3.** *Slang.* To cause to feel disappointed or depressed. **—bring-down** *n.*

brin·jal (brínjəl) *n.* Especially in India and Africa, the **aubergine** *(see).* [Portuguese *berinjela,* from Arabic. See **aubergine**.]

brink (bringk) *n.* **1. a.** The upper edge of a steep or vertical declivity: *the brink of a cliff.* **b.** The margin of land bordering a body of water. **2.** The verge of something: *on the brink of discovery.* **—See** Synonyms at **border.** [Middle English *brinke, brenk,* akin to Middle Dutch *brinkt,* slope.]

brink·man·ship (bríngk-mən-ship) *n.* Also **brinks·man·ship** (bríngks-). The practice of seeking advantage by forcing a dangerous situation to crisis point in the hope that one's opponent will back down first. [BRINK + (GAMES)MANSHIP.]

brin·ny, brin·nie (brínni) *n., pl.* **-nies.** *Australian Informal.* A small stone used for throwing, especially by children.

brin·y (brínī) *adj.* **-ier, -iest.** Of, pertaining to, or resembling brine; salty.
~*n.* The sea. Used humorously and with *the.* **—brin·i·ness** *n.*

bri·o (brée-ō) *n.* Vigour; vivacity. [Italian, "vivacity", from Gaulish *brigo-* (unattested), might, strength.]

bri·oche (bree-ósh, -ôsh) *n.* A soft, light-textured roll or bun made from eggs, butter, flour, and yeast. [French, from Old French, from *brier,* dialectal form of *broyer,* to knead, from Germanic.]

bri·o·lette (brée-ə-lét, -ô-) *n.* A pear-shaped gem, especially a diamond, cut with long triangular facets. [French, *bri(ll)olette,* probably an irregular diminutive of *brillant,* BRILLIANT.]

bri·quette, bri·quet (bri-két) *n.* A block of compressed coal dust or charcoal, used for fuel and kindling. [French *briquette,* from *brique,* BRICK.]

bri·sance (bréez'nss ‖ *U.S.* bri-záanss) *n.* The shattering effect of a sudden release of energy, as in an explosion. [French, from *brisant,* present participle of *briser,* to break, from Vulgar Latin *brisāre,* from Gaulish.] **—bri·sant** *adj.*

Bris·bane (bríz-bən, -bayn; *locally* -bən). Capital of the state of Queensland, Australia, a port and transport hub on the Brisbane river near its mouth on Moreton Bay, and the third largest city in Australia. The city began as a penal colony (1824), was incorporated as a town (1834), and was named after Sir Thomas Brisbane, the governor of New South Wales (1821–25).

brisk (brisk) *adj.* **brisker, briskest. 1.** Moving or acting quickly; lively; energetic: *a brisk walk.* **2.** Sharp or abrupt in speech or manner: *a brisk greeting.* **3.** Stimulating and invigorating: *a brisk wind.* **—See** Synonyms at **nimble.** [Probably a variant of BRUSQUE.] **—brisk·ly** *adv.* **—brisk·ness** *n.*

bris·ket (brískit) *n.* **1.** The chest of an animal. **2.** The ribs and meat from this part. [Middle English *brusket,* probably from a Scandinavian compound akin to Old Norse *brjóst,* breast + *ket†,* meat.]

bris·ling (bríss-ling, bríz-) *n.* A fish, the **sprat** *(see),* which is usually preserved and canned. [From Norwegian and Danish.]

bris·tle (bríss'l) *n.* A short, coarse, stiff hair or hairlike part.
~*v.* **bristled, -tling, -tles.** **—intr. 1.** To raise the bristles, as an angry, excited, or frightened animal does: *The dog bristled with fear.* **2.** To react with hostility or anger. **3.** To stand erect like bristles: *His hair bristled.* **4.** To be covered or thick with or as if with bristles: *The path bristled with thorns.* **—tr.** To furnish or supply with bristles; put bristles on. [Middle English *bristil, brustel,* from *brust,* bristle, Old English *byrst.*] **—bris·tly** *adj.*

bris·tle·cone pine (bríss'l-kōn) *n.* A small pine tree, *Pinus aristata,* native to the Rocky Mountains, that has the longest life span of any known conifer. Its annual rings are used in archaeological dating.

bris·tle·tail (bríss'l-tayl) *n.* Any of various wingless insects of the order Thysanura, such as the silverfish, having bristle-like posterior appendages.

bristle worm *n.* A type of worm, the **polychaete** *(see).*

Bris·tol (bríst'l). City, port, and Unitary Authority area in southwestern England, standing on the river Avon 11 kilometres

(7 miles) from its mouth on the Bristol Channel. It has been a trading centre since the 12th century, and is now a centre of nuclear and aeronautical engineering works.

Bristol board *n.* A smooth, heavy pasteboard of fine quality. Also called "Bristol paper".

Bristol Channel. An inlet of the Atlantic Ocean, about 137 kilometres (85 miles) long, broadening out from the mouth of the river Severn and separating Wales from southwestern England.

Bristol fashion *adj. British.* In good order; neat; tidy. Used especially in the phrase *all shipshape and Bristol fashion.* **—Bristol fashion** *adv.*

bris·tols (brist'lz) *pl. n. British Slang.* A woman's breasts. [From *Bristol City,* rhyming slang.]

brit, britt (brit) *n.* **1.** The young of herring and similar fish. **2.** Minute marine organisms, such as crustaceans of the genus *Calanus,* that are a major source of food for many fish and whales. [Perhaps from Cornish *brȳthel,* mackerel.]

Brit (brit) *n. Informal.* A British person.

Brit·ain (brítt'n). *Abbr.* **Br., Brit.** See **Great Britain.**

bri·tan·ni·a (bri-tán-yə, -i-ə) *n. Sometimes capital* **B.** A white alloy of tin with copper, antimony, and sometimes bismuth and zinc. It is used in the manufacture of tableware and light bearings. Also called "britannia metal".

Bri·tan·ni·a (bri-tán-yə, -i-ə). **1.** The ancient Roman province in Great Britain. **2.** *Poetic.* Great Britain. **3.** A female personification of Great Britain or the British Empire.

Bri·tan·nic (bri-tánnik) *adj. British.* Used chiefly in the phrase *His* (or *Her*) *Britannic Majesty.*

britch·es (bríchiz) *pl.n. Informal.* Breeches. **—too big for (one's) britches.** *Informal.* Overconfident; cocky; arrogant.

Brit·i·cism (brítti-siz'm) *n.* Also **Brit·ish·ism** (bríttish-iz'm). A word, phrase, or idiom characteristic of or peculiar to English as it is spoken in Great Britain.

Brit·ish (bríttish) *adj. Abbr.* **B., Br., Brit. 1.** Of, pertaining to, or characteristic of Great Britain, the United Kingdom, or the Commonwealth. **2.** Of, pertaining to, or characteristic of the ancient Britons.
~*n.* **1.** *Used with a plural verb.* The people of Great Britain. Preceded by *the.* **2.** The language spoken by the ancient Britons.

British Antarctic Territory. Area in the extreme Southern Hemisphere, bounded by latitude 60°S and longitudes 20°W and 80°W. It includes the South Orkney Islands, and Graham Land (on Antarctica) and the South Shetland Islands (parts of which are claimed by Argentina) and has been a colony administered from the Falkland Islands since 1962. Most of the small islands in the region are uninhabited, except for a transient population manning research stations.

British Anti-Lew·is·ite (ánti-lóo-i-sīt ‖ -léw-) *n.* A drug, **BAL** *(see).*

British Cameroons. See **Cameroon.**

British Co·lum·bi·a (kə-lúmbi-ə). The westernmost province of Canada, bordering on the Pacific Ocean and stretching to the Yukon in the north. The capital is Victoria, on Vancouver Island, but the largest city is Vancouver. The province is almost entirely mountainous, with the Rocky Mountains in the east and the Coast Mountains in the west. Timber and pulp and paper manufacture are its leading industries, but mining of silver, copper, gold, iron ore, lead, and zinc is also important. The silver mine at Kimberley is the largest in the world, and Kimberley also has the world's largest reserves of lead and zinc. **—British Co·lum·bi·an** *n. & adj.*

British Commonwealth of Nations *n.* See **Commonwealth** (sense 6).

British East Africa. Collectively, the former British territories in eastern Africa, including Kenya, Uganda, Tanganyika, and Zanzibar.

British Empire *n.* Collectively, all geographical and political units formerly under British control, including dominions, colonies, dependencies, trust territories, and protectorates.

British English *n.* The English language as spoken, pronounced, and written in Britain, as compared with the English spoken elsewhere.

Brit·ish·er (bríttishər) *n. Chiefly U.S. Informal.* A native or inhabitant of Great Britain or a person of British origin.

British Guiana. See **Guyana, Co-operative Republic of.**

British Honduras. See **Belize.**

British India. That part of the Indian subcontinent under direct British administration until 1947. See **India.**

British Indian Ocean Territory. British colony in the west Indian Ocean since 1965. The main islands include Diego Garcia, which has a U.S. base.

British Isles. An unofficial term for the United Kingdom and the Republic of Ireland.

British Legion *n.* An organisation founded in 1921 that provides assistance for former servicemen and -women. Also officially called the "Royal British Legion".

British Movement *n.* A modern British fascist splinter group, noted for its virulent racism.

British North America. *Abbr.* **B.N.A.** Formerly, the British possessions in North America north of the United States; specifically, Canada.

British Somaliland. See **Somalia.**

British Standards Institution *n. Abbr.* **BSI.** An association formed in 1901 that standardises units of measurement, technical terminology, the sizes of fittings, safety specifications, and the like, and ensures that products meet certain requirements for a wide variety of manufacturing industries.

British Summer Time *n. Abbr.* **B.S.T.** The time system that is used in Britain during the summer. It is one hour ahead of Greenwich Mean Time and is adopted in order to provide an extra hour of daylight in the evening.

British thermal unit *n. Abbr.* **btu, B.th.u.** The quantity of heat required to raise the temperature of one pound of water by one degree Fahrenheit.

British West Africa. *Abbr.* **B.W.A.** The former British possessions in western Africa, including Nigeria, Gambia, Sierra Leone, and the Gold Coast, and the trust territories of Togoland and Cameroons.

British West Indies. *Abbr.* **B.W.I.** The former name for the islands of the West Indies that were colonies or self-governing colonies of the United Kingdom.

Brit·on (brítt'n) *n.* **1.** A native or inhabitant of Britain. **2.** One of a Celtic people who inhabited Britain before the Roman invasion.

britt. Variant of **brit.**

Brit·tany (brĭttəni). *French* **Bre·tagne** (brə-tán-yə). Region and former province of northwest France, between the English Channel and the Bay of Biscay. It has a deeply indented rocky coast with deep natural harbours at Brest, Lorient, and St. Malo.

Brit·ten (brítt'n), **(Edward) Benjamin, Baron** (1913–76). British composer. His reputation rests chiefly on his vocal compositions which fall into two main categories: song cycles, such as *Les Illuminations* (1939) and the *Serenade* for tenor, horn, and string orchestra (1943); and the operas, including *Peter Grimes* (1945), *Albert Herring* (1947), and *Death in Venice* (1973). He was made a Companion of Honour (1953) and a life peer (1976).

brit·tle (brítt'l) *adj.* **1.** Likely to break; fragile: *brittle porcelain.* **2. a.** Difficult to deal with; touchy; snappish: *a brittle disposition.* **b.** Lacking warmth or friendliness. —See Synonyms at **fragile.** ~*n.* A hard toffee to which nuts are added: *peanut brittle.* [Middle English *brotel, britel,* Old English *brytel* (unattested), from Germanic.] —**brit·tle·ness** *n.*

brittle star *n.* Any of various marine organisms of the class Ophiuroidea, related to and resembling the starfish but having long, slender, whiplike arms.

Brix scale (briks) *n.* A density scale used in the sugar industry. A Brix hydrometer has a scale calibrated in units equivalent to the percentage of sugar in a pure sugar solution. [After A.F.W. *Brix,* 19th-century German inventor.]

Brno (búrnõ, brə-nő). *German* **Brünn** (brün). An industrial city in the Czech Republic. The Bren gun was developed there.

bro. brother.

broach¹ (brōch) *n.* **1.** A tapered and serrated tool used to shape or enlarge a hole. **2.** The hole made by such a tool. **3.** A spit for roasting meat. **4.** A narrow mason's chisel. **5.** A gimlet for tapping or broaching casks. **6.** Variant of **brooch.** ~*tr.v.* **broached, broaching, broaches. 1. a.** To begin to talk about: *broach a subject.* **b.** To announce: *"Ernest broached his plans for spending the next year or two"* (Samuel Butler). **2.** To pierce in order to draw off liquid: *broach a keg.* **3.** To draw off (a liquid) by piercing a hole in a cask, keg, or other container. **4.** To shape or enlarge (a hole) with a broach. **5.** To open and start using the contents of (a box, for example). —See Synonyms at **vent.** [Middle English *broche,* pointed rod or pin, from Old French, a spit, from Vulgar Latin *brocca* (unattested), a spike.] —**broach·er** *n.*

broach² *v.* **broached, broaching, broaches.** *Nautical.* —*tr.* To cause to veer broadside to the wind and waves. —*intr.* To veer broadside to the wind and waves. Used with *to.* [18th century : origin obscure.]

broad (brawd) *adj.* **broader, broadest. 1. a.** Extending a considerable distance from side to side. **b.** Of the specified extent from side to side; in breadth: *six feet broad.* **2.** Large in expanse; spacious: *a broad lawn.* **3.** Open to view; clear: *broad daylight.* **4.** Extensive in scope; generalised: *a broad rule.* **5.** Liberal; tolerant. **6.** Covering the essentials; comprehensive, but not detailed: *a broad outline of the problem.* **7.** Plain and clear; obvious: *a broad hint.* **8.** Outspoken; unrestrained. **9.** Vulgar; crude: *a broad joke.* **10.** Strongly marked by regional pronunciation: *a broad accent.* **11.** *Phonetics.* Designating a vowel that is pronounced with the tongue placed low and flat and with the oral cavity wide open, as in the Received Pronunciation of *a* in *father.* ~*n.* **1.** *British Regional.* A river that spreads over low-lying ground. **2.** *U.S. Slang.* **a.** A woman or girl. **b.** A prostitute. ~*adv.* Fully; completely: *broad awake.* [Middle English *brood,* Old English *brād,* from Germanic *braithaz* (unattested). For noun sense 2, compare obsolete (U.S.) *broadwife* (*abroad* + *wife*), female slave separated from her husband, who was owned by a different master.] —**broad·ly** *adv.*

broad arrow *n.* **1.** An arrow with a wide, barbed head. **2.** A wide arrowhead mark identifying British government property and, formerly, prison clothing.

broad·band (bráwd-band) *adj.* Designating a wide band of electromagnetic frequencies: *broadband communications.* —**broad·band** *n.*

broad bean *n.* **1.** A plant, *Vicia faba,* native to the Old World, cultivated for its edible pods and seeds. **2.** The somewhat flattened seed of this plant. Also called "horse bean".

broad·bill (bráwd-bil) *n.* **1.** Any of various birds of the family Eurylaimidae, of Africa and tropical Asia, having a short, wide bill and brightly coloured plumage. **2.** *U.S.* Any of several other broadbilled birds, such as the shoveler. **3.** *U.S.* The **swordfish** *(see).*

broad·brim (bráwd-brim) *n.* A hat with a broad, flat brim.

broad·cast (bráwd-kaast ‖ -kast) *v.* **-cast** or **-casted** (for sense 3), **-casting, -casts.** —*tr.* **1.** To transmit (a programme or signal) by radio or television. **2.** To make known over a wide area: *broadcast rumours.* **3.** To sow (seed) over a wide area, especially by hand. —*intr.* **1.** To transmit a radio or television programme. **2.** To participate in a radio or television programme. ~*n.* **1.** Transmission of a radio or television programme or signal. **2.** A radio or television programme, or the duration of such a programme. **3.** The act of scattering seed. ~*adj.* Scattered over a wide area. ~*adv.* In a scattered manner; far and wide. [BROAD (adverb), "widely" + CAST.] —**broad·cast·er** *n.*

Usage: The past tense and past participle for this verb is *broadcast* (as for *cast*), not *broadcasted,* as in *It was broadcast last week; The company have broadcast the news.* In the older sense meaning "to sow" (seed), *broadcasted* is acceptable.

Broad Church *n.* **1.** Those members of the Anglican Communion favouring liberalism in matters of doctrine and ritual. Compare **High Church, Low Church. 2.** Any group or party opposed to rigid dogma or exclusiveness, especially political. —**Broad-Church** (bráwd-chúrch) *adj.* —**Broad-Church·man** *n.*

broad·cloth (bráwd-kloth ‖ -klawth) *n.* **1.** A densely textured woollen cloth with a plain or twill weave and a lustrous finish. **2.** A closely woven silk, cotton, or synthetic fabric with a narrow crossways rib.

broad·en (bráwd'n) *v.* **-ened, -ening, -ens.** —*tr.* To make broad or broader. —*intr.* To become broad or broader.

broad gauge *n.* A railway line with a width between the rails greater than the standard gauge of 56½ inches. —**broad gauge, broad-gauged** (bráwd-gáyjd) *adj.*

broad·ie (bráwdi) *n. Australian Informal.* A U-turn.

broad jump *n. U.S.* A **long jump** *(see).*

broad·leaf (bráwd-leef) *n.* Any of various tobacco plants having broad leaves.

broad·leaved (bráwd-leevd) *adj.* Having relatively broad leaves. Said of trees other than conifers.

broad·loom (bráwd-lōom) *adj.* Designating carpet woven on a wide loom and measuring from 1.3 metres (4½ feet) to 5.5 metres (18 feet) in width. ~*n.* A broadloom carpet.

broad·mind·ed (bráwd-míndid) *adj.* Having or arising from liberal or tolerant views. —**broad·mind·ed·ly** *adv.* —**broad·mind·ed·ness** *n.*

broad·ness (bráwd-nəss, -niss) *n.* The state, quality, or aspect of being broad. Compare **breadth.**

broad seal *n.* The official public seal of a state or nation.

Broads (brawdz), **the.** Region of inland waterways in East Anglia, chiefly in Norfolk, but extending also in Suffolk. A great number of wide, shallow lakes are connected by the rivers Yare and Bure and their tributaries. The region is a wildlife sanctuary and recreational boating centre.

broad·sheet (bráwd-sheet) *n.* **1.** A large sheet of paper printed on one side, containing news or other matter. **2.** A large-format newspaper measuring approximately 38 by 61 centimetres (15 by 24 inches). Compare **tabloid.**

broad·side (bráwd-sīd) *n.* **1.** The side of a ship above the water line. **2. a.** All the guns on one side of a warship. **b.** Their simultaneous discharge. **3.** An explosive verbal attack or denunciation. **4.** A broadsheet. **5.** Any broad, unbroken surface. ~*adv.* With the side turned to a given object.

broadside ballad *n.* A rhymed popular tale of romance, adventure, or crime, printed on a broadsheet and sold by hawkers from the 16th to the 19th centuries.

broad-spec·trum (bráwd-spéktrəm) *adj.* Widely applicable or effective: *a broad-spectrum drug.*

broad·sword (bráwd-sawrd ‖ -sōrd) *n.* A cutting sword with a wide blade.

broad·tail (bráwd-tayl) *n.* **1.** A breed of sheep, the **karakul** *(see).* **2.** The pelt of a newborn karakul sheep, having a flat surface with wavy markings. Compare **Persian lamb.**

Broad·way (bráwd-way) *n.* **1.** The principal theatre district of New York City, located on or near the street called Broadway. **2.** This district thought of as representing the U.S. theatre: *a career in television and on Broadway.* Compare **off-Broadway.** —**Broad·way** *adj.*

Brob·ding·nag·i·an (bróbding-nággi-ən) *adj.* **1.** Gigantic; enormous. **2.** On a large scale; enlarged. [After *Brobdingnag,* the land of giants visited by Gulliver in *Gulliver's Travels* (1726), by Jonathan Swift.]

bro·cade (brə-káyd, brō-) *n.* A heavy fabric interwoven with a rich, raised design. ~*tr.v.* **brocaded, -cading, -cades.** To weave with a raised design. [Earlier *brocado,* from Spanish or Portuguese, from Italian *broccato,* embossed fabric, from *brocco,* twisted thread, shoot, from Vulgar Latin *brocca* (unattested), a spike, from Latin *brocchus,* in *brocci dentes,* "projecting teeth".]

broc·a·telle, *U.S.* **broc·a·tel** (bróckə-tél) *n.* A very heavy fabric resembling brocade, but with a more highly raised design. [French *brocatelle,* from Italian *brocatello,* diminutive of *broccato,* BROCADE.]

broc·co·li (bróckə-li, -lī) *n.* **1.** A plant, *Brassica oleracea,* closely related to the cabbage and the cauliflower, that bears dense green, white, or purple clusters of flowers (the curd) at the ends of the central axis and side shoots. There are two main forms, *sprouting broccoli,* with small, separate clusters of the flowers, and *curding* or *winter broccoli,* which is very similar to the cauliflower. **2.** The flower heads of this plant, eaten as a vegetable before the tightly clustered buds have opened. **3.** *Chiefly U.S.* A vegetable, the **calabrese** *(see).* [Italian, plural of *broccolo,* cabbage sprout, diminutive of *brocco,* shoot. See **brocade.**]

broch (brok, bruk, bro<u>kh</u>, bru<u>kh</u>) *n.* An ancient, round, dry-stone tower of a type found in northern Scotland, formerly used as a fortified dwelling. [From Old Norse *borg,* castle.]

bro·ché (bro-shay, bró-shay) *adj.* Woven with a raised pattern or design; brocaded. [French, past participle of *brocher,* to stitch, from *broche,* knitting needle, spit, from Old French, a spit, from Vulgar Latin *brocca* (unattested), a spike. See **brocade.**]

bro·chette (bro-shét ‖ brō-) *n.* **1.** A small spit or skewer upon which meat, fish, or vegetables are roasted or grilled. **2.** A dish cooked on a brochette. [French, from Old French, diminutive of *broche,* spit. See **broché.**]

bro·chure (brō-shər, -shoor, bro-shoór, bra- ‖ *U.S.* brō-shoór) *n.* A small pamphlet or booklet; especially, a promotional booklet, often lavishly illustrated, providing information about a service or product. [French, "a stitching" (from the former loose stitching of the pages), from *brocher,* to stitch.]

brock (brok) *n. British.* **1.** *Regional.* A badger. **2.** A name for a badger, especially in folklore and children's stories. [Old English *broc,* from Celtic *brokko-* (unattested), badger.]

Brock·en (bróckən). Also **Blocks·berg** (blóks-berg; *German* -bairk). A large granite dome in central Germany, the highest peak (1 142 metres; 3,747 feet) in the Harz Mountains. It is famous for the *Brocken Bow* (or *Brocken Spectre*), the hugely magnified shadow of an observer surrounded by bands of colour, projected against low-lying clouds when the sun is low. The colours are caused by the diffraction of the sun's rays by the clouds. The peak is also the legendary site of the witches' sabbath, held on Walpurgis Night.

brock·et (bróckit) *n.* **1.** A two-year-old stag with its first horns. **2.** Any of several small deer of the genus *Mazama,* of South America, having short, unbranched horns. [Middle English *broket,* from Old North French *brocard,* from *broque,* the horn of an animal, any pointed implement, variant of Old French *broche,* a spit.]

bro·de·rie an·glaise (brôdəri ON-gléz, -gláyz) *n.* Embroidery incorporating perforated patterns on fine white linen, cotton, or the like. [French, "English embroidery".]

Broe·der·bond (brôodər-bont, brôodər-, -bawnt) *n.* A secret society of Afrikaners in strategic positions in society, dedicated to upholding the interests of the Afrikaner community in South Africa. [Afrikaans, "band of brothers".]

bro·gan (brôgən) *n.* A heavy, ankle-high work shoe. [Irish-Gaelic *brōgan,* diminutive of *brōg,* BROGUE (shoe).]

Brog·lie (brôgli, broy), **Louis Victor, 7th Duc de** (1892-1987). French physicist. In 1927 he demonstrated by experiments that particles exhibit wavelike properties, thus establishing the field of wave mechanics. For this contribution to modern quantum theory he was awarded the Nobel prize in physics (1929).

brogue¹ (brōg) *n.* A strong regional accent; especially, a strong Irish accent. [From BROGUE (shoe), with reference to the shoes of Irish and Scottish peasants.]

brogue² *n.* **1.** A heavy shoe of untanned leather, formerly worn in Scotland and Ireland. **2.** A strong shoe, usually with ornamental perforations. [Irish and Scottish Gaelic *brōg,* from Old Irish *brōc,* shoe, apparently from Old Norse *brōk,* trousers.]

broil¹ (broyl) *v.* **broiled, broiling, broils.** —*tr.* **1.** To expose to great heat. **2.** *Chiefly U.S.* To cook by direct radiant heat; grill. —*intr.* To become broiled.
~*n.* **1.** The act or condition of broiling. **2.** Something broiled. [Middle English *broillen, brulen,* from Old French *brul(l)er,* earlier *brusler,* to burn, from Vulgar Latin *brustulāre* (unattested), perhaps from Germanic.]

broil² *n.* A rowdy argument; a brawl.
~*intr.v.* **broiled, broiling, broils.** To engage in a brawl. [From obsolete *broil,* to confound, disturb, from Middle English *broilen,* from Old French *brouiller,* perhaps from *breu,* broth.]

broil·er (bróylər) *n.* **1.** One who broils. **2.** *Chiefly U.S.* **a.** A small electric oven used for broiling. **b.** The part of a cooker used for broiling; the grill. **3.** A tender young chicken suitable for grilling or roasting. **4.** *Informal.* An extremely hot day.

broke (brōk). Past tense and *nonstandard* past participle of **break.**
~*adj. Informal.* Having no money.

bro·ken (brōkən). Past participle of **break.**
~*adj.* **1.** Shattered or snapped into two or more pieces. **2.** Disregarded; not honoured: *a broken promise.* **3.** Fragmentary; incomplete: *a broken set of books.* **4.** Disorganised; routed: *broken troops.* **5.** Intermittently stopping and starting; discontinuous. **6.** Varying abruptly, as in pitch: *broken sobs.* **7.** Spoken imperfectly: *broken English.* **8.** Rough; uneven: *broken ground.* **9.** Subdued; humbled: *a broken spirit.* **10.** Tamed and trained: *a broken stallion.* **11.** Weakened; exhausted: *broken health.* **12. a.** Crushed by grief: *a broken heart.* **b.** Utterly demoralised: *a broken man.* **13.** Financially ruined; bankrupt. **14.** In which the marriage partners or parents are separated or divorced: *a broken home.* **15.** Not functioning. —**bro·ken·ly** *adv.*

broken arrow *n.* An accident involving nuclear weapons.

bro·ken-down (brōkən-dówn ‖ *West Indies also* -dúng) *adj.* **1.** Out of working order. **2.** Debilitated; infirm.

bro·ken·heart·ed (brōkən-hártid) *adj.* Extremely sad, as through the loss of a loved one.

Broken Hill¹. Town in New South Wales, Australia, near the border with South Australia. It has one of the world's richest deposits of silver.

Broken Hill². See **Kabwe.**

broken reed *n.* A person whose former integrity or strength of character has been sapped, and who is now seen as pitiable, spineless, and ineffectual.

broken wind *n.* A disease of horses, the **heaves** *(see).*

bro·ker (brōkər) *n.* **1.** One who acts as an agent for others in negotiating contracts, purchases, or sales in return for a fee or commission. **2.** Formerly, a stockbroker. [Middle English, pedlar, pawnbroker, go-between, from Anglo-French *brocour†.*]

bro·ker·age (brōkərij) *n.* **1.** The business of a broker. **2.** A fee or commission paid to a broker.

broker-dealer *n.* One who acts as either a broker or a jobber in a stock exchange.

brol·ly (brólli) *n., pl.* **-lies.** *British Informal.* An umbrella.

bro·mate (brōmayt) *n.* A salt or ester of bromic acid.
~*tr.v.* **bromated, -mating, -mates.** **1.** To treat (a substance) chemically with a bromate. **2.** Loosely, to combine (a substance) chemically with bromine. [Probably German *Bromat* : BROM(O)- + -ATE.]

brome grass (brōm) *n.* Any grass of the genus *Bromus,* especially *B. mollis,* having spikelets in loose, often drooping clusters. Also called "brome". [New Latin *Bromus,* from Latin *bromos,* oats, from Greek *bromos†.*]

bro·me·li·ad (brə-méeli-ad, brō-) *n.* Any of various mostly epiphytic plants of the tropical American family Bromeliaceae, which includes the pineapple, Spanish moss, and many species grown as house plants. Typically, bromeliads have a rosette of fleshy, strap-shaped leaves and produce a long, central, often brightly coloured spike of flowers. [From New Latin *Bromelia* (type genus), after Olaf *Bromelius* (died 1705), Swedish botanist.]

bro·mic acid (brōmik) *n.* A corrosive, colourless unstable liquid, $HBrO_3$, used in making dyes and pharmaceuticals. [French *bromique* : BROM(O)- + -IC.]

bro·mide (brō-mīd) *n.* **1.** Any chemical compound in which the element bromine has a valency of one, either as a negative ion or as an atom linked to another by a covalent bond. **2.** A sedative, **potassium bromide** *(see).* **3.** A commonplace remark or notion; a platitude. **4.** A photographic print on paper that has been treated with bromine and silver. **5.** A photographic print on bromide paper of a typeset page of a book, magazine, or the like, to which artwork is attached before filming and platemaking. —See Synonyms at **cliché.** [BROM(INE) + -IDE.] —**bro·mid·ic** (-middik) *adj.*

bro·mi·nate (brōmi-nayt) *tr.v.* **-nated, -nating, -nates.** To combine (a substance) with bromine or a bromine compound. —**bro·mi·na·tion** (-náysh'n) *n.*

bro·mine (brō-meen, -min) *n. Symbol* **Br** A heavy, volatile, corrosive, reddish-brown, nonmetallic liquid element, having a highly irritating vapour. It is used in producing petrol antiknock mixtures, fumigants, dyes, and photographic chemicals. Atomic weight 79.909, atomic number 35, melting point –7.2°C, boiling point 58.78°C, relative density 3.119, valencies 1, 3, 5, 7. [French *brome,* from Greek *brōmos†,* stench + -INE.]

bro·mism (brōm-iz'm) *n.* Also **bro·min·ism** (-iniz'm). Poisoning from overuse of bromides. Symptoms include acne on the face, headache, sleepiness, apathy, and loss of strength. [Probably French *bromisme* : BROM(O)- + -ISM.]

bromo– *comb. form.* Indicates bromine as the principal element in a chemical compound; for example, **bromoacetone.** [Probably from French *brome,* BROMINE.]

bro·mo·ac·e·tone (brōmō-ássitōn) *n.* Also **brom·ac·e·tone** (brōm-). A colourless liquid, $CH_2BrCOCH_3$, used as a constituent of tear gas. Also called "bromomethane". [BROMO- + -ACETONE.]

bro·mo·form (brōmə-fawrm) *n.* A heavy, colourless liquid, $CHBr_3$, having a sweet taste and odour resembling chloroform, used in laboratory separations of minerals.

bron·chi. Plural of **bronchus.**

bron·chi·a (brόngki-ə) *pl.n. Singular* **-chium** (-əm). *Anatomy.* The bronchial tubes. [Late Latin, from Greek *bronkhia,* plural of *bronkhion,* diminutive of *bronkhos,* windpipe, BRONCHUS.]

bron·chi·al (brόngki-əl) *adj. Anatomy.* Of or pertaining to the bronchi or the bronchioles.

bronchial tube *n. Anatomy.* A bronchus or any of its branches. Also called "bronchium".

bron·chi·ec·ta·sis (brόngki-éktə-siss) *n. Pathology.* Chronic dilation of the bronchial tubes, with cough and formation of mucus and pus. [New Latin : BRONCH(O)- + *ectasis,* dilation, from Greek *ektasis,* stretching.]

bron·chi·ole (brόngki-ōl) *n. Anatomy.* Any of the fine, thin-walled, tubular extensions of a bronchus.

bron·chi·tis (brong-kítiss) *n.* Chronic or acute inflammation of the mucous membrane of the bronchial tubes. Symptoms include coughing and breathing difficulties. [New Latin : BRONCH(O)- + -ITIS.] —**bron·chi·tic** (-kíttik) *adj.*

broncho–, bronch– *comb. form.* Indicates the bronchi or bronchial tubes; for example, **bronchoscope, bronchitis.** [Late Latin, from Greek *bronkh(o)-,* from *bronkhos,* windpipe, BRONCHUS.]

bron·cho·di·la·tor (brόngkō-dī-láytər) *n.* Any of various drugs that relax bronchial muscles and therefore widen the air passages, used to treat asthma, bronchitis, and other breathing difficulties.

bronchopneumonia / brotherly

bron·cho·pneu·mo·ni·a (bróngkō-new-mṓni-ə ‖ -nōō-) *n.* Inflammation of the lungs spreading from and following infection of the bronchial tubes.

bron·cho·scope (bróngkə-skōp) *n.* A slender tubular instrument with a small light on the end for inspection of the interior of the bronchial tubes. [BRONCHO- + -SCOPE.]

bron·chus (bróng-kəss) *n., pl.* **-chi** (-kī, -kee). *Anatomy.* Either of the tubes, having walls thickened with cartilage and branching into smaller air passages, that convey air from the trachea to the lungs. [New Latin, from Greek *bronkhos*, trachea, windpipe, throat.]

bron·co (bróngkō) *n., pl.* **-cos.** A wild or semiwild horse of western North America. [Mexican Spanish, from Spanish, rough, wild.]

bron·co-bust·er (bróngkō-bustər) *n. U.S.* A cowboy who breaks wild horses to the saddle.

Bron·të (brónti), **Charlotte** (1816–55), **Emily** (1818–48), and **Anne** (1820–49). British novelists and poets, daughters of the Anglo-Irish clergyman and writer, Patrick Brunty, or Brontë, who was the curate at Haworth, Yorkshire, after 1820. In 1846 their first publication was issued, a volume of verse entitled *Poems by Currer, Ellis and Acton Bell.* In 1847 Charlotte published *Jane Eyre,* Emily *Wuthering Heights,* and Anne *Agnes Grey.* Anne's *The Tenant of Wildfell Hall* was published in 1848. Charlotte published *Shirley* in 1849 and *Villette* in 1853. Their brother, (Patrick) Branwell (1817–48), was an artist.

bron·to·sau·rus (bróntə-sáwrəss) *n., pl.* **-sauri** (-sáwrī). Also **bron·to·saur** (-sawr). A very large, plant-eating dinosaur of the genus *Apatosaurus* (or *Brontosaurus*) of the Late Jurassic period, having a long neck and tail and a small head. [New Latin *Brontosaurus* : Greek *brontē,* thunder + -SAUR.]

Bronx (brongks), **the.** Borough of New York City, the only one on the mainland. It is chiefly residential, except for the waterfront, which is crowded with warehouses and factories.

Bronx cheer *n. U.S. Slang.* An expression of derision or contempt, a **raspberry** *(see).*

bronze (bronz) *n.* **1. a.** Any of various alloys of copper and tin, sometimes with traces of other metals. **b.** Any of various alloys of copper, with or without tin, and antimony, phosphorus, or other components. **2.** A work of art made of bronze. **3.** A bronze medal. **4.** Metallic yellowish to olive brown. ~*tr.v.* **bronzed, bronzing, bronzes. 1.** To give the appearance of bronze to. **2.** To give a suntanned appearance to. [French, from Italian *bronzo,* perhaps from Persian *birinj,* copper.] —**bronze** *adj.* —**bronz·y** *adj.*

Bronze Age *n.* A period of human culture between the Stone Age and the Iron Age, characterised by weapons and implements made of bronze.

bronze medal *n.* A medal awarded for achieving third place in a race or similar competition.

brooch, broach (brōch ‖ *U.S. also* brōōch) *n.* An ornament worn on the clothing, attached by means of a pin and catch. [Middle English *broche,* brooch, BROACH (tool).]

brood (brōōd) *n.* **1.** The young of certain animals, such as birds or fish; especially, a group of young birds or fowl hatched at one time and cared for by the same mother. **2.** The children in one family. Often used humorously. **3.** A group with a common origin or purpose: *a brood of troublemakers.* —See Synonyms at **flock.** ~*v.* **brooded, brooding, broods.** —*tr.* To sit on or hatch (eggs). —*intr.* **1.** To sit on or hatch eggs. **2.** To hover envelopingly: *"that gentle heat that brooded on the waters"* (Thomas Browne). **3.** To ponder moodily. ~*adj.* Kept for breeding: *a brood mare.* [Middle English *brood,* Old English *brōd,* from Germanic *bro-* (unattested), heat.] —**brood·ing·ly** *adv.*

brood·er (brōōdər) *n.* **1.** One that broods. **2.** A heated enclosure in which young chickens, other fowl, or young farm livestock are raised.

brood·y (brōōdi) *adj.* **-ier, -iest. 1.** Moody; meditative. **2.** Inclined to sit on eggs to hatch them. Said of hens and other poultry. **3.** *Informal.* Being or typical of a woman who strongly desires to have a child.

brook¹ (brōōk ‖ brōōk) *n.* A small, natural freshwater stream. [Middle English *brook,* broke, Old English *brōc.*]

brook² *tr.v.* **brooked, brooking, brooks.** To put up with; bear; tolerate. Usually used in the negative: *I can't brook rudeness.* [Middle English *brouken,* broken, enjoy, to use (as food), to stomach, Old English *brūcan.*]

Brooke (brōōk), **Rupert (Chawner)** (1887–1915). British poet. His first volume of verse, *Poems,* was published in 1911. His *1914 and Other Poems* was published in 1915. The romantic patriotic lyricism of his war sonnets differs sharply in mood from the angry poems of the other leading war poets, Wilfred Owen and Siegfried Sassoon.

Brooke-bor·ough (brōōk-brə, -bərə ‖ brōōk-, -búrrə), **Sir Basil Stanlake Brooke, 1st Viscount** (1888–1973). Northern Irish politician. After serving in the Special Constabulary in its struggle against the I.R.A., he was a member of the Northern Irish Assembly at Stormont (1929–68), serving as Minister of Agriculture (1933–41), Minister of Commerce (1941–45), and prime minister (1943–63). An outspoken opponent of Irish reunification and a fierce upholder of Protestant ascendancy in the North, he was ennobled (1952). He retired from politics in 1968.

brook·ite (brōōk-īt ‖ brōōk-) *n.* A red-brown to black titanium dioxide mineral with characteristic orthorhombic crystals. [After Henry J. *Brooke* (died 1857), English mineralogist.]

brook·let (brōōk-lət, -lit ‖ brōōk-) *n.* A small brook.

brook·lime (brōōk-līm ‖ brōōk-) *n.* Either of two closely related trailing plants, *Veronica beccabunga,* native of Eurasia, and *V. americana,* of North America, growing in moist places and having small blue flowers resembling the speedwell. [Variant (influenced by LIME) of Middle English *brokelemke* : broke, BROOK + *lemke,* a kind of brooklime, Old English *hleomoce.*]

Brook·lyn (brōōklin). Borough of New York City, occupying the southwestern part of Long Island. It is both a residential and an industrial borough, and in population it is the city's largest. It includes Coney Island, famous for its beach and amusement park.

brook trout *n.* A freshwater game fish, *Salvelinus fontinalis,* of eastern North America, introduced in Europe. Also called "speckled trout".

brook·weed (brōōk-weed ‖ brōōk-) *n.* Either of two related plants, *Samolus valerandi* of Europe and *S. floribundus* of North America, both having small white flowers and growing in moist areas. Also called "water pimpernel".

broom (brōōm, brōōm) *n.* **1.** A sweeping implement consisting traditionally of a bundle of twigs or straw bound to a stick, but now usually of synthetic bristles fastened to a long handle. **2.** Any shrub of the genus *Sarothamnus (Cytisus),* especially *S. scoparius,* native to Eurasia, having compound leaves and usually yellow flowers. **3.** Any of several similar or related shrubs, especially of the genus *Genista.* ~*tr.v.* **broomed, brooming, brooms.** To sweep with a broom. [Middle English *broom,* broom made of broom twigs, broom plant, Old English *brōm,* broom plant.] —**broom·y** *adj.*

Broome (brōōm), **David** (1940–). British showjumper. He has won the European men's championship three times (1961, 1967, 1969) and the world championship, the first British jumper to do so, on Beethoven (1970). In 1991 he became the first rider to win the King George V Gold Cup six times.

broom·ie (brōō-mi) *n. Australian Informal.* A person who sweeps up wool in a shearing shed. [From BROOM.]

broom·rape (brōōm-rayp, brōōm-) *n.* Any of several leafless, parasitic plants of the genus *Orobanche,* yellow, purple, or reddish-brown in colour and living on the roots of other plants. [Partial translation of New Latin *rapum genistae,* "tuber of Genista (a genus of broom)" (from the resemblance of one of the parasitic growths to a tuber on the roots of broom).]

broom·stick (brōōm-stik, brōōm-) *n.* The long handle of a broom.

bros. brothers.

brose (brōz) *n.* A kind of oatmeal porridge eaten in Scotland. [Scottish form of BREWIS.]

broth (broth ‖ brawth) *n., pl.* **broths** (broths ‖ brawths, brawthz). **1.** The water in which meat, fish, or vegetables have been boiled; stock. **2.** A thin, clear soup based on stock, to which rice, barley, meat, or vegetables may be added. **3.** A nutrient medium for the culture of microorganisms and tissues. [Middle English, Old English, from Germanic.]

broth·el (bróth'l ‖ *U.S. also* bráwth'l) *n.* **1.** An establishment where men may have sex with prostitutes. **2.** *Australian Informal.* An untidy, disorganised place. [Shortened from *brothel-house,* from Middle English *brothel,* worthless person, prostitute, from Old English *brēothan,* fall into ruin.]

brothel creeper *n. Informal.* A man's thick-soled suede shoe.

broth·er (brúthər) *n., pl.* **brothers** or *archaic* **brethren** (bréthrin). *Abbr.* **b., B., br., bro. 1.** A male having the same mother and father as another person *(full brother),* having one parent in common with another person *(half brother),* having one parent in common with another person by marriage rather than by blood *(stepbrother),* or having the same father and mother after adoption *(foster brother).* **2.** One who shares a common ancestry, allegiance, character, or purpose with another or others, specifically: **a.** A kinsman. **b.** A fellow man. **c.** A fellow member, as of a trade union or profession: *a brother officer.* **d.** A close male friend; a comrade: *"Such a gallant set of fellows! Such a band of brothers!"* (Lord Nelson). **e.** *Informal.* A friend; a fellow. Used as a term of address. **3.** *Ecclesiastical. Abbr.* **Br. a.** A member of a men's religious order who is not in holy orders, but engages in the work of the order. **b.** A lay member of a religious order of men. **c.** *Capital* **B.** A title or form of address for such a person: *Brother Luke.* **4.** A black man or boy. Used as a term of address, especially by fellow blacks, to express solidarity. Compare **sister.** ~*interj.* Used to express despair, annoyance, or the like. [Middle English, Old English *brōthor,* from Germanic.]

broth·er·hood (brúthər-hōōd) *n.* **1.** The state or relationship of being a brother or brothers. **2.** The quality of being brotherly; fellowship. **3.** *Abbr.* **B.** An association of men united for common purposes; a union, society, or similar organisation. **4.** All the members of a specific profession or trade.

broth·er·in·law (brúthər-in-law) *n., pl.* **brothers·in·law. 1.** The brother of one's husband or wife. **2.** The husband of one's sister. **3.** The husband of the sister of one's husband or wife.

Brother Jon·a·than (jónnəthən) *n. British Archaic.* **1.** A personification of the people or government of the United States. **2.** An American. Also called "Jonathan". [Originally applied by British soldiers to American patriots during the American War of Independence (probably from the frequent use of Old Testament first names in the New England colonies).]

broth·er·ly (brúthərli) *adj.* **1.** Characteristic of or befitting brothers;

fraternal. **2.** Kind; generous. —**broth·er·li·ness** *n.* —**broth·er·ly** *adv.*

Brothers of the Christian Schools *pl. n.* The official name for the Christian Brothers *(see).*

Brough (bruff), **Althea Louise** (1923–). U.S. tennis player. Between 1948 and 1955 she won nine Wimbledon titles (four singles, three ladies' doubles, and two mixed doubles).

brough·am (brōōm, brōō-əm ‖ *U.S. also* brō-əm) *n.* **1.** A closed four-wheeled carriage with an open driver's seat in front. **2.** A car with an open driver's seat. **3.** An obsolete electrically powered car resembling a coupé. [After Henry Peter BROUGHAM.]

Brougham (brōōm, brōm), **Henry Peter, 1st Baron of Brougham and Vaux** (vawks) (1778–1868). British politician and educational reformer, born in Scotland. A Member of Parliament from 1810, he defended Queen Caroline in the divorce proceedings brought by George IV (1820) and, as Lord Chancellor (1830–34), played an important role in the passing of the 1832 Reform Act. He is remembered equally for his lifelong campaign against slavery, his great part in the extension of English education (he was a founder of London University and the mechanics' institutes), and his role as legal reformer.

brought. Past tense and past participle of **bring.**

brou·ha·ha (brōō-haa-haa ‖ brōō-háa-haa) *n.* An uproar; a hubbub. [French (imitative).]

Brou·wer (brów-ər), **Adriaen** (*c.*1606–38). Flemish genre and landscape painter, the pupil of Hals. He is famous for his lively treatment of everyday peasant life, and for his mastery of landscape.

brow (brow) *n.* **1.** *Anatomy.* **a.** The part of the face between the eyes and the hairline; the forehead. **b.** The **eyebrow** *(see).* **2.** A facial expression; a countenance: *"Speak you this with a sad brow?"* (Shakespeare). **3.** The edge of a steep place; the top of a slope or hill. —See Synonyms at **border.** [Middle English *brow,* Old English *brū,* eyelash, eyelid, eyebrow, from Germanic.]

brow·beat (brów-beet) *tr.v.* **-beat, -beaten** (-beet'n), **-beating, -beats.** To intimidate or bully with an overbearing manner.

brown (brown ‖ *West Indies also* brung) *n.* **1.** *Abbr.* **br. 1.** Any of a group of colours between red and yellow in hue that are medium to low in lightness, and low to moderate in saturation. **2.** Any of various butterflies of the family Satyridae, such as the mountain ringlets and the heaths. In this sense, also called **"satyr".**
~*adj.* **browner, brownest. 1.** *Abbr.* **br.** Of the colour brown. **2.** Deeply sun-tanned. **3.** Unprocessed and therefore retaining its natural brownish color: *brown flour.* Compare **white. 4.** *South African.* Of or pertaining to the Coloured community (of mixed racial descent) or a member of it.
~*v.* **browned, browning, browns.** —*tr.* To make brown; specifically, to cook until brown. —*intr.* To become brown. [Middle English *broun, brown,* Old English *brūn.*] —**brown·ish** *adj.* —**brown·ness** *n.*

Brown, Sir Arthur Whitten. See **Alcock, Sir John William.**

Brown, Ford Madox (1821–93). British painter, born in France. He trained in Paris and Rome before settling in England (1845). He was closely associated with the **Pre-Raphaelites,** but was never a member of the brotherhood. He painted chiefly historical subjects and scenes from contemporary life, of which the most famous is *Work* (1863).

Brown, George. See **George-Brown, Lord.**

Brown, (James) Gordon (1951–). British politician. He was rector of Edinburgh University (1972–75) while still a student there and was elected Labour M.P. in 1983. He was made Chancellor of the Exchequer in 1997, under Tony Blair, after Labour's general election victory of that year.

Brown, John (1800–59). U.S. abolitionist commemorated in the song, "John Brown's Body Lies A-mouldering in the Grave". A leading campaigner against black slavery in the American South, he enlisted men (1857) to give escaped slaves armed protection in a mountain stronghold. On 16 October 1859, they captured the U.S. arsenal at Harpers Ferry, Virginia. In the subsequent fighting his men were defeated, and Brown was hanged on 2 December.

Brown, Lancelot (1716–83). British landscape gardener, known as "Capability Brown" from his habit of assuring his patrons of the great capabilities of their estates. He broke with the convention of geometrically laid-out gardens, and planned parks and gardens in imitation of a natural landscape, as at Blenheim and Chatsworth. George III appointed him gardener at Hampton Court (1764).

Brown, Robert (1773–1858). British botanist. He discovered and named the nucleus of the cell, but he is most famous for his investigation of the sexual behaviour of plants. It was the microscopic observation of pollination which led to his discovery (1827) of the irregular movement of pollen grains. This observation led to the general physical concept known as **Brownian motion.**

brown algae *n.* Dark brown to olive green chiefly marine algae of the division Phaeophyta, which includes the bladderwracks and the kelps.

brown bear *n.* **1.** A very large bear, *Ursus arctos,* of Alaska and northern Eurasia, having brown to yellowish fur. Compare **grizzly bear, Kodiak bear. 2.** A brown variety of the American black bear.

brown bet·ty (bétti) *n.* A baked pudding consisting of apple, raisins, and spices covered with a topping of fried breadcrumbs, sugar, and butter.

brown bread *n.* Any bread made of flour darker than refined wheat flour.

brown coal *n.* A type of coal, **lignite** *(see).*

Browne (brown), **Hablot Knight** (1815–82). British illustrator and caricaturist, who worked under the pseudonym "Phiz". Dickens invited him to illustrate *Pickwick Papers* (1836), and thereafter he illustrated a number of Dickens' novels.

Browne, Sir Thomas (1605–82). English writer. He was an eminent physician, but his most successful, enduring work was *Religio Medici* (1642), in which he attempted to reconcile the faith of a Christian with the growing body of scientific knowledge.

brown earth *n.* A type of soil, typically found where there is a mild climate and moderate rainfall, usually supporting deciduous forest.

browned-off (brównd-óff ‖ -áwf; *West Indies also* brúngd-) *adj. British Informal.* **1.** Bored; fed up. **2.** Annoyed; irrated.

brown fat *n.* Adipose tissue whose oxidation is a major source of heat in mammals.

Brown·i·an motion (brówni-ən) *n.* The random motion of microscopic particles suspended in a liquid or gas, caused by collision with molecules of the surrounding medium. Also called "Brownian movement". [After Robert BROWN, who described it.]

brown·ie (brówni) *n.* **1.** *Folklore.* A small sprite supposed to do helpful work at night, especially domestic chores. **2.** *Chiefly U.S.* A small bar of flat, rich chocolate cake with nuts. [Diminutive of BROWN. The sprite was thought of as a "wee brown man".]

Brown·ie (brówni) *n.* A member of a junior branch of the Girl Guides. Also called "Brownie Guide". [From BROWNIE (sprite).]

Brown·ing (brówning), **Elizabeth Barrett** (1806–61). British poet. Her first volume of verse, *Poems* (1844), was read by Robert Browning; he subsequently married her and took her to live in Italy (1846) where she wrote *Sonnets from the Portuguese* (1850). Her verse novel *Aurora Leigh* was published in 1857.

Browning, Robert (1812–89). British poet. He published his first poem, *Pauline,* in 1833. After his first visit to Italy, he wrote *Sordello* (1840) and *Pippa Passes* (1841). The collection *Bells and Pomegranates* was published in 1846, the year that he married Elizabeth Barrett in secret. For the next 15 years they lived together in Italy, where Browning wrote *Christmas Eve and Easter Day* (1850) and the collection *Men and Women* (1855). After Elizabeth's death (1861), he returned to England. *The Ring and the Book* (1868–69) is considered his masterpiece, but he is more widely known for his dramatic monologues, such as *My Last Duchess, Andrea del Sarto,* and *The Italian in England.*

Browning automatic rifle *n. Abbr.* **BAR** A .30 calibre air-cooled, automatic or semiautomatic, gas-operated, magazine-fed rifle used in World Wars I and II. [After John Moses *Browning* (1855–1926), U.S. firearms designer.]

Browning machine gun *n.* A .30 or .50 calibre automatic machine gun capable of firing ammunition at a rate of more than 500 rounds per minute. [See **Browning automatic rifle.**]

brown-nose (brówn-nōz) *tr.v.* **-nosed, -nosing, -noses.** *Chiefly U.S. Slang.* **1.** To ingratiate oneself with; behave obsequiously towards. **2.** To achieve or attain by ingratiation: *brown-nosed her way to fame.* [Alluding to such taboo phrases as *to kiss someone's arse.*] —**brown-nose, brown-nos·er** *n.*

brown-out (brówn-owt) *n. Chiefly U.S. & Australian.* A partial extinguishing or dimming of lights in a city, especially as a defensive measure against enemy bombardment or as a means of conserving electricity. [After BLACKOUT.]

brown rat *n.* A common and very destructive rodent pest, *Rattus norvegicus,* found in both town and country. Also called "common rat", "Norway rat".

brown rice *n.* Unpolished rice grains, retaining the germ and the yellowish outer layer containing the bran.

brown rot *n.* **1.** A disease of ripe fruits, caused by fungi of the genus *Sclerotinia.* **2.** A disease of citrus trees, caused by fungi of the genus *Phytophthora.*

Brown Shirts *pl.n.* A Nazi militia, **Sturmabteilung** *(see).*

brown·stone (brówn-stōn) *n. U.S.* **1.** A brownish-red sandstone once widely used as a building material, especially for façades of houses. **2.** A house faced with such stone, especially in New York City. —**brown·stone** *adj.*

brown study *n.* A state of deep thought, melancholy, or reverie.

brown sugar *n.* **1. a.** Unrefined or partially refined sugar. **b.** Loosely, any sugar that is brown in colour. **2.** *Slang.* A coarse, low-grade variety of heroin from Southeast Asia.

brown trout *n.* A freshwater fish, *Salmo trutta,* native to Europe, having yellow-brown sides with black and red spots, the latter circled by pale rings. Compare **sea trout.**

browse (browz) *v.* **browsed, browsing, browses.** —*intr.* **1.** To look through or inspect something, such as a book or goods in a shop, in a leisurely and casual way. **2.** To feed on leaves, young shoots, and other vegetation. —*tr.* **1.** To nibble; crop. **2.** To graze on.
~*n.* **1.** An instance of browsing. **2.** Young twigs, leaves, and tender shoots of plants or shrubs that animals eat. [From Old French *broust, brost,* shoot, twig, from Germanic.] —**brows·er** *n.*

Bru·beck (brōō-bek), **Dave,** full name David Warren Brubeck (1920–). U.S. jazz pianist and composer. He was trained from the age of four as a classical pianist and studied composition under **Milhaud** and **Schoenberg,** but later turned entirely to jazz, forming an octet in 1946, and a quartet in 1951. He remains active.

Bruce, Robert the. See **Robert I.**

bru·cel·lo·sis (brōō-si-lô-siss ‖ brēw-) *n.* A contagious disease of certain livestock caused by bacteria of the genus *Brucella* and transmissible to humans, for example through infected milk. Symptoms in humans include fever, headache, weakness, and painful joints;

and in animals, abortions. Also called "Malta fever", "Mediterranean fever", "undulant fever", and in animals "contagious abortion". [New Latin : *Brucella*, after Sir David *Bruce* (1855–1931), Australian bacteriologist and physician + -OSIS.]

Bruch (brōokh), **Max (Carl August)** (1838–1920). German composer. He is remembered almost exclusively for his violin concerto in G minor and the *Scottish Fantasy*.

bruc·ine (brōō-seen, -sin ‖ brēw-) *n.* A poisonous white crystalline alkaloid, $C_{23}H_{26}O_4N_2 \cdot 2H_2O$, derived from nux vomica seeds. [After James *Bruce* (1730–94), Scottish explorer in Africa.]

Bruck·ner (brŏŏk-nər), **Anton** (1824–96). Austrian composer and organist. He did not write his first important work until he was in his forties, and it was not until his sixties that he became famous. His most important works are the nine symphonies and large choral works, especially the three masses and the *Te Deum*.

Brue·gel or **Breu·ghel** (brŏyg'l, brērg'l; *Dutch* brŏkh'l), **Jan** (1568–1625). Flemish painter, second son of Pieter the Elder. He painted landscapes and often put figures or landscape backgrounds into other artists' paintings, including some of **Rubens** and **Momper**. His reputation now rests mainly on his paintings of still lifes, especially flowers.

Bruegel, Pieter, the Elder (*c.*1530–69). Foremost of a family of Flemish painters, he was one of the first painters to treat landscape as a worthy subject of itself. He is best known for his genre paintings, especially of peasant scenes, in which he combined minute observation of the Flemish tradition with the somewhat fantastical manner of Bosch.

Bruegel, Pieter, the Younger (1564–1638). Flemish painter, son of Pieter the Elder. Many of his paintings are copies of his father's works. Owing to the scarcity of the latter's originals, Pieter the Younger is much better represented in museums and galleries.

Bruges (brōŏzh; *French* brüzh). *Flemish* **Brug·ge** (brōŏgə). Industrial city in northwestern Belgium, connected to the port of Zeebrugge on the North Sea by a canal. It was founded in the 9th century, and in the 13th century was a leading member of the **Hanseatic League** (*see*). In the High Middle Ages, at the zenith of its prosperity, it was one of the most important wool-processing towns and commercial hubs of Europe.

bru·in (brōŏ-in ‖ brēw-) *n.* A name for bear, used especially in folktales and children's stories. [Dutch *bruin*, "brown".]

bruise (brōŏz ‖ brewz) *v.* **bruised, bruising, bruises.** —*tr.* **1.** To damage the underlying tissue or bone of (part of the body) without breaking the skin. **2.** To damage or mar (fruit, for example). **3.** To pound into fragments; crush. **4.** To hurt psychologically; offend. —*intr.* To become discoloured, as the skin does after a hard blow. ~*n.* An area of skin discoloration, caused by the escape of blood from ruptured capillaries following a blow; a contusion. [Middle English *brusen, brisen,* to crush, mangle, from Old English *brȳsan* and Old French *bruisiert*, to break, crush.]

bruis·er (brōŏz-ər ‖ brēwz-) *n.* Slang. A rough-looking, powerfully built man.

bruit (brōōt ‖ brewt) *tr.v.* **bruited, bruiting, bruits.** To spread (a rumour, for example); report. Used with *about* or *abroad.* ~*n.* **1.** *Medicine.* An abnormal sound heard in the body during auscultation, especially a heart murmur. **2.** *Archaic.* A rumour. **3.** *Archaic.* A din; a clamour. [Middle English, noise, from Old French, from the past participle of *bruire,* to roar, from Vulgar Latin *brūgere* (unattested), variant of Latin *rugīre,* to roar.]

Brum (brum). *British.* A nickname for Birmingham. [See **brummagem.**]

bru·mal (brŏŏ-m'l ‖ brēw-) *adj. Archaic.* Of, pertaining to, or characteristic of winter; wintry. [Latin *brūmālis,* from *brūma,* winter solstice, "the shortest day", from *brevima* (unattested), the shortest, from *brevis,* short.]

brume (brŏŏm ‖ brewm) *n.* Heavy fog or mist; dense vapour. [French, mist, winter, from Old French, from Old Provençal *bruma,* from Latin *brūma.* See **brumal.**] —**bru·mous** *adj.*

brum·ma·gem (brúmmə-jəm) *adj.* Cheap and showy; tawdry. ~*n.* Any cheap and gaudy imitation, especially of jewellery. [Dialect form of BIRMINGHAM (with reference to counterfeit coins made there in the 17th century).]

Brum·mell (brúmm'l), **George Bryan,** known as Beau Brummell (1778–1840). British dandy and socialite. He became the close friend of the Prince of Wales and set the male fashion—dark, simply tailored clothes, trousers rather than breeches, and elaborate neckwear—of the Prince's society at Brighton. He came to lead society in London, but gambling brought him deeply into debt and he fled to France (1816) to escape his creditors. He died, after years of penniless squalor, in a lunatic asylum at Caen.

Brum·mie, Brum·my (brúmmi) *n., pl.* **-mies.** *British Informal.* A native or inhabitant of Birmingham. —**Brum·mie, Brum·my** *adj.*

brunch (brunch) *n. Informal.* A meal eaten late in the morning as a combination of breakfast and lunch. [*breakfast* + *lunch.*]

Brundisium. See **Brindisi.**

Bru·nei (brŏŏnī). Sultanate and former self-governing British protectorate on the north coast of Borneo. It is split into two sections, each of which is an enclave within Malaysian territory. The only British dependency inhabited by Malays not to have entered the Federation of Malaysia (1963), it became fully independent at the end of 1983. The economy is largely dependent on the export of oil. Area, 5 800 square kilometres (2,226 square miles). Population, 300,000. See map at **Malaysia.**

Brunei Town. See **Bandar Seri Begawan.**

Bru·nel (brŏŏ-nél, brŏŏ-), **Isambard Kingdom** (1806–59). British civil engineer, son of Sir Marc. He was an engineer with the Great Western Railway and also helped to build railways in Australia, Italy, and India. He worked with his father in the construction of the Thames Tunnel, but he is most famous for his design and construction of the three great ocean steamships, the *Great Western* (1838), which was the first transatlantic steamship, the *Great Britain* (1845), and the *Great Eastern* (1858).

Brunel, Sir Marc Isambard (1769–1849). British engineer and inventor, born in France. A royalist, he went to the United States in 1793 to escape the Terror and began his career as a civil engineer. By 1799 he had settled in England, where he patented a number of inventions, including a knitting machine. His greatest engineering achievement was the design and construction of the Thames Tunnel from Wapping to Rotherhithe, which was completed in 1843.

Bru·nel·les·chi (brŏŏ-ne-léski), **Filippo** (1377–1446). Italian architect, the most celebrated of the 15th century Florentine Renaissance. He reintroduced Roman forms of perspective and methods of construction, but his greatest architectural feat, the dome of Florence cathedral (completed after his death) is in Gothic style.

bru·nette (brŏŏ-nét) *n.* A woman with dark brown hair and dark eyes. Compare **blonde.** [French, from Old French, from *brun,* brown, from Germanic.]

Brun·hild (brŏŏn-hilt). In the *Nibelungenlied,* a legendary queen of Iceland who is won as a bride by Gunther.

Brünn. See **Brno.**

Brun·ner (brŏŏnnər), **Emil** (1889–1966). Swiss Protestant theologian. With Karl **Barth** he was one of the foremost opponents of the rational, liberal school of modern theology, and resolute in his insistence upon the importance of revelation in the relationship between God and humankind. Among his most influential writings were *The Divine Human Encounter* (1938) and *Christianity and Civilisation* (1948–49).

Brünn·hil·de (brŏŏn-hildə). The heroine of Wagner's *Ring of the Nibelung,* a Valkyrie who is placed in the circle of fire by Wotan and is eventually released by Siegfried. Compare **Brynhild.**

Bru·no (brŏŏnō), **Giordano** (*c.*1548–1600). Italian philosopher and cosmologist. He entered the Dominican order at the age of 15, but left it (1576) when he was charged with heresy, and thereafter travelled throughout Europe. He was delivered to the Inquisition by the Venetian authorities (1592) and, after refusing to recant, was burned at the stake (1600) for immoral conduct, blasphemy, and heresy. His most important works were the series of dialogues in which he argued for the indivisibility of all matter and all forms, and in which he extended Copernican thought to state that the universe is an infinite series of solar systems.

Bruno of Cologne, Saint (*c.*1050–1101). German monk, the founder of the **Carthusian** order. He was ordained a priest, but was deprived of his offices when he exposed the malpractices of an archbishop. In 1084 he retired with six fellow monks to the mountains of the Grande Chartreuse in southern France and founded a monastery.

Bruns·wick (brúnz-wik). German **Braun·schweig** (brówn-shvīk). Former German duchy, and then briefly, in reduced area, a West German state. The city of Brunswick, the former capital, is situated on the river Oker.

brunt (brunt) *n.* **1.** The main impact or force, as of a blow or attack. Used especially in the phrase *bear the brunt of.* **2.** *Obsolete.* A violent attack. [Middle English *brunt†.*]

Brusa. See **Bursa.**

brush[1] (brush) *n.* **1.** Any of various devices consisting of bristles, fibres, or other flexible material fastened into a handle, for such uses as scrubbing, polishing, applying paint, or grooming the hair. Often used in combination: *a toothbrush; a hairbrush.* **2.** An act of using such an implement. **3.** A light touch in passing; a graze. **4.** A brief, often unpleasant, contact or encounter: *had several brushes with the law.* **5.** The bushy tail of a fox, used especially as a hunting trophy. **6.** The art or profession of painting. Preceded by *the.* **7.** *Electricity.* A yielding or sliding connection completing a circuit between a fixed and a moving, especially rotating, conductor. **8.** *Australian & N.Z. Slang.* **a.** A girl or young woman. **b.** Women collectively. Preceded by *the.* —**tarred with the same brush.** Acquiring a bad reputation by associating with others who are already in disfavour. ~*v.* **brushed, brushing, brushes.** —*tr.* **1.** To use a brush on, so as to clean, polish, paint, or groom. **2.** To apply with or as if with motions of a brush. **3.** To remove with or as if with motions of a brush. **4.** To dismiss or rebuff abruptly or curtly. Used with *aside* or *off: brushed the matter aside.* **5.** To touch lightly in passing; graze against. —*intr.* **1.** To use or apply a brush. **2.** To move past something so as to touch it lightly. [Middle English *brusshe,* from Old French *broisse, brosse,* perhaps from *broce,* BRUSH (brushwood).] —**brush·er** *n.* —**brush·y** *adj.*

brush[2] *n.* **1. a.** A dense growth of bushes or shrubs. **b.** Land covered by such a growth. **2.** Sparsely populated woodland. **3.** Cut or broken branches. [Middle English *brusch(e),* from Anglo-French *brousse,* from Old French *broce,* from Vulgar Latin *bruscia* (unattested).] —**brush·y** *adj.*

brush discharge *n.* A faintly visible, relatively slow, crackling discharge of electricity without sparking.

brushed (brusht) *adj.* Of or designating knitted or woven fabrics that have a nap produced by brushing during manufacture.

brush-off (brúsh-off, -awf) *n. Informal.* An abrupt dismissal or snub; a rejection.

brush turkey *n.* Any of several Australian birds related to the domestic fowl; especially, *Alectura lathami.*

brush up *tr.v.* To refresh or improve one's knowledge of or one's skill at performing. —*intr.v.* To improve or refresh one's skills or knowledge. Used with *on.*

brush-up (brúsh-up) *n. Chiefly British.* An act of washing and tidying oneself up. Used chiefly in the phrase *a wash and brush-up.*

brush·wood (brúsh-wŏŏd) *n.* **1.** Cut or broken-off branches. **2. a.** Dense undergrowth. **b.** An area covered by such growth.

brush·work (brúsh-wurk) *n.* **1.** Work done with a brush. **2.** The manner in which a painter applies paint with the brush.

brusque (brŏŏsk, brŏ̄osk ‖ brusk) *adj.* Also *archaic* **brusk.** Abrupt and curt in manner or speech; discourteously blunt. See Synonyms at **gruff.** [French *brusque,* lively, fierce, harsh, from Italian *brusco,* sour, sharp, butcher's broom (as noun), from Vulgar Latin *bruscum†.*] —**brusque·ly** *adv.* —**brusque·ness** *n.*

brus·que·rie (brŏŏsk-ǝri, brŏ̄osk-, -ǝrée) *n.* Brusqueness; curtness.

Brus·sels (brúss'lz). *French* **Bru·xelles** (brüsél). Capital of Belgium, lying in Brabant province on the river Senne. Officially a bilingual (Flemish and French) city, it is the executive headquarters of the European Union.

Brussels carpet *n.* A machine-made carpet consisting of small, coloured woollen loops that form a heavy, patterned pile.

Brussels lace *n.* **1.** Fine needlepoint or bobbin lace worked in floral patterns. **2.** Net lace with an appliqué design made by machine.

Brussels sprout *n.* **1.** A variety of cabbage, *Brassica oleracea* or *B. gemmifera,* having a stout stem studded with budlike heads resembling miniature cabbages. **2.** The small edible heads of this plant. Also called "sprout".

brut (brŏŏt; *French* brüt) *adj.* Very dry. Said of wines, especially champagne. Compare **sec.** [French, raw, rough, from Old French, from Latin *brūtus,* heavy.]

bru·tal (brŏŏt'l ‖ bréwt'l) *adj.* **1.** Characteristic of a brute; cruel; inhumane. **2.** Crude or unfeeling in manner or speech; insensitive. **3.** Harsh; unrelenting; merciless: *brutal criticism.* —**bru·tal·ly** *adv.*

bru·tal·ise, bru·tal·ize (brŏŏ-t'l-īz ‖ bréw-) *tr.v.* **-ised, -ising, -ises.** **1.** To make brutal. **2.** To treat brutally. —**bru·tal·i·sa·tion** (-ī-záysh'n ‖ *U.S.* -i-) *n.*

bru·tal·ism (brŏŏt'l-iz'm ‖ bréw-) *n.* A style of architecture that uses stark, geometric lines and large areas of unrelieved concrete to create an impression of monolithic strength. —**bru·tal·ist** *n.*

bru·tal·i·ty (brŏŏ-tál-ǝti ‖ brew-) *n., pl.* **-ties. 1.** The state or quality of being brutal. **2.** A brutal act.

brute (brŏŏt ‖ brewt) *n.* **1.** Any animal other than a human being; a beast. **2. a.** *Informal.* A brutal person. **b.** *Informal.* A much disliked person.
~*adj.* **1.** Of or pertaining to beasts; animal: *"None of the brute creation requires more than food and shelter."* (Henry Thoreau). **2.** Characteristic of a brute: **a.** Entirely physical or instinctive: *brute force.* **b.** Lacking reason or intelligence. **3.** Savage; cruel. **4.** Gross; coarse. [Middle English, from Old French *brut,* rough. See **brut.**] —**brut·ism** *n.*

brut·ish (brŏŏt-ish ‖ bréwt-) *adj.* **1.** Of or characteristic of a brute. **2.** Crude in feeling or manner. **3.** Sensual; carnal. —**brut·ish·ly** *adv.* —**brut·ish·ness** *n.*

Bruttium. See **Calabria.**

Bru·tus (brŏŏtǝss), **Marcus Junius** (*c.*85–42 B.C.). Roman republican statesman and soldier. He joined Cassius in the successful plot to assassinate Caesar (44 B.C.), and began to rally forces for the coming war against Mark Antony, Octavian, and Marcus Lepidus. In Macedonia in 42 B.C. the opposing armies met; Brutus committed suicide at the Battle of **Philippi** on 23 October.

Bruxelles. See **Brussels.**

Bry·an (brí-ǝn), **William Jennings** (1860–1925). U.S. lawyer and Democratic politician. He was secretary of state in Woodrow Wilson's administration (1913–15). Many of the reforms of which he was a principal advocate—income tax, women's suffrage, prohibition—were later adopted.

Bryn·hild (brín-hild). *Norse Mythology.* A Valkyrie in the *Volsunga Saga* who is revived from an enchanted sleep by Sigurd.

bryo– *comb. form.* Indicates moss; for example, **bryophyte.** [New Latin, from Greek *bruon,* moss, akin to Greek *bruein,* to swell. See **embryo.**]

bry·ol·o·gy (brī-óllǝji) *n.* The study of mosses and liverworts. [BRYO- + -LOGY.] —**bry·o·log·i·cal** (brí-ǝ-lójik'l) *adj.*

bry·o·ny (brí-ǝni) *n., pl.* **-nies.** Either of two European plants, the **black bryony** or the **white bryony** (*both of which see*). [Latin *bryōnia,* from Greek *bruōnia,* akin to Greek *bruein,* to swell. See **embryo.**]

bry·o·phyte (brí-ǝ-fīt) *n.* Any plant of the major botanical division Bryophyta, which includes the mosses and liverworts. Bryophytes have stems and leaves but lack true roots and vascular tissue. [New Latin *Bryophyta* : BRYO- + -PHYTE.] —**bry·o·phyt·ic** (-fíttik) *adj.*

bry·o·zo·an (brí-ǝ-zó-ǝn) *n.* An invertebrate animal, a **polyzoan** (*see*). [New Latin *Bryozoa,* plural of *bryozoon* : BRYO- + -ZOON.] —**bry·o·zo·an** *adj.*

Bryth·on (bríth'n, -on) *n.* **1.** An ancient Celtic Briton of Cornwall, Wales, or Cumbria. **2.** One who speaks a Brythonic language.

Bry·thon·ic (bri-thónnik, brǝ-) *adj.* Of, pertaining to, or characteristic of the Brythons or their language.

~*n.* The branch of the Celtic languages that includes Welsh, Breton, and Cornish.

B.S. 1. British Standard. **2.** Bachelor of Surgery. **3.** Bachelor of Science (in the United States).

B.S.A. Birmingham Small Arms (company).

B.Sc. Bachelor of Science.

BSE Bovine spongiform encephalopathy (see).

B.S.I. British Standards Institution.

B. Special *n.* A member of a former auxiliary Protestant police force in Northern Ireland.

B.S.T. British Summer Time.

Bt. baronet.

B.Th. Bachelor of Theology.

Btu, btu. British thermal unit.

B.T.U. 1. Board of Trade Unit. **2.** British thermal unit.

bu, bu. bushel, bushels.

bub¹ (bub) *n. Slang.* A woman's breast. [Shortened from *bubby,* probably from Germanic; akin to German (dialect) *Bübbi,* teat.]

bub² *n. U.S. Informal.* Fellow. Used as a term of affectionate address. [From *bubby,* possibly a baby-talk variant of BROTHER.]

bub·ble (búbb'l) *n.* **1.** A thin transparent film of liquid, generally spherical, enclosing an accumulation of gas: *a soap bubble.* **2.** A small globule of gas trapped in a liquid or solid, as in a carbonated drink or in hardened glass. **3.** A sound made by or as if by the forming and bursting of bubbles. **4.** Anything insubstantial, groundless, or ephemeral, such as a scheme that comes to nothing. **5.** A glass or plastic dome, usually transparent.
~*v.* **bubbled, -bling, -bles.** —*intr.* **1.** To form or give off bubbles, as a boiling liquid does. **2.** To move or flow with a gurgling sound. **3.** To display irrepressible activity or animation. —*tr.* To cause to form bubbles. [Middle English *bobelen* (imitative).]

bubble and squeak *n. Chiefly British.* Leftover cabbage and mashed potatoes fried together, sometimes with meat added. [From the sounds it makes in cooking.]

bubble bath *n.* **1.** A perfumed liquid preparation added to bath water in order to make it foam. **2.** A bath to which such a preparation has been added.

bubble cap *n.* A perforated or slotted cap forming part of the plates of a distillation column that promotes the mixing of the condensate and the vapour.

bubble car *n.* A small car, usually a three-wheeler, having a transparent plastic dome for the top part of its body.

bubble chamber *n. Physics.* An apparatus for detecting the paths of charged particles, or inferring the paths of electrically neutral particles, by examination of trails of bubbles that form on ions produced in a superheated liquid. Compare **cloud chamber.**

bubble gum *n.* Chewing gum that can be blown into bubbles.

bubble memory *n.* A computer memory in which information is stored in the form of binary digits represented by the presence or absence of magnetic bubbles.

bub·bly (búbbli, búbb'l-i) *adj.* **-blier, -bliest. 1.** Containing bubbles; effervescent. **2.** Lively; vivacious.
~*n. Informal.* Champagne.

bubbly jock *n. Scottish.* A turkey.

Bu·ber (bŏ̄obǝr), **Martin** (1878–1965). Austrian-born philosopher and theologian. He was professor of the sociology of religion at the Hebrew University at Jerusalem (1938–51). Much of his writing was devoted to interpreting the mysticism of the Chassidim, the movement of extreme Jewish orthodoxy, but he was also greatly influenced by the Christian existentialism of **Kierkegaard.** His highly personal interpretation of the direct dialogue between God and man, expressed in *I and Thou* (1923), was much drawn upon by contemporary Christian writers.

bu·bo (béw-bō ‖ bŏ̄o-) *n., pl.* **-boes.** An inflamed swelling of a lymphatic gland, especially in the area of the armpit or groin. [Middle English, from Medieval Latin *bubo,* from Greek *boubōn,* groin, swollen gland.] —**bu·bon·ic** (bew-bónnik ‖ bŏ̄o-) *adj.*

bubonic plague *n.* A contagious, often fatal epidemic disease caused by the bacterium *Pasteurella pestis,* transmitted by fleas from infected rats and characterised by chills, fever, vomiting, diarrhoea, and buboes.

bu·bon·o·cele (bew-bónnǝ-seel ‖ bŏ̄o-) *n.* An incomplete hernia of the groin; a partial inguinal hernia. [Greek *boubōn,* groin + -CELE.]

buc·cal (búck'l) *adj.* Of or pertaining to the cheeks or mouth. [Latin *bucca,* cheek.]

buc·ca·neer (búckǝ-néer) *n.* A pirate, especially one of the freebooters who preyed upon Spanish shipping in the West Indies during the 17th century. [French *boucanier,* pirate, "one who cures meat on a barbecue frame" (as done by 17th-century French pirates), from *boucaner,* to cure meat, from *boucan,* barbecue frame, from Tupi *mukem.*]

buc·ca·neer·ing (búckǝ-néering) *adj.* Showing boldness and enterprise, as in business, often to the point of recklessness or unscrupulousness.

buc·ci·na·tor (búksi-naytǝr) *n.* A muscle of the cheek, important in chewing. [Latin, from *buccinare,* to blow a trumpet, from *buccina,* trumpet.]

Bu·ceph·a·lus (bew-séffǝ-lǝss). The war horse of Alexander the Great. [Latin *Būcephalus,* from Greek *Boukephalos,* "ox-headed" : *bous,* OX + -CEPHALOUS.]

Buch·an (búckǝn, búkhǝn), **Sir John, 1st Baron Tweedsmuir** (1875–1940). British writer and politician. He was Member of Parliament for the Scottish universities (1927–35), then was appointed governor-general of Canada and raised to the peerage. He wrote a number of historical works, including a four-volume account of World War I, but his fame rests chiefly on his novels, especially *Prester John* (1910) and *The Thirty-Nine Steps* (1915).

Bu·cha·rest (béwkə-rést, bóokə-, -rest). *Romanian* **Bu·cu·reş·ti** (bóokōō-réshti). Capital and largest city of Romania, lying in the southeastern region of Walachia, on the river Dîmboviţa. Founded in the 14th century, the town was a fortress and a trading centre on the trade route to Constantinople. It became the capital of Walachia in 1698 and, after the union of Walachia and Moldavia, the capital of Romania in 1861.

Buch·man (búk-mən, bóok-), **Frank (Nathan Daniel)** (1878–1961). U.S. evangelist, founder of the Moral Rearmament movement. A Lutheran minister, he preached "world-changing through life-changing" to Oxford undergraduates (1921). The movement, then known as the Oxford Group, spread to more than 60 countries. The MRA campaign (1938) emphasised the importance of purity, honesty, selflessness, and love, allied with reliance upon God. Buchman incurred criticism, however, by his admiration of Hitler.

Buch·man·ism (búk-mən-iz'm, bóok-) *n.* The doctrine of **Moral Rearmament** *(see).* —**Buch·man·ite** *n.*

Buch·ner (bóokhnər), **Eduard** (1860–1917). German chemist, famous for his discovery (1896) that the alcoholic fermentation of sugars is caused, not by the yeast cells themselves, but by enzymes in the yeast. In 1903 he discovered zymase, that part of the enzyme system which produces fermentation. He was awarded the Nobel prize for chemistry (1907).

Büch·ner (búkhnər), **Georg** (1813–37). German playwright, one of the early founders of the school of social realism in the theatre. He wrote only three plays, *Danton's Death* (1835), *Leonce and Lena* (1836), and the fragmentary *Woyzeck* (1836).

buck¹ (buk) *n., pl.* **bucks** or collectively **buck** (for 1 or 2). **1.** The adult male of some animals, such as the deer or hare. Also used adjectivally: *a buck rabbit.* **2.** A male or female antelope. **3.** *Informal.* **a.** A robust or high-spirited young man. **b.** *Archaic.* A fop. [Middle English *bukke,* Old English *buc,* stag, and *bucca,* he-goat, from Old Norse.]

buck² *v.* **bucked, bucking, bucks.** —*intr.* **1.** To jump upwards suddenly with a humped back. Used of a horse or mule. **2.** *U.S. & Australian.* To be obstinately opposed. Often used with *at* or *against.* —*tr.* **1.** To throw (a rider or burden) by bucking. Often used with *off.* **2.** To oppose or resist stubbornly: *buck the system.* —**buck up.** *Informal.* **1.** To summon one's courage or spirits; pull oneself together. Usually used in the imperative. **2.** To speed up; hurry. Usually used in the imperative. **3.** To improve or cheer up: *He had better buck up his methods a little.* —*n.* An act of bucking. [From BUCK (deer).] —**buck·er** *n.*

buck³ *n.* **1.** A vaulting-horse. **2.** *U.S.* A sawhorse. [Short for SAWBUCK.]

buck⁴ *n. U.S. & Australian Slang.* A dollar. [Short for BUCKSKIN (a unit of trade with the American Indians).]

buck⁵ *n.* A counter or marker formerly placed before a poker player to mark him as the next dealer. —**pass the buck.** To shift responsibility or blame to someone else. [Short for earlier *buckhorn knife,* from its use for this purpose.]

Buck, Pearl S(ydenstricker) (1892–1973). U.S. novelist, whose fiction deals mainly with life in China, where she lived until 1924. She wrote more than 85 books, including *The Good Earth* (1931), which won a Pulitzer prize. She won the Nobel prize for literature (1938).

buck·a·roo, (búckə-rōō) *n., pl.* **-roos.** *U.S.* A cowboy. [Variant of Spanish *vaquero,* VAQUERO, from *vaca,* cow, from Latin *vacca.*]

buck·bean (búk-been) *n.* A plant, the **bogbean** *(see).* [Translation of Dutch *boksboon.*]

buck·board (búk-bawrd ‖ -bōrd) *n.* A four-wheeled open carriage, especially in the United States, with the seat attached to a flexible board extending from the front to the rear axle. [From obsolete *buck,* body of a wagon, "trunk of a body", belly, Old English *būc,* from Germanic.]

bucked (bukt) *adj. British Informal.* Cheered up or encouraged: *They were very bucked by her praise.* [From BUCK (deer).]

buckeen (buckéen) *n.* Especially formerly, a young Irishman of the middle classes who imitates the manners and dress of the aristocracy. [BUCK (fop, dandy) + -*een,* from Irish -*ín,* diminutive suffix.]

buck·et (búckit) *n.* **1.** A cylindrical vessel with a semicircular handle and an open top used for holding or carrying liquids or solids; a pail. **2.** Any of various machine compartments that receive and convey material, such as the scoop of a steam shovel. **3.** A bucketful. **4.** *Plural. Informal.* Large quantities: *She's got buckets of money.* **5.** *Computing.* A region on a direct-access storage device from which data can be read. —**kick the bucket.** *Informal.* To die. [Referring to the death throes of a slaughtered animal, from obsolete *bucket,* beam (from which freshly killed animals were suspended).] —**empty** or **tip the bucket on.** *Australian Informal.* To heap criticism on or spread scandalous rumours about.

—*v.* **bucketed, -eting, -ets.** —*tr.* **1.** To hold, carry, or put in a bucket. **2.** *Archaic.* To ride (a horse) long and hard. —*intr.* **1.** To move or proceed rapidly and jerkily. **2.** To rain heavily (with *down*): *The rain bucketed down.* [Middle English *buket, boket,* from Anglo-French *buket,* bucket, tub, perhaps from Old English *būc,* belly, pitcher.]

buck·et·ful (búckit-fōol) *n., pl.* **-fuls** or **bucketsful.** The amount that a bucket will hold.

bucket seat *n.* A seat with a rounded or moulded back, as in sports cars and aircraft.

bucket shop *n.* **1.** A fraudulent brokerage operation that accepts orders to buy or sell shares or commodities but delays executing the orders on the gamble that prices will change adversely to the interests of the customer, so that it can pocket what the customer thinks he has lost. **2.** *Chiefly British.* An unlicensed travel agency that buys airline tickets in bulk and sells them to the public at a discount. [Originally a place where small amounts of commodity gambling transactions took place and where the customer could buy alcoholic drink in buckets.]

buck·eye (búk-ī) *n.* **1.** Any of several North American trees of the genus *Aesculus,* having compound leaves and erect clusters of white or reddish flowers. See **horse chestnut. 2.** The glossy brown nut of any of these trees. [BUCK (male deer) + EYE, referring to the appearance of the nut.]

buck·horn (búk-hawrn) *n.* The material of a buck's horn used for making handles for knives or other implements.

Buc·king·ham (búcking-əm ‖ -həm), **George Villiers, 1st Duke of** (1592–1628). English courtier, statesman, and favourite of James I.

Buckingham, George Villiers, 2nd Duke of (1628–87). English courtier and statesman, son of the 1st Duke. A staunch royalist during the Civil War, he fled to Holland (1648) and became a leading adviser to the exiled Charles II. On the restoration of Charles II (1660) he rose to prominence as a leading member of the royal administration, known as the **Cabal.**

Buckingham Palace. The official London residence of the British sovereign, situated at the western end of St James's Park between Birdcage Walk and the Mall.

Buck·ing·ham·shire (búck-ing-əm-shər, -sheer ‖ -həm-). County in central England, almost entirely agricultural. It has extensive parklands and a great number of country estates, of which the most famous is Cliveden. The county town is Aylesbury.

buck·ish (búckish) *adj. Archaic.* Foppish; dandified. —**buck·ish·ly** *adv.* —**buck·ish·ness** *n.*

buck·jump·er (búk-jumpər) *n.* **1.** A horse that bucks. **2.** *Australian.* A scone or small damper.

buck·le¹ (búck'l) *n.* **1.** A clasp, especially a metal frame with one or more movable tongues for fastening the two ends of a strap or belt. **2.** An ornament that resembles such a clasp.

—*v.* **buckled, -ling, -les.** —*tr.* To fasten or secure with a buckle. —*intr.* To become fastened or attached with a buckle. —**buckle down.** To apply oneself with determination. [Middle English *bocle,* from Old French *boucle,* metal ring, buckle, from Latin *buccula,* cheek strap of a helmet, diminutive of *bucca,* cheek.]

buck·le² *v.* **-led, -ling, -les.** —*intr.* **1.** To bend, warp, or crumple under pressure or heat. **2.** To collapse. —*tr.* To cause to bend, warp, or crumple. —**buckle under.** To surrender to another's authority; yield.

—*n.* A bend, bulge, or other distortion. [Middle English *boclen,* from Old French *boucler,* "to fasten with a buckle", from *boucle,* BUCKLE.]

buck·ler (búcklər) *n.* **1.** A small round shield either carried or worn on the arm. **2.** *Literary.* A means of protection; a defence. —*tr.v.* **bucklered, -lering, -lers.** *Archaic.* To shield with or as if with a buckler; protect. [Middle English *boc(e)ler,* from Old French *bocler, boucler,* from *boucle,* boss on a shield, BUCKLE.]

buckler fern *n.* Any of various ferns of the genus *Dryopteris,* such as *D. dilatata* (broad buckler fern). [Alluding to the shield-like shape of the foliage.]

Buck·ley's chance (búk-leez) *n. Australian & N.Z. Informal.* A very slim chance; little hope. Also "Buckley's", "Buckley's hope".

buck·ling (búckling) *n.* A smoked herring. [German *Bückling,* bloater.]

buck·min·ster·ful·ler·ene (búckminstər-fóollə-réen) *n.* The most symmetrical, C_{60}, of fullerene molecules, with a spherical shape like that of soccer balls or R. Buckminster Fuller's geodesic domes.

buck·o (búckō) *n., pl.* **-oes. 1.** *Slang.* A swaggering bully. **2.** *Chiefly Irish.* A young man; a lad. Often used as a term of address. [From BUCK (young man).]

buckra. Variant of **backra.**

buck·ram (búckrəm) *n.* **1.** A coarse cotton fabric heavily sized with glue, used for stiffening garments and in bookbinding. **2.** *Archaic.* Stiffness; formality.

—*adj.* Made of buckram or resembling it in stiffness.

—*tr.v.* **buckramed, -raming, -rams.** To stiffen with buckram. [Middle English *bokram,* a fine linen, from Old French *boquerant,* obscurely from BOKHARA, from where the fine linen was once imported.]

Bucks., Bucks Buckinghamshire.

buck·saw (búk-saw) *n. U.S.* A wood-cutting saw, usually set in an H-shaped frame. [From BUCK (vaulting-horse).]

buck·shee (búk-shée, -shee) *n. British Informal.* **1.** A windfall or gratuity. **2.** An extra ration.

—*adj. British Informal.* Free of charge; gratis. [Variant of BAKSHEESH.]

buck·shot (búk-shot) *n.* A large lead shot for shotgun shells. [Originally the distance at which a buck could be shot.]

buck·skin (búk-skin) *n.* **1.** The skin of a male deer. **2.** A strong, greyish-yellow leather once made from deerskins but now usually made from sheepskins. **3.** *Plural.* A pair of breeches or shoes made from this leather. **4.** A strong twilled woollen fabric.

—*adj.* Made of buckskin.

buck·thorn (búk-thawrn) *n.* Any of various shrubs or trees of the genera *Rhamnus, Frangula,* or *Hippophaë*; especially, *R. catharticus,* native to Eurasia, with small greenish flowers, black berries, and often thorny branches. See **sea buckthorn.**

buck·tooth (búk-tōoth || -tōoth) *n., pl.* **-teeth** (-téeth). A prominent, projecting upper front tooth. [From BUCK (deer).] **—buck·toothed** (-tōoth || -tōoth) *adj.*

buck·y·ball (búcki-bawl) *n. Informal.* A buckminsterfullerene molecule. [*Bucky* (from *Buck* + -Y³), short for *Buckminster* + BALL¹ (from the molecule's shape).]

buck·wheat (búk-weet, -hweet) *n.* **1.** Any plant of the genus *Fagopyrum;* especially, *F. esculentum,* native to Asia, having fragrant white or pink flowers and small triangular seeds. **2.** The edible seeds of this plant, often ground into flour. [Partial translation of Middle Dutch *boecweite,* "beech wheat" (because its seeds resemble beech nuts) : *boek,* beech + *weite,* wheat.]

bu·col·ic (bew-kóllik) *adj.* **1.** Of or characteristic of shepherds and flocks; pastoral. **2.** Of or characteristic of the countryside or its people; rustic. **—See Synonyms at rural.** **~***n. Plural.* A collection of pastoral poems. [Latin *būcolicus,* from Greek *boukolikos,* from *boukolos,* cowherd : *bous,* cow + *-kolos,* herd.] **—bu·col·i·cal·ly** *adv.*

Bucureşti. See **Bucharest.**

bud¹ (bud) *n.* **1.** *Botany.* **a.** An outgrowth on a stem or branch, often enclosed in protective scales, comprising a shortened stem and immature leaves or floral parts. **b.** The stage or condition of having buds. **c.** A partially opened flower. **2.** *Biology.* **a.** An asexually produced outgrowth, as on a polyp, that develops into a mature, complete organism. **b.** Any small, rounded organic part resembling a plant bud: *taste buds.* **—nip in the bud.** To stop (an idea, plan, or the like) in its initial stages. **~***v.* **budded, budding, buds.** *—intr.* **1.** To put forth or produce a bud or buds. **2.** To begin to develop or grow from or as if from a bud. *—tr.* **1.** To cause to put forth buds. **2.** To graft a bud onto (a plant). [Middle English *budde,* bud, perhaps from Low German *but,* perhaps from Old French *boter,* to push forth, from Germanic.] **—bud·der** *n.*

bud² *n. Chiefly U.S.* Fellow; mister. Used as an informal term of address. [Short for BUDDY.]

Bu·da·pest (béwdə-pést, bōodə-). Capital and largest city of Hungary, situated on the River Danube in northern Hungary. It was formed (1873) by the union of Buda and Óbuda, on the right bank of the Danube, with Pest, on the left bank. Buda was the capital of Hungary from 1361 to 1541, when it was captured by the Ottoman Turks. In 1686 both Buda and Pest passed to the Austro-Hungarian empire. The city was the site of the uprising of 1956.

Budd (bud), **Zola** (1966–). South African-born runner, who set a world record at 5000 metres in 1985.

Bud·dha¹ (bōōddə || *U.S. also* bōōdə), born Gautama Siddhartha (?c. 563–?c. 483 B.C.). Indian mystic, the founder of Buddhism. He was the son of a prince of the Sakya clan in northern India, and was brought up sheltered from the world, but at the age of 29 left the palace to wander about the world, deserting his wife and son. He studied yoga, then found a middle way between extreme asceticism and self-indulgence. He is said to have gained perfect spiritual enlightenment at Buddh Gaya at the age of 35. Having thereby become a Buddha, he lectured at Sarnath to five ascetic companions who became the first Buddhist disciples. He spent the rest of his life travelling through India preaching Buddhism to all listeners, regardless of caste. When he died, he was cremated and his ashes were distributed among eight Buddhist communities, who enshrined them in stupas.

Buddha² *n.* **1.** In Buddhism, one who has achieved a state of perfect spiritual enlightenment. **2.** A representation or likeness of Gautama Buddha. [Sanskrit, "awakened", past participle of *bōdhati,* he awakes, becomes aware.]

Bud·dhism (bōōd-iz'm || *U.S. also* bōōd-) *n.* **1.** The doctrine, attributed to Gautama Buddha, that suffering is inseparable from existence but that inward extinction of the self and of worldly desire culminates in a state of spiritual enlightenment beyond both suffering and existence. **2.** The religion represented by the many groups, especially numerous in Asia, that profess varying forms of this doctrine and venerate Gautama Buddha. **—Bud·dhist** (-ist) *n. & adj.* **—Bud·dhis·tic** (-ístik), **Bud·dhis·ti·cal** *adj.*

bud·ding (búdding) *adj.* Beginning to develop; promising: *a budding playwright.*

bud·dle (búdd'l) *n.* An inclined trough on which ore is separated from waste by washing with running water.

bud·dlei·a (búddli-ə || bud-lée-ə) *n.* Any ornamental shrub of the genus *Buddleia,* especially *B. davidii,* which has long, pyramidal spikes of small, scented, purple flowers that attract butterflies. Also called "butterfly bush". [After Adam *Buddle* (died 1715), British botanist.]

bud·dy (búddi) *n., pl.* **-dies. 1.** *Chiefly U.S. Informal.* A good friend. Often used as a term of address. **2.** Someone who befriends a person in need, such as one with AIDS. **~** *intr.v.* **buddied, buddying, buddies.** To act as a buddy. **~***adj. Informal.* Of, pertaining to, or representing a close, warm relationship between two tough men: *a buddy movie.* [Probably from a baby-talk variant of BROTHER.]

bud·dy-bud·dy (búddi-búddi) *adj. Chiefly U.S. Informal.* Showing great outward friendship.

budge¹ (buj) *v.* **budged, budging, budges.** *—intr.* **1.** To move or stir slightly. **2.** To alter a position or attitude. *—tr.* **1.** To cause or

persuade to move slightly. **2.** To cause to alter a position or attitude. Usually used in the negative in all senses. [Earlier *bouge,* from Old French *bouger, bougier,* from Vulgar Latin *bullicāre* (unattested), from Latin *bullīre,* to boil.]

budge² *n.* Fur, usually lambskin, treated to be worn with the wool outwards. **~***adj. Archaic.* Extremely formal; solemn; pompous. [Middle English *bugee, bogey*†.]

Budge (buj), **(John) Donald** (1915–). U.S. tennis player, the first to win the Grand Slam (Wimbledon, French, U.S., and Australian titles) in one year (1938). He won all three titles (men's singles, men's doubles and mixed doubles) at both Wimbledon and Forest Hills (1937, 1938).

budg·er·i·gar (bújəri-gaar) *n.* A parakeet, *Melopsittacus undulatus,* native to Australia, having green plumage in the wild. It is a popular cage bird and breeders have raised many different-coloured varieties. Also informally called "budgie". [Native Australian name : *budgeri,* good + *gar,* cockatoo.]

budg·et (bújit) *n.* **1.** An itemised summary of probable expenditures and income for a given period, usually embodying a systematic plan for meeting expenses. **2.** The total sum of money allocated for a particular purpose or time period. **—the Budget.** A statement presented annually by the British Chancellor of the Exchequer to the House of Commons outlining the government's probable expenditure for the ensuing financial year and the revenue, including proposed taxes, needed to meet this expenditure. **~***adj.* Designed to save money; cheap: *a budget holiday.* **~***v.* **budgeted, -eting, -ets.** *—tr.* To plan in advance the expenditure of (money or time, for example). *—intr.* **1.** To plan one's expenditure according to available resources: *Living on my income requires careful budgeting.* **2.** To allow for something in a budget. Used with *for: We've budgeted for the replacement of old machinery.* [Middle English *bouget,* wallet, from Old French *bougette,* diminutive of *bouge,* leather bag, from Latin *bulga,* from Gaulish.] **—budg·et·ar·y** (búji-tri, -təri) *adj.*

budget account *n.* An account at a large department store or a bank into which regular sums of money are paid to cover expenditures over a period of time.

budg·ie (búji) *n. Informal.* A budgerigar.

Bue·no (bwáynō), **Mária (Esther Andion)** (1939–). Brazilian tennis player who won the Wimbledon singles title three times (1959, 1960, 1964) and the U.S. championship four times between 1959 and 1966. She also won nine ladies' doubles titles at Wimbledon and Forest Hills.

Bue·nos Ai·res (bwáy-noss ír-iz, bwé-, -nəss, -nəz, aír-, aírz). The capital, chief port, and largest city of Argentina, at the mouth of the Río de la Plata. Situated at the edge of the Pampa, the intensely cultivated agricultural region, and connected by rivers to Brazil, Uruguay, and Paraguay, the city is one of the world's busiest ports. It is also one of the most heavily industrialised cities in South America. It was founded in 1536 by Spanish colonists and has been the capital since 1862.

buff¹ (buf) *n.* **1.** A soft, thick, undyed leather made chiefly from the skins of buffalo, elk, or oxen. **2.** The colour of this leather; pale creamy yellow to light yellowish brown. **3.** *Informal.* The bare skin. Used chiefly in the phrase *in the buff.* **4.** A polishing implement covered with a soft material, such as velvet or kid. **~***adj.* **1.** Made of buff. **2.** Of the colour of buff. **~***tr.v.* **buffed, buffing, buffs.** **1.** To polish or shine with a buff. **2.** To give (leather, for example) the velvety surface of buff, as with sandpaper. [Originally "buffalo", from Old French *buffle,* from Vulgar Latin *būfalus* (unattested), BUFFALO.]

buff² *n. Informal.* One who is enthusiastic and knowledgeable about a specified subject: *an opera buff.* [Originally a New York volunteer fireman, hence an enthusiast, from the firemen's buff uniforms.]

buf·fa·lo (búffəlō) *n., pl.* **-loes** or **-los** or collectively **buffalo. 1.** Any of several oxlike Old World mammals of the family Bovidae, having massive curved horns and humped backs, such as *Syncerus caffer* of Africa or the **water buffalo** (*see*). **2.** A related North American animal, the **bison** (*see*). [Portuguese *bufalo,* from Vulgar Latin *būfalus* (unattested), from Latin *būbalus,* from Greek *boubalos,* African antelope, buffalo, probably from *bous,* cow, ox.]

Buffalo Bill. See **Cody, William Frederick.**

buffalo gnat *n.* Any of various small, bloodsucking, North American insects of the genus *Simulium* and related genera. Also called "black fly".

buffalo grass *n.* A short grass, *Buchloë dactyloides,* of the plains east of the Rocky Mountains in North America.

buff·er¹ (búffər) *n.* An implement used to shine or polish, such as a soft cloth or a buffing wheel.

buffer² *n.* **1.** Something that lessens or absorbs the shock of an impact; especially, either of a pair of spring-loaded or hydraulically mounted steel pads attached to both ends of railway rolling stock and at the end of a railway line to reduce the shock of collision. **2.** One that protects by intercepting or moderating adverse pressures or influences. **3.** Something interposed between two rival powers, lessening the danger of conflict. Often used adjectively: *a buffer zone.* **4.** *Chemistry.* An ionic solution capable of maintaining the relative concentrations of hydrogen and hydroxyl ions in a solution by neutralising, within limits, added acids or bases. Also called "buffer solution". **5.** *Computing.* A memory device used for the temporary storage of data. **6.** *Electronics.* A circuit used to join two other circuits so as to minimise the reactance between them.

~*tr.v.* **buffered, -ering, -ers.** *Chemistry.* To treat (a solution) with a buffer. [Probably from obsolete *buff,* "to sound as a soft body when struck" (imitative).]

buffer³ *n. Informal.* A bumbling old man. [Probably from obsolete *buff* (imitative). See **buffer².**]

buf·fet¹ (bŏŏffay; *in sense 1 sometimes* bŭffit || bŭffi, bŏŏffi, *U.S.* bə-fáy, bŏŏ-) *n.* **1.** A large sideboard with drawers and cupboards. **2. a.** A counter or table from which meals or refreshments are served. **b.** A restaurant having such a counter. **c.** A buffet car. **3.** A meal at which guests serve themselves from various dishes displayed on a table or sideboard. Also used adjectivally: *a buffet lunch.* [French *buffet.*]

buf·fet² (bŭffit) *n.* **1.** A blow or cuff with the hand. **2.** A blast of wind or the impact of a wave. **3.** A blow; a setback.
~*v.* **buffeted, -feting, -fets.** —*tr.* **1.** To strike against forcefully or repeatedly; batter. **2.** To contend with; struggle against. —*intr.* **1.** To struggle; contend. **2.** To force one's way by struggling. [Middle English, from Old French, diminutive of *buffe,* blow (imitative).] —**buf·fet·er** *n.*

buf·fet car (bŏŏffay; *see* **buffet¹**) *n.* A railway coach serving light meals and refreshments. Also called "buffet".

buff·ing wheel (bŭffing) *n.* A wheel covered with a soft material, such as velvet or kid, for shining and polishing metal.

buf·fle·head (bŭff'l-hed) *n.* A small North American duck, *Bucephala albeola,* having black and white plumage and a densely feathered, rounded head. Also called "butterball". [From obsolete *buffle,* a buffalo (from the duck's large head), from Old French. See **buff** (leather).]

buf·fo (bŏŏffō || *U.S.* bŏŏfō) *n., pl.* **-fi** (bŏŏffee || *U.S.* bŏŏfee). A male singer of comic opera roles.
~*adj.* Characteristic of a buffo; comic. [Italian, "puff of wind", from *buffare,* to puff. See **buffoon.**]

Buf·fon (bŏŏ-fŏN, béw-, bŏŏ- || bŭ-fóN), **Georges-Louis Leclerc, Comte de** (1707-88). French biologist. In his 44-volume *Natural History* (1749), and in *Epochs of Nature* (1778), he contributed greatly to the development of modern science by stressing a materialist, geological explanation of the world's origin and history. Buffon also wrote a *Discourse on Style* (1753), an analysis of literary expression which features the famous phrase, "the style is the man".

buf·foon (bə-fŏŏn, bu-) *n.* **1.** A clown; a jester: *a court buffoon.* **2.** A bumbling, witless person; a fool. [French *bouffon,* from Italian *buffone,* from *buffare,* to puff (imitative).] —**buf·foon·er·y** *n.*

bug (bug) *n.* **1.** Any of various wingless or four-winged insects of the order Hemiptera, and especially the suborder Heteroptera, having mouthparts adapted for piercing and sucking. **2.** *Chiefly U.S.* Broadly, any insect or similar organism. **3.** *Informal.* **a.** A disease-producing microorganism. **b.** A disease so caused, often spreading as a minor epidemic: *The whole school was down with a tummy bug.* **4.** A mechanical, electrical, or other systemic defect or difficulty, as in a computer system. **5.** *Informal.* A craze; an obsessive hobby or enthusiasm. **6.** *Informal.* A small hidden microphone or other device used for eavesdropping or surveillance.
~*tr. v.* **bugged, bugging, bugs.** *Informal.* **1. a.** To annoy; pester. **b.** To worry; prey on: *That memory bugged me over the years.* **2.** To fit (a room, for example) with concealed electronic surveillance equipment. [17th century : origin obscure.]

bug·a·boo (búggə-bōō) *n., pl.* **-boos.** **1.** A bugbear. **2.** A steady source of concern. [Perhaps from Celtic; akin to Cornish *buccaboo,* the devil. Compare **bugbear** and **bogle.**]

Bu·gan·da (bōō-gándə, bōō-). **1.** A former kingdom in east Africa, occupying the northern shores of Lake Victoria, in present-day Uganda. It was ruled by the Ganda tribe until it became a British protectorate (1900). It was merged with Uganda when Uganda became an independent state (1962). **2.** An administrative region of Uganda which includes the capital, Kampala, and the chief commercial centre, Entebbe.

bug·bane (búg-bayn) *n.* Any of several plants of the genus *Cimicifuga;* especially, *C. foetida,* of Europe, having clusters of small white flowers supposed to repel insects.

bug·bear (búg-bair) *n.* **1.** An object of obsessive, but often groundless, dread. **2.** *Archaic.* A goblin reputed to eat naughty children. [Obsolete *bug,* from Middle English *bugge;* akin to Welsh *bwg(a),* ghost, and Cornish *buccaboo,* the devil.]

bug·ger¹ (búggər) *n.* **1.** A man who practises buggery. **2.** *Vulgar Slang.* A contemptible or disreputable person. **3.** *Slang.* A person, child, or animal. Used humorously or affectionately: *You daft bugger!* **4.** *Slang.* Something that is a problem or that causes difficulties. —**play silly buggers.** *Slang.* To be obstructive or uncooperative; mess about.
~*tr.v.* **buggered, -gering, -gers.** **1.** To practise buggery upon. **2.** *Slang.* To mess up or botch. Usually used with *up.* **3.** *Slang.* To tire; weary. **4.** *Slang.* Used in the passive, like *damned,* as an expression of surprise, annoyance, or determination. —**bugger about** or **around.** *Slang.* **1.** To behave stupidly. **2.** To cause difficulties for. —**bugger off.** *Vulgar Slang.* To go away.
~*interj. Vulgar Slang.* Used to express annoyance. [Middle English *bougre,* from Middle Dutch *bugger,* from Old French *bougre,* sodomite, heretic, from Medieval Latin *Bulgarus,* a Bulgarian; first applied to an heretical sect that came to France from Bulgaria in the 11th century.]

bugger² *n. Informal.* A person who plants an electronic eavesdropping or surveillance device. [BUG + -ER¹.]

bug·ger·y (búggəri) *n.* Anal intercourse practised by a man

on a woman, man, child, or animal. Usually considered vulgar when used in a nontechnical context.

Bug·gins' turn, Bug·gins's turn (búgginz, -iz) *n. British.* Someone's turn from the practice of assigning people to positions by rotation rather than on merit. [*Buggins,* used as a typical name.]

bug·gy¹ (búggi) *n., pl.* **-gies.** **1.** A small, light, horse-drawn carriage. **2.** A Baby Buggy *(see).* [18th century : origin obscure.]

buggy² *adj.* **-gier, -giest.** **1.** Infested with bugs. **2.** *U.S. Slang.* Crazy. —**bug·gi·ness** *n.*

bug·house (búg-howss) *n. U.S. Slang.* A lunatic asylum. [From BUGGY (crazy).]

bu·gle¹ (béwg'l) *n.* **1.** A brass wind instrument somewhat shorter than a trumpet, and without keys or valves. **2.** A hunting horn.
~*intr. v.* **bugled, -gling, -gles.** To play a bugle. [Middle English *bugle,* buffalo, horn, bugle, from Old French, from Latin *būculus,* diminutive of *bōs,* OX.] —**bu·gler** *n.*

bugle² *n.* A tubular glass or plastic bead used to trim clothing. Also called "bugle bead". [16th century : origin obscure.]

bugle³ *n.* Any of several plants of the genus *Ajuga,* especially *A. reptans,* native to Eurasia, having spikes or dense clusters of small blue or white flowers. Also called "bugleweed". [Middle English, from Old French, from Late Latin *bugula,* perhaps from Latin *bugillō,* from Gaulish.]

bu·gloss (béw-gloss || -glawss) *n.* Any of several plants of the genera *Lycopsis* and *Echium,* especially *L. arvensis,* having hairy stems and leaves and clusters of blue flowers. See **viper's bugloss.** [Middle English *buglosse,* from Old French, from Latin *būglōssa,* from Greek *bouglōssos,* "ox-tongued" (from the broad, rough leaves) : *bous,* ox + *glōssa,* tongue.]

bugong. Variant of **bogong.**

buhl, boule, boulle (bōōl) *n.* **1.** A style of furniture decoration in which elaborate designs are inlaid with tortoiseshell, ivory, and metals of various colours. **2.** A piece of furniture so decorated. Also called "buhlwork". [After André C. *Boulle* (1642-1732), French cabinetmaker.]

buhr·stone, burr·stone (búr-stōn) *n.* A tough limestone impregnated with silica, from which millstones were formerly made. [Variant of *bur(r)stone* : perhaps BUR + STONE.]

build (bild) *v.* **built** (bilt) *or archaic* **builded, building, builds.** —*tr.* **1.** To form by combining materials or parts; erect; construct. **2.** To develop and give form to according to a definite plan or process; fashion; mould; create. **3.** To order, finance, or supervise the building of: *The council stopped building council houses.* **4.** To establish and strengthen; create and add to: *build a savings account.* **5.** To establish a basis for; found or ground: *build an argument on fact.* —*intr.* **1.** To construct something or have something constructed: *"Each of the three architects built in a different style"* (Dwight Macdonald). **2.** To develop, progress, or advance. Used with *on* or *upon: building on our past success.* **3.** To progress towards a maximum, as of intensity, excitement, or the like. —**build in.** To construct as an integral or permanent part of. —**build into.** To make part of: *a clause built into the contract; fixtures built into the wall.*
~*n.* The physical make-up of a person or thing: *an athletic build.* [Middle English *bilden,* Old English *byldan,* from *bold,* a dwelling.]

build·er (bildər) *n.* **1.** One that builds; especially, a person who contracts for and supervises the construction of a building. **2.** An abrasive or filler used in a soap or a detergent.

build·ing (bilding) *n.* **1.** *Abbr.* **bldg.** Something that is built; a structure; an edifice. **2.** The act, process, or occupation of constructing.
Synonyms: building, structure, edifice.

building society *n.* An institution that lends money for house purchases and pays interest to investors who deposit money with it.

build up *tr. v.* **1.** To renew the strength or health of. **2.** To construct or develop in stages or by degrees; create and add to: *build up a business.* **3.** To magnify (a person or thing) by extravagant praise or publicity. —*intr.v.* **1.** To increase steadily; develop: *The tension built up.* **2.** To accumulate: *Scale has built up inside the pipes.*

build-up, build·up (bíld-up) *n.* **1.** The act of amassing or increasing. **2.** *Informal.* Extravagant praise; widely favourable publicity, especially by a systematic campaign. **3.** The result of building up: *the build-up of tension; the build-up of traffic.*

built. Past tense and past participle of **build.**
~*adj.* Having a physique or physical make-up of the specified type: *well built; heavily built.*

built environment *n.* The man-made part of the environment (such as buildings, roads, and public-transport facilities) by contrast with the natural environment.

built-in (bílt-in) *adj.* **1.** Constructed as part of a larger unit; not detachable: *a built-in wardrobe.* **2.** Forming a permanent or essential element or quality: *a built-in escape clause.*
~*n. Australian.* A built-in or fitted cupboard or wardrobe.

built-up (bilt-úp) *adj.* **1.** Occupied by or covered with many buildings. **2.** Made by fastening several layers or sections one on top of the other: *a built-up roof.*

Bu·jum·bu·ra (bōōjəm-bŏŏr-ə). Capital and largest city of **Burundi.**

Bu·kha·ra (bōō-khaárə, bōō-). Also **Bo·kha·ra** (bo-). A city in Uzbekistan, central Asia, situated in the Zeravshan river valley. It is one of the oldest cultural and trading centres of Asia and was the capital of the khanate, or state, of Bukhara during its heyday from the 16th to the 19th centuries.

Bukhara rug (bōō-kaárə, bōō- -khaárə) *n.* Also **Bokhara rug.** A kind of rug, usually having a black and white pattern of large and small octagons on a red, brownish-red, or sometimes tan ground.

Bu·kha·rin (boo-kha'arin), **Nikolai Ivanovich** (1888–1938). Soviet politician, theoretician, and editor of *Pravda* (1917–29). In 1923 he became a full member of the Politburo and in the power struggle that followed Lenin's death (1924) supported Stalin. Later his advocacy of gradual agricultural collectivisation and industrialisation lost him major posts in the party (1929), and he was executed for treason after the last of the Moscow "show trials" (1938).

Bu·la·wa·yo (boolla-wáy-o). Industrial city on the western border of Zimbabwe, lying on the Matsheumlope river. It is the second largest city in Zimbabwe, founded in 1893.

bulb (bulb) *n.* **1.** *Botany.* A modified underground stem, such as that of the onion or tulip, usually surrounded by scalelike modified leaves, and containing stored food for the undeveloped shoots of the new plant enclosed within it. **2.** Loosely, an underground stem resembling this, such as a corm, rhizome, or tuber. **3.** Any plant that grows from a bulb. **4.** A rounded projection or part of something: *the bulb of a syringe.* **5.** An incandescent lamp or its glass housing. Also called "light bulb". **6.** *Anatomy.* Any of various rounded, enlarged, or bulb-shaped structures, especially the **medulla oblongata** *(see).* [Latin *bulbus,* bulb, onion, from Greek *bolbos†,* name of various bulbous plants.]

bul·bar (búl-bər ‖ -baar) *adj. Anatomy.* Of, pertaining to, or characteristic of a bulb, especially of the medulla oblongata.

bul·bil (búlbil) *n. Botany.* A small bulblike part growing above ground on a flower stalk or in a leaf axil. [French *bulbille,* diminutive of *bulbe,* BULB.]

bul·bous (búlbəss) *adj.* **1.** Resembling a bulb in shape. **2.** *Botany.* Bearing bulbs or growing from a bulb.

bul·bul (boolbool) *n.* **1.** Any of various chiefly tropical Old World songbirds of the family Pycnonotidae, having greyish or brownish plumage. **2.** A songbird, thought to be a nightingale, often mentioned in Persian poetry. [Persian, from Arabic.]

Bul·ga·nin (bool-gaanin, bool-), **Nikolai Alexandrovich** (1895–1975). Soviet politician who distinguished himself as an administrator during World War II. After the war he was appointed a full member of the Politburo and deputy premier. In 1955 he replaced Malenkov as premier, but was dismissed by Khrushchev.

Bul·gar·i·a (bul-gaír-i-ə, bool-). Republic in the Balkan peninsula of southeastern Europe, bordered on the west by Yugoslavia and Macedonia (FYROM), on the north by Romania, on the east by the Black Sea, and on the south by Turkey and Greece. The centre of the country is crossed from west to east by the Balkan Mountains. Between these and the river Danube, which forms most of the northern boundary, lies a broad, fertile plateau. Although the country has been considerably industrialised since 1945, agriculture remains the leading sector of the economy. From the late 14th to the early 20th century, Bulgaria was ruled by Turkey. In 1946 it became a People's Republic. In 1989, the ruler Todor Zhivkov was ousted, and in 1990 free elections were held. Area, 110 994 square kilometres (42,855 square miles). Population, 8,360,000. Capital, Sofia.

Bul·gar·i·an (bul-gaír-i-ən ‖ bool-) *adj.* Of, pertaining to, or characteristic of Bulgaria, its inhabitants, or their language.
~*n.* Also **Bul·gar** (búl-gaar ‖ -gər) (for sense 1). **1.** A native or inhabitant of Bulgaria. **2.** The Slavonic language spoken by Bulgarians.

bulge (bulj) *n.* **1.** A protruding part; an outward curve or swelling. **2.** A sudden, often temporary increase in number or quantity.
~*v.* **bulged, bulging, bulges.** —*tr.* To cause to curve outwards. —*intr.* **1.** To swell up or outwards; grow larger or rounder. **2.** To be swollen because full: *a bulging wallet.* [Middle English, wallet, pouch, from Old French *bouge,* from Latin *bulga,* leather bag, probably from Gaulish.] —**bulg·i·ness** *n.* —**bulg·y** *adj.*

Bulge, Battle of the *n.* The last major German counteroffensive of World War II, launched December 16, 1944, and repulsed by January 25, 1945. [So called because the line of combat formed a large bulge deep into Belgium.]

bul·gur, bul·ghur (búl-gar, bool-) *n.* A cereal food prepared by boiling and drying coarsely ground wheat. Also called "bulgur wheat", "cracked wheat". [Turkish *burgul.*]

bu·lim·i·a (bew-limmi-ə, boo-) *n.* **1.** Insatiable appetite, especially if caused by a brain lesion. **2.** Bulimia nervosa *(see).* [New Latin, from Greek *boulimia* : *bous,* ox, cow + *limos,* hunger, famine.] — **bu·lim·ic** *adj. & n.*

bulimia ner·vos·a (ner-vō-sə) *n.* A psychological illness, often found in combination with **anorexia nervosa** *(see),* in which bouts of compulsive eating are followed by self-induced and ultimately involuntary vomiting. [New Latin "nervous bulimia".]

bulk (bulk) *n.* **1.** Size, mass, or volume, especially when very large. **2. a.** A distinct mass or portion of matter, especially a large one. **b.** The body of a human being or animal, especially a large and corpulent body. **3.** The major portion or greater part of something: *"the great bulk of necessary work can never be anything but painful"* (Bertrand Russell). **4.** Thickness of paper or cardboard in relation to weight. **5.** *Abbr.* **blk.** A ship's hold or the cargo stowed there. **6.** Any substance that stimulates the action of the intestines; roughage. —**in bulk. 1.** Unpackaged; loose. **2.** In large numbers, amounts, or volume.
~*v.* **bulked, bulking, bulks.** —*intr.* **1.** To appear to be, in terms of size, volume, or importance; loom: *"shopkeeping naturally bulks large among London occupations"* (G.D.H. Cole and Raymond Postgate). **2.** To grow or increase in size or importance. Usually used with *up.* **3.** To cohere or form a mass: *Certain paper pulps bulk well.* —*tr.* To gather together into a mass. [Middle English *bulke, bolke,* heap, mass, body, from Old Norse *bulki,* cargo.]

bulk buy *n.* A product bought in bulk. —**bulk-buy** *v.*

bulk density *n.* The mass of a substance divided by its volume when it is present in bulk. For example, the bulk density of coal is lower than its true density because of the air spaces between lumps.

bulk·head (búlk-hed) *n.* **1.** Any of the upright partitions dividing a ship into compartments and serving to prevent the spread of leakage or fire. **2.** A partition or wall serving a similar purpose in an aircraft, spacecraft, or other vehicle. [From BULK (ship's hold).]

bulk modulus *n.* A measure of the elasticity of a substance equal to the ratio of the stress applied to the resulting change in volume.

bulk·y (búlki) *adj.* **-ier, -iest. 1.** Extremely large; massive. **2.** Difficult to carry; unwieldy. —**bulk·i·ly** *adv.* —**bulk·i·ness** *n.*

bull[1] (bool) *n.* **1. a.** An adult male bovine mammal. **b.** The uncastrated adult male of domestic cattle. **2.** The male of certain other mammals, such as the elephant and whale. **3.** An exceptionally large, strong, and aggressive man. **4.** *Stock Market.* A person who buys stocks or shares in anticipation of a rise in prices or who tries by speculative purchases to effect such a rise, in order to sell later at a profit. Compare **bear. 5.** *Capital* B. The constellation and sign of the zodiac, **Taurus** *(see).* Preceded by *the.* **6.** A bull's eye *(see).* **7.** *Slang.* Empty, foolish, or boastful talk; nonsense. —**take the bull by the horns.** To deal with a problem directly and resolutely.
~*v.* **bulled, bulling, bulls.** —*tr.* **1.** *Stock Market.* To engage in speculative buying so as to raise the price of (stocks) or prices in (a market). Compare **bear. 2.** *U.S.* To push; force. —*intr. Stock Market.* To rise in price. Compare **bear.**
~*adj.* **1.** Male; masculine. **2.** Resembling a bull; large and strong.

3. *Stock Market.* Characterised by rising prices: *a bull market.* Compare **bear.** [Middle English *bule, bole,* from Old English *bula,* from Old Norse *boli.* Noun sense 7, from BULLSHIT; Stock Market senses, 18th century : term introduced to contrast with BEAR as descriptions of the two different types of speculators.]

bull² *n.* **1.** An official document issued by the pope and sealed with a bulla. **2.** The bulla itself. [Middle English *bulle,* from Old French *bulle,* from Medieval Latin *bulla,* seal, BULLA.]

Bull, John. See **John Bull.**

bul·la (bŏŏl-ə) *n., pl.* **bullae** (-ee). **1.** A round seal affixed to a papal bull. **2.** *Pathology.* A large blister or vesicle. Compare **bleb.** [Both senses, Medieval Latin, from Latin, bubble, seal.]

bul·lace (bŏŏlliss) *n.* A shrub or small tree, *Prunus institia,* the cultivated form of which is the **damson** *(see).* [Middle English *bolas,* from Old French *buloce, beloce,* sloe, probably from Medieval Latin *bolluca†.*]

bul·late (búl-ayt, bŏŏl-, -ət, -it) *adj.* Having a puckered or blistered appearance: *bullate leaves.* [New Latin *bulla,* bubble, from Latin.]

bull-bait·ing (bŏŏl-bayting) *n.* The setting of dogs upon bulls, once a popular sport in England.

bull bar *n.* A reinforced front motor-vehicle bumper in the form of a framework of metal bars.

bull·bat (bŏŏl-bat) *n.* A bird, the **nighthawk** *(see).* [From its roaring sound in flight.]

bull·dog (bŏŏl-dog ‖ -dawg) *n.* **1.** A short-haired dog of a breed characterised by a large head, strong, square jaws with dewlaps, and a stocky body. **2.** A short-barrelled revolver or pistol of a large calibre. **3.** *British Informal.* A proctor's assistant at the universities of Oxford or Cambridge.
~adj. Resembling or having the qualities of a bulldog; stubborn; tenacious.

bulldog ant *n.* A large Australian ant of the genus *Myrmecia* measuring up to one inch long, having powerful jaws and a painful sting. Also called "bull ant".

bulldog clip *n.* A strong, spring-operated metal clip for holding papers, documents, and the like.

bull·doze (bŏŏl-dōz) *tr.v.* **-dozed, -dozing, -dozes. 1.** To clear, dig up, or move with a bulldozer. **2.** *Informal.* To coerce by intimidation; bully. **3.** *Informal.* To force relentlessly or determinedly: *bulldozed his way to the top.* [Perhaps BULL + DOSE.]

bull·doz·er (bŏŏl-dōzər) *n.* A tractor, usually with caterpillar treads and a metal scoop in front for moving earth and rocks, used especially to clear land.

bull·dust (bŏŏl-dust) *n. Australian.* **1.** Coarse dust found on roads in the outback. **2.** *Informal.* Nonsense.
~intr.v. **bull-dusted, -dusting, -dusts.** *Australian Informal.* To brag or exaggerate.

bul·let (bŏŏllit) *n.* **1.** A spherical or pointed cylindrical metallic projectile that is fired from a pistol, rifle, or other relatively small firearm. **2.** Such a projectile in a metal casing; a cartridge. **3.** Any object of similar shape, action, or effect. **4.** *Printing.* A heavy dot (●) used to call attention to a particular passage. **5.** *Australian Informal.* A pop song that rises quickly up the charts. **—bite the bullet.** *Informal.* To endure a painful or difficult situation bravely and stoically. **—get** or **be given the bullet.** *Informal.* To be dismissed from employment. [French *boulette,* diminutive of *boule,* ball, from Old French, from Latin *bulla,* bubble, ball.]

bul·le·tin (bŏŏlli-tin) *n.* **1.** A brief, authoritative statement on a matter of public interest, intended for immediate broadcast or publication. **2.** A brief, periodically broadcast summary of the news. **3.** A periodical published by an organisation or society.
~tr.v. **bulletined, -tining, -tins.** To inform by bulletin. [French, probably from Old French *bullette,* from *bulle,* BULL (document).]

bulletin board *n. U.S.* A **notice board** *(see).*

bul·let-proof (bŏŏllit-prŏŏf ‖ -prŏŏf) *adj.* Impenetrable by bullets.
~tr.v. **bulletproofed, -proofing, -proofs.** To make impenetrable by bullets.

bullet train *n.* A high-speed Japanese passenger train.

bull·fight (bŏŏl-fīt) *n.* A public spectacle, especially in Spain and Latin America, in which a fighting bull is engaged in a series of traditional manoeuvres culminating usually with the matador's ceremonial execution of the bull by sword. **—bull·fight·er** *n.* **—bull·fight·ing** *n.*

bull·finch (bŏŏl-finch) *n.* **1.** A European bird, *Pyrrhula pyrrhula,* having a short, thick bill and, in the male, a red breast, black head, wings, and tail, and a grey and white back. **2.** Any of several other similar finches. [From its thick neck.]

bull·frog (bŏŏl-frog ‖ -frawg) *n.* Any of several large frogs, chiefly of the genus *Rana;* especially, *R. catesbeiana,* of North America, having a characteristic deep, resonant croak.

bull·head (bŏŏl-hed) *n.* **1.** Any of several North American freshwater catfishes of the genus *Ictalurus.* **2.** Any of several fishes of the family Cottidae, such as the **sculpin** and the **miller's thumb.**

bull·head·ed (bŏŏl-héddid) *adj.* Very stubborn; obstinate; headstrong. **—bull·head·ed·ly** *adv.* **—bull·head·ed·ness** *n.*

bul·li·on (bŏŏl-yən, -i-ən) *n.* **1.** Gold or silver considered with respect to quantity rather than value. **2.** Gold or silver in the form of bars, ingots, or plates. **3.** A heavy lace trimming made of twisted gold or silver threads. Also called "bullion fringe". [Middle English, from Anglo-French, "mint", perhaps variant of Old French *bouillon,* "a boiling", from *bouillir,* to BOIL.]

bull·ish (bŏŏl-ish) *adj.* **1.** Like a bull; brawny or bull-headed.

2. a. Causing, expecting, or characterised by rising stock-market prices. **b.** Optimistic or confident. Compare **bearish. —bull·ish·ly** *adv.* **—bull·ish·ness** *n.*

bull mastiff *n.* A heavy-set dog of a breed developed from the bulldog and the mastiff.

bull-necked (bŏŏl-nekt) *adj.* Having a short, thick neck.

bul·lock (bŏŏllək) *n.* **1.** A castrated bull; a steer. **2.** A young bull. [Middle English *bullok,* Old English *bulluc,* diminutive of *bula,* BULL.]

bul·lock·y (bŏŏlləki) *n. Australian Informal.* **1.** A person who drives a team of bullocks. **2.** Swearing or provocative language.

bull·ring (bŏŏl-ring) *n.* A circular arena for bullfights.

bull·roar·er (bŏŏl-rawrər ‖ -rōrər) *n.* A small wooden slat attached to a string that makes a roaring noise when whirled, used for example by Australian Aborigines in certain religious ceremonies. Also called "thunderstick".

bull session *n. U.S. Informal.* An informal group discussion.

bull's-eye, bull's eye (bŏŏlz-ī). **1. a.** The small central circle on a target. **b.** A shot that hits this circle. In both senses, also called "bull". **2.** Anything that precisely achieves a desired goal. **3.** A thick, circular piece of glass set in a roof, pavement, ship's deck, or the like, to admit light. **4.** Any circular opening or window. **5. a.** A plano-convex lens used to concentrate light. **b.** A lantern or lamp having such a lens. **6.** *Nautical.* A small round or oval wooden pulley. **7.** The boss set at the centre of a sheet of blown glass. **8.** A round, hard mint-flavoured sweet. **8.** In India, a fried egg.

bull·shit (bŏŏl-shit) *n. Vulgar Slang.* Foolish, uninformed, pretentious, or exaggerated talk; nonsense.
~intr. v. **bullshit** or **bullshitted, -shitting, -shits.** *Vulgar Slang.* To hold forth pretentiously on a subject one does not grasp; claim knowledge one lacks.

bull snake *n.* Any of several nonvenomous North American snakes of the genus *Pituophis,* having yellow and brown or black markings. Some species are also called "gopher snake".

bull terrier *n.* A dog of a breed developed by crossing a bulldog and the now extinct white English terrier, having a short, usually white coat and a tapering muzzle.

bull trout *n.* A large trout; especially, the **salmon trout** *(see).*

bull·whip (bŏŏl-wip, -hwip) *n.* A long, plaited rawhide whip with a knotted end.
~tr.v. **bullwhipped, -whipping, -whips.** To whip with a bullwhip.

bul·ly (bŏŏlli) *n., pl.* **-lies. 1.** A person who is habitually cruel or overbearing towards smaller or weaker people. **2.** A hired ruffian. Now used only adjectivally in the phrase *bully boy.* **3.** Bully beef. **4.** *Archaic.* A pimp. **5.** *Obsolete.* A sweetheart.
~v. **bullied, -lying, -lies.** *—tr.* **1.** To intimidate with superior size or strength. **2.** To induce or pressurise by intimidating. Used with *into: She bullied me into coming. —intr.* To behave like a bully.
~adj. Informal. **1.** Excellent; splendid. **2.** Dashing; gallant.
~interj. Used to express admiration or approval, especially ironically, in such phrases as *bully for you.* [Originally "sweetheart", probably from Middle Dutch *boele,* lover, from Middle High German *buole,* perhaps of baby-talk origin.]

bully beef *n.* Tinned corned beef, especially as part of military rations. Also called "bully". [French *bouilli,* boiled (beef), from the past participle of *bouillir,* to BOIL.]

bully off *intr. v.* Formerly, to start or restart a game of hockey. Two players hit each other's sticks and then the ground three times before trying to hit the ball.

bul·ly-off (bŏŏlli-óff, -áwf) *n.* The former procedure for starting or restarting a game of hockey.

bul·ly-rag (bŏŏl-i-rag) *tr.v.* **-ragged, -ragging, -rags.** Also **bal·ly·rag** (bál-). To mistreat or intimidate by bullying or teasing.

bully tree *n.* A tropical American tree, the **balata** *(see).* [By folk etymology, variant of BALATA.]

bul·rush (bŏŏl-rush) *n.* **1.** A tall grasslike sedge, *Scirpus lacustris,* growing in ponds and rivers and having oval reddish-brown flower spikes at the stem tip. **2.** A marsh plant, the **reed mace** *(see).* **3.** In the Old Testament, the **papyrus** *(see).* [Middle English *bulrish :* perhaps *bule,* BULL (in the sense "large") + *rish,* RUSH.]

bul·wark (bŏŏl-wark, -wurk ‖ búl-) *n.* **1.** A wall or wall-like structure raised as a defensive fortification; a rampart. **2.** Anything serving as a principal defence against attack or encroachment: *a bulwark against oppression.* **3.** A breakwater. **4.** *Usually plural.* The part of a ship's side that is above the upper deck.
~tr.v. **bulwarked, -warking, -warks. 1.** To fortify with a bulwark. **2.** To provide defence or protection for. [Middle English *bulwerke,* from Middle High German *bolwerc : bole,* plank + *werc,* WORK.]
    Synonyms: *bulwark, barricade, breastwork, earthwork, rampart, bastion, parapet.*

Bulwer-Lytton. See **Lytton, Bulwer-Lytton, 1st Baron.**

bum¹ (bum) *n. Chiefly British Slang.* The buttocks. [Middle English *bomt.*]

bum² *n. Chiefly U.S. Informal.* **1.** A tramp; a layabout. **2.** A person who avoids work and seeks to live off others. **3.** An incompetent or disagreeable person. **4.** One who is devoted to a specified activity: *ski bums.* **—on the bum.** *Slang.* **1.** Living as a tramp. **2.** Sponging or cadging.
~v. **bummed, bumming, bums.** *Informal. —intr.* **1.** To live by begging and scavenging from place to place. Often used with *around.* **2.** To loaf. *—tr.* To acquire by begging or sponging.
~adj. Slang. **1.** Of poor quality; worthless: *a bum deal.* **2.** Not in time: *a bum note.* [From earlier *bummer,* a loafer, probably from

German *bummler,* from *bummeln†,* to loaf.]

bum·bail·iff (búm-báyliff) *n. British.* Formerly, a court officer who pursued debtors. Used derogatorily. [From BUM (buttocks), since he pursues and catches from behind.]

bum·ble¹ (búmb'l) *v.* -bled, -bling, -bles. —*intr.* To speak or behave in a clumsy or faltering manner. —*tr.* To bungle; botch. [Variant of BUNGLE.] —**bum·bler** *n.* —**bum·bling·ly** *adv.*

bumble² *intr.v.* -bled, -bling, -bles. To make a humming or droning sound; buzz.
~*n.* A droning sound; a buzz. [Middle English *bomblen* (imitative).]

bum·ble·bee (búmb'l-bee) *n.* Any of various large, hairy, social bees of the genera *Bombres* and *Psithyrus.* Also called "humble-bee". [BUMBLE + BEE.]

bum·boat (búm-bōt) *n.* A small boat used to peddle provisions and small wares to ships anchored offshore. [Probably Dutch *bom†,* a kind of fishing boat + BOAT.]

Bu·mi·put·ra (bōōmi-pōōtrə) *n.* Any of the indigenous natives of Malaysia. —**Bu·mi·put·ra** *adj.*

bu·mi·pu·tra·i·sa·tion (bōōmi-pōōtrə-ī-záysh'n) *n.* In Malaysia, an official policy giving preference to Malays in areas such as business or education. [BUMIPUTRA + -ISATION.]

bum·ma·lo (búmmalō) *n., pl.* bummalo. A **bombay duck** (see). [Perhaps from Marathi *bombila.*]

bum·ma·ree (bumə-reé) *n. British.* 1. A dealer in Billingsgate fish market. 2. A porter at Smithfield meat market.

bum·mer (búmmər) *n. Slang.* 1. An idler. 2. Something which is inferior or disappointing. 3. An unpleasant experience, especially one caused by taking a hallucinatory drug. [BUM + -ER]

bump (bump) *v.* bumped, bumping, bumps. —*tr.* 1. To strike or collide with. 2. To cause to knock against an obstacle. 3. *British Informal.* To give (a child) the bumps. 4. *U.S.* To displace; dislodge. 5. In some rowing races at Oxford and Cambridge universities, to catch up with and touch (the boat ahead). —*intr.* 1. To hit or knock with force. Often used with *against* or *into.* 2. To proceed with jerks and jolts. Often used with *along.* 3. *Chiefly U.S.* To thrust the pelvis forward in a sensual way when dancing. Used chiefly in the phrase *bump and grind.* 4. To boil violently. —**bump into.** To meet by chance. —**bump off.** *Slang* To murder or kill. —**bump up.** *Informal.* To increase.
~*n.* 1. a. A light blow, collision, or jolt. b. The noise caused by this; a thud. 2. A slight swelling or lump. 3. A raised part on a generally even surface. 4. One of the natural protuberances of the human skull. 5. A sudden violent upward air current striking an aircraft in flight. 6. *Chiefly U.S.* A sensual forward thrust of the pelvis when dancing 7. *Plural.* A joke ceremony, specifically to celebrate a birthday, in which a person, usually a child, is held by the arms and legs, and swung up and down so that his buttocks touch the ground. Preceded by *the.* [Imitative.]

bump cap *n. Australian Informal.* A safety helmet.

bump·er¹ (búmpər) *n.* 1. One that bumps. 2. Either of two metal or rubber structures, typically horizontal bars, attached to the front and rear of a motor vehicle to absorb the impact of a collision. 3. A similar protective device on other objects. 4. In cricket, a **bouncer.**

bumper² *n.* A drinking vessel filled to the brim.
~*tr.v.* bumpered, -ering, -ers. 1. To fill to the brim. 2. To propose a toast to.
~*adj.* Unusually good, large, or abundant: *a bumper crop.* [Perhaps from BUMP (lump, hence something large).]

bumper³ *n. Australian Informal.* A cigarette butt. —**not worth a bumper.** *Australian Informal.* Useless; worthless. [Perhaps from BUTT + STUMP.]

bum·per·to·bum·per (búmpər-tə-búmpər, -tōō-) *adj.* Travelling close together, with bumpers almost touching. Said of motor vehicles. —**bum·per·to·bum·per** *adv.*

bumph, bumf (bumf) *n. Informal.* 1. Pamphlets, documents, memoranda, and the like, often bureaucratic and of little interest to the reader. 2. Toilet paper. [Shortened from *bum-fodder.* See bum (buttocks).]

bump·kin (búmp-kin, búm-) *n.* A **country bumpkin** (see). [Perhaps originally "Dutchman", probably from Dutch *boomken,* "little tree", squat person, diminutive of *boom,* tree, from Middle Dutch.]

bump start *n.* A method of starting a car or other vehicle by putting it in gear, pushing or rolling it with the clutch disengaged, and engaging the clutch when the car is moving. —**bump-start** *tr.v.*

bump·tious (búmpshəss) *adj.* Crudely arrogant and self-assertive in behaviour; pushy. [Perhaps a blend of BUMP and FRACTIOUS.] —**bump·tious·ly** *adv.* —**bump·tious·ness** *n.*

bump·y (búmpi) *adj.* -ier, -iest. 1. Covered with bumps or protuberances: *a bumpy road.* 2. Involving jerks and jolts: *a bumpy ride.* —**bump·i·ly** *adv.* —**bump·i·ness** *n.*

bum's rush *n. Slang.* Forcible ejection or dismissal. [From BUM (tramp).]

bun (bun) *n.* 1. A small bread roll; a bap. 2. A small round sweet bread roll, often made with dried fruit. 3. A roll of hair worn at the back of a woman's head. —**do (one's) bun.** *N. Z. Informal.* To get very angry. [Middle English *bunne†.*]

Bu·na (bōōnə, béwnə) *n.* A trademark for a type of synthetic rubber made by polymerisation of butadiene and sodium.

bunch (bunch) *n.* 1. A group of like items growing, fastened, or placed together; a cluster or tuft. 2. *Informal.* A small group of things or people. 3. *Rare.* A lump or swelling. 4. *Plural. British.* A hairstyle in which the whole head of hair is parted from forehead to

nape and fastened in two tresses, one on either side of the head.
~*v.* bunched, bunching, bunches. —*tr.* 1. To gather or form into a cluster or tuft. 2. To gather together in a group. 3. To gather (fabric) into folds. —*intr.* 1. To form a cluster or tuft. 2. To gather together in a group; cluster. 3. To be gathered up in folds. Used of fabric. [Middle English *bunche†.*] —**bunch·y** *adj.*

Bunche (bunch), **Ralph Johnson** (1904–71). U.S. civil servant and political scientist. He was the first black to become a divisional head in the Department of State (1945). At the United Nations (1946–70) he carried out detailed research into colonial administration and race relations and was awarded the Nobel peace prize (1950) for his work as principal secretary of the UN Palestine Commission.

bunch of fives *n. Slang.* A fist.

bun·co (búngkō) *n., pl.* -cos. Also **bun·ko** *pl.* -kos. *U.S. Informal.* A swindle; a confidence trick.
~*tr.v.* buncoed, -coing, -cos. Also **bunko.** *U.S. Informal.* To swindle; cheat. [Spanish *banca,* name of a card game, "bank" (in gambling), from Italian *banca,* BANK (financial establishment).]

buncombe. Variant of **bunkum.**

bund¹ (bund) *n.* In India and the Far East, an embankment or dyke. [Hindi *band,* from Persian.]

bund² (bōōnd, bund; German bōōnt) *n.* 1. A confederation or league. 2. *Often capital* B. A pro-Nazi German-American organisation of the 1930s. [German *Bund,* "league".] —**bund·ist** *n.*

Bun·des·rat, Bun·des·rath (bōōn-dəss-raat, -dəz-) *n.* 1. The upper house of the federal legislative body of Germany, made up of ministers from each of the states. 2. The federal council of certain countries, as of Switzerland and Austria. 3. Formerly, a federal legislative council composed of representatives from the 26 states of the German Empire. [*Bundes,* genitive of BUND + *Rat,* council.]

Bun·des·tag (bōōn-dəss-taag, -dəz-; German -dəss-taak) *n.* The lower house of the federal legislative body of Germany, elected by universal suffrage. [German : *Bundes,* genitive of BUND + *-tag,* meeting.]

bun·dle (búnd'l) *n.* 1. A number of objects bound, wrapped, or otherwise held together. 2. Anything wrapped or tied up for carrying; a package. 3. *Biology.* A cluster or strand of specialised cells. 4. *Botany.* A **vascular bundle** (see). 5. a. *Informal.* A large amount; a lot. Used in such phrases as *a bundle of laughs.* b. One who typifies a specified quality: *a bundle of fun; a bundle of nerves.* 6. *Mathematics.* A fibre bundle. —**drop (one's) bundle.** *Australian Informal.* To panic and give up. —**go a bundle on.** *Informal.* To be very keen on.
~*v.* bundled, -dling, -dles. —*tr.* 1. To tie, wrap, fold, or otherwise secure together. 2. To dispatch or cause to move quickly and unceremoniously; hustle. Usually used with *off* or *into.* 3. To stuff (clothes, for example) into a bag or other container. 4. To dress warmly. Used with *up.* —*intr.* To sleep in the same bed while fully clothed, a custom formerly practised by engaged couples in Wales and New England. [Middle English *bundel,* probably from Middle Dutch, sheaf of papers, bundle.] —**bun·dler** *n.*

bun·du (bōōndōō) *n. South African Slang.* A remote outback area. [Probably from Shona *bundo,* grasslands.]

bun·dy (bún-di) *n., pl.* -dies. *Australian Informal.* A time clock for workers.

bun·fight (bún-fīt) *n. British Informal.* A tea-party.

bung¹ (bung) *n.* 1. A stopper for a cask, flask, or the like. 2. The hole itself; a bunghole.
~*tr.v.* bunged, bunging, bungs. 1. To close (a bunghole) with a cork or stopper. 2. *Informal.* To stop up; clog; congest. Often, used with *up.* 3. *Informal.* To throw; toss. [Middle English *bunge,* from Middle Dutch *bonghe,* perhaps variant of *bonne,* perhaps from Late Latin *puncta,* hole, from the feminine past participle of Latin *pungere,* to prick.]

bung² *adj. Australian & N.Z. Slang.* Broken; out of order. —**go bung.** *Informal.* To fail. [From a native Australian language.]

bun·ga·low (búng-gə-lō) *n.* 1. A single-storey house. 2. In India, a thatched or tiled house having one storey and surrounded by a wide verandah. 3. *South African.* A barrack room or military domitory. [Earlier *bungale,* perhaps from Gujarati *bangalo,* from Hindi *bariglā,* "of Bengal".]

bungee (bún-ji) *jumping n.* Jumping from a great height while attached to a secured elasticated rope one hopes will not let one down. [From *bungee,* the rope (origin unknown).]

bung·hole (búng-hōl) *n.* The hole in a cask, keg, or barrel through which liquid is poured in or drained out.

bun·gle (búng-g'l) *v.* -gled, -gling, -gles. —*intr.* To work or act ineptly or inefficiently. —*tr.* To manage (a task) badly; botch. ~*n.* A clumsy or inept job or performance. [Perhaps from Scandinavian, akin to Swedish (dialectal) *bangla,* to work ineffectually.] —**bun·gler** *n.*

bun·gling (búng-gling) *adj.* Performing clumsily or ineptly; incompetent. See Synonyms at **awkward.** —**bun·gling·ly** *adv.*

bun hat *n. N.Z. Informal.* A bowler hat.

Bu·nin (bōōneen), **Ivan Alexeyevich** (1870–1953). Russian writer. He gained international recognition with the novel, *The Village* (1910), but he is best known for his short stories, especially *The Gentleman from San Francisco* (1915). He was awarded the Nobel prize for literature (1933).

bun·ion (bún-yən) *n.* A painful swelling at the first joint of the big toe, over which a bursa often forms. [Probably from earlier *bunny, bony,* swelling, from Old French *buignet†,* bump on the head.]

bunk¹ (bungk) *n.* **1.** A narrow bed attached like a shelf against a wall. **2.** Either of a pair of narrow beds stacked one on top of the other. Also called "bunk bed". **3.** *Informal.* Any place for sleeping. **—do a bunk.** *Slang.* To leave hurriedly, usually for dishonest reasons.
~*v.* **bunked, bunking, bunks.** —*intr.* **1.** To go to bed. Often used with *down.* **2.** *British Slang.* To play truant. Often used with *off.* —*tr. British Slang.* To play truant from (school). [Possibly short for BUNKER.]

bunk² *n. Slang.* Nonsense. [Short for BUNKUM.]

bun·ker (búngkər) *n.* **1.** A bin or tank for coal or other fuel. **2.** An obstacle on a golf course, consisting of a sand-filled pit, sometimes placed on a slope. Also *chiefly U.S.* "sand trap". **3.** A fortified underground defensive position, with an overground projection for gun emplacements. **4.** *Informal.* An entrenched, and often embattled, position. Also used adjectivally: *a bunker mentality.*
~*tr.v.* **bunkered, -kering, -kers.** **1.** To store (fuel) in a bunker. **2.** To drive (a golf ball) into a bunker. **3.** To place in a difficult position. [Earlier Scottish *bonker*†.]

bunk·house (búngk-howss) *n. U.S.* Sleeping quarters on a ranch or in a camp.

bunk·mate (búngk-mayt) *n.* A person with whom one shares rough sleeping quarters.

bunko. Variant of **bunco.**

bun·kum, bun·combe (búngkəm) *n.* Empty or meaningless talk, especially by a politician; claptrap. [After *Buncombe* County, North Carolina, from a remark made in about 1820 by its congressman, Felix Walker, who made a fatuous speech, calling it "a speech for Buncombe".]

bun·ny (búnni) *n., pl.* **-nies.** **1.** A rabbit. Used especially by and to children. **2.** A bunny girl. [From dialectal *bun*†, squirrel.]

bunny girl *n.* A hostess in a night club who wears a brief costume with a fluffy rabbit-like tail. Also called "bunny".

bun·ra·ku (boon-ráakoo) *n.* **1.** The traditional Japanese puppet theatre. **2.** One of the two schools of Japanese puppet theatre.

Bunsen burner *n.* A small laboratory burner consisting of a vertical metal tube connected to a gas source, and producing a hot flame from a mixture of gas and air let in through adjustable holes at the base. [After Robert Wilhelm *Bunsen*, its inventor.]

bunt¹ *n.* **1.** *Nautical.* The middle section of a square sail. **2.** The sagging middle part of a fishing net. [Perhaps from Middle Low German *bunt*, bundle.]

bunt² *n.* A disease of wheat, rye, and other cereal grasses, **stinking smut** *(see).* [18th century : origin obscure.]

bunt³ *v.* **bunted, bunting, bunts.** —*tr.* In baseball, to hit (a pitched ball) softly, without swinging the bat. —*intr.* In baseball, to hit a ball softly.
~*n.* An act of bunting. [Probably from Celtic, akin to Breton *bounta*, to butt.]

bunt·ing¹ (búnting) *n.* **1.** A light cotton or woollen cloth used for making flags. **2.** Flags collectively. **3.** Long, variously coloured strips of cloth or material hung along a string and used for festive decoration. [18th century : origin obscure.]

bunting² *n.* Any of various birds of the family Fringillidae, such as the **snow bunting** *(see),* having short, cone-shaped bills and brownish or greyish plumage. [Middle English *buntynge*†.]

bunt·line (búnt-lin, -līn) *n. Nautical.* A rope attached to a square sail when it is being hauled up for furling.

Bu·ñu·el (boonew-el, él), **Luis** (1900–83). Spanish film director. In the 1920s he collaborated with Dali in making a number of surrealist films, notably *Un Chien Andalou* (1929), but he is most highly regarded for his studies of social manners and social conditions, such as *Belle de Jour* (1966), and *The Discreet Charm of the Bourgeoisie* (1972).

bun·ya-bun·ya (bún-yə-bún-yə) *n.* Also **bun·ya** (bún-yə). An evergreen tree, *Araucaria bidwillii,* native to Australia, having sharp-pointed, close-set leaves and large cones. [From a native Australian language.]

Bun·yan (bún-yən), **John** (1628–88). English writer and preacher. As a Puritan, he served in the parliamentary army from 1644 to 1646 during the Civil War. He was imprisoned (1660–72) for unlicensed preaching. *The Pilgrim's Progress from This World to That Which Is to Come* was published in two parts in 1678 and 1684.

bun·yip (bún-yip) *n. Australian.* **1.** An imaginary monster that in Aboriginal legends is said to haunt swamps and lagoons. **2.** A fake; an impostor. [From a native Australian language.]

buoy (boy ‖ boo-i) *n.* **1.** *Nautical.* A float moored in water as a warning of danger under the surface or as a marker for a channel. See **bell buoy.** **2.** A device made of cork or other buoyant material for keeping a person afloat. In this sense, also called "lifebuoy".
~*tr.v.* **buoyed, buoying, buoys.** **1.** *Nautical.* To mark with a buoy. **2.** To keep afloat. Used with *up.* **3.** To uplift the spirits of; cheer; hearten. Used with *up.* [Middle English *boye,* probably from Old French *boie,* perhaps from Old High German *bouhhan.*]

buoy·an·cy (bóy-ən-si ‖ boo-yən-). *n.* **1. a.** The tendency or capacity to remain afloat in a liquid or to rise in air or gas. **b.** The upward force of a fluid upon a floating or immersed object. **2.** The ability to recover quickly from setbacks. **3.** Lightness of spirit; cheerfulness. **4.** A tendency, as of stock-market prices, to rise or to resist depressive influences.

buoy·ant (bóy-ənt ‖ boo-yənt) *adj.* Having or marked by buoyancy. [Spanish *boyante,* present participle of *boyar,* to float, from *boya,*

buoy, from Old French *boie,* BUOY.] **—buoy·ant·ly** *adv.*

BU·PA (boopə, béwpə) *n. British United Provident Association:* a medical insurance scheme offering private medical treatment and hospital accommodation.

bu·pres·tid (bew-préstid) *n.* Any of various often brightly coloured beetles of the family Buprestidae, many of which are destructive wood borers as larvae.

bur¹, burr (bur) *n.* **1. a.** The rough, prickly, or spiny fruit husk, seed pod, or flower of various plants, such as the chestnut or the burdock. **b.** A plant producing burs. **2.** A person or thing that clings persistently. **3.** Any of various rotary cutting tools designed to be attached to a drill. [Middle English *burre,* probably from Scandinavian, akin to Old Swedish *borre.*]

bur². **1.** Variant of **burr** (rough edge). **2.** Variant of **burr** (guttural trill). **3.** Variant of **burr** (washer).

Bur. **1.** *Chiefly U.S.* bureau. **2.** Burma.

bu·ran (boo-ráan) *n.* Also **bu·ra** (-ráa). A violent windstorm of the steppes of Russia, accompanied in summer by dust and in winter by snow. [Russian, *burya,* from Turkic; akin to Turkish and Kazan Tatar *buran.*]

Bur·bage (búrbij), **Richard** (*c.* 1567–1619). English actor, the leading tragedian of his age. As the leading player in Shakespeare's company, the Chamberlain's Men, he was the first to play the title roles in *Hamlet, King Lear, Othello,* and *Richard III.*

Bur·bank, (búr-bangk), **Luther** (1849–1926). U.S. biologist and plant breeder. He applied Mendel's laws of heredity to create new varieties of plants. Besides the Burbank potato, he produced hundreds of new varieties of fruit and roses and a spineless cactus for use as cattle fodder.

Bur·ber·ry (búr-bəri ‖ *U.S. also* -berri) *n., pl.* **-ries.** A trademark for a gabardine trench coat.

bur·ble (búrb'l) *n.* **1.** A rushing or bubbling sound. **2.** A rapid, excited flow of speech. **3.** *Aeronautics.* A separation in the boundary layer of air about a moving streamlined body, causing a breakdown in the smooth airflow and resulting in turbulence.
~*intr.v.* **burbled, -bling, -bles.** **1.** To bubble; gurgle. **2.** To speak quickly and excitedly. **3.** *Aeronautics.* To become turbulent. [Middle English *burblen,* to flow with a bubbling sound (imitative).]

bur·bot (búrbət) *n., pl.* **-bots** or collectively **burbot.** A freshwater fish, *Lota lota,* of the Northern Hemisphere, related to and resembling the cod. [Middle English *borbot,* from Old French *bourbotte, bourbete,* from *bourbeter,* to burrow in the mud, from *bourbe*†, mud.]

Burck·hardt (boork-haart), **Jacob Christoph** (1818–97). Swiss historian, one of the founders of the modern school of history-writing. His great achievement was to direct historians away from an almost exclusive concentration on political and military events to a consideration of wider cultural history, as in his work *The Civilisation of the Renaissance in Italy* (1860).

bur·den¹ (búrd'n) *n.* Also *archaic* **bur·then** (búrth'n). **1. a.** Something that is carried. **b.** Something that is difficult to bear physically or emotionally. **2.** A responsibility or duty. **3. a.** The amount of cargo that a vessel can carry. **b.** The weight of the cargo carried by a vessel at one time. **4.** The carrying of heavy loads: *a beast of burden.*
~*tr.v.* **burdened, -dening, -dens.** Also *archaic* **burthen.** **1.** To load or overload. **2.** To weigh down; oppress. [Middle English *burden, burthen,* Old English *byrthen.*]

burden² *n.* **1.** The chorus or refrain of a musical composition. **2.** A recurring idea or theme. **3.** The bass accompaniment to a song. **4.** The drone of a bagpipes. [Variant (influenced by BURDEN), load) of BOURDON, from the idea of the burden being carried along by the melody.]

burden of proof *n.* The responsibility of giving proof for a disputed charge or allegation. [Translation of Latin *onus probandi.*]

bur·den·some (búrd'n-səm) *adj.* Heavy; hard to bear; onerous. **—bur·den·some·ly** *adv.* **—bur·den·some·ness** *n.*
Synonyms: burdensome, onerous, oppressive, harsh, arduous, demanding, rigorous, exacting.

bur·dock (búr-dok) *n.* Any of several coarse, weedy plants of the genus *Arctium,* native to Eurasia, having large, heart-shaped leaves, purplish flowers surrounded by hooked bristles, and prickly fruits. [BUR + DOCK (plant).]

bu·reau (béwr-ō, -ŏ) *n., pl.* **-reaus** or **bureaux** (-ōz, -ŏz). **1.** *Chiefly British.* A writing desk or writing table with drawers. **2.** *U.S.* A chest of drawers. **3.** *Abbr.* **Bur.** **a.** An office, usually of a large organisation, that performs a specific duty: *a news bureau.* **b.** A business or office that offers information of a specified kind: *a travel bureau.* **c.** *Chiefly U.S.* A government department or subdivision of a department. [French, bureau, woollen material used to cover writing desks, from Old French, *burel,* from *bure,* dark brown, from Latin *burrus,* bright red, from Greek *purros,* red.]

bu·reauc·ra·cy (bewr-róckrə-si ‖ bew-) *n., pl.* **-cies.** **1. a.** Government administration through departments staffed by civil servants or similar officials. **b.** The officials in these departments. **2.** A form of administration in which authority is diffused among numerous offices and there is adherence to inflexible rules of operation. **3.** Any administration in which the need to follow complex procedures impedes effective action. [French *bureaucratie.*]

bu·reau·crat (béwr-ə-krat) *n.* **1.** An official of a bureaucracy. **2.** Any official who insists on rigid adherence to rules and routine, regardless of the needs of the situation. **—bu·reau·cratic** (-kráttik) *adj.* **—bu·reau·crat·i·cal·ly** *adv.*

bu·reauc·rat·ise, bu·reauc·rat·ize (bewr-róckrə-tīz ‖ bew-) *tr.v.*

ised, -ising, -ises. To foster bureaucracy in. —bu·reauc·rat·is·a·tion (-tī-záysh'n ‖ *U.S.* -ti-) *n.*

bureau de change (béwrō də shónzh) *n., pl.* **bureaux de change** (*same pronunciation*). *French.* A business office that sells and exchanges currency of more than one country, and cashes cheques.

bu·rette, bu·ret (bewr-rét ‖ bew-) *n.* **1.** A uniform-bore glass tube with fine graduations and a stopcock at the bottom, used especially in laboratory procedures for accurate dispensing and measurement of liquids. **2.** A similar device used for the experimental measurement of gas volumes. [French, originally "cruet", from Old French, cruet for sacramental wine, from *buire*, pitcher, variant of *buie*, from Frankish *būk* (unattested).]

burg (burg) *n.* **1.** A fortified town. **2.** *U.S. Informal.* A city or town. [Old English *burg, burh.*]

bur·gage (búrgij) *n.* A tenure in England and Scotland under which property of the king or a lord in a town was held in return for a yearly rent or other services. [Middle English, from Medieval Latin *burgāgium*, from *burgus*, fortified town, from Old English *burg*, BURG.]

bur·gee (búr-jee ‖ -jeé) *n.* A small distinguishing flag displayed by a ship or yacht. [Perhaps originally *burgee's flag*, from Channel Islands French *bourgeais*, shipowner, from Old French *burgeis*, owner, BURGESS.]

bur·geon, bour·geon (búrjən) *intr.v.* **-geoned, -geoning, -geons.** **1.** To put forth new buds, leaves, or greenery; begin to sprout, grow, or blossom. **2.** To emerge and develop rapidly; flourish. ∼*n.* A bud, sprout, or newly developing growth. [Middle English *burgenen*, from *burjon*, a bud, from Old French, from Vulgar Latin *burriō* (stem *burriōn*-) (unattested), from Late Latin *burra*, wool (probably from the down on some buds).]

burg·er (búrgər) *n.* **1.** A hamburger. **2.** A sandwich resembling a hamburger but with a specified filling: *a turkey burger.*

bur·gess (búr-jiss, *rarely* -jess) *n.* **1.** A freeman or citizen of an English borough. **2.** Formerly, a member of the English Parliament, representing a town, borough, or university. [Middle English *burgeis*, from Old French, from Vulgar Latin *burgensis* (unattested), from Late Latin *burgus*, fortified place, from Germanic.]

Bur·gess (búrjiss), **Anthony** (1917–93). British novelist and essayist. His fame rests chiefly on his novels, in which he exhibited a flamboyant range and command of language. His most successful novels were *A Clockwork Orange* (1962), *Nothing Like the Sun* (1964) and *End of the World News* (1982).

burgh (búrrə ‖ *U.S.* búrrō) *n.* A chartered town or borough in Scotland. Compare **borough.** [Scottish, variant of BOROUGH.] —**burgh·al** (búrg'l) *adj.*

burgh·er (búrgər) *n.* **1 a.** A member of the mercantile class of a medieval city. **b.** A citizen of a medieval city. **2.** A solid citizen. Sometimes used humorously. [Either German *Bürger*, from Middle High German *burgære*, from Old High German *burgāri*, towndweller, from *burg*, fortified place; or Dutch *burger*, from Middle Dutch *burgher*, from Middle High German *burgære*.]

Burgh·ley or **Bur·leigh** (búrli), **William Cecil, 1st Baron** (1520–98). English statesman, Elizabeth I's most important administrator and chief spokesman in the House of Commons. He had great influence in guiding Elizabeth to a middle religious course between the extreme Puritans and the Roman Catholics.

bur·glar (búrglər) *n.* One who commits burglary; a housebreaker. [Anglo-French *burgler*, from Anglo-Latin *burgulator*, probably from Medieval Latin *burg-* (unattested), plunder.]

bur·glar·i·ous (bur-gláir-i-əss) *adj.* Pertaining to burglary.

bur·glar·ise, bur·glar·ize (búrglər-īz) *tr.v.* **-ised, -ising, -ises.** *Chiefly U.S.* To burgle.

bur·glar·proof (búrglər-prōof ‖ -prôof) *adj.* Secure against burglary.

bur·gla·ry (búrgləri) *n., pl.* **-ries.** The crime or an act of breaking into and entering premises with intent to steal or commit any other offence.

bur·gle (búrg'l) *v.* **-gled, -gling, -gles.** —*tr.* To commit burglary in or on the premises of. See Synonyms at **rob.** —*intr.* To commit burglary. [Back-formation from BURGLAR.]

bur·go·mas·ter (búrg-ə-maastər, -ō- ‖ -mastər) *n.* In the Netherlands, Flanders, Austria, and Germany, the principal magistrate of a city or town, comparable to a mayor. [Partial translation of Dutch *burgemeester* : *burg*, town + MASTER.]

bur·go·net (búrgə-net) *n.* A light steel helmet with a peak and hinged flaps covering the cheeks. [French *bourguignotte*, feminine of *bourguignot*, "of Burgundy", from *Bourgogne*, Burgundy.]

bur·goo (búrgōō, bər-gōō) *n., pl.* **-goos.** **1.** Thick oatmeal gruel, originally served to sailors. **2.** *Southern U.S.* **a.** A thick, spicy soup or stew of meat and vegetables. **b.** A picnic or gathering where this dish is served.

Bur·gos (bóor-goss ‖ *U.S.* -gōss). A city in northern Spain, on a mountainous plateau, near the river Arlanzón. It was founded in *c.* 884 and was the capital of the kingdom of Castile from 1035 to 1087. It was the headquarters of the Nationalists during the Spanish Civil War of 1936–39. Its limestone cathedral (13th to 16th centuries) is one of the finest examples of Gothic architecture in Europe. The Spanish national hero, **El Cid,** is buried in the cathedral.

bur·grave (búr-grayv) *n.* **1.** In medieval Germany, the appointed governor of a town or military fortress. **2.** The hereditary lord of a German town and its surroundings. [Middle High German *burcgrāve* : *burc*, fortress, from Old High German *burg* + *grāve*, count.]

Bur·gun·dy (búrgəndi). *French* **Bour·gogne** (boor-gón-yə). A his-

toric region of eastern France. The region was first organised into a kingdom by the Burgundii tribe, from Savoy, in the late fifth century. The great age of Burgundian influence and power began (1364) when John II gave the duchy to his son Philip the Bold, who thus initiated the royal Valois-Bourgogne line. By the 15th century Burgundy had added most of present-day Belgium, Luxembourg, and the Netherlands to its territory and had become the most powerful duchy in France. Its historical importance and independence came to an end in the late 15th century, when Mary of Burgundy married the Emperor Maximilian I and so transferred Burgundy to the Habsburgs. Today Burgundy is famous for its wines, produced in the Chablis district, the mountains of Côte d'Or, and the Saône and the Rhône river valleys.

Burgundy² *n., pl.* **-dies.** *Often small* **b. 1. a.** Any of various red or white wines produced in Burgundy. **b.** Any of various similar fullbodied wines produced elsewhere. **2.** Blackish purple to dark purplish red.

bur·i·al (bérri-əl) *n.* The interment of a dead body or an instance of this. [Middle English *biriel, buryel*, grave, singular of *buriels*, Old English *byrgels*.] —**bur·i·al** *adj.*

bu·rin (béwr-in ‖ búr-) *n.* **1.** A pointed steel cutting tool used in engraving or in carving stone. **2.** The style or technique of an engraver's work. **3.** *Archaeology.* A primitive flint tool with a head like that of a chisel. [French, perhaps from Italian *burino*.]

bur·ka (bóorkə, búrkə) *n.* A full-length garment worn by Muslim women in public that covers the whole of the head except the eyes. [Hindi, from Arabic *burka'*.]

burke (burk) *tr.v.* **burked, burking, burkes. 1.** To murder by suffocation so as to leave the body intact and suitable for dissection. **2.** To suppress quietly and unceremoniously. [After William *Burke* (1792–1829), Irish murderer executed in Edinburgh for this crime.]

Burke (burk), **Edmund** (1729–97). British political writer and politician. As a Member of Parliament from 1765, he played a major part until the French Revolution in developing liberal policy for the Whigs and in formulating the constitutional notion of party responsibility and a loyal opposition (1770). He pleaded on behalf of the American colonists' appeal for independence, and in the 1780s led the campaign to reduce the influence of the Crown. He instigated the impeachment proceedings against Warren **Hastings.** The outbreak of the French revolution caused him to abandon the Whigs and support Pitt.

Burkina (bur-keénə). Formerly **Upper Volta,** *French* **Haute-Volta.** Landlocked state in the Sahel region of West Africa. It is one of the world's poorest countries, depending on aid, mostly from France. Over 90 per cent of its people are farmers, most at subsistence level. Some cattle and cotton are exported. A French colony from 1896, Burkina became independent in 1960. Area, 274 200 square kilometres (105,869 square miles). Population, 10,780,000. Capital, Ouagadougou. See map at **West African States.**

burl¹ (burl) *n.* **1.** A knot, lump, or slub in yarn or cloth. **2.** A large, rounded growth on the trunk or branch of a tree. **3.** The strongly marked wood from such a growth, especially walnut, usually cut into thin pieces and used as veneer.
∼*tr.v.* **burled, burling, burls.** To dress or finish (fabric) by removing burls or loose threads. [Middle English *burle*, from Old French *bourle*, diminutive of *bourre*, coarse wool, from Late Latin *burra†*, wool.] —**burl·er** *n.*

burl², birl *n. Australian.* An attempt; a try: *He'd give anything a burl.*
∼*tr.v.* **burled, burling, burls.** To jeer at; make fun of: *The other kids at school burl him mercilessly.* [Perhaps from northern English dialect *birl*, a twist, a turn.]

bur·lap (búrlap) *n.* A coarsely woven cloth made of fibres of jute, flax, or hemp, used to make bags, to reinforce linoleum, and in interior decoration. [17th century : origin obscure.]

bur·lesque (bur-lésk ‖ bər-) *n.* **1.** A literary or dramatic work that makes a subject appear ridiculous by treating it in an incongruous style, as by presenting a lofty subject with vulgarity, or the inconsequential with mock dignity. **2.** Any ludicrous or mocking imitation; a travesty. **3.** *U.S.* A variety show characterised by broad, ribald comedy, dancing, and striptease.
∼*v.* **burlesqued, -lesquing, -lesques.** —*tr.* To imitate mockingly: *"always bringing junk . . . home, as if he were burlesquing his role as provider"* (John Updike). —*intr.* To use the methods or techniques of burlesque.
∼*adj.* **1.** Mockingly and ludicrously imitative. **2.** Of, pertaining to, or characteristic of theatrical burlesque, especially in its ribald aspects. [French, from Italian *burlesco*, from *burla*, joke, ridicule, from Vulgar Latin *burrula* (unattested), diminutive of Late Latin *burra*, trifle, bit of nonsense, perhaps from *burra*, wool, shaggy garment.] —**bur·lesque·ly** *adv.* —**bur·les·quer** *n.*

bur·ly (búrli) *adj.* **-lier, -liest.** Heavy, strong, and muscular; thickset. [Middle English *burli, borlich*, stately, probably from Old English *būrlic* (unattested), exalted.] —**bur·li·ly** *adv.* —**bur·li·ness** *n.*

Bur·ma (búrmə). A republic in southeast Asia, officially called the Union of Myanmar. It is bordered on the west by the Indian Ocean, on the north by Bangladesh and India, and on the east by China, Laos, and Thailand. On both its northern and eastern borders it is cut off from its neighbours by large mountain ranges, between which lies the fertile Irrawaddy river valley, whose crops make Burma one of the world's largest producers of rice. Burma was made a province of British India (1886); it gained its independence in 1948. Area 676 552 square kilometres (261,218 square miles). Population, 45,920,000. Capital and largest city, Rangoon (Yangon).

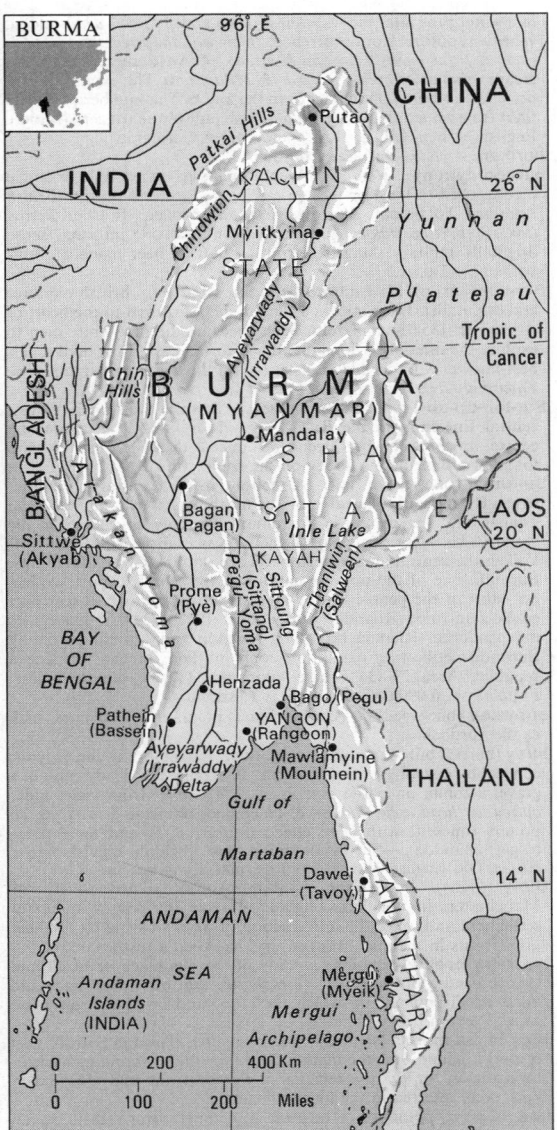

BURMA

CHINA

INDIA

KACHIN

Patkai Hills

•Putao

26° N

Chindwin

Myitkyina•

STATE

Yunnan

Plateau

Tropic of
Cancer

Chin
Hills

BURMA
(MYANMAR)

•Mandalay

SHAN

STATE

LAOS

20° N

Sittwe
(Akyab)

Bagan
(Pagan)

Inle Lake

KAYAH

Prome
(Pyè)

Thanlwin (Salween)

BAY
OF
BENGAL

Henzada•

Pathein
(Bassein)

Bago/(Pegu)

YANGON
(Rangoon)

Ayeyarwady
(Irrawaddy)
Delta

Mawlamyine
(Moulmein)

THAILAND

Gulf of

Martaban

Dawei
(Tavoy)

14° N

ANDAMAN

SEA

Mergui
(Myeik)

Andaman
Islands
(INDIA)

Mergui
Archipelago

0   200   400 Km

0   100   200 Miles

bur marigold *n.* Any of various plants of the genus *Bidens,* having yellow flowers and pointed seeds that cling to fur and clothing. Also called "beggar-ticks", "sticktight".

Bur·mese (búr-méez || *U.S. also* -méess) *adj.* Also **Bur·man** (búrmən). Of, pertaining to, or characteristic of Burma, its people, their language, or their culture.
~*n., pl.* **Burmese.** Also **Bur·man** *pl.* **-mans** (for sense 1). **1.** A native or inhabitant of Burma. **2.** The Sino-Tibetan language spoken in Burma.

Burmese cat *n.* A cat of a breed resembling the Siamese but having a dark-brown or blue-grey coat.

burn¹ (burn) *v.* **burnt** (burnt) or (especially for intransitive senses) **burned, burning, burns.** —*tr.* **1. a.** To cause to undergo combustion. **b.** To destroy or consume with fire. **2.** To damage or injure the surface of by fire, heat, or a heat-producing agent: *He burnt the toast.* **3.** To put to death by fire. **4.** To produce by fire or heat: *burn a clearing in the brush.* **5.** To use as a fuel. **6.** To impart a sensation of intense heat to: *The chilli burnt his mouth.* **7.** To brand (an animal). **8.** To harden or impart a finish to by subjecting to intense heat; fire. **9.** To let (oneself or part of one's body) become sunburnt. **10.** *Slang.* **a.** To sell inferior drugs to. **b.** To betray; inform on. **11.** *Chiefly U.S. Slang.* To execute in the electric chair; electrocute. —*intr.* **1.** To be on fire; undergo combustion; flame. **2.** To emit heat or light by or as if by means of fire. **3.** To be destroyed, injured, damaged, or changed by or as if by fire: *The house burnt down.* **4.** To feel or look hot: *Her cheeks burned.* **5.** To be consumed with strong emotion. **6.** *Chiefly U.S. Slang.* To be executed in the electric chair; be electrocuted. **7.** *Chiefly Australian & N.Z.* To go at speed, especially in a vehicle. —**burn ahead.** *Australian.* To spread very quickly and get out of control. Used of a bushfire. —**burn in.** To darken part of (a photographic print) by exposing unmasked areas. —**burn off.** To remove stubble from (land) by burning.

~*n.* **1.** An injury produced by fire, heat, light, chemicals, electricity, or radiation. **2.** A burnt place or area. **3.** *Aerospace.* One firing of a rocket. **4.** A **burn-up** *(see).* [Middle English *bernen, burnen,* from Old English *beornan, byrnan* (intransitive) and *bærnan.*]
Synonyms: burn, scorch, singe, sear, char, parch.

burn² *n. Chiefly Scottish.* A small stream; a brook. Often used in Scottish place names: *Bannockburn.* [Middle English *burn, burne,* Old English *burn, burna,* spring, fountain; from Germanic.]

burn-back (búrn-bak) *n. Australian.* The deliberate burning off of strips of land in order to prevent bushfires.

burn·er (búrnər) *n.* **1.** One that burns something. **2.** The part of a stove, furnace, or lamp that is lit to produce a flame. **3.** A device in which something is burnt: *an oil burner.*

bur·net (búr-nit || *U.S. also* -nét) *n.* **1.** Any of various plants of the genus *Sanguisorba,* especially the **salad burnet** *(see).* **2.** Any of various plants of the genus *Pimpinella,* especially *P. saxifraga* (burnet saxifrage), with umbrella-like clusters of white or pink flowers. **3.** Any of various red-and-black moths of the genus *Zygaena,* especially *Z. filipendulae* (six-spot burnet), that are active in the daytime. [Middle English, dark brown (from the brownish-red flowers), from Old French *burnete, brunette,* BRUNETTE.]

Bur·net (bər-nét, búrnit), **Sir Frank Macfarlane** (1899–1985). Australian virologist. For his work in the development of immunity against influenza and his research with P. B. Medawar into the tolerance of the body to the introduction of foreign living tissues, he shared with Medawar the Nobel prize for medicine (1960).

burnet rose *n.* A Eurasian wild rose, *Rosa pimpinellifolia,* having cream or sometimes pink flowers and dark purple or black fruits.

Bur·nett (bər-nét, bur-), **Frances (Eliza) Hodgson** (1849–1924). U.S. writer, born in England. She lived in the United States after 1865 and became world-famous for her children's books, especially *Little Lord Fauntleroy* (1886) and *The Secret Garden* (1911).

Bur·ney (búrni), **Fanny** (1752–1840). British diarist and novelist. Her diaries, begun in 1768 and continuing for more than 70 years, are a witty, sophisticated, and stylish record of the manners of the polished English society of her day.

Burn·ham scale (búrnəm) *n.* The scale used to grade the salaries of teachers in English and Welsh state schools. [After Lord *Burnham* (1862–1933), who chaired the committee which proposed it.]

burn·ing (búrning) *adj.* **1.** Characterised by intense emotion; passionate. **2.** Of immediate import; urgent; pressing: *burning issues.* —**burn·ing·ly** *adv.*

burning bush *n.* **1.** Any of several plants or shrubs having foliage that turns bright red, such as the **summer cypress** *(see).* **2.** the **gas plant** *(see).* **3.** Any of several plants or shrubs having bright red fruits or seeds. [So called from the burning bush in Exodus 3:2.]

burn·ing-glass (búrning-glaass || -glass) *n.* A convex lens used to focus the sun's rays and produce heat, especially for ignition. Also called "sunglass".

bur·nish (búrnish) *tr.v.* **-nished, -nishing, -nishes.** To polish or smooth by or as if by rubbing.
~*n.* A smooth, glossy metallic finish or appearance; lustre. [Middle English *burnischen,* from Old French *burnir* (present stem *burniss-*), variant of *brunir,* "to make brown", burnish, from *brun,* brown, shining, from Germanic.] —**bur·nish·er** *n.*

bur·nous, bur·nouse (bur-noóss, -noóz) *n.* A long hooded cloak worn by Arabs and Moors. [French, from Arabic *burnus,* from Greek *birros,* cloak.]

burn out *intr.v.* **1.** To stop burning or functioning from lack of fuel. Used of a fire, engine, or rocket. **2.** To become inoperative as a result of heat or friction. **3.** To become exhausted, especially as a result of overwork or dissipation. —*tr.v.* **1.** To exhaust or consume (oneself or itself), so as to cease to be active: *The disease burnt itself out.*

burn·out (búrn-owt) *n.* **1.** A failure attributable to burning, excessive heat, friction, or sheer exhaustion. **2.** *Aerospace.* The termination of a rocket or jet-engine operation because fuel has been shut off or exhausted.

Burns (burnz), **John Elliott** (1858–1943). British trade unionist and politician. He joined the Social Democratic Federation (1884) and was elected to the executive of the Amalgamated Society of Engineers. He helped to organise the London dock strike (1889) and was elected Member of Parliament for Battersea (1892).

Burns, Robert (1759–96). Scottish national poet. His first volume, *Poems, Chiefly in the Scottish dialect* (1786) won popularity through the humanity of its verse and through the use of the Lallans dialect.

burn·sides (búrn-sīdz) *pl.n. U.S.* Mutton-chop whiskers and a moustache. [After Ambrose E. *Burnside* (1824–81), U.S. General, who wore them.]

burnt (burnt). Past tense and past participle of **burn.**
~*adj.* **1.** Affected by or as if by burning; scorched. **2.** Treated by fire or calcined for a particular purpose. Said of bricks, certain pigments, or minerals, for example.

burnt offering *n.* An offering, such as a slaughtered animal, burnt on an altar as a religious sacrifice.

burnt orange *n.* A deep rust-coloured orange. —**burnt-or·ange** *adj.*

burnt orchid *n.* An orchid, *Orchis ustulata,* having dark maroon flowers resembling those of the lady orchid.

burnt-out (búrnt-ówt) *adj.* Exhausted; spent; extinguished.

burnt sienna 1. A reddish-brown pigment prepared by calcining raw sienna. **2.** Dark reddish orange. Also called "sienna".

burn-up (búrn-up) *n. Informal.* A fast ride in a car or on a motorcycle.

bu·roo (bə-rōō) n., pl. **-roos**. Scottish & Irish Informal. A social-security office. **—on the buroo**. Receiving unemployment benefit; on the dole. [From BUREAU.]

burp (burp) n. Informal. A belch.
~v. **burped, burping, burps.** Informal. —intr. To belch. —tr. To cause (a baby) to bring up wind after feeding. [Imitative.]

burr¹, bur (bur) n. **1.** A rough edge or area remaining on metal or other material after it has been cast, cut, or drilled. **2.** Any rough protuberance; especially, a burl on a tree. **3.** A part in a surgical drill used for cutting into teeth or bone.
~tr.v. **burred, burring, burrs. 1.** To form a rough edge on. **2.** To remove a rough edge or edges from. [Middle English burre, rough edge, BUR.]

burr², bur n. **1.** A rough trilling of the letter r, as in Scottish pronunciation. **2.** Any similar trilled pronunciation such as the retroflex r formed at the back of the mouth in the southwest of England, or the trilled uvular r of Northumbria. **3.** A buzzing or whirring sound.
~v. **burred, burring, burrs.** —tr. To pronounce with a burr. —intr. **1.** To speak with a burr. **2.** To make a buzzing or whirring sound. [Imitative, associated with BUR, from its roughness.] **—bur·ry** adj.

burr³, bur n. **1.** A washer that fits around the smaller end of a rivet. **2.** A blank punched from a sheet of metal. [Variant of obsolete burrow†.]

burr⁴. Variant of **bur.**

bur reed n. Any of various marsh plants of the genus Sparganium, having narrow leaves and round, prickly fruit.

bur·ro (búrrō) n., pl. **-ros**. Chiefly U.S. A small donkey, especially one used as a pack animal. [Spanish, from borrico, donkey, from Late Latin burricus†, small horse.]

Bur·roughs (búrrōz), **Edgar Rice** (1875-1950). U.S. novelist. He wrote many science-fiction and jungle tales, but is most famous for creating the character of Tarzan in Tarzan of the Apes (1914).

Bur·roughs, William S(eward) (1914–97). U.S. novelist. He became a cult figure of the beat generation with the publication of The Naked Lunch (1959), with its kaleidoscopic treatment of the brutality of contemporary life.

bur·row (búrrō) n. **1.** A hole or tunnel dug in the ground by a small animal, such as a rabbit or a mole, for habitation or refuge. **2.** Any similar narrow or snug place.
~v. **burrowed, -rowing, -rows.** —intr. **1.** To dig a burrow. **2.** To live or hide in a burrow. **3.** To move or progress through something as if by digging or tunnelling. —tr. **1.** To make by or as if by tunnelling or digging: burrowed his way through the hedge; burrow a hole. **2.** To dig a burrow in or through. **3.** To nestle; snuggle: The dog burrowed his head into the bedclothes. [Middle English borow, probably a variant of BOROUGH.] **—bur·row·er** n.

burr·stone. Variant of **buhrstone.**

bur·ry¹ (bŏŏrri) n., pl. **-ries**. Australian. An Aboriginal. Used derogatorily.

bur·ry² (búr-i) adj. **-rier, -riest. 1.** Like a bur; prickly. **2.** Full of or covered with burs.

bur·sa (búr-sə) n., pl. **-sae** (-see) or **-sas**. A saclike body cavity, especially one located between joints or at points of friction between moving structures. [New Latin, from Medieval Latin, bag, PURSE.]

Bur·sa (búr-sə). An industrial town and market centre in northwest Turkey, formerly called Brusa. It dates from the third century B.C., when it was founded by Prusias I, king of Bithynia. Its baths have been famous since ancient times and its importance as a silk-manufacturing centre dates from the Middle Ages. It was the capital of the Ottoman Empire from 1326 to 1413.

bur·sal (búrss'l) adj. **1.** Anatomy. Of or functioning as a bursa. **2.** Archaic. Pertaining to the public revenue; fiscal.

bur·sar (búr-sər ‖ U.S. also -saar) n. **1.** A treasurer or similar official in charge of funds and accounting, as at a school, college, or university. **2.** A scholarship student at a Scottish university. [Sense 1, Medieval Latin bursārius, from bursa, PURSE; sense 2, French boursier, from bourse, purse, from Medieval Latin bursa.]

bur·sa·ry (búrssəri) n., pl. **-ries. 1.** The office or room of a bursar. **2.** A scholarship, allowance, or award granted to a student at a school or university, especially at a Scottish university. [Medieval Latin bursāria, from bursa, purse.] **—bur·sar·i·al** (bur-sáir-i-əl) adj.

burse (burss) n. **1.** Ecclesiastical. A flat cloth case for carrying the piece of linen, or corporal, that is used in celebrating the Eucharist. **2.** A foundation or fund for providing bursaries.

bur·si·form (búrssi-fawrm) adj. Anatomy. Shaped like a pouch or sac. [Medieval Latin bursa, bag, purse + -FORM.]

bur·si·tis (bur-sítiss) n. Inflammation of a bursa, especially of one of the shoulder, elbow, or knee joints. [New Latin : BURS(A) + -ITIS.]

burst (burst) v. **burst, bursting, bursts.** —intr. **1.** To come open or fly apart suddenly or violently, especially from internal pressure. **2.** To be full to the point of almost breaking open; swell: a bag bursting with goodies. **3.** To come forth, emerge, or arrive suddenly and in full force: burst into the room; burst into flames. **4.** To give sudden utterance or expression, especially to an emotion or feeling. Used with into or out: burst into song; burst out laughing. —tr. **1.** To cause or experience the rupture or bursting apart of: burst a blood vessel. **2.** To bring or force into a breached or opened state: burst open the door. **—See Synonyms at break.**
~n. **1.** A sudden breaking open or flying apart; an explosion. **2.** The result of bursting; a breach or rupture; specifically, a rupture

of a water pipe after the water has frozen and thawed. **3.** A sudden, vehement outbreak or occurrence: "blow with the strength of a hurricane in fitful bursts" (Joseph Conrad). **4.** An abrupt, intense increase or spurt: a burst of speed. **5.** Military. **a.** The explosion of a projectile or bomb on impact or in the air. **b.** The number of bullets fired from an automatic weapon by one pull of the trigger. [Middle English bersten, Old English berstan, from Germanic.]

burthen. Archaic. Variant of **burden.**

bur·ton (búrt'n) n. Nautical. A light tackle having double or single blocks, used to hoist or tighten rigging. **—go for a burton**. British Informal. To become lost, destroyed, or broken. [Earlier Breton (takles), Brytton (takles), probably from BRETON; informal sense originally military slang, referring to bottled beer made at BURTON-UPON-TRENT.]

Bur·ton (búrt'n), **Sir Richard Francis** (1821-90). British explorer and orientalist. Disguised as a Pathan, he journeyed to the heart of Arabia. In 1858 he and John Speke became the first white men to explore the interior of Somaliland and to see Lake Tanganyika. His best-known work is his translation of the Arabian Nights, The Thousand Nights and a Night (1885-88).

Bur·ton-up·on-Trent (búrt'n-on-trént). Town in Staffordshire, west central England, on the River Trent. It is famous as a brewing centre, brewing having been introduced there by monks who founded a Benedictine abbey on the site in 1002.

Bu·run·di (bŏŏ-rŏŏndi, bə-). A republic in east central Africa, between Rwanda and Tanzania on the northeastern extremity of Lake Tanganyika. The capital is Bujumbura, the only large town in the country. The western edge of the country is in the East African Rift Valley; the central and eastern parts are dominated by mountains. Burundi, one of the poorest nations in the world, exports coffee, but most of the people live by subsistence agriculture. It was part of Belgian-ruled Ruanda-Urundi until 1962, when it gained its independence (Ruanda becoming **Rwanda** and Urundi becoming Burundi). Following a military coup in 1966 Burundi became a republic. Area 27 834 square kilometres (10,747 square miles). Population, 6,090,000. See map at **Tanzania.**

bur·weed (búr-weed) n. Any of various plants that bear burs, such as the burdock.

bur·y (bérri ‖ búrri) tr.v. **-ied, -ying, -ies. 1.** To place in the ground; conceal by covering over with earth. **2.** To place (a dead body) in a grave, a tomb, or in the sea; inter. **3.** To cover from view; hide: buried her head in her hands. **4.** To embed; immerse or sink. **5.** To occupy (oneself) with deep concentration. **6.** To put an end to; forget; abandon. **—See Synonyms at hide.** [Middle English berien, burien, Old English byrgan, from Germanic.] **—bur·i·er** n.

Bur·y (bérri). Town and Unitary Authority area north of Manchester, in northern England. It was the site of a Saxon settlement and, since the introduction of wool weaving by Flemish immigrants in the mid-14th century, has been a textile centre.

bur·y·ing beetle (bérri-ing) n. Any of various black or black and orange beetles of the genus Necrophorus, that bury dead mice and other small animals, on which they feed and lay their eggs. Also called "sexton beetle".

Bury St. Ed·munds (sənt édməndz ‖ -saynt-). Town in Suffolk, east central England. It is the market centre for the surrounding agricultural region. In 903 the remains of Edmund, the martyred Saxon king, were interred in the local monastery.

bus (buss) n., pl. **buses** or **busses. 1.** A long motor vehicle, sometimes with two decks, used as a means of public transport, usually along a fixed route. Also formally called "omnibus". **2.** Informal. A large car or aeroplane. **3.** Electricity. A bus bar. **—miss the bus.** To miss an opportunity; arrive too late.
~v. **bused or bussed, busing or bussing, buses or busses.** —tr. Chiefly U.S. To transport in a bus, especially to schools in different areas in order to encourage racial integration. —intr. To travel in a bus. [Short for OMNIBUS.] **—bus·ing, bus·sing** n.

bus. business.

bus bar n. **1.** A conducting bar that carries heavy currents to supply several electric circuits. **2.** A conducting bar in a computer used to carry data from one part to another. Also called "bus".

bus boy n. U.S. A waiter's assistant.

bus·by (búzbi) n., pl. **-bies**. A tall, fur hat with a plume and a bag hanging at one side worn in certain regiments of the British Army, especially the hussars. [18th century : origin obscure.]

bush¹ (bŏŏsh) n. **1.** Any low, branching, woody plant, usually smaller than a tree; a shrub. **2.** A thick growth of shrubs; a thicket. **3. a.** Land covered with a dense growth of shrubs. **b.** Land remote from settled or cultivated areas, especially in Australia, New Zealand, Canada, or Africa: bush dwellers. Usually preceded by the. **c.** Informal. The country as opposed to the city. Often preceded by the. **4.** A fox's tail. **5. a.** A clump of ivy formerly used as the sign of a tavern. **b.** Obsolete. A tavern. **—beat about the bush.** To delay in getting to the point. **—go bush.** Australian Informal. **1.** To go and live in the bush. **2.** To run wild, especially in a depraved manner. **—in the bush.** Australian. In surfing, out beyond the breakers. **—take to the bush.** Australian & N.Z. Informal. To disappear suddenly from one's usual social circles.
~adj. Australian & West African Informal. **1.** Backward, uncivilised, or unsophisticated. **2.** Rough; crude; makeshift: a bush breakfast; a bush cure; bush carpentry.
~v. **bushed, bushing, bushes.** —intr. **1.** To grow or branch out like a shrub or bush. **2.** To extend in a bushy growth. —tr. To decorate, protect, or support with shrubs or bushes. [Middle Eng-

lish *busshe*, Old English *bysc* (unattested); akin to Old Norse *buski*, Old French *bosc*, all of Germanic origin.]

bush² *n*. A metal lining used to constrain, guide, or reduce friction in a machine. Also called "bushing".
~*tr.v*. **bushed, bushing, bushes.** To furnish or line with a bush. [From Middle Dutch *busse*, bush of a wheel, wheel box, from Late Latin *buxis*, BOX.]

Bush, George (Herbert Walker) (1924-). U.S. diplomat and politician. A Republican, he was president of the U.S.A. 1988-93. He was Vice-President throughout Ronald Reagan's administration (1980-88). As well as holding various other public offices, he has also been a businessman, with interests in the petroleum industry.

bush baby *n*. Any of several small nocturnal primates of the genera *Galago* and *Euoticus*, having dense, woolly fur, large, round eyes, prominent ears, and a long tail. Also called "galago".

bush Baptist *n*. *Australian Informal*. A person who has strong religious beliefs but who does not belong to any particular sect.

bush-buck (bŏosh-buk) *n*. An African antelope, *Tragelaphus scriptus*, having a reddish-brown coat with white markings and twisted horns. Also called "harnessed antelope". [Translation of Afrikaans *bosbok*.]

bush-craft (bŏosh-kraaft ‖ -kraft) *n*. *Australian*. Experience or knowledge of life or survival in the bush.

bush cricket *n*. A grasshopper of the family Tettigoniidae having long, threadlike antennae and tarsi feet divided into four segments.

bushed (bŏosht) *adj*. *Informal*. **1.** Extremely tired; exhausted. **2.** *Chiefly Australian & Canadian*. Lost or confused. [Probably from BUSH (wilderness).]

bush-el (bŏosh'l *n*. *Abbr*. **bu, bu. 1. a.** A unit of volume or capacity in the British Imperial System, used in dry and liquid measure, and equal to 2,219.36 cubic inches (0.03637 cubic metre). **b.** A unit of volume or capacity in the U.S. customary system, used in dry measure and equal to 4 pecks or 2,150.42 cubic inches (0.03524 cubic metre). **2.** A container with the capacity of this unit. [Middle English *busshel*, *boyschel*, from Old French *boissel*, from *boisse*, one-sixth of a bushel, from Gaulish *bostia*† (unattested), handful.]

bush fly *n*. Any of the small and irritating flies that swarm about humans and animals in the bush.

bush hammer *n*. A hammer used for dressing stone, having a flat face with small pyramidal projections.

bush-house (bŏosh-howss) *n*. *Chiefly Australian*. **1.** A house or hut in the bush. **2.** A shed or hut in a garden.

Bu-shi-do, bu-shi-do (bŏoshi-dŏ) *n*. The traditional code of the Japanese samurai, stressing self-discipline, bravery, and simple living. [Japanese *bushidō*, "the way of the warrior".]

bush-ie, bush-y *n*., *pl*. **-ies.** *Australian & N.Z*. A person who lives in the bush, especially a person who is unsophisticated and ignorant of city life.

bush-ing (bŏoshing) *n*. **1.** A bush in a machine. **2.** An insulating lining for an aperture through which a wire or other conductor passes. **3.** An adaptor threaded to permit joining of pipes with different diameters. [From earlier BUSH (metal lining).]

bush jacket *n*. A light, belted jacket with four patch pockets.

bush-law-yer (bŏosh-láw-yər ‖ -lóy-ər) *n*. *Australian & N.Z*. **1.** A layman who pretends or claims to have knowledge of the law. **2.** Loosely, an argumentative person.

bush-league (bŏosh-leég) *adj*. *U.S. Informal*. Minor-league.

Bush-man (bŏosh-mən) *n*., *pl*. **-men** (-mən, -men) **1.** A member of a nomadic Negroid people of southwestern Africa, characteristically of short stature. **2.** Any of several Khoisan languages spoken by this people. **3.** *Small* **b.** *Chiefly Australian*. A person who lives in or knows the ways of life in the bush. [Translation of Afrikaans *boschjesman*.]

bush-mas-ter (bŏosh-maastər ‖ -mastər) *n*. A large, venomous snake, *Lachesis muta*, of tropical America, having brown and greyish markings.

bush oyster *n*. *Australian Informal*. A testicle, usually of a sheep, that is cooked and eaten.

bush pig *n*. A wild pig, *Potamochoerus porcus*, of southern Africa, having long tufts of hair on the face and ears. [Translation of Afrikaans *bosvark*.]

bush-rang-er (bŏosh-raynjər) *n*. **1.** *Australian*. Formerly, an escaped convict living in the bush; a fugitive. **2.** *N.Z*. Formerly, a European who volunteered to fight against the Maoris.

bush-sick (bŏosh-sik) *adj*. *Chiefly Australian*. Of or designating livestock that are rapidly losing energy and weight owing to mineral deficiencies in the soil. —**bush-sick-ness** *n*.

bush telegraph *n*. **1.** Word of mouth as a means by which rumours or gossip is rapidly spread. Also called "bush wire". **2.** Formerly, a means of disseminating information, especially amongst primitive tribes, as by beating drums.

bush-tit (bŏosh-tit) *n*. Either of two small, long-tailed songbirds, *Psaltriparus minimus* or *P. melanotis*, of western North America, having predominantly grey plumage.

bush-veld (bŏosh-felt, -velt) *n*. In South Africa, open country or veld whose flora consists predominantly of scrub or thorny bush.

bush week *n*. *Australian Informal*. **1.** A fictitious week during which bush dwellers come to town. **2.** A set of circumstances in which a person is easily duped: *What do you think this is—bush week?*

bush-whack (bŏosh-wak, -hwak) *v*. **-whacked, -whacking, -whacks.** —*intr*. **1.** *Australian*. To live in the bush. **2.** *N.Z*. To clear land of

timber. **3.** *U.S.* To make one's way through thick woods by cutting away bushes and branches. **4.** *U.S.* To fight as a guerrilla. —*tr.* To attack suddenly from a place of concealment; ambush. [Backformation from BUSHWHACKER.]

bush-whacked (bŏosh-wakt, -hwakt) *adj*. *Australian*. Bushed.

bush-whack-er (bŏosh-wackər, -hwackər) *n*. **1 a.** *Australian*. A person who lives in the bush; a bushie. **b.** *U.S.* A backwoodsman. **2.** *N.Z.* A person who clears land of timber. **3.** *U.S.* A guerrilla, especially a Confederate during the American Civil War. [BUSH + *whacker*, one who whacks, from WHACK.]

bush-y¹ (bŏoshi) *adj*. **-ier, -iest. 1.** Overgrown or thick with bushes. **2.** Shaggy and thick. —**bush-i-ly** *adv*. —**bush-i-ness** *n*.

bushy². Variant of **bushie**.

bus-i-ly (bízzili) *adv*. In a busy manner.

busi-ness (bíz-nəss, -niss) *n*. *Abbr*. **bus. 1.** The occupation, work, or trade in which a person is engaged. **2.** Commercial, industrial, or professional dealings; the buying and selling of goods or services: *business practices*. **3.** Any commercial establishment, such as a shop or factory. **4.** Volume or amount of commercial trade: *We're doing very good business*. **5.** Commercial policy or practice. **6.** One's rightful or proper concern or interest; responsibility: *Mind you own business; Make it your business to find out*. **7.** Serious work or endeavour, especially pertaining to one's job: *went to Tokyo on business*. **8.** An affair or matter: *tired of this silly business*. **9.** *Theatre*. Incidental actions performed by an actor on the stage to fill a pause between lines or to provide dramatic effect. Also called "stage business". **10.** A vague or unspecified area or subject: *astrology, magic, and all that business*. **11.** *Slang*. Prostitution. —**do business.** To come to a mutually agreeable arrangement. —**do (one's) business.** To defecate. Used euphemistically. —**get down to business.** To begin in earnest. —**in business. 1.** Ready for action; ready to start. **2.** Engaged in business: *in business for oneself*. —**like nobody's business.** Very much; extremely. —**mean business.** To be in dead earnest. [Middle English *bissinesse*, diligence, state of being busy, Old English *bisig*, BUSY.]

Synonyms: business, industry, commerce, trade, traffic.

business card *n*. A small card printed with one's name and position, the name of one's firm, and one's business address and telephone number. It is given to a person, especially a prospective client or customer, for information or as an introduction.

business end *n*. *Informal*. The end of something, such as a gun, knife, or the like, that actually performs the function for which the whole instrument has been designed.

business hours *pl.n*. The hours of the day during which a business, such as a shop, bank, or the like, conducts business.

busi-ness-like (bíz-nəss-līk, -niss-) *adj*. **1.** Methodical; systematic; efficient. **2.** Purposeful; earnest.

busi-ness-man (bíz-nəss-man, -niss-, -mən) *n*., *pl*. **-men** (-men, -mən). A man engaged in business, especially at an executive level.

business person *n*., *pl*. **business persons** or **business people.** A businessman or businesswoman.

busi-ness-wom-an (bíz-nəss-wŏoman, -niss-) *n*., *pl*. **-women.** A woman engaged in business, especially at an executive level.

busk *intr.v*. **busked, busking, busks.** *British*. To entertain by singing, playing music, or dancing, especially in streets and public places in return for money. [Perhaps from obsolete French *busquer*, to look for, seek.] —**busk-er** *n*.

bus-kin (búskin) *n*. **1.** A foot-and-leg covering reaching halfway to the knee, resembling a laced half-boot. **2.** A thick-soled laced half boot, worn by actors of tragedies in ancient Greece. Compare SOCK. **3.** *Formal & Poetic*. Tragedy. Usually preceded by *the*. [Old French *bouzequin, brouzequin*, akin to Spanish *borzeguí*, Italian *borzacchino*†.]

bus-man's holiday (búss-mənz) *n*. *Informal*. A holiday on which a person engages in recreation similar to his usual work. [A bus driver might go for a drive on a holiday.]

Bu-so-ni (bŏo-zóni), **Ferruccio Benvenuto** (1866-1924). Italian composer, conductor, and pianist. He achieved great fame as a pianist in the flamboyant manner of Liszt, and was a prolific composer, though few of his works are played today.

buss (buss) *v*. **bussed, bussing, busses.** *Archaic & Regional*. —*tr.* To kiss with a loud smacking sound. —*intr.* To kiss loudly.
~*n*. *Archaic & Regional*. A smacking kiss. [From earlier *bass*; akin to French *baiser*, Latin *basiare*.]

bus-shel-ter (búss-sheltər) *n*. A structure at a bus-stop designed to protect waiting passengers from wind and rain.

bus-stop (búss-stop) *n*. A place on a bus route, usually marked, where passengers alight from or board buses.

bust¹ (bust) *n*. **1. a.** A woman's bosom. **b.** *Archaic*. The human chest. **2.** A piece of sculpture representing a person's head, shoulders, and upper chest. [French *buste*, from Italian *busto*, piece of sculpture, origin obscure.]

bust² *v*. **busted** or **bust, busting, busts.** *Informal*. —*tr.* **1.** To burst or break. **2.** To cause to become bankrupt or short of money. **3. a.** To raid or search, especially for drugs. **b.** To place under arrest. **4.** *Chiefly U.S.* To reduce the rank of; demote. **5.** *U.S.* To hit or punch. —*intr.* **1.** To burst or break. **2.** To become bankrupt or short of money.
~*n*. *Slang*. **1.** An arrest or police raid. **2.** *Chiefly U.S.* A failure; a flop; bankruptcy. **3.** A spree.
~*adj*. **1.** Broken; burst. **2.** Bankrupt: *go bust*. [Variant of BURST.]

Bus-ta-man-te (bústə-mánti), **Sir William Alexander** (1884-1977). Jamaican politician, the first prime minister of independent Jamaica (1962-67). As a trade union leader he led the campaign for Jamaican independence and formed the Jamaica Labour Party (1943).

bus·tard (bústərd) *n.* Any of various large terrestrial Old World birds of the family Otididae, frequenting open, grassy regions. Bustards have long, strong legs, a stout body, and brown, mottled plumage. [Middle English *bustarde*, possibly from Anglo-French *bustarde* (unattested), blend of Old French *bistarde* and *oustarde*, both perhaps from Latin *avis tarda*, "slow bird" : *avis*, bird + *tarda*, feminine of *tardus*, slow (see **tardy**).]

bus·tee, bus·ti (bústi) *n.* A slum or shantytown in India.

bust·er (bústər) *n. Slang.* **1.** One who destroys or breaks up. Used in combination: *a crime-buster.* **2.** *Australian.* A strong gale. **3.** *U.S.* A spree. **4.** *Often capital* **B.** *U.S. & Australian.* A man or boy. Used as an informal term of address.

bus·tle[1] (búss'l) *v.* **-tled, -tling, -tles.** —*intr.* To hurry energetically and busily. —*tr.* To cause to hurry.
~*n.* Excited activity; commotion; stir. [Probably a variant of obsolete *buskle*, frequentative of dialectal *busk*, to prepare, from Middle English *busken*, from Old Norse *būask* : *būa*, to prepare + *-sk*, reflexive ending.]

bustle[2] *n.* A frame or pad worn, especially in the 19th and early 20th centuries, to support and extend the rear of a woman's skirt. [Perhaps from German *Buschel*†, a bunch, pad.]

bust·y (bústi) *adj.* **-ier, -iest.** *Informal.* Full-bosomed.

bu·sul·phan (bew-súlfən) *n.* A drug, $C_6H_{14}O_6S_2$, that destroys cancer cells and is used mainly to treat certain forms of leukaemia.

bus·y (bízzi) *adj.* **-ier, -iest.** **1.** Actively engaged in some form of work; occupied. **2.** Crowded with activity: *a busy morning.* **3.** Meddlesome; prying. **4.** *Chiefly U.S.* Engaged. Said of a telephone line. **5.** Cluttered with minute and distracting detail: *a busy design.*
~*n. Typically Plural. Northern English slang.* A policeman; copper.
~*tr.v.* **busied, -ying, -ies.** To make busy; occupy. Often used reflexively. [Middle English *bisy, busy*, Old English *bysig, bisig*, akin to Middle Low German *besicht*†.] —**bus·y·ness** *n.*
Synonyms: *busy, industrious, diligent, assiduous, sedulous.*

bus·y·bod·y (bízzi-boddi) *n., pl.* **-ies.** A person who meddles or pries into the affairs of others.

busy Liz·zie (lízzi) *n.* A fast-growing hybrid plant of the genus *Impatiens*, having red, pink, white, or orange flowers, widely cultivated as a pot plant.

but (but, *weak form* bət) *conj.* **1.** Contrary to expectation; even so: *He was very ill, but he recovered.* **2.** In spite of this; however: *I tried, but failed.* **3.** While on the other hand: *He left, but she stayed.* **4.** Were it not for the fact that: *I'd go, but it's raining.* **5.** Without the result that: *It never rains but it pours.* **6.** Other than: *I have no choice but to leave.* **7.** That. Often used after a negative: *There's no doubt but he'll win.* **8.** That . . . not. Used after a negative or question: *There never is a change made but someone complains.* **9.** Who . . . not; which . . . not: *None came to him but were treated well.* **10.** *Archaic.* Unless; if not: *"Beshrew me but I love her heartily"* (Shakespeare). **11.** *Archaic & Nonstandard.* Than: *"No sooner acquainted my brother, but he immediately wanted to propose it."* (Henry Fielding). **12.** Used to introduce: **a.** A conclusion: *But we must leave things there.* **b.** An objection or other observation: *But that's incredible!*
~*prep.* With the exception of; barring; save: *none but the brave.*
—**but for.** Were it not for: *But for luck, he would still be poor.*
~*adv.* **1.** No more than just: *but a month to live.* **2.** Only; simply: *If I had but known.* **3.** *Chiefly U.S. Informal.* Really: *rich, but rich!* **4.** *Australian & Regional.* Though; even so: *It's a nice day; cold, but.*
—**all but.** Nearly; almost: *His poem is all but finished.*
~*n.* An objection, restriction, or exception: *no ifs, ands, or buts.* [Middle English *bute, but* (conjunction and adverb), Old English *būtan, būte* (conjunction and preposition).]
Usage: Several common uses of *but* attract criticism, notably its use at the beginning of a sentence: *They should have gone. But they had no money.* As *but* is a conjunction, it should normally be used within a single sentence. By contrast, words like *however, still*, and *nevertheless* should follow a semicolon or full stop: *I was reluctant; however, I agreed.* There is a view that combinations like *but still, but nevertheless* are redundant and to be avoided, but many examples of their use can be found in recognised authors.
Doubt sometimes arises over which form of the personal pronoun to use after *but* in the sense of "except": *but I/me, but they/them.* Strict usage prefers the *I, he, she* forms before a verb, and the *me, him, her* forms after a verb: *No one but she saw it; I saw no one but her.* There is some tendency to find the subjective forms too formal and to use the objective forms in all cases.

but– *comb. form.* Indicates a chemical compound containing four carbon atoms; for example, *butane*. [From BUTYRIC.]

bu·ta·di·ene (bewtə-dî-een ‖ *U.S. also* -dî-éen) *n.* A colourless, highly flammable gaseous hydrocarbon, C_4H_6, obtained from petroleum and used in the manufacture of synthetic rubber. Also called "buta-1,3-diene". [BUTA(NE) + DI- + -ENE.]

bu·ta·nal bewtə-nal) *n.* A flammable liquid, $CH_3(CH_2)_2CHO$, used in synthesising resins. Also called "butyraldehyde".

bu·tane (bew-tayn, -táyn) *n.* A gaseous hydrocarbon, C_4H_{10}, produced synthetically from petroleum and used as a household fuel and refrigerant, and in the manufacture of synthetic rubber. Also called "*n*-butane". **2.** Formerly, either of the two isometric hydrocarbons with the formula C_4H_{10}, the straight-chain isomer **n-butane** and the

branched-chain isomer **isobutane (methylpropane)** *(both of which see).*

bu·ta·no·ate (bewtə-nó-ayt) *n.* A salt or ester of butanoic acid. Also called "butyrate".

bu·ta·no·ic acid (bewtə-nó-ik) *n.* A colourless solid acid occurring in animal-milk fats and used in disinfectants, emulsifying agents, and pharmaceuticals. Also called "butyric acid".

bu·ta·nol (bewtə-nol ‖ -nōl) *n.* **1.** An alcohol, C_4H_9OH, derived naturally from the bacterial fermentation of grain and used as a solvent for resins, in plasticisers, hydraulic fluids, and as a dehydrating agent. **2.** An isomeric alcohol derived from the cracking of petroleum or natural gas and used as a solvent in varnishes, lacquers, and paint removers.

bu·ta·none (bewtə-nōn) *n.* A colourless, flammable ketone, $CH_3COC_2H_5$, used in lacquers, paint removers, cements and adhesives, celluloid, and cleaning fluids. Also called "methyl ethyl ketone".

butch (booch) *n. Slang.* A woman who is masculine in appearance or manner; sometimes used of a lesbian assuming a pseudomasculine role.
~*adj. Informal.* **1.** Sturdily masculine in appearance. **2.** Assuming exaggeratedly masculine ways or appearance. Said of both male and female homosexuals. [From a boy's nickname, *Butch*, perhaps ultimately from BUTCHER.]

butch·er (boochər) *n.* **1.** One who slaughters and prepares animals for food or market. **2.** One who sells meat. **3.** One guilty of cruel or pointless killing. **4.** One who inflicts unnecessary suffering. Sometimes used humorously, as of a dentist. **5.** One who performs a task very unskilfully.
~*tr.v.* **butchered, -ering, -ers. 1.** To slaughter or dress (animals) for market. **2.** To kill cruelly or pointlessly. **3.** To spoil by botching; bungle. [Middle English *bo(u)cher*, from Anglo-French, from Old French *bouchier*, from *boc*, he-goat.] —**butch·er·er** *n.*

butch·er·bird (boochər-burd) *n.* A **shrike** *(see)*, especially one of the genus *Lanius*, which impales its prey on thorns.

butch·ers[1] (boochərz) *n. British Slang.* A look; a glance. [Short for *butcher's hook*, rhyming slang for *look.*]

butchers[2] *adj.* Also **butcher's hook.** *Australian Informal.* Unwell; crook. —**go butcher's (hook) at.** To become angry with.

butcher's broom *n.* A shrub, *Ruscus aculeatus*, native to Europe, having stiff, prickle-tipped, flattened stems resembling true leaves. [Formerly used as a broom by butchers.]

butch·er·y (boochəri) *n., pl.* **-ies. 1.** The trade of a butcher. **2.** A slaughterhouse. **3.** *South African.* A butcher's shop, where meat is sold. **4.** Wanton or cruel killing; carnage.

Bute (bewt). Also **Bute-shire** (-shər, -sheer, *locally* -shīr). Former county of Scotland, absorbed in 1996 into Argyll and Bute.

Bute, John Stuart, 3rd Earl of (1713–92). British politician. From 1751 he was tutor to the heir to the throne, later George III. In 1761 he was appointed secretary of state and helped to bring down the elder Pitt (1762). Bute succeeded Pitt as chief minister of the crown and worked to conclude peace with France (1763).

bu·tene (bewteen) *n.* Any of three isomeric colourless alkene hydrocarbons obtained from petroleum and used in manufacturing other organic compounds. The isomers are but-1-ene (CH_2:CHC_2H_5), isobutylene, and but-2-ene (CH_3CH:$CHCH_3$). See **butylene.**

bu·tene·di·o·ic acid (bewteen-dî-ō-ik) *n.* Either of two isomeric organic acids, cis-butenedioic acid (**maleic acid**) and trans-butanedioic acid (**fumaric acid**) *(both of which see).*

Bu·the·le·zi (boo-tə-láyzi, boo-, -te-laírzi) (**Mangosuthu**) **Gatsha** (1928–). Chief Minister of KwaZulu — one of the national states created as homelands for South Africa's blacks – who became minister of home affairs after the 1994 elections.

but·ler (búttlər) *n.* A male head servant in a household, in charge of the table and the wine cellar. [Middle English *buteler*, servant in charge of the wine cellar, from Old French *bouteillier*, a bottle bearer, from *bouteille, botele*, BOTTLE.]

But·ler (bútlər), **R(ichard) A(usten), Baron,** also known as Rab Butler (1902–82). British Conservative politician. He became Minister of Education in Churchill's coalition cabinet (1941). In 1944 he guided through Parliament the Education Act which provided free primary and secondary education for all. Between 1951 and 1964 he held the offices of Chancellor of the Exchequer, Home Secretary, and Foreign Secretary, but was twice (1957, 1963) passed over for the leadership of the Conservative Party. He retired from politics (1965) and was made a life peer. He was master of Trinity College, Cambridge (1965–78).

Butler, Samuel[1] (1612–80). English satirical poet. His reputation rests on one long poem, *Hudibras* (1663-78), a mock-heroic satire on the Puritans.

Butler, Samuel[2] (1835–1902). British novelist. He first gained literary notice with his novel, *Erewhon* (1872), a trenchant satire on English life and laws. Perhaps his greatest achievement was the semi-autobiographical novel, *The Way of all Flesh* (1903).

butler's pantry *n.* A serving and storage room between kitchen and dining room.

butt[1] (but) *v.* **butted, butting, butts.** —*tr.* To hit or push against with the head or horns; ram. —*intr.* **1.** To hit or push something with the head or horns. **2.** To project forwards or out. —**butt in.** *Informal.* **1.** To interfere or meddle. **2.** To intrude on a conversation. Used with *on.*
~*n.* A push or blow with the head or horns. [Middle English *butten*, from Anglo-French *buter, boter*, from Germanic.]

butt² *v.* **butted, butting, butts.** —*tr.* To join end to end; abut. —*intr.* To meet end on. —*n.* **1. a.** The act of joining two objects end to end. **b.** A **butt joint** *(see).* **2.** A **butt hinge** *(see).* [From BUTT (end).]

butt³ *n.* **1.** A person or thing serving as an object of ridicule or contempt. **2.** A target. **3.** *Plural.* A target range. **4.** A mound of earth, a wall, or another obstacle behind a target for stopping the shot. **5.** A low wall of turf or stone to conceal grouse-shooters. [Middle English *butte*, target, from Old French *but*†.]

butt⁴ *n.* **1.** The larger or thicker end of something: *the butt of a rifle.* **2.** An unburnt end, as of a cigarette. **3.** A short or broken remnant; a stub. **4.** *Chiefly U.S. Informal.* The buttocks. [Middle English *but, butte,* thicker end, from Germanic.]

butt⁵ *n.* **1.** A large cask. **2.** A unit of volume equal to 108 imperial gallons or 126 U.S. gallons. **3.** *Australian.* A standard size for a pack of greasy wool. [Middle English, from Anglo-French *but,* variant of Old French *bot, bout,* from Late Latin *buttis.* See **bottle**.]

butte (bewt) *n.* *Western U.S. & Canadian.* A hill rising abruptly above the surrounding area and having sloping sides and a flat top. [French, from Old French *but,* BUTT (mound behind targets).]

but·ter¹ (búttər) *n.* **1.** A soft, yellowish or whitish emulsion of butterfat, water, air, and sometimes salt, churned from milk or cream and processed for use in cooking and as a food. **2.** Any of various substances with a similar consistency, such as peanut butter or cocoa butter. —*tr.v.* **buttered, -tering, -ters. 1.** To put butter on or in. **2.** *Informal.* To flatter. Usually used with *up.* [Middle English *buter(e),* Old English *butere,* from West Germanic, from Latin *būtȳrum,* from Greek *bouturon,* "cow cheese" : *bous,* cow + *turos,* cheese.]

but·ter² *n.* One that butts with the head or horns.

but·ter-and-eggs (búttər-ən-égz, -ənd-) *n.* *Used with a singular or plural verb.* Any of various plants with yellow and orange flowers, especially **toadflax** *(see).*

but·ter·ball (búttər-bawl) *n.* **1.** A ball of butter. **2.** *Informal.* A fat or chubby person. **3.** A duck, the **bufflehead** *(see).*

butter bean *n.* A variety of Lima bean cultivated for its pale, flat, edible seeds. Also called "wax bean". [From the yellow pods of the wax bean.]

but·ter·bur (búttər-bur) *n.* Any of several plants of the genus *Petasites,* having woolly leaves and fragrant whitish or purple flowers. [Its leaves are said to have been used to wrap butter.]

but·ter·cup (búttər-kup) *n.* Any of various plants of the genus *Ranunculus,* characteristically having glossy yellow flowers, especially the meadow buttercup, *R. acris,* native to Europe, but widely introduced elsewhere.

but·ter·fat (búttər-fat) *n.* The oily fat of milk from which butter is made, consisting largely of the glycerides of oleic, stearic, and palmitic acids.

But·ter·field (búttər-feeld), **William** (1814–1900). British architect, important in the Gothic revival. His work is distinguished by the patterns which he made on façades with coloured bricks, stones, and tiles.

but·ter·fin·gers (búttər-fing-gərz) *n.* A clumsy or awkward person who drops things. —**but·ter·fin·gered** *adj.*

but·ter·fish (búttər-fish) *n., pl.* **-fishes** or collectively **butterfish.** Any of various fishes with slippery skins, such as the eel-like North Atlantic food fish *Pholis gunnellus.*

but·ter·fly (búttər-flī) *n., pl.* **-flies. 1.** Any of various diurnal insects of the order Lepidoptera, characteristically having slender bodies, knobbed antennae, and four broad, usually colourful wings that are closed over the back at rest. **2.** A frivolous pleasure-seeker: *a social butterfly.* **3.** The butterfly stroke. **4.** *Plural. Informal.* Nervous tremors in the stomach. [Middle English *butterflie,* from Old English *buttorflēoge : buter(e),* BUTTER + FLY, perhaps from the belief that butterflies steal milk and butter.]

butterfly bird *n.* A bird, the **wall creeper** *(see).*

butterfly bush *n.* A shrub, **buddleia** *(see).*

butterfly effect *n.* The subsequent, ever-increasing effect of an initially minute difference, change, or event, as when for want of a horseshoe nail a kingdom is eventually lost. [From the notion that the flutter of a butterfly's wings in one place might cause atmospheric turbulence that could grow to a hurricane elsewhere.]

butterfly fish *n.* Any of various tropical marine fishes of the family Chaetodontidae, having brightly coloured flattened bodies.

butterfly stroke *n.* A swimming stroke, a variation of the breast stroke, in which both arms are drawn upwards out of the water and forwards with a simultaneous up-and-down kick of the feet.

butterfly valve *n.* **1.** A disc turning on a diametrical axis inside a pipe, used as a throttle valve or damper. **2.** A valve composed of two semicircular plates hinged on a common spindle, used to permit flow in one direction only. [Its action somewhat resembles that of a butterfly's wings.]

but·ter·milk (búttər-milk) *n.* **1.** The sour liquid that remains after the butterfat has been removed from whole milk or cream by churning. **2.** Milk soured with certain microorganisms.

butter mountain *n.* A large surplus of butter periodically occurring as a result of overproduction by farmers within the European Community. Compare **wine lake.**

butter muslin *n.* A coarse loosely woven cotton gauze. [Formerly used for wrapping butter.]

but·ter·nut (búttər-nut) *n.* **1.** A tree, *Juglans cinerea,* of eastern North America, having compound leaves and egg-shaped nuts. Also called "white walnut". **2.** The edible, oily nut of this tree. **3.** The hard, greyish-brown wood of this tree. **4.** The bark of this tree, or an extract obtained from it, formerly used as a laxative. **5.** A brownish colour or dye obtained from butternut bark. [From the oiliness of the nut.]

but·ter·scotch (búttər-skoch) *n.* **1.** A syrup, sauce, or flavouring made by melting butter, brown sugar, and sometimes artificial flavourings. **2.** A hard, sticky sweet made from these ingredients. [Perhaps originally made in Scotland.]

but·ter·wort (búttər-wurt ‖ -wawrt) *n.* Any plant of the genus *Pinguicula;* especially, *P. vulgaris,* of wet places, having violet-blue, spurred flowers and fleshy, greasy leaves. [From the oiliness of the leaves.]

but·ter·y¹ (búttəri) *adj.* Resembling, containing, or spread with butter. —**but·ter·i·ness** *n.*

buttery² *n., pl.* **-ies.** *Chiefly British.* **1.** A pantry or wine cellar. **2.** A room or bar in colleges and universities where students can buy provisions. [Middle English *boteri, buttrie,* from Old French *boterie,* from *bot,* BUTT (cask).]

butt hinge *n.* A hinge composed of two plates attached to abutting surfaces of a door and door jamb and joined by a pin. Also called "butt". [From BUTT (abut).]

but·tin·ski (bu-tín-ski) *n.* *Australian & U.S. Informal.* An interfering busybody. [One who *butts in,* + *-ski,* surname suffix.]

butt joint *n.* A joint formed by two abutting surfaces placed squarely together. Also called "butt". [From BUTT (abut).]

but·tock (búttək) *n.* **1. a.** Either of the two rounded fleshy parts on the lower rear part of the human torso. **b.** The analogous part of the body of certain mammals. **2.** *Plural.* These two parts together; the bottom. [Middle English, from Old English *buttuc,* end, ridge, strip of land.]

but·ton (bútt'n) *n.* **1.** A fastener, usually disc-shaped, used to join two parts of a garment by fitting through a buttonhole or loop. **2.** Such an object used for decoration. **3.** Any of various objects of similar appearance, especially: **a.** A control switch, as on a bell or machine. **b.** *U.S. & Australian.* A badge. **c.** In fencing, the tip of a foil. **d.** A fused metal or glass globule. **4.** Any of various knoblike organic structures, especially: **a.** The head of a small mushroom. **b.** The tip of a rattlesnake's tail. —*v.* **buttoned, -toning, -tons.** —*tr.* **1.** To furnish with a button or buttons. **2.** To fasten with a button or buttons. Often used with *up.* —*intr.* **1.** To admit of being fastened with a button or buttons. Often used with *up.* **2.** *Informal.* To become uncommunicative. Used with *up.* [Middle English *boton,* from Old French *bouton,* bud, button, from *bouter,* to strike against, thrust, pierce, from Romance *bottare* (unattested), from Germanic.] —**but·ton·er** *n.* —**but·ton·y** *adj.*

button day *n.* *Australian.* A **flag day** *(see).*

but·ton·hole (bútt'n-hōl) *n.* **1.** A slit in a garment or piece of fabric for fastening a button. **2.** *Chiefly British.* A flower worn in a buttonhole on the lapel of a coat or jacket. —*tr.v.* **buttonholed, -holing, -holes. 1.** To make a buttonhole in. **2.** To sew with a buttonhole stitch. **3.** To accost and detain in conversation. —**but·ton·hol·er** *n.*

buttonhole stitch *n.* A loop stitch that forms a reinforced edge, as round a buttonhole.

but·ton·hook (bútt'n-hŏok ‖ -hōok) *n.* A small hook for buttoning shoes or gloves.

but·ton·quail (bútt'n-kwayl) *n.* Any of various small, quail-like birds of the family Turnicidae, occurring in warm grassland regions of the Old World. Also called "hemipode".

but·tons (bútt'nz) *n., pl.* **buttons.** *Informal.* A pageboy, especially in a pantomime. [From the buttons on his jacket.]

button tree *n.* A North American plane tree, *platanus occidentalis.* Also called "buttonwood".

butt plate *n.* A metal plate on the butt end of a gunstock.

but·tress (búttriss) *n.* **1.** A structure, usually brick or stone, built against a wall for support or reinforcement. See **flying buttress. 2.** Anything resembling a buttress, such as a projecting part of a hill. **3.** A horny growth on the heel of a horse's hoof. **4.** Anything that serves to support, prop, or reinforce. —*tr.v.* **buttressed, -tressing, -tresses. 1.** To support or reinforce with a buttress. **2.** To sustain, prop, or bolster: *buttress an argument with evidence.* [Middle English *butres, boteras,* from Old French *bouterez,* shortened from *(ars) bouterez,* thrusting (arch), from *bouter,* to strike against.]

buttress root *n.* A root growing from and supporting the trunk of a tree, as in the mangrove.

butt shaft *n.* A blunt, unbarbed arrow.

butt weld *n.* A welded butt joint.

butt-weld (bút-wéld) *tr.v.* **-welded, -welding, -welds.** To join by a butt weld.

but·ty¹ (bútti) *n., pl.* **-ties.** *Chiefly Welsh.* A miner's mate. [Perhaps from BOOTY, as in the phrase *play booty,* to share takings.]

butty² *n., pl.* **-ties.** *Northern English.* A sandwich or a slice of buttered bread: *a jam butty.*

bu·tyl (béw-tīl, -til) *n.* A hydrocarbon radical, C_4H_9, with the structure of butane and valency 1.

butyl alcohol *n.* Any of four isomeric alcohols widely used as solvents and in organic synthesis, each having the formula C_4H_9OH.

bu·ty·lene (béwtileen) *n.* Any of three gaseous isomeric ethylene hydrocarbons, C_4H_8, used principally in making synthetic rubbers.

The straight-chain isomers are *butenes*; the branched-chain isomer is *isobutylene* or *2-methylpropene.*

butyl rubber *n.* A synthetic rubber produced by copolymerisation of a butylene (98 per cent) with isoprene or butadiene (2 per cent), outstanding in gaseous impermeability and used in tyres, insulation, and as a binder fuel in solid propellants for rockets.

bu·ty·ra·ceous (béwti-ráyshəss) *adj.* Resembling butter in appearance, consistency, or chemical properties; buttery. [Latin *bútyrum,* BUTTER + -ACEOUS.]

bu·tyr·al·de·hyde (béwti-rál-di-hīd) *n.* An organic compound, **butanal** *(see).*

bu·ty·rate (béwti-rayt) *n.* A **butanoate** *(see).*

bu·tyr·ic (bew-tírrik) *adj.* 1. Of, pertaining to, containing, or derived from butter. 2. Of, pertaining to, or derived from butyric acid.

butyric acid *n.* An organic acid, **butanoic acid** *(see).*

bu·ty·rin (béwtirin) *n.* Any one of three isomeric glyceryl esters of butyric acid, naturally present in butter. [Earlier *butirine,* from French : Latin *bútyrum,* BUTTER + -INE.]

bux·om (búksəm) *adj.* Full-bosomed and plump. Said of a woman. [Earlier, flexible, gay, comely, Middle English *buhsum, buxum,* obedient, humble, bending, from Old English *gebūhsum* (unattested), easy to bend, pliable, from *būgan,* to bend.] **—bux·om·ly** *adv.* **—bux·om·ness** *n.*

Bux·te·hu·de (bŏókstə-hŏódə), **Dietrich** (1637–1707). Danish composer and organist. As church organist at Lübeck (1668–1707), he gained the admiration of Handel and Bach.

Bux·ton (búkstən). A town in Derbyshire, England, standing 300 metres (1000 feet) above sea level in the Peak District, overlooking the river Wye. It is famous for its mineral springs and baths.

buy (bī) *v.* **bought** (bawt), **buying, buys.** *—tr.* 1. To acquire in exchange for money or its equivalent; purchase. 2. To be a means of obtaining or procuring: *Money buys power.* 3. To acquire by sacrifice, exchange, or trade. 4. To bribe. 5. *Chiefly U.S. Slang.* To accept the truth, merit, or feasibility of. *—intr.* To purchase goods; act as a purchaser: *to buy in bulk.* **—buy in.** 1. To purchase (a supply of something) for future use. 2. To purchase back for the original owner, as at an auction when the bidding is low. 3. To purchase rather than manufacture (goods). **—buy into.** 1. To purchase shares or an interest in (a company, for example). 2. *Chiefly U.S. Slang.* To pay money in exchange for joining (a social or business group). 3. *Australian Informal.* To become involved in (an argument, for example). **—buy off.** To bribe in order to proceed without interference, or to be exempted from an obligation or from prosecution. **—buy out.** To purchase the controlling stock, business rights, or interests of. **—buy up.** To purchase all that is available of.
~n. Anything bought or capable of being bought; a purchase, especially something that is underpriced: *a good buy.* [Buy, bought (past tense), bought (past participle); Middle English *byen* (earlier *byggen*), *bo(g)hte, (i)bo(g)ht,* Old English *bycgan, bohte, geboht,* from Germanic *bugjan* (unattested).] **—buy·a·ble** *adj.*
    Usage: The correct form is to *buy* (something) *from* someone. To *buy* (something) *off* someone is an informal usage, and to *buy* (something) *off of* someone is nonstandard.

buy·er (bī-ər) *n.* 1. One who buys goods; a customer. 2. A purchasing agent, especially one who buys for a company or store.

buyers' market *n. Economics.* A market condition characterised by low prices, occurring when the supply of commodities exceeds market demand. Compare **sellers' market.**

Buys Bal·lot's law (bíss bál-əts, bə-lóts) *n. Meteorology.* The principle that in the northern hemisphere an observer standing with his back to the wind has a lower atmospheric pressure on his left. In the southern hemisphere the pressure is lower on his right. [After C.H.D. *Buys Ballot,* 19th-century Dutch meterologist.]

buzz (buz) *v.* **buzzed, buzzing, buzzes.** *—intr.* 1. To make a low droning or vibrating sound like that of a bee. 2. To talk excitedly in low tones. 3. To move quickly and busily; bustle. Often used with *about.* *—tr.* 1. To cause to buzz: *hornets buzzing their wings.* 2. To spread (gossip). Often used with *about.* 3. *Informal.* To fly low over: *The plane buzzed the control tower.* 4. To signal (a person) with a buzzer. 5. *Informal.* To telephone (a person). **—buzz off.** *Informal.* To go away. Usually used in the imperative.
~n. 1. A rapidly vibrating, humming, or droning sound. 2. A low murmur, as of many hushed voices speaking at once: *a buzz of talk.* 3. *Informal.* A telephone call. 4. A rumour 5. *Slang.* A pleasant euphoric feeling, as induced by drugs; a high. [Middle English *bussen* (attested only in the verbal noun *bussyng*), to drone (imitative).]

buz·zard (búzzərd) *n.* 1. Any hawk of the genus *Buteo,* having broad wings and a broad tail. 2. *U.S.* Any of various American vultures, such as the **turkey buzzard** *(see).* 3. An avaricious or unpleasant person. [Middle English *busard,* from Old French, alteration of *buson,* from Latin *būteō* (stem *būteōn-*).]

buzz bomb *n.* A **flying bomb** *(see)* of World War II. [From the buzzing noise made by its pulsejet engine.]

buzz·er (búzzər) *n.* Any of various electric signalling devices that make a buzzing sound, such as a doorbell.

buzz saw *n. U.S.* A **circular saw** *(see).* [From the sound it makes.]

buzz word *n. Informal.* A catchword; a jargon word, often one used to convey an impression of specialised knowledge. [From the meaninglessness or frequency of the word in question.]

B.V. Blessed Virgin.

B.V.M. Blessed Virgin Mary.

bwa·na (bwaánə) *n. East African.* A boss or employer. Often used as a term of respectful address. [Swahili, from Arabic *abūna,* our father.]

BWR boiling-water reactor.

by[1] (bī; *occasional weak forms* bi, bə.) *prep.* 1. Next to; close to: *the window by the door.* 2. Passing along or through: *He came by the back road.* 3. Up to and beyond; past: *He drove by the house.* 4. In the period of; during: *sleeping by day.* 5. Not later than: *by 3 o'clock.* 6. Used to indicate: **a.** Rate or amount: *letters by the thousand.* **b.** Units: *paid by the hour.* 7. To the extent of: *shorter by two inches.* 8. **a.** According to: *by his own admission.* **b.** In accordance with: *play by the rules.* 9. In the presence or name of. Used in oaths: *swear by the Bible.* 10. Used to indicate: **a.** A means: *done by machine.* **b.** A creator or originator: *a novel by Dickens.* **c.** The doer of an action: *The window was broken by some children.* 11. Used to indicate a cause or reason: *thrifty by necessity.* 12. Used to indicate a sign or piece of evidence: *I knew by his face that he was lying.* 13. Used to indicate a point of contact: *take by the hand.* 14. As regards; in respect of: *a plumber by trade.* 15. As far as it concerns: *It's all right by me.* 16. In succession to; after: *day by day.* 17. Used to link certain expressions to be taken together and indicating: **a.** Multiplication or division of quantities. **b.** Coordination of measurements: *a room 12 feet by 18.* **c.** Alternation of a compass direction: *north by northeast.*
~adv. 1. On hand; nearby: *stand by.* 2. Where one lives: *Come by if you're passing.* 3. Up alongside, and past: *The car raced by.* 4. Into the past: *as years go by.* **—by and by.** Soon enough; in good time. **—by and large.** Generally; on the whole. [Middle English *by,* Old English *bī, bi, be.*]

by[2]. Variant of **bye.**

by-, bye- *prefix.* Indicates: 1. Close at hand or near; for example, **bystander.** 2. Out of the way or aside; for example, **byroad, by-election.** 3. Secondary or incidental; for example, **by-product.** [Middle English *by-, bi-,* from BY.]

By·att (bī-ət), **A(ntonia) S(usan),** born Antonia Susan Drabble (1938–). British novelist, critic, and biographer. Her novels include *Shadow of a Sun* (1964), the richly allusive *The Virgin in the Garden* (1978), and *Possession* (1990), which won the Booker prize. She is the sister of the novelist Margaret Drabble.

by·bid·der (bī-biddər) *n.* A person who bids at an auction to raise prices for the owner.

Byb·los (bíb-loss ǁ *U.S.* -lòss). An ancient Phoenician port and the chief city of Phoenicia during the second millennium B.C. It stood northeast of present-day Beirut on the site of modern Jebeil (the biblical Gebal). It was also famous for its papyrus. See **Bible.**

by-blow (bī-blō) *n.* *Archaic.* 1. An indirect or chance blow. 2. An illegitimate child; a bastard. [Sense 2 from the idea of a child begotten incidentally or by chance.]

bye, by (bī) *n.* 1. A secondary matter; a side issue. 2. *Sports.* The position of one who draws no opponent for a round in a tournament and so advances to the next round. 3. In golf, one or more holes remaining unplayed at the end of a match. 4. In cricket, a run made off a ball not touched by the batsman. Compare **leg bye.** **—by the bye** or **by.** Incidentally; by the way. [From BY- (2,3).]

bye-bye (bī-bī, bī-bī) *interj. Informal.* Goodbye. [Baby-talk form.]

bye-byes (bī-bīz) *n. Informal.* Sleep; bed. Used especially to children. [From BYE-BYE.]

by-e·lec·tion, by·e·lec·tion, bye-e·lec·tion (bī-ileksh'n) *n.* A special election held between regular elections to fill a vacancy in a legislature; especially, in the United Kingdom and other Commonwealth countries, an election to Parliament occurring between general elections.

Byelorussia. See **Belarus.**

Byelorussian. Variant of **Belarussian.**

by·gone (bī-gon ǁ -gaan, -gawn) *adj.* Past; gone by; former.
~n. A past occurrence. **—let bygones be bygones.** To let past differences be forgotten; be reconciled.

by-lane (bī-layn) *n.* A side road; a byway.

by-law, by-law, bye-law (bī-law) *n.* 1. A regulation made by a local authority, corporation, or the like, having legal effect only in the area governed by that authority. 2. A law or rule governing the internal affairs of an organisation. [Middle English *bilawe, bylawe,* "village law", probably from Old Norse *bȳr,* village + *lǫg,* law.]

by-line (bī-līn) *n.* A line at the head or foot of a newspaper or magazine article with the author's name.
~tr.v. **by-lined, -lining, -lines.** To write (an article) under a by-line. **—by-lin·er** *n.*

Byng (bing), **George, Viscount Torrington** (1663–1733). English admiral. He persuaded the navy to support William of Orange against James II in 1688, and later repelled the attempted Jacobite invasions of 1708 and 1715. His greatest naval victory was the defeat of the Spanish fleet in the Strait of Messina (1718).

Byng, John (1704–57). English admiral, son of George, Viscount Torrington. After his failure to relieve Minorca from a French siege and his subsequent withdrawal from the island he was court-martialled and executed for neglect of duty, a severe punishment which Voltaire said was meted out "to encourage the others".

BYOB, b.y.o.b. Bring your own bottle; bring your own booze.

by·pass, by-pass (bī-paass ǁ -pass) *n.* 1. A road, especially a main road, that passes round or to one side of a town, town centre, or congested area. 2. A pipe or channel to conduct gas or liquid around another pipe or a fixture. 3. Any means of circumvention. 4. *Electronics.* A **shunt** *(see).* 5. *Medicine.* **a.** An apparatus used to keep the blood circulating and oxygenated while surgery is per-

formed on the heart. **b.** A surgical operation to pass round an obstructed passage, as in an artery or intestine. Also used adjectivally: *bypass surgery.* **c.** An alternative passage created in such an operation. **d.** A horseshoe-shaped length of tubing worn on the arm by a patient requiring regular treatment on a kidney machine.
~*tr.v.* **bypassed, -passing, -passes.** Also **by-pass. 1.** To go round instead of through; avoid (an obstacle). **2.** To proceed heedless of; ignore or circumvent: *bypassing office procedures.* **3.** To cause (a fluid or electricity, for example) to follow a bypass.
bypass engine *n.* A jet engine in which some of the air intake bypasses the combustion zone, flowing directly into or around the main exhaust gas flow to provide additional thrust.
by-path (bǐ-paath ‖ -path) *n., pl.* **-paths** (-paathz ‖ -paths, -pathz). An indirect or little-used path.
by-play (bǐ-play) *n.* Secondary action or speech taking place while the main action proceeds, especially in a play.
by-prod-uct (bǐ-prod-ukt, -əkt) *n.* **1.** Something, especially something useful, that is produced in the making of something else. **2.** A secondary result; a side effect.
Byrd (burd), **Richard E(velyn)** (1888 – 1957). U.S. aviator and polar explorer. In 1926 he made the first flight over the North Pole. Between 1929 and 1956 he led five scientific and exploratory air expeditions to the South Pole, voyages which established the basis of American claims to territory in Antarctica.
Byrd, William (*c.*1543–1623). English composer, one of the foremost of early English musicians. The best known of his works today are his settings of the Anglican service and his three masses.
byre (bīr) *n.* A cowshed or barn. [Middle English *byre,* Old English *bȳre,* stall, hut, perhaps variant of BOWER.]
by-road (bǐ-rōd) *n.* A side road; a minor road.
By-ron (bīr-ən), **George Gordon, 6th Baron (Lord)** (1788 – 1824). British poet, one of the leading figures of the English Romantic movement. The first two cantos of *Childe Harold's Pilgrimage,* which appeared in 1812, made him the darling of London society. In *Manfred* (1817) the full "Byronic hero" — lonely, rebellious, secretive — appeared. His last work, *Don Juan* (1819 – 24), considered by many to be the finest satirical and comic poem in the English language. In 1824 he sailed to Greece to help in the nationalist revolt against Turkish rule, but died of a fever.
By-ron-ic (bīr-rónnik, bī-) *adj.* Of or characteristic of Byron or his works; especially, adventurous and wildly romantic. **—By-ron-i-cal-ly** *adv.*
bys-sin-o-sis (bíssi-nṓ-siss) *n.* A lung disease affecting textile workers, caused by prolonged exposure to cotton dust and characterised by wheezing. [New Latin, from Greek *bussinos,* of BYSSUS + -OSIS.]
bys-sus (bíssəss) *n., pl.* **-suses** or **byssi** (bíssī). **1.** *Zoology.* A mass of filaments by means of which certain bivalve molluscs, such as mussels, attach themselves to fixed surfaces. **2.** A fine-textured linen of ancient times, used by the Egyptians as wrapping for mummies. [Latin, from Greek *bussos,* flax, linen.]
by-stand-er (bī-standər) *n.* A person who is present at some event without participating in it.
by-street (bī-street) *n.* A small side street; an alley.
byte (bīt) *n. Computing.* **1.** A group of bits of information, typically six or eight, treated as a unit in a computer process. **2.** The space occupied by a single character in a computer store. [Probably from BIT + BITE.]
by-way (bī-way) *n.* **1. a.** A small country road or lane. **b.** An unimportant or partially hidden side road. **2.** A secondary or unexplored field of study.
by-word (bī-wurd) *n.* **1.** A well-known saying; a proverb. **2.** One that proverbially represents a type, class, or quality. **3.** An object of contempt or notoriety. [Middle English *biword,* Old English *bīword* (translation of Latin *prōverbium,* PROVERB) : BY + WORD.]
by-your-leave (bī-yawr-léev, -yoor-, -yər-) *n.* A request for permission. Used chiefly in the phrase *without so much as a by-your-leave.*
byzant. Variant of **bezant.**
By-zan-tine (bī-zán-tīn, bi-, bízz'n-, -teen ‖ -tin) *adj.* **1.** Of, pertaining to, or characteristic of Byzantium, its inhabitants, or their culture. **2.** Of or designating the style of architecture developed from the fifth century A.D. in Byzantium, characterised by round arches, massive domes, intricate spires and minarets, and extensive use of mosaic. **3.** Of or designating the style of painting and design developed in Byzantium, characterised by formality of design, stylised presentation of figures, rich use of colour, especially gold, and generally religious subject matter. **4.** Of the Eastern Orthodox Church or the rites performed in it. **5.** *Sometimes small.* **b.** Complicated; labyrinthine; devious. **6.** *Sometimes small* **b.** Rigid; inflexible.
~*n.* A native or inhabitant of Byzantium.
Byzantine Empire *n. Arabic* **Rum** (rōōm). The successor to the Roman Empire, dating from A.D. 330, when Constantine I rebuilt Byzantium, named it Constantinople, and made it the capital of the Roman Empire. It was also called the Eastern Empire, especially after 395, when Honorius became emperor in the east and Arcadius emperor in the west, thus making permanent the split in the Roman Empire. Although its extent varied through the centuries, the core of the empire was always the Balkan peninsula and Asia Minor. The last Byzantine emperor was Constantine XI Palaeologus, who reigned from 1449–53. Constantinople fell to the Ottoman Turks in 1453, a defeat which marked the end of the empire.
By-zan-ti-um¹ (bī-zánti-əm, bi-, -zánshi-). The Byzantine Empire and its culture.
Byzantium². See **Constantinople.**

C

c, C (see) *n., pl.* **c's** or *rare* **cs, Cs** or **C's. 1.** The third letter of the modern English alphabet. **2.** Any of the speech sounds represented by this letter.
c, C, c., C. *Note:* As an abbreviation or symbol, *c* may be a small or a capital letter, with or without a full stop. Established forms or those generally preferred precede the definition. When no form is given, all four forms are in general use in that sense. **1.** C Canadian. **2.** C *Electricity.* capacitance. **3.** c., C. capacity. **4.** c., C. cape. **5.** c carat. **6.** C The symbol for the element carbon. **7.** c., C. carton. **8.** c., C. case. **9.** C. Catholic. **10.** c. caught (in cricket). **11.** C Celsius. **12.** C. Celtic. **13.** c., C. cent. **14.** c centi-. **15.** C centigrade. **16.** c., C. centime. **17.** c., C. century. **18.** C. chancellor. **19.** c., C. chapter. **20.** C *Physics.* charge conjugation. **21.** C. chief. **22.** c., C. church. **23.** c. circa (usually italic *c.*). **24.** C. city. **25.** c. cloudy. **26.** C. companion. **27.** c., C. congius. **28.** C. Congress. **29.** C. Conservative. **30.** c, C *Mathematics.* constant. **31.** c., C. consul. **32.** c., C. copy. **33.** c., C. copyright. **34.** c., C. corps. **35.** C coulomb. **36.** C. court. **37.** c cubic. **38.** c. cup. **39.** C The Roman numeral for 100. [Latin *centum.*] **40.** The third in a series.
C (see) *n., pl.* **Cs** or **C's. 1.** The third best or highest in quality, class, or rank; especially, the third highest mark awarded for academic work. **2. a.** The first note in the scale of C major, or the third note in the relative minor scale. **b.** The key or a scale in which C is the tonic. **c.** A written or printed note representing C. **d.** A string, key, or pipe tuned to C. **3.** Something shaped like the letter C.
© copyright.
C3, C-3 (sée-thrée) *adj.* **1.** Unhealthy; unfit. **2.** Inferior in status or quality. [From the lowest medical rating, *C3,* used in World War I.]
ca circa (usually italic *ca*).
Ca The symbol for the element calcium.
C.A. 1. Central America. **2.** chartered accountant. **3.** chief accountant. **4.** Consumer's Association.
C.A.A. Civil Aviation Authority.
Caaba. See **Kaaba.**

cab¹ (kab) *n.* **1.** A taxi *(see).* **2.** The covered compartment of a heavy vehicle or machine, such as a lorry or locomotive, in which the operator or driver sits. **3.** Formerly, a one-horse vehicle for public hire. [Short for CABRIOLET.]
cab², kab *n.* A Hebrew measure equal to roughly two litres (4 pints). [Hebrew *qabh,* "hollow vessel".]
CAB, C.A.B. Citizens Advice Bureau.
ca-bal (kə-bál, -báal) *n.* **1.** A conspiratorial group of plotters or intriguers. **2.** A secret scheme or plot. —See Synonyms at **conspiracy.**
~*intr.v.* **caballed, -balling, -bals.** To form a cabal; plot; conspire. [French *cabale,* from Medieval Latin *cabala,* CABALA. The term was popularised under Charles II, when applied to the ministry of Clifford, Arlington, Buckingham, Ashley, and Lauderdale.]
cab-a-la, cab-ba-la, kab-a-la, kab-ba-la (kə-báala, ka- ‖ kábbələ) *n.* **1.** *Often capital C.* An occult mystical philosophy of rabbinical origin, widely transmitted in medieval Europe, based on an esoteric interpretation of the Hebrew Scriptures. **2.** Any secret doctrine. [Medieval Latin, from Hebrew *qabbālāh,* received doctrine, tradition, from *qābal,* to receive.] —**cab-a-lism** *n.* —**cab-a-list** *n.*
cab-a-lis-tic (kábbə-lístik) *adj.* **1.** Of or pertaining to the Cabala. **2.** Having secret or hidden meaning; occult; mysterious.
Ca-bal-lé (kə-bī-yay, -bál-, káb-al-yáy), **Montserrat** (1933–). Spanish soprano, specialising in bel canto roles such as Norma in Bellini's opera of that name.
cab-al-le-ro (kábbəl-aír-ō; *Spanish* -yaír-ō) *n., pl.* **-ros.** In Spanish-speaking countries, a gentleman; a cavalier. [Spanish, from Late Latin *caballārius,* a horse groom, from Latin *caballus,* a horse. See **cavalier.**]
cab-a-ret (kábbə-ray ‖ *U.S.* -ráy) *n.* **1.** Live entertainment in a restaurant or nightclub, with performances by singers, comedians, dancers, and the like. **2.** A restaurant or nightclub that provides such entertainment. [French, tavern, from Old French, probably of dialect (Walloon) origin.]

cab·bage (kábbij) *n.* **1.** An edible plant, *Brassica oleracea capitata,* many varieties of which are grown in temperate climates throughout the world, having a short, thick stalk, and a large head formed by tightly overlapping green or reddish leaves. **2.** The head of a cabbage. **3.** An edible leaf bud of the **cabbage palm** *(see).* **4.** *Informal.* A person with no interests leading á stultifying life. **5.** *Informal.* A person who is severely mentally disabled, often as a result of serious brain damage. [Middle English *caboche,* from Old North French, variant of Old French *caboce†,* "head".] —**cab·ba·gy** *adj.*

cabbage moth *n.* A brown-grey moth, *Mamestra brassicae,* whose caterpillars are a horticultural pest.

cabbage palm *n.* **1.** A West Indian palm tree, *Roystonea oleracea,* having leaf buds that are edible when young. **2.** A similar Australian palm, *Livistonia australis.* Also called "cabbage tree".

cabbage palmetto *n.* See **palmetto.**

cabbage root fly *n.* A fly, *Erioischia brassicae,* whose larvae feed on and damage the roots of cabbages, turnips, and similar vegetables.

cabbage rose *n.* A prickly shrub, *Rosa centifolia,* native to the Caucasus, having large, fragrant, many-petalled pink flowers. It is cultivated in gardens in many varieties.

cabbage white *n.* Any of several white butterflies of the genus *Pieris,* having larvae that feed on cabbages and other brassicas.

cab·bage·worm (kábbij-wurm) *n.* Any of several caterpillars that feed on cabbage; especially, the bright green larva of the cabbage white.

cab·by, cab·bie (kábbi) *n., pl.* **-bies.** *Informal.* A taxi driver.

ca·ber (káybər ‖ ka'abər) *n.* A heavy wooden pole, usually the trunk of a young pine tree, thrown in the air as a trial of strength in Scottish highland games: *tossing the caber.* [Gaelic *cabar.*]

ca·ber·net sau·vi·gnon (kaber-náy) *n.* A variety of black grape grown in France and many other countries. It is the main variety used in claret. [French.]

cab·in (kábbin) *n.* **1.** A small, roughly or simply built house, cottage, or hut. **2. a.** In a ship, a room used as living quarters by an officer or passenger. **b.** In a boat, an enclosed compartment serving as a shelter or as living quarters. **c.** In an aircraft, the enclosed space for the crew, passengers, or cargo.
~*tr.v.* **cabined, -ining, -ins.** To confine, as in a cabin. [Middle English *cabane,* from Old French, from Old Provençal, from Late Latin *capanna†,* hut, cabin.]

cabin boy *n.* A boy servant aboard a ship.

cabin class *n.* A class of accommodation on some passenger ships, lower than first class and higher than tourist class. —**cab·in-class** *adj. & adv.*

cabin cruiser *n.* A motorboat with one or more cabins.

Ca·bin·da or **Ka·bin·da** (kə-bín-də, -béen-) *n.* A thickly forested district on the Atlantic seaboard of Angola, separated from the rest of the country by a strip of land along the Congo river belonging to Congo (Dem.Rep.). Offshore oil production, started in 1968, has led to expansion of the chief town, Cabinda.

cab·i·net (kábbi-nət, -nit) *n.* **1.** An upright cupboard or case with shelves, drawers, or compartments for the storage or display of a collection of objects or materials. **2.** A container for a record-player, television set, or the like. **3.** *Archaic.* A small or private room set aside for some specific activity. **4.** *Often capital* **C.** A powerful advisory and policy-making body appointed by a head of state or prime minister, and comprising those ministers who head the most important government departments.
~*adj.* **1.** Of suitable value, beauty, or size to be kept or displayed in a cabinet: *a cabinet edition.* **2.** *Often capital* **C.** Belonging or pertaining to a political cabinet: *a cabinet minister; a cabinet reshuffle.* **3.** Used for cabinetwork: *teak and other heavy cabinet woods.* [CABIN + -ET, after French *cabinet,* from *cabinet†,* a gambling house.]

cab·i·net-mak·er (kábbi-nət-maykər, -nit-) *n.* A craftsman specialising in making fine wooden furniture. —**cab·i·net-mak·ing** *n.*

cabinet pudding *n.* A steamed pudding made with breadcrumbs, custard, and dried fruit.

cab·i·net·work (kábbi-nət-wurk, -nit-) *n.* Finished woodwork made by a cabinet-maker.

ca·ble (káyb'l) *n.* **1.** A strong, large-diameter, heavy steel or fibre rope. **2.** *Electricity.* A bound or sheathed group of mutually insulated conductors. **3. a.** *Nautical.* A heavy rope or chain for mooring or anchoring a ship. **b.** A unit of nautical length equal to about 185 metres (608 feet) in the United Kingdom and 220 metres (720 feet) in the United States. Also called "cable's length". **4.** A cablegram. **5.** Cable stitch. **6.** Cable television: *cable broadcasting.*
~*v.* **cabled, -bling, -bles.** —*tr.* **1. a.** To send a cablegram to. **b.** To transmit (a message) by telegraph. **2.** To supply or fasten with a cable or cables. —*intr.* To send a cablegram. [Middle English, from Anglo-French, from Late Latin *capulum,* rope for fastening cattle, from Latin *capere,* to take.]

cable car *n.* A passenger car used on a cable railway.

ca·ble·gram (káyb'l-gram) *n.* An overseas telegram sent by submarine cable, radio, satellite, or the like.

ca·ble-laid (káyb'l-layd) *adj.* Made of three ropes of three strands each, twisted together anticlockwise.

cable railway *n.* A railway on which the cars are suspended on and moved by an endless cable driven by a stationary engine.

cable release *n.* A short length of flexible cable used to operate the shutter of a camera without moving or shaking the camera.

cable stitch *n.* A knitting technique or stitch that produces a twisted rope design. Also called "cable". —**ca·ble-stitch** *adj.*

ca·blet (káyb-lət, -lit) *n.* A cable-laid rope with a circumference of less than 25 centimetres (10 inches); a small cable. [Diminutive of CABLE.]

cable television *n.* A television system in which signals are delivered to subscribers' receivers by cable.

ca·ble·way (káyb'l-way) *n.* An overhead cable and apparatus for carrying materials, goods, passengers, and the like, normally secured between terminal towers.

cab·man (káb-mən) *n., pl.* **-men** (-mən, -men). The driver of a cab.

cab·o·chon (kábbə-shon) *n.* **1.** A highly polished, convex-cut, unfaceted gem. **2.** This style of cutting. [Old French, diminutive of Old North French *caboche, caboce,* head. See **cabbage.**]

ca·boo·dle (kə-bōōd'l) *n.* *Informal.* The lot, group, or bunch. Used chiefly in the phrase *the whole caboodle.* [19th century (U.S.) : perhaps contraction of phrase *kit and boodle.*]

ca·boose (kə-bōōss) *n.* **1.** A ship's kitchen on deck; a small galley. **2.** *U.S.* The last car on a goods train, having kitchen and sleeping facilities for the train crew. Compare **guard's van.** [Probably from Dutch *kabuis,* ship's supply room or galley, from Middle Low German *kabūse†.*]

Ca·bo·ra Bas·sa Dam (kə-báwrə bássə). See **Cahora Bassa Dam.**

Cab·ot (kábbət), **John** (*c.* 1455-98). *Italian* **Giovanni Ca·bo·to** (kä-bō'tō). Italian explorer from Genoa who settled in Bristol and led the first English expedition to America. In 1497, under letters patent from Henry VII, he set sail and discovered Newfoundland and Nova Scotia, thinking them to be part of Asia.

cab·o·tage (kábbə-taazh, -tij) *n.* **1.** Trade or navigation in coastal waters. **2.** The right of a country to operate exclusively the air traffic within its territory. [French, from *caboter,* to coast, probably from Spanish *cabo,* cape, headland, from Latin *caput,* head.]

cab rank *n.* A taxi rank *(see).*

Ca·bri·ni (kə-bréeni), **Saint Frances Xavier,** born Maria Francesca Cabrini (1850-1917). Italian-born founder of the Missionary Sisters of the Sacred Heart and the first citizen of the United States to be canonised (1946). Her feast day is December 22.

cab·ri·ole (kábbri-ōl, -ōl) *n.* A form of furniture leg, characteristic of Queen Anne and Chippendale furniture, that curves outwards and then narrows downwards into an ornamental foot. [French, "caper" (from its resemblance to the foreleg of a capering animal). See **capriole.**]

cab·ri·o·let (kábbri-ə-láy, -ō-) *n.* **1.** A two-wheeled, one-horse vehicle with two seats and a folding top. **2.** A car with a folding roof; a drophead coupé. [French, diminutive of *cabriole,* caper (in allusion to its bounding motion). See **capriole.**]

ca·ca·o (kə-káa-ō, -káy-ō) *n., pl.* **-os.** **1.** An evergreen tropical American tree, *Theobroma cacao,* having yellowish flowers and reddish-brown seed pods. **2.** The seed of this tree, used in making cocoa, and cocoa butter. In this sense, also called "cacao bean", "cocoa bean". [Spanish, from Nahuatl *cacahuatl,* cacao tree.]

cach·a·lot (kásha-lot ‖ -lō) *n.* The **sperm whale** *(see).* [French, from Spanish and Portuguese *cachalote†.*]

cache (kash) *n.* **1.** A hole or similar hiding place for the concealment and storage of provisions, weapons, or valuables. **2.** A store of goods or articles hidden in a cache.
~*tr.v.* **cached, caching, caches.** To store in a hiding place for future use. See Synonyms at **hide.** [French, from *cacher,* to hide, from Vulgar Latin *cŏacticāre* (unattested), to compress, from Latin *cŏactāre,* to constrain, from *cōgere* (past participle *cŏactus*), to drive together : *com-,* together + *agere,* to drive.]

ca·chet (káshay ‖ *U.S.* ka-sháy) *n.* **1.** Distinction; prestige: *social cachet.* **2.** A commemorative design stamped on an envelope to mark some postal or philatelic event. **3.** *Archaic.* A seal on a letter or document. **4.** A distinguishing mark or feature. **5.** A capsule formerly used by pharmacists for presenting an unpleasant drug. [Old French, from *cacher,* to hide, press together. See **cache.**]

ca·chex·i·a (ka-kéksi-ə) *n. Archaic.* A general wasting of the body or weakening of the brain during any debilitating chronic disease. [Late Latin, from Greek *kakhexia,* bad condition of the body : CAC(O)- + *hexis,* condition, from *ekhein,* to hold, be in a condition.] —**ca·chec·tic** (-kektik) *adj.*

cach·in·nate (kácki-nayt) *intr.v.* **-nated, -nating, -nates.** *Archaic.* To laugh loudly, hard, or convulsively; guffaw. [Latin *cachinnāre†.*] —**cach·in·na·tion** (-náysh'n) *n.*

ca·chou (káshōō, ka-shōō) *n.* **1.** An astringent, **catechu** *(see).* **2.** A pastille used to sweeten the breath. [French, from Portuguese *cachu,* from Malayalam *cāccu.*]

ca·chu·cha (kə-chōō-chə, ka- ‖ kaa-, -chaa) *n.* A Spanish solo dance in ¾ time. [Spanish, origin obscure.]

ca·cique (ka-séek, kə-) *n.* Also **ca·zique** (-zéek). **1.** An Indian chief, especially in the Spanish West Indies and other parts of Latin America during colonial and postcolonial times. **2.** A powerful local politician in Latin America or Spain. **3.** Any of various tropical American orioles. [Spanish, of Arawakan origin; akin to Arawak *kassequa,* chief, Taino *cacique.*]

cack-handed (kák-hándid) *adj. Informal.* **1.** Awkward; clumsy. **2.** Left-handed. [Dialect *cack,* to defecate, probably from Middle Low German *cacāre;* sense "clumsy" (hence, left-handed), probably alluding to the mess made by a clumsy person.]

cack·le (káck'l) *v.* **-led, -ling, -les.** —*intr.* **1.** To make the shrill, broken cry characteristic of a hen after laying an egg. **2.** To laugh

or talk in a similar manner. —*tr.* To utter in cackles.
~*n.* **1.** The act or sound of cackling. **2.** Shrill, brittle laughter. **3.** Foolish chatter. —**cut the cackle.** *Informal.* **1.** To stop foolish chatter or noise. **2.** To come to the point. Used in the imperative. [Middle English *cakelen,* probably from Middle Low German *kakeln* (imitative).] —**cack·ler** *n.*

caco- *comb. form.* Indicates bad, incorrect, or unpleasant; for example, **cacography.** [Greek *kako-,* from *kakos,* bad.]

cac·o·dyl (kácka-dīl, -dil) *n.* **Tetramethyldiarsine** *(see).* [Greek *kakōdēs,* bad-smelling : CACO- + -*ōdēs,* from *ozein,* to smell + -YL.] —**cac·o·dyl·ic** *adj.*

cac·o·e·thes (kácko̅-éetheez) *n. Archaic.* A mania or irresistible compulsion; a pernicious habit. [Latin, from Greek *kakoēthes,* from the neuter of *kakoēthēs,* ill-disposed, abominable, malignant : CACO- + *ēthos,* custom, disposition.]

cac·o·gen·ics (kácka-jénniks) *n.* **Dysgenics** *(see).* [CACO- + -GENIC(S).] —**cac·o·gen·ic** *adj.*

ca·cog·ra·phy (ka-kóggrafi, ka-) *n.* **1.** Bad handwriting. Compare **calligraphy. 2.** Incorrect spelling. Compare **orthography.** [CACO- + -GRAPHY.]

cac·o·mis·tle (kácka-miss'l) *n.* Also **cac·o·mix·le** (-miks'l). Either of two small, carnivorous mammals, *Bassariscus astutus,* of the southwest United States, or *Jentinkia sumichrasti,* of Central America, related to the raccoons and having greyish or brownish fur and a black-banded tail. Also called "ringtail", "ring-tailed cat". [Mexican Spanish, from Nahuatl *tlacomiztli : tlaco,* half + *miztli,* puma.]

ca·coph·o·ny (ka-kóffani, ka-) *n., pl.* **-nies. 1.** Jarring, discordant sound; dissonance. **2.** The use of harsh-sounding or unharmonious language. Compare **euphony.** [French *cacophonie,* from Greek *kakophōnia,* from *kakophōnos : kako-* + *phōnē,* sound.] —**ca·coph·o·nous** *adj.* —**ca·coph·o·nous·ly** *adv.*

cac·tus (kák-tass) *n., pl.* **-tuses** or **-ti** (-tī). Any of a large group of plants of the family Cactaceae, mostly native to arid regions of the New World. They are characterised by thick, fleshy, often prickly stems that function as leaves and in some species have showy flowers and edible fruit. [New Latin, from Latin, the cardoon, from Greek *kaktos†.*]

Usage: The regular English plural of this word, *cactuses,* is increasingly being used in formal contexts in place of *cacti.* In strictly technical usage, *cacti* remains the preferred form.

ca·cu·mi·nal (ka-kéwmin'l, ka-) *adj. Phonetics.* Pronounced with the tip of the tongue turned back and up towards the roof of the mouth; retroflex.
~*n. Phonetics.* A cacuminal consonant. [Latin *cacūmen* (stem *cacūmin-*), summit, treetop, point.]

cad (kad) *n.* An ungentlemanly man. Now usually used humorously. [Short for CADDIE (in earliest sense, "army cadet").] —**cad·dish** *adj.* —**cad·dish·ly** *adv.* —**cad·dish·ness** *n.*

ca·das·tre, ca·das·ter (ka-dástar) *n.* A public record, survey, or map of the value, extent, and ownership of land as a basis of taxation. [French *cadastre,* from Italian *catastro,* variant of Old Italian *catastico,* from Late Greek *katastikhon,* list, from *kata stikhon,* "line by line".] —**ca·das·tral** *adj.*

ca·dav·er (ka-dáavar, -dáyvar, -dávvar) *n.* A dead body, especially one considered for medical purposes or intended for dissection. [Latin, from *cadere,* to fall, "die".] —**ca·dav·er·ic** *adj.*

ca·dav·er·ine (ka-dávvareen) *n.* A syrupy, colourless fuming ptomaine, $NH_2(CH_2)_5NH_2$, formed from decaying animal flesh.

ca·dav·er·ous (ka-dávva-rass, -dáava-) *adj.* **1. a.** Corpselike. **b.** Sickly pale. **2.** Gaunt and haggard; emaciated: *a cadaverous face.* —**ca·dav·er·ous·ly** *adv.* —**ca·dav·er·ous·ness** *n.*

Cad·bur·y (kád-bri, -bari), **George** (1839–1922). British businessman, Liberal, and Quaker philanthropist. With his brother Richard (1835–99), he took over his father's cocoa and chocolate business and founded Cadbury Brothers. One of his principal concerns was to improve employees' working and living conditions.

cad·die, cad·dy (káddi) *n., pl.* **-dies.** A golfer's hired attendant, who carries his clubs.
~*intr.v.* **caddied, -dying, -dies.** To serve as a caddie. [French *cadet,* CADET.]

caddie car *n.* A light two-wheeled trolley used for carrying golf clubs. Also called "caddie cart".

cad·dis fly (káddiss) *n.* Any of various four-winged insects of the order Trichoptera, found near lakes and streams. [17th century: origin obscure.]

caddis worm *n.* The aquatic, wormlike larva of the caddis fly, commonly enclosed in a cylindrical case covered with grains of sand, fragments of shell, or the like.

cad·dy¹ (káddi) *n., pl.* **-dies.** A small box or other container, especially for holding tea. [Originally "a container of one caddy of tea", from Malay *kātī* (weight of 605 grams; 1⅓ pounds).]

caddy². Variant of **caddie.**

cade¹ (kayd) *adj.* Left by its mother and raised by hand: *a cade calf.* [Middle English *cad†.*]

cade² *n.* A juniper shrub, *Juniperus oxycedrus,* of the Mediterranean region, the wood of which yields an oily brown liquid *(oil of cade)* used to treat skin ailments. [French, from Old Provençal, from Medieval Latin *catanus,* probably from Gaulish *catānos* (unattested).]

Cade, Jack (died 1450). English rebel who led an unsuccessful Kentish rebellion against Henry VI (1450) and called for the return of Richard Plantagenet, the Duke of York, from Ireland.

-cade *n. comb. form.* Indicates procession or parade; for example, **motorcade.** [From CAVALCADE.]

ca·delle (ka-dél) *n.* A small blackish beetle, *Tenebroides mauritanicus,* both the larval and adult forms of which damage stored grain and packaged foods. [French, from Provençal *cadello,* from Latin *catella,* feminine of *catellus, catulus,* offspring.]

ca·dence (káyd'nss) *n.* **1.** Balanced, rhythmic flow, as of poetry or oratory. **2.** The measure or beat of movement, as in dancing or marching. **3. a.** A falling inflection of the voice, as at the end of a sentence. **b.** The general modulation of the voice; intonation. **4.** *Music.* A progression of chords moving to a harmonic close or point of rest. —See Synonyms at **rhythm.** [Middle English, from Old French, from Old Italian *cadenza,* from *cadere,* to fall, from Latin.] —**ca·denced** *adj.*

ca·dent (káyd'nt) *adj.* **1.** Having cadence or rhythm. **2.** *Archaic.* Falling. [Latin *cadēns* (stem *cadent-*), present participle of *cadere,* to fall.]

ca·den·za (ka-dénza) *n. Music.* **1.** An elaborate ornamental flourish interpolated into an aria or other vocal piece. **2.** An extended, virtuoso section for the soloist near the end of a movement of a concerto. [Italian, CADENCE.]

Ca·der Id·ris (ka'adar íddriss, káddar). Mountain ridge in south Gwynedd, Wales. Its highest peak, Pen-y-Gader, rises to 892 metres (2,927 feet). It is part of the Snowdonia National Park.

ca·det (ka-dét) *n.* **1.** A student training for service in the armed forces or police force, usually at a college. **2.** A younger son or brother.
~*adj.* Pertaining to or descended from a younger son: *the cadet branch of the family.* [French, from Gascon dialect *capdet,* captain, chief, from Late Latin *capitellum,* "small head", from Latin *caput,* head.] —**ca·det·ship** *n.*

cadet corps *n.* In Britain, a company of schoolboys receiving extracurricular military training, usually at a public school.

cadge (kaj) *v.* **cadged, cadging, cadges.** *Informal.* —*tr.* To get by begging or pretending to borrow. —*intr.* To beg or borrow something without intent to repay. [Back-formation from *cadger,* carrier, Middle English *cadgear,* from *caggen†,* to carry wares.] —**cadg·er** *n.*

ca·di (ka'adi, káydi) *n., pl.* **-dis.** A judge in a Muslim country. [Arabic *kādi,* from *kadā,* to judge.]

Ca·diz (ka-díz; *Spanish* ka'atheeth). Capital of Cadiz province in Spain. Situated at the entrance to the Bay of Cadiz, it is an important seaport, founded by the Phoenicians in c.1100 B.C. After the conquest of the Americas, it was used as a base for the Spanish treasure fleets.

cad·mi·um (kádmi-am) *n. Symbol* **Cd** A soft, bluish-white metallic element, occurring primarily in zinc, copper, and lead ores. It is easily cut with a knife and is used in low-friction, fatigue-resistant alloys, solders, dental amalgams, nickel-cadmium accumulators, neutron-absorbing control rods in nuclear reactors, and rust-proof electroplating. Atomic number 48, atomic weight 112.40, melting point 320.9°C, boiling point 765°C, relative density 8.65, valency 2. [New Latin, from Latin *cadmia,* zinc ore, CALAMINE (because cadmium is found together with calamine in the ore).] —**cad·mic** (kádmik) *adj.*

cadmium cell *n.* **1.** A photocell of a type having a cadmium electrode that is sensitive to ultraviolet radiation. **2.** A **Weston standard cell** *(see).*

cadmium sulphate *n.* A colourless crystalline solid, $CdSO_4$, used as an antiseptic.

cadmium sulphide *n.* An orange or yellow insoluble solid, CdS, used as a pigment in paints *(cadmium yellow).*

Cad·mus (kádmass). *Greek Mythology.* A Phoenician prince who killed a dragon and sowed its teeth, from which sprang up an army of men who fought one another until only five survived; with these Cadmus founded the Greek city of Thebes. —**Cad·me·an** *adj.*

cad·re (ka'adar || *chiefly U.S.* káddri) *n.* **1.** A nucleus of trained personnel, especially in a military or political organisation, around which a larger organisation can be built and trained. **2.** A member of such a nucleus. [French, from Italian *quadro,* from Latin *quādrum,* a square, from *quādrus.*]

ca·du·ce·us (ka-déwssi-ass, -déwshi- || -dōóssi-, -dōóshi-) *n., pl.* **-cei** (-ī). **1. a.** An ancient herald's wand or staff. **b.** *Mythology.* A winged staff with two serpents twined around it, carried by the Greek messenger-god Hermes. **2.** A similar staff used as the symbol of the medical profession. [Latin *cādūceus,* from Greek (Doric) *karukeion,* from *karux,* herald.] —**ca·du·ce·an** (-an) *adj.*

ca·du·ci·ty (ka-déwss-ati || -dōóss-) *n. Formal.* **1.** The frailty of old age; senility. **2.** Perishability; impermanence. [French *caducité,* from *caduc,* frail, falling, from Latin *cadūcus,* CADUCOUS.]

ca·du·cous (ka-déwk-ass || -dōók-) *adj. Biology.* Dropping off or shedding at an early stage of development. Said of the gills of amphibians or the leaves of certain plants. [Latin *cadūcus,* falling, frail, from *cadere,* to fall.]

cae·cil·i·an (see-sílli-an, si-, -séeli-) *n.* Any of various legless, burrowing, wormlike amphibians of the order Gymnophiona (formerly Apoda), of tropical regions. [New Latin *Caecilia,* type genus, from Latin *caecilia,* lizard, from *caecus,* blind (in allusion to a lizard's small eyes).]

cae·cum, *U.S.* **ce·cum** (sée-kam) *n., pl.* **-ca** (-ka). *Anatomy.* **1.** A blind-ended pouch marking the junction of the small and large intestines. Also called "blind gut". **2.** Any of various other anatomical pouches. [Latin, short for *intestinum caecum,* blind intestine, translation of Greek *tuphlon enteron.*] —**cae·cal** *adj.*

Caed·mon (kádmən) (died *c.* A.D. 680). The earliest known English poet, who, according to Bede, was a cowherd at the monastery of Whitby and who, as an old man, was told in a vision to sing "the beginning of all created things". He became a monk and spent the remainder of his days writing songs and poems based on the Scriptures.

Cae·li·an (seéli-ən) *n.* One of the seven hills of Rome.

Caen (koN). Port and administrative centre of the département of Calvados, northwest France, situated on the river Orne. It first came to prominence under William the Conqueror, who founded the Abbaye aux Hommes where he is buried. His wife Matilda founded the Abbaye aux Dames. Caen was a Huguenot stronghold in the 16th and 17th centuries and saw heavy fighting in World War II. Industries include machinery, textiles, and commerce.

cae·no·gen·e·sis, ce·no·gen·e·sis (seenō-jénnə-siss) *n.* The development of structural and organic adaptations in an embryo or larva that are not retained in the adult form. [Greek *kainos,* fresh, new + GENESIS.] —**cae·no·gen·etic** (-jə-néttik) *adj.* —**cae·nogen·e·tic·al·ly** *adv.*

Caer·le·on (kaar-leé-ən, kər-). Town in south Gwent, on the river Usk, in Wales. It was the site of the Roman fortress of Isca and has the best preserved Roman amphitheatre in Britain.

Caer·nar·fon or **Caer·nar·von** (kər-nárv'n). County town and port on the south shore of the Menai Strait, in north Wales. In 1284 Edward I built the castle, reputedly the birthplace of Edward II, the first Prince of Wales. Prince Charles, the 21st Prince of Wales, was invested here (1969).

Caer·nar·von·shire (kər-nárv'n-shər, -sheer || -shī). Formerly, a county in north Wales.

Caer·phil·ly[1] (kər-fílli, kaar-, kair-). *Welsh* **Caer·ffi·li.** Market and industrial centre in south Wales, and the home of Caerphilly cheese. Caerphilly Castle, built between the 13th and 14th centuries, is the largest in Wales.

Caer·phil·ly[2] *n.* A mild, crumbly white cheese originally from Wales. [After CAERPHILLY.]

Cae·sar (seézər) *n.* **1.** A surname of the early Roman emperors that after Hadrian became the title of the junior imperial colleague of the **Augustus** (*see*). **2.** A dictator or autocrat. **3.** *Small* **c.** *Informal.* A Caesarean section.

Caesar, (Gaius) Julius (*c.*100–44 B.C.). Roman general, statesman, and writer. During his Gaul campaign, he invaded Britain (55 B.C.) and returned to Rome a popular hero. He had, however, many political enemies, including Pompey, who persuaded the Senate to order Caesar to resign his army command. Instead, Caesar took his legions across the river Rubicon (49) and crushed Pompey at Pharsalus (48). In 47 B.C. he pursued his enemies to Egypt where he installed Cleopatra as queen. It is widely believed that Cleopatra later gave birth to his son, Caesarion. Returning to Rome (45), he was given a mandate by the people to rule, as dictator, for life. He introduced many reforms, including the **Julian calendar** (*see*) and public libraries. On 15 March, 44 B.C. (The Ides of March), Caesar was murdered in the Senate by a group of republicans, led by Cassius and Brutus, who feared that he was about to establish a monarchy with himself as king.

Cae·sar·e·an, Cae·sar·i·an (see-zaír-i-ən, si-) *adj.* Pertaining to Julius Caesar or the Caesars.
~*n.* A Caesarean section.

Caesarean section *n. Sometimes small* **c.** A surgical incision through the abdominal wall and uterus, performed to deliver a baby. Also called "Caesarean", informally "caesar". [From an unhistorical tradition that the eponymous ancestor of the Roman family *Caesar* (or Julius *Caesar* himself) was born by this operation, and named Caesar *ā caesō mātris ūtere,* "from the *incised* womb of his mother", from *caesus,* past participle of *caedere,* to cut.]

Cae·sa·re·a Pal·es·ti·nae (seézə-reér pál-i-stīni || -rée-ə). Ancient city in Israel, lying south of Haifa. It was founded by Herod the Great in 13 B.C. as a port on the Mediterranean coast. An early centre of Christianity, often referred to in the New Testament, Caesarea became the capital of Roman Judaea. The port declined after Muslim occupation (A.D. 638) and, though revived by the Crusaders, was destroyed by the Muslims (1265).

Cae·sar·ism (seézə-riz'm) *n.* Military dictatorship. —**Cae·sar·ist** *n.* —**Cae·sar·is·tic** (-rístik) *adj.*

caesar salad *n.* A salad made with lettuce, cheese, and croutons, and dressed with raw egg, oil, and lemon juice.

cae·si·um, *U.S.* **ce·si·um** (seé-zi-əm) *n. Symbol.* **Cs** A soft, silvery, very white ductile metal, used in photocells, and the radioisotope caesium-137 is used in radiotherapy. Atomic number 55, atomic weight 132.905, melting point 28.5°C, boiling point 690°C, relative density 1.87, valency 1. [Latin *caesius,* silvery white (referring to its spectrum lines).]

caesium clock *n.* A form of atomic clock based on the frequency of the radiation absorbed in changing the state of caesium nuclei in a magnetic field. It is used in the definition of the second.

caes·pi·tose, *U.S.* **ces·pi·tose** (séess-pi-tōss, séss-, -tōz) *adj. Botany.* Growing in dense tufts or turflike clumps; matted. [New Latin *caespitosus,* from Latin *caespes*† (stem *caespit*-), turf, grassy plain.] —**caes·pi·tose·ly** *adv.*

cae·su·ra, ce·su·ra (si-zéwr-ə, see- || -zhoór-, zoór-) *n., pl.* **-ras** or **-rae** (-ee). **1.** A pause in a line of verse dictated by sense or natural speech rhythm rather than by metre. It is conventionally indicated by an oblique stroke: "*Drink deep,* / *or taste not the Pierian Spring*" (Alexander Pope). **2.** In Latin and Greek verse, a break in a line caused by the ending of a word within a foot, especially when this coincides with a sense division: "*Arma virumque cano* / *Troiae qui primus ab oris*" (Virgil). **3.** *Music.* A pause or breathing at a point of rhythmic division in a melody. [Latin, "a cutting off", from *caedere,* to cut off.] —**cae·su·ral, cae·su·ric** *adj.*

Cae·ta·no (kī-taánō), **Marcello José das Neves Alves** (1906–80). Portuguese prime minister (1968–74). Following Salazar, he was comparatively liberal and reduced the harshness of the previous regime. He was overthrown by a military coup.

ca·fé, ca·fe (káffay, káffi || *U.S.* ka-fáy, kə-. *Note: there are also the informal pronunciations* kaf *and* kayf. *See* **caff**) *n.* **1.** In Britain, a small restaurant or coffee bar serving light meals or snacks, and non-alcoholic drinks. **2.** In Europe and elsewhere, a bar. **3.** In South Africa, a small shop selling sweets, cold drinks, and the like, and sometimes groceries. [French, COFFEE.]

Usage: The use of this word without the accent is now widespread in informal written English, and is increasingly to be found in shop signs and advertisements. In speech, the informal pronunciation is nowadays (káffi), with (káffay) restricted to careful use.

café au lait (ō láy) *n., pl.* **cafés au lait. 1.** Coffee served with hot milk. **2.** A light coffee colour. [French, "coffee with milk".]

café filtre (fíl-tr, -trə) *n.* Coffee made by pouring boiling water through a filter filled with ground coffee. [French.]

caf·e·te·ri·a (káffi-téer-i-ə) *n.* A restaurant in which the customers are served at a counter and carry their meals to tables. [American Spanish, coffee shop, from Spanish *cafetero,* coffee maker or seller, from *café,* COFFEE.]

caff (kaf) *n. British Informal.* A café.

caf·feine (káffeen, káffi-in) *n.* A bitter white alkaloid, $C_8H_{10}N_4O_2 \cdot H_2O$, derived from coffee, tea, and cocoa, and used as a stimulant and diuretic. [German *Kaffein,* from *Kaffee,* COFFEE.]

caf·tan, kaf·tan (káf-tan, -taan, -tən || *U.S. also* kaf-tán, kaaf-taán) *n.* **1.** In the Near East, a full-length tunic with long sleeves and a sash at the waist, worn under a coat. **2.** A westernised version of this consisting of a loose and often brightly coloured waist-length or ankle-length tunic. [Russian *kaftan,* from Turkish *kaftān.*]

cage (kayj) *n.* **1.** A structure for confining birds or animals, enclosed on at least one side by a grating of wires or bars in order to let in air and light. **2. a.** Any enclosure that serves as a means of confining prisoners. **b.** Anything that confines, physically or psychologically. **3.** Any framework having a cagelike appearance or construction. **4.** A rudimentary lift car, especially one used in a mine.
~*tr.v.* **caged, caging, cages.** To put in a cage; lock up or confine. [Middle English, from Old French, from Latin *cavea,* a hollow, enclosure, from *cavus,* hollow.]

Cage, John (1912–92). Avant-garde U.S. composer, whose works include *Sonatas and Interludes,* for a prepared piano with its strings damped by wood and metal (1946–48), *Imaginary Landscape No. 4,* for 12 randomly tuned radios (1951), and *4 minutes 33 seconds,* silence in three movements for any instrument or instruments (1954).

cage bird *n.* A bird of a type that is often kept in a cage.

cage·ling (káyjling) *n.* A caged bird.

cag·ey, cag·y (káyji) *adj.* **-ier, -iest.** *Informal.* Wary; careful; unwilling to disclose information. [20th century (U.S.) : origin obscure.] —**cag·i·ly** *adv.* —**cag·i·ness** *n.*

Ca·glia·ri (kal-yaári). Administrative and industrial centre of Sardinia, Italy. Also a seaport, it lies at the mouth of the river Mannu on the south side of the island. Founded by the Carthaginians, the city has a Roman amphitheatre, a basilica (fifth century), a massive tower (1304), and a university (1606).

Ca·glio·stro (kal-yóstrō), **Alessandro, Conte di,** born Giuseppe Balsamo (1743–95). Italian adventurer who became famous throughout Europe as an alchemist and magician. He died in Italy, following his incarceration for promoting freemasonry.

Cag·ney (kág-ni), **James** (1899–1986). U.S. actor famous for his portrayals of gangsters, hard characters injected with elements of humanity. His films include *Public Enemy* (1931), *Angels with Dirty Faces* (1938), *The Roaring Twenties* (1939), and *Yankee Doodle Dandy* (1942), for which he won an Academy Award.

ca·goule, ka·goule (kə-goól, ka-) *n.* A light, hooded, waterproof overgarment, generally of nylon, reaching to the waist or knees. [French, "cowl".]

ca·hoots (kə-hoóts) *pl.n. Informal.* Collaboration of a questionable nature. Used in the phrase *in cahoots.* [19th century : origin obscure.]

Ca·ho·ra Bas·sa Dam (kə-háwrə bássə). Hydroelectric project on the Zambezi river in Mozambique, completed in 1979.

Cai·a·phas (kí-ə-fass, -fəss || *chiefly U.S.* káy-), **Joseph.** Jewish High Priest; president of the council condemning Jesus.

caiman. Variant of **cayman.**

cain, kain, kane *n.* In former times in Scotland, tax or rent payments made in kind.

Cain[1]. The eldest son of Adam and Eve, who killed his brother Abel out of jealousy. Genesis 4. [Latin, from Greek *Kain,* from Hebrew *Qayin,* "creature".]

Cain[2] *n.* A murderer. —**raise Cain.** *Informal.* To create a great disturbance or uproar; make trouble. [From CAIN.]

-caine *n. comb. form.* Indicates a synthetic alkaloid in anaesthetic drugs; for example, **eucaine.** [From (CO)CAINE.]

Cainozoic. Variant of **Cenozoic.**

ca·ïque (kaa-éek, kī-) *n.* **1.** A long, narrow rowing boat used on the Bosporus. **2.** A small sailing vessel used in the eastern Mediterranean. [French, from Italian *caicco,* from Turkish *kayik.*]

caird (kaird) *n. Scottish.* A travelling tinker or handyman. [Scottish Gaelic *ceard,* artist, craftsman, from Old Irish *cerd,* art, artist.]

Cai·rene (kī-reen) *n.* A native or inhabitant of Cairo. —**Cai·rene** *adj.*

cairn (kairn) *n.* A mound of stones erected as a landmark or memorial. [Middle English *carne,* from Celtic *kar-n-, kr-ag-* (both unattested).] —**cairned** (kairnd) *adj.*

cairn·gorm (káirn-gawrm) *n.* A smoky-brown or yellow variety of quartz, used as a semiprecious gem. Also called "smoky quartz". [After *Cairngorm Mountains,* where it is found.]

Cairn·gorm Mountains (káirn-gawrm). Mountain range in northeast Scotland forming part of the Grampians. A favourite winter sports resort, includes Ben Macdhui, at 1309 metres (4,295 feet) the second highest peak in Scotland. The area was declared a nature reserve for arctic flora and fauna (1954).

Cairns (kairnz). Seaport on Trinity Bay in Queensland, Australia. It is a tourist centre for the Great Barrier Reef.

cairn terrier *n.* A small dog of a breed developed in Scotland, having a broad head and a rough, shaggy coat. [So called because it hunts among cairns.]

Cai·ro (kī-ō). *Arabic* **Al-Qahira.** Capital of Egypt, lying on the east bank of the river Nile. It is the largest city in Africa and the Middle East, and is one of the most important cultural, commercial, and political centres of the Arab world. The pyramids at Giza, 13 kilometres (8 miles) southwest of Cairo, and Egypt's many other monuments and treasures, ensure a busy tourist industry. Other industries include textiles, food processing, plastics, and motor vehicle assembly. Al-Fustat, now Old Cairo, was established by Arab conquerors as a military camp (A.D. 642). Al-Qahira was founded by the Fatimids as their capital (968). Saladin built the citadel (*c.*1176), and extended the city's walls against Crusader attack. Cairo prospered under the Mamelukes, but fell to the Ottoman Turks (1517). Following Napoleon's occupation (1798–1801), it became the capital of a virtually independent kingdom under the pasha Muhammad Ali (1805–49). The Al-Azhar university (970) is reputedly the world's leading centre for Koranic studies, and the city is also the headquarters of the Coptic church in Egypt.

cais·son (kə-sóon, káyss'n ‖ *chiefly U.S.* káy-son. *Note: engineers say* kə-sóon.) *n.* **1.** A watertight structure within which construction work is carried on. **2.** A watertight float, a **camel** *(see).* **3.** A floating structure used to close off the entrance to a dock or canal lock. **4.** A large box open at the top and one side, designed to fit against the side of a ship and used to repair damaged hulls under water. **5.** *Military.* **a.** A large box used to hold ammunition. **b.** A horse-drawn vehicle, usually two-wheeled, once used to carry ammunition. **6.** A sunken ceiling panel. [French, from Old French *casson,* from Italian *cassa,* chest, box, from Latin *capsa.*]

caisson disease *n.* **Decompression sickness** *(see).*

Caith·ness (káyth-néss). Former county in northeast Scotland, part of Highland Unitary Authority area. Mainly infertile moorland and mountains, it sustains sheep farming, fishing, and crofting. It includes the towns of Wick and Thurso, and Dunnet Head, the most northerly point of Scotland's mainland.

cai·tiff (káytif) *n. Archaic.* A base coward; a wretch.
~*adj.* Base and cowardly. [Middle English *caitif,* prisoner, captive, wretch, from Old French, from Latin *captīvus,* **CAPTIVE.**]

caj·e·put, caj·u·put (káj-ə-pŏot, -pət) *n.* **1.** A tree, *Melaleuca leucadendron,* native to Australia, having whitish flowers and leaves that yield an aromatic medicinal oil. **2.** The oil obtained from this tree. [Malay *kayu puteh* : *kayu,* tree + *puteh,* white.]

ca·jole (kə-jōl) *tr.v.* **-joled, -joling, -joles.** To persuade by means of flattery; coax; wheedle. [French *cajoler†.*] —**ca·jol·er** *n.* —**ca·jol·er·y** *n.* —**ca·jol·ing·ly** *adv.*

Ca·jun, Ca·jan (káyjən) *n.* **1.** A native of Louisiana believed to be descended from the French exiles from Acadia. **2.** The dialect of these people. **3.** Cajun music. [Alteration of **ACADIAN.**]

Cajun music *n.* A type of folk music originating among the Cajuns, typically using accordions and fiddles.

cake (kayk) *n.* **1.** A sweetened baked mixture of flour, liquid, eggs, and other ingredients, usually loaf- or layer-shaped. **2.** A flat, thin mass of dough or batter, baked or fried, such as a pancake or oatcake. **3.** A patty of fried food, such as a fishcake. **4.** A shaped or moulded piece, as of soap. **5.** An aggregate of benefits, especially financial benefits, that are to be divided up or to be distributed: *workers want a larger slice of the cake.* —**go** or **sell like hot cakes.** To be in great demand; sell in large quantities.
~*v.* **caked, caking, cakes.** —*tr.* To cause to dry out and harden around something; encrust. —*intr.* To form a hard, dried-out mass. [Middle English *cake, kake,* from Old Norse *kaka.*]

cake·hole (káyk-hōl) *n. Slang.* The mouth.

cakes and ale *pl.n.* Enjoyment of the good things in life.

cake·walk (káyk-wawk) *n.* **1.** Formerly, a promenade or walk in which those performing the most complex and unusual steps won cakes as prizes. **2. a.** A strutting dance based on this promenade. **b.** The music for this dance. **3.** *Informal.* Something easily done.
~*intr.v.* **cakewalked, -walking, -walks.** To perform a cakewalk.

cal calorie (small).

Cal calorie (large).

cal. **1.** calendar. **2.** calibre.

Cal·a·bar bean (kál-ə-baar) *n.* The dark brown poisonous seed of a woody vine, *Physostigma venenosum,* of tropical Africa. It is the source of the drug **physostigmine** *(see).* Also called "ordeal bean". [After *Calabar,* city in Nigeria.]

cal·a·bash (kál-ə-bash) *n.* **1.** A tropical American tree, *Crescentia cujete,* bearing large, rounded fruit. **2.** A vine, the **bottle gourd** *(see).* **3.** The hard-shelled fruit of either of these plants. **4.** A utensil, such as a dish, ladle, or tobacco pipe, made from the fruit of a calabash. [Obsolete French *calabasse,* from Spanish *calabaza†.*]

cal·a·boose (kál-ə-bŏoss) *n. U.S. Slang.* A jail. [Louisiana French *calabouse,* from Spanish *calabozo†,* a dungeon.]

cal·a·bre·se (kál-ə-bráy-say, -breez) *n.* **1.** An Italian variety of broccoli, *Brassica oleracea,* having a branched, greenish flower head. **2.** The flower head of this plant eaten as a vegetable before the green, tightly clustered buds have opened. [Italian, "Calabrian".]

Ca·lab·ri·a (kə-láb-ri-ə, -laáb-, -láyb-). Region in Italy comprising the provinces of Cosenza, Cantanzaro, and Reggio di Calabria, forming the "toe of Italy" between the Ionian and the Tyrrhenian Seas. It is mainly mountainous, with extensive forests. Crotone is an industrial centre, but the area is economically underdeveloped. The main sources of income are the cultivation of vines, citrus fruit, and olives, sheep and goat herding, and granite quarrying. Cantanzaro is the capital. —**Ca·lab·ri·an** *n. & adj.*

ca·la·di·um (kə-láydi-əm) *n.* Any of various tropical plants of the genus *Caladium,* widely cultivated as potted plants for their showy, variegated foliage. [New Latin *Caladium,* from Malay *kĕladi,* araceous plant.]

Ca·lais (kál-ay, -i; *formerly* -iss; *French* ka-láy). Industrial town and seaport in the Pas-de-Calais département, France. It lies 35 kilometres (22 miles) east-southeast of Dover, on the shortest crossing between England and France. Calais was conquered by Edward III (1347) after a siege in which six burghers offered their lives for the town, but intervention by Edward's queen, Philippa, saved them. Calais remained in English possession until 1558. It was almost destroyed in World War II, during the Dunkirk withdrawal. Industries include fishing, boatbuilding, textiles, and clothing.

cal·a·man·co (kál-ə-mángkō) *n., pl.* **-cos** or **-coes.** A glossy woollen fabric with a check pattern on only one side. [16th century : origin obscure.]

cal·a·man·der (kál-ə-mandər) *n.* The hard, black-and-brown-striped wood of certain tropical Asiatic trees of the genus *Diospyros,* used in furniture. [Probably from Dutch *kalamander(hout),* calamander (wood), perhaps metathetic variant of **COROMANDEL** (**COAST**).]

ca·la·ma·ri (kaá-lə-máree) *pl.n.* Squid as food. [Italian, plural of *calamaro.*]

cal·a·mine (kál-ə-mīn ‖ -min) *n.* **1.** A mineral, **smithsonite** *(see).* **2.** A white or sometimes iron- or copper-stained mineral, essentially $Zn_4Si_2O_7(OH)_2 \cdot H_2O$. Also called "hemimorphite". **3.** A pink, odourless, tasteless powder of zinc oxide with a small amount of ferric oxide, dissolved in mineral oils and used in skin lotions. [French, from Medieval Latin *calamīna,* alteration of Latin *cadmia,* from Greek *kadmeia,* "Cadmean (earth)" (first found near Thebes, city founded by Cadmus), from *kadmeios,* of **CADMUS.**]

cal·a·mint (kál-ə-mint) *n.* Any of several aromatic plants of the genus *Calamintha;* especially, *C. ascendens,* native to Eurasia, having clusters of purplish or pink flowers. [Middle English *calament,* from Old French, from Medieval Latin *calamentum,* variant of Late Latin *calaminthē,* from Greek *kalaminthē†.*]

cal·a·mite (kál-ə-mīt) *n.* Any of various extinct treelike Carboniferous plants of the genus *Calamites,* resembling the horsetails, but much larger, and found only as fossils. [New Latin *Calamites,* from Late Greek *kalamitēs,* reedlike, from Greek, of a reed, from *kalamos,* reed.]

ca·lam·i·tous (kə-lámmitəss) *adj.* Causing or involving a disaster. —**ca·lam·i·tous·ly** *adv.* —**ca·lam·i·tous·ness** *n.*

ca·lam·i·ty (kə-lámməti) *n., pl.* **-ties.** **1.** A disaster, especially one that leads to personal loss and suffering. **2.** Dire distress. —See Synonyms at **disaster.** [Middle English *calamite,* from Old French, from Latin *calamitās* (stem *calamitāt-).*]

Calamity (kə-lámməti) **Jane,** born Martha Cannary (*c.* 1852–1903). U.S. frontierswoman who has become a legend of the Wild West. Often dressing in men's clothes, she is reputed to have been a crack shot and a skilled horse-rider.

cal·a·mus (kál-ə-məss) *n., pl.* **-mi** (-mī). **1.** A plant, the **sweet flag** *(see),* or its aromatic root. **2.** Any of various tropical Asiatic palms of the genus *Calamus,* from some of which rattan is obtained. **3.** A part of a feather, a **quill** *(see).* [Latin, reed, cane, from Greek *kalamos.*]

ca·lan·do (kə-lándō, ka- ‖ *chiefly U.S.* kaa-laándō) *adj. Music.* Gradually diminishing in tempo and volume.
~*adv. Music.* In a calando manner. [Italian, from Latin *calandum,* a slackening, from *calāre, chalāre,* to let fall, slacken, from Greek *khalan.*]

cal·an·dri·a (kə-lándri-ə) *n.* A heat exchanger, as in the core of a nuclear reactor, consisting of a vessel with vertical tubes passing through it.

ca·lash (kə-lásh) *n.* Also **ca·lèche** (kə-lésh). **1.** A carriage with low wheels and a collapsible top. **2.** The top of such a carriage. **3.** A woman's folding bonnet, fashionable in the late 18th century. [French *calèche,* from German *Kalesche,* from Czech *kolesa,* plural of *koleso,* wheel, from *kolo* (stem *koles-*), wheel, from Old Church Slavonic.]

cal·a·thus (kál-ə-thəss) *n., pl.* **-thi** (-thī). A vase-shaped basket represented in ancient Greek painting and sculpture. [Latin, from Greek *kalathos†*.]

cal·a·ver·ite (kə-lávvərīt, kál-ə-vaír-īt) *n.* A rare ore of gold, essentially gold telluride, AuTe₂, often containing silver. [After *Calaveras*, county in California, where it was discovered.]

cal·ca·ne·us (kal-káy-ni-əss) *n., pl.* **-nei** (-ī). Also **cal·ca·ne·um** (-əm) *pl.* **-nea** (-ə). The quadrangular bone at the back of the tarsus, forming the projection of the heel. Also called "heel bone". [Latin, "heel", from *calx* (stem *calc-*), heel.] —**cal·ca·ne·al** *adj.*

cal·car (kál-kaar) *n., pl.* **calcaria** (kal-kaír-i-ə). *Biology.* A spur or spurlike projection. [Latin, spur, from *calx* (stem *calc-*), heel.]

cal·car·e·ous (kal-kaír-i-əss) *adj.* Composed of, containing, or characteristic of calcium carbonate, calcium, or limestone; chalky. [Latin *calcārius,* from *calx* (stem *calc-*), lime.]

cal·ce·i·form (kál-si-i-fawrm, kal-sée-) *adj. Botany.* Slipper-shaped; calceolate. [Latin *calceus,* shoe (see **calceolate**) + -FORM.]

cal·ce·o·lar·i·a (kál-si-ə-laír-i-ə) *n.* Any of various plants of the genus *Calceolaria,* native to tropical America and widely cultivated for their yellow, speckled, slipper-shaped flowers. [New Latin, from Latin *calceolārius,* shoemaker, from *calceolus,* small shoe. See **calceolate**.]

cal·ce·o·late (kál-si-ə-layt) *adj. Botany.* Shaped like a slipper, as the blossoms of some orchids are. [Latin *calceolus,* diminutive of *calceus†,* shoe.]

cal·ces. Alternative plural of **calx.**

calci-, calc- *comb. form.* Indicates lime or calcium; for example, **calciferous, calcite.** [Latin *calx* (stem *calc-*), lime, limestone.]

cal·cic (kál-sik) *adj.* Composed of, containing, derived from, or pertaining to calcium or lime.

cal·ci·cole (kál-si-kōl) *n. Botany.* A plant that thrives in soil rich in lime. [French : CALCI- + -*cole,* dweller, from Latin -*cola* (see -**colous**).] —**cal·cic·o·lous** (kal-síckələss) *adj.*

cal·cif·er·ol (kal-síffər-ol ‖ -ōl) *n.* One of the forms in which **vitamin D** *(see)* occurs. [*Calciferous* + ergo*sterol.*]

cal·cif·er·ous (kal-síffərəss) *adj.* Of, forming, or containing calcium or calcium carbonate. [CALCI- + -FEROUS.]

cal·cif·ic (kal-siffik) *adj.* Producing salts of lime, as in the formation of eggshells in birds.

cal·ci·fi·ca·tion (kál-sifi-káysh'n) *n.* **1.** Impregnation with calcium or calcium salts, as with calcium carbonate. **2.** Hardening, as of tissue, by such impregnation. **3.** A substance, such as petrified wood, or a part so impregnated.

cal·ci·fuge (kál-si-fewj) *n.* A plant that does not thrive in lime-rich soil, preferring acid soil. —**cal·cif·u·gal** (-síffewg'l, -si-féwg'l), **cal·cif·u·gous** (-síffewgəss, -si-féwgəss) *adj.*

cal·ci·fy (kál-si-fī) *v.* **-fied, -fying, -fies.** —*tr.* To make stony or chalky by deposition of calcium salts. —*intr.* To become stony or chalky by deposition of calcium salts. [CALCI- + -FY.]

cal·cine (kál-sīn, -sin ‖ *U.S. also* kal-sín) *v.* **-cined, -cining, -cines.** —*tr.* To heat (a substance) to a high temperature but below the melting or fusing point, causing loss of moisture, reduction, or oxidation. —*intr.* To undergo oxidation as a result of heating. [Middle English *calcinen,* from Old French *calciner,* from Medieval Latin *calcīnāre,* from Latin *calx,* lime. See **calcium**.] —**cal·ci·na·tion** (kál-si-náysh'n) *n.*

cal·cite (kál-sīt) *n.* A common crystalline form of natural calcium carbonate, the basic constituent of limestone, marble, and chalk. Also called "calcspar". —**cal·cit·ic** (kál-síttik) *adj.*

cal·ci·ton·in (kál-si-tōnin) *n.* A hormone secreted by the thyroid that lowers the amount of calcium in the blood to within normal limits. Also called "thyrocalcitonin". [CALCI- + TON(IC) + -IN.]

cal·ci·um (kál-si-əm) *n. Symbol* **Ca** A silvery, moderately hard metallic element, constituting approximately three per cent of the earth's crust; a basic component of bone, shells, and teeth. It occurs naturally in limestone, gypsum, and fluorite, and its compounds are used to make plaster, quicklime, Portland cement, and metallurgic and electronic materials. Atomic number 20, atomic weight 40.08, melting point 842 to 848°C, boiling point 1,487°C, relative density 1.55, valency 2. [New Latin, from Latin *calx* (stem *calc-*), lime, limestone, from Greek *khalix†,* pebble.]

calcium carbide *n.* A greyish-black crystalline compound, CaC₂, obtained by heating pulverised limestone or quicklime with carbon and used to generate acetylene, as a dehydrating agent, and in the manufacture of graphite and hydrogen. Also called "carbide".

calcium carbonate *n.* A colourless or white crystalline compound, CaCO₃, occurring naturally as chalk, limestone, marble, and other forms and used in a wide variety of manufactured products including commercial chalk, medicines, and toothpastes.

calcium chloride *n.* A white deliquescent compound, CaCl₂, used chiefly as a drying agent, refrigerant, and preservative.

calcium cyanamide *n.* A grey-black compound, Ca(CN)₂, used as a fertiliser and weedkiller.

calcium fluoride *n.* A white powder, CaF₂, used in emery wheels, carbon electrodes, and cements.

calcium hydroxide *n.* A soft white powder, Ca(OH)₂, used in making mortar, cements, calcium salts, paints, hard rubber products, and petrochemicals. Also called "slaked lime", "caustic lime", "calcium hydrate".

calcium hypochlorite *n.* A white crystalline solid, Ca(OCl)₂, used as a bactericide, fungicide, and bleaching agent.

calcium light *n.* An intense white light produced by incandescent lime, **limelight** *(see).*

calcium oxalate *n.* A white crystalline powder, CaC₂O₄, used to make oxalic acid and found in many plant cells.

calcium oxide *n.* A white caustic lumpy powder, CaO, used as a refractory, as a flux, in manufacturing steel, glassmaking, waste treatment, insecticides, and as an industrial alkali. Also called "lime", "quicklime", "unslaked lime", "calx".

calcium phosphate *n.* Any of several phosphate compounds, especially: **1.** A white crystalline powder, CaHPO₄ or CaHPO₄·2H₂O, used as a food, as a plastic stabiliser, and in glass; dibasic calcium phosphate. **2.** A colourless deliquescent powder, CaH₄(PO₄)₂·H₂O, used in baking powders, as a plant food, plastic stabiliser, and in glass; monobasic calcium phosphate. **3.** A white amorphous powder, Ca₃(PO₄)₂, used in ceramics, rubber, fertilisers, plastic stabilisers, and as a food supplement; tribasic calcium phosphate.

calc-sin·ter (kálk-sintər) *n.* Natural calcium carbonate, chiefly in the form of stalagmites or stalactites. See **travertine**. [German *Kalksinter : Kalk,* lime + *Sinter,* slag, SINTER.]

calc·spar (kálk-spaar) *n.* **Calcite** *(see).* [Partial translation of Swedish *kalkspar : kalk,* lime (see **calcium**) + SPAR (mineral).]

calc-tu·fa (kálk-tewfə ‖ -tōōfə) *n.* Also **calc-tuff** (-tuf). A porous or spongy deposit of calcium carbonate found in calcareous mineral springs. [*Calcareous* + *tufa.*]

cal·cu·la·ble (kál-kew-lə-b'l) *adj.* **1.** Capable of being calculated or estimated. **2.** That may be counted on or depended on. —**cal·cu·la·bil·i·ty** (-bílləti) *n.*

cal·cu·late (kál-kew-layt) *v.* **-lated, -lating, -lates.** —*tr.* **1.** To ascertain by computation; reckon. **2.** To make an estimate of; evaluate. **3.** To fit or plan for a purpose; design. Usually used in the passive: *His speech was cleverly calculated to stir up ill feeling against the government.* **4.** To rely or depend. Used with *on.* —*intr.* To execute a mathematical process. [Latin *calculāre,* from *calculus,* small stone (used in reckoning), diminutive of *calx* (stem *calc-*), lime, limestone, from Greek *khalix,* pebble.]

Synonyms: calculate, compute, reckon, estimate.

cal·cu·lat·ed (kál-kew-laytid) *adj.* **1.** Estimated with forethought: *a calculated risk.* **2.** Deliberately planned to achieve a particular purpose. —**cal·cu·lat·ed·ly** *adv.*

cal·cu·lat·ing (kál-kew-layting) *adj.* **1.** Performing calculations: *a calculating machine.* **2. a.** Shrewd; crafty. **b.** Coldly scheming or conniving.

cal·cu·la·tion (kál-kew-láysh'n) *n.* **1.** The act, process, or result of calculating. **2.** An estimate based upon probabilities. **3.** *Often plural.* **a.** Deliberation; foresight. **b.** Shrewd scheming. —**cal·cu·la·tive** (-lətiv, -laytiv) *adj.*

cal·cu·la·tor (kál-kew-laytər) *n.* **1.** A mechanical or electronic device for the automatic performance of arithmetical operations. **2.** A person who performs calculations. **3.** A set of mathematical tables used as an aid in calculating.

cal·cu·lous (kál-kew-ləss) *adj. Medicine.* Pertaining to, caused by, or having a calculus or calculi.

cal·cu·lus (kál-kew-ləss) *n., pl.* **-li** (-lī) or **-luses. 1.** *Pathology.* An abnormal concretion in the body, usually formed of mineral salts; a stone, as in the gall bladder, kidney, or urinary bladder. **2.** *Mathematics.* **a.** A method of analysis or calculation using a special symbolic notation. **b.** The combined mathematics of **differential calculus** and **integral calculus** *(both of which see).* [Latin, small stone (used in reckoning); reckoning. See **calculate**.]

calculus of variations *n.* The mathematical analysis of the maxima and minima of definite integrals, the integrands of which are functions of independent variables, dependent variables, and the derivatives of one or more dependent variables.

Cal·cut·ta (kal-kúttə). Capital city of West Bengal state, India. Built on the Hooghly river, it is India's largest city and one of the world's most densely populated. It was founded as a British East India Company trading post (*c.*1690). Captured by Siraj-ud-Dawlah, the Nawab of Bengal (1756), it was retaken by Clive (1757). During the campaign, the Nawab confined 146 prisoners overnight in a small guardhouse (see **Black Hole of Calcutta**). Calcutta is the chief port and industrial centre of east India.

Cal·der (káwl-dər ‖ kól-), **Alexander** (1898–1976). U.S. sculptor who created the mobile (moving sculpture) in Paris, in the early 1930s.

cal·de·ra (kal-daír-ə, -deér-ə, káwldərə) *n.* A large crater formed by the collapse of a volcanic cone, or by a volcanic explosion which removes the top of the original cone. [Spanish, "kettle", "boiler", from Late Latin *caldāria,* CAULDRON.]

caldron. *Chiefly U.S.* Variant of **cauldron.**

Ca·leb (káy-leb ‖ *chiefly U.S.* -ləb). A Hebrew leader. He and Joshua were the only two leaders allowed to enter the Promised Land. Numbers 14:24.

calèche. Variant of **calash.**

Cal·e·do·ni·a (kál-i-dōn-i-ə, -yə). The Roman name for Scotland. It was first used by Lucan, the Roman poet (1st century A.D.), to describe Britain north of the Antonine Wall, which reached from the Firth of Forth to the Firth of Clyde. Today, Caledonia is chiefly used in the names of many Scottish institutions, and in poetry.

Cal·e·do·ni·an (kál-i-dón-i-ən, -yən) *adj.* **1.** *Literary.* Of or pertaining to Scotland. **2.** *Geology.* Of or pertaining to the mountain-building episode that occurred in the late Silurian and Devonian periods.

~*n. Literary.* A native of Scotland.

Caledonian Canal. Waterway in Scotland, linking the North Sea with the Irish Sea through the Great Glen. It stretches 96 kilometres

(60 miles) from Loch Linnhe to the Moray Firth. Engineered by Thomas Telford, it was opened in 1822 and completed in 1847. It comprises a system of canals linking the lochs Ness, Oich, and Lochy, and is now used mainly by pleasure craft.

cal·e·fa·cient (kál-i-fáysh'nt) *adj.* Producing warmth.
~*n. Medicine.* An ointment or plaster applied to the skin to produce warmth. [Latin *calefaciēns* (stem *calefacient-*), present participle of *calefacere*, to make warm : *calēre*, be warm + *facere*, to make.] —**cal·e·fac·tion** (-fáksh'n) *n.*

cal·en·dar (kál-indər) *n. Abbr.* **cal.** **1.** Any of various systems of reckoning time in which the beginning, length, and divisions of a year are arbitrarily defined or otherwise established. **2.** A table showing the months, weeks, and days in at least one specific year. **3.** A list or schedule, especially one arranged in chronological order, as of court cases awaiting trial, sporting events, or the like: *the next big event in the racing calendar.* **4.** *Obsolete.* A guide; an example.
~*tr.v.* **calendared, -daring, -dars.** To enter on a calendar; list; schedule. [Middle English *calender*, from Anglo-French, from Medieval Latin *kalendārium*, from Latin, a moneylender's account book (because the monthly interest was due on the calends), from *kalendae*, the CALENDS.]

calendar month *n.* A month.

cal·en·der¹ (kál-indər) *n.* A machine in which paper or cloth is made smooth and glossy by being pressed through rollers.
~*tr.v.* **calendered, -dering, -ders.** To press in a calender. [French *calendre*, from Medieval Latin *calendra, celendra*, from Latin *cylindrus*, cylinder, roller, from Greek *kulindros*, from *kulindein*, to roll.] —**cal·en·der·er** *n.*

calender² *n.* A mendicant dervish. [Persian, *kalander.*]

ca·len·dri·cal (kə-léndrik'l) *adj.* Of, pertaining to, or used in a calendar.

cal·ends (kál-endz, -indz) *n., pl.* **calends.** Also **kal·ends.** *Used with a singular or plural verb.* In the ancient Roman calendar, the day of the new moon and the first day of the month. [Middle English *kalendes*, from Latin *kalendae.*] —**ca·len·dal** (kə-lénd'l) *adj.*

ca·len·du·la (kə-léndewlə) *n.* Any plant of the genus *Calendula*, having orange-yellow rayed flowers; especially, the **pot marigold** *(see).* [New Latin *Calendula*, from Medieval Latin *calendula*, marigold, from Latin *kalendae*, CALENDS (perhaps because it was thought to be a cure for menstrual disorders).]

cal·en·ture (kál-ən-tewr, -choor, -chər) *n.* A mild, brief, or sometimes persistent tropical fever. [Spanish *calentura*, from *calentar*, to heat, from Latin *calēns* (stem *calent-*), present participle of *calēre*, to be warm.]

calf¹ (kaaf ‖ *chiefly U.S.* kaf) *n., pl.* **calves** (kaavz ‖ *chiefly U.S.* kavz). **1.** A young cow or bull. **2.** The young of certain other mammals, such as the elephant or whale. **3.** Calfskin. **4.** A large, floating chunk of ice split from a glacier, iceberg, or floe. —**kill the fatted calf.** To prepare a feast of welcome; celebrate in grand style. [Middle English *calf, kelf*, Old English *cealf*, from West Germanic *kalbam* (unattested).]

calf² *n., pl.* **calves.** The fleshy, muscular back part of the human leg, between the knee and ankle. [Middle English, from Old Norse *kalfi†.*]

calf love *n.* An immature infatuation; puppy love.

calf's-foot jelly (kaavz-foot, kaafs-). Also **calves'-foot jelly** (kaavz-). A gelatinous food made by boiling calves' feet.

calf·skin (kaaf-skin ‖ *chiefly U.S.* káf-) *n.* **1.** The hide of a calf. **2.** *Abbr.* **cf.** Fine leather made from the hide of a calf. In this sense, also called "calf".

Cal·ga·ry (kálgəri). City of south Alberta, Canada. Situated at the confluence of the rivers Bow and Elbow, it is the market centre for south Alberta, and the heart of Canada's petroleum industry. It has a famous annual rodeo, the Calgary Stampede.

Cal·i·ban (kál-i-ban, -bən) *n.* A man of savage and brutish character. [After a character in Shakespeare's *The Tempest*, perhaps alteration of CARIBAN.]

cal·i·brate (kál-i-brayt) *tr.v.* **-brated, -brating, -brates. 1.** To check, adjust, or standardise systematically the graduations of a quantitative measuring instrument. **2.** To determine the calibre of (a tube). —**cal·i·bra·tion** (-bráysh'n) *n.* —**cal·i·bra·tor** (-braytər) *n.*

cal·i·bre, *U.S.* **cal·i·ber** (kál-i-bər) *n.* **1.** *Abbr.* **cal. a.** The diameter of the inside of a tube. **b.** The diameter of the bore of a gun. **c.** The diameter of a bullet or shell. **2.** Degree of excellence, worth, or distinction. [Old French *calibre*, from Old Italian *calibro*, from Arabic *qālib*, shoemaker's last, probably from Greek *kalapous*, "wooden foot" : *kalon*, wood, firewood, from *kaiein*, to burn + *pous*, foot.]

ca·li·che (ka-leechi, kə-) *n.* **a.** A crude sodium nitrate occurring naturally in Chile, Peru, and the southwest United States, used as fertiliser. **b. Sodium nitrate** *(see).* [American Spanish, from Spanish, chip of limestone, from *cal*, lime(stone), from Latin *calx*, from Greek *khalix*, pebble.]

cal·i·co (kál-i-kō) *n., pl.* **-coes** or **-cos. 1.** *British.* A plain white cotton cloth. **2.** A coarse cloth, usually printed with bright designs.
~*adj.* Made of calico. [Earlier *calicut*, after CALICUT.]

calico bush *n.* A shrub, the **mountain laurel** *(see).*

Cal·i·cut (kál-i-kət). Also **Ko·zhi·kode** (kōzhi-kōd). City on the southwest coast of India. Vasco da Gama made his first landfall in India on the site, where the Portuguese, British, French, and Danes later established trading posts. Finally ceded to Britain (1792), Calicut became the chief port of south India. It gave its name to calico, its main export in the 17th century.

calif. Variant of **caliph.**

Cal·i·for·ni·a (kál-i-fórn-yə, -i-ə). Pacific state of the United States. The third largest state and the most populous, it is known as the "Golden State" because of its sunny climate and the discovery of gold there in pioneering days. Its forested coastal ranges are noted for their giant redwood trees. The state's products include fruit, wine, natural gas, gold, silver, and copper, while its manufacturing includes aerospace and defence-linked industries. California was first colonised by the Spaniards from Mexico, and was ceded to the United States in 1848. Sacramento is the capital. —**Cal·i·for·ni·an** *n. & adj.*

California laurel *n.* An aromatic evergreen tree, *Umbellularia californica*, of the North American Pacific Coast, having yellowish-green fleshy fruit and attractively grained wood.

California lilac *n.* A shrub, *Ceanothus thyrsiflorus*, native to California but widely cultivated for its pyramid-shaped clusters of small blue flowers. Also called "ceanothus".

California poppy *n.* A plant, *Eschscholzia californica*, native to the Pacific Coast of North America but widely cultivated, having finely divided bluish-green leaves and orange-yellow flowers.

cal·i·for·ni·um (kál-i-fórni-əm) *n. Symbol* **Cf** A synthetic element produced in trace quantities, originally by helium isotope bombardment of curium. All isotopes are radioactive, chiefly by emission of alpha particles. Atomic number 98, mass numbers 240–255 of known isotopes, half-lives varying from 25 minutes to 800 years. [New Latin; discovered at the University of *California* (Berkeley).]

ca·lig·i·nous (kə-líjinəss) *adj. Archaic.* Dark; gloomy; shadowy. [Old French *caligineux*, from Latin *cālīginōsus*, dark, from *cālīgō†*, darkness.]

Ca·lig·u·la (kə-líggewlə), born Gaius Caesar Augustus Germanicus (A.D. 12–41). Emperor of Rome (A.D. 37–41). The son of Germanicus Caesar and Agrippina the Elder, he was adopted (A.D. 32) by Tiberius, on whose death he succeeded to the throne. He ennobled his favourite horse, claimed to be a manifestation of all the gods, and provoked a riot in Jerusalem by ordering a statue of himself to be erected in the Temple. He was assassinated after alienating the army and threatening to execute the members of the Senate. As a child, he wore military boots and was dubbed Caligula (little boot) by his father's soldiers.

cal·i·pash (kál-i-pash ‖ *U.S. also* -pásh) *n.* An edible, gelatinous, greenish substance lying beneath a turtle's upper shell. [Probably alteration of Spanish *carapacho*, CARAPACE.]

cal·i·pee (kál-i-pee, -pée) *n.* An edible, gelatinous, yellowish substance lying above a turtle's lower shell. [Probably alteration of CALIPASH.]

caliper. *Chiefly U.S.* Variant of **calliper.**

ca·liph, ca·lif, ka·lif, kha·lif (káyl-if, kál-, kaal-) *n.* The secular and religious head of a Muslim state. [Middle English *caliphe, califfe*, from Old French *calife*, from Arabic *khalīfa*, "successor" (of Muhammad), from *khalafa*, to succeed.]

ca·liph·ate (kál-i-fayt, -fət, -fit ‖ káyl-) *n.* The office, jurisdiction, or reign of a caliph.

cal·i·sa·ya (kál-i-sáy-ə) *n.* The bark of any tree of the genus *Cinchona*, from which quinine is obtained. Also called "calisaya bark", "yellowbark". [Spanish, probably after *Calisaya*, 17th-century Bolivian Indian who taught the Spanish the use of quinine contained in the bark.]

calisthenics. Variant of **callisthenics.**

calk¹ (kawk) *n.* A pointed extension on the toe or heels of a horseshoe designed to prevent slipping.
~*tr.v.* **calked, calking, calks. 1.** To supply with calks. **2.** To cut or injure with a calk. [Short for earlier *calkin*, Middle English *kakun*, from Middle Dutch *calcoen*, hoof of a horse, from Old French *calcain*, heel, from Latin *calcāneum, calcāneus*, from *calx†* (stem *calc-*).]

calk² (kawk, kalk) *tr.v.* **calked, calking, calks.** To reproduce (a pattern) by backing with rough colouring and tracing onto a surface or sheet of paper underneath. [French *calquer*, to trace. See CALQUE.]

calk³. Variant of **caulk.**

call (kawl) *v.* **called, calling, calls.** —*tr.* **1.** To cry out in a loud voice so as to attract attention. **2.** To summon. **3.** To convoke or convene (a meeting). **4.** To summon to a specified vocation or pursuit. **5.** To awaken. **6.** To telephone (someone). **7.** To name. **8.** To estimate as being; consider: *I call that fair.* **9.** To describe as; label: *Nobody calls me a liar!* **10.** *Law.* To bring to action or under consideration: *call a case to court.* **11.** To demand payment of (a loan or bond issue). **12. a.** In cricket, to declare (a bowler) to have bowled a no-ball. **b.** In billiards, to predict (the outcome of a shot) before playing. **c.** *Australian.* To give a running commentary on (a horse race). **d.** *U.S.* To stop (a baseball game) because of bad weather or darkness. **13. a.** In poker, to demand to see the hand of (an opponent) by equalling his bet. **b.** In bridge, to bid: *call no trumps.* **14.** To read aloud (a register or list) to ascertain any absences. **15.** To admit (a pupil lawyer) as a barrister: *called to the Bar.* —*intr.* **1.** To telephone. **2.** To pay a short visit. **3.** To attract attention by shouting. **4.** To urge one to go: *Duty calls.* **5.** To make a bid in bridge. **6.** To guess the result of the toss of a coin or spin of a racket. **7.** To make a characteristic cry. Used chiefly of birds. **8.** *Australian.* To commentate on a horse race. —**call back. 1.** To telephone in return. **2.** To retract or disavow. —**call down. 1.** To invoke, as from heaven. **2.** *Informal.* To find fault with or berate. —**call for. 1.** To go and get, or stop for. **2.** To be appropriate for; warrant: *this calls for a celebration.* **3.** To demand. **4.** To give orders for: *call for a strike.* —**call forth.** To evoke. —**call in. 1.** To collect or request payment of. **2.** To take out of circulation: *calling* *in half-crowns.* **3.** To recall to the factory (a defective product, such as a car). **4.** To summon for assistance or consultation: *call in a specialist.* **—call into being.** To create or cause to exist. **—call into question.** To raise doubt about. **—call off. 1.** To cancel or postpone. **2.** To restrain or recall. **3.** To read aloud, as from a list of names. **—call on** or **upon. 1.** To pay a short visit to. **2.** To request or order (someone) to do something. **—call out. 1.** To shout. **2.** To cause to assemble; summon: *call out the guard.* **3.** To instruct (workers) to strike.

~*n.* **1.** An act of calling. **2.** A shout or loud cry. **3. a.** The characteristic cry of an animal, especially a bird. **b.** An instrument or sound made to imitate such a cry, used as a lure. **4. a.** Need or occasion: *There was no call for that remark.* **b.** Demand: *There isn't much call for tiepins today.* **5. a.** A claim on a person's time or life: *the call of duty.* **b.** Attraction or appeal: *the call of the wild.* **6.** A short visit; especially, one made as a formality or for business or professional purposes. **7.** A summons or invitation. **8.** A signal, as made by a hunting horn, bugle, or bell. **9.** A vocation, as to the priesthood. **10.** An act of telephoning or instance of being telephoned. **11. a.** A notice summoning actors to rehearsal. **b.** A spoken message telling an actor to be ready to appear on stage. **12.** *Sports.* **a.** The decision of an umpire or linesman. **b.** In cricket, a shout by a batsman telling his partner whether or not to take a run. **13. a.** In poker, a demand to see an opponent's hand. **b.** In bridge, a bid or turn to bid. **14.** A demand or request for the payment of a debt. **15.** *Finance.* **a.** A call option *(see).* **b.** An unpaid part of the price of a share. **c.** A demand for this outstanding amount. **d.** A demand for the presentation of redeemable bonds or shares. **—on call. 1.** Payable on demand. **2.** Available whenever summoned. **—pay a call.** *Informal.* To go to the lavatory. **—within call.** Easily summoned; accessible. [Middle English *callen,* Old English *ceallian,* to call, shout, from Old Norse *kalla.*]

cal·la (kál-ə) *n.* **1.** Any of several tropical or semitropical plants of the genus *Zantedeschia*; especially, *Z. aethiopica*, widely cultivated for its large, showy white spathe that encloses a yellow spadix. Also called "arum lily". **2.** A marsh plant, *Calla palustris,* of the North Temperate Zone, having small, densely clustered greenish flowers partly enclosed in a spreading white spathe. [New Latin *Calla,* probably from Greek *kallaia,* wattle of a cock, from *kallos,* beauty.]

Cal·la·ghan (kál-ə-han, -hən, -gən), **(Leonard) James, Baron Callaghan of Cardiff** (1912-). British Labour prime minister (1976-79). He entered Parliament in 1945. He became Chancellor of the Exchequer (1964-67), Home Secretary (1967-70), and Foreign Secretary (1974-76).

Ca·llao (kə-yów). The major port of Peru, situated on the Pacific Ocean, and now part of Greater Lima. Founded in 1537, it was frequently raided by pirates and adventurers.

Cal·las (kál-ass, -əss), **Maria,** born Maria Anna Kalogeropoulos (1923-77). U.S.-born Greek coloratura soprano. She made her debut in Athens at the age of 14 in the opera *Cavalleria Rusticana.* She became the prima donna at Milan's La Scala (1950) and made her American debut in Chicago (1954) as Bellini's *Norma.*

call box *n.* **1.** A **telephone box** *(see).* **2.** A **payphone** *(see).*

call·boy (kául-boy) *n.* One who tells actors when it is time for them to go on stage.

call·er[1] (káwlər) *n.* **1.** Someone or something that calls or cries out. **2.** A person paying a short visit. **3.** A person making a telephone call. **4.** A person who calls numbers at bingo. **5.** In country dancing, a person who calls out the changing sequence of movements.

call girl *n. Informal.* A prostitute who takes appointments by telephone.

calli– *comb. form.* Indicates beauty; for example, **calliopsis.** [Latin, from Greek *kalli-,* from *kallos,* beauty.]

cal·lig·ra·phy (kə-líggrəfi, ka-) *n.* **1.** The art of fine handwriting. **2.** Penmanship; handwriting. Also called "chirography". Compare **cacography.** [French *calligraphie,* from Greek *kalligraphia* : CALLI- + -GRAPHY.] **—cal·lig·ra·pher, cal·lig·ra·phist** *n.* **—cal·li·graph·ic** (kál-i-gráffik) *adj.*

call·ing (káwling) *n.* **1.** An inner urge; a strong impulse. **2.** A vocation, profession, or career.

calling card *n.* U.S. A **visiting card** *(see).*

cal·li·o·pe (kə-lî-əpi || kál-i-ōp). *U.S.* A **steam organ** *(see).*

Cal·li·o·pe (kə-lî-əpi, ka-). *Greek Mythology.* The Muse of epic poetry. [Latin, from Greek *Kalliopē,* "beautiful-voiced" : CALLI- + *ops,* voice.]

cal·li·op·sis (kál-i-ópsiss) *n.* A plant, the **coreopsis** *(see).* [New Latin, "having a beautiful appearance" : Greek *kallos,* beauty + -OPSIS.]

cal·li·per (kál-i-pər) *n.* Also *chiefly U.S.* **cal·i·per. 1.** *Usually plural.* An instrument consisting essentially of two curved hinged legs, used to measure internal and external dimensions. **2.** A **vernier calliper** *(see).* **3.** *Medical.* Either of a pair of metal rods with straps and attachments for providing support to or exerting tension on a leg. ~*v.* **callipered, -pering, -pers.** —*tr.* To measure with callipers. —*intr.* To determine dimensions by using callipers. [Probably a variant of CALIBRE.]

calliper rule *n.* A measuring instrument consisting of a scale to which a set of jaws are attached at right angles. One of the jaws is fixed at the end of the scale, the other is adjustable and enables the dimensions of a workpiece to be read off on the scale.

cal·li·pyg·i·an (kál-i-píji-ən) *adj.* Also **cal·li·pyg·ous** (-pígəss). Having beautifully proportioned buttocks. [Greek *kallipugos* : CALLI- + *pugē,* buttocks.]

cal·lis·then·ics, cal·is·then·ics (kál-iss-thénniks) *pl.n.* **1.** Simple gymnastic exercises designed to develop muscular tone and improve general fitness. **2.** *Used with a singular verb.* The practice of such exercises. [Greek *kallos,* beauty + *sthenos,* strength.] **—cal·lis·then·ic** *adj.*

Cal·lis·to (kə-lístō) *n.* One of the satellites of Jupiter, shown by Voyager 2 to have an extremely smooth, icy surface. [After *Callisto,* in Greek mythology a nymph loved by Zeus.]

call loan *n.* A loan repayable on demand at any time.

call market *n.* The market for call money.

call money *n.* Money lent by banks, usually to stockbrokers, subject to repayment on demand at any time.

call number *n.* A number used in libraries to classify a book and indicate its place on the shelves.

call of nature *n.* A need to defecate or urinate. Used euphemistically: *left the party to answer a call of nature.*

call option *n.* An agreement in which a trader may, for a commission, buy a quantity of a stock or commodity for a specific price within a limited period of time. Also called "call".

cal·los·i·ty (ka-lóssəti, kə-) *n., pl.* **-ties. 1. a.** A callused area. **b.** The condition of being callused. **2.** *Formal.* Hard-heartedness; insensitivity. [Middle English *callosite,* from Old French, from Latin *callōsitās* (stem *callōsitāt-*), from *callōsus,* hardened, CALLOUS.]

cal·lous (kál-əss) *adj.* **1.** Emotionally hardened; insensitive; unfeeling. **2.** Having calluses; toughened. [Middle English, from Old French *calleuse,* from Latin *callōsus,* from *callum, callus,* hard skin, CALLUS.] **—cal·loused** *adj.* **—cal·lous·ly** *adv.* **—cal·lous·ness** *n.*

call-o·ver (káwl-ōvər) *n. British.* **1.** A roll call. **2.** An announcement of the betting prices for a horse race.

cal·low (kál-ō) *adj.* **1.** Immature; inexperienced. **2.** Not yet having feathers; unfledged. Said of birds. [Originally, "bald," hence unfledged, Middle English *calwe,* bald, Old English *calu,* probably from Latin *calvus,* bald.] **—cal·low·ness** *n.*

call rate *n.* The rate of interest charged on call loans.

call sign *n.* A signal, often using code words or letters, used by a radio station to identify itself.

call up *tr.v.* **1.** To summon for military service. **2.** To summon for assistance, for example. **3.** To telephone. **4.** To cause to remember; evoke: *calling up old times.*

call-up (káwl-up) *n.* **1.** A summons for military service. **2.** Those summoned for military service.

cal·lus (kál-əss) *n., pl.* **-luses. 1. a.** A localised thickening and enlargement of the horny layer of the skin, resulting from continual pressure or friction; callosity. **b.** The hard bony tissue that develops around the ends of a fractured bone during healing. **2.** *Botany.* Hardened tissue that develops over a wound or cut in a woody stem. ~*intr.v.* **callused, -lusing, -luses.** To form or develop a callus. [Latin *callus, callum†.*]

calm (kaam ‖ kaalm, kolm) *adj.* **calmer, calmest. 1.** Undisturbed by wind. **2.** Free from excitement or agitation. **3.** Not affected by anxiety or qualms. ~*n.* **1.** An absence of disturbance or agitation; peacefulness. **2.** *Meteorology.* A condition of no wind or a wind with a velocity of less than 1 knot; force 0 on the Beaufort scale. **3.** Freedom from anxiety or qualms. ~*v.* **calmed, calming, calms.** —*tr.* To make calm; quiet. Often used with *down.* —*intr.* To become calm or quiet. Often used with *down.* [Middle English *calme,* from Old French, from Late Latin *cauma,* heat of the day, hence, a rest or resting place in the heat of the day, from Greek *kauma,* burning heat, from *kaiein,* to burn.] **—calm·ly** *adv.* **—calm·ness** *n.*

Synonyms: calm, tranquil, placid, serene, still, quiet, peaceful.

calm·a·tive (káa-mətiv, kál- ‖ kaal-, kól-) *adj.* Having relaxing or pacifying properties; sedative. ~*n.* A sedative or tranquilliser. [From CALM (after SEDATIVE).]

cal·o·mel (kál-ə-mel, -məl) *n.* A white, tasteless compound, Hg_2Cl_2, used as a purgative. [French, from New Latin *calomelas,* "beautiful black" (calomel, though white, was originally developed from a black powder) : Greek *kalos,* beautiful + *melas,* black.]

Cal·or gas (kál-ər) *n.* A trademark in Britain for a domestic gas supplied in portable cylinders and consisting of butane liquefied under pressure.

ca·lor·ic (kə-lórrik, kál-ərik ‖ kə-láwrik) *adj.* Of or pertaining to heat or calories. ~*n.* A hypothetically indestructible, uncreatable, highly elastic, self-repellent, all-pervading fluid, formerly thought responsible for the production, possession, and transfer of heat.

cal·o·rie (kál-əri) *n.* **1.** *Abbr.* **cal** Any of several approximately equal units of heat, each measured as the quantity of heat required to raise the temperature of 1 gram of water by 1°C from a standard initial temperature, especially from 3.98°C, 14.5°C, or 19.5°C, at 1 atmosphere pressure. Also called "gram calorie", "small calorie". **2.** *Abbr.* **cal** The unit of heat equal to $^1/_{100}$ the quantity of heat required to raise the temperature of 1 gram of water from 0 to 100°C at 1 atmosphere pressure. Also called "mean calorie". **3.** *Abbr.* **Cal** The unit of heat equal to the amount of heat required to raise the temperature of 1 kilogram of water by 1°C at 1 atmosphere pressure. Also called "kilocalorie", "kilogram calorie", "large calorie". **4.** The unit of heat equal to 4.184 joules. Also called "thermochemical calorie". The calorie has been replaced by the joule for all scientific purposes. The calories used to express the energy value of foods are kilocalories (sense 3): 1 kilocalorie is equal to 4,184 joules.

[French, from Latin *calor*, heat.]

cal·o·rif·ic (kálǝ-riffik) *adj.* Pertaining to or generating heat or calories. [French *calorifique*, from Latin *calorificus* : *calor*, heat + -FIC.]

calorific value *n.* The quantity of heat, usually expressed in joules per kilogram, that will be produced by the complete combustion of a given mass of a fuel.

cal·o·rim·e·ter (kálǝ-rímmitǝr, -o-, -aw-) *n.* **1.** An apparatus for measuring heat. **2.** The part of such an apparatus, usually a sample container, in which the heat measured causes a change of state. [Latin *calor*, heat + -METER.]

cal·o·rim·e·try (kálǝ-rímmǝtri) *n.* The measurement of the quantity of heat evolved or absorbed by a chemical reaction, change of state, or formation of a solution. —**cal·o·ri·met·ri·cal** (-ri-méttrik'l) *adj.*

ca·loy·er (kál-oy-ǝr || -ǝ-yǝr, kǝ-lóy-ǝr) *n.* A monk of the Eastern Orthodox Church. [French, from obsolete Italian *caloiero*, from Medieval Greek *kalogēros*, venerable, "handsome old man" : Greek *kalos*, beautiful + *gēras*, old age.]

cal·pac, cal·pack, kal·pak (kál-pak || kal-pák) *n.* A large black cap, usually of sheepskin or felt, worn in Turkey, Armenia, and other Near Eastern regions. [Turkish *kalpāk*.]

calque (kalk) *n. Linguistics.* **1.** A form of semantic borrowing in which a word is given a special extended meaning by analogy with that of a word having the same basic meaning in another language. **2.** A **loan translation** *(see).*
~*tr.v.* **calqued, calquing, calques.** To model (the meaning of a word) upon that of an analogous word in another language. [French, tracing, imitation, close copy, from *calquer*, to trace, copy, from Italian *calcar*, to press, from Latin *calcāre*, to trample, stamp.]

cal·trop, cal·trap (kál-trǝp) *n.* **1.** *Military.* An iron ball with four projecting spikes so arranged that when three of the spikes were on the ground, the fourth pointed upwards. It was formerly used to delay the advance of mounted and unmounted troops. Also called "crowfoot", "crows-foot". **2.** Any of several plants having spiny burs or bracts, such as members of the genus *Tribulus*. See **water chestnut.** [Middle English *cal(ke)trap(pe)*, from Old French *chauchetrap*, iron ball with spikes, and Old English *calcatrippe*, spiny plant, brambles, both from Medieval Latin *calcatrappa*, *calcatrippa*, "foot trap" : Latin *calcāre*, to tread, from *calx*, heel + Medieval Latin *trappa*, trap, from Germanic.]

cal·u·met (kál-yōō-met || *U.S. also* -mǝt, -mét) *n.* A long-stemmed, ornamented pipe used by North American Indians for ceremonial purposes. Also called "peace pipe". [Canadian French, from French (Normandy dialect), variant of French *chalumeau*, a straw, from Late Latin *calamellus*, little reed, from *calamus*, a reed, from Greek *kalamos*.]

ca·lum·ni·ate (kǝ-lúm-ni-ayt) *tr.v.* **-ated, -ating, -ates.** To make false and damaging statements about; slander. See Synonyms at **malign.** [Latin *calumniārī*, from *calumnia*, CALUMNY.] —**ca·lum·ni·a·tion** (-áysh'n) *n.* —**ca·lum·ni·a·tor** (-aytǝr) *n.*

ca·lum·ni·ous (kǝ-lúm-ni-ǝss) *adj.* Also **ca·lum·ni·a·to·ry** (-ǝtri, -ǝtǝri, -áytǝri) Containing or implying calumny; slanderous; defamatory. —**ca·lum·ni·ous·ly** *adv.*

cal·um·ny (kál-ǝm-ni) *n.,* pl. **-nies. 1.** A false statement, maliciously or knowingly made to injure someone's reputation. **2.** The utterance of such statements; slander. [Middle English, from Old French *calomnie*, from Latin *calumnia*, "trickery", "deception", from *calvī*, to deceive, trick.]

cal·u·tron (kál-yoo-tron) *n. Physics.* A device for separating isotopes by deflecting ions in electric and magnetic fields. It is similar in action to a large mass spectrometer.

Cal·va·dos (kál-vǝ-doss || *U.S.* -dōss, -dáwss) *n.* A French brandy made from apples. [French; after *Calvados*, département in Normandy where it was originally made.]

cal·var·i·a (kal-vaír-i-ǝ) *n. Anatomy.* The top, rounded part of the skull. Also called "skullcap". [Late Latin, skull. See **Calvary.**]

cal·va·ry (kál-vǝri) *n.,* pl. **-ries. 1.** A sculptured depiction of the Crucifixion. **2.** A spiritual ordeal. [After CALVARY.]

Cal·va·ry (kál-vǝri). The hill outside the ancient city of Jerusalem where Jesus was crucified. [Middle English *Calvarie*, Old English *Calvarie*, from Late Latin *Calvāria*, from Latin *calvāria*, skull (translation of Greek *kranion*, translation of Aramaic *gulgūtha*, GOLGOTHA), from *calva*, scalp, from *calvus*, bald.]

Calvary cross *n. Heraldry.* A Latin cross set on three steps.

calve (kaav || *chiefly U.S.* kav) *v.* **calved, calving, calves.** —*intr.* **1.** To give birth to a calf. **2.** To break up and lose a mass of ice. Used of a glacier or an iceberg. —*tr.* **1.** To give birth to (a calf). **2.** To set loose (a mass of ice). [Middle English *calven*, Old English *cealfian*, from *cealf*, CALF (young cow).]

calves. Plural of **calf.**

calves'-foot jelly. Variant of **calf's-foot jelly.**

Cal·vin (kál-vin), **John** (1509–64). French Protestant reformer and theologian who, after breaking with the Roman Catholic Church (1533), settled in Geneva (1541). His brand of theology, published in his book *Institutes* and known today as presbyterianism or Calvinism, had a profound effect on the Christian world.

Cal·vin·ism (kál-vin-iz'm) *n.* **1.** The religious doctrines of John Calvin, which emphasise the supremacy of the Scriptures in the revelation of truth, the omnipotence of God, the sinfulness of man, the salvation of the elect by God's grace alone, and a rigid moral code. **2.** Agreement with or advocacy of such doctrines. —**Cal·vin·ist** *n. & adj.* —**Cal·vin·is·tic** (-ístik), **Cal·vin·is·ti·cal** *adj.*

caix (kalks) *n.,* pl. **calxes** or **calces** (kál-seez). **1.** The crumbly residue left after a mineral or metal has been calcined or roasted. **2.**

Lime; chalk. **3. Calcium oxide** *(see).* [Latin, lime, limestone, from Greek *khalix*, pebble.]

cal·y·cine (kál-i-sīn, káyl-) *adj.* Of, pertaining to, or resembling a calyx.

cal·y·cle (kál-ik'l || káyl-) *n.* **1.** *Botany.* An epicalyx *(see).* **2.** *Biology.* A calyculus. [French *calicule*, from Latin *calyculus*, diminutive of *calyx*, bud, CALYX.] —**ca·lyc·u·late** (kǝ-líckew-layt, -lǝt, -lit) *adj.*

ca·lyc·u·lus (kǝ-líckew-lǝss) *n.,* pl. **-li** (-lī). *Biology.* A small cupshaped structure. Also called "calycle". [Latin, CALYCLE.] —**ca·lyc·u·lar** *adj.*

ca·lyp·so¹ (kǝ-lípsō) *n.* An orchid, *Calypso bulbosa*, of the North Temperate Zone, having a pinkish flower with a slipper-shaped lip. [After CALYPSO.]

ca·lyp·so² *n.* **1.** A type of song originating in the West Indies, notably in Trinidad, characterised by improvised lyrics on topical or broadly humorous subjects and a syncopated rhythm. **2.** A dance to calypso music. [After CALYPSO.]

Ca·lyp·so (kǝ-lípsō). *Greek Mythology.* A sea nymph who delayed Odysseus on her island, Ogygia, for seven years. [Latin, from Greek *Kalupsō*, "she who conceals", from *kaluptein*, to cover, conceal.]

ca·lyp·tra (kǝ-líptrǝ) *n. Botany.* **1.** The protective cap covering the spore case of a moss or related plant. **2.** Any similar hoodlike or caplike structure. [New Latin, from Greek *kaluptra*, veil, covering, from *kaluptein*, to cover, conceal.] —**ca·lyp·trate** (-líptrayt) *adj.*

ca·lyp·tro·gen (kǝ-líptrǝ-jǝn) *n. Botany.* A layer of actively dividing cells at the end of a root tip, from which the root cap is formed.

ca·lyx (káyliks, kál-iks) *n.,* pl. **-lyxes** or **-lyces** (káyl-i-seez, kál-). **1.** The outer protective covering of a flower, consisting of a series of leaflike, usually green segments called sepals. Compare **corolla.** **2.** A cuplike or funnel-shaped animal structure, such as one of those forming part of the kidney. [Latin, from Greek *kalux*.]

cam (kam) *n.* A noncircular wheel mounted on a rotating shaft and used to produce variable or reciprocating motion in another engaged or contacted part. [Perhaps from French *came*, from German *Kamm*, "comb", from Old High German *kamb*.]

cam·an *n. Sports.* A **hurley** *(see).*

ca·ma·ra·de·rie (kámmǝ-raádǝ-ree, -ráddǝ- || *U.S. also* kaámǝ-) *n.* Goodwill and lighthearted rapport between or among friends; comradeship. [French, from *camarade*, COMRADE.]

Ca·margue, la (ka-márg, kǝ-). Island in the delta of the river Rhône, Bouches-du-Rhône département, southern France. Much of the once predominantly marshy land has been reclaimed and now supports livestock including cattle, bulls for the bullrings of Spain, and horses.

cam·a·ril·la (kámmǝ-rílla || -rée-yǝ) *n.* A group of confidential advisers; a cabal. [Spanish, "small room", from *cámara*, room, from Late Latin *camera*, from Latin, arched roof, from Greek *kamara*, vault.]

cam·ass, cam·as (kám-ass, -ǝss) *n.* Also **quam·ash** (kwaámǝsh). **1.** Any of several North American plants of the genus *Camassia*; especially, *C. quamash*, of western North America, having a showy cluster of blue or white flowers and an edible bulb. **2.** The **death camass** *(see).* [Chinook jargon *kamass*.]

cam·ber (kámbǝr) *n.* **1. a.** A slightly arched surface, as of a road, a ship's deck, or an aerofoil. **b.** The condition of being so arched. **2.** A setting of the front wheels of a road vehicle so that they are closer together at the bottom than at the top.
~*v.* **cambered, -bering, -bers.** —*tr.* To give a slight arch to. —*intr.* To arch slightly. [Middle English *ca(u)mber*, curved, from Old French *cambre*, from Latin *camur(us)*†, curved inwards.]

Cam·ber·well beauty (kámbǝrwel) *n.* A butterfly, *Nymphalis antiopa*, of temperate regions, having dark purple wings bordered with yellow. [After *Camberwell*, a district of south London.]

cam·bist (kámbist) *n.* **1.** A manual giving exchange rates of different currencies and equivalents of different weights and measures. **2.** A dealer in or expert on international exchange. [French *cambiste*, from Italian *cambista*, from *cambio*, exchange, from *cambiare*, to exchange, from Late Latin *cambiāre*.] —**cam·bis·try** *n.*

cam·bi·um (kámbi-ǝm) *n.* **1.** A layer of cells in the stems and roots of vascular plants that gives rise to phloem and xylem and thus increases the girth of the plant. Also called "vascular cambium". **2.** A similar tissue, **cork cambium** *(see).* [New Latin, "that which changes into new layers", from Medieval Latin, exchange, from Latin *cambium*.] —**cam·bi·al** *adj.*

Cam·bo·di·a (kam-bṓd-ǝ). Formerly **Kam·pu·che·a, People's Republic of** (kámpoo-chéer, -chée-ǝ). Kingdom of Southeast Asia. Its fertile basin is drained by the Mekong River, and the Khmer Empire flourished there (500–1450). Cambodia became part of French Indochina in 1863, and was a battleground for foreign powers after French withdrawal (1953). From 1971–75 it was known as the Khmer Republic. During the regime of Pol Pot, leader of the successful communist Khmer Rouge (1976–79), an estimated 3,000,000 people died of starvation or were murdered. The Vietnamese occupied the country between 1978 and 1989. In 1991 a peace agreement intended to end 13 years of civil war was concluded, and Cambodia was placed under UN supervision, but insurgency continued. Area, 181 035 square kilometres (69,880 square miles). Population, 10,270,000. Capital, Phnom Penh. —**Cam·bo·di·an** *n. & adj.*

cam·bo·gi·a (kam-bṓj-i-ǝ) *n.* A resin, **gamboge** *(see).* [New Latin, variant of GAMBOGE.]

Cam·bren·sis (kam-brén-sis), **Giraldus** (?1146–?1223). Welsh churchman, historian and patriot. He wrote a history of the Norman conquest of Ireland and an autobiography, but is best known

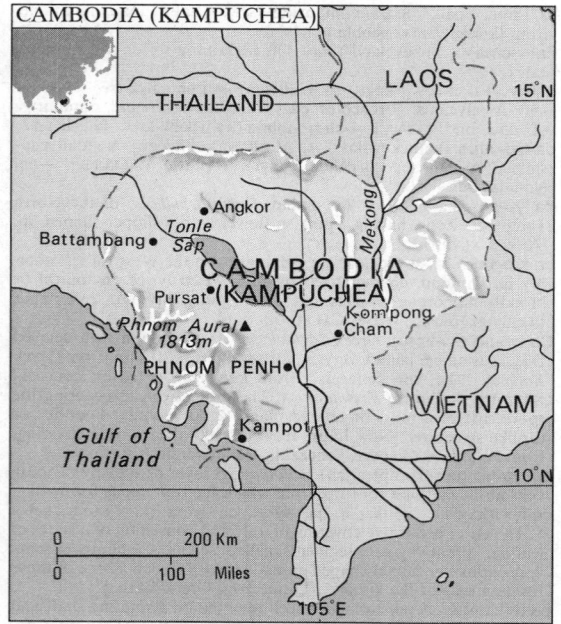

CAMBODIA (KAMPUCHEA)

LAOS

THAILAND

15°N

Angkor

Battambang   Tonle
                Sap

CAMBODIA
Pursat *(KAMPUCHEA)

Kŏmpong
Cham

Rhnom Aural
1813m

PHNOM PENH

VIETNAM

Gulf of
Thailand

Kampot

10°N

0   200 Km

0   100   Miles

105°E

for the contemporary picture of his homeland and people in his *Itinerary of Wales* (1191), and *Description of Wales* (1194), drawn from his travels.

Cam·bri·a (kámbri-ə). The Latin name for Wales. [Latin, from Welsh *Cymru,* from Old Welsh *kombroges* (unattested), Welshmen, "compatriots" : *kom-,* with + *bro,* border, region.]

Cam·bri·an¹ (kámbri-ən) *adj.* Of or pertaining to Wales; Welsh. ~*n.* A Welshman.

Cambrian² *adj.* ,Of, belonging to, or pertaining to the geological time or system of rocks of the first period of the Palaeozoic era, characterised by warm seas and desert land areas.
~*n. Geology.* The Cambrian period. Preceded by *the.* [After CAMBRIA (Wales), where rocks and fossils of this period were found.]

Cambrian Mountains. Mountains in Wales, extending north to south through the centre of the country and including Snowdonia and the Black Mountains.

cam·bric (káymbrik) *n.* A finely woven white linen or cotton fabric. [Earlier *cameryk,* from Flemish *Kameryk,* Cambrai, a French town where it was first made.] —**cam·bric** *adj.*

Cam·bridge¹ (káymbrij). City on the river Cam in Cambridgeshire. An important market centre for East Anglia, and the administrative centre of the county, the city is best known for its university, which dates back to 1284 when Peterhouse College was founded.

Cambridge². City on the Charles river, opposite Boston, in Massachusetts, United States, the seat of America's oldest and most famous university, Harvard (established 1636).

Cam·bridge·shire (káymbrij-shər, -sheer ‖ -shĭr). County in East Anglia, England. Consisting mainly of low-lying fens, it is chiefly agricultural and includes the former county of Huntingdonshire, the Soke of Peterborough, parts of west Suffolk, and the Isle of Ely. Its industries include engineering, brickmaking, cement, electronics, and printing.

Cambs. Cambridgeshire.

cam·cord·er (kám-kawrdər) *n.* A combined video camera and VCR. [Blend of CAMERA + RECORDER.]

Camden, William (1551–1623). English schoolmaster, historian and topographer. He was the author of *Britannia* (1586), the first full topographical survey of England. His *Annales* (published 1615–25) is important as the only contemporary political history of the reign of Elizabeth I.

came¹ (kaym) *n.* A slender, grooved lead bar used to hold together the panes in stained-glass or latticework windows. [Perhaps Scottish *calm,* casting-mould.]

came². Past tense of **come.**

cam·el (kámm'l) *n.* 1. A humped, long-necked ruminant mammal of the genus *Camelus,* domesticated in Old World desert regions as a beast of burden and as a source of wool, milk, and meat. See **Arabian camel, Bactrian camel, dromedary.** 2. A device used to raise a sunken vessel. In this sense, also called "caisson". 3. A light fawn or brownish yellow. [Middle English, from Old English, from Latin *camēlus,* from Greek *kamēlos,* from Semitic; akin to Hebrew and Phoenician *gāmāl,* Arabic *jamal.*]

cam·el·back (kámm'l-bak) *adj.* Having a shape characterised by a hump or upward curve.

cam·el·eer (kámmə-léer) *n.* A person who drives or rides a camel.

ca·mel·lia (kə-méel-i-ə, -yə) *n.* 1. Any of several shrubs or trees of the genus *Camellia,* native to Asia; especially, *C. japonica,* having shiny evergreen leaves and showy, usually white, pink, or red flowers. 2. The flower of a camellia. Also called "japonica". [New

Latin; first described by Georg Josef *Kamel* (1661–1706), Moravian Jesuit missionary.]

ca·mel·o·pard (kámmilə-paard, kə-méllə-) *n.* 1. *Archaic.* A giraffe. 2. *Heraldry.* A bearing resembling a giraffe, but represented with long curved horns. [Medieval Latin *camēlopardus,* from Latin *camēlopardalis,* from Greek *kamēlopardalis* : *kamēlos,* CAMEL + *pardalis,* variant of *pardos,* PARD (leopard), so called because the giraffe has a head like a camel's and the spots of a leopard.]

Cam·e·lot (kámmə-lot, kámmi-). The legendary site of King Arthur's court, and the Round Table. Among the places that claim it are Caerleon, Camelford, Winchester, and Cadbury Camp near Yeovil.

camel's hair *n.* Also **camel hair.** 1. The soft, fine hair of a camel or a substitute for it. 2. A soft, heavy cloth, usually light tan, made chiefly of camel's hair. —**cam·el's-hair** *adj.*

Cam·em·bert (kámməm-bair). Village in Normandy, northwest France, famous for the cheese originally made there.

Camembert *n. Sometimes small* **c.** A creamy French cheese that softens on the inside as it matures.

cam·e·o (kámmi-ō) *n., pl.* **-os.** 1. **a.** A technique of engraving in relief on a gem, stone, or shell, especially one with layers of different hues, cut so the raised design is of one colour and the background of another. Compare **intaglio. b.** A gem, stone, or shell so cut. 2. A medallion with a profile cut in raised relief. 3. A brief literary work or dramatic sketch. 4. A brief but dramatic appearance of a prominent actor or actress in a single scene in a television play or in a film. In this sense, also called "cameo role". [Middle English *cameu,* from Italian *cam(m)eo* and Old French *camaïeu,* perhaps from Arabic *qamā'īl,* plural of *qum'ūl,* flower bud.]

cameo ware *n.* Pottery having raised white figures on a contrasting background.

cam·er·a (kám-rə, kámmə-rə) *n., pl.* **-as** or **-ae** (-ree) (for sense 5). 1. Any apparatus for taking photographs, generally consisting of a lightproof enclosure having an aperture with a shuttered lens through which the image of an object is focused and recorded on a photosensitive film or plate. 2. The part of a television transmitting apparatus that receives the primary image on a light-sensitive cathode tube and transforms it into electrical impulses. 3. A camera obscura. 4. A **cine-camera** (see). 5. A room or chamber; specifically, a judge's private office. —**in camera.** *Law.* In court with only the judge and litigants or their representatives present. [Late Latin, room, from Latin *camera,* arched roof, from Greek *kamara,* vault.]

cam·er·al (kámmər'l) *adj.* 1. Pertaining to a judge's chamber and to the judicial affairs that take place there. 2. Pertaining to public finance and state business or to a council that manages such matters. [Medieval Latin *camerālis,* from *camera,* office, department of state, CAMERA.]

camera lu·ci·da (lŏo-síddə, léw-) *n.* An optical device that projects a virtual image of an object onto a plane surface, especially for tracing. [New Latin, "light chamber" : CAMERA + Latin *lūcīda,* feminine of *lūcīdus,* LUCID.]

cam·er·a·man (kám-rə-man, kámmə-, -mən) *n., pl.* **-men** (-men). A man who operates a cine-camera or television camera.

camera ob·scu·ra (ob-skéwr-ə, əb-) *n.* A darkened chamber in which the real image of an object is received through a small opening or lens and focused in natural colour onto a facing surface. Also called "camera". [New Latin, "dark chamber" : CAMERA + Latin *obscūra,* feminine of *obscūrus,* OBSCURE.]

cam·er·a-rea·dy copy (kám-rə-réddi, kámmə-) *n.* Typeset matter reproduced photographically onto bromide paper, with any illustrations pasted into position, so that it can be photographed to produce the film used in platemaking. Also *chiefly U.S.* "mechanical".

cam·er·a-shy (kám-rə-shī, kámmə-) *adj.* Reluctant or nervous about being photographed.

camera tube *n.* The part of a television camera that converts the optical image into electrical signals.

cam·er·a·wo·man (kám-rə-wŏoman, kámmə-) *n., pl.* **-women** (-wimmin). A woman who operates a cine-camera or television camera.

cam·er·lin·go (kámmər-ling-gō) *n., pl.* **-gos.** Also **cam·er·len·go** (-léng-gō). *Roman Catholic Church.* The cardinal who manages the pope's secular affairs. [Italian *camarlingo,* from Germanic *kamarling* (unattested), "chamber servant" : *kamar* (unattested), room, from Late Latin *camera,* CAMERA + -LING.]

Cam·er·on (kámmə-rən, kám- ‖ kámmərn), **Julia Margaret,** born J.M. Pattle (1815–79). British photographer noted for her pioneering work in artistic portrait photography. Tennyson, Darwin, and Ellen Terry were among her subjects.

Cam·e·roon, Republic of (kámmə-rŏon, -rŏon). Country in West central Africa. Originally the German colony of Kamerun, the country was divided between Britain and France (1919). French Cameroon was granted independence (1960) as the Cameroon Republic, and was joined by the southern part of the British Cameroons (when the remainder of the British territory joined Nigeria) to form the Federal Republic of Cameroon (1961). In 1984, it became the United Republic of Cameroon. Coffee, cocoa, and timber are the main exports. Off-shore oil deposits and large reserves of bauxite are being exploited. The main city and port is Douala. Area, 475 442 square kilometres (183,521 square miles). Population, 13,560,000. Capital, Yaoundé.

cam·i·knick·ers (kámmi-nickərz) *pl.n. British.* An undergarment worn by women, consisting of a pair of knickers combined with a camisole top. [*camisole* + *knickers.*]

cam·i·on (kámmi-ən; *French* kam-yóN) *n.* 1. A low, sturdy wagon.

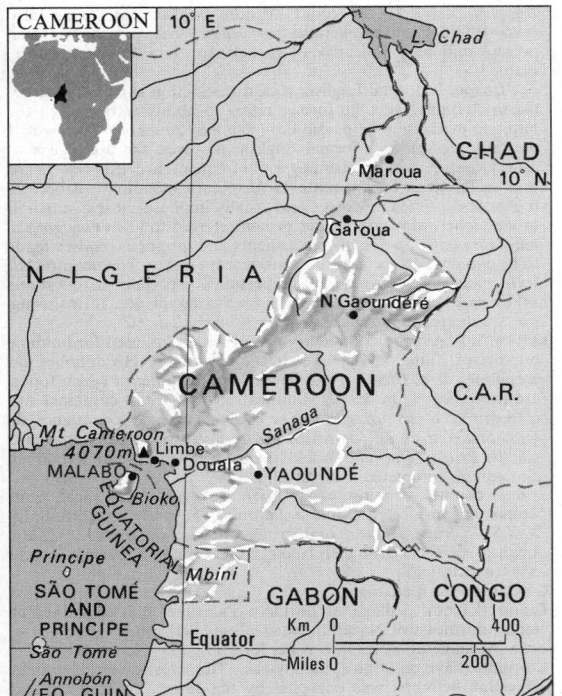

CAMEROON 10° E

2. A lorry. [French, from Old French *chamiont*.]

ca·mise (kə-méez || -méess) *n.* A loose shirt, shift, or tunic. [Arabic *qamīs*, from Late Latin *camīsia*, shirt.]

cam·i·sole (kámmi-sōl) *n.* 1. A woman's sleeveless underbodice. 2. A short negligee. [French, from Old Provençal *camisolla*, diminutive of *camisa*, shirt, from Late Latin *camīsia*.]

Cam·lan (kámlən). According to legend, the battlefield where King Arthur was mortally wounded.

cam·let (kám-lət, -lit) *n.* 1. A kind of rich cloth of Oriental origin, supposed to have been made formerly of camel's hair and silk, and later made of goat's hair and silk or other combinations. 2. A garment made from this cloth. [Middle English *chamelet*, from Old French *c(h)amelot*, from Arabic *ḥamlat*.]

Ca·mões (kə-móysh), **Luis Vaz de.** Also **Cam·o·ëns** (kámmō-enss) (1524–80). Portuguese poet and soldier noted for his book *Os Lusíadas* (1572), possibly the greatest of all Portuguese literary works.

camomile, chamomile (kámmə-mīl) *n.* 1. Any of various plants of the genus *Anthemis* or *Chamaemelum*; especially, *A. nobilis*, a Eurasian species with finely dissected leaves and white flowers. 2. Any of several similar plants of the related genus *Matricaria*; especially, *M chamomilla* of Eurasia. [Middle English, from Old French *camomille*, from Late Latin *chamomilla*, from Greek *khamaimēlon*, "earth-apple" (referring to the apple scent of the flowers).]

camomile tea *n.* A drink made by infusing the flowers or leaves of camomile plants, believed to have medicinal properties.

Ca·mor·ra (kə-mórrə || -máwrə) *n.* 1. A Neapolitan secret society organised about 1820, notorious for practising violence and blackmail. Compare **Mafia.** 2. Any unscrupulous, clandestine group. [Italian, perhaps from *camorra†*, a smock (supposedly worn by members of this society).] —**Ca·mor·rism** *n.* —**Ca·mor·rist** *n. & adj.*

cam·ou·flage (kámmə-flaazh, -flaaj) *n.* 1. *Military.* The method or materials used when concealing people or things from the enemy by making them appear to be part of the natural surroundings. 2. a. The condition of an animal being concealed from its predators or prey by means of protective coloration or shape. b. The protective coloration or shape of an animal. 3. Any means of concealment; dissimulation.
~*v.* **camouflaged, -flaging, -flages.** —*tr.* To conceal by disguise. —*intr.* To use camouflage. [French, from *camoufler*, to disguise, from Italian *camuffare†*, to disguise, trick.]

camp[1] (kamp) *n.* 1. a. A place where a body of people, such as soldiers, miners, or sportsmen, are temporarily lodged in tents, huts, or other makeshift shelters. b. The shelters in such a place or the persons using them. 2. A place where enemy aliens, political prisoners, and the like are detained. 3. A place consisting of more or less permanent cabins, caravans, tents, or other shelters, used for holidaying or other recreational purposes. 4. Military service; army life. 5. A group of persons, parties, or states favourable to a common cause, doctrine, or political system: *the socialist camp.*
~*adj.* 1. Pertaining to or used in a camp or camping. 2. Being portable and usually collapsible: *a camp bed.*
~*intr.v.* **camped, camping, camps.** 1. To make or set up a camp. 2. To live in or as if in a camp: *We camped in the flat until the furniture arrived.* —**camp out.** To sleep in the open. [French, from Italian *campo*, from Latin *campus†*, open field.]

camp[2] *adj.* 1. Theatrical, affected, or exaggerated in manner or style. 2. Effeminately homosexual. Said of a man. 3. In the style of an effeminate man; mannered.
~*intr.v.* **camped, camping, camps.** To act in a theatrical or effeminate manner. Used in the phrase *camp it up.* [20th century : origin obscure.] —**camp·y** *adj.*

cam·paign (kam-páyn, kám-) *n.* 1. A series of military operations undertaken to achieve a specific objective within a given area. 2. An operation undertaken, as by means of propaganda, to attain some political, social, commercial, or personal goal.
~*intr.v.* **campaigned, -paigning, -paigns.** To engage or serve in a campaign. [French *campagne*, from Old French, battlefield, from Italian *campania*, from Late Latin *campānia*, countryside, from *campus*, field.] —**cam·paign·er** *n.*

Cam·pa·ni·a (kam-páyni-ə, -pán-yə). Region in southern Italy spanning the provinces of Avellino, Benevento, Caserta, Napoli, and Salerno, with the islands of Capri, Ischia, Porcida, and the Pontine Islands. It joined Italy (1861) as part of the kingdom of Naples. The excavated Roman towns of Pompeii and Herculaneum and the region's many resorts give it a large tourist trade.

cam·pa·ni·le (kámpə-née-li) *n., pl.* **-les** (-liz) or **-li** (-lee). A bell tower, especially one near but not attached to a church. [Italian, from *campana*, bell, from Late Latin *campāna* (made of metal produced in Campania), from Latin *campānus*, of Campania.]

cam·pa·nol·o·gy (kámpə-nólləji) *n.* The art or study of bell ringing. [New Latin *campanologia* : Late Latin *campāna*, bell (see **campanile**) + -LOGY.] —**cam·pa·nol·o·gist** *n.*

cam·pan·u·la (kam-pánnew-lə) *n.* Any of various plants of the genus *Campanula*, usually having blue or white bell-shaped flowers. Also called "bellflower". See **Canterbury bell, harebell.** [New Latin, diminutive of Late Latin *campāna*, bell. See **campanile.**]

cam·pan·u·late (kam-pánnew-lət, -lit, -layt) *adj.* Also **cam·pan·i·form** (-pánni-fawrm). Bell-shaped: *campanulate flowers.* [New Latin *campanula*, small bell.]

Camp·bell (kámb'l), **Donald** (1921–67). British racing driver, son of Sir Malcolm. In Australia in 1964 he broke the world speed records both for wheel-driven cars and for speedboats. He died in 1967 during another attempt on the water speed record, when his jet-powered boat, Bluebird, was wrecked.

Campbell, (Ignatius) Roy(ston Dunnachie) (1901–57). South African poet and satirist, who spent part of his working life in England, where he was associated with the Bloomsbury Group. He also translated many European poets into English.

Campbell, Sir Malcolm (1885–1948). British motor engineer who held the land speed record nine times between 1924 and 1935, and the water speed record three times between 1937 and 1939.

Campbell, Mrs Patrick, born Beatrice Stella Tanner (1865–1940). Leading British actress, who played the original Eliza in *Pygmalion,* a part written especially for her by George Bernard Shaw. She also played roles in Shakespeare and Ibsen with great success.

Camp·bell-Ban·ner·man (kámb'l-bánnərmən), **Sir Henry** (1836–1908). British Liberal prime minister (1905–08). His government passed the Trades Disputes Act (1906), giving trade unionists greater freedom to strike.

Camp David. The official country retreat of the president of the United States, in the Appalachian Mountains, Maryland. It was here (1978) that President Carter mediated at a meeting between Anwar Sadat and Menachem Begin that led to the 1979 peace treaty between Egypt and Israel.

camp·er (kámpər) *n.* 1. A person who camps outdoors or who attends a camp for recreation. 2. A motor vehicle equipped for use as temporary living accommodation.

cam·pes·tral (kam-péstrəl) *adj.* Rare. Pertaining to or growing in uncultivated land or open fields. [Latin *campester*, of the fields, from *campus*, field.]

camp·fire (kámp-fīr) *n.* An outdoor fire in a camp.

camp follower *n.* 1. A civilian who follows an army from place to place to sell goods or services, especially sexual services. 2. One who sympathises with but does not belong to a main body or group.

cam·phene (kám-feen) *n.* A colourless crystalline compound, $C_{10}H_{16}$, used in the manufacture of synthetic camphor.

cam·phor (kámfər) *n.* A volatile crystalline compound, $C_{10}H_{16}O$, obtained from camphor tree wood or synthesised and used as an insect repellent, in the manufacture of film, plastics, lacquers, and explosives, and medicinally as a stimulant, expectorant, and diaphoretic. [Middle English *ca(u)mfre*, from Old French *camphre*, or Medieval Latin *camphora*, from Arabic *kāfūr*, from Sanskrit *karpūram*.] —**cam·phor·ic** (kam-fórrik) *adj.*

cam·phor·ate (kámfərayt) *tr.v.* **-ated, -ating, -ates.** To treat, fill, or saturate with camphor.

cam·pho·rat·ed oil (kámfəraytid) *n.* A liniment containing camphor and vegetable oil, used as a counterirritant.

camphor tree *n.* An evergreen tree, *Cinnamomum camphora,* native to eastern Asia, having aromatic wood that is a source of camphor.

cam·pi·on (kámp-i-ən) *n.* Any of various plants of the genus *Silene* (or *Lychnis*), having red, pink, or white flowers. See **bladder campion.** [Probably from *campion,* obsolete variant of CHAMPION; applied first to *lychnis coronaria,* "crowning lychnis" (whose leaves were formerly used to make crowns for athletic champions).]

Cam·pi·on (kámpi-ən), **Saint Edmund** (1540–81). English Jesuit martyr. Ordained an Anglican deacon, he was converted to Roman Catholicism (1571) in Douai. He was executed in England for circulating anti-Anglican literature (1581) and was canonised in 1970.

Campion (kámp-yən, -i-ən), **Thomas** (1567–1620). English composer, poet, and physician. The *Poemata* and his *Masques* are among his best-known works.

camp meeting *n. Chiefly U.S.* An evangelistic gathering held in a tent or outdoors and often lasting several days.

cam·po (kámpō) *n., pl.* **-pos** (-pōz). In South America and the Falkland Islands, a large, grassy plain with occasional bushes and small trees. [Portuguese, from Latin *campus*.]

camp·site (kámp-sīt) *n.* An area suitable for camping or pitching tents.

camp·stool (kámp-stōol) *n.* A light folding stool.

cam·pus (kámpəss) *n., pl.* **-puses.** **1. a.** The grounds of a college or university, especially when situated away from an urban centre. **b.** The college or university itself. **2.** In ancient Rome, a field used for various events, such as games, military exercises, and public meetings. [Latin *campus*, field, plain (sense 1, first used at Princeton University, United States).]

CAM·RA (kámrə) *n. Cam*paign for *R*eal *A*le.

Cam Ranh Bay (kám rán). Natural harbour in the South China Sea on the coast of south Vietnam. 20 kilometres (12 miles) wide, and protected by two peninsulas, it was a naval, military, and air base during the Vietnam War.

cam·shaft (kám-shaaft ‖ -shaft) *n.* An engine shaft fitted with a cam or cams, especially one used to operate the valves of an internal-combustion engine.

Ca·mus (kə-méw, kaa-, -mŭ), **Albert** (1913–60). French existentialist novelist. A member of the Algerian Communist Party (1934–35), he edited the French Resistance magazine *Combat* during the Nazi occupation of France. Among his best-known works are *The Outsider* (1946) and *The Plague* (1948). In 1957, he was awarded the Nobel prize for literature.

cam·wood (kám-wōod) *n.* **1.** An African tree, *Baphia nitida,* whose hard red-brown wood has been used as the source of a red dye. **2.** The wood of this tree.

can¹ (kan; *weak form* kən) *v.* Past tense **could,** present tense **can** or *archaic* **canst** (for second person singular). Used as an auxiliary, followed by an infinitive without *to,* or with the infinitive understood. It can indicate: **1. a.** Ability to do or perform: *I can meet you today.* **b.** With verbs of sense perception, ability plus achievement: *At last I can see the sun.* **2.** Possession of a specified power, right, or means: *Only the judge can save her from prison.* **3.** Possession of a specified capacity, faculty, or skill: *He can tune the harpsichord as well as play it.* **4.** Possibility or likelihood: *I wonder if she can be alive after all these years.* **5. a.** Right or sanction: *you can't drive without a licence.* **b.** Permission granted according to one's conscience or feelings. Used in the negative: *I can't let you take such a risk.* **6.** A requesting or granting of permission: *Can I be excused?*

No, you cannot. [Can, could; Middle English *can, coude* (also *couthe*), Old English *can* (also *con*), *cūthe,* first and third person present and past indicative of *cunnan,* to know how, from Germanic.]

Usage: In formal English, a clear distinction is maintained between *can* and *may:* the former refers to ability (*I can sing*), the latter to permission or possibility (*You may sing now; Tomorrow I may sing again*). In informal English, however, the use of *can* to refer to permission is becoming more frequent, and it is now heard even in relatively formal contexts. *May,* correspondingly, is becoming more restricted in its use, and usually implies a clear distinction in status between speaker and person referred to (*You may go; she may leave now*). In negative statements and questions, *mayn't* tends to be avoided, on account of its awkwardness, but the uncontracted form *may not* is also quite cumbersome, especially in questions (*Why may I not buy that book?*). As a consequence, forms using *can* are increasingly replacing *may: Why can't I...?*

can² *n.* **1. a.** A metal container, open or with a lid, used for holding oil, petrol, film, or the like. **b.** *Plural. Slang.* Headphones or earphones. **2. a.** *Chiefly U.S.* An airtight container in which foods are preserved; a tin. **b.** A cylindrical airtight metal container for cold drinks: *a can of lager.* **c.** The contents of such a container. **3.** *U.S. Slang.* **a.** A jail or prison. **b.** A lavatory. **—carry the can.** *Chiefly British Informal.* To take the blame. **—in the can.** Recorded and edited; completed. Said of film.

~tr.v. **canned, canning, cans. 1.** To seal (vegetables, meat, fruit, drinks, or jam) in a tin; tin. **2.** *Informal.* To make a recording of. **3.** *U.S. Informal.* To stop or dispense with: *can the chatter.* [Middle English *canne,* Old English *canne,* from Common Germanic *kannōn-* (unattested).]

Can. Canada; Canadian.

Ca·na (káynə). Village in northern Palestine, 6.5 kilometres (4 miles) northeast of Nazareth, where Jesus performed his first miracle by changing water into wine. John 2:1, 11.

Ca·naan (káyn-ən, -yən ‖ kə-náy-ən). The name given to ancient Palestine before it was occupied by the Jews. Covering an area approximately equal to that of Israel, western Jordan, and southern Syria, it was referred to in the Bible as the land promised by God to the Israelites.

Ca·naan·ite (káyn-ən-īt, -yən-) *n.* **1.** One of the Semitic inhabitants of the ancient land of Canaan before its conquest by the Israelites. **2.** The Semitic language of this people. **—Ca·naan·it·ic** (-íttik) *adj.*

Can·a·da (kánnədə). A country occupying (with the exception of Alaska) the northern part of North America. The second largest country in the world, it has six different time zones, ten provinces, two territories (the Northwest Territories and the Yukon), and two main languages (English and French). The population, concen-

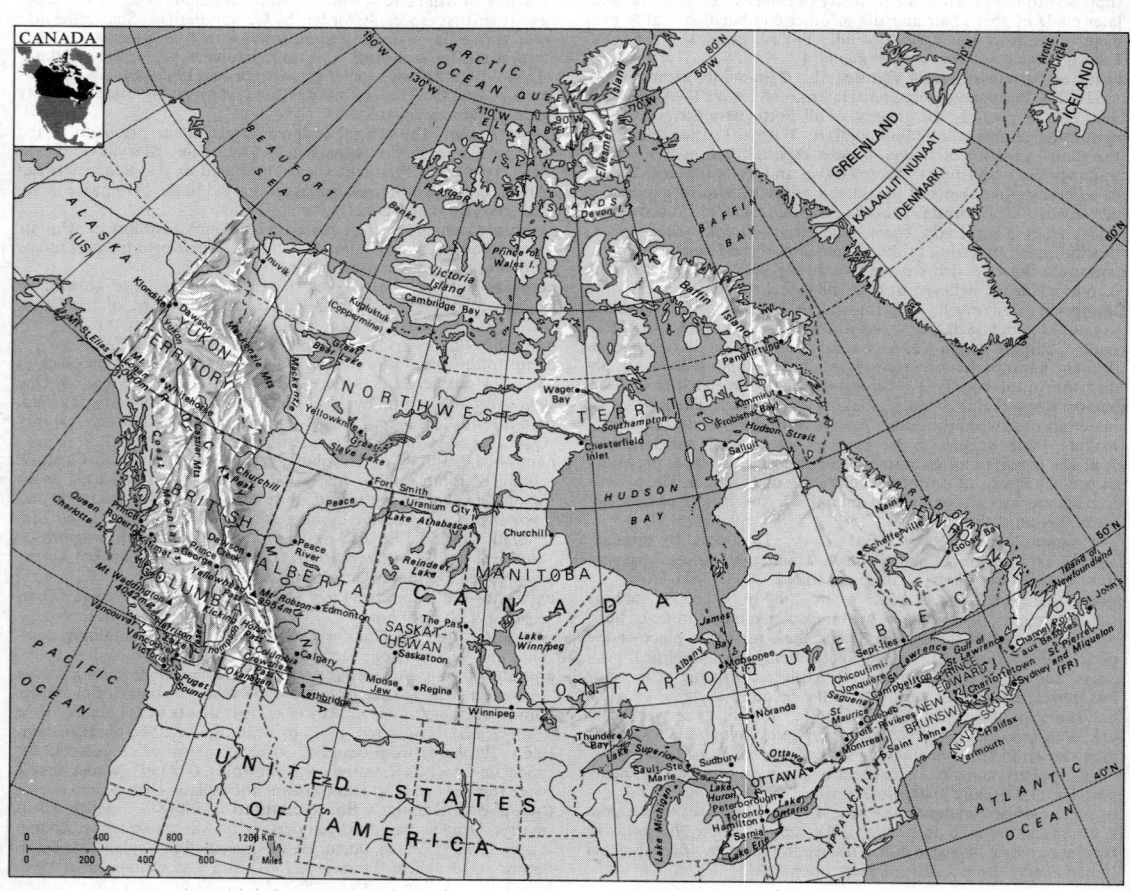

trated in the southeast, includes Europeans (the main ethnic group), about 250,000 Indians, mostly living in reserves, and 17,000 Eskimos. The Canadian coast was reached by John Cabot who sailed from Bristol (1497), but it was Samuel de Champlain who founded the first permanent settlement, at Quebec (1608). Quebec, known as New France, became a royal province of the French crown (1663). With the British Hudson's Bay Company establishing fur trading posts and strongholds in the Hudson Bay area, a seven-year war broke out between the British and the French (1756). In 1763 Canada was ceded to Britain. With the British North America Act (1867) the Dominion of Canada, a federation of the provinces of Lower Canada (Quebec), Upper Canada (Ontario), New Brunswick, and Nova Scotia, was formed. Between then and 1905, Rupert's Land (Northwest Territories) was acquired from the Hudson's Bay Company, and Manitoba, British Columbia, Prince Edward Island, Alberta, and Saskatchewan became part of the federation. The Statute of Westminster (1931) confirmed and defined Canada as an independent constitutional monarchy equal in status to Britain in the Commonwealth. Since Newfoundland joined the Federation (1949), Canada has had ten provinces, in spite of the autonomist Parti Québecois in the largely French-speaking province of Quebec. Fishing is Canada's oldest industry, and modern and effective farming methods produce spring wheat, oats, barley, and hay. Manufacturing industries include paper, motor vehicles, iron, steel, and food processing. Canada is rich in mineral resources and exports natural gas, petroleum, iron ore, nickel, zinc, copper, gold, and uranium. With forests covering a third of the country, Canada supplies the world with woodpulp, newsprint, and timber. The traditional fur trade still flourishes. Area, 9 958 319 square kilometres (3,844,928 square miles). Population, 29,960,000. Capital, Ottawa. **—Ca·na·di·an** (kə-náydi-ən) n. & adj.

Canada balsam n. **1.** A viscous, yellowish, transparent resin obtained from the balsam fir and used as a mounting cement for microscope specimens. **2.** A tree, the **balsam fir** (see).

Canada goose n. A common wild goose, *Branta canadensis,* originally of North America but introduced into Britain in the 17th century, having greyish plumage, a black neck and head, and a white face patch.

Canadian bacon n. Cured rolled bacon from the loin of a pig.

Canadian French n. The French language as spoken and written in Canada, chiefly in Quebec and the Maritime Provinces.

Canadian pondweed n. A North American water plant, *Elodea canadensis,* with dark green leaves, that is naturalised in Europe and planted in aquariums. Also called "pondweed".

ca·naille (kə-nī || -náyl) n. The masses; the rabble; the mob. [French, from Italian *canaglia,* "pack of dogs", from *cane,* dog, from Latin *canis.*]

ca·nal (kə-nál) n. **1.** A man-made waterway or artificially improved river used for irrigation, shipping, or travel. **2.** *Anatomy.* A tube or duct.
~tr.v. canalled or *U.S.* **-naled, -nalling** or *U.S.* **-naling, -nals. 1.** To dig an artificial waterway through. **2.** To provide with a canal or canals. [Middle English, tube, from Latin *canālis,* channel, from *canna,* reed, from Greek *kanna.*]

Can·a·let·to (kánnə-léttō), born Giovanni Antonio Canal (1697-1768). Venetian painter famous for his views of Venice and London. Canaletto was a master of light, flickering colours, and shadows, and his works influenced landscape artists for generations.

can·a·lic·u·lus (kánnə-líckew-ləss) n., pl. **-li** (-lī). *Anatomy.* A small bodily channel, such as any of those in bone. [Latin, diminutive of *canālis,* CANAL.] **—can·a·lic·u·lar** (-lər), **can·a·lic·u·late** adj.

ca·nal·i·sa·tion (kánn'l-ī-záysh'n || kə-nál-, *U.S.* -i-) n. **1.** The act or an instance of canalising. **2.** A system of canals.

ca·nal·ise, ca·nal·ize (kánn'l-īz || kə-nál-) tr.v. **-ised, -ising, -ises. 1.** To furnish with, build, or convert into a canal or canals. **2.** To channel into a particular direction; provide an outlet for.

canal rays pl.n. Positively charged ions formed in a gas by electrical discharge and attracted to the cathode of the discharge tube. Not in current technical usage. [Translation of German *Kanalstrahlen* (because the ions pass through fissures in the cathode).]

can·a·pé (kánnə-pay, -pi) n. A biscuit or small, thin piece of bread or toast spread with cheese, meat, or relish, and served as an appetiser. [French, "couch" ("seat" for the relish), from Medieval Latin *canapeum.* See **canopy.**]

ca·nard (kánnaard, ka-nárd, kə-) n. A false or unfounded story or item of news. [French "duck" (from the expression *vendre des canards à moitié,* "to half-sell ducks", swindle, deceive), from Old French *canart,* duck, from *caner,* to cackle (imitative).]

ca·nar·y (kə-naír-i) n., pl. **-ies. 1.** A songbird, *Serinus canaria,* native to the Canary Islands, that is greenish to yellow and has long been bred as a cage bird, being popular especially for its singing. **2.** A sweet white wine, similar to Madeira, from the Canary Islands. **3.** A lively 16th-century French and English court dance. [French *canari* (bird), *canarie* (wine, dance), from Old Spanish *canario,* "of the Canary Islands", from *Islas Canarias,* CANARY ISLANDS, from Latin *Canaria,* from *Canis,* dog (one of the islands was famous among the Romans for its breed of large dogs).]

canary creeper n. A climbing plant, *Tropaeolum peregrinum,* that is closely related, and similar, to the nasturtium. [After its yellow flowers.]

canary grass n. A grass, *Phalaris canariensis,* native to Europe, having straw-coloured seeds used to feed birds.

Ca·nar·y Islands (kə-naír-i). Also **Canaries;** *Spanish* **Islas Canarias.** Group of volcanic islands in the North Atlantic Ocean, 96 kilometres (60 miles) off the northwest coast of Africa. It comprises two provinces of Spain, each named after their capitals: Las Palmas de Gran Canaria has the islands of Fuerteventura, Lanzarote, Gran Canaria, and six uninhabited islands; Santa Cruz de Tenerife contains the islands of Tenerife, La Palma, Gomera, and Hierro. The islands were once possessions of Ferdinand and Isabella of Aragón-Castile (1476). After a treaty between Portugal and Aragón-Castile (1479), they became wholly subject to Spain. Having a mild climate, the islands are popular as a winter resort. With the help of irrigation citrus fruits, bananas, tomatoes, peaches, onions, and potatoes are grown for export.

canary yellow n. Vivid yellow with a slight greenish tinge.

ca·nas·ta (kə-nástə) n. **1.** A card game for two to six players, related to rummy and requiring two packs of cards. **2.** A meld of seven cards in this game. [Spanish, "basket" (from the use of two packs, or a "basketful", of cards), from *canasto, canastro,* basket, from Latin *canistrum,* CANISTER.]

can·as·ter (kánnəstər) n. Tobacco made from dried leaves that have been roughly shredded. [Spanish *canastro,* basket (referring to the rush baskets in which the tobacco was shipped). See **canister.**]

Ca·nav·er·al, Cape (kə-návvərəl). Known 1963–73 as Cape Kennedy. Cape on the east coast of Florida, United States. It is the site of NASA's Kennedy Space Center, the key launching site for all U.S. space missions.

Can·ber·ra (kán-berə, -brə). Capital of Australia. Situated on the Molongo river in the Australian Capital Territory, it was founded in 1824, chosen as capital (1908), and planned by the U.S. architect Walter Burley Griffin. It is the seat of the Australian National University and of the Commonwealth Parliament.

can·can (kán-kan) n. An exuberant dance popular especially in 19th-century France, performed by women and marked by high kicking. [French, earlier (16th century) "noise", "uproar", of obscure origin.]

can·cel (kánss'l) v. **-celled** or *U.S.* **-celed, -celling** or *U.S.* **-celing, -cels. 1.** To put off (an event, appointment, or the like); postpone indefinitely. **2.** To cross out with lines or other markings. **3. a.** To annul, revoke, or invalidate. **b.** To mark or perforate (a postage stamp or cheque, for example) to indicate that it may not be used again. **4.** To equalise or make up for; neutralise; offset. Usually followed by *out.* **5.** *Mathematics.* **a.** To remove (a common factor) from the numerator and denominator of a fractional expression. **b.** To remove (a common factor or term) from both members of an equation or inequality. **6.** *Printing.* To omit or delete. **—See Synonyms** at **erase, nullify.**
~n. *Abbr.* **canc. 1. a.** The omission or reprinting of a page of typed or printed matter. **b.** The page omitted or its replacement. **2.** Any part of a book used as a substitute for an original part of the book. **3.** *U.S.* In music, a **natural** (see). [Middle English *cancellen,* from Old French *canceller,* from Latin *cancellāre,* to make like a lattice, cross out, from *cancellī,* lattice, diminutive of *cancer, carcer,* jail.] **—can·cel·la·ble** adj. **—can·cel·ler** n.

can·cel·late (kán-sə-layt, kan-sé-) adj. Also **can·cel·lat·ed** (-laytid), **can·cel·lous** (-ləss). **1.** *Anatomy.* Having a coarse netlike or spongy structure. Said of bone. **2.** *Botany.* In the form of a network, as the vein pattern of some leaves is. [Latin *cancellātus,* past participle of *cancellāre,* to make like a lattice. See **cancel.**]

can·cel·la·tion (kán-sə-láysh'n) n. **1.** The act of cancelling. **2.** Marks or perforations indicating cancelling. **3.** Something that has been cancelled. **4.** Something, such as a ticket or hotel room, that becomes available after a reservation has been cancelled.

can·cer (kán-sər) n. **1. a.** Any of various malignant tumours, caused by abnormal division of cells, which invade surrounding tissues and often spread to other parts of the body through the blood or lymph. **b.** The pathological condition characterised by such growths. **2.** A pernicious, spreading evil. [Latin *cancer,* crab, creeping ulcer (formed after Greek *karkinōma,* CARCINOMA).] **—can·cer·ous** adj.

Can·cer (kán-sər) n. **1.** A constellation in the Northern Hemisphere near Leo and Gemini. **2.** The fourth sign of the **zodiac** (see). Also called the "Crab". **3.** One born under this sign. [Middle English, from Latin *cancer,* crab.] **—Can·cer·i·an** (kan-séer-i-ən) n. & adj.

can·croid (kángkroyd) adj. **1.** Similar to a cancer. **2.** Similar to a crab.
~n. A skin cancer. [Latin *cancer* (stem *cancr-*), crab, CANCER + -OID.]

can·del·a (kan-déela, -dáylə, -déllə) n. *Abbr.* **cd** The SI unit of luminous intensity equal to 1/600,000 of the luminous intensity per square metre of a black body radiating at the temperature of solidification of platinum (2,046°K) under a pressure of 101,325 newtons per square metre. Also called "candle", "standard candle". [Latin *candēla,* CANDLE.]

can·de·la·bra (kán-də-la'abrə, -də-, -lábrə) n., pl. **-bras.** A candelabrum.

can·de·la·brum (kándi-la'a-brəm, -lá-, -láy-) n., pl. **-bra** (-brə) or **-brums.** A large decorative candlestick having several arms or branches. [Latin *candēlābrum,* from *candēla,* CANDLE.]
Usage: Two different usage trends have affected this word. First, its original Latin-based plural, *candelabra,* has been in conflict with a later English-based plural, *candelabrums,* considered to be incorrect in formal speech or writing. Secondly, *candelabra* has increasingly come to be used as a singular form, from which a new English-based plural form has derived: *I bought a new candelabra*

today; The candelabras need cleaning. This second development is widespread in all but the most formal and technical contexts.

can·dent (kándənt) *adj. Rare.* Having a white-hot glow; incandescent. [Latin *candēns* (stem *candent-*), present participle of *candēre,* to shine, glow, be white.]

Candia. See **Iráklion.**

can·did (kándid) *adj.* **1.** Without pretence or reserve; straightforward; open. **2.** Without prejudice; impartial; fair. **3.** Not posed or rehearsed: *a candid snapshot.* —See Synonyms at **frank.** [French *candide,* from Latin *candidus,* glowing, white, pure, guileless, from *candēre,* to glow, be white.] —**can·did·ly** *adv.* —**can·did·ness** *n.*

can·di·date (kándi-dət, -dayt, -dit) *n.* **1.** A person who seeks or is nominated for an office, prize, honour, or the like. **2.** A person who seems likely to gain a certain position or undergo a certain state. **3.** Something which seems likely to be chosen. [Latin *candidātus,* "(Roman candidate) clothed in a white toga," from *candidus,* white, CANDID.] —**can·di·da·cy** (-də-si), **can·di·da·ture** (-də-chər, -choor, -tewr) *n.*

candid camera *n.* Any small, easily operated camera with a fast lens for taking unposed or informal photographs.

Can·dide (kón-deéd, kan-) *n.* An ingenuous youth whose views remain unaffected by the often adverse circumstances in which he finds himself. [After the hero of Voltaire's satire, *Candide* (1759).]

can·di·di·a·sis (kándi-dī-ə-siss) *n.* Infection with a fungus of the genus *Candida,* usually affecting moist areas of the body. Also called "moniliasis". [New Latin *Candida* (genus name), from Latin *candidus,* white + -IASIS.]

can·died (kán-did ‖ -deed) *adj.* **1.** Covered, encrusted, or cooked with sugar: *candied fruit.* **2.** Flattering or ingratiating.

Can·di·ot (kándi-ot) *adj.* Also **Can·di·ote** (-ōt). Of or pertaining to Candia (Iráklion) or Crete.

~ *n.* A native or inhabitant of Crete; Cretan.

can·dle (kánd'l) *n.* **1.** A block, usually a cylinder, of tallow, wax, or other fatty substance, containing a wick that is burnt to provide light. **2.** Anything resembling a candle in use or shape. **3. a.** *Physics.* An obsolete unit of luminous intensity, originally defined in terms of a wax candle with standard composition and equal to 1.02 candelas. Also called "international candle". **b.** *Symbol* **c.** A **candela** *(see).* —**burn the candle at both ends.** To exhaust oneself by leading too hectic a life. —**not hold a candle to.** To be not nearly so good as.

~ *tr.v.* **candled, -dling, -dles.** To examine (an egg) for freshness in front of a light. [Middle English *candel,* Old English *candel,* from Latin *candēla,* from *candēre,* to shine.] —**can·dler** *n.*

can·dle·ber·ry (kánd'l-bəri ‖ -berri) *n., pl.* **-ries.** A shrub or tree, the **wax myrtle** *(see),* or its fruit. [From the wax in the berry.]

can·dle·fish (kand'l-fish) *n., pl.* **-fishes** or collectively **candlefish.** An oily, edible fish, *Thaleichthys pacificus,* of northern Pacific waters, formerly dried and used as a torch. Also called "eulachon".

can·dle·light (kánd'l-līt) *n.* **1.** Illumination from a candle or candles. **2.** *Rare.* Dusk; twilight.

Can·dle·mas (kánd'l-məss) *n.* A church festival celebrated on February 2 as the feast of the purification of the Virgin Mary and the presentation of the infant Jesus in the temple. [Middle English *candelmasse,* Old English *candelmæsse* : CANDLE + -MAS (candles for church use were blessed at the feast).]

can·dle·nut (kánd'l-nut) *n.* **1.** A tree, *Aleurites moluccana,* of tropical Asia and Polynesia, bearing nuts that yield an oil used in paints and varnishes. **2.** The nut of this tree. [From the use of the oily nuts as candles.]

can·dle·pin (kánd'l-pin) *n.* A slender bowling pin used in a variation of the game of tenpins.

can·dle·pins (kánd'l-pinz) *n. Used with a singular verb.* A bowling game played with a ball smaller than that used in tenpins and a different scoring system.

can·dle·pow·er (kánd'l-powr) *n.* Luminous intensity of a light source in a given direction, expressed in candelas.

can·dle·stick (kánd'l-stik) *n.* A holder, often ornamental, with a cup or spike for a candle. Also called "candleholder".

can·dle·wick (kánd'l-wik) *n.* **1.** The wick of a candle. **2.** Soft, heavy cotton material into which cotton tufts are hooked to make a pattern. Also used adjectivally: *a candlewick bedspread.*

can·dle·wood (kánd'l-wŏŏd) *n.* **1.** A tree, the **ocotillo** *(see).* **2.** The resinous wood of this or similar trees. [After the use of the wood for torches and as a substitute for candles.]

can·do (kán-dōō) *adj.* Of, pertaining to, or designating a cast of mind according to which you can do anything because nothing is impossible: *a can-do mentality; a can-do kind of guy.*

can·dour, *U.S.* **can·dor** (kándər) *n.* **1.** Frankness of expression; sincerity; straightforwardness. **2.** Freedom from prejudice; impartiality. [Latin *candor,* whiteness, purity, frankness, from *candēre,* to glow, be white.]

C & W. country-and-western.

can·dy (kándi) *n., pl.* **-dies. 1.** A kind of boiled sweet. **2.** *U.S.* Confectionery. **3.** *U.S.* A piece of confectionery.

~ *v.* **candied, -dying, -dies.** —*tr.* **1.** To reduce to sugar crystals. **2.** To cook, preserve, saturate, or coat with sugar or syrup. —*intr.* **1.** To crystallise. Used of sugar. **2.** To become coated with sugar or syrup. [Short for *sugar candy,* from French *sucre candi,* from Arabic *sūkkar qandī,* from *qand,* sugar, from Persian, from Sanskrit *khanda,* sugar in lumps.]

candy floss *n. British.* Sugar spun into a fluffy mass and wound round a stick. Also *Australian* "fairy floss", *U.S.* "cotton candy".

can·dy-striped (kándi-strīpt) *adj.* Having narrow stripes, usually of pink and white.

can·dy-tuft (kándi-tuft) *n.* Any of various plants of the genus *Iberis,* cultivated for their clusters of white, red, or purplish flowers. [*Candy,* obsolete variant of *Candia,* Crete + TUFT.]

cane (kayn) *n.* **1. a.** A slender, jointed stem, woody but usually flexible, as of bamboo, rattan, or certain palm trees. **b.** Any plant having such a stem. **c.** Such stems, or strips of such stems, used for wickerwork. Also used adjectivally: *cane work; a cane chair.* **2.** Any of various grasses with long, stiff stems, especially of the genus *Arundinaria.* **3.** The long, woody stem of the raspberry, blackberry, certain roses, or similar plants. **4. Sugar cane** *(see).* **5.** A stick used as an aid in walking or carried as an accessory. **6.** A rod used for flogging, especially in schools.

~ *tr.v.* **caned, caning, canes. 1.** To make, supply, or repair with cane. **2.** To hit or beat with a cane. [Middle English, from Old French *cane,* from Latin *canna,* from Greek *kanna,* reed.] —**can·er** *n.*

Ca·ne·a or Kanea (kə-neé-ə, ka-). *Greek* see **Khan·iá** (khan-yaá).

cane·brake (káyn-brayk) *n. U.S.* A dense thicket of cane.

cane piece *n. West Indian.* A field of sugar cane.

cane rat *n.* A rodent, the **grass-cutter** *(see).*

ca·nes·cent (kə-néss'nt, ka-) *adj.* **1.** *Biology.* Covered with whitish or greyish down; hoary. **2.** Turning white or greyish. [Latin *canēscēns* (stem *canēscent-*), present participle of *canēscere,* to grow white, turn grey, from *canēre,* to be white or grey, from *canus,* white, grey.] —**ca·nes·cence** *n.*

cane spirit *n.* In South Africa, a colourless alcoholic drink distilled from sugar cane.

cane sugar *n.* A sugar yielded by sugar cane, **sucrose** *(see).*

Ca·nes Ve·nat·i·ci (káyneez vi-nátti-sī) *n.* A constellation in the Northern Hemisphere near Ursa Major and Boötes, under the handle of the Plough. [Latin, "hunting dogs".]

cane toad *n.* A large toad, *Bufo marinus,* with poison glands forming wart-like lumps behind each eye. Introduced to northeastern Australia in 1935 to control a beetle pest in the sugar cane fields, it became a nuisance by invading human settlements. Also called "giant" or "marine" toad.

cangue (kang) *n.* An old Chinese device for punishing petty criminals, consisting of a heavy wooden yoke enclosing the neck and hands of the offender. [French, from Portuguese *canga,* a yoke, from Vietnamese *gong.*]

Ca·nic·u·la (kə-níckewlə, ka-) *n.* A star, **Sirius** *(see).* [Latin, diminutive of *canis,* dog.]

ca·nic·u·lar (kə-níckewlər, ka-) *adj.* **1.** Of or pertaining to the Dog Star, Sirius. **2.** Pertaining to the dog days in July and August: *canicular heat.*

canikin. Variant of **cannikin.**

ca·nine (káy-nīn, kay-) *adj.* **1.** Of or resembling a dog. **2.** Of or belonging to the Canidae, a family of carnivores which includes the dogs, wolves, and foxes. **3.** Of or designating one of the conical teeth located between the incisors and the premolars.

~ *n.* **1.** A canine animal. Sometimes used humorously. **2.** A canine tooth. Also called "eyetooth". [Latin *canīnus,* from *canis,* dog.]

Ca·nis Major (káyniss) *n.* A constellation in the Southern Hemisphere near Puppis and Lepus. It contains the star Sirius. [Latin, "the larger dog".]

Canis Minor *n.* A constellation in the equatorial region of the Southern Hemisphere near Hydra and Monoceros. It contains the star Procyon. [Latin, "the smaller dog".]

can·is·ter (kánnistər) *n.* **1.** A container, usually of thin metal, for holding dry foods, chemicals, and the like. **2.** *Military.* A metallic cylinder that, when fired from a gun, bursts and scatters the shot packed inside it. Also called "canister shot", "case shot". **3.** The part of a gas mask containing a filter for removing poison gas from the air. [Latin *canistrum,* reed basket, from Greek *kanastron,* from *kanna,* reed.]

can·ker (kángkər) *n.* **1.** An ulcerous sore of the mouth and lips. **2.** An area of dead or decaying tissue in a plant surrounded by healthy wood or bark. **3.** Any of several animal diseases characterised by chronic inflammation of affected parts and attacking especially the ears of dogs and cats. **4.** Any source of spreading corruption or debilitation.

~ *v.* **cankered, -kering, -kers.** —*tr.* **1.** To attack or infect with canker. **2.** To cause to decay or become corrupt. —*intr.* To become infected with or as if with canker. [Middle English, from Old English *cancer* and Old Northern French *cancre,* both from Latin *cancer,* CANCER.] —**can·ker·ous** *adj.*

can·ker·worm (kángkər-wurm) *n.* The caterpillar of any of various moths that destroy leaves or buds.

can·na (kanna) *n.* Any of various tropical plants of the genus *Canna,* having broad leaves and showy red or yellow flowers for which they are widely grown for ornament. [New Latin *Canna,* from Latin *canna,* reed, CANE.]

can·na·bi·di·ol (kánnə-bíddi-ol ‖ -ōl) *n.* A dihydric alcohol, $C_{21}H_{29}(OH)_2$, present in cannabis.

can·na·bin (kánnəbin) *n.* A resinous material extracted from cannabis. Also called "cannabis resin". [CANNAB(IS) + -IN.]

can·na·bis (kánnəbiss) *n.* **1.** A plant of the genus *Cannabis,* **hemp** *(see).* **2.** A preparation made from the dried flowering tops of the hemp plant, and smoked, chewed, or drunk for its euphoric or relaxing effect. See **marijuana, hashish.** [New Latin, from Latin, hemp, from Greek *kannabis.*] —**can·na·bic** *adj.*

canned (kand) *adj.* **1.** Preserved and sealed in a can. **2.** *Informal.* Recorded or taped: *canned laughter.* **3.** *Slang.* Drunk.
can·nel (kánn'l) *n.* A type of bituminous coal that burns brightly with much smoke. Also called "cannel coal". [From *cannel coal,* dialectal form for *candle coal* (from its bright flame).]
can·nel·lo·ni (kánni-lṓni || *U.S. also* kaána-) *n.* An Italian pasta dish of large-sized macaroni stuffed with forcemeat or cheese mixture, baked, and served with tomato sauce. [Italian, plural of *cannellone,* from *cannello,* diminutive of *canna,* reed, CANE.]
can·ne·lure (kánnə-lewr, -loor) *n.* A groove or fluting, especially that round the cylindrical part of a bullet. [French, from *canneler,* to make a groove, channel, from *canne,* CANE.] **—can·ne·lured** *adj.*
can·ner (kánnər) *n.* Someone or something that cans.
can·ner·y (kánnəri) *n., pl.* **-ies.** An establishment where meat, vegetables, or other foods are canned.
Cannes (kan, kanz). Resort and port in the Alpes-Maritimes département, southern France. It has been a fashionable French Riviera resort since Lord Brougham (1778-1868) built a villa there. It has the oldest monastery in Western Europe (on the Île St. Honorat). Each spring, Cannes hosts an international film festival.
can·ni·bal (kánnib'l) *n.* **1.** A person who eats the flesh of human beings. **2.** Any animal that feeds on others of its own kind. [Spanish *Canibales* (plural), variant (recorded by Columbus) of *Caribes,* the allegedly man-eating Caribs of Cuba and Haiti.] **—can·ni·bal·ism** *n.* **—can·ni·bal·is·tic** (-ístik) *adj.*
can·ni·bal·ise, can·ni·bal·ize (kánnib'l-īz) *tr.v.* **-ised, -ising, -ises.** **1. a.** To remove serviceable parts from (damaged aircraft, cars, or other machinery) for use in the repair of other equipment. **b.** To extract material from (a book or magazine, for example) for use in another work. **2.** To deprive (an organisation) of personnel or equipment for use in another organisation. [Originally, "to eat human flesh", from CANNIBAL.] **—can·ni·bal·i·sa·tion** (-ī-záysh'n || *U.S.* -i-) *n.*
can·ni·kin, can·i·kin (kánnikin) *n.* A little can or cup. [Dutch *kanneken,* diminutive of CAN.]
Can·ning (kánning), **George** (1770-1827). British statesman, remembered for his achievements as foreign secretary (1807-09, 1822-27). After resigning (1809) over Castlereagh's handling of the Napoleonic Wars, he was wounded in the thigh by Castlereagh in a duel. During his second term as foreign secretary, he liberalised Tory politics, withdrew from Emperor Alexander I of Russia's Holy Alliance, and supported the rebellion of the Spanish-American colonies (1823) and the Greeks in their struggle for freedom from the Turks (1825-27). In 1827 he became prime minister, but half the cabinet and over 40 ministers refused to serve under him. He resigned, in failing health, after four months.
Canning Basin. Formerly **Desert Basin.** Structure in the northwest of Western Australia. Covering an area of 4 000 000 square kilometres (150,000 square miles), it underlies the Great Sandy Desert, which is largely unexplored.
Can·niz·za·ro, Stanislao (kánni-zaáro, kánnit-saárō) (1826-1910). Italian chemist whose ideas are the basis of much of modern chemistry. He expanded on Avogadro's work in distinguishing between molecular and atomic weights, and employed Avogadro's hypothesis to solve the problem of representing compounds by formulas.
can·non (kánnən) *n., pl.* **-nons** or collectively **cannon.** **1.** A weapon formerly used for firing projectiles, consisting of a heavy metal tube mounted on a carriage. **2. a.** Any modern large-calibre firearm on a mounting. See **gun, howitzer, mortar. b.** An automatic gun mounted on an aircraft. **3.** The loop at the top of a bell by which it is suspended. **4.** A round bit for a horse. Also called "cannon bit". **5.** The cannon bone. **6.** *British.* In billiards, a shot in which the cue ball strikes two other balls in succession.
~v. **cannoned, -noning, -nons.** *—tr.* To bombard or batter with cannon. *—intr.* **1.** To fire cannon. **2.** *British.* To make a cannon shot in billiards. **3.** To collide. Used with *into.* [Middle English *canon,* from Old French, from Italian *cannone,* "large tube, barrel", from *canna,* reed, tube, CANE.]
can·non·ade (kánnə-náyd) *v.* **-aded, -ading, -ades.** *—tr.* To assault or bombard with cannon fire. *—intr.* To deliver heavy artillery fire.
~n. An extended, usually heavy, discharge of artillery. [French *canonade,* discharge of artillery, from Italian *cannonata,* from *cannone,* CANNON.]
can·non·ball (kánnən-bawl) *n.* **1.** A round projectile fired from an early cannon. **2.** A jump into water made with the arms grasping the upraised knees. **3.** Something moving with great speed, such as a fast train. **4.** In tennis, a fast low serve.
~intr.v. **cannonballed, -balling, -balls.** **1.** To travel rapidly in the manner of a cannonball. **2.** To make a cannonball dive.
cannon bone *n.* The bone located between the back of the knee and the fetlock of a horse or ruminant, made up of fused, elongated metatarsals or metacarpals. [So called from its shape.]
can·non·eer (kánnə-néer) *n.* Formerly, a gunner or artilleryman. [Old French *canonier,* from *canon,* CANNON.] **—can·non·eer·ing** *n.*
cannon fodder *n.* Soldiers considered as expendable material of warfare. [Translation of German *Kanonenfutter.*]
can·non·ry (kánnənri) *n., pl.* **-ries.** **1.** Artillery; cannons collectively. **2.** Artillery fire.
cannon shot *n.* **1.** Ammunition for a cannon. **2.** A shot or shots fired by cannon. **3.** The firing distance of a cannon.
can·not (kánnot, kánnət, ka-nót) *v.* The negative form of **can.** See Usage note at **can**
can·nu·la, can·u·la (kánnew-lə) *n., pl* **-las** or **-lae** (-lee). A tube inserted into a bodily cavity to drain fluid or insert medication. [New Latin, from Latin, diminutive of *canna,* a reed, tube, CANE.]
can·nu·late (kánnew-layt) *tr.v.* **-lated, -lating, -lates.** To insert a cannula into.
~adj. (-layt, -lət, -lit). Also **can·nu·lar** (-lər). Tubular; hollow. **—can·nu·la·tion** (-láysh'n) *n.*
can·ny (kánni) *adj.* **-nier, -niest.** **1.** Shrewd; worldly-wise; prudent in looking after one's own interests. **2.** Cautious in spending money; thrifty. **3.** Susceptible of human understanding; explicable; natural. Used with a negative: *events not canny to strangers.* **4.** *Regional.* **a.** Pleasant; attractive. **b.** Good or remarkable.
~adv. Chiefly Scottish. Carefully; prudently. Used chiefly in the phrase *ca' canny* (go carefully). [From CAN (to know how, be able).] **—can·ni·ly** *adv.* **—can·ni·ness** *n.*
ca·noe (kə-nóo) *n.* A light, slender boat with pointed ends, propelled by paddles.
~v. **canoed, -noeing, -noes.** *—tr.* To carry or send by canoe, especially as a sport or hobby. *—intr.* To travel in or propel a canoe. [Earlier *canoa,* from Spanish, from Arawakan (recorded by Columbus), from Cariban.] **—ca·noe·ist** *n.*
can of worms *n. Informal.* A complicated situation or problem, likely to become more complicated with any attempt to resolve it.
can·on[1] (kánnən) *n. Abbr.* **can.** **1.** An ecclesiastical law or code of laws established by a church council. **2.** A secular law, rule, or code of law. **3.** A basis for judgment; a standard; a criterion. **4.** The books of the Bible officially recognised by the Church. **5.** *Often capital* **C.** In the Tridentine Mass, the part beginning after the Sanctus and ending just before the Lord's Prayer. Compare **Eucharistic Prayer. 6.** The calendar of saints accepted by the Roman Catholic Church. **7.** An authoritative list, as of the works of an author or authors: *the Shakespeare canon; Is she/her novel part of the canon?* **8.** *Music.* A composition or passage in which the same melody is repeated by one or more voices, overlapping in time in the same or a related key. See **fugue, round. 9.** *Printing.* A size of type, 48-point. [Middle English *cano(u)n,* from Old English and Old French *canon,* both from Late Latin *canōn,* from Latin, measuring line, rule, model, from Greek *kanōn,* rod, rule.]
canon[2] *n.* **1.** A member of a chapter of priests serving in a cathedral or collegiate church. **2.** A member of certain religious communities living under a common rule and bound by vows. [Middle English *cano(u)n,* from Anglo-French *canunie,* from Late Latin *canōnicus,* one living under a rule, from *canōn,* CANON (rule).]
can·on·ess (kánnən-iss, -ess) *n.* A member of a religious community of women, living under a common rule but not bound by vows.
ca·non·i·cal (kə-nónnik'l) *adj.* Also **ca·non·ic** (-nónnik). **1.** Pertaining to, required by, or abiding by canon law. **2.** Of or appearing in the Biblical canon. **3.** Authoritative; officially approved; orthodox. **4.** *Music.* Having the form of a canon. **5.** Pertaining or belonging to a cathedral chapter. **—ca·non·i·cal·ly** *adv.* **—can·on·ic·i·ty** (kánnə-níssəti) *n.*
canonical form *n.* **1.** *Mathematics.* A *diagonal matrix* (one in which all nondiagonal elements are zero), obtained by transformations on a given matrix. **2.** Loosely, the proper form of something.
canonical hours *pl.n.* **1.** In the Roman Catholic Church: **a.** A special set of prayers, prescribed by canon law, normally to be recited at specific times of the day. They are matins (with lauds), prime, terce, sext, nones, vespers, and compline. **b.** The times of day set aside for these prayers. **2.** *British.* The hours between 8 a.m. and 6 p.m., during which marriages may legally take place in parish churches.
ca·non·i·cals (kə-nónnik'lz) *pl.n.* The dress prescribed by canon law for officiating clergy.
ca·non·i·cate (kə-nónni-kayt, -kət, -kit) *n.* The office or dignity of a canon; canonry. [Medieval Latin *canōnicātus,* from Late Latin *canōnicus,* a canon, from *canōn,* CANON (rule).]
can·on·ise, can·on·ize (kánnən-īz-) *tr.v.* **-ised, -ising, -ises.** **1.** To declare (a deceased person) to be a saint and entitled to be fully honoured as such. Compare **beatify. 2.** To include in the Biblical canon. **3.** To approve as being within canon law. **4.** To glorify; exalt. **—can·on·i·sa·tion** (-ī-záysh'n || *U.S.* -i-) *n.* **—can·on·is·er** *n.*
can·on·ist (kánnən-ist) *n.* A person skilled in canon law. **—can·on·is·tic** (-ístik), **can·on·is·ti·cal** *adj.*
canon law *n.* The body of officially established rules governing the faith and practice of the members of a Christian church.
can·on·ry (kánnənri) *n., pl.* **-ries.** **1.** The position or benefice of one who is an ecclesiastical canon. **2.** Canons collectively.
ca·noo·dle (kə-nóod'l) *intr.v.* **-dled, -dling, -dles.** *Chiefly British Informal.* To engage in necking or petting. [19th century (U.S.) : origin obscure.] **—ca·nood·ler** *n.*
Ca·no·pic (kə-nṓpik, -nóppik) *adj.* Designating an ancient Egyptian vase, urn, or jar used to hold the remains of the dead. [Latin *Canopicus,* from *Canopus,* ancient Egyptian port east of Alexandria.]
Ca·no·pus (kə-nṓpəss) *n.* A star in the constellation Carina, 110 light-years from Earth, the second brightest star in the sky. [Latin, from Greek *Kanōpos*†.]
can·o·py (kánnəpi) *n., pl.* **-pies.** **1.** A cloth covering fastened or held horizontally above a person or an object for protection or ornamentation. **2.** *Architecture.* An ornamental, rooflike projection, as over an altar, pulpit, or the like. **3.** Any high covering: *a vast canopy of foliage.* **4. a.** The transparent, movable enclosure over the cockpit of an aircraft. **b.** The hemispherical fabric surface of a parachute.
~tr.v. **canopied, -pying, -pies.** To overhang with a canopy; form a canopy over: *Mist canopied the landscape.* [Middle English *canape,*

canope, from Medieval Latin *canopeum,* (couch with a) mosquito net, from Greek *kōnōpeion,* from *kōnōps,* gnat.]

ca·no·rous (kə-náwr-əss, kánnər- ‖ -nŏr-) *adj. Rare.* Tuneful. [Latin *canōrus,* from *canor,* tune, melody, from *canere,* to sing.] **—ca·no·rous·ly** *adv.* **—ca·no·rous·ness** *n.*

Ca·no·va (kə-nŏvə), **Antonio** (1757-1822). Italian neoclassical sculptor whose works include *The Tomb of Clement XIII* (1792) and *Pauline Borghese as Venus Victrix* (1807).

canst (kanst, *weak form* kənst). *Archaic.* The second person singular present tense of **can.** Used with *thou.*

cant¹ (kant) *n.* **1.** Angular deviation from a vertical or horizontal plane or surface; inclination; slant; slope. **2. a.** A thrust or motion that tilts something. **b.** The tilt caused by such a motion. **3.** An outer corner, as of a building. **4.** A slanted edge or surface.
~*v.* **canted, canting, cants.** —*tr.* **1.** To set at an oblique angle; cause to slant or tilt. **2.** To give a slanting edge to; bevel. **3.** To change the direction of suddenly. —*intr.* **1.** To tilt to one side; slant. **2.** To take an oblique direction or course; swing round. Used of a ship. [Middle English, side, edge, ultimately from Latin *cant(h)us,* iron tyre, rim of a wheel, from Celtic.]

cant² *n.* **1.** Hypocritically pious language. **2.** Platitudes uttered mindlessly. **3.** The special vocabulary peculiar to the members of a group on the fringe of society, such as thieves, for example; argot. **4.** The special terminology understood among the members of a profession, discipline, or class, but obscure to the general population; jargon. **5.** Whining speech, as used by beggars.
~*intr.v.* **canted, canting, cants. 1.** To speak in a whining, pleading tone. **2.** To speak tediously or sententiously; moralise. **3.** To use special jargon or argot. [Perhaps from Anglo-French *cant,* musical sound, singing, whining speech of beggars (sense perhaps derived from original application to the singing of religious mendicants), from *canter,* to sing, tell, from Latin *cantāre,* frequentative of *canere,* to sing.] **—cant·ing·ly** *adv.*

can't (kaant ‖ *chiefly U.S.* kant, kaynt). Contraction of *cannot.*

Cantab. Cambridge University.

can·ta·bi·le (kan-taabi-li, -lay ‖ *U.S. also* kaan-) *adv. Music.* In a smooth, lyrical, flowing style. Used as a direction to the performer.
~*n. Music.* A cantabile passage or movement. [Italian, from Late Latin *cantābilis,* singable, from Latin *cantāre,* frequentative of *canere,* to sing.] **—can·ta·bi·le** *adj.*

Can·ta·bri·an Mountains (kan-táybri-ən). Mountain range in the north of Spain stretching about 480 kilometres (300 miles) east to west along the Bay of Biscay. Its highest peak is Peña Cerredó (2 642 metres; 8,668 feet).

Can·ta·brig·i·an (kántə-bríji-ən) *adj.* **1.** Of or pertaining to Cambridge in England, or in Massachusetts, United States. **2.** Of or pertaining to Cambridge University.
~*n.* **1.** A native or resident of Cambridge. **2.** A student or graduate of Cambridge University. [Medieval Latin *Cantabrigia,* CAMBRIDGE.]

can·ta·loupe, can·ta·loup (kántə-loop ‖ *U.S.* -lōp) *n.* **1.** A variety of melon of the species *Cucumis melo,* having fruit with a ribbed, rough rind and aromatic orange flesh. **2.** Any of several similar melons. **3.** The fruit of any of these plants. [French *cantaloup,* from Italian *cantalupo,* first grown at *Cantalupo,* a papal villa.]

can·tank·er·ous (kan-tángkərəss) *adj.* Ill-tempered and quarrelsome. [Perhaps from Middle English *contekour,* rioter, brawler, from *contek,* quarrel, strife, from Anglo-French *contek†.*] **—cantank·er·ous·ly** *adv.* **—can·tank·er·ous·ness** *n.*

can·ta·ta (kan-taátə) *n., pl.* **-te** (-tay) *or* **-tas.** A vocal and instrumental composition comprising choruses, arias, and recitatives. [Italian *(aria) cantata,* "sung (aria)", from *cantare,* to sing, from Latin *cantāre.* See **cant** (jargon).]

can·teen (kan-téen, kán-) *n.* **1.** A cafeteria in a workplace. **2.** A temporary or mobile eating place, especially one set up in an emergency. **3.** *Military.* **a.** A shop selling provisions in a barracks. **b.** A recreational club for soldiers. **c.** A set of cooking and eating utensils. **4.** A box containing a set of cutlery. **5.** A flask for drinking water, of the kind carried by soldiers. [French *cantine,* from Italian *cantina,* a wine cellar, from *canto,* edge, from Latin *cant(h)us.* See **cant** (angle).]

can·ter (kántər) *n.* **1.** A horse's gait, slower than the gallop but faster than the trot, in which a three-time rhythm commences on the inside leg. **2.** A ride at this pace. **—win in a canter.** *Informal.* To win easily, without having to exert oneself.
~*v.* **cantered, -tering, -ters.** —*intr.* To move or ride at a canter. —*tr.* To make (a horse) go at a canter. [18th century : short for *Canterbury gallop, trot,* or the like, supposedly the slow pace at which mounted pilgrims rode to Canterbury in the Middle Ages.]

Can·ter·bur·y (kántər-bri, -bəri ‖ -berri). *Latin* **Durovernum.** City at the foot of the North Downs, on the river Stour, in east Kent, England. The 11th- to 15th- century cathedral, where Thomas Becket was martyred (1170), dominates the city, and is the seat of the Archbishop and Primate of the Anglican Communion. The original cathedral, founded by St. Augustine (597), was destroyed by fire (1067). The shrine erected to commemorate the canonisation of Becket was a focal point for pilgrims for three centuries, and inspired Chaucer's *Canterbury Tales.*

Canterbury bell *n.* A plant, *Campanula medium,* native to Europe, widely cultivated for its bell-shaped, violet-blue flowers. [The flowers resemble the bells on the horses of Canterbury pilgrims.]

Canterbury Plains. Low-lying area in the east central region of South Island, New Zealand. It supports sheep, dairy cattle, and arable farming. Christchurch is the chief town.

can·thar·i·des (kan-thárrideez) *pl.n* Singular **can·thar·is** (kánthəriss). *Used with a singular or plural verb.* A toxic preparation of the crushed, dried bodies of the beetle *Lytta* (or *Canthalis*) *vesicatoria,* formerly used as a counterirritant for skin blisters and as an aphrodisiac. Also called "Spanish fly". [Latin, plural of *cantharis,* from Greek *kantharis,* blister beetle, from *kantharos†,* dung beetle.]

cant hook *n.* A wooden pole with a hinged hook near the end, used for moving logs, similar to a peavey but with a blunt end. [From CANT (angle).]

can·thus (kán-thəss) *n., pl.* **-thi** (-thī). The corner at either side of the eye, formed by the meeting of the upper and lower eyelids. [Late Latin, from Greek *kanthos†.*]

can·ti·cle (kántik'l) *n.* A song or chant; specifically, a nonmetrical hymn with words taken directly from a Biblical text. [Middle English, from Latin *canticulum,* diminutive of *cantus,* song, from *canere,* to sing.]

Canticle of Canticles *n.* In the Douay Bible, the **Song of Solomon** *(see).*

can·ti·le·na (kánti-láynə) *n. Music.* A sustained, smooth-flowing melodic line. [Italian.]

can·ti·le·ver (kánti-leevər ‖ *U.S. also* -levvər) *n.* **1.** A projecting beam or other structure supported only at one end. **2.** A beam or other part projecting beyond a fulcrum and supported by a balancing part or a downward force behind the fulcrum. **3.** A bracket or block supporting a balcony or cornice.
~*v.* **cantilevered, -vering, -vers.** —*tr.* To build as a cantilever. —*intr.* To extend outwards as or like a cantilever. [17th century : origin obscure.]

cantilever bridge *n.* A bridge formed by two projecting beams or trusses that are joined in the centre by a connecting part and are supported on piers and anchored by counterbalancing parts.

can·til·late (kántil-layt) *v.* **-lated, -lating, -lates.** —*tr.* To chant or recite in a musical monotone, as in Jewish or other rituals. —*intr.* To recite in a musical monotone. [Latin *cantillāre,* to sing in a low voice, hum, from *cantāre,* frequentative of *canere,* to sing. **—can·til·la·tion** (-láysh'n) *n.*

can·ti·na (kan-téenə) *n.* In Spanish-speaking countries, a bar or wine shop. [Spanish, CANTEEN.]

cant·ing arms (kánting) *pl.n. Heraldry.* Arms which make a visual allusion to the bearer's name.

can·tle (kánt'l) *n.* **1.** The rear part of a saddle. **2.** A corner or portion, especially when cut off from something, such as a piece of land or cheese; a slice. [Middle English *cantel,* from Anglo-French, diminutive of *cant,* corner, CANT.]

can·to (kántō) *n., pl.* **-tos.** Any of the principal divisions of a long poem. [Italian, from Latin *cantus,* song, from *canere,* to sing.]

can·ton (kán-ton, -tón *in sense 1;* kán-tən *in senses 2 and 3) n.* **1. a.** A small territorial division of a country; especially, any of the constituent states of Switzerland. **b.** A subdivision of an arrondissement in France. **2.** *Heraldry.* A small, square division of a shield, usually in the upper left corner. **3.** A division of a flag, usually rectangular, occupying the upper corner next to the staff.
~*tr.v.* (kán-tón *in sense 1;* kan-tōon, kən- ‖ *U.S.* -tón, -tón *in sense 2*) **cantoned, -toning, -tons. 1.** To divide into parts, especially into cantons or territorial districts. **2.** To assign quarters to (troops); billet. [French, corner, subdivision, from Old French, from Italian *cantone,* augmentative of *canto,* CANT (corner).] **—can·ton·al** (kántən'l, kan-tónn'l) *adj.*

Canton. See **Guangzhou.**

Can·ton crepe (kán-ton, -tən) *n.* A soft fabric of silk or similar material with a finely crinkled texture. It is similar to crepe de Chine but heavier. [After CANTON, China, where it was originally made.]

Can·ton·ese (kántə-néez ‖ -néess) *n., pl.* **Cantonese. 1.** *Abbr.* **Cant.** The Chinese dialect spoken in Guangdong province in southern China, and in Hong Kong. Also called "Yüeh". **2.** A native or inhabitant of Guangdong province in southern China. **—Canton·ese** *adj.*

can·ton·ment (kan-tōon-mənt, kən- ‖ *U.S.* -tón-, -tón) *n.* **1.** A group of more or less temporary buildings for housing troops. **2.** The assignment of troops to temporary quarters.

can·tor (kán-tawr, -tər) *n.* **1.** The official soloist or chief singer of the liturgy in a synagogue. **2.** The person who leads a church choir or congregation in singing; a precentor. [Latin, singer, from *canere,* to sing.]

Can·tor (kán-tawr, -tər), **Georg** (1845-1918). Russian mathematician, noted for setting the concept of infinity on a mathematical foundation. Born in St. Petersburg, he moved to Germany with his family in 1856. His main achievements were in applying ideas of symbolic logic to sets of numbers and formulating his Theory of Sets. Attacked by many of his contemporaries, he had a breakdown (1884) and died in an asylum.

can·to·ri·al (kan-táwri-əl ‖ -tóri-) *adj.* **1.** Of or pertaining to a cantor. **2.** Situated to the north of the choir; on the precentor's side. Said of a side of a church or section of a choir. Compare **decanal.**

can·trip (kántrip) *n. Scottish.* **1.** A magic spell; a witch's trick. **2.** A mischievous trick; a prank. [18th century : origin obscure.]

can·tus fir·mus (kántəss fúr-məss, féer-) *n., pl.* **cantus firmi** (-mee). A pre-existing melody serving as the basis of a polyphonic composition by the addition of contrapuntal voices, as in 15th-century polyphony. [Medieval Latin, "fixed melody".]

Ca·nuck (kə-núk) *n. U.S. Slang.* A Canadian; specifically, a French

Canadian. Sometimes used derogatorily. [Perhaps from a mispronunciation (by Indians) of CANADIAN.] —**Ca·nuck** adj.

canula. Variant of **cannula**.

Ca·nute or **Cnut** (kə-néwt || -nōōt) (c. 994–1035). Danish King of England (from 1016), Denmark (from 1019), and Norway (from 1028). He repelled Viking attacks on England and temporarily subjugated Malcolm II and the Scots (1028). To prove to flatterers that even his powers were limited he is reputed to have taken his court to the seashore and commanded the incoming waves to recede.

can·vas (kánvəss) n. **1. a.** A heavy, coarse, closely woven fabric of cotton, hemp, or flax, used for making tents and sails. **2. a.** A piece of such material on which a painting, especially an oil painting, is executed. **b.** A painting of this kind. **3.** Sailcloth. **4.** A sail, or sails collectively. **5.** A tent, or tents collectively. **6.** A fabric of coarse open weave, used as a foundation for needlework. **7.** The floor of a ring in which boxing or wrestling takes place. **8.** In rowing, the enclosed section at the front or back of a racing boat: *They won by a canvas.* —**under canvas. 1.** In a tent or tents. **2.** With sails spread. [Middle English *canevas,* from Anglo-French, from Vulgar Latin *cannabāceus* (unattested), "made of hemp", from Latin *cannabis,* hemp, from Greek *kannabis.*]

can·vass (kánvəss) v. **-vassed, -vassing, -vasses.** —tr. **1. a.** To go through (a region) or go to (persons) to solicit votes, orders, subscriptions, or the like. **b.** To conduct a survey of (public opinion) on a given subject; poll. **2.** To examine carefully or discuss thoroughly; scrutinise. —intr. **1.** To solicit political support, sales orders, or opinions. **2.** To make a thorough examination or conduct a detailed discussion.
~n. **1. a.** A solicitation of votes, sales orders, or opinions. **b.** A survey of public opinion. **2.** An examination or discussion. [From CANVAS, probably from the idea of "tossing a person in a canvas sheet", hence to agitate, harangue.] —**can·vass·er** n.

can·yon (kán-yən) n. A narrow chasm with steep cliff walls, usually formed by running water; a gorge. [American Spanish *cañon,* from Spanish, pipe, tube, conduit, augmentative of *caña,* tube, cane, from Latin *canna,* a reed, from Greek *kanna.*]

can·zo·ne (kan-zōn-i, -tsōn-; Italian -tsōnay) n., pl. **-nes** (-iz) or **-ni** (-ee). **1.** A poetic form that was the dominant lyric genre of 13th-century Italy, consisting of a sequence of equal stanzas with various standard rhyme schemes developed as a synthesis of pre-existing Provençal forms by Dante and others. **2.** A polyphonic song form evolving from this and resembling the madrigal in style. [Italian, from Latin *cantiō* (stem *cantiōn-*), song, from *canere,* to sing.]

can·zo·net (kánzə-nét) n. Also **can·zo·net·ta** (-néttə). A short, light-hearted song or air. [Italian *canzonetta,* diminutive of CANZONE.]

caou·tchouc (ków-chōōk, -chōók, -chōō || U.S. -chōōk, -chōók) n. Natural **rubber** (see). [French, from obsolete Spanish *cauchuc,* from Quechua.]

cap (kap) n. **1.** A covering for the head, usually soft, close-fitting, and having a peak. **2.** A special head covering worn to indicate rank, occupation, or membership of a particular group: *a cardinal's cap.* **3.** Any of numerous objects that cover, protect, or seal: *a bottle cap.* **4.** Architecture. The capital of a column. **5.** The top part, or pileus, of a mushroom or toadstool. **6. a.** A **percussion cap** (see). **b.** A small explosive charge enclosed in paper for use in a toy gun. **7.** An academic mortarboard. Used especially in the phrase *cap and gown.* **8.** Sports. British. **a.** A token award made to a player on each appearance for a special team, especially an international football or cricket team. **b.** A sportsman awarded a cap. **9.** Any of several sizes of writing paper. See **foolscap, legal cap. 10.** A contraceptive device for women, the **diaphragm** (see). —**cap in hand.** Humbly, as a supplicant: *approach one's boss cap in hand.* —**If the cap fits (wear it),** used to invite the hearer to consider whether the speaker's words apply to him. —**set (one's) cap at.** To attempt to attract and win (a man) as a lover or husband.
~v. **capped, capping, caps.** —tr. **1.** To put a cap on: *a capped oil well.* **2.** To lie over or on top of; serve as a cap for; cover: *Snow capped the hills.* **3.** To apply the finishing touch to; complete: *cap a meal with dessert.* **4.** To surpass; outdo. **5.** To name (a sportsman) as member of a special team. **6.** To confer an academic degree on. —intr. To form a distinctive upper surface or layer (such as a particular hard one): *soil which dries out and "caps".* [Middle English *cappe,* Old English *cæppe,* from Late Latin *cappa,* hood, probably from Latin *caput,* head.]

cap. 1. capacity. **2.** capital (city). **3.** capital letter.

ca·pa·bil·i·ty (káypə-bílləti) n., pl. **-ties. 1.** The quality of being capable; physical, mental, or moral capacity; ability. **2.** Usually plural. Potential ability: *live up to one's capabilities.* **3.** The capacity to be used, treated, or developed for a specific purpose.

Ca·pa·blan·ca (y Grau·pe·ra) (káppə-bláɴɢkə ee grow-páir-ə), **José Raul** (1888–1942). Cuban chess master and diplomat. World champion (1921-27). His *Chess Fundamentals* was published in 1921.

ca·pa·ble (káypəb'l) adj. **1.** Having capacity or ability; competent; efficient; able: *a capable administrator.* **2.** Having the required mental or physical capacity; qualified. Used with *of.* **3.** Open; susceptible; Used with *of: an error capable of remedy.* [French, from Old French, from Late Latin *capābilis,* "able to hold", from *capere,* to hold.] —**ca·pa·ble·ness** n. —**ca·pa·bly** adv.

ca·pa·cious (kə-páyshəss) adj. Able to contain a large quantity; spacious; roomy. [Latin *capāx* (stem *capāc-*), able to hold, from *capere,* to hold, contain, take.] —**ca·pa·cious·ly** adv. —**ca·pa·cious·ness** n.

ca·pac·i·tance (kə-pássitənss) n. Symbol **C 1.** The ratio of charge to potential on an electrically charged, isolated conductor. **2.** The ratio of the electric charge transferred from one to the other of a pair of conductors to the resulting potential difference between them. Formerly called "capacity". [CAPACIT(Y) + -ANCE.] —**ca·pac·i·tive** adj. —**ca·pac·i·tive·ly** adv.

ca·pac·i·tate (kə-pássi-tayt) tr.v. **-tated, -tating, -tates. 1.** To render fit; make qualified; enable. **2.** To qualify legally: *capacitated to vote.* —**ca·pac·i·ta·tion** (-táysh'n) n.

ca·pac·i·tor (kə-pássitər) n. An electric circuit element used to store charge temporarily, consisting typically of two metallic plates separated by a dielectric. Formerly called "condenser".

ca·pac·i·ty (kə-pássəti) n., pl. **-ties.** Abbr. **c., C., cap. 1.** The ability to receive, hold, or absorb. **2.** A measure of this ability; volume. **3.** The maximum amount that can be contained: *a trunk filled to capacity.* **4.** The maximum or optimum amount of production: *factories operating below capacity.* **5.** The ability to learn or retain knowledge. **6.** The ability to do something; faculty; aptitude. Used with *of, for,* or an infinitive: *a capacity for self-expression.* **7.** The quality of being suitable for or receptive to specified treatment: *the capacity of elastic to be stretched.* **8.** The position in which one functions; a role: *in her capacity as hostess.* **9.** Legal qualification or authority: *the capacity to make an arrest.* **10.** Electricity. **a.** Capacitance. Not in current technical usage. **b.** A measure of the electric output of a generator. —See Synonyms at **ability.**
~adj. As large or numerous as possible: *a capacity crowd on opening night.* [Middle English *capacite,* from Old French, from Latin *capācitās* (stem *capācitāt-*), from *capāx,* CAPACIOUS.]

cap-a-pie, cap-à-pie (káppə-pée) adv. From head to foot. [Old French *(de) cap a pie,* from Old Provençal *de cap a pe* : *cap,* head, from Latin *caput* + *pe,* foot, from Latin *pēs.*]

ca·par·i·son (kə-párriss'n) n. **1.** A cover, usually ornamental, placed over a horse's saddle or harness; trappings. **2.** Richly ornamented clothing; finery.
~tr.v. **caparisoned, -soning, -sons.** To equip with a caparison. [Old French *caparaçon,* from Spanish *caparazón,* saddle blanket, "mantle with hood", probably from *capa,* CAPE (garment).]

cape¹ (kayp) n. A sleeveless garment fastened at the throat and worn hanging over the shoulders. [French, from Old Provençal *cape* and Spanish *capa,* both from Late Latin *cappa,* hood, cloak, from Latin *caput,* head.]

cape² n. Abbr. **c., C.** A point or head of land projecting into a sea or other body of water; a promontory. Compare **peninsula.** —**the Cape.** See **Cape of Good Hope.** [Middle English *cap,* from Old French, from Old Provençal, from Latin *caput,* head.]

Cape Breton Island. Island forming northern Nova Scotia, eastern Canada. A causeway links it to the mainland, and Sydney is the main town.

Cape Coast. Town on the Gulf of Guinea, Ghana. The capital of the British colony of the Gold Coast until 1877, it was formerly known as Cape Coast Castle after the castle built by the Swedes (1652). The Dutch followed the Swedes as the colonial power before handing over to the British (1664). Cocoa is its chief export.

Cape Cod. A low, sandy peninsula 105 kilometres (65 miles) long in Massachusetts Bay, in the United States. It encloses Cape Cod Bay, where the Pilgrim Fathers, in their ship *Mayflower,* first landed in America (1620).

Cape coloured n. A South African of mixed racial descent who lives in or near the Cape Peninsula.

Cape cowslip n. Any of various bulbous South African plants of the genus *Lachenalia,* having clusters of drooping red, green, or yellow flowers and widely cultivated as a potted plant.

Cape Dutch n., pl. **Cape Dutch. 1.** Plural. The early Dutch colonists at the Cape in South Africa. **2.** An early form of the Afrikaans language.
~adj. **1.** Of or pertaining to the Cape Dutch or their language. **2.** Of or pertaining to a style of architecture characterised by whitewashed gables, and a heavy style of furniture, both developed in the Cape in the 18th century.

Cape Horn. Most southerly point of South America, at Horn Island, Chile. It is also known as the Horn, and is notorious for storms and heavy seas.

Cape jasmine n. A species of **gardenia** (see).

cap·e·lin (káppə-lin, káp-) n. Also **cap·lin** (káp-). A small, edible marine fish, *Mallotus villosus,* of northern Atlantic and Pacific waters, related to and resembling the smelts. [French, from Provençal, "smelt", CHAPLAIN.]

Ca·pel·la (kə-péllə) n. A double star in Auriga, the brightest star in the constellation, approximately 46 light-years from Earth. [New Latin, from Latin, diminutive of *capra,* she-goat, from *caper,* goat.]

Cape of Good Hope, the. Southernmost point of South Africa's Cape Peninsula. It was first sighted and named Cábo Tormentoso ("Cape of Storms") by the Portuguese explorer Bartolemeu Dias (1488). The Dutch East India Company established a permanent post on the peninsula (1652), and it was eventually ceded by the Dutch to Britain (1814), which founded the Crown Colony of the Cape of Good Hope.

Cape Province. Former province of South Africa, now divided between the administrative provinces of Western Cape, Eastern Cape, and Northern Cape.

ca·per¹ (káypər) n. **1.** A playful leap or hop; a skip. **2.** A wild escapade. —**cut a caper.** To prance; frolic; strike a frivolous pose.

~*intr.v.* **capered, -pering, -pers.** To leap or frisk about; frolic; gambol. [Short for CAPRIOLE.] **—ca·per·er** *n.*

caper2 *n.* **1.** A spiny, trailing shrub, *Capparis spinosa,* of the Mediterranean region. **2. a.** A pickled flower bud of this shrub with a pungent taste, used as a condiment. **b.** Any similar pickled bud or pod. [From earlier *capres* (mistaken as plural), Middle English *caperis,* from Latin *capparis,* from Greek *kapparis*†.]

cap·er·cail·lie (káppər-káyl-i, -yi) *n.* Also **cap·er·cail·zie** (-i, -yi, -zi). A large grouse, *Tetrao urogallus,* of northern Europe, having dark plumage and, in the male, a fanlike tail. Also called "wood grouse". [Scottish Gaelic *capalcoille,* "horse of the wood" : *capall,* horse, probably from Latin *caballus* + *coille,* forest, probably from Old Irish *caill.*]

Ca·per·na·um (kə-pérni-əm). Also **Ca·phar·na·um** (-fáarni-). Ancient town on the northern shore of the Sea of Galilee, Israel. Closely associated with Christ's teachings, it is the scene of many Biblical events.

cape·skin (káyp-skin) *n.* Soft leather made from sheepskin. [After CAPE PROVINCE, where it was originally made.]

Ca·pe·tian (kə-péesh'n) *adj.* Pertaining or belonging to the dynasty (987–1328) founded by the French king Hugh Capet (ruled 987–996). **—Ca·pe·tian** *n.*

Cape Town. *Afrikaans* **Kaap·stad** (káap-stut). Legislative capital of South Africa, and the capital city of Western Cape. Founded by Jan van Riebeeck (1652) as a supply post on the Atlantic coast for the Dutch East India Company, it is the oldest white settlement in South Africa. The chief seaport and second largest city in the country (after Johannesburg), it is an important commercial and industrial centre producing chemicals, textiles, and motor vehicles.

Cape Verde, Republic of (verd, vaird). *Portuguese* **Ca·bo Ver·de.** Country occupying an archipelago in the North Atlantic Ocean. Settled by the Portuguese in the mid-15th century, the ten islands and five islets became a Portugese colony in 1495, an overseas province in 1951, and independent in 1975. The islands, of volcanic origin, have a poor economy based on subsistence farming. Area, 4 033 square kilometres (1,557 square miles). Population, 400,000. Capital, Praia. See map at **Atlantic Ocean.**

Cape York Peninsula. Northern part of Queensland, Australia, situated between the Gulf of Carpentaria and the Coral Sea. The low-lying peninsula, tipped by Cape York, the most northerly point of the Australian mainland, supplies bauxite to Australia's aluminium industries.

caph. Variant of **kaph.**

Cap Ha·ï·tien (káp īss-yáɴ, háysh'n). Also **Le Cap** (lə kap). Seaport and resort on the north coast of Haiti. Under French rule it was the capital of the colony until superseded by Port-au-Prince.

cap-height *n. Printing.* The height of a capital letter. Compare **x-height.**

ca·pi·as (káyp-i-ass, -i-əss, -yəss) *n. Law.* A writ authorising an officer to arrest the person named in it. [Middle English, from Latin *capias,* "you are to arrest" (first word of the writ), from *capere,* to seize, take.]

cap·il·lar·i·ty (káppi-lárrəti) *n., pl.* **-ties. 1.** The interaction between contacting surfaces of a liquid and a solid that, as a result of surface tension, distorts the liquid surface from a planar shape. Also called "capillary action". **2.** Movement of water as a result of this effect, for example upwards through soil.

cap·il·lar·y (kə-píllәri || *U.S.* káppə-lerri) *adj.* **1.** Pertaining to or resembling a hair; fine and slender. **2.** Having a very small internal diameter. Said of tubes. **3.** *Anatomy.* In, of, or pertaining to the capillaries. **4.** *Physics.* Of or pertaining to capillarity.
~*n., pl.* **capillaries. 1.** *Anatomy.* Any of the minute blood vessels that connect the arterioles and venules. **2.** Any tube with a small internal diameter. [Latin *capillāris,* from *capillus*†, hair.]

capillary attraction *n.* The force that results in the raising of the surface molecules of a liquid in contact with a solid surface, when the attraction between the solid and the liquid molecules is greater than that between the liquid molecules themselves.

capillary repulsion *n.* The force that results in the lowering of the surface molecules of a liquid in contact with a solid surface, when the attraction between the solid and the liquid molecules is less than that between the liquid molecules themselves.

capillary tube *n.* A tube with a narrow bore; especially, a glass tube with thick walls used in thermometers or similar devices.

capillary wave *n.* A water wave that has a length of less than one inch.

cap·i·tal1 (káppit'l) *n.* **1.** *Abbr.* **cap.** A town or city that is the official seat of government in a state, nation, or other political entity. **2.** Wealth in the form of money or property, owned, used, or accumulated in business by an individual, partnership, or corporation. **3.** Any form of material wealth used or available for use in the production of more wealth. **4. a.** *Accounting.* The remaining assets of a business after all liabilities have been deducted; net worth. **b.** The funds contributed to a business by the owners or stockholders. **5.** Capitalists considered as a group or class. **6.** Any asset or advantage. **7.** A **capital letter** *(see).*
~*adj.* **1.** First and foremost; chief; principal. **2.** Of or pertaining to a political capital; politically important. **3.** First-rate; excellent: *a capital fellow.* **4.** Extremely serious; fatal: *a capital blunder.* **5.** Involving death or calling for the death penalty: *a capital crime.* **6.** Of or pertaining to monetary capital. **7.** Designating an upper-case letter. [Middle English, from Old French, from Latin *capitālis,* "of the head", important, chief, from *caput,* head.]

capital2 *n. Architecture.* The top part, or head, of a pillar or column. [Middle English *capitale,* from Anglo-French *capitel,* from Late Latin *capitellum,* "small head," from Latin *caput,* head.]

capital account *n.* **1.** That part of a country's balance of payments which takes account of its international gold and currency movements rather than its trade. Compare **current account. 2.** *U.S.* An account stating the amount of funds and assets invested in a business by the owners or stockholders, including retained earnings; the owner's interest in the firm. **3.** *Accounting.* A statement of the net worth of a business enterprise at a given time.

capital assets *pl.n.* The fixed assets belonging to an individual, represented by shares or goodwill, for example.

capital expenditure *n.* Funds spent for additions or improvements to plant or equipment.

capital gains *pl.n.* Profits acquired by the sale of capital assets.

capital goods *pl.n.* Goods used in the production of commodities. Also called "producer goods". Compare **consumer goods.**

cap·i·tal·i·sa·tion (káppitə-lī-záysh'n || *U.S.* -li-) *n.* **1.** The act, practice, or result of capitalising. **2. a.** The total value of shares in a business firm; the total investment of shareholders. **b.** The authorised or outstanding stock or bonds in a corporation. **3.** The process of converting anticipated future income into present value.

cap·i·tal·ise, cap·i·tal·ize (káppitə-līz) *v.* **-ised, -ising, -ises.** —*tr.* **1.** To utilise as capital; convert into capital. **2.** To supply with capital or investment funds. **3.** To authorise the issue of a certain amount of capital stock of (a business). **4.** To convert (debt) into capital stock or shares. **5.** To estimate the present value of (a stock, annuity, or real estate, for example). **6.** *Accounting.* To include (expenditures) in business accounts as assets instead of expenses. **7. a.** To write or print in upper-case letters. **b.** To begin (a word) with an upper-case letter. —*intr.* To turn something to advantage; exploit an opportunity. Often used with *on*: *capitalise on an opponent's error.* **—cap·i·tal·is·a·ble** *adj.* **—cap·i·tal·i·ser** *n.*

cap·i·tal·ism (káppitə-liz'm) *n.* **1.** An economic system characterised by a free competitive market with private and corporate ownership of the means of production and distribution, and directed to the accumulation and reinvestment of profits. Also called "private enterprise". **2.** A political or social system regarded as being based on this. Compare **socialism.**

cap·i·tal·ist (káppitə-list) *n.* **1.** An investor of capital in business; especially, one having a major financial interest in an important enterprise. **2.** *Informal.* Any person of great wealth. **3.** A supporter of the capitalist system.
~*adj.* Of or pertaining to capitalism or capitalists. **—cap·i·ta·lis·tic** (-lístik) *adj.* **—cap·i·ta·lis·tic·al·ly** *adv.*

capital letter *n. Abbr.* **cap.** An upper-case letter; a letter written or printed in a size larger than and often in a form differing from its corresponding lower-case letter. Also called "capital".

capital levy *n.* A tax on capital assets or real property.

capital market *n.* A financial centre where capital can be raised for commercial ventures. Compare **money market.**

capital punishment *n.* The infliction of the death penalty for the commission of crimes.

capital ship *n.* A warship, such as a battleship or aircraft carrier, of the largest class.

capital stock *n.* **1.** The total amount of stock authorised for issue by a corporation. **2.** The total stated or par value of the physical capital of a firm or economy.

capital transfer tax *n.* A tax on gifts of money or property made during the benefactor's lifetime or on his death. It superseded **estate duty** *(see).*

cap·i·tate (káppi-tayt) *adj.* **1.** *Zoology.* Enlarged or globular at an end, as some tentacles and bones are. **2.** *Botany.* Forming a headlike mass or dense cluster. Said of certain flowers. [Latin *capitātus,* having a head, from *caput* (stem *capit-*), head.]

cap·i·ta·tion (káppi-táysh'n) *n.* **1.** A counting or assessing of individuals by head. **2.** A tax fixed at an equal sum per person; a per capita or poll tax. **3.** A payment or fee of a fixed amount per person. [Late Latin *capitātiō* (stem *capitātiōn-*), from *caput* (stem *capit-*), head, person.] **—cap·i·ta·tive** (-taytiv) *adj.*

Cap·i·tol (káppi-t'l || *U.S. also* -tol) *n.* **1.** The ancient temple of Jupiter on the Capitoline Hill in Rome. **2.** *U.S. Often small* **c.** The building in which a state legislature assembles. **3.** In the United States, the building in Washington, D.C., occupied by the Congress of the United States. [Middle English *Capitol(ie),* Jupiter's temple in Rome, from Latin *Capitōlium,* probably "the chief (temple)", from *caput* (stem *capit-*), head.]

Cap·i·to·line (kə-píttə-līn) *adj.* Of or pertaining to the Roman Capitol or to the Capitoline Hill.
~*n.* The highest of the seven hills of Rome.

ca·pit·u·lar (kə-píttewlər) *adj.* **1.** Pertaining or belonging to a chapter, especially an ecclesiastical chapter: *capitular clergy.* **2.** Of or pertaining to a capitulum. [Medieval Latin *capitulāris,* from *capitulum,* (ecclesiastical) chapter, from Late Latin, division (of a book), chapter. See **capitulate.**] **—ca·pit·u·lar·ly** *adv.*

ca·pit·u·lar·y (kə-píttew-ləri || *U.S.* -lerri) *n., pl.* **capitularies. 1.** A member of an ecclesiastical or similar chapter. **2.** *Plural.* Ordinances or a set of them; especially, those promulgated by Charlemagne and his successors.

ca·pit·u·late (kə-píttew-layt) *intr.v.* **-lated, -lating, -lates. 1.** To surrender under specified conditions; come to terms. **2.** To give up all resistance; acquiesce. —See Synonyms at **yield.** [Originally "to propose or make terms (of surrender)", from Medieval Latin *capitu-*

lāre, to draw up under heads or chapters, from Late Latin *capitulum,* chapter, from Latin, heading, from *caput,* head.] —**ca·pit·u·lant** *n.* —**ca·pit·u·la·tor** (-laytər) *n.*

ca·pit·u·la·tion (kə-píttew-láysh'n) *n.* **1.** The act of capitulating. **2.** A document containing terms of surrender. **3.** An enumeration of the main parts of a subject; an outline; a summary. —See Synonyms at **surrender.** —**ca·pit·u·la·to·ry** (-lətri, -láytəri) *adj.*

ca·pit·u·lum (kə-píttew-ləm) *n., pl.* **-la** (-lə). **1.** *Botany.* A dense, headlike cluster of stalkless flowers, seen in the daisy and related plants. **2.** *Anatomy.* A small knob or head-shaped part, such as the end of a bone or the knoblike tip of an insect's antenna. [New Latin, from Latin, diminutive of *caput,* head.]

caplin. Variant of **capelin.**

ca·po¹ (káypō, káppō) *n., pl.* **-pos.** A small movable bar placed across the fingerboard of a guitar or other similar instrument for altering the pitch of all the strings simultaneously. [Italian *capo (di tasto),* "cap (of the keys)", from Latin *caput,* head.]

ca·po² (káapō) *n., pl.* **capos.** The title of a divisional leader in the Mafia. [Italian, head, chief.]

ca·pon (káy-pən ‖ -pon) *n.* A cockerel castrated when young to improve the quality of its flesh for food. Compare **poulard.** [Middle English *capon,* Old English *capūn* and Anglo-French *capon,* both from Latin *capō* (stem *capōn-*).]

Ca·pone (kə-pōn) **Al(phonse),** also known as Scarface Al (1899–1947). Italian-born U.S. gangster. He ruled the Chicago underworld ruthlessly, as in the St. Valentine's Day Massacre (1929), when he had seven members of Bugs Moran's gang shot to death. Never successfully prosecuted for any of his gangland crimes, he was finally convicted of tax evasion and sent to Alcatraz prison (1931).

cap·o·ral (káppə-raál, -rəl) *n.* A strong, dark cigarette and pipe tobacco. [French *(tabac de) caporal,* "corporal's tobacco" (superior to *tabac de soldat,* private soldier's tobacco), from Italian *caporale,* corporal, from *capo,* head, chief, from Latin *caput,* head.]

ca·pote (kə-pōt) *n.* A long cloak or coat, usually hooded. [French, from Old French *cape,* CAPE (cloak).]

Ca·po·te (kə-pōti), **Truman** (1924–84). U.S. novelist and journalist best known for the book *In Cold Blood* (1966). *Breakfast at Tiffany's* (1958) enjoyed great success as a film.

Capp (kap), **Al,** born Alfred Gerald Caplin (1909–79). U.S. cartoonist who created the Li'l Abner comic strip, first published in the *New York Mirror* (1934). His characters satirised events and personalities of the time.

cap·puc·ci·no (káppoo-chée-nō) *n., pl.* **-nos** or **-ni** (-nee). **1.** Coffee prepared with frothed milk. **2.** A cup of such coffee. [Italian, Capuchin (alluding to the white hood).]

Cap·ra (kápprə), **Frank** (1897–1991). U.S. film director, born in Italy, whose comedies dealt with the individual's battles against corruption. His successful films included *Platinum Blonde* (1932), *It Happened One Night* (1934), *Mr. Smith Goes to Washington* (1939), and *It's a Wonderful Life* (1946).

cap·re·o·late (káppri-ə-layt, kə-prée-) *adj. Biology.* Having or like tendrils. [Latin *capreolus,* wild goat, wooden prop (suggesting horns) supporting tendrils of vines.]

Ca·pri (kə-prée, káppree, kaápree). Small island in the Bay of Naples, Italy. Warm and picturesque, it has been a tourist resort since Roman times. It has the remains of Emperor Tiberius' villas, and La Grotta Azzura (the Blue Grotto), discovered in 1826.

cap·ric acid (kápprik) *n. Chemistry.* An organic acid, $C_{10}H_{20}O_2$, derived from coconut oil by fractional distillation. It is chiefly used in the manufacture of esters for artificial fruit flavours and perfumes, and as a base for plasticisers and resins. Also called "decanoic acid". [Latin *caper,* goat (from the unpleasant odour of the acid).]

ca·pric·cio (kə-prée-chi-ō, -chō) *n., pl.* **-cios** or **-ci** (-chee). *Music.* An instrumental work with an improvisatory style and a free form. [Italian, CAPRICE.]

ca·pric·cio·so (kə-príchi-ṓ-sō, -zō ‖ *chiefly U.S.* -préechi-) *adv. Music.* Lively and free. Used as a direction. [Italian, from *capriccio,* CAPRICE.] **ca·pric·cio·so** *adj.*

ca·price (kə-préess) *n.* **1.** An impulsive change of mind. **2.** An inclination to make such changes. **3.** *Music.* A capriccio. [French, from Italian *capriccio,* "head with hair standing on end", hence horror, whim (in sense influenced by *capra,* goat, from Latin *caper*) : *capo,* head, from Latin *caput* + *riccio,* hedgehog, from Latin *ēricius,* hedgehog, from *ēr,* hedgehog.]

Synonyms: caprice, fancy, whim, notion, vagary.

ca·pri·cious (kə-prísh-əss ‖ *U.S. also* -préesh-) *adj.* Characterised by or subject to whim; impulsive and unpredictable; fickle. —**ca·pri·cious·ly** *adv.* —**ca·pri·cious·ness** *n.*

Cap·ri·corn (káppri-kawrn) *n.* **1. a.** The tenth sign of the **zodiac** *(see).* Also called the "Goat". **b.** One born under this sign. **2.** Variant of **Capricornus. 3.** The **Tropic of Capricorn** *(see).* —**Cap·ri·corn·i·an** (-kórni-ən) *n.* & *adj.*

Cap·ri·cor·nus (káppri-kórnəss) *n.* A constellation in the equatorial region of the Southern Hemisphere, near Aquarius and Sagittarius. [Latin (translation of Greek *aigokeros,* "goat-horned") : *caper,* goat + *cornū,* horn.]

cap·ri·fi·ca·tion (kápprifi-káysh'n) *n.* A method of assuring pollination of the edible fig by allowing certain wasps to carry pollen from the flowers of the caprifig to those of the edible variety. [Latin *caprificātio* (stem *caprificātion-*), from *caprificāre,* to ripen figs by caprification, from *caprificus,* CAPRIFIG.]

cap·ri·fig (káppri-fig) *n.* A wild variety of fig, *Ficus carica sylvestris,* of the eastern Mediterranean region, used in the caprification of the edible fig. [Middle English *caprifige, caprificus,* from Latin *caprificus,* "goat fig" : *caper,* goat + *fīcus,* FIG.]

cap·rine (kápprīn) *adj.* Of or like a goat. [Middle English, from Latin *caprīnus,* from *caper* (stem *capr-*), he-goat.]

cap·ri·ole (káppri-ōl) *n.* **1.** An upward leap in dressage made by a trained horse without going forward and with all feet off the ground. **2.** A leap or jump in ballet.
~*intr.v.* **caprioled, -oling, -oles.** To perform a capriole. [French, from Italian *capriola,* "leap of a goat", from *capriolo,* wild goat, roebuck, from Latin *capreolus,* diminutive of *caper,* goat.]

Ca·pri·vi Strip (kə-préevi). German **Ca·pri·vi Zip·fel** (tsípf'l). A strip of land in northeast Namibia giving the country access to the Zambezi river. 480 kilometres (300 miles) long and 48 kilometres (30 miles) wide, it was named after the German Chancellor, Graf Caprivi, who negotiated its cession from the British (1893).

cap rock *n. Geology.* **1.** A layer of rock covering a salt dome. **2.** A layer of rock covering an oil or gas deposit.

ca·pro·ic acid (ka-prō-ik, kə-) *n.* An organic acid, **hexanoic acid** *(see).* [Latin *caper* (stem *capr-*), goat (referring to its smell).]

cap·sa·i·cin (kap-sáy-ə-sin) *n.* A peppery, reddish-brown liquid, $C_{18}H_{27}O_3N,$ obtained from plants of the genus *Capsicum,* and used in flavouring vinegar and pickles and medicinally as a digestive stimulant. [CAPSIC(UM) + -IN.]

cap screw *n.* A screw with a head that has a shaped groove, usually six-sided, and is turned by a wrench that fits into this groove.

Cap·si·an (kápsi-ən) *adj.* Of or designating a Palaeolithic culture of northern Africa and southern Europe. [French *capsien,* after *Capsa,* ancient name of *Gafsa,* near which remains of the culture were found.]

cap·si·cum (kápsikəm) *n.* **1.** Any of various tropical plants of the genus *Capsicum.* See **pepper. 2.** The dried fruit of pungent varieties of *C. frutescens,* used medicinally as a gastric stimulant and counterirritant. [New Latin, probably from Latin *capsa,* box (from its podlike fruit). See **capsule.**]

cap·sid¹ (kápsid) *n.* Any bug of the family Miridae (formerly Capsidae), especially one that feeds on and damages crop plants. [New Latin *Capsus* (former genus name).]

capsid² *n.* The protein coat of a virus. [French *capside,* from Latin *capsa,* box.]

cap·size (kap-síz ‖ *Chiefly U.S.* káp-sīz) *v.* **-sized, -sizing, -sizes.** —*intr.* To overturn. Used typically of a boat or ship. —*tr.* To cause to capsize. [18th century : origin obscure.]

cap·stan (kapstən) *n.* **1.** *Nautical.* An apparatus consisting of a vertical cylinder rotated manually by a lever *(capstan bar)* or by motor, used for hoisting weights by winding in a cable. **2.** *Electronics.* A small cylindrical pulley used to regulate the speed of magnetic tape in a tape recorder. [Middle English, from Old Provençal *cabestan, cabestran,* from *cabestre,* rope noose, from Latin *capistrum,* halter, from *capere,* to take, seize.]

capstan lathe *n.* A lathe fitted with a rotatable head capable of holding a number of different tools.

capstan screw *n.* A screw with a number of radial holes through the head, turned by a bar that fits through one of these holes.

cap·stone (káp-stōn) *n.* Also **cope·stone** (kṓp-). **1.** The top stone of a structure or wall. Compare **coping. 2.** The crowning or final stroke; the culmination; the acme.

cap·su·lar (kápsew-lər ‖ kápsə-) *adj.* Of, pertaining to, or characteristic of a capsule.

cap·su·late (kápsew-layt, -lət, -lit ‖ kápsə-) *adj.* Also **cap·su·lat·ed** (-laytid). In or formed into a capsule. —**cap·su·la·tion** (-láysh'n) *n.*

cap·sule (kápsewl ‖ káps'l) *n.* **1.** *Pharmacology.* A soluble, gelatinous sheath enclosing a dose of an oral medicine. **2.** A seal or airtight cap, as for the mouth of a bottle. **3.** *Anatomy.* A fibrous, membranous, or fatty envelope enclosing an organ or part, such as the sac surrounding the kidney. **4.** *Microbiology.* A mucopolysaccharide layer enveloping certain bacteria. **5.** *Botany.* **a.** A dry fruit that contains two or more seeds that are released when it splits open. **b.** The spore case of a moss or other bryophyte. **6.** A pressurised modular compartment of an aircraft or spacecraft, especially one designed to accommodate a crew or to be ejected if required.
~*adj.* Condensed into a small or brief unit; concise; compact: *a capsule description.* [French, from Latin *capsula,* diminutive of *capsa,* box, chest.]

cap·sul·ise, cap·sul·ize (kápsew-līz ‖ kápsə-) *tr.v.* **1.** To express (a policy) very briefly; summarise; condense. **2.** To form into or encase within a capsule.

cap·tain (káptin ‖ *nonstandard also* káp'n) *n.* **1.** One who commands, leads, or guides others, specifically: **a.** The officer in command of a ship, aircraft, or spacecraft. **b.** The head girl or boy of a school or a subdivision of a school. **c.** The designated leader of a team or crew in sports. **2.** *Abbr.* **Capt. a.** A commissioned officer in the Army or Marine Corps who ranks below a major and above a first lieutenant. **b.** A commissioned officer in the Navy or Air Force who ranks below a commodore or air commodore and above a commander or wing commander. **3.** A figure in the forefront; a leader: *a captain of industry.* **4.** *U.S.* A head waiter.
~*tr.v.* **captained, -taining, -tains. 1.** To act as captain of (a team, for example). **2.** To command or direct. [Middle English *capitane, captein,* from Old French *capitain(e),* from Late Latin *capitāneus,* chief, from Latin *caput,* head.] —**cap·tain·cy** *n.* —**cap·tain·ship** *n.*

cap·tan (káp-tən, -tan) n. An agricultural fungicide, $C_9H_8CI_3NO_2S$. [Short for MERCAPTAN.]

cap·tion (kápsh'n) n. 1. A title, short explanation, or description accompanying an illustration or photograph. 2. A subtitle in a film. 3. A title or heading, as of a document or chapter in a book. 4. Law. The part of a legal document that states the time, place, and authority of its execution.
~tr.v. **captioned, -tioning, -tions.** To furnish a caption for. [Originally "arrest", hence record of execution of a commission, from Middle English capcioun, arrest, seizure, from Latin captiō (stem captiōn-), from capere, to seize, take.]

cap·tious (kápshəss) adj. 1. Marked by a disposition to find fault and make petty criticisms; carping. 2. Intended to entrap or confuse: a captious question. [Middle English capcious, from Old French captieux, from Latin captiōsus, "ensnaring", from captiō, seizure, CAPTION.] **—cap·tious·ly** adv. **—cap·tious·ness** n.

cap·ti·vate (kápti-vayt) tr.v. **-vated, -vating, -vates.** 1. To fascinate or hold the attention of by special charm, interest, or beauty. 2. Archaic. To capture. [Late Latin captīvāre, to capture, from Latin captīvus, CAPTIVE.] **—cap·ti·va·tion** (-váysh'n) n. **—cap·ti·va·tor** (-vaytər) n.

cap·tive (káptiv) n. 1. One that is forcibly confined, restrained, or subjugated, such as a prisoner. 2. One who is enslaved by a strong emotion or passion.
~adj. 1. Held as prisoner. 2. Under restraint or control. 3. Captivated; enraptured. 4. Obliged to be present: a captive audience. 5. Forced to buy from a particular source: a captive market. [Middle English captif, from Latin captīvus, from capere, to seize.]

cap·tiv·i·ty (kap-tívvəti) n., pl. **-ties.** The state or a period of being captive.

cap·tor (káp-tər; rarely -tawr) n. One who takes or keeps someone or something captive. [Late Latin, from Latin capere, to seize.]

cap·ture (kápchər) tr.v. **-tured, -turing, -tures.** 1. To take captive; seize or catch by force or craft. 2. To win possession or control of, as in a contest. 3. To succeed in preserving in a fixed form: capture a likeness in a painting.
~n. 1. The act of capturing; seizure. 2. One that is seized, caught, or won; a catch or prize. 3. Physics. **a.** The phenomenon whereby an atomic nucleus absorbs a subatomic particle, especially an orbiting electron, often with the subsequent emission of radiation. **b.** The phenomenon whereby an atom, molecule, or positive ion takes up an extra electron. [French, from Old French, from Latin captūra, from capere, to seize.]

captured rotation n. Astronomy. An orbit of a satellite in which the satellite's orbital period is equal to its rotation period. This means that the satellite always points the same hemisphere to its primary, as in the case of the Moon in relation to Earth. Also called "synchronous rotation".

Cap·u·a (káppew-ə; Italian ka'ap-wa). Market town in Campania, southern Italy, near Naples. It rose to prominence under the Romans when it was linked to Rome by the Appian Way.

ca·puche (kə-pōōsh ‖ -pōōch) n. A hood; especially, the long, pointed cowl worn by a Capuchin monk. [Italian cappuccio, from cappa, hood, from Late Latin, hood, cloak, from Latin caput, head.]

cap·u·chin (káppew-chin, -shin ‖ kə-péw-) n. 1. Capital C. A monk belonging to the Order of Friars Minor Capuchins, an independent branch of the Franciscans, founded in 1525, and licensed in 1619. 2. A hooded cloak worn by women. 3. Any of several long-tailed monkeys of the genus Cebus, of Central and South America, many of which have hoodlike tufts of hair on the head. In this sense, also called "sapajou". [French, from Old French, from Italian cappuccino, "hooded one", from cappuccio, CAPUCHE.]

cap·y·ba·ra (káppi-ba'arə ‖ U.S. also -bárrə) n. A large, short-tailed, semiaquatic rodent, Hydrochoerus hydrochaeris, of tropical South America, often attaining a length of four feet. [Portuguese capibara, from Tupi.]

car (kar) n. 1. A self-propelled land vehicle; especially, a four-wheeled passenger vehicle propelled by an internal-combustion engine. Also called "motor car", chiefly U.S. "automobile". 2. **a.** Chiefly U.S. A conveyance with wheels that runs along tracks, such as a railway carriage or tram. 3. Archaic. A chariot. 4. A box-like enclosure for passengers on a conveyance, such as a cable car. [Middle English car(re), cart, wagon, from Anglo-French, from Vulgar Latin carra (unattested), variant of Latin carrus, two-wheeled wagon.]

car. carat.

car·a·bao (kárrə-báy-ō ‖ -bów, U.S. also ka'arə-) n., pl. **-baos.** The water buffalo (see). [Visayan karabáw, akin to Malay karbaw.]

car·a·bid (kárrəbid) n. Any beetle of the family Carabidae, which includes the bombardier and other ground beetles.
~adj. Of or belonging to the Carabidae. [New Latin Carabidae, from Latin cārābus, from Greek karabos†, crayfish, horned beetle.]

carabin, carabine. Variants of **carbine.**

car·a·bi·neer, car·a·bi·nier (kárrəbi-néer) n. Also **car·bi·neer** (karbi-néer). A soldier armed with a carbine.

ca·ra·bi·nie·re (kárrabin-yaír-i) n, pl. **-ri** (-ee) An Italian policeman under military command. [Italian.]

car·a·cal (kárrə-kal) n. A wild cat, Lynx caracal, of Africa and western Asia, having short, fawn-coloured fur and long, tufted ears. Also called "desert lynx". [French, from Turkish kara kūlāk, "black ear" : kara, black + kūlāk, ear.]

ca·ra·ca·ra (kárrə-ka'arə, ka'arə- ‖ U.S. also -kə-ra'a) n. Any of several large carrion-eating or predatory birds of the subfamily Cara-

carinae, of South and Central America and the southern United States, related to the hawks and falcons. [Spanish caracara and Portuguese caracará, from Tupi caracara (imitative).]

Ca·ra·cas (kə-ráckəss, -ra'akəss). Capital of Venezuela. In a basin at 1 000 metres (3,280 feet) above sea level, it is connected to its port and airport at La Guaira by a tunnelled motorway 18 kilometres (11 miles) long. Caracas was founded by the Spanish in 1567. It now earns much of its wealth from oil.

car·a·cole (kárrə-kōl) n. Also **car·a·col** (-kol). A half turn to either side performed by a horse in dressage.
~intr.v. **caracoled, -coling, -coles.** To perform a caracole or caracoles. [French, from Spanish caracol†, snail, winding stair.]

car·a·cul (kárrə-kul) n. 1. A fur, **Persian lamb** (see). 2. Variant of **karakul.**

ca·rafe (kə-ráf, -ra'af) n. 1. A glass bottle for serving water or wine at the table; a decanter. 2. The amount a carafe will hold. [French, from Italian caraffa, from Spanish garaffa, from Arabic gharrāfa, from gharafa, to dip.]

car·a·mel (kárrə-mel, -məl ‖ kár-) n. 1. A smooth, chewy sweet made with sugar, butter, cream or milk, and flavouring. 2. Burnt sugar, used for colouring and sweetening foods. [French, from Old Spanish, probably from Late Latin calamellus, diminutive of Latin calamus, reed, cane, from Greek kalamos.]

car·a·mel·ise, car·a·mel·ize (kárrə-mel-īz, -məl-) v. **-ised, -ising, -ises.** —tr. To convert (sugar) into caramel. —intr. To change into caramel. **—car·a·mel·i·sa·tion** (-ī-záysh'n ‖ U.S. -i-) n.

car·an·gid (kə-ránjid, -ráng-gid) n. Any of various fishes of the family Carangidae, which includes the jacks, pilot fish, and pompanos, having a compressed body and forked tail.
~adj. Of or belonging to the Carangidae. [New Latin Carangidae : Caranx (stem Carang-) (genus), from French carangue, mackerel, from Spanish caranga† + -IDAE.]

car·a·pace (kárrə-payss) n. 1. Zoology. A hard bony or chitinous outer covering, such as the fused dorsal plates of a tortoise or the covering of the head and thorax of a crustacean. 2. Any similar protective covering. [French, from Spanish carapacho.]

car·at (kárrət) n. Also U.S. **kar·at** (for sense 2). 1. Abbr. c, car. A unit of weight for precious stones, equal to 200 milligrams. 2. A unit used to specify the proportion of pure gold in an alloy, on a scale of 1 to 24; for example, 12-carat gold is 50 per cent pure gold. [French, from Old French, from Medieval Latin carratus, from Arabic qīrāt, small weight, carat, from Greek keration, "little horn", carob fruit, carat, diminutive of keras, horn.]

Ca·rat·a·cus (kə-rátta-kəss) (first century A.D.). Also **Ca·rac·ta·cus** (-rákta-) or **Ca·rad·oc** (kə-ráddək). King of the Catuvellauni in the east of Britain. The son of Cunobelinus, he resisted the Roman invasion in A.D. 43, but was finally betrayed and taken by the Romans. Though freed by the Emperor Claudius, he died in exile.

Ca·ra·vag·gio (kárrə-váj-ō, ka'arə-, -va'aj-, -i-ō), born Michelangelo Merisi (1573–1610). Italian baroque painter, born in Caravaggio, Lombardy. Refusing to conform to the tradition of earlier European art with its idealised religious figures, he chose instead to use peasants and street people as the models for many of his sacred subjects. The altarpiece, Death of the Virgin, and the painting, Supper at Emmaus, are examples of his work. His mastery of light and shade influenced Velázquez and Rembrandt. He fled from Rome in 1606 after killing a man in a dispute over a tennis match and his final years were spent in exile in Naples, Malta, and Sicily.

car·a·van (kárrə-van, -ván) n. 1. Chiefly British. An unmotorised furnished vehicle, often attached as a trailer to a car or lorry, and used as living quarters, a temporary office, or a holiday home. 2. A company of travellers journeying together, especially across a desert. 3. A single file of vehicles or pack animals. 4. A large covered vehicle, especially one used by gypsies. In this sense, also called "van". [French caravane or Italian caravana, carovana, from Persian kārwān†.]

car·a·van·se·rai (kárrə-ván-sə-rī, -ri, -ray) n, pl. **-rais.** Also **car·a·van·sa·ry** (-sə-ri). 1. In the Near or Far East, an inn built round a large court for accommodating caravans. 2. Any large inn or hostelry. [Persian kārwānsarāī : kārwān, CARAVAN + sarāī, palace, inn.]

car·a·vel, car·a·velle (kárrə-vel) n. Also **car·vel** (kár-). A small, light sailing ship of the kind used by the Spanish and Portuguese in the 15th and 16th centuries. [French caravelle, carvelle, from Portuguese caravela, diminutive of cáravo, ship, from Latin cārabus, from Greek karabos†, crayfish, light ship.]

car·a·way (kárrə-way) n. 1. A plant, Carum carvi, native to Eurasia, having finely divided leaves and clusters of small, whitish flowers. 2. The pungent, aromatic seeds of this plant, used in baking and cooking. [Middle English car(a)way, probably from Old Spanish alcarahueya and Medieval Latin carvi, both from Arabic alkarāwiyā, probably from Greek karon†, cumin.]

car·ban·i·on (kárb-án-ī-ən) n. A negatively charged organic ion, such as H_3C^-, having one more electron than the corresponding free radical. [CARBO- + AN- + ION.]

car·bide (kárbīd) n. 1. A binary carbon compound consisting of carbon and a more electropositive element. 2. **Calcium carbide** (see). [CARB(O)- + -IDE.]

car·bine (kár-bīn) n. Also **car·a·bin** (kárrə-bin), **car·a·bine** (-bīn, -been). A light shoulder rifle with a short barrel, originally for cavalry use. [French carabine, carbine, carabineer, from Old French carabin, cavalryman, soldier armed with a musket, probably derisively from escarrabin, "one who lays out plague corpses", variant of *escarabilh, scarabée,* dung beetle, from Latin *scarabeus,* a beetle. See **scarab**.]

carbineer, carabinier. Variants of **carabineer.**

car·bi·nol (kárbin-ol ‖ -ōl) *n.* **1.** Wood alcohol, **methanol** *(see).* **2.** An alcohol derived from methanol by substitution of one or more hydrogen atoms by other hydrocarbon groups. [German *Karbinol* : CARB(O)- + -IN + -OL.]

carbo-, carb– *comb. form.* Indicates carbon; for example, **carbohydrate, carbolic acid.** [French, from *carbone,* CARBON.]

car·bo·hy·drate (kárb-ō-hídrayt, -ə-) *n.* Any of a group of chemical compounds, including sugars, starches, and cellulose, containing carbon, hydrogen, and oxygen only, with the ratio of hydrogen to oxygen atoms usually 2:1.

car·bo·lat·ed (kárbə-laytid) *adj.* Containing or treated with carbolic acid.

car·bol·ic acid (kaar-bóllik) *n.* An organic compound, **phenol** *(see).* [CARB(O)- + -OL + -IC.]

car·bon (kárbən) *n.* **1.** Symbol **C** A naturally abundant nonmetallic element that occurs in many inorganic and in all organic compounds, exists in amorphous, graphitic, and diamond forms, and is capable of chemical self-bonding to form an enormous number of chemically, biologically, and commercially important molecules. Atomic number 6; atomic weight 12.01115; sublimes above 3,500°C; boiling point 4,827°C; relative density of amorphous carbon 1.8 to 2.1, of diamond 3.15 to 3.53, of graphite 1.9 to 2.3; valency 4. **2. a.** A sheet of carbon paper. **b.** A copy made by using carbon paper. **3.** *Electricity.* **a.** Either of two rods through which current flows to form an arc in lighting or in welding. **b.** A carbonaceous electrode in an electric cell. ∼*adj.* **1.** Of, pertaining to, or like carbon. **2.** Treated with carbon. [French *carbone,* from Latin *carbō* (stem *carbōn-*), charcoal.] —**car·bon·ous** *adj.*

carbon 14 *n.* A naturally radioactive carbon isotope with atomic mass 14 and half-life 5,700 years, used in dating ancient carbon-containing objects. Also called "radiocarbon".

car·bo·na·ceous (kárbə-náyshəss) *adj.* Consisting of, containing, pertaining to, or yielding carbon.

car·bo·nade, car·bon·nade (kárbə-naad, -nayd) *n.* A rich stew of beef, onions, and beer, of Belgian origin. [French.]

car·bo·na·do¹ (kárbə-náydō, -náadō) *n., pl.* **-does** or **-dos.** A piece of scored and grilled fish, poultry, or meat. ∼*tr.v.* **carbonadoed, -doing, -dos. 1.** To score and grill (fish, poultry, or meat). **2.** *Archaic.* To slice; slash; chop. [Spanish *carbonada,* from *carbón,* charcoal, coal, from Latin *carbō,* CARBON.]

carbonado² *n., pl.* **-does.** A form of opaque or dark-coloured diamond, chiefly Brazilian, used for drills. Also called "black diamond", "bort". [Portuguese, "carbonated", from *carbone,* carbon, from French, CARBON.]

carbon arc *n.* An electric arc produced by a carbon electrode, as in an arc lamp or welder.

Car·bo·na·ri (kárb-ə-naá-ri, -ō-) *pl.n. Singular* **Carbonaro** (-rō). The members of a secret society originally organised in Naples in the early 19th century to establish a liberal, unified Italian republic. [Italian, "charcoal-burners", name adopted by members of the society apparently after disguising themselves as such after being driven into hiding in the forest of the Abruzzi.] —**Car·bo·na·rism** (-naár-iz'm) *n.* —**Car·bo·na·rist** (-naárist) *n. & adj.*

car·bon·ate (kárbə-nayt) *tr.v.* **-ated, -ating, -ates. 1.** To add carbon dioxide gas to (a cold drink, for example) to produce fizz. **2.** To burn to carbon; carbonise. **3.** To change into a carbonate. ∼*n.* (-nət, -nit, -nayt). A salt or ester of carbonic acid. —**car·bon·a·tion** (-náysh'n) *n.* —**car·bon·a·tor** (-naytər) *n.*

carbonated water *n.* **Soda water** *(see).*

carbon bisulphide *n.* Carbon disulphide. Not recommended in technical usage.

carbon black *n.* Any of various finely divided forms of carbon derived from the incomplete combustion of natural gas or petroleum and used principally in rubber and ink.

carbon copy *n.* **1.** *Abbr.* **C.C., c.c.** A replica, as of a letter, made by using carbon paper. **2.** *Informal.* Any duplicate or reproduction.

carbon cycle *n.* **1.** *Astrophysics.* The **carbon-nitrogen cycle** *(see).* **2.** *Biology.* The cycle of natural processes in which atmospheric carbon in the form of carbon dioxide is converted by photosynthesis in plants to carbohydrates which are eaten and metabolised by animals, and ultimately returned to the atmosphere as carbon dioxide through respiration or decomposition.

carbon dating *n.* **Radiocarbon dating** *(see).*

carbon dioxide *n.* A colourless, odourless, incombustible gas, CO_2, formed during respiration, combustion, and organic decomposition and used in food refrigeration, carbonated beverages, fire extinguishers, and aerosols.

carbon dioxide snow *n.* Solid carbon dioxide, used as a refrigerant.

carbon disulphide *n.* A clear flammable liquid, CS_2, used to manufacture viscose rayon and cellophane, as a solvent for fats, rubber, resins, waxes, and sulphur, and in fumigants and pesticides. Also called "carbon bisulphide".

carbon fibre *n.* A fine filament of almost pure crystalline carbon, made by heating stretched textile threads and extensively used in composite plastic and metal materials, as for aircraft parts.

car·bon·ic acid (kaar-bónnik) *n.* A weak, unstable acid, H_2CO_3, present only in solutions of carbon dioxide in water.

carbonic acid gas *n.* Carbon dioxide.

Car·bon·if·er·ous (kárbə-níffərəss) *adj.* **1.** *Geology.* Of, belonging to, or designating a period of the Palaeozoic era following the Devonian and preceding the Permian. It was characterised by swamp formation and deposition of plant remains that later hardened into coal. **2.** *Small* **c.** Producing coal or carbon. ∼*n. Geology.* The Carboniferous period. Preceded by *the.*

car·bon·i·sa·tion (kárbən-ī-záysh'n ‖ *U.S.* -i-) *n.* **1.** The process of carbonising. **2.** The decomposition by destructive distillation of bituminous coal to obtain coke and other by-products.

car·bon·ise, car·bon·ize (kárbənīz) *tr.v.* **-ised, -ising, -ises. 1.** To reduce or convert to carbon, as by partial burning. **2.** To coat or combine with carbon. —**car·bon·is·er** *n.*

car·bo·ni·um (kaar-bóni-əm) *n.* A positively charged organic ion, such as H_3C^+, having one electron fewer than a corresponding free radical and behaving chemically as if the positive charge were localised on the carbon atom.

carbon microphone *n.* A type of microphone in which an electric current passes through a diaphragm with carbon powder packed behind it. Sound waves vibrate the diaphragm, producing a varying pressure on the carbon and changing its electrical resistance.

carbon monoxide *n.* A colourless, odourless, highly poisonous gas, CO, formed by the incomplete combustion of carbon or any carbonaceous material.

car·bon·ni·tro·gen cycle (kárbən-nítrəjən) *n.* A chain of thermonuclear reactions in which nitrogen isotopes are formed in intermediate stages and carbon acts essentially as a catalyst to convert four protons into one helium nucleus. The sequence is thought to generate significant amounts of energy in certain classes of stars. Also called "carbon cycle", "nitrogen cycle", "CNO cycle".

carbon paper *n.* A lightweight paper faced on one side with a dark waxy pigment that is transferred by the impact of typewriter keys or by writing pressure to any copying surface, such as paper.

carbon process *n.* A photographic printing process using permanent pigments, such as carbon, contained in a sensitised tissue or film of gelatine.

carbon steel *n.* The normal type of steel, composed mainly of iron with added carbon. Compare **alloy steel.**

carbon tetrachloride *n.* A poisonous, nonflammable, colourless liquid, CCl_4, used as a solvent. Also called "tetrachloromethane".

car·bon·yl (kárbən-īl, -il ‖ *U.S. also* -eel) *n.* **1.** The bivalent radical CO. **2.** A metal compound containing the CO group bound directly to a metal atom or ion. —**car·bon·yl·ic** (-íllik) *adj.*

carbonyl chloride *n.* A poisonous gas, **phosgene** *(see).*

Car·bo·run·dum (kárbə-rúndəm) *n.* **1.** A trademark for a silicon carbide abrasive. **2.** *Small* **c.** A piece of this abrasive.

car·box·yl (kaar-bóks-īl, -il) *n.* A univalent radical, COOH, characteristic of all organic acids. [CARB(O)- + OX(Y)- + -YL.] —**car·box·yl·ic** (kárbok-síllik) *adj.*

car·box·yl·ase (kaar-bóksil-ayz, -ayss) *n.* An enzyme that produces an aldehyde and carbon dioxide from certain acids.

carboxylic acid *n. Chemistry.* An organic acid with the general formula RCOOH, where R is an organic group. See **fatty acid.**

car·boy (kárboy) *n.* A large glass or plastic bottle, usually encased in a protective basket or crate and often used to hold corrosive liquids. [Persian *qarāba,* from Arabic *qarrābah.*]

car·bun·cle (kár-bungk'l) *n.* **1.** An extensive skin eruption, resembling a boil but much larger and having multiple openings, usually caused by infection with *Staphylococcus aureus.* Compare **boil. 2.** A deep red precious stone, especially the garnet, unfaceted and convex. [Middle English, from Old French, from Latin *carbunculus,* small glowing ember, tumour, diminutive of *carbō* (stem *carbōn-*), charcoal, ember.] —**car·bun·cled** *adj.* —**car·bun·cu·lar** (-búng-kewlər) *adj.*

car·bu·ret (kár-bewr-ét, -bər-, -et ‖ -ayt) *tr.v.* **-retted** or *U.S.* **-reted, -retting** or *U.S.* **-reting, -rets.** To combine or mix with carbon or hydrocarbons. [From obsolete *carbure(t),* carbide, from French *carbure,* from Latin *carbō,* CARBON.]

car·bu·ret·tor, car·bu·ret·ter (kár-bewr-éttər, -bər-, -ettər) *n.* Also *chiefly U.S.* **car·bu·re·tor** (-aytər). A device used in petrol engines to produce an efficient explosive vapour of fuel and air. [From CARBURET.]

car·bu·rise, car·bu·rize (kár-bewr-īz, -bər-) *tr.v.* **-rised, -rising, -rises.** To treat (iron or steel, for example) with carbon. [CARBUR(ET) + -ISE.] —**car·bu·ri·sa·tion** (-ī-záysh'n ‖ *U.S.* -i-) *n.*

car·byl·amine (kárbil-ə-méen, -ámmin) *n.* A type of chemical compound, an **isocyanide** *(see).*

car·ca·jou (kárkə-jōo, -zhōo) *n. Canadian.* An animal, the **wolverine** *(see).* [Canadian French, from Algonquian *karkajou.*]

car·ca·net (kárkə-net, -nət, -nit) *n. Archaic.* A jewelled necklace, collar, or headband. [Old French *carcan,* collar, akin to Medieval Latin *carcannum†.*]

car·cass, car·case (kárkəss) *n.* **1.** The dead body of an animal or bird, especially one slaughtered and gutted. **2.** The body of a human being. Used humorously or derogatorily. **3.** Something from which the substance or character is gone: *the carcass of a once-glorious empire.* **4.** A framework or basic structure, as of a ruined building. [French *carcasse,* from Old French *c(h)arcois†.*]

Car·cas·sonne (kárkə-són). Capital of the Aude département on the Canal du Midi and the river Aude in southwest France. It includes an old fortified medieval hill town (la Cité) and a modern town (la Ville Basse).

Car·che·mish (kárkimish). Ancient city on the river Euphrates, south Turkey. A Hittite stronghold until the empire's collapse in the

12th century B.C., it survived as an independent kingdom until taken by the Assyrians, under Sargon II (717 B.C.). It was the scene of the Egyptians' defeat at the hands of Nebuchadnezzar and the Babylonians (605 B.C.).

car·cin·o·gen (kaar-sínnə-jən, kár-sinnə-, -jen) *n.* A cancer-causing substance. [Greek *karkinos,* cancer, crab + -GEN.] —**car·cin·o·gen·ic** (-jénnik) *adj.*

car·ci·no·ma (kár-si-nṓ-mə) *n., pl.* **-mas** or **-mata** (-mə-tə). A malignant tumour arising in epithelial tissue. [Latin *carcinōma,* cancerous ulcer, from Greek *karkinōma,* from *karkinos,* cancer, crab.] —**car·ci·no·ma·toid, car·ci·nom·a·tous** (-təss, *also* -nómmətəss) *adj.*

car·ci·no·ma·to·sis (kár-si-nṓmə-tṓ-siss) *n.* The existence of carcinomas at many bodily sites. [New Latin : Latin *carcinōma* (stem *carcinōmat-*), CARCINOMA + -OSIS.]

card¹ (kard) *n.* **1.** A small, flat piece of stiff paper, thin pasteboard, or plastic, usually rectangular, with numerous uses, as: **a.** Any of a set bearing significant numbers, symbols, and figures, used in numerous games and in fortune-telling. See **cards. b.** One used to send messages; especially, a postcard. **c.** One printed with a suitable illustration and greeting and sent in an envelope, as for Christmas. **d.** One bearing a person's name and other information, used for purposes of identification or classification, such as a visiting card or membership card. **e.** One used for cataloguing information in a file, such as a reference card. **f.** See **credit card. g.** See **cheque card. 2.** A notice or advertisement printed on cardboard. **3.** *Sports.* A list of events or competitors, such as: **a.** A scorecard *(see).* **b.** A racecard *(see).* **4.** See **compass card. 5.** *Computing.* A **punched card** *(see).* **6.** *Informal.* An amusing or eccentric person. —**have a card up (one's) sleeve.** To have a secret resource or plan held in reserve. [Middle English *carde,* from Old French *carte,* from Latin *charta,* leaf of papyrus, from Greek *khartēs,* probably from Egyptian.]

card² *n.* **1.** A wire-toothed brush or comblike machine used to disentangle fibres, as of wool, prior to spinning. **2.** A similar device used to raise the nap on a fabric.
~*tr.v.* **carded, carding, cards.** To comb out or brush with a card. [Middle English *carde,* from Old French, from *carder,* to card, from Old Provençal *cardar,* from Vulgar Latin *caritāre* (unattested), from Latin *cārere,* to card.] —**card·er** *n.*

Card. *Roman Catholic Church.* cardinal.

car·da·mom, car·da·mum (kárda-məm) *n.* Also **car·da·mon** (-mən). **1. a.** A tropical Asiatic perennial plant, *Elettaria cardamomum,* having large, hairy leaves and capsular fruit. **b.** The fruit and seeds of this plant, used as a condiment and in medicine. **2. a.** An East Indian plant, *Amomum cardamomum.* **b.** The fruit and seeds of this plant, used as an inferior substitute for true cardamom seed. [Latin *cardamōmum,* from Greek *kardamōmon : kardamon*†, cress + *amōmon*†, an Indian spice.]

card·board (kárd-bawrd ‖ -bôrd) *n.* A thin, stiff pasteboard made of paper pulp, used for making cartons and boxes.
~*adj.* **1.** Made of cardboard. **2.** Superficial; two-dimensional: *cardboard characters.*

cardboard city. *n.* An area where homeless people sleep rough, typically in discarded cardboard boxes.

card-car·ry·ing (kárd-karri-ing) *adj.* Designating a fully committed member, especially of a political organisation: *a card-carrying Communist.* [As if *carrying* a membership *card.*]

car·di·a (kárdi-ə) *n.* **1.** The opening of the oesophagus into the stomach. **2.** The heart. [New Latin, from Greek *kardia,* heart, cardiac orifice of the stomach.]

car·di·ac (kárdi-ak) *adj.* **1.** Of, near, or pertaining to the heart. **2.** Of or pertaining to the cardia.
~*n.* **1.** A person with a heart disorder. **2.** A drug that stimulates heart muscle. [Latin *cardiacus,* from Greek *kardiakos,* from *kardia,* heart.]

cardiac arrest *n.* The cessation of effective pumping of blood by the heart, resulting in loss of consciousness, absence of the pulse, and cessation of breathing.

cardiac massage *n.* A procedure to restore circulation in an individual by rhythmic manual compression either of the chest or of the heart through an opening in the chest wall.

cardiac muscle *n.* The striated muscle of the heart.

car·di·al·gi·a (kárdi-álji-ə) *n.* **1.** Heartburn *(see).* **2.** Pain in or close to the heart. [New Latin, from Greek *kardialgia* : CARDI(O)- + -ALGIA.]

Car·diff (kárdif). *Welsh* **Caer-dydd** (kīr-deéth, kaar-). Capital of Wales, situated on the river Taff. With the expansion of the South Wales coal and iron mines in the 19th century, Cardiff grew from a small market town into one of the world's leading coal exporters. It was chosen as the capital of Wales only in 1955. After World War II, the port declined and Tiger Bay, the quayside area, is now a residential suburb. Industries include general shipping, ship repairs, steel, engineering, chemicals, and cement.

car·di·gan (kárdigən) *n.* A sweater or knitted jacket worn by both sexes and opening down the front. [After the Earl of CARDIGAN.]

Car·di·gan. *Welsh* **A·ber·tei·fi** (ábbər-táyvi). Town on the river Teifi, south Wales, noted for its salmon and sea-trout angling. It is the main town of Ceredigion.

Car·di·gan (kárdigən), **James Thomas Brudenell, 7th Earl of** (1797–1868). British cavalry officer. He is remembered chiefly for leading the suicidal Charge of the Light Brigade at Balaclava (1854) in the Crimean War.

Car·di·gan·shire (kárdigən-shər, -sheer ‖ -shīr). *Welsh* **Cer·e·dig·**

ion (kérri-dig-yon). Former county in Wales and now a Unitary Authority area named Ceredigion.

Car·din (kár-daN ‖ kaar-dáN), **Pierre** (1922–). French fashion designer who made his mark in the 1950s with his slim-line coats, large collars, and Eastern-influenced designs.

car·di·nal (kárdin'l, kárd'n'l, kárdn'l) *adj.* **1.** Of foremost importance; pivotal. **2.** Of a dark to deep or vivid red colour.
~*n.* **1.** *Abbr.* **Card.** *Roman Catholic Church.* A member of the Sacred College or College of Cardinals. Members are appointed by the pope and elect a new pope when the Holy See is vacated. **2.** Dark to deep or vivid red. Also called "cardinal red". **3.** A North American bird, *Richmondena cardinalis,* having a crested head, a short, thick bill, and bright red plumage in the male. **4.** A short, hooded cloak, originally of scarlet cloth, worn by women in the 18th century. **5.** See **cardinal number.** [Middle English, from Old French, from Late Latin *cardinālis,* from Latin, principal, of a hinge, from *cardō*† (stem *cardin-*), hinge.]

car·di·nal·ate (kárdin'l-ayt, kárd'n'l-, -it) *n.* Also **car·di·nal·ship** (-ship). *Roman Catholic Church.* **1.** The College of Cardinals. **2.** The position, rank, dignity, or term of a cardinal.

cardinal beetle *n.* A bright red European beetle of the genus *Pyrodehroa,* especially *P. coccinea* and *P. serraticornis,* whose coloration and unpleasant taste help to protect it from predatory birds.

cardinal flower *n.* A plant, *Lobelia cardinalis,* of eastern North America, having a terminal cluster of brilliant scarlet flowers.

cardinal number *n.* **1.** A number, such as 3 or 11 or 412, used to indicate quantity but not order. Compare **ordinal number. 2.** A symbol denoting the size of a transfinite set.

cardinal point *n.* Any of the four principal directions on a compass: north, south, east, or west.

cardinal sins *pl.n.* The **seven deadly sins** *(see).*

cardinal virtues *pl.n.* The four qualities of justice, prudence, fortitude, and temperance. Also called "natural virtues".

cardio–, cardi– *comb. form.* Indicates the heart; for example, **cardiogram, cardioid.** [Greek *kardi(o)-,* from *kardia,* heart.]

car·di·o·gram (kárdi-ə-gram, -ō-) *n.* **1.** The curve traced by a cardiograph, used in the diagnosis of heart defects. **2.** An **electrocardiogram** *(see).* [CARDIO- + -GRAM.]

car·di·o·graph (kárdi-ə-graaf, -ō-, -graf) *n.* **1.** An instrument used to record the mechanical movements of the heart. **2.** An **electrocardiograph** *(see).* [French *cardiographe* : CARDIO- + -GRAPH.] —**car·di·og·raph·er** (-óggrəfər) *n.* —**car·di·o·graph·ic** (-gráffik), **car·di·o·graph·i·cal** *adj.* —**car·di·o·graph·i·cal·ly** *adv.* —**car·di·o·graph·y** (-óggrəfi) *n.*

car·di·oid (kárdi-oyd) *n.* A heart-shaped plane curve, the locus of a fixed point on a circle that rolls on the circumference of another circle with the same radius. [CARDI(O)- + -OID.]

car·di·ol·o·gy (kárdi-ólləji) *n.* The medical study of the diseases and functioning of the heart. [CARDIO- + -LOGY.] —**car·di·ol·o·gist** *n.*

car·di·o·meg·a·ly (kárdi-ō-méggəli) *n. Pathology.* **Megalocardia** *(see).* [CARDIO- + -megaly, from MEGALO-.]

car·di·o·res·pir·a·to·ry (kárdi-ō-ri-spírrə-tri, -spír-ə-, réspi-rə-, -təri) *adj.* Pertaining to the heart and the lungs.

car·di·o·vas·cu·lar (kárdi-ō-váskewlər) *adj.* Pertaining to or involving the heart and the blood vessels.

car·doon (kaar-dóon) *n.* A plant, *Cynara cardunculus,* of southern Europe, closely related to the artichoke, and having spiny leaves, purple flowers, and an edible leafstalk. [French *cardon,* from Provençal, from Late Latin *cardō* (stem *cardōn-*), thistle, from Latin *carduus,* thistle, artichoke.]

card punch *n. Computing.* A **key punch** *(see).*

card reader *n. Computing.* A device for reading data from punched cards into a computer or storage device.

cards (kardz) *n. Usually used with a singular verb.* **1.** Any game, such as bridge, whist, or poker, with playing cards, usually in packs of 52 cards divided into four suits: spades, hearts, diamonds, and clubs. **2.** The playing of such games. **3.** Formerly, an employee's documents, such as national insurance cards, held by an employer. —**get (one's) cards.** To be told to leave one's job; be dismissed. —**on the cards.** Likely to occur; probable. —**play (one's) cards right.** To carry out one's plans in the cleverest possible manner. —**put** or **lay (one's) cards on the table.** To make an open and honest declaration of one's position.

card·sharp (kárd-sharp) *n.* Also **card·sharp·er** (-sharpər). A person expert in cheating at cards. —**card·sharp·ing** *n.*

card vote *n.* A method of voting, used especially at trade union conferences, whereby the vote of each delegate counts for a specific number of his constituents; a process of deciding issues by **block vote** *(see).*

care (kair) *n.* **1.** Mental distress and uncertainty; worry. **2.** Mental suffering; grief. **3.** An object or source of worry, attention, or solicitude. **4.** Caution; heedfulness: *handle with care.* **5.** Protection; supervision; charge: *in the care of a nurse.* **6.** *British.* Supervision and protection of a child by a local authority: *taken into care while his mother was in prison.* **7.** Attentiveness to detail; painstaking application; conscientiousness: *a report prepared with great care.* —**care of.** *Abbr.* **c/o, c-o.** At the address of. Used in addressing letters and other post. —**take care.** To act prudently. —**take care of.** To look after or deal with.
~*v.* **cared, caring, cares.** —*intr.* **1.** To have a strong feeling or opinion; be concerned or interested. Often used with *about: I care about the Bomb.* **2.** To be fond; have regard. Used with *about* or *for: I care for her deeply; they really care about each other.* **3. a.** To wish;

be inclined. Used with an infinitive or *for: We don't care to come; would you care for some dessert?* **b.** To be pleased with. Used in the negative followed by *for: I don't care for your attitude.* **4.** To look after or nurse; provide help. Usually used with *for.* —*tr.* To be concerned to a specified degree. Often used in the negative: *I don't care a damn.* [Middle English *care,* Old English *caru, cearu.*]

ca·reen (kə-réen) *v.* **-reened, -reening, -reens.** —*intr.* **1.** To lean to one side; sway or heel, in the manner of a ship sailing in the wind. **2.** *Nautical.* To turn a ship on its side for cleaning, caulking, or repairing. **3.** *Chiefly U.S.* To move rapidly and erratically. —*tr. Nautical.* **1.** To cause to lean to one side; tilt. **2.** To lean (a ship) on one side for cleaning, caulking, or repairing. [French *(en) carène,* "(on) the keel", from Old French *carene,* keel, from Old Italian *carena,* from Latin *carīna,* keel of a ship, nutshell.] —**ca·reen·er** *n.*

Usage: Both *careen* and *career* may refer to rapid and uncontrolled movement, the similarity in their form having promoted their use as synonyms, especially in informal speech, with *career* being the more frequently used. Many people try to maintain a distinction in meaning between the words, restricting *career* to forward movement, and *careen* to leaning and tilting, as in the manner of a ship.

ca·reen·age (kə-réenij) *n.* **1.** A place for careening ships. **2.** The careening of ships. **3.** The charge for careening.

ca·reer (kə-réer) *n.* **1.** An occupation, especially one with the possibility of advancement; a profession that lasts most of one's working lifetime. **2.** A path, course, or progress through life or history; especially, the course of a working life. **3.** Rapid progress; swift movement; speed. Often used with *full: "My hasting days fly on with full career."* (Milton). —*adj.* Engaged in a specified occupation as a chosen career: *a career diplomat.* —*intr.v.* **careered, -reering, -reers.** To move or run at full speed; go headlong; rush. See Usage note at **careen.** [French *carrière,* racecourse, course, career, from Old French, from Old Provençal *carriera,* street, from Medieval Latin *(via) carrāria,* (road) for vehicles, from Latin *carrus,* a kind of vehicle.]

ca·reer·ism (kə-réer-iz'm) *n.* The practice of seeking one's professional advancement by all possible means. —**ca·reer·ist** *n. & adj.*

career woman *n.* A woman who successfully pursues a career or who places the demands of a career before those of her private life.

care·free (káir-free) *adj.* Free of worries and responsibilities.

care·ful (káirf'l) *adj.* **1.** Cautious in thought, speech, or action; circumspect; prudent. **2.** Thorough; painstaking; conscientious: *careful investigation.* **3.** Solicitous; protective. Used with *of.* **4.** *British Informal.* Frugal, often to the point of meanness. —**care·ful·ly** (*usually* káirfli) *adv.* —**care·ful·ness** *n.*

care·less (káir-ləss, -liss) *adj.* **1.** Inattentive; negligent. **2.** Marked by or resulting from lack of thought, thoroughness, or planning: *a careless mistake.* **3.** Inconsiderate: *a careless remark.* **4.** Unconcerned; unmindful: *careless about her health.* **5.** Unstudied; effortless: *careless grandeur.* —**care·less·ly** *adv.* —**care·less·ness** *n.*

Synonyms: careless, heedless, thoughtless, negligent, lax.

car·er (káirər) *n.* Someone who takes care of someone else, especially on a long-term or professional basis.

ca·ress (kə-réss) *n.* A gentle touch or gesture of fondness, tenderness, or love. —*tr.v.* **caressed, -ressing, -resses.** **1.** To touch or stroke in an affectionate or loving manner. **2.** To touch or stroke gently. [French *caresse,* from Italian *carezza,* endearment, from *caro,* dear, from Latin *cārus.*] —**ca·ress·er** *n.* —**ca·ress·ing·ly** *adv.*

car·et (kárrit, kárrət) *n.* A proofreading symbol used to indicate where something is to be inserted in printed or written matter. [Latin, "there is lacking", from *carēre,* to cut off, be without.]

care·tak·er (káir-taykər) *n.* **1.** A person employed to look after or take charge of goods, property, or a person; a custodian. **2.** One taking charge temporarily. Also used adjectively: *a caretaker government.*

care·worn (káir-wawrn ‖ -wörn) *adj.* Showing the effects of anxiety; weary from worry. See Synonyms at **haggard.**

car·go (kár-gō) *n., pl.* **-goes** or **-gos.** The freight carried by a ship, aeroplane, or other vehicle. [Spanish *cargo, carga,* load, cargo, from *cargar,* to load, from Late Latin *carricāre,* from Latin *carrus,* a kind of vehicle.]

cargo cult *n.* A religious cult, existing mainly in the South Pacific islands of Melanesia, based on a belief that suitable actions will bring the future arrival from boats and aeroplanes of rich and desirable goods.

Car·ib (kárrib) *n., pl.* **-ibs** or collectively **Carib.** **1.** A member of a group of American Indian peoples of northern South America and the Lesser Antilles. **2.** Any of the languages of these peoples. —**Car·ib** *adj.* —**Car·ib·an** *adj. & n.*

Car·ib·be·an (kárri-bée-ən ‖ kə-ríbbi-ən) *n.* **1.** The Caribbean Sea. Preceded by *the.* **2.** A Carib Indian. —*adj.* **1.** Of, pertaining to, or originating in the Caribbean Sea and its islands. **2.** Of or pertaining to the Carib or their language.

Caribbean Sea (kárri-bée-ən ‖ kə-ríbbi-ən). Part of the west Atlantic Ocean separated from the main part of the ocean by the West Indies. This tropical sea covering 2 590 000 square kilometres (1,000,000 square miles), has been an important shipping route since the opening of the Panama Canal in 1914. It takes its name from the original inhabitants of the area, the Caribs. See map at **Latin America.**

car·i·bou (kárri-bōō) *n., pl.* **-bous** or collectively **caribou.** A deer,

Rangifer tarandus, of arctic regions of the New World, having antlers in both sexes. It also occurs in Northern Europe and Asia, where it is called a **reindeer.** [Canadian French, probably from Algonquian.]

car·i·ca·ture (kárrikə-tewr, -choor, -téwr) *n.* **1.** A representation, especially pictorial, in which the subject's distinctive features or peculiarities are deliberately exaggerated or distorted to produce a comic or grotesque effect. **2.** The process or art of creating such representations. **3.** An imitation or copy so inferior as to be absurd. —*tr.v.* **caricatured, -turing, -tures.** To represent or imitate in or as in a caricature; satirise. [French, from Italian *caricatura,* caricature, "exaggeration", from *caricare,* to load, from Late Latin *carricāre,* from Latin *carrus,* a kind of vehicle.] —**car·i·ca·tur·ist** *n.*

Synonyms: caricature, parody, satire, lampoon, takeoff, spoof, travesty.

car·ies (káir-eez, -i-eez) *n.* Decay of a bone or a tooth (*dental caries*). [Latin *cariēs,* caries, decay.]

car·il·lon (kə-ríl-yən, kárril-, -on) *n.* **1.** A set of bells, usually housed in a tower, played from a keyboard or by some other mechanism. **2.** A stop on an organ that produces a bell-like sound. **3.** A tune played on a carillon. —*intr.v.* **carillonned, -lonning, -lons.** To play a carillon. [French, variant of Old French *carignon, quarregnon,* from Vulgar Latin *quadriniō* (stem *quadriniōn-*) (unattested), set of four bells, variant of Late Latin *quaterniō,* set of four, from *quaternī,* four each, from *quater,* four times.]

car·il·lon·neur (kə-ríl-yən-ér, kárril-, -on-, -ər) *n.* A person who plays a carillon.

ca·ri·na (kə-rée-nə, -rí-) *n., pl.* **-nae** (-nee). *Biology.* A keel-shaped ridge, such as that on the breastbone of a bird or in the petals of certain flowers. [New Latin, from Latin *carīna,* keel.]

Ca·ri·na (kə-rée-nə, -rí-) *n.* A constellation in the Southern Hemisphere near Vela containing the star Canopus. [Latin, "the Keel".]

car·i·nate (kárri-nayt, -nət, -nit) *adj.* Also **car·i·nat·ed** (-naytid). *Biology.* Having or shaped like a keel; ridged.

car·ing *adj.* Concerned; compassionate: *a more caring society.* —**car·ing·ly** *adv.*

Carinthia. See **Kärnten.**

car·i·o·ca (kárri-ŏkə) *n.* **1.** A South American ballroom dance that originated in Rio de Janeiro. **2.** The music for this dance. **3.** *Capital C.* A native or resident of Rio de Janeiro. [Portuguese *Carioca,* from Tupi.]

car·i·o·gen·ic (káir-i-ō-jénnik, -a-) *adj.* Producing caries, especially of the teeth. [CARIES + -GENIC.]

car·i·ole, car·ri·ole (kárri-ōl) *n.* **1.** A small, open, one-horse vehicle with two wheels. **2.** A light, covered cart. [French *carriole,* from Old Provençal *carriola,* diminutive of *carri,* chariot, from Vulgar Latin *carrium* (unattested), from Latin *carrus,* a kind of vehicle.]

car·i·ous (káir-i-əss) *adj.* Having caries; decayed. Said of teeth and bones. —**car·i·os·i·ty** (-óssəti), **car·i·ous·ness** *n.*

car·line[1] (kárlin) *n.* A thistle-like Eurasian plant, *Carlina vulgaris,* having spiny leaves and flower heads surrounded by slender, ray-like, straw-coloured bracts. Also called **"carline thistle".** [French, from Medieval Latin *carlina,* perhaps variant of *cardina* (through association with *Carolus (Magnus),* Charlemagne), from Latin *cardo,* thistle.]

car·line[2], **car·lin** *n.* **1.** *Scottish.* **a.** An old woman. **b.** A witch. **2.** Variant of **carling.** [See **carling**[1]]

car·ling[1] (kár-ling, -lin) *n.* Also **car·line** (-lin). *Nautical.* Any of the short timbers running fore and aft that connect the transverse beams supporting the deck of a ship. [French *carlingue,* from Old French *cal(l)ingue,* probably from Old Norse *kerling,* "old woman", from *karl,* man.]

car·ling[2] (kárling) *n. Northern English.* A type of dried pea, served stewed, and traditionally eaten on the fifth Sunday in Lent (*Care* or *Carling Sunday*). [From obsolete *carre,* Old English *care,* grief, CARE + -LING.]

Car·lisle (kaar-lïl, kár- ‖ *locally* kár-lïl). City in Cumbria, England, on the river Eden. Once a Roman fortress, it was destroyed by the Danes in A.D. 875 and rebuilt (1092) by William Rufus. Mary, Queen of Scots was imprisoned in its 11th-century castle.

Carl·ist (kárl-ist) *n.* In Spain, a supporter of Don Carlos (1788–1855), brother of Ferdinand VII (1784–1833), and pretender to the throne, or his heirs. The present Carlist pretender is Carlos Hugo de Bourbon-Parma (1930–). —**Carl·ism** *n.* —**Carl·ist** *adj.*

car·load (kár-lōd) *n.* The amount a car carries or is able to carry.

Carlovingian. Variant of **Carolingian.**

Car·low (kárlō). *Irish* **Ceatharlach.** A largely agricultural county in Leinster, southeast Republic of Ireland. Carlow is the chief town.

Carlsbad. See **Karlovy Vary.**

Carlsruhe. See **Karlsruhe.**

Car·lyle (kaar-lïl), **Thomas** (1795–1881). Scottish historian and essayist, well known for a literary style characterised by complex syntax and rich vocabulary. His book *Sartor Resartus* (1833–34), a blend of fiction, autobiography, and philosophy, was followed by *The French Revolution* (1837). His other works include *Past and Present* (1843), an attack on England's social and political ills.

car·man (kár-mən) *n., pl.* **-men** (-mən, -men). **1.** A man who drives a car or cart. **2.** *U.S.* A driver or conductor, as of a tram.

Car·mar·then (kər-márth'n). *Welsh* **Caer·fyr·ddin** (kīr-vúrthin). One of the oldest towns in Wales, situated on the river Towy in Carmarthenshire, south Wales. It was once the site of a Roman fort.

Car·mar·then·shire (kər-márth'nər, -sheer ‖ shïr). *Welsh* **Sir Gaer·**

fyr·ddin (seer gīr-vúr<u>th</u>in). Former county in Wales and now a Unitary Authority area.

Car·mel (kár-m'l, -mel), **Mount**. A limestone ridge, 546 metres (1,791 feet) at its highest, in northwest Israel. It was the scene of Elijah's struggle with the priests of Baal. The religious order of the Carmelites was founded there in the 12th century.

Car·mel·ite (kár-məl-īt, -mel-) *n*. **1.** A monk or mendicant friar belonging to the order of Our Lady of Mount Carmel, founded at Mount Carmel in about 1155. Also called "White Friar". **2.** A member of a community of nuns of this order, founded in 1452. —**Car·mel·ite** *adj*.

car·min·a·tive (kármin-ətiv || -aytiv) *adj*. Inducing expulsion of gas from the stomach and intestines.
~*n*. A carminative drug. [Middle English, from Medieval Latin *carmināтīvus*, from *carmināre* (past participle *carminātus*), to card wool, comb out impurities, from Latin *carmen*, a card for wool, from *cārere*, to card.]

car·mine (kár-mīn, -min) *n*. **1.** A deep vivid red colour with a purplish tinge. **2.** A crimson pigment derived from **cochineal** *(see)*. —*adj*. Vivid red or purplish-red. [French *carmin*, from Medieval Latin *carminium* : Arabic *qirmiz*, KERMES + Latin *minium*, MINIUM.]

Car·nac (kárnak). Small coastal village in Brittany, France, famous for its prehistoric standing stones extending in parallel rows for about 5 kilometres (3 miles).

car·nage (kárnij) *n*. **1.** Massive slaughter, as in war; massacre. **2.** *Archaic*. Corpses, especially of people killed in battle: *a battlefield bloody with carnage*. [Old French, from Medieval Latin *carnāticum*, slaughter of animals, from Latin *carō* (stem *carn-*), flesh, meat.]

car·nal (kárn'l) *adj*. **1.** Pertaining to the desires and appetites of the flesh or body; sensual; animal. **2.** Worldly or earthly; not spiritual; not holy or sanctified. [Middle English, from Medieval Latin *carnālis*, from Latin *carō* (stem *carn-*), flesh.] —**car·nal·ist** *n*. —**car·nal·i·ty** (kaar-nál-əti) *n*. —**car·nal·ly** *adv*.

carnal knowledge *n*. *Law*. Sexual intercourse.

car·nall·ite (kárn'l-īt) *n*. A white, brownish, or reddish mineral, KMgCl₃·6H₂O, used to manufacture potassium salts. [German *Carnallit*, after Rudolf von *Carnall* (1804–74), German mining engineer.]

Car·nap (kár-nap), **Rudolf** (1891–1970). German-born logical positivist philosopher, who was professor of philosophy at the universities of Vienna, Prague, Chicago, and California. To support his view that the purpose of philosophy is to analyse and clarify knowledge, he tried to create a formal language that would eliminate confusion and ambiguity in the empirical sciences.

Carnarvon. See **Caernarfon.**

Carnarvonshire. See **Caernarfonshire.**

car·nas·si·al (kaar-nássi-əl) *adj*. Adapted for tearing apart flesh. Said of teeth.
~*n*. A carnassial tooth, either the last upper premolar or the first lower molar in carnivorous mammals. [French *carnassier*, carnivorous, from Provençal, from *carnasso*, meat in abundance, from *carn*, flesh, from Latin *carō* (stem *carn-*), flesh.]

car·na·tion (kaar-náysh'n) *n*. **1. a.** Any of various ornamental cultivated plants derived from the **clove pink** *(see)*, having large, variously coloured double flowers. **b.** The flower of any of these plants. **2.** *Plural*. *Rare*. Flesh-coloured tints used in painting. [French, flesh-coloured, carnation, from Italian *carnagione*, complexion, from *carne*, flesh, from Latin *carō* (stem *carn-*), flesh.]

car·nau·ba (kaar-nówbə, -náwba) *n*. **1.** A palm tree, *Copernicia cerifera*, of tropical South America. **2.** A hard wax obtained from the leaves of this tree, used as a polish and in candles. In this sense, also called "carnauba wax". [Portuguese, probably of Tupi origin.]

Car·né (kárnay || kaar-náy), **Marcel** (1909–96). French director, noted for films made in collaboration with the screenwriter and poet Jacques Prévert. They include *Le Jour se lève* (1939) and *Les Enfants du paradis* (1944).

Car·neg·ie (kaar-náygi, -néggi, -néegi || *U.S. also* kárnəgi), **Andrew** (1835–1919). Scottish-born U.S. industrialist and philanthropist. Arriving in the United States as a penniless young boy, he became one of the world's richest men and gave more than £70 million to charities in the United States and in the United Kingdom.

car·nel·i·an (kaar-néeli-ən, -yən) *n*. Also **cor·nel·i·an** (kawr-). A reddish or reddish-brown variety of chalcedony, used in jewellery. [Middle English *corneline*, from Old French, probably "cherry-coloured", from *cornelle*, CORNEL (cherry).]

car·net (kárnay || *U.S.* kaar-náy) *n*. A permit or customs licence allowing a motor vehicle to be imported or driven across certain national frontiers. [French, "notebook".]

car·ney, car·ny (kárni) *n*. *British Regional*. Wheedling talk.
~*v*. **carneyed** or **carnied, -neying** or **-nying, -neys** or **-nies**. —*intr*. To behave or speak in a wheedling manner. —*tr*. To flatter; coax. [19th century : origin obscure.]

car·ni·val (kárniv'l) *n*. **1.** The season just before Lent celebrated in some Roman Catholic countries by processions, dancing, merry-making, and feasting. See **Mardi gras. 2.** Any time of revelry; a festival. **3.** *Chiefly U.S.* A travelling fair or circus. **4.** *Australian*. A large-scale sporting event: *a surfing carnival*. [Italian *carnevale*, from Old Italian *carnelevare*, "the putting away of flesh", Shrovetide, from Medieval Latin *carnelevāmen* : Latin *carō* (stem *carn-*), flesh + *levāre*, to raise, remove.]

car·ni·vore (kárni-vawr || -vōr) *n*. **1.** *Zoology*. Any animal belonging to the order Carnivora, which includes predominantly flesh-eating mammals such as dogs, cats, bears, and weasels. **2.** Any flesh-

eating or predatory organism, such as a bird of prey or an insectivorous plant. [French, from Latin *carnivorus*, CARNIVOROUS.]

car·niv·o·rous (kaar-nívvərəss) *adj*. **1.** Belonging or pertaining to the order Carnivora. **2.** Flesh-eating or predatory. **3.** *Botany*. Capable of trapping and absorbing insects or other small organisms; insectivorous. Said of plants such as the pitcher plant and the Venus's-flytrap. [Latin *carnivorus* : *carō* (stem *carn-*), flesh + -VO-ROUS.] —**car·niv·o·rous·ly** *adv*. —**car·niv·o·rous·ness** *n*.

Car·not (kárnō, kaar-nō), **(Nicolas Léonard) Sadi** (1796-1832). French physicist, engineer, and soldier who founded the science of thermodynamics. His investigations on the motive power of heat established that heat and work are reversible conditions. The **Carnot cycle** and **Carnot's principle** are described in his study *Réflexions sur la puissance motrice du feu* (1824).

Carnot, Lazare Nicolas Marguerite (1753-1823). Father of Sadi Carnot, and statesman and military engineer whose book *De la Défense des places fortes* (1810) became a classic study on fortifications.

Carnot cycle *n*. *Physics*. The thermodynamic cycle of an ideal heat engine, consisting of an adiabatic compression, an isothermal expansion, an adiabatic expansion, and an isothermal compression, the sequence restoring the initial conditions of the system. [After N.L.S. CARNOT.]

car·no·tite (kárnə-tīt) *n*. A yellow uranium ore with composition K₂(UO₂)₂(VO₄)₂nH₂O. [French, after M.A. *Carnot* (died 1920), French inspector general of mines.]

Carnot's principle *n*. *Physics*. The principle that the efficiency of a perfect heat engine does not depend on the substance used. [After N.L.S. CARNOT.]

car·ob (kárrəb) *n*. **1.** An evergreen tree, *Ceratonia siliqua*, of the Mediterranean region, having compound leaves and edible pods. Also called "algarroba", "locust". See **St. John's bread. 2.** The edible pod of the carob tree, used as animal fodder and to make a preparation resembling chocolate. [Obsolete French *caro(u)be*, from Medieval Latin *carrūbium*, from Arabic *kharrūbah.*]

ca·roche (kə-rósh || *U.S.* -rōch, -rōsh) *n*. A stately carriage of the 16th and 17th centuries. [French *carroche*, from Old Italian *carroccio*, augmentative of *carro*, vehicle, from Latin *carrus*.]

car·ol (kárrəl) *v*. **-olled** or *U.S.* **-oled, -olling** or *U.S.* **-oling, -ols.** —*tr*. **1.** To celebrate in song. **2.** To sing (something) joyously. —*intr*. **1.** To sing in a joyous manner; warble. **2.** To go from house to house singing Christmas carols.
~*n*. **1.** A song of praise or joy, especially one celebrating the birth of Christ. **2.** An old round dance often accompanied by singing. [Middle English *carolen*, from Old French *caroler*, of obscure origin.] —**car·oll·er** *n*.

Car·ol II (kárrəl) (1893–1953). King of Romania. Because of his love for a commoner, Magda Lupescu, he renounced his right to succession (1925) in favour of his son Michael, who became king in 1927. He returned to his country in 1930 and was proclaimed king, but his reign lasted only until 1940. After failure to prevent Nazi domination of the kingdom, he abdicated and settled in Mexico.

Car·o·le·an (kárrə-lée-ən) *adj*. Caroline. [Medieval Latin *Carolus*, CHARLES.]

Car·o·line (kárrəl-līn, -lin) *adj*. **1.** Of or pertaining to the life and times of Charles I or Charles II of England. **2.** Of or pertaining to Charlemagne or his time. [New Latin *Carolinius*, from Medieval Latin *Carolus*, CHARLES.]

Caroline Islands. Also **Carolines.** Archipelago in the west Pacific Ocean, whose main groups include Pohnpei, Chuuk, Yap and Palau. Formerly part of the United Nations Trust Territory of the Pacific Islands (1947–80), all but Palau joined the Federated States of Micronesia. Palau became an independent republic in 1994.

Caroline of Ans·bach (ánss-bakh, -baakh) (1683–1737). The wife of King George II of Great Britain and regent during her husband's absences. She was a patron of Sir Robert Walpole.

Car·o·lin·gi·an (kárrə-línji-ən) *adj*. Also **Car·lo·vin·gi·an** (kárlə-vínji-ən, kárlō-). Related to, designating, or belonging to the Frankish dynasty that was founded by Pepin the Short in A.D. 751 and that lasted until A.D. 987 in France and A.D. 911 in Germany. —*n*. Also **Car·lo·vin·gi·an**. A member of this dynasty. [French *Carolingien*, variant of *Carlovingien*, probably a blend of Medieval Latin *Carolus*, Charles and *Mérovingien*, MEROVINGIAN.]

car·om (kárrəm) *n*. *U.S.* In billiards, a cannon.
~*intr.v*. **caromed, -oming, -oms.** *U.S.* In billiards, to cannon. [Earlier *carambole*, from Spanish *carambola*, a kind of fruit, from Portuguese, from Marathi *karambal†*.]

Car·o's acid (kárrōz, káaróz) *n*. A strong acid, **peroxosulphuric acid** *(see)*. [After Heinrich *Caro* (died 1910), German chemist.]

car·o·tene (kárrə-teen) *n*. Also **car·o·tin** (-tin). An orange-yellow to red hydrocarbon, C₄₀H₅₆, existing in six isomeric forms, occurring in many plants as a pigment. Three of the isomers may be converted to vitamin A in the liver. [German *Karotin* : Latin *carōta*, CARROT + -ENE.]

ca·rot·e·noid, ca·rot·i·noid (kə-róttin-oyd) *n*. Any of a class of yellow to deep red pigments, such as the carotenes, occurring in many vegetable oils and animal fats.

ca·rot·id (kə-róttid) *n*. Either of the two major arteries in the neck that carry blood to the head.
~*adj*. Of or pertaining to either of the two carotid arteries. [French *carotide*, from Greek *karōtides*, from *karoun*, to stupefy (it was once thought that pressure on the carotids causes stupor).]

ca·rous·al (kə-rówz'l) *n.* A jovial, riotous drinking party; boisterous merrymaking; revelry.

ca·rouse (kə-rówz) *n.* A carousal. ~*intr.v.* **caroused, -rousing, -rouses.** To drink excessively; go on a drinking spree. [Old French *carrousse,* from *(boire) carous,* (to drink) all out, from German *garaus (trinken)* : *gar,* quite, entirely + *aus,* out.] —**ca·rous·er** *n.*

car·ou·sel (kárrə-sél, kárrōō-, -zél) *n.* Also chiefly U.S. **car·rou·sel. 1.** A tournament in which knights or horsemen engaged in various exercises and races. **2.** Chiefly U.S. A **merry-go-round** (see). **3.** Chiefly U.S. A rotating conveyor system, as for delivering luggage in an airport. [French *carrousel,* probably from Italian dialectal *carosello†,* a kind of tournament.]

carp¹ (karp) *intr.v.* **carped, carping, carps.** To find fault and complain constantly; harp on petty grievances; grumble. Often used with *at.* [Middle English *carpen,* from Old Norse *karpa,* to boast.] —**carp·er** *n.* —**carp·ing·ly** *adv.*

carp² *n., pl.* **carps** or collectively **carp. 1.** An edible freshwater fish, *Cyprinus carpio,* frequently bred in ponds and lakes. **2.** Any of various other fishes of the family Cyprinidae. [Middle English *carpe,* from Old French, from Late Latin *carpa†.*]

-carp *n. comb. form.* Botany. Indicates fruit or similar reproductive structure; for example, **mesocarp.** [New Latin *-carpium,* from Greek *-karpion,* from *karpos,* fruit.]

Car·pac·cio (kaar-páchi-ō, -pách-) **Vittore,** born Vittore Scarpazza (*c.* 1460–*c.*1525). Venetian painter noted for his views of the city and his narrative cycles. Influenced by Gentile and Giovanni Bellini, his works include the cycle *Scenes from the Life of St. Ursula,* and *The Miracle of the Cross.*

car·pal (karp'l) *adj.* Anatomy. Of, pertaining to, or near the carpus. ~*n.* Any bone of the carpus. [New Latin *carpalis,* from Greek *karpos,* wrist.]

carpal tunnel syndrome *n.* A syndrome of weakness, pain, and paraesthesia, principally in the hand, caused by compression of a nerve passing into the hand through the wrist.

car park *n.* British. A building or area in which cars can be parked, usually for a fee. Also U.S. "parking lot".

Car·pa·thi·an Mountains (kaar-páythi-ən) Also **Car·pa·thi·ans.** Mountain range extending through central and eastern Europe in an arc 1 400 kilometres (900 miles) long. It forms part of the Slovak-Polish border, crosses the southwest Ukraine into Romania and swings back to the Danube at the Iron Gates, on the Romanian-Yugoslav frontier. Sparsely inhabited, it is a resort area, and rich in mineral deposits.

car·pel (kár-p'l, -pel) *n.* Botany. The central, ovule-bearing female organ of a flower, consisting of an ovary, style, and stigma. Carpels may be separate or fused to form a single pistil. [New Latin *carpellum,* from Greek *karpos,* fruit.] —**car·pel·lar·y** (-əri ‖ -erri) *adj.* **car·pel·late** (kárpə-layt, -lət, -lit) *adj.* Botany. Having carpels.

Car·pen·tar·ia (kárpən-taír-i-ə), **Gulf of.** A large inlet of the Arafura Sea between Arnhem Land and Cape York Peninsula in north Australia. It is approximately 480 kilometres (300 miles) west to east, and 595 kilometres (370 miles) north to south.

car·pen·ter (kár-pin-tər, -pən-) *n.* One whose occupation is constructing and repairing wooden objects and structures, especially large solid ones, such as ships or houses. Compare **joiner.** ~*v.* **carpentered, -tering, -ters.** —*tr.* To make, build, or repair (wooden objects or structures). —*intr.* To work as a carpenter. [Middle English, from Anglo-French, from Latin *carpentārius (artifex),* carriage(-maker), from adjective, from *carpentum,* two-wheeled vehicle, wagon, from Celtic.] —**car·pen·try** (-tri) *n.*

carpenter moth *n.* Any of various moths of the family Cossidae, the larvae of which are harmful to the wood of various trees.

Car·pen·ti·er (kaar-pónti-ay, kár-poNt-yáy), **Georges** (1894–1975). French boxer who held the world light-heavyweight title (1920–22). His fight against Jack Dempsey (1921) was the first to realise a million dollars in takings.

car·pet (kárpit) *n.* **1. a.** A thick, heavy covering for a floor, usually made of wool or synthetic fibres, and typically larger than a rug. **b.** The fabric used for this. **2.** Any covering suggestive of a carpet in texture or appearance: *a carpet of leaves and pine needles.* —**on the carpet.** Informal. Being reprimanded by one in authority. ~*tr.v.* **carpeted, -peting, -pets. 1.** To cover with or as with a carpet. **2.** Informal. To reprimand. [Middle English *carpete,* from Old French *carpite,* from Old Italian *carpita,* from *carpire,* to pluck, tear, from Latin *carpere.*]

car·pet·bag (kárpit-bag) *n.* An old-fashioned kind of travelling bag made of carpet fabric.

car·pet·bag·ger (kárpit-baggər) *n.* **1.** A politician who for political interest seeks to represent an area with which he has no personal connections. **2.** U.S. A Northerner who went to the South after the Civil War for political or financial advantage. Compare **scalawag.** —**car·pet·bag·ger·y, car·pet·bag·gism** *n.*

carpet beetle *n.* Any of various small beetles of the genus *Anthrenus,* having larvae injurious to fabrics, furs, and other plant and animal products.

carpet shark *n.* Any of certain sharks of the family Orectolobidae, having a back patterned in brown and white and a fringe of fleshy growths round the sides of the head.

carpet snake *n.* A nonvenomous Australian snake, *Morelia variegata,* marked on its back with the pattern of a Persian carpet.

carpet-sweeper (kárpit-sweepər) *n.* A hand-operated household implement with a revolving brush, used for sweeping carpets.

car·phone (kár-fōn) *n.* A cordless telephone installed in a car.

carpo– *comb. form.* Indicates fruit or similar reproductive structure; for example, **carpogonium, carpology.** [Greek *karpos,* fruit.]

car·po·go·ni·um (kárpə-gōni-əm) *n., pl.* **-nia** (-ə). Botany. The female reproductive structure of red algae, comprising a swollen base enclosing the ovum and a long neck along which the male gametes pass. [New Latin : CARPO- + -GONIUM.] —**car·po·go·ni·al** *adj.*

car·pol·o·gy (kaar-póllə ji) *n.* The area of botany concerned with fruits and seeds. [CARPO- + -LOGY.]

car·po·met·a·car·pus (kárpō-méttə-kárpəss) *n.* A bone in a bird's wing made up of the metacarpal bones and some of the carpal bones fused together. [CARPO- + META- + CARPUS.]

car pool *n.* **1.** An arrangement whereby several commuters travel together in one car. **2.** A fleet of cars available for general use, for example by a firm's employees.

car·poph·a·gous (kaar-póffəgəss) *adj.* Feeding on fruit; fruit-eating. [Greek *karpophagos* : CARPO- + -PHAGOUS.]

car·po·phore (kárpə-fawr ‖ -fōr) *n.* Botany. **1.** The elongated part of the axis of certain flowers, to which the carpels and stamens are attached. **2.** A fruiting body or the stalk of a fruiting body in certain fungi. [CARPO- + -PHORE.]

car·port (kár-pawrt ‖ -pōrt) *n.* A roof projecting from the side of a building, used as a shelter for a motor vehicle.

car·po·spor·an·gi·um (kárpə-spaw-rán-ji-əm ‖ -spō-) *n., pl.* **-gia** (-ji-ə). A specialised sporangium in red algae, in which carpospores are formed. [New Latin : CARPO- + SPORANGIUM.]

car·po·spore (kárpə-spawr ‖ -spōr) *n.* Botany. A nonmotile haploid or diploid spore formed within the carposporangium of red algae.

-carpous, -carpic *adj. comb. form.* Indicates a specified number or kind of fruit; for example, **polycarpous, monocarpic.** [New Latin *-carpus,* from Greek *karpos,* fruit.]

car·pus (kár-pəss) *n., pl.* **-pi** (-pī). Anatomy. **1. a.** The **wrist** (see). **b.** The bones of the wrist. **2.** Any joint corresponding to the wrist in quadrupeds. [New Latin, from Greek *karpos,* wrist.]

carr (kaar) *n.* British Regional. An alder copse.

Carr E(dward) H(allett) (1892–1982). British historian. He is best known for his monumental history of the U.S.S.R.

Car·rac·ci (kə-ráachi). Family of Bolognese painters noted for reviving the Renaissance style of Raphael, Titian, and Corregio. In 1582, they established a teaching academy that was to influence many artists.

car·rack (kárrək) *n.* A type of merchant ship equipped for war and used in the 14th, 15th, and 16th centuries; a galleon. [Middle English *caryk, carrake,* from Old French *caraque,* from Old Spanish *carraca,* from Arabic *qarāqīr,* plural of *qurqūr,* carrack.]

car·ra·geen, car·ra·gheen (kárrə-geen) *n.* **1.** An edible red seaweed, *Chondrus crispus,* of rocky shores in northern Europe and North America, used in the preparation of jellies, blancmanges, and beverages. Also called "Irish moss". **2.** Any product made from this seaweed. [After *Carragheen,* near Waterford, Ireland, where it flourishes.]

Car·ran·tuo·hill (kárrən-tōō-əl). Mountain in Macgillicuddy's Reeks in County Kerry, Republic of Ireland. At 1 041 metres (3,415 feet), it is Ireland's highest peak.

Car·ra·ra (kə-ráarə). City in north central Italy famous for the white marble quarried nearby which was favoured by Michelangelo.

car·rel (kárrəl) *n.* A small separate enclosure, especially in a library, used for private study. [Variant of CAROL (in obsolete sense, "small enclosure").]

car·riage (kárrij; *in sense 5 rarely also* kárri-ij). *n.* **1.** A four-wheeled, horse-drawn passenger vehicle, often of an elegant design. **2.** British. A railway vehicle, or segment of a train, for carrying passengers. **3.** A wheeled support or frame for moving a heavy object, such as a cannon. **4.** A moving part of a machine for holding and moving another part, such as the moving part of a lathe that holds the cutting tools. **5. a.** The act or process of transporting or carrying. **b.** The cost or charge for transporting. Used especially in the phrases *carriage forward* and *carriage paid.* **6.** The manner of holding and moving one's head and body; deportment. —See Synonyms at **bearing.** [Middle English *cariage,* from Old North French, from *carier,* to transport in a vehicle, CARRY.]

carriage trade *n.* Wealthy patrons, as of a restaurant or theatre, especially in former times.

car·rick bend (kárrik) *n.* Nautical. A type of knot used to fasten two cables or hawsers together. [From obsolete *carrick,* carrack, from Middle English *caryk,* CARRACK.]

carrick bitt *n.* Nautical. Either of the two posts that support the windlass on a ship's deck. [See **carrick bend.**]

car·ri·er (kárri-ər) *n.* **1.** One that transports or conveys. **2.** An organisation or individual that deals in transporting passengers or goods. **3.** A mechanism or device by which something is conveyed or conducted. **4.** Medicine. A person or animal that shows no symptoms of a disease but transmits it directly or indirectly to others or, in the case of a hereditary disease, to offspring. **5.** Biology. A **vector** (see). **6.** Electronics. **a.** A **carrier wave** (see). **b.** A charge-carrying entity, especially an electron or a hole in a semiconductor. **7.** An **aircraft carrier** (see). **8. a.** Chemistry. A support, such as alumina or asbestos, for a solid catalyst. **b.** A molecule or ion that transports an atom or group between molecules. **c.** The solid that adsorbs a dyestuff in the formation of a lake. **d.** An inert substance containing a radioactive isotope, used to introduce the isotope into a system for tracer studies. **e.** See **carrier gas.**

carrier bag *n. Chiefly British.* A large plastic or paper bag used especially for carrying shopping.

carrier gas *n.* A gas, such as argon or hydrogen, used to sweep the sample through the column in gas chromatography.

carrier pigeon *n.* A **homing pigeon** *(see),* especially one trained to carry messages.

carrier wave *n.* A radio wave or other electromagnetic wave that can be modulated in frequency, amplitude, phase, or otherwise to transmit speech, music, images, or other signals.

Car·ring·ton (kárring-tən), **Peter (Alexander Rupert), 6th Baron** (1919–). British Conservative politician who served as foreign secretary (1979–82). His greatest political achievement is probably the Rhodesia settlement of 1979–80 which led to the establishment of Zimbabwe.

carriole. Variant of **cariole.**

car·ri·on (kárri-ən) *n.* Dead and decaying flesh.
~*adj.* **1.** Of or similar to carrion. **2.** Carrion-eating. [Middle English *carion, caroine,* from Anglo-French *caroine,* from Vulgar Latin *carōnia* (unattested), from Latin *carō* (stem *carn-*), flesh.]

carrion crow *n.* A common scavenging and predatory crow of Europe and Asia, *Corvus corone,* resembling the rook but having a pure black bill.

carrion flower *n.* **1.** A climbing vine, *Smilax herbacea,* of eastern North America, having clusters of small, greenish flowers with an odour of decaying flesh. **2.** Any of several other plants having flowers with an unpleasant odour.

Car·roll (kárrəl), **Lewis,** born Charles Lutwidge Dodgson (1832–98). English author of *Alice's Adventures in Wonderland* (1865) and *Through the Looking-Glass and What Alice Found There* (1872). A leading mathematician, he wrote *Euclid and his Modern Rivals* (1879) and *Curiosa Mathematica* (1888–93). He was ordained a deacon in the Church of England (1861) and was a pioneering portrait photographer, using as models mainly little girls. The Alice stories were written to amuse Alice Liddell, the daughter of the Dean of Christ Church, Oxford. His other works include the nonsense poem *The Hunting of the Snark* (1876).

car·rot (kárrət) *n.* **1.** A widely cultivated plant, *Daucus carota sativa,* having finely divided leaves, flat clusters of small white flowers, and an edible, yellow-orange root. **2.** The long, tapering root of this plant, eaten as a vegetable. **3.** Something offered as a means of persuasion; an incentive. [Old French *carotte,* from Latin *carōta,* from Greek *karōton.*]

car·rot·y (kárrəti) *adj.* **1.** Similar to a carrot, especially in colour. **2.** Having orange-red hair.

carrousel. *Chiefly U.S.* Variant of **carousel.**

car·ry (kárri) *v.* **-ried, -rying, -ries.** —*tr.* **1.** To bear or convey from one place to another; transport: *carry cargo.* **2.** To make known, take, bring, or communicate (a message, for example). **3.** To serve as a means for the conveyance or transmission of; transmit: *Flies carry disease.* **4.** To hold or bear while moving: *The plane carried us to safety.* **5. a.** To hold or be capable of holding: *The lift carries four people.* **b.** To sustain the weight of; support. **6.** To support or sustain the responsibility of. **7.** To keep or have on one's person. **8.** To be pregnant with. **9. a.** To hold and move (the body or a part of it) in a specified way. **b.** To behave or conduct (oneself) in a specified manner. **10.** To extend or continue in a certain direction or to a given point or degree: *carry a joke too far.* **11.** To cause to move; drive; impel. **12.** To take or seize, especially by force; capture: *"the Turks carried the defences of Jebel Subh"* (T.E. Lawrence). **13.** To gain victory, support, or acceptance for; especially, to secure the adoption of (a motion or bill). **14.** To be successful in; win. **15.** To include as part of a publication, broadcast, or the like. **16.** To sway; move; gain the interest of: *Her enthusiasm carried the audience.* **17.** To have as a customary, necessary, or characteristic attribute or accompaniment: *an appliance carrying a five-year guarantee; a critic whose views carry a lot of weight.* **18.** To involve necessarily as a condition, consequence, effect, or the like: *The crime carried a five-year sentence.* **19.** To keep in stock; offer for sale: *carry a large selection of china and glass.* **20.** *Mathematics.* To transfer (a number) from one column of digits for inclusion in the calculations of another. **21.** To include in another set of accounts: *carry a loss over to the following year.* **22.** To make up for the deficiencies of (a colleague, for example). **23.** To yield (a crop, for example). **24.** To support or sustain (livestock): *An acre can carry 60 sheep.* **25.** *Golf.* To cover (a distance) or advance beyond (a point or object) in one stroke. **26.** In hunting, to keep and follow (a scent). —*intr.* **1.** To act as a bearer: *She used to fetch and carry for her old aunt.* **2. a.** To reach; cover a distance or range: *a soprano voice that carries to the back of the hall; guns that carry for 500 metres.* **b.** To travel through the air. Used especially of golf and cricket balls. —See Synonyms at **convey.** —**carry all before (one).** To achieve a complete victory; gain unanimous support. —**carry away.** To move emotionally or excite greatly: *carried away by his beauty.* —**carry forward.** *Accounting.* To transfer (an entry) to the next column, page, book, or to another account. —**carry off. 1.** To cause the death of: *carried off by a fever.* **2.** To handle or cope with (a situation, for example) successfully. **3.** To win (a prize or award, for example). **4.** To seize and run away with; abduct. —**carry through. 1.** To accomplish; complete. **2.** To enable to endure; sustain: *Fortitude carried her through the ordeal.*
~*n., pl.* **carries. 1.** The act or process of carrying. **2. a.** The range of a gun or projectile. **b.** The distance travelled by a ball, especially a golf ball. [Middle English *carien,* from Old North French *carier,*

to transport in a vehicle, from *car(re),* vehicle, from Latin *carrus.*]

car·ry·all (kárri-awl) *n. U.S.* A holdall.

car·ry·cot (kárri-kot) *n.* A portable bed for a baby, usually made from canvas stretched over a metal frame or occasionally from wickerwork.

carrying charge *n.* The interest charged on the balance owed when paying in instalments.

car·ry·ings-on (kárri-ingz-ón ‖ -áwn) *pl.n.* **1.** Behaviour that is regarded as improper or frivolous: *Grandmothers do not generally hold with the carryings-on of the young.* **2.** Noisy or excitable behaviour.

carry on *tr.v.* To conduct; continue the process or activities of: *will carry on the business in my absence.* —*intr.v.* **1. a.** To persevere; continue: *carry on in the face of disaster.* **b.** To resume after stopping: *carry on where you left off.* **2.** *Informal.* To have a usually illicit sexual involvement: *Mrs. Brown is carrying on with the postman.* **3.** To behave in an excited or foolish manner; act hysterically or childishly.

car·ry-on (kárri-ón, -on ‖ -áwn) *n. Chiefly British Informal.* Carryings-on, or an instance thereof.

carry out *tr.v.* To put into practice or effect; accomplish.

car·ry-out (kárri-owt) *n. U.S. & Scottish.* **1.** Food or drink intended to be consumed off the premises where it is prepared or sold. **2.** A shop or restaurant selling such food or drink.

carry over *tr.v.* **1.** *Accounting.* To transfer (an entry) to another column, page, book, or account. **2.** To continue at another time; put off: *carry over a problem until the next meeting.*

car·ry-o·ver (kárri-ōvər) *n.* **1.** A part or quantity, as of goods or commodities, left over or held for future use. **2.** *Accounting.* A sum transferred to a new column, page, book, or account.

carse (karss) *n.* In Scotland, an alluvial plain beside a river or an estuary. [Middle English, of obscure origin.]

carsey. Variant of **carzey.**

car·sick (kár-sik) *adj.* Suffering nausea from motor travel, especially vehicular motion. —**car·sick·ness** *n.*

Car·son (kárss'n), **Kit,** born Christopher Carson (1809–68). U.S. frontiersman. Implementing the U.S. government policy of subjugating Indian peoples by forced mass migration, he destroyed the crops and livestock of about 8,000 Navajos and forced them into accepting reservation life.

Carson, Rachel Louise (1907–64). U.S. marine and genetic biologist and science writer. Her *The Sea Around Us* (1951) deals with the biology, chemistry, history, and geography of the sea. *Silent Spring* (1962) is a condemnation of the use of pesticides.

cart (kart) *n.* **1.** A two-wheeled vehicle usually drawn by a horse or other animal and used for transporting goods. **2.** A light open two-wheeled vehicle pulled by one horse. **3.** *Chiefly U.S.* **Trolley 1.** —*tr.v.* **carted, carting, carts. 1. a.** To convey in a cart. **b.** *Informal.* To convey laboriously, as in a cart; lug. **2.** To remove or transport (a person or thing) in an unceremonious manner or by force. Often used with *away* or *off*: *he was carted off to jail.* [Middle English *carte, cart,* partly from Old English *cræt,* partly from Old Norse *kartr.*] —**cart·a·ble** *adj.* —**cart·er** *n.*

cart·age (kártij) *n.* **1.** The act or process of transporting by cart. **2.** The cost of transporting by cart or other means.

Car·ta·ge·na[1] (kárta-jéena, -háyna, -kháyna). Capital of the Bolívar department on Colombia's Caribbean coast. The Spanish built a fortified stronghold here (1533) to export precious metals.

Cartagena[2]. A fortified naval base and seaport on the Mediterranean Sea, in the Spanish province of Murcia. The Carthaginian leader Hasdrubal founded it *c.* 225 B.C.

Carte, Richard D'Oyly. See **D'Oyly Carte, Richard.**

carte blanche (kárt blónsh ‖ blánch) *n.* Unrestricted power to act at one's own discretion; unconditional authorisation. [French, "blank card".]

car·tel (kaar-tél) *n.* **1.** A combination of independent business organisations formed to regulate production, pricing, and marketing of goods by the members. **2.** In some European countries, a political group united in a common cause; a bloc. [German *Kartell,* from French *cartel,* from Italian *cartello,* diminutive of *carta,* CARD.]

Car·ter (kártər), **Elliott (Cook)** (1908–). U.S. composer who studied in Paris under Nadia Boulanger. He won Pulitzer Prizes for his second (1960) and third (1973) string quartets.

Carter, Howard (1874–1939). British archaeologist, who excavated ancient Egyptian tombs, including that of the Pharaoh Tutankhamun (1922–32).

Carter, Jimmy (James Earl) (1924–). 39th President of the United States (1977–81). A Democrat, he was twice elected senator for Georgia (1962, 1964) and governor of Georgia (1970–74). He was elected President in the wake of the Watergate scandal. After promising a more "open" style of government, he lost popularity because of the failure of his economic measures and the lack of confidence in his social reforms. His main achievements were to cut national energy consumption and to negotiate the Camp David Agreement between Egypt and Israel (1979).

Car·te·si·an (kaar-téez-i-ən, -téezh-, -y-ən, -téezh'n) *adj.* **1.** Of or pertaining to the philosophy or methods of Descartes. **2.** Of or forming a Cartesian coordinate.
~*n.* A person who follows the philosophy or methods of Descartes. —**Car·te·si·an·ism** *n.*

Cartesian coordinate *n.* A coordinate in a Cartesian coordinate system.

Cartesian coordinate system *n. Mathematics.* **1.** A rectangular coordinate system, usually in two or three dimensions, in which the location of a point in rectangular space is identified by its distance from the mutually perpendicular axes. **2.** A three-dimensional coordinate system in which the coordinates of a point are its distances from each of three intersecting, often mutually perpendicular, planes along lines parallel to the intersection of the other two.

Car·thage (kárthij). *Punic* **Kart-Ha-dasht.** Ancient city-state in North Africa on the Bay of Tunis, near modern Tunis. Founded by the Phoenicians (9th century B.C.), it became the centre of Carthaginian power in the western Mediterranean from the 6th century B.C. Its trading empire included colonies in Senegal and Guinea, and it grew rich on the sale of slaves, ivory, and gold from the tropics of Africa. The three Punic Wars with Rome resulted in the complete destruction of Carthage (146 B.C.). In 45 B.C. Julius Caesar refounded the city and it became the commercial, cultural, and administrative centre of Roman Africa. The Vandals took it (A.D. 439) and made it their capital. Carthage was recaptured by the Byzantines (534), but virtually destroyed by Arabs (698). Only a few Punic and Roman ruins survive. **—Car·tha·gin·i·an** (kárthə-jínni-ən) *adj. & n.*

cart-horse (kárt-hawrss) *n.* A large, heavily built horse bred for pulling carts or similar vehicles.

Car·thu·si·an (kaar-théwz-i-ən, -thŏŏz-, -yən ‖ *U.S.* -thŏŏzh'n) *n. Roman Catholic Church.* A member of a contemplative order of monks founded in 1084 in Chartreuse, France, by St. Bruno. **—Car·thu·si·an** *adj.*

Car·ti·er-Bres·son (karti-áy-brəssón), **Henri** (1908–). French photographer and pioneer of photojournalism. He took up photography in 1931 and worked with the film director Jean Renoir (1936–39). Imprisoned by the Nazis (1940–43), he escaped and set up underground photographic units. He is the author of many photographic books, including *The Decisive Moment* (1952).

car·ti·lage (kártilij) *n.* A tough fibrous connective tissue attached at the joints between bones. It is a major constituent of the young vertebrate skeleton that is largely converted to bone with maturation. Also called "gristle". [Latin *cartilāgo* (stem *cartilāgin-*).]

cartilage bone *n.* A bone developed from cartilage. Compare **membrane bone.**

car·ti·lag·i·nous (kárti-lájinəss) *adj.* **1.** Of or pertaining to cartilage. **2.** Having a skeleton consisting mainly of cartilage.

cartilaginous fish *n.* Any fish of the class Chondrichthyes, which includes the sharks, skates, and rays, having a skeleton entirely made up of cartilage.

cartload (kárt-lōd) *n.* The amount that can be carried in a cart.

car·to·gram (kártə-gram) *n.* A presentation of statistical data in geographical distribution using lines, dots, and other marks on a map. [French *cartogramme* : *carte*, CARD + -GRAM.]

car·tog·ra·phy (kaar-tóggrəfi) *n. Abbr.* **cartog.** The art or technique of making maps or charts. [French *cartographie* : *carte*, map, CARD + -GRAPHY.] **—car·tog·ra·pher** *n.* **—car·to·graph·ic** (kártə-gráffik), **car·to·graph·i·cal** *adj.*

cart·o·man·cy (kárt-ə-man-si, -ō-) *n.* The telling of fortunes using playing cards, such as the tarot pack. [French *cartomancie* : *carte*, CARD + -*mancie*, -MANCY.]

car·ton (kárt'n) *n.* **1.** *Abbr.* **C., c., ctn.** A cardboard box or other container, especially: **a.** A box closed by flaps on the top or on one end, used for transporting goods. **b.** A small container for liquids: *a carton of milk.* **2.** The contents of such a box or container. [French, from Italian *cartone*, pasteboard, from *carta*, CARD.]

car·toon (kaar-tŏŏn, kár-) *n.* **1.** A drawing in a newspaper, magazine, or the like, often accompanied by a caption, which depicts a humorous situation or makes a satirical comment on a subject of current public interest. **2.** A preliminary sketch, similar in size to the fresco, mosaic, tapestry, or the like that is to be copied from it. **3.** An **animated cartoon** *(see).* [Italian *cartone*, pasteboard, CARTON.] **—car·toon·ist** *n.*

car·touche, car·touch (kaar-tŏŏsh) *n.* **1.** *Architecture.* A scroll-like tablet used either to provide space for an inscription or for ornamental purposes. **2.** In ancient Egyptian hieroglyphics, an oval or oblong figure that encloses characters expressing the names or epithets of royal or divine personages. **3.** A case containing the combustible materials in some varieties of fireworks. **4.** A panel on a map displaying the title, scale, and similar details. **5.** *Archaic.* A cartridge. [French, cartridge, from Italian *cartoccio*, from *carta*, paper, card. See **carton.**]

car·tridge (kártrij) *n.* **1. a.** A tubular metal or cardboard-and-metal case containing the propellant powder and primer of small arms ammunition or shotgun shells. **b.** Such a case loaded with shotgun pellets. **c.** Such a case fitted with a projectile, such as a bullet, for use in rifles, small arms, machine guns, or the like. Also called "round". **2.** A small modular unit of equipment, especially: **a.** A removable case containing the stylus and electric conversion circuitry in a record-player pickup. **b.** A large tape **cassette** *(see)* for use in tape recorders, video recorders, and the like. **c.** A case with photographic film that can be loaded directly into a camera. **d.** A disposable ink reservoir for a pen. [From earlier *cartage*, variant of French CARTOUCHE (cartridge).]

cartridge belt *n.* A belt for carrying ammunition, with loops or pockets for cartridges or clips of cartridges.

cartridge clip *n.* A metal container or frame for holding cartridges to be loaded into an automatic rifle or pistol.

cartridge paper *n.* A thick, heavy, smooth type of paper used for drawing or printing. [Originally used for making cartridges.]

cart track *n.* A rough lane or track in the country.

car·tu·lar·y (kár-tew-ləri ‖ -lerri) *n., pl.* **-ies.** Also **char·tu·lar·y** (kár-, chár-). A collection of deeds or charters; especially, a register of titles to all the property of an estate or monastery. [Medieval Latin *c(h)artulārium*, from Latin *chartula*, little paper, diminutive of *charta*, leaf of papyrus. See **card.**]

cart·wheel (kárt-weel, -hweel) *n.* **1.** The wheel of a cart. **2.** A somersault or handspring in which the body turns over sideways with the arms and legs spread like the spokes of a wheel.

cart·wright (kártrīt) *n.* A person who makes carts.

car·un·cle (kárrəngk'l, kə-rúngk'l) *n.* **1.** *Anatomy.* A fleshy, naked outgrowth, such as a cock's comb. **2.** *Botany.* An excrescence on a seed at or near the hilum. **3.** Any small fleshy mass on or in the body, either normal or abnormal. [Obsolete French *caruncule*, from Latin *caruncula*, diminutive of *carō* (stem *carn-*), flesh.] **—ca·run·cu·lar** (kə-rúngkew-lər) *adj.* **—ca·run·cu·late, ca·run·cu·lat·ed** *adj.*

Ca·ru·so (kə-rŏŏ-sō), **Enrico** (1873–1921). Italian tenor opera singer who made his debut at the Teatro Nuovo, Naples (1894). His final performance was with the Metropolitan Opera, New York (1920) when he ruptured a blood vessel in his throat while singing. He died of related complications. His most popular roles included Canio, in *Pagliacci*; Rodolpho, in *La Bohème*; and the Duke, in *Rigoletto*.

carve (karv) *v.* **carved, carving, carves.** *—tr.* **1.** To divide into pieces or slices by cutting: *carve a chicken.* **2.** To cut into a desired shape; fashion by cutting: *carve the wood into a figure.* **3.** To produce or form by cutting: *carve initials in the bark.* **4.** To decorate by carving. *—intr.* **1.** To engrave or cut figures as a hobby or trade. **2.** To slice and serve meat or poultry. **—carve out.** To achieve by exertion or ability: *carve out a career.* *~n.* An act or stroke of slicing or carving. [Middle English *kerven, carven*, Old English *ceorfan.*]

carvel. Variant of **caravel.**

car·vel-built (kárv'l-bilt) *adj.* Designating a boat or ship built with the hull planks lying flush or edge to edge, rather than overlapping. Compare **clinker-built.**

car·vel joint (kárv'l) *n.* A joining of wood planks so that they lie edge to edge; a flush joint.

car·ver (kárvər) *n.* **1.** One that carves. **2. a.** A carving knife. **b.** *Plural.* A carving knife and fork. **3.** A chair, with arms, belonging to a set of dining room chairs.

car·ver·y *n., pl.* **-ies.** A restaurant specialising in roast meats where one eats as much as one wishes for a fixed price.

carve up *tr.v.* **1.** To divide up by parcelling out: *carve up an estate.* **2.** *Informal.* To cause (the driver of a vehicle) to change course or slow down abruptly.

carve-up (kárv-up) *n. Slang.* **1.** A debate, business meeting, election, or the like, the outcome of which was already settled or known prior to its taking place. **2.** The distribution of ill-gotten gains.

carv·ing (kárving) *n.* A figure or design formed by carving.

carving knife *n.* A knife with a long, sharp blade for slicing up meat.

Car·y (káir-i), **(Arthur) Joyce (Lunel)** (1888–1957). British novelist, whose early works provide a sharp insight into the relationships between Africans and their British administrators. His major works, two trilogies: *Herself Surprised* (1941), *To Be a Pilgrim* (1942), and *The Horse's Mouth* (1944), and *Prisoner of Grace* (1952), *Except the Lord* (1953), and *Not Honour More* (1955), deal with the classic themes of conflict between the generations, the individual and society, and the artist and the middle classes.

car·y·at·id (kárri-áttid) *n., pl.* **-ids** or **-ides** (-eez). *Architecture.* A supporting column sculptured in the form of a woman in classical Greek dress. Compare **telamon.** [Latin *Caryātides* (plural), from Greek *Karuatidēs*, caryatids, priestesses of Artemis at *Karuai*, village in Laconia.]

caryo-. Variant of **karyo-.**

car·y·op·sis (kárri-óp-siss) *n., pl.* **-ses** (-seez) or **-sides** (-sideez). *Botany.* A one-seeded dry fruit, such as a grain of barley or wheat, having its outer coat fused to the seed coat. [New Latin : CARY(O)- + -OPSIS.]

car·zey, car·sey (kárzi) *n., pl.* **-zeys.** Also **kha·zi** *pl.* **-zis.** *British Regional Slang.* A lavatory. [Perhaps from Italian *casa* (plural, *case*), house.]

ca·sa·ba, cas·sa·ba (kə-sáabə) *n.* A variety of **winter melon** *(see)* having a yellow rind and sweet, whitish flesh. [From *Kassaba*, former name of Turgutlu, Turkey.]

Ca·sa·blan·ca (kássə-blángkə, kázzə-). *Arabic* Dar-al-Bei-da (daar-al-báydə). Seaport on the Atlantic coast of Morocco. It was founded by the Portuguese in the early 16th century and named *Casa Branca* (White House). Taken by the French in 1907, it remained for many years a centre of French influence in Africa. It is now Morocco's largest city.

Ca·sals (kə-sálz), **Pablo** (1876–1973). Spanish cellist, conductor, and composer. He founded the Barcelona Orchestra (1919) but left Spain in 1939 after Franco came to power. He was acclaimed as one of the greatest interpreters of Bach's unaccompanied cello suites and the cello concertos of Dvořák, Elgar, and Schumann.

Ca·sa·no·va (kássə-nōvə), **Giovanni Giacomo, Chevalier de Seingalt** (1725–98). Italian adventurer and legendary lover. After being expelled from a seminary for immoral conduct, he lived in many European cities and worked as a violinist, a spy, a writer, and a librarian. His adventures are chronicled in his memoirs, of which the first complete edition was published in 1960.

Casanova *n.* An ostentatiously promiscuous man; a ladykiller.

casbah. Variant of **kasbah.**

cas·cade (kass-káyd, káss-) *n.* **1. a.** A waterfall or a series of small waterfalls over steep rocks. **b.** Anything that falls loosely or freely: *a cascade of flowers.* **2.** *Physics.* An analogous structure or phenomenon, as: **a.** A cosmic-ray shower generated by the successive alternate production of electron–positron pairs by pair production and of photons by bremsstrahlung, continuing until the energy of each single particle is below the threshold for pair production. **b.** A process occurring in an electrical discharge in a gas by which at least one member of an ion pair is accelerated by the field to sufficiently high energy to produce another pair of ions in a collision. **c.** An **avalanche** *(see)* in a geiger counter. **3.** *Electricity.* A series of components or networks, the output of each of which serves as the input for the next. **4.** *Chemistry.* A series of compressed gases of successively lower boiling points, the expansion of which produces successively lower temperatures. This arrangement is used to liquefy gases.
~*intr.v.* **cascaded, -cading, -cades.** To fall from one level to another in a continuous series; fall loosely or freely. [French, from Italian *cascata,* from *cascare,* to fall, from Vulgar Latin *casicāre* (unattested), from Latin *cadere* (past participle *cāsus*).]

cas·car·a (kass-ká'arə, kəss-) *n.* **1.** The cascara buckthorn. **2.** Cascara sagrada. [Spanish *cáscara,* bark, from *cascar,* to break, break off, from Vulgar Latin *quassicāre* (unattested), from Latin *quassāre,* from *quatere* (past participle *quassus*), to shake.]

cascara buckthorn *n.* A shrub or tree, *Rhamnus purshiana,* of northwestern North America, the bark of which is the source of cascara sagrada.

cascara sa·gra·da (sə-grá'adə) *n.* The dried bark of the cascara buckthorn, used as a stimulant, cathartic, and laxative.

cas·ca·ril·la (káskə-rillə) *n.* **1.** A shrub, *Croton eluteria,* of the West Indies, having bitter, aromatic bark. **2.** The bark of this shrub, used as a tonic. In this sense, also called "cascarilla bark". [Spanish, diminutive of *cáscara,* bark. See **cascara.**]

case¹ (kayss) *n.* **1.** An instance or exemplification of the existence or occurrence of something. **2. a.** An occurrence of disease or disorder. **b.** A client, as of a doctor, psychiatrist, lawyer, or social worker. **3. a.** A particular set of circumstances or state of affairs: *will make an exception in this case.* **b.** The actual situation; the truth: *It simply isn't the case.* **4.** A set of circumstances subject to or requiring investigation: *Holmes's most famous case.* **5.** A set of reasons, arguments, or supporting facts offered in justification of a statement, action, situation, or thing: *the case for legalised abortion.* **6.** A question or problem; a matter: *a case of honour.* **7.** *Law.* **a.** An action or suit, or just grounds for legal action. **b.** The facts or evidence offered in support of a claim. **8.** *Informal.* A peculiar or eccentric person. **9.** *Linguistics.* **a.** The syntactic relationship of a noun, pronoun, or adjective to the other words of a sentence, indicated in inflected languages typically by endings, and in noninflected languages by word order or prepositions. **b.** The form or position of a word that indicates this relationship. **c.** Such forms, positions, or relationships collectively. —See Synonyms at **example.** —**in any case.** Regardless of what occurred or will occur. —**in case. 1.** To provide for the possibility that. **2.** *Chiefly U.S.* If. —**in case of.** In the event of; if there should happen. [Middle English *cas,* an occurrence, from Old French, from Latin *cāsus,* fall, event, occurrence, from the past participle of *cadere,* to fall.]

case² *n.* **1. a.** A container or receptacle. **b.** A suitcase. **2. a.** A decorative or protective covering or cover. **b.** A glass box for exhibiting items of interest. **3.** *Abbr.* **C., c., cs.** A box with its contents, especially when of a standard quantity; for example, a case of wine usually contains 12 bottles. **4.** A set or pair, as of pistols. **5.** The frame or framework of a window, door, or stairway. **6.** *Printing.* A shallow, compartmented tray for storing type or type matrices. **7.** A cover of stiff boards ready to be attached to a book.
~*tr.v.* **cased, casing, cases. 1.** To put into, cover, or protect with a case. **2.** *Slang.* To examine carefully, as in planning a crime: *case the bank before robbing it.* [Middle English, from Old North French *casse,* from Latin *capsa,* chest, case.]

ca·se·ate (káy-si-ayt) *intr.v.* **-ated, -ating, -ates.** To undergo caseation. [Latin *cāseus,* CHEESE.]

ca·se·a·tion (káy-si-áysh'n) *n.* **1.** The production of cheese from casein in the coagulation of milk. **2.** The degeneration of dead bodily tissue into a cheeselike substance. [From CASEATE.]

case·book (káyss-book) *n.* A book containing a record of medical or legal cases.

case·bound (káyss-bownd) *adj.* Hardback. Said of books.

case ending *n.* The letter or letters added to the stem of a noun, pronoun, or adjective in inflected languages to indicate case.

case·hard·en (káyss-hard'n) *tr.v.* **-ened, -ening, -ens. 1.** To harden the surface of (iron or steel) by high-temperature shallow infusion of carbon followed by quenching. **2.** To harden the spirit or emotions of; make callous. [From CASE (covering).]

case history *n.* An organised set of facts relevant to the development of an individual or group under study or treatment, especially in social work, psychiatry, or medicine.

ca·se·in (káy-see-in, -seen) *n.* A white, tasteless, odourless protein, precipitated from milk by rennin. It is the basis of cheese and is used to make plastics, adhesives, paints, and foods. [Probably French *caséine* : Latin *cāseus,* CHEESE + -IN.]

case law *n.* Law based on judicial decision and precedent rather than statute.

case load *n.* The number of cases for which a social worker, doctor,

or similar professional person is responsible at any one time.

case·mate (káyss-mayt) *n. Military.* **1.** On a warship, a fortified enclosure for artillery. **2.** A recess in a rampart with openings or embrasures, from which artillery can be fired. [Old French, from Italian *casamatta,* perhaps from Greek *khasmata,* plural of *khasma,* gap, CHASM.] —**case·mat·ed** *adj.*

case·ment (káyssmənt) *n.* **1.** A window frame that opens outwards or inwards by means of hinges along one side. **2.** A window with such frames. **3.** A case or covering. [Middle English *casement†.*] —**case·ment·ed** *adj.*

Case·ment (káyssmənt), **Sir Roger (David)** (1864–1916). British consular official and Irish nationalist, knighted in 1911. He retired to Ireland, his birthplace, in 1912, and with the outbreak of World War I, he attempted to obtain German help for the Irish nationalist cause. Caught returning to Ireland in a German submarine, he was tried, convicted for treason, and hanged.

ca·se·ous (káy-si-əss) *adj.* Resembling cheese. [Latin *cāseus,* CHEESE.]

ca·sern, ca·serne (kə-zérn) *n.* A military barracks. [French *caserne,* from Old French, small room for the night watch, from Old Provençal *cazerna,* group of four persons, from Vulgar Latin *quaderna* (unattested), from Latin *quater,* four times.]

Ca·ser·ta (kə-saír-tə, -zaír-). A market town in southern Italy, and capital of the Caserta province. In the 19th century, it was the centre of operations for Garibaldi's campaigns for the unification of Italy. The German forces in Italy in World War II surrendered to the Allied Command at Caserta (1945).

case shot *n.* **1.** A canister *(see).* **2.** The shot in a canister. **3.** A shrapnel shell.

case study *n.* A detailed analysis of an individual or group, especially as a model of medical, psychological, or social phenomena.

case·work (káyss-wurk) *n.* The part of a social worker's duties dealing with the problems of a particular case.

case·worm (káyss-wurm) *n.* An insect larva, such as a caddis worm, that constructs a protective case around its body.

Cash, Patrick Hart (1965-). Australian tennis player. He was Wimbledon men's singles champion in 1987.

cash¹ (kash) *n.* **1.** Ready money; currency or coins. **2.** Payment for goods or services in money or by cheque, as opposed to credit.
~*tr.v.* **cashed, cashing, cashes.** To exchange for or convert into ready money: *cash a cheque.* —**cash in. 1.** To convert to ready money. **2.** To take full advantage. Often used with *on.* **3.** *U.S. Slang.* To die. —**cash up.** *British.* To add up the money taken in a business, usually at the end of the day. [Old French *casse,* money box, CASE (box).]

cash² *n., pl.* **cash.** Any of various Oriental coins of small denomination; especially, a copper and lead coin with a square hole in its centre. [Portuguese *caixa,* from Tamil *kācu,* a small copper coin, from Sanskrit *karṣa,* a certain weight.]

cash-and-car·ry (kásh-ən-kárri) *n. Chiefly British.* A large warehouse or store selling goods, usually in bulk and at a discount, that may be paid for on the spot and removed by the purchaser. —**cash-and-carry** *adj.*

cash·book (káshbook) *n.* A book in which a record of cash receipts and expenditures is kept.

cash card *n.* A small plastic card issued to its customers by a bank, which can be used to obtain money and, sometimes, other services from a cash dispenser or service till.

cash crop *n.* A crop grown especially for sale, often to another country, rather than for consumption by the local population.

cash desk *n.* A counter, cash register, or till in a shop where cash payments are received.

cash discount *n. Abbr.* **c.d.** A reduction in the price of an item for sale allowed if payment is made within a stipulated period.

cash·ew (káshōō, ka-shōō) *n.* **1.** A widely cultivated tropical American evergreen tree, *Anacardium occidentale,* bearing kidney-shaped nuts that protrude from a fleshy receptacle. **2.** The nut of this tree, edible when roasted. In this sense, also called "cashew nut". [Portuguese *cajú, acajú,* from Tupi *acajú.*]

cash flow *n.* The movement of money into and out of a business. Often used adjectivally: *cash-flow problems.*

cash·ier¹ (ka-shéer) *n.* **1.** The person in a bank or business concern in charge of paying and receiving money. **2.** An employee whose major function is to handle cash transactions, usually at a cash desk, for any of various business operations, such as a restaurant or supermarket. [Dutch *cassier,* from French *caissier,* from *caisse,* money box, from Old French *casse,* CASE (box).]

cash·ier² (ka-shéer, ka-) *tr.v.* **-iered, -iering, -iers.** To dismiss from a position of command or responsibility, as in the armed forces, especially for disciplinary reasons. [Dutch *casseren,* from Old French *casser,* to discharge, annul, from Latin *quassāre,* to shake, break in pieces, from *quassus,* past participle of *quatere,* to shake.]

cash·less (kásh-ləss) *adj.* **1.** Having no money or no cash. **2.** Performed or functioning without cash: *a cashless transaction.*

cash·mere (kásh-méer, -meer ‖ *U.S.* also kázh-) *n.* **1.** Fine, downy wool growing beneath the outer hair of the Kashmir goat. **2.** A soft fabric made of wool from this goat, or from similar fibres.

Cashmere. Variant of **Kashmir.**

cash register *n.* A machine having a keyboard for tabulating the amount of sales transactions, a space for showing their amount, a paper tape for making a permanent and cumulative record of them, and a drawer or drawers in which cash may be kept.

cas·ing (káy-sing) *n.* **1.** Something that encases; an outer cover.

2. The cleaned intestines of cattle, sheep, or pigs used for wrapping sausage meat in. **3.** The frame or framework for a window or door. **4.** A metal pipe or tube used as a lining for water, oil, or gas wells. **5.** The outer cover of a pneumatic tyre.

ca·si·no (kə-seénō) *n., pl.* **-nos. 1.** A public room or building for entertainment, especially for gambling. **2.** Variant of **cassino. 3.** A summer or country house in Italy. [Italian, diminutive of *casa,* house, from Latin *casa†,* hut, cottage.]

cask (kaask || kask) *n. Abbr.* **ck., csk. 1.** A barrel of any size. **2.** The quantity contained in a barrel. [Spanish *casco,* helmet, cask, perhaps from *cascar,* to crack, break, from Vulgar Latin *quassicāre* (unattested), to shake, break, from Latin *quassāre.*]

cas·ket (kaáss-kit || káss-) *n.* **1.** A small case or chest for jewels or other valuables. **2.** *U.S.* A coffin. [Middle English, from Old French *cassette.* See **cassette.**]

Cas·par (káss-pər, -paar). Also **Gas·par** (gáss-, gaáss-). One of the three **Magi** *(see)* who travelled to see the infant Jesus.

Cas·par·i·an strip (kass-paír-i-ən) *n. Botany.* A band of thickening in the walls of certain cells in the plant stem surrounding the conducting tissues, forming a ring impervious to liquids and gases. Also called "Casparian band".

Cas·pi·an Sea (káspi-ən). The world's largest inland sea. It lies between southeast Europe and Asia, and covers 393 898 square kilometres (152,084 square miles). It is slowly shrinking, owing to dam construction on the Volga river which, together with the Ural, feeds the lake. Its fisheries produce the world's finest caviar.

casque (kask) *n.* **1.** A helmet or other piece of armour for the head. **2.** *Zoology.* A helmet-like structure or protuberance. [French, from Spanish *casco,* CASK.] **—casqued** (kaskt) *adj.*

cassaba. Variant of **casaba.**

Cas·san·dra¹ (kə-sándrə). A daughter of Priam, King of Troy, endowed with the gift of prophecy but fated by Apollo never to be believed.

Cassandra² *n.* A prophet of doom, especially one whose prophecies go unheeded. [After CASSANDRA.]

cas·sa·reep (kássə-reep) *n.* The boiled juice of the cassava root, used as a condiment in West Indian cookery. [Earlier *casserepo,* of Cariban origin.]

cas·sa·ta (kə-saátə, ka-) *n.* A type of Neapolitan ice cream containing nuts and fruit.

cas·sa·tion (ka-sáysh'n, kə-) *n.* Abrogation; annulment. [Middle English *cassacioun,* from Old French *cassation,* from *casser,* to annul. See **cashier** (dismiss).]

Cas·satt (kə-sát), **Mary** (1845–1926). U.S. painter. She is noted for her studies of mothers and their children, and was associated with the French impressionist movement.

cas·sa·va (kə-saávə) *n.* **1.** Any of various tropical American plants of the genus *Manihot*; especially, *M. utilissima,* having a large, starchy root which is eaten as a vegetable. Also called "manioc". **2.** A starch derived from the root of this plant, used to make tapioca and as a staple food in the tropics. [Spanish *cazabe,* cassava, from Taino *caçábi.*]

Cas·se·grain·i·an telescope (kássi-gráyni-ən) *n.* A reflecting telescope in which a concave primary mirror reflects incident light to a convex secondary mirror that in turn reflects the light back through a central hole in the primary mirror onto the focal plane. [After N. *Cassegrain,* 17th-century French physician, who invented it.]

Cassel. See **Kassel.**

cas·se·role (kássə-rōl') *n.* **1.** A dish, usually of earthenware, glass, or cast iron, in which food is both baked and served. **2.** Food prepared and served in such a dish. **3.** *Chemistry.* A small-handled, deep porcelain crucible used for heating and evaporating. *~tr.v.* **casseroled, -roling, -roles.** To cook in a casserole. [French, saucepan, from Old French, from *casse,* ladle, dripping pan, from Old Provençal *cassa,* from Medieval Latin *cattia,* dipper, from Greek *kuathion,* small ladle, diminutive of *kuathos†,* ladle.]

cas·sette (kə-sét, ka-) *n.* **1.** A case containing reeled magnetic tape, a pickup reel, and guide and feed mechanisms, used instead of separate reels in tape recorders, video recorders, and the like. **2.** A light-proof camera cartridge, for daylight loading of photographic film. [French, small box, from Old French, diminutive of *casse,* CASE (box).]

cas·si·a (kássi-ə || káshə) *n.* **1.** Any of various chiefly tropical trees, shrubs, and plants of the genus *Cassia,* having compound leaves, usually yellow flowers, and long pods. See **senna. 2.** A tree, *Cinnamomum cassia,* of tropical Asia, having bark similar to cinnamon but of inferior quality. **3.** The bark of *Cinnamomum cassia,* used as a spice. In this sense, also called "cassia bark". [Middle English *cassia,* Old English *cassia,* from Latin *cas(s)ia,* a kind of plant, from Greek *kas(s)ia,* from Hebrew *kesi'ah,* bark resembling cinnamon.]

Cas·si·ni's division (ka-seéniz, kə-). A gap 4 000 kilometres (2,500 miles) across, in the ring structure of Saturn. The Voyager missions have shown that it contains some ring particles which themselves are arranged in ring formations. [After Gian Domenico *Cassini* (1625–1712), Italian astronomer.]

cas·si·no, ca·si·no (kə-seénō) *n.* A card game for two to four players in which cards on the table are matched by cards in the hand. [From CASINO.]

Cas·si·no (ka-seénō, kə-). Town in Latium, central Italy. During World War II, the town and the Benedictine monastery of Monte Cassino were destroyed (1944).

Cas·si·o·pe·ia (kássi-ə-peé-ə) *n.* A W-shaped constellation in the Northern Hemisphere near Camelopardalis and Cepheus.

cas·sis (ka-seéss, kaa-) *n.* **1.** A syrup made from blackcurrants. **2.** A blackcurrant liqueur. [French, blackcurrant.]

cas·sit·e·rite (kə-síttə-rīt) *n.* A red-brown, or black mineral, SnO_2. It is the chief ore of tin, and most of the world's supply is mined in Malaysia. Also called "tinstone". [French *casiterite,* from Greek *kassiteros,* tin, from Elamite *kassi-ti-ra,* "coming from the land of the Kassi", an Elamite people.]

Cas·si·us Lon·gi·nus (kássi-əss lon-jīnəss), **Gaius** (*died* 42 B.C.). Roman general and politician. He was a leading member of the conspiracy to assassinate Julius Caesar. After the defeat of the Republican forces at Philippi, he comitted suicide.

Cas·si·ve·lau·nus (kássivə-láwnəss, -lównəss). King of the Catuvellauni, a people from north of the river Thames who temporarily resisted Julius Caesar's invasion of southeast Britain (54 B.C.) but finally agreed peace terms with the Romans.

cas·sock (kássək) *n.* A long garment, usually black, reaching to the feet and worn by members of the clergy, choristers, and others assisting in church services. [Old French *casaque,* from Persian *kazagand†,* padded jacket.]

Cas·son (káss'n), **Sir Hugh** (1910–). British architect and author. He was professor at the Royal College of Art (1953–75), and president of the Royal Academy of Arts (1976–).

cas·sou·let (káss-ōō-láy, -ə-) *n.* A stew originating in France made from haricot beans, sausages, and goose, pork, or duck. [French, diminutive of dialect *cassolo,* CASSEROLE (saucepan).]

cas·so·war·y (kássə-wair-i) *n., pl.* **-ies.** Any of several large, flightless birds of the genus *Casuarius,* of northern Australia, New Guinea, and adjacent islands, having a large, bony projection on the top of the head, coarse dark plumage, and a brightly coloured head, neck, and wattles. [Malay *kĕsuari.*]

cast (kaast || kast) *v.* **cast, casting, casts.** *—tr.* **1.** To throw, especially with violence or force; hurl; toss; fling. **2.** To throw off or away. **3.** To shed; moult. **4.** To throw forth or drop (a fishing net or anchor, for example). **5.** *Archaic.* **a.** To throw to the ground, as in wrestling. **b.** To overthrow; defeat. **6.** To put or place, especially with haste or violence. **7.** To throw aside; dismiss; discard: *cast one's doubts aside.* **8.** To deposit or register (a vote). **9.** To turn or direct (one's eyes). **10.** To cause (light, for example) to fall upon or over something or in a certain direction. **11.** *Archaic.* To bestow; confer. Used with *upon.* **12. a.** To draw (lots). **b.** To throw (dice). **13.** To express, utter, or give rise to (doubt or criticism, for example): *cast aspersions on his ability.* **14.** To cause (hounds) to scatter and circle in search of a lost scent. **15. a.** To choose actors for (a play or film). **b.** To assign a certain role to (an actor). **c.** To assign an actor to (a part). **16. a.** To form (liquid metal or plaster, for example) into a particular shape by pouring into a mould. **b.** To produce (an object) in this way. **17.** To arrange in some system. **18.** To contrive; formulate: *cast a spell.* **19.** To calculate or compute; add up (a column of figures). Often used with *up.* **20.** To calculate astrologically: *cast a horoscope.* **21.** To warp; twist. **22.** *Printing.* To stereotype or electrotype. **23.** *Nautical.* To turn (a ship); change to the opposite tack. *—intr.* **1.** To throw; especially, to throw out a lure or bait at the end of a fishing line. **2. a.** To add a column of figures; make calculations. **b.** To calculate horoscopes, tides, or the like. **3.** To receive form or shape in a mould. **4.** To spread out and search for a lost scent. Used of hunting hounds. **5.** *Nautical.* **a.** To veer to leeward from a former course; fall off. **b.** To put about; tack. **6.** To choose the actors for a play, film, or the like. **7.** To become warped. —See Synonyms at **throw. —cast about. 1.** To search or look. Often used with *for.* **2.** To devise means; contrive; scheme. **—cast back.** To refer or direct to something past: *cast your mind back to last summer.* **—cast down.** To make dejected or disappointed. **—cast on.** To make the first row of stitches in knitting. **—cast out.** To drive out by force; expel. *~n.* **1. a.** The act of casting or throwing. **b.** The distance thrown. **2. a.** The throwing of a fishing line or net into the water. **b.** The line or net thrown. **c.** The leader with flies or baited hooks attached. **3. a.** A throw of dice. **b.** The number thrown. **c.** A stroke of fortune or fate; one's lot. **4. a.** A slight squint in the eye. **b.** A turning of the eye; a glance in a particular direction. **5.** A quantity or thing thrown off, out, or away, such as the mass of waste and earth excreted by an earthworm, the skin shed by an insect, or a mass of feathers, bones, and other matter ejected from the crop of an owl. **6. a.** The addition of a column of figures; a calculation. **b.** A conjecture or forecast. **7. a.** The act of casting or founding. **b.** The amount of molten material poured into a mould at a single operation. **c.** Something formed by this means. **8. a.** An impression formed in a mould or matrix; a mould. **b.** *Geology.* A three-dimensional replica or solidified impression, as of ripple marks or footprints; especially, a fossil formed by a mineral substance that has filled a hole left by an object, such as a shell, that has been dissolved out of a rock or earth mass. **9.** The form in which something is made or constructed; an arrangement; a disposition. **10.** The actors in a play, film, or the like. **11.** A rigid dressing, usually made of gauze and plaster of Paris, for immobilising a broken bone, an arthritic joint, or part or all of the spine. Also called "plaster cast". **12. a.** A slight trace of colour. **b.** A tinge or shade of any quality. **13.** Outward form or aspect; appearance. **14.** A sort; a type. **15.** An inclination; a tendency. **16.** A distortion or twist. **17.** A pair of hawks released by a falconer at one time. **18.** The circling of hounds to pick up a scent. [Middle English *casten,* to throw, from Old Norse *kasta†.*]

cas·ta·nets (kástə-néts) *pl.n.* A pair of slightly concave shells of ivory or hardwood, held in the palm of the hand by a connecting cord over the thumb and clapped together with the fingers as a rhythmical accompaniment to dancing. [Spanish *castañeta*, from *castaña*, chestnut, from Latin *castanea*, CHESTNUT.]

cast away *tr.v.* **1.** To shipwreck; strand. Usually used in the passive. **2.** To throw away; squander.

cast·a·way (kaást-ə-way || kást-) *n.* **1.** One who has been shipwrecked. **2.** An outcast. **—cast·a·way** *adj.*

caste (kaast || kast) *n.* **1.** One of the four major hereditary classes into which Hindu society is divided. Each caste is distinctly separated from the others by restrictions placed upon occupation and marriage. See **Brahman, Kshatriya, Vaisya, Sudra. 2.** Any social class separated from others by distinctions of hereditary rank, profession, or the like. **3.** A social system or principle of social organisation based on these distinctions. Also used adjectivally: *a caste system.* **4.** The social position or status conferred by such a system: *lose caste.* **5.** *Zoology.* In social insects, any of the various kinds of specialised individuals, such as drones or workers. [Spanish and Portuguese *casta*, caste, race, breed, from the feminine of *casto*, pure, chaste, from Latin *castus*.]

Cas·tel Gan·dol·fo (kástel gan-dólfō). Village on the shore of Lake Albano, central Italy where the Pope has his summer residence.

cas·tel·lat·ed (káss-tə-laytid, -ti-, -te-) *adj.* Furnished with turrets and battlements in the style of a castle. [Medieval Latin *castellātus*, past participle of *castellāre*, to fortify as a castle, from Latin *castellum*, CASTLE.] **—cas·tel·la·tion** (-láysh'n) *n.*

cast·er (kaástər || kástər) *n.* Also **castor** (for sense 2). **1.** A person or thing that casts. **2. a.** A small container made of silver, glass, or the like, having a perforated top and used for sprinkling sugar or spices. **b.** A stand for holding a set of such containers. **3.** Variant of **castor.**

caster sugar *n.* A very finely granulated white sugar.

cas·ti·gate (kásti-gayt) *tr.v.* **-gated, -gating, -gates. 1.** To punish or chastise. **2.** To criticise severely. —See Synonyms at **punish.** [Latin *castīgāre*, to correct, punish : *castus*, pure + *agere*, to do, make.] **—cas·ti·ga·tion** (-gáysh'n) *n.* **—cas·ti·ga·tor** (-gaytər) *n.*

Cas·ti·glio·ne (kástəl-yōni, kaástəl-), **Baldassare** (1478–1529). Italian courtier, writer, and humanist. He is best known for *Il Cortegiano* (1528) which describes the perfect courtier.

Cas·tile (ka-steél). *Spanish* **Cas·til·la** (kas-teél-yə). Region in the high plateaux of central Spain. Stretching from the Bay of Biscay in the north to Sierra Morena in the south, it became an independent kingdom in 1035. In 1230, it joined the kingdom of León, and, in 1479, after the marriage of Isabella of Castile and Ferdinand II of Aragon, the nucleus of modern Spain was established. The name Castile probably derives from the number of castles that were built there against the Moorish invasions.

Castile soap *n. Sometimes small* **c.** A fine, hard, white, odourless soap made with olive oil and sodium hydroxide.

Cas·til·i·an (kass-tíl-i-ən, kəss-, -yən) *n.* **1.** The dialect of Spanish spoken in Castile, now the standard and official form of the Spanish language in Spain. **2. a.** A native or inhabitant of Castile. **b.** Broadly, a Spaniard. **—Cas·til·i·an** *adj.*

cast·ing (kaáss-ting || káss-) *n.* **1.** The act or process of one that casts. **2.** That which is cast in a mould, such as a metal piece. **3.** That which is cast off or out, such as skin, earth excreted by worms, or the like; a cast.

casting vote *n.* The vote of a presiding officer in an assembly or committee, given to decide a question when the votes of the members are tied.

cast iron *n.* A hard, brittle nonmalleable iron-carbon alloy containing 2.0 to 4.5 per cent carbon, 0.5 to 3 per cent silicon, and lesser amounts of sulphur, manganese, and phosphorus.

cast-i·ron (kaást-ī-ərn, -ī- || kást-) *adj.* **1.** Made of cast iron. **2.** Rigid; inflexible: *a cast-iron rule.* **3.** Tough; resilient: *a cast-iron stomach.* **4.** Unquestionable; indisputable: *a cast-iron alibi.*

cas·tle (kaáss'l || káss'l) *n.* **1.** A fortified building or group of buildings designed to defend a town, route, or territory, especially in medieval Europe. **2.** A former stronghold of this kind converted to residential use; a mansion. **3.** Something or somewhere that provides security or refuge; a stronghold. **4. a.** A small defensive tower on the deck of a medieval warship. Compare **forecastle. b.** A small tower carried on the back of an elephant in war. **5.** *Chess.* The **rook** *(see).* **—castles in the air** or **in Spain.** Daydreams; aspirations unlikely to be realised.

~v. **castled, -tling, -tles.** *—tr.* **1.** To place in or as if in a castle. **2.** *Chess.* To move (the king) from his own square two squares to one side and then, in the same move, bring the rook from that side to the square immediately past the king. *—intr. Chess.* To move the king and rook in this manner. [Middle English *castel*, from Old English *castel*, from Late Latin *castellum*, village, from Latin *castellum*, castle, diminutive of *castrum*, fortified place.]

cas·tled (kaáss'ld || káss'ld) *adj.* Castellated; fortified.

Cas·tle·maine (kaáss'l-mayn || káss'l-). Town in Victoria, Australia, on the northern flanks of the Great Dividing Range. It is one of the oldest gold-digging sites in the country, and now a farming centre.

cast off *tr.v.* **1.** To discard or reject. **2.** To set loose; especially, to detach (a boat) from its moorings. **3.** To estimate the space (a manuscript) will occupy when set into type. **4.** To loop (a knitted stitch or stitches) over the next, thus leaving a short finished edge. *—intr.v.* **1.** To finish the last row in a strip of knitting by looping each stitch in turn over the next. **2.** To detach a boat from its moorings.

cast-off (kaást-óff || kást-, -off, -áwf, -awf) *adj.* Discarded; rejected.

cast·off (kaást-off || kást-, -awf) *n.* **1.** Someone or something that has been discarded, especially an item of clothing. **2.** *Printing.* A calculation of the amount of space a manuscript will occupy when set into type.

cas·tor¹ (kaástər || kástər) *n.* **1.** An oily, brown, odorous substance obtained from glands in the groin of the beaver and used as a perfume fixative. **2.** A beaver hat. [Middle English, beaver, from Latin, from Greek *kastōr*, beaver.]

cas·tor², cas·ter *n.* **1.** A small wheel on a swivel attached to the underside of a piece of furniture or other heavy object to make it easier to move. **2.** Variant of **caster.**

Cas·tor (kaástər || kástər) *n.* A double star in the constellation Gemini, the brightest star in the group, approximately 46 light-years from Earth.

Castor and Pol·lux (póllәks). *Greek Mythology.* The twin sons of Leda, one by Tydareus, the other by Zeus. They were transformed by Zeus into the constellation Gemini so that they would not be separated. Also called "Dioscuri".

castor bean *n.* **1.** *U.S.* The castor-oil plant. **2.** A seed of this plant.

castor oil *n.* A colourless or yellowish oil extracted from castor-oil plant seeds and used as a laxative and a fine lubricant. [Probably from a mistaken connection with the substance CASTOR.]

cas·tor-oil plant (kaástər-óyl || kástər-) *n.* A large evergreen plant, *Ricinus communis*, native to tropical Africa and Asia, with lobed, bronze- or purple-flushed leaves, grown for ornament and for the commercial extraction of castor oil from its poisonous seeds.

cas·trate (kass-tráyt || *U.S.* kástrayt) *tr.v.* **-trated, -trating, -trates. 1.** To remove the testicles of; geld. **2.** To remove the ovaries of; spay. **3.** To deprive of strength or vigour. **4.** To bowdlerise. [Latin *castrāre*.] **—cas·tra·tion** *n.*

cas·tra·to (kass-traá-tō) *n., pl.* **-ti** (-tee) or **-tos.** A male singer castrated in boyhood so as to retain a soprano or alto voice. [Italian, "castrated (one)".]

Cas·tries (kass-treéss). Capital and the chief port of St. Lucia, in the Windward Islands, the West Indies.

Cas·tro (kástrō || *U.S. also* kaástrō), **Fidel,** born Fidel Castro Ruz (1927–). Cuban statesman and prime minister. He overthrew the corrupt regime of the dictator, Fulgencio Batista, and became the head of the Cuban government in February 1959. He seized U.S. and other foreign-owned property and established a socialist state. Under Castro, Cuba has become one of the leading Third World countries. **—Cas·tro·ism** *n.* **—Cas·tro·ist** *n.*

cast steel *n.* Carbon steel that has been cast into shape rather than wrought.

cas·u·al (kázhew-əl, kázzew-, kázhoo-, kázh-) *adj.* **1.** Resulting from or occurring by chance. **2.** Unpremeditated; not planned. **3. a.** Informal; relaxed. **b.** Suitable for informal occasions: *casual clothes.* **4.** Without specific purpose; aimless. **5. a.** Unconcerned; nonchalant. **b.** Careless; negligent. **6.** Pertaining to or associated with accidents. **7.** Irregular; occasional; part-time: *a casual labourer.* —See Synonyms at **chance.**

~n. **1.** A person who works at irregular intervals. **2.** A plant that occasionally occurs in the wild but never becomes naturalised. **3.** *Plural.* Casual clothes or footwear: *winter casuals.* [Middle English *casuel*, from Old French, from Late Latin *cāsuālis*, from Latin *cāsus*, fall, chance, CASE.] **—cas·u·al·ly** *adv.* **—cas·u·al·ness** *n.*

cas·u·al·ty (kázhew-əl-ti, kázzew-, kázhoo-, kázh-, -l-) *n., pl.* **-ties. 1.** One who is injured or killed in an accident. **2. a.** One injured, killed, captured, or missing in action against an enemy. **b.** *Usually plural.* Loss in numbers through injury, death, or other cause. **3.** A person or thing that has suffered injury, loss, or destruction as the result of a particular occurrence or circumstance: *one of the casualties of the recent cabinet reshuffle.* **4.** The department of a hospital to which people injured in accidents are initially admitted. [Middle English *casuelte*, from *casuel*, CASUAL.]

cas·u·a·ri·na (kázzew-ə-rīnə, kázhew-, kázhoo-, kássew-) *n.* Any of various tropical trees, with drooping jointed branches and rudimentary leaves, of the genus *Casuarina*, which includes the beefwoods and she-oaks. Known in Jamaica as "willow". [New Latin, from Malay *kĕsuari*, CASSOWARY (from the resemblance of its twigs to the drooping feathers of the cassowary).]

cas·u·ist (kázzew-ist, kázhew-, kázhoo-) *n.* **1.** One who argues plausibly but falsely; a sophist. **2.** One who determines what is right and wrong in matters of conscience or conduct. Often used derogatorily. [French *casuiste*, from Spanish *casuista*, from Latin *cāsus*, chance, CASE.] **—cas·u·is·tic** (-ístic) *adj.* **—cas·u·is·ti·cal·ly** *adv.*

cas·u·ist·ry (kázzew-istri, kázhew-, kázhoo-) *n.* **1.** Plausible but false reasoning; sophistry. **2.** The determination of right and wrong in questions of conduct or conscience by the application of general principles of ethics. [From CASUIST.]

ca·sus bel·li (kaá-səss bél-ee, káy-,-lī) *n., pl.* **casus belli** *(pronounced as singular, or* -sewss). An act or event that justifies or leads directly to a declaration of war. [Latin, "occasion of war".]

cat (kat) *n.* A small, furry, carnivorous mammal, *Felis catus* (or *F. domesticus*), domesticated since early times as a catcher of rats and mice and as a pet, and existing in several distinctive breeds and varieties. Also called "domestic cat". **2.** Any of the larger animals of the family Felidae, such as the lion, tiger, and leopard. Also called "big cat". **3.** Any other feline animal, such as a lynx or wildcat. **4.** The fur of a domestic cat. **5.** A spiteful woman. **6.** A cat-o'-nine-tails. **7.** *Nautical.* **a.** A cathead. **b.** A device for raising an anchor to the cathead. **c.** A catboat. **8.** *Slang.* A man. Used

especially among jazz musicians and enthusiasts. **—let the cat out of the bag.** To let a secret be known. **—play cat and mouse with.** To play with, tease, or keep in suspense in an unkind way. **—rain cats and dogs.** To rain heavily.
~*tr.v.* **catted, catting, cats.** **1.** To flog with a cat-o'-nine-tails. **2.** To hoist (an anchor) to the cathead. [Middle English *cat(te),* Old English *cat(t),* from Germanic *kattuz* (unattested).
CAT **1.** clear-air turbulence. **2.** computerised axial tomography. See **CAT scanner.**
cat. catalogue.
cata– *prefix.* Indicates: **1.** Reversing of a process; for example, **cataplasia. 2.** Lower in position or down from; for example, **cataphyll, catadromous.** [In borrowed Greek compounds *kata-* indicates: 1. Down, as in **catabolism.** 2. Down from, as in **catalepsy.** 3. Off or away, as in **catalectic.** 4. Against, as in **category.** 5. Wrongly or overly, as in **catachresis.** 6. According to, as in **catechise.** 7. Completely or thoroughly, as in **catalogue.** Greek *kata-,* from *kata,* down, down from, according to.]
ca·tab·o·lise, ca·tab·o·lize (kə-tábbə-līz) *v.* **-lised, -lising, -lises.** *—tr.* To break down (complex molecules) by metabolic processes. *—intr.* To undergo catabolism.
ca·tab·o·lism (kə-tábbə-liz'm) *n.* The metabolic change of complex into simple molecules with the release of energy; destructive metabolism. Compare **anabolism.** [Greek *katabolē,* a throwing down, from *kataballein,* to throw down : *kata-,* down + *ballein,* to throw.] **—cat·a·bol·ic** (kàttə-bóllik) *adj.* **—cat·a·bol·i·cal·ly** *adv.*
cat·a·caus·tic (kàttə-káwstik) *adj.* Designating a caustic curve or surface formed by reflected light rather than refracted light.
~*n.* A catacaustic curve or surface. Compare **diacaustic.**
cat·a·chre·sis (kàttə-krée-siss) *n., pl.* **-ses** (-seez) **1. a.** Strained use of a word or phrase, as for rhetorical effect. **b.** A deliberately paradoxical figure of speech. **2.** Incorrect use of a word. [Latin *catachrēsis,* from Greek *katakhrēsis,* excessive use, misuse, from *katakhrēsthai,* to misuse, use up : *kata-,* wrongly + *khrēsthai,* to use.] **—cat·a·chres·tic** (-kréstik) *adj.*
cat·a·cla·sis (kàttə-kláy-siss) *n., pl.* **-ses** (-seez). *Geology.* The process in which rocks are deformed by mechanical shearing, or in which selected rock minerals are granulated. [CATA- + -CLASIS.] **—cat·a·clas·tic** (-klástik) *adj.*
cat·a·clysm (kàttə-kliz'm) *n.* **1.** Any violent or destructive upheaval, especially one that brings fundamental change. **2.** A violent and sudden change in the earth's crust. **3.** A devastating flood. —See Synonyms at **disaster.** [French *cataclysme,* from Latin *cataclysmos,* deluge, flood, from Greek *kataklusmos,* from *katakluzein,* to deluge, inundate : *kata-,* down + *kluzein,* to wash.] **—cat·a·clys·mic** (-klízmik), **cat·a·clys·mal** (-klízməl) *adj.*
cat·a·combs (kàttə-kōōmz, -kōmz) *pl.n.* **1.** A series of underground chambers or tunnels with recesses for graves, especially those in Rome. **2.** *Singular.* An underground cemetery. [From Old French *catacombe,* a subterranean chamber, probably from Old Italian *catacomba,* from Late Latin *catacumba*†.]
cat·a·di·op·tric (kàttə-dī-óptrik) *adj.* Pertaining to or designating an optical instrument, such as a telescope, that uses both lenses and mirrors in its operation. [CATA- + DIOPTRIC.]
ca·tad·ro·mous (kə-táddrəməss) *adj.* Migrating down river to breed in marine waters, as some fishes do. Compare **anadromous.** [CATA- + -DROMOUS.]
cat·a·falque (kàttə-falk || -fawlk, -fawk) *n.* The raised structure upon which a coffin rests, as during a state funeral. [French, from Italian *catafalco*†.]
Cat·a·lan (kàttə-lan, -lən) *adj.* Of or pertaining to Catalonia, its people, language, or culture.
~*n.* **1.** A native or inhabitant of Catalonia. **2.** The Romance language of Catalonia.
cat·a·lase (kàttə-layz, -layss) *n.* An enzyme that catalyses the decomposition of hydrogen peroxide into water and oxygen. [CATAL(YSIS) + -ASE.]
cat·a·lec·tic (kàttə-léktik) *adj.* Designating a verse that lacks part of the last foot. [Late Latin *catalēcticus,* from Greek *katalēktikos,* incomplete, from *katalēgein,* to leave off : *kata-,* off, away + *lēgein,* to leave off, stop.]
cat·a·lep·sy (kàttə-lepsi) *n.* Muscular rigidity, lack of awareness of environment, and lack of response to external stimuli, often associated with encephalitis, schizophrenia, and hysteria. [Learned respelling of earlier *catalency,* from Middle English *cathalempsia,* from Medieval Latin *catalepsia,* from Late Latin *catalēpsis,* from Greek *katalēpsis,* "a seizing", from *katalambanein,* to seize : *kata-,* down from + *lambanein,* to take.] **—cat·a·lep·tic** (-léptik) *adj.*
cat·a·lo, cat·ta·lo (kàttəlō) *n., pl.* **-loes** or **-los.** A hardy, fertile hybrid breed resulting from a cross between the American buffalo, or bison, and domestic cattle. [CAT(TLE) + (BUFF)ALO.]
cat·a·logue, *U.S.* **cat·a·log** (kàttə-log || -lawg) *n. Abbr.* **cat. 1.** A systematised list, usually in alphabetical order, often with descriptions of the listed items. **2.** A list of all the publications contained in a library. **3.** A series; a succession: *a catalogue of disasters.*
~*v.* **catalogued** or *U.S.* **cataloged, -loguing** or *U.S.* **-loging, -logues** or *U.S.* **-logs.** *—tr.* **1.** To list in a catalogue; make a catalogue of. **2.** To add (a new item) to an existing catalogue. *—intr.* To make a catalogue. [Middle English *cateloge,* from Old French *catalogue,* from Late Latin *catalogus,* an enumeration, from Greek *katalogos,* from *katalegein,* to recount, enumerate : *kata-,* thoroughly + *legein,* to gather, speak.] **—cat·a·logu·er** *n.*
Cat·a·lo·ni·a (kàttə-lṓni-ə). *Spanish* **Ca·ta·lu·ña** (kàttə-lōōn-yə). *Catalan* **Ca·ta·lu·nya** (kàttə-lōōn-yə). A mountainous, industrialised region of northeast Spain, extending from the Pyrenees along the Mediterranean coast. It is an autonomous region comprising the provinces of Barcelona, Gerona, Lérida, and Tarragona.
ca·tal·pa (kə-tál-pə || *U.S. also* -táwl-) *n.* Any of several Asian or South American trees of the genus *Catalpa,* having large leaves, showy clusters of whitish flowers, and long, slender pods. Also called "Indian bean". [Creek *kutuhlpa,* "head with wings" (from the shape of its flowers).]
cat·a·lyse, *U.S.* **cat·a·lyze** (kàtta-līz) *tr.v.* **-lysed, -lysing, -lyses.** To modify the rate of (a chemical reaction) by catalysis. **—cat·a·lys·er** *n.*
ca·tal·y·sis (kə-tállə-siss) *n.* The action of a catalyst in modifying the rate of a chemical reaction. [Greek *katalusis,* dissolution, from *kataluein,* to dissolve : *kata-,* down + *luein,* to loosen, release.] **—cat·a·lyt·ic** (kàttə-líttik) *adj.* **—cat·a·lyt·i·cal·ly** *adv.*
cat·a·lyst (kàttəlist) *n.* **1.** *Chemistry.* A substance that modifies, and especially increases, the rate of a chemical reaction without being consumed or chemically changed in the process. **2.** One that precipitates a process or event, especially without being involved in or changed by the consequences. [From CATALYSIS (by analogy with ANALYST and ANALYSIS).]
catalytic converter *n.* A reaction chamber, typically containing a finely divided platinum-iridium catalyst, into which exhaust gases from a petrol engine are passed together with excess air so that carbon monoxide and hydrocarbon pollutants are oxidised to carbon dioxide and water.
catalytic cracker *n.* An oil-refinery unit in which catalytic **cracking** *(see)* of petroleum is performed. Also called "cat cracker".
cat·a·ma·ran (kàttəmə-rán, -ran) *n.* **1.** A boat with two parallel hulls. **2.** A raft of logs or floats lashed together. [Tamil *kaṭṭumaram* : *kaṭṭu-,* to tie + *maram,* tree, timber.]
cat·a·me·ni·a (kàttə-méeni-ə) *n. Physiology.* Menstruation. [New Latin, from Greek *katamēnia,* neuter plural of *katamēnios,* monthly : *kata-,* according to + *mēn,* month.] **—cat·a·me·ni·al** *adj.*
cat·a·mite (kàttə-mīt) *n.* A boy kept by a pederast. [Latin *catamītus,* from *Catamītus,* Ganymede, from Greek *Ganumēdēs,* GANYMEDE (cupbearer of the gods).]
cat·a·mount (kàttə-mownt) *n.* Also **cat·a·moun·tain** (-mówntin). Any of various wild felines, such as a mountain lion or a lynx. [Short for *catamountain,* variant of earlier *cat of the mountain.*]
Ca·ta·ni·a (kə-táyni-ə, -taán-). Capital city of Catania province in Sicily, situated at the foot of Mount Etna.
cat·a·pho·re·sis (kàttəfə-rée-siss) *n. Chemistry.* **Electrophoresis** *(see).* [New Latin : CATA- + -PHORESIS.] **—cat·a·pho·ret·ic** (-réttik) *adj.* **—cat·a·pho·ret·i·cal·ly** *adv.*
cat·a·phyll (kàttə-fil) *n. Botany.* A modified or rudimentary leaf, such as a bud scale. [CATA- + -PHYLL (translation of German *Niederblatt,* "lower leaf").]
cat·a·pla·si·a (kàttə-pláyzi-ə || -pláyzhi-, -pláyzh-) *n.* Degenerative reversion of cells or tissue to a less differentiated form. [New Latin : CATA- + -PLASIA.] **—cat·a·plas·tic** (-plástik) *adj.*
cat·a·plasm (kàttə-plaz'm) *n. Medicine.* A **poultice** *(see).* [Old French *cataplasme,* from Late Latin *cataplasma,* from Greek *kataplasma,* from *kataplassein,* to plaster over : *kata-,* thoroughly + *plassein,* to mould.]
cat·a·plex·y (kàttə-pleksi) *n.* A sudden temporary paralysis; especially, the hypnotic state assumed by animals when shamming death. [From Greek *kataplēxis* : *kata-,* CATA- + *plēxis,* from *plēssein,* to strike.] **—cat·a·plec·tic** (-pléktik) *adj.*
cat·a·pult (kàttə-pult) *n.* **1.** An ancient military machine for hurling large stones, or other missiles. **2.** A mechanism for launching aircraft without a runway, as from the deck of a ship. **3.** A forked twig or other Y-shaped implement with a piece of elastic fastened to the prongs, used by children for shooting small stones. In this sense, also *chiefly U.S.* "slingshot".
~*v.* **catapulted, -pulting, -pults.** *—tr.* **1. a.** To hurl or launch from or as if from a catapult. **b.** To shoot at with a catapult. **2.** To bring or move suddenly or abruptly: *catapulted to fame by the success of her first novel.* *—intr.* To become catapulted; spring up abruptly. [Old French *catapulte,* from Latin *catapulta,* from Greek *katapaltēs, katapeltēs* : *kata-,* down + *pallein,* to sway, brandish.]
cat·a·ract (kàttə-rakt) *n.* **1. a.** A very large waterfall, especially one with a sheer drop. **b.** A series of rapids on a stretch of river. **2.** A great downpour. **3.** *Pathology.* Opacity of the lens or capsule of the eye, causing partial or total blindness. [Middle English *cataracte,* floodgate, from Old French, portcullis, cataract (of the eye), from Latin *catarractēs,* waterfall, portcullis, from Greek *katar(rh)aktēs,* "a down-swooping", from *katarassein,* to dash down : *kata-,* down + *rassein,* to strike.]
ca·tarrh (kə-tár) *n.* Inflammation of mucous membranes, especially of the nose and throat, causing excessive secretion of phlegm or mucus. [Old French *catarrhe,* from Late Latin *catarrhus,* from Greek *katarrhous,* a flowing down, from *katarrhein,* to flow down : *kata-,* down + *rhein,* to flow.] **—ca·tarrh·al** (kə-taárəl) *adj.*
cat·arrh·ine (kàttə-rīn) *adj.* Of or designating a group of primates that includes the Old World monkeys, apes, and man, characterised by close-set nostrils directed forward or downwards.
~*n.* A catarrhine primate. [New Latin *Catarrhina,* from Greek *katarrhin,* hook-nosed : *kata-,* down + *rhis* (stem *rhin-*), nose.]
ca·tas·ta·sis (kə-tástə-siss) *n., pl.* **-ses** (-seez). **1.** In classical tragedy, the intensified part of the action directly preceding the catastrophe. **2.** The climax of a play. [Greek *katastasis,* settlement,

establishment, from *kathistanai,* to set in order, bring down : *kata-*, down + *histanai,* to set, place.]
ca·tas·tro·phe (kə-tástrəfi) *n.* **1.** A great and sudden calamity causing extreme, often widespread, ruin or destruction; a disaster. **2.** A sudden violent change in the earth's surface; a cataclysm. **3.** The dénouement of a play, especially a classical tragedy. —See Synonyms at **disaster.** [Greek *katastrophē,* from *katastrephein,* to turn down, overturn : *kata-*, down + *strephein,* to turn.] **—cat·a·stroph·ic** (káttə-stróffik) *adj.* **—cat·a·stroph·i·cal·ly** *adv.*
catastrophe theory *n.* A mathematical theory applied to a wide range of phenomena that show different structures or sudden discontinuous changes, such as biological differentiation, mechanical failure, social conflict, and the like. It depends on representation of different states of the system by geometrical shapes, and on topological analysis of shape and changes of shape.
ca·tas·tro·phism (kə-tástrə-fiz'm) *n. Geology.* The theory that geological changes in the past were caused by sudden catastrophic disturbances. The theory is also used to account for extinction of plant and animal species. Compare **uniformitarianism.**
cat·a·to·ni·a (káttə-tṓni-ə) *n.* A condition associated with schizophrenia and certain organic brain disorders and characterised by catalepsy and negativism. [New Latin, from German *Katatonie* : CATA- + -TONIA.] **—cat·a·ton·ic** (-tónnik) *adj. & n.*
cat·bird (kát-burd) *n.* **1.** Any of various Australian bowerbirds of the genera *Ailuroedus.* **2.** A North American songbird, *Dumetella carolinensis,* having predominantly slate-grey plumage. [After one of its calls, resembling the mewing of a cat.]
cat·boat (kát-bōt) *n.* A broad-beamed sailing boat carrying a single sail on a mast stepped well forward. Also called "cat".
cat brier *n.* A plant, the **greenbrier** *(see).*
cat burglar *n.* A burglar who enters buildings by climbing to the upper storeys.
cat·call (kát-kawl) *n.* A harsh or shrill call expressing disapproval or derision. **—cat·call** *v.*
catch (kach) *v.* **caught** (kawt), **catching, catches.** *—tr.* **1.** To capture or seize, especially after a chase. **2.** To take by trapping or snaring. **3.** To come upon suddenly, unexpectedly, or accidentally. **4. a.** To lay hold of forcibly or suddenly; grasp. **b.** To grab so as to stop the motion of. **5. a.** To reach; especially, to reach and overtake. **b.** To reach in time to board, attend, or otherwise make use of: *catch a plane; caught the last post.* **6. a.** To entangle; grip. **b.** To cause to become suddenly or accidentally hooked, entangled, or the like. **7.** To hit; strike. **8.** To check (oneself) in some sort of action. **9.** To become subject to or contract, as by exposure or contagion. **10.** To become affected by: *You've caught the sun.* **11.** To take or get suddenly, momentarily, or quickly. **12. a.** To grasp mentally; comprehend. **b.** To grasp by the senses; apprehend: *I didn't quite catch his last remark.* **13.** To apprehend and reproduce accurately, especially by artistic means; capture: *a novel that catches the flavour of the period.* **14.** To attract and fix; arrest: *catch the waiter's attention.* **15.** To watch or listen to (a show, a programme, or the like). **16.** In cricket, to dismiss (a batsman) by catching a ball struck by him before it touches the ground. **17.** *Informal.* To deceive; cheat. Used in the passive. **18.** *Informal.* To cause to become pregnant. Used in the passive. *—intr.* **1.** To become held, entangled, or fastened. **2.** To be communicable or infectious; spread. **3.** To take fire; kindle; burn. **—catch at. 1.** To try to catch; snatch or grab at. **2.** To clutch at gratefully or eagerly. **—catch it.** *Informal.* To receive some form of punishment or scolding. **—catch on.** *Informal.* **1.** To understand or perceive. **2.** To become popular. **—catch (one's) breath. 1.** To rest so as to be able to go on. **2.** To cease breathing briefly. **—catch out.** To detect (someone) in a mistake. **—catch up. 1.** To lift up suddenly; grab; snatch. **2.** To entangle: *caught up in some barbed wire.* **3. a.** To come up from behind and draw level. **b.** To reach the same level or amount. Used with *with*: *When will the supply catch up with the demand?* **c.** To have an expected, usually undesirable, effect, especially after a lapse of time. Used with *with*: *Years of riotous living finally caught up with him.* **4.** To cause to become involved, often unwillingly. Used in the passive: *caught up in the scandal.* **5. a.** To deal with an accumulation of work or the like. Used with *on* or *with*: *catch up on one's correspondence.* **b.** To become acquainted with the latest information. Used with *on* or *with*: *catch up on the gossip.* **6.** To absorb completely; engross. Used in the passive: *He is caught up in his work.*
~n. **1.** The act of catching; a taking and holding. **2.** Something that catches, especially a device for fastening or for checking motion. **3.** Something that is caught. **4.** The amount caught. **5.** A choking or stoppage of the breath or voice. **6.** *Informal.* One worth catching, especially as a partner in marriage. **7.** *Informal.* A tricky or unsuspected drawback or condition. **8.** A snatch or fragment. **9.** *Music.* A type of round for three or more voices, popular especially in the 17th and 18th centuries. **10. a.** The grabbing and holding of a thrown, kicked, or batted ball before it hits the ground; especially, in cricket, the dismissal of a batsman by means of a catch. **b.** A game of throwing and catching a ball. [Catch, caught, caught; Middle English *cacchen, cauhte, cauht,* to chase, catch, from Old North French *cachier,* to hunt, from Vulgar Latin *captiāre* (unattested), from Latin *captāre,* to chase, strive to seize, from *capere* (past participle *captus*), to take, seize.]
catch·all (kách-awl) *n.* Something, such as a phrase or law, that covers a variety of situations. **—catch·all** *adj.*
catch-as-catch-can (kách-əz-kach-kán) *n.* A style of wrestling in which a contestant is permitted to hold his opponent below the waist and to trip and tackle.
~adj. Chiefly U.S. Using any available means or opportunity.
catch crop *n.* **1.** A crop grown between two staple crops in consecutive seasons. **2.** A crop grown between the rows of a staple crop.
catch·er (káchər) *n.* One that catches, especially in a game.
catch·fly (káchflī) *n., pl.* **-flies.** Any of several plants of the genus *Silene* and related genera, having white, pink, or red flowers with characteristically sticky stems and calyxes.
catch·ing (káching) *adj. Informal.* **1.** Infectious. **2.** Attractive; alluring.
catch·ment (káchmənt) *n.* **1.** A catching or collecting of water. **2.** The intake from a particular area, as of a school or hospital.
catchment area *n.* **1.** The land bounded by watersheds that drains into a river, reservoir, or basin. Also called "catchment basin", "drainage area", "drainage basin". **2.** The geographical area from which people are drawn, as to attend a school or a hospital.
catch·pen·ny (kách-penni) *adj.* Designed and made to sell without concern for quality; cheap. **—catch·pen·ny** *n.*
catch phrase *n.* A phrase in popular use, such as one associated with a show-business personality.
catch points *pl.n.* Points on a railway designed to derail a train if it runs out of control.
catch·pole, catch·poll (kách-pōl) *n.* Formerly, a sheriff's officer, especially one who arrested debtors. [Middle English *cacchepol,* Old English *cæccepol,* from Old North French *cachepol,* "chicken chaser" : *cachier,* variant of Old French *chacier,* to hunt, CHASE + *poul, pol,* cock, from Latin *pullus,* young animal, young fowl.]
Catch-22 (kách-twenti-tōō) *n.* A paradox or predicament in which seeming alternatives actually cancel each other out, leaving no means of escape from a dilemma. [After *Catch-22* (1961), a novel by Joseph Heller (born 1923), U.S. author.]
catch·weight (kách-wayt) *adj. Sports.* Having no weight restriction. Used especially in wrestling.
catch·word (kách-wurd) *n.* **1.** An often repeated word or slogan, especially one associated with a political party. **2.** *Printing.* A word placed at the head of a column or page, as in a dictionary or encyclopedia, to indicate the first or last entry on the page. **3.** The first word of a page printed at the bottom of the preceding page. **4.** A cue for an actor or actress.
catch·y (káchi) *adj.* **-ier, -iest. 1.** Catching one's attention or interest; striking. **2.** Easily remembered and quickly popular.
cat cracker *n.* A **catalytic cracker** *(see).*
cat door *n.* A hole cut in a door, covered by a flap, through which a cat may pass. Also called "cat flap".
cat·e·che·sis (kátti-kée-siss) *n., pl.* **-ses** (-seez). Instruction of catechumens. [Late Latin *catēchēsis,* from Greek *katēkhēsis,* from *katēkhein,* to CATECHISE.] **—cat·e·chet·ic** (-kéttik), **cat·e·chet·i·cal** *adj.*
cat·e·chin (kátti-kin, -chin) *n.* A soluble yellow solid substance, $C_{15}H_{14}O_6$, derived from catechu and used in tanning and dyeing. [CATECH(U) + -IN.]
cat·e·chise, cat·e·chize (kátti-kīz) *tr.v.* **-chised, -chising, -chises. 1.** To instruct orally in the principles of a religious creed by means of questions and answers. **2.** To question searchingly or persistently. [Late Latin *catēchizāre,* from Late Greek *katēkhizein,* from Greek *katēkhein,* to teach by word of mouth : *kata-*, according to + *ēkhein,* to sound, from *ēkhē,* sound.] **—cat·e·chi·sa·tion** (-kī-záysh'n || *U.S.* -ki-) *n.* **—cat·e·chis·er** *n.*
cat·e·chism (kátti-kiz'm) *n.* **1.** A short book giving, in question-and-answer form, a brief summary of the basic principles of a religion, especially Christianity. **2.** A book of similar form giving instruction in other subjects. **3.** A question-and-answer examination, as of a political candidate. [Late Latin *catēchismus,* from Late Greek *katēkhismos,* from *katēkhizein,* to CATECHISE.] **—cat·e·chis·mal** (-kízm'l) *adj.*
cat·e·chist (kátti-kist) *n.* A person who catechises, especially one who instructs catechumens in preparation for baptism. [Late Latin *catēchista,* from Late Greek *katēkhistēs,* from *katēkhizein,* to CATECHISE.] **—cat·e·chis·tic** (-kístik), **cat·e·chis·ti·cal** *adj.*
cat·e·chol (kátti-kol, -chol) *n.* A colourless crystalline derivative of phenol, $C_6H_4(OH)_2$, used as a photographic developer. Also called "1,2-dihydroxybenzene". [CATECH(U) + -OL.]
cat·e·chol·a·mine (kátti-kóllə-meen, -kṓlə-) *n.* Any of a group of amine derivatives of catechol, which have important physiological effects on the central nervous system and include adrenaline, noradrenaline, and dopamine.
cat·e·chu (kátti-chōō) *n.* Any of several water-soluble, resinous, astringent substances used in tanning and dyeing, such as that obtained from a tree, *Acacia catechu,* of southern Asia. Also called "cachou", "cutch". [Probably from Malay *kachu,* probably from Dravidian, akin to Malayalam *kāccu,* CACHOU.]
cat·e·chu·men (kátti-kéw-men, -min) *n.* One who is being taught the principles of Christianity; a neophyte. [Middle English *cathecumyn,* from Old French *cathecumene,* from Late Latin *catēchūmenus,* from Greek *katēkhoumenos,* present passive participle of *katēkhein,* to CATECHISE.]
cat·e·gor·i·cal (kátti-górrik'l || *U.S.* -gáwrik'l, -gṓrik'l) *adj.* **1.** Without exception or qualification; absolute; certain. **2.** Of, concerning, or included in a category. **—cat·e·gor·i·cal·ly** *adv.*
categorical imperative *n.* In Kant's ethical system, an absolute and universally binding moral law derived from pure reason. Compare **hypothetical imperative.**

cat·e·go·rise, cat·e·go·rize (káttigə-rīz) *tr.v.* **-rised, -rising, -rises.** To put into categories; classify. **—cat·e·go·ri·sa·tion** (-rī-záysh'n ‖ *U.S.* -ri-) *n.*

cat·e·go·ry (kátti-gri, -gəri ‖ *U.S.* -gawri, -gōri) *n., pl.* **-ries. 1.** A specifically defined division in a system of classification; a class. **2.** *Philosophy.* Any of the basic classifications into which all knowledge can be placed. [Late Latin *catēgoria,* accusation, predicament, category of predicables, from Greek *katēgoria,* from *katēgorein,* to accuse : *kata-,* against + *-agorein,* to speak publicly, from *agora,* assembly.]

ca·te·na (kə-tée-nə) *n., pl.* **-nae** (-nee) or **-nas.** A closely linked series, especially of commentaries on the bible by church fathers. [Latin *catēna†,* chain.]

cat·e·nar·y (kə-téenəri ‖ *U.S. also* káttə-nerri) *n., pl.* **-ies. 1.** The curve theoretically formed by a perfectly flexible, uniformly dense and thick, inextensible cable suspended from two points. **2.** Anything having the shape of this curve. **3.** The overhead wire system of an electric railway. [New Latin *catenaria,* from Latin *catēnāria,* feminine of *catēnārius,* of a chain, from *catēna†,* chain.] **—cat·e·nar·y** *adj.*

catenary bridge *n.* A suspension bridge hanging from chains or cables.

cat·e·nate (kátti-nayt) *tr.v.* **-nated, -nating, -nates.** To connect in a series of ties or links; form into a chain. [Latin *catēnāre,* from *catēna†,* chain.] **—cat·e·na·tion** (-náysh'n) *n.*

cat·e·noid (káttinoyd) *n.* A geometrical solid generated by rotating a catenary about its axis.

ca·ten·u·late (kə-ténnew-layt, -lət, -lit) *adj. Biology.* Consisting or formed of chainlike links. [From Latin *catēnula,* little chain, diminutive of Latin *catēna†,* chain.]

ca·ter (káytər) *intr.v.* **-tered, -tering, -ters. 1.** To provide food or entertainment, usually for large dinners, banquets, and the like. Used with *for.* **2.** To provide anything wished for or needed. Used with *for.* **3.** To pander; minister: *caters to his every whim.* [From obsolete *cater,* a buyer of provisions, caterer, from Middle English *catour,* short for *acatour,* from Anglo-French, from *acater,* to buy, from Vulgar Latin *acceptāre* (unattested), to buy, procure, from Latin *acceptāre,* to ACCEPT.]

cat·er-cor·nered (káttər-kawr-nərd, -kaw-) *adj.* Also **cat·ty-cor·nered** (kátti-). *Chiefly U.S.* Diagonal. [From obsolete *cater,* four at dice, from Middle English, from Old French *quatre,* four, from Latin *quattuor.*] **—cat·er-cor·nered** *adv.*

cat·er·er (káytər-ər) *n.* One that caters; specifically, a person or company whose business is to supply and serve food and drinks for large social gatherings, banquets, and the like.

cat·er·pil·lar (káttər-pillər ‖ *also* káttə-) *n.* **1. a.** The wormlike, often brightly coloured, hairy or spiny larva of a butterfly or moth, having many legs and biting jaws. **b.** Any of various similar insect larvae. **2.** *Capital* **C.** A trademark for a tractor or bulldozer equipped with a pair of endless chain treads. [Middle English *catyrpel,* probably from Old French *catepelose,* "hairy cat" : *cate,* female cat, from Late Latin *catta,* CAT + *pelose, pelouse,* feminine of *pelous,* hairy, from Latin *pilōsus,* from *pilus,* hair.]

cat·er·waul (káttər-wawl) *intr.v.* **-wauled, -wauling, -wauls. 1.** To screech like a sexually aroused cat. **2.** To have a noisy argument. ~*n.* **1.** The cry of sexually aroused cats. **2.** Any similar cry. [Middle English *caterw(r)awen,* perhaps from Low German *katerwaulen* : *kater,* tomcat, from Germanic *kattuz* (unattested), CAT + *waulen,* to screech (perhaps imitative).] **—cat·er·waul·ing** *n.*

cat·fish (kát-fish) *n., pl.* **-fishes** or collectively **catfish.** Any of numerous scaleless, chiefly freshwater fishes of the order Siluriformes, characteristically having whisker-like barbels extending from the upper jaw.

cat flap *n.* A cat door *(see).*

cat·gut (kát-gut) *n.* A tough, thin cord or thread made from the dried intestines of certain animals (but not cat), used for stringing musical instruments and tennis rackets and for surgical ligatures. [16th century : origin obscure.]

Cath·ar (káthər, káthaar) *n., pl.* **-ars** or **-ari** (-i). An adherent of Catharism.

Cath·ar·ism (káthər-iz'm) *n.* The teachings of an ascetic sect of Gnostic heretics that existed in Europe between the 10th and 14th centuries, whose adherents regarded all matter as the creation of an evil deity opposed to God. **—Cath·ar·ist** *adj. & n.*

ca·thar·sis (kə-thár-siss, ka-) *n., pl.* **-ses** (-seez) **1.** A purifying or figurative cleansing of the emotions, especially as experienced by the audience of a drama. **2.** *Medicine.* Purgation, especially for the digestive system. **3.** *Psychoanalysis.* **a.** A technique used to relieve tension and anxiety by bringing repressed material to consciousness. **b.** The result of this process; abreaction. [New Latin, from Greek *katharsis,* from *kathairein,* to purge, purify, from *katharos†,* pure.]

ca·thar·tic (kə-thártik, ka-) *adj.* Inducing catharsis; purgative; cleansing. ~*n.* A cathartic agent, especially a laxative. [Late Latin *catharticus,* from Greek *kathartikos,* from *kathairein,* to purge, purify.]

Ca·thay (ka-tháy, kə-). An ancient and poetic name for China and east Tartary. Derived from the Khitan, the Mongol tribe who invaded the north of China in the 10th century, the name, still used in Russian (Kitai), was introduced to Europe by Marco Polo in the 13th century.

cat·head (kát-hed) *n.* A beam projecting outwards from the bow of a ship, and used as a support to lift the anchor. [CAT (nautical) + HEAD.]

ca·the·dra (kə-thée-drə, -thé-) *n., pl.* **-drae** (-dree). **1.** The official chair or throne of a bishop. **2.** The office or diocese of a bishop. See **ex cathedra.** [Latin, chair, from Greek *kathedra,* seat : *kata-,* down + *hedra,* seat.]

ca·the·dral (kə-théedrəl) *n. Abbr.* **cath.** The principal church of a bishop's diocese and one that contains his throne. Also used adjectivally: *a cathedral city.* [Originally *cathedral church,* from Middle English *cathedral,* of a cathedra, from Old French, from Late Latin *cathedrālis,* from Latin *cathedra,* CATHEDRA.]

ca·thep·sin (kə-thépsin, ka-) *n.* Any of a group of enzymes, found in animals, that digest proteins. [Greek *kathepsein,* "to boil down", soften.]

Cath·e·rine II (káth-rin, káthə-), known as Catherine the Great (1729–96). German-born Empress of Russia. She deposed her husband Peter III, who was later murdered. She encouraged the arts, public health, and a more liberal regime. During her reign, Russia extended its borders greatly.

Catherine de Me·di·ci (də méddichee) (1519–89). Wife of Henry II of France. She ruled France, as Regent during the minority of her son, Charles IX (1560–63) and, unofficially, until Charles' death (1574). Her plotting was largely responsible for the massacre of Protestants on St. Bartholemew's day, 1572.

Catherine of Ar·a·gon (árrəgon) (1485–1536). The first wife of Henry VIII of England and mother of Mary I. Henry's insistence on a divorce from her (1533), against the Pope's wishes, marked the beginning of the English Reformation.

Catherine of Bra·gan·za (brə-gánzə) (1638–1705). Portuguese princess and wife of Charles II of England. She married Charles in 1662, but her staunch Roman Catholicism and her failure to produce an heir led to unpopularity with the English people.

cath·e·rine wheel (káth-rin, -ərin) *n.* **1.** A circular firework that rotates around a pin, giving off sparks and coloured flames. Also called "pinwheel". **2.** A circular window with ribs radiating from its centre. [After St. *Catherine* of Alexandria (died A.D. 307), who was condemned to be tortured on a wheel.]

cath·e·ter (káthitər) *n. Medicine.* A slender, flexible tube of metal, rubber, or plastic inserted into a body channel, such as a vein, to introduce or remove fluid. [Late Latin *cathetēr,* from Greek *kathetēr,* something inserted, from *kathienai,* let fall, send down : *kata-,* down + *hienai,* to send.]

cath·e·ter·ise, cath·e·ter·ize (káthitə-rīz) *tr.v.* **-ised, -ising, -ises.** To introduce a catheter into (a bodily passage). **—cath·e·ter·i·sa·tion** *n.*

cath·e·tom·e·ter (káthi-tómmitər) *n.* An instrument that measures vertical distances, especially small differences in the level of liquids in tubes. [*catheto-* (see **catheter**) + -METER.]

ca·thex·is (kə-thék-siss) *n., pl.* **-es** (-seez). The concentration of emotional energy upon some object or idea. [New Latin (adopted to translate German *Besetzung,* the term used by Freud), from Greek *kathexis,* a holding, retention, from *katekhein,* to hold fast : *kata-,* down + *ekhein,* to have, hold.]

cath·ode (káthōd) *n.* **1.** Any negatively charged electrode, as of an electrolytic cell, accumulator, or electronic valve. **2.** The positively charged terminal of a primary cell or of an accumulator that is supplying current. [Greek *kathodos,* way down, descent : *kata-,* down + *hodos,* way.] **—ca·thod·ic** (ka-thóddik, kə-, -thōdik) *adj.* **—ca·thod·i·cal·ly** *adv.*

cathode ray *n.* A stream of electrons emitted by the cathode in an electrical discharge tube.

cath·ode-ray tube (káthōd-ráy ‖ -ray) *n.* A vacuum tube, used in television sets for example, in which a hot cathode emits electrons that are accelerated as a beam through a relatively high-voltage anode, further focused or deflected electrostatically or electromagnetically, and allowed to fall on a fluorescent screen to produce a visible spot of light. Also called "tube".

cath·o·lic (káth-lik, -əlik ‖ ká'ath-) *adj.* **1.** Universal; general; all-inclusive. **2.** Broad and comprehensive in interests, sympathies, or the like; liberal. [Old French *catholique,* from Late Latin *catholicus,* from Greek *katholikos,* from *katholou,* in general : *kata-,* according to + *holou,* neuter genitive of *holos,* whole.] **—ca·thol·i·cal·ly** (kə-thóllikli) *adv.*

Cath·o·lic (káth-lik, -əlik ‖ *West Indian also* ká'ath-) *adj. Abbr.* **C. 1.** Of, pertaining to, or designating the universal Christian church. **2.** Of, pertaining to, or designating the ancient undivided Christian church. **3.** Of, pertaining to, or designating any of those churches that have claimed to be representatives of the ancient undivided church, especially the Roman Catholic Church. **4.** Of, pertaining to, or designating the Western Church as opposed to the Eastern Orthodox Church. ~*n. Abbr.* **C.** A member of any Catholic church; specifically, a Roman Catholic.

Catholic Church *n.* The **Roman Catholic Church** *(see).*

Catholic Epistles *pl.n.* The seven epistles in the New Testament (James, Jude, Peter (two) and John (three)) that were addressed to the universal church rather than to particular Christian communities. Also called "Epistles General".

ca·thol·i·cise, ca·thol·i·cize (kə-thólli-sīz) *tr.v.* **-cised, -cising, -cises. 1.** To make catholic. **2.** To convert to Catholicism.

Ca·thol·i·cism (kə-thólli-siz'm) *n.* The faith, doctrine, system, and practice of a Catholic church, especially the Roman Catholic Church. See **Roman Catholicism.**

cath·o·lic·i·ty (káthə-lissəti) *n.* **1.** The condition or quality of being catholic; liberality; broad-mindedness. **2.** General prevalence or acceptance; universality. **3.** *Capital* **C.** Roman Catholicism.

ca·thol·i·con (kə-thólli-kən ‖ *U.S.* -kon) *n.* A universal remedy; a panacea. [French, from Medieval Latin, from Greek *katholikon*, neuter of *katholikos*, CATHOLIC.]

cat·i·on (kát-ī-ən) *n.* An ion having a positive charge and, in electrolytes, characteristically moving towards a negative electrode. Compare **anion**. [Greek *kation*, neuter of *kation*, present participle of *katienai*, to go down : *kata-*, down + *ienai*, to go.] —**cat·i·on·ic** (-ónnik) *adj.*

cat·kin (kátkin) *n. Botany.* A dense, often drooping flower cluster, such as that of a birch, consisting of small, scalelike flowers. Also called "ament". [Translation of obsolete Dutch *katteken*, "little cat" (the cluster resembles a kitten's tail).]

cat·lap (kát-lap) *n. British Regional & Slang.* Weak tea; slops.

cat·like (kát-līk) *adj.* Like a cat; especially, stealthy and silent.

cat litter *n.* A porous material, **litter** *(see).*

cat·mint (kát-mint) *n.* A hairy, aromatic blue-flowered plant, *Nepeta cataria*, native to Eurasia, to which cats are thought to be attracted. Also called "catnip".

cat nap *n.* A short nap; a light sleep.

Ca·to the Elder (káytō), **Marcus Porcius** (234–149 B.C.). Roman statesman who wrote the first history of Rome. As censor, he opposed luxury and decadence; and he continually warned the Senate of the threat posed by Carthage.

Cato the Younger, Marcus Porcius (95–46 B.C.). Roman politician and great-grandson of Cato the Elder. A conservative opponent of Julius Caesar's political ambitions he supported Pompey against Caesar in the civil war (49–46 B.C.).

cat-o'-nine-tails (káttə-nín-taylz) *n.* A whip consisting of nine knotted cords fastened to a handle, formerly used for flogging. [So called because it leaves marks like the scratches of a cat.]

ca·top·tric (kə-tóptrik) *adj.* Of or pertaining to mirrors and reflected images. [Greek *katoptrikos*, from *katoptron*, mirror : *kata-*, against, + *optos*, visible.] —**ca·top·trics** *n.*

CAT scanner (kat) *n.* A device that makes cross-sectional X-ray recordings of the soft tissues of the body which are then integrated by computer to give a three-dimensional image. See **computerised axial tomography.** —**CAT scan** *n. & v.*

cat's cradle *n.* A child's game in which an intricately looped string is transferred from the hands of one player to the next, resulting in a succession of different loop patterns.

cat-scratch fever (kát-skrach) *n.* A virus disease transmitted to humans following a skin injury, such as a cat scratch, characterised by fever and glandular swelling.

cats-ear (káts-eer) *n.* Any of various European plants of the genus *Hypochoeris*, having yellow dandelion-like flowers.

cat's-eye (káts-ī) *n.* **1.** Any of various semiprecious gems displaying a band of reflected light that shifts position as the gem is turned. **2.** *Capital* **C.** A trademark for a glass reflector set into the road to indicate traffic lanes at night.

cats-foot (káts-fŏŏt) *n.* A small European plant, *Antennaria dioica*, having woolly flowers that form a cluster resembling a cat's paw.

Cats·kill Mountains (kátskil). Mountain range in New York State, United States, west of the Hudson river and part of the Appalachians. The well-forested mountains rising to 1 281 metres (4,203 feet) at Slide Mountain, provide water and resorts for New York. It was the setting for Washington Irving's *"Rip van Winkle"*.

cat's-paw, cats-paw (káts-paw) *n.* **1.** A person used by another as a dupe or tool. **2.** A light breeze that ruffles small areas of a water surface. **3.** *Nautical.* A hitch in the bight of a rope, on which a tackle is hooked. [From the traditional tale of a monkey who used a cat's paw to retrieve nuts from the fire.]

cat's-tail (káts-tayl) *n.* A plant, the **reed mace** *(see).*

cat·suit (kát-sŏŏt, -sewt) *n.* A close-fitting, usually one-piece garment reaching from neck to ankles, worn by women.

catsup. *Chiefly U.S.* Variant of **ketchup.**

cat's whisker *n.* Also *U.S.* **cat whiskers. 1.** A fine, pointed wire formerly used to make electrical contact in a crystal radio receiver. **2.** A wire used to make contact with a semiconductor.

cat's whiskers *pl.n. Informal.* An excellent person or thing. Preceded by *the.*

cattalo. Variant of **catalo.**

Cattegat. See **Kattegat.**

cat·ter·y (káttəri) *n, pl.* **-ies.** A place where cats are bred or boarded out.

cat·tle (kátt'l) *pl.n.* **1.** Various bovid animals of the genus *Bos*, especially those of the domesticated species *B. taurus*, raised in many breeds for meat and dairy products. **2.** *Archaic.* Domestic animals; livestock. [Middle English *catel*, personal property, livestock, from Old North French, from Medieval Latin *capitāle*, property, from Latin, neuter of *capitālis*, chief, primary, from *caput*, head.]

cattle cake *n.* Concentrated cattle food made up into cake-shaped slabs.

cattle grid *n.* A ditch covered by a grid of parallel bars that prevents livestock crossing but allows the passage of vehicles and pedestrians.

cat·tle·man (kátt'l-mən, -man) *n., pl.* **-men** (-mən, -men). A man who tends or rears cattle.

cattle plague *n.* **Rinderpest** *(see).*

cattle stop *n. N.Z.* A cattle grid.

cattle truck *n.* **1.** A railway wagon used for transporting cattle. **2.** *Informal.* Any overcrowded vehicle.

cat·tle·ya (káttli-ə) *n.* Any orchid of the genus *Cattleya*, having showy rose-purple or white flowers. [New Latin, after William *Cattley* (died 1832), British patron of botany.]

cat·ty¹, cat·tie (kátti) *n., pl.* **-ties.** A unit of weight used in China and Southeast Asia generally equivalent to about 0.6 kilogram (1¹⁄₃ pounds avoirdupois). [Malay *kati.*]

catty² *adj.* **-tier, -tiest.** Also **cat·tish** (káttish). Subtly cruel or malicious; spiteful: *a catty remark.* —**cat·ti·ly** *adv.* —**cat·ti·ness** *n.*

catty-cornered. Variant of **cater-cornered.**

Ca·tul·lus (kə-túlləss), **Gaius Valerius** (*c.*84–54 B.C.). Roman lyric poet whose best-known poems tell of his love, from the beginning to the final disillusionment, for Lesbia, an aristocratic Roman woman whose real name was Clodia.

cat·walk (kát-wawk) *n.* A narrow platform or pathway, as on the sides of a bridge or along which models walk to display clothes in a fashion show.

Cau·ca·si·an (kaw-kávz-iən, -kávzh'n ‖ *U.S. also* -kázh'n, -káysh'n) *n.* **1.** A member of the Caucasoid ethnic division; especially, a white person. **2.** A native or inhabitant of the Caucasus. **3.** The group of languages spoken in the area of the Caucasus that are neither Indo-European nor Altaic, including Circassian and Georgian.

~*adj.* **1.** Of or pertaining to the Caucasus, its people, or their languages and culture. **2.** Caucasoid.

Cau·ca·soid (káwkə-soyd) *adj. Anthropology.* Of, pertaining to, characteristic of, or designating a major ethnic division of the human species having certain distinctive physical characteristics such as skin colour varying from very light to brown, and fine hair ranging from straight to wavy or curly. This division is considered to include groups of peoples indigenous to or inhabiting Europe, northern Africa, southwestern Asia, and the Indian subcontinent, and persons of this ancestry in other parts of the world.

~*n.* A member of the Caucasoid ethnic division.

Cau·ca·sus (káwkə-səss). *Russian* **Kav-kaz** (kuf-káss). Also **Cau·ca·si·a** (kaw-kávz-iə, -kázh-, -ə). Historic region between the Black Sea and Caspian Sea. Its earliest inhabitants before 2000 B.C., were Caucasoid peoples, and today, after many invasions, more than 40 languages are spoken, including Circassian, Armenian, Georgian, and Azerbaijani. It is divided in two by the Caucasus Mountains, whose highest peak is Mount Elbrus (5 642 metres; 18,510 feet), the highest mountain in Europe.

cau·cus (káwkəss) *n., pl.* **-cuses** or **-cusses. 1.** A group of activists within a political party, sometimes considered as unrepresentative or undemocratic. **2.** *Chiefly U.S.* **a.** A closed meeting of the members of a political party within a legislative body to decide upon questions of policy and the selection of candidates for office. **b.** These members as a group. **c.** A meeting of the members of a party at local level. [Perhaps from Algonquian *caucauasu*, counsellor (a term recorded by Captain John Smith).]

cau·dad (káwdad) *adv. Anatomy.* Towards the tail or posterior part of the body. Compare **cephalad.** [Latin *cauda*†, tail + -AD.]

cau·dal (káwd'l) *adj.* **1.** *Anatomy.* Of, at, or near the tail or hind parts; posterior. **2.** *Zoology.* Of or pertaining to the tail. [New Latin *caudalis*, from Latin *cauda*†, tail.] —**cau·dal·ly** *adv.*

caudal fin *n.* The tail fin of a fish.

cau·date (káw-dayt) *adj.* Also **cau·dat·ed** (kaw-dáytid ‖ *U.S.* káwdaytid). Having a tail or a tail-like part. [New Latin *caudatus*, from Latin *cauda*†, tail.]

cau·dex (káw-deks) *n., pl.* **-dices** (-di-seez) or **-dexes.** *Botany.* **1.** The thickened base of the stem of some perennial plants. **2.** A woody, trunklike stem, such as that of a tree fern. [Latin *caudex, cōdex*†, stem, tree trunk.]

cau·di·llo (kow-díllo, -díl-yō ‖ *U.S.* -thée-yō) *n., pl.* **-llos. 1.** In Spanish-speaking countries, a usually military leader who sets himself up as a dictator. **2.** *Capital* **C.** The title of general **Franco** as leader of fascist Spain. [Spanish, chieftain, from Late Latin *capitellum*, small head, diminutive of *caput*, head.]

cau·dle (káwd'l) *n.* A warm beverage formerly given to invalids, consisting of wine or ale mixed with sugar, eggs, bread, and various spices. [Middle English *caudel*, from Old North French *caudel, chaudel*, from *chaud*, warm, from Latin *cal(i)dus*.]

caught. Past tense and past participle of **catch.**

CAUCASUS

caul (kawl) *n.* **1.** A portion of the membrane that surrounds a foetus, which is sometimes found on its head at birth and considered a sign of good luck. **2.** The large omentum covering the intestines. [Middle English *calle,* probably from Old French *cale,* cap, from Germanic.]
caul·dron, cal·dron (káwl-drən || kól-) *n.* A large, deep pot or kettle for boiling liquids, often having a large hooped handle so that it can be suspended over an open fire. [Middle English, from Anglo-French and Old North French *caudron,* augmentative of Vulgar Latin *caldario* (unattested), from Latin *caldarium,* hot bath, from *calidus,* hot.]
cau·les·cent (kaw-léss'nt) *adj. Botany.* Having a stem showing above the ground. [Latin *caulis,* stem.]
cau·li·cle (káwlik'l) *n. Botany.* A small stem. [Latin *cauliculus,* diminutive of *caulis,* stem.]
cau·li·flow·er (kólli-flowr || káwli-) *n.* **1.** A plant, *Brassica oleracea botrytis,* related to the cabbage and broccoli and having an enlarged, crowded flower head. **2.** The compact, whitish flower head of this plant, eaten as a vegetable. [Earlier *colie-florie,* probably from Italian *caoli-fiori,* plural of *cavolo-fiore,* "flowered cabbage" : *cavolo,* cabbage, from Late Latin *caulus,* variant of Latin *caulis,* stem + *fiore,* flower, from Latin *flōs* (stem *flōr-*).]
cauliflower ear *n.* An ear swollen and deformed by repeated blows.
cau·line (káw-līn, -lin) *adj. Botany.* Of, having, or growing on a stem. [New Latin *caulinus,* from Latin *caulis,* stalk, stem.]
caulk, calk (kawk) *tr.v.* **caulked, caulking, caulks. 1.** *Nautical.* To make (a boat) watertight by packing seams with oakum or tar. **2.** To make (pipes, for example) watertight or airtight by filling in cracks. [Middle English *ca(u)lken,* from Old North French *cauquer,* to trample, tread, from Latin *calcāre,* from *calx* (stem *calc-*), a heel.] **—caulk·er** *n.*
caus·al (káwz'l) *adj.* **1.** Pertaining to, constituting, or involving a cause: *a number of causal factors.* **2.** Expressing a cause or reason. **—caus·al·ly** *adv.*
cau·sal·gi·a (kaw-zál-ji-ə, -jə) *n.* A burning pain felt in a limb along the course of a peripheral nerve that has been injured. It may be accompanied by changes in the appearance of the skin. [New Latin, from Greek *kausos,* fever, burning + -ALGIA.]
cau·sal·i·ty (kaw-zál-əti) *n., pl.* **-ties. 1.** The relationship between cause and effect. **2.** A causal agency, force, or quality.
cau·sa·tion (kaw-záysh'n) *n.* **1.** The act or process of causing. **2.** The relationship between cause and effect.
caus·a·tive (káwzətiv) *adj.* **1.** Functioning as a cause; effective. **2.** Designating a verb or verbal affix that expresses causation. In the phrase *to fell a tree, fell* is a causative verb.
~n. A word or form expressing causation. **—caus·a·tive·ly** *adv.*
cause (kawz) *n.* **1.** That which produces an effect, result, or consequence; the person, event, or condition responsible for an action or result. **2.** A basis for an action or decision; ground; reason; motive. **3.** Good or sufficient reason or ground. **4.** A goal, principle, or concern which is actively pursued: *the cause of mental health.* **5.** The interests of a person or group engaged in a struggle: *the cause of the oppressed.* **6.** *Law.* **a.** The ground for legal action. **b.** A lawsuit. **7.** *Archaic.* A subject under debate or discussion.
~tr.v. **caused, causing, causes.** To be the cause of; make happen; bring about. [Middle English, from Old French, from Latin *causa*†, reason, purpose, motive, lawsuit.] **—caus·a·ble** *adj.* **—cause·less** *adj.* **—caus·er** *n.*
Usage: *cause, reason, occasion.* These nouns denote things or prior conditions that bring about, or are associated with, certain effects. A *cause,* singly or as one of a series, must exist for an effect logically to occur: *Deficiency in vitamin C is the cause of scurvy. Reason* refers to what explains the occurrence or nature of an effect in terms of human thought rather than objective or external factors: *There was no reason to leave.* An *occasion* is the situation or time that permits existing causes to come into play: *The occasion for the robbery was the absence of the regular night watchman.*
cause cé·lè·bre (kōz se-lébr, say-, sə-, -léb) *n., pl.* **causes célèbres** *(pronounced as singular)* **1.** A celebrated legal case. **2.** A controversial issue arousing heated public debate and partisanship. [French.]
cause list *n. Law.* A list of cases awaiting trial.
cau·se·rie (kōz-əree, -əri || -ə-rée, -rée) *n.* **1.** An informal talk or chat. **2.** A short, conversational piece of writing. [French, from *causer,* to talk.]
cause·way (káwz-way) *n.* **1.** A raised roadway, as across water or marshland. **2.** A paved footpath. [Middle English *caucewei* : *cauce,* from Old North French *cauciee,* from Vulgar Latin *calciāta* (unattested), paved (as with limestone), from Latin *calx* (stem *calc-*), limestone, small stone, from Greek *khalix,* small stone + *wei,* WAY.]
caus·tic (káwstik, kóstik) *adj.* **1.** Able to burn, corrode, dissolve, or otherwise eat away by chemical action. **2.** Marked by sharp and bitter wit; cutting: *caustic comments.* **3.** *Optics.* Of or designating a curve or surface of revolution formed by rays of an initially parallel beam of light after they have been reflected or refracted by an optical system that does not bring the rays to a single focus. —See Usage Note at **sarcastic.**
~n. **1.** A caustic material or substance. **2.** A caustic curve or surface. [Latin *causticus,* from Greek *kaustikos,* from *kaiein,* to burn.] **—caus·ti·cal·ly** *adv.* **—caus·tic·i·ty** (kawss-tíssəti, koss-) *n.*
caustic lime *n.* **Calcium hydroxide** *(see).*
caustic potash *n.* **Potassium hydroxide** *(see).*
caustic soda *n.* **Sodium hydroxide** *(see).*
cau·ter·ise, cau·ter·ize (káwtər-īz) *tr.v.* **-ised, -ising, -ises.** To burn or sear with a cautery. [Old French *cauteriser,* from Late Latin *cautērizāre,* to brand, from Greek *kautēriazein,* from *kautērion,* branding iron.] **—cau·ter·i·sa·tion** (-ī-záysh'n || *U.S.* -i-) *n.*
cau·ter·y (káwtəri) *n., pl.* **-ies. 1.** A caustic agent or a very hot or very cold instrument used, especially in the treatment of wounds, to destroy abnormal tissue. **2.** The act of using a cautery. [Latin *cautērium,* branding iron, from Greek *kautērion,* from *kaiein,* to burn.]
cau·tion (káwsh'n) *n.* **1. a.** Forethought to avoid danger or harm. **b.** An instinctive avoidance of risks and danger. **2.** A warning; an admonishment. **3.** *British Law.* An official warning, given to a person suspected of or arrested for a crime, that if he chooses to speak, anything he says may be set down and used in evidence. **4.** *Informal.* Someone or something that is striking or amusing.
~tr.v. **cautioned, -tioning, -tions. 1.** To warn against danger; put on guard. **2.** *British Law.* To give a caution to (a person suspected of a crime). —See Synonyms at **warn.** [Middle English *caucion,* from Old French *caution,* from Latin *cautiō* (stem *cautiōn-*), a guarding, from *cavēre* (past participle *cautus*), to watch, take heed.]
cau·tion·ar·y (káwsh'n-əri, -ri || *U.S.* -erri) *adj.* Giving or serving as a warning.
caution money *n. British.* Money deposited as a surety, as for example against possible debts or damage.
cau·tious (káwshəss) *adj.* **1.** Showing or practising caution; wary; careful. **2.** Showing prudence and deliberation; guarded; tentative: *cautious optimism.* **—cau·tious·ly** *adv.* **—cau·tious·ness** *n.*
cav. cavalry.
cav·al·cade (kávv'l-káyd || -kayd) *n.* **1.** A ceremonial procession, especially of horsemen or carriages. **2.** A colourful procession or display. **3.** A succession: *a cavalcade of stars.* [French, from Italian *cavalcata,* from *cavalcare,* to ride on horseback, from Vulgar Latin *caballicāre* (unattested), from Latin *caballus,* horse.]
cav·a·lier (kávvə-léer) *n.* **1.** A gentleman accomplished in arms and horsemanship. **2.** A gallant courtly gentleman, especially one escorting a lady. **3.** *Capital* **C.** A supporter of Charles I in his struggles against the Parliamentarians; a Royalist.
~adj. **1.** Showing arrogant self-assurance; offhand. **2.** Carefree and gay. **3.** *Capital* **C.** Of or pertaining to the Cavaliers. [French, from Italian *cavaliere,* from Late Latin *caballārius,* horseman, rider, from Latin *caballus,* horse.] **—cav·a·lier·ly** *adv.*
Cavalier poets *pl.n.* A group of English poets, including Lovelace and Suckling, associated with the court of Charles I.
ca·val·la (kə-vál-ə) *n., pl.* **-las** or **cavalla.** Also **ca·val·ly** (-vál-i) *pl.* **-lies.** Any of various tropical marine food fishes of the family Carangidae. [Spanish *caballa,* horse mackerel, from Late Latin, feminine of Latin *caballus,* horse.]
cav·al·ry (kávv'l-ri) *n., pl.* **-ries.** *Abbr.* **cav. 1.** Troops mounted on horseback. **2.** A highly mobile army unit using armoured vehicles, helicopters, and the like. [French *cavallerie,* from Italian *cavalleria,* cavalry, chivalry, from *cavaliere,* CAVALIER.] **—cav·al·ry·man** *n.*
Cav·an (kávv'n). *Irish* **Cabhan.** County in the Republic of Ireland. It is a predominantly hilly region, infertile and boggy with many lakes.
cav·a·ti·na (kávvə-téenə) *n. Music.* **1.** An aria in a simple style. **2.** An instrumental piece or passage in a similar style. [Italian.]
cave[1] (kayv) *n.* **1.** A hollow beneath the earth's surface, often having an opening in the side of a hill or cliff. **2.** *British.* A dissident group formally seceding from a political party.
~v. **caved, caving, caves.** *—tr.* To hollow out. *—intr.* To explore caves. [Middle English, from Old French, from Latin *cava,* from the neuter plural of *cavus,* hollow.]
ca·ve[2] (káyvi) *n. British Slang.* A watch or lookout. Used by schoolchildren in the phrase *keep cave.*
~interj. (káy-vée) *British Slang.* Used by schoolchildren as a warning signal. [Latin, "beware!"]
ca·ve·at (kávvi-at, káyvi- || *U.S. also* kaávi-) *n.* **1.** *Law.* A formal application filed by an interested party to a court or officer, requesting the postponement of proceedings until he is heard. **2.** A warning or caution. [Latin, let him beware, from *cavēre,* to beware, take care.]
caveat emp·tor (émp-tawr) *n.* The principle in commerce that the buyer alone is responsible for assessing the quality of a purchase before buying it. [Latin, "let the buyer beware".]
cave·fish (káyv-fish) *n., pl.* **-fishes** or collectively **cavefish.** Any of various freshwater fishes of the family Amblyopsidae, of subterranean waters, having rudimentary eyes. Also called "blindfish".
cave in *intr.v.* **1.** To fall in; collapse, as from being undermined. **2.** *Informal.* To cease resistance. *—tr.v.* To cause to collapse.
cave-in (káyv-in) *n.* **1.** An act of caving in. **2.** A place where a structure, such as a mineshaft, has caved in.
Cav·ell (kávv'l; *also, wrongly,* kə-vél), **Edith** (1865–1915). British nurse who remained in Brussels after the German occupation (1915), helping to smuggle Allied troops to the Dutch border. Caught by the Germans, she was executed by firing squad.
cave·man (káyv-man) *n., pl.* **-men** (-men). **1.** A prehistoric man who lived in caves. **2.** *Informal.* A man who is crude or brutal, especially towards women.
cav·en·dish (kávv'ndish) *n.* Tobacco that has been sweetened and moulded into cakes. [Perhaps from the name of the first manufacturer.]
Cav·en·dish (kávv'ndish), **Henry** (1731–1810). English physicist and chemist, who discovered (1766) the properties of hydrogen and later established that water was a compound of hydrogen and oxy-

gen. Using the universal gravitational constant, he measured the density of the earth in 1798.

cave painting *n.* **1.** A painting made by prehistoric man on a cave wall. **2.** Prehistoric art found on cave walls.

cav·ern (kávvərn) *n.* **1.** A large cave. **2.** A large chamber in a cave, especially one hollowed out by the action of water.
~*tr.v.* **caverned, -erning, -erns. 1.** To enclose in or as if in a cavern. **2.** To hollow. Used with *out.* [Middle English *caverne*, from Old French, from Latin *caverna*, from *cavus*, hollow.]

cav·ern·ous (kávvər-nəss) *adj.* **1.** Filled with caverns. **2.** Like a cavern in depth, vastness, or darkness. **3.** Filled with cavities; porous. —**cav·ern·ous·ly** *adv.*

cav·es·son (kávviss'n) *n.* A strong noseband used when breaking in difficult horses. [French *caveçon,* from Italian *cavezzone,* augmentative of *cavezza,* halter, from Medieval Latin *capitium,* head-covering, from Latin *caput* (stem *capit-*), head.]

ca·vet·to (kə-véttō, ka-) *n., pl.* **-vetti** (-véttee) or **-tos.** A concave moulding for cornices, shaped like a circular quadrant. [Italian, from *cavo,* hollow, from Latin *cavus.*]

cav·i·ar, cav·i·are (kávvi-aar, -ár) *n.* The roe of a sturgeon, salted, seasoned, and eaten as a delicacy. [Earlier *caviari, cavialy,* probably from French *caviar,* from Italian *caviaro,* from Turkish *kãvyár.*]

cav·il (kávvil, kávv'l) *intr.v.* **-illed** or *U.S.* **-iled, -illing** or *U.S.* **-iling, -ils.** To raise unnecessary or trivial objections; carp. Used with *at, about,* or *with.*
~*n.* A captious or trivial objection. [French *caviller,* from Latin *cavillārī,* to satirise, criticise, from *cavilla,* a jeering.] —**cav·il·ler** *n.*

cav·ing (kávving) *n.* The exploration of caves as a sport or scientific pursuit. —**cav·er** *n.*

cav·i·ta·tion (kávvi-táysh'n) *n.* The sudden formation and collapse of low-pressure bubbles in liquids by means of mechanical forces, such as those resulting from rotation of a marine propeller. [From CAVITY.]

cav·i·ty (kávvəti) *n., pl.* **-ties. 1.** A hollow or hole. **2.** A hollow area within the body: *a sinus cavity.* **3.** A pitted area in a tooth caused by **caries** *(see).* —See Synonyms at **hole.** [French *cavité,* Old French *cavete,* from Late Latin *cavitās,* hollowness, from Latin *cavus,* hollow.]

cavity resonator *n. Electronics.* A microwave device containing an enclosed space in which an oscillating electromagnetic field can be maintained. The dimensions of the cavity determine the frequency of the oscillations. Also called "rhumbatron".

cavity wall *n.* A wall consisting of two layers separated by an air space for insulation. It is often an outside wall of a building using brick as the outer layer and breeze block as the inner layer.

ca·vort (kə-vórt) *intr.v.* **-vorted, -vorting, -vorts.** To bound or prance about in a sprightly manner; caper. [Perhaps variant of CURVET.]

Ca·vour (kə-vōōr), **Count Camillo Benso di** (1810–61). Italian liberal statesman who helped to unify Italy. Prime minister of Sardinia-Piedmont (1852–59, 1860–61), he made various alliances to oust the Austrians from Italy and, with Giuseppe **Garibaldi,** created the kingdom of Italy under the king of Sardinia-Piedmont, Victor Emmanuel II.

ca·vy (kávyi) *n., pl.* **-vies.** Any of various short-tailed or apparently tailless South American rodents of the family Caviidae, which includes the guinea pig. [New Latin *Cavia,* probably from Galibi *cabiai.*]

caw (kaw) *n.* The hoarse, raucous sound uttered by a crow or similar bird.
~*intr.v.* **cawed, cawing, caws.** To utter a caw. [Imitative.]

Caw·ley (káwli), **Evonne,** born Evonne Goolagong (1951–). Australian tennis player who won the Wimbledon ladies' singles championship twice (1971, 1980); the doubles championship (1974); and three Australian singles championships (1974, 1975, 1976).

Cawnpore. See **Kanpur.**

Cax·ton (kákstən), **William** (*c.*1422–91). The first English printer and publisher, previously a cloth merchant. *Recuyell of the Historyes of Troye* (1475) was the first book printed in English. He set up his own press (1476) at Westminster where he published and printed *Canterbury Tales* (1478) and the first illustrated English book, an encyclopedia, *Myrrour of the Worlde* (1481).

cay (kee, kay) *n.* A small, low islet composed largely of coral or sand; a key. [Spanish *cayo,* probably from Old French *quai, cay,* QUAY.]

Cay·enne (kay-én). The capital and chief seaport of French Guiana, situated on the coast of the Île de Cayenne. The French founded it in 1643, and it was a penal colony (1854–1938).

cay·enne pepper (kay-én || kī-) A condiment made from the very pungent fruit of various plants of the capsicum genus. Also called "cayenne", "red pepper". [Earlier *kian, chian* (influenced by CAYENNE), from Tupi *kyinha.*]

cay·man, cai·man (káymən) *n., pl.* **-mans.** Any of various tropical American crocodiles of the genus *Caiman* and related genera, resembling and closely related to alligators. [Spanish and Portuguese *caiman,* from Carib *acayuman.*]

Cay·man Islands (káy-mən || -mán). A group of three low-lying coral islands in the Caribbean Sea approximately 320 kilometres (200 miles) northwest of Jamaica. The largest, Grand Cayman, includes Georgetown, the capital. Little Cayman and Cayman Brac make up the rest of this British colony. Columbus discovered them in 1503.

Ca·yu·ga (kay-yōōgə, kī-) *n., pl.* **-gas** or collectively **Cayuga. 1.** A member of an American Indian people formerly living around Ca-

yuga and Seneca lakes in central New York State. **2.** The Iroquoian language spoken by this people. —**Ca·yu·ga** *adj.*

cay·use (kī-yōóss) *n. Western U.S.* A horse; especially, an Indian pony. [After the CAYUSE Indians.]

Cay·use (kī-yōóss) *n., pl.* **-uses** or collectively **Cayuse. 1.** A member of an American Indian people of Oregon. **2.** The Sahaptin language of this tribe. —**Cay·use** *adj.*

cazique. Variant of **cacique.**

Cb The symbol for the element columbium.

CB Citizens' Band (radio).

C.B. Companion of the (Order of the) Bath.

CBC Canadian Broadcasting Corporation.

C.B.D. cash before delivery.

C.B.E. Commander of the (Order of the) British Empire.

C.B.I. Confederation of British Industry.

cc cubic centimetre.

cc. chapters.

c.c., C.C. carbon copy.

C.C.A. County Councils Association.

C.C.F. 1. Combined Cadet Force. **2.** Cooperative Commonwealth Federation (of Canada).

C clef *n. Music.* A clef sign used to form any of three clefs, soprano, alto, or tenor, by locating middle C on, respectively, the lowest line of the staff, the middle line, or the fourth (next to the highest) line.

CCTV Closed Circuit TV.

cd *Physics.* candela.

Cd The symbol for the element cadmium.

c.d. cash discount.

C.D. 1. Civil Defence. **2.** Corps Diplomatique. **3. CD** Compact disc.

Cdr Commander.

Ce The symbol for the element cerium.

C.E. 1. chemical engineer. **2.** chief engineer. **3.** civil engineer. **4.** common Entrance. **5.** common era.

ce·a·no·thus (see-ə-nóthəss) *n.* Any shrub of the North American genus *Ceanothus,* often grown for ornament; especially, the **California lilac** *(see).* [New Latin, from Greek *keanōthos,* a type of thistle.]

cease (seess) *v.* **ceased, ceasing, ceases.** —*tr.* To put an end to; discontinue. —*intr.* **1.** To come to an end; stop. **2.** To desist; discontinue. Often used with *from.*
~*n.* Pause or end. Used in the phrase *without cease.* [Middle English *ces(s)en,* from Old French *cesser,* from Latin *cessāre,* to delay, stop, frequentative of *cēdere* (past participle *cessus*), to CEDE.]

cease-fire (seéss-fír, -fír) *n.* **1.** An order to cease firing. **2.** A suspension of active hostilities; a truce.

cease·less (seéss-ləss, -liss) *adj.* Without stop; endless. See Synonyms at **continual.** —**cease·less·ly** *adv.*

Ceau·şes·cu (chow-shéskōō), **Nicolae** (1918–89). Romanian statesman. As Romania's president (1974–89) he maintained close political ties with the U.S.S.R., but restricted its interference in Romania's national affairs. He was executed in 1989.

Cec·il (síss'l; *also, wrongly,* séss'l), **Lord (Edward Christian) David (Gascoyne)** (1902–86). British literary critic. Professor of English literature at Oxford University (1948–70), he was known for his biographies of literary figures, including Jane Austen and Sir Walter Scott.

Cecil, William. See **Burghley, William Cecil, 1st Baron.**

cecum. *U.S.* Variant of **caecum.**

ce·dar (seédər) *n.* **1.** Any of several coniferous evergreen trees of the genus *Cedrus,* native to the Old World and having spreading branches and barrel-shaped cones, such as the cedar of Lebanon and the **deodar** *(see).* **2.** Any of various similar evergreen trees, mostly of the genera *Thuja* and *Juniperus.* **3.** The durable, aromatic, often reddish wood of a cedar. [Middle English *cedre,* from Old French, from Latin *cedrus,* cedar, juniper, from Greek *kedros†.*]

cedar of Lebanon *n.* A tall evergreen tree, *Cedrus libani,* of Asia Minor, having level spreading branches, short dark needles, and fragrant hard wood. [Translation of Late Latin *cedrus libani* (translation of Hebrew *arzē Lәbānōn*).]

cede (seed) *tr.v.* **ceded, ceding, cedes. 1.** To surrender possession of officially or formally. **2.** To yield; grant. —See Synonyms at **relinquish.** [French *céder,* from Latin *cēdere,* to withdraw, yield.]

ce·di (seédi) *n.* **1.** The basic monetary unit of Ghana, equal to 100 pesewa. **2.** A note worth one cedi.

ce·dil·la (si-díllə) *n.* A mark ( ) placed beneath the letter *c* in the spelling of French, Portuguese, and older Spanish, to indicate that the letter is to be pronounced (s), as in the French word *garçon.* The cedilla is also used for various purposes in Turkish and Romanian spelling. [Obsolete Spanish *cedilla,* diminutive of *ceda,* the letter zed, from Late Latin *zēta,* ZETA (so called because a small *z* was formerly used to make a hard *c* sibilant).]

Cee·fax (see-faks) *n.* A trademark for a teletext service broadcast by the BBC, providing information on a wide variety of subjects.

C.E.G.B. Central Electricity Generating Board.

cei·ba (sáybə) *n.* Any of various large tropical trees of the genus *Ceiba,* which includes the kapok tree, the source of the silky fibre kapok. [New Latin, from Spanish, probably from Arawakan.]

ceil (seel) *tr.v.* **ceiled, ceiling, ceils. 1.** To line (a ceiling), as with plaster or panelling. **2.** To provide (a ship) with interior planking. [Middle English *celen,* perhaps a back-formation from CEILING.]

cei·lidh (káyli) *n.* An Irish or Scottish social gathering with traditional music, dancing, and storytelling. [Gaelic.]

ceil·ing (seeling) *n.* **1.** The interior upper surface of a room. **2.** The planking applied to the interior framework of a ship. **3.** A maximum limit, especially on wages or prices. **4.** Any of various vertical boundaries, especially of atmospheric visibility, cloud cover altitude, or operable aircraft altitude. [Middle English *celing†*.]

ceil·om·e·ter (see-lómmitər) *n.* A photoelectric instrument for ascertaining cloud heights. [CEIL(ING) + -METER.]

cel·a·don, cé·la·don (séllə-don, -d'n) *n.* **1.** Pale to very pale green. **2.** Celadon ware. [French *céladon,* from *Céladon,* wan character in d'Urfé's *L'Astrée* (1607–19).] **—cel·a·don** *adj.*

cel·a·don·ite (séllə-don-īt, -dən-) *n.* A soft mica having a green hue and a high iron content.

celadon ware *n.* A kind of pottery with a pale greyish-green glaze, originally produced in China.

Ce·lae·no¹ (si-léenō). *Greek Mythology.* One of the **Pleiades** *(see).*

Celaeno² *n.* One of the six stars in the Pleiades cluster visible to the naked eye. [After CELAENO.]

cel·an·dine (séllən-deen, -dīn) *n.* **1.** A plant, *Chelidonium majus,* native to Eurasia, having deeply divided leaves, yellow flowers, and yellow-orange juice. Also called "greater celandine". **2.** The **lesser celandine** *(see).* [Middle English *celidoine,* from Old French, from Medieval Latin *celidonia,* from Latin *chelidonia, chelidonium,* from Greek *khelidonion,* from *khelidōn,* swallow (the ancients associated the plant with the habits of the swallow).]

–cele¹ *n. comb. form.* Indicates a tumour or hernia; for example, **cystocele.** [From Greek *kēlē†,* tumour.]

–cele². *U.S.* Variant of **-coel.**

Celebes. See **Sulawesi.**

cel·e·brant (séllibrənt) *n.* **1.** The priest officiating at the celebration of the Eucharist or other religious ceremony. **2.** A person who participates in a religious ceremony or rite.

cel·e·brate (sélli-brayt) *v.* **-brated, -brating, -brates.** *—tr.* **1.** To mark or observe (a special day or event) with ceremonies of respect, festivity, or rejoicing. **2.** To perform (a religious ceremony). **3.** To extol; praise. *—intr.* **1.** To observe an occasion with appropriate ceremony, festivity, or merrymaking. **2.** To perform a religious ceremony. —See Synonyms at **observe.** [Latin *celebrāre,* to frequent, fill, celebrate, from *celeber,* numerous, much frequented.] **—cel·e·bra·tion** (-bráysh'n) *n.* **—cel·e·bra·tor** (-braytər) *n.*

cel·e·brat·ed (sélli-braytid) *adj.* Famous.

ce·leb·ri·ty (si-lébbrəti) *n., pl.* **-ties. 1.** A famous person. **2.** Notoriety or renown; fame. [Latin *celebritās* (stem *celebritāt-*), from *celeber,* numerous.]

ce·le·ri·ac (si-lérri-ak, sə-, -léer-i-) *n.* A variety of celery, *Apium graveolens rapaceum,* cultivated for its edible, turnip-like root. [Unexplained derivative of CELERY.]

ce·ler·i·ty (si-lérrəti, sə-) *n. Formal.* Swiftness; quickness; speed. [Middle English *celerite,* from Old French, from Latin *celeritās,* from *celer,* swift.]

cel·er·y (sélləri) *n.* A plant, *Apium graveolens dulce,* native to Eurasia and widely cultivated for its edible blanched stalks and its small seeds, used as seasoning. [French *céleri,* from Italian (Lombardy dialect) *seleri,* plural of *selero,* from Late Latin *selīnum,* from Greek *selinon†,* celery.]

ce·les·ta (si-léstə, sə-) *n.* Also **ce·leste** (-lést). A musical instrument having a keyboard and metal plates struck by hammers that produce bell-like tones. [French *célesta,* coined from *céleste,* celestial, from Latin *caelestis,* CELESTIAL.]

ce·les·ti·al (si-lésti-əl, sə- ‖ -léss-chəl) *adj.* **1.** Of or pertaining to the sky or the heavens. **2.** Of, from, or suggestive of heaven; divine; heavenly. **3.** *Usually capital* **C.** Of or pertaining to the Chinese people or to the former Chinese Empire. [Middle English, from Old French, from Latin *caelestis,* from *caelum†,* sky, heaven.]

celestial body *n.* Any object naturally occurring in space, especially a planet, star, or comet.

Celestial Empire *n.* The Chinese Empire. [Translation of Chinese *tiān cháo,* literally "celestial dynasty" (from the belief that the emperors were sons of Heaven).]

celestial equator *n.* A great circle on the celestial sphere in the same plane as the earth's equator. Also called "equinoctial", "equinoctial circle", "equinoctial line".

celestial globe *n.* A model of the celestial sphere showing the stars and other celestial bodies.

celestial guidance *n.* The guiding of missiles or spacecraft by reference to the positions of one or more celestial bodies.

celestial latitude *n.* The angular distance of a celestial body north (counted positive) or south (counted negative) of the ecliptic, measured on the great circle through the body and the poles of the ecliptic. Also called "ecliptic latitude".

celestial longitude *n.* The angular distance of a celestial body from the vernal equinox, measured eastwards along the ecliptic to its intersection with the great circle through the body and the poles of the ecliptic. Also called "ecliptic longitude".

celestial mechanics *n.* The science of the motion of celestial bodies under the influence of gravitational forces.

celestial navigation *n.* Ship or aircraft navigation based on the positions of celestial bodies. Also called "astronavigation".

celestial pole *n.* Either of two diametrically opposite points at which the extensions of the earth's axis intersect the celestial sphere.

celestial sphere *n.* An imaginary sphere of infinite extent with the earth as its centre. The stars, planets, and other celestial bodies appear to be located on its imaginary surface.

cel·es·tite (séllist-īt, si-lést-) *n.* A white, red-brown, or light-blue strontium ore, essentially strontium sulphate, $SrSO_4$. [German *Zölestin,* from Latin *caelestis,* CELESTIAL (from its blue colour).]

cel·i·ba·cy (séllibə-si) *n.* The condition of being unmarried or sexually chaste, especially by reason of religious vows. [Latin *caelibātus,* celibacy, from *caelebs†* (stem *caelib-*), unmarried.]

cel·i·bate (sélli-bət, -bit) *n.* One who remains unmarried, especially by religious vow.

~adj. **1.** Unmarried. **2.** Not having sexual intercourse; chaste. [From Latin *caelebs†* (stem *caelib-*), unmarried.]

cell (sel) *n.* **1.** A small, narrow room, as in a prison or monastic institution. **2.** Any small and humble dwelling. **3.** A small religious house dependent on a larger one, such as a priory within an abbey. **4.** The primary organisational unit of a subversive or revolutionary political group, consisting of a few members usually living or working in the same place. **5.** A small group of Christian lay persons working for the propagation of the faith. **6.** *Biology.* The smallest structural unit of an organism that is capable of independent functioning, consisting of one or more nuclei, cytoplasm, various organelles, and inanimate matter, all surrounded by a semipermeable plasma membrane. Plant cells have cellulose outer cell walls. **7.** *Biology.* A small, enclosed cavity or space, such as a compartment in a honeycomb or within a plant ovary, or an area bordered by veins in an insect's wing. **8. a.** A single unit for electrolysis or for conversion of chemical into electric energy, usually consisting of a container with electrodes and an electrolyte. **b.** A single unit that converts radiant energy into electric energy: *a solar cell.* **9.** *Computing.* The smallest unit of data, capable of storing a single bit in part of a computer store. [Middle English *celle,* from Old French, from Latin *cella,* cella, storeroom, chamber.]

cel·la (séllə) *n., pl.* **cellae** (séllee) The inner room of an ancient Greek or Roman temple. [Latin *cella,* cella, CELL.]

cel·lar (séllər) *n.* **1.** A room used for storage, usually beneath the ground or under a building. **2.** A dark, cool room for storing wines. **3.** A stock of wines.

~tr.v. **cellared, -laring, -lars.** To store in a cellar. [Middle English *celer,* from Anglo-French, from Late Latin *cellārium,* storehouse, larder, from Latin *cella,* storeroom, CELL.]

cel·lar·age (séllərij) *n.* **1.** A fee charged for storage in a cellar. **2.** The amount of storage space in a cellar.

cel·lar·er (séllərər) *n.* The member of a monastic community responsible for the maintenance of adequate supplies of food and drink. [Middle English *celerer,* from Anglo-French, from Late Latin *cellāriārius,* from *cellārium,* CELLAR.]

cel·lar·et (séllər-ét, -et) *n.* A cabinet used for storing bottles of wine. [Diminutive of CELLAR.]

cell division *n.* The process by which a cell gives rise to two daughter cells. See **amitosis, meiosis, mitosis.**

celled (seld) *adj.* Having cells of the specified type or number. Used in combination: *single-celled.*

Cel·li·ni (che-léeni, chə-), **Benvenuto** (1500–71). Italian goldsmith and sculptor, famous also for his *Autobiography,* which described court life in Rome, Florence, and Paris, and the siege of Rome (1527). *Perseus,* at the Loggia dei Lanzi, Florence, is considered his masterpiece as a sculptor.

cell membrane *n.* A **plasma membrane** *(see).*

cel·lo (chéllō) *n., pl.* **-los.** A four-stringed instrument of the violin family, pitched lower than the viola but higher than the double bass, and held upright between the knees. Also called "violoncello". [Short for VIOLONCELLO.] **—cel·list** (chéllist) *n.*

Usage: It is no longer standard practice to use an apostrophe with this word. *'Cello* and *'cellist* are occasionally used, but even in formal and technical contexts this spelling is old-fashioned.

cel·loi·din (sə-lóydin, se-) *n.* A pure pyroxylin in which specimens being sectioned for microscopical examination are embedded. [CELL(ULOSE) + -OID + -IN.]

cel·lo·phane (séllə-fayn) *n.* A thin, flexible, transparent cellulose material made from wood pulp and used as a moistureproof wrapping. [CELL(ULOSE) + -PHANE.]

cell·phone, cellular telephone *n.* A portable telephone, radio-operated within a small geographical unit or "cell".

cel·lu·lar (séllewlər) *adj.* **1.** Pertaining to or resembling a cell. **2.** Consisting of or containing a cell or cells. **3.** Containing a number of small compartments or cavities. Said of rock. **4.** Loosely woven: *a cellular blanket.*

cel·lu·lase (séllew-layz, -layss) *n.* Any of several enzymes found in fungi, bacteria, and lower animals, that hydrolyse cellulose. [CELLUL(OSE) + -ASE.]

cel·lule (séllewl) *n. Biology.* A small cell. [French, monk's cell, from Latin *cellula,* small apartment, diminutive of *cella,* CELL.]

cel·lu·lite (séllew-līt, -léet) *n.* A fatty deposit, found particularly around the thighs and buttocks and the tops of the arms. [CELLUL(E) + ITE.]

cel·lu·li·tis (séllew-lītiss) *n.* Inflammation of tissue between adjacent organs, causing pain and fever. [New Latin : Latin *cellula,* cell (see **cellule**) + -ITIS.]

Cel·lu·loid (séllew-loyd) *n.* A trademark for a colourless, flammable material made from cellulose nitrate and camphor and used for toys, toilet articles, and photographic film, and as a substitute for materials such as ivory and amber.

cel·lu·lose (séllew-lōss, -lōz) *n.* A polysaccharide, $(C_6H_{10}O_5)_x$, of high tensile strength, the main constituent of plant cell walls and used in the manufacture of many fibrous products, including paper, textiles, and explosives. [French, from *cellule,* biological cell, CELLULE.] **—cel·lu·los·ic** (-lō-sik, -zik) *adj.*

cellulose acetate *n.* A cellulose resin used in lacquers, photo-

graphic film, transparent sheeting, and cigarette filters.
cellulose nitrate *n.* A tough, thermoplastic ester of cellulose made by treating cellulose with nitric acid and sulphuric acid. It is used in explosives, plastics, and lacquers. In nontechnical usage, also called "nitrocellulose".
cell wall *n.* The rigid outermost layer of a plant cell, consisting of cellulose and other polysaccharides.
celom. *U.S.* Variant of **coelom.**
Cel·si·us (sél-se-əss || -shəss) *adj. Abbr.* **C** Of or pertaining to a temperature scale that registers the freezing point of water as 0°C and the boiling point as 100°C under normal atmospheric pressure. Also called "centigrade". The designation *Celsius* has been official since 1948, but *centigrade* remains in common use. [After Anders *Celsius* (1701–1744), Swedish astronomer who devised the scale.]
celt (selt) *n.* A prehistoric axelike tool. [Late Latin *celtis, celtes*†, chisel, a possible misreading of *certe,* surely, in a disputed text of the Vulgate (Job 19:24) (influenced in form by CELT).]
Celt (kelt, *rarely* selt) *n.* **1.** A member of an ancient people of western and central Europe, including the Britons, the Irish, and the Gauls. **2.** A speaker or a descendant of speakers of a Celtic language. [French *Celte,* singular of *Celtes,* from Latin *Celtae,* from Greek *Keltoi*†.]
Celt·ic (kéltik, *also (rarely except in the name of the Scottish football team)* séltik) *n. Abbr.* **C., Celt.** A subfamily of the Indo-European family of languages, subdivided into the Brythonic branch, consisting of Cornish, Welsh, and Breton, and the Goidelic branch, consisting of Irish Gaelic, Scottish Gaelic, and Manx.
~adj. Of or pertaining to the Celtic people and languages.
Celtic Church *n.* The Church as it existed throughout the British Isles until the late sixth century, and as it held out, at variance with the Church of Rome, in Wales and Ireland for some time.
Celtic cross *n.* An upright cross superimposed on a circle.
Celt·i·cism (kélti-siz'm, *rarely* sélti-) *n.* A Celtic custom or idiom.
Celt·i·cist (kélti-sist, *rarely* sélti-) *n.* A specialist in Celtic culture.
Celtic Sea. A section of the Atlantic Ocean bounded by southern Ireland, Wales, Cornwall, Brittany, and southwest England.
cem·ba·lo (chémbəlō) *n., pl.* **-los.** A harpsichord. [Italian, short for *clavicembalo,* from Medieval Latin *clāvicymbalum* : Latin *clāvis,* key + *cymbalum,* CYMBAL.] **—cem·ba·list** *n.*
ce·ment (si-mént, sə-) *n.* **1.** Any of various construction adhesives, consisting essentially of powdered, calcined rock and clay materials, that form a paste with water and can be moulded or poured to set as a solid mass, especially when mixed with sand and aggregate to form concrete. See **Portland cement, hydraulic cement. 2.** Any substance that hardens to act as an adhesive; glue. **3.** Any of various substances used in dentistry for example to form fillings or fix crowns in place. **4.** *Geology.* A chemically precipitated substance that binds particles of clastic rocks. **5.** Variant of **cementum.**
~v. **cemented, -menting, -ments.** *—tr.* **1.** To bind with or as if with cement. **2.** To cover or coat with cement. **3.** To make firm and united; bind closely: *cement a friendship.* *—intr.* To become cemented. [Middle English *siment, cyment,* from Old French *ciment,* from Latin *caementum,* rough quarried stone, and its plural *caementa,* marble chips (used to make lime), from *caedere,* to cut, hew.] **—ce·ment·er** *n.*
ce·men·ta·tion (séemen-táysh'n) *n.* **1.** The process or result of cementing. **2.** A metallurgical coating process in which iron or steel is immersed in a powder of another metal, such as zinc, chromium, or aluminium, and heated to a temperature below the melting point of either. **3.** A similar process in which wrought iron is heated in a bed of charcoal to produce steel.
ce·ment·ite (si-méntīt, sə-) *n.* A hard brittle iron carbide, Fe_3C, formed in steel with more than 0.85 per cent carbon.
cement mixer *n.* A machine with a revolving drum in which cement, sand, gravel, and water are combined into concrete. Also called "concrete mixer".
ce·ment·um (si-méntəm, sə-) *n.* Also **cement.** A bony substance covering the root of a tooth, which anchors the tooth in the socket. [New Latin, from Latin *caementum,* rough stone, CEMENT.]
cem·e·ter·y (sémmi-tri, -təri || *U.S.* -terri) *n., pl.* **-ies.** A place for burying the dead, usually not one attached to a church. [Middle English *cimitery,* from Late Latin *coemētērium,* from Greek *koimētērion,* sleeping room, burial place, from *koiman,* to put to sleep.]
cen. **1.** central. **2.** century.
cen·a·cle (sénnək'l) *n.* **1.** A small social group that meets to discuss shared interests; especially, a literary clique. **2.** *Archaic.* A small dining room, usually on an upper floor. [Middle English, from Old French, from Late Latin *cēnāculum,* dining room, the Cenacle of the Last Supper, from Latin *cēna,* dinner.]
-cene *adj. & n. comb. form.* Indicates a recent geological period; for example, **Neocene.** [From Greek *kainos,* new, fresh.]
C.Eng. Chartered Engineer.
Cen·ni·ni (che-néeni, chə-), **Cennino (di Drea)** (*c.*1370–*c.*1440). Florentine painter. Though his paintings have disappeared, he is remembered for his book *Il libro dell'arte* (*The Craftsman's Handbook*) which deals particularly with **tempera** painting *(see).*
cen·o·bite, coen·o·bite (séen-ə-bīt, -ō- || *U.S. also* sén-) *n.* A member of a monastic community. [Late Latin *coenobīta,* from *coenobium,* convent, from Greek *koinobion,* life in community : *koinos,* common + *bios,* life.] **—cen·o·bit·ic** (-bíttik), **cen·o·bit·i·cal** *adj.*
cenogenesis. Variant of **caenogenesis.**
ce·no·spe·cies (sée-nō-speesheez, -nə-) *n., pl.* **cenospecies.** Any of a group of species that are capable of interbreeding: *Donkeys and horses are cenospecies.* [From Greek *koinos,* common + SPECIES.]
cen·o·taph (sénnə-taaf, -taf) *n.* A monument erected in honour of a dead person or persons whose remains lie elsewhere. [French *cénotaphe,* from Latin *cenotaphium,* from Greek *kenotaphion,* empty tomb : *kenos,* empty + *taphos,* tomb.] **—cen·o·taph·ic** (-táffik) *adj.*
Ce·no·zo·ic (séen-ə-zō-ik, -ō- || *U.S. also* sén-) *adj.* Also **Cai·no·zo·ic** (kīn-, káyn-). Of, belonging to, or designating the latest era of geological time, which includes the Tertiary and Quaternary periods and is characterised by the evolution of mammals, birds, plants, modern continents, and glaciation.
~n. Geology. The Cenozoic era. Preceded by *the.* [Greek *kainos,* new, fresh + -ZOIC.]
cense (senss) *tr.v.* **censed, censing, censes. 1.** To perfume with incense. **2.** To offer incense to. [Middle English *censen,* short for *encensen,* to burn incense, from Old French *encenser,* from *encens,* INCENSE (noun).]
cen·ser (sén-sər) *n.* A vessel in which incense is burned, especially at religious ceremonies. Also called "thurible". [Middle English *censer,* from Old French *censier,* short for *encensier,* from *encens,* INCENSE (noun).]
cen·sor (sén-sər) *n.* **1.** An authorised examiner of literature, plays, films, or other material, who may prohibit what he considers morally, politically, or otherwise objectionable. **2.** An official, as in the armed forces or a prison, who examines personal mail and official dispatches to remove any information considered secret or improper. **3.** Any person who condemns or censures. **4.** In ancient Rome, either of two officials responsible for supervising the public census and public behaviour and morals. **5.** *Psychoanalysis.* The agent responsible for **censorship** *(see).*
~tr.v. **censored, -soring, -sors.** To examine and expurgate. [Latin *cēnsor,* from *cēnsēre,* to assess, estimate, judge.] **—cen·so·ri·al** (sen-sáwr-i-əl || -sṓr-) *adj.*
cen·so·ri·ous (sen-sáwr-i-əss || -sṓr-) *adj.* **1.** Tending to reprimand or censure; highly critical. **2.** Expressing censure. [Latin *cēnsōrius,* of a censor, from *cēnsor,* CENSOR.] **—cen·so·ri·ous·ly** *adv.* **—cen·so·ri·ous·ness** *n.*
cen·sor·ship (sén-sər-ship) *n.* **1.** The act or process of censoring. **2.** The office or authority of a censor. **3.** A programme or policy of censoring. **4.** *Psychoanalysis.* The inhibition, by either ego or superego, of conscious awareness of painful feelings or ideas.
cen·sur·a·ble (sénshər-əb'l) *adj.* Deserving censure. **—cen·sur·a·ble·ness, cen·sur·a·bil·i·ty** (-ə-bílləti) *n.* **—cen·sur·a·bly** *adv.*
cen·sure (sénshər) *n.* An expression of disapproval or severe criticism: *passed a vote of censure.*
~tr.v. **censured, -suring, -sures.** To criticise severely; express strong disapproval of. See Synonyms at **criticise.** [Latin *cēnsūra,* censorship, the office of a censor, from *cēnsor,* CENSOR.] **—cen·sur·er** *n.*
cen·sus (sén-səss) *n.* An official, periodic enumeration of population that usually also includes the collection of related demographic information. [Latin *cēnsus,* registration of citizens, from *cēnsēre,* to assess, tax.]
cent (sent) *n. Abbr.* **c., C., ct. 1. a.** *Symbol* **¢** A monetary unit equal to 1/100 of the U.S. dollar. **b.** A monetary unit equal to 1/100 of the dollar of various other countries such as Australia, Canada, New Zealand, Hong Kong, and Zimbabwe. **c.** A monetary unit equal to 1/100 of various standard monetary units, such as the leone of Sierra Leone, the rand of South Africa, the rupee of Sri Lanka, and the yuan of China. **d.** A monetary unit equal to 1/100 of the shilling of Kenya, Tanzania, Uganda, and Somalia. **2.** A coin or note worth one cent. [Old French, "hundred", from Latin *centum,* hundred.]
cent. **1.** centime. **2.** central. **3.** century.
cen·taur (sén-tawr) *n.* **1.** *Greek Mythology.* Any of a race of monsters, born of Ixion, having the head, arms, and trunk of a man and the body and legs of a horse. **2.** *Capital* **C.** Variant of **Centaurus.** [Middle English *Centaur,* from Latin *Centaurus,* from Greek *Kentauros*†, originally the name of a primitive Thessalian tribe.]
Cen·tau·rus (sen-táwrəss) *n.* Also **Centaur.** A constellation in the Southern Hemisphere near Vela and Lupus. [Latin, CENTAUR.]
cen·tau·ry (sén-tawri) *n., pl.* **-ries. 1.** Any of several plants of the genus *Centaurium,* native to Eurasia; especially, *C. erythraea,* having clusters of rose-purple flowers. **2.** A plant of the genus *Centaurea,* which includes the cornflower and knapweed. [Middle English *centaure,* from Old French *centauree,* from Late Latin *centaurea,* variant of Latin *centaureum,* from Greek *kentaureion,* centaury, from *Kentauros,* CENTAUR (its medicinal properties were supposedly discovered by the centaur Chiron, a physician).]
cen·ta·vo (sen-taávō) *n., pl.* **-vos. 1. a.** A monetary unit equal to 1/100 of the Portuguese escudo. **b.** A monetary unit equal to 1/100 of the standard monetary unit of various countries in Central and South America, such as the cruzeiro of Brazil or the peso of Mexico. **c.** A monetary unit equal to 1/100 of the escudo of Cape Verde. **2.** A coin worth one centavo. [Spanish, "a hundredth", from Latin *centum,* hundred.]
cen·te·nar·i·an (sénti-náir-i-ən) *n.* A person one hundred years old or older. [From Latin *centēnārius,* CENTENARY.] **—cen·te·nar·i·an** *adj.*
cen·ten·a·ry (sen-téen-əri, -tén-, séntin- || *U.S. also* séntə-nerri) *adj.* **1.** Of or pertaining to a 100-year period. **2.** Of or pertaining to a 100th anniversary.
~n., pl. **centenaries. 1.** A 100-year period. **2.** A 100th anniversary or a celebration of this. [Latin *centēnārius,* of a hundred, from *centēnī,* a hundred each, from *centum,* hundred.]

cen·ten·ni·al (sen-ténni-əl) *adj.* **1.** Of, pertaining to, or existing for a 100-year period. **2.** Occurring once every 100 years. **3.** Of or pertaining to a 100th anniversary.
~*n. Chiefly U.S.* A centenary. [Latin *centum,* hundred + (BI)ENNIAL.] —**cen·ten·ni·al·ly** *adv.*

center. *U.S.* Variant of **centre.**

centering. *U.S.* Variant of **centring.**

cen·tes·i·mal (sen-téssim'l) *adj.* Pertaining to or characterised by division into hundredths. [From Latin *centēsimus,* hundredth, from *centum,* hundred.] —**cen·tes·i·mal·ly** *adv.*

cen·tes·i·mo (sen-téssimō) *n., pl.* **-mos** A monetary unit equal to ¹/₁₀₀ of various standard monetary units, such as the Uruguayan nuevo peso or the Panamanian balboa. [Spanish, "hundredth", from Latin *centēsimus,* CENTESIMAL.]

–centesis *n. comb. form.* Indicates surgical puncture or perforation; for example, **amniocentesis.** [Greek *kentēsis,* a pricking, from *kentein,* to prick.]

centi-, cent-. *comb. form. Abbr.* **c** Indicates a hundred or hundredth; for example, **centinewton, centilitre.** [French, from Latin *centum,* hundred.]

cen·ti·grade (sénti-grayd) *adj.* **1.** Consisting of or divided into 100 degrees. **2.** *Abbr.* **C** Designating the **Celsius** temperature scale.
~*n.* A unit of angle equal to one hundredth (10^{-2}) of a grade. [French : CENTI- + GRADE.]

cen·ti·gram (senti-gram) *n. Abbr.* **cg** One hundredth (10^{-2}) of a gram.

cen·tile (sén-tíl ‖ *U.S. also* -til) *n.* **Percentile** *(see).*

cen·ti·li·tre (sénti-leetər) *n. Abbr.* **cl** One hundredth (10^{-2}) of a litre. [French : CENTI- + LITRE.]

cen·til·li·on (sen-tíl-yən, -i-ən) *n.* **1.** In British and German usage, the cardinal number represented by one followed by 600 zeros, usually written 10^{600}. **2.** In U.S. and French usage, the cardinal number represented by one followed by 303 zeros, usually written 10^{303}. [CENTI- + (MI)LLION.]

cen·time (són-teem, són-) *n. Abbr.* **c., C., cent. 1. a.** A monetary unit equal to ¹/₁₀₀ of the French franc. **b.** A monetary unit equal to ¹/₁₀₀ of the franc of various other countries, such as Belgium, Luxembourg, and Switzerland. **2.** A coin worth one centime. [French, from *cent,* hundred. See **cent.**]

cen·ti·me·tre (sénti-meetər ‖ *U.S. also* sáanti) *n. Abbr.* **cm** A unit of length equal to one hundredth (10^{-2}) of a metre or 0.3937 inch. [French *centimètre* : CENTI- + -METER.]

cen·ti·me·tre-gram-sec·ond system (sénti-meetər-grám-sékənd) *n. Abbr.* **cgs, CGS** A coherent system of units for mechanics, electricity, and magnetism, in which the basic units of length, mass, and time are the centimetre, gram, and second. It has now been replaced for scientific purposes by SI units.

cen·ti·mo (sénti-mō, thénti-) *n., pl.* **-mos. 1.** A monetary unit equal to ¹/₁₀₀ of various standard monetary units, such as the bolivar of Venezuela and the peseta of Spain. **2.** A coin worth one centimo. [Spanish *céntimo,* from French *centime,* CENTIME.]

cen·ti·new·ton (sénti-newt'n ‖ -nōōt'n) *n. Abbr.* **cN** One hundredth (10^{-2}) of a newton.

cen·ti·pede (sénti-peed) *n.* Any of various wormlike arthropods of the class Chilopoda, having numerous body segments, each with a pair of legs, the front pair modified into venomous biting organs. Compare **millipede.** [Latin *centipeda* : CENTI- + -PEDE.]

cen·ti·poise (sénti-poyz) *n. Abbr.* **cP** One hundredth (10^{-2}) of a poise.

cent·ner (sént-nər) *n.* A unit of weight corresponding to the hundredweight, equal to 50 kilograms (110.23 pounds), used in several European countries. [German *Zentner,* from Old High German *centenāri,* from Medieval Latin *centēnārius,* weighing a hundred pounds, from Latin, CENTENARY.]

cen·to (séntō) *n., pl.* **-tos.** A literary work pieced together from the works of several authors. [Latin *centō,* patchwork, cento.]

cen·tral (séntrəl) *adj. Abbr.* **cen., cent. 1.** At, in, near, or being the centre. **2.** Constituting that from which other things proceed or upon which they depend: *central government.* **3.** Dominant; essential: *the central theme of the book.* **4.** *Anatomy & Physiology.* **a.** Of or pertaining to the central nervous system. **b.** Of or pertaining to a centrum. **5.** *Phonetics.* Pronounced with the tongue in a neutral position, as *e* in *mister.* [Latin *centrālis,* from *centrum,* CENTRE.] —**cen·tral·ly** *adv.*

Central African Republic. A country in Central Africa. Known from 1976 to 1979 as the Central African Empire, it was, from 1894 to 1960, Ubangi-Shari, one of the four territories of French Equatorial Africa. It was granted independence in 1960, and in 1966 a coup brought Jean Bédel Bokassa to power. In 1976 he had himself crowned Emperor Bokassa I. Following allegations of corruption and massacres, he fled, and the short-lived empire became once again the Central African Republic. The country, one of the world's poorest, is covered by savanna. More than 90 per cent of its workers are subsistence farmers, but the republic does export diamonds, uranium, cotton, and coffee. Area, 622 984 square kilometres (240,472 square miles). Population, 3,340,000. Capital, Bangui. See map at **Chad.**

Central American States. Those states of Latin America (including Belize) lying between Mexico and Colombia.

central angle *n.* An angle having radii as sides, and the centre of a circle as its vertex.

central dogma *n.* The hypothesis of biochemical genetics that genetic information is carried only one way in the cell, from DNA to RNA to protein.

Central European Time *n. Abbr.* **CET, C.E.T.** The standard time adopted by some countries of Central Europe, Western Europe, and Africa. It is one hour ahead of Greenwich Mean Time. See map at **Time Zone.**

central heating *n. Abbr.* **c.h.** *Chiefly British.* A method of, or apparatus for, heating the rooms of a house, office, or other building by means of water-filled radiators or hot-air vents connected to a central boiler or heat source.

Central Intelligence Agency *n. Abbr.* **CIA** The coordinating agency for U.S. intelligence and espionage activities.

cen·tral·ise, cen·tral·ize (séntrəl-īz) *v.* **-ised, -ising, -ises.** —*tr.* **1.** To bring towards a centre. **2.** To bring under a single, central authority. —*intr.* To come together at a centre; concentrate. —**cen·tral·i·sa·tion** (-ī-záysh'n ‖ *U.S.* -i-) *n.* —**cen·tral·is·er** *n.*

cen·tral·ism (séntral-iz'm) *n.* The act or policy of concentrating control, as of decision-making or expenditure for example, in a central authority or organisation. —**cen·tral·ist** *n. & adj.* —**cen·tral·is·tic** (-ístik) *adj.*

cen·tral·i·ty (sen-trál-əti) *n.* **1.** The state or quality of being central. **2.** The tendency to be or remain at the centre.

central nervous system *n. Abbr.* **CNS.** The portion of the vertebrate nervous system consisting of the brain and spinal cord. Compare **autonomic nervous system.**

Central Powers *pl.n.* The alliance comprising Germany, Austria-

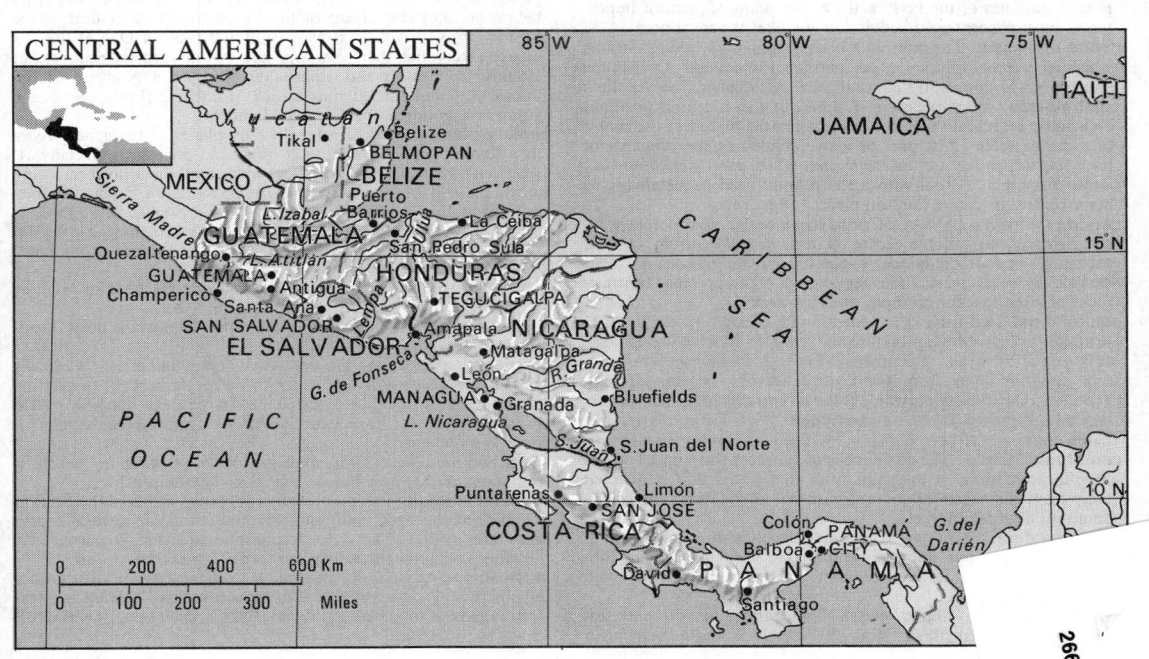

CENTRAL AMERICAN STATES

Hungary, Bulgaria, and Turkey in World War I.

central processing unit *n. Abbr.* **CPU** The central part of a computer, which performs all the logical and arithmetical operations.

Central Region. A Scottish local government region (1975–96), formed from Clackmannan, most of Stirling, south Perthshire, and a small part of West Lothian. Extending from the Grampian Mountains to the Central Lowlands, it includes the Forth valley, the towns of Stirling and Falkirk, and the Trossachs.

Central Standard Time *n. Abbr.* **CST, C.S.T.** The standard time adopted by parts of Canada, the United States, and Mexico, and some countries of Central America. It is six hours behind Greenwich Mean Time. See map at **Time Zone.** Also called "Central Time".

Central Sudanic *n.* A group of African languages of the Chari-Nile family, spoken in Chad, Central African Republic, Sudan, Congo, and Uganda.

cen·tre, *U.S.* **cen·ter** (séntər) *n. Abbr.* **ctr.** 1. A point equidistant or at the average distance from all points on the sides or outer boundaries of anything. 2. *Geometry.* **a.** A point equidistant from the vertexes of a regular polygon. **b.** A point equidistant from all points on the circumference of a circle or on the surface of a sphere. 3. A point round which something revolves; an axis. 4. A part of an object that is surrounded by the rest; a core: *a chocolate with a soft centre.* 5. An area that is roughly in the middle of a larger area: *the town centre.* 6. **a.** The main area in which a particular activity is concentrated: *the centre of the steel industry.* **b.** An area of special influence: *a centre of power.* **c.** A place used for a specified purpose or activity: *an arts centre.* 7. A person or thing that is the chief object of attention, interest, activity, or emotion. 8. A person, object, or group occupying a middle position. 9. A political group or a set of policies representing a compromise between the right and the left. 10. In some team sports, a player who holds a middle position on the field or court. 11. A collection of nerve cells in the central nervous system that controls a particular function: *the respiratory centre.* 12. A small conical hole made in a workpiece with a centre punch in order to centre a drill within it accurately. 13. A bar with a conical point used to support a workpiece, for example during turning, in a lathe. —*v.* **centred** or *U.S.* **centered, -tring** or *U.S.* **-tering, -tres** or *U.S.* **-ters.** —*tr.* 1. To place in or on a centre. 2. To concentrate at a centre. 3. In some team sports, especially football, to pass (the ball) into the centre of the field. —*intr.* To have a centre; be concentrated; focus. Often used with *on* or *upon* (*around* is nonstandard): *The dispute centred on the issue of overtime rates.* —*adj.* At the centre; middle. [Middle English, from Old French, from Latin *centrum,* centre, stationary point of a compass, from Greek *kentron,* sharp point, needle, from *kentein,* to prick.]

centre bit *n.* A drill bit having a sharp centre point, used in carpentry for boring holes.

cen·tre·board (séntər-bawrd ‖ -bôrd) *n. Nautical.* A flat board or metal plate that can be lowered through the bottom of a sailing boat to prevent drifting and provide stability.

cen·tre·fold (séntər-fōld) *n.* 1. An illustration that fills the middle pages of a magazine or newspaper. Also called "centre spread". 2. The sexy lady in a centrefold illustration.

centre of gravity *n.* 1. *Abbr.* **c.g.** The point in or near a body at which the gravitational potential energy of the body is equal to that of a single particle of the same mass located at that point and through which the resultant of the gravitational forces on the component particles of the body acts. 2. The point of greatest importance, most concentrated activity, or the like; the focal point.

centre of mass *n.* The point in a body or system of bodies through which all external forces may be considered to act and at which the entire mass is apparently concentrated. Also called "barycentre".

cen·tre·piece (séntər-peess) *n.* 1. Something in a central position; especially, a decorative object or arrangement placed at the centre of a dining table. 2. A part or item intended as the principal or most impressive feature: *the centrepiece of the party's manifesto.*

centre punch *n.* A tool with a sharp point used in metalwork to mark centres or centre lines on pieces to be drilled.

cen·tric (séntrik) *adj.* 1. At, of, or having a centre. 2. *Physiology.* Of or originating at a nerve centre. [Greek *kentrikos,* from *kentron,* CENTRE.] —**cen·tri·cal·ly** *adv.* —**cen·tric·i·ty** (sen-tríssəti) *n.*

–centric *adj. comb. form.* Indicates possession of a specified centre or focus of attention, for example, **anthropocentric.**

cen·trif·u·gal (sen-tríffewg'l, séntri-féwg'l, -fewg'l ‖ *chiefly U.S.* -tríffəg'l) *adj.* 1. Moving or directed away from a centre or axis. 2. Operated by means of centrifugal force. 3. *Physiology.* Transmitting impulses away from the central nervous system; efferent. 4. *Botany.* Developing outwards from a centre or axis. Said of certain inflorescences. Compare **centripetal.** [New Latin *centrifugus* : Latin *centrum,* CENTRE + *fugere,* to flee.] —**cen·trif·u·gal·ly** *adv.*

centrifugal force *n.* The component of apparent force on a body in curvilinear motion, as observed from that body, that is directed away from the centre of curvature or axis of rotation; the equilibrant of centripetal force.

cen·tri·fuge (séntri-fewj) *n.* Any apparatus consisting essentially of a compartment spun about a central axis, used to separate contained materials of different density or to simulate gravity with centrifugal force. —*tr.v.* **centrifuged, -fuging, -fuges.** To separate, dehydrate, or test ∨ means of a centrifuge. [French, from New Latin *centrifugus,*

CENTRIFUGAL.] —**cen·trif·u·ga·tion** (sen-tríffew-gáysh'n, séntri-few- ‖ *chiefly U.S.* -triffə-) *n.*

cen·tring, *U.S.* **cen·ter·ing** (séntring, séntəring) *n.* A wooden structure used to support an arch temporarily during its construction.

cen·tri·ole (séntri-ōl) *n. Genetics.* Either of two tiny cylindrical organelles in most animal cells that form the poles of the spindle during mitosis. [Latin *centrum,* CENTRE + -OLE.]

cen·trip·e·tal (sen-tríppit'l, séntri-péet'l, -peet'l) *adj.* 1. Directed or moving towards a centre or axis. 2. Operated by centripetal force. 3. *Physiology.* Transmitting impulses towards the central nervous system; afferent. 4. *Botany.* Developing inwards, towards the centre or axis. Said of some forms of inflorescence. Compare **centrifugal.** [New Latin *centripetus* : Latin *centrum,* CENTRE + -PETAL.] —**cen·trip·e·tal·ly** *adv.*

centripetal force *n.* The component of force acting on a body in curvilinear motion that is directed towards the centre of curvature or axis of rotation.

cen·trist (séntrist) *n.* One taking a position in the political centre; a moderate. [CENTR(O)- + -IST.] —**cen·trism** *n.*

centro-, centr- *comb. form.* Indicates centre; for example, **centromere, centrist.** [Greek *kentron,* CENTRE.]

cen·tro·bar·ic (séntrō-bárrik) *adj.* Of or relating to the centre of gravity. [Late Greek *kentrobarikos,* from Greek *kentrobarikē,* the theory of the centre of gravity : *kentron,* CENTRE + *bareos,* genitive of *baros,* weight.]

cen·tro·cli·nal (séntrō-klín'l) *n. Geology.* Designating a rock formation in which the strata slope down and inwards towards a central point or area. [CENTRO- + CLINE.]

cen·troid (séntroyd) *n.* The centre of mass of an object having uniform density. [CENTR(O)- + -OID.]

cen·tro·mere (séntrə-meer) *n. Genetics.* Region of a chromosome to which the spindle is attached during mitosis. [CENTRO + -MERE.]

cen·tro·some (séntrə-sōm) *n. Genetics.* A small mass of differentiated cytoplasm containing the centriole. [CENTRO- + -SOME (body).] —**cen·tro·so·mic** (-sómmik, -sōmik) *adj.*

cen·tro·sphere (séntrə-sfeer) *n. Genetics.* The mass of cytoplasm surrounding the centriole in a centrosome.

cen·trum (sén-trəm) *n., pl.* **-trums** or **-tra** (-trə). The major part of a vertebra, exclusive of the bases of the neural arch. [Latin, CENTRE.]

cen·tum (kéntəm) *adj.* Of, pertaining to, or designating those Indo-European languages that retained the velar *k,* and the labiovelar *kw* of primitive Indo-European. Compare **satem.** [From Latin *centum,* hundred (chosen as a typical word in which initial *c* represents initial Indo-European *k*).]

cen·tu·ple (séntewp'l ‖ sen-téw-p'l, -tóo-, séntə-) *adj.* Multiplied by a hundred; hundredfold. —*tr.v.* **centupled, -pling, -ples.** To increase a hundredfold; multiply by a hundred. [French, from Late Latin *centuplus* : Latin *centum,* hundred + *-plus,* "-fold".]

cen·tu·pli·cate (sen-téw-pli-kayt ‖ -tóo-) *tr.v.* **-cated, -cating, -cates.** To multiply by one hundred. —*adj.* (-kət, -kit, -kayt). Hundredfold. [Latin *centuplicāre,* from *centuplex,* hundredfold : *centum,* hundred + *-plex,* "-fold".] —**cen·tu·pli·ca·tion** (-káysh'n) *n.*

cen·tu·ri·on (sen-téwr-i-ən ‖ -tóor-) *n.* An officer commanding a century in the Roman army. [Middle English *centurioun,* from Old French *centurion,* from Latin *centuriō* (stem *centuriōn-*), from *centuria,* CENTURY.]

cen·tu·ry (sénch-əri, -ri) *n., pl.* **-ries.** *Abbr.* **C., c., cen., cent.** 1. A period of 100 years. 2. Each of the successive periods of 100 years before or since the advent of the Christian era. 3. A unit of the Roman army, originally consisting of 100 men. 4. One of the 193 groups into which the Roman people was divided for purposes of electing the consuls and other state officials. 5. A group of 100 things. 6. One hundred runs scored at cricket. [Latin *centuria,* a group of a hundred, from *centum,* hundred.]

century plant *n.* Any of several fleshy plants of the genus *Agave* that bloom only once in 10 to 20 years and then die; especially, *A. americana,* having large greyish leaves and greenish flowers.

ceorl (chairl ‖ *U.S.* cháy-awrl) *n.* In Anglo-Saxon England, a freeman of the lowest class. Also "churl". [Old English *ceorl,* CHURL.]

cep (sep) *n.* An edible mushroom, *Boletus edulis,* having a brown shiny cap. [French *cèpe,* from dialect (Gascon) *cep,* from Latin *cippus,* stake.]

ceph·a·lad (séffəlad) *adv. Anatomy.* Towards the head or anterior section. Compare **caudad.** [CEPHAL(O)- + -AD.]

ceph·al·al·gi·a (kéff'l-áljə, séff'l-, -álji-ə) *n.* Pain in the head; headache. [CEPHAL(O)- + -ALGIA.]

ce·phal·ic (si-fál-ik, sə-, ki-, ke-. *Note: in this and related words the medical profession generally prefer* ki- *or* ke-.) *adj.* 1. Of or relating to the head or skull. 2. Located on, in, or near the head. [Old French *cephalique,* from Latin *cephalicus,* from Greek *kephalikos,* from *kephalē,* head.]

–cephalic *adj. comb. form.* Indicates head or skull; for example, **orthocephalic.** [From Greek *-kephalos,* -CEPHALOUS.]

cephalic index *n.* The ratio of the maximum width of the head to its maximum length, multiplied by 100. Compare **cranial index.**

ceph·a·lin (séf-əlin, kéf-) *n.* A phospholipid that is particularly abundant in the brain and spinal cord. [CEPHAL(O)- + -IN.]

ceph·a·li·sa·tion (séffə-lī-záysh'n ‖ *U.S.* -li-) *n. Zoology.* The gradually increasing concentration of nervous tissue and feeding and sensory organs at the head end during animal evolution. [CEPHAL(O)- + -IS(E) + -ATION.]

cephalo-, cephal- *comb. form.* Indicates head; for example, **cephalopod, cephalad.** [Latin, from Greek *kephalo-*, from *kephalē*, head.]

ceph·a·lo·chor·date (séffəlō-kórdayt) *adj.* Of or belonging to the subphylum Cephalochordata, which includes primitive forerunners of the vertebrates such as the lancelet.
~*n.* A cephalochordate animal. [New Latin *Cephalochordata* : CEPHALO- + CHORDATE.]

ceph·a·lo·pod (séffə-lə-pod, -lō-) *n.* Any of various molluscs of the class Cephalopoda, such as an octopus or nautilus, having a beaked head, an internal shell in some species, and prehensile tentacles. ~*adj.* Also **ceph·a·lop·o·dous** (-lóppədəss). Of, pertaining to, or belonging to the Cephalopoda. [New Latin *Cephalopoda* : CEPHALO- + -POD.] —**ceph·a·lop·o·dan** (-lóppəd'n) *n. & adj.*

ceph·al·o·spo·rin (séffəlō-spáwr-in ‖ -spór-) *n.* Any one of a group of antibiotics, derived from the mould *Cephalosporium*, used to treat a wide variety of infections. [New Latin *Cephalosporium* : CEPHALO- + SPORE.]

ceph·a·lo·tho·rax (séffəlō-tháwr-aks ‖ -thór-) *n.* The anterior section of arachnids and many crustaceans, consisting of the fused head and thorax.

–cephalous *adj. comb. form.* Indicates a head; for example, **hydrocephalous.** [New Latin *-cephalus*, from Greek *-kephalos*, from *kephalē*, head.]

–cephalus *n. comb. form.* Indicates an abnormality of the head; for example, **hydrocephalus.** [New Latin *-cephalus*, -CEPHALOUS.]

–cephaly *n. comb. form.* Indicates a head; for example, **megalocephaly.** [From Greek *-kephalos*, CEPHALOUS.]

Ce·phe·id variable (séefi-id ‖ U.S. also séffi-) *n.* Either of two classes of intrinsically variable stars with exceptionally regular periods of light pulsation. Also called "Cepheid". [From CEPHEUS.]

Ce·pheus (sée-fewss, -fi-əss) *n.* A constellation in the Northern Hemisphere near Cassiopeia and Draco. [Latin *Cēpheus*, from Greek *Kēpheus*, a mythical king.]

ce·ra·ceous (si-ráyshəss, sə-) *adj.* Waxy or waxlike. [Latin *cēra*, wax (see **cerate**) + -ACEOUS.]

ce·ram·al (si-ráym'l, sə-, -rámm'l) *n.* An alloy, **cermet** (see). [CERAM(IC) + AL(LOY).]

ce·ram·ic (si-rámmik, sə-, ki-, ke-, kə-. *Note: experts prefer the pronunciations with initial k-.*) *n.* **1.** Any of various hard, brittle, heat-resistant and corrosion-resistant materials made by firing clay or other nonmetallic minerals. **2.** An object made of such materials. [Probably French *céramique*, "of pottery", from Greek *keramikos*, from *keramos*, potter's clay, earthenware.] —**ce·ram·ic** *adj.*

ce·ram·ics (si-rámmiks, kə-) *n. Used with a singular verb.* The art or technique of making objects from ceramic materials, especially from fired clay or porcelain. —**ce·ram·ist** (sérrəmist), **ce·ram·ic·ist** (-rámmi-sist) *n.*

ce·rar·gy·rite (si-rárji-rīt, sə-) *n.* A grey to yellow mineral, AgCl, used as a source of silver. Also called "horn silver". [From Greek *keras*, horn + *arguros*, silver + -ITE.]

ce·ras·tes (si-rásteez, se-, sə-) *n., pl.* **cerastes.** Either of the two species of desert-dwelling, venomous snakes of the genus *Cerastes*, especially the **horned viper** (see). [Middle English, from Latin *cerastēs*, from Greek *kerastēs*, horned (serpent), from *keras*, horn.]

ce·rate (séer-ət, -it, -ayt) *n.* A hard, oily, fat- or wax-based solid, sometimes medicated, formerly applied to the skin directly or on dressings. [Latin *cērātum*, a wax plaster, wax salve, from *cēra*, wax, akin to Greek *kēros†*, wax.]

ce·rat·o·dus (si-ráttədəss, sə-, sérra-tódəss) *n., pl.* **-duses.** Any of various extinct lungfishes of the genus *Ceratodus*, of the Triassic and Cretaceous periods. [New Latin *Ceratodus*, "horn-tooth" : Greek *keras* (stem *kerat-*), horn + *odous*, tooth.]

cer·a·toid (sérrətoyd) *adj.* Hornlike. [Greek *keratoeidēs* : *keras* (stem *kerat-*), horn + -OID.]

Cer·ber·us (sér-bərəss). *Greek & Roman Mythology.* A three-headed dog guarding the entrance of Hades. [Latin, from Greek *Kerberos†*.] —**Cer·be·re·an** (-béer-i-ən) *adj.*

cer·car·i·a (ser-káir-i-ə) *n., pl.* **-iae** (-i-ee) or **-as.** The parasitic larva of a trematode worm, having a tail that disappears in the adult stage. [New Latin, "the tailed one" : Greek *kerkos*, tail + -*aria*, from -*arius*, -ARY.] —**cer·car·i·al** *adj.*

cer·co·pi·the·coid (sérkō-pi-thée-koyd, -píthi-) *adj.* Of or belonging to the family Cercopithecidae, which includes Old World monkeys such as the baboons, mandrills, macaques, and langurs. ~*n.* Also **cer·co·pi·the·cid** (-sid). A member of the Cercopithecidae. [Latin *cercopithēcus*, long-tailed ape, from Greek *kerkopithēkos* : *kerkos*, tail + *pithēkos*, ape + -OID.]

cere[1] (seer) *tr.v.* **cered, cering, ceres.** To wrap (a corpse, for example) in or as if in cerecloth. [Middle English *ceren*, to cover with wax, from Old French *cirer*, from Latin *cērāre*, from *cēra*, wax. See **cerate**.]

cere[2] *n.* A fleshy or waxlike swelling at the base of the upper part of the beak in certain birds, such as parrots and some birds of prey. [Middle English *sere*, from Old French *cire*, from Medieval Latin *cēra*, from Latin, wax. See **cerate**.] —**cered** *adj.*

ce·re·al (séer-i-əl) *n.* **1.** An edible grain, such as wheat, oats, or maize. **2.** A grass producing such a grain. **3.** A food prepared from such a grain, especially one eaten at breakfast. [Latin *cereālis*, of grain, "of Ceres", from *Cerēs*, CERES.] —**ce·re·al** *adj.*

cer·e·bel·lum (sérri-béll-əm) *n., pl.* **-lums** or **-bella** (-béllə). The structure of the brain responsible for regulation and coordination of complex voluntary movement, lying below the occipital lobes of the

cerebral hemispheres. [Medieval Latin, from Latin, diminutive of *cerebrum*, brain.] —**cer·e·bel·lar** (-ər) *adj.*

ce·re·bral (sérri-brəl ‖ U.S. also sə-rée-) *adj.* **1.** Of or pertaining to the brain or cerebrum. **2.** Appealing to or involving the workings of the intellect, rather than of the emotions. —**ce·re·bral·ly** *adv.*

cerebral cortex *n.* The extensive outer layer of grey matter of the cerebral hemispheres, largely responsible for higher nervous functions. Also called "mantle", "pallium".

cerebral hemisphere *n.* Either hemisphere of the cerebrum of the brain, divided by a deep groove running lengthways.

cerebral palsy *n.* Impaired muscular power and coordination and weakness of the limbs resulting from brain damage usually occurring at or before birth.

cer·e·brate (sérri-brayt) *intr.v.* **-brated, -brating, -brates.** To think; ponder. Often used humorously. [Back-formation from CEREBRATION.]

cer·e·bra·tion (sérri-bráysh'n) *n.* The action of thinking; thought. [From Latin *cerebrum*, CEREBRUM.]

cerebro-, cerebr- *comb. form.* Indicates the brain or cerebrum; for example, **cerebral, cerebration.**

cer·e·bro·side (sérri-brō-sīd, -brō-) *n.* Any of a group of lipids found in the brain and other nerve tissue, yielding on decomposition a fatty acid, an unsaturated amino-alcohol, and a sugar. [CEREBR(UM) + -OS(E) + -IDE.]

ce·re·bro·spi·nal (sérri-brō-spīn'l, sə-rée-) *adj.* Of or pertaining to the brain and spinal cord. [CEREBR(UM) + SPINAL.]

cerebrospinal fever *n.* An acute infectious, epidemic meningitis that is caused by the bacterium *Neisseria meningitidis*. Also called "spinal meningitis", "cerebrospinal meningitis".

cerebrospinal fluid *n.* The serum-like fluid that bathes the ventricles of the brain and the cavity of the spinal cord.

ce·re·bro·vas·cu·lar (sérribrō-váskewlər) *adj.* Of or pertaining to the blood vessels supplying the brain or to the blood they carry.

cerebrovascular accident *n.* A sudden interruption of the supply of blood to the brain, caused by rupture (as in a cerebral haemorrhage) or blocking of a cerebral artery, and resulting in a stroke.

ce·re·brum (sérri-brəm ‖ U.S. also sə-rée-) *n., pl.* **-brums** or **-bra** (-brə). The large rounded structure of the brain occupying most of the cranial cavity, divided into two cerebral hemispheres and joined at the bottom by the corpus callosum. [Latin, brain.]

cere·cloth (séer-kloth ‖ -klawth) *n.* Cloth coated with wax, formerly used for wrapping the dead. [Earlier *cered cloth*, waxed cloth. See **cerate**.]

Cer·e·dig·ion (kérri-dig-yon). Unitary Authority area in west Wales established in 1996.

cere·ment (séermənt) *n. Usually plural. Archaic.* Cerecloth. [French *cirement*, from *cirer*, to wax. See **cerate**.]

cer·e·mo·ni·al (sérri-mōni-əl) *adj.* Of, appropriate to, or characterised by ceremony; formal; ritual.
~*n.* **1.** The ceremonies to be observed on an official or religious occasion; a rite. **2.** The observance of these ceremonies. —**cer·e·mo·ni·al·ism** *n.* —**cer·e·mo·ni·al·ist** *n.* —**cer·e·mo·ni·al·ly** *adv.*

Usage: The similarity in form between *ceremonial* and *ceremonious* often leads to a confusion of senses, but a clear distinction is maintained in standard English. *Ceremonial* relates primarily to what involves or is involved in ceremony (*ceremonial occasions, ceremonial dress*); *ceremonious* stresses formality and display, often in the unfavourable sense of pompousness (*He met me at the door and delivered a ceremonious greeting*).

cer·e·mo·ni·ous (sérri-mōni-əss) *adj.* Having, showing, or indicative of a fondness for ceremony; rigidly or elaborately formal. —See Usage note at **ceremonial.** —**cer·e·mo·ni·ous·ly** *adv.* —**cer·e·mo·ni·ous·ness** *n.*

cer·e·mo·ny (sérri-məni ‖ chiefly U.S. -mōni) *n., pl.* **-nies. 1. a.** A formal act or set of acts performed as prescribed by ritual, custom, or etiquette. **b.** Such acts collectively; pomp. **2.** A conventional social gesture or act without intrinsic purpose. **3.** Strict observance of formalities or etiquette. —**stand on ceremony.** To insist on or behave with excessive formality. [Middle English *ceremonie*, from Old French, from Latin *caerimōnia†*, sacredness, religious rite.]

Ce·ren·kov radiation, Che·ren·kov radiation (chə-réng-koff; *Russian* chi-ryén-kəff) *n. Physics.* The light emitted by a beam of high-energy particles passing through transparent, nonconducting material at a speed which is greater than the speed of light in that medium. [After P.A. *Cherenkov* (1904–90), Russian physicist.]

Ce·res[1] (séer-eez). *Roman Mythology.* The goddess of agriculture; identified with the Greek goddess Demeter. [Latin *Cerēs*.]

Ceres[2] *n.* The first asteroid to be discovered (1801), having an orbit between Mars and Saturn. [After CERES.]

ce·re·us (séer-i-əss) *n.* Any of several tall tropical American cacti of the genus *Cereus* or other genera, such as the **night-blooming cereus** (see). [New Latin, "candle" (from the shape), from Latin, taper, from *cēra*, wax. See **cerate**.]

ce·ric (séer-ik) *adj.* Of, pertaining to, or containing cerium, especially with valency 4.

ceric oxide *n.* A pale yellow-white powder, CeO_2, used in ceramics, to polish glass, and to sensitise photosensitive glass.

ce·rise (sə-réez, -réess) *n.* Purplish pink. [French, from Old French, CHERRY.] —**ce·rise** *adj.*

ce·ri·um (séer-i-əm) *n. Symbol Ce* A lustrous, iron-grey, malleable, metallic rare-earth element that occurs chiefly in the mineral monazite, exists in four allotropic states, is a constituent of lighter flint alloys, and is used in various metallurgical and nuclear applications. Atomic number 58, atomic weight 140.12, melting point 795°C, boiling point 3,468°C, relative density 6.67 to 8.23, valencies 3, 4. [New Latin, after the asteroid CERES, discovered shortly before the element.]

cer·met (sér-mit, -met) n. A material consisting of processed ceramic particles bonded with metal and used in high-strength and high-temperature applications. Also called "ceramal". [CER(AMIC) + MET(AL).]

CERN (sern) n. The research centre of the European Organisation for Nuclear Research in Geneva. [French *Conseil Européen Pour Recherches Nucléaires.*]

cer·nu·ous (sérnew-ǝss) adj. Botany. Hanging downwards; drooping; nodding. [Latin *cernuus†.*]

ce·ro·plas·tics (séer-ō-pláss-tiks, -pláass-) n. Used with a singular verb. The art of modelling in wax. [Latin *cēra,* wax (see **cerate**) + PLASTICS.] **—ce·ro·plas·tic** adj.

ce·ro·tic acid (si-róttik, sǝ-, -rōtik) n. An acid, $C_{25}H_{51}COOH$, occurring in waxes, such as beeswax and carnauba wax. Also called "hexacosanoic acid". [From Latin *cērōtum,* wax plaster, from Greek *kērōton,* from *kēros,* wax. See **cerate**.]

ce·ro·type (séer-ǝ-tīp, sérrǝ-) n. The process of preparing a printing surface for electrotyping by first engraving on a wax-coated metal plate. [Greek *kēros,* wax (see **cerate**) + -TYPE.]

ce·rous (séer-ǝss) adj. Of, pertaining to, or containing cerium, especially with valency 3. [CER(IUM) + -OUS.]

cert (sert) n. British Informal. A certainty; especially, a horse that is considered certain to win a race.

cert. certificate; certification; certified.

cer·tain (sért'n) adj. 1. Definitely known; determined beyond doubt. 2. a. Sure; destined; bound: *certain to be a best seller.* b. Sure to happen; inevitable: *At such speeds, an accident would mean certain death.* 3. Confident or convinced; having no doubt about something. 4. Sound; dependable; unerring. 5. Of a particular but unspecified character or identity: *has a certain rustic charm; a certain well-known politician.* 6. Designating a person not known or previously mentioned: *a certain Mr. Harvey.* 7. Some but not much; limited: *to a certain degree.* —See Synonyms at **sure**.
~pron. An indefinite but limited number; some. **—for certain.** Definitely; without doubt. [Middle English, from Old French, from Vulgar Latin *certānus* (unattested), from Latin *certus,* past participle of *cernere,* to decide, determine.]

Usage: Because *certain* implies an absolute lack of doubt, purists have criticised such constructions as *more certain, most certain, quite certain, fairly certain, very certain,* and so on. But such qualifications are widespread in all styles and dialects, and would generally be considered to be standard.

cer·tain·ly (sért'nli) adv. 1. Undoubtedly; indeed. 2. By all means; of course. 3. Admittedly.

cer·tain·ty (sért'nti) n., pl. -ties. 1. The fact, quality, or state of being certain. 2. A clearly established fact. 3. Something that is bound to happen.

Synonyms: certainty, certitude, assurance, conviction.

Cert. Ed. Certificate in Education.

cer·tes (sérteez) adv. Archaic. Certainly; truly; verily. [Middle English, from Old French, from Vulgar Latin *certās* (unattested), from Latin *certus,* CERTAIN.]

cer·ti·fi·a·ble (sérti-fī-ǝb'l, -fī-) adj. 1. Capable of being certified. 2. Fit to be declared insane. **—cer·ti·fi·a·bly** adv.

cer·tif·i·cate (sǝr-tiffi-kǝt, -kit) n. Abbr. **cert., ct., ctf.** 1. A document testifying to the truth of a given fact, such as a person's date of birth or ownership of shares. 2. a. A document issued to a person completing a course of study. b. A document certifying that a person may officially practise in certain professions.
~tr.v. (-kayt) **certificated, -cating, -cates.** To authorise by a certificate. [Middle English *certificat,* from Old French, from Medieval Latin *certificātum,* from the neuter past participle of Late Latin *certificāre,* to CERTIFY.]

cer·ti·fi·ca·tion (sértifi-káysh'n, sǝr-tíffi-) n. Abbr. **cert.** 1. The act of certifying or certificating. 2. The state of being certified. 3. A certified statement.

cer·ti·fied (sérti-fīd) adj. Abbr. **cert.** 1. Guaranteed in writing; vouched for; endorsed. 2. Holding a certificate. 3. Committed to a mental hospital.

certified cheque n. U.S. A **marked cheque** (see).

certified public accountant n. Abbr. **C.P.A.** In the United States, a public accountant who has received a certificate stating that he has met the state's legal requirements. Compare **chartered accountant**.

cer·ti·fy (sérti-fī) v. -fied, -fying, -fies. —tr. 1. a. To confirm formally as true, accurate, or genuine; testify to or vouch for in writing. b. To guarantee as meeting a standard; attest. 2. To declare or attest formally or authoritatively. 3. To declare legally insane. —intr. To testify. Usually used with *to.* —See Synonyms at **approve**. [Middle English *certifien,* from Old French *certifier,* from Late Latin *certificāre,* to make certain : Latin *certus,* CERTAIN + *facere,* to make.] **—cer·ti·fi·er** n.

cer·ti·o·ra·ri (sérshi-ǝ-raúr-ī, sérti-ǝ-, -aw-, -ráaree) n. Law. A writ from a higher court to a lower one requesting a transcript of the proceedings of a case for review. [Medieval Latin *certiōrārī volumus,* "we wish to be informed" (words used in the writ), from *certiōrāre,* to inform, certify, from *certior,* comparative of *certus,* CERTAIN.]

cer·ti·tude (sérti-tewd ‖ -tōōd) n. Complete assurance. See Synonyms at **certainty**. [Middle English, from Late Latin *certitūdō,* from Latin *certus,* CERTAIN.]

ce·ru·le·an (si-rōoli-ǝn, sǝ-) adj. Sky-blue; azure. [Latin *caeruleus,* dark-blue, azure, from *caelum,* sky. See **celestial**.]

ce·ru·men (si-rōō-men, sǝ-, -mǝn) n. A yellowish waxy secretion of the ear; earwax. [New Latin, from Latin *cēra,* wax. See **cerate**.]

ce·ruse (si-rōōss, sǝ-, séer-ōōss) n. **White lead** (see). [Middle English, from Old French, from Latin *cērussa,* perhaps from Greek *kēroessa* (unattested), white wax cosmetic, from *kēroun,* to wax, from *kēros,* wax. See **cerate**.]

ce·rus·site (séer-ǝ-sīt, si-rússīt, sǝ-) n. Natural lead carbonate, $PbCO_3$, a lead ore. [German *Zerussit* : Latin *cērussa,* CERUSE + -ITE.]

Cer·van·tes (ser-vánt-eez, -iz), **Miguel de** (1547–1616). Spanish writer. He is best known for *Don Quixote* (1605–15), the story of a middle-aged landowner who equips himself as a knight in armour and sets out into the world with his cunning squire, Sancho Panza, to right the wrongs of mankind.

cer·ve·lat (sérvǝ-laat, -láa, -lát) n. A kind of spiced smoked sausage made from pork or a mixture of beef and pork. [Obsolete French, from Italian *cervellata.*]

cer·vi·cal (ser-vík'l, sǝr-, sérvik'l) adj. Anatomy. Pertaining to the neck or the cervix. [New Latin *cervicalis,* from Latin *cervīx* (stem *cervic-*), CERVIX.]

cervical cap n. A contraceptive consisting of a thimble-shaped piece of rubber inserted at the neck of the cervix. Compare **diaphragm**.

cervical smear n. A specimen of material taken from the cervix of the uterus and examined for the presence of cancer.

cer·vi·ci·tis (sérvi-sítiss) n. Inflammation of the cervix of the uterus. [New Latin : CERVIX + -ITIS.]

cer·vine (sérvīn) adj. Pertaining to, resembling, or characteristic of a deer. [Latin *cervīnus,* from *cervus,* deer.]

cer·vix (sérviks) n., pl. **-vixes** or **-vices** (sérvi-seez, ser-vī-). Anatomy. 1. The neck. 2. Any neck-shaped anatomical structure; especially, the narrow outer end of the uterus. [Latin *cervīx,* neck.]

Cesarean. U.S. Variant of **Caesarean.**

cesium. U.S. Variant of **caesium.**

cespitose. U.S. Variant of **caespitose.**

cess¹ (sess) n. Any of various taxes or local rates formerly levied in Britain, Ireland, and British India. [Variant of *sess,* from obsolete *assess* (noun). See **assess**.]

cess² n. Irish. Luck: *Bad cess to him!* [Perhaps from CESS (tax).]

ces·sa·tion (se-sáysh'n) n. A ceasing; a discontinuance. [Middle English *cessacioun,* from Latin *cessātiō* (stem *cessātiōn-*), from *cessāre,* to CEASE.]

ces·ser (séssǝr) Law. The end of a term, annuity, or the like. [Anglo-French and Old French, from *cesser,* to CEASE.]

ces·sion (sésh'n) n. The act or an instance of giving up or ceding something to which one has a claim; especially, a surrendering of territory to another country by treaty. [Middle English, from Old French, from Latin *cessiō* (stem *cessiōn-*), from *cēdere* (past participle *cessus*), to yield.]

ces·sion·ar·y (sésh'n-ǝri ‖ chiefly U.S. -erri) n., pl. **-ies.** One to whom a cession is made; a transferee; an assignee.

cess·pool (séss-pōōl) n. 1. A covered hole or pit for receiving sediment or sewage from house drains. 2. A filthy or disgusting place. Also called "cesspit". [Variant (influenced by POOL) of earlier *cesperalle,* drainpipe, from Middle English *suspiral,* from Old French *souspirail,* breathing hole, from *sou(s)pirer,* to breathe, SUSPIRE.]

ces·tode (séss-tōd) n. Any flatworm of the class Cestoda, including tapeworms. [New Latin *Cestoda,* variant of *Cestoidea,* "ribbon-shaped ones" : Latin *cestus,* CESTUS (belt) + -OID.]

ces·tus¹ (séss-tǝss) n., pl. **-ti** (-tī). A belt or girdle, especially as formerly worn by a bride. [Latin *cestus,* girdle, belt, from Greek *kestos.*]

cestus² n., pl. **-tuses.** A covering for the hand, made of leather straps weighted with iron or lead, worn by ancient Roman boxers. [Latin *caestus, cestus,* boxing glove, from *caedere,* to strike.]

cesura. Variant of **caesura.**

CET, C.E.T. Central European Time.

ce·ta·ce·an (si-táysh'n, se-, -táyssi-ǝn, -táysh-) adj. Also **ce·ta·ceous** (-táyshǝss). Of or belonging to the order Cetacea, which includes fishlike aquatic mammals such as the whale and porpoise.
~n. Any mammal of the order Cetacea. [New Latin *Cetacea,* from the neuter plural of *cetaceus,* of whales : Latin *cētus,* whale, from Greek *kētos†* + -ACEOUS.]

ce·tane (sée-tayn) n. A colourless liquid, $C_{16}H_{34}$, used as a solvent and in standardised hydrocarbons to determine the cetane number of diesel fuels. [Latin *cētus,* whale (so called because it belongs to a series of compounds found in sperm whale oil) + -ANE.]

cetane number n. The performance rating of a diesel fuel, expressed as the percentage of cetane that must be mixed with liquid methylnaphthalene to produce the same ignition performance as the diesel fuel being rated. Also called "cetane rating". Compare **octane number**.

cete (seet) n. A company of badgers. [Probably from Latin *coetus, coitus,* meeting, reunion, assembly, COITUS.]

ce·te·ris pa·ri·bus (kéttǝ-riss páari-bǝss, káytǝ-, séttǝ-, -reess, párri-, -bōōss) adv. Abbr. **cet. par.** Latin. Other things being equal.

ce·tol·o·gy (see-tóllǝji, si-) n. The zoology of whales and related aquatic mammals. [Latin *cētus,* whale (see **cetacean**) + -LOGY.] **—ce·to·log·i·cal** (séetǝ-lójik'l) adj. **—ce·tol·o·gist** n.

ce·tri·mide (séttri-mīd) *n.* A detergent disinfectant, widely used for cleaning wounds, sterilising surgical instruments, and the like.

Ce·tshwa·yo (kech-wī-ō. *Note: the first sound, spelt C, is pronounced in Zulu as a voiceless dental click, like that of English "tut-tut".*) (c.1826–84). Zulu king. Although he held out against the British for a time and crushed them at Isandhlwana (1879), he was finally defeated at Ulundi (1879). He was taken prisoner and transported to London, but was later restored to his throne (1883).

Ce·tus (séetəss) *n.* A constellation in the equatorial region of the Southern Hemisphere near Aquarius and Eridanus. [Latin *cētus*, whale. See **cetacean**.]

ce·tyl alcohol (séetil) *n.* A waxy alcohol, $C_{16}H_{33}OH$, used in cosmetics and pharmaceutical products. Also called "hexadecanol".

Cé·vennes (say-vén). A mountain range at the extreme southeast of the Massif Central, France. Its highest peak is Mont Mézenc at 1 754 metres (5,753 feet). It is the source of many rivers, including the Allier, the Loire, the Lot, and the Tarn.

Ceylon. See **Sri Lanka, Democratic Socialist Republic of.**

Cey·lon moss (si-lon) *n.* A red seaweed of the genus *Gelidium,* of the East Indies, used for making agar.

Cé·zanne (si-zán, say-), **Paul** (1839–1906). French painter whose works led to the development of cubism and abstract art. His most famous paintings include a view of Mont Sainte-Victoire and *The Card Players.*

Cf The symbol for the element californium.

cf. 1. calfskin. 2. compare (Latin *confer*).

c.f., C.F. cost and freight.

C/F *Accounting.* carried forward.

CFC chlorofluorocarbon.

C.F.E. College of Further Education.

c.f.i., C.F.I. cost, freight, and insurance.

cg centigram.

c.g. 1. centre of gravity. 2. consul general.

C.G. 1. coastguard. 2. Coldstream Guards. 3. consul general.

cgs, CGS centimetre-gram-second (system of units).

ch chain (measurement).

ch. 1. chaplain. 2. chapter. 3. chief. 4. church.

Ch. 1. chaplain. 2. chief. 3. China; Chinese. 4. church.

c.h. 1. central heating. 2. clearing-house. 3. courthouse.

C.H. Companion of Honour.

Cha·blis (sháb-lee ‖ sha-blée). A very dry, white Burgundy wine produced in the region of Chablis, in east central France.

Cha·brol (sha-ból, shə- ‖ *U.S. also* -ból), **Claude** (1930–). French film director credited with having started the "nouvelle vague". A leading light of the New Wave of French directors of the late 1950s, his films include *Les Biches* (1968), *Le Boucher* (1970), and *L'Enfer* (1994). Much of his work is an examination of bourgeois social behaviour and relationships set against the tension of a Hitchcock-like thriller.

cha·cha (chaá-chaa) *n.* Also **cha·cha·cha** (chaá-chaa-chaá). 1. A rhythmic ballroom dance that originated in Latin America. 2. The heavily syncopated music for this dance.

~*intr.v.* **cha-chaed, -chaing, -chas.** To dance the cha-cha. [American Spanish *cha-cha-cha.*]

chac·ma (chákmə) *n.* A greyish-black baboon, *Chaeropithecus ursinus* (or *Papio ursinus*), of southern and eastern Africa. [Hottentot.]

cha·conne (shə-kón ‖ *U.S.* shaa-káwn) *n.* 1. A slow and stately dance of the 18th century. 2. The music for this dance. 3. A musical form consisting of variations based on a repeated harmonic pattern. Compare **passacaglia**. [French, from Spanish *chacona* (perhaps imitative of the castanets used for the music).]

chad (chad) *n.* The small discs of paper, card, or the like removed by punching from paper tape or computer cards. [Perhaps alteration of CHAFF (rubbish).]

Chad, Lake (chad). A shallow lake in north central Africa, partitioned between Chad, Cameroon, Nigeria, and Niger. It is watered by the Shari and has no outlet. It reaches 20 700 square kilometres (7,990 square miles) in extent during the wet season between May and October, but shrinks to half that size by April. The lake was first sighted by Europeans in 1823.

Chad, Republic of. *French* **Tchad.** A landlocked country in north central Africa, formerly a territory of French Equatorial Africa (1897–1960). The Sahara covers its northern half. Its population is predominantly Muslim in the north with Bantu peoples in the south, a cultural rift reflected from 1965 in costly civil war. In 1980, fighting broke out between a faction led by Hissené Habré and one supported by Colonel Gaddafi of Libya. Gaddafi declared a union of the two countries (1982), but when Libyan troops withdrew, Habré took the capital. Libyan forces occupied parts of northern Chad, but were expelled by Habré's troops with the help of the French. Chad is one of the world's poorest countries, and relies on foreign aid. Most of its people live as subsistence farmers, but some cotton is exported, and oil has been discovered. Area, 1 284 000 square kilometres (495,624 square miles). Population, 6,520,000. Capital, N'djamena. —**Chad·i·an** *n. & adj.*

cha·dor (cháadawr) *n.* A garment worn by women in some Muslim countries, especially Iran, made from a long, usually black, cloth covering the upper body, head, and part of the face. [Hindi, from Persian *chaddar.*]

Chad·wick (chádwik), **Sir James** (1891–1974). British physicist, who discovered the neutron (1932), pointing the way to the fission process which, in turn, led to the atom bomb. He was awarded the Nobel prize for physics (1935).

Chadwick, Lynn (Russell) (1914–). British sculptor and designer. His early work, influenced by Alexander Calder, consisted mainly of glass, bronze, and iron mobiles. He later concentrated on static constructions in iron.

chae·ta (kée-tə) *n., pl.* **-tae** (-tee). *Zoology.* A bristle, or seta, on the body of annelid worms, such as the earthworms, used in locomotion. [New Latin, from Greek *khaitē*, long hair.]

chae·tog·nath (kée-təg-nath, -tog-) *n.* Any of various marine worms of the phylum Chaetognatha, which includes the arrow worms. [New Latin *Chaetognatha*, "bristle-jaw" (so named from the spines at the jaws) : CHAETA + *gnathos*, jaw.]

chafe (chayf) *v.* **chafed, chafing, chafes.** —*tr.* 1. To wear away or irritate by rubbing. 2. To annoy; vex. 3. To heat or warm by rubbing. —*intr.* 1. To cause friction; rub. 2. To become worn or sore from rubbing. 3. To be or become irritated, impatient, or frustrated.

~*n.* 1. Warmth, wear, or soreness produced by friction. 2. Annoyance; irritation; vexation. [Middle English *chaufen*, from Old French *chauf(f)er*, to warm (by rubbing), from Vulgar Latin *calefāre* (unattested), variant of Latin *calefacere* : *calēre*, to be warm + *facere*, to make.]

cha·fer (cháyfər) *n.* Any of various beetles of the family Scarabaeidae, such as the cockchafer. [Middle English *cheaffer*, Old English *ceafor.*]

chaff¹ (chaaf, chaf) *n.* 1. The husks of grain after separation from the seed. 2. Finely cut straw or hay used as fodder. 3. Trivial or worthless matter. 4. Strips of metal foil released in the atmosphere to inhibit radar. [Middle English *chaf(f)*, Old English *ceaf.*]

chaff² *v.* **chaffed, chaffing, chaffs.** —*tr.* To make fun of goodnaturedly; tease. —*intr.* To engage in good-natured teasing.

~*n.* Good-natured teasing; banter. [Probably a blend of CHAFF (trivia) and CHAFE (to irritate).] —**chaff·er** *n.*

chaf·fer (cháffər) *intr.v.* **-fered, -fering, -fers.** 1. To bargain or haggle. 2. To bandy words; chatter.

~*n.* A bargaining or haggling. [Middle English *chaffare, cheapfare*, trade, merchandise, Old English *ceapfaru*, "bargain journey". See **cheap, fare.**] —**chaf·fer·er** *n.*

chaf·finch (cháffinch) *n.* A small European songbird, *Fringilla coelebs,* having predominantly reddish-brown plumage and black and white wings. [Middle English *chaffynche*, Old English *ceaffinc* : CHAFF + FINCH.]

chaf·ing dish (cháyfing) *n.* A dish set above a heating device, used to cook or maintain the warmth of food at the table.

Cha·gall (sha-gál, shə-, -gaál), **Marc** (1887–1985). Russian-born artist noted for his brilliant colours and dreamlike, fanciful imagery. Among his works is a huge painting, completed in 1964, for the ceiling of the Paris Opera House.

Cha·gas disease (shaágəss) *n.* A South American form of trypanosomiasis caused by the protozoan *Trypanosoma cruzi,* which is car-

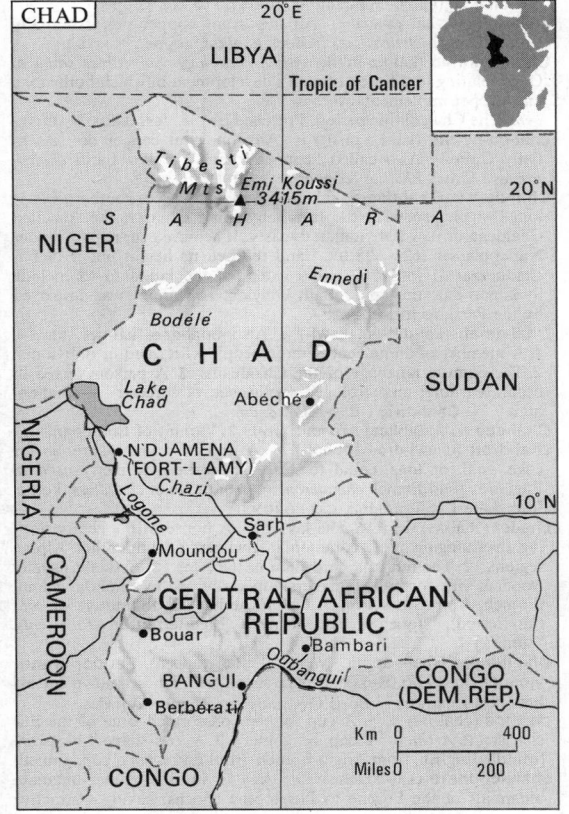

CHAD — 20°E — LIBYA — Tropic of Cancer — Tibesti Mts — Emi Koussi 3415m — 20°N — SAHARA — NIGER — Ennedi — Bodélé — CHAD — SUDAN — Lake Chad — Abéché — NIGERIA — N'DJAMENA (FORT-LAMY) — Chari — 10°N — Logone — Sarh — Moundou — CAMEROON — CENTRAL AFRICAN REPUBLIC — Bouar — Bambari — BANGUI — Oubangui — Berbérati — CONGO (DEM.REP.) — Km 0 400 — Miles 0 200 — CONGO

ried by a bloodsucking insect. [First described by Carlos *Chagas* (1879-1934), Brazilian physician.]

cha·grin (shággrin ‖ shə-grín) *n.* A feeling of embarrassment, annoyance, or humiliation caused by failure or disappointment. ~*tr.v.* **chagrined, -grining, -grins.** To cause to feel chagrin; discomfit. Usually used in the passive. [French, sadness, from *chagrin†*, sad.]

chain (chayn) *n.* **1. a.** A connected, flexible series of links, usually of metal, used for binding, connecting, or other purposes. **b.** Such a set of links, often of precious metal and with pendants attached, worn as an ornament or symbol of office. **2.** Anything that restrains or confines. **3.** *Plural.* Bonds, fetters, or shackles. **4.** *Plural.* Captivity or oppression; bondage. **5.** A number of events or processes that form a continuous or interconnected series: *a chain of coincidences; a food chain.* **6.** A number of establishments, such as stores, restaurants, or theatres, under common ownership or management. **7.** A mountain range. **8.** *Chemistry.* A group of atoms bonded in a spatial configuration resembling a chain. **9.** *Abbr.* **ch a.** A measuring instrument for surveying, consisting of 100 linked pieces of iron or steel. **b.** The length of this instrument as a unit of length, equal to 100 links or 66 feet. Also called "Gunter's chain". **10.** *Abbr.* **ch a.** A similar instrument used in engineering. **b.** The length of this instrument used as a unit of length, equal to 100 feet. Also called "engineer's chain". —See Synonyms at **series.** ~*tr.v.* **chained, chaining, chains.** To bind or confine with or as if with a chain or chains. [Middle English *chayne, cheyne,* from Old French *chaine, chaeine,* from Latin *catēna,* CATENA.]

Chain (chayn), **Sir Ernst Boris** (1906-79). British biochemist, born in Germany. He worked with Florey on antibiotic substances produced by various microorganisms and isolated and purified penicillin. With Alexander Fleming, who discovered penicillin, Chain and Florey were jointly awarded the Nobel prize for physiology or medicine for discovering the healing properties of the antibiotic (1945).

chain gang *n. Chiefly U.S.* A group of convicts chained together and set to outdoor labour.

chain letter *n.* A letter instructing the recipient to send out multiple copies, so that its circulation increases in a geometrical progression as long as the instructions are followed.

chain mail *n.* Flexible armour of joined metal links or scales.

chain·man (cháyn-mən) *n., pl.* **-men** (-mən, -men). In surveying, either of the two people who hold the measuring chain.

chain printer *n.* A printer used in computer systems in which the type is arranged in a continuous chain.

chain pump *n.* A pump that lifts water by means of containers, attached to an endless chain, that pass under water and up over a wheel.

chain reaction *n.* **1.** A series of events, each of which induces or otherwise influences its successor. **2.** *Physics.* A self-sustaining series of nuclear reactions; especially, a fission reaction in which neutrons are released and cause other nuclei to split, leading to a succession of fissions and an increasing amount of neutrons. —**chain-re·act** *intr.v.*

chain rule *n.* A mathematical theorem used in the differentiation of a function of a function: If y is a function of x and u is a function of y, then $du/dx = (du/dy) (dy/dx)$.

chain saw *n.* A power saw with teeth linked in an endless chain.

chain-smoke (cháyn-smŏk) *v.* **-smoked, -smoking, -smokes.** —*intr.* To smoke cigarettes or cigars in a continuous succession. —*tr.* To smoke (cigarettes or cigars) in a continuous succession. —**chain smoker** *n.*

chain stitch *n.* A decorative stitch in which loops are connected like the links of a chain. —**chain-stitch** *v.*

chain store *n.* **1.** A group of retail shops under the same ownership. Also *chiefly British* "chain". **2.** Any of the shops belonging to such a group.

chair (chair) *n.* **1. a.** A piece of furniture consisting of a seat, legs, and back, and often arms, designed to accommodate one person. **b.** Any of various types of seat designed for a particular purpose. Used in combination: *a deck chair; a sedan chair.* **2. a.** A seat of office, authority, or dignity, such as that of a bishop. **b.** A professorship. **3.** The office or position of a person having authority. **4.** A person who holds such an office or position; especially, one who presides over a meeting. **5.** A metal block for supporting and holding railway tracks in position. —**take** (or **be in**) **the chair.** To preside at a meeting. —**the chair.** *U.S.* The electric chair. ~*tr.v.* **chaired, chairing, chairs. 1.** To preside over (a meeting). **2.** To install in a position of authority, especially as a presiding officer. **3.** *British.* To carry (a person) aloft in triumph, usually in a chair. [Middle English *chaiere, chare,* from Old French *chaiere,* bishop's chair, from Latin *cathedra,* chair, from Greek *kathedra,* seat : *kata-,* down + *hedra,* seat.]

chair lift *n.* A cable-suspended, power-driven chair assembly used to transport people up or down mountains. See **ski lift.**

chair·man (chair-mən) *n., pl.* **-men** (-mən). *Abbr.* **chm. 1.** A person, especially male, who presides over an assembly, meeting, committee, or board. **2.** Formerly, one employed to carry a sedan chair. See Usage note at **-person.**

chair·man·ship (cháirmənship) *n.* The office or term of a chairman.

chair·per·son (cháir-perss'n) *n.* A person who presides over an assembly, meeting, committee, or board. See Usage note at **-person.**

chair·wom·an (chair-wŏomman) *n., pl.* **-women** (-wimmin). A female chairman. See Usage note at **-person.**

chaise (shayz) *n.* **1.** Any of various light, open carriages, often with a collapsible hood; especially, a two-wheeled carriage drawn by one horse. **2.** A **post chaise** (*see*). [French, chair, seat, from Old French, variant of *chaiere,* CHAIR.]

chaise longue (sháyz lóng, lóng ‖ *U.S.* láwng) *n., pl.* **chaise longues** or **chaises longues** (*pronounced as singular*). A reclining chair with a seat long enough to support the outstretched legs of the sitter. [French, "long chair".]

chak·ra (cháckra, chúckra, cháakra) *n.* In yogic philosophy, one of the seven centres of spiritual energy in the human body. [Sanskrit, wheel.]

Chak·kri (cháckri) (1737-). The ruling dynasty of Thailand, formerly Siam. First king of the dynasty was Phraya Chakkri (1737-1809) who became Rama I on his accession (1782). Under his rule, hostilities with neighbouring Burma were ended, and Bangkok was established as the new capital. The present king, Bhumibol Adulyadej (1927-), ascended the throne in 1946.

chalah. Variant of **challah.**

cha·la·za (kə-láyzə) *n., pl.* **-zae** (-zee) or **-zas. 1.** *Zoology.* Either of the two spiral bands of tissue in an egg, connecting the yolk to the lining membrane. **2.** *Botany.* The part of an ovule that is opposite the micropyle and that serves as a point of attachment for the integuments and the nucellus. [New Latin, from Greek *khalaza,* hailstone, small cyst.]

cha·la·zi·on (kə-láyzi-ən) *n.* A cyst in the eyelid, formed by a blocked and swollen sebaceous gland. [New Latin, diminutive of Greek *khalaza,* small cyst, hailstone, CHALAZA.]

chal·can·thite (kal-kánthīt) *n.* A blue mineral, $CuSO_4$·$5H_2O$, that occurs in some copper ores. [Latin *chalcanthum,* copper sulphate solution, from Greek *khalkanthon* : *khalkos,* CHALCO- + *anthos,* flower.]

chal·ced·o·ny (kal-séddəni) *n., pl.* **-nies.** A translucent to transparent milky or greyish quartz, SiO_2, with distinctive microscopic crystals arranged in slender fibres in parallel bands. [Middle English *calcedonie,* from Late Latin *chalcēdonius,* from Greek *khalkēdōn,* a mystical stone (Revelation 21:19), perhaps after *Khalkēdōn,* Chalcedon, town in Asia Minor.] —**chal·ce·don·ic** (kál-si-dónnik) *adj.*

chal·cid (kál-sid) *n.* Any of various minute insects of the superfamily Chalcidoidea, related to wasps, of which the larvae of many species are parasitic on the larval stages of other insects. Also called "chalcid fly." [New Latin *Chalcis* (genus), "copper (fly)" (from its metallic colour and sheen), from Greek *khalkos,* copper.]

Chal·cid·i·ce (kal-síddi-si). *Greek* **Khal·ki·dhi·ki** or **Hal·ki·di·kí** (khál-ki-theekeé, hál-). Mountainous peninsula of northeast Greece. It terminates in the three parallel promontories of Kassandra, Sithonia, and Akti. The latter is the site of Mount Athos, a monastic centre of the Greek Orthodox Church.

Chal·cis (kál-siss). *Greek* **Khal·kis** (khal-keéss). The principal town on the island of Euboea in eastern Greece. A prosperous city-state from the eighth century B.C., its traders established settlements in Italy, Sicily, Syria, and mainland Greece.

chalco-, chalc- *comb. form.* Indicates copper or bronze; for example, **chalcography, chalcolithic.** [Greek *khalkos,* copper.]

chal·co·cite (kál-kə-sīt) *n.* An important copper ore, essentially Cu_2S. [French *chalcos(ine)* : Greek *khalkos,* copper + -ITE.]

Chal·co·lith·ic (kál-kə-líthik) *adj. Archaeology. Sometimes small* **c.** Of or relating to a period of man's development in which both stone and copper implements were in use. ~*n.* The Chalcolithic period. Preceded by *the.* [CHALCO- + -LITH.]

chal·co·py·rite (kál-kə-pír-īt) *n.* An important copper ore, essentially $CuFeS_2$. Also called "copper pyrites". [New Latin *chalcopyrites* : Greek *khalkos,* copper + PYRITES.]

Chal·de·a or **Chal·dae·a** (kal-dée-a, kawl-). Area of southern Babylonia which produced the last Babylonian dynasty, the so-called Chaldean or new Babylonian dynasty. It achieved supremacy under Nabopolassar (626-605 B.C.) and reached its height under Nebuchadnezzar II (605-562), who extended the kingdom to include Syria and Palestine, and rebuilt Babylon. The empire was destroyed by the Persians in 539 B.C..

Chal·de·an (kal-dée-ən, kawl-) *n.* Also **Chal·dee** (kál-dee, káwl-). **1.** A member of an ancient Semitic people who ruled in Babylonia. **2.** The Semitic language of the Chaldeans. **3.** A person versed in occult learning; an astrologer, soothsayer, or sorcerer. —**Chal·de·an** *adj.* —**Chal·da·ic** (-dáy-ik) *n. & adj.*

Chal·dee *n.* **1. Biblical Aramaic** (*see*). **2.** Variant of **Chaldean.**

chal·dron (cháwl-drən ‖ chŏl-) *n.* A unit of dry measure, as for coke, coal, or lime, equal to 32 to 36 bushels, formerly used in England. [Old French *chauderon,* augmentative of *chaudiere,* kettle, from Late Latin *caldāria,* CAULDRON.]

cha·let (shál-ay, -i ‖ *U.S.* sha-láy) *n.* **1.** A house with a gently sloping overhanging roof, common in Switzerland and other Alpine regions. **2.** The hut of a herdsman in the Alps. **3.** A small, usually wooden, villa for holidaymakers, especially one in a holiday camp. [French, from Swiss French, cabin, perhaps a diminutive of *cala* (unattested), stone shelter, from a Mediterranean root *cal-,* "stone".]

Cha·li·a·pin (shál-i-áppin, -yáppin ‖ shəl-yápeen), **Feodor Ivanovich** (1873-1938). Russian opera singer. He is best known for his bass performances as Boris Godunov and Mephistopheles.

chal·ice (chál-iss) *n.* **1.** A cup for the consecrated wine of the Eucharist. **2.** *Archaic.* A cup or goblet. **3.** A cup-shaped blossom. [Middle English, from Anglo-French, from Latin *calix,* cup, goblet.]

chal·i·co·there (kál-ikō-theer) *n.* Any of various extinct ungulate mammals of the Eocene to Pleistocene epochs, having distinctive three-clawed, three-toed feet. [New Latin *Chalicotherium* (genus), "fossil beast" : Greek *khalix*, stone, pebble (see **calcium**) + Greek *thērion*, diminutive of *thēr*, beast.]

chalk (chawk ‖ chawlk) *n.* **1.** A soft, compact calcium carbonate, $CaCO_3$, a type of limestone, with varying amounts of silica, quartz, feldspar, or other mineral impurities, generally grey-white or yellow-white and derived chiefly from the remains of small marine organisms. **2.** A piece of chalk or chalklike substance, often calcium sulphate, frequently coloured, used for marking on a blackboard or other surface. **3.** A small cube of friction-enhancing material, usually blue chalk, used to coat the tip of a billiard cue. **—by a long chalk.** *Informal.* By a wide margin. Usually used in the negative. ~*tr.v.* **chalked, chalking, chalks. 1.** To mark, draw, or write with chalk. **2.** To smear or cover with chalk. **—chalk out.** To describe (a project) in broad terms; outline. **—chalk up. 1.** To earn or score: *chalk up points.* **2.** To credit: *Chalk that up to experience.* ~*adj.* Made with or consisting of chalk. [Middle English *chalk*, Old English *cealc*, from Latin *calx*, stone, pebble, from Greek *khalix*.] **—chalk·i·ness** *n.* **—chalk·y** *adj.*

chalk·board (cháwk-bawrd ‖ -bōrd) *n. U.S.* A **blackboard** (see).

chalk·stone (cháwk-stōn) *n. Medicine.* A **tophus** (see).

chalk·stripe (cháwk-strīp) *n.* A striped fabric in two colours, such that thin stripes of one colour alternate with thick stripes of the other. Compare **pinstripe. —chalk·stripe** *adj.*

chal·lah, cha·lah, hal·lah (háàlə, kháàlə) *n.* A yeast-leavened white bread made with egg, usually in a plaited loaf, traditionally eaten by Jews on the Sabbath and holidays. [Hebrew *hallâh.*]

chal·lenge (chál-inj) *n.* **1. a.** A call to engage in a contest or fight. **b.** Any act or statement likely to produce conflict or confrontation: *a challenge to the government's authority.* **2.** A demand for an explanation or justification. **3.** A sentry's call for identification. **4.** The quality of requiring full use of one's abilities, energy, or resources: *a career that offers plenty of challenge.* **b.** An undertaking having this quality. **5.** *Law.* A formal objection, especially to the qualifications of a juror or jury. **6. a.** A test of immunity following immunisation treatment. **b.** A dose of the antigen or substance administered in such a test. ~*v.* **challenged, -lenging, -lenges. —*tr.* 1.** To call to engage in a contest or fight. **2.** To call into question; dispute: *a book that challenges established beliefs.* **3.** To order to halt and be identified. **4.** *Law.* To object formally to (a juror or jury, for example). **5.** To claim; call for: *events that challenge our attention.* **6.** To present a challenge to; stimulate: *a problem that challenges the imagination.* **7.** To test (a patient or laboratory animal) for immunity following immunisation treatment. —*intr.* To make or give voice to a challenge. [Middle English *c(h)alenge*, accusation, challenge, from Old French *c(h)alenge*, from Latin *calumnia*, trickery, false accusation, from *calvī*, to deceive.] **—chal·lenge·a·ble** *adj.*

challenged *adj.* Handicapped; disabled; deficient. Used euphemistically (as when *mentally challenged* means "mentally deficient; stupid") or humorously and in sardonic mockery of such euphemisms (as when *vertically challenged* means "vertically handicapped; short").

chal·leng·er (chál-in-jər). **1.** One that challenges. **2.** One who takes part in a sporting contest against the holder of a title or championship.

chal·leng·ing (chál-in-jing) *adj.* Calling for full use of one's abilities and resources; difficult but stimulating.

chal·lis (shál-iss, -i) *n.* A light fabric usually printed and made of wool, cotton, or rayon. [Perhaps from the surname *Challis.*]

chal·one (kál-ōn) *n.* Any of a group of internal secretions that inhibit a metabolic process. [Greek *khalōn*, present participle of *khalan*, to slacken, let down.]

Châ·lons-sur-Marne (shál-ON-sewr-márn, shaa-lón-sür-). Capital of the Marne *département* of northeast France, situated on the river Marne. At the Battle of Châlons (A.D. 451), the Romans defeated Attila the Hun. The town is a champagne-producing centre.

cha·lyb·e·ate (kə-líbbi-ət, ka-, -it, -ayt) *adj.* **1.** Impregnated with or containing salts of iron. **2.** Tasting like iron. Said of mineral water. ~*n.* Water or medicine containing iron in solution. [New Latin *chalybeatus*, from Latin *chalybs*, steel, from Greek *khalups* (stem *khalub-*), from *Khalups*†, the Chalybes, ancient people in Asia Minor famous for their work in iron and steel.]

cham (kam) *n. Archaic.* A Tatar or Mogul khan. [French, from Persian *khān*, from Turkish, KHAN.]

cham·ae·phyte (kámmi-fīt) *n.* A plant whose winter buds are close to the soil surface. [Greek *khamai*, on the ground + -PHYTE.]

cham·ber (cháymbər) *n.* **1.** A room in a palace for the reception of visitors. **2.** A hall for the meeting of an assembly, especially a legislative assembly. **3.** A legislative, judicial, or deliberative assembly. **4.** *Archaic.* A room in a house, especially a bedroom. **5.** Formerly, a place where state or municipal funds were kept; a treasury. **6.** Any enclosed space or compartment, such as one in the body or in a piece of machinery; a cavity. **7. a.** An enclosed space in the bore of a gun that holds the charge. **b.** The part of a cylinder of a revolver that receives the cartridge. See **chambers.** ~*tr.v.* **chambered, -bering, -bers. 1.** To put in or as if in a chamber; enclose; confine. **2.** To furnish with a chamber. [Middle English *chambre*, from Old French, from Late Latin *camera, camara*, from Latin, vault, arched roof, from Greek *kamara.*]

cham·bered nautilus (cháymbərd) *n.* A cephalopod mollusc, *Nautilus pompilius*, of the Pacific and Indian oceans, having a parti-

tioned shell lined with a pearly layer. Also called "pearly nautilus".

cham·ber·lain (cháymbər-lin ‖ -layn) *n.* **1.** An official who manages the household of a sovereign or nobleman; a chief steward. **2.** An official who receives the rents and fees of a municipality; a treasurer. **3.** *Roman Catholic Church.* A papal attendant, usually honorary. [Middle English *chamberleyn*, from Old French *chamberlenc*, from Frankish *kamerling* (unattested), bedchamber servant : CHAMBER + -LING.]

Chamberlain (cháymbər-lin ‖ -layn), **(Arthur) Neville** (1869–1940). Son of Joseph Chamberlain by his second marriage. As Conservative prime minister (1937–40), he advocated a policy of appeasement towards the fascist regimes of Europe. In the hope of preventing war, he visited Hitler three times in 1938 before reaching the Munich Agreement which recognised Hitler's annexation of the Sudetenland. Germany's subsequent invasion of Czechoslovakia forced Chamberlain to abandon his policy. In September, 1939, he declared war on Germany after Hitler's invasion of Poland. He resigned as prime minister and joined Churchill's war cabinet (May 1940).

Chamberlain, Joseph (1836–1914). British politician. He was a Liberal M.P. from 1876 to 1886, after a period as mayor of Birmingham. He left the Liberals over the question of home rule for the Irish and organised the Unionist party, which allied itself with the Conservatives. He was Colonial Secretary (1895–1903) but split with the Conservatives over his proposals for tariff reforms.

Chamberlain, Sir (Joseph) Austen (1863–1937). Eldest son of Joseph Chamberlain, and a Liberal-Unionist M.P. from 1892. He was Chancellor of the Exchequer (1919–21) and Foreign Secretary (1924–29). He was awarded the Nobel peace prize (1925) for negotiating the **Locarno** Pact.

Chamberlain, Owen (1920–). U.S. physicist, who contributed to the development of the atom bomb. In 1955, he and Emilio Segrè discovered the antiproton by bombarding a copper target with high-energy protons. They were awarded the Nobel prize in physics (1959).

Cham·ber·lin (chámbərlin), **Thomas Chrowder** (1843–1928). U.S. geologist, who with the astronomer F.R. Moulton proposed the **planetesimal hypothesis** (1906) of the formation of the planets in the Solar System.

cham·ber·maid (cháymbər-mayd) *n.* A female servant who cleans and cares for bedrooms, now chiefly in hotels.

chamber music *n.* Music appropriate for performance in a private room or small concert hall and composed for a small group of instruments.

chamber of commerce *n. Abbr.* **C. of C.** An association of businessmen and merchants for the promotion of business interests in its community.

chamber orchestra *n.* A small orchestra, usually with only one instrument to a part, playing chamber music.

chamber pot *n.* A portable vessel used in a bedroom as a toilet.

cham·bers (cháymbərz) **1.** A room where a judge deals with minor cases. **2.** *British.* **a.** A set of rooms occupied by a group of barristers, especially in the Inns of Court. **b.** A set of rooms in an office building.

Cham·bé·ry (shón-be-rée). Capital of the Savoie *département* in the French Alps. It is popular with tourists.

cham·bray (shámbray) *n.* A fine, lightweight fabric, woven with white threads across a coloured warp. [After CAMBRAI.]

cham·bré (shómbray) *tr.v.* **-bréed, -bréing, -brés.** To bring (a wine) to room temperature after first opening it. [From the past participle of French *chambrer*, to put in a room, from *chambre*, room, CHAMBER.]

cha·me·le·on (kə-méel-i-ən) *n.* **1.** Any of various tropical Old World lizards of the family Chamaeleontidae, characterised by their ability to change colour. **2.** A changeable or inconstant person. [Middle English *camelion*, from Latin *chamaeleōn*, from Greek *khamaileōn*, "ground lion" : *khamai*, on the ground + *leōn*, LION.] **—cha·me·le·on·ic** (-ónnik) *adj.*

cham·fer (chámfər) *tr.v.* **-fered, -fering, -fers. 1.** To cut off the edge or corner of; bevel. **2.** To cut a groove in; flute. ~*n.* **1.** A flat surface made by cutting off the edge or corner of something, such as a block of wood. **2.** A furrow or groove, as in a piece of wood. [Perhaps a back-formation from *chamfering*, from French *chanfrein*, a bevel, from Old French *chanfrein(t)*, past participle of *chanfraindre*, to break the edge off : *chant*, edge, rim, from Latin *canthus*, iron ring of a wheel, from Celtic + *fraindre*, to break, from Latin *frangere.*]

cham·ois (shám-waa, *rarely* -waw; *in sense 2 only,* shámmi) *n., pl.* **chamois** (-z). Also (for sense 2) **cham·my, sham·my** (shámmi) *pl.* **-mies. 1.** A goat antelope, *Rupicapra rupicapra*, of mountainous regions of Europe, having upright horns with backward-hooked tips. **2. a.** The soft leather made from the hide of this animal or others such as deer or sheep. **b.** A piece of such leather, used for polishing windows and the like. [Old French, probably from Late Latin *camox*†.]

chamomile. Variant of **camomile.**

Cha·mo·nix (shámmə-nee ‖ -née). Tourist resort in the Haute-Savoie *département* of the French Alps. It is close to Mont Blanc and is a winter sports centre.

champ[1] (champ) *v.* **champed, champing, champs. —*tr.* To bite or chew upon noisily or impatiently. —*intr.* To work the jaws and teeth vigorously. **—champ at the bit.** To be impatient or frustrated at being held back. [Probably imitative.]

champ² *n. Informal.* A champion.

cham·pac, cham·pak (chámpak, chúmpuk) *n.* A tree, *Michelia champaca,* of India and the East Indies, having yellow flowers and yielding a camphor-like substance and an oil used in perfumes. [Hindi *campak,* from Sanskrit *campaka,* of Dravidian origin.]

cham·pagne (shám-páyn) *n.* **1.** A sparkling white wine produced in the Champagne region of France. **2.** Pale orange yellow to greyish yellow. —**cham·pagne** *adj.*

Cham·pagne (shám-páyn, shoN-páñ). Ancient province of northeast France, now falling chiefly in the Marne département. The sparkling wine which takes its name from the province was first produced around 1700, and comes from vineyards roughly bounded by Reims, Épernay, and Châlons-sur-Marne.

cham·paign (chámpayn, shám-páyn) *n. Literary.* A stretch of open country; a plain.
—*adj.* Pertaining to or like a champaign; level and open. [Middle English *champayn,* from Old French *champagne,* from Late Latin *campānia,* from Latin *Campānia,* Campagna (province in central Italy), from *campus,* plain, field. See **camp, campaign.**]

cham·pers (shámpǝrz) *n. British Slang.* Champagne. [CHAMP(AGNE) + -ERS (humorous suffix).]

cham·per·ty (chám-per-ti, -pǝr-) *n., pl.* -ties. *Law.* An illegal sharing in the proceeds of a lawsuit by an outside party who has promoted it. [Middle English *champartie,* from Anglo-French, from Old French *champart,* division of farm produce : *champ,* field, from Latin *campus* (see **camp**) + *part,* PART.]

cham·pi·gnon (sham-pín-yǝn, cham-, shámpin-yón) *n.* Any of various edible mushrooms, especially the common species *Agaricus campestris.* [French, from Old French *champigneul,* probably from Vulgar Latin *(fungus) campāniolus* (unattested), "(fungus) growing in the fields", from Late Latin *campānia,* countryside, CHAMPAIGN.]

cham·pi·on (chámpi-ǝn) *n.* **1.** One that holds first place or wins first prize in a contest, especially in sports. **2.** One who fights for, defends, or supports a cause or another person: *champion of the oppressed.* **3.** *Archaic.* One who fights; a warrior.
—*tr.v.* **championed, -oning, -ons.** To fight as champion of; defend; support. —See Synonyms at **support.**
—*adj.* **1.** Holding first place or prize; superior to all others. **2.** *British Regional.* Excellent; outstanding. [Middle English *champi(o)un,* from Old French *champion,* from Medieval Latin *campiō* (stem *campiōn-*), warrior, from Latin *campus,* field. See **camp.**]

cham·pi·on·ship (chámpi-ǝn-ship) *n.* **1.** The position or title of a champion. **2.** Defence or support; advocacy. **3.** *Often plural.* A competition or series of competitions to determine a winner.

Cham·plain (sham-pláyn), **Samuel de** (1567–1635). French explorer. In 1605, he founded the colony of Port Royal, and three years later he founded Stadacona, on the site of present-day Quebec.

champ·le·vé (shan-lǝ-váy) *n.* A technique of decorating silver and other metals in which hollowed-out areas are filled with coloured enamel. [From the French *champ* field, flat surface + *levé,* raised area.] —**champ·le·vé** *adj.*

Cham·pol·lion (shóN-pol-yón), **Jean François** (1790–1832). French Egyptologist. In 1822, working from the Rosetta stone, he became the first person to decipher Egyptian hieroglyphics.

chance (chaanss || chanss) *n.* **1. a.** The abstract nature or quality shared by unexpected, random, or unpredicted events; contingency. **b.** This quality regarded as a cause of such events; luck. **2. a.** A possibility: *There's just a chance that the letter has gone astray.* **b.** *Often plural.* Likelihood; probability: *What are the chances of our reaching the plane?* **3. a.** An opportunity. **b.** A risk, a gamble. **4.** An unexpected, random, or unpredicted event.
—*v.* **chanced, chancing, chances.** —*intr.* To happen by chance; occur by accident. —*tr.* To take the risk or hazard of. Often used in the phrase *chance it.* —See Synonyms at **happen.** —**chance on** or **upon.** To find or meet accidentally; happen upon.
—*adj.* Occurring as or in consequence of chance. [Middle English, from Old French, from Vulgar Latin *cadentia* (unattested), "a fall", happening, from Latin *cadere,* to fall.]

Synonyms: chance, random, casual, haphazard, desultory.

chan·cel (chaánss'l || chánss'l) *n.* The space around the altar of a church for the clergy and choir, often enclosed by a lattice or railing. [Middle English *chauncel,* from Old French *chancel,* from Late Latin *cancellus,* altar, from Latin *cancellī,* grating, lattice, plural diminutive of *cancer,* lattice.]

chan·cel·ler·y, chan·cel·lory (chaán-sǝlǝri, -slǝri, -sǝlri || chán-) *n., pl.* -ies. **1.** The rank or position of a chancellor. **2.** The office or department of a chancellor or the building in which it is located. **3.** *U.S.* The official place of business of an embassy, consulate, or legation. [Middle English *chancelerie,* from Old French, from *chancelier,* CHANCELLOR.]

chan·cel·lor (chaán-sǝlǝr, -slǝr || chán-) *n. Abbr.* **Chan., Chanc., C.**
1. Any of various officials of high rank; especially: **a.** In former times, a secretary to a king or nobleman. **b.** *British.* The chief secretary of an embassy. **c.** The chief minister of state in some European countries, such as West Germany. **2. a.** *British.* The honorary or titular head of a university. Compare **vice-chancellor.** **b.** *U.S.* The president of certain universities. **3.** A bishop's chief administrative officer, with responsibility for the temporal affairs of a diocese. [Middle English *cha(u)nceler,* from Anglo-French *chanceler,* from Old French *chancelier,* from Late Latin *cancellārius,* secretary, doorkeeper, from *cancellus,* grating, CHANCEL.] —**chan·cel·lor·ship** *n.*

Chancellor of the Duchy of Lancaster *n.* An officer of the British Crown, freed for duty as a government minister and doing work set by the prime minister, often of a financial nature.

Chancellor of the Exchequer *n.* The senior finance minister in the British Cabinet.

chance-med·ley (chaánss-méddli || chánss-) *n.* **1.** *Law.* An action, especially manslaughter, that is largely but not wholly accidental. **2.** A random or haphazard action. [Middle English, from Anglo-French *chance medlee,* "mixed chance" : Old French *chance,* CHANCE + *medlee,* past participle of *medler,* to MEDDLE.]

chan·cer (chaán-sǝr || chán-) *n. British Informal.* One who risks doing something, especially something likely to incur disapproval, in the hope of avoiding loss or discovery.

chan·cer·y (chaán-sǝri || chán-) *n., pl.* -ies. *Abbr.* **Chanc. 1.** *Often capital* **C.** One of the five divisions of the High Court of Justice, presided over by the Lord High Chancellor. Also called "Chancery Division". **2.** In the United States, a court of equity. Also called "court of chancery". **3.** *British.* The political section of a diplomatic mission. **4.** *Ecclesiastical.* A diocesan office controlling archives and legal matters. **5.** An office of public record; an archive. —**in chancery. 1.** *Law.* In litigation or pending in a court of chancery. **2.** In wrestling, having the head locked firmly in an opponent's arm and held against his chest. **3.** *Informal.* In an embarrassing or hopeless predicament. [Middle English *chancerie,* contraction of *chancelerie,* CHANCELLERY.]

chan·cre (shángkǝr) *n.* A dull-red, hard, insensitive lesion that is the first manifestation of syphilis. [French, from Latin *cancer,* ulcer, CANCER.] —**chan·crous** *adj.*

chan·croid (sháng-kroyd) *n.* A soft, nonsyphilitic, venereal lesion of the genital region, caused by infection with the bacterium *Haemophilus ducreyi.* Also called "soft sore". [French *chancroïde* : CHANCR(E) + -OID.]

chanc·y (chaán-si || chán-) *adj.* -ier, -iest. *Informal.* Uncertain or hazardous.

chan·de·lier (shándǝ-léér) *n.* A branched fixture that holds a number of light bulbs or candles, and is usually suspended from a ceiling. [French, from Old French, from Latin *candēlārum* (unattested), from Latin *candēlābrum,* CANDELABRUM.]

chan·delle (shan-dél) *n.* A sudden, steep climbing turn of an aircraft, executed to alter flight direction and gain altitude simultaneously. [French, "candle", from Old French. See **chandler.**] —**chan·delle** *intr.v.*

Chan·di·garh (chúndi-gǝr, chándi-, -gár). The joint capital of Punjab and Haryana states in northern India, situated below the foothills of the Himalayas. It was planned as the new Punjabi capital when Lahore became part of Pakistan (1947). The city, opened in 1953, was laid out in spacious rectangular blocks by a European team of architects under Le Corbusier.

chan·dler (chaándlǝr || chándlǝr) *n.* **1.** A person who makes or sells candles. **2.** A dealer in specified goods or equipment: *a ship's chandler.* [Middle English *chandeler,* from Old French *chandelier,* from *c(h)andelle,* candle, from Latin *candēla,* CANDLE.]

Chan·dler (chaándler || chándlǝr), **Raymond** (1888–1959). U.S. novelist noted for creating the character Philip Marlowe, a cynical and incorruptible private eye. His works include *The Big Sleep* (1939), *Farewell My Lovely* (1940), and *The Long Goodbye* (1953).

Chandler wobble *n.* A small periodical variation in the location of the geographic poles on the Earth's surface. It has an interval of about 14 months. [After *S. C. Chandler* U.S. astronomer.]

chan·dler·y (chaánd-lǝri || chánd-) *n., pl.* -ies. The stock or business of a chandler.

Chan·dra·se·khar (chándrǝ-sháykǝr, chúndrǝ-), **Subrahmanyan** (1910–95). Indian-born U.S. astronomer noted for his work on the evolution of stars, especially the small, low-mass white dwarf. In 1983 he was joint winner of the Nobel prize for physics.

Cha·nel (shǝ-nél, sha-), **Coco (Gabrielle)** (1883–1971). French fashion designer, noted for her classic dresses and suits, and later for her range of perfumes, particularly Chanel No. 5.

Changan. See **Xi'an.**

Chang-chow (cháng-chów) **1.** See **Zhangzhou. 2.** See **Changzhou.**

Chang-chun or **Ch'ang-ch'un** (cháng-choón). *Japanese* **Hsin-king.** Capital of Jilin province in northeast China. It grew in the early years of this century as a key station on the Chinese Eastern Railway, connecting the Trans-Siberian Railway with lines to Vladivostok and Port Arthur.

Chang-de or **Ch'ang-te** (cháng-dö, -dö). City of Hunan province, southeast China, situated on the Yuan river. The centre of a "rice bowl", it was formerly a treaty port.

change (chaynj) *v.* **changed, changing, changes.** —*tr.* **1. a.** To cause to be different; alter. **b.** To give a completely different form or appearance to; transform. **2.** To give and receive reciprocally; interchange. **3.** To exchange for or replace by another, usually of the same kind or category: *change one's name.* **4.** To lay aside or leave for another; switch: *change sides.* **5.** To transfer from (one vehicle) to another: *change planes.* **6.** To undergo or effect alterations in: *change one's mind; litmus paper changing colour.* **7.** To give or receive the equivalent of (money) in lower denominations or in foreign currency. **8.** To engage a higher or lower (gear), as in a motor vehicle. **9.** To put fresh clothes or coverings on: *change a baby.* —*intr.* **1.** To become different or altered. **2.** To go from one phase to another. Used of the Moon. **3.** To pass from one state or position to another according to an established pattern: *Wait till the traffic lights change; autumn changing to winter.* **4.** To transfer from one train, aeroplane, or the like to another. **5.** To put on other clothing. Often used with *into* or *out of*. —**change down** (or **up**). To change into a lower (or higher) gear.

~*n.* Also **'change** (for sense 9). **1. a.** The process or condition of changing. **b.** An instance of changing; an alteration or modification: *make a few changes.* **c.** The replacing of one thing for another; substitution. **2.** A transition from one state, condition, or phase to another: *the change of seasons.* **3. a.** Something different; a substitution. **b.** Variety; novelty. Used especially in the phrase *for a change.* **4.** A different or fresh set of clothing, especially one kept in reserve. **5.** The money of smaller denomination given or received in exchange for money of higher denomination. **6.** The balance of money returned when an amount given is more than what is due. **7.** Any coins, especially when of low value. **8.** A pattern or order in which bells are rung. **9.** *Archaic.* A market or exchange where business is transacted. —**get no change out of.** *Informal.* To fail to get information or help from. —**ring the changes. 1.** To ring bells with every possible variation. **2.** To do or say something familiar or routine in a new and different way. [Middle English *changen,* from Old French *changier,* from Late Latin *cambiāre,* probably from Celtic.] —**chang·er** *n.* —**change·less** *adj.*

    Synonyms: change, alter, vary, modify, transform, convert, transmute.

change·a·ble (cháynj-əb'l) *adj.* **1.** Liable or likely to change. **2.** Capable of being altered. **3.** Changing colour or appearance when seen from different angles or in different lights: *changeable taffeta.* —**change·a·bil·i·ty** (-ə-bílləti), **change·a·ble·ness** *n.* —**change·a·bly** (-əbli) *adv.*

change·ful (cháynjf'l) *adj. Poetic.* Changeable.

change·ling (cháynjling) *n.* **1.** A child believed to have been secretly exchanged for another, especially by fairies. **2.** *Archaic.* A changeable, fickle person.

change of life *n.* The **menopause** (*see*).

change over *intr.v.* **1.** To change completely; adopt a new system, position, or attitude. **2.** *Sports. Chiefly British.* To exchange ends of a playing field, especially at half time. Used of teams.

change·o·ver (cháynj-ōvər) *n.* **1.** A conversion to a different method, attitude, or system: *the changeover to decimal currency.* **2.** *Sports. Chiefly British.* The exchanging of ends of a playing field, especially at half time.

change ringing *n.* The ringing of a set of chimes or bells with every possible variation.

Chang Jiang or **Ch'ang Chiang** (cháng ji-áng). Also **Yang·tze Kiang** (yántsi ki-áng) or **Yang·tze.** Longest river of China. Rising in the Kunlun Shan in southwestern Qinghai province, it flows some 5 520 kilometres (3,430 miles) southeastwards along the Tibet-Sichuan border and then mainly eastwards to enter the East China Sea at Shanghai through a delta.

Chang·sha (cháng-shá). Capital of Hunan province, south China, situated on the Xiang river. This historic trade centre is set in rice-growing country and is famous for its handicrafts. Industries include engineering and chemicals, and zinc and lead mining.

Ch'ang·te. See **Changde.**

chan·nel¹ (chánn'l || *West Indies also* chánnil) *n.* **1.** The bed of a stream or river. **2.** The deeper part of a river or harbour; especially, a deep navigable passage. **3.** A broad strait, especially one that connects two seas: *the English Channel.* **4.** A tubular passage for liquids. **5.** A course or passage through which something may be moved or directed: *a channel of thought.* **6.** *Often plural.* A means of communication or access, especially one that is officially recognised: *went through the proper channels.* **7.** *Electronics.* **a.** A specific frequency band for the transmission and reception of electromagnetic signals, as of television signals. **b.** Loosely, a television station: *What channel is it on?* **c.** A thin layer of semiconductor between the source and the drain of a field-effect transistor. **d.** Any path along which signals, data, or the like can travel. **8.** A trench, furrow, or groove. **9.** A rolled metal bar with a bracket-shaped section. Also called "channel bar", "channel iron". **10.** *Computing.* Any of the rows of punched holes in a punched-paper tape used to store information. —**the Channel.** The English Channel.

~*tr.v.* **channelled** or *U.S.* **channeled, -nelling** or *U.S.* **-neling, -nels. 1.** To make or cut channels in: *"No more shall trenching war channel her fields."* (Shakespeare). **2.** To form a channel or flute in. **3.** To direct or guide along some desired course. [Middle English *chanel,* from Old French, from Latin *canālis,* CANAL.]

channel² *n. Nautical.* A wood or steel ledge projecting from a sailing vessel's sides to spread the shrouds and keep them clear of the gunwales. [Earlier *chainwale* : CHAIN (fastening) + WALE (plank).]

chan·nel·ise, chan·nel·ize (chánn'l-īz) *tr.v.* **-ised, -ising, -ises.** To channel. —**chan·nel·i·sa·tion** (-ī-záysh'n || U.S. -i-) *n.*

Channel Islands *French* **îles Anglo-Nor·mandes** (eelz ónglō nawr-mónd). An island group in the English Channel. They were settled by the Vikings and formed part of the duchy of Normandy, being united with the English crown in 1066. When England lost mainland Normandy in the 15th century, the islands remained possessions of the Crown. They have a measure of autonomy; U.K. laws do not apply until approved by their own legislative bodies. They were occupied by the Germans in World War II. Jersey and Guernsey are famous for early potato and tomato crops, woollen sweaters, and pedigree cattle. Tourism is a major industry.

chan·son de geste (shón-son də zhést, -són) *n., pl.* **chansons de geste** (*pronounced as singular*). A genre of Old French epic poem falling into cycles of poems celebrating the deeds of heroic or historical figures. [French, "song of heroic deeds".]

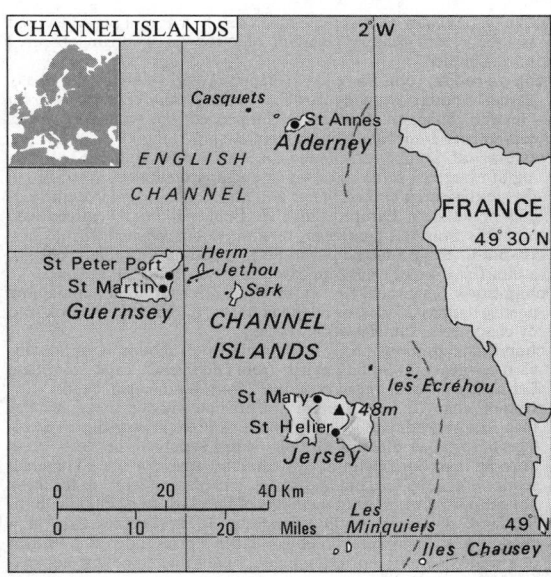

chant (chaant || chant) *n.* Also *archaic* **chaunt** (chawnt || chaant). **1.** A short, simple melody in which a number of syllables or words are sung on each note. **2.** A psalm or canticle sung in this manner. **3.** A repetitive rhythmic intonation of words or slogans, as by football supporters, demonstrators, or the like. **4.** A sing-song way of speaking.

~*v.* **chanted, chanting, chants.** —*tr.* To sing or intone as a chant. —*intr.* To sing; especially, to sing chants. **2.** To intone words or slogans in a repetitive, rhythmic manner. [Middle English, probably from *chanten,* to sing, from Old French *chanter,* from Latin *cantāre,* to sing, frequentative of *canere,* to sing.]

chant·er (chaántər || chántər) *n.* **1.** A person who chants; especially, a chorister or precentor. **2.** The pipe on a set of bagpipes on which the melody is played.

chan·te·relle (shánta-rél, chánta-) *n.* An edible yellow mushroom, *Cantharellus cibarius,* having a pleasant fruity odour. [French, from New Latin *cantharella,* "little cup" (from its shape), diminutive of Latin *cantharus,* drinking vessel, from Greek *kantharos†.*]

chan·teuse (shaán-térz, -tŏz || shán-, -tŏŏz) *n.* A woman singer, especially a nightclub singer. [French, feminine of *chanteur,* singer, from *chanter,* to sing, CHANT.]

chan·ti·cleer (shaán-tə-kleer, chaán-) *n.* Name for a cock or rooster. [Middle English *Chantecleer,* from Old French *Chantecler* (the cock in *Reynard the Fox*) : *chanter,* to CHANT + *cler,* CLEAR.]

chan·try (chaántri || chántri) *n., pl.* **-tries.** *Ecclesiastical.* **1.** In medieval times, an endowment to cover expenses for the saying of masses and prayers, usually for the soul of the founder of the endowment. **2.** An altar or chapel endowed for this purpose. [Middle English *chaunterie,* from Old French *chanterie,* from *chanter,* to CHANT.]

chanty, chantey. Variants of **shanty** (a song).

Cha·nuk·kah, Cha·nu·kah, Ha·nuk·kah, Ha·nu·kah (háa-nə-kə, khá-a-, -nŏŏ-, -kaa) *n.* A Jewish festival beginning on the 25th day of the month of Kislev and lasting eight days. It commemorates the victory of the Maccabees over the Syrians in 165 B.C. and the rededication of the Temple at Jerusalem. Also called "Feast of Lights", "Feast of Dedication". [Hebrew *hanukkāh,* "dedication", from *ḥānakh,* he dedicated.]

Chao Phra·ya (chów prə-yáa). River in north Thailand. It flows some 365 kilometres (225 miles) north to south, passing through Krung Thep (Bangkok) and emptying into the Gulf of Thailand.

cha·os (káy-oss) *n.* **1.** A condition of total disorder or confusion. **2.** *Often capital* **C.** The disordered state of unformed matter and infinite space supposed to have existed prior to the ordered universe according to some religious cosmological views. **3.** *Obsolete.* A vast abyss or chasm. [Latin, from Greek *khaos,* empty space, chaos.] —**cha·ot·ic** (kay-óttik) *adj.* —**cha·ot·i·cal·ly** *adv.*

chaos theory *n.* A branch of mathematics concerned with the principle of predictability. In computer science, minute differences in the way calculations are made can create vastly different results (See **butterfly effect**), so challenging the notion of predictability; but enigmatic patterns called *fractals* have been discerned in apparently chaotic results, and their study may offer insights into randomness in nature.

chap¹ (chap) *v.* **chapped, chapping, chaps.** —*tr.* **1.** To cause (the skin) to split or roughen, especially as a result of cold or exposure. **2.** To split or fissure (the ground). —*intr.* **1.** To split or become rough and sore. **2.** *Scottish.* To knock at a door.

~*n. Usually plural.* A sore roughening of the skin, caused by cold or exposure. [Middle English *chappen,* perhaps of Low German origin, akin to Middle Low German *kappen,* to chop off.]

chap² *n. Informal.* A man or boy; a fellow. [Short for CHAPMAN.]

chap³ *n.* The jaw or lower cheek, especially that of a pig when used as food. [16th century : variant of CHOP (jaw), origin obscure.]

chap. chapter.

cha·pa·re·jos, cha·pa·ra·jos (sháppə-ráy-ōz, -ōss) *pl.n.* Heavy leather trousers worn by cowboys, **chaps** *(see).* [Probably from Mexican Spanish *chaparreras* (influenced by Spanish *aparejo*, equipment), from *chaparro*, CHAPARRAL.]

chap·ar·ral (sháppə-rál, cháppə-) *n.* Dry scrub vegetation, consisting of evergreen scrub oaks, vines, and sparse grasses, especially in the southwestern United States and Mexico, and similar to the maquis of southern Europe. [Spanish, from *chaparro*, evergreen oak, probably from Basque *txapar*, diminutive of *saphar*, thicket.]

cha·pat·ti, cha·pa·ti (chə-pátti, -pútti, -paáti) *n.* In Indian cookery, a thin flat cake of coarse unleavened bread. [Hindi.]

chap·book (cháp-bŏŏk) *n.* A small book or pamphlet containing poems, ballads, stories, or religious tracts. [Originally, "a book sold by chapmen" : CHAP(MAN) + BOOK.]

chape (chayp, *rarely* chap) *n.* A metal tip or mounting on a scabbard or sheath. [Middle English, from Old French, cape, from Late Latin *cappa*, hood, "head covering", from Latin *caput*, head.]

chap·el (cháppʼl) *n.* **1.** A place of Christian worship that is smaller than and subordinate to a church. **2.** A place of worship in a college, hospital, or other institution, or in a stately home. **3.** A recess or room in a church with its own altar, set apart for special or small services. **4. a.** In England and Wales, any place of worship for those not connected with or not members of the established church. **b.** In Scotland, a Roman Catholic church. **5.** The services held in a chapel. **6. a.** An association of workers in a print shop. **b.** A branch of a trade union in a printing house, publishing company, newspaper office, or the like. ~*adj.* Belonging to a Nonconformist church. Compare **church**. [Middle English, from Old French *chapele*, from Medieval Latin *cappella*, originally a shrine containing the cape of St. Martin of Tours, diminutive of Late Latin *cappa*, cape. See **chape**.]

chapel of ease *n.* An Anglican church built for parishioners who live at a distance from the parish church.

chapel of rest *n.* A place on an undertaker's premises where a body is kept prior to burial.

chap·er·one, chap·er·on (sháppə-rōn) *n.* A person, especially an older or married woman, who for propriety supervises a group of young unmarried people or accompanies a young unmarried woman in public. ~*tr.v.* **chaperoned, -oning, -ones.** To act as chaperone to or for. See Synonyms at **accompany**. [French, "hood", protection, protectress, from Old French, from *chape*, CHAPE.] **—chap·er·on·age** (-ij) *n.*

chap·i·ter (cháppitər) *n. Architecture.* The capital of a column. [Middle English *chapitre*, from Latin *capitulum*. See **chapter**.]

chap·lain (cháppʼlin) *n. Abbr.* **ch., Ch. 1.** A clergyman attached to a chapel. **2.** A clergyman attached to a hospital, prison, university, or other institution. **3.** A clergyman attached to a military unit or on board a ship. [Middle English *chapeleyn*, from Old French *chapelain*, from Medieval Latin *cappellānus*, from *cappella*, CHAPEL.] **—chap·lain·cy, chap·lain·ship** *n.*

chap·let (cháp-lət, -lit, -let) *n.* **1.** A wreath or garland for the head. **2.** A string of beads; especially, a string of prayer beads having one third the number of a rosary's beads. **3.** *Architecture.* A small moulding carved in a way resembling a string of beads. [Middle English *chapelet*, from Old French, diminutive of *chapel*, CHAPEAU.] **—chap·let·ed** *adj.*

Chap·lin (cháp-lin), **Sir Charles,** known as Charlie Chaplin (1889–1977). British film star, director, producer, choreographer, and composer, knighted in 1975. His early films, in which he created the tramp in the baggy trousers, with bowler hat and twirling cane, made him an immediate success. His productions included *The Kid* (1920), *The Gold Rush* (1924), *City Lights* (1931), *Modern Times* (1936), and *The Great Dictator* (1940). His later films include *Monsieur Verdoux* (1947), in which he played a murderer; and *Limelight* (1952), in which he portrayed an ageing music-hall comic. A victim of the McCarthy anti-Communist witch hunt of the early 1950s, he left the United States for Switzerland in 1952.

chap·man (cháp-mən) *n., pl.* **-men** (-mən). *Archaic.* A dealer or merchant, especially a pedlar. [Middle English *chapman*, Old English *cēapman* : *cēap*, trade (see **cheap**) + MAN.]

Chapman (cháp-man), **George** (*c.*1560–1634). English poet, dramatist, and scholar noted for his translations of Homer's *Iliad* (1598–1611) and *Odyssey* (1616), which later prompted John Keats to compose his sonnet *On First Looking Into Chapman's Homer.*

chap·pal (chúppʼl) *n.* A type of Indian sandal, usually made of leather. [Hindi.]

chap·pie (cháppi) *n. Informal.* A fellow; a chap.

chaps (chaps, shaps) *pl.n.* Heavy leather trousers without a seat, worn over ordinary trousers by cowboys to protect their legs. Also called "chaparejos". [Short for Mexican Spanish *chaparreras*, CHAPAREJOS.]

chap·ter (cháptər) *n. Abbr.* **chap., ch., c., C. 1.** Any of the main divisions of a book or other piece of writing, usually numbered or titled. **2.** A distinct period or sequence of connected events, as in history or in a person's life. **3.** A numbered division of a session of Parliament relating to a specific Act of Parliament. **4.** *Ecclesiastical.* **a.** An assembly of the canons of a cathedral or collegiate church. **b.** The canons collectively. **5.** *Ecclesiastical.* An assembly of the members or representatives of a religious community or

knightly order. **6.** *U.S.* A local branch of a society, especially of a college fraternity or motorcycle gang. [Middle English *chapitre*, from Old French, from Late Latin *capitulum*, from Latin, small head, chapter, from *caput*, head.]

chapter and verse *n.* The exact source or authority for a statement or action. [Referring to citing the chapter and verses of Biblical books.]

chapter house *n.* A building in which the chapter of a cathedral or monastery assembles.

chapter of accidents *n. Chiefly British.* A series of unforeseen events or accidents.

char¹ (char) *v.* **charred, charring, chars.** *—tr.* **1.** To burn the surface of; scorch. **2.** To reduce to charcoal by incomplete combustion. *—intr.* To become charred. **—See Synonyms at burn.** ~*n.* A substance that has been charred; charcoal. [Back-formation from CHARCOAL.]

char² *n., pl.* **chars** or collectively **char.** Also **charr.** Any of several fishes of the genus *Salvelinus*, related to the trout; especially, the widely distributed species *S. alpinus*. [17th century : origin obscure.]

char³ *n. Informal.* A charwoman. ~*intr.v.* **charred, charring, chars.** *Informal.* To work as a charwoman. [Middle English *char(re)*, piece of work, Old English *cerr*, piece of work, a turning, from *cierran*, to turn, from Germanic.]

char⁴ (char, chaa) *n. Chiefly British Informal.* Tea. [Chinese *ch'a*.]

char·a·banc (shárrə-bang, -bоN) *n., pl.* **-bancs.** *British.* A large bus or coach, often used for sightseeing, group outings, or the like. [French *char à bancs*, "carriage with benches".]

char·a·cin (kárrə-sin) *n.* Also **char·a·cid** (-sid). Any of numerous chiefly tropical freshwater fishes of the family Characidae, related to the carp, many of which are popular aquarium fishes. [New Latin *Characinidae* (earlier family name) : *Charax* (genus), from Greek *kharax* (stem *kharak-*), a kind of fish, pointed stake + -IDAE.]

char·ac·ter (kárriktər ‖ kə-ráktər) *n.* **1.** The combination of qualities or features that distinguishes one person, group, or thing from another. **2.** One such distinguishing feature or attribute; a characteristic. **3.** The moral or ethical nature of a person or group. **4.** Moral or ethical strength; integrity; fortitude. **5.** The quality of being distinctive or outstanding: *an old house of great character.* **6.** Status; capacity; role: *in his character as a father.* **7.** *Informal.* **a.** A person: *There's some character at the door asking to see you.* **b.** A person who is amusing or eccentric. **8.** A person portrayed in a drama, novel, or other artistic piece. **9.** *Archaic.* A reference; a testimonial. **10.** A symbol or mark used in a writing system, such as a letter or a glyph. **11.** *Printing.* A letter, punctuation mark, numeral, or the like, cast in type and usually occupying a fixed amount of space. **12.** A style of printing or writing. **13.** *Genetics.* Any structure, function, or attribute determined by a gene or group of genes. **—See Synonyms at disposition, quality, type. —in** (or **out of) character.** Consistent (or inconsistent) with the usual nature of a person. ~*adj.* **1.** Specialising in roles portraying odd, eccentric, or unusual personality types: *a character actor.* **2.** Calling for the abilities of such an actor: *a character part.* ~*tr.v.* **charactered, -tering, -ters. 1.** To portray, describe, or represent. **2.** *Archaic.* To write, print, engrave, or inscribe. [Learned respelling of Middle English *caracter*, from Old French *caractere*, from Latin *charactēr*, character, mark, instrument for branding, from Greek *kharaktēr*, engraved mark, brand, from *kharassein*, to brand, sharpen, from *kharax* (stem *kharak-*), pointed stake.]

character assassination *n.* The malicious slandering of the reputation of a person, especially a public figure.

char·ac·ter·i·sa·tion (kárriktər-ī-záysh'n ‖ kə-ráktər-, *U.S.* -i-) *n.* **1.** The act of characterising; especially, a description of the qualities or peculiarities of a person or thing. **2.** The creation or delineation of a character or characters on the stage, in a film, or in writing, especially by imitating or describing actions, gestures, or speech.

char·ac·ter·ise, char·ac·ter·ize (kárriktər-īz ‖ kə-ráktər-) *tr.v.* **-ised, -ising, -ises. 1.** To describe the qualities or peculiarities of. **2.** To be a distinguishing trait or mark of.

char·ac·ter·is·tic (kárriktə-rístik) *adj.* Pertaining to, indicating, or constituting a distinctive character, quality, or disposition; typical. ~*n.* **1.** A distinguishing feature or attribute. **2.** *Mathematics.* The integral part of a logarithm as distinguished from the mantissa: *6 is the characteristic of the logarithm 6.3214.* **—char·ac·ter·is·ti·cal·ly** *adv.*

Synonyms: characteristic, individual, distinctive, peculiar, typical.

char·ac·ter·less (kárriktər-ləss, -liss ‖ kə-ráktər-) *n.* Without any distinguishing or interesting features or qualities.

character sketch *n.* A brief portrayal or summary of a person's qualities, distinguishing features, idiosyncrasies, or the like.

char·ac·ter·y (kárrik-təri, kə-rák-) *n., pl.* **-ies.** *Archaic.* **1.** The use of characters or symbols to express or convey thought and meaning. **2.** Such characters or symbols collectively.

cha·rade (shə-raád ‖ *chiefly U.S.* -ráyd) *n.* **1.** An episode or word represented in the game of charades. **2.** *Informal.* An absurd pretence; a farce.

cha·rades (shə-raádz ‖ *chiefly U.S.* -ráydz) *n.* *Used with a singular verb.* A game in which a word or phrase is acted out syllable by syllable, culminating with the whole thing, which is guessed at by the other players or team. [French, from Provençal *charrado*, chat, from *charra*, to chat (imitative).]

char·coal (chár-kōl) *n.* **1.** A black, porous carbonaceous material, produced by the destructive distillation of wood and used as a fuel, filter, and absorbent. **2.** A drawing pencil or crayon made from this substance. **3.** A drawing executed with such a pencil or crayon. **4.** Dark smoky grey to black.
—*tr.v.* **charcoaled, -coaling, -coals.** To draw, write, or blacken with charcoal. [Middle English *charcole* : perhaps Old French *charbon,* charcoal (see **carbon**) + COAL.]
char·coal-burn·er (chár-kōl-burnər) *n.* One who makes charcoal.
Char·cot (shárkō, shaar-kṓ), **Jean Martin** (1825–93). French physiologist noted for his research into the nervous system. Sigmund Freud was one of his students.
char·cu·te·rie (shaar-kéwt-əri, -kóot-) *n.* **1.** Cold cooked meats, especially ham, sausages, and the like. **2.** A shop selling such meats. [French, from *charcutier,* seller of cooked meat, from Old French, from *chair cuite,* "cooked meat" : *chair,* from Latin *caro* (stem *carn-*), flesh + *cuite,* past participle of *cuire,* from Latin *coquere,* to cook.]
chard (chard) *n.* A variety of beet, *Beta vulgaris cicla,* having large, leaves used as a vegetable. Also called "Swiss chard", "leaf beet". [French *carde,* edible stalks of the cardoon, from Old French, cardoon, from Late Latin *cardō,* from Latin *carduus,* artichoke.]
Char·din (shaar-dáɴ), **Jean-Baptiste Siméon** (1699-1779). French painter noted for the simplicity of his compositions and the textural qualities of his paintings. His themes were chiefly still lifes, interiors, and everyday scenes.
Chardin, Pierre Teilhard de. See **Teilhard de Chardin.**
char·don·nay (shaardonáy) *n.* A variety of white grape used for making fine white Burgundy wine. [French.]
Cha·rente (sha-róɴt). River in western France. It rises in the foothills of the Massif Central and flows 354 kilometres (220 miles) through Angoulême and Rochefort to the Bay of Biscay.
charge (charj) *v.* **charged, charging, charges.** —*tr.* **1.** To place a burden on; entrust with a duty, responsibility, task, or obligation. **2.** To command, instruct, or urge with authority: *The judge charged the court to be silent.* **3.** To blame or accuse; impute something to. Often used with *with*: *charged with murder.* **4.** To set or ask (a given amount) as a price. **5.** To hold financially liable; demand payment from: *Customers will be charged for any breakages.* **6.** To postpone payment on (a service or purchase) by recording as a debt: *charge the dress to my account.* **7.** To attack by rushing violently towards: *The soldiers charged the fort.* **8.** To load (a gun or other firearm). **9.** To fill (a vessel, for example): *Charge your glasses for the toast.* **10.** *Electricity.* **a.** To cause formation of a net electric charge on or in (a conductor, for example). **b.** To energise (an accumulator). Often used with *up*: *charge the battery up.* **11. a.** To cause to be saturated; impregnate: *The air was charged with perfume.* **b.** To fill so as to intensify: *The argument was charged with emotion.* **12.** *Heraldry.* To depict a heraldic charge on.
—*intr.* To make an attack by rushing forward: *the cows charged at the bulls; charged towards the door.* —See Synonyms at **command.**
—*n.* **1. a.** Care or custody: *children in the charge of their teacher.* **b.** Supervision; a position of responsibility or authority: *Who's in charge here?* **2.** An obligation or responsibility. **3.** A person or thing entrusted to one's care or management. **4.** An order, command, or injunction. **5.** An address, given by a judge to a jury at the end of a trial, of instruction about such matters as legal points and the weight of evidence. **6.** An accusation or indictment. **7.** *Abbr.* **chg.** The price set or demanded for an article or service: *bank charges.* **8.** *Archaic.* Expense: *gave the banquet at his own charge.* **9.** *Abbr.* **chg.** A debt or an entry in an account recording a debt. **10.** An attack or onset. **11.** The maximum quantity of anything that an apparatus or container can hold at one time. **12.** The quantity of explosive with which a firearm is loaded for one shot. **13.** *Electricity.* **a.** The intrinsic property of matter responsible for all electric phenomena, in particular for the force of the electromagnetic interaction, occurring in two forms arbitrarily designated *negative* and *positive.* **b.** A measure of this property. **c.** The net measure of this property possessed by a body or contained in a bounded region of space. **14.** *Heraldry.* Any device, figure, emblem, or the like depicted on a shield as part of a heraldic achievement. **15.** *Informal.* A feeling of excitement; a thrill. Used chiefly in the phrase *get a charge out of.* —See Synonyms at **price.** [Middle English *chargen,* to load, from Old French *charger,* from Late Latin *carricāre,* from Latin *carrus,* CAR.]
charge·a·ble (chárjəb'l) *adj.* **1.** That may be or is suitable to be charged, as to an account. **2.** Liable to be accused.
charge-capping (chárj-kapping). In Britain, the imposing by central government of an upper limit on the community charge that a local authority can levy.
charge conjugation *n. Symbol* **C** *Physics.* **1.** A mathematical operator that changes the sign of the charge and of the magnetic moment of every particle in the system to which it is applied. **2.** Loosely, the theoretical conversion of matter to antimatter or vice-versa.
char·gé d'af·faires (shár-zhay da-fáir, də-) *n., pl.* **chargés d'affaires** (-z, *or as singular).* **1.** A governmental official temporarily placed in charge of diplomatic affairs while the ambassador or minister is absent. **2.** A low-ranking diplomat representing his government in a country to which no higher-ranking diplomat has been appointed. [French, "(one) charged with affairs".]
charge density *n.* The electric charge per unit area or per unit volume of a body or of a region of space.
charge hand *n.* A workman, usually below the rank of a foreman, who is in charge of a particular section or group of workers.
charge nurse *n.* A nurse, especially a male nurse, in charge of a hospital ward.
charg·er[1] (chárjər) *n.* **1.** One that charges. **2.** A powerful horse trained for battle; a cavalry horse. **3.** An instrument that charges or replenishes batteries. Also called "battery charger".
charger[2] *n.* A large, shallow dish; a platter. [Middle English *chargeour,* from Anglo-French, probably from CHARGE, "to fill".]
charge sheet *n.* A document kept in a police station listing persons arrested and the charges made against them.
Char·ing Cross (chárring, cháir-ing). District in the London borough of the City of Westminster, where Whitehall and the Strand once met. There, in about 1290, Edward I set up the last of a series of crosses in memory of his queen, Eleanor. The cross was destroyed during the Civil War, but another was erected (1865) in front of Charing Cross station, a major railway terminus.
Cha·ri-Nile (chaári-nīl) *n.* A family of languages spoken in eastern and central Africa, including the East and Central Sudanic languages.
char·i·ot (chárri-ət) *n.* **1.** An ancient, horse-drawn, two-wheeled vehicle, used in war, races, and processions. **2.** A light, four-wheeled carriage used for ceremonial occasions or for pleasure.
—*v.* **charioted, -oting, -ots.** —*tr.* To convey or drive in a chariot. —*intr.* To ride in or drive a chariot. [Middle English, from Old French, augmentative of *char,* vehicle, from Latin *carrus,* CAR.]
char·i·o·teer (chárri-ə-téer) *n.* **1.** A person who drives a chariot. **2.** *Capital* **C.** The constellation **Auriga** *(see).*
cha·ris·ma (kə-ríz-mə) *n., pl.* **-mata** (-mətə, *also* kárriz-maátə). Also **char·ism** (kárriz'm) *pl.* **-isms** (for sense 2). **1.** An exceptional ability to attract and influence others; marked personal charm or magnetism. **2.** *Theology.* A divinely inspired gift or power, such as that of healing. [Greek *kharisma,* favour, divine gift, from *kharizesthai,* to favour, from *kharis,* grace, favour.]
char·is·mat·ic (kárriz-máttik) *adj.* **1.** Having charisma. **2.** *Theology.* **a.** Having a charisma. **b.** Inspired or bestowed by the Holy Spirit. **3.** Concerning or following the charismatic movement.
—*n.* A follower of the charismatic movement. **—char·is·mat·ic·al·ly** *adv.*
charismatic movement *n.* A movement among various Christian churches, seeking to reassert the influence of the Holy Spirit in the world and reviving certain practices of the early Church, such as the ministry of healing and speaking in tongues.
char·i·ta·ble (chárritəb'l) *adj.* **1.** Generous in giving money or other help to the needy. **2.** Mild or tolerant in judging others; lenient. **3.** Of, for, or concerned with charity: *a charitable organisation.* **—char·i·ta·ble·ness** *n.* **—char·i·ta·bly** *adv.*
char·i·ty (chárrəti) *n., pl.* **-ties.** **1.** The provision of help or relief to the poor. **2.** An institution, organisation, or fund established to help the needy or carry out other socially useful work. **3.** Something that is given up to help the needy; alms. **4.** An act or feeling of benevolence, goodwill, or affection. **5.** Indulgence or forbearance in judging others; leniency. **6.** *Theology.* **a.** The benevolence of God towards man. **b.** The love of man for his fellow men; brotherly love. [Middle English *charite,* Christian love, from Old French, from Latin *cāritās* (stem *cāritāt-*), love, regard, from *cārus,* dear.]
Charity Commissioners *pl.n.* Members of the body that registers institutional charities in Britain and oversees their administration.
cha·ri·va·ri (shaári-vaári ‖ *U.S.* shívvə-rée) *n., pl.* **-ris.** A noisy mock serenade to newly-weds. [French, from Late Latin *caribaria,* headache, from Greek *karēbaria,* "heavy head" : *karē, kara,* head + *barus,* heavy.]
char·kha, char·ka (chárkə, chúrka) *n.* In India, a spinning wheel, especially one used for cotton. [Hindi *carkha,* from Persian *charkha,* wheel.]
char·la·dy (chár-laydi) *n., pl.* **-dies.** *British.* A **charwoman** *(see).*
char·la·tan (shárlə-tən, *rarely* -tan) *n.* A person who claims to possess knowledge or skill that he does not have; especially, a quack. [French, from Italian *ciarlatano,* from *ciarlare,* to chatter, babble (as when peddling quick remedies), probably imitative. **—char·la·tan·ic** (-tánnik) *adj.* **—char·la·tan·ism** *n.*
Char·le·magne (shárlə-mayn, -máyn, -mīn), also called Charles the Great (*c.* 742–814). King of the Franks (768–814) and founder of the first empire in Western Europe since the fall of Rome. The elder son of King Pepin the Short, he built an empire that encompassed the entire heartland of Western Europe, stretching from the river Danube to the Pyrenees, from Rome to the North Sea. Pope Leo III crowned him emperor on Christmas Day 800. Charlemagne's court at Aix-la-Chapelle became the centre of a cultural rebirth in Europe, known as the Carolingian renaissance.
Charles (charlz), **Prince (Philip Arthur George)** (1948–). The eldest son of Elizabeth II, and heir to the British throne. He was invested as Prince of Wales (1969). He was educated at Gordonstoun and Cambridge, and later served in the Royal Navy and RAF. He married Lady Diana Spencer (1981). Marriage dissolved (1996).
Charles I (1600–49). King of England, Scotland, and Ireland (1625–49) and son of James I. His clashes with Parliament on constitutional issues led to the English Civil War. Conflict with three successive parliaments (1625, 1626, and 1628–9) on the issue of his right to raise taxes without Parliamentary consent led to 11 years' rule without Parliament. His arbitrary rule, High Church leanings, and indulgence in the Roman Catholic faith of his wife, Henrietta Maria, culminated in an attempt to force Archbishop Laud's Angli-

can prayer book on Presbyterian Scotland and led to the Bishops' Wars against Scotland (1639–40). Charles summoned a parliament which refused him financial support unless grievances were discussed. This so-called Short Parliament (April–May 1640) was dissolved, but a new one was summoned in November after a military defeat by the Scots. The Long Parliament vigorously opposed Charles and, following the failure of his attempt to have five of its members arrested for treason (January 1642), the king raised his standard against Parliament on 22 August. The battle of Naseby (1645) was decisive, and Charles surrendered to the Scots at Newark in the following year. In January 1647 he was handed over to Parliament. In November he escaped to the Isle of Wight, where he secretly enlisted the Scots against Parliament, a move that failed. Charles was tried for treason and executed in January 1649.

Charles II (1630–85). King of England, Scotland, and Ireland (1660–85). Exiled during the Commonwealth, Charles was invited to return in 1660. Seeking to free the monarchy from financial dependence on Parliament, he negotiated the secret Treaty of Dover (1670) with Louis XIV, agreeing to help the French against the Dutch. Parliament responded with the Test Act (1673) excluding dissenters and Roman Catholics from office. Fear of Roman Catholicism came to a head with the Popish Plot (1678), which fabricated a plan to place Charles's brother and heir, later James II, on the throne. Charles resisted Parliamentary attempts to exclude James from the succession and from 1681 ruled without Parliament.

Charles V (1500–58). Holy Roman Emperor (1519–56). The son of Philip of Burgundy, he inherited Burgundy with its Dutch possessions on his father's death in 1506, succeeded to the throne of Spain in 1516, and was elected Holy Roman Emperor on the death of his grandfather, Maximilian I.

Charles XIV, King of Sweden and Norway, born Jean Baptiste Jules Bernadotte (1763–1844). French Revolutionary general and King of Sweden and Norway (1818–44). He served brilliantly under Napoleon Bonaparte in the Italian campaign (1796–97), and became Minister of War (1799) and marshal of the empire (1804). Sweden was in need of an heir to the throne and approached Bernadotte. With Napoleon's support, he accepted, and was elected crown prince in 1810. In 1814 he marched into Denmark and forced the Danes to cede Norway to Sweden; both countries became united under the same crown. His reign was peaceful and marked by internal improvements, such as the building of the Göta Canal. He founded the present Swedish royal dynasty of Bernadotte.

Charles Mar·tel (maar-tél) (c.689–741). Frankish ruler of the eastern Frankish kingdom of Austrasia, who repulsed the Moors in Europe (732). He was the grandfather of Charlemagne.

Charles's law n. Physics. The law that the volume of a fixed mass of gas held at a constant pressure varies directly with the absolute temperature. Also called "Gay-Lussac's law". [After Jacques Charles (1746–1823), French physicist.]

Charles's Wain n. British. A constellation, the **Plough** (see).

Charles·ton[1] (chárl-stən). City in South Carolina, on the east coast of the United States, situated on a peninsula between the Ashley and Cooper rivers. It was founded in 1670, and is a major port and industrial centre.

Charleston[2] n. A fast dance in 4/4 time, characterised by kicks out to the side from the knee, and first popular during the 1920s. [After CHARLESTON, South Carolina.]

char·ley horse (chárli) n. U.S. Informal. Muscular cramp or stiffness, caused by injury or excessive exertion. [19th century : origin obscure.]

Char·lie (chárli) n. British Slang. 1. A fool. 2. Plural. A woman's breasts. [Unexplained use of Charlie, diminutive of Charles.]

char·lock (chár-lok, rarely -lək) n. A weedy plant, Sinapis arvensis (or Brassica kaber), native to Eurasia, having hairy stems, foliage, and yellow flowers. Also called "wild mustard". [Middle English cherlok, carlok, Old English cerlic†.]

char·lotte (shárlət) n. 1. Charlotte russe. 2. A dessert, served either hot or cold, consisting of a mould of sponge cake or bread with a filling of fruits. [French, from the name Charlotte.]

Charlotte A·ma·lia (ə-maál-yə). Capital of the U.S. Virgin Islands, a port situated on St. Thomas Island. See map at **Puerto Rico.**

Char·lot·ten·burg (shaar-lótt'n-burg, -boork). A residential area of Berlin in Germany. Once a city in its own right, it contains a 17th-century castle with museum and art gallery.

charlotte russe (rōōss, French rüss) n. A cold dessert of whipped cream or a custard mixture set in a mould lined with sponge fingers. [French, "Russian charlotte".]

Char·lotte·town (shaárlət-town). Capital city of Prince Edward Island, Canada. It was the site of the conference (1864), which laid the foundations of the confederation of Canada in 1867.

Charl·ton (chárltən), **Sir Robert (Bobby),** born Robert Charlton (1937–). British footballer. He scored a record 49 goals for England and was a member of the World Cup winning team (1966). He was knighted in 1994.

charm[1] (charm) n. 1. The power or quality of pleasing, attracting, or fascinating. 2. A particular quality or feature that fascinates or attracts: The painting's charm is its simplicity. 3. A trinket or small ornament worn on a bracelet or other piece of jewellery. 4. Anything that is worn for its supposed magical effect, as in warding off evil; an amulet. 5. Any action or formula thought to have magical power. 6. A chanting of a magic word or verse; an incantation. 7. Physics. A property of certain types of elementary particle, origi-

nally (1974) postulated to account for the long lifetime of the psi particle.
~v. **charmed, charming, charms.** —tr. 1. To attract or delight greatly or irresistibly; fascinate. 2. To act upon with or as if with magic; bewitch. —intr. 1. To be alluring or pleasing. 2. To act as an amulet or charm. 3. To employ spells. [Middle English charme, chant, magic spell, from Old French, from Latin carmen, song, incantation.] —**charm·less** n.

charm[2] n. Archaic. A confused sound of voices or bird calls. [Middle English cherme (influenced by charme, incantation, CHARM), Old English cirm, cierm, clamour, cry, of imitative origin.]

charmed[1] (charmd) adj. Affected or protected by or as if by a charm: a charmed life.

charmed[2] adj. Physics. Designating a quark with one unit of quantum number charm.

charmed circle n. An exclusive, glamorous circle of people.

charm·er (chármər) n. 1. One who charms or has the power to charm. 2. A **snake charmer** (see).

charm·ing (chárming) adj. 1. Having charm or a pleasant manner. 2. Delightful; appealing.
~interj. Used ironically to express indignation or distaste. —**charm·ing·ly** adv.

char·mo·ni·um (chaar-móni-əm) n. Physics. Any of various elementary particles consisting of a charmed quark and an antiquark. [CHARM + -onium, pseudoscientific suffix representing typical technical words (ammonium, plutonium, and so on).]

char·nel (chárnəl) n. A charnel house.
~adj. Resembling or suggesting a charnel house; sepulchral; deathlike. [Middle English, from Old French, from Medieval Latin carnāle, from Late Latin carnālis, carnal, from Latin carō (stem carn-), flesh.]

charnel house n. Formerly, a building, room, or vault in which the bones or bodies of the dead were placed.

Char·ol·lais, Char·o·lais (shárə-lay) n. Any of a breed of large, white beef cattle.

Char·on (kaír-ən, -on). Greek Mythology. The ferryman who conveyed the dead to Hades over the river Styx.

Char·pen·tier (shaar-pónti-ay), **Gustave** (1860–1956). French composer. He was a pupil of Massenet and is best known for his opera Louise (1900), describing the life of a Parisian working girl.

char·poy (chár-poy, -pī) n. A light bedstead used especially in India. [Urdu chārpāi.]

char·qui (chárki) n. Cured or jerked meat, especially beef. [Spanish, from Quechua ch'arki.]

charr. Variant of char (fish).

chart (chart) n. 1. a. A map showing coastlines, water depths, or other information of use to navigators. b. A map of the sky showing the positions of the stars. 2. An outline map on which special information, such as weather data, can be plotted. 3. A sheet presenting information in the form of graphs, tables, or other figures. 4. A **graph** (see). 5. Plural. The list of best-selling records of pop music. Preceded by the.
~tr.v. **charted, charting, charts.** 1. To make a chart of. 2. To plan in detail. 3. To record (progress, for example). [Old French charte, from Latin charta, papyrus leaf, paper, CARD.]

char·ter (chártər) n. 1. A document issued by a sovereign, legislative body, or other authority, creating a public or private corporation, such as a city, college, or bank, and defining its privileges and purposes. 2. A written grant from the sovereign power of a country conferring certain rights and privileges upon a person, a corporation, or the people. 3. Often capital C. A document outlining the principles, functions, and organisation of a corporate body; a statute; a constitution. 4. A document claiming or asserting certain rights. 5. A special privilege or immunity. 6. A licence to do wrong: a thieves' charter. 7. A charter party. 8. a. The hiring or leasing of an aircraft, vessel, or land vehicle. b. An agreement for such a hiring or leasing. 9. Any written instrument given as evidence of agreement, transfer, or contract; a deed.
~tr.v. **chartered, -tering, -ters.** 1. To grant a charter to; establish by charter. 2. To hire or lease by charter. 3. To hire (a vehicle). [Middle English chartre, from Old French, from Latin chartula, diminutive of charta, papyrus leaf, CARD.] —**char·ter·er** n.

char·ter·age (chártərij) n. 1. The act or business of chartering, especially of ships. 2. The fee charged by a ship broker.

char·tered accountant (chártərd) n. Abbr. **c.a., C.A.** In Britain, a member of an institute of accountants granted a royal charter. Compare **certified public accountant.**

charter flight n. A flight by a specially chartered aircraft; especially, one providing cheap fares for members of the chartering group.

char·ter·house (chártər-howss) n. A Carthusian monastery. [Middle English, altered (by assimilation to HOUSE) from Anglo-French Chartrous, (La Grande) Chartreuse. See **Carthusian.**]

charter member n. An original member or founder of an organisation.

charter party n. A contract for the commercial leasing of a vessel or space on a vessel.

Chart·ism (chártiz'm) n. The principles and practices of a movement of social and political reformers, chiefly working men, active in England from 1838 to 1848. Their views were stated in the People's Charter, published in 1838. —**Chart·ist** n. & adj.

Chartres (shártr). Capital of the Eure-et-Loir département of northwest France, situated on the river Eure. Its 12th-century cathedral is one of the masterpieces of Gothic architecture and is famous for its magnificent statuary and stained glass.

char·treuse (shär-trérz, -trŏz ‖ -trŏz, -trŏoss) *n.* **1.** Either of two liqueurs, green or yellow, made from herbs and spices by the Carthusian monks. **2.** Strong to brilliant greenish yellow to moderate or strong yellow green. [French, first made at *la Grande Chartreuse*, Carthusian monastery, near Grenoble.] —**char·treuse** *adj.*

chartulary. Variant of **cartulary**.

char·wom·an (chár-wŏoman) *n.*, *pl.* **-women** (-wimmin). *British.* A woman hired to do cleaning or similar work in an office or home. [CHAR (chore) + WOMAN.]

char·y (chaír-i) *adj.* **-ier, -iest. 1.** Careful; wary. **2.** Fastidious; finicky. **3.** Shy: *chary of meeting people.* **4.** Sparing: *chary of compliments.* [Middle English *charig, charry,* cherished, dear, Old English *cearig,* sorrowful, from Germanic *karō* (unattested), CARE.] —**char·i·ly** *adv.* —**char·i·ness** *n.*

Cha·ryb·dis (kə-ríbdiss). *Greek Mythology.* A whirlpool off the Sicilian coast, opposite the cave of **Scylla** *(see).*

Chas. Charles.

chase[1] (chayss) *v.* **chased, chasing, chases.** —*tr.* **1.** To pursue in order to catch or overtake. **2.** To follow (game) in order to capture or kill; hunt. **3. a.** To try to obtain. **b.** *Informal.* To pursue and force one's attentions on (a woman, for example). **4.** To put to flight; drive. Often used with *away, out,* or *off.* —*intr.* **1.** To go or follow in pursuit. **2.** *Informal.* To go hurriedly; rush. Often used with *after* or *off.* —**chase up. 1.** To seek out and find. **2.** To contact (someone from whom work is required) persistently to ensure that progress is maintained.
~*n.* **1.** The act of chasing; pursuit. **2.** The sport of hunting. Preceded by *the.* **3.** That which is hunted or pursued; a quarry. **4.** *British.* **a.** A privately owned, unenclosed game preserve. **b.** The right to hunt or keep game on the lands of others. **5.** A **steeplechase** *(see).* —**give chase.** To pursue; chase. [Middle English *chacen, chasen,* from Old French *chasser, chacier,* from Vulgar Latin *captiāre* (unattested), from Latin *captāre,* to seize, frequentative of *capere,* to take.]

chase[2] *n. Printing.* A rectangular steel or iron frame into which type is locked for printing or plate-making. [Probably from French *châsse,* a case, from Latin *capsa,* box, CASE.]

chase[3] *n.* **1. a.** A groove cut in any object; a slot. **b.** A trench or channel for drainpipes or wiring. **c.** A longitudinal groove for a tenon or tongue. **2.** The part of a gun which contains the bore. ~*tr.v.* **chased, chasing, chases. 1.** To decorate (metal) by engraving or embossing. **2. a.** To groove; indent. **b.** To cut or finish (the thread of a screw) using a chaser. [Old French *chas,* "enclosure", from Latin *capsus,* from *capsa,* box, CASE.]

chas·er[1] (cháyssər) *n.* **1.** One that chases or pursues. **2.** A gun on the bow or stern of a ship, used during pursuit or flight. Also called "chase gun". **3.** *Informal.* A drink of water, beer, or the like taken after spirits.

chaser[2] *n.* **1.** One who decorates metal by engraving or embossing. **2.** A steel tool for cutting or finishing screw threads.

chasm (kázz'm) *n.* **1.** A deep cleft or crack in the earth's surface; an abyss or narrow gorge. **2.** A sudden and considerable interruption of continuity; a gap; a hiatus. **3.** Any marked difference of opinion, interests, loyalty, or the like. [Latin *chasma,* from Greek *khasma,* akin to *khainein,* to gape.] —**chas·mal** (kázm'l) *adj.*

chas·sé (shássay ‖ U.S. sha-sáy) *n.* A dance movement consisting of one or more quick, gliding steps with the same foot always leading.
~*intr.v.* **chasséd, -séing, -sés.** To make or perform a chassé. [French, from the past participle of *chasser,* to CHASE.]

chasse·pot (sháss-pŏ) *n.* A type of breechloading rifle introduced into the French army in 1866. [French, after Antoine *Chassepot* (1833–1905), French gunsmith.]

chas·seur (sha-súr ‖ -sŏor) *n.* **1.** A soldier; especially, one of certain light cavalry or infantry troops of the French army, trained for rapid manoeuvres. **2.** A huntsman. **3.** A uniformed footman.
~*adj.* Served with a sauce of mushrooms and white wine: *chicken chasseur.* [French, "huntsman", from *chasser,* to CHASE.]

Chas·si·dim, Has·si·dim (hássi-deem, khássi-, -deem, -dim) *pl.n. Singular* **Chas·sid, Has·sid** (hássid, ha-séed, khá-). A sect of Jewish mystics founded in Poland (about 1750) in opposition to the formalistic Judaism of the period and to ritual laxity. [Hebrew *ḥasīdhīm,* "pious ones", from *ḥāsīdh,* pious.] —**Chas·si·dic** (hə-síddik, kha-) *adj.* —**Chas·si·dism** *n.*

chas·sis (shássi, -ee) *n., pl.* **chassis** (-z). **1.** The rectangular steel frame, supported on springs and attached to the axles, that holds the body and engine of a motor vehicle. **2.** The landing gear of an aircraft, including the wheels, floats, and other structures that support the aircraft on land or water. **3.** The frame on which a casement gun carriage moves forwards and backwards. **4.** The framework to which the functioning parts of a radio, television, record player, tape recorder, or other electronic equipment are attached. **5.** *Informal.* A woman's body. Used humorously. [French *châssis,* from Old French *chassis,* from Vulgar Latin *capsīcium* (unattested), from *capsa,* box, CASE.]

chaste (chayst) *adj.* **chaster, chastest. 1.** Sexually pure; decent; modest. **2. a.** Abstaining from unlawful sexual intercourse. **b.** Abstaining from all sexual activity. **3.** Pure or simple in literary or artistic style; not ornate or artificial. [Middle English, from Old French, from Latin *castus,* morally pure.] —**chaste·ly** *adv.*

—**chaste·ness** *n.*

chas·ten (cháyss'n) *tr.v.* **-tened, -tening, -tens. 1.** To punish or discipline, especially so as to effect moral improvement. **2.** To restrain; moderate. **3.** To refine; purify: *chasten one's style.* [From obsolete *chaste* (verb), from Middle English *chasten, chastien,* from Old French *chastier,* from Latin *castigāre,* to CASTIGATE.] —**chas·ten·er** *n.*

chaste tree *n.* A shrub, *Vitex agnus-castus,* of southern Europe, often cultivated for its spikes of lilac-blue flowers. [Translation of New Latin *agnus castus,* by folk etymology (influenced by Latin *agnus,* lamb) from Greek *agnos*† (confused with *hagnos,* holy, chaste).]

chas·tise (chass-tíz) *tr.v.* **-tised, -tising, -tises. 1.** To punish, usually by beating. **2.** To criticise severely. —See Synonyms at **punish.** [Middle English *chastisen,* variant of *chastien,* to CHASTEN.] —**chas·tise·ment** (chástiz-mənt, chastíz-) *n.* —**chas·tis·er** *n.*

chas·ti·ty (chástəti) *n.* **1.** The state or quality of being chaste or pure. **2.** Celibacy; virginity. [Middle English *chastete,* from Old French, from Latin *castitās* (stem *castitāt-),* from *castus,* CHASTE.]

chastity belt *n.* Any of various devices supposed to have been worn by medieval women to prevent sexual intercourse.

chas·u·ble (cházzewb'l ‖ U.S. also cházh-yəb'l, cháss-) *n.* A long, sleeveless vestment worn over the alb by the priest at Mass. [French, from Old French, from Late Latin *casubla,* hooded garment, irregularly from Latin *casula,* cloak, (literally, little house, cottage), diminutive of *casa,* house.]

chat (chat) *intr.v.* **chatted, chatting, chats.** To converse in an easy, informal, or familiar manner. —**chat up.** *British Informal.* To engage (a person) in friendly or flirtatious conversation, especially so as to win personal favour or strike up a sexual relationship.
~*n.* **1.** An informal or familiar conversation. **2.** Any of several birds known for their chattering call, such as: **a.** Any of several Old World birds of the genus *Saxicola.* See **stonechat, whinchat. b.** A North American bird, *Icteria virens.* **c.** Any of several Australian wrens of the genus *Ephthianura.* [Middle English *chatten,* short for *chatteren,* to CHATTER.]

cha·teau, châ·teau (sháttō ‖ chiefly U.S. sha-tŏ) *n., pl.* **chateaux** (-z, or as singular). **1.** A French castle or manor house. **2.** A country house; especially, one resembling a French castle. [French *château,* from Old French *chastel,* from Latin *castellum,* CASTLE.]

cha·teau-bot·tled (shátto-bott'ld ‖ sha-tŏ-) *adj.* Designating a wine coming from the vineyards attached to a chateau and bottled within its domain.

Cha·teau·bri·and[1] (sháttō-brée-ON, -bree-ónd), **François René, Vicomte de** (1768–1848). French author and diplomat, and a leading figure in the early Romantic movement in France. His autobiography, *Mémoires d'Outre-tombe* (1811–42), was published after his death.

Chateaubriand[2] *n. Sometimes small* **c.** A double-thick tender steak cut from the fillet. [Probably invented by the chef of the Vicomte de CHATEAUBRIAND.]

chat·e·lain (shátta-layn, -lan) *n.* The keeper of a castle; a castellan. [Middle English *chateleyn,* from Old French *chastelain,* from Latin *castellānus,* from *castellum,* CASTLE.]

chat·e·laine (shátta-layn, -len) *n.* **1.** The lady or mistress of a castle, chateau, or large, fashionable household. **2.** A clasp or chain worn at the waist for holding keys, a purse, or a watch.

Chat·ham (cháttəm). Town in Kent, England, at the mouth of the river Medway near the Thames estuary. Henry VIII established royal dockyards there, and the town remained a naval base until 1983.

Chatham Islands. Small Pacific island group forming part of New Zealand. They were discovered in 1791. Sheep farming is the main occupation. See map at **Pacific Ocean.**

chat line *n.* In Britain, a telephone service allowing subscribers to dial into a group conversation with others sharing the same interests.

cha·toy·ant (shə-tóy-ənt) *adj.* Having a changeable lustre.
~*n.* A chatoyant stone or gemstone, such as the cat's-eye. [French, present participle of *chatoyer,* gleam like a cat's eyes, from *chat,* CAT.]

chat show *n.* A radio or television show in which the presenter and invited guests engage in informal conversation. Also *U.S.* "talk show".

Chat·ta·noo·ga (chátta-nŏoga). City in Tennessee in the southeast of the United States, situated on the Tennessee river. It is a major rail terminus, celebrated in the song *Chattanooga Choo Choo.*

chat·tel (chátt'l) *n.* **1.** *Law.* An article of personal, movable property. **2.** A slave. [Middle English *chatel,* property, goods, from Old French. See **cattle.**]

chat·ter (cháttər) *intr.v.* **-tered, -tering, -ters. 1.** To utter a rapid series of short, inarticulate, speechlike sounds. Used of a bird or animal. **2.** To talk rapidly or incessantly, especially on a trivial subject; jabber. **3.** To click together quickly, as the teeth do from cold. **4.** To vibrate or rattle while in operation, as a power tool does. —See Synonyms at **speak.**
~*n.* **1.** Idle or trivial talk. **2.** The jabbering of an animal or bird. **3.** A rattling or clicking, as of the teeth. **4.** A rattling or vibration, as of a power tool in operation. [Middle English *chat(t)eren* (imitative).] —**chat·ter·er** *n.*

chat·ter·box (cháttər-boks) *n.* An extremely talkative person.

Chat·ter·jee (cháttər-jee), **Bankim Chandra** (1838–94). Bengalese civil servant who founded the *Bangadarshan,* a Hindu newspaper

(1872), and became a novelist. He grafted European rationalist thought onto Hindu traditions to create a new school of fiction.

chatter mark (chátter-maark) *n.* **1.** A riblike marking on wood or metal, caused by vibration of a cutting tool. **2.** *Geology.* Any of a series of short scars on a glaciated rock surface.

chat·ty (chátti) *adj.* **-tier, -tiest. 1.** Given to informal conversation. **2.** Marked by a familiar, conversational style: *a chatty letter.* —**chat·ti·ly** *adv.* —**chat·ti·ness** *n.*

Chau·cer (cháwssər), **Geoffrey** (*c.*1342–1400). English poet, considered the father of English poetry. He was also a diplomat and customs official, travelling widely in Europe under Richard II. *The Book of the Duchess* (1369), written in honour of the wife of John of Gaunt, was his first work, followed by others including the *Parliament of Fowls* and *Troilus and Criseyde.* His *Canterbury Tales,* a collection of stories supposedly told by a party of pilgrims travelling from London to Canterbury, is his most famous work.

Chau·ce·ri·an (chaw-séer-i-ən) *adj.* Of, pertaining to, or characteristic of Chaucer or his writings.
—*n.* **1.** A scholar specialising in the writings of Chaucer. **2.** An imitator of Chaucer.

chaud·froid (shŏ-frwáa) *n.* **1.** A jellied white or brown sauce used as an aspic for cold meats or fish. **2.** Moulded cold meat or fish dishes garnished with a chaudfroid sauce. [French, "hot-cold".]

chauf·feur (shŏfər, shō-fúr, shə-) *n.* One employed to drive a private or official car.
—*v.* **chauffeured, -feuring, -feurs.** —*tr.* To serve as a driver for. —*intr.* To serve as a chauffeur. [French, stoker, from *chauffer,* to warm. See **chafe.**]

chaul·moo·gra (cháwl-mŏogrə) *n.* Any of several trees of tropical Asia, especially *Taraktogenos kurzii* and those of the genus *Hydnocarpus,* having seeds that yield an oil formerly used in treating leprosy. [Bengali *cāulmugrā : cāul,* rice + *mugrā,* hemp.]

chaunt. *Archaic.* Variant of **chant.**

chausses (shŏss) *pl.n.* Medieval armour of mail for the legs and feet. [Middle English *chauces,* from Old French, from Medieval Latin *calcia,* clothing for the leg, from Latin *calceus,* shoe. See **calceate.**]

chau·vin·ism (shŏvin-iz'm) *n.* **1.** Militant devotion to and glorification of one's country; fanatical patriotism. **2.** Prejudiced belief in the superiority of one's own group: *male chauvinism.* [French *chauvinisme,* after Nicholas *Chauvin,* veteran of the First Republic and Empire noted for his patriotic fervour, popularised as a character in the play *La Cocarde tricolore* (1831).] —**chau·vin·ist** *n.* —**chau·vin·is·tic** (-ístik) *adj.* —**chau·vin·is·ti·cal·ly** *adv.*

chaw (chaw) *v.* **chawed, chawing, chaws.** *Regional.* —*intr.* To chew. —*tr.* To chew (something). —**chaw** *n.*

cha·zan, chaz·zen, haz·zan'n (háaz'n, kha-zán) *n.* A cantor in a synagogue. [Late Hebrew *ḥazzān,* officer, cantor.]

Ch.E. chemical engineer.

cheap (cheep) *adj.* **cheaper, cheapest. 1.** Relatively low in cost; inexpensive. **2.** Charging low prices: *a cheap restaurant.* **3.** Worth more than the price paid. **4.** Involving little effort or loss: *a cheap victory.* **5.** Of small value. **6.** Of poor quality; shoddy. **7.** Not worthy of respect; vulgar; despicable. **8.** Ashamed or abashed. **9.** *Economics.* **a.** Obtainable at a low rate of interest. **b.** Devalued, as in buying power.
—*adv.* Inexpensively. [Middle English *chep,* sale, bargain, purchase, Old English *cēap,* from West Germanic *kaupaz* (unattested), trader, from Latin *caupō,* innkeeper.] —**cheap·ly** *adv.* —**cheap·ness** *n.*

cheap·en (chéepən) *v.* **-ened, -ening, -ens.** —*tr.* **1.** To make cheap or cheaper. **2.** To lower in estimation; degrade. —*intr.* To become cheap or cheaper. —**cheap·en·er** *n.*

cheap·ie (chéepi) *n.* *Informal.* Something that is cheap and often of poor quality.

cheap·jack (chéep-jak) *adj.* **1.** Selling overpriced goods of poor quality. **2.** Of poor quality; worthless. [CHEAP + JACK (fellow), originally a hawker or dealer in shoddy goods.]

cheap·o (chéepō) *adj. Informal.* Cheap.

Cheap·side (chéep-sīd). Street in the City of London. It was the central market area of medieval London. St. Mary le Bow, built there by Wren in 1680, is the church of Bow Bells.

cheap·skate (chéep-skayt) *n. Informal.* A stingy person; a miser. [CHEAP + SKATE (chap).] —**cheap·skate** *adj.*

cheat (cheet) *v.* **cheated, cheating, cheats.** —*tr.* To deceive by trickery; swindle. **2.** To mislead; fool. **3.** To elude; escape: *cheat death.* —*intr.* **1.** To act dishonestly to gain some advantage: *cheat at cards.* **2.** To act fraudulently. **3.** *Informal.* To be unfaithful especially to one's spouse: *cheating on his wife.*
—*n.* **1.** A fraud or swindle. **2.** One who cheats. **3.** *Law.* The fraudulent acquisition of another's property. [Middle English *cheten,* to revert, short for *acheten,* variant of *escheten,* from *eschete,* ESCHEAT.] —**cheat·er** *n.* —**cheat·ing·ly** *adv.*

check (chek) *n.* **1.** An abrupt stopping or interruption of motion or progress; a delay or rebuff. **2.** Restraint or control. **3.** Someone or something that restrains or controls: *checks and balances.* **4.** An inspection or examination, as to assess or verify accuracy, efficiency, attendance, or the like. **5.** A standard of comparison used in such an inspection; a test. **6. a.** A pattern of small squares, as on a chessboard. **b.** Any of the squares of such a pattern. **c.** A fabric patterned with such squares. **7.** A small crack or fault, especially in a piece of timber. **8.** *Chess.* **a.** A move that directly attacks an opponent's king but does not constitute a checkmate. **b.** The posi-

tion or tactical condition of a king so attacked. **9.** A device in a piano to prevent a hammer from striking more than once when a key has been struck. **10.** In hunting, a loss of the scent by the hounds. **11.** *Chiefly U.S.* A ticket or slip of identification: *a baggage check.* **12.** *U.S.* **a.** Variant of **cheque. b.** A bill in a restaurant or bar. **c.** A mark indicating approval; a tick. **d.** A gambling chip or counter. —**in check.** Under restraint; in control.
—*interj.* **1.** *Chess.* A declaration made to an opponent that his king is in check. **2.** *U.S. Informal.* Used to express affirmation.
—*v.* **checked, checking, checks.** —*tr.* **1.** To arrest the motion or progress of abruptly; halt. **2.** To hold in restraint; curb. **3.** To slow the growth of; retard. **4.** *Informal.* To rebuke. **5. a.** To test or examine, as for accuracy or efficiency. **b.** To ascertain or verify: *I'll just check that I've locked the door.* **6.** *Chess.* To move so as to put (an opponent's king) under direct attack. **7.** *Ice Hockey.* To impede (an opponent) in control of the puck. **8.** *U.S.* To mark with a tick. **9.** *U.S.* To deposit in a cloakroom, left-luggage office, or the like. —*intr.* **1.** To come to an abrupt halt; stop; pause. **2.** To make an examination or investigation, as to verify something or to assess accuracy. Often used with *up, on,* or *upon.* **3.** *U.S.* To correspond accurately; agree. **4.** To pause to relocate a scent. Used of hunting dogs. **5.** *Chess.* To place an opponent's king in check. —See Synonyms at **restrain, delay.**
—*adj.* **1.** Marked in a pattern of checks or squares. **2.** Serving to verify or control. [Middle English *chek,* attack, quarrel, check at chess, from Old French *eschec, eschac,* from Arabic *shāh,* king, check at chess, from Persian, king.] —**check·a·ble** *adj.*

checked (chekt) *adj.* **1.** Having a pattern of checks or squares. **2.** *Phonetics.* **a.** Followed by a consonant in a closed syllable. Said of a vowel. **b.** Closed. Said of a syllable.

check·er[1] (chécker) *n.* **1.** One who checks, examines, or supervises. **2.** *U.S.* One who receives items for safekeeping: *a baggage checker.* **3.** *U.S.* A draught; draughtsman.

checker[2] Variant of **chequer.**

check·er·ber·ry (chécker-bri, -bəri, -berri) *n., pl.* **-ries.** *U.S.* **1.** A plant, the wintergreen *(see).* **2.** The red, edible, spicy berry of this plant. [CHECKER (a name for the fruit of the service tree) + BERRY.]

check·er·board (chécker-bawrd ‖ -bōrd) *n. U.S.* A **draughtboard** *(see).*

check·ers (chéckərz) *n. Used with a singular verb. U.S.* The game of **draughts** *(see).*

check in *intr.v.* To register on one's arrival, as at work or an airport. —*tr.v.* To register (passengers or luggage, for example) on arrival.

check-in (chék-in) *n.* **1.** Registration on one's arrival, as at an airport. **2.** The place where one registers. In this sense, also called "check-in desk."

check·ing account (chécking) *n. U.S.* A **current account** *(see).*

check·list (chék-list) *n.* Any list in which items can be compared, verified, or identified.

check·mate (chék-máyt, -mayt) *tr.v.* **-mated, -mating, -mates. 1.** *Chess.* To attack (an opponent's king) in such manner that no escape or defence is possible, thus ending the game. **2.** To defeat completely.
—*n.* **1.** *Abbr.* **chm.** *Chess.* **a.** A move that constitutes an inescapable and indefensible attack on an opponent's king. **b.** The position of a king so attacked. **2.** Utter defeat.
—*interj.* *Chess.* A call declaring the checkmate of an opponent's king. [Middle English *chekmate,* from Old French *eschec mat,* from Persian *shāh māt,* the king is dead.]

check out *intr.v.* **1.** To pay one's bill and depart, as from a hotel. **2.** To record one's departure, as from a workplace. **3.** *Chiefly U.S.* To correspond, upon investigation, to what is expected. —*tr.v.* **1.** To investigate or test, as for efficiency or safety. **2.** *Informal.* To look over or inspect.

check-out (chék-owt) *n.* **1.** A cash desk, as in a supermarket. **2.** The time by which a guest must vacate a hotel room or be charged for another day's occupancy. —**check-out** *adj.*

check·point (chék-poynt) *n.* A place where people or vehicles are stopped for inspection.

check·rein (chék-rayn) *n.* A **bearing rein** *(see).*

check·room (chék-rŏom, -rōom) *n. U.S.* A cloakroom or left-luggage office.

check up *intr.v.* To investigate or scrutinise a suspicious person or situation. Often used with *on.*

check·up (chék-up) *n.* **1.** A thorough examination, as for verification or accuracy. **2.** A medical examination.

check valve *n.* A valve that limits the flow of a fluid in a piping system to one direction and closes to prevent return flow.

Ched·dar[1] (chéddər). Town in Somerset in southwest England, situated in the valley of the Axe. Cheddar cheese was first produced there in the 17th century. Cheddar Gorge, cutting through the Mendip hills to the east, has limestone caverns and rare flora.

Cheddar[2] *n. Sometimes small* **c.** Any of several types of smooth, hard cheese varying in flavour from mild to extra sharp. [After CHEDDAR, Somerset, where it was originally made.]

ched·dite (chéd-īt, shéd-) *n.* An explosive consisting of a chlorate or perchlorate mixed with a fat or oil, such as castor oil. [After *Chedde,* a town in Savoy where it was first manufactured.]

che·der, he·der (kháy-dər) *n.* A class in which Jewish children are taught Hebrew and Jewish religious history and principles. [Hebrew, room.]

cheek (cheek) *n.* **1.** The fleshy part of either side of the face below the eye and between the nose and ear. **2.** Something resembling this in shape or position, such as either of two sides of a vice or door jamb. **3.** *Informal.* A buttock. **4.** Sauciness; impudence. —See Synonyms at **temerity.** —**cheek by jowl.** Side by side; intimate. —**turn the other cheek.** To submit to unjust treatment without retaliating.

~*tr.v.* **cheeked, cheeking, cheeks.** *Informal.* To speak impudently to. [Middle English *che(e)ke,* Old English *cēce, cēace,* from Germanic *kækōn-* (unattested).]

cheek·bone (cheék-bōn) *n.* A bone in the upper cheek, the **zygomatic bone** *(see).*

cheek pouch *n.* A pouch inside the mouth of many rodents and certain other animals, used for holding food.

cheek·y (cheéki) *adj.* **-ier, -iest.** Saucy; impudent; brazen. —**cheek·i·ly** *adv.* —**cheek·i·ness** *n.*

cheep (cheep) *n.* A faint, shrill sound like that of a young bird; a chirp.

~*v.* **cheeped, cheeping, cheeps.** —*tr.* To utter with a chirp. —*intr.* To chirp; peep. [Imitative.] —**cheep·er** *n.*

cheer (cheer) *n.* **1.** Gaiety; animation; happiness. **2.** A shout of approval, encouragement, or congratulation. **3.** *Archaic.* A comfort or encouragement. **4.** *Archaic.* Food or drink; refreshment.

~*v.* **cheered, cheering, cheers.** —*tr.* **1. a.** To fill with joy. **b.** To comfort. Often used with *up.* **2.** To encourage with or as if with cheers; urge. Often used with *on.* **3.** To salute or acclaim with cheers; applaud. —*intr.* **1.** To shout cheers; applaud. **2.** To become cheerful. Often used with *up.* [Middle English *cheere,* cheer, disposition, countenance, face, from Old French *ch(i)ere,* face, from Late Latin *cara,* from Greek *karē, kara,* head.] —**cheer·er** *n.* —**cheer·ing·ly** *adv.*

cheer·ful (cheérf'l) *adj.* **1.** Being in good spirits; happy. **2.** Promoting cheer; pleasant. —See Synonyms at **glad.** —**cheer·ful·ly** *adv.* —**cheer·ful·ness** *n.*

cheer·i·o (cheér-i-ō) *interj.* *Chiefly British Informal.* **1.** Used as a farewell greeting. **2.** Used as a toast. [From CHEER.]

cheer·lead·er (cheér-leedər) *n.* *Chiefly U.S.* One who leads group cheering, especially at sporting events.

cheer·less (cheér-ləss, -liss) *adj.* **1.** Gloomy and unwelcoming, as a room might be. **2.** Pessimistic; in low spirits. —**cheer·less·ly** *adv.* —**cheer·less·ness** *n.*

cheers (cheerz) *interj.* *Chiefly British.* **1.** Used as a toast. **2.** *Informal.* Used as a farewell. **3.** *Informal.* Used to express thanks.

cheer·y (cheér-i) *adj.* **-ier, -iest.** In good spirits; cheerful. —**cheer·i·ly** *adv.* —**cheer·i·ness** *n.*

cheese[1] (cheez) *n.* **1. a.** A solid or semisolid food prepared from the pressed curd of milk. **b.** A moulded mass of this substance. **2.** Something like cheese in shape, smell, or consistency. **3.** A fruit preserve with a spreading consistency. [Middle English *chese,* Old English *cēse,* from Germanic *kasjus* (unattested), from Latin *cāseus*†.] —**chees·y** (-i) *adj.*

cheese[2] *tr.v.* **cheesed, cheesing, cheeses.** *Slang.* To stop. Not in current usage. [19th century : origin obscure.]

cheese board *n.* **1.** The wooden board on which cheese is served. **2.** A selection of cheeses offered as an item on a menu.

cheese·burg·er (cheéz-burgər) *n.* A hamburger topped with melted cheese.

cheese·cake (cheéz-kayk) *n.* **1. a.** A cake made of sweetened curds, eggs, milk, sugar, and flavourings, usually cooked in a pastry base. **b.** A similar cake made of curds, flavourings, and whipped cream, having a biscuit base and set with gelatine. **2.** *Slang.* **a.** Photographs, as in advertisements, of sexually attractive women scantily clothed. **b.** Women who appear or who resemble those who appear in such photographs. Compare **beefcake.**

cheese·cloth (cheéz-kloth ‖ -klawth) *n.* A coarse, loosely woven cotton gauze, originally used for wrapping cheese.

cheese cutter *n.* **1.** A thin wire, often attached to a board, for cutting cheese. **2.** *Nautical.* A keel that can be raised and lowered. **3.** A peaked cap.

cheesed off (cheezd) *adj.* *British Slang.* Annoyed; fed up. [From CHEESE (to stop).]

cheese-head (cheéz-hed) *adj.* Designating a screw or bolt whose head is cylindrical and slotted.

cheese mite *n.* A white mite, *Tyrophagus longior,* sometimes found in mouldy cheese, on which it feeds.

cheese-par·ing (cheéz-pair-ing) *n.* Stinginess; parsimony.
~*adj.* Miserly; stingy.

cheese straw *n.* A stick of crusty pastry flavoured with cheese and served as an appetiser or with drinks.

chee·tah (cheétə) *n.* A long-legged, swift-running feline mammal, *Acinonyx jubatus,* of Africa and southwestern Asia, having black-spotted, tawny fur and partially retractile claws. It is sometimes trained to pursue game. Also called "hunting leopard." [Hindi *cītā,* from Sanskrit *citrakāya,* tiger : *citra,* speckled + *kāya,* body.]

chef (shef) *n.* A cook; especially, the chief cook of a large kitchen staff. [French, CHIEF.]

chef-d'oeu·vre (sháy-dérv, -rə ‖ she-, -dôvr) *n., pl.* **chefs-d'oeuvre** *(pronounced as singular).* *French.* A masterpiece. [French, "chief work".]

chef's salad *n.* *Chiefly U.S.* A green salad that usually includes raw vegetables, hard-boiled egg, and strips of cheese and meat.

chei·lo·sis (kī-lō-siss) *n.* Inflammation and cracking of the lips, a symptom of riboflavin (Vitamin B_2) deficiency and other nutritional disorders. [New Latin, from Greek *kheilos,* lip + -OSIS.]

cheiro-. Variant of **chiro.**

Che·ka (cháyk-ə, chék- ‖ -aa) *n.* The Soviet security service organised in 1918 by Lenin. Reorganised many times, it acquired in 1954 the designation **KGB** *(see).* [Russian, short for *Chrezvychaynaya Komissiya,* "extraordinary commission".]

Che·khov (chék-of; *Russian* chékh-əf), **Anton Pavlovich** (1860–1904). Russian playwright and short-story writer. Between 1898 and 1904 he had four plays produced at the Moscow Art Theatre: *The Seagull, Uncle Vanya, The Three Sisters,* and *The Cherry Orchard.* All are now acknowledged masterpieces.

Chekiang. See **Zhejiang.**

che·la[1] (cháyl-ə, -aa) *n.* *Hinduism.* A pupil of a guru. [Hindi *celā,* servant, from Sanskrit *ceṭa, ceṭaka*†, slave.]

che·la[2] (kée-lə) *n., pl.* **-lae** (-lee). A pincer-like claw of arthropods, as of a lobster, crab, or similar crustacean. [New Latin, from Latin *chēlē,* from Greek *khēlē*†, claw.]

che·late (kée-layt) *adj.* **1.** *Zoology.* Having or characteristic of a chela. **2.** *Chemistry.* Of or pertaining to a heterocyclic ring containing a metal ion attached by coordinate bonds to at least two non-metal ions in the same molecule.

~*tr.v.* (-layt, -láyt) **chelated, -lating, -lates.** To form a ring compound by joining a chelating agent to (a metal ion). —**che·late** *n.* —**che·la·tion** (kee-láysh'n) *n.*

che·lic·er·a (ki-líss-ər-ə) *n., pl.* **-erae** (-əree). Either of the first pair of appendages near the mouth of a spider or other arachnid, often modified for grasping food. [New Latin : CHELA (claw) + Greek *keras,* horn.] —**che·lic·er·ate** (-rayt) *adj.*

che·li·form (kéeli-fawrm) *adj.* Having the shape of a chela; pincer-like.

Chel·li·an, Chel·le·an (shélli-ən) *adj.* *Archaeology.* Abbevillian. [French *chelléen,* of *Chelles,* site near Paris where some archaeological specimens were found.]

cheloid. Variant of **keloid.**

che·lo·ni·an (ki-lṓni-ən) *adj.* *Zoology.* Of or belonging to the Chelonia, an order of reptiles which includes the turtles and tortoises. ~*n.* A member of the Chelonia. [New Latin *Chelonia,* from Greek *khelōnē,* tortoise.]

Chel·sea (chél-si). District in the west London royal borough of Kensington and Chelsea, on the north bank of the Thames, popular since the 18th century with writers and artists. It is now a fashionable residential and shopping area.

Chelsea bun *n.* A currant bun topped with sugar. [After CHELSEA in London.]

Chel·ten·ham (chélt'n-əm). Town in Gloucestershire in southwest England, situated on the river Chelt. It has three mineral springs which made it a fashionable spa in the 18th century.

Che·lyus·kin, Cape (chi-léw-skin). The northernmost promontory of the Asian continent, situated in Siberia in Russia.

chem-, chemi-. Variants of **chemo-.**

chem. chemical; chemist; chemistry.

chem·i·cal (kémmik'l) *adj. Abbr.* **chem. 1.** Of, used in, or pertaining to chemistry. **2.** Of, employing, or pertaining to the properties or actions of chemicals.

~*n.* A substance produced by or used in a chemical process. [Earlier *chimical,* from *chimic,* an alchemist, from New Latin *chimicus,* from Medieval Latin *alchimicus,* from *alchimia, alchymia,* AL-CHEMY.] —**chem·i·cal·ly** *adv.*

chemical bond *n.* Any of several forces or mechanisms, especially the **ionic bond, covalent bond, coordinate bond,** and **metallic bond** *(all of which see),* by which atoms or ions are bound in a molecule or crystal.

chemical engineering *n.* The technology of large-scale chemical and chemical materials production. —**chemical engineer** *n.*

chemical equation *n.* A representation of a chemical reaction using the chemical symbols of the elements taking part. The amount of substance of the reactants and products is usually given in moles.

Chemical Mace (-mayss) *n.* A trademark for a mixture of organic chemicals used in aerosol form as a weapon to disable. Also called "Mace".

chemical reaction *n.* An interaction between substances involving changes in the outer electron structure and energy content of their molecules, atoms, or ions.

chemical warfare *n.* Warfare using chemicals other than explosives, especially irritants, asphyxiants, contaminants, poisons, and incendiaries, as direct weapons.

chemical weathering *n.* The wearing away of rocks or soil; **leaching** or **corrosion** *(both of which see).*

chem·i·lu·mi·nes·cence (kémmi-lōōmi-néss'nss, -léwmi-) *n.* The emission of light as a result of a chemical reaction. —**chem·i·lu·mi·nes·cent** *adj.*

che·min de fer (shə-mán də fair) *n.* A gambling game, a variation of baccarat. [French, "road of iron", railway.]

che·mise (shə-méez) *n.* **1.** A woman's loose, shirtlike undergarment. **2.** A dress, a **shift** *(see).* [Middle English, from Old French, shirt, from Late Latin *camīsia,* linen shirt, nightgown.]

chem·i·sette (shémmi-zét) *n.* **1.** A short, sleeveless underbodice, formerly worn by women. **2.** A blouse front formerly worn by women to fill in the neckline of a dress. [French, diminutive of CHEMISE.]

chem·i·sorb (kémmi-sawrb) *tr.v.* **-sorbed, -sorbing, -sorbs.** Also **chem·o·sorb** (kémmə-). To take up and chemically bind (a substance) on the surface of another substance. [CHEMI- + (AB)SORB.] —**chem·i·sorp·tion** (-sórpsh'n) *n.*

chem·ist (kémmist) *n. Abbr.* **chem. 1.** A scientist specialising in chemistry. **2.** *British.* A pharmacist. **3.** *Obsolete.* An alchemist. [Earlier *chimist,* from New Latin *chimista,* short for Medieval Latin *alchymista,* ALCHEMIST.]

chem·is·try (kémmistri) *n., pl.* **-tries.** *Abbr.* **chem. 1.** The science of the composition, structure, properties, and reactions of matter, especially of atomic and molecular systems. **2.** The composition, structure, properties, and reactions of a substance. **3.** Spontaneous interaction, as between two individuals: *the chemistry of love.* [Earlier *chimistrie,* from *chimist,* CHEMIST.]

chemo–, chemi–, chem– *comb. form.* Indicates chemicals or chemical reactions; for example, **chemisorb, chemosmosis, chemotaxis.** [CHEM(ICAL) + -O-.]

chem·o·pro·phy·lax·is (kéemō-próffi-láksiss, kémmō-, -prófi-) *n.* The use of chemicals to prevent infectious disease. **—chem·o·pro·phy·lac·tic** *adj.*

chem·o·re·cep·tion (kéemō-ri-sépsh'n, kémmō-, -rə-) *n.* The reaction of a sense organ to a chemical stimulus. **—chem·o·re·cep·tive** *adj.* **—chem·o·re·cep·tiv·i·ty** (-rée-sep-tívvəti) *n.*

chem·o·re·cep·tor (kéemō-ri-séptər, kémmō-, -rə-) *n.* A nerve ending or sense organ, such as a taste bud, sensitive to chemical stimuli.

chem·os·mo·sis (kéem-oz-mō-siss ‖ -oss-) *n.* The phenomenon of ionic or molecular transport across a membrane. **—chem·os·mot·ic** (-móttik) *adj.*

chem·o·sphere (kéem-ō-sfeer, kém-, -ə-) *n.* The region of the atmosphere at an altitude of between 32 and 192 kilometres (20 and 120 miles) in which photochemical reactions initiated by solar radiation occur.

che·mo·sur·ge·ry (kéemō-súrjəri, kémmō-) *n.* The combined uses of surgery and chemotherapy to remove tumours of the skin.

chem·o·syn·the·sis (kéemō-síntha-siss, kémmō-) *n.* The synthesis of organic substances from carbon dioxide, by certain bacteria using the energy of chemical reactions. **—chem·o·syn·thet·ic** (-sin-théttik) *adj.* **—chem·o·syn·thet·i·cal·ly** *adv.*

chem·o·tax·is (kéemō-táksiss, kémmō-) *n.* Characteristic orientation or motion of a freely moving living organism in response to a chemical substance. [New Latin : CHEMO- + -TAXIS.] **—chem·o·tactic** (-táktik) *adj.* **—chem·o·tac·ti·cal·ly** *adv.*

chem·o·ther·a·py (kéemō-thérrəpi, kémmō-) *n.* The treatment of disease with chemicals; especially, the use of drugs (rather than radiotherapy) to treat cancer. **—chem·o·ther·a·peu·tic** (-thérrə-péwtik) *adj.* **—chem·o·ther·a·pist** *n.*

chem·ot·ro·pism (kem-óttrəpiz'm, kem-) *n.* Growth of an organism, especially a plant, in response to chemical stimuli. [German *Chemotropismus* : CHEMO- + -TROPISM.] **—chem·o·trop·ic** (-ə-tróp-pik) *adj.*

chem·ur·gy (kém-urji) *n.* The development of new industrial chemical products from organic raw materials, especially from those of agricultural origin. [CHEM(O)- + -URGY.] **—chem·ur·gic** (kem-úrjik), **chem·ur·gi·cal** *adj.*

Cheng-chou, Chengchow. See **Zhengzhou.**

Cheng-du (chéng-dōō), **Cheng-tu,** or **Ch'eng-too.** Capital of Sichuan province in central China, and one of the country's largest and oldest cities, founded before 770 B.C. It lies on the Min Jiang, on an irrigation system more than 2,000 years old.

che·nille (shə-néel) *n.* **1.** A soft, tufted cord of silk, cotton, or worsted used in embroidery or for fringing. **2.** Fabric made of this cord. [French, "caterpillar", from Latin *canīcula,* diminutive of *canis,* dog (from its hairy pile).]

che·no·pod (kéenə-pod, kénnə-) *n.* Any plant of the goosefoot family, Chenopodiaceae, which includes spinach and beetroot as well as many common weeds. [New Latin *Chenopodiaceae,* from *Chenopodium* (genus) : Greek *khēn,* goose + -PODIUM.] **—che·no·po·di·a·ceous** (-pōdi-áyshəss) *adj.*

cheong·sam (chóng-sám, chyóng-, -sáam ‖ cháwng-) *n.* A light tight-fitting dress with a high collar and a slit skirt, typically worn by Chinese women. [Cantonese *cheung saam,* "long gown".]

Cheops. See **Khufu.**

Chep·stow (chép-stō). Town in Monmouthshire in southeast Wales, situated near the estuary on the river Wye.

cheque, *U.S.* **check** (chek) *n. Abbr.* **chq.** A written order to a bank, usually in the form of a bill of exchange by the holder of a current account, to pay a stated amount from the drawer's funds. [From CHECK (something to verify accuracy), perhaps influenced in spelling by EXCHEQUER.]

cheque·book (chék-bōōk ‖ -bōōk) *n.* A group of blank cheques bound together, issued by a bank.

chequebook journalism *n.* Acquisition of news stories and interviews by means of large payments.

cheque card *n.* A card issued to a customer by a bank, as a guarantee to payees that a cheque will be honoured by the bank up to a stated amount. Also called "banker's card", "bank card".

cheq·uer, *U.S.* **checker** (chéckər) *n.* **1.** Any of the discs or counters used in the game of Chinese chequers. **2. a.** A pattern of checks or squares. **b.** Any of the squares in such a pattern.

~ *tr.v.* **chequered** or *U.S.* **checkered, -ering, -ers. 1.** To mark with a checked or square pattern. **2.** To diversify in colour, shading or character; variegate; alter. [Middle English, chess, chess-board, aphetic variant of EXCHEQUER.]

cheq·uer·board (chéckər-bawrd ‖ -bōrd) *n.* A draughtboard; chessboard.

cheq·uered (chéckərd) *adj.* Varying considerably in fortune or character: *a chequered career*

Cheq·uers (chéckərz). The country residence of the U.K. prime

minister, near Princes Risborough, Buckinghamshire. It was given to the nation by Lord Lee of Fareham (1917).

Cher·bourg (sháir-boorg, shér-, -burg). Port in the Manche département of northwest France, situated on the Cotentin peninsula. It serves cross-Channel lines to southern English ports.

cher·i·moy·a (chérri-móy-ə) *n.* **1.** A tropical American tree, *Annona cherimola,* having yellow flowers and edible fruit with white, soft, aromatic pulp. **2.** The fruit of this tree. [American Spanish *chirimoya,* from Quechua *chirimuya.*]

cher·ish (chérrish) *tr.v.* **-ished, -ishing, -ishes. 1.** To hold dear; treat with affection and tenderness. **2.** To keep fondly in mind; cling to. **—See Synonyms at appreciate.** [Middle English *cherissen, cherishen,* from Old French *cherir* (present stem *cheriss-*), from *cher,* dear, from Latin *cārus.*] **—cher·ish·er** *n.* **—cher·ish·ing·ly** *adv.*

cherished number plate *n.* A vehicle number plate containing the initials of the owner.

Cher·nen·ko (cher-nyéngkō), **Konstantin Ustinovich** (1911–85). Soviet politician, president of the U.S.S.R. (1984–85).

Cher·no·byl (chər-nóbbil, chər-nōbl). Town in Ukraine where in 1986 a nuclear reactor exploded, releasing a cloud of fallout that spread as far as Britain and Scandinavia.

cher·no·zem (chérn-ō-zem, -ə-, -zyóm) *n.* A black soil, rich in humus, typical of cool to temperate semiarid regions, such as the grasslands of European Russia. Also called "black earth". [Russian, contraction of *chërnaya zemlya,* "black earth" : *chërnyĭ,* black + *zemlya,* earth.]

Cher·o·kee (chérrə-kée, -kee) *n., pl.* **-kees** or collectively **Cherokee. 1.** A member of a North American Indian people, formerly inhabiting North Carolina and northern Georgia and now settled in Oklahoma. **2.** The Iroquoian language of this people. **—Cher·o·kee** *adj.*

Cherokee rose *n.* A climbing rose, *Rosa laevigata,* of Chinese origin, having large, white, fragrant flowers.

che·root (shə-rōōt ‖ chə-) *n.* A cigar with square-cut ends. [Tamil *curuṭṭu, śurruṭṭu,* from *śuruḷ,* a curl.]

cher·ry (chérri) *n., pl.* **-ries. 1.** Any of several trees of the genus *Prunus,* having small, fleshy, globe-shaped or heart-shaped fruit with a small, hard stone; especially, *P. avium,* the common wild cherry, and *P. cerasus,* the sour cherry. See **bird cherry. 2.** The fruit or wood of any of these trees. **3.** Strong red to purplish red. **4.** *Vulgar Slang.* The hymen considered as a symbol of virginity. [Middle English *chery,* from Old Northern French *cherise,* variant of Old French *cerise,* from Vulgar Latin *ceresia* (unattested), from Latin *cerasus,* cherry tree, from Greek *kerasos†.*] **—cher·ry** *adj.*

cherry brandy *n.* A liqueur made from brandy and crushed cherry stones.

cherry laurel *n.* An evergreen European shrub, *Prunus laurocerasus,* having white flowers, and blackish fruits.

cherry picker *n.* Any of various large, usually mobile cranes having a long, manoeuvrable, obliquely vertical boom often supporting a work platform.

cher·ry-pie (chérri-pī ‖ -pī) *n.* A widely cultivated garden heliotrope, *Heliotropium peruvianum.*

cherry plum *n.* A tree, the **myrobalan** *(see).*

chert (chert) *n.* Any of various microscopically crystalline mineral varieties of silica, usually occurring in bands or layers of nodules in sedimentary rocks. [17th century : origin obscure.]

cher·ub (chérrəb) *n., pl.* **cherubim** (chérroo-bim, chérrew-) (for senses 1, 2) or **-ubs** (for senses 3, 4). **1.** A winged celestial being. Genesis 3:24. **2.** In medieval angelology, any of the second order of angels. See **angel. 3.** A representation of an angelic cherub, portrayed as a winged child with a chubby, rosy face. **4.** A delightful or innocent-looking child. [Hebrew *kərūbh.*] **—che·ru·bic** (cherōōbik, chi- ‖ -réwbik) *adj.* **—che·ru·bi·cal·ly** *adv.*

cher·vil (chérvil) *n.* **1.** An aromatic plant, *Anthriscus cerefolium,* native to Eurasia, having aniseed-flavoured leaves used in soups and salads. **2.** Any of several related plants, especially *rough chervil, Chaerophyllum temulentum,* or *bur chervil, A. caucalis.* [Middle English *cherville,* Old English *cerfille,* from West Germanic *kervila* (unattested), from Latin *chaerephylla,* from Greek *khairephullon* : *khairein,* to delight in + *phullon,* leaf.]

Ches. Cheshire.

Ches·a·peake Bay (chéssə-peek ‖ *U.S. also* chéss-peek). An inlet 320 kilometres (200 miles) long on the eastern seaboard of the United States. Baltimore is its main port.

Chesapeake Bay retriever *n.* A hunting dog of a breed developed in the United States, having a thick, short, brownish coat.

Chesh·ire (chéshər, chésheer). County in western England, bounded by the Welsh border to the west and Derbyshire to the east. It is noted for dairy produce, including Cheshire cheese. Extensive salt beds supply an important chemical industry. Chester is the administrative centre.

Cheshire, (Geoffrey) Leonard, Baron (1917–92). British pilot and philanthropist who won the Victoria Cross in World War II. On leaving the R.A.F. he established the Cheshire Foundation Home for the Incurably Sick. He was married to Sue Ryder.

Cheshire cat *n.* In *Alice's Adventures in Wonderland,* by Lewis Carroll, a cat that faded until only its grin remained visible.

Cheshire cheese *n.* A fairly hard, crumbly English cheese. [From CHESHIRE.]

Chesh·van, Hesh·van (hésh-vən, khésh-, -vaan) *n.* The second month of the Hebrew civil year. Also called "Marcheshvan". [Hebrew.]

Ches·il Beach (chézz'l). Also **Chesil Bank.** A shingle spit in southern England, running some 29 kilometres (18 miles) along the Dorset coast from Abbotsbury to the Isle of Portland.

chess (chess) *n.* A board game for two players, each possessing an initial force of a king, a queen, two bishops, two knights, two rooks, and eight pawns, all manoeuvred following individual rules of movement with the objective of checkmating the opposing king. [Middle English *ches,* short for Old French *esches,* plural of *eschec,* CHECK (at chess).]

chess² *n. U.S.* Rye brome *(see).* [Perhaps akin to obsolete *chesses†* (plural), rows of grain in an ear of corn or grass.]

chess·board (chéss-bawrd ‖ -bôrd) *n.* A board used in playing chess, marked with 64 squares; draughtboard.

ches·sel (chéss'l) *n.* A mould used in the manufacture of cheese. [Probably CHEESE + WELL.]

chess·man (chéss-man, -mən) *n., pl.* **-men** (-men, -mən). Any of the pieces used in playing the game of chess. Also called "chess piece".

chest (chest) *n.* **1.** The part of the body between the neck and the abdomen, enclosed by the ribs and the breastbone. **2. a.** A sturdy box with a lid and often a lock, used for storage and protection of articles. **b.** A chest of drawers. **c.** *U.S.* A cupboard with shelves; a dresser. **3. a.** The treasury of a public institution. **b.** The funds kept there. **4. a.** A box for the shipping of certain goods, such as tea. **b.** The quantity packed in such a box. [Middle English *chest,* Old English *cest, cist,* box, from West Germanic *kistā* (unattested), from Latin *cista,* from Greek *kistē.*] **—chest·ed** *adj.*

Ches·ter (chéstər). City and administrative centre of Cheshire, situated on the river Dee. The Romans, who built a fort there to command the river crossing into Wales, called it Deva. It has an 11th-century cathedral.

ches·ter·field *n.* **1.** A single-breasted or double-breasted overcoat, usually with concealed buttons and a velvet collar. **2.** A large, overstuffed sofa with straight armrests of the same height as the back. [After an Earl of *Chesterfield* of the 19th century.]

Ches·ter·field (chéstər-feeld). Industrial town in Derbyshire in the north Midlands of England. George Stephenson lived there.

Ches·ter·ton (chéstər-tən), **G(ilbert) K(eith)** (1874–1936). British author, poet, and literary critic. His works include studies of *Robert Browning* (1903) and *Charles Dickens* (1906). His skills as a writer of mystery and fantasy were shown in *The Napoleon of Notting Hill* (1904), and *The Man Who Was Thursday* (1908). In 1911 he published the first of his popular Father Brown stories, featuring a Roman Catholic priest as a detective.

chest·nut (chéss-nut, -nət) *n.* **1.** Any of several trees of the genus *Castanea,* of the Northern Hemisphere, such as the sweet (or Spanish) chestnut, *C. sativa,* bearing nuts enclosed in a prickly bur. **2.** The nut of any of these trees, edible when cooked. **3.** The hard wood of these trees, used in furniture and as a building material. **4.** See **horse chestnut**. **5.** Greyish brown to rich reddish brown. **6.** A reddish-brown horse. **7.** A small, hard callus on the inner surface of a horse's foreleg. **8.** *Informal.* Anything lacking freshness or originality, as a joke, song, or story. [Earlier *chesten nut* : Middle English *chesten, chasteine,* chestnut, from Old French *chastaigne,* from Latin *castanea,* from Greek *kastanea†* + NUT.] **—chest·nut** *adj.*

chestnut soil *n.* A dark brown, friable type of chernozem, found in arid areas of steppe that have little grass.

chest of drawers *n.* A piece of furniture consisting of a set of drawers contained in a frame.

chest register *n.* The lowest register of the human voice. Also called "chest voice".

chest·y (chésti) *adj.* **-ier, -iest.** *Informal.* **1.** Having large or well-developed breasts. **2.** Symptomatic of or having excessive phlegm in the lungs and throat. **3.** *U.S.* Arrogant; proud; conceited. **—chest·i·ness** *n.*

cheth, heth (het, hess, k̲h̲et, k̲h̲ess) *n.* The eighth letter in the Hebrew alphabet. [Hebrew.]

Chet·nik (chét-nik) *n., pl.* **-niks** or **Chetnici** (chet-néetsi). A Serbian guerrilla fighter, especially in World War II. [Serbian *četnik,* from *četa†,* troop.]

che·val-de-frise (shə-vál-də-fréez) *n., pl.* **chevaux-de-frise** (-vô-). **1.** A defensive obstacle composed of barbed wire or spikes attached to a wooden frame. **2.** An obstacle in the form of jagged glass or spikes set in the masonry on the top of a wall. [French, "Frisian horse". It was first used in Friesland to compensate for a lack of cavalry.]

che·val glass (shə-vál) *n.* A long mirror mounted on swivels in a frame. [French *cheval,* support, "horse".]

chev·a·lier (shévvə-léer) *n.* **1.** A member of certain orders of knighthood or merit, such as the Legion of Honour in France. **2. a.** *Archaic.* A knight. **b.** A chivalrous, gallant man. [Middle English *chevaler,* from Old French *chevalier,* from Late Latin *caballārius,* horseman, CAVALIER.]

Che·va·lier (shə-vál-yay), **Maurice** (1888–1972). French singer and film actor. His career began in cabaret, but he moved to Hollywood to take part in screen musicals in the 1930s. *Gigi* (1958) is his best-known film.

che·vet (shə-váy) *n.* The rounded east end of a church, usually with apses. [French, "pillow", from Latin *capitium,* from *caput,* head.]

Chev·i·ot (chév-i-ət, -yət ‖ *chiefly Scottish* chéev-, chív-) *n.* **1.** A sheep of a breed with short, thick wool, originally bred in the Cheviot Hills. **2.** *Small* **c.** A woollen fabric with a coarse twill weave, originally made from the wool of the Cheviot sheep.

Cheviot Hills. Range of hills bordering England and Scotland. The

Cheviot (816 metres; 2,677 feet) is the highest peak.

chev·ron (shévvrən) *n.* **1.** A badge or insignia consisting of parallel stripes meeting at an angle, worn on the sleeve of a policeman or a noncommissioned officer in the armed forces, and indicating rank or length of service. **2.** *Heraldry.* A device shaped like an inverted V. **3.** Any V-shaped pattern, especially: **a.** A kind of architectural moulding. **b.** A symbol on road signs indicating a sharp bend. [Middle English, from Old French, beam, rafter, from Vulgar Latin *capriō* (unattested), from Latin *caper,* feminine of *capra,* goat.]

chev·ro·tain (shévvrə-tayn, -tin) *n.* Any of several small, hornless ruminants of the genera *Hyemoschus* and *Tragulus* of central Africa and southeastern Asia. The males have tusklike upper canine teeth. Also called "mouse deer". [French *chevrotin,* from Old French, diminutive of *chevrot,* kid, diminutive of *chevre,* goat, from Latin *capra.* See **chevron.**]

chevy. Variant of **chivvy.**

chew (cho͞o ‖ chew) *v.* **chewed, chewing, chews.** *—tr.* To bite and grind with the teeth; masticate. *—intr.* To make a crushing and grinding motion with the teeth. **—chew out.** *Chiefly U.S. Slang.* To scold or reprimand. **—chew over.** To meditate upon; ponder. **—chew up.** To grind, crush, or damage with or as if with the teeth: *heavy lorries that chew up the road.* ~ *n.* **1.** An act of chewing. **2.** That which is chewed or intended for chewing, such as a chewy sweet. [Middle English *chewen,* Old English *cēowan.*] **—chew·er** *n.*

chewing gum *n.* A sweetened, flavoured preparation with a rubbery texture for chewing, usually made of chicle.

chew·y (cho͞o-i ‖ chew-) *adj.* Having a texture such that it requires chewing.

Chey·enne¹ (shī-án, shī-, -én). Capital of Wyoming state in the west central United States. It was founded (1867) as a station of the Union Pacific Railway and became a cattle centre.

Cheyenne² *n., pl.* **-ennes** or collectively **Cheyenne. 1.** A member of a North American Indian people, formerly inhabiting central Minnesota and North and South Dakota, now settled in Montana and Oklahoma. **2.** The Algonquian language of this people. [Canadian French, from Dakota *šahíyena.*] **—Chey·enne** *adj.*

Cheyne-Stokes respiration (cháyn-stóks) *n.* An abnormal type of respiration, seen particularly in comatose patients, characterised by alternating shallow and deep breathing. [After John *Cheyne* (1777-1836), Scottish physician, and William *Stokes* (1804-78), Irish physician.]

chez (shay) *prep. French.* At the home of.

chg. charge.

chi, khi (kī) *n.* The 22nd letter in the Greek alphabet, written Χ, χ. Transliterated in English as *ch* or *kh,* and sometimes as *h,* especially for Modern Greek words. [Greek *khi.*]

Chiang Ch'ing. See **Jiang Qing.**

Chianghsi. See **Jiangxi.**

Chiang Kai-shek. **Jiang Jieshi.**

Chiang-su. See **Jiangsu.**

Chi·an·ti (ki-ánti ‖ *U.S. also* -áanti) *n. Often small* **c.** A fruity red wine produced in the Monte Chianti region of Tuscany in Italy.

chiao (tyow) *n., pl.* **chiao.** A monetary unit equal to ¹/₁₀ of the yuan of the People's Republic of China. [Chinese.]

chi·a·ro·scu·ro (ki-áarə-skoor-ō, -skéwr-) *n., pl.* **-ros. 1.** The technique of using light and shade in pictorial representation. **2.** The arrangement of light and dark elements in a pictorial work of art. **3.** The use of contrast in literary works. [Italian : *chiaro,* light, clear, from Latin *clārus,* clear + *oscuro,* dark, from Latin *obscūrus.*] **—chi·a·ro·scu·rist** *n.*

Chiarraighe. See **Kerry.**

chi·as·ma (kī-áz-mə) *n., pl.* **-mata** (-mətə) or **-mas.** Also **chi·asm** (kí-az'm). **1.** *Anatomy.* A crossing or intersection of two tracts, such as that of the two optic nerves in the brain. **2.** *Genetics.* A point of contact between homologous chromosomes, considered the cytological manifestation of *crossover (see).* [New Latin, from Greek *khiasma,* cross, from *khiazein,* to mark with the letter CHI.] **—chi·as·mal, chi·as·mic, chi·as·mat·ic** (kī-az-máttik) *adj.*

chi·as·mus (kī-áz-məss) *n., pl.* **-mi** (-mī). A rhetorical inversion of the second of two parallel structures, as in *He went onwards, but home went she.* [New Latin, from Greek *khiasmos,* from *khiazein,* to mark with the letter CHI.]

chi·as·to·lite (kī-ásto-līt) *n.* A mineral variety of andalusite with carbonaceous impurities symmetrically arranged along the longer axis of the crystal. In cross-section the crystals show a black cross, hence the name. Also called "macle". [German *Chiastolith* : Greek *khiastos,* crossed, past participle of *khiazein,* to mark with the letter CHI + -LITE.]

Chib·cha (chíbchə) *n., pl.* **-chas** or collectively **Chibcha. 1.** A member of an extinct Indian people once inhabiting Colombia. **2.** The extinct language of this people.

Chib·chan (chíbchən) *n.* **1.** A South American or Central American Indian ethnic stock including the Chibcha. **2.** The language spoken by these people. ~ *adj.* Of or pertaining to this ethnic stock or language.

chi·bouk, chi·bouque (chi-bo͞ok, shi-) *n.* A Turkish tobacco pipe with a long stem and a red clay bowl. [French *chibouque,* from Turkish *çubuk, çibuk,* tube.]

chic (sheek; *rarely* shik) *adj.* **1.** Sophisticated; stylish. **2.** Dressed smartly and fashionably; elegant. ~ *n.* **1.** Stylishness and sophistication in dress and manner; elegance. **2.** Fashionable elitism. [French, perhaps from German

Schick, skill, Middle High German *schicken†,* to arrange, prepare.] **—chic·ly** *adv.*

Chi·ca·go (shi-kaàgō; *rarely* chi-; *locally* -káwgō). Third largest city in the United States, and a major port on the Illinois shore of Lake Michigan. During the Prohibition years (1919–33), it became a notorious centre of gangsters and corruption. Chicago is a vital focus of U.S. industry, trade, finance, and communications.

chi·cane (shi-káyn) *v.* **-caned, -caning, -canes.** *—tr.* **1.** To trick; deceive. **2.** To quibble over. *—intr.* To use tricks or chicanery. *~n.* **1.** Chicanery. **2.** In bridge or whist, a hand without trumps. **3.** In motor racing, an obstacle on the track intended to slow the cars down. [French *chicaner,* from Old French *chicaner†,* to quibble.] **—chi·can·er** *n.*

chi·can·er·y (shi-káynəri) *n., pl.* **-ies. 1.** Deception by trickery or sophistry. **2.** A trick; a subterfuge.

Chi·ca·no (chi-kaànō) *n., pl.* **-nos.** *U.S.* A Mexican-American. [American Spanish *Chicano,* variant of *Mejicano,* a Mexican, from *Méjico,* MEXICO.] **—Chi·ca·no** *adj.*

Chich·es·ter (chíchistər). City in southern England, the administrative centre of West Sussex. Laid out by the Romans, it prospered in the medieval wool trade. Parts of its ancient walls and gates survive.

Chichester, Sir Francis (Charles), (1901–77). British pilot and yachtsman. He made the first long-distance seaplane flight (1931) and won the first solo transatlantic yacht race (1960). He sailed around the world singlehanded (1966–7).

chi·chi (shée-shee) *adj.* **1.** Elaborate; fussy; frilly. **2.** Pretentiously fashionable; precious. [French.]

chick (chik) *n.* **1.** A young hen. **2.** The young of any bird. **3.** *Archaic.* A child. **4.** *Slang.* A girl; a young woman. [Middle English *chike,* short for CHICKEN.]

chick·a·dee (chíckə-dee) *n.* Any of several small, plump North American birds of the genus *Parus,* having predominantly grey plumage and a dark-crowned head. [Imitative of its cry.]

Chick·a·saw (chícka-saw) *n., pl.* **-saws** or collectively **Chickasaw. 1.** A member of a North American Indian people, originally of Mississippi, later removed to Oklahoma. **2.** The Muskhogean language of this tribe. **—Chick·a·saw** *adj.*

chick·en (chíckin) *n.* **1.** A young bird, especially of the common domestic fowl. **2.** The flesh of the common domestic fowl. **3.** Any of various birds similar or related to the common domestic fowl, such as the **prairie chicken** *(see).* **—count (one's) chickens before they are hatched.** To rely on an outcome which is still uncertain. *~adj. Slang.* Cowardly; timid.

~intr.v. **chickened, -ening, -ens.** *Slang.* To act in a cowardly manner; lose one's nerve. Usually used with *out.* [Middle English *chiken,* Old English *cīcen,* from Germanic.]

chicken feed *n. Slang.* A trifling amount of money.

chick·en-heart·ed (chícken-hártid, -hartid) *adj.* Cowardly; timid.

chick·en-liv·ered (chíckin-lívvərd, -livvərd) *adj.* Cowardly; timid.

chicken louse *n.* A louse, *Menopon pallidum* (or *gallinae*), parasitic on domestic fowl.

chick·en·pox (chíckin-pox) *n.* An acute contagious viral disease, usually of children, characterised by skin eruption, slight fever, and mild constitutional symptoms. Also called "varicella". [Perhaps alluding to the mildness of the disease.]

chicken wire *n.* A light-gauge galvanised wire fencing, usually made with hexagonal mesh and used for hen runs and similar enclosures, and, crushed, in flower arranging.

chick·pea (chík-pee) *n.* **1.** A bushy plant, *Cicer arietinum,* grown in the Mediterranean region and central Asia and bearing edible seeds. **2.** Any of the pealike seeds of this plant, widely used as food. Also called "garbanzo". [Earlier *chich-pease* : Middle English *chiche,* chickpea, from Old French, from Latin *cicer†* + *pease,* PEA.]

chick·weed (chík-weed) *n.* Any of various plants of the genera *Cerastium* (mouse-ear chickweed) and *Stellaria;* especially, *S. media,* a weedy plant with white flowers. [So called because it is eaten by chickens.]

chic·le (chíck'l) *n.* The coagulated juice of the sapodilla, used as the main ingredient of chewing gum. [Spanish, from Nahuatl *chictli.*]

chic·o·ry (chíckəri) *n., pl.* **-ries. 1.** A widely cultivated plant, *Cichorium intybus,* having usually blue flowers, and leaves used in salads. **2.** The root of this plant, dried, roasted, and ground for mixing with coffee or as a coffee substitute. Also called "succory". See **endive.** [Middle English *cicoree,* from Old French, from Latin *cichorium,* from Greek *kikhora†.*]

chide (chīd) *v.* **chided** or **chid** (chid), **chided** or **chid** or **chidden** (chídd'n), **chiding, chides.** *—intr.* To scold; rebuke. *—tr.* **1.** To reprimand; rebuke. **2.** To state one's disapproval of. [Middle English *chiden,* Old English *cīdan,* from *cīd†,* strife.] **—chid·er** *n.* **—chid·ing·ly** *adv.*

chief (cheef) *n. Abbr.* **C., ch., Ch. 1.** One who is highest in rank or authority; a leader: *a meeting of party chiefs.* **2.** The headman of a tribe or clan. **3.** *Slang.* A boss. **4.** *Heraldry.* The upper section of a shield. **—in chief. 1.** Having the highest or most important position: *the commander in chief.* **2.** Chiefly.

~adj. **1.** Highest in rank, authority, or office. **2.** Principal; most important.

~adv. Archaic. Chiefly. [Middle English *chief, chef,* from Old French, from Vulgar Latin *capum* (unattested), from Latin *caput,* head.]

Synonyms: chief, foremost, leading, main, primary, principal.

chief constable *n.* In Britain, a high-ranking police officer in command of a regional police force.

chief·dom (cheef-dəm) *n.* The office or domain of a chief, especially of a tribal leader.

Chief Justice *n. Abbr.* **C.J.** The presiding judge of a court of several judges, especially the Supreme Court of the United States or of some Commonwealth countries. See **Lord Chief Justice.**

chief·ly (cheéfli) *adv.* **1.** Above all; especially. **2.** Mostly; mainly. *~adj.* Of, befitting, or similar to a chief.

chief of staff *n. Abbr.* **C. of S., C.S. 1.** The senior staff officer of a major military formation. **2.** The commanding officer of the U.S. Army, Navy, or Air Force.

chief petty officer *n.* The highest rank of noncommissioned officer in the navy.

Chief Rabbi *n.* The religious leader of the Jewish community within a country.

chief superintendent *n.* A police officer having a rank between superintendent and commander or assistant chief constable.

chief·tain (cheéf-tin, -tən) *n.* The leader of a clan or tribe. [Middle English *chieftaine, cheftaine,* from Old French *chevetain,* from Late Latin *capitāneus,* from Latin *caput,* head.]

chiff-chaff (chíf-chaf) *n.* A small European warbler, *Phylloscopus collybita,* with brownish-grey plumage. [Imitative of its cry.]

chif·fon (shiffon ‖ *chiefly U.S.* shi-fón) *n.* **1.** A fabric of sheer silk or rayon. **2.** *Usually plural. Rare.* Ribbons, laces, or other ornamental accessories for women's clothing.

~adj. **1.** Of or relating to chiffon. **2.** Having a light and fluffy consistency. Said of food. [French, "rag", from *chiffe,* old rag, variant of Old French *chipe,* from Middle English *chip,* CHIP.] **—chif·fon·y** *adj.*

chif·fo·nier (shiffə-néer) *n.* An ornamental cabinet, either a low cupboard with shelves above it, or a narrow, high chest of drawers, often with a mirror attached. [French *chiffonnier,* "bureau for rags", from CHIFFON.]

chig·ger (chíggər) *n.* **1.** The **harvest mite** *(see).* **2.** A flea, the **chigoe** *(see).* [Variant of CHIGOE.]

chi·gnon (sheén-yon, shi-nón) *n.* A roll or knot of hair worn at the back of the head by women. [French, variant of Old French *chaignon,* chain, from Vulgar Latin *catēniō* (unattested), from Latin *catēna,* CATENA.]

chig·oe (chíggō ‖ cheégō) *n.* A small tropical flea, *Tunga penetrans,* of which the fertile female burrows under the skin, causing intense irritation and sores that may become severely infected. Also called "chigger", "jigger". [Cariban *chigo.*]

Chi·hua·hua¹ (chi-waà-wə, -waà). Capital of Chihuahua state in northern Mexico. It is situated in a valley of the Sierra Madre.

Chihuahua² *n.* A very small dog of a breed originating in Mexico, having pointed ears and a smooth coat. [After CHIHUAHUA, Mexico.]

chil·blain (chíl-blayn) *n.* An inflammation followed by itchy irritation on the hands, feet, or ears, resulting from exposure to moist cold. [*Chill* + *blain.*] **—chil·blained** *adj.*

child (chīld) *n., pl.* **children** (chíldrən). **1.** Any person between birth and puberty. **2. a.** An unborn infant; a foetus. **b.** An infant; a baby. **3.** One who is childish or immature. **4.** A son or daughter. **5.** *Plural.* In Biblical usage, members of a tribe; descendants. **6.** A person being considered as the product of a specified influence or phenomenon: *a child of nature.* **—with child.** Pregnant. [Child, children; Middle English *child(e), childre(ns),* Old English *cild, cildra,* from Germanic *kiltham* (unattested).] **—child·less** *adj.* **—child·less·ness** *n.*

child·bear·ing (chíld-bair-ing) *n.* The process of pregnancy and childbirth. Also used adjectivally: *of childbearing age.*

child·bed (chíld-bed) *n.* The state of a woman in childbirth.

childbed fever *n.* **Puerperal fever** *(see).*

child benefit *n. British.* A regular welfare allowance payable for the maintenance of children.

child·birth (chíld-burth) *n.* The process of giving birth to a child; parturition.

child care *n.* Professional supervision, as by a local authority, of the welfare of children, especially in the absence or failure of parental supervision.

childe (chīld) *n. Archaic.* A young man of noble birth. [Middle English *child(e),* CHILD.]

Chil·ders (childərz), **(Robert) Erskine** (1870–1922). Irish nationalist. He was active in the cause of Irish Home Rule, and became a Sinn Fein deputy in the Irish Assembly (1921). He acted as publicity director for the I.R.A. during the Irish civil war. Arrested in 1922 for carrying arms, he was tried and shot. His son, Erskine Hamilton Childers (1905–74), became Irish president (1973–74).

child·hood (chíldhŏŏd) *n.* The time or state of being a child.

child·ish (chíldish) *adj.* **1.** Of, similar to, or suitable for a child. **2.** Foolishly immature. **—child·ish·ly** *adv.* **—child·ish·ness** *n.*

Usage: Standard English makes a distinction between *childish* and *childlike. Childish,* when applied to adults or older children, has a derogatory sense, suggesting immature or foolish behaviour. *Childlike* suggests endearing traits characteristic of children, such as innocence or simple charm.

child·like (chíld-līk) *adj.* Also *rare* **child·ly** (chíldli). Like or befitting a child, as in innocence or guilelessness. See Usage note at **childish.**

child·min·der (chíld-mīndər) *n.* One who looks after children, especially while their parents are at work.

child·proof (chíld-prŏŏf ‖ -prŏŏf) *adj.* Safe against tampering by children.

chil·dren. Plural of **child.**

Children of Israel *pl.n.* The Jews.

child's play *n. Informal.* Anything that is very easy to do.

Chil·e, Republic of (chílli). *Spanish* **Republica de Chile.** A long, narrow country, on the western seaboard of South America. The Spaniards colonised it from 1541, and the country declared its independence in 1818. After World War I cut off its markets and sources of manufactured goods, economic chaos ensued, and the military intervened in the government several times. Salvador Allende's Marxist coalition was elected (1970), and instituted sweeping reforms and nationalisation, but inefficiency and costly welfare schemes brought economic collapse and street violence. The armed forces staged a bloody coup in 1973, and under the harshly repressive regime of President Pinochet, the economy revived. A plebiscite in 1988 rejected Pinochet, and in 1989 a civilian, Patricio Aylwin of the centre-left opposition coalition, was elected president. Chile has large energy resources: oil and gas in Patagonia, hydroelectric power in the Andes, and coal. The fertile central valley is its economic heartland, with industries concentrated around Concepción and Santiago. Exports include copper, iron ore, and nitrates, wood products, and fruit and wine. Area, 756 626 square kilometres (292,135 square miles). Population 14,420,000. Capital, Santiago. —**Chil·e·an** *adj. & n.*

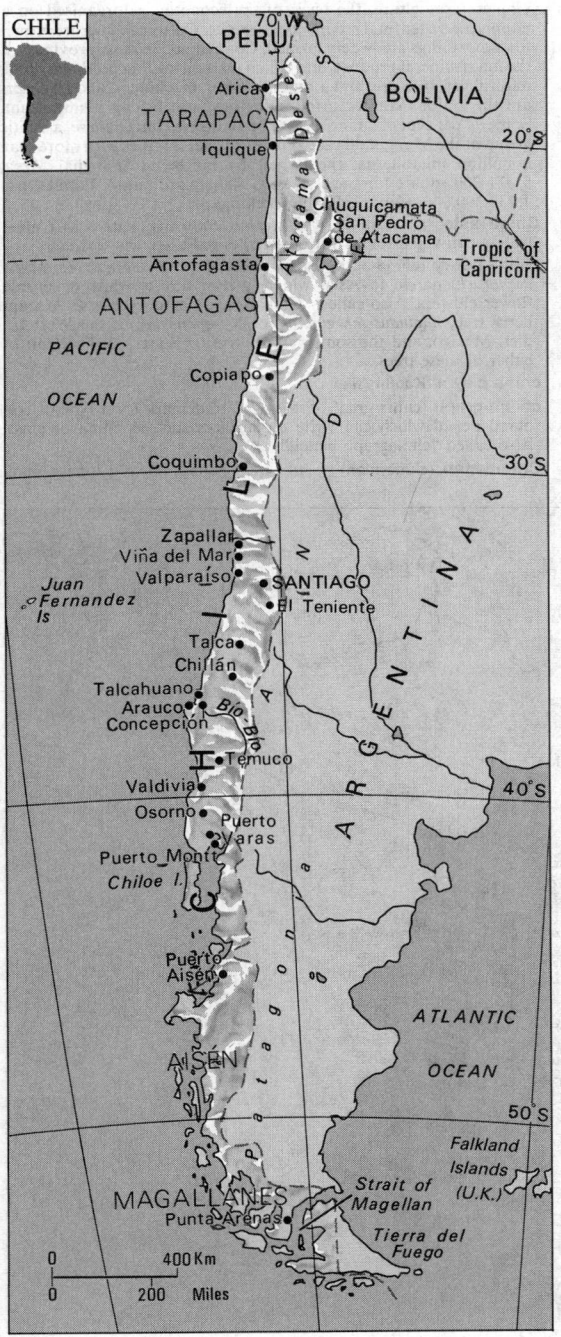

Chile saltpetre *n. Chemistry.* Sodium nitrate (see).

chil·i·ad (kílli-ad; *rarely* kī́li-, -əd) *n.* **1.** A group containing 1,000 elements. **2.** One thousand years. [Late Latin *chīliās* (stem *chīliad-*), from Greek *khilias,* thousand, from *khilioi,* thousand.]

chil·i·asm (kílli-az'm) *n.* **Millenarianism** *(see).* [New Latin *chilasmus,* from Greek *khiliasmos,* from *khilias,* CHILIAD.] —**chil·i·ast** (-ast) *n.* —**chil·i·as·tic** (-ástik) *adj.*

chill (chil) *n.* **1.** A moderate but penetrating coldness. **2. a.** A sensation of coldness, marked by shivering. **b.** An illness characterised by this: *catch a chill.* **3.** A checking or dampening of enthusiasm, spirit, or joy. **4.** A sudden numbing fear or dread. ~*adj.* **1.** Chilly. **2.** Depressing; discouraging. ~*v.* **chilled, chilling, chills.** —*tr.* **1.** To affect with cold. **2.** To discourage; dispirit. **3.** To cool, as in a refrigerator: *Serve the wine chilled.* **4.** *Metallurgy.* To harden (a metallic surface) by rapid cooling. —*intr.* **1.** To be seized with cold. **2.** To become cold. **3.** *Metallurgy.* To become hard by rapid cooling. [Middle English *chile, chele,* frost, Old English *c(i)ele.*] —**chill·er** *n.* —**chill·ing·ly** *adv.* —**chill·ness** *n.*

chil·li, chil·e, chil·i (chílli) *n., pl.* **-ies. 1. a.** The very pungent red fruit of several varieties of a woody plant, *Capsicum frutescens.* **b.** A condiment made from the dried fruits of this plant. In both senses, also called "chilli pepper". **2.** Chilli con carne. [Spanish *chile, chilli,* from Nahuatl *chilli.*]

chil·li con car·ne (chilli kon kárn-i, -ay). A highly spiced dish made of red peppers, meat, and usually beans. Also called "chilli". [Spanish, "chilli with meat".]

chilli sauce *n.* A spiced sauce made with chillies and tomatoes.

Chil·lon (shi-lón, shéeлON; *in Byron* shíllən). Castle in Switzerland, situated at the east end of Lake Geneva, near Montreux. Byron's poem *The Prisoner of Chillon* (1816) describes the fate of François de Bonnivard (1496–1570), a Genevan patriot imprisoned here.

chill·y (chílli) *adj.* **-ier, -iest. 1.** Cool or cold enough to cause shivering. **2.** Seized with cold; shivering. **3.** Distant and cool; unfriendly. —**chill·i·ly** *adv.* —**chill·i·ness** *n.*

chi·lo·pod (kílə-pod) *n.* Any of various arthropods of the class Chilopoda, which includes the centipedes. [New Latin *Chilopoda,* "foot jaws" (the foremost pair of legs are jawlike appendages) : Greek *kheilos,* lip + -POD.]

Chil·tern Hills (chíltərn). Also **Chilterns.** Range of chalk hills in southern England, running northeast from the Thames at the Goring Gap to the Bedfordshire-Hertfordshire border.

Chiltern Hundreds *pl.n. British.* A now merely formal Crown office applied for by Members of Parliament when they wish to resign from the House of Commons. [After a Crown manor in the CHILTERN HILLS, south-central England (the administration of which would require resignation from the House of Commons).]

chimaera (kī-méer-ə, ki-) *n.* **1.** Any deep-sea cartilaginous fish of the order *Chimaeriformes* having a smooth-skinned tapering body and a whiplike tail. See **rabbitfish. 2.** Variant of chimera.

chime (chīm) *n.* **1.** An apparatus for striking a bell or bells to produce a musical sound. **2.** *Usually plural.* A set of bells tuned to a scale and used as a musical instrument or in a clock. Compare **tubular bells. 3.** The musical sound produced by a bell or bells. **4.** Agreement; accord. ~*v.* **chimed, chiming, chimes.** —*intr.* **1.** To sound with a harmonious ring when struck. **2.** To make a musical sound by striking a chime. **3.** To agree; harmonise. Usually used with *with.* —*tr.* **1.** To produce (music) by striking, as a bell might, for example. **2.** To strike (a bell) to produce music. **3.** To make known (the hour) by chiming. —**chime in. 1.** To break into a conversation, especially to express agreement. **2.** To accord harmoniously. [Middle English *chime, chimbe,* cymbal, chime, perhaps from Old French *chimbe,* from Latin *cymbalum,* CYMBAL.] —**chim·er** *n.*

chi·me·ra, chi·mae·ra (kī-méer-ə, ki-) *n.* **1.** *Capital* **C.** *Greek Mythology.* A fire-breathing she-monster usually represented as a composite of a lion, a goat, and a serpent. **2.** A creation of the imagination; an impossible and foolish fancy. **3.** *Biology.* **a.** An organism, especially a cultivated plant, containing tissues from at least two distinct genetic types, often because of grafting. **b.** An animal or plant produced by genetic engineering, in which DNA from two distinct parent species is artificially combined to produce an individual with a double chromosone content. [Latin *Chimaera,* from Greek *khimaira,* chimera, "she-goat".]

chi·mere (chi-méer, shi-, chímmər) *n.* A long black or scarlet robe, with lawn sleeves, worn over a rochet by Anglican bishops. [Middle English, perhaps from Medieval Latin *chiméra,* "sheepskin" (see **chimera**); akin to Spanish *zamarra,* sheepskin cloak.]

chi·mer·i·cal (kī-mérrik'l, ki-) *adj.* **1.** Like a chimera; imaginary; unreal. **2.** Given to unrealistic fantasies. —**chi·mer·i·cal·ly** *adv.*

chim·ney (chímni) *n.* **1.** A passage through which smoke and gases escape from a fire or furnace; a flue. **2. a.** The usually vertical structure containing a flue. **b.** The part of such a structure that rises above a roof. **3.** A glass tube for enclosing the flame of a lamp. **4.** Anything resembling a chimney, such as a narrow cleft in a mountain by which a climber may ascend. **5.** *Geology.* **a.** The vent of a volcano. **b.** The most valuable part of a mineral deposit. [Middle English *chimenee,* from Old French *cheminee,* from Late Latin *caminata,* from Latin *camīnus,* furnace, from Greek *kaminos†.*]

chimney breast *n.* The projecting walls surrounding a fireplace and flue.

chimney corner *n.* A recessed seat inside or next to a large, old-fashioned fireplace.

chim·ney·piece (chímni-peess) *n.* **1.** The mantel of a fireplace. **2.** A decoration over a fireplace.

chimney pot *n.* A pipe placed on the top of a chimney to improve the draught.

chimney-stack *n.* **1.** The part of a chimney that rises above the roof of a building; stack. **2.** The masonry that encloses a number of flues.

chimney sweep *n.* Also **chimney sweeper**. A worker employed to clean soot from chimneys. Also called "sweep".

chimney swift *n.* A small, dark, swallow-like North American bird, *Chaetura pelagica*, that frequently nests in chimneys. Also called "chimney swallow".

chimp (chimp) *n. Informal.* A chimpanzee.

chim·pan·zee (chim-pan-zeé, -pən- ‖ *U.S. also* chim-pánzi) *n.* An anthropoid ape, *Pan troglodytes*, of tropical Africa, having dark hair, gregarious, somewhat arboreal habits, and a high degree of intelligence. [French *chimpanzé,* from Kongo.]

chin (chin) *n.* The central forward portion of the lower jaw. **—take it on the chin.** To accept misfortune or defeat stoically.
~*tr.v.* **chinned, chinning, chins. 1.** To place (a violin) under the chin. **2.** *Slang.* To hit on the chin. [Middle English *chin,* Old English *cin(n),* from Germanic.]

Ch'in or **Qin** (chin). A dynasty that ruled China from 221 to 206 B.C. See **China**.

chi·na¹ (chīnə) *n.* **1.** High quality porcelain or ceramic ware, originally made in China. **2.** Any porcelain ware. **3.** A collection of plates, cups, and the like made from porcelain. **—chi·na** *adj.*

china² *n. British Slang.* A friend; a mate. [From *china plate,* Cockney rhyming slang.]

Chi·na, People's Republic of (chīnə). The world's most populous and third largest country, lying in East Asia. Its heartland is formed by three giant river systems running west to east: the Huang He in the north, the Chang Jiang, and the Xi Jiang in the south. The country also includes the barren plateau of Tibet, and deserts in the north and west. China is the home of the oldest surviving civilisation, traditionally dated from the first emperor (*c.* 2700 B.C.). The Shang dynasty emerged *c.* 1525 B.C. on the North China Plain. Bronzeware had already evolved and a form of writing was in use. Under the Zhou dynasty (*c.* 1027–221 B.C.), Confucian and Taoist thought spread. The Ch'in dynasty (221–206 B.C.) founded the first unified empire and linked up the sections of the Great Wall against nomadic invasion. The Han dynasty (206 B.C.–A.D. 220) made great advances, and frontiers were extended, the "Silk Road" to Rome was opened up, and Buddhism introduced. The empire fell into decay, but was reunited by the Sui (581). Under the Tang (618–906) a golden age in the arts and great expansion in trade occurred. The Sung (960–1279) were removed by the Mongols, who set up the Yuan dynasty at Beijing (Peking), which Marco Polo visited. During the native Ming dynasty (1368–1644) the first European sea-farers reached China. The Manchus, a northern people, set up the Ch'ing dynasty (1644–1911), under which the eighteenth century was a period of relative stability, but in the later Ch'ing, isolation and stagnation led to backwardness. China was defeated in the Opium War (1839–42), and by Japan (1895), was humiliated in the Boxer Rising (1900), and was forced to accept treaty ports for foreign trade. After a popular revolution, Sun Zhong-shan inaugurated a republic (1912), but civil war between the nationalist Guomindang and the Chinese Communist Party broke out. Japanese encroachments from 1931 led to war (1937), and an uneasy alliance against the invader. After World War II, civil war (1946–49) established the People's Republic under chairman Mao Ze-dong, and the nationalists fled to Taiwan. China made great strides in modernisation and social and economic development, but Soviet aid ceased (1960) after an ideological break between the two countries, and Mao launched the Cultural Revolution (1966). In 1971 China was admitted to the United Nations, from which Taiwan was expelled. Mao's failing health led to a period of confusion during which the Gang of Four, led by his wife Jiang Qing, made a bid for power. Mao died in 1976, and was succeeded by Hua Guofeng. Under Hua and his successors as leader, Hu Yao-bang and Den Xiao-ping, modernisation was resumed, and relations with the West and Japan greatly improved in spite of the ruthless and bloody suppression of pro-democracy demonstrations in Beijing in 1989. Chinese agriculture, the basis of the economy, is organised on a commune system and is dependent on rice. Cotton and tea are grown for export. Pigs are widely farmed. Coal, mined in most provinces, is the main mineral product, and China is also a leading producer of oil, natural gas, iron ore, and antimony. Steel, machinery, and fertilisers are the major manufacturing industries, and fishing is important. Some 94 per cent of China's vast population is Han Chinese, a Sinitic group of the Mongoloid race. There are over 20 cities with more than a million inhabitants, the largest by far being Shanghai. Area, 9 571 300 square kilometres (3,695,500 square miles). Population, 1,238,390,000. Capital, Beijing (Peking).

China aster *n.* A plant, *Callistephus chinensis*, native to China, widely cultivated for its variously coloured aster-like flowers.

chi·na·ber·ry (chīnə-berri) *n., pl.* **-ries. 1.** A spreading tree, *Melia azedarach,* native to Asia, widely grown for its white or purple flower clusters. Also called "China tree", "azedarach". **2.** A soapberry tree, *Sapindus marginatus* (or *S. saponaria*), of the West Indies, Mexico, and the southwestern United States. **3.** The fruit of either of these trees.

china clay *n.* Kaolin (see).

chi·na·graph (chīnə-graaf, -graf) *n.* A trademark for a type of coloured pencil which can write on surfaces such as china or glass. Also called "chinagraph pencil".

Chi·na·man (chīnə-mən) *n., pl.* **-men** (-mən). **1.** A Chinese man.

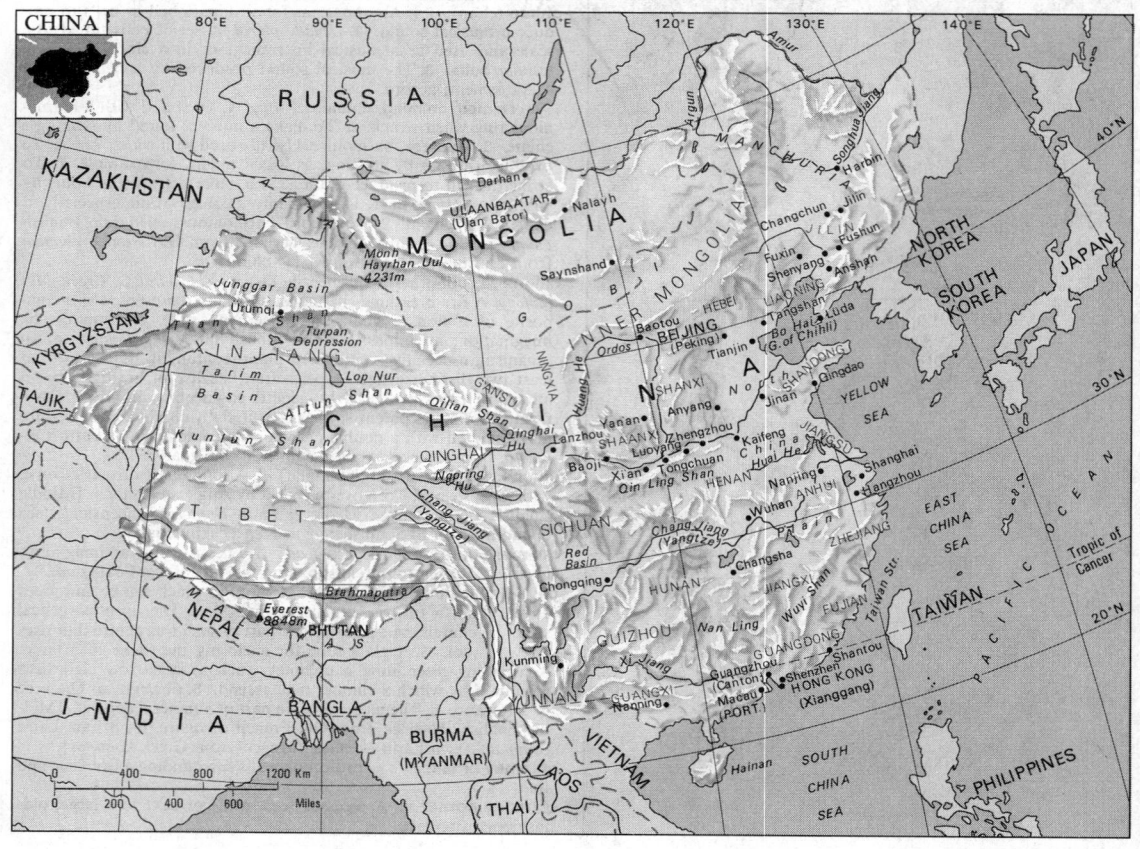

CHINA

Sometimes considered offensive. **2.** *small c.* In cricket, an **off break** *(see)* bowled by a left-handeder to a right-handed batsman.

China rose *n.* **1.** A shrub, *Rosa chinensis,* that has fragrant red or pink flowers and is the original ancestor of many cultivated hybrid roses. **2.** A dwarf, red-flowered rose, *Rosa semperflorens.*

China syndrome *n.* A hypothetical situation in which radioactive material from an uncontainable meltdown burns straight down through the Earth to emerge on the opposite side. [From the childish fantasy of digging a hole so deep that it extends all the way to China.]

Chi·na·town (chīnə-town) *n.* A district of a city inhabited mainly by Chinese people.

chi·na·ware (chīnə-wair) *n.* Porcelain or similar ware.

China wood oil *n.* **Tung oil** *(see).*

chinch bug *n.* **1.** A small black and white European insect, *Ischnodemus sabuleti,* that is very destructive to grains and grasses. **2.** A similar American insect, *Blissus leucopterus.* [Spanish *chinche,* from Latin *cīmex* (stem *cīmic-*), bug.]

chin·che·rin·chee (chínchə-rínchi, -rin-chée || *U.S. also* ching-kə-) *n.* Also **chin·ke·rin·chee** (chíng-kə-). A bulbous plant, *Ornithogalum thyrsoides,* of southern Africa, having long clusters or spikes of white or yellow flowers. [Imitative of the squeaky sound made by its stalks.]

chin·chil·la (chin-chíllə) *n.* **1.** A squirrel-like rodent, *Chinchilla laniger,* native to the mountains of South America and widely bred in captivity for its soft pale grey fur. **2.** The fur of this animal. **3.** A thick, twilled cloth of wool and cotton, used for overcoats. [Spanish, perhaps from Aymara.]

Chin·chil·la (chin-chíllə) *n.* **1.** A breed of domesticated rabbit having a thick bluish-grey coat. **2.** A breed of long-haired cat having silvery-white fur. [After the rodent, from the similarity of their coats.]

chin-chin (chin-chín) *interj. British.* Used as a toast or expression of farewell. [Pidgin English, from Chinese *qǐng qǐng,* "please please".]

Chin·dit (chíndit) *n.* In World War II, an Allied fighter behind the Japanese lines in Burma. [Burmese *chinthé,* a mythical lion; adoption of title perhaps influenced by the river CHINDWIN.]

chine¹ (chīn) *n.* **1.** The backbone; the spine. **2.** A cut of meat containing part of the backbone. **3.** A ridge or crest. **4.** The line of intersection between the side and bottom of a boat.
~*tr.v.* **chined, chining, chines.** To separate the backbone from the ribs in (a joint of meat). [Middle English *chyne,* from Old French *eschine,* probably from Germanic.]

chine² *n. British Regional.* A deep, narrow cleft in a cliff wall. [Old English *cinu,* cleft, chink, from Germanic.]

Chi·nese (chī-neéz || *U.S. also* -néess) *adj. Abbr.* **Ch., Chin.** Of or pertaining to China, its culture, people, or languages.
~*n., pl.* **Chinese. 1. a.** A native or inhabitant of China. **b.** A person of Chinese ancestry. **2.** Any of a group of Sino-Tibetan languages and dialects spoken in China, including Mandarin, Cantonese, Fujian, Amoy, and Shanghai. **3.** Mandarin, the standard language of China. See **Ancient Chinese.**

Usage: This is the normal term for someone of Chinese origin, other forms being generally considered derogatory or nonstandard. Many people find *a Chinese* and other singular uses awkward and somewhat formal, and prefer an adjective construction—*a Chinese man came in.*

Chinese anise *n.* A tree, the **star anise** *(see),* or its fruit.

Chinese cabbage *n.* **1.** A Chinese plant, *Brassica pekinensis,* related to the common cabbage, having a cylindrical head of crisp, edible leaves. Also called "pe-tsai", "celery cabbage". **2.** A similar plant, *B. chinensis.* Also called "pak-choi", "Chinese leaves". [Cantonese *baak choi,* "white vegetable".]

Chinese calendar *n.* The lunar calendar of the Chinese people, supposed to have begun in 2397 B.C. Years are reckoned in cycles of 60, each year having a name that is a combination of two characters derived schematically from two series of signs, the celestial and the terrestial. Months are reckoned also in cycles of 60 that are renewed every 5 years, and each month consists of 28 to 30 days.

Chinese chequers *n.* A game played on a six-pointed star-shaped board in which marbles or pegs are transferred, via holes or depressions on the boards, from one point to its opposite.

Chinese Chippendale *n.* Chippendale furniture characterised by certain Oriental influences.

Chinese date *n.* A tree, the **jujube** *(see),* or its fruit.

Chinese gooseberry *n.* A plant, the **kiwi** *(see),* or its fruit.

Chinese lantern *n.* **1.** A decorative, collapsible lantern of thin, brightly coloured paper. **2.** One of the papery, inflated seed cases of the Chinese lantern plant.

Chinese lantern plant *n.* An ornamental Asian plant, *Physalis alkekengii,* with inflated orange-red calyces. Also called "winter cherry".

Chinese puzzle *n.* **1.** A very intricate puzzle. **2.** Any very difficult problem.

Chinese red *n.* **Vermilion** *(see).*

Chinese restaurant syndrome *n.* A group of symptoms, including dizziness, facial pressure, sweating, and headache, that may occur after eating food containing large amounts of monosodium glutamate. [First noted by customers in Chinese restaurants.]

Chinese Revolution *n.* **1.** The revolution of 1911–12 in which the Republic of China was founded. **2.** The revolution culminating in the proclamation of the People's Republic of China (1949).

Chinese sacred lily *n.* A variety of the polyanthus narcissus, *Nar-*

cissus tazetta orientalis, that has fragrant yellow and white flowers.

Chinese Turkestan. See **Turkestan.**

Chinese wall *n.* A sharp or strict separation or barrier; specifically, a convention that prevents the passage between the parts of an organisation of information that might be used inappropriately (as for insider trading). [Perhaps from loan translation of German *Chinesische Mauer,* Great Wall of China.]

Chinese white *n.* A paint pigment, **zinc oxide** *(see).*

Chinese windlass *n. Machinery.* A **differential windlass** *(see).*

Ch'ing or **Qing** (ching). A Manchu dynasty which in 1644 took Beijing from the Ming and became the last ruling dynasty of China. See **China.**

chink¹ (chingk) *n.* A crack or fissure; a narrow opening.
~*tr.v.* **chinked, chinking, chinks.** *Chiefly U.S.* **1.** To fill cracks or chinks in. [Perhaps variant of earlier *chine,* from Middle English *chine,* crack, Old English *cinu, cine.*]

chink² *n.* A short, metallic sound.
~*v.* **chinked, chinking, chinks.** —*tr.* To strike (something) and make this sound. —*intr.* To produce this sound. [Imitative.]

chin·less (chin-ləss, -liss) *adj.* **1.** Having a small or receding chin. **2.** Ineffectual; lacking strength of character.

chinless wonder *n. British Informal.* An upper-class man, especially a stupid or ineffectual one.

Chin·ne·ret, Sea of. See **Galilee, Sea of.**

chi·no (chee-nō, shee-) *n., pl.* **-nos.** *U.S.* **1.** A coarse, twilled cotton fabric used for uniforms and sports clothes. **2.** *Plural.* Boys' and men's trousers of this material. [American Spanish *chino†,* "toasted" (from its original tan colour).]

Chino- *comb. form.* Indicates Chinese and; for example, **Chino-Soviet.** [From CHINA.]

chi·noi·se·rie (sheen-waˊazə-ri, -rée) *n.* **1.** A European style of the 17th and 18th centuries, found primarily in the decorative arts, employing real or, sometimes imagined motifs of Chinese art, such as the willow tree. **2.** An object in this style. [French.]

Chi·nook (chi-noŏk, shi-, -noŏk) *n., pl.* **-nooks** or collectively **Chinook. 1.** A member of a North American Indian people formerly inhabiting the Columbia river basin in Oregon and speaking one of the Chinookan languages. **2.** The language of this people. **3.** *Small c.* A moist, warm wind blowing from the sea on the Oregon and Washington coasts. **4.** *Small c.* A warm, dry wind that descends from the eastern slopes of the Rocky Mountains, causing a rapid rise in temperature.

Chi·nook·an (chi-noŏk-ən, shi-, -noŏk-) *n.* A North American Indian language family of Washington and Oregon.

Chinook jargon *n.* A language combining simple English, French, Chinookan, and other North American Indian languages, formerly used by Indians and fur traders of the Pacific Northwest.

Chinook salmon *n.* A salmon, *Oncorhynchus tshawytscha,* of northern Pacific waters, valued as a food fish.

chintz (chints) *n.* A printed and glazed cotton fabric, usually of bright colours. [Variant of earlier *chints,* plural of *chint,* from Hindi *chīṇt,* from Sanskrit *chitra* many-coloured, bright.]

chintz·y (chíntsi) *adj.* **-ier, -iest. 1.** Of, pertaining to, or decorated with chintz. **2.** Characterised by a bright, fussy, flowery style that attempts to evoke an old-fashioned, rustic atmosphere. **3.** *U.S.* Gaudy; trashy; cheap.

chin·wag (chín-wag) *n. British Informal.* A gossip or chat.

chip (chip) *n.* **1.** A small piece broken or cut off. **2.** A crack or other mark caused by chipping. **3.** A small disc or counter used in gambling to represent money. **4.** *Electronics.* A minute square of a thin semiconductor material, such as silicon or germanium, doped and otherwise processed to have specific electrical characteristics; especially, such a square before attachment of electrical leads and packaging as an electronic component or integrated circuit. **5. a.** A long, thin slice of potato, usually fried in deep fat. **b.** *Chiefly U.S.* A potato crisp. **6.** *Sports.* A short upward kick, shot, or the like that rises sharply. Also called "chip shot". **7.** Wood, palm leaves, straw, or similar material, cut and dried for weaving. —**chip off the old block.** *Informal.* One who resembles a parent, especially in behaviour. —**have a chip on (one's) shoulder.** To behave in an aggressive, truculent manner, especially owing to sensitivity about one's imagined social inferiority.
~*v.* **chipped, chipping, chips.** —*tr.* **1.** To break a small piece from; fragment. **2.** To chop or cut; especially, to chop (potatoes) to make chips. **3.** To shape or carve by cutting or chopping. **4.** *Sports.* To hit or kick (a ball) so that it rises sharply and travels only a short distance. —*intr.* To become broken off. —**chip in.** *Informal.* **1.** To contribute money, labour, or the like. **2.** To interject; interrupt. [Middle English *chip,* Old English *cipp†,* beam, piece cut off a beam.]

chip basket *n.* **1.** A wire basket for holding food during deep-frying. **2.** A basket made of woven wooden chips.

chip·board (chíp-bawrd || -bōrd) *n.* A hard, flat material made from sawdust and wood chips compressed and bound with resin, and used for making shelves, furniture, and the like.

chip·munk (chíp-mungk) *n.* A small rodent, *Tamias striatus,* of eastern North America, or any of several similar rodents of the genus *Eutamias,* of western North America and northern Asia, resembling a squirrel but smaller and having a striped back. [Variant of earlier *chitmunk,* from Algonquian.]

chip·o·la·ta (chippə-laˊatə) *n.* A very small sausage, often with a spicy flavour. [French, from Italian *cipollata,* "onion-flavoured (dish or mixture)", from *cipolla,* onion.]

Chip·pen·dale (chíppən-dayl), **Thomas** (1718–79). British furniture maker whose name is associated with elegant mid-18th century taste. His son, Thomas Chippendale (c.1749–1822), expanded the business to include fabrics and wallpaper.

chip·per (chíppər) adj. Informal. Active; cheerful; brisk; pert. [Perhaps from northern English dialect kipper, active, cheerful.]

chip·pings (chíppingz) pl.n. Small, roughly hewn pieces of stone, used in surfacing roads and railway tracks.

chip·py¹ (chíppi) n., pl. -pies. Also British regional chipper. Informal. A fish-and-chip shop. [From CHIP (fried potato).]

chippy² n., pl. -pies. Chiefly British Slang. A carpenter. [From CHIP (wood).]

chip shot n. Sports. A chip, especially in golf.

Chi·rac (sheér-ak, shee-rák), **Jacques (René)** (1932–). French politician and prime minister (1974–76). A Gaullist, he served as prime minister in the government of Giscard d'Estaing, but resigned (1976), reorganising Gaullist forces in the Rassemblement des Français pour la République. He became mayor of Paris (1977), prime minister again (1986–9), and president (1995).

chi·ral (kír-əl) adj. Of or pertaining to the handedness or chirality of an asymmetric molecule. [Greek kheir, hand.]

chi·ral·i·ty (kīr-ál-əti) n. Chemistry. The concept of left-or-right handedness applied to stereoisometric molecules. A figure representing the configuration of a molecule is said to have chirality if its image in a plane mirror cannot be superimposed on it.

chi·rho (kí-rố ‖ kée-) n. A monogram and symbol for Christ, consisting of the superimposed Greek letters chi (X) and rho (P), often embroidered on altar cloths and clerical vestments. [CHI + RHO, first two letters of Greek khristos, CHRIST.]

chiro– comb. form. Indicates of or with the hand; for example, **chiropractic**. [Latin, from Greek kheir, hand.]

Chi·ri·co (keér-i-kō), **Giorgio de** (1888–1978). Italian painter, born in Greece. He produced distinctive canvases which featured enigmatically arranged statues and objects set against semideserted backgrounds of Italian architecture.

chi·rog·ra·phy (kīr-óggrəfi) n. Calligraphy (see) or handwriting. [French chirographie : CHIRO- + -GRAPHY.] —**chi·rog·ra·pher** n. —**chi·ro·graph·ic** (-ə-gráffik), **chi·ro·graph·i·cal** adj.

chi·ro·man·cy (kír-ə-man-si) n. The art or practice of foretelling a person's future by studying the palm of his hand; palmistry. [CHIRO- + -MANCY.] —**chi·ro·man·cer** n.

Chi·ron (kír-ən ‖ -on). Greek Mythology. The wise centaur who tutored Achilles, Jason, and Asclepius.

chi·rop·o·dy (ki-róppədi, shi-) n. The paramedical speciality concerned with the care and treatment of the feet. [CHIRO- + -PODY.] —**chi·rop·o·dist** n.

chi·ro·prac·tic (kír-ə-praktik) n. A system of therapy in alternative medicine in which disease is considered the result of neural malfunction and manipulation of the spinal column and other bodily structures is the preferred method of treatment. [CHIRO- + Greek praktikos, effective, PRACTICAL.] —**chi·ro·prac·tor** (-praktər) n.

chi·rop·ter·an (kīr-óptərən) n. Also **chi·rop·ter** (kīr-óptər, kír-optər). Any flying mammal of the order Chiroptera, which includes the bats. [New Latin Chiroptera : CHIRO- + -PTER + -AN.] —**chi·rop·ter·an** adj.

chirp (churp) v. chirped, chirping, chirps. —intr. 1. To utter a short, high-pitched sound, like that of a small bird or grasshopper. 2. To speak in a quick, sprightly manner. —tr. To utter with a short, high-pitched sound.
~n. A short, high-pitched sound; a tweet. [Middle English chirpen (attested only in gerund chirpinge), to chirp, twitter (imitative).] —**chirp·er** n.

chirp·y (chúrpi) adj. -ier, -iest. Informal. Cheerful; bright; in a good or lively mood. —**chirp·i·ly** adv. —**chirp·i·ness** n.

chirr (chur) intr.v. chirred, chirring, chirrs. To make a harsh, trilled sound, as a cricket does. [Imitative.] —**chirr** n.

chir·rup (chírrəp ‖ chúrrəp) v. -ruped, -ruping, -rups. —intr. To utter a series of chirps; make a light, tremulous sound. —tr. To sound with chirps. [Variant of CHIRP.] —**chir·rup** n.

chis·el (chízz'l) n. A metal tool with a sharp, bevelled edge, used to cut and shape stone, wood, or metal.
~v. chiselled or U.S. chiseled, -elling or U.S. -eling, -els. —tr. 1. To shape or cut with or as if with a chisel. 2. Slang. To cheat or swindle. —intr. 1. To use a chisel. 2. Slang. To use unethical methods; cheat. [Middle English, from Old North French, from Vulgar Latin cīsellus, caesellus (both unattested), diminutive formation from caedere (past participle caesus), to cut.] —**chis·el·ler** n.

chi-square test (kí-skwair) n. Statistics. A test used in relation to a hypothesis concerning the discrepancy between observed and expected results. The result of the test, the chi-square distribution, is calculated as the sum of the squares of the differences between the observed and expected values divided by the expected values.

chit¹ (chit) n. Chiefly British. A small slip of paper, such as one carrying a memo, an order, a receipt, or a bill. Also called "chitty". [Short for earlier chitty, from Hindi ciṭṭhi, note, pass, from Sanskrit chitra, mark.]

chit² n. A child, girl, or young woman, especially one thought to be impertinent. [Middle English chittě, young animal.]

chi·tal (cheét'l) n. The axis deer (see). [Hindi cītal, from Sanskrit citrala, spotted, from chitra, bright, variegated.]

chit·chat (chít-chat) n. 1. Casual, light conversation. 2. Gossip. [Dissimilated reduplication of CHAT.] —**chit·chat** intr.v.

chi·tin (kítin) n. A semitransparent horny substance, primarily a mucopolysaccharide, forming the principal component of arthropod exoskeletons and the cell walls of certain fungi. [French chitine, from New Latin CHITON (mollusc).] —**chi·tin·ous** adj.

chi·ton (kí-t'n, -ton) n. 1. A tunic worn by men and women in ancient Greece. 2. Any of various marine molluscs of the class Amphineura, especially of the genus Chiton, living on rocks and having shells consisting of eight overlapping transverse plates. Also called "coat-of-mail shell". [New Latin, mollusc (with tunic-like shell), from Greek khitōn, tunic, from Semitic, akin to Hebrew kəthōnet.]

Chit·ta·gong (chítta-gong). Port and city in Bangladesh, near the mouth of the river Karnaphuli. It is the southern terminus of all the country's major land, river, and air routes, and Bangladesh's second largest industrial centre, processing cotton, jute, and tea.

chit·ta·ro·ne (kitə-rŏni) n. A large baroque lute. [Italian, augmentative of chittara, lute, GUITAR.]

chit·ter·lings (chíttər-lingz, chít-, -linz) pl.n. The small intestines of pigs, cooked and eaten as food. [Middle English chiterling, perhaps diminutive of Old English cieter (unattested), intestines.]

Chiu-lung. See Jiulong.

chiv·al·rous (shívv'l-rəss) adj. Also **chiv·al·ric** (shívv'l-rik). 1. a. Having the qualities of gallantry and honour attributed to an ideal knight. b. Courteous and protective, especially to the weak and to women. Said of men. 2. Of or pertaining to chivalry. —**chiv·al·rous·ly** adv. —**chiv·al·rous·ness** n.

chiv·al·ry (shívv'l-ri. Note: formerly chivv'l-) n., pl. -ries. 1. a. The medieval institution of knighthood. b. The principles and customs of this institution. 2. a. The qualities idealised by knighthood, such as bravery, courtesy, honesty, and readiness to help the weak and women. b. The manifestation of any of these qualities. 3. Archaic. A group of knights. [Middle English chivalrie, from Old French chevalerie, knightliness, from chevalier, knight, from Late Latin caballārius, horseman, CAVALIER.]

chivaree. U.S. Variant of charivari.

chive (chīv) n. 1. A plant, Allium schoenoprasum, native to Eurasia, having rose-pink flowers and hollow, grasslike leaves. 2. Plural. The leaves of this plant, used as a seasoning. [Middle English cyve, cheve, from Old French cive, from Latin cēpa, onion, perhaps akin to Greek kapia†, onions.]

chiv·vy, chiv·y (chívi) tr.v. -vied, -vying, -vies. Also **chev·y** (chévvi). British. To cause to act or move more quickly; chase or harass. [English dialectal chevy, short for chevy chase, confusion, pursuit, from Chevy Chase, name of a Middle English ballad about the battle of Otterburn (1388), which arose from a hunt (chase) near the CHEVIOT HILLS.]

chla·myd·e·ous (klə-míddi-əss) adj. Botany. Having or pertaining to a floral envelope. [Latin chlamys (stem chlamyd-), mantle, CHLAMYS.]

chla·myd·o·spore (klə-míddə-spawr ‖ -spōr) n. A thick-walled fungus spore derived from a hyphal cell; a resting spore. [Latin chlamys (stem chlamyd-), mantle, CHLAMYS + SPORE.]

chla·mys (klám-iss, kláym-) n., pl. -myses or chlamydes (-i-deez). A short mantle fastened at the shoulder, worn by men in ancient Greece. [Latin chlamys, from Greek khlamus†.]

chlo·as·ma (klō-ázmə) n. Brown patches on the skin, usually the face, that may occur during pregnancy and the menopause. [New Latin, from Late Greek khloasma, greenness, from khloazein, to be green, from khloos, light green colour.]

chlor·ac·ne (klaw-rákni ‖ klō-) n. An acne-like skin disorder caused by prolonged exposure to chlorinated hydrocarbons.

chlo·ral (kláwr-əl ‖ klŏr-) n. A colourless, mobile, oily liquid, CCl_3CHO, a penetrating lung irritant, used to manufacture DDT and chloral hydrate. [French : CHLOR(O)- + AL(COHOL).]

chloral hydrate n. A colourless crystalline compound, $CCl_3CH(OH)_2$, used medicinally as a sedative and hypnotic.

chlor·am·bu·cil (klaw-rámbew-sil ‖ klō-) n. A drug, $C_{14}H_{19}Cl_2NO_2$, administered orally in the treatment of cancers.

chlo·ra·mine (kláwr-ə-meen ‖ klŏr-) n. Any of several compounds containing nitrogen and chlorine; especially, an unstable colourless liquid, NH_2Cl, used to make hydrazine. [CHLOR(O)- + AM(MONIA) + -INE.]

chlo·ram·phen·i·col (kláwr-am-fénni-kol ‖ klŏr-, -kōl) n. An antibiotic, $C_{11}H_{12}O_2N_2Cl_2$, derived from the soil bacterium Streptomyces venezuelae or produced industrially by chemical synthesis. [CHLOR(O)- + AM(IDE) + PHE(NO)- + NI(TRO)- + (GLY)COL.]

chlo·rate (kláwr-ayt, -it ‖ klŏr-) n. The inorganic group ClO_3 or a compound containing it. [CHLOR(O)- + -ATE.]

chlor·dane (kláwr-dayn ‖ klŏr-) n. Also **chlor·dan** (-dan). An amber-coloured, odourless viscous liquid, $C_{10}H_6Cl_8$, used as an insecticide. [CHLOR(O)- + (IN)D(ENE) + -ANE.]

chlor·di·az·e·pox·ide (kláwr-dī-əzi-póksīd ‖ klŏr-) n. A drug used as a sedative and mild tranquilliser.

chlo·rel·la (klaw-réllə, klə- ‖ klō-) n. Any of various minute green algae of the genus Chlorella, widely used in studies of photosynthesis. [New Latin Chlorella : CHLOR(O)- + -ella, diminutive suffix.]

chlo·ren·chy·ma (klaw-réngkimə, klə- ‖ klō-) n. Plant tissue containing chlorophyll. [CHLOR(OPHYLL) + -ENCHYMA.]

chlo·ric (kláwr-ik ‖ klŏr-) adj. Of, pertaining to, or containing chlorine, especially with a valency of 5. [CHLOR(O)- + -IC.]

chloric acid n. A strongly oxidising, unstable acid, $HClO_3 \cdot 7H_2O$.

chlo·ride (kláwr- īd ‖ klŏr-) n. Any binary compound of chlorine. [CHLOR(O)- + -IDE.] —**chlo·rid·ic** (klaw-ríddik, klə- ‖ klō-) adj.

chlo·rin·ate (kláwr-i-nayt ‖ klŏr-) tr.v. -ated, -ating, -ates. To treat or combine with chlorine or with a chlorine compound. —**chlo·ri·na·tion** (-náysh'n) *n.* —**chlo·ri·na·tor** (-naytər) *n.*

chlorinated lime *n.* **Bleaching powder** (see).

chlo·rine¹ (klówr-een ‖ klṓr-, -in) *n. Symbol* **Cl** A highly irritating, greenish-yellow gaseous halogen, capable of combining with nearly all other elements, produced principally by electrolysis of sodium chloride and used widely to purify water, as a disinfectant, a bleaching agent, and in the manufacture of many important compounds including chloroform and carbon tetrachloride. Atomic number 17, atomic weight 35.45, freezing point −100.98°C, boiling point −34.0°C, relative density 1.56 (−33.6°C), valencies 1, 3, 5, 7. [CHLOR(O)- + -INE.]

chlo·rite¹ (klówr-īt ‖ klṓr-) *n.* A generally green or black secondary mineral, (Mg, Fe), Al (Al, Si₃)O₁₀ (OH)₉, often formed by metamorphic alteration of primary dark rock minerals. [Latin *chlorītis*, a green precious stone, from Greek *khlōritis*, from *khlōros*, greenish yellow.]

chlorite² *n.* The inorganic group ClO₂ or a compound containing it. [CHLOR(O)- + -ITE.]

chloro-, chlor- *comb. form.* Indicates: **1.** The colour green; for example, **chlorosis. 2.** The presence of chlorine; for example, **chloroform, chlorate.** [Greek *khlōros*, greenish yellow.]

chlo·ro·a·ce·tic acid (kláwrō-ə-seetik, -séttik ‖ klṓrō-) *n.* Also **chlor·a·ce·tic acid** (kláwr- ‖ klṓr-). **1.** A colourless crystalline solid, CH₂ClCOOH, prepared by chlorinating acetic acid and used as an intermediate. Also called "monochloracetic acid". **2.** A colourless liquid, CHCl₂COOH, used in the manufacture of dyes. Also called "dichloracetic acid." **3.** A deliquescent crystalline solid, CCl₃COOH. Also called "trichloracetic acid".

chlo·ro·ben·zene (kláwr-ō-bén-zeen ‖ klṓr-, -ben-zéen) *n.* A colourless, volatile flammable liquid, C₆H₅Cl, used to prepare phenol, DDT, aniline, and as a general solvent.

chlo·ro·eth·ene (kláwr-ō-étheen ‖ klṓr-) *n.* **Vinyl chloride** (see).

chlo·ro·flu·o·ro·car·bon (kláwr-ō-floͦor-ō-kárbən, -floͦo-ər-ō ‖ klṓr-) *n. Abbr.* **CFC.** A type of chemical compound, **Freon** (see), said to harm the ozonosphere. [CHLORO- + FLUOROCARBON.]

chlo·ro·form (klórrə-fawrm, kláwr- ‖ klṓrə-) *n.* A clear, colourless, heavy liquid, CHCl₃, used in refrigerants, propellants, and resins, and formerly as an anaesthetic.
~*tr.v.* **chloroformed, -forming, -forms. 1.** To anaesthetise or kill with chloroform. **2.** To apply chloroform to. [CHLORO- + FORM(YL).]

chlo·ro·hy·drin (kláwr-ō-hídrin ‖ klṓr-) *n.* An aliphatic organic chemical compound that is both an alkyl chloride and an alcohol, frequently containing a single chlorine atom and a single hydroxyl group on adjacent carbon atoms. [CHLORO- + HYDR(O)- + -IN.]

Chlo·ro·my·ce·tin (kláwr-ōmī-séetin ‖ klṓr-) *n.* A trademark for **chloramphenicol** (see).

chlo·ro·phyll, chlo·ro·phyl (klórrə-fil, kláwr- ‖ klṓrə-) *n.* Any of a group of related green pigments found in plants that trap energy from sunlight for use in photosynthesis, especially: **1.** *Chlorophyll a,* a waxy blue-black microcrystalline green-plant pigment, C₅₅H₇₂MgN₄O₅, with a characteristic blue-green alcohol solution. **2.** *Chlorophyll b,* a similar green-plant pigment, C₅₅H₇₀MgN₄O₆, having a brilliant green alcohol solution. [French *chlorophylle* : CHLORO- + -PHYLL.]

chlo·ro·pic·rin (kláwr-ō-píckrin, -ə- ‖ klṓr-) *n.* An oily colourless liquid, CCl₃NO₂, used to make poison gas, in dyestuffs, disinfectants, insecticides, and fumigants. Also called "nitrochloroform", "vomiting gas". [CHLORO- + PICR(O)- + -IN.]

chlo·ro·plast (kláwr-ō-plast, -ə-, -plaast ‖ klṓr-) *n.* Also **chlo·ro·plas·tid** (-plástid). *Botany.* A plastid containing chlorophyll in photosynthetic plants. [CHLORO- + -PLAST.]

chlo·ro·prene (kláwr-ō-preen, -ə- ‖ klṓr-) *n.* A colourless liquid, C₄H₅Cl, used as the monomer of neoprene rubber. [CHLORO- + (ISO)PRENE.]

chlor·o·quine (kláwr-ō-kween, -ə- ‖ klṓr-) *n.* A drug, C₁₈H₂₆ClN₃, used mainly in the treatment and prevention of malaria.

chlo·ro·sis (klaw-rṓ-siss ‖ klə-, klṓ-) *n.* **1.** *Botany.* An abnormal condition of plants, characterised by absence of or deficiency in green pigment and caused by lack of light, mineral deficiency, or genetic disorders. **2.** *Pathology.* An iron-deficiency anaemia chiefly affecting girls at puberty and characterised by greenish skin colour. [CHLOR(O)- + -OSIS.]

chlor·ous (kláwr-əss ‖ klṓr-) *adj.* Of, pertaining to, or containing chlorine, especially with a valency of 3.

chlor·prom·a·zine (kláwr-prṓmə-zeen, -prómmə- ‖ klṓr-) *n.* An oily liquid, C₁₇H₁₉ClN₂S, derived from phenothiazine and used as a sedative, tranquilliser, and antiemetic. [CHLOR(O)- + PRO(PYL) + METH(YL) + AZINE.]

chlor·tet·ra·cy·cline (kláwr-téttrə-sí-kleen ‖ klṓr-) *n.* An antibiotic, C₂₂H₂₃ClN₂O₈, obtained from the soil bacterium *Streptomyces aureofaciens* and used for treating a variety of infections.

cho·an·a (kṓ-ánnə, -áanə, kṓ-ənə) *n. Anatomy.* A funnel-shaped opening; especially, either of the two internal openings of the nose leading into the pharynx. [Greek *khoanē*, funnel, from *khein*, to pour.]

cho·an·o·cyte (kō-ánnə-sīt, kṓ-ənə-) *n. Biology.* Any of the flagellated cells that line the body cavity of a sponge. Also called "collar cell". [Greek *khoanē*, funnel, from *khein*, to pour + -CYTE.]

cho cho (chṓ-chō) *n.* The cucumber-like fruit of the cucurbitaceous vine, *Sechium edule,* eaten especially in the West Indies, Australia, and New Zealand. [Brazilian native name *chuchy*.]

choc-ice (chók-īss ‖ cháwk-) *n.* A small slab of ice-cream coated in chocolate.

chock (chok) *n.* **1.** A block or wedge placed under something, such as a boat, barrel, or wheel, to keep it from moving. **2.** *Nautical.* A heavy fitting of metal or wood with two jaws curving inwards, through which a rope or cable may be run.
~*tr.v.* **chocked, chocking, chocks.** To fit, secure, or wedge with a chock or chocks.

chock-a-block (chóckə-blók ‖ -blok) *adj.* **1.** Completely full; jammed: *chock-a-block with cars.* **2.** *Archaic.* Drawn so close that the blocks touch. Of a ship's hoisting tackle. —**chock-a-block** *adv.*

chock-full (chók-foͦol ‖ chúk-) *adj.* Completely filled; stuffed. Used with *of.* [Middle English *chokkeful,* probably from CHOCK (to ram tight with chocks).]

choc·o (chóckō) *n., pl.* **-os.** *Australian Slang.* During World War II, a military recruit. [Shortened from *chocolate soldier.*]

choc·o·late (chók-lət, chóckə-, -lit ‖ cháwk-, cháwkə-) *n.* **1.** Husked, roasted, and ground cacao seeds, often combined with a sweetener or flavouring agent. **2.** A sweet or drink made from this. **3.** Greyish to deep reddish brown. [Spanish, from Aztec *xocolatl* : *xococ,* bitter + *atl,* water.] —**choc·o·late** *adj.*

choc·o·late-box (chók-lət-boks; see **chocolate**) *adj.* Pretty in a sentimental or oversweet way. Usually said of pictures.

choc·taw (chók-taw) *n.* In ice-skating, a turn from either edge of one skate to the opposite edge of the other skate. [After CHOCTAW.]

Choc·taw (chók-taw) *n., pl.* **-taws** or collectively **Choctaw. 1.** A member of an American Indian people, formerly living in southern Mississippi and Alabama, now settled in Oklahoma. **2.** The Muskhogean language of this tribe.

chog·yal (chóg-yaal) *n.* The traditional title of the ruler of Sikkim.

choice (choyss) *n.* **1.** The act of choosing; selection; election. **2.** The power, right, or liberty of choosing; option. **3.** The person or thing chosen. **4. a.** A sufficient number or variety from which to choose. **b.** A supply chosen with care. **5.** The best part; the pick. **6.** An alternative.
~*adj.* **choicer, choicest. 1.** Of fine quality; select; excellent. **2.** Selected with care. **3.** Vulgar or strong: *her language was choice.* [Middle English *chois,* from Old French, from *choisir,* to CHOOSE.]
Synonyms: choice, alternative, option, preference, selection.

choir (kwīr) *n.* **1. a.** An organised company of singers, especially one performing church music or singing in a church. **b.** The part of a church used by such singers. **2.** *Architecture.* The part of a cruciform church between the nave and the main altar. Compare **chancel. 3.** Any of the orders of angels.
~*intr.v.* **choired, choiring, choirs.** To sing in chorus. [Earlier *quier, quire,* Middle English *quere,* from Old French *cuer,* from Medieval Latin *chorus,* CHORUS.]

choir·boy (kwīr-boy) *n.* A boy member of a choir.

choir loft *n.* A gallery for a church choir.

choke (chōk) *v.* **choked, choking, chokes.** —*tr.* **1.** To interfere with or terminate normal breathing of (a person, for example), especially by constricting or breaking the windpipe or by polluting the air. **2.** To stop by or as if by strangling; silence; suppress. Often used with *off, down,* or *back: choke back tears.* **3.** To reduce the air intake of (a carburettor), thereby enriching the fuel mixture. **4.** To check or slow down the movement, growth, or development of (plants, for example). **5.** To block up or obstruct by filling or crowding; clog; congest. **6.** To fill completely; jam; pack. Often used with *up.* **7.** To cause to be temporarily overcome with strong emotion. Usually used in the passive. —*intr.* **1. a.** To become suffocated; have difficulty in breathing, swallowing, or speaking. **b.** *Informal.* To do badly under pressure through loss of nerve or composure. **2.** *Slang.* To die.
~*n.* **1.** The act or sound of choking. **2.** That which constricts or chokes; a narrow part, such as the chokebore of a gun. **3.** A device used in an internal-combustion engine to enrich the fuel mixture by reducing the flow of air to the carburettor. **4.** *Electronics.* A coil of wire with a high impedance used to smooth the output of a rectifier or prevent the passage of high frequencies. Also called "choke coil". **5.** The inner part of a globe artichoke, composed of small inedible hairs. [Middle English *choken, cheken,* short for *achoken, acheken,* Old English *ācēocian,* from Germanic *kēkōn-* (unattested), CHEEK.]

choke-bore (chók-bawr ‖ -bōr) *n.* **1.** A shotgun bore which narrows towards the muzzle to prevent wide scattering of the shot. **2.** A gun with a bore of this kind.

choke-damp (chók-damp) *n.* A gaseous mixture, **black damp** (see). [So called because it causes suffocation in mines.]

chok·er (chṓkər) *n.* **1.** One that chokes. **2. a.** A necklace or band that fits closely round the throat. **b.** A high, tight collar.

chok·ey (chṓki) *n. British Slang.* Prison. [Hindi *chaukī,* (police) station, shed.]

cho·lan·gi·og·ra·phy (kōl-ánji-óggrəfi, kól-) *n.* X-ray examination of the bile ducts in order to detect obstruction or the presence of stones. [CHOLE- + ANGIO- + -GRAPHY.] —**chol·an·gi·o·graph·ic** (kōl-ánji-ə-gráffik, kól-) *adj.*

chole-, chol- *comb. form.* Indicates gall or bile; for example, **cholecyst, choline.** [Greek *kholē,* gall, bile.]

cho·le·cal·cif·er·ol (kōli-kal-síffər-ol, kólli- ‖ -awl, -ōl) *n.* One of the forms in which **Vitamin D** (see) occurs.

chol·e·cyst (kólli-sist, kṓli-) *n. Rare.* The gall bladder. [New Latin *cholecystis* : CHOLE- + CYST.]

chol·e·cyst·ec·to·my (kólli-sist-éktəmi, kṓli-) *n., pl.* **-mies.** Surgical removal of the gall bladder.

chol·er (kóllər ‖ *U.S. also* kôlər) *n.* **1.** *Archaic.* **a.** One of the four humours of the body, thought in the Middle Ages to cause anger and bad temper when present in excess; yellow bile. **b.** Biliousness. **2.** Anger; irritability. [Middle English *colre, coler(a),* from Old French *colere,* from Latin *cholera,* bilious diarrhoea, from Greek *kholera,* from *kholē,* bile, gall.]

chol·er·a (kóllə-rə) *n.* An acute infectious epidemic disease caused by the bacterium *Vibrio comma,* characterised by watery diarrhoea, vomiting, cramps, suppression of urine, and collapse. Also called "Asiatic cholera". [Latin *cholera,* bilious diarrhoea. See **choler.**] —**chol·e·ra·ic** (-ráy-ik) *adj.* —**chol·e·roid** (-royd) *adj.*

chol·er·ic (kóllərik, ko-lérrik, kə-) *adj.* Bad-tempered; irascible. —**chol·er·i·cal·ly, chol·er·ic·ly** *adv.*

cho·les·ter·ol (kə-léstər-ol, ko- ‖ -awl, -ōl) *n.* A glistening white soapy crystalline substance, $C_{27}H_{45}OH$, the most common animal sterol, a precursor of many hormones and a universal tissue constituent, occurring notably in bile, gallstones, the brain, blood cells, and plasma. Also called "cholesterin". [CHOLE- + Greek *stereos,* hard, solid + -OL. So called because first found in gallstones.]

cho·li (chóli) *n.* A short-sleeved woman's bodice, worn mainly by Indian women. [Hindi *coli.*]

cho·lic acid (kólik; *rarely* kóllik). *n.* An abundant crystalline bile acid, $C_{24}H_{40}O_5$. [Greek *kholikos,* bilious, from *kholē,* bile.]

cho·line (kôl-een, kól-, -in) *n.* A natural amine, $C_5H_{15}NO_2$, sometimes classed in the vitamin B complex and a precursor of various phospholipids and acetylcholine. [CHOL(E)- + -INE (from its function in preventing fat accumulation in the liver).]

cho·lin·er·gic (kōl-in-érjik, kól-) *adj.* **1.** Activated by or capable of liberating **acetylcholine** *(see).* Said of certain nerve fibres. **2.** Having physiological effects similar to acetylcholine. [(ACETYL)CHOLIN(E) + Greek *ergon,* work + -IC.]

cho·lin·es·ter·ase (kōl-in-éstər-ayz, kól-, -ayss) *n.* An enzyme that hydrolyses acetylcholine to form acetic acid and choline. Also called "acetylcholinesterase". [*Choline* + *esterase.*]

chol·la (chōl-yə, -yaa, chóv-ə) *n.* Any of several very spiny cacti of the genus *Opuntia,* characterised by cylindrical stem segments. See **prickly pear.** [Mexican Spanish, from Spanish *cholla,* head, possibly from Old French *cholle,* head, from Germanic.]

chomp (chomp) *v.* **chomped, chomping, chomps.** —*intr.v.* To chew noisily; champ. —*tr.v.* To chew (food) noisily. —**chomp** *n.*

Chom·sky (chóm-ski), **(Avram) Noam** (1928–). U.S. language theorist whose works revolutionised the study of linguistics. He argues that the structure of language is determined by the structure of the human mind, and that human language differs radically from the way animals communicate or machines may be programmed. —**Chom·sky·an** *adj. & n.*

chon (chŏn) *n., pl.* **chon.** A coin equal to $1/100$ of the won, the monetary unit of South Korea. [Korean.]

chon·dri·fy (kóndri-fī) *v.* **-fied, -fying, -fies.** —*tr.* To change into cartilage. —*intr.* To become cartilage. [CHONDRI- + -FY.] —**chon·dri·fi·ca·tion** (-fi-káysh'n) *n.*

chon·dri·o·some (kóndri-ə-sōm) *n. Biology.* A **mitochondrion** *(see).* [CHONDRI- + -SOME.]

chon·drite (kón-drīt) *n.* A stone of meteoric origin characterised by chondrules. [CHONDR(O)- + -ITE.] —**chon·drit·ic** (kon-dríttik) *adj.*

chondro-, chondr-, chondri– *comb. form.* Indicates: **1.** Cartilage; for example, **chondroma, chondrify. 2.** Granule or chondrule; for example, **chondrite.** [Greek *khondros,* granule, cartilage.]

chon·dro·cra·ni·um (kóndrō-kráy-ni-əm) *n., pl.* **-ums** or **-nia** (-ni-ə). The embryonic cartilaginous cranium, especially as distinguished from the **osteocranium** *(see).*

chon·dro·ma (kon-drô-mə) *n., pl.* **-mas** or **-mata** (-mətə). A benign cartilaginous tumour. [New Latin : CHONDR(O)- + -OMA.]

chon·drule (kóndrōōl) *n. Geology.* A small round granule of mineral or glass found embedded in some meteorites. [CHONDR(O)- + -ULE.]

Chong·qing, Ch'ung·ch'ing, or **Chung·king** (chōong-chíng, -kíng). City and river port in Sichuan province of central China, on the Chang Jiang. It was made capital of China (1937–46) during the war with Japan. Coal and iron are mined nearby.

choo·choo (chōō-chōō) *n. Informal.* A train. Used especially by or to children.

choose (chōōz) *v.* **chose** (chōz), **chosen** (chôz'n), **choosing, chooses.** —*tr.* **1.** To decide upon and pick out from a number of possible alternatives; select. **2.** To prefer to others. **3.** To want; desire: *choose to go.* —*intr.* To make a choice; select; decide. [Choose, Middle English *chosen,* Old English *cēosan* (later *ceōsan*). Chose, chosen; Middle English *chosen* (past plural), *chosen,* both from the infinitive *chosen.* All from Germanic *kiusan* (unattested).] —**choos·er** *n.*

Synonyms: choose, select, elect, pick.

choos·y (chōōzi) *adj.* **-ier, -iest.** Unwilling to settle for less than the best; hard to please. —**choos·i·ness** *n.*

chop¹ (chop) *v.* **chopped, chopping, chops.** —*tr.* **1.** To cut up by striking with a heavy, sharp tool, such as an axe. **2.** To make by cutting in this way. **3.** To cut into bits. **4.** *Sports.* To hit or hit at with a short, swift, downward stroke. **5.** *West African Informal.* To consume or make use of (food, money, or women, for example). —*intr.* **1.** To make heavy, cutting strokes. **2.** *West African Informal.* To eat.

~*n.* **1.** The act of chopping. **2.** A swift, short, cutting blow or stroke. **3.** A chopped-off piece; especially, a cut of meat, usually taken from the rib, shoulder, or loin and containing a bone. **4.** A

short, irregular motion of waves. **5.** *West African Informal.* Food. **6.** *Australian Slang.* A share, as of winnings. —**get the chop.** *British Slang.* To be dismissed from one's job. [Middle English *choppen,* variant of *chappen,* CHAP (to split).]

chop² *intr.v.* **chopped, chopping, chops.** To change direction suddenly; swerve. Used chiefly in the phrase *chop and change.* [Originally, "to exchange", from Middle English *choppen,* variant of *chappen, chepen,* to barter, trade, Old English *cēapian,* ultimately from Latin *caupō,* innkeeper; akin to CHEAP.]

chop³ *n.* In the Far East, an official stamp or permit. —**not much chop.** *Australian & N.Z. Informal.* Not much good; of poor quality. [Hindi *chhāp†,* seal.]

chop chop *adv. Informal.* Quickly. [Pidgin English, from Cantonese *gap gap,* "Quickly!"; reduplication of *gap,* corresponding to Mandarin *jí,* urgent.]

chop·house (chóp-howss) *n.* **1.** Formerly, a cheap restaurant. **2.** A restaurant that specialises in chops, steaks, and grills.

Chopin (shóppaN, shô-paN), **Frédéric (François)** (1810–49). Polish Romantic pianist and composer, of French parentage, known for his affair with the novelist George Sand, with whom he lived for nine years. His music, written chiefly for the piano, drew inspiration from the romance and melancholy of traditional Polish dance music.

chop·log·ic (chóp-lojik) *n.* Cunning but fallacious argument. —**chop·log·ic** *adj.*

chop·per (chóppər) *n.* **1.** One that chops. **2.** A small hand axe. **3.** A butcher's cleaver. **4.** A device that interrupts an electric current or beam of radiation. **5.** A motorcycle or bicycle with high handlebars. **6.** *Slang.* A helicopter. **7.** *Plural. Slang.* False teeth.

chop·py (chóppi) *adj.* **-pier, -piest.** Also **chop·ping** (chópping). Abruptly shifting or breaking, as waves or winds: *choppy seas.*

chops (chops) *pl.n.* The jaws, cheeks, or jowls of an animal or human being. [16th century : variant of *chap* (see **chapfallen**), origin obscure.]

chop·sticks (chóp-stiks) *pl.n.* A pair of slender sticks made of wood, ivory, or plastic and used as eating utensils by the Chinese, Japanese, and some other Asian peoples. [Pidgin English *chop,* fast (see **chop-chop**) + STICK(S), a loose translation of Cantonese *kuàizi,* "fast ones".]

chop su·ey (chóp sōō-i, séw-) *n.* A Chinese-style dish consisting of small pieces of meat or chicken cooked with bean sprouts and other vegetables and served with rice. [Cantonese *tsaap˙sui,* corresponding to *zá sui,* "mixed pieces".]

cho·ra·gus (kaw-ráy-gəss ‖ kə-, kō-) *n., pl.* **-gi** (-jī). **1.** In Greek drama: **a.** The leader of the chorus. **b.** An elected official supervising the production of dramatic performances in the festival of Dionysus at Athens. **2.** The leader of a choir. [Latin, from Greek *khoragos : khoros,* CHORUS + -*agos,* leader, from *agein,* to lead.] —**cho·rag·ic** (-rájik, -ráyjik) *adj.*

cho·ral (káwr-əl ‖ kór-) *adj.* **1.** Of or pertaining to a chorus or choir. **2.** Written for performance by a chorus. [Medieval Latin *chorālis,* from *chorus,* CHORUS.] —**cho·ral·ly** *adv.*

cho·rale, cho·ral (ko-raál, kə-, kaw- ‖ kō-) *n.* **1.** A Protestant hymn tune. **2.** A harmonised hymn, especially one for organ: *a Bach chorale.* **3.** *U.S.* A chorus or choir. [German *Choral(gesang),* "choral (song)", from Medieval Latin *chorālis,* CHORAL.]

chorale prelude *n. Music.* A composition for the organ, chiefly in baroque style, characterised by an elaborate contrapuntal structure based on the melody of a hymn or chorale.

chord¹ (kord) *n.* **1.** A combination of three or more usually concordant notes sounded simultaneously. **2.** An emotional feeling or response: *Her words struck a sympathetic chord.* [Alteration (influenced by Latin *chorda,* string, CORD) of Middle English *cord,* agreement, harmony, short for ACCORD.]

chord² (kord) *n.* **1.** *Geometry.* A straight line that joins two points on a curve. **2.** *Aeronautics.* An imaginary straight line connecting the leading and trailing edges of an aerofoil. **3.** *Archaic.* The string of a musical instrument. **4.** *Engineering.* A part of a truss, especially a member lying along the top or the bottom. [16th century : respelling (influenced by Latin *chorda,* string) of CORD.]

chord³. Variant of **cord.**

chord·al (kórd'l) *adj. Music.* **1.** Relating to or consisting of a harmonic chord. **2.** Giving prominence to harmonic rather than contrapuntal structure: *chordal music.*

chor·date (kórd-ayt) *n. Zoology.* Any of numerous animals belonging to the phylum Chordata, which includes all vertebrates and certain marine animals having a notochord, such as the lancelets. ~*adj. Zoology.* Of or belonging to the Chordata. [New Latin *Chordata,* from *chorda,* notochord, from Latin, CORD.]

chor·do·phone (kórdə-fōn) *n.* Any musical instrument producing its sound through the vibration of strings.

chore (chor ‖ chōr) *n.* **1.** A routine or minor task. **2.** An unpleasant or burdensome task. —See Synonyms at **task.** [Variant of CHARE, CHAR.]

–chore *n. comb. form.* Indicates a plant distributed by a specified agency; for example, **anemochore, zoochore.** [Greek *khōrein,* to move, spread abroad.]

cho·re·a (ko-réer, kə-, kaw-, -rée-ə ‖ kō-) *n.* Any of various nervous disorders marked by uncontrollable and irregular movements of the muscles of the arms, legs, and face, one of which is "St. Vitus' dance". [Latin *chorea,* dance, from Greek *khoreia,* choral dance, from *khoros,* dance, CHORUS.]

chor·e·o·graph (kórri-ə-graaf, káwri-, -graf ‖ kóri-) *v.* **-graphed, -graphing, -graphs.** —*tr.* To create the choreography of (a ballet or other stage work). —*intr.* To serve as a choreographer. [Back-formation from CHOREOGRAPHY.]

chor·e·og·ra·pher (kòrri-óggrəfər, káwri- ‖ kóri-) *n.* One who creates, arranges, or directs dances, especially ballets.

chor·e·og·ra·phy (kòrri-ógrafi, káwri- ‖ kóri-) *n.* **1.** The art of creating and arranging ballets or dances. **2.** The steps and movements of a dance or ballet. **3.** The art and technique of dance notation. **4.** The art of dancing. [French *chorégraphie* : Greek *khoreios*, of a dance, from *khoros,* dance, CHORUS + -GRAPHY.] —**chor·e·o·graph·ic** (-ə-gráffik) *adj.* —**chor·e·o·graph·i·cal·ly** *adv.*

chor·i·amb (kórri-am, káwri-, -amb ‖ kóri-) *n., pl.* **-ambs.** Also **cho·ri·am·bus** (-ám-bəss) *pl.* **-bi** (-bī) or **-buses.** In Greek and Latin verse, a metrical foot consisting of a trochee followed by an iamb, much employed in Aeolic poetry and in the choric odes of tragedy. [Late Latin *choriambus,* from Greek *khoriambos* : *khoreios,* of a chorus, hence trochee, from *khoros,* CHORUS + *iambos,* IAMBUS.] —**chor·i·am·bic** *adj.*

chor·ic (kórrik ‖ káwrik, kórik) *adj.* Of, pertaining to, or in the style of a singing or speaking chorus. Said of Greek poetry and drama: *choric dance.* [Late Latin *choricus,* from Greek *khorikos,* from *khoros,* CHORUS.]

cho·ri·on (káwri-ən ‖ kóri-, -on) *n.* The outer membrane enclosing the embryo in reptiles, birds, and mammals. Compare **amnion.** [Greek *khorion,* afterbirth.] —**cho·ri·on·ic** (-ónnik) *adj.*

chor·is·ter (kórri-stər ‖ káwri-, kóri-) *n.* A choir singer; especially, a choirboy. [Learned respelling of Middle English *queristre,* from Anglo-French *cueristre* (unattested), from Medieval Latin *chorista,* from *chorus,* CHORUS.]

cho·ri·zo (chə-rée-zō, chaw-, -sō) *n.* A spicy pork sausage, traditionally made in Spain. [Spanish.]

cho·rog·ra·phy (ko-rógrafi, kə-) *n.* **1.** The technique of mapping a region or district. **2.** *Archaic.* A description or map of a region. [Latin *chōrographia,* from Greek *khōrographia* : *khōros,* place, + -GRAPHY.] —**cho·rog·ra·pher** *n.* —**cho·ro·graph·ic** (kàwrə-gráffik, kòrrə-), **cho·ro·graph·i·cal** *adj.* —**cho·ro·graph·i·cal·ly** *adv.*

cho·roid (káwr-oyd ‖ kór-) *n.* The dark brown vascular coat of the eye between the sclera and the retina.

~*adj.* Also **cho·ri·oid** (káwri-oyd ‖ kóri-). *Anatomy.* **1.** Resembling the chorion. **2.** Resembling the corium. **3.** Of or pertaining to the choroid. [Greek *khoroeidēs,* scribal error for *khorioeidēs,* resembling an afterbirth : *khorion,* afterbirth, CHORION + -OID.]

choroid plexus *n.* A network of blood vessels in the ventricles of the brain that secretes cerebrospinal fluid.

cho·rol·o·gy (kə-rólləji, ko-) *n.* **1.** The study of the geographical distribution of plants and animals. **2.** The study of geographical features and their relationship within a particular region. [German *Chorologie* : Greek *khoros,* place + -*logie,* -LOGY.]

chor·tle (chórt'l) *intr.v.* **-tled, -tling, -tles.** To chuckle throatily: *"He chortled in his joy."* (Lewis Carroll).

~*n.* A snorting, joyful chuckle. [Blend of CHUCKLE and SNORT, coined by Lewis Carroll.] —**chor·tler** *n.*

cho·rus (káwr-əss ‖ kór-) *n., pl.* **-ruses. 1.** *Music.* **a.** A composition in four or more parts written for a large number of singers. **b.** A song refrain in which the audience joins the soloist. **c.** A solo section in jazz based on the main melody and played by a member of the group. **d.** A body of singers who perform choral compositions. **e.** A body of singers or dancers who support the soloists and leading actors in an opera, musical, or revue. **2. a.** In drama or poetry recitation, a group of persons who speak or sing a given part or composition in unison. **b.** In Elizabethan drama, an actor who recites the prologue and epilogue to a play and sometimes comments on the action. **c.** The lines spoken by this actor. **3.** In Greek poetry and drama: **a.** A ceremonial dance performed to the singing of odes. **b.** The portion of a drama consisting of choric dance and ode. **c.** The body of actors whose choric performance comments upon and accompanies the action of the play. **4. a.** Any speech, song, or other utterance made in concert by many people. **b.** Any simultaneous utterance by a number of persons or animals: *the dawn chorus.* —**in chorus.** With simultaneous utterance; all together.

~*v.* **chorused, -rusing, -ruses.** —*tr.* To sing or utter in chorus. —*intr.* To speak or sing in chorus. [Latin *chorus,* from Greek *khoros,* dance, chorus.]

chorus girl *n.* A girl who dances in a theatrical chorus.

chose[1] Past tense of **choose.**

chose[2] (shōz) *n. Law.* An item of personal property; a chattel. [French *chose,* "thing", from Old French, from Latin *causa,* thing, CAUSE.]

cho·sen (chóz'n) Past participle of **choose.**

~*adj.* **1.** Selected from or preferred above others. **2.** *Theology.* Elect.

~*n., pl.* **chosen. 1.** One of the elect. **2.** The elect collectively. Preceded by *the.*

Cho·sen (chō-sén). **1.** A name traditionally designating Korea since the second millennium B.C. **2.** The official name of Korea as a Japanese province (1910–45). See **Korea.**

chosen people *pl.n.* The Israelites regarded as the people chosen to receive God's revelation. Nehemiah 9:8.

Choson. See **Korea.**

cho·ta (chōtə) *adj. Indian.* Small; lesser in size or importance. [Hindi.]

chott. Variant of **shott.**

Chou or **Zhou** (jō) *n.* A Chinese dynasty that ruled from *c.* 1027 to 221 B.C., enlarging the empire and promoting philosophy.

chou·croute (shoō-kroōt, -kroōt) *n. French.* **Sauerkraut** (*see*). [From dialectal German *Surkrut.*]

Chou En-Lai. See **Zhou En-lai.**

chough (chuf) *n.* A crowlike Old World bird of the genus *Pyrrhocorax,* especially *P. pyrrhocorax,* having black plumage and red legs. [Middle English *choge, chowe,* from Germanic, proably imitative; akin to Old English *cēo,* jackdaw, jay, Middle Dutch *cauwe,* chough (imitative).]

choux pastry (shoō) *n.* A light glossy pastry made with eggs, typically used for making eclairs. [Partial translation of French *pâte choux,* "cabbage dough" (from its round shape), plural of *chou,* cabbage.]

chow[1] (chow) *n.* Also **chow-chow.** A heavy-set dog of a breed originating in China, having a long, dense, reddish-brown or black coat and a blackish tongue. [Pidgin English, perhaps from Cantonese *gao,* dog.]

chow[2] *n. Slang.* Food. [Pidgin English, probably from Cantonese *chaau,* to fry, cook.]

chow·chil·la (chow-chíllə) *n.* The **auctioneer bird** (*see*).

chow-chow (chów-chow, -chów) *n.* **1.** A relish consisting of chopped vegetables pickled in mustard. **2.** Variant of **chow.** [Pidgin English.]

chow·der (chówdər) *n. Chiefly U.S.* A thick soup or stew containing fish or shellfish, especially clams, and vegetables, often in a milk base. [French *chaudière,* stew pot, from Old French, from Late Latin *caldāria,* cauldron, from Latin *caldārius,* suitable for heating, from *caldus, calidus,* hot.]

chow mein (chów méen ‖ máyn) *n.* Also **chow mien** (chów myén). A Chinese-style dish consisting of any of various combinations of stewed vegetables and meat, served over fried noodles. [Cantonese *chaau min* or Mandarin *chăo mian* : *chăo,* to shallow fry + *mian,* noodles.]

chq. cheque.

Chr. Christ; Christian.

chres·ard (kréssərd) *n.* Water present in the soil and available for plant absorption. [Greek *khrēsis,* use, from *khrēsthai,* to use + *ardein*†, to water.]

chres·tom·a·thy (kress-tómməthi) *n., pl.* **-thies.** A selection of literary passages, used in studying literature or a language. [Greek *khrēstomatheia* : *khrēstos,* useful, from *khrēsthai,* to use + *-matheia,* learning, from *manthanein,* to learn.] —**chres·to·math·ic** (krésta-máthik) *adj.*

Chré·tien de Troyes (kráyt-yaN də trwa'a). (*c.*1135–*c.*1183). French poet, and author of the earliest surviving Arthurian romances, including *Lancelot, Knight of the Barrow.*

chrism (krízz'm) *n.* A mixture of oil and balsam consecrated by a bishop and used for anointing in various church sacraments, such as baptism and confirmation. [Middle English *crisme,* Old English *crisma,* from Late Latin *chrisma,* from Greek *khrisma,* ointment, from *khriein,* to anoint.] —**chris·mal** (krízm-əl) *adj.* —**chris·ma·tion** (kriz-máysh'n) *n.*

chris·om (krízz'm) *n.* **1.** A white cloth or robe worn by an infant at baptism. **2.** *Archaic.* An infant wearing a baptismal robe; a baby. [Middle English *crisom,* variant of *crisme,* CHRISM.]

Chris·sie (kríssi) *n. Chiefly Australian Informal.* Christmas.

Christ (krīst) *n. Abbr.* **Chr. 1.** The Anointed; the Messiah, as foretold by the prophets of the Old Testament. **2. Jesus** (*see*).

~*interj. Slang.* Used as an oath to express surprise, irritation, or the like. [Middle English *Crist,* Old English *Crist,* from Latin *Christus,* from Greek *Khristos,* "the anointed (one)", from *khriein,* to anoint.] —**Christ·li·ness** *n.* —**Christ·ly** *adj.*

Chris·ta·del·phi·an (krístə-délfi-ən) *n.* A member of a Christian sect, founded in the United States by Dr. John Thomas in the mid-19th century, that believes in the **millennium** (*see*) and rejects the doctrine of the Trinity. [From CHRIST + Greek *adelphos,* brother.] —**Chris·ta·del·phi·an** *adj.*

Christ·church[1] (kríst-church, kríss-). Capital of Canterbury province in New Zealand, situated on the Banks peninsula in the east of the South Island.

Christchurch[2]. Coastal resort in Dorset in southern England, situated at the mouths of the rivers Stour and Avon.

christ·cross (kríss-kross ‖ -krawss) *n. Archaic.* The cross, used as a signature by someone who cannot write. [From *Christ's cross.*]

chris·ten (kríss'n) *tr.v.* **-tened, -tening, -tens. 1.** To baptise into a Christian church. **2.** To give a name to at baptism. **3.** To name and dedicate ceremonially: *christen a ship.* **4.** *Informal.* To use for the first time. [Middle English *cristen, cristnen,* Old English *cristnian,* from *Crist,* CHRISTIAN.]

Chris·ten·dom (kríss'ndəm) *n.* **1.** Christians collectively. **2.** The Christian world. **3.** *Obsolete.* Christianity. [Middle English *Cristendom,* Old English *Cristendōm* : *Cristen,* CHRISTIAN + -DOM.]

chris·ten·ing (kríss'n-ing, kríssning) *n.* The Christian sacrament of baptism, including the bestowal of a name upon an infant.

Chris·tian (kríst-yən, kríss-chən, krish-) *adj.* **1.** Professing belief in Jesus as Christ or following the religion based on his teachings. **2.** Pertaining to or derived from Jesus or his teachings. **3.** Manifesting the qualities or spirit of Christ; Christlike. **4.** Pertaining to or characteristic of Christianity or its adherents. **5.** *Informal.* Kind, decent, or generous.

~*n.* **1.** *Abbr.* **Chr.** One who professes belief in Jesus as the Christ or follows the religion based on his teachings. **2.** One who lives according to the teachings of Jesus. **3.** *Informal.* A kind or generous human being. [Middle English *Cristen, Christen,* Old English *Crīs-*

ten, from Latin *Christiānus*, believer in Christ, from Greek *Khristianos*, from *Khristos*, CHRIST.] —**Chris·tian·ly** *adv*.

Christian X (1870–1947). King of Denmark (1912–47), notable for his passive resistance to the German occupation of his country during World War II. He rejected Nazi demands for anti-Jewish legislation (1942) and was kept in confinement until 1945.

Christian Brothers *pl.n*. An order of Roman Catholic brothers concerned with education of the poor. Also officially called "Brothers of the Christian Schools".

Christian era *n*. The period beginning with the birth of Jesus (conventionally in A.D. 1). Dates in this era are marked A.D., and dates before it, B.C. Also called "common era".

chris·ti·a·ni·a (kríss-ti-áani-ə ‖ -chi-) *n*. A ski turn in which the body is swung round with the skis parallel, to change direction or to make a stop. Also called "christie", "christy". [Norwegian, after CHRISTIANIA.]

Christiania. See **Oslo.**

Chris·tian·ise, Chris·tian·ize (kríst-yən-īz, kríss-chən-) *v*. **-ised, -ising, -ises.** —*tr*. **1.** To convert to Christianity. **2.** To imbue with Christian principles and qualities. —*intr. Rare*. To adopt Christianity. —**Chris·tian·i·sa·tion** (-ī-záysh'n ‖ *U.S*. -i-) *n*. —**Chris·tian·is·er** *n*.

Chris·ti·an·i·ty (kríss-ti-ánnəti ‖ -chi-) *n., pl*. **-ties. 1.** The Christian religion, founded on the teachings of Jesus. **2.** Christians as a group; Christendom. **3.** The state or fact of being a Christian.

Christian name *n*. A name other than a surname given to a person at birth or when he is christened.

Christian Science *n. Abbr*. **C.S.** The church and the religious system founded by Mary Baker **Eddy** *(see)*, emphasising healing through spiritual means as an important element of Christianity, and teaching pure divine goodness as underlying the scientific reality of existence. The church is also officially called "Church of Christ, Scientist". —**Christian Scientist** *n*.

Chris·tie (krísti), **Dame Agatha (Mary Clarissa)** (1890–1976). British author of detective fiction, who also wrote as Mary Westmacott. Her play *The Mousetrap* (1952) set a world record for the longest continuous run in one theatre.

Christie, Linford (1960–). Jamaican-born British sprinter who became the best sprinter in the Commonwealth. He won the Olympic 100 metres title in 1992 and the World title in 1993.

Christ·like (kríst-līk) *adj*. Having the spiritual qualities or attributes of Christ. —**Christ·like·ness** *n*.

Christ·mas (krissməss. *Note: there is also a pedantically careful pronunciation* kríst-məss) *n*. **1.** December 25, a holiday celebrated by Christians as the anniversary of the birth of Jesus. Christmas Day is one of the four quarter days in England and Wales. **2.** The Christian church festival extending from December 24 (Christmas Eve) to January 6 (Epiphany). In this sense, also called "Christmastide". [Middle English *Cristesmasse*, Old English *Cristesmæsse* : *Cristes*, genitive of *Crist*, CHRIST + *mæsse*, -MAS.]

Christmas box *n*. In Britain, a small gift, usually of money, given at Christmas to those who provide services, such as postmen.

Christmas cactus *n*. A spineless, epiphytic cactus, *Zygocactus truncatus*, of South America, cultivated as a house plant for its showy red flowers. Also called "crab cactus".

Christmas disease *n*. A disease very similar to haemophilia, caused by deficiency of one blood coagulation factor.

Christmas Eve *n*. The evening or the day before Christmas.

Christmas Island[1]. Part of the Republic of **Kiribati** *(see)*.

Christmas Island[2]. An island territory of Australia, situated in the Indian Ocean southwest of Java. Phosphates are mined here.

Christmas pudding *n*. A rich steamed pudding traditionally eaten at Christmas, made with flour, eggs, suet, spices, and dried fruit. Also called "plum pudding".

Christmas rose *n*. An evergreen plant, *Helleborus niger*, native to Europe, having white or pinkish-green flowers that bloom in late autumn or winter. Also called "hellebore".

Christmas stocking *n*. A stocking hung up by children on Christmas Eve, to be filled with presents by Father Christmas.

Christ·mas·sy (kríss-mə-si) *adj. Informal*. Characteristic of Christmas.

Christmas tree *n*. An evergreen or artificial tree decorated with lights and ornaments during the Christmas season.

Chris·toff, Boris (1919–93). Bulgarian bass opera singer, famous for his portrayals of Boris Godunov in Mussorgsky's opera and as King Philip in *Don Carlos*.

Chris·tol·o·gy (kriss-tóllǝji) *n., pl*. **-gies. 1.** The study of Christ's person, qualities, and deeds. **2.** Any doctrine or theory based on Christ or his teachings. —**Chris·to·log·i·cal** (krístə-lójik'l) *adj*.

Christ's-thorn (krísts-thawrn, kríss-, -thórn) *n*. Any of several plants of the Near East, such as the jujube or *Paliurus spina-christi*, having spiny thorns and popularly believed to have been used for Christ's crown of thorns.

chris·ty (krísti) *n., pl*. **-ties.** A ski turn, the **christiania** *(see)*.

chro·ma (krṓmə) *n*. That aspect of colour in the Munsell scale by which a sample appears to differ from a grey of the same lightness or brightness. Chroma corresponds to **saturation** *(see)* of the perceived colour. [Greek *khrṓma*, colour.]

chro·mate (krṓmayt) *n*. A salt or ester of chromic acid. [CHROM(O)- + -ATE.]

chro·mat·ic (krō-máttik, krə-) *adj*. **1. a.** Pertaining to colours or colour. **b.** Pertaining to colour perceived to have a saturation greater than zero. **2. a.** *Music*. Of, pertaining to, or based on the

chromatic scale. **b.** Pertaining to chords or harmonies based on nonharmonic notes. [Greek *khrōmatikos*, from *khrōma*, colour, modification of musical note.] —**chro·mat·i·cal·ly** *adv*. —**chro·mat·i·cism** *n*.

chromatic aberration *n*. Colour distortion in an image produced by a lens because of the focusing of light of different wavelengths by the lens at different points.

chro·ma·tic·i·ty (krōmə-tíssəti) *n*. The aspect of colour that includes consideration of its dominant wavelength and purity.

chro·mat·ic·ness (krō-máttik-nəss, krə-, -niss) *n. Physics*. Hue and saturation considered together as an attribute of colour.

chro·mat·ics (krō-máttiks, krə-) *n. Used with a singular verb*. The scientific study of colour. Also called "chromatology". —**chro·ma·tist** (krṓmətist) *n*.

chromatic scale *n. Music*. A scale consisting of 12 semitones.

chro·ma·tid (krṓmə-tid) *n. Genetics*. Either of two daughter strands of a duplicated chromosome while still joined by a single centromere. [CHROMAT(O)- + -ID.]

chro·ma·tin (krṓmə-tin) *n. Genetics*. A complex of nucleic acids and proteins in the nucleus of a cell, characterised by intense staining with basic dyes. [CHROMAT(O)- + -IN.]

chromato-, chromat– *comb. form*. Indicates: **1.** Colour, staining, or pigmentation; for example, **chromatophore, chromatid. 2.** Chromatin; for example, **chromatolysis.** [Greek *khrōma* (stem *khrōmat-*), colour.]

chro·mat·o·gram (krṓmətə-gram, krō-máttə-, krə-) *n*. **1.** The absorbent column or strip of material containing the stratographically differentiated constituents separated from a solution or mixture by chromatography. **2.** A graph or graphlike diagram indicating quantatively the substances present in a chromatographic analysis. [CHROMATO- + -GRAM.]

chro·ma·tog·ra·phy (krōmə-tóggrəfi) *n*. Any of several methods of separating chemical substances for analysis in which the substance is passed through a selectively absorbent medium such as treated filter paper (*paper chromatography*) or a column of powder (*column chromatography*). [CHROMATO- + -GRAPHY.] —**chro·ma·tog·ra·pher** *n*. —**chro·ma·to·graph·ic** (krṓmətə-gráffik, krō-máttə-) *adj*.

chro·ma·tol·y·sis (krṓmə-tóllə-siss) *n. Biology*. The disintegration of stainable material (chromatin) within a cell. [CHROMATO- + -LYSIS.]

chro·mat·o·phore (krṓmətə-fawr, krō-máttə- ‖ -fōr) *n. Biology*. A pigment-containing or pigment-producing cell; especially, a pigment-containing animal cell, as in certain lizards, that by expansion or contraction can change the overall colour of the skin. Also called "pigment cell". [CHROMATO- + -PHORE.] —**chro·ma·to·phor·ic** (-fórrik ‖ -fáwrik, -fōrik) *adj*.

chrome (krōm) *n*. **1. a.** Chromium. **b.** Anything plated with a chromium alloy. **2.** A pigment containing chromium. ~*tr.v.* **chromed, chroming, chromes. 1.** To plate with chromium. **2.** To tan or dye with a chromium compound. [French, from Greek *khrōma*, colour (from the brilliant colours of the chromium compounds).]

–chrome *n. & adj. comb. form*. Indicates pigment, colour, or coloured; for example, **autochrome.** [Greek *khrōma*, colour.]

chrome alum *n*. A violet-red crystalline compound, $CrK(SO_4)_2.12H_2O$, used in tanning, as a mordant, and in photography.

chrome green *n*. **1.** Any of a class of green pigments consisting of chrome yellow and iron blue in various proportions. **2.** Very dark yellowish green to moderate or strong green.

chrome red *n*. A light orange to red pigment consisting of basic lead chromate with varying proportions of $PbCrO_4$ and PbO.

chrome steel *n*. Any of various hard, rust-proof steels that contain chromium. Also called "chromium steel".

chrome yellow *n*. Lead chromate, $PbCrO_4$, a yellow pigment often combined with lead sulphate, $PbSO_4$, for lighter hues.

chro·mic (krṓmik) *adj*. Of, pertaining to, or containing chromium, especially with valency 3.

chromic acid *n*. **1.** A corrosive, oxidising acid, H_2CrO_4, known only in solution. **2.** The anhydride of this acid, CrO_3, a purplish crystalline material that reacts explosively with reducing agents and is used in chromium plating, and to colour glass and rubber.

chromic oxide *n*. A bright green, crystalline powder, Cr_2O_3, used in metallurgy and as a paint pigment.

chro·mi·nance (krṓmǝnǝnss) *n*. The quality of light that creates the sensation of colour and is determined by comparing it with a reference source of the same brightness and of known chromaticity. [CHROMO- + LUMINANCE.]

chro·mite (krṓmīt) *n*. **1.** A widely distributed black to brownish-black chromium ore, $FeCr_2O_4$. **2.** A salt of chromous acid. [CHROM(O)- + -ITE.]

chro·mi·um (krṓmi-əm) *n. Symbol* **Cr** A lustrous, hard, steel-grey metallic element, resistant to tarnish and corrosion, and found primarily in chromite. It is used as a catalyst, to harden steel alloys, to produce stainless steels, in corrosion-resistant decorative platings, and as pigment in glass.

chromium steel *n*. Chrome steel.

chromo-, chrom– *comb. form*. Indicates: **1.** Colour, coloured, staining, or pigment; for example, **chromophore, chromosome. 2.** Chromium or chromic acid; for example, **chromate.** [Greek *khrōma*, colour.]

chro·mo·dy·nam·ics *n. Used with a singular verb. Physics*. In quark theory, the study of the process by which various elementary particles interact. Also called "quantum chromodynamics". See **colour, gluon.**

chro·mo·gen (krṓmə-jən, -jen) *n.* **1.** *Chemistry.* A substance capable of chemical conversion into a pigment or dye. **2.** *Biology.* A strongly pigmented or pigment-generating organ, organelle, or microorganism. [CHROMO- + -GEN.] —**chro·mo·gen·ic** (-jénnik) *adj.*

chro·mo·lith·o·graph (krṓmō-líth-ə-graaf, -líth-, -graf. *Note: printers tend to say* -líth-, *others* -líth-) *n.* A coloured print produced by chromolithography.

chro·mo·li·thog·ra·phy (krṓmō-li-thóggrəfi, -lī-) *n.* The art or process of printing colour pictures from a series of stone or zinc plates by lithography. —**chro·mo·li·thog·ra·pher** *n.* —**chro·mo·lith·o·graph·ic** (-líthə-gráffik, -líthə-) *adj.*

chro·mo·mere (krṓm-ə-meer, -ō-) *n.* Any of the serially aligned chromatin granules forming a chromosome. [CHROMO- + -MERE.]

chro·mo·ne·ma (krṓmə-née-mə) *n., pl.* -**mata** (-mətə). The coiled threadlike core of a chromosome. [CHROMO- + Greek *nēma,* thread.] —**chro·mo·ne·mal** (-néem'l), **chro·mo·ne·mat·ic** (nimáttik), **chro·mo·ne·mic** (-néemik) *adj.*

chro·mo·phore (krṓmə-fawr ‖ -fōr) *n.* A molecular group capable of selective light absorption resulting in coloration of aromatic compounds. [CHROMO- + -PHORE.] —**chro·mo·phor·ic** (-fórrik ‖ -fáwrik, -fṓrik) *adj.*

chro·mo·plast (krṓmə-plast, -plaast) *n. Botany.* A coloured plastid containing a pigment other than or in addition to chlorophyll. [CHROMO- + -PLAST.]

chro·mo·pro·tein (krṓmō-prṓ-teen, -ti-in) *n.* A substance consisting of a protein forming a complex with a pigmented group.

chro·mo·scope (krṓmə-skōp) *n. Electronics.* A device used in sonar systems that displays information about objects detected by the sonar beam on a screen, in colours whose shade and intensity vary according to the density of the object.

chro·mo·some (krṓmə-sōm) *n.* Any of a number of threadlike structures in the cell nuclei of plants and animals, consisting of DNA, RNA, and protein, that carry genetic information in the form of genes and are responsible for the determination and transmission of hereditary characteristics. [CHROMO- + -SOME (body).] —**chro·mo·so·mal** (-sōm'l) *adj.* —**chro·mo·so·mal·ly** *adv.*

chro·mo·sphere (krṓmə-sfeer) *n.* **1.** An incandescent, transparent layer of gas, primarily hydrogen, several thousand miles in depth, that lies above and surrounds the photosphere of the sun but is distinctly separate from the corona. **2.** A similar gaseous layer around a star. [CHROMO- (from its rosy colour) + SPHERE.] —**chro·mo·spher·ic** (-sférrik ‖ -sféer-ik) *adj.*

chro·mous (krṓməss) *adj.* Of, pertaining to, or containing chromium, especially with valency 2.

chro·myl (krṓmil) *adj.* Of or designating a chemical compound that contains the divalent radical CrO_2. [CHROMO- (chromium) + -YL.]

chro·nax·y, chro·nax·ie (krṓn-aksi, krón-) *n., pl.* -**ies.** Also **chro·nax·i·a** (-ak-sée-ə). The time interval necessary to stimulate a muscle or nerve fibre electrically, using twice the minimum current needed to elicit a threshold response. [French *chronaxie* : CHRON(O)- + Greek *axia,* value, from *axios,* worthy.]

chron·ic (krónnik) *adj.* **1.** Of long duration; continuing; constant. **2.** Prolonged or developing slowly. Said of certain diseases. Compare **acute. 3.** Subject to a disease or habit for a long time; inveterate. **4.** *British Slang.* Dreadful; very bad: *The film was chronic.* [French *chronique,* from Latin *chronicus,* from Greek *khronikos,* pertaining to time, from *khronos†,* time.] —**chron·i·cal·ly** *adv.* —**chro·nic·i·ty** (kro-níssəti) *n.*

chron·i·cle (krónnik'l) *n.* A chronological record of events.
~*tr.v.* **chronicled, -cling, -cles.** To record in, or in the form of, a chronicle. [Middle English *cronicle,* from Anglo-French, from Old French *cronique,* from Latin *chronica,* from Greek *(biblia) khronika,* "chronological (books)", from *khronikos,* chronological. See **chronic.**] —**chron·i·cler** (krónniklər) *n.*

Chron·i·cles (krónnik'lz) *pl.n. Abbr.* **Chron.** In the Old Testament, either of two books, I and II Chronicles.

chrono-, chron- *comb. form.* Indicates time; for example, **chronaxy, chronometer.** [Greek *khronos,* time. See **chronic.**]

chron·o·bi·ol·o·gy (krónnə-bī-óllǝji, krōnə-) *n.* The branch of biology concerned with biorhythms.

chron·o·gram (krónnə-gram, krōnə-) *n.* **1.** The record produced by a chronograph. **2.** An inscribed phrase in which certain letters can be read as Roman numerals indicating a specific date. [CHRONO- + -GRAM.] —**chron·o·gram·mat·ic** (-grə-máttik) *adj.* —**chron·o·gram·mat·i·cal·ly** *adv.*

chron·o·graph (krónnə-graaf, krṓnə-, -graf) *n.* An instrument that registers or graphically records time intervals such as the duration of an event. [CHRONO- + -GRAPH.] —**chron·o·graph·ic** (krónnə-gráffik) *adj.* —**chron·o·graph·i·cal·ly** *adv.*

chron·o·log·i·cal (krónnə-lójik'l, krōnə-) *adj.* Also **chron·o·log·ic** (-lójik). *Abbr.* **chron., chronol. 1.** Arranged in order of time of occurrence. **2.** In accordance with or relating to chronology. —**chron·o·log·i·cal·ly** *adv.*

chronological age *n. Abbr.* **C.A.** The number of years a person has lived, used in psychometrics as a comparison standard for various performance measures. Compare **mental age.**

chro·nol·o·gy (krə-nóllǝji, kro-, krō-) *n., pl.* -**gies.** *Abbr.* **chron., chronol. 1.** The determination of dates and the sequence of events. **2.** The arrangement of events in time. **3.** A chronological list or table. [CHRONO- + -LOGY.] —**chro·nol·o·gist** *n.*

chro·nom·e·ter (krə-nómmitər) *n.* An exceptionally precise clock, watch, or other timepiece. [CHRONO- + -METER.] —**chron·o·met·ric** (krónnə-méttrik, krṓnə-) —**chron·o·met·ri·cal** *adj.* —**chron·o·met·ri·cal·ly** *adv.*

chro·nom·e·try (krə-nómmətri, kro-, krō-) *n.* The scientific measurement of time. [CHRONO- + -METRY.]

chro·non (krṓ-non) *n.* A unit of time equal to about 10^{-24} second, the time taken for a photon to traverse an electron. [CHRONO- + -ON.]

chron·o·scope (krónnə-skōp, krōnə-) *n.* An optical instrument for measuring minute time intervals. [CHRONO- + -SCOPE.] —**chron·o·scop·ic** (-skóppik) *adj.*

-chroous *adj. comb. form.* Indicates coloured; for example, **iso·chroous.** [Greek *khrōs,* flesh, complexion, colour.]

chrys·a·lid (kríssə-lid) *n. Entomology.* A chrysalis.
~*adj.* Also **chry·sal·i·dal** (kri-sállid'l). Pertaining to or resembling a chrysalis.

chrys·a·lis (kríssə-liss) *n., pl.* -**lises** or **chrysalides** (kri-sálli-deez). *Entomology.* **1.** A pupa; especially, the pupa of a moth or butterfly, enclosed in a firm case or cocoon. **2.** A state of incomplete development; a transitional stage. [Latin *chrȳsallis,* from Greek *khrusallis,* the golden pupa of a butterfly, from *khrusos,* gold. See **chryso-.**]

chry·san·the·mum (kri-zánthi-məm, -sánthi- ‖ -mum) *n.* Any of various plants of the genus *Chrysanthemum,* the cultivated forms of which have showy flowers of various sizes and colours, especially red, yellow, white, and brown. **2.** The flower of any of these plants. [Latin *chrȳsanthemum,* from Greek *khrusanthemon,* "gold flower" : CHRYS(O)- + *anthemon,* flower, from *anthos,* flower.]

chrys·a·ro·bin (kríssə-róbin) *n.* A medicine obtained from a deposit found in the wood of the araroba tree and formerly used to treat certain chronic skin conditions. [CHRYS(O)- (from its golden colour) + (AR)AROB(A) + -IN.]

chrys·el·e·phan·tine (kríss-eli-fán-tīn ‖ -əlǝ-, -teen) *adj.* Made of or overlaid with gold and ivory. Said especially of ancient Greek statues. [Greek *khruselephantinos* : CHRYS(O)- + *elephantinos,* of ivory, from *elephas,* ivory (see **elephant**).]

chryso-, chrys– *comb. form.* Indicates gold or the colour of gold; for example, **chrysotile, chrysarobin.** [Greek *khrusos,* gold, from Semitic; akin to Hebrew *ḥarūz,* gold.]

chrys·o·ber·yl (kríssə-bérril, -bérr'l) *n.* A green to yellow vitreous mineral, $BeAl_2O_4$, used as a gemstone. [Latin *chrȳsobēryllus* : CHRYSO- + BERYL.]

chrys·o·lite (kríssə-līt) *n.* A mineral, **olivine** *(see).* [Middle English *crisolite* : CHRYSO- + -LITE.]

chrys·o·prase (kríssə-prayz) *n.* An apple-green chalcedony used as a gemstone. [Middle English *crisopase,* from Old French *crisopace, crisopras,* from Latin *chrȳsoprasus,* from Greek *khrusoprasos,* "gold green" : CHRYSO- + *prason,* leek.]

Chrys·o·stom (kríssəstəm), **Saint John** (*c.* 347–407). Greek Church Father, Archbishop of Constantinople (398–407). He earned the name of *Chrysostom* (golden-mouthed) by preaching in Antioch.

chrys·o·ther·a·py (kríssə-thērrəpi) *n.* The treatment of certain diseases, especially rheumatoid arthritis, with gold compounds.

chrys·o·tile (kríssə-tīl, -til) *n.* A fibrous mineral variety of serpentine used as a variety of commercial asbestos. Also called "white asbestos". [CHRYSO- + Greek *tilos,* something plucked, fine hair, from *tillein†,* to pluck.]

chthon·ic (thónnik, kthónnik) *adj.* Also **chtho·ni·an** (thṓ-ni-ən, kthṓ-). Pertaining to the gods and spirits of the underworld. [Greek *khthonios,* under the earth, from *khthōn,* earth.]

chub (chub) *n., pl.* **chubs** or collectively **chub. 1.** Any of various freshwater fishes of the family Cyprinidae, related to the carps and minnows, especially a Eurasian species, *Leuciscus cephalus.* **2.** Any of various North American fishes, such as a whitefish of the genus *Coregonus* or a marine fish of the genus *Kyphosus.* [15th century : origin obscure.]

chub·by (chúbbi) *adj.* -**bier, -biest.** Rounded and plump. See Synonyms at **fat.** [Probably from CHUB, from the plumpness of the fish.] —**chub·bi·ness** *n.*

chuck¹ (chuk) *v.* **chucked, chucking, chucks.** —*tr.* **1.** To pat or squeeze fondly or playfully, especially under the chin. **2.** *Informal.* To throw; toss. **3.** *Informal.* To throw out; discard. Often used with *out.* **4.** *Informal.* To expel forcibly; eject. Used with *out.* **5.** *Informal.* To leave or give up. Usually used with *in* or *up*: *to chuck in one's job.* —*intr. U.S. & Australian & N.Z. Slang.* To vomit.
~*n.* **1.** An affectionate pat or squeeze under the chin. **2.** *Informal.* A throw, toss, or pitch. [Perhaps from Old French *choquer, chuquer,* to strike, SHOCK.]

chuck² *n.* **1.** A cut of beef extending from the neck to the ribs and including the shoulder blade. **2.** *Western U.S. Informal.* Food. **3.** A clamp with adjustable jaws that holds a tool, or the material being worked, in a machine such as a drill or a lathe. [Variant of CHOCK (wedge).]

chuck³ *intr.v.* **chucked, chucking, chucks.** To make a clucking sound. [Imitative.] —**chuck** *n.*

chuck⁴ *n. Archaic & Regional.* Used affectionately as a term of address.

chuck·er-out (chúckər-ówt) *n. Informal.* One who is employed to eject unwanted people, as from a meeting; a bouncer.

chuck·le (chúck'l) *intr.v.* -**led, -ling, -les.** To laugh quietly or to oneself.
~*n.* A quiet laugh of mild amusement or satisfaction. [Probably frequentative of CHUCK (to make a clucking sound).] —**chuck·ler** *n.*

chuck·le·head (chúck'l-hed) *n. Informal.* A stupid and gauche person; a blockhead. —**chuck·le·head·ed** *adj.*

chuck·wal·la (chúk-wollǝ) *n.* A lizard, *Sauromalus obesus,* of the southwestern United States and Mexico, related to the iguana. [Mexican Spanish *chacahuala,* from Shoshonean *tcaxxwal.*]

chu·fa (chōōfǝ) *n.* A sedge, *Cyperus esculentus,* native to warm regions of the Old World, having edible, nutlike tubers. [Spanish, fluff, nonsense, from Old Spanish, from *chufar, chuflar,* to hiss at, laugh at, from Vulgar Latin *sufilāre* (unattested), variant of Latin *sībilāre,* to whistle at, hiss down.]

chuff (chuf) *n.* A short, usually repeated, puffing sound. ~*intr.v.* **chuffed, chuffing, chuffs.** To make a regular puffing sound. Used especially of steam trains. [Imitative.]

chuffed (chuft) *adj. British Informal.* Very pleased; delighted. [From dialectal *chuff* (adjective), pleased, happy, chubby, from *chuff*† (obsolete noun), fat cheek.]

chug (chug) *n.* A dull, low sound, usually short and repeated, made by or as if by a labouring engine. ~*intr.v.* **chugged, chugging, chugs. 1.** To make such sounds. **2.** To travel or move while making such sounds. Often used with *along.* [Imitative.]

chu·kar (chu-kár) *n.* An Old World partridge, *Alectoris graeca,* having a black-striped brownish plumage and red legs and bill. [Hindi *chakor,* from Sanskrit *cakōra.*]

Chuk·chi (chŏŏk-chee) *n., pl.* **-chis** or collectively **Chukchi.** Also **Chuk·chee. 1.** A member of a Mongoloid people of northeastern Siberia. **2.** The language of this people, noted for being pronounced differently by men and women.

chuk·ka (chúkkǝ) *n.* A short, ankle-length boot, usually made of suede, having two pairs of eyelets. Also called "chukka boot". [From CHUKKER (polo players wear a kind of chukka boot).]

chuk·ker, chuk·kar (chúkkǝr) *n.* One of the periods of play, lasting 7 to 7½ minutes, in a polo match. [Hindi *cakkar,* circle, turn, from Sanskrit *cakra-,* wheel.]

chum (chum) *n.* An intimate friend or companion. ~*v.* **chummed, chumming, chums.** —*intr.* To be or become an intimate friend of. Often used with *up* or *up with.* —*tr. Scottish.* To accompany; escort. [17th century : Oxford University slang, probably from *chamber fellow,* "roommate".]

chum·my (chúmmi) *adj.* **-mier, -miest.** *Informal.* Intimate; friendly; amicable. —See Synonyms at **familiar.** ~*pron. Informal.* Him or her: *What about chummy here?* —**chum·mi·ly** *adv.* —**chum·mi·ness** *n.*

chump (chump) *n.* **1.** *Informal.* A blockhead; a dolt. **2.** A blunt end of something, such as a piece of wood. —**off (one's) chump.** *Chiefly British. Informal.* Out of one's mind; mad. [Probably a blend of CHUNK and LUMP or STUMP.]

chump chop *n.* A chop, especially of pork or lamb, cut from between the leg and loin.

chun·der (chúndǝr) *n. Chiefly Australian & N.Z. Slang.* Vomit. ~*intr.v.* **chundered, -dering, -ders.** *Chiefly Australian & N.Z. Slang.* To vomit. [20th century : origin obscure.] —**chun·der·ous** *adj.*

Ch'ung-ch'ing. See **Chongqing.**

Chungking. See **Chongqing.**

chunk (chungk) *n.* **1.** A thick mass or piece of something: *a chunk of bread.* **2.** *Informal.* A fair or substantial amount. [Probably a nasalised variant of CHUCK (wedge).]

chunk·y (chúngki) *adj.* **-ier, -iest. 1.** Short; thickset; stocky. **2.** In chunks. **3.** Being or knitted with thick wool: *a chunky sweater.* —**chunk·i·ness** *n.*

church (church) *n. Abbr.* **Ch., C., ch., c. 1.** *Capital* **C.** The body of all Christians throughout the world. **2.** A building for public worship, especially Christian worship. **3.** A congregation. **4.** Public divine worship in a church; a religious service. **5.** *Usually capital* **C.** A specified Christian denomination: *the Presbyterian Church.* **6.** Ecclesiastical power as distinguished from secular power. **7.** The clerical profession; the clergy. ~*tr.v.* **churched, churching, churches.** To conduct church services for; especially, to perform a religious service for (a woman after childbirth). ~*adj.* **1.** Of or pertaining to the church; ecclesiastical. **2.** Being a member of the Anglican church. Compare **chapel.** [Middle English *chirche,* Old English *cirice,* from West Germanic *kirika* (unattested), from Late Greek *kurikon,* variant of *(dōma) kuriakon,* the Lord's (house), from Greek *kuriakos,* of the Lord, from *kurios,* lord.]

Church Army *n.* A charitable organisation of the Church of England carrying out voluntary social work. Compare **Salvation Army.**

Church Commissioners *pl.n.* A body of people, representing both the church and the state, that manages the finances and property of the Church of England.

church·go·er (chúrch-gō-ǝr) *n.* One who attends church regularly. —**church·go·ing** *adj. & n.*

Church·ill[1] (chúrchil). River 1 610 kilometres (1000 miles) long in western Canada. It flows from Saskatchewan to Hudson Bay.

Churchill[2]. River in eastern Canada. It flows some 970 kilometres (600 miles) through Labrador into the Atlantic Ocean near Rigolet.

Churchill, Lord Randolph Henry Spencer (1849–95). British statesman and father of Winston Churchill. He was leader of the so-called Fourth Party, a group of Conservative M.P.s who pressed for social and constitutional reform.

Churchill, Sir Winston (Leonard Spencer) (1874–1965). British statesman and author. He became a Conservative M.P. (1900) but joined the Liberals over tariff reform (1904). He held office in sev-

eral Liberal governments and Lloyd George's coalition government, but rejoined the Conservative party (1924). As Chancellor of the Exchequer (1924–29) he forcefully opposed the **General Strike** (1926). With the rise of Nazism in Germany he urged British rearmament and on the outbreak of war (1939) became First Lord of the Admiralty and succeeded Neville Chamberlain as prime minister, heading the coalition government (1940–45). He was returned as prime minister (1951) and knighted (1953). He published several volumes including *The Second World War* (1948–53), and was awarded the Nobel prize for literature (1953). He resigned as prime minister in 1955, subsequently publishing his major study, *A History of the English Speaking Peoples* (1956–58).

Churchill Falls. A waterfall in Labrador in northeast Canada, on the upper Churchill river. The falls drop 75 metres (245 feet).

church·ly (chúrchli) *adj.* Of, pertaining to, or fit for a church. —**church·li·ness** *n.*

church·man (chúrch-mǝn) *n., pl.* **-men** (-mǝn). **1.** A clergyman; a priest. **2.** A male member of a church. —**church·man·ly** *adj.* —**church·man·ship** *n.*

Church militant *n.* The church on earth viewed as fighting against evil. Compare **Church triumphant.**

Church of Christ, Scientist *n.* The official name of the Christian Science Church. See **Christian Science.**

Church of England *n. Abbr.* **C. of E.** The episcopal and liturgical national church of England, which withdrew its recognition of papal authority in the 16th century. See **Anglican Church.**

Church of Jesus Christ of Latter-day Saints *n.* The official name of the Mormon Church. See **Mormon.**

Church of Rome *n.* The **Roman Catholic Church** *(see).*

Church of Scotland *n.* The established Presbyterian church in Scotland.

Church Slavonic *n.* The literary language of Slavonic manuscripts written after the early 11th century, still used as a liturgical language in the Eastern Orthodox Church.

church text *n. Printing.* A heavy black Gothic typeface.

Church triumphant *n.* That part of the Church which has overcome evil and reached heaven. Compare **Church militant.**

church·war·den (chúrch-wáwrd'n ‖ *U.S.* -wawrd'n) *n.* **1.** In the Anglican Church, a lay officer chosen annually by the vicar or the congregation to handle the secular and legal affairs of the parish. **2.** A clay pipe with a long stem.

church·wom·an (chúrch-wŏŏmǝn) *n., pl.* **-women** (-wimmin). **1.** A female member of a church. **2.** A clergywoman.

church·yard (chúrch-yaard) *n.* A yard adjacent to a church, often used as a graveyard.

chu·rin·ga (chǝ-ríng-gǝ) *n., pl.* **-gas** or collectively **churinga.** An Australian Aboriginal sacred amulet. [From a native Australian language.]

churl (churl) *n.* **1.** A rude, boorish person. **2.** A miser; a niggard. **3. a.** A **ceorl** *(see).* **b.** A medieval English peasant. [Middle English *churl, cherl,* man, husband, Old English *ceorl,* man, free man of the lowest rank, from West Germanic *kerl-* (unattested), man.]

churl·ish (chúrlish) *adj.* **1. a.** Rude; surly. **b.** Boorish. **2.** *Rare.* Difficult to work. Said especially of soil. —**churl·ish·ly** *adv.* —**churl·ish·ness** *n.*

churn (churn) *n.* **1.** A vessel or device in which cream or whole milk is agitated to separate the oily globules used to make butter. **2.** *British.* A large can used to carry milk. ~*v.* **churned, churning, churns.** —*tr.* **1.** To stir or agitate (milk or cream) in a churn in order to make butter. **2.** To make by the agitation of milk or cream: *churn butter.* **3.** To shake or agitate vigorously. —*intr.* **1.** To make butter by operating a churn. **2.** To move with great agitation: *My stomach churned at the prospect.* —**churn out.** To produce in large quantities, as if mechanically and usually at the expense of quality. [Middle English *chīrne, cherine,* Old English *cyrin, cyrn,* from Germanic *kernjōn* (unattested).] —**churn·er** *n.*

churn·ing (chúrning) *n.* The amount of butter churned at one time.

churr (chur) *n.* The sharp, whirring or trilling sound made by some insects and birds. [Imitative.] —**churr** *intr.v.*

chut (chu, chut) *interj. West Indian.* Used informally to express annoyance or impatience. [Imitative.]

chute (shōōt) *n.* **1.** An inclined trough, passage, or channel down which things may pass. **2.** A waterfall or rapid. **3.** *Informal.* A parachute. [French, a fall, from Old French *cheoite,* feminine past participle of *cheoir,* to fall, from Vulgar Latin *cadēre* (unattested), from Latin *cadere.*]

chut·ney (chútni) *n.* A pungent relish made of fruit, vinegar, spices, and herbs. [Hindi *catnī*†.]

chut·ty (chútti) *n. Australian & N.Z. Informal.* Chewing gum. Also called "chutty gum". [Perhaps from *chew it.*]

chutz·pah (khŏŏtspǝ) *n. Slang.* Shameless impudence; gall. [Yiddish.]

Chu·vash (chōō-vash, chōō-vaásh) *n., pl.* **-vashes** or collective **Chuvash. 1.** A member of a Tartar people living chiefly in Chuvashiya. **2.** The Turkic language of this people. [Russian, from Chuvash *čǎvaš,* akin to Turkish *yavaş,* gentle.]

Chuvashiya (chōō-vash-yǝ). Formerly an autonomous republic of the Soviet Union, now a republic within the Russian Federation. Capital: Cheboksary.

chyle (kīl) *n.* A thick white or pale yellow fluid, consisting of lymph and finely emulsified fat, that is taken up by the lacteals from the intestine in digestion. [Latin *chȳlus,* juice, from Greek *khulos,* from

khein, to pour.] **—chy·la·ceous** (kī-láyshəss), **chy·lous** (kíləss) *adj.*

chy·lo·mic·ron (kílə-míkron) *n.* Any of the microscopic fat particles present in the blood after fat has been digested and absorbed from the small intestine. [From *chylo-,* CHYLE + Greek *mikron,* particle, from *mikros,* small.]

chyme (kīm) *n.* The thick semifluid mass of partly digested food in the stomach that passes into the duodenum. [Late Latin *chȳmus,* from Greek *khumos,* juice, from *khein,* to pour. See **chyle.**] **—chy·mous** (kíməs) *adj.*

chy·mo·sin (kímə-sin) *n.* An enzyme, **rennin** *(see).* [CHYM(E) + -OS(E) + -IN.]

chy·mo·tryp·sin (kímə-trípsin) *n.* A protein-digesting enzyme secreted by the pancreas in an inactive form, which is activated by trypsin. [CHYM(E) + TRYPSIN.]

Ci curie.

C.I. Channel Islands.

CIA Central Intelligence Agency (in the United States).

cia·bat·ta (chə-báatə) *n.* Italian-style bread made with olive oil. [Italian "mule(slipper)", perhaps from the resemblance of the loaf to a flat or flattened shoe.]

ciao (chow) *interj.* Used informally to greet or take one's leave of somebody. [Italian.]

ci·bo·ri·um (si-báwri-əm || -bóri-) *n., pl.* **-ria** (-ə). A covered receptacle for holding the consecrated wafers of the Eucharist. [Medieval Latin *cibōrium,* from Latin, drinking vessel, from Greek *kibōrion,* the seed vessel of the Indian lotus, hence, a cup made from this, probably from Semitic.]

ci·ca·da (si-káa-də, -káy-) *n., pl.* **-das** or **-dae** (-dee). Any of various insects of the family Cicadidae, having a broad head, membranous wings, and, in the male, a pair of resonating organs that produce a characteristic high-pitched, droning sound. [Latin *cicāda,* probably of Mediterranean origin.]

ci·ca·trise, ci·ca·trize (síckə-trīz) *v.* **-trised, -trising, -trises.** *—tr.* To heal by the forming of a scar. *—intr.* To become healed or closed by the forming of a scar.

cic·a·trix (síckə-triks || *U.S. also* si-káy-) *n., pl.* **cicatrices** (-trí-seez || -tri-). Also **cic·a·trice** (síckə-triss). **1.** Recently formed connective tissue on a healing wound; scar tissue. **2.** *Botany.* A scar left where a leaf or a branch has been detached. [Middle English *cicatrice,* from Latin *cicātrix†.*] **—cic·a·tri·cial** (-trísh'l), **ci·cat·ri·cose** (si-kátri-kōss, síckətri-, -kōz) *adj.*

cic·e·ly (síssəli) *n., pl.* **-lies.** See **sweet cicely.** [Middle English *ciceli, seseli,* from Latin *seselis,* from Greek *seselis†.*]

cic·e·ro (síssərō) *n., pl.* **-ros.** *Printing.* A unit of measurement for type, slightly larger than the pica, used in Europe. [After an edition (1458) of Cicero, in which it was first used.]

Cic·e·ro (síssə-rō; *Latin* kíckə-), **Marcus Tullius** (106–43 B.C.). Roman orator and statesman, a leading figure during the last years of the Republic. **—Cic·e·ro·ni·an** (-rōni-ən) *adj.*

cic·e·ro·ne (chíchə-rṓ-ni, síssə-) *n., pl.* **-nes** or **-ni** (-ni, nee). A guide who conducts sightseers. [Italian *cicerone,* originally "a learned antiquarian", from *Cicerone,* CICERO.]

cich·lid (sícklid) *n.* Any of various tropical freshwater fishes of the family Cichlidae, many of which are popular as aquarium fish. *—adj.* Of or belonging to the Cichlidae. [New Latin *Cichlidae,* from *Cichla,* type genus, from Greek *kikhlē,* thrush, also, a sea fish.]

ci·cis·be·o (chíchiz-báy-ō) *n. pl.* **-bei** (-báy-ee). *Italian.* The male lover or companion of a married woman, especially in the 18th century. [Italian : origin obscure.]

C.I.D. *n.* *Criminal Investigation Department:* a division of the police force in the United Kingdom.

–cide *n. suffix.* Indicates: **1.** Killer of; for example, **insecticide. 2.** Murder or killing of; for example, **genocide, regicide.** [French, from Latin *-cīda,* killer, and *-cīdium,* killing, from *caedere,* to kill.]

ci·der, cy·der (sídər) *n.* **1.** The juice pressed from apples or, formerly, from other fruit, and fermented to produce an alcoholic drink. Also *U.S.* "hard cider". **2.** *U.S.* **Sweet cider** (sense 2). [Middle English *cidre, sidre,* from Old French *sidre, cisdre,* from Medieval Latin *sīcera,* from Greek (Septuagint) *sikera,* strong drink from Hebrew *shēkār.*]

CIE *n.* *Commission Internationale d'Eclairage:* a scientific organisation concerned with definitions, standards, and units in photometry.

c.i.f. cost, insurance, freight.

cig (sig) *n.* *Informal.* A cigarette.

ci·gar (si-gár) *n.* A small, compact roll of tobacco leaves prepared for smoking. [Spanish *cigarro.*]

cig·a·rette (síggə-rét || -ret) *n.* A small roll of finely cut tobacco for smoking, usually enclosed in a wrapper of thin paper. [French *cigarette,* diminutive of *cigare,* from Spanish *cigarro,* CIGAR.]

cigarette card *n.* A small illustrated card formerly given away with a packet of cigarettes.

cigarette holder *n.* A thin tube with a mouthpiece for holding a cigarette while smoking it.

cigarette paper *n.* A thin piece of gummed paper in which tobacco is rolled to make a cigarette.

cig·a·ril·lo (síggə-ríllō) *n., pl.* **-los.** A small, narrow cigar. [Spanish, diminutive of *cigarro,* CIGAR.]

cig·gy, cig·gie (síggi) *n.* *Informal.* A cigarette.

ci·lan·tro (si-lántrō) *n.* The parsley-like leaves of fresh coriander, used in Oriental cookery. [Spanish, coriander, from Late Latin *coliandrum,* from Latin *coriandrum,* CORIANDER.]

cil·i·a (sil-i-ə) *pl.n. Singular* **-ium** (-i-əm). **1.** Microscopic hairlike growths extending from the surface of a cell or organism. Their

rhythmical beating causes movement of the cell or of the surrounding medium. **2.** The eyelashes. [New Latin, plural of *cilium,* eyelash, hairlike process, from Latin, the lower eyelid.]

cil·i·ar·y (sílli-əri || *U.S.* -erri) *adj.* **1.** Of, pertaining to, or resembling cilia. **2.** Of or pertaining to the ciliary body.

ciliary body *n.* The thickened part of the vascular tunic of the eye that connects the choroid with the iris.

cil·i·ate (sílli-ayt, -ət, -it) *adj.* Also **cil·i·at·ed** (-aytid). **1.** Having cilia. **2.** Of or belonging to the protozoan class Ciliata. *~n.* Any of various protozoans of the class Ciliata, having numerous cilia. [New Latin *Ciliata,* plural of *ciliatus,* having cilia, from CILIA.]

cil·ice (síliss) *n.* **1.** A coarse cloth; haircloth. **2.** A garment made from this cloth. [French, from Latin *cilicium,* from Greek *kilikion,* coarse cloth made of Cilician goats' hair, from *Kilikia,* Cilicia.]

Ci·lic·i·an Gates (sī-líssi-ən, -líshi-) *n.* *Turkish* **Külek Boğazi.** Mountain pass through the Taurus range of southern Turkey.

cil·i·o·late (sílli-ə-layt, -lət, -lit) *adj.* Having minute cilia. [New Latin *ciliolum,* minute cilium, from *cilium,* singular of CILIA.]

Ci·ma·bu·e (chéemə-bóo-ay), **Giovanni (Cenni de Peppi)** (c. 1240 – c. 1302). Florentine artist, considered among the originators of the Italian Renaissance in painting. He worked within the tradition of Byzantine art but introduced a new expressiveness and sense of three-dimensional reality.

cim·ba·lom (símbə-ləm, tsímbə-) *n.* A type of dulcimer, used especially in Hungary. [Hungarian, from Italian (see **cembalo**).]

ci·met·i·dine (si-métti-deen) *n.* A drug that reduces acid secretion in the stomach and is used to treat peptic ulcers and other digestive disorders.

ci·mex (símeks) *n., pl.* **cimices** (símmi-seez). Any insect of the genus *Cimex,* which includes the bedbugs. [New Latin *Cimex,* from Latin *cīmex†,* bedbug.]

Cim·me·ri·an (si-méer-i-ən) *adj.* Gloomy; dark. *~n.* One of a mythical people described by Homer as inhabiting a land of perpetual darkness.

C in C, C-in-C commander in chief.

cinch (sinch) *n.* **1.** *Informal.* **a.** Something easy to accomplish. **b.** A certainty. **2.** *U.S.* A girth for a pack or saddle. **3.** *Chiefly U.S.* A firm grip. *~v.* **cinched, cinching, cinches.** *—tr.* **1.** *Informal.* To make certain of: *cinch a victory.* **2.** *U.S.* To put a saddle girth on. **3.** *Chiefly U.S. Informal.* To get a tight grip on. *—intr. U.S.* To tighten a saddle girth. Often used with *up.* [Spanish *cincha,* "girdle", from Latin *cingula,* from *cingere,* to gird.]

cin·cho·na (sing-kōnə || *U.S. also* sin-chōnə) *n.* **1.** Any of various trees and shrubs of the genus *Cinchona,* native to South America, whose bark yields quinine and other medicinal alkaloids. **2.** The dried bark of any of these trees. In this sense, also called "Peruvian bark". **3.** Any drug derived from this bark. [New Latin, after Francisca Henríquez de Ribera, countess of *Chinchón* (1576–1639), who introduced it into Europe after recovering from a fever through the use of cinchona bark.] **—cin·chon·ic** (-kónnik || -chónnik) *adj.*

cin·cho·nine (síng-kə-neen) *n.* An alkaloid, $C_{19}H_{22}N_2O,$ derived from the bark of various cinchona trees and used as an antimalarial agent.

cin·cho·nism (síng-kə-niz'm) *n.* A pathological condition resulting from an overdose of cinchona, marked by deafness, headache, giddiness, and dimming eyesight.

Cin·cin·na·tus (sín-si-náat-əss, -náyt- || -nát-), **Lucius Quinctius** (c.519–c.438 B.C.). A peasant farmer, twice called to assume the dictatorship of Rome during crises. He was regarded as a model of simple virtue, especially on account of his refusal to accept permanent dictatorship.

cinc·ture (síngk-chər, -tewr) *n.* **1.** A belt; a girdle. **2.** Something that encompasses or surrounds. *~tr.v.* **cinctured, -turing, -tures.** To gird or encompass. [Latin *cinctūra,* girdle, from *cingere* (past participle *cinctus),* to gird.]

cin·der (síndər) *n.* **1.** A burnt or partly burnt substance, such as coal or wood, that is not reduced to ashes, but is incapable of further combustion. **2.** A partly charred substance that can burn further, but without flame; an ember. **3.** *Plural.* Ashes. **4.** *Plural. Geology.* Volcanic scoria *(see).* **5.** *Metallurgy.* **Slag** *(see).* *~tr.v.* **cindered, -dering, -ders.** To burn or reduce to cinders. [Middle English *cinder, sinder,* Old English *sinder,* (iron) slag, dross.] **—cin·der·y** *adj.*

Cin·der·el·la (síndə-réllə) *n.* **1.** A person or thing that achieves recognition after a period of obscurity. **2.** A person or thing whose worth or beauty remains unrecognised. [After the fairy-tale character who, with the help of a fairy godmother, escaped from a life of drudgery and married a prince.]

cin·e (sínni) *adj.* Of, relating to, or used in the cinema or in making films. Often used in combination: *cinecamera, cinefilm.*

cin·e·aste (sínni-ast) *n.* A person who is enthusiastic and knowledgeable about the cinema; a film buff. [French : CINE- + *enthousiaste,* enthusiast.]

cin·e·cam·e·ra (sínni-kam-rə, -kám-, -ərə) *n.* A camera in which a strip of film passes the lens at a rate of 16 or more exposures per second, thus enabling a moving picture to be filmed.

cin·e·film (sínni-film) *n.* Photographic film suitable for use in a cinecamera.

cin·e·ma (sín-i-mə, -ə-, -maa) *n.* A theatre equipped with a screen and a projector for showing films. **—the cinema. 1. a.** Films collectively. **b.** The film industry. **c.** The art of making films. **2.** Cinematic quality. [French *cinéma,* shortened from *cinématographe,* CINEMATOGRAPH.] —**cin·e·mat·ic** (-máttik) *adj.* —**cin·e·mat·i·cal·ly** *adv.*

cin·e·ma·go·er (sín-i-mə-gō-ər, -ə-, -maa-) *n.* One who frequently attends the cinema.

Cin·e·ma·Scope (sín-i-mə-skōp, -ə-) *n.* A trademark for a process using an anamorphic lens to create films that can be projected onto a wide, curved screen.

cin·e·ma·theque (sín-i-mə-ték, -ə-, -tek) *n.* A small cinema showing experimental, artistic, and less commercially successful films. [French, originally "film library" : CINEMA + *bibliothèque,* library.]

cin·e·mat·o·graph (sín-i-máttə-graaf, -ə-, -graf) *n. British.* A camera or projector used in cinematography. [French *cinématographe* : Greek *kinēma* (stem *kinēmat-*), motion, from *kinein,* to move + -GRAPH.] —**cin·e·ma·tog·ra·pher** (-mə-tóggrəfər) *n.* —**cin·e·mat·o·graph·ic** (-gráffik) *adj.* —**cin·e·mat·o·graph·i·cal·ly** *adv.*

cin·e·ma·tog·ra·phy (sín-i-mə-tóggrafi, -ə-) *n.* The technique of making cinematic films.

cin·é·ma·vér·i·té (sín-i-mə-vérri-tay, -ə-, -táy) *n.* A style of filmmaking that tries to achieve an affect of realism and spontaneity by techniques such as the use of hand-held cameras and minimal editing of sound and image. [French, "cinema truth".]

cin·e·ol (sínni-ol || -ōl) *n.* Also **cin·e·ole** (-ōl). **Eucalyptol** *(see).* [New Latin *cina†,* wormseed + Latin *oleum,* OIL.]

cin·e·ra·di·og·ra·phy (sínni-ráydi-óggrəfi) *n.* Also **cin·e·mat·o·ra·di·og·ra·phy** (sínni-máttə-). A radiographic investigation of an organ or part in which a film is made from a series of successive X-rays to show the organ in motion.

cin·e·rar·i·a (sínnə-raír-i-ə) *n.* A plant, *Senecio cruentis,* native to the Canary Islands but widely cultivated as a house plant, having flat clusters of blue or purplish daisy-like flowers. [New Latin, from the feminine of Latin *cinerārius,* of ashes (from the ash-coloured down on its leaves). See **cinerarium.**]

cin·e·rar·i·um (sínnə-raír-i-əm) *n., pl.* **-ia** (-i-ə). A place for keeping the ashes of a cremated body. [Latin, from *cinerārius,* of ashes, from *cinis* (stem *ciner-*), ashes.] —**cin·er·ar·y** (-rəri || *U.S.* -rerri) *adj.*

ci·ne·re·ous (si-néer-i-əss) *adj.* **1.** Consisting of or like ashes. **2.** Of the colour of ashes; grey tinged with black. [Latin *cinereus,* from *cinis,* ashes.]

cin·gu·lum (síng-gew-ləm) *n., pl.* **-la** (-lə). *Biology.* A girdle-like structure or band. [New Latin, from Latin, girdle, from *cingere,* to gird.] —**cin·gu·la·te** (-lət, -lit, -layt) **cin·gu·la·ted** (-laytid) *adj.*

Cin·na (sínnə), **Lucius Cornelius** (died 84 B.C.). Roman consul, expelled by **Sulla** (87 B.C.). Joining forces with Marius he captured Rome, forcing Sulla's exile. He restored order as consul (86–84 B.C.), but was killed by his own troops.

cin·na·bar (sínnə-baar) *n.* **1.** A heavy reddish mineral form of mercuric sulphide, HgS, that is the principal ore of mercury. Also called "vermilion". **2.** Red mercuric sulphide used as a pigment. **3.** Bright red; vermilion. [Middle English *cynoper, cynabare,* from Old French *cenobre,* from Latin *cinnābaris,* from Greek *kinnabari,* of Oriental origin.]

cinnamic acid *n.* A white insoluble organic acid, $C_6H_5CH{:}CHCOOH$, existing in two isomeric forms and used in perfumes.

cin·na·mon (sínnəmən) *n.* **1.** Either of two trees, *Cinnamomum zeylanicum* or *C. loureirii,* of tropical Asia, having very aromatic bark. **2.** The yellowish-brown bark of either of these trees, dried and often ground, used as a spice. **3.** Any of several trees yielding a spice similar to this, such as cassia. **4.** A deep reddish brown. [Middle English *sinamome, cynamone,* from Old French *cinnamome,* from Latin *cinna(mo)mum, cinnamon,* from Greek *kinna(mō)mon,* from Hebrew *qinnāmown.*] —**cin·nam·ic** (si-námmik), **cin·na·mon·ic** (sínnə-mónnik) *adj.*

cinnamon bear *n.* A reddish-brown variety of the American black bear.

cinnamon stone *n.* A mineral, **essonite** *(see).*

cinque (singk, sangk) *n.* The number five, in cards or dice. [Middle English *cink,* from Old French *cinq,* from Latin *quīnque.*]

cin·que·cen·to (chíngkway-chéntō) *n.* The 16th century, especially in Italian art and architecture. [Italian, short for *(mil) cinquecento,* "(one thousand) five hundred".]

cinque·foil (sángk-foyl, síngk-) *n.* **1.** Any of various plants of the genus *Potentilla,* having compound leaves, often with five lobes. Also called "five-finger". **2.** *Architecture.* A design having five sides composed of converging arcs, usually used as a frame for glass or a panel. [Middle English *cincfoil,* from Old French *cincfoille,* from Latin *quīnquefolium,* "five leaves" (translation of Greek *pentaphullon*) : *quīnque,* five + *folium,* a leaf.]

Cinque Ports (singk). An association of ports in southeast England, formed in the 11th century to defend the English Channel coast. There were five original members: Sandwich, Dover, Hythe, Romney, and Hastings. Winchelsea and Rye joined later. The honorary title of Lord Warden of the Cinque Ports survives.

Cintra. See **Sintra.**

CIO, C.I.O. Congress of Industrial Organisations.

ci·pher, cy·pher (sífər) *n.* **1.** The mathematical symbol (0) denoting absence of quantity; zero. **2.** Any Arabic numeral or figure; a number. **3.** The Arabic system of numerical notation. **4.** A person or thing without influence or value; a nonentity. **5. a.** Any system of secret writing in which units of text of regular length, usually letters, are arbitrarily transposed or substituted according to a predetermined key. Compare **code. b.** The key to such a system. **6.** A mes-

sage in cipher. **7.** A design combining or interweaving letters or initials; a monogram. **8.** The continuous sounding of a pipe in an organ resulting from mechanical failure.

~*v.* **ciphered, -phering, -phers.** —*intr. Archaic.* To solve problems in arithmetic; calculate. —*tr.* **1.** To put (a message) in secret writing; encipher. **2.** To solve (a problem) by means of arithmetic. [Middle English *cifre,* zero, from Old French, from Medieval Latin *cifra,* from Arabic *ṣifr.*]

cir., circ. 1. circular. **2.** circulation. **3.** circumference.

cir·ca (súr-kə, -kaa) *prep. Abbr.* **ca, c.** About. Used before approximate dates or figures. [Latin *circā,* from *circum,* round about, from *circus,* circle.]

cir·ca·di·an (sur-káydi-ən, sər-) *adj. Biology.* Of or pertaining to endogenous or exogenous processes that exhibit approximately 24-hour periodicity: *circadian rhythm.* See **biorhythm.** [Latin *circā,* about, CIRCA + *diēs,* day.]

Cir·cas·sia (sər-kássi-ə, -káshi- || *U.S. also* -káshə). Region in the southwest of Russia, bordering the Black Sea northwest of the Great Caucasus mountains.

Cir·cas·sian (sər-kássi-ən || -káshi-, -kásh-) *n.* Also **Cir·cas·sic** (sər-kássik) **1.** An inhabitant of Circassia; especially, a member of a Caucasian people inhabiting Circassia, noted for their striking physical beauty. **2.** The North Caucasian language of this people. ~*adj.* Of or pertaining to the people, language, or region of Circassia.

Cir·ce (súr-si). An enchantress described in Homer's *Odyssey* who detains Odysseus for a year and turns his men into swine.

Cir·ce·an (sur-sée-ən, sər-) *adj.* Dangerously and deceptively beautiful; bewitching. [From CIRCE.]

cir·ci·nate (súr-si-nayt) *adj.* **1.** Ring-shaped. **2.** Rolled up from the tip, as a young fern frond or a butterfly's tongue is. [Latin *circinātus,* from *circināre,* to make circular, from *circinus,* pair of compasses, from *circus,* CIRCLE.] —**cir·ci·nate·ly** *adv.*

Cir·ci·nus (súr-si-nəss) *n.* A constellation in the Southern Hemisphere near Musca and Triangulum Australe. [Latin *circinus,* a pair of compasses. See **circinate.**]

cir·cle (súrk'l) *n.* **1.** A plane curve with the property that all points on the curve are equidistant from a given fixed point, the centre. See **great circle, small circle. 2.** A planar region bounded by such a curve. **3. a.** Anything shaped like a circle, such as a region or halo: *the Arctic Circle.* **b.** A group of things or people in a circle. **4.** A circular course, circuit, or orbit. **5.** An upper curved section or tier of seats in a theatre: *dress circle.* **6.** A series or process that finishes at its starting point or continuously repeats itself; a cycle. **7.** *Sometimes plural.* A group of people sharing an interest, activity, achievement, or the like: *publishing circles; circle of friends.* **8.** *Archaeology.* A ring of megalithic stones, such as Stonehenge, often thought to have some religious significance. **9.** A sphere of influence or interest; a domain. **10.** *Logic.* A fallacy in reasoning in which the premise is used to prove the conclusion, and the conclusion used to prove the premise. Also called "vicious circle". **11.** In hockey, a **striking circle** *(see).* —**come full circle.** To arrive back at a starting-point. —**go** or **run round in circles.** To expend effort fruitlessly.

~*v.* **circled, -cling, -cles.** —*tr.* **1.** To make or form a circle round; enclose. **2.** To move in a circle round. —*intr.* To move in circles; revolve: *Crows circled overhead.* —See Synonyms at **turn.** [Middle English *cercle,* from Old French, from Latin *circulus,* diminutive of *circus,* ring.] —**cir·cler** (súrklər) *n.*

Synonyms: circle, coterie, set, clique, club, society.

cir·clet (súrk-lit, -klət) *n.* A small circle; especially, a circular ornament worn on the head. [Middle English *cerclett,* band, from Old French, diminutive of *cercle,* CIRCLE.]

circs (surks) *pl.n. Informal.* Circumstances. Used chiefly in the phrases *in* or *under the circs.*

cir·cuit (súrkit) *n.* **1. a.** A closed, usually circular, curve. **b.** The area enclosed by such a curve. **2. a.** Any path or route, the complete traversal of which without local change of direction requires returning to the starting point. **b.** The act of following such a path. **c.** A journey made on such a path or route. **3.** *Electricity.* **a.** A closed path followed or capable of being followed by an electric current. **b.** Any configuration of electrically or electromagnetically connected components or devices. See **closed circuit, open circuit. 4. a.** A regular or accustomed course from place to place, such as that of a judge or salesman; a round. **b.** The area or district thus covered; especially, a territory under jurisdiction of a judge, in which he holds periodic court sessions. **5.** An administrative unit of the Methodist Church. **6.** An association of theatres or cinemas, usually under a single management, in which plays, acts, or films move from one to another for presentation. **7.** An association of teams or clubs, especially for the playing of a particular sport.

~*v.* **circuited, -cuiting, -cuits.** —*tr.* To make a circuit of. —*intr.* To move about in a circuit. [Middle English, from Old French, from Latin *circuitus,* from *circuīre, circumīre,* to go round : *circum-,* round + *īre,* to go.]

circuit breaker *n.* An automatic switch that stops the flow of electric current in a circuit when the current exceeds a preset safe value.

circuit court *n.* In Scotland, a lower criminal court presided over by a judge on circuit from the Scottish High Court.

circuit diagram *n.* A diagram representing the interconnections between elements of an electrical or electronic circuit.

circuit element *n.* A resistor, capacitor, inductor, transistor, or other device used in constructing electrical circuits.

circuit judge *n.* A judge assigned to a county court district to preside over the county court in civil cases and over a crown court in certain criminal cases.
cir·cu·i·tous (sər-kéw-itəss) *adj.* Being or taking a roundabout, lengthy course. [Medieval Latin *circuitōsus,* from Latin *circuitus,* CIRCUIT.] **—cir·cu·i·tous·ly** *adv.* **—cir·cu·i·ty, cir·cu·i·tous·ness** *n.*
cir·cuit·ry (súrkitri) *n.* **1.** The design of or a detailed plan for an electric circuit. **2.** Electric circuits collectively.
cir·cu·lar (súrkew-lər) *adj. Abbr.* **cir., circ. 1.** Of or pertaining to a circle. **2. a.** Having the shape of a circle. **b.** Having a shape approximately that of a circle; round. **3.** Moving in or forming a circle. **4.** Circuitous; indirect; roundabout. **5. a.** Addressed or distributed to a large number of persons. **b.** Using the premise to prove the conclusion, which is used in turn to prove the premise: *a circular argument.* **6.** *Mathematics.* **a.** Having a base in the shape of a circle: *a circular cone.* **b.** Designating a helix in which the distance from the curve to the axis is constant.
∼n. A printed advertisement, directive, or notice intended for distribution. [Middle English, from Anglo-French, from Old French *circulier,* from Late Latin *circulāris,* from *circulus,* CIRCLE.] **—cir·cu·lar·i·ty** (-lárrəti) *n.* **—cir·cu·lar·ly** *adv.*
circular file *n. Informal.* A wastepaper basket. Used humorously.
circular function *n. Mathematics.* A **trigonometric function** *(see).*
cir·cu·lar·ise, cir·cu·lar·ize (súrkewlər-īz) *tr.v.* **-ised, -ising, -ises. 1.** To make circular. **2.** To distribute circulars to. **—cir·cu·lar·i·sa·tion** (-ī-záysh'n || *U.S.* -i-) *n.* **—cir·cu·lar·is·er** *n.*
circular measure *n.* The measure of angles in **radians** *(see).*
circular mil *n. Abbr.* **c.m.** A unit of cross-sectional measurement, especially of wire, equal to the area of a circle with a diameter of one mil.
circular polarisation *n. Physics.* A type of polarisation of electromagnetic radiation in which the plane of polarisation rotates at a uniform rate about the direction of propagation of the radiation.
circular saw *n.* A power-driven saw consisting of a toothed steel disc rotated at high speed. Also *U.S.* "buzz saw".
cir·cu·late (súrkew-layt) *v.* **-lated, -lating, -lates.** *—intr.* **1.** To move in or flow through a circle or circuit. **2.** To move round, as from person to person, or place to place. **3.** To move about or flow freely; be diffused, like air. **4.** To spread widely among persons or places; disseminate. *—tr.* To cause to move about or be distributed. [Latin *circulāre,* from *circulus,* CIRCLE.] **—cir·cu·la·tive** (-lətiv, -laytiv) *adj.* **—cir·cu·la·tor** (-laytər) *n.* **—cir·cu·la·tor·y** (-láytəri, -lətri) *adj.*
circulating decimal *n. Mathematics.* A **repeating decimal** *(see).*
circulating medium *n.* Currency or coin that can be exchanged for goods without endorsement.
cir·cu·la·tion (súrkew-láysh'n) *n. Abbr.* **cir., circ. 1.** Movement in a circle or circuit. **2.** The movement of blood round the body through the arteries and veins as a result of the heart's pumping action. **3.** Any movement or passage through a system of vessels, as of water through pipes or sap through a plant. **4.** Free movement or passage. **5.** The passing of something like money or news, from place to place or from person to person. **6.** The condition of being passed about and widely known; distribution. **7.** The distribution of printed material, especially copies of newspapers or magazines, among readers. **8.** The number of copies sold or distributed of a given or an average issue of a publication.
circulatory system *n.* The system of vessels by which blood is circulated throughout the body by the heart.
circum- *prefix.* Indicates around or on all sides; for example, **circumlunar.** [Latin, from *circum,* round, from *circus,* circle.]
cir·cum·am·bi·ent (súrkəm-ámbi-ənt) *adj.* Surrounding; enclosing. [Latin *circumambiēns* (stem *circumambient-*) : CIRCUM- + AMBIENT.] **—cir·cum·am·bi·ence, cir·cum·am·bi·en·cy** *n.*
cir·cum·cen·tre (súrkəm-sentər) *n. Mathematics.* The centre of a circumscribed circle.
cir·cum·cir·cle (súrkəm-surk'l) *n. Mathematics.* A circumscribed circle.
cir·cum·cise (súrkəm-sīz) *tr.v.* **-cised, -cising, -cises. 1. a.** To remove the foreskin of (a male). **b.** To remove the clitoris of (a female). **c.** To perform the religious rite of circumcision for. **2.** To purify spiritually: *"Circumcise yourselves to the Lord"* (Jeremiah 4:4). [Middle English *circumcisen,* from Latin *circumcīdere* (past participle *circumcīsus*), "to cut round" (translation of Greek *peritemnein*) : CIRCUM- + *caedere,* to cut.] **—cir·cum·cis·er** *n.*
cir·cum·ci·sion (súrkəm-sízh'n) *n.* **1.** *Medicine.* The act of circumcising. **2.** A religious ceremony in which someone is circumcised. **3.** Spiritual purification.
cir·cum·fer·ence (sər-kúm-fərənss) *n. Abbr.* **cir., circ. 1. a.** The boundary line of a circle. **b.** The boundary line of any closed figure; a perimeter. **2.** The length of such a boundary. [Middle English, from Old French, from Latin *circumferentia,* from *circumferēns,* present participle of *circumferre,* to carry around : CIRCUM- + *ferre,* to carry.] **—cir·cum·fer·en·tial** (-fə-rénsh'l) *adj.*
cir·cum·flex (súrkəm-fleks) *n.* A mark (ˆ) used over a letter in certain languages, such as French, or in phonetic keys, to indicate quality of pronunciation, such as lengthening of a vowel.
∼adj. Marked with a circumflex.
∼tr.v. **circumflexed, -flexing, -flexes.** To mark with a circumflex. [Latin *circumflexus,* "a bending round", from *circumflectere,* to bend round : CIRCUM- + *flectere,* to bend, to FLEX.]
cir·cum·fuse (súrkəm-féwz) *tr.v.* **-fused, -fusing, -fuses. 1.** To pour or diffuse round; spread. **2.** To surround, as with liquid; suffuse. [Latin *circumfundere* (past participle *circumfūsus*), to pour round : CIRCUM- + *fundere,* to pour.] **—cir·cum·fu·sion** (-féwzh'n) *n.*
cir·cum·lo·cu·tion (súrkəm-lə-kéwsh'n, -lō- || *Irish & U.S.* -lō-) *n.* **1.** The use of prolix and indirect language. **2.** Evasion in speech or writing. **3.** A roundabout expression. [Middle English *circumlocucioun,* from Latin *circumlocūtiō* (stem *circumlocūtiōn-*), from *circumloquī,* "to speak in a roundabout way" : CIRCUM- + *loquī,* to speak.] **—cir·cum·loc·u·to·ry** (-lóckew-tri, -təri, -lə-kéwtəri || -lō-) *adj.*
cir·cum·lu·nar (súrkəm-lóō-nər, -léw-) *adj.* Revolving about or surrounding the moon.
cir·cum·nav·i·gate (súrkəm-návvi-gayt) *tr.v.* **-gated, -gating, -gates.** To sail or fly completely round. [Latin *circumnāvigāre* : CIRCUM- + *nāvigāre,* NAVIGATE.] **—cir·cum·nav·i·ga·tion** (-gáysh'n) *n.* **—cir·cum·nav·i·ga·tor** (-gaytər) *n.*
cir·cum·nu·tate (súrkəm-new-táyt, -néw-tayt || -nōō-, -nóō-) *intr.v.* **-tated, -tating, -tates.** *Botany.* To exhibit circumnutation. [CIRCUM- + Latin *nūtāre,* to nod, sway.]
cir·cum·nu·ta·tion (súrkəm-new-táysh'n || -nōō-) *n. Botany.* An elliptical or spiral direction of growth shown by certain plant parts, such as the apex of a growing tendril.
cir·cum·po·lar (súrkəm-pṓlər) *adj.* **1.** Located or found in one of the polar regions. **2.** *Astronomy.* Designating a star that from a given observer's latitude does not go below the horizon.
cir·cum·scis·sile (súrkəm-síss-īl || *U.S.* -síss'l) *adj. Botany.* Splitting or opening along a transverse circular line: *a circumscissile seed capsule.* [CIRCUM- + Latin *scissilis,* capable of being cut, from *scissus* (see **scission**).]
cir·cum·scribe (súrkəm-skrīb) *tr.v.* **-scribed, -scribing, -scribes. 1.** To draw a line round; encircle. **2.** To confine within bounds; limit; restrict. **3.** To determine the limits of. **4.** *Geometry.* To enclose (a geometric figure) within another geometric figure, so that the enclosed object touches but does not intersect with the enclosing figure. —See Synonyms at **limit.** [Middle English *circumscriben,* from Latin *circumscrībere* : CIRCUM- + *scrībere,* to write.] **—cir·cum·scrib·a·ble** *adj.* **—cir·cum·scrib·er** *n.*
cir·cum·scrip·tion (súrkəm-skríp-sh'n) *n.* **1. a.** The act of circumscribing. **b.** The state of being circumscribed. **2.** Something that circumscribes. **3.** A circumscribed space; a limited area. **4.** A circular inscription, as on a coin or medallion. **—cir·cum·scrip·tive** (-tiv) *adj.* **—cir·cum·scrip·tive·ly** *adv.*
cir·cum·spect (súrkəm-spekt) *adj.* Taking into account all circumstances or consequences; prudent. [Middle English, from Latin *circumspectus,* past participle of *circumspicere,* to look round, take heed : CIRCUM- + *specere,* to look.] **—cir·cum·spec·tion** (-spéksh'n) *n.* **—cir·cum·spect·ly** *adv.*
cir·cum·stance (súrkəm-stənss, -stanss, -staanss) *n.* **1.** One of the conditions or facts attending an event and having some bearing upon it; a determining or modifying factor. **2.** One of the conditions or facts that determine, or that must be considered in the determining of, a course of action. **3.** The sum of determining factors beyond wilful control: *a victim of circumstance.* **4.** *Usually plural.* Financial status or means: *living in reduced circumstances.* **5.** Additional or accessory information; detail. **6.** Formal display; ceremony: *pomp and circumstance.* —See Synonyms at **occurrence.** **—under no circumstances.** In no case; never. **—under** or **in the circumstances.** Given these conditions; such being the case. [Middle English, from Old French, from Latin *circumstāntia,* accessory details, from *circumstāns,* present participle of *circumstāre,* to stand round, be accessory : CIRCUM- + *stāre,* to stand.]
cir·cum·stanced (súrkəm-stənst, -stanst, -staanst) *adj.* Placed in specified circumstances, especially with regard to finance.
cir·cum·stan·tial (súrkəm-stánsh'l, -staánsh'l) *adj.* **1.** Of, pertaining to, or dependent upon circumstances. **2.** Of no primary significance; incidental; inessential. **3.** Complete and particular; full of detail. **—cir·cum·stan·ti·al·i·ty** (-stánshi-ál-əti, -staánshi-) *n.* **—cir·cum·stan·tial·ly** *adv.*
circumstantial evidence *n. Law.* Evidence not bearing directly on the fact in dispute, but on various attendant circumstances from which the judge or jury might infer the occurrence of the fact.
cir·cum·stan·ti·ate (súrkəm-stánshi-ayt, -staánshi-) *tr.v.* **-ated, -ating, -ates.** To support or verify with detailed evidence or proof. **—cir·cum·stan·ti·a·tion** (-áysh'n) *n.*
cir·cum·val·late (súrkəm-və-láyt, -va-, -vál-ayt) *tr.v.* **-lated, -lating, -lates.** To surround with a rampart or other defensive barrier.
∼adj. (-vál-ayt). Surrounded by or as if by a rampart. [Latin *circumvallāre* : CIRCUM- + *vallāre,* to wall, from *vallum,* wall.] **—cir·cum·val·la·tion** (-láysh'n) *n.*
cir·cum·vent (súrkəm-vént) *tr.v.* **-vented, -venting, -vents. 1.** To surround and entrap (an enemy, for example). **2.** To overcome by artful manoeuvring; outwit. **3.** To avoid by or as if by passing round; get round. [Latin *circumvenīre* (past participle *circumventus*) : CIRCUM- + *venīre, to come.*] **—cir·cum·vent·er, cir·cum·ven·tor** (-ər) *n.* **—cir·cum·ven·tion** (-vénsh'n) *n.* **—cir·cum·ven·tive** *adj.*
cir·cum·vo·lu·tion (súrkəm-və-lóō-sh'n, sər-kúm-, -léw- || -vō-) *n.* An act or instance of turning, coiling, or folding about a centre, core, or axis. [Middle English *circumvolucioun,* from Medieval Latin *circumvolūtiō* (stem *-volūtiōn-*), from Latin *circumvolvere* (past participle *circumvolūtus*), CIRCUMVOLVE.]
cir·cus (súrkəss) *n.* **1.** A public entertainment consisting typically of a variety of performances by acrobats, clowns, and trained animals. **2.** A travelling company that performs such entertainments. **3.** A circular arena for circuses, surrounded by tiers of seats and often covered by a tent. **4.** A roofless, oval enclosure surrounded by tiers

of seats and used in ancient times for public spectacles. **5.** *British.* An open circular place where several streets intersect. **6.** *Informal.* A place or activity given over to rowdy or noisy disorder. **7.** *Chiefly British.* A travelling group that performs exhibition sports matches: *a cricket circus.* Compare *flying circus.* [Latin *circus*, ring, CIRCLE.] —**cir·cus·y, cir·cus·sy** *adj.*

Ci·ren·ces·ter (sîr-ən-sestər. *Note: the old pronunciation* sissitər *is now hardly used*). Market town in Gloucestershire situated on the River Churn on the eastern edge of the Cotswolds, known as Corinium under the Romans. It has a fine Norman parish church.

cire per·due (seer pair-déw, per- || -doo) *n. French.* A bronze-casting technique, **lost-wax process** *(see)*. [Literally, "lost wax".]

cirque (surk) *n.* A steep-sided hollow, often containing a small lake, occurring on a mountainside or high above a valley. Also *Scottish* "corrie", *Welsh* "cwm". [French, from Latin *circus*, ring, CIRCLE.]

cir·rate (sírrayt) *adj.* Also **cir·rose** (sirróss), **cir·rous** (sírrəss). Having or of the nature of a cirrus or cirri. [Latin *cirrātus*, curled, from *cirrus*, curl, CIRRUS.]

cir·rho·sis (si-rṓ-siss) *n.* **1.** A chronic disorder of the liver, in which normal tissue is replaced by fibrous tissue similar to scar tissue, caused for example by alcoholism or hepatitis. **2.** Interstitial inflammation of any tissue or organ. [New Latin, "orange-coloured disease" (from the colour of the diseased liver) : Greek *kirrhos†*, orange tawny + -OSIS.] —**cir·rhot·ic** (si-róttik) *adj.*

cir·ri·pede (sírri-peed) *n.* Also **cir·ri·ped** (-ped). Any of various crustaceans of the subclass Cirripedia, which includes the barnacles and similar organisms that attach themselves to objects or become parasitic in the adult stage. [New Latin *Cirripedia*, "the cirrus-footed ones" : CIRR(US) + -ped.] —**cir·ri·ped** *adj.*

cir·ro·cu·mu·lus (sírrō-kéwmew-ləss) *n.* A high-altitude cloud composed of a series of small, regularly arranged cloudlets in the form of ripples or grains. [New Latin : CIRR(US) + CUMULUS.]

cir·ro·stra·tus (sírrō-stráa-təss, -stráy-) *n.* A high-altitude, thin, hazy, veil-like cloud, usually covering the sky and often producing a halo effect round the sun. [New Latin : CIRR(US) + STRATUS.]

cir·rus (sírrəss) *n., pl.* **cirri** (sírrī). **1.** A high-altitude cloud composed of narrow bands or patches of thin, generally white, wispy parts. **2.** *Botany.* A mass of coherent spores that are discharged through an ostiole. **3.** *Zoology.* A slender, flexible appendage, such as a tentacle. [New Latin, from Latin *cirrus†*, curl, filament, tuft.]

C.I.S. See **Commonwealth of Independent States.**

cis– *prefix.* **1.** Indicates location on this or the near side; for example, *cislunar.* **2.** *Chemistry.* Indicates an isomer in which two atoms or groups in a molecule occupy positions on the same side of a line, usually a chemical bond, or a centre. Compare **trans-.** [Latin, from *cis*, on this side of.]

Cis·al·pine Gaul (siss-álpīn, síss-). The part of ancient Gaul south of the Alps of northern Italy.

Cis·cau·ca·si·a (síss-kaw-káy-zi-ə, -zhi, -zhə). Also **North Caucasia.** A steppe-land region in the southwest of Russia.

cis·co (sískō) *n., pl.* **-coes** or **-cos.** Any of several North American whitefish, especially *Coregonus artedii*, of deep lake waters. Also called "lake herring". [Canadian French *ciscoette*, from Ojibwa *pemitewiskawet*, oily-skinned fish.]

Cis·kei (síss-kī). Formerly one of the segregated territories in South Africa known as Bantu homelands.

cis·lu·nar (siss-lṓō-nər, -léw-) *adj.* Of or pertaining to the region between the earth and the moon. Compare **translunar.**

cis·pon·tine (siss-póntīn) *adj.* On this (the speaker's) side of the bridge. [CIS- + *pontine*, from Latin *pons* (stem *pont*-), bridge.]

cis·soid (síssoyd) *n. Mathematics.* A type of geometric curve with a cusp and two branches, both asymptotic to a straight line. Its equation is $x^3 = y^2(2a - x)$, with the cusp at the origin and the asymptote being the line $x = 2a$. ~*adj.* Lying between the concave sides of two curves. Compare **sistroid.** [Greek *kissoeidēs*, ivy-shaped, from *kissos*, ivy.]

cissy (síssi) *British.* Variant of **sissy.**

cist (kist, sist) *n.* Also **kist** (kist). A Neolithic stone coffin. [Welsh, "chest", from Latin *cista*, basket, wicker receptacle, from Greek *kistē*.]

Cis·ter·cian (si-stérsh'n) *n.* A member of a contemplative monastic order founded by reformist Benedictines in France in 1098. ~*adj.* Of, pertaining to, or belonging to this order. [French *Cistertien*, from Medieval Latin *Cistercium*, Cîteaux, near Dijon, site of the original abbey.]

cis·tern (sístərn) *n.* **1.** A receptacle for holding water or other liquid, especially, a water tank in the roof of a house or connected to a lavatory. **2.** *Anatomy.* A cisterna. [Middle English *cisterne*, from Old French, from Latin *cisterna*, water tank, from *cista*, box, from Greek *kistē*, basket.] —**cis·ter·nal** (si-stérn'l) *adj.*

cis·ter·na (si-stér-nə) *n., pl.* **-nae** (-nee). Any fluid-containing sac or space in the body of an organism. Also called "reservoir". [New Latin, from Latin, CISTERN.]

cis-trans isomerism (síss-tráanz, -tránz) *n. Chemistry.* A type of isomerism in which two atoms or groups in a molecule can occupy positions on the same side (cis) or opposite sides (trans) of a line or centre. It is found especially in organic compounds containing double bonds and in inorganic square and octahedral coordination complexes. Also called "geometrical isomerism". —**cis-trans isomer** *n.*

cis·tron (síss-tron, -trən) *n.* A unit of genetic function: a section of DNA controlling the production of a single polypeptide chain of a protein molecule. [From *cis-trans* + -ON (molecular unit).]

cit. **1.** citation. **2.** cited. **3.** citizen.

cit·a·del (sítta-dəl, -del) *n.* **1.** A fortress in a commanding position in or near a city. **2.** Any stronghold or fortified place; a bulwark. **3.** A Salvation Army meeting-hall. [French *citadelle* or Italian *citadella*, diminutive of obsolete *cittade*, city, from Latin *cīvitās*, citizenry, state, CITY.]

ci·ta·tion (sī-táysh'n, si-) *n. Abbr.* **cit.** **1.** The act of citing. **2.** A quoting of an authoritative source for substantiation. **3.** A source so cited; a quotation. **4.** *Law.* A reference to previous court decisions or authoritative writings. **5.** An official commendation for meritorious action, especially in military service. **6.** A summons, especially one calling for appearance in court. —**ci·ta·to·ry** (sítə-tri, -təri, sī--táytəri) *adj.*

cite (sīt) *tr.v.* **cited, citing, cites. 1.** To quote as an authority or example. **2.** To mention or bring forward as support, illustration, or proof. **3.** To commend (a unit or individual in the armed forces) in dispatches, for meritorious action. **4.** To summon before a court of law. **5.** *Archaic.* To call to action; rouse. [Middle English *citen*, to summon, from Old French *citer*, from Latin *citāre*, frequentative of *ciēre*, to set in motion, summon.]

cith·a·ra (síthərə, kíthərə) *n.* An ancient musical instrument resembling the lyre. [Latin, from Greek *kithara†*.]

cith·er (síth-ər || síth-) *n.* Also **cith·ern** (-ərn). A musical instrument, a cittern *(see)*. [French *cithare*, from Latin *cithara*, CITHARA.]

cit·i·fied (sitti-fīd) *adj.* Having customs, manners, fashions, or other characteristics attributed to city people.

cit·i·fy (sítti-fī) *tr.v.* **-fied, -fying, -fies. 1.** To cause to become like a city; make urban. **2.** To cause to acquire the styles or manners of city people. —**cit·i·fi·ca·tion** (-fi-káysh'n) *n.*

cit·i·zen (síttiz'n) *n. Abbr.* **cit. 1.** A person owing loyalty to and entitled by birth or naturalisation to the protection of a given state. Used increasingly instead of "subject": *a British citizen.* **2.** A resident of a city or town, one entitled to vote and enjoy other privileges there. [Middle English *citisein*, from Anglo-French *citesein*, variant of Old French *citeien*, from *cite*, CITY.] —**cit·i·zen·ly** *adj.*

cit·i·zen·ry (síttiz'n-ri) *n., pl.* **-ries.** Citizens collectively.

Citizens Advice Bureau *n. Abbr.* **C.A.B.** An organisation staffed mainly by volunteers, that provides free information on a variety of subjects, especially on legal and social welfare rights.

citizen's arrest *n.* An arrest made by an ordinary member of the public, in accordance with the right of any citizen to arrest someone who has committed an arrestable offence or a breach of the peace.

citizens' band *n. Abbr.* **CB** A frequency band, in Britain 27 megahertz FM, officially allocated for radio communications between private individuals. Often used adjectivally: *citizens' band radio.*

cit·i·zen·ship (síttiz'n-ship) *n.* The status of a citizen with its attendant duties, rights, and privileges.

Ci·tlal·té·petl (séet-lal-táy-pett'l || -laal-). An extinct volcanic peak in southern Mexico, situated between Mexico City and Veracruz. At 5 699 metres (18,697 feet) it is Mexico's highest peak.

cit·ral (síttrəl, síttral) *n.* A free-flowing pale yellow liquid, $C_{10}H_{16}O$, derived from lemon-grass oil and used in perfumery and as a flavouring. It exists in two isomeric forms: the cis-isomer (*geranial*) and the trans-isomer (*neral*) [CITR(US) + -AL (aldehyde).]

cit·rate (síttrayt) *n.* A salt or ester of citric acid.

cit·ric (sittrik) *adj.* Of or obtained from citrus fruits.

citric acid *n.* A colourless translucent crystalline acid, $C_6H_8O_7$, principally derived by fermentation of carbohydrates or from lemon, lime, and pineapple juices, and used to prepare citrates, in flavourings, and in metal polishes.

citric acid cycle *n.* The **Krebs cycle** *(see)*.

cit·ri·cul·ture (sittri-kulchər) *n.* The cultivation of citrus fruits. [*citrus* + *culture*.] —**cit·ri·cul·tur·ist** (-kúlchərist) *n.*

cit·rine (síttrin, síttreen || *U.S. also* si-tréen) *n.* **1.** A pale yellow variety of quartz, resembling topaz. **2.** The greenish-yellow colour of a lemon. [Middle English, from Old French *citrin*, from Medieval Latin *citrīnus*, from Latin *citrus*, citron tree, CITRUS.] —**cit·rine** *adj.*

cit·ron (síttrən) *n.* **1.** A tree, *Citrus medica*, native to Asia, having lemon-like fruit with a thick, aromatic rind. **2.** The fruit of this tree. **3.** A variety of watermelon, *Citrullus vulgaris citroides*, having fruit generally considered inedible and a hard rind used as flavouring. In this sense, also called "citron melon". **4.** The preserved or candied rind of either of these fruits, used especially in baking. **5.** Greyish green yellow. [French, from Old French, from Latin *citrus†*, citron tree.] —**cit·ron** *adj.*

cit·ron·el·la (sittrə-néllə) *n.* **1.** A tropical Eurasian grass, *Cymbopogon nardus*, having bluish-green, lemon-scented leaves. Also called "citronella grass". **2.** A light yellow, aromatic oil obtained from this grass and used in insect repellents and perfumery. Also called "citronella oil". [New Latin, from French *citronnelle*, lemon oil, diminutive of *citron*, CITRON.]

cit·ron·el·lal (sittrə-nél-al) *n.* A colourless mixture of isomeric liquids, $C_9H_{17}CHO$, the chief constituent of citronella oil. [CITRONELL(A) + -AL (aldehyde).]

cit·rus (síttrəss) *adj.* Also **cit·rous. 1.** Of or pertaining to trees or shrubs of the genus *Citrus*, many of which bear edible fruit such as the orange, lemon, lime. and grapefruit. **2.** Of or characteristic of the fruits of these trees or shrubs.

~*n., pl.* **citruses** or collectively **citrus**. A citrus tree or shrub. [New Latin, from Latin *citrus*†, citron tree, citrus tree.]

Città del Vaticano. See **Vatican City.**

cit·tern (sittərn, sittern) *n.* A 16th-century guitar with a pear-shaped body. Also called "cither", "cithern". [Variant of CITHERN.]

cit·y (sítti) *n., pl.* **-ies.** *Abbr.* **C. 1.** A town of significant size. **2. a.** In Great Britain, a large incorporated town, usually the seat of a bishop, with its title conferred by the Crown. **b.** In various other countries, a large town, designated as a city according to population, the presence of a cathedral, or other factors. **3.** In the United States, an incorporated municipality with definite boundaries and legal powers set forth in a charter granted by the state. **4.** In Canada, a municipality of high rank, usually determined by population but varying according to province. **5.** The inhabitants of a city as a group. **—the City.** The commercial and financial district of London, in which the Stock Exchange and the Bank of England are situated.

~*adj.* Of, in, or belonging to a city. [Middle English *cite*, from Old French, from Latin *cīvitās* (stem *cīvitat-*), citizenry, state, (later) city, from *cīvis*, citizen.]

city editor *n.* **1.** *British.* The editor on a newspaper who handles commercial and financial news. **2.** *U.S.* The editor who handles local news.

city fathers *pl.n.* The members of the governing body of a city.

city hall *n. Chiefly U.S.* **1.** The offices or officials of a municipal government. **2.** A **town hall** *(see).*

city slicker *n. Informal.* A person with the sophisticated or smooth manners traditionally associated by rural people with city dwellers. Often used derogatorily.

cit·y-state (sítti-státyt) *n.* A sovereign state consisting of an independent city and its surrounding territory, especially as in ancient Greece.

Ciu·dad Bo·lí·var (sew-daád bo-leévaar, -dád, bə-). Port on the Orinoco River in eastern Venezuela, renamed Bolívar in 1849.

Ciu·dad Re·al (sew-daád ray-aál, -dád, -ál). Town in New Castile province in south central Spain, founded in the 13th century.

civ. civil; civilian.

civ·et (sívvit) *n.* **1.** Any of various catlike mammals of the family Viverridae, of Africa and Asia, having spotted or blotched fur and anal scent glands that secrete a fluid with a musky odour. Also called "civet cat". **2.** This fluid, used in the manufacture of perfumes. **3.** The fur of a civet. [French *civette*, from Old French, from Italian *zibetto*, from Arabic *zabād*.]

civ·ic (sívvik) *adj.* Of, pertaining to, or belonging to a city, to a citizen, or to citizenship; municipal or civil. [Latin *cīvicus*, from *cīvis*, citizen.] **—civ·i·cal·ly** *adv.*

civic centre *n.* A building or complex containing the municipal offices of a city, often with other facilities such as a hall.

civ·ics (sívviks) *n. Used with a singular verb.* **1.** The study of the rights and duties of a citizen. **2.** *U.S.* The branch of political science that deals with civic affairs.

civies. Variant of **civvies.**

civ·il (sívv'l, sívvil) *adj. Abbr.* **civ. 1.** Of, pertaining to, or befitting citizens or the citizen as an individual. **2.** Of or pertaining to citizens and their relations with one another or with the state. **3.** Of ordinary citizens or ordinary community life, as distinguished from the military or the ecclesiastical. **4.** Of or in accordance with organised society and government; civilised. **5.** Observing or befitting accepted social usages; proper; polite. **6.** Designating or according to legally recognised divisions of time: *a civil year.* **7.** *Law.* **a.** Of or in accordance with Roman civil law or with its medieval and modern derivatives. **b.** Pertaining to the rights of private individuals and to legal proceedings concerning these rights. Used to distinguish a court, proceeding, or rule which is not criminal, military, or international. **—See Synonyms at polite.** [Middle English, from Old French, from Latin *cīvīlis*, from *cīvis*, citizen.] **—civ·il·ly** *adv.*

civil day *n.* A mean solar day *(see).*

civil death *n. Law.* Formerly, the total deprivation of civil rights resulting from conviction for treason or other serious offences.

civil defence *n. Abbr.* **C.D. 1.** The activities of an organised body of civilian volunteers to protect life and property in the case of a natural disaster or an attack by an enemy. **2.** These civilian volunteers.

civil disobedience *n.* The refusal to obey civil laws that are regarded as unjust, usually by employing methods of passive resistance to bring about political change.

civil engineer *n. Abbr.* **C.E.** An engineer trained in the design and construction of public works.

ci·vil·ian (si-víl-yən) *n. Abbr.* **civ.** A person following the pursuits of civil life, as distinguished from one serving in the armed forces.

~*adj.* Of or pertaining to civilians or civil life; nonmilitary. [Middle English, practitioner of civil law, jurist, from *civile*, civil law, from Latin, from *(jūs) cīvīle*, from *cīvīlis*, CIVIL.]

civ·i·li·sa·tion (sívvil-ī-záysh'n) || *U.S.* -i-) *n.* **1.** A condition of human society marked by an advanced stage of development in the arts and sciences and by corresponding social, political, and cultural complexity. **2.** Those nations or peoples regarded as having arrived at this stage. **3.** The type of culture and society developed by a particular group, nation, or region, or by any of these in some particular epoch. **4.** The act or process of civilising or of reaching a civilised state. **5.** The state of being cultured or having good taste. **6.** Populated areas, especially urban areas, and the conveniences associated with them.

civ·i·lise, civ·i·lize (sívvil-īz, sívv'l-) *tr.v.* **-lised, -lising, -lises. 1.** To bring out of a primitive or savage state into a more developed one. **2.** To educate or enlighten. **—civ·i·lis·a·ble** *adj.* **—civ·i·lis·er** *n.*

civ·i·lised (sívvil-īzd, sívv'l-) *adj.* **1.** Having a highly developed society and culture. **2.** Of, pertaining to, or characteristic of a people or nation so developed. **3.** Polite or cultured; refined.

ci·vil·i·ty (si-víllэti) *n., pl.* **-ties. 1.** Politeness; courtesy. **2.** A courteous act or utterance.

civil law *n.* **1.** The body of law dealing with the rights of private citizens in a particular state or nation, as distinguished from criminal law, military law, or international law. Compare **criminal law. 2.** The law of ancient Rome, especially that which applied to private citizens. **3.** Any system of law having its origin in Roman law, as distinguished from common law or canon law.

civil liberty *n.* A liberty legally guaranteeing to the individual a right, such as free speech, thought, or action, limited only insofar as its use must not interfere with the rights of others.

civil list *n.* In Britain, the yearly provision by Parliament of funds for the personal and household expenses of the monarch.

civil marriage *n.* A marriage ceremony performed by a civil official, such as a registrar.

civil rights *pl.n.* Rights belonging to a person by virtue of his status as a citizen or as a member of civil society. Also used adjectivally: *the civil rights movement.*

civil servant *n.* A person employed in the civil service.

civil service *n. Abbr.* **C.S. 1.** All branches of government administration that are not legislative, judicial, military, or naval. **2.** Collectively, the persons employed by these branches of the government.

civil state *n.* Marital status. [Perhaps calqued in French *état civil.*]

civil time *n.* **Mean solar time** *(see).*

civil war *n.* A war between factions or regions of one country.

Civil War *n.* **1.** In Britain, the war between Charles I and Parliament. Hostilities commenced in 1642 and Charles finally surrendered at Naseby (1645). A Royalist uprising in 1648 prompted the second part of the Civil War and led to the execution of the king in 1649. A Commonwealth was established and the Civil War was concluded by the subjection of Ireland 1649–50 and the defeat of Charles's heir at Dunbar in 1650. Also called the "Great Rebellion". **2.** In the United States, the war between the Union (the North) and the Confederacy (the South) from 1861 to 1865. Also called "War of Secession".

Ci·vi·ta·vec·chia (chēevitэ-vék-yэ). Fishing port in Lazio on the west coast of central Italy. The old town was founded by Trajan, and Roman baths survive. Michelangelo designed the citadel.

civ·vies, civ·ies (sívviz) *pl.n. Slang.* Civilian clothes, as distinguished from military dress. [Short for CIVILIAN.]

Civ·vy Street (sívvi) *n. Informal.* Civilian life.

C.J. 1. chief justice. **2.** corpus juris.

CJD Creutzfeldt-Jakob disease.

ck. cask.

cl centilitre.

Cl The symbol for the element chlorine.

cl 1. class; classification. **2.** clause. **3.** clearance. **4.** clergyman; clergywoman. **5.** closet. **6.** cloth.

c.l. 1. carload. **2.** *Sports.* centre line. **3.** common law.

clab·ber (klábbər) *n.* Sour, curdled milk.

~*v.* **clabbered, -bering, -bers.** —*tr.* To cause to curdle. —*intr.* To become curdled. [Short for earlier *bonnyclabber*, from Irish : *bainne*, milk, from Middle Irish *banne*, a drop + *clabair*†, thick sour milk.]

clach·an (klákh'n, klaákh'n) *n. Scottish.* A village or hamlet. [Scottish Gaelic, from *clach*, stone.]

clack (klak) *v.* **clacked, clacking, clacks.** —*intr.* **1.** To make an abrupt, dry sound, as by the collision of two wooden surfaces. **2.** To chatter thoughtlessly or at length. **3.** To cackle or cluck, as a hen does. —*tr.* To cause to make an abrupt, dry sound.

~*n.* **1.** A clacking sound. **2.** Something that makes a clacking sound. **3.** Thoughtless, prolonged talk; chatter. [Middle English *clacken*, from Old Norse *klaka* (imitative).] **—clack·er** *n.*

Clack·man·nan (klak-mánnэn || *locally also* klэk-). Also **Clack·man·nan·shire.** (-shэr, -sheer, -shīr) Former county in central Scotland, now a Unitary Authority area.

clack valve *n.* A hinged or ball valve that permits fluids to flow in only one direction.

Clac·to·ni·an (klak-tóni-эn) *adj. Archaeology.* Of or pertaining to a lower Palaeolithic culture of northwestern Europe. [From *Clacton-on-Sea*, site of the discovery of artefacts from which the culture was classified.]

Clac·ton-on-Sea (kláktэn-on-seé). Coastal resort in Essex in southeast England.

clad[1] (klad) *tr.v.* **clad, cladding, clads.** To sheathe or cover (a metal) with a metal for decoration, protection, or the like. [Middle English *cladden*, from *cladde*, past participle of *clathen, clothen*, CLOTHE.]

clad[2] Alternative past tense and past participle of **clothe.**

clad-, clado- *comb. form.* Indicates a sprout or branch; for example, *cladistics.* [Greek *klados*, branch.]

clad·ding (kládding) *n.* **1.** A metal coating bonded onto another metal. **2.** A protective or insulating layer fixed to the outside of a building or other structure.

clade (klayd) *n.* A group of organisms that share a common ancestor. [Greek *klados*, branch.]

cla·dist (kláydist) *n.* One who practises cladistics.

cla·dis·tics (klə-dístiks) *n. Used with a singular verb.* A method of scientific classification in which organisms are placed in the same taxonomic group when they share features thought to indicate recent common ancestry. [CLAD- + -ISTICS.) —**cla·dis·tic** *adj.*

cla·doc·er·an (klə-dóssərən) *n.* Any of various small aquatic crustaceans of the order Cladocera, which includes the water fleas. ~*adj.* Of or belonging to the Cladocera. [New Latin *Cladocera* : Greek *klados*, branch, shoot + *keras*, horn.]

cla·do·gram (kláydə-gram) *n.* A diagram used in cladistics to show the relationships between organisms, consisting of a series of branches that repeatedly divide into two, each point of branching representing divergence from a common ancestor. [CLAD- + -GRAM.]

clad·o·phyll (kláddə-fil) *n.* A branch or portion of a stem that resembles a leaf. Also called "cladode", "phylloclade". [New Latin *cladophyllum* : Greek *klados*, twig + *phullon*, leaf, -PHYLL.]

clag (klag) *v.* **clagged, clagging, clags.** —*tr.* **1.** To clog. **2.** To stick, adhere. —*intr.* **1.** To become clogged. **2.** To become stuck. ~*n.* A clog or clot. [Middle English *claggen*, to daub with mud, from Scandinavian; akin to Danish *klagge*, mud.] —**clag·gy** *adj.*

claim (kláym) *v.* **claimed, claiming, claims.** —*tr.* **1.** To demand as one's due; assert one's right to. **2.** To take by or as if by right: *The war claimed many lives.* **3.** To state to be true; assert or maintain. **4.** To deserve or call for; require. **5.** To demand (money) under an insurance policy, as after an accident. —*intr.* To make a claim, especially an insurance claim. ~*n.* **1.** A demand for something as one's rightful due; affirmation of a right. **2.** A basis for demanding something; a title or right. **3.** Something claimed in a formal or legal manner; especially, a tract of land staked out by a miner or prospector. **4. a.** A sum of money demanded, as after an accident, in accordance with an insurance policy or other formal arrangement. **b.** A demand for such money. **5.** A statement of something as a fact; an assertion of truth. —**lay claim to.** To assert one's right to or ownership of. [Middle English *claimen*, from Old French *clamer* (present stem *claim-*), to cry, appeal, from Latin *clāmāre*, to call.] —**claim·a·ble** *adj.* —**claim·er** *n.*

claim·ant (kláymənt) *n.* **1.** A person making a claim. **2.** *British.* A person applying for or receiving social security payments.

Clair (klair), **René** (1898–1981). French film director. As an early exponent of sound productions, he directed the classics *Sous les Toits de Paris* (1929) and *Le Million* (1931).

clair·au·di·ence (klair-áwdi-ənss) *n.* The supposed faculty of hearing things outside the normal range of perception. [French *clair*, CLEAR + AUDIENCE, by analogy with CLAIRVOYANCE.] —**clair·au·di·ent** *n. & adj.*

clair de lune (klair də lǒon, léwn) *n.* **1.** A pale, greyish-blue glaze applied to various kinds of Chinese porcelain. **2.** The colour of this glaze. [French, "moonlight".] —**clair-de-lune** *adj.*

clair·schach, clar·sach (klá-shəkh, kláir-, -shaakh) *n.* An ancient Irish harp. [Middle English *clareschaw*, from Scottish Gaelic *clārsach†*.]

Clair·vaux (kláir-vô). Village in the Aube département of northeast France. Its abbey, founded by St. Bernard of Clairvaux in 1115, became the most influential centre of the Cistercian order.

clair·voy·ance (klair-vóy-ənss, kláir-) *n.* **1.** The supposed power to see or know things that are out of the natural range of human perception. **2.** Acute intuitive insight or perceptiveness. [French *clairvoyant*, "clear-seeing" : *clair*, clear, from Latin *clārus* + *voyant*, present participle of *voir*, to see, from Latin *vidēre*.] —**clair·voy·ant** *n. & adj.*

clam¹ (klam) *n.* **1.** Any of various usually burrowing marine and freshwater bivalve molluscs, including members of the genera *Venus*, *Mya*, and others, many of which are edible. See **quahog**. **2.** The soft, tasty, edible flesh of such a mollusc. **3.** *Informal.* An uncommunicative person. ~*intr.v.* **clammed, clamming, clams.** To hunt for clams. —**clam up.** To cease talking or remain silent. [Shortened from *clamshell*, "bivalve that shuts tight like a clamp", from CLAM (clamp).]

clam² *n.* A clamp or vice. [Middle English, Old English *clamm*, bond, fetter.]

cla·mant (kláymənt) *adj.* **1.** Clamorous; loud. **2.** Urgent; compelling. [Latin *clāmāns* (stem *clāmant-*), present participle of *clāmāre*, to cry out.]

clam·a·to·ri·al (klámmə-táw-ri-əl || -tô-) *adj. Ornithology.* Of or pertaining to the American flycatchers, a group of perching and singing birds. [New Latin *clamatores*, plural of Latin *clāmātor*, shouter, from *clāmāre*, to cry out.]

clam·bake (klám-bayk) *n. U.S.* **1.** A seashore picnic where clams, fish, and other foods are baked in layers on buried hot stones. **2.** *Informal.* A party, especially a noisy and lively one.

clam·ber (klámbər || *U.S. also* klámmər) *intr.v.* **-bered, -bering, -bers.** To climb with difficulty, especially on all fours; scramble. ~*n.* The act of clambering. [Middle English *clambren*, from Old Norse *klembra*, originally, "to grip".] —**clam·ber·er** *n.*

clam chowder *n.* Any of various soups made from shelled clams, salt pork, potatoes, and onions.

clam·my (klámmi) *adj.* **-mier, -miest. 1.** Disagreeably moist and usually cold. **2.** Humid; damp. Said of weather. [Middle English, from *clammen*, to stick, smear, Old English *clǣman*.] —**clam·mi·ly** *adv.* —**clam·mi·ness** *n.*

clam·or·ous (klámmər-əss) *adj.* Making, full of, or characterised by clamour. —**clam·or·ous·ly** *adv.* —**clam·or·ous·ness** *n.*

clam·our, *U.S.* **clam·or** (klámmər) *n.* **1.** A loud outcry or shouting; hubbub. **2.** A vehement expression of discontent or protest; a public outcry. **3.** Any loud and sustained noise; din; blare. —See Synonyms at **noise.** ~*v.* **clamoured** or *U.S.* **clamored, -ouring** or *U.S.* **-oring, -ours** or *U.S.* **-ors.** —*intr.* **1.** To make a clamour. **2.** To make vigorous demands or complaints. —*tr.* To exclaim insistently and noisily. [Middle English *clamour*, from Old French, from Latin *clāmor*, from *clāmāre*, to cry out.] —**clam·our·er** *n.*

clamp¹ (klamp) *n.* **1.** Any of various devices used to join, grip, support, or compress mechanical or structural parts. **2.** A wheel-clamp. ~*tr.v.* **clamped, clamping, clamps. 1.** To fasten, grip, or support with or as if with a clamp. **2.** To immobilise (an illegally parked vehicle) with a wheel-clamp. [Middle English, from Middle Dutch *clampe*.]

clamp² *British.* A pile of root vegetables stored under a mound of earth, turf, or the like. [Probably from Dutch *klamp*, heap; akin to CLUMP.]

clamp down *intr.v.* To repress, restrict, or prohibit something not approved of. Used with *on.* —**clamp-down** (klámp-down) *n.*

clamp·er (klámpər) *n.* **1.** A spiked plate attached to the sole of a shoe to prevent slipping on ice. **2.** One that clamps.

clam·shell (klám-shel) *n.* **1.** The shell of a clam. **2.** *Chiefly U.S.* A dredging bucket made of two hinged jaws. **3.** *Aeronautics.* An eye-lid *(see).*

clam·worm *n. U.S.* The **ragworm** *(see).*

clan (klan) *n.* **1.** A traditional social unit in Scotland, consisting of a number of families claiming a common ancestor and following the same hereditary chieftain. **2.** In some tribal societies, a division of a tribe tracing descent from a common ancestor. **3.** Any numerous group of relatives, friends, or associates. [Middle English, from Scottish Gaelic *clann*, children, family, from Latin *planta*, shoot, PLANT.]

clan·des·tine (klan-déss-tin, klándiss-, -tīn) *adj.* Concealed, usually for some secret or illicit purpose. See Synonyms at **secret.** [French *clandestin*, from Old French, from Latin *clandestīnus*, from *clam*, in secret (after *intestīnus*, inward, INTESTINE).] —**clan·des·tine·ly** *adv.* —**clan·des·tine·ness, clan·des·ti·ni·ty** (klán-dess-tínnəti, -diss-) *n.*

clang (klang) *n.* **1.** A loud, metallic, resonant sound. **2.** The strident call of a crane or goose. ~*v.* **clanged, clanging, clangs.** —*intr.* To make a clang. —*tr.* To cause to clang. [Latin *clangere*, to resound (imitative).]

clang·er (kláng-ər) *n. Informal.* An embarrassing or tactless blunder. [Imitative, also influenced by Latin *clangor*, resounding noise.]

clan·gour, *U.S.* **clan·gor** (kláng-gər, -ər) *n.* A clang or repeated clanging; a loud ringing; a din. [Latin, from *clangere*, CLANG.] —**clan·gor·ous** *adj.* —**clan·gor·ous·ly** *adv.* —**clangour** *intr.v.*

clank (klangk) *n.* A metallic sound, sharp and hard but not as resonant as a clang. ~*v.* **clanked, clanking, clanks.** —*intr.* To make a clank. —*tr.* To cause to clank. [Imitative.]

clan·nish (klánnish) *adj.* **1.** Of, pertaining to, or characteristic of a clan. **2.** Inclined to cling together in a group and exclude outsiders. —**clan·nish·ly** *adv.* —**clan·nish·ness** *n.*

clans·man (klánz-mən) *n., pl.* **-men** (-mən). A person belonging to a clan.

clans·wom·an (klánz-wǒomən) *n., pl.* **-women** (-wimmin). A woman belonging to a clan.

clap¹ (klap) *v.* **clapped, clapping, claps.** —*intr.* **1.** To strike the palms of the hands together with a sudden, explosive sound, as in applauding. **2.** To come together suddenly with a sharp noise. —*tr.* **1.** To strike (the hands, for example) together with a brisk movement and an abrupt, loud sound. **2.** To applaud (actors, for example) by clapping the hands. **3.** To strike lightly but firmly with the open hand, as in greeting: *clapped him on the shoulder.* **4.** To put or place quickly or firmly: *clapped him in irons.* **5.** To flap (the wings). —**clap eyes on.** *Informal.* To catch sight of. —**clap hold of.** *Informal.* To grip. ~*n.* **1. a.** The act or sound of clapping the hands. **b.** A loud, sharp, or explosive noise, especially that made by thunder. **2.** A sharp blow with the open hand; a slap. [Middle English *clappen*, from Old English *clappian*, to throb, beat, from Germanic *klap-* (unattested), imitative.]

clap² *n. Slang.* **Gonorrhoea** *(see).* Sometimes preceded by *the.* [Old French *clapoir*, venereal sore; akin to *clapier*, brothel, and Old Provençal *clap†*, heap of stones.]

clap·board (klábbərd, kláp-bawrd || -bôrd) *n. Chiefly U.S.* **Weatherboard** *(see).* [Partial translation of Middle Dutch *claphollt* : *clappen*, to crack, split, akin to Old English *clappian*, to CLAP + *holt*, board, wood.]

cla·po·tis (klə-pôtiss, kla-) *n.* A type of wave formation in which standing waves that have no horizontal motion of crests are formed by the approach of waves to a sea wall, breakwater, or other barrier. [French, from *clapoter*, (of a liquid) agitate with waves.]

clapped-out (klápt-ówt) *adj. Informal.* Worn out; no longer functioning effectively.

clap·per (kláppər) *n.* **1.** A person or thing that claps. **2.** The part of a bell that strikes the side. **3.** A rattle consisting of two pieces of wood that strike together to make a clapping sound. **4.** *Slang.* The tongue. —**like the clappers.** *British Informal.* Very fast: *run like the clappers.*

clap·per·board (kláppər-bawrd || -bôrd) *n.* A device used in film-making consisting of two hinged pieces of wood that are held before the camera bearing the scene number and clapped together to allow the synchronisation of the soundtrack and the image.

clap·per·claw (kláppər-klaw) *tr.v.* **-clawed, -clawing, -claws.** *Archaic.* **1.** To claw or scratch. **2.** To berate or revile. [Probably CLAPPER + CLAW.]

clap·trap (kláp-trap) *n. Informal.* Pretentious, insincere, or empty language. [CLAP + TRAP ("a trick to win applause").]

claque (klak) *n.* **1.** A group of persons hired to applaud at a performance. **2.** Any group of adulating or fawning admirers. [French, from *claquer*, to clap (imitative).]

clar·a·bel·la (klárrə-béllə) *n.* An eight-foot organ stop producing soft, sweet tones. [Latin *clāra*, feminine of *clārus*, CLEAR + *bella*, feminine of *bellus*, pretty.]

Clare (klair). *Irish* **Chlair.** A county in Munster province on the Atlantic coast of the Irish Republic. It is a farming district, with salmon fisheries in the Shannon estuary.

Clare, John (1793–1864). British poet, known for his lyrical evocations of the English countryside. His works, which include *The Shepherd's Calendar* (1827) and *The Rural Muse* (1835), sold poorly and he was destitute. From 1841, he spent his life in a mental hospital, where he produced some of his best poetry.

clar·ence (klárrənss) *n.* A four-wheeled closed carriage with seats for four passengers. [After the Duke of *Clarence* (1765–1837), later William IV.]

clar·en·don (klárrəndən) *n. Printing.* A variety of bold-face roman type. [After the *Clarendon* Press, printing house of Oxford University.]

Clarendon (klárrəndən), **Edward Hyde, 1st Earl of** (1609–74). English statesman and author. As an adviser to the future Charles II, he was instrumental in the restoration of the monarchy (1660). He was Lord Chancellor (1660–67).

Clare of Assisi (klair), **Saint** (1194–1253). Italian nun, who founded the first Franciscan order of nuns, the Poor Clares. She has become the patron saint of television because she is said to have witnessed a mass celebrated far away. Her feast day is August 12.

clar·et (klárrit) *n.* **1. a.** The dry red table wine from the Bordeaux region of France. **b.** Any of various similar red wines made elsewhere. **2.** Dark or greyish purplish red. [Middle English, from Old French, from Medieval Latin (*vīnum*) *clārātum*, "clarified (wine)", from Latin *clārāre*, to make clear, purify, from *clārus*, CLEAR.] **—clar·et** *adj.*

claret cup *n.* A chilled mixed drink of red wine with spirits, fruit, and other ingredients.

clar·i·fy (klárri-fī) *v.* **-fied, -fying, -fies.** *—tr.* **1.** To make clear or easier to understand; elucidate. **2.** To make clear by removing impurities, often by heating gently: *clarify butter.* *—intr.* To become clear. [Middle English *clarifien*, from Old French *clarifier*, from Late Latin *clārificāre* : Latin *clārus*, CLEAR + *facere*, to make.] **—clar·i·fi·ca·tion** (-fi-káysh'n) *n.* **—clar·i·fi·er** *n.*

clar·i·net (klárri-nét) *n.* Also *rare* **clar·i·o·net** (klárri-ə-nét) **1.** A woodwind instrument having a straight, cylindrical tube with a flaring bell and a single-reed mouthpiece, played by means of finger holes and keys. **2.** An eight-foot organ stop producing a sound suggestive of a clarinet. [French *clarinette*, from Italian *clarinetto*, diminutive of *clarino*, trumpet, from Latin *clārus*, CLEAR.] **—clar·i·net·ist, clar·i·net·tist** *n.*

cla·ri·no (kla-réeno, klə-) *n. Music.* **1.** The high register of the trumpet, especially in baroque music. **2.** A high, trumpet-like organ stop. [Italian, trumpet, probably from Spanish *clarín.*]

clar·i·on (klárri-ən) *n.* **1.** A medieval trumpet with a shrill, clear tone. **2.** The sound made by this instrument or any sound resembling it. **3.** An organ stop with a high, shrill tone. *~ adj.* Shrill and clear: *a clarion call for justice.* [Middle English *clarioun*, from Medieval Latin *clāriō* (stem *clārion-*) trumpet, from Latin *clārus*, CLEAR.]

clar·i·ty (klárrəti) *n.* **1.** Clearness. **2.** Plainness; lucidity: *clarity of style.* [Middle English *clarite*, from Latin *clāritās*, from *clārus*, CLEAR.]

Clark, Kenneth (Mackenzie), Baron (1903–83). British art critic and historian. *The Gothic Revival* (1929) was the first of his many influential books, and *The Nude* (1955) perhaps his most famous.

Clark cell *n. Physics.* A former standard voltaic cell with an emf of 1.4345 volts (15°C). It has a zinc cathode in zinc sulphate and a mercury anode in mercury sulphate. [After Josiah *Clark* (1822–98), English scientist.]

Clarke (klark), **Jeremiah** (c. 1673–1707). English organist and composer. The *Trumpet Voluntary* (*Suite in D*), attributed to Purcell, is an arrangement of one of Clarke's harpsichord pieces.

clark·i·a (klárki-ə) *n.* Any of several annual plants of the genus *Clarkia*, of western North America, especially *C. pulchella*, which is cultivated for its red, purple, and white flowers. [New Latin, after William *Clark* (1770–1838), U.S. explorer who discovered it.]

clarsach. Variant of **clairschach.**

clart (klart) *n. Northern British.* A smear of a dirty or sticky substance. *~tr.v.* **clarted, clarting, clarts.** *Northern British.* To smear or daub with a dirty or sticky substance. [Middle English, origin obscure.] **—clart·y** *adj.*

clar·y (klár-i) *n., pl.* **-ies.** Any of several European plants of the genus *Salvia*, especially *S. sclarea*, an aromatic herb with bluish-white flowers. Also called **clary sage.** [Middle English *clarye*, *sclarey*, from Old French *sclaree*, from Medieval Latin *sclareat*.]

–clase *n. comb. form.* Indicates a mineral with a specified cleavage; for example, **plagioclase.** [French, from Greek *klasis*, a breaking, from *klan*, to break.]

clash (klash) *v.* **clashed, clashing, clashes.** *—intr.* **1.** To collide with a loud, harsh noise. **2.** To conflict, as in a fight, contest, or debate; be in opposition. **3.** To create an unpleasant visual impression when combined. Used of colours. **4.** To occur at the same time; coincide: *The date of the meeting clashes with my dental appointment.* *—tr.* To strike together with a harsh, metallic sound. *~n.* **1.** A loud, resounding metallic noise, such as that made by two objects colliding. **2.** A conflict, opposition, or disagreement. **3.** An inharmonious grouping, for example of colours. **4.** A coincidence, of dates, for example. —See Synonyms at **discord.** [Imitative.]

clasp (klaasp ‖ klasp) *n.* **1.** A fastening, such as a hook or buckle, used to hold two objects or parts together. **2. a.** An embrace; a hug. **b.** A grip or grasp of the hand. **3.** A small metal bar attached to a military decoration indicating the action for which it was awarded. *~tr.v.* **clasped, clasping, clasps. 1.** To fasten with or as if with a clasp. **2.** To hold in a tight grasp; embrace. **3.** To grip firmly in or with the hand. [Middle English *claspe*, from *claspen*, *clapsen*, to grip, grasp, perhaps from Old English *clyppan*, to embrace.] **—clasp·er** *n.*

clas·pers (kláasp-ərz ‖ klásp-) *pl.n.* A pair of appendages, found in male insects and certain fish, that are specialised for the introduction of sperm into the female reproductive tract.

clasp knife *n.* A pocketknife with a single blade.

class (klaass ‖ klass) *n. Abbr.* **cl. 1. a.** A set, collection, group, or configuration containing members having or thought to have at least one attribute in common; a kind; a sort. **b.** *Statistics.* Any interval in a **frequency distribution** (*see*). See **set** (in mathematics). **2.** Any division of people or objects by quality, rank, or grade. **3.** A social stratum whose members share similar economic, social, and cultural characteristics. **4. a.** The division of society into relative strata or ranks: *discrimination on grounds of class.* **b.** Social rank or caste, especially high rank. **5. a.** A group of pupils or students studying the same subject or following the same course. **b.** The period during which such a group meets. **c.** In Britain, a grade of university degree. **d.** *U.S.* A group of students graduating in the same year. **6.** *Biology.* A taxonomic category ranking below a phylum (animals) or division (plants) and above an order. **7.** The quality of accommodation on a public vehicle: *travel in first class.* **8.** *Informal.* Good taste in manner or dress; stylishness: *a girl with class.* *~tr.v.* **classed, classing, classes.** To arrange, group, or rate according to qualities or characteristics; assign to a class; classify. [French *classe*, from Late Latin *classis*, from Latin, one of the six divisions of the Roman people, army, fleet.]

class. **1.** classic; classical. **2.** classification; classified; classify.

class-con·scious (kláass-kónshəss ‖ kláss-) *adj.* Aware of belonging to a particular socio-economic class, often to the extent of being hostile to or envious of other classes. **—class-con·scious·ness.**

clas·sic (klássik) *adj.* **1.** Of the highest rank or class. **2.** Serving as an outstanding representative of its kind; model. **3.** Having lasting significance or recognised worth. **4.** *Abbr.* **class.** Pertaining to ancient Greek or Roman literature or art; classical. **5. a.** Of or in accordance with established principles and methods in the arts and sciences. **b.** Having a simple and harmonious design unaffected by passing fashions. **6.** Of lasting historical or literary significance. **7.** *Informal.* Of a well-known or traditional type; remarkably typical: *a classic mistake.* *~n.* **1.** An artist, author, or work generally considered to be of the highest rank or excellence. **2.** *Plural.* The literature of ancient Greece and Rome. **3.** Something considered to be typical or traditional. **4.** In Britain, any of the five major races for three-year-old horses, including the Derby and St. Leger.

Usage: *Classic* and *classical* are sometimes interchangeable when used as adjectives, as in such phrases as *classic/classical design* or *look.* *Classical* is more common in senses pertaining to ancient Greek or Roman culture. *Classic* has a more general range of use, including the broad sense of "highest rank or excellence": *a classic story.* In this sense it would be different from *a classical story,* in that there is not necessarily any implication of historical origins. *Classic* has also undergone considerable semantic development in recent years, with its meaning of "typical", "appropriate", and its widespread ironic use in informal speech: *That's classic!* See also **-ic, -ical.**

clas·si·cal (klássik'l) *adj. Abbr.* **class. 1. a.** Of, pertaining to, or in accordance with the precedents of ancient Greek and Roman art, architecture, and literature. **b.** Learned in or studying Greek and Roman art, architecture, or literature. **2.** Of or concerning the most artistically developed stage of a civilisation: *Chinese classical poetry.* **3.** *Music.* **a.** Pertaining to or designating the European music, such as that of Haydn and Mozart, of the latter half of the 18th century. **b.** Designating any music in the educated European tradition, as distinguished from popular or folk music. **4.** Conventional and authoritative rather than new or experimental. **5.** Showing artistic restraint and respect for principles of traditional design. **6.** Of or pertaining to nonrelativistic or nonquantum physics: *classical mechanics.* See Usage note at **classic.** **—clas·si·cal·ism, clas·si·cal·ness** *n.* **—clas·si·cal·ly** *adv.*

Classical Greek *n.* The forms of Greek used in classical literature, chiefly Attic-Ionic, Doric, and Aeolic.

Classical Latin *n.* The form of Latin used in classical literature. Compare **Vulgar Latin.**

clas·si·cism (klássi-siz'm) *n.* **1.** Aesthetic attitudes and principles based on the culture, art, architecture, and literature of ancient Greece and Rome and characterised by emphasis on form, simplicity, proportion, and restraint. **2.** Classical scholarship. **3.** A Greek or Latin form or idiom.

clas·si·cist (klássi-sist) *n.* A student of classics.

clas·si·fi·a·ble (klássi-fī-əb'l, -fī-) *adj.* Capable of being classified.

clas·si·fi·ca·tion (klássi-fi-káysh'n) *n. Abbr.* **cl., class. 1.** The act or result of classifying. **2.** A category in which something may be classified. **3.** In South Africa: **a.** Any of various race groups as distinguished in law. **b.** The official registration of a person as a member of any such group. **4.** *Biology.* The systematic grouping of organisms into categories based on shared characteristics or traits; taxonomy. **5.** The designation of information as officially secret. —**clas·si·fi·ca·to·ry** (-fi-káytəri, -fickətri ‖ *U.S.* -fickə-tawri) *adj.*

classified advertisement *n.* An advertisement in a newspaper, usually brief and in small type. Also called "classified", "small ad".

clas·si·fy (klássi-fī) *tr.v.* **-fied, -fying, -fies. 1.** To arrange or organise according to class or category. **2.** In South Africa, to assign to or register under any of the various race groups. **3.** To designate (a document, for instance) as secret and available only to authorised persons: *classified information.* [Latin *classis,* CLASS + -FY.] —**clas·si·fi·er** *n.*

clas·sis (klássi-iss) *n., pl.* **classes** (-eez). *Ecclesiastical.* **1.** In certain Reformed churches, a governing body of pastors and elders having jurisdiction over local churches. **2.** The district or churches governed by such a body. [New Latin, from Latin, division, CLASS.]

class·less (kláass-ləss, -liss ‖ kláss-) *adj.* **1.** Not divided economically or socially; lacking class distinctions. **2.** Not belonging to any particular social class.

class mark *n. Statistics.* The numerical value given for computational convenience to a statistical observation falling within a number of intervals. Also called "mark".

class·mate (kláass-mayt ‖ kláss-) *n.* A member of the same class at school.

class·room (kláass-rōom, -rŏŏm ‖ kláss-) *n.* A room in which classes are conducted in a school.

class struggle *n.* Conflict between social classes; especially, in Marxist theory, the conflict for economic and political power between an exploiting class, like the capitalist bourgeoisie, and an exploited class, like the proletariat. Also called "class war".

class·y (kláassi ‖ klássi) *adj.* **-ier, -iest.** *Informal.* Stylish; elegant.

clast (klast) *n. Geology.* A fragment of rock. [Greek *klastos,* fragmented, from *klân,* to break.]

-clast *n. comb. form.* Indicates one that breaks or destroys; for example, **osteoclast, iconoclast.** [Medieval Latin -*clastēs,* from Medieval Greek -*klastēs,* breaker, from *klân,* to break.]

clas·tic (klástik) *adj.* **1.** Separable into parts or having removable sections: *a clastic anatomical model.* **2.** *Geology.* Made up of fragments; fragmental. **3.** *Biology.* Dividing into parts. [Greek *klastos,* broken, from *klân,* to break.]

clath·rate (kláth-rayt, -rət, -rit) *adj. Biology.* Having a lattice-like structure or appearance.
~ *n. Chemistry.* A compound in which atoms or molecules of one substance are trapped within the crystal structure of another. Also called "clathrate compound". [Latin *clāthrātus,* past participle of *clāthrāre,* to provide with a lattice, from *clāthrī, clātra,* lattice, from Greek *klēithra,* from *klēithron,* door bar, from *kleiein,* to close.]

clat·ter (kláttər) *n.* **1.** A loud rattling sound or sounds. **2.** A loud disturbance; a commotion.
~ *v.* **clattered, -tering, -ters.** —*intr.* **1.** To make a clatter; move with a clatter. —*tr.* **2.** To cause to clatter. [Middle English *clatren,* Old English *clatrian* (attested in gerund, *clatrung*) (imitative).] —**clat·ter·er** *n.*

Clau·di·an (kláwdi-ən), born Claudius Claudianus (c.A.D. 370–c.404). Roman poet, considered the last in the classical tradition. He is best known for his epic, *The Rape of Proserpine.*

clau·di·ca·tion (kláwdi-káysh'n) *n.* A halt in one's walk; a limp; lameness. [Middle English *claudicacioun,* from Latin *claudicātiō* (stem *claudicātiōn-*), from *claudicāre,* to limp, from *claudus†,* lame.]

Clau·di·us I (kláwdi-əss) (10 B.C.–A.D. 54). Roman emperor (A.D. 41–54) and historian. Physically disabled and considered weak in the head, he was excluded from public life until Caligula made him consul (A.D. 37). When Caligula was murdered (A.D. 41), Claudius became emperor and proved a sound, efficient ruler.

clause (klawz) *n. Abbr.* **cl. 1.** A group of words containing a subject and a predicate that forms part of a compound or complex sentence. See **subordinate clause, main clause. 2.** A section of a legal document, contract, or the like; a distinct article, stipulation, or provision in a document. [Middle English, from Old French, from Medieval Latin *clausa,* close of a rhetorical period, conclusion of a legal argument, hence section of a law, from *claudere* (past participle *clausus*), to close.] —**claus·al** (kláwz'l) *adj.*

Clau·se·witz (klówzə-vits), **Karl Marie von** (1780–1831). Prussian general and military theorist. In his *On War* (1833) he argued for the mobilisation of the national effort in a concept of total warfare which dominated Prussian and German military strategy up to World War I.

Clau·si·us (klówzi-ōōss, -əss), **Rudolph Julius Emanuel** (1822–88). German molecular physicist, who formulated the second law of thermodynamics (1850) that "heat cannot of itself pass from a colder to a hotter body". He developed the concept of entropy and a kinetic theory of gases.

claustral. Variant of **cloistral.**

claus·tro·pho·bi·a (kláwstrə-fŏb-yə, -i-ə) *n.* A pathological fear of confined spaces. [New Latin : Latin *claustrum,* enclosed place, CLOISTER + -PHOBIA.] —**claus·tro·pho·bic** (-fŏbik) *adj. & n.*

cla·vate (kláyv-ayt, -ət, -it) *adj.* Having one end thickened; club-shaped; claviform. [New Latin *clavatus,* from Latin *clāva,* club.] —**cla·vate·ly** *adv.*

clave. *Archaic.* **1.** Past tense of **cleave** (to split). **2.** Past tense of **cleave** (to cling).

cla·ver (kláyvər) *intr.v.* **-vered, -vering, -vers.** *Scottish.* To gossip or talk idly.
~ *n. Scottish.* Gossip; idle talk. [Scottish Gaelic *clabaire†,* babbler.]

clav·i·chord (klávvi-kawrd) *n.* An early musical keyboard instrument with a soft sound produced by brass pins (tangents) striking horizontal strings. [Medieval Latin *clāvichordium* : Latin *clāvis,* key + *chorda,* CHORD.]

clav·i·cle (klávvik'l) *n.* **1.** In human beings, either of the two bones connecting the upper part of the breastbone with the shoulder blades. Also called "collarbone". **2.** The corresponding structure in the pectoral girdle of certain other vertebrates. [Medieval Latin *clāvicula,* diminutive of Latin *clāvis,* key (referring to the shape).] —**cla·vic·u·lar** (klə-víckew-lər, kla-) *adj.* —**cla·vic·u·late** (-layt) *adj.*

clav·i·corn (klávvi-kawrn) *adj.* Belonging to or designating a group of beetles of the section Clavicornia, having club-shaped antennae, including the ladybirds and grain beetles. [New Latin *Clavicornia* (family name) : Latin *clāva,* club + Latin *cornū,* horn.]

cla·vier (klávvi-ər; *(especially in sense 2)* klə-véer; *rarely* kláyvi-ər) *n.* **1.** A keyboard. **2.** Any stringed keyboard instrument, such as a harpsichord or piano. [German *Klavier,* piano, from French *clavier,* keyboard, from Old French *clavier,* key-bearer, from Latin *clāvis,* key.]

clav·i·form (klávvi-fawrm) *adj.* Club-shaped; clavate. [Latin *clāva,* club + -FORM.]

claw (klaw) *n.* **1. a.** A sharp, often curved, nail on the toe of a mammal, reptile, or bird. **b.** The foot of a mammal, reptile, or bird having such nails. **2. a.** A chela or similar pincer-like structure on the limb of a crustacean or other arthropod. **b.** A limb terminating in such a structure. **3.** Anything resembling a claw, such as the cleft end of a hammerhead. **4.** *Botany.* The narrowed basal part of certain petals or sepals.
~ *v.* **clawed, clawing, claws.** —*tr.* To scratch, tear, grab, or pull with or as if with claws. —*intr.* To make scratching or digging motions with or as if with claws. [Middle English *clawe,* Old English *clawu,* from Germanic.]

claw back *tr.v.* **1.** To regain with difficulty. **2.** To get back (revenue lost by a particular measure, for example the introduction of a benefit or allowance) by measures such as increased taxation. —**claw-back** (kláw-bak) *n.*

claw hammer *n.* A hammer having a head with one end forked for removing nails.

claw hatchet *n.* A hatchet having one end of the head forked.

clay (klay) *n.* **1.** A fine-grained, firm, natural material, plastic when wet, that consists primarily of hydrated silicates of aluminium and is widely used in making bricks, tiles, and pottery. **2.** Any earth that forms a paste with water and hardens when heated or dried. **3.** Moist earth; mud. **4.** The human body as distinct from the spirit. Used in literary or poetic contexts. [Middle English *cley, clay,* Old English *clæg,* from Germanic.] —**clay·ey** (kláy-i), **clay·ish** (kláy-ish) *adj.*

Clay, Cassius. See **Muhammad Ali.**

clay court *n.* A tennis court having a surface made of clay or a synthetic substance resembling clay.

clay mineral *n.* Any of a group of hydrated silicates, mainly of aluminium and magnesium, present in clays and responsible for their plastic properties.

clay·more (kláy-mawr ‖ -mŏr) *n.* A large, double-edged broadsword formerly used by Scottish Highlanders. [Gaelic *claidheamh mōr,* "great sword" : *claidheamh,* sword + *mōr,* great.]

clay·pan (kláy-pan) *n.* **1.** *Geology.* A layer of compact clay beneath the surface soil, causing poor drainage and waterlogging. **2.** In Australia, a hollow or slight depression in the ground that has a bottom of clay and holds water after rain.

clay pigeon *n.* A clay disc thrown or propelled into the air as a flying target to be shot at for sport.

clay·to·ni·a (klay-tŏni-ə) *n.* Any North American or eastern Siberian succulent plant of the genus *Claytonia,* many of which are cultivated as ornamentals. [After John *Clayton* (1693–1773), American botanist.]

-cle *n. suffix.* Indicates small size; for example, **particle.** [Middle English, from Old French, from Latin -*culus.*]

clean (kleen) *adj.* **cleaner, cleanest. 1.** Free from dirt, stains, or impurities; unsoiled. **2. a.** Free from foreign matter; unadulterated. **b.** Not infected: *a clean wound.* **3.** Producing little radioactive fallout or contamination. **4. a.** Without imperfections or blemishes; regular; perfect: *a clean line.* **b.** Well-formed or elegant; streamlined. **5.** Free from clumsiness; deft; adroit: *a clean throw.* **6.** Without restrictions or encumbrances: *a clean bill of health.* **7.** Entire; thorough; complete: *a clean sweep.* **8.** Having few alterations or corrections; legible. **9.** Blank: *a clean page.* **10.** Morally pure; unsullied; sinless. **11.** Not ribald or obscene. **12.** Honest; fair, as in

sports: *a clean fighter.* **13.** *Slang.* **a.** Possessing no hidden drugs, weapon, stolen goods, or the like. **b.** Innocent of a crime. **14.** *Informal.* Having or showing no record or history of convictions for crimes or offences: *a clean driving licence.* **15.** In religious and biblical contexts: **a.** Free from defilement. **b.** Not prohibited by dietary law. **16.** Fresh; pleasantly sharp: *a clean taste.* **17.** *Informal.* Able to control urination and defecation.
~*adv.* **1.** In a clean manner; cleanly. **2.** *Informal.* Entirely; wholly; thoroughly. **—come clean.** *Slang.* To admit the truth; confess.
~*v.* **cleaned, cleaning, cleans.** —*tr.* **1.** To rid of dirt or other impurities. **2.** To remove (dirt or impurities) from something. **3.** To prepare (fowl or other food) for cooking. —*intr.* To undergo or perform the act of ridding of dirt and impurities. **—clean out. 1.** To rid of dirt, rubbish, or impurities. **2.** To rid or empty of contents or occupants. **3.** To drive or force out. **4.** *Informal.* To deprive completely of money or material wealth: *The robbery cleaned her out.* **5.** *Informal.* To exhaust (a supply of goods or money).
~*n.* An act or instance of cleaning. [Middle English *clene,* Old English *clǣne,* from West Germanic *klaini* (unattested).] **—clean·a·ble** *adj.* **—clean·ness** *n.*

clean bowled *adj.* In cricket, bowled out by a ball that hit the wicket without touching the batsman or the bat.

clean-cut (kléen-kút) *adj.* **1.** Clearly and sharply defined or outlined. **2.** Wholesome; neat and well-dressed.

clean·er (kléenər) *n.* **1.** A person who is employed to clean houses, offices, and the like. Also called, if female, "cleaning woman". **2.** A machine, device, or chemical agent that cleans.

clean·ers (kléenərz) *n.* *Used with a singular or plural verb.* A commercial establishment providing a dry-cleaning service. **—take to the cleaner's.** *Slang.* **1.** To swindle or rob. **2.** To take all the money or possessions of; ruin. **3.** To subject to withering criticism.

clean·ly (klénli || *Australian also* kléenli) *adj.* **-lier, -liest.** Habitually and carefully neat and clean.
~*adv.* (kléenli). **1.** In a clean manner. **2.** Smoothy; deftly or easily: *cut the wood cleanly.* **—clean·li·ness** (klénli-nəss, -niss) *n.*

cleanse (klenz) *tr.v.* **cleansed, cleansing, cleanses. 1.** To free from dirt, defilement, or guilt; purge or clean. **2.** To clean (a wound). **3.** To use a cleanser on. [Middle English *clensen,* Old English *clǣnsian.*]

cleans·er (klénzər) *n.* **1.** One that cleans. **2.** A detergent, powder, or other chemical agent that removes dirt, grease, or stains. **3.** A skin lotion or cream that is used to clean the face.

clean-shav·en (kleeén-sháyv'n) *adj.* **1.** Having the beard or hair shaved off. **2.** Having recently shaved.

clean·skin (kléen-skin) *n.* *Australian.* **1.** A cow or horse that has not been branded. **2.** *Slang.* A person who has no criminal record.

clean up *intr.v.* **1.** To rid a place of dirt or disorder. **2.** To make oneself clean, neat, or presentable. **3.** *Informal.* To finish; conclude. **4.** *Informal.* To make a large profit. —*tr.v.* **1.** To clean and make tidy (a room or oneself, for example); remove dirt or debris from. **2.** *Informal.* To rid (a town, for example) of corruption.

clean-up (kléen-up) *n.* **1.** A thorough cleaning or tidying. **2.** *Informal.* The process of ridding a place of corruption or dishonesty. **3.** *Informal.* A large profit.

clear (kleer) *adj.* **clearer, clearest. 1.** Free from anything that dims, obscures, or darkens; unclouded. **2.** Free from flaw, blemish, or impurity. **3.** Free from impediment, obstruction, or hindrance; open. **4.** Plain or evident. **5.** Easily perceptible to the eye or ear; distinct. **6.** Free of guilt; untroubled: *a clear conscience.* **7. a.** Free from doubt or confusion; certain; sure. **b.** Logical and incisive: *a clear thinker.* **8.** Free from qualification or limitation; absolute: *a clear winner.* **9.** Resonant; ringing, like certain sounds. **10.** Freed from contact or connection; disengaged. Used with *of*: *We are now clear of danger.* **11.** Free from roughness or protrusions, as timber. **12.** Freed from burden or obligation. **13.** Without charges or deductions; net: *She earns a clear £15,000.* **14.** Transparent: *clear soup.* **15.** Not cloudy or raining. Said of weather. **16.** Empty: *a clear desk; a clear ship.* **17.** In show jumping, having incurred no penalties: *a clear round.* **—in the clear.** Free from burdens, dangers, difficulties, or suspicion.
~*adv.* **1.** Distinctly; clearly. **2.** *Informal.* All the way; completely; entirely: *He cried clear through the night.* **3.** Out of the way; completely away: *stand clear of the doors.*
~*v.* **cleared, clearing, clears.** —*tr.* **1.** To make clear, light, or bright. **2.** To rid of impurities, blemishes, muddiness, or foreign matter. **3.** To free from confusion, doubt, or ambiguity; make plain or intelligible. **4. a.** To rid of obstructions or entanglements: *clear the road of snow.* **b.** To make (a way, path, clearing, or the like) by removing obstacles or entanglements: *clear a space in the snow.* **c.** To remove or get rid of (obstacles or entanglements): *clear snow from the road.* **5.** To free from a legal charge or imputation of guilt; acquit. **6.** To pass by, under, or over without contact. **7.** To settle (a debt). **8.** To gain (a given amount) as net profit or earnings. **9. a.** To pass (a cheque or other bill of exchange) through a clearing-house. **b.** To pass (a cheque) through the banking system and debit and credit the relevant accounts. **10.** To free (a ship or cargo) from legal detention at a harbour by fulfilling the customs and harbour requirements. **11.** To free (the throat) of phlegm by coughing. **12.** To empty; remove objects from: *clear the cupboard.* **13.** To leave; evacuate: *If the fire alarm goes off, everyone must clear the building.* **14.** To declare (a person) fit to see secret or classified documents or to take part in confidential matters. **15.** To pass through by complying with or satisfying certain conditions: *clear customs.* **16.** *Sports.* To kick, hit, throw, or carry (a ball or puck) away from the defended goal. **17.** *Computing.* To remove (stored data) from a storage device. **18.** To make (a microscope specimen) transparent by immersing in a fluid such as xylene. —*intr.* **1.** To become clean, fair, or bright. **2.** To exchange cheques and bills or settle accounts, through a clearing-house. **3.** To pass through the banking system and be debited and credited to the relevant accounts. Used of a cheque. **4.** To be enabled to pass through by satisfying certain conditions; especially, to comply with customs regulations. **5.** To become empty or unblocked. **6.** To stop raining or become less cloudy; brighten. **7.** To go away; disappear. Used of fog, mist, rain, or the like. **—clear off.** *Slang.* To go away; leave quickly. Often used in the imperative. **—clear up. 1.** To make clear. **2.** To become fair and sunny after having been cloudy. **3.** To rid of confusion or mystery; explain. [Middle English *clere,* from Old French *cler,* from Latin *clārus,* bright, clear.] **—clear·a·ble** *adj.* **—clear·er** *n.* **—clear·ly** *adv.* **—clear·ness** *n.*

clear-air turbulence (kléer-áir) *n.* *Abbr.* **CAT** A type of turbulence encountered by aircraft at high altitudes, caused by waves formed at the interface between two unmixed air layers.

clear·ance (kléer-ənss) *n.* **1.** The act of clearing. **2.** A space cleared; a clearing. **3.** *Abbr.* **cl.** The amount by which a moving object clears something. **4.** An intervening distance or space enabling free play, such as that between machine parts. **5.** Permission for an aeroplane, ship, or other vehicle to proceed, as after an inspection of equipment or cargo or during certain traffic conditions. **6.** Official certification of blamelessness, trustworthiness, or suitability. **7.** A sale, generally at reduced prices, to dispose of old merchandise. **8.** *Abbr.* **cl.** The passage of cheques and other bills of exchange through a clearing-house.

clear·cole (cléerkōl) *n.* A primer or size that contains whiting. **—clear·cole** *tr.v.*

clear-cut, clear cut (kléer-kút) *adj.* **1.** Distinctly and sharply defined or outlined. **2.** Plain; evident. —See Synonyms at **incisive.**

clear-eyed (kléer-īd) *adj.* **1. a.** Having sharp, bright eyes. **b.** Keen-sighted. **2.** Mentally acute or perceptive.

clear-head·ed (kléer-héddid) *adj.* Having a clear, orderly mind; sensible. **—clear-head·ed·ly** *adv.* **—clear-head·ed·ness** *n.*

clear·ing (kléer-ing) *n.* **1.** A tract of land within a wood or other overgrown area from which the trees and other obstructions have been removed. **2.** In banking, the exchange among banks of cheques, drafts, and notes, and the settlement of differences arising from it.

clearing bank *n.* **1.** A bank that is a member of the London Bankers' Clearing House. **2.** *Informal.* A commercial or joint stock bank that issues chequebooks. Compare **merchant bank.** See **transmission.**

clear·ing-house (kléer-ing-howss) *n.* *Abbr.* **c.h., C.H.** An office where banks exchange cheques and drafts and settle accounts.

clear out *tr.v.* To tidy or empty by removing rubbish or unwanted articles. —*intr.v.* *Informal.* To leave. **—clear·out** (cléer-owt) *n.*

clear-sight·ed (kléer-sītid) *adj.* **1.** Having sharp, clear vision. **2.** Perceptive; discerning. **—clear-sight·ed·ly** *adv.* **—clear-sight·ed·ness** *n.*

clearstory. *Chiefly U.S.* variant of **clerestory.**

clear·way (kléer-way) *n.* In Britain, a road or a stretch of road in which cars are not allowed to stop except in an emergency.

clear·wing (kléer-wing) *n.* Any of various moths of the family Sesiidae (or Aegeriidae), having scaleless, transparent wings and resembling wasps.

cleat (kleet) *n.* **1.** A strip of wood or iron used to strengthen or support the surface to which it is attached. **2.** A piece of iron, rubber, or leather attached to the underside of a shoe to preserve the sole or prevent slipping. **3.** A piece of metal or wood having projecting arms or ends on which a rope can be wound or secured. **4.** A wedge-shaped piece of wood or other material fastened onto something such as a spar to act as a support or to prevent slipping. **5.** A spurlike device used in gripping a tree or pole in climbing. **6.** *Mining.* A joint or system of joints developed in a coal seam. [Middle English *clete,* Old English *clēat* (unattested), lump, wedge.]

cleav·age (kléevij) *n.* **1.** The act of splitting or cleaving. **2.** The state of being split or cleft; a fissure or division. **3.** *Mineralogy.* The splitting of a crystal, or the tendency to split, along definite crystalline planes *(cleavage planes)*, yielding smooth surfaces. **4.** *Zoology.* The process of cell division that produces a blastula (hollow ball of cells) from a fertilised ovum. Also called "segmentation". **5.** *Informal.* The hollow or line between a woman's breasts, especially that exposed by a low neckline.

cleave¹ (kleev) *v.* **cleft** (kleft) or **cleaved** or **clove** (klōv) or *archaic* **clave** (klayv), **cleft** or **cleaved** or **cloven** (klṓv'n) or *archaic* **clove, cleaving, cleaves.** —*tr.* **1.** To split or separate, as with an axe. **2.** To make or accomplish as if by cutting: *cleave a path through the forest.* **3.** To pierce or penetrate. —*intr.* **1.** To split or separate, especially along a natural line of division. **2.** To make one's way; penetrate; pass. Used with *through.* —See Synonyms at **tear.** [Cleave, clove, cloven; Middle English *cleven, clave, cloven,* Old English *clēofan, clēaf* (past singular), *clofen.* The weak form *cleft,* Middle English *cleved, cleft,* from the infinitive *cleven.*]

cleave² *intr.v.* **cleaved** or *archaic* **clave** or **clove, cleaved, cleaving, cleaves.** *Archaic.* **1.** To adhere, cling, or stick fast. Used with *to.* **2.** To be faithful. Used with *to*: *"Cleave to that which is good."* (Romans 12:9). [Middle English *clevien,* Old English *cleofian.*]

cleav·er (kléevər) *n.* A heavy, axelike knife or hatchet used especially by butchers.

cleav·ers (kléevərz) *n., pl.* **-ers.** Any of several plants of the genus *Galium*; especially, *G. aparine,* having small white flowers and prickly stems and fruits. This species is also called "goose grass". [Middle English *clivre* (probably influenced by *clivres,* claws), Old English *clīfe,* "the clinging plant", from *cleofian,* CLEAVE (cling).]

cleek (kleek) *n.* **1.** A number-one golf iron, having very little loft to the club face. **2.** *Scottish.* A large hook. [Middle English *cleche, cleike,* "grasping", from *clechen,* to grasp, seize, Old English *clǣcan* (unattested), probably akin to CLUTCH (verb).]

clef (klef) *n.* A symbol on a musical staff, indicating the pitch of the notes. See **alto clef, bass clef, treble clef.** [French, key, musical key, from Old French, from Latin *clāvis,* key.]

cleft (kleft) *n.* A past tense and past participle of **cleave** (to split). ~*adj.* **1.** Divided; split; separated. **2.** *Botany.* Having deeply divided lobes or divisions: *a cleft leaf.* ~*n.* **1.** A crack; a crevice; a split. **2.** A split or indentation between two parts, as of the chin. **3.** A moon rille *(see).* [Middle English *clift,* rift, fissure, Old English *geclyft.*]

cleft palate *n.* A congenital fissure in the roof of the mouth, often associated with a cleft in the upper lip (a harelip).

cleg (kleg) *n.* The **horsefly** *(see).* [Old Norse *kleggi.*]

clei·do·ic egg (klī-dó-ik) *n.* An egg with a tough shell that limits water loss but permits gas exchange, characteristic of reptiles, birds, and insects. [Greek *kleidoun,* to lock in, from *kleis* (stem *kleid-*), key.]

cleis·tog·a·mous (klī-stóggəməss) *adj.* Also **cleis·to·gam·ic** (klīstə-gámmik). *Botany.* Characterised by self-fertilisation in an unopened, budlike state, as in the violet. [Greek *kleistos,* closed + -GAMOUS.] —**cleis·tog·a·mous·ly** *adv.* —**cleis·tog·a·my** *n.*

cleis·to·the·ci·um (klīstə-thée-si-əm ‖ -shī-) *n. Botany.* In fungi, a type of ascocarp in which the ascospores are completely enclosed and released by decay of its wall. [Greek *kleistos,* closed + New Latin *-thecium,* case, from Greek *thēkē,* case.]

Cle·land (kéllənd, kléeländ), **John** (1709–89). English author, best known for the racy novel *Fanny Hill* (1748–49).

clem·a·tis (klémmə-tiss, kli-máy-) *n.* Any of various northern temperate plants or vines of the genus *Clematis,* many of which are cultivated as ornamentals, having white or variously coloured flowers and plumelike seeds. Also **traveller's joy.** [New Latin *Clematis,* from Latin *clēmatis,* from Greek *klēmatis,* from *klēma,* twig.]

Cle·men·ceau (klém-ən-sō, -ON- ‖ -sṓ), **Georges (Eugène Benjamin)** (1841–1929). French statesman and prime minister (1906–09, 1917–20), whose polemical style earned him the nickname "The Tiger". He played a key role in negotiating the Treaty of Versailles (1919).

clem·en·cy (klémmən-si) *n., pl.* **-cies. 1.** Mildness of temper, especially towards an offender or enemy; leniency; mercy. **2.** Mildness, especially of weather. —See Synonyms at **mercy.**

clem·ent (klémmənt) *adj.* **1.** Lenient or merciful in disposition. **2.** Mild. Said of weather or climate. [Middle English, from Latin *clēmēns†* (stem *clēment-*), gentle.] —**clem·ent·ly** *adv.*

Cle·men·ti (kli-ménti, kle-), **Muzio** (1752–1832). Italian pianist and composer, noted for his many piano studies and sonatas.

clem·en·tine (klémmən-teen, -tīn) *n.* A type of citrus fruit resembling a tangerine, possibly a hybrid between a tangerine and an orange. [French *clémentine,* probably from the feminine name.]

clench (klench) *tr.v.* **clenched, clenching, clenches. 1.** To bring together (hands or teeth) tightly; close up: *a clenched fist.* **2.** To grasp or grip tightly. **3.** To clinch (a nail or bolt, for example). **4.** *Nautical.* To fasten with a clinch. ~*n.* **1.** A tight grip or grasp. **2.** Anything that clenches or holds fast, such as a mechanical device. **3.** *Nautical.* A kind of knot, a **clinch** *(see).* [Middle English *clenchen,* Old English *beclencan.*]

cle·o·me (kli-ṓmi) *n.* Any of various mostly tropical plants of the genus *Cleome;* especially, *C. spinosa,* cultivated for its clusters of white or purplish flowers with long, conspicuous stamens. [New Latin *Cleome†.*]

Cle·on (klée-ən, -on) (died 422 B.C.). Athenian statesman and orator, known for his vigorous opposition to Sparta and its allies in the Peloponnesian War.

Cle·o·pat·ra VII (klée-ə-páttrə, -paátrə) (69–30 B.C.). Queen of Egypt (51–48 B.C., 47–30 B.C.) noted for her beauty and charisma. She had Julius Caesar and Mark Antony as lovers.

clepe (kleep) *tr.v.* **cleped** (klept, kleept) or **clept, cleping, clepes.** Also *past participle* **ycleped** or **yclept** (i-klépt, -kléept). *Archaic.* To call by the name of; name. [Middle English *clepen,* to speak, call out, Old English *cleopian, clipian†,* to call out, call by name.]

clep·sy·dra (klépsid-rə, klep-sid-) *n., pl.* **-dras** or **-drae** (-ree). An ancient device that measured time by marking the regulated flow of water through a small opening. Also called "water clock". [Latin, from Greek *klepsudra,* "water stealer" (from the "stealthy" flow of the water): *kleps-,* stem of *kleptein,* to steal + *hudōr,* water.]

clere·sto·ry (kléer-stəri, klérrə-, -tawri ‖ -stōri) *n., pl.* **-ries.** Also *chiefly U.S.* **clear·sto·ry. 1.** The upper part of the nave, transepts, and choir of a church, containing windows. **2.** Any similar windowed wall or construction used for light and ventilation. [Middle English : *clere,* lighted, CLEAR + STOREY (of a building).]

cler·gy (klérji) *n., pl.* **-gies.** The body of women and men ordained for religious service. Compare **laity.** [Middle English *clergie,* from Old French (influenced by *clerge,* body of clerks), from *clerc,* ecclesiastic, CLERK.]

cler·gy·man (klérji-mən) *n., pl.* **-men** (-mən). *Abbr.* **cl.** A male member of the clergy.

clergyman's throat *n.* Hoarseness after a long period of talking, especially as suffered by professional speechmakers.

cler·gy·wom·an (klérji-wŏŏmən) *n., pl.* **-women** (-wimmin). A female member of the clergy.

cler·ic (klérrik) *n.* A member of the clergy. [Medieval Latin *clēricus,* CLERK.]

cler·i·cal (klérrik'l) *adj.* **1. a.** Of or pertaining to clerks or office workers. **b.** Of, pertaining to, or designating office work such as filing and correspondence. **2.** Of, pertaining to, or characteristic of the clergy or a member of the clergy. **3.** Advocating clericalism. ~*n.* **1.** A member of the clergy. **2.** *Plural.* The distinctive garb of a member of the clergy. **3.** A person or party advocating clericalism. —**cler·i·cal·ly** *adv.*

clerical collar *n.* A stiff white collar in the shape of a band fastening at the back of the neck, worn by clerics. Also informally called "dog collar".

cler·i·cal·ism (klérrik'l-iz'm) *n.* A policy of supporting the power or influence of the clergy in secular matters. —**cler·i·cal·ist** *n.*

cler·i·hew (klérri-hew) *n.* A humorous rhyming quatrain about a person whose name generally serves as one of the rhymes. [After Edmund *Clerihew* BENTLEY, writer who invented it.]

cler·i·sy (klérri-si) *n.* Educated people as a class; the literati. [German *Klerisei,* from Medieval Latin *clērica,* the clergy, from Late Latin *clēricus,* CLERK.]

clerk (klark ‖ *U.S.* klerk) *n.* **1.** A person who works in an office performing such tasks as keeping records, attending to correspondence, or filing. **2.** A person who keeps the records and performs the regular business of a court or legislative body. **3.** A person who oversees building works. Also called "clerk of (the) works". **4.** A judge's secretary at a racecourse or racetrack. Also called "clerk of the course". **5.** *Anglican Church.* A lay minister who helps the parish clergyman to perform his duties. **6.** *Archaic.* A clergyman. **7.** *Archaic.* **a.** A literate person. **b.** A scholar. ~*intr.v.* **clerked, clerking, clerks.** To work or serve as a clerk. [Middle English, from Old English and Old French *clerc,* from Late Latin *clēricus,* a cleric, from Greek *klērikos,* belonging to inheritance, cleric (with reference to the Levites whose only inheritance was the Lord), from *klēros,* allotment, inheritance.] —**clerk·dom** *n.* —**clerk·ship** *n.*

clerk·ess (klaar-késs ‖ kler-) *n. Rare.* A female clerk.

clerk·ly (klárk-li ‖ *U.S.* klérk-li) *adj.* **-lier, -liest. 1.** Of or pertaining to a clerk or clerks. **2.** *Archaic.* Scholarly. —**clerk·li·ness** *n.*

Cleve·land (kléev-lənd). From 1974 to 1997 a small county in N.E. England, centred on the industrial region of Teesside.

clev·er (klévvər) *adj.* **cleverer, cleverest. 1.** Mentally quick and original; bright. **2.** Nimble with the hands; dexterous. **3.** Showing quick-wittedness; ingenious: *a clever story.* **4.** *Informal.* Superficial or contrived. —See Synonyms below and at **intelligent.** [Probably from Middle English *cliver,* expert to seize, dexterous, perhaps from Scandinavian; akin to Old Norse *kleyfr.*] —**clev·er·ly** *adv.* —**clev·er·ness** *n.*

Synonyms: *clever, cunning, ingenious, shrewd.*

clev·er-clev·er (klévvər-klévvər) *adj. Informal.* Ostentatiously clever. Used derogatorily.

clever dick, clever Dick *n. Informal.* An ostentatiously clever or knowing person. Used derogatorily.

clev·is (klévviss) *n.* A U-shaped metal piece with holes in each end through which a pin or bolt is run, used for attaching a drawbar to a plough, for example. [Probably plural of *clevi,* "cleft instrument", from Scandinavian, akin to Old Norse *klofi,* cleft, fissure.]

clew¹ (klōō ‖ klew) *n.* **1.** *Archaic.* A ball of yarn or thread. **2.** *Greek Mythology.* The ball of thread used by Theseus as a guide through the labyrinth of Minos on Crete. **3.** *Plural.* The cords by which a hammock is suspended. **4.** *Nautical.* **a.** One of the two lower corners of a square sail. **b.** The lower aft corner of a fore-and-aft sail. ~*tr.v.* **clewed, clewing, clews. 1.** To roll or coil into a ball. **2.** *Nautical.* To raise the lower corners of (a square sail) by means of clew lines. Used with *up.* [Middle English *clewe(n),* Old English *cliewen, clewe(n).*]

clew² Variant of **clue.**

clew line *n.* A rope used to raise the clew of a sail up to the yard or mast.

cli·an·thus (kli-ánthəss) *n.* Any of several plants of the genus *Clianthus,* native to Indochina, Australia, and New Zealand, having showy clusters of elongated scarlet flowers.

cli·ché (kléeshay ‖ *U.S.* klee-sháy) *n.* **1.** A trite or overused expression or idea. **2.** *Printing.* A stereotype or electrotype plate. [French, "stereotyped", from *clicher,* to stereotype (imitative of the sound made when the matrix is dropped into the molten metal to make a stereotype plate).]

Synonyms: *cliché, bromide, truism, commonplace, banality.*

cli·chéd (kléeshayd ‖ *U.S.* klee-sháyd) *adj.* Hackneyed; trite.

click (klik) *n.* **1.** A brief, sharp, nonresonant sound: *the click of a door latch.* **2.** A mechanical device that snaps into position, such as a detent or pawl. **3.** *Phonetics.* An oral ingressive speech sound, common in some African languages, which is produced by drawing air into the mouth and clicking the tongue. Also called "suction stop". ~*v.* **clicked, clicking, clicks.** —*intr.* **1.** To produce one or a series of clicks. **2.** *Slang.* **a.** To become a success. **b.** To establish an immediate rapport. **c.** To become clear; fall into place. —*tr.* To cause to click. [Imitative.] —**click·er** *n.*

click beetle *n.* Any of various beetles of the family Elateridae, characterised by the ability to right itself from an overturned position by flipping into the air with a clicking sound. Also called "snapping beetle", "skipjack".

click languages *pl.n.* A set of African languages employing the phonetic click, including the **Khoisan** *(see)* family and the Nguni group.

cli·ent (klī-ənt) *n.* **1.** One for whom services, usually professional services, are rendered. **2.** A customer or patron. **3.** One dependent on the patronage of another. **4.** One receiving the attention and care of a social worker or doctor. [Middle English, from Old French, from Latin *cliēns* (stem *client-*), dependent, follower, earlier *cluēns*, from *cluere*, to follow, obey.] —**cli·en·tal** (klī-ént'l) *adj.* —**cli·ent·ship** *n.*

cli·en·tele (klée-ON-tél, -ən-, -tayl ‖ klī-) *n.* Customers, patrons, or clients of a shop, restaurant, professional person, or the like, considered collectively. [French *clientèle*, from Latin *clientēla*, from *cliēns*, CLIENT.]

client state *n.* A country that is economically or politically dependent on a larger or more powerful state.

cliff (klif) *n.* A high, steep, or overhanging face of rock. [Middle English *clif*, Old English *clif*, from Germanic *klibam* (unattested).] —**cliff·y** *adj.*

cliff dweller *n.* **1.** A member of certain prehistoric Indian tribes of the southwestern United States who lived in caves in the sides of cliffs. **2.** *U.S. Slang.* A person who lives in a block of flats, especially in a city. —**cliff-dwel·ling** *adj.*

cliff·hang·er (klíf-hang-ər) *n.* **1.** A situation of great suspense occurring usually at the end of a chapter in a book, scene in a film, or episode in a serial. **2.** A serial in which each episode ends in suspense. **3.** A situation, as in a competition or election, in which the outcome is uncertain until the very end. —**cliff·hang·ing** *adj.*

cli·mac·ter·ic (klī-máktərik, klímak-térrik) *n.* **1. a.** The **menopause** *(see).* **b.** A corresponding period in the male, marked by a reduction in sexual activity. **2.** *Archaic.* A critical period or year in a person's life when major changes in health or fortune take place. **3.** *Botany.* The increase in respiration rate associated with fruit ripening and senescence. **4.** Any critical period. ~*adj.* Also **cli·mac·ter·i·cal** (klímak-térrik'l). Pertaining to a critical stage, period, or year. [Latin *clīmactēricus*, from Greek *klimaktērikos*, from *klimaktēr*, rung of a ladder, crisis, from *klimax*, ladder. See **climax**.]

cli·mac·tic (klī-máktik) *adj.* Pertaining to or constituting a climax. —**cli·mac·ti·cal·ly** *adv.*

cli·ma·gram, cli·mo·gram (klímə-gram) *n.* A **climograph**.

climagraph. Variant of **climograph**.

cli·mate (klīm-ət, -it) *n.* **1.** The meteorological conditions, including temperature, rainfall, and wind, that characteristically prevail in a particular region. **2.** A region having particular meteorological conditions. **3.** A prevailing set of attitudes or opinions in human affairs: *the political climate.* [Middle English *climat*, from Old French, from Late Latin *clīma*, climate, zone of latitude, from Greek *klima*, sloping surface of the earth.] —**cli·mat·ic** (klī-máttik), **cli·ma·tal** (klímət'l), **cli·mat·i·cal** *adj.* —**cli·mat·i·cal·ly** *adv.*

cli·mat·o·graph (klī-máttə-graaf, klímətə-, -graf) *n.* *Meteorology.* A circular graph showing the yearly variations of average temperature (as distance from centre) against time of year (as angular position). [CLIMATE + -GRAPH.]

cli·ma·tol·o·gy (klī-mə-tólləji) *n.* The meteorological study of climate. [CLIMATE(E) + -LOGY.] —**cli·ma·to·log·ic** (-tə-lójik), **cli·ma·to·log·i·cal** *adj.* —**cli·ma·tol·o·gist** (-tóllǝjist) *n.*

cli·max (klí-maks) *n.* **1. a.** The point of greatest intensity, excitement, or interest in any series or progression of events; the culmination. **b.** Such a point in a literary or dramatic work. **2.** An orgasm. **3.** *Rhetoric.* **a.** A series of statements or ideas in an ascending order of force or intensity. **b.** The final statement in such a series. **4.** The stage in ecological development or evolution in which the community of organisms becomes stable. —See Synonyms at **summit**. ~*v.* **climaxed, -maxing, -maxes.** —*intr.* To reach a climax. —*tr.* To bring to a climax. [Latin, rhetorical climax, from Greek *klimax*, ladder.]

climax community *n.* *Ecology.* The mature or stabilised stage in a successional series of communities, usually associated with maximum complexity, when dominant species are completely adapted to environmental conditions, as in tropical rain forests.

climb (klīm) *v.* **climbed** or *archaic* **clomb** (klōm), **climbing, climbs.** —*tr.* To move up or mount, especially by using the hands and feet; ascend. —*intr.* **1.** To rise to a higher position; move upwards: *The sun climbed in the sky.* **2.** To rise slowly or with effort in rank, status, or fortune. **3.** To slant or slope upwards. **4.** To grow in an upward direction, as some plants do, by twining about or clinging to another object for support. **5.** To move in a specified direction by or as if by clambering: *climbed out of the window.* —See Synonyms at **rise**. ~*n.* **1.** An act of climbing; an ascent. **2.** A place to be climbed. [Climb, clomb; Middle English *climben, clomb*, Old English *climban, clamb* (or *clomb*).] —**climb·a·ble** (klímǝb'l) *adj.*

Usage: Both *up* and *down* are used with this verb in standard English. *Climb up* has been said to contain an unnecessary element, in that climbing implies ascent. By the same token, *climb down* is said to be self-contradictory, but both uses are well-established.

climb down *intr.v.* **1.** To move downwards or descend by using the limbs. **2.** To retreat from a position one has taken up; back down in an argument or dispute. ~*tr.v.* To descend by using the limbs.

climb-down (klīm-down) *n.* An act of yielding or backing down in an argument or dispute.

climb·er (klímǝr) *n.* **1.** Something or someone that climbs; especially, a person who climbs mountains. **2.** *Informal.* A person seeking to gain a higher social or professional position. Used derogatorily. **3.** A plant that grows upwards by clinging to or twining about something.

climb·ing frame (klíming) *n.* A structure, usually of metal tubing, for children to climb on.

climbing irons *pl.n.* Iron bars with spikes or spurs attached, which are strapped to a shoe or boot and used in climbing telegraph poles, trees, or ice slopes.

clime (klīm) *n.* *Poetic.* Climate or region. [Middle English, region of the earth, zone, from Late Latin *clīma*, CLIMATE.]

–clinal *adj. comb. form.* Indicates a slope or inclination; for example, **anticlinal, synclinal.** [CLINE + -AL.]

cli·mo·graph, cli·ma·graph (klímə-graaf, -graf) *n.* *Meteorology.* A graph in which one climatic feature at a location is plotted against another, for example temperature against humidity. Also called "climagram", "climogram". [CLIMATE + -GRAPH.]

clin-. Variant of **clino-**.

cli·nan·dri·um (kli-nán-dri-əm) *n., pl.* **-dria** (-dri-ə). *Botany.* A hollow containing the anther in the upper part of the column of an orchid. [New Latin, "stamen bed" : CLIN(O)- + *-andrium*, "stamen", from Greek *anēr* (stem *andr-*), man.]

clinch (klinch) *v.* **clinched, clinching, clinches.** —*tr.* **1.** To fix or secure (a nail or bolt, for example) by bending down or flattening the end that has been driven through something. **2.** To fasten together in this way. **3.** To settle definitely and conclusively; make final. **4.** *Nautical.* To fasten with a clinch. —*intr.* **1.** In boxing and wrestling, to hold the opponent's body with one or both arms to prevent or hinder his movements. **2.** *Informal.* To embrace. ~*n.* **1.** The act of clinching. **2.** Something that clinches, such as a clinched nail or clamp. **3.** The clinched part of a nail, bolt, rivet, or the like. **4.** In boxing and wrestling, the act or an instance of clinching. **5.** *Nautical.* A knot in a rope made by a half hitch with the end of the rope fastened back by seizing. Also called "clench". **6.** *Informal.* An amorous or romantic embrace. [Variant of CLENCH.]

clinch·er (klínchǝr) *n.* **1.** One that clinches; specifically, a tool for clinching nails or bolts. **2.** *Informal.* A decisive point, fact, or remark, as in an argument.

clincher-built. Variant of **clinker-built.**

cline (klīn) *n.* **1.** *Ecology.* A continuous variation in form within members of a species or population, resulting from gradual changes or transitions in the environment over a wide range. **2.** Loosely, a continuum. [Greek *klinein*, to slope, lean.]

–cline *n. comb. form.* Indicates slope; for example, **anticline, syncline.** [Greek *klinein*, to slope.]

cling (kling) *intr.v.* **clung** (klung), **clinging, clings. 1.** To hold fast or adhere to something, as by grasping, sticking, or entwining. **2. a.** To stay near; remain close. **b.** To resist separation. **3.** To hold on, often stubbornly; remain attached: *cling to old-fashioned ideas.* [Cling, clung (past tense), clung (past participle); Middle English *clingen, clung* (past singular), *clungen* (past plural), *clungen,* Old English *clingan, clang, clungon, clungen.*] —**cling·er** *n.*

Cling Film *n.* A trademark for a type of thin transparent plastic film that readily clings to any surface and is used especially for covering food to keep it fresh.

cling·fish (kling-fish) *n., pl.* **-fishes** or collectively **clingfish.** Any of various small marine fishes of the family Gobiesocidae, having an adhesive disc under the front part of the body, by which it fastens itself to rocks and seaweed.

cling peach *n.* A clingstone peach.

cling·stone (klíng-stōn) *n.* A fruit, especially a peach, having pulp that adheres partially to the stone. Compare **freestone.** —**cling·stone** *adj.*

cling·y (klíng-i) *adj.* **-gier, -giest.** Tending to cling: *a clingy dress; a clingy husband.*

clin·ic (klínnik) *n.* **1.** An establishment, often a department of a hospital specialising in a particular branch of medicine, devoted to the treatment and care of out-patients. **2.** A private hospital or nursing home. **3.** *Chiefly U.S.* A group meeting or seminar devoted to the study of problems in a particular field, or an institution where such meetings take place: *a writers' clinic.* [French *clinique*, originally "a bedridden person", from Greek *klinikē*, medical treatment at sickbed, from *klinikos*, "of a bed", doctor who visits bedridden persons, from *klinē*, bed.]

–clinic *adj. comb. form.* Indicates: **1.** Inclination or slope; for example, **isoclinic. 2.** A specified number of oblique axial intersections; for example, **triclinic.** [-CLINE + -IC.]

clin·i·cal (klínnik'l) *adj.* **1.** Pertaining to or connected with a clinic. **2.** Of or pertaining to direct observation and treatment of patients: *a clinical lecture.* **3.** Analytical; highly objective; rigorously scientific: *clinical details.* **4.** Suggestive of a hospital or clinic; austere; antiseptic: *a clinical style of decor.* ~*n.* A class in which medical students are instructed in the examination and treatment of patients at the bedside. —**clin·i·cal·ly** *adv.*

clinical thermometer *n.* A thermometer used to measure body temperature; especially, a small mercury-in-glass thermometer designed with a kink in the base so that the mercury thread stays in position when the instrument is removed from the body.

cli·ni·cian (kli-nísh'n) *n.* A doctor, psychologist, or psychiatrist specialising in clinical studies or practice. [French *clinicien,* from *clinique,* CLINIC.]

clink[1] (klingk) *n.* A soft, sharp, ringing sound.
~*v.* **clinked, clinking, clinks.** —*intr.* To make a clink. —*tr.* To cause to clink. [Middle English, from Middle Dutch *klinken.*]

clink[2] *n. Slang.* Prison. [16th century (as *the Clink,* name of former prison in Southwark) : origin obscure.]

clink·er (klíngkər) *n.* **1.** The incombustible residue, fused into irregular lumps, that remains after the combustion of coal. **2.** A partially vitrified brick or a mass of bricks fused together. **3.** An extremely hard burnt brick. **4.** Vitrified matter expelled by a volcano. **5.** *U.S. Slang.* A mistake or fault, especially in music.
~*intr.v.* **clinkered, -ering, -ers.** To form clinker while burning. [Earlier *clincart, klincard,* from obsolete Dutch *klinckaerd,* "one that clinks" (from its clinking sound when struck), from Middle Dutch *klinken, clinken,* CLINK.]

clink·er-built (klíngkər-bilt) *adj.* Also **clinch·er-built** (klínchər-). Built with overlapping planks or boards. Said of ships or boats. Compare **carvel-built.** [From *clinker,* a fastening or clinching with nails, from Middle English *clinken,* probably variant of *clenchen,* CLENCH.]

clino–, clin– *comb. form.* Indicates slope or slant; for example, **clinometer, clinandrium.** [New Latin, from Greek *klinein,* to slope, and *klinē,* bed.]

cli·nom·e·ter (klī-nómmitər, kli-) *n.* An instrument for measuring the angle of an incline, as of an embankment. Also called "inclinometer". [CLINO- + -METER.] —**cli·no·met·ric** (-nə-méttrik), **cli·no·met·ri·cal** *adj.* —**cli·nom·e·try** (-nómmətri) *n.*

cli·no·stat (klīnō-stat) *n. Botany.* An apparatus used to study plant growth, consisting of a rotating disc to which the plant is attached. Rotation ensures that all parts of the plant receive identical stimulation, for example from light or gravity. [CLINO- + -STAT.]

clin·quant (klíngkənt) *adj. Archaic.* Adorned with gold or silver.
~*n. Archaic.* Imitation gold leaf; tinsel. [French, "glistening", from *clinquer,* to glitter, clink, from Middle Dutch *clinken,* CLINK.]

clint (klint) *n. Geology.* Any of a number of irregularly shaped blocks making up a type of flat, exposed limestone formation. [Middle English, perhaps from Scandinavian; akin to Danish and Swedish *klint,* Old Norse *klettr,* cliff.]

Clin·ton (klíntən), **William Jefferson,** known as Bill Clinton (1946–). U.S. Democratic politician, 42nd President of the United States (1993–). He rose from an impoverished childhood to become State Governor of Arkansas in 1979; at the age of 32, the country's youngest sitting governor. At 46 he became the third youngest president in U.S. history. Re-elected 1996.

clin·to·ni·a (klin-tōni-ə) *n.* Any plant of the genus *Clintonia,* having narrow leaves, white, greenish-yellow, or purplish flowers, and usually blue berries. [New Latin, after De Witt *Clinton* (1769–1828), U.S. statesman.]

Cli·o (klī-ō). *Greek Mythology.* The Muse of history. [Latin *Clīō,* from Greek *Kleiō,* "teller", from *kleiein, kleein,* to tell, praise.]

cli·o·met·rics (klī-ə-méttriks) *n. Used with a singular verb.* The use of statistics in the study of history. —**cli·o·met·ric** *adj.*

clip[1] (klip) *tr.v.* **clipped, clipping, clips. 1.** To cut off or cut out with or as if with scissors or shears: *clip an article from a newspaper; clipped three seconds off the record.* **2.** To make shorter by cutting; trim. **3.** To cut off the edge of: *clip a coin.* **4. a.** To cut short (a word or words) by leaving out letters or syllables. **b.** To enunciate with clarity and precision: *clipped speech.* **5.** *British.* To punch a hole in (a ticket). **6.** *Informal.* To hit with a sharp blow. **7.** *Chiefly U.S. Slang.* To cheat or overcharge.
~*n.* **1.** The act of clipping. **2.** A short extract from a film, especially when shown on television. **3. a.** The wool shorn at one shearing. **b.** A season's shearing. **4.** *Informal.* A quick, sharp blow: *a clip on the ear.* **5.** *Informal.* A brisk pace. [Middle English *clippen,* from Old Norse *klippa*†, to cut short.]

clip[2] *n.* **1.** A device for holding things together; a clasp; a fastener. **2.** A piece of jewellery fastened by a clip; a brooch. **3.** A **cartridge clip** *(see).* **4.** A **hairclip** *(see).*
~*tr.v.* **clipped, clipping, clips.** To fasten with a clip. [Middle English *clipp,* from *clippen,* to embrace, fasten, Old English *clyppan.*]

clip·board (klíp-bawrd ‖ -bōrd) *n.* A small writing board with a spring clip at the top for holding papers or a writing pad.

clip joint *n. Slang.* A restaurant or place of public entertainment where customers are overcharged or otherwise defrauded.

clip-on (klíp-on) *adj.* Designating an article that is attached by means of a clip: *clip-on earrings; a clip-on bow tie.*

clip·per (klíppər) *n.* **1.** One who cuts, clips, or shears. **2.** *Plural.* An instrument or tool for cutting, clipping, or shearing: *nail clippers.* **3.** A sharp-bowed sailing vessel of the mid-19th century, having tall masts and sharp lines and built for great speed. **4.** *Electronics.* A **limiter** *(see).*

clip·ping (klípping) *n.* **1.** Something that is cut off or out: *nail clippings.* **2.** *Chiefly U.S.* An item cut out of a newspaper; a cutting.

clique (kleek ‖ klik) *n.* An exclusive group of friends or associates. See Synonyms at **circle.** [French, from Old French, probably "a group of applauders", from *cliquer,* to click, clap (imitative).]

cli·quish (kléekish ‖ klíckish) *adj.* Also **cli·quey, cli·quy** (kléeki ‖ klicki). Of, like, or characteristic of a clique; exclusive. —**cli·quish·ly** *adv.* —**cli·quish·ness** *n.*

cli·tel·lum (kli-téllәm, klī-) *n., pl.* **-tella** (-téllə). A swollen, glandular, saddle-like region in the epidermis of certain annelid worms, such as the earthworm, serving to bind worms together during copulation. [New Latin, from Latin *clītellae,* packsaddle.]

clit·o·rid·ec·to·my (klíttərid-éktəmi) *n.* The ritualistic mutilation of the clitoris, as performed on prepubertal girls in certain cultures. [New Latin *clitoris* (stem *clitorid-*), CLITORIS + -ECTOMY.]

clit·o·ris (klíttə-riss; *rarely* klītə-) *n.* A part of the female genitalia lying in front of the vagina and urethra, consisting of a small, highly sensitive, erectile organ, which plays a major role in the female orgasm. [New Latin, from Greek *kleitoris,* "little hill", diminutive of *kleitor-* (unattested), hill, from *klinein,* to incline.] —**clit·o·ral** (-rəl) *adj.*

Clive of Plassey (klīv), **Robert, Baron,** also known as Clive of India (1725–74). British soldier and statesman, famous for securing British interests in India.

clo·a·ca (klō-áy-kə) *n., pl.* **-cae** (-see, -kee). **1.** *Zoology.* The cavity into which the intestinal, genital, and urinary tracts open in vertebrates such as fish, reptiles, birds, and some primitive mammals. **2.** A sewer. [Latin *cloāca,* sewer, canal.] —**clo·a·cal** (-k'l) *adj.*

cloak (klōk) *n.* **1.** A loose outer garment, usually sleeveless. **2.** Anything that covers or conceals.
~*tr.v.* **cloaked, cloaking, cloaks. 1.** To cover with a cloak. **2.** To cover up; hide; conceal. —See Synonyms at **hide.** [Middle English *cloke,* from Old French *cloque,* bell, "bell-shaped garment". See **clock.**]

cloak-and-dagger (klōk-ən-dággər) *adj.* Concerned with or suggestive of melodramatic intrigue.

cloak·room (klōk-rŏŏm, -rōōm) *n.* **1.** A room where coats and other articles may be left temporarily, as in a school or theatre. Also *U.S.* "checkroom". **2.** *British.* A lavatory. Used euphemistically.

clob·ber[1] (klóbbər) *tr.v.* **-bered, -bering, -bers.** *Slang.* **1.** To strike violently and repeatedly; batter or maul. **2.** To defeat completely. **3.** To criticise or condemn harshly. [20th century : origin obscure; perhaps akin to *club* (to beat).]

clobber[2] *n. British Slang.* **1.** Belongings; equipment. **2.** Clothes. [19th century : origin obscure.]

cloche (klosh, klōsh) *n.* **1.** A semicylindrical or bell-shaped cover, usually of glass, used to protect young plants. **2.** A close-fitting woman's hat with a bell-like shape. [French, bell, from Old French, bell, CLOCK.]

clock[1] (klok) *n.* **1.** An instrument for measuring or indicating time; especially, a mechanical device with a numbered dial and moving hands or pointers. **2.** Any of various scientific devices for the accurate measurement or standardisation of time. **3.** *Informal.* Any of various instruments that indicate measurement by a dial and pointer or by a digital display, such as a mileometer, speedometer, or the meter on a taxi. **4.** An electronic circuit that produces regular pulses. See **clock pulse. 5.** A **time clock** *(see).* **6.** *Botany.* The downy flower head of a dandelion that has gone to seed. —**put the clock back. 1.** To revert to outmoded practices or ideas; regress. **2.** To revert to a former, preferable, and idealised state of affairs.
~*v.* **clocked, clocking, clocks.** —*tr.* **1.** To record the time or speed of, as with a stopwatch. **2.** To register or record (a distance travelled, a speed attained, or the like). Used with *up.* **3.** *Electronics.* To regulate (a circuit) with clock pulses. **4.** *British Slang.* To punch; hit. —*intr.* **1.** To register the time of arrival at work. Used with *on* or *in.* **2.** To register the time of departure from work. Used with *off* or *out.* [Middle English *clok,* from Middle Dutch *clocke,* bell, clock, from Old French *cloche, cloque,* bell, from Late Latin *clocca* (imitative).] —**clock·er** *n.*

clock[2] *n.* An embroidered or woven decoration on the side of a stocking or sock. [Perhaps originally "a bell-shaped ornament", from Middle Dutch *clocke,* bell, CLOCK.]

clock radio *n.* An appliance that combines an alarm clock with a radio that can be set to start playing at a particular time.

clock-watch·er (klók-wochər) *n.* A person who continually checks the time while at work. —**clock-watch·ing** *n.*

clock·wise (klók-wīz) *adv.* In the same direction as the rotating hands of a clock. —**clock·wise** *adj.*

clock·work (klók-wurk) *n.* A mechanism of gears driven by a wound spring, as in a mechanical clock, toy, or the like. —**like clockwork.** With machine-like regularity and precision; perfectly. —**clock·work** *adj.*

clod (klod) *n.* **1.** A lump of earth or clay. **2.** Earth or soil. **3.** A dull, ignorant, or stupid person; an oaf. **4.** A cut of the shoulder of beef. [Middle English *clodde,* Old English *clod-* (only in compounds), variant of *clott,* lump.] —**clod·dish** *adj.* —**clod·dish·ness** *n.*

clod·hop·per (klód-hoppər) *n.* **1.** A clumsy, coarse person; a lout or bumpkin. **2.** *Plural.* Big, heavy shoes. [Originally "farmer" : CLOD (earth) + HOPPER.] —**clod·hop·ping** *adj.*

Cloe·te, (Edward Fairlie) Stuart (Graham) (klŏŏ-ti, -tə) (1897–1976). South African author. He produced a number of popular novels, including *Turning Wheels* (1937), *Rags of Glory* (1963), and *The Abductors* (1966). His non-fiction works include *African Portraits* and *The African Giant.*

clog (klog) *n.* **1.** A heavy wooden or wooden-soled shoe. **2.** A block or other weight attached to the leg of an animal to hinder movement. **3.** *Archaic.* An obstacle or hindrance. —**pop (one's) clogs.** *Slang.* To die.
~*v.* **clogged, clogging, clogs.** —*tr.* **1.** To block up; obstruct. **2.** To impede or encumber; hamper. —*intr.* **1.** To become obstructed or choked up. **2.** To thicken or stick together; coagulate.

[Middle English *clog, clogge*†, block of wood.] **—clog·gy** *adj.*
clog dance *n.* A dance performed wearing clogs and characterised by heavy, stamping steps.
cloi·son·né (klwa̋a-zónnay, klóy-, -zə-náy) *n.* **1.** A kind of enamelware in which the surface decoration is formed by different colours of enamel separated by thin strips of metal. **2.** The process or method of producing such enamelware.
∼*adj.* Of or designating this ware or method. [French, past participle of *cloisonner,* to partition, from Old French *cloison,* partition, from Vulgar Latin *clausiō* (unattested), enclosure, from Latin *claudere,* to close.]
clois·ter (klóystər) *n.* **1.** *Plural.* A covered walk with an open colonnade on one side, running along the walls of buildings that face a quadrangle. **2.** A place devoted to religious seclusion; especially, a monastery or convent. **3.** *Literary.* Life in a monastery or convent. Preceded by *the.*
∼*tr.v.* **cloistered, -tering, -ters.** **1.** To shut away from the world in or as if in a cloister; seclude. **2.** To furnish (a building) with a cloister. [Middle English *cloistre,* from Old French, variant of *clostre* (influenced by *cloison,* partition, CLOISONNÉ), from Medieval Latin *claustrum,* from Latin, enclosed place, from *claudere,* to close.]
clois·tral (klóystrəl) *adj.* Also **claus·tral** (kláwstrəl). Of, resembling, or suggesting a cloister; secluded. [Middle English *claustral,* from Medieval Latin *claustrālis,* from *claustrum,* CLOISTER.]
clomb. *Archaic.* Past tense and past participle of **climb.**
clomp (klomp). Variant of **clump.**
clone (klōn) *n.* **1.** A group of genetically identical cells descended from a single common ancestor. **2.** One or more organisms descended asexually from a single ancestor. **3.** An exact copy of a person or thing; a duplicate. Often used derogatorily.
∼*v.* **cloned, cloning, clones.** *—intr.* To create a genetic duplicate of an individual organism through asexual reproduction, as by stimulating a single cell or taking cuttings of plants. *—tr.* **1.** To duplicate (an organism) asexually by cloning. **2.** To create (a new organism) in this way. **3.** To create a duplicate of. [Greek *klōn,* twig, shoot.] **—clon·al** (klṓn'l) *adj.* **—clon·al·ly** *adv.*
clonk (klongk) *n.* A dull, metallic sound.
∼*v.* **clonked, clonking, clonks.** *—intr.* To make a clonk. *—tr.* **1.** To cause to clonk. **2.** *Informal.* To hit; punch.
clo·nus (klṓnəss) *n., pl.* **-nuses.** A convulsion characterised by rapidly alternating muscular contraction and relaxation. [New Latin, from Greek *klonos,* agitation, turmoil.] **—clo·nic** (klónnik; *rarely* klṓnik) *adj.* **—clo·nic·i·ty** (klo-níssəti, klō-), **clo·nism** (klónniz'm, klṓniz'm) *n.*
clop (klop) *n.* The sound of a horse's hoof striking a paved surface.
∼*intr.v.* **clopped, clopping, clops.** To make or move with this sound. [Imitative.]
close (klōss) *adj.* **closer, closest.** **1.** A small distance away or apart; not far off in space or time; near. **2.** Near in relationship: *close relatives.* **3.** Having all elements or parts near to each other; compact; dense: *a close weave.* **4.** Near the surface; short: *a close haircut.* **5.** Nearly even; decided by a narrow margin: *a close finish.* **6.** Fitting tightly. **7.** Not deviating substantially from an original or model: *a close resemblance.* **8.** Complete; thorough; rigorous: *a close examination.* **9.** Bound by mutual interests, loyalties, or affection: *close friends.* **10.** Enclosed or confined. **11.** Confined to specific persons or groups; restricted: *a close secret.* **12.** Heavily guarded; allowing no means of escape: *under close arrest.* **13.** Secretive in manner; reticent. **14.** Not generous; miserly. **15.** Airless; stuffy; oppressive. **16.** *Phonetics.* Spoken with the tongue near the palate. Said of vowels. —See Synonyms at **familiar, stingy.**
∼*v.* (klōz) **closed, closing, closes.** *—tr.* **1.** To shut. **2.** To bar or obstruct: *The road is closed for repairs.* **3.** To bring together all the elements of; end; finish. **4.** To bring to an end, temporarily or permanently, the operations of (a business establishment, factory, or the like). **5.** To settle (an account) finally, by withdrawing any money credited to it and settling outstanding debts. **6.** To join or unite; bring into contact: *close a circuit.* **7.** *Archaic.* To enclose on all sides. *—intr.* **1.** To become shut. **2.** To finish or conclude. **3.** To cease operations, temporarily or permanently. **4.** To engage at close quarters; begin to fight. Used with *with.* **5.** To reach an agreement; come to terms. Used with *with.* **6.** To have a specified value at the end of the day's trading: *Gold closed at 520 dollars an ounce.* —See Synonyms at **complete.** **—close in.** To surround and advance upon, so as to eliminate the possibility of escape. Often used with *on* or *upon.* **—close out.** *U.S.* To dispose of (goods) usually at greatly reduced prices.
∼*n.* (klōz *for senses 1,2,3;* klōss *for senses 4,5*). **1.** A conclusion; a finish. **2.** The concluding part of a musical phrase or theme; a cadence. **3.** *Archaic.* A fight at close quarters. **4.** An enclosed place, especially land surrounding a cathedral. **5. a.** *Scottish.* A narrow passage or alley leading to the back of a house or to a common stairway in a block of flats. **b.** *British.* A cul-de-sac.
∼*adv.* (klōss). Closely. **—close on.** Approximately; practically. [Middle English *clos,* from Old French, from Latin *clausus,* past participle of *claudere,* to close.] **—close·ly** (klṓssli) *adv.* **—close·ness** (klṓss-nəss, -niss) *n.* **—clos·er** (klṓzər) *n.*
close call (klōss) *n. Informal.* A narrow escape.
close company (klōss) *n. British.* For the purposes of corporation tax, a company that is under the control of five or fewer shareholders, or of any number of shareholders who are directors.
closed (klōzd) *adj.* **1.** Having complete boundaries; enclosed. **2.** Blocked or barred to passage or entry. **3.** Having explicitly limited membership; restricted; exclusive. **4.** *Phonetics.* Ending in a consonant. Said of a syllable. **5.** *Geometry.* **a.** Of or pertaining to a curve, such as a circle, having no end points. **b.** Of or pertaining to a surface having no boundary curves.
closed book *n. Informal.* A person or matter that is not known or understood.
closed chain *n.* A chemical **ring** *(see).* Compare **open chain.**
closed circuit *n.* **1.** A television transmission circuit with a limited number of reception stations and no broadcasting facilities. **2.** An electric circuit providing an uninterrupted, endless path for the flow of current. Compare **open circuit.**
close down (klōz) *intr.v.* **1.** To stop or cease operations entirely. **2.** To end transmission for the day. Used of a radio or television station. **—close-down** (klṓz-down) *n.*
closed scholarship *n.* A scholarship for which only certain people, such as the children of servicemen, are eligible to compete.
closed shop *n.* A business or industrial establishment in which the employers have a contractual agreement with a particular trade union only to employ members of that union. Compare **open shop, union shop.**
close-fist·ed (klṓss-fístid) *adj.* Miserly; tight-fisted.
close-grained (klṓss-gráynd) *adj.* Dense or compact in structure or texture: *close-grained wood.*
close harmony (klōss) *n.* A singing arrangement in which the three upper parts lie close together, usually within an octave.
close-hauled (klṓss-háwld) *adv. Nautical.* With sails trimmed flat for sailing as close to the wind as possible. **—close-hauled** *adj.*
close-knit (klṓss-nít) *adj.* Bound together by social or cultural ties: *a close-knit village community.*
close packing (klōss) *n.* An arrangement of objects, such as spheres or atoms in a crystal, such that the total occupies the minimum possible volume. In the close packing of equal spheres each sphere has 12 near neighbours. **—close packed** *adj.*
close quarters (klōss) *pl.n.* Close range; close proximity. Used chiefly in the phrase *at close quarters.*
close season (klōss) *n.* The period in the year when the law prohibits the killing for sport of certain animals, birds, and fish. Compare **open season.**
close shave (klōss) *n. Informal.* A narrow escape.
close stitch (klōss) *n.* The **buttonhole stitch** *(see).*
clos·et (klózzit || *U.S. also* kláwzit) *n. Abbr.* **cl.** **1.** *Chiefly U.S.* A small room, cabinet, or recess for storing linens or supplies, hanging clothes, or the like. **2.** *Archaic.* A small private chamber for studying, meditating, praying, or the like. **3.** A water closet; a toilet. **—come out of the closet.** To give up concealing proclivities, opinions, or affiliations considered undesirable by others.
∼*tr.v.* **closeted, -eting, -ets.** To enclose or shut up in a private room, as for discussion or meditation. Usually used reflexively.
∼*adj.* **1.** Secret; covert: *a closet queen.* **2.** *U.S.* Based upon theory and speculation rather than practice: *closet plans.* [Middle English, from Old French, diminutive of *clos,* enclosure, from Medieval Latin *clausum,* from Latin *clausus,* enclosed, CLOSE.]
close up (klōz) *tr.v.* **1.** To close entirely. **2.** To bring nearer together. *—intr.v.* To come nearer together.
close-up (klṓss-up) *n.* **1.** A picture, such as a film or television shot, taken at close range. **2.** A close or intimate view or description.
clos·ing time (klṓzing) *n.* In Britain, the time at which pubs or bars close business every afternoon and evening. Compare **opening time.**
clos·trid·i·um (kloss-tríddi-əm) *n., pl.* **-tridia** (-tríddi-ə). Any of various rod-shaped, spore-forming, chiefly anaerobic bacteria of the genus *Clostridium,* including some of the nitrogen-fixing bacteria found in soil and those causing botulism and tetanus. [New Latin, "small spindle", from Greek *klōstēr,* spindle, from *klōthein,* to spin. See **Clotho.**]
clo·sure (klṓzhər) *n.* **1.** The act of closing or the condition of being closed. **2.** Something that closes or shuts. **3.** A finish; a conclusion. **4.** In the House of Commons or other deliberative bodies, a procedure whereby a debate may be ended by majority agreement, and the question put to the vote, even though some members may still wish to speak. In this sense, also *U.S.* "cloture". **5.** *Geology.* The vertical distance from the highest point of a structure and the lowest surrounding contour. **6.** *Mathematics.* The property of an algebraic structure, such as a group, by which combinations of elements produce other elements that belong to the set.
∼*tr.v.* **closured, -suring, -sures.** To end (a debate) by closure. [Middle English, from Old French, from Latin *clausūra,* from *clausus,* enclosed, CLOSE.]
clot (klot) *n.* **1.** A thick, viscous, or coagulated mass or lump, as of blood. **2.** *British Slang.* A stupid person; an idiot.
∼*v.* **clotted, clotting, clots.** *—intr.* To form into clots. *—tr.* To cause to clot; fill or cover with clots. [Middle English *clot,* Old English *clott,* lump.]
cloth (kloth || klawth) *n., pl.* **cloths** (kloths || klawthz, klawths, klothz). **1.** *Abbr.* **cl.** Fabric or material formed by weaving, knitting, pressing, or felting natural or synthetic fibres. **2.** A piece of fabric or material used for a specific purpose. Often used in combination: *tablecloth; dishcloth.* **3.** *Nautical.* **a.** Canvas. **b.** A sail. **4.** Professional attire or mode of dress. **—the cloth.** The clergy. [Middle English *cloth,* Old English *clāth,* from Germanic.] **—cloth** *adj.*
cloth·bound (klóth-bownd || kláwth-) *adj.* Designating a book bound in boards and covered with cloth.
cloth-cap (klóth-káp || kláwth-) *adj. British.* Of or considered as

characteristic of the working class: *a cloth-cap mentality.*
clothe (kloth) *tr.v.* **clothed** or **clad** (klad), **clothing, clothes. 1.** To put clothes on; dress. **2.** To cover as if with clothes. [Middle English *clothen, clathen,* Old English *clāthian,* from *clāth,* CLOTH.]
cloth-eared (klóth-eerd || kláwth-) *adj. Informal.* Hard of hearing.
clothes (klōthz; *sometimes* klōz) *pl.n.* **1.** Articles of dress; garments. **2. Bedclothes** *(see).* [Middle English, from Old English *clāthas,* plural of *clāth,* CLOTH.]
clothes·hanger (klōthz-hang-ər, klōz-) *n.* A **coat hanger** *(see).*
clothes horse *n.* **1.** A frame on which clothes are hung to dry or air. **2.** A person considered to be excessively concerned with dress.
clothes line *n.* A cord, rope, or wire on which clothes are hung to dry or air.
clothes moth *n.* Any of various moths of the family Tineidae, the larvae of which feed on wool, hair, fur, and feathers.
clothes·peg (klōthz-peg, klōz-) *n.* A clip of wood or plastic for fastening clothes to a clothes line. Also *U.S.* "clothes pin".
clothes pole *n.* A pole to which a clothes line is attached.
clothes prop *n.* A wooden or metal support, usually notched at one end, used to raise a clothes line.
cloth·ier (klōth-yər, -i-ər) *n.* One who deals in clothing, especially men's clothing.
cloth·ing (klōthing) *n.* **1.** Clothes collectively; attire. **2.** A covering.
Clo·tho (klōthō). *Greek Mythology.* One of the three **Fates** *(see).* [Greek *klōthō,* "spinner", from *klōthein,* to spin, akin to *kalathos,* CALATHUS.]
cloth of gold *n.* Silk or woollen cloth interwoven with gold threads.
clot·ted cream (klóttid) *n.* Thick cream made by scalding milk.
clo·ture (klōchər) *n. U.S.* A **closure** (debate procedure) *(see).*
cloud (klowd) *n.* **1.** A visible body of very fine droplets of water or particles of ice dispersed in the atmosphere above the earth's surface at various altitudes ranging up to several kilometres. **2.** Any visible mass in the air, as of steam, smoke, or dust. **3.** A large mass of things moving in the air; a swarm. **4.** Anything that darkens, threatens, or fills with gloom. **5.** A dark region or blemish on a polished stone or gem. **6.** An appearance of dimness or milkiness, as in glass or a liquid. **—have (one's) head in the clouds.** To be unpractical; live in a world of fantasy. **—under a cloud.** Under suspicion or out of favour.
~*v.* **clouded, clouding, clouds.** —*tr.* **1.** To cover with or as if with clouds; darken; dim. **2.** To make gloomy, sullen, or troubled. —*intr.* To become cloudy or overcast. Often used with *over* or *up.* [Middle English *cloud,* hill, mass of earth, cloud, Old English *clūd,* rock, hill.] **—cloud·less** *adj.* **—cloud·let** *n.*
cloud·ber·ry (klówd-berri, -bəri) *n., pl.* **-ries. 1.** A creeping plant, *Rubus chamaemorus,* of northern regions, having white flowers and edible fruit. **2.** The reddish-orange fruit of this plant.
cloud·burst (klówd-burst) *n.* A sudden rainstorm; a downpour.
cloud chamber *n.* A device for detecting charged subatomic particles by the formation of small droplets of liquid along the paths of the particles as they pass through supersaturated vapour. The droplets condense on ions produced by the particles. Compare **bubble chamber.**
cloud-cuckoo-land (klówd-kóokoo-land) *n.* An ideal realm of imagination or fantasy. Often used derogatorily. [Translation of Greek *Nephelokokkugia* (*nephelē,* cloud + *kokkux,* cuckoo), a comic utopia in Aristophanes's comedy *The Birds* (414 B.C.).]
cloud nine *n. Informal.* A state of great happiness. Used in the phrase *on cloud nine.* [Originally *on cloud seven;* the phrase is perhaps related to *in the seventh heaven* (in some Jewish and Muslim literature the seventh and final heaven is the abode of God).]
cloud seeding *n.* A technique of stimulating rainfall, especially by distributing quantities of dry-ice crystals or silver iodide smoke through clouds. Also informally called "rainmaking".
cloud·y (klówdi) *adj.* **-ier, -iest. 1.** *Abbr.* **c.** Full of or covered with clouds; overcast. **2.** Of or like a cloud or clouds. **3.** Marked with indistinct masses or streaks: *cloudy marble.* **4.** Not transparent; milky. Said of liquids. **5.** Obscure; vague. **6.** Troubled; gloomy. **—cloud·i·ly** *adv.* **—cloud·i·ness** *n.*
clough (kluf) *n. British Regional.* A steep-sided narrow valley; a ravine. [Old English *clōh,* from Germanic *klanh-* (unattested).]
clout (klowt) *n.* **1.** A blow, especially with the open hand. **2.** *Informal.* Power, prestige, or influence; pull: *political clout.* **3.** An archery target. **4.** *Archaic & Regional.* A piece of cloth. **5.** A short nail with a wide flat head. Also called "clout nail".
~*tr.v.* **clouted, clouting, clouts. 1.** To hit. **2.** *Archaic & Regional.* To patch. [Middle English *clout,* from Old English *clūt* (noun), lump, piece of material, patch, *clūtian,* to patch.]
clove[1] (klōv) *n.* **1.** An East Indian evergreen tree, *Eugenia aromatica,* of which the aromatic unopened flower buds are used, whole or ground, as a spice. **2.** The small dried flower bud of this tree. [Middle English *clowe (of gilofre),* "nail-shaped bud (of clove)", from Old French *clou (de girofle)* : *clou,* nail, from Latin *clāvus* + *girofle,* clove tree (see **gillyflower**).]
clove[2] *n.* Any of the small sections of a separable bulb, such as that of garlic. [Middle English *clove,* Old English *clufu.*]
clove[3]. **1.** Alternative past tense and *archaic* past participle of **cleave** (to split). **2.** *Archaic.* Past tense of **cleave** (to cling).
clove hitch *n.* A knot used to secure a line to a spar, post, or other object, consisting of two turns with the second held under the first. [*Clove,* from CLOVEN (split).]
clo·ven (klōv'n). Alternative past participle of **cleave** (to split).
~*adj.* Split; divided.
cloven foot *n.* A cloven hoof. **—clo·ven-foot·ed** (klōv'n-fóotid) *adj.*
cloven hoof *n.* **1.** A divided or cleft hoof, as in deer or cattle. **2.** The symbol of Satan, who is often depicted with such hooves. **—clo·ven-hoofed** (klōv'n-hóoft), **clo·ven-hooved** (-hóovd) *adj.*
clove pink *n.* A plant, *Dianthus caryophyllus,* having pink flowers from which the garden carnations have been bred.
clo·ver (klōvər) *n.* **1.** Any plant of the genus *Trifolium,* having compound leaves with usually three leaflets and tight heads of small flowers. Many species provide valuable pasturage. **2.** Any of several related plants, such as the sweet clover, or **melilot** *(see).* **—in clover.** Living a carefree life of ease, comfort, or prosperity. [Middle English *clover, claver,* Old English *clǣfre,* clover, from Germanic *klaibrōn* (unattested).]
clo·ver·leaf (klōvər-leef) *n., pl.* **-leaves** (-leevz) or **-leafs.** A road junction in the shape of a four-leafed clover at which two roads crossing each other on different levels are provided with curving access and exit roads, enabling vehicles to go in any of four directions.
Clo·vis (klōviss) (*c.* A.D. 466–511). King of the Franks (481–511), the greatest of the early Merovingian dynasty, who united Gaul as a single kingdom and set up his capital in Paris. His name, gallicised as "Louis", was given to 19 later French monarchs.
clown (klown) *n.* **1.** A buffoon or jester, often wearing outlandish clothes and make-up, who entertains by jokes, antics, and tricks, in a circus, play, or other presentation. **2.** A person who acts the fool or behaves in a comic way. **3.** An ignorant or boorish person. **4.** *Archaic.* A rustic or peasant.
~*intr.v.* **clowned, clowning, clowns. 1.** To behave in a silly, clownlike fashion. Often used with *around.* **2.** To perform as a clown. [Probably from Scandinavian, akin to Icelandic *klunni,* clumsy person.] **—clown·ish** *adj.* **—clown·ish·ly** *adv.* **—clown·ish·ness** *n.*
cloy (kloy) *v.* **cloyed, cloying, cloys.** —*tr.* To supply with too much of something, especially with something too rich or sweet; surfeit. —*intr.* To cause a feeling of surfeit. [Short for obsolete *accloy,* to nail, hence, to clog, satiate, Middle English *acloien,* to obstruct, hamper, from Old French *encloer,* to nail, from Vulgar Latin *inclā vāre* (unattested) : Latin *in,* in + *clāvāre,* to nail, from *clāvus,* nail.] **—cloy·ing** *adj.* **—cloy·ing·ly** *adv.* **—cloy·ing·ness** *n.*
club[1] (klub) *n.* **1.** A stout, heavy stick, usually thicker at one end than at the other, suitable for use as a weapon; a cudgel. **2.** A bat or stick used in certain games to drive a ball; especially, a stick with a curved head used in golf. **3.** *Botany.* A club-shaped structure or organ. **4. a.** The black symbol appearing on one of the four suits of playing cards, in the shape of a trefoil or cloverleaf. **b.** A card bearing this symbol. See **clubs. 5.** *Nautical.* A spar.
~*tr.v.* **clubbed, clubbing, clubs. 1.** To strike or beat with or as with a club. **2.** *Rare.* To gather or combine (hair, for example) into a clublike mass; tangle: *clubbed roots.* [Middle English *clubbe,* from Old Norse *klubba,* billet, club.]
club[2] *n.* **1. a.** A group of people organised for a common purpose; especially, a group that meets regularly. **b.** An association of people formed for social purposes, having premises providing meals, accommodation, and other facilities. **c.** *Sports.* An association that organises and provides teams, matches, facilities, and events, in a particular game or sport: *a tennis club; a golf club.* **2.** The room, building, or other facilities used by such a group or association. **3.** *Chiefly British.* An arrangement by which people, especially customers of a shop, can save up money. **—in the club.** *British Slang.* Pregnant. —See Synonyms at **circle.**
~*v.* **clubbed, clubbing, clubs.** —*tr.* To contribute for a joint or common purpose. —*intr.* To join or combine for a common purpose. Used with *together: They clubbed together to buy her a leaving present.* **—club up.** To join forces for self-protection or attack; close ranks: *They clubbed up against the traitor in their midst.* [Probably from CLUB[1] (in rare sense, to gather into a mass).]
club·ba·ble (klúbbəb'l) *adj. Informal.* Sociable.
club chair *n.* An upholstered easy chair with arms and a low back.
club·foot (klúb-fòot) *n., pl.* **-feet** (-feet). **1.** Congenital deformity of the foot, with a misshapen appearance often like a club. Also called "talipes". **2.** A foot so deformed. **—club·foot·ed** *adj.*
club·house (klúb-howss) *n.* A building occupied by a club, especially a sports club or team.
club·land (klúb-land) *n.* **1.** *British.* The area around St. James's in London where many famous clubs are situated. **2.** Any district containing a large number of clubs or nightclubs.
club·man (klúb-mən, -man) *n., pl.* **-men** (-mən, -men). A man who is an active member of a fashionable club or clubs.
club moss *n.* Any of various erect or creeping mosslike plants of the genus *Lycopodium,* having tiny, scalelike, overlapping leaves. Some species are also called "ground pine". Also called "lycopodium". [After the club-shaped strobiles on some species.]
club root *n.* A disease of cabbage and related plants, caused by a fungus of the genus *Plasmodiophora,* and resulting in large, distorted swellings on the roots.
clubs (klubz) *n. Used with a singular or plural verb.* One of the four suits of playing cards distinguished by black trefoil figures printed on the face of each card.
club sandwich *n.* A sandwich, usually of three slices of toast, with a filling of various meats, tomato, lettuce, and dressing.
club soda *n. U.S.* Soda water.
club·wom·an (klúb-wòomən) *n., pl.* **—women** (-wimmin). A female clubman.
cluck (kluk) *v.* **clucked, clucking, clucks.** —*intr.* To utter a cluck

or clucks. —*tr.* To express by clucking: *He clucked his disapproval.* ~*n.* **1. a.** The characteristic sound made by a hen when brooding or calling her chicks. **b.** Any sound resembling this. **2.** *Informal.* A stupid or foolish person: *a dumb cluck.* [Imitative.]

clue (klōō ‖ klew) *n.* Anything that guides or directs in the solution of a problem or mystery. —**not have a clue.** *Informal.* To be ignorant or incapable. ~*tr.v.* **clued, clueing** or **cluing, clues.** To give (someone) guiding information. Used with *in* or *up.* [Variant of CLEW.]

clue·less (klōō-ləss, -liss ‖ kléw-) *adj. Slang.* Stupid.

Clum·ber spaniel (klúmbər) *n.* A dog of a breed developed in England, having short legs and a silky, predominantly white coat. [After *Clumber Park,* a country estate in Nottinghamshire.]

clump (klump) *n.* **1.** A clustered mass; a lump. **2.** A thick grouping, as of plants. **3.** A heavy dull sound; a thud, as of footsteps. ~*v.* **clumped, clumping, clumps.** —*intr.* **1.** To walk with a heavy dull sound. **2.** To form clumps. —*tr.* **1.** To gather into or form clumps of. **2.** To cause (blood cells, bacteria, and the like) to form clumps. [Low German *klump,* from Middle Low German *klumpe.*] —**clump·y** *adj.*

clum·sy (klúmzi) *adj.* **-sier, -siest. 1.** Lacking physical coordination, skill, or grace; awkward. **2.** Awkwardly made; unwieldy. **3.** Gauche; inept: *a clumsy excuse; a clumsy compliment.* —See Synonyms at **awkward.** [From obsolete *clumse,* to be numb with cold, probably from Scandinavian *klumsen,* benumbed, from Germanic *klum-* (unattested).] —**clum·si·ly** *adv.* —**clum·si·ness** *n.*

clunch (klunch) *n.* **1.** Any of several types of stiff English clay. **2.** A soft white English limestone sometimes used in building and decorating. [Possibly from Dutch *klont,* clod, lump.]

clung. Past tense and past participle of **cling.**

clunk. Variant of **clonk.**

Clu·ny (klōōni, klü-née). Town in Saône-et-Loire *département* of east central France, situated on the river Grosne. The Cluniac order of Benedictine monks was established here in 910.

clu·pe·id (klōō-pi-id ‖ kléw-) *n.* Any of various fishes of the family Clupeidae, which includes herrings, sardines, and sprats. [New Latin *Clupeidae,* from Latin *clupea†,* a kind of small fish.] —**clu·pe·id** *adj.*

clus·ter (klústər) *n.* **1.** Any configuration of elements gathered or occurring closely together; a group; a loose bunch. **2.** Two or more successive consonants in a word; for example, *cl* and *st* in the word *cluster.* **3.** *Astronomy.* A group of stars or galaxies moving together. ~*v.* **clustered, -tering, -ters.** —*intr.* To gather or grow in clusters. —*tr.* To cause to grow or form into clusters. [Middle English *cluster,* Old English *clyster, cluster†.*]

cluster bomb *n.* A bomb consisting of a collection of **fragmentation bombs** (*see*) that are dispersed on impact.

cluster fly *n.* A fly of the family Calliphoridae that gathers with others of its kind in crevices or corners of buildings.

cluster pine *n.* A tree, the **pinaster** (*see*).

clutch¹ (kluch) *v.* **clutched, clutching, clutches.** —*tr.* **1.** To grasp and hold tightly. **2.** To seize or snatch. —*intr.* To attempt to grasp or seize. Used with *at.* ~*n.* **1.** The hand, claw, talon, paw, or the like, used in the act of grasping. **2.** A tight grasp. **3.** *Usually plural.* Control or power: *We had them in her clutches.* **4.** *Machinery.* **a.** Any of various devices for engaging and disengaging two working parts of a shaft or of a shaft and a driving mechanism, as in a car. **b.** The apparatus that activates such a device. [Middle English *clicchen, clucchen,* Old English *clyccan,* from Germanic *klukjan* (unattested).]

clutch² *n.* **1.** The number of eggs produced or incubated by one bird or in one nest, at one time. **2.** A brood of chickens. **3.** *Informal.* A group of people or things. ~*tr.v.* **clutched, clutching, clutches.** To hatch (chicks). [18th century : variant of dialectal *cletch,* from Middle English *clecken,* to hatch, give birth, from Old Norse *klekja†.*]

clutch bag *n.* A handbag without a strap or handles.

clut·ter (klúttər) *n.* **1.** A confused or disordered state or collection; a jumble. **2.** *Archaic.* A confused noise; a clatter. **3.** *Electronics.* Noise, echoes, or other unwanted signals on a radar display. ~*tr.v.* **cluttered, -tering, -ters.** To litter or pile in a disordered state. Used with *up.* [Middle English *clotteren,* to clot, coagulate, heap, from *clot,* lump, CLOT.]

Clwyd (klōō-id). From 1974 to 1996, county in northeast Wales.

Clyde (klīd). River in western Scotland. It rises in the Southern Uplands and flows 170 kilometres (106 miles) northwest through Glasgow and Clydebank to the sea at the Firth of Clyde.

Clyde·bank (klīd-bangk). Town in West Dunbartonshire Unitary Authority area, situated on the lower Clyde. Many ocean liners were built in its shipyards, including the *Queen Mary* and *Queen Elizabeth.*

Clydes·dale (klīdz-dayl) *n.* **1.** A large, powerful draught horse of a breed developed in the Clyde valley in Scotland. **2.** A type of small terrier.

clyp·e·ate (klíppi-ət, -ayt, -it) *adj.* Also **clyp·e·i·form** (-i-fawrm). **1.** Shaped like a round shield. **2.** Having a clypeus.

clyp·e·us (klíppi-əss) *n., pl.* **-ei** (klíppi-ī). *Biology.* A shieldlike structure, especially a plate on the front of the head of an insect. [New Latin, from Latin *clipeus, clupeus†,* round shield.] —**clyp·e·al** *adj.*

clys·ter (klístər) *n. Medicine. Rare.* An enema. [Middle English *clister,* from Old French *clistere,* from Latin *clystēr,* from Greek *klustēr,* "liquid for washing out", from *kluzein,* to wash out.]

Cly·tem·nes·tra (klītəm-néestrə, klítim-, -néstrə). In Greek legend, the consort of Agamemnon, and mother of Orestes and Electra. With her lover Aegisthus she murdered Agamemnon and was killed by her son in revenge.

cm centimetre; centimetres.

Cm The symbol for the element curium.

c.m. 1. circular mil. **2.** court-martial.

Cmd. Command Paper (fourth series, 1918–56).

Cmdr. commander.

C.M.G. Companion (of the Order) of St. Michael and St. George.

cml commercial.

Cmnd. Command Paper (fifth series, 1956–86).

cN centinewton.

C/N credit note.

C.N.A.A., CNAA *n.* Council for National Academic Awards: a degree-awarding body for polytechnics and other institutions apart from the universities.

CND Campaign for Nuclear Disarmament.

cni·dar·i·an (nī-dáir-i-ən, knī-) *n.* Any of various aquatic invertebrates of the Cnidaria, a chiefly marine subphylum of the Coelenterata that includes the jellyfish, sea anemones, and corals. ~*adj.* Of or belonging to the Cnidaria. [New Latin *Cnidaria,* from Greek *knidē,* nettle.]

Cnossos. See **Knossos.**

CNS central nervous system.

Cnut. See **Canute.**

Co The symbol for the element cobalt.

co– *prefix.* Indicates: **1.** Joint, jointly, together, or mutually; for example, **co-education, cooperate, copilot. 2.** Same, similar; for example, **cosconscious. 3.** Complement of an angle; for example, **cosine, coaltitude.** [In borrowed Latin compounds, *co-* is the reduced form of *com-* (see **com-**), used before *h, gn,* and usually before vowels, as in COHERE, COGNATE, and COALESCE.]

co., Co. 1. company. **2.** county.

c.o. 1. care of. **2.** *Accounting.* carried over. **3.** cash order.

C.O. 1. commanding officer. **2.** conscientious objector.

c/o care of.

co·ac·er·vate (kō-ássər-vayt, -vət, -vit) *n. Chemistry.* A cluster of droplets separated out of a lyophilic colloid. [Latin *coacervātus,* past participle of *coacervāre,* to heap together : *co-,* together + *acervāre,* to heap, ACERVATE.] —**co·ac·er·va·tion** (-váysh'n) *n.*

coach (kōch) *n.* **1.** *Chiefly British.* A comfortable single-decker long-distance motor bus. **2.** A large, closed horse-drawn carriage with four wheels. **3.** A railway carriage. **4.** *U.S.* Economy-class seating on a train or aeroplane. **5.** A person who trains athletes or sports teams. **6.** A private tutor employed to prepare a student for an examination. **7.** *Australian.* A tame bullock used as a decoy to trap wild cattle. ~*v.* **coached, coaching, coaches.** —*tr.* To tutor or train. —*intr.* To act as a coach. —See Synonyms at **teach.** [French *coche,* from German *Kutsche,* from Hungarian *kocsi,* after *Kocs,* Hungary, where such carriages originated. Sense 6; 19th-century : university slang use of *coach* (carriage).] —**coach·er** *n.*

coach-built (kōch-bílt) *adj.* Designating a vehicle body built specially by craftsmen.

coach dog *n.* The **Dalmatian** (*see*). [Formerly trained as a fashionable pet to run behind a coach.]

coach·ing inn (kōching) *n.* An inn where the horses pulling a long-distance coach could be changed for a fresh team.

coach·man (kōch-mən) *n., pl.* **-men** (-mən). **1.** A person who drives a horse-drawn coach. **2.** A type of artificial fishing fly.

coach screw *n.* A large screw with a square head used for joining large pieces of wood.

coach·wood (kōch-wŏŏd) *n.* An Australian tree yielding closely grained wood suitable for making furniture.

coach·work (kōch-wurk) *n.* The bodywork of a motor vehicle.

co·ac·tion (kō-áksh'n) *n.* **1.** Joint action. **2.** *Archaic.* Compulsion. [Middle English *coaccioun,* from Old French *coaction,* from Latin *coactiō,* from *cōgere* (past participle *cōactus*), to drive together, force. See **coagulum.**] —**co·ac·tive** *adj.* —**co·ac·tive·ly** *adv.*

co·ad·ju·tant (kō-ájōōtənt) *adj.* Helping each other. ~*n.* A coworker; an assistant.

co·ad·ju·tor (kō-ájōōtər ‖ kŏ-ə-jōōtər) *n. Abbr.* **coad. 1.** The assistant to a bishop. **2.** Any coworker; an assistant. [Middle English *coadjutour,* from Old French *coadjuteur,* from Latin *coadjūtor : cō-,* together + *adjūtor,* assistant, from *adjūtāre,* to assist, AID.]

co·ad·u·nate (kō-áddew-nət, -nit, -nayt) *adj.* Closely joined by growing together; connate. [Late Latin *coadūnāre : cō-,* together + *adūnāre,* to unite to : Latin *ad-,* to + *ūnāre,* to unite, from *ūnus,* one.] —**co·ad·u·na·tion** (-náysh'n) *n.* —**co·ad·u·na·tive** (-naytiv, -nətiv) *adj.*

co·ag·u·lant (kō-ággewlənt) *n.* An agent that causes coagulation. —**co·ag·u·lant** *adj.*

co·ag·u·lase (kō-ággew-layz, -layss) *n.* An enzyme, such as thrombin, that causes blood clotting. [COAGUL(ATE) + -ASE.]

co·ag·u·late (kō-ággew-layt) *v.* **-lated, -lating, -lates.** —*tr.* To cause transformation of (a liquid or solid, such as blood) into a soft, semisolid, or solid mass. —*intr.* To become such a mass. [Middle English *coagulaten,* from Latin *coāgulāre,* to curdle, from COAGULUM.] —**co·ag·u·la·ble** (-ləb'l) *adj.* —**co·ag·u·la·bil·i·ty** (-lə-bílləti) *n.* —**co·ag·u·la·tion** (-láysh'n) *n.* —**co·ag·u·la·tive** (-laytiv, -lətiv) *n.* —**co·ag·u·la·tor** (-laytər) *n.*

coagulation factor *n.* Any factor in the blood or plasma that contributes to the clotting of blood.

co·ag·u·lum (kō-ággew-ləm) *n., pl.* **-la** (-lə). A coagulated mass; a clot; a curd. [Latin *coāgulum,* from *cōgere,* to drive together, condense : *cō-,* together + *agere,* to drive.]

coal (kōl) *n.* **1.** A natural dark brown to black solid used as a fuel, formed from fossilised plants, and consisting of carbon with various organic and some inorganic compounds. **2.** A piece of this substance. **3.** A glowing or charred piece of coal, wood, or other solid fuel; an ember. **—haul** or **drag over the coals.** To reprimand; scold. **—take coals to Newcastle.** To take something to a place where it is already plentiful.
~*v.* **coaled, coaling, coals.** —*tr.* To provide (a ship, for example) with coal. —*intr.* To take on coal. [Middle English *cole,* Old English *col,* coal, live coal.]

coal·er (kṓlər) *n.* A ship that transports coal.

co·a·lesce (kō-ə-léss) *intr.v.* **-lesced, -lescing, -lesces. 1.** To grow together; fuse. **2.** To come together so as to form one whole; unite. —See Synonyms at **mix.** [Latin *coalēscere,* to grow together : *cō-,* together + *alēscere,* to grow, inceptive of *alēre,* to nourish.] **—co·a·les·cence** (-léss'nss) *n.* **—co·a·les·cent** (-léss'nt) *adj.*

coal bunker *n.* A place for storing coal outside a house or in a ship.

coal·face (kṓl-fayss, -fáyss) *n.* **1.** The exposed seam in a mine from which the coal is cut. **2.** *Chiefly British Informal.* The sharp end; front line: *the practical problems of lexicographers working at the coalface.*

coal·field (kṓl-feeld) *n.* An area with large deposits of coal.

coal·fish (kṓl-fish) *n., pl.* **-fishes** or collectively **coalfish.** An edible deep-water marine fish, *Gadus virens,* closely related to the cod, with a blackish back and chin barbel. Also called "coley", "saithe".

coal gas *n.* A gaseous mixture produced by the destructive distillation of bituminous coal and formerly used as a commercial fuel.

co·a·li·tion (kṓ-ə-lísh'n) *n.* **1.** An alliance, especially a temporary one, of factions, parties, or nations. **2.** A combination or fusion into one body. [French, from Medieval Latin *coalitiō* (stem *coalitiōn-*), from Latin *coalēscere,* COALESCE.] **—co·a·li·tion·ist** *n.*

coal·i·fy (kṓli-fī) *v.* **-fied, fy·ing, -fies.** —*tr.* To cause (plant material) to form coal. —*intr.* To form coal. Used of plant material. **—coal·i·fi·ca·tion** (-fi-káysh'n) *n.*

coal measures *pl.n. Geology.* **1.** *Capital* **C,** *capital* **M.** A stratigraphic unit equivalent to the uppermost division of the Upper Carboniferous period. **2.** Strata of the Carboniferous period containing coal deposits.

coal oil *n.* **1.** An oil formed during the distillation of coal. **2.** *U.S.* **Kerosene** *(see).*

Coal·port (kṓlpawrt) *n.* An antique type of translucent bone china, decorated with brightly coloured patterns on a white base. [After *Coalport,* Shrewsbury, where it was made.] **—Coal·port** *adj.*

coal scuttle *n.* A metal container, usually with a handle, in which coal is kept by a hearth.

coal tar *n.* A viscous black liquid obtained by the destructive distillation of coal, used as a raw material for many dyes, drugs, medications, and organic chemicals and for waterproofing, paints, roofing, and insulation materials. **—coal-tar** (kṓl-tár) *adj.*

coal-tar pitch *n.* A heavy black pitch produced by the distillation of coal tar, used as a binder in smokeless fuels and in road surfacing.

coal tit *n.* A small songbird, *Parus ater,* native to Europe, having a black head and a white patch on the back of the neck.

co·al·ti·tude (kō-ál-ti-tewd, kṓ-, -áwl- || -ól-, -tōōd) *n. Astronomy.* The **zenith distance** *(see).*

coam·ing (kṓming) *n.* A raised rim or curb around an opening in a ship's deck or the roof of a building, designed to keep out water. [17th century : origin obscure.]

co·ap·ta·tion (kṓ-ap-táysh'n) *n.* The adjustment of parts to each other; especially, the joining of broken bones or the edges of a wound. [Late Latin *coaptātiō* (stem *coaptātiōn-*), a careful fitting together, from Latin *co-,* together + *aptāre,* to fit.]

co·arc·tate (kō-árktayt) *adj. Entomology.* Describing an insect pupa in which the final larval cuticle remains to form a hardened shell around the body. [Latin *coarctātus,* past participle of *coarctāre, coartāre,* to press together : *cō-,* together + *artāre,* to press, from *artus,* narrow, tight.] **—co·arc·ta·tion** (kṓ-aark-táysh'n) *n.*

coarse (korss || kōrss) *adj.* **coarser, coarsest. 1.** Of low, common, or inferior quality. **2. a.** Lacking in delicacy or refinement. **b.** Obscene or improper. Said of language. **3.** Consisting of large particles; not fine in texture. **4.** Rough; harsh. [Middle English *co(a)rs,* ordinary, coarse, probably from *co(u)rs,* COURSE ("the usual practice").] **—coarse·ly** *adv.* **—coarse·ness** *n.*

Synonyms: *coarse, gross, crass, vulgar, obscene, ribald.*

coarse fish *n.* Any freshwater fish that does not belong to the salmon or trout families. **—coarse fishing** *n.*

coarse-grained (kórss-gráynd || kṓrss-) *adj.* **1.** Having a rough or coarse texture. **2.** Not refined; indelicate; crude.

coars·en (kórss'n || kṓrss'n) *v.* **-ened, -ening, -ens.** —*intr.* To become coarse. —*tr.* To make coarse.

coast (kōst) *n.* **1.** The land next to the sea; the seashore. **2.** *British.* The seaside. **3.** The act of sliding or coasting; a slide. **4.** *U.S.* A hill or other slope down which one may coast, as on a toboggan. **—the coast is clear.** *Informal.* There are no dangers or hindrances.
~*v.* **coasted, coasting, coasts.** —*intr.* **1. a.** To move along without power, as a freewheeling car does. **b.** To progress effortlessly, at an unhurried pace. **2.** *U.S.* To slide down a slope, on a toboggan for example. **3.** To sail near or along a coast. —*tr.* To sail or move along the coast or border of. [Middle English *cost,* from Old French *coste,* from Latin *costa,* rib, side.] **—coast·al** (kṓst'l) *adj.*

coast·er (kṓstər) *n.* **1.** A ship engaged in coastal trade. **2.** A disc placed under a bottle or glass to protect a table top. **3.** A small tray for passing a wine decanter round a table, for example. **4.** *U.S.* A toboggan for coasting.

coast·guard (kṓst-gaard) *n.* **1.** A body officially responsible for the protection of life and property at sea, the enforcement of customs laws, and the like. **2.** *Chiefly British.* Any member of this body.

coast·line (kṓstlīn) *n.* The shape or boundary of a coast.

coast·ward (kṓstwərd) *adj.* Directed towards a coast. **—coast·wards** (-wərdz) *adv.*

coast·wise (kṓst-wīz) *adj.* Following the coast.
~*adv.* By way of or along the coast.

coat (kōt) *n.* **1.** An outer garment covering the body from the shoulders to the waist or below, worn primarily for protection from cold or bad weather. **2. a.** A woman's garment extending to just below the waist and usually forming the top part of a suit. **b.** *Chiefly U.S.* The jacket of a man's suit. **3.** A natural integument or outer covering, such as the fur of an animal. **4.** A layer of some material covering something else; a coating: *a coat of dust; a coat of paint.*
~*tr.v.* **coated, coating, coats. 1.** To provide or cover with a coat. **2.** To cover with a layer, as of paint or chocolate. [Middle English *cote,* from Old French, from Frankish *kotta* (unattested), from West Germanic *kotta* (unattested).]

coat·ed (kṓtid) *adj.* **1.** Having an outer layer, coat, or covering. **2.** Being or designating paper which has a highly polished surface suitable for halftone printing. **3.** *Optics.* Having a thin layer to minimise reflection; bloomed. Said of a lens.

co·a·ti (kō-aáti) *n.* Any of several omnivorous mammals of the genus *Nasua,* of South and Central America and the southwestern United States, related to and resembling the raccoon but having a longer snout and tail. Also called "coatimundi". [Portuguese *coatí,* from Tupi *coatí, coatim,* "belt-nosed" : *cua,* belt, band + *tim,* nose.]

coat·ing (kṓting) *n.* **1.** A layer of any substance spread over a surface for protection or decoration. **2.** Cloth for making coats.

coat of arms *n.* **1.** Formerly, a tabard or surcoat blazoned with heraldic bearings. **2.** The heraldic bearings of a family, city, or the like, usually represented on a shield and accompanied by the crest and motto.

coat of mail *n., pl.* **coats of mail.** An armoured coat made of chain mail, interlinked rings, or overlapping metal plates.

coat·tails (kṓt-taylz) *pl.n.* The long divided part at the back of a formal or dress coat. **—on (someone's) coattails.** *Chiefly U.S.* Benefitting from someone else's advancement.

co-au·thor (kṓ-áwthər) *n.* A collaborating or joint author. —*tr.v.* **co-authored, -thoring, -thors.** To be a co-author of.

coax[1] (kōks) *v.* **coaxed, coaxing, coaxes.** —*tr.* **1.** To persuade or try to persuade by pleading or flattery; cajole; wheedle. **2.** To obtain by persistent persuasion. —*intr.* To use persuasion or inducement. —See Synonyms at **urge.** [Earlier *coaks, cokes,* to fool, from *cokes*†, fool.] **—coax·er** *n.* **—coax·ing·ly** *adv.*

co·ax (kṓ-aks) *n.* A **coaxial cable** *(see).*

co·ax·i·al (kō-áksi-əl, kṓ-) *adj.* Having or mounted on a common axis.

coaxial cable *n.* A high-frequency cable used for telephone, telegraph, or television transmission, consisting of a conducting metal tube enclosing and insulated from a central conducting wire core.

cob[1] (kob) *n.* **1.** The central core of an ear of maize: *eat corn on the cob.* **2.** A male swan. Compare **pen. 3.** A thick-set, stocky, short-legged horse. **4.** A tree, the **hazel** *(see),* or its edible nut. Also called "cobnut". **5.** *British.* A type of round loaf. [Middle English *cobbe*†, lump, round object.]

cob[2] *n. British.* A mixture of clay and straw formerly used as a building material. [17th century : origin obscure.]

co·balt (kṓ-bawlt || -bolt) *n. Symbol* **Co** A hard, brittle metallic element, found associated with nickel, silver, lead, copper, and iron ores and resembling nickel and iron in appearance. It is used chiefly for magnetic alloys, high-temperature alloys, and in the form of its salts for blue glass and ceramic pigments. Atomic number 27, atomic weight 58.9332, melting point 1 495°C, boiling point 3 100°C, relative density 8.9, valencies 1, 2, 3. [German *Kobalt, Kobold,* from Middle High German *kobolt,* an underground goblin (cobalt was thought to be injurious to silver ores).]

cobalt-60 *n.* A radioactive isotope of cobalt with mass number 60 and exceptionally intense gamma-ray activity, used in radiotherapy, metallurgy, and materials testing.

cobalt blue *n.* **1.** A blue to green pigment consisting of a variable mixture of cobalt and aluminium oxides. Also called "Thénard's blue". **2.** Vivid or strong greenish blue. **—co·balt-blue** *adj.*

cobalt bomb *n.* **1.** An apparatus for producing a beam of gamma rays from a cobalt-60 source, used in medical radiation treatment. **2.** A nuclear weapon designed to release large amounts of radioactive cobalt-60 into the atmosphere.

co·bal·tic (kō-báwlt-ik || -bólt-) *adj.* Of or containing cobalt. Said especially of chemical compounds containing cobalt with valency 3.

co·bal·tite (kṓ-bawlt-īt || -bolt-) *n.* Also **co·balt·ine** (-een). A silver-white to grey mineral, CoAsS, that is an important cobalt ore and is used in ceramics.

co·bal·tous (kō-báwlt-əss || -bólt-) *adj.* Of or containing cobalt. Said especially of chemical compounds containing cobalt with valency 2.

cob·ber (kóbbər) *n. Australian & N. Z.* Comrade; mate. [Origin unknown.]

Cob·bett (kóbbit), **William** (1763–1835). British radical author known for his *Weekly Political Register* (1802–35). His *Rural Rides* (1830) described horseback tours of England, charting the decline of traditional values and liberties with industrialisation.

cob·ble¹ (kŏbb'l) *n.* **1.** A cobblestone. **2.** *Plural.* Coal in lumps about the size of cobblestones. **3.** *Geology.* A rock fragment with a diameter of 64–256 milometres (2½–10 inches). ∼*tr.v.* **cobbled, -bling, -bles.** To pave with cobblestones. [Back-formation from COBBLESTONE.]

cobble² *tr.v.* **-bled, -bling, -bles.** **1.** To make or mend (boots or shoes). **2.** To put together quickly and roughly. Often used with *together*: *cobbled together a short story.* [Probably back-formation from COBBLER.]

cob·bler¹ (kŏbblər) *n.* **1.** One who mends boots and shoes. **2.** *Archaic.* One who is clumsy at his work; a bungler. **3.** *Australian & N.Z. Slang.* A sheep that is difficult to shear and is therefore shorn last. [Middle English *cobelere†.*]

cobbler² *n.* **1.** An iced drink made of wine or liqueur, sugar, and citrus fruit. **2.** *U.S.* **Crumble** *(see).* [Perhaps from COBBLER (mender).]

cob·blers (kŏbblərz) *pl.n.* **1.** *Vulgar Slang.* The testicles. **2.** *Slang.* Nonsense. Used chiefly in the phrase *a load of old cobblers.* [Perhaps from *cobblers' awls*, rhyming slang for *balls*.]

cob·ble·stone (kŏbb'l-stōn) *n.* A naturally rounded stone, formerly used for paving streets and walls. Also called "cobble". [Middle English *cobelston* : *cobel-*, probably diminutive of *cobbe*, COB (lump) + STONE.]

Cob·den (kŏb-dən), **Richard** (1804–65). British economist and a leading spokesman for Free Trade. He was a leading member of the Anti-Corn-Law League (1838–46), which brought about the repeal of protectionist legislation.

co·bel·lig·er·ent (kō-bi-líjərənt, -bə-) *n.* A nation associated with another or others in waging war.

co·bi·a (kŏbi-ə) *n.* A large game fish, *Rachycentron canadum*, of tropical and subtropical seas. [Origin obscure.]

co·ble (kŏb'l) *n. British.* A small, flat-bottomed fishing boat with a lugsail on a raking mast. [Old English *cobel*, from Celtic; akin to Old Breton *caubal*.]

Coblenz. See **Koblenz.**

cob·nut (kŏb-nut) *n.* A tree, the **cob** *(see)*, or its edible nut.

CO·BOL (kō-bol ‖ *U.S.* -bawl) *n.* A computer language based on English words and phrases, used for various business applications. [*common business oriented language.*]

co·bra (kŏbrə, kōbrə) *n.* Any of several venomous snakes of the genus *Naja* and related genera, of Asia and Africa, capable of expanding the skin of the neck to form a flattened hood. [Short for Portuguese *cobra (de capello)*, "snake (with a hood)", from Latin *colubra*, feminine of *coluber†*, snake.]

cob·web (kŏb-web) *n.* **1.** A disused spider's web. **2.** A single thread of such a web. **3.** Something resembling a cobweb in flimsiness, diaphanousness, or intricacy. **4.** *Plural.* **a.** Any musty accumulation, especially as a result of disuse or neglect. **b.** A feeling of staleness or fustiness: *to go for a walk in the fresh air and blow away the cobwebs.* ∼*tr.v.* **cobwebbed, -webbing, -webs.** To cover with or as if with cobwebs. [Middle English *coppeweb* : *coppe*, spider, Old English *(āttor)coppe* + WEB.] —**cob·web·by** *adj.*

co·ca (kōkə) *n.* **1.** A South American tree, *Erythroxylon coca*, having leaves that contain cocaine and related alkaloids. **2.** The dried leaves of this shrub or related plants, chewed by people of the Andes as a stimulant. [Spanish, from Quechua *kúka, cuca.*]

Co·ca·Co·la (kōkə-kōlə) *n.* A trademark for a dark-coloured aerated soft drink.

co·caine (kə-káyn, kō-, *rarely* ko- ‖ *U.S. also* kōkayn) *n.* A colourless or white crystalline narcotic alkaloid, $C_{17}H_{21}NO_4$, extracted from coca leaves and used as a stimulant or local anaesthetic. [COCA + -INE.]

co·cain·ism (kə-káyn-iz'm, kō-) *n.* **1.** The habitual use of cocaine. **2.** Mental and physical deterioration resulting from misuse of cocaine.

coc·cid (kŏksid) *n.* An insect of the family Coccidae, which includes the scale insects and mealybugs. [New Latin Coccidae, from *Coccus* (genus), from Greek *kokkos*, kermes berry, pit.]

coc·cid·i·o·sis (kok-síddi-ō-siss) *n.* A disease of many animals, including cattle, pigs, sheep, dogs, cats, and poultry, but rarely of humans, resulting from an infection of the digestive tract by parasitic protozoa of the order Coccidia. [New Latin : *Coccidia*, from COCCUS + -OSIS.]

coc·cus (kŏksəss) *n., pl.* **cocci** (kŏksī, kōksī). **1.** A bacterium with a spherical or spheroidal shape. **2.** *Botany.* A division that contains a single seed and splits apart from a many-lobed fruit. **3.** Any scale insect of the genus *Coccus.* [New Latin, from Greek *kokkos*, kermes berry, pit.] —**coc·coid, coc·cal** *adj.*

-coccus *n. comb. form.* Indicates a microorganism that is spheroidal in shape; for example, **streptococcus.** [New Latin, from COCCUS.]

coc·cyx (kŏk-siks) *n., pl.* **coccyges** (-sijeez, kok-sījeez). In humans and certain apes, a small bone at the base of the spinal column, consisting of several fused rudimentary vertebrae, which represents a vestigial tail. [New Latin, from Greek *kokkux*, cuckoo, coccyx (bone shaped like the cuckoo's beak) (imitative).] —**coc·cyg·e·al** (kok-síji-əl) *adj.*

Co·chin¹ (kō-chin, -chín) Port on the Malabar coast of southwest India. It was the first European settlement in India, colonised by the Portuguese from 1502.

Co·chin² (kŏchin, kōchin) *n.* A large domestic fowl of a breed developed in Asia, having thickly feathered legs. Also called "Cochin China". [After COCHIN CHINA.]

Coch·in Chi·na (kóch-in chínə, kóch-). The European name for a historic region of central and southern Vietnam. It was incorporated into the French Union of Indochina (1887–1945) and now forms part of Vietnam.

coch·i·neal (kóchi-neèl, -neel) *n.* **1.** A tropical American scale insect, *Dactylopius coccus*, that feeds on certain species of cacti. Also called "cochineal insect". **2.** A brilliant red dye, used especially in cookery, made by drying and pulverising the bodies of the females of this insect. **3.** Vivid red. [French *cochenille*, from Spanish *cochinilla*, from Latin *coccinus*, scarlet, from Greek *kokkinos*, from *kokkos*, kermes berry.] —**coch·i·neal** *adj.*

coch·le·a (kŏckli-ə) *n., pl.* **-leae** (-ee). A spiral tube of the inner ear resembling a snail shell and containing nerve endings essential for hearing. [New Latin, from Latin, snail shell, from Greek *kokhlias*, from *kokhlos*, land snail.] —**coch·le·ar** (-ər) *adj.*

cochlear implant *n.* An electronic implant in the cochlea to facilitate hearing by stimulating the acoustic nerve.

cochlear nerve *n.* The nerve connecting the cochlea to the brain, responsible for the nerve impulses relating to hearing. It is a division of the **acoustic nerve** *(see).*

coch·le·ate (kŏckli-ət, -it, -ayt) *adj.* Also **coch·le·at·ed** (-aytid). Shaped like a snail shell; spirally twisted. [Latin *cochleātus*, from *cochlea*, snail. See **cochlea.**]

cock¹ (kok) *n.* **1.** The adult male of the domestic fowl. **2. a.** The male of various other birds. **b.** The male of certain other animals, such as the lobster and the salmon. **3.** A weathervane in the shape of a cock; a weathercock. **4.** A tap or valve by which the flow of a liquid or gas can be regulated. **5. a.** The hammer in a firearm. **b.** Its position when ready for firing. **6.** *British Slang.* A mate; a fellow. Used as a familiar term of address. **7.** *British Slang.* Nonsense. **8.** *Vulgar Slang.* The penis. ∼*v.* **cocked, cocking, cocks.** —*tr.* **1.** To set the hammer of (a firearm) in a position ready for firing. **2.** To tilt or turn (the ears, for example) up or to one side, usually in a jaunty or alert manner. —*intr.* **1.** To cock the hammer of a firearm. **2.** To turn or stick up. ∼*adj.* Male. Said of birds and, sometimes, other animals: *a cock lobster.* [Middle English, Old English *cocc*, probably from Medieval Latin *coccus* (imitative).]

cock² *n.* A cone-shaped pile of straw or hay. ∼*tr.v.* **cocked, cocking, cocks.** To arrange (straw or hay) in such piles. [Middle English *cok*, Old English *cocc* (attested only in place names), perhaps from Scandinavian.]

cock·ade (kok-áyd) *n.* A rosette or knot of ribbon worn especially on the hat as a badge. [Originally *cockard*, from French *cocarde*, jauntily tilted hat, from Old French *coquard*, strutting, vain, from *coq*, COCK.] —**cock·ad·ed** (-id) *adj.*

cock·a·doo·dle·doo (kŏckə-dōōd'l-dōō) *n.* A representation of the characteristic crow of a cock. [Imitative.]

cock·a·hoop (kŏckə-hōōp ‖ -hoōp) *adj.* **1.** In a state of elation or exultation. **2.** Boastful. [From the expression *set cock a hoop*, perhaps "to set a cock on a hoop or measure of grain".] —**cock·a·hoop** *adv.*

Cock·aigne, Cock·ayne (ko-káyn, kə-) *n.* An imaginary land of easy and luxurious living. [Middle English *cockayne*, from Old French *(pais de) quoquaigne*, "(land of) delicacies", probably from Middle Low German *kōkenje*, small fancy sugar cake, diminutive of *kōke*, cake.]

cock·a·leek·ie, cock·ie·leek·ie (kŏckə-léeki) *n.* A cream soup made with leeks and chicken, of Scottish origin.

cock·a·lo·rum (kŏckə-láwrəm ‖ -lórəm) *n.* **1.** A little man with an unduly high opinion of himself. **2.** A children's jumping game like leapfrog. [Pseudo-Latin : COCK ("strutting leader") + Latin *-orum*, genitive plural ending.]

cock-and-bull story (kŏk-ən-boól) *n.* An absurd or highly improbable tale. [Originally a rambling animal fable about a cock changed into a bull.]

cock·a·tiel (kŏckə-téel) *n.* A crested parrot, *Nymphicus hollandicus*, of Australia, having grey and yellow plumage. Also called "quarrion". [Dutch *kaketielje*, probably from Portuguese *cacatilha*, diminutive of *cacatua*, COCKATOO.]

cock·a·too (kŏckə-tóo) *n., pl.* **-toos. 1.** Any of various parrots of the genus *Cacatuinae* and related genera, of Australia and adjacent areas, characterised by a long, erectile crest. **2.** *Australian & N. Z. Informal.* A small farmer. Also called ("cocky"). [Dutch *kaketoe*, from Malay *kakatua.*]

cock·a·trice (kŏckə-trīss, -triss) *n.* A mythical serpent reputed to be hatched from a cock's egg and supposed to have the power of killing by its glance. Compare **basilisk.** [Middle English *cocatrice*, basilisk, crocodile, from Old French *cocatris*, from Medieval Latin *cocātrix*, variant of Late Latin *calcātrix*, "the tracker" (translation of Greek *ikhneumōn*, ICHNEUMON), from *calcāre*, to track, from *calx*, heel.]

cock·boat (kŏck-bōt) *n.* A small rowing boat kept on a ship. [Middle English *cokbote* : *cok*, cockboat, from Old French *coque, coche*, probably from Late Latin *caudica*, canoe (made from the trunk of a tree), from Latin *caudex*, trunk of a tree + BOAT.]

cock·chaf·er (kŏck-chayfər) *n.* Any of various Old World beetles of the Scarabaeidae family; especially, *Melolontha melolontha*, the larvae of which often destroy plant roots. Also called "May bug".

[COCK (bird) + CHAFER (so called probably from its large size).]

Cock·croft (kók-kroft), **Sir John Douglas** (1897–1967). British pioneer of atomic physics. He invented, with E.T.S. Walton, the first machine to split the atom (1932). He contributed to the wartime development of the atomic bomb and was director of the Atomic Energy Research Establishment at Harwell (1946–59). He and Walton were awarded the 1951 Nobel prize for physics.

Cockcroft·Walton accelerator n. An early linear accelerator consisting of an ion source and a series of cylindrical high-voltage electrodes to accelerate the ions on to a target. It was used in producing the first artificial disintegration of an atomic nucleus. Also called "Cockcroft-Walton generator". [After Sir John Douglas COCKCROFT and Ernest Thomas Sinton WALTON, the inventors.]

cock·crow (kók-krō) n. The time of day when the cock crows; early morning; dawn.

cocked hat (kokt) n. A hat with the brim turned up in two or three places; especially, a three-cornered hat; a tricorn. —**knock into a cocked hat.** Informal. To defeat or nullify utterly.

cock·er¹ (kóckər) n. 1. A cocker spaniel. 2. A person who keeps or trains fighting cocks.

cocker² tr.v. **-ered, -ering, -ers.** To pamper, spoil, or coddle. [Middle English cokerenägger.]

cock·er·el (kóck-rəl, -ərəl) n. 1. A young domestic cock. 2. Loosely, a domestic cock. [Middle English cokerelle, diminutive of COCK.]

cocker spaniel n. A dog of a breed originally developed in England, having long, drooping ears and a variously coloured silky coat. [Originally used for hunting woodcocks.]

cock-eyed (kók-īd, -īd) adj. 1. Cross-eyed. 2. Slang. a. Crooked; askew. b. Foolish; ridiculous; absurd. c. Drunk.

cock·fight (kók-fīt) n. A fight between gamecocks that are often fitted with metal spurs. —**cock·fight·ing** adj. & n.

cock·horse (kók-hórss, -hawrss) n. A hobbyhorse.
~adv. Also **a-cock-horse** (ə-). On horseback.

cockieleekie. Variant of **cock-a-leekie.**

cock·le¹ (kóck'l) n. 1. Any of various bivalve molluscs of the family Cardiidae, especially Cardium edule, having rounded or heart-shaped shells with radiating ribs. 2. The shell of any of these molluscs; a cockleshell. 3. A wrinkle or pucker. 4. A small and shallow boat. —**the cockles of (one's) heart.** One's innermost feelings.
~v. **cockled, -ling, -les.** —tr. To cause to wrinkle or pucker. —intr. To become wrinkled or puckered. [Middle English cokille, from Old French coquille, shell, from Vulgar Latin conchīlia (unattested), variant of Latin conchȳllium, from Greek konkhullion, diminutive of konkhē, mussel, conch.]

cockle² n. Any of several plants often growing as weeds in grain fields, especially the corn cockle. [Middle English cok(k)el, Old English coccel, from Medieval Latin cocculus (unattested), diminutive of Latin coccus, kermes berry.]

cock·le·bur (kóck'l-bur) n. 1. Any of several coarse weeds of the genus Xanthium, especially X. spinosum, bearing prickly burs. 2. The bur of any of these plants.

cock·le·shell (kóck'l-shel) n. 1. a. The shell of a cockle. b. A shell similar to that of a cockle. 2. A small, light boat.

cock·loft (kók-loft || -lawft) n. A small loft. [16th century : perhaps COCK (fowl) + LOFT, from its use as a roosting place.]

cock·ney (kók-ni) n., pl. **-neys.** 1. Often capital C. A native of the East End of London or adjacent areas. 2. The dialect or accent of cockneys.
~adj. Of or like cockneys or their dialect. [Middle English cokeney, "cock's egg", pampered brat, effeminate youth, townsman (of London) : cokene, genitive plural of cok, COCK + ey, egg, Old English æg.]

cock of the north n. The brambling (see).

cock-of-the-rock (kók-əv-thə-rók) n., pl. **cocks-of-the-rock.** Either of two South American birds, Rupicola rupicola or R. peruviana, having a distinctive crest and bright-orange or reddish plumage in the male. [From its habit of nesting on rocks.]

cock of the walk n. 1. The leader or most important person in a group. 2. An overbearing or domineering person.

cock·pit (kók-pit) n. 1. A pit or enclosed space for cockfights. 2. A site of many battles. 3. a. In old warships, a section used as quarters for junior officers and as a station for the wounded during a battle. b. In small decked vessels, an area from which the vessel is steered. 4. a. The space for the pilot, and sometimes passengers, in the fuselage of a small aircraft. b. The space set apart for the pilot and crew in a large airliner; the flight deck. 5. The place where the driver of a racing car sits.

cock·roach (kók-rōch) n. Any of various oval, flat-bodied insects of the family Blattidae, several species of which are common household pests. [Earlier cacarootch, from Spanish cucaracha†.]

cocks·comb (kóks-kōm) n. Also **cox·comb** (for sense 4). 1. The comb of a cock. 2. The cap of a jester, decorated to resemble this. 3. Any of several plants of the genus Celosia; especially, C. argentea cristata, having a showy crested or rolled flower cluster. 4. A pretentious fop.

cocks·foot (kóks-foot) n., pl. **-foots.** A perennial grass, Dactylis glomerata, sown as a pasture grass in North America and South Africa. [From its appearance.]

cock·shy (kók-shī) n., pl. **-shies.** British. 1. A target aimed at in throwing contests. 2. The throw itself. 3. A target for abuse or ridicule. [In the earliest form of this game, the contestants shied or threw sticks at a cock.]

cock·spur (kók-spur) n. 1. An annual grass, Echinochloa crus-galli, widely distributed in warm temperate and tropical areas. 2. A small, thorny North American tree, Crataegus crus-galli, having white flowers and small red fruit. [From the resemblance of its thorn to a cock's spur.]

cock·sure (kók-shoor, -shawr || -shewr) adj. Too sure of oneself or one's opinions; overconfident. [16th century : from cock, euphemistic for GOD + SURE.] —**cock·sure·ly** adv. —**cock·sure·ness** n.

cock·tail¹ (kók-tayl) n. 1. Any of various mixed alcoholic drinks, often served chilled, consisting usually of a spirit combined with fruit juices or other ingredients, such as bitters or vermouth. 2. An appetiser typically consisting of seafood or mixed fruits: a prawn cocktail. 3. A mixture of medicinal drugs in drinkable form. 4. A mixture of potent ingredients: a heady cocktail of threats and promises.
~adj. 1. Of, pertaining to, or served with cocktails: cocktail sausages. 2. Suitable for wear on semiformal occasions: a cocktail dress. [19th-century (U.S.) : apparently COCKTAIL (horse), but the reason for the name is obscure.]

cocktail² n. A horse that has had its tail docked. [Earlier, "docked tail (of horse)", from COCK (fowl) + TAIL.]

cocktail party n. A drinks party, usually in the early evening.

cock up tr.v. British Slang. To cause (a plan or project) to fail. [From COCK¹ (nonsense).]

cock·up (kók-up) n. 1. British Slang. a. A blunder. b. Something that has been bungled; a mess. 2. Archaic. A hat or cap with upturned front.

cock·y¹ (kócki) adj. **-ier, -iest.** Informal. Cheerfully self-assertive or self-confident; conceited. Said especially of or about males. —**cock·i·ly** adv.

cocky² n., pl. **-ies.** Australian & N. Z. Informal. A small farmer, a **cockatoo** (see). [Diminutive of COCKATOO.]

co·co (kókō) n., pl. **-cos.** adj. Made of fibres from the coconut shell: coco matting. [Spanish, from Portuguese coco, goblin, grimace (referring to the base of the coconut shell, which resembles a face).]

co·coa (kókō) n. 1. A powder made from cocoa beans after they have been roasted, ground, and freed of most of their fatty oil. 2. A beverage made by combining this powder with water or milk and sugar. 3. Moderate brown to reddish brown. [Variant of CACAO, by confusion with COCO (nut).] —**co·coa** adj.

cocoa bean n. The seed of the cacao.

cocoa butter n. A yellowish-white, waxy solid obtained from cocoa beans and used in the manufacture of pharmaceuticals, confections, and soap. Also called "cacao butter".

coco de mer (-də-maír) n. 1. A Seychelles palm tree, Lodoicea maldivica, bearing a large fruit that contains a two-lobed edible nut. 2. The nut of this palm. [French, "sea coconut".]

co·con·scious (kō-kónshəss) adj. Being aware or conscious of the same things.
~n. Also **co·con·scious·ness** (-nəss, -niss). Psychiatry. Mental processes outside the realm of conscious activity or awareness, as with schizophrenic individuals.

co·co·nut, co·coa·nut (kókə-nut || -nət) n. The fruit of the coconut palm, a large seed with a thick, hard shell that encloses edible white meat and has a milky fluid, coconut milk, filling the hollow centre.

coconut butter n. A solid form of coconut oil used for making soap, candles, and other products.

coconut crab n. The **robber crab** (see).

coconut matting n. A type of coarse matting made from the outer fibres of the coconut.

coconut oil n. The oil obtained from the white flesh of the coconut, used especially in the manufacture of soaps and cosmetics.

coconut palm n. A tall palm tree, Cocos nucifera, native to the East Indies, bearing coconuts as fruit. Also called "coco", "coco palm", "coconut tree".

coconut shy n. A sideshow at a fair in which balls are thrown at coconuts to knock them off their stands and win a prize.

co·coon (kə-kóōn) n. 1. A covering of silk or similar fibrous material spun by the larvae of moths and other insects as protection for their pupal stage. 2. Any similar protective covering or structure, such as that of a spider or earthworm. 3. A protective plastic coating placed over stored inactive military or naval equipment.
~v. **cocooned, -cooning, -coons.** —tr. To cover or envelop in, or as if in, a cocoon. —intr. To form a cocoon. [French cocon, from Provençal cocoun, from coco, eggshell, hence, cocoon, from Latin coccum, coccus, kermes berry, from Greek kokkos.]

co·co·pan (kō-ko-pan) n. In South Africa, a small truck on a mine railway. [Possibly from Zulu nqukumbana, small cart.]

Co·cos Islands (kō-koss, -kəss). Also **Keel·ing Islands** (kéeling). A group of coral island territories of Australia in the east Indian Ocean. They were discovered in 1609 and settled from 1826.

co·cotte (ko-kót, kō- || U.S. kaw-káwt) n. 1. A prostitute or demimondaine. 2. A small dish used for baking individual portions, especially of egg dishes. [French, originally a baby's word for hen, from coq, cock.]

co·co·yam (kókō-yam) n. A tropical plant, the taro (see).

Coc·teau (kók-tō, -tō), **Jean** (1889–1963). French artist, poet, and dramatist. His works, including the film Orphée (1950) and the play La Machine infernale (1934), made use of dreams and myths.

Co·cy·tus (kō-sī-təss) n. Greek Mythology. One of the six rivers of Hades. [Latin, from Greek Kōkutos, "river of lamentation", from kōkuein, to wail, lament.]

cod¹ (kod) n., pl. **cod** or **cods.** Any of various marine fishes of the family Gadidae; especially, *Gadus morhua* (or *G. callarias*), an important food fish of Northern Atlantic waters and a source of cod-liver oil. Also called "codfish". [Middle English.]

cod² *n. British Informal.* Nonsense. [Shortened from CODSWALLOP.]

cod³ *n. British Informal.* A hoax or trick; a piece of humorous deception.
~*adj.* Mock; pastiche: *cod French.*
~*v.* **codded, codding, cods.** *British Informal.* —*tr.* To play a joke on; trick in a humorous way. —*intr.* To play jokes; hoax; tease. [19th century : origin obscure.]

COD, C.O.D. 1. cash on delivery. 2. *U.S.* collect on delivery.

Cod. codex.

co·da (kṓdə) *n.* 1. *Music.* A passage added on to the end of a movement or composition that brings it to a formal close. 2. In ballet, the closing part of a pas de deux. [Italian, "tail", from Latin *cōda, cauda.*]

cod·dle (kŏd'l) *tr.v.* **-dled, -dling, -dles.** 1. To cook in water just below boiling point. 2. To treat indulgently; pamper. —See Synonyms at **pamper.** [Variant of CAUDLE.] —**cod·dler** *n.*

code (kōd) *n.* 1. **a.** A systematically arranged and comprehensive collection of laws. **b.** Any systematic collection of regulations and rules of procedure or conduct: *the military code.* 2. A generally accepted set of principles: *a code of conduct.* 3. A system of signals used to represent letters or numbers in transmitting messages. 4. A system of symbols, letters, or words given certain arbitrary meanings, used for transmitting messages requiring secrecy or brevity. Compare **cipher.** 5. A system of symbols used to identify something for classification or selection. See **genetic code.**
~*v.* **coded, coding, codes.** —*tr.* 1. To systematise and arrange (laws and regulations) into a code; codify. 2. To encode. 3. To carry the genetic information for (a specific amino acid, for example). —*intr.* To be or carry genetic information. Used with *for.* [Middle English, from Old French, from Latin *cōdex,* CODEX.] —**cod·er** *n.*

co·deine (kṓ-deen, -di-een, -in) *n.* An alkaloid narcotic, $C_{18}H_{21}NO_3$, derived from opium or morphine, used for relieving coughing, as an analgesic, and as a hypnotic. [French *codéine* : Greek *kōdeia,* poppyhead, from *koos,* hollow place, cavity + -INE.]

Code Napoléon *n.* The code of French civil law, prepared under the direction of Napoleon Bonaparte between 1804 and 1807.

co·dex (kṓdeks) *n., pl.* **codices** (kṓ-di-seez, kŏddi-). *Abbr.* **Cod.** A manuscript volume, especially of the Scriptures. [Latin *cōdex, caudex,* tree trunk, board, writing tablet, book (of laws).]

Codex Ju·ris Ca·non·i·ci (jŏŏr-iss kə-nónni-sī, -chee) *n.* The code of law that has governed the Roman Catholic Church since 1918. [Latin, "book of canon laws".]

cod·fish (kŏd-fish) *n., pl.* **-fishes** or collectively **codfish.** The **cod¹** *(see).*

codg·er (kójər) *n. Informal.* An old man; especially, an eccentric one. Used in the phrase *old codger.* [Perhaps a variant of *cadget.* See **cadge.**]

cod·i·cil (kŏdi-sil, kóddi-) *n.* 1. *Law.* A supplement or appendix to a will. 2. Any supplement or appendix. [Middle English, from Old French *codicille,* from Latin *cōdicillus,* diminutive of *cōdex,* CODEX.] —**cod·i·cil·la·ry** (-síllóri) *adj.*

cod·i·fy (kŏdi-fī, kóddi-) *tr.v.* **-fied, -fying, -fies.** 1. To reduce to a code: *codify laws.* 2. To arrange or systematise. —**cod·i·fi·ca·tion** (-fi-káysh'n) *n.* —**cod·i·fi·er** *n.*

cod·ling¹ (kŏd-ling) *n.* Also **cod·lin** (-lin). *British.* 1. A long, tapering apple. 2. An unripe apple. [Middle English *querdlyng,* from Anglo-French *quer de lion,* "lion's heart", from its elongated shape.]

codling² *n., pl.* **-lings** or collectively **codling.** A young cod.

codling moth *n.* Also **codlin moth.** A small greyish moth, *Laspreyresia pomonella,* the larvae of which are destructive to various fruits, especially apples.

cod·lins-and-cream (kŏdlinz-ən-kreém) *n.* A Eurasian plant, *Epilobium hirsutum,* having hairy stems and leaves and purple-red flowers in a stalked spike. [From CODLING (apple).]

cod-liv·er oil (kŏd-livvər) *n.* An oil obtained from the livers of cod and containing a rich supply of vitamins A and D.

co·do·main (kṓ-do-máyn, -dō-, -mayn) *n. Mathematics.* The **range** *(see)* of a function.

co·don (kṓd-on) *n. Genetics.* A sequence of three adjacent nucleotides on a DNA molecule that specifies the insertion of an amino acid in a specific structural position during protein synthesis. [COD(E) + -ON.]

cod·piece (kŏd-peess) *n.* A pouch at the crotch of the tight-fitting breeches worn by men in the 15th and 16th centuries. [Middle English.]

co-driv·er (kō-drĪvər, -drĪvər) *n.* One who takes turns with another to drive a car, especially in a race or rally.

cods·wal·lop (kŏdz-wolləp) *n. British Slang.* Nonsense, especially when put forward as a serious statement. [20th century : origin obscure.]

Co·dy (kṓdi), **William F(rederick),** known as Buffalo Bill. (1846–1917). U.S. frontiersman and showman, who from 1883 toured the United States and Europe with his Wild West Show.

Coe (kō), **Sebastian (Newbold)** (1956–). British runner. He has been the only athlete to hold world records at 800 metres, 1000 metres, 1500 metres, and mile simultaneously, and he has been a Tory M.P. (1992–97).

co-ed, co·ed (kṓ-ed) *U.S. Informal.* A woman student attending a co-educational school, college, or university.

~*adj. Informal.* Co-educational. [Short for *co-educational student.*]

co-ed·u·ca·tion (kṓ-eddew-káysh'n) *n.* The system of education in which both male and female pupils or students attend the same institution or classes. —**co-ed·u·ca·tion·al** *adj.*

co·ef·fi·cient (kṓ-i-fish'nt) *n.* 1. *Mathematics.* **a.** A numerical factor of an elementary algebraic term, such as 4 in the term 4*x.* **b.** The product of all but one of the factors of an expression, the product being regarded as a distinct entity with respect to the excluded factor and to a designated operation. See **correlation coefficient.** 2. A numerical measure of a physical or chemical property that is constant for a system under specified conditions. [New Latin *coefficiens* : CO- (together) + EFFICIENT.]

coefficient of self-induction *n.* Self-inductance *(see).*

coel- *comb. form.* Indicates a cavity within a body or bodily organ; for example, **coelenterate.** [New Latin, from Greek *koilos,* hollow.] **-coel, -cele, -coele** *n. comb. form.* Indicates the body cavity; for example, **haemocoel.**

coe·la·canth (seélə-kanth) *n.* Any of various fishes of the order Coelacanthiformes, known only in fossil form until a living species, *Latimeria chalumnae,* of African marine waters, was identified in 1938. [New Latin *coelacanthus,* "hollow-spined" : COEL- + Greek *akanthos,* spine, thorn, from *akantha,* thorny plant.] —**coe·la·can·thine** (-kánth-īn, -in) *adj.* —**coe·la·can·thous** (-kánthəss) *adj.*

coe·len·ter·ate (see-léntər-ayt, si-, -ət, -it) *n.* Any invertebrate animal of the phylum Coelenterata, characterised by a radially symmetrical body with a saclike internal cavity, and including the jellyfishes, hydras, sea anemones, and corals. See **cnidarian, ctenophoran.**
~*adj.* Of or belonging to the Coelenterata. [New Latin *coelenterata,* "hollow-intestined ones" : COEL- + ENTER(ON) + -ATE.] —**coe·len·ter·ic** (seélen-térrik) *adj.*

coe·len·ter·on (see-léntər-on, si-, -ən) *n., pl.* **-tera** (-ə). *Zoology.* The saclike body cavity of a coelenterate. [New Latin : COEL- + ENTERON.]

coe·li·ac, *U.S.* **ce·li·ac** (seéli-ak) *adj.* Of or pertaining to the abdomen. [Latin *coeliacus,* from Greek *koiliakos,* from *koilia,* belly.]

coeliac disease *n.* A chronic condition of young children in which the small intestine fails to absorb and digest fats and other food, resulting in distension of the abdomen, malnutrition, and foul-smelling stools.

coe·lom (seéləm) *n., pl.* **-loms** or **-lomata.** Also *chiefly U.S.* **ce·lom.** The body cavity in all animals higher than the coelenterates and certain primitive worms, formed by the splitting of the mesoderm into two layers. [German *Koelom,* from Greek *koilōma,* cavity, from *koilos,* hollow.]

coe·lo·stat (seélə-stat) *n. Astronomy.* A movable mirror that rotates slowly so as to compensate for the earth's rotation, used to direct light from a fixed region of the sky into a telescope or other optical instrument.

coeno-, ceno- *comb. form.* Also **coen-, cen-.** Indicates common; for example, **coenurus.** [New Latin, from Greek *koino-,* from *koinos,* common.]

coen·o·bi·um (see-nṓbi-əm) *n. Botany.* A colony of motile cells formed by certain green algae. [New Latin, from Greek *koinobion,* convent : *koinos,* common + *bios,* life.]

coe·no·cyte (seénə-sīt) *n. Botany.* An organism consisting of a multinucleate protoplasmic mass resulting from nuclear division without the formation of a new cell wall or membrane, as in slime moulds and certain fungi and algae. [COENO- + -CYTE.] —**coe·no·cyt·ic** (-síttik) *adj.*

coe·no·sarc (seén-ə-saark, -ō-) *n.* The system of tissues connecting the polyps of compound zoophytes such as corals. [COENO- + Greek *sarx* (stem *sark-*), flesh.]

coe·nu·rus (see-néwr-əss, si-) *n., pl.* **-ri** (-ī). The encysted larval stage of a tapeworm, *Taenia multiceps* (or *Multiceps multiceps*) that attacks the central nervous system of ruminant animals. [New Latin, "having a common tail" (because it has many heads and only one tail) : COEN(O)- + -UR(O)US.]

co·en·zyme (kṓ-énzīm) *n.* A heat-stable organic molecule that must be loosely associated with certain enzymes for them to function.

co·e·qual (kṓ-éekwəl) *adj. Archaic & Literary.* Equal with one another, as in rank or size.
~*n.* An equal. —**co·e·qual·i·ty** (kṓ-ee-kwólləti) *n.* —**co·e·qual·ly** *adv.*

co·erce (kō-érss) *tr.v.* **-erced, -ercing, -erces.** 1. To compel by force or the threat of force. 2. To dominate, restrain, or control forcibly. 3. To achieve by means of force; enforce: *coerce an agreement.* —See Synonyms at **force.** [Middle English *cohercen,* from Old French *cohercier,* from Latin *coercēre,* to constrain : *cō-,* together + *arcēre,* to restrain, confine.] —**co·erc·er** *n.* —**co·erci·ble** *adj.*

co·er·cion (kō-érsh'n) *n.* 1. The act or practice of coercing. 2. Government by coercion. —**co·er·cion·ar·y** (-əri ‖ -erri) *adj.*

co·er·cive (kō-ér-siv) *adj.* Characterised by or inclined to coercion. —**co·er·cive·ly** *adv.* —**co·er·cive·ness** *n.*

coercive force *n. Physics.* The external magnetic field strength required to demagnetise a given sample.

co·er·civ·i·ty (kṓ-er-sívvəti) *n. Physics.* The external magnetic field strength required to demagnetise a given sample that has been magnetised to saturation.

co·es·sen·tial (kṓ-i-sénsh'l) *adj. Theology.* Having the same nature or essence. —**co·es·sen·ti·al·i·ty** (-sénshi-ál-əti), **co·es·sen·tial·ness** *n.* —**co·es·sen·tial·ly** *adv.*

co·e·ta·ne·ous (kṓ-ee-táyni-əss, -i-) *adj.* Of equal age, duration, or period; contemporary. [Latin *coaetāneus* : *co-*, same + *aetās*, age.] —**co·e·ta·ne·ous·ly** *adv.* —**co·e·ta·ne·ous·ness** *n.*

co·e·ter·nal (kō-ee-térn'l, -i-) *adj.* Equally eternal; eternally existing with one another. —**co·e·ter·nal·ly** *adv.* —**co·e·ter·ni·ty** *n.*

Coeur de Lion. See **Richard I.**

co·e·val (kō-éev'l) *adj.* Originating or existing during the same period of time; lasting through the same era. [Latin *coaevus* : *cō-*, same + *aevum*, age.] —**co·e·val** *n.* —**co·e·val·ly** *adv.*

co·ex·ist (kō-ig-zíst, -eg- ‖ -ik-) *intr.v.* **-isted, -isting, -ists.** **1.** To exist together, at the same time, or in the same place. **2.** To exist together in peace.

co·ex·is·tence (kō-ig-zístɘnss, -eg- ‖ -ik-) *n.* **1.** The condition of existing together. **2.** The concurrent but separate existence of two or more nations of great ideological disparity. —**co·ex·is·tent** *adj.*

co·ex·ten·sive (kō-iks-tén-siv, -eks-) *adj.* Extending over the same space or time; having the same scope. —**co·ex·ten·sive·ly** *adv.*

co·fac·tor (kō-faktɘr) *n.* **1.** *Mathematics.* A determinant associated with a given element of a matrix, formed by removing the row and column containing this element. **2.** *Biochemistry.* A nonprotein portion of certain enzymes, essential for their activity, such as a coenzyme or a metal ion, as of sodium or potassium.

C. of E. Church of England.

cof·fee (kóffi ‖ *chiefly U.S.* káwfi) *n.* **1.** Any of several trees of the genus *Coffea,* native to eastern Asia and Africa, bearing berries containing beans used in the preparation of a beverage; especially, *C. arabica,* the chief commercial source of these beans. **2. a.** The seeds or beans of the coffee tree. **b.** Such beans roasted and ground. **3. a.** An aromatic, mildly stimulating beverage prepared from ground coffee beans. **b.** A cup of coffee. **4.** Moderate to dark yellowish brown.
~*adj.* **1.** Of, pertaining to, or accompanied by the drink coffee: *a coffee morning.* **2.** Having the colour coffee. [Italian *caffè,* from Turkish *kahve,* from Arabic *qahwah.*]

coffee bar *n.* A place that serves coffee and other refreshments.

coffee cup *n.* A usually small cup from which coffee is drunk.

cof·fee-house (kóffi-howss ‖ káwfi-) *n.* An establishment serving coffee and other refreshments, popular especially in the 17th and 18th centuries as a rendezvous for fashionable people.

coffee mill *n.* A device for grinding roasted coffee beans.

cof·fee·pot (kóffi-pot ‖ káwfi-) *n.* A pot for making or serving coffee.

coffee shop *n.* **1.** A shop that sells or serves coffee. **2.** *Chiefly U.S.* A small restaurant in which light meals are served.

coffee table *n.* A long, low table, often placed before a sofa.

cof·fee-ta·ble book (kóffi-tayb'l ‖ káwfi-) *n.* A large, expensive, illustrated book, for looking through rather than reading.

cof·fer (kóffɘr ‖ *chiefly U.S.* káwfɘr) *n.* **1. a.** A chest or a strong-box. **b.** *Plural.* Funds; a treasury. **3.** A decorative sunken panel in a soffit, ceiling, dome, or vault. **4.** A cofferdam.
~*tr.v.* **coffered, -fering, -fers.** **1.** To supply with decorative sunken panels. **2.** *Archaic.* To put in a coffer. [Middle English *cof(f)re,* box, chest, from Old French, from Latin *cophinus,* basket. See **coffin.**]

cof·fer·dam (kóffɘr-dam ‖ káwfɘr-) *n.* *Engineering.* **1.** A temporary watertight enclosure built in the water and pumped dry to expose the bottom so that construction, as of piers, may be undertaken. **2.** A watertight chamber attached to a ship's side to facilitate repairs below the water line.

cof·fin (kóffin ‖ *chiefly U.S.* káwfin) *n.* **1.** An oblong box in which a corpse is buried or cremated. **2.** A horse's hoof. **3.** A thick, usually lead, container for transporting radioactive materials.
~*tr.v.* **coffined, -fining, -fins.** To place in or as if in a coffin. [Middle English, box, basket, from Old French *cofin,* from Latin *cophinus,* from Greek *kophinus†,* basket, measure of capacity.]

coffin bone *n.* The bone inside the hoof of a horse or similar animal.

cof·fle (kóff'l ‖ *U.S. also* káwf'l) *n.* A file of animals, prisoners, or slaves, chained together in transit. [Arabic *qāfilah,* caravan.]

cog¹ (kog) *n.* **1.** Any of a series of teeth on the rim of a wheel which by engagement transmit motive force to a corresponding wheel or toothed rack. **2.** A cogwheel. **3.** A subordinate member within a given organisation.
~*tr.v.* **cogged, cogging, cogs.** To roll (steel ingots) to convert into blooms. [Middle English *cogge,* probably from Scandinavian, akin to Swedish *kugge.*]

cog² *v.* **cogged, cogging, cogs.** *Archaic Slang.* —*tr.* To load or manipulate (dice) fraudulently. —*intr.* To cheat, especially at dice. [16th century : origin obscure.]

cog³ *n.* A tenon projecting from a wooden beam and fitting into an opening in another beam to form a joint.
~*tr.v.* **cogged, cogging, cogs.** To join with such tenons. [19th century : origin obscure.]

cog. cognate.

co·gent (kōjɘnt) *adj.* **1.** Forcibly convincing. **2.** Compelling; powerful. [Latin *cōgens* (stem *cogent-*), present participle of *cōgere,* to force, drive together : *cō-*, together + *agere,* to drive.] —**co·gen·cy** (kōjɘn-si) *n.* —**co·gent·ly** *adv.*

cog·i·tate (kóji-tayt) *v.* **-tated, -tating, -tates.** —*intr.* To take long and careful thought; meditate; ponder. —*tr.* To think carefully about; consider intently. [Latin *cōgitāre* : *cō-* (intensive) + *agitāre,* to turn to mind, consider, AGITATE.] —**cog·i·ta·ble** (-tɘb'l) *adj.* —**cog·i·ta·tor** (-taytɘr) *n.*

cog·i·ta·tion (kóji-táysh'n) *n.* **1.** Thoughtful consideration; meditation. **2.** A serious thought; a reflection.

cog·i·ta·tive (kóji-tɘtiv, -taytiv) *adj.* Meditative. —**cog·i·ta·tive·ly** *adv.* —**cog·i·ta·tive·ness** *n.*

cog·i·to (kóggi-tō, kōgi-) *n.* *Philosophy.* The principle that establishes a person's existence from the fact of his thinking and awareness. [Latin, "I think" (abstracted from Descartes' phrase, *cogito, ergo sum,* "I think, therefore I am").]

co·gnac (kón-yak, kōn-) *n.* *Sometimes capital* **C.** A brandy produced in the vicinity of Cognac.

Co·gnac. Town in the Charente département of western France, situated on the river Charente. Only brandy produced in a limited area around the town can be called cognac.

cog·nate (kóg-nayt, -náyt) *adj.* *Abbr.* **cog.** **1.** Related by blood; having a common ancestor, especially a maternal one. **2.** *Linguistics.* Akin. Said especially of languages or of words in different languages derived from the same root. **3.** Related or analogous in nature, character, or function.
~*n. Abbr.* **cog.** A person or thing cognate with another. [Latin *cōgnātus* : *cō-*, same + *gnātus,* born, from *gnāscī, nāscī,* to be born.] —**cog·na·tion** (kog-náysh'n) *n.*

cog·ni·sa·ble (kóg-niz-ɘb'l, kónniz- ‖ kog-níz-) *adj.* **1.** Knowable or perceptible. **2.** Within a court's jurisdiction. —**cog·ni·sa·bly** *adv.*

cog·ni·sance (kóg-niz'nss, kónniz'nss) *n.* **1.** Conscious knowledge or awareness. **2.** The range of what one can know or understand. **3.** *Law.* **a.** The examination of a case by a court. **b.** The right or power of a court's jurisdiction. **4.** *Heraldry.* A crest or badge worn to distinguish the bearer. —**have cognisance of.** To know, especially in an official context. —**take cognisance of.** To take notice of; acknowledge. [Middle English *co(g)nisaunce,* from Old French *conoissance,* from *conoistre,* to know, from Latin *cognōscere,* to learn. See **cognition.**]

cog·ni·sant (kóg-niz'nt, kónniz'nt) *adj.* **1.** Fully informed; conscious. Used with *of.* **2.** *Philosophy.* Having cognition. [From COGNISANCE.]

cog·nise, cog·nize (kɘg-nīz, kóg-nīz) —*tr.v.* **-nised, -nising, -nises.** *Philosophy.* To have cognition of. [Back formation from COGNISANCE, by analogy with *recognise,* and so on.]

cog·ni·tion (kog-nísh'n) *n.* **1.** The mental process or faculty by which knowledge is acquired. **2.** That which comes to be known, as through perception, reasoning, or intuition; knowledge. [Middle English *cognicioun,* from Latin *cognitiō* (stem *cognition-*), from *cognōscere,* to get to know, learn : *cō-* (intensive) + *gnōscere,* to know.] —**cog·ni·tion·al, cog·ni·tive** (kógnitiv) *adj.*

cog·no·men (kog-nō-men ‖ -mɘn, kógnɘmɘn) *n., pl.* **-mens** or **-nomina** (-nómminɘ, -nóminɘ) **1.** A family name; a surname. **2.** The third and usually last name of a citizen of ancient Rome, such as *Caesar* in *Caius Julius Caesar.* Compare **nomen, praenomen.** **3.** Any name, especially a descriptive nickname. [Latin *cōgnōmen,* "additional name" (formed after *cognōscere,* to learn) : *cō-*, together + *nōmen,* name.] —**cog·nom·i·nal** (-nómmin'l) *adj.*

co·gno·scen·te (kón-yɘ-shén-ti, -yō-, kónnō-, kóg-nō-) *n., pl.* **-ti** (-tee). A person of expert knowledge or superior taste; a connoisseur. [Obsolete Italian, "the knowing one", from Latin *cognōscēns* (stem *cognōscent-*), present participle of *cognōscere,* to get to know. See **cognition.**]

cog·no·vit (kog-nóvit) *n.* *Law.* A written admission by a defendant of his liability, made to avoid the expense of a trial. [Latin, "he has acknowledged", from *cognōscere,* to get to know, recognise, acknowledge. See **cognition.**]

cog railway *n.* A railway designed to operate on steep slopes, having locomotives with a centre cogwheel that engages with a cogged centre rack to provide traction. Also called "rack railway".

cog·wheel (kóg-weel, -hweel) *n.* Any of a set of cogged wheels within a given mechanism.

co·hab·it (kō-hábbit) *intr.v.* **-ited, -iting, -its.** To live together in a sexual relationship when not legally married. Used with *with.* [Late Latin *cohabitāre* : *cō-*, together + *habitāre,* to inhabit.] —**co·hab·it·ant, co·hab·it·ee** *n.* —**co·hab·i·ta·tion** *n.*

co·here (kō-héer) —*intr.v.* **-hered, -hering, -heres.** **1.** To stick or hold together. **2.** To be logically or contextually connected or consistent. [Latin *cohaerēre* : *cō-*, together + *haerēre,* to cling to.]

co·her·ence (kō-héer-ɘnss ‖ -herrɘnss) *n.* Also **co·her·en·cy** (-i). The quality or state of logical or orderly relationship of parts; consistency; logical or contextual congruity.
Usage: Standard English makes a clear distinction between *coherence* and *cohesion. Coherence* refers to the logical or orderly relationship of parts, especially in speech or writing. *Cohesion* refers to the literal sticking together of objects or substances, or figuratively to a close connection established between people.

co·her·ent (kō-héer-ɘnt ‖ -hérrɘnt) *adj.* **1.** Sticking together; cohering. **2.** Marked by an orderly or logical relation of parts that allows comprehension or recognition: *coherent speech.* **3.** *Physics.* Of or pertaining to waves with a continuous relationship among phases. **4.** Designating or pertaining to a system of units of measurement in which a small number of basic units are defined from which all others in the system are derived by multiplication or division only. —**co·her·ent·ly** *adv.*

co·he·sion (kō-héezh'n) *n.* **1.** The process or condition of cohering; a becoming or remaining united, especially in a tangible or explicit way. **2.** *Physics.* The mutual attraction by which the elements of a body are held together. Compare **adhesion.** **3.** *Botany.* The congenital joining of two parts, such as flower petals. —See Usage note at **coherence.** [Latin *cohaesus,* past participle of *cohaerēre,* COHERE.]

co·he·sive (kō-hée-siv ‖ -ziv) *adj.* Showing or producing cohesion or unity. —**co·he·sive·ly** *adv.* —**co·he·sive·ness** *n.*

co·hort (kō-hawrt) *n.* **1.** Any of the ten divisions of a Roman legion, consisting of 300 to 600 men. **2.** A group or band united in some struggle. **3.** *U.S. Informal.* An associate. [Middle English, from Old French *cohorte,* from Latin *cohors* (stem *cohort-*), enclosed yard, company of soldiers, multitude.]

co·ho salmon (kō-hō) *n.* A food and game fish, *Oncorhyncus kisutch,* originally of Pacific waters. Also called "silver salmon". [*Coho,* probably from an American Indian language.]

co·hune (kō-hōon) *n.* A tropical American palm tree, *Attalea cohune,* having long feather-like leaves and oily nuts. Also called "cohune palm". [American Spanish, from Mosquito *ókhún.*]

C.O.I. Central Office of Information.

coif (koyf) *n.* **1.** A tight-fitting cap worn under a veil, as by nuns. **2. a.** A white skullcap formerly worn by English lawyers and serjeants at law. **b.** The office or rank of serjeant at law.
~*tr.v.* (koyf; *also* kwof *for sense* 2) **coifed, coifing, coifs. 1.** To cover with or as if with a coif. **2.** To arrange or dress (the hair, especially of women). [Middle English *coyfe,* from Old French *coiffe, coife,* from Late Latin *cofia†.*]

coif·feur (kwa-fér, kwaa-, kwo-, -fôr) *n.* Feminine **coif·feuse** (-férz, -fōz). A hairdresser. [French, from COIF.]

coif·fure (kwa-féwr, kwaa-, kwo-, -fúr) *n.* A way of arranging the hair; a woman's hairstyle.
~*tr.v.* **coiffured, -furing, -fures.** To arrange or dress (women's hair). [French, from *coiffer,* to COIF.]

coign (koyn) *n.* A projecting corner, a **quoin** *(see).* [Variant of COIN (quoin).]

coil (koyl) *n.* **1.** A series of connected spirals or concentric rings formed by gathering or winding: *a coil of rope.* **2.** An individual spiral or ring within such a series. **3.** A spiral pipe or series of spiral pipes, as in a radiator. **4.** *Electricity.* **a.** A wound spiral of two or more turns of insulated wire, used to introduce inductance into a circuit or to provide a magnetic field. **b.** Any device of which such a spiral is the major component. **5.** An **intrauterine device** *(see)* shaped like a coil. **6.** A transformer in a petrol engine that supplies the high voltage to the sparking plugs through the distributor.
~*v.* **coiled, coiling, coils.** —*tr.* **1.** To wind in loops, spirals, or concentric rings. **2.** To wind into a shape resembling a coil. —*intr.* **1.** To form coils. **2.** To move in a spiral course. **3.** To move in a sinuous way. [Middle English *coilen,* to collect, cull, from Old French *coillir,* from Latin *colligere* : *com-,* together + *legere,* to gather.] —**coil·er** *n.*

coil spring *n.* A spring formed from a helical coil of wire.

Coim·bra (kwéem-brə, kwím-). City in central Portugal, situated on the Mondego River. It has the oldest university in the country and a fine Romanesque cathedral.

coin (koyn) *n.* **1.** A small piece of metal, usually flat and circular, authorised by a government for use as money. **2.** Metal money collectively. **3.** *Architecture.* A cornerstone, a **quoin** *(see).*
~*tr.v.* **coined, coining, coins. 1. a.** To make (coins) from metal; mint; strike: *coin fifty-pence pieces.* **b.** To make coins from (metal): *coin gold.* **2.** *Informal.* To earn (money) quickly and in large quantities: *coining it in.* **3.** To invent (a word or phrase). [Middle English *coyne,* wedge, design stamped on a coiner's die, coin, from Old French *coing, coin,* wedge, from Latin *cuneus†,* wedge.] —**coin·a·ble** *adj.* —**coin·er** *n.*

coin·age (kóynij) *n.* **1.** The act or process of making coins. **2. a.** Metal currency. **b.** A system of metal currency. **3. a.** A coined word or phrase. **b.** The invention of new words.

co·in·cide (kō-in-síd) *intr.v.* **-cided, -ciding, -cides. 1. a.** To occupy the same position simultaneously. **b.** To have identical dimensions. **2.** To happen at the same time or during the same period. **3.** To correspond exactly; be identical. **4.** To concur; agree. —See Synonyms at **agree.** [Medieval Latin *coincidere* : *cō-,* together + *incidere,* to happen.]

co·in·ci·dence (kō-ín-si-d'nss ‖ -denss) *n.* **1.** The state or fact of coinciding. **2.** An accidental sequence of events that appear to have a causal relationship. —**co·in·ci·dent** *adj.*

coincidence gate *n. Electronics.* A circuit or device that produces an output only when both its input terminals receive pulses within a specific short interval; a **gate** *(see).*

co·in·ci·den·tal (kō-ín-si-dént'l, kō-ín-) *adj.* Occurring as or resulting from coincidence. —**co·in·ci·den·tal·ly** *adv.*

coin-op (kóyn-op) *n.* A launderette in which the machines are operated by the insertion of coins. Also called "coin-op laundry".

co·in·sur·ance (kō-in-shóor-ənss, -shór- ‖ -shéwr-) *n.* **1.** Insurance held jointly with another or others. **2.** A form of insurance in which a person insures property for less than its full value and agrees to be responsible for the difference. —**co·in·sure** *v.* —**co·in·sur·er** *n.*

Coin·treau (kwéen-trō, kwáan-) *n.* A trademark for a colourless liqueur made from brandy and oranges.

coir (kóy-ər, koyr) *n.* The fibre obtained from the husk of a coconut, used in making rope and matting. [Malayalam *kāyar,* cord.]

co·i·tus (kō-itəss) *n.* Also **co·i·tion** (kō-ísh'n). Sexual intercourse. [Latin *coitus,* "meeting", from *coīre,* to come together : *cō-,* together + *īre,* to go.]

coitus in·ter·rup·tus (íntə-rúptəss) *n.* Sexual intercourse deliberately interrupted by withdrawal of the penis prior to ejaculation. Also called "withdrawal". [Latin, "interrupted intercourse".]

coke¹ (kōk) *n.* **1.** The solid carbonaceous residue obtained from coal after removal of volatile material by destructive distillation, used as fuel. **2.** A similar material formed in different ways; espe-

cially, the layer of carbon formed within an engine as a result of incomplete combustion of the fuel.
~*v.* **coked, coking, cokes.** —*tr.* To convert or change into coke. —*intr.* To become coke. [Middle English *coke†.*]

coke² *n. Slang.* Cocaine.

Coke *n.* A trademark for Coca-Cola.

Coke (kŏŏk; *also, incorrectly,* kōk), **Thomas William, Earl of Leicester** (1752–1842). British statesman and pioneer of agricultural improvement. Also known as "Coke of Holkham" (his family seat in Norfolk).

col (kol) *n.* **1.** A pass between two peaks or a gap in a ridge. **2.** *Meteorology.* A region of intermediate pressure between two anticyclones and two depressions. [French, from Old French, neck, from Latin *collum.*]

col. 1. collector. **2.** college; collegiate. **3.** colonial; colony. **4.** colour. **5.** column.

Col. 1. Colombia. **2.** Colonel. **3.** Colossians (New Testament).

col-¹. Variant of **com-.**

col-². Variant of **colo-.**

co·la, ko·la¹ (kốlə) *n.* **1.** Either of two African trees, *Cola nitida* or *C. acuminata,* cultivated in the tropics for their seeds. See **cola nut. 2.** A soft carbonated drink flavoured with an extract from cola nuts. [Probably a variant of Mandingo *kolo,* nut.]

co·la². Alternative plural of **colon.**

col·an·der (kúl-in-dər, kól-, -ən-) *n.* A bowl-shaped kitchen utensil with a perforated bottom for draining off liquids and rinsing food. [Middle English *colyndore, culatre,* from Old Provençal *colador* (unattested), from Vulgar Latin *cōlātor* (unattested), from Latin *cōlāre,* to strain, from *cōlum,* sieve, filter.]

cola nut, kola nut *n.* The seed of the cola tree, containing caffeine and theobromine and yielding an extract used in carbonated drinks and in pharmaceutical products.

co·lat·i·tude (kō-látti-tewd ‖ -tōod) *n. Astronomy.* The complement of the celestial latitude; (90°-β), where β is the celestial latitude.

Col·bert (kol-báir, kōl-), **Claudette,** born Lily Claudette Chauchoin (1903–96). French film actress, later a U.S. citizen. She made her name with vivacious performances in comedies such as *It Happened One Night* (1934) and *Midnight* (1939).

Col·bert, Jean-Baptiste (1619–83). French statesman and leading adviser to Louis XIV. To encourage trade, he reformed taxes, centralised the administration, and improved road and canal networks. He also developed the French navy and codified laws.

col·can·non (kəl-kánnən, kol-, kól-kannən) *n.* An Irish dish of mashed potatoes and cabbage. [Irish Gaelic *cal ceannan,* "white-headed cabbage" : *cal,* cabbage, from Old Irish from Latin *caulis* + *ceannan,* white-headed, from *ceann,* head.]

Col·ches·ter (kól-chistər ‖ kól-, -chestər). Town in Essex in southeast England, situated on the River Colne. Parts of the old Roman town, called Camulodunum, have been excavated, and relics are displayed in a fine Norman castle.

col·chi·cine (kól-chi-seen, -ki-, -sin) *n.* A poisonous alkaloid, $C_{22}H_{25}NO_6$, used experimentally to induce chromosome doubling and medicinally to treat gout. [German *Kolchizin,* from New Latin *colchicum,* COLCHICUM.]

col·chi·cum (kól-chi-kəm, -ki-) *n.* **1.** Any of various bulbous plants of the genus *Colchicum,* such as the **autumn crocus** *(see).* **2.** The dried seeds or corms of the autumn crocus, a source of colchicine. [New Latin, from Latin, a poisonous root, from Greek *Kolkhikon,* from *Kolkhikos,* of Colchis, belonging to the witch Medea of Colchis, from *Kolkhis, Colchis,* ancient region on the Black Sea.]

col·co·thar (kól-kə-thaar) *n.* A brownish-red iron oxide obtained as a residue after heating ferrous sulphate, used in glass polishing and as a pigment. [French *colcotar,* from Spanish, from Arabic *qolqoṭār.*]

cold (kōld) *adj.* **colder, coldest. 1. a.** Having a low or lower than usual temperature. **b.** Lacking heat: *the cold light of the moon.* **2.** Feeling no warmth; uncomfortably chilled. **3.** Designating a colour or tone that suggests little warmth, such as pale grey. **4.** Cooked and allowed to cool: *cold chicken.* **5.** *Informal.* **a.** Unconscious; insensible: *knocked cold.* **b.** Dead. **6.** Not affected by emotion; objective: *cold logic.* **7.** Without appeal to the senses or feelings; depressing: *cold decor.* **8.** Not affectionate or friendly: *a cold reception.* **9.** Without sexual desire; frigid. **10.** Unenthusiastic; apathetic: *The prospect left him cold.* **11.** Without freshness; faint; weak. Said of a scent in hunting. **12.** *Informal.* In guessing and searching games, far removed from the object sought.
~*adv. Informal.* **1.** Completely; thoroughly: *turned our offer down cold.* **2.** Without preparation or rehearsal.
~*n.* **1.** The relative lack of warmth. **2.** The sensation resulting from lack of warmth. **3.** A viral infection characterised by inflammation of the mucous membranes of the respiratory passages and accompanying fever, chills, coughing, and sneezing: *the common cold.* **4.** A condition of low air temperature; cold weather. —**catch a cold.** To get into difficulties. —**out in the cold.** Neglected; ignored. [Middle English *cold, cald,* Old English *ceald,* from Germanic.] —**cold·ly** *adv.* —**cold·ness** *n.*

cold-blood·ed (kōld-blúddid) *adj.* **1.** Ruthless; unfeeling; heartless. **2.** *Zoology.* Having a body temperature that varies with the external environment; poikilothermic. **3.** *Informal.* Likely to feel the cold. —**cold-blood·ed·ly** *adv.* —**cold-blood·ed·ness** *n.*

cold cathode *n.* An electrode from which electrons are emitted at ambient temperatures as a result of a high surface potential gradient.

cold chisel *n.* A chisel made of hardened, tempered steel and used for cutting cold metal.

cold comfort *n.* Something that gives little consolation or cheer.

cold cream *n.* An emulsion for cleansing and softening the skin.

cold cuts *pl.n. Chiefly U.S.* Slices of assorted cold meats.

cold desert *n.* **1.** A polar area with no vegetation. **2.** A tundra. **3.** A high plateau in a continental interior, cut off from moist maritime influences.

cold-drawn (kṓld-dráwn) *adj.* Designating a metal wire, bar, or the like that has been pulled through a die without heating to reduce its thickness or change its toughness or appearance.

cold duck *n.* An alcoholic drink combining champagne and burgundy. [Perhaps alluding to a dish suitable to accompany it.]

cold feet *n. Informal.* Failure of nerve.

cold frame *n.* A structure consisting of a frame with a glass top, used for protecting young plants from the cold.

cold front *n.* The leading portion of a cold atmospheric air mass moving into the base of, and eventually replacing, a warm air mass.

cold-heart-ed (kṓld-hártid) *adj.* Unkind; stern.

Col-ditz (kṓl-dits, kól-). Town in eastern Germany, situated on the river Mulde. A clifftop castle there was used as a prison camp (Oflag VII C) for persistent Allied escapers in World War II.

cold light *n.* **1.** Light producing little or no heat. **2.** Light emitted by a process other than incandescence.

cold pack *n.* **1.** *Medicine.* A therapeutic pack consisting of a cold, damp sheet, used to lower body temperature. **2.** A tinning process in which uncooked food is packed in tins, then sterilised by heat.

cold rubber *n.* A durable, strong, synthetic rubber polymerised at low temperatures.

cold shoulder *n. Informal.* Deliberately unkind or unfriendly treatment; a slight; a snub. Preceded by *the.*

cold-shoul-der (kṓld-shṓldər) *tr.v.* **-dered, -dering, -ders.** *Informal.* To give (someone) the cold shoulder; slight; snub.

cold snap *n.* A sudden, brief spell of cold weather.

cold sore *n.* A small sore on the lips that often accompanies a fever or cold and is caused by a viral infection. In technical usage, also called "herpes simplex".

cold storage *n.* **1.** The protective storage of foods, furs, or the like in a refrigerated place. **2.** *Informal.* A state of temporary suspension.

Cold-stream (kṓld-streem). Town in Borders area of southeast Scotland, situated on the river Tweed. The regiment of Coldstream Guards, for which it is famous, was first formed there in 1660.

cold sweat *n.* A reaction to extreme nervousness, characterised by a cold, moist skin.

cold turkey *n. Informal.* Immediate, complete withdrawal from something on which one has become dependent, such as an addictive drug. [Originally, a blunt statement, with reference to a plain ungarnished dish of cold meat; hence, a "blunt" withdrawal from drugs.]

cold type *n.* Typesetting, such as photocomposition, done without the casting of metal.

cold war *n.* **1.** A state of political tension and rivalry between nations, stopping short of actual full-scale war. **2.** *Capital C, capital W.* The state of such rivalry existing between the Soviet and Western blocs, following World War II. **—cold warrior** *n.*

cold wave *n.* **1.** An abrupt onset of unusually cold weather brought by a cold air mass following a depression. **2.** A form of permanent wave in which the hair is set by chemicals rather than heat. See **perm.**

cold-weld (kṓld-wéld) *tr.v.* **-welded, -welding, -welds.** To join (two metals) together without heat by forcing their surfaces together under pressure.

cold-work (kṓld-wúrk) *tr.v.* **-worked, -working, -works.** To shape or form (metal) in the absence of heat.

cole (kōl) *n. Rare.* Any of various plants of the genus *Brassica,* such as the cabbage or rape. Also called "colewort". [Middle English *col, coole,* Old English *cāl, cāul,* from Latin *caulis,* plant stalk, cabbage.]

co-lec-to-my (kə-léktəmi) *n., pl.* **-mies.** Surgical removal of part or all of the colon. [COL(O)- + -ECTOMY.]

cole-man-ite (kṓlmən-īt) *n.* A natural white or colourless hydrated calcium borate, $Ca_2B_6O_{11}\cdot5H_2O$, a principal source of borax. [After William T. *Coleman* (1824–93), U.S. pioneer, owner of the mine where it was discovered.]

co-le-op-ter-an (kólli-óptər-ən, kóli-) *n.* Any insect of the order Coleoptera, characterised by forewings modified to form tough protective covers for the hind wings, and including the beetles. *—adj.* Also **co-le-op-ter-ous** (-əss). Of or belonging to the Coleoptera. [New Latin *Coleoptera,* "sheath-winged ones", from Greek *koleopteros,* sheath-winged : *koleon,* sheath + -PTEROUS.] **—co-le-op-ter-ist** *n.*

co-le-op-tile (kólli-óp-tīl, kóli- ‖ *U.S.* -til) *n. Botany.* A leaflike structure in grasses and similar monocotyledons, forming a protective sheath around the plumule. [New Latin *coleoptilum,* "sheathed plume" : Greek *koleon,* sheath + *ptilon,* plume, down.]

co-le-o-rhi-za (kólli-ə-rī-zə, kóli-) *n., pl.* **-zae** (-zee). *Botany.* A protective sheath around the embryonic root of grasses and similar monocotyledons. [New Latin, "root sheath" : Greek *koleon,* sheath + *rhiza,* root.]

Co-le-ridge (kṓlə-rij, kól-), **Samuel Taylor** (1772–1834). British poet and critic. With William Wordsworth he published *Lyrical Ballads* (1798) which contained *The Rime of the Ancient Mariner,* his best-known poem. Other works include the visionary poem

Kubla Khan (published 1816), and the critical and philosophical *Biographia Literaria* (1817).

Co-le-ridge-Tay-lor (kṓlə-rij táylər, kól-), **Samuel** (1875–1912). British composer, of joint British and West African parentage. He is best remembered for his choral trilogy *Hiawatha* (1898–1900).

cole-slaw (kṓl-slaw) *n.* Also **cole slaw.** A salad consisting mainly of finely shredded raw cabbage with a dressing. [Dutch *koolsla* : *kool,* cabbage, from Middle Dutch *cōle,* from Latin *caulis* + *sla,* short for *salade,* SALAD.]

Col-et (kóllit), **John** (*c.* 1466–1519). English humanist theologian and champion of Renaissance scholarship within the Catholic Church. He founded St. Paul's School, London (1509) to promote classical as well as scriptural learning.

Co-lette (ko-lét), born Sidonie Gabrielle Claudine Colette (1873–1954). French novelist, famous especially for her sensuous and idyllic evocations of childhood and nature. Her works include *Gigi* (1944) and the series of *Claudine* books.

co-le-us (kṓli-əss) *n.* Any of various plants of the genus *Coleus,* of Eurasia and Africa, cultivated for their showy leaves, which are often marked with red, yellow, or white. [New Latin *Coleus,* from Greek *koleos, koleon,* sheath (from the way its filaments are joined).]

cole-wort (kṓl-wurt ‖ -wawrt) *n.* A plant, **cole** (*see*).

co-ley (kṓli) *n., pl.* **-leys** or collectively **coley.** Any of several edible fishes, especially the **coalfish** (*see*). [Probably shortened from *coalfish.*]

col-ic (kóllik) *n.* **1.** Acute, paroxysmal pain in the abdomen, caused by spasm, obstruction, or distension of the intestine. **2.** Severe abdominal pain in infants, usually resulting from accumulation of gas in the alimentary canal. In this sense, also called "infantile colic". [Middle English *colike,* from Old French *colique,* from Latin *cōlicus,* from Greek *kōlikos,* suffering in the colon, from *kōlon,* variant of *kolon,* COLON (intestine).] **—col-ick-y** (kólliki) *adj.*

col-i-cin (kól-i-sin, kól-) *n.* A protein produced by some strains of coliform bacteria such as *Escherichia coli* that is lethal to other strains of the same species. [New Latin, *coli* (specific name of the bacterium) + *-c-* (connective) + -IN.]

co-li-form bacteria (kólli-fawrm, kóli-) *pl.n.* A group of rod-shaped bacteria most commonly occurring in the intestines of man and other vertebrates, some of which can cause disease. [COL(ON) + -FORM.]

col-i-se-um (kólli-sée-əm) *n. Chiefly U.S.* A large stadium, theatre, or exhibition hall for public entertainment. [After the COLOSSEUM in Rome.]

Coliseum. Variant of **Colosseum.**

co-lis-tin (kō-listin, kó-) *n.* An antibiotic produced by the bacterium *Bacillus colistinus* that is used mainly in treating gastrointestinal infections. [New Latin *colistinus* (specific name of the bacterium).]

co-li-tis (ko-lītiss, kə-, kō-) *n.* Inflammation of the mucous membrane of the colon. [New Latin : COL(O)- + -ITIS.]

coll. 1. collateral. **2.** collection; collector. **3.** college; collegiate. **4.** colloquial; colloquialism.

coll-. Variant of **collo-.**

col-lab-o-rate (kə-lábbə-rayt) *intr.v.* **-rated, -rating, -rates. 1.** To work together, especially in a joint intellectual or artistic effort. **2.** To cooperate treasonably, especially with an enemy occupying one's country. [Late Latin *collabōrāre* : Latin *com-,* together + *labōrāre,* to work, from *labor,* labour.] **—col-lab-o-ra-tion** (-ráysh'n) *n.* **—col-lab-o-ra-tor** (-raytər) *n.*

col-lab-o-ra-tion-ist (kə-lábbə-ráysh'n-ist) *n.* A person who collaborates with an occupying enemy. **—col-lab-o-ra-tion-ism** *n.*

col-lage (ko-láazh, kə- ‖ *U.S. also* kō-) *n.* **1.** An artistic composition of materials and objects pasted over a surface. **2.** Such compositions as an art form. **3.** An assemblage of images or sounds on a theme. [French, from *coller,* to glue, paste, from *colle,* glue, from Vulgar Latin *colla* (unattested), from Greek *kolla.*]

col-la-gen (kóllə-jən) *n.* A fibrous protein occurring in bone, cartilage, and connective tissue. [Greek *kolla,* glue + -GEN.] **—col-la-gen-ic** (-jénnik), **col-lag-e-nous** (kə-lájinəss) *adj.*

col-lap-sar (kə-lápsar) *n.* A star which has collapsed on its own Schwarzschild radius; a black hole.

col-lapse (kə-láps) *v.* **-lapsed, -lapsing, -lapses.** *—intr.* **1.** To fall down or inwards suddenly; cave in. **2.** To break down suddenly in health or strength; lose consciousness or energy. **3.** To suffer a complete loss of power, effectiveness, or the like: *Opposition to the proposals has collapsed.* **4.** To fold compactly. *—tr.* To cause to collapse.
—n. **1.** The act of falling down or inwards, as from external pressure or loss of supports. **2.** An abrupt failure of function, strength, or health. [Back-formation from *collapsed,* from Latin *collāpsus,* past participle of *collābī,* to fall together, fall in ruin : *com-,* together + *lābī,* slide, fall.] **—col-laps-a-ble, col-laps-i-ble** *adj.* **—col-laps-i-bil-i-ty** (-ə-bílləti) *n.*

col-lar (kóllər) *n.* **1.** The part of a garment that encircles the neck. **2.** A necklace, choker, or similar ornament for the neck. **3.** A restraining or identifying band of leather or metal put round the neck of an animal. **4.** The cushioned part of a harness that presses against the shoulders of a draught animal. **5.** A cut of meat, usually bacon, from the neck. **6.** *Biology.* An encircling structure or bandlike marking suggestive of a collar. **7.** Any of various ringlike devices or parts used to limit, guide, or secure a machine part. **—hot under the collar.** *Informal.* Angry; annoyed.
—tr.v. **collared, -laring, -lars. 1.** To furnish with a collar. **2.** To

seize by the collar. **3.** *Informal.* To seize or detain. [Middle English *coler,* from Anglo-French, from Latin *collāre,* necklace, collar, from *collum,* neck.]

collar beam *n.* A timber beam connecting the midpoints of the sloping rafters of a pitched roof.

col·lar·bone (kóllər-bōn) *n. Anatomy.* The **clavicle** *(see).*

collar cell *n. Biology.* A **choanocyte** *(see).*

col·lard (kóllərd) *n.* A variety of kale, *Brassica oleracea acephala,* having a crown of edible leaves. [Variant of COLEWORT.]

col·lared dove (kóllərd) *n.* A common European dove, *Streptopelia decaocto,* having a pale, brownish-grey plumage with a black band round the back of the neck.

col·late (ko-láyt, kə- || kō-) *tr.v.* **-lated, -lating, -lates. 1.** To examine and compare carefully (texts) in order to note points of difference and agreement. **2.** In bookbinding, to examine (gathered signatures) in order to arrange them in proper sequence before binding. **3.** To verify the order and completeness of (the pages of a volume). **4.** To assemble in proper numerical or logical sequence. **5.** *Ecclesiastical.* To admit (a cleric) to a benefice. [Latin *collātus* (past participle of *conferre,* to bring together) : *com-,* together + *lātus,* "carried".] **—col·la·tor** (-ər) *n.*

col·lat·er·al (kə-láttrəl, ko-, -láttərəl) *adj. Abbr.* **coll. 1.** Situated or running side by side; parallel. **2.** Coinciding in tendency or effect; concomitant; accompanying. **3.** Serving to support or corroborate: *collateral evidence.* **4.** Of a secondary nature; subordinate. **5.** *Finance.* Of, designating, or guaranteed by a security pledged against the performance of an obligation: *a collateral loan.* **6.** Descended from the same ancestor, but through a different line: *a collateral branch of the family.* In this sense, compare **lineal.**

~n. **1.** *Finance.* Property acceptable as security for a loan or other obligation. **2.** A collateral relative. [Middle English, from Medieval Latin *collaterālis* : *com-,* together + *laterālis,* of the side, LATERAL.] **—col·lat·er·al·ly** *adv.*

col·la·tion (ko-láysh'n, kə- || kō-) *n.* **1.** The act or process of collating. **2.** A description of the material aspects of a book. **3.** In the Roman Catholic Church, a light meal permitted on fast days. **4.** Any light meal. [Middle English, from Old French, from Latin *collātiō* (stem *collātiōn-*), a bringing together (see **collate**). Senses 3, 4 : from the custom in Benedictine monasteries of reading from Cassian's *Collationes Patrum (Lives of the Fathers)* before taking a light meal on fast days.]

col·league (kólleeg) *n.* A fellow member, typically of a profession, staff, or academic faculty; an associate. See Synonyms at **partner.** [French *collègue,* from Old French, from Latin *collēga,* one chosen to serve with another : *com-,* together + *lēgāre,* to choose.] **—col·league·ship** *n.*

Usage: This word was traditionally used to refer to fellow members of the various professions (ecclesiastical, academic, medical, and so on) or to office-workers in business. In recent years, however, it has come to be used by other groups of workers, especially those involved in trade-union negotiations.

col·lect[1] (kə-lékt) *v.* **-lected, -lecting, -lects.** *—tr.* **1.** To bring together in a group; assemble. **2.** To accumulate as a hobby or for study. **3.** To obtain payment of (rents or taxes, for example). **4.** To recover control of. **5.** To call for; go and fetch. **6.** *Informal.* To win or receive (money, for example). **7.** *Australian Informal.* To run into or collide with. *—intr.* **1.** To gather together; congregate. **2.** To take in payments or donations. **—**See Synonyms at **gather.**

~adj. U.S., Australian, & N.Z. With payment to be made by the receiver.

~adv. U.S., Australian, & N.Z. So that the receiver is charged: *phone collect.* [Middle English *collecten,* from Latin *colligere* (past participle *collectus*), to gather together : *com-,* together + *legere,* to gather.] **—col·lect·i·ble, col·lect·a·ble** *adj. & n.*

col·lect[2] (kól-ekt, -ikt) *n. Ecclesiastical.* A brief formal prayer used in various Western liturgies before the epistle at Mass or Holy Communion and varying with the day. [Middle English *collecte,* from Old French, from Medieval Latin *collēcta,* from *ōrātiō ad collēctam,* "prayer at the congregation", from Late Latin *collēcta,* assembly, from Latin *collēctus,* collected. See **collect**[1].]

col·lec·ta·ne·a (kóllek-táyni-ə) *pl.n.* A selection of passages from one or more authors; an anthology. [Latin, "things collected", from *collēctāneus,* collected, from *collēctus.* See **collect**[1].]

collect call *n. U.S., Australian, & N.Z.* A **reverse-charge call** *(see).*

col·lect·ed (kə-léktid) *adj.* **1.** Self-possessed; composed. **2.** Brought or placed together from various sources: *the collected poems of W.H. Auden.* **—**See Synonyms at **cool. —col·lect·ed·ly** *adv.* **—col·lect·ed·ness** *n.*

col·lec·tion (kə-léksh'n) *n. Abbr.* **coll. 1.** The act or process of collecting. **2.** A group of things that have been brought together, especially: **a.** A set of like objects collected as a hobby or for exhibition: *a postcard collection.* **b.** A set of literary works assembled in a single volume: *a collection of short stories.* **c.** A range of clothes exhibited by a fashion designer. **3.** An accumulation; a deposit. **4. a.** A collecting of money, as in church. **b.** The sum collected. **5.** A removal of letters for delivery from a postbox.

col·lec·tive (kə-léktiv) *adj.* **1.** Formed by collecting; assembled or accumulated into a whole. **2.** Of, pertaining to, characteristic of, or made by a number of individuals taken or acting as a group: *a collective decision.*

~n. **1.** A collective enterprise, such as a **workers' cooperative** *(see),* or the persons working in it. **2.** A group of people working together for mutual support or advancement: *a women's collective.* **3.** *Grammar.* A collective noun. **—col·lec·tive·ly** *adv.* **—col·lec·tive·ness** *n.*

collective bargaining *n.* Negotiation between trade-union representatives and employers to determine wages, hours, rules, and working conditions.

collective farm *n.* A farm or a group of farms organised as a unit, managed and worked cooperatively by a group of workers, typically under government supervision. See **kibbutz, kolkhoz.**

collective fruit *n. Botany.* A **multiple fruit** *(see).*

collective noun *n. Grammar.* A noun, such as *family* or *committee,* that denotes a collection of persons or things regarded as a unit.

Usage: A collective noun takes a singular verb when it refers to the collection as a whole and a plural verb when it refers to the members of the collection as separate persons or things: *The orchestra was playing* but *The orchestra have all gone home.* A collective noun should not be treated as both singular and plural in the same construction. Thus: *The family is determined to press its (*not *their) claim.*

collective pitch lever *n.* A control in a helicopter that changes the angle of attack of all the rotor blades simultaneously to make the craft rise or fall.

col·lec·tiv·ise, col·lec·tiv·ize (kə-léktiv-īz) *tr.v.* **-ised, -ising, -ises.** To organise (an economy, industry, or enterprise) on the basis of collectivism. **—col·lec·tiv·i·sa·tion** (-ī-záysh'n || *U.S.* -i-) *n.*

col·lec·tiv·ism (kə-léktiviz'm) *n.* The principle or system of ownership and control of the means of production and distribution by the people collectively. **—col·lec·tiv·ist** *adj. & n.* **—col·lec·tiv·i·ty** (kól-lek-tívvəti, kə-lék-) *n.*

col·lec·tor (kə-léktər) *n.* **1.** A person or thing that collects. **2.** *Abbr.* **col., coll.** A person employed to collect taxes, duties, or other payments. **3.** A person who collects things as a hobby, such as stamps. **4.** Formerly, the chief administrative officer of a district in British India. **5. a.** *Electricity.* A conducting contact between moving and stationary parts of an electric circuit. **b.** *Electronics.* The output terminal of a three-terminal semiconducting device, especially of a transistor. **—col·lec·tor·ship** *n.*

col·leen (kólleen, ko-leén) *n. Note: in Ireland generally* ko-leén) *n.* An Irish girl. [Irish *cailīn,* diminutive of *caile,* girl, from Old Irish *calé,* probably from Latin *pellex,* concubine, akin to Greek *pallakē,* Sanskrit *pallavaki,* of non-Indo-European origin.]

col·lege (kóllij) *n. Abbr.* **col., coll. 1.** An institution offering courses in higher education, especially: **a.** One specialising in a particular field of learning: *a college of art.* **b.** A self-governing body of scholars incorporated within a university. **c.** *U.S.* A university offering undergraduate degrees only. **2.** A secondary school, often outside the state education system. **3.** The building or buildings occupied by such an institution or school. **4.** A company or assemblage; especially, a body of persons having a common purpose, common professional interests, or common duties. **5.** A body of clergymen living together on an endowment. [Middle English, from Old French, from Latin *collēgium,* corporate institution, partnership, from *collēga,* COLLEAGUE.]

College of Arms *n.* A royal corporation in Britain that deals with matters of heraldry. Also called "Heralds' College", "College of Heralds".

College of Cardinals *n. Roman Catholic Church.* A body comprising all the cardinals that elects the pope, assists him in governing the church, and administers the Holy See when vacant. Also called "Sacred College".

college of education *n.* A college that trains teachers.

col·le·gi·al·i·ty (kə-leéji-ál-əti, ko-) *n. Roman Catholic Church.* The principle that the bishops, together with the pope, share collectively the responsibility of ruling the Church.

col·le·gian (kə-leéj-ən, ko-, -yən, -i-ən) *n.* A student or recent graduate of a college.

col·le·giate (kə-leéj-ət, ko-, -yət, -i-ət, -it) *adj.* Also **col·le·gi·al** (-i-əl). *Abbr.* **col., coll. 1.** Of, pertaining to, or resembling a college. **2.** Made up of colleges. Said of universities. **3.** Of, for, or typical of college students. Also "college". **4.** Of or pertaining to a collegiate church. [Medieval Latin *collēgiātus,* from Latin *collēgium,* COLLEGE.]

collegiate church *n.* **1.** A Roman Catholic or Anglican church other than a cathedral, having a chapter of canons and presided over by a dean or provost. **2.** In the United States: **a.** A church associated with others under a common body of pastors. **b.** An association of such churches. **3.** In Scotland, a church served by two or more ministers at the same time.

col·le·gi·um (ko-leéji-əm) *n., pl.* **-gia** (-ə) or **-giums.** An executive council or committee of equally empowered members; specifically, one supervising an industry, commissariat, or other organisation in the U.S.S.R. [Russian *kollegya,* from Latin *collēgium,* COLLEGE.]

col·lem·bo·lan (kə-lémbələn) *n.* Any small wingless insect of the order Collembola; a springtail. [New Latin *Collembola, from* Greek *kolla,* glue + *embolon,* wedge, peg (referring to a projecting pouch characteristic of all members of the order).] **—col·lem·bo·lan** *adj.*

col·len·chy·ma (kə-léngkimə) *n. Botany.* Supportive tissue of plants, consisting of elongated, approximately rectangular cells with cell walls thickened with cellulose and pectin. [New Latin, "glue tissue" : COLL(O)- + -ENCHYMA.] **—col·len·chym·a·tous** (kól-lin-kímmətəss) *adj.*

Col·les' fracture (kólliss) *n.* A fracture of the wrist, at the lower end of the radius, in which the hand is displaced backwards. [After Abraham *Colles* (1773–1843), Irish surgeon.]

col·let (kóllit) *n.* **1.** A cone-shaped sleeve used for holding circular or rodlike machine pieces. **2.** A metal collar used in watchmaking

to join one end of a balance spring to the balance staff. **3.** A circular flange or rim, as in a ring, into which a gem is set.
~*tr.v.* **colleted, -leting, -lets.** To set in or supply with a collet. [French, diminutive of *col,* neck, collar, from Latin *collum,* neck.]
col·lide (kə-lī́d) *intr.v.* **-lided, -liding, -lides. 1.** To come into contact with violent, direct impact. **2.** To meet in opposition; clash; conflict. [Latin *collīdere* : *com-,* together + *laedere,* to strike.]
col·lie (kólli) *n.* A large dog of a breed originating in Scotland and widely used as a sheep dog, having long hair and a long, narrow muzzle. [Scottish, possibly from *colly,* "black like coal" (its original colour), from *coll,* variant of COAL.]
col·li·er (kólli-ər, kól-yər) *n. British.* **1.** A coal miner. **2.** A coal ship. [Middle English *colier,* from *col, cole,* COAL.]
col·lier·y (kól-yəri) *n., pl.* **-ies.** *British.* A coal mine.
col·li·gate (kólli-gayt) *tr.v.* **-gated, -gating, -gates. 1.** To tie together. **2.** *Logic.* To bring (isolated observations) together by an explanation or hypothesis that applies to them all. [Latin *colligāre* : *com-,* together + *ligāre,* to tie.] **—col·li·ga·tion** (-gáysh'n) *n.*
col·lig·a·tive (kə-líggətiv, kólli-gətiv, -gaytiv) *adj.* Designating the physical properties of a substance that depend on the concentrations of molecules, atoms, or ions present rather than on their nature: *colligative properties.*
col·li·mate (kólli-mayt) *tr.v.* **-mated, -mating, -mates. 1.** To make parallel; line up. **2.** To adjust the line of sight of (a transit, telescope, or other optical device). [New Latin *collimare,* to adjust, misreading of Latin *collīneāre,* to direct in a straight line : *com-* (intensive) + *līneāre,* to make straight, from *līnea,* LINE.] **—col·li·ma·tion** (-máysh'n) *n.*
col·li·ma·tor (kólli-maytər) *n.* **1.** Any device capable of collimating radiation, such as a long narrow tube in which strongly absorbing or reflecting walls permit only radiation travelling parallel to the tube axis to traverse the entire length. **2.** A small telescope attached to a larger one as an aid to adjusting its line of sight.
col·lin·e·ar (ko-línni-ər, kə- || kō-) *adj.* **1.** Lying on the same line. **2.** Containing a common line; coaxial. [COM- + LINEAR.]
col·lins (kóllinz) *n.* A tall iced drink made with gin, vodka, rum, or other spirits, and lemon or lime juice, soda water, and sugar. [20th century : origin obscure.]
Collins *n.* A letter written to thank a host for his hospitality. [After William *Collins,* a character in Jane Austen's *Pride and Prejudice* (1813).]
Collins, Michael (1890–1922). Irish nationalist. He took part in the Easter Rising in Dublin (1916) and was elected a Sinn Fein member of the Dàil (1919). He helped to negotiate the establishment of the Irish Free State (1921) but was killed in an ambush by republican opponents.
Collins, (William) Wilkie (1824–89). British novelist, a pioneer of the mystery story, best remembered for *The Woman in White* (1860) and *The Moonstone* (1868).
col·li·sion (kə-lízh'n) *n.* **1.** A direct, violent striking together; a crash. **2.** A clash of ideas or interests; a conflict. **3.** *Physics.* A dynamic event consisting of the interaction between two or more bodies, usually of very brief duration, resulting in a change of momentum of at least one participating body. [Middle English, from Latin *collīsiō* (stem *collīsiōn-*), from *collīdere,* COLLIDE.]
collision course *n.* A course, as of moving objects or ideas, that will end in collision or conflict if continued unchanged.
collo-, coll- *comb. form.* Indicates: **1.** Glue; for example, **collenchyma. 2.** Colloid; for example, **collotype.** [New Latin, from Greek *kolla,* glue.]
col·lo·cate (kól-ə-kayt, -ō-) *v.* **-cated, -cating, -cates.** *—tr.* To place together or in proper order; arrange. *—intr. Linguistics.* To occur habitually and naturally together; for example, *quick* collocates with *temper,* but *fast* does not. [Latin *collocāre* : *com-,* together + *locāre,* to place, LOCATE.]
col·lo·ca·tion (kól-ə-káysh'n, -ō-) *n.* **1. a.** The act of collocating. **b.** The state of being collocated. **2.** An arrangement or juxtaposition; especially, a group of words habitually occurring together.
col·loc·u·tor (kə-lóckew-tər, kóllə-kewtər) *n. Formal.* A partner in conversation. [Late Latin, from *colloquī* (participial stem *collocut-*), to talk with. See **colloquy.**]
col·lo·di·on (kə-lṓdi-ən) *n.* Also **col·lo·di·um** (-əm). A highly flammable, colourless or yellowish syrupy solution of **pyroxylin** *(see)* in ether and alcohol, used to hold surgical dressings, as a coating for certain skin diseases, and for making photographic plates. [New Latin *collodium,* from Greek *kollōdēs,* gluelike, from *kolla,* glue.]
col·logue (ko-lṓg, kə-) *intr.v.* **-logued, -loguing, -logues.** *British Regional.* To confer secretly; conspire. [Probably from obsolete verb *colleague,* to be a colleague, ally, conspire (influenced by Latin *colloquī,* to converse), from Old French *colleguer,* from Latin *colligāre,* to tie together, COLLIGATE.]
col·loid (kól-oyd) *n.* **1.** *Chemistry.* **a.** A dispersion of finely divided particles in a continuous medium (a gaseous, liquid, or solid substance), such as an atmospheric fog, a paint, or foam rubber, containing suspended particles that are approximately 1 to 1 000 nanometres in size, do not settle out of the medium rapidly, and are not readily filtered. **b.** The particulate matter so suspended. See **sol, gel, emulsion, foam. 2.** *Physiology.* A clear gelatinous secretion of the thyroid gland. Also called "thyroid colloid". **3.** *Pathology.* Gelatinous material resulting from tissue degeneration.
~*adj.* Also **col·loi·dal** (kə-lóyd'l, ko-). Of, pertaining to, or having the nature of a colloid. [French *colloïde* : COLL(O)- + -OID.]
col·lop (kólləp) *n. British Regional.* **1.** A small portion or slice, especially of meat. **2.** A roll of flesh on the body. [Middle English *coloppe, colhoppe*†.]
col·lo·qui·al (kə-lṓkwi-əl) *adj. Abbr.* **coll., colloq. 1.** Characteristic of or appropriate to the spoken language or to writing that seeks its effect; informal in diction or style of expression. **2.** Pertaining to conversation; conversational. [From COLLOQUY.] **—col·lo·qui·al·ly** *adv.* **—col·lo·qui·al·ness** *n.*
col·lo·qui·al·ism (kə-lṓkwi-əl-iz'm) *n. Abbr.* **coll., colloq. 1.** Colloquial style or quality. **2.** A colloquial expression.
col·lo·qui·um (kə-lṓ-kwi-əm) *n., pl.* **-ums** or **-quia** (-ə). An academic seminar on some broad field of study, usually led by a different lecturer at each meeting. [Latin *colloquium,* COLLOQUY.]
col·lo·quy (kólləkwi) *n., pl.* **-quies. 1.** A conversation, especially one that is formal or mannered. **2.** A written dialogue. [Latin *colloquium,* conversation, from *colloquī,* to converse : *com-,* together + *loquī,* to speak.]
col·lo·type (kól-ə-tīp, -ō-) *n.* **1.** A printing process utilising a glass plate with a gelatine surface carrying the image to be reproduced. Also called "photogelatine process". **2.** A print made by this process. [COLLO- + -TYPE.]
col·lude (kə-lṓōd, ko-, -léwd) *intr.v.* **-luded, -luding, -ludes.** To be in collusion; act together secretly. [Latin *collūdere* : *com-,* together + *lūdere,* to play, deceive, from *lūdus,* game.] **—col·lud·er** *n.*
col·lu·sion (kə-lṓōzh'n, -léwzh'n) *n.* **1.** Secret agreement between two or more persons for a deceitful or fraudulent purpose. **2.** A secret agreement between the parties in a lawsuit to obtain a specific verdict. —See Synonyms at **conspiracy.** [Middle English *collucioun,* from Old French *collusion,* from Latin *collūsiō* (stem *collūsiōn-*), from *collūdere,* COLLUDE.]
col·lu·sive (kə-lṓō-siv, -léw- || -ziv) *adj.* Secretly arranged for fraudulent purposes. **—col·lu·sive·ly** *adv.* **—col·lu·sive·ness** *n.*
col·lu·vi·um (kə-lṓō-vi-əm, -léw-) *n., pl.* **-via** (-ə) or **-ums.** A loose deposit of rock debris accumulated at the base of a cliff or slope. [Latin *colluvium, colluviō,* collection of filth, washings, from *colluere,* to wash thoroughly, wash out : *com-* (intensive) + *lavere,* to wash.] **—col·lu·vi·al** *adj.*
col·lyr·i·um (kə-lírri-əm, ko-) *n., pl.* **-ums** or **-lyria** (-ə). A medicinal lotion applied to the eye; eyewash. [Latin, from Greek *kollurion,* poultice, diminutive of *kollura*†, roll of bread.]
col·ly·wob·bles (kólli-wobb'lz) *pl.n. Informal.* **1.** A pain in the stomach, especially due to nervousness. **2.** A state of apprehension. [19th century: fanciful coinage, from COLIC + WOBBLE.]
colo-, col- *comb. form.* Indicates the colon; for example, **colostomy, colitis.** [New Latin, from Latin *colon,* COLON (intestine).]
col·o·bo·ma (kóllə-bṓmə) *n.* Any of various defects of the eye or eyelid, including notches or fissures. [New Latin, from Greek *kolobōma,* a mutilation, from *kolobos,* cut, docked.]
col·o·bus (kólləbəss) *n.* Any Old World monkey of the genus *Colobus* of West and Central Africa, having a long tail, long silky fur, and short thumbs. [New Latin, from Greek *kolobos,* cut short (referring to its reduced thumbs).]
col·o·cynth (kóllə-sinth) *n.* **1.** A vine, *Citrullus colocynthis,* of the Mediterranean region, bearing a small, bitter fruit. **2.** The fruit of this plant, used as a cathartic. Also called "bitter apple". [Latin *colocynthis,* from Greek *kolokunthis,* from *kolokunthē*†, round gourd.]
co·log·a·rithm (kō-lóggə-rith'm) *n.* The logarithm of the reciprocal of a number, expressed with a positive mantissa.
co·logne (kə-lṓn) *n.* A scented liquid made of alcohol and various fragrant oils. Also called "cologne water", "eau de cologne". [French *eau de cologne,* "water of Cologne"; see **Köln.**]
Cologne. See **Köln.**
Co·lom·bi·a, Republic of (kə-lómbi-ə, -lúmbi-). *Spanish* **República de Colombia.** Country in northwest South America. It was settled by the Spaniards in 1510. In 1740 it became part of the viceroyalty of New Granada, which was liberated from Spain by Simón Bolívar (1819). By 1903 Colombia had its present boundaries, and had suffered 27 civil wars. Land and other reforms were slow, and strife led to military intervention (1953). However, agreements in 1957 and 1974 left Colombia a fragile democracy. The country, formerly dependent on coffee, is diversifying, and coffee now accounts for about half its official exports. Illicit cocaine amounts to much more; and the government is trying to suppress the aggressive, violent and destabilising activities of the drug cartels. With industrialisation, Colombia has become an importer instead of an exporter of oil. It also has large reserves of coal and emeralds. Area, 1 141 748 square kilometres (440,831 square miles). Population, 35,630,000. Capital, Bogotá. **—Co·lom·bi·an** *adj. & n.*
Co·lom·bo (kə-lúm-bō, -lóm-). Capital of Sri Lanka, a port on the west coast of the island near the mouth of the river Kelani. It is noted for gem cutting and ivory carving.
Colombo, Cristoforo. See Christopher **Columbus.**
co·lon¹ (kṓ-lən, -lon) *n., pl.* **-lons** or **-la** (-lə) (for sense 2). **1. a.** A punctuation mark (:) used after a word introducing a quotation, explanation, example, or series, or, in the United States, after the salutation of a formal letter. **b.** The sign (:) used between numbers or groups of numbers, as in ratios (1:2), biblical references (Genesis 4:1-5), or, chiefly in the United States, expressions of time (8:45). **2.** A section of a rhythmical period in Greek and Latin verse, consisting of two to six feet and having one principal accent. [Latin *cōlon,* unit of verses, from Greek *kōlon,* "limb".]
co·lon² (kṓ-lən, -lon) *n., pl.* **-lons** or **-la** (-lə). The section of the large intestine extending from the caecum to the rectum. [Middle Eng-

COLOMBIA

Caribbean Sea
70°W
10°N
Barranquilla
Cartagena
PANAMA
VENEZUELA
Cúcuta
Medellín
Bucaramanga
PACIFIC
Manizales
OCEAN
SANTA FÉ
DE BOGOTÁ
Cali
COLOMBIA
Equator
ECUADOR
Caqueta
PERU
BRAZIL
400 Km
200 Miles

lish, from Latin, from Greek *kolont*, large intestine.] —**co·lon·ic** (kə-lónnik, kō-) *adj.*

co·lón (kō-lón || *U.S.* -lón) *n., pl.* **-lóns** or *Spanish* **colones** (-ló-ness || -nayss). **1. a.** The basic monetary unit of Costa Rica, equal to 100 céntimos. **b.** The basic monetary unit of El Salvador, equal to 100 centavos. **2.** A coin or note worth one colón. [Spanish *colón*, after *Cristóbal Colón,* Christopher Columbus.]

Colón, Cristóbal. See Christopher **Columbus.**

colo·nel (kúrn'l) *n. Abbr.* **Col. 1.** An officer of the British Army or Royal Marines, generally in command of a regiment, and ranking between a brigadier and a lieutenant-colonel, equivalent in rank to a captain in the Navy and a group captain in the Royal Air Force. **2.** An officer of similar rank in other military or paramilitary organisations. [French, from Italian *colonnello,* "commander of a column", diminutive of *colonna,* column (of soldiers), from Latin *columna.*] —**colo·nel·cy, colo·nel·ship** *n.*

Colonel Blimp (blimp) *n.* An elderly, pompous, reactionary man, especially an army officer or government official. [After *Colonel Blimp,* character in cartoons by David Low.]

co·lo·ni·al (kə-lōni-əl) *adj. Abbr.* **col. 1.** Of, pertaining to, possessing, or inhabiting a colony or colonies, especially those of the British Empire. **2.** *Often capital* **C. a.** Of or pertaining to the 13 British colonies that became the original United States of America. **b.** Of or pertaining to the colonial period before American independence. **3.** *Often capital* **C.** Designating an architectural style prevalent in the American colonies in the 17th and 18th centuries. ~*n.* An inhabitant of a colony, especially a settler or one descended from settlers. —**co·lo·ni·al·ly** *adv.*

co·lo·ni·al·ism (kə-lōni-əliz'm) *n.* A policy by which a nation maintains or extends its control over foreign dependencies. —**co·lo·ni·al·ist** *n. & adj.*

colonic irrigation *n.* The washing out of the contents of the large intestine by injecting large quantities of fluid through the rectum.

col·o·ni·sa·tion (kólla-nī-záysh'n || *U.S.* -ni-) *n.* The act or process of establishing a colony or colonies.

co·lo·nise, co·lo·nize (kóllanīz) *v.* **-nised, -nising, -nises.** —*tr.* **1. a.** To establish a colony or colonies in. **b.** To migrate to and settle in; occupy as a colony. **2.** *U.S.* To register party supporters as votes in (a district) so as to influence an election there. —*intr.* **1.** To set up or form a colony. **2.** To settle in a colony or colonies. —**col·o·nis·er** *n.*

col·o·nist (kóllanist) *n.* **1.** An original settler or founder of a colony. **2.** An inhabitant of a colony; a colonial.

col·on·nade (kólla-náyd) *n.* **1.** *Architecture.* A series of columns placed at regular intervals. **2.** A series of trees placed at regular intervals. [French, from Italian *colonnato,* from *colonna,* column, from Latin *columna.*] —**col·on·nad·ed** *adj.*

col·o·ny (kólləni) *n., pl.* **-nies. 1.** A group of emigrants or their descendants who settle in a distant land but remain subject to or intimately connected with the parent country. **2.** A territory thus settled. **3.** *Abbr.* **col.** Any region politically controlled by a distant country; a dependency. **4.** *Capital* **C.** Any of the 13 British colonies that became the original United States of America. **5. a.** A group of people with the same interests or ethnic origin, concentrated in a particular area. **b.** The area or place occupied by such a group. **6.** An area or institution in which a specified group of people is kept apart from others: *a leper colony.* **7.** *Biology.* **a.** A group of the same kind of animals or plants living or growing together. **b.** A group of individuals structurally connected and functioning as a single unit, as in sponges and corals. **8.** *Microbiology.* A visible growth of microorganisms in a nutrient medium. [Middle English *colonie,* from Old French, from Latin *colōnia,* farm, settlement, from *colōnus,* farmer, settler, from *colere,* to cultivate, inhabit.]

col·o·phon (kólla-fən, -fon) *n.* **1.** Formerly, an inscription placed at the end of a book, giving facts pertaining to its publication. **2.** A publisher's emblem or trademark placed usually on the title page of a book. [Latin *colophōn,* from Greek *kolophōn,* summit, finishing.]

co·loph·o·ny (kə-lóffəni) *n.* **Rosin** (see). [Latin *Colophonia rēsina,* "resin of *Colophon*" (ancient city in Lydia).]

color. *U.S.* Variant of **colour.**

Col·o·ra·do[1] (kólla-ráadō || *U.S. also* -ráddō). State in the west central United States, where the Rocky Mountains meet the Great Plains. The Rocky Mountains contain reserves of molybdenum and uranium, and oil. Denver is the state capital. It joined the Union in 1876.

Colorado[2]. River in the west of the United States. It rises in the Rocky Mountains of Colorado state and flows 2 336 kilometres (1,450 miles) southwest through Utah and Arizona, reaching the sea in Mexico at the Gulf of California. It supplies the Hoover Dam.

Colorado beetle *n.* A small black-and-yellow striped beetle, *Leptinotarsa decemlineata,* native to Central America but now widespread in Europe, that is a major pest of potatoes. Also called "Colorado potato beetle", "potato beetle". [After COLORADO, where it first became a major pest of potatoes.]

col·or·ant (kúllərənt) *n.* Anything that colours or modifies the colour of something else, especially a dye, pigment, ink, or paint.

col·o·ra·tion (kúlla-ráysh'n) *n.* Arrangement of colours.

col·o·ra·tu·ra (kól-ərə-toór-ə, -téwr- || kúl-) *n.* **1.** Florid ornamental trills and runs in vocal music. **2.** Music characterised by such ornamentation. **3.** A singer, especially a soprano, specialising in this. [Obsolete Italian, "colouring", from Late Latin *colōrātūra,* from Latin *colōrāre,* to COLOUR.]

col·or·if·ic (kúlla-ríffik) *adj.* **1.** Producing or imparting colour. **2.** Of or pertaining to colour.

col·or·im·e·ter (kúlla-rímmitər) *n.* **1.** Any of various instruments used to determine or specify colours, as by comparison with spectroscopic or visual standards. **2.** An instrument that measures the concentration of a known solution constituent by comparison with colours of standard solutions of that constituent. —**col·or·i·met·ric** (-ri-métrik) *adj.* —**col·or·i·met·ri·cal·ly** *adv.* —**col·or·im·e·try** (-rímmətri) *n.*

Co·los·sae (ko-lóss-ī). An ancient city in western Asia Minor, the seat of a congregation to which St. Paul addressed the Epistle to the Colossians. —**Co·los·sian** (kə-lósh'n, -lóssi-ən) *adj. & n.*

co·los·sal (kə-lóss'l) *adj.* **1.** Enormous in size or extent; gigantic. **2.** *Informal.* Great in degree; enormous: *a colossal waste of time.* —See Synonyms at **enormous.** [French, from Latin *colossus,* COLOSSUS.] —**co·los·sal·ly** *adv.*

Col·os·se·um, Col·i·se·um (kólla-sée-əm) *n.* An amphitheatre in Rome built by Vespasian and Titus (A.D. *c.*75–80). [Latin, from *colosseus,* huge, from *colossus,* COLOSSUS.]

Co·los·sians (kə-lósh'nz, -lóssi-ənz) *n. Used with a singular verb. Abbr.* **Col.** A book of the New Testament, an epistle of Saint Paul to the Christians of Colossae.

co·los·sus (kə-lóss-əss) *n., pl.* **-si** (-ī) *or* **-suses. 1.** A huge statue. **2.** Any person or thing of outstanding size or importance. [Latin, from Greek *kolossos,* probably of Mediterranean origin.]

Colossus of Rhodes. A huge statue of Apollo, about 36 metres (120 feet) high, built about 280 B.C. and later destroyed by an earthquake. It was set at the entrance to the harbour of Rhodes.

co·los·to·my (kə-lóstəmi, ko-) *n., pl.* **-mies.** The surgical construction of an artificial excretory opening from the colon onto the surface of the abdomen. [COLO- + -STOMY.]

co·los·trum (kə-lóstrəm) *n.* The first secretion of the mammary glands immediately after childbirth, lasting for a few days and consisting of serum, white blood cells, and antibodies. [Latin *colostrum, colostrat.*]

col·our, *U.S.* **col·or** (kúllər) *n. Abbr.* **col. 1.** That aspect of things that is caused by differing qualities of the light reflected or emitted by them. It may be defined in terms of the observer (sense **a.**) or by the light (sense **b.**): **a.** The appearance of objects or light sources described in terms of the individual's perception of them, involving hue, lightness, and saturation for objects, and hue, brightness, and saturation for light sources. **b.** The characteristics of light by which the individual is made aware of objects or light sources through the receptors of the eye, described in terms of dominant frequency, luminance, and purity. **2.** Any of the gradations of this aspect, conventionally divided into shades as, for example, red, green, or brown. See **primary colour, secondary colour. 3.** A dye, pigment, paint, or other substance that imparts colour. **4. a.** A redness of complexion, considered as a sign of normal health. **b.** A reddening of the face, as from indignation or embarrassment. **5.** The complexion of a person not classed as a Caucasian. **6.** *Plural.* **a.** An identifying flag or banner, as of a country, organisation, or military unit. **b.** A ceremony of lowering or raising military colours. **7.** *Plural.* **a.** Any distinguishing symbol, badge, ribbon, or mark: *the colours of a college.* **b.** *British.* Such a badge or ribbon awarded for representing one's school, for example at sport. **8.** Character or nature: *appear in one's true colours.* **9.** Outward, often deceptive, appearance. Used chiefly in the phrase *under colour of.* **10.** Appearance of truth or authenticity; plausibility. **11.** *Chiefly U.S. Plural.* An opinion or position. **12.** Variety of effect or expression. **13.** Picturesque and authentic detail, as in a film or novel, for example. **14.** Vitality; exuberance: *She loved the colour of Mediterranean life.* **15.** In art, the use or effect of colour as distinct from form. **16.** *Music.* Tonal quality. **17.** *Printing.* The amount, shade, or tone of ink used. **18.** *Obsolete. Law.* An apparent or prima-facie right, pretext, or ground. **19.** *U.S.* A particle or bit of gold found in auriferous gravel or sand. **20.** *Physics.* A hypothetical property associated with quark theory. Each quark may exist in any of three states designated red, blue, and green. The combination of certain colour and quark types produces the various baryons and mesons. **—man** or **woman of colour.** *Chiefly U.S.* A male (or female) member of a coloured ethnic minority. **—nail (one's) colours to the mast.** To persist in pursuing one's goal. **—with flying colours.** With great success. ~*v.* **coloured, -ouring, -ours.** —*tr.* **1.** To impart colour to or change the colour of. **2.** To give a distinctive character or quality to; modify or influence. **3.** To misrepresent, especially by distortion or exaggeration. —*intr.* **1.** To take on colour or become coloured. **2.** To change colour. **3.** To become red in the face, as from embarrassment or indignation. [Middle English, from Old French, from Latin *color.*] **—col·our** *adj.* **—col·our·er** *n.*

col·our·a·ble (kúllər-əb'l) *adj.* **1.** Seemingly true or genuine. **2.** Feigned; pretended. **—col·our·a·bil·i·ty** (-ə-bílləti), **col·our·a·ble·ness** *n.* **—col·our·a·bly** *adv.*

colour bar *n.* Statutory or social and economic discrimination on the basis of race, especially as practised by white people against nonwhite people. Also *chiefly U.S.* "colour line".

col·our-blind (kúllər-blīnd) *adj.* Partially or totally unable to distinguish certain colours. See **deuteranopia, protanopia, tritanopia.** **—colour blindness** *n.*

colour code *n.* A method of distinguishing items, such as parts, components, wires, or resistors using distinctive colours for identification. **—col·our-cod·ed** (kúllər-kŏdid) *adj.*

col·oured (kúllərd) *adj.* **1.** Having colour. **2.** *Often capital* **C.** Designating a dark-skinned person, especially a Negro. **3.** Distorted or biased, as by irrelevant or incorrect information. ~*n.* **1.** A coloured person. **2.** In South Africa, a person of racially mixed descent belonging to a population grouping that is distinct from Asians, blacks, and whites.

col·our-fast (kúllər-faast ‖ -fast) *adj.* Having colour that will not run or fade with washing or wear. Said of fabrics. **—col·our-fast·ness** *n.*

colour filter *n.* A photographic filter used to increase contrast or in taking photographs through haze.

col·our·ful (kúllər-f'l, -fŏŏl) *adj.* **1.** Full of colour; abounding in colours. **2.** Characterised by rich variety; vivid; distinctive. **—col·our·ful·ly** *adj.* **—col·our·ful·ness** *n.*

colour index *n.* **1.** *Astronomy.* The numerical difference between the apparent photographic magnitude and the apparent visual magnitude of a star, as an indication of its colour and temperature. **2.** *Geology.* The percentage of dark and coloured minerals in a rock, calculated on the basis of its total mineral content.

col·our·ing (kúllɐring) *n.* **1.** Any substance used to colour something. **2.** Appearance with regard to colour. **3.** The arrangement of or patterns created by colours. **4.** A false or misleading appearance.

col·our·ist (kúllər-ist) *n.* An artist skilled in achieving special effects with colour. **—col·our·is·tic** (-ístik) *adj.*

col·our·less (kúllər-ləss, -liss) *adj.* **1.** Without colour. **2.** Weak or dull in colour; pallid. **3.** Lacking animation, variety, or distinction; uninteresting; dull. **4.** Without bias; neutral; objective. **—col·our·less·ly** *adv.* **—col·our·less·ness** *n.*

colour line *n. Chiefly U.S.* A **colour bar** *(see).*

col·our·man (kúllər-man) *n., pl.* **-men** (-men). A person who prepares an artist's colours.

colour phase *n.* **1.** A seasonal variation in the colour of the fur or feathers of some animals, especially those living in arctic regions. **2.** Variation in the colour of animals of the same species.

colour scheme *n.* An arrangement of colours, especially one planned for a certain effect, as in interior decorating.

colour supplement *n. British.* A magazine with many advertisements and colour photographs that accompanies a newspaper, especially a Sunday newspaper.

col·our·way (kúllər-way) *n.* A **colour scheme** *(see).*

-colous *adj. comb. form.* Indicates habitat in or among; for example, **arenicolous.** [Latin *-cola,* inhabitant.]

col·pi·tis (kol-pītiss) *n.* **Vaginitis** *(see).* [New Latin : Greek *kolpos,* bosom, womb, vagina + -ITIS.]

col·por·teur (kól-pawr-tér, -tór, -pawr-tər ‖ -pōr-) *n.* A pedlar of devotional literature. [French, from Old French *comporteur* (influenced by *col,* neck), from *comporter,* to peddle, COMPORT.]

col·po·scope (kólpə-skōp) *n.* An instrument used to examine the vagina and the cervix of the uterus. [Greek *kolpos,* womb, vagina + -SCOPE.] **—col·pos·co·py** (kol-póskəpi) *n.*

colt (kōlt) *n.* **1.** A young male horse. **2. a.** A youthful or inexperienced person; a novice or beginner. **b.** *Sports.* An inexperienced player; a player in a junior team. **3.** A rope whip formerly used for shipboard discipline. [Middle English *colt,* Old English *colt,* young ass or camel, perhaps from Scandinavian; akin to Swedish dialectal *kult, kulter†,* half-grown animal, boy.]

Colt *n.* A trademark for a type of revolver.

colter. *U.S.* Variant of **coulter.**

colt·ish (kōltish) *adj.* **1.** Of or like a colt. **2.** Lively and playful;

frisky. **—colt·ish·ly** *adv.* **—colt·ish·ness** *n.*

colts·foot (kōlts-fŏŏt) *n., pl.* **-foots.** A plant, *Tussilago farfara,* native to the Old World, having yellow, daisy-like flowers that appear before the heart-shaped leaves. [From the shape of its leaves.]

col·u·brid (kóllew-brid) *n.* Any of numerous chiefly nonvenomous snakes of the family Colubridae, which includes the grass snake. ~*adj.* Of or belonging to the Colubridae. [New Latin *Colubridae,* from Latin *coluber,* snake.]

col·u·brine (kóllew-brīn) *adj.* **1.** Of or like a snake. **2.** Of or belonging to the Colubrinae, a subfamily of nonvenomous colubrid snakes. [Latin *colubrīnus,* from *coluber,* snake.]

co·lu·go (kə-lŏŏ-gō, -léw-) *n., pl.* **-gos.** A mammal, the **flying lemur** *(see).* [Malay.]

Co·lum·ba (kə-lúmbə) *n.* A constellation in the Southern Hemisphere near Caelum and Puppis. Also called the "Dove". [New Latin, from Latin *columba,* dove.]

Columba, Saint (A.D. *c.*521–597). Irish saint and missionary. He founded a church and monastery on the island of Iona (563). This became the centre of evangelical activity in Scotland, from which the northern Picts were converted. His feast day is June 9.

col·um·bar·i·um (kólləm-báır-i-əm) *n., pl.* **-baria** (-ə). **1. a.** A vault with niches for urns containing ashes of the dead. **b.** Any of the niches in such a vault. **2.** A dovecote. [Middle English *columba(i)re,* dovecote, from Latin *columbārium,* from *columba,* dove.]

Columbia. River in western Canada and the northwestern United States. It rises in British Columbia and flows 1 950 kilometres (1,210 miles) southwest to the Pacific in Oregon.

Columbia, District of. See **District of Columbia.**

col·um·bine (kólləm-bīn) *n.* Any of several plants of the genus *Aquilegia,* having variously coloured flowers with five conspicuously spurred petals. [Middle English, from Medieval Latin *(herba) columbīna,* from Latin *columbīnus,* dovelike (from the resemblance of the inverted flower to a cluster of five doves), from *columba,* dove.]

Columbine *n.* In pantomime, the partner or sweetheart of Harlequin.

co·lum·bite (kə-lúmbīt) *n.* A black mineral, essentially (Fe, Mn)(Nb, Ta)$_2$O$_6$, used as a source of niobium and tantalum. [COLUMB(IUM) + -ITE.]

co·lum·bi·um (kə-lúmbi-əm) *n. Symbol* **Cb** Formerly, the element **niobium** *(see).* [New Latin, after *Columbia* (name of a personification of the United States), because it was discovered in a mineral found in Connecticut.] **—co·lum·bic** *adj.*

Columbus, Christopher, *Italian* Cristoforo Colombo, *Spanish* Cristóbal Colón (1451–1506). Italian explorer in the service of Spain, the first modern European to discover America. Believing that the earth was not flat, Columbus concluded that it must be possible to reach the east by sailing westwards. He reached the Bahamas (1492) and discovered Puerto Rico, Jamaica, and other islands (1493–96). On a third voyage (1498–1500) he reached Trinidad and the mouth of Orinoco in South America. Having set up colonies in the New World, he was charged with mismanaging them and returned to Spain in chains (1500). On a fourth voyage (1502–04), he landed at Honduras, Costa Rica, and Panama.

col·u·mel·la (kóllew-méllə) *n., pl.* **-lae** (-méllee). Any of several small, column-like structures in various plants and animals, such as the central part of the sporangium of certain fungi and mosses. [New Latin, from Latin, diminutive of *columna,* COLUMN.] **—co·lu·mel·lar** (-méllər) *adj.*

col·umn (kólləm) *n. Abbr.* **col. 1.** A pillar consisting of a base, a cylindrical shaft, and a capital, used as a support or standing alone as a monument. **2.** Anything resembling a pillar in form or function: *a column of smoke.* **3.** Any of two or more vertical sections of printed lines lying side by side on a page and separated by a rule or blank space. **4.** A section of a newspaper or magazine that regularly contains an article by a particular writer, or is devoted to a particular subject: *the personal column.* **5.** A vertical row of numbers on a page. **6.** A formation, as of troops, vehicles, ships, or aircraft, in which the elements follow one behind the other. **7.** *Botany.* An organ in an orchid flower formed by the fusion of stamens and style. [Middle English *columpne,* from Old French *colomne,* from Latin *columna.*] **—co·lum·nar** (kə-lúm-nər), **col·umned** (kólləmd) *adj.*

column inch *n.* A unit used to measure advertising space in newspapers or magazines, one column wide and one inch deep.

col·um·nist (kólləm-nist, -ist) *n.* A writer of a regular column in a newspaper or periodical.

co·lure (kə-léwr, -lóor, kŏ-lewr, -loor) *n. Astronomy.* Either of two great circles passing through the celestial poles on the celestial sphere: one passing through the equinoxes (*equinoctial colure*) and the other through the solstices (*solstitial colure*). [Middle English, from Late Latin, from Greek *kolouros,* "dock-tailed", truncated (because the view of the lower part of the circles is cut short) : *kolos,* docked + *oura,* tail.]

col·za (kól-zə ‖ kŏl-) *n.* A plant, **rape** *(see).* [French, from Dutch *koolzaad,* "cabbage seed".]

COM (kom) *n.* computer *o*utput on *m*icrofilm: a process that enables computer output to be presented directly in the form of photographic film or fiche.

com– *prefix.* Indicates with, together, jointly; for example, **commeasure, commingle.** [In borrowed Latin compounds, *com-* indicates: 1. With, together, joint, jointly, mutually, collectively, as in **compose, compact.** 2. Altogether, comprehensively, inclusively, intensively, as in **comfort, combust.** 3. Same, similar, as in **concord,**

consubstantial. 4. Together in mind, mentally, as in **compute, comprehend.** (The semantic function of *com-* is often so indistinct as to be indefinable, as in **concave.**) Before *l* and *r*, *com-* is assimilated to *col-* and *cor-;* before *h, gn,* and usually before vowels, it is reduced to *co-* (hence English **co-**); before all other consonants except *b, p,* and *m,* it becomes *con-*. *Com-* is the preverbal form of the Old Latin preposition *com,* which in classical Latin became *cum,* with.]

com. 1. comedy; comic. **2.** commerce; commercial. **3.** committee.

Com. 1. commander. **2.** commission; commissioner. **3.** committee. **4.** commodore. **5.** communist.

co·ma[1] (kṓmə) *n., pl.* **-mas.** A state of deep, prolonged unconsciousness, usually the result of injury, disease, or poison. [New Latin, from Greek *kōma,* deep sleep, lethargy.]

coma[2] *n., pl.* **-mae** (kṓmee). **1.** *Astronomy.* The nebulous luminescent cloud containing the nucleus and constituting the major portion of the head of a comet. **2.** *Botany.* A tuft of hairs, as on some seeds. **3.** *Optics.* The distorted image of a point source, appearing as a diffuse, pear-shaped spot. It is the result of errors in an optical system. [Latin, hair, from Greek *komḗ*†.] **—co·mal** *adj.*

Coma Ber·e·ni·ces (kṓmə bérri-nī́-seez) *n.* A constellation in the northern sky near Boötes and Leo. It contains the coma cluster of galaxies.

Co·man·che (kə-mánchi) *n., pl.* **-ches** or collectively **Comanche. 1.** A member of a Uto-Aztecan-speaking North American Indian people, formerly ranging over the western plains from Wyoming to Texas, now living in Oklahoma. **2.** The language of this people. **—Co·man·che** *adj.*

Co·ma·neci (kómmə-nech), **Nadia** (1961–). Romanian gymnast. Olympic golds (1976, 1980). To U.S. (1989).

co·mate (kṓ-mayt) *adj.* Also **co·mose** (-mōz, -mōss). *Botany.* Having or resembling a tuft of hairs. [Latin *comātus,* from *coma,* hair, from Greek *komḗ.*]

co·ma·tose (kṓmə-tōz, -tōss ‖ *U.S* also kómmə-) *adj. Pathology.* **1.** Of, pertaining to, or affected with coma; unconscious. **2.** Lethargic or torpid. **—co·ma·tose·ly** *adv.*

co·mat·u·lid (kə-máttew-lid) *n.* Also **co·mat·u·la** (-lə) *pl.* **-lae** (-lee). Any of several marine invertebrates of the order Crinoidea, including the feather stars, that are attached to a surface by a stalk when young but are free-swimming as adults. [New Latin *Comatulidae* (former designation), from Late Latin *comātulus,* with neatly curled hair, from Latin *comātus,* having hair, COMATE.]

comb (kōm) *n.* **1.** A thin, toothed strip of plastic, bone, rubber, or other material, used to smooth, arrange, or fasten the hair. **2.** Something resembling a comb in shape or use, such as: **a.** A card for dressing and cleansing wool or other fibres. **b.** A toothed part, as in a shearing device, guiding hair or fleece towards the blade. **3.** A **currycomb** *(see).* **4.** The fleshy crest or ridge that grows on the crown of the head of domestic fowl and other birds and is most prominent in the male. **5.** Something suggesting a fowl's comb in appearance or position. **6.** A **honeycomb** *(see).* **~v. combed, combing, combs. —tr. 1.** To dress or arrange with or as if with a comb. **2.** To card (wool or other fibres). **3.** To search thoroughly; look through. *—intr.* To roll and break. Used of waves. **—comb out. 1.** To remove tangles from (the hair). **2.** To isolate and get rid of (something unwanted). [Middle English *comb,* Old English *comb, camb.*]

comb. 1. combination. **2.** combining.

com·bat (kəm-bát, kóm-bat, kúm-) *v.* **-batted** or **-bated, -batting** or **-bating, -bats.** *—tr.* **1.** To fight against; contend with; oppose in battle. **2.** To oppose vigorously; resist. *—intr.* To engage in fighting; content; struggle. Used with *with* or *against*: combat against laziness. **—See Synonyms at oppose.**

~n. (kóm-bat, kúm-, -bət). Fighting, especially armed battle; strife. Also used adjectivally: *combat troops.* **—See Synonyms at conflict.** [Old French *combattre,* from Vulgar Latin *combattere* (unattested), to fight with : Latin *com-,* with + *battuere,* beat.]

com·bat·ant (kóm-bətənt, kúm- ‖ kəm-bátt'nt) *n.* One taking part in armed combat. **—com·bat·ant** *adj.*

combat fatigue (kóm-bat) *n.* A nervous disorder, usually temporary but sometimes leading to a permanent neurosis, brought on by the exhaustion and stress of combat or similar situations, and characterised by deep anxiety, depression, irritability, and other related symptoms. Also called "battle fatigue". Compare **shell shock.**

com·bat·ive (kóm-bətiv, kúm- ‖ kəm-báttiv) *adj.* Eager or disposed to fight. **—com·bat·ive·ly** *adv.* **—com·bat·ive·ness, com·ba·tiv·i·ty** (kóm-bə-tívvəti, kúm-) *n.*

combe. Variant of **coomb.**

comb·er (kṓmər) *n.* **1.** One that combs. **2.** A long, cresting wave; a breaker.

com·bi·na·tion (kómbi-náysh'n) *n. Abbr.* **comb. 1. a.** The act of combining. **b.** The state of being combined. **2.** Something resulting from combining; a compound; an aggregate: *passed the exam through a combination of luck and hard work.* **3.** An alliance or association of persons or parties for a common purpose. **4.** A sequence of numbers or letters used to open a combination lock. **5.** *Plural.* A one-piece undergarment consisting of an undershirt or chemise and drawers. **6.** *Mathematics.* One or more elements selected from a set without regard to order of selection. **7.** *Chemistry.* The union of two or more compounds, as a result of chemical reaction, to form another compound. **—com·bi·na·tion·al** *adj.*

combination lock *n.* A lock that will open only when its dial is turned through a predetermined sequence of positions identified on the dial face by numbers or letters.

com·bi·na·tive (kómbi-ətiv, -naytiv ‖ kəm-bínətiv) *adj.* **1.** Of, pertaining to, or resulting from combination. **2.** Tending, serving, or able to combine.

com·bi·na·to·ri·al (kómbinə-táwri-əl, kəm-bínə- ‖ -tóri-) *adj.* **1.** Pertaining to or involving combinations. **2.** *Mathematics.* Pertaining to the arrangement and manipulation of combinations and permutations and mathematical elements in sets: *combinatorial analysis.* **—com·bi·na·to·ry** *adj.*

com·bine (kəm-bín ‖ kom-) *v.* **-bined, -bining, -bines.** *—tr.* **1.** To bring into a state of unity; join; merge; blend. **2.** To possess or exhibit in combination. *—intr.* **1.** To become united; coalesce. **2.** To join forces for a common purpose; enter into an alliance. **3.** *Chemistry.* To form a chemical compound. **—See Synonyms at join, mix.**

~n. (kóm-bīn). **1.** An association of persons or firms united for commercial interests, such as control of prices. **2.** A combine harvester. [Middle English *combinen,* from Old French *combiner,* from Late Latin *combīnāre* : Latin *com-,* together + *bīnī,* two at a time.] **—com·bin·er** *n.*

combined operation (kəm-bínd ‖ kom-) *n. Often plural.* A military exercise involving more than one of the services, for example the army and the air force.

combine harvester (kóm-bīn) *n.* A harvesting machine that cuts, threshes, and cleans grain. Also called "combine".

comb·ings (kṓmingz) *pl.n.* Hairs, wool, or other material removed with a comb.

combining form *n. Grammar.* A word element that can form new words by combining with complete words, other combining forms, or sometimes with affixes; for example, **-logy,** as in **gynaecology; macro-,** as in **macrochemistry; Sino-,** as in **Sino-Soviet.**

combining weight *n.* Equivalent weight *(see).*

comb jelly *n.* A marine organism, a **ctenophore** *(see).*

com·bo (kóm-bō) *n., pl.* **-bos. 1.** *Informal.* A small group of musicians, usually jazz musicians. **2.** *Australian Slang.* A white man who lives with an Aboriginal woman. [Short for COMBINATION.]

combs (kombz) *pl.n. Informal.* Combinations (undergarment).

com·bust (kəm-búst ‖ kom-) *adj. Astrology.* Not visible, because of proximity to the sun. Said of a star or planet.

~v. combusted, -busting, -busts. *—tr.* To cause to burn. *—intr.* To burn; undergo combustion. [Middle English, "burned", from Old French, from Latin *combustus,* past participle of *combūrere,* to burn up (infixed *b* probably influenced by *ambūrere,* to burn up) : *com-* (intensive) + *ūrere,* to burn.] **—com·bus·tive** (-bústiv) *adj.*

com·bus·ti·ble (kəm-bústəb'l ‖ kom-) *adj.* **1.** Capable of igniting and burning. **2.** Easily aroused or excited.

~n. A combustible substance. **—com·bus·ti·bil·i·ty** (-bústə-bílləti) *n.* **—com·bus·ti·bly** *adv.*

com·bus·tion (kəm-búss-chən ‖ kom-) *n.* **1.** The act or process of burning. **2.** *Chemistry.* A chemical change, especially oxidation, accompanied by the production of heat and light. [Middle English, from Old French, from Late Latin *combustiō* (stem *combustiōn-*), from Latin *combustus.* See **combust.**]

combustion chamber *n.* An enclosure in which combustion, especially of a fuel or propellant, is initiated and controlled.

com·bus·tor (kəm-bústər ‖ kom-) *n.* The combustion system of a jet engine or gas turbine, consisting of a combustion chamber together with its igniter and fuel injection system.

comdg. commanding.

Comdr. commander.

Comdt. commandant.

come (kum) *v.* **came** (kaym), **coming, comes.** *—intr.* **1. a.** To advance towards the speaker or towards a specified place; approach. **b.** To advance in a specified manner. **2.** To arrive as a result of moving or making progress. **3.** To reach a particular point in a series or as a result of orderly progression. **4.** To move into view; appear. **5.** To occur in time. **6. a.** To arrive at a particular result or end: *come to an understanding.* **b.** To arrive at or reach a particular state or condition: *came to like him; didn't come to any harm.* **c.** To move or be brought to a particular position: *The bus came to an abrupt halt.* **7.** To extend; reach: *hair coming to the waist.* **8.** To exist at a particular point or place: *The letter* T *comes before* U. **9. a.** To happen: *How did you come to know that? No harm will come to it if you leave it here.* **b.** To happen as a result: *This comes of your carelessness.* **10.** To be allotted or given: *On my death the jewels will come to you.* **11.** To occur in the mind: *An idea came to him.* **12. a.** To issue forth: *A loud scream came from the next room.* **b.** To descend; originate: *comes of an old Scottish family.* **c.** To be derived. **13.** To be a native or have been a resident of. **14.** To be moving towards a concluding or culminating stage; develop; evolve: *The project is coming along very well.* **15.** To become: *The knot came loose.* **16.** To be available as specified; be offered for sale: *Houses here don't come cheap; It comes in two sizes.* **17.** To prove or turn out to be: *His wish came true.* **18.** To be achieved or mastered as specified: *Maths comes easily to some people.* **19.** *Informal.* To have an orgasm. *—tr. Informal.* **1.** To act the part of; behave like. **2.** To perform or produce: *He'll only come that spiel about his bad leg again.* **—come about. 1.** To occur; take place; happen. **2.** *Nautical.* To change tack. **—come across. 1.** To encounter or find by chance. **2.** To leave an impression: *He comes across as a very pushy young man.* **3.** *Slang.* To do or give what is wanted. **—come again. 1.** To come or go back; return. **2.** *Informal.* To repeat what one has just said. Used in the imperative.

—come along. 1. To improve; progress; advance. **2.** To appear;

arrive: *Don't just take the first job that comes along.* —**come at.**
1. *Australian Informal.* To agree to do. **2.** To attack; rush at.
—**come between.** To cause the separation or estrangement of.
—**come by.** To acquire or get, especially by chance. —**come down on** or **upon. 1.** To descend upon; attack. **2.** *Informal.* To criticise; scold. —**come forward.** To volunteer one's services. —**come good.** *Informal.* **1.** To fulfil potential. **2.** To recover after a setback. —**come in. 1.** To turn out to be: *Some matches would come in handy.* **2.** To become popular or fashionable. **3.** To be received as income. **4.** To finish a race: *My horse came in last as usual.* **5.** To rise; flow. Used of the tide. —**come in for.** *Informal.* **1.** To be eligible for. **2.** To get; receive; acquire. —**come into.** To inherit. —**come off. 1.** To happen; occur. **2.** To have an intended effect; succeed: *My plans to excuse myself didn't come off.* —**come off it.** *Informal.* To stop talking nonsense. Used in the imperative. —**come out. 1.** To be disclosed or made public. **2.** To declare oneself openly to be something, especially a homosexual or lesbian. **3.** To make a formal social debut. **4.** To result; end up. **5.** *Chiefly British.* To go on strike. **6.** To become available; be published: *His new book is coming out next month.* **7.** To be developed successfully. Used of photographic film: *Our holiday photos didn't come out.* —**come out in.** To be covered with: *come out in a rash.* —**come out with. 1.** To disclose publicly; declare. **2.** To put into words; say. —**come over. 1.** To seize; possess: *Strange feelings came over me.* **2.** To change sides. **3.** To give a specified impression: *His speech came over well.* **4.** To be communicated: *His voice came over the loudspeaker.* **5.** *Informal.* To visit. —**come round** or **around. 1.** To recover; revive. **2.** To change one's opinion; accede to a particular position. **3.** To regain one's temper: *He'll soon come round.* —**come through. 1.** To recover; survive. **2.** *Informal.* To do as expected. —**come to. 1.** To recover consciousness. **2.** To amount to. **3.** To be a matter of; concern: *When it comes to mending radios, he's in a class of his own.* *Nautical.* **a.** To bring a ship's bow into the wind. **b.** To anchor. —**come to light with.** *Australian Informal.* To produce. —**come to that.** One could go further and say. —**come up.** To be regurgitated. —**come up against. 1.** To struggle or do battle with. **2.** To encounter (a problem, for example). —**come upon. 1.** To meet by accident. **2.** To attack. —**come up to. 1.** To reach or extend to; meet. **2.** To equal. —**come up with.** *Informal.* To propose; produce. —**how come.** *Informal.* Why.
~*interj.* Used to express anger, impatience, or remonstrance: *Come now, that's enough.*
~*prep.* As from; by: *Come next Friday, our financial problems will be solved.* [Come, came, come; Middle English *comen* or *cumen* (infinitive), *com* or *cam* (past singular), *comen* or *camen* (past plural), *comen* or *cumen* (past participle), Old English *cuman*, *cōm*, *c(w)ōmon*, *cumen*, from Germanic.]

come back *intr.v.* **1.** To return to popularity; become fashionable again. **2.** To return to memory. **3.** To retort. Usually used with *at.*
come·back (kúm-bak) *n.* **1.** A return to former prosperity or status. **2.** A retort; a piece of repartee. **3.** A recourse; a means of redress.
Com·e·con (kóm-ee-kon, -i-) *n.* An association of Communist states for economic cooperation, from 1949 until the early 1990s. Its members included the U.S.S.R. and its eastern European allies, Cuba, Mongolia, and Vietnam. [*Council for Mutual Economic Assistance.*]
co·me·di·an (kə-méed-i-ən) *n.* **1.** A professional entertainer who tells jokes, does impersonations, or performs various other comic acts. **2.** An actor in comedy. **3.** An amusing person; a clown. **4.** A stupid person; a fool.
co·me·di·enne (kə-méedi-én) *n.* A female comedian. [French.]
com·e·do (kómmi-dō) *n., pl.* -**dos** or -**dones** (-dōneez). A blackhead (*see*). Used in technical contexts. [New Latin, from Latin *comedo*, glutton, from *comedere*, to eat up : *com*- (intensive) + *edere*, to eat.]
come down *intr.v.* **1.** To lose status or wealth. **2.** To become ill. Used with *with: come down with measles.* **3.** To move to a lower position; drop. **4.** To reach a decision about a matter: *They came down on the side of the union.* **5.** To be transmitted through history; be passed down. Often used with *to.* **6.** To rebuke harshly or punish. Used with *on.* **7.** To amount to. Used with *to: It comes down to this.* **8.** *British.* To leave university. **9.** *Slang.* To come out of a drug-induced state.
come·down (kúm-down ‖ *West Indian also* -dung) *n.* **1.** A decline or drop to a lower status or level. **2.** *Informal.* A disappointment.
com·e·dy (kómmədi) *n., pl.* -**dies.** *Abbr.* **com. 1.** A play, film, or other work that is humorous in its treatment of theme and character and usually has a happy ending. **2.** Any literary composition with humorous themes or characters. **3.** The branch of literature dealing with comedies. **4.** The art or technique of composing or acting in comedy. **5.** A comic element of literature or life. **6.** A comic occurrence. [Middle English *comedie*, from Old French, from Latin *cōmoedia*, from Greek *kōmōidia*, from *kōmōidos*, originally "a singer in the revels" : *kōmos†*, revel + *ōidos*, *aoidēs*, singer, from *aeidein*, to sing.] —**com·e·dic** (kə-méedik, ko-) *adj.*
comedy of manners *n.* A comedy satirising fashionable society.
come·hith·er (kúm-híthər) *adj.* Seductive; alluring.
come·ly (kúmli) *adj.* -**lier,** -**liest.** Having a pleasing appearance; attractive. See Synonyms at **beautiful.** [Middle English *comli*, *comeli(ch)*, Old English *cȳmlic*, lovely, splendid, from *cȳme†*, beautiful.] —**come·li·ness** *n.*
Co·me·ni·us (kə-máyni-əss), **John Amos,** *Czech* Jan Amos Komenský (1592–1670). Czech theologian and educational reformer,

who believed that science exalted divine majesty rather than threatened it. He held that learning should be by observation rather than through authoritarian dogma.
come on *intr.v.* **1.** To make progress; improve; develop. **2.** To enter or appear, as on a theatre stage or sports pitch **3.** To begin: *I feel a cold coming on.* **4.** *Informal.* To try to attract; allure. —*tr.v.* To find or encounter; happen on.
come-on (kúm-on ‖ -awn) *n.* Something offered to allure or attract; an inducement. —**give (someone) the come-on.** To behave towards (someone) in a sexually provocative manner.
com·er (kúmmər) *n.* **1.** One that arrives or comes. Usually used in combination: *a latecomer; a newcomer.* **2.** *Chiefly U.S. Informal.* One showing great promise.
co·mes·ti·ble (kə-méstib'l) *adj.* Edible.
~*n. Plural.* Food. [Old French, from Medieval Latin *comestibilis*, from Latin *comedere* (past participle *comestus*), to eat up : *com*- (intensive) + *edere*, eat.]
com·et (kómmit) *n. Astronomy.* A celestial body, observed only in that part of its orbit that is relatively close to the sun, having a head consisting of a solid nucleus surrounded by a nebulous coma, an elongated curved vapour tail arising from the coma when sufficiently close to the sun, and thought to consist chiefly of ammonia, methane, carbon dioxide, and water. [Middle English *comete*, Old English *cōmēta*, from Latin *cōmēta*, *cōmētēs*, from Greek (*astēr*) *komētēs*, "long-haired (star)", from *koman*, to wear long hair, from *komē†*, hair.] —**com·et·ar·y** (kómmi-təri ‖ *U.S.*-terri), **co·met·ic** (kə-méttik) *adj.*
come·up·pance (kúm-úppənss) *n. Informal.* Punishment or retribution that one deserves; one's just deserts. [From phrase *come up*, sense development obscure.]
com·fit (kúm-fit, kóm-) *n.* A sugar-coated sweet. [Middle English *confit*, from Old French, from Latin *confectum*, "preparation", from Latin *conficere*, to prepare : *com*- (intensive) + *facere*, to make.]
com·fort (kúmfərt) *tr.v.* -**forted,** -**forting,** -**forts. 1.** To soothe in time of grief or fear; console. **2.** To ease physically; relieve of pain or discomfort. —See Synonyms at **relieve.**
~*n.* **1.** A state of ease or well-being; freedom from pain or anxiety. **2.** Relief; consolation; solace. **3.** A source of consolation or support. **4.** A source of physical well-being: *home comforts.* **5.** Capacity to give physical ease and well-being: *enjoying the comfort of his favourite chair.* —See Synonyms at **rest.** [Middle English *comforten*, from Old French *conforter*, from Late Latin *confortāre*, to strengthen : Latin *com*- (intensive) + *fortis*, strong.] —**com·fort·ing·ly** *adv.*
com·fort·a·ble (kúmftərb'l, kúmfərtəb'l) *adj.* **1.** Providing or giving comfort. **2.** Being in a state of comfort; at ease. **3.** *Informal.* **a.** Providing adequately for one's material needs: *a comfortable income.* **b.** Having an adequate income. —**com·fort·a·ble·ness** *n.* —**com·fort·a·bly** *adv.*
    Synonyms: comfortable, cosy, snug, restful.
com·fort·er (kúmfərtər) *n.* **1.** One that comforts. **2.** *Capital* **C.** The Holy Spirit. **3.** *Chiefly British.* A woollen neck scarf. **4.** *Chiefly U.S.* A baby's dummy. **5.** *U.S.* A quilted bedcover.
comfort station *n. U.S.* A **public convenience** (*see*). Used euphemistically.
com·frey (kúmfri) *n., pl.* -**freys.** Any of several usually hairy or bristly plants of the genus *Symphytum*, native to the Old World, having clusters of blue, purplish, or white flowers. [Middle English *conferie*, from Old French *cumfirie*, *confire*, from Latin *conferva*, a water plant, "healer", from *confervēre*, to boil together, heal : *com*-, together + *fervēre*, to boil.]
com·fy (kúmfi) *adj.* -**fier,** -**fiest.** *Informal.* Comfortable.
com·ic (kómmik) *adj. Abbr.* **com. 1.** Of, characteristic of, or pertaining to comedy. **2.** Amusing; humorous.
~*n. Abbr.* **com. 1.** A comedian. **2.** A person who is comical. **3.** A magazine that contains mainly comic strips. **4.** *Plural. Chiefly U.S.* Comic strips. [Latin *cōmicus*, from Greek *kōmikos*, from *kōmos*, revelry, merrymaking. See **comedy.**]
com·i·cal (kómmik'l) *adj.* **1.** Provoking mirth; funny; amusing. **2.** Amusing in an odd way; ludicrous. —**com·i·cal·i·ty** (kómmi-kál-əti), **com·i·cal·ness** *n.* —**com·i·cal·ly** *adv.*
comic opera *n.* An opera or operetta with a humorous plot, spoken dialogue, and, usually, a happy ending.
comic strip *n.* A narrative series of cartoons. Also *British* "strip cartoon".
com·ing (kúmming) *adj.* **1.** Approaching; next. **2.** Showing promise of fame or success; up-and-coming.
~*n.* Arrival; advent.
com·ing-out (kúmming-ówt) *n. Informal.* A social debut. Also used adjectivally: *a coming-out party.*
Com·in·tern (kómmin-tern) *n.* The Third **International** (*see*) or, especially, its executive committee in Moscow. [*Communist International.*]
com·i·ty (kómməti) *n., pl.* -**ties.** *Formal.* Civility; courtesy. [Latin *cōmitās*, from *cōmis*, courteous.]
comity of nations *n.* **1.** Courteous recognition accorded by one nation to the laws and institutions of another. **2.** The nations observing such courtesy.
comm. 1. commerce. **2.** commission; commissioner. **3.** commonwealth. **4.** communication.
com·ma (kómmə) *n.* A punctuation mark (,) used to indicate a separation of ideas or of elements within the structure of a sentence, and, in some countries, to precede a decimal fraction. [Latin, from

Greek *komma,* a cut, section, clause, from *koptein,* to cut.]
comma bacillus *n.* A bacillus, *Vibrio comma,* that causes cholera. [From its comma-like shape.]
comma butterfly *n.* A European butterfly, *Polygonia c-album,* having orange-brown wings with white comma-shaped markings on the underside.
com·mand (kə-maánd ‖ -mánd) *v.* **-manded, -manding, -mands.** —*tr.* **1.** To direct with authority; give orders to. **2.** To have control or authority over; rule. **3.** To have at one's disposal: *The country commands enormous mineral resources.* **4.** To deserve and receive as due; require: *His bravery commanded respect.* **5.** To dominate by position; overlook. —*intr.* **1.** To give commands. **2.** To exercise authority as a commander; be in control.
~*n.* **1.** The act of commanding or giving orders. **2.** An order so given. **3.** The authority to command. **4.** Possession; power of disposal: *using all the skill at his command.* **5.** Ability to control; mastery: *an impressive command of the language.* **6.** Dominance by location; extent of view. **7. a.** The jurisdiction of a commander. **b.** *Military.* A unit, post, or region under the control of one officer. **8.** *British.* An invitation from the reigning monarch. **9.** *Computing.* An instruction. Also used adjectivally: *a command file.* [Middle English *com(m)aunden,* from Anglo-French *comaunder,* from Old French *comander,* from Late Latin *commandāre,* to COMMEND.]
  Synonyms: *command, order, bid, enjoin, direct, instruct, charge.*
com·man·dant (kómmən-dánt, -daánt) *n. Abbr.* **Comdt. 1.** A commanding officer of a military organisation. **2.** *South African.* A lieutenant-colonel.
com·man·deer (kómmən-deér) *tr.v.* **-deered, -deering, -deers. 1.** To force into military service. **2.** To seize (property) for military use; confiscate. **3.** *Informal.* To take arbitrarily or by force. [Afrikaans *kommandeer,* from French *commander,* to COMMAND.]
com·mand·er (kə-maándər ‖ -mándər) *n.* **1.** A person who commands; a leader. **2.** *Abbr.* **Comdr., Cdr., Com., Cmdr.** An officer of the Royal Navy ranking between a captain and a lieutenant commander, equivalent in rank to a lieutenant colonel in the army and a wing commander in the Royal Air Force. **3.** The chief commissioned officer of a military unit, regardless of his rank. **4.** An officer in charge of a Metropolitan Police district. **5.** A chief or an officer in certain knightly or fraternal orders.
commander in chief *n., pl.* **commanders in chief. 1.** *Abbr.* **C-in-C, C in C.** The supreme commander of all the armed forces of a nation. **2.** The officer commanding a major armed force.
command guidance *n.* A form of missile guidance in which instructions are transmitted to a missile by radio during its flight.
com·mand·ing (kə-maánding ‖ -mánding) *adj.* **1.** *Abbr.* **comdg.** Having command; controlling. **2.** Impressive. **3.** Dominating, as by height or position. —**com·mand·ing·ly** *adv.*
commanding officer *n. Abbr.* **C.O.** An officer in charge of any military unit.
com·mand·ment (kə-maánd-mənt ‖ -mánd-) *n.* **1.** A command; an edict; specifically, a divine command or edict. **2.** *Sometimes capital* **C.** Any of the **Ten Commandments** *(see).*
command module *n.* The portion of a spacecraft in which the astronauts live and operate controls during a flight.
com·man·do (kə-maándō ‖ -mándō) *n., pl.* **-dos** or **-does. 1.** A small fighting force trained for quick raids against enemy-held areas. Also used adjectivally: *a commando unit.* **2.** A member of such a force. **3.** Originally, in South Africa, an organised force of Boer troops. [Afrikaans *kommando,* from Dutch *commando,* unit of troops, from Spanish *comando,* from *comandar,* to command, from Vulgar Latin *commandāre* (unattested), COMMAND.]
command paper *n. Abbr.* **Cmd., Cmnd.** In Britain, a paper presented to Parliament, technically at the command of the sovereign.
command performance *n.* A theatrical performance, entertainment, or the like, given at the request of a head of state.
command post *n. Abbr.* **C.P.** The field headquarters used by the commander of a military unit.
com·me·dia dell'ar·te (ko-máydi-ə del-árti, kə-) *n.* A type of comedy developed in Italy in the 16th century, characterised by improvisation from a plot outline and by the use of stock characters. [Italian, "comedy of art".]
comme il faut (kóm eel fő ‖ kúm, *U.S. also* káwm) *adj. French.* As one or it should be; proper.
com·mem·o·rate (kə-mémmə-rayt) *tr.v.* **-rated, -rating, -rates. 1.** To honour the memory of (a person or event) in speech or writing, or with a ceremony. **2.** To serve as a memorial to. —See Synonyms at **observe.** [Latin *commemorāre,* to call to mind clearly : *com-* (intensive) + *memor,* to remind, speak of, from *memor,* mindful.] —**com·mem·o·ra·tor** (-raytər) *n.*
com·mem·o·ra·tion (kə-mémmə-ráysh'n) *n.* **1.** The act of commemorating. **2.** Something that commemorates. **3.** A commemorative celebration.
com·mem·o·ra·tive (kə-mémmə-rətiv, -mém-, -raytiv) *adj.* **1.** Serving to commemorate. **2.** Issued to commemorate a notable person or event. Said of coins, stamps, or the like.
~*n.* Anything that commemorates.
com·mence (kə-ménss) *v.* **-menced, -mencing, -mences.** —*tr.* To begin; start. —*intr.* To come into existence; have a beginning. —See Synonyms at **begin.** [Middle English *commencen,* from Old French *comencer,* from Vulgar Latin *cominitiāre* (unattested) : Latin *com-* (intensive) + *initiāre,* to INITIATE.] —**com·menc·er** *n.*
com·mence·ment (kə-ménssmənt) *n.* **1.** A beginning; a start. **2.** *Chiefly U.S.* A ceremony at which academic degrees or diplomas

are conferred.
com·mend (kə-ménd) *tr.v.* **-mended, -mending, -mends. 1.** To represent as worthy, qualified, or desirable; recommend. **2.** To express approval of; praise. **3.** To commit to the care of another; entrust. —See Synonyms at **praise.** [Middle English *commenden,* from Latin *commendāre,* to commit to one's charge, commend, recommend : *com-* (intensive) + *mandāre,* to entrust.] —**com·mend·a·ble** *adj.* —**com·mend·a·bly** *adv.*
com·men·da·tion (kóm-en-dáysh'n, -ən-) *n.* **1.** The act of commending; recommendation; approval. **2.** An award or honour: *a commendation for bravery.* —**com·men·da·to·ry** (-dáytəri, kə-ménd-ə-tri, -təri) *adj.*
com·men·sal (kə-ménss'l) *adj.* **1.** *Rare.* Eating at the same table. **2.** *Biology.* Pertaining to or characterised by commensalism.
~*n.* **1.** *Rare.* A mealtime companion. **2.** *Biology.* An organism participating in commensalism. [Middle English, from Medieval Latin *commensālis* : Latin *com-,* together + *mēnsa,* table.] —**com·men·sal·ly** *adv.*
com·men·sal·ism (kə-ménss'l-iz'm) *n. Biology.* A relationship in which two or more organisms live in close association, and in which one may derive some benefit, but in which neither harms or is parasitic on the other. Compare **symbiosis.**
com·men·su·rate (kə-mén-sewr-ət, -shər-, -it) *adj.* **1.** Of the same size, extent, or duration; coextensive. **2.** Corresponding in scale or measure; proportionate: *a salary commensurate with the job's responsibilities.* [Late Latin *commēnsūrātus* : *com-,* same + *mēnsūrātus,* past participle of *mēnsūrāre,* to MEASURE.] —**com·men·su·rate·ly** *adv.* —**com·men·su·ra·tion** (-áysh'm) *n.*
com·ment (kóm-ent) *n.* **1. a.** A remark, as in criticism or observation. **b.** A brief statement of fact or opinion, especially one that expresses a personal reaction or attitude. **2.** *Usually plural.* A written note intended as an explanation, illustration, or criticism of a passage in a book or other writing; an annotation. **3.** Talk; gossip: *caused a lot of comment.* **4.** Something that exemplifies; an illustration: *The match was a sad comment on the present state of cricket.*
~*intr.v.* **commented, -menting, -ments.** To make a comment; remark. Often used with *on.* [Middle English, from Latin *commentum,* contrivance, interpretation, from *commentus,* past participle of *comminīscī,* to contrive by thought.]
com·men·tar·y (kómmən-tri, -təri ‖ *U.S.* -terri) *n., pl.* **-ies. 1.** A series of annotations, explanations, or interpretations of a literary text. **2.** *Often plural.* An expository treatise or essay; an exegesis. **3.** A series of descriptive observations of an event, especially a sports event, as it happens in a radio or television broadcast. **4.** An illustration; a comment. —**com·men·tar·i·al** (-táir-i-əl) *adj.*
com·men·tate (kóm-ən-tayt, -en-) *intr.v.* **-tated, -tating, -tates.** To serve as a commentator; make a commentary, especially for a film or a radio or television broadcast. Used with *on.* Also, *chiefly U.S., tr.v.*
com·men·ta·tor (kóm-ən-taytər, -en-) *n.* **1.** An author of commentaries, especially on current or political events. **2.** A person who makes radio or television commentaries.
com·merce (kóm-erss ‖ -ərss) *n.* **1.** *Abbr.* **com., comm.** The buying and selling of goods, especially on a large scale, as between cities or nations; business; trade. **2.** Intellectual exchange or social intercourse. **3.** *Archaic.* Sexual intercourse. Used with **business.** [Old French, from Latin *commercium* : *com-* (collective) + *merx* (stem *merc-*), merchandise.]
com·mer·cial (kə-mérsh'l) *adj. Abbr.* **com., cml. 1. a.** Of, pertaining to, or engaged in commerce. **b.** Suitable for commerce; profitable: *valuable minerals in commercial quantities.* **2.** Produced in large quantities for use by industry; unrefined. Said especially of chemicals. **3.** Viewed purely in terms of financial returns: *The play was a commercial success.* **4.** Having profit, success, or immediate results as chief aim: *a commercial painter.* **5.** Financed by advertising revenue: *commercial television.*
~*n.* An advertisement on radio or television.
commercial bank *n.* A privately owned bank, usually with a large number of branches, the principal functions of which are to operate deposit and current accounts, and to make loans.
com·mer·cial·ise, com·mer·cial·ize (kə-mérsh'l-īz) *tr.v.* **-ised, -ising, -ises. 1.** To make commercial; apply methods of business to. **2. a.** To exploit, do, or make mainly for financial gain. **b.** To sacrifice the quality of for profit. —**com·mer·cial·i·sa·tion** (-ī-záysh'n ‖ *U.S.* -i-) *n.*
com·mer·cial·ism (kə-mérsh'l-iz'm) *n.* **1.** The practices, methods, aims, and spirit of commerce or business. **2.** An attitude that emphasises or overemphasises tangible profit or success. —**com·mer·cial·ist** *n.* —**com·mer·cial·is·tic** (-ístik) *adj.*
commercial traveller *n.* A **travelling salesman** *(see).*
commercial vehicle *n.* A vehicle used for transporting merchandise by road.
Com·mie (kómmi) *n. Often small* **c.** *Informal.* A Communist. Used derogatorily. —**Com·mie** *adj.*
com·mi·na·tion (kómmi-náysh'n) *n.* **1.** A formal denunciation; a threatening. **2.** In the Anglican liturgy, a recital of God's judgment and anger against sinners, read on Ash Wednesday. [Middle English *comminacioun,* from Old French *commination,* from Latin *comminātiō* (stem *comminātiōn-*), from *comminārī,* to threaten : *com-* (intensive) + *minārī,* threaten, from *minae,* threats.] —**com·min·a·to·ry** (kómmin-ətri, -ətəri, -aytəri) *adj.*
com·min·gle (kom-míng-g'l) *v.* **-gled, -gling, -gles.** —*intr.* To blend together; mix. —*tr.* To mix together; combine.
com·mis·er·ate (kə-mízzə-rayt) *v.* **-ated, -ating, -ates.** —*intr.* To

feel or express sorrow or pity for someone; sympathise with someone. Used with *with.* —*tr. Archaic.* To grieve in sympathy. [Latin *commiserārī* : *com-*, with + *miserārī,* to pity, from *miser,* wretched, pitiable.] **—com·mis·er·a·tive** (-rətiv, -raytiv) *adj.* **—com·mis·er·a·tive·ly** *adv.* **—com·mis·er·a·tor** (-raytər) *n.*

com·mis·er·a·tion (kə-mízzə-ráysh'n) *n.* A feeling or expression of sorrow or sympathy for the distress of another; compassion. See Synonyms at **pity.**

com·mis·sar (kómmi-sár, -saar) *n.* **1.** An official of a Communist Party charged with teaching and enforcing party principles. **2.** Formerly, the head of a commissariat in the U.S.S.R. [Russian *kommissar,* from French *commissaire,* COMMISSARY.]

com·mis·sar·i·at (kómmi-sáir-i-ət, -at) *n.* **1.** A department of an army in charge of providing food and other supplies for the troops. **2.** The officers in charge of this. **3.** A food supply. **4.** Formerly, any major government department in the U.S.S.R. [Russian *kommissariat,* from French and Medieval Latin *commissariatus,* from *commissārius,* COMMISSARY.]

com·mis·sar·y (kómmiss-əri, kə-míss- || *U.S.*-erri) *n., pl.* **-ies. 1.** A person to whom a special duty is given by a higher authority; a representative; a deputy. **2.** *Chiefly U.S.* **a.** A supermarket for the use of soldiers in a camp, employees, diplomatic personnel, or the like. **b.** A cafeteria on a film set or in a television studio. **3.** Formerly, an army officer in charge of supplying provisions. [Middle English *commissarie,* from Medieval Latin *commissārius,* commissioner, agent, from *committere,* to entrust, commission, COMMIT.]

com·mis·sion (kə-mísh'n) *n.* **1. a.** An act of committing or giving authority to carry out a particular task or duty, or granting certain powers; an entrusting. **b.** A document conferring such an authority. **2.** The authority, duty, or task conferred in this way. **3.** The state of being authorised to perform certain functions. **4.** *Abbr.* **Com., comm.** A group of people lawfully authorised to perform certain duties or functions, such as a government agency: *the Forestry Commission.* See **High Commission, Royal Commission. 5.** A committing or perpetrating: *commission of a crime.* **6.** A fee or percentage allowed to a salesman or agent for his services. **7.** *Abbr.* **Com., comm. a.** An official document issued by a government, conferring the rank of a commissioned officer in the armed forces. **b.** The rank and powers so conferred. **—in (or out of) commission. 1.** In (or out of) active service. Said of a ship. **2.** In (or out of) working condition or use.

~*tr.v.* **commissioned, -sioning, -sions. 1.** To grant a commission to. **2.** To place an order for. **3.** *Nautical.* To put (a ship) into active service. [Middle English *commissioun,* from Old French *commission,* from Latin *commissiō* (stem *commissiōn-*), from *committere* (past participle *commissus*), COMMIT.] **—com·mis·sion·al, com·mis·sion·ar·y** (-əri || *U.S.* -erri) *adj.*

com·mis·sion·aire (kə-mísh'n-áir) *n. Chiefly British.* A uniformed doorman. [French *commissionnaire,* from Old French *commission,* COMMISSION.]

commissioned officer *n.* Any officer in the armed forces who holds a commission, ranking as second lieutenant, or its equivalent, and above. Compare **noncommissioned officer, warrant officer.**

com·mis·sion·er (kə-mísh'n-ər) *n. Abbr.* **Com., Comr., comm. 1.** A person authorised by a commission to perform certain duties. **2.** A member of a commission. **3.** An official in charge of a particular department: *commissioner of police.* **—com·mis·sion·er·ship** *n.*

Commisioner for Local Administration *n.* See **ombudsman.**

commissioner for oaths *n.* A solicitor authorised to certify statements sworn to under oath.

com·mit (kə-mít) *v.* **—mitted, -mitting, -mits.** —*tr.v.* **1.** To do, perform, or perpetrate (especially something bad or wrong): *commit a murder.* **2.** To place in trust or charge; consign; entrust. **3.** To place officially in confinement or custody; especially, to place in a mental institution. **4.** To consign for future use or reference or for preservation: *commit a poem to memory.* **5.** To put in some place to be kept safe or be disposed of: *commit old love-letters to the flames.* **6. a.** To pledge (oneself) to a position on some issue. **b.** To bind or obligate, as by a pledge. **c.** To assign for a particular purpose; pledge. **7.** To refer (a bill, for example) to a committee. —*intr.v. Chiefly U.S.* To commit oneself: *He won't commit to marriage.* [Middle English *committen,* from Latin *committere,* to join, connect, entrust : *com-*, together + *mittere,* to send, put.] **—com·mit·ta·ble** *adj.*

Synonyms: *commit, consign, entrust, confide, assign.*

com·mit·ment (kə-mít-mənt) *n.* Also **com·mit·tal** (-mítt'l) (for senses 1, 2, 3, 8). **1. a.** The act of committing; a giving in charge or entrusting. **b.** The state of being committed. **2.** Official consignment, as to a prison or mental hospital. **3.** *Law.* A court order authorising consignment to a prison; a mittimus. **4. a.** A pledge to do something. **b.** Something pledged. **5.** An engagement by contract involving financial obligation. **6.** The state of being bound emotionally or intellectually to some way of thinking or course of action: *a deep commitment to liberal policies.* **7.** A perpetration, as of a crime. **8.** The act of referring a legislative bill to a committee.

com·mit·tee (kə-mítti) *n. Abbr.* **com., Com. 1.** A group of people, usually appointed from a larger body, delegated to perform a function, such as investigating, considering, or acting on a matter. **2.** *Law.* Formerly, a person to whom the care of an estate or incompetent person is committed; a trustee; a guardian. **—in committee.** Under consideration by a committee. Said of a legislative measure. [Middle English *committe,* trustee, from *committen,* COMMIT.]

Usage: Standard English allows the use of both *is* and *are* with this word, depending on the meaning intended. The singular is used when the committee is viewed as a unitary group; the plural, when viewed as a collection of individuals. *The committee has decided* is therefore more likely, as is *The committee are making up their minds.* See also **collective noun.**

committee of the whole house *n.* The whole of the membership of a legislative body, especially the British House of Commons, sitting as a committee to consider the details of a legislative proposal.

committee stage *n.* The stage in the progress of a bill through Parliament between the second and third readings, during which the finer details of the bill are considered by a committee appointed by Parliament for that purpose.

com·mix (kə-míks, ko-) *v.* **-mixed, -mixing, -mixes.** *Rare.* —*tr.* To mix together. —*intr.* To mix; blend. [Middle English, back-formation from *commixt,* from Latin *commixtus,* past participle of *commiscēre,* to mix together : *com-*, together + *miscēre,* mix.]

com·mix·ture (kə-míks-chər, ko-, -tewr) *n.* **1.** The act or process of mixing together. **2.** The result of this; a mixture.

com·mode (kə-mṓd) *n.* **1.** A low cabinet or chest of drawers, often elaborately decorated and usually on legs or short feet. **2.** Formerly: **a.** A movable stand or cupboard containing a washbowl. **b.** A chair containing a concealed chamber pot. **3.** A woman's ornate lace headdress, fashionable around 1700. [French, "convenient," from Latin *commodus,* COMMODIOUS.]

com·mo·di·ous (kə-mṓdi-əss) *adj.* **1.** Spacious; roomy. **2.** *Archaic.* Convenient; suitable. [Middle English, from Old French *commodieux,* from Medieval Latin *commodiōsus,* from Latin *commodus,* convenient, "(conforming) with (due) measure" : *com-*, with + *modus,* measure.] **—com·mo·di·ous·ly** *adv.* **—com·mo·di·ous·ness** *n.*

com·mod·i·ty (kə-móddəti) *n., pl.* **-ties. 1.** Anything useful or that can be turned to commercial or other advantage. **2.** *Economics.* **a.** An article of trade or commerce that can be transported, especially an agricultural or mining product. **b.** Any economic unit that can be exchanged, such as a service or a product. **3.** *Obsolete.* **a.** Convenience; profit; expediency. **b.** A quantity of goods. [Middle English *commodite,* profit, income, property, from Old French *commodite,* from Latin *commoditās* (stem *commoditāt-*), advantage, convenience, from *commodus,* convenient, COMMODIOUS.]

com·mo·dore (kómmə-dawr || -dōr) *n. Abbr.* **Com., Como. 1.** *British.* An officer in the Royal Navy ranking semi-officially between a rear admiral and a captain; a senior naval captain. **2.** *U.S.* Formerly, a naval officer ranking between a rear admiral and a captain. **3. a.** The senior captain of a naval squadron or merchant fleet. **b.** The presiding officer of a yacht club. [Dutch *komandeur,* commander, from French *commandeur,* commander.]

com·mon (kómmən) *adj.* **-moner, -monest. 1.** Belonging equally to two or more; shared by all alike; joint: *common interests.* **2.** Pertaining to the community as a whole; public: *the common good.* **3.** Generally known: *common knowledge.* **4.** Widespread; prevalent; general. **5.** Of frequent or habitual occurrence; usual. **6.** Most widely known or occurring most frequently; ordinary: *the common crow.* **7.** Without special designation, status, or rank: *a common sailor.* **8.** Not distinguished by superior or other characteristics; average: *the common spectator/man/people.* **9.** Of no special quality; standard; plain: *common courtesy.* **10.** Of mediocre or inferior quality; not costly or rare: *common cloth.* **11.** Vulgar; unrefined; coarse. **12.** Of variable length; either short or long. Said of a syllable in verse. **13.** *Grammar.* **a.** Either masculine or feminine in gender. **b.** Representing one or all the members of a class; not designating a unique entity. **14.** *Anatomy.* Having several branches: *common bile duct.* —See Usage note at **mutual.**

~*n.* **1.** *Sometimes plural.* A tract of land belonging to or used by a community as a whole. **2.** *Law.* The right of a person to use the lands or waters of another, as for fishing or grazing cattle. **3.** *Sometimes capital* **C.** A church service used for a particular class of festivals. **—in common.** Equally with or by all; jointly. [Middle English *commun(e),* from Old French, from Latin *commūnis.*] **—com·mon·ness** *n.*

Synonyms: *common, ordinary, familiar, prevalent.*

com·mon·age (kómmənij) *n.* **1.** The right to pasture animals on common land. **2.** The use of this right. **3.** The state of being held in common. **4.** That which is held in common, especially land.

com·mon·al·i·ty (kómmən-ál-əti) *n.* **1.** The state of being held in common or shared by numerous people or things. **2.** An object or attribute so shared. **3.** A common occurrence. **4.** The common people; the commonalty.

com·mon·al·ty (kómmənəlti) *n., pl.* **-ties. 1.** The common people, as opposed to the upper classes. **2.** A body corporate; a corporation. [Middle English *communalte,* from Medieval Latin *commūnālitās* (stem *commūnālitat-*), from *commūnālis,* COMMUNAL.]

common carrier *n.* A carrier by land, water, or air, such as a railway or coach company, which is prepared to accept any passengers or goods that require transport. Compare **private carrier.**

common denominator *n.* **1.** A quantity into which all the denominators of a set of fractions may be evenly divided. **2.** A quality or belief common to all the members of a particular group, and considered to characterise them as a group.

Common Entrance *n. Abbr.* **C.E.** The entrance examination for British public schools, taken at the age of about 13.

com·mon·er (kómmənər) *n.* **1.** One of the common people. **2.** One who is not a noble. **3.** In certain British universities and public schools, a student who does not hold a scholarship or similar award.

common era *n. Abbr.* **C.E.** The **Christian era** *(see).* Used especially by non-Christians.

common factor *n.* A quantity that is a factor of two or more quantities. Also called "common divisor".

common fraction *n.* A **simple fraction** *(see).*

common gender *n.* Gender that may refer to either masculine or feminine categories; for example, *child, person.* Compare **natural gender, grammatical gender.**

common ground *n.* Points of agreement between the parties in a discussion providing a basis for argument or negotiation.

common law *n. Abbr.* **c.l. 1.** The system of laws originated and developed in England, based on court decisions, on the doctrines implicit in those decisions, and on customs and usages, rather than on codified written laws. Compare **statute law. 2.** The part of a system of laws of any state or nation that is of a general and universal application. —**com·mon-law** (kómmən-láw) *adj.*

common law marriage *n.* **1.** In English law, a marriage contracted in circumstances not allowing an official ceremony. **2.** In Scots law, a form of marriage existing by mutual agreement between a man and a woman, based on having lived together for a number of years. **3.** Loosely, a relationship between a man and a woman involving regular cohabitation.

common logarithm *n.* A logarithm to the base 10. Compare **natural logarithm.**

com·mon·ly (kómmənli) *adv.* **1.** Generally; ordinarily. **2.** In a common manner.

Common Market *n.* **1.** The **European Economic Community** *(see).* **2.** *Usually small* c, *small* m. Any economic union between countries in which trade barriers are removed.

common multiple *n.* A quantity that is a multiple of each of two or more given quantities.

common noun *n. Grammar.* A noun that represents one or all of the members of a class; for example, *book, woman.* Compare **proper noun.**

common-or-garden *adj.* Unexceptional; ordinary.

com·mon·place (kómmən-playss) *adj.* Ordinary; uninteresting; common. See Synonyms at **trite.**

~*n.* **1.** A trite or obvious remark; a platitude. **2.** Something ordinary or common. **3.** A passage in a book marked for reference or entered in a commonplace book. —See Synonyms at **cliché.** [Translation of Latin *locus commūnis,* translation of Greek *koinos topos,* "common place", literary passage of universal application.] —**com·mon·place·ness** *n.*

commonplace book *n.* A personal journal in which quotable passages, literary excerpts, and comments are written.

Common Prayer *n.* **1.** The liturgy for public worship in the Church of England. **2.** The **Book of Common Prayer** *(see).*

common room *n. Chiefly British.* A sitting room in an educational or similar institution, where newspapers and light refreshments are usually available.

com·mons (kómmənz) *n.* **1.** *Used with a plural verb.* The common people. **2.** *Used with a singular verb.* A building or hall for dining. **3.** *Used with a singular verb. Rare.* Food; daily rations. **4. a.** *Used with a singular or plural verb.* The political class comprising the commoners. **b.** *Often capital* **C.** The representatives of this class in Parliament. **c.**

Often capital **C.** The House of Commons.

common salt *n.* **1. Salt** *(see).* **2. Sodium chloride** *(see).* **3. Table salt** *(see).*

common sense *n.* **1.** Native good judgment. **2.** A set of general unexamined assumptions as distinguished from specially acquired concepts. [Translation of Latin *sensus commūnis* and Greek *koinē aisthēsis,* total perception of the five senses.] —**com·mon-sense, com·mon-sense** (kómmən-sénss) *adj.*

com·mon·weal (kómmən-weel) *n. Archaic.* The public good.

com·mon·wealth (kómmən-welth) *n.* **1.** The people of a nation or state; the body politic. **2.** *Abbr.* **comm.** A nation or state governed by the people; a republic. **3.** *Obsolete.* The public welfare; the commonweal. —**the Commonwealth. 1.** The political community consisting of the United Kingdom, its dependencies, and certain former colonies that are now sovereign nations. Also officially called the "Commonwealth of Nations", formerly the "British Commonwealth of Nations". **2. a.** The period of republican government in Britain between 1649 and 1660. **b.** The parts of this period that preceded (1649–53) and followed (1659–60) Oliver Cromwell's personal protectorship. **c.** The form or forms of government during these periods. Also called the "Commonwealth of England". **3. Australia** *(see).* **4.** The official title of various U.S. states, such as Kentucky or Virginia. **5. Puerto Rico,** Northern Marianas *(see).*

Commonwealth of Independent States. A political and economic association, established in 1992, of countries that had been part of the U.S.S.R. Of the 15 former Soviet republics, only Estonia, Latvia and Lithuania have chosen to remain outside the new association.

com·mo·tion (kə-mōsh'n) *n.* **1.** Violent or turbulent motion; agitation. **2.** Political disturbance or insurrection; disorder. **3.** A confused noise, suggesting upheaval; a tumult. [Middle English *commocioun,* from Latin *commōtiō* (stem *commōtiōn-*), from *commovēre* (past participle *commōtus*), to move violently : *com-* (intensive) + *movēre,* to move.] —**com·mo·tion·al** *adj.*

com·mu·nal (kómmew-n'l, kə-méw-) *adj.* **1.** Of or pertaining to a commune or community. **2.** Of, pertaining to, or shared by the people of a community or members of a group; common: *communal washing facilities.* **3.** Of or concerning different and opposed communities, especially in India: *communal riots between Hindus and Muslims.* [French, from Old French *comunal,* from Medieval Latin *commūnālis,* from *commūna, commūnia,* COMMUNE (community).] —**com·mu·nal·i·ty** (-nál-əti) *n.* —**com·mu·nal·ly** *adv.*

com·mu·nal·ise, com·mu·nal·ize (kómmewnəl-īz, kə-méwnəl-) *tr.v.* **-ised, -ising, -ises.** To convert into municipal or community property.

com·mu·nal·ism (kómmewnəl-iz'm, kə-méwnəl-) *n.* **1.** A theory or system of government in which virtually autonomous local communities are loosely bound in a federation. **2.** Belief in or practice of communal ownership, as of goods and property. **3.** Strong devotion to one's own cultural or ethnic group rather than society as a whole. —**com·mu·nal·ist** *n.* —**com·mu·nal·is·tic** (-istik) *adj.*

Com·mu·nard (kómmew-nárd) *n.* **1.** A member or supporter of the **Paris Commune** *(see).* **2.** *Small* **c.** A member of a commune. [French, from *commune,* COMMUNE (division).]

com·mune[1] (kə-méwn; *rarely* kómmewn) *intr.v.* **-muned, -muning,**

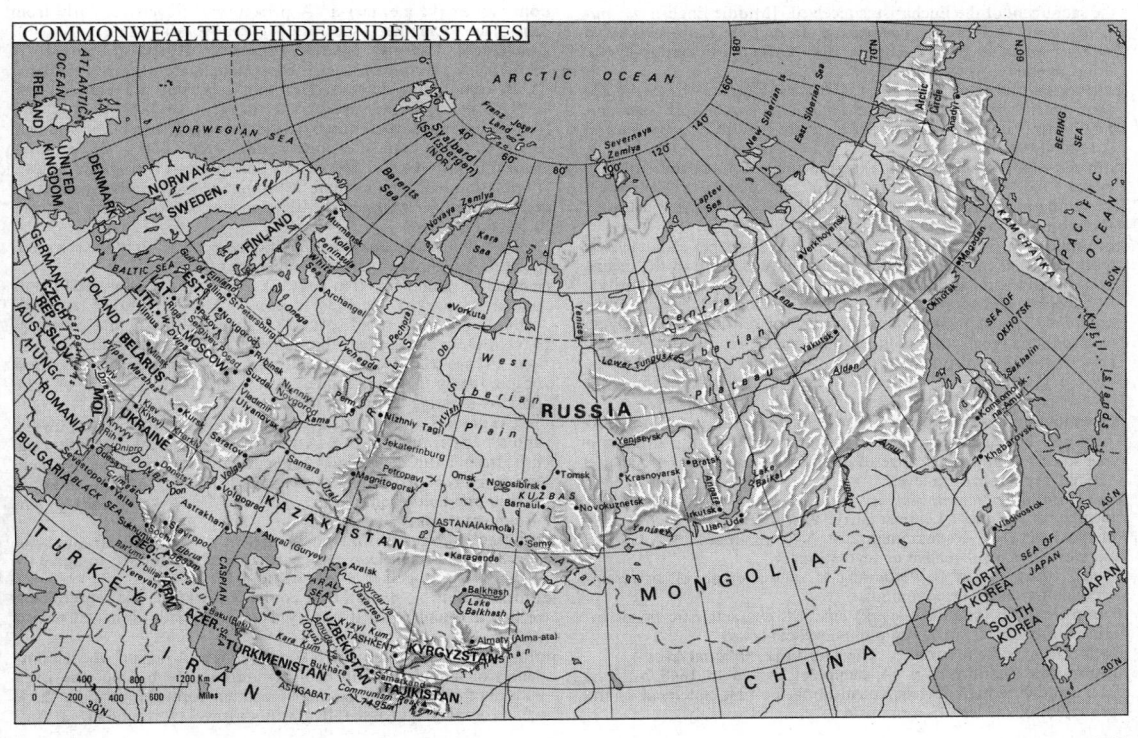

COMMONWEALTH OF INDEPENDENT STATES

-munes. 1. To have close or intimate rapport or communication. Often used with *with.* **2.** *Chiefly U.S.* To receive Communion. ~*n.* (kómmewn). Intimate conversation or communion. [Middle English *communen,* to distribute, share, communicate, from Old French *comuner,* from *comun, commun,* COMMON. Sense 2 of verb : back-formation from COMMUNION.]

com·mune² (kómmewn) *n.* **1.** The smallest local political division of France, Belgium, Italy, and Switzerland, governed by a mayor and municipal council. **2. a.** A local community organised legally for promoting local interests. **b.** A municipal corporation in the Middle Ages. **3.** A small, often rural, community whose members have common interests and in which property is often shared or owned jointly. **4.** The people of a commune. —**the Commune. 1.** The revolutionary committee that governed Paris from 1789 to 1795. **2.** The **Paris Commune** *(see).* [French, from Medieval Latin *commūnia,* community, from Latin *commūnis,* public, COMMON.]

com·mu·ni·ca·ble (kə-méwnik-əb'l) *adj.* **1.** Able to be communicated. **2.** *Medicine.* Liable to be passed on from one person to another; infectious. Said of a disease. —**com·mu·ni·ca·bil·i·ty** (-ə-bílləti) —**com·mu·ni·ca·ble·ness** *n.* —**com·mu·ni·ca·bly** *adv.*

com·mu·ni·cant (kə-méwnikənt) *n.* **1.** A person who receives, or is entitled to receive, Communion. **2.** One who communicates. ~*adj.* Communicating.

com·mu·ni·cate (kə-méwni-kayt) *v.* **-cated, -cating, -cates.** —*tr.* **1.** To make known; impart: *communicate information.* **2.** To transmit (a disease, for example). —*intr.* **1.** To share or convey information. **2. a.** To have an interchange, as of ideas. **b.** To have mutual sympathy or good mutual understanding. **3.** To express oneself in such a way that one is readily and clearly understood. **4.** To receive Communion. **5.** To be connected or form a connecting passage. [Latin *commūnicāre,* "to make common", make known, from *commūnis,* COMMON.] —**com·mu·ni·ca·tor** (-kaytər) *n.*

com·mu·ni·ca·tion (kə-méwni-káysh'n) *n. Abbr.* **comm. 1.** The act of communicating; transmission. **2.** The exchange of thoughts, messages, or the like, as by speech, signals, or writing. **3.** Something communicated. **4.** *Plural.* A means of communicating, especially: **a.** A system for sending and receiving messages, as by post, telephone, or telegram. **b.** Any method by which human beings pass information to one another, including publishing, broadcasting, and telecommunications. **c.** *Military.* A network of routes for sending messages and transporting troops and supplies. **5.** Any connective passage or channel. **6.** *Plural.* The art and technology of communicating in all its forms.

communication cord *n. British.* A cord or chain in a carriage of a passenger train that can be pulled to stop the train in an emergency.

communications satellite *n.* A satellite used to aid communications, as by reflecting a radio signal. Also called "comsat."

com·mu·ni·ca·tive (kə-méwni-kətiv, -kaytiv) *adj.* **1.** Inclined to communicate readily; talkative. **2.** Of communication.

com·mun·ion (kə-méwn-yən, -i-ən) *n.* **1.** A possessing or sharing in common; participation. **2.** The act of communing; the sharing of thoughts or feelings; close rapport: *in communion with nature.* **3. a.** A religious or spiritual fellowship. **b.** A body of Christians with a common religious faith who practise the same rites; a denomination. **4. a.** *Capital* **C.** The **Eucharist** *(see).* **b.** The consecrated elements of the Eucharist. **c.** The part of the Mass in which the sacrament of the Eucharist is received. [Middle English *communioun,* from Old French *communion,* from Late Latin *commūnio* (stem *commūnion-*), the Eucharist, from Latin, participation by all, from *commūnis,* COMMON.]

com·mu·ni·qué (kə-méwni-kay ‖ *U.S. also* -káy) *n.* An official announcement made to the press and public. [French, from *communiquer,* to inform, announce, from Latin *commūnicāre,* COMMUNICATE.]

com·mu·nise, com·mu·nize (kómmew-nīz) *tr.v.* **-nised, -nising, -nises. 1.** To make public property of; nationalise. **2.** To convert to communist principles or control. [Latin *commūnis,* COMMON.] —**com·mu·ni·sa·tion** (-nī-záysh'n ‖ *U.S.* -ni-) *n.*

com·mu·nism (kómmew-niz'm) *n.* **1.** A social system characterised by the absence of classes and by common ownership of the means of production and subsistence. **2. a.** A political, economic, and social doctrine aiming at the establishment of such a society. **b.** *Often capital* **C.** The Marxist-Leninist doctrine of revolutionary struggle towards this goal, the political movement representing it, or, loosely, socialism as practised in countries ruled by communist parties. **c.** Communalism. **3.** Loosely, left-wing activity aiming at revolution. [French *communisme,* from *commun,* COMMON.]

Communism Peak. *Russian* **Pik Kommunizma** (péek kommoŏ-néezmə). The highest mountain in the former U.S.S.R., situated in the south in the Pamir range of Tajikistan. It rises to 7 495 metres (24,590 feet) above sea level.

com·mu·nist (kómmew-nist) *n.* **1.** *Often capital* **C.** *Abbr.* **Com.** A member of a Marxist-Leninist party. **2.** A supporter of such a party or movement. **3.** A communalist. **4.** A Communard. **5.** Any radical viewed as a subversive or revolutionary. ~*adj. Often capital* **C.** Pertaining to, characteristic of, or resembling communism or communists.

com·mu·nis·tic (kómmew-nístik) *adj.* Of, characteristic of, or inclined to communism. —**com·mu·nis·ti·cal·ly** *adv.*

Communist International *n.* The Third **International** *(see).*

Communist Manifesto *n.* A pamphlet, issued in 1848 by Karl Marx and Friedrich Engels, constituting the first statement of the principles of modern Communism.

com·mu·ni·ty (kə-méwnəti) *n., pl.* **-ties. 1. a.** A group of people living in the same locality or under the same local government. **b.** The district in which they live. **2.** A social group or class having common characteristics. **3.** Any group having common interests: *the scientific community.* **4.** Joint participation or common ownership: *community of property.* **5.** Similarity or identity: *a community of interests.* **6.** Society as a whole; the public. Preceded by *the.* **7.** *Ecology.* **a.** A group of plants and animals living in a specific region under similar conditions, and interacting through food webs and other relationships. **b.** The region in which they live. [Middle English *communite,* from Old French *comunete,* from Latin *commūnitās* (stem *commūnitat-*), from *commūnis,* COMMON.]

community architecture *n.* The concept of a close partnership between the architect and the community for whom he or she is creating homes, usually involving the restoration of existing buildings, and of a sense of community where it is lost.

community centre *n.* A meeting place used by members of a community for social, cultural, or recreational purposes.

community charge *n.* In Britain, a poll tax that till 1993 replaced rates as a way of financing local government.

community home *n.* In Britain, since 1969, a residential centre for young offenders, replacing the approved school and remand home.

community medicine *n.* The branch of medicine concerned with disease and health care of populations, rather than of individuals.

community singing *n.* Singing, especially of popular songs, by a group of people.

com·mut·a·ble (kə-méwt-əb'l) *adj.* **1.** Capable of being commuted; interchangeable. **2.** *Law.* Capable of being reduced in length or severity. Said of a sentence. —**com·mut·a·bil·i·ty** (-ə-bílləti) *n.*

com·mu·tate (kómmew-tayt) *tr.v.* **-tated, -tating, -tates. 1.** To reverse the direction of (an alternating electric current) each half-cycle. **2.** To convert (an alternating electric current) into a direct current. [Back-formation from COMMUTATION.]

com·mu·ta·tion (kómmew-táysh'n) *n.* **1.** A substitution, exchange, or interchange. **2. a.** The substitution of one kind of payment for another. **b.** The payment substituted. **3. a.** The conversion of alternating to direct electric current. **b.** The reversing of current direction. **4.** *Law.* A reduction of a penalty to a less severe one. [Middle English, from Old French, from Latin *commutātiō* (stem *commutā-tiōn-*), from *commutāre,* COMMUTE.]

com·mu·ta·tive (kómmew-taytiv, kə-méwtətiv) *adj.* **1.** Pertaining to, involving, or characterised by substitution, interchange, or exchange. **2.** *Mathematics & Logic.* Independent of the order of terms. Said of a combining operation, such as multiplication.

com·mu·ta·tor (kómmew-taytər) *n.* A cylindrical arrangement of insulated metal bars connected to the coils of an electric motor or generator to provide a unidirectional current from the generator or a reversal of current into the coils of the motor.

com·mute (kə-méwt) *v.* **-muted, -muting, -mutes.** —*tr.* **1.** To substitute; exchange; interchange. **2.** To convert; change; transform. **3.** To change (a penalty, debt, or payment) to a less severe one. —*intr.* **1.** *Archaic.* To compensate. **2.** To serve as a substitute. **2.** To travel as a commuter. **3.** *Mathematics & Logic.* To satisfy or engage in a commutative operation. [Middle English *commuten,* from Latin *commutāre,* to exchange : *com-,* mutually + *mutāre,* to change.]

com·mut·er (kə-méwtər) *n.* A person who travels regularly from one place to another, especially between work and home.

Com·o·ros, Federal Islamic Republic of the (kómmə-rōz). Country in the Indian Ocean. Most people are of mixed African, Arab, and Malay descent. The islands became a French colony (1912), and a French overseas territory in 1947. In 1974 all the islands except Mayotte voted for independence, which was attained in 1975. The islands export vanilla, sisal, copra, coffee, and perfume oils. Area, 1 862 square kilometres (719 square miles). Population, 630,000. Capital, Moroni. See map at **Madagascar.**

comp (komp) *n. Informal.* **1.** A compositor. **2.** An accompaniment. **3.** A competition. ~*intr.v. Informal.* **comped, comping, comps. 1.** To work as a compositor. **2.** To play a jazz accompaniment.

com·pact¹ (kəm-páct, kóm-pakt ‖ *kom-*) *adj.* **1.** Closely and firmly united or packed together; dense. **2.** Packed into or arranged within a relatively small space. **3.** Expressed briefly and concisely. **4.** *U.S.* Designating a car that is small and cheap to run. ~*tr.v.* (kəm-pákt ‖ *kom-*) **compacted, -pacting, -pacts. 1.** To press or join firmly together; condense; consolidate. **2.** To make or compose by pressing or joining together. ~*n.* (kóm-pakt). **1.** A small case containing a mirror, face powder, and a powder puff. **2.** *U.S.* A small economical car. [Middle English, from Latin *compactus,* past participle of *compingere,* to join together : *com-,* together + *pangere,* to fasten.] —**com·pact·er** *n.* —**com·pac·tion** (kəm-páksh'n ‖ *kom-*) *n.* —**com·pact·ly** *adv.* —**com·pact·ness** *n.*

com·pact² (kóm-pakt) *n.* An agreement or covenant. [Latin *compactum,* from *compactus,* past participle of *compacīscī,* to agree together : *com-,* together + *pacīscī,* to agree.]

compact disc *n. Abbr.* **CD** A compact laser disc for reproducing recorded sound when it is played on a specially designed record player.

com·pan·ion (kəm-pán-yən ‖ *kom-*) *n.* **1. a.** A person who accompanies or associates with another; a comrade. **b.** One who lives with another as an intimate, but without formal legal ties. **2.** A person employed to assist, live with, or travel with another. **3.** Any of two or more matching or complementary things; a mate; a match. Also used adjectively: *a companion volume.* 4. A guidebook or handbook. 5. *Abbr.* **C.** A member of the lowest rank or grade in certain orders of knighthood. 6. The fainter part of a double star. ~*tr.v.* **companioned, -ioning, -ions.** *Rare.* To be a companion to; associate with; accompany. [Middle English *compai(g)noun*, from Old French *compaignon*, from Vulgar Latin *compāniō* (stem *compāniōn-*), "one who eats bread with another" : Latin *com-*, together + *pānis*, bread.]

com·pan·ion·a·ble (kəm-pán-yənəb'l ‖ kom-) *adj.* Suited to be a good companion; sociable; friendly. **—com·pan·ion·a·bly** *adv.*

com·pan·ion·ship (kəm-pán-yən-ship ‖ kom-) *n.* The relationship existing between companions; fellowship.

com·pan·ion·way (kəm-pán-yən-way ‖ kom-) *n.* A stairway leading from a ship's deck to the cabins or deck below.

com·pa·ny (kúmp-əni ‖ -ni) *n., pl.* **-nies.** 1. A group of people; an assembly; a gathering. 2. People assembled for a social purpose. 3. A guest or guests. 4. a. Companionship; fellowship. b. A source of companionship: *She'll be company for you.* c. A person's companions: *bad company.* 5. A social environment; society: *she's rather shy in company.* 6. A business enterprise; a firm. See **limited company.** 7. *Abbr.* **co., Co.** A partner or partners not specifically named in a firm's title: *John Rogers and Company.* 8. A troupe of dancers or dramatic or musical performers: *a repertory company.* 9. *Military.* A subdivision of a regiment or battalion, usually under the command of a captain. 10. A ship's crew and officers. 11. A medieval guild. —See Synonyms at **visitor.** **—keep company.** To associate, as in courtship. **—keep (someone) company.** To accompany. **—part company.** To end an association or friendship. ~*v.* **companied, -nying, -nies.** *Archaic.* —*tr.* To accompany or associate with. —*intr.* To keep company; associate. [Middle English *compaignie*, from Old French *compagnie*, from *compain*, **COMPANION.**]

company secretary *n. British.* The officer of an incorporated company who carries out the detailed administration of the company and is its legal representative.

com·pa·ra·ble (kómpərə-b'l ‖ kəm-párrə-, kom-, -paír-ə-) *adj.* 1. Able to be compared; similar or equivalent. 2. Worthy of comparison. **—com·pa·ra·bil·i·ty** (-bílləti), **com·pa·ra·ble·ness** *n.* **—com·pa·ra·bly** *adv.*

com·par·a·tive (kəm-párrətiv) *adj. Abbr.* **comp., compar.** 1. Pertaining to, based on, or involving comparison: *comparative studies.* 2. Estimated by comparison; relative: *a comparative failure.* 3. *Grammar.* Expressing or involving the intermediate degree of comparison of adjectives and adverbs. Compare **positive** and **superlative.** ~*n. Grammar.* 1. The comparative degree. 2. An adjective or adverb expressing the comparative degree; for example, *brighter* is the comparative of *bright; more keenly* is the comparative of *keenly.* **—com·par·a·tive·ly** *adv.*

comparative linguistics *n.* The study of two languages or linguistic varieties which are usually synchronous, with the emphasis on common features or divergence from a common source. Compare **historical linguistics.**

com·pa·ra·tor (kəm-párrətər, kómpə-ráytər ‖ kom-) *n.* 1. Any of various devices for comparing an aspect of an object, such as shape, colour, or brightness, with a standard. 2. An electrical device containing a circuit for comparing two signals.

com·pare (kəm-paír) *v.* **-pared, -paring, -pares.** —*tr.* 1. To represent as similar, equal, or analogous; liken. Used with *to.* 2. *Abbr.* **cf., cp.** To examine in order to note similarities or differences. Used with *with* or *and.* 3. *Grammar.* To form the positive, comparative, or superlative degrees of (an adjective or adverb). —*intr.* To be worthy of comparison; be considered as similar or equal. Used with *with: Nothing can compare with real silk.* ~*n.* Comparison. Used chiefly in the phrase *beyond compare.* [Middle English *comparen*, from Old French *comparer*, from Latin *comparāre*, to pair, match, from *compar*, like, equal : *com-*, mutually + *pār*, equal.] **—com·par·er** *n.*

Usage: In formal usage, *compare to* and *compare with* have different interpretations. In the sense "represent as similar", *compare to* is usual: *He compared the meeting to a battlefield.* In the sense "examine in order to note similarities and differences", *compare with* is usual: *He compared Shelley's poetry with Wordsworth's.*

com·par·i·son (kəm-párriss'n ‖ kom-) *n.* 1. A comparing or being compared; a statement or estimate of similarities and differences. 2. The quality of being capable or worthy of being compared; similarity; likeness. 3. *Grammar.* The modification or inflection of an adjective or adverb to denote the three degrees (positive, comparative, and superlative). [Middle English *comparisoun*, from Old French *comparaison*, from Latin *comparātiō* (stem *comparātiōn-*), from *comparāre*, **COMPARE.**]

com·part·ment (kəm-pártmənt ‖ kom-) *n.* 1. Any of the parts or spaces into which an area is subdivided. 2. Any separate room, section, or chamber: *a storage compartment.* 3. Any separate part or division. 4. A separate section of a railway carriage. [French, *compartiment*, from Italian *compartire*, from Late Latin *compartīrī*, to divide, share with : *com-*, with + *partīrī*, to share, from *pars* (stem *part-*), a part + -MENT.] **—com·part·ment·ed** *adj.*

com·part·men·tal·ise, com·part·men·tal·ize (kóm-paart-mént'l-īz ‖ kəm-párt-) *tr.v.* **-ised, -ising, -ises.** To divide or partition into compartments or categories. **—com·part·men·tal·i·sa·tion** (-ī-záysh'n ‖ U.S. -i-) *n.*

com·pass (kúm-pəss ‖ kóm-) *n.* 1. a. A device used to determine geographical direction, usually consisting of a magnetic needle horizontally mounted or suspended and free to pivot until aligned with the magnetic field of the earth. b. Any other device for determining geographical direction, such as a **radio compass** or a **gyrocompass** *(both of which see).* 2. *Sometimes plural.* A V-shaped device for drawing circles or circular arcs, consisting of a pair of rigid, hinged arms, one of which is equipped with a pen or pencil and the other with a sharp point providing a central anchor or pivot about which the drawing arm is turned. Also called "pair of compasses". 3. An enclosing line or boundary; a circumference. 4. An enclosed space or area. 5. A range or scope; an extent. 6. *Music.* The range of a voice or instrument; a register. **—box the compass.** To recite all the points of the compass in order, from North, clockwise. ~*tr.v.* **compassed, -passing, -passes.** 1. To go round; circle. 2. *Literary.* To surround; encircle. 3. To understand; comprehend. 4. To achieve; obtain; accomplish. 5. *Archaic.* To contrive, especially by scheming or plotting. —See Synonyms at **reach.** [Middle English *compas*, measure, circle, compasses, compass, from Old French, from *compasser*, to measure (with compasses), from Vulgar Latin *compassāre* (unattested), "to measure off by steps" : Latin *com-* (intensive) + *passus*, PACE.] **—com·pass·a·ble** *adj.*

compass card *n.* A freely pivoting circular disc carrying the magnetic needles of a compass and marked with the 32 points of the compass and the 360 degrees of the circle.

com·pas·sion (kəm-pásh'n ‖ kom-) *n.* A deep feeling of pity for the suffering of another, and an inclination to give aid or support, or to show mercy. See Synonyms at **pity.** [Middle English *compassioun*, from Old French *compassion*, from Late Latin *compassiō* (stem *compassiōn-*), from *compatī* (past participle *compassus*), to sympathise with : *com-*, with + *patī*, to suffer.]

com·pas·sion·ate (kəm-pásh'n-ət, -it ‖ kom-) *adj.* Feeling or showing pity or compassion; sympathetic. See Synonyms at **kind.** **—com·pas·sion·ate·ly** *adv.* **—com·pas·sion·ate·ness** *n.*

compassionate leave *n. British.* Leave granted to a serviceman or employee for compassionate reasons, such as a death in the family.

compass rose *n.* A circle resembling a compass card, often decorated, printed onto a chart or map to indicate the points of the compass relative to the land depicted in the map or chart.

com·pat·i·ble (kəm-páttə-b'l ‖ kom-) *adj.* 1. Capable of living or performing in harmonious, consistent, or congenial combination with another or others. 2. Capable of efficient integration and operation with each other or with other elements in a system. Said of pieces of machinery, electronic equipment, or the like. 3. Consistent: *His lifestyle is hardly compatible with his political views.* 4. Capable of forming a chemically or biochemically stable system. 5. *Botany.* Capable of being successfully grafted. Said of plants. [Middle English, from Old French, from Medieval Latin *compatibilis*, from Late Latin *compatī*, to sympathise with. See **compassion.**] **—com·pat·i·bil·i·ty** (-bílláti), **com·pat·i·ble·ness** *n.* **—com·pat·i·bly** *adv.*

com·pa·tri·ot (kəm-páttri-ət ‖ kom-; *chiefly U.S.* -páytri-, -ot) *n.* A fellow countryman or countrywoman. [French *compatriote*, from Late Latin *compatriōta* : *com-*, together + *patriōta*, PATRIOT.] **—com·pa·tri·ot·ic** *adj.*

com·peer (kóm-peer ‖ kəm-péer) *n.* 1. A person of equal status, ability, or rank; a peer or equal. 2. A comrade, companion, or associate. [Middle English *comper*, from Old French, from Latin *compār* : *com-*, with + *pār*, an equal, PEER.]

com·pel (kəm-pél ‖ kom-) *tr.v.* **-pelled, -pelling, -pels.** 1. To force, drive, or constrain. 2. To obtain or bring about by or as if by force; exact: *compel obedience; compel respect.* 3. *Archaic.* To gather or unite by force; herd. —See Synonyms at **force.** [Middle English *compellen*, from Old French *compeller*, from Latin *compellere*, "to drive (cattle) together", force : *com-*, together + *pellere*, drive.] **—com·pel·la·ble** *adj.* **—com·pel·la·bly** *adv.* **—com·pel·ler** *n.*

com·pel·ling (kəm-pélling ‖ kom-) *n.* Arousing serious attention or interest; convincing. **—com·pel·ling·ly** *adv.*

com·pen·di·ous (kəm-péndi-əss ‖ kom-) *adj.* Containing or stating briefly and concisely all the essentials of something; terse; succinct. See Synonyms at **concise.** [Middle English, from Latin *compendiōsus*, from *compendium*, COMPENDIUM.] **—com·pen·di·ous·ly** *adv.* **—com·pen·di·ous·ness** *n.*

com·pen·di·um (kəm-péndi-əm ‖ kom-) *n., pl.* **-ums** or **-dia** (-ə). 1. A short, complete summary; an abridgment. 2. *British.* A collection of useful information. 3. *British.* A collection, especially of assorted games, stored together. [Latin, "that which is weighed together", gain, saving, abridgment, from *compendere*, to weigh together : *com-*, together + *pendere*, to weigh.]

com·pen·sate (kóm-pen-sayt, -pən-) *v.* **-sated, -sating, -sates.** —*tr.* 1. To make up for or offset; counterbalance. 2. To make equivalent or satisfactory reparation to; recompense or reimburse. 3. To provide (a pendulum, for example) with a mechanism to offset the effects of variations such as expansion. —*intr.* 1. To provide or serve as a substitute or counterbalance. 2. *Biology & Psychology.* To make up for a failing or defect by cultivating some other characteristic: *compensated for his lack of height by an aggressive manner.* [Latin *compensāre*, to weigh one thing against another, counterbalance : *com-*, mutually, reciprocally + *pensāre*, frequentative of *pendere*, to weigh.] **—com·pen·sa·tive** (-saytiv, kəm-pén-sətiv ‖ kom-), **com·pen·sa·to·ry** (-saytəri, -sáytəri, kəm-pén-sətri, -sətəri) *adj.* **—com·pen·sa·tor** (-saytər) *n.*

com·pen·sa·tion (kóm-pen-sáysh'n, -pən-) *n.* 1. a. The act of compensating or making amends. **b.** The state of being compensated. **2.** Something given or received as an equivalent or as reparation for a loss, service, or debt; a recompense; an indemnity. **3.** *Biology.* The counterbalancing of any functional defect in one organ by the supplementary development or activation of another organ or another part of the defective structure. **4.** *Psychology.* Behaviour designed to compensate for real or imagined defects. **—com·pen·sa·tion·al** *adj.*

com·pere (kóm-pair) *n. British.* The master of ceremonies of a variety show, cabaret, or the like. [Old French, "godfather" : *com-* (joint) + *père,* father.] **—com·pere** *v.*

com·pete (kəm-péet ‖ kom-) *intr.v.* **-peted, -peting, -petes.** To strive or contend with another or others for profit, prize, position, or the necessities of life; vie. See Synonyms at **rival.** [Latin *competere,* "to strive together" : *com-,* together + *petere,* to seek, strive.]

com·pe·tence (kómpi-tənss) *n.* Also **com·pe·ten·cy** (-tən-si). **1.** The state or quality of being capable or competent; adequate skill or ability. **2.** Sufficient means for a comfortable existence. **3.** *Law.* The quality or condition of being legally qualified, eligible, or admissible; legal authority, qualification, or jurisdiction. **4.** *Linguistics.* The knowledge underlying an individual's ability to speak or understand a language. Compare **langue, performance. 5.** The ability possessed by embryonic cells at an early stage of development to differentiate into any of various types of cells. **—See** Synonyms at **ability.**

com·pe·tent (kómpitənt) *adj.* **1.** Properly or well qualified; having adequate skill or ability; capable. **2.** *Law.* Legally qualified or fit; admissible. **3.** Rightly or properly belonging; permissible. Used with *to.* **4.** Adequate for the purpose; suitable. **5.** Able to differentiate in any of various ways. Said of embryonic cells at an early stage of development. [Middle English, from Old French, from Latin *competēns* (stem *competent-*), present participle of *competere,* to be competent, COMPETE.] **—com·pe·tent·ly** *adv.*

com·pe·ti·tion (kómpi-tísh'n) *n.* **1. a.** The action of competing with another or others for profit, prize, position, or the necessities of life; rivalry. **b.** The person or persons competing; one's competitors considered collectively. **2. a.** A contest, match, or other trial of skill or ability. **b.** A series of such contests. **3.** The rivalry between two or more businesses striving for the same customer or market: *Competition tends to keep prices down.* **4.** *Ecology.* The struggle between organisms in a community for scarce resources.

com·pet·i·tive (kəm-péttətiv ‖ kom-) *adj.* **1.** Of, involving, or determined by competition. **2.** Comparatively low in price. **3.** Having an urge to compete; inclined to rivalry. **4.** Relatively generous or high: *competitive salaries.* **—com·pet·i·tive·ly** *adv.* **—com·pet·i·tive·ness** *n.*

com·pet·i·tor (kəm-péttitər ‖ kom-) *n.* Someone or something that competes, as in sports or business; a rival. See Synonyms at **opponent.**

Com·piègne (koNp-yáyn). Town in the Oise département of north France, situated on the river Oise. The Armistice which ended World War I (1918), and the agreement by which France fell to the Germans (1940), were signed in a railway carriage in Compiègne forest.

com·pi·la·tion (kóm-pi-láysh'n, -pī-) *n.* **1.** The act of collecting or compiling. **2.** Something compiled, such as a set of data, a report, or an anthology.

com·pile (kəm-pīl ‖ kom-) *tr.v.* **-piled, -piling, -piles. 1.** To gather (facts, literature, or other material) into one book or corpus. **2.** To put together or compose (a book, outline, or other collection) from materials gathered from several sources. [Middle English *compilen,* from Old French *compiler,* from Latin *compīlāre,* "to heap together", plunder, plagiarise : *com-,* together + *pīlāre,* to plunder, "pile up (booty)", from *pīla,* "pile", PILLAR.]

com·pil·er (kəm-pīlər ‖ kom-) *n.* **1.** A person who compiles something. **2.** A computer program that converts from a high-level language into machine language. Each language needs its own compiler for each type of computer.

com·pla·cen·cy (kəm-pláyss'n-si ‖ kom-) *n.* Also **com·pla·cence** (-ss). **1. a.** A feeling of contentment or satisfaction; gratification. **b.** Equanimity, sometimes excessive, in the face of real or potential problems. **2.** Self-satisfaction; smugness.

com·pla·cent (kəm-pláyss'nt ‖ kom-) *adj.* **1.** Having or showing complacency. **2.** *Archaic.* Complaisant. [Originally "pleasing", from Latin *complacēns* (stem *complacent-*), present participle of *complacēre,* to please : *com-* (intensive) + *placēre,* to please.] **—com·pla·cent·ly** *adv.*

com·plain (kəm-pláyn ‖ kom-) *intr.v.* **-plained, -plaining, -plains. 1.** To express feelings of pain, dissatisfaction, or resentment. **2.** To describe one's pains, problems, or dissatisfactions. Used with *of.* **3.** To make a formal accusation or report a grievance officially: *to complain to the police about a neighbour's dog.* **—See** Synonyms at **object.** [Middle English *compleinen,* from Old French *complaindre,* from Vulgar Latin *complangere* (unattested) : Latin *com-* (intensive) + *plangere,* to lament.] **—com·plain·er** *n.*

com·plain·ant (kəm-pláynənt ‖ kom-) *n. Law.* A person who makes a complaint or files a formal charge, as in a court of law; a plaintiff.

com·plaint (kəm-pláynt ‖ kom-) *n.* **1.** An expression of pain, dissatisfaction, resentment, discontent, or grief. **2.** A cause or reason for complaining; a grievance. **3.** A cause of physical pain; a malady; an illness. **4.** A literary outpouring of grief, typically a poem lamenting lost love. **5.** *Law.* A formal allegation made by the plaintiff in a civil action in a magistrate's court. [Middle English *com-*

pleint(e), from Old French *complainte,* from *complaint,* past participle of *complaindre,* COMPLAIN.]

com·plai·sance (kəm-pláyz'nss ‖ kom-; *U.S. also* -pláyss'nss, kóm-play-zánss) *n.* Willing compliance with the wishes of others; obligingness.

com·plai·sant (kəm-pláyz'nt ‖ kom-; *U.S. also* -pláyss'nt, kóm-play-zánt) *adj.* Showing a desire or willingness to please; cheerfully obliging. [French, pleasing, agreeable, from Old French, present participle of *complaire,* to please, from Latin *complacēre.* See **complacent.**] **—com·plai·sant·ly** *adv.*

com·pleat (kəm-pléet ‖ kom-) *adj. Archaic.* Complete: *"The Compleat Angler"* (Izaak Walton). Often used humorously.

com·plect (kəm-plékt ‖ kom-) *tr.v.* **-plected, -plecting, -plects.** *Archaic.* To join by weaving or twining together; interweave. [Latin *complectī, complectere* : *com-,* together + *plectere,* to entwine.]

com·ple·ment (kómpli-mənt ‖ -ment) *n.* **1.** Something that completes, makes up a whole, or perfects. **2.** The quantity or number needed to make up a whole. **3.** Either of two parts that complete the whole or mutually complete each other. **4.** The full quantity, allowance, or amount; a complete set. **5.** *Mathematics.* An angle related to another so that the sum of their measures is 90 degrees. **6.** *Grammar.* A word or words used after a verb to complete a predicate construction; for example, *their best player* acts as the complement in the sentence *They considered her their best player.* **7.** An interval in music that completes an octave when added to a given interval. **8.** The full crew of officers and men required to man a ship. **9.** *Biochemistry.* The heat-sensitive substance found in normal blood serum that helps to destroy pathogenic bacteria and other materials. In this sense, formerly called "alexin". *~tr.v.* (-ment, -mént ‖ -mənt) **complemented, -menting, -ments.** To add or serve as a complement to. [Middle English, from Latin *complēmentum,* from *complēre,* to COMPLETE.]

Usage: *Complement* and *compliment* are often confused because of their identical pronunciations, as are the adjectival pair *complementary* and *complimentary.* The former has the sense of completion, the latter the sense of praising.

com·ple·men·ta·ry (kómpli-mént-ri, -əri) *adj.* Also **com·ple·men·tal** (-mént'l). **1.** Forming or serving as a complement; completing. **2.** Complementing each other; supplying what is needed to make whole or complete. **3.** *Genetics.* Producing effects when in combination that are different from those produced separately. Said of genes. **—com·ple·men·ta·ri·ness** *n.*

complementary angles *pl.n.* Two angles whose sum is 90 degrees.

complementary colour *n.* Either of a pair of colours, such as blue-green and red, that appear as white or grey when mixed in the correct proportions.

complement fixation *n. Biochemistry.* The joining of a complement to the antigen-antibody pair for which it is specific. It is used as a test for the presence of specific antigens and antibodies and hence used in the diagnosis of certain infections.

com·plete (kəm-pléet ‖ kom-) *adj. Abbr.* **comp. 1.** Having all necessary or normal parts; entire; whole. **2.** *Botany.* Having all characteristic floral parts, including sepals, petals, stamens, and a pistil. **3.** Brought to a satisfactory conclusion; ended: *Work on the new bridge is almost complete.* **4.** Thorough; exhaustive: *a complete report on the accident.* **5.** Total; absolute: *a complete stranger.* **6.** Fully supplied or equipped: *comes complete with its own instruction manual.* **7.** *Archaic.* Skilled; accomplished. *~v.* **completed, -pleting, -pletes.** *—tr.* **1.** To make whole or complete. **2.** To fill in (a form). **3.** To conclude. *—intr. Chiefly British.* To conclude all legal formalities in the sale and purchase of a house or land. [Middle English *complet(e),* from Old French, from Latin *complētus,* past participle of *complēre,* to fill up : *com-* (intensive) + *plēre,* to fill.] **—com·plete·ly** *adv.* **—com·plete·ness** *n.* **—com·ple·tive** *adj.*

Synonyms: *complete, close, end, finish, conclude, terminate.*

Usage: In formal English, anything that is *complete* is absolutely so. It is therefore incorrect to use such qualifying words as *more, most, very, quite,* and so on, unless the implication is one of comprehensiveness of scope or thoroughness of treatment (where degrees of completeness are felt to exist), as in *Her report is a more complete account of the situation than is mine.*

com·ple·tion (kəm-pléesh'n ‖ kom-) *n.* **1.** The act of concluding, perfecting, or making entire. **2.** The state of being completed. **3.** Accomplishment; realisation; fulfilment. **4.** *Chiefly British.* The conclusion of all legal formalities in the sale and purchase of a house or land.

com·plex (kóm-pleks ‖ kəm-pléks) *adj.* **1.** Consisting of interconnected or interwoven parts; composite; compound. **2.** Involved or intricate, as in structure; complicated. **3.** *Grammar.* **a.** Pertaining to or designating a word consisting of at least one bound form, such as *slowly.* **b.** Pertaining to a **complex sentence** *(see).* **4.** *Mathematics.* Of, pertaining to, or designating a number or variable that has both a real and an imaginary part. *~n.* (kóm-pleks). **1.** A whole composed of intricate or interconnected parts. **2.** *Psychology.* A connected group of repressed ideas that compel characteristic or habitual patterns of thought, feeling, and action. **3.** *Informal.* An exaggerated or obsessive concern or fear. **4.** A group of buildings designed for a particular purpose or supplying a variety of related facilities: *a leisure complex; an industrial complex.* **5.** *Chemistry.* **a.** A complex ion. **b.** Any compound in which two molecules or groups are linked to each other by a coordinate bond. [Latin *complexus,* past participle of *complectī,*

complectere, to entwine : *com-*, together + *plectere*, to twine, plait.]
—**com·plex·ly** *adv.* —**com·plex·ness** *n.*
   Synonyms: *complex, complicated, intricate, involved, knotty.*
complex conjugate *n. Mathematics.* **1.** A complex number that differs from another complex number only by the reversal of the sign of the imaginary part. For example, *a* + *bi* has as complex conjugate *a* – *bi*.
complex fraction *n.* A fraction in which the numerator or denominator or both contain fractions, such as ³¹⁴/₁₇/₁₁, ¹/₅/₆. Also called "compound fraction".
com·plex·i·fy (kəm-pléksi-fī ‖ kom-) *v.* **-fied, -fying, -fies.** —*tr.* To make more complex. —*intr.* To become more complex. —**com·plex·i·fi·ca·tion** (-fi-káysh'n) *n.*
complex ion *n. Chemistry.* An ion or radical in which several groups or ions are attached to a central atom by coordinate bonds. Also called "complex", "coordination compound".
com·plex·ion (kəm-pléksh'n ‖ kom-) *n.* **1.** The natural colour, texture, and appearance of the skin, especially on the face. **2.** General character, aspect, or appearance. **3.** In medieval physiology, the combination of the four humours of cold, heat, moistness, and dryness in specific proportions, thought to control the temperament and the constitution of the body. [Middle English *complexioun*, physical constitution, temperament, from Old French *complexion*, from Medieval Latin *complexiō* (stem *complexiōn-*), "combination of corporeal humours", from Latin, connection, combination, from *complexus*. See *complexus*.] —**com·plex·ion·al** *adj.*
com·plex·ioned (kəm-pléksh'nd ‖ kom-) *adj.* Of or having a specified complexion. Used in combination: *fair-complexioned*.
com·plex·i·ty (kəm-pléksəti) *n., pl.* **-ties. 1.** The state or condition of being intricate or complex. **2.** Something intricate or complex.
complex number *n.* A number consisting of a real and imaginary part, usually expressed in the form *a* + *bi* where *a* and *b* are real numbers and i is the imaginary unit such that $i^2 = -1$.
complex salt *n.* A salt containing one or more complex ions.
complex sentence *n. Grammar.* A sentence containing one main clause and one or more subordinate clauses; for example, the sentence *When the rain stops, we'll leave* is a complex sentence. Compare **simple sentence.**
complex variable *n.* An expression of the form $x+iy$, where *x* and *y* are real variables and $i^2=-1$.
com·pli·ance (kəm-plī́-ənss ‖ kom-) *n.* Also **com·pli·an·cy** (-i). **1.** The act of yielding to a wish, request, or demand; acquiescence. **2.** A disposition or tendency to yield to others. **3. a.** *Mechanics.* The extension or displacement of a loaded structure per unit load. **b.** Flexibility. Not in technical usage.
com·pli·ant (kəm-plī́-ənt ‖ kom-) *adj.* Also *archaic* **com·pli·a·ble** (-əb'l). Yielding; submissive. See Synonyms at **obedient.** [COM-PL(Y) + -ANT.] —**com·pli·ant·ly** *adv.*
com·pli·ca·cy (kómplikə-si ‖ kəm-plíckə-) *n., pl.* **-cies.** *Rare.* **1.** The state of being complicated. **2.** A complication.
com·pli·cate (kómpli-kayt) *tr.v.* **-cated, -cating, -cates. 1.** To make intricate or perplexing. **2.** To combine so as to produce a more complex result. **3.** *Pathology.* To aggravate (an existing disease). ~*adj.* (-kət, -kit, -kayt). **1.** *Biology.* Folded longitudinally on one or several times, as certain leaves or the wings of some insects are. **2.** *Archaic.* Complex; intricate; involved. [Latin *complicāre*, to fold together : *com-*, together + *plicāre*, to fold.]
com·pli·cat·ed (kómpli-kaytid) *adj.* Containing intricately combined or involved parts; not easily understood or untangled. See Synonyms at **complex.** —**com·pli·cat·ed·ly** *adv.* —**com·pli·cat·ed·ness** *n.*
com·pli·ca·tion (kómpli-káysh'n) *n.* **1.** The act of complicating. **2.** A confused or intricate relationship of parts. **3.** Any factor, condition, or event that is complicated or that complicates. **4.** *Pathology.* A condition occurring during the course of or as a consequence of another disease and often aggravating it.
com·plice (kómpliss) *n. Archaic.* An associate or accomplice. [Middle English, from Old French, from Latin *complex*, closely connected, hence a confederate : *com-*, together + *-plex*, -fold.]
com·plic·i·ty (kəm-plíssəti ‖ kom-) *n., pl.* **-ties. 1.** The state of being an accomplice in a wrongful act. **2.** *Rare.* Complexity.
com·pli·ment (kómpli-mənt ‖ -ment) *n.* **1.** An expression of praise, admiration, or congratulation. **2.** A formal act of civility, courtesy, or respect. **3.** *Usually plural.* A formal or ceremonious greeting, now given especially as an accompaniment to a present, brochure, polite request for payment, or the like. **4.** *Archaic.* A gift presented for services rendered; a gratuity.
~*tr.v.* (-ment, -mént ‖ -mənt) **complimented, -menting, -ments. 1.** To pay a compliment to. **2.** To show fondness, regard, or respect for (someone) by giving a gift or performing a favour. —See Usage note at **complement.** [French, from Spanish *cumplimiento*, from *cumplir*, to complete, behave properly, be courteous, from Latin *complēre*, to fill up : *com-* (intensive) + *plēre*, to fill.]
com·pli·men·ta·ry (kómpli-mént-ri, -əri) *adj.* **1.** Expressing, using, or resembling a compliment. **2.** Given free of charge to repay a favour, as an act of courtesy, or for publicity purposes. —**com·pli·men·ta·ri·ly** *adv.*
com·pline, com·plin (kóm-plin; *rarely* -plīn) *n. Ecclesiastical.* **1.** The last of the seven **canonical hours** *(see).* **2.** The time of day set aside for this prayer, usually just before retiring to bed. [Middle English *compline*, from Old French *complie*, from Medieval Latin *(hōra) complēta*, "completed (hour)", from Latin *complētus*, past participle of *complēre*, COMPLETE.]

com·ply (kəm-plī́ ‖ kom-) *intr.v.* **-plied, -plying, -plies. 1.** To act in accordance with a command, request, rule, wish, or the like. Used with *with.* **2.** *Obsolete.* To be courteous or obedient. [Italian *complire*, from Spanish *cumplir*, to complete, do what is proper, be courteous, from Latin *complēre*, to fill up : *com-* (intensive) + *plēre*, to fill.]
com·po¹ (kómpō) *n., pl.* **-pos.** Any of various combined substances, such as mortar or plaster, formed by mixing ingredients. [Short for COMPOSITION.]
compo² *n. Australian Informal.* Compensation, especially for injury received at work.
com·po·nent (kəm-pṓnənt ‖ kom-) *n.* **1.** A constituent part of a complex whole, especially of a mechanical or electrical device. **2.** *Mathematics.* Any of a set of two or more vectors having a sum equal to a given vector. **3.** *Chemistry.* Any of the minimum number of substances required to specify completely the composition of all phases of a chemical system.
~*adj.* Being or functioning as a component; constituent. [Latin *compōnens* (stem *compōnent-*), present participle of *compōnere*, to place together : *com-*, together + *pōnere*, to put.]
com·po·ny (kəm-pṓni ‖ kom-) *adj. Heraldry.* Composed of a row of squares in alternating tinctures. [Old French *componé*, "made of pieces", from *compon, copon*, piece. See **coupon.**]
com·port (kəm-pórt ‖ kom-, -pṓrt) *v.* **-ported, -porting, -ports.** —*tr.* To conduct or behave (oneself) in a specified manner. —*intr.* To agree, correspond, or harmonise. Used with *with.* [Old French *comporter*, to support, conduct, from Latin *comportāre*, to bring together, later to support : *com-*, together + *portāre*, to carry, bear.] —**com·port·ment** *n.*
com·pose (kəm-pṓz ‖ kom-) *v.* **-posed, -posing, -poses.** —*tr.* **1.** To make up or be the constituent parts of; constitute or form. See Usage note at **comprise. 2.** To create or make by putting together parts or elements. **3.** To create or produce (a literary or musical piece). **4.** To make (someone, especially oneself) calm or tranquil; quiet. **5.** To settle (arguments or differences); reconcile. **6. a.** To arrange aesthetically or artistically (the constituents of a painting, for example). **b.** To put in order; arrange (one's thoughts, for example). **7.** *Printing.* To arrange or set (type or matter to be printed). —*intr.* **1.** To create literary or musical pieces. **2.** *Printing.* To set type. [Middle English, from Old French *composer* : *com-*, together, from Latin + *poser*, to place, from Latin *pausāre*, to cease, repose, hence to place, from *pausa*, a pause, from Greek *pausis*, from *pauein*, to stop.]
com·posed (kəm-pṓzd ‖ kom-) *adj.* Calm; serene; self-possessed. See Synonyms at **cool.** —**com·pos·ed·ly** (-pṓzidli) *adv.* —**com·pos·ed·ness** (-pṓzid-nəss, -niss) *n.*
com·pos·er (kəm-pṓzər ‖ kom-) *n. Abbr.* **comp.** A person who composes, especially one who composes music.
composing stick *n. Printing.* Especially formerly, a small shallow tray, usually metal and with an adjustable end, in which a compositor sets type before it is placed in the galley.
com·pos·ite (kómpə-zit ‖ -sit, -zīt, -sīt; *chiefly U.S.* kəm-pózzit) *adj. Abbr.* **comp. 1.** Made up of distinct components; compound. **2.** *Mathematics.* Having factors; factorisable. **3.** *Botany.* Of, belonging to, or characteristic of the Compositae, a large plant family characterised by flower heads consisting of both **ray flowers** and **disc flowers** *(both of which see),* as in the daisy, of disc flowers only, as in wormwood, or of ray flowers only, as in the dandelion. **4.** *Capital* C. *Architecture.* Pertaining to or designating the Composite order.
~*n.* **1.** A composite structure or entity. **2.** A complex material, such as wood or fibreglass, in which two or more distinct, structurally complementary substances, especially metals, ceramics, glasses, and polymers, combine to produce some structural or functional properties not present in any individual component. **3.** A plant belonging to the Compositae, a composite plant.
~*tr.v.* (-zīt, -sīt, kəm-pózzit) **composited, -iting, -ites.** To combine (several resolutions or motions) into a single resolution or motion. [Latin *compositus*, past participle of *compōnere*, to put together : *com-*, together + *pōnere*, to put.] —**com·pos·ite·ly** *adv.* —**com·pos·ite·ness** *n.*
composite number *n.* An integer exactly divisible by at least one number other than itself or 1.
Composite order *n. Architecture.* A late Roman style of capital formed by superimposing Ionic volutes on a Corinthian capital.
com·po·si·tion (kómpə-zísh'n) *n. Abbr.* **comp. 1.** A putting together of parts or elements to form a whole; a combining. **2.** The manner in which such parts are combined or related; constitution; make-up. **3.** The result or product of composing; a mixture; a compound. **4.** The arrangement of artistic parts so as to form a unified whole. **5.** The art or act of composing a literary or musical work. **6.** Any work of art, literature, or music, or its structure and arrangement. **7. a.** An essay; especially, one written as a school exercise. **b.** An exercise or class in writing poetry or prose. **8.** *Linguistics.* The formation of compound words from separate words. **9.** *Printing.* Typesetting. **10.** *Law.* **a.** A settlement whereby the creditors of a debtor about to enter bankruptcy agree to accept partial payment in lieu of full payment for debts. **b.** The sum thus agreed upon. **11.** *Archaic.* Settlement by mutual agreement or compromise. [Middle English *composicioun*, from Old French *composition*, from Latin *compositiō* (stem *compositiōn-*), from *compōnere*, to put together, arrange : *com-*, together + *pōnere*, to put.] —**com·po·si·tion·al** *adj.*
composition of forces *n.* The finding or determination of a vector

that is the resultant of a given set of forces.

com·pos·i·tor (kəm-pózzi-tər ‖ kom-) *n. Abbr.* **comp.** *Printing.* A typesetter. —**com·pos·i·to·ri·al** (-táwri-əl ‖ -tóri-) *adj.*

com·pos men·tis (kóm-pəss méntiss ‖ -poss) *adj.* Of sound mind; sane. [Latin, having control of one's mind.]

com·post (kóm-post ‖ *U.S.* -pōst) *n.* **1.** A mixture of decaying organic matter, such as leaves and manure, used as fertiliser. **2.** A composition; a mixture.
~*tr.v.* **composted, -posting, -posts. 1.** To fertilise with compost. **2.** To change (vegetable matter) to compost. [Middle English, stew, compote, from Old French *composte,* stewed fruit, and *compost,* mixture, respectively from Latin *composita* and *compositum,* feminine and neuter of *compositus,* put together, COMPOSITE.]

com·po·sure (kəm-pṓzhər ‖ kom-) *n.* Self-possession; calmness; tranquillity. See Synonyms at **equanimity.** [From COMPOSE.]

com·pote (kóm-pot, -pōt) *n.* Fruit stewed or cooked in syrup. [French, from Old French *composte,* stewed fruit, COMPOST.]

com·pound[1] (kəm-pównd, kom- ‖ *West Indies also* -púngd) *v.* **-pounded, -pounding, -pounds.** —*tr.* **1.** To combine; mix. **2.** To produce or create by combining ingredients or parts. **3.** *Pharmacology.* To mix (drugs) according to prescription. **4.** To settle (a debt, for example) by agreeing on an amount less than the claim; adjust. **5.** To compute (compound interest). **6.** *Law.* To agree, for payment or other consideration, not to prosecute: *compound a felony.* **7.** To add to or intensify (a difficulty, an error, or the like). —*intr.* **1.** To come to terms; agree. **2.** To settle or compromise with a creditor. —See Synonyms at **mix.**
~*adj.* (kóm-pownd ‖ *West Indian also* -pungd; *U.S. also* kompównd). Consisting of two or more substances, ingredients, elements, or parts.
~*n.* (kóm-pownd ‖ *West Indian also* -pungd). *Abbr.* **comp., cpd. 1.** A combination of two or more elements or parts. **2.** *Linguistics.* **a.** A word formed either from other words, for example *racehorse,* or by the addition or combination of affixes or combining forms, for example *geography* or *isometric.* **b.** An intonational pattern exhibiting a primary stress and a terminal juncture. **c.** A verb form, in any of various tenses, the passive mood, or the like, consisting of a main verb and at least one auxiliary verb; for example, *may have been eaten.* **d.** In transformational grammar, a sequence of words not connected by a functional element in surface structure but functioning as a grammatical unit in deep structure. **3.** *Chemistry.* A pure, macroscopically homogeneous substance consisting of atoms or ions of two or more different elements in definite proportions, and usually having properties unlike those of its constituent elements. [Middle English *compounen,* from Old French *compon(d)re,* from Latin *compōnere,* to put together : *com-,* together + *pōnere,* to put.] —**com·pound·a·ble** *adj.* —**com·pound·er** *n.*

com·pound[2] (kóm-pownd ‖ *West Indian also* -pungd) *n.* **1.** In the Orient, an enclosure for a factory or group of European residences. **2.** In South Africa, living quarters, usually inside an enclosure, for black workers. **3.** A large enclosed area inside a prison, concentration camp, or the like. [Portuguese *campon* or Dutch *kampoeng,* from Malay *kampong,* village, cluster of buildings.]

com·pound-com·plex sentence (kóm-pownd-kómpleks) *n.* A sentence consisting of at least two coordinate main clauses and one or more subordinate clauses.

compound engine *n.* **1.** A steam engine in which the steam is expanded in two or more stages in different cylinders. **2.** A petrol or diesel engine in which the exhaust gases are used to drive a turbine-powered supercharger.

compound eye *n.* The eye of most insects and some crustaceans, composed of many light-sensitive elements, each with its own refractive system and each forming a portion of an image.

compound flower *n.* A flower head of a composite plant, such as a daisy, consisting of numerous small flowers appearing as a single bloom.

compound fraction *n. Mathematics.* A **complex fraction** *(see).*

compound fracture *n.* A fracture in which broken bone lacerates soft tissue.

compound interest *n.* Interest computed on the accumulated unpaid interest as well as on the original principal. Compare **simple interest.**

compound leaf *n.* A leaf consisting of two or more separate leaflets borne on a single leafstalk.

compound microscope *n.* A microscope consisting of an objective and an eyepiece, that is, two lenses or lens systems, at opposite ends of an adjustable tube.

compound number *n.* A quantity, such as 10 pounds 5 ounces or 3 feet 4 inches, involving different units of measure.

compound pendulum *n.* See **pendulum.**

compound tense *n. Grammar.* A tense in which the verb is associated with at least one auxiliary; for example, the present perfect tense of "go", *I have gone,* as opposed to the simple past tense, *I went.* Compare **simple tense, compound**[1] (sense 2c).

compound time *n. Music.* Time in which each beat in a bar is divisible into thirds, sixths, and so on; for example, ⁶/₈ time.

com·pra·dor, com·pra·dore (kómprə-dór) *n.* Formerly, in China and certain other Asian countries, a native agent for a foreign business. [Portuguese, "buyer", from Late Latin *comparātor,* from Latin *comparāre,* provide, buy, prepare : *com-* (collectively) + *parāre,* to prepare.]

com·pre·hend (kómpri-hénd) *tr.v.* **-hended, -hending, -hends. 1.** To grasp mentally; understand or fathom. **2.** To take in; include;

embrace. —See Synonyms at **apprehend, include.** [Middle English *comprehenden,* from Latin *comprehendere,* to grasp mentally : *com-,* together in mind, mentally + *prehendere,* to seize, grasp.]

com·pre·hen·si·ble (kómpri-hén-sib'l) *adj.* Capable of being comprehended or understood; intelligible. —**com·pre·hen·si·bil·i·ty** (-si-bílləti), **com·pre·hen·si·ble·ness** *n.* —**com·pre·hen·si·bly** *adv.*

com·pre·hen·sion (kómpri-hénsh'n) *n.* **1.** The act or capacity for comprehending or understanding. **2.** Comprehensiveness. **3.** *Logic.* The attributes making up a concept; intension. **4.** An exercise designed to test students' powers of comprehension.

com·pre·hen·sive (kómpri-hén-siv) *adj.* **1.** Including or comprehending much; large in scope or content. **2.** Designating a type of motor-vehicle insurance that provides wide-ranging cover. **3.** Designating a system in Britain of secondary education, or a school within such a system, that aims to provide for pupils of all abilities.
~*n.* A comprehensive school. Compare **grammar school, public school, secondary modern school.** —**com·pre·hen·sive·ly** *adv.* —**com·pre·hen·sive·ness** *n.*

com·pre·hen·siv·ise, com·pre·hen·siv·ize (kómpri-hén-sivīz) *v.* **-ised, -ising, -ises.** —*tr.* To make (a school) comprehensive. —*intr.* To adopt the comprehensive system of education. —**com·pre·hen·siv·i·sa·tion** (-siv-ī-záysh'n ‖ *U.S.* -i-) *n.*

com·press (kəm-préss ‖ kom-) *tr.v.* **-pressed, -pressing, -presses.** To press together or force into a smaller space; condense; compact. See Synonyms at **contract.**
~*n.* (kóm-press). *Medicine.* **1.** A soft pad of gauze or other material applied to a part of the body, either hot or cold, dry or moistened with water or medication, to alleviate pain or reduce inflammation. **2.** A soft pad of gauze or other material applied with force to reduce bleeding. [Middle English *compressen,* from Old French *compresser,* from Late Latin *compressāre,* frequentative of Latin *comprimere* (past participle *compressus*), to press together : *com-,* together + *premere,* to press.] —**com·press·i·bil·i·ty** (-ə-bílləti), **com·press·i·ble·ness** *n.* —**com·press·i·ble** *adj.*

com·pressed (kəm-prést ‖ kom-) *adj.* **1.** Pressed together or into less space; made compact. **2.** *Biology.* Flattened laterally or lengthways. Said of certain seed pods or the bodies of many fish.

compressed air *n.* Air under greater than atmospheric pressure, especially when used to power a mechanical device or provide a portable supply of oxygen.

compressed air illness *n.* **Decompression sickness** *(see).*

com·pres·sion (kəm-présh'n ‖ kom-) *n.* **1. a.** The act or process of compressing. **b.** The state of being compressed. **2. a.** The process by which the working substance in a heat engine, such as the vapour mixture in the cylinder of an internal-combustion engine, is compressed. **b.** The engine cycle during which this process occurs.

compression-ignition engine (kəm-présh'n-ig-nísh'n ‖ kom-) *n.* A **diesel-engine** *(see).*

compression ratio *n.* The ratio of the volume of the combustion chamber of an internal-combustion engine with the piston at the bottom of its stroke to the volume when the piston has reached the top of its stroke.

com·pres·sive (kəm-préssiv ‖ kom-) *adj.* Compressing or capable of compressing. —**com·pres·sive·ly** *adv.*

com·pres·sor (kəm-préssər ‖ kom-) *n.* **1.** A device or machine for compressing a gas. **2.** The part of a gas turbine that compresses the air before it enters the combustion chambers. **3.** *Electronics.* A device for reducing the variation in signal amplitude in a communication channel. **4.** *Anatomy.* Any muscle that acts to compress an organ or part. **5.** *Medicine.* An instrument used for holding down a tissue or part of the body.

com·prise (kəm-príz ‖ kom-) *tr.v.* **-prised, -prising, -prises. 1.** To consist of; be composed of. **2.** To include; contain. **3.** To constitute; make up. —See Synonyms at **include.** [Middle English *comprisen,* from Old French *comprendre* (past participle *compris*), to comprehend, include, from Latin *comprehendere,* to grasp mentally : *com-,* together, in mind, mentally + *prehendere,* to seize.] —**com·pris·a·ble** *adj.*

Usage: In formal usage, *comprise* is restricted to sentences of the form "the whole comprises the parts", as in *this country comprises four main administrative areas.* A common mistake, in both written and spoken English, is to say *is comprised of,* instead of *consists of* or *is composed of.*

com·pro·mise (kómprə-mīz) *n.* **1.** A settlement of differences in which each side makes concessions. **2.** Anything resulting from such a settlement. **3.** Something midway between different things or courses of action, combining certain of their qualities, but often in a way that is felt to be unsatisfactory. Also used adjectivally: *a compromise proposal.* **4.** Loosely, a concession, especially one involving one's principles or integrity: *She had to make a lot of compromises to keep this job.*
~*v.* **compromised, -mising, -mises.** —*tr.* **1.** To settle by concessions. **2.** To expose or make liable to scandal, suspicion, or disrepute. **3.** To make concessions damaging to (one's interests, principles, or integrity). —*intr.* To make a compromise. [Middle English *compromis,* from Old French, from Latin *comprōmissum,* from *comprōmittere,* to promise mutually (to abide by an arbiter's decision) : *com-,* mutually + *prōmittere,* to PROMISE.] —**com·pro·mis·er** *n.*

compte ren·du (kont-ron-dóō; *French* -dü) *n., pl.* **comptes rendus** *(pronounced as singular). French.* **1.** A statement of account. **2.** A short review or criticism, especially of a book. **3.** An official statement or report.

Comp·tom·e·ter (komp-tómmitər) *n.* A trademark for a high-speed calculating and adding machine.

Comp·ton (kómptən), **Arthur Holly** (1892-1962). U.S. physicist, noted for his research into radiation. In 1923 he discovered the **Compton effect**, an important step towards the development of quantum mechanics. He was awarded the Nobel prize for physics with C.T.R. Wilson (1927).

Comp·ton (kúmp-tən, kómp-), **Denis (Charles Scott)** (1918–97). British cricketer. He was an outstanding batsman in the years before and after World War II. He played for Middlesex and England, and scored a record 3,816 runs in a single season (1947). He also played football for Arsenal and England.

Comp·ton-Bur·nett (kúmp-tən-burnét, kómp-, -búrnit), **Dame Ivy** (1892-1969). British novelist. She is best remembered for a series of popular novels about life in the wealthy households of England, at the turn of the century.

Compton effect *n.* The increase in wavelength of electromagnetic radiation, especially of an X-ray or gamma-ray photon, scattered by an electron. [After A.H. COMPTON, who discovered it.]

comp·trol·ler (kən-trólər ‖ kon-, *U.S. also* komp-) *n. Rare.* A controller. Used as a title for various financial executives. [Variant of *controller*, through erroneous association with COUNT and with Latin *computus*, calculation.] —**comp·trol·ler·ship** *n.*

com·pul·sion (kəm-púlsh'n ‖ kom-) *n.* **1.** The act of compelling or forcing; coercion; constraint. **2.** The state of being compelled. **3.** *Psychology.* **a.** An irresistible impulse to act in a certain way, regardless of the rationality of the motivation. **b.** An act or acts performed in response to such an impulse. [Middle English *compulsioun*, from Old French *compulsion*, from Late Latin *compulsiō* (stem *compulsiōn-*), from Latin *compellere* (past participle *compulsus*), COMPEL.]

com·pul·sive (kəm-púl-siv ‖ kom-) *adj.* **1.** Having the power to or tending to compel. **2.** *Psychology.* Acting from or conditioned by compulsion or obsession: *a compulsive gambler.* —**com·pul·sive·ly** *adv.* —**com·pul·sive·ness** *n.*

com·pul·so·ry (kəm-púl-səri ‖ kom-) *adj.* **1.** Obligatory; required; enforced. **2.** Employing or exerting compulsion; coercive; compelling. [Medieval Latin *compulsōrius*, from Latin *compellere*, to COMPEL.] —**com·pul·so·ri·ly** *adv.* —**com·pul·so·ri·ness** *n.*

com·punc·tion (kəm-púngk-sh'n ‖ kom-) *n.* **1.** A strong uneasiness caused by a sense of guilt; remorse. **2.** A slight uneasiness or feeling of regret. —See Synonyms at **qualm.** [Middle English *compunccion*, from Old French *componction*, from Late Latin *compunctiō* (stem *compunctiōn-*), "prick of conscience", from Latin, puncture, from *compungere*, to prick hard : *com-* (intensive) + *pungere*, to prick, sting.] —**com·punc·tious** (-shəss) *adj.* —**com·punc·tious·ly** *adv.*

com·pur·ga·tion (kóm-pur-gáysh'n) *n. Law.* The former practice, especially in the Middle Ages, of clearing an accused person of a charge by having a number of people swear to a belief in his innocence or good character. [Late Latin *compurgātiō* (stem *compurgatiōn-*), from Latin *compurgāre*, to purify completely : *com-* (intensive) + *purgāre*, to purify.] —**com·pur·ga·tor** (-gaytər) *n.*

com·pu·ta·tion (kómpew-táysh'n) *n.* **1.** The act, process, or method of computing. **2.** The result of computing.

com·pute (kəm-péwt ‖ kom-) *v.* **-puted, -puting, -putes.** —*tr.* To determine by mathematics, especially by numerical methods or with the aid of a computer. —*intr.* **1.** To determine an amount or number. **2.** To perform mathematical or logical calculations. Used of a computer. —See Synonyms at **calculate.** ~*n.* Computation; calculation. Used in the phrase *beyond compute.* [Latin *computāre*, to reckon together : *com-*, together in mind, mentally + *putāre*, to think, reckon.] —**com·put·a·bil·i·ty** (-ə-bílləti) *n.* —**com·put·a·ble** *adj.*

com·put·er (kəm-péwtər ‖ kom-) *n.* One that computes; specifically, an electronic machine that performs high-speed mathematical or logical calculations or that assembles, stores, correlates, or otherwise processes and prints information derived from coded data in accordance with a predetermined **program** (*see*). See **digital computer, analog computer.**

com·put·er·ise, com·put·er·ize (kəm-péwtər-īz ‖ kom-) *tr.v.* **-ised, -ising, -ises. 1.** To perform (an operation) or process (information) with an electronic computer or system of computers. **2.** To furnish with a computer or computer system. —**com·put·er·i·sa·tion** (-ī-záysh'n ‖ *U.S.* -i-) *n.*

com·put·er·ised axial tomography (kəm-péwtərīzd ‖ kom-) *n. Abbr.* **CATS** A radiological technique for examining the soft tissues of the body. X-ray slices are recorded by a **CAT scanner** (*see*) and integrated by computer to give a three-dimensional image of the tissue or organ.

computer language *n.* A code used to provide data and instructions to computers; a code for programming computers.

computer typesetting *n.* A method of setting type using the output of a computer to drive the typesetting machine. Also called "automatic typesetting".

Comr. commissioner.

com·rade (kóm-rayd, kúm-, -rid ‖ -rad) *n.* **1.** A friend, associate, or companion. **2.** A person who shares one's interests, occupation, or activities. **3.** *Often capital* **C.** A fellow member; especially, a fellow member of a Communist or socialist party. [Earlier *camerade, cumrade*, from Old French *camarade*, roommate, soldier sharing the same room, from Spanish *camarada*, from *camara*, room, from Late Latin *camera*, from Latin, arched roof, from Greek *kamara*, vault.] —**com·rade·ship** *n.*

com·sat (kóm-sát) *n.* A **communications satellite** (*see*).

Comte (koNt), **(Isidore) Auguste (Marie François)** (1798-1857). French philosopher and the founder of modern sociology, a term he coined. He believed that intellectual life had developed through three stages: theological, metaphysical, and positivist. Sociology, he held, formed the apex of a hierarchy of sciences, and would help to build a better future.

Com·tism (kóm-tiz'm, koN-) *n.* The philosophy of Auguste Comte; positivism. —**Com·tist** (-tist) *adj. & n.*

Co·mus (kōməss). In Roman mythology, a god or the spirit of revelry. [Latin, from Greek *Kōmos*, personification of *kōmos*, revel, festival procession. See **comedy.**]

con¹ (kon) *n. Informal.* **1.** One that votes or argues against. **2.** An argument against. Used in the phrase *pros and cons.* [Middle English, short for *contra*, against, from Latin *contrā*.]

con² *tr.v.* **conned, conning, cons.** *Archaic & Literary.* **1.** To study, peruse, or examine carefully. **2.** To learn or commit to memory. [Middle English *connen, cunnen*, to know how, be able, master, Old English *cunnan.*] —**con·ner** *n.*

con³, conn *tr.v.* **conned, conning, cons.** *Nautical.* To direct the steering or course of (a ship). [Earlier *cond, cund*, from Middle English *conduen, condien*, to guide, from Old French *conduire*, to conduct, from Latin *condūcere*, "to bring together" : *com-*, together + *dūcere*, to lead.]

con⁴ *tr.v.* **conned, conning, cons.** *Slang.* To swindle or defraud by first winning the confidence of; dupe. ~*n. Slang.* A swindle; a trick. [Short for CONFIDENCE TRICK.]

con⁵ *n. Slang.* A convict.

con. **1.** concerto. **2.** *Law.* conclusion. **3.** connection. **4.** consolidated.

Con. **1.** conformist. **2.** Conservative. **3.** consul.

Co·na·kry or **Ko·na·kry** (kón-ə-krée, -ə-). Capital and chief port of Guinea, situated on Tombo island off the west coast of Africa. It is connected by a causeway to the mainland.

con a·mo·re (kón a-máwr-ay, ə-, -i ‖ -mŏr-; *U.S. also* kŏn aa-) *adv. Music.* Lovingly; tenderly. Used as a direction. [Italian, "with love".]

Conan Doyle, Sir Arthur. See **Doyle, Sir Arthur Conan.**

co·na·tion (kō-náysh'n) *n. Psychology.* The aspect of mental processes or behaviour directed towards action or change and including impulse, desire, volition, and striving. [Latin *cōnātiō* (stem *cōnātiōn-*), endeavour, effort, from *cōnātus*, past participle of *cōnārī*, to endeavour.] —**co·na·tion·al** *adj.*

co·na·tive (kóna-tiv, kónnə-) *adj.* **1.** *Psychology.* Of, pertaining to, or involving conation. **2.** *Grammar.* Being or designating a verb, verb form, verbal aspect, or affix in certain inflected languages, such as Russian, that expresses an attempt to perform an action that is not necessarily achieved. ~*n.* A conative linguistic form.

co·na·tus (kō-náytəss) *n., pl.* **conatus.** Any natural tendency, impulse, or directed effort. [Latin *cōnātus*, attempt, effort, from the past participle of *cōnārī*, to endeavour. See **conation.**]

con bri·o (kon brée-ō ‖ *U.S. also* kŏn) *adv. Music.* With spirit and vigour. Used as a direction. [Italian, "with vigour".]

conc. concentrate; concentrated.

con·cat·e·nate (kən-kátti-nayt, kon-) *tr.v.* **-nated, -nating, -nates.** To connect or link in a series or chain. ~*adj.* (-nət, -nit, -nayt). Connected or linked in a series. [Late Latin *concatēnāre* : *com-*, together + *catēnāre*, to link, chain, from Latin *catēna*, CATENA.] —**con·cat·e·na·tion** (-náysh'n) *n.*

con·cave (kón-káyv, -kayv) *adj.* Curved like a section of the inner surface of a sphere: *a concave mirror.* Compare **convex.** ~*n.* A concave surface, structure, or line. [Middle English, from Old French, from Latin *concavus*, vaulted, hollow : *com-* (intensive) + *cavus*, hollow.] —**con·cave·ly** *adv.* —**con·cave·ness** *n.*

con·cav·i·ty (kon-kávvəti, kən-) *n., pl.* **-ties. 1.** The condition or state of being concave. **2.** A concave surface or structure.

con·ca·vo-con·cave (kon-káyvō-kon-káyv) *adj.* Concave on both surfaces, as certain lenses are.

con·ca·vo-con·vex (kon-káyvō-kon-véks) *adj.* **1.** Concave on one side and convex on the other; convexo-concave. **2.** Designating a lens with greater concave than convex curvature.

con·ceal (kən-séel ‖ kon-) *tr.v.* **-cealed, -cealing, -ceals. 1.** To prevent from being noticed or discovered: *couldn't conceal her disgust.* **2.** To keep out of sight; hide: *a concealed entrance.* See Synonyms at **hide.** [Middle English *concelen*, from Old French *conceler*, from Latin *concēlāre* : *com-* (intensive) + *cēlāre*, to hide.] —**con·ceal·a·ble** *adj.* —**con·ceal·er** *n.* —**con·ceal·ment** *n.*

con·cede (kən-séed ‖ kon-) *v.* **-ceded, -ceding, -cedes.** —*tr.* **1.** To acknowledge as true, just, or proper; admit. **2.** To yield or grant (a privilege or right, for example). **3.** To allow an opponent to score (a goal, points, or the like). —*intr.* **1.** To make a concession. **2.** To admit defeat, as in an election. —See Synonyms at **acknowledge.** [French *concéder*, from Latin *concēdere*, to yield : *com-* (intensive) + *cēdere*, to go away, withdraw.] —**con·ced·ed·ly** *adv.* —**con·ced·er** *n.*

con·ceit (kən-séet ‖ kon-) *n.* **1.** A high, often exaggerated, opinion of one's own abilities, worth, or personality; vanity. **2.** An ingenious, fanciful, or witty thought or expression. **3. a.** A far-fetched or exaggerated metaphor. **b.** The use of such metaphors. **c.** A poem or verse constructed entirely around an elaborate conceit. **4.** *Archaic.* A thought or idea; an opinion. ~*tr.v.* **conceited, -ceiting, -ceits.** *Archaic.* **1.** To imagine or consider. **2.** To take a fancy to. [Middle English *conceite,* concept, notion, from *conceiven,* to CONCEIVE (by analogy with DECEIVE, DECEIT).]

con·ceit·ed (kən-séetid || kon-) *adj.* **1.** Holding too high an opinion of oneself; vain. **2.** *Archaic.* Inclined to be fanciful or whimsical. **—con·ceit·ed·ly** *adv.* **—con·ceit·ed·ness** *n.*

con·ceiv·a·ble (kən-séevəb'l || kon-) *adj.* Capable of being conceived or imagined; possible. **—con·ceiv·a·bil·ity** (-ə-bílləti), **con·ceiv·a·ble·ness** *n.* **—con·ceiv·a·bly** *adv.*

con·ceive (kən-séev || kon-) *v.* **-ceived, -ceiving, -ceives.** *—tr.* **1. a.** To become pregnant with. **b.** To begin or induce the conception of: *a test-tube baby conceived outside the womb.* **2. a.** To form in the mind; become possessed by: *conceived an instant dislike for her.* **b.** To formulate; devise: *conceive a plan.* **3.** To apprehend mentally; imagine or understand. Often followed by a clause. **4.** To think or consider. Often followed by a clause. *—intr.* **1.** To form an idea. Used with *of.* **2.** To become pregnant. [Middle English *conceiven,* from Old French *conceivre,* from Latin *concipere,* to take to oneself, hence to be impregnated, to take into the mind : *com-,* comprehensively + *capere,* to take.] **—con·ceiv·er** *n.*

con·cel·e·brate (kən-séllibrayt, kón-) *intr.v.* **-brated, -brating, -brates.** To take part in a concelebration. [Latin *concelebrāre* : *com-,* together + *celebrāre,* to CELEBRATE.]

con·cel·e·bra·tion (kən-sélli-bráysh'n, kón) *n.* The celebration of the Eucharist by two or more clergy.

con·cen·trate (kón-s'n-trayt, -sen-) *v.* **-trated, -trating, -trates.** *—tr.* **1.** To direct or draw towards a common centre, purpose, or the like; focus: *tried to concentrate her mind on her work.* **2.** *Chemistry.* To increase the concentration of (a solution or mixture). *—intr.* **1.** To converge towards a centre. **2. a.** To focus one's thoughts or attention. Often used with *on* or *upon.* **b.** To keep one's attention closely on a matter in hand.

~n. Abbr. **conc.** *Chemistry.* A product of concentration.

~adj. Abbr. **conc.** Concentrated. [French *concentrer* : *com-,* same + *centre,* CENTRE.] **—con·cen·tra·tor** (-traytər) *n.*

con·cen·tra·tion (kón-s'n-tráysh'n, -sen-) *n.* **1.** The act or process of concentrating or the condition of being concentrated. **2.** A concentrated mass; an accumulation. **3.** Closely directed thoughts or attention. **4.** *Chemistry.* The amount of a given substance in a unit amount of another substance, usually expressed as the number of moles of solute in a litre or a cubic decimetre of solvent.

concentration camp *n.* An internment camp of a type first used by the British in the Boer War, where prisoners of war, enemy aliens, and political prisoners are confined and sometimes, as in those of Nazi Germany, subjected to brutal treatment. [Referring to the *concentration* of large numbers of such prisoners in one area.]

con·cen·tre (kon-séntər) *v.* **-tred, -tring, -tres.** *—tr.* To direct towards a common centre. *—intr.* To come together at a common centre. [French *concentrer,* to CONCENTRATE.]

con·cen·tric (kən-séntrik, kon-) *adj.* Having a common centre. Compare **eccentric.** [Middle English *concentrik,* from Old French *concentrique,* from Medieval Latin *concentricus* : Latin *com-,* same + *centrum,* CENTRE.] **—con·cen·tri·cal·ly** *adv.* **—con·cen·tric·i·ty** (kón-sen-tríssəti, -sən-) *n.*

con·cept (kón-sept) *n.* **1.** A general idea or understanding, especially one derived from specific instances or occurrences. **2.** A thought or notion, especially one that is abstract or theoretical. **3. a.** A way of thinking about something. **b.** The structure or design of something, considered in the abstract. **—**See Synonyms at **idea.** [Late Latin *conceptus,* a thing conceived, thought, from past participle of *concipere,* to take to oneself, CONCEIVE.]

con·cep·ta·cle (kən-séptək'l || kon-) *n.* A cavity in certain algae and fungi that opens to the exterior and contains reproductive structures. [French, from Latin *conceptāculum,* from *concipere,* to receive, contain, CONCEIVE.]

con·cep·tion (kən-sépsh'n || kon-) *n.* **1. a.** The fertilisation of an egg cell by a sperm in the uterus to form an embryo capable of survival and maturation in normal conditions. **b.** The entity so formed; an embryo. **2.** A beginning. **3.** The ability to form mental concepts; invention. **4.** That which is mentally conceived; a concept, plan, design, idea, or thought. **—**See Synonyms at **idea.** [Middle English *concepcioun,* from Old French *conception,* from Latin *conceptiō* (stem *conceptiōn-*), from *concipere,* to take to oneself, CONCEIVE.] **—con·cep·tion·al** *adj.*

con·cep·tive (kən-séptiv || kon-) *adj.* Able to conceive mentally.

con·cep·tu·al (kən-sép-tew-əl, -choo- || kon-, -chōōl) *adj.* Of or pertaining to concepts or mental conception. **—con·cep·tu·al·ly** *adv.*

conceptual art *n.* Art that is intended to convey an idea or concept to the perceiver and need not involve the creation or appreciation of a traditional art object such as a painting or sculpture.

con·cep·tu·al·ise, con·cep·tu·al·ize (kən-sép-tew-əl-īz, -choo- || kon-, -chōōl-) *v.* **-ised, -ising, -ises.** *—tr.* To form concepts or a concept of. *—intr.* To form concepts, theories, or ideas. **—con·cep·tu·al·i·sa·tion** (-ī-záysh'n || *U.S.* -i-) *n.*

con·cep·tu·al·ism (kən-sép-tew-əl-iz'm, -choo- || kon-, -chōōl-) *n.* *Philosophy.* The doctrine that universals, or abstract concepts, exist only within the mind and have no external or substantial reality. **—con·cep·tu·al·ist** *n.* **—con·cep·tu·al·is·tic** (-ístik) *adj.*

con·cern (kən-sérn || kon-) *tr.v.* **-cerned, -cerning, -cerns.** **1. a.** To pertain or relate to. **b.** To be of interest or importance to; affect. **2.** To engage or involve the mind or interests of. Used reflexively or in the passive: *concern oneself with trivia.* **3.** To cause anxiety or uneasiness in; trouble.

~n. **1. a.** A matter that relates to or affects one. **b.** Something of interest or importance. **2.** Regard for or interest in someone or something: *concern for her well-being.* **3.** A matter about which one is concerned. **4.** Anxiety; worry. **5.** A business establishment or enterprise; a company. **—**See Synonyms at **anxiety.** [Middle English *concernen,* from Old French *concerner,* from Medieval Latin *concernere,* to relate to, involve with, from Latin, to mix in a sieve (before sifting) : *com-,* together + *cernere,* to sift.]

Usage: In the senses "engage in", "relate to", the usual preposition used with *concern* is *with,* less often *in*: *Her work is concerned with aviation.* In the sense "cause anxiety", both *for* and *about* are used, *for* being somewhat more formal: *John was concerned about Sarah; John felt concern for Sarah.*

con·cerned (kən-sérnd || kon-) *adj.* **1.** Interested or affected; involved. **2.** Anxious; troubled; disturbed. **—con·cern·ed·ly** (-sérnidli) *adv.* **—con·cern·ed·ness** (-sérnid-nəss, -niss) *n.*

con·cern·ing (kən-sérning || kon-) *prep.* With reference to; regarding; about.

con·cern·ment (kən-sérn-mənt || kon-) *n. Archaic.* **1.** A matter that concerns one; an affair. **2.** Reference, relation, or importance.

con·cert (kón-sərt; *in sense* 2 *also* -sert) *n.* **1.** A musical performance in which a number of singers or players participate. **2.** Agreement in purpose, feeling, or action. **—in concert.** **1.** All together; in agreement. **2.** Playing or singing live, at a concert.

~adj. Pertaining to, playing in, or designed for concerts.

~tr.v. (kən-sért) **concerted, -certing, -certs.** **1.** To plan or arrange by mutual agreement. **2.** To contrive or devise. [French, from Italian *concerto,* from Old Italian *concertare*†, to bring into agreement, harmonise.]

con·cert·ed (kən-sértid || kon-) *adj.* **1.** Planned or accomplished together; combined: *a concerted effort.* **2.** *Music.* Arranged in parts for voices or instruments. **—con·cert·ed·ly** *adv.*

concert grand *n.* The largest type of grand piano, being roughly 2.8 metres (9 feet) in length.

con·cer·ti·na (kón-sər-téenə) *n.* A small, hexagonal accordion with bellows, and buttons for keys.

~v. **concertinaed** (-téenəd), **-naing** (-téenəring, -téenə-ing), **-nas.** *—intr.* To fold up like a concertina; collapse in folds. *—tr.* To cause to fold up or collapse. [CONCERT + Italian *-ina* (feminine diminutive suffix).]

con·cer·ti·no (kón-chair-tée-nō, -chər-) *n., pl.* **-nos** or **-ni** (-nee). *Music.* **1.** A short concerto. **2.** The solo instrument group in a concerto grosso. [Italian, diminutive of *concerto,* concerto, CONCERT.]

con·cert·mas·ter (kón-sərt-maastər || -mástər) *n. Chiefly U.S.* The leader of an orchestra.

con·cer·to (kən-cháir-tō, -chér- || kon-) *n., pl.* **-tos** or **-ti** (-tee). *Abbr.* **con.** A composition for an orchestra and one or more solo instruments, typically in three movements. [Italian, CONCERT.]

concerto gros·so (gróssō || *U.S.* grō-sō) *n., pl.* **concerti grossi** (gróssee). A composition for a small group of solo instruments and a full orchestra. [Italian, "great concerto".]

concert pitch *n.* **1.** *Music.* A pitch to which orchestral instruments are tuned with the A above middle C at 440 hertz. Also called "international pitch". **2.** *Informal.* The state of being ready and tensely alert.

con·ces·sion (kən-sésh'n || kon-) *n.* **1.** The act of conceding, granting, or yielding. **2.** Any thing or point so conceded. **3.** Something granted by a government or controlling authority, such as a right to land or exploration, to be used for a specific purpose. **4.** *Chiefly U.S.* **a.** The right to operate a subsidiary business within a larger establishment. **b.** The space allotted for such a business. [Middle English, from Old French, from Latin *concessiō* (stem *concessiōn-*), from *concēdere* (past participle *concessus*), to CONCEDE.]

con·ces·sion·aire (kən-sésh'n-áir || kon-) *n.* The holder of a concession; especially, a company having special trading rights.

con·ces·sion·ar·y (kən-sésh'n-əri || kon-; *U.S.* -erri) *adj.* Of the nature of or granted by a concession.

con·ces·sive (kən-séssiv || kon-) *adj.* **1.** Of the nature of or containing a concession; tending to concede. **2.** *Grammar.* Expressing concession, as can the conjunction *although.* [Latin *concessīvus,* from *concessus,* past participle of *concēdere,* to CONCEDE.]

conch (kongk, konch) *n., pl.* **conchs** (kongks) or **conches** (kónchiz). **1.** Any of various tropical marine gastropod molluscs of the genus *Strombus* and other genera, having large, often brightly coloured spiral shells and, in some species, edible flesh. **2.** The shell of any of these molluscs, used for ornament, in making cameos, or as a horn. **3.** A concha. [Middle English *conche, conk,* from Latin *concha,* from Greek *konkhē.*]

con·cha (kóng-kə) *n., pl.* **-chae** (-kee). **1.** *Anatomy.* A shell-like structure, such as the external ear. **2.** *Architecture.* The half dome over an apse. [Latin, CONCH.]

con·chie, con·chy (kónchi) *n., pl.* **-chies.** *British Slang.* A **conscientious objector** *(see).* Usually used derogatorily.

con·chif·er·ous (kong-kíffərəss) *adj.* **1.** Having or forming a shell. **2.** Containing shells. Said of certain rocks. [CONCH(O)- + -FEROUS.]

con·chi·o·lin (kong-kī-ə-lin, kon-) *n.* A fibrous protein, $C_{32}H_{98}N_2O_{11}$, that is the principal constituent of mollusc shells. [From CONCH.]

concho-, conch-, conchi- *comb. form.* Indicates shell; for example, **conchology.** [Greek *konkho-,* from *konkhē,* shell.]

con·choid (kóng-koyd) *n.* In geometry, a curve having two branches with a common asymptote, so that a line from a fixed point that intersects both branches is of constant length between the asymptote and either branch. [CONCH + -OID (referring to the shape of the curve).]

con·choi·dal (kong-kóyd'l) *adj.* Of or designating rocks, such as flint or obsidian, having bivalve shell-like surfaces when fractured. [Greek *konkhoeidēs*, shell-like : CONCH(O)- + -OID.]

con·chol·o·gy (kong-kóllǝji) *n.* The study of molluscs and their shells. [CONCHO- + -LOGY.] —**con·cho·log·i·cal** (kóngkǝ-lójik'l) *adj.* —**con·chol·o·gist** (-kóllǝjist) *n.*

con·ci·erge (kón-si-airzh, kón-, -airzh) *n.* A person who attends the entrance of a building and acts as caretaker. [French, from Old French *cumcerges*, from Vulgar Latin *conservius* (unattested), variant of Latin *conservus*, a fellow slave : com-, together + *servus*, slave.]

con·cil·i·ar (kǝn-sílli-ǝr ‖ kon-) *adj.* Of or pertaining to a council, especially an ecclesiastical council.

con·cil·i·ate (kǝn-sílli-ayt ‖ kon-) *tr.v.* **-ated, -ating, -ates. 1.** To overcome the distrust or animosity of; win over; placate; soothe. **2.** To gain, win, or secure (favour, friendship, or goodwill, for example) by friendly overtures. **3.** To reconcile. —See Synonyms at **pacify.** [Latin *conciliāre*, to bring together, unite, from *concilium*, union, gathering, meeting.] —**con·cil·i·a·ble** (-ǝb'l) *adj.* —**con·cil·i·a·tor** (-aytǝr) *n.* —**con·cil·i·a·to·ry** (-ǝtri, -ǝtǝri, -áytǝri) *adj.*

con·cil·i·a·tion (kǝn-sílli-áysh'n ‖ kon-) *n.* **1.** The act or process of conciliating; placation; propitiation. **2.** The process of settling differences between employers and employees through the good offices of a third party but without resort to arbitration. —See Synonyms at **mediation.**

con·cin·ni·ty (kǝn-sínnǝti ‖ kon-) *n., pl.* **-ties. 1.** A skilful, harmonious arrangement of parts. **2.** Elegance of literary style. [Latin *concinnitās*, from *concinnus*, placed fitly together, from *concinnāre*, to place fitly together, arrange in good order : com-, together + *cinnus†*, a mixed drink.]

con·cise (kǝn-síss ‖ kon-) *adj.* Expressing much in few words; short and to the point; succinct. [Latin *concīsus*, past participle of *concīdere*, to cut up : com- (intensive) + *caedere*, to cut.] —**con·cise·ly** *adv.* —**con·cise·ness** *n.*

Synonyms: concise, terse, laconic, pithy, succinct, summary, compendious, epigrammatic.

con·ci·sion (kǝn-sízh'n ‖ kon-) *n.* The quality of being concise; terseness; brevity; succinctness. [Middle English *concisioun*, from Latin *concīsiō* (stem *concīsiōn-*), from *concīsus*, CONCISE.]

con·clave (kóng-klayv, kón-) *n.* **1.** A confidential or secret meeting. **2. a.** The private rooms in which the cardinals of the Roman Catholic Church meet to elect a pope. **b.** The meeting so held. [Middle English, from Old French, from Latin *conclāve*, "room locked with a key" : com-, together + *clāvis*, key.]

con·clude (kǝn-kloōd ‖ kon-, -kléwd) *v.* **-cluded, -cluding, -cludes.** —*tr.* **1.** To bring to an end; wind up; finish. **2.** To arrive finally at (an agreement or settlement); settle: *conclude a peace treaty.* **3.** To infer or deduce. **4.** To determine; decide. —*intr.* **1.** To come to an end; close. **2.** To form a final judgment; come to a decision or an agreement. —See Synonyms at **complete, decide.** [Middle English *concluden*, from Latin *conclūdere*, to shut up closely : com- (intensive) + *claudere*, to shut.] —**con·clud·er** *n.*

con·clu·sion (kǝn-kloōzh'n ‖ kon-, -kléwzh'n) *n.* **1.** The close or termination of something; the end; the finish. **2.** The closing or last part, as of a speech, paper, or the like, often containing a summing up. **3.** A final outcome or result: *Their election victory was a foregone conclusion.* **4.** A judgment, inference, or decision reached after deliberation. **5.** A final arrangement or settlement, as of a treaty. **6.** *Law. Abbr.* **con.** a. The close of a plea or deed. **b.** An estoppel *(see).* **7.** *Logic.* **a.** In a syllogism, the proposition that must follow from the major and minor premises. **b.** The proposition concluded from one or more premises; a deduction. —**jump** or **leap to conclusions.** To form an opinion or judgment over-hastily and prematurely. —**try conclusions with.** To engage in a contest or argument. [Middle English *conclusioun*, from Old French *conclusion*, from Latin *conclūsiō* (stem *conclūsiōn-*), from *conclūdere*, to shut up closely, CONCLUDE.]

con·clu·sive (kǝn-kloō-siv ‖ kon-, -kléw-, -ziv) *adj.* Serving to put an end to doubt or question; decisive; final. See Synonyms at **valid.** —**con·clu·sive·ly** *adv.* —**con·clu·sive·ness** *n.*

con·coct (kǝn-kókt ‖ kon-) *tr.v.* **-cocted, -cocting, -cocts. 1.** To prepare by mixing ingredients, as in cookery. **2.** To invent or fabricate; contrive: *concoct a plausible story.* [Latin *concoquere* (past participle *concoctus*), to cook together : com-, together + *coquere*, to cook.] —**con·coct·er, con·coc·tor** (-ǝr) *n.* —**con·coc·tion** (-kóksh'n) *n.* —**con·coc·tive** *adj.*

con·com·i·tance (kǝn-kómmi-tǝnss ‖ kon-) *n.* Also **con·com·i·tan·cy** (-tǝn-si) *pl.* **-cies. 1.** Occurrence together or in connection with another; coexistence. **2.** *Theology.* The coexistence of the body and blood of Christ in both elements of the Eucharist.

con·com·i·tant (kǝn-kómmi-tǝnt ‖ kon-) *adj.* Existing or occurring concurrently as an attendant feature or circumstance; accompanying. See Synonyms at **contemporary.**
~*n.* A concomitant state, circumstance, or thing. [Latin *concomitāns* (stem *concomitant-*), present participle of *concomitārī*, to accompany : com-, together + *comitārī*, to accompany, from *comes* (stem *comit-*), companion.]

con·cord (kóng-kawrd, kón-) *n.* **1.** Harmony or agreement of interests or feelings; concurrence; accord. **2.** A treaty establishing peaceful relations. **3.** *Grammar.* Agreement between words in person, number, gender, or case. **4.** A harmonious combination of si-multaneously sounded notes; consonance. Compare **discord.** [Middle English, from Old French *concorde*, from Latin *concordia*, from *concors*, "of the same mind" : com-, same, mutually + *cors* (stem *cord-*), the heart, mind.]

con·cor·dance (kǝn-kórd'nss ‖ kon-) *n.* **1.** A state of agreement; harmony; concord. **2.** An index of all the words in a text or corpus of texts, showing every contextual occurrence of a word.

con·cor·dant (kǝn-kórd'nt ‖ kon-) *adj.* Harmonious; agreeing; corresponding. [Middle English *concordaunt*, from Old French *concordant*, from Latin *concordāns* (stem *concordant-*), present participle of *concordāre*, to agree, from *concors*, agreed. See **concord.**] —**con·cor·dant·ly** *adv.*

con·cor·dat (kǝn-kór-dat, kǝn-) *n.* A formal agreement; especially, an agreement between the pope and a government for the regulation of church affairs. [French, from Medieval Latin *concordātum*, from Latin *concordāre*, to agree. See **concordant.**]

Con·corde (kóng-kawrd, kón-). An Anglo-French supersonic airliner, capable of flying at speeds greater than Mach 2. [French, *concord*, unity, referring to Anglo-French cooperation in producing it.]

Concord grape (kóng-kǝrd, kón-, -kawrd) *n.* A variety of grape having purple-black fruit with a bluish bloom. [Discovered (1846) at *Concord,* Massachusetts.]

con·cours (kóng-koor, kón-) *adj. Chiefly British.* Superb; worthy of exhibition. Said of motor vehicles, in the phrase *in concours condition.* [From French *concours d'élégance,* "contest of elegance".]

con·course (kóng-kawrss, kón- ‖ -kōrss) *n.* **1.** A great crowd; a throng; a multitude. **2.** A coming, moving, or flowing together. **3. a.** A large open space for the gathering or passage of crowds, as in a railway station. **b.** A broad thoroughfare. [Middle English, from Old French *concours,* from Latin *concursus,* from the past participle of *concurrere,* to run together : com-, together + *currere,* to run.]

con·cres·cence (kǝn-kréss'nss ‖ kon-) *n.* The uniting, especially the growing together, of related parts, as of physical particles or anatomical structures. [Latin *concrēscentia,* from *concrēscēns* (stem *concrēscent-*), present participle of *concrēscere,* to grow together : com-, together + *crēscere,* to grow.]

con·crete (kón-kreet, kóng- ‖ kǝn-kréet, kon-) *adj.* **1.** Pertaining to an actual, specific thing or instance; not general; particular. **2.** Existing in reality or in real experience; perceptible by the senses; real. **3.** Designating a material object or thing as opposed to an abstraction or quality. **4.** Formed by the coalescence of separate particles or parts into one mass; solid. **5.** Made of concrete. —See Synonyms at **real.**
~*n.* (kóng-kreet, kón- ‖ *U.S. also* kon-kréet). **1.** A construction material consisting of sand, gravel, pebbles, broken stone, or the like in a mortar or cement matrix. **2.** A mass formed by the coalescence of particles.
~*v.* (kǝn-kréet ‖ kon-; *but in sense 2* kóng-kreet, kón-) **concreted, -creting, -cretes.** —*tr.* **1.** To form into a mass by coalescence or cohesion of particles. **2.** To build, treat, or cover with concrete. —*intr.* To coalesce; solidify. [Middle English *concret,* from Old French, from Latin *concrētus,* past participle of *concrēscere,* to grow together, harden : com-, together + *crēscere,* to grow.] —**con·crete·ly** *adv.* —**con·crete·ness** *n.*

concrete mixer *n.* A **cement mixer** *(see).*

concrete noun *n.* A noun designating a material object as opposed to an abstract idea or quality. Compare **abstract noun.**

concrete poetry *n.* Poetry in which the physical representation or arrangement of the words conveys or adds meaning.

con·cre·tion (kǝn-kréesh'n ‖ kon-) *n.* **1.** The act or process of growing together or becoming united in one mass; coalescence. **2.** A solid or concrete mass. **3.** *Geology.* A rounded or irregular mass of mineral matter found in sedimentary rock. **4.** *Pathology.* A solid mass of inorganic material formed in a cavity or tissue of the body; a calculus. —**con·cre·tion·ar·y** (-ǝri ‖ -erri) *adj.*

con·cre·tise, con·cre·tize (kón-kreet-īz, kóng-, -krit-) *tr.v.* **-tised, -tising, -tises.** To render concrete; make real or specific. —**con·cre·ti·sa·tion** (-ī-záysh'n ‖ *U.S.* -i-) *n.*

con·cu·bi·nage (kon-kéwbīnij, kǝn-, -kéwbinij) *n.* **1.** Cohabitation without legal marriage. **2.** The state of being a concubine.

con·cu·bine (kóng-kew-bīn, kón-) *n.* **1.** A woman who cohabits with and is supported by a man without being married to him. **2.** In certain polygamous societies, a secondary wife, usually of inferior legal and social status. [Middle English, from Old French, from Latin *concubīna,* "one to sleep with" : com-, together + *cubāre,* to lie down.] —**con·cu·bi·nar·y** *adj.*

con·cu·pis·cence (kǝn-kéwpiss'nss, kónkew-píss'nss) *n.* **1.** Sexual desire; lust. **2.** Any abnormally strong desire. [Latin *concupīscēns,* present participle of *concupīscere,* inceptive of *concupere,* to have a strong desire for : com- (intensive) + *cupere,* to desire.] —**con·cu·pis·cent** *adj.*

con·cur (kǝn-kúr ‖ kon-) *intr.v.* **-curred, -curring, -curs. 1.** To have the same opinion; agree. **2.** To act together; cooperate. **3.** To occur at the same time; coincide. —See Synonyms at **assent.** [Middle English *concurren,* from Latin *concurrere,* to run together : com-, together + *currere,* to run.]

Usage: Concur in is generally used to express approval or joint action: *concur in a plan. Concur with* expresses agreement: *concur with her view.*

con·cur·rence (kǝn-kúrrǝnss ‖ kon-) *n.* **1.** Agreement in opinion; accord. **2.** Cooperation or combination, as of agents, causes, circumstances, or events. **3.** Simultaneous occurrence; coincidence. **4.** In geometry, the intersection of three or more lines. **5.** *Rare.* Competition; rivalry.

con•cur•rent (kən-kúrrənt || kon-) *adj.* **1. a.** Happening at the same time or place. **b.** Intended to run simultaneously. **2.** Operating in conjunction. **3.** Meeting at or tending to meet at the same point. **4.** In accordance or agreement; harmonious. **5.** Exercising equal authority or having the same jurisdiction. —See Synonyms at **contemporary.** [Middle English, from Old French, from Latin *concurrēns* (stem *concurrent-*), present participle of *concurrere,* to run together, CONCUR.] **—con•cur•rent•ly** *adv.*

con•cuss (kən-kúss || kon-) *tr.v.* **-cussed, -cussing, -cusses. 1.** To injure by concussion. **2.** *Rare.* To shake or agitate; disturb severely. [Late Latin *concutere* (past participle *concussus*), to shake violently : Latin *com-* (intensive) + *-cutere,* from *quatere,* to shake, dash.]

con•cus•sion (kən-kúsh'n || kon-) *n.* **1.** An injury of a soft structure, especially of the brain, resulting from a violent blow and usually causing loss of consciousness. **2.** Any violent jarring shock. **—con•cus•sive** (-kússiv) *adj.*

Con•dé (kóN-day, koN-dáy), **Louis I de Bourbon, Prince de** (1530–69). Leader of the Huguenots during the French Wars of Religion.

Condé, Louis II de Bourbon, Prince de, also known as the Great Condé (1621–86). Great-grandson of Louis Condé I. He was a brilliant general for France during the Thirty Years' War.

con•demn (kən-dém || kon-) *tr.v.* **-demned, -demning, -demns. 1.** To express disapproval of; censure; criticise. **2. a.** To pronounce judgment against; sentence. **b.** To doom; force into an undesirable state. **3.** To demonstrate the guilt of; convict. **4.** To judge or declare to be unfit for use or consumption, usually by official order. —See Synonyms at **criticise.** [Middle English *condem(p)nen,* from Old French *condem(p)ner,* from Latin *condemnāre* : *com-* (intensive) + *damnāre,* to damage, condemn, from *damnum,* damage, fine.] **—con•dem•na•ble** (-dém-nəb'l) *adj.* **—con•demn•er** *n.*

con•dem•na•tion (kón-dem-náysh'n, -dəm-) *n.* **1.** The act of condemning. **2.** The state of being condemned. **3.** Severe reproof; strong censure. **4.** A reason or occasion for condemning. **—con•dem•na•to•ry** (kən-dém-nə-tri, -təri, kón-dem-náytəri, -dəm-) *adj.*

con•demned cell (kən-démd || kon-) *n.* The prison cell of a person who has been condemned to death.

con•den•sate (kón-den-sayt, -dən-, kən-dén-) *n.* A liquid formed by condensation. [Latin *condēnsātus,* past participle of *condēnsāre,* to CONDENSE.]

con•den•sa•tion (kón-den-sáysh'n, -dən-) *n.* **1.** The act of condensing. **2.** The state of being condensed. **3.** A product of condensing, especially, abridgment. **4.** *Physics.* **a.** The physical process by which a liquid is removed from a vapour or vapour mixture. **b.** The liquid so removed; a condensate, especially water droplets forming on cold glass as air cools. **5.** *Chemistry.* A chemical reaction in which water or another simple substance is released by the combination of two or more molecules. **6.** *Psychoanalysis.* The process by which a single idea or word is invested with the emotional content of a group of ideas.

condensation trail *n.* A **vapour trail** *(see).*

con•dense (kən-dénss || kon-) *v.* **-densed, -densing, -denses.** *—tr.* **1.** To reduce the volume of; compress. **2.** To abridge (a literary work, for example). **3. a.** To form a condensate from (a vapour, for example). **b.** To subject (a vapour, for example) to condensation. *—intr.* **1.** To become more compact. **2.** To undergo condensation. —See Synonyms at **contract.** [Middle English *condensen,* from Old French *condenser,* from Latin *condēnsāre* : *com-* (intensive) + *dēnsāre,* to make dense, from *dēnsus,* dense.] **—con•dens•a•ble** *adj.* **—con•dens•a•bil•i•ty** (-ə-bílləti) *n.*

con•densed (kən-dénst || kon-) *adj.* **1. a.** Made more compact. **b.** Abridged: *a condensed book.* **2.** *Printing.* Narrower than normal in proportion to its height. Said of type. Compare **expanded. 3.** *Botany.* Having stalkless or nearly stalkless flowers tightly crowded together. Said of certain inflorescences.

condensed milk *n.* Cow's milk with sugar added, and reduced by evaporation to a thick consistency. Compare **evaporated milk.**

con•dens•er (kən-dénssər || kon-) *n.* **1.** One that condenses. **2.** *Physics.* An apparatus used to condense vapour. **3.** *Electricity.* A **capacitor** *(see).* **4.** A mirror, lens, or combination of lenses used to gather light and direct it upon an object or projection lens.

con•de•scend (kón-di-sénd) *intr.v.* **-scended, -scending, -scends. 1.** To come down voluntarily to the level of inferiors with whom one is dealing; deign. **2.** To behave in a patronising manner. [Middle English *condescenden,* from Old French *condescendre,* from Medieval Latin *condēscendere,* to stoop to : Latin *com-* (intensive) + *dēscendere,* to descend : *dē-,* down + *scandere,* to climb.] **—con•de•scend•er** *n.*

con•de•scen•dence (kóndi-séndənss) *n.* **1.** *Scottish Law.* A list of facts or grounds presented by the plaintiff. **2.** Condescension.

con•de•scend•ing (kóndi-sénding) *adj.* Showing or assuming an air of superiority; patronising. **—con•de•scend•ing•ly** *adv.*

con•de•scen•sion (kóndi-sénh'n) *n.* **1. a.** The act of condescending. **b.** An instance of this. **2.** Patronising behaviour or manner.

con•dign (kən-dīn || kon-, kóndīn) *adj.* Deserved; adequate; merited. Said of punishment or censure. [Middle English *condigne,* from Old French, from Latin *condignus,* wholly worthy : *com-* (intensive) + *dignus,* worthy.] **—con•dign•ly** *adv.*

Con•dil•lac (kóN-dee-yák), **Étienne Bonnot de** (1715-80). French philosopher, a leading figure in the Enlightenment. He developed Locke's view that all knowledge derives from the senses.

con•di•ment (kóndi-mənt) *n.* A seasoning for food, such as mustard, vinegar, or a spice. [Middle English, from Old French, from Latin *condīmentum,* from *condīre,* to season, preserve by pickling, perhaps variant of *condere,* to bring together, store up.] **—con•di•men•tal** (-mént'l) *adj.*

con•di•tion (kən-dísh'n || kon-) *n.* **1.** The particular mode or state of being of a person or thing, especially: **a.** State of health. **b.** State of readiness or preparation: *out of condition for the race.* **c.** State of repair or fitness for use. **d.** Rank or social position. **2.** A disease or ailment: *a heart condition.* **3.** Something indispensable to the appearance or occurrence of something else; a prerequisite: *The Moon's atmosphere lacks the essential conditions for supporting human life.* **4.** Something required as prerequisite to the fulfilment or performance of something else; a stipulation. **5.** Something that restricts or modifies something else; a qualification. **6.** *Usually plural.* The existing or external circumstances: *poor driving conditions.* **7.** *Grammar.* The dependent clause of a conditional sentence. **8.** *Logic.* A proposition upon which another proposition depends; the antecedent of a conditional proposition. **9.** *Law.* **a.** A provision making the effect of a legal instrument contingent upon the occurrence of some uncertain future event. **b.** The event itself. —See Synonyms at **state. —in an interesting condition.** Pregnant. Used euphemistically or humorously.
~*tr.v.* **conditioned, -tioning, -tions. 1.** To make conditional; govern. Often used in the passive. **2.** To render fit; put into the desired condition. **3. a.** *Psychology.* To cause to respond in a specific manner to a specific stimulus. **b.** To accustom (a person) to adopt or conform to certain attitudes, modes of behaviour, or the like. **4.** To treat with conditioner: *conditioned his hair.* [Middle English *condicioun,* from Old French *condicion,* from Latin *conditiō* (stem *conditiōn-*), agreement, stipulation, probably (irregularly) from *condīcere,* to talk together, agree : *com-,* together + *dīcere,* to talk.]

con•di•tion•al (kən-dísh'n-əl || kon-) *adj.* **1.** Imposing, depending on, or containing a condition or conditions. **2.** *Grammar.* Stating or implying a condition.
~*n. Grammar.* A mood, tense, clause, or word expressing a condition. **—con•di•tion•al•i•ty** (-ál-əti) *n.* **—con•di•tion•al•ly** *adv.*

conditional probability *n.* The probability that an event will take place provided that some other event has occurred or will occur.

con•di•tioned (kən-dísh'nd || kon-) *adj.* **1.** Subject to or dependent upon conditions or stipulations. **2. a.** Physically fit; in good physical condition. **b.** Prepared for a specific action or process. **3.** *Psychology.* Exhibiting or trained to exhibit a conditioned response.

conditioned response *n. Psychology.* A response, elicited by conditioning, to a stimulus that does not really cause it. Also called "conditioned reflex".

conditioned stimulus *n. Psychology.* A stimulus rendered capable of eliciting a response like that of a specific **unconditioned stimulus** *(see)* by conditioning.

con•di•tion•er (kən-dísh'n-ər || kon-) *n.* **1.** A person or thing that conditions. **2.** An additive or application that improves the condition of something: *a soil conditioner; a hair conditioner.*

con•di•tion•ing (kən-dísh'n-ing || kon-) *n. Psychology.* The process of altering behaviour by modifying the stimuli associated with it. In *classical conditioning* the stimulus that normally causes the response is paired with a different stimulus until a conditioned response is elicited by the second stimulus alone. In *operant,* or *instrumental, conditioning* the response is modified by reinforcement (reward or punishment).

con•dole (kən-dṓl || kon-) *v.* **-doled, -doling, -doles.** *—intr.* To mourn or express sympathy with someone in pain, grief, or misfortune. Used with *with.* *—tr. Archaic.* To commiserate with or grieve over. [Late Latin *condolēre,* to feel another's pain : Latin *com-,* together + *dolēre,* to feel pain, grieve.] **—con•do•la•to•ry** (-ətri, -ətəri) *adj.* **—con•dol•er** *n.*

con•do•lence (kən-dṓlənss || kon-) *n.* **1.** Sympathy with a person in pain, grief, or misfortune. **2.** *Plural.* A formal declaration of such sympathy. —See Synonyms at **pity. —con•do•lent** *adj.*

con•dom (kón-dəm, -dom) *n.* A sheath, usually made of thin rubber, designed to cover the penis during sexual intercourse, for contraception or as protection against venereal disease or AIDS. [18th century : origin obscure.]

con•do•min•i•um (kóndə-mínni-əm) *n.* **1. a.** Joint sovereignty; especially, the joint rule of a territory by two or more states. **b.** The territory so governed. **2.** *U.S.* **a.** A block of flats in which the flats are owned individually. **b.** A flat in such a building. Also informally called "condo". [New Latin : CON- + DOMINIUM.]

con•do•na•tion (kón-dō-náysh'n, -də-) *n.* **1.** The condoning or overlooking of an offence. **2.** *Law.* A forgiving by a wife or husband of an offence by the other, especially adultery.

con•done (kən-dṓn || kon-) *tr.v.* **-doned, -doning, -dones.** To forgive, overlook, or disregard (an offence) without protest or censure. —See Synonyms at **forgive.** [Latin *condōnāre,* to give up, forgive : *com-* (intensive) + *dōnāre,* to give away, from *dōnum,* gift.] **—con•don•er** *n.*

con•dor (kón-dawr, -dər) *n.* **1.** Either of two very large, black and white New World vultures, *Vultur gryphus* of the Andes or *Gymnogyps californianus* of the mountains of California. **2.** Any of several gold coins of some South American countries bearing the figure of a condor. [Spanish *cóndor,* from Quechua *kúntur.*]

con•dot•tie•re (kón-dotti-aír-i, -dot-yaír-, -ay) *n., pl.* **-tieri** (-ee). **1.** A leader of mercenary soldiers in Europe between the 14th and 16th centuries. **2.** A mercenary soldier. [Italian, leader, from *condotto,* conduct, leadership, from Latin *conductum,* from *condūcere,* to lead together, CONDUCT.]

con·duce (kən-déwss ‖ kon-, -dŏŏss) *intr.v.* **-duced, -ducing, -duces.** To contribute or lead to a particular end or result. Used with *to* or *towards.* [Middle English *conducen,* from Latin *condūcere,* to lead together, be useful, contribute : *com-,* together + *dūcere,* to lead.] —**con·duc·er** *n.*

con·du·cive (kən-déw-siv ‖ kon-, -dŏŏ-) *adj.* Conducing; promoting; contributive. Used with *to.* See Synonyms at **favourable.** —**con·du·cive·ness** *n.*

con·duct (kən-dúkt ‖ kon-) *v.* **-ducted, -ducting, -ducts.** —*tr.* **1.** To direct the course of; manage; carry out: *conduct an opinion poll.* **2.** To guide or escort: *a conducted tour.* **3.** To direct or guide (an orchestra or other musical group), with movements of the hands or a baton. **4.** To serve as a medium or channel for conveying; transmit (heat or electricity, for example). **5.** To behave. Used reflexively. —*intr.* **1.** To act as a conductor. **2.** To be capable of transmitting heat, electricity, or other forms of energy. —See Synonyms at **accompany.**
~*n.* (kón-dukt). **1.** The way a person acts; behaviour. **2.** The act of directing or controlling; management; administration. **3.** *Obsolete.* A guide or escort. —See Synonyms at **behaviour.** [Middle English *conducten,* from Medieval Latin *condūcere,* to escort, from Latin, to lead together : *com-,* together + *dūcere,* to lead.] —**con·duct·i·bil·i·ty** (-dúktə-bílləti) *n.* —**con·duct·i·ble** (-dúktəb'l) *adj.*

Synonyms: *conduct, direct, manage, control, steer, supervise, oversee.*

con·duc·tance (kən-dúktənss ‖ kon-) *n.* A measure of a material's ability to conduct electric charge, the real part of the complex representation of **admittance** *(see).*

con·duc·tim·e·try (kón-duk-tímmətri, kən-dúk-) *n.* The study of chemical analyses that involve titrations based on changes in the electrical conductance of a solution.

con·duc·tion (kən-dúksh'n ‖ kon-) *n.* The transmission or conveying of something through a medium or passage, especially: **1.** The transmission of electric charge or heat through a conducting medium without perceptible motion of the medium itself. **2.** The transmission of a nerve impulse along a nerve fibre.

con·duc·tive (kən-dúktiv ‖ kon-) *adj.* Exhibiting conductivity.

con·duc·tiv·i·ty (kón-duk-tívvəti) *n. Symbol* σ **1.** A measure of the ability of a material to conduct an electric charge, the reciprocal of **resistivity** *(see).* See **thermal conductivity. 2.** The ability or power to conduct or transmit.

con·duc·tor (kən-dúktər ‖ kon-) *n.* **1.** A person who conducts or leads. **2.** The person who collects the fares on a bus or train. **3.** One who conducts an orchestra or other musical ensemble. **4.** *Physics.* A substance or medium that conducts heat, sound, or an electric current. —**con·duc·tor·ship** *n.* —**con·duc·tress** *n.*

con·duit (kón-dit, kún-, -dew-it ‖ -doo-it, -dwit) *n.* **1.** A channel or pipe for conveying water or other fluids. **2.** A tube or duct for enclosing electric wires or cable. **3.** *Archaic.* A fountain. [Middle English, from Old French, conveyance, from Medieval Latin *conductus,* escort, transportation, from Latin, past participle of *condūcere,* to lead together, CONDUCT.]

con·du·pli·cate (kon-déwpli-kət, -kit, -kayt ‖ -dŏŏpli-) *adj. Botany.* Folded in half lengthways. Said especially of unopened leaves. [Latin *conduplicātus,* past participle of *conduplicāre,* to double, fold together : *com-,* together + *duplicāre,* to double, DUPLICATE.] —**con·du·pli·ca·tion** (-káysh'n) *n.*

con·dyle (kón-dil, -dīl) *n.* A rounded articulatory prominence at the end of a bone. [French, from Latin *condylus,* knuckle, from Greek *kondulos†.*] —**con·dy·lar** (-ər) *adj.* —**con·dy·loid** *adj.*

con·dy·lo·ma (kóndi-lṓ-mə) *n., pl.* **-mas** or **-mata** (-mətə). A wart-like growth near the anus or external genitalia, usually a result of venereal infection. [New Latin, from Greek *kondulōma* : *kondulos,* knuckle, CONDYLE + -OMA.] —**con·dy·lom·a·tous** (-lómmə-təss, -lṓmə-) *adj.*

cone (kōn) *n.* **1.** *Geometry.* **a.** A surface generated by a straight line, the *generator,* passing through a fixed point, the *vertex,* and moving along the intersection with a fixed curve, the *directrix.* **b.** The surface generated by such a generator passing through a vertex lying on the perpendicular axis of a circular directrix. Also called "right circular cone". **2. a.** The figure formed by such a surface bound, or regarded as bound, by its vertex and a plane section taken anywhere above or below the vertex. **b.** Anything having the shape of this figure. **3. a.** A conical, spheroidal, or cylindrical structure borne by certain trees, such as the pines, firs, and cypresses, consisting of clusters of stiff, overlapping, woody scales, between which are the naked ovules. **b.** Any similar structure, such as the fruit of the magnolia or hop or the reproductive structure of pteridophytes. Also called "strobilus". **4.** A photoreceptor in the retina of the eye that is sensitive to colour and bright light. Compare **rod. 5.** Any of various gastropod molluscs of the family Conidae, of tropical seas, having a conical, often vividly marked shell. Also called "cone shell". **6.** A volcanic peak with a wide base. **7.** An **ice-cream cone** *(see).*
~*tr.v.* **coned, coning, cones.** To shape like a cone or cone segment. [French *cône,* from Latin *cōnus,* from Greek *kōnos.*]

cone-flow·er (kṓn-flowr) *n.* Any of various North American plants of the genera *Rudbeckia, Ratibida,* and *Echinacea,* having rayed flowers with a conelike centre of tubular florets.

coney. Variant of **cony.**

conf. conference.

con·fab (kón-fab, *rarely* -fáb) *n. Informal.* A confabulation; a chat. ~*intr.v.* (*also* kən-fáb) **confabbed, -fabbing, -fabs.** *Informal.* To talk informally; confabulate.

con·fab·u·late (kən-fábbew-layt ‖ kon-) *intr.v.* **-lated, -lating, -lates. 1.** To talk informally; chat. **2.** *Psychiatry.* To replace fact with fantasy in memory. [Latin *confābulārī* : *com-,* together + *fābulārī,* to talk, from *fābula,* story, conversation, from *fārī,* to speak.] —**con·fab·u·la·tion** (-láysh'n) *n.* —**con·fab·u·la·to·ry** (-lə-tri, -təri, -láytəri) *adj.*

con·fect (kən-fékt ‖ kon-) *tr.v.* **-fected, -fecting, -fects.** To put together; make.
~*n.* (kón-fekt). *Archaic.* A sweet confection; a comfit. [Middle English *confecten,* from Latin *conficere* (past participle *confectus*), to prepare : *com-* (intensive) + *facere,* to make.]

con·fec·tion (kən-féksh'n ‖ kon-) *n.* **1.** The act or a product of compounding, mixing, or preparing. **2.** A sweet preparation, such as a cake or a preserve. **3.** A sweetened medicinal compound. **4.** Especially formerly, a stylish article of women's clothing.

con·fec·tion·ar·y (kən-féksh'n-əri ‖ kon-, *U.S.* -erri) *adj.* Pertaining to or resembling confections or their preparation.

con·fec·tion·er (kən-féksh'n-ər ‖ kon-) *n.* One who makes or sells confections, especially sweets.

confectioners' sugar *n. U.S.* **Icing sugar** *(see).*

con·fec·tion·er·y (kən-féksh'n-əri, -nəri ‖ kon-, *U.S.* -erri) *n., pl.* **-ies. 1.** Sweets and other confections collectively. **2.** The art or occupation of a confectioner. **3.** A confectioner's shop; a sweetshop.

con·fed·er·a·cy (kən-féddrə-si, -féddərə- ‖ kon-) *n., pl.* **-cies. 1.** A union of persons, parties, or states; an alliance; a league. **2.** A combination for unlawful practices; a conspiracy. **3.** *Capital* C. The Confederate States of America. [Middle English *confederacie,* from Anglo-French, from Latin *confoederātiō,* union, from *confoederāre,* to unite. See **confederate.**]

con·fed·er·ate (kən-féd-rət, -féddə-, -rit ‖ kon-, -rayt) *n.* **1.** A member of a confederacy; an ally. **2.** One who assists in a plot; an accomplice. **3.** *Capital* C. Formerly, a supporter of the Confederate States of America. —See Synonyms at **partner.**
~*adj.* **1.** United in a confederacy; allied. **2.** *Capital* C. Of or pertaining to the Confederate States of America.
~*v.* (-féddərayt) **confederated, -ating, -ates.** —*tr.* To form into a confederacy. —*intr.* To unite into, or become part of, a confederacy. [Middle English *confederat,* from Latin *confoederātus,* from past participle of *confoederāre,* to unite in a league : *com-,* together + *foederāre,* to unite, from *foedus,* league.] —**con·fed·er·a·tive** (-rətiv) *adj.*

Confederate States of America *n. Abbr.* **C.S.A.** The confederation of 11 Southern states that seceded from the United States (1860–65), comprising Alabama, Arkansas, Florida, Georgia, Louisiana, Mississippi, North Carolina, South Carolina, Tennessee, Texas, and Virginia. Also called the "Confederacy", "Southern Confederacy".

con·fed·er·a·tion (kən-féddə-ráysh'n, kón-) *n. Abbr.* **confed. 1.** An act of confederating or a state of being confederated. **2.** A group of confederates, especially of states or nations, united for a common purpose; a league. Compare **federation.** —**con·fed·er·a·tion·ism** *n.* —**con·fed·er·a·tion·ist** *n.*

con·fer (kən-fér ‖ kon-) *v.* **-ferred, -ferring, -fers.** —*tr.* **1.** To bestow (an honour or degree, for example). Used with *on* or *upon.* **2.** *Archaic.* To compare. —*intr.* To hold a conference; compare views; consult together. [Latin *conferre,* to bring together, contribute, bestow : *com-,* together + *ferre,* to bring, bear.] —**con·fer·ment, con·fer·ral** *n.* —**con·fer·ra·ble** *adj.* —**con·fer·rer** *n.*

con·fer·ee (kón-fer-ée, *in sense 1 also* -fər-) *n.* **1.** A participant in a conference. **2.** One upon whom something is conferred.

con·fer·ence (kón-frənss, -fərənss) *n. Abbr.* **conf. 1.** A meeting for consultation or discussion. **2.** A formal meeting, especially one held annually, at which delegates representing different states or organisations, or different branches of the same organisation, discuss and debate matters of common interest. **3.** In the Methodist and some other Protestant churches, the annual assembly of clerical and lay members that constitutes the governing body of such churches. **4.** An association for mutual benefit. **5.** The act of conferring, as of a degree; bestowal or conferral. —**in conference.** Taking part in a meeting or discussion. [Old French, from Medieval Latin *conferentia,* from Latin *conferēns* (stem *conferent-*), present participle of *conferre,* to CONFER.] —**con·fer·en·tial** *adj.*

conference call *n.* A conference by telephone in which three or more people in different places participate by means of a central switching unit.

conference pear *n.* A cultivated pear with sweet, juicy flesh and a dark green skin flushed with russet.

con·fer·va (kən-fér-və ‖ kon-) *n., pl.* **-vae** (-vee) or **-vas.** Any of various bright green, threadlike freshwater algae, especially any of the genus *Tribonema.* [New Latin, from Latin *conferva,* COMFREY.] —**con·fer·void** *n. & adj.*

con·fess (kən-féss ‖ kon-) *v.* **-fessed, -fessing, -fesses.** —*tr.* **1.** To disclose or acknowledge (something damaging or inconvenient to oneself). **2.** To concede the truth or validity of; admit. **3.** To acknowledge belief or faith in. **4. a.** To make known (one's sins), especially to a priest for absolution. **b.** To confess thus the sins of (oneself). **c.** To hear the confession of. Used of a priest. —*intr.* **1.** To admit or acknowledge a crime or deed. Sometimes used with *to.* **2.** To tell one's sins to a priest. —See Synonyms at **acknowl-**

edge. [Middle English *confessen,* from Old French *confesser,* from Late Latin *confessāre,* frequentative of *confitērī* (past participle *confessus*), to acknowledge : *com-* (intensive) + *fatērī,* to admit.]
con·fess·ed·ly (kən-féss-idli || kon-) *adv.* By one's own admission; admittedly.
con·fes·sion (kən-fésh'n || kon-) *n.* **1.** The act or an instance of confessing; an acknowledgment; an avowal; an admission. **2.** A formal declaration of guilt. **3.** The disclosure of sins to a priest for absolution. **4.** An avowal of belief in the doctrines of a particular faith. Also called "confession of faith". **5.** A church or group of worshippers adhering to a particular creed.
con·fes·sion·al (kən-fésh'nəl || kon-) *adj.* Of, pertaining to, or resembling confession.
~*n.* **1.** A small enclosed stall in a church, in which a priest hears confessions. **2.** The act of confessing to a priest.
con·fes·sor (kən-féssər || kon-) *n.* **1.** A priest who hears confession and gives absolution. **2.** One who confesses. **3.** One who confesses faith in Christianity in the face of persecution but does not suffer martyrdom: *King Edward the Confessor.*
con·fet·ti (kən-fétti, kon-) *n. Used with a singular verb.* Small pieces of coloured paper thrown during festive celebrations, especially at the bride and groom after a wedding. [Italian, plural of *confetto,* confection, from Medieval Latin *confectum,* from Latin *confectus,* past participle of *conficere,* to put together, prepare, CONFECT.]
con·fi·dant (kónfi-dánt, -dant, -dóN || *U.S. also* -daánt, -daant) *n.* One to whom secrets or private matters are confided. [French *confident,* from Italian *confidente,* from Latin *confīdēns* (stem *confīdent-*), present participle of *confīdere,* to CONFIDE.]
con·fi·dante (kónfi-dánt, -dant, -dóNT || *U.S. also* -daánt, -daant) *n.* A female confidant. [French *confidente,* feminine of *confident,* CONFIDANT.]
con·fide (kən-fīd || kon-) *v.* **-fided, -fiding, -fides.** —*tr.* **1.** To tell (something) in confidence. **2.** To entrust (something) to another. —*intr.* To tell private matters to another in confidence. Used with *in.* —See Synonyms at **commit.** [Middle English *confiden,* from Old French *confider,* from Latin *confīdere* : *com-* (intensive) + *fīdere,* to trust.] **—con·fid·er** *n.*
con·fi·dence (kónfidənss) *n.* **1.** Trust in a person or thing. **2.** A trusting relationship in which secrets may be imparted: *took us into her confidence.* **3.** Something confided, such as a secret. **4.** A feeling of assurance or certainty, especially in oneself and one's capabilities. **—in confidence** As a secret. —See Synonyms below and at **trust.**
Synonyms: *confidence, assurance, aplomb, self-confidence, self-possession, self-reliance.*
confidence interval *n.* A statistical range, bounded by confidence limits, with a stipulated probability that a given parameter lies within the range.
confidence limit *n.* One of the two values reasonably chosen to specify the limits of a confidence interval.
confidence man *n.* One who swindles by using a confidence trick or tricks. Also informally called "con man".
confidence trick *n.* A swindle in which the victim is defrauded after his confidence has been won. Also *U.S.* "confidence game". **—confidence trickster** *n.*
con·fi·dent (kónfi-dənt || *U.S. also* -dent) *adj.* **1.** Having or indicating assurance or certainty, as of success. **2.** Having confidence in oneself; self-assured. **3.** *Archaic.* Very bold; presumptuous. **4.** *Obsolete.* Confiding; trustful. —See Synonyms at **sure.**
~*n.* A confidant. [Latin *confīdēns* (stem *confīdent-*), present participle of *confīdere,* to CONFIDE.] **—con·fi·dent·ly** *adv.*
con·fi·den·tial (kónfi-dénsh'l) *adj.* **1.** Done or communicated in confidence; told in secret. **2.** Entrusted with the confidence of another; intimate: *a confidential secretary.* **3.** Denoting trust or intimacy: *a confidential tone of voice.* **—con·fi·den·ti·al·i·ty** (-dénshi-ál-əti), **con·fi·den·tial·ness** *n.* **—con·fi·den·tial·ly** *adv.*
con·fid·ing (kən-fīding || kon-) *adj.* Trusting; unsuspicious. **—con·fid·ing·ly** *adv.* **—con·fid·ing·ness** *n.*
con·fig·u·ra·tion (kən-fíggewr-áysh'n, kón-, -fíggər-) *n.* **1. a.** The arrangement of the parts or elements of something. **b.** The form of a figure as determined by the arrangement of its parts; an outline; a contour. **2.** *Psychology.* A **gestalt** *(see).* **3.** *Chemistry.* **Conformation** *(see).* [Late Latin *configūrātiō* (stem *configūrātiōn-*), from Latin *configūrāre,* "to form together", fashion after : *com-,* together + *figūrāre,* to form, from *figūra,* shape, FIGURE.] **—con·fig·u·ra·tive** (-ətiv || -aytiv), **con·fig·u·ra·tion·al** *adj.* **—con·fig·u·ra·tion·al·ly** *adv.*
con·fine (kən-fīn || kon-) *v.* **-fined, -fining, -fines.** —*tr.* **1.** To keep within bounds; restrict. **2.** To shut within an enclosure; imprison. **3.** To keep (a woman who is about to give birth) in bed. Used in the passive. —*intr. Archaic.* To border; be adjacent. —See Synonyms at **limit.**
~*n.* (kón-fīn; *also* kən-fīn *for sense 2*). **1.** *Usually plural.* A border or limit; a boundary. **2.** *Archaic.* Confinement. **3.** *Obsolete.* A place of confinement. —See Synonyms at **boundary.** [Old French *confiner,* from *confin,* boundary, limit, from Latin *confīne,* from *confīnis,* having the same border : *com-,* together + *fīnis,* border, end.] **—con·fin·a·ble, con·fine·a·ble** *adj.* **—con·fin·er** *n.*
con·fine·ment (kən-fīn-mənt || kon-) *n.* **1.** The act of confining or the state of being confined. **2.** The state of being confined prior to and during childbirth. **3.** *Physics.* The theory that the attractive force between two quarks increases as the quarks are pulled apart as a result of the exchange of gluons, used to explain why quarks cannot be found as free particles.
con·firm (kən-fúrm || kon-) *tr.v.* **-firmed, -firming, -firms. 1.** To assure the certainty or validity of; corroborate; verify. **2.** To make more firm; strengthen: *She confirmed my suspicions.* **3.** To make valid or binding by a formal or legal act; ratify. **4.** To administer the religious rite of confirmation to. [Middle English *confirmen,* from Old French *confirmer,* from Latin *confirmāre* : *com-* (intensive) + *firmāre,* to make firm, strengthen, from *firmus,* firm.] **—con·firm·a·ble** *adj.* **—con·firm·er** *n.*
Synonyms: *confirm, corroborate, substantiate, authenticate, validate, prove, establish, ratify, verify.*
con·fir·ma·tion (kón-fər-máysh'n) *n.* **1.** An act of confirming. **2.** That which confirms; corroboration or verification. **3.** A rite admitting a baptised person to full membership in a church. **—con·firm·a·to·ry** (kən-fúrmə-tri, -təri, kón-fər-máytəri), **con·firm·a·tive** (kən-fúrmətiv || kon-) *adj.*
con·firmed (kən-fúrmd || kon-) *adj.* Firmly established in a given state or habit, and unlikely to change; inveterate: *a confirmed bachelor.* **—con·firm·ed·ly** (-fúrmidli) *adv.*
con·fis·ca·ble (kən-fískəb'l || kon-) *adj.* Subject to confiscation.
con·fis·cate (kón-fiss-kayt || -viss-) *tr.v.* **-cated, -cating, -cates. 1.** To seize (private property) for a public treasury, especially by way of penalty. **2.** To seize by or as by authority.
~*adj.* Confiscated; appropriated. [Latin *confiscāre,* to lay up in a chest, confiscate : *com-* (collective) + *fiscus,* chest, the treasury.] **—con·fis·ca·tion** (-káysh'n) *n.* **—con·fis·ca·tor** (-kaytər) *n.*
Con·fit·e·or (kən-fítti-awr || kon-, -féeti-) *n. Roman Catholic Church.* A prayer in which confession of sins is made. [Latin, "I confess" (first word of the prayer).]
con·fla·grant (kən-fláygrənt || kon-) *adj. Archaic.* Burning intensely; blazing. [Latin *conflagrāns* (stem *conflagrant-*), present participle of *conflagrāre,* to burn up. See **conflagration.**]
con·fla·gra·tion (kón-flə-gráysh'n) *n.* A large, blazing, and destructive fire. [Latin *conflagrātiō* (stem *conflagrātiōn-*), from *conflagrāre,* to burn up : *com-* (intensive) + *flagrāre,* to burn, blaze.]
con·flate (kən-fláyt || kon-) *tr.v.* **-flated, -flating, -flates.** To fuse or blend into a single unit (especially two versions of a text).
con·fla·tion (kən-fláysh'n, kon-) *n.* **1.** A combining, as of two variant texts into one text. **2.** A product of this; especially, a text or reading arrived at by fusing material from different sources. [Middle English *conflacioun,* from Late Latin *conflātiō* (stem *conflātiōn-*), from Latin *conflāre,* "to blow together", combine two readings : *com-,* together + *flāre,* to blow.]
con·flict (kón-flikt) *n.* **1.** A prolonged battle; a struggle. **2.** The clash of opposing ideas or forces; disagreement; opposition. **3.** *Psychology.* Inner struggle resulting from the opposition of irreconcilable impulses, desires, or tendencies. **4.** A crashing together; a collision. —See Synonyms at **discord.**
~*intr.v.* (kən-flíkt || kon-) **conflicted, -flicting, -flicts. 1.** To come into opposition; collide; differ. **2.** To fight; do battle. [Middle English, from Latin *conflīctus,* from the past participle of *conflīgere,* to clash together, contend : *com-,* together + *flīgere,* to strike.] **—con·flic·tion** (-fliksh'n) *n.* **—con·flic·tive** *adj.*
Synonyms: *conflict, contest, combat, fight, affray, melee, scuffle.*
con·flic·ting (kən-flíkting || kon-) *adj.* Mutually incompatible or contradictory: *conflicting ideologies; conflicting reports.* **—con·flic·ting·ly** *adv.*
con·flu·ence (kón-floo-ənss || -flew-) *n.* Also **con·flux** (-fluks). **1.** A flowing together, as of two or more streams. **2.** The point of juncture of such streams. **3.** A gathering together; a crowd.
con·flu·ent (kón-floo-ənt || -flew-) *adj.* **1.** Flowing together; blended into one. **2.** *Pathology.* Merging together so as to form a mass. Said of sores in a rash. **3.** *Anatomy.* Coalesced. Said for example of two originally separate bones.
~*n.* **1.** A confluent stream. **2.** A tributary. [Middle English, from Latin *confluēns* (stem *confluent-*), present participle of *confluere,* to flow together : *com-,* together + *fluere,* to flow.]
con·fo·cal (kón-fōk'l) *adj.* Having the same focus or foci.
con·form (kən-fórm || kon-) *v.* **-formed, -forming, -forms.** —*intr.* **1.** To come to have the same form or character as another or each other. **2.** To act or be in accord or agreement; comply. Used with *to* or *with.* **3.** To act in accordance with current customs or modes. **4.** To comply with the usages of an established church, especially the Church of England. —*tr.* **1.** To make similar. **2.** To bring into agreement or correspondence. Often used reflexively. —See Synonyms at **agree.** [Middle English *conformen,* from Old French *conformer,* from Latin *conformāre,* "to have the same form" : *com-,* same, similar + *formāre,* to shape, from *forma,* form, shape.] **—con·form·er** *n.*
con·form·a·ble (kən-fórm-əb'l || kon-) *adj.* **1.** In harmony or agreement; corresponding; consistent. Often used with *to* or *with.* **2.** Quick to comply; submissive. **3.** *Geology.* Designating strata that are parallel to each other without interruption. **—con·form·a·bil·i·ty** (-ə-bílləti), **con·form·a·ble·ness** *n.* **—con·form·a·bly** *adv.*
con·for·mal (kən-fórm'l || kon-) *adj.* **1.** *Mathematics.* Designating a depiction of a surface or region upon another surface so that all angles between intersecting curves remain unchanged. **2.** Of, pertaining to, or designating a map projection in which angles around any point are true, and at any point the scale is the same in any direction, so that small areas are rendered with true shape. [Late Latin *confōrmālis,* having the same form : Latin *com-,* same, similar + *fōrmālis,* having a form, FORMAL.] **—con·for·mal·ly** *adv.*
con·for·ma·tion (kón-fawr-máysh'n, -fər-) *n.* **1.** The structure or outline of something as determined by the arrangement of its parts. **2.** The act of conforming or state of being conformed; adjustment;

adaptation. **3.** *Chemistry.* The shape of a molecule or an atom as determined by the three-dimensional arrangement of its constituents. Also called "configuration".

conformation theory *n. Chemistry.* The theory that the stability and reactivity of a molecule can be predicted from its three-dimensional structure, especially with respect to the conformation of organic molecules and their substituents.

con·form·ist (kən-fórmist || kon-) *n.* **1.** One who conforms to current standards or customs. **2.** *Abbr.* **Con.** One who complies with the usages of an established church, especially the Church of England. Compare **dissenter, nonconformist** —**con·form·ism** *n.*

con·form·i·ty (kən-fórməti || kon-) *n., pl.* **-ties.** Also **con·form·ance** (-fórmənss). **1.** Similarity in form or character; correspondence; agreement. **2.** Action or behaviour in correspondence with current customs, rules, or styles. **3.** Compliance with the usages of an established church, especially the Church of England.

con·found (kən-fównd; *in sense 6 also* kón- || kon-, *West Indies also* -fúngd) *tr.v.* **-founded, -founding, -founds. 1.** To cause to become confused or disordered; bewilder. **2.** To mix up (incompatible elements or ideas). **3.** To fail to distinguish; confuse; mix up. **4.** To cause to be ashamed; abash. **5.** To defeat; overthrow. **6.** To damn. Used in mild oaths: *Confound it!* —See Synonyms at **puzzle.** [Middle English *confounden,* from Old French *confondre,* from Latin *confundere,* to pour together, mix up : *com-,* together + *fundere,* to pour.] —**con·found·er** *n.*

con·found·ed (kən-fówndid, kón- || kon-) *adj.* **1.** Confused; befuddled. **2.** Damned. Used as a mild oath: *a confounded fool.* —**con·found·ed·ly** *adv.* —**con·found·ed·ness** *n.*

con·fra·ter·ni·ty (kón-frə-térnəti) *n., pl.* **-ties.** An association of men united by profession or in some common purpose, usually of a religious or charitable nature. [Middle English *confraternite,* from Old French, from Medieval Latin *confrāternitās* (stem *confrāternitāt-*), from *confrāter,* colleague, CONFRERE.]

con·frere (kón-frair) *n.* A fellow member of a fraternity or profession; a colleague. [Middle English, from Old French, from Medieval Latin *confrāter,* colleague, fellow member : Latin *com-,* together + *frāter,* brother.]

con·front (kən-frúnt || kon-) *tr.v.* **-fronted, -fronting, -fronts. 1.** To come face to face with; stand in front of. **2.** To face with hostility or defiance. **3.** To bring close together for comparison; compare. **4.** To cause to meet or face: *confronted them with the evidence of their guilt.* **5.** To come up against; encounter. [Old French *confronter,* from Medieval Latin *confrontāre,* to have a common border : Latin *com-,* together + *frōns* (stem *front-*), forehead, FRONT.] —**con·front·er** *n.*

con·fron·ta·tion (kón-frun-táysh'n, -frən-) *n.* The act of confronting; especially, a condition or stance of conflict and rivalry rather than of conciliation. —**con·fron·ta·tion·ist** *adj.*

Con·fu·cian·ism (kən-féwsh'n-iz'm || kon-) *n.* The ethical system based on the teachings of Confucius, emphasising personal virtue, devotion to family (including the spirits of one's ancestors), and justice. —**Con·fu·cian** *adj. & n.* —**Con·fu·cian·ist** *n.*

Con·fu·cius (kən-féwshəss) (*c.* 551-479 B.C.). *Chinese* **Kong-zi** (kŏŏng-dzə), **Kong-fu-zi** (kŏŏng-fōō-dzə). Chinese philosopher, who was a statesman and adviser to various feudal lords. When none would implement his philosophy of perfecting one's own moral character, he became a teacher. Many books and sayings have been attributed to him, but few can be authenticated.

con·fuse (kən-féwz || kon-) *tr.v.* **-fused, -fusing, -fuses. 1.** To disturb the thought process, perceptions, or purpose of; perplex. **2.** To assemble without order or sense; jumble. **3.** To make less clearcut; blur: *confuse an important issue.* **4.** To fail to distinguish: *confuse a word with a near synonym.* [Back-formation from Middle English *confused,* from Old French *confus,* from Latin *confūsus,* past participle of *confundere,* to mix up, CONFOUND.] —**con·fus·ed·ly** (-idli) *adv.* —**con·fus·ed·ness** *n.* —**con·fus·er** *n.* —**con·fus·ing·ly** *adv.*

con·fu·sion (kən-féw<u>zh</u>'n || kon-) *n.* **1.** The act of confusing or state of being confused. **2.** Disorder; jumble. **3.** Distraction; bewilderment. —**con·fu·sion·al** *adj.*

con·fu·ta·tion (kón-few-táysh'n) *n.* **1.** An act of confuting. **2.** Something that confutes. —**con·fu·ta·tive** (kən-féwtətiv || kon-, kón-few-taytiv) *adj.*

con·fute (kən-féwt || kon-) *tr.v.* **-futed, -futing, -futes.** To prove conclusively that (a person or argument) is wrong or in error. [Latin *confūtāre,* to check, restrain.] —**con·fut·a·ble** *adj.* —**con·fut·er** *n.*

Cong. Congregational.

con·ga (kóng-gə) *n.* **1.** A dance of Latin-American origin in which the dancers form a long, winding line. **2.** Music for this dance. ~*intr.v.* **congaed, -gaing, -gas.** To dance the conga. [American Spanish *(danza) Conga,* "the Congo (dance)", from CONGO.]

conga drum *n.* A tall, narrow bass drum beaten with the hands.

con·gé (kón-<u>zh</u>ay, KÓN- || *U.S. also* kon-<u>zh</u>áy, KON-) *n.* Also **con·gee** (kón-jee). **1.** Formal or authoritative permission to depart. **2.** An abrupt dismissal. **3. a.** *Archaic.* A formal bow. **b.** A leave-taking. **4.** *Architecture.* A kind of concave moulding.
~*intr.v.* **congéed, -géeing, -gées.** *Archaic.* **1.** To take ceremonious leave. **2.** To make a formal bow. [French, from Old French *congie,* from Latin *commeātus,* "a going to and fro", from *commeāre,* to go to and fro : *com-,* mutually, back and forth + *meāre,* to go.]

con·geal (kən-jéel || kon-) *v.* **-gealed, -gealing, -geals.** —*intr.* **1.** To solidify, as by freezing. **2.** To coagulate; jell. —*tr.* To cause to solidify or coagulate. [Middle English *congelen,* from Old French *congeler,* from Latin *congelāre,* to freeze solid : *com-,* together + *gelāre,* to freeze.] —**con·geal·a·ble** *adj.* —**con·geal·er** *n.* —**con·geal·ment** *n.* —**con·ge·la·tion** (kón-ji-láysh'n) *n.*

con·ge·ner (kónji-nər, kən-jéenər) *n.* **1.** A member of the same kind, class, or group. **2.** An organism belonging to the same genus as another or others. [Latin, of the same race : *com-,* same + *genus* (stem *gener-*), race, kind.] —**con·ge·ner·ic** (-nérrik), **con·gen·er·ous** (-jénnərəss) *adj.*

con·gen·i·al (kən-jéen-i-əl, -yəl || kon-) *adj.* **1.** Having the same tastes, habits, or temperament; sympathetic. **2.** Suited to one's needs or tastes; agreeable. [CON- (same) + GENIAL.] —**con·ge·ni·al·i·ty** (-i-ál-əti), **con·gen·ial·ness** *n.* —**con·gen·ial·ly** *adv.*

con·gen·i·tal (kən-jénnit'l || kon-) *adj.* **1.** Existing at birth but not hereditary: *a congenital defect.* **2.** Having a specified character as if by nature: *a congenital thief.* —See Synonyms at **innate.** [Latin *congenitus,* born together with : *com-,* together + *genitus,* born, past participle of *gignere,* to beget.] —**con·gen·i·tal·ly** *adv.*

con·ger (kóng-gər) *n.* Any of various large marine eels of the family Congridae; especially, *Conger conger,* of northern waters. Also called "conger eel". [Middle English *congre,* from Old French, from Latin *conger, congrus,* from Greek *gongros,* of Mediterranean origin.]

con·ge·ries (kon-jéer-eez, -jérri-, -iz) *n. Used with a singular verb.* A collection of things heaped together; an aggregation. [Latin *congeriēs,* heap, pile, from *congerere,* to bring together, CONGEST.]

con·gest (kən-jést || kon-) *v.* **-gested, -gesting, -gests.** —*tr.* **1.** To overfill or overcrowd. **2.** *Pathology.* To cause excessive blood to accumulate in (a vessel or organ). **3.** To block (the nose). Used of mucus. —*intr.* To become congested. [Latin *congerere* (past participle *congestus*), to bring together, heap up : *com-,* together + *gerere,* to carry.] —**con·ges·tive** *adj.*

con·ges·tion (kən-jéss-chən, -jésh- || kon-) *n.* **1. a.** An accumulation of blood in a bodily organ. **b.** An accumulation of mucus in the nose. **2.** A congested or overcrowded condition, especially as caused by traffic.

con·glo·bate (kóng-glō-bayt, -glə- || kon-glṓ-) *v.* **-bated, -bating, -bates.** Also **con·globe** (kon-glṓb) **-globed, -globing, -globes.** —*intr.* To become a globe or globule. —*tr.* To gather into a globe or ball.
~*adj.* Shaped like or formed into a ball. [Latin *conglobāre* : *com-,* together + *globāre,* to make into a globe, from *globus,* globe.] —**con·glo·ba·tion** (-báysh'n) *n.*

con·glom·er·ate (kən-glómmər-ayt || kon-) *v.* **-ated, -ating, -ates.** —*tr.* To collect into a cohesive mass. —*intr.* To form into an adhering or rounded mass.
~*n.* (-ət, -it, -ayt). **1.** A collected heterogeneous mass; a cluster. **2.** *Geology.* A rock consisting of pebbles and gravel embedded in fine-grained material. Also called "pudding stone". **3.** A business concern made up of a number of different companies that operate in widely diversified fields.
~*adj.* (-ət, -it, -ayt). **1.** Gathered into a cohesive mass; clustered. **2.** *Geology.* Made up of cemented heterogeneous material. [Latin *conglomerāre,* to roll together : *com-,* together + *glomerāre,* to roll into a ball, from *glomus,* ball.] —**con·glom·er·at·ic** (-áttik) *adj.*

con·glom·er·a·tion (kən-glómmər-áysh'n, kón-) *n.* **1.** The process of conglomerating or state of being conglomerated. **2.** A collection or mass of miscellaneous things. **3.** A cohesive mass.

con·glu·ti·nate (kən-glṓōti-nayt || kon-, -gléw-) *v.* **-nated, -nating, -nates.** —*intr.* **1.** To become stuck or glued together; adhere. **2.** *Medicine.* To become reunited. Used of bones or tissues. —*tr.* **1.** To stick or glue together. **2.** *Medicine.* To cause (bones or tissues) to reunite. [Middle English *conglutinaten,* from Latin *conglūtināre,* to glue together : *com-,* together + *glūtināre,* to glue, from *glūten,* glue.] —**con·glu·ti·nant** *adj.* —**con·glu·ti·na·tion** (-náysh'n) *n.* —**con·glu·ti·na·tive** (-nətiv, -naytiv) *adj.*

Congo. River of Central Africa, also known as the Zaire from 1971 to 1997. Formed by the confluence of the rivers Lualaba and Luvua near the Congo (Dem.Rep.)-Zambian border, it flows 4 667 kilometres (2,900 miles) west and southwest, forming the Congo (Dem.Rep.)-Congo (Rep. of) border, to enter the Atlantic Ocean through a wide delta at Boma. It was explored by Captain J. Tuckey (1816), David Livingstone (1871) and Henry Stanley (1874–77). It is navigable by shipping to Matadi and is the second longest river of Africa.

Congo, Democratic Republic of the. Formerly Belgian Congo, Congo (Kinshasa), Zaire. Republic of Central Africa. Situated almost entirely in the basin of the Congo river, with a small coastline on the Atlantic Ocean. It is largely equatorial rainforest with the Ruwenzori Mountains in the southeast and savannah in the north and south. Discovered by the Portuguese (15th century), it was a source of slaves (17th–19th century) and in 1908 was annexed by Belgium from whom independence was gained in 1960. In 1965 Mobutu Sese Seko seized power and in ensuing years ruthlessly put down any insurrection. His corrupt rule came to an end in 1997 when Laurent Kabila seized power. The country is impoverished but has potential for growing tea, coffee, rubber, cocoa, palm oil and cotton and there are reserves of copper, zinc, cobalt, diamonds, oil and natural gas. Area, 2 344 885 square kilometres (905,365 square miles). Population, 46,810,000. Capital, Kinshasa.

Congo, Republic of the. Formerly Congo (Brazzaville) or French Congo. Country in west Central Africa. Oil from offshore fields and timber are the main exports. The Portuguese encountered the powerful Kongo kingdom in the 15th and 16th centuries. The area

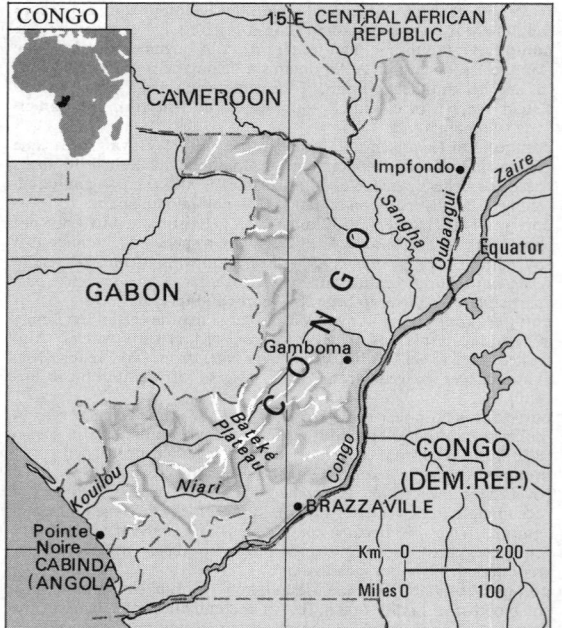

was claimed by France, and in 1910 became the Middle Congo, a territory of French Equatorial Africa. In 1960 it was granted independence as the Republic of the Congo (Brazzaville). The country became Africa's first Marxist state in 1970. In 1977 a military junta assumed control. Multi-party democracy was eventually restored in 1992. Area, 342 000 square kilometres (132,047 square miles). Population, 2,670,000. Capital, Brazzaville.

Congo (Brazzaville), Republic of the. See **Congo, Republic of the.**

Congo (Kinshasa), Republic of the. See **Congo, Democratic Republic of.**

Con·go·lese (kóng-gə-léez) *adj.* Of or pertaining to the region of the Congo and the two Congo republics or their inhabitants.
~*n., pl.* **Congolese.** An inhabitant of the region of the Congo or of either of the two Congo republics.

Congo peacock *n.* A variety of **peacock** (*see*).

Congo red *n.* A brownish-red powder, $C_{32}H_{22}N_6O_6S_2Na_2$, used as a diagnostic indicator, dye, chemical indicator, and biological stain.

congou. Variant of **conggou.**

con·grat·u·late (kən-gráttew-layt, -grácha- || kon-, *U.S. also, nonstandard,* -grája-) *tr.v.* **-lated, -lating, -lates. 1.** To acknowledge or express one's pleasure at the achievement or good fortune of. Usually used with *on* or *upon*. **2.** To take pride in (oneself) for an achievement. [Latin *congrātulārī,* to rejoice with someone : *com-*, with + *grātulārī,* to express one's joy, rejoice, from *grātus,* pleasing.] —**con·grat·u·la·tor** (-laytər) *n.*

con·grat·u·la·tion (kən-gráttew-láysh'n, -grácha-, || kon-; *U.S. also, nonstandard,* -grája-) *n.* **1.** The act of congratulating. **2.** *Plural.* Acknowledgment of the achievement or good fortune of another. Often used as an interjection. Also *informal* "congrats".

con·grat·u·la·to·ry (kən-gráttew-lə-tri, -grácha-, -təri, -láytəri || kon-) *adj.* Conveying or expressing congratulations.

con·gre·gant (kóng-gri-gənt) *n.* A member of a congregation, especially a Jewish one.

con·gre·gate (kóng-gri-gayt) *v.* **-gated, -gating, -gates.** —*intr.* To come together in a crowd; assemble. —*tr.* To bring together in a crowd or an assembly; collect. [Middle English *congregaten,* from Latin *congregāre,* to assemble : *com-,* together + *gregāre,* to flock together, from *grex* (stem *greg-*), herd, flock.] —**con·gre·ga·tor** (-gaytər) *n.*

con·gre·ga·tion (kóng-gri-gáysh'n) *n.* **1.** An act of congregating. **2.** A body of assembled people or things; a gathering. **3. a.** A group of people gathered for religious worship. **b.** The members of a specific religious group who regularly worship at a particular church. **4.** *Roman Catholic Church.* Any of several committees of the **Curia** (*see*). **5.** *Chiefly British.* An assembly of the senior members of a university. Compare **convocation.**

con·gre·ga·tion·al (kóng-gri-gáysh'n-'l) *adj.* **1.** Of or pertaining to a congregation. **2.** *Capital* **C.** *Abbr.* **Cong.** Of or pertaining to Congregationalism or Congregationalists.

Congregational Church *n.* An evangelical Protestant denomination practising Congregationalism and, since 1972, part of the United Reformed Church.

Con·gre·ga·tion·al·ism (kóng-gri-gáysh'n-'l-iz'm) *n.* The system of government and religious beliefs of the Congregational Church, in which each member church is self-governing. —**Con·gre·ga·tion·al·ist** *n. & adj.*

Congregation of the Holy Office *n.* The official name for the **Holy Office** (*see*).

con·gress (kóng-gress || *chiefly U.S.* -griss) *n.* **1.** A formal assembly of representatives, as of various nations or of an association, to discuss problems and policy. **2.** The national legislative bodies of certain nations. **3.** *Capital* **C.** *Abbr.* **Cong., C. a.** The national legislative body of the United States, consisting of the Senate and the House of Representatives. **b.** The two-year session of this legislature between elections of the House of Representatives. **4.** *Capital* **C.** Any of certain political parties, such as the Indian National Congress and the African National Congress. **5.** Sexual intercourse. [Middle English *congresse,* a coming together, from Latin *congressus,* from *congredī,* to come together : *com-,* together + *gradī,* to go.]

con·gres·sion·al (kən-grésh'n-'l || kon-) *adj.* **1.** Of or pertaining to a congress. **2.** *Capital* **C.** *Abbr.* **Cong.** Of or pertaining to the Congress of the United States.

con·gress·man (kóng-gress-mən || -griss-) *n., pl.* **-men** (-mən, -men). *Often capital* **C.** A member of a Congress, especially the U.S. Congress and in particular its House of Representatives.

con·gress·wom·an (kóng-gress-wŏomən || -griss-) *n., pl.* **-women** (-wimmin). *Often capital* **C.** A female member of a Congress, especially the House of Representatives of the U.S. Congress.

Con·greve (kóng-greev), **William** (1670–1729). English dramatist, brought up in Ireland. He is best known for his witty comedies, including *Love for Love* (1695) and *The Way of the World* (1700).

con·gru·ence (kóng-groo-ənss || kən-gróō-, -gréw-) *n.* Also **con·gru·en·cy** (-i). **1.** Agreement; conformity. **2.** *Mathematics.* **a.** The state of being congruent. **b.** A mathematical statement that two quantities are congruent.

con·gru·ent (kóng-groo-ənt || kən-gróō-, -gréw-) *adj.* **1.** Corresponding; congruous. **2.** *Mathematics.* **a.** Coinciding exactly when superimposed: *congruent triangles.* **b.** Having a difference divisible by a modulus: *congruent numbers.* [Middle English, from Latin *congruēns* (stem *congruent-*), present participle of *congruere†,* to meet together, agree.] —**con·gru·ent·ly** *adv.*

con·gru·i·ty (kon-gróō-əti, kən- || -gréw-) *n., pl.* **-ties. 1.** The quality or fact of being congruous. **2.** A point of agreement. **3.** *Geometry.* Exact coincidence when superimposed.

con·gru·ous (kóng-groo-əss) *adj.* Corresponding in character or kind; appropriate; harmonious. [Latin *congruus,* from *congruere†,* to meet together, agree.]

con·ic (kónnik). Also **con·i·cal** (kónnik'l). **1.** Shaped like a cone. **2.** Pertaining to a cone.
~*n. Mathematics.* A conic section. [New Latin *conicus,* from Greek *kōnikos,* from *kōnos,* CONE.]

conic projection *n.* In cartography, a method of projecting pictures of parts of the earth's spherical surface onto a tangent cone, which is then flattened to a plane surface having concentric circles as parallels of latitude and radiating lines from the apex as meridians. Also called "conical projection".

con·ics (kónniks) *n. Used with a singular verb.* The study of conic sections.

conic section *n.* One of a group of plane curves, including the circle, ellipse, hyperbola, and parabola, generated by: **1.** An intersection of a right circular cone and a plane. **2.** The plane locus of a point that moves so that the ratio of its distance to a fixed point to its distance from a fixed line is a positive constant. **3.** A graph of the general quadratic equation in two variables.

co·nid·i·o·phore (kō-níddi-ə-fawr, kə- || -fōr) *n.* A specialised hyphal filament in certain fungi, bearing conidia. [CONIDI(UM) + -PHORE.]

co·nid·i·um (kō-níddi-əm, kə-) *n., pl.* **-ia** (-ə). An asexual spore in certain fungi that is produced at the tip of a conidiophore. [New Latin (diminutive), from Greek *konis,* dust.] —**co·nid·i·al** *adj.*

con·i·fer (kónni-fər, kóni-) *n.* Any gymnosperm tree of the order Coniferales, typically evergreen and bearing cones, such as the pine, spruce, cypress, yew, or fir. [New Latin *Coniferae* (family name), from Latin *cōnifer,* cone-bearing : *cōnus,* CONE + -FER.]

co·nif·er·ous (kō-níffərəss, ko-, kə-) *adj.* **1.** Bearing cones. **2.** Of or composed of conifers.

co·ni·ine (kóni-een, kóneen) *n.* A poisonous, colourless liquid alkaloid, $C_8H_{17}N$, obtained from the poison hemlock and formerly used in the treatment of spasmodic disorders. Also called "Z-propylpiperidine". [German *Koniin* : CONIUM + -IN.]

con·i·sa·tion (kón-ī-záysh'n || *U.S.* -i-) *n.* Surgical removal of a cone of tissue, especially from the cervix of the uterus. [CON(E) + -IS(E) + -ATION.]

co·ni·um (kóni-əm) *n.* Any of several poisonous plants of the genus *Conium,* including the **hemlock** (*see*). [New Latin *Conium,* from Late Latin *cōnīum,* poison hemlock, from Greek *kōneion,* perhaps from *kōnos,* cone (from its indented, pinnatifid leaves suggesting pine cones).]

conj. 1. conjugation. **2.** *Grammar.* conjunction; conjunctive. **3.** *Astronomy.* conjunction.

con·jec·tur·al (kən-jék-chər-əl, -choor- || kon-) *adj.* **1.** Involving conjecture. **2.** Inclined to conjecture. —**con·jec·tur·al·ly** *adv.*

con·jec·ture (kən-jékchər || kon-) *v.* **-tured, -turing, -tures.** —*tr.* To infer from inconclusive evidence; guess. —*intr.* To make a conjecture.
~*n.* **1.** Inference based on inconclusive or incomplete evidence; guesswork. **2.** An opinion or conclusion based on incomplete evidence. [Middle English, from Old French, from Latin *conjectūra,* conclusion, interpretation, from *conjicere,* "to throw together", put together mentally, conjecture, interpret : *com-,* together + *jacere,* to throw.] —**con·jec·tur·a·ble** *adj.* —**con·jec·tur·a·bly** *adv.* —**con·jec·tur·er** *n.*

Synonyms: *conjecture, surmise, guess, speculate, presume, infer.*

con·join (kən-jóyn, kon-) *v.* **-joined, -joining, -joins.** *—tr.* To join together; connect; unite. *—intr.* To become joined or connected. [Middle English *conjoinen,* from Old French *conjoindre,* from Latin *conjungere* : *com-,* together + *jungere,* to join.] **—con·join·er** *n.*

con·joint (kón-joynt, kən-jóynt, kon-) *adj.* **1.** Joined together; connected; associated. **2.** Of, pertaining to, or involving two or more associated parties; joint. [Middle English, from Old French, past participle of *conjoindre,* to CONJOIN.] **—con·joint·ly** *adv.*

con·ju·gal (kónjōōg'l || kən-jōōg'l, kon-) *adj.* Of or pertaining to marriage or the marital relationship. [Old French, from Latin *conjugālis,* from *conjux* (stem *conjug-*), a spouse, from *conjungere,* to join together (in marriage) : *com-,* together + *jungere,* to join.] **—con·ju·gal·i·ty** (kónjōō-gál-əti) *n.* **—con·ju·gal·ly** *adv.*

conjugal rights *pl.n.* A right to sexual intercourse with one's husband or wife.

con·ju·gant (kónjōōgənt) *n.* Either of a pair of organisms, cells, or gametes undergoing conjugation. [Latin *conjugāns* (stem *conjugant-*), present participle of *conjugāre,* to CONJUGATE.]

con·ju·gate (kón-jōō-gayt, -jə-) *v.* **-gated, -gating, -gates.** *—tr. Grammar.* To inflect (a verb) in the forms corresponding to person, number, tense, mood, and voice. *—intr.* **1.** *Biology.* To undergo conjugation. **2.** *Grammar.* **a.** To inflect or admit of inflection. Used of a verb. **b.** To inflect a verb.

~adj. (-gət, -git, -gayt). **1.** Joined together, especially in a pair or pairs; coupled. **2.** *Mathematics & Physics.* Inversely or oppositely related with respect to one of a group of otherwise identical properties; especially, designating either or both of a pair of complex numbers differing only in the sign of the imaginary term. **3.** *Grammar.* Designating words that have the same derivation and usually a related meaning. **4.** *Geometry.* Designating two angles that together have a sum of 360°.

~n. (-gət, -git, -gayt). **1.** *Grammar.* One of two or more conjugate words. **2.** *Mathematics & Physics.* Either of a pair of conjugate quantities. [Middle English *conjugat,* joined, from Latin *conjugātus,* past participle of *conjugāre,* to yoke or join together : *com-,* together + *jugāre,* to yoke, from *jugum,* yoke.] **—con·ju·ga·tive** (-gətiv, -gaytiv) *adj.* **—con·ju·ga·tor** (-gaytər) *n.*

con·ju·gat·ed (kón-jōō-gaytid, -jə-) *adj. Chemistry.* **1.** Designating a double bond that is separated from another double bond in a molecule by one single bond. **2.** Designating a molecule or compound containing two or more double bonds that alternate with single bonds. **3.** Designating a substance that is formed by the combination of two compounds.

conjugated protein *n.* A compound consisting of a protein attached to a nonprotein group, such as a lipid or a carbohydrate.

con·ju·ga·tion (kón-jōō-gáysh'n, -jə-) *n. Abbr.* **conj. 1.** *Grammar.* **a.** The inflection of a particular verb. **b.** A presentation of the complete set of inflected forms of a verb. **c.** A class of verbs having similar inflected forms. Compare **declension. 2.** *Biology.* **a.** A process of sexual reproduction in ciliate protozoans, certain algae, and some bacteria, in which two individuals of the same species temporarily couple and exchange genetic material. **b.** Chromosome pairing in the first meiotic division. **c.** The fusion of gamete nuclei; karyogamy. **d.** The union of sex cells; syngamy. **—con·ju·ga·tion·al** *adj.* **—con·ju·ga·tion·al·ly** *adv.*

conjugation tube *n.* A slender protoplasmic tube formed between two algae undergoing conjugation, through which exchange of gametes between the individuals occurs.

con·junct (kón-jungkt, kon-júngkt) *adj.* **1.** Joined together; united. **2.** Associated with another; joint. [Middle English, from Latin *conjunctus,* past participle of *conjungere,* to join together : *com-,* together + *jungere,* to join.] **—con·junct·ly** *adv.*

con·junc·tion (kən-júngksh'n || kon-) *n.* **1.** The act of joining or state of being joined; combination. **2.** Simultaneous occurrence; coincidence. **3.** *Abbr.* **conj.** *Grammar.* A part of speech comprising words such as, in English, *and, but, because, as,* that connect other words, phrases, clauses, or sentences. See **coordinating conjunction, correlative conjunction, subordinate conjunction. 4.** *Abbr.* **conj.** *Astronomy.* The position of two celestial bodies on the celestial sphere when they have the same celestial longitude. **5.** *Logic.* **a.** A compound proposition in which the components are joined by the word *and,* which is true only if both or all the components are true. **b.** The relationship between the components of such a proposition. **—con·junc·tion·al** *adj.* **—con·junc·tion·al·ly** *adv.*

con·junc·ti·va (kón-jungk-tī-və) *n., pl.* **-vas** or **-vae** (-vee). The mucous membrane that lines the inner surface of the eyelid and the exposed surface of the eyeball. [Middle English, from Medieval Latin *(membrāna) conjunctīva,* "the connective (membrane)", from Late Latin *conjunctīvus,* CONJUNCTIVE.] **—con·junc·ti·val** *adj.*

con·junc·tive (kən-júngk-tiv || kon-) *adj.* **1.** Joining; connective. **2.** Joined together; combined. **3.** *Abbr.* **conj.** *Grammar.* **a.** Designating or used as a conjunction. **b.** Serving to connect elements of meaning and construction in a sentence, as do *and* and *but.*

~n. Abbr. **conj.** *Grammar.* A connective word, especially a conjunction. [Late Latin *conjunctīvus,* from Latin *conjunctus,* CONJUNCT.] **—con·junc·tive·ly** *adv.*

con·junc·ti·vi·tis (kən-júngkti-vī-tiss || kon-) *n. Pathology.* Inflammation of the conjunctiva. See **pinkeye.** [New Latin : CONJUNCTIV(A) + -ITIS.]

con·junc·ture (kən-júngkchər || kon-) *n.* A combination of circumstances or events, especially one of a critical nature; a crisis.

con·ju·ra·tion (kónjoor-áysh'n) *n.* **1. a.** A solemn invocation. **b.** A magic spell or incantation. **2.** Magic; legerdemain.

con·jure (*in tr. sense 1* kən-jóor || kon-; *in other senses* kún-jər || kon-) *v.* **-jured, -juring, -jures.** *—tr.* **1.** To call upon or entreat solemnly, especially by an oath. **2.** To summon (a devil or spirit) by incantation or magic spell. **3.** To cause or effect by or as by magic. *—intr.* **1.** To practise magic; especially, to perform tricks using sleight of hand. **2.** To summon a devil by incantation or magic spell. **—conjure up. 1.** To bring into existence as if by magic. **2.** To bring to the mind's eye; evoke. [Middle English *conjuren,* from Old French *conjurer,* from Medieval Latin *conjūrāre,* to invoke with oaths or incantations, from Latin, to swear together, conspire : *com-,* together + *jūrāre,* to swear.]

con·jur·er, con·jur·or (kún-jərər || kón-) *n.* One who practises magic tricks or legerdemain, especially as an entertainer.

conk (kongk) *n. Slang.* **1.** The nose. **2.** The head. **3.** A blow, especially on the head.

~tr.v. **conked, conking, conks.** *Slang.* To hit, especially on the head. **—conk out. 1.** To fail suddenly. **2.** To tire, fall asleep, or faint after exertion. **3.** To die. [Probably alteration of CONCH.]

con·ker (kóngkər) *n.* The brown shiny nut of the **horse chestnut** *(see).* [From dialect *conker,* snail shell (later replaced by horse chestnuts in the game), perhaps (through influence of CONQUER) an alteration of CONCH.]

con·kers (kóngkərz) *n. Used with a singular verb.* A children's game in which each contestant swings a conker threaded on a string and tries to hit and break that held by the opponent.

con man *n. Slang.* A **confidence man** *(see).*

con moto (kon mōtō) *adv. Music.* With movement; spiritedly. Used as a direction. [Italian.]

Conn. Connecticut.

Con·nacht (kónnəkht, kónnət). Formerly **Con·naught** (kónnawt). Province in the northwest of the Republic of Ireland. It consists of counties Galway, Leitrim, Mayo, Roscommon, and Sligo.

con·nate (kónnayt) *adj.* **1.** Part of or existing in someone or something from birth; inborn; innate. **2.** Coexisting since birth or origin; cognate; related. **3.** *Biology.* Congenitally or firmly united. Said of similar parts or organs. [Late Latin *connātus,* past participle of *connascī,* to be born together : *com-,* together + Latin *nascī,* to be born.] **—con·nate·ly** *adv.* **—con·na·tion** (kə-náyshən) *n.*

con·nat·u·ral (kə-náchərəl) *adj.* **1.** Innate; congenital; natural. **2.** Related or similar in nature; cognate. [Medieval Latin *connātūrālis* : *com-,* together + Latin *nātūrālis,* NATURAL.] **—con·nat·u·ral·ly** *adv.* **—con·nat·u·ral·ness** *n.*

con·nect (kə-nékt) *v.* **-nected, -necting, -nects.** *—tr.* **1.** To join or fasten together; link; unite. **2.** To associate or consider as related. **3.** To establish communication between, especially by telephone. **4.** To join to a communications circuit. *—intr.* **1.** To be or become joined or united. **2.** To operate so that passengers can easily transfer from one route or mode of transport to another. Used of means of public transport. **3.** *Informal. Sports.* To make a successful hit, kick, or stroke; make contact. **4.** *Slang.* To be successful; have the desired effect. —See Synonyms at **join.** [Middle English *connecten,* from Latin *connectere* : *com-,* together + *nectere,* to bind, tie.] **—con·nect·ed·ly** *adv.* **—con·nect·i·ble, con·nect·a·ble** *adj.* **—con·nec·tor** (-néktər), **con·nect·er** *n.*

Usage: *Connect* may be used with either *to* or *with* in standard English. Informally, *up* is also often used (*Connect X up with Y*), but it is considered unnecessary in formal speech or writing.

Con·nect·i·cut (kə-nétti-kət). State in the northeastern United States, in the area known as New England. Connecticut was one of the 13 founder states of the Union.

con·nect·ing rod (kə-nékting) *n.* **1.** A rod linking rotating parts of a machine in reciprocating motion. **2.** Such a rod connecting the crankshaft of an internal-combustion engine to a piston.

con·nec·tion (kə-néksh'n) *n.* Also *British* **con·nex·ion.** *Abbr.* **con. 1.** The act of joining or state of being joined; union. **2.** Anything that joins, relates, or connects; a bond; a link. **3. a.** The fact of being related or associated: *wanted in connection with a series of robberies.* **b.** A point of relationship or association: *What was her connection with the deceased?* **4.** The logical ordering of words or ideas; coherence. **5.** The relation of a word or idea to the surrounding text; context. **6.** A person with whom one is associated, especially by professional or family ties: *has some useful connections in the City.* **7. a.** The meeting of various means of transport for the transfer of passengers. **b.** A connecting train, plane, or the like: *missed my connection.* **8.** A line of communication between two points in a telephone system. **9.** A point of contact in an electrical circuit: *a loose connection.* **10.** A religious organisation or denomination. **11.** *Slang.* **a.** A dealer in illegal drugs. **b.** A major supply route for illegal drugs. **—in this** or **that connection.** Relating to this (or that) matter. **—con·nec·tion·al** *adj.*

con·nec·tive (kə-néktiv) *adj.* Serving or tending to connect.

~n. **1.** Anything that connects. **2.** *Grammar.* A word, such as a conjunction, that connects words, phrases, clauses, and sentences. **3.** *Botany.* The tissue of a stamen that forms the division between the two lobes of an anther. **—con·nec·tive·ly** *adv.* **—con·nec·tiv·i·ty** (kónnek-tívvəti) *n.*

connective tissue *n.* Tissue arising chiefly from the embryonic mesoderm, consisting typically of a jelly-like matrix in which are embedded collagen and elastic fibres, fat cells, fibroblasts, mast cells, and the like. It supports and separates organs and occurs in tendons, ligaments, cartilage, and bone.

Con·ne·ma·ra (kónni-maarə). Region of County Galway in the west of the Republic of Ireland, between the Atlantic Ocean and loughs Mask and Corrib.

con·ning tower (kónning) n. 1. The armoured wheelhouse of a warship. 2. A raised, enclosed observation post in a submarine, also usually used as a means of entrance and exit. [From CON (to steer).]

con·nip·tion (kə-nípsh'n) n. U.S. Informal. A fit of anger or hysteria. [19th century : origin obscure.]

con·niv·ance (kə-nîv'nss) n. 1. The act of conniving. 2. Law. Knowledge of, and tacit consent to, the commission of an illegal act by another.

con·nive (kə-nîv) intr.v. -nived, -niving, -nives. 1. To feign ignorance of a wrong, thus implying tacit encouragement or consent. Used with at. 2. To cooperate secretly or conspire. Used with with. [French conniver, from Latin connivēre, cōnivēre, to close the eyes, be indulgent.] —con·niv·er n.

Usage: In is sometimes used to replace *at* in informal English: *I connived in what he did.*

con·ni·vent (kə-nîv'nt) adj. Biology. Converging and touching, but not fused together. Said especially of stamens or an insect's wings. [Latin connivēns (stem connivent-), present participle of connivēre, "to bend together", close the eyes, CONNIVE.]

con·nois·seur (kónnə-sér, -soor, -séwr) n. A person with informed and astute discrimination, especially concerning the arts or matters of taste. [Obsolete French, from Old French connoisseor, from connoistre, to know, from Latin cognōscere, to get acquainted with, know thoroughly : co-, together + gnōscere, nōscere, to know.] —con·nois·seur·ship n.

Con·nors (kónnərz), **(James Scott) "Jimmy"** (1952-). U.S. tennis player. He twice won both the U.S. and the Wimbledon men's singles titles (1974, 1982), and also won the U.S. title in 1976, 1978 and 1983.

con·no·ta·tion (kónnō-táysh'n, kónnə-) n. 1. The fact or quality of connoting. 2. What is implied or suggested by a word or thing, beyond its literal or explicit sense. 3. Logic. The total of the attributes constituting the meaning of a term; intension. —See Usage note at, and compare, **denotation.** —con·no·ta·tive (-taytiv, kə-nôtətiv) adj. —con·no·ta·tive·ly adv.

con·note (ko-nôt, kə-) tr.v. -noted, -noting, -notes. 1. To suggest or imply in addition to literal meaning. 2. To involve as a condition or consequence. [Medieval Latin connotāre, "to mark in addition" : Latin com-, together with + notāre, to mark, note, from nota, a mark, note.]

con·nu·bi·al (kə-néwbi-əl, ko- ‖ -nóōbi-) adj. Of marriage or the married state; conjugal. [Latin connūbiālis, from connūbium, marriage : com-, together + nūbere, to marry.] —con·nu·bi·al·i·ty (-ál-əti) n. —con·nu·bi·al·ly adv.

co·no·dont (kónə-dont, kónnə-) n. Any of various small, toothlike fossils of the Palaeozoic era, of unknown origin. [Greek kōnos, cone + -ODONT.]

co·noid (kónoyd) adj. Also **co·noid·al** (kō-nóyd'l). Cone-shaped; conical.
~n. 1. Something that is cone-shaped. 2. A geometric surface obtained when a parabola, ellipse, or hyperbola is rotated about one axis. [CON(E) + OID.]

con·quer (kóngkər) v. -quered, -quering, -quers. —tr. 1. To defeat or subdue by force, especially by force of arms. 2. To gain or secure control of by or as if by force of arms. 3. To overcome or surmount by physical, mental, or moral force: conquer one's fear of flying. 4. To climb (a mountain) successfully. —intr. To be victorious; win. —See Synonyms at **defeat.** [Middle English conqueren, from Old French conquerre, from Vulgar Latin conquaerere (unattested), variant of Latin conquīrere, to search for, procure, win : con- (intensive) + quaerere, to seek.] —con·quer·a·ble adj.

con·quer·or (kóngkərər) n. Someone who conquers.

con·quest (kóng-kwest, kón-) n. 1. The act or process of conquering. 2. Something acquired by conquering, especially territory. 3. A successful amorous exploit: boasting about his latest conquest. 4. Someone whose love or favour has been captured. —the **Conquest.** The **Norman Conquest** (see). [Middle English conquest(e), from Old French, from Vulgar Latin conquaesītus (unattested), past participle of conquaerere (unattested), to CONQUER.]

con·qui·an (kóng-ki-ən) n. A card game resembling rummy, for two players. Also called "cooncan". [(Mexican) Spanish con quién, with whom?]

con·quis·ta·dor (kon-kwístə-dawr, kən-, -kéestə-dór) n., pl. -dores (-dórez) or -dors. A conqueror; specifically, any of the Spanish conquerors of Central and South America, especially Mexico and Peru, in the 16th century. [Spanish, from conquistar, to conquer, from Medieval Latin conquestāre, frequentative of Vulgar Latin conquaerere (unattested). See **conquer.**]

Con·rad (kón-rad), **Joseph,** born Teodor Josef Konrad Korzeniowski (1857-1924). Polish-born novelist who became a major English literary figure. His masterpieces include Lord Jim (1900), The Heart of Darkness (1902), and Under Western Eyes (1911).

Con·ran (kón-rən), **Sir Terence Orby** (1931-). British interior designer. Combining a practical flair for design with a keen business sense, he brought good interior design to the public at reasonable prices in his Habitat stores, the first of which opened in 1964.

con rod n. Informal. A connecting rod.

cons. 1. consigned; consignment. 2. consonant. 3. constable. 4. constitution; constitutional. 5. construction.

Cons. 1. Conservative. 2. Constable. 3. Consul.

con·san·guin·e·ous (kón-sang-gwinni-əss) adj. Also **con·san·guine** (kon-sáng-gwin). Of the same lineage or origin; especially, related by blood. [Latin consanguineus : com-, joint + sanguineus, of blood, SANGUINE.] —con·san·guin·e·ous·ly adv.

con·san·guin·i·ty (kón-sang-gwínnəti) n. 1. Blood relationship. 2. Any close connection or affinity.

con·science (kónsh'nss) n. 1. The faculty of recognising the distinction between right and wrong in regard to one's own conduct, together with the feeling that one ought not to do wrong. 2. a. A feeling or consciousness of conformity to one's own sense of right conduct: a clear conscience. b. Informal. A feeling of remorse; a bad conscience. 3. Archaic. Consciousness. —in all conscience. 1. In fairness; reasonably. 2. Certainly. —on (one's) conscience. Causing remorse. [Middle English, from Old French, from Latin conscientia, from consciēns (stem conscient-), present participle of conscīre, to be conscious, know well : com- (intensive) + scīre, to know.] —con·science·less adj.

conscience clause n. A clause in a law that recognises or exempts persons whose moral scruples forbid compliance.

conscience money n. Money paid to atone for some concealed dishonest or morally wrong act.

con·science-stric·ken (kónsh'nss-strickən) adj. Feeling guilty or remorseful about something one has done or failed to do.

con·sci·en·tious (kónshi-énshəss) adj. 1. Governed by or accomplished according to conscience; scrupulous. 2. Thorough and painstaking; careful and diligent. —See Synonyms at **meticulous.** [French conscientieux, from Medieval Latin conscientiōsus, from Latin conscientia, CONSCIENCE.] —con·sci·en·tious·ly adv. —con·sci·en·tious·ness n.

conscientious objector n. Abbr. CO, C.O. One who on the basis of his religious or moral principles refuses to bear arms or participate in military service.

con·scion·a·ble (kónsh'n-əb'l) adj. In accordance with conscience. [From conscions, obsolete variant of CONSCIENCE + -ABLE.]

con·scious (kónshəss) adj. 1. a. Characterised by awareness of one's own existence, sensations, and thoughts, and of one's environment. b. Having a particular preception; aware: conscious of having offended her. 2. Not asleep; awake. 3. Subjectively known and felt: She spoke with conscious pride. 4. Intentionally conceived or done; deliberate: a conscious insult. 5. Self-conscious. 6. Concerned about or interested in something. Often used in combination: fashion-conscious.
~n. That component of waking awareness perceptible by an individual at any given instant; the conscious mind; consciousness. [Latin conscius, knowing with others, participating in knowledge, aware of : com-, with + scīre, to know.] —con·scious·ly adv.

Usage: Conscious, subconscious, preconscious, and *unconscious.* These are psychological terms referring to aspects of the workings of the mind. *Conscious* refers to mental processes, such as thoughts or emotional reactions, of which a person is aware. *Subconscious* pertains to thoughts or feelings outside the immediate awareness either wholly or partly. *Preconscious* refers to mental processes that are outside the consciousness, but are easily brought into the conscious mind. *Unconscious* alludes to all mental processes that a person is not aware of, including thoughts or feelings that have been forgotten or repressed, and also images, instincts, desires, and the like. It is often used interchangeably with *subconscious.*

con·scious·ness (kónshəss-nəss, -niss) n. 1. The state or condition of being conscious. 2. The essence or totality of attitudes, opinions, and sensitivities held or thought to be held by an individual or group: national consciousness. 3. The conscious. 4. A critical awareness of one's own indentity and situation.

con·scious·ness-rais·ing (kónshəss-nəss-rayzing, -niss-) n. The gaining or facilitating of greater awareness of oneself and one's situation so as to be able to achieve one's full potential.

con·script (kón-skript) n. One who is compulsorily enrolled for service in the armed forces.
~adj. (kón-skript). Enrolled compulsorily.
~tr.v. (kən-skrípt ‖ kon-) conscripted, -scripting, -scripts. 1. To enrol compulsorily for service in the armed forces. 2. To force into service. [Old French, enlisted, from Latin conscriptus, past participle of conscrībere, to write together, enter in a list, enrol : com-, together + scrībere, to write.]

con·scrip·tion (kən-skrípshən ‖ kon-) n. Compulsory enlistment in the armed forces.

con·se·crate (kón-si-krayt) tr.v. -crated, -crating, -crates. 1. To make, declare, or set apart as sacred: consecrate a church. 2. a. To change (bread and wine) into the body and blood of Christ, according to the doctrines of orthodox Christianity. b. To sanctify (bread and wine) to be taken as a memorial of Christ, according to the beliefs of the Reformed churches. 3. To initiate (a priest) into the order of bishops. 4. To dedicate to some service or goal. 5. To make venerable: a tradition consecrated by time. —See Synonyms at **devote.**
~adj. Archaic. Consecrated. [Middle English consecraten, from Latin consecrāre : com- (intensive) + sacrāre, to make sacred, from sacer, sacred.] —con·se·cra·tive (-kraytiv) adj. —con·se·cra·tor (-kraytər) n. —con·se·cra·to·ry (-kráytəri ‖ U.S. -krə-tawri) adj.

con·se·cra·tion (kón-si-kráysh'n) n. 1. The act, process, or ceremony of consecrating. 2. The state of being consecrated.

con·se·cu·tion (kón-si-kéwsh'n) n. 1. A sequence or succession. 2. The relation of consequent to antecedent; deduction; inference. [Latin consecūtiō (stem consecūtiōn-), sequence, from consequī, to follow up. See **consequent.**]

con·sec·u·tive (kən-séckew-tiv || kon-) *adj.* **1.** Following successively without interruption. **2.** Marked by logical sequence. **3.** *Music.* Designating harmonic intervals of a similar kind. **4.** *Grammar.* Expressing a consequence. [French *consécutif,* Medieval Latin *consecūtīvus,* from Latin *consequī,* to follow up. See **consequent.**] **—con·sec·u·tive·ly** *adv.* **—con·sec·u·tive·ness** *n.*

con·sen·su·al (kən-sén-sew-əl || kon-, -shoo-) *adj.* **1.** Based on or involving mutual consent or consensus. **2.** *Physiology.* Responding to reflex stimulation. Said especially of certain reflex actions by parts of the body that respond to stimulation of another part. [From CONSENSUS (after SENSUAL).] **—con·sen·su·al·ly** *adv.*

con·sen·sus (kən-sén-səss, kon-) *n.* Collective opinion or concord; general agreement or accord; a majority view. Also used adjectivally: *consensus politics.* [Latin, from *consentīre,* to agree, CONSENT.]

Usage: The phrase *consensus of opinion* is widely used in informal speech and writing, and is sometimes used in formal speech. But people aware of the definition of *consensus* (which already contains the notion of "opinion") avoid the phrase, on the grounds that it contains a redundant element.

con·sent (kən-sént || kon-) *intr.v.* **-sented, -senting, -sents. 1.** To give assent or permission; accede; agree. **2.** *Archaic.* To agree in opinion; be of the same mind. —See Synonyms at **assent.**

~n. **1.** Voluntary acceptance or allowance of what is planned or done by another; permission. **2.** Agreement as to opinion or a course of action: *by common consent.* [Middle English *consenten,* from Old French *consentir,* from Latin *consentīre,* to feel together, agree : *com-,* together + *sentīre,* to feel.] **—con·sent·er** *n.*

con·sen·ta·ne·ous (kón-sen-táyni-əss) *adj.* **1.** Consistent; accordant. **2.** Unanimous. [Latin *consentāneus,* from *consentīre,* to feel together, CONSENT.] **—con·sen·ta·ne·i·ty** (kən-séntə-neé-əti, -náy- || kon-), **con·sen·ta·ne·ous·ness** *n.* **—con·sen·ta·ne·ous·ly** *adv.*

con·sen·tient (kən-sénsh'nt, -sénti-ənt) *adj.* United in agreement.

con·se·quence (kón-si-kwənss || -kwenss) *n.* **1.** That which rationally or naturally follows from an action or condition; an effect; a result. **2.** A logical result or inference. **3.** Importance in rank: *someone of consequence.* **4.** Significance: *a matter of little consequence.* —See Synonyms at **effect, importance.**

con·se·quen·ces (kón-si-kwən-siz || -kwen-) *n. Used with a singular verb.* A party game in which a story is made up from contributions written by all the players, each player being ignorant of what the others have written.

con·se·quent (kón-si-kwənt || -kwent) *adj.* **1. a.** Following as a natural effect, result, or conclusion. **b.** Following as a logical conclusion. **2.** Logically correct or consistent. **3.** *Geology.* Having a position or direction resulting from the original slope of the earth's surface: *consequent rivers.* In this sense, compare **obsequent, subsequent.**

~n. **1.** Anything that follows something else, usually with causal relation. **2.** An outcome or result. **3.** *Logic.* The second part of a conditional proposition, whose truth is dependent on the truth of the antecedent. **4.** *Mathematics.* The second term of a ratio. [Middle English, from Old French, from Latin *consequēns* (stem *consequent-*), present participle of *consequī,* to follow up, accompany : *com-,* together + *sequī,* to follow.]

Usage: The usual prepositions following the adjectival sense of this word are *on* or *upon. To* is also common, but this usage increases the likelihood of confusion with *subsequent to. Consequent* usually implies a causal or logical relationship with what has gone before; *subsequent* has no such meaning, being equivalent to "after".

con·se·quen·tial (kón-si-kwén-sh'l) *adj.* **1.** Following as an effect, result, or conclusion; resultant; consequent. **2.** Self-important; pompous. **3.** Important; significant. **—con·se·quen·ti·al·i·ty** (-shi-ál-əti), **con·se·quen·tial·ness** *n.* **—con·se·quen·tial·ly** *adv.*

con·se·quent·ly (kón-si-kwənt-li || -kwent-) *adv.* As a result; therefore.

con·ser·van·cy (kən-sérv'nssi || kon-) *n., pl.* **-cies. 1.** Conservation, especially of natural resources. **2.** *British.* A commission supervising fisheries, navigation, forests, or the like.

con·ser·va·tion (kón-sər-váysh'n) *n.* **1.** The act of conserving; preservation from loss, depletion, waste, or harm. **2.** The systematic preservation of the environment, especially of natural resources such as topsoil, forests, and waterways. **—con·ser·va·tion·al** *adj.*

con·ser·va·tion·ist (kón-sər-váysh'n-ist) *n.* One who practises or advocates the conservation of natural resources, and the protection of plant and animal species and the natural environment.

conservation law *n.* **1.** *Physics.* A law stating that a given quantity, such as mass, energy, or charge, cannot be created or destroyed regardless of changes of distribution of that quantity within a system. **2.** A law by which a government seeks to prohibit certain stipulated actions in order to preserve a natural amenity or resource.

conservation of energy *n. Physics.* An exact conservation law stating that the total energy of an isolated system remains constant regardless of changes within the system.

conservation of mass *n. Physics.* The classical principle that the total mass of an isolated system is unchanged by interaction of its parts.

conservation of momentum *n. Physics.* An exact conservation law stating that the total linear or angular momentum of an isolated system remains constant regardless of changes within the system.

con·ser·va·tism (kən-sérvətiz'm || kon-) *n.* **1.** The disposition in politics or culture to maintain the existing order and to resist or oppose change or innovation. **2.** The principles and practises of persons or groups so disposed. **3.** *Capital* **C.** The principles and practises of the Conservative Party.

con·ser·va·tive (kən-sérvətiv || kon-) *adj.* **1.** Tending to favour the preservation of the existing order; averse to and distrustful of change. **2.** *Capital* **C.** *Abbr.* **Con.** Belonging to, supporting, or characteristic of the Conservative Party. **3.** *Capital* **C.** *Chiefly U.S.* Adhering to or characteristic of Conservative Judaism. **4.** Moderate; prudent; cautious. **5.** Traditional in manner or style; not showy. **6.** Tending to conserve; conserving; preservative.

~n. **1.** A conservative person; especially, one who supports or belongs to a conservative political party. **2.** *Capital* **C.** *Abbr.* **C.** A member or supporter of the Conservative Party. **—con·ser·va·tive·ly** *adv.* **—con·ser·va·tive·ness** *n.*

Conservative Judaism *n. Chiefly U.S.* A grouping within Judaism that holds a modified view of the sanctity of the Torah and is flexible in its submission to the authority of the Rabbinical Law, accepting some liturgical and ritual changes in the light of the needs of modern life. Compare **Orthodox Judaism, Reform Judaism.**

Conservative Party *n.* The major right-wing British political party, which supports private enterprise and privatisation and opposes state control and nationalisation. Also officially called "Conservative and Unionist Party".

con·ser·va·toire (kən-sérvə-twaar, -saírvə- || kon-, -twawr) *n.* A school where musical and, sometimes, other artistic training is given. Also *U.S.* "conservatory". [French.]

con·ser·va·tor (kən-sérvətər, kón-sər-vaytər) *n.* **1.** Someone who preserves from injury or violation; a protector. **2.** A custodian of an art gallery or museum. **3.** *Law.* A guardian; a keeper.

con·ser·va·to·ry (kən-sérvə-tri, -təri || kon-) *n., pl.* **-ries. 1.** A glass-enclosed room or greenhouse, usually forming part of a dwelling, in which plants are grown and displayed. **2.** *U.S.* A conservatoire.

con·serve (kən-sérv || kon-) *tr.v.* **-served, -serving, -serves. 1.** To protect from loss or wasteful depletion; preserve. **2.** To preserve (fruits) with sugar.

~n. (*also* kón-serv). *Often plural.* A jam containing whole fruit or whole pieces of fruit. [Middle English *conserven,* from Old French *conserver,* from Latin *conservāre* : *com-* (intensive) + *servāre,* to keep, preserve.] **—con·serv·a·ble** *adj.* **—con·serv·er** *n.*

con·sid·er (kən-síddər || kon-) *v.* **-ered, -ering, -ers.** *—tr.* **1.** To deliberate upon; examine; study. **2.** To regard as; think or deem to be. **3.** To believe, especially after careful deliberation; judge. **4.** To take into account; make allowance for. **5.** To have regard for; pay attention to. **6.** To regard highly; esteem. **7.** To think about as possible or acceptable: *refused to consider the other possibilities.* *—intr.* To think carefully; reflect. [Middle English *consideren,* from Old French *considerer,* from Latin *consīderāre,* to observe (originally a term of augury meaning "to observe the stars carefully").] **—con·sid·er·er** *n.*

Synonyms: *consider, deem, regard, account, reckon.*

con·sid·er·a·ble (kən-síddrə-b'l, -síddərə- || kon-) *adj.* **1.** Fairly large in amount, extent, or degree: *a man of considerable influence.* **2.** Worthy of consideration; important; significant: *a considerable poet.* **—con·sid·er·a·bly** *adv.*

con·sid·er·ate (kən-síddər-ət, -síddrət, -it || kon-) *adj.* **1.** Having regard for the needs or feelings of others. **2.** *Archaic.* Characterised by careful thought; deliberate. —See Synonyms at **thoughtful.** [Latin *consīderātus,* past participle of *consīderāre,* to be considerate, CONSIDER.] **—con·sid·er·ate·ly** *adv.* **—con·sid·er·ate·ness** *n.*

con·sid·er·a·tion (kən-síddə-ráysh'n || kon-) *n.* **1.** The act or process of considering; deliberation; meditation. **2.** A circumstance to be considered; a factor in forming a judgment or decision. **3.** Thoughtfulness; solicitude. **4.** Something given in exchange for a service rendered; a recompense. **5.** *Law.* Something promised, given, or done that has the effect of making an agreement a legally enforceable contract. **6.** *Archaic.* High regard. **—in consideration of. 1.** In view of; on account of. **2.** In return for.

con·sid·ered (kən-síddərd || kon-) *adj.* **1.** Reached after deliberation or careful thought. **2.** Regarded; esteemed.

con·sid·er·ing (kən-síddəring, -síddring || kon-) *prep.* In view of; taking into consideration.

~adv. Informal. All things considered.

~conj. Informal. In view of the fact that: *Considering he's only six, he reads very well.*

con·sign (kən-sín || kon-) *tr.v.* **-signed, -signing, -signs. 1.** To give over to the care of another; entrust. **2.** To turn over permanently; commit irrevocably. **3.** To hand over (goods) to another for transport by sea, rail, or the like, and eventual delivery. —See Synonyms at **commit.** [Middle English *consignen,* to certify by a seal, from Old French *consigner,* from Latin *consignāre* : *com-* (intensive) + *signāre,* to seal, from *signum,* seal, mark.] **—con·sign·a·ble** *adj.* **—con·sig·na·tion** (kón-sī-náysh'n || *U.S. also* -sig-) *n.* **—con·sign·or** (-ər, kón-sī-nór), **con·sign·er** *n.*

con·sign·ee (kón-sī-neé, kən-sí-) *n.* A person to whom goods are consigned.

con·sign·ment (kən-sín-mənt || kon-) *n. Abbr.* **cons. 1.** The consigning of goods or cargo, especially to an agent for sale or custody. **2.** That which is consigned; a shipment of goods.

con·sist (kən-síst || kon-) *intr.v.* **-sisted, -sisting, -sists. 1.** To be made up or composed. Used with *of.* **2.** To have a basis; lie; rest. Used with *in.* **3.** To be compatible; accord. [Old French *consister,* from Latin *consistere,* to stand still, exist : *com-* (intensive) + *sistere,* to cause to stand, place.]

con•sis•ten•cy (kən-sístən-si || kon-) *n., pl.* **-cies.** Also **con•sis•tence** (-sístənss). **1.** Agreement or logical coherence among things or parts. **2.** Compatibility or agreement among successive acts, ideas, or events. **3.** The condition of holding together; firmness. **4.** The degree or texture of firmness or viscosity.

con•sis•tent (kən-sístənt) *adj.* **1.** Agreeing; compatible; not contradictory. Often used with *with.* **2.** Conforming to the same principles, course of action, or standards. [Latin *consistens* (stem *consistent-*), present participle of *consistere,* to stand firmly, CONSIST.] **—con•sis•tent•ly** *adv.*

con•sis•to•ry (kən-sístəri || kon-) *n., pl.* **-ries.** **1.** *Roman Catholic Church.* A gathering, either of cardinals alone, *secret consistory,* or with others present, *public consistory,* presided over by the pope for the solemn promulgation of papal acts, such as the appointment of cardinals or bishops or the canonisation of a saint. **2.** In certain Reformed churches, a governing body of a local congregation, composed of the ministers and elders. **3.** In Lutheran churches, a court appointed to regulate ecclesiastical affairs. **4.** In the Anglican Church, a diocesan court presided over by the bishop's chancellor or commissary. **5.** The meeting place, or the meeting itself, of any such body. **6.** *Archaic.* A council or tribunal. [Middle English *consistorie,* from Old French, from Medieval Latin *consistōrium,* from Late Latin, place of assembly, from Latin *consistere,* to take one's place (at a meeting), stand, CONSIST.] **—con•sis•to•ri•al** (kón-siss-táwri-əl || -tōri-), **con•sis•to•ri•an** (-táwri-ən || -tōri-) *adj.*

con•so•ci•ate (kən-sṓ-si-ayt, -shi- || kon-) *v.* **-ated, -ating, -ates.** *—tr.* To bring into friendly association. *—intr.* To come into friendly association.
~*adj.* (-ət, -it, -ayt). Associated; united.
~*n.* (-ət, -it, -ayt). An associate; a companion; a partner. [Middle English *consociat,* associated, from Latin *consociātus,* past participle of *consociāre,* to associate, join : *com-,* together + *sociāre,* to join, from *socius,* ally, companion.]

con•so•ci•a•tion (kən-sṓ-si-áysh'n, kon-, -shi-) *n.* **1.** The act of consociating. **2.** A subdivision of an ecological association having one dominant species of plant. An example is a beech wood in a deciduous forest association.

consol. consolidated.

con•so•la•tion (kón-sə-láysh'n, -sō-) *n.* **1. a.** The act or an instance of consoling. **b.** The state of being consoled. **2.** Someone or something that consoles; a comfort. **—con•sol•a•to•ry** (kən-sól-ə-tri, -sṓl-, -təri || kon-) *adj.*

consolation prize *n.* A prize given to a competitor who loses.

con•sole[1] (kən-sṓl || kon-) *tr.v.* **-soled, -soling, -soles.** To cheer in time of grief, disappointment, or trouble; comfort; solace. [French *consoler,* from Old French, from Latin *consōlārī* : *com-* (intensive) + *sōlārī,* to comfort.] **—con•sol•a•ble** *adj.* **—con•sol•er** *n.* **—con•sol•ing•ly** *adv.*

con•sole[2] (kón-sōl) *n.* **1.** A decorative bracket for supporting a cornice, shelf, bust, or other object. **2.** A console table. **3.** The desklike part of an organ that contains the keyboard, stops, and pedals. **4.** A cabinet for a radio, television set, or record player, designed to stand on the floor. **5.** A panel housing the controls for electrical, electronic, or mechanical equipment; especially, the control panel of a computer. [French, short for *consolateur,* a carved human figure used to support cornices, from Latin *consōlātor,* one that consoles, hence a support, from *consōlārī,* to CONSOLE.]

con•sole table (kón-sōl) *n.* **1.** A table supported by decorative consoles fixed to a wall. **2.** A small table, often with curved legs resembling consoles, designed to be set against a wall. Also called "console".

con•sol•i•date (kən-sólli-dayt || kon-) *v.* **-dated, -dating, -dates.** *—tr.* **1.** To make firm or coherent; form into a compact mass; solidify. **2.** To make strong or secure; strengthen: *consolidate an empire.* **3.** To unite into one system or body; combine; merge. *—intr.* To become solidified or united. —See Synonyms at **join.** [Latin *consolidāre* : *com-* (intensive) + *solidāre,* to make solid or firm, from *solidus,* solid.] **—con•sol•i•da•tor** (-daytər) *n.*

Con•sol•i•dat•ed Fund (kən-sóllidaytid) *n. British.* A fund into which certain tax revenue is paid and from which certain recurrent expenses, notably interest on the national debt, are met.

con•sol•i•da•tion (kən-sólli-dáysh'n || kon-) *n.* **1.** The act of consolidating or the state of being consolidated. **2.** The process of combining or uniting, as of separate companies to form a single whole, or of several related enactments into a single statute. **3.** *Geology.* The process by which a loose deposit is compressed and cemented into solid rock.

con•sols (kón-solz, kən-sólz) *pl.n.* The perpetual governmental securities of Great Britain. Also called "bank annuities". [Short for *consolidated annuities.*]

con•so•lute (kón-sə-lōōt, -lewt) *adj.* Designating two or more liquids that are mutually soluble in all proportions. [Latin *consolūtus* : *con-,* together + *solūtus,* past participle of *solvere,* to dissolve.]

con•som•mé (kən-sómmay, kón-so-may || *U.S.* -sə-máy) *n.* A clear soup made of meat, fish, or vegetable stock or a combination of these. [French, "concentrate", from Old French *consommer,* to consume, from Latin *consummāre* : *com-* (intensive) + *summa,* SUM.]

con•so•nance (kón-sənənss) *n.* **1.** Agreement; harmony; accord. **2. a.** Correspondence of sounds. **b.** In poetry, a similarity of terminal consonants but not of vowels, in two or more syllables, words, or lines. Compare **assonance.** **3.** *Music.* A simultaneous combination of sounds conventionally regarded as pleasing and final in effect. Compare **dissonance.**

con•so•nant (kón-sənənt) *adj.* **1.** In agreement or accord. Often used with *with* or *to.* **2.** Corresponding in sound. Often used with *with* or *to.* **3.** Harmonious in sound. **4.** Consonantal.
~*n. Abbr.* **cons.** *Phonetics.* **1. a.** A speech sound produced by a partial or complete obstruction of the air stream by any of various constrictions of the speech organs. **b.** A subordinate or less distinctive sound within a syllable, such as a glide in a diphthong. **2.** A letter or character representing such a sound, such as *p, t, g, k*; a letter that is not a vowel. [Middle English from Old French, from Latin *(littera) consonāns* (stem *consonant-*), "(letter) sounded with (a vowel)", from the present participle of *consonāre,* to sound at the same time, harmonise, agree : *com-,* together + *sonāre,* to sound.] **—con•so•nant•ly** *adv.*

con•so•nan•tal (kón-sə-nánt'l) *adj.* **1.** Of, relating to, or having the nature of a consonant. **2.** Containing a consonant or consonants. **—con•so•nan•tal•ly** *adv.*

con sor•di•no (kón sawr-deénō) *adv. Music.* Using the mute. Used as a direction. [Italian.]

con•sort (kón-sawrt) *n.* **1.** A husband or wife; especially, the spouse of a monarch. **2.** A companion or partner. **3.** A ship accompanying another. **4. a.** *Archaic.* A harmonious combination of voices or musical instruments. **b.** A group of singers or instrumentalists.
~*v.* (kən-sórt || kon-) **consorted, -sorting, -sorts.** *—intr.* **1.** To keep company; especially, to associate with undesirable characters. **2.** To be in accord or agreement. *—tr.* To bring together; associate. [Middle English, from Old French, from Latin *consors* (stem *consort-*), "one who shares the same fate", companion, partner : *com-,* together + *sors,* fate, share.]

con•sor•ti•um (kən-sór-ti-əm || kon-, -shi-) *n., pl.* **-tia** (-ti-ə || -shi-ə). **1.** An association of business organisations or financial institutions for carrying out a project requiring extensive financial resources, especially in international finance. **2.** Any association or partnership. **3.** *Law.* A married person's right to the company, help, and affection of his or her spouse. [Latin, fellowship, participation, from *consors,* partner, companion, CONSORT.]

con•spe•cif•ic (kón-spi-síffik) *adj. Biology.* Of the same species.

con•spec•tus (kən-spéktəss || kon-) *n.* **1.** A general survey of a subject. **2.** A brief résumé; a synopsis. [Latin, "view", "survey", from the past participle of *conspicere,* to observe (see **conspicuous**).]

con•spic•u•ous (kən-spíckew-əss || kon-) *adj.* **1.** Easy to notice; obvious. **2.** Attracting attention by being unusual or remarkable. [Latin *conspicuus,* from *conspicere,* to look at closely, observe : *com-* (intensive) + *specere,* to look.] **—con•spic•u•ous•ly** *adv.* **—con•spic•u•ous•ness** *n.*

conspicuous consumption *n.* Ostentatious extravagance pursued in order to enhance one's prestige in society.

con•spir•a•cy (kən-spírrə-si || kon-) *n., pl.* **-cies.** **1.** An agreement to perform together an illegal, treacherous, or evil act. **2.** A combining or acting together, as if by evil design: *a conspiracy of natural forces.* **3.** *Law.* An agreement between two or more persons to commit a crime or to accomplish a legal purpose through illegal action. [Middle English *conspiracie,* from Anglo-French, variant of Old French *conspiration,* from Latin *conspīrātiō,* from *conspīrāre,* to CONSPIRE.]
Synonyms: *conspiracy, plot, collusion, intrigue, cabal.*

conspiracy of silence *n.* An agreement that nothing should be said on a particular matter, usually in order to promote the interests of those who know of the matter against those who do not.

con•spir•a•tor (kən-spírrətər || kon-) *n.* A person engaged in a conspiracy; a plotter.

con•spir•a•to•ri•al (kən-spírrə-táwri-əl || kon-, -tōri-) *adj.* Pertaining to or suggestive of conspirators or a conspiracy: *gave me a conspiratorial wink.* **—con•spir•a•to•ri•al•ly** *adv.*

con•spire (kən-spír || kon-) *v.* **-spired, -spiring, -spires.** *—intr.* **1.** To plan together with another or others secretly, especially to commit an illegal or evil act. **2.** To combine or act together, especially to do harm. *—tr.* To plan or plot secretly. [Middle English *conspiren,* from Old French *conspirer,* from Latin *conspīrāre,* "to breathe together", agree, unite, plot : *com-,* together + *spīrāre,* to breathe, blow.] **—con•spir•er** *n.* **—con•spir•ing•ly** *adv.*

con spi•ri•to (kon spírri-tō) *adv. Music.* With spirit and vigour. Used as a direction.

const. **1.** constable. **2.** constant. **3.** constitution. **4.** construction.

Const. **1.** constable. **2.** constitution.

con•sta•ble (kún-stəb'l, kón-) *n. Abbr.* **cons., Cons., const., Const.** **1.** In Britain and various other countries, a police officer; especially, a policeman or policewoman of the lowest rank. **2.** Formerly, a local officer responsible for keeping the peace and suppressing riots, prior to the establishment of modern police forces. **3.** In medieval monarchies, an officer of high rank, usually serving as military commander in the ruler's absence. **4.** The governor of a royal castle. [Middle English, from Old French, from Late Latin *comes stabulī,* "count of the stable" : Latin *comes,* companion, count + *stabuli,* genitive of *stabulum,* STABLE.] **—con•sta•ble•ship** *n.*

Constable, John (1776–1837). British landscape painter. His direct observations of nature and free use of broken colour were original and influential. *The Hay Wain* (1821) is his best-known work.

con•stab•u•lar•y (kən-stábbew-ləri || kon-, -lerri) *n., pl.* **-ies.** The police force of a district or city.
~*adj.* Of or pertaining to constables or to constabularies.

Constance. See **Konstanz.**

Constance, Lake (kón-stənss). *German* **Bo•den•see** (bṓd'n-zay). Alpine lake on the river Rhine.

con•stan•cy (kón-stən-si) *n.* **1.** Steadfastness in purpose or loyalty;

faithfulness. **2.** An unchanging quality or state.
con·stant (kón-stənt) *adj.* **1. a.** Continuous; unremitting: *constant noise.* **b.** Continually recurring; persistent: *a constant worry.* **2.** Unchanging in nature, value, or extent; invariable. **3.** Steadfast in purpose, loyalty, or affection; faithful. —See Synonyms at **continual, faithful, steady.**
~*n.* **1.** A thing that is unchanging or invariable. **2.** *Abbr.* **const.** *Symbol* **c, C a.** A quantity taken to have a fixed value in a specific mathematical context. **b.** An experimental or theoretical condition, factor, or quantity that occurs or is regarded as invariant in specific circumstances. [Middle English, from Old French, from Latin *constāns* (stem *constant-*), present participle of *constāre,* to stand together, remain steadfast : *com-,* together + *stāre,* to stand.] **—con·stant·ly** *adv.*
Con·stant (kóN-stoN, koN-stóN), **Benjamin,** pseudonym of Henri Benjamin Constant de Rebecque (1767–1830). French writer and political figure who wrote defending the French Revolution, but opposed Napoleon and went into exile (1803). His long affair with Madame de Staël underlies his novel, *Adolphe* (1816).
Con·stant·an (kón-stən-tan) *n.* A trademark for an alloy of copper containing up to 45 per cent nickel, used chiefly in electrical instruments because of its constant resistance. [Coined from CONSTANT.]
Con·stan·tine (kón-stən-tīn), **Learie Nicholas, Baron** (1902–1971). Trinidadian cricketer and statesman. He won fame as a great all-round cricketer, playing for the West Indies. He served as high commissioner of Trinidad and Tobago (1962–64) and was made a peer in 1969.
Constantine II (1940–). King of Greece (1964–67). He went into exile after a right-wing coup by army officers (1967). Greece became a republic (1973).
Constantine the Great (*c.*285–337). Roman emperor who ruled the western empire (312–24) and became sole emperor (324–37). He adopted the Christian faith (312), and suspended the persecution of Christians. He rebuilt Constantinople (modern Istanbul) as the new Rome (330).
Con·stan·ti·no·ple (kón-stánti-nṓp'l). Capital of the Byzantine Empire (330–1453), and of Turkey (1453–1923). Originally called Byzantium, the city was founded by Greeks in 667 B.C., captured by Roman forces in A.D. 196, and rebuilt by Constantine (330), who changed its name to Constantinople. The city enjoyed a golden age under Justinian the Great (532–62), when the church of Hagia Sophia was built. Constantinople finally fell to the Ottoman Turks (1453) and, as their capital, expanded across the Bosporus, and Hagia Sophia became a mosque. In 1923 the Turkish capital was moved to Ankara, and Constantinople was renamed Istanbul (1930).
con·sta·ta·tion (kón-stə-táysh'n, -sta-) *n.* **1.** The act of ascertaining or verifying. **2.** A statement or fact that has been ascertained. [French, from *constater,* to verify, from Latin *constat,* it is certain.]
con·stel·late (kón-ste-layt, -stə-) *v.* **-lated, -lating, -lates.** *—tr.* To cause to form a group or cluster. *—intr.* To form a group or cluster. [Back-formation from CONSTELLATION.]
con·stel·la·tion (kón-stə-láysh'n, -ste-) *n.* **1.** *Astronomy.* **a.** Any of the 88, scientifically arbitrary, groupings of stars as seen from Earth, considered to resemble and named after various mythological characters, inanimate objects, and animals. **b.** An area of the celestial sphere occupied by such a group. **2.** *Astrology.* The position of the stars at the time of one's birth, regarded as determining one's character or fate. **3.** A brilliant gathering or assemblage. **4.** A set or configuration of usually related objects, properties, or individuals. [Middle English *constellacioun,* from Old French *constellation,* from Late Latin *constellātiō* (stem *constellātiōn-*), group of stars : Latin *com-,* together + *stellātus,* starred, from *stella,* star.] **—con·stel·la·to·ry** (-láytəri, kən-stéllə-tri, -təri) *adj.*
con·ster·nate (kón-stər-nayt) *tr.v.* **-nated, -nating, -nates.** To fill with consternation. Usually used in the passive. [Latin *consternāre,* to stretch out, overcome, perplex : *com-* (intensive) + *sternere,* to spread out.]
con·ster·na·tion (kón-stər-náysh'n) *n.* Sudden confusion, amazement, or frustration.
con·sti·pate (kón-sti-payt) *tr.v.* **-pated, -pating, -pates. 1.** To cause constipation in. **2.** To repress; restrain. Used in the passive. [Latin *constīpāre,* to press or crowd together (in Medieval Latin, "to confine the bowels") : *com-,* together + *stīpāre,* to press, cram.]
con·sti·pa·tion (kón-sti-páysh'n) *n.* Difficult, incomplete, or infrequent evacuation of the bowels.
con·stit·u·en·cy (kən-stíttew-ən-si || kon-) *n., pl.* **-cies. 1. a.** The body of voters represented by an elected member of a legislative body. **b.** The area so represented. **2.** Any group of supporters or people whose wishes must be considered.
con·stit·u·ent (kən-stíttew-ənt || kon-) *adj.* **1.** Serving as part of a whole; component. **2.** Authorised to make or amend a constitution. **3.** Empowered to elect representatives.
~*n.* **1.** Someone represented by an elected official. **2.** Someone represented by another; a client. **3.** A constituent part; a component. **4.** *Grammar.* Any of the functional elements into which a construction or compound may be divided by analysis. [Latin *constituēns* (stem *constituent-*), present participle of *constituere,* to CONSTITUTE.] **—con·stit·u·ent·ly** *adv.*
con·sti·tute (kón-sti-tewt || -tōōt) *tr.v.* **-tuted, -tuting, -tutes. 1. a.** To be the elements or parts of; make up; compose. **b.** To be equivalent or tantamount to: *Does this constitute a precedent?* **2.** To give legal form to (an assembly, court, or the like). **3.** To establish formally; found (an institution, for example). **4.** To appoint to an office or task; designate. [Middle English *constituten,* from Latin *constituere,* to cause to stand, set, fix : *com-* (intensive) + *statuere,* to set up.] **—con·sti·tut·er, con·sti·tu·tor** (-ər) *n.*
con·sti·tu·tion (kón-sti-téwsh'n || -tōōsh'n) *n. Abbr.* **cons., const., Const. 1.** The act or process of constituting or establishing. **2.** The composition of something made of a number of parts; make-up. **3.** A person's physical make-up as it relates to his characteristic state of health and strength: *a strong constitution.* **4. a.** The system of fundamental laws and principles that prescribes the nature, functions, and limits of a government or other institution. **b.** The document in which this system is recorded. **5.** In former times, a decree or enactment.
con·sti·tu·tion·al (kón-sti-téwsh'n-'l || -tōōsh'n-) *adj. Abbr.* **cons. 1.** Of or proceeding from the basic structure or nature of a person or thing; essential. **2.** Contained in or consistent with the constitution. **3.** Established by or operating under a constitution. **4.** For the sake of one's general health.
~*n.* A walk taken for the sake of one's health. **—con·sti·tu·tion·al·i·ty** (-ál-əti) *n.* **—con·sti·tu·tion·al·ly** *adv.*
con·sti·tu·tion·al·ism (kón-sti-téwsh'n-'l-iz'm || -tōōsh'n-) *n.* **1.** Government in which power is distributed and limited by a system of laws that must be obeyed by the rulers. **2.** Advocacy of such government. **—con·sti·tu·tion·al·ist** *n.*
constitutional monarchy *n.* A monarchy in which the powers of the ruler are restricted to those granted under the constitution and laws of the nation.
con·sti·tu·tive (kón-sti-tewtiv, kən-stíttewtiv || -tōōtiv) *adj.* **1.** Making a thing what it is; essential. **2.** Having power to institute, establish, or enact. **—con·sti·tu·tive·ly** *adv.*
constitutive enzyme *n.* An enzyme that is always present in a cell, being synthesised at a constant rate regardless of the presence or absence of substrate.
constr. construction.
con·strain (kən-stráyn || kon-) *tr.v.* **-strained, -straining, -strains. 1. a.** To compel by physical, moral, or circumstantial force; oblige. **b.** To bring about by compulsion; enforce. **2.** To keep within close bounds; confine. **3.** To check the freedom or mobility of; restrain. —See Synonyms at **force.** [Middle English *constreinen,* from Old French *constraindre,* from Latin *constringere,* to draw or bind tightly together : *com-,* together + *stringere,* to draw tight.] **—con·strain·a·ble** *adj.* **—con·strain·er** *n.*
con·strained (kən-stráynd || kon-) *adj.* **1.** Resulting from constraint; restrained. **2.** Forced; unnatural. **—con·strain·ed·ly** (-stráynidli) *adv.*
con·straint (kən-stráynt || kon-) *n.* **1.** The threat or use of force to prevent, restrict, or dictate the action or thought of others. **2.** The state, quality, or sense of being restricted to a given course of action or inaction. **3.** Something that restricts, limits, or regulates. **4.** A lack of ease; embarrassed reserve or reticence. [Middle English *constreint(e),* from Old French *constrainte,* from *constraindre,* to CONSTRAIN.]
con·strict (kən-stríkt || -kon-) *tr.v.* **-stricted, -stricting, -stricts. 1.** To make smaller or narrower, as by shrinking or contracting. **2.** To squeeze or compress by or as if by narrowing or tightening. **3.** To limit; inhibit. —See Synonyms at **contract.** [Latin *constringere* (past participle *constrictus*), to draw or bind tightly together, CONSTRAIN.] **—con·stric·tive** *adj.* **—con·stric·tive·ly** *adv.*
con·stric·tion (kən-stríksh'n || kon-) *n.* **1. a.** The act or process of constricting. **b.** The condition of being constricted. **2.** A feeling of pressure or tightness. **3.** A constricted or narrow part.
con·stric·tor (kən-stríktər || kon-) *n.* **1.** Something that constricts. **2.** *Anatomy.* Any muscle that compresses an organ or causes narrowing of a duct or passage. **3.** Any of various snakes, such as a python or boa, that coil around and crush their prey.
con·stringe (kən-strínj || kon-) *tr.v.* **-stringed, -stringing, -stringes.** *Archaic.* To cause to contract; constrict. [Latin *constringere,* to CONSTRAIN.] **—con·strin·gen·cy** *n.* **—con·strin·gent** *adj.*
con·struct (kən-strúkt || kon-) *tr.v.* **-structed, -structing, -structs. 1.** To form by assembling parts; build; erect. **2.** To create (an argument or sentence, for example) by systematically arranging ideas or expressions; devise with the mind. **3.** *Mathematics.* To draw (a geometric figure) that meets specific requirements, usually with instruments limited to a ruler and compass.
~*n.* (kón-strukt). Something synthesised or constructed from simple elements; especially, a concept constructed by the mind to form part of a theory. [Latin *construere* (past participle *constructus*), to pile up together, build : *com-,* together + *struere,* to pile up.] **—con·struc·tor** (-strúktər), **con·struct·er** *n.* **—con·struct·i·ble** *adj.*
con·struc·tion (kən-strúksh'n || kon-) *n. Abbr.* **cons., const., constr. 1. a.** The act or process of constructing. **b.** The science or business of building. Also used adjectivally: *the construction industry.* **2.** That which is constructed; a structure or building. **3.** The way in which a thing is put together; structure. **4.** The interpretation or explanation given to an action or statement. **5.** *Grammar.* The arrangement of words to form a phrase, clause, or sentence that makes sense. **—con·struc·tion·al** *adj.* **—con·struc·tion·al·ly** *adv.*
con·struc·tive (kən-strúktiv || kon-) *adj.* **1.** Serving to advance a good purpose; helpful. **2.** Of or pertaining to construction; structural. **3.** *Law.* Based on an interpretation; inferred but not directly expressed. **—con·struc·tive·ly** *adv.* **—con·struc·tive·ness** *n.*
con·struc·tiv·ism (kən-strúktiv-iz'm || kon-) *n. Sometimes capital* **C.** A movement in modern art that developed in Russia around 1920,

in which industrial materials are used to create nonrepresentational, often geometric objects. **—con·struc·tiv·ist** *adj.* & *n.*

con·strue (kən-strōō ‖ kon-, -strēw) *v.* **-strued, -struing, -strues.** —*tr.* **1.** *Grammar.* **a.** To analyse the structure of (a clause or sentence). Compare **parse. b.** To use syntactically: *The noun "fish" can be construed as singular or plural.* **2.** To deduce and explain the meaning of; especially, to put a particular construction or interpretation upon. **3.** *Archaic.* To translate, especially aloud. —*intr.* **1.** To analyse grammatical structure. **2.** To be capable of grammatical analysis. Used of a phrase or sentence.
~*n.* (kón-strōō ‖ -strew). An interpretation or translation. [Middle English *construen,* from Late Latin *construere,* from Latin, to CONSTRUCT.] **—con·stru·al** *n.*

con·sub·stan·tial (kón-səb-stán-sh'l, -stáən- ‖ -sub-) *adj. Theology.* Having the same substance, nature, or essence. Said of the three persons of the Trinity. [Middle English *consubstancial,* from Late Latin *consubstantiālis* : Latin *com-,* same + *substantiālis,* SUBSTANTIAL.]

con·sub·stan·ti·ate (kón-səb-stán-shi-ayt, -stáən- ‖ -sub-) *v.* **-ated, -ating, -ates.** —*tr.* To unite in one common substance, nature, or essence. —*intr.* To become united in one common substance. [New Latin *consubstantiare* : *com-,* together + SUBSTANTIATE.]

con·sub·stan·ti·a·tion (kón-səb-stán-shi-áysh'n, -stáən- ‖ -sub-) *n. Theology.* **1.** The doctrine that the body and blood of Christ coexist with the elements of bread and wine during the Eucharist. **2.** The process by which this coexistence is believed to take place. Compare **transubstantiation.**

con·su·e·tude (kón-séw-i-tewd, -sōō-, kón-swi- ‖ -tōōd) *n. Chiefly Law.* Custom; usage; habit. [Middle English, from Latin *consuē- tūdo,* from *consuēscere,* to accustom : *com-* (intensive) + *suēscere,* to become accustomed.] **—con·su·e·tu·di·nar·y** (-tewd-i-nəri ‖ -tōōd-, *chiefly U.S.* -nerri) *adj.*

con·sul (kón-s'l) *n. Abbr.* **c., C., Con., Cons. 1.** An official appointed by a government to reside in a foreign city and represent its commercial interests and give assistance to its citizens there. **2.** Either of the two chief officials of the Roman Republic, elected for a term of one year. **3.** Any of the three chief officials of the French Republic from 1799 to 1804. [Middle English, Roman magistrate, from Old French, from Latin *consul,* akin to *consulere,* to CONSULT.] **—con·su·lar** (kón-sew-lər ‖ -sə-, -shə-) *adj.* **—con·sul·ship** *n.*

consular agent *n.* A member of one of the lower grades into which the British consular service is divided.

con·su·late (kón-sew-lət, -lit ‖ -sə-, -shə-) *n.* **1.** The official premises occupied by a consul. **2.** The office or term of office of a consul. **3.** Government by, or the period of government by, consuls. [Middle English *consulat,* from Old French, from Latin *consulātus,* from *consul,* CONSUL.]

consul general *n., pl.* **consuls general.** *Abbr.* **c.g., C.G.** A consular officer of the highest rank.

con·sult (kən-súlt ‖ kon-) *v.* **-sulted, -sulting, -sults.** —*tr.* **1.** To seek advice or information from. **2.** To have regard for; consider. —*intr.* **1.** To exchange views; confer. Often used with *with.* **2.** To give expert advice as a professional. [Old French *consulter,* from Latin *consultāre,* frequentative of *consulere†,* to take counsel.]

con·sul·tan·cy (kən-súltən-si ‖ kon-) *n., pl.* **-cies.** The business or position of a consultant.

con·sul·tant (kən-súltənt ‖ kon-) *n.* **1. a.** *Chiefly British.* A physician or surgeon who holds the highest hospital appointment in his speciality and is ultimately responsible for the patients in his care. **b.** A specialist physician who is asked to confirm a diagnosis. **2.** A person who gives expert or professional advice. **3.** A person who consults another person or source of information.

con·sul·ta·tion (kón-s'l-táysh'n, -sul-) *n.* **1.** The act or procedure of consulting. **2.** A conference at which advice is given or views are exchanged.

con·sult·a·tive (kən-súltətiv ‖ kon-) *adj.* Of or pertaining to consultation; advisory.

con·sul·ting (kən-súlting ‖ kon-) *adj.* Acting in an advisory capacity in one's special field: *a consulting engineer.*

consulting room *n.* A room in which a doctor sees his patients.

con·sume (kən-séwm, -sōōm ‖ kon-, -shōōm) *v.* **-sumed, -suming, -sumes.** —*tr.* **1.** To eat or drink up; ingest. **2.** To use up; expend (resources, time, or the like). **3.** To waste; squander. **4.** To destroy, especially by fire. **5.** To preoccupy; engross: *consumed by jealousy.* —*intr.* To be destroyed or expended; waste away. [Middle English *consumen,* from Old French *consumer,* from Latin *consūmere,* to take completely, consume : *com-* (intensive) + *sūmere,* to take up.] **—con·sum·a·ble** *adj.* & *n.*

con·sum·ed·ly (kən-séwm-idli, -sōōm- ‖ kon-, -shōōm-) *adv. Archaic.* Excessively.

con·sum·er (kən-séwm-ər, -sōōm- ‖ kon-, -shōōm-) *n.* **1.** One that consumes. **2.** *Economics.* One who acquires goods or services; a buyer. **3.** *Ecology.* An organism, such as an animal or insectivorous plant, that feeds on other organisms. Compare **producer.**

consumer credit *n. Economics.* Credit granted to a consumer, permitting him to own or use goods while he is paying for them.

consumer goods *pl.n. Economics.* Goods directly used by a consumer to satisfy a need, such as food, clothing or household appliances, as distinguished from those used in the production of other goods. Compare **capital goods.**

con·sum·er·ism (kən-séwm-ər-iz'm, -sōōm- ‖ kon-, -shōōm-) *n.* **1.** Public demand for the protection of the interests of the consumer, as through fair advertising, improved safety standards, and

similar measures. **2.** *Economics.* The advocacy of a high level of consumption as economically desirable. **3.** Excessive, materialistic concern with the acquisition of consumer goods. **—con·sum·er·ist** *n.* & *adj.*

consumer research *n.* Investigation into what purchasers of goods and services buy and what they require.

consumer society *n.* A society greatly, perhaps excessively, concerned with the marketing and acquisition of consumer goods.

consumer terrorism *n.* Terrorism directed against consumers, as by tampering with goods so as to make them unsafe. **—consumer terrorist** *n.*

con·sum·mate (kón-sə-mayt, -su-, -sew-) *tr.v.* **-mated, -mating, -mates. 1.** To bring to completion, perfection, or fulfilment; achieve. **2.** To fulfil (a marriage) with the first act of sexual intercourse after the ceremony.
~*adj.* (kən-súm-ət, kon-səm-, -it ‖ kon- *Note: the widespread tendency to pronounce the adjective like the verb is condemned by purists*). **1.** Supremely accomplished or skilled. **2.** Complete; perfect. [Middle English *consummaten,* from Latin *consummāre,* to bring together, sum up : *com-,* together + *summa,* a SUM.] **—con·sum·mate·ly** *adv.* **—con·sum·ma·tive** (kón-sə-maytiv, -su-, -sew-, kən-súmmətiv), **con·sum·ma·to·ry** (kən-súmmə-tri, -təri ‖ kon-) *adj.* **—con·sum·ma·tor** (kón-sə-maytər, -su-, -sew-) *n.*

con·sum·ma·tion (kón-sə-máysh'n, -su-, -sew-) *n.* **1.** The act of consummating, especially consummating a marriage; completion. **2.** An ultimate end or goal.

con·sump·tion (kən-súmpsh'n ‖ kon-) *n.* **1. a.** The act or process of consuming. **b.** The state of being consumed. **2.** The amount consumed. **3.** *Economics.* The using up of consumer goods and services. **4.** Any disease causing wasting of tissues, especially (formerly) tuberculosis of the lungs. [Middle English *consumpcioun,* from Old French *consumption,* from Latin *consūmptiō,* from *consūmere,* to CONSUME.]

con·sump·tive (kən-súmptiv ‖ kon-) *adj.* **1.** Tending to consume; wasteful; destructive. **2.** Pertaining to or afflicted with consumption, especially tuberculosis of the lungs.
~*n.* A person afflicted with consumption.

cont. 1. containing. **2.** contents. **3.** continent; continental. **4.** continue; continued. **5.** contract. **6.** contraction.

con·tact (kón-takt) *n.* **1. a.** The coming together of two or more objects, surfaces, or parts of objects so that there is no space between them. **b.** The fact or relation of not being separated by space or another object. **2.** The state of being in communication. **3.** An acquaintance who might be of use; a connection. **4.** *Electricity.* **a.** A connection between two conductors that permits a flow of current. **b.** A part or device that makes or breaks such a connection. **5.** *Medicine.* A person recently exposed to a contagious disease and therefore potentially able to transmit it.
~*v.* (kón-takt, kən-tákt) **contacted, -tacting, -tacts.** —*tr.* **1.** To bring or put in contact. **2.** *Informal.* To get in touch with. —*intr.* To be in or come into contact.
~*adj.* (kón-takt). **1.** Of, sustaining, or making contact. **2. a.** Caused or transmitted by contact: *a contact skin rash.* **b.** Activated or operating by means of contact: *a contact insecticide.* [Latin *contāctus,* from the past participle of *contingere,* to touch, border upon, attain to : *com-,* together + *tangere,* to touch.] **—con·tac·tu·al** (kən-táktew-əl ‖ kon-) *adj.* **—con·tac·tu·al·ly** *adv.*

contact dermatitis *n.* Inflammation of the skin caused by direct contact with an irritating substance, especially a chemical.

contact flight *n.* Aircraft navigation by visual reference to the horizon or to landmarks. Also called "contact flying".

contact lens *n.* A thin lens worn directly against the eye to correct visual defects.

contact print *n.* A print made by exposing a photosensitive surface in direct contact with a photographic negative.

con·ta·gion (kən-táyjən ‖ kon-) *n.* **1.** Disease transmission by direct or indirect contact. **2.** A disease that is or may be so transmitted. **3.** A contagium. **4.** A harmful or corrupting influence. **5.** The tendency to spread, as of an idea or emotional state: *the contagion of laughter.* [Middle English *contagioun,* from Old French *contagion,* from Latin *contāgiō* (stem *contāgiōn-*), from *contingere,* to touch, touch with pollution, CONTACT.]

con·ta·gious (kən-táyjəss ‖ kon-) *adj.* **1.** Transmissible by direct or indirect contact; communicable. Said of certain diseases. **2.** Carrying or capable of carrying disease. **3.** Spreading or tending to spread from one to another; catching. Compare **infectious. —con·ta·gious·ly** *adv.* **—con·ta·gious·ness** *n.*

contagious abortion *n.* **Brucellosis** *(see)* of cattle.

con·tain (kən-táyn ‖ kon-) *tr.v.* **-tained, -taining, -tains. 1.** To have within; enclose. **2.** To have as component parts; comprise; include. **3.** To be able to hold; have capacity for. **4.** *Mathematics.* To be exactly divisible by. **5.** To hold or keep within limits; restrain; confine: *contain one's emotions.* **6.** To prevent the expansion of (a country or power bloc, for example), as by encircling it with hostile alliances. [Middle English *conteinen,* from Old French *contenir,* from Latin *continēre,* to hold together, enclose, contain : *com-,* together + *tenēre,* to hold.] **—con·tain·a·ble** *adj.*
Synonyms: contain, hold, accommodate.

con·tain·er (kən-táynər ‖ kon-) *n.* **1.** One that contains; especially, something such as a box or crate, used for holding or carrying. **2.** A large, usually rectangular, receptacle of standard size, used for transporting cargo. **3.** A container ship or lorry.
~*adj.* Equipped with, able to transport, or designed to handle con-

tainers: *a container ship; a container port.*

con·tain·er·ise, con·tain·er·ize (kən-táynər-īz || kon-) *tr.v.* **-ised, -ising, -ises. 1.** To package (cargo) in large, standardised containers to facilitate shipping and handling. **2.** To adapt (shipping or other transport facilities) to handle and transport cargo in containers. **—con·tain·er·i·sa·tion** (-ī-záysh'n || *U.S.* -i-) *n.*

con·tain·ment (kən-táyn-mənt || kon-) *n.* The act of containing; especially, the act or policy of keeping a hostile power or bloc within existing limits of influence.

con·tam·i·nate (kən-támmi-nayt || kon-) *tr.v.* **-nated, -nating, -nates. 1.** To make impure or corrupt by contact or mixture. **2.** To expose to radioactivity.
~*adj. Archaic.* Contaminated. [Middle English *contaminaten,* from Latin *contāmināre.*] **—con·tam·i·na·tive** (-nətiv, -naytiv) *adj.* **—con·tam·i·nant, con·tam·i·na·tor** (-naytər) *n.*

con·tam·i·na·tion (kən-támmi-náysh'n || kon-) *n.* **1. a.** The act or process of contaminating. **b.** The state of being contaminated. **2.** One that contaminates; an impurity. **3.** *Linguistics.* The alteration of a form through misunderstood association with another. For example, "miniscule" is a contamination of *minuscule* under the influence of *miniature.*

con·tan·go (kən-táng-gō || kon-) *n., pl.* **-gos. 1.** An arrangement on the London Stock Exchange whereby the settlement for the delivery of stock is carried forward from one account to the next. **2.** The fee paid for this postponement. Also called "continuation". [19th century : arbitrary coinage apparently based on *continuation.*]

contd. continued.

conte (KONT) *n., pl.* **contes** (KONT). *French.* A short story, especially one full of adventure. [French, from Old French *conter, compter,* COUNT (to relate).]

con·temn (kən-tém || kon-) *tr.v.* **-temned, -temning, -temns.** *Literary.* To view with contempt; despise. [Middle English *contempnen,* from Old French *contem(p)ner,* from Latin *contemnere* : *com-* (intensive) + *temnere*†, to despise.] **—con·temn·er** *n.*

con·tem·plate (kón-tem-playt, -təm-) *v.* **-plated, -plating, -plates.** —*tr.* **1.** To look at pensively. **2.** To ponder or consider thoughtfully. **3.** To have in mind as a purpose; intend: *contemplate marriage.* **4.** To regard or take account of as a possibility. —*intr.* To ponder or concentrate on, especially spiritual matters; meditate. —See Synonyms at **see.** [Latin *contemplārī,* to observe carefully (originally a team of augury) : *com-* (intensive) + *templum,* open space and marked out by augurs for observation.] **—con·tem·pla·tor** (-ər) *n.* **—con·tem·pla·tion** (-pláysh'n) *n.*

con·tem·pla·tive (kən-témplətiv, kón-tem-playtiv, -təm-) *adj.* **1.** Disposed to or characterised by contemplation. **2.** Devoted to religious contemplation. —See Synonyms at **pensive.**
~*n.* **1.** A person given to contemplation. **2.** A member of a religious order dedicated to meditation. **—con·tem·pla·tive·ly** *adv.* **—con·tem·pla·tive·ness** *n.*

con·tem·po·ra·ne·ous (kən-témpə-ráyni-əss || kon-) *adj.* Originating, existing, or happening during the same period of time. Often used with *with.* See Synonyms at **contemporary.** [Latin *contemporāneus* : *com-,* same + *tempus* (stem *tempor-*), time.] **—con·tem·po·ra·ne·i·ty** (-rə-née-əti, -náy-), **con·tem·po·ra·ne·ous·ness** *n.* **—con·tem·po·ra·ne·ous·ly** *adv.*

con·tem·po·rar·y (kən-témp-rəri, -ərəri || -əri, -ri, kon-, *U.S.* -ərerri) *adj.* **1.** Belonging to the same period of time. **2.** Of about the same age. **3. a.** Belonging to the present time; current. **b.** Very modern; up-to-date.
~*n., pl.* **contemporaries. 1.** Something or someone of the same period of time. **2.** A person of about the same age. [Medieval Latin *contemporārius* : Latin *com-,* together + *tempus* (stem *tempor-*), time (see **temporal**).]

Synonyms: *contemporary, contemporaneous, simultaneous, synchronous, concurrent, coincident, concomitant.*

Usage: The use of *contemporary* to mean "modern" can be confusing. There is no problem when it used to refer to the present day, but when it refers to a past time, it may be unclear whether it refers to the past or to the current situation. For example, *They put on the play in contemporary dress* could mean that either old-fashioned (belonging to the historical period in which the play was written) or modern (contemporary now) dress was used.

con·tem·po·rise, con·tem·po·rize (kən-témpərīz || kon-) *tr.v.* **-rised, -rising, -rises.** To relate in time; synchronise. [From CONTEMPORARY (after TEMPORISE).]

con·tempt (kən-témpt || kon-) *n.* **1.** Reproachful disdain, as for something vile or dishonourable; bitter scorn. **2.** The state of being scorned, despised, or dishonoured: *hold someone in contempt.* **3.** Open disrespect or wilful disobedience of the authority of a court of law or a legislative body. Also called "contempt of court". [Middle English, from Latin *contemptus,* from the past participle of *contemnere,* to CONTEMN.]

con·tempt·i·ble (kən-témptə-b'l || kon-) *adj.* Deserving contempt; despicable. **—con·tempt·i·bil·i·ty** (-bílləti), **con·tempt·i·ble·ness** *n.* **—con·tempt·i·bly** *adv.*

con·temp·tu·ous (kən-témptew-əss || kon-) *adj.* Manifesting or feeling contempt; scornful; disdainful. Often used with *of.* **—con·temp·tu·ous·ly** *adv.* **—con·temp·tu·ous·ness** *n.*

con·tend (kən-ténd || kon-) *v.* **-tended, -tending, -tends.** —*intr.* **1.** To strive, as in battle; fight. **2.** To strive, as in competition; vie. **3.** To strive in controversy or debate; dispute. —*tr.* To maintain or assert. —See Synonyms at **discuss.** [Middle English *contenden,* from Old French *contendre,* from Latin *contendere,* to strain, strive with : *com-,* with + *tendere,* to stretch, strain, strive.]

con·tend·er (kən-téndər) *n.* One participating or likely to participate in a contest, as for a championship or political office.

con·tent¹ (kón-tent) *n.* **1.** *Abbr.* **cont.** *Usually plural.* That which is contained in a receptacle. **2. a.** *Sometimes plural.* The subject matter, as of a book or speech. **b.** *Plural.* A list printed at the beginning of a book or other publication giving a summary of its subject matter. **3.** The meaning or significance of a literary or artistic work, as distinguished from its form. **4.** Ability to receive and hold; capacity. **5.** The amount held; volume. **6.** The proportion of a specified substance: *a high fat content.* [Middle English, from Medieval Latin *contentum,* from Latin *contentus,* past participle of *continēre,* to CONTAIN.]

con·tent² (kən-tént || kon-) *adj.* **1.** Not desiring more than what one has; satisfied. **2.** Willing; prepared.
~*tr.v.* **contented, -tenting, -tents.** To make content or satisfied. **—content (oneself) with.** To limit oneself to; wish for no more than.
~*n.* **1.** Contentment; satisfaction. **2.** *British.* An affirmative vote or voter in the House of Lords. [Middle English, from Old French, from Latin *contentus,* restrained, satisfied, past participle of *continēre,* to restrain, CONTAIN.] **—con·tent·ment** *n.*

con·tent·ed (kən-téntid || kon-) *adj.* Satisfied with things as they are; content. **—con·tent·ed·ly** *adv.* **—con·tent·ed·ness** *n.*

con·ten·tion (kən-ténsh'n || kon-) *n.* **1.** A verbal struggling; dispute; controversy. **2.** A striving to win in competition; a state of rivalry. **3.** An assertion put forward in argument. —See Synonyms at **discord.** [Middle English *contencioun,* from Old French *contention,* from Latin *contentiō* (stem *contentiōn-*), from *contendere,* CONTEND.]

con·ten·tious (kən-ténshəss || kon-) *adj.* **1.** Given to contention; quarrelsome. **2.** Involving contention; controversial. —See Synonyms at **belligerent. —con·ten·tious·ly** *adv.* **—con·ten·tious·ness** *n.*

con·ter·mi·nous (kon-térmi-nəss, kən-) *adj.* Also **con·ter·mi·nal** (-n'l) Having a common boundary; coextensive; coterminous. [Latin *conterminus* : *com-,* together + *terminus,* boundary, limit.] **—con·ter·mi·nous·ly** *adv.*

con·tes·sa (kon-téssə) *n.* An Italian countess. [Italian.]

con·test (kón-test) *n.* **1.** A struggle for superiority or victory between rivals. **2.** A dispute; a debate. **3.** Any competition; especially, one in which entrants perform separately and are rated by judges. —See Synonyms at **conflict.**
~*v.* (kən-tést || kón-test) **contested, -testing, -tests.** —*tr.* **1.** To compete or strive for: *Six candidates contested the seat at the last election.* **2.** To attempt to disprove or invalidate; dispute; challenge: *contest a will.* —*intr.* To struggle or compete; contend. —See Synonyms at **oppose.** [Old French *conteste,* from *contester,* from Latin *contentus,* restrained, satisfied, past participle of *continēre,* to restrain, CONTAIN.] **—con·tent·ment** *n.*
a witness.] **—con·test·a·ble** *adj.* **—con·test·er** *n.*

con·test·ant (kən-téstənt || *U.S. also* kón-testənt) *n.* **1.** One who takes part in a contest; a competitor. **2.** One who contests something, such as an election or a will.

con·tes·ta·tion (kón-tess-táysh'n) *n.* Controversy; disputation.

con·text (kóntekst) *n.* **1.** The part of a written or spoken statement that leads up to and follows a particular word or passage, and often specifies its meaning, or without which the meaning cannot be understood. **2.** The circumstances in which a particular event occurs; a background. [Middle English, from Latin *contextus,* coherence, sequence of words, from the past participle of *contexere,* to join together, weave : *com-,* together + *texere,* to join, weave, plait.]

con·tex·tu·al (kən-tékstew-əl || kon-) *adj.* Of, pertaining to, making use of, or depending upon the context. **—con·tex·tu·al·ly** *adv.*

con·tex·tu·al·ise, con·tex·tu·al·ize (kən-tékstew-əl-īz || kon-) —*tr.v.* **-ised, -ising, -ises.** To place (a word, an idea, or an activity, for example) in an appropriate context. **—con·tex·tu·al·i·sa·tion** (-ī-záysh'n || *U.S.* -i-) *n.*

con·tex·ture (kən-téks-chər || kon-) *n.* **1.** The act of weaving or assembling parts. **2.** An arrangement of interconnected parts; a structure. **—con·tex·tur·al, con·tex·tured** *adj.*

Con·ti·board (kónti-bawrd || -bōrd) *n.* A trademark for a type of board covered in melamine and used for shelving.

con·tig·u·ous (kən-tíggew-əss || kon-) *adj.* **1.** Sharing an edge or boundary; touching. **2.** Nearby; neighbouring; adjacent. **3.** Adjacent in time; immediately preceding or following. [Latin *contiguus,* from *contingere,* to touch on all sides, CONTACT.] **—con·ti·gu·i·ty** (kónti-géw-əti) *n.* **—con·tig·u·ous·ly** *adv.* **—con·tig·u·ous·ness** *n.*

con·ti·nence (kóntinənss) *n.* **1.** Self-restraint; moderation. **2.** Control of the bodily functions of urination and defecation. **3.** Partial or complete abstention from sexual activity. —See Synonyms at **abstinence.**

con·ti·nent¹ (kóntinənt || *U.S. also* kónt-nənt) *n.* **1.** *Abbr.* **cont.** Any of the principal landmasses of the earth, usually regarded as including Africa, Antarctica, Asia, Australia, Europe, and North and South America. **2.** *Rare.* A thing that holds or retains. **—the Continent.** The mainland of Europe. [Latin *(terra) continēns* (stem *continent-*), "continuous (land)," from the present participle of *continēre,* to hold together, continue. See **continent** (adjective).]

continent² *adj.* **1.** Self-restrained; moderate. **2.** Able to control the bodily functions of urination and defecation. **3.** Partially or completely abstaining from sexual activity. [Middle English, from Old French, from Latin *continēns* (stem *continent-*), present participle of *continēre,* to hold together, CONTAIN.] **—con·ti·nent·ly** *adv.*

con·ti·nen·tal (kónti-nént'l) *adj.* **1.** Of, pertaining to, or characteristic of a continent. **2.** *Often capital* **C.** Of or relating to the mainland of Europe; European. **3.** Designating a climate characteristic of large landmasses, with hot summers, cold winters, and low rainfall. ∼*n. Usually capital* **C.** An inhabitant of the mainland of Europe; a European. —**con·ti·nen·tal·ism** *n.* —**con·ti·nen·tal·ist** *n.* —**con·ti·nen·tal·i·ty** *n.* —**con·ti·nen·tal·ly** *adv.*

continental breakfast *n.* A light breakfast consisting of rolls, usually with butter and jam, and coffee.

continental divide *n.* **1.** An extensive stretch of high ground from each side of which the river systems of a continent flow in opposite directions. **2.** *Capital* **C,** *capital* **D.** In North America, such a stretch formed by the crests of the Rocky Mountains. In this sense, also called "Great Divide".

continental drift *n.* The theory that the earth's continents are not fixed in position but move slowly over the surface of the earth, their present positions resulting from the break-up of a single landmass about 200 million years ago. See **plate tectonics.**

continental quilt *n.* A **duvet** *(see).*

continental shelf *n.* A generally shallow, flat submerged portion of a continent, extending to a point of steep descent to the ocean floor. Also called "shelf".

con·tin·gence (kən-tínjəns ‖ kon-) *n.* **1.** A joining or touching. **2.** The condition of contingency.

con·tin·gen·cy (kən-tínjən-si ‖ kon-) *n., pl.* **-cies. 1. a.** An event that may occur but that is not likely or intended; a possibility. **b.** A possibility that must be prepared against; a future emergency. Sometimes used adjectivally: *a contingency fund.* **2.** The condition of being dependent upon chance; uncertainty; fortuitousness. **3.** Something incidental to something else. **4.** *Statistics.* The degree of association between theoretical and observed frequencies of certain types of variable.

con·tin·gent (kən-tínjənt ‖ kon-) *adj.* **1.** Liable to occur, but not with certainty; possible. **2.** Dependent upon conditions or events not yet established; conditional. Often used with *on* or *upon.* **3.** Happening by chance or accident; fortuitous. **4.** *Philosophy.* Neither necessarily true nor necessarily false. Said of a proposition. —See Synonyms at **accidental.** ∼ *n.* **1.** A contingency. **2.** A share or quota, as of troops, contributed to a general effort. **3.** A representative group forming part of a larger group. [Middle English, from Old French, from Latin *contingēns* (stem *contingent-*), present participle of *contingere,* to touch on all sides, happen, CONTACT.] —**con·tin·gent·ly** *adv.*

con·tin·u·al (kən-tínnew-əl ‖ kon-, -tínnewl, -tín-yəl) *adj.* **1.** Repeated regularly and frequently; recurring often: *continual interruptions.* **2.** Unending; incessant: *a source of continual worry.* —**con·tin·u·al·ly** *adv.*

    Synonyms: continual, continuous, constant, ceaseless, incessant, perpetual, eternal, perennial, interminable.

con·tin·u·ance (kən-tínnew-ənss ‖ kon-) *n.* **1.** The act or fact of continuing. **2.** The time during which something exists or lasts; duration. **3.** A continuation; a sequel. **4.** *U.S. Law.* Adjournment.

    Usage: Continuance, except in its legal sense, and continuation are sometimes interchangeable; but usually the former emphasises the duration of a condition (*a machine's continuance in working order*), whereas the latter stresses prolongation or resumption of action (*the continuation of the story*).

con·tin·u·ant (kən-tínnew-ənt ‖ kon-) *n. Phonetics.* A consonant, such as *s, z,* or *f,* that may be prolonged as long as the breath lasts without a change in quality. Compare **stop.** [French, from Latin *continuāns* (stem *continuant-*), present participle of *continuāre,* to CONTINUE.]

con·tin·u·a·tion (kən-tínnew-áysh'n ‖ kon-) *n.* **1. a.** The act or fact of continuing. **b.** The state of being continued. See Usage note at **continuance. 2.** A part by which something is carried on or extended; a supplement or sequel. **3.** A **contango** *(see).*

con·tin·u·a·tive (kən-tínnew-ətiv ‖ kon-, -aytiv) *adj.* **1.** Serving to continue or cause continuation. **2.** *Grammar.* Expressing or producing continuation. Said of a word or clause. ∼*n.* Something that expresses or causes continuation. —**con·tin·u·a·tive·ly** *adv.*

con·tin·u·a·tor (kən-tínnew-aytər ‖ kon-) *n.* One that continues; especially, a person who resumes the work of another.

con·tin·ue (kən-tínnew ‖ kon-) *v.* **-ued, -uing, -ues.** —*intr.* **1.** To exist over a prolonged period; last; persist. **2.** To exist over an extended space; extend. **3.** To remain in the same state, capacity, or place. **4.** To go on after an interruption; resume. —*tr.* **1.** To carry forward; keep up; persist in. **2.** To carry further in time, space, or development; extend. **3.** To carry on after an interruption; resume. **4.** *U.S. Law.* To adjourn. [Middle English *continuen,* from Old French *continuer,* from Latin *continuāre,* from *continuus,* from *continēre,* to hold together, be continuous, CONTAIN.] —**con·tin·u·a·ble** *adj.* —**con·tin·u·er** *n.*

con·ti·nu·i·ty (kónti-néw-əti ‖ -nóō-) *n., pl.* **-ties. 1.** The state or quality of being continuous. **2.** An uninterrupted succession; an unbroken course. **3.** A detailed film scenario designed to create the impression of continuous action and to prevent discrepancies from shot to shot. **4.** Connecting items or announcements serving to link radio or television programmes so that no break occurs.

con·tin·u·o (kən-tínnew-ō ‖ kon-) *n., pl.* **-os. 1.** A bass part, typically played on a stringed or keyboard instrument, in which numerals indicate the successive chords, the actual notes played being left to the performer. Also called "basso continuo", "figured bass".

2. The instrument or instruments playing this. [Italian, "continuous".]

con·tin·u·ous (kən-tínnew-əss ‖ kon-) *adj.* **1.** Extending or prolonged without interruption or cessation; unceasing. **2.** *Mathematics.* Designating a function in which no sudden changes in value occur as the variable increases or decreases gradually. **3.** *Grammar.* **Progressive** *(see).* —See Synonyms at **continual.** [Latin *continuus,* from *continēre,* to hold together, CONTINUE.] —**con·tin·u·ous·ly** *adv.* —**con·tin·u·ous·ness** *n.*

continuous assessment *n.* A method of assessing a student's work in which the work is constantly monitored and evaluated throughout his or her course, as opposed, for example, to an assessment based solely on performance in a final examination.

continuous creation *n.* The hypothesis that the universe did not start at a particular instant but has been continuously created throughout time. This hypothesis is a part of the **steady-state theory** *(see).*

continuous stationery *n.* Joined sheets of paper that are separated only by perforations and folded in alternate directions, used especially for computer print-out.

continuous wave *adj. Abbr.* **cw, CW** Emitting or capable of emitting continuously; not pulsed. Said especially of lasers.

con·tin·u·um (kən-tínnew-əm ‖ kon-) *n., pl.* **-tinua** (-tínnew-ə) or **-tinuums. 1.** A continuous extent, succession, or whole, no part of which can be distinguished from neighbouring parts except by arbitrary division. **2.** *Mathematics.* A set having the same number of points as all the real numbers in an interval. [Latin, neuter of *continuus,* CONTINUOUS.]

con·tort (kən-tórt ‖ kon-) *v.* **-torted, -torting, -torts.** —*tr.* To twist, wrench, or bend severely out of normal shape. —*intr.* To become twisted into a strained shape or expression. —See Synonyms at **distort.** [Latin *contorquēre* (past participle *contortus*), to twist together : *com-,* together + *torquēre,* to twist.] —**con·tor·tion** *n.* —**con·tor·tive** *adj.*

con·tort·ed (kən-tórtid ‖ kon-) *adj.* **1.** Twisted or strained out of shape. **2.** *Botany.* Twisted or bent upon itself. —**con·tort·ed·ly** *adv.* —**con·tort·ed·ness** *n.*

con·tor·tion·ist (kən-tórsh'n-ist ‖ kon-) *n.* An acrobat who can contort his body and limbs into extraordinary positions. —**con·tor·tion·is·tic** (-ístik) *adj.*

con·tour (kón-toor) *n.* **1.** The outline of a figure, body, or mass; shape. **2.** A line that represents such an outline; a contour line. —See Synonyms at **form.** ∼*tr.v.* **contoured, -touring, -tours. 1.** To make or shape the outline of; represent in contour. **2.** To build (a road, for example) to follow the contour of the land. ∼*adj.* **1.** Following the contour lines of uneven terrain to limit erosion of topsoil: *contour ploughing.* **2.** Shaped to fit the outline or form of something. [French, from Italian *contorno,* from *contornare,* to go around, draw in outline : *con-* (intensive), from Latin *con-, com-* + *tornare,* to turn in a lathe, from Latin *tornāre,* from *tornus,* lathe, from Greek *tornos.*]

contour feather *n.* Any of the outermost feathers of a bird, forming the visible body contour and plumage.

contour line *n.* An imaginary line, or its representation on a contour map, joining points of equal elevation.

contour map *n.* A map showing elevations and surface configuration by means of contour lines.

contr. 1. contract. **2.** contraction. **3.** contralto.

con·tra (kón-trə, -traa) *prep.* **1.** Against. Used chiefly in the phrase *pro and contra.* **2.** Contrary to the view or evidence of: *believe, contra recent opinion polls, that they can still win the election.* [Latin.]

Contra *n., pl.* **-tras.** An opponent of the Sandinista government of Nicaragua. [Spanish, probably from *contra-Sandinista,* from *contra,* against, akin to English CONTRA.] —**Contra** *adj.*

contra– *comb. form.* Indicates: **1.** Against, opposing, or contrary; for example, **contradistinction, contraindicate. 2.** Pitched next below a specified musical instrument; for example, **contrabassoon.** [Middle English, from Latin *contrā-,* from *contrā,* against.]

con·tra·band (kóntrə-band) *n.* **1.** Goods prohibited by law or treaty from being imported or exported. **2. a.** Illegal traffic in such goods; smuggling. **b.** Smuggled goods. **3.** *International Law.* Goods that may be confiscated by a belligerent if supplied to another belligerent by a neutral. Also called "contraband of war". [French *contrebande,* from Italian *contrabbando* : *contra-,* against, from Latin *contrā-* + *bando,* proclamation, from Late Latin *bannus, bannum.*] —**con·tra·band** *adj.* —**con·tra·band·ist** *n.*

con·tra·bass (kóntrə-bayss) *n. Music.* A **double bass** *(see).* ∼*adj. Music.* Pitched an octave below the normal bass range. [Obsolete Italian *contrabasso* : *contra-,* pitched below, from Latin *contrā-,* against + *basso,* low, bass, from Late Latin *bassus.*] —**con·tra·bass·ist** *n.*

con·tra·bas·soon (kóntrə-bə-sóōn) *n.* The largest and lowest-pitched of the double-reed wind musical instruments, sounding an octave below the bassoon. Also called "double bassoon".

con·tra·cep·tion (kóntrə-sépsh'n) *n.* The prevention of unwanted pregnancy. [CONTRA- + (CON)CEPTION.]

con·tra·cep·tive (kóntrə-séptiv) *adj.* Capable of preventing conception. ∼*n.* A contraceptive agent or device, such as a condom.

con·tract (kón-trakt) *n. Abbr.* **contr., cont. 1.** An agreement between two or more parties, especially one that is written and enforceable by law. **2.** The writing or document containing such an

agreement. **3.** The branch of law dealing with contracts. **4.** An agreement by which property is transferred; a conveyance. **5.** Marriage as a formal agreement; betrothal. **6.** In the game of bridge: **a.** The last and highest bid of one hand. **b.** The number of tricks thus bid. **7.** *Slang.* An undertaking to kill someone for a fee.
~*v.* (kən-trákt || kón-trakt) **contracted, -tracting, -tracts.** —*tr.* **1.** To enter into by contract; establish or settle by formal agreement. **2. a.** To acquire or incur (a debt, for example). **b.** To catch (a disease). **3.** To reduce in size by drawing together; shrink. **4.** To pull together; wrinkle. **5.** To shorten (a word or words) by omitting or combining some of the letters or sounds; for example, *I'm* for *I am.* —*intr.* **1.** To enter into or make a contract. **2.** To become reduced in size by or as if by being drawn together. **—contract out.** To arrange formally not to participate in a scheme or to be exempt from an obligation. [Middle English, from Old French, from Latin *contractus,* from the past participle of *contrahere,* to draw together, bring about, enter into an agreement : *com-,* together + *trahere,* to draw.] **—con·tract·i·bil·i·ty** (-ə-bílləti) *n.* **—con·tract·i·ble** *adj.*
Synonyms: *contract, condense, compress, constrict, shrink.*

contract bridge *n.* A form of auction bridge in which tricks in excess of the contract may not count towards game. Compare **auction bridge.**

con·trac·tile (kən-trákt-īl || kon-, *U.S.* -əl) *adj.* Capable of contracting or causing contraction. **—con·trac·til·i·ty** (kón-trak-tílləti) *n.*

contractile root *n.* A specialised root formed by certain bulbs and corms that pulls the bulb or corm down to the appropriate depth in the soil.

con·trac·tion (kən-tráksh'n || kon-) *n. Abbr.* **cont., contr. 1.** The act of contracting or the state of being contracted. **2.** *Grammar.* **a.** A shortened word or words formed by omitting or combining some of the letters or sounds; for example, *isn't* for *is not.* **b.** The formation of such a word. **3.** *Physiology.* The shortening, and often thickening, of functioning muscle; especially, that which occurs immediately preceding childbirth. **4.** *Medicine.* Any abnormal, often irreversible, shrinking or shortening of a body or part. **5.** *Physics.* A decrease in size caused by a reduction in temperature.

con·trac·tor (kən-tráktər || kon-, *U.S. also* kón-traktər) *n.* **1.** One who agrees to furnish materials or perform services at a specific price, especially in the building trade. **2.** Something that contracts, especially a muscle.

con·trac·tu·al (kən-tráktew-əl || kon-) *adj.* Of, connected with, or having the nature of a contract.

con·trac·ture (kən-trák-chər || kon-) *n.* **1.** A drawing together of skeletal muscle, usually due to fibrosis, resulting in distortion or deformity. **2.** A deformity resulting from such shortening.

con·tra·dict (kóntrə-díkt) *v.* **-dicted, -dicting, -dicts.** —*tr.* **1.** To assert or express the opposite of (a statement). **2.** To deny the statement of. **3.** To be contrary to; be inconsistent with. —*intr.* To utter a statement that contradicts. [Latin *contrādīcere,* to speak against : *contrā-,* against + *dīcere,* to speak.] **—con·tra·dict·a·ble** *adj.* **—con·tra·dict·er, con·tra·dic·tor** (-ər) *n.*

con·tra·dic·tion (kóntrə-díksh'n) *n.* **1. a.** The act of contradicting. **b.** The state of being in disagreement or opposition. **2.** A statement that contradicts; a denial. **3.** Inconsistency or discrepancy. **4.** Something that contains contradictory elements: *a contradiction in terms.*

con·tra·dic·tious (kóntrə-díkshəss) *adj.* Tending to contradict; argumentative.

con·tra·dic·to·ry (kóntrə-díktəri, -díktri) *adj.* **1.** Involving or having the nature of a contradiction; mutually inconsistent. **2.** Given to contradicting. —See Synonyms at **opposite.**
~*n., pl.* **contradictories.** *Logic.* Either of two propositions related in such a way that it is impossible for both to be true or both to be false. Compare **contrary. —con·tra·dic·to·ri·ly** *adv.* **—con·tra·dic·to·ri·ness** *n.*

con·tra·dis·tinc·tion (kóntrə-di-stíngk-sh'n) *n.* Distinction by contrast or opposing qualities. **—con·tra·dis·tinc·tive** (-tiv) *adj.* **—con·tra·dis·tinc·tive·ly** *adv.*

con·tra·dis·tin·guish (kóntrə-di-stíng-gwish) *tr.v.* **-guished, -guishing, -guishes.** To distinguish by contrasting qualities.

con·tra·flow (kóntrə-flō) *adj. British.* Relating to a system whereby traffic is allowed to move in a direction opposite to that of its usual movement (as to facilitate bus travel or to keep two-way traffic on a motorway one of whose carriageways is closed). [CONTRA- + *flow* (of traffic).]

con·trail (kón-trayl) *n.* A visible trail of water droplets or ice crystals sometimes forming in the wake of an aircraft. Also called "vapour trail". [CON(DENSATION) + TRAIL.]

con·tra·in·di·cate (kóntrə-índi-kayt) *tr.v.* **-cated, -cating, -cates.** *Medicine.* To indicate the inadvisability of: *Allergic reactions contraindicated the use of penicillin.* **—con·tra·in·di·cant** (-kənt) *n.* **—con·tra·in·di·ca·tion** (-káysh'n) *n.*

con·tral·to (kən-traál-tō, -trál- || kon-) *n., pl.* **-tos** or **-ti** (-tee). *Abbr.* **contr.** *Music.* **1.** The lowest female voice or voice part, intermediate in range between soprano and tenor. **2.** A woman having such a voice. [Italian : *contra-,* pitched below, from Latin *contrā-,* against + ALTO.]

con·trap·tion (kən-trápsh'n || kon-) *n.* A contrivance; a device or machine. [Humorous blend of CONTRIVE and TRAP + -TION.]

con·tra·pun·tal (kóntrə-púnt'l) *adj. Music.* Of, pertaining to, or incorporating counterpoint. [From Italian *contrapunto* : *contra-,* against + *punto,* POINT.] **—con·tra·pun·tal·ly** *adv.*

con·tra·pun·tist (kóntrə-puntist, -púntist) *n.* A specialist in contrapuntal music.

con·tra·ri·e·ty (kóntrə-rī́-əti) *n., pl.* **-ties. 1.** The quality or condition of being contrary. **2.** Something contrary; a discrepancy or inconsistency. [Middle English, from Old French *contrarieté,* from Late Latin *contrārietās* (stem *contrārietāt-*), from *contrārius,* CONTRARY.]

con·trar·i·ous (kən-traír-i-əss) *adj. Archaic.* Perverse; contrary; adverse. [Middle English, from Medieval Latin *contrāriōsus,* from *contrārius,* CONTRARY.] **—con·trar·i·ous·ly** *adv.*

con·trar·i·wise (kón-trəri-wīz, kən-traír-i-) *adv.* **1.** From a contrasting point of view. **2.** In the opposite way or reverse order. **3.** Contrarily; perversely.

con·tra·ry (kón-trəri; *in sense 4 also* kən-traír-i || *U.S.* -trerri) *adj.* **1.** Opposed, as in character or purpose; completely different. **2.** Opposite in direction or position. **3.** Adverse; unfavourable. Said of weather conditions. **4.** Given to acting or speaking in opposition to others; obstinate; wilful. —See Synonyms at **opposite.**
~*n., pl.* **contraries. 1.** That which is contrary; the opposite. **2.** Either of two contrary, opposing, or incompatible things or conditions. **3.** *Logic.* A proposition related to another in such a way that if the latter is true, the former must be false, but if the latter is false, the former is not necessarily true. In this sense, compare **contradictory. —by contraries.** In opposition to what is expected. **—on the contrary.** Quite the opposite; in complete disagreement; conversely. **—to the contrary.** To a contrasting or opposite effect: *in the absence of any evidence to the contrary.*
~*adv.* In opposition; contrariwise. [Middle English *contrarie,* from Old French *contraire,* from Latin *contrārius,* from *contrā,* against.] **—con·tra·ri·ly** *adv.* **—con·tra·ri·ness** *n.*
Synonyms: *contrary,obstinate, stubborn, perverse, adverse, wayward, wilful.*

con·trast (kən-traást || kon-, -trást, kón-traast, -trast) *v.* **-trasted, -trasting, -trasts.** —*tr.* To set in opposition or juxtapose in order to show or emphasise differences. —*intr.* To show differences or differing qualities when compared. Used with *with.*
~*n.* (kón-traast, -trast). **1.** The act of contrasting or the state of being contrasted. Often used in the phrases *by contrast, in contrast with,* and *in contrast to.* **2.** A quality of dissimilarity, often striking, between things compared. **3.** Something that shows a dissimilarity, often striking, when compared to something else. **4.** In a work of art, the use of opposing elements, such as colours, forms, or lines, in proximity to produce an effect. **5.** The extent to which different parts of a photographic image differ in density. **6.** The extent to which different parts of a television picture differ in brightness. [French *contrester, contraster,* to contrast, resist, from Italian *contrastare,* from Medieval Latin *contrāstāre* : Latin *contrā-,* against + *stāre,* to stand.] **—con·trast·a·ble** *adj.* **—con·trast·ing·ly** *adv.* **—con·trast·ive** *adj.* **—con·trast·ive·ly** *adv.*
Usage: As a verb, *contrast* is usually followed by *with.* As a noun the usual preposition is *between* (*the contrast between X and Y*), but *with* and *to* are also used (*the contrast with last year; as a contrast to his father.*). The phrase *in contrast* is usually followed by *with,* but *to* is also used, especially when the notion of opposition is being stressed.

con·trast·y (kón-traast-i || -trast-, kən-traásti, -trásti) *adj. Photography.* Having or producing sharp contrasts between light and dark.

con·tra·sug·gest·ible (kóntrə-sə-jéstəb'l) *adj. Psychology.* Having or showing a tendency to do or believe the opposite in response to a suggestion. **—con·tra·sug·gest·i·bil·i·ty** (-jéstə-bílləti) *n.*

con·tra·vene (kóntrə-véen) *tr.v.* **-vened, -vening, -venes. 1.** To act or be counter to (especially laws or regulations); violate; infringe. **2.** To oppose in argument. [Old French *contravenir,* from Late Latin *contrāvenīre,* to come against, oppose : Latin *contrā-,* against + *venīre,* to come.] **—con·tra·ven·er** *n.*

con·tra·ven·tion (kóntrə-vénsh'n) *n.* The act or instance of contravening; a violation; an infringement.

con·tre·danse, con·tra·dance (kóntrə-daanss || -danss) *n.* **1.** A folk dance performed in two lines with the partners facing each other. **2.** The music for such a dance. [French, from English COUNTRY DANCE (influenced by French *contre,* against, opposite, on account of the partners' facing each other).]

con·tre·temps (kón-trə-toN, kóN-) *n., pl.* **contretemps. 1.** An inopportune or embarrassing occurrence; a mishap. **2.** An argument or confrontation. [French : *contre-,* against, from Latin *contrā-* + *temps,* time, from Latin *tempus.*]

con·trib·ute (kən-tríbbewt || kon-, kóntri-bewt. *Note: the last-mentioned pronunciation, although very widely used, is condemned by purists.*) *v.* **-uted, -uting, -utes.** —*tr.* **1.** To give or supply in common with others; give to a common fund or for a common purpose. **2.** To submit (an article, for example) for inclusion in a publication. —*intr.* **1.** To make a contribution. **2.** To act as a significant factor; play an important part. Used with *to*: *We have all contributed to his failure.* **3.** To join in a discussion, debate, or the like. [Latin *contribuere,* to bring together, unite, collect : *com-,* together + *tribuere,* to allot, grant (see **tribute**).] **—con·trib·ut·a·ble** *adj.* **—con·trib·u·tive** *adj.* **—con·trib·u·tive·ly** *adv.* **—con·trib·u·tive·ness** *n.*

con·tri·bu·tion (kóntri-béwsh'n) *n.* **1.** The act of contributing. **2.** Something contributed, especially a written article contributed to a publication or money contributed to a cause. **3.** *Archaic.* An impost or levy for a special, especially military, purpose.

con·trib·u·tor (kən-tríbbewtər || kon-) *n.* One who contributes; especially, one who contributes articles or features to a newspaper or magazine.

con·trib·u·to·ry (kən-tríbbew-tri, -təri || kon-, kóntri-béwtəri) *adj.* **1.** Of, involving, or making a contribution. **2.** Contributing towards a result. **3.** *British.* Designating an employees' pension scheme to which both employer and employee make contributions.
~n., pl. **contributories.** **1.** One that contributes. **2.** *Law.* A person who is obliged to contribute towards the payment of a company's debts if the company is wound up.
contributory negligence *n. Law.* Carelessness on the part of the injured party in a legal case that has contributed to the injury or harm that he has suffered.
con trick *n. Informal.* A confidence trick.
con·trite (kón-trīt, kən-trīt) *adj.* **1.** Humbled by guilt and repentant for one's sins; penitent; remorseful. **2.** Arising from contrition: *contrite resolutions.* [Middle English *contrit,* from Old French, from Medieval Latin *contrītus,* "broken in spirit", repentant, from Latin, past participle of *conterere,* to bruise, grind : *com-* (intensive) + *terere,* to rub, grind.] **—con·trite·ly** *adv.* **—con·trite·ness** *n.*
con·tri·tion (kən-trísh'n || kon-) *n.* **1.** Sincere remorse for wrongdoing. **2.** *Theology.* Repentance for sin, as *perfect contrition,* repentance with a sincere desire to amend, arising from pure love of God, or *imperfect contrition,* repentance arising from a motive less than the pure love of God. Compare **attrition.**
con·tri·vance (kən-trívənss || kon-) *n.* **1. a.** The act or manner of contriving. **b.** The ability to contrive; inventiveness. **2.** Something contrived, such as a mechanical device or a clever plan.
con·trive (kən-trīv || kon-) *v.* **-trived, -triving, -trives.** *—tr.* **1.** To plan or devise with cleverness or ingenuity. **2.** To plot with evil intent; scheme. **3.** To invent or fabricate, especially by improvisation: *have to contrive excuses on the spur of the moment.* **4.** To manage or succeed in, as by scheming. *—intr.* To plot or scheme. [Middle English *contreven, controven,* from Old French *controver,* from Late Latin *contropāre,* to represent figuratively, compare : Latin *com-,* together + *tropus,* figure of speech, trope, from Greek *tropos,* turn, manner, style.] **—con·triv·a·ble** *adj.* **—con·triv·er** *n.*
con·trived (kən-trīvd || kon-) *adj.* Achieved by artifice; unnatural. **—con·triv·ed·ly** *adv.*
con·trol (kən-trōl || kon-) *tr.v.* **-trolled, -trolling, -trols. 1. a.** To exercise authority or a dominating influence over; direct: *control an empire.* **b.** To regulate; operate: *This button controls the lights.* **2.** To hold in restraint; check. **3.** To verify or regulate (a scientific experiment) by conducting a parallel experiment in which the variable whose effects are to be tested is absent or held constant or by comparing with some other standard. **4.** To verify (an account or figures, for example). —See Synonyms at **conduct.**
~n. **1.** Authority or ability to regulate, direct, restrain, or dominate: *under the control of the local authority; lost control of her temper.* **2.** An act or means of regulating or verifying; a check or curb: *go through passport control; price controls.* **3. a.** A standard of comparison for checking or verifying the results of an experiment. **b.** An individual or group used as a standard of comparison in a control experiment. Also used adjectivally: *a control group.* **4.** Any of a set of instruments used to operate, regulate, or guide a machine or vehicle. Also used adjectivally: *control panel.* **5.** The organisation, personnel, and equipment used in running and controlling an operation such as a space flight: *ground control to Major Tom.* **6.** In spiritualism, a spirit presumed to act through a medium. [Middle English *controllen,* from Old French *cont(r)eroller,* from Medieval Latin *contrārotulāre,* to check by a counter roll or duplicate register, from *contrārotulus,* counter roll, duplicate register : Latin *contrā-,* against, opposite + *rotulus,* roll, "little wheel", from *rota,* wheel.] **—con·trol·la·bil·i·ty** (-ə-bílləti) *n.* **—con·trol·la·ble** *adj.*
control chart *n. Statistics.* A graph of a quantitative characteristic of a manufacturing process, usually determined from small, periodically repeated samples and evaluated with respect to control limits rendered as parallel horizontal lines above and below a line representing the expected or average value of the characteristic.
control experiment *n.* An experiment designed to check or verify a parallel experiment or as part of a set of experiments testing the effects of a variable or variables, in which the variable factors are controlled so that the effects of changing one at a time can be observed.
control grid *n. Electronics.* A **grid** *(see)* in a vacuum tube.
con·trolled response (kən-trōld || kon-) *n.* A response to a military attack by limited military means in an effort to avoid nuclear war.
con·trol·ler (kən-trōl-ər || kon-) *n.* Also **comp·trol·ler** (for sense 2). **1.** One who controls. **2.** An officer who audits accounts and supervises the financial affairs of a corporation or government body. **3.** A regulating mechanism, as in a vehicle or electrical device.
control rod *n. Physics.* Any of a number of rods that can be moved into or out of the core of a nuclear reactor, used to control the rate of the reaction. They are made of a material that absorbs neutrons, such as boron.
control stick *n.* A lever used in small aircraft to control the angle of the elevators and ailerons; a joystick. Also called "control column.".
control surface *n.* A movable aerofoil, especially a rudder, aileron, or elevator, used to control or guide an aircraft, guided missile, or rocket.
control tower *n.* A usually glass-enclosed tower at an airport from which air traffic is controlled by radio.
con·tro·ver·sial (kóntrə-vérsh'l) *adj.* **1.** Subject to, surrounded by, or likely to produce controversy. **2.** Fond of controversy; disputatious. **—con·tro·ver·sial·ist** *n.* **—con·tro·ver·sial·ly** *adv.*
con·tro·ver·sy (kóntrə-versi, -vərsi, kən-tróvvərsi) *n., pl.* **-sies. 1.** A dispute or debate, especially a lengthy and public one, between sides holding opposing views. **2.** Disputation; contention: *an affair surrounded by controversy.* —See Synonyms at **argument.** [Middle English *controversie,* from Latin *contrōversia,* from *contrōversus,* turned against, disputed : *contrō-,* variant of *contrā-,* against + *versus,* past participle of *vertere,* to turn.]
Usage: This word continually attracts attention, because of the way in which its stress pattern has begun to change in British English in recent years. From an original pronunciation (still universal in the United States) in which *con-* carries the main stress, there has been a change to a main stress on *-trov-.* The reasons for the change are not altogether clear, but may be connected with the fact that most English people no longer pronounce an *r-* sound in the penultimate syllable *-vers-.* Previously, *controversy* followed the regular pattern for words of its general shape, as exemplified by *ádmiralty, dífficulty, éxcellency, présidency,* all with a double consonant sound before the final vowel. The new pattern is that of words with a single consonant sound at this point, as exemplified by *apólogy, epítome, facílity, rhinóceros.* The same change, presumably for the same reason, may also be observed in *metallurgy.*
con·tro·vert (kóntrə-vért, -vert) *tr.v.* **-verted, -verting, -verts. 1.** To raise arguments against; voice opposition to; deny. **2.** To argue or dispute about; debate. [From CONTROVERSY (by analogy with CONVERT, REVERT).] **—con·tro·vert·i·ble** *adj.*
con·tu·ma·cious (kón-tew-máyshəss || -tōō-) *adj.* Obstinately disobedient or rebellious; insubordinate. **—con·tu·ma·cious·ly** *adv.* **—con·tu·ma·cious·ness** *n.*
con·tu·ma·cy (kón-tew-mə-si || -tə-, -chə-) *n., pl.* **-cies. 1.** Obstinate or contemptuous resistance to authority. **2.** Wilful disobedience to a court order. [Middle English *contumacie,* from Latin *contumācia,* from *contumāx,* stubborn, disobedient.]
con·tu·me·ly (kón-tewm-li, -tewmi-, kən-téwmi- || -tōōm-, -təm-) *n., pl.* **-lies. 1.** Rudeness or contempt in behaviour or speech; insolence. **2.** An insulting remark or act. [Middle English *contumelie,* from Old French, from Latin *contumēlia,* insult, reproach.] **—con·tu·me·li·ous** (kóntew-meéli-əss) *adj.* **—con·tu·me·li·ous·ly** *adv.*
con·tuse (kən-téwz || kon-, -tōōz) *tr.v.* **-tused, -tusing, -tuses.** To injure without breaking the skin; bruise. [Middle English *contusen,* from Old French *contuser,* from Latin *contundere* (past participle *contūsus*), to beat, pound : *com-* (intensive) + *tundere,* to beat.] **—con·tu·sion** (-téwzh'n || -tōōzh'n) *n.*
co·nun·drum (kə-nún-drəm) *n.* **1.** A riddle in which a fanciful question is answered by a pun. **2.** A puzzling problem or question admitting of no satisfactory solution. [16th century : perhaps originally a mock-Latin university slang word.]
con·ur·ba·tion (kón-ur-báysh'n, -ər-) *n.* A large urban sprawl including smaller towns that have spread and joined together. [CON- + Latin *urbs,* city (see **urban**) + -ATION.]
con·va·lesce (kón-və-léss) *intr.v.* **-lesced, -lescing, -lesces.** To return to health after illness, particularly by resting; recuperate. [Latin *convalēscere* : *com-* (intensive) + *valēscere,* to grow strong, from *valēre,* to be strong or well.]
con·va·les·cence (kón-və-léss'nss) *n.* **1.** Gradual return to health and strength after illness, particularly by resting. **2.** The period needed for this.
con·va·les·cent *n.* One who is regaining health and strength after illness, particularly through resting. **—con·va·les·cent** *adj.*
con·vect (kən-vékt || kon-) *v.* **-vected, -vecting, -vects.** *—tr.* To transfer (heat) by convection. *—intr.* To undergo convection.
con·vec·tion (kən-véksh'n || kon-) *n.* **1.** The act or process of transmitting or conveying. **2.** *Physics.* **a.** Heat transfer by fluid motion between regions of unequal density that result from nonuniform heating. Also called "natural convection". **b.** Fluid motion caused by an external force such as a fan. Also called "forced convection". **3.** *Meteorology.* The transfer of heat or other atmospheric properties by massive motion within the atmosphere, especially by such motion directed upwards. [Late Latin *convectiō* (stem *convectiōn-*), from *convehere,* to carry together, bring along : *com-,* together + *vehere,* to carry.] **—con·vec·tion·al** *adj.* **—con·vec·tive** *adj.* **—con·vec·tive·ly** *adv.*
con·vec·tor heater (kən-véktər || kon-) *n.* A portable room heater, typically having an enclosed electrically heated element from which warm air circulates by natural convection. Also called "convector".
con·vene (kən-veén || kon-) *v.* **-vened, -vening, -venes.** *—intr.* To assemble, usually for an official or public purpose; meet formally. *—tr.* **1.** To cause to come together or assemble; convoke. **2.** To summon to appear, as before a court of law. [Middle English *convenen,* from Old French *convenir,* to come together, meet, hence agree, be suitable, from Latin *convenīre* : *com-,* together + *venīre,* to come.] **—con·ven·a·ble** *adj.*
con·ven·er, con·ven·or (kən-veénər || kon-) *n.* A person, often elected, who convenes or is the chairperson of a meeting, committee, or the like.
con·ven·i·ence (kən-veén-i-ənss || kon-) *n.* Also *archaic* **con·ven·i·en·cy** (-i) *pl.* **-cies. 1.** The quality of being convenient; suitability or handiness. **2.** Personal comfort or advantage. **3.** Anything that increases comfort or makes work less difficult; a convenient appliance, service, condition, or circumstance. **4.** *Chiefly British.* A lavatory. **—at (someone's) convenience.** At a convenient time for someone.
convenience food *n.* Packaged food requiring minimal preparation before being ready to eat.

con·ven·i·ent (kən-véen-i-ənt || kon-) *adj.* **1.** Suited or favourable to one's comfort, purpose, or needs. **2.** Easy to reach; accessible. **3.** *Obsolete.* Fitting and proper; appropriate. [Middle English, from Latin *conveniēns* (stem *convenient-*), present participle of *convenīre,* to be suitable. See **convene.**] **—con·ven·ient·ly** *adv.*
con·vent (kón-vənt || -vent) *n.* **1.** A community, especially of nuns, bound by vows to a religious life under a superior. **2.** The building or buildings occupied by such a community; especially, a nunnery. **3.** A convent school. [Middle English *covent,* from Old French, from Medieval Latin *conventus,* from Latin, a coming together, assembly, from *convenīre,* to come together, CONVENE.]
convent school *n.* A school in which the teaching staff are nuns.
con·ven·ti·cle (kən-véntik'l) *n.* **1.** A religious meeting, especially a secret or illegal one, such as those held by dissenters in England and Scotland in the 16th and 17th centuries. **2.** A building used for such a meeting. [Middle English, from Latin *conventiculum,* a place of meeting, diminutive of *conventus,* assembly, CONVENT.] **—con·ven·ti·cler** *n.*
con·ven·tion (kən-vénsh'n || kon-) *n.* **1.** A formal assembly or meeting of members, representatives, or delegates of a group, such as a political party or trade union. **2.** The body of persons attending such an assembly. **3.** An agreement or compact; especially, an international agreement, less formal than a treaty, dealing with a specific subject such as the treatment of war prisoners. **4.** General agreement on or acceptance of certain practices or attitudes. **5.** A practice or procedure widely observed in a group, especially to facilitate social intercourse. **6.** A widely used and accepted device or technique, as in drama, literature, or painting. **7.** In card games, a prearranged method of bidding or play in order to convey information to partners. [Middle English *convencioun,* from Old French *convention,* from Latin *conventiō* (stem *conventiōn-*), assembly, agreement, from *convenīre,* to come together, CONVENE.]
con·ven·tion·al (kən-vénsh'n'l || kon-) *adj.* **1.** Developed, established, or approved by general usage; customary. **2.** Conforming to or rigidly following established practice or accepted standards; not adventurous or spontaneous. Often used derogatorily. **3.** Marked by or dependent upon conventions, to the point of artificiality. **4.** *Art.* Represented in simplified or abstract form. **5.** *Law.* Based upon mutual consent or agreement; contractual. **6.** Of or having to do with an assembly. **7.** Designating non-nuclear weapons or warfare. **—con·ven·tion·al·ly** *adv.*
conventional current *n. Electronics.* An electric current that is considered to flow from a positive point to a negative, as distinguished from the actual current, which is a flow of electrons in the opposite direction.
con·ven·tion·al·ise, con·ven·tion·al·ize (kən-vénsh'n'l-īz || kon-) *tr.v.* **-ised, -ising, -ises.** **1.** To make conventional. **2.** To represent in a simplified or abstract manner. **—con·ven·tion·al·i·sa·tion** (-ī-záysh'n || *U.S.* -i-) *n.*
con·ven·tion·al·ism (kən-vénsh'n'l-iz'm) *n.* **1.** Advocacy of or adherence to existing conventions. **2.** *Philosophy.* The view that principles and laws, especially scientific laws, are formulated and adopted according to convention and conventional ways of interpreting evidence rather than purely by reason. **—con·ven·tion·al·ist** *n.* **—con·ven·tion·al·i·ty** (-ál-əti) *n.*
conventional wisdom *n.* A body of established, received ideas accepted uncritically. Preceded by *the.*
con·ven·tu·al (kən-véntew-əl || kon-) *n.* **1.** A member of a convent. **2.** *Capital* **C.** A member of a branch of the Franciscan order that permits the accumulation and possession of common property. **—con·ven·tu·al** *adj.*
con·verge (kən-vérj || kon-) *v.* **-verged, -verging, -verges.** *—intr.* **1.** To approach the same point from different directions; tend towards a meeting or intersection. **2.** To tend or move towards union or towards a common conclusion or result. **3.** *Mathematics.* To approach a limit. *—tr.* To cause to converge or meet. [Late Latin *convergere,* to incline together : Latin *com-,* together + *vergere,* to bend, turn, incline.]
con·ver·gence (kən-vérjənss || kon-) *n.* Also **con·ver·gen·cy** (-i) *pl.* **-cies.** **1.** The act, condition, quality, or fact of converging. **2.** *Mathematics.* The property or manner of approaching a limit such as a point, line, surface, or value. **3.** The point or degree of converging. **4.** *Physiology.* The coordinated turning of the eyes inwards to focus on a nearby point. **5.** *Biology.* The adaptive evolution of superficially similar structures, such as the wings of birds and insects, in unrelated species subjected to similar environments. Also called "convergent evolution". **6.** *Meteorology.* A condition characterised by a horizontal net inflow of air over a region, which may be compensated by an upward air current giving rise to cloud and rain. **—con·ver·gent** *adj.*
convergent thinking *n. Psychology.* A type of thinking operation characterised by the use of logical reasoning to arrive at a single correct solution to a problem. Compare **divergent thinking.** **—convergent thinker** *n.*
con·vers·a·ble (kən-vérssəb'l) *adj.* Affable and chatty. **—con·vers·a·ble·ness** *n.*
con·ver·sant (kən-vérss'nt, kónvər-s'nt || kon-) *adj.* Familiar, as by study or experience. Used with *with.* [Middle English *conversaunt,* from Old French *conversant,* from Latin *conversāns* (stem *conversant-*), present participle of *conversārī,* to associate with, CONVERSE.] **—con·ver·sance, con·ver·san·cy** *n.* **—con·ver·sant·ly** *adv.*
con·ver·sa·tion (kónvər-sáysh'n) *n.* **1.** An informal spoken exchange of thoughts and feelings; a familiar talk. **2.** *Archaic.* Close acquaintance or association. **3.** *Archaic.* Manner of life; behaviour. **4.** *Archaic.* Sexual intercourse. **—make conversation.** To talk for the sake of politeness.
con·ver·sa·tion·al (kónvər-sáysh'n'l) *adj.* **1.** Of, pertaining to, or in the style of conversation; informal. **2.** Adept at or given to conversation. **—con·ver·sa·tion·al·ly** *adv.*
con·ver·sa·tion·al·ist (kónvər-sáysh'n'l-ist) *n.* Also **con·ver·sa·tion·ist** (-sáysh'n-ist). One given to or skilled at conversation.
conversation piece *n.* **1.** A type of painting, especially popular in the 18th century, depicting a group of fashionable people. **2.** An unusual object that arouses comment or interest.
con·ver·sa·zi·o·ne (kónvər-sátsi-ṓ-ni) *n., pl.* **-nes** or **-ni** (-nee). A meeting for conversation or for discussion, especially of the arts. [Italian, "conversation".]
con·verse[1] (kən-vérss || kon-) *intr.v.* **-versed, -versing, -verses.** **1.** To engage in spoken exchange of thoughts and feelings; talk. **2.** *Archaic.* To consort; associate. **—See Synonyms at speak.**
~*n.* (kón-verss). *Literary.* Spoken interchange of thoughts and feelings; conversation. [Middle English *conversen,* to dwell, associate with, from Old French *converser,* from Latin *conversārī,* to associate with : *com-,* with + *versārī,* to live, occupy oneself, from *versāre,* frequentative of *vertere,* to turn.]
con·verse[2] (kón-verss, kən-vérss) *adj.* Reversed, as in position, order, or action; contrary.
~*n.* (kón-verss). **1.** Something that is contrary; the opposite. **2.** *Logic.* A proposition obtained by conversion. [Latin *conversus,* past participle of *convertere,* to turn around. See **convert.**] **—con·verse·ly** (kən-vérss-li, kón-) *adv.*
con·ver·sion (kən-vérsh'n || kon-, -vérzh'n) *n.* **1.** The act of converting or the state of being converted. **2.** Something, such as a building, that has been converted, as from one use to another. **3.** A change in which one adopts a new religion. **4.** A change from one belief, opinion, or practice to another. **5.** *Law.* **a.** The unlawful appropriation of another's property. **b.** The changing of real property to personal property or vice versa. **6.** *Finance.* The exchange of one type of security or currency for another. **7.** *Logic.* The interchange of the subject and predicate of a proposition. **8. a.** In Rugby football, a score made after a try, for kicking the ball over the crossbar. **b.** In American football, a successful attempt for an extra score after making a touchdown. **9.** *Psychiatry.* The symbolic manifestation of repressed ideas or impulses in motor or sensory abnormalities such as paralysis. Also called "conversion hysteria". **10.** *Physics.* The process in which an atomic nucleus in an excited state of energy changes to a lower state, the energy being taken up by an orbiting electron which is ejected from the atom. Also called "internal conversion". **11.** The act, method, or result of converting a quantity in one system of units into another system of units, as metres into feet and inches. [Middle English *conversioun,* from Old French *conversion,* from Latin *conversiō* (stem *conversiōn-*), from *convertere,* to turn about, CONVERT.] **—con·ver·sion·al, con·ver·sion·ar·y** (-əri || -erri) *adj.*
conversion factor *n.* A numerical factor used to multiply or divide a quantity in order to convert it from one system of units into another.
con·vert (kən-vért || kon-) *v.* **-verted, -verting, -verts.** *—tr.* **1.** To change into another form, substance, state, or product; transform; transmute: *convert water into ice.* **2.** To persuade or induce to adopt a particular religion, belief, or practice. **3. a.** To change from one use, function, or purpose to another; adapt to a new or different purpose. **b.** To make structural alterations to (a building). **4.** To exchange for something of equal value. **5.** *Finance.* To exchange (a security or bond, for example) by substituting an equivalent in another form. **6.** To express (a quantity) in alternative units. **7.** *Logic.* To transform (a proposition) by conversion. **8.** *Law.* **a.** To appropriate without right (another's property) to one's own use. **b.** To change (property) from real to personal, from joint to separate, or vice versa. *—intr.* **1.** To be converted or convertible; change: *My sofa converts into a bed; convert to Buddhism.* **2.** In Rugby and American football, to make a conversion. —See Synonyms at **change.**
~*n.* (kón-vert). One who has been converted, especially from one religion or belief to another. [Middle English *converten,* from Old French *convertir,* from Medieval Latin *convertere,* to convert religiously, from Latin, to turn around, transform : *com-* (intensive) + *vertere,* to turn.]
con·vert·er (kən-vértər || kon-) *n.* Also *chiefly U.S.* **con·ver·tor.** **1.** One that converts. **2.** A furnace in which pig iron is converted into steel by the Bessemer process. **3. a.** A machine that changes electric current from one kind to another, especially one that converts direct current into alternating current. **b.** A device that changes one frequency to another. **c.** A device that transforms information from one code to another. **4.** A converter reactor.
converter reactor *n.* A nuclear reactor designed to change one type of nuclear fuel into another. Also called "converter". Compare **breeder reactor.**
con·vert·i·ble (kən-vértə-b'l || kon-) *adj.* **1.** Capable of being converted. **2.** Having a top that may be folded back or removed. Said of a car. **3.** *Finance.* Capable of being lawfully exchanged for gold or another currency: *dollars convertible into pounds.*
~*n.* A convertible car. **—con·vert·i·bil·i·ty** (-bílləti), **con·vert·i·ble·ness** *n.* **—con·vert·i·bly** *adv.*
con·vert·i·plane, con·vert·a·plane (kən-vértə-playn) *n.* An aeroplane that is designed to fly vertically as well as forwards. [CONVERTI(BLE) + (AERO)PLANE.]

con·vex (kón-véks, kən-, -veks) *adj.* **1.** Having a surface or boundary that curves or bulges outwards, as the exterior of a sphere does. Compare **concave**. **2. a.** Thicker at the centre than at the edges. Said of a lens. **b.** Having a convex reflecting surface. Said of a mirror. **3.** *Mathematics.* Designating a set in which the line segment between any two points is also contained in the set. [Latin *convexus*, arched, convex.] —**con·vex·ly** *adv.*

con·vex·i·ty (kən-véksəti, kon-) *n., pl.* **-ties. 1.** The state of being convex. **2.** A convex surface, body, part, or line.

con·vex·o·con·cave (kən-véksō-kon-káyv, kon-, -kən-) *adj.* **1.** Concavo-convex *(see).* **2.** *Optics.* Having greater convex than concave curvature. Said of a lens.

con·vex·o·con·vex (kən-véksō-kon-véks, kon-, -kən-) *adj.* Convex on both sides; doubly convex; biconvex.

con·vey (kən-váy ‖ kon-) *tr.v.* **-veyed, -veying, -veys. 1.** To take or carry from one place to another; transport. **2.** To serve as a medium of transmission for; conduct; transmit. **3.** To communicate or make known: *"a look intended to convey sympathetic comprehension"* (Saki). **4.** *Law.* To transfer ownership of or title to. **5.** *Archaic.* To steal. [Middle English *conveien*, from Old French *conveier*, from Medieval Latin *conviāre*, to go with, escort : Latin *com-*, with + *via*, way.] —**con·vey·a·ble** *adj.*

Synonyms: convey, carry, bear, transport, transmit, transfer.

con·vey·ance (kən-váy-ənss ‖ kon-) *n.* **1.** The act of transporting, transmitting, or communicating. **2.** A means of conveying; especially, a vehicle such as a bus. **3.** *Law.* **a.** The transfer of title to property from one person to another. **b.** The document by which this transfer is effected.

con·vey·anc·ing (kən-váy-ənss-ing ‖ kon-) *n.* **1.** The branch of legal practice dealing with the conveyance of property. **2.** An act or instance of conveying property. —**con·vey·anc·er** *n.*

con·vey·er (kən-váy-ər ‖ kon-) *n.* Also **con·vey·or** (especially for sense 2). **1.** One that conveys. **2.** Any mechanical contrivance, especially a conveyor belt, that transports materials.

conveyor belt *n.* A continuous moving belt, usually driven by rollers, that transports objects or packages from one place to another, as on an assembly line in a factory. Also called "belt".

con·vict (kən-víkt ‖ kon-) *tr.v.* **-victed, -victing, -victs. 1.** To find or prove (someone) guilty of an offence, especially by the verdict of a court. **2.** To convince (someone) of his own guilt or sinfulness. ~*n.* (kón-vikt). **1.** A person found or declared guilty of an offence or crime. **2.** A person serving a sentence of imprisonment. [Middle English *convicten*, from Latin *convincere* (past participle *convictus*), to prove guilty, CONVINCE.]

con·vic·tion (kən-víksh'n ‖ kon-) *n.* **1.** The act or process of finding or proving guilty. **2.** The state or an instance of being convicted: *a string of previous convictions.* **3.** The act or process of convincing. **4.** The state of being convinced or persuaded. **5.** A fixed or strong belief. **6.** The quality of being convincing; plausibility: *His defence of government policy doesn't carry much conviction.* —See Synonyms at **certainty, opinion.** —**con·vic·tion·al** *adj.*

con·vince (kən-vinss ‖ kon-) *tr.v.* **-vinced, -vincing, -vinces.** To bring by argument and evidence to belief; cause to believe something; persuade. Often used in the passive with a clause, or with *of*: *I am convinced that he's evil; convince them of our superiority.* —See Synonyms at **persuade.** [Latin *convincere*, to overcome, refute, prove guilty : *com-* (intensive) + *vincere*, to conquer, overcome.] —**con·vince·ment** *n.* —**con·vinc·er** *n.* —**con·vin·ci·ble** *adj.*

con·vinc·ing (kən-vinss-ing ‖ kon-) *adj.* **1.** Persuading or satisfying by evidence or argument. **2.** Believable; plausible. **3.** Providing decisive proof of superiority. —See Synonyms at **valid.** —**con·vinc·ing·ly** *adv.* —**con·vinc·ing·ness** *n.*

con·viv·i·al (kən-vívvi-əl ‖ kon-) *adj.* **1.** Fond of feasting, drinking, and good company; sociable; jovial. **2.** Appropriate to or of the nature of a jolly social occasion; festive: *a convivial atmosphere at the office party.* —See Synonyms at **jolly.** [Late Latin *convīviālis*, from Latin *convīvium*, "a living together", banquet : *com-*, together + *vīvere*, to live.] —**con·viv·i·al·i·ty** (-ál-əti) *n.* —**con·viv·i·al·ly** *adv.*

con·vo·ca·tion (kón-və-káysh'n, -vō-) *n.* **1.** The act of convoking or calling together. **2.** A group of people assembled by summons. **3.** *Anglican Church.* A clerical assembly or synod, especially in the provinces of Canterbury and York. **4.** In certain British universities, a deliberative or legislative assembly, typically composed of graduates of the university. Compare **senate, congregation.** —**con·vo·ca·tion·al** *adj.*

con·voke (kən-vók ‖ kon-) *tr.v.* **-voked, -voking, -vokes.** To cause to assemble; convene. [Old French *convoquer*, from Latin *convocāre*, to call together, summon : *com-*, together + *vocāre*, to call.] —**con·vok·er** *n.*

con·vo·lute (kónvə-lōōt, -lewt) *adj.* Rolled or folded together with one part over another; twisted; coiled. ~*v.* (also -lōōt, -léwt) **convoluted, -luting, -lutes.** —*tr.* To coil round or wind. —*intr.* To coil up. [Latin *convolūtus*, past participle of *convolvere*, to CONVOLVE.] —**con·vo·lute·ly** *adv.*

con·vo·lut·ed (kónvə-lōōt-id, -lōōt-, -lewt-, -léwt-) *adj.* **1.** Exhibiting convolutions; coiled; twisted. **2. a.** Intricate; complicated. **b.** Difficult to understand or grasp because lengthy, roundabout, or tortuous: *a convoluted explanation.*

con·vo·lu·tion (kónvə-lōōsh'n, -léwsh'n) *n.* **1. a.** A coiling or twisting together. **b.** An entangling or interlacing, so as to make intricate. **2.** Any of the convex folds of the surface of the brain. See **gyrus. 3.** *Mathematics.* A function that measures how the shape of one function affects another, defined by the integral of the product $g(t)f(x-t)$ with respect to the variable t.

con·volve (kən-vólv ‖ kon-, -vólv) *v.* **-volved, -volving, -volves.** —*tr.* To roll together; coil up. —*intr.* To form convolutions. [Latin *convolvere*, to roll together, enwrap : *com-*, together + *volvere*, to roll.]

con·vol·vu·lus (kən-vól-vew-ləss ‖ kon-, -vól-) *n., pl.* **-luses** or **-li** (-lī). Any of several trailing or twining plants of the genus *Convolvulus*, which includes the bindweeds. [New Latin *Convolvulus*, from Latin *convolvulus*, bindweed, from *convolvere*, to interweave, CONVOLVE.]

con·voy (kón-voy ‖ kən-vóy) *tr.v.* **-voyed, -voying, -voys.** To accompany on the way for protection, either by sea or land; escort. ~*n.* (kón-voy). **1.** An accompanying and protecting force; a convoying vessel, fleet, or troop. **2.** That which is convoyed, such as ships or troops. **3.** The act of convoying. **4.** A group, as of vehicles, travelling together. [Middle English *convoyen, conveien*, from Old French *convoier, conveier*, to CONVEY.]

con·vul·sant (kən-vúlss'nt) *n.* A drug or other agent that produces convulsions. —**con·vul·sant** *adj.*

con·vulse (kən-vúlss ‖ kon-) *tr.v.* **-vulsed, -vulsing, -vulses. 1.** To shake or agitate violently. **2.** To cause to laugh uproariously. **3.** To affect with irregular and involuntary muscular contractions; throw into convulsions. [From Latin *convellere* (past participle *convulsus*), to pull violently, wrest : *com-* (intensive) + *vellere*, to pull.]

con·vul·sion (kən-vúlsh'n ‖ kon-) *n.* **1.** *Pathology.* An intense paroxysmal involuntary muscular contraction. **2.** *Often plural.* An uncontrolled fit of laughter. **3.** A violent turmoil.

con·vul·sion·ar·y (kən-vúlsh'n-əri ‖ kon-, -erri) *adj.* Of, pertaining to, affected with, or of the nature of convulsions. ~*n., pl.* **convulsionaries.** A person affected with convulsions, especially as a result of religious fervour.

con·vul·sive (kən-vúl-siv) *adj.* **1.** Marked by or of the nature of convulsions. **2.** Having or producing convulsions. —**con·vul·sive·ly** *adv.* —**con·vul·sive·ness** *n.*

Con·wy (kón-wi). Formerly **Con·way** (-way). *Welsh* **Ab·er·conwy** (ábber-kónwi). Unitary Authority area, and situated near the mouth of the river Conwy in northwest Wales.

co·ny (kóni ‖ *U.S. also* kúnni) *n., pl.* **-nies.** Also **co·ney** *pl.* **-neys. 1.** A rabbit, especially the Old World species *Oryctolagus cuniculus.* **2.** The fur of a rabbit. **3.** A mammal, the **pika** *(see).* **4.** In the Old Testament, a mammal, the **hyrax** *(see).* Deuteronomy 14:7. [Middle English *coni(n)g, cunin,* from Old French *conin, conil,* from Latin *cunīculus,* rabbit.]

coo (kōō) *v.* **cooed, cooing, coos.** —*intr.* **1.** To utter the characteristic murmuring sound of a dove or pigeon, or a sound resembling this. **2.** To talk amorously or fondly in murmurs. Usually used in the phrase *bill and coo.* —*tr.* To express or utter gently or amorously, as with a murmuring sound. ~*n., pl.* **coos.** The murmuring sound made by a dove or pigeon, or a sound resembling this. ~*interj. Chiefly British.* Used to express surprise, admiration or the like. [Imitative.] —**coo·er** *n.*

Coo·ber Pe·dy (kōōbər péedi). A small town in central South Australia, in the Stuart Range. More than half of the world's annual output of opals is mined there.

coo·ee (kōō-ee, -i ‖ *Australian also* kōō-ée) *n., pl.* **-ees.** Also **coo·ey** *pl.* **-eys.** A prolonged shrill cry used as a signal or to attract attention. [Used originally by the Australian Aborigines and later adopted by the settlers.]

cook (kōōk ‖ *Northern & Irish also* kōōk) *v.* **cooked, cooking, cooks.** —*tr.* **1.** To prepare for eating by applying heat, as by boiling, frying, or baking. **2.** To subject to heat. **3.** *Informal.* To falsify (accounts, records, or statistics). Used chiefly in the phrase *cook the books.* —*intr.* **1.** To prepare food for eating by applying heat. **2.** To undergo cooking. **3.** *Slang.* To happen, develop, or take place. Used chiefly in the phrase *What's cooking?* —**cook up.** *Informal.* To fabricate; concoct. ~*n.* A person who prepares food for eating. [Middle English *coken*, from *cok(e)*, a cook, Old English *cōc*, from Vulgar Latin *cōcus* (unattested), from Latin *cocus, coquus*, from *coquere*, to cook.]

Cook (kōōk), **Captain James** (1728–79). British explorer and navigator. From 1768–71 in his ship *Endeavour*, Cook charted the coasts of New Zealand, reached eastern Australia, landed at Botany Bay, and skirted the Great Barrier Reef. On the voyage he conquered scurvy by providing fresh vegetables for his crew. His second voyage (1772–75) reached as far south as the Antarctic Circle, charting Easter Island and most of the major island groups in the South Pacific. On his third voyage (1776–79) he discovered the Hawaiian islands and charted the Bering Strait.

Cook, Mount. *Maori* **Aorangi.** The highest mountain in New Zealand, situated on the west of South Island, in the Southern Alps. It is 3 763 metres (12,346 feet) high.

cook·er (kōōkər ‖ .kōōkər) *n.* **1.** An apparatus used for cooking, typically including an oven, a grill, and a number of gas rings or electric hotplates. **2.** An appliance or vessel for cooking: *a pressure cooker.* **3.** A cooking apple.

cook·er·y (kōōk-əri ‖ kōōk-) *n.* The art or practice of preparing food.

cookery book *n.* A book containing recipes and other information about the preparation of food. Also called "cook book".

cook·gen·e·ral (kōōk-jénrəl, -jénnərəl ‖ kōōk-) *n., pl.* **cooks-ge-**

neral. *British.* Formerly, a servant paid to do the cooking and general household tasks.

cook·house (kǒok-howss ‖ kǒk-) *n.* A place, usually on a camp or ranch, where the cooking is done.

cook·ie, cook·y (kǒoki) *n., pl.* **-ies.** 1. *U.S.* A sweet biscuit. 2. *Scottish.* A bun. 3. *Chiefly U.S. Slang.* A person. [Dutch *koekje*, diminutive of *koek*, cake, from Middle Dutch *koeke*.]

cook·ing (kǒok-ing ‖ kǒok) *adj.* 1. Used in or for cooking: *cooking utensils.* 2. More suitable for use in cooking than for consuming uncooked: *cooking sherry; cooking apples.*

cooking apple *n.* Any large sour apple used in cooking. Also called "cooker".

Cook Islands. An associated state of New Zealand, in the southwest Pacific Ocean. Discovered by Captain Cook (1773), the group comprises 15 islands, including Rarotonga, with Avarua, the administrative centre.

cook·out (kǒok-owt) *n. U.S.* An outing with a meal cooked and served outdoors.

Cook Strait. *Maori Raukawa.* Sea channel between North Island and South Island, New Zealand, 26 to 145 kilometres (16 to 90 miles) wide.

cool (kǒol) *adj.* **cooler, coolest.** 1. Moderately cold; neither warm nor very cold. 2. Reducing discomfort in hot weather; allowing a feeling of coolness: *a cool blouse.* 3. Not excited; calm; controlled. 4. Showing dislike, disdain, or indifference; unenthusiastic; not cordial: *a cool greeting.* 5. Calmly audacious or bold. 6. Designating or characteristic of colours, such as blue and green, that produce the impression of coolness. 7. *Informal.* Having or showing a quietly self-possessed, unruffled attitude. 8. *Chiefly U.S. Slang.* **a.** Excellent; first-rate. **b.** Acceptable; O.K.: *Tonight, if that's cool with you.* 9. *Informal.* Without exaggeration; entire; full: *He lost a cool million.* 10. *Music.* Slow and relaxed. Said of music, especially jazz. —*v.* **cooled, cooling, cools.** —*tr.* 1. To make less warm. 2. To make less ardent, intense, or zealous. —*intr.* 1. To become less warm. Often used with *down.* 2. To become less ardent, intense, or zealous. 3. To become calm. Used with *down* or *off.* —**cool it.** *Slang.* To calm down; relax. —*n.* 1. A cool atmosphere: *the cool of early morning.* 2. The state or quality of being cool. 3. *Slang.* Composure: *recover one's cool.* [Middle English *col,* Old English *cōl,* from Germanic.] —**cool·ly** *adv.* —**cool·ness** *n.*

Synonyms: cool, composed, collected, unruffled, nonchalant, imperturbable, detached.

coo·la·bah, coo·li·bah (kǒolə-baa) *n.* An Australian eucalyptus tree, *Eucalyptus microtheca*, found near rivers. [From a native Australian language.]

cool·ant (kǒolənt) *n.* An agent that produces cooling; especially, a fluid that draws off heat by circulating through a machine or by bathing a mechanical part. [COOL + *-ant,* by analogy with *lubricant.*]

cool·drink (kǒol-dringk) *n. South African.* Any cold drink.

cool·er (kǒolər) *n.* 1. A device or container that cools something or keeps it cool. 2. Anything that cools, such as a cold drink. 3. *Chiefly U.S. Slang.* A jail or prison cell.

Coo·ley's anaemia (kǒo-liz ‖ -leez) *n.* **Thalassaemia** *(see).* [After Thomas *Cooley* (1871–1945), American paediatrician.]

cool·head·ed (kǒol-héddid, -heddid) *adj.* Not easily excited or flustered.

Coo·lidge (kǒolij), **(John) Calvin** (1872–1933). U.S. Republican statesman, 30th president (1923–29). He succeeded Warren Harding (1923), and helped to restore public trust after the scandals of his predecessor's administration.

coo·lie, coo·ly (kǒoli) *n., pl.* **-lies.** In India and the Far East, an unskilled labourer. 2. In South Africa, Guyana, or the West Indies, someone of Indian ancestry. Used derogatorily. [Hindi *kulī, qulī,* perhaps from *Kulī, Kolī,* an aboriginal tribe of Gujarat, India.]

cool·ing-off period (kǒoling-off, -awff) *n.* A relatively calm or inactive interval, occurring especially during or after a dispute, in which people can calmly take stock of their position.

cool·ing tow·er (kǒoling) *n.* A large tower used to condense steam to water for reuse in power stations and the like, typically having a conical shape with inward-curving sides to assist the upward draught.

Coomassie. See **Kumasi.**

coomb, combe (kǒom) *n. British.* A short valley, especially in coastal areas. [Old English *cumb,* probably from Celtic.]

coon (kǒon) *n.* 1. *U.S. Informal.* A raccoon. 2. *Slang.* A black person. An offensive term used derogatorily. [Short for RACCOON.]

coon·can (kǒon-kan) *n.* A card game, **conquian** *(see).*

coon·skin (kǒon-skin) *n. U.S.* 1. The pelt of the raccoon. 2. An article made of coonskin, such as a hat. —**coon·skin** *adj.*

coop (kǒop ‖ *U.S. also* kǒop) *n.* 1. An enclosure or cage, as for poultry or small animals. 2. *Slang.* Any place of confinement. 3. A basket used to catch fish. —**fly the coop.** *Informal.* To escape. —*tr.v.* **cooped, cooping, coops.** To confine in a limited space. Usually used with *up.* [Middle English *c(o)upe,* wicker basket, chicken coop, probably from Middle Low German *kūpe,* basket, cask, tub, barrel.]

co-op (kǒ-op ‖ kǒ-óp) *n.* A cooperative.

coop·er (kǒopər ‖ *U.S. also* kǒopər) *n.* One who makes or repairs wooden tubs and barrels. —*v.* **coopered, -ering, -ers.** —*tr.* To repair or make (casks or barrels). —*intr.* To work as a cooper. [Middle English *couper,* prob-

ably from Middle Low German *kūper,* from *kūpe,* cask, COOP.]

Coop·er (kǒopər ‖ *U.S. also* kǒopər), **Gary,** born Frank James Cooper (1901–1961). U.S. film actor, who specialised in "strong, silent" hero roles in Hollywood westerns, such as the classic *High Noon* (1952).

Cooper, James Fenimore (1789–1851). U.S. novelist. He is best remembered for his novels of frontier life such as *The Last of the Mohicans* (1826).

coop·er·age (kǒop-ərij) *n.* A cooper's work, shop, or products.

co·op·er·ate, co-op·er·ate (kō-óppərayt) *intr.v.* **-ated, -ating, -ates.** 1. To work together towards a common end or purpose. 2. To adopt a helpful and willing attitude. [Latin *cooperārī : co-,* together + *operārī,* to work, from *opus,* work.] —**co·op·er·a·tor** (-ər) *n.*

co·op·er·a·tion, co-op·er·a·tion (kō-óppə-ráysh'n) *n.* 1. The act of cooperating. 2. Help or a helpful attitude. 3. The principle or practice of associating in an economic cooperative. —**co·op·er·a·tion·ist** *n.*

co·op·er·a·tive, co-op·er·a·tive (kō-ópprə-tiv, -óppərə- ‖ -óppəray-tiv) *adj.* 1. Working together. 2. Helpful; inclined to cooperate. 3. Functioning as a cooperative: *a cooperative farm.* —*n.* Any enterprise, such as a farm, factory, shop, or set of houses or dwellings, that is collectively owned and operated for mutual benefit. Also called "co-op". —**co·op·er·a·tive·ly** *adv.* —**co·op·er·a·tive·ness** *n.*

Cooper pair *n. Physics.* A pair of interacting electrons responsible for carrying the electric current in a superconductor. [After Leon N. *Cooper* (born 1930), American physicist.]

Coo·pers Creek (kǒopərz). Intermittent watercourse in eastern Australia, whose upper course is the Barcoo river. It flows 1 420 kilometres (880 miles) southwest from the Great Dividing Range into Lake Eyre.

co-opt (kō-ópt ‖ *U.S. also* kō-ópt) *tr.v.* **-opted, -opting, -opts.** 1. To elect into a group by the votes of the group's existing members. 2. To absorb or take over, especially by assimilation into an established group or culture. [Latin *cooptāre : co-,* together + *optāre,* to choose, elect.] —**co-op·ta·tion** (kō-op-táysh'n), **co-op·tion** (kō-ópsh'n) *n.* —**co-op·ta·tive** (kō-óptətiv), **co-op·tive** (kō-óptiv) *adj.*

co·or·di·nate, co-or·di·nate (kō-órdi-nət, -nit ‖ -nayt) *n.* 1. One that is equal in importance, rank, or degree. 2. *Mathematics.* **a.** Any of a set of numbers that determines the location of a point in a space of a given dimension. **b.** Any of a set of two or more magnitudes used to determine the position of a point, line, curve, or plane. 3. *Plural.* Items of clothing or accessories designed to match and be worn together. —*adj.* (-nət, -nit, -nayt). 1. Of equal importance, rank, or degree; not subordinate. 2. Of or involving coordination. 3. Of or based on coordinates. —*v.* (-nayt) **coordinated, -nating, -nates.** —*tr.* 1. To place in the same order, class, or rank. 2. To arrange in the proper relative position. 3. To bring together in a common and harmonious action or effort. 4. *Chemistry.* To cause (an atom, ion, or the like) to form a coordinate bond. —*intr.* 1. To work together harmoniously. 2. *Chemistry.* To form a coordinate bond. [Back-formation from COORDINATION.] —**co·or·di·nate·ly** *adv.* —**co·or·di·nate·ness** *n.* —**co·or·di·na·tive** (-nətiv, -naytiv) *adj.* —**co·or·di·na·tor** (-aytər) *n.*

coordinate bond *n.* A covalent chemical bond in which both electrons forming the bond are supplied by one atom. Also called "semipolar bond", "dative bond".

coordinate geometry *n.* A branch of geometry, **analytical geometry** *(see).*

coordinate system *n. Mathematics.* A method of specifying the positions of points in space by reference to fixed points, lines, or planes. See **Cartesian coordinates, cylindrical coordinates, polar coordinates.**

co·or·di·na·ting conjunction (kō-órdinayting) *n.* Also **coordinate conjunction.** *Grammar.* A conjunction that connects parallel grammatical elements; for example, *or* in *She doesn't know whether she's coming or going.* Compare **subordinate conjunction.**

co·or·di·na·tion, co·or·di·na·tion (kō-órdi-náysh'n) *n.* 1. The act of coordinating. 2. The state of being coordinated; harmonious adjustment or interaction. 3. *Physiology.* The coordinated functioning of muscles or groups of muscles in the execution of a complex task. [French, from Late Latin *coōrdinātiō* (stem *coōrdinātiōn-*), arrangement in the same order : Latin *co-,* same + *ōrdinātiō,* arrangement, from *ōrdināre,* to arrange in order, from *ōrdō,* order.]

coordination compound *n.* A chemical compound or complex ion formed by joining independent molecules or ions to a central metallic atom. Also called "coordination complex".

coot (kǒot) *n.* Any of several dark-grey aquatic birds of the genus *Fulica;* especially, the Eurasian species *F. atra.* [Middle English *cote,* probably from Middle Dutch *coet, cuut*†.]

cop[1] (kop) *n.* 1. A cone-shaped or cylindrical roll of yarn or thread wound on a spindle. 2. *Archaic.* A summit or crest. Now used in place names. [Middle English *cop,* coppe, summit, top, tip, Old English *copp,* from Late Latin *cuppa,* from Latin *cūpa,* tub.]

cop[2] *n. Slang.* 1. A policeman. 2. An arrest. Used chiefly in the phrase *a fair cop.* 3. *British.* Value; usefulness. Used chiefly in the phrase *not much cop.* —*tr.v.* **copped, copping, cops.** *Slang.* 1. To seize; catch. 2. To receive (a punishment). —**cop it.** *Slang.* To suffer a punishment or misfortune. [Probably from obsolete *cap,* to arrest, from Old French *caper,* to seize.]

cop. copyright.

co·pa·ce·tic, co·pa·se·tic (kŏpə-séttik, -séetik) *adj. U.S. Slang.* Excellent; first-rate. [20th century : origin obscure.]

co·pai·ba (kō-pība, ko-, -pấybə) *n.* A transparent, yellowish, viscous resin from South American trees of the genus *Copaifera*, used in varnishes and tracing papers and as an expectorant, diuretic, and stimulant. Also called "copaiba balsam". [Spanish, from Portuguese *copaíba*, from Tupi *copaíba*.]

co·pal (kŏp'l, kō-pal) *n.* A brittle, aromatic, yellow to red resin of recent or fossil origin, obtained from various tropical trees and used in varnishes. [Spanish, from Nahuatl *copalli*, resin.]

Co·pán (kō-pán, -paˊan). A ruined city of the ancient Maya on the Copán river in western Honduras, discovered by the Spanish in the early 16th century. Copán, second largest of the great Maya cities, flourished from *c.* 300 B.C.–A.D. 900.

co·par·ce·nar·y (kō-párss'n-əri ‖ *U.S.* -erri) *n., pl.* **-ies. 1.** *Law.* Joint ownership of inherited property. Also called "parcenary". **2.** Any joint ownership. **—co·par·ce·nar·y** *adj.*

co·par·ce·ner (kō-párss'n-ər) *n. Law.* Any of two or more persons sharing an undivided inheritance. Also called "parcener".

co·part·ner, co·part·ner (kō-pártnər, kō-) *n.* A partner, as in a business enterprise; an associate. **—co·part·ner·ship** *n.*

cope[1] (kōp) *intr.v.* **coped, coping, copes. 1.** To contend or struggle successfully. Used with *with.* **2.** To deal successfully or competently with a difficult situation. Often used with *with.* [Middle English *co(u)pen*, to contend with, join in battle with, from Old French *couper*, to strike, from *coup*, a blow, from Late Latin *colpus*, from Latin *colaphus*, from Greek *kolaphos*.]

cope[2] *n.* **1.** A long cloaklike ecclesiastical vestment worn over the alb or surplice. **2.** Any covering resembling a cloak or mantle. **~tr.v. coped, coping, copes.** To provide (a wall, for example) with coping. [Middle English *cope*, Old English *(cantel)cāp*, from Late Latin *cāpa, cappa*, cloak, hood, from Latin *caput*, head.]

copeck. Variant of **kopeck.**

Co·pen·ha·gen (kŏpən-háygən ‖ -haygən, -haˊagən, -haagən). *Danish* **Kø·ben·havn** (kōbən-hówn). The capital of Denmark, situated on the Baltic coast of Sjælland.

co·pe·pod (kŏpi-pod) *n.* Any of numerous small marine and freshwater crustaceans of the subclass *Copepoda.* [New Latin *Copepoda*, "oar-footed ones" (from their oarlike legs) : Greek *kōpē*, oar handle, oar + POD.]

co·per (kŏpər) *n. British.* A horse dealer. [From obsolete *cope*, to buy, exchange, from Low German; akin to Dutch *koopen*, German *kaufen*, to buy.]

Co·per·ni·can system (kə-pérnikən, kō-) *n.* The description of the solar system published by Copernicus in 1543, with the Sun at the centre and the planets moving around it in, as originally formulated, circular orbits and epicycles. Compare **Ptolemaic system.**

Co·per·ni·cus (kə-pérnikəss), **Nicolaus** (1473–1543). Polish name **Mikołaj Kopernik.** Polish astronomer. The difficulties he encountered in trying to calculate the position of the planets within the framework of the well-established Ptolemaic system led him to reject Ptolemy's belief that the heavenly bodies moved around the Earth, and to place the Sun at the centre of the universe. **—Co·per·ni·can** *adj.*

cope·stone (kŏp-stōn) *n.* **1.** A capstone *(see).* **2.** A coping stone.

cop·i·er (kŏppi-ər) *n.* **1.** Any of various office machines that make copies. **2.** A copyist or transcriber. **3.** An imitator.

co·pi·lot, co·pi·lot (kō-pīlət, -pílət) *n.* The relief pilot of an aircraft.

cop·ing (kŏping) *n.* The top part of a wall or roof, usually slanted. [From COPE (vestment).]

coping saw *n.* A narrow, short-bladed saw with a thin blade in a U-shaped frame, used for cutting designs in wood.

coping stone *n.* A stone used in or as a coping.

co·pi·ous (kŏpi-əss) *adj.* **1.** Yielding or containing plenty; affording ample supply. **2.** Large in quantity; abundant. **3.** Abounding in matter, thoughts, or words; wordy. [Middle English, from Old French *copieux*, from Latin *cōpiōsus*, from *cōpia*, abundance.] **—co·pi·ous·ly** *adv.* **—co·pi·ous·ness** *n.*

co·pi·ta (kə-péetə, ko-, kō-) *n.* The traditional tulip-shaped sherry glass. [Spanish, diminitive of *copa*, cup.]

co·pla·nar (kō-plāynər) *adj.* Lying or occurring in the same plane.

Cop·land (kŏpland), **Aaron** (1900–90). U.S. pianist and composer. His works include the ballets *Rodeo* (1942) and *Appalachian Spring* (1944), and his highly acclaimed *Third Symphony* (1946).

co·pol·y·mer (kō-pólli-mər) *n.* A polymer of two or more different monomers. **—co·pol·y·mer·ic** (-mérrik) *adj.*

co·pol·y·mer·ise, co·pol·y·mer·ize (kō-póllimər-īz) *v.* **-ised, -ising, -ises.** *—tr.* To polymerise (different monomers) together. *—intr.* To react to form a copolymer. **—co·pol·y·mer·i·sa·tion** (-ī-záysh'n ‖ *U.S.* -i-) *n.*

cop out *intr.v. Slang.* **1.** To evade a difficult question, situation, or commitment. **2.** To compromise one's principles. [From COP (to seize).]

cop-out (kŏp-owt) *n. Slang.* An act of copping out; a failure to commit oneself or abide by one's principles.

cop·per[1] (kŏppər) *n.* **1.** *Symbol* **Cu** A ductile, malleable, reddishbrown metallic element that is an excellent conductor of heat and electricity and is widely used for electrical wiring, water piping, and corrosion-resistant parts either pure or in alloys such as brass and bronze. Atomic number 29, atomic weight 63.54, melting point 1,083°C, boiling point 2,595°C, relative density 8.96, valencies 1, 2. ?. **a.** A coin of low value made of copper or a copper alloy. **b.** Such ins collectively. **3.** *Chiefly British.* A large boiler made of copper

or often of iron, especially one used for laundry. **4.** Any of various small butterflies of the subfamily Lycaeninae, having predominantly copper-coloured wings.

~tr.v. coppered, -pering, -pers. To coat or finish with a layer of copper. [Middle English, Old English *coper, copor*, from Common Germanic *kupar* (unattested), from Late Latin *cuprum*, from Latin *Cyprium (aes)*, "(copper) of Cyprus" (Cyprus was known in ancient times as the source of the best copper).] **—cop·per·y** *adj.*

copper[2] *n. Slang.* A policeman. [From COP (to seize).]

cop·per·as (kŏppərəss) *n.* A greenish, crystalline, hydrated ferrous sulphate, $FeSO_4 \cdot 7H_2O$, used in the manufacture of fertilisers and inks and in water purification. [Middle English *coperose*, from Old French *co(u)perose*, from Medieval Latin *cup(e)rosa*, probably short for *aqua cup(e)rosa*, "copper water".]

copper beech *n.* A cultivated variety of the European beech, *Fagus sulvatica* var. *atropunicea*, having purple- or copper-coloured leaves.

Cop·per·belt (kŏppər-belt). A region of central Africa, extending in an arc from Dem. Rep. of the Congo (Shaba province) into northern Zambia (Copperbelt province). It has the largest copper deposits in Africa.

cop·per-bot·tomed (kŏppər-bóttəmd) *adj.* Thoroughly reliable or free of risk, especially in financial terms.

cop·per·head (kŏppər-hed) *n.* **1.** A venomous snake, *Agkistrodon contortrix* (or *Ancistron contortrix*), of eastern United States, having reddish-brown markings. **2.** A large, venomous snake, *Denisonia superba*, found in Australian marshes.

copper nickel *n.* A nickel ore, **niccolite** *(see).*

cop·per·plate (kŏppər-playt, -playt) *n.* **1.** A copper printing plate, engraved or etched to form a recessed pattern of the matter to be printed. **2.** A print or engraving made by using such a plate. **3.** An ornate, cursive handwriting style based on copperplate engraved models and characterised by a slant to the right, regular loops, and vertical strokes thicker than horizontal strokes.

copper pyrites *n.* A copper ore, **chalcopyrite** *(see).*

cop·per·smith (kŏppər-smith) *n.* **1.** A worker or manufacturer of objects in copper. **2.** A brightly coloured bird, *Megalaima haemacephala*, of southeastern Asia, having a ringing, metallic call.

copper sulphate *n.* A poisonous crystalline copper salt, $CuSO_4$, used in agriculture, textile dyeing, leather treatment, electroplating, and the manufacture of germicides. It is white when anhydrous; the hydrate, $CuSO_4 \cdot 5H_2O$, is blue.

cop·pice (kŏppiss) *n. Chiefly British.* A thicket or copse. **~tr.v. coppiced, -picing, -pices.** To cut down (a tree in a coppice) leaving enough of the trunk to allow the regrowth of branches. [From Old French *copeiz*, from Vulgar Latin *colpaticium* (unattested), from *colpare* (unattested), to cut, from Medieval Latin *colpus*, blow. See cope (to contend).]

cop·ra (kŏprə) *n.* Dried coconut meat from which coconut oil is extracted. [Portuguese, from Malayalam *koppara*.]

copro– *comb. form.* Indicates dung, excrement, or faeces; for example, **coprolite.** [From Greek *kopros*, dung.]

cop·ro·lite (kŏprə-līt) *n.* Fossilised excrement. [COPRO- + -LITE.] **—cop·ro·lit·ic** (-líttik) *adj.*

cop·rol·o·gy (kop-róllǝji) *n.* Scatology. [COPRO- + -LOGY.]

cop·roph·a·gous (kop-róffə-gəss) *adj.* Feeding on excrement: coprophagous insects. [New Latin *coprophagus*, from Greek *koprophagos* : COPRO- + -PHAGOUS.] **—cop·roph·a·gy** (-ji) *n.*

cop·ro·phil·i·a (kŏprə-fílli-ə) *n.* An abnormal attraction to faecal matter. [New Latin : COPRO- + -PHILIA.]

copse (kops) *n.* A thicket of small trees or shrubs, especially one grown for periodic cutting. [Short for COPPICE.]

cop shop *n. British Slang.* A police station.

Copt (kopt) *n.* **1.** A native of Egypt descended from ancient Egyptian stock. **2.** A member of the Coptic Church. [French *Copte*, from New Latin *Coptus*, from Arabic *quft, qubt*, the Copts, from Coptic *gyptios*, from Greek *Aiguptios*, from *Aiguptos*, EGYPT.]

cop·ter (kŏptər) *n. Informal.* A helicopter.

Cop·tic (kŏptik) *n.* The Afro-Asiatic language of the Copts, used today only in the liturgy of the Coptic Church. **—Cop·tic** *adj.*

Coptic Church *n.* The Christian church of Egypt, adhering to the Monophysite doctrine.

cop·u·la (kŏppew-lə) *n., pl.* **-las** or **-lae** (-lee). **1.** A verb, such as *feel, become, seem*, or any form of *be*, that identifies the predicate of a sentence with the subject. In the sentence *The child seems unhappy*, the copula is *seems.* **2.** *Logic.* The word or set of words that serves as a link between the subject and predicate of a proposition. [Latin *cōpula*, link, bond.] **—cop·u·lar** *adj.*

cop·u·late (kŏppew-layt) *intr.v.* **-lated, -lating, -lates.** To engage in sexual intercourse. [Latin *cōpulāre*, to fasten together, link, from *cōpula*, link, bond.] **—cop·u·la·tion** (-láysh'n) *n.*

cop·u·la·tive (kŏppew-lətiv, -laytiv) *adj.* **1.** Joining or uniting. **2.** *Grammar.* **a.** Serving to connect coordinate words or clauses. Said of a conjunction such as *and.* **b.** Serving as a copula. **3.** Of or pertaining to copulation.

~n. *Grammar.* A copulative word or group of words. **—cop·u·la·tive·ly** *adv.*

co·punc·tal (kō-púngktəl) *adj. Mathematics.* Having a point in common. Said of three or more intersecting planes or surfaces.

cop·y (kŏppi) *n., pl.* **-ies. 1.** An imitation or reproduction of something original; a duplicate. **2.** One specimen or example of a printed text or picture. **3.** *Abbr.* **c., C. a.** Manuscript or other material to be set in type. **b.** Text, especially advertising material, as distinct from graphic material. **4.** Suitable source material, as for a newspaper story.

~*v.* **copied, -ying, -ies.** —*tr.* **1.** To make a copy or copies of; transcribe or reproduce. **2.** To follow as a model or pattern; imitate. —*intr.* **1.** To make one or more copies or reproductions. **2.** To cheat, as in an examination, by copying another's work. **3.** To admit of being reproduced. —See Synonyms at **imitate.** [Middle English *copie,* from Old French, from Medieval Latin *cōpia,* transcript, right of reproduction, from Latin, abundance, power.]

cop·y·book (kóppi-böök ‖ -böök) *n.* A book of models for imitation, especially models of handwriting.

~*adj.* **1.** Unoriginal; trite: *a copybook phrase.* **2.** Model; exemplary: *played a copybook shot.*

cop·y·cat (kóppi-kat) *n. Informal.* One who imitates, especially in a slavish way. —**cop·y·cat** *adj.*

copy desk *n. Chiefly U.S.* The desk in a newspaper office where copy is edited and prepared for typesetting.

cop·y·ed·it (kóppi-edit) *tr.v.* **-ited, -iting, -its.** To correct and prepare (a manuscript, for example) for typesetting and printing. —**copy editor** *n.*

cop·y·graph (kóppi-graaf, -graf) *n.* A **hectograph** *(see).*

cop·y·hold (kóppi-höld) *n.* **1.** Formerly in England, tenure based on the customs of the local manor. **2.** Land held in this way.

cop·y·hold·er (kóppi-höldər) *n.* **1.** An assistant who reads manuscript aloud to a proofreader. **2.** A device that holds copy in place for the typesetter. **3.** Formerly, one holding land by copyhold.

cop·y·ist (kóppi-ist) *n.* One who makes written copies.

cop·y·read·er (kóppi-reedər) *n.* One who edits and corrects newspaper copy for publication.

cop·y·right (kóppi-rīt) *n. Abbr.* **c., C., cop.** The right granted by law to an author, composer, playwright, publisher, or distributor, to exclusive publication, production, sale, or distribution of a literary, musical, dramatic, or artistic work. In Britain this right extends for a period of 50 years after the death of the artist concerned.

~*adj.* Protected by copyright.

~*tr.v.* **copyrighted, -righting, -rights.** To secure a copyright for. —**cop·y·right·a·ble** *adj.* —**cop·y·right·er** *n.*

copyright deposit library *n.* Any of the five British libraries (the British Library, the Bodleian Library in Oxford, Cambridge University Library, the Scottish National Library, and the National Library of Wales) entitled to receive automatically a free copy of every book published in the United Kingdom, in accordance with the copyright laws.

copy taster *n.* One who reads copy and selects material for printing or publication. —**copy tasting** *n.*

copy typist *n.* One who types out written rather than dictated material. Compare **audio typist.**

cop·y·writ·er (kóppi-rītər) *n.* One who writes advertising copy.

coq au vin (kóckō-ván) *n.* Chicken cooked in red wine, with mushrooms, onions, and other ingredients. [French, "cock in wine".]

co·quet (ko-két, kō-, kə-) *intr.v.* **-quetted, -quetting, -quets. 1.** To play the coquette; flirt. **2.** To trifle; dally. [French *coqueter,* to flirt, from *coquet,* flirtatious man. See **coquette.**]

co·quet·ry (kócki-tri, kōki-, ko-kétri) *n., pl.* **-ries.** Dalliance; flirtation. [French *coquetterie,* from COQUETTE.]

co·quette (ko-két, kō-, kə-) *n.* A woman who flirts with men. [French, feminine of *coquet,* flirtatious man, diminutive of *coq,* cock, from Old French *coc,* from Late Latin *coccus,* from Latin *coco,* cackle. See **cock.**] —**co·quet·tish** *adj.* —**co·quet·tish·ly** *adv.* —**co·quet·tish·ness** *n.*

co·quil·la nut (ko-kéel-yə, kō-, -kée-) *n.* The nut of a South American palm tree, *Attalea funifera,* having a hard oval shell used for decorative carving or turning. [Portuguese *coquilho,* diminutive of *côco,* COCO.]

co·qui·to (ko-kéetō, kō-) *n., pl.* **-tos.** A Chilean palm tree, *Jubaea spectabilis,* whose sap gives a sweet edible syrup. [Spanish, diminutive of *coco,* coco palm, from Portuguese *côco,* COCO.]

cor (kaw) *interj. Informal.* Used to express surprise or appreciation. [Variant of *God!*]

cor. 1. corner. **2.** cornet. **3.** coroner. **4.** corpus. **5.** correction. **6.** correspondence; correspondent; corresponding.

Cor. Corinthians (New Testament).

cor·a·ci·i·form (kórrə-sí-i-fawrm, kə-rássi-) *adj.* Of, belonging to, or pertaining to the Coraciiformes, an order of birds that includes the kingfishers, hornbills, hoopoes, and bee-eaters. [From New Latin *Coracias* (genus), from Greek *korakias,* chough.]

cor·a·cle (kórrək'l ‖ káwrək'l) *n.* A small, rounded boat made of waterproof material stretched over a wicker or wooden frame. Also *Scottish & Irish* "currach". [Earlier *corougle,* from Welsh *corwgl, cwrwgl.* See **currach.**]

cor·a·coid (kórrə-koyd ‖ káwrə-) *n.* A paired cartilage bone projecting from the scapula towards the sternum in teleost fish and quadrupeds. In mammals it is reduced to a peg, the *coracoid process.* [New Latin *coracoides,* "(bone) shaped like a crow's beak", from Greek *korakoeidēs,* like a raven : *korax,* raven + -OID.] —**cor·a·coid** *adj.*

cor·al (kórrəl ‖ káwrəl) *n.* **1.** Any of numerous chiefly colonial marine coelenterates of the class Anthozoa, characterised by calcareous skeletons massed in a wide variety of shapes, and often forming reefs or islands. **2.** The often hard, rocklike structure formed by such organisms. **3.** The material forming such a structure; especially, the red-orange, pinkish, or white stony substance secreted by corals of the genus *Corallium,* used to make jewellery

and ornaments. **4.** An object made of coral. **5.** Deep or strong pink to moderate red or reddish orange. [Middle English, from Old French, from Latin *corallum,* from Greek *korallion,* probably of Semitic origin, akin to Hebrew *gōrāl,* a pebble.] —**cor·al** *adj.*

cor·al·line (kórrə-līn ‖ káwrə-, -lin) *adj.* **1.** Of, consisting of, or producing coral. **2.** Resembling coral; especially, coral-coloured.

~*n.* **1.** A coral-like animal, such as certain polyzoans or hydrozoans. **2.** Any of various red algae, especially of the genus *Corallina,* covered with a calcareous substance and forming stony deposits.

cor·al·loid (kórrə-loyd) *adj.* Resembling coral.

coral reef *n.* A marine ridge or mound consisting chiefly of compacted coral together with algal material and biochemically deposited magnesium and calcium carbonates.

cor·al·root (kórrəl-rōōt ‖ -rōot) *n.* Any of several saprophytic orchids of the genus *Corallorhiza,* having small yellow-green or purplish flowers and branched roots that resemble coral.

Coral Sea. A region of the South Pacific Ocean, between northeast Australia and the New Britain-New Caledonia island chain. It contains the Great Barrier Reef, the largest coral reef in the world.

coral snake *n.* **1.** Any of various venomous snakes of the genus *Micrurus,* of tropical America and the southern United States, characteristically having brilliant red, black, and yellow banded markings. **2.** Any of various venomous snakes of the genus *Aspidelaps,* of southern Africa. **3.** A small, venomous snake, *Brachyurophis australis,* of eastern Australia.

cor an·glais (kór óNglay) *n., pl.* **cors anglais** (kórz). A double-reed woodwind musical instrument similar to but larger than the oboe, and pitched lower by a fifth. Also *chiefly U.S.* "English horn". [French, "English horn".]

cor·beil (kórb'l) *n.* Also **cor·beille** (kawr-báy). A sculptured basket of flowers or fruits used as an architectural ornament. [French *corbeille,* from Late Latin *corbicula,* diminutive of Latin *corbis,* basket. See **corf.**]

cor·bel (kórb'l) *n.* A bracket of stone, wood, brick, or other building material, projecting from the face of a wall and generally used to support a cornice or an arch.

~*tr.v.* **corbelled** or *U.S.* **corbeled, -belling** or *U.S.* **-beling, -bels.** To provide with or support by a corbel or corbels. [Middle English, from Old French, diminutive of *corp,* raven (early corbels were wedge-shaped, like ravens' beaks), from Latin *corvus.*]

cor·bel·ling (kórb'l-ing) *n.* An overlapping arrangement of bricks or stones in which each course extends farther out from the vertical of the wall than the course below.

cor·bie (kórbi) *n. Scottish & Regional.* A raven, crow, or rook. [Middle English, diminutive of Old French *corb,* from Latin *corvus,* crow.]

corbie gable *n.* A gable roof with corbie-steps.

cor·bie-step (kórbi-step) *n.* Also **corbel step.** Any of a series of steps or steplike projections on the top of a gable wall. [From Middle English *corbie,* raven (the steps being accessible only to birds), from Old French *corbin,* from Latin *corvīnus,* raven-like.]

cor blimey. Variant of **gorblimey.**

Corbusier, Le. See **Le Corbusier.**

Cor·by (kórbi). New town in Northamptonshire in the Midlands of England, largely dependent on its steelworks until these closed in 1980 because of the decline of the British steel industry.

cord (kord) *n.* Also **chord** (for sense 5 only). **1.** A string or small rope of twisted strands or fibres. **2.** A length of plaited fibres, made of fine material such as silk, used as decoration on clothing, as a belt, or the like. **3.** An insulated, flexible electric wire fitted with a plug or plugs; a flex. **4.** An influence, feeling, or force that binds or restrains. **5.** Any anatomical structure resembling a cord. **6.** A raised rib on the surface of cloth, as on corduroy. **7.** A fabric with such ribs. **8.** *Plural.* Trousers made of corduroy. **9.** A unit of quantity for cut fuel wood, equal to about 3.625 cubic metres (128 cubic feet) in a stack measuring 4 by 4 by 8 feet.

~*tr.v.* **corded, cording, cords. 1.** To fasten or bind with a cord or cords. **2.** To pile (wood) in cords. [Middle English, from Old French *corde,* from Latin *chorda,* catgut, cord, from Greek *khordē.*] —**cord·er** *n.*

cord·age (kórdij) *n.* **1.** The ropes in the rigging of a ship. **2.** The amount of wood in an area, as measured in cords.

cor·date (kórdayt) *adj. Biology.* Having a heart-shaped outline: *a cordate leaf.* [New Latin *cordatus,* from Latin *cor* (stem *cord-*), heart.] —**cor·date·ly** *adv.*

Cor·day (kór-day, kawr-dáy), **Charlotte,** born Marie Charlotte de Corday d'Armont (1768–93). French noblewoman who assassinated Jean-Paul Marat. Of an impoverished Norman aristocratic family, she sympathised with the Girondins in the French Revolution. She was guillotined in 1793.

cord·ed (kórdid) *adj.* **1. a.** Made of cords. **b.** Tied with cords. *"corded bales"* (Matthew Arnold). **2.** Ribbed or twilled, as corduroy. **3.** Standing out like tightened cords. Said of muscles.

cor·di·al (kórdi-əl ‖ *U.S.* kórjəl) *adj.* **1.** Hearty; warm; sincere. **2.** Invigorating; stimulating; reviving.

~*n.* **1.** A fruit-based, sweet, non-alcoholic drink. **2.** A stimulant. **3.** *U.S.* A liqueur. [Middle English, of the heart, from Medieval Latin *cordiālis,* from Latin *cor* (stem *cord-*), heart.] —**cor·di·al·i·ty** (-ál-əti ‖ *U.S.* kórj-), **cor·di·al·ness** *n.* —**cor·di·al·ly** *adv.*

cor·di·er·ite (kórdi-ər-īt) *n.* A dichroic violet-blue to grey mineral silicate of magnesium, aluminium, and sometimes iron. Also called "dichroite". [French, "iolite" after Pierre L.A. *Cordier* (1777–1861), French geologist who first described it.]

cor·di·form (kórdi-fawrm) *adj.* Heart-shaped. [French *cordiforme* : Latin *cor* (stem *cord-*), heart + -FORM.]

cor·dil·le·ra (kórdil-yaír-ə, -aír- || *U.S. also* kawr-díllərə) *n.* **1.** A series of broadly parallel mountain ranges; especially, the principal mountain system of a large land mass. **2.** In South America, a small mountain range. [Spanish, from *cordilla*, diminutive of *cuerda*, cord, chain, from Latin *chorda*, CORD.] —**cor·dil·le·ran** *adj.*

cord·ite (kórdīt) *n.* A smokeless explosive powder consisting of nitrocellulose, nitroglycerin, and petrolatum dissolved in acetone, dried, and extruded in cords. [From CORD.]

cordless (kórd-ləss, -liss) *adj.* Without cord or flex; especially, operated by a usually rechargeable battery.

cór·do·ba (kórdəbə) *n.* **1.** The basic monetary unit of Nicaragua, equal to 100 centavos. **2.** A note worth one córdoba. [After Francisco de *Córdoba* (1475–1526), Spanish explorer.]

Cór·do·ba[1] (kórdəbə). Capital of Córdoba province, southern Spain, situated on the river Guadalquivir. As a Moorish capital (756–1031) it was a brilliant cultural centre.

Córdoba[2]. Capital of Córdoba province in central Argentina. It lies on the river Primero, and was founded in 1573.

cor·don (kórd'n, *rarely* kór-don) *n.* **1.** A line of people, military posts, ships, or the like stationed around an area to enclose or guard it. **2.** A cord or braid worn as a fastening or an ornament. **3.** A ribbon, usually worn diagonally across the chest as a badge of honour or a decoration. **4.** *Architecture.* An ornamental band of stone or masonry, a **stringcourse** *(see)*. **5.** *Horticulture.* A fruit tree trained and pruned to grow along wires or other supports.

~*tr.v.* **cordoned, -doning, -dons.** To form a cordon round (an area) so as to prevent movement in or out. Often used with *off.* [French, from Old French, diminutive of *corde*, CORD.]

cor·don bleu (kór-doɴ blúr, -doɴ, blǒ || *U.S.* kawr-dóɴ) *n., pl.* **cordons bleus** (*pronounced as singular*). **1.** The blue ribbon worn as a decoration by members of the Order of the Holy Ghost, the highest order of French chivalry under the Bourbon monarchy. **2.** A person highly distinguished in his field; especially, a master chef.

~*adj.* Of or designating the highest standard of cooking. [French, "blue ribbon".]

cor·don sa·ni·taire (kór-doɴ sánni-taír, -don, -d'n || *U.S.* kawr-dóɴ) *n., pl.* **cordons sanitaires** (*pronounced as singular*). **1.** A chain of buffer states organised around a nation considered ideologically dangerous or potentially hostile. **2.** Any comprehensive barrier, physical or figurative, devised so as to keep off some potential danger. [French, "quarantine line".]

cor·do·van (kórdəvən) *n.* A fine leather made originally at Córdoba, Spain, first of goatskin but now more frequently of split horsehide. Also called "cordovan leather".

~*adj.* Made of this leather. [Spanish *cordobán*, from CÓRDOBA.]

Cor·do·van (kórdəvən) *n.* An inhabitant or native of Córdoba. [Old Spanish *Cordován*, from *Córdova*, CÓRDOBA.] —**Cor·do·van** *adj.*

cor·du·roy (kór-dew-roy, -də- || *U.S. also* -róy) *n.* **1.** A durable cut-pile fabric, usually made of cotton, with vertical raised ribs. **2.** *Plural.* Corduroy trousers; cords.

~*adj.* **1.** Made of or resembling corduroy. **2.** Made of logs laid together transversely: *a corduroy road.*

~*tr.v.* **corduroyed, -roying, -roys.** To build (a road) of logs laid together transversely. [Probably from CORD (ribbed cloth) + obsolete *duroy, deroy†*, a coarse woollen fabric.]

cord·wood (kórd-wǒod) *n.* Wood piled or sold in cords.

core (kor || kōr) *n.* **1.** The hard or fibrous central part of certain fruits, such as the apple or pear, containing the seeds. **2. a.** The innermost or most important part of anything; the heart; the centre; the essence. **b.** A group or body forming the essential basis of something, such as an organisation. **3.** *Electricity.* A soft iron rod in the coil of an electromagnet or transformer that intensifies and provides a path for the magnetic field produced by the windings. **4.** A mass of dry sand placed within a mould to provide openings or shape to a casting. **5.** The base, usually of soft or inferior wood, to which veneer woods are glued. **6.** *Computing.* Any of the small magnetic rings used to store a bit of information in a magnetic memory. Also called "magnetic core". **b.** A computer memory made up of such magnetic rings. **7.** The central part of the earth lying below the mantle. **8. a.** The central part of any planet that is differentiated into layers. **b.** The central part of a star, in which the energy is produced. **9.** *Physics.* The part of a nuclear reactor in which the reaction occurs, containing the fuel and control rods. **10.** *Geology.* A cylindrical sample of the earth's crust obtained by a hollow drill or piston.

~*tr.v.* **cored, coring, cores.** To remove the core of: *core apples.* [Middle English *core, coor†*.] —**cor·er** *n.*

core dump *n.* A listing in the form of a print-out or a display on a screen, for example, of the data stored in a computer core.

core-dump (kór-dump || kōr-) *tr.v.* **-dumped, -dumping, -dumps.** To list (the data in a computer core), as by printing out or displaying on a screen.

corelate. *Chiefly British.* Variant of **correlate.**

co·re·lig·ion·ist (kǒ-ri-lijənist, -rə-) *n.* One having the same religion as another.

Co·rel·li (kə-rélli, ko-), **Arcangelo** (1653–1713). Italian composer and violinist, and an important innovator of violin technique in the baroque era. As a composer, he is best remembered for his 12 con-

certi grossi which shaped the development of the concerto.

Corelli, Marie, born Mary Mackay (1855–1924). British novelist, whose works of melodrama and high moral tone appealed to Victorian taste. Her best-selling titles included *Barabbas* (1893) and *The Sorrows of Satan* (1895).

co·re·op·sis (kórri-ópsiss || *U.S.* káwri-, kǒri-) *n.* Any of several plants of the genus *Coreopsis*, having daisy-like yellow or variegated flowers. Also called "tickseed" and sometimes "calliopsis". [New Latin, "resembling a bedbug" (from the shape of the seed) : Greek *koris*, bedbug + -OPSIS.]

co·re·spon·dent (kǒ-ri-spóndənt, -rə-) *n. Law.* A person cited in a divorce case as having committed adultery with the partner (respondent) being sued by the petitioner.

~*adj.* Patterned with two different shades, usually of leather. Said of shoes, usually humorously. —**co·re·spon·den·cy** *n.*

core store *n.* The main store in a computer, the **memory** *(see).*

corf (korf) *n., pl.* **corves** (korvz). *British.* A wagon, tub, or basket used in a mine. [Middle English, basket, from Middle Dutch *corf* or Middle Low German *korf*, probably from Latin *corbis†*.]

Cor·fam (kór-fam) *n.* A trademark for a synthetic leather, used especially for shoes.

Cor·fu (kór-fǒo, -féw, -fǒo). *Greek* **Kér·ki·ra** (kaírki-rə). Island in the Ionian Sea off northwest Greece. It is probably the Scheria of Homer and was later called Corcyra. The island passed through the hands of Rome, Byzantium, Sicily, and Venice, and was under British protection from 1815 to 1864, when it was ceded to Greece. Corfu's beaches attract many tourists.

cor·gi (kórgi) *n.* A dog belonging to either of two long-bodied, short-legged breeds, the *Cardigan corgi* or the *Pembroke corgi*. Also called "Welsh corgi". [Welsh : *cor*, dwarf + *ci*, dog.]

co·ri·a·ceous (kórri-áyshəss || *U.S.* káwri-, kǒri-) *adj.* Of or like leather, especially in texture; tough. [Late Latin *coriāceus*, from Latin *corium*, leather, hide.]

co·ri·an·der (kórri-ándər || *U.S.* káwri-, kǒri-, *also* -andər) *n.* **1.** A herb, *Coriandrum sativum*, widely cultivated for its aromatic seeds. **2.** The dried ripe seeds of this plant, used especially to flavour food. [Middle English *coriandre*, from Old French, from Latin *coriandrum*, from Greek *koriandron, koriannon*, perhaps of Mediterranean origin.]

Cor·inth (kórrinth). *Greek* **Kórinthos.** Port in southern Greece, on the Isthmus of Corinth. As a city-state it became rich and influential in the seventh and sixth centuries B.C. as the region's leading pottery producer and maritime power, but it was later overshadowed by Athens. Medieval exports included currants, which get their name from the city.

Co·rin·thi·an (kə-rínthi-ən) *adj.* **1.** Of or pertaining to ancient Corinth. **2.** Given to luxury; licentious; profligate. **3.** Elegantly or elaborately ornate. **4.** Pertaining to the Corinthian order.

~*n.* **1.** A native or inhabitant of Corinth. **2.** One who excels in both sporting and intellectual pursuits. **3.** *Archaic.* A man-about-town. **4.** Plural. *Abbr.* **Cor.** Either of two epistles addressed by Saint Paul to the Christian community at Corinth, each forming a book of the New Testament. In this sense, also called "Epistle to the Corinthians".

Corinthian order *n.* The most ornate of the three classical orders of architecture, characterised by a slender fluted column having an ornate bell-shaped capital decorated with acanthus leaves. Compare **Doric order, Ionic order.**

Cor·i·o·la·nus (kórri-ō-láynəss, -ə- || káwri-), **Gaius Marcius** (5th century B.C.). Roman general, commemorated in Shakespeare's play *Coriolanus*. Of noble birth, he is alleged to have won his name at the siege of Corioli in the war against the Volscians (493 B.C.).

Cor·i·o·lis force (kórri-ōliss || *U.S.* káwri-, kǒri-) *n. Physics.* A fictitious force used mathematically to describe motion relative to a non-inertial, uniformly rotating frame of reference. It is used, for example, to describe the motion of air relative to the rotating earth. [After Gaspard G. de *Coriolis* (1792–1843), French mathematician.]

co·ri·um (káwri-əm || kǒri-) *n., pl.* **coria** (-ə). The **dermis** *(see).* [New Latin, from Latin, skin, hide.]

cork (kork) *n.* **1.** The light, porous, elastic outer bark of the cork oak, used widely as an insulator and a stopper for bottles. **2.** Something made of cork, especially a bottle stopper. **3.** A bottle stopper made of other material, such as plastic, glass, or rubber. **4.** A small float used on a fishing line or net to buoy up the line or to indicate when a fish bites. **5.** *Botany.* Cork cambium.

~*tr.v.* **corked, corking, corks. 1.** To stop or seal with or as if with a cork. **2.** To hold back; restrain or check. Usually used with *up.* [Middle English, from Dutch *kurk* or Low German *korck*, from Spanish *alcorque*, cork sole or shoe, probably from Spanish Arabic *al-qūrq*.]

Cork[1] (kork). *Irish* **Cor·caigh** (kórki). A county in Munster in the southwest of the Republic of Ireland. Its hills are scattered with fortified castles, including the 15th-century Blarney Castle, famous for the Blarney Stone.

Cork[2]. *Irish* **Corcaigh.** The administrative centre of County Cork at the mouth of the River Lee in the southwest of the Republic of Ireland. It is Ireland's second largest city.

cork·age (kórkij) *n.* A charge exacted at a restaurant for opening and serving bottles of wine or other alcoholic beverages not bought on the premises.

cork·board (kórk-bawrd || -bōrd) *n.* A construction and insulating sheet material made of compressed and baked granules of cork.

cork cambium *n. Botany.* A layer of continually dividing cells situated near the surface of woody plant stems and roots, which forms cork to the outside and secondary cortical cells to the inside. Also called "cork", "phellem".

corked (korkt) *adj.* **1.** Designating wine or spirits that have been impaired in some way by a poor or decaying cork: *corked port.* **2.** Blackened by burnt cork. **3.** *British Slang.* Drunk.

cork·er (kórkər) *n.* **1.** One that inserts corks, as in bottles. **2.** *Slang.* Someone or something that is remarkable or astounding. **3.** *Slang.* An unanswerable fact or argument.

cork·ing (kórking) *adj. Informal.* Excellent; splendid; fine. [From CORK (verb), probably influenced in meaning by CORKER.] —**corking** *adv.*

cork oak *n.* An evergreen oak tree, *Quercus suber,* of the Mediterranean region, having a porous outer bark that is the source of cork. Also called "cork tree".

cork·screw (kórk-skrōō || -skrew) *n.* A device for drawing corks from bottles, consisting typically of a pointed metal spiral attached to a handle. ~*adj.* Resembling a corkscrew in shape; spiral; helical. ~*v.* **corkscrewed, -screwing, -screws.** —*tr.* To cause to move in a spiral or winding course. —*intr.* To move spirally.

cork·wood (kórkwōōd) *n.* **1.** A small tree or shrub, *Leitneria floridana,* of the southeastern United States, having wood lighter than cork which is used for fishing-net floats. **2.** Any of several other trees having light, porous wood. **3.** The wood of these.

cork·y (kórki) *adj.* **-ier, -iest. 1.** Of or like cork. **2.** *Informal.* Lively; buoyant. **3.** Tasting of cork; corked. —**cork·i·ness** *n.*

corm (korm) *n. Botany.* An underground stem, such as that of the gladiolus, similar to a bulb but having papery, rather than fleshy, scale leaves. [New Latin *cormus,* from Greek *kormos,* a trimmed tree trunk, from *keirein,* to shear.]

cor·mel (kórm'l) *n. Botany.* A young corm that arises at the base of a fully developed corm.

cor·mo·phyte (kórmə-fīt) *n.* Any of a former botanical division, Cormophyta, consisting of plants having roots, stems, and foliage. [New Latin *Cormophyta* : Greek *kormos,* tree trunk (see **corm**) + -PHYTE.] —**cor·mo·phyt·ic** (-fíttik) *adj.*

cor·mo·rant (kórmə-rənt || *U.S.* also -rant) *n.* Any of several widely distributed aquatic birds of the genus *Phalacrocorax,* especially *P. carbo,* having dark plumage, webbed feet, a hooked bill, and a distensible pouch. [Middle English *cormeraunt,* from Old French *cormoran, cormaran, cormareng* : *corp,* raven, from Latin *corvus* + *marenc,* of the sea, from Latin *marīnus,* MARINE.]

corn¹ (korn) *n.* **1. a.** Any of several cereal plants producing edible seed, especially when the main crop of a region, such as wheat in England, oats in Scotland, or maize in Australia and the United States. **b.** The seeds of such a plant or crop; grain. **2.** *U.S.* A crop. **maize** *(see).* **3. a.** A single seed of a cereal plant; a grain. **b.** A seed or fruit of various other plants. **4.** *U.S. Informal.* Corn whiskey. **5.** *Slang.* Anything considered trite, dated, or unduly sentimental. ~*tr.v.* **corned, corning, corns. 1. a.** To preserve and season with granulated salt. **b.** To preserve in brine. **2.** To feed (animals) with corn or grain. [Middle English *corn,* Old English *corn.*]

corn² *n.* A horny painful thickening of the skin, usually on or near a toe, resulting from pressure or friction. —**tread on (someone's) corns.** *Informal.* To offend; hurt the feelings of. [Middle English *corne,* from Old French *corne,* corn on the foot, horn, from Latin *cornū,* horn.]

Corn. Cornwall.

Corn Belt. An extensive region of the United States, stretching across Ohio, Indiana, Illinois, Iowa, Minnesota, South Dakota, Missouri, Kansas, and Nebraska. About two thirds of the country's maize (corn) output is grown there.

corn borer *n.* **1.** The larva of a moth, *Pyrausta nubilalis,* native to the Old World, that feeds on and destroys maize and other plants. **2.** Any of various similar insect larvae that infest maize.

corn bunting *n.* A European songbird, *Emberiza calandra,* with streaked brown plumage.

corn·cob (kórn-kob) *n.* **1.** The hard core of an ear of maize to which the kernels are attached. **2.** A corncob pipe.

corncob pipe *n.* A pipe with a bowl made of a dried corncob. Also called "corncob".

corn cockle *n.* A plant, *Agrostemma githago,* native to Europe, having red flowers and growing in cornfields and by roadsides.

corn·crake (kórn-krayk) *n.* A common Old World bird, *Crex crex,* having brownish plumage and frequenting cornfields and meadows. Also called "land rail".

cor·ne·a (kórni-ə) *n., pl.* **-as** *or* **-ae** (-ee). The transparent anterior portion of the outer fibrous coat of the vertebrate eye, a uniformly thick, nearly circular, convex structure that refracts light onto the lens. [Medieval Latin *cornea (tēla),* "horny (tissue)", from Latin, feminine of *corneus,* horny, from *cornū,* horn.] —**cor·ne·al** *adj.*

corned beef *n.* A type of salted cooked beef, generally tinned.

Cor·neille (kawr-náy), **Pierre** (1606–84). French playwright, the pioneer of French classical drama. His plays, including *Le Cid* (1637) and *Horace* (1640), dramatise grand moral themes within measured and elegant verse.

cor·nel (kórn'l) *n.* Any of various plants of the genus *Cornus,* which includes the dogwoods. [German *Kornel(beere), Kornel(baum),* cornel (berry), cornel (tree), from Old High German *kornul-,* from Medieval Latin *corna* (unattested), from Latin *cornus†,* cornel tree.]

cornelian. Variant of **carnelian.**

cor·nel·i·an cherry (kawr-néeli-ən, kər- || *U.S.* also -nél-yən) *n.* A shrub or small tree, *Cornus mas,* native to Eurasia, having very small yellow flowers and bright-red edible fruit. [From CORNEL.]

cor·ne·ous (kórni-əss) *adj.* Made of horn or a hornlike substance; horny. [Latin *corneus,* from *cornū,* horn.]

cor·ner (kórnər, káwnər) *n. Abbr.* **cor. 1.** The position at which two lines or surfaces meet. **2.** The immediate interior or exterior region of the angle formed at this position, bounded by the two lines or surfaces. **3.** The point or place where the sides of roads, streets, or walls join, meet, or intersect. **4.** A threatening or embarrassing position, especially one from which escape is difficult or impossible. **5.** Any part, quarter, or region: *from every corner of the globe.* **6.** A remote, secluded, or secret place, area, or part. **7.** A guard or decoration fitted on various kinds of corners, as of a bookbinding. **8.** A speculative monopoly of a stock or commodity, created by purchasing all or most of the available supply, in order to raise its price. **9.** *Sports.* A free kick or shot, taken from a corner of the field next to the defending team's goal, awarded to the attacking team when the ball has gone behind the goal line after having been touched last by a defender. **10.** In boxing and wrestling, either of two diagonally opposite corners of the ring in which opponents rest between rounds. —**cut corners.** *Informal.* **1.** To take the shortest route around obstacles, often dangerously or illegally. **2.** To reduce expenditure; economise. —**fight (one's) corner.** To defend one's position or interests vigorously. —**stand (one's) corner.** To contribute one's share, as in an undertaking. —**turn the corner.** To get over or come through the worst part of an illness, financial difficulty, or the like; pass the critical point. ~*v.* **cornered, -nering, -ners.** —*tr.* **1.** To furnish with corners. **2.** To place or drive into a corner. **3.** To get a corner in (a stock or commodity). —*intr.* **1.** To get a corner in a stock or commodity. **2.** To turn, as at a corner. ~*adj.* **1.** On or at a corner. **2.** Designed for or used in a corner. [Middle English, from Old French *cornere, corniere,* from Vulgar Latin *cornārium* (unattested), from Latin *cornū,* horn, extremity.]

corner shop *n.* A local shop, usually small, selling food and other provisions, and typically situated at the corner of a street.

cor·ner·stone (kórnər-stōn) *n.* **1.** A stone at the corner of a building uniting two intersecting walls; a quoin. **2.** Such a stone ceremonially laid and often inscribed. **3.** The indispensable and fundamental basis of something.

cor·net (kórnit || *U.S.* kawr-nét *for sense 1 only*) *n.* **1.** *Abbr.* **cor.** A musical wind instrument of the trumpet class, having three valves operated by pistons. **2.** A cornet player. **3.** *British.* **a.** A wafer, usually cone-shaped, holding ice cream. **b.** The wafer itself. **4.** The large white headdress worn by certain nuns. **5.** A headdress, often cone-shaped, worn by women in the late Middle Ages. **6. a.** Formerly, the fifth commissioned officer in a British cavalry troop. **b.** The standard carried by such an officer. [Middle English, from Old French, diminutive of *corn,* horn, from Latin *cornū.*]

cor·net·cy (kórnit-si) *n., pl.* **-cies.** Formerly, the rank or commission of a cornet cavalry officer.

cor·net·ist, cor·net·tist (kawr-néttist) *n.* One who plays a cornet.

corn exchange *n.* **1.** A place where corn is bought and sold, usually wholesale. **2.** A building formerly used for this purpose.

corn factor *n.* A person who buys and sells corn for a living.

corn·field (kórn-feeld) *n.* A field planted with corn.

corn·flakes (kórn-flayks) *pl.n.* A crisp, flaky commercially prepared cold cereal made from toasted maize.

corn·flour (kórn-flowr) *n.* A starchy flour made from maize, rice, or other cereal and used as a thickening in cookery. Also *U.S.* "cornstarch".

corn·flow·er (kórn-flowr) *n.* A weed of cultivation, *Centaurea cyanus,* native to Eurasia, having bright blue flowers resembling those of knapweeds. Also called "bluebottle". [So called because it is found in cornfields.]

corn·husk (kórn-husk) *n. U.S.* The leafy husk surrounding an ear of maize. Also called "corn shuck".

cor·nice (kórniss) *n.* **1.** *Architecture.* **a.** A horizontal moulded projection that crowns or completes a building or wall. **b.** The uppermost part of an entablature. **2.** A moulding at the top of the walls of a room, between the walls and ceiling. **3.** An overhanging mass of snow at a precipice. ~*tr.v.* **corniced, -nicing, -nices.** To supply, decorate, or finish with, or as with, a cornice. [French *corniche,* from Italian *cornice,* perhaps from Latin *cornix* (stem *cornic-*), crow, also influenced by Greek *korōnis,* curved line, coping stone, from *korōnē,* anything curved, from *korōnos,* curved.]

cor·niche (kór-neesh, -nish) *n.* A coast road, often along the side of a cliff. [French. See **cornice.**]

cor·nic·u·late (kawr-níckew-layt, -lət, -lit) *adj.* Having horns or hornlike projections. [Latin *corniculātus,* from *corniculum,* little horn, diminutive of *cornū,* horn.]

Cor·nish (kórnish) *adj.* Of or pertaining to Cornwall in southwest England, its inhabitants, or their language. ~*n.* **1.** The Brythonic Celtic language of Cornwall. **2.** *Used with a plural verb.* The natives or inhabitants of Cornwall. —**Cor·nish·man** *n.* —**Cor·nish·wo·man** *n.*

Cornish pas·ty (pásti) *n.* A kind of pie, often semicircular in shape, with a forcemeat and vegetable filling.

Corn Laws *pl.n.* A series of British laws in force before 1846 regulating the grain trade and restricting imports of grain.

corn lily *n.* Any of several bulbous plants of the genus *Ixia,* native to southern Africa, having variously coloured lily-like flowers.

corn marigold *n.* A Eurasian plant, *Chrysanthemum segetum,* having yellow daisy-like flowers; a common weed in fields.

corn·meal (kórn-meel) *n.* Meal made from corn. **—corn·meal** *adj.*

corn poppy *n.* An Old World plant, *Papaver rhoeas,* having bright-red flowers, frequently a weed. Also called "Flanders poppy".

corn rose *n.* Formerly, any of several red-flowered plants growing in cornfields, such as the corn poppy or the corn cockle.

corn rows *pl.n.* A hairstyle popular especially among West Indian women and black Americans in which the hair is plaited in parallel rows close to the head.

corn rule *n. Chemistry.* A rule for indicating the optical activity of amino acids with the formula $RCH(NH_2)$ (COOH). If the molecule were observed along the H–C direction, the COOH, R, and NH_2 groups would be arranged clockwise in dextrorotatory acids and anticlockwise in laevorotatory acids. [From the acronym, COO(H) R N(H_2).]

corn salad *n.* Any of several plants of the genus *Valerianella;* especially, *V. locusta* (or *V. olitoria*), native to Europe, having small bluish flowers, and leaves used for salad. Also called "lamb's-lettuce". [So called because it is found in cornfields.]

corn shuck *n. U.S.* A cornhusk *(see).*

corn silk *n. U.S.* The silky tuft on an ear of maize, **silk** *(see).*

corn·stalk (kórn-stawk) *n.* A stalk or stem of corn.

corn·starch (kórn-staarch) *n. U.S.* **Cornflour** *(see).*

corn·stone (kórn-stōn) *n.* A mottled red-and-green limestone.

corn syrup *n. U.S.* A syrup prepared from maize.

cor·nu (kórnew) *n., pl.* **-nua** (-ə). *Anatomy.* A structure resembling a horn. [Latin *cornū,* horn.] **—cor·nu·al** *adj.*

cor·nu·co·pi·a (kór-new-kŏpĭ-ə ‖ *chiefly U.S.* -nə-) *n.* **1.** A goat's horn overflowing with fruit, flowers, and corn, signifying prosperity; a horn of plenty. **2.** An overflowing store; an abundance. **3.** Any cone-shaped receptacle or ornament. [Late Latin *cornūcōpia,* horn of plenty, from Latin *cornū cōpiae* : *cornū,* horn + *cōpiae,* genitive of *cōpia,* plenty.] **—cor·nu·co·pi·an, cor·nu·co·pi·ate** *adj.*

cor·nute (kawrn-néwt ‖ -nóōt) *adj.* Also **cor·nut·ed** (-id). **1.** Horn-shaped. **2.** Having horns or horn-shaped anatomical processes. [Latin *cornūtus,* horned, from *cornū,* horn.]

Corn·wall (kórn-wəl, -wawl). County in the extreme southwest of England. At its extremity is Land's End, the westernmost point of the English mainland. Tin was mined in Cornwall in ancient times and was still mined until recently. Following the Roman and Saxon invasions of Britain, Cornwall became a bastion of Celtic culture, and its language, of Celtic origin, has been revived. Truro is the administrative centre and county town.

Corn·wal·lis (kawrn-wólliss), **Charles, 1st Marquess** (1738–1805). British soldier and statesman who commanded British forces in South Carolina during the War of American Independence. His surrender at Yorktown on October 19, 1781, marked the final British defeat. As governor-general of India (1786–93), he introduced a series of land reforms (the Cornwallis code) to secure administrative control of India for the East India Company.

corn whiskey *n. U.S.* Whiskey distilled from maize.

corn·y (kórni) *adj.* **-ier, -iest.** *Informal.* **1.** Trite or sentimental. **2.** Using well-worn jokes or comic devices. [From CORN (from the supposedly unsophisticated humour of farmers).]

co·rol·la (kə-róllə) *n. Botany.* The inner envelope of a flower, consisting of fused or separate petals. Compare **calyx.** [New Latin, from Latin, diminutive of *corōna,* garland, CORONA.]

cor·ol·lar·y (kə-rólləri ‖ *U.S.* kórrə-lerri, káwrə-) *n., pl.* **-ies. 1.** A proposition that follows with little or no proof from one already proved. **2.** A deduction or inference. **3.** A natural consequence or effect.

~*adj.* Consequent or resultant. [Middle English *corolarie,* from Latin *corollārium,* money paid for a garland, gratuity, from *corolla,* small garland, diminutive of *corōna,* garland, CORONA.]

Cor·o·man·del Coast (kórrə-mánd'l). The southern reaches of India's eastern seaboard, stretching from Cape Calimere in the south to the mouth of the Krishna river in the north. It is lashed by rough seas and monsoons.

co·ro·na (kə-rŏ-nə) *n., pl.* **-nas** or **-nae** (-nee). **1.** *Astronomy.* **a.** A faintly coloured luminous ring around a celestial body visible through a haze or thin cloud, especially such a ring around the Moon or Sun, caused by diffraction of light from small suspended ice crystals in the Earth's upper atmosphere. **b.** The luminous irregular envelope of highly ionised gas outside the chromosphere of the Sun. **2.** *Architecture.* The top projecting part of a cornice. **3.** A cigar having a long tapering body and blunt ends. **4.** A circular chandelier hanging from the ceiling of a church. **5.** *Anatomy.* A crownlike or upper part or structure, such as the top of the head. **6.** *Botany.* A crownlike part of a flower, usually between the petals and stamens, but sometimes an appendage of the corolla, as in daffodils. Also called "crown". **7.** *Electricity.* A faint glow enveloping the high-field electrode in a **corona discharge** *(see),* often accompanied by streamers directed towards the low-field electrode. [Latin *corōna,* garland, crown, from Greek *korōnē,* something curved, kind of crown, from *korōnos,* curved.]

Corona Aus·tra·lis (o-stráyliss, aw-) *n.* A constellation in the Southern Hemisphere near Telescopium and Sagittarius. Also called the "Southern Crown".

Corona Bo·re·al·is (báwri-aliss, bórri- ‖ bŏri-, *U.S.* -állis) *n.* A constellation containing the Corona Borealis cluster of galaxies, in the Northern Hemisphere near Hercules and Boötes. Also called the "Northern Crown".

co·ro·nach (kórrə-nəkh, -nək, -nak) *n.* In Ireland or the Highlands of Scotland, a Gaelic funeral dirge. [Irish *coranach* and (Scottish) Gaelic *corranach* : *comh-,* together + *rānach,* a crying.]

corona discharge *n.* An electrical discharge characterised by a corona and occurring when one of two electrodes in a gas has a shape such that the electric field strength close to its surface is significantly greater than that between the electrodes.

co·ro·na·graph, co·ro·no·graph (kə-rŏnə-graaf, -graf) *n. Astronomy.* A type of refracting telescope designed for study of the Sun's corona, having a central disc to block light from the Sun's surface. **—co·ro·na·graph·ic** (-gráffik) *adj.*

co·ro·nal (kórrən'l, kə-rŏn'l ‖ *U.S. also* káwrən'l) *n.* **1.** A garland, wreath, or circlet. **2.** *Anatomy.* The coronal suture. **3.** *Phonetics.* A coronal speech sound.

~*adj.* **1.** Of or pertaining to a coronal. **2.** *Anatomy.* Of, designating, or having the direction of the coronal suture. **3.** *Phonetics.* Articulated with the blade of the tongue raised. [Middle English, from Old French *coronal,* from Latin *corōnālis,* of a crown, from CORONA.]

coronal suture *n.* The line of union of the two parietal bones with the frontal bone of the skull. Also called "coronal".

cor·o·nar·y (kórrən-ri, -əri ‖ *U.S.* káwrə-nerri, kórrə-) *adj.* **1.** Encircling. Said of arteries, ligaments, nerves, and the like that encircle a structure. **2.** Loosely, of or pertaining to the heart.

~*n., pl.* **coronaries.** *Informal.* A coronary thrombosis. [Latin *corōnārius,* of a wreath or garland, from *corōna,* garland, crown, CORONA.]

coronary artery *n.* Either of the two arteries that originate in the aorta and supply blood to the heart.

coronary thrombosis *n.* The obstructing of a coronary artery by a blood clot, often leading to destruction of heart muscle and causing severe pain in the chest. Also informally called "coronary".

cor·o·na·tion (kórrə-náysh'n) *n.* The act or ceremony of crowning a sovereign or a sovereign's consort. [Middle English *coronacioun,* from Old French *coronation,* from Medieval Latin *corōnātiō* (stem *corōnātiōn-*), from Latin *corōnāre* (past participle *corōnātus*), to crown, from CORONA.]

cor·o·ner (kórrə-nər) *n. Abbr.* **cor. 1.** A public officer, normally a doctor, whose primary function is to investigate by inquest any death which may not have been from natural causes. **2.** *British.* An official who examines cases of treasure trove. [Middle English, officer charged with maintaining the record of the Crown's pleas, from Anglo-French *corouner,* from *coro(u)ne,* CROWN.] **—cor·o·ner·ship** *n.*

coroner's jury *n.* A group of people summoned to a coroner's inquest to determine the cause of the death under investigation.

cor·o·net (kórrə-nit, -net) *n.* **1.** A small crown worn by princes and other nobles below the rank of sovereign. **2.** A chaplet or headband decorated with gold or jewels. **3.** The upper margin of a horse's hoof. [Middle English *coronette,* from Old French, diminutive of *coro(u)ne,* CROWN.]

Co·rot (kórrō, ko-rŏ), **Jean Baptiste Camille** (1796–1875). French landscape painter. His early informal sketches of the Italian countryside are today among his most highly regarded works, though they were never exhibited in his lifetime. His larger compositions are somewhat more mannered, characterised by soft contours and muted, silvery tones.

corp. corporation.

cor·po·ra. Plural of **corpus.**

cor·po·ral¹ (kórp-ərəl, -rəl) *adj.* Of the body; bodily. [Middle English *corporal, corporel,* from Old French, from Latin *corporālis,* from *corpus* (stem *corpor-*), body.] **—cor·po·ral·i·ty** (-ə-rál-əti) *n.* **—cor·po·ral·ly** *adv.*

Usage: The similarity in form between *corporal* and *corporeal* sometimes leads to confusion. *Corporal* means simply "of the body" and is used in many phrases where the physical form of the body is involved (*corporal punishment, corporal needs*). *Corporeal* adds the implication of "bodily as opposed to spiritual or intangible" (*corporeal substance*). For *body* in the sense of "group of people united for some common end", the related adjective is *corporate.*

corporal² *n. Abbr.* **Cpl.** A noncommissioned officer of the lowest rank in the army, air force, or marines. [Obsolete French, variant (probably influenced by *corporal,* bodily, as if meaning "leader of a body of troops") of CAPORAL.]

corporal³ *n.* Also **cor·po·ra·le** (-ə-ráyli). *Ecclesiastical.* A white linen cloth on which the consecrated elements are placed during the celebration of the Eucharist. [Middle English *corporale,* from Old French *corporal,* from Medieval Latin *corporāle,* from the neuter of Latin *corporālis,* of the body, CORPORAL.]

corporal punishment *n.* Physical punishment, such as beating.

cor·po·rate (kórpə-rət, -rit) *adj.* **1.** Formed into a corporation; incorporated. **2.** Of a corporation. **3.** United or combined into one body; collective. **4.** Considered as, pertaining to, or shared by a united body. See Usage note at **corporal. 5.** Variant of **corporative.** [Latin *corporātus,* past participle of *corporāre,* to make into a body, from *corpus* (stem *corpor-*), CORPUS.] **—cor·po·rate·ly** *adv.*

cor·po·ra·tion (kórpə-ráysh'n) *n. Abbr.* **corp. 1.** A body of persons granted a charter legally recognising them as a separate entity having its own rights, privileges, and liabilities distinct from those of its members. Also called "body corporate". **2.** Such a body created for purposes of government, especially that of a city. **3.** Any group of people acting as one body. **4.** *Informal.* A fat belly.

cor·po·ra·tive (kórpə-rətiv, -raytiv) *adj.* Also **cor·po·rate** (-rət, -rit).

1. Of, pertaining to, or associated with a corporation. 2. Of or designating a government or political system in which the principal economic functions, such as banking, industry, labour, and government, are organised as corporate entities with some official status. —**cor·po·rat·iv·ism** n.

cor·po·re·al (kawr-páwri-əl ‖ -pŏ́ri-) adj. 1. Of, pertaining to, or characteristic of the body. 2. Of a material rather than spiritual nature; tangible. See Usage note at **corporal**. [From Latin corporeus, of the body, from corpus (stem corpor-), CORPUS.] —**cor·po·re·al·ly** adv. —**cor·po·re·al·ness** n.

cor·po·re·i·ty (kórpə-rée-əti, -ráy-) n. Also **cor·po·re·al·i·ty** (kawr-páwri-ál-əti ‖ -pŏ́ri-). The state of being material or corporeal.

cor·po·sant (kórpə-zant, -sant) n. A luminous electrical phenomenon, **St. Elmo's fire** (see). [Portuguese corpo-santo, "holy body".]

corps (kor ‖ kōr) n., pl. **corps** (korz ‖ kōrz). 1. Abbr. **c.**, **C.** Military. **a.** A separate branch or department of the armed forces having a specialised function. **b.** A tactical unit of ground combat forces, composed of two or more divisions and auxiliary service troops. 2. A body of persons acting together or associated in a common calling or purpose. [French, from Latin corpus, CORPUS.]

corps de bal·let (kór də báll-ay, -i ‖ kŏ́r, ba-láy) n. The dancers in a ballet troupe who perform as a group and have no solo parts. [French, "ballet troupe".]

corpse (korps) n. A dead body, especially of a human being. ~v. **corpsed, corpsing, corpses.** Slang. intr. To laugh inadvertently on stage. —tr. To cause (an actor) to corpse. [Middle English corps, cors, from Old French, from Latin corpus, body.]

cor·pu·lence (kórpewlənss) n. Fatness; obesity. [Middle English, from Latin corpulentia, from corpulentus, from corpus, body, CORPUS.] —**cor·pu·lent** adj. —**cor·pu·lent·ly** adv.

cor·pus (kór-pəss) n., pl. **-pora** (-pərə) Abbr. **cor.** 1. A large collection of writings or other artistic compositions of a specific kind or having a specific theme. 2. Anatomy. **a.** A structure constituting the main part of an organ. **b.** Any distinct mass or body. 3. The principal or capital, as distinguished from the interest or income, of a fund, estate, investment, or the like. 4. A human or animal body, especially when dead. [Middle English, from Latin, body, substance.]

corpus cal·lo·sum (kə-lŏ́-səm, ka-) n., pl. **corpora callosa** (-sə). Anatomy. A wide arched band of white matter connecting the cerebral hemispheres of the brain at the base of the longitudinal fissure. [New Latin, "callous body".]

Cor·pus Chris·ti (kórpəss krísti) n. Roman Catholic Church. A festival celebrated in honour of the Eucharist ten or fourteen days after Pentecost. [Middle English, from Medieval Latin, "body of Christ".]

cor·pus·cle (kór-puss'l, kawr-púss'l ‖ -pəss'l) n. 1. Biology. A cell, such as an erythrocyte or leucocyte, that is capable of free movement in a fluid or matrix, as distinguished from a cell fixed in tissue. 2. Anatomy. The encapsulated ending of a secondary nerve. 3. A discrete particle such as a photon or electron. 4. Any minute globular particle. In this sense, also called "corpuscule". [Latin corpusculum, diminutive of CORPUS.] —**cor·pus·cu·lar** (kawr-púskewlər) adj.

corpuscular theory n. Physics. The theory that light consists of streams of small particles. Compare **wave theory**. See **light**.

corpus de·lic·ti (di-líktī) n. 1. Law. **a.** The material substance upon which a crime has been committed. **b.** The material evidence of the fact that a crime has been committed, such as the discovered corpse of a murder victim. 2. Loosely, the victim's corpse in a murder case. [New Latin, "body of the crime".]

corpus ju·ris (jòoriss) n. Abbr. **C.J.** The collective body of all the laws of a nation or state. [Late Latin, "body of law".]

Corpus Juris Ca·non·i·ci (kə-nónni-sī) n. Roman Catholic Church. The body of decrees and canons constituting the standard of ecclesiastical law until replaced in 1918 by Codex Juris Canonici. [Late Latin, "body of canon law".]

Corpus Juris Ci·vil·is (si-ví-liss, -vée-) n. The body of civil or Roman law comprising the Digest, the Institutes, the Code, and the Novels, assembled and issued (A.D. 529–535) during Justinian's reign and forming the basis of most continental European law. [Latin, "body of civil law".]

corpus lu·te·um (lŏo-ti-əm, léw-) n., pl. **corpora lutea** (-ə). A yellow mass of endocrine cells in a ruptured mature Graafian follicle of the ovary, formed after the release of an ovum. It secretes the hormone progesterone, which maintains pregnancy. [New Latin, "yellowish body".]

corpus stri·a·tum (strī-áy-təm) n., pl. **corpora striata** (-tə) n. Either of two grey-and-white, striated ganglionic masses of the brain stem in the lower lateral wall of each cerebral hemisphere. [New Latin, "striated body".]

corpus vi·le (víli) n., pl. **corpora vilia** (vílli-ə). Something only fit to serve as an object in an experiment. [Latin, "worthless body".]

corr. 1. correction. 2. correspondence; correspondent.

cor·rade (kə-ráyd) v. **-raded, -rading, -rades.** —tr. To wear away by friction of objects such as sand and gravel moving by gravity or carried in waves, running water, wind, or ice. —intr. To be worn away in this way. [Latin corrādere, to scrape together : com-, together + rādere, to scrape.] —**cor·ra·sion** (kə-ráyzh'n) n. —**cor·ra·sive** (-ráy-siv ‖ -ziv) adj.

cor·ral (kə-ra̍al, ko- ‖ U.S. -rál) n. U.S. 1. An enclosure for confining livestock. 2. An enclosure formed by a circle of wagons for defence against attack while encamped.

~tr.v. **corralled, -ralling, -rals.** U.S. 1. To drive into and hold in a corral. 2. To arrange (wagons) in a corral. 3. Informal. To seize; capture. [Spanish and Portuguese, of Latin origin. See also **kraal**.]

cor·rect (kə-rékt) tr.v. **-rected, -recting, -rects.** 1. To remove the errors or mistakes from. 2. To indicate or mark the errors of. 3. To admonish or punish for the purpose of improving. 4. To remove, remedy, or counteract (a malfunction, for example). 5. To adjust so as to meet a standard or other required condition.
~adj. 1. Free from error or fault; true or accurate. 2. Conforming to accepted standards; proper: correct behaviour. [Middle English correcten, from Latin corrigere (past participle correctus), to make straight, correct : com- (intensifier) + regere, to lead straight, rule.] —**cor·rect·a·ble, cor·rect·i·ble** adj. —**cor·rect·ly** adv. —**cor·rect·ness** n. —**cor·rect·or** n.

Synonyms: correct, rectify, remedy, redress, reform, revise, amend.

cor·rec·tion (kə-réksh'n) n. Abbr. **cor., corr.** 1. The act or process of correcting. 2. That which is offered or substituted for a mistake, fault, or abnormality; an improvement. 3. Punishment. 4. An amount or quantity that is added or subtracted in making exact or accurate. —**cor·rec·tion·al** adj.

correction fluid n. Liquid used to cover a written or typed error that dries to form a new surface on which corrections may be made.

cor·rec·ti·tude (kə-rékti-tewd ‖ -tŏod) n. The state or quality of being correct, especially in manners and behaviour; propriety.

cor·rec·tive (kə-réktiv) adj. Tending or intended to correct. ~n. Something that corrects. —**cor·rec·tive·ly** adv.

Cor·reg·gio (kə-réji-ō, ko-, -réj-), born Antonio Allegri (c.1494–1534). Italian painter, a master of the High Renaissance, whose name derived from his home town in northern Italy. He produced devotional pictures which include Holy Night, and frescoes, such as those in the convent of S. Paolo, Parma (1518).

correl. correlative.

cor·re·late (kórrə-layt, kórri- ‖ kŏ́-ri-) v. **-lated, -lating, -lates.** Also chiefly British **co·re·late.** —tr. 1. To put or bring into causal, complementary, parallel, or reciprocal relation. 2. To establish or demonstrate as having a correlation. —intr. To be related by a correlation.
~adj. Related by a correlation; especially, having corresponding characteristics. ~n. Either of two correlate entities; a correlative. [Back-formation from CORRELATION.]

cor·re·la·tion (kórrə-láysh'n, kórri- ‖ kŏ́-ri-) n. 1. A causal, complementary, parallel, or reciprocal relationship; especially, a structural, functional, or qualitative correspondence between two comparable entities. 2. Statistics. **a.** The simultaneous increase or decrease in value of two numerically valued random variables. Also called "positive correlation". **b.** The simultaneous increase in the value of one and decrease in the value of the other of two numerically valued random variables. Also called "negative correlation". 3. The act of correlating or the condition of being correlated. [Medieval Latin correlātiō (stem correlātiōn-): com-, together + relātiō, relation, from Latin relātus, "carried back" (see relate).] —**cor·re·la·tion·al** adj.

correlation coefficient n. Statistics. A measure of the interdependence of two random variables that ranges in value from −1 to +1, indicating perfect negative correlation at −1, absence of correlation at 0, and perfect positive correlation at +1.

cor·rel·a·tive (kə-réllə-tiv, ko-) adj. Abbr. **correl.** 1. Related; corresponding. 2. Reciprocally related.
~n. Abbr. **correl.** 1. Either of two correlative entities; a correlate. 2. Grammar. A correlative word or expression. —**cor·rel·a·tive·ly** adv. —**cor·rel·a·tive·ness, cor·rel·a·tiv·i·ty** (-tívvəti) n.

correlative conjunction n. Either of a pair of conjunctions indicating a reciprocal or complementary grammatical relation. Neither and nor are correlative conjunctions.

cor·re·spond (kórri-spónd, kórrə-) intr.v. **-sponded, -sponding, -sponds.** 1. To be in agreement, harmony, or conformity; be consistent or compatible. 2. To be similar or equivalent in some way, such as character, meaning, or function. Used with to or with: English "navel" corresponds to Greek "omphalos". 3. To communicate by letter, usually over a period of time. —See Synonyms at **agree.** [Old French correspondre, from Medieval Latin correspondēre : com-, together, mutually + respondēre, RESPOND.]

cor·re·spon·dence (kórri-spóndənss, kórrə-) n. Abbr. **cor., corr., corresp.** 1. The act, fact, or state of agreeing or conforming. 2. Similarity or analogy. 3. **a.** Communication by the exchange of letters. **b.** The letters written or received.

correspondence principle n. Physics. The principle that predictions of quantum theory approach those of classical physics in the limit of large quantum numbers.

correspondence school n. A school that offers instruction by post, sending lessons and examinations to students at home.

cor·re·spon·dent (kórri-spóndənt, kórrə-) n. Abbr. **cor., corr.** 1. One who communicates by means of letters. 2. Someone employed by a newspaper, magazine, or broadcasting company to supply news or articles from a distant place or on a specific subject. 3. A person who writes letters to a newspaper or magazine. 4. A person or firm having regular business relations with another, especially at a distance. 5. A thing that corresponds; a correlative.
~adj. Corresponding; consistent. —**cor·re·spon·dent·ly** adv.

cor·re·spond·ing (kórri-spónding, kórrə-) adj. Abbr. **cor.** 1. Agree-

ing or conforming; consistent. **2.** Analogous or equivalent. **—cor·re·spond·ing·ly** *adv.*
corresponding angle *n. Mathematics.* Either of a pair of angles formed when two lines are cut by a third (the transversal). The pairs of corresponding angles are angles that lie on the same side of each line and the same side of the transversal. If the two lines are parallel the corresponding angles are equal.
corresponding member *n.* A member living abroad.
cor·re·spon·sive (kórri-spón-siv, kórrə-) *adj.* Corresponding. **—cor·re·spon·sive·ly** *adv.*
cor·ri·da (ko-reédə, kə-, -reéthə || kaw-) *n.* A bullfight. [Spanish, "a running", from the feminine past participle of *correr,* to run, from Latin *currere.* See **corridor.**]
cor·ri·dor (kórri-dawr, -dər) *n.* **1.** A narrow hallway, passageway, or gallery, generally with rooms opening onto it. **2.** A similar passageway alongside the compartments of a train. **3.** A tract of land forming a passageway, such as that which allows an inland country access to the sea through another country. [French, from Italian *corridore,* "a run", from *correre,* to run, from Latin *currere.*]
cor·rie (kórri || káwri) *n. Scottish.* A **cirque** *(see).* [Scottish Gaelic *coire,* cauldron, hollow, whirlpool.]
cor·ri·gen·dum (kórri-jén-dəm, -gén-) *n., pl.* **-da** (-də). **1.** An error to be corrected, especially a printer's error. **2.** *Plural.* A list of errors with their corrections, in a book. [Latin, gerundive of *corrigere,* to CORRECT.]
cor·ri·gi·ble (kórri-jə-b'l) *adj.* Capable of being corrected, reformed, or improved. [Middle English, from Old French, from Medieval Latin *corrigibilis,* from Latin *corrigere,* to CORRECT.] **—cor·ri·gi·bil·i·ty** (-bílləti) *n.* **—cor·ri·gi·bly** *adv.*
cor·ri·val (kə-rív'l, ko-, kō-) *n.* A rival or opponent.
~adj. Rival or opposing. [Old French *corrival,* from Latin *corrīvālis,* joint rival : *com-,* together + *rīvālis,* RIVAL.] **—cor·ri·val·ry** *n.*
cor·rob·o·rant (kə-róbbərənt) *adj. Archaic.* **1.** Corroborating. **2.** Strengthening.
~n. Archaic. Something that corroborates.
cor·rob·o·rate (kə-róbbə-rayt) *tr.v.* **-rated, -rating, -rates.** To strengthen or support (other evidence); attest the truth or accuracy of. See Synonyms at **confirm.** [Latin *corrōborāre* : *com-* (intensive) + *rōborāre,* to strengthen, from *rōbur,* hard kind of oak, strength.] **—cor·rob·o·ra·tion** (-ráysh'n) *n.* **—cor·rob·o·ra·tor** (-raytər) *n.*
cor·rob·o·ra·tive (kə-róbbə-rətiv, -raytiv) *adj.* Also **cor·rob·o·ra·to·ry** (-rə-tri, -təri) Confirming or tending to confirm. **—cor·rob·o·ra·tive·ly** *adv.*
cor·rob·o·ree (kə-róbbə-ri, -ree) *n. Australian.* **1.** An aboriginal dance festival held at night to celebrate tribal victories or other events. **2.** Any large or noisy celebration. [Native name *korobra.*]
cor·rode (kə-rōd) *v.* **-roded, -roding, -rodes.** *—tr.* **1.** To dissolve or wear away gradually, especially by chemical action. **2.** To impair; consume; slowly destroy. *—intr.* To be eaten or worn away; become corroded. [Middle English *corroden,* from Latin *corrōdere,* to gnaw to pieces : *com-* (intensive) + *rōdere,* to gnaw.] **—cor·rod·ent** *n.* **—cor·rod·i·ble, cor·ro·si·ble** (kə-rṓ-səb'l, -zəb'l) *adj.*
cor·ro·sion (kə-rṓzh'n) *n.* **1.** The act or process of dissolving or wearing away; especially, the wearing away of metals. **2.** A substance, such as rust, resulting from such a process. **3.** The condition produced by such a process. **4.** *Geology.* The wearing down of rocks by chemical means such as solution or oxidation. Also called "chemical weathering". **5.** Slow destruction, as of a relationship. [Middle English *corosioun,* from Old French *corrosion,* from Late Latin *corrōsiō* (stem *corrōsiōn-*), from Latin *corrōsus,* past participle of *corrōdere,* to CORRODE.]
cor·ro·sive (kə-rṓ-siv, -ziv) *adj.* **1. a.** Capable of corroding. **b.** Inclined to produce corrosion. **2.** Spiteful, malicious, or malevolent. **3.** Insidiously destructive.
~n. A corrosive substance. **—cor·ro·sive·ly** *adv.* **—cor·ro·sive·ness** *n.*
corrosive sublimate *n. Chemistry.* An inorganic compound, **mercuric chloride** *(see).* Not in current technical usage.
cor·ru·gate (kórrŏŏ-gayt, kórrə-, *rarely* kórrew-) *v.* **-gated, -gating, -gates.** *—tr.* To shape into folds or parallel and alternating ridges and grooves. *—intr.* To become corrugated. [Latin *corrūgāre,* to make full of wrinkles : *com-,* together + *rūgāre,* to wrinkle, from *rūga,* wrinkle.] **—cor·ru·gate, cor·ru·gat·ed** (-gaytid) *adj.* **—cor·ru·ga·tion** (-gáysh'n) *n.*
corrugated iron *n.* A structural sheet steel, usually galvanised, shaped in parallel grooves and ridges for rigidity.
cor·rupt (kə-rúpt) *adj.* **1.** Immoral; perverted; depraved. **2.** Marked by or guilty of venality and dishonesty, especially bribery. **3.** Decaying; putrid. **4.** Impure; contaminated; unclean. **5.** Containing errors or alterations, as a text might; debased.
~v. **corrupted, -rupting, -rupts.** *—tr.* **1.** To destroy or subvert the honesty or integrity of, especially by bribery. **2.** To ruin morally; pervert. **3.** To taint; contaminate; infect. **4.** To cause to become rotten; spoil. **5.** To change the original form of (a text, language, or the like). **6.** *Computing.* To change (stored data) so that it cannot be used. *—intr.* To become corrupt. [Middle English, from Old French, from Latin *corruptus,* past participle of *corrumpere,* break to pieces, destroy, ruin : *com-,* completely + *rumpere,* to break.] **—cor·rup·ter, cor·rup·tor** (-ər) *n.* **—cor·rup·tive** *adj.* **—cor·rupt·ly** *adv.* **—cor·rupt·ness** *n.*
cor·rupt·i·ble (kə-rúpt-əb'l) *adj.* Able to be corrupted, as by bribery, depravity, or decay. **—cor·rupt·i·bil·i·ty** (-ə-bílləti), **cor·rupt·i·ble·ness** *n.* **—cor·rupt·i·bly** *adv.*
cor·rup·tion (kə-rúpsh'n) *n.* **1.** The act or result of corrupting. **2.** The state of being corrupt. **3.** Any altered or debased form of a word. **4.** Anything that corrupts.
cor·rup·tion·ist (kə-rúpsh'n-ist) *n.* One who defends or practises corruption.
cor·sage (kawr-saázh, kór-saazh) *n.* **1.** The bodice or waist of a dress. **2.** *Chiefly U.S.* A small bouquet of flowers pinned to a woman's dress. [Middle English, from Old French, torso, bust, from *cors, corps,* body, from Latin *corpus,* CORPUS.]
cor·sair (kór-sair) *n.* **1.** A privateer, especially along the Barbary Coast of North Africa. **2.** A swift pirate ship. **3.** A pirate. [Old French *corsaire,* pirate, from Old Provençal *corsari,* from Old Italian *corsaro,* from Medieval Latin *cursārius,* from *cursus,* plunder, from Latin, "a run", from the past participle of *currere,* to run.]
corse (korss) *n. Archaic.* A corpse. [Middle English *cors,* CORPSE.]
corse·let (kórss-lət, -lit; *in sense 2 also* -ə-lét) *n.* Also **cors·let** (for sense 1 only). **1.** Body armour; especially, a breastplate. **2.** A light corset incorporating a brassiere. [Old French *corselet,* diminutive of *cors,* body. See **corpse.**]
cor·set (kór-sit) *n.* **1.** A close-fitting undergarment, often reinforced by elastic or stays, worn especially by women to support or shape the waistline, hips, and upper abdomen. **2.** A medieval outer garment, especially a laced jacket or bodice.
~tr.v. **corseted, -seting, -sets.** To enclose in or as if in a corset; fit a corset on. [Middle English, from Old French, diminutive of *cors,* body. See **corpse.**]
cor·se·tière (kór-sət-yaír, -set-) *n. Masculine* **corsetier** (-yáy). A maker, fitter, or seller of corsets. [French, from CORSET.]
Cor·si·ca (kórssikə). *French* **Corse** (korss). A rugged Mediterranean island forming two départements of France. Napoleon Bonaparte was born there. The landscape and poor communications have contributed to a tradition of banditry. Sheep and goats are raised, and vines, olives, lemons, and tobacco are grown. Ajaccio is the capital, and Bastia the largest city. **—Cor·si·can** *adj. & n.*
cor·tege, cortège (kawr-táyzh, -tézh) *n.* **1. a.** A ceremonial procession. **b.** A funeral procession. **2.** A train of attendants; a retinue, as of a distinguished person. [French *cortège,* from Italian *corteggio,* from *corteggiare,* to pay honour, court, from *corte,* court, from Latin *cohors* (stem *cohort-*), enclosure, court.]
Cor·tes (kór-tess, -tez, -tiz) *n.* The legislative assembly of Spain. [Spanish, plural of *corte,* COURT.]
Cor·tés (kór-tez; *Spanish* kawr-téss), **Hernán** (1485–1547). Spanish soldier and explorer who won Aztec Mexico for Spain. With an army of native Tlaxcalans he reached the Aztec capital, Tenochtitlán (1519), and took their ruler, Montezuma, hostage. In his absence, the Aztecs rebelled and drove the Spaniards out. Cortés besieged the city (1521) and razed it to the ground. Appointed governor of Mexico, or New Spain, he reorganised land tenure and launched expeditions to Central America (1524–26).
cor·tex (kór-teks) *n., pl.* **-tices** (-ti-seez) or **-texes.** **1.** *Anatomy.* The outer layer of an organ or part, as of the kidney, adrenal gland, cerebrum, or cerebellum. **2.** *Botany.* **a.** A layer of tissue in roots and stems lying between the epidermis and the vascular tissue. **b.** An external layer such as bark or rind. [Latin, bark, shell, rind.]
cor·ti·cal (kórtik'l) *adj.* **1.** Of, pertaining to, or consisting of cortex. **2.** Of, pertaining to, associated with, or depending on the cerebral cortex. [New Latin *corticalis,* from Latin *cortex* (stem *cortic-*), bark, shell, CORTEX.] **—cor·ti·cal·ly** *adv.*
cor·ti·cate (kórti-kət, -kit, -kayt) *adj.* Also **cor·ti·cat·ed** (-kaytid). Having a bark, rind, or similar specialised outer layer. [Latin *corticātus,* covered with bark, from *cortex* (stem *cortic-*), bark, CORTEX.]
cortico–, cortic– *comb. form.* Indicates cortex; for example, **corticotrophin, corticoid.** [Latin *cortex* (stem *cortic-*), CORTEX.]
cor·tic·o·lous (kawr-tíckələss) *adj. Biology.* Growing or living on tree bark. [French *corticicole* : CORTI(CO)- + -COLOUS.]
cor·ti·co·ster·oid (kórtikō-steér-oyd, -stérroyd) *n.* Any of the steroid hormones of the adrenal cortex. Also called "corticoid".
cor·ti·co·ster·one (kórti-kóstərōn) *n.* A corticoid, $C_{21}H_{30}O_4$, that induces hyperglycaemia and depositing of glycogen in the liver. [CORTICO- + STER(OL) + -ONE.]
cor·ti·co·tro·phin (kórtikō-trṓfin) *n.* Also *chiefly U.S.* **cor·ti·co·tro·pin** (-trṓpin, -tróppin). An anterior pituitary hormone, **ACTH** *(see).* [CORTICO- + -TROP(IC) + -IN.]
cor·ti·sol (kórti-sol || -sōl) *n.* A corticosteroid, **hydrocortisone** *(see).* [CORTIS(ONE) + -OL.]
cor·ti·sone (kórti-zōn, -sōn) *n.* A corticosteroid, $C_{21}H_{28}O_5$, active in carbohydrate metabolism and used to treat rheumatoid arthritis, adrenal insufficiency, certain allergies, diseases of connective tissue, and gout. [Short for CORTICOSTERONE.]
co·run·dum (kə-rúndəm) *n.* An extremely hard mineral, aluminium oxide, sometimes containing iron, magnesia, or silica, occurring in gem varieties such as ruby and sapphire and in a common grey, brown, or blue form used chiefly in abrasives. [Tamil *kuruntam,* probably ultimately from Sanskrit *kuruvinda*†, ruby.]
Co·run·na. See **La Coruña.**
cor·us·cate (kórrə-skayt) *intr.v.* **-cated, -cating, -cates.** **1.** To give forth flashes of light; sparkle; glitter; scintillate. **2.** To make a brilliant display, as of wit. [Latin *coruscāre,* to thrust, vibrate, glitter.] **—cor·us·ca·tion** (-skáysh'n) *n.*
cor·vée (kórvay || *U.S. also* kawr-váy) *n.* **1.** Formerly, a day of unpaid work required of a vassal by his feudal lord. **2.** A former system of exacting labour for little or no pay or instead of taxes, used especially in the maintenance of roads. [Middle English *corve,*

from Old French, from Late Latin *(opera) corrogāta,* "(works) collected", feminine past participle of Latin *corrogāre,* to summon together, collect : *com-,* together + *rogāre,* to ask.]

corves. Plural of **corf.**

cor·vette (kawr-vét) *n.* Also **cor·vet** (*also* kór-vet). **1.** A fast, lightly armed warship, smaller than a destroyer. **2.** Formerly, a warship, smaller than a frigate, usually armed with one tier of guns. [French, from Old French, probably from Middle Dutch *corf,* basket, kind of small ship, CORF.]

cor·vine (kór-vīn ‖ -vin) *adj.* Of, resembling, or characteristic of crows, ravens, or related birds. [Latin *corvīnus,* from *corvus,* raven.]

Corvo (kórvō), **Baron.** See **Rolfe, Frederick William.**

Cor·vus (kórvəss) *n.* A constellation in the Southern Hemisphere near Crater and Virgo. [Latin, from Latin, raven.]

Cor·y·bant (kórri-bant) *pl.* **-bants** or **Corybantes** (-bánteez). *Greek Mythology.* A priest of the ancient Phrygian goddess Cybele whose rites were celebrated with music and ecstatic dances. [Latin *Corybas* (stem *Corybant-*), from Greek *Korubas,* probably of Phrygian origin.] —**Cor·y·ban·tian** (-bánti-ən), **Cor·y·ban·tic** (-bántik) *adj.*

co·ryd·a·lis (kə-ríddəliss, ko-) *n.* Any of various plants of the genus *Corydalis,* having finely lobed leaves and spurred two-lipped yellow, cream, or pinkish flowers. [New Latin, from Greek *korudallis,* crested lark (the shape of the flowers resembles the bird's spur), variant of *korudos.*]

Cor·y·don (kórri-d'n, -don). A conventional name for a shepherd in many pastoral poems. [Latin, from Greek *Korudōn†,* proper name.]

cor·ymb (kórrim, -b) *n. Botany.* A flat-topped flower cluster in which the individual stalks grow upwards from various points of the main stem to approximately the same height. It is found in the cow parsley. [French *corymbe,* from Latin *corymbus,* cluster, from Greek *korumbos,* uppermost point, cluster of fruits or flowers.] —**co·rym·bose** (kə-rím-bōss, -bōz), **co·rym·bous** (-bəss) —**co·rym·bose·ly** *adv.*

cor·y·phae·us (kórri-fée-əss) *n., pl.* **-phaei** (-ī). **1.** The leader of the chorus in ancient Greek drama. **2.** Any leader or spokesman. [Latin *coryphaeus,* leader, chief, from Greek *koruphaios,* leader, leader of the chorus, from *koruphē,* head, top.]

cor·y·phée (kórri-fay) *n.* A ballet dancer ranking above the ordinary members of the corps de ballet but below the principal soloists. [French, from Latin *coryphaeus,* leader, CORYPHAEUS.]

co·ry·za (kə-rīzə) *n.* An acute inflammation of the nasal mucous membrane marked by discharge of mucus, sneezing, and watering of the eyes. Also called "head cold". [Late Latin *corȳza,* from Greek *koruza†,* catarrh.]

cos¹ (koss) *n.* A variety of lettuce having a long slender head and crisp leaves. Also called "cos lettuce". [After Cos (Kos), Aegean island where it originated.]

cos² (koz). cosine.

Cos (koss ‖ *U.S. also* kōss). *Greek* **Kos.** Greek island in the Dodecanese group. It joined the Delian League in the fifth century B.C., and was a seat of learning.

COS, C.O.S. cash on shipment.

'cos. *Informal.* Contraction of *because.*

Co·sa Nos·tra (kō-zə nóstrə ‖ -sə, nōstrə) *n.* A crime syndicate active throughout the United States, hierarchic in structure and comprising locally independent units known as families; it is often believed to have an important relationship with the Sicilian Mafia. [Italian, "our thing", "our enterprise".]

co·se·cant (kō-séekənt) *n. Abbr.* **cosec, csc** *Trigonometry.* The secant *(see)* of the complement of a directed angle or arc.

co·seis·mal (kō-síz-m'l ‖ -síss-) *adj.* Also **co·seis·mic** (-mik). Pertaining to or designating a line connecting the points on a map that indicate the places simultaneously affected by an earthquake shock. —*n.* A coseismal line. [CO- (together) + SEISM(O)- + -AL.]

co·set (kō-set) *n. Mathematics.* A set associated with a subgroup of a group and formed by the products of elements of the group and elements of the subgroup.

Cos·grave (kóz-grayv), **William (Thomas)** (1880–1965). Irish statesman. A Sinn Fein supporter, he fought in the Easter Rising (1916) and was imprisoned. Released the next year, he was elected to the Dáil and served in the illegal Republican ministry (1918–21). He was the first president of the Irish Free State (1922–32).

cosh¹ (kosh) *n. British.* **1.** A heavy stick, such as a truncheon or bludgeon, used as a weapon. **2.** An attack with such a weapon. —*tr.v.* **coshed, coshing, coshes.** *British.* To bludgeon. [19th century : origin obscure.]

cosh² (kosh). hyperbolic cosine.

cosh·er (kóshər) *tr.v.* **-ered, -ering, -ers.** To coddle; pamper. [19th century : origin obscure.]

co·sign (kō-sīn) *tr.v.* **-signed, -signing, -signs. 1.** To sign (a document) jointly with another or others. **2.** To endorse (a signature), as for a loan or mortgage. —**co·sign·er** *n.*

co·sig·na·to·ry (kō-sígnə-tri, -təri, kō-) *adj.* Signed jointly with another or others.

—*n., pl.* **cosignatories.** One who cosigns, such as a state or person; a cosigner.

co·sine (kō-sīn) *n. Abbr.* **cos 1.** In a right-angled triangle, the function of an acute angle that is the ratio of the adjacent side to the hypotenuse. **2.** A trigonometric function of an angle, given by the X-coordinate of the end of a line of unit length drawn from the origin at the stated angle to the positive X-axis. [CO- + SINE.]

cosine rule *n. Mathematics.* The rule that in any triangle $a^2 = b^2 +$

$c^2 - 2bc \cos A$, where *a, b,* and *c* are the lengths of the sides and *A* is the angle opposite side *a.*

cos·met·ic (koz-méttik) *n.* A preparation, such as a skin cream or lipstick, designed to beautify the body, especially the face, by direct application.

—*adj.* **1.** Serving to beautify the body, especially the face. **2.** Serving to improve or modify the appearance of the body: *cosmetic surgery.* **3.** Decorative or superficial only; not having any significant effect or function. [French *cosmétique,* from adjective, "of adornment", from Greek *kosmētikos,* skilled in arranging, from *kosmētos,* well ordered, from *kosmein,* to arrange, from *kosmos,* order, COSMOS.] —**cos·met·i·cal·ly** *adv.*

cos·me·ti·cian (kóz-mi-tísh'n, -me-) *n.* A person whose occupation is manufacturing, selling, or applying cosmetics.

cos·me·tol·o·gy (kóz-mi-tóllǝji, -me-) *n.* The study or art of cosmetics and their use. [French *cosmétologie : cosmétique,* COSMET(IC) + -LOGY.] —**cos·me·tol·o·gist** *n.*

cos·mic (kózmik) *adj.* Also **cos·mi·cal** (-'l). **1. a.** Of or pertaining to the entire universe. **b.** Of or pertaining to the universe as distinct from the Earth and its atmosphere or, sometimes, from the Solar System. **2.** Infinitely or inconceivably extended, as in space or time; vast. **3.** *Rare.* Harmonious; orderly. [Greek *kosmikos,* of the universe, from *kosmos,* COSMOS.] —**cos·mi·cal·ly** *adv.*

cosmic background *n.* The **microwave background** *(see).*

cosmic censorship *n. Astronomy.* The principle that, in a black hole, the point at which the density could become infinite (the singularity) can never be observed because of a surrounding spherical boundary (the event horizon) preventing the passage of information.

cosmic dust *n.* Fine solid particles of matter in interstellar space.

cosmic radiation *n.* Streams of ionising radiation; cosmic rays.

cosmic ray *n.* Any of a number of high-energy ionising particles or photons that can be observed moving through the Earth's atmosphere or reaching the surface of the Earth. Cosmic rays originate as primary radiation from space (mainly protons and atomic nuclei with some electrons) which interact with atoms in the atmosphere to produce secondary radiation (pions, muons, electrons, and gamma rays).

cosmic year *n.* The time taken for the Sun to make one complete revolution about the centre of the Galaxy (about 220 million years). Also called "galactic year".

cosmo-, cosm- *comb. form.* Indicates world or universe; for example, *cosmology.* [Greek *kosmos,* COSMOS.]

cos·mo·chem·is·try (kózmō-kémmistri) *n.* The branch of astronomy concerned with the chemical composition of the universe. —**cos·mo·chem·i·cal** (-kémmik'l) *adj.*

cos·mo·drome (kózmə-drōm) *n.* A Soviet spacecraft-launching centre. [COSMO- + -DROME.]

cos·mo·gen·ic (kóz-mə-jénnik, -mō-) *adj.* Of or produced by cosmic rays. [COSMO- + -GENIC.]

cos·mog·o·ny (koz-móggəni) *n., pl.* **-nies. 1.** The astrophysical study of the evolution of the universe. **2.** A specific theory or model of this evolution. [Greek *kosmogonia,* the creation of the world : COSMO- + *gonos,* creation.] —**cos·mo·gon·ic** (kózmə-gónnik), **cos·mo·gon·i·cal** *adj.* —**cos·mog·o·nist** (-móggənist) *n.*

cos·mog·ra·phy (koz-móggrəfi) *n., pl.* **-phies. 1.** The study of the constitution of nature. **2.** A description of the world or universe. [Greek *kosmographia,* description of the world : COSMO- + -GRAPHY.] —**cos·mog·ra·pher** (-móggrəfər) *n.* —**cos·mo·graph·ic** (kózmə-gráffik), **cos·mo·graph·i·cal** *adj.*

cos·mol·o·gy (koz-móllǝji) *n.* **1.** A branch of philosophy dealing with the origin, processes, and structure of the universe. **2. a.** The astrophysical study of the structure and constituent dynamics of the universe. **b.** A specific theory or model of such structure and dynamics. See **big-bang theory, steady-state theory.** [New Latin *cosmologia* : COSMO- + -LOGY.] —**cos·mo·log·ic** (kózmə-lójik), **cos·mo·log·i·cal** *adj.* —**cos·mo·log·i·cal·ly** *adv.* —**cos·mol·o·gist** (koz-móllǝjist) *n.*

cos·mo·naut (kózmə-nawt) *n.* An astronaut, especially of the former U.S.S.R. [Russian *kosmonavt* : COSMO- + Greek *nautēs,* sailor.]

cos·mo·pol·i·tan (kózmə-póllitən) *adj.* **1. a.** At home in or familiar with many parts of the world or many spheres of interest. **b.** Sophisticated and broadminded. **2.** Inhabited by or composed of many races of people with differing cultural backgrounds. **3.** Common to the whole world. **4.** *Biology.* Growing or occurring in all or most parts of the world; widely distributed.

—*n.* A person who has lived or travelled in many parts of the world and is free from national prejudices. [French *cosmopolitain,* from Old French, from Greek *kosmopolitēs,* COSMOPOLITE.] —**cos·mo·pol·i·tan·ism** *n.*

cos·mop·o·lite (koz-móppəlīt) *n.* **1.** A cosmopolitan. **2.** *Biology.* A cosmopolitan organism. [Greek *kosmopolitēs,* citizen of the world : COSMO- + *politēs,* citizen, from *polis,* city.] —**cos·mop·o·lit·ism** *n.*

cos·mo·ra·ma (kózmə-ra'amə ‖ -rámmə) *n.* A series of scenes and pictures from all over the world viewed through an eyehole using mirrors, lenses, or the like. [COSM(O)- + (PAN)ORAMA.] —**cos·mo·ram·ic** (-rámmik, -ra'amik) *adj.*

cos·mos (kóz-moss ‖ *U.S. also* -məss, -mōss) *n.* **1.** The universe regarded as an orderly, harmonious whole. **2.** Any system regarded as ordered, harmonious, and whole. **3.** Harmony and order as distinct from chaos. **4.** Any of various tropical American plants of the genus *Cosmos,* having variously coloured rayed flowers; especially,

C. bipinnatus, widely cultivated as a garden plant. [Greek *kosmos,* order, the universe, the world.]

Cos·mo·tron (kózmə-tron) *n. Physics.* A large synchrotron designed to produce high-energy protons. [COSMO- + -TRON.]

Cos·sack (kóss-ak ‖ -ək) *n.* A member of a people of the southern part of the former U.S.S.R. in Europe and adjacent parts of Asia, noted as cavalrymen, especially under the tsars. **—Cos·sack** *adj.*

cos·set (kóssit) *tr.v.* **-seted, -seting, -sets.** To pamper; spoil. **—**n. A pet; especially, a pet lamb. [Noun ("pet lamb"), from Anglo-French *cozet, coscet,* from Old English *cotsæta,* cottager.]

cos·sie (kózzi) *n. Chiefly British Informal.* A swimming costume. [Shortened from COSTUME.]

cost (kost ‖ kawst) *n.* **1.** An amount paid or required in payment for a purchase or for the production or upkeep of something, often measured in terms of effort and time expended. **2.** A loss or sacrifice. **3.** *Plural. Law.* The charges fixed for litigation, usually payable by the losing party. **—**See Synonyms at **price.**

~v. **cost, costing, costs. —**intr. To require a specified payment, expenditure, effort, or loss. **—**tr. **1.** To estimate or determine the cost of. **2.** *Informal.* To be costly to. [Middle English, from Old French, from *coster,* to cost, from Latin *constāre,* to stand with, stand at a particular price : *com-,* with + *stāre,* to stand.]

cos·ta (kóss-tə) *n., pl.* **-tae** (-tee). *Biology.* A rib or a riblike part, such as the midrib of a leaf or a thickened anterior vein or margin of an insect's wing. [Latin, rib.] **—cos·tal** *adj.*

Cos·ta Bra·va (kóstə bráavə ‖ *U.S. also* kŏ́stə). The Mediterranean coastline in eastern Spain, stretching from Barcelona to the French border. It is a popular tourist area.

cost accountant *n.* An accountant who keeps records of all the costs of production and distribution of an enterprise. **—cost ac·counting** *n.*

co·star (kŏ́-staar) *n.* A starring actor or actress given equal status with another or others in a play or film.

~v. *(also* kŏ́-stár). **costarred, -starring, -stars. —**intr. To act as a costar. **—**tr. To present or feature as a costar.

cos·tard (kúss-tərd, kóss-) *n.* **1.** An English variety of apple tree or the fruit of this tree. **2.** *Archaic Slang.* The head. [Middle English, from Anglo-French, "ribbed one" (from its appearance), from *coste,* rib, from Latin *costa.*]

Cos·ta Ri·ca, Republic of (kóstə réekə ‖ *U.S. also* kŏ́stə). Country in Central America. Its heartland is a broad, upland plateau amid volcanic ranges. The country was discovered by Christopher Columbus (1502) and became a territory of Spain. Its native Indian population almost disappeared under colonial rule, and the people are now of Spanish or mixed descent. Costa Rica became independent in 1821. In 1948, it abolished its army to make military coups impossible. Attempts are being made to stimulate industrial growth and tourism, but the economy is chiefly agricultural, and coffee and bananas are still the leading exports. Area, 51 100 square kilometres (19,730 square miles). Population, 3,400,000. Capital, San José. See map at **Central America.**

cost benefit analysis *n.* An analysis that takes into account the losses or benefits in economic and social welfare that will be incurred if a particular project is undertaken.

cost-effective (kóst-i-féktiv, -ə- ‖ káwst-) *adj.* Of or resulting in a profit or return that justifies the initial outlay.

cos·ter·mon·ger (kóstər-mung-gər ‖ -mong-) *n. British.* One who sells fruit, vegetables, fish, or other goods from a cart, barrow, or stall in the streets, especially in London. Also called "coster". [Originally *costardmonger,* "apple seller" : COSTARD + MONGER.]

cos·tive (kóstiv) *adj.* **1. a.** Constipated. **b.** Causing constipation. **2.** Slow; sluggish. **3.** Stingy. [Middle English *costif,* from Old French *costive,* past participle of *costiver,* to bind, constipate, from Latin *constīpāre,* to CONSTIPATE.]

cost·ly (kóst-li ‖ káwst-) *adj.* **-lier, -liest. 1.** Of high price or value; expensive. **2.** Entailing loss or sacrifice. **—cost·li·ness** *n.*

 Synonyms: costly, expensive, dear, valuable, precious, invaluable, priceless.

cost·mar·y (kóst-mair-i ‖ káwst-) *n.* A herb, *Chrysanthemum balsamita,* native to Asia, having aromatic foliage sometimes used as seasoning. [Middle English *costmarie* : *cost,* costmary, Old English *cost,* from Latin *costum,* from Greek *kostos,* from Arabic *kust* + *Mary* (so named because regarded as sacred to the Virgin Mary).]

cost of living *n.* The average cost of those goods and services considered necessary to provide a person with a basic or average standard of living.

cost-plus (kóst-plúss ‖ káwst-) *adj.* Of or designating a method of calculating prices based on the cost of production plus a fixed rate of profit.

cost price *n.* The price at which a merchant or retailer buys goods.

cost-push (kóst-póosh ‖ káwst-) *adj.* Designating a type of inflation in which increased production costs, as from higher wages, tend to drive up prices. Compare **demand-pull.**

cos·trel (kóstrəl) *n. Archaic.* A flat, pear-shaped drinking vessel with loops for attachment to the belt of the user. [Middle English, from Old French *costerel,* perhaps from *costier,* "that which is at the side", from *coste,* side, rib, from Latin *costa.*]

cos·tume (kóss-tewm ‖ -tōom, -chōom, -təm) *n.* **1.** A complete style of dress including clothes, accessories, and often hairstyle, characteristic of a particular country, period, or people. **2.** A set of clothes worn for a play, film, fancy-dress ball, or the like, designed to give the wearer the appearance of the role that he or she is playing. **3.** A

woman's suit. **4.** A set of clothes appropriate for a usually specified occasion or season, such as a swimming costume.

~tr.v. **costumed, -tuming, -tumes. 1.** To put a costume on; dress. **2.** To furnish a costume or costumes for (a play or film, for example). [French, from Italian, custom, dress, from Latin *consuētūdō* (stem *consuētūdin-*), CUSTOM.]

costume drama *n.* A stage or television play, or a film, set in a specific era, in which the actors wear the appropriate dress.

costume jewellery *n.* Inexpensive jewellery made from cheap materials such as glass, diamante, or the like.

cos·tum·i·er (koss-téwm-i-ər, -ay ‖ -tōom-) *n.* Also **cos·tum·er** (koss-téwm-ər ‖ -tōom-). A person or company that makes or supplies plies costume.

co·sy, *U.S.* **co·zy** (kŏ́zi) *adj.* **-sier** or *U.S.* **-zier, -siest** or *U.S.* **-ziest. 1.** Snug and comfortable; warm. **2.** Marked by friendly intimacy. **—**See Synonyms at **comfortable.**

~n., *pl.* **cosies** or *U.S.* **cozies.** A padded or knitted covering placed over a teapot, for example, to keep the contents hot. [18th century (Scottish) : origin obscure.] **—cos·i·ly** *adv.* **—cos·i·ness** *n.*

cot[1] (kot) *n.* **1.** *British.* A bed for a small child, usually with sides of vertical bars. Also *U.S.* "crib". **2.** A narrow bed; especially, a camp bed. **3.** *Nautical.* A canvas bed resembling a hammock. [Anglo-Indian, from Hindi *khāṭ,* bedstead, couch, from Sanskrit *khātvā,* from Dravidian, akin to Tamil *kaṭṭil.*]

cot[2] *n.* **1.** A shelter or protective covering, especially a cote. **2.** *Archaic & Poetic.* A small house; a cottage. [Middle English *cot(e),* Old English *cot.*]

co·tan·gent (kŏ́-tánjənt) *n. Abbr.* **ctn, cotan.** *Trigonometry.* The tangent of the complement of a directed angle or arc. **—co·tan·gen·tial** (-tan-jénsh'l) *adj.*

cot case *n. Australian Informal.* A person who is too drunk or exhausted to move. Used humorously.

cot death *n.* The sudden and unexplained death of a baby during sleep. Also called "sudden infant death syndrome".

cote[1] (kŏt) *n.* **1.** A small shed or shelter for sheep or birds. **2.** *Regional.* A cottage; a hut. [Middle English *cote,* Old English *cote.*]

cote[2] *tr.v.* **coted, coting, cotes.** *Archaic.* To go round by the side of; pass. [Origin obscure.]

co·ten·ant (kŏ́-ténənt) *n.* One of two or more tenants sharing common property. [CO- + TENANT.] **—co·ten·an·cy** *n.*

co·te·rie (kŏ́təri) *n.* A small, usually select, group of persons who associate frequently, especially because of shared artistic interests. Sometimes used derogatorily. See Synonyms at **circle.** [French, from Old French, an association of peasant tenants, probably from *cotier,* cottager, from *cote* (unattested), cottage, perhaps from Middle English *cot,* COT (cottage).]

co·ter·min·ous (kŏ́-términəss) *adj.* **1.** Having a boundary in common; contiguous. **2.** Contained within the same boundaries; coextensive in space, time, or meaning. **—co·ter·min·ous·ly** *adv.*

coth (koth). hyperbolic cotangent.

co·thur·nus (ko-thúr-nəss, kŏ-) *n., pl.* **-ni** (-nī). Also **co·thurn** (kŏ́thurn, kŏ-thúrn). A buskin or thick-soled boot worn by actors of classical tragedy. [Latin, from Greek *kothornos,* perhaps from Lydian.]

co·ti·dal (kŏ́-tíd'l) *adj.* **1.** Of or pertaining to a coincidence of the tides. **2.** Designating lines on a map that join places at which high or low tides occur simultaneously.

co·til·lion, co·til·lon (kə-tíl-yən, ko- ‖ kŏ-) *n.* **1.** A lively dance originating in France in the 18th century, with varied, intricate patterns and steps. **2.** *U.S.* A quadrille. **3.** *U.S.* A formal ball. [French *cotillon,* peasant dress, country dance, from Old French, petticoat, diminutive of *cote,* COAT.]

co·to·ne·as·ter (kə-tŏ́ni-ástər, kŏ-, ko-) *n.* Any of various Old World shrubs of the genus *Cotoneaster,* having small white or pinkish flowers and frequently cultivated for their showy red fruit. [New Latin *Cotoneaster,* from Latin *cotōneum,* QUINCE.]

Cot·o·pax·i (kóttə-páksi ‖ *U.S. also* kŏ́tə-, -páaksi). One of the highest active volcanoes in the world, situated in the Andes mountains of northern Ecuador. It has erupted periodically since the first recorded outburst in 1532, and rises to 5 896 metres (19,457 feet).

cot·quean (kót-kween) *n. Archaic.* **1.** A vulgar woman; a hussy. **2.** A man who does domestic work considered more suitable for women. [COT (cottage) + QUEAN.]

Cots·wold (kóts-wŏld, -wəld) *n.* A sheep of a breed known for its long wool and originally developed in the Cotswolds.

Cots·wolds (kóts-wŏldz, -wəldz). Range of limestone hills in southwest England, chiefly in Gloucestershire.

cot·ta (kóttə) *n., pl.* **cottae** (kóttee) or **-tas.** A short ecclesiastical surplice, often sleeveless or short-sleeved. [Medieval Latin, from West Germanic *kotta* (unattested), COAT.]

cot·tage (kóttij) *n.* **1.** A small house, typically in the suburbs or the country. **2.** *British Slang.* A public convenience. Used by male homosexuals. **3.** *Australian.* A single-storeyed house. [Middle English *cotage,* from *cot(e),* COT (cottage).] **—cot·tag·ey** *adj.*

cottage cheese *n.* A soft, white cheese made of strained and seasoned curds of skimmed milk.

cottage hospital *n. Chiefly British.* A small hospital serving a local, often rural, community and providing only basic medical facilities, that is staffed usually by local doctors and part-time specialists.

cottage industry *n.* An industry, such as weaving or sewing, carried out in the home by individual workers rather than in a factory.

cottage loaf *n.* A loaf of bread made of two round masses, with the smaller on top of the larger.

cottage piano n. An upright, usually small, piano.

cottage pie n. A dish made from cooked minced meat, usually beef, covered with sliced or mashed potato and baked.

cot·tag·er (kóttijər) n. A person, especially a farm labourer, who lives in a cottage.

cot·tag·ing (kóttijing) n. British Slang. The practice of soliciting by male homosexuals in public conveniences.

cot·tar, cot·ter (kóttər) n. 1. A medieval villein who occupied a cottage with a small piece of land in return for his labour. 2. Scottish. A farm worker who, in return for a cottage, gives labour at a fixed rate when required. 3. A cottier. [From COT (house).]

cot·ter (kóttər) n. 1. A bolt, wedge, key, or pin inserted through a slot in order to hold parts together. 2. A cotter pin. [17th century : shortened from dialectal cotterel†.]

cotter pin n. A split cotter inserted through holes in two or more pieces and bent at the ends to fasten and prevent excessive sliding and rotation. Also called "cotter".

cot·ti·er (kótti-ər) n. 1. In Ireland in former times, a peasant renting and cultivating a small piece of land directly from its owner, the rate having been fixed by public competition. Also called "cotter". 2. A cottager. [Middle English, from Old French cotier, cottager, from cote (unattested), cottage, perhaps from Middle English cot, COT (cottage).]

cot·ton (kótt'n) n. 1. Any of various plants or shrubs of the genus Gossypium, cultivated in warm climates for the fibre surrounding their seeds. 2. The soft, white, downy fibre attached to the seeds of the cotton plant, used in making textiles and other products. 3. Cotton plants collectively. 4. The crop of these plants. 5. Thread or cloth manufactured from cotton fibre. 6. Any of various soft, downy substances found in other plants.
~adj. Of, pertaining to, or made from cotton.
~intr.v. **cottoned, -toning, -tons.** U.S. Informal. To become friendly. Used with to or with. **—cotton on.** Informal. To understand; grasp. Used with to. [Middle English cotoun, from Old French, from Arabic (dialectal) qoṭon, variant of Arabic quṭn.]

cotton bush n. Any of various Australian shrubs, such as Kochia aphylla, having leaves and other parts covered with cottony down.

cot·ton cake n. A fodder for livestock made out of compressed cottonseeds.

cotton candy n. U.S. **Candy floss** (see).

cotton flannel n. A soft, warm, napped fabric woven of cotton.

cotton gin n. A machine that separates the seeds, seed hulls, and other small objects from the fibres of cotton. Also called "gin".

cotton grass n. Any of various grasslike bog plants of the genus Eriophorum that grow in colder north temperate zones, having densely tufted, cottony flower heads.

cot·ton·mouth (kótt'n-mowth) n. A snake, the **water moccasin** (see). [Its mouth is lined with a white cottony substance.]

cot·ton·seed (kótt'n-seed) n., pl. **-seeds** or collectively **cottonseed.** The seed of cotton, used as a source of oil and meal.

cottonseed meal n. Meal made from the residue of cottonseed after the oil has been removed, used as animal feed and fertiliser.

cottonseed oil n. A yellowish to dark red oil obtained by crushing cottonseed and used in cooking and as salad oil and in the manufacture of paints, soaps, and other products.

cot·ton·tail (kótt'n-tayl) n. Any of several New World rabbits of the genus Sylvilagus, having greyish or brownish fur and a tail with a white underside.

cotton tree n. A **silk cotton tree** (see).

cotton waste n. Refuse cotton fibre, used especially for cleaning machinery.

cot·ton·weed (kótt'n-weed) n. A creeping perennial coastal plant, Otanthus maritimus, covered with a thick white down and having button-like yellow flowers.

cot·ton·wood (kótt'n-wŏŏd) n. Any of several softwood trees of the genus Populus, having seeds with cotton-like tufts; especially, P. deltoides, of eastern and central North America.

cotton wool n. 1. Chiefly British. Loose cotton that is sterilised, pressed into wads, and used as an absorbent or protective material, for example in dressing wounds. Also U.S. "absorbent cotton". 2. Cotton in its natural or raw state.

cot·ton·y (kótt'n-i) adj. 1. Of or resembling cotton; downy; fluffy. 2. Covered with fibres resembling cotton; nappy.

cot·ton·y-cush·ion scale (kótt'n-i-kŏŏsh'n) n. A scale insect, Icerya purchasi, that attacks citrus trees.

cot·y·le·don (kótti-léed'n) n. 1. Botany. A simple leaf of a plant embryo, which in some species is the first or one of the first to appear from the sprouting seed and acts as a food store in many seeds. Also called "seed leaf". See **dicotyledon, monocotyledon.** 2. Anatomy. A lobule of the placenta, especially of ruminants. [Latin cotylēdon, navelwort, from Greek kotulēdōn, cup-shaped hollow, navelwort, from kotulē†, anything hollow, cup.] **—cot·y·le·don·al, cot·y·le·do·nous** adj.

cot·y·loid (kótti-loyd) adj. Also **cot·y·loi·dal** (-lóyd'l). Anatomy. 1. Shaped like a cup. 2. Of or relating to the acetabulum. [Greek kotuloeidēs, cup-shaped : kotulē, anything hollow, cup (see cotyledon) + -OID.]

couch (kowch) n. 1. **a.** A long piece of upholstered furniture with a back and arms that more than one person may sit on; a sofa. **b.** A bed, especially one with a headrest and low back, used by a psychoanalyst's patients, for example. 2. **a.** The frame or floor on which grain, usually barley, is spread in malting. **b.** A layer of grain, usually barley, spread to germinate. 3. Couch grass. 4. In papermak-

ing, a board or felt blanket on which sheets of paper are laid to dry. 5. Archaic. The lair of a wild beast.
~v. **couched, couching, couches.** —tr. 1. To cause to lie down. Usually used in the passive. 2. To express in a certain context or style. 3. To embroider by laying thread flat on a surface and fastening by stitches at regular intervals. 4. To spread (grain) on a frame or floor to germinate, as in malting. 5. Archaic. To lower (a spear, lance, or the like) to the position of attack. 6. Medicine. To remove (a cataract) by downward and backward displacement of the lens. —intr. 1. To lie in ambush or concealment; lurk. 2. Archaic. **a.** To lie down; recline. **b.** To crouch. 3. To be in a heap or pile. Used especially of leaves for decomposition or fermentation. [Middle English couche, from Old French, from coucher, to lay down, from Latin collocāre, to place together, put : com-, together + locāre, to place, LOCATE.] **—couch·er** n.

couch·ant (kówchənt) adj. Heraldry. Lying down with the head raised. Used after the noun: a lion couchant. [Middle English, from Old French, present participle of coucher, to lay down, COUCH.]

cou·chette (kŏŏ-shét) n. A folding bunk in a railway carriage. [French, diminutive of couche, bed, COUCH.]

couch grass (kŏŏch, kowch) n. A grass, Agropyron repens, having whitish-yellow rootstocks by means of which it multiplies rapidly, becoming a troublesome weed. Also called "couch", "scutch grass", "twitch grass". [Originally quitch grass, Middle English quicche (unattested), Old English cwice; perhaps akin to cwicu, alive, QUICK.]

couch·ing (kówching) n. Embroidery work in which heavy thread is attached at intervals to a material with minute stitches. [Middle English, from couchen, to embroider, COUCH.]

couch potato n. Informal. Chiefly U.S. A person who stays at home in a passive, vegetable-like way, typically on a couch watching television, rather than being more enterprising.

cou·dé (kŏŏday, kŏŏ-dáy) adj. Astronomy. Of or pertaining to a system of deflecting light from the primary mirror of a reflecting telescope into the eyepiece. [French, "bent like an elbow", past participle of couder, to bend at right angles, from coude, elbow, from Latin cubitum, elbow, CUBIT.]

Cou·é (kŏŏ-áy), **Émile** (1857–1926). French psychologist and pioneer of autosuggestion in psychotherapy. **—Cou·é·ism** n.

cou·gar (kŏŏ-gər, -gaar) n. The **puma** (see). [French couguar, from Portuguese cuguardo, from Tupi suasuarana, "like a deer" (from its colour) : suasú, deer + ran, rã, similar to.]

cough (kof ‖ kawf) v. **coughed, coughing, coughs.** —intr. 1. To expel air from the lungs suddenly and noisily. 2. To make a noise like coughing. —tr. To expel or utter with a cough. Usually used with up or out. **—cough up.** Slang. To hand over (money, information, or the like) reluctantly.
~n. 1. A sudden and noisy effort to expel the air from the lungs. 2. An illness marked by coughing. [Middle English coughen, Old English cohhian (unattested), from an imitative root kokh-.]

cough drop n. A small, often medicated and sweetened lozenge taken to ease coughing or soothe a sore throat.

cough mixture n. A liquid medicine, taken to relieve coughing.

could. Past tense of **can,** but often used as an auxiliary verb for various shades of associated meanings indicating: 1. Possibility: This could be a world record. 2. Advice: You could always take a taxi if you're in a hurry. 3. A polite appeal or request: Could I ask you a favour? 4. Condition: If you could just be more tolerant, people like you better.

could·n't (kŏŏd'nt). Contraction of could not.

cou·lée, cou·lee (kŏŏ-lay, -li) n. 1. A sheet of solidified lava. 2. U.S. A stream of molten lava. 3. In the western United States and Canada: **a.** A deep gulch or ravine formed by rainstorms or melting snow, often dry in summer. **b.** A stream in such a gulch. [Canadian French coulée, from French, a flow, a flow of lava, from the past participle of couler, to flow, from Latin cōlāre, to strain, filter, from cōlum, a sieve.]

cou·lisse (kŏŏ-léess) n. 1. A grooved piece of timber in which a frame or panel slides. 2. Theatre. **a.** Any of the side scenes in the wings of a stage; a stage flat. **b.** The space between two side scenes. 3. A body of unofficial dealers on a stock exchange, especially the Paris Stock Exchange. [French, groove, corridor (see **portcullis**); sense 3, after the dealers' corridors in the Paris Bourse.]

cou·loir (kŏŏl-waar ‖ U.S. kŏŏl-waár) n. A steep, narrow mountainside gully, especially in the Alps. [French, colander, passageway, ravine, from couler, to slide, flow. See **coulée.**]

cou·lomb (kŏŏ-lom ‖ U.S. also -lōm, -lóm, -lŏm) n. Abbr. **C** A metre-kilogram-second unit of electrical charge equal to the quantity of charge transferred in one second by a steady current of one ampere. [After Charles A. de COULOMB.]

Cou·lomb (kŏŏ-lom; French kŏŏ-lón), **Charles Augustin de,** (1736–1806). French physicist who pioneered research into magnetism and electricity and formulated **Coulomb's law.**

Coulomb field n. An electric field equivalent to one produced by a point charge, substituted for a charged body so that the force due to the body at every point is described by Coulomb's law.

Coulomb force n. An attractive or repulsive electrostatic force described by Coulomb's law.

cou·lomb·me·ter, cou·lom·e·ter (kŏŏ-lom-méetər, kŏŏ-lommitər) n. An instrument for measuring electricity in coulombs.

cou·lomb·me·tric, cou·lo·me·tric (kŏŏlə-méttrik) adj. Chemistry. Of or pertaining to measurement of electric current. **— cou·lomb·me·try** (kŏŏ-lómmətri) n.

Coulomb potential *n.* The potential at any point in a Coulomb field.

Coulomb scattering *n.* The scattering of a charged particle from another charged particle, especially from an atomic nucleus, principally or exclusively as a result of Coulomb forces.

Coulomb's law *n.* The principle that the force between two charged particles is directly proportional to the product of their charges and inversely proportional to the square of the distance between them.

coul·ter, *U.S.* **col·ter** (kṓltər || *Scottish* kōōtər) *n.* A blade or wheel on the front of a plough that makes a preliminary cut through the soil. [Middle English, from Old English *culter,* from Latin, ploughshare.]

cou·ma·rin (kōṓmərin) *n.* A toxic fragrant organic compound, $C_9H_6O_2$, present in many plants including sweet clover and tonka beans. It is usually produced synthetically and used in perfumery. [French *coumarine,* from *coumarou,* tonka bean tree, from Spanish *coumarú,* from Tupi *cumaru, comarú.*] —**cou·ma·ric** *adj.*

coun·cil (kówn-s'l || *West Indies also* kúng-) *n.* **1.** An assembly of persons called together for consultation, deliberation, or discussion. **2. a.** A body of people elected or appointed to serve in an administrative, legislative, or advisory capacity. **b.** Such a body elected to serve as a local government authority. **3.** The discussion or deliberation that takes place in a council. **4.** An assembly of church officials and theologians convened for regulating matters of doctrine and discipline. **5.** The **Sanhedrin** *(see).* [Middle English *co(u)nceil,* from Anglo-French *concilie, cuncile,* assembly, from Latin *concilium,* meeting, assembly..]

Usage: Identity of pronunciation and relatedness of meaning between *council* and *counsel, councillor* and *counsellor,* lead to regular spelling confusions. *Council* refers to a deliberative assembly; *councillor* to its member. *Counsel* may be either noun or verb, referring to advice and guidance in general; *counsellor* or, in law, *counsel,* refers to the person who provides it.

coun·cil·lor, *U.S.* **coun·cil·or** (kówn-sələr, -sillər || *West Indies also* kúng-) *n.* A member of a council, especially the local governing body of a city or town. See Usage note at **council.**

council tax *n.* In Britain, the replacement for the **community charge** *(see).* The tax is levied by local councils on households divided into bands according to their property value.

coun·sel (kówn-s'l || *West Indies also* kúng-) *n., pl.* **-sels** or **counsel** (for sense 5). **1.** The exchanging of opinions and ideas; consultation; discussion. **2.** Advice or guidance, especially as given by a knowledgeable or qualified person. **3.** A deliberate resolution; a plan; a scheme. **4.** A private purpose or opinion: *keep one's own counsel.* **5.** A lawyer, group of lawyers, or others giving legal advice; especially, a barrister engaged to conduct a case in court. —See Usage notes at **council, lawyer.**

~*v.* **counselled** or *U.S.* **counseled, -selling** or *U.S.* **-seling, -sels.** —*tr.* **1.** To give counsel to; advise. **2.** To give professional help to on social or psychological problems. **3.** To urge the adoption of; recommend. —*intr.* To give or take counsel or advice. —See Usage note at **council.** [Middle English *counseil, conseil,* from Old French *conseil,* from Latin *consilium,* deliberation, consultation.]

coun·sel·lor, *U.S.* **coun·sel·or** (kówn-sələr || *West Indies also* kúng-) *n.* **1. a.** A person who gives counsel; an adviser. **b.** Such a person employed to advise on personal or other problems as a social service. **2.** *U.S.* A lawyer, especially one appearing in court. Also called "counsel-at-law". **3.** A high-ranking diplomat. **4.** *U.S.* A person supervising children at a summer camp. —See Usage notes at **council, lawyer.** —**coun·se·llor·ship** *n.*

count¹ (kownt || *West Indies also* kungt *(and in derivatives)*) *v.* **counted, counting, counts.** —*tr.* **1.** To find out the total number of units by listing the individual units. **2.** To recite numerals in ascending order up to and including: *count three before firing.* **3.** To include in a reckoning; take account of: *ten dogs, counting the puppies.* **4.** To believe or consider to be; deem: *He counts himself lucky.* —*intr.* **1.** To recite or list numbers in order or enumerate items by units or groups: *count by tens; count to three.* **2.** To have importance, especially when a judgment is being made: *His ill-health counted against him.* **3.** To have a specified value or importance; amount. Usually used with *for: His opinions count for little.* **4.** *Music.* To keep time by counting beats. **5.** *Informal.* To rely. Used with *on.* —See Synonyms at **rely.** —**count in.** To include. —**count off.** To separate into groups by or as if by counting. —**count out. 1.** To exclude or discount. **2.** To count to ten and thereupon declare beaten (a boxer who has fallen to the floor).

~*n.* **1.** The act of counting or calculating. **2.** A number reached by counting. **3.** A reckoning; an accounting. **4.** *Law.* Any of the separate and distinct charges in an indictment. **5.** A counting from one to ten seconds, during which time a boxer who is down must rise or be declared the loser. [Middle English *counten,* from Old French *conter, compter,* from Latin *computāre;* see **compute.**]

count² *n. Abbr.* **Ct.** In some European countries, a nobleman whose rank corresponds to that of an earl in Britain. [Middle English *counte,* from Old French *conte, comte,* from Late Latin *comes* (stem *comit-*), occupant of any state office, from Latin, companion.]

count·a·ble (kówntəb'l) *adj.* **1.** Capable of being counted. **2.** *Mathematics.* Capable of being put in a one-to-one correspondence with the positive integers. **3.** *Grammar.* Designating nouns that can be preceded by the indefinite article or a cardinal number and take a plural; for example, *cat* and *bag* are countable. Compare **noncountable.** —**count·a·bly** *adv.*

count·down (kównt-down) *n.* **1.** The act or process of counting

backwards aloud to indicate the time elapsing before an imminent deadline that will initiate an event or operation. **2.** *Aerospace.* The act or process of making a timed scheduled series of successive checks during the preparation of a missile or space vehicle for launching. **3.** The time leading up to an important event.

coun·te·nance (kówn-ti-nənss || *West Indies also* kúng-) *n.* **1.** Aspect; appearance; especially, the expression of the face. **2.** The face or facial features. **3.** Support or approval in general. **4.** Composure; bearing; self-control. —**out of countenance.** Visibly disconcerted or embarrassed.

~*tr.v.* **countenanced, -nancing, -nances.** To give approval to; condone. [Middle English *contenaunce,* behaviour, demeanour, from Old French *contenance,* from *contenir,* to behave, CONTAIN.] —**coun·te·nanc·er** *n.*

count·er¹ (kówn-tər || *West Indies also* kúng-) *adj.* Contrary; opposing.

~*n.* **1.** One that is counter; an opposite; a contrary. **2.** *Boxing.* A blow given while receiving or parrying another. **3.** *Fencing.* A parry in which one foil follows the other in a circular fashion. **4.** A stiff piece of leather around the heel of a shoe. **5.** The portion of a ship's stern extending from the water line to the end of the curved part. **6.** The part of a horse's chest between the shoulders and under the neck. **7.** The depression between the raised lines of a typeface.

~*v.* **countered, -ering, -ers.** —*tr.* **1.** To meet or return (a blow) by another blow. **2.** To oppose; act counter to. **3.** To respond to by retaliating in kind. —*intr.* **1.** To give a return blow while receiving or parrying one, as in boxing. **2.** To retaliate.

~*adv.* In a contrary manner or direction. [Middle English *countre,* from Old French *contre,* from Latin *contrā,* contrary to, against.]

counter² *n.* **1.** A table or similar flat surface on which money is counted, business transacted, or food served. **2.** A piece used for keeping a count or a place in games. **3.** An imitation coin; a token. —**over the counter.** See **over-the-counter.** —**under the counter.** See **under-the-counter.** [Middle English *contour,* from Old French *comptouer, conteoir,* from Medieval Latin *computātōrium,* place of accounts, from Latin *computāre,* to COUNT.]

counter³ *n.* **1.** A person who counts. **2.** Any electronic or mechanical device that automatically counts occurrences or repetitions of phenomena or events. **3.** *Physics.* An apparatus that detects individual particles or photons.

counter– (kówntər- || *West Indian also* kúngtər-, *not shown in individual entries below*) *prefix.* Indicates: **1.** Opposition, as in direction or purpose; for example, **countermarch, counteract. 2.** Reciprocation; for example, **countersign. Note:** Many compounds other than those entered here may be formed with *counter-.* In forming compounds, *counter-* is normally joined to the following element without a space or hyphen. [Middle English *countre-,* from Anglo-French, from Old French *contre-,* from Latin *contrā,* opposite to, COUNTER.]

coun·ter·act (kówntər-ákt) *tr.v.* **-acted, -acting, -acts.** To oppose and mitigate the effects of by contrary action; check. See Synonyms at **neutralise.** —**coun·ter·ac·tion** *n.* —**coun·ter·ac·tive** *adj.* —**coun·ter·ac·tive·ly** *adv.*

coun·ter·at·tack (kówntər-ə-tak) *n.* A return attack.

~*v.* **counterattacked, -tacking, -tacks.** —*intr.* To deliver a counterattack. —*tr.* To make a counterattack against.

coun·ter·at·trac·tion (kówntər-ə-tráksh'n) *n.* A rival or alternative attraction.

coun·ter·bal·ance (kówntər-bal-ənss) *n.* **1.** Any force or influence equally counteracting another. **2.** A weight that acts to balance another; a counterpoise.

~*tr.v.* (*also* -bál-) **counterbalanced, -ancing, -ances. 1.** To act as a counterbalance to; counterpoise. **2.** To oppose with an equal force; offset.

coun·ter·blast (kówntər-blaast || -blast) *n.* **1.** A vehement declaration or statement in response to an earlier one. **2.** A return blast, as of air or gunfire.

coun·ter·change (kówntə-cháynj) *tr.v.* **-changed, -changing, -changes. 1.** To exchange; transpose. **2. a.** To chequer. **b.** *Heraldry.* To reverse (colours and metals) on a field so that colour comes next to metal and metal next to colour.

coun·ter·charge (kówntər-chaarj) *n.* A charge in opposition to a charge made by another.

~*v.* (-chárj) **countercharged, -charging, -charges.** —*tr.* To bring a charge against (one's accuser). —*intr.* To make a countercharge.

coun·ter·check (kówntər-chek) *n.* **1.** Something that serves to check or verify something else. **2.** Something that confirms or denies the correctness of a previous check. **3. a.** A restraint that reinforces another check. **b.** A restraint that counteracts another check.

~*tr.v.* (-chék) **counterchecked, -checking, -checks. 1.** To oppose or check by a counteraction. **2.** To check again.

coun·ter·claim (kówntər-klaym) *n.* A claim made in opposition to a claim made by another.

~*v.* (-kláym) **counterclaimed, -claiming, -claims.** —*tr.* To make a counterclaim to the effect that. —*intr.* To make a counterclaim. —**coun·ter·claim·ant** *n.*

coun·ter·clock·wise (kówntər-klók-wīz) *adv. U.S.* Anticlockwise. —**coun·ter·clock·wise** *adj.*

coun·ter·coup (kówntər-kōō) *n.* A coup staged to reverse the effects of a previous coup.

coun·ter·cul·ture (kówntər-kulchər) *n.* A culture created by or for the alienated young in opposition to traditional lifestyles, values, and assumptions. —**coun·ter·cul·tur·al** (-kúlchərəl) *adj.*

coun·ter·cur·rent (kówntər-kúrrənt) *n.* An opposing current or flow.
~*adj. Chemistry.* Involving or pertaining to an opposing flow. Said of certain analytical or industrial separation techniques.

coun·ter·es·pi·o·nage (kówntər-éspi-ə-naazh, -nij) *n.* Espionage undertaken to detect and counteract enemy espionage.

coun·ter·ex·am·ple (kówntər-ig-zaamp'l, -eg- ‖ -ik-, zámp'l) *n.* An example that goes against a previous one or a theory.

coun·ter·feit (kówntər-feet, -fit) *v.* **-feited, -feiting, -feits.** —*tr.* **1.** To make a copy of, usually with the intent to defraud; forge. **2.** To imitate. **3.** To make a pretence of; feign. —*intr.* **1.** To carry on a deception; feign; dissemble. **2.** To make imitations or forgeries.
~*adj.* **1.** Made in imitation of what is genuine with the intent to defraud. **2.** Simulated; feigned. —See Synonyms at **artificial**.
~*n.* **1.** A fraudulent imitation or facsimile. **2.** *Obsolete.* A portrait; an image. [Middle English *countrefeten,* from Old French *contrefaire* (past participle *contrefait*), from Medieval Latin *contrāfacere,* to make in contrast to, hence to make in imitation : Latin *contrā-,* opposite to + *facere,* to make.] —**coun·ter·feit·er** *n.*

coun·ter·flow (kówntər-flō) *n.* Fluid flow in opposite directions, as in adjacent parts of an apparatus, such as a heat exchanger, or in biological systems, such as the gills of a fish.

coun·ter·foil (kówntər-foyl) *n.* The part of a cheque or other commercial paper retained by the issuer as a record of a transaction.

coun·ter·glow (kówntər-glō) *n.* **1. Gegenschein** *(see).* **2.** A coloured band or bands seen above the earth's shadow just above the eastern horizon after sunset, and the western horizon before sunrise.

coun·ter·in·sur·gen·cy (kówntər-in-súrjən-si) *n.* Measures taken by a state against the activities of terrorists or other rebels.

coun·ter·in·tel·li·gence (kówntər-in-téllijənss) *n.* The branch of an intelligence service charged with keeping valuable information from enemy spies, preventing subversion and sabotage, and gathering political and military information.

coun·ter·in·tu·i·tive (kówntər-in-téw-i-tiv ‖ -tōō-) *adj.* Contrary to what is perceived intuitively.

coun·ter·ir·ri·tant (kówntər-írri-tənt) *n. Medicine.* An agent that induces local irritation to counteract general or deep irritation. —**coun·ter·ir·ri·ta·tion** (-táysh'n) *n.*

coun·ter·jum·per (kówntər-jumpər) *n. Informal.* A shop assistant. Used derogatorily.

coun·ter·man (kówntər-man, -mən) *n., pl.* **-men** (-men, -mən). *U.S.* One who serves at a counter, as in a cafeteria.

coun·ter·mand (kówntər-maánd, -maand ‖ -mánd, -mand) *tr.v.* **-manded, -manding, -mands.** **1.** To cancel or reverse (a command or order). **2.** To recall by a contrary order.
~*n.* An order or command reversing an earlier one. [Middle English *countremaunden,* from Old French *contremander* : COUNTER- + *mander,* to command, from Latin *mandāre.*]

coun·ter·march (kówntər-maarch) *n.* **1.** A march back or in a reverse direction. **2.** A complete reversal of method or conduct.
~*v.* (-márch) **countermarched, -marching, -marches.** —*tr.* To conduct in a countermarch. —*intr.* To execute a countermarch.

coun·ter·mea·sure (kówntər-mezhər) *n.* A measure or action taken to oppose or compensate for another.

coun·ter·mine (kówntər-mīn) *n.* **1. a.** A mine or tunnel dug by the defenders of a fortress to intercept and destroy a tunnel made by the besiegers. **b.** A mine or charge of explosive placed so as to explode an enemy's mines. **2.** A counterplot.
~*v.* (-mín) **countermined, -mining, -mines.** —*tr.* **1.** To make or use a countermine against. **2.** To defeat or frustrate by secret measures. —*intr.* To make or lay down countermines.

coun·ter·move (kówntər-mōōv) *n.* A move countering another move.

coun·ter·move·ment (kówntər-mōōvmənt) *n.* A movement in an opposing direction.

coun·ter·of·fen·sive (kówntər-ə-fén-siv, -fen-) *n.* A large-scale attack by an army, designed to stop the offensive of an enemy force.

coun·ter·pane (kówntər-payn) *n.* A coverlet for a bed; a bedspread. [Earlier *counterpoint,* from Middle English, from Old French *contrepointe, coultepointe,* from Medieval Latin *culcita puncta,* "stitched quilt" : Latin *culcita,* QUILT + *puncta,* stabbed; see **point**.]

coun·ter·part (kówntər-paart) *n.* **1.** One that closely or exactly resembles another, in function or relation. **2. a.** One of two parts that fit and complete each other, such as a seal and its impression. **b.** One that is a natural complement to another.

coun·ter·plot (kówntər-plot) *n.* A plot intended to frustrate another plot.
~*v.* (-plót) **counterplotted, -plotting, -plots.** —*tr.* To oppose and frustrate by another plot. —*intr.* To devise a counterplot.

coun·ter·point (kówntər-poynt) *n.* **1. a.** Melodic material that is added above or below an existing melody. **b.** The musical technique of combining two or more melodic lines in such a way that they establish a harmonic relationship while retaining their linear individuality. **c.** Music incorporating or consisting of composition in counterpoint. **2.** A contrasting but parallel element, item, or theme.
~*tr.v.* **counterpointed, -pointing, -points.** **2.** To compose in counterpoint. **2.** To emphasise by means of contrasting detail.

coun·ter·poise (kówntər-poyz) *n.* **1.** A counterbalancing weight. **2.** Any force or influence that balances or equally counteracts another. **3.** The state of being balanced or in equilibrium.
~*tr.v.* (-póyz) **counterpoised, -poising, -poises.** **1.** To oppose with an equal weight; counterbalance. **2.** To act against with an equal force or power; offset.

coun·ter·pro·duc·tive (kówntər-prə-dúktiv) *adj.* Tending to hinder rather than serve one's purpose; harmful.

coun·ter·pro·pos·al (kówntər-prə-pōz'l, -póz'l) *n.* A proposal offered to nullify or substitute for a previous one.

coun·ter·ref·or·ma·tion (kówntər-réffər-máysh'n) *n.* A reformation in opposition to previous reformation.

Counter Reformation. *n.* A reform movement within the Roman Catholic Church during the 16th century and the first half of the 17th century organised in reaction to the Protestant Reformation.

coun·ter·rev·o·lu·tion (kówntər-révvə-lōōsh'n, -léwsh'n) *n.* A movement arising in opposition to a revolution and aiming to restore the prerevolutionary state of affairs. —**coun·ter·rev·o·lu·tion·ar·y** (-əri ‖ -erri) *adj. & n.* —**coun·ter·rev·o·lu·tion·ist** *n.*

coun·ter·scarp (kówntər-skaarp) *n.* The outer wall of a ditch in a fortification.

coun·ter·shaft (kówntər-shaaft ‖ -shaft) *n.* An intermediate shaft between the powered and driven shafts in a belt drive or gear train.

coun·ter·sign (kówntər-sīn) *tr.v.* **-signed, -signing, -signs.** To sign (a previously signed document), as for authentication.
~*n.* **1.** A second or confirming signature, as on a previously signed document; a countersignature. **2.** *Military.* A secret sign or signal to be given to a sentry in order to obtain passage; a password. **3.** A secret sign or signal given in answer to another.

coun·ter·sig·na·ture (kówntər-sígnichər) *n.* A signature made in countersigning.

coun·ter·sink (kówntər-singk) *tr.v.* **-sunk** (-sungk), **-sinking, -sinks.** **1.** To enlarge the top part of (a hole) so that a screw or bolthead will lie flush with or below the surface. **2.** To fit (a screw or bolt) in this way.
~*n.* **1.** A tool for making a countersunk hole. **2.** A countersunk hole.

coun·ter·spy (kówntər-spī) *n.* A spy working in opposition to enemy espionage.

coun·ter·stain (kówntər-stayn) *n.* A dye used to treat microscope specimens that have already been treated with another dye. The stain and the counterstain colour different parts of the specimen.
~*tr.v.* **counterstained, -staining, -stains.** To treat with a counterstain.

coun·ter·ten·or (kówntər-tennər) *n.* **1.** An adult male voice with a range above that of tenor. **2.** A part written for such a voice. **3.** A singer with such a voice.

coun·ter·vail (kówntər-váyl, -vayl) *v.* **-vailed, -vailing, -vails.** —*tr.* **1.** To act against with equal force. **2.** To compensate for; offset. —*intr.* To avail. Used with *against.* [Middle English *countrevaillen,* to be equal in value, from Old French *contrevaloir* : COUNTER- + *valoir,* to be worth, from Latin *valēre,* to be strong, be worth.]

coun·ter·weigh (kówntər-wáy) *v.* **-weighed, -weighing, -weighs.** —*tr.* To cause to counterbalance; counterpoise. —*intr.* To counterbalance.

coun·ter·weight (kówntər-wayt) *n.* A counterbalance. —**coun·ter·weight·ed** (-waytid) *adj.*

coun·ter·word (kówntər-wurd) *n.* A word commonly used without regard to its precise meaning, as *nice* or *awful.*

count·ess (kównt-iss, -ess) *n.* **1. a.** In various European countries, the wife or widow of a count. **b.** In Britain, the wife or widow of an earl. **2.** A woman holding the title of count or earl in her own right. [Middle English *countes(se),* from Old French *contesse,* feminine of *conte,* COUNT.]

counting house *n.* An office in which a business firm carries on operations such as accounting and correspondence. Also called "counting room".

counting number *n.* Any of the numbers 0, 1, 2, 3, ... used in counting objects.

count·less (kównt-ləss, -liss) *adj.* Too many to be counted; innumerable; very many. See Synonyms at **infinite**.

count noun *n.* A countable (sense 3) noun. Compare **mass noun.**

count palatine *n., pl.* **counts palatine** A noble originally exercising certain royal powers within his domain, a **palatine** *(see).*

coun·tri·fied, coun·try·fied (kúntri-fīd) *adj.* Resembling or having the characteristics of country life; rural; rustic.

coun·try (kúntri) *n., pl.* **-tries. 1.** A large tract of land distinguishable by features of topography, biology, or culture. **2.** A district outside cities and towns; a rural area. **3.** The territory of a nation or state; land. **4.** The people of a nation or state. **5.** The land of a person's birth or citizenship or to which a person owes allegiance. **6.** *Music.* Country-and-western. —See Synonyms at **nation.** —**go to the country.** *British.* To resign and hold a general election.
~*adj.* **1.** Of or pertaining to rural areas. **2.** Unsophisticated; rustic. [Middle English *cuntree, contre,* from Old French *contree,* from Medieval Latin *(terra) contrāta,* "(land) lying opposite or before one", from *contrātus,* lying opposite, from Latin *contrā,* against, opposite.]

coun·try-and-west·ern (kúntri-ən-wéstərn) *n. Abbr.* **C & W.** A type of commercialised folk music originating in the southern or southeastern United States. Also called "country music". —**country-and-western** *adj.*

country bumpkin *n.* A simple country dweller; a yokel.

country club *n.* A club in the country or suburbs with facilities for outdoor sports and social activities.

country cousin *n.* One whose lack of familiarity with the ways of urban life is regarded as laughable by city dwellers.

country dance *n.* A folk dance, typically one in which two lines of dancers face each other. **—country dancing** *n.*
country gentleman *n.* The proprietor of a country estate.
country house *n.* A mansion or other grand dwelling on a country estate.
coun·try·man (kúntri-mən) *n., pl.* **-men** (-mən). **1.** A man from one's own country. **2.** A man from a particular region. **3.** A man who lives in the country and knows the countryside well.
country rock *n. Geology.* An existing rock within which a new rock, such as an igneous intrusion, is formed.
country seat *n.* **1.** An estate in the country. **2.** A mansion on such an estate.
coun·try·side (kúntri-sīd) *n.* **1.** The rural areas of a country. **2.** The inhabitants of a rural area.
coun·try·wom·an (kúntri-wŏŏmən) *n., pl.* **-women** (-wimmin). **1.** A woman from one's own country. **2.** A woman from a particular region. **3.** A woman who lives in the country and knows it well.
coun·ty (kówn-ti ‖ *West Indian also* kúng-) *n., pl.* **-ties.** *Abbr.* **co.** **1.** In Britain and Ireland, any of the largest administrative divisions of local government. **2.** In some Commonwealth countries, an administrative division. **3.** In the United States, a political subdivision of a state. **4.** The people living in a county. **5.** *Obsolete.* **a.** The territory under the jurisdiction of a count or earl. **b.** A count or earl.
~adj. **1.** Of or pertaining to a county. **2.** *Chiefly British.* Belonging to or characteristic of the landed gentry in its interest in outdoor pursuits such as hunting and riding. [Middle English *co(u)nte,* from Anglo-French *counté,* from Medieval Latin *comitātus,* territory of a count, from Late Latin, retinue of a count, from *comes* (stem *comit-*), COUNT.]
county borough *n.* In Britain, a large area including a town, formerly considered as a county.
county council *n.* The local government body administering a county; especially, in Britain, a nonmetropolitan county council.
county court *n.* In England and Wales, a court on the lowest tier of those hearing civil actions.
county palatine *n.* **1.** The domain of a count palatine. **2.** A modern county, such as Lancashire or Cheshire, which was formerly such a domain.
county town *n.* A town or city which is the seat of a county council. Also *U.S.* "county seat".
coup (kōō) *n., pl.* **coups** (kōōz; *French* kōō). **1.** A brilliantly executed stratagem; a masterstroke. **2.** A coup d'état. [French, from Old French, from Late Latin *colpus,* from Latin *colaphus,* blow, from Greek *kolaphos,* a blow.]
coup de grâce (kōō də gráass) *n., pl.* **coups de grâce** *(pronounced as singular). French.* **1.** The mortal or finishing stroke, as delivered to someone mortally wounded. **2.** Any finishing or decisive stroke. ["Stroke of mercy".]
coup de main (kōō də máɴ) *n., pl.* **coups de main** *(pronounced as singular). French.* A sudden action undertaken to surprise an enemy. ["Stroke of hand".]
coup d'é·tat (kōō day-taá, de-) *n., pl.* **coups d'état** *(pronounced as singular).* A sudden overthrowing of government and seizure of power by others. See Synonyms at **rebellion.** ["Stroke of state".]
coup de thé·â·tre (kōō də tay-aátr) *n., pl.* **coups de théâtre** *(pronounced as singular). French.* An unexpected and dramatic event that overturns some given situation. ["Stroke of theatre".]
coup d'oeil (kōō dú-i, dō-i) *n., pl.* **coups d'oeil** *(pronounced as singular). French.* A glance; a quick survey. ["Stroke of eye".]
coupe[1] (kōōp) *n.* **1.** A dessert of ice cream or fruit-flavoured ice, variously garnished with nuts, fruit, whipped cream, and the like, served in a special dessert glass. **2. a.** The stemmed glass in which such a dessert is served. **b.** A shallow, bowl-shaped dessert dish. [French, "cup", from Late Latin *cuppa,* CUP.]
coupe[2] *U.S.* Variant of **coupé** (a two-door car).
cou·pé (kōō-pay ‖ *U.S.* kōō-páy) *n.* Also **coupe** (*U.S.* kōōp) (for sense 1). **1.** A closed streamlined two-door car. **2.** A closed four-wheel carriage with two seats inside and one outside. [French, short for *(carrosse) coupé,* "cut-off (carriage)", from the past participle of *couper,* to cut off, from Old French *coup,* COUP.]
Cou·pe·rin (kōōpə-raɴ, -ráɴ), **François** (1668–1733). The most famous of a family of French musicians, known as "The Great". He was a court organist at Versailles under Louis XIV, and wrote songs, chamber music, choral works, and organ pieces.
cou·ple (kúpp'l) *n.* **1.** Two items of the same kind; a pair. **2.** Something that joins two things together; a connection; a link. **3.** Two people, especially a man and a woman, joined in a stable relationship such as marriage or cohabitation. **4.** Two people engaged in some joint activity, such as dancing. **5.** *Informal.* A few; several: *a couple of days.* **6.** *Physics.* A pair of forces of equal magnitude acting in parallel but opposite directions, capable of causing rotation but not translation. **7.** *Physics.* **a.** A pair of metals or semiconductors in direct contact developing an electromotive force across their junction, as in a thermocouple. **b.** A pair of metals in an electrolyte forming a galvanic cell. Also called "galvanic couple". **8. a.** A pair of hunting dogs. **b.** A double leash joining them.
~v. **coupled, -ling, -les.** *—tr.* **1.** To link together; attach; join. **2.** To form into pairs. **3.** To join as man and wife; marry. **4.** To combine. **5.** *Electricity.* To link (two circuits or currents) as by magnetic induction. *—intr.* **1.** To form pairs. **2.** To copulate. **3.** *Physics.* To interact as by electromagnetic interaction. Used of electrons or other elementary particles. [Middle English, pair, bond, from Old French *co(u)ple,* from Latin *cōpula,* bond, link.]
Synonyms: *couple, pair, duo, brace, yoke.*
Usage: In informal usage, the meaning of *couple* has extended so that it is no longer restricted to two, but has the general sense of "a few". As the earlier meaning of "two" is still very much alive, however, the word is often ambiguous. *I've got a couple of pounds in my wallet* does not necessarily mean only two (though it might). On the other hand, *Lend me a couple of pounds* is likely to be interpreted in a precise way.
cou·pler (kúpplər) *n.* **1.** A device for coupling. **2.** A device connecting two organ keyboards so that they may be played together. **3.** A device for linking two electronic circuits.
cou·plet (kúpplit) *n.* **1.** A unit of verse consisting of two successive lines, usually rhyming and having the same meter. **2.** Two similar things; a pair. [Old French *couplet,* diminutive of *co(u)ple,* COUPLE.]
cou·pling (kúppling) *n.* **1.** The act of forming a couple or pair. **2.** A device for connecting railway carriages or wagons. **3.** The part of the body connecting the hindquarters and forequarters of a four-footed animal. **4.** *Physics.* Interaction between elementary particles, especially between their magnetic moments.
cou·pon (kōō-pon ‖ kéw-) *n.* **1.** Any of a number of small, negotiable certificates attached to a bond that represent sums of interest due at stated maturities. **2.** A certificate or detachable part of an advertisement entitling the bearer to certain stated benefits, such as a cash discount or a gift, or for use as an order or enquiry form. **3.** Any of a number of detachable slips used when making instalment payments. **4.** *British.* An entry form for a football pool. **5.** A ration voucher. [French, from Old French *colpon,* "a piece cut off", from *colper, couper,* to cut off, from *coup,* a blow. See **coup.**]
cour·age (kúrrij) *n.* **1.** The state or quality of mind or spirit that enables one to face danger and overcome fear. **2.** *Obsolete.* Heart; mind; disposition. [Middle English *corage,* heart as the seat of feeling, courage, from Old French, from Vulgar Latin *corāticum* (unattested), from Latin *cor,* heart.]
Synonyms: *courage, heroism, bravery, valour, mettle, fortitude, resolution, tenacity, backbone.*
cou·ra·geous (kə-ráyjəss) *adj.* Having or characterised by courage; valiant. See Synonyms at **brave.** **—cou·ra·geous·ly** *adv.* **—cou·ra·geous·ness** *n.*
cou·rante (kōō-róɴt ‖ kōō-) *n.* **1.** A French dance of the 17th century, characterised by running and gliding steps to an accompaniment in triple time. **2.** The second movement of the classical suite, typically following the allemande. [French, "running (dance)", from *courir,* to run, from Old French *courre,* from Latin *currere.*]
Cour·bet (kóor-bay, koor-báy), **(Jean Désiré) Gustave** (1819–77). French painter who headed the realist school. He developed an earthy and uncompromising style, as in *Burial at Ornans* (1850), *Bonjour M. Courbet* (1854), and *The Artist's Studio* (1855).
cour·gette (koor-zhét, kawr-) *n.* **1.** A variety of marrow bred to bear many small fruits. **2.** The fruit of this plant, cooked and eaten as a vegetable. Also called "zucchini". [French, diminutive of *courge,* marrow, gourd.]
cour·i·er (kōōrri-ər, kúrri-) *n.* **1.** A messenger employed on urgent business; especially, one working for a parcel delivery service. **2.** An official diplomatic messenger. **3.** A person who carries information back and forward between members of a secret service. **4.** A person employed to make arrangements for and attend to the requirements of travellers or holidaymakers. **5.** Used in the title of certain newspapers: *Dundee Courier.* [Middle English, from Old French *courrier,* from Italian *corriere,* "runner", from *correre,* from Latin *currere,* to run.]
cour·lan (kóor-lən) *n.* A bird, the **limpkin** *(see).* [French, variant of *courliri,* from Galibi *kurliri.*]
course (korss ‖ kōrss, koorss) *n.* **1.** Onward movement in a particular direction; progress; advance. **2.** The direction of continuing movement. **3.** The route or path taken by something that moves, such as a stream. **4. a.** A designated area of land or water on which a race is held or a sport played. **b.** A **golf course** *(see).* **5.** Movement in time; duration: *in the course of a year.* **6.** A mode of action or behaviour. **7.** A typical or natural manner of proceeding; customary passage from stage to stage; regular development: *The fad ran its course.* **8.** A systematic or orderly succession regarded as a unit: *a course of treatment.* **9.** *Architecture.* A continuous layer of building material, such as brick or tile, on a wall or roof of a building. **10.** *Education.* **a.** A prescribed body of studies to be followed by students. **b.** The subject matter studied. **11.** A part of a meal served as a unit at one time. **12.** The lowest sail on any mast of a square-rigged ship. **13.** A point on the compass; especially, the one towards which a ship is sailing. **14.** A hunt by hounds pursuing the quarry by sight rather than scent. —See Synonyms at **way.** **—in due course.** In proper order; at the right time. **—lay a course.** *Nautical.* **1.** To go in a particular course or direction without tacking. **2.** To plan some action or project. **—of course.** **1.** In the natural order of things; naturally. **2.** Without any doubt; certainly.
~v. **coursed, coursing, courses.** *—tr.* **1.** To move swiftly through or over; traverse. **2.** To pursue or hunt, especially with hounds chasing the quarry by sight rather than scent. **3.** To set (hounds) to chase game; send into pursuit. *—intr.* **1.** To proceed on a course; follow a direction. **2. a.** To move swiftly; race. **b.** To run; flow: *"big tears now coursed down her face"* (Iris Murdoch). **3.** To hunt game with hounds. [Middle English *cours, course,* from Old French, from Latin *cursus,* from the past participle of *currere,* to run.]

cours·er¹ (kórss-ər ‖ kórss-, koórss-) n. 1. A dog trained for coursing. 2. A person who courses hounds.

courser² n. Poetic. A swift horse.

courser³ n. Any of various plover-like birds of the family Glareolidae, found mainly in warm regions of Africa and Asia and characterised by the ability to run fast. [From New Latin *Cursorius* (genus), from Late Latin, "adapted for running", from Latin *cursus*, COURSE (forward movement).]

cours·ing (kórss-ing ‖ kórss-, koórss-) n. The sport of hunting with dogs trained to chase game by sight instead of scent.

court (kort ‖ kōrt) n. Abbr. **C., ct.** 1. An extent of open ground partially or completely enclosed by walls or buildings; a courtyard. 2. A short street; especially, an alley walled by buildings on three sides. 3. A large, open section of a building, often with a glass roof or skylight. 4. a. Formerly, a mansion or other large building standing in a courtyard. Now used only in proper names. b. British. A large block of flats. 5. A level area, marked with appropriate lines, upon which tennis, squash, basketball, or some other game is played. 6. The place of residence of a sovereign or dignitary; a royal mansion or palace. 7. The retinue of a sovereign, including the royal family and his personal servants, advisers, ministers, and the like. 8. A sovereign's governing body, including the council of ministers and state advisers. 9. A formal meeting called for and presided over by a sovereign. 10. a. A person or body of persons appointed to hear and submit a decision on legal cases. b. The building, hall, or room in which cases are heard and determined. c. The regular session of a judicial assembly. 11. Any similar authorised tribunal having military or ecclesiastical jurisdiction. 12. a. The body of directors of a corporation, company, or other organisation. b. The governing body in certain British universities. —**out of court.** 1. Without a trial. 2. Being regarded as too trivial, rash, or ridiculous for discussion or consideration. —**pay court to.** 1. To flatter with solicitous overtures in an attempt to obtain something. 2. To woo. ~v. **courted, courting, courts.** —tr. 1. To attempt to gain the favour of by flattery or attention. 2. To attempt to gain the affections or love of; woo. 3. To attempt to gain; seek. 4. To invite, often unwittingly or foolishly: *court disaster.* —intr. To be involved in regular social activities with a view to eventual marriage. ~adj. Of, pertaining, or appropriate to a court. [Middle English, from Old French *cort*, from Latin *cohors* (stem *cohort-*), enclosure, court, cohort.]

court bouillon (koór) n. A light stock made from vegetables, herbs, and white wine, used for poaching fish. [French, "short bouillon".]

court card n. A playing card bearing a jack, queen, or king of any suit. Also called "picture card", U.S. "face card". [Folk-etymological alteration of earlier *coat card.*]

court circular n. In Britain, a column in a newspaper announcing the social engagements of the Royal Family.

Cour·telle (kawr-tél, koor- ‖ kōr-) n. A trademark for a synthetic fabric.

cour·te·ous (kúrti-əss, rarely kórti- ‖ kórti-) adj. Characterised by graciousness and good manners; considerate towards others. See Synonyms at **polite.** [Middle English *curteis, corteis,* having manners befitting a courtly gentleman, from Old French, from *cort*, COURT.] —**cour·te·ous·ly** adv. —**cour·te·ous·ness** n.

cour·te·san, cour·te·zan (kórti-zán, -zan ‖ kórti, kúrti-, -zən) n. A prostitute or kept woman, especially one associating with men of rank or wealth. [Old French *courtisane*, from Old Italian *cortigiana*, "female courtier", from *cortigiano*, courtier, from *corte*, court, from Latin *cohors* (stem *cohort-*), COURT.]

cour·te·sy (kúrtə-si, kórtə- ‖ kórtə-) n., pl. **-sies.** 1. Polite behaviour; gracious manner or manners. 2. A polite gesture or remark. 3. Consent or favour; indulgence: *called "doctor" by courtesy.* —**courtesy of.** 1. With the permission of. 2. Paid for by. [Middle English *curteisie*, from Old French, from *curteis*, COURTEOUS.]

courtesy light n. An inside light in a car that is switched on automatically by the opening of a door.

courtesy title n. British. A title of nobility that has no official or legal status.

court hand n. A style of handwriting formerly used in English legal papers.

court·house (kórt-howss ‖ kórt-) n. Abbr. **c.h., C.H.** A building housing judicial courts.

court·i·er (kórt-i-ər, -yər ‖ kórt-) n. 1. An attendant at the court of a sovereign. 2. One who seeks favour, especially by flattery or obsequious behaviour. [Middle English *courteour*, from Anglo-French, from Old French *corteier*, to be at court, to court, from *cort*, court, COURT.] —**cour·ti·er·ly** adv.

court-leet (kórt-léet ‖ kórt-) n. A former court in Britain, a **leet** (see).

court·ly (kórt-li ‖ kórt-) adj. **-lier, -liest.** 1. Suitable for a royal court; stately; dignified. 2. Elegant in manners; polite; refined. 3. Flattering; obsequious. —**court·li·ness** n.

courtly love n. A code of chivalrous devotion to an idealised beloved, usually a married lady, that became a regular theme of medieval and Renaissance literature.

court-mar·tial (kórt-mársh'l ‖ kórt-, U.S. also -maarsh'l) n., pl. **courts-martial.** Abbr. **c.m.** 1. A military or naval court of officers appointed by a commander to try persons for offences under military law. 2. A trial by court-martial. ~tr.v. **court-martialled** or U.S. **-tialed, -tialling** or U.S. **-tialing, -tials.** To try by court-martial.

Court of Appeal n. A superior court to which appeals are made on points of law resulting from the judgment of a trial court. Compare **High Court of Justice.** See **Supreme Court of Judicature.**

Court of Common Pleas n. 1. Formerly, a court in Britain to hear civil cases between commoners. 2. In some states of the United States, a court having general jurisdiction.

Court of Exchequer n. Formerly, a court in Britain with jurisdiction in equity and common law, dealing originally with matters of revenue and later all kinds of cases, now merged with the High Court.

court of first instance n. A civil or criminal court that conducts the initial hearing of a case.

court of inquiry n. British. A tribunal specially appointed to investigate an accident, breach of discipline, or other matter of concern.

Court of Queen's Bench n. A superior court of common law in Britain, now merged with the High Court as the Queen's Bench Division. Called during the reign of a king "Court of King's Bench".

Court of Sessions n. The superior court of civil justice in Scotland, hearing both appeal cases and cases at first instance.

Court of St. James's n. The British royal court to which ambassadors are formally accredited.

court plaster n. An adhesive plaster formerly used to cover cuts or scratches on the skin. [Originally, referring to the black silk plaster used by ladies at court to make beauty spots.]

Cour·trai. See **Kortrijk.**

court·room (kórt-rōom, -rŏom ‖ kórt-) n. A room in which court proceedings are carried on.

court·ship (kórt-ship ‖ kórt-) n. 1. The act or period of courting before marriage. 2. Mating rituals between animals.

court tennis n. U.S. **Real tennis** (see).

court·yard (kórt-yaard ‖ kórt-) n. An open space surrounded by walls or buildings, adjoining or within a large building.

cous·cous (kŏoss-kŏoss) n. A North African dish of crushed semolina steamed and served with various meats, spices, and vegetables. [French, from Arabic *kouskous.*]

cous·in (kúzz'n) n. 1. A child of one's aunt or uncle. Also called "cousin-german", "first cousin", "full cousin". 2. A relative descended from a common ancestor, such as a grandfather, by two or more steps in a diverging line; for example, one's first cousin's child is one's *first cousin once removed,* and the child of one's parent's first cousin is one's *second cousin.* 3. Obsolete. A person related by descent from a common ancestor, but not a brother or sister. 4. Loosely, any relative by blood or marriage. 5. A member of a kindred group or country: *our Canadian cousins.* 6. A title of address used by a sovereign to a nobleman or to another sovereign. [Middle English *cosin(e)*, from Old French *cosin, cousin,* from Latin *consōbrīnus*, maternal first cousin : *com-*, together + *sōbrīnus*, maternal cousin.] —**cous·in·ly** adj.

Cou·sin, Jean (kŏo-zán), known as the Younger (c. 1522–94). French artist, son of Jean Cousin the Elder (c. 1490–1560). His *Last Judgment* was among the first French thematic paintings. He designed stained glass windows and produced fine woodcuts and engravings.

cous·in-ger·man (kúzz'n-jérmən) n., pl. **cousins-german.** A first cousin. See **cousin.**

Cou·steau (kŏo-stó, kŏo-stô), **Jacques (Yves)** (1910–97). French pioneer of underwater exploration. He helped to invent the aqualung (1943) and later developed underwater laboratories.

cou·ter (kŏotər) n. A piece of armour protecting the elbow. [Middle English, from Old French *coute* (modern French *coude*), elbow, from Latin *cubitum;* see **cubit.**]

couth (kŏoth) adj. 1. Refined; suave; cultured. Used humorously as a back-formation from "uncouth". 2. Obsolete. Friendly; familiar. [Middle English *couth*, familiar, known, Old English *cūth.*]

couth·y, couth·ie (kŏothi) adj. Scottish. Characterised by homeliness or affability. [Middle English. See **couth, uncouth.**]

cou·ture (kŏo-téwr, kŏo- ‖ -tóor) n. The business of a couturier, the designing and making of fashionable clothes for women. [French, tailoring, sewing, from Old French *cousture*, from Vulgar Latin *consūtūra* (unattested), from the feminine past participle of Latin *consuere*, to sew together : *com-*, together + *suere*, to sew.]

cou·tu·rier (kŏo-téwr-i-ay, kŏo- ‖ -tóor-, U.S. -áy) n. Feminine **cou·tu·rière** (-air ‖ -aír). 1. One who designs, makes, and sells fashionable, usually custom-made, women's clothing. 2. An establishment engaged in this business. [French, from COUTURE.]

cou·vade (kŏo-vaʾad) n. A practice among certain peoples in which the husband of a woman in labour takes to his bed as if he were bearing the child. [French, "a hatching", from *couver*, to hatch, sit on (eggs), from Latin *cubāre*, to lie down (on).]

cou·vert (kŏo-vaír, kŏo-) n. 1. A table setting at a restaurant table. 2. A cover charge (see). [French, "cover".]

co·va·lency (kō-váylən-si) n. Chemistry. 1. The process of forming covalent bonds. 2. The number of electron pairs an atom can share with other atoms in such bonds. Also called "covalence". —**co·va·lent** (-váylənt) adj.

covalent bond n. A chemical bond formed by the sharing of one or more electrons, especially pairs of electrons, between atoms.

covalent crystal n. Chemistry. A crystal in which all the atoms are linked together by covalent bonds.

co·var·i·ance (kō-vaír-i-ənss) n. 1. Physics. The principle that the laws of physics have the same form regardless of the system of coordinates in which they are expressed. 2. Statistics. The expected

value of the product of the deviations of corresponding values of two variables from their respective means.
co·var·i·ant (kō-vair-i-ənt) *adj.* **1.** *Physics.* Expressing, exhibiting, or pertaining to covariance. **2.** *Mathematics.* Varying with another variable quantity in a manner that leaves a specified relationship unchanged.
cove[1] (kōv) *n.* **1.** A small, sheltered bay in the shoreline of a sea, river, or lake. **2. a.** A steep-walled mountain hollow. **b.** A steep-walled semicircular recess, especially one forming the head of a valley. **c.** A cave or cavern. **3.** *Architecture.* A concave moulding. ~*tr.v.* **coved, coving, coves.** To cause to arch over or curve inwards. [Middle English *cove,* closet, chamber, cave, Old English *cofa.*]
cove[2] *n. British Slang.* A man; a chap. No longer in current usage. [16th century cant, perhaps from Romany *cofe, kova*†, man.]
co·vel·lite (kō-vel-īt, -vəl-) *n.* An indigo-blue mineral form of copper sulphide, CuS; an important source of copper. [After Nicholas *Covelli* (died 1829), Italian chemist who discovered it.]
cov·en (kúvv'n || kōv'n) *n.* **1.** An assembly of witches. **2.** A group of 13 witches. [Perhaps from Middle English *covent,* a gathering, CONVENT.]
cov·e·nant (kúvvə-nənt) *n.* **1.** A binding agreement made by two or more parties; a compact; a contract. **2.** A solemn agreement or vow made by members of a church to defend and support its faith and doctrine. **3.** *Theology.* God's promises to man, as recorded in the Old and New Testaments. **4.** *Law.* **a.** A formal sealed agreement or contract, especially one to pay regular sums, as to a charity or relative. **b.** A particular clause of such a contract.
~*v.* **covenanted, -nanting, -nants.** —*tr.* To promise by a covenant. —*intr.* To enter into a covenant; contract. [Middle English, from Old French, from the present participle of *co(n)venir,* to agree, CONVENE.] **—cov·e·nant·al** (-nánt'l) *adj.* **—cov·e·nant·al·ly** *adv.*
cov·e·nant·ee (kúvvənən-tée) *n.* The participant in a covenant to whom the promise is made.
cov·e·nant·er (kúvvə-nəntər, -nántər) *n.* **1.** One who makes a covenant. **2.** *Capital* **C.** A Scottish Presbyterian who supported either of the agreements (National Covenant, 1638, or Solemn League and Covenant, 1643) intended to defend and extend Presbyterianism.
cov·e·nant·or (kúvvənəntər) *n.* The party to a covenant by whom the obligation expressed in it is to be performed.
Cov·en·try (kóvv'n-tri, kúvv'n-). Industrial city in the Midlands, central England. A new cathedral, designed by Sir Basil Spence, was opened in 1962 and incorporates bombed ruins of the old, bombed in 1940. **—send to Coventry.** To refuse to associate with; ostracise. [*Send to Coventry,* from the sending of Royalist prisoners to Coventry during the English Civil War.]
cov·er (kúvvər) *v.* **-ered, -ering, -ers.** —*tr.* **1.** To place something upon, over, or in front of, so as to protect, shut in, or conceal; overlay or spread with something. **2.** To put a covering on; clothe. **3.** To put a cap, hat, or the like on (one's head). **4.** To bring upon (oneself or one's reputation). Used reflexively: *He covered himself in glory.* **5.** To serve as a covering for; occupy the surface of: *Dust covered the table.* **6.** To extend over; occupy: *a farm covering more than 100 acres.* **7.** To copulate with (a female). Used of animals, especially horses. **8.** To sit on (eggs); incubate; brood. **9.** To screen from view or detection; conceal. **10.** To protect or shield from harm, injury, or danger; shelter. **11.** To protect by insurance; insure against a specified risk or loss. **12.** To include; comprise: *a broad category that covers a variety of species.* **13.** To be sufficient to defray (a charge or expense); meet or offset (a liability). **14.** To make provision for; allow for: *This law does not cover such cases.* **15.** To deal with; treat of. **16.** To travel or pass over; traverse. **17.** To have as one's territory or sphere of work: *A single doctor has to cover the whole region.* **18.** To overwhelm; fill. Used in the passive: *covered in confusion.* **19.** *Military.* **a.** To overlook and dominate from a strategic position; have within range. **b.** To protect (a soldier, unit, or position, for example) by occupying a position from which enemy troops can be fired upon. **20.** *Journalism.* To be responsible for securing and reporting the details of (an event or situation): *cover a test match.* **21.** *Sports.* To be responsible for marking (an opponent) or for defending (an area or position): *cover the midfield.* **22.** To match (an opponent's stake) in a wager. **23.** *Card Games.* To play a higher-ranking card than (the one previously played). **24.** *Obsolete.* To pardon or remit: *"Thou hast covered all their sins".* (Psalms 85:2). —*intr. Informal.* To act as a substitute or replacement during someone's absence. Often used with *for.*
~*n.* **1.** Something that covers or is laid, placed, or spread over or upon something else, especially: **a.** A blanket or sheet on a bed. **b.** The lid or top of a container. **c.** The binding at the front or back of a book. **d.** The front outer page of a magazine, or its outer front and back pages. **2.** *Military.* Natural or artificial shelter or protection by other armed units: *under a cover of mortar fire.* **3. a.** Vegetation covering an area, often serving to provide shade or prevent erosion. **b.** Undergrowth or other vegetation serving as protective concealment for wild animals. **4. a.** Something that screens or hides: *a heavy cloud cover.* **b.** Something that conceals or keeps secret, such as a pretext or disguise: *The secret agent's job in the bank is just a cover.* **5.** A table setting for one person. **6.** A cover charge. **7.** *Philately.* **a.** An envelope or wrapper for mail. **b.** An envelope, postcard, or the like bearing a stamp and postal markings of special interest to stamp collectors. **8.** *Finance.* **a.** Funds sufficient to meet an obligation or secure against loss. **b.** Coverage (sense 2). **9.** *Mathematics.* A collection of sets associated with a given set such that every point in the given set belongs to at least one other set in the collection. **10.** *Plural.* In cricket, the area parallel to the pitch and roughly halfway to the boundary on the batsman's off side. —See Synonyms at **shelter. —break cover.** To come out of hiding. **—take cover.** To seek concealment or protection, as from enemy fire. **—under cover. 1.** Operating secretly or under a guise; covert. **2.** Hidden; protected. [Middle English *coveren,* from Old French *covrir,* from Latin *cooperīre,* to cover completely : *co-,* completely + *operīre,* to cover.] **—cov·er·er** *n.*
Usage: In formal English, *covered* is used with *in* when describing the state of something: *His face was covered in spots. With* is used to refer to an action or the result of an action: *The desk was covered with a large cloth.* In informal usage, no distinction is made, and in the latter example even *by* can be used.
cov·er·age (kúvvərij) *n.* **1.** The reporting and analysis of a news item. **2.** The extent of protection afforded by an insurance policy. **3.** The amount of funds reserved to meet liabilities. **4.** The way in which a subject is treated. **5.** The range achieved by a transmitter or communication medium.
cov·er·all (kúvvər-awl) *n. Usually plural.* A loose-fitting one-piece garment worn by workmen to protect their clothes.
~*adj.* Covering all instances or possibilities; comprehensive.
cover charge *n.* A fixed service charge added to a restaurant bill. Also called "cover", "couvert".
cover crop *n.* A temporary crop planted to protect the soil from erosion in winter and provide humus or nitrogen when ploughed under in the spring.
Cov·er·dale (kúvvər-dayl), **Miles** (1488–1568). English Protestant theologian and translator of the Bible (1535). Revised in 1538–39, this formed the Great Bible to be issued to every English church.
covered smut *n.* A disease of wheat, **stinking smut** *(see).*
covered wagon *n.* A large wagon covered with an arched canvas top, used by American pioneers for prairie travel.
cover girl *n.* An attractive female model whose picture appears on magazine covers.
cov·er·ing (kúvvəring) *n.* Something that covers for protection, concealment, or warmth.
covering board *n. Nautical.* A **plank-sheer** *(see).*
covering letter *n.* An explanatory letter enclosed with goods or other documents.
cov·er·let (kúvvər-lət, -lit) *n.* An ornamental cloth covering for a bed; a bedspread.
cover note *n.* A temporary document providing the holder with motor insurance until an official policy is issued.
cover point *n.* In cricket, a fielding position or fielder in the covers.
covers versed cosine.
co·ver·sine (kō-vér-sīn) *n. Trigonometry.* A **versed cosine** *(see).*
cover slip *n.* A small, usually square, thin piece of glass used to cover a specimen on a microscope slide.
cov·ert (kúvvərt || kō-vert, -vərt) *adj.* **1.** Concealed; hidden; secret. **2.** *Rare.* Covered or covered over; sheltered. See **feme covert.** —See Synonyms at **secret.**
~*n.* (*in senses 1–4 also* kúvvər) **1.** A covering or cover. **2.** A covered place or shelter; a hiding place. **3.** Thick undergrowth or woodland affording cover for game; cover. **4.** Covert cloth. **5.** *Zoology.* Any of the feathers covering the bases of the longer main feathers of a bird's wings or tail. [Middle English, from Old French, from the past participle of *covrir,* to COVER.] **—cov·ert·ly** *adv.* **—cov·ert·ness** *n.*
covert cloth (kúvvərt, kúvvər) *n.* A twilled cloth made of woollen or worsted yarn with cotton, silk, or rayon. It has a speckled appearance and is used for clothing. Also called "covert".
cov·er·ture (kúvvər-tewr, -choor || -chər) *n.* **1.** *Literary.* A covering; shelter; concealment; disguise. **2.** *Law.* The legal status of a married woman.
cover up *tr.v.* **1.** To put a cover over. **2.** To conceal or attempt to conceal (a crime, for example). —*intr.v.* To conceal or attempt to conceal a crime, scandal, or the like.
cov·er-up (kúvvər-up) *n.* An effort or strategy designed to conceal something, such as a crime or scandal, that could be harmful or embarrassing if known. **—cov·er-up** *adj.*
cov·et (kúvvit) *tr.v.* **-eted, -eting, -ets. 1.** To desire (that which is another's). **2.** To wish for excessively and culpably; crave. [Middle English *coveiten,* from Old French *coveitier,* from Vulgar Latin *cupiditāre* (unattested), to desire, from Latin *cupiditās,* desire, CUPIDITY.] **—cov·et·a·ble** *adj.* **—cov·et·er** *n.*
cov·et·ous (kúvvitəss) *adj.* **1.** Excessively desirous, especially of someone else's possessions; avaricious; greedy. **2.** Very desirous; eager for acquisition: *covetous of learning.* **—cov·et·ous·ly** *adv.* **—cov·et·ous·ness** *n.*
cov·ey (kúvvi) *n., pl.* **-eys. 1.** A family or small flock of partridges. **2.** A small group of people or things. [Middle English *covei(e),* from Old French *covee,* a brood, from *cover, couver,* to hatch, sit on (eggs), from Latin *cubāre,* to lie down (on).]
cov·in (kúvvin) *n. Law.* A secret arrangement to defraud or injure another person. [Middle English, from Old French *covin(e),* from Medieval Latin *convenium,* "a coming together", agreement, collusion, from Latin *convenīre,* to CONVENE.]
cov·ing (kōving) *n. Architecture.* **1.** A concave moulding, often ready-made, used to form a junction between a ceiling and a wall. **2.** A curved part of a wall where it joins a ceiling.
cow[1] (kow) *n., pl.* **cows** or *archaic* **kine** (kīn). **1.** The mature female of cattle of the genus *Bos.* **2.** The mature female of other animals,

such as whales, elephants, or moose. **3.** Broadly, any domesticated bovine. **4.** *Slang.* **a.** A fat or unpleasant woman. **b.** A woman. Used derogatorily. **5.** *Australian Slang.* An unpleasant or annoying thing, person, or situation. [Cow, kine; Middle English *cou, kin,* Old English *cū, cȳ(e).*]

cow² *tr.v.* **cowed, cowing, cows.** To frighten with threats or a show of force; intimidate. [Originally dialectal (as Scottish *kow*), perhaps ultimately from Old Norse *kūga,* to oppress.]

cow·ard (ków-ərd) *n.* One who lacks courage in the face of danger, pain, or an unpleasant situation; an ignobly frightened or timid person. [Middle English *couherde, coward,* from Old French *couard, coward,* perhaps "one with his tail between his legs", from *coue,* tail, from Latin *cauda,* tail.]

Cow·ard (może, jest) (ków-ərd), **Sir Noël (Pierce)** (1899–1973). British dramatist, composer, and entertainer. He began as an actor and won fame as a playwright, becoming especially noted for his witty and worldly comedies which include *Hay Fever* (1925) and *Private Lives* (1930).

cow·ard·ice (ków-ər-diss) *n.* Lack of courage in the face of danger, pain, difficulty, or opposition.

cow·ard·ly (ków-ərd-li) *adj.* **1.** Lacking courage; ignobly fearful. **2.** Showing cowardice; befitting a coward. ~*adv.* In the manner of a coward; basely; meanly. —**cow·ard·li·ness** *n.*

cow·bane (ków-bayn) *n.* **1.** A poisonous perennial plant, *Cicuta virosa,* bearing small white flowers in an umbel, found in and near water. **2.** A similar plant, *Oxypolis rigidior,* of the southeastern and central United States. **3.** Any other plant in the family Umbelliferae reputed to be poisonous to cattle.

cow·bell (ków-bel) *n.* A bell hung from a collar around a cow's neck to aid in locating her.

cow·ber·ry (ków-bri, -bəri, -berri) *n., pl.* **-ries. 1.** A creeping evergreen shrub, *Vaccinium vitis-idaea,* having pink or reddish flowers and edible, slightly acid red berries. **2.** A berry of this plant. Also called "red whortleberry".

cow·bird (ków-burd) *n.* Any of various American orioles of the genus *Molothrus* and related genera, that lay their eggs in the nests of other birds. [The birds feed on cattle vermin.]

cow·boy (ków-boy) *n.* **1. a.** A boy who tends cows. **b.** A hired man, especially in the western United States, who tends cattle, as on a ranch, and performs many of his duties on horseback. **2.** In the United States, a performer who demonstrates feats of horsemanship, as at a rodeo. **3.** A figure from the era of the Wild West, conventionally represented as fighting Indians. **4.** *British Informal.* **a.** Someone in a business or trade who provides shoddy, overpriced goods or services. Also used adjectivally: *cowboy firms.* **b.** A reckless, irresponsible person.

cow·catch·er (ków-kachər) *n.* An iron grille or frame that projects from the front of a locomotive and serves to clear the track of obstructions.

Cow·drey (ków-dri, -dray), **(Michael) Colin, Baron** (1932–). British cricketer. An outstanding batsman, he played for Kent and England (1950–76). He captained the English team 27 times; in Test cricket he scored 22 centuries and 7,624 runs.

cow·er (kowr, ków-ər) *intr.v.* **-ered, -ering, -ers.** To cringe or shrink away, as from cold or in fear. See Synonyms at **recoil.** [Middle English *couren,* from Middle Low German *kūren†,* lie in wait.]

Cowes (kowz). A town on the river Medina in the north of the Isle of Wight, off southern England. A yachting club was founded there in 1812 and the town stages an international regatta each August.

cow·fish (ków-fish) *n., pl.* **-fishes** or collectively **cowfish.** Any of various small whales, porpoises, or similar aquatic mammals; especially, a whale of the genus *Mesoplodon,* having a pointed snout.

cow·girl (ków-gurl) *n.* A female cowboy (senses 1, 2).

cow·hand (ków-hand) *n.* A cowboy (senses 1, 2).

cow·herd (ków-herd) *n.* A person who herds or tends cattle.

cow·hide (ków-hīd) *n.* **1. a.** The hide of a cow. **b.** The leather made from this hide. **2.** A strong, heavy, flexible whip, usually made of braided leather.

cowl (kowl) *n.* **1. a.** A hood worn by monks. **b.** The hooded robe of a monk or a similar garment. **c.** A loose collar that can be worn as a hood. **2.** A hood-shaped covering used to increase the draught of a chimney. **3.** A cowling. ~*tr.v.* **cowled, cowling, cowls.** To put a cowl on or cover with a cowl. [Middle English *coule,* Old English *cugele, cūle,* from Late Latin *cuculla,* from Latin *cucullus†,* hood.]

cowled (kowld) *adj.* **1.** Wearing or supplied with a cowl; hooded. **2.** Having the shape of a cowl.

cow·lick (ków-lik) *n.* A projecting tuft of hair on the head that will not lie flat. [It appears to have been licked by a cow.]

cowl·ing (ków-ling) *n.* A removable metal covering for the engine of an aircraft or motor vehicle. Also called "cowl".

cow·man (ków-mən) *n., pl.* **-men** (-mən, -men). **1.** *British.* A man who tends cows. **2.** The owner of a cattle ranch.

co·work·er (kō-wúrkər, -wurkər) *n.* A fellow worker.

cow parsley *n.* A common hedgerow plant, *Anthriscus sylvestris,* having small white flowers in an umbrella-shaped flower head.

cow parsnip *n.* A plant, the **hogweed** (*see*).

cow pat *n.* A mass of cow dung.

cow·pea (ków-pee) *n.* **1.** A tropical vine, *Vigna sinensis,* bearing long, hanging pods and grown in the southern United States for soil improvement and as animal feed. **2.** The edible, pealike seed of this plant. In this sense, also called "black-eyed pea".

Cow·per (koʊpər; *also* kówpər), **William** (1731–1800). British poet.

His works include *Table Talk* (1782), *John Gilpin* (1783), and *On the Loss of the Royal George* (published posthumously).

Cow·per's glands (koʊ-pərz, ków-) *pl.n.* A pair of small glands lying near the prostate gland that secrete mucus into the male urethra, thus contributing to the semen. [After William *Cowper* (1666–1709), English anatomist who discovered them.]

cow·poke (ków-pōk) *n. U.S. Informal.* A cowboy, as on a ranch.

cow·pox (ków-poks) *n.* A contagious viral disease of cattle characterised by vesicles on the skin, especially the udder. Inoculation of humans with cowpox virus confers temporary immunity to smallpox. Also called "vaccinia".

cow·punch·er (ków-punchər) *n. U.S. Informal.* A cowboy, as on a ranch.

cow·rie, cow·ry (ków-ri) *n., pl.* **-ries. 1.** Any of various tropical marine molluscs of the family Cypraeidae, having glossy, often brightly marked shells, some of which are used as money in the South Pacific and parts of Africa. **2.** The shell of any of these molluscs. [Hindi *kaurī,* from Sanskrit *kaparda,* from Dravidian; akin to Tamil *kōṭu,* shell.]

cow shark *n.* Any of several sharks of the family Hexanchidae, of warm and temperate seas.

cow·slip (ków-slip) *n.* An Old World primrose, *Primula veris,* having yellow flowers borne in a cluster. [Middle English *cowslyppe,* Old English *cūslyppe,* "cow dung" (probably because some varieties are found in cow pastures): *cū,* cow + *slyppe, slypa,* slime, paste.]

cox (koks) *n. Informal.* A coxswain. ~*v.* **coxed, coxing, coxes.** *Informal.* —*tr.* To serve as coxswain for (a boat). —*intr.* To act as coxswain. —**cox·less** *adj.*

cox·a (kók-sə) *n., pl.* **coxae** (-see). **1.** *Anatomy.* The hip or hip joint. **2.** *Zoology.* The first segment of the leg of an insect or other arthropod, adjoining and attached to the body. [Latin *coxa,* the hip.]

cox·al·gi·a (kok-sál-ji-ə, -jə) *n.* Pain in or disease of the hip. [New Latin: COXA(A) + -ALGIA.] —**cox·al·gic** *adj.*

cox·comb (kóks-kōm) *n.* **1.** A conceited dandy; a fop. **2.** A cap resembling a cock's comb, formerly worn by jesters. **3.** Variant of **cock's comb.** [Middle English *cokkes comb,* "cock's comb".]

cox·comb·ry (kóks-kōm-ri) *n., pl.* **-ries.** Arrogance and pretension in manner or behaviour; foolishness; foppery.

Cox·sack·ie virus (koʊk-saáki, kook-sácki) *n.* Any of a group of enteroviruses, some of which produce a disease resembling poliomyelitis without paralysis. [After *Coxsackie,* a town in New York state; the virus was first identified in a resident of the town.]

Cox's orange pippin (kóksiz) *n.* A variety of eating apple, having crisp flesh and a red-tinged green skin. Also called "Cox", "Cox's". [19th century: after R. *Cox,* Englishman who propagated it.]

cox·swain (kók-s'n, -swayn) *n.* A person who steers a boat or racing shell or has charge of its crew. Also informally called "cox". [Middle English *cok swain: cok,* COCKBOAT + *swain,* servant, SWAIN.]

coy (koy) *adj.* **coyer, coyest. 1.** Shy and demure; retiring. **2.** Pretending shyness or modesty; coquettishly shy. **3.** Annoyingly unwilling to commit oneself; affectedly reticent. —See Synonyms at **shy.** [Middle English, from Old French *coi,* shy, quiet, from Vulgar Latin *quētus* (unattested), variant of Latin *quiētus,* QUIET.] —**coy·ly** *adv.* —**coy·ness** *n.*

coy·o·te (kī-ṓti, koy-, kī-ṓt, kóy-) *n.* A wolflike carnivorous animal, *Canis latrans,* common in desert and prairie regions of western North America. Also called "prairie wolf". [Mexican Spanish, from Nahuatl *coyotl.*]

coy·pu (kóy-poo, -pew) *n., pl.* **-pus. 1.** A large, beaverlike South American rodent, *Myocaster coypu,* valued for its fur. **2.** The fur of this animal. Also called "nutria". [American Spanish *coipú,* from Araucanian *kóypu.*]

coz (kuz) *n. Archaic Informal.* Cousin.

coz·en (kúzz'n) *v.* **-ened, -ening, -ens.** —*tr.* To deceive, by means of a petty trick or fraud. —*intr.* To act with intent to deceive. [16th century cant: perhaps akin to COUSIN.] —**coz·en·er** *n.*

coz·en·age (kúzz'n-ij) *n.* **1.** The art or practice of cozening; cheating. **2.** A deception; a fraud.

cozy. *U.S.* Variant of **cosy.**

cp. compare.

c.p. 1. candle power. **2.** chemically pure.

C.P. 1. Cape Province. **2.** command post. **3.** also **CP** Communist Party. **4.** Country party (in Australia). **5.** Court of Probate.

C-parity *n. Physics.* A quantum conserved in strong and electromagnetic interactions by elementary particles that have zero charge, strangeness, and baryon number. Also called "charge conjugation parity". [charge conjugation *parity.*]

cpd. compound.

Cpl. corporal.

C.P.O. chief petty officer.

cps cycles per second.

CPU central processing unit.

CQ code letters used at the beginning of radio messages intended for all receivers: Call to Quarters.

Cr The symbol for the element chromium.

cr. credits.

craal. Variant of **kraal.**

crab¹ (krab) *n.* **1. a.** Any of various predominantly marine crustaceans of the section Brachyura within the order Decapoda, characterised by a broad, flattened cephalothorax covered by a hard shell with the small abdomen concealed beneath it, and five pairs of legs, of which the front pair are large and pincer-like. **b.** The flesh of any edible variety of crab. **2.** Any of various similar related crustaceans,

such as the **hermit crab** *(see).* **3.** See **horseshoe crab.** **4. a.** The crab louse. **b.** *Plural. Informal.* Infestation by crab lice. **5.** *Capital* **C.** The constellation and sign of the zodiac, **Cancer** *(see).* **6.** The manoeuvring of an aircraft partially into a crosswind in order to compensate for drift. **7.** Any of various machines for handling or hoisting heavy weights. **8.** *Plural. Informal.* The lowest throw, usually a two or three, of a pair of dice. **—catch a crab.** In rowing, to strike the water with an oar in recovering a stroke or to miss it in making one.
~*v.* **crabbed, crabbing, crabs.** *—intr.* **1.** To hunt or catch crabs. **2.** *Nautical.* To drift diagonally or sideways. **3.** To move sideways. *—tr. Aviation.* To direct (an aircraft) partly into a crosswind to eliminate drift. [Middle English *crab(be),* Old English *crabba,* from Germanic.]

crab[2] (krab) *n.* **1.** The crab apple or its fruit. **2.** A quarrelsome, ill-tempered person.
~*v.* **crabbed** (krabd), **crabbing, crabs.** *Informal.* *—intr.* To criticise; find fault. *—tr.* **1.** To interfere with and ruin. **2.** To find fault with. [16th century : originally, (of hawks) to claw, fight, from Middle Low German *krabben;* akin to CRAB (crustacean).]

crab apple *n.* **1.** Any of several trees of the genus *Malus,* especially *M. sylvestris,* having white, pink, or red flowers and small, sour apple-like fruit. **2.** The tart fruit of any of these trees, used for making jelly. [Middle English, perhaps alteration (through influence of CRAB) of earlier *scrab,* probably from Scandinavian.]

Crabbe (krab), **George** (1754–1832). British poet. His first major poem was *The Village* (1783), in which he portrayed the ugliness of rural life, a theme taken up in subsequent works including *The Parish Register* (1807) and *The Borough* (1810).

crab·bed (krábbid) *adj.* **1.** Irritable and perverse in disposition; ill-tempered. **2.** Difficult to understand; complicated. Said of a writer or his style. **3.** Difficult to read. Said of handwriting. [Middle English, partly from *crabbe,* CRAB, referring to the perversity of its gait, and partly from *crabbe,* CRAB (apple), referring to its sourness.] **—crab·bed·ly** *adv.* **—crab·bed·ness** *n.*

crab·ber (krábbər) *n.* **1.** A person whose occupation is fishing for crabs. **2.** The boat used in fishing for crabs.

crab·by (krábbi) *adj.* **-bier, -biest.** Irritable; bad-tempered.

crab·grass (kráb-graass || -grass) *n.* Any of various coarse grasses of the genus *Digitaria,* that tend to spread and displace other grasses in lawns.

crab louse *n.* A body louse, *Phthirus pubis,* that generally infests the pubic region and causes severe itching. Also called "crab".

Crab Nebula *n.* An expanding nebula of dust and gas about 5,000 light-years away in the constellation Taurus. It contains a pulsar and is the remnant of a supernova recorded in 1504. [So called from its shape.]

crab·stick (kráb-stik) *n.* **1.** A stick made of crab-apple wood. **2.** A bad-tempered person.

crabwise (kráb-wīz) *adv.* Sideways; in a manner like a crab.

crack (krak) *v.* **cracked, cracking, cracks.** *—intr.* **1.** To break with a sharp, snapping sound. **2.** To make such a sound; snap. **3.** To break without dividing into parts; split slightly. **4.** To change sharply in pitch or timbre, as from hoarseness or emotion. Used of the voice. **5. a.** To break down; fail; give out. **b.** To give in to pressure. **6.** *Chemistry.* To decompose into simpler compounds. Used especially of large-molecule hydrocarbons from petroleum, which are broken by heat or catalysis to smaller molecules suitable for use as fuel. **7.** *Regional.* To gossip; talk. *—tr.* **1.** To cause to make a sharp, snapping sound; snap: *crack the whip.* **2.** To cause to break or split slightly or completely. **3.** To break with a sharp, snapping sound: *crack an egg.* **4.** To strike with a sudden, sharp sound. **5.** To break open or into. **6.** To discover the solution to, especially after considerable effort: *crack a problem.* **7.** To cause (the voice) to crack. **8.** *Informal.* To tell (a joke). **9.** To impair or diminish (a reputation, for example). **10.** *Chemistry.* To reduce (petroleum, for example) to simpler compounds by cracking. **11.** *Informal.* To open and drink (a bottle of wine, can of lager, or the like). **12.** *Informal.* To deal with successfully. Often used in such phrases as *crack it.* —See Synonyms at **break.** **—cracked up to be.** *Informal.* Praised or lauded as; believed to be.
~*n.* **1.** A sharp, snapping sound, such as the report of a firearm. **2.** A partial split or break; a flaw; a fissure. **3.** A slight, narrow space: *The window was open a crack.* **4.** A sharp, resounding blow. **5.** A mental or physical impairment; a defect. **6.** A cracking vocal tone or sound, as in hoarseness. **7.** *Informal.* An attempt; a chance: *gave him a crack at the job.* **8.** *Informal.* **a.** A flippant or sarcastic remark. **b.** A humorous remark; a joke. **9.** A moment; an instant: *at the crack of dawn.* **10.** *Regional.* Gossiping talk; chat. **11.** *Informal.* One that is good at doing something: *That horse is a crack over that distance.* **12.** *Slang.* A mixture containing cocaine: *"The mixture of cocaine with baking powder known as 'crack'"* (Auberon Waugh). **—a fair crack of the whip.** A fair chance; a reasonable opportunity. —See Synonyms at **joke.**
~*adj.* Excelling in skill or achievement; superior; first-rate: *a crack marksman.* [Middle English *craken,* Old English *cracian,* to resound, from Germanic.]

crack·brain (krák-brayn) *n.* A foolish or insane person. **—crack·brained** *adj.*

crack down *intr.v.* To become more demanding, severe, or strict. Often used with *on: crack down on student absences.*

crack·down (krák-down) *n.* Sudden punitive action.

cracked (krakt) *adj.* **1.** Having a crack or cracks. **2.** *Informal.* Crazy; foolish.

cracked wheat *n.* A cereal, **bulgur** *(see).*

crack·er (kráckər) *n.* **1.** A thin, crisp wafer or biscuit, usually made of unleavened, unsweetened dough. **2.** A firecracker. **3.** A small cardboard cylinder covered with decorative paper and containing a joke, a small toy, or the like and a weak explosive that makes a sharp popping noise when a paper strip is pulled at one or both ends and torn. **4.** *Chemistry.* A piece of apparatus in an oil refinery for cracking petroleum. **5.** *British Slang.* **1.** An exceptionally good-looking person, especially a woman. **2.** Something very good: *A cracker of a goal.*

crack·er-bar·rel (kráckər-barrəl) *adj. U.S.* Resembling or characteristic of the extended informal discussions carried on by persons habitually assembled at a general store; homespun and unsophisticated: *cracker-barrel theories.* [Cracker barrels were common fixtures in country stores.]

crack·er·jack (kráckər-jak) *adj. Slang.* Of fine quality or ability. ~*n. Slang.* Someone or something with excellent skills or abilities. [From CRACK (proficient) + JACK (man).]

crack·ers (kráckərz) *adj. Chiefly British Slang.* Insane.

crack·ing (krácking) *n. Chemistry.* Thermal decomposition, sometimes with catalysis, of a complex substance; especially, such decomposition of petroleum to extract low-boiling fractions.
~*adj. Informal.* Very good: *had a cracking time.* **—crack·ing** *adv.* **—get cracking.** *Informal.* To set about something promptly.

crack·le (krák'l) *v.* **-led, -ling, -les.** *—intr.* To make a succession of slight sharp, snapping noises, as a small fire may. *—tr.* **1.** To crush (paper, for example) with such sounds. **2.** To cause (china, for example) to become covered with a network of fine cracks.
~*n.* **1.** The act or sound of crackling. **2.** A network of fine cracks on the surface of glazed pottery, china, or glassware. **3.** Ware bearing this network of cracks. Also called "crackleware". [Frequentative of CRACK.]

crack·ling (kráckling) *n.* **1.** A succession of slight sharp, snapping noises. **2.** The crisp browned rind of roasted pork. **3.** *Plural.* The crisp bits that remain of pork fat after rendering.

crack·ly (krákli) *adj.* Likely to crackle; crisp.

crack·nel (krák-n'l) *n.* **1.** A hard, crisp biscuit. **2.** *Plural. U.S.* Crisp bits of fried pork fat. [Middle English *crak(e)nel,* probably from Old French *craquelin,* from Middle Dutch *krākelinc,* from *krāken,* to crack.]

crack·pot (krák-pot) *n. Informal.* An eccentric person, especially one espousing bizarre ideas. **—crack·pot** *adj.*

crack up *intr.v. Informal.* **1.** To have a mental or physical breakdown. **2.** To laugh boisterously. **3.** *Chiefly U.S.* To crash; collide.

crack-up (krák-up) *n. Informal.* **1.** A mental or physical breakdown. **2.** *Chiefly U.S.* A collision.

Cracow. See **Krakow.**

-cracy *n. comb. form.* Indicates government or rule; for example, **aristocracy, mobocracy.** [Old French *-cratie,* from Late Latin *-cratia,* from Greek *-kratia,* from *kratos,* strength, power.]

cra·dle (kráyd'l) *n.* **1.** A small, low bed for an infant, often furnished with rockers. **2. a.** A place of origin; a birthplace. **b.** Infancy; the earliest phase of one's life. Preceded by *the.* **3.** A framework of wood or metal used to support something, such as a ship undergoing construction or repair. **4.** A framework used to protect an injured limb. **5.** The part of a telephone upon which the handset rests. **6. a.** A frame projecting above a scythe, used to catch grain as it is cut so that it can be laid flat. **b.** A scythe equipped with such a frame. **7.** A low, flat framework that rolls on castors, for use by a mechanic working beneath a motor vehicle. Also called "creeper". **8.** A movable platform suspended by cables down the side of a building or ship, used by painters, window-cleaners, and the like. **9.** A boxlike device fitted with rockers, used for washing gem or gold-bearing dirt. **10.** A metal frame inserted under bedclothes to keep them from touching an injured part of the body.
~*v.* **cradled, -dling, -dles.** *—tr.* **1.** To place into, rock, or hold in or as if in a cradle. **2.** To care for or nurture in infancy. **3.** To reap (grain) with a cradle. **4.** To place or support (a ship) in a cradle. **5.** In lacrosse, to rock (the ball) in the net of the stick while running in order to retain possession. **6.** *Mining.* To wash (gem- or gold-bearing dirt) in a cradle. *—intr. Rare.* **1.** To lie in or as if in a cradle. **2.** To reap grain with a cradle. [Middle English *cradel;* probably akin to Old High German *kratto,* basket.] **—cra·dler** *n.*

cradle cap *n.* Crusting of the scalp occurring in young babies. It is a type of seborrhoea.

cra·dle-snatch (kráyd'l-snach) *v.* **-snatched, -snatching, -snatches.** *—tr.* To take (a much younger person) as a lover or spouse. *—intr.* To practise cradlesnatching. **—cra·dle·snatch·er** *n.*

cra·dle·song (kráyd'l-song || *U.S. also* -sawng) *n.* A lullaby.

craft (kraaft || kraft) *n., pl.* **crafts** or **craft** (for sense 5). **1.** Skill or ability in something, especially in handiwork or the arts; proficiency; expertness. **2.** Skill in evasion or deception; cunning; guile. **3.** An occupation, art, or trade, especially one requiring manual dexterity. **4.** The membership of such an occupation or trade; a guild. **5.** A boat, ship, aircraft, or spacecraft.
~*tr.v.* **crafted, crafting, crafts.** **1.** To make by hand. **2.** To make, produce, or create with painstaking skill and attention to detail. [Middle English *craft,* strength, skill, device, Old English *cræft,* from West Germanic *kraftaz, krab-taz* (both unattested), strength.]

-craft *n. comb. form.* Indicates work, art, or practice of; for example, **woodcraft, stagecraft.** [From CRAFT.]

crafts·man (kraáfts-mən || kráfts-) *n., pl.* **-men** (-mən). **1.** A skilled worker who practises a craft by occupation. **2.** An artist considered with regard to technical skill. **—crafts·man·ly** *adj.* **—crafts·man· ship** *n.* **—crafts·wom·an** *n.*

craft union *n.* A trade union limited in membership to workers engaged in the same type of work. Compare **industrial union.**

craft·y (kráːfti ‖ kráfti) *adj.* **-ier, -iest. 1.** Skilled in underhandedness and deception; shrewd; cunning. **2.** *Archaic.* Skilful; ingenious; dexterous. —See Synonyms at **sly. —craft·i·ly** *adv.* **—craft·i·ness** *n.*

crag¹ (krag) *n.* A steeply projecting mass of rock forming part of a rugged cliff or headland. [Middle English, from Celtic *kar-n-, krag-* (both unattested). See **cairn.**]

crag² *n. Geology.* **1.** A shelly deposit of sandstone, found especially in East Anglia. **2.** Strata containing this deposit. [18th century : perhaps specialised use of CRAG¹.]

crag·gy (krági) *adj.* **-gier, -giest.** Also **crag·ged** (krággid). **1.** Having crags; steep and rugged. **2.** Uneven; rugged: *craggy features.* **—crag·gi·ly** *adv.* **—crag·gi·ness** *n.*

crake (krayk) *n.* Any of several birds of the family Rallidae, such as the corncrake, or a marsh bird of the genus *Porzana.* [Middle English *crak, crake,* crow, raven, from Old Norse *krāka* (imitative).]

cram (kram) *v.* **crammed, cramming, crams.** —*tr.* **1.** To force, press, or squeeze into an insufficient space; stuff. **2.** To fill too tightly. **3.** To gorge with food. **4.** *Informal.* To prepare (a person) hastily or revise and study (a subject) intensively for an examination. —*intr.* **1.** To gorge oneself with food. **2.** *Informal.* To make a concentrated last-minute revision of a given academic subject, as in studying for an examination. ~*n.* **1.** The act of, or condition resulting from, cramming. **2.** *Informal.* The knowledge acquired by cramming. [Middle English *crammen,* Old English *crammian* from Germanic.]

Cram (kram), **Stephen** (1960-). British middle-distance runner. He set three world records in 19 days in 1985, when already World champion at 1 500 metres.

cram·bo (krámbō) *n., pl.* **-boes. 1.** A word game in which a player or team must find and express a rhyme for a word or line presented by the opposing player or team. **2.** Doggerel. [Obsolete *crambe,* "stale cabbage", tedious repetition, from Latin *crambē (repetīta),* "cabbage (served up again)" (expression used by Juvenal), from Greek *krambē.*]

cram-full (krám-fóol) *adj.* Filled to the maximum; stuffed.

cram·mer (krámmər) *n.* A person or establishment that crams students in preparation for an examination.

cramp¹ (kramp) *n.* **1.** A sudden involuntary muscular contraction causing severe pain, often occurring in the calf or foot as the result of overexertion, chill, or salt loss. **2.** A temporary partial paralysis of habitually or excessively used muscles: *writer's cramp.* **3.** Sharp, persistent pains in the abdomen. Also *U.S.* "cramps". ~*tr.v.* **cramped, cramping, cramps.** To affect or cause to be affected with or as if with a cramp. [Middle English *crampe,* from Old French, probably from Old High German *krampho.*]

cramp² *n.* **1.** A bar, usually of steel, with right-angle bends at both ends, used for permanently holding together stones, timber, and other building materials. Also called "cramp iron". **2.** A frame with an adjustable part to hold pieces together; a clamp. **3.** Anything that compresses or restrains. **4.** A confined position or part. ~*tr.v.* **cramped, cramping, cramps. 1.** To hold together with a cramp. **2.** To confine; restrict; hamper. [Middle English, from Middle Dutch *crampe,* hook, from Germanic; akin to CRAMP¹.]

cramped (krampt) *adj.* **1.** Restricted; contracted; narrowed. **2.** Difficult to read or decipher: *cramped handwriting.*

cram·pon (krám-pən, -pon) *n.* **1.** Either of a hinged pair of curved metal bars for raising heavy objects, such as stones or timber. **2.** An iron spike or spiked frame attached to the sole of a boot to prevent slipping when climbing or walking on ice. [Old French *crampon,* perhaps from Frankish *kramp* (unattested); akin to CRAMP².]

cran (kran) *n.* A unit of measure for fresh herring, equal to 37.5 gallons in volume. [18th century : from Gaelic *crann*†.]

Cra·nach (kráːa-nakh), **Lucas** also known as Cranach the Elder, (1472–1553). German painter and engraver. His works include a famous *Adam and Eve* (1526), as well as portraits of Elector John Frederick, Martin Luther, and others. His work was carried on by his son, Lucas Cranach the Younger (1515–86).

cran·age (kráynij) *n.* **1.** The hire, loan, or use of a crane. **2.** The amount of money charged or paid for such use.

cran·ber·ry (krán-bri, -bəri ‖ -berri) *n., pl.* **-ries. 1.** A creeping evergreen shrub, *Vaccinium oxycoccus,* with pink flowers and edible red berries. **2.** Any of certain other shrubs of the genus *Vaccinium.* **3.** The berry of any of these plants, often made into a sauce or jelly. [Partial translation of (American colonial) Low German *kraanbere,* "crane-berry" (from the stamens which resemble a beak).]

crane (krayn) *n.* **1.** Any of various large wading birds of the family Gruidae, having a long neck, long legs, and a long bill. **2.** Loosely, a similar bird, such as a heron. **3.** A machine for hoisting and moving heavy objects by means of cables attached to a movable boom. **4.** A movable arm on which a film or television camera is mounted. ~*v.* **craned, craning, cranes.** —*tr.* **1.** To hoist or move with or as if with a crane. **2.** To strain and stretch (the neck). —*intr.* **1.** To stretch one's neck for a better view. **2. a.** To baulk and lean forward, as a horse does before jumping. **b.** To hesitate. [Middle English *crane,* Old English *cran,* from Germanic; akin to Latin *grus.*]

Crane (krayn), **(Harold) Hart,** (1899–1932). U.S. poet.

His mature work is characterised by a passionate spiritual affirmation of America's democratic potential.

Crane, Stephen (1871–1900). U.S. novelist. He won fame with *The Red Badge of Courage* (1895), set in the American Civil War.

crane fly *n.* Any of various flies of the family Tipulidae, having a slender body, long delicate wings, and long legs. Also *chiefly British* "daddy longlegs".

cranes·bill (kráynz-bil) *n.* Any of various plants of the genus *Geranium* with fruits ending in a long, straight, pointed beak. See **wild geranium.**

cra·ni·al (kráyni-əl) *adj.* Of or pertaining to the skull. [From CRANIUM.]

cranial index *n.* The ratio of the maximum width to the maximum length of the cranium, multiplied by 100. Compare **cephalic index.**

cranial nerve *n.* Any of several nerves that arise in pairs from the brainstem and reach the periphery through openings in the skull.

cra·ni·ate (kráyni-ət, -it, -ayt) *adj.* Having a skull. ~*n.* Any animal having a skull; a vertebrate. [CRANI(O)- + -ATE.]

cranio-, crani- *comb. form.* Indicates cranium or cranial; for example, **craniology, craniate.** [From CRANIUM.]

cra·ni·ol·o·gy (kráyni-óllə ji) *n.* The scientific study of the characteristics of the skull, such as size and shape, especially in humans. [CRANIO- + -LOGY.] **—cra·ni·o·log·i·cal** (-ə-lójik'l) *adj.* **—cra·ni·o· log·i·cal·ly** *adv.* **—cra·ni·ol·o·gist** (-óllə jist) *n.*

cra·ni·om·e·ter (kráyni-ómmitər) *n.* An instrument for measuring skulls. [CRANIO- + -METER.] **—cra·ni·o·met·ric** (-ə-méttrik), **cra·ni· o·met·ri·cal** *adj.* **—cra·ni·om·e·try** (-ómmətri) *n.*

cra·ni·ot·o·my (kráyni-óttəmi) *n., pl.* **-mies.** *Surgery.* **1.** The cutting or removal of part of the skull to relieve pressure or to expose the brain for examination. **2.** The cutting or breaking of the skull of a dead foetus to reduce its size for removal when normal delivery is not possible. [CRANIO- + -TOMY.]

cra·ni·um (kráyni-əm) *n., pl.* **-ums** or **-nia** (-ə). **1.** The skull of a vertebrate. **2.** The portion of the skull enclosing the brain comprising eight bones connected by immovable joints. [Medieval Latin *crānium,* from Greek *kranion.*]

crank¹ (krangk) *n.* **1.** A device for transmitting rotary motion, consisting of a handle or arm attached at right angles to a shaft. **2.** An angled steel bar used as a crank to start car engines. Also called "starting handle". ~*v.* **cranked, cranking, cranks.** —*tr.* **1.** To start or operate (an engine, for example) by turning a crank. **2.** To make into the shape of a crank; twist; bend. **3.** To provide with a crank. —*intr.* **1.** To turn a crank. **2.** *Obsolete.* To twist; wind. [Middle English *crank,* Old English *cranc* (only in *crancstæf,* a weaving instrument), perhaps from *crincan,* to curl, twist, variant of *cringan,* to fall in a battle.]

crank² *n.* **1.** An eccentric person, especially one with obsessive behaviour or opinions. **2.** *Rare.* A turn of speech; a verbal conceit. **3.** *Rare.* A peculiar or eccentric idea or action. **4.** *U.S. Informal.* A bad-tempered person. [Back-formation from CRANKY (eccentric).]

crank³ *adj. Nautical.* Liable to capsize; unstable. [Short for earlier *crank-sided*†, lopsided.]

crank·case (krángk-kayss) *n.* The metal case enclosing the crankshaft and associated parts in a reciprocating engine.

Cran·ko (kráng-kō), **John** (1927–73). British choreographer, born in South Africa. From 1946 he worked in London, producing his first full-length work, *The Prince of the Pagodas* (1956), at Covent Garden. He later won fame with the Stuttgart Ballet.

crank·pin (krángk-pin) *n.* A bar or cylinder in the arm of a crank to which a reciprocating member or connecting rod is attached.

crank·shaft (krángk-shaaft ‖ -shaft) *n.* A shaft that turns or is turned by a crank.

crank·y¹ (krángki) *adj.* **-ier, -iest. 1.** *Informal.* Odd; ecentric. **2.** *Informal.* Ill-tempered; peevish. **3.** Full of bends and turns; crooked. **4.** Unreliable; mechanically faulty. [Perhaps from obsolete cant *crank,* a rogue pretending sickness; akin to Dutch *krank,* ill, weak.] **—crank·i·ly** *adv.* **—crank·i·ness** *n.*

crank·y² (krángki) *adj.* **-ier, -iest. 1.** *Nautical.* Liable to capsize. **2.** Rickety; loose; shaky.

Cran·mer (krán-mər), **Thomas** (1489–1556). English churchman, Archbishop of Canterbury (1533–53). A leading Reformer, he worked on the English Prayer Books (1549 and 1552). He was burned at the stake during the Catholic reaction under Mary I.

cran·nog (kránnəg) *n.* Also **cran·noge** (kránnəj). A lake or bog dwelling, often fortified, used in Scotland and Ireland from ancient times up to the late Middle Ages. [Irish, from Old Irish *crann,* beam, timber, tree.]

cran·ny (kránni) *n., pl.* **-nies.** A small opening, as in a wall or rock face; a crevice; a fissure. [Middle English *crani,* from Old French *cran, cren,* notch, perhaps from Late Latin *crēna.*] **—cran·nied** *adj.*

Cran·well (krán-wəl, -wel). A village in Lincolnshire, east England. The Royal Air Force College was founded there in 1919.

crap (krap) *n.* **1.** *Vulgar.* Faeces. **2.** *Vulgar Slang.* Foolish or dishonest speech or writing; nonsense; rubbish. ~*intr.v.* **crapped, crapping, craps.** *Vulgar.* To defecate. [15th century: "chaff", from Dutch *krappe,* probably from *krappen,* to break off.]

crape myrtle (krayp) *n.* An Oriental shrub, *Lagerstroemia indica,* widely cultivated in warm climates for its showy flowers.

crap·pie (kráppi) *n., pl.* **-pies.** Either of two edible North American freshwater fishes, *Pomoxis nigromaculatus,* (the black crappie), or *P.*

annularis, (the white crappie), related to the sunfishes. [Canadian French *crapet†*.]

craps (kraps) *n. Usually used with a singular verb.* A U.S. gambling game played with two dice in which a first throw of 7 or 11 wins, a first throw of 2, 3, or 12 loses the bet, and a first throw of any other number (a point) must be repeated to win before a 7 is thrown, which loses both the bet and the dice. [Louisiana French, from French *crabs, craps,* from obsolete English slang *crabs,* the lowest throw at hazard, plural of CRAB.]

crap·shoot·er (kráp-shōōtər) *n. U.S.* One who plays craps.

crap·u·lent (kráppew-lənt) *adj.* Also **crap·u·lous** (-ləss). **1.** Overindulgent; intemperate. **2.** Ill as a result of overeating or excessive drinking. **3.** Drunk. [Late Latin *crāpulentus,* drunk, from Latin *crāpula,* intoxication, from Greek *kraipalē,* intoxication, hangover.] —**crap·u·lence, crap·u·lous·ness** *n.* —**crap·u·lent·ly** *adv.*

cra·que·lure (krácka-loor, -lewr) *n.* A pattern of tiny cracks on an old or deteriorated painting or its varnish. [French, from *craqueler,* to crackle, from *craquer,* to crack (imitative).]

crash¹ (krash) *v.* **crashed, crashing, crashes.** —*intr.* **1.** To fall or break noisily; smash. **2. a.** To collide. **b.** To undergo sudden damage or destruction on impact. **3.** To make a sudden loud noise. **4.** To move noisily or so as to cause damage. **5.** To fail suddenly, as a business or an economy might. **6.** *Computing.* To break down as a result of a malfunction of hardware or software. Used of computers and storage disks. **7.** *Slang.* To lodge temporarily; stay over: *Can I crash at your place tonight?* —*tr.* **1.** To cause to crash. **2.** To dash to pieces; smash. **3.** *Informal.* To join or enter without invitation; gate-crash. —**crash out.** *Slang.* To fall asleep; collapse with tiredness.

~*n.* **1.** A sudden loud noise, as of something breaking. **2.** A sudden accidental wrecking, smashing, or collision, especially of a car, train, or aircraft. **3.** A sudden business failure. **4.** *Computing.* An instance of crashing.

~*adj.* **1.** *Informal.* Of or characterised by an intensive effort to produce or accomplish something: *a crash programme.* **2.** Abrupt or violent: *a crash tackle.* [Middle English *crashen* (imitative).] —**crash·er** *n.*

crash² *n.* **1.** A coarse, light, unevenly woven fabric of cotton or linen, used for towels and curtains. **2.** Starched reinforced fabric used to strengthen a book binding or the spine of a bound book. [Russian *krashenina,* a kind of coloured linen, from *krashenie,* colouring, from *krasit',* to colour, from *krasa,* beauty.]

crash barrier *n.* A barrier set up between traffic lanes, around racetracks, and the like, to limit the damage in the event of an accident.

crash cymbal *n.* A cymbal that produces an especially loud crashing sound when struck.

crash dive *n.* **1.** A rapid submerging of a submarine, especially in an emergency. **2.** A steep, uncontrolled fall to earth by an aircraft. —**crash-dive** *v.*

crash helmet *n.* A padded helmet, as worn by motorcyclists and pilots, to protect the head.

crash·ing (kráshing) *adj. Informal.* Complete; utter; absolute: *a crashing bore.*

crash-land (krásh-lánd, -land) *v.* **-landed, -landing, -lands.** —*tr.* To land (an aircraft) in emergency conditions so as to minimise damage. —*intr.* To crash-land an aircraft. —**crash landing** *n.*

crash pad *n.* **1.** A padded area inside cars or other vehicles for protecting occupants in the event of an accident, sudden stop, or the like. **2.** *Slang.* A temporary lodging.

crash truck *n.* A truck specially designed and equipped to rescue victims of an aeroplane crash. Also called "crash wagon".

cra·sis (kráy-siss) *n., pl.* **-ses** (-seez). Vowel contraction at the beginning and end of two adjacent words. [New Latin, from Greek *krasis,* "a mixture".]

crass (krass) *adj.* **crasser, crassest. 1.** Grossly ignorant; unfeeling; stupid. **2.** *Rare.* Thick; coarse. —See Synonyms at **coarse, stupid.** [Latin *crassus†,* fat, gross, dense.] —**crass·ly** *adv.* —**crass·ness** *n.*

-crat *n. comb. form.* Indicates a participant in or supporter of a class or form of government; for example, **democrat, technocrat.** [French *-crate* from Greek *-kratēs,* from *-kratia,* -CRACY.] —**-cratic** *adj. comb. form.*

cratch (krach) *n.* A frame for holding fodder, used for feeding farm animals out of doors. [Middle English, from Old French *creche,* crib, CRÈCHE.]

crate (krayt) *n.* **1.** A container for storing or transporting objects, usually consisting of a slatted wooden case or box or a wicker basket. **2.** *Slang.* An old, rickety vehicle, especially a car or aircraft. ~*tr.v.* **crated, crating, crates. 1.** To pack into a crate. Often used with *up.* **2.** To transport (goods) in a crate. [Latin *crātis,* wickerwork, hurdle.] —**crat·er** *n.*

cra·ter (kráytər) *n.* **1.** A bowl-shaped depression at the mouth of a volcano or geyser. **2.** Any of numerous round, bowl-shaped depressions with raised rims covering the surface of the moon and various planets. **3.** Any bowl-shaped pit, especially when formed by an exploded projectile or by the impact of a meteor. **4.** A wide, two-handled bowl used in ancient Greece and Rome for mixing wine and water. ~*tr.v.* **cratered, -tering, -ters.** To cause craters to form on (the moon or a planet, for example). [Latin *crātēr,* bowl, crater, from Greek *kratēr,* mixing vessel.]

Cra·ter (kráytər) *n.* A constellation in the Southern Hemisphere near Hydra and Corvus.

cra·ton, kra·ton (kráy-ton, kra-, -tən) *n.* A large part of the Earth's crust which has not been significantly deformed for many millions of years. Also called "shield".

cra·vat (krə-vát) *n.* **1.** A small, light scarf, often of silk, worn round the neck and knotted at the front, usually by men. **2.** *U.S.* A necktie. [French *cravate,* originally a neckband worn by Croatian mercenaries in the service of France, from *Cravate,* a Croatian, from Flemish *Krawaat,* from Serbo-Croatian *Hrvat,* a CROAT.]

crave (krayv) *v.* **craved, craving, craves.** —*tr.* **1.** To have an intense desire for. **2.** To need urgently; require. **3.** To beg earnestly for; implore. —*intr.* To have an eager or intense desire. Used with *for* and *after.* —See Synonyms at **beg.** [Middle English *craven,* Old English *crafian,* to beg, demand, from West Germanic *krabjan* (unattested), to demand, from the stem of *krab-taz* (unattested); strength.] —**crav·er** *n.* —**crav·ing·ly** *adv.*

cra·ven (kráyv'n) *adj.* Characterised by abject fear; cowardly. ~*n.* A coward. [Middle English *cravant,* perhaps from Old French *crevant,* dying, from *crever,* to burst, die, from Latin *crepāre,* to crack, burst.] —**cra·ven·ly** *adv.* —**cra·ven·ness** *n.*

crav·ing (kráyving) *n.* A consuming desire; a longing; a yearning.

craw (kraw) *n.* **1.** The crop of a bird. **2.** The stomach of an animal. —**stick in** (one's) **craw.** To be unacceptable or offensive. [Middle English *crawe,* Old English *craga* (unattested). from Germanic.]

Craw·ford (kráwfərd), **Joan,** born Lucille Le Sueur (1906–77). U.S. film actress. She portrayed tough ambitious women in films like *The Women* (1939) and *Mildred Pierce* (1945; Oscar).

crawl¹ (krawl) *intr.v.* **crawled, crawling, crawls. 1.** To move slowly on the hands and knees or by dragging the body along the ground; creep. **2.** To advance slowly, feebly, or laboriously: *Time crawls.* **3.** To proceed or act servilely. **4.** To be or feel as if covered with crawling things: *Her flesh crawled in horror; the place was crawling with journalists.* **5.** To swim the crawl. ~*n.* **1.** The action of crawling. **2.** A rapid swimming stroke consisting of alternating overarm strokes and a flutter kick. See **Australian crawl.** [Middle English *craulen,* from Old Norse *krafla,* to crawl, creep.] —**crawl·ing·ly** *adv.*

crawl² *n.* A pen in shallow water, as for confining fish or turtles. [Dutch *kraal,* KRAAL.]

crawl·er (kráwlər) *n.* **1.** One that crawls, especially an insect. **2.** *Slang.* A toady; a fawning flatterer. —See Synonyms at **sycophant. 3.** A tractor with caterpillar tracks instead of wheels. **4.** *Plural.* A one-piece garment worn by a baby.

crawl·y (kráwli) *adj.* **-ier, -iest.** *Informal.* **1.** Feeling as if insects are crawling over one's skin. **2.** Producing a crawly feeling.

Crax·i (krák-si), **Bettino** (1934-). Italian politician. General Secretary of the PSI (Italian Socialist Party) since 1976, Craxi became Prime Minister in 1983. He lost office in 1987, having held it continuously for four years: longer than any other Italian Prime Minister since World War II.

cray·fish (kráy-fish) *n., pl.* **-fishes** or collectively **crayfish.** Also chiefly *U.S.* **craw·fish** (kráw-). **1.** Any of various, mostly freshwater, crustaceans of the genera *Cambarus* and *Astacus,* resembling a lobster but considerably smaller. **2.** Broadly, a similar crustacean, such as the **spiny lobster** (*see*). [Alteration (influenced by FISH) of earlier *crevis, cravis,* Middle English *crevise,* from Old French, from Frankish *krabītja* (unattested), CRAB.]

cray·on (kráy-ən, -on) *n.* **1.** A stick or pencil of coloured wax, charcoal, or chalk, used for drawing. **2.** A drawing made with crayons. ~*tr.v.* **crayoned, -oning, -ons.** To draw, colour, or decorate with crayons. [French, crayon, pencil, from *craie,* chalk, from Latin *crēta†.*] —**cray·on·ist** *n.*

craze (krayz) *v.* **crazed, crazing, crazes.** —*tr.* **1.** To cause to become mentally deranged or obsessed; make insane. **2.** To produce a network of fine cracks in (a ceramic, metal, or painted surface). —*intr.* **1.** To become mentally deranged or obsessed; go insane. **2.** To become covered with fine cracks. ~*n.* **1.** A short-lived popular fashion; a rage; a fad. **2.** *Rare.* Insanity; mania. **3.** A pattern of fine cracks. [Middle English *crasen,* to shatter, render insane, from Old Norse *krasa* (unattested), to shatter (probably imitative).]

cra·zy (kráyzi) *adj.* **-zier, -ziest. 1.** *Informal.* Affected with or suggestive of madness; insane. **2.** *Informal.* Departing from proportion or moderation, especially: **a.** Possessed by enthusiasm or excitement. **b.** Immoderately fond; infatuated. **c.** Not sensible; impractical. **3.** *U.S. Slang.* Excellent or very appealing. **4.** *Archaic.* Rickety or dilapidated. ~*n., pl.* **zies.** *U.S. Slang.* A mad or eccentric person. [From CRAZE.] —**cra·zi·ly** *adv.* —**cra·zi·ness** *n.*

Crazy Horse, *Sioux* Ta-Sunko-Witko (*c.* 1849–1877). Sioux Indian chief. Resisting U.S. settlement in Dakota, he joined Sitting Bull at Little Big Horn and led the force which defeated General Custer's U.S. cavalry (1876). He surrendered (1877), but was killed in custody in Fort Robinson, Nebraska.

crazy paving *n. Chiefly British.* Paving, especially on driveways or garden paths, consisting of irregularly shaped stone slabs laid together in a random pattern.

crazy quilt *n.* A patchwork quilt of pieces of cloth of various shapes, colours, and sizes, arranged in no definite pattern.

creak (kreek) *v.* **creaked, creaking, creaks.** —*intr.* **1.** To make a grating or squeaking sound. **2.** To move with such a sound or sounds. —*tr.* To cause to make a creaking sound. ~*n.* A grating or squeaking sound. [Middle English *creken* (imitative).] **—creak·ing·ly** adv.

creak·y (krée̱ki) adj. -ier, -iest. 1. Tending or liable to creak. 2. Dilapidated; decrepit. 3. Suspect; unreliable: a creaky argument. **—creak·i·ly** adv. **—creak·i·ness** n.

cream (kreem) n. 1. The yellowish fatty component of unhomogenised milk that tends to accumulate at the surface. 2. The colour of cream; pale yellow to yellowish white. 3. Any of various substances resembling cream, such as certain cosmetics. 4. The choicest part: the cream of the crop. 5. A soup, dessert, or other dish containing cream or resembling cream in consistency. 6. Chiefly British. A three-layer sweet biscuit with a middle sweet creamy layer.
~v. **creamed, creaming, creams.** —intr. 1. To form cream. 2. To form foam or scum at the top. 3. Chiefly U.S. Vulgar Slang. To ejaculate semen. —tr. 1. To allow the cream to separate from (milk). 2. To remove the cream from; skim. 3. a. To select or remove the best part from. b. To select or remove (the best part) of something. Used with off. 4. To beat (butter and sugar, for example) into a creamy consistency. 5. To prepare or cook (a vegetable, for example) in or with a cream sauce. 6. To add or apply cream or a similar substance to. 7. U.S. Slang. To defeat overwhelmingly. [Middle English creme, creime, from Old French cresme, craime, blends of Late Latin chrisma, ointment, CHRISM, and Late Latin crāmum†, cream.] **—cream** adj.

cream caramel n. A dessert, **crème caramel** (see).
cream cheese n. A soft white cheese made of cream and milk.
cream cracker n. British. A light, crisp, unsweetened biscuit, often eaten with cheese.
cream·er (krée̱mər) n. 1. A machine or device for separating cream from milk. 2. Chiefly U.S. A small jug or pitcher for cream.
cream·er·y (krée̱məri) n., pl. -ies. An establishment where dairy products are prepared or sold.
cream of tartar n. A chemical compound used in cookery, **potassium bitartrate** (see).
cream puff n. 1. A shell of light pastry filled with whipped cream, custard, or ice cream. 2. Slang. A sissy; an effeminate man.
cream sauce n. A white sauce made by heating a mixture of flour and butter and adding milk or cream.
cream soda n. A sweet soft drink flavoured with vanilla.
cream tea n. British. An afternoon meal consisting of scones, or sometimes bread, with jam and whipped or clotted cream.
cream·y (krée̱mi) adj. -ier, -iest. Rich in cream or resembling cream. **—cream·i·ly** adv. **—cream·i·ness** n.
crease (kreess) n. 1. A line made by pressing, folding, or wrinkling. 2. In cricket any of the lines marking off the positions of the bowler and batsman or the space bounded by these lines. 3. In ice hockey, the rectangular area marked off in front of each goal cage. 4. In lacrosse, the circular area around each goal.
~v. **creased, creasing, creases.** —tr. 1. To make a fold or wrinkle in. 2. To graze with a bullet; wound superficially. 3. Slang. To cause to laugh heartily. Often used with up. —intr. 1. To become wrinkled or creased. 2. Slang. To laugh heartily. [Earlier creast, from Middle English crest, ridge, CREST.] **—creas·er** n. **—creas·y** adj.

cre·ate (kree-áyt, kri- ‖ krée-ayt) v. -ated, -ating, -ates. —tr. 1. a. To cause to exist; bring into being; originate. b. To make or produce (something, especially an artistic work). 2. To give rise to; bring about; produce: Her remark created a stir. 3. To invest with office or title; appoint. 4. To be first to portray and give character to (a role or part). —intr. 1. To be occupied in painting or a similar creative activity. 2. British Slang. To make trouble; cause a fuss. ~adj. Poetic. Created. [Middle English createn from Latin creāre.]
cre·a·tine (krée-ə-teen, -tin) n. Also **cre·a·tin** (-tin). A nitrogenous organic acid, $C_4H_9N_3O_2$, found, combined with phosphoric acid, mainly in the muscle tissue of many vertebrates and acting in muscular contraction. [Greek kreas (stem kreat-), flesh + -INE.]
cre·at·i·nine (kree-átti-neen, kri-) n. The creatine anhydride $C_4H_7N_3O$, a normal metabolic waste. [CREATIN(E) + -INE.]
cre·a·tion (kree-áysh'n, kri-) n. 1. a. The act of creating. b. The fact or process of being created. 2. Capital C. God's primal act of bringing the world into existence. Usually preceded by the. 3. a. The world or universe and all things in it. b. All creatures or a class of creatures: all creation. 4. An original product of human invention or imagination; a work. 5. A specially designed garment or other article of fashion. **—cre·a·tion·al** adj.
cre·a·tion·ism (kree-áysh'n-iz'm, kri-) n. 1. The doctrine ascribing the origin of all matter and living forms as they now exist to distinct acts of creation by God. Compare **evolutionism**. 2. The doctrine that each human soul is a distinct and new creation by God. Compare **infusionism, traducianism**. **—cre·a·tion·ist** n.
cre·a·tive (kree-áytiv, kri-) adj. 1. Having the ability or power to create things. 2. Creating; productive. Often used with of. 3. Characterised by originality and expressiveness; imaginative. 4. Stimulating to the imagination: creative tension. 5. Extending its scope beyond normal limits, often for questionable purposes: creative accounting. **—cre·a·tive·ly** adv. **—cre·a·tiv·i·ty** (kree-ay-tívvəti), **cre·a·tive·ness** n.
cre·a·tor (kree-áytər, kri-) n. 1. One that creates. 2. Capital C. God.
crea·ture (krée̱chər) n. 1. Anything created. 2. A living being, especially an animal. 3. A human being. Often used with a suggestion of pity or contempt. 4. One dependent upon or subservient to another; a tool. **—crea·tur·al, crea·ture·ly** adj.
creature comforts pl.n. Material possessions that help ensure bodily comfort.

crèche (kraysh, kresh) n. 1. Chiefly British. A day nursery for very young children, in a place of work or study. 2. A foundling hospital. 3. A representation of the Nativity scene. [French, from Old French, from Vulgar Latin creppja (unattested), from Germanic krippja (unattested), manger, CRIB.]
Cré·cy, Battle of (kréssi ‖ kráy-si, kray-sée). The first major land battle of the Hundred Years' War, fought near Crécy-en-Ponthieu in the Somme département, northern France (August 26, 1346). English longbowmen outdistanced French crossbowmen and inflicted a crushing defeat on the French.
cre·dence (kréed'nss) n. 1. Acceptance as true or valid; belief. 2. Claim to acceptance; trustworthiness. 3. Recommendation; credential: a letter of credence. 4. Ecclesiastical. A small shelf or table to hold the bread and wine used in the Eucharist. In this sense, also called "credence table". [Middle English, from Old French, from Medieval Latin crēdentia, belief, trust, hence a table holding food for tasting in order to detect poison, from Latin crēdere, to believe.]
cre·den·dum (kri-dén-dəm ‖ kree-) n., pl. -da (-də). Ecclesiastical. An article or matter of faith. [Latin crēdundum, from the neuter gerundive of crēdere, to believe.]
cre·den·tial (kri-dénsh'l) n. 1. That which entitles one to confidence, credit, or authority. 2. Usually plural. a. A letter attesting one's right to credit, confidence, or authority. b. Written evidence of qualifications. [From Medieval Latin crēdentiālis, giving authority, from crēdentia, trust, CREDENCE.]
cre·den·za (kri-dénzə) n. A cupboard or sideboard, especially one without legs, sometimes used as a credence table. [Italian, from Medieval Latin crēdentia, CREDENCE (table).]
cred·i·bil·i·ty (kréddi-bílləti, krédda-) n. Worthiness of belief.
credibility gap n. 1. An inability to carry conviction because of previous failure to live up to promises; especially, the improbability of official claims and pronouncements when viewed against the apparent facts. 2. Public scepticism about official claims.
cred·i·ble (kréddib'l, kréddəb'l) adj. 1. Capable of being believed; believable; plausible. 2. Worthy of confidence; reliable. [Middle English, from Latin crēdibilis, from crēdere, to believe, entrust.] **—cred·i·ble·ness** n. **—cred·i·bly** adv.
Usage: Credible, credulous, and creditable are sometimes confused. Credible means "believable": a credible story. Credulous is used to refer to someone who is disposed to believe too readily: a credulous person. Creditable has nothing to do with the notion of belief; it means "deserving commendation": a creditable result.
cred·it (kréddit) n. Abbr. **cr.** 1. Belief or confidence in the truth of something; trust. 2. The quality or state of being trustworthy or credible. 3. A reputation for sound character or quality; standing; repute. 4. A source of honour or distinction: He is a credit to his family. 5. Approval for some act, ability, or quality; praise. 6. Influence based on the good opinion or confidence of others. 7. Usually plural. a. An acknowledgment of sources or contributors as in the production of a film, play, or book. b. A list appearing at the beginning or end of a film or broadcast, naming all those who have taken part. 8. Chiefly U.S. a. Official certification that a student has successfully completed a course of study. b. A unit of study so certified. c. A distinction awarded for a high mark in a course of study. 9. Reputation for solvency and integrity, entitling a person to be trusted in buying or borrowing. 10. a. Confidence in a buyer's ability and intention to fulfil financial obligations at some future time. b. The commercial practice which allows such future payments. c. The time allowed for payment for anything sold on trust. 11. Accounting. a. The acknowledgment of payment by a debtor by entry of the sum in an account. b. The right-hand side of an account on which such amounts are entered. c. An entry on this side. d. The sum of such entries. Compare **debit**. 12. The positive balance or amount remaining in a person's account. 13. An amount placed by a bank, shop, or the like, at the disposal of a client, against which he may draw. **—on credit**. With payment to be made at some time in the in the future.
~tr.v. **credited, -iting, -its.** 1. To believe; trust: "she refused steadfastly to credit the reports of his death" (Agatha Christie). 2. Archaic. To bring honour or distinction to. 3. a. To give credit to (a person) for something. Used with with: credit him with the invention. b. To ascribe (something) to a person; attribute. Used with to: credit the invention to him. 4. Accounting. a. To give credit for (a sum paid). b. To give credit to (a payer). c. To make an entry in the right-hand side of (an account). Compare **debit**. 5. Chiefly U.S. To give or award credits to (a student). —See Synonyms at **attribute**. [French, from Italian credito, from Latin crēditum, "something entrusted", loan, from the past participle of crēdere, to believe, entrust.]
cred·it·a·ble (krédditə-b'l) adj. 1. Deserving commendation. 2. Capable of being credited or assigned; assignable. See Usage note at **credible**. **—cred·it·a·bil·i·ty** (-bílləti), **cred·it·a·ble·ness** n. **—cred·it·a·bly** adv.
credit account n. British. A financial scheme offered by a business, allowing a customer to buy goods or services on credit.
credit card n. A card issued by banks and business concerns authorising the holder to buy goods or services on credit.
credit limit n. The maximum amount of credit to be extended to a customer. Also U.S. "credit line", "line of credits".
credit line n. 1. A line of copy acknowledging the source or origin of a news report, published article, film, or other work. 2. U.S. A credit limit.
credit note n. A note issued by a shop or business concern indicating a specific amount of credit due to a customer, especially one

given in exchange for goods returned by the customer.

cred·i·tor (krédditər) *n.* A person or firm to whom money or its equivalent is owed. Compare **debtor**.

credit rating *n.* An estimate of the amount of credit that can be extended to a company or individual without undue risk.

credit squeeze *n.* **1.** The restriction by government of the availability of credit facilities by means of regulations limiting bank loans, overdrafts, and the like. **2.** A period of such restriction.

credit union *n.* A cooperative organisation that makes loans to its members at low interest rates.

credit·wor·thy (kréddit-wúrthi) *adj.* Designating a person or company to whom credit may be safely extended. —**cred·it·wor·thi·ness** *n.*

cre·do (krée-dō, kráy-) *n., pl.* **-dos. 1.** A statement of belief; a creed. **2.** *Often capital* C. **a.** The **Apostles' Creed** or the **Nicene Creed** (*both of which see*). **b.** A musical setting for either of these. [Latin *crēdo*, "I believe", the first word of the Apostles' Creed, from *crēdere*, to believe.]

cre·du·li·ty (kri-déw-ləti, kre- ‖ -dōō-) *n.* A disposition to believe too readily; gullibility. [Middle English *credulite*, from Old French, from Latin *crēdulitās* (stem *crēdulitāt-*), from *crēdulus*, CREDULOUS.]

cred·u·lous (kréddewləss) *adj.* **1.** Disposed to believe too readily; gullible. **2.** Arising from or characterised by credulity. [Latin *crēdulus*, from *crēdere*, to believe.] —**cred·u·lous·ly** *adv.* —**cred·u·lous·ness** *n.* See Usage note at **credible**.

Cree (kree) *n., pl.* **Crees** or collectively **Cree. 1.** A member of an American Indian people formerly living in Ontario, Manitoba, and Saskatchewan. **2.** The language of this people, of the Algonquian family or languages. [Shortened from Canadian French *Christianaux*, by folk etymology from Ojibwa *Kenistenoag*, earlier *Kilistino* (unattested), tribal name.]

creed (kreed) *n.* **1.** A formal statement of religious belief; a confession of faith. **2.** An authoritative statement of certain articles of Christian faith that are considered essential; for example, the Apostles' Creed or the Nicene Creed. **3.** Any statement or system of belief, principles, or opinions. [Middle English *crede*, Old English *crēda*, from Latin *crēdo*, "I believe".] —**creed·al** *adj.*

creek (kreek ‖ *U.S. also* krik) *n.* **1.** *British.* A small tidal inlet in a shoreline. **2.** A small stream. **3.** An intermittent stream. —**up the creek.** *Slang.* In a difficult or unfortunate position. [Middle English *creke, crike*, possibly from Old Norse *kriki*, a bend, nook.]

Creek (kreek) *n., pl.* **Creeks** or collectively **Creek. 1.** A member of any of several confederated American Indian peoples, formerly inhabiting parts of Georgia, Alabama, and northern Florida. **2.** Any of the languages of these peoples.

creel (kreel) *n.* **1.** A wicker basket, especially one used by anglers for carrying fish. **2.** A wickerwork trap for fish or lobsters. **3.** A frame for holding bobbins or spools in a spinning machine. [Middle English (Scottish) *crel, crelle†*.]

creep (kreep) *intr.v.* **crept** (krept), **creeping, creeps. 1.** To move with the body close to the ground, as a reptile does. **2.** To move stealthily, cautiously, or very slowly. **3.** To behave obsequiously; fawn. **4.** *Botany.* To grow along a surface, rooting at intervals or clinging by means of suckers or tendrils. **5.** To slip out of place from pressure or wear; shift gradually. **6.** *Metallurgy.* To undergo slow deformation as a result of applied stress or high temperature. **7.** To have a tingling sensation: *made my flesh creep.*
~*n.* **1.** The action of creeping; a creeping motion or progress. **2.** *Slang.* An obnoxious or insignificant person. **3.** *Metallurgy.* A slow flow of metal when under high temperature or great stress. **4.** *Geology.* The slow movement of rock debris and soil, lubricated by rainwater, down a slope. **5.** Any slow deformation of an object, or slow distortion of the relative positions of two or more objects. —**the creeps.** *Informal.* A sensation of fear or repugnance, as if things were crawling on one's skin. [Creep: Middle English *crepen*, Old English *crēopan*. Crept: Middle English *creped, crept*, analogous formation from the infinitive *crepen*.]

creep·er (kréepər) *n.* **1.** One that creeps. **2.** *Slang. Plural.* Shoes with thick soft soles. Also called "brothel creeper". **3.** *Botany.* A plant having stems that grow along a surface, either rooting at intervals or clinging for support. **4. a.** Any of various birds that creeps about in bushes looking for food. **b.** A treecreeper (*see*). **5.** A grappling device for dragging lakes and river. **6.** In cricket, a **daisycutter** (*see*). **7.** A small platform on wheels for working underneath a car; a cradle. **8.** *Usually plural.* A metal frame with spikes, attached to a shoe or boot to prevent slipping.

creeping bent grass (kréeping) *n.* A perennial grass, *Agrostis stolonifera*, of temperate regions. Also called "fiorin".

creeping eruption *n.* An intensely irritating skin disease caused by larvae burrowing beneath the skin and characterised by spreading eruptions in the form of reddish lines.

creeping Jenny, creeping Jennie *n.* A low-growing, creeping plant, *Lysimachia nummularia*, with yellow bell-like flowers, found in damp and shady places and grown in gardens. Also called "creeping Charlie", "moneywort".

creeping thistle *n.* A perennial plant, *Cirsium arrense*, having brushlike lilac flowers with purple bracts, found in waste places.

creep·y (kréepi) *adj.* **-ier, -iest. 1.** Creeping; slow-moving. **2.** *Informal.* Inducing or having a sensation of repugnance or fear, as of insects crawling on one's skin. —**creep·i·ness** *n.*

creep·y-crawl·y (kréepi-kráwli) *n., pl.* **-crawlies.** *British Informal.* A small crawling animal, especially an insect.
~*adj.* Having or causing a feeling as if insects are crawling over one's skin.

creese. Variant of **kris**.

cre·mate (kri-máyt ‖ *U.S. also* kréemayt) *tr.v.* **-mated, -mating, -mates.** To burn (a corpse) to ashes. [Latin *cremāre*, to burn, consume by fire.] —**cre·ma·tion** (-máysh'n) *n.*

cre·ma·tor (kri-máytər ‖ *U.S. also* krée-maytər) *n.* **1.** One that cremates. **2.** *Chiefly British.* A furnace used for cremating.

cre·ma·to·ri·um (krémmə-táwri-əm ‖ kréemə-, -tóri-) *n., pl.* **-ums** or **-toria** (-ə). A furnace, building, or place for the cremation of corpses.

crem·a·to·ry (krémmə-tri, -təri ‖ *U.S. also* kréemə-tawri, -tóri) *adj.* Of or pertaining to cremation.
~*n., pl.* **crematories.** *Chiefly U.S.* A crematorium. [New Latin *crematorium*, from Latin *cremāre*, CREMATE.]

crème brû·lée (kráym brōōlay, krém brü-láy) *n.* A rich, soft cream or custard dessert coated with a layer· of hard caramelised sugar. [French, "burnt cream".]

crème caramel (kráym kárrə-mel, krém, -mél) *n.* A solid but soft baked custard with a caramel sauce. Also called "cream caramel". [French.]

crème de ca·ca·o (kráym də kaa-kaʹa-ō, krém, kə-, kőkō ‖ kréem) *n.* A sweet, chocolate-flavoured liqueur. [French, "cream of cacao".]

crème de la crème (krém də laa krém, kráym) *n.* **1.** The essence of excellence. **2.** The very best of a given kind. [French, "cream of the cream", but perhaps coined in English.]

crème de menthe (kráym də mónth, krém, mónt, ménth) *n.* A sweet green or white liqueur, well flavoured with mint. [French, "cream of mint".]

Cre·mo·na[1] (kri-mónə). A city in Lombardy in northern Italy, famous for the making of fine stringed instruments.

Cremona[2] *n.* Any of the fine violins or other stringed instruments made in Cremona, from the 16th to the 18th century, especially by the Amati family, Antonio Stradivari, or Giuseppe Guarneri.

cre·nate (krée-nayt) *adj.* Also **cre·nat·ed** (kri-náytid ‖ *U.S.* krée-naytid). *Biology.* Having a margin with rounded or scalloped projections: *a crenate leaf.* [New Latin *crenatus*, probably from Late Latin *crēna†*, notch.] —**cre·nate·ly** *adv.*

cre·na·tion (kri-náysh'n) *n.* **1.** A rounded projection; a crenature. **2.** The condition or fact of being crenate.

cren·a·ture (krénnə-tewr, kréenə-, -choor) *n.* **1.** A crenation. **2.** A notch between crenations, as on a leaf.

cren·el·lat·ed, *U.S.* **cren·e·lat·ed** (krénnə-laytid) *adj.* **1.** Having battlements. **2.** Having square indentations: *a crenellated moulding.* [French *crenel*, a crenellation, from Old French, perhaps from Vulgar Latin *crenellus* (unattested), diminutive of Late Latin *crēna*, notch.] —**cren·el·late** —*tr.v.* —**cren·e·lla·tion** (-láysh'n) *n.*

cren·u·late (krénnew-layt, -lət, -lit) *adj.* Also **cren·u·lat·ed** (-laytid). Having minutely notched or scalloped projections: *a crenulate shell.* [New Latin *crenulatus*, from *crenula*, perhaps diminutive of Late Latin *crēna*, notch.] —**cren·u·la·tion** (-láysh'n) *n.*

cre·o·dont (krée-ə-dont) *n.* Any of various extinct carnivorous mammals of the suborder Creodonta, of the Tertiary period. [New Latin *Creodonta*, "flesh-toothed ones" : Greek *kreas*, flesh + -ODONT.]

Cre·ole (krée-ōl, *sometimes* kráy-) *n.* **1.** Any person of European descent born in the West Indies or Spanish America. **2.** A person descended from or culturally related to the original French settlers of the southern United States, especially Louisiana. **3.** The French patois spoken by these people. **4.** A person descended from or culturally related to the Spanish and Portuguese settlers of the Gulf States. **5.** A person of Negro descent born in the West Indies or Spanish America, as distinguished from a Negro brought from Africa. Also called "Creole Negro". **6.** Any person of mixed European and Negro ancestry who speaks a Creole dialect. **7.** *Often small* c. A creolised language.
~*adj.* **1.** Of, relating to, or characteristic of creole or the Creoles. **2.** *Small* c. Cooked with a spicy sauce containing tomatoes, onions, and peppers. [French *créole*, from Spanish *criollo*, from Portuguese *crioulo*, slave born in his master's house, from *criar*, to bring up, from Latin *creāre*, to create, beget.]

cre·ol·ise, cre·ol·ize (krée-ə-līz, -ō-, *sometimes* kráy-) —*tr.v.* **-ised, -ising, -ises.** To establish as a creolised language. —**cre·ol·i·sa·tion** (-lī-záysh'n ‖ *U.S.* -li-) *n.*

cre·o·lised language (krée-ə-līzd, kráy-) *n.* Any of several mixed languages of a kind that develops through contact between two language communities, incorporating the basic vocabulary of the dominant or colonial language with the grammar and an admixture of words from the subordinate or indigenous language. It then becomes the native tongue of the indigenous people. Compare **pidgin.**

Cre·on (krée-ən ‖ -on) *n.* In Greek legend, King of Thebes, successor to his nephew Oedipus and uncle of Antigone.

cre·o·sol (krée-ə-sol ‖ -sōl) *n.* A colourless to yellow aromatic liquid, $C_8H_{10}O_2$, that is a constituent of creosote and is obtained from beechwood tar. [CREOS(OTE) + -OL.]

cre·o·sote (krée-ə-sōt) *n.* **1.** A colourless to yellowish oily liquid, obtained by the distillation of wood tar, especially from beechwood, and formerly used to treat chronic bronchitis. **2.** A yellowish to greenish-brown oily liquid obtained from coal tar and used as a wood preservative and disinfectant.
~*tr.v.* **creosoted, -soting, -sotes.** To treat or paint (wood or other material) with creosote. [German *Kreosot*, "flesh preserver" (from its antiseptic qualities) : Greek *kreas*, flesh + *sōtēr*, preserver, from *sōzein*, to preserve, save, from *saos*, safe.]

creosote bush *n.* A resinous shrub, *Larrea tridentata*, of the western United States and Mexico, exuding an odour like that of creosote. Also called "greasewood".

crepe, crêpe (krayp ‖ krep) *n.* Also **crape** (for senses 1-4). **1.** A light, soft, thin fabric of silk, cotton, wool, or other fibre, with a crinkled surface. **2.** A black band of this fabric, originally displayed or worn on the sleeve or hat as a sign of mourning. **3.** Crepe paper. **4.** Crepe rubber. **5.** A very thin pancake. ~*tr.v.* **creped, creping, crepes.** Also **crape, crape.** To cover or drape with crepe. [French *crêpe,* from Old French *crespe,* crisp, curly, from Latin *crispus.*] —**crep·y, crepe·y** *adj.*

crepe de Chine (də shéen) *n.* A silk crepe used for women's dresses and blouses. [French, "crepe of China".]

crepe hair *n.* False hair used in theatrical make-up for making artificial beards, sideboards, and the like.

crepe myrtle. Variant of **crape myrtle.**

crepe paper *n.* Crinkled tissue paper, resembling crepe, used for decorations. Also called "crepe".

crepe rubber *n.* A white or yellowish natural or synthetic rubber with a crinkled texture, used for shoe soles. Also called "crepe".

crêpe su·zette (kráyp soo-zét, krép) *n., pl.* **crêpe suzettes** or **crêpes suzette.** A thin pancake usually rolled with hot orange or tangerine sauce and served with a flaming brandy or curaçao sauce. [French : CREPE (pancake) + *Suzette,* pet form of the name *Suzanne.*]

crep·i·tate (kréppi-tayt) *intr.v.* **-tated, -tating, -tates.** To make a creaking or rattling sound; crackle. [Latin *crepitāre,* to crackle, frequentative of *crepāre* (past participle *crepitus*), to crack, creak.] —**crep·i·ta·tion** (-táysh'n) *n.*

cre·pi·tus (kréppitəss) *n.* **1.** A rattling sound heard in the chest of someone suffering from a lung disease such as pneumonia. **2.** A grating sound produced by the rubbing together of the two edges of a broken bone. [Latin, from *crepāre,* to creak.]

crept. Past tense and past participle of **creep.**

cre·pus·cu·lar (kri-púskewlər, kre-) *adj.* **1.** Of or like twilight; hazy; dim. **2.** *Zoology.* Becoming active at twilight or before sunrise. Said of certain insects and birds. [From Latin *crepusculum,* twilight, from *creper,* dusky, dark.]

cres·cen·do (kri-shén-dō ‖ -sén-) *n., pl.* **-dos** or **-di** (-dee). *Abbr.* **cresc. 1.** A gradual increase in the volume or intensity of sound. **2.** The direction or symbol indicating this in music. The sign < is displayed above the notes. **3.** A musical passage played in a crescendo. Compare **decrescendo.** ~*adj. Abbr.* **cresc.** Gradually increasing in volume or intensity. ~*adv. Abbr.* **cresc., cres.** With a crescendo. Often used as a direction. ~*intr.v.* **crescendoed, -doing, -do** To increase gradually in volume. [Italian, "increasing", from *crescere,* to increase, from Latin *crēscere,* to grow.]

Usage: *Rise in a crescendo* is considered better than *rise to a crescendo.*

cres·cent (krézz'nt, kréss'nt) *n.* **1.** The figure of the moon as it appears in its first or last quarters, with concave and convex edges terminating in points. **2.** Something shaped like this. **3.** *Often capital* C. **a.** The Turkish emblem. **b.** Turkish or Muslim power. Often preceded by *the.* **4.** *British. Abbr.* **Cres.** A crescent-shaped street, often lined with Georgian houses. **5.** *Heraldry.* A crescent moon, especially with horns pointing upwards, indicating a second son. ~*adj.* **1.** Crescent-shaped. **2.** Increasing; waxing, as does the moon. [Middle English *cressaunt,* from Old French *creissant,* "waxing", "increasing", from Latin *crēscēns* (stem *crēscent-*), present participle of *crēscere,* to increase, grow.] —**cres·cen·tic** (kri-séntik) *adj.*

cre·sol (krée-sol ‖ -sōl) *n.* Any of three isomeric phenols, $CH_3C_6H_4OH$, found in coal tar and used in resins and as a disinfectant. [Variant of CREOSOL.]

cress (kress) *n.* Any of various plants of the cabbage family, such as those of the genera *Cardamine* and *Arabis,* having pungent leaves often used in salads and as a garnish. See **watercress, garden cress.** [Middle English *cresse,* from Old English *cresse, cærse.*]

cres·set (kréssit) *n.* A metal cup, often suspended on a pole, containing burning oil or pitch and used as a torch. [Middle English, from Old French *cresset, craisset,* from *craisse,* oil, grease, from Vulgar Latin *crassia* (unattested), animal fat, from Latin *crassus,* fat, thick.]

Cres·si·da (kréssidə). Also **Cri·sey·de, Cres·seid, Cres·sid.** In medieval romances and in Shakespeare, a Greek lady who first returns the love of the Trojan Troilus but later forsakes him for the Greek Diomedes.

crest (krest) *n.* **1.** A tuft, ridge, or similar projection on the head of a bird or other animal. **2. a.** A plume used as decoration on top of a helmet. **b.** A helmet. **c.** The ridge or raised part on a helmet. **3.** *Heraldry.* An emblem placed above the shield on a coat of arms and also used by itself on seals, stationery, and the like. **4. a.** The top of something, as a mountain or wave; a peak; a summit. **b.** A ridge. **5.** The ridge of an animal's neck or the mane growing on it. **6.** The ridge of a bone. **7.** *Architecture.* Cresting. ~*v.* **crested, cresting, crests.** —*tr.* **1.** To serve as or decorate or furnish with a crest. **2.** To reach the crest of (a hill, for example). —*intr.* To form into a crest, as a wave might. [Middle English *creste,* from Old French, from Latin *crista,* crest, plume.] —**crest·ed** *adj.* —**crest·less** *adj.*

crest·fall·en (krést-fawlən) *adj.* Dejected; dispirited; depressed. —**crest·fall·en·ly** *adv.*

crest·ing (krésting) *n. Architecture.* An ornamental ridge, as on top of a wall or roof.

cre·syl·ic (kri-síllik, kre-) *adj. Chemistry.* Of or pertaining to creosote or cresol. [CRES(OL) + -YL + -IC.]

Cre·ta·ceous (kri-táyshəss, kre-) *adj.* **1.** Of, belonging to, or designating the geological time, system of rocks, and sedimentary deposits of the third and last period of the Mesozoic era, characterised by the deposition of chalk, the development of flowering plants, and the disappearance of dinosaurs. **2.** *Small* **c.** Of, containing, or resembling chalk. ~*n. Geology.* The Cretaceous period. Preceded by *the.* [Latin *crētāceus : crēta†,* chalk, clay (see also **crayon**) + -ACEOUS.]

Crete (kreet). *Greek* **Krí·ti** (krée-tee). The largest of the Greek islands, lying southeast of the mainland between the Mediterranean and Aegean seas. The Minoan civilisation flourished in the mountainous island in *c.* 3500–1400 B.C., and was celebrated in Greek mythology through the legends of King Minos, the Labyrinth, and Minotaur. Modern excavation at Knossos has shown it to have been an advanced bronze-age culture and a sea power. The civilisation perished in the 15th century B.C., partly, it is thought, because of a catastrophic eruption. Crete was subsequently occupied by Romans, Byzantines, Muslims, Venetians and Turks. It was ceded to Greece (1913), following unrest between its Christian and Muslim populations. In the World War II Battle of Crete (1941), Germany won the island through the world's first major airborne landing, using paratroops and troop-carrying gliders to defeat an Allied force which had been evacuated there from Greece. Crete was liberated in 1945. Sheep and goats are raised, and grapes, olives, and citrus fruits grown. Khania is the capital; Iráklion the chief port and centre of the tourist industry. —**Cret·an** *n. & adj.*

cre·tic (kréetik) *n. Prosody.* A metrical foot consisting of one long syllable followed by a short and long syllable. [From Latin *crēticus,* from Greek *krētikos,* "Cretan (foot)", from *Krētē,* Crete.]

cre·tin (kréttin ‖ *chiefly U.S.* kréetin) *n.* **1.** One afflicted with cretinism. **2.** A fool; an idiot. [French *crétin,* from Swiss French *crestin,* CHRISTIAN, hence human being (an idiot being nonetheless human).] —**cre·tin·oid** *adj.* —**cre·tin·ous** *adj.*

cre·tin·ism (kréttin-iz'm ‖ kréetin-) *n.* A condition caused by congenital deficiency of thyroid hormone and characterised by dwarfism and mental retardation.

cre·tonne (krétton ‖ *U.S. also* kri-tón) *n.* A heavy unglazed cotton, linen, or rayon fabric, colourfully printed and used for curtains and chair covers. [French, first made in *Creton,* village in Normandy.]

Creutz·feldt-Ja·kob disease (króytz-felt-yákob ‖ -yaákob) *n. Abbr.* **CJD.** A spongiform encephalopathy of humans that is typically fatal and is held to be linked in some cases to the consumption of beef from cattle with BSE. [After H.G. *Creutzfeldt* (1885–1964) and A. *Jakob* (1882–1927), the German neurologists who first described it.]

cre·vasse (kri-váss) *n.* **1.** A deep fissure, as in a glacier; a chasm. **2.** A crack in a dyke or embankment. ~*tr.v.* **crevassed, -vassing, -vasses.** To make crevasses in; fissure. [French, from Old French *crevace,* CREVICE.]

crev·ice (krévviss) *n.* A narrow crack or opening; a cleft. [Middle English *crevice, crevace,* from Old French *crevace,* from *crever,* to split, from Latin *crepāre,* to rattle, crack.] —**crev·iced** *adj.*

crew¹ (kroo ‖ krew) *n.* **1.** *Nautical.* **a.** All personnel manning a ship. **b.** All of a ship's personnel except the officers. **2.** All personnel manning an aircraft in flight. **3.** Any group of people working together; a team. **4.** A company; a crowd. Often used derogatorily. **5.** A team of oarsmen. **6.** Crew members: *twenty crew.* ~*v.* **crewed, crewing, crews.** —*tr.* To be a member of the crew on (a ship, aircraft, or boat in rowing). —*intr.* To work as a member of a crew. [Middle English *creue,* military reinforcement, from Old French *creue,* an increase, from the feminine past participle of *creistre,* to grow, from Latin *crēscere.*]

crew². *Archaic.* A past tense of **crow.**

crew cut *n.* A close-cropped man's haircut. [Oarsmen formerly had this kind of haircut.] —**crew-cut** *adj.*

crew·el (króo-əl ‖ kréw-) *n.* A loosely twisted worsted yarn used for embroidery, crochet, and the like. [Middle English *crule†.*]

crew neck *n.* A round, slightly raised neckline on a sweater. [After the style of sweaters worn by boat crews.]

crib (krib) *n.* **1. a.** A child's bed; a cradle. **b.** *U.S.* A baby's cot. **2.** *Chiefly U.S.* A small building, bin, or box for storing grain. **3.** A rack or trough for fodder; a manger. **4.** A cattle stall. **5.** A small, crude cottage or room. **6.** A framework to support or strengthen a mine or shaft. **7.** A representation of the Nativity scene. **8.** *Informal.* **a.** A petty theft. **b.** Plagiarism. **9.** *Informal. Chiefly British.* A translation or summary of a text, used by students, usually illicitly, as an aid in understanding the text or in answering examination questions. Also *U.S.* "pony", "trot". **10.** *Informal.* Cribbage. **11.** Cribwork. **12.** *U.S. & Canadian.* A dam or group of rafts made of logs. **13.** *Australian & N. Z.* A light meal; a snack. **14.** In cribbage, a set of cards made up from discards by each player, used by the dealer. ~*v.* **cribbed, cribbing, cribs.** —*tr.* **1.** To confine in or as in a crib. **2.** To furnish with a crib. **3.** *Informal.* To steal (something, especially an idea); plagiarise. **4.** To reinforce a mine or shaft with a wooden framework. —*intr. Informal.* To use a crib or copy from a neighbour in lessons or examinations; cheat. [Middle English *crib,* manger, stall, basket, Old English *cribb,* manger.] —**crib·ber** *n.*

crib·bage (kribbij) *n.* A card game for from two to four players, in which the object is to score a given number of points with certain combinations of cards. [Perhaps from CRIB (noun), "basket", hence discard pile.]

crib·bing (kríbbing) *n.* **1.** A supporting framework, as of timber lining a shaft; a crib. **2.** Crib-biting.

crib-bit·ing (kríb-bīting) *n.* A harmful habit of horses of biting at the edge of a feed trough or other object and swallowing air at the same time. —**crib-bite** *intr.v.* —**crib-bit·er** *n.*

crib death *n. U.S.* **Cot death** (see).

cri·bel·lum (kri-bél-əm) *n., pl.* **-la** (-ə). An additional, sievelike, silk-spinning organ possessed by certain spiders, located between the spinnerets. [New Latin, diminutive of Latin *cribrum*, sieve.]

crib·ri·form (kríbbri-fawrm) *adj. Anatomy.* Perforated like a sieve. [Latin *cribrum*, sieve + -FORM.]

crib tin *n. Australian & N.Z.* A container for a packed lunch.

crib·work (kríb-wurk) *n.* A structural framework made of logs stacked one above the other, with the logs in each layer at right angles to those in the layer below, used in constructing mines, foundations, and the like.

crick (krik) *n.* A painful cramp or muscle spasm, as in the back or neck.
~ *tr.v.* **cricked, cricking, cricks.** To cause a crick in by turning or wrenching. [Middle English *crike, crykke*†.]

Crick (krik), **Francis Harry Compton** (1916–). British biophysicist who, with the U.S. geneticist J.D. Watson, pioneered the study of DNA, proposing a spiral model for the molecular structure of DNA (1953). Crick subsequently investigated protein synthesis in the DNA molecule. He shared the Nobel prize for physiology or medicine with Watson and Maurice Wilkins (1962).

crick·et¹ (kríckit) *n.* **1.** Any of various insects of the family Gryllidae, having long antennae and legs adapted for leaping. The males of many species produce a shrill, chirping sound by rubbing their front wings together. **2.** Any of various similar insects, such as the bush cricket, or the mole cricket. [Middle English *criket*, from Old French *criquet*, from *criquer*, to click, creak (imitative).]

cricket² *n.* A field game, popular in Britain and many of its former colonies, played with bats and a ball on a large field with a 22-yard pitch between the wickets. The object is to score more runs than the opposing team. A full game consists of two innings by each team, and can last up to five days. —**not cricket** *Informal* Unfair; unsporting.
~ *intr.v.* **cricketed, -eting, -ets.** *Rare.* To play cricket. [16th century : origin obscure.] —**crick·et·er** *n.*

cricket³ *n.* A small, low wooden stool. [Origin obscure.]

cri·coid (kríkoyd) *n. Anatomy.* A ring-shaped cartilage of the lower larynx. [Greek *krikoeidēs*, ring-shaped : *krikos*, ring + -OID.] —**cri·coid** *adj.*

cri de coeur (kreé də kér, kōr) *n., pl.* **cris de coeur.** A cry from the heart; a heartfelt appeal or utterance. [Alteration of French *cri du cœur*.]

cri·er (krí-ər) *n.* **1.** One that cries. **2.** A person who shouts out public announcements; especially, a **town crier** (see). **3.** A hawker who advertises his wares by shouting.

cri·key (kríkī) *interj. British Slang.* Used to express surprise or dismay. [Euphemistic for *Christ!*]

crime (krīm) *n.* **1.** An act committed or omitted in violation of a law forbidding or commanding it, and for which punishment is imposed upon conviction. **2.** Unlawful activity in general. **3.** Any serious wrongdoing or offence. **4.** *Informal.* An unjust or senseless act or condition. [Middle English, from Old French, from Latin *crimen*, verdict, judgment, crime.]

Cri·me·a (krī-méer, -meé-ə). *Russian* **Krym** (krim). A peninsula and autonomous region of Ukraine. In 1475 the Crimea was conquered by the Ottoman Turks and was governed as a tributary Tatar Khanate until annexed by Russia in 1783. At the outset of the Crimean War much of the Tatar population was deported. After 1944 the remaining Tatars were exiled, accused of collaborating with occupying German troops. Control of the Crimea passed from the Russian to the Ukrainian S.S.R. in 1954. Simferopol is the capital; Sevastopol the major port. —**Cri·me·an** *adj. & n.*

Crimean War *n.* A war (1853–56) conducted mainly in the Crimea, in which Britain, France, Turkey, and Piedmont defeated Russia.

crime passionel (kreém páss-yə-nél, pásha-) *n. French.* A crime prompted by passion, usually unpremeditated and connected with sexual jealousy. Also called "crime of passion".

crim·i·nal (krímmin'l) *adj. Abbr.* **crim. 1.** Of, involving, or having the nature of crime. **2.** Pertaining to the administration of penal law as distinguished from civil law. **3.** Guilty of crime. **4.** *Informal.* Regrettable; senseless: *a criminal waste of space.*
~ *n.* **1.** A person who has committed or been legally convicted of a crime. **2.** A person who habitually commits crime, usually theft. [Middle English, from Old French *criminel*, from Late Latin *criminālis*, from Latin *crimen* (stem *crimin-*), CRIME.] —**crim·i·nal·ly** *adv.*

criminal conversation *n. Law.* Adultery.

crim·i·nal·i·ty (krímmi-nál-əti) *n., pl.* **-ties. 1.** The state, quality, or fact of being criminal. **2.** *Rare.* A criminal action or practice.

criminal law *n.* Law involving crime and its punishment. Compare civil law.

crim·i·nol·o·gy (krímmi-nólləji) *n.* The study of crime, criminals, and policing. See **penology.** [Italian *criminologia* : CRIME + -LOGY.] —**crim·i·no·log·i·cal** (-nə-lójik'l) *adj.* —**crim·i·no·log·i·cal·ly** *adv.* —**crim·i·nol·o·gist** (-nólləjist) *n.*

crimp¹ (krimp) *tr.v.* **crimped, crimping, crimps. 1.** To press into small, regular folds or ridges; pleat; corrugate. **2.** To bend or

mould (leather) into shape. **3.** To gash (the flesh of a raw fish, for example) to make it crisper and firmer when cooked. **4.** To form (hair) into tight curls or waves. **5.** To bend the edges of (metal) before joining. **6.** *U.S.* To hamper; obstruct.
~ *n.* **1. a.** The act of crimping. **b.** Something that has been crimped. **2.** *Usually plural.* Tightly curled or waved hair. **3.** The natural curliness of wool fibres. **4.** A fold or bend in sheet metal to provide stiffness or form a joint. —**put a crimp in.** *U.S. Informal.* To obstruct; hamper. [Middle English *crimpen*, to wrinkle, shrivel, Old English *gecrympan*, to curl.] —**crimp·er** *n.* —**crimp·y** *adj.*

crimp² *n.* Formerly, a person who procured men to serve as sailors or soldiers by tricking or coercing them.
~ *tr.v.* **crimped, crimping, crimps.** To procure (sailors or soldiers) by trickery or coercion; pressgang. [17th century : origin obscure.]

Crimp·lene (krímpleen) *n.* A trademark for a synthetic, crease-resistant fabric.

crim·son (krímz'n) *n.* A deep to vivid purplish red to vivid red.
~ *v.* **crimsoned, -soning, -sons.** —*intr.* **1.** To become crimson. **2.** To blush. —*tr.* To make crimson. [Middle English *cremesin*, from Old Spanish, from Arabic *qirmizī*, from *qirmiz*, kermes insect (from which red dye was obtained).] —**crim·son** *adj.*

cringe (krinj) *intr.v.* **cringed, cringing, cringes. 1.** To shrink back, as with fear, revulsion, or distate. **2.** To behave in a servile manner; fawn. —See Synonyms at **recoil.**
~ *n.* An act or instance of cringing. [Middle English *crengen*, probably ultimately from Old English *cringan*, to fall dead.]

crin·gle (kríng-g'l) *n. Nautical.* A small ring or eyelet of rope or metal fastened to the edge of a sail. [Low German *kringel*, diminutive of *kring*, ring, circle, from Middle Low German *krink, kring.*]

cri·nite (krí-nīt) *adj. Biology.* Covered with delicate hairs or hairlike tufts. [Latin *crīnītus*, past participle of *crīnīre*, to provide with hair, from *crīnis*, hair.]

crin·kle (kríngk'l) *v.* **-kled, -kling, -kles.** —*intr.* **1.** To form into wrinkles or ripples. **2.** To make a soft, crackling sound; rustle. —*tr.* To cause to wrinkle or rustle.
~ *n.* **1.** A wrinkle or ripple; a fold. **2.** A rustling sound. [Middle English *crinkelen*, akin to Middle Dutch *crinkelen.*] —**crin·kly** *adj.*

cri·noid (krínoyd) *n.* Any of various marine invertebrates of the class Crinoidea, which includes the sea lilies and feather stars, characterised by feathery, radiating arms and a stalk by which they are attached to a surface.
~ *adj.* **1.** Of or belonging to the Crinoidea. **2.** Resembling a lily in shape. [New Latin *Crinoidea* : Greek *krinon*, lily + -OID.]

crin·o·line (krínnə-lin, -leen) *n.* **1.** A coarse, stiff cotton fabric, formerly made of horsehair and linen, used to line and stiffen garments. **2.** A petticoat made of this fabric. **3.** A **hoop skirt.** [French, from Italian *crinolino* : *crino*, horsehair, from Latin *crīnis*, hair + *lino*, flax, from Latin *līnum.*] —**crin·o·line** *adj.*

cri·num (krínəm) *n., pl.* **-nums.** Any of several mostly tropical plants of the genus *Crinum*, having long, strap-shaped leaves and clusters of lily-like flowers. Also called "crinum lily". [New Latin *Crinum*, from Greek *krinon*†, lily.]

cri·ol·lo (kree-óló, -ōl-) *n., pl.* **-los. 1.** A native of Latin America of Spanish descent. Compare **Creole. 2.** Any of various domestic animals belonging to South American breeds. **3.** A high-grade type of cocoa. [Spanish, "native, local". See **Creole.**] —**cri·ol·lo** (-ə) *adj.*

cripes (krīps) *interj. British Slang.* Used to express surprise or dismay. [Euphemistic for *Christ!*]

crip·ple (krípp'l) *n.* **1.** One who is partly disabled or lame. **2.** One who is deficient in a specified way: *an emotional cripple.*
~ *tr.v.* **crippled, -pling, -ples. 1.** To make into a cripple. **2.** To disable or damage. [Middle English *crepel*, Old English *crypel*, from Germanic.] —**crip·pler** *n.*

Cripps (krips), **Sir (Richard) Stafford** (1889–1952). British lawyer and statesman. As a Labour M.P., he helped to form the Socialist League. In World War II he was ambassador to Moscow (1940–42) and minister of aircraft production (1942–45). In the postwar government he was Chancellor of the Exchequer (1947–50).

cris. Variant of **kris.**

Criseyde. Variant of **Cressida.**

cri·sis (krí-siss) *n., pl.* **-ses** (-seez). **1. a.** A crucial point or situation in the course of anything; a turning point. **b.** An unstable condition in political, international, or economic affairs in which an abrupt or decisive change is impending. **2.** *Medicine.* A sudden change in the course of an acute disease, towards either improvement or deterioration. **3.** The point in a story or drama at which hostile forces are at their most tense state of opposition. [Latin, from Greek *krisis*, turning point, from *krinein*, to separate, decide.]

crisis centre *n.* **1.** A place used as headquarters during an emergency for organising relief work. **2.** A place providing advice or psychological support, as, for example, to victims of rape or assault.

crisp (krisp) *adj.* **crisper, crispest. 1.** Firm but easily broken or crumbled; brittle. **2.** Firm and fresh: *crisp celery.* **3.** Brisk; invigorating; bracing. **4.** Animated; stimulating. **5.** Terse; pithy; sharp. **6.** Well defined; neat. **7.** Having small curls, waves, or ripples. —See Synonyms at **incisive.**
~ *v.* **crisped, crisping, crisps.** —*tr.* To make crisp. —*intr.* To become crisp.
~ *n.* **1.** A crisp part. **2.** *Chiefly British.* A thin, dry, often salted, potato slice. Also *chiefly U.S.* "potato chip". [Middle English *crisp*, Old English *crisp*, curly, from Latin *crispus*, crisped, curly.] —**crisp·ly** *adv.* —**crisp·ness** *n.*

cris·pate (kríss-payt) *adj.* Also **cris·pat·ed** (kriss-páytid). Crimped, curled, or tightly waved. [Latin *crispātus,* from *crispāre,* to curl, from *crispus,* curly, CRISP.]

cris·pa·tion (kriss-páysh'n) *n.* **1. a.** The act of crisping or curling. **b.** The state of being crisped or curled. **2.** A slight involuntary contraction or constriction, as of the skin. **3.** A minute undulation on the surface of a liquid, produced by vibration.

crisp·bread (krísp-bred) *n.* A flat, dry, unsweetened biscuit made of wheat or rye flour, popular with slimmers.

crisp·er (kríspər) *n.* One that crisps; especially, a compartment in a refrigerator, used for storing vegetables to keep them fresh.

crisp·y (kríspi) *adj.* **-ier, -iest.** Crisp. **—crisp·i·ly** *adv.* **—crisp·i·ness** *n.*

criss·cross (kríss-kross ‖ -krawss) *v.* **-crossed, -crossing, -crosses.** **—tr.** **1.** To mark with crossing lines. **2.** To move crossways through or over. **—intr.** To move crossways or in crisscrosses.
~n. **1.** A mark or pattern made of crossing lines. **2.** *U.S.* A game, **noughts and crosses** (*see*).
~adj. Crossing one another or marked by crossings.
~adv. In a crisscross manner; in crossing directions. [Variant of CHRISTCROSS.]

cris·sum (kríss-əm) *n., pl.* **crissa** (-ə). *Zoology.* The feathers or area surrounding a bird's cloacal opening. [New Latin, from Latin *crissāre, crisāre,* to move the haunches.] **—cris·sal** *adj.*

cris·ta (kríss-tə) *n., pl.* **-tae** (-tee). *Biology.* A crest or ridge; especially, any of the infoldings of the inner membrane of a mitochondrion, or a sensory structure in the semicircular canal of the ear. [Latin, CREST.]

cris·tate (kríss-tayt) *adj.* Also **cris·tat·ed** (kriss-táytid) Having or forming a crest. [Latin *cristātus,* from *crista,* tuft, crest.]

cris·to·bal·ite (kriss-tṓbəlīt) *n.* A white mineral form of silica, SiO₂, found in volcanic rocks. [From German, after Cerro San *Cristóbal,* Mexico, where it was discovered.]

cri·te·ri·on (krī-téer-i-ən) *n., pl.* **-ria** (-ə). A standard, rule, or test on which a judgment or decision can be based. [Greek *kritērion,* a means for judging, standard, from *krites,* a judge, umpire, from *krinein,* to separate, choose.]

Usage: Criteria is used only as a plural form in standard English. Constructions such as *a criteria* or *the criteria is* are not acceptable in educated usage.

crit·ic (kríttik) *n.* **1.** One who forms and expresses judgments of the merits and faults of anything. **2.** *Abbr.* **crit.** A professional specialist in the explication and judgment of literary or artistic works. **3.** A person who finds fault; a severe judge. **4.** *Obsolete.* A critique; a criticism. [Latin *criticus,* from adjective, "decisive", from Greek *kritikos,* able to discern, critical, from *kritos,* separated, chosen, from *krinein,* to separate, choose.]

crit·i·cal (kríttik'l) *adj. Abbr.* **crit.** **1.** Inclined to judge severely; given to censuring. **2.** Characterised by careful and exact evaluation and judgment. **3.** Of, pertaining to, or characteristic of critics or criticism: *critical acclaim.* **4.** Forming, or of the nature of, a crisis; crucial. **5.** Fraught with danger or risk; perilous. **6.** Designating materials and products essential to some condition or project but in short supply. **7.** *Medicine.* Of or pertaining to a crisis. **8.** *Mathematics.* Of or pertaining to a point at which a curve has a maximum, minimum, or point of inflection. **9.** *Chemistry & Physics.* Of or pertaining to a condition causing an abrupt change in a quality, property, or phenomenon. **—go critical.** To produce a self-sustaining nuclear reaction, as when becoming operational. Used especially of a nuclear power station. **—crit·i·cal·ly** *adv.*

Synonyms: critical, acute, crucial, serious.

critical angle *n.* **1.** *Optics.* The smallest angle of incidence at which a light ray passing from one medium to another less refractive medium can be totally reflected from the boundary between the two. **2.** *Aviation.* The **stalling angle** (*see*).

critical apparatus *n.* An **apparatus criticus** (*see*).

critical constants *pl.n.* *Physics.* Constants, such as critical temperature, pressure, and volume, that characterise the critical point of a given substance.

critical mass *n.* The smallest mass of a fissionable material that will sustain a nuclear chain reaction.

critical-path analysis (kríttik'l-paáth ‖ -páth) *n.* A technique for finding the best way of completing a complex process in the minimum time by analysing alternative combinations of stages.

critical point *n.* **1.** *Physics.* The condition in which the liquid and vapour phases of a pure stable substance have the same density. Also called "critical state". **2.** *Mathematics.* **a.** A maximum, minimum, or point of inflection. **b.** A point at which the derivative of a function is zero or infinite.

critical pressure *n.* The least applied pressure required at the critical temperature to liquefy a gas.

critical speed *n.* *Physics.* The speed above which fluid flow changes from smooth laminar flow to turbulent flows.

critical temperature *n.* The temperature above which a gas cannot be liquefied, regardless of the pressure applied.

critical volume *n.* The volume of one mole of a substance at its critical point.

crit·i·cise, crit·i·cize (kríttì-sīz) *v.* **-cised, -cising, -cises.** **—tr.** **1.** To judge the merits and faults of someone or something; analyse and evaluate. **2.** To judge with severity; find fault with; censure. **—intr.** **1.** To find fault. **2.** To act as a critic. **—crit·i·cis·a·ble** *adj.* **—crit·i·cis·er** *n.*

Synonyms: blame, reprehend, censure, condemn, denounce.

crit·i·cism (krítti-siz'm) *n. Abbr.* **crit.** **1.** The act of making judgments or criticising. **2. a.** The passing of unfavourable judgment; censure; disapproval. **b.** An instance of this; a critical comment or observation. **3.** The art, skill, or profession of making discriminating judgments and evaluations, especially of literary or other artistic works. **4.** A review or other article expressing such judgment and evaluation; a critique. **5.** The detailed investigation of the origin and history of literary documents, especially in order to produce the most authentic possible text. Also called "textual criticism".

cri·tique (kri-téek) *n.* **1.** A critical review or commentary, especially one dealing with a literary or other artistic work. **2.** A critical discussion of some specified topic. **3.** The art of criticism.
~ tr.v. **critiqued, -tiquing, -tiques.** To do a critique of; review. [French, from Greek *kritikē,* the art of criticism, from *kritikos,* critical. See **critic.**]

crit·ter (kríttər) *n. U.S. Regional.* **1.** A creature, especially a domestic animal. **2.** A person. [Variant of CREATURE.]

CRO **1.** cathode-ray oscilloscope. **2.** Criminal Records Office.

croak (krōk) *v.* **croaked, croaking, croaks.** **—intr.** **1.** To utter the low, hoarse sound characteristic of frogs and crows. **2.** To speak with a low, hoarse voice. **3.** To talk discontentedly or dolefully. **4.** *Slang.* To die. **—tr.** **1.** To utter by croaking. **2.** *Slang.* To kill. **~n.** A croaking sound. [Middle English *croken* (imitative).] **—croak·i·ly** *adv.* **—croak·y** *adj.*

croak·er (krṓkər) *n.* **1. a.** A croaking animal. **b.** A person who grumbles or habitually predicts evil. **2.** Any of various chiefly marine fishes of the family Sciaenidae, that make croaking sounds.

Croat (krṓ-at, -ət ‖ krōt) *n.* **1.** A native or inhabitant of Croatia. **2.** The Slavonic language of the Croats; Croatian.

Cro·a·tia, Republic of (krō-áysh-ə, -yə). *Serbo-Croat* **Hrvatska.** Former constituent republic of Yugoslavia, situated in the northwest of the country. The Croats, a Slav people, occupied the area in the seventh century. In 1102, it became associated with the Hungarian crown, and largely remained so until the collapse of Austria-Hungary (1918), when the kingdom of Serbs, Croats, and Slovenes (later Yugoslavia) was formed. In 1992, after civil war between Croats and minority Serbs, and conflict with Serbia, Croatia declared its independence. Area, 56 610 square kilometres (21,857 square miles). Population, 4,500,000. Capital, Zagreb.

Cro·a·tian (krō-áysh'n) *adj.* Of or pertaining to Croatia, the Croats, their language, or their culture.
~n. **1.** A Croat. **2.** A form of the Serbo-Croatian language written using the Latin alphabet.

cro·ce·in (krṓ-see-in) *n.* Any of various red or orange acid azo dyes. [Latin *croceus,* saffron-coloured, from *crocus,* saffron, CROCUS + -IN.]

cro·chet (krṓ-shay, -shi ‖ -shər, *U.S.* krō-sháy) *v.* **-cheted** (-shayd, -shid ‖ -shərd, *U.S.* -sháyd), **-cheting** (-shay-ing, -shi- ‖ -shər-, *U.S.* -sháy-), **-chets** (shayz, -shiz ‖ -shərz, *U.S.* -sháyz). **—intr.** To make a piece of needlework by looping thread with a hooked needle. **—tr.** To make or decorate (a fabric) by looping thread with a hooked needle.
~n. A kind of needlework made by crocheting. [French, a hook, from Old French, diminutive of *croc(he),* a hook, from Frankish *krōk* (unattested).]

cro·cid·o·lite (krō-síddə-līt) *n.* A fibrous, lavender-blue or greenish mineral, a sodium iron silicate that is used as a commercial form of asbestos. Also called "blue asbestos". [German *Krokydolith,* "fibrous stone" : Greek *krokus* (stem krokud-), nap of cloth + -LITE.]

crock¹ (krok) *n.* **1.** An earthenware vessel. **2.** A piece of broken earthenware; a potsherd. [Middle English *crokke,* Old English *crocc(a).*]

crock² *n. British Regional.* **1.** Soot. **2.** Colouring matter that rubs off from poorly dyed cloth.
~v. **crocked, crocking, crocks.** *British Regional.* **—tr.** To stain with or as with crock. **—intr.** To give off soot or colour. [Possibly

CROATIA

from CROCK (pot, hence "soot on a cooking pot").]

crock³ *n. Chiefly British. Informal.* One that is worn-out, decrepit, or impaired, especially a car.
~*v.* **crocked, crocking, crocks.** *Chiefly British Slang.* —*intr.* To get sick; become weak or disabled. Often used with *up.* —*tr.* To cause to collapse; disable. Sometimes used with *up.* [Middle English *crok,* perhaps from Scandinavian.]

crocked (krokt) *adj.* **1.** *British Slang.* Disabled through injury. **2.** *U.S. Slang.* Drunk. [Perhaps from CROCK (to become disabled).]

crock·er·y (krókəri) *n.* Plates, cups, and the like collectively; china or earthenware.

crock·et (krókit) *n. Architecture.* An ornamental device, usually in the form of a cusp or curling leaf, placed along outer angles of pinnacles and gables, especially in the Gothic style. [Middle English *croket,* from Old North French *croquet,* variant of Old French *crochet,* hook. See **crochet**.]

Crock·ett (krókit), **Davy** (1786-1836). U.S. frontiersman and political figure renowned as a shrewd, homespun backwoodsman. He became a Congressman (1827-31, 1833-35) and later fought for Texas against Mexico. He died at the siege of the Alamo.

croc·o·dile (krókə-dīl) *n.* **1.** Any of various large aquatic reptiles of the genus *Crocodylus* and related genera, of tropical regions, having thick, armour-like skin and long, tapering jaws. **2.** Broadly, any crocodilian reptile, such as an alligator, cayman, or gavial. **3.** Leather made from crocodile skin. [Middle English *cocodril,* from Old French, from Medieval Latin *cocodrillus,* from Latin *crocodīlus,* from Greek *krokodilos,* "worm of the pebbles" (from its habit of basking in the sun) : *krokē*†, pebbles + *drilos*†, worm.]

crocodile clip *n.* A small spring clip with long-toothed jaws, used to make temporary electrical connections.

crocodile tears *pl.n.* False tears; an insincere display of grief. [From the belief that crocodiles weep after eating their victims.]

croc·o·dil·i·an (krókə-dílli-ən) *n.* Any of various reptiles of the order Crocodilia, which includes the alligators, crocodiles, caymans, and gavials. [New Latin *Crocodylia,* from Latin *crocodīlus,* CROCODILE.] —**croc·o·dil·i·an** *adj.*

cro·co·ite (krókō-īt) *n.* A rare orange to reddish mineral of lead chromate, PbCrO₄, found in oxidised lead deposits. [Earlier *crocoisite* : French *crocoise,* from Greek *krokoeis,* saffron-like, from *krokos,* saffron, CROCUS + -ITE.]

cro·cus (krō-kəss) *n., pl.* **-cuses** or **-ci** (-sī). Any plant of the genus *Crocus,* widely cultivated in gardens, and having showy, variously coloured flowers and grasslike leaves. See **autumn crocus.** [New Latin *Crocus,* from Latin *crocus,* saffron, from Greek *krokos,* from Semitic, akin to Hebrew *karkōm.*]

Croe·sus (krée-səss), (died *c.* 546 B.C.). Last King of Lydia (*c.* 560-546 B.C.). He allied himself with Babylonia and Egypt and extended his kingdom, building a legendary prosperity on commerce.

croft (kroft ‖ krawft) *n. British.* **1.** A small enclosed field or pasture. **2.** An agricultural smallholding, especially in the Highlands and islands of Scotland. [Middle English *croft,* Old English *croft.*]

croft·er (króftər ‖ kráwftər) *n. British & Scottish.* A person who rents or owns a croft, especially in Scotland.

Crohn's disease (krōnz) *n. Medicine.* **Regional ileitis** *(see).* [After B. B. Crohn (1884 – 1983), U.S. gastroenterologist.]

crois·sant (krwaá-soɴ, krwa- ‖ *U.S.* krwaa-sóɴ) *n.* A rich, crescent-shaped roll of leavened dough or puff pastry. [French, from Old French *croissant, creissant,* CRESCENT.]

Croix de Guerre (krwaá də gaír) *n.* A French military decoration for bravery in battle. [French, "cross of war".]

Cro-Mag·non (krō-mán-yon, -yən ‖ -mág-nən) *adj.* Of, relating to, or designating an early form of modern man, *Homo sapiens sapiens,* inhabiting Europe in the late Palaeolithic era, characterised by a tall stature and known from skeletal parts found in the Cro-Magnon cave in southern France. —**Cro-Magnon** *n.*

Cromarty. See **Ross and Cromarty.**

crom·lech (króm-lek, -lekh) *n.* **1.** A prehistoric monument consisting of monoliths encircling a mound. **2.** A **dolmen** *(see).* [Welsh : *crom,* feminine of *crwn,* arched + *llech,* flat stone.]

Cromp·ton (krómp-tən, krúmp-), **Richmal,** born Richmal Crompton Lamburn (1890-1969). British novelist. She is best remembered for her children's novels with the anarchic schoolboy, William Brown, as hero. *Just—William* (1922) was the first of many titles.

Crompton, Samuel (1753-1827). British inventor of the spinning mule (1779), which combined the principles of Hargreaves's spinning jenny and Arkwright's water frame.

Crom·well (króm-wəl, krúm-, -wel), **Oliver** (1599-1658). English soldier and statesman, Lord Protector of England (1653-58). A Puritan and critic of Charles I, he founded the New Model Army (1644). Originally working for reconciliation between army, Crown, and Parliament he eventually sided with the army. During the second Civil War (1648) he came to support demands for Charles's execution (1649). As Lord Lieutenant of Ireland (1649-50), he ruthlessly suppressed rebellion and defeated the royalist rising of Scots at Worcester (1651). In 1653 he dismissed the governing Rump parliament, and after the failure of the Barebones parliament accepted leadership of a kingless Protectorate. As Lord Protector he pursued a vigorous foreign policy against Spain and conquered Jamaica (1655). At home he tried to restrain the excess of Puritan zeal but was beset by constitutional difficulties.

Cromwell, Richard (1626-1712). Son of Oliver, he succeeded him briefly as Lord Protector (1658-59) before the restoration of the monarchy under Charles II.

Cromwell, Thomas, Earl of Essex (*c.* 1485-1540). English lawyer and statesman who devised the legislation that made the English church independent of Rome, culminating in the Act of Supremacy (1534). From 1536 he supervised the dissolution of the monasteries. He lost favour, was accused of treason and executed.

Crom·wel·li·an (króm-wélli-ən, krúm-) *adj.* Of, pertaining to, or characteristic of Oliver Cromwell or his time; especially, austere or puritanical. —**Crom·wel·li·an** *n.*

crone (krōn) *n.* A withered old woman. [Middle English, from Middle Dutch *caroonje, croonje,* old ewe, dead body, from Old North French *carogne,* CARRION.]

Cron·os, Kron·os (krón-oss, krōn-). *Greek Mythology.* A Titan who ruled the universe until dethroned by his son Zeus; identified with the Roman god Saturn.

cro·ny (krōni) *n., pl.* **-nies.** **1.** A close friend or companion. **2.** An associate in some dishonest or questionable activity. [Earlier *chrony* (Cambridge University slang), "old companion," from Greek *khronios,* long-lasting, from *khronos,* time.]

crook (krŏŏk ‖ krŏŏk) *n.* **1.** Something bent or curved; a hook or hooked part. **2.** An implement or tool with a bent or curved part, such as a bishop's crosier or a shepherd's staff. **3.** A curve or bend; a turn. **4.** *Informal.* A person who makes his living by dishonest methods; a thief.
~*v.* **crooked, crooking, crooks.** —*tr.* To give a crook to or make a crook in; curve; bend. —*intr.* To become crooked.
~*adj. Australian & N. Z. Informal.* **1.** Unwell or disabled. **2.** Faulty; out of order. **3.** Poor in quality. **4.** Dishonest. **5.** Unpleasant. —**go (off) crook (at).** *Australian & N. Z. Informal.* To become angry with or reproach (a person). [Middle English *crok,* from Old Norse *krōkr,* a hook.]

crook·back (krŏŏk-bak ‖ krŏŏk-) *n. Archaic.* A hunchback. —**crook·backed** *adj.*

crook·ed (krŏŏkid ‖ krŏŏkid) *adj.* **1.** Having bends, curves, or angles; not straight. **2.** *Informal.* Dishonest or unscrupulous; fraudulent. **3.** Misshapen; deformed. **4.** *Australian & N. Z. Informal.* Opposed to or angry with. Used with *on.* —**crook·ed·ly** *adv.* —**crook·ed·ness** *n.*

Crookes (krŏŏks), **Sir William** (1832-1919). British chemist and physicist. He discovered the element thallium (1861) and invented the radiometer. He pioneered research into cathode rays.

Crookes dark space *n.* A small dark region near the cathode in a luminous gas discharge. [After Sir William CROOKES.]

Crookes glass *n.* A type of glass containing cerium, which cuts down the transmission of ultraviolet radiation. It is used in sunglasses and protective goggles. [After Sir William CROOKES.]

Crookes radiometer *n.* A device consisting of a small, evacuated glass bulb containing a set of four light, vertical metal vanes, each blackened on one side and mounted on a vertical, rotating spindle. When light or other radiation falls on the tube, the vanes rotate. [After Sir William CROOKES.]

Crookes tube *n.* A low-pressure discharge tube used to study the properties of cathode rays. [After Sir William CROOKES.]

croon (krŏŏn) *v.* **crooned, crooning, croons.** —*intr.* **1.** To sing or hum softly; murmur. **2.** To sing popular songs in a soft, sentimental manner. **3.** *British Regional.* **a.** To wail or cry softly, as when lamenting. **b.** To utter a deep, loud sound; roar. —*tr.* To sing by crooning.
~*n.* A soft singing, humming, or murmuring. [Middle English *croynen,* to boom, sing, from Middle Dutch *krōnen,* to groan, lament (imitative).] —**croon·er** *n.*

crop (krop) *n.* **1.** Cultivated plants or agricultural produce, such as grain, vegetables, or fruit. **2.** The quantity or quality of such produce of a particular season, place, or kind. **3.** A group, quantity, or supply appearing at one time: *this year's crop of students.* **4.** A short haircut. **5.** An animal hide, tanned and complete. **6. a.** A short whip used in horse-riding, with a loop serving as a lash. **b.** The stock of a whip. **7.** *Zoology.* **a.** A pouchlike enlargement of a bird's oesophagus, in which food is stored or partially digested. **b.** A similar organ in earthworms, insects, and other invertebrates. **8.** The mark produced by cropping the ears of a domestic animal.
~*v.* **cropped, cropping, crops.** —*tr.* **1.** To cut off the stems or top of (a plant). **2.** To cut (hair, for example) very short. **3.** To clip (an animal's ears or a photograph, for example). **4.** To reap; harvest. **5.** To cause to grow or yield a crop or crops. —*intr.* To plant, grow, or yield a crop or crops. —**crop out.** To project above the ground. Used of rock formations. —**crop up.** To appear or develop unexpectedly. [Middle English *crop,* Old English *cropp,* cluster, bunch, ear of corn, from Germanic.]

crop-dusting (króp-dusting) *n.* The spraying of crops with insecticidal or fungicidal dust, usually from a light aircraft.

crop-eared (króp-eerd) *adj.* **1.** Having the ears cropped. **2.** With the hair cut so short that the ears show.

crop·per¹ (króppər) *n.* **1.** A person, animal, or machine that crops. **2.** A person who works land in return for a share of the yield; a sharecropper. **3.** *Informal.* A plant that yields a crop of the specified type: *a generous cropper; a late cropper.*

cropper² *n.* **1.** A heavy fall; a tumble. **2.** A disastrous failure; a fiasco. —**come a cropper.** **1.** To fall heavily. **2.** To fail miserably; come to grief. [From the phrase *neck and crop,* "completely", perhaps from CROP (to cut off).]

crop rotation *n.* The practice of growing different crops successively on a piece of land so as to conserve the fertility of the soil.

cro·quet (krō-kay, -ki ‖ *U.S.* krō-káy) *n.* **1.** An outdoor game in which the players drive wooden balls through a series of loops using long-handled mallets. **2.** The act of driving away an opponent's croquet ball by hitting one's own ball when the two are in contact. ~*v.* **croqueted** (-kayd, -kid ‖ -káyd), **-queting** (-kay-ing, -ki- ‖ -káy-), **-quets** (-kayz, -kiz ‖ -káyz). —*tr.* To drive away (an opponent's ball) with a croquet. —*intr.* To croquet an opponent's ball. [Perhaps dialect form of French *crochet,* a hook. See **crochet.**]

cro·quette (kro-két, krō-, krə-) *n.* A small cake of savoury minced or moulded food, coated with bread crumbs and deep-fried. [French, from *croquer,* to crunch, crack (imitative).]

crore (kror ‖ krōr) *n. Indian.* Ten million, or a set containing ten million units. Compare **lakh.** [Hindi *k(ā)rōr,* from Prakrit *krodi,* from Sanskrit *koti,* apex.]

Cros·by (krózbi), **Bing,** born Harry Lillis Crosby (1904–77). U.S. singer, actor, and entertainer. He popularised a new, softer, and more relaxed style of singing, and starred with Bob Hope in the *Road* series of comedy films.

cro·sier, cro·zier (krō-zhər, -zi-ər) *n.* **1.** A staff with a crook at the end, carried by or before an abbot, bishop, or archbishop as a symbol of office. Also called "pastoral staff". **2.** *Botany.* A coiled tip of a plant stalk, as of a young fern frond. [Middle English *crocer,* from Old French *crossier,* staff-bearer, from *crosse,* bishop's staff, from Germanic.]

cross (kross ‖ krawss) *n.* **1.** A structure, mark, or pattern formed typically by the intersection of two lines of equal length or two lines at right angles. **2.** An upright post with a transverse piece near the top, upon which condemned persons were executed in ancient times. **3.** Any of several representations of the cross upon which Jesus was crucified. **4.** A sign made of the cross. **5.** A crucifix. **6. a.** Any of various symbolic or ornamental figures or structures in the form of a cross or modified cross, such as a medal or emblem. **b.** A monument in the form of a cross, often at a central place in a town or village. **7.** A source of trouble or sorrow; an affliction: *She too has her cross to bear.* **8.** A mark (X) used as a signature, or to indicate an error, point of intersection, and the like. **9.** A pipe fitting with four branches in the form of a cross, used as a junction for intersecting pipes. **10.** *Biology.* **a.** A plant or animal produced by crossbreeding; a hybrid. **b.** The process of crossbreeding; hybridisation. **11.** A combination of the qualities of two things or people. **12.** *Slang.* A swindle or fraud; especially, a contest whose outcome has been dishonestly prearranged. **13.** *Sports.* **a.** In boxing, a punch launched from the side, usually the right. **b.** In soccer, a shot that sends the ball across the pitch: *a long cross to the centre.* —**the Cross. 1.** The cross upon which Jesus was crucified. **2.** Christianity; the Christian religion. ~*v.* **crossed, crossing, crosses.** —*tr.* **1.** To go across; pass from one side of to the other. **2.** To carry or convey across. **3.** To extend or pass across, through, or over; intersect. **4.** To make or put a line across. **5.** To lay across or over; place crosswise: *cross one's legs.* **6.** To make the sign of the cross upon (oneself) or over (another) as a sign of devotion. **7.** To encounter in passing: *His path crossed mine.* **8.** To thwart or obstruct; interfere with: *Do not cross me.* **9.** *Biology.* To crossbreed or cross-fertilise (plants or animals). **10.** *British.* To draw two parallel lines across (a cheque), thus making it payable only through the payee's bank account. —*intr.* **1.** To lie or pass across each other; intersect. **2.** To move or extend from one side to another. **3.** To encounter each other in passing: *Our paths crossed.* **4.** *Biology.* To crossbreed or cross-fertilise. **5.** To be in the post simultaneously. Used of two letters addressed to each other's senders. —**cross off** or **out.** To cancel or eliminate by or as if by drawing a line or lines through. ~*adj.* **1.** Lying or passing crosswise; intersecting. **2.** Contrary or counter; opposing. **3.** Showing ill humour; annoyed. **4.** Crossbred; hybrid. [Middle English *cros,* Old English *cros,* from Old Irish *cross,* from Latin *crux* (stem *cruc-*), perhaps from Phoenician.] —**cross·er** *n.* —**cross·ly** *adv.* —**cross·ness** *n.*

cross·bar (króss-baar ‖ kráws-) *n.* A horizontal beam or bar, as on a hurdle, on a bicycle, or on goalposts.

cross·beam (króss-beem ‖ kráwss-) *n.* A beam that links or rests on two supports.

cross bedding *n. Geology.* The formation of laminations within a stratum at a different angle to that of the main bed. Also called "current bedding", "false bedding".

cross·bench (króss-bench ‖ kráwss-) *n. British.* A bench in Parliament occupied by members who belong to neither government nor opposition. —**cross·bench·er** (-bénchər, -benchər) *n.*

cross·bill (króss-bil ‖ kráwss-) *n.* Any of several birds of the genus *Loxia,* having bills whose upper and lower parts curve and cross at their narrow tips.

cross·bones (króss-bōnz ‖ kráwss-) *n.* See **skull and crossbones.**

cross·bow (króss-bō ‖ kráwss-) *n.* A medieval weapon consisting of a bow fixed crosswise on a wooden stock, with grooves on the stock to direct the arrow or other projectile. —**cross·bow·man** (-mən) *n.*

cross·breed (króss-breed ‖ kráwss-) *v.* **-bred** (-bred), **-breeding, -breeds.** —*tr.* **1.** To make individuals of (different varieties or breeds); hybridise. **2.** To produce (a hybrid) by crossbreeding. —*intr.* To mate so as to produce a hybrid; interbreed. ~*n.* A hybrid produced by crossbreeding. Also called "crossbred".

cross·check (króss-chék ‖ kráwss-) *tr.v.* **-checked, -checking, -checks.** To verify by comparing with supplementary data. ~*n.* (-chek). An act of crosschecking.

cross·coun·try (króss-kúntri ‖ kráwss-) *adj.* **1.** Moving or directed

across open country, rather than following roads. **2.** From one side of a country to the opposite side. ~*n.* A long running race over open country. —**cross-coun·try** *adv.*

cross-cul·tur·al (króss-kúlchərəl ‖ kráwss-) *adj.* Dealing with or involving two or more different cultures: *a cross-cultural study of marriage customs.*

cross-cur·rent (króss-kurrənt ‖ kráwss-) *n.* **1.** A current flowing across another current. **2.** A conflicting movement, tendency, or inclination.

cross-cut (króss-kut ‖ kráwss-) *v.* **-cut, -cutting, -cuts.** —*tr.* **1.** To cut across transversely. **2.** In film-making, to intercut. —*intr.* To cut or run crosswise. ~*adj.* **1.** Used or constructed for cutting crosswise: *a crosscut saw.* **2.** Cut on the bias or across the grain. ~*n.* **1.** A course or cut going crosswise. **2.** A path more direct than the main path; a short cut. **3.** In mining, a level driven so that it intersects a vein of ore.

cross-dres·ser (króss-dréssər ‖ kráwss) *n.* A **transvestite** *(see).* —**cross-dres·sing** *n.*

crosse (kross ‖ krawss) *n.* A lacrosse stick. [French, from Old French *crosse,* staff. See **crosier.**]

crossed line (krost ‖ krawst) *n.* A telephone connection between two callers in which another call can be heard.

cross-ex·am·ine (króss-ig-zámmin, -eg- ‖ kráwss-, -ik-) *v.* **-ined, -ining, -ines.** —*tr.* **1.** To question (someone) closely, especially in order to check the resulting answers against answers previously made. **2.** *Law.* To question (a witness already examined by the opposing side). —*intr.* To question a person closely. —**cross-ex·am·i·na·tion** (-áysh'n) *n.* —**cross-ex·am·in·er** *n.*

cross-eye (króss-ī, -ī ‖ kráwss-) *n.* An eye defect in which one or both eyes turn towards the nose; a squint. See **strabismus.** —**cross-eyed** *adj.*

cross-fer·ti·li·sa·tion (króss-fértil-ī-záysh'n ‖ kráwss-, -fért'l-, *U.S.* -i-) *n.* **1.** *Biology.* The union of gametes from different individuals, usually of the same species. Cross-fertilisation in plants is also called "allogamy". **2.** An interchange, as of ideas or methods, between different groups. —**cross-fer·tile** *adj.*

cross-fer·ti·lise, cross-fer·ti·lize (króss-fértil-īz ‖ kráwss-, -fért'l-) *v.* **-lised, -lising, -lises.** —*tr.* To fertilise by means of cross-fertilisation. —*intr.* To be fertilised by means of cross-fertilisation.

cross-fire (króss-fīr ‖ kráwss-) *n.* **1.** *Military.* Lines of fire from two or more positions crossing one another at or near a single objective. **2.** Any situation in which things originating from different sources meet in conflict. **3.** A heated exchange of conflicting ideas.

cross-grained (króss-gráynd, -graynd ‖ kráwss-) *adj.* **1.** Having an irregular, transverse, or diagonal grain. **2.** Stubborn; contrary.

cross hairs *pl.n.* Cross **wires** *(see).*

cross·hatch (króss-hách, -hach ‖ kráwss-) *tr.v.* **-hatched, -hatching, -hatches.** In drawing, to shade with two or more sets of intersecting parallel lines. —**cross·hatch·ing** *n.*

cross·head (króss-hed ‖ kráwss-) *n.* **1.** *Engineering.* A beam that connects the piston rod to the connecting rod of a reciprocating engine. **2.** *Printing.* A subheading. ~*adj.* **1.** Designating a screw that has a cross-shaped notch in its head. **2.** Designating a screwdriver designed to fit such a screw.

cross·ing (króss-ing ‖ kráwssing) *n.* **1.** A place at which roads, lines, or tracks intersect; an intersection. **2.** A place at which something, such as a river or road, may be crossed. **3.** An act or instance of crossing, especially in a ship: *a rough crossing from Dover to Calais.* **4.** The intersection of the nave and transept in a cruciform church. **5.** The act of crossbreeding.

crossing over *n.* The exchange of genetic material between homologous chromosomes during the formation of gametes. Also called "crossover".

cross·jack (króss-jak ‖ kráwss-) *n.* The square sail below the lowest mizzenmast spar on a ship. [CROSS + JACK (flag).]

cross-legged (króss-legd, -légd, -léggid ‖ kráwss-) *adj.* With one leg crossed over the other. —**cross-legged** *adv.*

cross·let (króss-lit, -lət ‖ kráwss-) *n. Heraldry.* A cross with a smaller cross at each of the four tips. [16th century *croslet,* diminutive of CROSS.]

cross-link (króss-lingk, -língk ‖ kráwss-) *Chemistry.* Also **cross·link·age** (-línk-ij). A short chain of atoms joined across two long chains in certain types of polymer. ~*v.* **cross-linked, -linking, -links.** —*tr.* To cause the formation of cross-links in (a polymer). —*intr.* To polymerise with cross-links.

Cross·man (króss-mən ‖ kráwss-), **Richard (Howard Stafford)** (1907–74). British Labour politician and writer. He became minister of housing and local government (1964–66) and of social services (1968–70). He was editor of the *New Statesman* (1970–72). His posthumous *Diaries of a Cabinet Minister* (4 vols, 1975–81) controversially revealed secrets of Cabinet meetings.

cross matching *n.* The process by which blood compatibility between donor and recipient is tested before transfusion.

cros·sop·te·ryg·i·an (króssop-tə-ríji-ən) *n.* A member of the Crossopterygii, a group of mostly extinct bony fishes including the coelacanths, believed to have been the possible ancestors of terrestrial vertebrates. [New Latin *Crossopterygii,* "the fringed-winged ones" : Greek *krossoi†,* fringe + Greek *pterux,* wing, from *pteron,* feather, wing.] —**cros·sop·te·ryg·i·an** *adj.*

cross·o·ver (króss-ōvər ‖ kráwss-) *n.* **1.** A place at which or the means by which a crossing is made. **2.** A short connecting track by which a train can be transferred from one line to another. **3.** *Genet-*

ics. a. A crossing over. **b.** A character combination resulting from crossing over.

cross-patch (króss-pach ‖ kráwss-) *n. Informal.* A peevish, irascible person. [CROSS (angry) + obsolete *patch,* jester, probably from Italian *pazzo†.*]

cross-piece (króss-peess ‖ kráwss-) *n.* A transverse piece, such as a beam in a building.

cross-ply (króss-plī ‖ kráwss-) *adj.* Designating car tyres that have fabric cords lying crosswise to stiffen the sidewalls. Compare **radial-ply.**
~*n.* A cross-ply tyre.

cross-pol·li·na·tion (króss-pólli-náysh'n ‖ kráwss-) *n.* The transfer of pollen from the stamens of a flower of one plant to the stigma of a flower of another plant, either naturally by insects or wind, or artificially by hand. —**cross-pol·li·nate** (-nayt) *v.* —**cross-pol·li·na·tor** (-naytər) *n.*

cross product *n. Mathematics.* A vector product *(see).*

cross-pur·pos·es (krósiz-púrpəs-iz ‖ kráwss-) *pl.n.* Conflicting or contrary purposes; mutual misunderstanding. Used in the phrase *be at cross-purposes.*

cross-ques·tion (króss-kwés-chən ‖ kráwss-) *tr.v.* **-tioned, -tioning, -tions.** To cross-examine; question closely.
~*n.* A question asked in the process of cross-examination.

cross-re·fer (króss-ri-fér, -rə- ‖ kráwss-, -ree-) *v.* **-ferred, -ferring, -fers.** —*tr.* **1.** To refer (the reader) from one part or passage to another. **2.** To refer (one item or section in a text) to another. —*intr.* To make a cross-reference.

cross-ref·er·ence (króss-réf-rənss, -réffə- ‖ kráwss-) *n.* A reference from one part of a book, index, catalogue, or file to another part containing related information.
~*tr.v.* **cross-referenced, -encing, ences.** To supply (a text) with cross-references.

cross-roads (króss-rōdz ‖ kráwss-) *n., pl.* **crossroads. 1.** A place where two or more roads meet. **2.** A place where different cultures meet. **3.** A crucial point or place.

cross-ruff (króss-rúf, -ruf ‖ kráwss-) *n.* A series of plays in card games such as bridge and whist where partnership hands alternately trump the other's lead.
~*v.* **crossruffed, -ruffing, -ruffs.** —*intr.* To perform a crossruff or a series of crossruffs. —*tr.* To trump (one's partner's lead or a lead from the dummy) in alternating plays.

cross-section (króss-séksh'n) *n.* **1.** A section formed by a plane cutting through an object, usually at right angles to an axis. **2.** A piece so cut or a graphic representation of such a piece. **3.** *Physics.* A measure of the probability of occurrence of a particular atomic or nuclear reaction. **4.** A representative sample meant to be typical of the whole. —**cross-sec·tion·al** (króss-séksh'n'l ‖ kráwss-) *adj.*

cross-slide (króss-slīd ‖ kráwss-) *n.* The part of a lathe that moves the tool post at right angles to the bed of the lathe.

cross-stitch (króss-stich ‖ kráwss-) *n.* **1.** In sewing and embroidery, a double stitch forming an X. **2.** Needlework made with this stitch. —**cross-stitch** *v.*

cross-sub·si·dise (króss-súb-si-dīz ‖ kráwss-) *v.* **-dised, -dising, -dises.** —*tr.* To give financial support to (an unprofitable section of a firm or similar operation) from the profits of another. —*intr.* To cross-subsidise a financial operation. —**cross-sub·si·dy** *n.*

cross-talk (króss-tawk ‖ kráwss-) *n.* **1.** Noise or garbled sounds heard on a telephone or other electronic receiver, caused by interference from another channel. **2.** *British.* Exchange of repartee; witty conversation.

cross-tie (króss-tī ‖ kráwss-) *n.* **1.** A transverse beam or rod serving as a support or connection. **2.** *U.S.* A railway sleeper.

cross-town (króss-town ‖ kráwss-) *adj. Chiefly U.S.* Running across a city or town; specifically, running across the principal direction of traffic flow: *a cross-town bus.* —**cross-town** *adv.*

cross-tree (króss-tree ‖ kráwss-) *n. Nautical.* Either of the two horizontal crosspieces at the upper ends of the lower masts in fore-and-aft-rigged vessels, serving to spread the shrouds.

cross-ways (króss-wayz ‖ kráwss-) *n. Archaic.* A crossroads.
~*adv.* Across; crosswise.

cross-wind (króss-wind ‖ kráwss-) *n.* A wind blowing more or less at right angles to a given direction, as to an aircraft's line of flight.

cross wires *n.* Two fine wires at right angles to each other, mounted in the focal plane of optical measuring instruments, such as theodolites, and used for sighting. Also called "cross hairs".

crosswise (króss-wīz ‖ kráwss-) *adv.* Transversely; across; diagonally.

cross-word puzzle (króss-wurd ‖ kráwss-) *n.* A puzzle in which an arrangement of numbered squares has to be filled with words running across and down in answer to correspondingly numbered clues.

cross-wort (króss-wurt ‖ kráwss-) *n.* A herbaceous perennial plant, *Galium cruciata,* having small yellow flowers borne at the leaf bases.

crotch (kroch) *n.* **1.** The angle, or region of the angle, formed by the junction of parts or members, as by two branches, limbs, steps, or legs. **2.** *Informal.* The human genital area. Also called "crutch". **3.** The fork of a pole or other support. [Perhaps a variant of Middle English and Old French *croche,* hook. See **crochet.**] —**crotched** (krocht) *adj.*

crotch·et (króchit) *n.* **1.** A small hook or hooklike structure. **2.** An odd, whimsical, or stubborn notion. **3.** *Music.* A note with the time value of a quarter of a semibreve. Also *U.S.* "quarter note". [Middle English *crochet,* small hook, from Old French. See **crochet.**]

crotch·et·y (króchiti) *adj.* **1.** Irritable; snappish. **2.** Capriciously stubborn or eccentric; perverse. —**crotch·et·i·ness** *n.*

cro·ton (krōt'n) *n.* **1.** Any of various chiefly tropical plants, shrubs, or trees of the genus *Croton.* See **croton oil. 2.** Any of various tropical plants of the genus *Codiaeum;* especially, *C. variegatum pictum,* frequently grown as a house plant for its showy, varicoloured foliage. [New Latin *Croton,* from Greek *krotōn†.*]

croton oil *n.* A yellowish-brown, violently cathartic oil obtained from the seeds of a tree, *Croton tiglium,* of southeastern Asia.

crouch (krowch) *v.* **crouched, crouching, crouches.** —*intr.* **1.** To bend low with the limbs pulled close to the body. **2.** To bend servilely or timidly; cringe. —*tr.* To cause to bend low, as in fear or humility.
~*n.* The act or posture of crouching. [Middle English *cro(u)chen,* from Old French *crochir,* to be bent, from *croc(he),* a hook. See **crochet.**] —**crouch·ing·ly** *adv.*

croup[1] (krōōp) *n.* A disorder affecting the throat in children, characterised by difficulty in breathing and a harsh cough, and associated with inflammation and obstruction of the larynx. [Probably imitative of coughing.] —**croup·ous** (krōōpəs), **croup·y** *adj.*

croup[2], **croupe** *n.* The rump of certain animals, especially the horse. [Middle English *croupe,* from Old French, from Frankish *kruppa* (unattested).]

crou·pi·er (krōōpi-ay, -ər) *n.* An attendant at a gaming table who deals the cards, and collects and pays bets. [French, originally "rider on the rump (behind a rider)", from *croupe,* rump, CROUP.]

crou·ton (krōō-ton, -TON ‖ *U.S. also* krōō-tón) *n.* A small crisp cube of toasted or fried bread, often served in soup. [French *croûton,* from *croûte,* crust, from Old French *crouste,* from Latin *crusta,* CRUST.]

crow[1] (krō) *n.* **1.** Any of several large, glossy, black birds of the genus *Corvus,* having a characteristic raucous call; especially, *C. corone,* the carrion crow, of Eurasia. **2.** Loosely, any similar bird. **3.** A crowbar. —**as the crow flies.** In a straight line. [Middle English *croue,* Old English *crāwe,* akin to *crāwan,* to CROW.]

crow[2] (krō) *intr.v.* **crowed** or **crew** (krōō ‖ krew) (for sense 1), **crowing, crows. 1.** To utter the shrill cry characteristic of a cock. **2. a.** To boast, especially over the misfortune of another. **b.** To exult. **3.** To make a sound expressive of pleasure or well-being, like that of a baby. —See Synonyms at **boast.**
~*n.* **1.** The shrill cry of a cock. **2.** An inarticulate sound expressive of pleasure or delight. [Middle English *crouen,* Old English *crāwan* (imitative).]

Crow (krō) *n., pl.* **Crows. 1.** A member of an American Indian people, formerly inhabiting the region between the Platte and Yellowstone rivers and now settled in southeastern Montana. **2.** The language of this people, of the Siouan family of languages.

crow·bar (krō-baar) *n.* A straight bar of iron or steel, with the working end shaped like a forked chisel, used as a lever. Also called "crow". [From the resemblance of the forked end to a crow's foot.]

crow·ber·ry (krō-bəri, -berri) *n., pl.* **-ries.** A low-growing evergreen shrub, *Empetrum nigrum,* of cool regions of the Northern Hemisphere, having small, purplish flowers and black, berry-like fruit. **2.** Any of several similar or related plants. **3.** The fruit of any of these plants.

crow blackbird *n.* The **grackle** *(see).*

crowd[1] (krowd) *n.* **1. a.** A large number of people gathered together; a throng. **b.** The mass of spectators, as at a football match. **2.** Ordinary people; people in general. Used with *the.* **3.** A specified social group; a clique: *the usual crowd; the arty crowd.* **4.** A large number of things grouped or considered together.
~*v.* **crowded, crowding, crowds.** —*intr.* **1.** To throng, congregate closely. Often used with *round.* **2.** To advance by shoving. —*tr.* **1.** To press, cram, or force tightly together; compress. **2.** To fill or occupy to overflowing. **3.** *Informal.* To put pressure on; harass. **4.** *Nautical.* To crowd on (sail). —**crowd on.** *Nautical.* To spread a large amount of (sail) to increase speed. [Middle English *crouden, crowden,* to crowd, press, Old English *crūdan,* to hasten.] —**crowd·ed·ness** *n.* —**crowd·er** *n.*

crowd[2] (krowd, krōōd) *n.* An ancient Celtic musical instrument, stringed and played with a bow. [Middle English *croud, crouth,* from Welsh *crwth.*]

crowd puller *n. Informal.* A very popular person, event, or the like, that is assured of a large audience.

crow·foot (krō-fŏŏt) *n., pl.* **-foots** (for senses 1, 2) or **-feet** (-feet) (for sense 3). **1.** Any of various plants of the genus *Ranunculus,* related to the buttercups, such as *R. aquatilis* and *R. sceleratus,* having small, inconspicuous yellow flowers and divided leaves. **2.** Loosely, any of various other plants having leaves or other parts resembling a bird's foot. **3.** *Nautical.* **a.** A block used in supporting the middle section of an awning. **b.** A set of small lines passed through holes of a batten or fitting to help support the backbone of an awning.

crown (krown ‖ *West Indies also* krung) *n.* **1.** An ornamental circlet or head covering, often made of precious metal set with jewels, and worn as a symbol of sovereignty. **2.** The power, position, or empire of a monarch. **3. a.** A decorative garland or wreath worn on the head as a symbol of victory, honour, or distinction. **b.** A championship title in a sport: *Borg's fifth Wimbledon crown.* **4.** Distinction or reward for achievement: *the crown of martyrdom.* **5.** Anything resembling a crown in shape, such as a badge, emblem, or heraldic bearing. **6.** A coin stamped with a crown or crowned head on the reverse side. **7. a.** A former British coin worth five shillings. **b.** Any of several European coins with a name that means

crown, such as the koruna, krona, and krone. **8. a.** The top or highest part of the head. **b.** The head itself. **9.** The top or upper part of a hat. **10.** The highest point of anything, especially: **a.** The summit of a hill or mountain. **b.** The highest point of a curved structure or surface, such as an arch or a cambered road. **11.** The highest or most outstanding state or point; the culmination: *the crown of her athletics career.* **12.** The most outstanding attribute or exemplar; the chief ornament. **13.** *Dentistry.* **a.** The part of a tooth that is covered by enamel and projects beyond the gum line. **b.** A gold, porcelain, or plastic substitute for the natural crown of a tooth. **14.** The lowest part of the shank of an anchor, where the arms are joined to it. **15. a.** The upper part of a tree, including the leaves and living branches. **b.** The part of a plant, usually at ground level, between the root and the stem. **c.** A flower part, the **corona** *(see).* **16.** The crest of an animal, especially of a bird. **17.** The portion of a cut gem above the girdle. **18.** A size of paper, approximately 50 by 38 centimetres (20 by 15 inches). **—the Crown.** **1.** The monarch as the head of state or sovereign governing power. **2.** The power, position, or empire of a monarch.
~*tr.v.* **crowned, crowning, crowns.** **1.** To put a crown or garland upon the head of. **2.** To invest with regal power; make a monarch of; enthrone. **3.** To confer honour, dignity, or reward on. **4. a.** To cover or occupy the top of. **b.** To surmount or be the highest part of. **5.** To form the crown, top, or chief ornament of. **6.** To bring to completion or successful conclusion; complete; consummate. **7.** To put a crown on (a tooth). **8.** In draughts, to make (a piece that has reached the last row) into a king by placing another piece upon it. **9.** *Informal.* To hit on the head. [Middle English *crowne, coroune,* from Old French *corone,* from Latin *corōna,* garland, from Greek *korōnē,* anything curved, from *korōnos,* curved.] **—crown** *adj.*

Crown Agent *n. British.* **1.** An appointed agent providing financial and commercial advice and assistance to crown colonies. **2.** *Law.* In Scotland, the solicitor to the Lord Advocate's department, who is effectively in charge of the administration of criminal justice.

crown cap *n.* An airtight bottle-top for beer and soft drink bottles, consisting of a lined metal disc with its edge crimped over the mouth of the bottle.

crown colony *n.* A British colony in which the sovereign has control of legislation, usually administered by an appointed governor.

Crown Court *n. Law.* A criminal court in towns in England and Wales where cases are heard by a circuit judge or recorder.

Crown Derby *n.* A fine porcelain, marked with a crown, made in Derby in the late 18th and early 19th centuries.

crown gall *n.* A disease of plants caused by a bacterium, *Agrobacterium tumefaciens,* and characterised by warty, usually woody growths on roots and stems, especially near the soil line.

crown glass *n.* **1.** A clear soda-lime-silica optical glass with low refraction. Compare **flint glass.** **2.** A form of window glass made by whirling a glass bubble to make a flat circular disc with a lump in the centre formed by the craftsman's rod.

crown graft *n.* A horticultural graft in which the scion is grafted onto the crown of the stock.

crown imperial *n.* A garden plant, *Fritillaria imperialis,* with a terminal cluster of orange bell-shaped flowers.

crown jewels *pl.n.* The jewels belonging to the regalia of a sovereign or royal family, used on state occasions.

crown lens *n.* The crown glass element in an achromatic lens.

crown-of-thorns (krown-əv-thórnz || *West Indies also* krúng-) *n.* **1.** A spiny, vinelike desert plant, *Euphorbia splendens* (or *E.milii*), often grown as a potted plant for its flowers, which have scarlet bracts. **2.** A starfish, *Acanthaster planci,* that is covered with spines and feeds on living coral.

crown prince *n.* The male heir apparent to a throne.

crown princess *n.* **1.** The wife of a crown prince. **2.** A female heir apparent to a throne.

crown roast *n.* Two or more rib sections of veal, pork, or especially lamb, secured together at the ends to form a circle and roasted.

crown saw *n.* A cylindrical saw with teeth on the bottom edge of the cylinder.

crow's-foot (krōz-fŏŏt) *n., pl.* **-feet** (-feet). **1.** *Plural.* The wrinkles at the outer corner of the eye, common in many adults. **2.** A three-pointed embroidery stitch used as finishing, as at the end of a seam. **3.** The set of ropes or strands of a rope attached to a single rope, used in sailing, ballooning, and the like. **4.** *Military.* A defensive device, a **caltrop** *(see).*

crow's-nest (krōz-nest) *n.* **1.** A small lookout platform with a high protective railing and wind screen, located near the top of a ship's mast. **2.** Any similar lookout platform located ashore.

Croy·don (króyd'n). Borough of Greater London since 1965; it was formerly an important market town in Surrey. Croydon Aerodrome, closed in 1959, was London's airport until after World War Two.

croze (krōz) *n.* **1.** The groove at the ends of the staves of a barrel or cask into which the head is set. **2.** A cooper's tool, such as a plane, for making such a groove. [French *creux,* from Old French *crues,* socket, groove, perhaps from Gallo-Roman *crosus*† (unattested).]

crozier. Variant of **crosier.**

CRT Cathode-ray tube.

cru (krōō, krü) *n.* A wine produced by certain superior French vineyards. [French, growth, from *crû,* past participle of *croître,* to grow.]

cru·ces. Alternative plural of **crux.**

cru·cial (krōō-sh'l || kréw-) *adj.* **1.** Of supreme importance in determining an outcome; critical; decisive: *a crucial election.* **2.** *Informal.* Very important or significant. **3.** *Rare.* Having the form of a cross; cross-shaped. —See Synonyms at **critical.** [French, from Latin *crux* (stem *cruc-*), CROSS.] **—cru·cial·ly** *adv.*

cru·ci·ate (krōō-shi-ayt || kréw-) *adj.* **1.** Cross-shaped. **2.** Overlapping or crossing, as are the wings of some insects when at rest. [New Latin *cruciatus,* from Latin *crux,* CROSS.]

cru·ci·ble (krōō-sib'l || kréw-) *n.* **1.** A vessel made of a refractory substance, such as graphite or porcelain, used for melting and calcining materials at high temperatures. **2.** The bottom of an ore furnace, in which the molten metal collects. **3.** A severe test or trial. [Middle English *crusible,* from Medieval Latin *crucibulum,* perhaps originally a lamp kept burning in front of a crucifix, from Latin *crux,* CROSS.]

crucible steel *n.* A high-grade steel made by fusing low-carbon steel with charcoal or cast iron in a graphite crucible and used in tools and dies.

cru·ci·fer (krōō-si-fər || kréw-) *n.* **1.** One who bears a cross in a religious procession. **2.** *Botany.* Any plant of the family Cruciferae, such as a mustard or cress, having four-petalled flowers suggestive of a cross. [Late Latin : Latin *crux,* CROSS + -FER.] **—cru·cif·er·ous** (krōō-síffərəss || kréw-) *adj.*

cru·ci·fix (krōō-si-fiks || kréw-) *n.* A cross with an image of Christ on it. [Middle English, from Old French, from Late Latin *crucifixus,* from the past participle of *crucifīgere,* CRUCIFY.]

cru·ci·fix·ion (krōō-si-fíksh'n || kréw-) *n.* **1.** The action of putting to death on a cross. **2.** A representation, as in painting or carving, of Christ on the Cross. **—the Crucifixion.** The crucifying of Christ on Calvary.

cru·ci·form (krōō-si-fawrm || kréw-) *adj.* Cross-shaped.
~*n.* A cross-shaped geometric curve having four branches forming similar asymptotes with two mutually perpendicular pairs of lines. [Latin *crux* (stem *cruc-*), CROSS + -I- + -FORM.]

cru·ci·fy (krōō-si-fī || kréw-) *tr.v.* **-fied, -fying, -fies.** **1.** To put to death by nailing or binding to a cross. **2.** To mortify or subdue (the passions, for example). **3.** To torment; torture, especially mentally. **4. a.** *Slang.* To defeat overwhelmingly, as in a sporting contest. **b.** *Informal* To criticise or ridicule mercilessly. [Middle English *crucifien,* from Old French *crucifier,* from Late Latin *crucifīgere* : Latin *crux* (stem *cruc-*), CROSS + *fīgere,* to fasten.] **—cru·ci·fi·er** *n.*

cruck (kruk) *n. Architecture.* Either of a pair of sloping timbers, often curved, that help support a roof. [19th century : variant of CROOK (noun).]

crud (krud) *n. Slang.* **1.** A coating or incrustation of filth or refuse. **2.** A contemptible or disgusting person or thing. **3.** Nonsense; rubbish. **4.** *Chiefly U.S.* Any disease, imaginary or real, especially one affecting the skin. [Middle English *crudde,* CURD.] **—crud·dy** *adj.*

crude (krōōd) *adj.* **cruder, crudest.** **1.** In an unrefined or natural state; raw. **2.** *Archaic.* Unripe; immature. **3.** Lacking finish, tact, or polish. **4.** Not carefully, skilfully, or completely made; rough. **5.** *Statistics.* Not corrected, analysed, or tabulated. Said of data. **6.** Undisguised or unadorned; blunt. **7.** Offensive tasteless; vulgar.
~*n.* Crude oil. [Middle English, from Latin *crūdus,* bloody, raw.] **—crude·ly** *adv.* **—cru·di·ty, crude·ness** *n.*

crude oil *n.* **Petroleum** *(see)* in its unrefined state.

cru·el (krōō-əl, -il || krōōl) *adj.* **-eler** or *chiefly British* **-eller, -elest** or *chiefly British* **-ellest.** **1.** Disposed to inflict pain or suffering. **2.** Causing suffering; painful: *a cruel hoax.* [Middle English, from Old French, from Latin *crūdēlis,* morally unfeeling, cruel; akin to *crūdus,* bloody, CRUDE.] **—cru·el·ly** *adv.*

Synonyms: *cruel, ferocious, barbarous, inhuman, sadistic, vicious, pitiless, ruthless.*

cru·el·ty (krōō-əl-ti, -il- || krōōl-, kréw-) *n., pl.* **-ties.** **1.** The quality or condition of being cruel. **2.** Something that causes pain or suffering, such as a cruel action or remark. **3.** *Law.* Behaviour that damages or endangers the physical or mental health of a spouse, and constitutes grounds for divorce.

cru·et (krōō-it) *n.* **1. a.** A small glass bottle for holding vinegar or oil. **b.** A small container for other condiments, such as a salt cellar, a pepper pot, or a mustard bowl. **2.** A pair or set of cruets, often on a tray or rack. **3.** Either of two small vessels used for wine and water at the Eucharist. [Middle English, from Anglo-French *cruet,* diminutive of Old French *crue,* flask, from Germanic.]

Cruik·shank (krŏŏk-shangk), **George** (1792–1878). British caricaturist and illustrator, best remembered for his illustrations of Dickens and other novelists. His own collections include his *Comic Almanack* (1835–53).

cruise (krōōz || krewz) *v.* **cruised, cruising, cruises.** —*intr.* **1.** To sail or travel about, as for pleasure or reconnaissance. **2.** To travel at a speed (cruising speed) that provides maximum operating efficiency for a sustained period. **3.** *Informal.* To wander about the street, frequent bars, and so on, in search of a sexual partner. —*tr.* **1.** To cruise or journey over. **2.** *Slang.* To appraise sexually.
~*n.* A sea voyage for pleasure, usually in a liner stopping at numerous ports. [Perhaps Dutch *kruisen,* to sail to and fro, from Middle Dutch *crucen,* to cross, from *crūce,* a cross, from Latin *crux,* CROSS.]

cruise missile *n.* A subsonic, long-range guided missile armed with a nuclear warhead, which can fly low towards its target to avoid radar detection and which uses inbuilt computerised navigation equipment.

cruis·er (krōōzər || kréwzər) *n.* **1.** One that cruises. **2.** Any of a class of fast warships of medium tonnage with a long cruising radius and less armour and firepower than a battleship. **3.** A large motorboat

whose cabin is equipped with living facilities. Also called "cabin cruiser", "cruising yacht". **4.** *Informal.* A cruiserweight boxer.
cruis·er·weight (kro͞ozər-wayt || kréwzər-) *n.* A professional boxer weighing between 12 stone 7 pounds and 13 stone 8 pounds (79.4 to 86.2 kilograms).
cruise·way (kro͞oz-way || kréwz-) *n. British.* A stream or canal used in pleasure boating.
cruising radius *n.* The longest distance a ship or aircraft can go and return at cruising speed without refuelling.
crul·ler (krúllər) *n. U.S.* A small cake of sweet dough fried in deep fat, usually ring-shaped or twisted. [Dutch *krulle,* from *krullen,* to curl, from *krul,* curly, from Middle Dutch *crulle.*]
crumb (krum) *n.* **1.** A small piece broken or fallen from cake, bread, or other baked goods. **2.** Any small fragment or scrap. **3.** The soft inner portion of bread. Compare **crust. 4.** *Slang.* A contemptible, untrustworthy, or loathsome person.
~*v.* **crumbed, crumbing, crumbs.** —*tr.* **1.** To break into small pieces or crumbs; crumble. **2.** In cookery, to cover or prepare with breadcrumbs; bread. —*intr.* To break apart in crumbs. [Middle English *crome,* Old English *cruma.*]
crum·ble (krúmb'l) *v.* **-bled, -bling, -bles.** —*tr.* To break or cause to break into small parts or crumbs. —*intr.* To fall into tiny pieces; disintegrate. —See Synonyms at **decay.**
~*n. British.* A baked dessert of stewed fruit topped with a sweet, crumblike misture of flour, fat, and sugar. [Earlier *crimble,* from Middle English *cremelen,* perhaps from Old English *gecrymian,* from *cruma,* CRUMB.]
crum·bly (krúmbli) *adj.* **-blier, -bliest.** Easily crumbled.
crumbs (krumz) *interj. British Slang.* Used to express surprise or dismay. [Euphemistic for *Christ!*]
crum·horn, krumm·horn (krúm-hawrn) *n.* A medieval musical instrument, with a deep pitch, curving tube, and double reed. [From German *Krummhorn,* "carved horn".]
crum·my (krúmmi) *adj.* **-mier, -miest.** *Slang.* Also **crumb·y.** Inferior, worthless, or unpleasant. [From CRUMB.]
crump (krump) *v.* **crumped, crumping, crumps.** —*tr.* **1.** To crush or crunch with the teeth. **2.** To bombard or strike heavily with a crunching or thudding sound. —*intr.* To make a crunching sound.
~*n.* **1.** A crunching sound. **2.** The sound of a bomb or shell exploding [Imitative.]
crum·pet (krúmpit) *n. Chiefly British.* **1.** A light, round teacake with holes in the top, made from a yeast batter, which is poured into special rings *(crumpet rings)* and cooked on one side on a heated baking sheet or a griddle and often toasted. **2.** *Slang.* Women collectively when considered sexually attractive. [Probably from Middle English *crompid (cake),* "curled cake", from *crampen, crumpen,* to curl, from *crump, crumb,* crooked, Old English *crump.*]
crum·ple (krúmp'l) *v.* **-pled, -pling, -ples.** —*tr.* To crush together or press into wrinkles; rumple. —*intr.* **1.** To become wrinkled; shrivel. Often used with *up.* **2.** To collapse; break down.
~*n.* An irregular fold, crease, or wrinkle. [Frequentative of obsolete *crump,* to curl up, from Middle English *crampen.* See **crumpet.**]
crunch (krunch) *v.* **crunched, crunching, crunches.** —*tr.* **1.** To chew with a noisy crackling sound. **2.** To crush, grind, or walk on noisily. —*intr.* **1.** To chew noisily with a crackling sound. **2.** To move with a crushing sound. **3.** To produce a crushing sound.
~*n.* **1.** The act or sound of crunching. **2. a.** A decisive confrontation. **b.** A critical situation.
~*adj.* Decisively important; crucial: *a crunch issue.* [Earlier *craunch* (imitative), assimilated to *munch.*]
crup·per (krúppər) *n.* **1.** A leather strap looped under a horse's tail and attached to a harness or saddle to keep it from slipping forwards. **2.** The rump of a horse. [Middle English *crouper, cropier,* from Old French *cropiere,* from *croupe,* rump, CROUP.]
cru·ral (kro͝or-əl) *adj.* Of or pertaining to the leg, shank, or thigh. [Latin *crūrālis,* from *crūs* (stem *crūr-*), leg, CRUS.]
crus (kruss || kro͞oss) *n., pl.* **crura** (kro͝or-ə). **1.** The section of the leg or hind limb between the knee and foot; the shank. **2.** A leglike part. [Latin *crūs*†, leg.]
cru·sade (kro͞o-sáyd || krew-) *n.* **1.** *Often capital* **C.** Any of the military expeditions undertaken by European Christians in the 11th, 12th, and 13th centuries to recover the Holy Land from the Muslims. **2.** Any holy war undertaken with papal sanction: *the Albigensian Crusade.* **3.** Any vigorous concerted movement for a cause or against an abuse.
~*intr.v.* **crusaded, -sading, -sades.** To engage in a crusade. [Earlier forms: (a) *croisade,* from Old French, variant of *croisée,* from the past participle of *croiser,* to bear the cross, from *crois,* cross, from Latin *crux;* (b) *crusado,* from Spanish *cruzada,* from *cruzar,* to bear the cross, from *cruz,* cross, from Latin *crux,* CROSS.] **—cru·sad·er** *n.*
cruse (kro͞oz || krewz, *U.S. also* kro͞oss) *n.* A small jar or pot for holding water, wine, or oil. [Middle English *crouse,* perhaps from Middle Dutch *cruyse,* pot.]
crush (krush) *v.* **crushed, crushing, crushes.** —*tr.* **1.** To press between opposing bodies so as to break, injure, or damage. **2. a.** To obtain juice from (a fruit). **b.** To obtain (juice) by crushing fruit thus. **3.** To crumple or rumple. **4.** To break, pound, or grind into small fragments or powder. **5.** To press upon, shove, or crowd. **6.** To put down; subdue. **7.** To overwhelm or humiliate, as in an argument or contest. **8.** To oppress severely: *Debt was crushing them.* —*intr.* **1.** To be or become crushed. **2.** To proceed or move by crowding or pressing. —See Synonyms at **break.**
~*n.* **1.** The act of crushing; extreme pressure. **2.** The state of being crushed. **3.** A great crowd or throng. **4.** A drink prepared from crushed fruit, or one tasting like this. **5.** *Informal.* **a.** An infatuation. Used with *on.* **b.** A person as the object of an infatuation. [Middle English *crushen,* from Old French *croissir,* probably from Vulgar Latin *cruscīre*† (unattested).] **—crush·a·ble** *adj.* **—crush·er** *n.*
crush bar *n. British.* A bar in a theatre for interval drinks. [Perhaps from CRUSH (crowd).]
crush barrier *n.* A safety barrier used to hold back a crowd.
Crusoe, Robinson. See **Robinson Crusoe.**
crust (krust) *n.* **1.** The hard outer portion or surface area of bread. Compare **crumb. 2.** A piece of bread consisting mostly of this part. **3.** A pastry shell, as of a pie or tart. **4.** Any hard, crisp covering or surface. **5.** A hard deposit produced by maturing wine on the interior of bottles. **6. a.** *Geology.* The solid exterior portion of the Earth that lies above the Mohorovičić discontinuity. **b.** The outermost solid layer of a planet or moon. **7.** The hard outer covering or integument of certain plants and animals, such as lichens and crustaceans. **8.** *Pathology.* A coating or dry outer layer, as of pus or blood; a scab. **9.** *Informal.* Insolence; audacity; gall.
~*v.* **crusted, crusting, crusts.** —*tr.* **1.** To cover with a crust; encrust. **2.** To form (dough) into a crust. —*intr.* **1.** To become covered with a crust. **2.** To harden into a crust. [Middle English *cruste,* from Old French *crouste,* from Latin *crusta*†, shell.]
crus·ta·cean (kruss-táysh'n) *n.* Any of various predominantly aquatic arthropods of the class Crustacea, including lobsters, crabs and shrimps, having a segmented body, a chitinous exoskeleton, and paired, jointed limbs. [From New Latin *crustacea,* "the shelled ones", from *crustaceus,* CRUSTACEOUS.] **—crus·ta·cean** *adj.*
crus·ta·ceous (kruss-táyshəss) *adj.* **1.** Having, resembling, or constituting a hard crust or shell. **2.** Crustacean. [New Latin *crustaceus* : Latin *crusta,* shell, CRUST + -ACEOUS.]
crus·tal (krúst'l) *adj.* Of or pertaining to a crust, especially that of the Earth or the Moon.
crusted port *n.* Blended port wine that has been kept in cask for several years, and deposits a crust after bottling.
crust·y (krústi) *adj.* **-ier, -iest. 1.** Like or having a crust. **2.** Surly or short-tempered. —See Synonyms at **gruff. —crust·i·ness** *n.*
crutch (kruch) *n.* **1.** A staff or support used by the lame or infirm as an aid in walking, usually having a crosspiece to fit under the armpit and often used in pairs. **2.** Any device similar to this in form or function. **3.** A forked support for the boom of a sailing vessel when the sails are furled. **4.** Anything or anyone depended upon for support; a prop. **5.** The human genital area; crotch.
~*tr.v.* **crutched, crutching, crutches. 1.** To support on or as on crutches. **2.** *Australian.* To cut (wool) from a sheep's hind quarters. [Middle English *crucche,* Old English *crycc,* from Germanic.]
crux (kruks, kro͝oks) *n., pl.* **cruxes** or **cruces** (kro͞osēz). **1.** A crucial or vital moment; a critical point. **2.** The basic or essential feature: *the crux of our argument.* **3.** A puzzling problem. [Latin, CROSS.]
Crux (kruks) *n.* A constellation in the Southern Hemisphere near Centaurus and Musca. Also called "Southern Cross".
crux an·sa·ta (krúks an-sáytə, -saátə) *n.* An **ansate cross** *(see).*
Cruyff (kroyf), **Johann** (1947–). Dutch footballer. A brilliant centre forward, he played for Ajax (Amsterdam), Barcelona, and Holland, captaining Holland in the final of the World Cup (1974).
cruzado. Variant of **crusado.**
cru·zei·ro (kro͞o-zaírō, -ro͞o) *n., pl.* **-ros. 1.** The basic monetary unit of Brazil, equal to 100 centavos. **2.** A coin worth one cruzeiro. [Portuguese, "(coin) bearing the figure of a cross", from *cruz,* cross, from Latin *crux,* CROSS.]
cry (krī) *v.* **cried, crying, cries.** —*intr.* **1.** To make inarticulate sobbing sounds expressing grief, sorrow, or pain. **2.** To produce moisture from the eyes; shed tears; weep. **3.** To call aloud; shout. Often used with *out.* **4.** To utter a characteristic sound or call. Used of an animal. **5.** To withdraw from an undertaking or back out of an agreement or promise. Used with *off.* —*tr.* **1.** To utter loudly. **2.** To proclaim or announce (especially goods for sale) in public. **3.** To beg for; beseech; implore: *cry forgiveness.* **4. a.** To bring into a specified condition by weeping: *cry oneself to sleep.* **b.** To weep or shed (tears). **5.** To belittle or disparage. Used with *down.* **6.** To break or withdraw from a promise, agreement, or undertaking. Used with *off.* **7.** To praise highly; extol. Used with *up.* **—cry out for.** To be in urgent need of; demand.
~*n., pl.* **cries. 1.** A loud utterance of some emotion, such as fear or anger. **2.** Any loud exclamation or utterance; a shout; a call. **3.** A fit of weeping. **4.** An urgent entreaty or appeal. **5.** A public or general demand or complaint; a clamour; an outcry. **6.** *Archaic.* An advertising of wares by calling out. **7.** A rallying call or signal as in a battle or election campaign. **8.** A political slogan. **9.** The characteristic call or utterance of an animal or bird. **9.** A pack of hounds. **—a far cry. 1.** A very different state of affairs. **2.** A long way. **—in full cry.** In hot pursuit, as hounds hunting. [Middle English *crien,* from Old French *crier,* from Latin *quirītāre,* to cry out, to implore the aid of the Roman citizens, from *Quirītēs,* plural of *Quirīs*†, a Roman citizen.]
Synonyms: *cry, weep, wail, moan, whimper, sob, blubber.*
cry·ba·by (krī-baybi) *n., pl.* **-bies.** A person who cries or complains frequently with little cause.
cry·ing (krī-ing) *adj.* Demanding or requiring immediate action or remedy: *a crying shame; a crying need.*
crymotherapy. Variant of **cryotherapy.**
cryo-. *comb. form.* Indicates cold, freezing, or frost; for example,

cryometer. [From Greek *kruos†*, icy cold, frost.]

cry·o·bi·ol·o·gy (krī-ō-bī-ólləji) *n.* The study of the effects of very low temperatures on living organisms.

cry·o·gen (krī-ə-jen, -jən) *n.* A refrigerant used to obtain very low temperatures. [CRYO- + -GEN.]

cry·o·gen·ics (krī-ə-jénniks) *n.* The science of low-temperature phenomena. [From CRYO- + -GENIC.] —**cry·o·gen·ic** *adj.*

cry·o·hy·drate (krī-ō-hídrayt, -ə-) *n.* A eutectic that crystallises below the temperature of freezing water. It consists of water and a specific proportion of a salt.

cry·o·lite (krī-ə-līt) *n.* A white, vitreous natural fluoride of aluminium and sodium, Na₃AlF₆, used chiefly as an electrolyte in aluminium refining and in the production of glass, enamel, and ceramics. Also called "Greenland spar". [CRYO- + -LITE.]

cry·om·e·ter (krī-ómmitər) *n.* A thermometer capable of measuring very low temperatures. [CRYO- + -METER.]

cry·o·plank·ton (krī-ə-plángktən, -ō-) *n. Biology.* Minute organisms living in snow, ice, or perpetually icy waters.

cry·o·scope (krī-ə-skōp) *n.* An instrument used to measure the freezing point of a substance. [Back-formation from CRYOSCOPY.]

cry·os·co·py (krī-óskəpi) *n.* The study of the freezing points of solutions. [CRYO- + -SCOPY.] —**cry·o·scop·ic** (krī-ə-skóppik) *adj.*

cry·o·stat (krī-ə-stat, -ō-) *n.* An apparatus used to maintain constant low temperature. [CRYO- + -STAT.]

cry·o·sur·ger·y (krī-ə-súrjəri, -ō-) *n.* Surgery performed by local or general application of extreme cold to destroy unwanted tissue.

cry·o·ther·a·py (krī-ə-thérrəpi, -ō-) *n.* Also **cry·mo·ther·a·py** (krīmō-). The use of low temperatures in medical therapy.

cry·o·tron (krī-ə-tron) *n.* A small electronic switch that is based on the phenomenon of superconductivity. It works at the temperature of liquid helium, switching the conducting wire from a superconducting state to a nonsuperconducting state. [CRYO- + -TRON.]

crypt (kript) *n.* **1.** An underground vault or chamber, especially one beneath a church that is used as a burial place. **2.** *Anatomy.* Any of various small pits, recesses, glandular cavities, or follicles in the body. [Latin *crypta*, from Greek *kruptē*, from *kruptos*, hidden, from *kruptein*, to hide.]

cryp·taes·the·sia, *Chiefly U.S.* **cryp·tes·the·sia** (krípt-eess-thée-zi-ə ‖ -əss-, -zhə) *n. Psychology.* A term describing the various modes of supposed paranormal perception, such as clairvoyance. [New Latin : CRYPT(O)- + AESTHESIA.]

cryp·ta·nal·y·sis (kríptə-nál-ə-siss) *n.*, *pl.* **-ses** (-seez). The analysis and deciphering of cryptograms, ciphers, codes, or other secret writings. [CRYPT(OGRAM) + ANALYSIS.] —**cryp·tan·a·lyst** (-tánnəlist) *n.* —**cryp·tan·a·lyt·ic** (krípt-ánnə-líttik) *adj.*

cryp·tic (kríptik) *adj.* Also **cryp·ti·cal** (-'l). **1. a.** Mysterious; enigmatic. **b.** Intentionally obscure. **2.** Hidden; concealed. **3.** Having esoteric or hidden meaning; mystifying. **4.** *Biology.* Tending to conceal or camouflage: *cryptic colouring.* —See Synonyms at **ambiguous.** [Late Latin *crypticus*, from Greek *kruptikos*, from *kruptos*, hidden. See **crypt.**]

crypto-, **crypt-.** *comb. form.* Indicates hidden or secret; for example, **cryptoclastic.** [New Latin, from Greek *kruptos*, hidden, from *kruptein*, to hide.]

cryp·to·clas·tic (kríptō-klástik) *adj.* Composed of microscopic fragments. Said of rocks.

cryp·to·crys·tal·line (kríptō-kríst'l-īn ‖ -in) *adj.* Having a microscopic crystalline structure. Said of rocks and minerals.

cryp·to·gam (krípt-ō-gam, -ə-) *n. Botany.* In former classification systems, any of the flowerless and seedless plants that reproduce by spores, such as fungi, algae, mosses, and ferns. Compare **phanerogam.** [French *cryptogame*, from New Latin *cryptogamia* : CRYPTO- + -GAMY.] —**cryp·to·gam·ic** (-gámmik), **cryp·tog·a·mous** (kríp--tóggəməss) *adj.*

cryp·to·gen·ic (kríptə-jénnik) *adj.* Also **cryp·tog·e·nous** (krip-tójə-nəss). Of obscure or unknown origin. Said of diseases.

cryp·to·gram (kríptə-gram) *n.* **1.** Something written in code or cipher; a cryptograph. **2.** A figure having a secret or occult significance. [French *cryptogramme* : CRYPTO- + -GRAM (written).] —**cryp·to·gram·mic** (-grámmik) *adj.*

cryp·to·graph (kríptə-graaf, -graf) *n.* **1.** A cryptogram. **2.** A system of secret or cipher writing; a cipher. **3. a.** A device for translating plain text into cipher. **b.** A device for deciphering codes and ciphers. [Back-formation from CRYPTOGRAPHY.]

cryp·tog·ra·phy (krip-tóggrəfi) *n.* **1.** The art or process of writing in or deciphering secret code. **2.** Any system of secret writing. [New Latin *cryptographia* : CRYPTO- + -GRAPHY.] —**cryp·tog·ra·pher** (-tóggrəfər), **cryp·tog·ra·phist** *n.* —**cryp·to·graph·ic** (kríptə-gráffik) *adj.* —**cryp·to·graph·i·cal·ly** *adv.*

cryp·tol·o·gy (krip-tólləji) *n.* **1.** The study of the use of secret codes or ciphers; cryptography. **2.** Cryptanalysis. [CRYPTO- + -LOGY.]

cryp·to·me·ri·a (kríptə-méer-i-ə) *n.* An evergreen tree, *Cryptomeria japonica*, native to Japan, having short, inward-curving needles and soft, durable, fragrant wood. Also called "Japanese cedar". [New Latin : CRYPTO- + Greek *meros*, part, -MERE.]

cryp·to·nym (kríptə-nim) *n.* A secret name. [French *cryptonyme* : CRYPT(O)- + -ONYM.] —**cryp·ton·ym·ous** (krip-tónniməss) *adj.*

crypt·or·chid·ism (kript-órkid-iz'm) Also **crypt·or·chism** (kript-ór-kiz'm) *n.* The condition in which the testes fail to descend into the scrotum at puberty. [CRYPTO- + Greek *orkhis* (stem *orkhid*-), testicle + -ISM.]

cryp·to·zo·ite (kríptə-zō-īt) *n.* A sporozoite such as a malarial parasite as it exists in its host's tissues prior to invasion of the red blood cells. [CRYPTO- + (SPORO)ZOITE.]

cryst. 1. crystalline. **2.** crystallography.

crys·tal (kríst'l) *n.* **1. a.** A three-dimensional atomic, ionic, or molecular structure consisting of periodically repeated, identically constituted, congruent unit cells. **b.** The unit cell of such a structure. **2.** A body, such as a piece of quartz, having such a structure, often characterised by external planar faces visible without magnification. **3.** An oscillator, detector, or other electronic device based on crystalline piezoelectricity, magnetism, semiconductivity, or other electric properties. **4. a.** A high-quality clear, colourless glass. **b.** An object, especially a vessel or ornament, made of such glass. **c.** Such objects collectively. **5.** A clear glass or plastic protective cover for the face of a watch or clock.
~*adj.* **1.** Of, pertaining to, made of, or based on crystal. **2.** Designating an electronic device operated by a crystal. **3.** Clear; transparent. [Middle English *cristal*, from Old French, from Latin *crystallum*, rock crystal, crystal, from Greek *krustallos†*.]

crystal ball *n.* A glass globe used in crystal gazing.

crystal counter *n.* A high-energy radiation detector in which particles strike a crystal, causing a brief increase in conductivity.

crystal detector *n.* A rectifying detector used especially in early radio receivers and consisting of a semiconducting crystal in point contact with a fine metal wire.

crystal gazing *n.* A foretelling or attempt to foretell the future by or as if by seeing future events in a crystal ball. —**crys·tal gaz·er** *n.*

crystal lattice *n.* A regular network of fixed points about which the ions, atoms, or molecules forming a crystal vibrate.

crys·tal·lif·er·ous (krístə-lifførəss) *adj.* Also **crys·tal·lig·er·ous** (-lijərəss). Producing or containing crystals.

crys·tal·line (krístə-līn ‖ *U.S.* -lin) *adj.* **1.** *Abbr.* **cryst.** Pertaining to or made of crystal or crystals. **2.** Pertaining to crystals or their structure. **3.** Resembling crystal; transparent. [Middle English *cristallin*, from Old French, from Latin *crystallinus*, from Greek *krustallinos*, from *krustallos*, CRYSTAL.] —**crys·tal·lin·i·ty** (-línnəti) *n.*

crystalline lens *n.* The **lens** (*see*) of the vertebrate eye.

crys·tal·lise, **crys·tal·lize** (krístə-līz) *v.* **-lised**, **-lising**, **-lises.** —*tr.* **1.** To cause to form crystals or to assume a crystalline structure. **2.** To give a definite and permanent form to. **3.** To coat with sugar. —*intr.* **1.** To assume a crystalline form. **2.** To take on a definite and permanent form. [CRYSTAL(L)O- + -ISE.] —**crys·tal·lis·a·bil·i·ty** (-līzə-bílləti) *n.* —**crys·tal·lis·a·ble** (-līz-əb'l ‖ -līz-) *adj.* —**crys·tal·li·sa·tion** (-lī-záysh'n ‖ *U.S.* -li-) *n.* —**crys·tal·lis·er** *n.*

crys·tal·lite (krístə-līt) *n.* Any of numerous minute rudimentary, crystalline bodies found in glassy igneous rocks. [German *Kristallit* : CRYSTALL(O)- + -ITE.] —**crys·tal·lit·ic** (-líttik) *adj.*

crystallo-, crystall-. *comb. form.* Indicates crystal; for example, **crystallography, crystalloid.** [Greek *krustallos*, CRYSTAL.]

crys·tal·log·ra·phy (krístə-lóggrəfi) *n. Abbr.* **cryst., crystall.** The science of the structure, form, and properties of crystals. [French *crystallographie*, from New Latin *crystallographia* : CRYSTALLO- + -GRAPHY.] —**crys·tal·log·ra·pher** (-lóggrəfər) *n.* —**crys·tal·lo·graph·ic** (lə-gráffik, -lō-), **crys·tal·lo·graph·i·cal** *adj.* —**crys·tal·lo·graph·i·cal·ly** *adv.*

crys·tal·loid (krístə-loyd) *n.* **1.** *Chemistry.* A water-soluble crystalline substance capable of diffusion through a semipermeable membrane. **2.** *Botany.* Any of various minute crystalline particles consisting of protein, found in certain plant cells, especially oily seeds.
~*adj.* Also **crys·tal·loi·dal** (-lóyd'l). Resembling or having the properties of a crystal or crystalloid. [CRYSTALL(O)- + -OID.]

crystal pickup *n.* A record-player pickup that uses a piezoelectric crystal to convert stylus vibrations into electric impulses. Compare **magnetic pickup.**

crystal set *n.* An early radio receiver using a crystal detector.

crystal system *n.* Any of seven classifications into which crystals fall, depending on their symmetry: cubic, tetragonal, hexagonal, trigonal (sometimes regarded as a subsystem of hexagonal), orthorhombic, monoclinic, and triclinic.

crystal violet *n.* A dye derived from rosaniline and used as a general biological stain and as an antiseptic for some skin infections. Also called "gentian violet".

Cs The symbol for the element caesium.

cs. case.

c/s cycles per second.

C.S. 1. chief of staff. **2.** Christian Science; Christian Scientist. **3.** civil service. **4.** chartered surveyor.

csardas. Variant of **czardas.**

csc cosecant.

C.S.C. Civil Service Commission.

CSE, C.S.E. *n.* Certificate of Secondary Education: a certificate awarded to secondary-school pupils who passed an examination generally of a lower academic standard than GCE O level. See **GCSE.**

CS gas *n.* A tear gas, *ortho*-chlorobenzylidine malonitrile C₆H₄ClCH: C(CN)₂, used in the control of civil disturbances. It causes tears, salivation, and breathing difficulties. [*CS*, after Ben *C*arson and Roger *S*taughton, its U.S. inventors (1928).]

C.S.I.R.O. Commonwealth Scientific and Industrial Research Organisation (in Australia).

CST, C.S.T. Central Standard Time.

ct. 1. carat. **2.** cent. **3.** court.

Ct. count (title).

C.T. Central Time.

cte·nid·i·um (ti-níddi-əm) *n., pl.* **-ia** (-ə). *Zoology.* A comblike structure, such as the respiratory apparatus of a mollusc. [New Latin : Greek *kteis* (stem *kten-*), a comb.]

cten·oid (téen-oyd, tén-) *adj. Biology.* Having narrow segments or spines resembling the teeth of a comb: *fishes with ctenoid scales.* [Greek *ktenoeidēs*, like a comb : *kteis* (stem *kten-*), comb + -OID.]

cten·o·phore (téenə-fawr, ténnə- || -fōr) *n.* Any of various marine coelenterate animals of the subphylum Ctenophora, having transparent, gelatinous bodies bearing eight rows of comblike cilia used for locomotion. Also called "comb jelly". [New Latin *Ctenophora* : Greek *kteis* (stem *kten-*), a comb + -PHORE.] —**cte·noph·o·ran** (tee-nóffərən, ti-) *adj. & n.*

ctn cotangent.

ctr. centre.

Cu The symbol for the element copper [Latin *cuprum*].

cu. cubic.

cub (kub) *n.* **1.** The young of certain carnivorous animals, such as the bear, wolf, or lion. **2.** An inexperienced, awkward, or ill-mannered youth. **3.** A novice or learner, particularly in journalism. Also used adjectivally: *a cub reporter.* **4.** Capital **C.** A Cub Scout *(see).* [16th century : origin obscure.]

Cu·ba, Republic of (kéwbə; *Spanish* kóoba). Country in the Caribbean Sea and the largest island in the West Indies. Cuba was discovered by Columbus (1492) and was a Spanish colony until 1898. Then it became nominally independent under the United States, which reserved the right to intervene in its affairs until 1934. From 1935, the dictator Fulgencio Batista dominated Cuba until he was overthrown by Fidel Castro (1959). Cuba began to import Soviet arms and a U.S.-backed attempt to topple the regime resulted in disaster at the Bay of Pigs (1961). The Soviet installation of rocket bases caused a U.S. naval blockade and acute international tension until the missiles were withdrawn (1962). From the 1970s, Cuba supplied troops to help liberation movements in Africa. Since the break-up of the Soviet Union, economic aid has not reached Cuba and this, with ongoing US embargoes, has resulted in poverty. Sugar is the mainstay of the economy, while nickel and tobacco are also exported. Area, 110 860 square kilometres (42,803 square miles). Population, 11,020,000. Capital, Havana. —**Cu·ban** *adj. & n.*

Cuban heel *n.* A moderately high heel for a man's boot or shoe.

cu·ba·ture (kéwbə-tewr, -chər) *n.* Also **cub·age** (kéwbij). **1.** The determination of the cubic contents of a solid. **2.** Cubic contents. [*Cube* + quad*rature.*]

cub·by (kúbbi) *n., pl.* **-bies.** A small room; a cubbyhole. [obsolete English *cub*, a stall, perhaps from Dutch *kub, kubbe,* trap, basket, from Middle Dutch *cubbe.*]

cub·by·hole (kúbbi-hōl) *n.* **1.** A snug or cramped space or room. **2.** A small compartment. **3.** A small cupboard.

cube (kewb) *n.* **1.** *Geometry.* A regular solid having six congruent square faces. **2.** Anything having such a shape. **3.** *Mathematics.* The third power of a number or quantity; the result of multiplying something by itself twice: *27 is the cube of 3.*
—*tr.v.* **cubed, cubing, cubes. 1.** To raise (a quantity or number) to the third power. **2.** To determine the cubic contents of. **3.** To form or cut into cubes or the shape of a cube; dice. [French, from Latin *cubus,* a dice, cube, from Greek *kubos.*]

cu·bé, cu·be (kéwbay || *U.S. also* kew-báy) *n.* **1.** Any of various tropical American shrubs or plants, especially of the genus *Lonchocarpus,* whose roots yield the chemical compound rotenone. **2.** An extract from the roots of these plants, used as a fish poison and insecticide. [American Spanish *cubé†.*]

cu·beb (kéw-beb) *n.* **1.** A treelike woody vine, *Piper cubeba,* of southeastern Asia, bearing brownish berries. **2.** The dried, unripe, fruit of this plant, used medicinally as a stimulant and diuretic and sometimes smoked in cigarettes. [Middle English *cubibe,* from Old French *cubebe,* from Medieval Latin *cubēba,* from Arabic *kabābah.*]

cube root *n.* The number that when cubed produces a given number: *3 is the cube root of 27.*

cu·bic (kéwbik) *adj.* **1. a.** Having the shape of a cube. **b.** Having a shape similar to or approximating that of a cube. **2.** *Abbr.* **c, cu. a.** Having three dimensions. **b.** Having a volume equal to a cube whose edge is of a stated length: *a cubic metre.* **3.** *Mathematics.* Of the third power, order, or degree. **4.** *Crystallography.* Isometric.
—*n. Mathematics.* A cubic expression, curve, or equation.

cu·bi·cal (kéwbik'l) *adj.* **1.** Cubic. **2.** Of or pertaining to volume. —**cu·bi·cal·ly** *adv.* —**cu·bi·cal·ness** *n.*

cu·bi·cle (kéwbik'l) *n.* **1.** A small sleeping compartment, especially one partitioned off from a larger room. **2.** Any small compartment or partitioned-off part: *a shower cubicle.* [Latin *cubiculum,* sleeping chamber, from *cubāre,* to lie down, sleep.]

cubic measure *n.* A unit, such as a cubic metre or a cubic foot, or a system of units used to measure volume or capacity.

cu·bi·form (kéwbi-fawrm) *adj.* Having the shape of a cube.

cub·ism (kéwb-iz'm) *n. Often capital* **C.** A movement in painting and sculpture, initiated in Paris in the early 20th century by Picasso and Braque, that emphasised the structure of objects by combining lines, planes, and geometrical shapes to represent several viewpoints of an object simultaneously. [French, from CUBE (from a remark by Henri Matisse concerning the "small cubes" that predominated in a painting by Georges Braque).] —**cub·ist** *adj. & n.* —**cu·bis·tic** (kew-bístik) *adj.* —**cu·bis·ti·cal·ly** *adv.*

cu·bit (kéwbit) *n.* An ancient unit of linear measure, originally equal to the length of the forearm from the tip of the middle finger to the elbow, or from 43 to 56 centimetres (17 to 22 inches). [Middle English *cubite,* from Latin *cubitum,* cubit, elbow.]

cu·bi·tal (kéwbit'l) *adj.* **1.** Of, pertaining to, or situated near the forearm or elbow. **2.** Of or pertaining to measurement by cubits.

cu·boid (kéwboyd) *adj.* Also **cu·boi·dal** (kew-bóyd'l). **1.** Having the shape or approximate shape of a cube. **2.** *Anatomy.* Designating the bone on the side of the tarsus between the calcaneus and the fourth and fifth metatarsal bones of the foot.
—*n.* **1.** *Anatomy.* The cuboid bone. **2.** *Geometry.* A rectangular parallelepiped.

Cub Scout *n.* A member of the junior division of the Scout Association. Also called "cub".

Cu·chul·ain, Cu·chul·ainn (kōo-kúllin). *Celtic Mythology.* A tribal

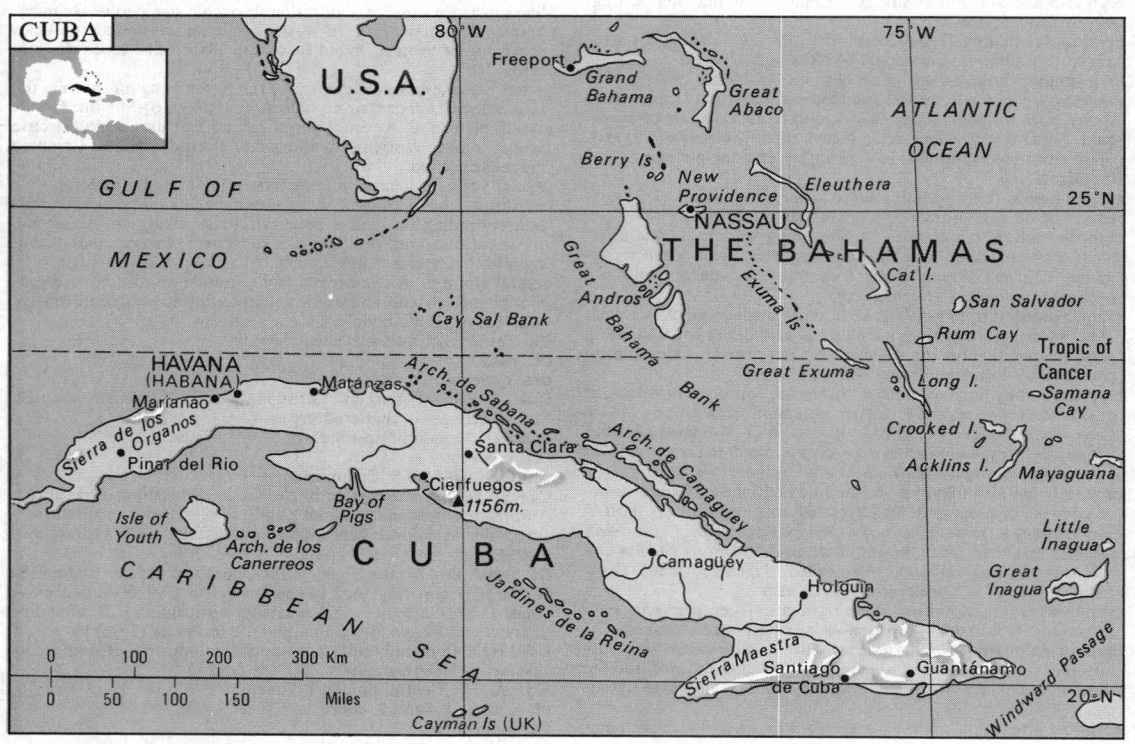

CUBA

80°W · 75°W

U.S.A.

Freeport · Grand Bahama · Great Abaco · ATLANTIC OCEAN

Berry Is · New Providence · Eleuthera · 25°N

GULF OF MEXICO

NASSAU · THE BAHAMAS · Cat I.

Andros · Great Bahama Bank · Exuma Is · San Salvador · Rum Cay

Cay Sal Bank

HAVANA (HABANA) · Matanzas · Arch. de Sabana · Great Exuma · Long I. · Tropic of Cancer

Marianao · Samana Cay

Sierra de los Organos · Pinar del Rio · Santa Clara · Arch. de Camaguey · Crooked I. · Acklins I. · Mayaguana

Cienfuegos · 1156m.

Isle of Youth · Bay of Pigs · Arch. de los Canerreos · C U B A · Camagüey · Little Inagua

CARIBBEAN · Jardines de la Reina · Holguin · Great Inagua

0 · 100 · 200 · 300 Km

0 · 50 · 100 · 150 Miles

SEA · Sierra Maestra · Santiago de Cuba · Guantánamo · 20°N

Cayman Is (UK) · Windward Passage

hero of Ulster who single-handedly defended it against the rest of Ireland.

cuck·ing stool (kúcking) *n.* A former instrument of punishment for prostitutes or dishonest tradesmen, consisting of a chair in which the offender was tied and exposed to public derision or ducked in water. Compare **ducking stool**. [Middle English *cucking stol,* "excreting stool" : *cucking,* present participle of *cukken,* to defecate, from Old Norse *kūka* (unattested) + *stol,* STOOL.]

cuck·old (kúck'ld, kúk-ōld) *n.* A man whose wife has committed adultery.
~*tr.v.* **cuckolded, -olding, -olds.** To make a cuckold of. [Middle English *cukeweld, cokewold,* from Anglo-French *cucuald* (unattested), variant of Old French *cucuault,* pejorative form of *cucu,* cuckoo (perhaps because cuckoos leave their eggs in the nests of other birds).] —**cuck·old·ry** (-ri) *n.*

cuck·oo (kŏokŏo ‖ *U.S. also* kŏo-kŏo) *n.* **1. a.** A European bird, *Cuculus canorus,* having greyish plumage and a characteristic two-note call. It lays its eggs in the nests of other birds. **b.** Any of various related birds of the family Cuculidae. **2.** The call or cry of a cuckoo. **3.** A foolish person; a simpleton.
~*v.* **cuckooed, -ooing, -oos.** —*tr.* To repeat again and again. —*intr.* To utter or imitate a cuckoo's call.
~*adj. Informal.* Demented; foolish. [Middle English *cuccu* (imitative).]

cuckoo clock *n.* A wall clock having a mechanical cuckoo announcing intervals of time.

cuck·oo·flow·er (kŏokŏo-flowr ‖ kŏo-kŏo-) *n.* **1.** A plant, *Cardamine pratensis,* of the North Temperate Zone, having white or rose-pink flowers. Also called "lady's-smock". **2.** A plant, the **ragged robin** (see).

cuck·oo·pint (kŏokŏo-pīnt, -pint ‖ kŏokŏo-) *n.* A European plant, *Arum maculatum,* having arrow-shaped leaves and a spadix enclosed in a purple-spotted spathe. Also called "lords-and-ladies". [Short for obsolete *cuckoo-pintle,* from Middle English *cokkupyntel* : *cokku, cuccu,* CUCKOO + *pintel,* penis, PINTLE (from the shape of the spadix).]

cuckoo shrike *n.* Any songbird of the family Campephagidae, of the Old World Tropics, having long pointed wings and mainly grey plumage.

cuckoo spit *n.* A frothy mass of liquid secreted on plant stems as a protective covering by nymphs of the froghopper. Also called "frog spit".

cu·cu·li·form (kew-kŏowli-fawrm) *adj.* Of or belonging to the order Cuculiformes, which includes the cuckoos and related birds. [New Latin *Cuculiformes* : Latin *cuculus,* cuckoo (imitative) + -FORM.]

cu·cul·late (kékwəl-ayt, kew-kúl-, -ət, -it) *adj.* Having the shape of a cowl or hood: *cucullate sepals.* [Medieval Latin *cucullātus,* from Latin *cucullus,* cap, hood. See COWL.] —**cu·cul·late·ly** *adv.*

cu·cum·ber (kéw-kumbər) *n.* **1.** A vine, *Cucumis sativus,* cultivated for its edible fruit. **2.** The usually cylindrical fruit of this vine, having a hard green rind and firm, white, succulent flesh. [Middle English *cucumer, cocumber,* from Old French *cocombre,* from Latin *cucumis,* of Mediterranean origin.]

cucumber tree *n.* **1.** A tree, *Magnolia acuminata,* of eastern and central North America, having cup-shaped greenish-yellow flowers and brown or scarlet cucumber-shaped fruit. **2.** A tree, *Averrhoa bilimbi,* of eastern Asia, having reddish-purple flowers and edible fruit that resemble small cucumbers.

cu·cur·bit (kew-kúrbit) *n.* **1.** A gourd-shaped flask forming the body of an alembic, formerly used in distillation. **2.** Any of various vines of the family Cucurbitaceae, which includes the marrow, pumpkin, and cucumber. [Middle English *cucurbite,* from Old French, from Latin *cucurbita,* GOURD.] —**cu·cur·bit·a·ceous** *adj.*

cud (kud) *n.* Food regurgitated from the first stomach to the mouth of a ruminant and chewed again. —**chew the cud.** *Informal.* To ponder. [Middle English *cud(de),* Old English *cwudu, cudu,* from Germanic; akin to Old High German *kuti,* glue.]

cud·bear (kúd-bair) *n.* A dye, orchil (see). [From the name of Dr. *Cuthbert* Gordon, 18th-century Scottish chemist who patented the substance.]

cud·dle (kúd'l) *v.* **-dled, -dling, -dles.** —*tr.* To fondle in the arms; hug tenderly. —*intr.* To nestle; snuggle. Often followed by *up.*
~*n.* The act of cuddling; a hug or embrace. [16th century : origin obscure.] —**cud·dle·some** *adj.* —**cud·dly** *adj.*

cud·dy¹ (kúddi) *n., pl.* **-dies.** **1.** A small cabin or the cook's galley on a ship. **2.** A small room or cupboard. [Origin obscure.]

cud·dy² *n., pl.* **-dies.** *Scottish.* **1.** A donkey. **2.** A fool. [Perhaps from *Cuddy,* pet form of *Cuthbert.*]

cudg·el (kújəl) *n.* A short, heavy club. —**take up the cudgels.** To join in a dispute, especially in defence of a participant.
~*tr.v.* **cudgelled** or *U.S.* **cudgeled, -elling** or *U.S.* **-eling, -els.** To beat or strike with a cudgel. —**cudgel (one's) brains.** To think hard. [Middle English *cuggel,* Old English *cycgel.*] —**cudg·el·ler** *n.*

cud·weed (kúd-weed) *n.* **1.** Any of various woolly plants of the genus *Gnaphalium,* having clusters of brownish or yellow button-like flowers. **2.** Any of several similar or related plants, especially a European plant, *Filago germanica.*

cue¹ (kew) *n.* **1.** In billiards, snooker, and the like, the long, tapered rod used to propel the ball. **2.** *Archaic.* A queue of hair; a long braid.
~*v.* **cued, cuing, cues. 1.** To strike (a ball) with a cue. **2.** *Archaic.* To braid or twist (hair) into a cue. —*intr.* To strike a ball with a

cue. [French *queue,* "tail" (from the shape of the cue), from Old French *coue,* from Latin *cauda,* tail.]

cue² *n.* **1. a.** A word or bit of stage action signalling the beginning of another action or speech. **b.** Any guide to a performer, such as a musician or singer, that serves as a signal for subsequent action. **2.** A hint or reminder; a prompting. **3.** *Psychology.* A perceived signal for action, especially one that produces an operant response. —**on cue.** Precisely at the right moment. —**take (one's) cue from.** To imitate the style of behaviour of.
~*tr.v.* **cued, cuing, cues.** To give (an actor or other performer) a cue. [16th century : origin obscure.]

cue ball *n.* In billiards, snooker, and the like, the ball that is hit directly with the cue.

cues·ta (kwéstə) *n.* A land elevation with a gentle slope on one side and a much steeper one on the other. [Spanish, sloping side, from Latin *costa,* side.]

cuff¹ (kuf) *n.* **1. a.** The bottom of a sleeve. **b.** A fold or band used as trimming at the bottom of a sleeve. **2.** *U.S. & Australian.* A trouser **turn-up** (see). **3.** A band of linen, lace, or other fabric attached about the wrist, either under or over a sleeve. **4.** The part of a gauntlet that extends over the wrist. **5.** *Informal.* A **handcuff** (see). —**off the cuff.** *Informal.* Extemporaneously. [Middle English *cuffe†,* glove, mitten.]

cuff² *tr.v.* **cuffed, cuffing, cuffs.** To strike with the open hand; slap.
~*n.* A blow or slap with the open hand. [16th century : perhaps imitative.]

cuff link *n.* Either of a pair of linked buttons, used to fasten the cuffs of a shirt.

Cufic. Variant of **Kufic.**

cui·rass (kwi-ráss) *n.* **1.** A piece of armour for protecting the breast and back. **2.** The breastplate alone. **3.** *Zoology.* A protective covering of bony plates, scales, or shell.
~*tr.v.* **cuirassed, -rassing, -rasses.** To protect with a cuirass. [Middle English *curace,* cuirass (especially one of leather), from Old French *cuirasse,* from Vulgar Latin *coriāca* (unattested), "leather buckler", from Latin *coriāceus,* of leather, from *corium,* hide, skin.]

cui·ras·sier (kwirrə-séer) *n.* Formerly, a horse soldier in European armies whose equipment included the cuirass.

cuir bouil·li (kwéer bŏo-yee, bŏo-yée) *n.* Leather soaked and left to harden, used as an early form of armour. [French, "boiled leather".]

cui·sine (kwi-zéen) *n.* **1.** A characteristic manner or style of preparing food. **2.** Food prepared by a hotel, restaurant, or the like. [French, from Late Latin *coquīna,* a kitchen, cookery, from *coquere,* to cook.]

cuisine min·ceur (maN-sér, -sôr) *n.* A style of French cooking that seeks to minimise the use of rich ingredients such as flour, butter, and cream. [French, "slenderness cuisine".]

cuisse (kwiss) *n.* Also **cuish** (kwish). A piece of plate armour worn to protect the thigh. [Back-formation from Middle English *cussues, cushies,* from Old French *cuissaux,* plural of *cuissel,* from *cuisse,* thigh, from Latin *coxa,* thigh, hip.]

culch, cultch (kulch) *n.* **1.** A natural bed for oysters, consisting of gravel or crushed shells to which oyster spawn may adhere. **2.** The spawn of the oyster. **3.** Rubbish or refuse. [Perhaps from Old French *culche, couche,* bed, COUCH.]

cul-de-sac (kúl-də-sak, kŏol-, -sák) *n., pl.* **cul-de-sacs** or **culs-de-sac. 1.** A dead-end street; a road closed at one end. **2.** *Anatomy.* A saclike cavity or tube open only at one end. [French, "bottom of sack", blind alley.]

–cule *n. suffix.* Indicates smallness; for example, **molecule.** [French, from New Latin *-cula,* diminutive suffix from Latin *-culus, -cula, -culum.* See also **-cle.**]

cu·let (kéwlit) *n.* **1.** The flat face of a gem cut as a brilliant. **2.** One of the plates of medieval armour covering the lower back. [French, diminutive of *cul,* the rump, from Latin *cūlus.*]

cu·lex (kéw-leks) *n., pl.* **-lices** (-li-seez). Any of various mosquitoes of the genus *Culex,* which includes the house mosquito, *C. pipiens.* [New Latin, from Latin *culex†,* gnat.]

Cul·ham (kúlləm). Village in Oxfordshire, England, where the U.K. Atomic Energy Authority and the Joint European Torus (J.E.T.) programme on nuclear fusion do research.

cu·li·cide (kéwli-sīd) *n.* A chemical used to destroy mosquitoes or gnats. [Latin *culex* (stem *culic-),* gnat + -CIDE.]

cu·li·nar·y (kúlli-nəri ‖ kéwli-, *U.S.* -nerri) *adj.* Of or pertaining to a kitchen or to cookery. [Latin *culīnārius,* from *culīna,* kitchen.] —**cu·li·nar·i·ly** *adv.*

cull (kul) *tr.v.* **culled, culling, culls. 1.** To pick out from others; select. **2.** To gather; collect. **3. a.** To remove and kill (weak or surplus animals in a herd or flock). **b.** To search through (a herd or flock) in order to remove and kill weak or surplus animals.
~*n.* **1.** The act of culling. **2.** The amount culled. **3.** Something picked out from others; especially, something rejected because of inferior quality. [Middle English *coilen,* from Old French *cuillir,* from Latin *colligere,* to COLLECT.] —**cull·er** *n.*

cul·let (kúllit) *n.* Scraps of broken or waste glass gathered for re-melting. [Perhaps variant of earlier *collet,* from French *collet,* "little neck" (the neck of glass broken off a newly blown vessel), diminutive of *col,* neck, from Old French, from Latin *collum.*]

cul·lis (kúlliss) *n., pl.* **-lises.** A gutter or groove in a roof. [Middle English *colis,* from Old French *coleïs,* channel, from *coler,* to pour, strain, from Latin *cōlāre,* to filter, strain, from *cōlum,* a sieve.]

Culloden Moor / cumshaw

Cul·lod·en Moor (kə-lódd'n, -lŏd'n). The site near Inverness, Scotland, of the last battle to be fought on British soil. The Jacobite forces of Charles Edward Stuart were defeated by an army commanded by the Duke of Cumberland (1746). The battle marked the final defeat of the Jacobite cause and was followed by savage repression in the Highlands.

culm[1] (kulm) *n.* The jointed stem of a grass or sedge. [Latin *culmus*, stalk.]

culm[2] *n.* **1.** Waste from anthracite coal mines, consisting of fine coal, coal dust, and dirt. **2. a.** *Often capital* **C.** *Geology.* A Lower Carboniferous formation consisting of shale and sandstone. Also called "culm measures". **b.** Inferior anthracite coal. [Middle English *colme*, coal dust, perhaps akin to *col*, COAL.]

cul·mi·nant (kúlmi-nənt) *adj.* Culminating; highest.

cul·mi·nate (kúlmi-nayt) *intr.v.* **-nated, -nating, -nates. 1.** To reach the highest point or degree; come to full effect; climax. Usually used with *in.* **2.** *Astronomy.* To cross the meridian of the observer; reach the highest point above an observer's horizon. Used of stars and other celestial bodies. [Late Latin *culmināre*, from Latin *culmen* (stem *culmin-*), top, summit.] —**cul·mi·na·tion** (-náysh'n) *n.*

cu·lottes (kew-lóts ‖ kōō-) *pl.n.* A woman's full trousers, usually knee-length, cut to resemble a skirt. [French, breeches, diminutive of *cul*, backside, from Latin *cūlus.*] —**cu·lotte** (-lót) *adj.*

cul·pa·ble (kúlpə-b'l) *adj.* Responsible for wrong or error; deserving censure. [Middle English *coupable*, from Old French, from Latin *culpābilis*, from *culpāre*, to blame, from *culpa.*] —**cul·pa·bil·i·ty** (-bílləti) *n.* —**cul·pa·ble·ness** *n.* —**cul·pa·bly** *adv.*

Cul·pep·er (kúl-peppər), **Nicholas** (1616-54). English herbalist and physician. He set up as an apothecary in 1640 and in 1649 angered the London College of Physicians by producing a popular translation from Latin of their official *Pharmacopoeia.* He is best remembered for *Culpeper's Herbal* (1653), describing properties of herbs.

cul·prit (kúlprit) *n.* **1.** A person guilty of a fault or crime. **2.** *Archaic.* A person charged with an offence or crime. [From the 17-century legal phrase "Culprit, how will you be tried?", perhaps a mistake for Anglo-French "*Culpable. Prit d'averrer . . .*", "Guilty. (I am) ready to prove . . .", the prosecutor's response to a plea of not guilty, which might have been abbreviated as "*Cul. prit, etc.*": CULPABLE + *prit, prist*, ready, from Latin *praestus* (see **presto**).]

cult (kult) *n.* **1.** A system or community of religious worship and ritual, especially one focusing upon a single deity or spirit. **2. a.** Obsessive devotion or veneration for a person, principle, or ideal. **b.** The object of such devotion. **3. a.** An exclusive group of persons sharing an esoteric interest. **b.** The object of such an interest. **4.** Any fashion or fad. Often used derogatorily. ~*adj.* Pertaining to or characteristic of a cult: *a cult figure.* [French *culte*, from Latin *cultus*, cultivation, a labouring, worship, from the past participle of *colere*, to CULTIVATE.] —**cul·tic** *adj.* —**cult·ism** *n.* —**cult·ist** *n. & adj.*

cultch. Variant of **culch.**

cul·ti·gen (kúlti-jen, -jən) *n.* An organism, especially a cultivated plant such as maize, of a kind not known to have a wild or uncultivated counterpart. [CULTI(VATED) + -GEN.]

cul·ti·va·ble (kúlti-vəb'l) *adj.* Also **cul·ti·vat·a·ble** (-vaytəb'l). Capable of being cultivated. —**cul·ti·va·bil·i·ty** (-və-bílləti) *n.*

cul·ti·var (kúlti-vaar, -vair) *n.* A horticulturally or agriculturally derived variety of a plant, as distinguished from a natural variety. [*Cultivated* + *variety.*]

cul·ti·vate (kúltivayt) *tr.v.* **-vated, -vating, -vates. 1. a.** To improve and prepare (land), as by ploughing or fertilising, for raising crops; till. **b.** To loosen or dig (soil) around growing plants. **2.** To grow or tend (a plant or crop). **3.** To promote the growth of (a biological culture, for example). **4.** To nurture; foster. **5.** To form and refine, as by education. **6.** To seek the acquaintance or goodwill of. [Medieval Latin *cultīvāre*, from (*terra*) *cultīva*, tilled (land), from *cultīvus*, tilled, from Latin *cultus*, past participle of *colere*, to till, cultivate.]

cul·ti·vat·ed (kúlti-vaytid) *adj.* **1.** Cultured; refined. **2.** Specially nurtured or improved by cultivation. Said of plants.

cul·ti·va·tion (kúlti-váysh'n) *n.* **1. a.** The act of cultivating. **b.** The state of being cultivated. **2.** Refinement; social polish. —See Synonyms at **culture.**

cul·ti·va·tor (kúlti-vaytər) *n.* **1.** One who cultivates. **2.** An implement or machine for loosening the earth and destroying weeds around growing plants.

cul·trate (kúltrayt) *adj.* Also **cul·trat·ed** (kul-tráytid). Sharp-edged and pointed; knifelike: *a cultrate beak.* [Latin *cultrātus*, knifelike, from *culter* (stem *cultr-*), knife.]

cul·tur·al (kúl-chər-əl, -chōōr-) *adj.* **1.** Of or relating to culture, especially social, intellectual, or artistic pursuits. **2.** Obtained by specialised breeding, as certain plant varieties are.

cultural anthropology *n.* The scientific study of human culture based on archaeological, ethnologic, ethnographic, linguistic, social, and psychological data and methods of analysis. Compare **physical anthropology.**

Cultural Revolution *n.* A political movement in China (1966-68), thought to have been launched by Mao Ze-dong, aimed at overthrowing entrenched bureaucracy and rekindling revolutionary fervour and ideals.

cul·ture (kúlchər) *n.* **1.** Social and intellectual formation. **2. a.** The totality of socially transmitted behaviour patterns, arts, beliefs, institutions, and all other products of human work and thought characteristic of a community or population. **b.** The set of shared beliefs, attitudes, values, and behavioural patterns characteristic of a group or an organisation: *towards a more dynamic corporate culture.* **3.** A style of social and artistic expression peculiar to a society or class. **4. a.** Intellectual and artistic activity. **b.** Intellectual and social refinement resulting from such activity. **5.** The cultivation of the soil; tillage. **6.** The breeding of animals or growing of plants, especially to produce improved stock. **7.** *Biology.* **a.** The growing of microorganisms in a nutrient medium for scientific research or medical use. **b.** Such a growth or colony, as of bacteria. ~*tr.v.* **cultured, -turing, -tures. 1.** To cultivate. **2.** To develop (microorganisms or tissues, for example) in a culture medium. [Middle English, cultivation, tillage, from Old French, from Latin *cultūra*, from *cultus*, cultivation. See **cultivate.**]
Synonyms: culture, cultivation, refinement, taste.

cul·tured (kúlchərd) *adj.* **1.** Cultivated; refined. **2.** Produced under artificial and controlled conditions.

cultured pearl *n.* A pearl made to grow in the shell of an oyster or clam by inserting a small bead of mother of pearl, around which layers of nacre are deposited.

culture medium *n.* A substance, such as agar or blood, on which colonies of microorganisms, such as bacteria, are grown.

culture shock *n.* Severe and often distressing feelings of disorientation and isolation felt by a person on coming into contact with a completely alien society or foreign way of life.

culture vulture *n.* A person whose interest in art, literature, and the like is considered excessive or overzealous.

cul·tus (kúl-təss) *n., pl.* **-tuses** or **-ti** (-tī). A religious cult. [New Latin, from Latin *cultus*, worship, CULT.]

cul·ver (kúlvər) *n. Poetic.* A dove; a pigeon. [Middle English *culver*, Old English *culufre*, from Vulgar Latin *columbra* (unattested), from Latin *columbula*, diminutive of *columba*, dove.]

cul·ver·in (kúlvərin) *n.* **1.** A type of early musket. **2.** A heavy cannon used in the 16th and 17th centuries. [Middle English, from Old French *couleurine*, "serpentine", from *couleuvre*, snake, from Vulgar Latin *colobra* (unattested), from Latin *colubra*, feminine of *coluber*, snake.] —**cul·ver·i·neer** (-éer) *n.*

Cul·ver's root (kúlvərz) *n.* **1.** A North American plant, *Veronicastrum virginicum*, having spikes of small white or purplish flowers. **2.** The root of this plant, formerly used as a cathartic and emetic. [After a Dr. Culver, 18th-century U.S. physician.]

cul·vert (kúlvərt) *n.* **1.** A sewer or drain crossing under a road or embankment. **2.** A pipe or channel for an electric cable. [18th century : origin obscure.]

cum (kum, kōōm) *prep.* Together with; plus. Used in combination and names to indicate a dual nature or function: *her attic-cum-studio; Charlton-cum-Hardy, Lancs.* [Latin.]

cum·ber (kúmbər) *tr.v.* **-bered, -bering, -bers.** *Archaic.* **1.** To weigh down; burden. **2.** To hamper; obstruct. ~*n. Archaic.* A hindrance; an encumbrance. [Middle English *combren*, perhaps from Old French *combrer*, from *combre†*, hindrance.]

Cum·ber·land (kúmbər-lənd). Former county of northwest England. Since 1974 has been a part of the new county of Cumbria.

Cumberland, William Augustus, Duke of, known as The Butcher (1721–65). British general, the third son of George II. Made commander in chief of the British army (1745), he crushed the Jacobite rebellion at the battle of Culloden (1746).

Cum·ber·nauld (kúmbər-náwld). Town in North Lanarkshire, Scotland. It was designated a new town (1955) to house excess population from Glasgow, 22 kilometres (14 miles) away.

cum·ber·some (kúmbər-səm) *adj.* **1.** Clumsy; unwieldy. **2.** Burdensome; onerous. —See Synonyms at **heavy.** —**cum·ber·some·ly** *adv.* —**cum·ber·some·ness** *n.*

cum·brance (kúmbrənss) *n.* **1.** An encumbrance. **2.** Trouble. [Middle English *cumbraunce*, from *cumbren*, to CUMBER.]

Cum·bri·a (kúmbri-ə). County in northwest England, formed (1974) from Cumberland and Westmoreland with parts of Yorkshire and Lancashire. It encompasses the Lake District with the Cumbrian mountains, which rise to 977 metres (3,205 feet) at Scafell, the highest point in England. There are nuclear plants at Windscale and Calder Hall. Carlisle is the administrative centre. —**Cum·bri·an** *adj. & n.*

cum gra·no sa·lis (kum gráynō sáyliss, kōōm gráanō sáaliss) *adv. Latin.* With a grain of salt; with scepticism.

cum·in, cum·min (kúmmin) *n.* **1.** An Old World plant, *Cuminum cyminum*, having finely divided leaves and small white or pinkish flowers. **2.** The aromatic seeds of this plant, used as a condiment. [Middle English *comin*, from Old French *cumin*, from Latin *cumīnum*, from Greek *kuminon*, from Semitic, akin to Hebrew *kammōn*, Akkadian *kamūnu.*]

cum lau·de (kum láwdi, kōōm lówday) *adv.* With praise. Used on university and college diplomas to designate the third-highest degree of academic distinction. Compare **magna cum laude, summa cum laude.** [New Latin.]

cum·mer·bund (kúmmər-bund) *n.* A broad, pleated sash worn round the waist in men's formal dress. [Hindi *kamarband*, from Persian, loinband, waistband : *kamar*, loins, waist + *band*, band.]

cum·mings (kúmmingz), **e(dward) e(stlin)** (1894-1962). U.S. poet, noted for his lyricism and unconventional use of punctuation and typography.

cumquat. Variant of **kumquat.**

cum·shaw (kúm-shaw) *n.* A tip; a gratuity; a present. [Pidgin English, from Chinese dialect (Amoy) *kam sia*, to thank.]

cu·mu·late (kéwmew-layt) *tr.v.* **-lated, -lating, -lates.** To accumulate.
~*adj.* (*also* (-lǝt, -lit). Amassed; accumulated; heaped up. [Latin *cumulāre*, from *cumulus*, heap.] —**cu·mu·la·tion** (-láysh'n) *n.*
cu·mu·la·tive (kéwmew-lǝtiv, -laytiv) *adj.* **1.** Increasing or enlarging by successive addition. **2.** Acquired by or resulting from accumulation. **3.** *Finance.* **a.** Of or pertaining to interest or a dividend that increases if not paid when due. **b.** Designating shares that entitle holders to be paid arrears of dividend before any other payment is made to ordinary shareholders. **4.** *Law.* Designating additional or supporting evidence. **5.** *Statistics.* **a.** Of, pertaining to, or designating the sum of the frequencies of experimentally determined values of a random variable that are less than or equal to a given value. **b.** Of, pertaining to, or designating experimental error that increases in magnitude with each successive measurement. —**cu·mu·la·tive·ly** *adv.* —**cu·mu·la·tive·ness** *n.*
cumulative voting *n.* A system of voting, used, for example, by shareholders, in which each voter has as many votes as there are representatives to be elected and may give them all to one candidate or distribute them among several candidates.
cu·mu·li·form (kéwmewli-fawrm) *adj. Meteorology.* Having the shape of a cumulus cloud. [CUMUL(US) + -I- + -FORM.]
cu·mu·lo·nim·bus (kéwmewlō-ním-bǝss) *n., pl.* **-buses** or **-bi** (bī). *Meteorology.* An extremely dense cumulus cloud developed vertically to a great height, usually producing heavy rains, thunderstorms, or hailstorms. [New Latin : CUMUL(US) + -O- + NIMBUS.]
cu·mu·lus (kéwmew-lǝss) *n., pl.* **-li** (-lī). **1.** *Meteorology.* A dense, white, flat-based cloud with a multiple rounded top and a well-defined outline, occurring at heights of 600 to 900 metres (2,000 to 3,000 feet), and usually formed by the ascent of thermally unstable air masses. Also called "cumulus cloud". **2.** A pile, mound, or heap. [New Latin, from Latin, heap, mass.] —**cu·mu·lous** *adj.*
cunc·ta·tion (kúngk-táysh'n) *n. Rare.* Delay; procrastination. [Latin *cūnctātiō* (stem *cunctātiōn-*), from *cūnctātus*, past participle of *cūnctārī*, to delay.] —**cunc·ta·tive** (-tǝtiv, -táytiv) *adj.* —**cunc·ta·tory** (-táytǝri) *adj.* —**cunc·ta·tor** (-táytǝr) *n.*
cu·ne·al (kéwni-ǝl) *adj.* Wedge-shaped. [New Latin *cunealis*, from Latin *cuneus*, wedge. See **coin.**]
cu·ne·ate (kéwni-ayt, -ǝt, -it) *adj.* Wedge-shaped. Said especially of leaves that are narrow and triangular, and taper towards the base. [Latin *cuneātus*, from *cuneus*, wedge. See **coin.**] —**cu·ne·ate·ly** *adv.*
cu·ne·i·form (kéw-ni-fawrm, -ni-i- ‖ kew-née-i-) *adj.* **1.** Wedge-shaped. **2.** Designating: **a.** The wedge-shaped characters used in ancient Sumerian, Akkadian, Assyrian, Babylonian, and Persian writing. **b.** Documents, stone tablets, or inscriptions written or engraved in such characters. **3.** *Anatomy.* Designating any of the three wedge-shaped bones in the tarsus of the foot.
~*n.* **1.** Cuneiform writing. **2.** A cuneiform bone. [French *cunéiforme* : Latin *cuneus*, wedge (see **coin**) + -FORM.]
Cu·ne·ne or **Ku·ne·ne** (kōō-náy-nǝ, -nay). River of southern Africa. It rises in central Angola and flows some 1 200 kilometres (about 750 miles) to the Atlantic, its lower course forming much of the Angola-Namibia border. The South-African-financed Cunene River Scheme will provide power and water for both countries.
cun·ni·lin·gus (kúnni-líng-gǝss) *n.* Also **cun·ni·linc·tus** (-lingk-tǝss). Sexual stimulation of the female genitals by the lips and tongue. Compare **fellatio.** [New Latin : Latin *cunnus*, vulva + *lingere*, to lick.]
cun·ning (kúnning) *adj.* **1.** Shrewd; crafty; artful. **2.** Executed with or exhibiting ingenuity. —See Synonyms at **clever, sly.**
~*n.* **1.** Skill in deception; craftiness; guile. **2.** *Archaic.* Skill or adeptness in performance; adroitness; dexterity. [Middle English *conning*, perhaps from the present participle of *connen*, to know, Old English *cunnan.*] —**cun·ning·ly** *adv.* —**cun·ning·ness** *n.*
Cun·ning·ham (kúnning-ǝm, -ham), **Merce** (1919–). U.S. choreographer, a pioneer of experimental ballet. He danced with Martha Graham's company (1939–45) and from 1942 often worked with John Cage. Own company since 1953.
Cu·no·be·li·nus (kéwnō-bǝ-lī-nǝss, -lée-) (died c. A.D. 42). *English* **Cym·be·line** (símbǝleen). Ancient British ruler, chief of the Catuvellauni tribe who ruled a territory corresponding to modern Hertfordshire.
cunt (kunt) *n. Vulgar.* **1.** The female genitals. **2.** The vagina. [Middle English, from Germanic; akin to Middle Dutch *kunte*, Old Norse *kunta.*]
cup (kup) *n.* **1.** A small, rounded, open container, typically with a flat bottom and a handle, used for drinking. **2. a.** Such a container and its contents. **b.** The contents alone. **3.** *Abbr.* **c. a.** A British measure of capacity equal to ½ pint, 10 fluid ounces, or 284 millitres. **b.** A chiefly U.S. measure equal to 8 fluid ounces or 237 millilitres. In both senses, also called "cupful". **4.** The bowl of a drinking vessel. **5.** The chalice or the wine used in the celebration of the Eucharist. **6.** An ornamental cup-shaped vessel, usually two-handed, to commemorate an event or as a prize or trophy. **7.** A sporting contest, often an elimination competition lasting several rounds, played for a cup as the prize. Also used adjectivally: *cup final; cup winner.* **8.** Either of the two rounded, hollow parts of a brassiere that contain or support the breasts. **9.** *Golf.* A hole or the metal container inside a hole. **10.** Any of various beverages, usually combining wine, fruit, and spices. **11.** Anything resembling a cup. **12.** *Biology.* A cuplike structure or organ. **13.** A lot or portion to be suffered or enjoyed. —**in (one's) cups.** Drunk. —**not (one's) cup of tea.** *Informal.* Not to one's taste; not agreeable.

~*tr.v.* **cupped, cupping, cups.** **1.** To place in or as in a cup. **2.** To shape like a cup: *cup one's hand.* **3.** *Medicine.* To practise cupping on. [Middle English *cuppe*, Old English *cuppe*, from Late Latin *cuppa†*, drinking vessel.] —**cup·py** *adj.*
cup·bear·er (kúp-bair-ǝr) *n.* One who serves wine, as in a royal household.
cup·board (kúbbǝrd) *n.* A cabinet or recessed portion of a room enclosed by a door, usually with shelves for storing food, crockery, and the like.
cupboard love *n.* Love shown or simulated in order to gain material goods or advantages.
cup·cake (kúp-kayk) *n.* A small cake baked in a cup-shaped container.
cu·pel (kéwp'l, kew-pél) *n.* **1.** A shallow, porous vessel used in assaying to separate precious metals from less valuable elements. **2.** The bottom or receptacle in a silver-refining furnace.
~*tr.v.* **cupelled** or *U.S.* **cupeled, -pelling** or *U.S.* **-peling, -pels.** To separate from base metals in a cupel. [French *coupelle*, diminutive of *coupe*, cup, from Late Latin *cuppa*, CUP.] —**cu·pel·ler** *n.*
cu·pel·la·tion (kéw-pi-láysh'n, -pe-) *n.* A refining process for non-oxidising metals, such as silver and gold, in which the components of a metallic mixture oxidised at high temperatures are separated by absorption into the walls of a cupel.
cup final *n. Often capital* **C,** *capital* **F.** The final match in a sporting competition with a cup as the prize.
cup·ful (kúp-fōōl) *n., pl.* **-fuls** or **cupsful. 1.** The amount a cup will hold. **2.** *Cooking. U.S.* A measure of capacity; a cup.
cu·pid (kéwpid) *n.* A representation of the god Cupid as a winged boy holding a bow and arrow.
Cu·pid (kéwpid). The Roman god of love, identified with the Greek Eros. [Latin *Cupīdō*, personification of *cupīdō*, desire, from *cupere*, to desire.]
cu·pid·i·ty (kew-píddǝti) *n.* Avarice; greed; strong desire for gain. [Middle English *cupidite*, from Old French, from Latin *cupiditās* (stem *cupiditāt-*), from *cupidus*, desiring, from *cupere*, to desire.]
cu·po·la (kéwpǝlǝ) *n.* **1. a.** A domed roof or ceiling. **b.** A small, usually domed structure surmounting a roof. **2.** A cylindrical vertical type of blast furnace used for remelting metals, usually iron, before casting. Also called "cupola furnace". **3.** A protective revolving dome on the guns of a warship. **4.** *Geology.* A small dome-shaped igneous intrusion. [Italian *cupola*, from Late Latin *cūpula*, diminutive of Latin *cūpa*, tub, vat.]
cup·pa (kúppǝ) *n. British Informal.* A cup of tea. [From *cup of.*]
cup·ping (kúpping) *n.* A therapeutic process, rarely used in modern medicine, in which glass cups (*cupping glasses*), partially evacuated by heating, are locally applied to the skin in order to draw blood towards or through the surface.
cu·pre·ous (kéwpri-ǝss) *adj.* Of, resembling, or containing copper; coppery. [Late Latin *cupreus*, from *cuprum*, COPPER.]
cu·pric (kéwprik) *adj.* Of or containing divalent copper. [Late Latin *cuprum*, COPPER.]
cu·prif·er·ous (kew-príffǝrǝss) *adj.* Yielding copper. [Late Latin *cuprum*, COPPER + -FEROUS.]
cu·prite (kéwprīt) *n.* A natural red copper ore, essentially Cu_2O. [German *Kuprit* : Late Latin *cuprum*, COPPER + -ITE.]
cupro-, cupri-, cupr- *comb. form.* Indicates copper; for example, **cupronickel, cupriferous.** [Late Latin *cuprum*, copper.]
cu·pro·nick·el (kéwprō-níck'l) *n.* An alloy of copper with up to 40 per cent of nickel, highly resistant to corrosion.
cu·prous (kéwprǝss) *adj.* Of, pertaining to, or containing univalent copper. [Late Latin *cuprum*, COPPER.]
cup tie *n.* An elimination match in a sporting contest being played for a cup as a prize.
cu·pu·la (kéwpew-lǝ) *n., pl.* **-lae** (-lee). *Anatomy.* A cup-shaped or domed structure, such as the apex of the cochlea. [New Latin, CUP-ULE.]
cu·pu·late (kéwpew-layt, -lǝt, -lit) *adj.* Also **cu·pu·lar** (-lǝr). **1.** Resembling a small cup; cup-shaped. **2.** Having or bearing a cupule.
cu·pule (kéwpewl) *n. Biology.* A cup-shaped part, structure, or indentation; especially, the cuplike base of an acorn. [New Latin *cupula*, from Late Latin *cūpula*, little cask or tub, diminutive of Latin *cūpa*, a tub, vat.]
cur (kur) *n.* **1.** A dog considered to be inferior, vicious, or undesirable; a mongrel. **2.** A base or cowardly person. [Middle English *curre*, short for *kur(dogge)*, "growling dog", perhaps from Old Norse *kurra*, to growl.] —**cur·rish** *adj.*
cur. currency.
cur·a·ble (kéwr-ǝb'l) *adj.* Capable of being healed or cured. —**cur·a·bil·i·ty** (-ǝ-bíllǝti), **cur·a·ble·ness** *n.* —**cur·a·bly** *adv.*
cu·ra·çao (kéwr-ǝ-só) *n.* Also **cu·ra·çoa** (-só-ǝ). A liqueur flavoured with the peel of the sour Curaçao orange. [From CURAÇAO.]
Cu·ra·çao (kéwr-ǝ-só, kóor-, -só, -sów, -sow). The largest island in the Netherlands Antilles group, situated in the south Caribbean Sea. It was discovered and settled by Spain (1499) and occupied by the Dutch in the 17th century. It received autonomy under the Dutch Crown (1954). Willemstad is the administrative centre.
cu·ra·cy (kéwr-ǝ-si) *n., pl.* **-cies.** The office, duties, or term of office of a curate.
curagh, curragh. Variants of **currach.**
cu·ra·re, cu·ra·ri (kewr-áari ‖ *U.S. also* kōō-ráari) *n.* **1.** A resinous substance obtained from several species of South American trees. It is used medicinally as a muscle relaxant and by some South American Indians as an arrow poison. **2.** Any of the trees from which this

substance is obtained. [Portuguese and Spanish, from Carib *kurari*.]

cu·ra·rine (kewr-a'ar-een ‖ -in) *n.* A poisonous alkaloid, $C_{19}H_{26}N_2O$, obtained from curare. [CURAR(E) + -INE.]

cu·ra·rise, cu·ra·rize (kewr-a'ar-īz) *tr.v.* -rised, -rising, -rises. 1. To poison with curare. 2. To treat with curare so as to paralyse the motor nerves. —**cu·ra·ri·sa·tion** (-ī-záysh'n ‖ *U.S.* -i-) *n.*

cu·ras·sow (kéwr-ə-sō) *n.* Any of several long-tailed, crested tropical American birds of the family Cracidae, related to the pheasants and domestic fowl. [Variant of CURAÇAO (island).]

cu·rate (kéwr-ət, -it) *n.* 1. A clergyman who assists or deputises for a rector or vicar. 2. *Archaic.* A clergyman who has charge of a parish. [Middle English *curat*, from Medieval Latin *cūrātus*, "one having a (spiritual) cure or charge", from *cūra*, CURE.]

curate's egg *n.* *British.* Something that is bad, but is said to have both good and bad aspects or parts. [From a cartoon in *Punch* (November, 1895) showing a shy curate dining with his bishop. He has been served a bad egg and when asked how it is, he replies that parts of it are excellent.]

cur·a·tive (kéwr-ətiv) *adj.* 1. Serving or tending to cure. 2. Of or relating to the cure of disease.
~*n.* Something that cures; a remedy. —**cur·a·tive·ly** *adv.* —**cur·a·tive·ness** *n.*

cu·ra·tor (kewr-áytər ‖ *chiefly U.S.* kéwr-ətər, -aytər) *n.* 1. The administrative director of a museum, library, zoo, or other similar institution. 2. In Scots law, a guardian. [Middle English *curatour*, from Old French *curateur*, from Latin *cūrātōr*, overseer, manager, from *cūrāre*, to take care of, from *cūra*, care, CURE.] —**cu·ra·to·ri·al** (kéwr-ə-táwri-əl ‖ -tóri-) *adj.* —**cu·ra·tor·ship** *n.*

curb (kurb) *n.* 1. Anything that checks or restrains. 2. A chain or strap serving, with the bit, to restrain a horse. 3. An enclosing structure, framework, or fender. 4. *U.S.* Variant of **kerb.**
~*tr.v.* **curbed, curbing, curbs.** 1. To check, restrain, or control. 2. To place a curb on (a horse). 3. *U.S.* To lead (a dog) off the pavement kerb into the adjacent part of the road to defecate or urinate. —See Synonyms at **restrain.** [Middle English, from Old French *courber*, from Latin *curvāre*, bend, CURVE.] —**curb·er** *n.*

curb roof *n.* A roof having two slopes on each side, the lower slope being the steeper.

cur·cu·li·o (kur-kéwli-ō) *n.,* pl. **-os.** Any of several American weevils of the family Curculionidae, many of which are destructive to fruit and other plants. [New Latin, from Latin *curculiō†*, weevil.]

cur·cu·ma (kúrkewmə) *n.* Any of various Old World tropical plants of the genus *Curcuma*, having aromatic rootstocks. *C. longa* provides turmeric (*see*). [New Latin, from Arabic *kurkum*, saffron.]

curd (kurd) *n.* 1. *Often plural.* The coagulated part of milk, formed by the action of rennet or acid and used especially to make cheese. 2. Any coagulation resembling this. 3. The edible flower head of the cauliflower or the broccoli.
~*v.* **curded, curding, curds.** —*tr.* To form into curd; cause to thicken; curdle. —*intr.* To become curd; curdle; coagulate. [Middle English *curd, crudde†*.] —**curd·y** *adj.*

curd cheese *n.* A soft, mild cheese made from skimmed milk curds.

cur·dle (kúrd'l) *v.* **-dled, -dling, -dles.** —*intr.* 1. To congeal; become curd; coagulate. 2. To go sour. —*tr.* 1. To cause to congeal or change into curd. 2. To make sour. [Frequentative of CURD.]

cure (kewr) *n.* 1. Restoration of health; recovery from disease. 2. A method or course of medical treatment used to restore health. 3. **a.** An agent, such as a drug, that restores health; a remedy. **b.** A remedy for a harmful or troublesome condition: *a cure for unemployment.* 4. *Ecclesiastical.* Spiritual charge or care of souls, as of a priest for his congregation. Also called "cure of souls". 5. The office or duties of a curate. 6. The act or process of preserving a product such as fish, meat, or tobacco.
~*v.* **cured, curing, cures.** —*tr.* 1. To restore to health; heal. 2. To get rid of; remedy: *cure an evil.* 3. To preserve (meat, fish, or the like), as by salting or smoking. 4. To prepare, preserve, or finish (a substance) by a chemical or physical process. 5. To vulcanise (rubber). —*intr.* 1. To effect a cure or recovery. 2. To be prepared, preserved, or finished by a chemical or physical process. [Middle English, care, spiritual charge, cure, from Old French, from Latin *cūra*, care, charge, healing.] —**cure·less** *adj.* —**cur·er** *n.*

cu·ré (kéwr-ay ‖ kewr-áy) *n.* *French.* A parish priest.

cure-all (kéwr-awl) *n.* That which cures all diseases or evils; a panacea.

cu·ret·tage (kéwr-i-ta'a̱zh, kewr-éttij) *n.* Surgical scraping of a bodily cavity, as of the uterus, with a curette. Also called "curettement". See **dilatation and curettage.** [French, from CURETTE.]

cu·rette, cu·ret (kewr-ét) *n.* A surgical instrument shaped like a scoop or spoon, used to remove dead tissue or growths from a bodily cavity. [French, from *curer*, to clean, from Old French, from Latin *cūrāre*, from *cūra*, CURE.]

cur·few (kúrfew) *n.* 1. An order or regulation enjoining most people or specific members of the population to retire from the streets or from public premises at a prescribed hour. 2. A similar medieval regulation requiring fires to be extinguished. 3. **a.** The period during which any such regulation is in effect. **b.** The signal, such as a bell, announcing a curfew. **c.** The hour at which a curfew comes into effect. [Middle English *curfeu, coeverfu*, from Old French *cuevrefeu*, "a covering of the fire" : *co(u)vrir*, to COVER + *feu*, fire, from Latin *focus*, hearth (see **fuel**).]

cu·ri·a (kéwr-i-ə) *n.,* pl. **curiae** (-ee). 1. **a.** The Senate or any of the various buildings in which it met in republican Rome. **b.** The place

of assembly of high councils in various Italian cities under Roman administration. 2. The ensemble of central administrative and governmental services in imperial Rome. 3. *Often capital* **C.** The central administration governing the Roman Catholic Church. 4. In medieval Europe: **a.** A feudal assembly or council. **b.** A royal court of justice. [Latin *cūria*, curia, council.] —**cu·ri·al** *adj.*

cu·rie (kéwr-i ‖ *U.S. also* kew-rée) *n. Abbr.* **Ci** A unit of radioactivity, the amount of any nuclide that undergoes exactly 3.7×10^{10} radioactive disintegrations per second. [After Marie CURIE.]

Cu·rie (kéwr-i, -ée), **Marie,** born Maria Sklodowska (1867–1934). Polish chemist, famous for her discovery of radium (1898). She studied science in Paris and in 1895 married Pierre Curie (1859–1906), a French professor of physics. From 1896, the Curies investigated radioactivity and laid the foundations of nuclear physics. They were awarded the Nobel prize for physics jointly with Henri Becquerel (1903). After her husband's death, Marie Curie continued her work and was awarded a second Nobel prize, this time in chemistry for her discovery of radium and polonium and their properties (1911). The Curies' daughter, Irène Joliot-Curie (1897–1956) and her husband the French physicist Frédéric Joliot (1900–58) won the Nobel prize for chemistry (1935).

Curie law *n.* The law that magnetic susceptibility varies inversely with thermodynamic temperature in a paramagnetic substance. Also called "Curie's law". [After Pierre CURIE.]

Curie point *n.* A transition temperature marking a change in the magnetic properties of a substance, especially the change from ferromagnetism to paramagnetism. Also called "Curie temperature". [After Pierre CURIE.]

Cu·rie-Weiss law (kéwr-i-vîss ‖ *U.S. also* kew-rée-, -wîss) *n.* The law that the magnetic susceptibility of a paramagnetic substance above the Curie point varies inversely with the excess of temperature above that point. [After Pierre CURIE and Pierre *Weiss* (1865–1940), French physicist.]

cu·ri·o (kéwr-i-ō) *n.,* pl. **-os.** A curious or unusual object of art or bric-a-brac. [Short for CURIOSITY.]

cu·ri·o·sa (kéwr-i-ó-sə, -zə) *pl.n.* Books, writings, or objects dealing with unusual, especially pornographic, topics; erotica. [New Latin, from Latin *cūriōsa*, neuter plural of *cūriōsus*, CURIOUS.]

cu·ri·os·i·ty (kéwr-i-óssəti) *n.,* pl. **-ties.** 1. **a.** A desire to know or learn, especially about something new or strange. **b.** Excessive interest or eagerness to know; inquisitiveness. 2. That which arouses interest, as by being novel or extraordinary. 3. Strangeness; novelty. Also used adjectivally: *curiosity value.*

cu·ri·ous (kéwr-i-əss) *adj.* 1. Eager to acquire information or knowledge. 2. Unduly inquisitive; prying; nosy. 3. Interesting because of novelty or rarity; singular; odd. 4. *Archaic.* Accomplished with skill or ingenuity. [Middle English, from Old French *curios,* from Latin *cūriōsus,* careful, diligent, inquisitive, from *cūra,* care, CURE.] —**cu·ri·ous·ly** *adv.* —**cu·ri·ous·ness** *n.*
   Synonyms: *curious, inquisitive, nosy, intrusive.*

cu·ri·um (kéwr-i-əm) *n. Symbol* **Cm** A silvery, metallic, synthetic, radioactive, transuranic element having 13 isotopes with mass numbers from 238 to 250 and half-lives from 64 minutes to 16.4 million years. Atomic number 96. [New Latin, after Marie and Pierre CURIE.]

curl (kurl) *v.* **curled, curling, curls.** —*tr.* 1. To twist (the hair, for example) into ringlets or coils. 2. To form into the spiral or curved shape of a ringlet or coil. —*intr.* 1. To form ringlets or coils. 2. To assume a spiral or curved shape. Often used with *up.* 3. To move in a curve or spiral. 4. To play the game of curling. —**curl up.** 1. To assume a position with the legs drawn up. 2. To make oneself comfortable. 3. *Informal.* To react with horror, shame, or distaste.
~*n.* 1. Something with a spiral or coiled shape. 2. A coil or ringlet of hair. 3. **a.** The act of curling. **b.** The state of being curled. 4. *Mathematics.* The vector product of the del operator and a vector function. Compare **divergence.** [Middle English *curlen, crullen,* from *crulle,* curly, from Middle Dutch.]

curl·er (kúrlər) *n.* 1. One that curls. 2. A pin, roller, or the like on which hair is wound for curling. 3. A player of the game of curling.

cur·lew (kúr-lew, -lōō) *n.* Any of several brownish, long-legged shore birds of the genus *Numenius,* having long, slender, downward-curving bills. [Middle English *curleu,* from Old French *courlieu* (imitative).]

curl·i·cue, curl·y·cue (kúrli-kew) *n.* A fancy twist or curl, such as a flourish made with a pen. —**curl·i·cued, curl·y·cued** (-kewd) *adj.* [CURLY + CUE (rod).]

curl·ing (kúrling) *n.* A game originating in Scotland and played on ice, in which two four-man teams slide heavy, flat, round stones (*curling stones*) towards a fixed mark in the centre of a circle.

curling tongs *pl.n.* A scissor-like metal device, usually rod-shaped, that is heated and used to curl individual locks of hair. Also *U.S.* "curling irons".

curl paper *n.* A piece of soft paper on which a lock of hair is rolled up in order to make it curl.

curl·y (kúrli) *adj.* **-ier, -iest.** 1. Having curls. 2. Having the tendency to curl. 3. Having a wavy grain. Said of wood: *curly maple.* —**curl·i·ly** *adv.* —**curl·i·ness** *n.*

cur·mudg·eon (kur-mújən, kər-) *n.* 1. A surly person. 2. A miser. [16th century : origin obscure.] —**cur·mudg·eon·ly** *adj.*

cur·rach, cur·agh, cur·ragh (kúrrə, -kh) *n. Scottish & Irish.* A kind of boat, a **coracle** (*see*). [Middle English *currok,* from Scottish Gaelic *curach* and Irish Gaelic *currach;* akin to Welsh *corwgl, cwrwgl†.*]

cur·rant (kúrrənt) *n.* **1.** A small, dried seedless grape of the Mediterranean region, used in cooking. **2.** Any of various shrubs of the genus *Ribes,* bearing clusters of red, black, or greenish fruit. See **blackcurrant, redcurrant. 3.** The small, sour fruit of any of these plants, used chiefly for making jam and jelly. [Middle English *raysons of coraunce,* from Anglo-French *raisins de corauntz,* grapes of CORINTH (from where they were originally exported).]

cur·ra·wong (kúrrə-wong) *n.* Any Australian bird of the genus *Strepera,* usually having a black plumage with white markings. Also called "bell magpie". [From a native Australian name.]

cur·ren·cy (kúrrən-si) *n., pl.* **-cies. 1.** *Abbr.* **cur.** Any form of money in actual use as a medium of exchange. **2.** A passing from hand to hand; circulation. **3.** Common acceptance; prevalence. [Medieval Latin *currentia,* "a flowing", from Latin *currēns* (stem *current-*), present participle of *currere,* to run. See **current.**]

cur·rent (kúrrənt) *adj.* **1. a.** Belonging to the time now passing; now in progress. **b.** Most recent: *the current issue.* **2.** Passing from one to another; circulating, as money does. **3.** Commonly accepted; prevalent. —See Synonyms at **prevailing.**
∼n. **1.** A steady and smooth onward movement, as of water. **2.** The part of any body of liquid or gas that has a continuous movement in a specific direction: *a river current.* **3.** A general tendency, movement, or course. **4.** *Symbol* **i, I** *Electricity.* **a.** A flow of electric charge. **b.** The amount of electric charge flowing past a specific circuit point per unit time. In this sense, also called "electric current". —See Synonyms at **tendency.** [Middle English *curraunt,* from Old French *corant,* present participle of *courre,* to run, from Latin *currere.*] **—cur·rent·ly** *adv.* **—cur·rent·ness** *n.*

current account *n.* **1.** A bank account, usually one that does not earn interest and against which cheques may be written and from which money can be drawn at any time. **2.** *Economics.* The part of the balance of payments recording noncapital transactions. Compare **capital account.**

current affairs *pl.n.* **1.** Topical news, usually of serious issues such as politics or international affairs. **2.** Discussion of such news, as on television. Also used adjectivally: *current affairs programmes.* Also called "current events".

current assets *pl.n.* Cash or other assets convertible into cash at short notice.

current bedding *n.* **Cross bedding** *(see).*

current density *n. Symbol* **J 1.** *Electricity.* The ratio of the magnitude of current flowing in a conductor to the cross-sectional area perpendicular to the current flow. **2.** *Physics.* The number of subatomic particles per unit time crossing a unit area in a designated plane perpendicular to the direction of motion of the particles.

cur·ri·cle (kúrrik'l) *n.* A light, open two-wheeled vehicle, drawn by two horses abreast. [Latin *curriculum,* a running, racecourse, racing chariot. See **curriculum.**]

cur·ric·u·lum (kə-ríckew-ləm) *n., pl.* **-la** (-lə) or **-lums. 1.** All the courses of study offered by an educational institution. **2.** A particular course of study, often in a special field. [New Latin, from Latin, a running, course, from *currere,* to run.] **—cur·ric·u·lar** (-lər) *adj.*

curriculum vi·tae (vītee, véetī) *n., pl.* **curricula vitae.** *Abbr.* **c.v.** A short résumé of one's educational background and career, as for a prospective employer. [Latin, the course of one's life.]

cur·ri·er (kúrri-ər) *n.* One who curries something, especially leather. [Middle English *curr(e)iour,* from Old French, from Latin *coriārius,* a tanner, from *corium,* leather.]

cur·ri·er·y (kúrri-əri) *n., pl.* **-ies.** The trade, work, or shop of a leather currier.

cur·ry[1] (kúrri) *tr.v.* **-ried, -rying, -ries. 1.** To groom (a horse) with a currycomb. **2.** To prepare (tanned hides) for use by soaking, colouring, or other processes. **—curry favour.** To seek or gain favour by fawning or flattery. [Middle English *curreien,* from Old French *co(n)reer,* to prepare, equip, from Vulgar Latin *conrēdāre* (unattested) : *com-* (intensive), with + *rēdāre* (unattested), to prepare, from Germanic. Sense 2 is partly a back-formation from CURRIER.]

curry[2] *n., pl.* **-ries. 1.** A dish originating in India, consisting of meat, fish, or vegetables prepared and cooked in a sauce made of various spices that give it a hot or piquant flavour. **2.** Curry powder or curry paste. **3.** A dish seasoned with curry powder or curry paste. **—give (someone) curry.** *Australian Slang.* To hurl insults at.
∼tr.v. **curried, -rying, -ries. 1.** To make a curry of. **2.** To season with curry. [Tamil *kari,* sauce.]

Cur·ry (kúrri), **John (Anthony)** (1949–94). British ice skater, who brought the expressiveness of ballet to his art. He won the European, Olympic, and World figure-skating championships in a single season (1976).

cur·ry·comb (kúrri-kōm) *n.* A comb with metal teeth, used for grooming horses.
∼tr.v. **currycombed, -combing, -combs.** To groom with a currycomb.

curry paste *n.* A condiment prepared from pungent spices, as in curry powder, blended with oil, tomatoes, onions, and the like.

curry powder *n.* A blended condiment prepared from turmeric and other pungent spices such as cumin, coriander, and chilli.

curse (kurss) *n.* **1.** An appeal to a supernatural power for evil or injury to befall someone or something. **2.** The evil or injury thus invoked. **3.** Someone or something accursed. **4.** That which brings or causes evil; a scourge. **5.** Any profane oath, swearword, or obscenity. **6.** *Ecclesiastical.* A censure, ban, or anathema. **7.** *Informal.* Menstruation. Preceded by *the.*
∼v. **cursed** or **curst, cursing, curses.** *—tr.* **1.** To invoke evil, calamity, or injury upon; damn. **2.** To swear at; abuse profanely. **3.** To bring harm upon; afflict. **4.** *Ecclesiastical.* To put under ban or anathema; excommunicate. *—intr.* To utter curses; swear. [Middle English *curs(e),* Old English *curs*†.] **—curs·er** *n.*

curs·ed (kúr-sid, kurst) *adj.* Also **curst** (for senses 1, 2). **1.** Deserving to be cursed; wicked; detestable. **2.** Damned; under a curse. **3.** Variant of **curst. —curs·ed·ly** *adv.* **—curs·ed·ness** *n.*

cur·sive (kúr-siv) *adj.* Designating writing or printing in which the letters are joined together; flowing.
∼n. **1.** A cursive character or letter. **2.** A manuscript written in cursive characters. **3.** *Printing.* A kind of type that imitates handwriting. [Medieval Latin *(scripta) cursīva,* "flowing (script)", from Latin *cursus,* past participle of *currere,* to run.]

cur·sor (kúr-sər) *n.* **1.** The point of a measuring or calculating instrument that slides; especially, the movable window on a slide rule. **2.** A visual indicator, such as a movable point of light, that is used to indicate a specific position on a visual display unit, such as where a deletion or insertion is to be made. [Latin, "runner", from *currere* (past participle stem *curs-*), to run.]

cur·so·ri·al (kur-sáwri-əl ‖ -sōri-) *adj. Zoology.* Adapted to or specialised for running: *cursorial birds; cursorial legs.* [Late Latin *cursōrius,* of running. See **cursory.**]

cur·so·ry (kúr-səri) *adj.* Hasty and superficial; not thorough. See Synonyms at **superficial.** [Late Latin *cursōrius,* of running, from Latin *cursor,* a runner, from *cursus.* See **cursive.**] **—cur·so·ri·ly** *adv.* **—cur·so·ri·ness** *n.*

curst (kurst) *adj.* Also **curs·ed** (kúr-sid, kurst) (for sense 1). **1.** *Archaic & Regional.* Ill-tempered. **2.** Variant of **cursed.**

curt (kurt) *adj.* **1.** Rudely brief or abrupt, as in speech or manner. **2.** Terse; concise. **3.** Shortened. —See Synonyms at **gruff.** [Latin *curtus,* cut short.] **—curt·ly** *adv.* **—curt·ness** *adj.*

cur·tail (kur-táyl) *tr.v.* **-tailed, -tailing, -tails.** To reduce by or as if by cutting short. [Variant of obsolete *curtal,* to dock the tail of a horse, from CURTAL.] **—cur·tail·er** *n.* **—cur·tail·ment** *n.*

curtail step *n.* The widened step or steps at the foot of a flight of stairs. [Origin obscure.]

cur·tain (kúrt'n) *n.* **1.** A piece of cloth or similar material hanging in a window or other opening as a decoration, shade, or screen. **2.** *Theatre.* **a.** A hanging barrier that rises at the beginning of a scene and falls at the end of a scene. **b.** A line, speech, or situation in a play that occurs at the very end or just before the curtain falls. **3.** The part of a rampart or parapet connecting two bastions or gates. **4.** Any barrier to visibility: *a curtain of fog.* **5.** Any barrier, such as a restriction on communication. See **bamboo curtain, iron curtain. 6.** *Plural. Informal.* The end; ruin.
∼tr.v. **curtained, -taining, -tains. 1.** To shut off with or as if with a curtain. Often used with *off.* **2.** To provide with curtains. [Middle English *curtin(e),* from Old French, from Late Latin *cortīna,* enclosure, curtain, translation of Greek *aulaia,* from *aulē,* court.]

curtain call *n.* The appearance of a performer or performers at the end of a performance in response to applause.

curtain raiser *n.* **1.** A short entertainment presented before the principal dramatic production. **2.** Any preliminary event.

curtain speech *n.* **1.** A talk given in front of the curtain at the conclusion of a theatrical performance. **2.** The final speech of a play or of an act of a play.

cur·tain-up (kúrt'n-úp) *n. British.* The start of a theatrical performance.

curtain wall *n.* **1.** An enclosing wall connecting two towers or similar structures. **2.** An external wall not supporting a roof.

cur·tal (kúrt'l) *n. Obsolete.* **1.** An animal with a docked tail. **2.** Anything cut short or docked.
∼adj. Obsolete. **1.** Cut short or docked, as an animal's tail may be. **2.** Wearing a short frock: *a curtal friar.* [Old French *courtault,* horse with a cropped tail or mane, from *court,* short, from Latin *curtus,* shortened.]

cur·tate (kúrtayt) *adj.* Shortened; abbreviated. [Latin *curtātus,* past participle of *curtāre,* to shorten, from *curtus,* short, CURT.]

cur·ti·lage (kúrtilij) *n. Law.* The enclosed land surrounding a house or dwelling. [Middle English, from Old French *courtillage,* from *courtil,* little court, diminutive of *cort,* COURT.]

curt·sy (kúrtsi) *n., pl.* **-sies.** Also **curt·sey** *pl.* **-seys.** A gesture of respect or reverence made by women by bending the knees with one foot forward and lowering the body.
∼intr.v. **curtsied, -sying, -sies.** Also **curtsey, -seyed, -seying, -seys.** To make a curtsy. [Variant of COURTESY.]

cu·rule (kéwr-ōōl, -yōōl) *adj.* Privileged to sit in a curule chair; of superior rank. [Latin *curūlis,* "of a chariot", of a curule chair (originally a throne mounted on a chariot), from *currus,* a chariot, from *currere,* to run.]

curule chair *n.* A seat with heavy, curved legs and no back, reserved for the use of the highest officials in ancient Rome. Also called "curule seat".

cur·va·ceous (kur-váyshəss) *adj.* **1.** Curving. **2.** *Informal.* Of, pertaining to, or designating a woman having a full or voluptuous figure; shapely. [CURV(E) + -ACEOUS.] **—cur·va·ceous·ly** *adv.*

cur·va·ture (kúrvə-tewr, -choor, -chər) *n.* **1. a.** An act of curving. **b.** The state of being curved. **2.** *Mathematics.* **a.** The ratio of the change in tangent inclination over a given arc to the length of the arc. Also called "average curvature". **b.** The limit of this ratio as the length of the arc approaches zero. **3.** *Medicine.* A curving or bending, especially an abnormal one: *curvature of the spine.* [Latin *curvātūra,* from *curvātus,* past participle of *curvāre,* to bend, from *curvus,* curved.]

curve (kurv) *n.* **1. a.** A line that deviates from straightness in a smooth, continuous fashion. **b.** A surface that deviates from a flat plane in a smooth, continuous fashion. **2.** A curved part, object, or region, such as a part of the human body. **3. a.** A line representing data on a graph. **b.** A trend derived from or as if from such a graph. **4.** *Mathematics.* **a.** The graph of a function on a coordinate plane. **b.** The intersection of two surfaces in three dimensions.
~*v.* **curved, curving, curves.** —*intr.* To move in or take the shape of a curve. —*tr.* To cause to curve. [From earlier *curve (line),* "curved (line)", from Middle English *curve,* curved, from Latin *curvus.*] —**curv·ed·ly** (-idli) *adv.* —**curv·ed·ness** *n.* —**curv·y** *adj.*

cur·vet (kur-vét) *n.* A light leap by a horse in dressage, in which both hind legs leave the ground just before the forelegs are set down.
~*v.* **curvetted** or **-veted, -vetting** or **-veting, -vets.** —*intr.* **1.** To leap in a curvet. **2.** To prance; frolic. —*tr.* To cause to leap in a curvet. [Italian *corvetta,* "curving leap", from Old Italian, diminutive of *corva,* a curve, from Latin *curva,* feminine of *curvus,* curved, bent.]

cur·vi·lin·e·ar (kúrvi-línni-ər) *adj.* Also **cur·vi·lin·e·al** (-əl). Formed, bounded, or characterised by curved lines. [Latin *curvus,* curved (see **curve**) + LINEAR.] —**cur·vi·lin·e·ar·ly** *adv.*

Cus·co (kŏŏsko, kŏŏskō). City in southern Peru, situated in the Andes range. The capital of the Inca empire before the Spanish conquests, it contains the ruins of many impressive Inca temples.

cus·cus (kúskəss) *n.* Any of several marsupials of the genus *Phalanger,* of New Guinea and adjacent areas, having protruding eyes, a yellow nose, and a long, prehensile tail. [New Latin, probably from the native New Guinean name.]

cu·sec (kéw-sek) *n.* A unit of volumetric flow of liquids, equal to one cubic foot per second. [*Cu*bic *sec*ond.]

cush (kŏŏsh) *n. Informal.* A cushion on a billiard table.

Cush[1] (kush, kŏŏsh). The eldest son of Ham. Genesis 10:6.

Cush[2], **Kush.** **1.** A legendary ancient region of northeastern Africa where the Biblical descendants of Cush settled, often identified with Ethiopia. **2.** An ancient kingdom of Nubia in northern Sudan. It flourished from the 11th century B.C. until the 4th century A.D. when its capital, Merowe, fell to the Ethiopians.

Cush·ing's disease (kŏŏshingz) *n.* A disease resulting from excess corticosteroid hormones in the body, characterised by obesity, high blood pressure, and loss of minerals from the bones. Also called "Cushing's syndrome". [After Harvey *Cushing* (1869–1939), U.S. neurologist.]

cush·ion (kŏŏsh'n) *n.* **1.** A pad or pillow with a soft filling, used for resting or reclining against or on. **2.** Anything resilient used as a rest, support, or shock absorber. **3.** Something that provides protection against harmful or distressing effects: *her savings were a cushion against inflation.* **4.** The edge of the playing area on a billiard table. **5.** A pillow used in lacemaking. **6.** An **air cushion** *(see).*
~*tr.v.* **cushioned, -ioning, -ions.** **1.** To provide with a cushion. **2.** To place or seat on a cushion. **3.** To cover or hide with or as if with a cushion. **4.** To protect against or absorb the shock or adverse effects of something. [Middle English *cuisshen,* from Old French *coissin,* from Vulgar Latin *coxīnus* (unattested), "hip rest", cushion, from Latin *coxa,* hip.] —**cush·ion·y** *adj.*

Cush·it·ic, Kush·it·ic (kŏŏ-shíttik) *n.* A group of Hamitic languages, including Somali and other languages spoken in Somalia and Ethiopia.
~*adj.* Of or pertaining to this group of languages.

cush·y (kŏŏshi) *adj.* **-ier, -iest.** *Slang.* Comfortable; undemanding: *a cushy job.* [Anglo-Indian, from Hindi *khūsh,* from Persian *khōsh*†, pleasant.]

cusp (kusp) *n.* **1.** A point or pointed end. **2.** *Anatomy.* **a.** A prominence or projection on the chewing surface of a tooth. **b.** A fold or flap of a heart valve. **3.** *Geometry.* A point at which a curve crosses itself and at which the two tangents to the curve coincide. In this sense, also called "spinode". **4.** *Architecture.* The pointed figure formed by two intersecting arcs or foils. **5.** *Astronomy.* Either point of: **a.** A crescent moon. **b.** A satellite or inferior planet in a similar phase. **6.** *Astrology.* The transitional first or last part of a house or sign. —**on the cusp.** At a transition point. [Latin *cuspis*†, a point, spear.]

cus·pate (kúspayt) *adj.* Also **cus·pat·ed** (kuss-páytid), **cusped** (kuspt). **1.** Having a cusp or cusps. **2.** Shaped like a cusp.

cus·pid (kúspid) *n.* A tooth having one point; a canine tooth. [Back-formation from BICUSPID.]

cus·pi·date (kúspi-dayt) *adj.* Also **cus·pi·dat·ed** (-id), **cus·pi·dal** (-d'l). **1.** Having a cusp or cusps. **2.** *Biology.* Terminating in or tipped with a sharp point: *a cuspidate leaf.* [Latin *cuspidātus,* from the past participle of *cuspidāre,* to make pointed, from *cuspis* (stem *cuspid-*), point, CUSP.]

cus·pi·da·tion (kúspi-dáysh'n) *n. Architecture.* Decoration with cusps.

cus·pi·dor (kúspi-dawr || -dōr) *n. Chiefly U.S.* A **spittoon** *(see).* [Portuguese, from *cuspir,* to spit, from Latin *conspuere,* to spit upon: *com-* (intensive), with + *spuere,* to spit.]

cuss (kuss) *v.* **cussed, cussing, cusses.** *Informal.* —*intr.* To curse. —*tr.* To shout curses at.
~*n. Informal.* **1.** A curse. **2.** An odd or perverse creature. [Variant of CURSE.]

cuss·ed (kússid) *adj. Informal.* **1.** Cursed. **2.** Perverse; obstinate. **3.** Irritating; vexatious. —**cuss·ed·ly** *adv.* —**cuss·ed·ness** *n.*

cus·tard (kústərd) *n.* **1. a.** A thick, sweet, yellow sauce for desserts and puddings, made of sweetened milk and eggs, heated together and sometimes thickened with cornflour. **b.** A similar preparation made with sweetened milk and custard powder. **2.** A dessert of milk, sugar, sometimes cream, eggs, and, usually, flavouring, baked until set. [Middle English *crustade,* a kind of pie, from Anglo-French *crustade* (unattested), from *crute,* CRUST.]

custard apple *n.* **1.** A tropical American tree, *Annona reticulata,* bearing large, heart-shaped fruit. **2.** The fruit of this tree, having edible, fleshy pulp. **3.** Any of several related trees or fruit; especially, the **papaw** *(see).* [So called as its pulp resembles custard.]

custard powder *n.* A commercially prepared powder, usually made from cornflour and, often, dried eggs, used for making custard.

Cus·ter (kústər), **George A(rmstrong)** (1839–76). U.S. cavalry officer, made a brigadier general at the age of 23. Facing Sioux opposition under Sitting Bull and Crazy Horse, he rashly divided his force and led a party of 264 men to annihilation by an overwhelmingly larger Indian force at Little Bighorn (1876).

cus·to·di·al (kuss-tṓdi-əl) *adj.* **1.** Of or pertaining to guarding or guardianship. **2.** Involving or necessitating imprisonment.

cus·to·di·an (kuss-tṓdi-ən) *n.* **1.** One who has charge of something; a warder or caretaker. **2.** A keeper, especially of a public building, art collection, or the like. —**cus·to·di·an·ship** *n.*

cus·to·dy (kústədi) *n., pl.* **-dies.** **1.** The act or right of guarding, especially such a right granted by a court to a guardian of a minor. **2.** The state of being kept or guarded. **3.** The state of being detained or held under guard, especially by the police. [Middle English *custodie,* from Latin *custōdia,* from CUSTOS.]

cus·tom (kústəm) *n.* **1.** A practice followed as a matter of course among a people or society; a conventional mode or form of action. **2.** A habitual practice of an individual. **3.** *Law.* A common tradition or usage so long established that it has the force or validity of law. **4. a.** Habitual patronage, as of a shop or business. **b.** Collectively, those who patronise a shop or business; customers. **5.** Tribute, service, or rent paid by a feudal tenant to his lord. —See Synonyms at **habit.**
~*adj.* Made to the specifications of an individual purchaser: *a custom car.* [Middle English *custume,* from Old French *costume,* from Latin *consuētūdō,* a being accustomed, from *consuēscere,* to accustom : *com-* (intensive), with + *suēscere,* to become accustomed.]

cus·tom·a·ble (kústəməb'l) *adj.* Subject to tariffs.

cus·tom·ar·y (kústəm-əri || -erri) *adj.* **1.** Commonly practised or used as a matter of course; usual. **2.** Based on custom or tradition rather than written law or contract. —See Synonyms at **usual.**
~*n., pl.* **customaries.** A written record of the customary laws of a community. —**cus·tom·ar·i·ly** *adv.* —**cus·tom·ar·i·ness** *n.*

cus·tom-built (kústəm-bílt) *adj.* Built according to the specifications of the buyer.

cus·tom·er (kústəmər) *n.* **1.** A person or organisation who buys goods or services. **2.** *Informal.* A person with whom one must deal: *a tough customer.*

cus·tom·ise, cus·tom·ize (kústəm-īz) *tr.v.* **-ised, -ising, -ises.** To alter (a standard car model, for example) to the tastes of the buyer.

cus·tom-made (kústəm-máyd) *adj.* Made according to the specifications of an individual purchaser.

cus·toms (kústəmz) *n. Used with a singular or plural verb.* **1.** A duty or tax imposed on imported and, less commonly, exported goods. Also called "customs duty". **2.** The government department authorised to collect such duties. **3. a.** The procedure for inspecting goods and baggage entering a country. **b.** The place, as at an airport or frontier, where this inspection takes place.

customs house *n.* Also **cus·tom-house** (kústəm-howss). A government building or office where customs are collected and ships are cleared for entering or leaving the country.

customs union *n.* An international association organised to eliminate customs restrictions on goods exchanged between member nations and to establish a uniform tariff policy towards nonmember nations.

cus·tos (kústoss) *n., pl.* **custodes** (kuss-tṓdeez). **1.** A guardian or keeper; a custodian. **2.** A superior in certain monastic orders. [Middle English, from Latin *custōs*†, guard, protector.]

cus·tu·mal (kústewm'l) *n.* A written record of the customs of a monastery or community. [Medieval Latin *custumāle,* from the neuter of *custumālis,* customary, from Old French *custumel,* from *custome,* CUSTOM.]

cut (kut) *v.* **cut, cutting, cuts.** —*tr.* **1.** To penetrate with a sharp edge; strike a narrow opening in. **2.** To separate into parts with or as if with a sharp-edged instrument; sever: *cut cloth with scissors.* **3.** To sever the edges or outer extensions of; shorten; trim. **4.** To reap; harvest. **5.** To fell by sawing; hew. Often used with *down.* **6.** To have (a new tooth) grow through the gums. **7.** To form or shape by severing or incising: *a doll cut from paper.* **8.** To form by penetrating, probing, or digging. **9.** To separate or dissociate from a main body; detach: *cut off a chicken drumstick.* **10.** To pass through or across; cross. **11.** *Card Games.* To divide (a pack of cards) in two, as before dealing. **12. a.** To curtail the size, extent, or duration of; abridge. **b.** To reduce; diminish: *cut expenditure.* **13.** *Chiefly U.S.* To lessen the strength of; dilute: *cut whisky with water.* **14.** To dissolve by breaking down the fat of: *Soap cuts grease.* **15.** To injure the feelings of; hurt keenly. **16.** *Chiefly U.S. Informal.* To deliberately fail to attend: *cut a class.* **17.** *Informal.* To cease; stop. **18. a.** *Sports.* To strike (a ball) with a slicing stroke so that it spins irregularly or is deflected. **b.** In cricket, to hit (a ball), usually with the bat held horizontally, on the off side in a direction between third man and cover. **19.** To perform: *cut a caper.* **20.** To terminate (a scene in a film). **21.** To record a performance on (a gramophone record). **22.** To edit (film or audio tape). **23.** *Informal.* To snub; refuse to acknowledge: *he cut his wife dead.* **24.** *Informal.* To switch off (a car engine, for example). **25.** *Geometry.* To meet across (a line or curve). **26.** To castrate. *—intr.* **1.** To make an incision or separation. **2.** To allow incision or severing: *Butter cuts easily.* **3.** To use a sharp-edged instrument. **4.** To grow through the gums. Used of teeth. **5.** To penetrate so as to cause injury. **6. a.** To change direction abruptly: *cut to the left.* **b.** In cricket, to turn abruptly on pitching. Used of a bowled ball. **7.** To go directly and often hastily: *cut across the field.* **8.** To divide a pack of cards into two parts in order, for example, to make a decision on the basis of the card or cards displayed. **9.** *Geometry.* To intersect. Used of lines. **10.** To stop filming or recording. Often used in the imperative. **—cut along.** To go away. Usually used in the imperative. **—cut and run.** *Informal.* To escape in a hurry. **—cut both ways. 1.** To have equally good and bad effects. **2.** To affect equally (two sides of an argument, for example). **—cut corners.** To do something quickly or cheaply to the detriment of quality; skimp. **—cut loose.** To become independent; break free. **—cut no ice with.** To fail to have an effect on; make no impression on. **—cut (one's) teeth on.** To gain early experience from. **—cut up.** *Informal.* **1.** To hurt the feelings of. **2.** To behave; act: *He cut up rough about having been sacked.*

∼n. **1.** The act of incising, severing, or separating. **2.** The result of cutting; an incision; especially, a smallish wound or gash. **3.** A part that has been severed from a main body: *a cut of beef.* **4. a.** A passage or channel resulting from excavating or probing. **b.** *British.* A canal. **c.** *British.* A railway cutting. **5. a.** An elimination or excision of a part: *a cut in a speech.* **b.** The eliminated part. **6. a.** A reduction: *a salary cut.* **b.** *Often plural.* Reduction in government expenditure. **7.** The style in which hair or a garment is cut. **8.** *Informal.* A share of profits or earnings. **9.** *Informal.* **a.** A wounding remark; an insult. **b.** A snub. **10.** *Chemistry.* A fraction obtained by distilling. **11.** *Printing.* **a.** An engraved block or plate. **b.** A print made from such a block. **12.** *Sports.* A stroke played by cutting. **13.** In card games, the act of dividing a pack of cards into two parts, as before dealing. **14.** A sharp transition between shots or scenes in a film. **15.** A **power cut** *(see).* **—a cut above.** A little better than. [Middle English *cutten, kitten,* probably from late Old English *cyttan* (unattested), akin to Icelandic *kuta,* to cut with a knife, of North Germanic origin.]

cut-and-dried (kútt'n-dríd) *adj.* **1.** Prepared and arranged in advance; settled. **2.** Ordinary; routine; lacking spontaneity.

cut and thrust *n.* **1.** *Fencing.* Play that uses both the edge and the point of the sword. **2.** Spirited exchange, as of arguments, ideas, and the like.

cu·ta·ne·ous (kew-táyni-əss) *adj.* Of, pertaining to, or affecting the skin. [New Latin *cutaneus,* from Latin *cutis,* skin.] **—cu·ta·ne·ous·ly** *adv.*

cut·a·way (kúttə-way) *n.* **1.** A diagram, as of a building or machine, that shows the interior by omitting the outer shell. **2.** A man's formal daytime coat, with front edges sloping diagonally from the waist and forming tails at the back. Also called "cutaway coat".

cut back *tr.v.* **1.** To prune severely; shorten (the stem of a plant, for example). **2.** To reduce; curtail. *—intr.v.* To make reductions; economise. Used with *on.*

cut·back (kút-bak) *n.* A decrease; a curtailment: *a cutback in production.*

cutch (kuch) *n.* A resinous substance, **catechu** *(see).* [Malay *kachu,* CATECHU.]

cut down *intr.v.* To reduce consumption, expenditure, or the like. Used with *on.* *—tr.v.* To kill, especially suddenly.

cut-down (kút-down) *n.* **1.** An act of cutting down; a reduction. **2.** Something reduced in size or extent.

∼adj. (-dówn). Shortened, abridged.

cute (kewt) *adj.* **cuter, cutest. 1.** Delightfully pretty or dainty. **2.** *Chiefly U.S.* Obviously contrived to charm; affected. **3.** Shrewd; clever. [Short for ACUTE.] **—cute·ly** *adv.* **—cute·ness** *n.*

cut glass *n.* Glassware shaped or decorated by cutting instruments or abrasive wheels.

cut-glass (kút-glaàss || -gláss) *adj.* **1.** Of cut glass: *a cut-glass bowl.* **2.** *British.* Exaggeratedly precise in pronunciation: *a cut-glass R.P. accent.*

cut-grass (kút-graass || -grass) *n.* Any of several swamp and marsh grasses of the genus *Leersia,* having leaves with very rough margins.

Cuth·bert (kúthbərt), **Saint** (*c.* A.D. 635–687). English saint and missionary, who converted the Northumbrians to Christianity. His allegedly uncorrupted body was moved from the Farne Islands for burial in Durham Cathedral in the 10th century.

cu·ti·cle (kéwtik'l) *n.* **1.** The strip of hardened skin at the base of a fingernail or toenail. **2.** The epidermis. **3.** *Zoology.* The noncellular, often horny protective outer covering in many invertebrates. **4.** *Botany.* The protective layer of cutin covering the epidermis of plants. [Latin *cutīcula,* diminutive of *cutis,* skin.] **—cu·tic·u·lar** (kew-tíckewlər) *adj.*

cu·tie, cu·tey (kéwti) *n., pl.* **-ies.** *Slang.* An attractive or charming person.

cut in *intr.v.* **1.** To move in front of another car too sharply, thus endangering or inconveniencing another motorist. **2.** To interrupt. **3.** To interrupt a dancing couple in order to dance with one of them. **4.** To take another player's place in a card game. *—tr.v. Informal.* To share with; give a share to: *cut him in.*

cut-in (kút-in) *n.* An inserted shot, often a still close-up, interrupting the continuity of the main action of a film.

cu·tin (kéwtin) *n. Botany.* A waxlike, water-repellent material present in the walls of some plant cells, and forming the cuticle which covers the epidermis. [Latin *cut(is),* skin + -IN.]

cu·tin·ise, cu·tin·ize (kéwtin-īz) *v.* **-ised, -ising, -ises.** *Botany.* *—tr.* To coat or impregnate with cutin. *—intr.* To become coated or impregnated with cutin. **—cu·tin·i·sa·tion** (-ī-záysh'n || *U.S.* -i-) *n.*

cu·tis (kéwtiss) *n. Anatomy.* The **dermis** *(see).* [Latin *cutis,* skin.]

cut·lass, cut·las (kút-ləss || -lass) *n.* A short, heavy sword with a curved single-edged blade, once used as a weapon by sailors. [Variant of earlier *coutelace,* from Old French *coutelas,* from *coutel,* knife, from Latin *cultellus,* diminutive of *culter,* knife.]

cutlass fish *n. U.S.* The **hairtail** *(see).*

cut·ler (kút-lər) *n.* A person who makes, repairs, or sells knives, cutlery, or other cutting instruments. [Middle English, from Old French *coutelier,* from *coutel,* knife. See **cutlass.**]

cut·ler·y (kút-ləri || *U.S.* -lerri) *n.* **1.** Cutting instruments and tools. **2.** Implements used as tableware. **3.** The occupation of a cutler.

cut·let (kút-lit) *n.* **1.** A small chop, usually veal or lamb, cut from the best end of neck. **2.** A piece of fish cut across from between the head and middle part of the body of a large fish such as cod or halibut; a fish steak. **3.** A flat, cutlet-shaped croquette of chopped meat or fish. [French *côtelette,* from Old French *costelette,* diminutive or *coste,* rib, from Latin *costa,* rib.]

cut off *tr.v.* **1.** To detach by severing. **2.** To discontinue; stop. **3.** To interrupt or intercept. **4.** To separate; isolate. **5.** To disinherit. **6.** To disconnect (a power supply, for example).

cut-off (kút-off || -awf) *n.* **1.** A designated limit or point of termination. **2.** A new channel cut by a river across the neck of an oxbow lake. **3. a.** A checking or cutting off of a flow of steam, water, or other fluid. **b.** The device that cuts off.

∼adj. Of or pertaining to a cut-off: *a cut-off point.*

cut out *tr.v.* **1.** To shape or fashion by cutting. **2.** To remove the background from behind a figure (as in a photograph or painting). **3.** *Informal.* To be temperamentally suited or fitted: *cut out for city life.* **4.** *Informal.* To cease or give up: *cut out cigarettes.* **5.** To outdo or take the place of (a rival). *—intr.v.* **1.** To cease functioning; switch off. **2.** To leave or be excluded from a card game.

cut-out (kút-owt) *n.* **1.** Something cut out or intended to be cut out. **2.** *Electricity.* A device that interrupts, bypasses, or disconnects a circuit or circuit element, especially as a safety measure.

cut-price (kút-prīss) *adj.* **1.** Sold or on sale at a reduced price. **2.** Offering goods for sale at reduced prices: *a cut-price store.* Also *chiefly U.S.* "cut-rate".

cut·purse (kút-purss) *n. Archaic.* A pickpocket. [Originally one who cut off purses that were attached to a girdle.]

cut·ter (kúttər) *n.* **1.** One who cuts, especially in tailoring or hairdressing. **2.** A device or machine that cuts. **3.** *Nautical.* **a.** A single-masted fore-and-aft-rigged sailing vessel with a running bowsprit, a mainsail, and two or more headsails. Compare **sloop. b.** A ship's boat, powered by a motor or oars, and used for transporting stores or passengers. **c.** A small, lightly armed motorboat.

cut·throat (kút-thrōt) *n.* **1.** One who cuts throats; a murderer. **2.** *Chiefly British.* A razor having a long blade that folds into the handle. Also called "cutthroat razor".

∼adj. **1.** Cruel; murderous. **2.** Relentless or merciless in competition. **3.** *Games & Sports.* Of or designating a form of game in which each of three players acts and scores for himself.

cut·ting (kútting) *adj.* **1.** Capable of or designed for incising, shearing, or severing. **2.** Sharply penetrating; piercing and cold. **3.** Bitterly sarcastic or insulting. —See Synonyms at **incisive.**

∼n. **1.** A part cut off from a main body. **2.** An excavation made through high ground in the construction of a road, railway, or the like. **3.** *Chiefly British.* An article, story, or other item cut out from a newspaper or magazine. **4.** *Horticulture.* **a.** A twig, leaf, or plant part removed in order to form roots and propagate a new plant. **b.** Propagation by means of cuttings.

cut·tle·bone (kútt'l-bōn) *n.* The calcareous internal shell of a cuttlefish, used as a dietary supplement for cage birds or ground into powder for use as a polishing agent.

cut·tle·fish (kútt'l-fish) *n., pl.* **-fishes** or collectively **cuttlefish.** Any of various squidlike cephalopod marine molluscs of the genus *Sepia,* having ten arms and a calcareous internal shell, and secreting a dark, inky fluid. Also called "cuttle". [Middle English *codel,* Old English *cudele;* akin to *cod,* bag (see **codpiece**), referring to its ink-sac.]

cut·ty (kútti) *adj. Scottish & Northern English.* Short; cut short.

∼n. A short-stemmed tobacco pipe. [From CUT (verb).]

cut·wa·ter (kút-wawtər) *n.* **1.** The forward part of a ship's prow. **2.** The wedge-shaped end of a bridge pier, designed to divide the current and break up ice floes.

cut·work (kút-wurk) *n.* Openwork embroidery in which the ground fabric is cut away from the design.

cut·worm (kút-wurm) *n.* The larva of any of various moths of the family Noctuidae, feeding on a wide variety of plants. [So called because many species eat through stems of plants.]

Cuxhaven. See **Hamburg.**

Cuz·co. See **Cusco.**

c.v. *n.* curriculum vitae.

CVA cerebrovascular accident.

cw, CW continuous wave.

cwm (kōōm; *also* kŏŏm) *n. Welsh.* **1.** A valley. **2.** A steep hollow, a **cirque** *(see).*

CWO chief warrant officer.

c.w.o. cash with order.

CWS Chemical Warfare Service.

cwt. hundredweight.

–cy *n. suffix.* Indicates: **1.** A quality or condition; for example, **bankruptcy, infancy. 2.** Office or rank; for example, **baronetcy, magistracy.** [Middle English *-cie,* from Old French, from Latin *-cia, -tia,* and Greek *-kiā, -tiā,* both abstract noun suffixes.]

cy·an (sí-ən, -an) *n.* Greenish blue; one of the subtractive primary colours; a complement of red. [Greek *kuanos,* CYANO-.]

cy·an·a·mide (sī-ánnə-mīd, -mid) *n.* Also **cy·an·a·mid** (-mid). **1.** An irritating caustic acidic crystalline compound, $NCNH_2$, prepared by continuous carbonation of calcium cyanamide in water. **2.** A compound, **calcium cyanamide** *(see).* **3.** A salt or ester of cyanamide. [French : CYAN(O)- + AMIDE.]

cy·a·nate (sī-ən-ayt, -ət, -it) *n.* A salt or ester of cyanic acid. [CYAN(O)- + -ATE.]

cy·an·ic (sī-ánnik) *adj.* **1.** Pertaining to or containing cyanogen. **2.** Blue or bluish. [CYAN(O)- + -IC.]

cyanic acid *n.* A poisonous, unstable, highly volatile organic acid, HOCN, used to prepare certain cyanates.

cy·a·nide (sí-ə-nīd) *n.* Also **cy·an·id** (-nid). Any of various salts or esters of hydrogen cyanide containing a CN group; especially, the extremely poisonous compounds **potassium cyanide** and **sodium cyanide** *(both of which see).*

~*tr.v.* **cyanided, -niding, -nides. 1.** To treat (a metal surface) with cyanide to produce a hard surface. **2.** To treat (an ore) with cyanide to extract gold or silver. [CYAN(O)- + -IDE.]

cyanide process *n.* A process of extracting gold or silver from ores treated with a solution of sodium or calcium cyanide.

cy·a·nine (sí-ə-neen ‖ -nin) *n.* Any of various blue dyes, used to extend the range of colour sensitivity of photographic emulsions. [CYAN(O)- + -INE.]

cyanite. Variant of **kyanite.**

cyano-, cyan– *comb. form.* Indicates: **1.** A blue or dark-blue colouring; for example, **cyanine, cyanic. 2.** *Chemistry.* Cyanide or cyanogen; for example, **cyanate, cyanotype.** [German *zyan-,* from Greek *kuanos,* dark-blue enamel, the colour blue, from an unknown language of Asia Minor.]

cy·a·no·ac·ry·late (sī-anō-áckri-layt, -lət, -lit) *n.* An industrial and medical adhesive with an acrylic base.

cy·a·no·co·bal·a·min (sī-anō-kō-bál-əmin, -báwl-) *n.* **Vitamin B_{12}** *(see).* [CYANO- + COBAL(T) + (VIT)AMIN.]

cy·an·o·gen (sī-ánnə-jen, -jən) *n. Chemistry.* A colourless, flammable, highly poisonous gas, C_2N_2, used as a rocket propellant, fumigant, military weapon, and in welding. [French *cyanogène* : CYANO- + -GEN.]

cyano group (sī-ánnō) *n.* The univalent radical CN, found in simple and complex cyanide compounds.

cy·a·no·hy·drin (sī-ənō-hídrin) *n. Chemistry.* Any of a class of organic compounds containing both CN and OH groups attached to the same carbon atom. [CYANO- + HYDRO- + -IN.]

cy·a·nosed (sī-ə-nōzd) *adj. Pathology.* Afflicted with cyanosis. [From CYANOSIS.]

cy·a·no·sis (sī-ə-nō-siss) *n. Pathology.* A bluish discoloration of the skin, resulting from inadequate oxygenation of the blood. [New Latin, from Greek *kuanōsis,* dark blue : CYAN(O)- + -OSIS.] —**cy·a·not·ic** (-nóttik) *adj.*

cy·an·o·type (sī-ánnə-tīp) *n.* A blueprint *(see).*

cy·a·nu·ric acid (sī-ə-néwr-ik ‖ -nŏŏr-) *n.* A white crystalline acid, $C_3N_3(OH)_3$, that decomposes with heating to form cyanic acid. [CYAN(O)- + URIC ACID.]

Cyb·e·le (síbbəli) *n.* The Phrygian goddess of nature and mother of all living things.

cyber– *comb. form.* Indicates cybernetics, computers, the Internet, or virtual reality; for example, **cyberspace.** [From CYBER(NETICS).]

cy·ber·nate (sībər-nayt) *v.* **-nated, -nating, -nates.** —*tr.* To control (an industrial process) automatically by computer. —*intr.* To become so controlled. [From CYBERNET(ICS) + -ATE.] —**cy·ber·na·tion** (-náysh'n) *n.*

cy·ber·net·ics (sībər-néttiks) *n. Used with a singular verb.* The theoretical study of control processes in electronic, mechanical, and biological systems; especially, the mathematical analysis of the flow of information in such systems. [Coined by Norbert Wiener from Greek *kubernētēs,* pilot, governor, from *kubernan,* to steer, guide, GOVERN.] —**cy·ber·net·ic** *adj.* —**cy·ber·ne·tic·ian** (-ne-tísh'n), **cy·ber·net·i·cist** (-nétti-sist) *n.*

cy·ber·space (síbər-spayss) *n.* **1. Virtual reality** *(see).* **2.** The environment in which Internet communication takes place likened to the physical space between people conversing.

cy·borg (síborg) *n.* A hypothetical being, part machine part human; bionic person. Compare **android.** [CYB(ERNETIC) + ORG(ANISM).]

cy·cad (sí-kad) *n.* Any seed-bearing gymnosperm plant of the family Cycadaceae, resembling a palm tree but surmounted by fernlike leaves. [New Latin *Cycas* (stem *Cycad-*), genus name, from Greek *kukas,* manuscript error for *koïkas,* accusative plural of *koïx,* doom palm, perhaps from Egyptian.] —**cy·cad·a·ceous** (-áyshəss) *adj.*

cycl–. Variant of **cyclo–.**

Cyc·la·des (sícklə-deez). *Greek* **Ki·klá·dhes** (kee-klᷛáthess). A group of more than 200 Greek islands, in the Aegean Sea southeast of the mainland. They include Naxos, the largest, Páros, and Delos. Hermoupolis, on Syros, is the capital.

cyc·la·mate (sícklə-mayt, síklə-) *n.* A salt or ester of cyclamic acid; especially, either of two very sweet crystalline compounds: **a.** Sodium cyclamate *(see).* **b.** Calcium cyclamate, $C_{12}H_{24}N_2O_6S_2Ca$.

cyc·la·men (sícklə-mən ‖ síklə-, -men) *n.* Any of several plants of the genus *Cyclamen,* widely cultivated for their showy white, pink, or red flowers with reflexed petals. [New Latin, from Greek *kuklaminos,* probably from *kuklos,* meaning a circle (from the bulbous roots).]

cyc·la·mic acid (si-klámmik, sī-) *n.* A sour-sweet crystalline acid, $C_6H_{13}NO_3S$.

cy·cle (sík'l) *n.* **1.** A time interval in which a characteristic, especially regularly repeated, event or sequence of events occurs. **2. a.** A single complete execution of a periodically repeated phenomenon. **b.** A periodically repeated sequence of events. **c.** The time taken for the phenomenon or sequence to be completed. **3.** The orbit of a celestial body. **4.** A long period of time; an age; an eon. **5. a.** The aggregate of traditional legends, stories, or tales concerning a central theme or hero: *the Arthurian cycle.* **b.** A series of poems or songs on the same theme. **6.** A bicycle, tricycle, or the like. **7.** *Botany.* A circular arrangement of flower parts such as petals or sepals. ~*intr.v.* **cycled, -cling, -cles. 1.** To occur in or pass through a cycle. **2.** To move in, or as if in, a circle. **3.** To ride a bicycle, tricycle, or similar vehicle. [French, from Late Latin *cyclus,* from Greek *kuklos,* circle.]

cy·cle·way (sík'l-way) *n. Chiefly British.* A path or track reserved for the use of bicycles, usually alongside a dual carriageway. Also called "cycletrack".

cy·clic (sícklik, síklik) *adj.* Also **cy·cli·cal** (-'l). **1. a.** Of, relating to, or characterised by cycles. **b.** Recurring or moving in cycles. **2.** *Chemistry.* Of or pertaining to compounds having atoms arranged in a ring or closed-chain structure. **3.** *Botany.* **a.** Having parts arranged in a whorl. **b.** Forming a whorl. **4.** *Geometry.* Designating a polygon whose vertices lie on the circumference of a circumscribing circle: *a cyclic quadrilateral.* —**cy·cli·cal·ly** *adv.*

cyclic AMP *n. Biochemistry.* A cyclic form of adenosine monophosphate that has an important role in regulating metabolic processes, including the action of many hormones, in animals and humans.

cyclic pitch lever *n.* A helicopter control lever that alters the angle of attack of individual rotor blades, causing the aircraft to move forwards, backwards, or sideways.

cy·clist (síklist) *n.* One who rides a bicycle, tricycle, or similar vehicle. Also *U.S.* "cycler".

cyclo-, cycl– *comb. form.* Indicates: **1.** Circle; for example, **cyclometer, cyclorama. 2.** A cyclic compound; for example, **cyclohexane.** [Greek *kuklos,* circle, CYCLE.]

cy·clo·al·kane (síklō-ál-kayn) *n.* Any of a class of hydrocarbons, including cyclopropane, cyclopentane, and cyclohexane, in which at least three carbon atoms per molecule are joined in a ring structure and each such carbon in the ring is bonded to two hydrogen atoms or alkyl groups. Also called "cycloparaffin".

cy·clo·cross (síklō-kross ‖ -krawss) *n.* **1.** A cross-country bicycle race. **2.** The sport of cross-country bicycle-racing.

cy·clo·hex·ane (síklō-héksayn) *n.* An extremely flammable, colourless, mobile liquid, C_6H_{12}, obtained from petroleum and benzene and used as a solvent, paint and varnish remover, and in the manufacture of nylon.

cy·clo·hex·i·mide (síklō-héksi-mīd) *n. Chemistry.* A compound, $C_{15}H_{23}NO_4$, that is used as an agricultural fungicide.

cy·cloid (síkloyd) *adj.* **1.** Resembling a circle. **2.** *Zoology.* Thin, rounded, and smooth-edged; disclike. Said of fish scales, such as those of the salmon. **3.** *Psychiatry.* Designating a person suffering from cyclothymia. ~*n. Geometry.* The curve traced by a point on the circumference of a circle that rolls on a straight line. [French *cycloïde,* from Greek *kukloeidēs* : CYCL(O) + -OID.] —**cy·cloi·dal** (sī-klóyd'l) *adj.*

cy·clom·e·ter (sī-klómmitər) *n.* **1.** An instrument that records the revolutions of a wheel in order to indicate distance travelled. **2.** An instrument that measures circular arcs. [CYCLO- + -METER.] —**cy·clo·met·ric** (-klə-méttrik, -klō-) *adj.* —**cy·clom·e·try** (-klómmətri) *n.*

cy·clone (síklōn) *n.* **1.** *Meteorology.* **a.** A type of tropical atmospheric disturbance characterised by masses of air rapidly circulating clockwise in the southern and anticlockwise in the northern hemisphere, about a low-pressure centre, usually accompanied by stormy, often destructive, weather. **b.** Formerly, a depression. **2.** Loosely, any violent, rotating windstorm, such as a **tornado** *(see).* [Probably from Greek *kuklōma,* coil, wheel, from *kuklos,* circle, CYCLE.] —**cy·clon·ic** (sī-klónnik), **cy·clon·i·cal** *adj.*

cy·clo·pe·an (sī-klōpiən, síklə-pée-ən) *adj.* **1.** *Often capital* **C.** Pertaining to or suggestive of the Cyclopes. **2.** Pertaining to or designating a primitive style of masonry characterised by the use of massive stones of irregular shape and size.

cy·clo·pe·di·a, cy·clo·pae·di·a (síklə-péedi-ə) *n.* An encyclopedia. —**cy·clo·pe·dic** (-péedik) *adj.* —**cy·clo·pe·dist** (-péedist) *n.*

cy·clo·pen·tane (síklō-péntayn, sícklō-) *n.* A colourless flammable liquid, C_5H_{10}, derived from petroleum and used as a solvent and motor fuel.

cy·clo·ple·gi·a (síklə-plée'j-ə, -i-ə) *n.* Loss of ability to focus vision because of paralysis of the ciliary muscles of the eye. [New Latin :

CYCLO- + -PLEGIA.]

cy·clo·pro·pane (sī́klō-prṓpayn) *n.* A highly flammable, explosive, colourless gas, C₃H₆, used as an anaesthetic.

Cy·clops (sī́klops), *pl.* **Cyclopes** (sī-klṓpeez), **Cyclopses, Cyclops.** *Greek Mythology.* 1. Any of the three one-eyed Titans who forged thunderbolts for Zeus. 2. Any of a race of one-eyed giants, reputedly descended from these Titans, inhabiting the island of Sicily.

cy·clo·ram·a (sī́klə-ráámə ‖ -rámmə) *n.* 1. A large composite picture placed on the interior walls of a cylindrical room so as to appear in natural perspective to a spectator standing in the centre. 2. A large curtain or wall, usually concave, placed or hung at the rear of a stage. [CYCL(O)- + (PAN)ORAMA.] —**cy·clo·ram·ic** (-rámmik) *adj.*

cy·clo·ser·ine (sī́klō-séér-een, -in) *n.* An antibiotic active against a wide range of bacteria, used chiefly in the treatment of tuberculosis and infections of the urinary tract.

cy·clo·sis (sī-klṓ-siss) *n., pl.* **-ses** (-seez). The circulatory motion of protoplasm or organelles within certain cells and single-celled animals. [New Latin, from Greek *kuklōsis,* a surrounding, from *kukloun,* to surround, from *kuklos,* a circle, CYCLE.]

cy·clo·stome (sī́klō-stōm) *n.* Any of various primitive eel-like vertebrates of the class Agnatha, such as the lamprey, lacking jaws and true teeth and having a circular, sucking mouth. [New Latin *Cyclostomi,* "round-mouths" and *Cyclostomata,* "round-mouthed" : CYCLO- + -STOME.] —**cy·clos·to·mate** (sī-klṓstə-mayt, -mət, -mit ‖ si-), **cy·clos·to·a·tous** (-stómmətəss) *adj.*

cy·clo·style (sī́klō-stīl) *n.* A device consisting of a pen with a small toothed wheel producing a stencil from which copies can be made. ~*tr.v.* **cyclostyled, -styling, -styles.** To produce (copies) using a cyclostyle. [CYCLO- + Latin *stylus,* writing implement.]

cy·clo·thy·mi·a (sī́klō-thími-ə) *n. Psychiatry.* A form of mental disorder characterised by alternating periods of activity and excitement and periods of inactivity and depression. [New Latin, from German *Zyklothymie* : CYCLO- + -THYMIA.] —**cy·clo·thy·mic** (-thímik) *adj. & n.*

cy·clo·tron (sī́klə-tron) *n. Physics.* A circular particle accelerator capable of generating particle energies between a few million and several tens of millions of electronvolts, in which charged particles generated at a central source are accelerated spirally outwards in a plane at right angles to a fixed magnetic field by an alternating electric field. [CYCLO- + -TRON.]

cyder. *Chiefly British.* Variant of **cider.**

cyg·net (síg-nit) *n.* A young swan. [Middle English *sygnett,* diminutive of Old French *cygne,* swan, from Latin *cycnus, cygnus,* from Greek *kuknos.*]

Cyg·nus (síg-nəss) *n.* A constellation in the Northern Hemisphere near Lacerta and Lyra in the Milky Way. Also called "Northern Cross", "Swan". [Latin *cygnus,* swan. See **cygnet.**]

cyl·in·der (síllindər) *n. Abbr.* **cyl.** 1. *Geometry.* **a.** A surface generated by a straight line moving parallel to a fixed straight line and intersecting a plane curve. **b.** The portion of such a surface bounded by two parallel planes and the regions of the planes bounded by the surface. **c.** A solid consisting of two parallel planes bounded by two identical closed curves, usually circles. 2. Any cylindrical container or object. 3. *Engineering.* **a.** The chamber in which the piston of a reciprocating engine moves. **b.** The chamber of a pump from which fluid is expelled by a piston. 4. The rotating chamber of a revolver that holds the cartridges. 5. Any of the rotating cylinders in a printing press that carry the paper or the curved printing plate, or receive the ink or impression. 6. *Archaeology.* A cylindrical stone or clay object with an engraved design or inscription. 7. A cylindrical copper tank in which the hot water of a domestic hot-water system is stored. Also called "hot-water cylinder". ~*tr.v.* **cylindered, -dering, -ders.** To provide (a system) with a cylinder. [Old French *cylindre,* from Latin *cylindrus,* from Greek *kulindros,* roller, cylinder, from *kulindein,* to revolve, roll.]

cylinder block *n.* The casting containing the cylinders and cooling channels of an internal-combustion engine.

cylinder head *n.* The closed, often detachable, end of a cylinder or cylinders in an internal-combustion engine.

cy·lin·dri·cal (si-líndrik'l) *adj. Abbr.* **cyl.** Also **cy·lin·dric** (-líndrik). 1. Having the shape of a cylinder, especially of a circular cylinder. 2. Of or pertaining to a cylinder. 3. Of or pertaining to the coordinate system, or to any of three coordinates in it, formed by two polar coordinates in a plane and a rectangular coordinate measured perpendicularly from the plane. —**cy·lin·dri·cal·i·ty** (-líndri-kál-əti) *n.* —**cy·lin·dri·cal·ly** *adv.*

cylindrical projection *n.* A map projection in which points on the globe are projected onto a cylinder placed at a tangent to or intersecting its surface, which is then opened and laid flat.

cyl·in·droid (síllin-droyd, si-lín-) *n.* A cylindrical surface or solid that is elliptical in cross-section. ~*adj.* Resembling a cylinder.

cylix. Variant of **kylix.**

cy·ma (sī́-mə) *n., pl.* **-mae** (-mee) or **-mas.** 1. *Architecture.* A moulding for a cornice, having a partly concave and partly convex curve in profile. A *cyma recta* has the concave curve uppermost, a *cyma reversa* the convex. 2. *Botany.* A cyme. [Greek *kuma,* anything swollen, waved moulding, from *kuein,* to swell, be pregnant.]

cy·ma·ti·um (si-máy-ti-əm, sī-, -shi-) *n., pl.* **-tia** (-ə). 1. A cyma. 2. The topmost moulding of a classical cornice. [Latin *cȳmatium,* from Greek *kumation,* diminutive of *kuma,* moulding, CYMA.]

cym·bal (símb'l) *n.* 1. One of a pair of concave brass plates that are struck together as percussion instruments. 2. A single brass plate, sounded by hitting with a drumstick and often part of a set of drums. [Middle English, from Old French *symbale,* from Latin *cymbalum,* from Greek *kumbalon,* from *kumbē,* hollow of a vessel, a cup.] —**cym·bal·ist** *n.*

cym·ba·lo (símbəlō) *n., pl.* **-los.** A dulcimer *(see).* [Italian. See **cymbal.**]

Cymbeline. See **Cunobelinus.**

cym·bid·i·um (sim-bíddi-əm) *n.* Any orchid of the genus *cymbidium,* cultivated as ornamentals for their sprays of long-lasting flowers. [New Latin, from Greek *kumbē,* cup.]

cyme (sīm) *n. Botany.* An often flat-topped flower cluster that blooms from the centre towards the edges, and whose main axis always terminates in a flower. Also called "cyma". [New Latin *cyma,* from Latin *cȳma,* young cabbage sprout, from Greek *kuma,* anything swollen, CYMA.] —**cy·mif·er·ous** (sī-míffərəss) *adj.*

cy·mene (sī́meen) *n. Chemistry.* Any of three colourless isomeric liquid hydrocarbons, C₁₀H₁₄, obtained chiefly from the essential oils of various plants and used in the manufacture of synthetic resins. [French *cymène,* from Greek *kuminon,* CUMIN.]

cy·mo·gene (sī́mə-jeen) *n.* A flammable gaseous fraction of petroleum, chiefly butane. [CYM(ENE) + -GENE.]

cy·moid (sī́moyd) *adj.* Resembling a cyma or cyme. [CYM(E) + CYM(A) + -OID.]

cy·mo·phane (sī́mə-fayn) *n.* A variety of chrysoberyl having an undulating lustre. [French : Greek *kuma,* undulation, CYMA + -PHANE.]

cy·mose (sī́-mōss, -mōz) *adj. Botany.* 1. Pertaining to or resembling a cyme. 2. Bearing a cyme or cymes. [CYM(E) + -OSE.] —**cy·mose·ly** *adv.*

Cym·ric, Kym·ric (kúm-rik, kím- ‖ sim-) *adj.* Of or pertaining to the Cymry or their languages, especially Welsh. ~*n.* 1. The Welsh language. 2. The Brythonic branch of the Celtic languages, including Welsh, Breton, and Cornish.

Cymru. See **Wales.**

Cym·ry, Cym·ri, Kym·ry (kúm-ri, kím- ‖ sím-) *n.* 1. The Welsh. 2. The branch of the Celtic people to which the Welsh, the Cornish, and the Bretons belong.

cyng·ha·nedd (kəng-háa-neth) *n.* Consonantal patterning, as practised in Welsh versification. [Welsh.]

cyn·ic (sínnik) *n.* 1. **a.** One who believes that people are insincere and motivated by selfishness and who consequently expects the worst of human behaviour. **b.** A scornful or mocking person. 2. *Capital* **C.** A member of a sect, founded by Antisthenes of Athens, of ancient Greek philosophers who believed virtue to be the only good and self-control to be the only means of achieving virtue. ~*adj.* 1. *Rare.* Cynical. 2. *Capital* **C.** Of or pertaining to the Cynics or their doctrines. [Latin *cynicus,* from Greek *kunikos,* "doglike", currish (perhaps mistaken by the Greeks from the first part of *kunosarge,* the gymnasium where Antisthenes taught), from *kuōn* (stem *kun*-), dog.]

cyn·i·cal (sínnik'l) *adj.* 1. **a.** Scornful or sceptical of the motives or virtue of others. **b.** Bitterly mocking; sneering. 2. Showing contempt for accepted morality or values: *a cynical cover-up by the authorities.* 3. *Capital* **C.** Of or pertaining to the Cynics or their doctrines. —**cyn·i·cal·ly** *adv.* —**cyn·i·cal·ness** *n.*

cyn·i·cism (sínni-siz'm) *n.* 1. A cynical attitude or character. 2. A cynical comment or act. 3. *Capital* **C.** The beliefs and doctrines of the Cynics.

cy·no·sure (sī́nə-sewr, -zewr, -shoor, -zhoor ‖ sínnə-) *n.* 1. An object or person that serves as a focal point of attention and admiration. 2. Anything that serves to guide. [French, Ursa Minor, "the guiding star", from Latin *cynosūra,* from Greek *kunosoura,* "the dog's tail", Ursa Minor : *kunos,* genitive of *kuōn,* dog + *-ura,* plural of *-urus,* -UROUS.] —**cy·no·sur·al** *adj.*

Cyn·thi·a¹ (sínthi-ə). *Greek Mythology.* Artemis, goddess of the moon. [Artemis was born on Mount *Cynthus,* on the island of Delos, Greece.]

Cynthia² *n. Poetic.* The moon or its personification.

cypher. Variant of **cipher.**

cy pres (sée práy) *n. Law.* A doctrine relating to charitable trusts whereby a condition or instruction of a donor or testator that cannot be legally complied with will be followed as closely as is practicable. [Anglo-French, "so near" (that is, as closely as is practicable).]

cy·press (sī́prəss) *n.* 1. Any evergreen coniferous tree of the genus *Cupressus,* having small, scalelike leaves and rounded cones. 2. Any similar and related tree of the genus *Chamaecyparis,* such as *C. lawsoniana,* (Lawson's cypress). Also called "false cypress". 3. The wood of any of these trees. 4. Cypress branches used as a symbol of mourning. [Middle English *cipres,* from Old French, from Late Latin *cypressus,* from Greek *kuparissos,* of Mediterranean origin.]

cypress spurge *n.* A plant, *Euphorbia cyparissias,* native to Eurasia, having densely crowded, narrow leaves, and clusters of yellow-green flowers. [Probably because its narrow leaves suggest the needles of the cypress.]

Cyp·ri·an (síppri-ən) *adj.* 1. Of or pertaining to Cyprus, its people, their customs, or their language. 2. Characteristic of or resembling the ancient worship of Aphrodite on Cyprus; licentious; wanton. ~*n.* 1. A Cypriot *(see).* 2. *Obsolete. Often small* **c.** A wanton person, especially a prostitute.

cy·pri·nid (sípprinid, si-prínid) *n.* Any of numerous freshwater fishes of the family Cyprinidae, which includes the minnows, carps, and tench. [New Latin *Cyprinidae* : *Cyprinus* (genus name), from Latin *cyprīnus*, a carp, from Greek *kuprinos*, from *kupros*, "the henna plant", from Semitic, akin to Hebrew *kōpher* + -ID.] **—cy·pri·nid** *adj*.

cy·prin·o·dont (sí-prínnə-dont, -prī́nə-) *n*. Any of various soft-finned fishes of the family Cyprinodontidae, which includes the killifishes, and many species popular in home aquariums. [New Latin *Cyprinodon* : Latin *cyprinus*, carp (see **cyprinid**) + -ODONT.]

cyp·ri·noid (síppri-noyd, si-prī́-) *adj*. Of, pertaining to, or resembling a carp or related fish. [New Latin *Cyprinoidea* : *Cyprinus*, genus (see **cyprinid**) + -OID.] **—cyp·ri·noid** *n*.

Cyp·ri·ot, Cyp·ri·ote (síppri-ət ‖ *U.S.* -ōt) *n*. **1**. A native or inhabitant of Cyprus. Also called "Cyprian". **2. a**. The ancient Greek dialect of Cyprus, belonging to the Arcado-Cyprian branch. **b**. The dialect of Modern Greek spoken in Cyprus. **—Cyp·ri·ot** *adj*.

cyp·ri·pe·di·um (síppri-peédi-əm) *n*. Any orchid of the genus *Cypripedium*, which includes the lady's-slippers. [New Latin, probably "Venus' slipper" : Late Latin *Cypris*, Venus, from Greek *Kupris*, Aphrodite, from *Kupros*, CYPRUS (supposedly her birthplace) + New Latin *-pedium*, probably a variant of Greek *pedilon*, sandal.]

Cy·prus, Republic of (sī́prəss). *Turkish* Ki·bris (kee-bréess); *Greek* Ky·pros (keé-pross). Island state in the east Mediterranean Sea. Dominated in turn by ancient Egypt, Assyria, Greece, Persia, the Romans, and Byzantium, it fell to the Ottoman Empire (1571), and passed to Britain (1878). Some Greek Cypriots sought *enosis* ("union") with Greece, and violence erupted in 1931, and again in 1955 under the EOKA movement. The island became an independent Commonwealth republic (1960), but violence between Greeks and Turks (the latter making up 18 per cent of the population) continued. President Makarios was temporarily overthrown (1974) by an army coup supported by Greece, and Turkey invaded the north. The island was partitioned, the northern part becoming known internally as the Turkish Federated State of Cyprus. This part declared itself an independent republic (1983). Economic recovery in the south led to resumed exports of clothing, copper, vegetables, fruit, and wine, and a renewed tourist industry. Area, 9 251 square kilometres (3,572 square miles). Population, 760,000. Capital, Nicosia.

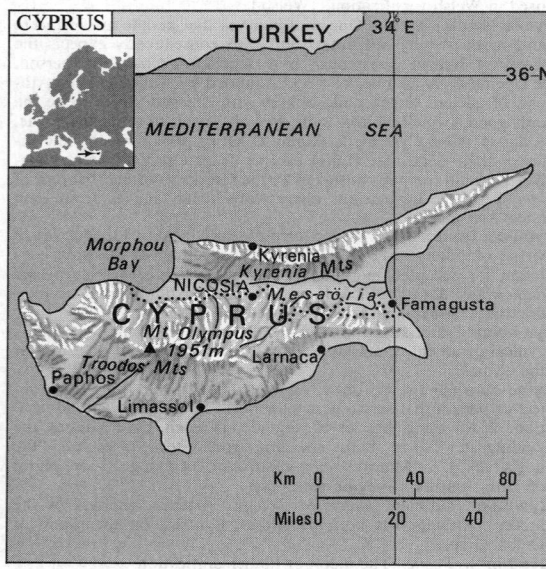

cyp·se·la (sípsə-lə) *n., pl.* **-lae** (-lee). *Botany*. A small dry fruit that resembles an achene but does not separate from its calyx, characteristic of composite plants. [New Latin, from Greek *kupselē*, hollow vessel, chest.]

Cy·ra·no de Ber·ge·rac (sírrənō də bér-zhə-rak, baír-), **Savinien de** (1619–55). French dramatist and novelist, whose spirited dramas *Le Pédant Joué* (*c.* 1654) and *La Mort d'Agrippine* (1653) ran counter to the classical taste of his day. He was the subject of Edmond Rostand's play *Cyrano de Bergerac* (1897), which depicted him as a chivalric duellist with a comically long nose.

Cyr·e·na·ic (sír-ə-náy-ik ‖ *U.S. also* sírrə-) *adj*. **1**. Of or pertaining to Cyrenaica or its major city, Cyrene. **2**. Of or pertaining to the hedonistic school of philosophy founded in Cyrene by Aristippus, who believed that pleasure is the only good in life.
~*n*. **1**. A native or inhabitant of Cyrenaica or Cyrene. **2**. A disciple of the Cyrenaic school of philosophy.

Cy·re·na·ica (sír-ə-náy-i-kə ‖ *U.S. also* sírrə-). Region of eastern Libya, extending from the Mediterranean coast into the desert.

Cy·re·ne (sī-eéeni). Ancient city in northeast Libya. Founded by Greeks from Thera (*c.* 630 B.C.), it became the chief city of Cyrenaica.

Cyr·il (sírrəl), **Saint** (*c.* A.D. 827–869). Macedonian missionary to

the Slavs, the alleged inventor of the Cyrillic alphabet. From 863 he and his brother St. Methodius (825–884) worked among the Khazars of Moravia, translating the scriptures into the local language through an adaptation of the Greek alphabet.

Cyr·il·lic (si-ríllik) *adj*. **1**. Of or pertaining to St. Cyril, the ninth-century missionary to the Moravians. **2**. Of or designating the Cyrillic alphabet.
~*n*. The Cyrillic alphabet.

Cyrillic alphabet *n*. An old alphabet ascribed to St. Cyril, presently used in modified form for Russian, Bulgarian, Serbo-Croat, Macedonian, and certain languages of the former U.S.S.R., such as Ukrainian. Also called "Cyrillic".

Cy·rus (II) The Great (sī́r-əss) (died 529 B.C.). King of Persia (559–529 B.C.) and founder of the Achaemenid empire. Having seized the empire of the Medes, he went on to conquer Lydia, the Ionian cities, and Babylon with its subject states in Syria. He was tolerant in religious matters, permitting the worship of native gods, and allowing the Jews to return to Jerusalem (537).

cyst (sist) *n*. **1**. *Pathology*. An abnormal membranous sac containing a liquid or semisolid substance. **2**. *Anatomy*. Any sac or vesicle in the body. **3**. *Biology*. A capsule-like membrane enclosing certain organisms in a resting stage. [New Latin *cystis*, from Greek *kustis*, bladder, pouch.]

cys·tec·to·my (sist-éktəmi) *n., pl.* **-mies**. **1**. Surgical excision of the gall bladder or of a portion of the urinary bladder. **2**. Surgical removal of a cyst.

cys·te·ine (síst-een, -i-in) *n*. An amino acid, $C_3H_7NO_2S$, found in most proteins, especially in keratin. [From CYSTINE.]

cys·tic (sístik) *adj*. **1**. Of, pertaining to, or like a cyst. **2**. Having or containing a cyst or cysts. **3**. Enclosed in a cyst. **4**. *Anatomy*. Pertaining to the gall bladder or urinary bladder.

cys·ti·cer·coid (sisti-sérkoyd) *n*. The larval stage of certain tapeworms, like a cysticercus but having a smaller sac. [CYSTICERC(US) + -OID.]

cys·ti·cer·cus (sísti-sér-kəss) *n., pl.* **-ci** (-sī́). The larval stage of many tapeworms, consisting of a scolex, or head, enclosed in a fluid-filled sac. [New Latin, "bladder tail" : CYST(O)- + Greek *kerkos*, tail.]

cystic fibrosis *n*. A hereditary disease of mucous and sweat glands throughout the body, usually developing during childhood and causing pancreatic insufficiency and pulmonary disorders.

cys·tine (sisteen) *n*. A white crystalline compound, $C_6H_{12}N_2O_4S_2$, the principal sulphur-containing amino acid of protein. [CYST(O)- + -INE.]

cys·ti·tis (siss-tī́tiss) *n*. Inflammation of the urinary bladder. [New Latin : CYST(O)- + -ITIS.]

cysto-, cyst- *comb. form*. Indicates a bladder or cyst; for example, **cystocele, cystoid**. [Greek *kustis*, bladder.]

cys·to·carp (síst-ō-kaarp, -ə-) *n*. *Botany*. A structure consisting of fertile filaments and carpospores, developed after fertilisation of the carpogonium in red algae. [CYSTO- + -CARP.]

cys·to·cele (síst-ō-seel, -ə-) *n*. A hernia of the bladder. [CYSTO- + -CELE (hernia).]

cys·toid (sístoyd) *n*. A structure resembling a cyst but lacking an enclosing membrane. [CYST(O)- + -OID.] **—cys·toid** *adj*.

cys·to·lith (síst-ō-lith, -ə-) *n*. **1**. *Botany*. A mineral concretion, usually calcium carbonate, formed in the cellulose wall of certain plant cells. **2**. *Pathology*. A urinary calculus. [CYSTO- + -LITH.]

cys·to·scope (sísto-skōp) *n*. A tubular instrument fitted with a light and used to examine the urinary bladder and ureter. [CYSTO- + -SCOPE.] **—cys·to·scop·ic** (-skóppik) *adj*.

cys·tos·co·py (siss-tóskəpi) *n*. Examination of the urinary bladder using a cystoscope in order to detect and remove polyp, take tissue specimens, or the like. [CYSTO- + -SCOPY.]

cys·tot·o·my (siss-tóttəmi) *n*. Surgical cutting of the urinary bladder, usually through the abdominal wall. [CYSTO- + -TOMY.]

–cyte *n. comb. form*. Indicates a cell; for example, **leucocyte**. [New Latin *-cyta*, from Greek *kutos*, hollow vessel.]

Cytherea. See **Aphrodite**.

cyto-, cyt- *comb. form*. Indicates cell; for example, **cytokinesis, cytology**. [Greek *kutos*, hollow vessel.]

cy·to·chem·is·try (sītō-kémmistri) *n*. The chemistry of plant and animal cells. **—cy·to·chem·i·cal** *adj*.

cy·to·chrome (sīto-krōm) *n*. Any of a class of compounds containing iron and protein, important for oxidation-reduction reactions in cells. [CYTO- + -CHROME.]

cy·to·gen·e·sis (sītō-jénna-siss) *n*. Also **cy·tog·e·ny** (sī-tójəni). The formation and development of cells. [CYTO- + -GENESIS.] **—cy·to·ge·net·ic** (-jə-néttik) *adj*.

cy·to·ge·net·ics (sītō-jə-néttiks) *n*. *Used with a singular verb*. The study of heredity by cytological and genetic methods, particularly involving the study of chromosomes. **—cy·to·ge·net·i·cal** *adj*. **—cy·to·ge·net·i·cal·ly** *adv*. **—cy·to·ge·net·i·cist** (-nétti-sist) *n*.

cy·to·ki·ne·sis (sītō-kī-née-siss, -ki-) *n*. The cleavage of cytoplasm during cell division. [New Latin : CYTO- + -KINESIS.]

cy·tol·o·gy (sī-tólləji) *n*. *Abbr.* **cytol**. The branch of biology dealing with the study of the formation, structure, and function of cells. [CYTO- + -LOGY.] **—cy·to·log·i·cal** (sītə-lójik'l) *adj*. **—cy·to·log·i·cal·ly** *adv*. **—cy·tol·o·gist** (sī-tólləjist) *n*.

cy·tol·y·sin (sī-tólli-sin) *n*. A substance capable of destroying an animal cell partially or completely. [CYTOLYS(IS) + -IN.]

cy·tol·y·sis (sī-tólla-siss) *n*. The dissolution of a cell. [New Latin : CYTO- + -LYSIS.] **—cy·to·lyt·ic** (sītə-líttik) *adj*.

CZECH REPUBLIC & SLOVAKIA

cy·toph·a·gy (sī-tóffəji) *n.* The devouring of other cells by the phagocytes. [CYTO- + -PHAGY.] —**cy·to·phag·ic** (sītə-fájik), **cy·toph·a·gous** (-tóffəgəss) *adj.*

cy·to·plasm (sītə-plaz'm) *n.* The protoplasm outside a cell nucleus. [CYTO- + -PLASM.] —**cy·to·plas·mic** (-plázmik) *adj.* —**cy·to·plas·mi·cal·ly** *adv.*

cy·to·plast (sītə-plast, -plaast) *n.* The cytoplasm within a single cell. [CYTO- + -PLAST.] —**cy·to·plas·tic** (-plástik) *adj.*

cy·to·sine (sītə-sin, -seen, -zeen) *n.* A pyrimidine base, $C_4H_5N_3O$, that is an essential constituent of both RNA and DNA. [CYT(O)- + -OS(E) + -INE.]

cy·to·tax·on·o·my (sītō-tak-sónnəmi) *n.* The classification of organisms based on cellular structure, especially on the comparative morphology of chromosomes. —**cy·to·tax·o·nom·ic** (-táksə-nómmik) *adj.* —**cy·to·tax·on·o·mist** (-tak-sónnəmist) *n.*

cy·to·tox·ic (sītō-tóksik) *adj.* Destructive to cells. Said particularly of drugs that destroy cancer cells and are used in chemotherapy. [CYTO- + TOXIC.] —**cy·to·tox·ic·i·ty** (-íssəti) *n.*

czar (zar) *n.* **1.** Variant of **tsar**. **2.** *U.S. Informal.* A supremo.

czar·das, csar·das (chár-dash, -dəss ‖ *U.S.* -daash) *n.* **1.** An intricate Hungarian dance characterised by variations in tempo. **2.** Music for this dance. [Hungarian *csárdás.*]

Czech (chek) *n.* **1.** A native or inhabitant of the Czech Republic. **2.** The West Slavonic language of these people. Formerly called "Bohemian". —**Czech** *adj.*

Czech·o·slo·vak·i·a (chéck-ə-slō-vácki-ə, -ō-, -slə-, -va'aki-ə). Official name **Czech and Slovak Federal Republic.** *Czech* **Československo.** Former country in central Europe, federation of the Czech and Slovak republics. Czechoslovakia was created (1918) out of the former Austrian territories of Bohemia and Moravia, with parts of Silesia and Hungary. Ruthenia was added in 1920. The nation's name derives from the two main language groups: Czech in the west and Slovak in the east. Czechoslovakia developed in the interwar years under the democratic leadership of Tomáš **Masaryk** and Edvard **Beneš**. Tensions grew among its component nationalities, especially the German-speakers in the areas known as the **Sudetenland,** and the region was ceded to Germany by the Munich Agreement (1938). Hitler occupied the rest of the country (1939). After World War II, the country fell within the Soviet orbit. In 1968 a liberal programme was introduced by the new secretary of the Communist Party, Alexander **Dubček**. The experiment ended when Warsaw Pact tanks invaded and Dubček was dismissed. A return to rigid pro-Soviet orthodoxy ended in 1989 when sustained pro-democracy demonstrations forced the communists to give most government positions to the non-communists. The former dissident playwright Václav **Havel** was elected president and democractic parties triumphed in free elections held in 1990. Since 1993, following pressure in Slovakia for greater autonomy, the two consituent republics have, by agreement, independent status as the Czech Republic and Slovakia. —**Czech·o·slo·vak** (-slóvak), **Czech·o·slo·va·ki·an** *adj. & n.*

Czech Republic. Country formed in 1993 from the constituent republic of former Czechoslovakia of the same name. It consists of the natural regions of Bohemia and Moravia, and is a highly industrialised nation producing iron and steel, machinery, cars, textiles, glass and ceramics. Cereals, sugar beet, potatoes and hops are the chief crops, and timber is an important product. Area, 78 864 square kilometres (30,442 square miles). Population, 10,320,000. Capital, Prague.

Czę·sto·cho·wa (cheinsto-khóva). *Russian* **Chen·sto·khov** (chin-stə-kháwf). City of south-central Poland, on the river Warta, the site of Poland's most famous Marian Shrine.

d, D (dee) *n., pl.* **d's** or *rare* **ds, Ds** or **D's. 1.** The fourth letter of the modern English alphabet. **2.** Any of the speech sounds represented by this letter.

d, D, d., D. *Note:* As an abbreviation or symbol, *d* may be a small or a capital letter, with or without a full stop. Established forms or those generally preferred precede the definition. When no form is given, all four forms are in general use in that sense. **1. d.** *Genealogy.* dam. **2. d.** date. **3. d.** daughter. **4. d** day. **5. D.** December. **6. d** deci–. **7. D, D** democrat; democratic. **8. d** *Physics.* density. **9. D.** department. **10. d** departs. **11. d., D** deputy. **12. D** *Mathematics.* derivatives. **13. D.** Deus. **14. D** The symbol for deuterium. **15. d** *Physics.* deuteron. **16. d** dextro–. **17. d.** died. **18. D** dimension. **19. D.** *Optics.* diopter. **20. D.** director. **21. D.** doctor (in academic degrees). **22. D.** Dominus. **23. D.** Don (title). **24. d., D.** dose. **25. d** down quark. **26. d., D.** drachma. **27. D.** duchess. **28. D.** duke. **29. D.** Dutch. **30. D** The Roman numeral for 500. **31. d.** *British.* old penny (Latin *denarius*). **32.** The fourth in a series.

D *n., pl.* **Ds** or **D's. 1.** The fourth-highest mark awarded for academic work. **2.** A socioeconomic classification representing semi-skilled manual workers. **3. a.** The second note in the scale of C major. **b.** The key or a scale in which D is the tonic. **c.** A written or printed note representing D. **d.** A string, key, or pipe tuned to the pitch of D.

d– *comb. form. Chemistry.* Indicates a dextrorotatory compound; for example, *d*–**glucose.** Compare *l*–.

D– *comb. form. Chemistry.* Indicates an optically active compound with a molecular structure derived from or related to the structure of dextrorotatory glyceraldehyde; for example, **D–alanine.** Compare **L–.** An isomer designated D– may itself be dextrorotatory (*d*–) but is not necessarily so.

–'d. 1. Contraction of *had, should, would,* or *did,* as in *Who'd you see?* **2.** Contraction of *-ed,* as in *martyr'd.*

da (daa) *n. Regional.* Father. [Of baby-talk origin.]

D.A. 1. Deposit account. **2.** *U.S.* district attorney.

dab¹ (dab) *v.* **dabbed, dabbing, dabs.** —*tr.* **1.** To apply with short, poking strokes. **2.** To cover or press on lightly with or as if with something moist. **3.** To strike or hit lightly, as with a quick pat of the hand. —*intr.* **1.** To touch or poke gingerly at something. **2.** To tap gently; pat. ~*n.* **1. a.** A small amount. **b.** A small mass or lump of a moist substance: *a dab of jam.* **2.** A quick, light pat, as with the hand. **3.** *Chiefly British Slang.* A fingerprint. [Middle English *dabben,* probably from Middle Dutch *dabben,* to tap (imitative).]

dab² *n.* Any of various small flatfishes, chiefly of the genera *Li-*

manda and *Hippoglossoides.* The European species *L. limanda* is an important food fish. [16th century : origin obscure.]

dab³ *n. British Informal.* An expert. [17th century : origin obscure.]

dab·ber (dábbər) *n.* **1.** One that dabs. **2.** *Printing.* A cushioned pad used with a brayer by printers and engravers to apply ink.

dab·ble (dább'l) *v.* **-bled, -bling, -bles.** —*tr.* **1.** To splash or spatter, as with a liquid. **2.** To move (a part of the body) in water. —*intr.* **1.** To splash liquid gently and playfully. **2.** To undertake something superficially or without serious intent: *dabble in antiques.* [Probably from Dutch *dabbelen,* frequentative of *dabben,* to strike, tap, DAB.] —**dab·bler** *n.*

dab·bling duck (dábbling) *n.* Any duck of the genus *Anas* that feeds near the surface of the water or on land, including the mallard, teal, and wigeon. Compare **diving duck.**

dab·chick (dáb-chik) *n.* Any of various small grebes of the genus *Podiceps,* such as the Eurasian species *P. ruficollis.* [Earlier *dapchick, dopchick* : *dop-,* probably from Middle English *doppe,* diving bird, Old English *-doppa* + CHICK.]

dab hand *n. British Informal.* An expert; a skilful person: *a dab hand at sewing.*

da ca·po (daa ká'apō) *adv. Abbr.* **D.C.** *Music.* From the beginning. Used as a direction to repeat a passage: *da capo al fine.* [Italian.]

Dac·ca or **Dhākā** (dáckə). Capital of Bangladesh, on a branch of the Dhaleswari river in the south of the country. Formerly capital of Mogul Bengal (1608–1704), it came under British rule and was capital of the province of East Bengal and Assam (1905–12). After Indian independence (1947), Dacca was made capital of East Pakistan (1956), which became Bangladesh in 1971.

dace (dayss) *n., pl.* **daces** or collectively **dace.** Any of various small freshwater fishes of the family Cyprinidae, such as the European species *Leuciscus leuciscus,* related to and resembling the roach. [Middle English *dars, dase,* from Old French *dars,* probably from *dart,* DART (from its swift motion).]

da·cha (dáchə ‖ dá'achə) *n.* A Russian country house; a villa. [Russian *dacha,* gift, portion, land (granted by a prince), country or holiday house.]

Dach·au (dáckow ‖ German dákhow) Town in southern Germany, near Munich in Bavaria. A Nazi concentration camp was built there in 1935, and an estimated 70,000 inmates died.

dachs·hund (dáks-hōont, -hōond ‖ dáaks-) *n.* A small dog of a breed developed in Germany for hunting badgers, having a long body with a usually short-haired brown or black and brown coat, drooping ears, and very short legs. [German *Dachshund* : *Dachs,* badger + *Hund,* dog.]

Da·cia (dáy-si-ə, -shi-, -shə). An ancient name for the area roughly corresponding to modern Romania. —**Da·cian** *adj. & n.*

da·coit, da·koit (də-kóyt) *n.* A member of any of the robber bands of India and Burma that live in the hills and attack in armed gangs, usually on horseback. [Hindi *ḍakait,* from *ḍākā,* "gang-robbery", from Sanskrit *daṣṭaka*†, crowded.]

da·coit·y (də-kóyti) *n., pl.* **-ties.** Gang robbery in India or Burma. [Hindi *dakaiti.* See **dacoit.**]

Da·cron (dáyk-ron, dák-) *n.* A trademark for a synthetic polyester textile fibre resistant to stretching and wrinkling.

dac·tyl (dák-til ‖ -t'l) *n.* Also **dac·ty·lus** (-ti-əss) *pl.* **-li** (-lī) (for sense 2). **1.** *Prosody.* **a.** In modern verse, a metrical foot consisting of one accented syllable followed by two unaccented. **b.** In classical verse, one long syllable followed by two short. **2.** *Zoology.* A finger, toe, or similar part or structure; a digit. [Middle English *dactil,* from Latin *dactylus,* from Greek *daktulos*†, finger, hence dactyl (the three syllables of which correspond to the three joints of a finger).] —**dac·tyl·ic** (dak-tíllik) *adj. & n.* —**dac·tyli·cal·ly** *adv.*

dactylo–, dactyl–. *comb form.* Indicates finger or toe; for example, **dactylogram.** [Greek *daktulos,* finger, DACTYL.]

dac·tyl·o·gram (dak-tíllagram) *n. Chiefly U.S.* A fingerprint. [DACTYLO- + -GRAM.]

dac·ty·log·ra·phy (dák-ti-lóggrəfi) *n. Chiefly U.S.* The study of fingerprints as a method of identification. [DACTYLO- + -GRAPHY.] —**dac·ty·lo·graph·er** *n.* —**dac·ty·lo·graph·ic** (-lə-gráffik) *adj.*

dac·ty·lol·o·gy (dák-ti-lólləji) *n.* The use of the fingers and hands to communicate, as in the manual alphabet used by deaf or dumb people. [DACTYLO- + -LOGY.]

dad (dad) *n.* **1.** *Informal.* A father. **2.** *Slang.* A term of address used to an older male person other than one's father. [Of baby-talk origin.]

Da·da, da·da (dáadaa) *n.* Also **Da·da·ism** (-iz'm). A western European artistic and literary movement (1916–24) that reacted against traditional cultural aesthetic values by emphasising irrationality. [French *dada,* hobbyhorse, from baby talk (a name arbitrarily adopted first as the title of a Dadaist review of 1916).] —**Da·da·ist** *n. & adj.* —**Da·da·is·tic** (-ístik) *adj.*

Dadd (dad), **Richard** (1817–87). British painter. Of unstable temperament, he murdered his father and produced much of his best work in a lunatic asylum. He is known for his extraordinarily dense and intricate fantasy scenes of fairies, goblins, and sprites.

dad·dy (dáddi) *n., pl.* **-dies.** *Informal.* Father; dad. Used familiarly, especially by children. [Diminutive of **dad.**]

daddy long·legs *n., pl.* **daddy longlegs. 1.** *Chiefly British.* An insect, the crane fly *(see).* **2.** *U.S.* An arachnid, the **harvestman** *(see).*

da·do (dáydō) *n., pl.* **-does. 1.** *Architecture.* The section of a pedestal between the base and cornice. **2.** The lower portion of the wall of a room, decorated differently from the upper section, as with panels. —*tr.v.* **dadoed, -doing, -does.** To provide with a dado. [Italian, a

die, cube, probably from Latin *datum,* gift, pawn (chesspiece), from the past participle of *dare,* to give.]

dae·dal (déed'l) *adj. Poetic.* Wonderfully skilful; inventive. [Latin *daedalus,* from Greek *daidalos,* skilful.]

Daed·a·lus (dée-d'ləss, dé-). In Greek legend, a sculptor and inventor, father of Icarus and builder of the Labyrinth. —**Dae·da·li·an,** **Dae·da·le·an** (dee-dáyli-ən) *adj.*

dae·mon (déemən) *n.* Also **dai·mon** (dī-mən, -mon). **1.** *Greek Mythology.* A minor divinity, such as a deified hero. **2.** An attendant or guiding spirit; a genius. **3.** Variant of **demon.**

daf·fo·dil (dáffədil) *n.* **1.** A bulbous plant, *Narcissus pseudonarcissus,* having yellow flowers with a trumpet-shaped central crown. **2.** Its flower. **3.** Brilliant to vivid yellow. [Probably from Dutch *de affodil,* the asphodel : *de,* the + *affodil,* from Medieval Latin *asphodilus,* from Latin *asphodelus,* ASPHODEL.]

daf·fy (dáffi) *adj.* **-fier, -fiest.** *Informal.* Silly; foolish; zany. [Obsolete English *daff,* fool, Middle English *daffe,* probably related to *dafte,* gentle, foolish, DAFT.]

daft (daaft ‖ daft) *adj.* **1.** Mad; crazy. **2.** Foolish; stupid. [Middle English *dafte,* gentle, modest, foolish, Old English *gedæfte,* mild, meek.] —**daft·ly** *adv.* —**daft·ness** *n.*

Da·fydd ap Gruffydd (dá-vith ap gríffith, dáa) (died 1283). The last native Prince of Wales (1282–3), he fought his brother Llywelyn ap Gruffydd for the title, claiming it when his brother died (1282). He was captured by the English under Edward I, and executed.

Dafydd ap Gwil·ym (gwíllim) (*c.*1320–*c.*1380). Welsh poet. He was influenced by the troubadours of Europe and wrote in a tone more personal than the conventions of his day. He also popularised a new metrical form adopted by later bardic writers.

dag (dag) *n.* **1.** A lock of matted or dung-coated wool. **2.** *Archaic.* A loosely hanging end or shred. **3.** *Australian & N. Z. Slang.* An odd or eccentric person. [Middle English *dagge*†, shred, tag.]

dag decagram.

Da·gan (dáa-gən ‖ -gaan). The Babylonian god of the earth, considered by some to be identified with Baal.

Dag·en·ham (dággənəm). An industrial and residential district in east Greater London. It has a large car factory.

Da·ge·stan (daagi-staan, dággi-). A republic within the Russian Federation, bounded to the east by the Caspian Sea. It was annexed by Russia in 1813. Though comprising over 30 different nationalities, the region's population is chiefly Muslim. Its capital is Makhachkala.

dag·ga (dúkhə, dákhə) *n. South African.* Indian hemp used as a narcotic; cannabis. [Afrikaans, from Hottentot *dachab.*]

dag·ger (dággər) *n.* **1.** A short pointed weapon with sharp edges, used for stabbing. **2.** Something that agonises, torments, or wounds. **3.** *Printing.* **a.** An **obelisk** *(see).* **b.** A **double dagger** *(see).* —**at daggers drawn.** Hostile; ready for confrontation. —**look daggers at.** To glare angrily or hatefully at. ~*tr.v.* **daggered, -gering, -gers. 1.** To stab with a dagger. **2.** To mark with a dagger. [Middle English *daggere,* from obsolete *dag,* to pierce, influenced by Old French *dague,* from Old Provençal or Old Italian *daga,* perhaps from Vulgar Latin *daca* (unattested), "Dacian knife", feminine of Latin *Dācus,* Dacian, from DACIA.]

dag·lock (dág-lok) *n.* A lock of wool; a dag.

da·go (dáygō) *n., pl.* **-gos** or **-goes.** *Sometimes capital* **D.** *Slang.* **1.** A Spaniard or Portuguese. Used derogatorily. **2.** Broadly, any foreigner of Latin extraction. Used derogatorily. [Alteration of common Spanish name *Diego,* from Latin *Jacōbus,* JACOB.]

Da·gon (dáy-gon, -gən). The chief god of the ancient Philistines and later the Phoenicians, represented as half man and half fish. [Middle English, from Latin, from Greek *Dagōn,* from Hebrew *Dāgōn,* "small fish", diminutive of *dāg,* fish.]

Da·guerre (da-gáir, də-), **Louis (-Jacques-Mandé)** (1789–1851). French inventor of a photographic method in which sunlight formed a permanent image on a copper plate treated with silver iodide.

da·guerre·o·type (də-gérrə-tīp) *n.* **1.** An early photographic process with the impression made on a light-sensitive silver-coated metallic plate and developed by mercury vapour. **2.** A photograph made by this process. ~*tr.v.* **daguerreotyped, -typing, -types.** To photograph by this process. [After Louis DAGUERRE.] —**da·guerre·o·typ·er** *n.* —**da·guerre·o·typ·y** (-tīpi) *n.*

dah (daa) *n.* A dash in Morse code. Compare **dit.**

da·ha·be·ah, da·ha·bee·yah, da·ha·bi·ah (dáahə-bée-ə) *n.* A houseboat used on the Nile, having sails and sometimes an engine. [Arabic *dahabīya,* "the golden" (that is, gilded barge), originally with reference to those used by Egyptian rulers.]

Dahl (daal), **Roald** (1916–90). British author, born in Wales of Norwegian parents. He wrote suspense stories and children's books, such as *Charlie and the Chocolate Factory* (1964).

dahl·i·a (dáyli-ə ‖ *U.S.* dáali-ə, dál-i-ə) *n.* **1.** Any of several plants of the genus *Dahlia,* native to Mexico and Central America, having tuberous roots and showy, variously coloured flowers; especially, any of the horticultural forms derived from *D. pinnata* and *D. juarezii.* **2.** The flower of any of these plants. [New Latin *Dahlia;* named in honour of Anders *Dahl* (1751–87), 18th-century Swedish botanist.]

Dahomey. See **Benin, People's Republic of.**

Dáil Éireann (dóyl áir-ən). The lower legislative house of the Irish parliament. Also called "Dáil". See **Oireachtas.** [Irish : *dáil,* assembly, from Old Irish *dāl* + *Ēireann,* genitive of *Ēire,* Ireland, from Old Irish *Ēriu,* "land".]

dai·ly (dáyli) *adj.* Of, pertaining to, occurring, or published every day or every weekday.
~*n., pl.* **dailies. 1.** A daily publication, especially a newspaper. **2.** *British.* A servant, especially a cleaning woman, who lives off the premises.
~*adv.* Each day; day after day. [Middle English *daili,* Old English *dæglīc,* from *dæg,* DAY.]

daily double *n.* In horse racing, a bet won by choosing both winners of two specified races on one day.

dai·mio, dai·myo (dĭm-yō) *n., pl.* **daimio, dai·myo, -mios,** or **-myos.** A hereditary nobleman in feudal Japan. [Japanese *daimyō,* "great name".]

Daim·ler (dáymlər ‖ *German* dīmlər), **Gottlieb (Wilhelm)** (1834–1900). German inventor who developed the petrol-driven internal-combustion engine. He produced one of the first practical motor cars, and in 1890 founded the German Daimler Motor Company.

daimon. 1. Variant of **demon. 2.** Variant of **daemon.**

dain·ty (dáynti) *adj.* **-tier, -tiest. 1.** Delicately beautiful or charming; exquisite: *dainty fingers.* **2.** Delicious; choice. **3.** Of refined taste or manners. **4.** Too fastidious; fussy.
~*n., pl.* **dainties.** Something delicious; a delicacy. [Middle English *deinte,* delicious, pleasant, from *deinte,* pleasure, delicacy, from Old French *deintie,* from Latin *dīgnitās* (stem *dīgnitāt-,* dignity, worth, from *dīgnus,* worthy).] —**dain·ti·ly** *adv.* —**dain·ti·ness** *n.*

dai·qui·ri (dĭk-iri, dáck-, -əri) *n., pl.* **-ris.** An iced cocktail of rum, lime or lemon juice, and sugar. [After *Daiquirí,* Cuba, source of the rum originally used in this drink.]

dair·y (dáir-i) *n., pl.* **dairies. 1.** A commercial establishment that processes or sells milk and milk products. **2.** A place where milk and cream are stored and processed, such as a specially equipped building on a farm.
~*adj.* **1.** Of, pertaining to, producing, or made from milk: *dairy produce; dairy cream.* **2.** Of or pertaining to a dairy. [Middle English *daierie,* from *daie,* dairymaid, Old English *dæge,* dough-kneader.] —**dairy** *adj.*

dairy cattle *pl.n.* Cows bred and raised for the production of milk rather than meat.

dairy farm *n.* A farm for producing milk and milk products.

dair·y·ing (dáir-i-ing) *n.* **1.** The business of a dairy. **2.** Dairy farming. —**dair·y·ing** *adj.*

dair·y·maid (dáir-i-mayd) *n.* A female dairy worker.

dair·y·man (dáir-i-mən, -man) *n., pl.* **-men** (-mən, -men). **1.** A male dairy worker. **2.** A dairy manager or owner.

da·is (dáy-iss, dayss) *n., pl.* **-ises** (-issiz). A raised platform, as in a lecture hall or dining hall, used by speakers, dignitaries, or the like. [Middle English *deis,* from Old French, table, platform, from Latin *discus,* dish, quoit, DISC.]

dai·sy (dáyzi) *n., pl.* **-sies. 1.** A low-growing European plant, *Bellis perennis,* having flowers with pink or white rays. **2.** Any of various other composite plants with central disc flowers surrounded by large ray flowers, such as the oxeye daisy, Michaelmas daisy, and Shasta daisy. **3.** The flower of any of these plants. **4.** *Slang.* Something excellent or notable. —**push up (the) daisies.** To be dead and in the grave. [Middle English *daisie, dayeseye,* Old English *dægeseage,* "day's eye" (the flower of some species opens to reveal a yellow disc in the morning and closes again in the evening) : *dæges,* genitive of *dæg,* DAY + *ēage,* eye.]

daisy chain *n.* A number of daisies strung together head through stalk.

dai·sy·cut·ter (dáyzi-kuttər) *n. Informal.* A ball in cricket, tennis, or similar games, struck or thrown so that it skims along the ground. Also called "creeper".

daisy wheel *n.* A printing device, used especially in the printing machines attached to computers and word processors, consisting of printing characters fixed at the end of spokes on a wheel.

dak (dawk) *n.* In India, the post or mail delivery service. [Hindi and Marathi.]

Da·kar (dáckər, dákaar). Capital of Senegal, a port situated on Cape Verde peninsula. A fort was built there by the French in 1857, and the city was the capital of French West Africa (1904–59).

dak bungalow *n.* In India, a place providing lodging for travellers.

Da·kin's solution (dáykinz) *n.* A dilute solution of sodium hypochlorite in water, used as a surgical disinfectant. [Developed by Henry Drysdale *Dakin* (1880–1952), British biochemist.]

dakoit. Variant of **dacoit.**

Da·ko·ta (də-kótə) *n., pl.* **-tas** or collectively **Dakota. 1.** A member of any of a large group of Siouan-speaking people of North American Plains Indians, now living on reservations in North and South Dakota, Minnesota, and Montana. **2.** The Siouan language of these Indians. —**Da·ko·tan** *adj. & n.*

dal. See **dhal.**

Da·la·dier (dál-ad-yáy), **Edouard** (1884–1970). French statesman and prime minister (1933, 1934, 1938–40). Daladier signed the Munich agreement (1938) for France. He was arrested after France fell to the Germans in 1940, and remained in captivity until 1945.

Da·lai La·ma (dál-ī-láamə, daál-, də-lī-) The traditional ruler and highest priest of the Buddhist religion in Tibet and Mongolia. The position is not hereditary or elective, but said to be held by the same individual in successive incarnations. Also called "Grand

Lama". [Tibetan : Mongolian *dalai,* ocean, great + Tibetan *bla-ma,* superior one, a Buddhist monk, LAMA.]

da·la·pon (dál-ə-pon) *n.* A selective weedkiller used on unwanted grasses. [Probably *di-* + *alpha* + *propionic* acid.]

da·la·si (də-láa-si ‖ daa-) *n.* The basic monetary unit of Gambia, equivalent to 100 bututs. [Native name in Gambia.]

dale (dayl) *n.* A broad valley, especially in north Yorkshire. [Middle English *dale,* Old English *dæl.*]

Da·lek (dáalek) *n.* **1.** A hostile science-fictional robot-like creature with a harsh, monotonous voice. **2.** A person who behaves in a dehumanised, automatic manner. [After a group of sinister robot-like creatures in the television series *Dr. Who.*]

d'A·lem·bert (dál-oN-báir), **Jean le Rond** (1717–83). French mathematician and philosopher, who defined the laws of dynamics governing equilibrium and centrifugal force, known as *d'Alembert's principle.* A friend of Voltaire and Diderot, he contributed to the *Encyclopédie.*

dales·man (dáylz-mən, -man) *n., pl.* **-men** (-mən, -men). A person who lives in a dale, especially in north Yorkshire.

da·leth (dáa'l-əth, -eth, -et) *n.* The fourth letter of the Hebrew alphabet. [Hebrew *dāleth,* from *dālt,* door, daleth.]

Da·li (dáali ‖ *Spanish* da-lée), **Salvador** (1904–89). Spanish painter. He went to Paris in 1929 and joined the Surrealist movement. Influenced by Freud's psychoanalytic theories of the unconscious, he painted disturbing images whose quasi-photographic finish heightens their disquieting effect, as in *Persistence of Memory* (1931).

Dal·la·pic·co·la (dál-ə-píck-ō-lə, -ə-, -la), **Luigi** (1904–75). Italian pianist and composer. He wrote *Songs of Captivity* (1941) in protest against Italy's Fascist regime, and the opera *Ulysses* (1968).

Dal·las (dál-əss ‖ *U.S. also* -iss). City on the Trinity river in north-east Texas, south United States. It grew on the site of Peter's Colony (founded 1841), becoming Dallas in 1845. The town prospered as a cotton centre, and expanded from 1915 with the discovery of oil nearby, becoming the largest city in Texas. President John F. Kennedy was assassinated in the city in November, 1963.

dal·li·ance (dál-i-ənss) *n.* **1.** Frivolous spending of time; dawdling. **2.** Amorous play; flirtation.

dal·ly (dál-i) *v.* **-lied, -lying, -lies.** —*intr.* **1.** To play amorously; flirt. **2.** To trifle; toy. **3.** To waste time; dawdle. —*tr.* To waste (time). Used with *away.* [Middle English *dalien,* from Old French *dalier†,* to chat.] —**dal·li·er** *n.* —**dal·ly·ing·ly** *adv.*

Dal·ma·tia (dal-máyshə). A region on the eastern shore of the Adriatic. It is mountainous and the population mostly Croatian. It was dominated by Venice in the 15th to 18th centuries, then fell to Austria. Italy claimed Dalmatia in World War I, but it joined the Kingdom of Serbs, Croats, and Slovenes (1918), which became Yugoslavia (1929). During World War II, much of it was held by Italy, but was subsequently restored to Yugoslavia. Most of it is now in Croatia. Dalmatia has a scenic coastline, and the region produces wines and liqueurs. Split is the chief town.

Dal·ma·tian (dal-máysh'n) *n.* **1.** A dog of a breed believed to have originated in Dalmatia, having a short, smooth, white coat covered with black or dark brown spots. Also called "coach dog", "carriage dog". **2.** A native or inhabitant of Dalmatia.
~*adj.* Of or pertaining to Dalmatia or its inhabitants.

dal·mat·ic (dal-máttik) *n.* **1.** *Roman Catholic Church.* A wide-sleeved garment formerly worn over the alb by the deacon at the celebration of High Mass, and now worn by bishops and other prelates. **2.** A similar garment worn by an English monarch as a coronation robe. [Middle English *dalmatik,* from Old French *dalmatique,* from Late Latin *dalmatica (vestis),* "Dalmatian (garment)" (originally of Dalmatian wool), from *dalmaticus,* of DALMATIA.]

dal se·gno (dál-sényō, daál-sáynyō) *adv. Abbr.* **d.s., D.S.** *Music.* From the sign. Used as a direction to repeat from the place marked by the sign (·S·) to a designated point. [Italian, "from the sign".]

Dal·ton (dáwl-tən ‖ dól-), **John** (1766–1844). British chemist, whose pioneer work on the properties of gases led to his discovery in 1803 that the atoms of chemical elements differed in weight, and his formulation of the atomic theory.

dal·to·ni·an (dawl-tón-i-ən ‖ dol-) *adj.* Also **Dal·to·ni·an,** especially for sense 1. **1.** Of or pertaining to John Dalton or his atomic theory. **2.** Of or pertaining to daltonism.

dal·ton·ism (dáwl-tən-iz'm ‖ dól-) *n. Sometimes Capital* **D. 1.** Red-green colour blindness. **2.** Any form of colour blindness. [After John DALTON, who was colour blind.] —**dal·ton·ic** (-tónnik) *adj.*

Dalton plan *n.* An educational system in which pupils learn by completing long-term study projects. [After *Dalton,* Massachusetts, where the plan was introduced.]

Dalton's law *n. Chemistry.* The principle that the pressure of a mixture of gases is the sum of the partial pressures of the components of the mixture. Also called "Dalton's law of partial pressures". [After John DALTON.]

dam¹ (dam) *n.* **1.** A barrier constructed across a waterway to control the flow or raise the level of water. **2.** A natural barrier, such as an ice dam, across a water course. **3.** A body of water controlled by such a barrier. **4.** Any obstruction or hindrance.
~*tr.v.* **dammed, damming, dams. 1.** To construct a dam across; hold back by means of a dam. **2.** To obstruct or restrain; confine. Usually used with *up.* —See Synonyms at **hinder.** [Middle English, probably from Middle Low German *dam,* from Germanic *dammjan* (unattested), to impede, dam.]

dam² *n.* **1.** *Abbr.* **d.** A female parent of a quadruped, such as a sheep or horse. **2.** *Archaic.* A mother. [Middle English, variant of DAME.]

damage / damselfish

dam·age (dámmij) *n.* **1.** Harm done to a person or thing, usually reducing usefulness, value, soundness, or standing. **2.** *Plural. Law.* Money paid or ordered to be paid as compensation for injury or loss. **3.** *Informal.* Cost; price: *What's the damage?*
~*v.* **damaged, -aging, -ages.** —*tr.* To cause injury to; impair; harm. —*intr.* To suffer or be susceptible to damage. —See Synonyms at **injure, ruin.** [Middle English, from Old French, from *dam(me)*, loss, damage, from Latin *damnum*, loss, harm, fine.] —**dam·age·a·ble** *adj.* —**dam·ag·ing·ly** *adv.*

da·man (da-má·an, dámmən) *n. Rare.* The hyrax, a small mammal of Africa and Asia Minor. [Arabic *damān (Isrā'īl)*, "sheep of Israel".]

Da·man (daa-má·an, də-). *Portuguese* **Damāo** (damŏ̃N). Region of northwest India, on the eastern shore of the Gulf of Khambar (Cambay). It was a Portuguese territory from the 16th century, and was occupied by India in 1961. It now forms part of the Union Territory of Daman and Diu.

damar. Variant of **dammar.**

Da·ma·ra·land (də-má·arə-land). Also **He·re·ro·land** (herá·iro-land). Region of north central Namibia (South West Africa), home of the pastoralist Herero and Damara peoples.

dam·as·cene (dámmə-seén, -seen) *tr.v.* **-cened, -cening, -cenes.** To decorate (metal) with wavy patterns of inlay, usually of gold or silver, or etching.
~*n.* Work decorated by damascening.
~*adj.* Of or pertaining to damascening or damask. [Middle English, from Old French *damasquiner*, "to decorate in the manner of Damascus blades or steel", from *damasquin*, of Damascus, from Italian *damaschino*, from Latin *Damascēnus*, from Greek *Damaskēnos*, from *Damaskos*, DAMASCUS.] —**dam·a·scen·er** *n.*

Dam·a·scene (dámmə-seén, -seen) *n.* A native or inhabitant of Damascus. —**Dam·a·scene** *adj.*

Da·mas·cus (də-másk-əss, -maásk-) *French* **Da·mas** (da-má); *Arabic* **Ash Sham** or **Di·mash.** Capital of Syria, on the Barada river in the southwest of the country. A city of great antiquity, it is mentioned in the Bible. Damascus fell to the Arabs (635); and was the capital of the Islamic empire under the Umayyad caliphs (661–750). A Saracen stronghold in the Crusades, the city was in Ottoman hands (1516–1918) and then occupied by the French before becoming the capital of independent Syria (1941). The city was once famous for its blades and armour, and still produces fine metalware, textiles, glass, and leather goods.

Damascus steel *n.* An early form of steel having wavy markings, developed in Near Eastern countries, especially Persia, and used chiefly in sword blades. Also called "damask steel".

dam·ask (dámməsk) *n.* **1.** A rich patterned fabric of cotton, linen, silk, or wool. **2.** A fine, twilled table linen. **3.** Damascus steel. **4.** The wavy pattern on Damascus steel. **5.** *Archaic & Poetic.* A colour, perhaps that of the damask rose.
~*tr.v.* **damasked, -asking, -asks. 1.** To damascene. **2.** To decorate or weave with rich patterns.
~*adj.* **1.** Of or from Damascus. **2.** Made from damask or damask steel. **3.** Of the colour damask. [Middle English *damask (cloth)*, from Medieval Latin *(pannus de) damasco*, "(cloth of) Damascus".]

damask rose *n.* A rose, *Rosa damascena*, native to Asia, having fragrant red or pink flowers used as a source of attar. [Medieval Latin *rosa Damascēna*, from Latin *Damascēnus*, of DAMASCUS, its supposed place of origin.]

dame (daym) *n.* **1.** A title formerly given to a woman in authority or to the mistress of a household. Now only used in expressions such as *Dame Fortune.* **2.** *Archaic.* A married woman; a matron. **3.** *Chiefly U.S. Slang.* A woman; a female. **4.** *British. Capital* D. A woman member equivalent in status to a knight, of the Order of the British Empire or any of several other orders. **5.** *British.* A stock pantomime figure of a middle-aged or elderly woman, usually fat and swathed in layers of garish clothes, played by a man. See **principal boy.** [Middle English, from Old French, from Latin *domina*, feminine of *dominus*, master, lord.]

dame school *n.* Formerly, a small local school run by an elderly woman, usually for children of primary school age.

dame's rocket *n.* A plant, *Hesperis matronalis*, native to Europe, having clusters of fragrant purple or white flowers. Also called "dame's violet", "damewort". [Translation of its Latin name.]

Da·mien (dáymi-ən, *French* dam-yáN), **Father (Joseph de Veuster)** (1840–89). Belgian Roman Catholic missionary who volunteered in 1873 to supervise Hawaii's leper colony on Molokai Island. He died there of leprosy in 1889.

dam·mar, da·mar, dam·mer (dámmər) *n.* Any of various hard resins obtained from Indo-Malayan trees of the genera *Agathis* and *Shorea*, used in varnishes and lacquers. [Malay *damar*, resin.]

dam·mit (dámmit) *interj.* Damn it.

damn (dam) *v.* **damned, damning, damns.** —*tr.* **1.** To pronounce an adverse judgment upon; criticise adversely. **2.** To bring about the failure of; ruin. **3.** To condemn as harmful, illegal, or immoral: *damn gambling and strong drink.* **4.** *Theology.* To condemn to everlasting punishment or a similar fate. **5.** To swear at by using the word "damn"; curse. —*intr.* To swear; curse.
~*interj.* Used to express anger, irritation, or disappointment.
~*n.* **1.** The saying of "damn"; a curse. **2.** *Informal.* The least valuable bit; a jot: *don't give a damn; not worth a damn.*
~*adj.* Damned.
~*adv. Informal.* Damned. Used as an intensive. [Middle English *dam(p)nen*, from Old French *dam(p)ner*, from Latin *damnāre*, to

inflict loss upon, condemn, from *damnum*, loss, damage.]

dam·na·ble (dám-nəb'l) *adj.* **1.** Deserving condemnation; odious; hateful. **2.** Disagreeable; unpleasant: *damnable weather.* —**dam·na·ble·ness** *n.* —**dam·na·bly** *adv.*

dam·na·tion (dam-náysh'n) *n.* **1.** The act of damning or condition of being damned. **2.** *Theology.* **a.** Condemnation to everlasting punishment; doom. **b.** Everlasting punishment. **3.** Failure or ruination incurred by adverse criticism.
~*interj.* Used to express anger or annoyance.

dam·na·to·ry (dám-nə-təri, -tri, *rarely* -náytəri) *adj.* Threatening with damnation; condemning; damning.

damned (damd) *adj.* **1.** Condemned, especially to eternal punishment; doomed. **2.** *Informal.* **a.** Deserving condemnation; detestable. Used as an expression of irritation or disappointment: *this damned weather!* **b.** Absolute; utter. Used as an intensive: *a damned fool.* **3.** *Informal.* Used as an expression of surprise or refusal: *I'm damned if I'll lend her my car!*
~*adv. Informal.* Very; extremely: *a damned poor excuse.*

damned·est (dám-dist) *adj. Informal.* Most extraordinary: *the damnedest thing I've ever heard.* —**do one's damnedest.** To do all one possibly can.

dam·ni·fy (dám-ni-fī) *tr.v.* **-fied, -fying, -fies.** *Law.* To cause loss or damage to. [Old French *damnifier*, from Late Latin *damnificāre*, from Latin *damnificus*, causing loss, harmful : *damnum*, loss, harm + *-ficus, -*FIC.] —**dam·ni·fi·ca·tion** (-fi-káysh'n) *n.*

damn·ing (dámming) *adj.* **1.** That condemns or criticises: *a damning review.* **2.** That incriminates or gives proof of guilt: *damning evidence.* —**damn·ing·ly** *adv.*

Dam·o·cles (dámmə-kleez). (4th century B.C.) A member of the court of Dionysius the Elder, tyrant of Syracuse, who was forced by Dionysius to sit at a banquet under a sword suspended by a single hair, to demonstrate the precariousness of a king's fortunes. See **Sword of Damocles.** —**Dam·o·cle·an** (-kleé-ən) *adj.*

Da·mon and Pyth·i·as (dáymən; píthi-əss, -ass). In classical legend, two friends so devoted that Damon pledged his life as a hostage for the condemned Pythias.

dam·o·sel, dam·o·zel (dámmə-zel) *n.* Also **dam·oi·selle** (-zél). *Archaic.* A damsel. [Variant of DAMSEL.]

damp (damp) *adj.* **damper, dampest. 1.** Slightly wet; moist; humid. **2.** *Archaic.* Dejected. —See Synonyms at **wet.**
~*n.* **1. a.** Moisture; humidity; mist. **b.** Moisture on the inside walls of a building caused by condensation, by rain entering through an outside wall, or by water seeping up from the ground *(rising damp).* **2.** Foul or poisonous gas that sometimes pollutes the air in mines. See **afterdamp, black damp, firedamp. 3.** *Archaic.* Lowness of spirits; depression. **4.** A restraint or check; discouragement.
~*tr.v.* **damped, damping, damps. 1.** To make damp or moist; moisten. **2.** To cut off the flow of air to (a fire) to reduce combustion. Often used with *down.* **3.** To restrain or check; discourage. Often used with *down.* **4.** To provide (the strings of a keyboard instrument) with dampers as a means of deadening the sound. **5.** *Physics.* To decrease the amplitude of (an oscillation or wave). —**damp off.** *Botany.* To be affected by **damping off** *(see).* [Middle English, poison gas, choke-damp, from Middle Low German and Middle Dutch, smoke, vapour, from Germanic *damp-* (unattested).] —**damp·ish** *adj.* —**damp·ly** *adv.* —**damp·ness** *n.*

damp course *n.* A strip of plastic or layer of other waterproof material placed between two courses of bricks close to the ground in a wall in order to prevent rising damp. Also called "damp-proof course".

damp·en (dámpən) *v.* **-ened, -ening, -ens.** —*tr.* **1.** To moisten; make damp. **2.** To deaden; depress: *dampen one's spirits.* —*intr.* To become wet or moist. —**damp·en·er** *n.*

damp·er (dámpər) *n.* **1.** One that damps, restrains, or depresses. **2.** An adjustable plate in the flue of a furnace or stove for controlling the draught. **3.** *Music.* **a.** A device in various keyboard instruments for deadening the vibrations of the strings. **b.** A mute for various brass instruments. **4.** Any device that eliminates or progressively diminishes oscillations. **5.** *Australian & N.Z.* An unleavened bread made from flour and water and cooked in an open fire. —**put a damper on.** *Informal.* To suppress; discourage.

Dam·pi·er (dámpi-ər), **William** (1652–1715). British pirate who later became an explorer and circumnavigated the globe, which he described in his *Voyage Round the World* (1697). In 1699 he was sent by the Admiralty to the South Seas. He discovered the Dampier archipelago off northwest Australia.

damp·ing off (dámping) *n.* A disease of planted seeds or very young seedlings caused by fungi, particularly those of the genus *Pythium*, and resulting in death of the newly sprouted plants due to softening and collapse of the stem base.

damp-proof (dámp-prŏ̃of || -prŏ̃of) *adj.* Resistant to damp.
~*tr.v.* **damp-proofed, -proofing, -proofs.** To make damp-proof, especially by providing a damp course.

damp squib *n.* Something that fails to live up to expectations: *The office party was a bit of a damp squib.*

dam·sel (dámz'l) *n. Archaic & Poetic.* A young woman or girl; a maiden. [Middle English *damisele*, from Old French *dameisele*, from Vulgar Latin *dominicella* (unattested), diminutive of Latin *domina*, lady, DAME.]

dam·sel·fish (dámz'l-fish) *n., pl.* **-fishes** or collectively **damselfish.** Any of various small tropical marine fishes of the family Pomacentridae, having laterally compressed, usually brightly coloured bodies. Also called "demoiselle".

dam·sel·fly (dámz'l-flī) *n., pl.* **-flies.** Any of various slender-bodied, often brightly coloured insects of the order Odonata, related to the dragonflies but differing in having wings that are folded together over the back when at rest. Also called "demoiselle".

dam·son (dámz'n) *n.* **1.** A plum tree, *Prunus institia* (or *P. domestica institia*), native to Eurasia, cultivated since ancient times for its edible fruit. Also called "bullace". **2.** The oval, bluish-black, juicy plum borne by this tree. Also called "damson plum". [Middle English *damascene, damson,* from Latin *(prūnum) Damascēnum,* "(plum) of Damascus".]

dan (dan) *n. Sometimes capital* **D.** **1.** In the oriental martial arts such as judo, any of twelve levels of proficiency at the grade of **black belt** (*see*). **2.** One who has achieved such a level: *a fourth dan.* [Japanese.]

Dan¹ (dan). **1.** The fifth son of Jacob. Genesis 30:6. **2.** One of the 12 tribes of Israel, descended from Dan.

Dan² *n. Archaic.* A title of honour equivalent to *master* or *sir:* "*Dan Chaucer, well of English undefiled*" (Spenser). [Middle English *Dan, Daunz,* "master", "mister", originally a title of respect for a monk or priest, from Old French *Dan, Danz,* from Medieval Latin *Domnus,* contracted from Latin *dominus,* master, lord.]

Dan. **1.** Daniel (Old Testament). **2.** Danish.

Dan·a·e, Dan·a·ë (dán-ay-ee, -i-). *Greek Mythology.* The mother of Perseus by Zeus, who visited her in the form of a shower of gold during her imprisonment by her father.

Dan·a·id, Dan·a·ïd (dán-ay-id, -i-) *n.* Any of the Danaides.

Da·na·i·des, Dan·a·i·des (də-náy-i-deez) *pl.n. Greek Mythology.* The fifty daughters of Danaus who, with one exception, murdered their bridegrooms on their wedding night and were condemned in Hades to fill sieves with water from leaky jars. —**Dan·a·id·e·an** (-i-dée-ən) *adj.*

Da Nang (dáa náng). Formerly **Tou·rane** (tōo-ráan). City and port on the South China Sea coast of Vietnam. A U.S. airforce base was sited there during the Vietnam War. The chief product is textiles.

Dan·a·us, Dan·a·üs (dán-i-əss). *Greek Mythology.* A king of Argos, father of the Danaides.

dance (daanss ‖ danss) *v.* **danced, dancing, dances.** —*intr.* **1.** To move rhythmically, usually to music, using prescribed or improvised steps and gestures. **2. a.** To leap or skip about excitedly; caper; frolic. **b.** To move lightly or nimbly. **3.** To bob up and down. **4.** To be a dancer by profession. —*tr.* **1.** To engage in or perform (a dance). **2.** To cause to dance. **3.** To bring to a specified state or condition by dancing: *She danced him off his feet.* —*n.* **1.** A series of rhythmical motions and steps, usually to music. **2.** A particular set of such prescribed movements. **3.** The art of dancing. Often preceded by *the.* **4.** A party or gathering of people for dancing. **5.** One round or turn of dancing. **6.** An act of dancing; a dance performance. **7.** A musical or rhythmical accompaniment composed or played for dancing. —**lead (someone) a (merry) dance.** To exasperate by unpredictable and unreasonable behaviour. [Middle English *dansen, dauncen,* from Old French *danser,* from Vulgar Latin *dansāre†.*] —**danc·er** *n.* —**danc·ing·ly** *adv.*

dance·a·ble (dáanss-əb'l ‖ dánss-) *adj.* Suitable for dancing. Said of music.

Dance of Death *n.* In the art, music, and literature of medieval Europe, the concept of death as all-powerful, represented by a dance in which the living are led off to their graves in order of rank. Also called "danse macabre".

D and C *n.* **Dilatation and curettage** (*see*).

dan·de·li·on (dándi-lī-ən) *n.* **1.** A plant, *Taraxacum officinale,* native to Eurasia and widely naturalised as a weed having many-rayed yellow flowers and deeply notched basal leaves, the leaves of which are sometimes used in salads. **2.** Any of several similar, related plants. [Middle English *dent-de-lion,* from Old French, translation of Medieval Latin *dēns leōnis,* "lion's tooth" (from its sharply indented leaves) : Latin *dēns* (stem *dent-*), tooth + *leōnis,* genitive of *leō,* LION.] —**dan·de·li·on** *adj.*

dandelion and burdock *n.* A soft carbonated drink with a dark colour and strong liquorice flavour.

dan·der¹ (dándər) *n. Informal.* Temper. —**get one's dander up.** *Informal.* To become angry or roused to vigorous action. [19th century : origin obscure.]

dander² *n.* Scurf from the coat of various animals, such as dogs, cats, or horses, often of an allergenic nature. [Short for DANDRUFF.]

dander³ *n. Scottish.* A saunter; a stroll.

~*intr.v.* **dandered, -dering, -ders.** *Scottish.* To go for a stroll. [19th century : origin obscure.]

Dan·die Din·mont (dándi dín-mont) *n.* A small terrier of a breed having a rough greyish or brownish coat and short legs. [After *Dandie Dinmont,* owner of two such dogs in *Guy Mannering* (1815), a novel by Sir Walter Scott.]

dan·di·fy (dándi-fī) *tr.v.* **-fied, -fying, -fies.** To dress up or make resemble a dandy or fop. —**dandi·fi·cation** (-fi-káysh'n) *n.*

dan·di·prat (dándi-prat) *n.* **1.** *Archaic.* A little, insignificant, or contemptible fellow. **2.** A small 16th-century English coin. [16th century : origin obscure.]

dan·dle (dánd'l) *tr.v.* **-dled, -dling, -dles.** To move (a small child) up and down, usually on the knees or in the arms. [16th century : perhaps related to Italian *dandolare,* to dandle, swing (expressive formation).] —**dan·dler** (dándlə) *n.*

dan·druff (dán-druf, -drəf) *n.* A scaly, whitish scurf formed on and shed from the scalp, often caused by seborrhoea. [16th century : unexplained first element + *-ruff,* perhaps from Middle English

roufe, scab, from Old Norse *hrufa.*]

dan·dy¹ (dándi) *n., pl.* **-dies.** **1.** A man who affects extreme elegance in his clothes and manners. **2.** *Nautical.* A yawl (*see*).

~*adj.* **dandier, -diest.** **1.** Like or dressed like a dandy; foppish. **2.** *Informal.* Fine; good. [Perhaps short for *jack-a-dandy,* pert person, fop : JACK (person) + A- (of) + *dandy,* probably from *Dandy,* Scottish nickname for the name *Andrew.*] —**dan·dy·ism** *n.*

dandy-brush (dándi-brush) *n.* A stiff brush used for grooming horses.

dandy roll *n.* Also **dandy roller.** *Printing.* A cylinder of wire gauze pressed on drained but moist paper pulp before it starts through the rollers. Produces watermarks in the paper. [From DANDY (fine).]

Dane (dayn) *n.* A native or inhabitant of Denmark or a person of Danish ancestry. [Middle English *Dan* (replacing *Dene,* from Old English *Dene,* the Danes), from Old Norse *Danr.*]

Dane-geld (dáyn-geld) *n.* Also **Dane-gelt** (-gelt). A tax levied in England from the 10th to the 12th century, initially to finance protection against Danish invasion. It was later continued as a land tax. [Middle English (modelled upon some Scandinavian compound such as Old Danish *Danegield*) : *Dane,* genitive plural of *Dan,* DANE + *geld,* tribute, payment, Old English *gield.*]

Dane-law, Dane-lagh (dáyn-law) *n.* **1.** The body of law established by the Danish invaders and settlers in northeastern England in the ninth and tenth centuries. **2.** The area of northern and eastern England under jurisdiction of this law, roughly encompassing present-day Yorkshire, the east Midlands, and East Anglia. [Middle English *Dene laue,* Old English *Dena lagu,* "Danes' law" : *Dena,* genitive of *Dene,* the Danes + *lagu,* law.]

dane-wort (dáyn-wurt ‖ -wawrt) *n.* A Eurasian shrub, *Sambucus ebulus,* similar and related to the elder.

dan·ger (dáynjər) *n.* **1.** Exposure or vulnerability to harm or evil; risk; peril. **2.** A source or instance of risk or peril. **3.** *Obsolete.* Power, especially power to harm. —**on** (or **off**) **the danger list.** In (or out of) serious danger of death. [Middle English *daunger,* power, dominion, peril, damage, from Old French *dangier, dongier,* from Vulgar Latin *dom(i)niārium* (unattested), authority, from Latin *dominium,* sovereignty, from *dominus,* lord, master.]

Synonyms: danger, jeopardy, peril, hazard, risk.

danger money *n. Chiefly British.* A payment made, in addition to basic wages, for work involving risk or danger.

dan·ger·ous (dáynjərəss) *adj.* **1.** Involving or fraught with danger; perilous. **2.** Able or apt to do harm. —**dan·ger·ous·ly** *adv.* —**dan·ger·ous·ness** *n.*

dan·gle (dáng-g'l) *v.* **-gled, -gling, -glings.** —*intr.* **1.** To hang loosely and swing or sway to and fro. **2.** To hover around someone; follow; be a hanger-on. Usually used with *after.* —*tr.* **1.** To cause to dangle. **2.** To offer (something enticing) as an inducement or temptation.

~*n.* **1.** The act of dangling. **2.** Something that is dangled. [Perhaps from Danish *dangle* or Swedish *dangla,* from Germanic *dang-* (unattested).] —**dan·gler** (dáng-glər) *n.* —**dan·gly** *adj.*

dangling participle *n. Grammar.* A **misrelated participle** (*see*).

Dan·iel¹ (dán-yəl). An Old Testament prophet during the Babylonian captivity whose faith protected him from death in a lions' den.

Daniel² *n. Abbr.* **Dan.** The book in the Old Testament containing the story and prophecies of Daniel.

Dan·iell (dán-yəl), John Frederic (1790–1845). British chemist. In 1836 he invented the Daniell cell and the dewpoint hygrometer, which measures atmospheric humidity.

Daniell cell *n.* A type of electric cell in which the anode is a zinc rod in sulphuric acid and the cathode is a copper rod in copper sulphate solution, the two electrodes being separated by porous pot. It has an emf of about 1.1 volts. [After J. F. DANIELL.]

da·ni·o (dáyni-ō) *n., pl.* **-os.** Any of various small, often brightly coloured freshwater fishes of the genera *Danio* and *Brachydanio,* native to Asia and popular as aquarium fish. [New Latin *Danio†.*]

Dan·ish (dáynish) *adj. Abbr.* **Dan., Da.** Of or pertaining to Denmark, the Danes, their language, or their culture.

~*n.* **1.** *Abbr.* **Dan., Da.** The North Germanic language of the Danes. **2.** *Informal.* A Danish pastry. [Middle English *Danish,* Old English *Denisc,* from *Dene,* the Danes.]

Danish blue *n.* A pungent, soft, blue-veined white cheese.

Danish pastry *n.* A sweet, buttery pastry made with raised dough, filled with fruit or marzipan and topped with icing, nuts, or other decoration. Also informally called "Danish".

Danish West In·dies (ín-diz ‖ -deez). The former possessions of Denmark in the Lesser Antilles, since 1917 the Virgin Islands of the United States.

Dan·ite (dánnīt) *n.* A descendant of Dan. Judges 13:2.

~*adj.* Of or pertaining to the Hebrew tribe descended from Dan.

dank (dangk) *adj.* **danker, dankest.** Unpleasantly damp; chilly and wet: *a dank cellar.* See Synonyms at **wet.** [Middle English *dank†.*] —**dank·ly** *adv.* —**dank·ness** *n.*

Danmark. See **Denmark.**

D'An·nun·zio (da-nóonts-yō), Gabriele (1863–1938). Italian writer and nationalist. His first novel, *The Child of Pleasure,* appeared in 1898. In the same year his play, *City of Death,* written for Sarah Bernhardt, was first performed. He became a leading nationalist. In 1919 he headed an unofficial Italian expedition to seize the Dalmatian port of Fiume (now Rijeka), and held the city for 15 months, in defiance of his government. He encouraged Mussolini's movement, helping to set up a Fascist seamen's union.

Da·no-Nor·we·gian (dáynō-nawr-wéejən) *n.* A form of the Norwegian language, **Bokmål** *(see)*.

danse ma·ca·bre (dónss makább-rə, -ə) *n. French.* The **dance of death** *(see)*.

dan·seur (don-sér, -sōr ‖ -séwr) *n., pl.* **-seurs** (-sérz, -sōrz ‖ -séwrz). A male ballet dancer. [French, from Old French, from *danser*, to DANCE.]

dan·seuse (don-sérz, -sōz ‖ -sōoz, -sōoss) *n. pl.* **-seuses** *(pronounced as singular).* A female ballet dancer. [French.]

Dan·te A·li·ghie·ri (dán-ti ál-ig-yaír-i, daán-, -tay) (1265-1321). Italian poet. Son of a noble burgher family in Florence, he remained in exile from the city after political rivals took over in 1302. He wrote *La Vita Nuova* (1292), the story of his boyhood love for a girl named Beatrice. *La Divina Commedia* (The Divine Comedy) he dates from a vision in 1300. It describes his progress through Hell and Purgatory (guided by Virgil), and Heaven (guided by Beatrice).

Dan·te·an (dánti-ən, dan-tée-ən) *adj.* **1.** Of or pertaining to Dante or his writings: *Dantean scholarship.* **2.** Dantesque.
~*n.* A scholar specialising in the life and writings of Dante.

Dan·tesque (dán-tésk) *adj.* Resembling or having the exalted, visionary literary style of Dante.

dan·tho·ni·a (dan-thóni-ə) *n.* Any grass of the genus *Danthonia*, of the Southern Hemisphere. See **wallaby grass**. [New Latin, after E. *Danthoine*, 19th-century French botanist.]

Dan·ton (don-tón), **Georges Jacques** (1759-94). French lawyer and revolutionary leader. He took part in the storming of the Bastille in 1789, became Minister of Justice in 1792, and a member of the Committee for Public Safety. Danton supported the execution of Louis XVI in 1793. He was president of the Jacobin Club but tried to moderate the Terror. Robespierre brought him before the revolutionary tribunal in 1794, and he was guillotined.

Dan·ube (dánnewb). *German* **Donau**; *Czech* **Dunaj** (dōonī); *Serbo-Croat* **Dunav** (dōonaav); *Romanian* **Dunărea**; *Hungarian* **Duna**. The largest river in Europe, exceeding the Volga in volume though not in length. It rises in the Black Forest of southwestern Germany and flows 2 850 kilometres (1,770 miles) through central and southeastern Europe into the Black Sea in Romania. During the Middle Ages it was the chief route from Central Europe to Constantinople (Istanbul), and remains a major trade artery. It passes through three European capitals, Vienna, Budapest, and Belgrade, and is connected to the rivers Rhine, Main, Oder, and Tisza by canals. —**Dan·u·bi·an** (dan-yōobi-ən) *adj.*

Danzig. See **Gdańsk**.

Dao. Variant of **Tao**.

Daoism. Variant of **Taoism**.

dap[1] (dap) *intr.v.* **dapped, dapping, daps.** **1.** To fish by letting a baited hook fall gently on the water. **2.** To dip lightly or quickly into water, as a bird does. **3.** To skip or bounce, especially over the surface of water. [Probably alteration of DAB (to strike lightly), influenced by DIP.]

dap[2] *n. Welsh & Southwest English.* A plimsoll. [Probably special use of DAP (in the sense, "to bounce").]

daph·ne (dáfni) *n.* Any of several shrubs of the genus *Daphne*, native to Eurasia, cultivated for their glossy evergreen foliage and clusters of bell-shaped flowers. See also **spurge laurel**. [New Latin *Daphne*, from Latin *daphnē*, laurel, from Greek. See **Daphne**.]

Daph·ne (dáfni). *Greek Mythology.* A nymph who chose to be turned into a laurel in order to escape rape by Apollo. [Latin *Daphnē*, from Greek, from *daphnē*, laurel, probably related to Latin *laurus*, LAUREL.]

daph·ni·a (dáfni-ə) *n., pl.* **daphnia.** Any of various small freshwater crustaceans of the genus *Daphnia*, some species of which are commonly used as food for aquarium fish. See also **water flea**. [New Latin *Daphnia*, perhaps from Latin *Daphnē*, DAPHNE.]

Da Pon·te (da póntay), **Lorenzo** (1749-1838). Italian author. He wrote the librettos for Mozart's operas *The Marriage of Figaro* (1786), *Don Giovanni* (1787), and *Così fan Tutti* (1790).

dap·per (dáppər) *adj.* **1.** Neatly dressed; trim. **2.** Small, compact, and active. [Middle English *dapyr*, elegant, probably from Middle Low German or Middle Dutch *dapper*, quick, nimble.] —**dap·per·ly** *adv.* —**dap·per·ness** *n.*

dap·ple (dáppّl) *n.* **1. a.** Mottled or spotted marking, as on a horse's coat. **b.** An individual spot. **2.** An animal, especially a horse, with a mottled or spotted coat.
~*tr.v.* **dappled, -pling, -ples.** To mark or mottle with spots: *Sunlight dappled the lawn.*
~*adj.* Also **dap·pled** (-d). Spotted or mottled. [Probably from DAPPLE-GREY.]

dap·ple-grey (dáppّl-gráy) *adj.* Grey with a mottled pattern of darker grey markings.
~*n.* A dapple-grey horse. [Middle English *dappel-grey*, perhaps alteration (influenced by Old Norse *depill*, a spot) of *appel-grey* (unattested), "apple-grey", probably from Old Norse *apalgrár* : *apall-, epli,* apple + *grār,* grey.]

D.A.R. Daughters of the American Revolution.

dar·af (dárrəf) *n. Physics.* A unit of elastance; a reciprocal farad. [Reverse spelling of FARAD.]

Dar-al-Beida. See **Casablanca**.

dar·by (dárbi) *n. British Slang.* A handcuff. [Originally *darbies* (plural), alluding to the phrase *Father Darby's bands,* a harsh binding agreement between a moneylender and a debtor.]

Dar·by and Joan (dárbi) *n.* An elderly married couple who live a placid, harmonious life together and are seldom apart. [After the elderly couple in a popular 18th-century English ballad.]

Dar·by-and-Joan club *n.* A special club for elderly people.

Dard (dard) *n., pl.* **Dards** or collectively **Dard.** A member of any of various Indo-European peoples speaking a Dardic language.

Dar·dan (dárd'n) *n.* Also **Dar·da·ni·an** (daar-dáyni-ən). A Trojan. [After DARDANUS.] —**Dar·dan** *adj.*

Dar·da·nelles (dárd'n-élz). *Turkish* **Çannakale Boğazi.** A strait linking the Aegean Sea with the Sea of Marmara, and separating Europe from Asia Minor. It was known to antiquity as the Hellespont. It was the site of the Dardanelles campaign (1915-16) of World War I. Allied landings were made at Gallipoli and Suvla Bay to try to secure the straits and open a route to Russia, forcing Turkey from the war. The attempt failed with the loss of many lives.

Dar·da·nus (dárdən-əss). *Greek Mythology.* The son of Zeus and Electra and founder of Troy.

Dar·dic (dárdik) *n.* The group of Indic languages of the upper Indus Valley.

dare (dair) *v.* **dared** or *archaic* **durst** (durst), **daring, dare** or **dares.**
—*tr.* **1.** To have the courage or boldness required for. Often used with an infinitive, with or without *to: No one dared oppose the dictator's wishes.* **2.** To challenge (a person) to do something requiring boldness: *I dare you to climb that tree.* —*intr.* To be courageous or bold enough to do or try something. —**dare say.** Also **dare·say** (dáirsay, déssay). To consider very likely or almost certain. Used only in the first person.
~*n.* A challenge, especially to give proof of bravery; an act of taunting or defying. [*Dare, durst*; Middle English *dar, dorste* (also *durste*), Old English *dear, dorste* (also *durste*), first and third person present and past indicative of *durran,* to venture, dare.] —**dar·er** *n.*

dare·dev·il (dáir-devv'l) *n.* One who is recklessly bold.
~*adj.* Recklessly bold. —**dare·dev·il·ry, dare·dev·il·try** *n.*

Dar es Sa·laam (dár ess sə-laám). Former capital of Tanzania, an Indian Ocean port. It was founded by the Sultan of Zanzibar (1862), and its name means "haven of peace". The German East Africa Company made it capital of German East Africa (1891–1916). It was later capital of Tanganyika, then of Tanzania from 1964. The city lies at the terminus of the TanZam Railway from Zambia (1975).

darg (darg) *n. Chiefly British Regional.* **1.** A full day's work. **2.** An amount of work to be completed. [Middle English, syncopated form of *daywerk,* day-work.]

dar·ic (dárrik) *n.* A gold coin of ancient Persia. [Greek *Dār(e)ikos,* probably after *Dāreios,* DARIUS I.]

Da·ri·én (dáir-i-ən, dárri-, -én). Spanish colony founded by Vasco Núñez de Balboa (1510) in what is now Panama, on the west coast of the Gulf of Darién.

Darién, Gulf of. A wide bay of the Caribbean Sea between eastern Panama and northwestern Colombia.

Darién, Isthmus of. See **Panama, Isthmus of.**

dar·ing (dáir-ing) *adj.* Willing to take risks; fearless; bold; adventurous. See Synonyms at **brave, reckless.**
~*n.* Active bravery; boldness; intrepidity. —**dar·ing·ly** *adv.* —**dar·ing·ness** *n.*

dar·i·ole (dárri-ōl) *n.* A small, cup-shaped mould used for making savoury or sweet puddings, jellies, or the like. [French, from Old French, perhaps a diminutive formation from *dorer,* to gild, from Latin *dēaurāre* : *dē-* (intensive) + *aurāre,* to gild, from *aurum,* gold.]

Da·ri·us I (də-rī-əss; *commonly also* dáir-i-əss). (c.558–486 B.C.). King of Persia (521–486 B.C.). He seized the throne after murdering a usurper, then divided the Persian empire into provinces known as satrapies. Following unrest among subject Greek states, he invaded mainland Greece. A long war ended in defeat of the Persians at Marathon (490 B.C.).

Dar·jee·ling[1] (daar-jéeling). Town in West Bengal, India, in the lower Himalayas. It is a tourist centre 2 290 metres (7,500 feet) above sea level, with fine views of mounts Everest and Kangchenjunga. The surrounding district is famous for its tea.

Darjeeling[2] *n.* A fine variety of black tea from Darjeeling in India. Also called "Darjeeling tea".

dark (dark) *adj.* **darker, darkest.** *Abbr.* **dk. 1.** With very little or no light. **2.** Reflecting only a small fraction of the incident light. **3.** Lacking light or brightness; shaded; obscure: *a dark day.* **4.** Of a shade tending towards black or brown by comparison with *light, pale,* or *white: dark hair; dark green.* **5.** Characterised by or producing gloom; dreary; dismal. **6.** Sullen; threatening: *a dark scowl.* **7.** Hard to understand; obscure. **8.** Concealed; secret; mysterious. **9.** Unenlightened; uncivilised: *a dark era in history.* **10.** Evil or wicked; sinister: *a dark purpose.* **11.** *Phonetics.* Designating an (l) that has the characteristics of a back vowel.
~*n.* **1.** Absence of light. **2.** A place having little light. **3.** Night; nightfall. Used chiefly in the phrases *after dark* and *before dark.* **4.** A dark hue or colour. —**in the dark. 1.** In secret: *things done in the dark.* **2.** In a state of ignorance; uninformed. —**whistle in the dark.** To put on a brave show to hide one's fears. [Middle English *derk,* Old English *deorc;* probably from Germanic.] —**dark·ish** *adj.*
Synonyms: dark, dim, murky, dusky, obscure, shady, shadowy.

dark adaptation *n.* The physical and chemical adjustments of the eye, including dilation of the pupil, that make vision possible in relative darkness. —**dark-a·dapt·ed** *adj.*

Dark Ages *n.* **1.** The early part of the Middle Ages from the fall of the Roman Empire in A.D. 476 until the coronation of Charlemagne in A.D. 800. **2.** The entire period from the end of classical civilisation to the revival of learning in the West in about A.D. 1000, formerly regarded as a period lacking in cultural development.

Dark Continent *n.* Africa. Preceded by *the.* [So called because its hinterland was largely unknown until the late 19th century.]

dark·en (dárkən) *v.* **-ened, -ening, -ens.** —*tr.* **1.** To shut out the light of; make dark or darker. **2.** To impart a darker hue to; render less white or clear. **3.** To fill with sadness; make gloomy. **4.** To obscure or cloud the meaning of; render vague. **5.** To strike with blindness. —*intr.* **1.** To become dark or darker. **2.** To become dark in colour. **3.** To become obscure, vague, or uncertain. **4.** To grow clouded, gloomy, or sullen. **5.** To become blind. —**dark·en·er** *n.*

dark-field microscope (dárk-feeld) *n.* A microscope used for studying minute objects, such as colloidal particles, using the Tyndall effect, in which high-intensity illumination makes the image of the specimen appear bright against a dark background.

dark glasses *pl. n.* Glasses with tinted lenses worn to protect the eyes from glare.

dark horse *n.* **1.** A little-known entrant in a horse race, contest, or the like. **2.** A secretive person, especially one whose capabilities or talents are not yet revealed. **3.** *U.S.* One who receives unexpected support as a candidate for the nomination in a political convention.

dark lantern *n.* A lantern whose light can be blocked by a sliding panel or other device.

dark·ling (dárkling) *adv. Poetic.* In the dark.
~*adj. Poetic.* **1.** Being or happening in the dark or the night. **2.** Dim; obscure. [Middle English *derkeling* : DARK + -LING (becoming).]

darkling beetle *n.* Any of various nocturnal, black or dark brown beetles of the widely distributed family Tenebrionidae.

dark·ly (dárkli) *adv.* **1.** So as to appear dark; in a dark manner. **2. a.** Mysteriously. **b.** In a sinister manner. **3.** Dimly; obscurely: *"For now we see through a glass, darkly."* (I Corinthians 13:12).

dark matter *n.* Matter in the universe that, though itself invisible, is thought to exist because its existence could account for otherwise inexplicable gravitational and astronomical phenomena. [DARK²·⁷ + MATTER¹.]

dark·ness (dárk-nəss, -niss) *n.* **1.** Total or almost total absence of light. **2.** The quality of being dark in colour. **3.** Blindness. **4.** Lack of enlightenment; ignorance. **5.** Evil; wickedness. **6.** Secrecy; concealment. **7.** Lack of clearness; obscurity.

dark·room (dárk-room, -room) *n.* A room in which photographic materials are processed, either in complete darkness or illuminated by sources of light to which the materials are not sensitive.

dark·some (dárk-s'm) *adj. Poetic.* Dark; darkish; sombre.

dark star *n.* A star that is normally obscured or too faint to see; especially, the component of an eclipsing binary detectable by spectral analysis or in the eclipse of the bright component.

dar·ling (dárling) *n.* **1.** One who is very dear; a much-loved person. Often used as a term of address. **2.** One that is greatly liked or preferred; a favourite. **3.** A charming or attractive person or thing. ~*adj.* **1.** Regarded with great affection and tenderness; very dear; beloved. **2.** Regarded with special favour; favourite: *"Metaphysics and poetry . . . are my darling studies."* (S. T. Coleridge). **3.** *Informal.* Charming; amusing; pleasing: *a darling hat.* [Middle English *dereling,* Old English *dēorling* : DEAR + -LING (diminutive).]

Dar·ling (dárling). River in New South Wales, in southeast Australia. It flows 2 739 kilometres (1,702 miles) from the Great Dividing Range to join the Murray river.

Darling, Grace (Horsley) (1815–42). Daughter of the keeper of the Longstone lighthouse, Northumberland, who braved the sea in a small boat to help her father rescue four men and a woman shipwrecked off the Farne Islands in 1838.

Dar·ling·ton (dárlingtən). Town in County Durham in northeast England. The Stockton and Darlington Railway, the world's first public locomotive-drawn railway to carry both freight and passengers, opened in 1825.

Darm·stadt (dárm-stat ‖ *German* -shtat). City in Hessen in central Germany. In the 16th to 19th centuries it was the seat of the Hesse-Darmstadt royal house.

darn¹ (darn) *v.* **darned, darning, darns.** —*tr.* To mend by weaving thread or wool across a gap or hole. —*intr.* To mend or repair a hole or garment by darning.
~*n.* **1.** A hole repaired by darning. **2.** The act of darning. [Perhaps from obsolete *dern,* to hide, Old English *derne, dierne,* concealed, from Germanic.] —**darn·er** *n.*

darn² *interj. Informal.* Damn. Used euphemistically. —**darn** *adj. & adv.*

darned (darnd) *adj. Informal.* Damned. Used euphemistically and as an intensive: *a darned good player.* —**darned** *adv.*

dar·nel (dárn'l) *n.* Any of several grasses of the genus *Lolium,* native to Europe and Asia; especially, *L. tementulum.* [Middle English, akin to French dialect *darnelle†,* cockle.]

darning mushroom *n.* An object with a flattish, rounded end used to hold the shape of material being darned.

darning needle *n.* A long, large-eyed needle used in darning.

Darn·ley (dárnli), **Henry Stuart, Lord** (1545–67). Scottish earl, who was, by lineage, a possible successor to Elizabeth I of England. He married Mary, Queen of Scots, in 1565, chiefly to cement their joint claims to the throne. He became jealous of his wife's Italian secretary, Rizzio, and connived at his murder in 1566. Darnley himself was found murdered the following year, probably by Mary's lover, the Earl of Bothwell. His son by Mary became James VI of Scotland and the first Stuart king of England.

da·ro·gha (də-rǒ-gə, daa-, -gaa) *n.* In India, an overseer, manager, or governor. [Urdu.]

dar·shan (dárshaan) *n. Hinduism.* A spiritual feeling experienced in the presence of a holy or revered person. [Hindi, from Sanskrit *darśana,* view.]

dart¹ (dart) *n.* **1.** A slender, pointed missile, often having tail fins, to be thrown by the hand or shot, as from a blowgun. **2.** Anything like a dart in shape, use, or effect. **3.** *Zoology.* Any of various slender, pointed structures, such as an insect's sting. **4.** A rapid, sudden movement. **5.** In sewing, a tapered tuck to adjust the fit of a garment.
~*v.* **darted, darting, darts.** —*intr.* To move suddenly and swiftly. —*tr.* To throw or thrust suddenly or swiftly; shoot. [Middle English, from Old French, from Germanic *darōdhaz* (unattested), spear.]

dart² *n. Australian Informal.* A plan or scheme.

dart·board (dárt-bawrd ‖ -bŏrd) *n.* A circular board divided into numbered segments with a small circle (bull's eye) at the centre, used as the target in the game of darts.

dar·ter (dártər) *n.* **1.** One that moves suddenly and swiftly. **2.** Any of several long-necked, long-billed birds of the genus *Anhinga,* occurring in tropical and subtropical inland waters. Also called "snakebird". **3.** Any of various small, often brightly coloured freshwater fishes of the family Percidae, of eastern North America.

Dart·ford (dártfərd). Town in Kent on the southeast periphery of the London conurbation, England. The Dartford Tunnel under the river Thames connects the town with Purfleet, Essex.

dar·tle (dárt'l) *tr.v.* **-tled, -tling, -tles.** To thrust or shoot out repeatedly. [Frequentative of DART.]

Dart·moor (dárt-moor, -mawr). An expanse of high moorland in southwest Devon, England. Its many tors include High Willhays (621 metres; 2,038 feet), and there are ancient megalithic sites. Hardy ponies graze freely on the moor, which was made a national park in 1951. The prison at Princetown was built (1806–09) for French prisoners of war, and later housed American prisoners from the war 1812–14. Since 1850 it has held long-term civilian prisoners.

Dartmoor pony *n.* A pony of a breed originating in the Dartmoor region of England.

Dart·mouth (dártməth). Seaport on the Dart estuary in Devon, southwest England. Richard I's crusaders embarked there in 1190. In 1905, the Royal Naval College for naval cadets was opened.

darts (darts) *n. Used with a singular verb.* An indoor game in which darts are thrown at a target (a dartboard).

Dar·win (dár-win). Capital and seaport of Northern Territory, Australia. Founded as Palmerston (1869), it was renamed Port Darwin (1911). The modern city is an important stopover point on international air routes, and is the terminus of the transcontinental telegraph and Stuart Highway from Adelaide.

Darwin, Charles Robert (1809–82). British naturalist who revolutionised biological theory by putting forward his theory of evolution based on natural selection. His views, formed after his comprehensive observations of fossils and the diverse plant and animal life during his voyage (1831–36) round South America and the Pacific as naturalist on H.M.S. Beagle, were published in *On the Origin of Species* (1859). His conclusions conflicted with received Christian opinion on the creation of the world, and caused much controversy, especially where, as in his *The Descent of Man* (1871), evolutionary theories were applied to human origins.

Dar·win·ism (dár-win-iz'm) *n.* A theory of biological evolution developed by Charles Darwin and others. It states that species of plants and animals develop through **natural selection** *(see)* of variations that increase the organism's ability to survive and reproduce. —**Dar·win·ist** *adj. & n.* —**Dar·win·is·tic** (-istik) *adj.*

Darwin's finches *pl. n.* The finches of the subfamily Geospizinae, found only on the Galapagos Islands. Variations in their bill structure and feeding habits provided Charles Darwin with evidence to support his theory of evolution.

dash¹ (dash) *v.* **dashed, dashing, dashes.** —*tr.* **1.** To break or smash by striking violently. **2.** To hurl, knock, or thrust with sudden violence: *He was dashed to the ground.* **3.** To splash; bespatter. **4.** To write or execute hastily. Used with *off* or *down.* **5.** To destroy; frustrate: *His dreams were dashed.* **6.** To confound; abash: *She was dashed by the criticism.* **7.** To add an enlivening or altering element to; mix; adulterate: *"Some truth there was, but dash'd and brew'd with lies."* (John Dryden). —*intr.* **1.** To strike violently or with great force; smash. **2.** To move with haste; rush; race.
~*n.* **1.** A swift, violent blow or stroke. **2.** A splashing sound. **3.** A small amount of an added ingredient: *a dash of salt.* **4.** A quick stroke, as with a pencil or brush. **5.** A sudden movement; a rush. **6.** *Athletics.* A sprint. **7.** Spirited action or style; vigour; verve. **8.** A punctuation mark (—) used in writing and printing. See Usage note below. **9.** In Morse code and similar codes, the long sound or signal used in combination with the dot, a shorter sound, to represent letters or numbers. —**cut a dash.** To make a striking impression. [Middle English *daschen, dashen,* perhaps from Scandinavian, akin to Danish *daske,* to beat (imitative).]

Usage: The dash as a mark of punctuation has the following uses: 1. To set off a parenthetical clause: *Her face—or so it seemed to me—was never more radiant.* 2. To indicate a break in thought: *Then he ran—the fool.* 3. To mark an omission: *She doesn't give a d——.* 4. To mark a summing up: *Study and practice—this is the only solution.* 5. To do the work of a colon: *Ten were chosen—five girls and five boys.* In modern writing, the dash is not used in combination with the colon or comma. Indiscriminate use of the dash often leads to choppiness and confusion of expression.

dash² *Interj.* Damn. Used euphemistically.

dash³ *n. West African.* A tip or gratuity.

~*tr.v.* **dashed, dashing, dashes.** *West African.* To give a tip or gratuity to. [Probably from Fanti.]

dash·board (dásh-bawrd ‖ -bórd) *n.* A panel under the windscreen of a car, aircraft, or the like, containing indicator displays, compartments, and control instruments.

dashed (dasht) *adj. Informal.* Damned. Used euphemistically and as an intensive: *it's a dashed shame.* —**dashed** *adv.*

da·sheen (da-sheén) *n.* A plant, **taro** *(see).* [Perhaps alteration of French *de Chine,* of China.]

dash·er (dáshər) *n.* **1.** One that dashes. **2.** The plunger of a churn or ice-cream freezer. **3.** *Archaic. Informal.* A spirited person.

da·shi·ki (daa-sheéki, də-) *n.* A loose, often brightly coloured African tunic, usually worn by men. [Yoruba *danshiki.*]

dash·ing (dáshing) *adj.* **1.** Audacious and gallant; bold; spirited. **2.** Marked by showy elegance; splendid: *a dashing new coat.* —**dash·ing·ly** *adv.*

dash·pot (dásh-pot) *n.* A mechanical device for damping vibration in a machine, consisting of a piston moving in a cylinder of liquid.

dash·y (dáshi) *adj.* **-ier, -iest.** Stylishly showy; dashing.

das·sie (dássi) *n.* A mammal, the **hyrax** *(see).* [Afrikaans, diminutive of *das,* badger, hyrax, from Middle Dutch.]

das·tard (dáss-tərd, daáss-) *n.* A base, sneaking coward. [Middle English, perhaps from obsolete *dasart,* dull person, influenced by *dotard.*]

das·tard·ly (dáss-tərdli, daáss-) *adj.* Cowardly and mean-spirited; base. —**das·tard·li·ness** *n.*

das·y·ure (dássi-yoór) *n.* Any of various marsupial mammals of the family Dasyuridae, of Australia and adjacent regions, ranging in size and appearance from that of a mouse to that of a dog. See **Tasmanian devil.** [New Latin *Dasyurus* (genus), "hairy-tailed" : Greek *dasus,* hairy, shaggy + -UROUS.]

DAT (*often* dat). Digital audio tape.

da·ta (dáy-tə, daá- ‖ *U.S. also* dáttə) *pl.n. Singular* **da·tum** (dáy-təm, daá- ‖ *U.S. also* dáttəm). **1.** Information; especially, information organised for analysis or used as the basis for a decision. **2.** Numerical information in a form suitable for processing by computer. [Latin, plural of DATUM.]

Usage: Originally, data was used solely as the plural of *datum,* but it has increasingly come to be used as a singular, in such constructions as *the data is, this data, much data, two items of data.*

data base A store of information; especially, a large store from which information can be selected by computer. Also called "data bank".

data capture *n.* The process of converting data into a form in which it can be stored in or processed by a computer, as by keyboarding or optical character recognition (OCR).

data processing *n.* **1.** The preparation of information for processing by computers. **2.** The storing or processing of raw data by a computer. —**data processor** *n.*

da·ta·ry (dáytəri) *n., pl.* **-ries.** *Roman Catholic Church.* **1.** The duty, formerly an official office of the curia, of investigating the fitness of candidates for papal benefices. **2.** A cardinal assuming the duty of datary. [Medieval Latin *datārius,* official who dated all papal letters, from Late Latin *data* (time).]

date¹ (dayt) *n. Abbr.* **d. 1.** A particular point or period of time at which something happened or existed or is to happen. **2.** The time during which something lasts; duration. **3.** The time or historical period to which something belongs: *artefacts of a later date.* **4.** *Plural.* The years of a person's birth and death. **5.** The day of the month. **6.** An inscription or statement, as on a coin or letter, indicating when it was made or written. **7.** *Informal.* **a.** An appointment to meet, or a meeting or outing with, a partner for romantic purposes. **b.** *Chiefly U.S.* A person so met. —**to date.** Up to the present time; as yet.

~*v.* **dated, dating, dates.** —*tr.* **1.** To mark or supply (a letter, for example) with a date. **2.** To assign a date to; determine the date, occurrence, or origin of. **3.** To betray the age of. **4.** *Chiefly U.S. Informal.* **a.** To go on a date with. **b.** To go on dates regularly with. —*intr.* **1.** To have origin in a particular time in the past. Usually used with *back to* or *from*: *dates from 500 B.C.* **2.** To become old-fashioned. **3.** *Chiefly U.S. Informal.* To have social engagements with persons of the opposite sex. [Middle English, from Old French, from Medieval Latin *data,* "given", "issued" (used for Latin *datum* in the letter-dating formula, e.g. *datum Romae,* issued at Rome) from Latin *datus,* past participle of *dare,* to give.] —**dat·able, date·able** *adj.* —**date·less** *adj.* —**dat·er** *n.*

date² *n.* **1.** The sweet, oblong, edible fruit of the date palm containing a narrow, hard seed. **2.** The date palm. [Middle English, from Old French, from Old Provençal *datil,* from Latin *dactylus,* from Greek *daktulos,* "finger" (from the shape of the fruit). See **dactyl.**]

dat·ed (dáytid) *adj.* **1.** Marked with or displaying a date. **2.** Old-fashioned; antiquated; out-moded. —**dat·ed·ness** *n.*

date line *n. Sometimes capital* D, *capital* L. An imaginary line through the Pacific Ocean roughly corresponding to 180 degrees longitude, to the east of which, by international agreement, the calendar date is one day earlier than to the west. Called in full "International Date Line".

date-line (dáyt-līn) *n.* A phrase at the beginning of a newspaper or magazine article that gives the date and place of its origin.

date palm *n.* A palm tree, *Phoenix dactylifera,* of tropical and sub-tropical areas, having feather-like leaves and bearing clusters of dates.

date stamp *n.* A device with adjustable numerals and letters for marking a date on documents, goods, and other objects.

date-stamp (dáyt-stamp) *tr.v.* **-stamped, -stamping, -stamps.** To mark a date on with a date stamp.

da·tive (dáytiv) *n.* **1.** The grammatical case in certain Indo-European languages, such as Greek or Russian, that denotes the indirect object of a verb and the object of any of certain verbs and prepositions. **2.** A form or construction in this case.

~*adj.* Also **da·ti·val.** Designating, pertaining to, or inflected in the dative. [Middle English *datif,* from Latin (*cāsus*) *datīvus,* "(case) of giving" (translation of Greek *ptōsis dotikē*), from *dare,* to give.] —**da·tive·ly** *adv.*

dative bond *n. Chemistry.* A **coordinate bond** *(see).*

da·to (daátō) *n., pl.* **-tos.** Also **dat·to** (dáttō). **1.** The chief of a Muslim Moro tribe in the Philippines. **2.** The head man of a barrio or Malay tribe. [Spanish *dato,* from Tagalog *datò,* from Malay *dato',* "grandfather".]

da·tum (dáy-təm, daá- ‖ *U.S. also* dá-) *n., pl.* **-ta** (-tə) or **-tums** (for sense 3). **1.** An assumed, given, measured, or otherwise determined single fact or proposition used to draw a conclusion or make a decision; a single piece of information. **2.** The real or assumed point from which any reckoning or scale begins. **3.** A point, line, or level used as a reference, as in surveying or geology. [Latin, "something given", from the neuter past participle of *dare,* to give.]

da·tu·ra (də-téwr-ə, da-, -tóor-) *n.* Any of several plants of the genus *Datura,* including the **thorn apple** *(see),* having large trumpet-shaped flowers. [New Latin *Datura,* from Hindi *dhatūrā,* from Sanskrit *dhattūrā*†.]

daub (dawb ‖ daáb) *v.* **daubed, daubing, daubs.** —*tr.* **1.** To cover, coat, or smear with an adhesive substance, such as plaster, mud, or grease. **2.** To apply paint to with hasty or crude strokes. —*intr.* To apply paint or colouring with crude, unskilful strokes.

~*n.* **1.** The act or a stroke of daubing. **2.** Any soft adhesive coating material that is daubed on, such as plaster or mud. See **wattle and daub. 3.** A crude or amateurish painting. [Middle English *dauben,* from Old French *dauber,* from Latin *dēalbāre,* to whitewash : *dē-,* completely + *albāre,* to whiten, from *albus,* white.] —**daub·er** *n.* —**daub·er·y** (-əri) *n.* —**daub·ing·ly** *adv.*

daube (dōb) *n.* **1.** A method of cooking in which meat, usually beef, is braised in red wine. **2.** A stew so prepared. [French, from Spanish *doba* (unattested), from *dobar*†, to stew.]

Dau·bi·gny (dōbeen-yée), **Charles-François** (1817–78). French landscape painter whose delight in the fleeting effects of light in the 1850s strongly influenced the young Impressionists.

Dau·det (dōday, dō-dáy), **Alphonse** (1840–97). French novelist. He wrote *Lettres de mon moulin,* a collection of scenes from Provençal life in 1868. His novels include *le Petit Chose* (1868) and *Tartarin de Tarascon* (1872). His son, **Leon Daudet** (1867–1942), helped to found the royalist paper *Action Française.*

daugh·ter (dáwtər) *n. Abbr.* **d. 1.** A female child considered in relation to her parents. **2.** Any female descendant. **3.** A girl or woman attached to a country, organisation, or the like as a child is to a parent: *a daughter of the nation.* **4.** Anything personified or regarded as a female descendant: *regarded Japan as a daughter of Chinese civilisation.* Also used adjectively: *a daughter cell.* **5.** A term of address used to a girl or woman by an older man other than her father, especially a priest. **6.** *Physics & Chemistry.* A particle, nucleus, ion, or the like produced by the decay or breakdown of another entity (the parent). Also used adjectively: *a daughter nucleus.* [Middle English *doughter,* Old English *dohtor.*] —**daugh·ter·ly** *adj.*

daugh·ter-in-law (dáwtər-in-law) *n., pl.* **daughters-in-law** (dáwtərz-). The wife of one's son.

Daughters of the American Revolution *n. Abbr.* DAR, D.A.R. A society of women descended from American patriots of the Revolutionary War, organised in 1890.

Dau·mier (dōmi-ay, dōm-yáy), **Honoré** (1808–79). French caricaturist and painter. His lithographs in *La Caricature* and *Le Charivari* satirised French government and society.

daunt (dawnt ‖ daant) *tr.v.* **daunted, daunting, daunts. 1.** To intimidate. **2.** To discourage; dishearten. —See Synonyms at **dismay.** [Middle English *daunten,* from Old French *danter, donter,* from Latin *domitāre,* frequentative of *domāre,* to tame, subdue.] —**daunt·er** *n.* —**daunt·ing·ly** *adv.*

daunt·less (dáwnt-ləss, -liss ‖ daánt-) *adj.* Incapable of being intimidated or discouraged; fearless; bold. See Synonyms at **brave.** —**daunt·less·ly** *adv.* —**daunt·less·ness** *n.*

dau·phin (dáwfin, dō-faɴ, *French* dō-fáɴ) *n.* The eldest son of the king of France. Used as a title from 1349 to 1830. [French, from Old French *dalphin, dalfin,* DOLPHIN. This title (originally borne by the lords of Viennois, whose coat of arms bore three dolphins) was adopted by the French crown princes as a condition when the Viennois province of Dauphiné was ceded to the crown.]

dau·phin·e (dáw-feen, dō-, *French* dō-féen) *n.* Also **dau·phin·ess** (-iss, -ess). The wife of the dauphin.

Dau·phi·né (dōfee-náy). Region in southeast France, comprising the present départements of Drôme, Hautes-Alpes, and Isère. Before 1343 it was ruled by a count known as a dauphin. It was then sold to Charles of Valois the future Charles V of France. The king gave the province to his eldest son, and thereafter all eldest sons of the French kings inherited it with the title of dauphin.

dav·en·port (dávv'n-port ‖ -pōrt) *n.* **1.** *British.* A small writing desk with drawers and a hinged shelf to write on. **2.** *U.S.* A large sofa, often convertible into a bed. [After *Davenport,* name of the original manufacturer of the desk.]

David (dáyvid) (died *c.* 962 B.C.). King of Judah and Israel, who founded the Jewish royal dynasty at Jerusalem. He was born in Bethlehem and was acclaimed for his legendary boyhood feat of killing the Philistine giant, Goliath. Later outlawed by Saul, he seized the southern kingdom (Judah) on the king's death, and gradually subdued the north (Israel), uniting the Israelites. He was succeeded by his son, Solomon.

David I (1084–1153). King of Scotland (1124–1153). When Stephen took the English throne in 1135, David invaded northern England, but he was defeated at the Battle of the Standard (1138).

David II (1324–71). King of Scotland (1329–71). He succeeded his father Robert the Bruce at the age of five. At French instigation, David invaded England in 1346, but was defeated and remained a prisoner of the English king, Edward III, from 1346 to 1357.

Da·vid (da-véed), **Jacques Louis** (1748–1825). French painter and leading figure in the neoclassical movement. David welcomed the French revolution in 1789, and painted pictures including *The Oath of the Horatii* (1784) and *Death of Marat* (1793) to promote republican feeling. He was elected to the national convention 1792. He survived the downfall of his friend Robespierre, to become court painter to Napoleon in 1804. His style became more richly decorative in such paintings as *Napoleon crowning Josephine* (1805–07). With the fall of Napoleon, David was exiled and died in Brussels.

David, Saint (C.A.D. 520–601). Patron saint of Wales. He was the primate of the Celtic church in south Wales, and set up his seat of government at Mynyw (now St. David's). His feast day is March 1.

David, Star of. A symbol of Judaism, the **Magen David** *(see).*

Da·vies (dáy-viss, -veez), **Sir Peter Maxwell** (1934–). British composer. He founded and has written numerous works for the Fires of London ensemble, including *Le Jongleur de Notre Dame* (1978). Since moving to Orkney he has also composed works for performances by local children and for the Orkney festival.

Davies, W(illiam) H(enry) (1871–1940). British poet, a tramp, pedlar, and street entertainer in England and the United States. His first volume was *The Soul's Destroyer, and Other Poems* (1905) and his prose includes *The Autobiography of a Super Tramp* (1908).

da Vinci, Leonardo. See **Leonardo da Vinci.**

Da·vis (dáyviss), **Bette,** born Ruth Elizabeth Davies (1908–89). U.S. film actress. She made her screen debut in *The Man Who Played God* (1932) and twice won Oscars, for *Dangerous* (1935) and *Jezebel* (1938). She was acclaimed as an old and embittered former child star in *Whatever Happened to Baby Jane?* (1962).

Davis, Sir Colin Rex (1927–). British conductor. He is noted for his interpretations of Mozart and Tippett, and his promotion of the music of Berlioz. He was knighted in 1980.

Davis, Jefferson (1808–89). President of the Confederate states during the American Civil War (1861–65). A graduate of West Point Military Academy, he served seven years (1828–35) as a soldier before taking up cotton farming in Mississippi. He was state senator (1847–51). Back in the senate in 1857, he led the Southern Democrats in upholding slavery and state rights against federal interference. After the election of Abraham Lincoln (1860), he withdrew his state from the Union (1861). As president of the Southern confederacy, Davis ordered the offensive which resulted in disaster at Gettysburg (1863). He was captured at Irwinville, Georgia (May 1865), and was imprisoned for two years on a charge of treason.

Davis, Miles (Dewey) (1926–91). U.S. jazz trumpeter and composer. After playing with Charlie Parker in the 1940s he became one of the most influential musicians in jazz. Important recordings include *Birth of the Cool* (1949–50) and *Bitches Brew* (1970).

Davis Cup *n.* **1.** A trophy awarded to the nation whose team is the winner of the annual International Lawn Tennis Championship for men. **2.** The competition held for this cup. [After Dwight F. *Davis* (1879-1945), American civic leader and government official who donated the trophy in 1900.]

dav·it (dávv-it, dáyv-) *n.* Any of various small cranes, usually one of a pair and made of shaped steel tubing, used on ships to hoist lifeboats, anchors, and cargo. [Middle English *daviot,* from Old French *daviot, daviet,* diminutive of the name *David,* also the name given to a carpenter's tool.]

Dav·itt (dávvit), **Michael** (1846–1906). Irish nationalist politician. He joined the Fenian brotherhood in 1865. In 1870 he was arrested for treason and spent seven years in prison. In 1895, after two further periods of imprisonment, he was elected to parliament.

Da·vos (daa-vóss). *Romansch* **Tavau.** An Alpine town in the Graubünden canton in east Switzerland. It is a tourist centre, especially for winter sports.

Da·vy (dáyvi), **Sir Humphry** (1778–1829). British chemist, and inventor of the Davy miner's safety lamp. He joined the Royal Institution in London and became a pioneer of electrochemistry. Davy was appointed president of the Royal Society (1820), and gave much encouragement to Michael Faraday.

Davy Jones *n.* The spirit of the sea. [Perhaps *Davy,* nickname for David + *Jones,* alteration of *Jonas, Jonah* (the prophet, with allusion to the whale in Jonah 1:17).]

Davy Jones's locker *n.* The bottom of the sea, especially as the grave of all who perish at sea.

Davy lamp *n.* An early safety oil lamp having a gauze surrounding the flame to prevent ignition of gas, used by coal miners. Also

called "davy". [Invented by Sir Humphry DAVY.]

daw (daw) *n. Archaic & Poetic.* A bird, the **jackdaw** *(see).* [Middle English *dawe,* probably from Old English *dāwe* (unattested), from West Germanic *dǣgw-* (unattested).]

daw·dle (dáwd'l) *v.* **-dled, -dling, -dles.** —*intr.* **1.** To move slowly; loiter; lag behind. **2.** To waste time by trifling; linger. —*tr.* To waste (time) in this manner. Usually used with *away: dawdling away the hours.* [17th century : probably of dialect origin.] —**daw·dler** (dáwdlər) *n.* —**daw·dling·ly** *adv.*

Dawes (dawz), **Charles G(ates)** (1865–1951). U.S. financier and statesman. His report, known as the Dawes Plan (1924), provided a system for Germany to pay reparations for World War I damage. The plan helped the reconstruction of the German economy, and Dawes received the Nobel peace prize (1925). He became Republican vice-president under Calvin Coolidge (1925–29).

dawn (dawn) *n.* **1.** The time each morning when daylight first appears. **2.** A first appearance; a beginning: *the dawn of history.* ~*intr.v.* **dawned, dawning, dawns. 1.** To begin to become light in the morning. **2.** To begin to appear or develop; emerge. **3.** To begin to be perceived or understood. Used with *on* or *upon: "the suspicion dawning on him that he was not a welcome visitor"* (Somerset Maugham). [Middle English *daunen,* probably back-formation from *dauninge,* daybreak, alteration of *dauinge,* Old English *dagung,* from *dagian,* to dawn.]

dawn chorus *n.* The singing of birds when they awaken at first light. Preceded by *the.*

dawn raid *n.* A swift purchase in the stock market of a large shareholding in a company, as by a rival company or an investor planning a takeover.

dawn redwood *n.* A Chinese deciduous coniferous tree, *Metasequoia glyptostroboides,* discovered as an extant species after having long been considered extinct. It is often grown for ornament.

Daw·son (dáwss'n). A town in Yukon Territory, northwest Canada. It was founded (1896) during the Klondike gold rush, and was the territory's capital (1898–1951).

day (day) *n. Abbr.* **d 1. a.** The period of light between dawn and nightfall; the interval from sunrise to sunset. **b.** The light of day; daylight. **2.** The 24-hour period during which the earth completes one rotation on its axis. See **mean solar day, sidereal day. 3.** The portion of a day devoted to work: *the eight-hour day.* **4.** A day reserved for a certain activity: *a day of rest.* **5.** *Usually capital* D. A particular day connected with a special event or observance: *Mother's Day.* **6. a.** *Often plural.* One's lifetime. **b.** The period of activity or prominence in one's lifetime: *a writer who has had his day.* **c.** A period of opportunity: *Every dog has his day.* **7. a.** *Often plural.* A period of time; an age; an era: *in Napoleon's day; in days of old.* **b.** A day considered as a point in time: *same day.* **8.** A unit of distance travelled in an ordinary day's journey. **9.** The contest or issue at hand: *carry the day.* **10.** *Astronomy.* The period during which a heavenly body completes one turn on its axis. —**call it a day.** *Informal.* **1.** To stop one's work or activity for the day. **2.** To terminate after any period of time. —**day after day.** Continuously; for many days. —**day in, day out.** Every day without fail; continuously. —**late in the day.** At a regrettably late stage. [Middle English *dai, day,* Old English *dæg, from Germanic.*]

Dayak. Variant of **Dyak.**

Da·yan (dī-án, -yán), **Moshe** (1915–81). Israeli general and politician. He was chief of the general staff (1953–58), and minister of defence (1967, 1969–74). He became a national hero for directing Israel's victory in the Six Day War (1967). In 1977 he was made foreign minister, resigning two years later.

day bed *n.* A couch or sofa that can be used as a bed, especially during the day.

day blindness *n. Pathology.* **Hemeralopia** *(see).*

day·book (dáy-bŏŏk ‖ -bōōk) *n.* **1.** *Abbr.* **D.B.** Bookkeeping. A book in which daily transactions are recorded. **2.** A diary.

day·boy (dáy-boy) *n. British.* A schoolboy who attends a boarding school but lives at home. Compare **boarder.**

day·break (dáy-brayk) *n.* Dawn.

day care *n.* The providing of daytime supervision, training, or the like, for young children or for the elderly or handicapped.

day-care (dáy-kair) *adj.* Of, relating to, or providing day care: *a day-care centre.*

day·dream (dáy-dreem) *n.* A dreamlike musing or fantasy while awake; idle reverie, especially of the fulfilment of wishes or hopes. ~*intr.v.* **daydreamed** or **-dreamt** (-dremt), **-dreaming, -dreams.** To have daydreams. —**day·dream·er** *n.*

day-flow·er (dáy-flowr) *n.* Any of various plants of the genus *Commelina,* having blue or purplish flowers that wilt quickly.

day·fly (dáy-flī) *n., pl.* **-flies.** An insect, the **mayfly** *(see).*

day·girl (dáy-gurl) *n. British.* A schoolgirl who attends a boarding school but lives at home. Compare **boarder.**

Day-Glo *n.* A trademark for a type of fluorescent paint that glows brightly in daylight.

day hospital *n.* A hospital as for the elderly or mentally ill, in which patients receive medical supervision but do not stay overnight.

day labour *n.* Labour hired and paid by the day. —**day labourer** *n.*

Day Lew·is (dáy lóō-iss ‖ léw-), **Cecil** (1904–72). British poet and author. In *Revolution in Writing* (1935), he attempted to reconcile Marxism with the liberal artistic tradition. He also wrote detective stories under the pseudonym of Nicholas Blake. He was appointed poet laureate (1968).

day·light (dáy-līt) *n.* **1.** The light of day; direct light of the sun.

2. a. Daybreak. **b.** Daytime. **3.** Exposure to public notice. **4.** *Plural. Slang.* Sense; wits: *scared the living daylights out of him.* —see **daylight. 1.** To approach the end of a difficult endeavour. **2.** To begin to understand what was formerly obscure.

daylight robbery *n. Informal.* Blatant swindling or overcharging.

day·light-sav·ing time (dáylĭt-sáyving) *n. Abbr.* **DST, D.S.T.** Time during which clocks are set one hour or more ahead of standard time to provide more daylight at the end of the working day during late spring, summer, and early autumn. See **British Summer Time.**

day lily *n.* **1.** Any of various plants of the genus *Hemerocallis,* native to Eurasia, having sword-shaped leaves and yellow to red funnel-shaped blooms. Also called "hemerocallis". **2.** The **plantain lily** *(see).*

day·long (dáy-long ‖ -lawng) *adj.* Lasting the whole day. ∼*adv.* Through the whole day.

day-neutral (dáy-néwtrəl ‖ -nōōtrəl) *adj.* Of or designating plants whose ability to flower is not affected by the length of the day.

day nursery *n.* A nursery providing daytime care for children of preschool age, especially while their mothers are at work.

Day of Atonement *n.* Yom Kippur *(see).*

Day of Judgment *n.* The **Judgment Day** *(see).*

day release *n. British.* A system whereby a worker is given regular, paid time off to attend an educational course. Compare **block release.**

day return *n. British.* A ticket, usually at a reduced fare, used when travelling to a place and back again on the same day.

day room *n.* A communal sitting room used for recreation, especially in institutions such as schools, hospitals, and prisons.

day school *n.* **1.** A private or state school for pupils living at home. Compare **boarding school. 2.** A school that holds classes during the day, as opposed to the evening, or on weekdays, as opposed to Sunday.

days of grace *pl. n.* Extra days, usually three, allowed for payment of a note or bill after it has fallen due. [Translation of Latin *diēs grātiae.*]

day·spring (dáy-spring) *n. Poetic.* The early dawn; daybreak.

day·star (dáy-staar) *n.* **1.** The morning star. **2.** *Poetic.* The Sun.

day·time (dáy-tīm) *n.* The time between dawn and dark; day. ∼*adj.* During the day.

day-to-day (dáy-tə-dáy) *adj.* **1.** Occurring daily or on successive days. **2.** Routine or regular; mundane.

Day·ton (dáyt'n). A city in the United States on the Miami river in Ohio. It was the home of the aircraft pioneers Orville and Wilbur Wright.

Day·to·na Beach (day-tṓnə béech). An Atlantic coastal city in Florida, United States. It is a beach resort, and its hard sands have been the venue for speed trials since 1903. The city is also the site of an international speedway circuit.

day-trip (dáy-tríp) *n.* An excursion to a place and back again completed in one day. —**day-tripper** *n.*

daze (dayz) *tr.v.* **dazed, dazing, dazes. 1.** To stun, as with a heavy blow or shock; stupefy. **2.** To dazzle, as with strong light. ∼*n.* A stunned or bewildered condition: *wandering about in a daze.* [Middle English *dasen,* from Old Norse *dasa* (attested in the reflexive form *dasask,* to become weary).] —**daz·ed·ly** (-idli) *adv.*

daz·zle (dázz'l) *v.* **-zled, -zling, -zles.** —*tr.* **1.** To dim the vision of; blind temporarily with intense light. **2.** To bewilder, amaze, impress or overwhelm with some spectacular display. —*intr.* **1.** To inspire admiration or wonder: *dazzling wit and repartee.* **2.** *Archaic.* To become blinded: *"thy sight is young,/ And thou shalt read when mine begin to dazzle"* (Shakespeare). ∼*n.* The act or quality of dazzling: *"the dazzle of league after league of featureless sand"* (T.E. Lawrence). [Frequentative of DAZE.] —**daz·zler** (dázzlər) *n.* —**daz·zling·ly** *adv.*

dB, db decibel.

D.B. daybook.

D.B.E. Dame Commander of the Order of the British Empire.

D.Bib. Douay Bible.

dbl. double.

dc, DC direct current.

D.C. **1.** *Music.* da capo. **2.** District of Columbia. **3.** District Commissioner.

D.C.B. Dame Commander of the Order of the Bath.

D.C.L. Doctor of Civil Law.

D.C.M. Distinguished Conduct Medal.

D.C.M.G. Dame Commander of the Order of St. Michael and St. George.

D.C.V.O. Dame Commander of the Royal Victorian Order.

D.D. **1.** demand draft. **2.** dishonourable discharge. **3.** Doctor of Divinity. [Latin *Divinitatis Doctor*].

D-Day (dée-day) *n.* The unnamed day on which a military offensive or other operation is to be launched; specifically, June 6, 1944, the day on which the Allied forces invaded France during World War II. [*D* (abbreviation for DAY) + DAY.]

D.D.R. Deutsche Demokratische Republik (East Germany).

D.D.S., D.D.Sc. Doctor of Dental Science; Doctor of Dental Surgery.

DDT *n.* A colourless contact insecticide, $(ClC_6H_4)_2CHCCl_3$, toxic to man and animals when swallowed or absorbed through the skin. [From *di*chloro*di*phenyltrichloroethane.]

de, De (də) *prep. French.* Of; from. Used in personal names, originally to show place of origin: *Guy de Maupassant.* [French, from Latin *dē,* from.]

de– *prefix.* Indicates: **1.** Reversal or undoing; for example, **decode, denationalise. 2.** Removal; for example, **decapitate, delouse. 3.** Degradation, reduction; for example, **debase, demean. *Note:*** Many compounds other than those entered here may be formed with *de*-. In forming compounds, *de*- is normally joined with the following element without space or hyphen: *decarbonise.* However, if the second element begins with *e,* it is separated with a hyphen: *de-escalate.* It is also preferable to use the hyphen if the compound brings together three or more vowels: *de-aerate.* In the rare case that the second element begins with a capital letter, it is separated with a hyphen: *de-Americanise.* [In borrowed Latin and French compounds, Latin *dē-* (French *dé-,* Old French *des-*) indicates: **1.** Down, downwards, as in **declivity, deject. 2.** Away, away from, off, as in **decide, deprecate. 3.** Reversal, undoing, as in **decrease, destroy. 4.** Removal, riddance, as in **defoliate, decapitate. 5.** Completely, carefully, intensively, as in **denominate, declare. 6.** Pejorative sense, as in **deride, deceive.** Latin *dē-,* from.]

de·ac·ces·sion (dée-ak-sésh'n) *v.* **-sioned, -sioning, -sions.** *Chiefly U.S.* —*tr.* To remove (an article) from the collection in a museum or gallery, and sell it off in order to raise funds. —*intr.* To remove an article or articles in this way.

dea·con (deékən) *n.* **1.** In the Anglican, Greek Orthodox, and Roman Catholic churches, a clergy member ranking just below a priest. **2.** In various other Christian churches, a lay person who assists the minister in various functions. ∼*tr.v.* **deaconed, -coning, -cons.** *U.S. Informal.* **1.** To read aloud lines or verses of (a hymn) to help the congregation in singing. **2.** To arrange (fruit and vegetables) for sale so that inferior items are concealed. [Middle English *dek(e)n,* Old English *dīacon,* from Late Latin *diāconus,* from Greek *diakonos,* "servant".] —**dea·con·ship** *n.*

dea·con·ess (deékən-iss, -ess) *n.* A woman appointed or elected to serve as an assistant in a church.

dea·con·ry (deékənri) *n., pl.* **-ries. 1.** The office or position of a deacon. **2.** Deacons collectively.

de·ac·ti·vate (dée-ák-ti-vayt) *tr.v.* **-vated, -vating, -vates. 1.** To render inactive; especially, to make (a bomb or radioactive sample, for example) harmless or ineffective. **2.** *U.S. Military.* To remove from active status. —**de·acti·va·tion** (-váysh'n) *n.*

dead (ded) *adj.* Sometimes **deader, deadest. 1.** No longer alive; lifeless. Compare **brain dead. 2.** Not having the capacity to live; inanimate: *as dead as a stone.* **3. a.** Lacking feeling; numb: *My leg's gone dead.* **b.** Lacking sensitivity; unresponsive: *dead to all our entreaties.* **4.** No longer in existence, use, force, or operation: *a dead language.* **5.** Devoid of animation, interest, or excitement. **6.** Not productive; idle: *dead capital.* **7.** *Informal.* Weary and worn-out; exhausted. **8.** Without brightness or lustre. Said of colours. **9.** Without resonance. Said of sounds. **10.** Extinguished: *a dead match.* **11.** Lacking elasticity or resilience. **12.** Suggestive of the finality or absoluteness of death, especially: **a.** Abrupt: *dead stop.* **b.** Complete; utter: *dead silence.* **c.** Exact; unerring: *the dead centre.* **13.** *Sports.* Out of play. Said of a ball. **14. a.** Lacking connection to a source of electric current or voltage. **b.** Drained of electric charge; discharged. Said of a battery. **15.** *Printing.* No longer needed for use. Said of type. **16.** *Informal.* Empty or finished with: *a dead glass.* ∼*n.* The period of greatest intensity, as of cold or darkness: *the dead of winter.* ∼*adv.* **1.** Absolutely; altogether. **2.** Directly; exactly: *dead ahead.* —**dead on.** Exactly right. [Middle English *ded,* Old English *dēad,* from Germanic.] —**dead·ness** *n.*

Synonyms: *dead, deceased, departed, lifeless, inanimate.*

dead air *n.* Unprogrammed silence during air time.

dead-air space (déd-air) *n.* An unventilated space.

dead-and-alive (dédd'n-ə-lív) *adj. British Informal.* Dull; quiet: *This place is a dead-and-alive hole.*

dead ball line *n.* In Rugby football, a line behind the goal line, beyond which the ball is out of play (dead).

dead-beat (déd-beet) *n.* **1.** *Informal.* Someone with no money; a destitute person. **2.** A lazy or lethargic person; a loafer. **3.** *U.S.* A person who does not pay his debts. ∼*adj. Informal.* Completely exhausted. [Probably DEAD (completely) + BEAT (exhausted).]

dead·beat (déd-beet) *adj.* **1.** *Physics.* Lacking recoil, as the mechanism of a clock may be. **2.** Stopping without oscillation. [DEAD + BEAT (oscillation).]

dead centre *n.* Either of two points in the path of a moving crank and connecting rod at the ends of a stroke when the two lie in a straight line. Also called "dead point".

dead duck *n. Slang.* A failure or a person or thing doomed to failure.

dead·en (dédd'n) *v.* **-ened, -ening, -ens.** —*tr.* **1.** To render less sensitive, intense, or vigorous: *pills to deaden the pain.* **2.** To make soundproof. **3.** To make less colourful. —*intr.* To become dead or as if dead. —**dead·en·er** *n.*

dead end *n.* **1.** An end of a passage, such as a street or pipe, that affords no outlet or exit. **2.** Any point beyond which no movement or progress can be made; an impasse.

dead-end (déd-end, -énd) *adj.* **1.** Affording no progress or prospects: *a dead-end job.* **2.** Having no prospects or hopes for future success: *dead-end kids.*

dead·en·ing (dédd'ning) *n.* Material used for soundproofing.

dead·eye (dĕd-ī) n. **1.** Nautical. A flat hardwood disc with a grooved perimeter, pierced by three holes through which the lanyards are passed, used to fasten the shrouds. **2.** Chiefly U.S. Slang. An expert marksman. [Sense 1 : perhaps because the holes on the disc resemble the empty sockets in a human skull.]

dead·fall (dĕd-fawl) n. U.S. A trap for large animals, in which a heavy weight is arranged to fall on and kill or disable the prey.

dead ground n. Land obscured from view by an intervening landform or landforms.

dead hand n. **1.** Law. Mortmain (see). **2.** A persisting oppressive influence. [Middle English dede hond, translation of Old French mortemain, MORTMAIN.]

dead·head¹, dead-head (dĕd-hĕd, -hed) v. British. -headed, -heading, -heads. —tr. To remove the dead flowers from (a plant) to tidy it or prevent seeding. —intr. To remove the dead flowers from a plant. —**dead·head·ing** n.

dead·head² (dĕd-hed) n. **1.** A vehicle, such as a railway carriage or aeroplane, carrying no passengers or freight. **2.** A dull-witted or sluggish person. **3.** U.S. Informal. A person who uses a free ticket for admittance, accommodation, or entertainment.
~tr.v. **deadheaded, -heading, -heads.** U.S. Informal. To drive (a train, bus, or lorry) carrying no passengers or freight.
~adv. U.S. Informal. Without passengers or freight; empty.

dead heart n. Australian. The arid interior of Australia.

dead heat n. A race in which two or more contestants finish at the same time; a tie.

dead letter n. **1.** An unclaimed or undelivered letter that after a period of time is destroyed or returned to the sender by the post office. **2.** A law or directive still formally in effect but no longer valid or enforced.

dead·light (dĕd-līt) n. **1.** Nautical. **a.** A strong shutter or plate fastened over a ship's porthole or cabin window in stormy weather. **b.** A thick window set in a ship's side or deck. **2.** A skylight made so that it cannot be opened.

dead·line (dĕd-līn) n. **1.** A time limit, as for payment of a debt or completion of an assignment. **2.** The time after which copy for a newspaper, periodical, or the like will not be accepted.

dead load n. Engineering. The fixed weight of a structure or piece of equipment, such as a bridge on its supports. Also called "dead weight". Compare **live load.**

dead·lock (dĕd-lok) n. **1.** A stoppage or standstill resulting from the opposition of two unrelenting forces. **2.** A door lock that combines the features of a **Yale lock** and a **mortise lock** (both of which see). ~v. **deadlocked, -locking, -locks.** —tr. To bring to a deadlock. —intr. To come to a deadlock.

dead loss n. Informal. A useless or ineffectual person, thing, or activity.

dead·ly (dĕddli) adj. **-lier, -liest. 1.** Causing or tending to cause death; lethal. **2.** Suggestive of death; deathly: deadly white. **3.** Implacable; mortal: deadly enemies. **4.** Destructive in effect. **5.** Absolute; unqualified: deadly accuracy. **5.** Informal. Extremely dull and boring: How deadly! —See Synonyms at **fatal.**
~adv. **1.** So as to suggest death. **2.** To an extreme: deadly earnest. —**dead·li·ness** n.

deadly nightshade n. A Eurasian plant, Atropa belladonna, having purple or greenish bell-shaped flowers and extremely poisonous black berries. Also called "belladona".

deadly sins pl. n. **seven deadly sins.**

dead·man's fingers (dĕd-manz) n. Used with a singular verb. **1.** A soft coral, Alcyonium digitatum, consisting of a colony of flesh-pink, finger-like polyps. **2.** A fungus, **devil's fingers** (see).

dead man's handle n. British. A safety feature fitted to a train or other vehicle. It is used to control speed and, when not depressed, it will bring the vehicle to a stop.

dead march n. A slow, solemn march played for a funeral.

dead nettle n. Any of several weedy plants of the genus Lamium, native to the Old World, having nettle-like leaves and clusters of small purplish, white, or yellow flowers. [Because it does not sting.]

dead·pan (dĕd-pan, -pán) adj. Characterised by a blank or expressionless face or manner. —**dead·pan** adv.

dead point n. Machinery. **Dead centre** (see).

dead reckoning n. **1.** Navigation. A method of determining the position of an aircraft or ship without external aids, such as astronomical observations or radio, by calculating from the direction and speed of travel from a known point. **2.** Calculation based on inference or guesswork.

Dead Sea. Arabic **Bah·ret Lut.** Lake at the outlet of the River Jordan partitioned between Israel and Jordan to the east. It is the lowest point on the Earth's surface, its surface being 396 metres (1,299 feet) below sea level. The surface waters have a salt content nearly nine times the average salinity of the ocean, allowing humans to float like corks. The sea contains no living things, has no outflow, its inflow being lost through evaporation.

Dead Sea Scrolls pl.n. A number of scrolls, dated from about 250 B.C. to about A.D. 70, containing Hebrew and Aramaic Scriptural texts and the liturgical writings of an ascetic community. The first scrolls were found in 1947 in caves near the Dead Sea.

dead-set (dĕd-sĕt) adj. Determined; resolved: dead-set on winning.

dead weight n. **1.** The unrelieved weight of a heavy, motionless mass. **2.** An oppressive burden or difficulty affording no advantage whatever. **3.** Engineering. A **dead load** (see).

dead wood n. **1.** Dead branches or wood on a tree or shrub. **2.** Anything burdensome or superfluous. **3.** Useless or superfluous

personnel, as in a company. **4.** Nautical. The vertical planking between the keel of a vessel and the sternpost, serving merely as a reinforcement.

deaf (def) adj. **deafer, deafest. 1.** Partially or completely incapable of hearing. **2.** Unwilling or refusing to listen; heedless. [Middle English de(a)f, Old English dēaf, from Germanic.] —**deaf·ly** adv. —**deaf·ness** n.

deaf-aid (déf-ayd) n. A hearing aid (see).

deaf·en (déff'n) tr.v. **-ened, -ening, -ens. 1.** To make deaf, especially momentarily, by a loud noise. **2.** To make soundproof.

deaf·en·ing (déff'n-ing) adj. Stunning to the ears; resounding loud. —**deaf·en·ing·ly** adv.

deaf-mute (déf-méwt) n. Also **deaf mute.** A person who can neither speak nor hear.
~adj. Unable to speak or hear.

Dea·kin (deékin), **Alfred** (1857–1919). Australian prime minister (1903–04, 1905–08, and 1909–10). He was Australia's first attorney-general when the Commonwealth of Australia was formed (1901), and became Australia's second prime minister (1903).

deal¹ (deel) v. **dealt** (delt), **dealing, deals.** —tr. **1.** To give to someone as a share; apportion. **2.** To distribute or pass out among several people. **3.** To administer; deliver (a blow, for example). **4.** In card games: **a.** To distribute (playing cards) among players. **b.** To give (a specific card) to a player while so distributing. —intr. **1.** To be occupied or concerned; treat. Used with in or with: a book dealing with the Middle Ages. **2.** To behave in a specified way towards another or others; have transactions. Used with with: deal honestly with competitors. **3.** To take action. Used with with: The committee will deal with this complaint. **4.** To do business; trade: dealing in diamonds. **5.** In card games, to distribute playing cards. —See Synonyms at **distribute.**
~n. **1.** The act or a round of apportioning or distributing. **2.** In card games: **a.** The distribution of the playing cards. **b.** The cards so distributed; a hand. **c.** The right or turn of a player to distribute the cards. **d.** The playing of one hand. **3.** An indefinite quantity, extent, or degree: a great deal of experience. **4.** An agreement arranged secretly, as in business or politics. **5.** Informal. Any agreement or business transaction. **6.** Informal. An exchange or bargain. **7.** Informal. Treatment received, especially as the result of an agreement: a raw deal. **8.** A programme, such as a political platform, that offers some specified treatment for those participating; especially, President Roosevelt's **New Deal** (see). [Middle English delen, Old English dǣlan, to divide, distribute, from Germanic.]

deal² n. **1.** A board of fir, pine, or similar wood cut to standard dimensions. **2.** Such boards or planks collectively. **3.** Fir, pine, or similar wood. [Middle English dele, from Middle Low German or Middle Dutch dele.]

Deal (deel). Channel port in Kent, southeast England. In the 17th century it became one of the Cinque Ports. Its castle was built by Henry VIII (1539).

deal·er (deélər) n. **1.** A person or group engaged in buying and selling: a used car dealer. **2.** In card games, the person who distributes the cards. **3.** Informal. One who deals in illegal drugs.

deal·fish (deél-fish) n., pl. **-fishes** or collectively **dealfish.** A marine fish, Trachipterus arcticus, of Atlantic waters, resembling the ribbonfishes. [DEAL (plank), from its long, thin body + FISH.]

deal·ing (deéling) n. **1.** Usually plural. Transactions or relations with others, usually in business. **2.** Method or manner of conduct in relation to others; treatment: honest dealing.

de·am·i·nate (dée-ámm-i-nayt) tr.v. **-nated, -nating, -nates.** Also **de·am·i·nise, de·am·i·nize** (-nīz), **-nised, -nising, -nises.** To remove an amino group from (an organic compound, especially an amino acid). —**de·am·i·na·tion** (-náysh'n), **de·am·i·ni·sa·tion** (-nī-záysh'n ǁ U.S. -ni-) n.

dean¹ (deen) n. **1. a.** An administrative officer in charge of a college, faculty, or division in a university. **b.** In some universities and colleges, a member of staff who counsels students and supervises the enforcement of rules. **2.** Ecclesiastical. The head of the chapter of canons governing a cathedral or collegiate church. **3.** Chiefly British. A priest appointed to oversee a group of parishes within a diocese. Also called "rural dean". **4.** Roman Catholic Church. **a.** A high-ranking official, usually a cardinal, who runs a department in the Vatican. **b.** The head of the college of cardinals. **5.** The senior member of any body. [Middle English deen, den, from Anglo-French, from Late Latin decānus, "(one) set over ten", from Greek dekanos, from deka, ten.] —**dean·ship** n.

dean². A valley. See **dene.**

Dean, Forest of (deen). Woodland region of Gloucestershire in the west of England. Formerly an ancient royal hunting preserve, it became the first of Britain's National Forest Parks (1938).

Dean, James (Byron) (1931–55). U.S. film actor. He was a youth hero of the rock'n'roll era, whose screen image was one of moody rebellion. His films include East of Eden (1955) and Rebel Without a Cause (1955). He was killed in a car crash.

dean·er·y (deénəri) n., pl. **-ies. 1.** The office, jurisdiction, or authority of a dean. **2.** A dean's official residence.

dear (deer) adj. **dearer, dearest. 1.** Beloved; loved; precious. **2.** Highly esteemed or regarded. Used as a conventional form of address at the beginning of a letter: Dear Sir. **3. a.** Expensive; costly. **b.** Charging high prices. **4.** Earnest; ardent: fulfilled his dearest wishes. **5. a.** Sweet; lovely: a dear little kitten. **b.** Obsolete. Noble; worthy. —See Synonyms at **costly.**

~*n.* A greatly loved person; a darling. Often used as a term of affectionate address: *my dear.*

~*adv.* **1.** Fondly or affectionately. **2.** At a high cost: *Her mistake will cost her dear.*

~*interj.* Used as a polite exclamation, as of dismay: *Oh dear; dear me.* [Middle English *dere*, Old English *dēore*, from Germanic *deur-jaz* (unattested), worthy, costly, dear.] —**dear·ness** *n.*

Dear John letter *n. Informal.* A letter from a woman to her fiancé or lover informing him that their relationship is ended.

dear·ly (déerli) *adv.* **1.** With deep affection; fondly. **2.** At great cost or price. **3.** Earnestly; ardently.

dearth (derth) *n.* **1.** Scarcity; lack; paucity. **2.** Shortage of food; famine. [Middle English *dearth(e)*, costliness, scarcity, from *dere*, DEAR (expensive).]

dear·y, dear·ie (déer-i) *n., pl.* **-ies.** *Informal.* Darling; dear. Used as a term of address.

death (deth) *n.* **1. a.** The act of dying; termination of life. See **brain death. b.** An instance of dying or killing: *a number of deaths on the road.* **2.** The state of being dead. **3.** *Often capital* **D.** A personification of the destroyer of life, usually represented as a skeleton holding a scythe. **4.** Termination; extinction: *the death of imperialism.* **5.** The cause of dying. **6.** A manner of dying: *a hero's death.* **7.** Loss or absence of spiritual life. **8.** *Law.* Civil death *(see).* —**be the death of (someone).** To irritate or distress someone to an intolerable degree. —**catch one's death (of cold).** *Informal.* To catch a bad cold. —**do** or **put to death.** To kill or execute. —**like death warmed up.** Very ill, or looking very ill. —**to death.** To an intolerable degree: *worried to death.* [Middle English *de(e)th*, Old English *dēath*, from Germanic.]

death adder *n.* A venomous Australian snake, *Acanthophis antarcticus*, resembling an adder.

death·bed (déth-bed) *n.* **1.** The bed on which a person dies. **2.** The last hours before death. Also used adjectivally: *a deathbed plea.*

death·blow (déth-blō) *n.* **1.** A blow or stroke that causes death. **2.** Any fatal event or occurrence.

death camp *n.* An **extermination camp** *(see).*

death cap *n.* A deadly poisonous, usually white mushroom, *Amanita phalloides*, having white gills and a prominent bulbous base. Also called "death angel".

death cell *n.* A prison cell in which one who is condemned to death awaits execution.

death certificate *n.* An official document, signed by a doctor, giving details of the date, place, and cause of a person's death.

death duty *n. British.* A tax on inherited property. Not in technical usage. The official term in Britain was formerly **estate duty** and is now (since 1975) **capital transfer tax** *(both of which see).*

death knell *n.* **1.** A bell tolled to announce a death. **2.** Anything that signals imminent death, as of a person or of hopes or plans.

death·less (déth-ləss, -liss) *adj.* Not subject to death; immortal. —**death·less·ly** *adv.* —**death·less·ness** *n.*

death·ly (déthli) *adj.* **1.** Resembling or characteristic of death. **2.** Causing death; fatal; deadly. **3.** *Poetic.* Of death.

~*adv.* **1.** In the manner of death. **2.** Extremely; very: *deathly quiet.* —**death·li·ness** *n.*

death mask *n.* A cast of a person's face taken after death.

death penalty *n.* **1.** A sentence of death. **2.** Capital punishment.

death rate *n.* **1.** The ratio of total deaths to total population, usually expressed as deaths per 1,000, 10,000, or 100,000 population, in a specified community. Also called "mortality rate". **2.** The number of deaths per 100 persons having the same disease. In this sense, also called "fatality rate".

death rattle *n.* A rare respiratory gurgling or rattling in the throat of a dying person, caused by loss of the cough reflex and by the passage of breath through accumulating mucus in the throat.

death row *n. U.S.* A prison building containing death cells. Also called "death house". —**on death row.** Under sentence of death.

death's-head (déths-hed) *n.* The human skull or a representation of it, symbolising mortality or death.

death's-head moth *n.* A large Eurasian hawk moth, *Acherontia atropos*, having a skull-like marking on the upper part of the thorax.

death squad *n.* Any of several unofficial groups of vigilantes, especially in Latin America, whose members kill criminals, political agitators, or others considered hostile to society.

death tax *n. U.S.* A tax on inherited property. Compare **death duty.**

death·trap (déth-trap) *n.* **1. a.** An unsafe building or structure, especially one susceptible to fire. **b.** An unsafe train, motor vehicle, or the like. **2.** Any perilous circumstance or situation.

Death Valley. An arid desert basin in east California, United States. It acquired its name after a party crossing the valley in the 1849 gold rush died there. The valley is about 225 kilometres (140 miles) long, and is the hottest and deepest spot on the North American continent, 85 metres (282 feet) below sea level. The valley was made a national monument in 1933.

death warrant *n.* **1.** *Law.* An official order authorising a person's execution. **2.** Anything that destroys hope, joy, or expectation.

death·watch (déth-woch) *n.* **1.** A vigil kept beside a dying or dead person. **2. a.** Any of several beetles of the family Anobiidae, especially *Xestobium rufovillosum*, that strike their heads with a hollow, clicking sound against the wood into which they burrow. Also called "deathwatch beetle". **b.** A booklouse that makes a similar sound.

death wish *n. Psychology.* A conscious or unconscious wish for one's own, or someone else's, death.

Deau·ville (dṓ-vil, -veel). Coastal resort in the Calvados département of Normandy, northwest France. It has a casino, yachting harbour, and racecourse.

deave (deev) *tr.v.* **deaved, deaving, deaves.** *Chiefly Scottish.* To deafen or confuse with noise. [Middle English *deven*, Old English *ādēafian*, from *dēaf*, DEAF.]

deb (deb) *n. Informal.* A debutante.

de·ba·cle, dé·bâcle (day-baák'l, di- || *U.S. also* -bák'l) *n.* **1.** A sudden, disastrous overthrow or collapse; a rout. **2.** The breaking up of ice in a river. **3.** A violent flood. —See Synonyms at **disaster.** [French *débâcle*, from *débâcler*, to unbar, from Old French *desbacler*: *des-*, from Latin *dē-* (removal) + *bacler*, to bar, from Old Provençal *baclar*, from Vulgar Latin *bacclāre* (unattested), from Latin *baculum*, rod, stick.]

de·bag (dee-bág, dée-) *tr.v.* **-bagged, -bagging, -bags.** *British Slang.* To remove the trousers of (someone) as a joke or humiliation.

de·bar (di-bár, dée-) *tr.v.* **-barred, -barring, -bars. 1.** To exclude or bar; shut out. **2.** To forbid, hinder, or prevent. [Middle English *debarren*, from Old French *desbarrer*, to unbar : *des-*, from Latin *dē-* (removal) + *barrer*, to bar, from BAR.] —**de·bar·ment** *n.*

de·bark (di-bárk, dée-) *v.* **-barked, -barking, -barks.** —*tr.* To unload, as from a ship. —*intr.* To disembark. [French *débarquer*, from Old French *desbarquer* : *de-*, from Latin *dē-* (removal) + *barque*, ship, BARK.] —**de·bar·kation** (dee-baar-káysh'n) *n.*

de·base (di-báyss, dée-) *tr.v.* **-based, -basing, -bases. 1.** To reduce the value of (a coin) by adulterating with base metal. **2.** To lower in character, quality, or value; degrade; adulterate. [DE- (down) + BASE (low).] —**de·base·ment** *n.* —**de·bas·er** *n.*

de·bat·a·ble (di-báytəb'l) *adj.* **1.** Capable of being argued or discussed. **2.** In dispute; questionable. See Synonyms at **doubtful.** —**de·bat·a·bly** *adv.*

de·bate (di-báyt) *v.* **-bated, -bating, -bates.** —*intr.* **1.** To deliberate; consider. **2.** To engage in argument; discuss opposing points. **3.** To engage in a formal discussion or argument. **4.** *Obsolete.* To fight; quarrel. —*tr.* **1.** To dispute or argue about. **2.** To discuss or argue (a question, for example) formally, as in a legislative assembly. **3.** To deliberate upon; consider. **4.** *Obsolete.* To fight or argue for or over. —See Synonyms at **discuss.**

~*n.* **1. a.** A discussion involving opposing points as in a legislative assembly. **b.** An argument; a dispute. **2.** Deliberation; consideration. **3.** A formal argument in which two opposing teams defend and attack a given proposition. **4.** *Obsolete.* Conflict; strife; contention. [Middle English *debaten*, from Old French *debattre* : *de-*, *des-*, from Latin *dis-*, apart, against each other + *battre*, to fight, beat, from Latin *battere, battuere*.] —**de·bat·er** *n.*

de·bauch (di-báwch) *v.* **-bauched, -bauching, -bauches.** —*tr.* **1.** To corrupt morally; lead into a life of dissipation; pervert. Usually used in the passive. **2.** To seduce (especially an innocent woman or girl). —*intr.* To indulge in dissipation.

~*n.* An act or period of dissipation. [French *débaucher*, Old French *desbaucher†*.] —**de·bauch·ed·ly** (-idli) *adv.* —**de·bauch·er** *n.*

deb·au·chee (dé-baw-chée, dée-, -shée || *U.S. also* -sháy) *n.* A person who habitually indulges in debauchery; a libertine.

de·bauch·er·y (di-báwch-əri) *n., pl.* **-ies. 1.** Extreme indulgence in sensual pleasures; intemperance; dissipation. **2.** *Archaic.* Seduction from morality, allegiance, or duty.

de·ben·ture (di-bénchər, də-) *n. Abbr.* **deb., deben. 1.** A certificate or voucher acknowledging a debt. **2.** An unsecured bond, issued by a company or government corporation or agency and backed only by the credit standing of the issuer. **3.** A customs certificate providing for the repayment of duty. [Middle English *debentur*, from Latin *dēbentur*, "they are due", from *dēbēre*, to owe.]

de·bil·i·tate (di-bill-i-tayt) *tr.v.* **-tated, -tating, -tates.** To make feeble; enervate. [Latin *dēbilitāre*, from *dēbilis*, weak.] —**de·bil·i·ta·tion** (-táysh'n) *n.* —**de·bil·i·ta·tive** (-tətiv, -taytiv) *adj.*

de·bil·i·tat·ed (di-bíll-i-tayt-id) *adj.* Tired; worn-out.

de·bil·i·ty (di-bílləti) *n.* A state of abnormal bodily weakness; feebleness. [Middle English *debilite*, from Old French, from Latin *dēbilitās*, from *dēbilis*, weak.]

deb·it (débbit) *n. Abbr.* **dr.** *Accounting.* **1.** An item of debt as recorded in an account. **2. a.** An entry of a sum in the left-hand side of an account, recording money paid out or goods supplied. **b.** The sum of such entries. Compare **credit. 3.** The left-hand side of an account or ledger where bookkeeping entries are made.

~*tr.v.* **debited, -iting, -its. 1.** To enter (a sum) on the left-hand side of an account or ledger. **2.** To charge with a debt. Compare **credit.** [Middle English *debite*, from Old French, from Latin *dēbitum*, DEBT.]

debit card *n.* A card authorising the holder's bank account to be debited to pay for purchases made with the card.

deb·o·nair, deb·o·naire, deb·on·naire (débbə-naír) *adj.* **1.** Suave; nonchalant; urbane. **2.** Affable; genial. **3.** Carefree; jaunty. [Middle English *debonaire*, from Old French, from *de bon aire*, "of good disposition".] —**deb·o·nair·ly** *adv.* —**deb·o·nair·ness** *n.*

Deb·o·rah (débbərə). A prophetess and judge of Israel who helped the Israelites free themselves from the Canaanites. Judges 4:4.

de·bouch (di-bówch, -bóosh) *v.* **-bouched, -bouching, -bouches.** —*intr.* **1.** *Military.* To march from a narrow or confined area into the open. **2.** To emerge or issue, especially into a less restricted space, as a river might. —*tr.* To cause to emerge or issue.

~*n.* A débouché. [French *déboucher* : *dé-*, from Latin *dē-*, out of +

bouche, mouth, opening, from Old French, from Latin *bucca,* puffed-out cheek, mouth.]

dé·bou·ché (day-bōōshay, dáy-bōō-sháy) *n.* **1.** An opening in military works for the passage of troops. **2.** An outlet, as for goods. Also called "debouch". [French, from *déboucher,* DEBOUCH.]

de·bouch·ment (di-bówch-mənt, -bōōh-) *n.* **1.** The act or an instance of emerging or debouching. **2.** A debouchure.

de·bou·chure (dáybōō-shóor) *n.* A mouth or opening, especially of a river or channel.

De·bray (də-bráy), **(Jules) Regis** (1940–). French author. He was a Marxist supporter of Castro's Cuban regime, and wrote on Latin America in *Revolution in the Revolution?* (1967). He visited Che Guevara in Bolivia, and when Guevara was killed in 1967, Debray was arrested and sentenced to 30 years' imprisonment. He was released after three years, and went to Chile. Appointed a foreign affairs adviser by President Mitterrand of France (1981–4).

De·bré (də-bráy), **Michel** (1912–96). French statesman, and first prime minister (1959–62) of De Gaulle's Fifth Republic. Debré, a French Resistance fighter in World War II, drafted the constitution of the Fifth Republic (1958). Successively minister of finance, foreign affairs, and defence 1966–9; 1979, M.E.P.

De·brett (di-brét), **John** (1752–1822). British publisher, and founder of *Debrett's Peerage and Baronetage* (also known as "Debrett"). He took over a directory of the nobility in 1802, and made it into an authoritative guide to the British nobility and royalty.

dé·bride·ment (di-brééd-mənt, day-, -MON) *n.* The surgical excision of dead and devitalised tissue and the removal of all foreign matter from a wound. [French, from *débrider,* "to unbridle", from Old French *desbrider* : *des-,* from Latin *dē-* (removal) + *bride,* bridle, from Middle High German *brīdel.*]

de·brief (dée-bréef) *v.* **-briefed, -briefing, -briefs.** —*tr.* **1.** To question or interrogate (a diplomat, spy, or astronaut, for example) to obtain knowledge or intelligence gathered on a mission. **2.** To instruct (a government agent or similar employee) not to reveal secret information after his employment has ceased. —*intr.* To answer questions and provide information after returning from a mission.

de·brief·ing (dée-brééfing) *n.* **1.** The act or process of being debriefed. **2.** The information conveyed during this procedure.

de·bris, dé·bris (dáy-bree, dé-, -bri ‖ *U.S. also* də-brée) *n.* **1.** The scattered remains of something broken or destroyed; ruins; fragments. **2.** *Geology.* An accumulation of loose material produced by disintegration of rocks. It includes rock fragments, sands, and clays. [French *débris,* from Old French *de(s)brisier,* to break to pieces : *des-,* from Latin *dē-* (intensive) + *brisier,* to break, from (unattested) Vulgar Latin *brīsāre.*]

de Broglie wave (də-brŏgli) *n. Physics.* A wave associated with a particle that represents its wavelike behaviour under certain conditions, such as electron diffraction by crystals. The wavelength is given by *h/mv,* where *h* is the Planck constant, *m* is the particle's mass, and *v* its velocity, interpreted in quantum mechanics as a wave of probability, in which the probability of finding the particle at a given point depends on the square of the wave function. [After L. V. DE BROGLIE.]

debt (det) *n.* **1.** Something owed, such as money, goods, or services. **2.** An obligation or liability to pay or render something to someone else. **3.** The condition of having such an obligation in debt. **4.** *Archaic.* An offence requiring forgiveness or reparation; a sin; a trespass. [Middle English *det(te),* from Old French *dette,* from Vulgar Latin *dēbita* (unattested), feminine of Latin *dēbitum,* debt, from *dēbitus,* past participle of *dēbēre,* to owe.]

debt of honour *n.* A debt that is morally binding but not legally recoverable, such as a gambling debt.

debt·or (déttər) *n. Abbr.* **dr.** A person who owes something to another. Compare **creditor.** [Middle English *det(t)our,* from Old French *det(t)or,* from Latin *dēbitor,* from *dēbēre,* to owe. See **debt.**]

de·bug (dée-búg) *tr.v.* **-bugged, -bugging, -bugs. 1.** To remove insects from. **2.** To search for and eliminate malfunctioning elements in. **3.** To search for and eliminate sources of error in (a computer program, for example). **4.** To search for and remove concealed microphones from (a room, for example).

de·bunk (dée-búngk, di-) *tr.v.* **-bunked, -bunking, -bunks.** *Informal.* To expose or ridicule the falseness, sham, or exaggerated claims of. [DE- + BUNK (nonsense).] —**de·bunk·er** *n.*

De·bus·sy (də-bōōss-i, -béwss- ‖ *French* -büss-eé), **Claude (Achille)** (1862–1918). French composer. He was the first exponent of musical impressionism, using unusual tone patterns to communicate mood and emotion. His works include *L'Après-midi d'un faune* (1894), and the opera *Pelléas and Mélisande* 1892–1902).

de·but, dé·but (dáy-bew, débbew ‖ *U.S. also* di-béw, day-) *n.* **1.** A first public appearance, as of an actor on the stage. **2.** The formal presentation of a girl to society. **3.** The beginning of a career or course of action.
~ *v.* **-buted, -buting, -buts.** *(silent t).* —*intr.* To make a debut: *debuted in Carmen.* —*tr.* To cause to debut: *debuted her as/in Carmen.* [French *début,* from *débuter,* to make one's debut, "give the first stroke in a game" : *dé,* from Latin *dē,* away + *but,* BUTT (target).]

deb·u·tant (dèbbew-taant) *n.* A person making a debut, such as a sportsman playing in a team for the first time.

deb·u·tante, dé·bu·tante (dèbbew-taant, dáybew-, -tant, -toNt) *n.* A young lady making a debut into society. Also informally called "deb". [French *débutante,* from *débuter,* to make one's DEBUT.]

Dec. December.

deca-, dec-, deka-, dek- *comb. form. Abbr.* **da** Indicates ten; for

example, **decahedron, decane, decapod.** [Greek *deka-,* from *deka,* ten.]

dec·ade (dékkayd, di-káyd) *n.* **1.** A period of ten years. **2.** A group or series of ten. [Middle English, from Old French, from Late Latin *decas* (stem *decad-*), from Greek *dekas,* from *deka,* ten.]

de·ca·dence (dékkədənss, di-káyd'nss) *n. Also* **de·ca·den·cy** (-i) *pl.* **-cies. 1.** A process, condition, or period of deterioration or decline, as in morals or art; decay. **2.** *Usually capital* **D.** The period during which the Decadents flourished. Preceded by *the.* [Old French, from Medieval Latin *decadentia,* from Vulgar Latin *dēcadere* (unattested), to DECAY.]

de·ca·dent (dékkədənt, di-káyd'nt) *adj.* **1.** In a state or condition of decline or decay. **2.** Of or pertaining to the Decadents.
~*n.* **1.** A person in a condition or process of mental or moral decay. **2.** *Usually capital* **D.** A member of a group of French and English writers of the 19th century who often sought inspiration in the morbid, neurotic, or macabre and tended towards overrefinement of style. [From DECADENCE.] —**de·ca·dent·ly** *adv.*

de·caff (dée-kaff) *n.* A trademark for decaffeinated coffee.
~ *adj.* Decaffeinated.

de·caf·fein·ate (dée-káffi-nayt) *tr.v.* **-ated, -ating, ates.** To remove most of the caffeine from (coffee).

dec·a·gon (dékkə-gən ‖ -gon) *n.* A polygon with ten angles and ten sides. [New Latin *decagonum,* from Greek *dekagōnon,* "(one) having ten angles" : DECA- + -GON.] —**de·cag·o·nal** (di- kággən'l, de-) *adj.* —**de·cag·o·nal·ly** *adv.*

dec·a·gram, dec·a·gramme (dékkə-gram) *n. Abbr.* **dag** Ten grams. [French *décagramme* : DECA- + GRAM.]

dec·a·he·dron (dékkə-hée-drən, -hé-) *n., pl.* **-drons** or **-dra** (-drə). A polyhedron with ten faces. [New Latin : DECA- + -HEDRON.] —**dec·a·he·dral** *adj.*

de·cal (dée-kál, di-) *n. Chiefly U.S.* A picture or design transferred by the process of decalcomania.

de·cal·ci·fy (dée-kál-si-fī,) *tr.v.* **-fied, -fying, -fies.** To remove calcium or calcareous matter from (bones or teeth, for example). —**de·cal·ci·fi·ca·tion** (-fi-káysh'n) *n.* —**de·cal·ci·fi·er** *n.*

de·cal·co·ma·ni·a (di-kál-kə-máyni-ə, dée-) *n. Chiefly U.S.* **1.** The process of transferring pictures or designs printed on specially prepared paper to glass, metal, or other material. **2.** A picture so transferred; a decal. [French *décalcomanie* : *décalquer,* to transfer by tracing : *dé-,* from, from Latin *dē-* + *calquer,* to trace, from Italian *calcare,* to trace, trample, from Latin, to tread, from *calx* (stem *calc-*), heel (see **calk**[1]) + *manie,* madness, from Late Latin *mania,* MANIA (from its mid-19th-century popularity).]

de·ca·les·cence (dée-kə-léss'nss, -ka-) *n.* In a metal being heated, a sudden slowing in the rate of temperature increase, as a result of an endothermic change in crystal structure. [DE- + Latin *calescere,* to become warm, from *calēre,* to be warm.] —**de·ca·les·cent** *adj.*

Dec·a·logue (dékkə-log ‖ -lawg) *n. Sometimes small* **d.** Also *chiefly U.S.* **Dec·a·log.** The **Ten Commandments** *(see).* [Middle English *decalog,* from Old French *decalogue,* from Late Latin *decalogus,* from Greek *dekalogos* : DECA- + *logos,* speech, word.]

dec·a·me·tre (dékkə-meetər) *n. Abbr.* **dam** Ten metres.

de·camp (di-kámp, dée-) *intr.v.* **-camped, -camping, -camps. 1.** To depart from a camping ground; break camp. **2.** To depart secretly or suddenly; run away. [French *décamper,* from Old French *descamper* : *des-,* from Latin *dē-* (reversal) + *camper,* to camp, from *camp,* CAMP.] —**de·camp·ment** *n.*

dec·a·nal (di-káyn'l ‖ déckən'l) *adj.* **1.** Of or pertaining to a dean or deanery. **2.** On the south side of a cathedral choir. Compare **cantorial.** [Late Latin *decānus,* DEAN.] —**dec·a·nal·ly** *adv.*

dec·ane (déckayn) *n.* **1.** A straight-chain liquid hydrocarbon, $C_{10}H_{22}$, of the alkane series. Also called "normal decane". **2.** Any of various isomeric liquid alkanes with the formula $C_{10}H_{22}$. [DEC(A)- + -ANE.]

dec·ane·di·o·ic acid (deekãn-dī-ŏ-ik) *n.* **Sebacic acid** *(see).* [DEC-ANE + DI + -OIC.]

de·ca·no·ic acid (dékkə-nŏ-ik) *n. Chemistry.* An organic acid, **capric acid** *(see).* [DECAN(E) + -OIC.]

de·cant (di-kánt) *tr.v.* **-canted, -canting, -cants. 1.** To pour off (wine, for example) without disturbing the sediment. **2.** To pour (a liquid) from one container into another. **3.** *Informal.* To transfer (offices, for example) from one location to another. [Medieval Latin *dēcanthāre* : Latin *dē-,* from + *canthus,* rim of a vessel, from Latin, rim of a wheel, tyre.] —**de·can·ta·tion** (déekan-táysh'n) *n.*

de·cant·er (di-kántər) *n.* **1.** A decorative bottle used for serving wine or other drinks. **2.** A vessel used for decanting.

de·cap·i·tate (di-kápp-i-tayt, dée-) *tr.v.* **-tated, -tating, -tates.** To cut off the head of; behead. [Late Latin *dēcapitāre* : Latin *dē-* (removal) + *caput,* head.] —**de·cap·i·ta·tion** *n.* —**de·cap·i·ta·tor** (-taytər) *n.*

dec·a·pod (dékkə-pod) *n.* **1.** Any crustacean of the order Decapoda, such as a crab, lobster, or shrimp, characteristically having five pairs of walking legs, each pair joined to a segment of the thorax. **2.** A cephalopod mollusc, such as a squid or cuttlefish, having ten armlike tentacles.
~*adj.* Of or pertaining to the Decapoda or a decapod. [New Latin *Decapoda,* "the ten-footed ones" : DECA- + -POD.] —**de·cap·o·dal** (di-káppəd'l), **de·cap·o·dan, de·cap·o·dous** *adj.*

de·car·bon·ate (dée-kárbə-nayt) *tr.v.* **-ated, -ating, -ates.** To remove carbon dioxide or carbonic acid from.

de·car·bon·ise, de·car·bon·ize (dée-kárbən-īz) *tr.v.* **-ised, -ising, -ises.** Also **de·car·bu·rise** (-kárbewr-īz) **-ised, -ising, -ised.** To remove carbon from. —**de·car·bon·i·sa·tion** (-ī-záysh'n ‖ *U.S.* -i-) *n.* —**de·car·bon·is·er** *n.*

de·car·box·y·late (dée-kar-bóksi-layt) *v.* **-ated, -ating, -ates.** *Chemistry.* —*tr.* To remove a carboxyl group (−COOH) from (a chemical compound), usually with replacement by hydrogen. —*intr.* To lose a carboxyl group. —**de·car·box·y·la·tion** (-láysh'n) *n.*

dec·are (déckair, de-káir ‖ *U.S. also* déckaar) *n.* A metric unit of area equal to 1 000 square metres. [French *décare* : DECA- + ARE.]

de·ca·style (déckə-stīl) *n. Architecture.* A portico with ten columns.

dec·a·syl·la·ble (dékkə-silləb'l) *n.* A word or line of verse having ten syllables. —**dec·a·syl·lab·ic** (-si-lábbik) *adj.*

de·cath·lon (di-káth-lon, de-, -lən) *n.* An athletic contest in which each contestant participates in ten different events. [French *décathlon* : DECA- + Greek *athlon*, contest (see **athlete**).] —**de·cath·lete** (-leet) *n.*

de·cay (di-káy) *v.* **-cayed, -caying, -cays.** —*intr.* **1.** *Biology.* To decompose; rot. **2.** *Physics.* To fall away; diminish in magnitude. Used of such effects as radioactivity, phosphorescence, and magnetism. **3.** *Aerospace.* To decrease in orbit. Used of an artificial satellite. **4.** To become a ruin; fall into ruin. **5.** *Pathology.* To decline in health or vigour; waste away. **6.** To decline from a state of normality, excellence, or prosperity. —*tr.* To cause to decay. —*n.* **1. a.** The destruction or decomposition of organic matter as a result of bacterial or fungal action; rot. **b.** Decaying matter. **2.** *Physics.* **a.** A reduction in or falling away of an effect such as radioactivity. **b.** A process in which an atomic nucleus disintegrates or emits a particle or gamma ray, and transforms into a different nucleus. **c.** A process in which an elementary particle transforms spontaneously into one or more other particles. **3.** The decrease in orbital altitude of an artificial satellite owing to conditions such as atmospheric drag. **4. a.** A gradual deterioration to an inferior state, as of health or mental capability. **b.** The state reached in this process. [Middle English *decayen*, from North French *decair*, from Vulgar Latin *dēcadere* (unattested), to fall down, decay : Latin *dē-*, down + *cadere*, to fall.]

Synonyms: decay, rot, putrefy, spoil, crumble, moulder, disintegrate, decompose.

decay chain *n.* **Radioactive series** *(see).*

Dec·can[1] or **Dek·kan** (déck-ən, -aan). India south of the river Narmada. Its population is mostly Dravidian.

Deccan[2], **The.** The central plateau of southern India, bounded by the Eastern and Western Ghats. It is an ancient rock shield, and its fertile volcanic soils produce cotton and tea.

decd. deceased.

de·cease (di-séess) *intr.v.* **-ceased, -ceasing, -ceases.** *Formal.* To die. —*n. Formal.* Death. [Middle English *decesen*, to die, from *deces*, death, from Old French, from Latin *dēcessus*, departure, death, from the past participle of *dēcēdere*, to depart : *dē-*, away + *cēdere*, to go.]

de·ceased (di-séest) *adj. Abbr.* **decd.** *Formal.* No longer living; dead. See Synonyms at **dead.** —*n., pl.* **deceased.** A dead person. Preceded by *the.*

de·ce·dent (di-séedn't) *n. Chiefly U.S. Law.* A deceased person. [Latin *dēcēdēns* (stem *dēcēdent-*), present participle of *dēcēdere*, to die, DECEASE.]

de·ceit (di-séet) *n.* **1.** An act of deceiving; misrepresentation; deception. **2.** A stratagem; a trick; a wile. **3.** A tendency to deceive or habit of deceiving; falseness; deceitfulness. [Middle English *deceit(e)*, from Old French, from Latin *dēcepta*, feminine of *dēceptus*, past participle of *dēcipere*, DECEIVE.]

de·ceit·ful (di-séetf'l) *adj.* **1.** Given to cheating or deceiving. **2.** Misleading; deceptive. —See Synonyms at **dishonest.** —**de·ceit·ful·ly** *adv.* —**de·ceit·ful·ness** *n.*

de·ceive (di-séev) *v.* **-ceived, -ceiving, -ceives.** —*tr.* **1.** To trick into believing something false; mislead. **2.** *Archaic.* To catch by guile; ensnare. —*intr.* To practise deceit. [Middle English *deceiven*, from Old French *deceive*, *decevoir*, from Latin *dēcipere*, to take in, deceive : *dē-* (pejorative) + *capere*, to take, seize.] —**de·ceiv·a·bil·i·ty** (-ə-billəti) *n.* —**de·ceiv·a·ble** (-əb'l) *adj.* —**de·ceiv·a·bly** *adv.* —**de·ceiv·er** *n.* —**de·ceiv·ing·ly** *adv.*

Synonyms: deceive, betray, mislead, beguile, delude, dupe, fool, hoodwink, bamboozle, outwit, double-cross.

de·cel·er·ate (dée-séllə-rayt) *v.* **-ated, -ating, -ates.** —*tr.* **1.** To decrease the velocity of. **2.** To cause (a process, such as a chemical reaction) to slow down. —*intr.* **1.** To decrease in velocity. **2.** To be slowed down. [DE- + (AC)CELERATE.] —**de·cel·er·a·tion** (-ráysh'n) *n.* —**de·cel·er·a·tor** *n.*

de·cel·e·rom·e·ter (dée-séllə-rómmitər) *n.* Any instrument used to measure decrease in velocity. [DECELER(ATE) + -METER.]

de·cel·er·on (dée-sélləron) *n.* An aileron speed brake used primarily on jet aircraft. [*deceleration* + *aileron*.]

De·cem·ber (di-sémbər) *n. Abbr.* **Dec., D.** The 12th and last month of the year according to the Gregorian calendar. December has 31 days. [Middle English *decembre*, from Old French, from Latin *December*, "the tenth month", from *decem*, ten.]

De·cem·brist (di-sémbrist) *n.* Any of the conspirators or participants in the attempted overthrow of Tsar Nicholas I of Russia in December, 1825.

de·cem·vir (di-sém-vər, -vur) *n., pl.* **-virs** or **-viri** (-və-ree, və-rī). A member of a body of ten Roman magistrates; especially, a member of either of two such bodies appointed in 451 and 450 B.C. to draw up a code of laws. **2.** A member of any commission or governing body which has ten members. [Middle English, from Latin, singular of *decemvirī*, from *decem virī*, ten men : *decem*, ten + *virī*, plural of *vir*, man.] —**de·cem·vi·ral** *adj.* —**de·cem·vi·rate** (-ayt, -ət, -it) *n.*

de·cen·a·ry, de·cen·na·ry (di-sénnəri) *adj.* Of or pertaining to a tithing. —*n., pl.* **decenaries.** A tithing. [Middle English *decennare*, tithing man, from Medieval Latin *decennārius*, from *decenna*, tithing, from Latin *decem*, ten.]

de·cen·cy (dée-s'n-si) *n., pl.* **-cies. 1.** The state or condition of being decent; propriety. **2.** Conformity to prevailing standards of propriety or modesty. **3.** *Plural.* The things considered necessary for leading a decent life. **4.** *Plural.* The proprieties.

de·cen·na·ry[1] (di-sénnəri) *adj.* Pertaining to a ten-year period. —*n., pl.* **decennaries.** A decennium; a decade. [Latin *decennis*, of ten years. See **decennium.**]

decennary[2]. Variant of **decenary.**

de·cen·ni·al (di-sénni-əl) *adj.* **1.** Pertaining to or lasting for ten years. **2.** Occurring every ten years. —*n.* **1.** An anniversary celebrated every ten years. **2.** The celebration of such an anniversary. [Latin *decennium*, DECENNIUM.] —**de·cen·ni·al·ly** *adv.*

de·cen·ni·um (di-sénni-əm) *n., pl.* **-niums** or **-cennia** (-sénni-ə). A period of ten years; a decade. [Latin, from *decennis*, of ten years : *decem*, ten + *annus*, year.]

de·cent (dée-s'nt) *adj.* **1.** Honest and respectable; conforming to recognised standards of morality and propriety. **2.** Proper; fitting. **3.** Free from indelicacy; modest. **4.** Adequate; passable: *a decent salary.* **5.** *Informal.* Kind; obliging; generous. **6.** *Informal.* Properly or modestly dressed. [Latin *decēns* (stem *decent-*), present participle of *decēre*, to be fitting, suit.] —**de·cent·ly** *adv.* —**de·cent·ness** *n.*

de·cen·tral·ise, de·cen·tral·ize (dee-séntrə-līz, dée-) *tr.v.* **-ised, -ising, -ises.** —*tr.* **1.** To distribute the administrative functions or powers of (a central authority) among regional authorities. **2.** To cause to withdraw from an area of concentration: *decentralise an industry.* —*intr.* To disperse across a greater area or range of authorities. —**de·cen·tral·i·sa·tion** (-lī-záysh'n ‖ *U.S.* -li-) *n.*

de·cep·tion (di-sépsh'n) *n.* **1.** An act of deceiving; the use of deceit. **2.** The fact or state of being deceived. **3.** An act intended to deceive; a trick. [Middle English *decepcioun*, from Old French *deception*, from Late Latin *dēceptiō* (stem *dēceptiōn-*), from Latin *dēcipere* (past participle *dēceptus*), DECEIVE.]

de·cep·tive (di-séptiv) *adj.* **1.** Intended or tending to deceive. **2.** Likely to confuse; misleading. —**de·cep·tive·ly** *adv.* —**de·cep·tive·ness** *n.*

de·ce·re·brate (dée-sérri-brayt) *tr.v.* **-brated, -brating, -brates.** To eliminate the cerebral functions of (an experimental animal) by removing a large part of the brain or cutting across the brain below the cerebrum. [DE- + CEREBRO- + -ATE.] —**de·ce·re·bra·tion** (-bráysh'n) *n.*

deci– *comb. form. Symbol* **d** Indicates one-tenth; for example, **decimetre.** [French *déci-*, from Latin *decimus*, tenth, from *decem*, ten.]

de·ci·bel (déssi-bel, -b'l) *n. Abbr.* **dB.** A unit used to express relative difference in power, usually between acoustic or electric signals, equal to ten times the common logarithm of the ratio of the two levels. [DECI- + BEL.]

de·cide (di-síd) *v.* **-cided, -ciding, -cides.** —*tr.* **1.** To conclude or settle: *He decided his plans.* **2.** To influence or determine the conclusion of: *Sheer firepower decided the battle.* **3.** To cause to make a decision: *Your nagging decided me to buy it.* —*intr.* **1.** To pronounce a judgment; announce a verdict. Often used with *for* or *against.* **2.** To make up one's mind. [Middle English *deciden*, from Old French *decider*, from Latin *dēcīdere*, to cut off, determine : *dē-*, off + *cædere*, to cut.] —**de·cid·a·ble** *adj.* —**de·cid·er** *n.*

Synonyms: decide, determine, settle, rule, conclude, resolve.

de·cid·ed (di-sídid) *adj.* **1.** Unquestionable; definite. **2.** Resolute; unhesitating. —**de·cid·ed·ly** *adv.* —**de·cid·ed·ness** *n.*

Usage: Decided and *decisive* both have the sense "unquestionable" or "resolute". But *decided* usually means simply "definite", whereas *decisive* emphasises the notion of decision-making or settling an issue beyond doubt. If John has a *decided advantage*, he is in a very strong position; but if he has a *decisive advantage*, he is in the strongest possible position and cannot lose.

de·cid·er (di-sídər) *n.* In a contest, a round that determines the winner.

de·cid·ing (di-síding) *adj.* **1.** Settling, or able to settle, a matter in dispute or doubt; decisive; conclusive: *the deciding vote.*

de·cid·u·a (di-síddew-ə) *n.* A mucous membrane that lines the uterus, modified during pregnancy and cast off during menstruation or at parturition. [New Latin *(membrana) decidua*, "(membrane) that falls off", from Latin *dēcidua*, feminine of *dēciduus*, DECIDUOUS.] —**de·cid·u·al** *adj.*

de·cid·u·ate (di-síddew-ayt) *adj.* **1.** Characterised by or having a decidua. **2.** Characterised by shedding.

de·cid·u·ous (di-síddew-əss) *adj.* **1.** Falling off or shed at a specific season or stage of growth: *deciduous antlers; deciduous leaves.* **2.** Shedding or losing foliage at the end of the growing season: *deciduous trees.* Compare **evergreen.** **3.** Not lasting; temporary. [Latin *dēciduus*, from *dēcidere*, to fall off : *dē-*, off + *cadere*, to fall.] —**de·cid·u·ous·ly** *adv.* —**de·cid·u·ous·ness** *n.*

dec·i·gram (déssi-gram) *n. Abbr.* **dg** One-tenth (10^{-1}) of a gram.

dec·i·li·tre (déssi-leetər) *n. Abbr.* **dl** One-tenth (10^{-1}) of a litre.

de·cil·lion (di-síl-yən, de-) *n.* **1.** *British.* The cardinal number represented by 1 followed by 60 zeros, usually written 10^{60}. **2.** The cardinal number represented by 1 followed by 33 zeros, usually written 10^{33}. [Latin *decem,* ten + (M)ILLION.] **—de·cil·lion** *adj.*

de·cil·lionth (di-síl-yənth, de-) *n.* **1.** The ordinal number decillion in a series. **2.** Any of a decillion equal parts. **—de·cil·lionth** *adj. & adv.*

dec·i·mal (déssim'l) *n.* **1.** A linear array of integers that represents a fraction, every decimal place indicating a multiple of a positive or negative power of 10; for example, the decimal .1 = 1/10, .003 = 3/1000. Also called "decimal fraction". **2.** Any number written using base 10. In this sense, also called "decimal number".
~adj. **1.** Expressed or expressible as a decimal. **2. a.** Based on ten. **b.** Numbered or ordered by tens. **3.** Loosely, not integral; fractional. [Medieval Latin *decimālis,* of tithes, from Latin *decimus,* tenth, from *decem,* ten.] **—dec·i·mal·ly** *adv.*

decimal currency *n.* A system of currency in which the monetary units are divided into or multiplied by further units of 10 or 100.

dec·i·mal·ise, dec·i·mal·ize (déssim'l-īz) *tr.v.* **-ised, -ising, -ises.** To change to a decimal system. **—dec·i·mal·i·sa·tion** (-ī-záysh'n ‖ *U.S.* -i-) *n.*

decimal place *n.* The position of a digit to the right of a decimal point, identified as an ordinal number, the digit immediately to the right of the decimal point being first. For example, in the decimal number 1.021, 2 is in the second decimal place.

decimal point *n.* A full stop, centred dot, or, in some countries, a comma, placed to the left of a decimal fraction.

decimal system *n.* **1.** A number system using the base 10. **2.** A measurement system in which all derived units are multiples of ten of basic units. **3.** A classification system using decimals.

dec·i·mate (déssi-mayt) *tr.v.* **-mated, -mating, -mates. 1.** To destroy or kill a large part of. **2. a.** To destroy or kill a tenth of. **b.** Especially in the ancient Roman army, to select by lot and kill one in every ten of, as a punishment for mutiny or cowardice: *decimate a cohort.* [Latin *decimāre,* from *decimus,* tenth, from *decem,* ten.] **—dec·i·ma·tion** (-máysh'n) *n.* **—dec·i·ma·tor** (-maytər) *n.*
Usage: The earlier meaning of *decimate* is, literally, "to kill one tenth of", but the word is now generally used to mean "to kill many of"—a change in usage still criticised by purists.

dec·i·me·tre (déssi-meetər) *n. Abbr.* **dm** One-tenth (10^{-1}) of a metre. [French *décimètre* : DECI- + METRE.]

de·ci·pher (di-sīfər) *tr.v.* **-phered, -phering, -phers. 1.** To read or interpret (something ambiguous, obscure, or illegible). **2.** To convert from a code or cipher to plain text; decode. [DE- (reversal) + CIPHER (after Old French *deschiffrer*).] **—de·ci·pher·a·ble** *adj.* **—de·ci·pher·er** *n.* **—de·ci·pher·ment** *n.*

de·ci·sion (di-sízh'n ‖ -zísh'n) *n.* **1.** The passing of judgment on an issue under consideration. **2.** The act of reaching a conclusion or making up one's mind. **3.** A conclusion or judgment reached or pronounced; a verdict. **4.** Firmness of character or action; determination. **5.** In boxing, a victory won on points when no knockout has occurred. [Middle English *decisioun,* from Old French *decision,* from Latin *dēcīsiō* (stem *dēcīsiōn-*), from *dēcīdere,* DECIDE.]

de·ci·sion-mak·er (di-sízh'n-maykər) *n.* One who has the responsibility for making decisions; especially, an important administrator in business or government. **—de·ci·sion-mak·ing** *n. & adj.*

de·ci·sive (di-sī-siv, -ziv) *adj.* **1.** Able to settle a matter in dispute or doubt; conclusive. **2.** Characterised by firm decision; resolute; determined. **3.** Beyond doubt; unquestionable. See Usage note at **decided.** **—de·ci·sive·ly** *adv.* **—de·ci·sive·ness** *n.*

deck[1] (dek) *n. Abbr.* **dk. 1. a.** *Nautical.* A platform extending horizontally from one side of a ship to the other. **b.** The space between two such platforms. **2.** Any similar platform or surface, as on a bus. **3.** The roadway on a bridge. **4.** The surface in a hi-fi system incorporating a turntable, cassette player, or the like. **5.** *Informal.* The floor or ground. **6.** *Chiefly U.S.* A pack of playing cards. **7.** A pile of punched computer cards. **8.** *Chiefly U.S.* A packet of narcotic drugs. **—clear the decks.** *Informal.* To prepare for action. **—hit the deck.** *Slang.* **1.** To fall or drop to the floor or ground. **2.** To get out of bed. **3.** To prepare for action. **—on deck.** *Slang.* **1.** On hand; present. **2.** *U.S.* Waiting to take one's turn.
~ tr.v. **decked, decking, decks. 1.** To furnish with a deck. **2.** *Informal.* To knock down; floor. [Middle English *dekke,* from Middle Dutch *dec, decke,* roof, covering.]

deck[2] *tr.v.* **decked, decking, decks.** To clothe with finery; decorate; adorn. Often used with *out: decked out for a party.* [Middle Dutch *dekken,* to cover.]

deck chair *n.* A folding chair, usually made of wood and canvas, found on the decks of passenger ships and now used generally for sitting outdoors, as in parks and gardens.

deck hand *n.* A member of a ship's crew who works on deck; an ordinary seaman..

deck·house (dék-howss) *n.* A superstructure on the upper deck of a ship.

deck·le, deck·el (déck'l) *n.* **1.** A frame used in making paper by hand to form paper pulp into sheets of a desired size. **2.** A deckle edge. **3.** A device for trimming mechanically made paper to the desired width. [German *Deckel,* diminutive of *Decke,* "a cover", from Old High German *decchī,* from *decchen,* to cover.]

deckle edge *n.* **1.** The rough, crimped edge of handmade paper formed in a deckle. Also called "featheredge". **2.** A similar edge produced by a machine. **—deck·le-edged** (déck'l-éjd) *adj.*

de·claim (di-kláym) *v.* **-claimed, -claiming, -claims.** *—intr.* **1.** To deliver an elocutionary recitation. **2.** To speak loudly and vehemently; inveigh. Used with *against.* *—tr.* To utter or recite with rhetorical effect. [Middle English *declamen,* from Latin *dēclāmāre* : *dē-* (intensive) + *clāmāre,* to cry out.] **—de·claim·er** *n.*

dec·la·ma·tion (décklə-máysh'n) *n.* **1.** An elocutionary recitation. **2. a.** Vehement oratory. **b.** A harangue; a tirade. **3. a.** Correct and expressive delivery of words to a musical accompaniment. **b.** The art or action of reading or reciting a literary text with the proper intonation and expression. [Middle English *declamacioun,* from Latin *dēclāmātiō* (stem *dēclāmātiōn-*), from *dēclāmāre,* DECLAIM.]

de·clam·a·to·ry (di-klámmə-təri, -tri) *adj.* **1.** Having the quality of a declamation; loudly demanding attention. **2.** Pretentiously rhetorical; meaninglessly bombastic. **—de·clam·a·to·ri·ly** *adv.*

de·clar·a·ble (di-kláir-əb'l) *adj.* Such as can or should be declared, as for payment of customs duty.

de·clar·ant (di-kláir-ənt) *n.* **1.** *Law.* One making a declaration. **2.** *U.S.* One who has signed a declaration of intention of becoming a U.S. citizen.

dec·la·ra·tion (décklə-ráysh'n) *n.* **1.** An explicit or formal statement or announcement. **2.** Such a statement in written form. **3.** The act or process of declaring. **4.** A statement of taxable goods or of properties subject to duty. Used especially in the phrase *a customs declaration.* **5.** *Law.* **a.** Formerly, a formal statement by a plaintiff specifying the facts and circumstances constituting his cause of action. **b.** An unsworn statement of facts that may be admissible as evidence. **c.** A ruling or a point of law made in the High Court, especially in the Chancery division. **6.** In card games: **a.** A bid, especially the final bid of a hand. **b.** An announcement by a player of points made. **7.** In cricket, a decision by the captain of the batting side to end an innings before all the batsmen are out.

Declaration of Independence *n.* **1.** A proclamation by the Second Continental Congress declaring the 13 American colonies politically independent from Great Britain, formally adopted on July 4, 1776. **2.** The document in which this proclamation is recorded.

de·clar·a·tive (di-klárrə-tiv, *also* -kláir-ə-) *adj.* Serving to declare or state. **—de·clar·a·tive·ly** *adv.*

de·clar·a·to·ry (di-klárrə-təri, -tri) *adj.* **1.** Declarative. **2.** *Law.* Explaining a point of law or setting out the rights of the parties.

de·clare (di-kláir) *v.* **-clared, -claring, -clares.** *—tr.* **1.** To bring into being by announcing officially or formally; decree: *declare war; declare an amnesty.* **2.** To admit to: *declare an interest.* **3.** To pronounce as being in a specified condition: *I declared him fit and well.* **4.** To state with emphasis or authority; affirm: *declare one's loyalty.* **5.** To reveal or manifest; prove: *His face declares his guilt.* **6.** To make a full statement of (dutiable goods, for example). **7.** To announce (a dividend) as payable. **8.** In bridge, to designate (a trump suit or no-trump) with the final bid of a hand. **9.** In various card games: **a.** To reveal (cards). **b.** To announce (points scored by such cards). *—intr.* **1.** To make a declaration. **2.** To proclaim one's choice, opinion, or resolution; act. Used with *for* or *against.* **3.** In cricket, to decide to end an innings before all one's batsmen are out. —See Synonyms at **assert.** [Middle English *declaren,* from Old French *declarer,* from Latin *dēclārāre,* to make clear : *dē-* (intensive) + *clārāre,* to make clear, from *clārus,* clear.] **—de·clar·er** *n.*

de·class (dée-klaáss ‖ -kláss) *tr.v.* **-classed, -classing, -classes.** To lower in class or standing; degrade; debase.

dé·clas·sé (day-klássay) *adj.* Also **de·classed** (dée-klaást ‖ -klást). Lowered in social standing. [French, from *déclasser,* to lower in class : *dé-,* from Latin *dē-,* down + *classe,* CLASS.]

de·clas·si·fy (dée-klássi-fi) *tr.v.* **-fied, -fying, -fies.** To remove official security classification from (information, documents, and the like); make (information) no longer secret. **—de·clas·si·fi·a·ble** *adj.* **—de·clas·si·fi·ca·tion** (-fi-káysh'n) *n.*

de·clen·sion (di-klénsh'n) *n.* **1.** *Grammar.* **a.** In certain languages, the inflection of nouns, pronouns, and adjectives in such categories as case, number, and gender. **b.** A class of nouns, pronouns, and adjectives with the same or a similar system of inflections, such as the first declension in Latin. Compare **conjugation.** **2.** A descending slope; a descent. **3.** *Literary.* A decline or decrease; deterioration: *empires in their declension.* **4.** A deviation, as from a standard or practice. [Learned respelling of Middle English *declinson,* from Old French *declinaison,* from Late Latin *dēclīnātiō* (stem *dēclīnātiōn-*), grammatical declension, from Latin, DECLINATION.] **—de·clen·sion·al** *adj.*

dec·li·na·tion (déckli-náysh'n) *n.* **1.** A sloping or bending downwards. **2.** A falling off, especially from prosperity or vigour; a decline. **3.** A deviation, as from a specific direction or standard. **4.** A formal refusal to accept. **5. Magnetic declination** *(see).* **6.** *Astronomy. Symbol* δ The angular distance to a point on the celestial sphere, measured north or south from the celestial equator along the **hour circle** *(see).* [Middle English *declinacioun,* from Old French *declination,* from Latin *dēclīnātiō* (stem *dēclīnātiōn-*), from *dēclīnāre,* DECLINE.] **—dec·li·na·tion·al** *adj.*

de·cline (di-klīn) *v.* **-clined, -clining, -clines.** *—intr.* **1.** To refuse to do or accept something. **2.** To slope downwards. **3.** To deteriorate gradually; fail. **4.** To draw to a gradual close; wane. **5.** *Grammar.* To have inflected forms. Used of nouns, pronouns, and adjectives in certain languages. *—tr.* **1.** To refuse (an offer or request; for example). **2.** To cause to slope downwards. **3.** *Grammar.* In certain languages, to give the inflected forms of (a noun, pronoun, or adjective). Compare **conjugate.** —See Synonyms at **refuse.**
~n. **1.** The process or result of declining; especially, gradual deterioration. **2.** A downward movement. **3.** The period when something is tending towards an end. **4.** A downward slope. **5.** *Archaic.* Any disease, such as tuberculosis, that gradually weakens or wastes

the body or a bodily part. [Middle English *declinen,* from Old French *decliner,* from Latin *dēclīnāre,* to turn aside, go down, inflect grammatically : *dē-,* away, aside + *clīnāre,* to bend.] —**de·clin·a·ble** *adj.* —**de·clin·er** *n.*

dec·li·nom·e·ter (déckli-nómmitər) *n.* An instrument for measuring magnetic declination. [DECLIN(ATION) + -METER.]

de·cliv·i·tous (di-klívvitəss) *adj.* Rather steep.

de·cliv·i·ty (di-klívvəti) *n., pl.* -**ties.** A descending slope, as of a hill. Compare **acclivity.** [Latin *dēclīvitās,* from *dēclīvis,* sloping down : *dē-,* down + *clīvus,* a slope.]

de·clutch (dée-klúch, di-) *intr.v.* -**clutched, -clutching, -clutches.** To disengage the clutch of an engine.

de·coct (di-kókt) *tr.v.* -**cocted, -cocting, -cocts.** 1. To extract (the flavour, essence, or other desired substance of) by boiling. 2. To concentrate by boiling; boil down. [Middle English *decocten,* from Latin *dēcoquere* (past participle *dēcoctus*), to boil to the dregs : *dē-* (intensive) + *coquere,* to cook.] —**de·coc·tion** *n.*

de·code (dée-kōd) *tr.v.* -**coded, -coding, -codes.** To convert from code into plain, understandable language; decipher. —**de·cod·er** *n.*

de·coke (dée-kōk, di-) *tr.v. British.* To decarbonise (an engine). ~*n.* (dée-kōk) An act of decarbonising.

de·col·late (dée-kə-láyt, dé-, -ko-, -kō-) *tr.v.* -**lated, -lating, -lates.** To separate out into individual copies. Used of documents produced in multiple copies. [DE- + COLLATE.]

dé·colle·tage (dáy-kol-ta'azh, day-kól-taazh, -kóllə-) *n.* 1. a. A low neckline on a garment. b. The exposure of the breast and, often, shoulders caused by a low neckline. 2. A décolleté garment. [French, from *décolleter.* See **décolleté.**]

dé·colle·té (day-kól-tay, de-, di-, -kóllə- ‖ U.S. dáy-kol-táy) *adj.* 1. Having a low neckline: *a décolleté dress.* 2. Wearing a garment with a low neckline. [French, past participle of *décolleter,* to uncover the neck, cut a low neckline : *dé-* (removal) + *collet,* collar, diminutive of *col,* neck, collar, from Old French, from Latin *collum,* neck.]

de·col·o·nise, de·col·o·nize (dée-kóllə-nīz, di-) *tr.v.* -**nised, -nising, -nises.** To give independence to (a former colony). —**de·col·o·ni·sa·tion** (-nī-záysh'n ‖ U.S. -ni-) *n.*

de·col·or·ant (dée-kúllərənt) *adj.* Able to remove colour or to bleach. ~*n.* A bleaching agent.

de·col·or·ise, de·col·or·ize (dée-kúllər-īz) *tr.v.* -**ised, -ising, -ises.** Also *chiefly British* **de·col·our·ise.** To decolour. —**de·col·or·i·sa·tion** (-ī-záysh'n ‖ U.S.-i-) *n.* —**de·col·or·is·er** *n.*

de·col·our (dée-kúllər) *tr.v.* -**oured, -ouring, -ours.** To deprive of colour; bleach. —**de·col·or·a·tion** (-áysh'n) *n.*

de·com·pose (dée-kəm-pōz ‖ -kom-) *v.* -**posed, -posing, -poses.** —*tr.* 1. To separate into component parts or basic elements. 2. To cause to rot. —*intr.* 1. To break down into component parts; disintegrate. 2. To break down into constituent parts by the action of bacteria or decay; putrefy. Used of organic matter. —See Synonyms at **decay.** [French *décomposer* : *dé-* (reversal) + *composer,* to COMPOSE, from Old French.] —**de·com·pos·a·ble** *adj.*

de·com·pos·er (dée-kəm-pōzər ‖ -kom-) *n.* Something that decomposes or causes decomposition; especially, an organism such as a bacterium or fungus that breaks down dead organic matter.

de·com·po·si·tion (dée-kompə-zísh'n) *n.* The act or result of decomposing; especially: 1. *Chemistry.* Separation into constituents by chemical reaction. 2. *Biology.* Organic decay. 3. *Geology.* Chemical breakdown of rock minerals with the resultant disintegration of the rocks themselves.

de·com·pound¹ (dée-kəm-pównd ‖ -kom-) *tr.v.* -**pounded, -pounding, -pounds.** 1. To create (compounded things) by combining various elements. ~*adj.* 1. Compounded or consisting of things or parts already compound. 2. Having or consisting of subdivided or compound leaflets: *a decompound leaf.*

de·com·pound² *tr.v.* -**pounded, -pounding, -pounds.** To decompose.

de·com·press (dée-kəm-préss ‖ -kom-) *tr.v.* -**pressed, -pressing, -presses.** 1. To relieve of pressure. 2. To bring (a diver, for example) back to normal air pressure by means of an air lock or a decompression chamber. —**de·com·pres·sion** (-présh'n) *n.*

decompression chamber *n.* An apparatus in which the air pressure can be artificially varied, for the use of divers and others while they gradually readjust from the high pressure of their working environment to normal pressure.

decompression sickness *n.* A disorder in divers and caisson and tunnel workers caused by a too rapid return from high pressure to atmospheric pressure and characterised by pains in the joints, cramps, paralysis, and eventual death unless treated by gradual decompression. Also called "compressed air illness", the "bends", "caisson disease", "tunnel disease".

de·con·gest·ant (dée-kən-jéstənt ‖ -kon-) *adj.* Able to relieve congestion, especially in the nasal passages. ~*n.* A decongestant drug. [DE- + CONGEST + -ANT.]

de·con·se·crate (dée-kón-si-krayt) *tr.v.* -**crated, -crating, -crates.** To transfer (a church, for example) legally from religious to lay use or ownership. —**de·con·se·cra·tion** (-kraysh'n) *n.*

de·con·struc·tion (dée-kən-strúksh'n ‖ -kon-) *n.* 1. The act or process of dismantling. 2. A method of analysis, as in philosophy or literary criticism, that attempts to uncover hidden assumptions or contradictions in the work. —**de·con·struc·tion·ism** *n.* —**de·con·struc·tion·ist** *adj. & n.* —**de·con·struct** *tr. v.*

de·con·tam·i·nate (dée-kən-támmi-nayt ‖ -kon-) *tr.v.* -**nated, -nating, -nates.** 1. To eliminate contamination in. 2. To make safe by eliminating harmful substances, such as noxious chemicals or radioactive material. —**de·con·tam·i·nant** (-nənt) *n.* —**de·con·tam·i·na·tion** (-náysh'n) *n.* —**de·con·tam·i·na·tor** (-naytər) *n.*

de·con·trol (dée-kən-trōl ‖ -kon-) *tr.v.* -**trolled, -trolling, -trols.** To free from control, especially from government control.

de·cor, dé·cor (dáykawr, déckawr, di-kór, day-) *n.* 1. a. A decorative style or scheme, as of a room or stage setting. b. The decorations and furnishings of a place. 2. A stage setting; scenery. [French, from *décorer,* to DECORATE, from Latin *decorāre.*]

dec·o·rate (déckərayt) *tr.v.* -**rated, -rating, -rates.** 1. To furnish or adorn with fashionable or beautiful things; embellish; ornament. 2. To apply paint or wallpaper to (a room, for example). 3. To confer a medal or other honour upon; present with a decoration. [Latin *decorāre,* from *decus* (stem *decor-*), ornament.]

dec·o·rat·ed (décka-raytid) *adj. Architecture. Often capital* D. Designating a style of English Gothic architecture of the 13th and 14th centuries, characterised by the use of the **ogee** *(see)* and elaborate tracery and carving.

dec·o·ra·tion (décka-ráysh'n) *n.* 1. The act, process, technique, or art of decorating. 2. An object or group of objects used to decorate; an ornament; an embellishment. 3. A medal, badge, or other emblem of honour.

dec·o·ra·tive (décka-rətiv ‖ -raytiv) *adj.* Serving to decorate; ornamental. —**dec·o·ra·tive·ly** *adv.* —**dec·o·ra·tive·ness** *n.*

decorative arts *pl.n.* The arts or crafts, such as pottery or cabinetmaking, producing objects used as decoration or furnishings.

dec·o·ra·tor (décka-raytər) *n.* 1. *British.* A person who decorates walls with paint or wallpaper. 2. An **interior decorator** *(see).*

dec·o·rous (décka-rəss, di-káw-) *adj.* Characterised by or exhibiting decorum; proper. [Latin *decōrus,* from *decor,* seemliness, elegance, beauty.] —**dec·o·rous·ly** *adv.* —**dec·o·rous·ness** *n.*

de·cor·ti·cate (dée-kórti-kayt) *tr.v.* -**cated, -cating, -cates.** 1. To remove the cortex from (an organ or structure), especially in surgery. 2. To remove the bark, husk, or outer layer from; strip; peel. [Latin *dēcorticāre* : *dē-* (removal) + *cortex* (stem *cortic-*), bark.] —**de·cor·ti·ca·tion** (-káysh'n) *n.* —**de·cor·ti·ca·tor** (-kaytər) *n.*

de·co·rum (di-káwr-əm ‖ -kór-) *n.* Respect for social convention and good manners; propriety. See Synonyms at **etiquette.** [Latin *decōrum,* from *decōrus,* DECOROUS.]

de·cou·page, dé·cou·page (dáy-kōō-pa'azh) *n.* 1. The technique of decorating with paper cutouts. 2. Something produced by decoupage. [French, from Old French *decouper,* to cut out : *de-,* from Latin *dē-,* away + *couper,* to cut, strike, from *coup,* stroke, COUP.]

de·cou·ple (dee-kúpp'l) *tr.v.* -**pled, -pling, -ples.** *Electronics.* 1. To remove (unwanted signals or interference produced by coupling) from a signal or circuit. 2. To rid (a signal or circuit) of interference caused by coupling. 3. To **uncouple** *(see):* to decouple the provision of health care from the patient's ability to pay.

de·coy (dée-koy, di-kóy) *n.* 1. An enclosed place, such as a pond or a large trap, into which wildfowl are lured for capture. 2. A living or artificial bird or other animal used to entice game into a trap or within shooting range. 3. One that misleads or leads into danger or a trap, especially by diverting attention from the real danger. ~*v.* (di-kóy) **decoyed, -coying, -coys.** —*tr.* To lure into danger or a trap; entrap by or as if by a decoy. —*intr.* To be lured by or as if by a decoy; fall into a trap. See Synonyms at **lure.** [Perhaps from Dutch *de kooi,* "the cage" : *de,* the, from Middle Dutch + *kooi,* cage, from Middle Dutch *cōie,* from Latin *cavea,* from *cavus,* hollow.] —**de·coy·er** *n.*

de·crease (di-kréess, dée-, dée-kreess) *v.* -**creased, -creasing, -creases.** —*intr.* To grow or become gradually less or smaller; diminish gradually; dwindle. —*tr.* To cause to grow or become less or smaller; make less; reduce. ~*n.* (dée-kreess, -kréess, di-) *Abbr.* **dec.** 1. The act or process of decreasing, or the resulting condition. 2. The amount by which something has been reduced. [Middle English *decresen,* from Old French *de(s)creistre* (present stem *decreiss-*), from Vulgar Latin *discrēscēre* (unattested), variant of Latin *dēcrēscere* : *dē-* (reversal) + *crēscere,* to grow, increase.] —**de·creas·ing·ly** *adv.*

Synonyms: decrease, reduce, lessen, dwindle, abate, diminish.

de·cree (di-krée) *n.* 1. An authoritative order having the force of law. 2. a. In English law, either of two judgments made in divorce proceedings, the first being the provisional *decree nisi,* and the second a *decree absolute,* which follows unless there is some reason to prevent it. b. In Scots law, the final order of a court, either granting or refusing the application or remedy being sought. Also called "decreet". 3. *Roman Catholic Church.* a. A doctrinal or disciplinary act of an ecumenical council. b. An administrative act applying or interpreting articles of canon law. ~*v.* **decreed, -creeing, -crees.** —*tr.* To ordain, establish, or decide by decree. —*intr.* To issue a decree. [Middle English *decre(t),* from Old French, from Latin *dēcrētum,* from *dēcrētus,* past participle of *dēcernere,* to decide : *dē-* (removal) + *cernere,* to sift.] —**de·cree·a·ble** *adj.* —**de·cre·er** *n.*

dec·re·ment (déckri-mənt) *n.* 1. The act or process of decreasing or becoming gradually less. 2. The amount lost by gradual diminution or waste. 3. *Mathematics.* The amount by which a variable is decreased; a negative increment. 4. *Physics.* The ratio of the amplitude of an oscillation to the amplitude after one period, used as a measure of damping. ~*tr.v.* (-ment) **decremented, -menting, -ments.** To make or show a

decrement in or on. [Latin *dēcrēmentum,* from *dēcrēscere,* to DECREASE.]
de·crep·it (di-kréppit) *adj.* Weakened by age, illness, or hard use; broken-down. See Synonyms at **weak.** [Middle English, from Old French, from Latin *dēcrepitus,* probably "cracked" : *dē-* (intensive) + *crepitus,* past participle of *crepāre,* to crack, creak.] **—de·crep·it·ly** *adv.* **—de·crep·i·tude** (di-kréppi-tewd || -tōōd) *n.*
de·crep·i·tate (di-kréppi-tayt) *v.* **-tated, -tating, -tates.** *—tr.* To roast or calcine (crystals) until they emit a crackling sound or until this sound stops. *—intr.* To crackle when roasted. [Medieval Latin *dēcrepitāre* : Latin *dē-* (intensive) + *crepitāre,* frequentative of *crepāre,* to creak, crack.] **—de·crep·i·ta·tion** (-táysh'n) *n.*
de·cre·scen·do (dée-kri-shéndō) *n., pl.* **-dos.** *Abbr.* **decresc. 1.** A gradual decrease in force or loudness. **2.** A musical passage marked or performed in a decrescendo. Also called "diminuendo".
~adj. Abbr. **decresc.** Gradually diminishing in force or loudness; diminuendo.
~adv. Abbr. **decresc.** With a decrescendo; diminuendo. [Italian, from Latin *dēcrescendum,* gerund of *dēcrēscere,* to DECREASE.]
de·cres·cent (di-krézz'nt, -kréss'nt) *adj.* Decreasing; waning. Said of the moon. Compare **increscent.** [Latin *dēcrescēns* (stem *dēcrescent-*), present participle *dēcrescere,* to DECREASE.]
de·cre·tal (di-kréet'l) *n. Roman Catholic Church.* **1.** A decree; especially, a letter from the pope giving a decision on some point of canon law. **2.** *Capital* **D.** *Plural.* The body of papal laws and decrees forming a part of canon law. [Middle English, from Old French, from Medieval Latin *(epistola) dēcrētālis,* (letter) of decree, from Latin *dēcrētum,* DECREE.] **—de·cre·tal** *adj.*
de·cre·tive (di-kréetiv) *adj.* Having the force of a decree.
dec·re·to·ry (di-krée-təri || *U.S.* déckrə-tawri, -tōri) *adj.* Of or resulting from a decree.
de·crim·i·nal·ise, de·crim·i·nal·ize (dée-krímminə-līz, dee-) *tr.v.* **-ised, -ising, -ises.** To cause to be no longer illegal; regulate rather than prohibit: *decriminalise the use of marijuana.* **—de·crim·i·nal·i·sa·tion** (-lī-záysh'n || *U.S.* -li-) *n.*
de·cry (di-krī́) *tr.v.* **-cried, -crying, -cries. 1.** To belittle or disparage openly; censure. **2.** To depreciate or devalue (currency, for example) by official proclamation or by rumour. [French *décrier,* from Old French *descrier,* "to cry down" : *des-,* from Latin *dē-,* down + *crier,* to CRY.] **—de·cri·er** *n.*
Synonyms: *decry, disparage, belittle, depreciate.*
de·crypt (di-krípt, dée-) *tr.v.* **-crypted, -crypting, -crypts.** To decode a cipher, especially without knowledge of the key. [DE- + CRYPT(O-GRAM).]
de·cu·bi·tus ulcer (di-kéwbitəss) *n. Medicine.* A **bedsore** *(see).* [Latin *dēcubitus,* past participle of *dēcumbere,* to lie down. See **decumbent.**]
de·cum·bent (di-kúm-bənt) *adj.* **1.** Reclining; lying down or lying flat; prostrate. **2.** *Botany.* Lying or growing along the ground but turning upwards at or near the apex: *decumbent stems.* [Latin *dēcumbēns* (stem *dēcumbent-*), present participle of *dēcumbere,* to lie down : *dē-,* down + *cumbere,* to lie.] **—de·cum·bence, de·cum·ben·cy** (-bən-si) *n.*
dec·u·ple (déckewp'l) *adj.* Ten times as great; tenfold.
~n. A tenfold amount.
~tr. v. **decupled, -cupling, -cuples.** To multiply by ten or increase tenfold. [Middle English, from Old French, from Late Latin *decuplus* : Latin *decem,* ten + *-plus,* -fold.]
de·cu·plet (déckew-plət, de-kéw-, -plet) *n.* A set of ten items of the same type. [From DECUPLE, by analogy with *triplet.*]
de·cu·ri·on (de-kéwr-i-ən, di-) *n.* **1.** A commander in the Roman army in charge of ten men, especially in the cavalry. **2.** A member of the senate of a Roman colony or town. **3.** A member of a council in certain Italian towns. [Latin *decuriō* (stem *decuriōn-*), from *decuria,* company of ten, from *decem,* ten.]
de·cur·rent (di-kúrrənt) *n. Botany.* A leaf base prolonged down the stem forming a wing or ridge. [Latin *dēcurrēns* (stem *dēcurrent-*), present participle of *dēcurrere,* to run down : *dē-,* down + *currere,* to run.] **—de·cur·rent·ly** *adv.*
dec·u·ry (déckewr-i) *n.* **1.** A division of the Roman army consisting of ten men. **2.** In ancient times, any group of ten men. [Latin *decuria.* See **decurion.**]
de·cus·sate (di-kúss-ayt) *v.* **-sated, -sating, -sates.** *—tr.* To intersect so as to form an X. *—intr.* To cross each other; intersect.
~adj. (-ayt, -ət, -it) **1.** Intersected or crossed in the form of an X. **2.** *Botany.* Arranged on a stem in opposite pairs at right angles to those above or below. [Latin *decussāre* (past participle *decussātus*), from *decussis,* number ten, symbol X, coin worth ten asses : *decem,* ten + *ās,* AS (coin).] **—de·cus·sate·ly** *adv.*
de·cus·sa·tion (dée-kuss-áysh'n) *n.* **1.** A crossing in the shape of an X. **2.** *Anatomy.* An X-shaped crossing of nerve fibres connecting corresponding parts on the two sides of the spinal cord or brain.
de·dans (də-dóɴ) *n., pl.* **dedans. 1.** A screened gallery for spectators at the service end of a real-tennis court. **2.** The spectators at a real-tennis match. [French, "inside", "interior", from Old French, "from within" : *de,* from + *dans,* in, within, from Late Latin *deintus* : Latin *dē,* from + *intus,* within.]
ded·i·cate (déddi-kayt) *tr.v.* **-cated, -cating, -cates. 1.** To set apart for a deity or for religious purposes; consecrate. **2.** To set apart for some special use; appropriate; devote. **3.** To address or inscribe (a literary work or artistic performance, for example) to someone as a mark of respect or affection. **4.** To commit (oneself) to a particular course of thought or action. **5.** To open (a building, for example) for public use or unveil (a monument), especially with a ceremony. —See Synonyms at **devote.**
~adj. Archaic. Devoted; dedicated. [Middle English *dedicaten,* from Latin *dēdicāre,* to give out tidings, proclaim : *dē-,* away from oneself + *dicāre,* to say, proclaim.] **—ded·i·ca·tee** (-kə-tée) *n.* **—ded·i·ca·tor** (-kaytər) *n.*
ded·i·cat·ed (déddi-kaytid) *adj.* **1.** Devoted to a particular vocation, aim, or cause. **2.** *Computing.* Designed to perform one particular function. Said of computer programs or equipment.
ded·i·ca·tion (déddi-káysh'n) *n.* **1. a.** The act of dedicating. **b.** The state of being dedicated. **2.** A note prefixed to a literary, artistic, or musical work dedicating it to someone as a token of affection or esteem. **3.** A rite or ceremony of dedicating. **—ded·i·ca·tive** (-kaytiv), **ded·i·ca·to·ry** (-kə-tri, -təri, -kaytəri || *U.S.* -kə-tawri, -tōri) *adj.*
de·dif·fer·en·ti·a·tion (dée-díffə-rén-shi-áysh'n, -si-) *n. Biology.* The loss of specialised cellular form, especially prior to redifferentiation.
de·duce (di-déwss || -dōōss) *tr.v.* **-duced, -ducing, -duces. 1.** To reach (a conclusion) by reasoning. **2.** To infer from a general principle; reason deductively. **3.** *Archaic.* To trace the origin or derivation of. [Middle English *deducen,* from Latin *dēdūcere,* to lead away, deduce : *dē-,* away + *dūcere,* to lead.] **—de·duc·i·ble** *adj.*
de·duct (di-dúkt) *tr.v.* **-ducted, -ducting, -ducts.** To take away (a quantity from another); subtract. [Latin *dēdūcere* (past participle *dēductus*), to lead or take away, DEDUCE.]
de·duct·i·ble (di-dúktəb'l) *adj.* **1.** Capable of being deducted. **2.** *Chiefly U.S.* Tax-deductible.
de·duc·tion (di-dúksh'n) *n.* **1.** The act of deducting; subtraction. **2.** That which is or may be deducted: *These expenses are legitimate tax deductions.* **3. a.** The act of deducing; the drawing of a conclusion by reasoning. **b.** *Logic.* The process of reasoning in which a conclusion follows necessarily from the stated premises; inference by reasoning from the general to the specific. **c.** *Logic.* A conclusion reached by this process. In this sense, compare **induction.**
de·duc·tive (di-dúktiv) *adj.* **1.** Of or based on deduction. **2.** Involving deduction in reasoning. **—de·duc·tive·ly** *adv.*
Dee (dee), **John** (1527–1608). English mathematician, astronomer, astrologer (as to Elizabeth I), and magician.
Dee. River in Aberdeenshire, northeast Scotland. It flows 140 kilometres (87 miles) from the Grampian Mountains into the North Sea at Aberdeen. *Dee* is an ancient British word for river: there is another one in southern Scotland, one in North Wales, and a fourth in county Limerick in the Republic of Ireland.
deed (deed) *n.* **1.** An act. **2.** A feat; an exploit. **3.** Action or performance in general, especially as distinguished from words: *bold in deed as well as in speech.* **4.** *Law.* A document sealed as an instrument of bond, contract, or conveyance, especially one pertaining to property.
~tr.v. **deeded, deeding, deeds.** *Chiefly U.S.* To transfer by means of a deed. [Middle English *dede,* Old English *dǣd.*]
deed poll *n. Law.* A deed made by one party, especially by a person changing his name.
dee·jay (dée-jáy, -jay) *n. Informal.* A **disc jockey** *(see).* [From the initials *d* and *j.*]
deem (deem) *v.* **deemed, deeming, deems.** *Formal. —tr.* To judge; consider; think: *We deem it advisable to wait. —intr.* To have an opinion; suppose. —See Synonyms at **consider.** [Middle English *demen,* Old English *dēman.*]
de·em·pha·sise, de·em·pha·size (dée-émfə-sīz) *tr.v.* **-ised, -ising, -ises. 1.** To remove emphasis from. **2.** To reduce the emphasis on.
deem·ster (déem-stər) *n.* Also **demp·ster** (démp-). Either of the two justices of the Isle of Man. [DEEM + -STER.]
deep (deep) *adj.* **deeper, deepest. 1.** Extending to or located at: **a.** An unspecified, usually considerable, distance below a surface. **b.** A specified distance below a surface. **2.** Extending from front to rear, or inwards from the outside, for: **a.** An unspecified distance. **b.** A specified distance. **3.** Arising from or penetrating to a depth. **4. a.** Far distant. **b.** In cricket, far from the pitch. **5. a.** Difficult to fathom or understand; obscure. **b.** Learned; understanding; wise. **c.** Cunning; crafty; sly. **6. a.** Profound; intense; extreme. **b.** Profoundly absorbed or immersed. **7.** Dark rather than pale in shade. **8.** Low in pitch; resonant. **—deep down.** *Informal.* In fact rather than in appearance; truthfully.
~n. **1.** Any deep place on land or in a body of water, especially in the ocean and over 6 000 metres (3 000 fathoms) in depth. **2.** The most intense or extreme part. **3.** *Nautical.* A distance estimated in fathoms between successive marks on a sounding line: *by the deep, 11.* **4.** *Plural. Military Slang.* Submarines. **—the deep. 1.** *Poetic.* The ocean. **2.** In cricket, that part of the field far from the pitch.
~adv. **1.** Deeply; profoundly. **2.** Well on in time: *worked deep into the night.* [Middle English *dep,* Old English *dēop,* from Germanic.] **—deep·ly** *adv.* **—deep·ness** *n.*
deep-drawn (déep-dráwn) *adj.* Shaped by forcing through a die while cold. Said of metals.
deep-dyed (déep-dī́d) *adj.* Unmitigated; absolute.
deep·en (déepən) *v.* **-ened, -ening, -ens.** *—tr.* To make deep or deeper. *—intr.* **1.** To become deep or deeper. **2.** To become more intensive: *a deepening depression.* **—deep·en·er** *n.*
deep end *n. Informal.* The most difficult or complex part, as of a project. **—go off the deep end.** *Informal.* **1.** To become distraught or hysterical, especially with anger. **2.** *U.S.* To behave or proceed in an impulsive or reckless way.
deep-end (déep-énd) *tr.v. Informal.* To oblige to enter a project at the deep end, without enough preparation.

deep-freeze (déep-fréez, -freez) *n.* **1. a.** A refrigerator designed to freeze and store food for long periods; a freezer. **b.** *U.S. Capital D.* A trademark for such a refrigerator. **2.** *Informal.* Storage or preservation in, or as if in, a deepfreeze. **3.** A state of suspended activity. —**deep-freeze** (-fréez) *tr.v.*

deep-fry (déep-frī) *tr.v.* **-fried, -frying, -fries.** To fry by immersing in a deep pan of fat or oil.

deep-laid (déep-láyd) *adj.* Elaborately worked out and kept secret. Said of a plan or scheme.

deep-root-ed (déep-róōt-id ‖ -róōt-) *adj.* Firmly implanted; ingrained.

deep-sea (déep-sée) *adj.* **1.** Abyssal. **2.** Of or pertaining to distant waters: *deep-sea fishing.*

deep-seat-ed (déep-séetid) *adj.* Deeply rooted; ingrained.

Deep South *n.* The southeast part of the United States, especially the states of Alabama, Georgia, Louisiana, Mississippi, and South Carolina.

deep space *n.* The regions beyond the moon, encompassing interplanetary, interstellar, and intergalactic space.

deep structure *n. Linguistics.* In the standard theory of transformational grammar, an explicit representation of the parts of a sentence and their relations in a form that allows the meaning of the sentence to be understood. For example, the deep structure of the sentence *Children want to play* may be displayed as *Children want (children play).* See **surface structure.**

deep therapy *n.* A type of radiotherapy using penetrating, high-frequency X-rays.

deep throat *n. Chiefly U.S.* **1.** A secret but authoritative informer on corrupt or dubious official activities. **2.** Fellatio.

deep water *n.* A situation that is extremely complicated to deal with or resolve.

deer (deer) *n., pl.* **deers** or collectively **deer.** **1.** Any of various hoofed ruminant mammals of the family Cervidae, characteristically having deciduous antlers usually borne only by the males. **2.** Any of various smaller deerlike mammals, such as the mouse deer. [Middle English *der,* animal, beast, deer, Old English *dēor.*]

deer-hound (déer-hownd) *n.* A dog of a breed developed in Scotland, resembling a greyhound but larger and having a wiry coat.

deer ked *n.* See **ked.**

deer-lick (déer-lik) *n.* A salty spring or patch of ground, to which deer come to lick the salt and other minerals.

deer mouse *n.* Any of various New World mice of the genus *Peromyscus,* having large ears, white feet and underparts, and a long tail. Also called "white-footed mouse". [From its deerlike agility.]

deer-skin (déer-skin) *n.* **1.** Leather made from the hide of a deer. **2.** A garment made from such leather.

deer-stalk-er (déer-stawkər) *n.* **1.** A person who stalks deer, usually with the intention of killing them. **2.** A soft cloth hat, with peaks at the front and back and with earflaps that can be tied on its top.

de-es-ca-late (dée-ėska-layt, dee-) *tr.v.* **-lated, -lating, -lates.** To decrease the scope or intensity of (a war, for example). —**de-es-ca-la-tion** (-láysh'n) *n.*

def. 1. defective. **2.** defence. **3.** defendant. **4.** deferred. **5.** definite. **6.** definition.

de-face (di-fáyss) *tr.v.* **-faced, -facing, -faces.** **1.** To spoil or mar the surface or appearance of. **2.** To impair the usefulness, value, or influence of. **3.** To efface or obliterate. [Middle English *defacen,* from Old French *desfacier : des-,* from Latin *dē-* (undoing, ruin) + *face,* FACE.] —**de-face-a-ble** *adj.* —**de-face-ment** *n.* —**de-fac-er** *n.*

de fac-to (dee-fáktō, day-) *adj.* **1.** In reality or fact; actually. **2.** Actually exercising power. Compare **de jure.** —**de fac-to** *adv.*
~*n. Australian & N.Z.* A lover whom one lives with. [Latin, "from the fact".]

defaecate. Variant of **defecate.**

de-fal-cate (dée-fal-kayt ‖ *Chiefly U.S.* di-fál-, -fáwl-, déff'l-) *intr.v.* **-cated, -cating, -cates.** *Law.* To misuse funds; embezzle. [Medieval Latin *dēfalcāre,* to cut off : Latin *dē-,* off + *falx* (stem *falc-*), sickle.] —**de-fal-ca-tion** (-káysh'n) *n.* —**de-fal-ca-tor** (-kaytər) *n.*

def-a-ma-tion (déffa-máysh'n) *n. Law.* Calumny; slander or libel. —**de-fam-a-to-ry** (di-fámmə-tri, -tôri) *adj.*

de-fame (di-fáym) *tr.v.* **-famed, -faming, -fames.** To attack the good name of by slander or libel. See Synonyms at **malign.** [Middle English *diffamen, defamen,* from Old French *diffamer, defamer,* from Latin *diffāmāre : dis-* (undoing, ruin) + *fāma,* report, fame.] —**de-fam-er** *n.*

de-fault (di-fáwlt ‖ -fólt) *n.* **1.** A failure to perform a task or fulfil an obligation; especially, failure to meet a financial obligation. **2.** Failure to make a required appearance in court. **3.** The failure of one or more competitors or teams to participate in a contest: *win by default.* **4.** Lack or need. —**go by default.** To be ignored because absent or inconspicuous. —**in default of.** Through the failure, absence, or lack of.
~*v.* **defaulted, -faulting, -faults.** —*intr.* **1.** To fail to do that which is required. **2.** To fail to pay money when it is due. Often used with *on* or *in.* **3.** *Law.* **a.** To fail to appear in court when summoned. **b.** To lose a case by not appearing. **4.** *Sports.* To fail to compete in or complete a scheduled contest. —*tr.* **1.** To fail to perform or pay. **2. a.** To fail to take part in or complete (a contest, for example). **b.** To forfeit (a match, for example) through such failure. **3.** *Law.* **a.** To lose (a case) by failing to take part in it. **b.** To give judgement against (a defendant) because of his failure to participate in the case. [Middle English *defaut(e),* from Old French *defaute,* from Vulgar Latin *dēfallita* (unattested), from *dēfallīre* (unattested), to

fail : *dē-* (intensive) + *fallīre* (unattested), variant of Latin *fallere,* to FAIL.] —**de-fault-er** *n.*

de-fea-sance (di-féez'nss) *n.* **1.** An annulment or rendering void. **2.** *Law.* The voiding of a contract or deed. **3.** *Law.* A clause within a contract or deed providing for annulment. [Middle English *defesaunce,* from Old French *de(s)fesance,* from *de(s)fesant,* present participle of *de(s)faire,* to destroy, DEFEAT.]

de-fea-si-ble (di-féezə-b'l) *adj. Law.* Capable of being annulled or forfeited. —**de-fea-si-bil-i-ty** (-bílləti), **de-fea-si-ble-ness** *n.*

de-feat (di-féet) *tr.v.* **-feated, -feating, -feats.** **1.** To win a victory over; vanquish. **2.** To prevent the success of; thwart. **3.** *Law.* To annul or make void.
~*n.* **1.** The act of defeating or state of being defeated. **2.** Failure to win; overthrow. **3.** A coming to naught; frustration. **4.** *Law.* A making null and void. [Middle English *defeten,* from Old French *de(s)faire* (past participle *desfait*), from Medieval Latin *disfacere,* to undo, destroy : Latin *dis-* (reversal) + *facere,* to do, make.] —**de-feat-er** *n.*

Synonyms: *defeat, conquer, vanquish, beat, rout, subdue, subjugate, overcome.*

de-feat-ism (di-féet-iz'm) *n.* Acceptance of, or resignation to, the prospect of defeat. —**de-feat-ist** *n.*

def-e-cate (déffi-kayt) *v.* **-cated, -cating, -cates.** Also *chiefly British* **def-ae-cate.** —*intr.* To discharge faeces from the bowels. —*tr.* To clarify (a chemical solution). [Latin *dēfaecāre : dē-* (removal) + *faex,* dregs, FAECES.] —**def-e-ca-tion** (-káysh'n) *n.* —**def-e-ca-tor** (-kaytər) *n.*

de-fect (dée-fekt, di-fékt) *n.* **1.** The lack of something necessary or desirable; a deficiency. **2.** An imperfection; a failing; a fault. **3.** *Physics.* An irregularity in a crystal lattice, such as a vacancy or line of missing atoms. —See Synonyms at **blemish.**
~*intr.v.* (di-fékt) **defected, -fecting, -fects.** **1.** To desert one's proclaimed allegiance, political party, or the like. **2.** To leave one's country after disowning allegiance to it and take residence in another. [Middle English, from Old French, from Latin *dēfectus,* deficiency, lack, from the past participle of *dēficere,* to remove from, desert, fail, be wanting : *dē-,* away from + *facere,* to do, set.] —**de-fec-tion** (-féksh'n) *n.* —**de-fec-tor** (-féktər) *n.*

de-fec-tive (di-féktiv) *adj. Abbr.* **def. 1.** Lacking perfection; having a defect; faulty. **2.** Below average or below an acceptable standard, especially in mental powers. Said of a person. **3.** *Grammar.* Lacking one or more of the inflected forms normal for a particular category of word. In English, *may* is a defective verb.
~*n.* **1.** Something imperfect or damaged. **2.** Someone mentally incapacitated. —**de-fec-tive-ly** *adv.* —**de-fec-tive-ness** *n.*

Usage: The similarity in form and meaning between *defective* and *deficient* sometimes leads to a confusion in usage. *Defective* applies especially to what has a discernible fault, and is therefore primarily concerned with quality: *a defective electric light; defective intelligence. Deficient* refers to insufficiency or incompleteness, and is basically a quantitative term, associated with deficit: *a deficient account; deficient in intelligence.*

de-fence *U.S.* **de-fense** (di-fénss ‖ *for senses,* 7a, b, *U.S. also* déefenss) *n. Abbr.* **def. 1.** The act or policy of defending against attack, danger, or injury; protection. **2.** Anyone or anything that defends or protects. **3.** Military resources and activities designed to discourage or defend against enemy attack: *increased spending on defence.* **4. a.** An argument or set of arguments in support or justification of something. **b.** The speech, document, or the like, giving such arguments. **5.** *Law.* **a.** The defendant's opposition to the complaints or allegations against him. **b.** The defendant and his legal counsel. **6.** *Psychology.* An unconsciously acquired and involuntary mental process such as regression, repression, or projection, that protects one from shame or anxiety. **7.** *Sports.* **a.** The action or policy of defending oneself or one's goal against the opposition's attacks. **b.** The team or those of its players attempting to do this. **c.** In cricket, the guarding by a batsman of his wicket. **d.** The participation in a contest or match against a challenger, to retain one's title or championship. —**de-fence-less** *adj.* —**de-fence-less-ly** *adv.* —**de-fence-less-ness** *n.*

defence mechanism *n.* **1.** *Biology.* Any reaction of an organism used in defending itself, as against germs. **2.** *Psychology.* A defence, or the psychic structure or mechanism underlying a defence.

de-fend (di-fénd) *v.* **-fended, -fending, -fends.** —*tr.* **1.** To protect from danger, attack, or harm; shield; guard. **2.** To support or maintain, as by argument or action; justify. **3.** *Law.* **a.** To represent (the defendant) in a civil or criminal case. **b.** To contest (a legal action or claim). **4.** *Sports.* **a.** To protect (oneself or one's goal) against the opposition's attacks. **b.** To compete in order to retain (a title or championship) against a challenger. —*intr.* To make a defence. [Middle English *defenden,* from Old French *defendre,* from Latin *dēfendere,* to ward off.] —**de-fend-a-ble** *adj.* —**de-fend-er** *n.*

Synonyms: *defend, protect, guard, preserve, shield, safeguard.*

de-fen-dant (di-féndənt) *n. Abbr.* **def.** *Law.* A person against whom an action is brought. Compare **plaintiff.**

Defender of the Faith *n.* A title of English sovereigns, originally conferred upon Henry VIII by Pope Leo X (1521).

de-fen-es-tra-tion (dée-fénni-stráysh'n, dee-) *n.* An act of throwing something or someone out of a window. [DE- + FENESTRA + -TION.]

defense. *U.S.* Variant of **defence.**

de-fen-si-ble (di-fén-səb'l) *adj.* Capable of being defended, protected, or justified. —de·fen·si·bil·i·ty (-sə-bíllәti), de·fen·si·ble· ness n. —de·fen·si·bly adv.

Usage: Defensible and defensive come from the same root, but have distinct meanings. Defensible means "capable of being defended": a defensible position; defensive means "intended for or providing a defence", and is frequently used with pejorative connotations: You're very defensive.

de·fen·sive (di-fén-siv) adj. 1. Intended or appropriate for defence. 2. Done for defence; defending. 3. Of or pertaining to defence. —See Usage note at defensible.
~n. 1. A means of defence. 2. An attitude of defence. —on the defensive. Ready to defend or justify oneself. —de·fen·sive·ly adv. —de·fen·sive·ness n.

de·fer¹ (di-fér) v. -ferred, -ferring, -fers. —tr. To put off until a future time; postpone. —intr. To procrastinate; delay. [Middle English differen, from Old French differer, from Latin differre : dis-, away + ferre, to carry.] —de·fer·rer n.

defer² intr.v. -ferred, -ferring, -fers. To comply with or submit to the opinion or decision of another; be deferential. Used with to. See Synonyms at yield. [Middle English deferren, from Old French def(f)erer, from Latin dēferre, to carry away, bring to, submit : dē-, away + ferre, to carry.] —de·fer·rer n.

def·er·ence (défféranss) n. 1. Submission or courteous yielding to the opinion, wishes, or judgment of another. 2. Courteous respect. —See Synonyms at honour.

def·er·ent¹ (défférant) adj. Showing deference; deferential.

deferent² adj. 1. Carrying down or away. Said of nerves, blood vessels, and similar channels conveying impulses, fluids, or the like. 2. Adapted to carry or transport.
~n. Astronomy. A circle with the earth at its centre, marking the path of the centre of a planet's epicycle in the Ptolemaic model of the universe. [Latin dēferēns, stem dēferent-), present participle of dēferre, to bring to, DEFER (to comply).]

def·er·en·tial (déffa-rénsh'l) adj. Marked by courteous respect: "Mr. Bulstrode had also a deferential, bending attitude in listening." (George Eliot). —def·er·en·tial·ly adv.

de·fer·ment (di-fér-mant) n. Also de·fer·ral (-'l). The act or an instance of delaying or putting off; postponement.

de·fer·ra·ble, de·fer·a·ble (di-fér-ab'l) adj. Suitable for being postponed: deferrable plans.

de·ferred (di-férd) adj. Abbr. def. 1. Postponed; delayed. 2. With benefits or payments withheld until a future date.

de·fer·ves·cence (dée-far-véss'nss, -fer-) n. The abatement of a fever. [DE- + Latin fervescere, inceptive of fervēre, to boil, be hot + -ENCE.]

de·fi·ance (di-fí-anss) n. 1. The disposition to defy or resist an opposing force or authority; resolute resistance. 2. Intentionally provocative behaviour or attitude; a challenge. [Middle English defiaunce, from Old French desfiance, from desfier, DEFY.]

de·fi·ant (di-fí-ant) adj. Marked by defiance. —de·fi·ant·ly adv.

de·fib·ril·la·tion (dée-fíbbri-láysh'n) n. Medicine. The administration of an electric shock to restore normal heart rhythm in cases of fibrillation. Electrodes from the apparatus used, a defibrillator, are placed over the chest wall or directly on the heart.

de·fi·cien·cy (di-físh'n-si) n., pl. -cies. Also rare de·fi·cience (-fish'nss). 1. The quality or condition of being deficient. 2. A lack; a shortage; an insufficiency. 3. Genetics. A deletion (see).

deficiency disease n. A disease caused by the lack of essential substances, especially vitamins, in the diet.

de·fi·cient (di-físh'nt) adj. 1. Lacking an essential quality or element; incomplete; defective. 2. Inadequate in amount or degree; insufficient. —See Usage note at defective. [Latin dēficiēns (stem dēficient-), present participle of dēficere, to remove from, desert, fail, lack : dē-, away + facere, to make, do.] —de·fi·cient·ly adv.

def·i·cit (déffi-sit, rarely déefi-, di-físsit) n. 1. The amount by which a sum of money falls short of the required or expected amount; a shortage. 2. Finance. An excess of liabilities over assets, or expenditures over income. [French déficit, from Latin dēficit, it is lacking, from dēficere, to lack. See deficient.]

deficit spending n. Government spending of money obtained by borrowing, resulting in a deficit in the budget.

de fi·de (dee fídi, day féeday) adj. Latin. Roman Catholic Church. Designating a doctrine that is an essential part of the faith, especially when so ruled by the pope. [Literally, of faith.]

def·i·lade (déffi-láyd || U.S. -layd) tr.v. -laded, -lading, -lades. Military. To arrange (fortifications) so as to give protection from enfilading and other fire.
~n. The act or procedure of defilading, or the protection so provided. [DE- + (EN)FILADE.]

de·file¹ (di-fíl) tr.v. -filed, -filing, -files. 1. To make filthy or dirty. 2. To tarnish the lustre of; render impure; corrupt. 3. To profane or sully (a good name or reputation, for example). 4. To make unclean or unfit for ceremonial use; desecrate. 5. To violate the chastity of. [Middle English defilen, probably alteration (influenced by filen, to sully) of defoulen, to trample down, injure, from Old French defouler : de-, from Latin dē-, down + fouler, to trample, FULL (verb).] —de·file·ment n. —de·fil·er n. —de·fil·ing·ly adv.

de·file² (di-fíl) intr.v. -filed, -filing, -files. 1. To march in single file. 2. To march in files or columns.
~n. (dée-fíl, di-fíl) 1. A narrow pass that restricts lateral movement, as of troops. 2. A marching in line, as of a single column of soldiers or travellers. [French défiler : dé-, off, away

+ filer, to march by files, from Old French, to spin, from Late Latin fīlāre, from Latin fīlum, thread.]

de·fine (di-fín) v. -fined, -fining, -fines. —tr. 1. To state the precise meaning of (a word or sense of a word, for example). 2. To describe the nature or basic qualities of; explain: define the properties of a new drug. 3. To delineate the outline or form of; make clear: a shape defined by a line. 4. To specify distinctly; fix definitely: define the weapons to be used in limited warfare. 5. To serve to distinguish; characterise. —intr. To make a definition. [Middle English diffinen, from Old French definer, from Vulgar Latin dēfīnāre (unattested), variant of Latin dēfīnīre, to set bounds to : dē, off + fīnis, end, boundary.] —de·fin·a·bil·i·ty (-a-bíllati) n. —de·fin·a·ble adj. —de·fin·a·bly adv. —de·fine·ment n. —de·fin·er n.

de·fin·i·en·dum (di-fínni-én-dəm) n., pl. -da (-də). That which is defined by a definiens. [Latin, neuter of dēfīnīendus, gerundive of dēfīnīre, to set bounds to, DEFINE.]

de·fin·i·ens (di-fínni-enz) n., pl. definientia (-én-shi-ə, -shə). The word or words serving to define another word or expression, as in a dictionary entry. [Latin dēfīniēns, present participle of dēfīnīre, DEFINE.]

def·i·nite (déffi-nət, -nit) adj. 1. Having distinct limits: definite restrictions on wine and spirit sales. 2. Known positively; for certain; sure: a definite victory. 3. Clearly defined; precise; explicit: a definite statement of the terms of the will. 4. Abbr. def. Grammar. Limiting or particularising. 5. Botany. a. Of a specified number not exceeding 20. Said of floral organs, especially stamens. b. Determinate. [Middle English diffinite, from Latin dēfīnītus, past participle of dēfīnīre, to determine, DEFINE.] —def·i·nite·ness n.

Usage: Definite and definitive both apply to what is precisely defined or explicitly set forth. But definitive more often refers, in addition, to what is unalterably final, and is not therefore usually interchangeable with definite. A definite decision is firm and clear-cut, and might come at any time and be provided by anyone. A definitive decision, by contrast, usually implies the conclusion of a process of decision-making ("less definite" decisions having previously been made), and suggests that the issues are complex or important, and have received the attention of an authority.

definite article n. Grammar. The article which restricts or particularises the noun or noun phrase following it; in English, the article the. Compare indefinite article.

definite integral n. An integral that is calculated between two specified limits, usually expressed in the form $\int_a^b f(x)dx$. The result of performing the integral is a number which represents the area under the curve of function $f(x)$ between the limits and the x-axis. Compare indefinite integral.

def·i·nite·ly (déf-nət-li, déffi-, -nit-) adv. 1. In a definite way. 2. Certainly; undoubtedly.
~interj. Used to express emphatic confirmation.

def·i·ni·tion (déffi-nísh'n) n. Abbr. def. 1. The act of stating a precise meaning or significance, as of a word, phrase, or term. 2. The statement of such a meaning. 3. The act or an instance of making clear and distinct: a definition of one's intentions. 4. The state of being closely outlined or determined. 5. A determining of outline, extent, or limits: the definition of my authority. 6. In telecommunications, the degree of clarity with which a televised image is received or a radio receives a given station. 7. The clarity of detail in an optically produced image, as in a photograph, produced by a combination of resolution and contrast. [Middle English diffinicioun, from Old French definition, from Latin dēfīnītiō (stem dēfīnītiōn-), from dēfīnīre, DEFINE.] —def·i·ni·tion·al adj.

de·fin·i·tive (di-fínnə-tiv) adj. 1. Precisely defining or outlining; explicit. 2. Determining finally; conclusive; decisive. 3. Designating a statement or work that can stand as the most complete and authoritative: the definitive biography of Lawrence. 4. Zoology. In a complete, fully developed form. Said especially of parasites. 5. Issued for permanent rather than commemorative or other use. Said of a postage stamp. —See Usage note at definite.
~n. 1. Grammar. A word that defines or limits, such as the definite article or a demonstrative pronoun. 2. A definitive postage stamp. —de·fin·i·tive·ly adv. —de·fin·i·tive·ness n.

de·fin·i·tude (di-fínni-tewd || -tood) n. The quality of being definite or exact; precision.

def·la·grate (défflə-grayt, dééflə-) v. -grated, -grating, -grates. —tr. To cause to burn with great heat and intense light. —intr. To burn with great heat and intense light. [Latin dēflagrāre : dē- (intensive) + flagrāre, to burn.] —def·la·gra·tion (-gráysh'n) n.

de·flate (di-fláyt, dée-) v. -flated, -flating, -flates. —tr. 1. a. To release contained air or gas from. b. To collapse by releasing contained air or gas. 2. To reduce or lessen the confidence, pride, self-esteem, or certainty of. 3. Economics. a. To reduce the amount or availability of (currency or credit), effecting a decline in prices. b. To produce deflation in (an economy). In these senses, compare reflate. —intr. To be or become deflated. [DE- (reversal) + (IN)-FLATE.] —de·fla·tor (-fláytər) n.

de·fla·tion (di-fláysh'n, dée-) n. 1. a. The act of deflating. b. The state of being deflated. 2. Economics. A reduction in the general price level, brought on by a decrease in the amount of money in circulation or in the total volume of spending. Compare inflation. 3. Geology. The blowing away of loose rock particles by the wind. —de·fla·tion·ar·y (-ri, -əri || -erri) adj. —de·fla·tion·ist n.

de·flect (di-flékt) v. -flected, -flecting, -flects. —tr. To cause to swerve or turn aside. —intr. To swerve or turn aside. [Latin dēflec-

tere : *dē-*, away + *flectere,* to bend, FLEX.] **—de·flec·ta·ble** *adj.* **—de·flec·tive** *adj.* **—de·flec·tor** (-fléktər) *n.*

de·flec·tion (di-flékshʼn) *n.* Also *British* **de·flex·ion. 1. a.** The act of deflecting. **b.** The condition of being deflected. **2.** Deviation or the amount of deviation. **3.** The deviation from zero shown by the indicator of a measuring instrument. **4.** The movement of a structure or structural part as a result of stress.

de·flexed (di-flékst, dée-flekst) *adj. Botany.* Bent or turned downwards at a sharp angle: *deflexed petals.* [Latin *dēflexus,* past participle of *dēflectere,* DEFLECT.]

de·floc·cu·late (dée-flóckew-layt, di-) *v.* **-lated, -lating, -lates.** *—tr.* **1.** To disperse (an aggregate, such as clay or soil) into fine particles. **2.** To prevent or hinder (a suspension or colloid) from forming an aggregate. *—intr.* To be dispersed into fine particles. **—de·floc·cu·la·tion** (-láyshʼn) *n.*

de·flo·ra·tion (dée-flaw-ráyshʼn, défflə-) *n.* The act of deflowering.

de·flow·er (di-flówr, dée-, -flów-ər) *tr.v.* **-ered, -ering, -ers. 1.** To strip of flowers. **2.** *Literary.* To rupture the hymen of (a virgin) by sexual intercourse. Sometimes used humorously. **3.** To spoil the appearance or nature of; mar. **4.** To destroy the innocence of; violate. [Middle English *deflouren,* from Old French *deflorer,* from Late Latin *dēflōrāre* : Latin *dē-* (removal) + *flōs* (stem *flōr-*), flower.] **—de·flow·er·er** *n.*

De·foe (di-fṓ), **Daniel** (1660–1731). English author. He took part in Monmouth's rebellion (1685) and later became a journalist. *Robinson Crusoe,* the most famous of his many novels, was published in 1719. Three major works appeared in 1722 alone: the novels *Moll Flanders* and *The History of Colonel Jack,* and the pseudo-documentary *Journal of the Plague Year.*

de·fo·li·ant (dee-fṓli-ənt, di-) *n.* A chemical sprayed or dusted on plants to cause the leaves to fall off.

de·fo·li·ate (dee-fṓli-ayt, di-) *v.* **-ated, -ating, -ates.** *—tr.* To deprive (a tree or other plant) of leaves, as by the use of a chemical spray or dust. *—intr.* To lose foliage. [Late Latin *dēfoliāre* : Latin *dē,* removal + *folium,* leaf.] **—de·fo·li·ate** (-ət, -it, -ayt) *adj.* **—de·fo·li·a·tion** (-áyshʼn) *n.* **—de·fo·li·a·tor** (-aytər) *n.*

de·force (di-fórss || -fṓrss) *tr.v.* **-forced, -forcing, -forces.** *Law.* **1. a.** In English feudal property law, to withhold by force from the rightful owner. **b.** To deprive (a rightful owner) of property by force. **2.** In Scots law, to resist an officer of the law in the performance of his duty. [Middle English *deforcen,* from Anglo-French *deforcer,* variant of Old French *de(s)forcier* : *des-* (reversal) + *forcier,* to force, from Vulgar Latin *fortiāre* (unattested), from Latin *fortis,* strong.] **—de·force·ment** *n.*

de·for·ciant (di-fór-si-ənt || -fṓr-, -shənt) *n. Law.* One who deforces a rightful owner.

de·for·est (dée-fórrist, di- || *U.S. also* -fáwrist) *tr.v.* **-ested, -esting, -ests.** To cut down and clear away the trees or forests from. **—de·for·es·ta·tion** (-áyshʼn) *n.* **—de·for·est·er** *n.*

de·form (di-fórm, dée-) *v.* **-formed, -forming, -forms.** *—tr.* **1.** To spoil the natural form of; misshape. **2.** To deface; disfigure. **3.** To spoil the nature of; pervert. **4.** To alter the shape of by pressure or stress. *—intr.* To become deformed. —See Synonyms at **distort.** [Middle English *deformen,* from Old French *deformer,* from Latin *dēformāre* : *dē-* (reversal) + *formāre,* to form, from *forma,* FORM.] **—de·form·a·bil·i·ty** (-ə-bílləti) *n.* **—de·form·a·ble** *adj.* **—de·for·ma·tion** (dée-fawr-máyshʼn, déffər-) *n.*

de·formed (di-fórmd) *adj.* Misshapen; disfigured.

de·form·i·ty (di-fórməti) *n., pl.* **-ties. 1.** The state or condition of being deformed. **2.** A bodily malformation, such as a clubfoot or hunchback. **3.** A deformed person or thing. **4.** Gross ugliness or distortion, especially in art or morals.

de·fraud (di-fráwd) *tr.v.* **-frauded, -frauding, -frauds.** To deprive (a person) of property by fraud; swindle. [Middle English *defrauden,* from Old French *defrauder,* from Latin *dēfraudāre* : *dē-* (intensive) + *fraudāre,* to cheat, from *fraus* (stem *fraud-*), FRAUD.] **—de·fraud·a·tion** (dée-fraw-dáyshʼn) *n.* **—de·fraud·er** *n.*

de·fray (di-fráy) *tr.v.* **-frayed, -fraying, -frays.** To meet or satisfy (costs or expenses) by payment; pay: *defray the cost of a trip.* [French *défrayer,* from Old French *deffrayer, desfrayer* : *des-* (removal) + *frai* (attested only in the plural *frais*), expense, cost, "damage", from Latin *fractum,* from *fractus,* past participle of *frangere,* to break.] **—de·fray·a·ble** *adj.* **—de·fray·al** *n.*

de·frock (dée-frók) *tr.v.* **-frocked, -frocking, -frocks.** To unfrock.

de·frost (dée-fróst, di- || -fráwst) *v.* **-frosted, -frosting, -frosts.** *—tr.* **1.** To remove ice or frost from (a refrigerator, for example). **2.** To cause to thaw. *—intr.* **1.** To become free of ice or frost. **2.** To become unfrozen; thaw.

de·frost·er (dée-fróst-ər, di- || -fráwst-) *n.* **1.** A device to help remove ice or prevent its formation in a refrigerator. **2.** *U.S.* A demister.

deft (deft) *adj.* Skilful; adroit. See Synonyms at **dexterous.** [Middle English *defte,* originally "gentle", "meek", variant of *dafte,* DAFT.] **—deft·ly** *adv.* **—deft·ness** *n.*

de·funct (di-fúngkt) *adj.* **1.** Having ceased to live or exist; extinct; dead. **2.** No longer operative, effective, or respected. [Latin *dēfunctus,* past participle of *dēfungī,* to discharge, finish, die : *dē-* (intensive) + *fungī,* to discharge.] **—de·func·tive** *adj.* **—de·funct·ness** *n.*

de·fuse (dée-féwz, di-) *tr.v.* **-fused, -fusing, -fuses. 1.** To remove the fuse from (an explosive device). **2.** To make less dangerous, tense, or hostile: *defuse an international crisis.*

de·fy (di-fī́) *tr.v.* **-fied, -fying, -fies. 1.** To confront or stand up to; challenge: *defying convention.* **2.** To resist (an attempt, for example) successfully; withstand, especially in a puzzling way: *"so the plague defied all medicines"* (Daniel Defoe). **3.** To challenge or dare (a person) to perform something considered impossible. [Middle English *defien, diffien,* from Old French *desfier,* from Vulgar Latin *disfīdāre* (unattested), to renounce one's faith : *dis-* (reversal) + *fīdāre* (unattested), variant of Latin *fīdere,* to trust.] **—de·fi·er** *n.*

deg, deg. degree (thermometric).

dé·ga·gé (dáy-gaa-zháy) *adj.* Free and relaxed in manner; casual. [French, past participle of *dégager,* to disengage, release, from Old French *desgagier,* "to redeem a pledge" : *des-* (reversal) + *gage,* a pledge, gage, from Frankish (unattested) *wadi.*]

de·gas (dée-gáss) *tr.v.* **-gassed, -gassing, -gasses** or **-gases. 1.** To remove poisonous gases from (a place or person). **2.** To evacuate gas from (a substance or device). **—de·gas·ser** *n.*

De·gas (dáygaa; *French* də-gaá), **(Hilaire Germain) Edgar** (1834–1917). French painter and sculptor. He was noted for his portrayal of movement, as in his paintings of ballet dancers.

De Gaulle (də gṓl, gáwl), **Charles (André Joseph Marie)** (1890–1970). French soldier and statesman, president of France (1958–69). Based in London during World War II, he was made head of the Free French forces in exile, and became the acknowledged leader of the Resistance movement in France. He led the provisional government briefly after the liberation (1944–46). With the Algerian crisis (1958), De Gaulle's supporters brought him out of retirement. He was made prime minister, empowered to redraw the constitution, and became president of the new Fifth Republic (1959). Despite violent hostility, he supervised Algeria's path to independence in 1962. He defended the French nuclear deterrent, and reduced France's participation in NATO (1966). His leadership was severely tested by strikes and student riots in 1968, and he resigned the following year after proposed constitutional reforms were rejected in a referendum.

de·gauss (dée-gówss) *tr.v.* **-gaussed, -gaussing, -gausses.** To remove or neutralise the magnetic field of (a ship, piece of electronic apparatus, or the like). [DE- + GAUSS.]

de·gen·er·a·cy (di-jénnərə-si) *n., pl.* **-cies. 1.** The state or condition of being degenerate. **2.** The process of degenerating. **3.** *Physics.* The number of quantum states with the same energy.

de·gen·er·ate (di-jénnə-rayt) *intr.v.* **-ated, -ating, -ates. 1.** To become degenerate; deteriorate. **2.** *Biology.* To undergo degeneration. *~adj.* (-rət, -rit || -rayt). **1.** Characterised by deterioration; having declined in condition or quality. **2.** Having become debased or depraved; having declined morally. **3.** *Physics.* **a.** Having the same energy. Said of quantum states that are distinct but of equal energy: *degenerate orbitals.* **b.** Designating or pertaining to a semiconductor in which the number of conduction electrons approaches that in a metallic conductor. **c.** Having modes with equal frequencies. Said of a resonance device. **d.** Composed of nuclei and electrons; fully ionised. Said of matter in neutron stars.
~n. (-rət, -rit || -rayt). **1.** A morally degraded person. **2. a.** A person lacking or having progressively lost normative biological or psychological characteristics. **b.** A person exhibiting antisocial, especially sexually deviant, behaviour. [Latin *dēgenerāre,* to fall from one's ancestral quality : *dē-,* away from + *genus* (stem *gener-*), race.] **—de·gen·er·ate·ly** *adv.* **—de·gen·er·ate·ness** *n.* **—de·gen·er·a·tive** (-rətiv) *adj.*

de·gen·er·a·tion (di-jénnə-ráyshʼn) *n.* **1.** The process of degenerating. **2.** The state or condition of being degenerate. **3.** *Biology.* **a.** The usually irreversible deterioration of specific cells or organs with corresponding loss of function, caused by injury or disease and often resulting in necrosis or death. **b.** The loss of function of a part or organ over a period of time, as in the evolutionary development of vestigial organs. **4.** *Electronics.* Negative feedback of output power to an input signal in an amplifying circuit.

de·glu·ti·nate (dée-glóō-ti-nayt, di- || -gléw-) *tr.v.* **-nated, -nating, -nates.** To extract the gluten from (wheat flour, for example). [Latin *dēglūtināre* : *dē* (removal) + *glūtināre,* to glue, from *glūten,* glue.] **—de·glu·ti·na·tion** (-náyshʼn) *n.*

de·glu·ti·tion (dée-glóō-tíshʼn || -glew-) *n.* The process or act of swallowing. [French, from Latin *dēglūtīre,* to swallow down : *dē-,* down + *glūtīre,* to swallow.] **—de·glu·ti·to·ry** (-ti-tri, -təri) *adj.*

deg·ra·da·tion (déggrə-dáyshʼn) *n.* **1.** The act or process of degrading; specifically: **a.** A deposition, removal, or dismissal from rank or office. **b.** A reduction in worth or standing. **2.** A process of transition from a higher to a lower quality or level. **3.** The state or condition of being degraded; deterioration; degeneration. **4.** *Geology.* **a.** A general lowering of the earth's surface by erosion and removal of the eroded material. **b. Denudation** *(see).* **c.** The downward cutting action of a stream as it carves its bed. **5.** The changes in the nature of a soil as its chemicals are washed away. **6.** *Chemistry.* Decomposition of a compound into simpler compounds; especially, decomposition by stages exhibiting well-defined intermediate products. —See Synonyms at **disgrace.**

de·grade (di-gráyd) *tr.v.* **-graded, -grading, -grades. 1.** To reduce in grade, rank, or status; especially, to deprive of an office or dignity. **2.** To lower in moral or intellectual character; debase; corrupt. **3.** To reduce, divert, or pervert. **4.** To expose to contempt, dishonour, or disgrace. **5.** To impair or reduce in quality. **6.** *Geology.* To lower by erosion. Compare **aggrade. 7.** *Chemistry.* To cause (a compound) to undergo degradation. [Middle English *degraden,* from Old French *degrader,* from Late Latin *dēgradāre* : Latin *dē-,* down + *gradus,* rank, step.] **—de·grad·er** *n.* **—de·grad·a·ble** *adj.*

Synonyms: degrade, abase, demean, humble, humiliate, discredit, mortify.

de·grad·ed (di-gráydid) adj. **1.** Reduced in rank, honour, or position. **2.** Reduced in quality or value; distorted; vulgarised: a degraded level of art. **3.** Having declined in moral qualities; depraved; degenerate. **4.** Considered as below normal standards of civilisation. —**de·grad·ed·ly** adv. —**de·grad·ed·ness** n.

de·grad·ing (di-gráyding) adj. **1.** Debasing; giving rise to embarrassment or humiliation. **2.** Geology. Eroding to a lower level; wearing down. —**de·grad·ing·ly** adv.

de·grease (dée-gréess ‖ -gréez) tr.v. **-greased, -greasing, -greases.** To remove the grease from.

de·gree (di-grée) n. **1.** Any of a series of steps or stages in a process, course of action, progression, or retrogression. **2.** The relative distance, or a step, in a direct hereditary line of descent or ascent. **3.** Archaic. Relative social or official rank, dignity, or position. **4.** Relative intensity or amount of a quality, attribute, or the like. **5.** Relative condition or extent; capacity; manner. **6.** The extent or measure of a state of being, action, or the like. **7.** Abbr. **deg, deg.** Symbol ° **a.** A unit division of a temperature scale. **b.** A unit division of various other scales of measurement, such as scales of hardness or relative density. **8.** Symbol ° A unit of angular measure equal in magnitude to the central angle subtended by 1/360 of the circumference of a circle. **9.** Geography. A unit of latitude or longitude, 1/360 of a great circle. **10.** In algebra: **a.** The greatest sum of the exponents of the variables in a term of a polynomial or polynomial equation. **b.** The exponent of the derivative of highest order in a differential equation in standard form; for example, the polynomial $ax^2 + bx + c$ is of the second degree. Compare **order.** **11. a.** An academic title given by a college or university to a student who has completed a course of study. **b.** A similar title conferred as an honorary distinction. **12.** Law. **a.** In the United States, a division or classification of a specific crime according to its seriousness. **b.** In Britain, either of the two classifications formerly applied to a felony. **13.** Grammar. Any of the three forms used in the comparison of adjectives and adverbs. See **positive, comparative, superlative. 14.** Music. **a.** Any of the seven notes of a diatonic scale. **b.** A space or line of the staff. **15.** Any of the three former classifications of a burn according to seriousness. —**by degrees.** Little by little; gradually. —**to a degree. 1.** To a great extent. **2.** Somewhat. [Middle English degre, from Old French, from Vulgar Latin dēgradus (unattested), "a step down" : Latin dē-, down + gradus, a step.]

de·gree-day (di-grée-dáy) n. **1.** An indication of the extent of departure of the mean daily temperature from a standard. **2.** A unit used in estimating quantities of fuel and power consumption, based on a daily ratio of consumption and the mean temperature below 18°C (65°F).

degree of freedom n. **1.** Statistics. Any of the unrestricted, independent random variables that constitute a statistic. **2.** Any of the minimum number of coordinates required to specify completely the motion of a mechanical system. **3.** In thermodynamics, any of the independent variables, such as pressure, temperature, or composition, required to specify a system with a given number of phases and components. See **phase rule.**

de·gres·sion (di-grésh'n, dée-) n. **1.** A going down by stages or steps; a descent. **2.** The progressive reduction of the rate of tax on sums below a certain limit. [Middle English degressioun, from Medieval Latin dēgressiō (stem dēgressiōn-), from Latin dēgredī (past participle dēgressus), to step down : dē-, down + gradī, to go, step.] —**de·gres·sive** adj.

de·gum (dée-gúm) tr.v. **-gummed, -gumming, -gums.** To free from gum.

de·gust (di-gúst, dée-) v. **-gusted, -gusting, -gusts.** Rare. —tr. To taste with relish or care. —intr. To have a taste; be relishing. [Latin dēgustāre : dē- (intensive) + gustāre, to taste.] —**de·gus·ta·tion** (dée-guss-táysh'n) n.

De Hav·il·land (di hávvilənd), Sir Geoffrey (1882–1965). British aircraft designer. He taught himself to fly in a plane of his own design (1910). His company produced the Moth biplane (1925), the Mosquito of World War II, and the Comet (1949), which in 1952 became the world's first commercial jet airliner.

de·hisce (di-híss) intr.v. **-hisced, -hiscing, -hisces.** To burst or split open along a line or slit, as do the ripe capsules or pods of some plants. [Latin dēhiscere : dē-, off + hiscere, to open, split, inceptive of hiāre, to be open, gape.]

de·his·cent (di-híss'nt) adj. Opening at pores or by splitting to release seeds within a fruit or pollen from an anther. Compare **indehiscent.** —**de·his·cence** n.

de·horn (dée-hórn) tr.v. **-horned, -horning, -horns. 1.** To remove the horns from. **2.** To prevent growth in the horns of (cattle, for example), as by cauterisation.

Deh·ra Dun (dáir-ə dŏon, dáy-ərə). City in Uttar Pradesh, north India. It was founded by a 17th-century Sikh community whose temple (1669) survives. The Indian Military Academy and Forestry Department have their headquarters there.

de·hu·man·ise, de·hu·man·ize (dée-héwmən-īz ‖ -yŏomən-) tr.v. **-ised, -ising, -ises. 1.** To deprive of human qualities or attributes. **2.** To offend human dignity or personality: dehumanising conditions. **3.** To render mechanical and routine. —**de·hu·man·i·sa·tion** (-ī-záysh'n ‖ U.S. -i-) n.

de·hu·mid·i·fy (dée-hew-míddi-fī ‖ -yŏo-) tr.v. **-fied, -fying, -fies.** To remove atmospheric moisture from; decrease the humidity of. —**de·hu·mid·i·fi·ca·tion** (-fi-káysh'n) n. —**de·hu·mid·i·fi·er** n.

de·hy·drate (dée-hí-drayt, -hī-dráyt) v. **-drated, -drating, -drates.** —tr. **1.** Chemistry. To eliminate water from or make anhydrous. **2.** To remove water from (vegetables, for example) for preservation. **3.** To cause to lose body fluids. **4.** Informal. To make dull or uninteresting. Usually used in the passive. —intr. **1.** To lose moisture; become dry. **2.** To become dehydrated. —**de·hy·dra·tor** (-ər) n.

de·hy·dra·tion (dée-hī-dráysh'n) n. **1.** The process of removing water from a substance or compound. **2.** Pathology. Excessive loss of water from the body or from an organ or bodily part.

de·hy·dro·gen·ase (dée-hī-drójən-ayz, -hídrəjən-, -ayss) n. An enzyme that removes hydrogen from a substrate in oxidation-reduction reactions.

de·hy·dro·ge·nate (dée-hī-drója-nayt, -hídrəjə-) tr.v. **-nated, -nating, -nates.** Chemistry. To remove hydrogen from; dehydrogenise. —**de·hy·dro·ge·na·tion** (-náysh'n) n.

de·hy·dro·ge·nise, de·hy·dro·ge·nize (dée-hī-drójə-nīz, -hídrəjə-) tr.v. **-nised, -nising, -nises.** To dehydrogenate. —**de·hy·dro·ge·ni·sa·tion** (-nī-záysh'n ‖ U.S. -ni-) n.

de·hyp·no·tise (dée-hípnə-tīz) tr.v. **-tised, -tising, -tises.** To arouse from a hypnotic state.

de-ice (dée-íss) tr.v. **-iced, -icing, -ices.** To keep free of ice; remove ice from.

de-ic·er (dée-í-sər) n. **1.** Any device, such as an electric heater, used to keep surfaces free from ice or remove ice after it has formed. **2.** Any compound used to prevent the formation of ice on windows, windscreens, and the like.

de·i·cide (dée-i-sīd, dáy-) n. **1.** The killing of a god. **2.** One who kills a god. [New Latin deicida : Latin deus, god, DEITY + -CIDE.]

deic·tic (díktik) adj. **1.** Logic. Directly proving by argument. Compare **elenctic. 2.** Grammar. Designating a word, such as this or you, that specifies the object, person, or time referred to; demonstrative. [Greek deiktikos, from deiktos, able to show directly, from deiknunai, to show.] —**deic·ti·cal·ly** adv.

de·if·ic (dee-iffik, day-) adj. **1.** Making or tending to make divine. **2.** Divine; godlike. [Old French deifique, from Late Latin deificus : Latin deus, god, DEITY + -FIC.]

de·i·fi·ca·tion (dée-i-fi-káysh'n, dáy-) n. **1.** The act or process of deifying. **2.** The condition of having been deified.

de·i·form (dée-i-fawrm, dáy-) adj. Embodying the qualities of a god; godlike. [Medieval Latin deiformis : dei-, genitive of deus, god + -formis, -FORM.]

de·i·fy (dée-i-fī, dáy-) tr.v. **-fied, -fying, -fies. 1.** To raise to divine rank. **2.** To worship, revere, or personify as a god. **3.** To idealise; exalt. [Middle English deifien, from Old French deifier, from Late Latin deificāre, from deificus, DEIFIC.] —**de·i·fi·er** n.

deign (dayn) v. **deigned, deigning, deigns.** —intr. **1.** To think it appropriate or suitable to one's dignity to do something. **2.** To agree in a condescending way to do something. —tr. To condescend to give or grant. [Middle English deinen, from Old French deignier, to regard as worthy, from Latin dignārī, from dignus, worthy.]

Dei gratia adv. Abbr. **D.G.** Latin. By the grace of God.

deil (deel) n. Scottish. A devil.

Dei·mos (dáy-moss, dí-) n. The smaller and more distant from the primary of the two moons of Mars. [After Deimos, a son of Ares, from Greek deimos, fear.]

deip·nos·o·phist (dīp-nóssəfist) n. Rare. A person who is skilled in dinner-table conversation. [Greek deipnosophistai (plural), title of work by Athenaeus (3rd century) describing learned conversations at banquets: deipnon, meal + sophistai, wise men (see **sophist**).]

Deir·dre (déer-dri ‖ -drə, -dray). Irish Mythology. A beautiful harper's daughter of Ulster who killed herself after her husband, Naoise, was murdered by the king Conchobar, the man she had originally been meant to marry.

de·ism (dée-iz'm, dáy-) n. The belief that the truth of the existence of God can be discovered only by the individual through the evidence of reason and nature without resort to any particular church or to revelation. Compare **pantheism, theism.** [French déisme, from Latin deus, god.] —**de·ist** n. —**de·is·tic** (-ístik) adj. —**de·is·ti·cal·ly** adv.

de·i·ty (dée-əti, dáy-) n., pl. **-ties. 1.** A god or goddess. **2.** Divinity. —**the Deity.** God. [Middle English deite, from Old French, from Late Latin deitās (stem deitāt-), from Latin deus, god.]

deix·is (díksiss) n. Grammar. The use of a deictic word.

dé·jà vu (dáyzhaa vŏo, vŭ) n. The illusion or feeling of having already experienced something actually being experienced for the first time. [French, "already seen".]

de·ject (di-jékt) tr.v. **-jected, -jecting, -jects.** To dishearten; dispirit. [Middle English dejecten, from Latin dējicere (past participle dējectus), to cast down : dē-, down + jacere, to throw.]

de·jec·ta (di-jéktə) pl.n. Excremental matter; faeces. [New Latin, from Latin, neuter plural of dējectus, past participle of dējicere, to cast down, DEJECT.]

de·ject·ed (di-jéktid) adj. Depressed; disheartened. See Synonyms at **sad.** —**de·ject·ed·ly** adv. —**de·ject·ed·ness** n.

de·jec·tion (di-jéksh'n) n. **1.** A state of depression; melancholy. **2. a.** Evacuation of the bowels. **b.** Excrement. —See Synonyms at **despair.**

de ju·re (dee-jŏor-i, day-). adj. By legal or constitutional right. Compare **de facto.** [Latin, "according to law".] —**de ju·re** adv.

deka-. Variant of **deca-.**

dekameter. Variant of **decameter.**

Dekkan. See **Deccan.**

Dek·ker (déckər), **Thomas** (c. 1572–1632). British dramatist and author. He wrote more than 40 plays, *The Shoemaker's Holiday* (1600), being the best known today.

dek·ko (déckō) *n., pl.* **-kos.** *British Slang.* A look; a glance. [Hindi *dekho*, imperative of *dekhnā*, to look.]

De Klerk (də-klairk), **F(rederik) W(illem)** (1936–). South African president (1989–94). He removed the ban on black opposition groups, released Nelson Mandela, and confirmed through the referendum of 1992 the ending of apartheid. He shared the 1993 Nobel peace prize with Mandela, and after the 1994 elections became Second Deputy President. Leader of the opposition (1996–97), retired 1997.

De Koo·ning (də kṓ-ning, kōō-) **Willem** (1904–97). Dutch-born U.S. painter. He emigrated to the United States in 1926, and became connected with action painters. From 1950, he produced a series of female figures with distorted bodies and grimacing faces.

del (del) *n. Symbol* ∇ *Mathematics.* The vector differential operator, having as components in three-dimensional Cartesian coordinates the first partial derivative operators with respect to each coordinate direction. Also called "nabla". [Short for DELTA (because it appears like an inverted delta).]

De·la·croix (délla-krwaa, də-la-krwaa), **(Ferdinand Victor) Eugène** (1798–1863). French painter and leading figure in the Romantic movement in art. His dramatic *Massacre at Chios* caused a sensation when exhibited at the Salon of 1824. Delacroix exalted colour and tumult, as in the voluptuous *Death of Sardanapalus* (1827), and *Liberty Leading the People* (1830) celebrating the French revolution of that year.

de·laine (də-láyn) *n.* A light fabric of wool or cotton and wool. [French *(mousseline) de laine*, "(muslin) of wool", from Latin *lāna*, wool.]

De la Mare (délla máir), **Walter (John)** (1873–1956). British poet and novelist. He published his first collection of poetry, *Songs of Childhood* (1902), under the pseudonym Walter Ramal.

de·lam·i·nate (dee-lámminayt) *intr.v.* **-nated, -nating, -nates.** To split into thin layers.

de·lam·i·na·tion (dee-lámmi-náysh'n, dee-) *n.* 1. A splitting or separating into layers. 2. *Embryology.* The splitting of the blastoderm into two layers of cells.

de·late (di-láyt, dee-) *tr.v.* **-lated, -lating, -lates.** *Archaic.* 1. To report (an offence). 2. To inform against (a person). [Latin *dēlātus*, past participle of *dēferre* to bring down, report, indict : *dē-*, down + *ferre*, to bear.] **—de·la·tion** (-láysh'n) *n.* **—de·la·tor** (-láytər) *n.*

De·lau·nay (də-láwnay), **Robert** (1885–1941). French painter and a leading cubist. His preoccupation with the pure aesthetics of colour and structure was christened Orphism by the poet Apollinaire.

Del·a·ware[1] (délla-wair). The second smallest of the United States, on the Atlantic seaboard; capital, Dover. It covers 5 328 square kilometres (2,057 square miles) on the Delaware river. In 1776, it was one of the 13 U.S. founder states, and although a Slave State fought on the Union side in the American Civil War (1861–65). Wilmington is the administrative and industrial centre.

Delaware[2] *n., pl.* **-wares** or collectively **Delaware.** 1. A member of a group of North American Indian peoples, formerly inhabiting the Delaware river valley. 2. Their language, of the Algonquian family of languages. **—Del·a·war·e·an** (-wáir-i-ən) *adj.*

de·lay (di-láy) *v.* **-layed, -laying, -lays.** *—tr.* 1. To postpone until a later time; defer. 2. To cause to be late or detained; hinder. *—intr.* To be unduly slow in doing something; linger.
~n. 1. The act of delaying; postponement. 2. The condition of being delayed; detainment. 3. The period of time during which one is delayed. 4. The time interval between any two events. [Middle English *delaien*, from Old French *delaier, deslaier : des-*, from Latin *dē-*, off + *laier*, variant of *laissier*, to leave, let, from Latin *laxāre*, to slacken, undo, from *laxus*, slack, loose.] **—de·lay·er** *n.*
Synonyms: *delay, slow, retard, detain, check.*

de·layed-ac·tion (di-láyd-áksh'n) *adj.* Also **de·lay-ac·tion** (-láy-). 1. Acting only after a predetermined time interval elapses. 2. Detonating after impact.

delayed drop *n.* 1. A parachute jump in which the parachutist delays opening the parachute for a certain period of time. 2. A way of writing or presenting a story, as in a newspaper or a television news item, so that the main point of the story is held back until several sentences have been read or heard.

delayed neutron *n.* A neutron emitted by a product of nuclear fission several seconds or minutes after the fission occurs. Compare **prompt neutron.**

delay line *n. Electronics.* Any of various devices used to cause a controlled delay in the passage or action of a signal.

del cre·de·re (dél-kréddəri, -kráydəri) *adj.* 1. Designating a selling agent who guarantees the solvency of a buyer. 2. Designating goods that are subject to an extra charge in return for the provision of a del credere agent's guarantee.
~n. The charge made for such a guarantee. [Italian, "of trust".]

de·le (dée-lee) *n.* A sign indicating that something is to be removed from typeset matter.
~tr.v. **deled, -leing, -les.** 1. To take out or delete. 2. To mark with a dele. Compare **stet.** [Latin *dēle*, imperative singular of *dēlēre*, DELETE.]

de·lec·ta·ble (di-léktə-b'l) *adj.* Greatly pleasing, especially to the sense of taste; enjoyable. [Middle English, from Old French, from Latin *dēlectābilis*, from *dēlectāre*, to please, DELIGHT.] **—de·lec·ta·bil·i·ty** (-bílləti), **de·lec·ta·ble·ness** *n.* **—de·lec·ta·bly** *adv.*

de·lec·ta·tion (dée-lek-táysh'n) *n.* Pleasure; delight.

del·e·ga·cy (délligə-si) *n., pl.* **-cies.** 1. The authority, office, or position of a delegate. 2. The act of delegating or being delegated. 3. A body of delegates; a delegation.

del·e·gate (délli-gət, -git, -gayt) *n. Abbr.* **del.** 1. A person authorised to act as representative for another or others, especially one elected or appointed to be a representative at a conference. 2. *U.S.* An elected or appointed representative of a Territory in the House of Representatives who is entitled to speak but not vote.
~v. (-gayt) **delegated, -gating, -gates.** *—tr.* 1. To authorise or send (a person) as one's representative. 2. To commit to one's agent or representative. 3. To assign (work or duties) to employees or others over whom one has authority. 4. *Law. Chiefly U.S.* To appoint (one's debtor) as a debtor to one's creditor to replace oneself in satisfying a claim. *—intr.* To assign work or duties to employees or others over whom one has authority: *A manager must know how to delegate effectively.* [Middle English *delegat*, from Medieval Latin *dēlēgātus*, from Latin, past participle of *dēlēgāre*, to send away, dispatch : *dē-*, away + *lēgāre*, to send.]

del·e·ga·tion (délli-gáysh'n) *n.* 1. **a.** The act of delegating. **b.** The condition of being delegated; appointment; deputation. 2. *Abbr.* **del.** A person or group of persons officially elected or appointed to represent another or others.

de·lete (di-léet) *tr.v.* **-leted, -leting, -letes.** *Abbr.* **del.** 1. To cross out or erase (written or printed matter). 2. To cancel (information stored in a computer, for example). 3. To remove (a recording) from a recording company's catalogue. —See Synonyms at **erase.**
~n. Computing. An operation to delete stored information. [Latin *dēlēre†*, to wipe out, efface.]

del·e·te·ri·ous (délli-téer-i-əss, dílli-, déeli-) *adj.* Having a harmful effect; injurious. [Medieval Latin *dēlētērius*, from Greek *dēlētērios*, from *dēleisthai†*, to harm, injure.] **—del·e·te·ri·ous·ly** *adv.* **—del·e·te·ri·ous·ness** *n.*

de·le·tion (di-léesh'n) *n.* 1. An act of deleting; an omission or erasing. 2. A word, passage, or the like that has been deleted from written, printed, or recorded matter. 3. *Genetics.* A type of mutation in which part of a chromosome is missing. In this sense, also called "deficiency". 4. A recording deleted from a recording company's catalogue.

delft (delft) *n.* Also **delf** (delf). 1. A style of glazed earthenware, usually blue and white, originally made in Delft. Also called "delftware". 2. A piece of pottery in this style. 3. Any pottery made in imitation of this style.

Delft (delft; *Dutch also* délləft). Town in South Holland province, southern Netherlands. A fine pottery has been produced here since the late 16th century. The artist Vermeer lived and worked in Delft.

Del·hi (délli). Capital of India, on the right bank of the river Yamuna (Jumna), a tributary of the Ganges. Delhi was an ancient capital of Hindu legend. Under its 17th-century Muslim ruler, Shah Jahan, Old Delhi was laid out within defensive walls 9 kilometres (5½ miles) long. Chief among its monuments are the huge Red Fort (1638–48) and Great Mosque (1644–58). New Delhi was founded under the British in 1912, to replace Calcutta as the capital of India. It was laid out by Sir Edwin Lutyens.

del·i (délli) *n., pl.* **-is.** *Informal.* A delicatessen.

de·lib·er·ate (di-líbbə-rayt) *v.* **-ated, -ating, -ates.** *—intr.* 1. To take careful thought; reflect. 2. To consult with another or others as a process in reaching a decision. *—tr.* To consider (a matter) carefully.
~adj. (-ət, -it). 1. Premeditated; intentional. 2. **a.** Careful and slow in deciding or determining. **b.** Not rashly or hastily determined: *a deliberate choice.* 3. Leisurely or slow in motion or manner; not hurried or impulsive. —See Synonyms at **voluntary.** [Latin *dēlīberāre*, to weigh well, ponder : *dē-*, completely + *lībrāre*, to weigh, from *lībra*, a scale, pound.] **—de·lib·er·ate·ly** *adv.* **—de·lib·er·ate·ness** *n.* **—de·lib·er·a·tor** *n.*

de·lib·er·a·tion (di-libbə-ráysh'n) *n.* 1. The process of deliberating; thoughtful and lengthy consideration. 2. *Often plural.* Formal discussion and debate of all sides of an issue. 3. Thoughtfulness or care in decision or action.

de·lib·er·a·tive (di-líb-rətiv, -ərətiv ‖ -ə-raytiv) *adj.* 1. Assembled or organised for deliberation or debate: *a deliberative legislature.* 2. Characterised by or being the result of deliberation or debate. 3. *Grammar.* Expressing doubt or deliberation. **—de·lib·er·a·tive·ly** *adv.* **—de·lib·er·a·tive·ness** *n.*

De·libes (də-léeb), **(Clément Philibert) Léo** (1836–91). French composer. He was second chorus master at the Grand Opera for many years. His compositions include the ballet *Coppélia* (1870) and the opera *Lakmé* (1883).

del·i·ca·cy (déllikə-si) *n., pl.* **-cies.** 1. The quality of being delicate. 2. Frailty of bodily constitution or health. 3. Sensitivity of perception, feeling, appreciation, or the like; refinement. 4. **a.** Consideration of the feelings of others. **b.** Aversion to what is considered morally distasteful or injurious. 5. A need of taste and tact in treating or handling: *a topic of some delicacy.* 6. Softness or fineness of touch. 7. Fineness or keenness of response or reaction. 8. Something pleasing and appealing, especially a choice food. [Middle English *delicacie*, from *delicat*, DELICATE.]

del·i·cate (délli-kət, -kit) *adj.* 1. **a.** Exquisitely or pleasingly fine. **b.** Beautiful in a graceful or tender way. **c.** Characterised by precise skill, as in execution or workmanship. 2. Frail in constitution or health. 3. Easily broken or damaged. 4. Requiring tasteful and tactful treatment. 5. Keen in sense discrimination or perception. 6. Manifesting extreme sensitivity and distaste towards anything immodest, impolite, or morally reprehensible; squeamish. **7.** Mindful of the feelings of others. **8.** Keenly accurate in response or reaction. **9.** Soft or gentle in touch or skill. **10.** Very subtle in difference or distinction. —See Synonyms at **fragile.** [Middle English *delicat,* from Latin *dēlicātus*†, alluring, charming, dainty.] **—del·i·cate·ly** *adv.* **—del·i·cate·ness** *n.*

del·i·ca·tes·sen (déllikə-téss'n) *n.* A shop that sells cooked or prepared foods ready for serving, especially foreign or unusual foods. [German *Delikatessen,* plural of *Delikatesse,* delicacy, from French *délicatesse,* from Italian *delicatezza,* from *delicato,* delicate, dainty, from Latin *dēlicātus,* DELICATE.]

de·li·cious (di-líshəss) *adj.* **1.** Highly pleasing or agreeable to the senses of taste or smell. **2.** Very pleasant; enjoyable; delightful. [Middle English, from Old French, from Late Latin *dēliciōsus,* pleasing, delightful, from Latin *dēlicia,* pleasure, from *dēlicere,* to entice away, DELIGHT.] **—de·li·cious·ly** *adv.* **—de·li·cious·ness** *n.*

de·lict (di-líkt) *n.* **1.** In Scots and South African law, the branch of law corresponding to the English law of tort. **2.** In Roman law, the obligation to pay or make compensation for any wrong committed. [Latin *dēlictum,* from *dēlictus,* past participle of *dēlinquere,* to fail in duty, offend. See **delinquent.**]

de·light (di-lít) *n.* **1.** Great pleasure; gratification; joy. **2.** Something that gives enjoyment. —See Synonyms at **ecstasy.**
~*v.* **delighted, -lighting, -lights.** —*intr.* **1.** To take great pleasure or joy. **2.** To give great pleasure or joy. —*tr.* To please greatly. [Middle English *deliten,* from Old French *deleitier,* from Latin *dēlectāre,* frequentative of *dēlicere,* to allure, entice away : *dē-,* away + *lacere*†, to allure.]

de·light·ed (di-lítid) *adj.* **1.** Filled with delight. **2.** *Obsolete.* Delightful. **—de·light·ed·ly** *adv.* **—de·light·ed·ness** *n.*

de·light·ful (di-lít-f'l) *adj.* Affording keen satisfaction; greatly pleasing. **—de·light·ful·ly** *adv.* **—de·light·ful·ness** *n.*

de·light·some (di-lít-səm) *adj. Literary.* Delightful. **—de·light·some·ly** *adv.* **—de·light·some·ness** *n.*

De·li·lah[1] (di-lílə). A Philistine woman who betrayed Samson, her lover, to the Philistines by having his hair shorn as he slept, thus depriving him of his strength. Judges 16.

Delilah[2] *n.* A seductive, treacherous woman. [After DELILAH.]

de·lim·it (dee-límmit, di-) *tr.v.* **-ited, -iting, -its.** Also **de·lim·i·tate** (-ayt) **-tated, -tating, -tates.** **1.** To establish the limit or boundaries of; demarcate. **2.** To define: *Their authority is delimited in the constitution.* [French *délimiter,* from Latin *dēlīmitāre* : *dē-,* completely + *līmitāre,* to limit, from *līmes* (stem *līmit-*), LIMIT.] **—de·lim·i·ta·tion** (-áysh'n) *n.* **—de·lim·i·ta·tive** (-ətiv || -aytiv) *adj.*

de·lin·e·ate (di-línni-ayt) *tr.v.* **-ated, -ating, -ates.** **1.** To draw or trace the outline of; sketch out. **2.** To represent pictorially; depict. **3.** To depict in words or gestures; portray. [Latin *dēlīneāre* : *dē-,* completely + *līnea,* thread, LINE.] **—de·lin·e·a·tion** (-áysh'n) *n.* **—de·lin·e·a·tive** (-ətiv, -aytiv) *adj.*

de·lin·e·a·tor (di-línni-aytər) *n.* **1.** One that delineates. **2.** An adjustable pattern used by tailors for cutting garments of various sizes.

de·lin·quen·cy (di-língkwən-si) *n., pl.* **-cies.** **1.** A tendency to indulge in antisocial behaviour, especially petty crime. See **juvenile delinquency.** **2.** An offence or minor crime; a misdeed. **3.** Negligence or failure in doing what is required.

de·lin·quent (di-língkwənt) *adj.* **1.** Engaging in delinquency. **2.** Failing to do what is required by law or obligation. **3.** *Chiefly U.S.* Overdue in payment: *a delinquent account.*
~*n.* **1.** A delinquent person, especially a **juvenile delinquent** *(see).* **2.** A person who neglects or fails to do what law or obligation requires. [Latin *dēlinquēns* (stem *dēlinquent-*), present participle of *dēlinquere,* to fail in duty, offend, "leave undone" : *dē-* (intensive) + *linquere,* to leave.] **—de·lin·quent·ly** *adv.*

del·i·quesce (délli-kwéss) *intr.v.* **-quesced, -quescing, -quesces.** **1.** *Chemistry.* To dissolve and become liquid by absorbing moisture from the air. **2.** *Botany.* **a.** To divide into numerous branches. **b.** To become fluid or soft on maturing, as do certain fungi. **3.** To melt away or disappear as if by melting. Usually used humorously. —See Synonyms at **melt.** [Latin *dēliquēscere* : *dē-,* completely + *liquēscere,* to melt, from *liquēre,* to be liquid.]

del·i·ques·cence (délli-kwéss'nss) *n.* **1.** The act or process of deliquescing. **2.** The liquid resulting from the process of deliquescing. **—del·i·ques·cent** *adj.*

de·lir·i·ous (di-lírri-əss, *also* -léer-i-) *adj.* **1.** Affected by delirium. **2.** Characteristic of or pertaining to delirium: *delirious speech.* **—de·lir·i·ous·ly** *adv.* **—de·lir·i·ous·ness** *n.*

de·lir·i·um (di-lírri-əm, *also* -léer-i-) *n., pl.* **-ums** or **-ia** (-ə). **1.** A state of temporary mental confusion and clouded consciousness resulting from high fever, intoxication, or shock, and characterised by anxiety, tremors, hallucinations, delusions, and incoherence. **2.** A state of uncontrolled excitement or emotion. [Latin *dēlīrium,* from *dēlīrāre,* to deviate from a straight line, be deranged : *dē-,* away from + *līrā,* a furrow.] **—de·lir·i·ant** *adj.*

delirium tre·mens (trée-menz, tré- || -mənz) *n.* A severe psychotic delirium caused by the withdrawal of alcohol from an alcoholic or similar symptoms occurring when there is severe organic or functional brain disorder. Also informally called "D.T.'s". [New Latin, "trembling delirium".]

De·li·us (déeli-əss), **Frederick** (1862–1934). British composer, of German parentage. He emigrated to Florida as an orange planter, and was influenced by Negro songs. He moved to France, composing there operas, concertos, orchestral music, songs, and chamber music. He wrote *On Hearing the First Cuckoo in Spring* (1912).

de·liv·er (di-lívvər) *v.* **-ered, -ering, -ers.** —*tr.* **1.** To put into another's possession or power; hand over. **2.** To take to the intended recipient: *deliver groceries.* **3.** To release or rescue from bondage, danger, or evil of any kind; set free. See Synonyms at **save.** **4. a.** To assist (a female) in giving birth: *The doctor delivered her of twins.* **b.** To assist or aid in the birth of: *The midwife delivered the twins.* **5.** To send forth (a blow or ball, for example) by releasing, discharging, or throwing. **6.** To utter or pronounce. **7.** To produce or perform (something promised): *delivered the contract on time.* **—deliver (oneself) of.** To pronounce; utter. —*intr.* **1.** To take goods to the intended recipient: *Our grocer delivers.* **2.** *Informal.* To produce results as promised or expected. [Middle English *deliv(e)ren,* from Old French *delivrer,* from Late Latin *dēlīberāre* : Latin *dē-,* completely + *līberāre,* to set free, from *līber,* free.] **—de·liv·er·a·bil·i·ty** (-ə-bílləti) *n.* **—de·liv·er·a·ble** *adj.* **—de·liv·er·er** *n.*

de·liv·er·ance (di-lívvərənss) *n.* **1.** The act of delivering; especially, rescue from bondage or danger. **2.** The state of being so delivered. **3.** A publicly expressed opinion, such as the verdict of a jury.

de·liv·er·y (di-lívvri, -lívvəri) *n., pl.* **-ies.** **1.** The act of delivering or conveying. **2.** That which is delivered. **3.** The act of releasing or rescuing. **4.** The act of giving birth; parturition. **5.** *Law.* The act of transferring possession of an article from one person to another. **6.** A giving up; a surrender. **7. a.** Utterance. **b.** A manner of speaking or singing. **8.** The act or manner of throwing or discharging; especially, the act or an instance of bowling in cricket or pitching in baseball.

delivery room *n.* A room in a hospital equipped to deliver babies.

dell (del) *n.* A small, secluded wooded hollow. [Middle English *del,* Old English *dell,* from Germanic.]

del·la Rob·bi·a (déllə róbbi-ə, rób-yə), **Luca** (1400–82). Italian sculptor of the early Renaissance. One of his best-known works is a marble relief, *Cantoria,* in the Duomo, Florence. Much of his work was done with enamelled terracotta.

de·lo·cal·i·sa·tion (dée-lōkə-lī-záysh'n || *U.S.* -li-) *n.* **1.** The act of delocalising or the condition of being delocalised. **2.** *Physics & Chemistry.* The overlap of orbitals with the free movement of electrons throughout these orbitals, resulting in stronger bonds and a more stable structure.

de·lo·cal·ise, de·lo·cal·ize (dée-lṓkə-līz, dee-) *tr.v.* **-ised, -ising, -ises.** **1.** To remove (something) from its native or usual locality. **2.** To broaden the range or scope of.

De·lorme or **de l'Orme** (də-lórm), **Philibert** (*c.* 1510–1570). French architect. He was in charge of work at Fontainebleau, and later commissions included extending the palace of the Tuileries in 1565.

De·los (déeloss). *Greek* **Dhí·los.** Greek island, virtually uninhabited, in the Aegean. It is the smallest of the Cyclades group, covering an area of barely 3 square kilometres (one square mile). In Greek myth, it was the birthplace of Apollo and temples dedicated to the god have been excavated on the island.

de·louse (dée-lówss) *tr.v.* **-loused, -lousing, -louses.** To rid (a person or animal) of lice by physical or chemical means.

Del·phi (dél-fī, -fi). Ancient site in central Greece, 10 kilometres (6 miles) inland from the Gulf of Corinth. It was the most important sanctuary of Apollo, lying in a secluded glade overlooked by Mount Parnassus. The site, discovered in 1890, included Apollo's temple, where his oracle was consulted, a theatre, and treasuries. The oracle fell into disuse with the rise of Christianity.

Del·phic (délfik). Also **Del·phi·an** (délfi-ən). **1.** Of or pertaining to Delphi or to the oracle of Apollo at Delphi. **2.** *Sometimes small* **d.** Ambiguous; obscure in meaning; oracular.

del·phin·i·um (del-fínni-əm) *n.* Any plant of the genus *Delphinium;* especially, any of several tall cultivated varieties having spikes of variously coloured, especially blue, spurred flowers, such as the larkspur. [New Latin *Delphinium* (genus), from Greek *delphinion,* larkspur, diminutive of *delphis* (stem *delphin-*), DOLPHIN (from the shape of the nectary).]

Del·phi·nus (del-fínəss) *n.* A constellation in the Northern Hemisphere near Pegasus and Aquila. [New Latin, from Latin *delphīnus,* DOLPHIN.]

del·ta (déltə) *n.* **1.** The fourth letter in the Greek alphabet, written Δ, δ, transliterated in English as *d, D,* or for some modern Greek words, *dh* or *th.* **2.** A usually triangular alluvial area at the mouth of a river, where the river branches into several channels. **3.** Anything resembling the shape of a triangle. **4.** *Mathematics.* A finite increment in a variable. [Middle English, from Greek, from Semitic; akin to Hebrew *dāleth.*] **—del·ta·ic** (del-táy-ik), **del·tic** *adj.*

delta connection *n. Electricity.* A method of connecting a three-phase supply by joining three components in a triangle and connecting the inputs and outputs across each arm. Compare **star connection.** [After the shape of the Greek capital delta.]

delta wing *n.* An aircraft with sweptback wings that give it the appearance of a triangle.

del·ti·ol·o·gy (délti-ólləji) *n.* The study and collecting of postcards, especially picture postcards. [From Greek *deltion,* small writing-tablet + -O- + -LOGY.] **—del·ti·ol·o·gist** *n.*

del·toid (déltoyd) *n.* A thick, triangular muscle covering the shoulder joint, used to raise the arm from the side.
~*adj.* **1.** Triangular. **2.** Pertaining to the deltoid. [New Latin *deltoides,* from Greek *deltoeidēs,* triangular : DELTA + -OID.]

de·lude (di-lóod, -léwd) *tr.v.* **-luded, -luding, -ludes.** **1.** To deceive the mind or judgment of; mislead. **2.** *Obsolete.* To elude or evade. **3.** *Obsolete.* To frustrate the hopes or plans of. —See Synonyms at

deceive. [Middle English *deluden,* from Latin *dēlūdere,* to play false, deceive : *dē-* (pejorative) + *lūdere,* to play, from *lūdus,* game.] **—de·lud·a·ble** *adj.* **—de·lud·er** *n.* **—de·lud·ing·ly** *adv.*

del·uge (déllewj) *tr.v.* **-uged, -uging, -uges. 1.** To overrun with water; flood. **2.** To inundate in overwhelming numbers: *deluged with enquiries.* ~*n.* **1.** A great flood; a heavy downpour. **2.** Anything that overwhelms as if by a great flood. **—the Deluge.** The great flood that occurred in the time of Noah. Genesis 7–10. [Middle English, from Old French, from Latin *dīluvium,* flood, from *dīluere,* to wash away : *dis-,* apart + *-luere,* from *lavere,* to wash.]

de·lu·sion (di-lóozh'n) *n.* **1. a.** The act or process of deluding; deception. **b.** The state of being deluded. **2. a.** A mistaken belief or idea. **b.** *Psychiatry.* A false belief, strongly held in spite of invalidating evidence. [Middle English *delusioun,* from Latin *dēlūsio* (stem *dēlūsiōn-*), from *dēlūdere* (past participle *dēlūsus*), DELUDE.] **—de·lu·sion·al** *adj.*

de·lu·sive (di-lóo-siv, -lēw-) *adj.* Also **de·lu·so·ry** (-səri). **1.** Tending to deceive or mislead; deceptive. **2.** Having the nature of a delusion; false. **—de·lu·sive·ly** *adv.* **—de·lu·sive·ness** *n.*

de luxe, de·luxe (di-lúks, də-, -lóoks) *adj.* Of special elegance or luxury; superior : *a de luxe model.* [French, "of luxury", from Latin *luxus,* extravagance, LUXURY.]

delve (delv) *v.* **delved, delving, delves.** —*intr.* **1.** To search deeply and painstakingly. **2.** *Archaic.* To dig the ground, as with a spade. —*tr. Archaic.* To dig (ground) with a spade. [Middle English *delven,* to dig, Old English *delfan.*] **—delv·er** *n.*

Dem. Democrat; Democratic.

de·mag·net·ise, de·mag·net·ize (dée-mágni-tīz, dee-) *v.* **-ised, -ising, -ises.** —*tr.* To remove magnetic properties from. —*intr.* To lose magnetisation. **—de·mag·net·i·sa·tion** (-tī-záysh'n ‖ *U.S.* -ti-) *n.* **—de·mag·net·is·er** *n.*

de·mag·ni·fy (dée-mág-ni-fī) *tr.v.* To reduce to a very small size; miniaturise.

dem·a·gog·ic (démmə-gójik, -góggik) *adj.* Also **dem·a·gog·i·cal** (-'l). Relating to, of the nature of, or characteristic of a demagogue. **—dem·a·gog·i·cal·ly** *adv.*

dem·a·gogue, *U.S.* **dem·a·gog** (démmə-gog) *n.* **1.** A leader who obtains power by means of impassioned appeals to the emotions and prejudices of the populace. **2.** A leader of the common people in ancient times. [Greek *dēmagōgos,* popular leader : *dēmos,* common people + *agōgos,* leading, from *agein,* to lead.]

dem·a·gogu·er·y (démmə-góggəri) *n.* The practices or rhetoric of a demagogue. Also called "demagogism".

dem·a·go·gy (démmə-goji, -goggi) *n.* **1.** The quality or character of demagogues. **2.** Rule by a demagogue. **3.** Demagogues collectively.

de·man (dée-mán) *v.* **-manned, -manning, -mans.** —*tr.* **1.** *British.* To reduce the number of employees in (a factory or industry). **2.** *Chiefly U.S.* To emasculate. —*intr. British.* To de-man a factory or industry.

de·mand (di-maánd ‖ -mánd) *v.* **-manded, -manding, -mands.** —*tr.* **1.** To ask for urgently or firmly, leaving no chance for refusal or denial. **2.** To claim as a right or due. **3.** To ask to be informed of: *demand the cause of his action.* **4.** To need or require as useful, just, proper, or necessary. **5.** *Law.* To claim formally; lay legal claim to. —*intr.* To make a demand. ~*n.* **1.** The act of demanding. **2.** Something that is demanded. **3. a.** The state of being sought after. **b.** An urgent requirement, need, or claim: *an ever-growing demand for investment.* **4.** *Archaic.* An emphatic question or enquiry. **5.** *Law.* A formal claim. **6.** *Economics.* **a.** The desire to possess something combined with the ability to purchase it. **b.** The amount of any commodity that people are ready and able to buy at a given time for a given price. Compare **supply.** **—in demand.** Much sought after. **—on demand.** Immediately obtainable on presentation or request. [Middle English *demaunden,* from Old French *demander,* to ask, charge with doing, from Latin *dēmandāre,* to give in charge, entrust : *dē-* (intensive) + *mandāre,* to entrust.] **—de·mand·a·ble** *adj.* **—de·mand·er** *n.*

Usage: *Demand,* the verb, is used in several constructions: with a direct object (*demand payment*), with an infinitive (*demand to know*), with a dependent clause (*demand that you leave,* where *that* is sometimes omitted), and with a double object (*demand a lot of him,* where *from* can be a less formal alternative for *of*). The noun *demand* is used with both *on* and *upon* (*make a demand (up)on him*).

demand deposit *n.* A bank deposit that can be withdrawn by the depositor immediately and without advance notice.

de·mand·ing (di-maán-ding ‖ -mán-) *adj.* Making rigorous or excessive demands, as on one's time, attention, or effort. —See Synonyms at **burdensome. —de·mand·ing·ly** *adv.*

demand note *n.* A bill or draft payable in lawful money on presentation or demand.

de·mand-pull (di-maánd-póol ‖ -mánd-) *adj.* Designating a type of inflation in which increased demand for a limited amount of goods and services tends to drive up prices. Compare **cost-push.**

de·man·toid (di-mántoyd) *n.* A transparent, green variety of garnet, used as a gem. [German *Demantoid* : *Demant* (obsolete), diamond, from Middle High German *diemant,* from Old French *diamant,* DIAMOND + -OID.]

de·mar·cate (dée-maar-kayt ‖ di-már-) *tr.v.* **-cated, -cating, -cates. 1.** To set the boundaries of; delimit. **2.** To separate clearly as if by boundaries; discriminate. [Back-formation from DEMARCATION.] **—de·mar·ca·tor** (-ər) *n.*

de·mar·ca·tion (dée-maar-káysh'n) *n.* **1.** The setting or marking of boundaries or limits. **2.** A separation; a distinction: *a line of demarcation.* **3. a.** The practice of strictly differentiating the type of work carried out by members of individual trade unions. **b.** An instance of this practice. [Spanish *demarcación,* from *demarcar,* to mark out the boundary : *de-,* completely + *marcar,* to mark, from Italian *marcare,* from Old Italian, from Germanic.]

dé·marche (dáy-maarsh, day-mársh) *n.* **1.** An initiative or manoeuvre; a step. **2.** A diplomatic representation or protest. **3.** A statement or protest addressed to public authorities. [French.]

de·ma·te·ri·al·ise, de·ma·te·ri·al·ize (dée-mə-téer-i-ə-līz) *v.* **-ised, -ising, -ises.** —*tr.* To divest of material qualities or characteristics. —*intr.* To lose material character or form; disappear. **—de·ma·te·ri·al·i·sa·tion** (lī-záysh'n ‖ *U.S.* -li-) *n.*

deme (deem) *n.* **1.** Any of the townships of ancient Attica. **2.** *Biology.* A local, usually stable population of organisms having common genetic or cytological characteristics. [Greek *dēmos,* common people, deme.]

de·mean[1] (di-méen) *tr.v.* **-meaned, -meaning, -means. 1.** To debase in dignity or stature. **2.** To humble (oneself). —See Synonyms at **degrade.** [DE- (pejorative) + MEAN (base).]

demean[2] *tr.v.* **-meaned, -meaning, -means.** To conduct or behave (oneself) in a particular manner. ~*n. Archaic.* Behaviour; demeanour. [Middle English *demeinen,* from Old French *demener* : *de-,* completely + *mener,* to lead, conduct, from Latin *mināre,* to drive (herds), from *minārī,* to threaten, from *minae,* threats.]

de·mean·our, *U.S.* **de·mean·or** (di-méenər) *n.* The way in which a person behaves or conducts himself; deportment; manner. See Synonyms at **bearing.**

de·ment (di-mént) *tr.v.* **-mented, -menting, -ments.** *Rare.* To make demented. [Late Latin *dēmentāre,* from Latin *dēmēns* (stem *dēment-*), mad : *dē-* (undoing) + *mēns,* mind.]

de·ment·ed (di-méntid) *adj.* **1.** Insane. **2.** Suffering from dementia. **3.** Crazed, as through grief or worry. **—de·ment·ed·ly** *adv.* **—de·ment·ed·ness** *n.*

dé·men·ti (day-món-tee, dáy-мoN-tée) *n., pl.* **démentis** (-z, *or as singular*). *French.* An official denial, as of a rumour or news story.

de·men·tia (di-mén-shi-ə, -shə) *n.* Deterioration of mental faculties combined with emotional disturbances, resulting from organic brain disorder. See **senile dementia.** See Synonyms at **insanity.** [Latin *dēmentia,* madness, from *dēmēns,* mad. See **dement.**]

dementia prae·cox (prée-koks) *n.* **Schizophrenia** *(see).* Not in current technical usage. [New Latin, "premature dementia".]

dem·e·rar·a (démmə-raír-ə) *n.* **1.** A type of brown crystallised cane sugar. **2.** A type of blended rum. [After *Demerara,* Guyana, the main source of the sugar.]

Dem·e·ra·ra (démmə-raárə). River in Guyana. It flows 290 kilometres (180 miles) north from the Guiana Highlands to the Atlantic Ocean at Georgetown, which as Stabroek, was the administrative centre of the Dutch colony of Demerara.

de·mer·it (dee-mérrit, dée-merrit ‖ di-) *n.* **1. a.** A quality or characteristic that deserves blame or censure; a fault. **b.** Absence of merit. **2.** *U.S.* A mark made on one's record by a superior, implying some loss of status or privileges for bad conduct or failure. [Middle English *demerite,* offence, guilt, originally "merit", "desert", from Old French, probably from Latin *dēmerēre,* to deserve : *dē-* (intensive) + *merēre, merērī,* to deserve, MERIT.] **—de·mer·i·tor·i·ous** (-áwri-əss ‖ -óri-) *adj.* **—de·mer·i·tor·i·ous·ly** *adv.*

de·mer·sal (di-mérss'l, dée-) *adj.* Designating animal life in deep water, as at the bottom of the sea or a lake. [Latin *dēmergere* (past participle *dēmersus*), to plunge : *dē-,* down + *mergere,* to dip.]

de·mesne (di-máyn, -méen) *n.* **1.** *Law.* Possession and use of one's own land. **2.** Lands retained by a feudal lord for his own use. **3.** The grounds belonging to a mansion or country house. **4.** An extensive piece of landed property; an estate. **5.** Any district; a territory. **6.** A realm; a domain. [Middle English *demesne, demeine,* from Old French *demaine,* DOMAIN.]

De·me·ter (di-méetər). *Greek Mythology.* The goddess of agriculture, fertility, and marriage, identified with the Roman goddess Ceres.

demi– *prefix.* Indicates: **1.** Half; for example, **demisemiquaver. 2.** Less than full status; for example, **demigod.** [French, from *demi,* half, from Medieval Latin *dīmedius,* from Latin *dīmidius,* half, divided in half : *dis-,* apart + *medius,* half.]

dem·i·god (démmi-god) *n.* **1. a.** A mythological semidivine being, such as the offspring of a god and a mortal. **b.** An inferior deity; a minor god. **2.** A man with godlike attributes.

dem·i·god·dess (démmi-god-iss, -ess) *n.* A female demigod.

dem·i·john (démmi-jon) *n.* A large, narrow-necked bottle made of glass or earthenware, often encased in wickerwork. [Probably a variant of French *dame-Jeanne,* "Lady Jane", assimilated to DEMI- + the name *John.*]

de·mil·i·ta·rise, de·mil·i·ta·rize (dee-míllitə-rīz, dee-) *tr.v.* **-rised, -rising, -rises. 1.** To eliminate the military character of. **2.** To prohibit military forces or installations in. **3.** To replace military control of with civilian control. **—de·mil·i·ta·ri·sa·tion** (-rī-záysh'n ‖ *U.S.* -ri-) *n.*

demilitarised zone *n. Abbr.* **DMZ** A region, defined by diplomatic or political agreement, wherein military forces and installations may not be established.

De Mille, (də-míl), **Cecil B(lount)** (1881–1959). U.S. film producer and director, known for spectacular epics. He popularised religious and Biblical stories through the cinema with *The Ten Command-*

ments (1923) and *Samson and Delilah* (1949). His other films include *The Plainsman* (1936), *Union Pacific* (1939), and *The Greatest Show on Earth,* (1952), which won an Academy Award.

dem·i·lune (démmi-lōōn, -lewn) *n.* **1.** A crescent or half-moon. **2.** *Military.* A crescent-shaped outwork to defend the entrance of a fort. **3.** A crescent-shaped mass of protoplasm found in salivary glands. [French *demi-lune* : DEMI- + *lune,* moon, from Latin *lūna.*]

dem·i·mon·daine (démmi-món-dayn, -dáyn) *n.* A woman belonging to the demimonde.

dem·i·monde (démmi-mond, -MOND, -móND) *n.* **1.** The social class of those women kept by wealthy lovers or protectors, especially as it existed in the 19th century. **2.** Any group existing on the margin of success or respectability: *the literary demimonde.* [French *demimonde,* "half-world", coined (1855) by Alexandre Dumas fils to designate "the class of the déclassé".]

de·min·er·al·ise, de·min·er·al·ize (dée-mínrə-līz, -mínnərə-) *tr.v.* **-ised, -ising,-ises.** To remove salts from (a liquid). **—de·min·er·al·i·sa·tion** (-lī-záysh'n || *U.S.* -li-) *n.*

demi-pension (démmi-PÓNSS-YON, də-mée-PONSS-YÓN) *n.* **Half board** *(see).* [French.]

dem·i·pique (démmi-peek) *n.* A military saddle used during the 18th century, having a pommel about half the height of those on earlier saddles. [Earlier *demipeak* : DEMI- + PEAK.]

dem·i·re·lief (démmi-ri-léef) *n. Sculpture.* **Mezzo-relievo** *(see).*

dem·i·rep (démmi-rep) *n. Archaic.* A demimondaine.

de·mise (di-míz, -méez) *n.* **1.** Death. **2.** An ending or failure. **3.** The transfer of an estate by lease or will. **4.** The transfer of a ruler's authority by death or abdication: *demise of the crown.*
~v. **demised, -mising, -mises.** *—tr.* **1.** To transfer (an estate) by will or lease. **2.** To transfer (sovereignty) by abdication or will. *—intr.* **1.** To be transferred by will or descent. **2.** *Archaic.* To die. [Middle English *dimise, demise,* transfer of property, from Old French, from feminine past participle of *demettre,* DEMIT.] **—de·mis·a·ble** *adj.*

dem·i·sem·i·qua·ver (démmi-semmi-kwayvər) *n. Music. British.* A note which has a time value equivalent to one thirty-second of a semibreve. [DEMI- + SEMI- + QUAVER.]

de·mis·sion (di-mísh'n) *n. Rare.* The relinquishment of an office or function. [Middle English *dimissioun,* from Latin *dīmissiō* (stem *dīmissiōn-*), dismissal, from *dīmittere* (past participle *dīmissus*), to send away, DEMIT.]

de·mist (dée-míst) *v.* **-misted, -misting, -mists.** *Chiefly British. —tr.* To clear condensation from (a surface, especially a car windscreen). *—intr.* To become clear of condensation.

de·mist·er (dée-místər) *n. Chiefly British.* A heating device designed to clean condensation from a car windscreen or similar surface.

de·mit (di-mít) *v.* **-mitted, -mitting, -mits.** *—tr. Archaic.* **1.** To relinquish (an office or function). **2.** *Obsolete.* To dismiss. *—intr. Archaic.* To resign. [Middle English *dimitten,* to release, deliver, Old French *demettre,* from Latin *dīmittere,* to dismiss, renounce, send away : *dis-,* away + *mittere,* to send.]

dem·i·tasse (démmi-tass) *n.* **1.** A small coffee cup. **2.** The strong black coffee drunk from such a cup. [French : DEMI- + *tasse,* cup, from Old French, from Arabic *ṭašt,* basin, from Persian *ṭašt*†.]

dem·i·urge (démmi-urj, déemi-) *n.* **1.** *Often capital* **D.** The name used by Plato to designate the deity who fashions the material world. **2.** *Often capital* **D.** In Gnostic philosophy, the creator of the material world. **3.** A public magistrate in some ancient Greek states. [Late Latin *dēmiūrgus,* from Greek *dēmiourgos,* "public craftsman" : *dēmios,* public, from *dēmos,* people + *ergon,* work.] **—dem·i·ur·geous, dem·i·ur·gic** (-úrjik), **dem·i·ur·gi·cal** *adj.*

dem·i·vierge (démmi-vi-áirzh) *n.* A woman who engages in sexual activities but who retains her physiological virginity. [French, "half virgin".]

dem·i·volt, dem·i·volte (démmi-volt) *n.* In dressage, a half-turn performed by a horse on its hind legs.

dem·i·wave (démmi-wayv) *n.* A mild perm for the hair, making it wavy rather than curly.

dem·o (démmō) *n., pl.* **-os.** *Informal.* **1.** A demonstration, especially a political one. **2.** A record or tape recording presented to an agent, concert promoter, or the like to advertise a song or group.

de·mob (dée-mób) *tr.v.* **-mobbed, -mobbing, -mobs.** *British Informal.* To demobilise.
~n. British Informal. Demobilisation.

de·mo·bil·ise, de·mo·bil·ize (dee-mṓbi-līz, di-, dée-) *v.* **-ised, -ising, -ises.** *—tr.* To discharge from military service or use; disband or dismiss (troops, for example). *—intr.* To be demobilised. **—de·mo·bil·i·sa·tion** (-lī-záysh'n || *U.S.* -li-) *n.*

de·moc·ra·cy (di-móckrə-si) *n., pl.* **-cies.** **1.** Government by the people, exercised either directly or through elected representatives. **2.** A political or social unit based upon this form of rule. **3.** A social condition of equality and respect for the individual within the community. **4.** Control of an institution, such as a company, by all those employed or involved in it. **5.** The people considered as a source of political authority. [Old French *democratie,* from Late Latin *dēmocratia,* from Greek *dēmokratia* : *dēmos,* common people + -CRACY.]

dem·o·crat (démmə-krat) *n.* **1.** An advocate of democracy. **2.** *Capital* **D.** *Abbr.* **D, D., a.** A member or supporter of the Democratic Party in the U.S.A. **b.** A member or supporter of the Social and Liberal Democrats in Britain.

dem·o·crat·ic (démmə-kráttik) *adj.* **1.** Of, characterised by, or advocating democracy. **2.** Pertaining to, encompassing, or promoting the interests of the people. **3.** In favour of or practising social equality; not snobbish. **4.** *Capital* **D.** *Abbr.* **D, D., Dem.** *Chiefly U.S.* Pertaining to or characteristic of the Democratic Party. **—dem·o·crat·i·cal·ly** *adv.*

Democratic Party *n.* One of the two major political parties in the United States. It owes its origin to a split in the Democratic-Republican Party under Andrew Jackson in 1828.

Dem·o·crat·ic-Re·pub·li·can Party (démmə-kráttik-ri-púbblikən) *n.* A U.S. political party opposed to the Federalist Party, founded by Thomas Jefferson in 1792 and dissolved in 1828.

Democratic Saharan Arab Republic. See **Western Sahara.**

de·moc·ra·tise, de·moc·ra·tize (di-móckrə-tīz) *v.* **-tised, -tising, -tises.** *—tr.* To make democratic. *—intr.* To become democratic. **—de·moc·ra·ti·sa·tion** (-tī-záysh'n || *U.S.* -ti-) *n.*

De·moc·ri·tus (di-móckritəss) (*c.* 460–370 B.C.). Greek philosopher and scientist. He developed an atomist theory of the universe, holding that it was made up of minute particles, or atoms, multifariously arranged to account for the differing properties of matter.

dé·mo·dé (dáy-mṓ-day || -mō-dáy) *adj. French.* Outmoded.

de·mod·u·late (dee-móddew-layt) *tr.v.* **-lated, -lating, -lates.** *Electronics.* To extract (information) from a modulated carrier wave. **—de·mod·u·la·tion** (-láysh'n) *n.*

de·mod·u·la·tor (dee-móddew-laytər) *n.* A device used in demodulating radio signals. Also called "detector".

de·mog·ra·phy (di-móggrəfi) *n.* The study of the characteristics of human populations, such as size, growth, density, distribution, and vital statistics. [French *démographie* : Greek *dēmos,* people + -GRAPHY.] **—de·mog·ra·pher** *n.* **—dem·o·graph·ic** (démmə-gráffik), **dem·o·graph·i·cal** *adj.* **—dem·o·graph·i·cal·ly** *adv.*

dem·oi·selle (dém-waa-zél) *n.* **1.** *Literary.* A young lady or damsel. **2.** A small Old World crane, *Anthropoides virgo,* having grey and black plumage, long black breast feathers, and white plumes at the sides of the head. Also called "demoiselle crane". **3.** *Rare.* A **damselfly** *(see).* **4.** A **damselfish** *(see).* [French, from Old French *dameisele,* DAMSEL.]

de·mol·ish (di-móllish) *tr.v.* **-ished, -ishing, -ishes.** **1.** To tear down completely; wreck; level. **2.** To do away with completely; put an end to. **3.** To destroy or defeat utterly: *demolish the prosecution's case.* **4.** *Informal.* To eat up completely. —See Synonyms at **ruin.** [Old French *demolir* (present stem *demoliss-*), from Latin *dēmōlīrī,* to throw down, demolish : *dē-* (reversal) + *mōlīrī,* to endeavour, strive, build, from *mōlēs,* mass.]

dem·o·li·tion (démmə-lísh'n) *n.* **1.** The act or process of wrecking or destroying; specifically, the destruction of a redundant building. **2.** *Military.* **a.** Destruction by explosives. **b.** *Plural.* Explosives used to demolish. [Old French, from Latin *dēmōlītiō* (stem *dēmōlītiōn-*), from *dēmōlīrī,* DEMOLISH.] **—dem·o·li·tion·ist** *n.*

de·mon (déemən) *n.* Also **dae·mon, dai·mon** (déé-mən, dí- || -mon) (for senses 3, 4). **1.** A devil or evil being; especially, in the New Testament, an unclean spirit that possesses and afflicts a person. **2.** A persistently tormenting person, force, or passion. **3.** *Greek Mythology.* An inferior divinity, such as a deified hero. **4.** An attendant spirit; a genius. **5.** One who is extremely zealous, skilful, or engrossed in a given activity. **6.** *Australian Slang.* A policeman or detective. [Middle English, from Late Latin *daemōn,* evil spirit, from Latin, spirit, from Greek *daimōn,* divine power, fate, god.]

demon. *Grammar.* demonstrative.

de·mon·e·tise, de·mon·e·tize (dee-múnni-tīz, di-, -mónni-) *tr.v.* **-tised, -tising, -tises.** **1.** To divest (a coin, for example) of monetary value. **2.** To stop using (a metal) as a monetary standard. [French *démonétiser* : *dé-,* away from + *monēta,* coin, MONEY.] **—de·mon·e·ti·sa·tion** (-tī-záysh'n || *U.S.* -ti-) *n.*

de·mo·ni·ac (di-mṓni-ak) *adj.* Also **de·mo·ni·a·cal** (déemə-nī-ək'l). **1.** Arising or seeming to arise from possession by a demon. **2.** Befitting or suggestive of a devil; fiendish; frenzied.
~n. One who is or seems to be possessed by a demon. [Middle English *demoniak,* from Late Latin *daemoniācus,* from Greek *daimoniakos,* from *daimonios,* of a spirit, from *daimōn,* DEMON.] **—de·mo·ni·a·cal·ly** *adv.*

de·mon·ic (di-mónnik, dee-) *adj.* **1.** Befitting a demon; fiendish. **2.** Motivated by a spiritual force or genius; inspired. **3.** Showing a frenetic enthusiasm.

de·mon·ise, de·mon·ize (déemən-īz) *tr.v.* **-ised, -ising, -ises.** **1.** To turn into or as if into a demon. **2.** To possess. Used of a demon.

de·mon·ism (déemən-iz'm) *n.* **1.** Belief in demons. **2.** The worship of demons. **3.** Demonology. **—de·mon·ist** *n.*

de·mon·ol·o·gy (déemə-nólləji) *n.* **1.** The study of demons. Also called "demonism". **2.** A treatise on demons or demon worship. **—de·mon·ol·o·gist** *n.*

de·mon·stra·ble (démmən-strəb'l, di-món-) *adj.* Capable of being shown or proved. **—de·mon·stra·bil·i·ty** (-strə-billəti), **de·mon·stra·ble·ness** *n.* **—de·mon·stra·bly** *adv.*

dem·on·strate (démmən-strayt) *v.* **-strated, -strating, -strates.** *—tr.* **1.** To prove or make manifest by reasoning or adducing evidence. **2.** To describe or illustrate by experiment or practical application. **3.** To manifest or reveal. **4.** To display the advantages of (a product, for example) to a prospective buyer, as by operation or explanation. *—intr.* To present or participate in a demonstration, especially a public rally for a particular cause. [Latin *dēmonstrāre,* to point out : *dē-,* completely + *monstrāre,* to show, from *mōnstrum,* divine portent, from *monēre,* to warn.]

dem·on·stra·tion (démmən-stráysh'n) *n.* **1.** The act of making evident or proving. **2.** Conclusive evidence; proof. **3.** An illustration or explanation, as of a theory or product, by exemplification or practical application. **4.** A manifestation, as of one's feelings. **5.** A public display of group opinion, as by a rally or march. **6.** A show of military strength.

de·mon·stra·tive (di-mónstrətiv) *adj.* **1.** Serving to manifest or prove. **2.** Involving or characterised by demonstration. **3.** Given to or marked by the open expression of emotion, especially affection. **4.** *Abbr.* **demon.** *Grammar.* Designating a word, such as *these* or *then,* that specifies or singles out the person, thing, or time referred to. Compare **interrogative, relative.**
~*n. Abbr.* **demon.** *Grammar.* A demonstrative pronoun or adjective. —**de·mon·stra·tive·ly** *adv.* —**de·mon·stra·tive·ness** *n.*

dem·on·stra·tor (démmən-straytər) *n.* **1.** One who demonstrates something. **2.** A vehicle, domestic appliance, or the like used to demonstrate a product to a potential customer. **3.** A person who demonstrates experiments and other practical work to students in a laboratory. **4.** One who takes part in a public demonstration.

dem·o·pho·bi·a (démmō-fóbi-ə) *n.* Abnormal fear of crowds. [Greek *dēmos,* people, DEMOS + -PHOBIA.] —**dem·o·pho·bic** *adj.*

de·mor·al·ise, de·mor·al·ize (di-mórrə-līz || -máwrə-) *tr.v.* **-ised, -ising, -ises. 1.** To debase the morals of; corrupt. **2.** To undermine the confidence or morale of; dishearten. **3.** To put into disorder. —**de·mor·al·i·sa·tion** (-lī-záysh'n || *U.S.* -li-) *n.* —**de·mor·al·is·er** *n.*

de·mos (déemoss) *n.* **1.** The people of an ancient Greek state, considered as a social class or as a political entity. **2.** The common people; the populace. [Greek *dēmos,* district, people.]

De·mos·the·nes (di-mósthə-neez) (384–322 B.C.). Athenian orator and statesman. He is famous for the *Philippics,* a series of orations attacking the political ambitions of Philip of Macedon.

de·mote (di-mōt, dée-) *tr.v.* **-moted, -moting, -motes.** To lower in rank or grade. [DE- (reversal) + (PRO)MOTE.] —**de·mo·tion** *n.*

de·mot·ic (di-móttik, dee-) *adj.* **1. a.** Of or pertaining to the common people; in common use; popular. Said especially of language. **b.** Of the masses; unsophisticated or unrefined: *demotic tastes in food.* **2.** Of, pertaining to, or written in the simplified form of ancient Egyptian hieratic writing. **3.** *Often capital* **D.** Of or pertaining to Dhimotiki.
~*n.* **1.** Demotic language. **2.** *Capital* **D.** The popular form of modern Greek, **Dhimotiki** *(see).* [Greek *dēmotikos,* from *dēmotēs,* commoner, from *dēmos,* common people, DEMOS.] —**de·mot·ist** *n.*

de·mo·ti·vate (dée-mōti-vayt, dee-) *tr.v.* **-ated, -ating, -ates.** To cause (a person) to lose motivation.

de·mount (dée-mównt) *tr.v.* **-mounted, -mounting, -mounts. 1.** To remove (a gun or motor, for example) from a position on a mounting or other support. **2.** To dismantle. —**de·mount·a·ble** *adj.*

Demp·sey (démpsi), **Jack,** born William Harrison Dempsey (1895–1983). U.S. heavyweight boxer; world champion (1919–26).

dempster. Variant of **deemster.**

de·mul·cent (di-múlss'nt) *adj.* Soothing.
~*n.* A soothing, usually mucilaginous or oily substance, used especially to relieve pain in inflamed or irritated mucous surfaces. [Latin *dēmulcēns* (stem *dēmulcent-*), present participle of *dēmulcēre,* to stroke down, caress, soothe : *dē-,* down + *mulcēre†,* to stroke.]

de·mur (di-múr) *intr.v.* **-murred, -murring, -murs. 1.** To take exception; raise objections; object. **2.** *Law.* To enter or interpose a demurrer. **3.** To delay. —See Synonyms at **object.**
~*n.* Also **de·mur·ral** (di-múr-əl). **1.** The act of demurring. **2.** An objection. **3.** A delay. [Middle English *demeoren, demuren,* to delay, from French *demorer, demurer,* from Latin *dēmorārī* : *dē-* (intensive) + *morārī,* to delay, from *mora,* delay.] —**de·mur·ra·ble** *adj.*

de·mure (di-méwr) *adj.* **-murer, -murest. 1.** Sedate or self-possessed in manner or behaviour; reserved. Said especially of women and children. **2.** Feigning modesty or shyness. —See Synonyms at **shy.** [Middle English, from Old French *demore,* quiet, sedate, "settled", past participle of *demorer,* to stay, delay, DEMUR.] —**de·mure·ly** *adv.* —**de·mure·ness** *n.*

de·mur·rage (di-múrrij) *n.* **1. a.** The detention of a ship or other cargo conveyance during loading or unloading beyond the scheduled time of departure. **b.** The compensation paid for this detention. **2.** A fee charged by the Bank of England when changing bullion into notes.

de·mur·rer (di-múr-ər for sense 1; for senses 2 and 3 di-múrrər) *n.* **1.** A person who demurs; an objector. **2.** *Obsolete. Law.* A plea to dismiss a lawsuit on the grounds that although the opposition's statements may be true, they are insufficient to sustain the claim. **3.** An objection.

de·my (di-mí) *n., pl.* **-mies. 1.** Any of several standard sizes of paper, especially: **a.** In Britain, paper measuring 394 by 572 millimetres (15½ by 20 inches) or 445 by 572 millimetres (17½ by 22½ inches). **b.** In the United States, paper measuring 406 by 533 millimetres (16 by 21 inches). **2.** A size of book, 8½ by 5½ inches. Also called "demy octavo". **3.** A size of book, 11¾ by 8⅝ inches. Also called "demy quarto". [From DEMI-.]

de·mys·ti·fy (dée-místi-fī, dee-) *tr.v.* **-fied, -fying, -fies.** To make less complex or less ambiguous; make less difficult to understand. —**de·mys·ti·fi·ca·tion** (-fi-káysh'n) *n.*

de·my·thol·o·gise, de·my·thol·o·gize (dée-mi-thóllə-jīz) *tr.v.* **-gised, -gising, -gises. 1.** To remove the mythical elements from (a piece of writing) so that the essential meaning may be made clear. **2.** To reinterpret mythical elements in (a piece of writing), especially in a way held to be more rational. **3.** To do away with the spurious reverence surrounding (a figure or institution).

den (den) *n.* **1.** The shelter or retreat of a wild animal; a lair. **2.** A cave considered as a refuge or hiding place. **3.** A residence or abode, especially if hidden or squalid. **4.** A small secluded room for study or relaxation. **5.** *Scottish.* A small wooded dell.
~*intr.v.* **denned, denning, dens.** To inhabit or hide in a den. [Middle English *den(ne),* Old English *denn,* from Germanic.]

Den. Denmark.

de·nar·i·us (di-naír-i-əss, de-, -naʹar-) *n., pl.* **-narii** (-i-ī, -i-ee). **1.** An ancient Roman silver coin, originally equivalent to four sesterces. **2.** An ancient Roman gold coin valued at 25 silver denarii. [Middle English, from Latin *dēnārius,* from adjective, "consisting of ten", from *dēnī,* by tens.]

den·a·ry (déenəri || *U.S. also* dénnəri) *adj.* **1.** Tenfold. **2.** Divided or counted by tens; decimal. [Latin *dēnārius.* See **denarius.**]

de·na·tion·al·ise, de·na·tion·al·ize (dée-násh'n-ə-līz) *tr.v.* **-ised, -ising, -ises. 1.** To return (a nationalised industry or service) to private ownership. **2.** To deprive of national rights, status, or characteristics. —**de·na·tion·al·i·sa·tion** (-lī-záysh'n || *U.S.* -li-) *n.*

de·nat·u·ral·ise, de·nat·u·ral·ize (dee-nách-rə-līz, -náchōo-) *tr.v.* **-ised, -ising, -ises. 1.** To make unnatural. **2.** To deprive of the rights of naturalisation or citizenship. —**de·nat·u·ral·i·sa·tion** (-lī-záysh'n || *U.S.* -li-) *n.*

de·na·tur·ant (dée-náychərənt) *n.* An evil-tasting chemical substance or vivid colouring that is added to a product to make it unfit for human consumption. [DENATURE + -ANT.]

de·na·ture (dée-náychər) *tr.v.* **-tured, -turing, -tures.** Also **de·na·tur·ise** (-īz), **-ised, -ising, -ises. 1.** To change the nature or natural qualities of. **2.** To render unfit to eat or drink; especially, to add methanol to (ethanol) for this purpose. **3.** *Physics.* To add nonfissionable matter to (fissionable material) to prevent use in an atomic weapon. **4.** *Biochemistry.* To cause (a protein) to unfold by subjecting it to a change of temperature, acidity, or the like. —**de·na·tur·a·tion** (-áysh'n) *n.*

de·na·zi·fy (dée-naátsi-fī, dee-, naʹazi- || *U.S. also* -nátsi-) *tr.v.* **-fied, -fying, -fies.** To make or declare free of Nazi influence. —**de·na·zi·fi·ca·tion** (-fi-káysh'n) *n.*

Den·bigh (dénbi). *Welsh* **Din-bych** (dín-bikh). Town in Denbighshire, Wales, formerly in Clwyd. Its castle was built in 1282 for Edward I.

Den·bigh·shire (dén-bi-shər, -sheer || -shīr) *Welsh* **Sir Ddin-bych** (sheer thín-bikh). Welsh Unitary Authority area, divided 1974–96 between Clwyd (to the east) and Gwynedd (to the west).

den·dri·form (déndri-fawrm) *adj.* Having the characteristic form or structure of a tree. [DENDRI- + -FORM.]

den·drite (déndrīt) *n.* **1.** A mineral crystallisation in a branching or treelike form inside another mineral bearing such a crystal formation. **2.** In a nerve cell, a fine branch of a dendron. [DENDR(O)- + -ITE.]

den·drit·ic (den-dríttik) *adj.* Also **den·drit·i·cal** (-'l). **1.** Of, pertaining to, or resembling a dendrite. **2.** Tree-shaped; dendriform. [DENDRIT(E) + -IC.] —**den·drit·i·cal·ly** *adv.*

dendro-, dendri-, dendr- *comb. form.* Indicates tree; for example, **dendrology, dendriform, dendrite.** [New Latin, from Greek, from *dendron,* tree.]

den·dro·chro·nol·o·gy (déndrō-krə-nóllə ji) *n.* The study of the growth rings in trees as an aid in determining and dating past events. —**den·dro·chro·no·log·i·cal** (-krónnə-lójik'l) *adj.*

den·dro·cli·ma·tol·o·gy (déndrō-klīmə-tóllə ji) *n.* The determination of past climates and climatic conditions from a study of tree rings.

den·droid (déndroyd) *adj.* Also **den·droi·dal** (-'l). Shaped like a tree. [Greek *dendroeidēs* : DENDR(O)- + -OID.]

den·drol·o·gy (den-dróllə ji) *n.* The botanical study of trees. [DENDRO- + -LOGY.] —**den·dro·log·ic** (déndrə-lójik), **den·dro·log·i·cal** *adj.* —**den·drol·o·gist** (-dróllə jist) *n.*

den·dron (déndrən) *n.* A protoplasmic process of a nerve cell, which conducts impulses towards the cell body. [Greek, tree.]

dene¹, dean (deen) *n. British Regional.* A sandy tract of land or low hill near the sea. [Probably akin to low German *düne.* See **dune.**]

dene² or **den.** Variant of **dean** (valley).

De·neb (dénneb) *n.* The brightest star in the constellation Cygnus, approximately 1630 light years from Earth. [Arabic *dhanab,* tail.]

den·e·ga·tion (dénni-áysh'n || dee-neg-áysh'n) *n. Archaic.* A denial. [Middle English *denegacioun,* from Old French *denegation,* from Latin *dēnegātiō* (stem *dēnegātiōn-*), from *dēnegātus,* past participle of *dēnegāre,* to DENY.]

dene hole *n. Archaeology.* A type of excavation found in chalk soils in Britain and France, consisting of a vertical shaft which widens out into several chambers. [Perhaps from DANE + HOLE.]

den·gue (déng-gi, -gay) *n.* An infectious, virulent, tropical and subtropical viral disease transmitted by mosquitoes and characterised by fever, rash, and severe pains in the joints. Also called "breakbone fever". [Spanish, of African origin, akin to Swahili *kidinga.*]

Deng Xiao-ping or **Teng Hsiao-p'ing** (dóng syów píng), also called Gan Ze-gao or Kan Tse-kao (1904–97). Vice-premier of the State Council of the People's Republic of China (1975–76, 1977–80) and vice-chairman of the Chinese Communist Party (1977–87). Dismissed during the Cultural Revolution as a "capitalist roader", he was rehabilitated in 1973 and became acting chairman in 1974. Disgraced again, in 1976, he was rehabilitated a year later.

Den Haag. See the **Hague.**

de·ni·a·ble (di-ní-əb'l) *adj.* Capable of being denied; questionable. —**de·ni·a·bly** *adv.*

de·ni·al (di-nī-əl) *n.* **1.** A negative reply, as to a request; a refusal to comply or satisfy. **2. a.** Refusal to grant the truth of a statement or allegation; contradiction. **b.** An assertion that a statement or allegation is untrue. **3. a.** A rejection, as of a doctrine or belief. **b.** *Psychology.* A state of inability to face painful realities: *You can't change if you're in denial.* **4.** A disowning or disavowal; repudiation. **5.** Abstinence; self-denial. [From DENY.]

de·nic·o·tin·ise, de·nic·o·tin·ize (dée-nícka-teen-īz, dee-, -tin-) *tr.v.* **-ised, -ising, -ises.** To remove nicotine from (tobacco, for example).

den·i·er¹ (dénni-ər, *also* -ay ‖ *U.S.* -áy *for sense 1; also* di-néer *for sense 2*) *n.* **1.** A unit of fineness for rayon, nylon, and silk yarns, based on a standard of 50 milligrams per 450 metres of yarn. **2.** A small coin of very low value current in France and western Europe from the eighth century until the French Revolution. [Middle English *denere,* a small coin, from Old French *denier,* from Latin *dēnārius,* DENARIUS.]

de·ni·er² (di-nī-ər) *n.* One who denies.

den·i·grate (dénni-grayt, *sometimes* dée-nī-) *tr.v.* **-grated, -grating, -grates.** **1. a.** To defame; calumniate. **b.** To belittle; undervalue. **2.** *Archaic.* To blacken. [Latin *dēnigrāre* (past participle *dēnigrātus*), to blacken : *dē-,* completely + *nigrāre,* blacken, from *niger,* black.] —**den·i·gra·tion** *n.*

den·im (dénnim) *n.* **1. a.** A coarse twilled cloth used for jeans, overalls, and work uniforms. **b.** *Plural.* A garment, especially trousers, made of coarse, often blue, denim. **2.** A finer grade of material used in draperies and upholstery. [French *(serge) de Nîmes,* serge of Nîmes.]

De·nis (dénniss, də-née), **Saint** (died A.D. 270). Patron saint of France. He was sent to preach the Gospel to the Gauls and became the first Bishop of Paris. He was martyred during the reign of Valerian. His feast day is October 9.

de·ni·tri·fy (dée-nītri-fī, dee-) *tr.v.* **-fied, -fying, -fies.** To remove nitrogen from (a material or chemical compound), as by bacterial action on soil. —**de·ni·tri·fi·ca·tion** (-fi-káysh'n) *n.*

de·ni·tri·fy·ing bacteria (dée-nītri-fī-ing, dee-) *pl.n. Singular.* **denit·rifying bacterium.** The soil bacteria that reduce nitrate to ammonia, including species of *Thiobacillus* and *Escherichia.*

den·i·zen (dénniz'n) *n.* **1.** An inhabitant; a resident. **2.** *British.* A foreigner permitted certain rights and privileges of citizenship. **3.** *Ecology.* An animal or plant naturalised in a region to which it is not indigenous.
~*tr.v.* **denizened, -zening, -zens.** *British.* To make a denizen. [Middle English *denisein,* from Old French *denzein,* from *deinz,* within, from Late Latin *dēintus,* from within : Latin *dē-,* from + *intus,* within.] —**den·i·zen·a·tion** (-áysh'n) *n.*

Den·mark, Kingdom of (dén-maark). *Danish* **Dan·mark** (dánmaarg). A low-lying country on the Jutland peninsula and islands, in northern Europe. It also has sovereignty over Greenland and the Faeroe Islands. In the tenth century Denmark was unified under the Viking king, Harald Bluetooth, who converted the people to Christianity. His expansionist policy was continued by his successors who also brought England temporarily into the Danish fold (1013) under King Canute (*c.* 994–1035). Norway and Sweden came under the Danish crown, in a union cemented at Kalmar in 1397. Sweden broke away (1523), and Denmark later lost Norway to Sweden (1815). It joined the European Economic Community in 1973. The country is intensively farmed, and is noted for its beer, bacon, and butter. Its other exports include livestock, fish products, transport equipment, and fine ceramics and glassware. Area, 43 094 square kilometres (16,639 square miles). Population, 5,260,000. Capital, Copenhagen.

den mother *n. Chiefly U.S.* A woman who supervises a group of Cub Scouts.

Denning (dénning), **Alfred Thompson, Baron** (1899–). British jurist. As Master of the Rolls (1962–82) he took a radical approach to the interpretation in the law which sometimes brought him into conflict with the House of Lords.

de·nom·i·nate (di-nómmi-nayt) *tr.v.* **-nated, -nating, -nates.** To give a name to; designate. [Latin *dēnōmināre : dē-,* completely + *nōmināre,* to name, from *nōmen,* name.] —**de·nom·i·na·ble** (-nəb'l) *adj.*

de·nom·i·nate number (di-nómmi-nət, -nit, -nayt) *n.* A number that designates a quantity as a multiple of a unit. In the expression *12 metres, 12* is a denominate number.

de·nom·i·na·tion (di-nómmi-náysh'n) *n.* **1.** The act of naming. **2.** A name; a designation. **3.** The name of a class or group; a classification. **4.** A class of units having specific values, as in a system of currency or weights. **5.** A religious grouping with a common organisation and name. —See Synonyms at **name.** —**de·nom·i·na·tion·al** *adj.* —**de·nom·i·na·tion·al·ly** *adv.*

de·nom·i·na·tion·al·ism (di-nómmi-náysh'n-ə-liz'm) *n.* **1.** The tendency to separate into religious sects or denominations. **2.** Advocacy of such separation. **3.** Strict adherence to a denomination; sectarianism. —**de·nom·i·na·tion·al·ist** *n.*

de·nom·i·na·tive (di-nómmi-nətiv; *in sense 2 and as n., also* dée-). Also **de·nom·i·nal.** *adj.* **1.** Giving or constituting a name; naming; appellative. **2.** *Grammar.* Formed from a noun or adjective.
~*n.* A word, especially a verb, that is derived from a noun or adjective, such as the verb *to bus* from the noun *bus,* or *to mushroom* from the noun *mushroom.*

de·nom·i·na·tor (di-nómmi-naytər) *n.* The quantity below the line indicating division in a fraction; the quantity that divides the numerator; the divisor. Compare **numerator.**

de nos jours (də nō zhoor) *adj. French.* Of or pertaining to the present time: *the Shakespeare de nos jours.* ["Of our days".]

de·no·ta·tion (dée-nō-táysh'n, -nə-) *n.* **1.** The act of denoting; indication. **2.** A sign, symbol, or reference that denotes; an indicator. **3.** Something signified or referred to; a particular meaning of a symbol. **4.** The explicit meaning of a word, as opposed to its connotation.

Usage: The distinction between *denotation* and *connotation* is sometimes confused in informal speech, with the latter being used in contexts where only the former is appropriate. The most important distinction is between *denotation* in the sense of "explicit, literal, objective meaning of a word" and *connotation* in the sense of "associations or emotions attached to a word". A given word has a literal meaning, but in addition it may have pleasant, unpleasant, or other connotations. The verbs *denote* and *connote* are also sometimes confused in this way: *A chair connotes a piece of furniture* is inappropriate, because a *chair* really *is* a piece of furniture; whereas if someone said (the offer of) *a chair connotes politeness,* this would be an appropriate use of *connote* because politeness is not part of the literal meaning of *chair,* but is a personal association stemming from the speaker's experience. Note, however, that *connotation* has a technical meaning in logic.

de·no·ta·tive (di-nōtə-tiv, dée-nō-tay-) *adj.* 1. Able to denote; designative. 2. Explicit. —**de·no·ta·tive·ly** *adv.*

de·note (di-nōt) *tr.v.* **-noted, -noting, -notes.** 1. To reveal or indicate; mark. 2. To serve as a symbol or name for; signify. 3. To refer to specifically; mean explicitly. —See Synonyms at **mean** (convey sense). See Usage note at **denotation.** [French *dénoter,* from Latin *dēnotāre* : *dē-,* completely + *notāre,* mark, from *nota,* NOTE.] —**de·not·a·ble** *adj.* —**de·no·tive** *adj.*

dé·noue·ment, de·noue·ment (day-nōō-moN ‖ *U.S.* dáy-nōō-móN) *n.* 1. The solution, clarification, or unravelling of the plot of a play or novel. 2. Any outcome or final solution. [French, "an untying", from Old French *desnouement,* from *desno(u)er,* undo : *des-, de-,* reversing + *no(u)er,* to tie, from Latin *nōdāre,* from *nōdus,* knot.]

de·nounce (di-nownss ‖ *West Indies also* -núngss) *tr.v.* **-nounced, -nouncing, -nounces.** 1. To condemn openly; censure, especially as evil. 2. To accuse formally; inform against. 3. To give formal announcement of the ending of (a treaty). —See Synonyms at **criticise.** [Middle English *denouncen,* from Old French *denoncier,* announce, from Latin *dēnūntiāre,* make an official announcement of : *dē-,* completely + *nūntiāre,* announce, from *nūntius,* messenger.] —**de·nounce·ment** *n.* —**de·nounc·er** *n.*

de nouveau (də nōōvō, nōō-vō) *adv. French.* Starting afresh; anew.

de no·vo (dee nōvō, day) *adv. Latin.* Afresh; anew.

dense (denss) *adj.* **denser, densest.** 1. **a.** Having relatively high density. **b.** Crowded closely together; compact. 2. Thick; impenetrable. 3. Thickheaded; dull. 4. Comprehensible only through intellectual effort: *a dense argument.* 5. *Photography.* Opaque, with good contrast between light and dark areas. Said of a developed negative. —See Synonyms at **stupid.** [Latin *dēnsus.*] —**dense·ly** *adv.* —**dense·ness** *n.*

den·sim·e·ter (den-símmitər) *n.* An instrument used to determine density. [DENSE + -METER.] —**den·si·met·ric** (dén-si-méttrik) *adj.*

den·si·tom·e·ter (dén-si-tómmitər) *n.* An apparatus for measuring the optical density of a material, such as a photographic negative. [DENSITY + METER.]

den·si·ty (dénssəti) *n., pl.* **-ties.** 1. **a.** The degree or a measure of the degree to which anything is filled or occupied. **b.** The condition or quality of being dense. 2. *Physics.* **a.** The mass per unit volume of a substance under stipulated or standard conditions of pressure and temperature. See **relative density. b.** The amount of something per unit measure, especially per unit length, area, or volume. See **charge density, current density, energy density.** 3. **Population density** *(see).* 4. The degree of optical opacity of a medium or material, such as a photographic negative. 5. *Statistics.* A **probability density function** *(see).* Also called "density function".

dent¹ (dent) *n.* 1. A depression in a surface made by pressure or a blow. 2. A lessening or weakening effect: *a dent in his confidence.* ~*v.* **dented, denting, dents.** —*tr.* To make a dent in. —*intr.* To become dented. [Middle English *dent,* variant of *dint,* strike, blow, Old English *dynt,* from Germanic *dunti-* (unattested).]

dent² *n.* 1. A toothlike protuberance, such as that on a gearwheel. 2. The space between two wires on a loom through which a warp thread is drawn. [French, tooth.]

dent. dental; dentist; dentistry.

den·tal (dentl) *adj. Abbr.* **dent.** 1. Of, pertaining to, or for the teeth. 2. Of, pertaining to, or for dentistry. 3. *Phonetics.* Produced with the tip of the tongue near or against the upper front teeth. ~*n. Phonetics.* A dental consonant. [New Latin *dentalis,* from Latin *dēns* (stem *dent-*), tooth.]

dental appliance *n.* A brace *(see).*

dental caries *n.* Tooth decay.

dental floss *n.* A strong waxed thread used to clean areas between the teeth. Also called "floss".

dental hygiene *n.* The maintenance of healthy teeth and gums, especially by scaling and regular brushing. Also called "oral hygiene".

dental hygienist *n.* A person trained in dental hygiene, who cleans and scales the teeth of dental patients and gives advice on general care. Also called "hygienist".

den·ta·li·um (den-táyli-əm) *n., pl.* **-lia** (-ə) or **-liums.** Any tusk shell of the genus *Dentalium.* [New Latin, from Late Latin *dentālis,* of a tooth, DENTAL.]

dental plaque *n.* A film containing bacteria and other substances that forms on the surface of a tooth. Also called "plaque".

dental plate *n.* 1. A plate fixed to the palate with a fitting used to correct the position of the teeth. 2. A **denture** *(see).*

dental surgeon *n.* A **dentist** *(see).*

dental technician *n.* A person who repairs dentures and makes plaster casts of teeth.

den·tate (déntayt) *adj.* Edged with toothlike projections; toothed. [Latin *dentātus,* from *dēns* (stem *dent-*), tooth.] —**den·tate·ly** *adv.*

den·ta·tion (den-táysh'n) *n.* 1. The condition of being dentate. 2. A toothlike part or projection.

dent corn *n.* A tall-growing variety of corn, *Zea mays indentata,* having yellow or white kernels that are indented at the tip. Also called "dent maize".

denti–, dent– *comb. form.* Indicates tooth; for example, **dentiform, dentoid.** [Latin *dēns* (stem *dent-*), tooth.]

den·ti·cle (déntik'l) *n.* A small tooth or toothlike projection. [Middle English, from Latin *denticulus,* diminutive of *dēns* (stem *dent-*), tooth.]

den·tic·u·late (den-tíckew-lət, -lit, -layt) *adj.* Also **den·tic·u·lat·ed** (-laytid). 1. Finely toothed; minutely dentate. 2. *Architecture.* Having dentils. [Latin *denticulātus,* from *denticulus,* DENTICLE.] —**den·tic·u·late·ly** *adv.* —**den·tic·u·la·tion** (-láysh'n) *n.*

den·ti·form (dénti-fawrm) *adj.* Shaped like a tooth. [DENTI- + -FORM.]

den·ti·frice (dénti-friss) *n.* A substance, such as a powder or paste, for cleaning the teeth; toothpaste or tooth powder. [French, from Latin *dentifricium* : DENTI- + *fricāre,* to rub.]

den·til (déntil) *n. Architecture.* Any of a series of small rectangular blocks forming a moulding or projecting beneath a cornice. [Obsolete French *dentille,* from Old French, diminutive of *dent,* tooth, from Latin *dēns* (stem *dent-*), tooth.]

den·ti·la·bi·al (dénti-láybi-əl) *adj. Phonetics.* Labiodental. —**den·ti·la·bi·al** *n.*

den·ti·lin·gual (dénti-líng-gwəl) *adj. Phonetics.* Interdental. —**den·ti·lin·gual** *n.*

den·tine (dén-teen) *n.* Also chiefly *U.S.* **den·tin** (-tin) The calcareous part of a tooth, beneath the enamel, containing the pulp chamber and root canals. [DENT(I)- + -INE.] —**den·ti·nal** (-tin'l) *adj.*

den·tist (déntist) *n. Abbr.* **dent.** A person whose profession is dentistry. [French *dentiste,* from *dent,* tooth.]

den·tist·ry (déntistri) *n. Abbr.* **dent.** The diagnosis, prevention, and treatment of diseases of the teeth and related structures, including the repair or replacement of defective teeth.

den·ti·tion (den-tísh'n) *n.* 1. *Biology.* The type, number, and arrangement of teeth, especially in humans and other animals. 2. The process of cutting new teeth; teething. [Latin *dentītiō* (stem *dentītiōn-*), from *dentītus,* past participle of *dentīre,* to teethe, from *dēns* (stem *dent-*), tooth.]

dent maize *n.* **Dent corn** *(see).*

den·toid (déntoyd) *adj.* Toothlike. [DENT(I)- + -OID.]

den·tu·lous (déntewləss) *adj.* Possessing teeth; toothed.

den·ture (dénchər) *n.* 1. A set of artificial teeth for a single jaw or part of it. Also called "dental plate". 2. *Plural.* A set of removable artificial teeth for both jaws. [French, from Old French, from *dent,* tooth.]

de·nu·cle·ar·ise, de·nu·cle·ar·ize (dée-néwkli-ə-rīz, dee- ‖ -nōōkli-) *tr.v.* **-ised, ising, -ises.** To remove nuclear installations from (a country or area).

de·nu·da·tion (dée-new-dáysh'n ‖ -noo-) *n.* 1. *Geology.* The combined processes of erosion, weathering, and transporting away of the material removed. Also called "degradation". 2. The act or process of denuding.

de·nude (di-néwd ‖ -nōōd) *tr.v.* **-nuded, -nuding, -nudes.** 1. **a.** To strip of covering; make bare. **b.** To divest; deprive completely. 2. To cause to undergo denudation. —See Synonyms at **strip.** [Latin *dēnūdāre* : *dē-,* thoroughly + *nūdāre,* to make bare, from *nūdus,* NUDE.]

de·nu·mer·a·ble (di-néw-mərəb'l ‖ -nōō-) *adj.* Capable of being put into one-to-one correspondence with the positive integers; countable. —**de·nu·mer·a·bly** *adv.*

de·nun·ci·ate (di-nún-si-ayt, -shi-) *tr.v.* **-ated, -ating, -ates.** *Rare.* To denounce. [Latin *dēnūntiāre,* to DENOUNCE.]

de·nun·ci·a·tion (di-nún-si-áysh'n, -shi-) *n.* 1. The act or an instance of denouncing; open condemnation or censure. 2. *Archaic.* The act of accusing another of a crime before a public prosecutor. 3. A formal declaration of the termination of a treaty.

Den·ver (dénvər). Capital of Colorado state, in the United States. It lies where the Rocky Mountains meet the Great Plains, a natural stopping-point for early 19th-century settlers. The population boomed in 1859, during a gold rush. It is a railway interchange, and industrial, tourist, and marketing centre.

de·ny (di-ní) *tr.v.* **-nied, -nying, -nies.** 1. To declare untrue; assert the contrary of; contradict. 2. To refuse to believe; reject. 3. To refuse to recognise or acknowledge; disavow; disown. 4. To refuse to grant; withhold. —**deny (oneself).** To abstain from indulging in. [Middle English *denien,* from Old French *denier,* from Latin *dēnegāre* : *dē-,* completely + *negāre,* to say no.]

deoch an dor·is (dókh ən dórriss) *n. Scottish & Irish.* A drink, usually of whisky, which is taken before departure. [Gaelic *deoch an doruis,* drink at the door.]

de·o·dand (dée-ə-dand, -ō-) *n.* Formerly in English law, an object which caused the death of a person, either accidentally or intentionally, and which was then confiscated by the Crown to be used for charitable purposes. [Anglo-French *deodande,* from Latin *Deō dandum,* something to be given to God : *Deus,* God + *dare,* to give.]

de·o·dar (dée-ō-daar, -ə-) *n.* A tall cedar, *Cedrus deodara,* native to the Himalayas, having drooping branches. [Hindi *dē' odār,* from

Sanskrit *devadāru* : *devás*, divine + *dāru*, tree.]
de·o·dor·ant (dee-ódərənt) *n.* **1.** A substance applied to counteract body odours. **2.** A chemical exposed to or sprayed into the air to counteract staleness. [DE- (removal) + Latin *odor*, odour + -ANT.] **—de·o·dor·ant** *adj.*
de·o·dor·ise, de·o·dor·ize (dee-ódər-īz) *tr.v.* **-ised, -ising, -ises.** To disguise or absorb the odour of. **—de·o·dor·i·sa·tion** (-ī-záysh'n ‖ *U.S.* -i-) *n.* **—de·o·dor·is·er** *n.*
De·o gra·ti·as (dáy-ō graáti-əss, -ass). *Abbr.* **D.G.** *Latin.* Thanks be to God.
de·on·tic (dee-óntik) *adj.* **1.** *Logic & Philosophy.* Of or pertaining to such ethical concepts as obligation or commitment. **2.** *Linguistics.* Of or pertaining to the representation in language of obligation and permission, especially through various uses of the modal auxiliaries, for example, *must* and *may.* [Greek *deont-*, participial stem of *dei* (impersonal), it behoves, it is right.]
de·on·tol·o·gy (deé-on-tólləji, -ón-) *n. Philosophy.* The theory or study of moral obligation or commitment. [Greek *deon* (stem *deont-*), that which is binding or needful (influenced in meaning by *dein*, to bind), from *dei*, it is right + -LOGY.] **—de·on·to·log·i·cal** (-tə-lójik'l) *adj.* **—de·on·tol·o·gist** *n.*
De·o vo·len·te (deé-ō və-lénti, vō-; dáy-ō vo-léntay) *adv. Abbr.* **D.V.** *Latin.* God willing.
de·ox·i·dise, de·ox·i·dize (dee-óksi-dīz, deé-) *tr.v.* **-dised, -dising, -dises.** To remove oxygen, especially chemically combined oxygen, from. **—de·ox·i·di·sa·tion** *n.* **—de·ox·i·dis·er** *n.*
deoxy–, desoxy– *comb. form.* Indicates that a molecule contains less oxygen than another to which it is related; for example, **deoxyribonucleic acid.**
de·ox·y·cor·ti·co·ster·one (dee-óksi-korti-kóstə-rōn, -kō-steér-ōn) *n.* A steroid hormone, $C_{21}H_{30}O_3$, derived from the adrenal cortex, that regulates water and salt balance and is used to treat adrenal insufficiency.
de·ox·y·gen·ate (dee-óksijə-nayt, deé-) *tr.v.* **-ated, -ating, -ates.** To remove oxygen from. **—de·ox·y·gen·a·tion** (-náysh'n) *n.*
de·ox·y·ri·bo·nu·cle·ic acid (dee-óksi-rībō-new-kleé-ik, deé-, -kláy- ‖ -nōō-) *n.* Also **des·ox·y·ri·bo·nu·cle·ic acid** (déz-). **DNA** *(see).*
de·ox·y·ri·bose (dee-óksi-rī-bōz, deé-, -bōss) *n.* Also **des·ox·y·ri·bose** (déz-). A sugar, $C_5H_{10}O_4$, that is a constituent of DNA.
dep. 1. depart; departure. **2.** department. **3.** deponent. **4.** deposed. **5.** deposit. **6.** depot. **7.** deputy.
de·part (di-párt) *v.* **-parted, -parting, -parts.** *—intr.* **1.** To go away; set forth; leave. **2.** To diverge, as from an established course; deviate: *depart from custom.* *—tr.* To leave. Used chiefly in the phrase *depart this life.* [Middle English *departen*, divide, from Old French *departir* : *de-*, away + *partir*, to go, divide, from Latin *partīre*, from *pars* (stem *part-*), PART.]
de·part·ed (di-pártid) *adj.* **1.** Bygone; past. **2.** Dead. —See Synonyms at **dead.**
dé·parte·ment (dáy-paart-móN, -paartə-) *n.* The largest administrative subdivision of France and some of her colonies.
de·part·ment (di-pártmənt) *n. Abbr.* **D., dep., dept., dpt. 1.** A distinct division of a large organisation, such as a company or shop, having a specialised function and personnel and often housed separately. **2.** *Usually capital* **D.** Any of the principal administrative divisions of the government: *the Department of Energy.* **3.** A département. **4.** A division of a school, college, or university dealing with a particular field of study. **5.** *Informal.* An area of special knowledge or activity. [French *département*, from Old French, departure, from *departir*, divide, DEPART.]
de·part·men·tal (deé-paart-mént'l) *adj.* Pertaining to a department or departments. **—de·part·men·tal·ism** *n.* **—de·part·men·tal·ly** *adv.*
de·part·men·tal·ise, de·part·men·tal·ize (deé-paart-mént'l-īz) *tr.v.* **-ised, -ising, -ises.** To organise into departments. **—de·part·men·tal·i·sa·tion** (-ī-záysh'n ‖ *U.S.* -i-) *n.*
department store *n.* A large retail establishment offering a wide variety of merchandise and services, and organised into departments according to the kinds of goods sold.
de·par·ture (di-párchər) *n. Abbr.* **dep. 1.** The act of leaving; a going away. **2.** A starting out, as on a trip or a new course of action. **3.** A deviation or divergence, as from an established rule, plan, or procedure. **4.** *Nautical.* **a.** The distance sailed due east or west by a ship on its course. **b.** A ship's bearing at the start of a voyage, used as a basis for dead reckoning.
de·pas·ture (dee-paáss-chər ‖ -páss-) *v.* **-tured, -turing, -tures.** *—tr.* **1.** To put out (cattle, for example) to graze. **2.** To empty or denude (a field, for example) by grazing. *—intr.* To graze in a pasture.
de·pend (di-pénd) *intr.v.* **-pended, -pending, -pends. 1.** To rely, as for support or aid. Used with *on* or *upon.* **2.** To be assured; place trust. Used with *on* or *upon.* **3. a.** To be determined, conditioned, or dependent. Usually used with *on* or *upon*: *It depends upon your taste.* **b.** To depend on something unspecified: "*Will you do it?*" "*That depends*". **4.** *Archaic.* To hang down. Used with *from.* **5.** *Archaic.* To be pending or undecided. —See Synonyms at **rely.** [Middle English *dependen*, from Old French *dependre*, to hang down, from Latin *dēpendēre* : *dē-*, down + *pendēre*, to hang.]
Usage: *Depend,* expressing condition or contingency, is usually followed by *on* or *upon*: *It depends (up)on what he does.* In informal speech, the preposition is often omitted.
de·pend·a·ble (di-péndə-b'l) *adj.* Capable of being depended upon; trustworthy. See Synonyms at **faithful. —de·pend·a·bil·i·ty** (-bílləti), **de·pend·a·ble·ness** *n.* **—de·pend·a·bly** *adv.*
de·pend·ant (di-péndənt) *n.* Also *chiefly U.S.* **de·pend·ent.** One who relies on another for support, especially for financial support.
de·pend·ence (di-péndənss) *n.* Also *chiefly U.S.* **de·pend·ance. 1.** The state or fact of being dependent; especially, subjection to, control by, or reliance upon someone or something else: *drug dependence.* **2.** Trust; reliance. —See Synonyms at **trust.**
de·pend·en·cy (di-péndən-si) *n., pl.* **-cies.** Also *chiefly U.S.* **de·pend·an·cy. 1. a.** Dependence. **b.** Dependence on state benefits or charity regarded as detrimental to self-reliance and initiative. Often used attributively: *"The dependency theorists argue that welfare ... actually generates apathy and a sense of 'being trapped within welfare'." (The Times)* . **2.** Anything dependent or subordinate. **3.** *Abbr.* **Dep.** A territory under the jurisdiction of another country from which it is separated geographically.
de·pend·ent (di-péndənt) *adj.* Also *chiefly U.S.* **dependant. 1.** Contingent upon something or someone else. **2.** Subordinate. **3.** Unable to exist or function satisfactorily without the aid or use of someone or something. **4.** *Archaic.* Hanging down.
~n. Chiefly U.S. Variant of **dependant. —de·pend·ent·ly** *adv.*
dependent clause *n. Grammar.* A **subordinate clause** *(see).*
de·per·son·al·ise, de·per·son·al·ize (dee-pérss'n-ə-līz, deé-) *tr.v.* **-ised, -ising, -ises. 1.** To deprive of personal or individual character. **2.** To render impersonal. **—de·per·son·al·i·sa·tion** (-lī-záysh'n ‖ *U.S.* -li-) *n.*
de·phleg·ma·tor (dee-flég-maytər, deé-fleg-) *n.* A device used in distillation to condense the higher boiling constituents of a mixed vapour. [DE- + PHLEGM + -ATOR.]
de·pict (di-píkt) *tr.v.* **-picted, -picting, -picts. 1.** To represent in a picture or sculpture. **2.** To represent in words; describe. [Latin *dēpingere* (past participle *dēpictus*) : *dē-*, completely + *pingere*, to picture.] **—de·pic·tion** *n.*
dep·i·late (déppi-layt) *tr.v.* **-lated, -lating, -lates.** To remove hair from (the body). [Latin *dēpilāre* (past participle *dēpilātus*) : *dē-*, completely + *pilāre*, to deprive of hair, from *pilus*, hair.] **—dep·i·la·tion** (-láysh'n) *n.* **—dep·i·la·tor** (-laytər) *n.*
de·pil·a·to·ry (di-píllə-tri, de-, -təri) *adj.* Capable of removing hair. *~n., pl.* **depilatories.** A liquid or cream used to remove unwanted hair from the body.
de·plane (deé-pláyn, dee-) *intr.v.* **-planed, -planing, -planes.** *Chiefly U.S.* To disembark from an aeroplane.
de·plete (di-pleét) *tr.v.* **-pleted, -pleting, -pletes. 1.** To reduce significantly in amount, numbers, or extent; exhaust. **2.** To empty totally or partially. [Latin *dēplēre* (past participle *dēplētus*), to empty : *de-* (reversal) + *plēre*, to fill.] **—de·plet·a·ble** *adj.* **—de·ple·tion** *n.*
Synonyms: *deplete, drain, exhaust, impoverish.*
depletion layer *n. Physics.* A region in a semiconductor in which the mobile carrier charge density is sufficient to neutralise the net fixed charge density of donors and acceptors.
de·plor·a·ble (di-pláwrə-b'l ‖ -plṓrə-) *adj.* **1.** Worthy of severe reproach. **2.** Lamentable; grievous. **3.** Wretched; bad. **—de·plor·a·ble·ness, de·plor·a·bil·i·ty** (-bílləti) *n.* **—de·plor·a·bly** *adv.*
de·plore (di-plór ‖ -plṓr) *tr.v.* **-plored, -ploring, -plores. 1.** To feel or express deep sorrow over; lament. **2.** To feel or express strong disapproval of; censure. [French *déplorer*, from Latin *dēplōrāre* : *dē-*, completely + *plōrāre*†, to wail.]
de·ploy (di-plóy) *v.* **-ployed, -ploying, -ploys.** *—tr.* **1.** *Military.* **a.** To station (persons, weapons, or forces) systematically over an area. **b.** To spread out (troops) to form an extended front. **c.** To bring (forces or weapons) into action. **2.** To use or arrange for a particular effect. *—intr.* To be or become deployed. [French *déployer*, from Latin *displicāre*, to scatter : *dis-* (reversal) + *plicāre*, to fold.] **—de·ploy·ment** *n.*
de·plume (deé-plōōm, dee- ‖ -pléwm) *tr.v.* **-plumed, -pluming, -plumes. 1.** To pluck the feathers from. **2.** To deprive of honour or pride. [Middle English *deplumen*, from Old French *deplumer*, from Medieval Latin *deplumāre* : Latin *de-*, removal + *plūma*, feather.] **—de·plu·ma·tion** (-áysh'n) *n.*
de·po·lar·i·sa·tion, de·po·lar·i·za·tion (deé-pōlə-rī-zaysh'n, dee- ‖ *U.S.* -ri-) *n.* **1.** An instance or the process of depolarising. **2.** The sudden diffusion of ions across the membrane of a nerve cell that accompanies the passage of a nerve impulse and produces an action potential.
de·po·lar·ise, de·po·lar·ize (deé-pṓlərīz, dee-) *tr.v.* **-ised, -ising, -ises.** To eliminate or counteract the polarisation of.
de·pone (di-pṓn) *v.* **-poned, -poning, -pones.** *Archaic.* *—tr.* To testify or declare under oath. *—intr.* To give testimony. [Medieval Latin *dēpōnere*, from Latin, to put down : *dē-*, down + *pōnere*, put.]
de·po·nent (di-pṓnənt) *adj. Abbr.* **dep., dpt.** *Grammar.* Designating a verb of active meaning but passive form, such as certain Latin and Greek verbs.
~n. Abbr. **dep., dpt. 1.** A deponent verb. **2.** *Law.* A person who testifies under oath, especially in writing. [Late Latin *dēpōnēns* (stem *dēpōnent-*), "laying aside" (in grammar, referring to the idea that the verb had "laid aside" its passive meaning), from Latin, present participle of *dēpōnere*, to put down, lay aside. See **depone.**]
de·pop·u·late (deé-póppew-layt, dee-) *v.* **-lated, -lating, -lates.** *—tr.* To reduce the population of. *—intr.* To be reduced in population. [Latin *dēpopulāre*, ravage : *dē-*, completely + *populāre*, to ravage, from *populus*, people.] **—de·pop·u·la·tion** (-láysh'n) *n.* **—de·pop·u·la·tor** (-laytər) *n.*
de·port (di-pórt ‖ -pṓrt) *tr.v.* **-ported, -porting, -ports. 1.** To expel from a country. **2.** To behave or conduct (oneself). [(Sense 1, from French *déporter*), Old French *deporter*, behave, from Latin *dēpor-*

tāre, to carry off, carry away : *dē-,* away, off + *portāre,* to carry.]
de·por·ta·tion (dée-pawr-táysh'n || -pōr-) *n.* Banishment from a country; especially, the expulsion of an undesirable alien.
de·por·tee (dée-pawr-tée || -pōr-) *n.* A deported person.
de·port·ment (di-pórt-mənt || -pṓrt-) *n.* **1.** Conduct; demeanour. See Synonyms at **bearing, behaviour**. **2.** Posture; carriage.
de·pos·al (di-pṓz'l) *n.* Deposition (senses 1, 2).
de·pose (di-pṓz) *v.* **-posed, -posing, -poses.** —*tr.* **1.** To remove from office or a position of power. **2.** *Law.* To declare under oath, especially in writing. —*intr. Law.* To testify, especially in writing. [Middle English *deposen,* from Old French *deposer* : *de-,* away + *poser,* to put, POSE.] —**de·pos·a·ble** *adj.*
de·pos·it (di-pózzit) *v.* **-ited, -iting, -its.** —*tr.* **1.** To put down; place. **2.** To lay down or cause to settle, especially in a layer or layers, by a natural process. **3.** To give (money) as partial payment or security. **4.** To entrust (money) to a bank or other institution, especially so as to earn interest. —*intr.* To become deposited; precipitate; settle.
∼*n. Abbr.* **dep. 1.** Something entrusted for safekeeping, such as a sum of money in a bank. **2.** The condition of being entrusted for safekeeping. Used chiefly in the phrase *on deposit.* **3.** A partial or initial payment of a cost or debt. **4.** A sum of money given as security for an item acquired for temporary use. **5.** A depository. **6.** Something deposited, especially by a natural process, as: **a.** *Geology.* Material which results from the process of deposition. **b.** *Biology.* A sediment in a bodily fluid or a localised bodily accretion, such as calcium. **c.** A sediment or precipitate that has settled out of a solution. **7.** A coating or layer formed on a metal surface by electrolysis or by some other process, such as hot dipping. [Latin *dēpōnere* (past participle *dēpositus*), to put aside : *dē-,* aside + *pōnere,* put.] —**de·pos·i·tor** (-ər) *n.*
deposit account *n. Chiefly British.* A bank account in which the money deposited earns interest and notice of withdrawal is sometimes required.
de·pos·i·tar·y (di-pózzi-tri, -təri || -terri) *n., pl.* **-ies. 1.** A person or group entrusted with the preservation or safekeeping of something. **2.** A repository; a depository.
dep·o·si·tion (déppə-zísh'n, deépə-) *n.* **1.** The act of deposing, as from high office. **2.** The act of depositing. **3.** Something deposited; a deposit. **4.** *Law.* Testimony under oath; especially, a written statement by a witness for use in court in his absence. **5.** *Geology.* The laying down of material by natural processes, such as matter transported by wind or water, or that resulting from the decay of living matter or organisms. **6.** *Capital* **D. a.** The taking down of Christ from the cross. **b.** A work of art depicting this scene.
de·pos·i·to·ry (di-pózzi-tri, -təri) *n., pl.* **-ries. 1.** A place where something is deposited for safekeeping; a repository. **2.** A trustee; a depositary.
de·pot (déppō || *U.S.* deépō) *n. Abbr.* **dep. 1. a.** A building where trains or buses are cleaned, serviced and repaired. **b.** A bus station. **2.** A warehouse or storehouse. **3.** *Military.* **a.** A centrally located installation for the storage, repair, or distribution of military equipment and materials. **b.** The headquarters of a regiment, where new recruits and replacements are received and trained. [French *dépôt,* from Old French *depost,* from Latin *dēpositum,* deposit, from the neuter past participle of *dēpōnere,* to DEPOSIT.]
de·prave (di-práyv) *tr.v.* **-praved, -praving, -praves.** To deprive of rectitude; debase morally; corrupt. [Middle English *depraven,* from Old French *depraver,* to pervert, from Latin *dēprāvāre* : *dē-,* completely + *prāvus*†, distorted, crooked.] —**dep·ra·va·tion** (déprə-váysh'n) *n.* —**de·prav·er** *n.*
de·praved (di-práyvd) *adj.* Morally corrupt; debased; perverted.
de·prav·i·ty (di-právvəti) *n., pl.* **-ties. 1. a.** Moral corruption. **b.** *Theology.* The innate corruption of human nature due to original sin. **2.** A wicked or perverse act.
dep·re·cate (déppri-kayt) *tr.v.* **-cated, -cating, -cates. 1.** To express disapproval of; protest or plead against. **2.** To depreciate; belittle. [Latin *dēprecārī,* to ward off by prayer : *dē-,* away + *precārī,* pray.] —**dep·re·ca·tion** (-káysh'n) *n.* —**dep·re·ca·tor** *n.*
Usage: Similarity in form and meaning between *deprecate* and *depreciate* has led to a semantic development that is already well established. *Deprecate* means "express disapproval of": *He deprecated the use of force. Depreciate* means "belittle" or "lessen the value of": *depreciated my achievements.* However, examples such as *He deprecated my achievements,* and associated forms (such as *deprecation, self-deprecatory*), are increasingly found and accepted.
dep·re·ca·to·ry (déppri-kə-tri, -təri, -káytəri) *adj.* Also **dep·re·ca·tive** (-kətiv, -kaytiv). **1.** Expressing deprecation; disapproving. **2.** Expressing apology, or regret; apologetic.
de·pre·ci·a·ble (di-preé-shi-əb'l, -shəb'l) *adj.* Liable to depreciation.
de·pre·ci·ate (di-preé-shi-ayt, -si-) *v.* **-ated, -ating, -ates.** —*tr.* **1.** To lessen the price or value of. **2.** To make to seem less in value or importance; belittle. —*intr.* To diminish in value or price. —See Synonyms at **decry**. See Usage note at **deprecate**. [Medieval Latin *dēpreciāre,* manuscript error for Late Latin *dēpretiāre* : *dē-,* down from + *pretium,* price.] —**de·pre·ci·a·tor** (-aytər) *n.*
de·pre·ci·a·tion (di-preé-shi-áysh'n, -si-) *n.* **1.** A decrease or loss in value because of wear, age, or other cause. **2.** *Accounting.* An allowance made for this loss. **3.** A reduction in the purchasing power of money. **4.** A disparaging; a belittling.
de·pre·ci·a·to·ry (di-preé-shi-ə-tri, -si-, -təri, -áytəri) *adj.* Also **de·pre·ci·a·tive** (-ətiv, -aytiv). **1.** Diminishing in value. **2.** Disparaging.
dep·re·da·tion (déppra-dáysh'n) *n.* An act of plundering or ravaging; devastation. [Latin *dēpraedātiō,* from *dēpraedārī* : *dē,* completely + *praedārī,* to plunder, from *praeda,* booty.] —**dep·re·date** *intr.v.* —**de·pred·a·to·ry** (di-préddə-tri, -təri) *adj.*
De·prés. See **des Prés.**
de·press (di-préss) *tr.v.* **-pressed, -pressing, -presses. 1.** To dispirit; sadden. **2.** To press down; lower: *depress a pedal.* **3.** To lower prices in (a stock market). [Middle English *depressen,* from Old French *depresser,* from Latin *deprimere* (past participle *depressus*) : *de-,* down + *premere,* to press.]
de·pres·sant (di-préss'nt) *adj.* **1.** *Medicine.* Serving to lower the rate of vital activities. **2.** Causing dejection; depressing.
∼*n. Medicine.* A depressant drug.
de·pressed (di-prést) *adj.* **1.** Lacking energy and enthusiasm; melancholy; gloomy. **2.** *Botany.* Flattened downwards, as if pressed from above. **3.** *Zoology.* Flattened along the dorsal and ventral surfaces. **4.** Sunk below the surrounding region: *the depressed centre of a crater.* **5.** Economically and socially disadvantaged; marked by widespread poverty and unemployment: *a depressed area.* —See Synonyms at **sad.**
de·pres·sion (di-présh'n) *n.* **1. a.** The act of depressing. **b.** The condition of being depressed. **2. a.** *Pathology.* An abnormal lowering of the rate of any physiological function or activity, such as heart beat. **b.** *Psychology.* A state of gloom and melancholy often accompanied by feelings of inadequacy and usually by a lack of energy. **3.** An area that is below or has sunk below its surroundings; a hollow. **4.** *Meteorology.* A region of low barometric pressure in high or mid-latitudes. Also called "low", "disturbance", and formerly a "cyclone". **5.** In surveying, the angular distance below the horizontal plane through the point of observation. **6.** *Astronomy.* The angular distance of a celestial body below the horizon. **7.** *Economics.* **a.** A period of drastic decline in an economy, characterised by decreasing business activity, falling prices, and unemployment. **b.** *Capital* **D.** The period during the 1930s when such a decline occurred, in most industrialised countries. Preceded by *the.* —See Synonyms at **despair.**
de·pres·sive (di-préssiv) *adj.* **1.** Causing depression. **2.** *Psychology.* Of or characterised by depression.
∼*n. Psychology.* A person suffering from depression. —**de·pres·sive·ly** *adv.* —**de·pres·sive·ness** *n.*
de·pres·so·mo·tor (di-préssō-mṓtər) *adj.* Retarding physiological motor activity: *depressomotor nerves.*
∼*n.* A drug that causes such a retardation.
de·pres·sor (di-préssər) *n.* **1.** Something that depresses or is used to depress. **2.** A depressor nerve. **3.** Any of several muscles that cause depression or contraction of a part. **4.** Any instrument, such as a tongue depressor, used to depress a part. **5.** *Phonetics.* A consonant that has the effect of lowering the tone of a following vowel.
depressor nerve *n.* A nerve that lowers arterial blood pressure. Also called "depressor".
de·pres·sur·ise, de·pres·sur·ize (deé-préshərīz, dee-) *tr.v.* **-ised, -ising, -ises.** To reduce the pressure of air or gas within (a sealed container, room, or vehicle). —**de·pres·sur·i·sa·tion** (-ī-zaysh'n || *U.S.* -i-) *n.*
dep·ri·va·tion (déppri-váysh'n) *n.* Also **de·priv·al** (di-prī́v'l). **1. a.** The act of depriving. **b.** The condition of being deprived. **2.** Privation. **3.** A taking away of rank or office.
de·prive (di-prī́v) *tr.v.* **-prived, -priving, -prives. 1.** To take something away from; dispossess; divest. **2.** To keep from the possession or enjoyment of something; deny. **3.** To take a position from; depose from office. [Middle English *depriven,* from Old French *depriver,* from Medieval Latin *dēprīvāre* : Latin *dē-,* completely + *prīvāre,* to deprive, from *prīvus,* individual, private.] —**de·priv·a·ble** *adj.*
de·prived (di-prī́vd) *adj.* **1.** Lacking the financial means, education, family environment, or social ties considered necessary to achieve a fulfilling life: *a deprived childhood.* **2.** Lacking adequate housing, educational facilities, industry, and the like.
de pro·fun·dis (day prə-fo͝on-deess, pro-) *adv. Latin.* Out of the depths of misery or grief.
de·pro·gramme, *U.S.* **de·pro·gram** (deé-prṓ-gram, dee- || -grəm) *tr.v.* **-grammed** or *U.S.* **-gramed, -gramming** or *U.S.* **-graming, -grammes,** or *U.S.* **-grams.** To counteract the effects of previous programming or indoctrination. —**de·pro·gram·mer** *n.*
dept. 1. department. **2.** deputy.
Dept·ford (dét-fərd). District in Lewisham, Greater London, on the south bank of the River Thames. In 1513, Henry VIII founded a royal dockyard on the site.
depth (depth) *n.* **1.** The condition or quality of being deep; deepness. **2.** The extent, measurement, or dimension downwards, backwards, or inwards. **3.** *Often plural.* A deep part of or place in something. **4.** *Often plural.* The middle, inner, or most remote or inaccessible part. **5.** *Often plural.* The most profound or intense part or stage: *the depths of despair.* **6.** *Often plural.* The severest or worst part: *in the depth of winter.* **7.** Intellectual penetration; profundity. **8.** The range of one's understanding or competence: *out of one's depth.* **9.** *Plural.* An immoral condition; disgrace: *sink to such depths.* **10.** Richness; intensity; darkness: *depth of colour.* **11.** Lowness in pitch, as of a voice or musical instrument. —**in depth.** Marked by thorough coverage or treatment: *a study in depth.* [Middle English *depthe,* from DEEP.]
depth charge *n.* Any explosive charge designed for detonation under water, especially such a charge dropped or catapulted from a ship and used against submarines. Also called "depth bomb".

depth of field *n.* The distance in front of and behind an object focused by a camera, microscope, or the like, within which other objects would appear in focus. Compare **depth of focus.**
depth of focus *n.* The amount by which the distance between a camera lens and the film or plate can be varied without altering the sharpness of the image. Compare **depth of field.**
depth perception *n.* Perception of spatial relationships, especially of distances between objects, in three dimensions.
depth psychology *n.* **1.** Any psychology of the unconscious, especially as distinguished from the psychology of conscious behaviour. **2.** Loosely, psychoanalysis.
dep·u·rate (déppewr-ayt) *v.* **-rated, -rating, -rates.** *—tr.* To cleanse or purify. *—intr.* To become cleansed or purified. [Medieval Latin *dēpūrāre* : Latin *dē-*, removal + *pūrāre*, to purify, from *pūrus*, pure.] **—dep·u·ra·tion** (-áysh'n) *n.* **—dep·u·ra·tive** (-ətiv, -aytiv) *n. & adj.* **—dep·u·ra·tor** (-aytər) *n.*
dep·u·ta·tion (déppew-táysh'n) *n.* **1.** A person or group appointed to represent another or others; a delegation. **2. a.** The act of deputing. **b.** The state of being deputed.
de·pute *tr.v.* (di-péwt). **-puted, -puting, -putes. 1.** To appoint or authorise as an agent or representative. **2.** To appoint to carry out a particular job. **3.** To assign (authority or duties) to another or others; delegate.
~n. (déppewt). In Scotland, an assistant to a procurator fiscal. See **advocate-depute, sheriff-depute.** [Middle English *deputen*, from Old French *deputer*, from Late Latin *dēputāre*, to allot, from Latin, "to cut off", consider : *dē-*, off + *putāre*, to prune, cut, esteem.]
dep·u·tise, dep·u·tize (déppew-tīz) *v.* **-tised, -tising, -tises.** *—intr.* To serve as a deputy. *—tr. Chiefly U.S.* To appoint as a deputy.
dep·u·ty (déppewti) *n., pl.* **-ties.** *Abbr.* **d., D., dep., dept. 1.** A person named or empowered to act for another. **2.** An assistant exercising full authority in the absence of his superior and equal authority in emergencies. **3.** A representative in a legislative body in certain countries, such as France. **4.** A mining official who is responsible for safety precautions.
~adj. Acting as deputy. [Middle English *depute*, from Old French, from the past participle of *deputer*, to DEPUTE.]
Deputy Secretary *n.* An administrative officer in the British government service in the grade between Permanent Under Secretary and Under Secretary.
De Quin·cey (də kwín-si), **Thomas** (1785–1859). British writer and critic. At Oxford he took opium, ostensibly to cure a toothache, and became addicted to the drug for the rest of his life. He is best known for his *Confessions of an English Opium Eater* (1821).
der. derivation; derivative.
de·rac·i·nate (di-rássi-nayt) *tr.v.* **-nated, -nating, -nates. 1.** To pull out by the roots; uproot. **2.** To displace from a natural environment; dislocate. [French *déraciner*, from Old French *desraciner* : *des-, de-* (undoing) + *racine*, root, from Late Latin *rādīcīna*, from Latin *rādix* (stem *rādīc-*).] **—de·rac·i·na·tion** (-náysh'n) *n.*
dé·rac·i·né (day-rássi-nay || -náy) *adj.* Uprooted or rootless; having no ties with one's home or origins. [French.] **—dé·rac·i·né** *n.*
de·rail (di-ráyl, dée-) *v.* **-railed, -railing, -rails.** *—tr.* To cause (a train) to run off the rails. *—intr.* To run off the rails. [French *dérailler* : *dé-*, off + *rail*, RAIL.] **—de·rail·ment** *n.*
de·rail·leur (di-ráyl-yər, -ər) *n.* A device for changing gear on bicycles. [French, switch (for gears, rails), from *dérailler*, to go off rails, DERAIL.]
de·range (di-ráynj) *tr.v.* **-ranged, -ranging, -ranges. 1.** To disturb the order or arrangement of; disorder; disarrange. **2.** To disturb the normal condition or functioning of; upset. **3.** To disturb the mental stability of; make insane. [French *déranger*, from Old French *desrengier* : *de-* (sense of undoing) + *reng, renc*, line, RANK.]
de·range·ment (di-ráynjmənt) *n.* **1.** Severe mental disorder; insanity. **2.** The act or an instance of deranging. **3.** Disarrangement; confusion; disorder.
Der·by[1] (dárbi || dérbi, *especially for sense 5*) *n.* **1.** A horse race for three-year-olds, held annually at Epsom Downs in Surrey. Preceded by *the.* **2.** Any of various other horse races, especially the Kentucky Derby in the United States. **3.** *Small* **d.** Any race with a more or less open field of contestants: *a soapbox derby.* **4.** A football, cricket, or other sports match held between two teams from the same area: *a local Derby.* **5.** *Small* **d.** *U.S.* A bowler hat. [After the 12th Earl of *Derby* (died 1834).]
Derby[2] *n.* A mild cheese originally made in Derby, often flavoured with sage.
Derby[3] City and Unitary Authority area at the foot of the Pennines in central England. The country's first silk mill was founded there in 1719. The making of the porcelain known as *Derbyware* or *Crown Derby* was begun by William Duesbury (1725–86), and is still a major concern. Derby also produces jet engines for Rolls-Royce.
Der·by, Edward (George Geoffrey Smith), Stanley, 14th Earl of (1799–1869). British statesman. Initially a Whig, Derby led a protectionist Conservative government in 1852 and served again as prime minister (1858–59) and (1866–68).
Der·by·shire (dárbi-shər, -sheer || dérbi-, -shīr). A county in north central England. The Peak District in the north is largely a National Park supporting sheep farming and tourism. Coal is mined around Chesterfield and Derby.
de·reg·u·late (dée-réggew-layt, dee-) *tr.v.* **1.** To remove rules or restrictions from: *deregulate the media.* **2.** To remove price controls from: *deregulate air fares.* **—de·reg·u·la·tion** (-láysh'n) *n.*
der·e·lict (dérri-likt) *adj.* **1.** Deserted by an owner or guardian; abandoned; forsaken. **2.** Dilapidated; falling into ruins; neglected. **3.** *Chiefly U.S.* Neglectful of duty; remiss.
~n. **1.** An item of abandoned property; especially, a ship abandoned at sea. **2.** A social outcast; a vagrant. **3.** *Law.* Land left dry by a permanent recession of the water line. **4.** *Chiefly U.S.* One neglectful of duty or obligation. [Latin *dērelictus*, past participle of *dērelinquere*, to abandon : *dē-*, completely + *relinquere*, to leave behind : *re-*, behind + *linquere*, to leave.]
der·e·lic·tion (dérri-liksh'n) *n.* **1.** Wilful neglect, as of duty. **2.** Abandonment. **3.** *Law.* **a.** A gaining of land by the permanent recession of the water line. **b.** The land so gained.
de·re·strict (dée-ri-strikt) *tr.v.* To free from restriction; especially, to free (a road or area) from speed limits. **—de·re·stric·tion** *n.*
Dergue (derg) *n.* The ruling council established in Ethiopia after the overthrow of Haile Selassie in 1974.
de·ride (di-rīd, də-) *tr.v.* **-rided, -riding, -rides.** To speak of or treat with contemptuous mirth; scoff at. See Synonyms at **ridicule.** [Latin *dērīdēre* : *dē-* (pejorative) + *rīdēre*, to laugh at.] **—de·rid·er** *n.*
de ri·gueur (də ri-gér, -gőr || -géwr) *adj. French.* Required by the current fashion or custom; socially obligatory.
de·ri·sion (di-rízh'n) *n.* **1. a.** Scoffing; ridicule. **b.** A state of being derided. **2.** An object of ridicule; a laughing stock. [Middle English *derisioun*, from Old French *derision*, from Late Latin *dērīsiō* (stem *dērīsiōn-*), from Latin *dērīsus*, past participle of *dērīdēre*, to DERIDE.] **—de·ris·i·ble** (di-rizzib'l) *adj.*
de·ri·sive (di-rī-siv, -ziv, -rízziv) *adj.* **1.** Mocking; scoffing. **2.** Liable to derision; absurd. **—de·ri·sive·ly** *adv.* **—de·ri·sive·ness** *n.*
de·ri·so·ry (di-rī-sə-ri, də-, -zə-) *adj.* **1.** Derisive. **2.** So small or inadequate as to be ridiculous: *a derisory pay offer.*
der·i·va·tion (dérri-váysh'n) *n. Abbr.* **der., deriv. 1.** The act or process of deriving. **2.** The condition or fact of being derived. **3.** Something derived; a derivative. **4.** The form or source from which something is derived; the origin; the descent. **5.** The historical origin and development of a word; an etymology. **6.** *Linguistics.* The morphological process by which new words are formed from existing words, chiefly by the addition of affixes to roots, stems, or words. **7.** *Mathematics.* A logical or mathematical process indicating through a sequence of statements that a result, such as a theorem or a formula, necessarily follows from the initial assumptions. **—der·i·va·tion·al** *adj.*
de·riv·a·tive (di-rívvətiv, də-) *adj.* Also **der·i·vate** (dérri-vayt). *Abbr.* **der. 1.** Resulting from derivation; derived. **2.** Copied or adapted from others; lacking originality.
~n. **1.** Something derived. **2.** *Linguistics.* A word formed from another by derivation. Compare **primitive. 3.** *Mathematics.* The limit, as the increment in the argument of a function approaches zero, of the ratio of the increment in its value to the corresponding increment in the argument; loosely, the instantaneous rate of change of a function with respect to a variable. Also called "differential coefficient". **4.** *Chemistry.* Any compound derived or obtained from known or hypothetical substances and containing essential elements of the parent substance. **5.** *Plural.* Futures, options, and the like, whose price derives from the price of other things, such as commodities, currencies, or shares. **—de·riv·a·tive·ly** *adv.*
de·rive (di-rīv, də-) *v.* **-rived, -riving, -rives.** *—tr.* **1.** To obtain or receive from a source. **2.** To arrive at by reasoning; deduce; infer: *derive a conclusion from facts.* **3.** To trace the origin or development of (a word, for example). **4.** *Chemistry.* To produce or obtain (a compound) from another substance by chemical reaction. *—intr.* To issue from a source; originate. [Middle English *deriven*, to conduct water from a source, spring from, from Old French *deriver*, from Latin *dērīvāre*, to draw off, derive : *dē-*, away, off + *rīvus*, stream.] **—de·riv·a·ble** *adj.* **—de·riv·er** *n.*
de·rived unit (di-rīvd, də-) *n.* A unit of measurement obtained by multiplying or dividing two or more base units of a system of units without the introduction of numerical factors.
-derm *n. comb. form. Biology.* Indicates skin; for example, **endoderm, echinoderm.** [French *-derme*, from Greek *derma*, skin.]
der·ma[1] (dérmə) *n.* Also **derm** (derm). *Anatomy.* A layer of skin, the **dermis** *(see).* [New Latin *derma, dermis*, from Greek *derma*, skin.]
derma[2] *n.* Beef or poultry casing stuffed with a seasoned mixture of matzo meal or flour, onion, and suet, that is boiled and then roasted. Also called "stuffed derma", "kishke". [Yiddish *derme*, plural of *darm*, intestine, from Middle High German, from Old High German.]
-derma *n. comb. form.* Indicates skin or skin disease; for example, **scleroderma.** [New Latin, from Greek *derma*, skin.]
der·mal (dérm'l) *adj.* Also **der·mic** (dérmik). Of or pertaining to the skin. [DERM(ATO)- + -AL.]
der·ma·ti·tis (dérmə-tītiss) *n. Medicine.* Inflammation of the skin. [New Latin : DERMAT(O)- + -ITIS.]
dermato-, derm-, derma-, dermat- *comb. form.* Indicates skin; for example, **dermatology, dermal, dermatome, dermatoid.** [Greek, from *derma*, skin.]
der·mat·o·gen (der-máttə-jen, -jən) *n. Botany.* The outer layer of a root meristem, from which the epidermis is formed.
der·ma·toid (dérmə-toyd) *n.* Also **der·moid** (dér-moyd). Resembling skin; skinlike. [DERMAT(O)- + -OID.]
der·ma·tol·o·gy (dér-mə-tólləji) *n.* The branch of medicine concerned with the physiology and pathology of the skin and treatment of skin diseases. [DERMATO- + -LOGY.] **—der·ma·to·log·i·cal**

(-tə-lójik'l) *adj.* —**der·ma·tol·o·gist** (-tóllǝjist) *n.*

der·ma·tome (dérmǝ-tōm) *n.* **1.** An area of skin with sensory fibres from a single spinal nerve. **2.** An instrument used in cutting thin slices of the skin, as in skin grafting. **3.** *Biology.* The part of a somite that develops into the dermis. [DERMA(TO)- + -TOME.]

der·ma·to·phyte (dér-mǝtǝ-fīt ‖ der-máttǝ-) *n.* Any of various fungi that cause skin disease. [DERMATO- + -PHYTE.]

der·ma·to·phy·to·sis (dér-mǝ-tŏfī-tō-siss) *n.* Any fungal infection of the skin, especially of the feet, such as athlete's foot. [DERMATO-PHYT(E) + -OSIS.]

der·ma·to·plas·ty (dérmǝtō-plasti) *n.* The use of skin grafts in plastic surgery to correct defects or replace skin loss. [DERMATO- + -PLASTY.]

der·ma·to·sis (dérmǝ-tŏ-siss) *n., pl.* **-ses** (-seez). A skin disease. [DERMAT(O)- + -OSIS.]

dermic. Variant of **dermal.**

der·mis (dérmiss) *n.* The living part of the skin that forms a thick layer below the epidermis and is made up of connective tissue containing blood and lymph vessels, nerve endings, sweat and sebaceous glands, and smooth muscle. Also called "corium", "derma", "derm". [New Latin, abstracted from EPIDERMIS.]

Der·mot Mac·Mur·rough (dérmǝt mǝk-múrrō), also known as Diarmaid MacMurchada (*c.* 1110–71). King of Leinster. Defeated by his rivals, he regained his kingdom with the aid of the English. Even today he is unpopular with Irish nationalists for introducing the English into Ireland.

der·nier cri (dérn-yay krée) *n. French.* The latest thing; the newest fashion. [French, "last cry".]

de·ro (dérrō) *n., pl.* **deros.** Also **der·ro.** *Australian Slang.* A vagabond; a tramp. [From DERELICT.]

der·o·gate (dérrǝ-gayt) *v.* **-gated, -gating, -gates.** —*intr.* **1.** To detract; take away. Used with *from.* **2.** To deviate from a standard or expectation; go astray. Used *from.* —*tr.* To disparage; belittle. [Latin *dērogāre*, repeal, restrict, disparage : *dē-*, away + *rogāre*, ask.] —**der·o·ga·tion** (-gáysh'n) *n.* —**der·o·ga·tive** (di-róggǝtiv) *adj.*

de·rog·a·to·ry (di-róggǝ-tri, -tǝri) *adj.* Deliberately offensive; detracting or disparaging. —**de·rog·a·to·ri·ly** *adv.* —**de·rog·a·to·ri·ness** *n.*

der·rick (dérrik) *n.* **1.** A large crane for hoisting and moving heavy objects, consisting of a movable boom equipped with cables and pulleys and connected to the base of an upright stationary beam. **2.** A tall framework over the opening of an oil well or other drilled hole, used to support boring equipment or to hoist and lower pipe lengths. [Originally, "hangman", "gallows", after *Thomas Derick*, noted hangan at Tyburn, *c.* 1600.]

der·ri·ère (dérri-aír, -air) *n. Informal.* The buttocks; the rear. [French, "the rear".]

der·ring-do (dérring-dōō) *n. Poetic.* Daring spirit and action; valour. [Middle English *during don,* daring to do (mistaken for a noun phrase by Edmund Spenser and later by Sir Walter Scott) : *durring,* present participle of *durren,* Old English *durran,* to DARE + *don,* to DO.]

der·rin·ger (dérrinjǝr) *n.* A short-barrelled pistol with a large bore. [After Henry *Deringer* (1786–1868), 19th century U.S. gunsmith who invented it.]

der·ris (dérriss) *n.* **1.** Any of various woody vines of the genus *Derris,* of tropical Asia, whose roots yield rotenone. **2.** The extract from the roots of such plants, which is a powerful insecticide. [New Latin, from Greek, covering, skin.]

der·ry[1] (dérri) *n., pl.* **-ries.** A meaningless word used as a refrain or chorus in old songs.

derry[2] *n. Australian & N.Z. Informal.* A grudge; an aversion: *have a derry on a rival.* [Probably shortened from *derry down,* common refrain in folk songs, with allusion to the phrase *have a down on.*]

Derry. See **Londonderry.**

derv (derv) *n. British.* Diesel fuel for road vehicles. [From *d*iesel *e*ngine *r*oad *v*ehicle.]

der·vish (dérvish) *n.* A member of any of various Muslim orders of ascetics, some of which practise the achievement of collective ecstasy through whirling dances and the chanting of religious formulas. [Turkish *derviş,* mendicant, from Persian *darvēsh*†.]

Der·went (dérwǝnt). The name of several rivers in England, from a Celtic word meaning "clear water". The longest is in Derbyshire, flowing 96 kilometres (60 miles) into the River Trent.

Derwent Water. Small lake in Cumbria, in the Lake District, England.

D.E.S. Department of Education and Science.

De·sai (de-sí), **(Shri) Morarji (Ranchhodji)** (1896–1995). Indian statesman. A disciple of Mahatma Gandhi, he later came to lead the Congress Party against Indira Gandhi, who as prime minister imprisoned him during a state of emergency. He defeated her in the 1977 elections and as prime minister led the newly formed Janata Party, but resigned in 1979.

de·sal·i·nate (dée-sál-i-nayt) *tr.v.* **-nated, -nating, -nates.** Also **de·sal·i·nise** (-nīz), **de·salt** (-sáwlt ‖ -sólt). To remove (salts and other chemicals) from sea water or saline water. —**de·sal·i·na·tion** *n.*

des·cant (déss-kant) *n.* Also **dis·cant** (díss-) (for sense 1). *Music.* **a.** An ornamental melody or counterpoint sung or played above a musical theme. **b.** The highest part sung in part music. **2.** A discussion or discourse on a theme.

~*intr.v.* (dess-kánt) **descanted, -canting, -cants.** Also **discant** (for sense 2). **1.** To comment at length; discourse. Used with *on* or *upon.* **2. a.** To sing or play a descant. **b.** To sing melodiously. [Middle

English *discant,* from Old North French *descant,* from Medieval Latin *discantus,* refrain : *dis-,* apart + *cantus,* song, from the past participle of *canere,* to sing.] —**des·cant·er** *n.*

descant recorder *n. Music.* A recorder having the highest pitch of those in common use.

Des·cartes (dáy-kaart ‖ *French* day-kárt), **René** (1596–1650). French philosopher. Having rejected all his previously held beliefs, he built his philosophy on the one premise he held to be indisputable, the existence of himself as a thinking subject: "Cogito ergo sum" ("I think, therefore I am"), which he argued in his *Discourse on Method* (1637), and his *Meditations* (1641). As a mathematician, he introduced coordinates and the method of undetermined coefficients.

de·scend (di-sénd) *v.* **-scended, -scending, -scends.** —*intr.* **1.** To move from a higher to a lower place, rank, pitch, or the like; come or go down. **2.** To slope, extend, or incline downwards: *"a rough path descended like a steep stair into the plain"* (J.R.R. Tolkien). **3.** To come or be derived from ancestors. **4.** To have hereditary derivation. **5.** To lower oneself in behaviour; stoop. **6.** To arrive in an overwhelming manner. Used with *on* or *upon.* **7.** To move down towards the horizon. Used of the Sun and Moon. —*tr.* To move from a higher to a lower part of; go down. [Middle English *descenden,* from Old French *descendre,* from Latin *dēscendere* : *dē-,* down + *scandere,* to climb.] —**de·scend·i·ble, de·scend·a·ble** *adj.*

de·scen·dant (di-séndǝnt) *n.* **1.** A person, animal, or plant descended from an individual, race, species, or earlier form; an immediate or remote offspring. **2.** Anything descended from an earlier form.

~*adj.* Variant of **descendent.**

Usage: There is a clear distinction between the noun *descendant* "offspring" and the adjective *descendent* "moving downwards", though it is easy to confuse the two in spelling.

de·scen·dent (di-séndǝnt) *adj.* Also **descendant.** **1.** Moving downwards; descending. **2.** Proceeding by descent from an ancestor. Often used with *from.* See Usage note at **descendant.**

~*n.* In astrology, the point on the ecliptic which lies directly opposite the **ascendant** *(see).*

de·scend·er (di-séndǝr) *n.* **1.** One that descends. **2.** *Printing.* **a.** The part of certain letters, such as *g, p,* or *y,* that extends below the bottom of most lower-case letters. **b.** Any such letter.

de·scent (di-sént) *n.* **1.** The act or an instance of descending; a coming or going down. **2.** A way down; a downward incline or passage. **3.** Hereditary derivation; ancestral extraction; lineage. **4.** A generation of a specific lineage. **5.** A lowering or decline, as in status or level. **6.** A sudden attack; an onslaught. **7.** *Law.* Transference of property by inheritance. [Middle English *descent,* from Old French, from *descendre,* to DESCEND.]

de·scribe (di-skrīb) *tr.v.* **-scribed, -scribing, -scribes.** **1.** To give a verbal account of; tell about in detail. **2.** To transmit a mental image or impression of with words; picture verbally. **3.** To characterise succinctly; label; call. Used with *as: I should describe him as an idiot.* **4.** To trace or draw the figure of; outline: *describe a circle with a compass.* [Latin *dēscrībere,* to copy off, write down : *dē-,* down + *scrībere,* to write.] —**de·scrib·a·ble** *adj.* —**de·scrib·er** *n.*

de·scrip·tion (di-skrípsh'n) *n.* **1.** The act, process, or technique of describing. **2.** A statement or account describing someone or something. **3.** A kind; a sort: *costumes of every description.* [Middle English *descripcioun,* from Old French *description,* from Latin *dēscriptiō* (stem *dēscriptiōn-*), from *dēscriptus,* past participle of *dēscrībere,* to DESCRIBE.]

de·scrip·tive (di-skríptiv) *adj.* **1.** Involving or characterised by description; serving to describe. **2.** Concerned with description or classification rather than explanation: *descriptive science.* **3.** *Grammar.* Expressing an attribute of the qualified noun; for example, *green* in *green grass.* Said of an adjective or adjectival clause. **4.** *Linguistics.* Of or pertaining to descriptive linguistics. Compare **prescriptive.** —**de·scrip·tive·ly** *adv.* —**de·scrip·tive·ness** *n.*

descriptive geometry *n. Mathematics.* The collection of graphic techniques used in problems relating to three-dimensional structures.

descriptive linguistics *n.* The study of a language or languages as they exist, or as they existed at a specific stage of development, with the emphasis on constructing a complete grammatical analysis without the use of standards of usage.

de·scrip·ti·vism (di-skrípti-viz'm) *n.* **1.** *Philosophy.* The doctrine that ethical propositions describe something about the real world and are true or false. Compare **emotivism, prescriptivism.** **2.** *Linguistics.* The practice or advocacy of the methods of descriptive linguistics. Compare **prescriptivism.**

de·scry (di-skrí) *tr.v.* **-scried, -scrying, -scries.** **1.** To discern (something difficult to catch sight of): *descried a ship through the mists.* **2.** To discover by careful observation or investigation. —See Synonyms at **see.** [Middle English *descrien,* to cry out, proclaim, catch sight of, from Old French *descrier,* to decry : *des-,* used in pejorative sense, DIS- + *crier,* to CRY.] —**de·scri·er** *n.*

des·e·crate (déssi-krayt) *tr.v.* **-crated, -crating, -crates.** To abuse the sacredness of; subject to sacrilege; profane. [DE- + (CON)SECRATE.] —**des·e·crat·er, des·e·cra·tor** *n.* —**des·e·cra·tion** (-kráysh'n) *n.*

de·seg·re·gate (dée-séggri-gayt) *v.* **-gated, -gating, -gates.** —*tr.* To abolish racial segregation in (a school, for example). —*intr.* To become desegregated. —**de·seg·re·ga·tion** (-gáysh'n) *n.* —**de·seg·re·ga·tion·ist** (-gáysh'n-ist) *adj. & n.*

de·se·lect (dée-si-lékt) tr.v. **-lected, -lecting, -lects.** British. To withdraw official party support from (a candidate who had previously been selected to contest an election). —**de·se·lec·tion** n.

de·sen·si·tise, de·sen·si·tize (dee-sén-si-tīz) tr.v. **-tised, -tising, -tises.** To render less sensitive, as to what provokes an allergy or phobia. —**de·sen·si·ti·sa·tion** (-áysh'n) n. —**de·sen·si·tis·er** n.

des·ert[1] (dézzərt) n. **1.** A region rendered barren or partially barren by low precipitation (typically less than 250 millimetres or 10 inches a year), or by its exceptionally permeable surface. **2.** A place which lacks aesthetic or cultural appeal: an architectural desert. ~adj. Of, pertaining to, or characteristic of a desert; barren and uninhabited; desolate: a desert island. [Middle English, from Old French, from Late Latin dēsertum, from Latin, neuter past participle of dēserere, to abandon, DESERT.]

de·sert[2] (di-zért) n. **1.** Usually plural. That which is deserved or merited, especially a punishment: received his just deserts. **2.** The state or fact of deserving reward or punishment. [Middle English deserte, from Old French, from desert, from deservir, to DESERVE.]

de·sert[3] (di-zért) v. **-serted, -serting, -serts.** —tr. **1.** To forsake or leave; abandon. **2.** To leave (one's post, for example) in violation of orders or oath. —intr. To forsake one's duty or post; especially, to be absent without leave from the armed forces with no intention of returning. [French déserter, from Late Latin dēsertāre, from Latin dēsertus, past participle of dēserere, to abandon : dē-, reversal + serere, to join.] —**de·sert·er** n.

de·ser·tion (di-zérsh'n) n. **1. a.** The act of deserting. **b.** The state of being deserted. **2.** Law. Wilful abandonment of one's spouse or children, or both, without their consent and with the intention of forsaking all legal obligation.

desert rat n. **1.** A jerboa, Jaculus orientalis, inhabiting North African deserts. **2.** British Informal. A soldier who served in North Africa (1941–42) with the Allied Seventh Armoured Division.

de·serve (di-zérv) v. **-served, -serving, -serves.** —tr. To be worthy of; have a right to; merit. —intr. To be worthy. [Middle English deserven, to be entitled to in return for services, deserve, from Old French deservir, from Latin dēservīre, serve well : dē-, completely + servīre, to SERVE.]

de·served (di-zérvd) adj. Merited or earned. Often used in combination: a well-deserved holiday. —**de·serv·ed·ly** (di-zérvid-li) adv. —**de·serv·ed·ness** n.

de·serv·ing (di-zérving) adj. Worthy of support, reward or praise; meritorious. ~n. Merit; deserts. —**de·serv·ing·ly** adv. —**de·serv·ing·ness** n.

de·sex (dée-séks) tr.v. **-sexed, -sexing, -sexes.** To remove part or all of the reproductive organs of; spay or castrate.

déshabillé. Variant of dishabille.

De Si·ca (de séeka), **Vittorio** (1901–74). Italian film director and actor. Among his best films are Shoeshine (1946), Bicycle Thieves (1948), and Umberto D (1952).

des·ic·cant (déssikənt) n. A substance, such as calcium oxide or sulphuric acid, that has a high affinity for water and is used as a drying agent to absorb moisture. [Latin dēsiccāns (stem dēsiccant-), present participle of dēsiccāre, to DESICCATE.] —**des·ic·cant** adj.

des·ic·cate (déssi-kayt) v. **-cated, -cating, -cates.** —tr. **1.** To make thoroughly dry; dry out. **2.** To preserve (foods) by removing the moisture. **3.** To divest of spirit, spontaneity, or animation; make dry or uninteresting. —intr. To become dry. ~adj. Also **des·ic·cat·ed.** Lacking spirit, spontaneity, or animation; arid. [Latin dēsiccāre : dē-, completely + siccāre, to dry up, from siccus, dry.] —**des·ic·ca·tion** (-káysh'n) n. —**des·ic·ca·tive** (-kətiv, -kaytiv) adj.

des·ic·ca·tor (déssi-kaytər) n. **1.** A jar or box, especially one used in laboratories, that contains a desiccant and protects substances from atmospheric moisture. **2.** An apparatus for drying milk, fruit, or other natural products.

de·sid·er·ate (di-zíddə-rayt, -síddə-) tr.v. **-ated, -ating, -ates.** To long for. [Latin dēsīderāre, to DESIRE.]

de·sid·er·a·tive (di-zíddə-rətiv, -síddə- ‖ -raytiv) adj. **1.** Of or pertaining to desire. **2. a.** Designating a category of verbs in some Indo-European languages, such as Latin, expressing a wish to perform the action denoted by the given verb. **b.** Being a verb, verb form, or affix in this category. ~n. A desiderative verb.

de·sid·er·a·tum (di-zíddə-ráa-təm, -síddə-, -ráy-) n., pl. **-ta** (-tə). Something needed and desired. [Latin desiderātum, neuter past participle of dēsīderāre, to DESIRE.]

de·sign (di-zín) v. **-signed, -signing, -signs.** —tr. **1.** To conceive; invent; contrive. **2.** To form a plan for. **3.** To be responsible for the design of (a building or stage set, for example). **4.** To have as a goal or purpose; intend. —intr. **1.** To make or execute plans. **2.** To create designs. ~n. **1.** The invention, description, depiction, or disposition of the forms, parts, or details of something according to a plan. **2.** A drawing or sketch. **3.** A decorative or artistic work. **4.** A visual composition; a pattern. **5.** The art of creating designs. **6.** A plan; a project; an undertaking. **7.** A reasoned purpose; an intention. **8.** Often plural. **a.** A sinister or hostile scheme; a crafty plot. Used with on, upon, or against. **b.** Sexual intentions. [French désigner, from Latin dēsignāre, to DESIGNATE.] —**de·sign·a·ble** adj. —**de·sign·er** n.

des·ig·nate (dézzig-nayt) tr.v. **-nated, -nating, -nates. 1.** To indicate or specify; point out. **2.** To give a name or title to; characterise. **3.** To select for a particular duty, office, or purpose; appoint. ~adj. (dézzig-nit,-nayt). Appointed but not yet installed in office. Used after the noun: the chairwoman designate. [Latin dēsignāre, designate, mark out : dē-, out + signāre, mark, from signum, sign.] —**des·ig·na·to·ry, des·ig·na·to·ry** (-nə-tri, -təri, -náytəri) adj. —**des·ig·na·tor** (-naytər) n.

des·ig·na·tion (dézzig-náysh'n) n. **1.** The act of designating; a marking or pointing out. **2.** Nomination or appointment. **3.** A distinguishing name or mark; a title.

de·sign·ed·ly (di-zínidli) adv. On purpose; intentionally.

de·sign·er (di-zínər) n. **1.** A person who creates designs, usually commercial designs, as of clothing, fabrics, furniture, or machinery. **2.** A person who has designs; a schemer; a plotter. ~adj. **1.** Designed by a well-known designer or manufacturer: a designer dress. **2.** Designed, created, or altered especially: designer drugs; designer plants thanks to genetic engineering. **3.** As if so designed; as if customised or custom-made to be chic and/or trendy: "Sloane Ranger accents and designer bone-structure to match." (The Spectator.)

de·sign·ing (di-zíning) adj. **1.** Conniving; artful; crafty. **2.** Showing or exercising forethought. —**de·sign·ing·ly** adv.

des·i·nence (déssinəns) n. **1.** A termination; a finishing. **2.** Grammar. An inflectional ending. [French, from Medieval Latin dēsinentia, from Latin dēsinere, present participle of dēsinere, to cease, leave off : dē-, off + sinere, to leave.]

de·sir·a·ble (di-zír-əb'l) adj. **1.** Worth seeking or deserving preference; pleasing; fine. **2.** Arousing desire, especially sexual desire. **3.** Worth wanting or doing; beneficial: a desirable reform. ~n. A desirable person or thing. —**de·sir·a·bil·i·ty** (-ə-bíllətí) —**de·sir·a·ble·ness** n. —**de·sir·a·bly** adv.

de·sire (di-zír) tr.v. **-sired, -siring, -sires. 1.** To wish or long for; want; crave. **2.** To express a wish for. ~n. **1.** A wish, longing, or craving. **2.** A request as expressed; a petition. **3.** Something or someone longed for: my heart's desire. **4.** Sexual appetite; lust. [Middle English desiren, from Old French desirer, from Latin dēsīderāre.] —**de·sir·er** n.

de·sir·ous (di-zír-əss) adj. Having, expressing, or characterised by desire; desiring. Often used with of : desirous of quick promotion. —**de·sir·ous·ly** adv. —**de·sir·ous·ness** n.

de·sist (di-zíst, -síst) intr.v. **-sisted, -sisting, -sists.** To cease doing something; forbear; abstain. Often used with from. [Old French desister, from Latin dēsistere, cease, stand off : dē-, from + sistere, to stop, stand.]

desk (desk) n. **1.** A piece of furniture typically having a flat or sloping top for writing, and often drawers or other compartments. **2.** A table, counter, or booth at which specified services or functions are performed: an information desk. **3.** A department of a large organisation, such as a government agency or newspaper, in charge of a specified operation: city desk. **4. a.** A music stand in an orchestra. **b.** Two string players using the same music stand in an orchestra. **5.** A bookrest for the service book in a church. [Middle English deske, from Medieval Latin desca, variant of Italian desco, table, from Latin discus, quoit, DISC.]

de·skill (dee-skill) tr.v. **-skilled, -skilling, -skills.** To remove the need for skilled labour in (an industry), especially by introducing machines and computers: Printing has been deskilled.

desk·top (désk-top) adj. Compact and light enough to be used when placed on a desk or similar supporting surface: a desktop computer.

des·man (déz-mən, déss-) n., pl. **-mans.** Either of two aquatic, insectivorous, molelike mammals, Desmana moschata of eastern Europe and western Asia, or Galemys pyrenaicus of southwestern Europe, having dense, brownish fur, a long snout, and a flattened, scaly tail. [Short for Swedish desman(srätta), musk(rat).]

des·mid (déz-mid, déss-) n. Any of various green, unicellular freshwater algae of the family Desmidiaceae, often forming chainlike colonies. [New Latin Desmidiaceae, from Desmidium (genus) : Greek desmos, bond, from dein, to bind.]

Des Moines (di-móyn, də-, -móynz). Capital of Iowa, United States. It is the centre of the Iowa Corn Belt, a maize growing and stock-raising region.

des·mo·some (dézmə-sōm) n. Zoology. A strengthened area of contact between an epithelial cell and a smooth-muscle cell at which the cell membranes become thickened and fibrils extend into the cytoplasm. [Greek desmos, bond, from dein, to bind + -SOME.]

des·o·late (déssə-lət, dézzə-, -lit) adj. **1.** Devoid of inhabitants; deserted: "streets which were usually so thronged now grown desolate" (Daniel Defoe). **2.** Rendered unfit for habitation; laid waste; devastated. **3.** Dreary; dismal; gloomy. **4.** Without friends or hope; forlorn; lonely. —See Synonyms at sad. ~tr.v. (-layt) **desolated, -lating, -lates. 1.** To rid or deprive of inhabitants. **2.** To devastate. **3.** To forsake; abandon. **4.** To make lonely, forlorn, or wretched. [Middle English desolat, from Latin dēsōlātus, past participle of dēsōlāre, abandon : dē-, completely + sōlus, alone.] —**des·o·late·ly** adv. —**des·o·late·ness** n. —**des·o·lat·er, des·o·la·tor** n.

des·o·la·tion (déssə-láysh'n, dézzə-) n. **1.** The act of rendering desolate. **2.** The state of being desolate; ruin. **3.** A wasteland. **4.** Loneliness or misery; wretchedness.

de·sorb (di-sórb, -zórb) v. **-sorbed, -sorbing, -sorbs.** Chemistry. —intr. To change from an adsorbed state to a liquid or gaseous state. —tr. To change (a substance) from an adsorbed state to a liquid or gaseous state. [DE- + (AD)SORB.] —**de·sorp·tion** n.

de·spair (di-spáir) intr.v. **-spaired, -spairing, -spairs. 1.** To lose all

hope; be overcome by a sense of futility or defeat. **2.** To lack trust or confidence, as in a favourable outcome or a person's abilities. Used with *of*.
~*n.* **1.** Utter lack of hope. **2.** That which destroys all hope. [Middle English *despeiren*, from Old French *desperer*, from Latin *dēspērāre* : *dē-* (reversal) + *spērāre*, to hope.] —**de·spair·ing·ly** *adv.*
Synonyms: *despair, hopelessness, desperation, despondency, depression, discouragement, dejection.*

despatch. Variant of **dispatch.**

des·per·a·do (désspə-raádō, -ráydō) *n.* **-does** or chiefly *U.S.* **-dos.** A desperate, dangerous criminal. [Pseudo-Spanish variant of DESPERATE.]

des·per·ate (désp-rət, déspə-, -rit) *adj.* **1.** Reckless or violent through despair; driven to take any risk. **2.** Undertaken as a last resort. **3.** Nearly hopeless; critical; grave: *a desperate illness.* **4.** Marked by, arising from, or showing despair; despairing: *the desperate look of hunger.* **5.** In an unbearable situation because of need or anxiety: *an artist desperate for recognition.* **6.** Extreme because of fear, danger, or suffering; very great: *in desperate need.* [Latin *dēspērātus,* past participle of *dēspērāre,* to DESPAIR.] —**des·per·ate·ly** *adv.* —**des·per·ate·ness** *n.*

des·per·a·tion (déspə-ráysh'n) *n.* **1.** The condition of being desperate. **2.** Recklessness arising from despair. —See Synonyms at **despair.**

des·pi·ca·ble (di-spík-əb'l, déss-pik-) *adj.* Deserving of contempt or disdain; mean; vile. [Late Latin *dēspicābilis,* from Latin *dēspicārī,* to despise.] —**des·pi·ca·bil·i·ty,** (-ə-bílləti), **des·pi·ca·ble·ness** *n.* —**des·pi·ca·bly** *adv.*

de·spise (di-spíz) *tr.v.* **-spised, -spising, -spises.** To regard with contempt or disdain. [Middle English *despisen,* from Old French *despire* (present stem *despis-*), from Latin *dēspicere,* to look down on : *dē-,* down + *specere,* to look.] —**de·spis·er** *n.*

de·spite (di-spít) *prep.* In spite of: *won despite overwhelming odds.*
~*n.* **1.** Contemptuous defiance. **2.** An act of such defiance; an insult; an offence. —**in despite of.** In spite of. [Preposition, short for *in despite of;* Middle English *despit,* spite, from Old French, from Latin *dēspectus,* past participle of *dēspicere,* to DESPISE.]

de·spite·ful (di-spítf'l) *adj. Archaic.* Full of malice; spiteful. —**de·spite·ful·ly** *adv.* —**de·spite·ful·ness** *n.*

de·spoil (di-spóyl) *tr.v.* **-spoiled, -spoiling, -spoils.** To deprive of possessions or contents by force; plunder; ravage. [Middle English *despoilen,* from Old French *despoiller,* from Latin *dēspoliāre* : *dē-,* sense of undoing + *spoliāre,* to plunder, from *spolium,* booty, spoil.] —**de·spoil·er** *n.* —**de·spoil·ment** *n.*

de·spo·li·a·tion (di-spóli-áysh'n) *n.* The act of despoiling or the condition of being despoiled. [Late Latin *dēspoliātiō* (stem *dēspoliātiōn-*), from Latin *dēspoliātus,* past participle of *dēspoliāre,* to DESPOIL.]

de·spond (di-spónd) *intr.v.* **-sponded, -sponding, -sponds.** To become disheartened.
~*n. Archaic.* Despondency. [Latin *dēspondēre,* to despond, promise to give, give up : *dē-,* away + *spondēre,* to promise.] —**de·spond·ing·ly** *adv.*

de·spon·den·cy (di-spón-dən-si) *n., pl.* **-cies.** Also **de·spon·dence** (-dənss). Lowness of spirits from loss of hope, confidence, or courage; dejection. See Synonyms at **despair.**

de·spon·dent (di-spóndənt) *adj.* Feeling or expressing despondency; disheartened; dejected. [Latin *dēspondēns* (stem *dēspondent-*), present participle of *dēspondēre,* to DESPOND.] —**de·spon·dent·ly** *adv.*

des·pot (déss-pot, -pət) *n.* **1.** An autocratic ruler; a tyrant. **2.** Any autocratic or domineering person. **3.** A Greek title borne by Byzantine emperors and princes, by Christian rulers in the Balkans under the Turks, and by Eastern Orthodox bishops. [French, from Medieval Latin *despota,* from Greek *despotēs,* lord.] —**des·pot·ic** (di-spóttik) *adj.* —**des·pot·i·cal·ly** *adv.*

des·pot·ism (déspə-tiz'm) *n.* **1.** Rule by or as if by a despot; absolute power or authority. **2.** The actions of a despot; tyranny. **3. a.** A government or political system in which the ruler exercises absolute power. **b.** A state so ruled.

des·qua·mate (déskwə-mayt) *intr.v.* **-mated, -mating, -mates.** *Pathology.* To shed, peel, or come off in scales. Used of skin. [Latin *dēsquāmāre* : *dē-,* removal + *squāma,* scale.] —**des·qua·ma·tion** (-máysh'n) *n.*

Des·sa·lines (de-sa-léen), **Jean Jacques** (*c.*1758–1806). Emperor of Haiti. A former slave, he rose in the slave revolt led by Toussaint-L'Ouverture against the French and took over the leadership on Toussaint's capture in 1802. In 1803, with British help, he defeated the French, and later declared himself emperor. His tyrannical rule provoked dissent, and he was assassinated.

des·sert (di-zért) *n.* **1.** The last course of a lunch or dinner, consisting of a serving of a sweet food, such as fruit, ice cream, or pastry. **2.** *Chiefly British.* Especially formerly, fresh fruit, nuts, or sweetmeats served after the sweet course of a dinner. [French, from *desservir,* clear the table : *des-, de-,* reversal + *servir,* to SERVE.]

des·sert·spoon (di-zért-spoōn) *n.* A spoon intermediate in size between a tablespoon and a teaspoon. —**des·sert·spoon·ful** (-foōl) *n.*

dessert wine *n.* A wine intended to be drunk with dessert.

de·sta·bil·ise, de·sta·bil·ize (dée-stáybi-līz) *tr.v.* **-ised, -ising, -ises.** To undermine and reduce the effective functioning of (a government or other political authority). —**de·sta·bil·i·sa·tion** (-záysh'n) *n.*

de Stijl (də stíl, stáyl) *n.* A school of art originating in the Netherlands in 1917 and characterised by the use of rectangular shapes and primary colours. [Dutch, "the style".]

des·ti·na·tion (désti-náysh'n) *n.* **1.** The place or point to which someone or something is going or directed. **2.** The ultimate goal or purpose for which anything is created or intended.

des·tine (déstin) *tr.v.* **-tined, -tining, -tines.** **1.** To determine beforehand; preordain to or as if to an inevitable outcome. Usually used with the infinitive: *destined to rule.* **2.** To assign or intend for a specific end, use, or purpose. **3.** To direct towards a given destination. [Middle English *destinen,* from Old French *destiner,* from Latin *dēstināre,* to determine, destine.]

des·tined (déstind) *adj.* **1.** Preordained; assured through destiny. **2.** Intended for. **3.** Bound for a particular destination.

des·ti·ny (déstini) *n., pl.* **-nies.** **1.** The inevitable or necessary fate to which a particular person or thing is destined; one's lot. **2.** The preordained or inevitable course of events considered as something beyond human power or control. **3.** The power or agency thought to predetermine events; fate. **4.** *Capital* D. This power personified or regarded as a goddess. [Middle English *destine,* from Old French *destinee,* from the feminine past participle of *destiner,* to DESTINE.]

des·ti·tute (désti-tewt ‖ -tōot) *adj.* **1.** Utterly impoverished. **2.** Altogether lacking; devoid. Used with of: *destitute of experience.* **3.** *Obsolete.* Abandoned; deserted. —See Synonyms at **poor.** [Middle English *destitut,* from Latin *dēstitūtus,* past participle of *dēstituere,* to set down, desert : *dē-,* down, away from + *statuere,* to place.]

des·ti·tu·tion (désti-téw-sh'n ‖ -tōo-) *n.* Extreme want of resources or the means of subsistence; complete poverty.

de-stock·ing (dée-stócking) *n.* The selling off of existing stocks to produce a cash flow, as during an economic recession. —**de-stock** *intr.v.*

des·tri·er (déstri-ər) *n. Archaic.* A warhorse; a charger. [Middle English, from Old French, from Vulgar Latin *dextrārius* (unattested), from Latin *dexter,* right (the squire managed his own horse with his left hand and led his knight's horse with his right).]

de·stroy (di-stróy) *v.* **-stroyed, -stroying, -stroys.** —*tr.* **1.** To ruin completely; spoil so that restoration is impossible; consume: *The fire destroyed the ancient manuscripts.* **2.** To tear down or break up; raze; demolish. **3.** To put an end to; bring to nothing: *a speech that destroyed any chance of a settlement.* **4.** To kill; especially, to put down (an animal that cannot be cured). **5.** To subdue or defeat completely; crush. —*intr.* To be destructive or harmful. —See Synonyms at **ruin.** [Middle English *destruyen,* from Old French *destruire,* from Vulgar Latin *dēstrūgere* (unattested), from Latin *dēstruere,* past participle *dēstructus* : *dē-* (reversal) + *struere,* to build, pile up.]

de·stroy·er (di-stróy-ər) *n.* **1.** One that destroys. **2.** A medium-sized, fast warship armed with guns, torpedoes, and depth charges, and noted for its high manoeuvrability.

destroyer escort *n.* A warship, usually smaller than a destroyer, used to convoy merchant vessels.

de·stroy·ing angel (di-stróying) *n.* An extremely poisonous white toadstool, *Amanita virosa.*

de·struct (di-strúkt) *n. Chiefly U.S.* The intentional destruction of a space vehicle, rocket, or missile after launching.
~*v.* **destructed, -structing, -structs.** —*tr.* To destroy (a defective missile or space vehicle) after launching. —*intr.* To be destroyed deliberately, as a safety measure; self-destruct. Used of a missile or space vehicle. [Back-formation from DESTRUCTION.]

de·struc·ti·ble (di-strúkta-b'l) *adj.* Subject to destruction; capable of being destroyed: *destructible machine parts.* —**de·struc·ti·bil·i·ty** (-billəti), **de·struc·ti·ble·ness** *n.*

de·struc·tion (di-strúksh'n) *n.* **1.** The act of destroying. **2.** The fact of being destroyed. **3.** A cause or means of destroying. [Middle English *destruccioun,* from Old French *destruction,* from Latin *dēstructiō* (stem *dēstructiōn-*), from *dēstructus,* past participle of *dēstruere,* to DESTROY.]

de·struc·tion·ist (di-strúksh'n-ist) *n.* A person who favours destruction, especially of existing social institutions.

de·struc·tive (di-strúktiv) *adj.* **1.** Tending to destroy; causing or wreaking destruction; ruinous. Often used with *of* or *to: destructive to national safety.* **2.** Designed or tending purely to disprove or discredit; negative; not constructive: *destructive criticism.* —**de·struc·tive·ly** *adv.* —**de·struc·tive·ness** *n.*

destructive distillation *n. Chemistry.* The simultaneous decomposition by heat and distillation of substances such as wood, coal, and oil shale to produce useful by-products such as coke, charcoal, oils, and gases. Also called "dry distillation".

de·struc·tor (di-strúktər) *n.* **1.** A furnace for disposing of rubbish, especially one which generates power from the heat so produced. **2.** A device which causes defective rockets and other space vehicles to explode.

des·ue·tude (di-séw-i-tewd, -sōo-, désswi-, dée-swi- ‖ -tōod) *n.* The state or condition of disuse: *words fallen into desuetude.* [French *désuétude,* from Latin *dēsuētūdō,* from *dēsuēscere,* to put out of use, become unaccustomed : *dē-* (reversal) + *suēscere,* to become accustomed.]

de·sul·phur·ise, de·sul·phur·ize (dée-súlfər-īz) *tr.v.* **-ised, -ising, -ises.** To eliminate sulphur from. —**de·sul·phu·ri·sa·tion** (-ī-záysh'n ‖ *U.S.* -i-) *n.*

des·ul·to·ry (déss'l-tri, -təri ‖ dézz'l-) *adj.* **1.** Moving or jumping from one thing to another; disconnected; rambling. **2.** Occurring haphazardly; random. —See Synonyms at **chance.** [Latin *dēsultōrius,* of a leaper, from *dēsultor,* a leaper, from *dēsultus,* past participle of *dēsilīre,* to leap down : *dē-,* down + *salīre,* to jump.] **—des·ul·to·ri·ly** *adv.* **—des·ul·to·ri·ness** *n.*

det. 1. *Military.* detachment. 2. detail.

de·tach (di-tách) *tr.v.* **-tached, -taching, -taches.** 1. To separate, usually without violence or damage; disconnect. 2. *Military.* To send (troops or ships, for example) on a special mission. [French *détacher,* from Old French *destachier* : *des-, de-,* apart + *atachier,* variant of *estachier,* to ATTACH.] **—de·tach·a·bil·i·ty** (-ə-bílləti) *n.* **—de·tach·a·ble** *adj.* **—de·tach·a·bly** *adv.*

de·tached (di-tácht) *adj.* 1. Standing apart from others; disconnected; separate: *a detached house.* 2. Free from emotional, intellectual, social, or other involvement; without bias; disinterested. —See Synonyms at **cool, indifferent.**

de·tach·ment (di-táchmənt) *n.* 1. The act or process of disconnecting or detaching; separation. 2. The state or condition of being separate or apart. 3. Dissociation from or lack of involvement in wordly affairs or one's environment; aloofness. 4. Absence of prejudice or bias; disinterest. 5. *Military.* a. The dispatch of troops or ships selected from a larger unit for a special duty or mission. b. *Abbr.* **det.** The unit of troops or ships so dispatched. c. *Abbr.* **det.** A permanent unit, usually smaller than a platoon, organised for special duties.

de·tail (dée̱tayl || *chiefly U.S.* di-táyl) *n. Abbr.* **det.** 1. An individually considered part, portion, or item; a particular. 2. Such an item considered as trivial or not worth attending to. 3. Particulars considered separately and in relation to a whole: *careful attention to detail.* 4. A small or secondary part of a painting, statue, building, or other work of art, especially when considered or represented in isolation. 5. *Military.* a. The selection of one or more troops for a particular duty, usually a fatigue duty. b. The personnel so selected. c. The duty assigned. **—go into detail(s).** To discuss the finer points; cover most of the particulars. **—in detail.** With particulars; item by item.

~tr.v. **detailed, -tailing, -tails.** 1. To report or relate minutely or in detail. 2. *Military.* To select and dispatch for a particular duty. [French *détail,* from Old French *detail,* piece cut off, from *detailler,* to cut up : *de-,* thoroughly + *tailler,* to cut, from Vulgar Latin *tāliāre* (unattested), to cut off.]

de·tain (di-táyn) *tr.v.* **-tained, -taining, -tains.** 1. To keep from proceeding; delay or retard. 2. To keep in custody; confine. 3. *Obsolete.* To retain or withhold. —See Synonyms at **delay.** [Middle English *deteynen,* from Old French *detenir,* from Latin *dētinēre,* to keep back : *dē-,* away + *tenēre,* to hold.] **—de·tain·ment** *n.*

de·tain·er (di-táynər) *n. Law.* 1. a. The unlawful withholding of the property of another. b. The detention of a person, especially in custody or confinement. 2. A writ authorising the further detention of a person in custody pending action.

de·tect (di-tékt) *tr.v.* **-tected, -tecting, -tects.** 1. To discover or discern the existence, presence, or fact of. 2. To find out the true nature of. 3. *Electronics.* To demodulate. [Middle English *detecten,* from Latin *dētegere* (past participle *dētectus*), to uncover : *dē-* (reversal) + *tegere,* to cover.] **—de·tect·a·ble, de·tect·i·ble** *adj.* **—de·tect·er** *n.*

de·tec·tion (di-téksh'n) *n.* 1. The act of finding out or the fact of being found out; discovery, as of something hidden or obscure. 2. *Electronics.* Demodulation.

de·tec·tive (di-téktiv) *n.* A person, usually a police officer, whose work is investigating crimes and obtaining evidence.

~adj. 1. Of or pertaining to detectives or their work. 2. Suited for or used in detection.

de·tec·tor (di-téktər) *n.* 1. Any apparatus that detects; especially, a mechanical, electrical, or chemical device that automatically identifies and records or registers a stimulus such as an environmental change in pressure or temperature, an electric signal, or radiation from a radioactive material. 2. A **demodulator** *(see).*

de·tec·tor·ist (di-téktərist) *n.* One who uses a metal detector.

de·tent (di-tént) *n. Engineering.* A **pawl** *(see).* [French *détente,* a loosening, a trigger, from Old French *destente,* from *destendre,* to release : *des-, de-,* apart + *tendre,* to stretch, from Latin *tendere.*]

dé·tente (day-tóNt) *n.* A relaxing or easing, as of tension between nations. [French. See **detent.**]

de·ten·tion (di-ténsh'n) *n.* 1. a. The act of detaining. b. The state of being detained. 2. A form of punishment in schools, by which a pupil is made to remain in class after hours. 3. A keeping in custody or confinement; especially, a period of temporary custody while awaiting trial. [French, from Late Latin *dētentiō* (stem *dētentiōn-*), from Latin *dētentus,* past participle of *dētinēre,* to DETAIN.]

detention centre *n.* In Britain, a place where young offenders are detained by order of a court for up to four months.

de·ter (di-tér) *tr.v.* **-terred, -terring, -ters.** To prevent or discourage (someone) from acting because of fear, doubt, or the like. [Latin *dēterrēre,* to frighten from : *dē-,* away from + *terrēre,* to frighten.] **—de·ter·ment** *n.*

de·terge (di-térj) *tr.v.* **-terged, -terging, -terges.** To wash or wipe off; cleanse. [French *déterger,* to cleanse, from Latin *dētergēre,* to wipe off : *dē-,* off, away + *tergēre*†, to wipe.]

de·ter·gen·cy (di-térjən-si) *n.* Cleansing power or quality.

de·ter·gent (di-térjənt) *n.* A cleansing substance, especially one that acts as a wetting agent and emulsifier and is made from a chemical compound such as an alkyl sulphonate, rather than from fats and lye. Compare **soap.**

~adj. Having cleansing power. [Latin *dētergēns* (stem *dētergent-*), present participle of *dētergēre,* to DETERGE.]

de·te·ri·o·rate (di-tée̱r-i-ə-rayt) *v.* **-rated, -rating, -rates.** *—intr.* To decline or grow worse in quality, condition, or value. *—tr.* To cause to deterioriate. [Late Latin *dēteriōrāre,* from Latin *dēterior,* worse, comparative of *dēter* (unattested).] **—de·te·ri·o·ra·tive** (-rətiv, -raytiv) *adj.*

de·te·ri·o·ra·tion (di-tée̱ri-ə-ráysh'n) *n.* 1. The act or an instance of deteriorating. 2. The state or condition of being deteriorated. 3. *Linguistics.* A change in the sense of a word to a less favourable sense; for example, the word *silly* has undergone deterioration from its earlier sense of "humble" and its still earlier sense of "blessed". Also called "pejoration". Compare **amelioration.**

de·ter·mi·na·ble (di-términəb'l) *adj.* 1. Capable of being settled, fixed, or determined. 2. *Law.* Liable to be terminated.

de·ter·mi·nant (di-términənt) *adj.* Tending or serving to determine; determinative.

~n. 1. An influencing or determining factor. 2. *Mathematics.* A square array of quantities, or elements, having a value determined by a rule of combination for the elements and used especially in solving certain classes of simultaneous equations.

de·ter·mi·nate (di-términ-ət, -nit) *adj.* 1. Precisely limited or defined. 2. Settled; final. 3. Firm in purpose; resolute. 4. a. Capable of being deduced or predicted. b. In accordance with the laws of causality. 5. *Botany.* a. Terminating in a flower, and blooming in a sequence beginning with the uppermost or central flower: *a determinate inflorescence.* b. Not continuing indefinitely at the tip of an axis: *determinate growth.* [Middle English *determinat,* from Latin *dēterminātus,* past participle of *dēterminare,* to DETERMINE.]

de·ter·mi·na·tion (di-términ-náysh'n) *n.* 1. a. The act of making or arriving at a decision. b. The decision arrived at; a strong resolve. 2. The quality of being resolute or firm in purpose; resoluteness. 3. a. The act of settling a dispute, suit, or other question by an authoritative decision or pronouncement. b. The decision or pronouncement made. 4. a. The ascertaining or establishing of the extent, quality, position, or character of anything. b. The result of such ascertaining. 5. A fixed movement or tendency towards some object or end. 6. *Logic.* a. The rendering of a concept or proposition more definite by further qualification. b. The factor or factors that so qualify. c. The defining of a concept through its constituent elements.

de·ter·mi·na·tive (di-términ-ətiv || -naytiv) *adj.* Tending, able, or serving to determine or settle; limiting; deciding.

~n. 1. Something that determines. 2. *Grammar.* A determiner. **—de·ter·mi·na·tive·ness** *n.*

de·ter·mine (di-términ) *v.* **-mined, -mining, -mines.** *—tr.* 1. a. To decide or settle (a dispute, for example) conclusively and authoritatively. b. To end or decide by judicial or other final action. 2. To establish or ascertain definitely, as after consideration, investigation, or calculation. 3. To cause (someone) to come to a conclusion or resolution. 4. To influence decisively; regulate. 5. To give direction to; decide the course of. 6. To limit in scope or extent; fix the bounds of. 7. *Mathematics.* In geometry, to fix or define the position, form, or configuration of. 8. *Logic.* To explain or limit (a concept or notion) by adding or requiring certain features or characteristics. 9. *Law.* To put an end to; terminate. *—intr.* 1. To reach a decision; resolve. 2. *Law.* To come to an end. —See Synonyms at **decide.** [Middle English *determinen,* from Old French *determiner,* from Latin *dēterminare,* to limit : *dē-,* off + *termināre,* to limit, from *terminus,* boundary line.]

de·ter·mined (di-términd) *adj.* Marked by or showing determination or fixed purpose; resolute; unwavering; firm. **—de·ter·mined·ly** *adv.* **—de·ter·mined·ness** *n.*

de·ter·min·er (di-términər) *n.* 1. One that determines. 2. *Grammar.* A word, such as an article or a possessive adjective, that limits the meaning of a noun or noun phrase and precedes other adjectives that accompany it; for example, in the phrases *the new house, her young daughters,* and *both girls,* the words *the, her,* and *both* are determiners.

de·ter·min·ism (di-términiz'm) *n.* The philosophical doctrine that every event, act, and decision is the inevitable consequence of antecedents, such as physical, psychological, or environmental conditions, that are independent of the individual human will. **—de·ter·min·ist** *n. & adj.* **—de·ter·min·ist·ic** *adj.*

de·ter·rence (di-térrənss || -tér-ənss) *n.* 1. The action or a means of deterring. 2. A defensive policy or strategy involving the deployment of weapons at a level believed likely to deter potential aggressors.

de·ter·rent (di-térrənt || -tér-ənt) *n.* 1. Something that deters: *a deterrent to theft.* 2. Power of retaliation, especially in the form of weapons, considered as a means of discouraging enemy attack: *a nuclear deterrent.* **—de·ter·rent** *adj.*

de·test (di-tést) *tr.v.* **-tested, -testing, -tests.** To dislike intensely; abhor; loathe. [Latin *dētestārī,* to execrate : *dē-* (pejorative) + *testārī,* to invoke, from *testis,* a witness.] **—de·test·er** *n.*

de·test·a·ble (di-téstə-b'l) *adj.* Deserving abhorrence or execration; odious; abominable. See Synonyms at **hateful.** **—de·test·a·bil·i·ty** (-bílləti), **de·test·a·ble·ness** *n.* **—de·test·a·bly** *adv.*

de·tes·ta·tion (dée̱te-stáysh'n) *n.* 1. Strong dislike; hatred or abhorrence. 2. Someone or something that is detested.

de·throne (dee-thrṓn) *tr.v.* **-throned, -throning, -thrones.** To remove from a throne or high position; depose. **—de·throne·ment** *n.*

det·i·nue (détti-new) *n. Law.* 1. a. An action to recover possession or the value of property wrongfully detained. b. The writ authorising such action. 2. *Obsolete.* The act of unlawfully detaining personal property. [Middle English *detenewe,* from Old French *detenue,* detention, from the past participle of *detenir,* to DETAIN.]

det·o·nate (déttə-nayt) *v.* **-nated, -nating, -nates.** —*intr.* **1.** To explode; go off. Said of a bomb, explosive charge, or the like. **2.** To burn spontaneously and prematurely. Said of the mixture in an internal-combustion engine. —*tr.* To cause to detonate. [Latin *dētonāre,* to thunder down : *dē-,* down + *tonāre,* to thunder.] —**de·to·na·tive** (-naytiv) *adj.*

det·o·na·tion (déttə-náysh'n) *n.* **1.** The act of detonating or exploding. **2.** A violent explosion.

det·o·na·tor (déttə-naytər) *n.* **1.** A device, such as an electric generator, fuse, or percussion cap, used to set off explosives. **2.** An explosive.

de·tour (dée-toor, day-, -toor) *n.* **1.** A roundabout way or course; especially, a byroad used temporarily instead of a main route. **2.** Deviation from the direct or shortest road, route, or course of action.
~*v.* **detoured, -touring, -tours.** —*intr.* To go by a roundabout way. —*tr.* To cause to go by a roundabout way or detour. [French *détour,* from Old French *destor,* from *destorner,* to turn away : *des-, de-,* away + *torner,* to TURN.]

de·tox (di-trákt) *t.v.* *Informal.* **-toxed, -toxing, -toxes.** To detoxify.
~ (dée-toks) *n. Informal.* Detoxification.

de·tox·i·fy (dée-tók-si-fī) *tr.v.* **-fied, -fying, -fies.** Also **de·tox·i·cate** (-kayt) **-cated, -cating, -cates. 1.** To counteract or destroy the toxic properties of. **2.** To remove the effects of poison from. [DE- (reversal) + TOXI(C) + -FY.] —**de·tox·i·fi·ca·tion** (-fi-káysh'n), **de·tox·i·ca·tion** *n.*

de·tract (di-trákt) *v.* **-tracted, -tracting, -tracts.** —*intr.* To take away a desirable or valuable quality; diminish. Used with *from.* —*tr.* To distract. [Middle English *detracten,* from Latin *dētrahere* (past participle *dētractus*), to pull down, draw away : *dē-,* away + *trahere,* to pull.]

de·trac·tion (di-tráksh'n) *n.* **1.** A person or thing that detracts. **2.** The act of detracting or taking away; disparagement; depreciation. —**de·trac·tive** *adj.* —**de·trac·tor** *n.*

de·train (dée-tráyn) *v.* **-trained, -training, -trains.** —*tr.* To cause to leave a railway train. —*intr.* To leave a railway train. —**de·train·ment** *n.*

de·trib·al·ise, de·trib·al·ize (dée-trīb'l-īz) *tr.v.* **-ised, -ising, -ises.** To cause to lose tribal customs or habits, or tribal organisation. —**de·trib·al·i·sa·tion** (-ī-záysh'n ‖ *U.S.* -i-) *n.*

det·ri·ment (déttrimənt) *n.* **1.** Damage, harm, or loss. **2.** Something that causes damage, harm, or loss. [Middle English, from Old French, from Latin *dētrīmentum,* from *dēterere,* to wear away : *dē-,* away + *terere,* to rub.]

det·ri·men·tal (déttri-mént'l) *adj.* Causing damage or harm; injurious. Often used with *to.* —**det·ri·men·tal·ly** *adv.*

de·trit·ed (di-trītid) *adj.* **1.** Worn down. **2.** *Geology.* Formed as detritus. [Latin *dētrītus,* past participle of *dēterere,* to wear down. See detriment.]

de·tri·tion (di-trísh'n) *n.* The act of wearing away by friction or rubbing. [Medieval Latin *dētrītiō* (stem *dētrītiōn-*), from Latin *dētrītus,* past participle of *dēterere,* to rub away. See detriment.]

de·tri·tus (di-trītəss) *n.* **1.** Loose fragments, particles, or grains that have been formed by the disintegration of rocks. **2.** Any disintegrated matter; debris. [French *détritus,* from Latin *dētrītus,* past participle of *dēterere,* to wear away. See detriment.]

De·troit (di-tróyt). City in Michigan, United States, on the Canadian border. It was founded by French settlers in 1701. In the 20th century it became the centre of the U.S. car industry. It is also a rail and shipping centre serving the Great Lakes.

de trop (də trō). *adj. French.* **1.** Too much; too many; excessive. **2.** Not wanted; superfluous: *I felt distinctly de trop with the honeymoon couple.*

de·tu·mes·cence (dée-tew-méss'nss ‖ -toō-) *n.* Subsidence of swelling; especially, restoration of an erect penis to the flaccid state. [Latin *dētumescere,* to cease swelling : *dē-* (reversal) + *tumescere,* to swell up, from *tumēre,* to be swollen.] —**de·tu·mes·cent** *adj.*

Deu·ca·li·on (dew-káyli-ən ‖). *Greek Mythology.* A son of Prometheus who, with his wife Pyrrha, survived a deluge sent by Zeus by building an 'ark' and became the ancestor of the renewed human race.

deuce¹ (dewss ‖ doōss) *n.* **1. a.** A playing card or side of a dice bearing two marks, symbols, or spots. **b.** A cast of the dice totalling two. **2.** In tennis and various similar games, a score in which each player or side is just one point short of the usual winning total, and either player or side must win two successive points to win the game. [Old French *deus,* two, from Latin *duōs,* accusative of *duo.*]

deuce² *n. Informal.* Bad luck; the devil.
~*interj.* Used to express annoyance, impatience, or surprise. Often preceded by *the* or *what the.* [Probably from Low German *duus,* deuce, two at dice (from the exclamation of the player making the lowest throw), ultimately from Latin *duōs,* two.]

deu·ced (déw-sid, -st ‖ doō-) *adj. Chiefly British Informal.* Darned; confounded; extreme. Not in current usage. [From DEUCE (devil).] —**deu·ced, deu·ced·ly** *adv.*

deuces wild *n.* A variation of certain card games, such as poker, in which each deuce may represent any card the holder chooses.

De·us (dáy-əss, dée-, -ōōss) *n. Abbr.* **D.** *Latin.* God.

de·us ex mach·i·na (eks mácki-nə, -naa) *n.* **1.** A deity in ancient Greek and Roman drama who was brought in by stage machinery to intervene in a difficult situation. **2.** Any unexpected, artificial, or improbable character, device, or event suddenly intervening to resolve a situation or untangle a plot. [New Latin, "god from a machine" (translation of Greek *theos ek mēkhanēs*).]

Deut. Deuteronomy (Old Testament).

deu·ter·a·no·pi·a (déw-tərə-nōpi-ə ‖ doō-) *n.* A form of colour blindness characterised by confusion of green, red, and yellow. [New Latin : DEUTER(O)- + AN- (lack of) + -OPIA.] —**deu·ter·a·nope** (-nōp) *n.*

deu·ter·ide (déw-tə-rīd ‖ doō-) *n.* A compound of deuterium and another element, analogous to a hydride.

deu·te·ri·um (dew-tēeri-əm ‖ doō-) *n. Symbol* **D** An isotope of hydrogen having an atomic weight of 2.0141. Also called "heavy hydrogen". [New Latin : DEUTER(O)- (because it is the second in the series of possible hydrogen isotopes) + -IUM.]

deuterium oxide *n.* An isotopic form of water with composition D_2O, present in natural water as approximately 1 part in 6,500 and isolated for use as a moderator in certain nuclear reactors. Also called "heavy water".

deutero-, deuter-, deuto- *comb. form.* **1.** Indicates second or secondary; for example, **deuterocanonical, deuteranopia, deutoplasm. 2.** *Chemistry.* Indicates the presence of deuterium. [Greek *deuteros,* second.]

deu·ter·o·ca·non·i·cal (déwt-ərō-kə-nónnik'l ‖ doō-) *adj.* **1.** Pertaining to or designating books or sections of books in the New Testament whose authority was once contested but later accepted. **2.** Pertaining to or designating books or sections of books in the Old Testament, considered canonical by Eastern Orthodox Christians and Roman Catholics, and apocryphal by many Protestants. See **Apocrypha.** [DEUTERO- + CANONICAL.]

deu·ter·og·a·my (déw-tə-róggəmi ‖ doō-) *n.* **Digamy** (*see*).

Deu·ter·o·I·sa·iah (déw-tərō-īzí-ə ‖ doō-, -īzáy-). The author of chapters 40–66 of Isaiah, who was a Hebrew writer during the Babylonian captivity (586–538 B.C.).

deu·ter·on (déw-tərən ‖ doō-) *n. Symbol* **d** The nucleus of a deuterium atom, a composite of a proton and a neutron, regarded as a subatomic particle with unit positive charge. [DEUTER(IUM) + -ON.]

Deu·ter·on·o·my (déw-tə-rónnəmi ‖ doō-) *n. Abbr.* **Deut.** The fifth book of the Old Testament, in which the law of Moses is stated completely for the second time. [Middle English, from Late Latin *deuteronomium,* from Greek *deuteronomion,* from the Septuagint mistranslation (Deuteronomy 16:18) of Hebrew *mishnēh hattōrah hazzō'th,* "a copy of this law", as *deuteronomion (touto),* "(this) second law" : DEUTERO- + *nomos,* law.]

deu·to·plasm (déw-tə-plaz'm ‖ doō-) *n.* Also **deu·ter·o·plasm** (-tərō-). Food substance or yolk in the cytoplasm of an ovum or other cell. [DEUT(ERO)- + -PLASM.]

Deutschland. See **Germany.**

Deutsch·mark (dóych-maark) *n.* Also **Deut·sche mark** (dóycha márk). *Abbr.* **DM 1.** The basic monetary unit of Germany, equal to 100 pfennigs. **2.** A coin worth one Deutschmark. See **mark²** (money). [German, "German mark".]

deut·zi·a (déwt-si-ə, dóyt- ‖ doōt-) *n.* Any of various shrubs of the genus *Deutzia,* cultivated for their clusters of white or pinkish flowers. [New Latin *Deutzia,* after Jean Deutz (died c. 1784), Dutch patron of botany.]

de·va (dáyvə) *n. Sometimes capital* **D.** In Buddhism and Hinduism, any of various gods or divinities. [Sanskrit, god.]

De Va·lér·a (de və-laír-ə, də, -léer-), **Eamon** (1882–1975). Irish statesman. He was a battalion commander in the 1916 Easter Rising, and was imprisoned by the British. He served as president of Sinn Fein (1917–26), prime minister of the Irish Free State (1932–48, 1951–54, 1957–59), and president of the Republic (1959–73).

De Val·ois (də vál-waa), **Dame Ninette,** born Edris Stannus (1898–). Irish-born British dancer and choreographer. After dancing with Diaghilev's Ballets Russes from 1923 to 1926, she opened a ballet school in London. She choreographed many ballets, including *The Rake's Progress* (1935), and founded the Sadler's Wells Ballet, which became the Royal Ballet at Covent Garden in 1956.

de·val·ue (dée-vál-yoo) *v.* **-ued, -uing, -ues.** Also **de·val·u·ate** (-ayt) **-ated, -ating, -ates.** —*tr.* **1.** To lessen or annul the importance or value of. **2.** To lower the exchange value of (currency) against gold or other currencies, by government action. Compare **revalue.** —*intr.* To institute an official reduction in the value of a currency. —**de·val·u·a·tion** (-áysh'n) *n.*

De·va·na·ga·ri (dáyvə-naàgəri) *n.* The script in which Sanskrit and many modern Indian languages are written. [Sanskrit *devanāgarī,* "the divine script of the city" : *deváh,* god + *nāgarī,* (script) of the city, from *nāgaram,* town, city, probably from Dravidian.]

dev·as·tate (dévvə-stayt) *tr.v.* **-tated, -tating, -tates. 1.** To reduce to a state of desolation; ravage; lay waste. **2.** *Informal.* To defeat, overwhelm, or confound. —See Synonyms at **ruin.** [Latin *dēvāstāre* : *dē-* (intensive) + *vāstāre,* to lay waste, from *vāstus,* waste.] —**dev·as·tat·ing·ly** *adv.* —**dev·as·ta·tion** (-stáysh'n) *n.* —**dev·as·ta·tor** *n.*

de·vel·op (di-véllǝp) *v.* **-oped, -oping, -ops.** —*tr.* **1.** To expand or realise the potentialities of; bring gradually to a fuller, greater, or better state. **2.** To elaborate or enlarge. **3.** *Music.* To unfold (a theme) with rhythmic and harmonic variations. **4.** To disclose (a plot, for example) gradually. **5.** To bring into being; make active; generate. **6.** To make more available; put to use. **7.** To convert (a tract of land) to a new function, and to increase its value, as by building extensively. **8.** To come to have gradually; acquire. **9.** To become affected with (a disease); contract. **10.** In photography, to process (a photosensitive material), especially with chemicals, in order to render a recorded image visible. **11.** In chess, to bring (a piece) into play from its starting position. **12.** *Mathematics.* To expand (a function) into a series. —*intr.* **1.** To grow; expand; progress to a more advanced state. **2.** To come gradually into existence or activity. **3.** To be disclosed. **4.** *Biology.* **a.** To progress from earlier to later stages of individual maturation. **b.** To progress from earlier to later or from simpler to more complex stages of evolution. [French *développer*, from Old French *desveloper* : *des-* (reversal) + *voloper*, to wrap up, perhaps from Celtic *vol-* (unattested), to roll.] —**de·vel·op·a·ble** *adj.*

de·vel·op·er (di-vélləpər) *n.* **1.** One that develops; especially, a person who develops property. **2.** A person who matures at a specified time or rate: *a late developer.* **3.** In photography, a chemical used to render visible the image recorded on a photosensitive surface.

de·vel·op·ing (di-véllopíng) *adj.* In the process of improving living standards and attaining an economically viable level of industrial production: *developing countries.*

de·vel·op·ment (de-vélləpmənt) *n.* **1.** The act, process, or result of developing. **2.** A developed state, condition, or form. **3.** Something, such as an event, factor, or piece of information, that has come into existence or been disclosed: *the latest developments in the police corruption scandal.* **4.** A group of dwellings built by the same contractor or in the same scheme. **5.** *Music.* A section in a movement in which various thematic variations are exploited. **6.** In chess, the moving of pieces from their starting positions, or the state of play resulting from this. —**de·vel·op·men·tal** (-mént'l) *adj.* —**de·vel·op·men·tal·ly** *adv.*

development area *n.* An area where the setting up of new factories and businesses is encouraged, usually by means of government subsidies, to ease unemployment.

de·verb·al (dee-vérb'l) *adj.* Also *chiefly U.S.* **de·verb·a·tive** (-vérbətiv). **1.** Designating a word or word form derived from a verb; for example, *variable* is a deverbal adjective derived from the verb *vary.* **2.** Designating an element added to a verb form to produce a derivative; for example, the suffix *-er* in *worker* is a deverbal suffix. —*n.* Also *chiefly U.S.* **de·verb·a·tive.** A deverbal word or element.

devest. Variant of **divest.**

De·vi (dáyvi) *n. Hinduism.* The most powerful of the Hindu goddesses, mother and consort of Siva. She combines benevolence with ferocity. See **Durga, Kali, Parvati, Sati.**

de·vi·ant (deevi-ənt) *adj.* Differing from a norm or from the accepted standards of society; deviating. —*n.* **1.** A person whose attitude or behaviour differs from the norm or from accepted social or moral standards. **2.** A sexual pervert. Also called "deviate". [Middle English *deviaunt*, from Late Latin *dēviāns* (stem *dēviant-*), present participle of *dēviāre*, to DEVIATE.] —**de·vi·ance** *n.*

de·vi·ate (deevi-ayt) *v.* **-ated, -ating, -ates.** —*intr.* To differ, depart, or turn aside from a designated norm, as from a specific course or prescribed mode of behaviour. —*tr.* To cause to turn aside or differ. —*n.* (-ayt, -ət). A deviant. [Late Latin *dēviāre* : Latin *dē-*, away from + *via*, road, way.] —**de·vi·a·tor** (-aytər) *n.*

de·vi·a·tion (deevi-áysh'n) *n.* **1.** The act or result of deviating or turning aside. **2.** An abnormality; a departure: *That outburst was a deviation from her usual serenity.* **3.** *Statistics.* **a.** The difference, especially the absolute difference, between one of a set of numbers and their mean. **b.** Any variation from a trend. **4.** Divergence from an accepted or dominant policy or ideology. **5.** The deflection of a compass needle due to local magnetic disturbances. —**de·vi·a·tion·ism** *n.* —**de·vi·a·tion·ist** *n.*

de·vice (di-víss) *n.* **1.** Something devised or constructed for a particular purpose; especially, a machine used to perform one or more relatively simple tasks. **2.** An artistic contrivance in a literary or dramatic work used to achieve a particular effect. **3.** A plan or scheme, especially a malign one. **4.** A decorative design or pattern, such as one used in embroidery. **5.** A graphic symbol, emblem, or design, especially in heraldry. **6.** *Archaic.* The act, state, or power of devising. —**leave (someone) to his** or **her own devices.** To allow (someone) to do as he or she pleases. [Middle English *devis, devise*, from Old French *devis*, division, contrivance, invention, and *devise*, difference, design, plan, both from *deviser*, to divide, DEVISE.]

dev·il (dévv'l) *n.* **1.** *Often capital* **D.** *Theology.* The major spirit of evil, ruler of Hell, and foe of God, often depicted as a man with horns, a tail, and cloven hoofs; Satan. **2.** A subordinate evil spirit. **3.** A wicked, malevolent, or ill-tempered person or animal. **4.** An unfortunate person or animal; a wretch: *poor devil.* **5.** A person who is energetic, mischievous, daring, or clever. **6.** The personification of something evil or undesirable. **7.** A junior barrister working for an established barrister in order to gain a reputation and experience. **8.** A printer's devil *(see).* **9.** Any of various mechanical devices with sharp teeth or spikes, as for tearing up rags. **10.** *Informal.* Anything difficult or hard to manage: *a devil of a job.* —**(caught) between the devil and the deep blue sea.** Having to make a choice between two equally unsatisfactory options. —**give the devil his due.** To acknowledge the ability or success of an evil or disliked person. —**go to the devil. 1.** To become thoroughly dissipated. **2.** Used as an exclamation of anger or annoyance to a person who has annoyed one. —**(let the) devil take the hindmost.** To look after one's own interests and leave others to manage as best they can. —**the devil.** *Informal.* **1.** An exclamation or expletive used to express surprise, anger, disgust, vexation, or the like. **2.** Used as an

intensive: *Where the devil is the waiter?* —**talk** or **speak of the devil.** Used when a person who has been the subject of conversation in his absence suddenly appears. —**the devil to pay.** Trouble to be faced as a result of some action.

~*v.* **devilled** or *U.S.* **deviled, -villing** or *U.S.* **-viling, -vils.** —*tr.* **1.** To prepare (food) with pungent seasoning or condiments, such as mustard or cayenne pepper. **2.** To tear up (cloth or rags) in a toothed machine. **3.** *Chiefly U.S.* To annoy, torment, or harass. —*intr.* **1.** To serve as a printer's devil. **2.** To work for a barrister or carry out research for an author, often with little remuneration. [Middle English *devel*, Old English *dēofol*, from Late Latin *diabolus*, from Late Greek *diabolos*, from Greek, slanderer, from *diaballein*, to slander, "throw across" : *dia-*, across + *ballein*, to throw.]

dev·il·fish (dévv'l-físh) *n., pl.* **-fishes** or collectively **devilfish.** The **manta** *(see).*

dev·il·ish (dévv'l-ish, dévvlish) *adj.* **1.** Of, resembling, or characteristic of a devil; fiendish: *devilish cruelty.* **2.** *Informal.* Excessive; extreme: *devilish heat.* ~*adv. Informal.* Extremely; very. Not in current usage. —**dev·il·ish·ly** *adv.* —**dev·il·ish·ness** *n.*

dev·il-may-care (dévv'l-may-káir) *adj.* Careless; reckless.

dev·il·ment (dévv'lmənt) *n.* **1.** Mischief; pranks. **2.** Devilish dealings.

dev·il·ry (dévv'l-ri) *n., pl.* **-ries.** Also *regional* **dev·il·try** (-tri). **1.** Wickedness; evil. **2.** Mischief; high spirits. **3.** Black magic; diabolism.

devil's advocate *n.* **1.** *Roman Catholic Church.* An official appointed to present arguments against a proposed canonisation or beatification. Also officially called "Promoter of the Faith". **2.** A person who opposes an argument with which he does not necessarily disagree, to determine its validity or be provocative. **3.** An adverse critic, especially of a good cause.

devil's bit *n.* **1.** A dark blue-to-purple flowered scabious plant, *Succisa pratensis.* **2.** A plant, the **blazing star** *(see).* [So called from the ragged bitten-off appearance of the roots.]

devil's darning needle *n. Informal.* A **dragonfly** *(see).*

devil's dozen *n. Informal.* Thirteen. [Alluding to the unluckiness of the number thirteen.]

devil's fingers *n. Usually used with a singular verb.* An ascomycete fungus, *Xylaria polymorpha*, which grows in blackish, club-shaped tufts on the stumps of deciduous trees. Also called "dead man's fingers".

dev·il's-food cake (dévv'lz-fōōd, -fóod) *n. Chiefly U.S.* A rich, dark, dense-textured chocolate cake. [From the contrast with the white colour of ANGEL FOOD CAKE.]

Devil's Island. *French* **île du Diable** (eel dü dee-a'abl). Small island in the south Caribbean Sea, off French Guiana. A French penal colony for political prisoners from the late 19th century, it held Alfred Dreyfus (1894–99), and Henri Charrière ("Papillon"), who claimed to have made the first successful escape from it (1941). It was finally closed in 1945.

dev·ils-on-horse·back (dévv'lz-on-hórss-bak) *n.* A savoury dish of prunes stuffed with chutney, wrapped in bacon rashers, and then placed on buttered bread and grilled. Compare **angels-on-horse-back.** [Fanciful name coined to contrast with ANGELS-ON-HORSE-BACK.]

De·vine (di-veen), **George (Alexander Cassady)** (1910–66). British theatre manager, producer, director, and actor. He founded the English Stage Company at the Royal Court Theatre, London in 1956 and produced the works of modern playwrights.

de·vi·ous (deevi-əss) *adj.* **1.** Done, planned, used, or acting in an underhand manner; not straightforward; shifty: *a devious plot.* **2.** Straying or deviating from the usual, straight, or direct course or way; circuitous; roundabout. **3.** Straying or departing from the correct or proper way; erring. **4.** Remote; sequestered. [Latin *dēvius*, off the main road : *dē-*, away from + *via*, way.] —**de·vi·ous·ly** *adv.* —**de·vi·ous·ness** *n.*

de·vis·a·ble (di-vízəb'l) *adj.* **1.** *Law.* Capable of being transmitted by will. Said of real property. **2.** Capable of being invented or contrived.

de·vi·sal (di-víz'l) *n.* The act of devising.

de·vise (di-víz) *tr.v.* **-vised, -vising, -vises. 1.** To form or arrange in the mind; plan; invent; contrive. **2.** *Law.* To transmit or give (real property) by will. **3.** *Archaic.* To imagine; conceive. ~*n. Law.* **1.** The act of transmitting or giving real property by will. **2.** The property or lands so transmitted. **3.** A will or clause in a will devising real property. [Middle English *devisen*, to divide, distinguish, examine, design, from Old French *deviser*, from Vulgar Latin *dīvīsāre* (unattested), frequentative of Latin *dīvīdere* (past participle *dīvīsus*), to divide.] —**de·vis·er** *n.*

de·vi·see (di-ví-zée) *n. Law.* One to whom property is devised.

de·vi·sor (di-vízər) *n. Law.* One who devises property.

de·vi·tal·ise, de·vi·tal·ize (dee-vít'l-īz) *tr.v.* **-ised, -ising, -ises.** To reduce or destroy the vitality of.

de·vit·ri·fy (dee-víttri-fī) *tr.v.* **-fied, -fying, -fies. 1.** To deprive of or destroy the glassy quality of. **2.** To treat (material such as glass) so as to cause crystallisation, brittleness, and loss of transparency. —**de·vit·ri·fi·ca·tion** (-fi-káysh'n) *n.*

de·vo·cal·ise, de·vo·cal·ize (dee-vōkə-līz) *tr.v.* **-ised, -ising, -ises.** *Phonetics.* To devoice (a speech sound). —**de·vo·cal·i·sa·tion** (-lī-záysh'n ‖ *U.S.* -li-) *n.*

de·voice (dee-vóyss) *tr.v.* **-voiced, -voicing, -voices.** *Phonetics.* To produce (a speech sound, especially one usually voiced) without vibration of the vocal cords.

de·void (di-vóyd) *adj.* Completely lacking; destitute; empty; without. Used with *of.* [Middle English *devoide,* from *devoiden,* to get rid of, from Old French *desvuidier* : *des-,* from Latin *dē-,* completely + *vuidier,* to empty, from Vulgar Latin *vocitāre* (unattested), from *vocitus* (unattested), empty, from Latin *vacāre,* to be empty.]

de·voir (də-vwár, dé-vwaar) *n.* **1.** *Usually plural.* Courteous attentions; compliments; respects: *pay one's devoirs to the host.* **2.** *Archaic.* Duty. [Middle English *dever, devoir,* duty, from Old French *devoir,* "that which is due", from *devoir,* to owe, from Latin *dēbēre.*]

dev·o·lu·tion (dee-və-lōōsh'n, dé-, -lewsh'n) *n.* **1.** A passing down through successive stages. **2.** The passing to a successor of anything, such as properties, rights, or qualities. **3. a.** A delegating of authority or duties to a subordinate or substitute. **b.** The transfer of a certain amount of legislative or executive power from a central to a regional authority. **4.** Biological degeneration, as distinguished from evolution. [Medieval Latin *dēvolūtiō* (stem *dēvolūtiōn-*), from Latin *dēvolvere* (past participle *dēvolūtus*), to roll down, DEVOLVE.] —**dev·o·lu·tion·ar·y** (-ri, -əri ‖ -erri) *adj.*

de·volve (di-vólv ‖ *South of England also* -vólv) *v.* **-volved, -volving, -volves.** —*tr.* To pass on, delegate, or transfer (duty or authority, for example) to a successor or substitute. —*intr.* To fall or be passed on to a substitute or successor; be conferred. Used with *on, to,* or *upon.* [Middle English *devolven,* from Latin *dēvolvere,* to roll down : *dē-,* down + *volvere,* to roll.] —**de·volve·ment** *n.*

Dev·on[1] (dévv'n). County in southwest England, spanning the western peninsula between the Bristol Channel and English Channel. The land is hilly, rising to Dartmoor in the south and Exmoor to the northeast. The county is agricultural and famous for its cattle, clotted cream, and cider. Tourism is important. The main town and administrative centre is Exeter.

Devon[2] *n.* Any of a breed of reddish cattle developed in Devon and raised primarily for beef.

De·vo·ni·an (di-vóni-ən) *adj.* **1.** Of or pertaining to Devon. **2.** Of, belonging to, or designating the geological time or system of rocks of the fourth period of the Paleozoic era, preceded by the Silurian and followed by the Carboniferous period.
—*n.* **1.** *Geology.* The Devonian period or system of rocks. Preceded by *the.* **2.** A native or inhabitant of Devon.

Devonshire cream *n.* A rich yellow clotted cream.

de·vote (di-vót) *tr.v.* **-voted, -voting, -votes. 1.** To give or apply (one's time, attention, or self) entirely to a particular activity, pursuit, cause, or person. **2. a.** To dedicate by a vow or solemn act; consecrate. **b.** To set apart; give over to a particular purpose: *a broadcast devoted to Ireland.* **3.** *Archaic.* To doom to destruction; curse. [Latin *dēvovēre* (past participle *dēvotus*), to vow, devote : *dē-,* completely + *vovēre,* to vow.] —**de·vote·ment** *n.*
Synonyms: devote, dedicate, consecrate, pledge.

de·vot·ed (di-vótid) *adj.* **1.** Feeling or displaying strong affection or attachment: *devoted friends.* **2.** Selflessly loyal or zealously committed; ardent. —See Synonyms at **faithful.** —**de·vot·ed·ly** *adv.* —**de·vot·ed·ness** *n.*

dev·o·tee (dévvə-tée, dévvō- ‖ *U.S. also* -táy) *n.* **1.** One ardently devoted or attached to anything; an enthusiast: *a devotee of sports.* **2.** One ardently devoted to a religion.

de·vo·tion (di-vósh'n) *n.* **1.** Ardent attachment or affection, as to a person or cause; faithfulness; loyalty. **2.** Religious ardour or zeal; piety. **3.** *Usually plural.* An act of religious observance or prayer, especially when private. **4.** The act of devoting or the state of being devoted. —See Synonyms at **love, fidelity.**

de·vo·tion·al (di-vósh'n'l) *adj.* **1.** Of or pertaining to devotion. **2.** Used in worship. —**de·vo·tion·al·ly** *adv.*

de·vour (di-vówr) *tr.v.* **-voured, -vouring, -vours. 1.** To swallow or eat up greedily. **2.** To destroy, consume, or waste. **3.** To take in greedily with the senses or mind: *devour a novel.* **4.** To engross, absorb, or preoccupy. [Middle English *devouren,* from Old French *devourer,* from Latin *dēvorāre* : *dē-,* completely + *vorāre,* to swallow, devour.] —**de·vour·er** *n.* —**de·vour·ing·ly** *adv.*

de·vout (di-vówt) *adj.* **1.** Deeply religious; pious. **2.** Expressing reverence or piety. **3.** Sincere; earnest; devoted. [Middle English *devo(u)t,* from Old French *devot,* from Late Latin *dēvōtus,* from Latin, past participle of *dēvovēre,* to vow, DEVOTE.] —**de·vout·ly** *adv.* —**de·vout·ness** *n.*

de Vries (də vrées), **Hugo Marie** (1843–1935). Dutch botanist noted for his mutation theory, which concluded that new species of plants and animals evolve through mutations.

dew (dew ‖ dōō) *n.* **1.** Water droplets condensed from the air, usually at night, forming on cool surfaces, such as grass. **2.** Anything resembling or suggestive of dew; something moist, refreshing, or pure. **3.** Any moisture appearing in small drops, especially tears. —*tr.v.* **dewed, dewing, dews.** To wet with or as with dew; moisten; bedew. [Middle English *deu, de(a)w,* Old English *dēaw,* from Germanic.]

DEW distant early warning.

de·wan, di·wan (di-waán) *n.* Any of certain government officials in India, especially a finance minister, or the prime minister of a state. [Hindi *dīwān,* from Persian *dīvān†,* register, account book, hence office of accounts, council of state. See also **divan.**]

Dew·ar flask (déw-ər ‖ dōō-) *n.* A type of vacuum flask used especially to store liquefied gases, having a double wall with evacuated space between the walls and silvered surfaces. [After Sir James *Dewar* (1842–1923), Scottish physicist who invented it.]

dew·ber·ry (déw-bəri, -bri ‖ dōō-, -berri) *n., pl.* **-ries. 1.** Any of several trailing forms of the blackberry, such as *Rubus caesius,* of Europe, and *R. hispidus,* of North America. **2.** The fruit of any of these plants.

dew·claw (déw-klaw ‖ dōō-) *n.* A vestigial digit, claw, or hoof on the foot of certain mammals. [Because it reaches only the dewy surface of the ground.]

dew·drop (déw-drop ‖ dōō-) *n.* A drop of dew, or anything that resembles one.

Dew·ey (déw-i ‖ dōō-), **John** (1859–1952). U.S. philosopher and educationalist, one of the main exponents of philosophical pragmatism. He held that education should be as much concerned with physical and moral welfare as with intellectual development. His writings include *Democracy and Education* (1916), *Reconstruction in Philosophy* (1920), and *Experience and Nature* (1925).

Dewey decimal system *n.* A system of classification of books and other publications in a library into ten major categories, each category being further subdivided by number. Also called "Dewey classification". Compare **Library of Congress classification.** [After Melvil *Dewey* (1851–1931), U.S. librarian who devised it.]

dew·fall (déw-fawl ‖ dōō-) *n.* **1.** The formation of dew. **2.** The time of evening when dew begins to form. [From the erroneous assumption that dew falls like rain.]

De Wint (də wínt), **Peter** (1784–1849). British watercolourist. Much of his best work was produced in the Lincolnshire countryside. *The Cornfield* (1815) is probably his best-known painting.

dew·lap (déw-lap ‖ dōō-) *n.* **1.** A fold of loose skin hanging from the neck region of certain animals, especially cattle. **2.** A similar pendulous part, such as the wattle of a bird or a fold of skin hanging from the throat of an old person. [Middle English *dewlappe* : DEW + *lappe,* LAP (loose flap). Compare **dewclaw.**]

DEW line (dew ‖ dōō) *n.* A line of radar stations in North America at about the latitude of 70° North, designed to give advance warning of approaching aircraft and missiles. See **DEW.**

dew point *n.* The temperature at which air becomes saturated and produces dew.

dew pond *n.* A manmade hollow, usually lined with clay or cement, found on chalk downs. Most of the water in it comes from rainfall.

dew·worm (déw-wurm ‖ dōō-) *n.* Any earthworm found on or near the surface of the ground and used as fishing bait.

dew·y (déw-i ‖ dōō-) *adj.* **-ier, -iest. 1.** Wet or moist with or as if with dew. **2.** Of, resembling, or suggestive of dew. —**dew·i·ly** *adv.* —**dew·i·ness** *n.*

dew·y-eyed (déw-i-íd ‖ dōō-) *adj.* Characterised by childlike innocence and faith; naive.

dex (deks) *n. Slang.* Dextroamphetamine.

dex·ter[1] (dékstər) *adj.* **1.** *Archaic.* Of or located on the right side. **2.** *Heraldry.* Located on the wearer's right and the observer's left. Compare **sinister. 3.** *Obsolete.* Auspicious; favourable. [Latin, on the right side.]

dexter[2] *n.* Any of a breed of small, hardy cattle originating in Ireland. [Perhaps from the surname of the breeder.]

dex·ter·i·ty (dek-stérrəti) *n.* **1.** Skill in the use of the hands or body; adroitness. **2.** Mental skill or adroitness; cleverness. **3.** *Rare.* Right-handedness. [French *dextérité,* from Latin *dexteritās* (stem *dexteritāt-*), from *dexter,* skilful, DEXTER.]

dex·ter·ous, dex·trous (déks-trəss, -tərəss) *adj.* **1.** Adroit or skilful in the use of the hands, body, or mind; artful; clever. **2.** Done with dexterity. [Latin *dexter,* skilful, DEXTER.] —**dex·ter·ous·ly** *adv.* —**dex·ter·ous·ness** *n.*
Synonyms: dexterous, deft, adroit, handy, nimble.

dex·tral (dékstral) *adj.* **1.** Of, pertaining to, or located on the right side; right. **2.** Right-handed. Compare **sinistral. 3.** *Zoology.* Designating or pertaining to a gastropod shell that has its aperture to the right when facing the observer with the apex uppermost. [Medieval Latin *dextrālis,* from Latin *dexter,* DEXTER.] —**dex·tral·i·ty** (dek-strál-əti) *n.* —**dex·tral·ly** *adv.*

dex·tran (dékstrən) *n.* Any of various heavy long-chain polymers of glucose that are used, depending on molecular weight, as a blood-plasma substitute, in confections, lacquers, and food additives. [DEXTR(O)- + -AN.]

dex·trin (dék-strin) *n.* Also **dex·trine** (-strin, -streen). A white or yellow powder formed by the hydrolysis of starch, having colloidal properties, and used mainly as an adhesive and thickening agent. [DEXTR(O)- + -IN.]

dex·tro (dékstrō) *adj. Chemistry.* Dextrorotatory.

dextro–, dextr– *comb. form. Abbr.* **d** Indicates on or towards the right-hand side; for example, **dextrorotatory, dextran.** [Latin, from *dexter,* on the right side.]

dex·tro·am·phet·a·mine (dékstrō-am-féttə-min, -meen) *n.* A drug, ($C_9H_{13}N$), that is the dextrorotatory form of amphetamine, acting as a stimulant on the central nervous system. It is commonly used as a sulphate or phosphate salt.

dex·tro·glu·cose (dékstrō-glōō-kōz, -kōss ‖ -glēw-) *n.* Dextrose.

dex·tro·gy·rate (dékstrō-jír-ət, -it, -ayt) *adj.* Dextrorotatory.

dex·tro·ro·ta·tion (dékstrō-rō-táysh'n) *n. Optics.* A turning to the right. Said especially of the plane of polarisation of light.

dex·tro·ro·ta·to·ry (dékstrō-rō-táy-təri, -tri, -rōtə-) *adj.* Also **dex·tro·ro·ta·ry** (-rótəri). **1.** *Optics.* Turning or rotating the plane of polarisation of light to the right or clockwise: *dextrorotatory crystals.* **2.** *Chemistry.* Of, pertaining to, or designating a solution that so rotates the plane of polarised light; dextrogyrate. Compare **laevorotatory.**

dex·trorse (dék-strawrss, dek-strórss) *adj.* Growing upwards in a spiral that turns from left to right: *a dextrorse vine.* Compare **sinistrorse**. [New Latin *dextrorsus,* from Latin, turned towards the right side : DEXTRO- + *versus,* past participle of *vertere,* to turn.] —**dextrorse·ly** *adv.*

dex·trose (dék-strōz, -strōss) *n.* A dextrorotatory sugar, $C_6H_{12}O_6 \cdot H_2O$, found in animal and plant tissue and derived synthetically from starch. Also called "corn sugar", "dextroglucose", "D-glucose", "grape sugar". [DEXTR(O)- + -OSE.]

dey (day) *n.* **1.** The title of the governor of Algiers before the French conquest in 1830. **2.** Formerly, a title held by a ruler of Tunis or Tripoli. [French, from Turkish *dayı,* maternal uncle.]

D.F. direction finder.

DFC, D.F.C. Distinguished Flying Cross.

DFM, D.F.M. Distinguished Flying Medal.

D.G. 1. Dei gratia. **2.** Deo gratias. **3.** director-general.

dhak (daak, dawk) *n.* A tree, *Butea frondosa,* of tropical Asia, that yields a red resin used as an astringent. [Hindi *ḍhāk†.*]

Dhākā. See **Dacca.**

dhal, dal (daal, dal) *n.* **1.** A tropical shrub of the genus *Cajanus,* cultivated for its pealike seeds. Also called "pigeon pea". **2.** The edible seed of this shrub. **3.** An Indian dish made from dhal or other pulses, onions, and various spices. [Hindi *dāl,* (split) pulse, from Sanskrit *dal,* to split.]

dhar·ma (dár-mə, dér-) *n. Hinduism & Buddhism.* **1.** The ultimate law of all things. **2.** Individual right conduct in conformity to this law. [Sanskrit, law.]

Dhau·la·gi·ri (dówlə-géer-i). Himalayan peak in central Nepal. At 8 172 metres (26,811 feet) it is the sixth highest mountain in the world.

Dhi·mo·ti·ki (thee-mótti-kée, -kee ‖ -mōti-) *n.* The colloquial form of Modern Greek. Also called "Demotic". Compare **Katharevusa.** [Greek, "demotic".]

dho·bi (dōbi) *n.* In India, a man who washes clothes. [Hindi, from *dhōb,* washing.]

dhobi's itch *n.* Also **dhobi itch.** A fungal skin disease, *Tinea cruris.* [The disease being common in the tropics, and supposedly contracted from other people's dirty clothes.]

dhole (dōl) *n.* A doglike, carnivorous mammal, *Cuon alpinus,* of Asia, having brownish fur, and often hunting in packs. [Of Anglo-Indian origin, akin to Kanarese *tōla,* wolf.]

dho·ti (dóti) *n., pl.* **-tis.** A long cloth worn round the waist and lower half of the body by Hindu men in India. [Hindi *dhōtī†.*]

dhow (dow) *n.* A lateen-rigged Arabian vessel. [Arabic *dāw†.*]

DHSS Department of Health and Social Security.

Dhul-Hij·ja (dool-híjaa) *n.* Also **Dul-heg·gia** (-héjaa). The 12th month of the Muslim year. Dhul-Hijja has 29 days. [Arabic *dhū'l-ḥijja,* "the one of the pilgrimage".]

Dhul-Qa·dah, Dul-kaa·da (dool-ka'adaa) *n.* The 11th month of the Muslim year. Dhul-Qadah has 30 days. [Arabic *dhū'l-ga'dah,* "the one of the sitting".]

Di The symbol for didymium.

di– *comb. form.* Indicates: **1.** Twice, double, or two; for example, **dicotyledon. 2.** *Chemistry.* Having two atoms, molecules, or radicals; for example, **diacetylmorphine.** [Greek *di-,* two, twice.]

dia. diameter.

dia-, di– *prefix.* Indicates: **1.** Through or throughout; for example, **diachronic. 2.** Across or by transmission; for example, **diapophysis, diactinic. 3.** *Botany.* Over, across, or at right angles; for example, **diatropism. 4.** In opposite or different directions; for example, **diamagnetic.** [In borrowed Greek compounds, *dia-* indicates: **1.** Through, throughout, as in **diapason. 2.** Across, as in **diagonal. 3.** Between, as in **diapause. 4.** Apart, as in **dialysis. 5.** From one to another, mutually, as in **dialogue. 6.** In different directions, as in **diathesis. 7.** Completely, as in **diaphragm. 8.** Made of, as in **diatessaron.** Greek *dia-* is the preverbal form of the preposition *dia†,* through.]

di·a·base (dí-ə-bayss) *n.* **1.** Dolerite in which the pyroxene has been altered to amphibole. **2.** *U.S.* **Dolerite** (see). [French, from Greek *diabasis,* a crossing over, from *diabainein,* to cross over : *dia-,* across + *bainein,* to go.]

di·a·be·tes (dí-ə-bée-teez, -tiz) *n.* Any of several metabolic disorders marked by excessive discharge of urine and persistent thirst, especially diabetes mellitus. [Middle English *diabete,* from Medieval Latin *diabētēs,* from Greek *diabētēs,* "a crossing over or passing through" (from the symptomatic excessive urination), from *diabainein,* to cross over : *dia-,* across + *bainein,* to go.]

diabetes in·sip·i·dus (in-síppidəss) *n.* A disease characterised by intense thirst and excessive urination. It is caused by a deficiency of the pituitary hormone vasopressin. [New Latin, "insipid diabetes".]

diabetes mel·li·tus (mə-lítəss) *n.* A chronic disease of pancreatic origin, characterised by insulin deficiency, subsequent inability to utilise carbohydrates, excess sugar in the blood and urine, excessive thirst, hunger, and urination, weakness, emaciation, imperfect combustion of fats resulting in acidosis, and, in the absence of regular injection of insulin, eventual coma and death. [New Latin, "honey-sweet diabetes".]

di·a·bet·ic (dí-ə-béttik) *adj.* **1.** Of, pertaining to, or having diabetes. **2.** For the use of diabetics.
~*n.* One afflicted with diabetes mellitus.

di·a·ble·rie (dí-aáblari) *n.* **1.** Dealings with demons or the devil; sorcery; witchcraft. **2. a.** The representation of devils or demons, as in paintings or fiction. **b.** Devil lore; demonology. **3.** Devilish conduct; devilry. [French, from *diable,* DEVIL.]

di·a·bol·ic (dí-ə-bóllik) *adj.* Also **di·a·bol·i·cal** (-'l). **1.** Of, concerning, or characteristic of the devil; satanic; hellish. **2.** Appropriate to a devil; extremely wicked; fiendishly cruel. [Middle English *deabolik,* from Old French *diabolique,* from Late Latin *diabolicus,* from *diabolus,* DEVIL.] —**di·a·bol·i·cal·ly** *adv.* —**di·a·bol·i·cal·ness** *n.*

di·a·bol·i·cal (dí-ə-bóllik'l) *adj.* **1.** Variant of **diabolic. 2.** Very annoying or offensive. Used as an intensive: *a diabolical insult.* **3.** *Informal.* Inferior; of miserably low quality.

di·a·bo·lise, di·a·bo·lize (dí-ábbə-līz) *tr.v.* **-lised, -lising, -lises. 1.** To turn into a devil. **2.** To bring under the influence of the devil. [Greek *diabolos,* devil.]

di·a·bo·lism (dí-ábbə-liz'm) *n.* **1.** Dealings with or worship of the devil or demons; sorcery; witchcraft. **2.** Devilish conduct or character. —**di·a·bo·list** *n.*

di·a·bo·lo (dí-ábbə-lō, -aábə-) *n., pl.* **-los. 1.** A game in which an hourglass-shaped top is spun and caught on a string held at each end by a stick. **2.** The top used in this game. [Italian, devil (the name of the top).]

di·a·caus·tic (dí-ə-káwstik) *n. Optics.* A caustic curve or surface formed by refracted rather than reflected light. Compare **catacaustic.** —**di·a·caus·tic** *adj.*

di·ac·e·tyl·mor·phine (dí-ássətil-mór-feen) *n.* A drug, **heroin** (see).

di·a·chron·ic (dí-ə-krónnik) *adj.* **1.** Considering phenomena as they occur or develop through time. **2.** *Linguistics.* Pertaining to or designating an approach to the study of language and linguistic phenomena from a historical perspective. Compare **synchronic.** [DIA- (through) + Greek *khronos,* time.]

di·ac·id (dí-ássid, dí-) *adj.* **1.** Capable of combining with two monoprotic acid molecules or one diprotic acid molecule to form a salt or ester. Said especially of bases. **2.** Possessing two hydrogen atoms replaceable by metal atoms. Said of a salt.
~*n.* An acid possessing two readily replaceable hydrogen atoms.

di·a·cid·ic (dí-ə-síddik) *adj.* Designating a base, such as calcium hydroxide, that is able to neutralise two protons. See **dibasic.**

di·ac·o·nal (dí-áckən'l) *adj.* Of or concerning a deacon or the diaconate. [Late Latin *diācōnālis,* from *diāconus,* DEACON.]

di·ac·o·nate (dí-áckə-nət, -nit, -nayt) *n.* **1.** The rank or office of a deacon. **2.** A body of deacons. [Late Latin *diācōnātus,* from *diāconus,* DEACON.]

di·a·crit·ic (dí-ə-kríttik) *adj.* **1.** Diacritical. **2.** *Medicine.* Diagnostic or distinctive.
~*n.* A diacritical mark.

di·a·crit·i·cal (dí-ə-kríttik'l) *adj.* Marking a distinction; distinguishing. [Greek *diakritikos,* distinguishing, from *diakrinein,* to distinguish : *dia-,* apart + *krinein,* to separate.] —**di·a·crit·i·cal·ly** *adv.*

diacritical mark *n.* A mark added to a letter to indicate a special phonetic value; for example, in French *façon,* the cedilla indicates that the *c* does not have its regular value before back vowels (k), but a sibilant value (s).

di·ac·tin·ic (dí-ak-tínnik) *adj.* Capable of transmitting chemically active, or actinic, radiation. Said of a lens filter, for example. [DI(A)- (across) + ACTINIC.] —**di·ac·tin·ism** (-ákti-niz'm) *n.*

di·a·del·phous (dí-ə-délfəs) *adj. Botany.* Having stamens in two bundles owing to the fusion of filaments. Compare **monadelphous.** [DI- (two) + -ADELPHOUS.]

di·a·dem (dí-ə-dem, -dəm) *n.* **1.** A crown or cloth headband, worn as a sign of royalty. **2.** Royal power or dignity. [Middle English *diademe,* from Old French, from Latin *diadēma,* from Greek *diadēma,* from *diadein,* to bind on either side : *dia-,* across + *dein,* to bind.] —**di·a·demed** (-demd, -dəmd) *adj.*

di·aer·e·sis (dí-éer-ə-siss, -i-) *n., pl.* **-ses** (-seez). Also *chiefly U.S.* **di·er·e·sis. 1.** A mark (¨) placed over the second of two adjacent vowels, and occasionally over a vowel following a consonant, to indicate: **a.** That two separate sounds are to be pronounced; for example, **Noël. b.** That a vowel which might otherwise have been interpreted as mute is to be pronounced; for example, **Brontë.** See **umlaut. 2.** The separation of two adjacent vowels into separate syllables. **3.** In poetry, a slight pause at the end of a line that occurs when the end of a word and the end of a metric foot coincide. Compare **synaeresis.** [Late Latin, from Greek *diairesis,* division, separation; from *diairein,* to separate : *dia-,* apart + *hairein,* to take.] —**di·ae·ret·ic** (dí-ə-réttik) *adj.*

di·a·gen·e·sis (dí-ə-jénni-siss) *n.* The changes that occur in sediments by which they become consolidated into rock, excluding weathering and metamorphism. [DIA- (through) + -GENESIS.]

di·a·ge·ot·ro·pism (dí-ə-jee-óttrə-piz'm) *n. Botany.* The tendency of certain parts, such as rhizomes, to become orientated at right angles to the direction of gravitational force. [DIA- (over across) + GEOTROPISM.] —**di·a·ge·o·trop·ic** (-jée-ə-tróppik) *adj.*

Di·agh·i·lev or **Di·ag·i·lev** (dee-ággi-lef ‖ -aági-), **Sergei (Pavlovich)** (1872–1929). Russian director and ballet impresario. He started his own company, Les Ballets Russes, in 1909 and influenced the evolution of the ballet as an art form. Among his collaborators were Picasso, Cocteau, Stravinsky, and Milhaud.

di·ag·nose (dí-əg-nōz, -nōz, -nōss, -nōss) *v.* **-nosed, -nosing, -noses.** —*tr.* **1.** To distinguish or identify (a disease or fault) by diagnosis. **2.** To diagnose a disease or fault in: *diagnosed him as diabetic.* —*intr.* To make a diagnosis. [Back-formation from DIAGNOSIS.] —**di·ag·nos·a·ble** *adj.*

di·ag·no·sis (dí-əg-nō-siss) *n., pl.* **-ses** (-seez). **1.** *Medicine.* **a.** The act or process of identifying or determining the nature of a disease or injury through examination. **b.** The opinion derived from such an examination. **2. a.** The process of investigating and determining the nature of a condition or problem; especially, the identification and analysis of faults in a machine: *a computer diagnosis of faults in a car's electrical system.* **b.** The conclusion reached by such an investigation. **3.** *Biology.* A precise and detailed description of the characteristics of an organism for taxonomic classification. [New Latin, from Greek *diagnōsis,* discernment, from *diagignōskein,* to distinguish, discern : *dia-,* apart + *gignōskein,* to perceive.]

di·ag·nos·tic (dī́-əg-nóstik) *adj.* Of, pertaining to, or used in a diagnosis.

~n. Medicine. A symptom serving as supporting evidence in a diagnosis. [Greek *diagnōstikos,* from *diagnōstos,* to be distinguished, from *diagignōskein,* to distinguish. See **diagnosis.**] **—di·ag·nos·ti·cal·ly** *adv.*

di·ag·nos·ti·cian (dī́-əg-no-stísh'n) *n.* A person who diagnoses; especially, a medical practitioner specialising in medical diagnoses.

di·ag·nos·tics (dī-əg-nóstiks) *n. Used with a singular verb.* The science or practice of making medical diagnoses.

di·ag·o·nal (dī-ággən'l) *adj.* **1.** *Geometry.* **a.** Joining two nonadjacent vertices of a polygon. **b.** Joining two vertices of a polyhedron not in the same face. **2.** Having a slanted or oblique direction. **3.** Having oblique lines or markings.

~n. **1.** A diagonal line or plane. **2. a.** Anything arranged obliquely, such as a row, course, pattern, or part. **b.** A diagonal direction. **3.** A fabric woven with diagonal lines. [Latin *diagōnālis,* from Greek *diagōnios,* from angle to angle : *dia-,* across + *gōnia,* angle.] **—di·ag·o·nal·ly** *adv.*

di·a·gram (dī́-ə-gram) *n.* **1.** A plan, sketch, drawing, or outline, not necessarily representational, designed to demonstrate, describe, or explain something or clarify the relationship existing between the parts of a whole. **2.** A graphic representation of an algebraic or geometric relationship. **3.** A chart or graph.

~tr.v. **diagrammed** or *U.S.* **diagramed, -gramming** or *U.S.* **-graming, -grams.** To indicate or represent by or as if by a diagram. [Latin *diagramma,* from Greek, from *diagraphein,* to mark out : *dia-,* apart + *graphein,* to write.] **—di·a·gram·mat·ic** (-grə-máttik), **di·a·gram·mat·i·cal** *adj.* **—di·a·gram·mat·i·cal·ly** *adv.*

di·a·graph (dī́-ə-graf, -graaf) *n.* **1.** An instrument used to draw copies of other drawings, such as maps, according to a desired scale. **2.** A protractor and scale combined. [French *diagraphe,* from Greek *diagraphein,* to mark out (in lines). See **diagram.**]

di·a·ki·ne·sis (dī-ə-ki-nee̍-siss, -kī-) *n., pl.* **-ses** (-seez). *Genetics.* The final stage of the prophase in meiosis, characterised by the separation of homologous chromosomes after chiasmata formation and the disappearance of the nucleoli and nuclear membrane. [DIA- (across) + -KINESIS (division).] **—di·a·ki·ne·tic** *adj.*

di·al (dī́-əl, dīl) *n.* **1.** Any graduated, usually circular face or disc on which some measurement, as of speed, pressure, or temperature, is indicated by a moving needle or pointer. **2. a.** The face of a clock. **b.** A **sundial** *(see).* **3. a.** The panel or face on a radio or television receiver on which the frequencies or channels are indicated. **b.** The control on a radio or television receiver used to change the frequency or channel. **4.** A rotatable disc on a telephone with numbers and sometimes letters used to make connections. **5.** A miner's compass with sights, a spirit level, and a vernier, used for underground surveying. **6.** *British Slang.* The face.

~v. **dialled** or *U.S.* **dialed, -alling** or *U.S.* **-aling, -als.** *—tr.* **1.** To measure or survey with or as with a dial. **2.** To point to, indicate, or register by means of a dial. **3.** To telephone (the number of another telephone) by means of a dial. *—intr.* To use a dial, as on a telephone. [Middle English *diall,* sundial, from Medieval Latin *diāle,* clock dial, from *diālis,* daily, from Latin *diēs,* day.] **—di·al·ler, di·al·er** *n.*

dial. dialect; dialectal.

di·a·lect (dī́-ə-lekt) *n. Abbr.* **dial. 1.** A regional variety of a language, distinguished from other varieties by pronunciation, grammar, or vocabulary, especially: **a.** A variety of speech differing from the standard literary language or speech pattern of the culture in which it exists. Also used adjectivally: *a dialect word.* **b.** A variety of language that, with other varieties, constitutes a single language of which no single variety is standard: *the dialects of Ancient Greek.* **2.** The spoken language peculiar to the members of an occupational or professional group, an immigrant or minority group, or a particular social class. **3.** A manner or style of expressing oneself; idiom. **4.** A language considered as part of a larger family of languages or a linguistic branch: *Spanish and French are Romance dialects.* [Old French *dialecte,* from Latin *dialectus,* from Greek *dialektos,* speech, language, dialect, from *dialegesthai,* to converse : *dia-,* one with another + *legesthai,* middle voice of *legein,* to tell.]

di·a·lec·tal (dī́-ə-lékt'l) *adj. Abbr.* **dial.** Pertaining to, characteristic of, or of the nature of a dialect. **—di·a·lec·tal·ly** *adv.*

di·a·lec·tic (dī́-ə-léktik) *n.* **1.** The art of arriving at the truth by exposing the contradictions in an opponent's argument or beliefs and overcoming them; especially, the Socratic method of question and answer to elicit the truth. **2. a.** The process, formulated by Hegel, of reaching the truth or the absolute through change, whereby a proposition or idea (thesis) is transformed into its opposite (antithesis) and preserved and fulfilled by it, the combination of the two being resolved in a higher form of truth (synthesis), the ultimate synthesis being for Hegel the mind or thought. **b.** Hegel's critical method for the investigation of this process. **3.** The contradiction between two conflicting forces viewed as the determining factor in their continuing interaction. [Middle English *dialetik,* from Old French *dialetique,* from Latin *dialectica,* from Greek *dialektikē (tekhnē),* "(the art) of debate", from *dialektikos,* of conversation or discussion, from *dialektos,* discussion, debate, DIALECT.] **—di·a·lec·tic, di·a·lec·ti·cal** *adj.* **—di·a·lec·ti·cian** (-lek-tísh'n) *n.*

dialectical materialism *n.* The Marxist interpretation of reality, viewing matter as the primary subject of change and all change as the product of a constant conflict between opposites arising from the internal contradictions inherent in all things, these contradictions being resolved at higher levels and fresh contradictions arising. This theory has been applied to various areas of thought and scholarship, and especially to history. See **historical materialism.**

di·a·lec·tics (dī-ə-léktiks) *n. Used with a singular verb.* **1.** Any method of argument or exposition that systematically weighs contradictory facts or ideas with a view to the resolution of their real or apparent contradictions. **2.** *Sometimes singular.* **a.** The Marxist doctrine, adopted from Hegel, of the process of change through the conflict of opposing forces, but asserting that matter, not mind, is the primary reality. **b.** The Marxist critique of this process. **3.** *Sometimes singular.* Logic, especially as used to expose invalid reasoning.

di·a·lec·tol·o·gy (dī́-əlek-tólləji) *n.* The study of dialects. **—di·a·lec·to·log·i·cal** (dī́-ə-léktə-lójik'l) *adj.* **—di·a·lec·tol·o·gist** (-tólləjist) *n.*

dial gauge *n.* A measuring instrument, the **indicator** *(see).*

di·al·ling code (dī́-əling, dīling) *n. British.* A series of numbers that are dialled before a local telephone number in order to reach a particular town, region, or country.

dialling tone *n.* Also *U.S.* **dial tone.** A low, steady tone on lifting a telephone receiver that indicates to the user that a telephone number may be dialled and connected.

di·a·log·ic (dī́-ə-lój-ik) *adj.* Of, pertaining to, or written in dialogue. **—di·a·log·i·cal·ly** *adv.*

di·al·o·gism (dī́-ələ-jiz'm) *n.* **1.** *Archaic.* A dialogue, especially an imaginary one contrived as a means of presenting divergent viewpoints. **2.** *Logic.* A form of argument having a single premise and resulting in a disjunctive conclusion.

di·al·o·gist (dī-ál-əjist, dī́-ə-loggist) *n.* **1.** One who writes dialogue. **2.** One who speaks in a dialogue. **—di·a·lo·gis·tic** (dī́-ələ-jístik), **di·a·lo·gis·ti·cal** *adj.*

di·a·logue (dī́-ə-log || -lawg) *n.* Also *chiefly U.S.* **di·a·log. 1.** A conversation between two or more people. **2.** A conversational passage in a play or narrative. **3.** The lines spoken by the characters in a play or narrative. **4.** A literary or philosophical work written in the form of a conversation: *the dialogues of Galileo.* **5.** An exchange of ideas or opinions. **6.** Diplomatic contact, negotiation, or discussion, especially between opposing nations or groups.

~v. **dialogued, -loguing, -logues.** *—tr.* To express as or as in a dialogue. *—intr.* To converse in a dialogue. [Middle English *dialog(ue),* from Old French *dialogue,* from Latin *dialogus,* from Greek *dialogos,* from *dialegesthai,* to converse : *dia-,* one with another + *legesthai,* middle voice of *legein,* to tell, talk.] **—di·a·log·uer** *n.*

di·a·lyse, *U.S.* **di·a·lyze** (dī́-ə-līz) *v.* **-lysed, -lysing, -lyses.** *— tr.* To subject to dialysis; separate by dialysis. *—intr.* To undergo dialysis. [Back-formation from DIALYSIS.]

di·a·lys·er (dī́-ə-līzər) *n.* An apparatus for performing dialysis, especially a kidney machine.

di·al·y·sis (dī-ál-ə-siss) *n., pl.* **-ses** (-seez). **1.** The separation of smaller molecules from larger molecules, or of crystalloid particles from colloidal particles, in a solution by selective diffusion through a semipermeable membrane. **2. Haemodialysis** *(see).* [New Latin, from Greek *dialusis,* from *dialuein,* to tear apart : *dia-,* apart + *luein,* to loosen.] **—di·a·lyt·ic** (dī́-ə-líttik) *adj.* **—di·a·lyt·i·cal·ly** *adv.*

diam diameter.

di·a·mag·net (dī́-ə-magnit) *n.* A diamagnetic substance.

di·a·mag·net·ic (dī́-ə-mag-néttik || -məg-) *adj.* Pertaining to or designating substances exhibiting diamagnetism.

di·a·mag·net·ism (dī́-ə-mágni-tiz'm) *n.* The type of magnetism occurring in substances with a small negative magnetic susceptibility and a relative permeability of less than unity. It is caused by changes in the orbital motion of the electrons in the atoms of the substance and sometimes masked by the much stronger paramagnetism and ferromagnetism.

di·a·man·té (dee̍-ə-món-tay, -móɴ-, -ti) *adj.* Decorated with or made from powdered glass or crystal, artificial jewels, or the like, in order to give the glittering effect of diamonds.

~n. **1.** Jewellery made from diamanté paste. **2.** Fabric having diamanté decoration or decorations. [French, past participle of *diamanter,* to stud with diamonds, from *diamant,* DIAMOND.]

di·a·man·tine (dī́-ə-mán-tīn) *adj.* Of, pertaining to, or resembling diamonds. [French, from *diamant,* DIAMOND.]

di·am·e·ter (dī-ámmitər) *n. Abbr.* **dia., diam 1.** *Mathematics.* **a.** A straight line passing through the centre of a figure, especially of a circle or sphere, and terminating at the periphery. **b.** The length of such a line. **2.** Loosely, the thickness or width of anything. [Middle English *diametre,* from Old French, from Latin *diametros,* from Greek *diametros (grammē),* "(line) which measures through" : *dia-,* through + *metron,* measure.] **—di·am·e·tral** *adj.*

di·a·met·ri·cal (dī́-ə-méttrik'l) *adj.* Also **di·a·met·ric** (-méttrik) (for sense 2). **1.** Of, pertaining to, or along a diameter. **2.** Exactly opposite; contrary.

di·a·met·ri·cal·ly (dī́-ə-méttrikəli, -méttrikli) *adv.* **1.** Along a diameter; straight across a circle or other figure. **2.** Absolutely; irreconcilably: *diametrically opposed ideologies.*

di·am·ine (dī́-ə-meen, -min, -meen || *U.S. also* dī́-ámm-een, -in) *n.* Any of various chemical compounds containing two amino groups, especially **hydrazine** *(see)*. [DI- (two) + -AMINE.]

di·a·mond (dī́əmənd || dī́mənd) *n.* **1.** A highly refractive, colourless crystalline allotrope of carbon, used as a gemstone and in rock drills, abrasives, and cutting tools. It is the hardest naturally occurring substance and may be coloured yellow, orange, blue, brown, or black by impurities. **2.** A figure with four equal sides forming two inner obtuse angles and two inner acute angles; a rhombus or lozenge. **3. a.** The red symbol appearing on one of the four suits of playing cards, in the shape of a diamond. **b.** A card bearing this symbol. See **diamonds. 4.** *Baseball.* **a.** The infield. **b.** The whole playing field. **5.** *Printing.* A small type size, 4½-point.
~*adj.* **1.** Of, resembling, or made with diamonds. **2.** Designating a 60th, or sometimes a 75th, anniversary: *diamond jubilee.*
~*tr.v.* **diamonded, -monding, -monds.** To adorn with or as with diamonds. [Middle English *diamaunt,* from Old French *diamant,* from Late Latin *diamas* (stem *diamant-*), variant of Vulgar Latin *adimas* (unattested), variant of Latin *adamas,* from Greek. See **adamant.**]

dia·mond·back (dī́-əmənd-bák || dī́mənd-) *n.* **1.** Any of several large, venomous rattlesnakes of the genus *Crotalus,* of the southern and western United States and Mexico, having diamond-shaped markings. Also called "diamondback rattlesnake". **2.** Any of several turtles of the genus *Malaclémys,* of the southern Atlantic and Gulf coasts of the United States, having edible flesh and a carapace with roughly diamond-shaped, ridged or knobbed markings. Also called "diamondback terrapin". **3.** A moth, *Plutella maculipennis,* that is highly destructive to vegetables.

diamond bird *n.* Any bird of the species *Pardalotus,* found in Australia and Tasmania. Also called "pardalote". [From the diamond-shaped pattern of its plumage.]

dia·mond·if·er·ous (dī́-əmən-dífərəss || dī́mən-) *adj.* Bearing or yielding diamonds.

diamond point *n.* A diamond-tipped stylus used for engraving.

di·a·monds (dī́əməndz || dī́məndz) *n. Used with a singular or plural verb.* One of the four suits of playing cards, distinguished by red diamond-shaped figures printed on the face of each card.

Di·an·a¹ (dī-ánnə). *Roman Mythology.* The goddess of chastity, hunting, and the moon; identified with the Greek goddess Artemis.

Diana² *n. Poetic.* The moon. [From DIANA (moon goddess).]

Diana³**, Princess of Wales,** born Lady Diana Frances Spencer (1961–1997). She married Charles, Prince of Wales, in 1981. They had two children, Princes William (Arthur Philip Louis) (1982–) and Harry (properly Henry Charles Albert David) (1984–). Noted for her work for charities, which she continued after the marriage was dissolved in 1996. She died in a car crash in Paris.

di·an·drous (dī-ándrəss) *adj. Botany.* Having two stamens. [DI- (two) + -ANDROUS.]

di·a·net·ics (dī́-ə-néttiks) *n. Used with a singular verb.* A system of therapy originated by L. Ron Hubbard (1911–86), aimed at achieving total mental health by cleansing the mind, especially by the process of recollecting all one's past experience. See **scientology.** [From *dianetic,* variant of DIANOETIC.]

di·a·no·et·ic (dī-ənō-éttik) *adj.* Of or pertaining to reasoning; intellectual. [Greek *dianoētikos,* from *dianoia,* thought, process of thinking : *dia-,* through + *nous,* mind.]

di·an·thus (dī-ánthəss) *n.* Any plant of the genus *Dianthus,* which includes carnations and pinks. [New Latin *Dianthus* : DI- (two) + Greek *anthos,* flower.]

di·a·pa·son (dī́-ə-páy-z'n, -s'n) *n. Music.* **1.** Either of the two principal stops on a pipe organ, the *open diapason* and the *stopped diapason,* which form the tonal basis for the entire scale of the instrument. **2. a.** The full range of notes; the compass of a voice or instrument. **b.** Range; breadth; scope. **3.** A former standard indication of pitch fixed in 1859 by the French Commission at the note A. Also called "diapason normal". See **concert pitch. 4.** A swelling burst of harmonious sound. [Middle English *dyapason,* from Latin *diapāsōn,* from Greek *(hē) dia pasōn (khordōn sumphonia),* (concord) through all (the notes) : *dia-,* through + *pasōn,* feminine genitive plural of *pas,* all.]

di·a·pause (dī́-ə-pawz) *n. Biology.* A period during which growth or development is suspended, as in certain insects. [Greek *diapausis,* pause, from *diapauein,* to rest between times, pause : *dia-,* between + *pauein,* to stop, cease.]

di·a·pe·de·sis (dī-əpə-dée-siss) *n.* The passing of blood or any constituents, especially erythrocytes, through intact blood-vessel walls. [New Latin, from Greek *diapēdēsis,* "a leaping through", from *diapēdan,* to leap through, ooze : *dia-,* through + *pēdan,* to leap.] **—di·a·pe·det·ic** (-déttik) *adj.*

di·a·pen·te (dī́-ə-pénti) *n.* In Greek and medieval music, the interval or consonance of a fifth. [Latin, from Greek *(hē) dia pente (khordōn sumphōnia),* (concord) through five (notes): *dia,* through + *pente,* five.]

di·a·per (dī́əpər || dī́pər) *n.* **1.** A white cotton or linen fabric patterned with small diamond-shaped figures. **2.** A piece of such cloth, or such a pattern. **3.** *U.S.* A baby's nappy.
~*tr.v.* **diapered, -pering, -pers.** To weave or decorate in a diamond-shaped pattern. [Middle English, from Old French *dia(s)pre,* from Medieval Latin *diasprum,* from Greek *diaspros,* ecclesiastical : DIA- (intensive) + *aspros,* white.]

di·aph·a·nous (dī-áffənəss) *adj.* **1.** Allowing light to show through; transparent or translucent. **2.** Characterised by lightness or delicacy of form. [Medieval Latin *diaphanus,* from Greek *diaphanēs,* from *diaphanein,* to show through : *dia-,* through + *phainein,* to show.] **—di·aph·a·nous·ly** *adv.* **—di·aph·a·nous·ness** *n.*

di·aph·o·ny (dī-áffəni) *n., pl.* **-nies.** *Music.* A simple form of polyphony; organum. [Medieval Latin *diaphonia,* from Greek *diaphōnia,* discord, dissonance, from *diaphōnos,* dissonant : *dia-,* apart + *phōnē,* sound.] **—di·a·phon·ic** (dī-ə-fónnik) *adj.*

di·a·pho·re·sis (dī-əfə-rée-siss) *n.* Perspiration, especially when copious and medically induced. [Late Latin *diaphorēsis,* from Greek, from *diaphorein,* to disperse abroad (by perspiration) : *dia-,* in different directions + *phorein,* frequentative of *pherein,* to carry.]

di·a·pho·ret·ic (dī-əfə-réttik) *adj.* Producing perspiration.
~*n.* A diaphoretic medicine or agent.

di·a·phragm (dī́-ə-fram) *n.* **1.** *Anatomy.* A muscular membranous partition separating the abdominal and thoracic cavities and functioning in respiration. **2.** Any similar membranous part that divides or separates, such as a semipermeable membrane separating two solutions. **3.** A thin disc, especially in a microphone or telephone receiver, the vibrations of which convert electric to acoustic signals or acoustic to electric signals. **4.** A contraceptive consisting of a flexible cap that covers the uterine cervix. Also called "cap", "Dutch cap". Compare **cervical cap. 5.** A disc having a fixed or variable opening used to restrict the amount of light traversing a lens or optical system. [Middle English *diafragma,* from Late Latin *diaphragma,* from Greek, from *diaphrassein,* to barricade : *dia-,* completely + *phrassein,* to enclose.] **—di·a·phrag·mat·ic** (-frag-máttik) *adj.* **—di·a·phrag·mat·i·cal·ly** *adv.*

di·aph·y·sis (dī-áffi-siss) *n., pl.* **-ses** (-seez). The shaft of a long bone. [New Latin, from Greek *diaphusis,* spinous process of the tibia, from *diaphuesthai,* to grow between : *dia-,* between + *phuesthai,* middle voice of *phuein,* to bring forth, beget.] **—di·a·phys·i·al** (-ə-fízzi-əl) *adj.*

di·ap·sid (dī-ápsid) *n.* In some classifications, a reptile of the subclass *Diapsidia,* having the upper and lower temporal regions of the skull distinct. [New Latin : DI- + Greek *hapsis* (stem *hapsid-*), arch.] **—di·ap·sid** *adj.*

di·ar·chy, dy·ar·chy (dī́-aarki) *n., pl.* **-chies.** Government by two joint rulers or ruling bodies. [DI- (two) + -ARCHY.] **—di·ar·chic** (dī-árkik) *adj.*

di·a·rist (dī́-ərist, dī́r-ist) *n.* A person who keeps a diary recording personal experiences and observations.

di·ar·rhoe·a (dī́-ə-réer, -rée-ə) *n.* Also *chiefly U.S.* **di·ar·rhe·a. 1.** Excessive and frequent evacuation of watery faeces. **2.** Such faeces themselves. **3.** Any uncontrolled, excessive outpouring: *verbal diarrhoea.* [Middle English *diaria,* from Late Latin *diarrhœa,* from Greek *diarrhoia,* "a flowing through", from *diarrhein,* to flow through : *dia-,* through + *rhein,* to flow.] **—di·ar·rhoe·al, di·ar·rhoe·ic, di·ar·rhoet·ic** (-réttik) *adj.*

di·ar·thro·sis (dī-ar-thrṓ-siss) *n., pl.* **-ses** (-seez). Any of several types of bone articulation permitting free motion in a joint. [New Latin, from Greek *diarthrōsis,* from *diarthroun,* to fasten by a joint, articulate : *dia-,* between + *arthroun,* to fasten, from *arthron,* joint.] **—di·ar·thro·di·al** *adj.*

di·a·ry (dī́-əri, dī́r-i) *n., pl.* **-ries. 1.** A daily record, especially a personal record of events, experiences, and observations, or of engagements and appointments. **2.** A book for keeping such a record; a journal. [Latin *diārium,* daily allowance, journal, from *diēs,* day.]

di·a·scope (dī́-ə-skōp) *n.* **1.** A projector used to throw an optical image of a transparency onto a screen. Compare **epidiascope. 2.** *Pathology.* A flat glass plate that is pressed against the skin in order to examine superficial lesions. [DIA- + -SCOPE.]

Di·as·po·ra (dī-áss-pərə, -prə) *n.* **1. a.** The dispersion of the Jews after the Babylonian captivity. Also called the "Dispersion". **b.** The body of Jews living dispersed among the Gentiles after the Babylonian captivity. **2.** The aggregate of Jews living outside Israel. **3.** In the New Testament, the body of Christians living outside Palestine. **4.** *Often small* **d.** A dispersion, as of any originally homogeneous people. [Greek, "dispersion" (Deuteronomy 28:25), from *diaspeirein,* to disperse : *dia-,* apart + *speirein,* to scatter.]

di·a·spore (dī́-ə-spawr || -spōr) *n.* A white, pearly hydrous aluminium oxide, $Al_2O_3{\cdot}H_2O$, found with corundum and emery and in bauxite. It is used as a refractory and abrasive. [Greek *diaspora,* scattering, DIASPORA (from the strong decrepitation of the mineral before the blowpipe).]

di·a·stase (dī́-ə-stayss, -stayz) *n.* An amylase or a mixture of amylases that converts starch to maltose, found in certain germinating grains such as malt. [French, from Greek *diastasis,* separation, DIASTASIS.] **—di·a·sta·sic** (-stáy-sik, -zik), **di·a·stat·ic** (-státtik) *adj.*

di·a·sta·sis (dī-ástə-siss) *n., pl.* **-ses** (-seez). **1.** *Pathology.* Separation of certain muscles during pregnancy, or of normally adjacent, unjoined bones without fracture. **2.** *Physiology.* The last stage of diastole in the heart, occurring prior to contraction and during which little blood enters the filled ventricle. [New Latin, from Greek, separation, from *diistanai,* to set apart : *dia-,* apart + *histanai,* to cause to stand, set.] **—di·a·stat·ic** (dī-ə-státtik) *adj.*

di·a·ste·ma (dī-ə-stée-mə) *n., pl.* **-mata** (-mətə). **1.** Any bodily fissure or cleft, especially if congenital. **2.** An abnormally large space between teeth. [New Latin, from Late Latin *diastēma,* from Greek, interval, aperture, from *diistanai,* to set apart. See **diastasis.**]

di·as·ter (dī-ástər) *n. Biology.* **Anaphase** *(see).* Not in current technical usage. [DI- (two) + Greek *astēr,* star.] **—di·as·tral** *adj.*

di·as·to·le (dī-ástəli) *n. Physiology.* The normal rhythmically occurring relaxation and dilation of the heart cavities, during which the cavities are filled with blood. [Greek *diastolē*, dilatation, separation, from *diastellein*, to expand, separate : *dia-*, apart + *stellein*, to put.] —**di·a·stol·ic** (dī-ə-stóllik) *adj.*

di·as·tro·phism (dī-ástrə-fiz'm) *n.* The process or series of processes by which the major features of the Earth's crust, including continents, mountains, and ocean basins, are formed. [Greek *diastrophē*, twisting, distortion, from *diastrephein*, to twist different ways, distort : *dia-*, in different directions + *strephein*, to turn, twist.] —**di·a·stroph·ic** (dī-ə-stróffik) *adj.*

di·a·style (dī-ə-stīl) *adj. Architecture.* Having intervals of three to four diameters between the columns.
~ *n. Architecture.* A diastyle building or arrangement of columns. [Latin, from Greek *diastūlos*, having spaced pillars : *dia-*, apart, through + *stūlos*, column, STYLE.]

di·a·tes·sa·ron (dī-ə-téssə-ron, -rən) *n.* **1.** In Greek and medieval music, the interval of a fourth. **2.** A single narrative made by conflating the four gospels. [Middle English, from Late Latin, from Greek *dia tessarōn*, consisting of four : *dia*, made out of + *tessarōn*, genitive of *tessares*, four.]

di·a·ther·mic (dī-ə-thérmik) *adj.* **1.** Capable of transmitting heat or infrared radiation. **2.** Of or pertaining to diathermy.

di·a·ther·my (dī-ə-thermi) *n.* The therapeutic generation of local heat in body tissues by high-frequency electromagnetic waves. [DIA-, across, by transmission + Greek *thermē*, heat (see therm).]

di·ath·e·sis (dī-áthi-siss) *n., pl.* **-ses** (-seez). A familial predisposition of the body to a disease, group of diseases, or structural or metabolic abnormality. [New Latin, from Greek, disposition, bodily state, from *diatithenai*, to dispose : *dia-*, in different directions + *tithenai*, to put, set.] —**di·a·thet·ic** (dī-ə-théttik) *adj.*

di·a·tom (dī-ə-tom, -təm) *n.* Any of various minute, unicellular or colonial algae of the class Bacillariophyceae, having siliceous cell walls consisting of two overlapping, symmetrical parts. [New Latin *diatoma*, from Greek *diatomē*, feminine of *diatomos*, cut in half, from *diatemnein*, to cut through, cut in half : *dia-*, through + *temnein*, to cut.]

di·a·to·ma·ceous (dī-ətə-máyshəss) *adj.* Consisting of diatoms or their siliceous skeletons.

diatomaceous earth *n.* Diatomite.

di·a·tom·ic (dī-ə-tómmik) *adj.* **1.** Made up of two atoms. Said of a molecule. **2.** Having two replaceable atoms or radicals.

di·at·o·mite (dī-áttə-mīt) *n.* A fine, powdered siliceous earth, composed of the skeletons of diatoms, used in industry as a filler, filtering agent, absorbent, clarifier, and insulator. Also called "diatomaceous earth", "kieselguhr".

diatom ooze *n.* A siliceous sediment composed largely of the skeletons of diatoms, found on the deep (abyssal) ocean floor and on lake beds.

di·a·ton·ic (dī-ə-tónnik) *adj. Music.* Of or using only the eight notes of a standard major or minor scale without chromatic variations. [French *diatonique*, from Late Latin *diatonicus*, from Greek *diatonikos*, from *diatonos*, "at the interval of a tone" : *dia-*, throughout, at the interval of + *tonos*, TONE.] —**di·a·ton·i·cal·ly** *adv.* —**di·a·ton·i·cism** (-tonni-siz'm) *n.*

di·a·tribe (dī-ə-trīb) *n.* A bitter and abusive criticism or denunciation; an invective. [Latin *diatriba*, learned discourse, from Greek *diatribē*, "a wearing away", from *diatribein*, to rub hard, rub away, consume (time) : *dia-*, completely + *tribein*, to rub, wear out.]

di·at·ro·pism (dī-áttrə-piz'm) *n.* The tendency of certain organisms or their parts to arrange themselves at right angles to the direction of a stimulus. [DIA- (over across, at right angles) + -TROPISM.] —**di·a·trop·ic** (dī-ə-tróppik) *adj.*

Dí·az (dée-az, -ass), **Porfirio** (1830–1915). Mexican soldier and politician. He became president of Mexico in 1876 following a coup and remained in office until 1880. He served a second term as president (1884–1911) but was forced to flee and died in exile.

di·az·e·pam (dī-ázzə-pam) *n.* A tranquilliser, **Valium** (*see*).

di·a·zine (dī-ə-zeen, dī-ázz-, -in) *n.* A compound containing a benzene ring in which two of the carbon atoms have been replaced by nitrogen atoms; especially, any of three compounds so structured and having the composition $C_4H_4N_2$. [DIAZ(O) + -INE.]

di·a·zo (dī-áyzō || *U.S.* -ázzō) *adj.* Of, pertaining to, or consisting of a pair of nitrogen atoms bonded to each other and to an organic radical. [DI- (two) + A- (not) + Greek *zoē*, life.]

di·a·zole (dī-áy-zōl || -ázzōl) *n.* An organic chemical in which the molecules contain a five-membered ring consisting of three carbon atoms and two nitrogen atoms.

di·az·o·me·thane (dī-áyzō-méethayn || -ázzō-) *n.* A yellow explosive gas, $CH_2:N:N$, used as a methylating agent.

di·a·zo·ni·um (dī-ə-zóni-əm) *adj.* Of, pertaining to, or containing the univalent cation $RN\,N^+$, where R is an aromatic hydrocarbon radical. [DIAZ(O) + (AMM)ONIUM.]

diazonium salt *n.* An organic compound with the general formula $RN\,N^+X^-$, where R is an aromatic hydrocarbon and X^- is an anion, such as the chloride ion, Cl^-.

di·a·zo·tise, di·a·zo·tize (dī-áyzə-tīz || -ázzə-) *tr.v.* **-tised, -tising, -tises.** To cause (an aromatic hydrocarbon) to react with nitrous acid to produce a diazonium salt. —**di·a·zo·ti·sa·tion** (-tī-záysh'n || *U.S.* -ti-) *n.*

di·ba·sic (dī-báy-sik) *adj. Chemistry.* **1.** Containing two replaceable hydrogen atoms. **2.** Designating salts, or acids forming salts, with two atoms of a univalent metal. See **diacidic**. [DI- + BASIC.]

dib·ber (díbbər) *n.* Also **dib·ble** (díbb'l). A pointed gardening im-

plement used to make holes in soil, especially for planting bulbs or seedlings. [See dibble[1].]

dib·ble[1] (díbb'l) *tr.v.* **-bled, -bling, -bles. 1.** To make holes in (soil) with a dibber. **2.** To plant by means of a dibber.
~ *n.* A dibber. [Middle English *debyllet*.]

dib·ble[2] *intr.v.* **-bled, -bling, -bles.** Also **dib** (dib), **dibbed, dibbing, dibs.** In angling, to dip bait gently up and down in the water. [Probably variant of obsolete *dib*, to tap, dip, variant of DAB.]

di·bran·chi·ate (dī-brángki-ət, -it, -ayt) *n.* Any of various two-gilled cephalopod molluscs of the former order Dibranchiata, which includes the octopuses, cuttlefish, and squids.
~ *adj.* Of or belonging to the Dibranchiata. [New Latin *Dibranchiata* : DI- + BRANCHIATE.]

di·bro·mide (dī-brō-mīd || -mid) *n.* A binary chemical compound containing two bromine atoms per molecule.

dibs (dibz) *pl.n. Slang.* Money, especially in small amounts. [Short for *dibstones*, a children's game played with knucklebones, hence knucklebones, counters used in a game, money, probably from *dib*, to tap, dip, variant of DAB.]

di·car·box·yl·ic (dī-kárbok-síllik) *adj.* Designating an acid that contains two carboxyl groups per molecule.

dic·ast (dickast || dī-kast) *n.* In ancient Athens, one of the 6,000 citizens chosen each year to sit in the law courts, with functions resembling those of a judge and juror. [Greek *dikastēs*, judge, from *dikazein*, to judge, from *dikē*, custom, right, lawsuit.] —**di·cas·tic** (dī-kástik || dī-) *adj.*

dice (dīss) *n., pl.* **dice.** Also *chiefly U.S. & archaic* **die** (dī). **1.** A small cube, as of ivory, bone, or plastic, marked on each side with a pattern of small dots, numbering from one to six, and used, usually in pairs, in games of chance. **2.** Any game of chance using dice. **3.** Any small cube. —**no dice.** *Slang.* **1.** Used to express a refusal. **2.** No luck or success. —See Usage note at **die** (noun).
~ *v.* **diced, dicing, dices.** —*intr.* **1.** To play or gamble with dice. **2.** To take risks: *dice with death.* —*tr.* **1.** To win or lose (money) by gambling with dice. **2.** To cut (food) into small cubes. **3.** To decorate with a pattern of squares. [Plural of DIE (cube).] —**dic·er** *n.*

di·cen·tra (dī-séntrə) *n.* Any plant of the genus *Dicentra*, which includes the **bleeding-heart** and **Dutchman's-breeches** (*both of which see*). [New Latin *Dicentra*, "two-spurred" (from its dissected leaves) : di- (two) + Greek *kentron*, spur, point, centre, from *kentein*, to prick.]

di·cey (dīssi) *adj.* **-cier, -ciest.** *British Informal.* Risky; unreliable. [From DICE (hence, risky).]

di·cha·si·um (dī-káy-zi-əm, -zhəm) *n., pl.* **-sia** (-zi-ə, -zhə). *Botany.* A cyme in which two lateral branches occur at approximately the same level. Compare **monochasium**. [New Latin, from Greek *dikhasis*, division, from *dikhazein*, to divide in two, from *dikha*, in two.] —**di·cha·si·al·ly** *adv.*

di·chlo·ride (dī-klōr-īd || -klōr-) *n.* A binary chemical compound containing two chloride atoms per molecule. Also called "bichloride".

di·chlo·ro·di·fluo·ro·me·thane (dī-kláwrō-dī-flóor-ō-méethayn || -klōrō-) *n.* A colourless nonflammable gas, CCl_2F_2, used as an aerosol propellant, fire extinguisher, and refrigerant. See **Freon**.

di·chlor·o·di·phen·yl·tri·chlor·o·eth·ane (dī-kláwrō-dī-fée-nīl-trī-kláwrō-éethayn || -klōrō-, -éthayn) *n.* An organic compound, **DDT** (*see*).

dicho- *comb. form.* Indicates two parts or a division into two parts; for example, **dichotomy, dichogamous.** [Late Latin, from Greek *dikho-*, from *dikha*, in two.]

di·chog·a·mous (dī-kóggəməss) *adj.* Having pistils and stamens that mature at different times, thus ensuring cross-fertilisation rather than self-pollination. [DICHO- + -GAMOUS.] —**di·chog·a·my** *n.*

di·chot·o·mise, di·chot·o·mize (dī-kóttə-mīz) *v.* **-mised, -mising, -mises.** —*tr.* To separate into two parts or classifications. —*intr.* To be or become divided into parts or branches; fork. —**di·chot·o·mi·sa·tion** (-mī-záysh'n || *U.S.* -mi-) *n.* —**di·chot·o·mist** *n.*

di·chot·o·mous (dī-kóttəməss) *adj.* Also **di·cho·tom·ic** (dīkə-tómmik). **1.** Divided or dividing into two parts or classifications. **2.** Characterised by dichotomy. —**di·chot·o·mous·ly** *adv.*

di·chot·o·my (dī-kóttəmi, di-) *n., pl.* **-mies. 1. a.** Division into two usually contradictory parts or opinions; schism. **b.** Loosely, a lack of agreement or correspondence; a discrepancy: *a dichotomy between their election promises and their performance.* **2.** *Logic.* The division or subdivision of a class into two mutually exclusive groups: *the dichotomy of truth and falsehood.* **3.** *Astronomy.* The phase of the Moon, Mercury, or Venus when half of the disc is illuminated. **4.** *Botany.* Branching characterised by successive forking into two approximately equal divisions. [Greek *dikhotomia*, from *dikhotomos*, divided : DICHO- + *temnein*, to cut.]

di·chro·ic (dī-krō-ik) *adj.* Also **di·chro·it·ic** (dīkrō-ittik). **1.** Manifesting dichroism. **2.** Dichromatic. [Greek *dikhroos*, two-coloured : DI- (two) + -CHROOUS.]

di·chro·ism (dīkrō-iz'm) *n.* **1.** *Chemistry.* The property of showing different colours depending on the thickness of the medium or the relative concentration of colouring matter in it. **2.** The property possessed by some crystals of exhibiting different colours, especially two different colours, when viewed along different axes. Compare **pleochroism**. [Greek *dikhroos*, two-coloured, DICHROIC.]

di·chro·ite (dīkrō-īt) *n.* A mineral, **cordierite** (*see*). [DICHRO(IC) + -ITE.]

di·chro·mate (dī-krō-mayt) *n.* Any chemical compound which is a salt of the hypothetical acid, dichromic acid. A dichromate usually has a characteristic red-orange colour. Also called "bichromate".

di·chro·mat·ic (dī-krō-máttik, -krə-) *adj.* **1.** Possessing or exhibiting two colours. **2.** *Zoology.* Having two distinct colour phases in the adult. Said of certain species of birds. **3.** *Pathology.* Capable of distinguishing only two colours. Also "dichroic", "dichromic".

di·chro·ma·tism (dī-krōmə-tiz'm) *n.* The quality or condition of being dichromatic.

di·chro·mic (dī-krōmik) *adj.* **1.** Dichromatic. **2.** *Chemistry.* Containing two chromium atoms per molecule.

dichromic acid *n.* An acid, $H_2Cr_2O_7$, known only in solution.

dick¹ (dik) *n.* **1.** *British Slang.* A fellow. **2.** *Vulgar Slang.* A penis. [From *Dick,* nickname for *Richard.*]

dick² *n.* A detective. [Shortened from DETECTIVE.]

dick·ens (díckinz) *n.* Deuce; devil: *"I cannot tell what the dickens his name is"* (Shakespeare). [16th century : perhaps euphemistic for *(Old) Nick.*]

Dick·ens (díckinz), **Charles** (1812–70). British novelist. The son of an admiralty clerk who was imprisoned for debt, he was sent to work in a blacking factory at the age of 12. This, together with his school experiences, provided much of the material for his largely autobiographical *David Copperfield* (1849–50). After working in a solicitor's office, he became a journalist, going on to write sketches under the pen name "Boz" for the *Monthly Magazine. The Pickwick Papers,* published from 1836 to 1837, established his popularity. His novels became an influential protest against the squalor and vices of Victorian society. Among his best-known books are *Oliver Twist, A Christmas Carol, Bleak House, A Tale of Two Cities, The Old Curiosity Shop, Nicholas Nickleby,* and *Great Expectations.*

Dick·en·si·an (di-kénzi-ən) *adj.* Of or characteristic of Charles Dickens, his novels, settings, and characters, or his literary style; especially, reminiscent of: **a.** The grim conditions of urban squalor and deprivation described in some of Dickens' novels: *the factory's Dickensian working conditions.* **b.** The cosy Victorian jollity of Dickens' sentimental family scenes.

dick·er (díckər) *v.* **-ered, -ering, -ers.** —*intr.* **1.** *Chiefly British.* To dither; vacillate. **2.** *Chiefly U.S.* To bargain; barter; haggle. —*tr. Chiefly U.S.* To trade or exchange.
~*n. Chiefly U.S.* Barter or bargaining. [Probably from obsolete *dicker,* ten, ten hides (used as a unit of trade), Middle English *dyke,* Old English *dicor* (unattested), from West Germanic *dicura* (unattested), from Latin *dicuria,* set of ten, from *decem,* ten. Verb sense 1, probably variant of **dither.**]

Dick·in·son (díckin-s'n), **Emily (Elizabeth)** (1830–86). U.S. poet. She wrote over 1,700 poems though only seven were ever published in her lifetime. The first volume of her work appeared in 1890.

Dick test *n.* A skin test for susceptibility to scarlet fever. [After Gladys and George Dick U.S. medical practitioners.]

dick·y¹, dick·ie (dicki) *n., pl.* **-ies.** Also **dick·ey** *pl.* **-eys. 1.** A detachable shirt front. **2.** *Informal.* A bow tie. Also called "dicky bow". **3.** A child's bib. **4.** A donkey. **5.** *Informal.* Any small bird. Also called "dickybird". **6. a.** Either of two seats on a carriage, the forward outside driver's seat or a rear seat for servants. **b.** *British.* An extra open seat at the back of a car. [From *Dick,* nickname for *Richard.*]

dicky² *adj.* **-ier, -iest.** Also **dickey.** *British Informal.* Not in good health or condition: *She suffers from a dicky heart.* [Perhaps from the phrase *as queer as Dick's hatband.*]

di·cli·nous (dīkli-nəss, di-klī-) *adj. Botany.* **1.** Having stamens and pistils in separate flowers: *a diclinous plant.* **2.** Having pistils but not stamens, or stamens but not pistils: *diclinous flowers.* [DI- (two) + Greek *klinē,* bed.] —**di·cli·ny** (dīkli-ni, dī-klī-) *n.*

di·cot·y·le·don (dī-kotti-léed'n) *n.* Also **di·cot** (dīkot). Any plant of the Dicotyledonae, one of the two major divisions of angiosperms, characterised by a pair of embryonic seed leaves that appear at germination, and including many trees, shrubs, and other flowering plants. Compare **monocotyledon.** —**di·cot·y·le·don·ous** *adj.*

di·cro·tism (dīkrə-tiz'm) *n.* A pathological doubling of the pulse with each beat of the heart. [From Greek *dikrotos,* double-beating : DI- (two) + *krotein,* to strike.] —**di·crot·ic** (dī-króttik) *adj.*

dict. 1. dictation. **2.** dictionary.

dic·ta. Plural of **dictum.**

Dic·ta·phone (díktə-fōn) *n.* A trademark for a recording apparatus used for office dictation.

dic·tate (dik-táyt || *U.S. also* dík-tayt) *v.* **-tated, -tating, -tates.** —*tr.* **1.** To say or read aloud (something to be recorded or written by another). **2.** To prescribe expressly and with authority: *dictate a command.* **3.** To influence decisively; determine: *The choice of computer was dictated by the company's special needs.* —*intr.* **1.** To say or read aloud material to be transcribed by another. **2. a.** To issue orders or commands. **b.** To adopt an authoritarian attitude.
~*n.* (díktayt). A directive or command: *the dictates of common sense.* [Latin *dictāre,* frequentative of *dīcere,* to say, tell.]

dic·ta·tion (dik-táysh'n) *n. Abbr.* **dict. 1.** The process of dictating material to another for transcription. **2.** The material dictated. **3.** *Formal.* Authoritative command or prescription; dictate.

dic·ta·tor (dik-táytər || *U.S.* dík-taytər) *n.* **1.** A ruler having absolute authority and supreme jurisdiction over the government of a state; especially, one who is considered tyrannical or oppressive. **2.** One who has absolute authority or control in a particular sphere. **3.** One who dictates. **4.** In ancient Rome, a government official temporarily invested with absolute authority to deal with an immediate crisis or emergency.

dic·ta·to·ri·al (dík-tə-táwri-əl || -tóri-) *adj.* **1.** Tending to dictate; overbearing; domineering. **2.** Characteristic of or pertaining to a dictator; autocratic. —**dic·ta·to·ri·al·ly** *adv.* —**dic·ta·to·ri·al·ness** *n.*
Synonyms: *dictatorial, arbitrary, dogmatic, doctrinaire, imperious, overbearing.*

dic·ta·tor·ship (dik-táy-tər-ship || *U.S. also* díktay-) *n.* **1.** The office or tenure of office of a dictator. **2.** A state or government under dictatorial rule. **3.** Government by a dictator. **4.** Absolute or despotic control or power.

dic·tion (diksh'n) *n.* **1.** Choice and use of words in speech or writing; manner of expression. **2.** The degree of distinctness of speech; the manner of enunciation. [Latin *dictiō* (stem *dictiōn-*), from *dictus,* past participle of *dīcere,* to say.]
Synonyms: *diction, articulation, enunciation.*

dic·tion·ar·y (dík-sh'n-ri, -əri || -erri) *n., pl.* **-ies.** *Abbr.* **dict. 1.** A reference book containing an explanatory alphabetical list of words, as: **a.** A book listing a comprehensive or restricted selection of the words of a language, identifying usually the pronunciation, grammatical function, and meanings of each word, often with other information on its origin and use. **b.** Such a book listing the words or other units of a particular category within a language: *a slang dictionary.* **2.** A book listing the words of a language with translations into another language. **3.** A book listing words or other linguistic items from particular fields, with specialised information about them: *a medical dictionary.* **4.** A reference book dealing with a particular subject: *a dictionary of modern history.* [Medieval Latin *dictiōnārium,* from Latin *dictiō,* DICTION.]

Dic·to·graph (díktə-graaf, -graf) *n.* A trademark for an instrument used as an internal telephone that reproduces or records sounds from a transmitter by means of a small microphone.

dic·tum (díktəm) *n., pl.* **dicta** (díktə) or **-tums. 1.** A dogmatic and authoritative pronouncement. **2.** *Law.* An obiter dictum *(see).* **3.** A popular saying; a maxim. [Latin, from *dictus,* past participle of *dīcere,* to say.]

did. Past tense of **do.**

Did·a·che (díddə-kee) *n.* **1.** An anonymous church treatise of the second century or possibly the first century A.D., known as the "Teaching of the Twelve Apostles". **2.** *Small* **d.** *Theology.* The didactic element in early Christian teaching. Compare **kerygma.** [Greek *didakhē,* "a teaching", from *didaskein,* to teach.]

di·dac·tic (dī-dáktik, di-) *adj.* **1.** Intended to instruct; expository. **2.** Inclined to teach or moralise; pedantic. **3.** Intended to provide moral instruction, sometimes without regard for interest or style. Said especially of works of literature. [Greek *didaktikos,* skilful in teaching, from *didaktos,* taught, from *didaskein,* to teach.] —**di·dac·ti·cal·ly** *adv.* —**di·dac·ti·cism** (-dákti-siz'm) *n.*

di·dac·tics (dī-dáktiks, di-) *n. Used with a singular verb.* The art or science of teaching or instruction; pedagogy.

di·dap·per (dī-dappər) *n. Regional.* A small grebe, such as the dabchick. [Middle English *didopper,* variant of *divedap, dovedop,* Old English *dūfedoppa,* pelican : *dūfan,* DIVE + *-doppa,* dapper.]

did·dle¹ (dídd'l) *v.* **-dled, -dling, -dles.** Also *regional* **dad·dle** (dádd'l). —*tr. Informal.* To cheat; swindle. —*intr. Archaic.* To waste time; dawdle.
~*n. Informal.* A swindle. [Probably back-formation from Jeremy *Diddler,* a dawdling, swindling character in *Raising the Wind* (1803), a farce by James Kenney, perhaps ultimately related to Old English *dydrian,* to delude, deceive.] —**did·dler** *n.*

diddle² *v.* **-dled, -dling, -dles.** *Scottish.* —*tr.* To jerk back and forth. —*intr.* To move jerkily from side to side; shake. [Perhaps variant of dialectal *didder,* to quiver, Middle English *dideren,* probably variant of *doderen,* perhaps from Middle Low German.]

Did·e·rot (déedə-rō), **Denis** (1713–84). French philosopher and writer who helped to create the philosophical movement known as the Enlightenment through the *Encyclopédie* which he edited. This project ran to 28 volumes, from 1751 to 1772.

did·ger·i·doo (díjəri-dóō) *n.* An Australian Aboriginal wind instrument, made from a long hollow wooden tube and blown to produce a droning sound. [Imitative.]

di·di·coy, di·di·koi (díddi-koy) *n.* In Britain, an itinerant tinker or scrap-metal dealer, typically living in a caravan and often supposed to be of Gypsy origin. [Romany.]

did·n't (díd'nt). Contraction of *did not.*

di·do (dídō) *n., pl.* **-dos** or **-does.** *U.S. Informal.* A mischievous prank or antic; a caper. [19th century : origin obscure.]

Di·do (dídō). In Virgil's *Aeneid,* a Tyrian princess, founder and queen of Carthage, and lover of Aeneas.

didst (didst). *Archaic.* Second person singular, past tense, of **do.** Used with *thou.*

di·dy (dídi) *n., pl.* **-dies.** *U.S. Informal.* A baby's nappy. Typically said by or to children. [Variant of DIAPER.]

di·dym·i·um (dī-dímmi-əm, di-) *n. Symbol* **Di 1.** A metallic mixture, once considered an element, composed of neodymium and praseodymium. **2.** A mixture of rare-earth elements and oxides used chiefly in manufacturing and colouring various forms of glass. [New Latin, from Greek *didumos,* twin (so named from its association with lanthanum). See **didymous.**]

did·y·mous (diddiməss) *adj. Botany.* Arranged or occurring in pairs; twin. [Greek *didumos,* twin.]

Didymus. See Saint **Thomas.**

di·dyn·a·mous (dī-dínnəməss) *adj. Botany.* Having four stamens arranged in pairs that differ from one another, especially in length. [New Latin *Didynamia,* a former class of didynamous plants, "having two stamens stronger than the others" : DI- (two) + Greek *dunamis,* power (see **dynamic**).]

die¹ (dī) *v.* **died, dying, dies.** —*intr.* **1.** To cease living; become dead; expire. **2.** To cease existing, especially by degrees; fade or pass away: *The sunlight died in the west.* **3.** To lose vitality, activity, or force; become faint or weak. Often used with *away, out,* or *down: The storm died down.* **4.** To cease existing completely; become extinct. Often used with *off* or *out.* **5.** To cease functioning suddenly. **6.** To experience the agony or suffering associated with death. **7.** To lose all attachment: *She died to the world.* **8.** *Informal.* To be completely overcome. Often used with *of: We died laughing. They were dying of thirst.* **9.** *Informal.* To desire something greatly or longingly: *dying for a drink; dying to go to the party.* **10.** *Theology.* To experience spiritual death. **11.** *Slang.* To get a very poor reception from an audience. —*tr.* To experience (a specified kind of death): *They died a gruesome death.* [Middle English *d(e)ien, deighen,* from late Old English *diegan,* from Old Norse *deyja.*]

Usage: Die, in its primary sense, it usually followed by *of* when expressing cause: *She died of a heart attack. From* is quite often used in informal speech.

die² *n., pl.* **dies** (for senses 1, 2) or **dice** (dīss) (for sense 3). **1.** Any of various devices used for cutting out, forming, or stamping material, especially: **a.** An engraved metal piece used for impressing a design upon a softer metal, as in minting coins. **b.** Any of several component pieces that are fitted into a diestock to cut threads on screws or bolts. Compare **tap. c.** A part on a machine that punches shaped holes in, cuts, or forms sheet metal, cardboard, or other material. **d.** A metal block containing small conical holes through which plastic, metal, or other ductile material is extruded or drawn. **2.** *Architecture.* The dado of a pedestal, especially when cube-shaped. **3.** *Chiefly U.S. & Archaic.* A dice. —**the die is cast.** The decision has been made and is irrevocable.

~*tr.v.* **died, dieing, dies.** To cut, form, or stamp with or as with a die. [Middle English *dee,* from Old French *de,* from Vulgar Latin *datum* (unattested), "playing piece", from Latin, neuter past participle of *dare,* to give, "play"; idiom, translation of Latin *alea jacta est,* supposedly said by Julius Caesar upon crossing the Rubicon into Italy.]

Usage: In British English, the relationship between this word and its plural *dice* (in the sense of "cube used in game of chance") is now wholly obscure in everyday use. It is found only in the idiom *The die is cast. Dice* is now the noun for both singular and plural contexts.

die back *intr.v.* To be affected by dieback.

die-back (dī-bak) *n.* A condition leading to the gradual dying of plant shoots, starting at the tips, as a result of various diseases or climatic conditions.

die-cast (dī-kaast ‖ -kast) *tr.v.* **-cast, -casting, -casts.** To form by pressing molten metal into a die under pressure. —**die-caster** *n.*

diecious. Variant of **dioecious.**

dief·fen·bach·i·a (deef'n-bácki-ə) *n.* Also **dif·fen·bach·i·a** (diff'n-). Any of various erect evergreen plants of the genus *Dieffenbachia,* native to tropical America, often kept as house plants for their attractive spotted foliage. Also called "dumb cane", after its speech-inhibiting qualities after being chewed. [New Latin, after J.F. *Dieffenbach* (1794-1847), German botanist.]

Diego Garcia. See **British Indian Ocean Territory.**

die-hard, die·hard (dī-haard) *n.* One who stubbornly refuses to abandon a position or resists apparently inevitable change. —**die-hard** *adj.* —**die-hard·ism** *n.*

diel·drin (deéldrin) *n.* A contact insecticide based on a chlorinated naphthalene derivative, $C_{12}H_8OCl_6$, which was widely used for such purposes as mothproofing furnishings. [From *Diels-Alder* reaction + -IN.]

di·e·lec·tric (dī-i-léktrik) *n.* A nonconductor of electricity; especially, a substance with electrical conductivity of less than a millionth (10^{-6}) of a siemens. [DI(A)- (through) + ELECTRIC.] —**di·e·lec·tric** *adj.* —**di·e·lec·tri·cal·ly** *adv.*

dielectric constant *n.* Relative permittivity. See **permittivity.**

dielectric heating *n.* The heating of electrically nonconducting materials by means of a rapidly varying electrostatic field, widely used in the manufacture of furniture, plastics, foam rubber, and other products.

Diels (deelss), **Otto Paul Herman** (1876-1954). German chemist whose work with Kurt Alder (1902-58) on converting linear organic molecules into cyclic molecules earned them the 1950 Nobel prize for chemistry.

Diels-Al·der reaction (deélss-ál-dər, -áwl-) *n.* A chemical reaction in which an aromatic compound is formed from a diene and a compound containing a single double bond. [After Otto DIELS and Kurt *Alder* (1902-58), German chemists.]

Dien Bien (dyén byén). Formerly **Dien Bien Phu** (foo). A village in northeast Vietnam, where in 1954 a French fortress fell to Vietminh troops after two months of almost continuous fighting. The defeat led to the French withdrawal from Vietnam.

di·en·ceph·a·lon (dī-en-séff'l-on) *n.* The posterior part of the forebrain that connects the midbrain with the cerebral hemispheres and contains the thalamus, hypothalamus, and pituitary gland. Also called "interbrain", "thalamencephalon". [New Latin : DI(A)- (between) + ENCEPHALON.]

di·ene (dī-een) *n.* An unsaturated hydrocarbon containing two double bonds. [DI- + -ENE.]

–diene *n. comb. form. Chemistry.* Indicates a compound containing

two double bonds; for example, **butadiene.** [DI- (two) + -ENE.]

Di·eppe (di-ép ‖ *French* dyep). Channel port and resort in Seine-Maritime, northern France.

dieresis. *Chiefly U.S.* Variant of **diaeresis.**

die·sel (deéz'l) *n.* **1.** A diesel engine. **2.** A vehicle, especially a locomotive, using a diesel engine. **3.** Diesel fuel. [After Rudolf *Diesel* (1858-1913), German engineer.] —**die·sel** *adj.*

diesel cycle *n.* A four-stroke engine cycle in which combustion takes place at constant pressure and heat is rejected at constant volume. Compare **Otto cycle.**

die·sel·e·lec·tric (deéz'l-i-léktrik) *adj.* Designating a locomotive in which a diesel engine drives an electric generator, the current from which is used to drive electric motors. ~*n.* A diesel-electric locomotive.

diesel engine *n. Sometimes capital* **D.** An internal-combustion engine that uses heat caused by high compression, rather than a spark plug, to ignite the fuel mixture. Also called "diesel motor", "diesel". [See **diesel.**]

diesel fuel *n.* A petroleum-based fuel used for diesel engines. Also called "diesel".

die·sel·hy·drau·lic (deéz'l-hī-dráw-lik ‖ -dróllik) *adj.* Designating a locomotive in which a diesel engine drives the wheels through a hydraulic transmission system using torque converters. ~*n.* A diesel-hydraulic locomotive.

die·sel·ise, die·sel·ize (deéz'l-īz) *tr.v.* **-ised, -ising, -ises.** To equip with a diesel engine or machinery using diesel engines.

Di·es I·rae (dee-ayz ĕeray, dī-ezz īr-ee, -ī) *n.* A medieval Latin hymn describing the Day of Judgment, used in some Masses for the dead. [Latin, "day of wrath".]

di·e·sis (dī-i-siss) *n., pl.* **-ses** (-seez). **1.** *Printing.* The double dagger *(see).* **2.** *Music.* **a.** The interval between four minor thirds and an octave. **b.** The interval between three major thirds and an octave. [Middle English, semitone, interval of a semitone (often indicated by a double dagger), from Latin, quarter tone, from Greek, "a letting through", from *diienai,* send through, discharge : *dia-,* through + *hienai,* to send.]

di·es non (dī-eez nón) *n. Law.* A day on which courts may not convene nor any legal business be transacted. Also called "dies non juridicus". Compare **juridical days.** [Latin, short for *dies non juridicus,* "day without courts".]

die·stock (dī-stok) *n.* An apparatus for holding dies that cut threads on screws, bolts, pipes, or rods.

di·et¹ (dī-ət) *n.* **1.** The usual food and drink of a person or animal. **2.** A regulated selection of foods, especially as prescribed for gaining or losing weight or for other medical reasons: *a high-protein diet.* **3.** Anything taken or provided regularly: *her usual diet of thrillers.* ~*v.* **dieted, -eting, -ets.** —*tr.* To regulate or prescribe food and drink for. —*intr.* **1.** To eat and drink according to a regulated system, especially in order to lose weight. **2.** *Archaic.* To eat or feed. [Middle English *diete,* from Old French, from Latin *diaeta,* from Greek *diaita,* mode of life, regimen, diet, from *diaitan,* to lead one's life.] —**di·et·er** *n.*

di·et² *n.* **1.** *Sometimes capital* **D.** A legislative assembly in certain countries, such as Japan. **2.** *Scottish.* **a.** A single daily session of a court or local legislature. **b.** A day upon which a court convenes. **3.** *Capital* **D.** The semiannual general assembly of the estates of the former Holy Roman Empire. [Middle English *diete, dyet,* day's journey, day for meeting, from Medieval Latin *diēta,* from Latin *diēs,* day.]

diet. dietetics.

di·e·tar·y (dī-ə-təri, -tri ‖ -terri) *adj.* Of or pertaining to diet. ~*n., pl.* **dietaries. 1.** A system or regimen of dieting. **2.** A regulated daily food allowance.

dietary fibre *n.* Roughage *(see).*

dietary laws *pl.n.* In certain religions such as Judaism or Islam, a body of regulations prescribing the kinds and combinations of food that may be eaten by the orthodox.

di·e·tet·ic (dī-ə-téttik) *adj.* **1.** Of or pertaining to diet or its regulation. **2.** Specially prepared or processed for restrictive diets. [Late Latin *diaetēticus,* from Greek *diaitētikos,* from *diaita,* DIET.] —**di·e·tet·i·cal·ly** *adv.*

di·e·tet·ics (dī-ə-téttiks) *n. Used with a singular verb. Abbr.* **diet.** The study of diet and dieting as it relates to health and hygiene.

di·eth·y·lene glycol (dī-éthi-leen) *n.* A clear, colourless, extremely hygroscopic, syrupy liquid, $CH_2OHCH_2OCH_2CH_2OH$, widely used as an antifreeze, solvent, softening agent, and herbicide.

di·eth·yl ether (dī-éthil) *n.* **Ether** *(see).*

di·e·ti·cian, di·e·ti·tian (dī-ə-tísh'n) *n.* A person specialising in dietetics.

Die·trich (deétrikh), **Marlene,** born Maria Magdalena von Losch (1901-92). German actress, singer, and film star. Her international reputation was made in 1930 with Josef von Sternberg's German film *The Blue Angel.* Her Hollywood films include *Morocco* (1930), *Shanghai Express* (1932), and *Destry Rides Again* (1939).

dif., diff. difference; different.

diffenbachia. Variant of **dieffenbachia.**

dif·fer (diffər) *intr.v.* **-fered, -fering, -fers. 1.** To be unlike or dissimilar in nature, quality, amount, or form. Often used with *from.* **2.** To be of a different opinion; disagree; dissent. Often used with *with.* **3.** *Archaic.* To quarrel. [Middle English *differen,* from Old French *differer,* from Latin *differre,* to carry in different directions, be different : *dis-,* apart + *ferre,* to carry.]

dif·fer·ence (diff-ərənss, -rənss) *n. Abbr.* **dif., diff. 1.** The condition or degree of being unlike, dissimilar, or diverse; disparity; variation. **2.** A specific point of disparity or unlikeness; an instance of variation. **3.** *Archaic.* A distinct mark or peculiarity. **4.** A disagreement; a quarrel. **5.** A distinction or discrimination. **6. a.** A substantial change: *Do you see a difference in her these days?* **b.** A critical factor in determining an outcome: *A good pension can be the difference between hardship and comfort in old age.* **7.** *Mathematics.* **a.** The amount by which one quantity is greater or less than another. **b.** The amount that remains after one quantity is subtracted from another. Also called "remainder". **8.** *Logic.* A differentia. **9.** *Heraldry.* A distinguishing mark on a coat of arms to differentiate branches of the same family. **—make a difference.** To alter matters significantly.

~tr.v. **differenced, -encing, -ences. 1.** To make or cause to make a difference between or in; distinguish. **2.** *Heraldry.* To add a distinguishing mark to (a coat of arms).

Synonyms: *difference, dissimilarity, unlikeness, divergence, variation, distinction, discrepancy.*

dif·fer·ent (diff-ərənt, -rənt) *adj. Abbr.* **dif., diff. 1.** Characterised by a difference; unlike. **2.** Distinct; separate. **3.** Differing from the ordinary; special or unusual.

~adv. Nonstandard. Differently. [Middle English, from Old French, from Latin *differēns* (stem *different-*), present participle of *differre,* to DIFFER.] **—dif·fer·ent·ly** *adv.* **—dif·fer·ent·ness** *n.*

Usage: A long-standing usage dispute focuses on the correct choice of word to use following *different* and *differently,* in such sentences as *This book is different . . . that, She behaves differently . . . Joan. From* is the traditional standard form, in both British and American English, but the use of *than* as an alternative to *from* is particularly common in informal American English. A British alternative is the use of *to*—a usage that dates back to the 16th century. Purists criticise *to* on the grounds that it contradicts the etymological meaning of *diff-* (separation), in view of which *from* is felt to be more appropriate (as in the verb *differ from).* Other problems involving *different* include: its emphatic use following a number, where it is sometimes criticised as unnecessary (*Three different doctors examined him*); and its adverbial use, where standard English recommends *differently* (*They do it different at home* would not be regarded as correct).

dif·fer·en·ti·a (diffə-rén-shi-ə) *n., pl.* **-tiae** (-shi-ee, -shi-ī). *Logic.* An attribute that characterises and distinguishes a species from others of the same genus. [Latin, difference.]

dif·fer·en·ti·a·ble (diffə-rén-shi-əb'l, -shəb'l) *adj.* **1.** Capable of being differentiated. **2.** *Mathematics.* Possessing a derivative. **—dif·fer·en·ti·a·bil·i·ty** (-ə-bílləti) *n.*

dif·fer·en·tial (diffə-rénsh'l) *adj.* **1.** Pertaining to or showing a difference or differences. **2.** Constituting or making a difference; distinctive. **3.** Dependent on or making use of a difference or distinction. **4.** *Mathematics.* Of or pertaining to differentiation. **5.** Involving differences in speed or direction of motion: *a differential pulley.*

~n. **1.** A factor that constitutes or makes a difference. **2.** *Mathematics.* **a.** An infinitesimal increment in a variable. **b.** The product of the derivative of a function of one variable multiplied by the independent variable increment. **3.** A differential gear. **4.** A difference in costs, charges, or rates; especially, a difference in rates of pay, as between different types of work in the same industry or profession, or similar work done in different places or circumstances. **—dif·fer·en·tial·ly** *adv.*

differential analyser *n.* A mechanical or electronic analog computer used to solve especially complicated differential equations.

differential calculus *n.* The mathematics of the variation of a function with respect to changes in independent variables; loosely, the study of slopes of curves, accelerations, maxima, and minima by means of derivatives and differentials.

differential coefficient *n. Mathematics.* A **derivative** *(see).*

differential diagnosis *n. Medicine.* The process or an instance of distinguishing between different diseases with similar signs or symptoms.

differential equation *n.* An equation containing derivatives or differentials of an unknown function.

differential gear *n.* An arrangement of gears in an epicyclic train permitting the rotation of two shafts at different speeds, used on the drive axle of motor vehicles to allow different rates of wheel rotation on curves.

differential operator *n. Symbol* ∇ A mathematical operator used in vector analysis.

differential windlass *n.* A hoisting device that has two drums of different sizes on the same axis. A line wound on the larger and unwound from the smaller provides extra lifting power. Also called "Chinese windlass".

dif·fer·en·ti·ate (diffə-rénshi-ayt) *v.* **-ated, -ating, -ates.** *—tr.* **1.** To constitute the difference in or between; serve to make a distinction between: *subspecies differentiated by the markings on their wings.* **2.** To perceive or show the difference in or between; discriminate; distinguish. **3.** To cause differences to develop in (something) by alteration or modification. Usually used in the passive. **4.** *Mathematics.* To calculate the derivative or differential of. *—intr.* **1.** To become distinct or specialised; acquire a different character. **2.** To make distinctions; discriminate. **3.** *Biology.* To develop into more specialised organs. Used especially of embryonic cells or tissues. **—dif·fer·en·ti·a·tion** (-áysh'n) *n.*

dif·fi·cult (díffi-k'lt || -kult) *adj.* **1.** Requiring effort or skill to do or achieve: *a difficult task.* **2.** Requiring mental effort to comprehend or solve: *a difficult puzzle.* **3.** Not easy to persuade, control, or manage ; stubborn; obstinate: *a difficult child.* —See Synonyms at **hard.** [Middle English, back-formation from DIFFICULTY.] **—dif·fi·cult·ly** *adv.*

dif·fi·cul·ty (díffi-k'lti || -kulti) *n., pl.* **-ties. 1.** The condition, fact, or quality of being difficult. **2.** Something not easily done, accomplished, comprehended, or solved. **3. a.** A problem; problems; trouble: *I had difficulty catching her accent.* **b.** *Usually plural.* A troublesome or embarrassing state of affairs, especially one resulting from a shortage of money. **4.** A lack of normal ease: *Asthma can cause breathing difficulties.* **5.** A disagreement; a dispute. **6.** An objection or impediment: *to make difficulties for someone.* [Middle English *difficulte,* from Latin *difficultās* (stem *difficultāt-*), from *difficilis* (earlier *difficul*), difficult : *dis-,* not + *facilis,* easy.]

dif·fi·dent (díffi-dənt || -dent) *adj.* **1.** Lacking self-confidence; timid. **2.** Not self-assertive. See Synonyms at **shy.** [Middle English, from Latin *diffīdens* (stem *diffīdent-*), present participle of *diffīdere,* to mistrust : *dis-,* not + *fīdere, to trust.*] **—dif·fi·dence** *n.* **—dif·fi·dent·ly** *adv.*

dif·fract (di-frákt) *tr.v.* **-fracted, -fracting, -fracts.** To cause to undergo diffraction. [Back-formation from DIFFRACTION.] **—dif·frac·tive** *adj.* **—dif·frac·tive·ly** *adv.* **—dif·frac·tive·ness** *n.*

dif·frac·tion (di-fráksh'n) *n.* **1.** Modification of the intensity distribution of wave phenomena that are incident upon an object or aperture whose size is similar to that of the wavelength, resulting in dispersion and interference patterns. **2.** Any phenomenon resulting from such modification. [New Latin *diffractiō* (stem *diffractiōn-*), "a breaking up", from Latin *diffractus,* past participle of *diffringere,* to break to pieces : *dis-,* apart + *frangere,* to break.]

diffraction grating *n.* A usually glass or polished metal surface having a large number of very fine parallel grooves or slits cut in the surface and used to produce optical spectra by diffraction of transmitted or reflected light.

dif·fuse (di-féwz) *v.* **-fused, -fusing, -fuses.** *—tr.* **1.** To pour out and cause (a gas or liquid, for example) to spread or disperse. **2.** To spread about or scatter; disseminate. **3.** To make less brilliant; soften. *—intr.* **1.** To spread out; become widely dispersed. **2.** *Physics.* To undergo diffusion.

~adj. (di-féwss). **1.** Characterised by excessive wordiness and poor organisation; lacking conciseness. Said of speech or writing. **2.** Widely spread or scattered; dispersed. [Middle English, dispersed, from Old French *diffus,* from Latin *diffūsus,* past participle of *diffundere,* to pour out, spread : *dis-,* apart + *fundere,* to pour.] **—dif·fuse·ly** *adv.* **—dif·fuse·ness** *n.* **—dif·fus·ible** (di-féwzəb'l) *adj.* **—dif·fus·i·bly** *adv.*

dif·fused junction (di-féwzd) *n.* A semiconductor junction formed by the diffusion of impurity atoms into semiconducting material to create p-type or n-type regions.

dif·fus·er, dif·fu·sor (di-féwzər) *n.* **1.** One that diffuses. **2.** A lighting fixture, such as a frosted globe or optically rough reflector, that diffuses light. **3.** A flow passage in a wind tunnel that decelerates a stream of gas or liquid from a high to a low velocity. **4.** A device, such as a cone or baffle, placed in front of a loudspeaker diaphragm to diffuse the sound waves. **5.** A medium that scatters light, used in photography to soften shadows.

dif·fu·sion (di-féwzh'n) *n.* **1.** The process of diffusing or the condition of being diffused. **2.** *Physics.* The angular redistribution of radiation by a scattering, reflecting, or refracting system, ideally producing an isotropic distribution of intensity. **3.** *Physics.* The gradual mixing of the molecules of two or more substances, as a result of random thermal motion. **4. a.** Excessive wordiness; verbosity. **b.** Poor organisation of material, as in a literary work, for example. **5.** *Anthropology.* The spreading of customs, skills, or the like from one group to another.

diffusion coefficient *n.* Diffusivity (sense 1).

dif·fu·sive (di-féw-siv || -ziv) *adj.* Characterised by diffusion; tending to diffuse. **—dif·fu·sive·ly** *adv.* **—dif·fu·sive·ness** *n.*

dif·fu·siv·i·ty (diffew-sívvəti) *n. Physics.* **1.** The rate at which a substance diffuses between the opposite sides of a unit cube when there is unit concentration difference between them. Also called "diffusion coefficient". **2.** The ratio of the thermal conductivity of a substance to the product of its specific heat capacity and its density. **3.** The ability of a substance to undergo diffusion.

dig (dig) *v.* **dug** (dug) or *archaic* **digged** (digd), **digging, digs.** *—tr.* **1.** To break up, turn over, or remove (earth or sand, for example) with a spade, the hands, or other tools; excavate. **2.** To make (a hole) by or as if by digging: *dig a grave.* **3.** To obtain by digging: *dig coal.* **4.** To mix with the earth when digging. Used with *in.* **5.** To learn or discover by careful research or investigation; unearth. Often used with *up* or *out.* **6. a.** To force or thrust into or against. Used with *into.* **b.** To prod or poke: *dug me in the ribs.* **7.** *Slang.* To comprehend, appreciate, or enjoy. *—intr.* **1.** To loosen or turn over the earth. **2.** To make one's way by or as if by digging. Used with *through, into,* or *under.* **3.** *U.S. Informal.* To study or work hard and diligently. **—dig in. 1.** *Military.* To dig holes or trenches. **2.** To entrench (oneself). **3.** *Informal.* To eat heartily.

~n. **1.** A poke; a thrust: *a dig in the ribs.* **2.** A sarcastic, taunting remark; a gibe. **3.** An archaeological excavation. **4.** *Plural. Chiefly British Informal.* Lodgings: *student digs.* [Middle English *diggen,* from Old French *diguer,* "to make a dyke or ditch", from *digue,* ditch, from Germanic.]

dig. digest (compilation).

di·gam·ma (dī-gammə, -gámmə) *n.* A letter, written *F*, occurring in certain early forms of Greek and transliterated in English as *w*. [Latin, from Greek : DI- (two) + GAMMA (from its resemblance to two capital gammas placed one above the other).]

dig·a·my (díggəmi) *n.* Remarriage after the death or divorce of one's first wife or husband. Also called "deuterogamy". [Late Latin *digamia*, from Late Greek : DI- (two) + -GAMY.] **—dig·a·mous** *adj.*

di·gas·tric (dī-gásstrik) *adj.* Having two fleshy ends connected by a thinner tendinous portion. Said of certain muscles.
~n. A lower jaw muscle that assists in lowering the jaw. [New Latin *digastricus*, "having two bellies" : DI- (two) + GASTRIC.]

di·gen·e·sis (dī-jénni-siss) *n.* **Alternation of generations** *(see).*

di·gest (di-jést, dī-) *v.* **-gested, -gesting, -gests.** *—tr.* **1.** To transform (food) into an assimilable condition, as by chemical and muscular action in the alimentary canal. **2.** To absorb or assimilate mentally. **3.** To organise into a systematic arrangement, usually by summarising or classifying. **4.** *Archaic.* To endure or bear patiently. **5.** *Chemistry.* To soften or disintegrate by means of chemical action, heat, or moisture. *—intr.* **1.** To become assimilated into the body. **2.** To assimilate food substances. **3.** *Chemistry.* To undergo exposure to heat, liquids, or chemical agents.
~n. (dī-jest). **1.** *Abbr.* **dig.** A systematic organisation or arrangement of summarised literary, scientific, or statistical materials or data; a synopsis. **2.** A periodical containing literary abridgments, brief accounts of current affairs, and the like. **3.** *Law.* A systematic arrangement of statutes or court decisions. **—the Digest.** *Roman Law.* The **Pandects** *(see).* [Middle English *digesten*, from Latin *dīgerere* (past participle *dīgestus*), to divide, distribute, digest : *di-*, apart + *gerere*, to bear, carry.]

di·gest·ant (di-jéstənt, dī-) *n.* Also **digester.** A substance taken to aid digestion.

di·gest·er (di-jéstər, dī-) *n.* **1.** A person who makes a digest. **2.** Variant of **digestant. 3.** *Chemistry.* An apparatus in which substances are softened or decomposed, usually for further processing.

di·gest·i·ble (di-jéstə-b'l, dī-) *adj.* Capable of being digested. **—di·gest·i·bil·i·ty** (-billəti), **di·gest·i·ble·ness** *n.* **—di·gest·i·bly** *adv.*

di·gest·if (dizhes-teéf) *n.* A drink, especially a brandy or liqueur, taken after a meal to aid digestion.

di·ges·tion (di-jésschən, dī-) *n.* **1.** *Physiology.* **a.** The primarily enzymatic bodily process by which foods are decomposed into simple, assimilable substances. **b.** The ability to digest food. **2.** The process of decomposing organic matter in sewage by bacteria. **3.** The assimilation of ideas or information; understanding.

di·ges·tive (di-jéstiv, dī-) *adj.* **1.** Pertaining to or aiding digestion. **2.** Functioning to digest food.
~n. **1.** Any substance that aids digestion. **2.** A digestive biscuit. **—di·ges·tive·ly** *adv.*

digestive biscuit *n.* A kind of semisweet biscuit made from wholemeal flour.

digestive system *n.* The alimentary canal together with accessory glands including the salivary glands, liver, and pancreas, regarded as an integrated system responsible for digestion.

dig·ger (diggər) *n.* **1.** A person who digs, especially one who digs for gold. **2.** A machine with an attachment for excavating earth. **3.** *Informal.* A person, especially a soldier, from New Zealand or Australia. [Sense 3 with allusion to Australian gold-miners.]

digger wasp *n.* Any of various wasps of the family Sphecidae, that burrow into the ground to build their nests.

dig·gings (díggingz) *pl.n.* **1.** An excavation site. **2.** Materials dug out. **3.** *Chiefly British.* Lodgings; digs. No longer in current usage.

dight (dīt) *tr.v.* **dight** or **dighted, dighting, dights.** *Archaic.* To dress; adorn. [Middle English *dighten*, Old English *dihtan*, to arrange, compose, from Latin *dictāre*, to DICTATE.]

dig·it (díjit) *n.* **1. a.** A finger or toe. **b.** Any of the corresponding parts of other vertebrates, the number of which may be reduced. In the horse, for example, there is a single digit on each leg. **2.** The breadth of a finger, used as a unit of measure, equal to about two centimetres (3/4 inch). **3.** Any one of the ten Arabic number symbols, 0 to 9. [Middle English, from Latin *digitus*, finger.]

dig·i·tal (díjit'l) *adj.* **1.** Of, pertaining to, or resembling a digit, especially a finger. **2.** Done with the fingers. **3.** Having digits. **4.** Displaying measurements by means of changing numbers rather than by hands on a dial: *a digital clock.* **5.** *Computing.* Using digits to represent quantities. Compare **analog. 6.** Of or pertaining to digital recording or broadcasting.
~n. Any key played or operated with the finger, as on a piano. **—dig·i·tal·ly** *adv.*

digital audio tape *n. Abbr.* **DAT.** An **audio tape** with sound signals digitally recorded, giving more faithful sound reproduction than a conventional recording.

digital broadcasting *n.* The broadcasting of digitised signals for higher-fidelity reproduction.

digital computer *n.* A computer that performs operations with quantities represented electronically as digits, usually in the binary system. Compare **analog computer.**

dig·i·tal·in (díji-táyl-in) || *U.S.* -tál-) *n.* A poisonous white powder, $C_{36}H_{56}O_{14}$, used to treat heart disease. [DIGITAL(IS) + -IN.]

dig·i·tal·is (díji-táyl-iss || *U.S.* -tál-) *n.* **1.** Any plant of the genus *Digitalis*, which includes the foxgloves. **2.** A drug prepared from the seeds and dried leaves of this plant, used as a cardiac stimulant. [New Latin, from Latin *digitālis*, digital (from the finger-shaped corollas of foxglove), from *digitus*, DIGIT.]

dig·i·tal·ise, dig·i·tal·ize (díjit'l-īz) *tr.v.* **-ised, -ising, -ises. 1.** To treat medically with digitalis. **2.** To digitise. **—dig·i·tal·i·sa·tion** (-ī-záysh'n || *U.S.* -i-) *n.*

digital recording *n.* **1.** A method of tape-recording in which the signal is not recorded in a continuously variable way, but in bits, as many as 30,000 per second, resulting in greater precision and therefore lower distortion. **2.** A similar method of recording images, such as photographs or maps, used for example in facsimile systems. **3.** A recording produced by this method.

dig·i·tate (díjit-ayt) *adj.* Also **dig·i·tat·ed** (-aytid). **1.** Having digits or finger-like parts. **2.** *Botany.* Having radiating finger-like lobes or leaflets. **—dig·i·tate·ly** *adv.*

dig·i·ta·tion (díji-táysh'n) *n.* **1.** Division into finger-like parts; the condition of being digitate. **2.** A finger-like part or projection.

dig·i·ti·grade (díjiti-grayd) *adj.* Walking so that only the digits touch the ground, as do horses, cats, and dogs.
~n. A digitigrade animal. Compare **plantigrade.** [Latin *digitus*, finger, toe, DIGIT + -GRADE.]

dig·it·ise, dig·it·ize (díjit-īz) *tr.v.* **-ised, -ising, -ises.** To convert (continuous data) into digital form for computer processing, recording, or broadcasting. **—dig·it·i·sa·tion** (-ī-záysh'n || *U.S.* -i-) *n.*

dig·i·tox·in (díji-tóksin) *n.* A highly active glycoside, $C_{41}H_{64}O_{13}$, derived from digitalis. [DIGI(TALIS) + TOXIN.]

dig·i·tron (díji-tron) *n.* An electronic display tube consisting of an anode and a series of cathodes, each shaped as a number or letter, which can be separately lit by a glow discharge. Also called "Nixie tube". [DIGIT + -TRON.]

dig·ni·fied (díg-ni-fīd) *adj.* Having or expressing dignity. **—dig·ni·fied·ly** (díg-ni-fīd-li, -fī-id-li) *adv.*

dig·ni·fy (díg-ni-fī) *tr.v.* **-fied, -fying, -fies. 1.** To confer dignity or honour upon. **2.** To impart a sense of dignity to. **3.** To elevate with the semblance of dignity. [Middle English *dignifien*, from Old French *dignifier*, from Late Latin *dignificāre* : Latin *dignus*, worthy + *facere*, to make, do.]

dig·ni·tar·y (díg-ni-təri, -tri || -terri) *n., pl.* **-ies.** A person of high rank. [From DIGNITY.]

dig·ni·ty (díg-nəti, -niti) *n., pl.* **-ties. 1. a.** The presence of poise, self-control, and seriousness in one's deportment to a degree that inspires respect. **b.** Inherent nobility and worth: *the dignity of labour.* **c.** An imposing, formal quality; grandeur; stateliness. **2.** The respect and honour associated with an important position. **3. a.** A high office or rank. **b.** Standing or rank in relation to others. **4.** Self-esteem. **5.** *Plural.* The ceremonial symbols and observances attached to high office: *the dignities of office.* [Middle English *dignite*, from Old French, from Latin *dignitās* (stem *dignitāt-*), from *dignus*, worthy.]

di·graph (dī-graaf, -graf) *n.* **1.** A pair of letters that represents a single speech sound, such as the *ph* in *pheasant* or the *ea* in *beat.* **2.** Two letters run together to represent a special sound, such as Old English *æ.* [DI- + -GRAPH.] **—di·graph·ic** (dī-gráffik) *adj.*

di·gress (dī-gréss, di-) *intr.v.* **-gressed, -gressing, -gresses. 1.** To stray from the main subject in writing or speaking. **2.** To turn aside. [Latin *dīgredī* (past participle *dīgressus*), to go aside : *dis-*, apart, aside + *gradī*, to go.]

di·gres·sion (dī-grésh'n, di-) *n.* **1.** The act of digressing. **2.** An instance of digressing; especially, a written or spoken passage not bearing directly on the main subject. **—di·gres·sion·al** *adj.*

di·gres·sive (dī-gréssiv, di-) *adj.* Characterised by digression; rambling. **—di·gres·sive·ly** *adv.* **—di·gres·sive·ness** *n.*

di·he·dral (dī-heédrəl) *adj.* **1.** Formed by or having two plane faces; two-sided. **2.** Pertaining to, having, or forming a dihedral angle.
~n. **1.** A dihedral angle. **2.** The upward or downward inclination of an aircraft wing from true horizontal. [DI- + -HEDRAL.]

dihedral angle *n.* **1.** *Geometry.* The angle formed by two intersecting planes. **2.** The acute angle between an aircraft wing and true horizontal. Also called "dihedral".

di·hy·brid (dī-hībrid) *n. Genetics.* **1.** A cross whose parents differ in two distinct characters. **2.** An organism that is heterozygous for two pairs of alleles.

di·hy·dric (dī-hīdrik) *adj.* Containing two hydroxyl radicals.

Dijon (deé-zhoN; *French* dee-zhóN). City in east central France, capital of the Côte d'Or, and once the capital of Burgundy. It is a railway junction, and gastronomic and industrial centre, best known for mustard and cassis, a blackcurrant liqueur.

dik-dik (dík-dik) *n.* Any of several very small African antelopes of the genus *Madoqua.* [Native name in East Africa, imitative of its cry.]

dike. *Chiefly U.S.* Variant of **dyke.**

dik·kop (díckop) *n. South African.* A bird, the **stone curlew** *(see).* [Afrikaans : *dik*, thick + *kop*, head.]

dik·tat (dík-taat, -tat || *U.S.* -taát) *n.* **1.** A unilaterally imposed settlement that deals harshly with a defeated party. **2.** An authoritative or dogmatic statement; a command. [German, "dictation", "command", from Latin *dictātum*, neuter past participle of *dictāre*, to DICTATE.]

Di·lan·tin (dī-lántin) *n.* A trademark for diphenylhydantoin sodium, used to treat epilepsy.

di·lap·i·date (di-láppi-dayt) *v.* **-dated, -dating, -dates.** *—tr.* To bring into a state of ruin, decay, or disrepair. *—intr.* To fall into partial ruin or decay. [Latin *dīlapidāre*, to throw away, destroy : *dis-*, apart + *lapidāre*, to throw stones, from *lapis*, stone.]

di·lap·i·dat·ed (di-láppi-daytid) *adj.* Fallen into a state of disrepair; shabby; broken-down.

di·lap·i·da·tion (di-láppi-dáysh'n) *n.* **1.** The state of being or the process of becoming dilapidated. **2.** *Often plural. Law.* Damage or disrepair to rented property for which a tenant is liable.

di·la·tan·cy (dī-láyt'n-si, di-) *n.* **1.** The increase in volume of a fixed amount of certain materials, such as wet sand, when it is subjected to a deformation that increases the interparticle distances of its constituents. **2.** Any of various related phenomena, such as increase in viscosity or solidification, resulting from such deformation.

di·la·tant (dī-láyt'nt, di-) *adj.* **1.** Tending to dilate; dilating. **2.** Exhibiting dilatancy.
~n. A dilator.

dil·a·ta·tion (dī́-lay-táysh'n, dí-, -lə-) *n.* **1.** The act or process of dilating; expansion; dilation. **2.** The state or condition of being dilated or stretched. **3.** *Medicine.* The condition of being abnormally enlarged or dilated. **4.** Lengthy explanation or elaboration of a subject in writing or speech. **—dil·a·ta·tion·al** *adj.*

dilatation and curettage *n. Abbr.* **D and C.** A surgical operation in which the cervix is opened using a dilator and the lining of the uterus is removed with a curette, performed after an incomplete miscarriage, for example.

di·late (dī-láyt, di- || *U.S. also* dī́-layt) *v.* **-lated, -lating, -lates.** *—tr.* To make wider or larger; cause to expand. *—intr.* **1.** To become wider or larger; expand. **2.** To write or speak at length on a subject; elaborate. Used with *on* or *upon.* [Middle English *dilaten,* from Old French *dilater,* from Latin *dīlātāre,* to enlarge, extend : *dis-,* apart + *lātus,* wide.] **—di·lat·a·bil·i·ty** (-láytə-bílləti) **—di·lat·a·ble** *adj.* **—di·la·tion** (-láysh'n) *n.* **—di·la·tive** (-láytiv || *U.S. also* dī́lətiv) *adj.*

di·lat·ed (dī-láytid, di- || dī́-laytid) *adj.* **1.** Widened; expanded. **2.** Distended.

dil·a·tom·e·ter (dìllə-tómmitər, dī́lə-) *n.* An instrument used to measure thermal expansion in solids, liquids, and gases. [DILATE + -METER.] **—dil·a·to·met·ric** (-tə-métrik) *adj.* **—dil·a·tom·e·try** *n.*

di·la·tor, di·la·ter (dī-láytər, di- || dī́-laytər) *n.* Something that dilates an object, organ, or part; especially, a drug, surgical instrument, or muscle that induces dilation.

dil·a·to·ry (dìllə-təri, -tri || dī-láytəri, di-) *adj.* **1.** Intended to cause delay. **2.** Characterised by a tendency to postpone or delay. —See Synonyms at **tardy.** [Middle English *dilatorie,* from Latin *dīlātōrius,* from *dīlātor,* delayer, from *dīlātus* (past participle of *differre,* to postpone, DEFER) : *dis-,* apart + *-lātus,* "carried".] **—dil·a·to·ri·ly** *adv.* **—dil·a·to·ri·ness** *n.*

dil·do (díl-dō) *n., pl.* **-dos** or **-does.** An object shaped like an erect penis, usually used for sexual penetration. [17th century : origin obscure.]

di·lem·ma (di-lémmə, dī-) *n.* **1.** A situation that requires one to choose between two equally balanced and often equally unpleasant alternatives. **2.** A predicament that seemingly defies a satisfactory solution. —See Synonyms at **predicament.** [Latin, from Greek *dilēmma,* ambiguous proposition : DI- (double) + *lēmma,* proposition, LEMMA.] **—dil·em·mat·ic** (dìllə-máttik, dī́lə-) *adj.*

dil·et·tante (dìlli-tánti, -taánti || *U.S. also* -taánt, -tánt, -taant, -tant) *n., pl.* **-tantes** or **-tanti** (-tántee, -taántee). **1.** One whose interest in a subject is not serious or professional; a dabbler, especially in the arts. **2.** *Archaic.* A lover of the fine arts; a connoisseur.
~adj. Superficial or amateurish. [Italian *dilettante,* "amateur", from *dilettarsi,* to take pleasure in, from Latin *dēlectāre,* to DELIGHT.] **—dil·et·tan·tish** *adj.* **—dil·et·tan·tism** *n.*

dil·i·gence[1] (dìllijənss) *n.* **1.** Earnest and persistent application to a matter in hand; steady effort; assiduity. **2.** Attentive care; heedfulness.

dil·i·gence[2] *n.* In former times, a large public stagecoach. [French, from *diligence,* "speed", from *diligent,* DILIGENT.]

dil·i·gent (dìllijənt) *adj.* **1.** Industrious; hard-working. **2.** Characterised by persevering, painstaking effort. —See Synonyms at **busy.** [Middle English, from Old French, from Latin *dīligēns* (stem *diligent-*), "loving", attentive, careful, from *dīligere,* to "single out", "choose", esteem highly, love : *dis-,* apart + *legere,* to choose, gather.] **—dil·i·gent·ly** *adv.*

dill (dil) *n.* **1.** An aromatic herb, *Anethum graveolens,* native to the Old World, having finely dissected leaves and small yellow flowers. **2.** The leaves or seedlike fruits of this plant, used as seasoning. Also called "dill weed". [Middle English *dile,* from Old English *dile,* from West Germanic *dilja* (unattested).]

dill pickle *n.* A cucumber pickled and flavoured with dill.

dil·ly (dìlli) *n., pl.* **-lies.** *Informal.* An excellent person or thing.
~adj. Informal. Mad or scatterbrained. [Noun, from *delightful* or *delicious;* adjective, perhaps from *delirious.*]

dilly bag *n. Australian.* A bag or basket, especially one made of woven rushes or bark. [From *dilli,* a native word in Queensland.]

dil·ly·dal·ly (dìlli-dal-i) *intr.v.* **-lied, -lying, -lies.** *Informal.* **1.** To dawdle. **2.** To vacillate. [Reduplication of DALLY.]

dil·u·ent (díllew-ənt) *adj.* Capable of diluting or serving to dilute.
~n. A substance used to dilute. [Latin *dīluēns* (stem *dīluent-*), present participle of *dīluere,* to DILUTE.]

di·lute (dī-léwt, di-, -lōōt) *tr.v.* **-luted, -luting, -lutes. 1.** To thin or reduce the strength or concentration of by adding water or a similar fluid. **2.** To lessen the force, strength, purity, or brilliance of, especially by admixture.
~adj. **1.** Weakened; diluted. **2.** Designating a solution of a substance in which the substance is present in a low concentration. [Latin *dīluere* (past participle *dīlūtus*), to wash away, dilute : *dis-,* apart + *-luere,* from *lavere,* to wash.] **—di·lut·er** *n.*

di·lu·tion (dī-lōōsh'n, di-, -léwsh'n) *n.* **1. a.** The process of diluting or being diluted. **b.** A dilute or weakened condition. **2.** A diluted substance.

di·lu·vi·al (dī-lōōvi-əl, di-, -léwvi-) *adj.* Also **di·lu·vi·an** (-ən). Of or produced by a flood, especially the Biblical Flood. [Late Latin *dīluviālis,* from Latin *dīluvium,* flood, from *dīluere,* to wash away, DILUTE.]

dim (dim) *adj.* **dimmer, dimmest. 1.** Faintly lit. **2.** Shedding a small amount of light; faint. **3.** Lacking brightness or lustre; subdued; dull. **4.** Faintly outlined; indistinct; obscure. **5.** Lacking keenness of the senses, especially sight. **6.** *Informal.* Mentally slow; stupid. **7.** *Informal.* Negative, unfavourable, or disapproving: *She took a dim view of the plan.* —See Synonyms at **dark.**
~v. **dimmed, dimming, dims.** *—tr.* **1.** To make dim. **2.** *U.S.* To dip (headlights). *—intr.* To become dim. [Middle English *dim(me),* Old English *dimm,* from Germanic *dim-* (unattested).] **—dim·ly** *adv.* **—dim·ness** *n.*

dime (dīm) *n.* **1.** A U.S. coin worth ten cents or $^1/_{10}$ of a dollar. **2.** A similar coin in Canadian currency. [Middle English, a tenth part, tithe, from Old French *dime, disme,* from Latin *decima (pars),* tenth (part), tithe, from *decimus,* tenth, from *decem,* ten.]

di·men·hy·dri·nate (dī́men-hī́dri-nayt) *n.* An antihistamine, $C_{24}H_{28}ClN_5O_3$, used to treat travel sickness and allergic disorders.

di·men·sion (di-ménsh'n, dī-) *n. Abbr.* **dim. 1.** A measure of spatial extent, especially width, height, or length. **2.** *Often plural.* Extent; magnitude; size; scope. **3.** *Mathematics.* **a.** Any of the least number of independent coordinates required to specify a point in space uniquely. **b.** The range of any of these coordinates. **4.** *Physics.* A physical property, often mass, length, time, or some combination thereof, regarded as a fundamental measure, or as one of a set of fundamental measures, of a physical quantity: *Velocity has the dimensions of length divided by time.* **5.** An aspect of or way of regarding a whole: *This adds a whole new dimension to the problem.*
~tr.v. **dimensioned, -sioning, -sions.** *Chiefly U.S.* To cut or shape to specific dimensions. [Middle English *dimensio(u)n,* from Old French *dimension,* from Latin *dīmēnsiō* (stem *dīmēnsiōn-*), "a measuring", from *dīmētīrī* (past participle *dīmēnsus*), to measure carefully : *dis-* (intensive) + *mētīrī,* to measure.] **—di·men·sion·al** *adj.* **—di·men·sion·al·i·ty** (-ál-əti) *n.* **—di·men·sion·al·ly** *adv.*

di·mer (dī́mər) *n. Chemistry.* **1.** A molecule consisting of two identical simpler molecules. **2.** A chemical compound consisting of such molecules. [DI- + Greek *meros,* part.]

di·mer·ic (dī-mérrik) *adj.* **1.** *Biology.* Composed of two parts or divisions. **2.** *Chemistry.* Composed of dimers.

dim·er·ous (dímmərəss) *adj.* **1.** Consisting of two parts or segments, as does the tarsus in certain insects. **2.** *Botany.* Having flower parts, such as petals, sepals, and stamens, in sets of two. Also written *2-merous.* [New Latin *dimerus* : DI- + -MEROUS.] **—dim·er·ism** *n.*

dim·e·ter (dímmitər) *n.* A verse consisting of two metrical feet or of two groups of two feet. [Late Latin, (verse) of two measures or metres, from Greek *dimetros,* having two metres : DI- + *metron,* METRE.]

di·meth·yl·sulph·ox·ide (dī-méth'l-sul-fóksīd, -meéthīl-) *n. Abbr.* **DMSO.** A colourless hygroscopic liquid $(CH_3)_2SO$, obtained from lignin, used as a solvent and in medicine as a skin penetrant to convey medications into the tissues.

di·min·ish (di-mínnish) *v.* **-ished, -ishing, -ishes.** *—tr.* **1. a.** To reduce the size of; make smaller or less. **b.** To detract from the authority, rank, or prestige of. **2.** *Architecture.* To cause to taper. **3.** *Music.* To reduce (a perfect or minor interval) by a semitone. Compare **augment.** *—intr.* **1.** To become smaller or less. **2.** To become narrower; taper. —See Synonyms at **decrease.** [Middle English *deminishen,* blend of (a) *diminuen,* to reduce, lessen, from Old French *diminuer,* from Latin *dīminuere,* variant of *dēminuere* : *dē-,* from + *minuere,* to lessen; and (b) *minishen, minuisen,* to make smaller, from Old French *menuiser,* from Vulgar Latin *minūtiāre* (unattested), from Latin *minūtia,* smallness, from *minūtus,* small, from the past participle of *minuere,* to lessen.] **—di·min·ish·a·ble** *adj.* **—di·min·ish·ment** *n.*

diminished responsibility *n. Law.* Grounds on which responsibility and punishment for a crime, especially murder, can be lessened by taking into account mental weakness or abnormality.

diminishing returns *pl. n.* **1.** *Economics.* The principle that, after a certain point, further increases in a particular factor of production lead to progressively smaller increases in output. **2.** The idea that, after a certain point, more effort or investment in a project brings less reward or profit. Also called "law of diminishing returns".

di·min·u·en·do (di-mínnew-éndō) *n., pl.* **-dos** or **-does.** *Abbr.* **dim., dimin.** *Music.* A **decrescendo** *(see).* [Italian, "diminishing", from Latin *dīminuendum,* gerund of *dīminuere,* to DIMINISH.] **—di·min·u·en·do** *adj. & adv.*

dim·i·nu·tion (dìmmi-néwsh'n || -nōōsh'n) *n.* **1. a.** The act or process of diminishing. **b.** The resulting reduction; decrease. **2.** *Music.* The repetition of a theme in notes of shorter duration than those of the original. Compare **augmentation.** [Middle English *diminucioun,* from Old French *diminution,* from Latin *dīminūtiō* (stem *dīminūtiōn-*), *dēminūtiō,* from *dēminuere,* to DIMINISH.]

di·min·u·tive (di-mínnew-tiv) *adj. Abbr.* **dim., dimin. 1.** Of extremely small size; tiny. **2.** Designating certain affixes that denote smallness, youth, familiarity, affection, or contempt, such as *-let* in *booklet.* Compare **augmentative.** —See Synonyms at **small.**
~n. Abbr. **dim., dimin. 1.** A diminutive word or affix. **2.** *Heraldry.* A smaller form of an ordinary when repeated on a shield. [Middle English *diminutif,* from Old French, from Latin *dīminūtīvus, dēmi-*

nūtīvus, from *dēminūtus,* past participle of *dēminuere,* to DIMINISH.]
—**di·min·u·tive·ly** *adv.* —**di·min·u·tive·ness** *n.*

dim·i·ty (dímmiti) *n., pl.* **-ties.** A sheer, crisp cotton fabric with raised woven stripes or checks, used chiefly for curtains and dresses. [Middle English *demyt,* from Medieval Latin *dimitum,* from Medieval Greek *dimitos,* double-threaded : DI- + *mitos,* thread.]

dim·mer (dímmər) *n.* A rheostat or other device used to vary the electric current to a light bulb, thereby altering the intensity of illumination.

di·morph (dī-mawrf) *n.* Either of two forms of something exhibiting dimorphism.

di·mor·phic (dīmór-fik) *adj.* Also **di·mor·phous** (-fəss). Exhibiting dimorphism.

di·mor·phism (dī-mórfiz'm) *n.* **1.** *Botany.* The occurrence of two distinct forms of the same parts, such as leaves, flowers, or stamens, in a single plant or in plants of the same kind. **2.** *Chemistry & Physics.* Crystallisation in two distinct forms. **3.** *Zoology.* The state of having two distinct forms in the same species, especially when these forms serve to distinguish two sexes. [Greek *dimorphos,* having two forms : DI- + -MORPHOUS.]

dim-out (dím-owt) *n.* **1.** The restricted use or exposure of lights in wartime or as a stage effect. **2.** The semidarkness resulting from this. Compare **blackout.**

dim·ple (dímp'l) *n.* **1.** A small natural indentation in the flesh on a part of the human body, especially on the chin or cheek. **2.** Any slight depression or indentation in a surface.
~*v.* dimpled, -pling, -ples. —*tr.* To produce dimples in. —*intr.* To form dimples, as by smiling. [Middle English *dimple,* Old English *dympel* (unattested), pool, dimple.] —**dim·ply** *adj.*

dim sum (dím súm, dím sőom) *n. Used with a plural or singular verb.* A Chinese meal consisting of a variety of snacks that, typically, are hot, including dumplings with various fillings, and are ordered separately. [Cantonese, "light refreshment(s)"; literally, "dot of the heart", from *dim* dot, speck, drop + *sem* heart, centre.]

dim-wit (dím-wit) *n. Informal.* A stupid person. —**dim·wit·ted** (-wíttid) *adj.* —**dim·wit·ted·ly** *adv.* —**dim·wit·ted·ness** *n.*

din (din) *n.* A medley of resounding and discordant sounds; a continuing and unpleasant loud noise. See Synonyms at **noise.**
~*v.* dinned, dinning, dins. —*tr.* **1.** To stun or assail with deafening noise. **2.** To teach or instil by wearying repetition. Usually used with *into: din an idea into someone's head.* —*intr.* To make a din. [Middle English *dine, dune,* Old English *dyne.*]

DIN (din) *n.* A logarithmic scale used to express the speed of a photographic emulsion, film, or the like. The speed is equal to $-10 \log_{10}E$, where *E* is the exposure of a point 0.1 density units above the fog level. [German *Deutsche Industrie-Norm,* German Industry Standard.]

di·nar (dee-naar, dee-naár) *n. Abbr.* **din. 1. a.** The basic monetary unit of Iraq, Jordan, Kuwait, and South Yemen, equal to 1,000 fils. **b.** The basic monetary unit of Algeria, equal to 100 centimes. **c.** The basic monetary unit of Tunisia, equal to 1,000 millimes. **d.** The basic monetary unit of Yugoslavia, Bosnia-Herzegovina, Macedonia, and Croatia, equal to 100 paras. **2.** A monetary unit equal to 1/100 of the rial of Iran. **3.** A coin or note worth one dinar. **4.** Any of several units of gold and silver currency used in the Middle East from the 8th to the 19th century. [Arabic *dīnār,* from Late Greek *dēnarion,* DENARIUS.]

Di·nar·ic Alps (di-nárrik, dī-). *Serbo-Croat* **Dinara Planina.** Eastern European mountain range, stretching 700 kilometres (435 miles) from the Julian Alps of Slovenia southeastwards along the Adriatic coast to the Balkan Mountains of Albania.

Dinbych. See **Denbigh.**

dine (dīn) *v.* **dined, dining, dines.** —*intr.* **1.** To eat dinner. **2.** To eat something for dinner: *"They dined upon mince and slices of quince"* (Edward Lear). —*tr.* To entertain at dinner; give dinner to. —**dine out.** To dine away from home. —**dine out on.** To be invited to a meal or other social occasion largely because of (an interesting anecdote or experience one has to relate). [Middle English *dinen,* from Old French *di(s)ner,* to dine, breakfast, from Vulgar Latin *disjējūnāre* (unattested), to break one's fast : Latin *dis-* (reversal) + Latin *jējūnus†,* fasting, hungry.]

din·er (dīnər) *n.* **1.** A person taking dinner. **2.** A railway dining car. **3.** *U.S.* A restaurant with a long counter and booths, originally shaped like a railway carriage.

di·ner·ic (di-nérrik, dī-) *adj.* Of or pertaining to the interface between two immiscible liquids. [DI- + Late Greek *nēron,* water + -IC.]

Din·e·sen (dínni-s'n), **Isak,** pen name of Karen Dinesen, Baroness Blixen-Finecke (1885-1962). Danish author who lived in Kenya, East Africa, from 1914 to 1933. Among her books are *Winter's Tale* (1942), *Last Tales* (1957), *Anecdotes of Destiny* (1958), and two collections of her memoirs, *Out of Africa* (1938) and *Shadow on the Grass* (1961).

di·nette (dī-nét) *n.* **1.** A nook or alcove for informal meals. **2.** The table and chairs used in a dinette. [From DINE.]

ding[1] (ding) *v.* **dinged, dinging, dings.** —*intr.* **1.** To ring; clang. **2.** *Informal.* To speak persistently and repetitiously. —*tr.* **1.** To cause to clang, as by striking. **2.** *Informal.* To hammer into or at with repetitious talk.
~*n.* A ringing sound. [Probably imitative, but influenced by *ding,* to strike. See **dingbat.**]

ding[2] *n. Australian Slang.* A party. [Shortened from WINGDING].

Din·gaan (díng-gaan), also called Udingane (*c.* 1795-1843). Para-

mount chief of the Zulu nation at the height of the conflict between the Zulus and South Africa's white settlers. He is remembered as the man responsible for the massacre of Voortrekker leader Piet Retief and 101 of his followers on February 6, 1838.

ding·bat (díng-bat) *n. U.S. Informal.* **1.** Any unspecified gadget or other article; a thingamabob. **2.** A beggar; a tramp. [Probably obsolete *ding,* to strike, Middle English *dingen,* probably from Old Norse *dengja,* to cudgel, from Germanic *ding-* (unattested) + BAT (cudgel).]

ding·bats (díng-bats) *pl. n. Australian & N.Z. Informal.* **Delirium tremens** *(see).* Preceded by *the.* —**give (someone) the dingbats.** To make nervous or uncomfortable.
~*adj. Australian & N.Z. Informal.* Mad; stupid. [Perhaps from *ding,* to strike, beat + BAT (as in sports).]

ding-dong (díng-dòng, -dong) *n.* **1.** The peal of a bell. **2.** Any similar repeating sound. **3.** *Informal.* A violent argument or brawl.
~*intr.v.* **ding-donged, -donging, -dongs.** To ring; peal.
~*adj.* Characterised by a vigorous exchange, as of blows or insults. [Imitative.]

din·ghy (díng-gi, -i) *n., pl.* **-ghies.** Also **din·gey** *pl.* **-eys.** Any small open boat. [Hindi *dĩngī, dẽngī,* diminutive of *dẽṅgā†,* boat.]

din·gle (díng-g'l) *n.* A small, wooded valley; a dell. [Middle English *dingle†.*]

din·go (díng-gō) *n., pl.* **-goes. 1.** A wild dog, *Canis dingo,* of Australia, having a yellowish-brown coat. **2.** *Australian Slang.* A cowardly or treacherous person. [From a native Australian name.]

din·gus (díng-gəss, -əss) *n. Informal.* A gadget or other article whose name eludes one or is not known. [Dutch *dinges,* probably from German *Dinges,* genitive of *Ding,* thing, from Old High German *ding.*]

din·gy (dínji) *adj.* **-gier, -giest. 1.** Dark and dull, as from smoke, grime, or lack of daylight; dim, dirty, or discoloured. **2.** Shabby; worn. [Possibly from Middle English *dinge,* rare variant of *dung, dong,* DUNG.] —**din·gi·ly** *adv.* —**din·gi·ness** *n.*

dining car *n.* A railway carriage in which meals are served. Also called "restaurant car".

dining room *n.* A room in which meals are eaten.

di·ni·tro·ben·zene (dī-nítrō-bén-zeen, ‖ -ben-zéen) *n.* Any of three isomeric compounds, $C_6H_4(NO_2)_2$, made from a mixture of nitric acid, sulphuric acid, and benzene and used in celluloid manufacture, in dyes, and in organic syntheses.

di·ni·tro·gen tetroxide (dī-nítrə-jən, -nítrō-) *n.* **Nitrogen tetroxide** *(see).*

Din·ka (dingkə) *n., pl.* **-kas** or collectively **Dinka. 1.** A member of a group of Nilotic tribes of the southern Sudan. **2.** The East Sudanic language of this people. [Dinka *jieng,* "people".]

din·kum (díngkəm) *adj. Australian & N.Z. Informal.* True; genuine; real. Often used interjectionally in the phrase *fair dinkum.*
~*adv. Australian & N.Z. Informal.* Truly; honestly. [19th century : origin obscure.]

dinkum oil *n. Australian & N.Z. Informal.* The truth; trustworthy information.

dink·y (díngki) *adj.* **-ier, -iest. 1.** *Informal.* Dainty; small and neat; cute. **2.** *U.S. Informal.* Of small size or consequence; insignificant. [Probably from Scottish *dink†,* trim, neat.]

dink·y-di (díngki-dī) *adj. Australian & N.Z. Informal.* Genuine; real; dinkum. [Variant of DINKUM.]

din·ner (dínnər) *n.* **1.** The chief meal of the day, eaten at midday or in the evening. **2.** A banquet or formal meal, especially one in honour of some person or commemorating an occasion. [Middle English *diner,* from Old French *di(s)ner,* from *di(s)ner,* to DINE.]

dinner jacket *n.* A man's jacket, usually black with satin lapels, worn on formal occasions. Also *chiefly U.S.* "tuxedo".

dinner service *n.* A set of matching plates, saucers, and other china or crockery, used in serving a dinner. Also called "dinner set".

di·no·flag·el·late (dīnō-flájə-lət, -flə-jé-, -lit, -layt) *n.* Any of numerous minute, chiefly marine organisms, characteristically having two flagella and a cellulose outer envelope, and forming one of the chief constituents of plankton. They can be classified as protozoans (group Dinoflagellata) or algae (group Dinophyceae). [New Latin *Dinoflagellata,* "ones having whirling flagella" : Greek *dinos,* whirlpool, eddy, from *dinein†,* to whirl + FLAGELLUM.]

di·no·saur (dīnə-sawr) *n.* **1.** Any of various extinct, often gigantic reptiles of the orders Saurischia and Ornithischia, that existed during the Mesozoic era. **2.** An outmoded person or thing. [New Latin : Greek *deinos,* fearful, monstrous + -SAUR.] —**di·no·sau·ri·an** (-sáwri-ən) *adj. & n.* —**di·no·sau·ric** (-sáwrik) *adj.*

di·no·there (dīnə-theer) *n.* Any of various extinct elephant-like mammals of the genus *Dinotherium,* that existed during the Miocene, Pliocene, and Pleistocene epochs. [New Latin *dinotherium* : Greek *deinos,* fearful, monstrous + -THERE.]

dint (dint) *n.* **1.** Force or effort; power; exertion. Used in the phrase *by dint of.* **2.** A dent.
~*tr.v.* **dinted, dinting, dints.** To put a dent or dents in. [Middle English *dint, dunt,* Old English *dynt.* See **dent.**]

di·nu·cle·o·tide (dī-néw-kli-ə-tīd ‖ -nóo-) *n.* A compound consisting of two linked nucleotides, such as the coenzyme NAD.

Di·o Cas·si·us (dī-ō kássi-əss) (*c.* A.D. 155-235). Roman historian. His 80 books, written in Greek, traced the history of Rome from the legendary arrival of Aeneas in Italy up to A.D. 229.

di·oc·e·san (dī-óss-iss'n, -iz'n ‖ *US also* dī-ə-séez'n) *adj.* Of or pertaining to a diocese.
~*n.* **1.** A bishop of a diocese. **2.** A member of a diocese.

di·o·cese (dī́-ə-siss, -seess, -seez) *n. Abbr.* **dioc.** The district or churches under the jurisdiction of a bishop; a bishopric. [Middle English *diocise,* from Old French, from Late Latin *diocēsis,* from Latin *dioecēsis,* jurisdiction, district, from Greek *dioikēsis,* "housekeeping", administration, from *dioikein,* to keep house, administer : *dia-,* completely + *oikein,* to inhabit, from *oikos,* house.]

Di·o·cle·tian (dī-ə-kléesh'n), born Gaius Aurelius Valerius Diocletianus (A.D. 254–313). Roman emperor (284–305). In 286 he appointed Maximian as his co-emperor and divided the empire into east and west in order to govern more effectively. In 303, in a bid to revive the old religion he instituted the last major persecution of the Christians. Two years later, he and Maximian abdicated and retired to his grand palace at Salona (now Split, Croatia).

di·ode (dī́-ōd) *n.* **1.** An electronic component having one semiconductor junction, used chiefly as a rectifier. **2.** A simple thermionic valve having two electrodes: a cathode and an anode. [DI- + -ODE.]

di·oe·cious, di·e·cious (dī-éeshəss) *adj.* Also **di·oi·cous** (dī-óykəss). *Botany.* Having male and female flowers borne on separate plants. Compare **monoecious.** [New Latin *Dioecia* : DI- + Greek *oikia,* dwelling, from *oikos,* house.] **—di·oe·cious·ly** *adv.*

di·oe·strus (dī-ée-strəss) *n.* *Biology.* A stage in the oestrous cycle when the follicles and the uterus are small in size, and the epithelium layer surrounding the vagina is thin.

Di·og·e·nes (dī-ójineez), known as the Cynic (412–322 B.C.). Greek philosopher. Exiled with his father from Cinope, he settled in Athens and founded the Cynic school of philosophy, promoting self-control, acceptance of suffering, the avoidance of physical pleasure, and a return to nature.

di·ol (dī́-ol || -ōl) *n.* *Chemistry.* An alcohol that has two hydroxyl groups in its molecules; a dihydric alcohol. Also called "glycol".

Di·o·me·des (dī-ə-méedeez). Also **Di·o·med** (dī́-ə-med), **Di·o·mede** (-meed). *Greek Mythology.* A king of Argos and, in the Homeric poems, one of the chief heroes at Troy.

Di·o·nys·i·a (dī-ə-nízzi-ə, -níssi-, -nízhi-) *pl.n.* Any of various festivals of ancient Attica, held in honour of the god Dionysus, especially: **1.** The lesser festival, held in the autumn, in which the tragedy as a dramatic and literary form is thought to have had its origin. **2.** The great spring festival in Athens, at which competing plays were presented from the time of Pisistratus.

Di·o·nys·i·ac (dī-ə-nízzi-ak, -níssi-, -nízhi-) *adj.* **1.** Of or pertaining to Dionysus or the Dionysia. **2.** *Sometimes small* **d.** Dionysian, as opposed to Apollonian. **—Di·o·ny·si·a·cal·ly** *adv.*

Di·o·nys·i·an (dī-ə-nízzi-ən, -níssi-, -nízhi-) *adj.* **1.** Of or pertaining to any of several historical persons named Dionysius. **2.** Of or pertaining to Dionysus or the Dionysia. **3.** *Often small* **d. a.** Of an ecstatic, orgiastic, or irrational character. **b.** Filled with tremendous creative energy. **4.** *Sometimes small* **d.** In the philosophy of Nietzsche, characteristic of the spontaneous, irrational, creative, passionate qualities of human nature. Compare **Apollonian.**

Di·o·nys·i·us the Areopagite (dī-ə-níssi-əss || -níshəss), **Saint** (1st century A.D.). Greek martyr. A judge of the Areopagus, he was converted to Christianity by St. Paul and became the first Bishop of Athens.

Di·o·ny·sus, Di·o·ny·sos (dī-ə-nī́-səss). *Greek Mythology.* The god of wine and ecstasy, idol of an orgiastic religion celebrating the power and fertility of nature. Also called "Bacchus".

Di·o·phan·tine equation (dī-ō-fán-tīn, -ə-, -tin) *n.* *Mathematics.* An equation of two or more variables with integral coefficients, for which sets of possible integer solutions are required. [After DIOPHANTUS of Alexandria.]

Di·o·phan·tus of Alexandria (dī-ō-fántəss) (third or fourth century A.D.). Greek mathematician, credited with inventing algebra. His work, preserved by Arabic mathematicians, was translated into Latin in the 16th century.

di·op·side (dī-óp-sīd, -sid) *n.* A monoclinic pyroxene mineral, $CaMgSi_2O_6$, used as a gemstone and as a refractory. [French : DI- (two) + Greek *opsis* (stem *opsid-*), appearance, sight.]

di·op·tom·e·ter (dī-op-tómmitər) *n.* An instrument for measuring ocular refraction. [DI- + Greek *optos,* visible (see **optic**) + -METER.] **—di·op·tom·e·try** *n.*

di·op·tre, *U.S.* **di·op·ter** (dī-óptər) *n.* *Optics.* A unit, equal to a reciprocal metre, of curvature and of the power of lenses, refracting surfaces, and other optical systems. [French, from Latin, from Greek *dioptra,* an optical instrument : *dia-,* through + *opsesthai,* to see.] **—di·op·tral** *adj.*

di·op·tric (dī-óptrik) *adj.* Also **di·op·tri·cal** (-'l). *Optics.* **1.** Of or pertaining to dioptrics. **2.** Pertaining to optical refraction; refractive.

di·op·trics (dī-óptriks) *n.* *Used with a singular verb.* The study of the refraction of light, especially within the eye. [Greek *dioptrikos,* from *dioptra,* optical instrument : *dia-,* through + *optos,* visible.]

Di·or (dée-awr; *French* dee-ór), **Christian** (1905–57). French fashion designer noted for his "new look" for women's fashions in 1947. His styling featured fitted bodices and long, full skirts.

di·o·ram·a (dī-ə-ráa-mə || -rá-) *n.* **1.** A three-dimensional miniature scene with painted model or wax figures or stuffed animals against a background. Dioramas are often used for museum exhibits. **2.** A scene reproduced on cloth transparencies with various lights shining through the cloths to produce changes in effect, and viewed through a small aperture. [French : DI(A)- (through) + (PAN)ORAMA.] **—di·o·ram·ic** (dī-ə-rámmik) *adj.*

di·o·rite (dī́-ə-rīt) *n.* Any of various coarse-textured, crystalline igneous rocks rich in plagioglase and having little quartz, being intermediate between acid and basic rock. [French, from Greek *diorizein,* to distinguish : *dia-,* apart + *horizein,* to divide, from *horos,* boundary.] **—di·o·rit·ic** (-ríttik) *adj.*

Di·o·scor·i·des Pe·dan·i·us (dī-ə-skórrideez pe-dánni-əss) (*c.* A.D. 40–90). Greek physician. His *De Materia Medica* catalogued and described more than 600 plants and plant principles.

Di·os·cu·ri (dī-oss-kéwr-ī, dī-óskewr-ī). *Greek Mythology.* **Castor and Pollux** *(see).* [Greek *Dioskouroi,* "sons of Zeus" : *Dios,* genitive of ZEUS + *kouroi,* plural of *kouros,* boy, son.]

di·ox·an (dī-óks-an, -'n) *n.* Also **di·ox·ane** (-ayn). A flammable, potentially explosive, colourless liquid, $C_4H_8O_2$, used as a solvent for fats, greases, and resins and in various products including paints, lacquers, and fumigants.

di·ox·ide (dī-óksīd, dī-) *n.* An oxide with two oxygen atoms per molecule.

di·ox·in (dī-óksin) *n.* An extremely toxic substance that causes chloracne and genetic mutation, formed as a by-product in the manufacture of the herbicide 2,4,5 – T. Also called "tetrachlorodibenzo-p-dioxin", "TCDD".

dip (dip) *v.* **dipped, dipping, dips.** *—tr.* **1.** To plunge briefly in or into a liquid, usually in order to wet, coat, or saturate. **2.** To colour or dye in this manner. **3.** To immerse (livestock) in a disinfectant solution. **4.** To make (a candle) by repeatedly immersing a wick in melted wax or tallow. **5.** To galvanise or plate (metal) by immersion. **6.** To scoop up by plunging the hand or a container into and out of a liquid; bail; ladle. **7.** To lower and raise (a flag) in salute. **8.** *Chiefly British.* To put (vehicle headlights) on low beam. *—intr.* **1.** To plunge into water or other liquid and come out quickly. **2.** To plunge the hand or a container into a liquid or another container, especially for the purpose of taking something up or out: *dipped into her pocket.* **3.** To drop or sink suddenly. **4.** To appear to sink. **5.** To slope downwards; decline. **6.** *Geology.* To lie at an angle to the horizontal plane, as a rock stratum may. **7.** To read here and there in a book or magazine; browse. Used with *into.* **8.** To investigate a subject superficially; dabble. **9.** To use up money, especially one's savings. Used with *into.*

~n. **1.** A brief plunge or immersion; especially, a brief swim. **2.** A liquid into which something is dipped; especially, a **sheep dip** *(see).* **3.** A smooth creamed preparation, as of softened cheese, into which potato crisps, carrots, or the like may be dipped. **4.** An amount taken up by dipping. **5.** A container for dipping. **6.** A candle made by repeated dipping in tallow or wax. **7.** A downward slope; a decline. **8.** *Geology.* The downward inclination of a rock stratum in reference to the plane of the horizontal. **9.** *Surveying.* The angular difference between eye level and the lower level of the horizon. **10. Magnetic dip** *(see).* **11.** A hollow; a depression. **12.** In gymnastics, an exercise on the parallel bars in which the body is lowered by bending the elbows until the chin reaches the level of the bars and then is raised by straightening the arms. **13.** A lowering or loss of altitude, as of an aeroplane. **14.** *Slang.* A pickpocket. [Middle English *dippen,* Old English *dyppan,* from Germanic.]

Dip. A.D. Diploma in Art and Design (in Britain).

Dip. Ed. Diploma in Education (in Britain).

di·pep·tide (dī-péptīd) *n.* Any compound consisting of two amino acids linked by a peptide bond.

di·pet·al·ous (dī-pét'l-əss) *adj.* *Botany.* Having two petals.

di·phase (dī́-fayz) *adj.* Also **di·pha·sic** (dī-fáyzik). *Physics.* Having two phases.

di·phen·hy·dra·mine (dīfen-hī́drəmeen) *n.* An antihistamine drug used to treat hay fever and other allergic conditions.

di·phen·yl (dī-fée-nīl, -n'l, -fén'l) *n.* *Chemistry.* **Biphenyl** *(see).*

di·phen·yl·a·mine (dī-fée-nīl-ə-méen, -n'l-, -fén'l-, -ámmin) *n.* A colourless crystalline compound, $(C_6H_5)_2NH$, used as a stabiliser for plastics and in the manufacture of dyes, explosives, pesticides, and pharmaceuticals.

di·phen·yl·hy·dan·to·in sodium (dī-fée-nīl-hī-dántō-in, -fé-, -n'l-) *n.* A white powder, $C_{15}H_{11}N_2O_2Na$, used as an anticonvulsant in the treatment of grand mal epilepsy. Trademark: Dilantin.

di·phe·nyl·meth·a·none (di-pheen'l-méthənōn) *n.* **Benzophenone** *(see).*

di·phos·gene (dī-fóss-jeen || -fóz-) *n.* A colourless mobile liquid, $ClCOOCCl_3$, with a vapour used as a military poison gas, especially in World War I.

diph·the·ri·a (dif-théer-i-ə, dip-) *n.* An acute contagious disease caused by infection with the bacillus *Corynebacterium diphtheriae,* and characterised by the formation of a false membrane in the throat, causing difficulty in breathing, high fever, and weakness. [New Latin, from French *diphthérie,* from Greek *diphthera,* piece of leather (from the rough false membrane).] **—diph·the·rit·ic** (dífthə-ríttik), **diph·ther·ic** (-thérrik), **diph·the·ri·al, diph·ther·oid** *adj.*

diph·thong (díf-thong, díp-) *n.* *Phonetics.* **1.** A complex speech sound beginning with one vowel sound and moving to another vowel or semivowel position within the same syllable. For example, *oy* in the word *boy* is a diphthong. **2.** Either of the two ligatures *æ* or *œ,* originally pronounced as diphthongs in Classical Latin but in modern English rendered as single vowels. [Middle English *diptonge,* from Old French *diptongue,* from Late Latin *dipthongus,* from Greek *diphthongos* : DI- (two) + *phthongos*†, voice, sound. See also **monophthong, apothegm.**] **—diph·thon·gal** *adj.*

diph·thong·ise, diph·thong·ize (díf-thong-gīz, díp-, -īz) *v.* **-ised, -ising, -ises.** *—tr.* To pronounce as a diphthong. *—intr.* To become a diphthong. **—diph·thong·i·sa·tion** (-ī-záysh'n || *U.S.* -i-) *n.*

di·phy·cer·cal (díffi-sérk'l) *adj.* *Zoology.* Designating or having a tail fin in which the vertebral column extends to the tip, with symmetrical upper and lower parts. [Greek *diphuēs,* double, twofold + *kerkos,* tail.]

di·phy·let·ic (dī-fī-léttik) *adj.* Descended from two ancestral lines.

di·phyl·lous (dī-fíllǝss) *adj. Botany.* Having two leaves. [New Latin *diphyllus* : DI- + -PHYLLOUS.]

di·phy·o·dont (diffi-ō-dont, dī-fi-, -ǝ-) *adj. Zoology.* Having two successive sets of teeth, as do humans and most other mammals. [Greek *diphuēs,* double, twofold : DI- (two) + *phuein,* to bring forth, grow + -ODONT.]

dipl. diplomat; diplomatic.

dip·la·cu·sis (dípplǝ-kōō-siss, -kèw-) *n.* The hearing of a single sound as two sounds, due to a defect in the inner ear. [New Latin : DIPL(O)- + Greek *akousis,* hearing, from *akouein,* to hear.]

di·ple·gia (dī-plée-jǝ, -ji-ǝ) *n.* Paralysis of corresponding parts on both sides of the body. [DI- + -PLEGIA.]

di·plex (dípleks) *adj.* Capable of simultaneous transmission or reception of two messages in the same radio channel. [DI- + (DU)-PLEX.]

diplo-, dipl- *comb. form.* Indicates double; for example, **diploid.** [Greek, from *diploos,* double : DI- (two) + -*ploos,* "-fold".]

dip·lo·blas·tic (dípplō-blástik) *adj.* Having two distinct cellular layers. Said of lower invertebrate animals such as sponges and coelenterates. Compare **triploblastic.** [DIPLO- + -BLASTIC.]

dip·lo·car·di·ac (dípplō-kárdi-ak) *adj.* Having or characterising a heart in which the two sides are distinctly separated, as in birds and mammals. [DIPLO- + Greek *kardia,* heart.]

dip·lo·coc·cus (dípplō-kóckǝss) *n., pl.* **-cocci** (-kók-sī, -kóckī). Any of various paired spherical bacteria, including those of the genus *Diplococcus,* some of which are pathogenic. [New Latin : DIPLO- + -COCCUS.] **—dip·lo·coc·cal** (-kóck'l), **dip·lo·coc·cic** (-kók-sik, -kóckik) *adj.*

dip·lod·o·cus (di-plóddǝkǝss, díp-lǝ-dókǝss, -lō-) *n.* A very large, extinct, long-necked, herbivorous dinosaur of the genus *Diplodocus,* that existed during the Jurassic period. [New Latin : DIPLO- + Greek *dokos,* beam.]

dip·lo·ë (dípplō-ee) *n.* The spongy, bony tissue between the outer and inner bone layers of the cranium. [New Latin, from Greek *diploë,* "doubling", "fold", from *diploos,* double. See diplo-.]

dip·loid (dípp-loyd) *adj.* **1.** Double or twofold. **2.** *Genetics.* Having a homologous pair of chromosomes for each characteristic except sex, the total number of chromosomes being twice that of a gamete. Compare **haploid.**
~*n. Genetics.* **1.** A diploid cell. **2.** An individual characterised by a diploid chromosome number. [DIPL(O)- + -OID.]

di·plo·ma (di-plōmǝ) *n.* **1. a.** A document or certificate issued by a university, college, school, or other educational institution indicating that a certain level of proficiency has been reached, examinations passed, or a particular course of study successfully completed. **b.** The course of study followed in preparation for a diploma. **2.** A certificate conferring a privilege or honour. **3.** An official document or charter. [Latin, from Greek *diplōma,* something doubled, folded paper, document, from *diploos,* double. See diplo-.]

di·plo·ma·cy (di-plōmǝ-si) *n., pl.* **-cies. 1.** The art or practice of conducting international relations, as in negotiating alliances, treaties, and agreements. **2.** Tact or skill in dealing with people. —See Synonyms at **tact.**

dip·lo·mat (dípplǝ-mat) *n.* **1.** *Abbr.* **dipl.** A person appointed to represent one government in its relations with others, such as an ambassador. **2.** One who possesses skill or tact in dealing with others. [French *diplomate,* back-formation from *diplomatique,* DIPLOMATIC.]

dip·lo·mate (dípplǝ-mayt) *n.* One who has received a diploma; especially, a medical practitioner certified as a specialist by a board of examiners.

dip·lo·mat·ic (dípplǝ-máttik) *adj.* **1.** *Abbr.* **dipl.** Of, pertaining to, or involving diplomacy or diplomats. **2.** Characterised by tact and sensitivity in dealing with people; discreet; politic. **3. a.** Of or pertaining to diplomatics. **b.** Being an exact copy of an original: *a diplomatic edition.* —See Synonyms at **suave.** [French *diplomatique,* connected with the documents that regulate international relations, from New Latin *diplomaticus,* connected with documents or diplomatics, from Latin *diplōma,* document. See **diploma.**] **—dip·lo·mat·i·cal·ly** *adv.*

diplomatic corps *n.* The entire body of diplomatic personnel in residence at the capital of a nation.

diplomatic immunity *n.* Exemption from taxation and the ordinary processes of law afforded to diplomatic personnel in a foreign country.

dip·lo·mat·ics (dípplǝ-máttiks) *n. Used with a singular verb.* **1.** Diplomacy. **2.** The branch of palaeography devoted to the study of ancient documents and the determination of their age and authenticity. [Sense 1, see **diplomatic;** sense 2, see **diploma.**]

di·plo·ma·tist (di-plōmǝtist) *n.* A diplomat.

dip·lont (dípp-lont) *n. Biology.* An organism having somatic cells with diploid chromosomes. [DIPLO- + -*ont,* cell, from Greek *ōn* (stem *ont*-), present participle of *einai,* to be.]

di·plo·pi·a (di-plōpi-ǝ) *n. Pathology.* A disorder of vision which causes objects to appear double; double vision. [New Latin : DIPL(O)- + -OPIA.] **—di·plo·pic** (di-plóppik, -plōpik) *adj.*

dip·lo·pod (dípplǝ-pod) *n.* Any of various segmented, cylindrical arthropods of the class Diplopoda, which includes the millipedes. [New Latin *Diplopoda* : DIPLO- + -POD.] **—dip·lo·pod** *adj.*

di·plo·sis (di-plō-siss) *n.* The formation of the full (diploid) number of chromosomes found in a somatic cell by the fusion of gamete

nuclei containing haploid sets in fertilisation. [New Latin, from Greek *diplōsis,* a doubling, from *diploun,* to double, from *diploos,* double. See **diplo-.**]

dip·lo·tene (dípplō-teen) *n. Genetics.* A stage of the first prophase of meiosis during which crossing over occurs and the paired homologous chromosomes begin to separate. [DIPLO- + -*tene,* from Greek *tainia,* band.]

dip needle *n.* **1.** *Physics.* A magnetic needle balanced and pivoted to rotate freely in a vertical plane to indicate the local inclination of the earth's magnetic field. **2.** An instrument, the **inclinometer** *(see).*

dip·no·an (dip-nō-ǝn, dípnō-ǝn) *n.* Any of various fishes of the group Dipnoi, which includes the lungfishes, characterised by modified lungs that enable them to breathe atmospheric air. ~*adj.* Of or belonging to the Dipnoi. [New Latin *Dipnoi,* from *dipnous,* having two apertures for breathing, from Greek *dipnoos* : DI- + *pnoē,* breath, from *pnein,* to breathe.]

dip·o·dy (díppǝdi) *n., pl.* **-dies.** A metrical unit in poetry consisting of two feet. [Late Latin *dipodia,* from Greek, from *dipous* (stem *dipod*-), two-footed : DI- + -POD.]

di·po·lar (dī-pōlǝr, dī-pōlǝr) *adj.* Of or having a dipole.

di·pole (dī-pōl) *n.* **1.** *Physics.* A pair of electric charges or magnetic poles, of equal magnitude but of opposite sign or polarity, separated by a small distance. **2.** *Electronics.* An aerial, usually fed from the centre, consisting of two equal rods extending outwards in a straight line. In this sense, also called "dipole antenna".

dipole moment *n.* **1.** The product of either charge in an electric dipole with the distance separating them. Also called "electric dipole moment". **2.** The product of the strength of either pole in a magnetic dipole with the distance separating them. Also called "magnetic dipole moment".

dip·per (díppǝr) *n.* **1.** One that dips. **2.** A container used for dipping, such as a long-handled cup for taking up water. **3.** *Capital D. U.S.* Either of two star groups shaped like a ladle, the Plough (Big Dipper) and the smaller, similarly shaped group in Ursa Minor (Little Dipper). **4.** Any of several small diving birds of the genus *Cinclus.* Also called "water ouzel".

dip·py (díppi) *adj.* **-pier, -piest.** *Informal.* Foolish; not sensible. [20th century : origin obscure.]

di·pro·pel·lant (dīprǝ-péllǝnt) *n.* A **bipropellant** *(see).*

dip·sas (dip-sǝss) *n., pl.* **-sades** (-sǝ-deez). A serpent whose bite was fabled to produce a great thirst. [Middle English, from Latin, from Greek, from *dipsa†,* thirst.]

dip slope *n.* A land surface whose degree and direction of slope corresponds roughly with the dip of the underlying rock strata.

dip·so (dípsō) *n., pl* **-sos.** *Slang.* An alcoholic; a dipsomaniac.

dip·so·ma·ni·a (dípsǝ-máyni-ǝ, dipsō-) *n.* An insatiable, often periodic craving for alcoholic drink. [New Latin : Greek *dipsa†,* thirst + -MANIA.] **—dip·so·ma·ni·ac** (-máyni-ak) *n. & adj.* **—dip·so·ma·ni·a·cal** (-mǝ-nī-ǝk'l) *adj.*

dip·stick (díp-stik) *n.* **1.** A graduated rod for measuring the depth or amount of liquid in a container, as of oil in a crankcase. **2.** *Slang.* Someone crazy or foolish.

dip·switch (díp-swich) *n.* A switch, lever, or button for putting the headlights of a car on low beam.

dip·ter·al (díptǝrǝl) *adj.* **1.** *Architecture.* Built with two rows of columns. **2.** Variant of **dipterous.**

dip·ter·an (díp-tǝr-ǝn) *n.* Also **dip·ter·on** (-tǝ-ron). A dipterous insect. [New Latin *Diptera,* plural of *dipterus,* DIPTEROUS.] **—dip·ter·an** *adj.*

dip·ter·ous (díptǝrǝss) *adj.* Also **dipteral. 1.** Of, pertaining to, or belonging to the Diptera, a large order of insects which includes the true flies and mosquitoes, characterised by a single pair of membranous wings and a pair of club-shaped balancing organs, the halteres. **2.** *Botany.* Having two winglike parts: *the dipterous fruit of the maple.* [New Latin *dipterus,* from Greek *dipteros,* having two wings : DI- + -PTEROUS.]

dip·tych (díptik) *n.* **1.** An ancient writing tablet having two leaves hinged together. **2.** A pair of painted or carved panels hinged together. [Late Latin *diptycha,* from Greek *diptukha,* from *diptukhos,* double-folded : DI- + *ptukhē,* a fold, from *ptussein,* to fold.]

Di·rac (di-rák), **Paul Adrien Maurice** (1902–84). British mathematician and physicist. He received, with Erwin Schrödinger, the Nobel prize (1933) for his work on the quantum theory. In 1930, he introduced an equation that predicted the existence of antiparticles.

Dirac constant *n. Symbol* $\hbar$ A physical constant: the Planck constant divided by 2π. It is equal to 1.0544×10^{-34} joule seconds. [After P.A.M. DIRAC.]

dire (dīr) *adj.* **direr, direst. 1.** Having dreadful or terrible implications or consequences; calamitous. **2.** Extreme; urgent: *in dire need.* **3.** *Informal.* Hard to bear; tiresome or unpleasant. [Latin *dīrus,* fearful, ill-omened.] **—dire·ly** *adv.* **—dire·ness** *n.*

di·rect (di-rékt, dǝ-, dī-) *v.* **-rected, -recting, -rects.** —*tr.* **1.** To conduct the affairs of; manage; regulate. **2.** To take charge of with authority; control; give commands to. **3. a.** To guide (musicians, especially a small group) while playing oneself. **b.** *Chiefly U.S.* To conduct (musicians or a choir). **4.** To move (something or someone) towards a goal; aim; point. **5.** To give instructions to (someone) for finding a place. **6.** To address (mail) to a destination. **7.** To address (a speech, remark, or the like) to a person or audience. **8. a.** To give guidance and instruction to (actors, camera technicians, or the like) in the rehearsal and performance of a play or the making of a film. **b.** To supervise the performance of actors in. **c.** To supervise the creative aspects of the making of a (film). —*intr.* **1.** To give commands or directions. **2.** To supervise a performance, rehearsal, or the making of a film. —See Synonyms at **command, conduct.**

~*adj.* (*also* dĭr-ekt). **1.** Proceeding or lying in a straight course or line; not deviating or swerving. **2.** Straightforward; candid; frank. **3.** Without intervening persons, conditions, or agencies; immediate. **4.** By action of the voters, rather than through elected representatives or delegates: *direct elections to the European Parliament.* **5.** Of unbroken descent; lineal. **6. a.** Consisting of the exact words of the writer or speaker: *a direct crib.* **b.** *Grammar.* Repeated or reported exactly as originally spoken; addressed straight to the hearer or reader. Compare **indirect. 7.** Absolute; total: *direct opposites.* **8.** *Mathematics.* Varying in the same manner as another quantity; especially, increasing if another quantity increases or decreasing if it decreases. Compare **inverse. 9.** *Astronomy.* Designating a west-to-east motion of a planet or other celestial body in the same direction as the Sun's movement among the stars. Compare **retrograde.**

~*adv.* **1.** In a direct manner; straight; directly. **2.** Without going through a telephone operator: *dial direct.* [Middle English *directen,* from Latin *dīrigere* (past participle *dīrectus*), to arrange in distinct lines, direct : *dis-,* apart + *regere,* to guide.]

direct access *n. Computing.* **Random access** (see).

direct action *n.* The use of strikes, demonstrations, sabotage, and similar methods to exert pressure on a government, employer, or any other established authority. —**direct actionist** *n.*

di·rect-ac·tion (di-rékt-áksh'n, dĭr-ekt) *adj.* Operating without intermediate ingredients, components, stages, or processes.

Direct Broadcast Satellite *n.* **1.** A satellite that broadcasts television directly into the home. **2.** The system using such satellites.

direct current *n. Abbr.* **dc, D.C.** An electric current flowing in one direction only.

direct drive *n.* A mechanism in which the drive shaft is directly connected to the part to be driven.

di·rec·ted angle (di-réktid, dī-) *n.* An angle having an indicated positive sense.

directed distance *n.* A segment of a line having an indicated positive sense.

direct evidence *n. Law.* Evidence that bears directly on the fact in dispute, such as that of an eye-witness. Compare **circumstantial evidence.**

di·rect-grant school (di-rékt-graánt, dī- || -gránt) *n. British.* Formerly, a type of school for fee-paying pupils which received a central government grant conditional upon its acceptance of a percentage of pupils whose fees were paid by local councils.

di·rec·tion (di-réksh'n, dī-) *n.* **1.** The act or function of directing. **2.** Management, supervision, or guidance of some action or operation. **3.** The art or process of film or theatrical directing. **4.** A word or phrase in a musical score indicating how a particular passage is to be played or sung. **5.** *Usually plural.* An instruction or series of instructions for doing something. **6.** An order or command; an authoritative indication. **7. a.** The distance-independent relationship between two points that specifies the angular position of either with respect to the other; the relationship by which the alignment or orientation of any position with respect to any other position is established. **b.** A position to which motion or another position is referred. **c.** A line leading to a place or point. **d.** The line, course, or angle along which a person or thing moves. **e.** The destination of a person or thing. **8.** The statement, in degrees, of the angle measured between due north and a given line or course on a compass. Used to indicate the course of a ship, aircraft, or the like. **9.** A course or area of development or action. [Middle English, arrangement, management, from Old French, from Latin *dīrectiō* (stem *directiōn-*), from *dīrigere,* to DIRECT.]

di·rec·tion·al (di-réksh'n-əl, dī-) *adj.* Of or pertaining to spatial direction, especially one particular direction. —**di·rec·tion·al·i·ty** -ál-əti) *n.*

directional aerial *n.* An aerial adapted for receiving signals from or sending signals in a particular direction.

direction angle *n. Mathematics.* One of the three angles that a given line makes with the axes of a three-dimensional Cartesian coordinate system.

direction cosine *n. Mathematics.* The cosine of a direction angle of a given line.

direction finder *n.* A device for determining the source of a transmitted signal, consisting mainly of a radio receiver and a coiled rotating antenna.

direction indicator *n.* A compass used in aircraft navigation to compare an intended course to the actual course.

direction ratio *n. Mathematics.* One of three numbers that are proportional to the direction cosines of a given line.

di·rec·tive (di-réktiv, dī-) *n.* An order or instruction, especially one issued by a central authority.

~*adj.* Serving to direct, indicate, or point out; directing.

direct labour *n.* The hiring of labour directly, especially by a local authority, as opposed to using independent contractors.

di·rect·ly (di-réktli, dī-; *for sense 4 and conj., also* drékkli) *adv.* **1.** In a direct line or manner; straight. **2.** Without anyone or anything intervening; immediately. **3.** Exactly; totally; absolutely. **4.** At once; instantly. —See Synonyms at **immediately.**

~*conj. Chiefly British.* As soon as: *We'll go directly she's ready.*

direct mail *n.* **1.** A method of advertising by which a business or organisation approaches prospective customers or patrons directly through the post. **2.** The advertising matter so sent.

direct method *n.* A method of teaching a foreign language using

only the language being taught and introducing only a minimal amount of formal grammar.

direct object *n.* In English and some other languages, the word or words in a sentence designating the person or thing undergoing the action of a transitive verb and required to complete its syntactic function. The direct object in English is usually a noun, nominal clause or phrase, or pronoun, and generally follows the verb. In *The girl broke the dish,* the direct object is *the dish.* Compare **indirect object** *n.* See **object.**

Di·rec·toire (dée-rek-twár) *n.* The executive body in charge of the French government from 1795 to 1799. Also called "Directory".

~*adj.* Of or in the ornate style characteristic of the period of the Directoire in France.

di·rec·tor (di-réktər, dī-) *n.* **1.** One who supervises, controls, or manages. **2.** A member of a board of persons which controls or governs the affairs of a business concern, institution, or the like. **3. a.** A person who supervises the creative aspects of a dramatic production and instructs the actors on stage. Compare **producer. b.** The person who supervises the creative aspects of the making of a film. **4.** *U.S.* The conductor of an orchestra or chorus. **5.** A surgical instrument used to control the direction and extent of an incision. —**di·rec·tor·ship** *n.*

di·rec·tor·ate (di-réktər-ət, dī-, -it) *n.* **1.** The office or position of a director. **2.** A board of directors.

di·rec·tor-gen·e·ral (di-réktər-jénnərəl, dī-, -jénrəl) *n., pl.* **directors-general.** *Abbr.* **D.G.** The person appointed overall head of a large institution or organisation.

di·rec·to·ri·al (di-rek-táwri-əl, dī- || -tóri-) *adj.* **1.** Of or pertaining to a director or directorate. **2.** Serving to direct; directive. —**di·rec·to·ri·al·ly** *adv.*

Director of Public Prosecutions *n. Abbr.* **DPP, D.P.P.** The chief government prosecutor in England and Wales, to whom the police must refer certain cases.

director's chair *n.* A type of light folding chair, usually of canvas on a wooden frame, as used typically by film directors.

di·rec·to·ry (di-rék-təri, də-, dī-, -tri) *n., pl.* **-ries.** **1.** One that directs. **2.** A book listing names, addresses, and telephone numbers of: **a.** Persons living in a particular area, usually listed alphabetically. **b.** A specific group of persons or firms, listed according to a trade or service offered. **3.** A book of rules or directions, especially for use in church worship. **4.** A directorate.

~*adj.* Serving to direct.

Di·rec·to·ry (di-rék-təri, dī-, -tri) *n.* The **Directoire** (see).

direct primary *n. U.S.* A preliminary election in which a party's candidates for public office are nominated by popular vote.

di·rec·tress (di-réktrəss, dī-) *n. Rare.* A female director.

di·rec·trix (di-rék-triks, dī-) *n., pl.* **-trixes** or **-trices** (-tri-seez). **1.** *Geometry.* **a.** The straight reference line used in generating a conic. **b.** The curve about which the generator moves in forming a cone, cylinder, or other surface. **2.** *Military.* The median line in the trajectory of fire. [New Latin, "directress", from Late Latin *dīrector,* DIRECTOR.]

direct speech *n.* Speech or writing that is reported in its exact original form. Compare **indirect speech.**

direct tax *n.* A tax, such as an income or property tax, levied directly on the taxpayer. Compare **indirect tax.**

dire·ful (dīrf'l) *adj.* Dreadful; frightful; dire. —**dire·ful·ly** *adv.* —**dire·ful·ness** *n.*

dirge (durj) *n.* **1.** A funeral hymn or lament. **2.** *Ecclesiastical.* The office for the dead; a funeral service that is sung. [Middle English *dirige, derge,* from the first word in Medieval Latin *dīrige, Domine, Deus meus, in conspectu tuo viam meam,* "Direct, O Lord, my God, my way in thy sight" (an antiphon in the office of the dead, adopted from Psalms 5:9), from Latin, singular imperative of *dīrigere,* to DIRECT.] —**dirge·ful** *adj.*

dir·ham (déer-am, -əm || di-rám) *n.* **1.** The basic monetary unit of Morocco, divided into 100 centimes. **2.** The basic monetary unit of the United Arab Emirates, divided into 100 fils. **3.** A coin of various North African and Middle Eastern countries. [Arabic *dirham,* from Greek *drakhmē,* DRACHMA.]

dir·i·gi·ble (dírrij-ib'l, di-ríj-) *n.* An early steerable airship.

~*adj.* Able to be guided or steered. [Latin *dīrigere,* to guide, DIRECT.] —**dir·i·gi·bil·i·ty** (dírri-ji-bíllәti) *n.*

dir·i·ment (dírrimənt) *adj.* Rendering totally void; nullifying. Used especially in common law in the phrase *diriment impediment of marriage* to signify any sufficient cause for voiding a marriage. [Latin *dīrimēns* (stem *dīriment-*), present participle of *dīrimere,* to take apart, separate, interrupt : *dis-,* apart + *emere,* to take, buy.]

dirk (durk) *n.* A dagger, especially as worn by Scottish Highlanders. ~*tr.v.* **dirked, dirking, dirks.** To stab with a dirk. [Earlier *durk, dork,* probably related to or altered from German *Dolch,* dagger.]

dirn·dl (dúrnd'l) *n.* **1.** A full-skirted dress with a tight bodice, patterned after Tyrolean peasant wear. **2.** A gathered skirt in this style. [German, short for *Dirndlkleid : Dirndl,* diminutive of *Dirne,* girl, from Old High German *thiorna,* maid + *Kleid,* dress.]

dirt (durt) *n.* **1.** Earth or soil. **2.** A filthy or soiling substance, such as mud, dust, or excrement. **3.** Something or somebody mean, contemptible, or vile. **4.** Obscene language. **5.** Malicious or scandalous gossip. **6.** Gravel, slag, or other material from which metal is extracted in mining. **7.** Earth, gravel, or the like that has been pressed down to create a road surface.

~*adj.* Made of dirt: *a dirt track.* [Middle English *dirt,* variant of *drit,* excrement, mud, filth, from Old Norse *drit,* from Germanic *drit-* (unattested).]

dirt-cheap (dúrt-chéep) *adj. Informal.* Very cheap. **—dirt-cheap** *adv.*

dirt farmer *n. U.S. Informal.* A farmer who does all his own work.

dirt-y (dúrti) *adj.* **-ier, -iest. 1.** Soiled, as with dirt; grimy; unclean. **2.** *Informal.* **a.** Obscene or scatological. **b.** Sexually abusive. **3.** Contemptibly contrary to honour or rules; underhand; nasty: *a dirty trick.* **4.** Of a clouded or muddy appearance. Said especially of colours. **5.** Designating a nuclear weapon that produces an excessive amount of radioactive fallout. **6.** Stormy; rough: *dirty weather.* **7.** Tending to soil or make grubby: *dirty work.* **8.** Expressing hostility or ill-will: *a dirty look.* **—do the dirty on.** *Informal.* To act in an underhand or unfair way towards. **~v. dirtied, -ying, -ies.** *—tr.* To make soiled; stain; tarnish. *—intr.* To become dirty. [Middle English *dritti, dirti,* from *drit,* DIRT.] **—dirt-i-ly** *adv.* **—dirt-i-ness** *n.*
Synonyms: *dirty, filthy, foul, nasty, squalid, soiled, grimy.*

dirty linen *n. Informal.* Potentially embarrassing private affairs, such as those of a married couple. Used chiefly in the phrase *wash one's dirty linen in public.*

dirty old man *n. Abbr.* **D.O.M. 1.** A man, usually middle-aged or elderly, who makes furtive and unwelcome sexual advances to women and children. **2.** Any man seen as entertaining lewd or lecherous thoughts.

dirty protest *n.* A protest, as by prisoners, involving the deliberate neglect of personal hygiene and sometimes the smearing of cell walls with faeces.

dirty tricks *pl.n. Chiefly U.S.* Underhand political activities; especially, dishonest practices used in an election campaign to discredit opponents or subvert the electoral process.

dirty weekend *n.* An illicit weekend spent with a lover.

dirty word *n.* **1.** A swearword; an obscenity. **2.** Something disapproved of or regarded as objectionable.

dirty work *n. Informal.* **1.** Foul play; deceit. **2.** A difficult or distasteful chore or task, especially when delegated to a subordinate.

dis. Variant of **diss.**

dis- *prefix.* Indicates: **1.** Negation, lack, invalidation, or deprivation; for example, **distrust, disuse. 2.** Reversal; for example, **disengage, disunite. 3.** Removal or rejection; for example, **discard, disbar. 4.** Intensification or completion of negative action; for example, **disrupt.** [In borrowed Latin and French compounds, Latin *dis-* (Old French *des-*) indicates: 1. Apart, asunder, aside, as in **digress, distrain. 2.** Away, abroad, in different directions, as in **dismiss, divulge, disseminate. 3.** Negation, deprivation, as in **diffident, disparage. 4.** Reversal, as in **dissimulate. 5.** Removal, as in **dismantle. 6.** Intensification or completion of divisive action, as in **disturb, dissever. 7.** Pejoration, as in **disaster.** Latin *dis-* (sometimes *di-*) is the preverbal form of *dis†,* apart, asunder.]

dis-a-bil-i-ty (diss-ə-billəti) *n., pl.* **-ties. 1.** A disabled state or condition; incapacity. **2.** Something that disables; a handicap. **3.** A legal incapacity or disqualification.

dis-a-ble (diss-áyb'l) *tr.v.* **-bled, -bling, -bles. 1.** To weaken or destroy the normal physical or mental abilities of; cripple; incapacitate. **2.** To render legally disqualified. **3.** To make (a machine, for example) inoperative. **—dis-a-ble-ment** *n.*

dis-a-bled (diss-áyb'ld) *adj.* Physically handicapped; especially, lacking full use of one's limbs.

dis-a-buse (diss-ə-béwz) *tr.v.* **-bused, -busing, -buses.** To free from a false impression or misconception; undeceive.

di-sac-cha-ride (dī-sáckə-rīd, -rid) *n. Chemistry.* Any of a class of carbohydrates, including lactose and sucrose, that yield two monosaccharides on hydrolysis.

dis-ac-cord (diss-ə-kórd) *n.* Lack of accord; disagreement. **~intr.v. disaccorded, -cording, -cords.** *Rare.* To disagree.

dis-ac-cus-tom (diss-ə-kústəm) *tr.v.* **-tomed, -toming, -toms.** To cause to become unaccustomed.

dis-ad-van-tage (diss-əd-vaàn-tij ‖ -ván-) *n.* **1.** An unfavourable condition or circumstance; a handicap. **2.** Detriment. **~tr.v. disadvantaged, -taging, -tages.** To put at a disadvantage; set back.

dis-ad-van-taged (diss-əd-vaàn-tijd ‖ -ván-) *adj.* Subjected to severe economic and social disadvantage.

dis-ad-van-ta-geous (diss-ad-vaan-táyjəss, -əd-, diss-ád-, -vən- ‖ -van-) *adj.* Detrimental; unfavourable; harmful. **—dis-ad-van-ta-geous-ly** *adv.* **—dis-ad-van-ta-geous-ness** *n.*

dis-af-fect (diss-ə-fékt) *tr.v.* **-fected, -fecting, -fects.** To cause to lose affection or loyalty; alienate.

dis-af-fect-ed (diss-ə-féktid) *adj.* No longer contented and loyal; alienated. **—dis-af-fect-ed-ly** *adv.*

dis-af-fec-tion (diss-ə-féksh'n) *n.* Absence or withdrawal of affection or loyalty.

dis-af-fil-i-ate (diss-ə-fílli-ayt) *v.* **-ated, -ating, -ates.** *—tr.* To disassociate (oneself or another) from an alliance. *—intr.* To sever an affiliation or association. **—dis-af-fil-i-a-tion** (diss-ə-filli-áysh'n) *n.*

dis-af-firm (diss-ə-fúrm) *tr.v.* **-firmed, -firming, -firms. 1.** To deny or contradict. **2.** *Law.* **a.** To repudiate. **b.** To set aside; reverse. **—dis-af-fir-mance** (-ənss), **dis-af-fir-ma-tion** *n.*

dis-a-gree (diss-ə-grée) *intr.v.* **-greed, -greeing, -grees. 1.** To be different or inconsistent; fail to correspond. **2.** To have a different opinion; fail to agree; dissent. **3.** To dispute; quarrel. **4.** To cause adverse effects; be incompatible: *Something I ate disagreed with me.*

dis-a-gree-a-ble (diss-ə-grée-əb'l) *adj.* **1.** Unpleasant; offensive;

distasteful. **2.** Quarrelsome; bad-tempered. **—dis-a-gree-a-ble-ness** *n.* **—dis-a-gree-a-bly** *adv.*

dis-a-gree-ment (diss-ə-gréemənt) *n.* **1.** A failure or refusal to agree. **2.** Disparity; inconsistency. **3.** A conflict or difference of opinion.

dis-al-low (diss-ə-lów) *tr.v.* **-lowed, -lowing, -lows. 1.** To refuse to allow. **2.** To reject as invalid, untrue, or improper. **—dis-al-low-a-ble** *adj.* **—dis-al-low-ance** *n.*

dis-am-big-u-ate (diss-am-bíggew-ayt) *tr.v.* **ated, -ating, -ates.** To remove the ambiguity from (an ambiguous word or statement). **—dis-am-big-u-a-tion** *n.*

dis-an-nul (diss-ə-núl) *tr.v.* **-nulled, -nulling, -nuls.** To annul completely; make void; cancel. **—dis-an-nul-ment** *n.*

dis-ap-pear (diss-ə-péer) *intr.v.* **-peared, -pearing, -pears. 1. a.** To pass out of sight, either suddenly or gradually; vanish. **b.** To cease to be perceived by the senses: *the pain has disappeared.* **2.** To die out; become extinct. **3.** To become lost or absent, often in a mysterious or sinister way. **—dis-ap-pear-ance** *n.*

dis-ap-point (diss-ə-póynt) *tr.v.* **-pointed, -pointing, -points. 1.** To fail to satisfy the hope, desire, or expectation of. **2.** To frustrate; thwart. *—intr. Informal.* To cause disappointment: *His latest play disappoints.* [Middle English *disappointen,* to remove from office, dispossess, from Old French *desapointier* : *des-,* from Latin *dis-* (reversal) + *apointier,* to APPOINT.] **—dis-ap-point-er** *n.* **—dis-ap-point-ing-ly** *adv.*

dis-ap-point-ed (diss-ə-póynt-id) *adj.* Made unhappy by the failure of hopes or expectations; frustrated. **—dis-ap-point-ed-ly** *adv.*

dis-ap-point-ment (diss-ə-póynt-mənt) *n.* **1. a.** The act of disappointing. **b.** The condition or feeling of being disappointed. **c.** An instance of disappointing or being disappointed. **2.** A person, thing, or state of affairs that disappoints.

dis-ap-pro-ba-tion (diss-ápprə-báysh'n, diss-) *n.* Moral disapproval; condemnation.

dis-ap-prov-al (diss-ə-próov'l) *n.* The act of disapproving; condemnation; censure.

dis-ap-prove (diss-ə-próov) *v.* **-proved, -proving, -proves.** *—tr.* **1.** To have an unfavourable opinion of; censure; condemn. **2.** To refuse to approve. *—intr.* To regard something as wrong, especially morally wrong; have an unfavourable opinion. Used with *of.* **—dis-ap-prov-ing-ly** *adv.*

dis-arm (diss-árm ‖ diz-) *v.* **-armed, -arming, -arms.** *—tr.* **1.** To deprive of weapons; divest of arms. **2.** To deprive of the means of attack or defence; render helpless or harmless. **3.** To overcome or allay the suspicion, hostility, or antagonism of; win the confidence of. **4.** To win the affection of; charm. *—intr.* **1.** To lay down arms. **2.** To reduce or abolish one's stock of weapons, armaments, or armed forces. **—dis-arm-er** *n.*

dis-ar-ma-ment (diss-árm-ə-mənt ‖ diz-) *n.* **1.** The act of laying down arms; especially, the reduction or abolition of military forces and armaments by a national government. **2.** The condition of being disarmed.

dis-arm-ing (diss-árm-ing ‖ diz-) *adj.* Tending to remove suspicion or hostility; winning; endearing. **—dis-arm-ing-ly** *adv.*

dis-ar-range (diss-ə-ráynj) *tr.v.* **-ranged, -ranging, -ranges.** To upset the arrangement of; disorder. **—dis-ar-range-ment** *n.*

dis-ar-ray (diss-ə-ráy) *n.* **1.** A state of disorder; disarrangement; confusion. **2.** Disordered or untidy dress. **~tr.v. disarrayed, -raying, -rays.** To throw into confusion; upset.

dis-ar-tic-u-late (diss-ar-tíckew-layt) *v.* **-lated, -lating, -lates.** *—tr.* To separate at the joints; disjoint. *—intr.* To come apart at the joints; become disjointed. **—dis-ar-tic-u-la-tion** (-láysh'n) *n.* **—dis-ar-tic-u-la-tor** (-laytər) *n.*

dis-as-sem-ble (diss-ə-sémb'l) *tr.v.* **-bled, -bling, -bles.** To take apart. **—dis-as-sem-bly** *n.*

dis-as-so-ci-ate (diss-ə-sṓ-shi-ayt, -si-) *tr.v.* **-ated, -ating, -ates.** To dissociate. See Usage note at **dissociate.** **—dis-as-so-ci-a-tion** (-áysh'n) *n.*

dis-as-ter (di-zaàstər ‖ -zástər) *n.* **1. a.** An occurrence inflicting widespread destruction and distress. **b.** A grave misfortune. **2.** *Informal.* A total failure. **3.** *Obsolete.* An unfavourable influence of a celestial body. [French *désastre,* from Italian *disastro,* back-formation from *disastrato,* "ill-starred" : *dis-,* from Latin (pejorative) + *astro,* star, from Latin *astrum,* from Greek *astron.*]
Synonyms: *disaster, calamity, catastrophe, cataclysm, debacle.*

disaster area *n.* **1.** An area where a major disaster has occurred; especially, one officially designated as such and thus eligible for government or international aid. **2.** *Informal.* A person who is prone to accidents or misfortune. **3.** *Informal.* An untidy or disordered place.

dis-as-trous (di-zaàstrəss ‖ -zástrəss) *adj.* Calamitous; ruinous. **—dis-as-trous-ly** *adv.* **—dis-as-trous-ness** *n.*

dis-a-vow (diss-ə-vów) *tr.v.* **-vowed, -vowing, -vows.** To disclaim knowledge of, responsibility for, or association with; disown. **—dis-a-vow-al** *n.* **—dis-a-vow-er** *n.*

dis-band (diss-bánd) *v.* **-banded, -banding, -bands.** *—tr.* To break up (a group or unit, such as an army); dissolve. *—intr.* To become disbanded. **—dis-band-ment** *n.*

dis-bar (diss-bár) *tr.v.* **-barred, -barring, -bars. 1.** To expel (a barrister) from an Inn of Court, so that he no longer has the right to practise. **2.** Broadly, to expel from the legal profession. **—dis-bar-ment** *n.*

dis-be-lief (diss-bi-léef) *n.* Refusal or reluctance to believe.

dis-be-lieve (diss-bi-léev) *v.* **-lieved, -lieving, -lieves.** *—tr.* To refuse to believe; reject. *—intr.* To withhold belief. Used with *in.* **—dis·be·liev·er** *n.* **—dis·be·liev·ing·ly** *adv.*

Usage: In standard English this verb is not a simple opposite to *believe,* but has the specific meaning of "refuse to believe".

dis·branch (diss-bra̋anch || -bránch) *tr.v.* **-branched, -branching, -branches. 1.** To cut or break a branch or branches from (a tree). **2.** To remove (a limb or branch).

dis·bud (diss-búd) *tr.v.* **-budded, -budding, -buds. 1.** *Horticulture.* To remove buds from (a plant) to promote better blooms from remaining buds or to control the shape of the plant. **2.** To remove newly developing horns from (livestock).

dis·bur·den (diss-búrd'n) *v.* **-dened, -dening, -dens.** *—tr.* **1.** To relieve of a burden; especially, to relieve (oneself) of a feeling of anxiety or guilt. **2.** To unload or remove (a burden). *—intr.* To remove or unload a burden. **—dis·bur·den·ment** *n.*

dis·burse (diss-búrss) *tr.v.* **-bursed, -bursing, -burses.** To pay out; expend, as from a fund. [Old French *desbourser* : *des-,* from Latin *dis-* (reversal) + *bourse,* purse, from Medieval Latin *bursa,* from Greek.] **—dis·burs·a·ble** *adj.* **—dis·burs·er** *n.*

dis·burse·ment (diss-búrss-mənt) *n.* Also **dis·bur·sal** (-búrss'l). **1.** The act of disbursing. **2.** Money paid out; expenditure.

disc (disk) *n.* Also *chiefly U.S.* **disk. 1.** Any thin, flat, circular plate. **2.** Anything resembling such a plate, such as a star or planet seen from Earth, or an anatomical structure. See **intervertebral disc, slipped disc. 3.** *Botany.* The enlarged receptacle containing numerous tiny flowers in the flower head of many composite plants, such as the daisy. **4.** *Informal.* A gramophone record. **5.** *Computing.* Variant of **disk.**

Usage: In American English, the spelling *disk* is standard, *disc* being an infrequent variant. In British English, *disc* is standard, *disk* being encountered only in certain contexts, such as computing.

dis·calced (diss-kálst) *adj.* Barefoot. Said of certain orders of monks. [Latin *discalceātus* : *dis-,* not + *calceātus,* shod, from *calceus,* shoe.]

discant. Variant of **descant.**

dis·card (diss-kárd) *v.* **-carded, -carding, -cards.** *—tr.* **1.** To throw away; reject; dismiss as useless or unwanted. **2.** In card games: **a.** To throw out (an undesired card or cards) from one's hand. **b.** To play (a card other than a trump and different in suit from the card led). *—intr.* In card games, to discard a card.

~n. (*usually* díss-kard). **1.** The act of discarding. **2.** A person or thing that is discarded; especially, the card or cards discarded in a card game. **—dis·card·er** (diss-kárdər) *n.*

disc brake *n.* A type of brake that works by bringing hydraulically operated friction pads into contact with a disc that is fixed to, and rotates with, the road wheel of a motor vehicle.

dis·cern (di-sérn, -zérn) *v.* **-cerned, -cerning, -cerns.** *—tr.* **1.** To perceive (something obscure or concealed); detect. **2.** To perceive as distinct; discriminate. *—intr.* To perceive differences; make distinctions. —See Synonyms at **see.** [Middle English *discernen,* from Old French *discerner,* from Latin *discernere,* to "separate by sifting", distinguish between : *dis-,* apart + *cernere,* to sift, separate, perceive.] **—dis·cern·er** *n.*

dis·cern·i·ble (di-sérn-əb'l, -zérn-) *adj.* Perceptible; distinguishable. See Synonyms at **perceptible. —dis·cern·i·bly** *adv.*

dis·cern·ing (di-sérn-ing, -zérn-) *adj.* **1.** Astute; perceptive. **2.** Having or showing good taste or judgment. **—dis·cern·ing·ly** *adv.*

dis·cern·ment (di-sérn-mənt, -zérn-) *n.* **1.** The act or process of discerning. **2.** Keenness of discrimination; good judgment. —See Synonyms at **reason.**

disc flower *n.* Any of the tiny, tubular flowers forming the centre of the flower head of certain composite plants, such as the daisy. Also called "disc floret". Compare **ray flower.**

dis·charge (diss-chárj) *v.* **-charged, -charging, -charges.** *—tr.* **1.** To relieve of a burden or of contents; unload. **2.** To unload or empty (contents, such as ship's cargo). **3.** To release, as from confinement or hospital, or from duty. **4.** To dismiss from employment. **5.** To send or pour forth; emit. **6.** To shoot or fire (a projectile or weapon). **7.** To perform the obligations or demands of (an office, duty, or task). **8.** To acquit oneself of (a debt or promise); comply with the terms of. **9.** *Law.* **a.** To release (a defendant, for example). **b.** To set aside; dismiss; annul: *discharge a court order.* **10.** To remove (colour) from cloth, as by chemical bleaching. **11.** *Electricity.* To cause electrical discharge in (a battery, for example). **12.** *Architecture.* **a.** To apportion (weight) evenly, as over a door. **b.** To relieve (a part) of excess weight by distribution of pressure. *—intr.* **1.** To get rid of a burden, load, or weight. **2.** To fire a projectile or weapon. **3.** To pour forth contents. **4.** To become blurred; run. Used of dye or dyed cloth. **5.** To undergo electrical discharge. —See Synonyms at **perform.**

~n. (díss-charj, diss-chárj). **1.** The act of removing a load or burden; an unloading. **2.** The act of shooting or firing a projectile or weapon. **3.** A pouring forth; an emission; an ejection. **4.** The amount or rate of emission or ejection. **5.** Something that is discharged, released, or emitted: *vaginal discharge.* **6.** A relieving from or elimination of an obligation, burden, or responsibility. **7.** Fulfilment or performance. **8. a.** Dismissal or release from employment, service, or confinement. **b.** A document certifying such release, especially from military service. **9.** A legal annulment or acquittal; a dismissal, as of a court order. **10.** *Electricity.* **a.** The release of stored energy in a capacitor by the flow of electric current between its terminals. **b.** The conversion of chemical energy to electric energy in a battery. **c.** A flow of electricity in a gas, especially a continuous luminous flow in a gas at low pressure. **d.** The elimination of net electric charge from any charged body. [Middle English *dischargen,* from Old French *deschargier,* from Vulgar Latin *discarricāre* (unattested), to unload : *dis-* (reversal) + *carricāre* (unattested), to load, CHARGE.] **—dis·charge·a·ble** *adj.* **—dis·charg·er** *n.*

discharge lamp *n.* A lamp that generates light by means of an internal electrical discharge in a gas.

discharge tube *n.* A closed insulating tube fitted with electrodes and containing a gas in which an electrical discharge is induced by a high applied potential difference.

disc harrow *n.* A harrow equipped with a series of discs set on edge or at an angle on one or more axles.

disci. Alternative plural of **discus.**

dis·ci·ple (di-sīp'l) *n.* **1. a.** A person who subscribes to the doctrines and teachings of another, especially of a great teacher or leader. **b.** Any active adherent, as of a movement or philosophy. **2.** Any of Christ's personal followers. **3.** Loosely, any of the 12 Apostles. [Middle English *disciple,* Old English *discipul,* from Latin *discipulus,* pupil, from *discere,* to learn.] **—dis·ci·ple·ship** *n.*

Disciples of Christ *n.* A Christian denomination, founded in the United States in 1809, that accepts only the Bible as the rule of Christian faith and practice.

dis·ci·pli·nar·i·an (dissipli-naír-iən) *n.* A person who enforces or believes in strict discipline.

dis·ci·pli·nar·y (díssi-plin-əri, -plín-, -plīn- || -erri) *adj.* Also **dis·ci·pli·nal** (dissi-plīn'l, díssi-plin'l). Promoting or used for discipline.

dis·ci·pline (díssiplin || di-sípplin) *n.* **1.** Training that is expected to produce a particular character or pattern of behaviour, especially that which is expected to produce moral or mental improvement. **2.** Controlled behaviour resulting from such training; self-discipline. **3.** A systematic method of obtaining obedience: *military discipline.* **4.** A state of order based upon submission to rules and authority. **5.** Punishment intended to correct or train. **6.** In some religions, the mortification of the flesh as a penance. **7.** A set of rules or methods, such as those regulating the practice of a church or monastic order. **8.** A branch of knowledge or teaching.

~tr.v. **disciplined, -plining, -plines. 1.** To train by instruction and control; teach to obey rules or accept authority. **2.** To punish or penalise. **3.** To organise thoroughly; set in order: *a disciplined mind.* —See Synonyms at **teach, punish.** [Middle English, from Old French, from Latin *disciplīna,* instruction, knowledge, from *discipulus,* pupil, DISCIPLE.] **—dis·ci·plin·a·ble** *adj.* **—dis·ci·plin·er** *n.*

disc jockey *n. Abbr.* **DJ** A person who presents and comments on recordings of popular music, especially on the radio.

dis·claim (diss-kláym) *v.* **-claimed, -claiming, -claims.** *—tr.* **1.** To deny or renounce any claim to or connection with; disown. **2.** To deny the validity of; repudiate. **3.** *Law.* To renounce one's right or claim to. *—intr. Law.* To renounce a legal right or claim.

dis·claim·er (diss-kláymər) *n.* **1.** A repudiation or denial of a claim. **2.** A statement denying responsibility for something.

dis·cla·ma·tion (díss-klə-máysh'n) *n.* Disavowal; renunciation.

dis·cli·max (diss-klīmaks) *n.* A normally stable ecological community that has been altered by human or other influences, such as a grassland community that has been turned into desert by overgrazing.

dis·close (diss-klṓz) *tr.v.* **-closed, -closing, -closes. 1.** To expose to view, as by removing a cover; uncover. **2.** To make known; divulge (a secret, for example). —See Synonyms at **reveal. —dis·clos·er** *n.*

disclosing tablet *n.* A tablet used to show the presence of plaque on the teeth, reacting with it to produce a red stain.

dis·clo·sure (diss-klṓzhər) *n.* **1.** The act or process of disclosing. **2.** Something that is disclosed; a revelation.

dis·co (dískō) *n.* **1.** A **discotheque** *(see).* Also used adjectivally: *disco music.* **2.** A style of music or dancing as found in discotheques.

disco- *prefix.* Indicates a gramophone record; for example, **discophile.** [From DISC.]

dis·cob·o·lus (diss-kóbbə-ləss) *n., pl.* **-li** (-lī). A discus-thrower, or a statue of one, in ancient Greece or Rome. [Latin, from Greek *diskobolos* : *diskos,* quoit, DISC + *-bolos,* thrower, from *ballein,* to throw.]

dis·cog·ra·phy (diss-kóggrəfi) *n., pl.* **-phies.** A catalogue of gramophone records; especially, a comprehensive list of the recordings made by a particular performer or of a particular composer's works. [French *discographie* : DISCO- + -GRAPHY.] **—dis·cog·ra·pher** *n.*

dis·coid (díss-koyd) *adj.* Also **dis·coi·dal** (diss-kóyd'l). **1.** Having the shape of a disc. **2.** *Botany.* Having disc flowers but no ray flowers. Said of the flower head of a tansy and similar composite plants.

~n. A disc or an object shaped like a disc. [Late Latin *dīscoides,* disc-shaped, from Greek *diskoeidēs* : *diskos,* DISC + -OID.]

dis·col·or·a·tion (diss-kúllə-ráysh'n, diss-) *n.* **1. a.** The act of discolouring. **b.** The condition of being discoloured. **2.** A stain.

dis·col·our, *U.S.* **dis·co·lor** (diss-kúllər) *v.* **-oured, -ouring, -ours.** *—tr.* To alter or spoil the proper colour of; stain. *—intr.* To become changed or spoilt in colour.

dis·com·bob·u·late (díss-kəm-bóbbew-layt) *tr.v.* **-lated, -lating, -lates.** *Chiefly U.S. Slang.* To throw into a state of confusion; disconcert; upset. [Mock-Latin formation.]

dis·com·fit (diss-kúmfit) *tr.v.* **-fited, -fiting, -fits. 1.** To make uneasy or perplexed; disconcert; embarrass. **2.** To thwart the plans or purposes of; frustrate; foil. **3.** *Archaic.* To defeat in battle; rout; vanquish. [Middle English *discomfiten,* from Old French *desconfire* (past participle *disconfit*), to defeat, from Vulgar Latin *disconficere* (unattested) : Latin *dis-* (reversal) + *conficere*, to prepare, accomplish : *com-*, together + *facere*, to make.] **—dis·com·fi·ture** *n.*

dis·com·fort (diss-kúmfərt) *n.* **1.** The condition of being uncomfortable in body or mind; mild pain. **2.** Something that disturbs one's comfort; an annoyance.
~*tr.v.* **discomforted, -forting, -forts.** To make uneasy or uncomfortable.

dis·com·fort·a·ble (diss-kúm-fərtəb'l, -kúmftəb'l) *adj. Rare.* Not comfortable; distressed or distressing.

dis·com·mend (diss-kə-ménd) *tr.v.* **-mended, -mending, -mends.** *Formal.* To show or voice disapproval of. **—dis·com·mend·a·ble** *adj.*

dis·com·mode (diss-kə-mṓd) *tr.v.* **-moded, -moding, -modes.** *Formal.* To put to inconvenience; disturb. [French *discommoder* : Latin *dis-* (reversal) + *commode*, convenient (see **commode**).]

dis·com·pose (diss-kəm-pṓz ‖ -kom-) *tr.v.* **-posed, -posing, -poses. 1.** To disturb the composure or calm of; agitate; perturb. **2.** *Archaic.* To put into a state of disorder; disarrange. **—dis·com·pos·ed·ly** (-pṓzidli) *adv.* **—dis·com·pos·ing·ly** *adv.*

dis·com·po·sure (diss-kəm-pṓzhər ‖ -kom-) *n.* Absence of composure; a state of agitation.

dis·con·cert (diss-kən-sért ‖ -kon-) *tr.v.* **-certed, -certing, -certs. 1.** To upset the self-possession of; perturb; ruffle. **2.** To frustrate by throwing into disorder; upset; rout. [Obsolete French *disconcerter*, from Old French *desconcerter* : *des-*, from Latin *dis-* (reversal) + *concerter*, to bring into agreement, from Italian *concertare* (see **concert**).] **—dis·con·cert·ing·ly** *adv.*

dis·con·cert·ed (diss-kən-sértid ‖ -kon-) *adj.* Deprived of one's composure; thrown into confusion or embarrassment. **—dis·con·cert·ed·ly** *adv.* **—dis·con·cert·ed·ness** *n.*

dis·con·form·i·ty (díss-kən-fórməti ‖ -kon-) *n., pl.* **-ties.** *Geology.* A break in a stratigraphical sequence, caused by an interruption of sedimentation due to denudation. Compare **unconformity**.

dis·con·nect (díss-kə-nékt) *tr.v.* **-nected, -necting, -nects. 1.** To break or interrupt the connection of or between. **2.** To shut off the current in (an electrical appliance) by removing its connection with the power source. **3.** *Informal.* To cut off a power supply to the premises of: *If we don't pay the gas bill by Tuesday, we'll be disconnected.* **—dis·con·nec·tion** *n.*

dis·con·nect·ed (díss-kə-néktid) *adj.* **1.** Not connected; detached. **2.** Marked by a lack of logical connections; confused; incoherent. **—dis·con·nect·ed·ly** *adv.* **—dis·con·nect·ed·ness** *n.*

dis·con·so·late (diss-kón-sə-lət, -lit) *adj.* **1.** Too unhappy to be consoled; hopelessly sad. **2.** Cheerless; gloomy; dismal. [Middle English, from Medieval Latin *disconsōlātus* : Latin *dis-* (negative) + *consōlātus*, past participle of *consōlārī*, to CONSOLE.] **—dis·con·so·late·ly** *adv.* **—dis·con·so·late·ness, dis·con·so·la·tion** (-láysh'n) *n.*

dis·con·tent (díss-kən-tént ‖ -kon-) *n.* **1.** Absence of contentment; dissatisfaction. **2.** A sense of resentment and grievance.
~*adj.* Discontented.
~*tr.v.* **discontented, -tenting, -tents.** To cause dissatisfaction in; make discontented.

dis·con·tent·ed (díss-kən-téntid ‖ -kon-) *adj.* Restlessly unhappy; dissatisfied. **—dis·con·tent·ed·ly** *adv.* **—dis·con·tent·ed·ness** *n.*

dis·con·tin·u·ance (díss-kən-tínnew-ənss ‖ -kon-) *n.* **1.** The act of discontinuing or the condition of being discontinued; cessation. **2.** *Law.* The termination of an action by the plaintiff.

dis·con·tin·u·a·tion (díss-kən-tínnew-áysh'n ‖ -kon-) *n.* Discontinuance; cessation.

dis·con·tin·ue (díss-kən-tínnew ‖ -kon-) *v.* **-ued, -uing, -ues.** *—tr.* **1.** To cause to cease; put a stop to; terminate. **2.** To cease from; give up; abandon. **3.** *Law.* To terminate (an action) by discontinuance. **4.** To cease production of: *a sale of discontinued lines.* *—intr.* To come to an end. **—dis·con·tin·u·er** *n.*

dis·con·ti·nu·i·ty (díss-konti-néw-əti, diss-kónti- ‖ -nóō-əti) *n., pl.* **-ties. 1.** A lack of continuity, logical sequence, or cohesion. **2.** A break or gap. **3.** *Mathematics.* **a.** The property of being discontinuous. **b.** A point at which a function is defined but is not continuous. **c.** A point at which a function is undefined. **4.** *Geology.* A boundary across which the internal character of the earth changes abruptly, such as the Mohorovičić discontinuity. **5.** *Meteorology.* A **front** (*see*) or frontal zone.

dis·con·tin·u·ous (díss-kən-tínnew-əss ‖ -kon-) *adj.* **1.** Marked by breaks or interruptions; intermittent. **2.** *Mathematics.* Possessing one or more discontinuities. **—dis·con·tin·u·ous·ly** *adv.* **—dis·con·tin·u·ous·ness** *n.*

disc·o·phile (dískə-fīl) *n.* A collector of or specialist in gramophone records. [DISCO- + -PHILE.]

dis·cord (díss-kord) *n.* **1.** Lack of agreement among persons, groups, or things; dissension. **2.** A confused or harsh mingling of sounds; a din. **3.** *Music.* **a.** The inharmonious combination of simultaneously sounded notes; dissonance. Compare **concord**. **b.** Any chord exemplifying this.
~*intr.v.* (diss-kórd) **discorded, -cording, -cords.** To fail to agree or harmonise; clash. [Middle English, from Old French *descorde*, from Latin *discordia*, strife, from *discors*, disagreeing : *dis-*, apart + *cor* (stem *cord-*), heart.]

Synonyms: discord, strife, contention, dissension, conflict, clash, variance.

dis·cor·dant (diss-kórdənt) *adj.* **1.** Not in accord; conflicting. **2.** Disagreeable in sound; harsh or dissonant. **—See Synonyms at**

inconsistent. **—dis·cor·dance, dis·cor·dan·cy** *n.* **—dis·cor·dant·ly** *adv.*

dis·co·theque, dis·co·thè·que (díss-kə-tek ‖ -ték) *n.* **1.** A nightclub featuring dancing to amplified recorded music. **2.** Portable equipment for providing such music, as at a party. [French : DISCO- + -THÈQUE, record library, by analogy with *bibliothèque*, library.]

dis·count (diss-kównt, díss-kownt) *v.* **-counted, -counting, -counts.** *—tr.* **1.** To deduct or subtract (a specified sum or percentage) from a cost or price. **2. a.** To buy or sell (a promissory note such as a treasury bill) after deducting the amount of interest that will accumulate before it matures. **b.** To advance money as a loan on (a promissory note not immediately payable) after deducting the interest. **3.** To reduce in cost, quantity, or value. **4.** To leave out of account as being untrustworthy or exaggerated; disregard; ignore. **5.** To anticipate and make allowance for. *—intr.* To lend money after deduction of interest.
~*n.* (díss-kownt). **1.** A reduction from the full or standard amount of a price or debt. **2.** The interest deducted in advance in purchasing, selling, or lending a promissory note such as a treasury bill. **3.** The rate of interest deducted in such a transaction. Also called "discount rate". **4.** The act or an instance of discounting a bill of exchange, treasury bill, or the like.
~*adj.* Selling at prices below those set by manufacturers. [Obsolete French *descompte, descompter,* from Medieval Latin *discomputāre* : Latin *dis-* (reversal) + *computāre*, to add, sum up, COMPUTE.] **—dis·count·a·ble** (diss-kówntəb'l, díss-kowntəb'l) *adj.* **—dis·count·er** (diss-kowntər, -kówntər) *n.*

dis·coun·te·nance (diss-kówntinənss) *tr.v.* **-nanced, -nancing, -nances. 1.** To view or treat with disfavour. **2.** To embarrass; abash; disconcert.
~*n.* Disfavour; disapproval.

discount house *n.* **1.** *Finance.* An institution, especially one in the City of London, that deals in bills of exchange, treasury bills, and other securities. **2.** A shop selling goods, such as electrical appliances, at prices below those recommended by the manufacturers.

dis·cour·age (diss-kúrrij) *tr.v.* **-aged, -aging, -ages. 1.** To deprive of confidence, hope, or spirit; dishearten; daunt. **2.** To hamper or hinder. **3.** To dissuade or deter. Used with *from.* **4.** To try to prevent by expressing disapproval or raising objections: *The report discourages smoking.* **—dis·cour·ag·er** *n.* **—dis·cour·ag·ing·ly** *adv.*

dis·cour·age·ment (diss-kúrrij-mənt) *n.* **1. a.** The act of discouraging. **b.** The condition of being discouraged. **2.** Something that courages; a deterrent. **—See Synonyms at despair.**

dis·course (díss-kawrss ‖ -kórss) *n.* **1.** Verbal expression in speech or writing. **2.** Verbal exchange; conversation. **3.** A formal and lengthy discussion of a subject, either written or spoken. **4.** *Archaic.* The process or power of reasoning.
~*v.* (diss-kórss ‖ -kórss) **discoursed, -coursing, -courses.** *—intr.* **1.** To speak or write formally and at length. Used with *on* or *upon.* **2.** To engage in conversation or discussion; converse. *—tr. Archaic.* **1.** To narrate or discuss. **2.** To give forth (musical sounds); perform. **—See Synonyms at speak.** [Middle English *discours,* from Late Latin *discursus,* conversation, from Latin, "a running back and forth", from the past participle of *discurrere,* to run back and forth, speak at length : *dis-*, in different directions + *currere,* to run.] **—dis·cours·er** *n.*

dis·cour·te·ous (diss-kúrti-əss, -kórti-) *adj.* Lacking courtesy; impolite; rude. **—dis·cour·te·ous·ly** *adv.* **—dis·cour·te·ous·ness** *n.*

dis·cour·te·sy (diss-kúrtə-si, -kórtə-) *n., pl.* **-sies. 1.** Lack of courtesy; rudeness. **2.** A discourteous act or statement.

dis·cov·er (diss-kúvvər) *tr.v.* **-ered, -ering, -ers. 1.** To obtain knowledge of; arrive at through search or study. **2.** To be the first to find, learn of, or observe. **3.** To learn of or experience for the first time: *discover the pleasures of music.* **4.** *Informal.* To find that a (previously unknown person) has marketable talents. **5.** *Archaic.* To reveal; expose. **—dis·cov·er·er** *n.*

dis·cov·ert (diss-kúvvərt) *adj. Law.* Having no husband, and therefore not subject to coverture. Said of a woman. **—dis·cov·er·ture** *n.*

dis·cov·er·y (diss-kúvvəri) *n., pl.* **-ies. 1.** The act or an instance of discovering. **2. a.** Something that has been discovered. **b.** A person recently found to have a special talent. **3.** *Law.* The process whereby parties in an action are obliged to disclose any documents relevant to the case.

dis·cred·it (diss-kréddit) *tr.v.* **-ited, -iting, -its. 1.** To damage in reputation; disgrace; dishonour. **2.** To cast doubt on; cause to be distrusted. **3.** To give no credence to; disbelieve. **—See Synonyms at degrade.**
~*n.* **1.** Loss of or damage to one's reputation; dishonour; disgrace. **2.** Lack or loss of trust or belief; doubt. **3.** Anything damaging to one's reputation or stature. **—See Synonyms at disgrace.**

dis·cred·it·a·ble (diss-kréddit-əb'l) *adj.* Deserving of or resulting in discredit; blameworthy. **—dis·cred·it·a·bly** *adv.*

dis·creet (diss-kréet) *adj.* **1.** Showing a judicious reserve in one's speech or behaviour; especially, able to keep other people's secrets. **2.** Lacking ostentation or pretension; unobtrusive; modest. [Middle English, from Old French *discret,* from Medieval Latin *discrētus,* "showing good judgment", from Latin, past participle of *discernere,* to separate, DISCERN.] **—dis·creet·ly** *adv.* **—dis·creet·ness** *n.*

dis·crep·an·cy (diss-kréppən-si) *n., pl.* **-cies.** Also **dis·crep·ance** (-kréppənss). **1.** Divergence or disagreement, as between facts or claims; inconsistency. **2.** An instance of such disagreement. **—See Synonyms at difference.**

dis·crep·ant (diss-kréppənt) *adj.* Marked by discrepancy; not consistent or matching; disagreeing. [Middle English *discrepaunt,* from Latin *discrepāns* (stem *discrepant-*), present participle of *discrepāre,* to sound different, vary : *dis-,* apart + *crepāre,* to rattle, sound.] **—dis·crep·ant·ly** *adv.*

dis·crete (diss-kréet, díss-) *adj.* **1.** Constituting a separate thing; individual; distinct. **2.** Consisting of unconnected distinct parts. [Middle English, from Latin *discrētus,* separate. See **discreet.**] **—dis·crete·ly** *adv.* **—dis·crete·ness** *n.*

dis·cre·tion (diss-krésh'n) *n.* **1.** The quality of being discreet; prudent or cautious reserve. **2.** Freedom to act or judge on one's own; latitude of choice and action: *the age of discretion.* **—at (someone's) discretion.** In accordance with the wishes or judgment of.

dis·cre·tion·ar·y (diss-krésh'n-əri, -ri || -erri) *adj.* Also **dis·cre·tion·al** (diss-krésh'n-əl). **1.** Left to or regulated by one's own discretion or judgment. **2.** Based on consideration of a particular case, not on a general regulation: *a discretionary grant.* **—dis·cre·tion·ar·i·ly** *adv.*

dis·cri·mi·nant (diss-krímminənt) *n. Mathematics.* A value or function related to a polynomial equation, giving information about the nature of the roots of the equation. It is the product of the squares of all the differences of the roots taken in pairs; for a quadratic equation $ax^2 + bx + c = 0$, the discriminant is $b^2 - 4ac$. [Latin *discrīminans* (stem *discrīminant-*), present participle of *discrīmināre,* to DISCRIMINATE.]

dis·crim·i·nate (diss-krímmi-nayt) *v.* **-nated, -nating, -nates.** *—intr.* **1.** To make a clear distinction; differentiate. Often used with *between.* **2.** To act on the basis of prejudice. *—tr.* **1.** To perceive the distinguishing features of; recognise as distinct. **2.** To serve to mark; differentiate: *The ability to reason discriminates humans from animals.*

~adj. (-nət, -nit). Discriminating. [Latin *discrīmināre,* to divide, distinguish, from *discrīmen,* distinction.] **—dis·crim·i·nate·ly** *adv.*

dis·crim·i·nat·ing (diss-krímmi-nayting) *adj.* **1.** Able or tending to draw fine distinctions; discerning. **2.** Fastidiously selective. **3.** Serving to differentiate; distinctive. **4.** Showing favouritism or prejudice; differential, as a tariff may be. **—dis·crim·i·nat·ing·ly** *adv.*

dis·crim·i·na·tion (diss-krímmi-náysh'n) *n.* **1.** The act of discriminating. **2.** The ability or power to see or make fine distinctions; discernment. **3.** Attitude, behaviour, or treatment based on prejudice. **4.** *Electronics.* The use of a circuit to pass signals of one characteristic while rejecting others. See **discriminator.**

dis·crim·i·na·tive (diss-krímmi-nətiv || -naytiv) *adj.* **1.** Drawing distinctions; discriminating. **2.** Discriminatory. **—dis·crim·i·na·tive·ly** *adv.*

dis·crim·i·na·tor (diss-krímmi-naytər) *n.* **1.** One that discriminates. **2.** *Electronics.* A device that converts a property of a signal, such as frequency or phase, into an amplitude variation.

dis·crim·i·na·to·ry (diss-krímmi-nə-təri, -náy-, -tri) *adj.* **1.** Marked by or showing prejudice; biased. **2.** Discriminating. **—dis·crim·i·na·to·ri·ly** *adv.*

dis·crown (diss-krówn) *tr.v.* **-crowned, -crowning, -crowns.** To deprive of a crown; dethrone; depose.

dis·cur·sive (diss-kúr-siv) *adj.* **1.** Covering a wide field of subjects; rambling; digressive. **2.** Proceeding to a conclusion through reason rather than intuition. [Medieval Latin *discursīvus,* from Latin *discursus,* "a running back and forth". See **discourse.**] **—dis·cur·sive·ly** *adv.* **—dis·cur·sive·ness** *n.*

dis·cus (díss-kəss) *n., pl.* **-cuses** or **disci** (díss-kī, -ī). **1.** A disc, usually wooden with a metal rim and weighing 2 kilograms (4½ pounds), thrown for distance in athletic competitions. **2.** The field event in which this disc is thrown. **3.** A small, brilliantly coloured South American freshwater fish, *Symphysodon discus,* that has a disc-shaped body and is popular in home aquariums. [Latin, DISC.]

dis·cuss (diss-kúss) *tr.v.* **-cussed, -cussing, -cusses. 1.** To discourse about in speech or writing; treat of. **2.** To consider (a matter) by speaking together about it; debate. **3.** *Literary.* To consume (food or drink) with relish. Used humorously. [Middle English *discussen,* from Late Latin *discutere* (past participle *discussus*), to investigate, discuss, from Latin, to break up, scatter : *dis-,* apart + *quatere,* to shake.] **—dis·cuss·er** *n.* **—dis·cuss·i·ble** *adj.*

Synonyms: *discuss, argue, debate, dispute, contend.*

dis·cuss·ant (diss-kússənt) *n.* One who takes part in a discussion.

dis·cus·sion (diss-kúsh'n) *n.* **1.** The consideration of a subject by a group; an earnest conversation. **2.** A discourse by one person upon a topic; an exposition.

dis·dain (diss-dáyn) *tr.v.* **-dained, -daining, -dains. 1.** To regard or treat with haughty contempt; despise. **2.** To consider unworthy of oneself; refuse with scorn.

~n. A feeling, attitude, or show of scornful superiority; aloof contempt: *"a cold stare of lionlike disdain"* (Bram Stoker). [Middle English *desdeynen,* from Old French *desdeignier,* from Vulgar Latin *disdignāre* (unattested), variant of Latin *dēdignārī,* to scorn : *dē-* (reversal) + *dīgnāre,* to deem worthy, from *dignus,* worthy.]

dis·dain·ful (diss-dáynf'l) *adj.* Feeling or showing disdain; scornful and haughty. See Synonyms at **proud. —dis·dain·ful·ly** *adv.* **—dis·dain·ful·ness** *n.*

dis·ease (di-zéez) *n.* **1.** An abnormal condition of an organism or part, especially as a consequence of infection, inherent weakness, or environmental stress, that impairs normal physiological functioning. **2.** A condition or tendency, as of society, regarded as abnormal and pernicious. **3.** *Obsolete.* Lack of ease.

dis·eased (di-zéezd) *adj.* **1.** Affected with disease. **2.** Unhealthy; unsound; disordered.

dis·em·bark (diss-im-bárk, -em-) *v.* **-barked, -barking, -barks.** *—intr.* To go ashore from a ship. *—tr.* To put or cause to go ashore from a ship. **—dis·em·bar·ka·tion** (díss-im-bar-káysh'n, diss-ém-) *n.*

dis·em·bar·rass (díss-im-bárrəss, -em-) *tr.v.* **-rassed, -rassing, -rasses.** To free from something embarrassing, bothersome, or encumbering; relieve. **—dis·em·bar·rass·ment** *n.*

dis·em·bod·ied (díss-im-bóddid, -em-, -deed) *adj.* **1.** No longer connected with the body; ghostly. **2.** Unrelated to the real world.

dis·em·bod·y (díss-im-bóddi, -em-) *tr.v.* **-ied, -ying, -ies.** To free (the soul or spirit) from the body. **—dis·em·bod·i·ment** *n.*

dis·em·bogue (díss-im-bṓg, -em-) *v.* **-bogued, -boguing, -bogues.** *—intr.* To empty at the mouth. Used of a river. *—tr.* To discharge (waters) at the mouth. Used of a river. [Alteration of Spanish *desembocar* : *des-,* from Latin *dis-* (reversal) + *embocar,* to put into the mouth : *em-,* from Latin *in-,* in + *boca,* mouth, from Latin *bucca,* cheek.] **—dis·em·bogue·ment** *n.*

dis·em·bow·el (díss-im-bów-əl, -em-, -bówl) *tr.v.* **-elled** or *U.S.* **-eled, -elling** or *U.S.* **-eling, -els.** To remove the bowels from. **—dis·em·bow·el·ment** *n.*

dis·em·broil (díss-im-bróyl, -em-) *tr.v.* **-broiled, -broiling, -broils.** To free from a condition of complexity or confusion; disentangle.

dis·en·chant (díss-in-chaánt, -en- || -chánt) *tr.v.* **-chanted, -chanting, -chants.** To free from enchantment or illusion; undeceive. **—dis·en·chant·er** *n.* **—dis·en·chant·ment** *n.*

dis·en·chant·ed (díss-in-chaántid, -en- || -chántid) *adj.* Disappointed; disillusioned. Used with *with.*

dis·en·cum·ber (díss-in-kúmbər, -en-) *tr.v.* **-bered, -bering, -bers.** To relieve of encumbrances. **—dis·en·cum·ber·ment** *n.*

dis·en·dow (díss-in-dów, -en-) *tr.v.* **-dowed, -dowing, -dows.** To deprive of endowments.

dis·en·franch·ise (díss-in-fránchīz, -en-) *tr.v.* **-ised, -ising, -ises.** Also **dis·fran·chise** (diss-frán-chīz). **1.** To deprive (an individual) of a right to citizenship, especially of the right to vote. **2.** To deprive (a company, for example) of a privilege or franchise. **—dis·en·fran·chise·ment, dis·fran·chise·ment** (-chiz-mənt || -chīz-) *n.* **—dis·en·fran·chis·er, dis·fran·chis·er** *n.*

dis·en·gage (díss-in-gáyj, -en-) *v.* **-gaged, -gaging, -gages.** *—tr.* **1.** To release from something that holds fast, connects, or entangles, especially in a mechanical device. **2.** To unfasten; detach. **3.** *Archaic.* To release from an engagement, pledge, or obligation. *—intr.* To become disengaged; get loose, break contact with.

dis·en·gage·ment (díss-in-gáyjmənt, -en-) *n.* **1. a.** The act of disengaging. **b.** The condition of being disengaged. **2.** *Military.* Withdrawal of forces from a particular military theatre. **3.** Freedom from obligation; ease of manner.

dis·en·tail (díss-in-táyl, -en-) *tr.v.* **-tailed, -tailing, -tails.** *Law.* To release (an estate) from entail. **—dis·en·tail·ment** *n.*

dis·en·tan·gle (díss-in-táng-g'l, -en-) *v.* **-gled, -gling, -gles.** *—tr.* **1.** To extricate from entanglement or involvement; free. **2.** To clear up or resolve (a mystery, for example). *—intr.* To become disentangled. **—dis·en·tan·gle·ment** *n.*

dis·en·tomb (díss-in-tóom, -en-) *tr.v.* **-tombed, -tombing, -tombs.** To remove from or as if from a tomb. **—dis·en·tomb·ment** *n.*

dis·en·twine (díss-in-twín, -en-) *v.* **-twined, -twining, -twines.** *—tr.* To disentangle; untwine. *—intr.* To become untwined.

dis·e·qui·lib·ri·um (díss-ekwi-líbbri-əm, -eekwi- || diss-ékwi-, -éekwi-) *n.* Loss or lack of equilibrium or stability.

dis·es·tab·lish (díss-i-stábblish, -e-) *tr.v.* **-lished, -lishing, -lishes. 1.** To alter the status of (something established by authority or general acceptance). **2.** To deprive (a church) of the status of an **established church** *(see).* **—dis·es·tab·lish·ment** *n.*

dis·es·teem (díss-i-stéem) *tr.v.* **-teemed, -teeming, -teems.** To have little regard for; hold in disfavour.

~n. Lack of esteem.

dis·fa·vour (diss-fáyvər) *n.* **1.** Unfavourable opinion or regard; disapproval. **2.** The condition of being regarded with disapproval. **3.** A disservice.

~tr.v. **disfavoured, -vouring, -vours. 1.** To view or treat with dislike or disapproval. **2.** To withhold favour from.

dis·fig·ure (diss-fíggə || *U.S.* -fíg-yər) *tr.v.* **-ured, -uring, -ures.** To blemish or spoil the appearance or shape of. **—dis·fig·ur·er** *n.*

dis·fig·ure·ment (diss-fíggər-mənt || *U.S.* fíg-yər-) *n.* Also **dis·fig·u·ra·tion** (-fíg-yə-ráysh'n). **1. a.** The act of disfiguring. **b.** The condition of being disfigured. **2.** A deformity; a flaw.

disfranchise. Variant of **disenfranchise.**

dis·frock (diss-frók) *tr.v.* **-frocked, -frocking, -frocks.** To unfrock.

dis·gorge (diss-górj) *v.* **-gorged, -gorging, -gorges.** *—tr.* **1.** To bring up and expel from the throat or stomach; vomit. **2.** To discharge in a violent or confused manner; spew out. **3.** To yield up reluctantly. *—intr.* To discharge or pour forth contents. **—dis·gorge·ment** *n.*

dis·grace (diss-gráyss || diz-) *n.* **1.** Loss of honour, respect, or reputation; shame. **2.** The condition of being out of favour or badly thought of. **3.** Something that brings shame, dishonour, or disfavour. **4.** *Informal.* Something that is shocking in its poor quality or appearance.

~tr.v. **disgraced, -gracing, -graces. 1.** To bring shame or dishonour upon. **2.** To cause (someone) to lose favour or reputation. **—dis·grac·er** *n.*

Synonyms: *disgrace, dishonour, shame, infamy, ignominy, odium, scandal, obloquy, opprobrium, disrepute, discredit, degradation.*

dis·grace·ful (diss-gráyss-f'l || diz-) *adj.* Bringing or deserving disgrace; shameful. **—dis·grace·ful·ly** *adv.* **—dis·grace·ful·ness** *n.*

dis·grun·tle (diss-grúnt'l ‖ diz-) *tr.v.* **-tled, -tling, -tles.** To make discontented or cross; put in a disagreeable mood. [DIS- (intensive) + dialectal *gruntle,* to grumble, Middle English *gruntlen,* frequentative of *grunten,* to GRUNT.] **—dis·grun·tled** *adj.* **—dis·grun·tle·ment** *n.*

dis·guise (diss-gíz ‖ diz-) *tr.v.* **-guised, -guising, -guises. 1.** To modify the appearance or manner of in order to prevent recognition. **2.** To conceal or obscure by false pretences; misrepresent. ~*n.* **1. a.** The act of disguising. **b.** The condition of being disguised. **2.** Something that serves to disguise, such as a mask, costume, or pretence. [Middle English *disg(u)isen,* from Old French *desguisier : des-,* from Latin *dis-* (reversal) + *guise,* manner, GUISE.] **—dis·guis·er** *n.*

dis·gust (diss-gúst ‖ diz-) *tr.v.* **-gusted, -gusting, -gusts. 1.** To be so unpleasant as to excite nausea in; sicken. **2.** To offend the taste or moral sense of; repel. ~*n.* A strong feeling of distaste excited by something physically revolting or offensive to one's moral or aesthetic values. [Old French *desgouster : des-,* from Latin *dis-* (negative) + *goust,* taste, from Latin *gustus.*]

dis·gust·ed (diss-gústid ‖ diz-) *adj.* Filled with disgust or irritated impatience. **—dis·gust·ed·ly** *adv.*

Usage: Three prepositions are used after *disgusted* in standard English. One is *disgusted at* someone's action or behaviour, especially when one is giving an immediate reaction; one is *disgusted with* a person or his action, especially when one's attitude is being maintained over a period of time; and one may also be *disgusted by* someone or something.

dis·gust·ful (diss-gúst-f'l ‖ diz-) *adj.* **1.** Causing disgust; repugnant. **2.** Full of or marked by disgust. **—dis·gust·ful·ly** *adv.*

dis·gust·ing (diss-gústing ‖ diz-) *adj.* Deeply offensive to one's taste or moral values; acutely repugnant. **—dis·gust·ing·ly** *adv.*

dish (dish) *n.* **1. a.** An open container, generally shallow and concave, for holding or serving food. **b.** Loosely, any container on which food is placed or served, such as a plate or bowl. **c.** The portion a dish holds. **2.** A particular variety, preparation, or article of food. **3. a.** A concavity or depression like that in a dish. **b.** The degree of such a concavity. **4.** A large dish-shaped aerial, as in a radio telescope or radar apparatus. **5.** *Slang.* A good-looking person. ~*tr.v.* **dished, dishing, dishes. 1.** To serve (food) in or from a dish, cooking pot, pan, or the like. Usually used with *up* or *out.* **2.** To hollow out; make concave. **3.** *British Slang.* To foil; ruin. **4.** *Informal.* To give out; dispense; distribute. Used with *out.* **—dish it out.** *Slang.* To hand out abuse or punishment. **—dish up. 1.** To serve food or a meal. **2.** *Informal.* To present (a proposal, for example) in an attractive manner. [Middle English *dish,* Old English *disc,* plate, bowl, platter, from West Germanic *diskaz* (unattested), from Latin *discus,* quoit, DISC.]

dis·ha·bille (diss-a-béel, -ə-, -bée) *n.* Also **dés·ha·bil·lé** (dáy-za-bée-ay, -zə-, -béelay). The state of being partially or very casually dressed; a state of undress. [French *déshabillé,* from the past participle of *déshabiller,* to undress : *dés-,* from Latin *dis-* (reversal) + *habiller,* to dress.] **—dis·ha·bille** *adj.*

dis·har·mo·ny (diss-hármoni) *n., pl.* **-nies.** Lack of harmony; discord. **—dis·har·mo·ni·ous** (diss-haar-môni-əss) *adj.*

dish·cloth (dísh-kloth ‖ -klawth) *n., pl.* **-cloths** (-kloths ‖ -klawths, -klawthz, -klothz). **1.** A cloth used for washing dishes or wiping surfaces. Also called "dishrag". **2.** A drying-up cloth; a tea towel.

dishcloth gourd *n.* **1.** Any of several tropical vines of the genus *Luffa;* especially, *L. cylindrica,* cultivated for its cucumber-like fruits. **2.** The fruit of any of these plants, the fibrous skeleton of which is used as a **loofah** (see). Also called "vegetable sponge".

dis·heart·en (diss-hárt'n) *tr.v.* **-ened, -ening, -ens.** To shake or destroy the courage or resolution of; dispirit. **—dis·heart·en·ing·ly** *adv.* **—dis·heart·en·ment** *n.*

dished (disht) *adj.* **1.** Slanting towards one another at the bottom. Said of a pair of wheels. **2.** Dish-shaped.

di·shev·el (di-shévv'l) *tr.v.* **-elled** or *U.S.* **-eled, -elling** or *U.S.* **-eling, -els. 1.** To loosen and let fall (hair or clothing) in disarray. **2.** To disarrange the hair or clothing of (a person). [Back-formation from DISHEVELLED.] **—dis·hev·el·ment** *n.*

di·shev·elled (di-shévv'ld) *adj.* **1.** In a state of disarray; unkempt; untidy. [Middle English *discheveled,* from Old French *deschevele,* past participle of *descheveler,* to disarrange the hair : *des-,* from Latin *dis-,* apart + *chevel,* hair, from Latin *capillus.*]

dis·hon·est (diss-ónnist, diz-) *adj.* **1.** Disposed to lie, cheat, or deceive. **2.** Involving deception or untruthfulness. **3.** Obtained illegally or unfairly. **—dis·hon·est·ly** *adv.*

Synonyms: dishonest, lying, untruthful, deceitful, mendacious, tricky, shady, underhand.

dis·hon·es·ty (diss-ónnisti, diz-) *n., pl.* **-ties. 1.** Lack of honesty; inclination to deceive or cheat. **2.** A dishonest act or statement.

dis·hon·our (diss-ónnər, diz-) *n.* **1.** Loss of honour, respect, or reputation; disgrace; shame. **2.** Something that causes loss of honour. **3.** An offence or insult. **4.** Failure to honour a cheque or bill of exchange, or to meet a commercial obligation. **—See Synonyms at disgrace.** ~*tr.v.* **dishonoured, -ouring, -ours. 1.** To deprive of honour; disgrace. **2.** To offend the dignity of; slight. **3.** To violate the chastity of. **4.** To fail to honour (a cheque, for example). **—dis·hon·our·er** *n.*

dis·hon·our·a·ble (diss-ónnərəb'l ‖ diz-) *adj.* **1.** Characterised by or causing dishonour or discredit. **2.** Lacking integrity; unprincipled. **—dis·hon·our·a·bly** *adv.*

dish·rag (dísh-rag) *n.* A **dishcloth** (see).

dish·tow·el (dísh-tow-əl) *n.* *U.S.* A tea towel (see).

dish·wash·er (dísh-woshər ‖ -wawshər) *n.* **1.** An electric machine that washes crockery, cutlery, and utensils automatically. **2.** A person who washes dishes; specifically, one employed to do this in a restaurant.

dish·wa·ter (dísh-wawtər ‖ *U.S. also* -wottər) *n.* **1.** Water in which dishes are being or have been washed. **2.** *Informal.* An unpleasantly weak-tasting drink.

dish·y (díshi) *adj.* **-ier, -iest.** *Informal.* Very attractive. [From DISH (attractive person).]

dis·il·lu·sion (diss-i-lóo-zh'n, -léw-) *tr.v.* **-sioned, -sioning, -sions. 1.** To free or deprive of illusions or misconceptions. **2.** To undermine or destroy the ideals of; disenchant. ~*n.* **1.** The act of disillusioning. **2.** The condition or fact of being disillusioned. **—dis·il·lu·sion·ment** *n.* **—dis·il·lu·sive** (-siv ‖ -ziv) *adj.*

dis·il·lu·sioned (diss-i-lóozh'nd, -léwzh'nd) *adj.* **1.** No longer contented or satisfied. **2.** No longer idealistic; cynical.

dis·in·cen·tive (diss-in-séntiv) *n.* Something that discourages or dissuades; a deterrent. **—dis·in·cen·tive** *adj.*

dis·in·cli·na·tion (diss-inkli-náysh'n ‖ diss-in-) *n.* Lack of willingness or disposition; reluctance; aversion.

dis·in·cline (diss-in-klín) *v.* **-clined, -clining, -clines.** —*tr.* To make reluctant or unwilling. —*intr.* To be reluctant or unwilling.

dis·in·clined (diss-in-klínd) *adj.* Unwilling; reluctant.

dis·in·fect (diss-in-fékt) *tr.v.* **-fected, -fecting, -fects.** To cleanse of disease-carrying microorganisms. **—dis·in·fec·tion** *n.*

dis·in·fec·tant (diss-in-féktənt) *n.* An agent that disinfects by destroying, neutralising, or inhibiting the growth of disease-carrying microorganisms. ~*adj.* Serving to disinfect.

dis·in·fest (diss-in-fést) *tr.v.* **-fested, -festing, -fests.** To rid of vermin. **—dis·in·fes·ta·tion** (diss-in-fest-áysh'n) *n.*

dis·in·fla·tion (diss-in-fláysh'n) *n.* The downward movement of inflated prices to a more normal level, without necessarily entailing a reduction in the level of economic activity.

dis·in·form (diss-in-fórm) *tr.v.* **-formed, -forming, -forms.** To supply with disinformation.

dis·in·for·ma·tion (diss-infər-máysh'n, diss-infər-) *n.* False or misleading information deliberately spread by a propaganda agency.

dis·in·gen·u·ous (diss-in-jénnew-əss) *adj.* Not straightforward or candid; insincere; crafty. **—dis·in·gen·u·ous·ly** *adv.* **—dis·in·gen·u·ous·ness** *n.*

dis·in·her·it (diss-in-hérrit) *tr.v.* **-ited, -iting, -its.** To deprive of inheritance or the right to inherit, especially by excluding members of one's family. **—dis·in·her·i·tance** *n.*

dis·in·te·grate (diss-ínti-grayt) *v.* **-grated, -grating, -grates.** —*intr.* **1.** To separate into components or fragments, especially after a physical shock. **2.** To weaken or collapse, especially in the face of difficulties. —*tr.* To cause (a body) to separate into components; destroy. **—See Synonyms at decay. —dis·in·te·gra·tor** (-graytər) *n.*

dis·in·te·gra·tion (diss-ínti-gráysh'n, diss-inti-) *n.* **1.** The process of disintegrating or the state of being disintegrated. **2.** *Physics.* The break-up of an atomic nucleus or an unstable elementary particle into smaller fragments, either spontaneously or as a result of bombardment with radiation. See **decay.**

dis·in·ter (diss-in-tér) *tr.v.* **-terred, -terring, -ters. 1.** To dig up or remove, as from a grave or tomb; exhume. **2.** To remove from obscurity; expose. **—dis·in·ter·ment** *n.*

dis·in·ter·est (diss-íntrist, -intər-ist, -əst, -est) *n.* **1.** Freedom from selfish bias or self-interest; impartiality. **2.** *Nonstandard.* Lack of interest.

dis·in·ter·est·ed (diss-íntrəstid, -íntristid, -íntə-restid) *adj.* **1.** Not influenced by self-interest; impartial: *disinterested praise.* **2.** *Nonstandard.* Uninterested; indifferent. **—dis·in·ter·est·ed·ly** *adv.* **—dis·in·ter·est·ed·ness** *n.*

Usage: Standard English attempts to maintain a clear distinction between *disinterested* meaning "impartial", "unbiased" and *uninterested* meaning "indifferent". The former implies a lack of self-interest, whereas the latter indicates a lack of any interest. In fact, the use of *disinterested* to mean "uninterested" came *earlier* than its sense of "impartial"; and conversely, the early use of *uninterested* was in the sense of "impartial". Both of these were recorded in the early 17th century.

dis·in·vest·ment *n.* A reduction of investment, as through the withdrawal or disposal of foreign assets, or through a failure to replace capital stock such as machinery. **—dis·in·vest** *intr.v.*

dis·ject (diss-jékt) *tr.v.* **-jected, -jecting, -jects.** To split or disperse with force; scatter. [Latin *disjicere* (past participle *disjectus*) : *dis-,* apart + *jacere,* to throw.]

dis·join (diss-jóyn) *v.* **-joined, -joining, -joins.** —*tr.* To undo the joining of; separate. —*intr.* To become disconnected. [Middle English, from Old French *desjoindre,* from Latin *disjungere : DIS-* + *jungere,* to JOIN.]

dis·joint (diss-jóynt) *v.* **-jointed, -jointing, -joints.** —*tr.* **1.** To put out of joint; dislocate. **2.** To take apart at the joints; separate. **3.** To destroy the coherence or connections of. —*intr.* **1.** To come apart at the joints. **2.** To become dislocated. ~*adj.* *Mathematics.* Having no elements in common. Said espe-

cially of sets. [Middle English *disjointen,* from Old French *desjoindre* (past participle *desjoint*), to DISJOIN.]
dis·joint·ed (diss-jóyntid) *adj.* **1.** Separated at the joints. **2.** Out of joint; dislocated. **3.** Lacking order or coherence; disconnected. **—dis·joint·ed·ly** *adv.* **—dis·joint·ed·ness** *n.*
dis·junct (diss-júnkt, díss-jungkt) *adj.* **1.** Separated; disconnected. **2.** *Music.* Pertaining to progression by intervals larger than major seconds. **3.** *Zoology.* Having the head, thorax, and abdomen separated by deep constrictions. Said of insects.
~n. Logic. Any of the propositions in a disjunction. [Middle English *disjuncte,* from Latin *disjunctus,* past participle of *disjungere,* to DISJOIN.]
dis·junc·tion (diss-júngk-sh'n) *n.* Also **dis·junc·ture** (-chər) (for sense 1). **1.** The act of disjoining or the condition of being disjointed. **2.** *Logic.* A compound proposition that presents two or more alternative terms, with the assertion that only one is true. **3.** *Genetics.* The separation of homologous pairs of chromosomes during meiosis.
dis·junc·tive (diss-júngktiv) *adj.* **1.** Serving to separate or divide. **2.** *Grammar.* **a.** Serving to establish a relationship of contrast or opposition. The conjunction *but* in the phrase *beautiful but smelly* is disjunctive. **b.** Able to stand in isolation; syntactically independent; for example, the word *honestly* in *Honestly, I don't know,* is disjunctive. **3.** *Logic.* **a.** Presenting two or more alternative propositions. Said of a compound proposition. **b.** Containing a disjunction as one premise. Said of a syllogism.
~n. **1.** *Grammar.* A disjunctive word. **2.** *Logic.* A disjunction. **—dis·junc·tive·ly** *adv.*
disk (disk) *n.* **1.** *U.S.* Variant of **disc.** **2.** *Computing.* A random-access storage device consisting of a flat rotatable circular disc with a magnetic coating. See **floppy disk.** —See Usage note at **disc.**
disk crash *n. Computing.* A **crash** *(see)* involving a disk.
disk drive *n. Computing.* A device with read/write heads used for retrieving information from or storing information on a magnetic disk or tape.
dis·kette (diss-két) *n.* A **floppy disk** *(see).*
dis·like (diss-lík) *tr.v.* **-liked, -liking, -likes.** To regard with distaste or aversion; find unpleasant.
~n. An attitude or feeling of distaste or aversion.
dis·lo·cate (díss-lə-kayt || *U.S. also* diss-lṓ-) *tr.v.* **-cated, -cating, -cates.** **1.** To put out from the usual or proper relationship with contiguous parts; displace; shift. **2.** *Pathology.* To displace (a limb or organ) from the normal position; especially, to displace (a bone) from its joint. **3.** To throw into confusion or disorder; upset.
dis·lo·ca·tion (díss-lə-káysh'n || -lō-) *n.* **1.** The act of dislocating or the state or condition of being dislocated. **2.** *Geology.* A **fault** *(see).* **3.** *Crystallography.* A line or plane in a crystal in which there is a deviation from the regular repeating order of the crystal lattice. An *edge dislocation* is a straight line marking the edge of an incomplete plane of atoms. A *screw dislocation* is a line about which atoms are arranged in helices.
dis·lodge (diss-lój) *v.* **-lodged, -lodging, -lodges.** *—tr.* To remove or force out from a previously occupied position. *—intr.* To move or go from a dwelling or former position. **—dis·lodg·ment, dis·lodge·ment** *n.*
dis·loy·al (diss-lóy-əl) *adj.* Lacking in loyalty. See Synonyms at **faithless.** **—dis·loy·al·ly** *adv.*
dis·loy·al·ty (diss-lóy-əlti) *n., pl.* **-ties.** **1.** The quality of being disloyal; faithlessness. **2.** A disloyal act.
dis·mal (dízməl) *adj.* **1.** Causing dismay or depression; dreary; drab. **2.** *Informal.* Incompetent; inadequate; disappointing: *a dismal effort.*
~n. Plural. Rare. Low spirits: *in the dismals.* [Middle English, unlucky days (two days in each month that were considered unpropitious), from Medieval Latin *diēs malī* : Latin *diēs,* plural of *diēs,* day + *malī,* plural of *malus,* evil.] **—dis·mal·ly** *adv.* **—dis·mal·ness** *n.*
dis·man·tle (diss-mánt'l) *tr.v.* **-tled, -tling, -tles.** **1.** To strip (a house, for example) of furnishings or equipment. **2.** To take apart; disassemble. **3.** To tear down; destroy. **4.** To strip of clothing or covering. **—dis·man·tle·ment** *n.*
dis·mast (diss-maást || -mást) *tr.v.* **-masted, -masting, -masts.** *Nautical.* To remove or break off the mast or masts of.
dis·may (diss-máy, diz-) *tr.v.* **-mayed, -maying, -mays.** **1.** To fill with dread or apprehension; make anxious or afraid. **2.** To discourage or trouble greatly; dishearten.
~n. **1.** A feeling of discouragement or disappointment. **2.** A loss of courage or confidence in the face of trouble or danger; consternation. [Middle English *dismayen,* from Old French *desmayer* (attested only in past participle *dismaye*) : *des-,* from Latin *dis-* (intensive) + *esmayer,* to frighten, be frightened, from Vulgar Latin *exmagāre* (unattested), to deprive of power, from Germanic.]
dis·mem·ber (diss-mémbər) *tr.v.* **-bered, -bering, -bers.** **1.** To cut, tear, or pull off the limbs of. **2.** To hack or cut to pieces. **3.** To divide into sections; partition: *To dismember an organisation.* **—dis·mem·ber·er** *n.* **—dis·mem·ber·ment** *n.*
dis·miss (diss-míss || diz-) *tr.v.* **-missed, -missing, -misses.** **1.** To discharge, as from employment. **2.** To direct or allow to leave: *dismiss troops.* **3.** To rid one's mind of; dispel. **4.** To reject; repudiate: *dismiss an allegation.* **5.** To refuse to consider seriously: *They dismissed her great invention as a toy.* **6.** *Law.* To put (a claim or action) out of court without further hearing. **7.** In cricket, to end the innings of. [Middle English *dismissen,* from Medieval Latin *dismittere* (past participle *dismissus*), variant of Latin *dīmittere* : *dīs-,* away + *mittere,* to send.] **—dis·miss·i·ble** *adj.*
dis·miss·al (diss-míss'l || diz-) *n.* Also *archaic* **dis·mis·sion** (-mísh'n). **1. a.** The act of dismissing. **b.** The condition of being dismissed. **2.** An order or notice of discharge.
dis·miss·ive (diss-míssiv || diz-) *adj.* **1.** Contemptuous or disparaging. **2.** Showing little inclination to give due consideration to other people or their views. **—dis·miss·ive·ly** *adv.* **—dis·miss·ive·ness** *n.*
dis·mount (diss-mównt, díss-) *v.* **-mounted, -mounting, -mounts.** *—intr.* To get off or down, as from a horse or bicycle; alight. *—tr.* **1.** To remove (a thing) from its support, setting, or mounting. **2.** To unseat, as from a horse. **3.** To take apart (a mechanism).
Dis·ney (dízni), **Walt** (1901–66). U.S. film producer and animator. He founded a film empire in the 1920s and 1930s with his creation of the cartoon characters Mickey Mouse and Donald Duck. He produced feature-length cartoon films, nature documentaries, and adventure films. In 1955 He opened Disneyland, a vast amusement park with attractions based on the characters and settings of his films, in Anaheim, California. His films include *Snow White and the Seven Dwarfs* (1937), *Fantasia* (1940), and *Mary Poppins* (1964).
Dis·ney·land (dízni-land) *n.* A bright, quaint world of childish fantasy. [After *Disneyland* in California. See Walt **Disney.**]
dis·o·be·di·ence (díss-ə-beédi-ənss || -ō-) *n.* The condition or fact of not obeying; deliberate failure to obey; insubordination. **—dis·o·be·di·ent** *adj.* **—dis·o·be·di·ent·ly** *adv.*
dis·o·bey (díss-ə-báy || -ō-) *v.* **-beyed, -beying, -beys.** *—intr.* To refuse or fail to follow an order or rule. *—tr.* To refuse or fail to obey. **—dis·o·bey·er** *n.*
dis·o·blige (díss-ə-blíj || -ō-) *tr.v.* **-bliged, -bliging, -bliges.** **1.** To refuse or neglect to act in accord with the wishes of. **2.** *Regional.* To inconvenience. **—dis·o·blig·ing·ly** *adv.*
dis·or·der (diss-órdər, diz-) *n.* **1.** A lack of order or regular arrangement; confusion. **2.** A breach of civic order or peace; a public disturbance. **3.** Imperfect functioning of part of the body or mind. **4.** A breakdown, as in a system.
~tr.v. **disordered, -dering, -ders.** **1.** To throw into disorder; muddle. **2.** To disturb the normal physical or mental health of; derange.
dis·or·dered (diss-órdərd, diz-) *adj.* **1.** In a condition of disorder; disarranged. **2.** Physically or mentally ill; deranged.
dis·or·der·ly (diss-órdərli, diz-) *adj.* **1.** Lacking regular or logical order or arrangement; irregular; unsystematic. **2.** Undisciplined; unruly; riotous. **3.** *Law.* Disturbing the public peace or decorum: *drunk and disorderly.* **—dis·or·der·li·ness** *n.*
disorderly conduct *n. Law.* Any of various petty offences of a kind likely to cause a breach of the peace.
disorderly house *n. Law.* Any house, such as a house of prostitution, whose visitors regularly violate public order or decency.
dis·or·gan·ise, dis·or·gan·ize (diss-órgə-nīz, diz-) *tr.v.* **-ised, -ising, -ises.** To destroy the organisation, systematic arrangement, or unity of; throw into confusion. **—dis·or·gan·i·sa·tion** (nī-záysh'n || *U.S.* -ni-) **—dis·or·gan·is·er** *n.*
dis·o·ri·en·tate (diss-áwri-ən-tayt || -óri-) *tr.v.* **-tated, -tating, -tates.** Also *chiefly U.S.* **dis·o·ri·ent** (-ent, -ənt), **-ented, -enting, -ents.** **1. a.** To cause to lose one's sense of direction or location, as by removing from a familiar environment. **b.** *Psychology.* To cause to lose one's awareness of time, place, or self in relation to one's environment. **2.** To confuse; perplex. **—dis·o·ri·en·ta·tion** (-táysh'n) *n.*
dis·own (diss-ṓn) *tr.v.* **-owned, -owning, -owns.** **1.** To refuse to acknowledge or accept as one's own. **2.** To renounce; repudiate.
dis·par·age (diss-párrij) *tr.v.* **-aged, -aging, -ages.** **1.** To speak of slightingly or dismissively. **2.** To reduce in esteem; discredit. —See Synonyms at **decry.** [Middle English *disparagen,* to degrade, disgrace, humble, from Old French *desparager,* "to deprive someone of his rank" : *des-,* from Latin *dis-* (privative) + *parage,* rank, from *per,* PEER.] **—dis·par·ag·er** *n.* **—dis·par·ag·ing·ly** *adv.*
dis·par·age·ment (diss-párrijmənt) *n.* **1.** The act of disparaging; detraction. **2.** A lowering of dignity or esteem; discredit. **3.** Something that lowers dignity or esteem.
dis·pa·rate (díss-pər-ət, -it || diss-párrət) *adj.* Completely distinct or different in kind; entirely dissimilar. [Latin *disparātus,* past participle of *disparāre,* to separate : *dis-,* apart + *parāre,* to prepare.] **—dis·pa·rate·ly** *adv.* **—dis·pa·rate·ness** *n.*
dis·par·i·ty (diss-párrəti) *n., pl.* **-ties.** **1.** The condition or fact of being unequal in age, rank, degree, or other measure; difference. **2.** Unlikeness; incongruity; dissimilarity.
dis·pas·sion (diss-pásh'n) *n.* Freedom from passion, bias, or emotion; objectivity.
dis·pas·sion·ate (diss-pásh'n-ət, -it) *adj.* Devoid of or unaffected by passion, emotion, or bias; impartial; calm: *dispassionate judgment.* See Synonyms at **fair.** **—dis·pas·sion·ate·ly** *adv.* **—dis·pas·sion·ate·ness** *n.*
dis·patch, des·patch (diss-pách) *tr.v.* **-patched, -patching, -patches.** **1.** To send off to a specific destination or on specific business. **2.** To complete or dispose of promptly. **3.** To put to death summarily.
~n. (|| díss-pach). **1.** The act of dispatching or sending off. **2.** A putting to death. **3.** Efficient speed or promptness; expeditious performance. **4.** An official communication, sent with speed; especially, a report of military operations. **5.** A news item sent to a newspaper, as by a correspondent. [Spanish *despachar* or Italian *dispacciare,* perhaps from Old French *despeechier,* to set free, unshackle : *des-,* from Latin *dis-* (reversal) + *(em)peechier,* to hinder,

from Late Latin *impedicāre,* to entangle : Latin *in-* + *pedica,* shackle.] **—dis·patch·er** *n.*
dispatch box *n.* **1.** A container for holding documents. **2.** A box on the table of the House of Commons, at which senior government or opposition spokesmen stand when addressing the House.
dispatch rider *n.* One who carried dispatches, usually on a motorcycle.
dis·pel (diss-pél) *tr.v.* **-pelled, -pelling, -pels.** To rid of by or as if by driving away or scattering; dispense with: *"the effect of his tone was to dispel her shyness"* (Henry James). [Middle English *dispellen,* from Latin *dispellere* : *dis-,* away + *pellere,* to push, drive, strike.] **—dis·pel·ler** *n.*
dis·pen·sa·ble (diss-pénss-əb'l) *adj.* **1.** Capable of being dispensed with; unimportant. **2.** Able to be dispensed, administered, or distributed. **3.** Subject to exemption in particular cases, as a sin may be; condonable. **—dis·pen·sa·bil·i·ty** (-ə-bílləti), **dis·pen·sa·ble·ness** *n.*
dis·pen·sa·ry (diss-pénss-əri) *n., pl.* **-ries. 1.** An office in a hospital or other institution from which medical supplies and preparations are dispensed. **2.** Any other place where medicines are dispensed.
dis·pen·sa·tion (díss-pen-sáysh'n, -pən-) *n.* **1.** The act of dispensing or giving out; distribution; apportionment. **2.** Something that is dispensed or given out. **3.** A specific arrangement or system by which something is dispensed or administered. **4.** Any exemption or release from an obligation or rule, granted by or as if by an authority. **5. a.** An exemption from a church law, a vow, or other similar obligation, granted in a particular case by an ecclesiastical authority. **b.** The document containing this exemption. **6.** *Theology.* **a.** The divine ordering of worldly affairs. **b.** A religious system or code of commands considered to have been divinely revealed or appointed: *the Muslim dispensation.* **—dis·pen·sa·tion·al** *adj.*
dis·pen·sa·to·ry (diss-pén-sə-təri, -tri || díss-pen-sáytəri) *adj.* Of, pertaining to, or granted by dispensation.
~*n., pl.* **dispensatories. 1.** A book in which the preparation, uses, and contents of medicines are described; a pharmacopoeia. **2.** *Archaic.* A dispensary.
dis·pense (diss-pénss) *v.* **-pensed, -pensing, -penses.** —*tr.* **1.** To deal out or distribute in parts or portions. **2.** To prepare and give out (medicines) according to a doctor's prescription. **3.** To administer (justice, for example). **4.** To exempt, as from a duty or religious obligation. —*intr.* To grant dispensation or exemption. **—dispense with. 1.** To manage without; forgo. **2.** To do away with; make unnecessary. —See Synonyms at **distribute.** [Middle English *dispensen,* from Medieval Latin *dispensāre,* to grant dispensation to, exempt, condone, from Latin, to pay out, distribute, frequentative of *dispendere,* to weigh out : *dis-,* away + *pendere,* to weigh.]
dis·pens·er (diss-pén-sər) *n.* One that dispenses or gives out; specifically: **1.** A device that dispenses goods in measured amounts or single units: *a paper-cup dispenser.* **2.** A person who dispenses medicines.
dis·per·sal (diss-pérss'l) *n.* The act or process of dispersing or the condition of being dispersed; distribution.
Usage: *Dispersal* and *dispersion* are often interchangeable, but there is a tendency for the former to be more commonly used for the act or process of dispersing (*the dispersal of a crowd by the troops*), and the latter for the resulting situation (*the dispersion of the rioters throughout the town*).
dis·per·sant (diss-pér-sənt) *n.* A liquid or gas in which something is dispersed, such as the liquid used as a propellant in an aerosol can.
dis·perse (diss-pérss) *v.* **-persed, -persing, -perses.** —*tr.* **1.** To scatter in various directions; distribute widely. **2.** To cause to vanish or evaporate; dispel. **3.** To disseminate (knowledge, for example). **4.** To separate (light or other radiation) into components with different wavelengths. —*intr.* To move or scatter in different directions. [Middle English *dispersen,* from Old French *disperser,* from Latin *dispergere* (past participle *dispersus*), to scatter on all sides : *dis-,* in different directions + *spargere,* to strew, scatter.] **—dis·pers·ed·ly** (-pérss-idli) *adv.* **—dis·pers·er** *n.* **—dis·pers·i·ble** *adj.*
disperse system *n.* Any continuous medium containing dispersed entities of any size or state.
dis·per·sion (diss-pérsh'n || -pérzh'n) *n.* **1. a.** The state of being dispersed. **b.** The act or process of dispersing. **2.** *Statistics.* The degree of scatter of data, usually about some mean or median value. **3.** *Physics.* The separation of a complex wave into component parts according to some characteristic, such as frequency or wavelength; for example, separation of visible light into its colour components by refraction or diffraction. **4.** *Chemistry.* A suspension, such as smog or homogenised milk, of solid, liquid, or gaseous particles, of colloidal size or larger, in a liquid, solid, or gaseous medium. **5.** *Capital* **D.** The **Diaspora** (*see*). —See Usage note at **dispersal.**
dis·per·sive (diss-pér-siv || -ziv) *adj.* **1.** Tending to become dispersed. **2.** Tending to produce dispersion.
dis·per·soid (diss-pér-soyd) *n. Chemistry.* A colloid in which one substance is dispersed in another. Also used adjectivally: *a dispersoid sol.*
dis·pir·it (di-spírrit) *tr.v.* **-ited, -iting, -its.** To lower in spirit; dishearten. [DI(S)- (negative) + SPIRIT.]
dis·pir·it·ed (di-spírritid) *adj.* Characterised by low spirits; disheartened; dejected. **—dis·pir·it·ed·ly** *adv.* **—dis·pir·it·ed·ness** *n.*
dis·place (diss-pláyss) *tr.v.* **-placed, -placing, -places. 1.** To change the place or position of; move from the usual place. **2.** To take the place of; supplant. **3.** To discharge from an office or position. **4.** To cause a displacement of (a body, for example). —See Synonyms at **replace. —dis·place·a·ble** *adj.* **—dis·plac·er** *n.*
dis·placed person (*usually* díss-playst) *n. Abbr.* **DP, D.P.** A person living in a foreign country who has been driven from his homeland, especially by war or political unrest.
dis·place·ment (diss-pláyss-mənt) *n.* **1. a.** The act of displacing. **b.** The condition of being displaced. **2.** *Chemistry.* A reaction in which one kind of atom or group is removed from a molecule and replaced by another. See **substitution. 3.** *Physics.* **a.** The weight or volume of a fluid displaced by a floating body, used especially as a measurement of the weight or bulk of ships. **b.** A vector, or the magnitude of a vector, from the initial position to a subsequent position assumed by a body. **4.** *Psychology.* **a.** The shifting of a feeling, such as anger, from an appropriate to an inappropriate object. **b.** Engagement in inappropriate or irrelevant behaviour during situations of extreme emotion or conflict. Often used adjectivally: *displacement activity.*
displacement ton *n. Nautical.* A unit for measuring the displacement of a ship afloat, equivalent to one long ton or about 35 cubic feet of salt water.
dis·play (diss-pláy) *tr.v.* **-played, -playing, -plays. 1.** To hold up to view; make visible; expose; exhibit. **2.** To make manifest or noticeable; show evidence of. **3.** To exhibit ostentatiously; show off; flaunt. **4.** To spread out; unfurl: *a peacock displaying its tail.* **5.** *Printing.* To give prominence to (printed letters or words, for example), as by using large type. —See Synonyms at **show.**
~*n.* **1.** The act of displaying; exhibition. **2.** Anything that is exhibited or displayed. **3.** Vulgar ostentation. **4.** *Printing.* **a.** An arrangement or style of type designed to give prominence to printed matter. **b.** Printed matter that is set off prominently. **c.** An advertisement designed to catch the eye, as distinguished from a classified advertisement. Also used adjectivally: *display advertisements.* **5.** *Zoology.* A type of behaviour characterised by gestures that act as specific signals in courtship and aggression. It is shown particularly by birds and fishes. **6. a.** An electronic device for representing text, numbers, or diagrams visually. **b.** The material represented on such a device. [Middle English *displayen,* to unfold, unfurl, exhibit, from Old French *despleier,* from Medieval Latin *displicāre,* from Latin, to scatter : *dis-* (reversal) + *plicāre,* to fold.]
dis·played (diss-pláyd) *adj. Heraldry.* Standing erect with wings extended.
dis·please (diss-pleéz) *v.* **-pleased, -pleasing, -pleases.** —*tr.* To cause annoyance or vexation to; offend. —*intr.* To cause annoyance or offence. **—dis·pleas·ing·ly** *adv.*
dis·pleas·ure (diss-plézhər) *n.* **1.** The condition or fact of being displeased or dissatisfied; annoyance; anger. **2.** *Archaic.* Discomfort; uneasiness. **3.** *Archaic.* An annoying or injurious offence.
~*tr.v.* **displeasured, -uring, -ures.** *Archaic.* To displease.
dis·port (diss-pórt || -pōrt) *v.* **-ported, -porting, -ports.** —*intr.* To play; frolic. —*tr.* To occupy (oneself) with diversion or amusement.
~*n.* Diversion; play; sport. [Middle English *disporten,* from Old French *desporter,* "to carry away", divert : *des-,* from Latin *dis-,* apart + *porter,* to carry, PORT.]
dis·pos·a·ble (diss-pōzə-b'l) *adj.* **1.** Designed to be disposed of after use. **2.** Available for use.
~*n.* Something intended to be disposed of after use. **—dis·pos·a·bil·i·ty** (-bílləti) *n.*
disposable income *n.* The residue of one's income that is available for use after all direct taxes have been paid.
dis·pos·al (diss-pōz'l) *n.* **1.** A particular order, distribution, or arrangement. **2.** A particular method of attending to or settling matters. **3.** The transference of something by gift or sale. **4.** A throwing out or away. **5.** An apparatus or device for disposing of something, such as household waste. Also used adjectivally: *a disposal unit.* **6.** The liberty or power to dispose of or use someone or something: *funds at our disposal.*
dis·pose (diss-pōz) *v.* **-posed, -posing, -poses.** —*tr.* **1.** To place in a particular order; arrange. **2.** To put (business affairs, for example) into correct, definitive, or conclusive form. **3.** To make willing or receptive; incline. Often used in the passive. —*intr.* To settle or decide a matter. **—dispose of. 1.** To attend to; arrange; settle. **2.** To transfer or part with, as by giving or selling. **3.** To get rid of; throw away. **4.** To eat or drink (food or liquid). [Middle English *disposen,* from Old French *disposer,* reshaped (after *poser,* to POSE), from Latin *dispōnere,* to place here and there, arrange : *dis-,* in different directions + *pōnere,* to put.] **—dis·pos·er** *n.*
dis·po·si·tion (díss-pə-zísh'n) *n.* **1.** One's customary manner of emotional response; temperament: *"She had a lively, playful disposition, which delighted in anything ridiculous."* (Jane Austen). **2.** A tendency or inclination, especially when habitual: *a disposition to heavy drinking.* **3. a.** The act or manner of disposing. **b.** The condition or fact of being disposed. **4.** The power or liberty to control, direct, or dispose.
Synonyms: *disposition, temperament, character, personality, nature.*
dis·pos·sess (díss-pə-zéss || -séss) *tr.v.* **-sessed, -sessing, -sesses.** To deprive (someone) of the possession of something, especially property. **—dis·pos·ses·sion** (-zésh'n) *n.* **—dis·pos·ses·sor** (-ər) *n.* **—dis·pos·ses·so·ry** (-zéssəri) *adj.*
dis·po·sure (diss-pōzhər) *n. Rare.* Disposal.
dis·praise (diss-práyz) *tr.v.* **-praised, -praising, -praises.** To express disapproval of; disparage; censure.
~*n.* Reproach; censure. [Middle English *dispreisen,* from Old

French *despreiser,* from Vulgar Latin *dispretiãre* (unattested), variant of Latin *dẽpretiãre,* to DEPRECIATE.] —**dis·prais·er** *n.* —**dis·prais·ing·ly** *adv.*

Dis·prin (dísprin) *n.* A trademark for a preparation of aspirin, calcium carbonate, and anhydrous citric acid, taken, in the form of water-soluble tablets, for the relief of pain.

dis·prize (diss-príz) *tr.v.* **-prized, -prizing, -prizes.** *Archaic.* To hold in low esteem. [Middle English *disprisen, dispreisen,* to DISPRAISE.]

dis·proof (diss-proof ‖ -proof) *n.* **1.** The act of disproving or refuting. **2.** Evidence that disproves or refutes.

dis·pro·por·tion (diss-pra-pórsh'n ‖ -pórsh'n) *n.* **1.** The absence of due proportion; disparity. **2.** An instance of a disproportionate relation, as in size. —*tr.v.* **disproportioned, -tioning, -tions.** To make disproportionate.

dis·pro·por·tion·ate (diss-pra-pórsh'n-ət, -it ‖ -pórsh'n-) *adj.* Also **dis·pro·por·tion·al** (díss-pra-pórsh'n-əl ‖ -pórsh'n-). Not proportionate; out of proportion, as in relative size, shape, or amount. —*intr.v.* **-ated, -ating, -ates.** *Chemistry.* To undergo disproportionation. —**dis·pro·por·tion·ate·ly** *adv.* —**dis·pro·por·tion·ate·ness** *n.*

dis·pro·por·tion·a·tion (díss-pra-pórsh'n-áysh'n ‖ -pórsh'n-) *n. Chemistry.* A type of chemical reaction in which one molecule of reactant is reduced and another is oxidised.

dis·prove (diss-proov) *tr.v.* **-proved, -proving, -proves.** To prove to be false, invalid, or in error; refute. —**dis·prov·a·ble** *adj.* —**dis·prov·al** *n.*

dis·put·a·ble (diss-péw-təb'l, díss-pew-) *adj.* Capable of being disputed or challenged; debatable. —**dis·put·a·bil·i·ty** (-tə-bíllăti) *n.* —**dis·put·a·bly** *adv.*

dis·pu·tant (diss-péw-tənt, díss-pew-) *adj.* Engaged in argument or dispute. —*n.* A person who disputes; a debater.

dis·pu·ta·tion (díss-pew-táysh'n) *n.* **1.** The act of disputing; a debate. **2.** A formal academic debate or an oral defence of a thesis.

dis·pu·ta·tious (díss-pew-táyshəss) *adj.* Argumentative; contentious. —**dis·pu·ta·tious·ly** *adv.* —**dis·pu·ta·tious·ness** *n.*

dis·pute (diss-péwt) *v.* **-puted, -puting, -putes.** —*tr.* **1.** To argue about; debate. **2.** To question the truth or validity of; doubt. **3.** To strive to win (a prize, for example); contend for. **4.** To strive against; oppose; resist. —*intr.* **1.** To argue; discuss; debate. **2.** To quarrel vehemently. —See Synonyms at **discuss.** —*n.* (*also* diss-pewt) **1.** A verbal controversy; an argument; a debate. **2.** A quarrel. **3.** *British.* A state of official disagreement between management and workers in an industry or company, usually following the breakdown of preliminary negotiations and preceding further action, such as a strike. —See Synonyms at **argument.** [Middle English *disputen,* from Old French *desputer,* from Late Latin *disputãre,* from Latin, to reckon, discuss : *dis-,* separately + *putãre,* to clean, prune, settle an account, hence to reckon, think.] —**dis·put·er** *n.*

Usage: Traditionally, the stress is on the second syllable, for both the verb and the noun. In recent years, however, many people have begun to put the stress on the first syllable in the case of the noun, but there is a great deal of inconsistency; for example, the phrase *in dispute* usually retains the stress on the second syllable, even in the speech of people who often say *dispute.*

dis·qual·i·fi·ca·tion (diss-kwóllifi-káysh'n, díss-) *n.* **1.** The act of disqualifying, or the condition of being disqualified. **2.** Something that disqualifies.

dis·qual·i·fy (diss-kwólli-fī, díss-) *tr.v.* **-fied, -fying, -fies. 1.** To render unfit or unqualified; disable. **2.** To declare ineligible or unqualified. **3.** To deprive of a legal right, power, or privilege: *disqualified from driving for 12 months.* **4.** To debar from a sports event, as for misconduct.

dis·qui·et (diss-kwí-ət) *tr.v.* **-eted, -eting, -ets.** To deprive of peace or rest; trouble. —*n.* The absence of mental peace or rest; restlessness; anxiety. —**dis·qui·et·ing** *adj.* —**dis·qui·et·ing·ly** *adv.*

dis·qui·e·tude (diss-kwí-ə-tewd ‖ -tood) *n.* A state of worry or uneasiness; anxiety.

dis·qui·si·tion (díss-kwi-zísh'n) *n.* A formal discourse or treatise, often in writing; a dissertation. [Latin *disquĩsĩtiõ* (stem *disquĩsĩtiõn-*), enquiry, from *disquĩrere,* to enquire diligently : *dis-* (intensive) + *quaerere,* to search for.]

Dis·rae·li (diz-ráyli, diss-), **Benjamin,** 1st Earl of Beaconsfield (1804–81). British statesman. The grandson of a Venetian Jew, he became a Christian in 1817. In 1837 he entered Parliament and from 1842 led the Young England group of Conservatives. He was three times Chancellor of the Exchequer in Derby's cabinet, and in 1867 was responsible for the Reform Bill which gave household suffrage in the boroughs and extended the county franchise. Disraeli succeeded Lord Derby as Prime Minister in 1868, but lost office in the autumn to Gladstone and the Liberals. He returned to power in 1874. He bought Britain a major share in the Suez Canal, proclaimed Queen Victoria Empress of India (1876), and annexed Cyprus. He established the Conservative Party as a political force upholding monarchy, the Anglican Church, and the Empire.

dis·rate (diss-ráyt) *tr.v.* **-rated, -rating, -rates.** To reduce in rating or rank; especially, to demote (a petty officer in the navy or noncommissioned officer in the marines).

dis·re·gard (díss-ri-gárd, -rə-) *tr.v.* **-garded, -garding, -gards. 1.** To pay no attention or heed to; fail to consider; ignore. **2.** To treat without proper respect or attentiveness. —*n.* Lack of thoughtful attention or due regard, especially when

wilful. —**dis·re·gard·er** *n.* —**dis·re·gard·ful** *adj.*

dis·rel·ish (diss-réllish) *tr.v.* **-ished, -ishing, -ishes.** To have distaste for; dislike. —*n.* Distaste; aversion.

dis·re·mem·ber (díss-ri-mémbər, -rə-) *v.* **-bered, -bering, -bers.** *Chiefly Irish & Regional.* —*tr.* To fail to remember. —*intr.* To forget.

dis·re·pair (díss-ri-paír, -rə-) *n.* The condition of being in need of repairs; a state of neglect; dilapidation: *a house in disrepair.*

dis·rep·u·ta·ble (diss-réppew-təb'l) *adj.* **1.** Lacking a good reputation; not esteemed. **2.** Not respectable in character or appearance. **3.** Disgraceful; discreditable. —**dis·rep·u·ta·bil·i·ty** (-tə-bílləti), **dis·rep·u·ta·ble·ness** *n.* —**dis·rep·u·ta·bly** *adv.*

dis·re·pute (díss-ri-péwt) *n.* Also *archaic* **dis·rep·u·ta·tion** (diss-réppew-táysh'n). The absence or loss of reputation; discredit; disgrace. See Synonyms at **disgrace.**

dis·re·spect (díss-ri-spékt, -rə-) *n.* Lack of respect, esteem, or courteous regard; rudeness. —*tr.v.* **disrespected, -specting, -spects.** To show a lack of respect for or to.

dis·re·spect·a·ble (díss-ri-spékta-b'l, -rə-) *adj.* Lacking respectability; not worthy of respect. —**dis·re·spect·a·bil·i·ty** (-bílləti) *n.*

dis·re·spect·ful (díss-ri-spéktf'l, -rə-) *adj.* Having or demonstrating a lack of respect; rude; discourteous. —**dis·re·spect·ful·ly** *adv.* —**dis·re·spect·ful·ness** *n.*

dis·robe (diss-rōb) *v.* **-robed, -robing, -robes.** *Formal.* —*tr.* To remove the clothing from. —*intr.* To undress oneself. —**dis·robe·ment** *n.* —**dis·rob·er** *n.*

dis·rupt (diss-rúpt) *tr.v.* **-rupted, -rupting, -rupts. 1.** To upset the order of; throw into confusion or disorder. **2.** To interrupt or impede the progress, movement, or procedure of. **3.** To break or burst; rupture. [Latin *disrumpere* (past participle *disruptus*), to break asunder : *dis-,* asunder + *rumpere,* to break.] —**dis·rupt·er, dis·rup·tor** (-rúptər) *n.*

dis·rup·tion (diss-rúpsh'n) *n.* **1.** The act of disrupting or the state of being disrupted. **2.** *Capital* **D.** The breaking away of the Free Church from the Established Church of Scotland in 1843.

dis·rup·tive (diss-rúptiv) *adj.* Pertaining to, causing, or produced by disruption. —**dis·rup·tive·ly** *adv.* —**dis·rup·tive·ness** *n.*

diss, dis (diss) *n. Slang.* Disrespect. —*tr.v. Slang.* To disrespect; badmouth. [From DIS(RESPECT).]

dis·sat·is·fac·tion (díss-sáttiss-fáksh'n, diss-) *n.* **1.** The condition or feeling of being displeased or not satisfied; discontent. **2.** Anything that causes discontent.

dis·sat·is·fac·to·ry (díss-sáttiss-fák-təri, diss-, -tri) *adj.* Unsatisfactory.

dis·sat·is·fied (díss-sáttiss-fīd) *adj.* Affected by a sense of inadequacy, discontent, or displeasure, or by an insufficiency of something; not content. —**dis·sat·is·fied·ly** *adv.*

dis·sat·is·fy (díss-sáttiss-fī, diss-) *tr.v.* **-fied, -fying, -fies.** To fail to meet the expectations or fulfil the desires of; disappoint.

dis·sect (di-sékt, dī- ‖ dī-sékt) *tr.v.* **-sected, -secting, -sects. 1.** To cut open or apart (plant or animal tissue), especially for scientific study or in surgery. **2.** To examine, analyse, or criticise in minute detail: *dissected her motives.* **3.** *Geology.* To carve up (a land form, especially a plateau) by erosion. Used of a river. [Latin *dissecãre* (past participle *dissectus*), to cut apart : *dis-,* apart + *secãre,* to cut.] —**dis·sec·ti·ble** *adj.* —**dis·sec·tor** (-séktər) *n.*

dis·sect·ed (di-séktid, dī-) *adj. Botany.* Divided into numerous narrow segments or lobes: *dissected leaves.*

dis·sec·tion (di-séksh'n, dī-) *n.* **1.** The act or process of dissecting. **2.** Something that has been dissected, such as tissue under study. **3.** A detailed examination or analysis.

dis·seise, dis·seize (diss-séez) *tr.v.* **-seised, -seising, -seises.** *Law.* To dispossess (a person) of property unlawfully. [Middle English *disseisen,* from Anglo-French *desseisir,* variant of Old French *dessaisir* : *des-,* from Latin *dis-* (reversal) + *saisir,* to SEIZE.] —**dis·sei·see** (diss-see-zee, diss-sée-zee) *n.* —**dis·sei·sor** (-ər) *n.*

dis·sei·sin (diss-séezin) *n.* Also **dis·sei·sure** (-séezhər). *Law.* Wrongful usurpation of the powers and privileges of ownership; ejection of the lawful holder of a freehold. [Middle English *dysseysyne,* from Anglo-French *disseisine,* variant of Old French *dessaisine* : *des-,* from Latin *dis-* (reversal) + SEIZIN.]

dis·sem·blance (di-sémblənss) *n.* **1.** The act of dissembling or disguising; dissimulation. **2.** *Archaic.* Absence of resemblance; dissimilarity.

dis·sem·ble (di-sémb'l) *v.* **-bled, -bling, -bles.** —*tr.* **1.** To disguise the real nature of; hide with a false appearance or semblance: *dissemble one's fears with laughter.* **2.** To make a false show of; feign. —*intr.* To conceal one's real motives, nature, or feelings under a pretence. —See Synonyms at **pretend.** [Middle English *dissemblen,* from Old French *dessembler,* to be different (influenced by *dissimuler,* to pretend, dissimulate) : *des-,* from Latin *dis-* (reversal) + *sembler,* to be like, appear, seem.] —**dis·sem·bler** *n.* —**dis·sem·bling·ly** *adv.*

dis·sem·i·nate (di-sémmi-nayt) *v.* **-nated, -nating, -nates.** —*tr.* **1.** To scatter widely, as in sowing seed; distribute; disperse. **2.** To spread abroad (information, for example); promulgate widely. —*intr. Rare.* To become diffused; spread. [Latin *dissẽminãre* : *dis-,* in different directions + *sẽminãre,* to sow, from *sẽmen,* seed.] —**dis·sem·i·na·tion** (-náysh'n) *n.* —**dis·sem·i·na·tive** (-nətiv, -naytiv) *adj.* —**dis·sem·i·na·tor** *n.*

disseminated sclerosis *n. British.* **Multiple sclerosis** (*see*).

dis·sem·i·nule (di-sémmi-newl || -nōōl) *n.* A plant part, such as a seed, fruit, or spore, that propagates and spreads the species. [DIS-SEMIN(ATE) + -ULE.]
dis·sen·sion (di-sénsh'n) *n.* Disagreement or quarrelling caused by a difference of opinion. See Synonyms at **discord.** [Middle English *dissencioun,* from Old French *dissension,* from Latin *dissensiō* (stem *dissensiōn-*), from *dissentīre,* to DISSENT.]
dis·sent (di-sént) *intr.v.* **-sented,-senting, -sents. 1.** To think or feel differently; disagree; differ. **2.** To refuse to conform to the authority or doctrine of an established church. **3.** To withhold assent or approval. —See Synonyms at **object** (verb).
~*n.* **1.** Difference of opinion or feeling; disagreement. **2.** The refusal to conform to the authority or doctrine of an established church; nonconformity. [Middle English *dissenten,* from Latin *dissentīre* : *dis-,* apart + *sentīre,* to feel.] **—dis·sent·ing·ly** *adv.*
dis·sent·er (di-séntər) *n.* **1.** One who dissents. **2.** *Often capital* **D.** One who refuses to accept the doctrines or usages of an established or national church; especially, a Protestant who dissents from the Church of England. Compare **conformist.**
dis·sen·ti·ent (di-sén-shi-ənt, -shənt) *adj.* Dissenting, especially from the view or policies of a majority.
~*n.* One who dissents. **—dis·sen·tience** *n.*
dis·sen·tious (di-sénshəss) *adj.* Given to dissension.
dis·sep·i·ment (di-séppi-mənt) *n.* A membranous or calcareous partition between organs or parts; a septum. [Latin *dissaepīmentum,* partition, from *dissaepīre,* to separate, divide : *dis-,* apart + *saepīre,* to fence in, enclose, from *saepes,* fence, hedge.] **—dis·sep·i·men·tal** (mént'l) *adj.*
dis·ser·tate (díssər-tayt) *intr.v.* **-tated, -tating, -tates.** Also **dis·sert** (di-sért), **-serted, -serting, -serts.** *Rare.* To discourse formally, learnedly, or at some length. [Latin *dissertāre,* frequentative of *disserere,* to discuss (translation of Greek *dialegesthai,* to discuss, converse, "pick out", "separate"; see **dialogue**) : *dis-,* apart + *serere,* to connect, join (in speech), discuss.] **—dis·ser·ta·tor** (-ər) *n.*
dis·ser·ta·tion (díssər-táysh'n) *n.* A lengthy and formal treatise or discourse, especially one written by a candidate for a higher university degree; a thesis.
dis·serve (diss-sérv, diss-) *tr.v.* **-served, -serving, -serves.** To treat badly; do a disservice to; harm.
dis·ser·vice (díss-sérviss, diss-) *n.* A harmful action; an ill turn.
dis·sev·er (di-sévvər, díss-) *v.* **-ered, -ering, -ers.** *—tr.* **1.** To separate; sever. **2.** To divide into parts; break up. *—intr.* To become separated or disunited. [Middle English *dis(s)everen,* from Old French *des(s)evrer,* from Late Latin *dissēparāre* : Latin *dis-* (intensive) + *sēparāre,* to SEPARATE.] **—dis·sev·er·ance, dis·sev·er·ment** *n.*
dis·si·dence (díssidənss) *n.* Disagreement, as of opinion or belief; difference; dissent.
dis·si·dent (díssidənt) *adj.* Disagreeing, as in opinion or belief; differing; dissenting.
~*n.* One who disagrees; especially, a citizen of a one-party state who is in fundamental disagreement with the prevailing politics or ideology. [Latin *dissidēns* (stem *dissident-*), present participle of *dissidēre,* "to sit apart", dissent : *dis-,* apart + *sedēre,* to sit.]
dis·sim·i·lar (di-símmilər, díss-) *adj.* Distinct; unlike; different. **—dis·sim·i·lar·ly** *adv.*
dis·sim·i·lar·i·ty (díssimi-lárrəti, díss-simmi-) *n., pl.* **-ties. 1.** The quality of being distinct or unlike; difference. **2.** A point of distinction or difference. —See Synonyms at **difference.**
dis·sim·i·late (di-símmilayt, dí-) *v.* **-lated, -lating, -lates.** *—tr.* **1.** To make dissimilar or unlike. **2.** *Linguistics.* To cause to undergo dissimilation. *—intr.* **1.** To become dissimilar. **2.** *Linguistics.* To undergo dissimilation. [DIS- + (AS)SIMILATE.]
dis·sim·i·la·tion (di-símmi-láysh'n, díssimi-) *n.* **1.** The act or process of making or becoming dissimilar. **2.** *Linguistics.* The process by which one of two similar phonemes is displaced or changed by the other, as in the English form *marble* from French *marbre.*
dis·si·mil·i·tude (díssi-mílli-tewd, díss-si- || -tōōd) *n.* **1.** Lack of resemblance; difference. **2.** A point of difference; a dissimilarity. [Middle English, from Latin *dissimilitūdō,* from *dissimilis,* different : *dis-,* not + *similis,* like, SIMILAR.]
dis·sim·u·late (di-símmew-layt) *v.* **-lated, -lating, -lates.** *—tr.* To disguise (one's intentions, for example) under a feigned appearance. *—intr.* To conceal one's true feelings or intentions. **—dis·sim·u·la·tion** (-láysh'n) *n.* **—dis·sim·u·la·tive** (-lətiv, -laytiv) *adj.* **—dis·sim·u·la·tor** (-ər) *n.*
dis·si·pate (díssi-payt) *v.* **-pated, -pating, -pates.** *—tr.* **1.** To drive away or dispel by or as if by dispersing; rout; scatter. **2.** To spend or use up; waste; squander. *—intr.* **1.** To vanish by dispersion; scatter. **2.** *Physics.* To lose (energy) through conversion into another form, especially into heat. **3.** To indulge excessively in the pursuit of pleasure or debauchery. [Middle English *dissipaten,* from Latin *dissipāre,* to disperse, squander.] **—dis·si·pat·er, dis·si·pa·tor** (-ər) *n.* **—dis·si·pa·tive** (-paytiv) *adj.*
dis·si·pat·ed (díssi-paytid) *adj.* **1.** Unrestrained in the pursuit of pleasure; dissolute. **2.** Wasted; squandered. **—dis·si·pat·ed·ly** *adv.* **—dis·si·pat·ed·ness** *n.*
dis·si·pa·tion (díssi-páysh'n) *n.* **1. a.** The act of dissipating. **b.** The condition of being dissipated; dispersion. **2.** Wasteful consumption or expenditure. **3.** Dissolute indulgence in pleasure; intemperance. **4.** Amusement; diversion.
dis·so·cia·ble (di-sṓ-shi-əb'l) *adj.* Capable of being dissociated; separable. **—dis·so·cia·bil·i·ty, dis·so·cia·ble·ness** *n.* **—dis·so·cia·bly** *adv.*
dis·so·ci·ate (di-sṓ-shi-ayt, -si-) *v.* **-ated, -ating, -ates.** *—tr.* **1.** To remove from association; separate: *"Marx never dissociated man from his social environment"* (Sidney Hook). **2.** *Chemistry.* To cause to undergo dissociation. **3.** *Psychology.* To cause to undergo dissociation. *—intr.* **1.** To cease associating; part. **2.** *Chemistry.* To undergo dissociation. **3.** *Psychology.* To undergo dissociation. [Latin *dissociāre* : *dis-* (reversal) + *sociāre,* to join, associate, from *socius,* companion.] **—dis·so·ci·a·tive** (-ətiv, -aytiv) *adj.*
Usage: Dissociate is traditionally used as the opposite of *associate,* but *disassociate* is increasing in use. Less commonly, *disassociation* is used for *dissociation.*
dis·so·ci·a·tion (di-sṓ-si-áysh'n, -shi-) *n.* **1. a.** The act of dissociating. **b.** The condition of being dissociated; separation. **2.** *Chemistry.* The chemical process, especially a reversible process, by means of which a change in physical condition, as in pressure, temperature, or the action of a solvent, causes a molecule to split into simpler groups of atoms, single atoms, or ions. **3.** *Psychology.* The separation of a belief or attitude, or a group of related psychological activities, from the rest of the personality so that they function independently, as in cases of multiple ("split") personalities.
dis·sol·u·ble (di-sóllew-b'l) *adj.* Capable of being dissolved; soluble. [Latin *dissolūbilis,* from *dissolvere,* to DISSOLVE.] **—dis·sol·u·bil·i·ty** (-bílləti), **dis·sol·u·ble·ness** *n.*
dis·so·lute (díssə-lōōt, -lewt) *adj.* Lacking in moral restraint; debauched. [Middle English, from Latin *dissolūtus,* loose, licentious, past participle of *dissolvere,* to DISSOLVE.] **—dis·so·lute·ly** *adv.* **—dis·so·lute·ness** *n.*
dis·so·lu·tion (díssə-lōōsh'n, -léwsh'n) *n.* **1.** Decomposition into fragments or constituent parts; disintegration. **2.** Termination or extinction by deconcentration or dispersion. **3.** Extinction of life; death. **4.** Annulment or termination of a formal or legal bond, tie, or contract. **5.** Formal dismissal of an assembly or legislature. **6.** Reduction to a liquid form; liquefaction. **—dis·so·lu·tive** (-lōōt-iv, -lewt-, di-sóllewtiv) *adj.*
dis·solve (di-zólv) *v.* **-solved, -solving, -solves.** *—tr.* **1.** To cause to pass into solution. **2.** To reduce to liquid form; melt. **3.** To break into component parts; cause to disintegrate or disappear. **4.** To bring to an end by or as if by breaking up; terminate. **5.** To dismiss (a meeting or parliament, for example). **6.** To cause to give way emotionally or psychologically; upset. **7.** To cause to lose definition; blur; confuse. **8.** *Law.* To render null; abrogate; annul. *—intr.* **1.** To pass into solution; be mixed or dispersed in another substance. **2.** To become liquid; melt. **3.** To break up or disperse. **4.** To disintegrate or disappear. **5.** To collapse emotionally or psychologically. **6.** To lose clarity or definition; fade away. **7.** To change scenes in a film or television programme by having one scene fade out while the next appears behind it and grows clearer as the first dims. —See Synonyms at **melt.**
~*n.* A scene transition in a film or on television, made by dissolving. [Middle English *dissolven,* from Latin *dissolvere* : *dis-,* apart + *solvere,* to loosen, untie.] **—dis·solv·a·ble** *adj.* **—dis·solv·er** *n.*
dis·sol·vent (di-zólv'nt) *adj.* Capable of dissolving.
~*n.* A solvent.
dis·so·nance (díssənənss) *n.* **1.** A harsh or disagreeable combination of sounds; discord. **2.** An absence of agreement or consistency; disparity. **3.** *Music.* A combination of notes conventionally considered to suggest unrelieved tension and to require resolution. Compare **consonance. 4.** *Psychology.* An aversive state which arises when an individual is aware of inconsistency or conflict within himself. See **cognitive dissonance.**
dis·so·nant (díssənənt) *adj.* **1.** Harsh or inharmonious in sound; discordant. **2.** Disagreeing or at variance: *"Jerome's new presumption, so dissonant from his former meekness"* (Horace Walpole). **3.** *Music.* Constituting or producing a dissonance. [Middle English, from Old French *dissonant,* from Latin *dissonāns* (stem *dissonant-*), present participle of *dissonāre,* to disagree in sound, be inharmonious : *dis-,* apart + *sonāre,* to sound.] **—dis·so·nant·ly** *adv.*
dis·suade (di-swáyd) *tr.v.* **-suaded, -suading, -suades.** To discourage or deter (a person) from a purpose or course of action by persuasion or exhortation. Used with *from.* [Latin *dissuādēre* : *dis-* (reversal) + *suādēre,* to advise, persuade.] **—dis·suad·er** *n.*
dis·sua·sion (di-swáyzh'n) *n.* The act or an instance of dissuading; exhortation against a course of action. [Latin *dissuāsiō* (stem *dissuāsiōn-*), from *dissuādēre,* to DISSUADE.] **—dis·sua·sive** (-swáy-siv || -ziv) *adj.* **—dis·sua·sive·ly** *adv.* **—dis·sua·sive·ness** *n.*
dis·syl·la·ble (di-síllәb'l, dí-, dī́-) *n.* Also **di·syl·la·ble** (dī́-). A word with two syllables. **—dis·syl·lab·ic** (díssi-lábbik, dī́-si-) *adj.*
dis·sym·me·try (di-símmətri, díss-) *n., pl.* **-tries. 1.** Lack or absence of symmetry. **2.** Mirror-image symmetry, as of a left hand and a right hand. **—dis·sym·met·ric** (díssi-métrik), **dis·sym·met·ri·cal** *adj.* **—dis·sym·met·ri·cal·ly** *adv.*
dist. 1. distance; distant. **2.** distinguish; distinguished. **3.** district.
dis·taff (díss-taaf || -taff) *n., pl.* **-taffs** or *rare* **-taves** (-tayvz). **1.** A rod or stick with a cleft end in which is held the unspun flax, wool, or tow from which thread is drawn in spinning. **2.** *Archaic.* A woman's work and concerns. [Middle English *distaf,* Old English *distæf,* "flax staff" : *dis-,* bunch of flax, akin to Middle Low German *dise* (see **dizen**) + STAFF.]
distaff side *n.* The female line or maternal branch of a family. Used humorously. Also called "spindle side". Compare **spear side.**
dis·tal (díst'l) *adj. Anatomy.* Located far from the origin, point of

attachment, or median line of the body: *The fingers are at the distal end of the arm.* Compare **proximal.** [DIST(ANT) + -AL.] —**dis·tal·ly** *adv.*

dis·tance (dístənss) *n. Abbr.* **dist.** **1.** The fact or condition of being apart in space or time. **2.** *Geometry.* **a.** A nonnegative number designating the magnitude of a path along a straight line or curve. **b.** The length of a line segment joining two points. **c.** The length of the perpendicular from a given point to a given line or plane. **3. a.** The space between any two locations or points. **b.** The interval separating any two specified instants in time. **4. a.** The degree of deviation or difference that separates two things in relationship. **b.** The extent to which difference has arisen between two points in a trend or course: *The campaign moved some distance from its original objectives.* **5.** A stretch of linear space without designation of limit. **6. a.** A point removed in space or time. **b.** A position of being uninvolved or apart: *always kept himself at a distance.* **7.** Chilliness of manner; aloofness. **8.** The scheduled duration of a race, boxing match, or other sporting contest. Used chiefly in the phrases *go the distance* and *last the distance.* **9.** Any running race of 1 500 metres or more. Also used adjectivally: *a distance race*; *a distance runner.* —**keep (one's) distance.** To remain reserved or aloof.
~ *tr.v.* **distanced, -tancing, -tances.** **1.** To place or keep at a distance. **2.** To cause to appear at a distance. **3.** To leave behind, as in a race; outrun; outstrip. [Middle English *distaunce,* from Old French *destance,* from Latin *distantia,* from *distāns,* DISTANT.]

dis·tant (dístənt) *adj. Abbr.* **dist.** **1.** Separate or apart in space or time. **2.** Far removed in space or time. **3.** Located at, coming from, or going to a distance. **4.** Far apart in relationship; remote: *a distant cousin.* **5.** Far removed from the present situation: *distant thoughts.* **6.** Aloof or chilly in manner; reserved. [Middle English *distaunt,* from Old French, from Latin *distāns* (stem *distant-*), present participle of *distāre,* to be remote : *dis-,* apart + *stāre,* to stand.] —**dis·tant·ly** *adv.*
Synonyms: *distant, far, far-off, faraway, remote, removed.*

dis·taste (diss-táyst) *n.* Dislike or aversion. Often used with *for.*
~ *tr.v.* **distasted, -tasting, -tastes.** *Archaic.* **1.** To feel repugnance for; dislike. **2.** To offend; displease.

dis·taste·ful (diss-táystf'l, díss-) *adj.* Unpleasant; disagreeable. —**dis·taste·ful·ly** *adv.* —**dis·taste·ful·ness** *n.*

dis·tem·per¹ (di-stémpər) *n.* **1. a.** An infectious virus disease occurring in certain mammals, especially dogs, characterised by loss of appetite, a catarrhal discharge from the eyes and nose, and often partial paralysis and death. **b.** Any of various similar mammalian diseases. **2.** *Archaic.* Any illness or disease of the body or mind; an ailment. **3.** *Archaic.* Ill humour; testiness. **4.** *Archaic.* Disorder or disturbance, especially of a social or political nature.
~ *tr.v.* **distempered, -pering, -pers.** *Archaic.* To upset or disturb; disorder. [Middle English *distemperen,* to upset the proper balance of the humours, vex, be ill, from Old French *destemprer,* from Medieval Latin *distemperāre* : Latin *dis-* (reversal) + *temperāre,* to mingle in due proportion, TEMPER.]

distemper² *n.* **1.** A process of painting in which pigments are mixed with water and a glue-size or casein binder, used for flat wall decoration or for scenic and poster painting. **2. a.** The paint used in this process. **b.** Any of various heavily pigmented matt paints, such as whitewash, that can be thinned with water. **3.** A painting done in distemper.
~ *tr.v.* **distempered, -pering, -pers.** **1.** To mix (powdered pigments or colours) with water and size. **2.** To paint using distemper. [Middle English *distemperen,* to dilute, mix, from Medieval Latin *distemperāre* : *dis-* (intensive) + *temperāre,* to mingle, TEMPER.]

dis·tend (di-sténd) *v.* **-tended, -tending, -tends.** —*intr.* To become bloated and swollen from or as if from internal pressure; swell out. —*tr.* **1.** To cause to expand by or as if by internal pressure; dilate. **2.** To stretch out; extend in all directions. [Middle English *distenden,* from Latin *distendere* : *dis-,* apart + *tendere,* to stretch.]

dis·ten·si·ble (di-stén-səb'l) *adj.* Capable of being distended. —**dis·ten·si·bil·i·ty** (-sə-bíllǝti) *n.*

dis·ten·sion, dis·ten·tion (di-sténsh'n) *n.* The act of distending or the condition of being distended. [Middle English *distensioun,* from Latin *distentiō* (stem *distensiōn-*), from *distendere* (past participle *distentus*), to DISTEND.]

dis·tich (dístik) *n., pl.* **-tichs.** In poetry, a couplet, especially one used in a Latin or Greek elegy. [Latin *distichon,* from Greek *distikhon,* neuter of *distikhos,* having two rows or verses : DI- + *stikhos,* row, line, verse.]

dis·ti·chous (dístikəss) *adj. Botany.* Arranged in two vertical rows or ranks on opposite sides of an axis. Said of leaves. [Late Latin *distichus,* with two rows, from Greek *distikhos.* See **distich.**] —**dis·ti·chous·ly** *adv.*

dis·til, *U.S.* **dis·till** (di-stíl) *v.* **-tilled, -tilling, -tils** or *U.S.* **-tills.** —*tr.* **1.** To subject (a substance) to distillation. **2.** To extract (a distillate) by distillation. **3.** To purify or refine by or as if by distillation. **4.** To separate or extract (an essential idea or characteristic, for example) from its context, as if by distillation. **5.** To exude or give off (a substance) in drops or small quantities. —*intr.* **1.** To undergo or be produced by distillation. **2.** To fall or exude in drops or small quantities. [Middle English *distillen,* to trickle, drip, distil, from Old French *distiller,* from Latin *dēstīllāre, dīstīllāre* : *dē-,* down + *stīllāre,* to drip, from *stīlla*†, drop.] —**dis·til·la·ble** *adj.*

dis·til·late (dístil-ət, -it, -ayt ‖ *U.S. also* di-stíl-) *n.* **1.** The liquid condensed from vapour in distillation. **2.** Anything regarded as an essence or purified form. Also called "distillation".

dis·til·la·tion (dísti-láysh'n) *n.* **1.** Any of various heat-dependent processes used to purify or separate a fraction of a mixture; especially, the vaporisation of a liquid mixture with subsequent collection of components by differential cooling to condensation. **2.** A distillate.

distillation column *n.* A tall cylindrical metal shell fitted inside with perforated horizontal plates used to promote separation of miscible liquids ascending in the shell as vapour.

dis·till·er (di-stíllər) *n.* A producer or maker of alcoholic drinks by the process of distillation.

dis·till·er·y (di-stílləri) *n., pl.* **-ies.** An establishment or plant for distilling alcohol to produce spirits, such as whisky or gin.

dis·tinct (di-stíngkt) *adj.* **1.** Not identical; individual; discrete. **2.** Not similar; different; unlike. **3.** Easily perceived by the senses or intellect; clear. **4.** Well-defined; unmistakable; unquestionable: *a distinct improvement.* —See Synonyms at **evident.** [Middle English, separated, different, from Old French, from Latin *distinctus,* past participle of *distinguere,* to DISTINGUISH.] —**dis·tinct·ly** *adv.* —**dis·tinct·ness** *n.*
Usage: *Distinct* and *distinctive* are seldom interchangeable. *Distinct* has the meaning "unmistakable" or "clear" in most of its uses; *distinctive* has the meaning "distinguishing", "setting something apart from others". The contrast can be seen in such phrases as *a distinct smell,* where the smell is pronounced, compared with a *distinctive smell,* where the smell is uniquely identifiable.

dis·tinc·tion (di-stíngk-sh'n) *n.* **1.** The action of distinguishing; differentiation. **2.** The condition or fact of being dissimilar or distinct; a difference. **3.** A distinguishing factor, attribute, or characteristic. **4.** Excellence or eminence, as of performance, character, or reputation: *a man of distinction.* **5. a.** Recognition of achievement or superiority: *She graduated with distinction.* **b.** An honour conferred in recognition of achievement or superiority: *the V.C., a distinction reserved for very few.* —See Synonyms at **difference.**

dis·tinc·tive (di-stíngk-tiv) *adj.* **1.** Serving to identify; distinguishing: *distinctive tribal tattoos.* **2.** Characteristic: *distinctive habits.* **3.** *Linguistics.* Serving to distinguish meaning. Said of a phonological feature. —See Synonyms at **characteristic.** —See Usage note at **distinct.** —**dis·tinc·tive·ly** *adv.* —**dis·tinc·tive·ness** *n.*

dis·ting (díss-ting) *n. West African Informal.* An object whose name is unknown or forgotten; a thingummyjig. [From *this thing.*]

dis·tin·gué (di-stáng-gay, déess-taN-gáy) *adj.* Distinguished in appearance, manner, or bearing. [French, "distinguished".]

dis·tin·guish (di-stíng-gwish) *v.* **-guished, -guishing, -guishes.** —*tr.* **1.** To recognise as being different or distinct. **2.** To perceive distinctly; discern; make out. **3.** To detect or recognise; pick out. **4.** To make noticeable or different; set apart, characterise. **5.** To cause to be eminent or recognised. Usually used reflexively: *He distinguished himself in the exam.* —*intr.* To perceive or indicate differences; discriminate. Usually used with *among* or *between.* [Middle English *distinguen,* from Old French *distinguer* (present stem *distinguiss-*), from Latin *distinguere,* to separate, distinguish.] —**dis·tin·guish·a·ble** *adj.* —**dis·tin·guish·a·bly** *adv.*

dis·tin·guished (di-stíng-gwisht) *adj. Abbr.* **dist.** **1.** Characterised by excellence or distinction; eminent; renowned. **2.** Having an air of distinction and dignity in conduct or appearance.

dis·tort (di-stórt) *tr.v.* **-torted, -torting, -torts.** **1.** To twist out of a proper or natural relation of parts; misshape; contort. **2.** To cast false light on; alter misleadingly; misrepresent. **3.** To cause to work in a twisted or disordered manner; pervert. **4.** To alter the original or ideal form of (an electronic signal, sound wave, or the like). [Latin *distorquēre* (past participle *distortus*) : *dis-,* apart, aside + *torquēre,* to twist.] —**dis·tort·er** *n.*
Synonyms: *distort, twist, deform, contort, warp, gnarl.*

dis·tor·tion (di-stórsh'n) *n.* **1. a.** The act or an instance of distorting. **b.** A product of distorting; a distorted feature: *The newspaper article was full of distortions.* **2.** The condition of being distorted. **3.** *Optics.* A distorted image resulting from imperfections in an optical system, such as a lens. **4. a.** An undesired change in the waveform of an electronic signal, sound wave, or the like. **b.** Any consequence of such a change; especially, diminished clarity in reception or reproduction. **5.** *Psychoanalysis.* The modification of unconscious impulses into acceptable forms by conscious or dreaming perception. —**dis·tor·tion·al** *adj.*

distr. distributor.

dis·tract (di-strákt) *tr.v.* **-tracted, -tracting, -tracts.** **1.** To cause to turn away from the original focus of attention or interest; sidetrack; divert. **2.** To pull in conflicting directions; bewilder. [Middle English *distracten,* from Latin *distrahere* (past participle *distractus*), to pull apart, draw away, perplex : *dis-,* apart, aside + *trahere,* to draw.] —**dis·tract·ing·ly, dis·trac·tive·ly** *adv.* —**dis·trac·tive** *adj.*

dis·tract·ed (di-stráktid) *adj.* **1.** Having the attention diverted or not paying attention. **2.** Suffering conflicting emotions; confused. **3.** Distraught; made mad; *distracted by grief.* —See Synonyms at **forgetful.** —**dis·tract·ed·ly** *adv.*

dis·trac·tion (di-stráksh'n) *n.* **1.** The act of distracting or the condition of being distracted; a diversion from an original focus. **2.** Anything that compels attention or distracts; especially, an amusement. **3.** Extreme mental or emotional disturbance; obsession: *"I loved Dora Spenlow to distraction!"* (Charles Dickens).

dis·train (di-stráyn) *v.* **-trained, -training, -trains.** *Law.* —*tr.* To seize and hold (property) to compel payment or reparation, as of debts. —*intr.* To seize a person's goods in order to compel payment of his debts to the distrainer; levy a distress. Often used with *upon.* [Middle English *distreinen,* to seize, compel, detain, from Old French *destreindre* (present stem *destreign-*), from Medieval Latin *distringere,* to seize, compel, from Latin, to draw apart, detain, hinder : *dis-,* apart + *stringere,* to draw tight.] **—dis·train·a·ble** *adj.* **—dis·train·ment** *n.* **—dis·trai·nor** (-ər), **dis·train·er** *n.*

dis·train·ee (dístray-née) *n. Law.* One whose property has been distrained.

dis·traint (di-stráynt) *n. Law.* The act or process of distraining property; a distress. [From DISTRAIN (by analogy with *restraint, restrain*).]

dis·trait (dístray, di-stráy) *adj.* **1.** Inattentive; distracted. **2.** Agitated; worried. [Middle English, from Old French *destrait,* past participle of *destraire,* to DISTRACT.]

dis·traught (di-stráwt) *adj.* **1.** Extremely anxious or agitated; harried; frantic with worry. **2.** Crazed; mad. —See Synonyms at **abstracted.** [Middle English, alteration of *distract,* distracted, from Latin *distractus,* past participle of *distrahere,* to perplex, DISTRACT.]

dis·tress (di-stréss) *tr.v.* **-tressed, -tressing, -tresses. 1.** To cause anxiety or suffering to; worry or upset. **2.** To bring into difficult circumstances, especially difficult financial circumstances. **3.** *Archaic.* To constrain by harassment; force. **4.** *Law.* To hold the property of (a person) against the payment of debts; distrain upon.
~*n.* **1.** Mental or physical suffering; anxiety; sorrow; unhappiness. **2.** Severe strain resulting from exhaustion, accident, or the like. **3.** The condition of being in need of immediate assistance: *a damsel in distress; a ship in distress.* Also used adjectivally: *a distress signal.* **4.** *Law.* **a.** The seizing of goods belonging to a debtor, as security or in reparation; the act of distraining. **b.** The goods thus seized. [Middle English *distressen, destressen,* from Old French *destresser,* from *destresse,* "narrow passage", strait, constraint, from Vulgar Latin *districtia* (unattested) narrowness, from Latin *districtus,* past participle of *distringere,* to "draw tight", detain, hinder. See **distrain.**] **—dis·tress·ing·ly** *adv.*

dis·tressed (di-strést) *adj.* **1.** Upset or worried; made anxious; made to suffer. **2.** Impoverished; poor in comparison to one's former circumstances: *distressed gentlefolk.* **3.** Deliberately treated to give an impression of age and wear. Said of furniture and leather.

dis·tress·ful (di-stréssf'l) *adj.* **1.** Causing distress. **2.** Experiencing distress. **—dis·tress·ful·ly** *adv.* **—dis·tress·ful·ness** *n.*

dis·trib·u·tar·y (di-stríbbew-tri, -təri || -terri) *n., pl.* **-ies.** A branch of a river that flows away from the main stream and does not return to it; especially, such a branch in the delta of a large river. Compare **tributary.**

dis·trib·ute (di-stríbbewt || dístri-bewt. *See note at* **contribute**) *tr.v.* **-uted, -uting, -utes. 1.** To divide and dispense in portions; parcel out. **2.** To deliver or pass out: *distribute leaflets.* **3.** To spread or diffuse over an area. Often used in the passive: *a widely distributed species.* **4.** To separate into groups or categories; arrange or classify. **5.** *Logic.* To use (a term) so as to include all individuals or entities of a given class. **6.** *Printing.* To separate (type) and replace in the proper boxes. [Middle English *distributen,* from Latin *distribuere* : *dis-,* apart + *tribuere,* to allot, grant (see **tribute**).]
Synonyms: *distribute, divide, dispense, dole out, deal, ration.*

dis·tri·bu·tion (dístri-béwsh'n) *n.* **1.** The act of distributing or the condition of being distributed; apportionment. **2.** Something distributed; an allotment. **3.** The act of dispersing or the condition of being dispersed; a diffusion. **4.** The geographical occurrence or range of an organism. **5.** Division into categories; classification. **6.** *Law.* The division of an estate or property among rightful heirs. **7.** *Commerce.* The process of getting goods from the manufacturer to the consumer, including marketing, handling of orders, and transport of goods. **8.** Any spatial or temporal array of objects or events: *the distribution of theatres in the West End.* **9.** *Statistics.* Symbol **+** The particular way in which numbers representing a given characteristic are distributed amongst the members of a group, usually arranged according to frequency. See **frequency distribution. —dis·tri·bu·tion·al** *adj.*

dis·trib·u·tive (di-stríbbewtiv || dístri-bewtiv) *adj.* **1.** Of or pertaining to distribution. **2.** Serving to distribute. **3.** *Grammar.* Referring to each individual or entity of a group separately rather than collectively; for example, *every* in the sentence *Every employee attended the meeting.* **4.** *Mathematics.* Of, pertaining to, or designating an operation having the same effect whether performed before or after another operation; for example, multiplication is *distributive* with respect to addition; that is, $a \times (b + c) = (a \times b) + (a \times c)$.
~*n.* A distributive word or term. **—dis·trib·u·tive·ly** *adv.* **—dis·trib·u·tive·ness** *n.*

dis·trib·u·tor, dis·trib·u·ter (di-stríbbewtər || dístri-bewtər) *n. Abbr.* **distr. 1.** One that distributes: *film distributors.* **2.** One that markets or sells a commodity; especially, a wholesaler. **3.** In the ignition system of an internal-combustion engine, a device for applying electric current in proper sequence to the spark plugs.

dis·trict (dístrikt) *n. Abbr.* **dist. 1.** A division of an area or geographical unit either created arbitrarily, as for administrative purposes, or existing as a division by virtue of a characteristic: *an electoral district; a residential district; the Lake District.* **2.** In England, any subdivisions of a county or Unitary Authority area, with an elected council. **3.** In Scotland and Wales, any subdivisions of a Unitary Authority area, with an elected council. —See Synonyms at **area.**
~*tr.v.* **districted, -tricting, -tricts.** *Chiefly U.S.* To mark off or divide into districts. [French, from Medieval Latin *districtus,* (area of) jurisdiction, distraint, from Latin, past participle of *distringere,* to detain, hinder. See **distrain.**]

district attorney *n. Abbr.* **D.A.** In the United States, the state's prosecuting officer in a given judicial district.

district council *n. Chiefly British.* A council, elected by the voters of a district, that has many statutory powers and duties and deals with such matters as water, sewerage, town planning, rates, and licensing.

district court *n.* **1.** In Scotland, the lowest criminal court dealing with minor offences. **2. a.** A U.S. Federal trial court serving a judicial district. **b.** In some U.S. states, a court of general jurisdiction.

district nurse *n.* **1.** A nurse assigned to care for patients within a certain area, especially a rural district. **2.** A **home nurse** *(see).*

District of Columbia. Federal area in the east United States, whose boundaries are those of Washington, the nation's capital.

district officer *n.* A representative of the British government, especially formerly, in a district of a colony.

dis·trust (diss-trúst, díss-) *n.* Lack of trust; doubtfulness or misgiving; suspicion.
~*tr.v.* **distrusted, -trusting, -trusts.** To lack confidence in; doubt or suspect.
Usage: *Distrust* and *mistrust* are usually interchangeable, but the *dis-* prefix carries greater emphasis or strength of feeling. The *mis-* form is generally the one used when reference is to oneself: *I mistrusted my first reactions to her.*

dis·trust·ful (diss-trústf'l, díss-) *adj.* Doubting; suspicious. **—dis·trust·ful·ly** *adv.* **—dis·trust·ful·ness** *n.*

dis·turb (di-stúrb) *tr.v.* **-turbed, -turbing, -turbs. 1.** To break up or destroy the tranquillity or settled state of. **2.** To trouble emotionally or mentally; upset or alarm. **3.** To intrude upon; interrupt: *disturb one's sleep.* **4.** To disarrange; put out of order. **5.** To put (oneself) out; inconvenience (oneself): *She need not have disturbed herself on my account.* [Middle English *destourben,* from Old French *destorber,* from Latin *disturbāre* : *dis-* (intensive) + *turbāre,* to throw into disorder, disturb, from *turba,* confusion, probably from Greek *turbē,* disorder.] **—dis·turb·er** *n.* **—dis·turb·ing·ly** *adv.*

dis·tur·bance (di-stúrbənss) *n.* **1.** The act of disturbing or the condition of being disturbed. **2.** Something that disturbs; an interruption; an intrusion. **3.** A commotion, brawl, or riot; especially, a public breach of the peace. **4.** Unbalance or disorder, as of the mind. **5.** A variation in a normal course or condition. **6.** *Law.* The infringement of or interference with another's incorporeal property interests, such as easements, tenancies, franchises, or the like. **7.** *Meteorology.* A **depression** *(see),* usually one of low intensity.

dis·turbed (di-stúrbd) *adj.* Mentally unbalanced; emotionally unstable.

di·sul·fi·ram (dī-sul-féer-əm) *n.* A drug used in the treatment of chronic alcoholism. It acts by producing unpleasant effects, such as nausea and vomiting, when taken with alcohol. [From tetraethyltriu*ram disulf*ide *(disulphi*de*).*]

di·sul·phide (dī-súlfīd, dī-) *n.* A chemical compound containing two sulphur atoms combined with other elements or radicals. Also called "bisulphide".

dis·un·ion (díss-yóon-yən, diss-) *n.* **1.** The state of being disunited; separation. **2.** Lack of unity; discord. **—dis·un·ion·ist** *n. & adj.*

dis·u·nite (díss-yoo-nīt) *v.* **-nited, -niting, -nites.** —*tr.* **1.** To disrupt the union of; separate. **2.** To estrange; put at odds. —*intr.* To become separate.

dis·u·ni·ty (díss-yóonəti, diss-) *n., pl.* **-ties.** Lack of unity; dissension.

dis·use (díss-yóoss, diss-) *n.* The state of not being used or of being no longer in use; desuetude. **—dis·used** (-yóozd) *adj.*

dis·u·til·i·ty (díss-yoo-tílləti) *n.* The negative or harmful aspects of something; disadvantage.

disyllable. Variant of **dissyllable.**

dit (dit) *n.* The oral representation of the dot in radio and telegraphic codes, as in Morse code. Compare **dah.** [Imitative.]

ditch (dich) *n.* A long narrow trench or furrow dug in the ground, as for irrigation or drainage, or as a boundary line.
~*v.* **ditched, ditching, ditches.** —*intr.* To make or repair ditches. —*tr.* **1.** To dig or make a ditch in. **2.** To surround with a ditch. **3. a.** To drive (a vehicle) into a ditch. **b.** *U.S.* To derail (a train). **c.** To bring (an aircraft) down on water in an emergency. **4.** *Slang.* To throw aside; discard; desert. [Middle English *dich,* Old English *dīc†,* moat, ditch.] **—ditch·er** *n.*

ditch·water (dích-wáwtər) *n.* Foul, stagnant water, such as that found in ditches.

di·the·ism *n.* **1.** A belief in two supreme gods. **2.** The belief that good and evil govern the world as two supreme principles.

dith·er (díthər) *n.* **1.** *Chiefly British.* A state of nervous indecision or uncertainty. **2.** A state of agitation, excitement, or confusion.
~*intr.v.* **dithered, -ering, -ers. 1.** To be in a dither. **2.** To quiver or tremble, as with excitement. [Earlier *didder,* Middle English *didderen,* to DODDER.] **—dith·er·er** *n.* **—dith·er·ing, dith·er·y** *adj.*

dith·y·ramb (díthi-ram, -ramb) *n.* **1.** A frenzied and impassioned choric hymn and dance of ancient Greece, in honour of Dionysus. **2.** An irregular poetic expression suggestive of the ancient Greek dithyramb. **3.** Any piece of writing or speech in a frenzied and impassioned style. [Latin *dīthyrambus,* from Greek *dithurambos,* of non-Indo-European origin; akin to *thriambos,* TRIUMPH, and *iambos,* IAMB.] **—dith·y·ramb·ic** (-rámbik) *adj.*

dit·ta·ny (díttəni) *n., pl.* **-nies. 1.** An aromatic Cretan plant, *Origanum dictamnus,* with pink flowers, formerly believed to have magical powers. **2.** The **gas plant** *(see).* [Middle English *ditane, diteyne,* from Old French *ditan, ditain,* from Medieval Latin *di(p)tamnus,* variant of Latin *dictamnus,* from Greek *diktamnon,* perhaps after *Diktē,* mountain in Crete.]

dit·to (dítto) *n., pl.* **-tos.** *Abbr.* **do. 1.** The aforesaid; the above; the same as before. Used to avoid repetition and indicated by a pair of small *ditto marks* (") placed under the word that would otherwise be repeated. **2.** A duplicate or copy.
~*adv.* As before; likewise.
~*tr.v.* **dittoed, -toing, -tos.** To duplicate or repeat.
~*interj.* Used to express agreement. [Italian dialectal (Tuscan) *ditto,* "said", from Latin *dictus,* past participle of *dīcere,* to say.]

dit·ty (dítti) *n., pl.* **-ties.** A simple song. [Middle English *dite, ditti,* from Old French *ditie,* "composition", from Latin *dictātum,* "thing dictated", from *dictāre,* to dictate, compose, frequentative of *dīcere,* to say.]

ditty bag, ditty box *n.* A bag or box used by sailors to carry small items such as sewing implements. [Possibly from obsolete *dutty,* coarse calico, from Hindi *dhōtī,* loincloth, DHOTI.]

Di·u (dée-ōō). Island and seaport, now part of the Indian territory of Daman and Diu.

di·u·re·sis (dī-yoor-ée-siss) *n.* Excessive discharge of urine. [New Latin, from Late Latin *diūrēticus,* DIURETIC.]

di·u·ret·ic (dī-yoor-éttik) *adj.* Tending to increase the production and discharge of urine.
~*n.* A diuretic drug. [Middle English *diuretik,* from Late Latin *diūrēticus,* from Greek *diourētikos,* from *diourein,* to pass urine : *dia-,* through + *ourein,* to urinate, from *ouron,* urine.]

di·ur·nal (dī-úrn'l) *adj.* **1.** Pertaining to or occurring in a day or each day; daily. **2.** Occurring or active during the daytime rather than at night. Said especially of animals. Compare **nocturnal. 3.** Opening during daylight hours and closing at night. Said of flowers. [Middle English, from Latin *diurnālis,* from *diurnus,* of a day, daily : *diēs,* day + *-urnus,* adjective suffix.] **—di·ur·nal·ly** *adv.*

diurnal parallax *n. Astronomy.* **Parallax** *(see)* caused by the Earth's daily rotation, defined by the angle subtended at a celestial body by the radius of the Earth. Also called "geocentric parallax".

diurnal rhythm *n.* A **circadian rhythm** *(see).*

di·u·tur·nal (dī-ōō-túrn'l) *adj.* Long-lasting. [From Latin *diūturnus,* from *diū,* long.] **—di·u·tur·ni·ty** *n.*

div. 1. *Mathematics.* divergence. **2.** divided; division; divisor. **3.** dividend. **4.** divorced.

di·va (dée-və) *n., pl.* **-vas** or *Italian* **-ve** (-vay). **1.** An operatic prima donna. **2.** A female pop star. [Italian, "goddess", from Latin, feminine of *dīvus,* god.]

divagate (dívə-gayt || U.S. also dívvə-) *intr. v.* **-gated, -gating, -gates.** *Literary.* **1.** To a wander or drift about. **2.** To ramble; digress. [Late Latin *dīvagārī* : Latin *dis-,* apart + *vagārī,* to wander, from *vagus,* wandering, VAGUE.] **—di·va·ga·tion** (-gáysh'n) *n.*

di·va·lent (dī-váylənt) *adj.* Having a valency of two; bivalent.

di·van (di-ván, dī-, dī-van; *also* -vaán *for senses 2, 3, 4, 5*) *n.* Also **di·wan** (di-waán) (for senses 2, 5). **1. a.** A long backless couch, especially one against a wall with pillows. **b.** A low bed without a headboard or footboard. **2.** In Muslim countries: **a.** A council that constitutes or is a part of the government. **b.** A room where such a council is held; a court of justice; a council chamber. **3.** Any council. **4.** Formerly, a coffee house or smoking room furnished with divans. **5.** In the Middle East, a book of poems by one author. [French, from Turkish *dīvān,* from Persian *dīvān*†, register, account, hence office of accounts, council of state.]

di·var·i·cate (dī-várri-kayt, di-) *intr.v.* **-cated, -cating, -cates.** To diverge at a wide angle; branch off; spread apart. Used especially of branches.
~*adj.* (-kət, -kit, -kayt). *Biology.* Branching or spreading widely from a point or axis; diverging. [Latin *dīvāricāre,* to spread apart : *dis-,* apart + *vāricāre,* to straddle, from *vāricus,* with the feet spread apart, from *vārus,* bent, knock-kneed.] **—di·var·i·cate·ly** *adv.*

di·var·i·ca·tion (dī-várri-káysh'n, di-) *n.* **1.** The act of divaricating; a branching off. **2.** A divergence of opinion. **3.** The point at which branching occurs.

di·var·i·cat·or (dī-várri-kaytər, di-) *n.* **1.** A muscle that effects the opening and closing of the shell in brachiopods. **2.** A surgical instrument used to divide tissue into two separate parts.

dive (dīv) *v.* **dived** or *U.S. Informal* **dove** (dōv), **dived, diving, dives.** —*intr.* **1. a.** To plunge headfirst into water, often as a sport. **b.** To go towards the bottom of a body of water: *dive for pearls.* **c.** To submerge under power. Used of a submarine. **d.** To fall head down through the air. **e.** To descend nose down at an acceleration usually exceeding that of free fall. Used of an aeroplane. **f.** To engage in the sport of skydiving. **g.** To drop sharply and rapidly; plummet. **2. a.** To rush headlong, usually downwards or out of sight: *dived into an alley.* **b.** To plunge one's hand into something: *dived into my handbag for a coin.* **3.** To lunge; throw oneself. Used with *at* or *for*: *We dived for the best seats.* **4.** To plunge or rush with great enthusiasm or vigour. Used with *in* or *into*: *The children all dived in and helped themselves to the food.* —*tr.* To cause (an aircraft or a submarine, for example) to dive.
~*n.* **1. a.** A headlong plunge into water, especially one executed deliberately. **b.** A nearly vertical descent at an accelerated speed through water, air, or space. **c.** A quick, pronounced drop. **2.** *Slang.* A disreputable or run-down bar or nightclub. **3.** *Slang.* A knockout feigned by prearrangement between boxers. Used chiefly in the phrase *to take a dive.* [Middle English *diven, duven,* to dive, to submerge, Old English *dȳfan* (transitive), to dip, immerse, and *dūfan* (intransitive), to sink, dive.]

dive-bomb (dīv-bom) *tr.v.* **-bombed, -bombing, -bombs.** *Aviation.* To release a bomb at the end of a steep dive towards the target. **—dive-bomber** *n.*

div·er (dīvər) *n.* **1.** One that dives. **2.** One who dives for something or goes under water for work or pleasure, especially one equipped with breathing apparatus and weighted clothing. **3. a.** Any of several aquatic birds of the family Gaviidae, having black and white plumage and small, pointed wings and noted for their ability to dive deeply under water in search of prey. Also *U.S.* "loon". **b.** Any of various other diving birds.

di·verge (dī-vérj, di-) *v.* **-verged, -verging, -verges.** —*intr.* **1.** To tend in different directions from a common point. **2.** To differ in opinion or manner. **3.** To depart from a set course or norm; deviate. *Mathematics.* To fail to approach a limit. Compare **converge.** —*tr.* To cause to diverge; deflect. —See Synonyms at **separate.** [Late Latin *dīvergere,* to turn aside : Latin *dis-,* apart + *vergere,* to bend, turn.]

di·ver·gence (dī-vérjənss, di-) *n.* Also **di·ver·gen·cy** (-vérjən-si) *pl.* **-cies.** *Abbr.* **div. 1. a.** The act of diverging. **b.** The state of being divergent. **c.** The degree by which things diverge. **2.** Departure from a norm; deviation. **3.** Difference, as of opinion. **4.** *Mathematics.* **a.** The property or manner of diverging; failure to approach a limit. **b.** The scalar product of the del operator and a vector function. In this sense, compare **curl. 5.** *Meteorology.* A condition characterised by a net horizontal outflow of air from a region, often compensated for by a descending air current, usually accompanied by fine dry weather. —See Synonyms at **difference.**

di·ver·gent (dī-vérjənt, di-) *adj.* **1. a.** Drawing apart from a common point; diverging. **b.** Causing divergence of radiation. **2.** Departing from convention; deviant. **3.** Differing from each other: *divergent opinions.* **4.** *Mathematics.* Failing to approach a limit; not convergent. **—di·ver·gent·ly** *adv.*

divergent thinking *n. Psychology.* A type of thinking operation characterised by breadth of vision and the use of imagination to arrive at a variety of possible solutions to a problem. Compare **convergent thinking. —divergent thinker** *n.*

di·vers (dīvərz) *adj. Archaic.* Various; several; sundry. [Middle English *divers(e).* See **diverse.**]

di·verse (dī-vérss, dī-verss || di-) *adj.* **1.** Distinct in kind; disparate; unlike. **2.** Having variety in form; diversified; multiform. [Middle English *divers(e),* from Old French *divers,* from Latin *dīversus,* contrary, diverse, from the past participle of *dīvertere,* to turn aside, DIVERT.] **—di·verse·ly** *adv.* **—di·verse·ness** *n.*

di·ver·si·form (dī-vér-si-fawrm, di-) *adj.* Having a variety of forms; variform. [DIVERS(E) + -I- + -FORM.]

di·ver·si·fy (dī-vér-si-fī, di-) *v.* **-fied, -fying, -fies.** —*tr.* **1.** To make diverse; give variety to; vary. **2. a.** To extend (activities) into various different disparate fields in order to increase profits, spread the risk of loss, or the like. Used of a business enterprise. **b.** To distribute (investments) among several companies in order to reduce the risk of loss. —*intr.* To engage in a wide range of activities. Used especially of a business enterprise. [Middle English *diversifien,* from Old French *diversifier,* from Medieval Latin *dīversificāre* : Latin *dīversus,* DIVERSE + *facere,* to make.] **—di·ver·si·fi·a·ble** *adj.* **—di·ver·si·fi·ca·tion** (-fi-káysh'n) *n.*

di·ver·sion (dī-vérsh'n, di- || -vérzh'n) *n.* **1.** An act or instance of diverting; a turning aside. **2.** Something that distracts the mind and relaxes or entertains. **3.** In military strategy, a manoeuvre that draws the attention of the enemy away from the planned point of attack. **4.** A detour created for traffic. **—di·ver·sion·ar·y** *adj.*

di·ver·sion·ist (dī-vérsh'n-ist, di- || -vérzh'n-) *n. Politics.* One engaged in diversionary, disruptive, or subversive activities, especially from within and against a Communist state. **—di·ver·sion·ist** *adj.*

di·ver·si·ty (dī-vérssəti, di-) *n., pl.* **-ties. 1. a.** The fact or quality of being diverse; difference. **b.** A point or respect in which things differ. **2.** Variety; multiformity: *a healthy diversity in one's diet.*

di·vert (dī-vért, di-) *v.* **-verted, -verting, -verts.** —*tr.* **1.** To turn aside from a usual course or direction; deflect. **2.** To distract. **3.** To amuse or entertain. —*intr.* To turn aside. [Middle English *diverten,* to turn aside, digress, escape, from Old French *divertir,* from Latin *dīvertere,* to turn aside : *dis-,* aside + *vertere,* to turn.] **—di·vert·er** *n.* **—di·vert·ing·ly** *adv.*

diverticular disease *n.* A condition in which diverticula in the colon are associated with lower abdominal pain.

di·ver·tic·u·li·tis (dī-ver-tíckew-lītiss, -vər-) *n. Pathology.* Inflammation of a diverticulum.

di·ver·tic·u·lum (dī-vert-tíckew-ləm, -vər-) *n., pl.* **-la** (-lə). A pouch or sac branching out from a hollow organ or structure, especially the intestine. Diverticula may occur as abnormal structures formed at weak points in the intestinal wall. [New Latin, from Latin *dēverticulum,* bypath, from *dēvertere,* to turn aside : *dē-,* away + *vertere,* to turn.] **—di·ver·tic·u·lar** (-lər) *adj.*

di·ver·ti·men·to (di-vérti-méntō, -vairti-) *n., pl.* **-ti** (-tee). *Music.* A chiefly 18th-century form of instrumental chamber music having several short movements. [Italian, "diversion", "amusement", from *divertire,* to DIVERT.]

di·ver·tisse·ment (déevair-teéss-mon, -món, di-vértiss-mənt) *n.* **1.** A short ballet or other performance given as an interlude in the opera or theatre. **2. a.** *Music.* A divertimento. **b.** A fantasia composed using well-known melodies. **3.** A diversion; an amusement. [French, from *divertir,* to DIVERT.]

Di·ves (dī́veez) *n.* A man of wealth. [Middle English, from Latin *Dīvēs,* the rich man in the parable of Lazarus, Luke 16:19–31, from *dīvēs,* rich, costly.]
di·vest (dī-vést, di-) *tr.v.* **-vested, -vesting, -vests. 1.** To strip, as of clothes. **2.** To deprive, as of rights or property; dispossess. **3.** *Law.* To take away from a person (an interest or estate previously vested in him); devest. —See Synonyms at **strip.** [Alteration of DEVEST.]
divi. Variant of **divvy.**
di·vide (di-vī́d) *v.* **-vided, -viding, -vides.** *—tr.* **1. a.** To separate into parts, sections, groups, or branches. **b.** To sector into units of measurement; graduate. **c.** To separate and group according to kind; classify. **2. a.** To separate into opposing factions; disunite: *The issue of unemployment divided the party.* **b.** *British.* To cause (Members of Parliament) to vote by separating into groups for and against a motion. **3.** To separate from; cut off; serve as a boundary between. **4.** To apportion among a number; share out. **5.** *Mathematics.* **a.** To subject to the process of division. **b.** To be an exact divisor of. *—intr.* **1. a.** To become separated into parts. **b.** To branch out. Used of a river, for example. **c.** To form into factions; take sides. **d.** *British.* To vote by being divided. **2.** To perform the mathematical operation of division. —See Synonyms at **distribute, separate.**
~n. **1.** A dividing point or line. **2.** *Chiefly U.S.* A ridge of land forming a watershed. **3.** See **Great Divide.** [Middle English *dividen,* from Latin *dīvidere.*] **—di·vid·a·ble** *adj.*
di·vid·ed (di-vī́did) *adj. Abbr.* **div. 1.** Separated into parts or pieces. **2.** In disagreement; disunited. **3.** Pulled by conflicting interests or activities. **4.** *Botany.* Having indentations extending to the midrib or base and forming distinct divisions: *divided leaves.*
divided highway *n. U.S.* A dual carriageway.
divided road *n. Australian.* A dual carriageway.
div·i·dend (dívvi-dend, *rarely* -dənd) *n. Abbr.* **div. 1.** *Mathematics.* A quantity to be divided. **2. a.** A pro rata share of net profits distributed to a shareholder in a company. **b.** A share of profits received by a member of a cooperative society or by a policyholder in a mutual insurance society. **c.** A pro rata payment to a creditor of a person adjudged bankrupt. **3.** A benefit; a bonus: *Our decision to buy a computer paid handsome dividends.* —See Synonyms at **bonus.** [French, from Latin *dīvidendum,* "thing to be divided", neuter gerundive of *dīvidere,* to DIVIDE.]
di·vid·er (di-vī́dər) *n.* **1. a.** One that divides. **b.** A screen or other partition. **2.** *Plural.* A device resembling a compass with two points, used for dividing lines and transferring measurements.
div·i·div·i (dívvi-dívvi) *n., pl.* **-is. 1.** A tropical American tree, *Caesalpina coriaria,* having compound leaves and long pods. **2.** The dried pods of this tree, yielding an extract used in tanning leather. [Spanish *dividivi,* from Cariban.]
div·i·na·tion (dívvi-náysh'n) *n.* **1.** The art or act of foretelling events or revealing occult knowledge by means of augury or alleged supernatural agency. **2.** Inspired insight; intuition. **3.** That which has been divined; a prophecy. **—di·vin·a·to·ry** (di-vínnə-tri, -təri) *adj.*
di·vine[1] (di-vī́n) *adj.* **-viner, -vinest. 1. a.** Being or having the nature of a deity. **b.** Of, pertaining to, emanating from, or being the expression of a deity. **c.** In the service or worship of a deity or god; sacred; holy. **2.** Superhuman; godlike. **3.** Supremely good; magnificent. **4.** *Informal.* Heavenly; perfect.
~n. A clergyman, religious, or priest, especially one knowledgeable in theology. [Middle English, from Old French *devin,* from Latin *dīvīnus,* from *dīvus,* divine, god.] **—di·vine·ly** *adv.* **—di·vine·ness** *n.*
divine[2] *v.* **-vined, -vining, -vines.** *—tr.* **1.** To know, foresee, predict, or come to conjecture, as by inspiration, intuition, or reflection. **2.** To locate (water, minerals, or the like) with a divining rod or pendulum.
~intr. **1.** To practise divination. **2.** *Formal.* To guess. —See Synonyms at **foretell.** [Middle English *divinen,* from Old French *deviner,* from Latin *dīvīnāre,* from *dīvīnus,* soothsayer, "(one) inspired by the gods", DIVINE (adjective).] **—di·vin·er** *n.*
Divine Liturgy *n.* The Eastern Orthodox Eucharistic ceremony.
Divine Office *n. Roman Catholic Church.* The prayers and readings for the daily canonical hours; the offices and prayers in the breviary.
divine right *n.* **1.** The right of a monarch to rule, supposed to have come directly from God and to be independent of the will or consent of his subjects. Also called "divine right of kings". **2.** *Informal.* Any right or claim regarded by its holder as incontestable.
Divine Service *n.* A public service in a Christian church for the worship of God.
diving beetle *n.* Any of various predatory aquatic beetles of the family Dytiscidae, having streamlined bodies and flattened hind legs.
diving bell *n.* A large vessel for underwater work, open on the bottom and supplied with air under pressure.
diving board *n.* A flexible board or platform from which a dive may be executed, secured at one end and projecting over water at the other.
diving duck *n.* Any duck that dives to the bottom of a river or lake to feed. Diving ducks include the pochard, scaup, and goldeneye. Compare **dabbling duck.**
diving suit *n.* A heavy waterproof suit with a large detachable helmet supplied with air, used for underwater work.
divining rod *n.* A forked branch or stick that allegedly indicates subterranean water or minerals by bending downwards when held over a source. Also called "dowsing rod".
di·vin·i·ty (di-vínnəti) *n., pl.* **-ties. 1.** The state or quality of being divine; especially, the state of being a deity. **2. a.** *Capital* **D.** God; the godhead. **b.** A god or goddess; a deity. **3.** Theology.
di·vis·i·ble (di-vízzə-b'l) *adj.* Capable of being divided, especially of being divided evenly with no remainder. **—di·vis·i·bil·i·ty** (-bílləti) *n.* **—di·vis·i·bly** *adv.*
di·vi·sion (di-vízh'n) *n. Abbr.* **div. 1. a.** The act or process of dividing. **b.** The state of being divided. **2.** The act or process of sharing out; distribution. **3.** Something that serves to divide or keep separate, such as a boundary or partition. **4.** One of the parts, sections, or groups into which something is divided. **5. a.** An area of governmental, judicial, or business activity organised as an administrative or functional unit. **b.** A territorial section marked off, as for political, governmental, or policing purposes. **6.** *Military.* **a.** The major autonomous administrative and tactical unit of an army that is larger than a regiment but smaller than a corps. It is the smallest self-contained unit of an army that can engage independently in prolonged combat. **b.** A corresponding unit in any of the other armed forces. **7.** *Botany.* A major taxonomic category corresponding approximately to a phylum. **8. a.** Variance of opinion; disagreement. **b.** A splitting into factions; disunion. **9.** *British.* The physical separation of Members of Parliament into groups according to their stand on an issue put to the vote. Also used adjectivally: *the division bell.* **10.** *Mathematics.* The operation of determining how many times one quantity is contained in another. Compare **multiplication. 11.** A type of plant propagation in which a part separated from the parent grows into a new plant. **12.** *Sports.* **a.** Any of various competitive categories in a particular sport, organised according to age, ability, sex, or the like. **b.** Any of the subsections of a league into which soccer teams are grouped according to ability. [Middle English *divisioun,* from Old French *division,* from Latin *dīvīsiō* (stem *dīvīsiōn-*), from *dīvidere* (past participle *dīvīsus*), to DIVIDE.] **—di·vi·sion·al** *adj.*
di·vi·sion·ism (di-vízh'n-iz'm) *n.* A branch of neo-impressionism in which colours are divided into their primary components and arranged in dabs so that the eye organises the shape. Compare **pointillism. —di·vi·sion·ist** *n. & adj.*
division lobby *n.* A **lobby** *(see)* in a legislative chamber.
division sign *n.* The symbol (÷) placed between two quantities to indicate the division of the first by the second.
di·vi·sive (di-vī́-siv || -ziv, -víssiv) *adj.* Creating discord or dissension. **—di·vi·sive·ly** *adv.* **—di·vi·sive·ness** *n.*
di·vi·sor (di-vī́zər) *n. Abbr.* **div. 1.** The quantity by which another quantity, the dividend, is to be divided. **2.** A number that divides another number exactly; a factor.
di·vorce (di-vórss || dī-, -vṓrss) *n.* **1. a.** The dissolution of a marriage by the legal judgment of a court, or in some societies, by established custom. **b.** The legal declaration of such a dissolution. **2.** A complete or radical separation of things formerly closely connected.
~v. **divorced, -vorcing, -vorces.** *—tr.* **1.** To dissolve the marriage bond between. **2.** To end one's marriage to (one's spouse) by legal divorce. **3.** To separate or detach; disunite. *—intr.* To become divorced. —See Synonyms at **separate.** [Middle English, from Old French, from Latin *dīvortium,* separation, divorce, fork in a road, from *dīvortere, dīvertere,* to turn aside, separate, DIVERT.]
di·vor·cée (di-vór-see, dívvawr-, -say || -vṓr-, *U.S.* -sáy, -sée) *n. Masculine* **di·vor·cé.** A divorced woman. [French, "divorced".]
div·ot (dívvət) *n.* **1.** A piece of turf torn up by a golf club in striking a ball, or by a horse's hoof. **2.** *Scottish.* A thin square of turf or sod, used especially for roofing. [Scottish *deva(i)t, dewot, duvat*†.]
di·vulge (dī-vúlj, di-) *tr.v.* **-vulged, -vulging, -vulges. 1.** To disclose (something previously kept secret); reveal; make known. **2.** *Archaic.* To proclaim publicly. —See Synonyms at **reveal.** [Middle English *divulgen,* from Latin *dīvulgāre,* to spread abroad among the people : *dis-,* abroad + *vulgāre,* to make common, publish, from *vulgus,* multitude, public. See **vulgar.**] **—di·vul·gence, di·vulge·ment** *n.* **—di·vulg·er** *n.*
di·vul·sion (dī-vúlsh'n) *n.* A tearing apart; a violent separation. [Latin *divulsiō* (stem *divulsiōn-*), from *dīvellere* (past participle *dīvulsus*), to tear apart : *dis-,* apart + *vellere,* to tear, pluck.] **—di·vul·sive** *adj.*
div·vy[1], di·vi dívvi) *n., pl.* **-vies. 1.** *Informal.* A dividend, especially one from a cooperative society. **2.** *Chiefly U.S. Informal.* A share or portion.
~tr.v. **divvied, -vying, -vies.** *Informal.* To divide. Usually used with *up.* [Short for DIVIDEND.]
divvy[2] *adj.* **divvier, divviest.** *Northern English Slang.* silly; foolish.
~n. Northern English Slang. A silly fool. [20th century : origin obscure.]
diwan. 1. Variant of **dewan. 2.** Variant of **divan.**
Dix·ie (díksi) *n.* The Southern states of the United States that joined the Confederacy during the American Civil War. Also called "Dixieland". [Perhaps from *dixie,* a ten-dollar bill issued by a New Orleans bank prior to the Civil War, with a large *Dix* printed on each side, from French *dix,* ten.]
Dix·ie·land (díksi-land) *n.* **1.** A style of instrumental jazz based on the traditional New Orleans style of jazz with a relatively fast, strongly accented two-beat rhythm and group improvisation, but having a more regular melodic structure. **2.** Dixie.
D.I.Y., d.i.y. *n.* Do-it-yourself. **—D.I.Y., d.i.y.** *adj.*
di·zen (dī́z'n, dízz'n) *tr.v.* **-ened, -ening, -ens.** *Archaic.* To deck out, especially vulgarly, in fine clothes or adornments; bedizen. [Earlier *disen,* to dress a distaff with flax, perhaps from Low German *dise*†,

bunch of flax on a distaff.] —**di·zen·ment** *n.*

di·zy·got·ic (dī-zī-góttik) *adj.* Derived from two separate and separately fertilised ova. Said especially of fraternal twins.

diz·zy (dízzi) *adj.* **-zier, -ziest. 1.** Having a sensation of whirling or feeling a tendency to fall; giddy. **2.** Bewildered or confused. **3. a.** Producing or tending to produce giddiness or a whirling sensation: *the dizzy heights of success.* **b.** Characterised by giddiness; reeling: *a dizzy spell.* **4.** *Informal.* Scatterbrained; silly; foolish. ~*tr.v.* **dizzied, -zying, -zies.** To make dizzy; confuse; bewilder. [Middle English *dusie,* foolish, giddy, from Old English *dysig,* foolish, stupid.] —**diz·zi·ly** *adv.* —**diz·zi·ness** *n.*

DJ *n., pl.* **DJ's** or **DJs. 1.** A disc jockey. **2.** A dinner jacket.

Djakarta. See **Jakarta.**

djellaba. Variant of **jellaba.**

Dji·bou·ti, Republic of (ji-bóoti). Small, arid country on the northeast coast of Africa, on the Gulf of Aden. The population, mostly Muslim, is concentrated on the port of Djibouti, which was developed by the French when the area became the colony of French Somaliland in 1888. From 1967 until independence ten years later, Djibouti was administered as the French Territory of the Afars and Issas—the two main population groups. Area, 23 200 square kilometres (8,958 square miles). Population, 620,000. Capital, Djibouti. See map at **Ethiopia.**

Dji·las (jee-lɔss, -lass), **Milovan** (1911–95). Yugoslav politician and writer. He was a member of Tito's resistance group in World War II and served in the postwar Communist government, but was demoted for criticising the regime. He wrote *The New Class* (1957), *Land Without Justice* (1958), and *Conversations with Stalin* (1962).

djinni, djinny. Variants of **jinni.**

Djokjakarta. See **Jogjakarta.**

dk. 1. dark. **2.** deck. **3.** dock.

dl decilitre.

D layer *n. Meteorology.* The weakly ionised layer of the ionosphere, approximately 50 to 90 kilometres (30 to 55 miles) above the Earth. Also called "D region".

D line *n. Physics.* One of two closely spaced lines in the yellow region of the spectrum of sodium, used as a standard for optical measurement. The lines occur at wavelengths of 589.6 and 589.0 nanometres.

D.Lit., D.Litt. Doctor of Letters; Doctor of Literature. [Latin *Doctor Lit(t)erarum.*]

D.L.P. Democratic Labor Party (in Australia).

dm decimetre.

DM 1. *Chemistry.* adamsite. **2.** Deutschmark.

DMA *Computing.* direct memory access.

DMSO dimethylsulphoxide.

D. Mus. Doctor of Music.

DMZ demilitarised zone.

DNA *n.* Deoxyribonucleic acid, a nucleic acid that is the chief constituent of chromosomes, can replicate itself, and is responsible for transmitting genetic information, in the form of genes, from parents to offspring. It consists of a double helix of two long chains of linked **nucleotides** *(see),* connected by hydrogen bonds between the bases adenine and thymine or cytosine and guanine.

DNB Dictionary of National Biography.

Dnepr or **Dnie·per** (dnéepɔr, néeɔpr; *Russian* dnyepr). *Ukrainian* **Dni·pro** (dnee-pró, -práw). River in Russia, Belarus, and Ukraine, flowing from the Valdai Hills 2 286 kilometres (1,420 miles) to the Black Sea. It is the third-longest river entirely within Europe. Kiev is the biggest city on its banks. The river is an important source of hydroelectric power.

Dnestr or **Dnie·ster** (dnéestɔr, néestɔr; *Russian* dnyestr). River in Ukraine and Moldova. It flows 1 411 kilometres (877 miles) from the Carpathian mountains to the Black Sea near Odessa.

Dnipro. See **Dnepr.**

D notice *n. British.* An official notice from the government, circulated among news editors, requesting that certain information be withheld from publication or broadcasting for security reasons.

do¹ (dōo; *weak forms* dōo, dɔ, d) *v.* **did** (did), **done** (dun), **doing, does** (duz; *weak forms* dɔz, dz). Present tense, first person, **do;** second person, **do** or (for singular) *archaic* **doest** (dōo-ist), **dost** (dust; *weak form* dɔst); third person singular, **does** or *archaic* **doeth** (dōo-ith), **doth** (duth; *weak form* dɔth); third person plural, **do.** Used as an auxiliary in the past or present tense followed by the infinitive without *to,* or, in reply to a question or suggestion, with this infinitive understood. Its function can be: **1.** To indicate the tense of the infinitive in questions, negative statements, and inverted phrases: *Do you understand?; I did not sleep well; Little did she suspect.* **2.** To intensify or emphasise: *Do be still!* **3.** To represent an antecedent verb, and thus avoid its repetition: *She tries as hard as they do; Jane arrived late, and so did I.* **4.** To serve as an extra word, in verse or poetic prose, which improves the sound but does not change the sense of a line, or to express certain nuances of irony or humour: *Well, I do declare.* —*tr.* **1.** To perform or execute (an action, procedure, or piece of work): *She did the driving; Have you done your homework?* **2.** To carry out; fulfil what is involved in: *We did all that was necessary.* **3.** To produce or make (a piece or amount of work): *did a portrait.* In this sense, often used in place of verbs such as *write, paint,* or *compose.* **4. a.** To bring about; achieve: *It won't do any good.* **b.** To effect (an improvement): *That hat doesn't do anything for her.* **5.** To attend to, deal with, or treat in an appropriate way: *do the dinner; The school doesn't do Latin; I must get the car done.* In this sense, often used in place of a wide

variety of common verbs. **6.** To render or give: *do justice to her abilities.* **7.** To work at as an occupation or study. **8.** To work out the details of; solve: *do a crossword.* **9.** To present (a play or dramatic reading, for example); perform; stage. **10.** To have the role of; play. **11. a.** To travel over (a specified distance): *do a mile in four minutes; do 40 miles to the gallon.* **b.** To travel at or be capable of attaining (a specified speed). **12.** To travel about; visit; tour: *do Europe in five weeks.* **13.** To meet the needs of sufficiently; be suitable or convenient for; suffice: *This room will do us very nicely.* **14.** To groom or beautify (the hair, for example). **15.** To translate: *Homer's Iliad, done into English verse.* **16.** *Informal.* To serve (a term of imprisonment). **17.** *British Informal.* To treat: *They did us very well.* **18.** *Informal.* **a.** To imitate; mimic. **b.** To behave in a manner that is characteristic of: *did a Houdini and escaped through the bars.* **19.** *Slang.* To cheat or swindle: *do someone out of her inheritance.* **20.** *Slang.* To have sexual intercourse with. **21.** *Chiefly British Slang.* **a.** To attack; beat up. **b.** To rob. **c.** To arrest and prosecute. —*intr.* **1.** To behave or conduct oneself; act: *Do as you are told; You would do well to leave.* **2.** To act effectively or energetically; strive: *Do or die.* **3.** To get along; fare: *doing well at school.* **4.** To be suitable; serve the purpose: *This coat will do for another season.* **5.** To be sufficient or appropriate in a given situation: *That will do!* **6.** *Informal.* To happen; take place: *Was there anything doing in town yesterday?* —**do away with. 1.** To dispose of; eliminate. **2.** To destroy; kill. —**do by.** To behave with respect to; deal with. —**do down.** To get the better of (someone). —**do for.** *Informal.* **1.** To take care of; specifically, to do housework for. **2.** To cause to fail or die. —**do in.** *Slang.* **1.** To tire completely; exhaust. **2.** To kill. —**do over.** *Slang.* **1.** To attack. **2.** To rob. —**do up. 1.** *Informal.* To groom or adorn lavishly. **2.** To wrap and tie (a package). **3.** To tie up or arrange (the hair) so that it is off the neck. **4.** *Informal.* To refurbish or renovate. **5.** To fasten; button or zip up. —**do with.** To be glad to have; need or want: *I could do with a drink.* —**do without.** To manage easily without; be able to dispense with. —**have** or **be to do with. 1.** To have a relation to or relationship with. **2.** To be concerned with; have as subject matter: *a book that has* or *is to do with religion.* —**make do.** To manage with whatever one has or whatever is available.

~*n., pl.* **do's** or **dos** (dōoz). **1.** *Informal.* An entertainment; a party. **2.** *Informal.* A hoax or swindle; a cheat. **3.** A statement of what should be done: *do's and don'ts.* **4.** *Informal.* Share or deal. Used in the phrase *fair do's.* **5.** *Archaic.* Duty. Used chiefly in the phrase *to do one's do.* [Do, did, done, dost, does (or doth), didst; Middle English *don, did(d)e, idon, dost, does* (regularly *doth*), *diddest,* Old English *dōn, dyde, gedōn, dēst, dēth* (plural *dōth*), *dydest,* from Germanic; akin to Greek *tithēnai,* to place, Sanskrit *dádhāmi,* to put.]

Usage: Do is sometimes used informally in ways that formal standard English constructions would avoid, for example: *I said she would leave and she did do* (where majority use would omit the *do*); *Those who have seen such fighting as I have done* (where again it would be usual to omit *done*); *You've been to a comprehensive school, as we've done* (where the use of *do* to refer back to the main verb *be* is open to criticism). The use of *do* with the verb *have* presents special problems. See Usage note at **have.**

The use of *don't* (*She just don't care*) for *doesn't* is nonstandard in both British and American English, but it is an extremely widespread form in regional dialects.

do² *Music.* Variant of **doh.**

do. ditto.

D.O. Diploma in Ophthalmology.

D.O.A. *Medicine.* dead on arrival.

do·a·ble (dōo-ɔb'l) *adj.* Able to be done.

doat. Variant of **dote.**

dob·bin (dóbbin) *n.* A horse, especially a workhorse. Used mainly by and to children. [From *Dobbin,* alteration of *Robin,* pet form for the name *Robert.*]

Do·bell's solution (dó-belz, -b'lz) *n.* An aqueous solution of sodium borate, sodium bicarbonate, glycerol, and phenol, used as an antibacterial agent for the mucous membranes, of the nose and throat. [After Horace B. *Dobell* (1828–1917), British doctor.]

Do·ber·man pin·scher (dōbɔr-mɔn pínshɔr, -man) *n.* A fairly large dog of a breed originating in Germany, having a smooth, short, usually black coat with rust-red markings and often used for guard or police work. [German *Dobermann,* after Ludwig *Dobermann,* 19th-century German dog-breeder + *Pinscher,* terrier, probably from English PINCH (in allusion to its cropped ears and docked tail).]

doc (dok) *n. Informal.* A doctor.

doc. document.

do·cent (dō-sént, dó-sɔnt) *n.* In the United States, a teacher or lecturer at certain universities who is not a full faculty member. [Obsolete German *Docent,* from Latin *docēns* (stem *docent-*), present participle of *docēre,* to teach.]

Do·ce·tism (dō-séet-iz'm ‖ *U.S. also* dó-sɔt-) *n.* The doctrine, espoused by a sect considered heretical in the early Christian Church, that Christ had no human body and only appeared to suffer and die on the cross. [Late Latin *Docētae,* the sect advocating this doctrine, from Late Greek *Dokētai,* from Greek *dokein,* to seem, appear.] —**Do·ce·tic** (dō-séetik, -séttik) *adj.* —**Do·ce·tist** *n. & adj.*

do·cile (dō-sīl ‖ *U.S.* dóss'l) *adj.* **1.** Submissive to another's will; easily handled. **2.** Yielding to handling or treatment; easily shaped or formed: *"metal is so docile that it will submit to any formal conception a sculptor may have"* (Herbert Read). **3.** Capable of being

dock¹ / dodger

taught; ready and willing to learn. —See Synonyms at **obedient**. [Latin *docilis*, from *docēre*, to teach.] —**doc·ile·ly** *adv.* —**do·cil·i·ty** (dō-síllǝti) *n.*

dock¹ (dok) *n. Abbr.* **dk.** **1.** The area of water between two piers or alongside a pier that receives a ship for loading, unloading, or repairs. See **dry dock.** **2.** A pier or wharf. **3.** *Often plural.* A group of piers, often enclosed, on a protected basin or other waterway serving as a general landing area for ships or boats. **4.** *U.S.* A platform at which lorries or trains discharge or pick up freight.
~*v.* **docked, docking, docks.** —*tr.* **1.** To manoeuvre (a vessel) into or next to a dock. **2.** *Aerospace.* To couple (two or more spacecraft, for example) in space. —*intr.* **1.** To move or come into a dock. **2.** To join with another spacecraft while in space. [Middle Low German and Middle Dutch *docke*, probably from Vulgar Latin *ductia* (unattested), conduit, aqueduct, from Latin *dūcere*, to lead.]

dock² *n.* **1.** The solid or bony part of an animal's tail. **2.** The tail of an animal after it has been cut short.
~*tr.v.* **docked, docking, docks.** **1.** To cut short or cut off (an animal's tail, for example). **2.** To deduct a part from (someone's salary or wages). **3.** To withhold or cut an amount, as of wages or salary, from. [Middle English *dok*, trimmed hair (of a tail), perhaps Old English *docca* (attested only in *fingerdocca*, finger muscle), from Germanic *dukk-* (unattested), bundle. See also **doxy.**]

dock³ *n.* An enclosed place where the defendant stands or sits in a criminal court. [Flemish *docke, dok*†, cage, pen.]

dock⁴ *n.* Any of various weedy plants of the genus *Rumex*, having large leaves and clusters of small greenish or reddish flowers. [Middle English *dock, docke,* Old English *docce*.]

dock·age (dóckij) *n.* **1.** A charge for docking vessels. **2.** Facilities for docking vessels. **3.** The docking of ships.

dock brief *n. British.* A consultation occurring in the court buildings between a duty solicitor and a defendant who is not otherwise represented.

dock·er (dóckǝr) *n. British.* A worker at a dock who loads and unloads ships from the wharf. Also *U.S.* "longshoreman".

dock·et (dóckit) *n.* **1.** A label on or ticket affixed to a package listing the contents or directions for assembling or operating. **2.** *British.* A receipt from the Customs authorities. **3.** A voucher or chit. **4.** *Law.* **a.** A brief record of the proceedings in a court of justice. **b.** The book containing such records. **5.** *U.S.* **a.** A list of the cases awaiting action in a court. **b.** Any list of things to be done; an agenda. **6.** *Archaic.* A summary or other brief statement of the contents of a document; an abstract.
~*tr.v.* **docketed, -eting, -ets.** **1.** To provide with a brief identifying statement. **2.** To enter in a docket. **3.** To label or ticket (a parcel). [Middle English *doggette*†.]

dock·hand (dók-hand) *n.* A dock worker.

dock·land (dók-land) *n. Often plural.* The district surrounding a city's docks.

dock·yard (dók-yaard) *n.* **1.** An area, with facilities for building, repairing, or dry-docking ships. **2.** *British.* A government shipyard; a navy yard.

doc·tor (dóktǝr) *n.* **1.** *Abbr.* **D.** A person who holds the highest academic degree awarded by a college or university in any specified discipline: *a Doctor of Music.* **2.** *Abbr.* **Dr.** A person qualified to practise medicine; especially, a physician or surgeon, and in the United States, a dentist or vet. **3.** *Abbr.* **Dr.** The title used in addressing a medical practitioner or a person who holds the degree of doctor. **4. a.** A Doctor of the Church. **b.** *Archaic.* Any learned person; a teacher. **5.** A person who repairs things or puts right an undesirable situation. **6.** Any device designed to repair a defect or do a special task. **7.** Any of several brightly coloured artificial flies used in fly fishing: *a silver doctor.* —**the Doctor.** Any of several local winds in different parts of the world that mitigate extreme (unhealthy) weather conditions; the harmattan of West Africa is such a wind.
~*v.* **doctored, -toring, -tors.** *Informal.* —*tr.* **1.** To give medical treatment to. **2.** To repair, especially in a makeshift manner. **3.** To change or falsify (evidence or data) so as to make it favourable to oneself or one's cause. **4.** To add ingredients to (food) either to improve its taste or appearance or to make it poisonous. **5.** To castrate or spay (an animal). —*intr.* To practise medicine. [Middle English, Church Father, theologian, canonist, medical doctor, scholar, from Old French *docteur*, from Medieval Latin *doctor*, from Latin, teacher, from *docēre*, to teach.]

doc·tor·al (dóktǝrǝl) *adj.* Of, belonging, or pertaining to an academic doctor: *doctoral robes; a doctoral thesis.*

doc·tor·ate (dóktǝr-ǝt, -it) *n.* The degree or status of a doctor as conferred by a university.

Doctor of Philosophy *n. Abbr.* **Ph.D., D.Ph., D.Phil.** The highest academic degree granted in most arts and sciences. Compare **Bachelor of Arts, Master of Arts.**

Doctor of the Church *n.* One of the saints recognised by the Church as being especially important in the development of Christian doctrine, including four Doctors of the Western Church, St. Ambrose, St. Augustine, St. Jerome, and St. Gregory, or four Doctors of the Eastern Church, St. Athanasius, St. Basil, St. Gregory of Nyssa, and St. John Chrysostom.

doc·tri·naire (dóktri-naír) *adj.* Having or showing an inflexible commitment to a particular theory or principle, and seeking to apply it without regard to practicality or individual circumstances; excessively and impractically dogmatic. —See Synonyms at **dictatorial.**

~*n.* One who adopts a doctrinaire approach; an impractical, dogmatic theorist. —**doc·tri·nair·ism** *n.* —**doc·tri·nar·i·an** *n.*

doc·tri·nal (dok-trín'l ‖ *chiefly U.S.* dóktrin'l) *adj.* Belonging to, characterised by, or concerning doctrine. —**doc·tri·nal·ly** *adv.*

doc·trine (dóktrin) *n.* **1.** Something that is taught; a principle or body of principles taught or advocated in instruction. **2.** A principle or system of principles presented for acceptance or belief, as by a religious, political, scientific, or philosophic group; dogma; received theory. [Middle English, from Old French, from Latin *doctrīna*, teaching, learning, from *doctor*, teacher, DOCTOR.]

doc·u·dra·ma (dóckew-draámǝ) *n.* A television or film presentation of political, social, or historical events or circumstances made like a documentary but recreating events in a fictionalised way, as by using actors to portray the protagonists.

doc·u·ment (dóckew-mǝnt. *Note: not all speakers maintain the distinction between -mǝnt (noun) and -ment (verb).*) *n.* **1.** *Abbr.* **doc.** A paper, such as a deed, letter, or report, which gives evidence or information, especially of an official or legal nature. **2.** A record; historical or sociological evidence: *The archaeologists' discoveries are a fascinating document of Viking civilisation.* **3.** Anything serving as evidence or proof, as a material substance bearing a revealing symbol or mark.
~*tr.v.* (-ment) **documented, -menting, -ments.** **1.** To furnish with a document or documents. **2.** To support (an assertion or claim, for example) with documentary evidence or decisive information. **3.** To support (statements in a book, for example) with written references or citations, annotate. **4.** To record or provide evidence of. [Middle English, precept, instruction, from Old French, from Latin *documentum*, lesson, example, warning, from *docēre*, to teach.]

doc·u·men·tal·ist (dóckew-mént'l-ist) *n.* A person who conserves and studies documents.

doc·u·men·ta·ry (dóckew-mént-ri, -ǝri) *adj.* Also **doc·u·men·tal** (-mént'l). **1.** Consisting of, concerning, or based upon documents. **2.** Presenting facts objectively without inserting fictional matter, as in a book, newspaper account, or film.
~*n., pl.* **documentaries.** A television or film presentation of political, social, or historical events or circumstances, often consisting of news film accompanied by narration.

doc·u·men·ta·tion (dóckew-men-táysh'n, -mǝn-) *n.* **1.** The supplying of documents or supporting references or records. **2.** The documents or references supplied. **3.** The process or science of gathering, classifying, and storing information.

dod·der¹ (dóddǝr) *intr.v.* **-dered, -dering, -ders.** **1.** To shake or tremble, as from old age; totter. **2.** To progress in a feeble, unsteady manner. [17th century : variant of obsolete *dadder*, Middle English *dadiren*, perhaps from Scandinavian; akin to Norwegian *dudra*, to quiver.]

dodder² *n.* Any of various parasitic vines of the genus *Cuscuta*, having slender, twining yellow or reddish stems with a few minute, scalelike leaves, and small whitish flowers. [Middle English *doder*, perhaps from Low German; akin to Middle Low German *dod(d)er.*]

dod·dered (dóddǝrd) *adj.* Lacking the top branches as a result of age or decay. [Alteration of *doddard* : *dod*, to lop off, Middle English *dodent* + -ARD.]

dod·der·ing (dóddǝring) *adj.* Also **dod·der·y** (dóddǝri). Feebleminded or unsteady from age; senile.

dod·dle (dódd'l) *British Informal. n.* Something easily done. [Perhaps a variant of TODDLE.]

do·dec·a·gon (dō-déckǝ-gǝn ‖ -gon) *n.* A polygon having 12 sides and 12 angles. [Greek *dōdekagōnon* : *dōdeka, duódeka,* twelve : *duo,* two + *deka,* ten + -GON.] —**do·de·cag·o·nal** (dō-de-kággǝn'l) *adj.*

do·dec·a·he·dron (dō-deckǝ-hée-drǝn, -hé-) *n., pl.* **-drons** or **-dra** (-drǝ). A polyhedron with 12 plane surfaces. A *regular dodecahedron* has faces that are equal regular pentagons. [Greek *dōdekaedron* : *dōdeka,* twelve (see **dodecagon**) + -HEDRON.] —**do·dec·a·he·dral** *adj.*

Do·dec·a·nese (dō-deckǝ-néess, -néez). *Greek* **Dho·dhe·ka·ni·sos** (thōthéká-neesoss). Group of Greek islands in the southeast Aegean, forming part of the southern Sporades. The name means "twelve islands", and there are twelve main ones, including Cos and Rhodes, and several islets. The city of Rhodes is the administrative centre, and the islands are noted for tourism and sponge-diving.

do·dec·a·no·ic acid (dō-deckǝ-nóik) *n.* **Lauric acid** (*see*).

do·dec·a·phon·ic (dō-deckǝ-fónnik) *adj.* Pertaining to, composed in, or consisting of 12-note music. [Greek *dōdeka,* twelve (see **dodecagon**) + PHONIC.] —**do·dec·a·phon·ist** (-fónnist, -fōnist, dōde-káffǝnist, -déckǝfǝni) *n.* —**do·dec·a·phon·ism, do·dec·a·phon·y** (-fónni, -fōni, dō-de-káffǝni, -déckǝfǝni) *n.*

do·dec·a·syl·la·ble (dō-deckǝ-síllǝb'l) *n.* A metrical line of 12 syllables.

dodge (doj) *v.* **dodged, dodging, dodges.** —*tr.* **1.** To avoid (a blow, for example) by moving or shifting quickly aside. **2.** To evade (an obligation or issue, for example) by cunning, trickery, or deceit. —*intr.* **1.** To move aside quickly, as to avoid a blow; shift or twist suddenly. **2.** To practise trickery or cunning; prevaricate.
~*n.* **1.** An act of dodging; a quick move or shift. **2.** A clever or evasive plan or device; a stratagem. **3.** An ingenious method of doing something; a shortcut. —See Synonyms at **artifice.** [16th century : origin obscure.]

dodg·em (dójǝm) *n.* A small electrically powered car in a funfair, which bumps into other similar cars as it is driven round an enclosure. Also called "dodgem car". [DODGE + 'EM.]

dodg·er (dójǝr) *n.* **1.** A person who dodges or evades: *fare-dodgers.*

2. A shifty or dishonest person; a cheat; a trickster. **3.** A shelter on the bridge of a ship providing protection against rain and sea-spray. **4.** *British Regional.* Food. **5.** *U.S.* A small printed handbill.

dodg·y (dŏji) *adj.* **-ier, -iest.** *Informal.* **1.** Risky or dangerous. **2.** Unreliable; deceitful. **3.** Not in good health or condition; likely to give way under stress.

do·do (dōdō) *n., pl.* **-does** or **-dos. 1.** A large flightless bird, *Raphus cucullatus,* of the island of Mauritius in the Indian Ocean, that has been extinct since the late 17th century. **2.** *Informal.* One whose ideas, dress, or manner of living are hopelessly out-of-date. [Portuguese *doudo,* from *doudo†,* stupid (from its clumsy appearance).]

Do·do·ma (dōdŏ-maa). City and capital of Tanzania, situated in the centre of the country. The transfer of government from the old capital, Dar es Salaam, was completed during the 1990s.

doe (dō) *n., pl.* **does** or collectively **doe. 1.** The female of a deer or related animal. **2.** The female of certain other animals, such as the hare or kangaroo. [Middle English *do,* Old English *dā†.*]

D.O.E. Department of the Environment.

doek (dōōk) *n. South African.* A scarf or cloth used for covering the head. [Afrikaans.]

do·er (dōō-ər) *n.* **1.** A person who does something. **2.** A particularly active and energetic person, who is able to achieve things.

does. Present tense, third person singular of **do.**

doe·skin (dō-skin) *n.* **1.** The skin of a doe, deer, or goat. **2.** Leather made from this. **3.** A fine, soft, smooth woollen fabric.

does·n't (dúzz'nt). Contraction of *does not.*

do·est. *Archaic.* Second person singular, present tense of **do.** Used with *thou.*

do·eth. *Archaic.* Third person singular, present tense of **do.**

doff (dof || dawf) *tr.v.* **doffed, doffing, doffs. 1.** To remove or take off: *doff one's clothes.* **2.** To lift or remove (one's hat) in salutation. **3.** To throw out or away; discard. [Middle English *doffen,* from *don off :* **do,** to **do** + **off.**]

dog (dog || dawg) *n.* **1.** A domesticated carnivorous mammal, *Canis familiaris,* developed in a wide variety of breeds and probably originally derived from several wild species. **2.** Any of various other animals of the family Canidae, such as the dingo. **3.** A male canine animal, especially of a domesticated breed or of the fox. **4.** Any of various other animals, such as the prairie dog. **5. a.** *Informal.* A fellow: *you lucky dog.* **b.** A contemptible, worthless fellow. **c.** *Informal.* A dashing fellow; a playboy: *a gay dog.* **6.** *U.S. Slang.* **a.** An uninteresting or unattractive person: *a date with a real dog.* **b.** A hopelessly inferior product or creation. **7.** *Plural. Informal.* Greyhound races. Preceded by *the.* **8.** *Plural. Slang.* The feet. **9.** A firedog; an andiron. **10. a.** Any of various hooked or U-shaped mechanical devices used for gripping or holding heavy objects. **b.** A pawl or other device engaging a gear or ratchet wheel. **11.** *Astronomy.* A **sun dog** (*see*). **—go to the dogs.** *Informal.* To go to ruin; degenerate. **—like a dog's dinner.** *Informal.* Dressed or arranged in an eye-catching, but rather flashy manner.
~*adj.* Inferior; not genuine: *dog Latin.*
~*adv.* Totally; completely. Used in combination: *dog-tired.*
~*tr.v.* **dogged, dogging, dogs. 1. a.** To follow after like a dog; pursue relentlessly. **b.** To trouble persistently; hound. **2.** To hold or fasten with a mechanical dog. [Middle English *dog, dogge,* Old English *docga†.*]

dog·bane (dóg-bayn || dáwg-) *n.* Any of several plants of the genus *Apocynum,* mostly of tropical or subtropical regions, having bell-shaped white or pink flowers. [Said to be poisonous to dogs.]

dog·ber·ry (dóg-bəri, -berri || dáwg-) *n., pl.* **-ries. 1.** Any of several European shrubs bearing berry-like fruit, such as the dogwood. **2.** The fruit of any of these plants.

dog·cart (dóg-kaart || dáwg-) *n.* **1.** A vehicle drawn by one horse and accommodating two persons seated back to back. **2.** A small cart pulled by dogs.

dog·catch·er (dóg-kachər || dáwg-) *n.* A **dog warden** (*see*).

dog collar *n.* **1.** A collar for a dog. **2.** *Informal.* A clerical collar.

dog days *pl. n.* **1.** In the Northern Hemisphere, the hot, sultry period between mid-July and September. **2.** A period of inactivity. [Translation of Late Latin *diēs canīculārēs,* "Dog Star days" (so called because Sirius rises and sets with the Sun during this time).]

doge (dōj; *sometimes, wrongly,* dōzh) *n.* The elected chief magistrate of the former republics of Venice and Genoa. [French, from Italian (Venetian dialect), from Latin *dux,* leader, from *dūcere,* to lead.]

dog-ear (dóg-eer || dáwg-) *n.* Also **dog's-ear** (dógz-eer || dáwgz-). A turned-down corner of the page of a book.

dog-eared (dóg-eerd, -éerd || dáwg-) *adj.* **1.** Having pages with the corners turned down. Said of a book. **2.** Worn from overuse.

dog-eat-dog (dóg-eet-dóg || dáwg-eet-dáwg) *adj.* Ruthlessly competitive or acquisitive: *a dog-eat-dog society.*

dog-end (dóg-énd, -end || dáwg-) *n. Slang.* A cigarette butt.

dog·face (dóg-fayss || dáwg-) *n. U.S. Slang.* An infantryman in the U.S. Army in World War II.

dog fennel *n.* Any of various strong-smelling plants of the genus *Anthemis,* such as the stinking mayweed.

dog·fight (dóg-fīt || dáwg-) *n.* **1.** A violent fight between or as if between dogs; a brawl. **2.** An aerial battle, especially between fighter planes.

dog·fish (dóg-fish || dáwg-) *n., pl.* **-fishes** or collectively **dogfish. 1.** Any of various small sharks, chiefly of the families Scyliorhinidae (*spotted dogfish*), Squalidae (*spiny dogfish*), and Triakidae (*smooth dogfish,* or *smooth hounds*). **2.** the **bowfin** (*see*).

dog·ged (dóggid) *adj.* Not yielding readily; tenacious;

stubborn and persistent: *dogged self-assertion.* See Synonyms at **obstinate. —dog·ged·ly** *adv.* **—dog·ged·ness** *n.*

Dog·ger Bank (dóggər). A sandbank and fishing ground in the North Sea, off northeast England.

dog·ger·el (dóg-rəl, -ərəl || dáwg-) *n.* Verse of a loose, irregular rhythm or of a trivial nature and poor quality. **—dog·ger·el** *adj.* [Middle English *dogerel,* poor, worthless, perhaps from *dogge,* **dog.**]

dog·ger·y (dóg-əri || dáwg-) *n., pl.* **-ies. 1.** Surly behaviour; meanness. **2.** Undesirable elements; riffraff.

dog·gish (dóg-ish || dáwg-) *adj.* **1.** Pertaining to or suggestive of a dog. **2.** Surly. **—dog·gish·ly** *adv.* **—dog·gish·ness** *n.*

dog·go (dóggō) *adv.* Quiet and out of sight. Used in the phrase *lie doggo.* [Probably from **dog.**]

dog·gone (dóg-gón || dáwg-, -gáwn) *adj. U.S.* Damn. Used euphemistically. [Euphemistic for *God damn (it).*] **—dog·gone** *interj.* **—dog·gone** *tr.v.*

dog·gy, dog·gie (dóggi || dáwgi) *n., pl.* **-gies.** A dog, especially a small one. Used by or to children.
~*adj.* **doggier, -giest. 1.** Of or like a dog. **2.** Liking and caring for dogs. Used humorously.

doggy bag *n. Informal.* A bag for leftover food that a diner in a restaurant may take home. [As if saving it for a pet.]

dog·house (dóg-howss || dáwg-) *n. U.S.* A kennel. **—in the doghouse.** *Slang.* In disfavour; in trouble.

do·gie (dōgi) *n. U.S.* A motherless or stray calf. [19th century : origin obscure.]

dog in the manger *n.* One who prevents others from enjoying what he himself has no use for. [From a fable of Aesop.]

dog·leg (dóg-leg || dáwg-) *n.* Something that has a sharp bend; especially, a golf hole in which the fairway is abruptly angled. **—dog·leg·ged** (-léggid, -légd, -legd) *adj.*

dog·ma (dóg-mə || dáwg-) *n., pl.* **-mas** or **-mata** (-mətə). **1.** *Theology.* A doctrine or system of doctrines proclaimed true by a religious sect: *Christian dogma.* **2.** A principle, belief, or statement of an idea or opinion, especially one that is authoritatively, sometimes arrogantly, asserted as absolute truth: *party dogma.* **3.** A system of such principles or beliefs. [Latin, from Greek, opinion, belief, public decree, from *dokein,* to seem, think.]

dog·mat·ic (dog-máttik || dawg-) *adj.* Also **dog·mat·i·cal** (-máttik'l). **1.** Pertaining to or characteristic of dogma. **2.** Characterised by an authoritative, arrogant assertion of unproved or unprovable principles. **—See** Synonyms at **dictatorial.** [Late Latin *dogmaticus,* from Greek *dogmatikos,* from *dogma* (stem *dogmat-*), **dogma.**] **—dog·mat·i·cal·ly** *adv.*

dog·mat·ics (dog-máttiks || dawg-) *n.* Used with a singular verb. The study of religious dogmas, especially those of the Christian church. Also called "dogmatic theology".

dog·ma·tise, dog·ma·tize (dóg-mə-tīz || dáwg-) *v.* **-tised, -tising, -tises.** *—intr.* To express oneself dogmatically in writing or speech. *—tr.* To proclaim as dogma. **—dog·ma·ti·sa·tion** (-tī-záysh'n || *U.S.* -ti-) *n.*

dog·ma·tism (dóg-mə-tiz'm || dáwg-) *n.* Dogmatic assertion of opinion or belief.

dog·ma·tist (dóg-mə-tist || dáwg-) *n.* **1.** An arrogantly assertive person. **2.** One who expresses or sets forth dogma.

do·good·er (dōō-gōōdər || *U.S.* -gōōdər) *n. Informal.* A person who does charitable work or supports good causes, often considered as naively patronising or unrealistic. **—do-good·ism** *n.*

dog paddle, doggy paddle *n.* A stroke in which the swimmer's arms are bent in front of him and paddle (as a dog's forepaws do in swimming), while the legs kick vigorously in alternation.

dog rose *n.* A prickly wild rose, *Rosa canina,* native to Europe and Asia, having scentless pink or white flowers.

Dogs, Isle of. District in Tower Hamlets, London, bounded on three sides by the River Thames. It was formerly the heart of dockland and is now a redeveloped commercial and business centre.

dogs·bod·y (dógz-boddi || dáwgz-) *n., pl.* **-ies.** A person who is required to perform dreary tasks that others consider beneath them: *a general dogsbody.* [Originally naval slang, midshipman, from *dog's body,* slang for *pease pudding.*]

dog's breakfast *n. Informal.* A mess; a shambles.

dog's-ear. Variant of **dog-ear.**

dog's life *n. Informal.* An unhappy, slavish existence.

dog's mercury *n.* An ill-smelling Eurasian weed, *Mercurialis perennis,* having small greenish flowers and creeping rhizomes.

dog's-tail (dógz-tayl || dáwgz-) *n.* Any grass of the genus *Cynosurus,* native to Europe; especially, *C. cristatus,* having spikelets in a densely crowded, narrow cluster.

Dog Star *n.* The star **Sirius** (*see*).

dog's tongue (dógz-tung || dáwgz-, -tong) *n.* A plant, **hound's-tongue** (*see*).

dog's tooth violet *n.* Any of several plants of the genus *Erythronium,* having nodding, lily-like yellow or purple flowers and sometimes grown as garden ornamentals. Also called "adder's-tongue".

dog tag *n.* **1.** A metal identification disc attached to a dog's collar. **2.** *U.S.* An identification tag worn by soldiers in duplicate on a chain around the neck.

dog-tired (dóg-tírd || dáwg-) *adj.* Extremely tired; exhausted.

dog-tooth (dóg-tōōth || dáwg-, -tōōth) *n., pl.* **teeth** (-teeth). Also **dog tooth** (for sense 1). **1.** A canine tooth; an eyetooth. **2.** *Architecture.* A medieval architectural ornament consisting of four leaflike projections radiating from a raised centre.

dogtooth check, dog's tooth check *n.* **Hound's tooth check** (*see*).

dog·trot (dóg-trot ‖ dáwg-) *n.* A steady trot like that of a dog.
dog violet *n.* A Eurasian violet, *Viola canina,* having blue-and-yellow flowers.
dog warden *n. British.* A person employed to impound stray dogs. Also called "dog catcher".
dog·watch (dóg-woch ‖ dáwg-) *n. Nautical.* Either of two short periods of watch duty, from 4 to 6 p.m. or from 6 to 8 p.m.
dog·wood (dóg-wŏŏd ‖ dáwg-) *n.* Any of various shrubs of the genus *Cornus,* such as the European dogwood, *C. sanguinea,* which has red stems, white flowers, and black berries.
doh, do (dō) *n. Music.* In tonic sol-fa, a syllable representing the first note of a diatonic scale.
Do·ha (dŏ-haa). *Arabic* **Ad Daw·hah.** Capital of Qatar. Since 1949, the country's oil revenues have converted it from a tiny fishing village to a large city.
Doh·ná·nyi (dok-naʹan-yee, dokh-; *Hungarian* dóh-naan-yi), **Ernö** (1877–1960). Hungarian concert pianist and composer. Emigrating for political reasons in 1948, he settled in the United States in 1949. His works include *Variations on a Nursery Song* (1913), based on the tune known as *Twinkle Twinkle Little Star.*
doi·ly, doy·ly (dóyli) *n., pl.* **-lies.** Also **doy·ley** *pl.* **-leys.** A small ornamental mat made of lace, linen, paper, or other material, and used on plates or to protect or adorn furniture. [After *Doyly* or *Doily,* a London draper, *c.* 1712.]
do·ings (dŏŏ-ingz) *pl.n. Informal.* **1.** Events or activities. **2.** Used to designate something which one cannot or does not wish to name.
do-it-your·self (dŏŏ-it-yər-sélf, -yoor-, -yawr-) *n.* The hobby or practice of carrying out work such as home decoration or repairs oneself, as opposed to employing a professional person.
~adj. Designed for or concerning work done in this way.
do-it-your·self·er (dŏŏ-it-yər-sélfər, -yoor-, -yawr-) *n.* A keen amateur handyman.
dol (dol) *n.* A unit used to measure pain, or by inference analgesia, based on application of heat to the skin. See **dolorimetry.** [Latin *dolor,* pain, DOLOUR.]
dol. 1. *Music.* dolce. **2.** dollar.
do·lab·ri·form (dō-lábbri-fawrm) *adj.* Also **do·lab·rate** (-lábbrayt). *Biology.* Having the shape of the head of an axe. [Latin *dolābra,* pickaxe, from *dolāre,* to hew + -FORM.]
Dol·by (dólbi) *adj.* Of or designating circuitry that reduces noise inherent in the tape recording process. During quiet passages the level of the incoming signal is increased; the compensating decrease during playback reduces noise (tape hiss) to below audibility. [The Dolby system (trademark) invented *c.* 1966 by R.M. *Dolby* (1933-), U.S. electronic engineer.] **—Dol·by·ise** *tr.v.*
dol·ce (dól-chi, dōl-, -chay) *adv. Abbr.* **dol.** *Music.* Gently and sweetly. Used as a direction. [Italian, "sweet", from Latin *dulcis.*]
—dol·ce *adj.*
dol·ce far nien·te (dól-chi faar nyén-ti, dōl-, -chay, -tay) *n. Italian.* Delicious inactivity. [Italian, "sweet doing nothing".]
Dol·ce lat·te (dól-chi láttay, -chay) *n.* A trademark for a smooth, blue-veined Italian cheese. [Italian, "sweet milk".]
dol·ce vi·ta (dól-chay véetə, -chi) *n.* A life of comfort or luxury. [Italian, "sweet life".]
Dol·ci (dól-chi, -chee), **Danilo** (1924–97). Italian writer and social reformer. The author of some 13 books, including *Waste* (1963), he has worked since 1959 to reform the social conditions of the Sicilian poor. He won the Lenin peace prize (1958).
dol·drums (dól-drəmz, dōl-) *n. Used with a singular verb.* **1. a.** Ocean regions near the equator, characterised by calms or light winds. **b.** The calms characteristic of these areas. **2.** A period of inactivity, listlessness, or depression. **3.** A condition of stagnation or recession: *The motor industry is in the doldrums.* In all three senses, usually preceded by *the.* [Dialect, perhaps ultimately from Old English *dol,* dull (probably influenced in form by TANTRUM).]
dole[1] (dōl) *n.* **1.** The distribution or dispensing of goods, especially of money, food, or clothing as charity. **2.** A gift or share of money, food, or clothing distributed as charity. **3.** *Chiefly British.* **Unemployment benefit** (see) or other social security payments to the unemployed. **4.** *Archaic.* One's fate. **—on the dole.** *Chiefly British.* Unemployed and receiving unemployment benefit or other social security payments from the government.
~tr.v. **doled, doling, doles.** To distribute, especially in small portions. Usually used with *out.* See Synonyms at **distribute.** [Middle English *dol(e),* part, division, Old English *dāl,* share, portion.]
dole[2] *n. Archaic.* Grief; sorrow; dolour. [Middle English *dol,* from Old French *dol, duel,* from Late Latin *dolus,* pain, grief, from Latin *dolēre,* to feel pain, grieve for.]
dole·ful (dŏl-fʹl) *adj.* Filled with grief; mournful; melancholy. See Synonyms at **sad. —dole·ful·ly** *adv.* **—dole·ful·ness** *n.*
dol·er·ite (dóllə-rīt) *n.* A basic, medium-grained, intrusive igneous rock, mainly composed of feldspar, pyroxene, and sometimes olivine. Also *U.S.* "diabase". [Greek *doleros,* deceitful, from *dolos,* bait, trick (so named from the difficulty in analysing it) + -ITE.]
dol·i·cho·ce·phal·ic (dólikō-si-fál-ik, -se-, -ki-, -ke-) *adj.* Also **dol·i·cho·ceph·a·lous** (-séffə-ləss, -kéffə-). Having a relatively long head; designating a skull that is longer than it is broad, with a cephalic index of 75 or less. Compare **brachycephalic, mesocephalic.** [New Latin *dolichocephalus* : Greek *dolikhos,* long + -CEPHALOUS.] **—dol·i·cho·ceph·a·lism** (-séffə-liz'm, -kéffə-), **dol·i·cho·ceph·a·ly** (-séffəli, -kéffəli) *n.*
do·li·ne, do·li·na (də-léenə, dō-) *n.* A saucer-shaped or shallow funnel-shaped hollow in the ground, large enough to be cultivable,

formed by dissolution of limestone. [Slavonic *dolina,* valley.]
doll (dol) *n.* **1. a.** A child's toy representing a baby or other human being. **b.** A dummy used by a ventriloquist. **2.** A pretty child. **3.** *Slang.* An attractive woman. **4.** *Informal.* Any person regarded with fond familiarity. **5.** *Chiefly U.S. Slang.* A pep pill, sleeping pill, or other drug in capsule or tablet form.
~v. **dolled, dolling, dolls.** *Informal.* *—intr.* To dress up or adorn oneself smartly, as for a special occasion. Used with *up.* *—tr.* **1.** To dress up smartly, especially for ostentation. Used with *up.* **2.** To apply make-up to (one's face), especially too thickly. [From *Doll,* pet name for *Dorothy.*]
dol·lar (dóllər) *n. Abbr.* **dol.** *Symbol* **$ 1. a.** The basic monetary unit of the United States, equal to 100 cents. **b.** The basic monetary unit, equal to 100 cents, of numerous countries, including Australia, Canada, Fiji, Guyana, Hong Kong, Liberia, Malaysia, New Zealand, Singapore, Trinidad and Tobago, and Western Samoa. **2.** A coin or note worth one dollar. **3.** *British Informal.* Five shillings. No longer in current usage. [Low German *daler,* from German *Taler,* taler, short for *Joachimstaler,* a coin made with metal from *Joachimsthal,* Jachymov, town in the Erzgebirge Mountains, Czech Republic.]
dol·lar·bird (dóllər-burd) *n.* A bird, *Eurystomus orientalis,* of southeast Asia and Australia, having a round white spot on each wing.
dollar diplomacy *n.* **1.** A foreign policy aimed at furthering the commercial interests and political influence of the United States by encouraging the investment of U.S. capital in foreign countries. **2.** A policy designed to safeguard such investments.
dol·lar·fish (dóllər-fish) *n., pl.* **-fishes** or collectively **dollarfish.** Any of several rounded silvery fishes, such as the **moonfish** (see).
dol·lop (dóllop) *n. Informal.* A large measure, helping, lump, or portion, as of cream. [19th century (earlier sense, tuft) : perhaps from Scandinavian.]
doll's house *n.* Also *U.S.* **doll·house** (dól-howss). A small-scale model of a house, used as a child's toy.
dol·ly (dólli) *n., pl.* **-lies. 1.** A doll. Used by or to children. **2.** A low mobile platform that rolls on casters, used for moving heavy loads. **3.** A similar wheeled apparatus used to move a film or television camera about a set. **4.** *U.S.* A small locomotive for use in a railway yard, building site, or the like. **5.** A tool used to hold one end of a rivet while the opposite end is being hammered to form a head. **6.** A small piece of wood or metal placed on the head of a pile to prevent damage while the pile is being driven. **7.** *Cricket.* An easy catch. **8.** *Chiefly British Informal.* A dolly bird. **9.** *British.* **a.** A stick used to stir washing in a dolly tub. **b.** A dolly tub.
~intr.v. **dollied, -lying, -lies.** To move the dolly on which a film or television camera is mounted towards or away from the scene of action. Often used with *back, in,* or *out.* [From DOLL.]
dolly bird *n. Chiefly British Informal.* A pretty, flashily dressed young woman.
dolly tub *n. British.* A wooden tub formerly used for washing clothes. [From DOLLY (stick used in washing clothes).]
Dol·ly Var·den (dólli várd'n) *n.* **1.** A woman's large hat, trimmed with flowers. **2.** A colourfully spotted trout, *Salvelinus malma,* of northwestern North America. [After *Dolly Varden,* a character who wore such a hat in Charles Dickens' *Barnaby Rudge.*]
dol·ma (dól-mə, -maa) *n.* Also **dol·ma·des** (dol-maʹa-dess, -thess). A dish of Turkish origin, consisting of vine leaves stuffed with various mixtures. [Turkish, from *dolaman,* wrapping.] See **dolman.**
dol·man (dól-mən ‖ -dōl-) *n.* **1.** A long Turkish outer robe. **2.** A woman's cloak or coat with capelike arm pieces. **3.** A jacket, usually elaborately decorated, often worn like a cape as part of a hussar's uniform. [French, from German *Dolman,* from Turkish *dolaman,* wrapping, from *dolamak,* to wind.]
dolman sleeve *n.* A full sleeve that is very wide at the armhole and narrow at the wrist. [See **dolman.**]
dol·men (dól-men ‖ dōl-, -mən) *n.* Any prehistoric megalithic structure consisting of two or more vertical stones supporting a horizontal one, typically forming a chamber. Also called "cromlech". Compare **menhir.** [French, probably coined from Breton *tol,* table, from Old Breton, from Latin *tabula,* TABLE + *men,* stone, from Celtic *magino-* (unattested); compare **menhir.**]
dol·o·mite (dóllə-mīt) *n.* **1.** A light-tinted, especially yellowish, brownish, or white mineral, essentially $CaMg(CO_3)_2$, used as a furnace refractory, construction, and ceramic material, and in fertilisers. **2.** A type of limestone consisting largely of the mineral dolomite. Also called "dolomitic limestone", "magnesian limestone". [French, after Déodat de *Dolomieu* (1750–1801), French geologist.] **—dol·o·mit·ic** (-mittik) *adj.*
Dol·o·mites (dóllə-mīts). *Italian* **Do·lo·mi·ti** (dollo-méeti). Dolomitic limestone mountain range in the Alps of northeast Italy, rising to 3 342 metres (10,965 feet) at Marmolada. Cortina d'Ampezzo is its principal tourist resort.
dol·or·im·e·try (dóllə-rímmətri) *n.* A technique for measuring the intensity of pain perception ranging from unpleasant to unbearable, by applying heat to the skin. [DOLOUR + -METRY.]
do·lo·ro·so (dòllə-rō-sō) *adj. Music.* Mournful; plaintive.
~adv. Music. With a mournful or plaintive tempo or quality. Used as a direction. [Italian, from Latin *dolōrōsus,* DOLOROUS.]
dol·or·ous (dóllər-əss, dōllər-) *adj.* **1.** Sorrowful; sad. **2.** Painful; distressing. [Middle English, from Late Latin *dolōrōsus,* from Latin *dolor,* DOLOUR.] **—dol·or·ous·ly** *adv.* **—dol·or·ous·ness** *n.*
do·lour, *U.S.* **do·lor** (dóllər, dōlər) *n. Poetic.* Sorrow; grief. [Middle

English *dolour*, pain, suffering, grief, from Old French, from Latin *dolor*, from *dolēre*, to feel pain, grieve.]

dol·phin (dól-fin) *n.* **1.** Any of various marine mammals, chiefly of the family Delphinidae, related to the whales but generally smaller and having a beaklike snout; especially, the common, widely distributed species *Delphinus delphis*. Sometimes called "porpoise". **2.** Either of two marine food fishes of tropical or temperate seas, *Coryphaena hippurus* or *C. equisetus*, having iridescent colouring. Also called "dolphin fish". **3.** A post, bollard, or the like, for mooring a boat. [Middle English *dolphin, dalphin*, from Old French *daufin, dalfin*, from Vulgar Latin *dalfīnus* (unattested), from Latin *delphīnus*, from Greek *delphis* (stem *delphin-*).]

dolt (dōlt) *n.* A stupid person; a blockhead. [Perhaps from obsolete *dol*, a variant of DULL.] —**dolt·ish** *adj.* —**dolt·ish·ly** *adv.* —**dolt·ish·ness** *n.*

Dom (dom) *n.* **1.** A title formerly bestowed in Portugal and Brazil on a man of high rank. Compare **don**. **2.** *Roman Catholic Church.* A title used before the names of monks of certain orders, especially Benedictines. [Portuguese, from Latin *dominus*, lord.]

Dom. Dominican.

D.O.M. *n.* A dirty old man *(see)*.

–dom *n. suffix.* Indicates: **1.** The condition of being; for example, **boredom**. **2.** The domain, position, or rank of; for example, **dukedom**. **3.** The people who comprise a group, or their general character; for example, **officialdom, Afrikanerdom**. [Middle English *-dom*, Old English *-dōm*.]

do·main (də-máyn, dō-) *n.* **1.** A territory or range of rule or control; a realm. **2.** A sphere of interest, special knowledge, or action; field: *the domain of history*. **3.** *Physics.* Any of numerous contiguous regions in a ferromagnetic material in which the direction of spontaneous magnetisation is uniform and different from that in neighbouring regions. Also called "magnetic domain". **4.** *Law.* **a.** The ownership and right of disposal of property. **b.** The right of **eminent domain** *(see)*. **5.** *Mathematics.* **a.** The set of possible values of an independent variable of a function. Also called "region". Compare **range**. **b.** Any open connected set that contains at least one point. [French *domaine*, from Old French *demaine*, from Latin *dominium*, property, ownership rights, from *dominus*, lord.]

do·maine (də-máyn, dō-, do-mén) *n.* A vineyard: *domaine-bottled wine.* [French, "domain".]

dome (dōm) *n.* **1.** A generally hemispherical roof or vault. **2. a.** Any object or structure resembling the shape of this, such as a **geodesic dome** *(see)*. **b.** A natural formation resembling a dome: *the dome of the sky*. **3.** *Poetic.* A large, stately building. **4.** *Slang.* The head. **5.** *Crystallography.* A form of crystal in which two similarly inclined faces intersect in a line parallel to the horizontal axis. **6.** *Geology.* **a.** A **pericline** *(see)*. **b.** A **salt dome** *(see)*. ~*v.* **domed, doming, domes.** —*tr.* **1.** To cover with or as if with a dome. **2.** To shape like a dome. —*intr.* To assume the shape of a dome by rising or swelling. [French *dôme*, from Italian *duomo*, (domed) cathedral, from Latin *domus*, house.]

domesday. Variant of **doomsday**.

Domes·day Book (dŏomz-day ‖ *U.S. also* dōmz-) *n.* Also **Doomsday Book.** The written record of a census and survey of English landowners and their property, made by order of William the Conqueror in 1085–86.

do·mes·tic (də-méstik, dō-) *adj.* **1.** Of or pertaining to the family or household: *domestic chores*. **2.** Fond of home life and competent in household management. **3.** Tame; domesticated. Said of animals. **4.** Of or pertaining to a country's internal affairs: *domestic politics*. **5.** Produced in or indigenous to a particular country: *domestic wine*. ~*n.* A household servant. [French *domestique*, from Latin *domesticus*, from *domus*, house.] —**do·mes·ti·cal·ly** *adv.*

do·mes·ti·cate (də-mésti-kayt, dō-) *v.* **-cated, -cating, -cates.** Also **do·mes·ti·cise** (-sīz), **-cised, -cising, -cises.** —*tr.* **1.** To train to live with and be of use to man; tame. **2.** To bring into cultivation. **3.** To cause to feel comfortable at home; make domestic. **4.** To accommodate to an environment. —*intr.* To become domestic. [DOMESTIC + -ATE.] —**do·mes·ti·ca·tion** (-káysh'n) *n.*

domestic fowl *n.* A domesticated bird of the genus *Gallus*, most probably derived from the red jungle fowl *G. gallus*, which exists in several different forms.

do·mes·tic·i·ty (dóm-ess-tíssəti, dŏm-) *n., pl.* **-ties. 1.** The quality or condition of being domestic. **2.** Home life or devotion to it.

domestic science *n.* The study of skills pertaining to cookery, dressmaking, and household management.

do·mi·cal (dŏm-ik'l, dóm-) *adj.* Pertaining to, having, or shaped like a dome. —**do·mi·cal·ly** *adv.*

dom·i·cile (dómmi-sīl, dŏmi-, -sil) *n.* Also **dom·i·cil** (-sil). **1.** A residence; a home. **2.** One's legal residence. **3.** *Finance.* The place where a bill of exchange is payable. ~*v.* **domiciled, -ciling, -ciles.** Also **dom·i·cil·i·ate** (-sílli-ayt) **-ated, -ating, -ates.** —*tr.* **1.** To establish (a person or oneself) in a residence. **2.** *Finance.* To make (a bill of exchange) payable at a particular place. —*intr.* To reside or dwell. [Middle English, from Old French, from Latin *domicilium*, habitation, abode.] —**dom·i·cil·i·ar·y** (-sílli-əri ‖ -erri, -sílləri) *adj.*

dom·i·nance (dómmi-nənss) *n.* Also **dom·i·nan·cy** (-i). The condition or fact of being dominant; ascendancy.

dom·i·nant (dómmi-nənt) *adj.* **1. a.** Exercising the most influence or control. **b.** Seeking or tending to exert control or occupy a pre-eminent position. **2.** Providing a view from above; in a commanding position. **3.** Most noticeable or prevalent. **4.** *Genetics.* Producing the same phenotypic effect whether paired with an identical or a dissimilar gene. Compare **recessive. 5.** *Ecology.* Designating or pertaining to the species that is most abundant in a particular habitat and that may determine the presence and type of other species. **6.** *Music.* Pertaining to or based upon the fifth note of a diatonic scale. ~*n.* **1.** *Genetics.* A dominant gene or characteristic. **2.** *Ecology.* A dominant species. **3.** *Music.* The fifth note of a diatonic scale. [Old French, from Latin *domināns* (stem *dominant-*), present participle of *domināri*, to DOMINATE.] —**dom·i·nant·ly** *adv.*

Synonyms: dominant, predominant, preponderant, paramount, pre-eminent.

dominant wavelength *n.* The wavelength of the light that, when combined in specific proportions with an achromatic standard light, matches a given colour.

dom·i·nate (dómmi-nayt) *v.* **-nated, -nating, -nates.** —*tr.* **1.** To control, govern, or exert influence over by superior authority or power. **2.** To occupy the pre-eminent or most noticeable position in or over: *A large painting dominated the room.* **3.** To overlook from a height. —*intr.* To be dominant in position or authority. [Latin *domināri*, to be lord and master, from *dominus*, master, lord.] —**dom·i·na·tive** (-nətiv, -naytiv) *adj.* —**dom·i·na·tor** (-ər) *n.*

dom·i·na·tion (dómmi-náysh'n) *n.* **1.** The act of dominating or the condition of being dominated; rule; control. **2.** *Plural.* In medieval angelology, the fourth of the nine orders of angels. Also called "dominions". See **angel.**

dom·i·nee (dŏo-mini) *n.* In South Africa, a minister of the Dutch Reformed Church. [Dutch, from Latin *dominus*, master, teacher.]

dom·i·neer (dómmi-néer) *v.* **-neered, -neering, -neers.** —*tr.* To rule over arbitrarily or arrogantly; tyrannise. [Dutch *domineren*, from French *dominer*, from Latin *domināri*, to DOMINATE.] —**dom·i·neer·ing·ly** *adv.*

Do·min·go (do-míng-gō, də-), **Placido** (1941–). Spanish operatic tenor. He emigrated to Mexico as a child, and made his debut at the Metropolitan Opera, New York, in 1968.

Dom·i·nic (dómminik), **Saint**, born Dominic de Guzman (*c.* 1170–1221). Spanish churchman and founder of the Dominican Order. He became prior at Osma Cathedral in Castile, and backed the crusade of Simon de Montfort against the heretical Albigenses in southern France. He founded his order in 1216, and his zeal earned him the reputation "burner and slayer of heretics". His pursuit of them was ruthlessly followed by the Dominican-dominated Spanish Inquisition.

Dom·i·ni·ca, Commonwealth of (dómmi-néekə; *also, wrongly,* də-mínnikə). Island country of the West Indies. The largest of the Windward Islands, it was discovered by Columbus, who named it after the day of its discovery, *Dies Dominica*, Sunday, November 3, 1493. After alternating between British and French rule, it became British in 1783. In 1978, it became an independent Commonwealth republic. Following devastating hurricanes in 1979 and 1980, government development of tourism and light industry is taking place to reduce dependence on the export of bananas. Area, 751 square kilometres (290 square miles). Population, 70,000. Capital, Roseau. See map at **Latin America.**

do·min·i·cal (də-mínnik'l, do-, dō-) *adj.* **1.** Of or associated with the Lord (Christ). **2.** Pertaining to Sunday as the Lord's day. [Medieval Latin *dominicālis*, from Latin *dominicus*, of a lord, from *dominus*, lord.]

dominical letter *n.* One of the first seven letters of the alphabet applied to Sundays in order to determine the ecclesiastical calendar for a given year, the letter being the one that corresponds with the first Sunday in January when the first seven days of the month are lettered in order; for example, if the first Sunday is January 2, *B* will be the dominical letter for the year.

Do·min·i·can (də-mínnikən, do-, dō-. *Also* dómmi-néek'n *for* n. & adj. sense 3) *adj.* **1.** *Abbr.* **Dom.** Of, pertaining to, or designating the order of preaching friars established in 1216 by St. Dominic. **2.** Of or pertaining to the Dominican Republic. **3.** Of or pertaining to Dominica. ~*n.* **1.** *Abbr.* **Dom.** A friar of the order of Saint Dominic. **2.** A native or inhabitant of the Dominican Republic. **3.** A native or inhabitant of Dominica.

Do·min·i·can Republic (də-mínnikən, do-, dō-). Mountainous country on the West Indian island of Hispaniola, discovered by Columbus in 1492. The present republic was established in 1844. This has been prone to economic and political instability and civil strife, and U.S. forces have intervened twice (1916–24; 1965–66). The ruthless dictator General Trujillo came to power in 1930. He was assassinated (1961), and succeeded by Joaquín Balaguer. A year later, the leftist Juan Bosch was elected president—only to be deposed by a military coup (1963). A leftist revolt was put down with U.S. help in 1965, and Balaguer was re-elected in 1966, 1970, 1974 and 1986. Sugar is the main industry, and supplies 33 per cent of the country's exports. However, after hurricane damage in 1979, tourism and mining are being developed rapidly, and gold, silver, and bauxite are also exported. Area, 48 422 square kilometres (18,696 square miles). Population, 8,050,000. Capital, Santo Domingo. See map, next page.

dom·i·nie (dómmi-ni ‖ *U.S. also* dōmi-ni) *n.* **1.** *Chiefly Scottish.* A schoolmaster. **2.** In the United States, a clergyman of the Dutch Reformed Church. [From obsolete *domine*, form of address to ministers and schoolmasters, from Latin *dominē*, vocative of *dominus*, lord, master.]

do·min·ion (də-mín-yən, dō-) *n.* **1.** Control or the exercise of control; rule; sovereignty. **2.** A territory or sphere of influence or control; a realm; a domain. **3.** *Often capital* D. A term formerly applied to any of the larger self-governing nations within the British Commonwealth, such as Canada or Australia. **4.** *Law.* Dominium. **5.** *Plural.* An order of angels, dominations. [Middle English *dominioun,* from Old French *dominion,* from Medieval Latin *dominiō* (stem *dominiōn-*), from Latin *dominium,* property, ownership rights, lordship, from *dominus,* lord, master.]

Dominion Day *n.* July 1, a national holiday in Canada, the anniversary of the Dominion's formation in 1867.

do·min·i·um (də-mínni-əm) *n. Law.* Ownership of property, especially of land, and the right to its disposition. Also called "dominion". [Latin, property, DOMINION.]

dom·i·no[1] (dómmi-nō) *n., pl.* **-noes** or **-nos. 1.** A hooded robe worn with an eye mask at a masquerade. **2.** The mask itself, worn with such a robe. [French, probably from Latin *dominus,* lord, but the reason for the name is unknown.]

domino[2] *n., pl.* **-noes.** A small, rectangular block, the face of which is divided into halves, used in games of dominoes. Each half is marked by one to six dots or is blank. [French, obscurely from DOMINO (hooded robe).]

Dom·i·no (dómmi-nō), **Fats,** born Antoine Domino (1928–). U.S. R & B singer, pianist, and songwriter. His songs, popular especially in the 1950s, include *Ain't That A Shame, I'm In Love Again, Blue Monday,* and *Blueberry Hill.*

dom·i·noes (dómmi-nōz) *n. Used with a singular verb.* Any of several games played with a set of usually 28 dominoes, in which they are laid flat on a surface so that their corresponding halves match.

domino theory *n.* A theory that one event, if allowed to happen, will inevitably lead to a succession of similar events, as a row of upright dominoes will fall if the first one is knocked down; especially, the theory that if one vulnerable nation, as in Southeast Asia, comes under Communist domination, the neighbouring nations will naturally follow.

Do·mi·nus (dómmi-nəss, dṓmi-) *n. Abbr.* **D.** *Latin.* The Lord. Used with reference to God or Christ.

Do·mi·tian(us) (də-mísh'n, do- dō-; -mítti-áanəss), **Titus Flavius** (A.D. 51–96). Roman emperor. He succeeded his brother Titus in A.D. 81 and completed the conquest of Britain. After A.D. 89 his government became dictatorial and with the Senate firmly in his control, he instigated a reign of terror. He was murdered in his bed-chamber by a freedman with the connivance of his wife.

don[1] (don) *n.* **1.** *Capital* D. *Abbr.* **D.** Sir. A title formerly placed before the Christian name of a Spaniard of high rank, now used generally as a courtesy title. **2.** A Spanish gentleman. **3.** *British.* **a.** A fellow of a college at Oxford or Cambridge. **b.** Any university lecturer. [Spanish, from Latin *dominus,* lord, master.]

don[2] *tr.v.* **donned, donning, dons.** To put on; dress in. [Contraction of *do on.*]

Don[1] (don). Tributary of the Ouse, in South Yorkshire, England, 112 kilometres (69 miles) long.

Don[2]. River of European Russia. It flows 1 930 kilometres (1,224 miles) south to the Sea of Azov.

do·ña (dón-yə, -yaa || *U.S. also* dṓn-) *n.* **1.** A Spanish gentlewoman. **2.** *Capital* D. A title of courtesy placed before a woman's Christian name in Spanish-speaking countries. [Spanish, "lady", from Latin *domina.* See **dame.**]

do·nate (dō-náyt, də- || *chiefly U.S.* dṓ-nayt) *tr.v.* **-nated, -nating, -nates.** To present as a gift, especially to a fund or cause; contribute. [Back-formation from DONATION.] —**do·na·tor** (-ər) *n.*

Do·na·tel·lo (dónnə-téllō), born Donato di Niccolo di Betto Bardi (1386–1466). Florentine sculptor who was a pioneer of the Renaissance style, breaking all traditions with his natural, life-like figures, such as the marble sculptures of *St. Mark* and *St. George.* Michelangelo is reputed to have been so impressed with *St. Mark* that he asked the statue why it did not speak to him.

do·na·tion (dō-náysh'n, də-) *n.* **1.** The act of making a gift, especially to a fund or cause. **2.** A gift or grant; a contribution. [Middle English *donacioun,* from Old French, from Latin *dōnātiō* (stem *dō-nātiōn-*), from *dōnātus,* past participle of *dōnāre,* to give, from *dōnum,* gift.]

Do·na·tist (dṓnə-tist || *U.S. also* dónnə-) *n.* A member of a schismatic Christian sect that arose in North Africa in the fourth century A.D. and held sanctity essential to church membership and administration of sacraments. [Medieval Latin *Dōnātista,* from *Dōnātus,* probably bishop of Carthage in the fourth century.] —**Do·na·tism** *n.* —**Do·na·tist** *adj.*

do·na·tive (dṓnə-tiv || *U.S. also* dónnə-) *n.* **1.** A gift or donation. **2.** A benefice that can be bestowed by its founder or patron without reference to the diocesan authorities. ~*adj.* Constituting such a benefice. [Latin *dōnātīvum,* neuter of *dōnātīvus,* of a donation, from *dōnātus.* See **donation.**]

Donau. See **Danube.**

Don·bas (dón-baáss). Major industrial region of Ukraine and Russia in the lower Dnepr, Donets, and Don valleys. It produced more than a third of the U.S.S.R.'s coal and has extensive chemical industries based on local salt deposits. Donetsk and Rostov are the main centres. Also called "Donets Basin".

Don·cas·ter (dóng-kəstər || -kaastər, -kastər). Industrial town and Unitary Authority area in northern England, on the river Don, once the Roman station, Danum. The St. Leger horse race is run every September on the nearby Town Moor course.

done (dun). Past participle of **do.** ~*adj.* **1.** Finished. **2.** Cooked adequately. **3.** Socially acceptable: *not done in polite society.* —**done for. 1.** Doomed. **2.** Dead or dying. **3.** Exhausted. ~*interj.* Used to express agreement when concluding a deal.

do·nee (dō-née) *n.* **1.** *Chiefly Law.* A recipient of a gift. **2.** *Medicine.* The recipient of an organ transplanted from a donor. [DON(OR) + -EE.]

Don·e·gal (dónni-gáwl, dúnni-). *Irish* **Dún na nGall.** Mountainous county on the northwest Atlantic coast of the Republic of Ireland. Its chief occupations are sheep and cattle rearing, and potato farming. Donegal tweed and linen are also produced.

do·ner kebab (dṓnər) *n.* A kebab made from meat, mostly mutton, sliced from a large compressed loaf which turns on an upright spit. Also called "kebab".

Do·nets'k (də-nyétsk). Industrial city in southeast Ukraine, founded by Thomas Hughes, a Welshman, in the 1870s. This city has a population of over 1 million.

dong[1] (dong) *n.* Symbol **D 1.** The basic monetary unit of Vietnam, equal to 100 hao. **2.** A coin or note worth one dong. [Vietnamese.]

dong[2] *v.* **donged, donging, dongs.** —*intr.* To make a deep, bell-like sound. —*tr. Australian & N.Z. Informal.* To strike; punch. [Imitative.] —**dong** *n.*

dong[3] *n. Vulgar Slang.* A penis. [20th century : origin obscure.]

don·ga (dong-gə, -ə) *n. South African.* **1.** A **wadi** (see). **2.** A gully resulting from soil erosion. [Nguni.]

Dö·nitz (dér-nits, dö-), **Karl** (1891–1980). German admiral. He developed the highly effective "pack" system of U-boat attacks in World War II. In 1943, he became grand admiral and commander-in-chief of the navy. Hitler nominated Dönitz as his successor, and he was briefly chancellor on Hitler's death. At the Nuremberg trials in 1946 he was sentenced to 10 years' imprisonment.

Do·ni·zet·ti (dónni-zétti, -dzétti || *U.S. also* dṓni-), **Gaetano** (1797–1848). Italian composer of about 75 operas. His best-known work is *Lucia di Lammermoor* (1835).

don·jon (dón-jən, dún-) *n.* The fortified main tower of a castle; a keep. Also called "dungeon". [Variant of DUNGEON.]

Don Ju·an (dón jō̄-ən || waán) *n.* **1.** A man obsessed with seducing women. **2.** A libertine; a profligate. [After *Don Juan,* legendary Spanish nobleman and libertine.]

don·key (dóng-ki || dúng-) *n., pl.* **-keys. 1.** The domesticated ass, probably descended from the wild ass *Equus asinus.* **2.** An obstinate, sluggish, or stupid person. [Perhaps from DUN (dark) + diminutive suffix *-ey* (influenced by MONKEY).]

donkey engine *n.* A small auxiliary steam engine used for hoisting or pumping, especially aboard ship.

donkey jacket *n.* A workman's thick jacket, usually with a piece of plastic or leather over each shoulder. [Alluding to the donkey as an animal associated with drudgery.]

donkey's years *n. British Informal.* A very long time. [Perhaps alteration of *donkey's ears,* hence, very long.]

donkey vote *n. Australian Informal.* A vote in which an uncritical elector records his order of preference simply by following the order in which the candidates are listed. [Alluding to one animal following another in a line.]

don·key·work (dóngki-wurk) *n.* **1.** The laborious, uninteresting part of an operation. **2.** Monotonous work; drudgery.

Don·lea·vy (don-léevi), **J(ames) P(atrick)** (1926–). Irish-American novelist. Born in New York City, he later settled in Ireland. *The Ginger Man* (1955) won acclaim for its comic and irreverent style.

don·na (dónnə) *n.* **1.** An Italian gentlewoman or lady. **2.** *Capital* **D.** A title of courtesy placed before a woman's Christian name in Italian-speaking countries. [Italian, "lady", from Latin *domina.* See **dame.**]

Donne (dun, don), **John** (1572–1631). English poet and divine, one of the great Metaphysical poets. In 1601, he married a 16-year-old girl without her father's consent and was briefly imprisoned. He joined the Anglican Church and took holy orders (1615), becoming chaplain to King James before being appointed Dean of St. Paul's (1621). Among his poems are *The Ecstasie, Hymn to God the Father,* and the sonnet sequence *La Corona.*

don·nish (dónnish) *adj.* Resembling or characteristic of a university don; bookish; pedantically erudite.

don·ny·brook (dónni-brŏŏk || -brŏŏk) *n.* A brawl or uproar; a free-for-all. [After *Donnybrook* fair, held yearly at *Donnybrook,* near Dublin, at which such uproars were common.]

do·nor (dṓn-ǝr, -awr) *n.* **1.** One who contributes something, such as money to a cause or fund. **2. a.** One who donates blood, tissue, or an organ for use in a transfusion or transplant. **b.** One that provides semen for artificial insemination. **3.** *Chemistry.* The atom in a coordinate bond that supplies both electrons. Compare **acceptor. 4.** *Physics.* An impurity atom added to a semiconductor to increase the n-type conductivity. Compare **acceptor.** [Middle English, from Anglo-French *donour,* from Old French *doneur,* from Latin *dōnātor,* from *dōnātus.* See donation.]

Don Qui·xo·te (dón kwík-sǝt, -sōt; dón-ki-hṓ-ti, -tay) *n.* An impractical idealist bent on righting incorrigible wrongs. [After *Don Quixote,* hero of a satirical chivalric romance by Cervantes, published 1605–15.]

don't (dōnt). Contraction of *do not.*

don't know *n.* One who has not yet arrived at a definite viewpoint, as in replying to an opinion poll, questionnaire, or the like.

donut. Variant of **doughnut.**

doo·dah (dṓo-daa) *n.* Also *U.S.* **doo·dad** (-dad). *Informal.* **1.** An unnamed gadget or trinket. **2.** Any article whose name one has forgotten or does not know. [20th century : origin obscure.]

doo·dle (dṓod'l) *v.* **-dled, -dling, -dles.** *Informal.* —*intr.* To scribble mechanically or absent-mindedly. —*tr.* To draw (figures) while preoccupied.
~*n. Informal.* A figure, design, or scribble drawn or written absent-mindedly. [17th century (originally, simpleton) : perhaps from Low German; current sense perhaps related to dialect *doodle*†, to fritter away time.]

doo·dle·bug (dṓod'l-bug) *n.* **1.** *British Informal.* A V-1 flying bomb. **2.** *U.S.* **a.** An insect, the **ant lion** *(see),* in its larval stage. **b.** Loosely, any of various other similar insect larvae. **3.** *U.S.* A divining rod. [Perhaps English dialect *doodle,* to waste time (see **doodle**) + BUG.]

doo·lal·ly (dṓo-lal-i) *adj. British Slang.* Mentally unbalanced; mad. [Originally military slang, shortened from *dolally tap,* after *Deolali,* near Bombay, town and camp where soldiers waited to be shipped home; it symbolised boredom.]

doom (dṓom) *n.* **1.** A predestined end in ruin or tragedy; a terrible fate. **2.** Disaster; ruin; extinction. **3.** The Last Judgment. **4.** *Archaic.* Condemnation to a severe penalty.
~*tr.v.* **doomed, dooming, dooms.** To condemn or destine to ruination or death. [Middle English *doom,* Old English *dōm.*]

doom palm. Variant of **doum palm.**

dooms·day (dṓomz-day) *n.* Also **domes·day** (dṓomz- || *U.S.* also dōmz-). **1.** The day of the Last Judgment. **2.** Any dreaded day of judgment or reckoning. [Middle English *domesday,* Old English *dōmes dæg* : *dōmes,* genitive of *dōm,* DOOM + *dæg,* DAY.]

Doomsday Book. Variant of **Domesday Book.**

doom·watch (dṓom-woch) *n.* A state of watching for and warning of impending disaster; especially, vigilance to protect the environment from possible destruction. —**doom·watch·er** *n.*

door (dor || dôr) *n.* **1.** Any movable structure used to close off the entrance to a room, building, vehicle, cupboard, or the like, typically consisting of a panel of wood, glass, or metal that swings on hinges. **2.** The entranceway to a room, building, or passage. **3.** Any means of approach or access. **4.** The room or building to which a door belongs: *three doors down the hall.* —**by the back door.** Going through unofficial channels; secretly or deceitfully. —**lay (something) at (someone's) door.** To blame (something) on (someone). —**show (someone) the door.** To tell (someone) to leave. [Middle English *dor,* Old English *dor, duru,* gate, door.]

door·bell (dór-bel || dôr-) *n.* A buzzer or bell outside a door, used as a signal for admission.

door·jamb (dór-jam || dôr-) *n.* Either of the two vertical pieces framing a doorway and supporting the lintel. Also called "doorpost".

door·keep·er (dór-keepǝr || dôr-) *n.* **1.** A person employed to guard an entrance or gateway. **2.** *Roman Catholic Church.* One of the **minor orders** *(see).*

door·knob (dór-nob || dôr-) *n.* A knob-shaped handle for opening and closing a door.

door·man (dór-man, -mǝn || dôr-) *n., pl.* **-men** (-men, -mǝn). A man employed to stand watch at the entrance of a hotel, block of flats, or other large building.

door·mat (dór-mat || dôr-) *n.* **1.** A mat placed before a doorway for wiping the shoes. **2.** *Informal.* A person who unprotestingly allows himself to be mistreated by others.

door·nail (dór-nayl || dôr-) *n.* A large-headed nail formerly used as a stud on doors. —**dead as a doornail.** Undoubtedly dead.

Doornik, Doornijk. See **Tournai.**

door·sill (dór-sil || dôr-) *n.* The threshold of a doorway.

door·step (dór-step || dôr-) *n.* **1.** A step leading to a door. Also used adjectively: *a doorstep salesman.* **2.** *Informal.* A very thick slice of bread: *a doorstep sandwich.*
~*v.* **doorstepped, -stepping, -steps.** —*intr.* To go from door to

door as a way of selling, canvassing for a political party, investigating a news story, or the like. —*tr.* To hound persistently (someone who is the subject of a news story), especially by waiting outside the person's house. Used of journalists.

door·stop (dór-stop || dôr-) *n.* **1.** A wedge inserted beneath a door to hold it open at a desired position. **2.** A weight or spring that prevents a door from slamming. **3.** A rubber-tipped projection attached to a wall to protect it from the impact of an opening door.

door-to-door (dór-tǝ-dór) *adj.* **1.** Calling at every dwelling in a particular area: *a door-to-door salesman.* **2.** Moving directly from one place to another, especially from a place of collection or purchase to a specific address for delivery.
~*adj.* Directly from one place to another: *15 miles door-to-door.*

door·way (dór-way || dôr-) *n.* The entrance to a room or building.

dop (dop) *n. South African.* A tot of cheap spirits, especially brandy. [Afrikaans; akin to DIP.]

do·pa (dṓpa) *n.* An intermediate compound in the synthesis of catecholamines from the amino acid tyrosine. It is needed for certain brain functions and the form L-dopa is used to treat Parkinsonism. [From German, from *dioxyphenylalanine.*]

do·pa·mine (dṓpǝ-meen) *n.* A catecholamine that is an intermediate in the synthesis of noradrenaline and possibly acts as a neurotransmitter. [DOPA + AMINE.]

dop·ant (dṓpǝnt) *n.* A small quantity of a substance, such as phosphorus, added to another substance, such as a semiconductor, to alter the latter's properties. [DOP(E) + -ANT.]

dope (dōp) *n.* **1.** Any viscid substance or liquid; especially: **a.** A lubricant, such as axle grease. **b.** An absorbent material used in manufacturing dynamite. **c.** Any of various preparations resembling varnish formerly used to protect, waterproof, and tauten the cloth surfaces of aeroplane wings. **2.** *Informal.* **a.** A drug, especially a narcotic. **b.** Any illegal drug, such as cannabis. **3.** *Slang.* A very stupid person. **4.** *Slang.* Factual information, especially of a confidential nature.
~*tr.v.* **doped, doping, dopes. 1.** To add or apply dope to. **2.** *Informal.* To administer a narcotic to; drug. **3.** *Electronics.* To add an impurity to (a semiconductor). **4.** *Chiefly U.S. Informal.* To work out (an outcome or puzzle) by calculation and guesswork. Often used with *out.* [Dutch *doop,* sauce, from *doopen,* to dip, mix, from Middle Dutch *dōpen.*]
Usage: The use of *dope* as a noun, in the context of narcotics, is widespread informally, and may be found even in relatively formal contexts in U.S. English. The verb use is more established formally in British English (*The horse was doped*), although many people prefer to use a verb with no slang associations (such as *drug*).

dope-fiend (dṓp-feend) *n. Slang.* A drug addict.

dope sheet *n. U.S. Slang.* A publication giving information on the horses running in the day's races.

do·pey, do·py (dṓpi) *adj.* **-ier, -iest.** *Slang.* **1.** Dazed or lethargic, as if drugged. **2.** Stupid; silly.

Dop·pel·gäng·er (dóppᵊl-gang-ǝr, -geng-) *n.* **1.** A ghostly double of a living person, especially one that haunts its own fleshly counterpart. **2.** Loosely, a double of a person. [German, "double-goer".]

Dop·pler effect (dópplǝr) *n.* An apparent change in the frequency of sound or electromagnetic waves occurring when the source and observer are in motion relative to one another, the frequency increasing when the source and observer approach one another and decreasing when they move apart. Also called "Doppler shift". — See **red shift.** [After Christian *Doppler* (1803–53), Austrian physicist, who discovered the effect for sound waves.]

Doppler radar *n.* A radar system which uses the Doppler effect to measure velocity.

dor (dor) *n.* Any of various insects that fly with a droning sound, such as a dorbeetle. [Middle English *dorre, dore,* Old English *dora,* bumblebee (probably imitative).]

Dor. Dorian; Doric.

do·ra·do (dǝ-ráa-dō) *n., pl.* **-dos.** A large marine fish, *Coryphaena hippurus.* See **dolphin.**

Do·ra·do (dǝ-ráadō) *n.* A constellation of the Southern Hemisphere near Reticulum and Pictor, containing a portion of the larger **Magellanic Cloud** *(see).*

dor·bee·tle (dór-beet'l) *n.* An Old World dung beetle, *Geotrupes stercorarius,* that flies with a droning sound.

Dor·ches·ter (dór-chistǝr || -chestǝr) *n.* Market town in the south of England, the administrative centre of Dorset. Thomas Hardy, born nearby, made it the model for Casterbridge in his *Wessex Tales.*

Dor·dogne (dawr-dóyn). **1.** River in southwest France. It flows 467 kilometres (290 miles) from the Auvergne Mountains to form the Gironde estuary with the river Garonne, crossing the Dordogne département on the way. Its lower banks are lined with vineyards, like those of St. Emilion. **2.** Département in Aquitaine.

Do·ré (dáwray, daw-ráy), **(Paul) Gustave** (1832–83). French engraver and lithographer who illustrated Dante, La Fontaine, Balzac, and scenes of London poverty. His drawings of eerie fantasy inspired a vogue for illustrated books. He illustrated Balzac's *Droll Stories,* La Fontaine's *Fables,* and Dante's *Divine Comedy.*

Do·ri·an (dáwri-ǝn || dóri-ǝn) *n. Abbr.* **Dor.** A member of a Hellenic people that invaded Greece around 1100 B.C. and remained culturally and linguistically distinct within the Greek world, especially in Sparta, Corinth, and Argos.
~*adj.* **1.** Of or pertaining to the Dorians. **2.** *Music.* Of or designating a mode represented by the white notes of the scale D to D on the piano keyboard.

Dor·ic (dórrik ‖ dáwrik) *n. Abbr.* **Dor.** **1.** One of the four main dialects of Ancient Greece spoken chiefly in the Peloponnese, in various Aegean islands, and in Magna Graecia. Compare **Aeolic, Arcado-Cyprian, Attic-Ionic.** **2.** Any broad dialect of English; especially, the dialect of northeast Scotland.
~adj. Abbr. **Dor.** **1.** Belonging to, characteristic of, or designating the Doric dialect. **2.** In the style of or designating the Doric order. **3.** Rustic. Said of a dialect. [Latin *Dōricus,* from Greek *Dōrikos,* from *Dōris,* area of Ancient Greece, the traditional home of the Dorians.]

Doric order *n.* The oldest and simplest of the three orders of classical Greek architecture, characterised by heavy, fluted columns having no base, plain, saucer-shaped capitals, and a bold, simple cornice. Compare **Corinthian order, Ionic order.**

Dor·king (dórking) *n.* A domestic fowl of a breed having a heavy body and five toes, reared chiefly for table use. [After *Dorking,* Surrey, where it was bred.]

dorm (dorm) *n. Informal.* A dormitory in a school or college.

dor·mant (dórmənt) *adj.* **1.** Asleep or lying as if asleep; not awake or active. **2. a.** Latent but capable of being activated. **b.** Temporarily inactive. **3.** Designating a volcano that has not erupted within recorded history but is thought not to be extinct. **4.** *Biology.* In a relatively inactive or resting condition in which some processes are slowed down or suspended. **5.** *Heraldry.* Lying in a sleeping position, with head on paws: *a lion dormant.* —See Synonyms at **inactive, latent.** [Middle English *dormaunt,* from Old French *dormant,* from the present participle of *dormir,* to sleep, from Latin *dormīre.*] —**dor·man·cy** *n.*

dor·mer (dórmər) *n.* **1.** A window set vertically in a small gable projecting from a sloping roof. Also called "dormer window." **2.** The gable holding such a window. [Old French *dormeor,* "bedroom window", from *dormir,* to sleep. See **dormant.**]

dor·mi·to·ry (dórmi-tri, -təri) *n., pl.* **-ries.** **1.** A room providing sleeping quarters for a number of persons, especially in a boarding school. **2.** *U.S.* A hall of residence in a college or university. **3.** A suburb or small town, many of whose inhabitants commute to work in a nearby urban centre. Also used adjectivally: *a dormitory town.* [Latin *dormītōrium,* from *dormītōrius,* of sleep, from *dormītus,* past participle of *dormīre,* to sleep.]

Dor·mo·bile (dór-mə-beel, -mō-) *n.* A trademark for a type of motorised caravan.

dor·mouse (dór-mowss) *n., pl.* **-mice** (-mīss). Any of various small Old World rodents of the family Muscardinidae; especially, *Muscardinus avellanarius,* of Europe. [Middle English *dormowse†.*]

dor·my (dórmi) *adj. Golf.* Ahead of an opponent by as many holes as remain to be played. [19th century : origin obscure.]

dor·nick (dórnik) *n.* A coarse damask cloth. [Middle English *dornewick,* first manufactured in *Doornik* (French *Tournai*), city in Belgium.]

dorp (dorp) *n. South African.* A small township; a village. [Dutch; akin to THORP.]

Dorpat. See **Tartu.**

dor·sad (dór-sad) *adv. Anatomy.* In the direction of the back. [DORS(O)- + -AD (towards).]

dor·sal (dórss'l) *adj.* **1.** *Anatomy.* Of, towards, on, in, or near the back. **2.** *Botany.* Of or on the surface of an organ directed away from the main axis. [Late Latin *dorsālis,* from Latin *dorsuālis,* from *dorsum,* back.] —**dor·sal·ly** *adv.*

dorsal fin *n.* The main unpaired fin on the dorsal surface of fishes or certain marine mammals.

Dor·set (dór-sit) *n.* A county in southwest England. Agriculture is the main occupation, with sheep-rearing on the downs and dairy cattle and crops in the lowlands. Tourism flourishes on the coast, especially in the towns of Bournemouth, Swanage, and Weymouth. Thomas Hardy portrayed the area in his Wessex Tales.

Dorset Down *n.* A domestic sheep of a hornless breed with a brown face and legs, and fine-textured wool.

Dorset Horn *n.* A domestic sheep of a breed having large horns and fine-textured wool.

dor·si·ven·tral (dór-si-véntrəl) *adj.* **1.** Having distinct upper and lower surfaces, as most leaves do. **2.** Dorsoventral.

dorso-, dorsi-, dors- *comb. form.* Indicates the dorsal area; for example, **dorsoventral, dorsiventral, dorsad.** [Latin *dorsum,* back.]

dor·so·ven·tral (dór-sō-véntrəl) *adj.* Extending from a dorsal to a ventral surface. [DORSO- + VENTRAL.]

dor·sum (dór-səm) *n., pl.* **-sa** (-sə). *Anatomy.* **1.** The back. **2.** Any part of an organ analogous to the back: *the dorsum of the hand.* [Latin, back.]

Dort·mund (dórt-mōond, -mōont). Industrial city and port at the end of the Dortmund-Ems Canal, in the Ruhr, western Germany. Other canals connect it to the Weser and Elbe rivers. Dortmund became part of the Hanseatic League in the 13th century.

Dort·mund-Ems Canal (dórt-mōond-émz, -mōont-émss). An important industrial waterway in western Germany. It is some 270 kilometres (168 miles) long, and links the Ruhr with the Ems river and the North Sea.

dor·ty (dórti) *adj.* **-tier, -tiest,** *Scottish.* Sullen; bad-tempered. [From Scottish *dort,* sullenness.]

do·ry¹ (dáwri ‖ dōri) *n., pl.* **-ries.** *Chiefly U.S.* A small, narrow, flat-bottomed fishing boat with high sides and a sharp prow. [18th century : origin obscure.]

dory² *n., pl.* **-ries.** Any of various marine fishes of the family Zeidae; especially, the **John Dory** *(see).* [Middle English *dorre,* from Old

French *doree,* gilded (from its metallic shine), from the feminine past participle of *dorer,* to gild, from Late Latin *dēaurāre* : Latin *dē-,* thoroughly + *aurum,* gold.]

dos-à-dos (dō-zaa-dō, -zə-) *n., pl.* **dos-à-dos** (-dōz, *or as singular*) Also **do-si-do** (dō-si-dō, -sī-) (for sense 2) *pl.* **-dos.** **1.** A sofa or carriage that accommodates two people seated back to back. **2.** A movement in country dancing in which two dancers approach each other and circle back to back, then return to their original positions. *~adj.* Bound together back to back with one central board. Said of two books. [French, "back to back".]

dos·age (dō-sij) *n.* **1.** The administration of a therapeutic agent in prescribed amounts. **2.** The amount administered. **3.** A dose of ionising radiation. **4.** A dose added to wine.

dose (dōss) *n.* **1.** *Abbr.* **d., D.** A prescribed quantity of a therapeutic agent prescribed to be taken at one time or at stated intervals. **2.** *Informal.* An amount, especially of something unpleasant, to which one is subjected: *You need a dose of hard work.* **3.** An ingredient added to wine to impart flavour or strength. Also called "dosage". **4.** *Physics.* The energy imparted to a unit mass of matter by ionising radiation. Also called "absorbed dose". **5.** The recommended upper limit of absorbed dose that a person should receive in a particular period. Also called "maximum permissible dose". **6.** *Slang.* A venereal infection.
~tr.v. **dosed, dosing, doses.** **1.** To give (someone) a dose, as of medicine. **2.** To give or prescribe (medicine) in doses. **3.** To treat (wine) with an ingredient, such as syrup, during bottling. [French, from Late Latin *dosis,* from Greek, a giving, dose, from *didonai,* to give.] —**dos·er** *n.*

do·sim·e·ter (dō-símmitər) *n.* A device that measures and indicates the amount of X-rays or other radiation absorbed by matter, or the intensity of a radioactive source. [DOS(E) + -METER.]

do·sim·e·try (dō-símmətri) *n. Medicine.* The accurate measurement of doses, especially of radiation for cancer treatment. [DOS(E) + -METRY.]

Dos Pas·sos (dəss pássəss), **John (Roderigo)** (1896–1970). U.S. novelist. His writing combines narrative, stream-of-consciousness passages, and newspaper quotations. His best-known work is the trilogy called collectively *U.S.A.* (1930–36).

doss (doss) *n. British Slang.* **1.** A makeshift bed. **2.** A sleep.
~intr.v. **dossed, dossing, dosses.** *British Slang.* To bed down; sleep. Often used with *down.* [Variant of earlier *dorse,* from Latin *dorsum,* back.]

dos·sal, dos·sel (dóss'l) *n.* **1.** An ornamental hanging of rich fabric, as behind an altar or at the sides of a chancel. **2.** *Archaic.* An ornamental covering for the back of a chair or throne. In this sense, also called "dosser". [Medieval Latin *dossāle,* neuter of *dossālis,* of the back, from Late Latin *dorsālis,* DORSAL.]

dos·ser¹ (dóssər) *n.* **1.** *Rare.* A large pack basket; a pannier. **2.** A dossal. [Middle English *doser,* from Old French *dossier,* from Medieval Latin *dorsārium,* from Latin *dorsum,* back.]

dosser² *n. British Slang.* **1.** A vagrant. **2.** An idle person. [From DOSS.]

doss·house (dóss-howss) *n. British Slang.* A cheap lodging house used by vagrants. Also *U.S.* "flophouse".

dos·si·er (dóssi-ay, -ər ‖ dáwssi-) *n.* A collection of papers or documents pertaining to a particular person or subject; a file. [French, from Old French, bundle of papers having a label on the back, from *dos,* back, from Latin *dorsum.*]

dost *v. Archaic.* Second person singular present tense of **do.** Used with *thou.*

Dos·to·yev·sky (dóss-toy-éff-ski, -tə-yéff-), **Fyodor Mikhailovich** (1821–81). Russian novelist, whose works combine religious mysticism with profound psychological and social insight; he is often considered a forerunner of the Existentialists. In 1849 he was found guilty of revolutionary activities and was sent to a penal colony in Siberia for four years. The experience produced *Notes from The House of the Dead* (1862). His four great novels were *Crime and Punishment* (1866), *The Idiot* (1868), *The Possessed* (1871–72), and *The Brothers Karamazov* (1879–80).

dot¹ (dot) *n.* **1. a.** A tiny round mark made by or as if by a pointed instrument; a spot; a point. **b.** Such a mark used in orthography, such as the dot above an *i.* **2.** A tiny amount; a speck. **3.** In Morse and similar codes, a short sound or signal used in combination with the dash and written as a dot to represent letters, numbers, or punctuation. Compare **dit.** **4.** *Mathematics.* **a.** A decimal point. **b.** A symbol of multiplication. **5.** *Music.* **a.** A dot after a note or rest indicating an increase in time value by half. **b.** A dot above or below a note indicating that it should be played or sung staccato. —**on the dot.** *Informal.* Absolutely punctual; on time.
~v. **dotted, dotting, dots.** *—tr.* **1.** To mark with a dot or dots. **2.** To form or make with dots. **3.** To cover at intervals with or as if with dots. **4.** *Slang.* To punch; hit. *—intr.* To make a dot or dots. [16th century : perhaps from Old English *dott,* head of a boil, perhaps akin to Old English *titt,* teat, TIT.] —**dot·ter** *n.* —**dot·ted** *adj.*

dot² (dot; *French* dō) *n.* A woman's marriage portion; a dowry. [French, from Latin *dōs* (stem *dōt-*), dowry.] —**do·tal** (dōt'l) *adj.*

do·tage (dōtij) *n.* **1. a.** Senility. **b.** Feeble-mindedness. **2.** Foolish or excessive fondness. [Middle English, from *doten,* to DOTE.]

do·tard (dōtərd) *n.* A senile person. [Middle English, from *doten,* to DOTE.]

dote, doat (dōt) *intr.v.* **doted** or **doated, doting** or **doating, dotes** or **doats.** **1.** To lavish excessive love or fondness. Used with *on* or *upon.* **2.** To be foolish or feeble-minded, especially as a result of

senility. [Middle English *doten,* from Middle Dutch, to be silly.]
—**dot·er** *n.*

doth *v. Archaic.* Third person singular present tense of **do.**

dot product *n. Mathematics.* The **scalar product** *(see).* [So called because it is written **x.y**]

dot-se-quen-tial (dót-si-kwénsh'l) *adj.* Pertaining to or designating a colour-television system in which the primary colours red, green, and blue are transmitted as dots in sequence and exhibited in the same sequence to produce a complete colour image.

dot·ted line (dóttid) *n.* A line of dots, on a legal document for example, where a signature is placed to indicate formal agreement or ratification.

dot·ter·el, dot·trel (dóttrəl, dóttərəl) *n.* A small Eurasian plover, *Eudromias morinellus,* having a grey breast and a chestnut-brown belly. [Middle English, dotard, plover (apparently referring to its supposed stupidity) : DOTE + suffix *-rel,* as in *wastrel.*]

dot·tle, dot·tel (dótt'l) *n.* The plug of tobacco left in the bowl of a pipe after it has been smoked. [From DOT (in the obsolete sense "lump").]

dot·ty (dótti) *adj.* **-tier, -tiest.** *Informal.* **1.** Daft; crazy; eccentric: *a dotty old lady.* **2.** Infatuated. Used with *about.* [Variant of Scottish *dottle,* silly, from Middle English *doten,* to DOTE.] —**dot·ti·ness** *n.*

Dou·ai (dōō-ay; *French* dway). *Formerly* **Dou·ay.** Industrial town in the Nord département, France. A college for English Catholics was established there in 1568, where the Old Testament of the Douay Bible was published in 1610.

Dou·a·la, Du·a·la (dōō-áalə). Chief seaport and largest town of Cameroon. It is one of West Africa's major industrial centres with brewing, flour-milling, textiles, food-processing, and timber industries.

Dou·ay Bible, Dou·ai Bible (dów-i, dōō-, -ay). *Abbr.* **D.Bib., D.V.** An English translation of the Latin Vulgate Bible by Roman Catholic scholars. Also called "Douay Version".

dou·ble (dúbb'l) *adj. Abbr.* **dbl. 1.** Of a size, strength, number, or amount that is exactly or roughly twice as great as is usual: *a double dose.* **2.** Composed of two like parts; in a pair: *double doors.* **3.** Composed of two unlike parts; combining two; dual: *a double meaning.* **4.** Accommodating or designed for two: *a double sleeping bag.* **5. a.** Acting two parts: *a double agent.* **b.** Characterised by duplicity; deceitful: *speak with a double tongue.* **6.** *Botany.* Having many more than the usual number of petals, usually in a crowded or overlapping arrangement: *a double chrysanthemum.* **7.** *Music.* Producing pitches one octave lower than the notes written on the score: *a double bass.*

~*n. Abbr.* **dbl. 1.** Something increased twofold; a double quantity or amount. **2. a.** One that is exactly like a thing or person. **b.** An apparition; a wraith. **3.** An actor's understudy. **4. a.** A sharp turn in running, as of a hunted animal or a river; a reversal. **b.** An evasive reversal or shift in argument. **5. a.** In darts, the space between the two outer rings on a dartboard. **b.** A score made from a dart that lands in this space. **6.** A bet on two horses in different races, any winnings from the first being placed on the second. **7.** *Bridge.* **a.** A bid indicating strength to one's partner; a request for a bid. **b.** A bid doubling one's opponent's bid, thus increasing the penalty for failure to fulfil the contract. **c.** A hand justifying such a bid. —**at** or **on the double. 1.** *Military.* In double time. **2.** *Informal.* Immediately.

~*v.* **doubled, -bling, -bles.** —*tr.* **1.** To make twice as great. **2.** To be twice as much as. **3.** To fold in two. **4.** *Bridge.* To challenge (an opponent's bid) with a double. **5.** *Music.* To duplicate (another part or voice) an octave higher or lower or in unison. **6.** *Nautical.* To sail round: *double a cape.* —*intr.* **1.** To be increased twofold. **2.** To turn sharply backwards; reverse one's direction. Often used with *back: double back on one's trail.* **3.** To serve in an additional capacity: *The postman doubled as a gardener in his spare time.* **4.** To replace an actor in the execution of a given action or in the actor's absence: *doubled for the star in the chase scene.* **5.** *Bridge.* To announce a double. —**double up. 1.** To bend in two: *doubled up with laughter.* **2.** To share the same living or sleeping accommodation. **3.** To cause to double up. **4.** To stake (the winnings from one horse race) on a second race.

~*adv.* **1. a.** To twice the extent; doubly. **b.** To twice the amount: *win double your money back.* **2.** Two together: *sleeping double.* **3.** In two: *bent double; fold the paper double.* —**see double.** To see two images of a single object, usually as a result of visual aberration. [Middle English, from Old French, from Latin *duplus,* twofold, double.] —**dou·ble·ness** *n.* —**dou·bler** *n.*

doub·le-act·ing (dúbb'l-ácting) *adj.* Designating a steam engine in which the pistons are pressurised at either end of the cylinders. Compare **single-acting.**

double agent *n.* A spy working overtly for one country or organisation while secretly working for a rival country or organisation.

double-bank (dúbb'l-bángk) *intr.v.* **1.** To double-park. **2.** *Australian & N.Z.* To ride two on a horse or bicycle.

double bar *n.* A double vertical or heavy black line drawn through a staff to indicate the end of any of the main sections of a musical composition.

dou·ble-bar·relled (dúbb'l-bárrəld) *adj.* **1.** Having two barrels mounted side by side: *a double-barrelled shotgun.* **2.** Serving two purposes; twofold; ambiguous. **3.** *British.* Comprising two hyphenated parts. Said of a surname: *Smythe-Green.*

double bass *n.* The largest member of the violin family, shaped like a cello, played with a bow or, especially in jazz, plucked, and having

a deep range of about three octaves. Also called "bass", "bass fiddle", "contrabass", "string bass".

double bassoon *n.* The **contrabassoon** *(see).*

double bed *n.* A bed wide enough to accommodate two people.

double bill *n.* A programme such as a film show or concert in which there are two main items.

double bind *n.* **1.** *Psychology.* A sense of impasse caused by contradictory injunctions, especially when these are uttered by the same authority. A child hearing *"You're a bad girl!"* and *"Be a good girl!"* is in a double bind, since the first statement may function subconsciously as an order. **2.** A situation that cannot be resolved; a dilemma.

double blind *adj.* Of, designating, or pertaining to an experiment in which neither the experimenter nor the subjects know, at the time of testing, which are the items or substances being tested and which are the controls. Compare **single-blind.** See **control experiment.**

double boiler *n.* A saucepan consisting of an upper removable saucepan that fits into a lower pan. Water simmering in the lower pan gently cooks the contents of the upper pan. Also called "double saucepan".

double bond *n.* A chemical bond that characterises unsaturated organic molecules in which two atoms are linked by two covalent bonds.

dou·ble-breast·ed (dúbb'l-bréstid) *adj.* **1.** Fastened by lapping one half over the other, and usually having a double row of buttons with a single row of buttonholes: *a double-breasted jacket.* **2.** Having a jacket of this type: *a double-breasted suit.*

double check *n.* A careful reinspection or re-examination to ensure accuracy or efficiency; a verification.

dou·ble-check (dúbb'l-chék) *v.* **-checked, -checking, -checks.** —*tr.* To inspect or examine again; verify. —*intr.* To make a double check.

double chin *n.* A fold of fatty flesh beneath the chin.

dou·ble-coat·ed (dúbb'l-kótid) *adj.* Designating a mammal such as a rat or dog having two layers of hair, one longer than the other, which may give a two-tone colour effect.

double coconut *n.* **1.** A tall palm tree, *Lodoicea maldivica* (or *L. seychellarum*), of the Seychelles Islands, having broad, fanlike foliage and large fruit. **2.** The two-lobed fruit of this tree, containing one enormous seed, the largest of any plant, sometimes weighing 22 kilograms (48 pounds) each. Also called "coco-de-mer".

double concerto *n. Music.* A concerto composed for two solo instruments.

double cream *n.* Thick cream with a high fat content.

dou·ble-cross (dúbb'l-króss ‖ -kráwss) *tr.v.* **-crossed, -crossing, -crosses.** To deceive or betray by acting in contradiction to an agreed course of action. See Synonyms at **deceive.**

~*n.* An instance of such betrayal; treachery. —**double-cross** *n.* —**dou·ble-cross·er** *n.* —**dou·ble-cross·ing** *adj.*

double dagger *n.* In writing and printing, a reference mark (‡). Also called "dagger", "diesis".

dou·ble-deal·ing (dúbb'l-déeling) *adj.* Characterised by duplicity; deceitful; treacherous.

~*n.* An act of treachery or duplicity. —**dou·ble-deal·er** *n.*

dou·ble-deck·er (dúbb'l-déckər) *n.* **1.** A bus with two decks or tiers for passengers. **2.** *Chiefly U.S. Informal.* A sandwich having three slices of bread and two layers of filling.

dou·ble-de·clutch (dúbb'l-di-klúch, -dee-) *intr.v.* **-clutched, -clutching, -clutches.** To change to a lower gear in a motor vehicle by moving the gear lever into neutral, then increasing the engine speed before changing into the required gear. Also *U.S.* "double clutch", *Australian* "double-shuffle".

double decomposition *n.* A chemical reaction between two compounds in which the first and second parts of one reactant are united, respectively, with the second and first parts of the other reactant. Also called "metathesis".

dou·ble-dig·it (dúbb'l-dijit) *adj.* Relating to percentage rates between 10 and 99 per cent: *double-digit inflation.*

dou·ble-dot·ted (dúbb'l-dóttid) *adj. Music.* Having two dots added so as to increase the time value by three quarters. Said of a note.

double Dutch *n. Sometimes small* **d.** Language that cannot be understood; gibberish.

dou·ble-edged (dúbb'l-éjd) *adj.* **1.** Having two cutting edges: *a double-edged sword.* **2.** Capable of being effective or interpreted in two ways: *double-edged praise.*

dou·ble en·ten·dre (dōōb'l ON-tóndrə, -tóndr ‖ dúbb'l-) *n.* **1.** A word or phrase having a double meaning, especially when the second meaning is risqué. **2.** The use of such expressions. [From obsolete French, "double meaning".]

double entry *n.* A method of bookkeeping in which a transaction is entered both as a debit to one account and a credit to another account, so that the totals of debits and credits are equal. Compare **single entry.**

dou·ble-faced (dúbb'l-fáyst) *adj.* **1.** Having two faces, aspects, or sides. **2.** Characterised by duplicity; hypocritical. **3.** Finished on both sides. Said of fabric.

double fault *n.* In tennis, the serving of two faults in succession, resulting in the loss of a point.

double feature *n.* A cinema programme consisting of two full-length films.

double first *n. British.* A first-class honours degree in two subjects or in two sets of examinations.

double glazing *n.* Glazing consisting of two panes of glass separated by an air space, used to provide protection against heat loss and noise. **—dou·ble-glaze** *tr.v.*

Double Gloucester *n.* A type of mild, orange-coloured cheese.

double helix *n. Biochemistry.* The structure of a DNA molecule, consisting of two spiral chains of polynucleotides coiled around the same axis.

double integration *n. Mathematics.* Two separate integrations performed on an integrand containing two independent variables. In each integration one of the independent variables is kept constant.

dou·ble-joint·ed (dúbb'l-jóyntid) *adj.* Having unusually flexible joints permitting connected parts, such as limbs or fingers, to be bent at unusual angles.

double knit *n.* A jersey-like fabric knitted on a machine equipped with two sets of needles so that a double thickness of fabric is produced in which the two sides of the fabric are interlocked. **dou·ble-knit** (dúbb'l-nít) *adj.* Of or made of double knit.

double negative *n.* **1.** A syntactic construction that employs two negatives, especially to express a single negation. **2.** A similar construction in which the repetition of negation produces an affirmative.

Usage: There are several constructions in English in which two negative forms are used together in the same clause to express a single "positive" or "negative" meaning. The most commonly used type, illustrated by *He never said nothing* (to mean "He said nothing"), is not an acceptable standard form. However, its use is widespread in regional dialects as an emphatic expression of negation and it has considerable literary precedent in earlier periods of English. Within standard English, certain types of double negative are acceptable: when the negatives do "cancel out", or "make a positive", as in *I can't not go* (that is, I have to go); to express understatement, as in *He's a not unattractive man;* between main and subordinate clauses of certain kinds, as in *I shouldn't be surprised if he doesn't go;* and as a means of reinforcement later in the sentence, as in *He wouldn't surrender, not even after several appeals.*

double or quits *n.* A betting game that decides whether a player's existing losses will be doubled or cancelled.

dou·ble-park (dúbb'l-párk) *v.* **-parked, -parking, -parks.** *—tr.* To park (a vehicle) alongside another vehicle already parked parallel to the kerb. *—intr.* To park a vehicle in such a manner.

double pneumonia *n.* Pneumonia afflicting both lungs.

dou·ble-quick (dúbb'l-kwík) *adj. & adv.* Very quick; fast.

dou·ble-reed (dúbb'l-réed) *adj.* Pertaining to or designating any of a group of wind instruments, such as the oboe, that have a mouthpiece formed of two joined reeds that vibrate against each other.

double refraction *n. Optics.* **Birefringence** *(see).*

doubles *n.* Used with a singular verb. A game, especially of tennis, having two players on each side.

double salt *n. Chemistry.* A salt consisting, or regarded as consisting, of a molecular combination of two simple salts.

double saucepan *n.* A **double boiler** *(see).*

double-shuffle *intr.v. Australian.* To double-declutch.

dou·ble-space (dúbb'l-spáyss) *v.* **-spaced, -spacing, -spaces.** *—intr.* To type so that there is a full line space between lines. *—tr.* To type (copy) in this way.

dou·ble-speak (dúbb'l-speek) *n.* Complicated and ambiguous language, often meaning the opposite of what is said.

double standard *n.* A set of inconsistent ethical principles in which something regarded as reprehensible in one person or in some circumstances may be condoned or approved in others.

double star *n.* A **binary star** *(see).*

dou·ble-stop (dúbb'l-stóp) *v.* **-stopped, -stopping, -stops.** *—tr.* To play (two parts or notes) at the same time on a stringed instrument. *—intr.* To play a stringed instrument in this way. **—dou·ble-stop·ping** *n.*

dou·blet (dúbblit) *n.* **1.** A close-fitting jacket, with or without sleeves, worn by men between the 15th and 17th centuries: *doublet and hose.* **2.** A counterfeit gem made of a piece of coloured glass covered with crystal or with a thin face of real gemstone. **3. a.** A pair of similar things. **b.** One of a pair. **c.** *Physics.* A multiplet with two members. **4.** *Linguistics.* One of two words derived from the same source by different routes of transmission, such as *fragile* and *frail.* **5.** *Plural.* A throw of two dice in which the same number of dots appears on the upper face of each. [Middle English, from Old French, from *double,* DOUBLE.]

double take *n.* A delayed reaction to an unusual remark or circumstance, often used in an exaggerated form as a comic device.

double talk *n.* **1.** Meaningless speech that consists of nonsense syllables mixed with intelligible words; gibberish. **2.** Ambiguous or evasive language.

dou·ble-think (dúbb'l-thingk) *n.* The belief in two contradictory ideas or points of view at the same time, usually leading to a double standard. [1949: from Orwell's *Nineteen Eighty-Four.*]

double time *n. Abbr.* **d.t.** **1.** A wage rate that is double the normal rate. **2.** *Music.* Duple time. **3.** *Military.* A regulation running pace. **dou·ble-time** (dúbb'l-tím) *v.* **-timed, -timing, -times.** *—tr.* To march (troops) in double time. *—intr.* **1.** To march in double time. **2.** To jog or run.

dou·ble-tongu·ing (dúbb'l-túnging) *n.* The playing of a series of notes on a wind instrument by rapidly covering and uncovering the air passage with the tongue. Compare **single-tonguing, triple-tonguing. —double-tongue** *v.*

dou·ble-tree (dúbb'l-tree) *n.* A crossbar on a wagon or coach to which two swingletrees are attached for harnessing two animals

abreast.

double vision *n.* The simultaneous perception of two images of the same object as a result of poor coordination of the muscles that move the eyeball.

double wedding *n.* A wedding of two couples at the same time.

dou·bloon (dub-lóon) *n.* An obsolete Spanish gold coin. [Spanish *doblón,* augmentative of *dobla,* Spanish coin, from Latin *dupla,* feminine of *duplus,* DOUBLE.]

dou·blure (dōō-blóor, də- || -bléwr) *n.* An ornamental lining, as of vellum or leather, on the inside face of a book cover. [French, lining, from Old French, from *doubler,* to double, line, from Latin *duplāre,* to double, from *duplus,* DOUBLE.]

dou·bly (dúbbli) *adv.* **1.** To a double degree; twice. **2.** Twofold.

doubt (dowt) *v.* **doubted, doubting, doubts.** *—tr.* **1.** To be uncertain or sceptical about; be undecided about. **2.** To tend to disbelieve; distrust. **3.** *Archaic.* To suspect; fear: *I doubt that Thackeray did not write the Latin epitaph"* (A. Trollope). *—intr.* To be undecided, unconvinced, or sceptical.

~n. **1. a.** *Often plural.* A lack of conviction or certainty. **b.** An instance of this; a point about which one is uncertain or sceptical. **2.** An uncertain condition or state of affairs: *an outcome still in doubt.* **—See Synonyms at uncertainty. —beyond doubt.** Unquestionably; definitely. **—no doubt. 1.** Certainly. **2.** Probably. **—without doubt.** Certainly. **—See Usage note at doubtless.** [Middle English *d(o)uten,* from Old French *douter,* from Latin *dubitāre,* to waver, vibrate.] **—doubt·er** *n.*

Usage: Doubt (and *doubtful*) may be followed by *whether, that,* or *if.* In positive statements intended to convey real uncertainty, *whether* is the usual choice, especially in formal contexts (*I doubt whether they can win*). *If* is acceptable, but is less formal. The use of *that* in such contexts has been criticised as being "weak" in meaning, but it is quite widely used informally. In negative or interrogative constructions, where there is clear denial of doubt, *that* is appropriate (*Do you doubt that he will come?; I don't doubt you're right*).

doubt·ful (dówtf'l) *adj.* **1.** Subject to or tending to give rise to doubt; uncertain; unclear. **2.** Experiencing doubt. **3.** Of uncertain outcome; undecided. **4.** Questionable; suspect: *a ruler with a doubtful past.* **—doubt·ful·ly** *adv.* **—doubt·ful·ness** *n.*

Synonyms: doubtful, dubious, questionable, arguable, debatable.

doubting Thomas *n.* One who habitually expresses or feels doubts and requires concrete proof. [After St. THOMAS, who doubted Christ's resurrection until he had proof.]

doubt·less (dówt-ləss, -liss) *adj. Literary.* Certain; assured: *doubtless of ultimate victory.*

~adv. **1.** Certainly. **2.** Presumably; probably. **—doubt·less·ly** *adv.*

Usage: Doubtless and *no doubt* are relatively weak in expressing certainty, since they can also indicate mere presumption or probability (*He's doubtless been caught in the traffic*) or concession (*No doubt you're right*). In contrast, *undoubtedly* and *without doubt* express only certainty and conviction (*You are undoubtedly/without doubt correct*).

douce (dōōss) *adj. British Regional.* Sedate; sober; gentle. [Middle English, sweet, pleasant, from Old French, from Latin *dulcis,* sweet.]

dou·ceur (dōō-sér, -sôr) *n.* Money given as a tip, gratuity, or bribe. [French, "sweetness", from Late Latin *dulcor,* from Latin *dulcis,* sweet.]

douche (dōōsh) *n.* **1.** A stream of water or air applied to a part or cavity of the body for cleansing or medicinal purposes. **2.** The application of a douche. **3.** A syringe or other instrument for applying a douche.

~v. **douched, douching, douches.** *—tr.* To cleanse or treat by means of a douche. *—intr.* To be cleansed or treated by a douche. [French, douche, shower, from Italian *doccia,* conduit pipe, douche, probably from *doccione,* tube, from Latin *ductiō* (stem *ductiōn-*), a leading away, from *ductus,* past participle of *dūcere,* to lead.]

dough (dō) *n.* **1.** A soft, thick mixture of flour or meal, liquids, and various dry ingredients that is baked as bread, pastry, or the like. **2.** Any similar pasty mass. **3.** *Slang.* Money. [Middle English *dogh,* Old English *dāg;* from Germanic.]

dough·boy (dō-boy) *n.* **1.** Bread dough that is rolled thin and cut into various shapes, then fried in deep fat, or that is made into a dumpling and boiled. **2.** *U.S Informal.* An infantryman in World War I. [Sense 2, origin obscure.]

dough·nut (dō-nut) *n.* Also *chiefly U.S.* **do·nut. 1.** A small, ringshaped or round cake made of rich, light dough that is fried in deep fat. **2.** Anything shaped like a ring; especially, a **torus** *(see).*

dough·ty (dówti) *adj.* **-tier, -tiest.** Stout-hearted; courageous. See Synonyms at **brave.** [Middle English *doughty,* Old English *dohtig, dyhtig,* from Germanic.] **—dough·ti·ly** *adv.* **—dough·ti·ness** *n.*

dough·y (dō-i) *adj.* **-ier, -iest.** Having the consistency or appearance of dough.

Doug·las (dúggləss). Capital of the Isle of Man. Its buildings include the House of Keys (the parliament), and the Manx Museum. Douglas was the first seaport in the British Isles to be fitted with radar (1948).

Douglas fir *n.* A tall evergreen timber tree, *Pseudotsuga menziesii,* of northwestern North America, having short needles and eggshaped cones. Also called "Oregon fir". [After David *Douglas* (1798–1834), Scottish botanist.]

Doug·las-Home (dúggləss-héwm), **Alex(ander) Frederick, Baron Home of the Hirsel** (1903–95). British politician. He was elected as a Conservative M.P. in 1931. He lost his seat at the 1945 elections, and was returned again in 1950. In 1951, he succeeded his father as the 14th Earl of Home. In 1963 he renounced his hereditary peerage in order to become Prime Minister and returned to the Commons as Sir Alec Douglas-Home. The Conservatives lost the election of 1964, and he resigned as leader in July, 1965. He was foreign secretary from 1970 to 1974, when he returned to the Lords as a life peer.

Douma. Variant of **Duma.**

doum palm, doom palm (do͞om) *n.* An African palm tree, *Hyphaene thebaica,* having a trunk which branches into two. [From Arabic *dawm.*]

Doun·reay (do͞on-ray). The site, in Caithness, on the northern coast of Scotland, where the world's first fast breeder nuclear reactors were built.

dour (door || *chiefly U.S.* dowr) *adj.* **1.** Silently ill-humoured; gloomy. **2.** Marked by intractable sternness or harshness; forbidding. —See Synonyms at **glum.** [Middle English, perhaps from Latin *dūrus,* hard.]

doura, dourah. Variants of **durra.**

dou·rine (do͝or-een || *U.S.* do͞o-re͞en) *n.* A contagious disease of horses, asses, and mules, caused by the microorganism *Trypanosoma equiperdum,* which is transmitted during copulation. [French, from Arabic *darina,* to be dirty.]

Dou·ro (do͝or-ō; *Portuguese* dṓ-ro͞o). *Spanish* **Duero.** River in Portugal and Spain. It flows 722 kilometres (480 miles) from the Sierra de Cebollera, forming part of the Spanish and Portuguese border.

dou·rou·cou·li (do͝or-o͞o-ko͞oli, -ə-) *n., pl.* **-lis.** Also **dou·ro·cou·li** (-ō-, -ə-). Any of various nocturnal monkeys of the genus *Aotus,* of Central and South America, having very large, round eyes. [Native South American name.]

douse¹, dowse (dowss) *v.* **doused** or **dowsed, dousing** or **dowsing, douses** or **dowses** —*tr.* **1.** To plunge into liquid; immerse. **2.** To wet thoroughly; drench. —*intr.* To become thoroughly wet; soak.
∼*n.* A drenching. [16th century : *douse*†, to strike, smite.] —**douser** *n.*

douse² *tr.v.* **doused, dousing, douses.** To put out (a light or fire); extinguish. [Perhaps from earlier sense (to strike, smite) of DOUSE (immerse).]

douse³ *tr.v.* **doused, dousing, douses.** *Nautical.* **1.** To lower (a sail). **2.** To close (a porthole). [Perhaps from Low German; akin to Middle Dutch *dossen,* to beat, strike.]

DOVAP (dṓ-vap) *n. Electronics.* A system for determining the velocity and position of a long-range missile using the **Doppler effect** *(see).* [*D*oppler *v*elocity *a*nd *p*osition.]

dove¹ (duv) *n.* **1.** Any of various birds of the family Columbidae, which also includes the pigeons; especially, an undomesticated species, such as the **turtle dove** *(see).* **2.** A gentle or innocent child or woman. Used especially as a term of endearment. **3.** A messenger of peace or deliverance from care by allusion to the dove of Genesis 8:8–12. **4.** One advocating a policy of conciliation or moderation. **5.** *Sometimes capital* **D.** The Holy Spirit. **6.** A warm pale grey or greyish-brown colour. **7.** *Capital* **D.** The constellation **Columba** *(see).* [Middle English *do(u)ve,* Old English *dūfe* (unattested), from Germanic.] —**dove** *adj.*

dove². *Chiefly U.S.* Alternative past tense of **dive.**

dove·cote (dúv-kot, -kōt) *n.* Also **dove·cot** (-kot). A roost for domesticated pigeons.

dove·kie (dúv-ki) *n.* Also **dove·key** *pl.* **-keys.** A sea bird, the **little auk** *(see).* [Diminutive of DOVE.]

Do·ver (dṓvər). Port in Kent, southeast England, the only one of the Cinque Ports that still has a major dock. It is the United Kingdom's principal ferry and hovercraft terminus for the continent, with Calais only 35 kilometres (22 miles) away. The Norman castle which overlooks the town has in its precincts a Roman lighthouse (pharos), used to guide the legions across the Channel.

Dover, Strait of. A stretch of water between England and France, connecting the English Channel with the North Sea. Its narrowest point, 34 kilometres (21 miles) between Dover and Cap Gris Nez, is the route taken by Channel swimmers following the first successful crossing by Captain Webb in 1875.

Dover sole *n.* A **sole** (sense 1) *(see).*

Do·ver's powder (dṓvərz) *n.* A powdered drug, made essentially of ipecac and opium, formerly used to relieve pain and induce perspiration. [After Thomas *Dover* (1660–1742), English physician.]

dove·tail (dúv-tayl) *n.* **1.** In carpentry, a fan-shaped tenon that forms a tight interlocking joint when fitted into a corresponding mortise. **2.** A joint formed by interlocking one or more such tenons and mortises. In this sense, also called "dovetail joint".
∼*v.* **dovetailed, -tailing, -tails.** —*tr.* **1.** To cut into or join by means of dovetails. **2.** To connect or combine precisely or harmoniously. —*intr.* To combine or interlock into a unified whole. [From its supposed resemblance to a dove's tail.]

dow·a·ger (dów-əjər) *n.* **1.** A widow who holds a title or property derived from her dead husband. Often used in combination with the title. **2.** An elderly woman of means or status. [Old French *douagiere,* from *douage,* dower, from *douer,* to portion, endow, from Latin *dōtāre,* from *dōs* (stem *dōt-*), dowry.]

dow·dy (dówdi) *adj.* **-dier, -diest.** Lacking in stylishness or neatness; shabby; old-fashioned: *dowdy clothes.*
∼*n., pl.* **dowdies.** A dowdy woman; a frump. [From Middle English *doude*†, slut.] —**dow·di·ly** *adv.* —**dow·di·ness** *n.*

dow·el (dów-əl) *n.* **1.** A usually round pin that fits tightly into a corresponding hole to fasten or align two adjacent pieces of wood or stone. **2.** A round stick or rod from which dowels are cut. In this sense, also called "dowelling". **3.** A piece of wood driven into a wall to act as an anchor for nails.
∼*tr.v.* **dowelled** or *U.S.* **-eled, -elling** or *U.S.* **-eling, -els. 1.** To fasten or align with dowels. **2.** To equip with dowels. [Middle English *dowle,* from Middle Low German *dovel,* peg, block, nail.]

dow·er (dowr, dów-ər) *n.* **1.** The part or interest of a deceased man's real estate allotted by law to his widow for her lifetime. Also *archaic* "dowry". **2.** A marriage portion, **dowry** *(see).* **3.** A natural endowment or gift.
∼*tr.v.* **dowered, -ering, -ers.** To assign a dower to; endow. [Middle English *dowere,* from Old French *douaire,* from Medieval Latin *dōtārium,* from Latin *dōs* (stem *dōt-*), dowry.]

dower house *n.* A smaller house, often near a manor house, intended for occupation by a dowager.

Dow-Jones average (dów jōnz) *n.* The daily index of prices on the New York stock exchange, based on the average price of 30 selected shares. Also called "Dow-Jones index". Compare **FT index.** [After C.H. *Dow* (died 1902) and E.D. *Jones* (died 1920), U.S. economists.]

Dow·land (dówlənd), **John** (1562–1626). Anglo-Irish composer, born in Dublin. He was the most celebrated lute player of his time and served the King of Denmark and Charles I of England. His *Songs or Ayres* (1597–1603) were known throughout Europe.

down¹ (down || *West Indies also* dung) *(and so also in compounds) adv.* **1. a.** From a higher to a lower place or position. **b.** Downstairs. **c.** Towards, to, or on the ground, floor, or bottom. **d.** Towards a point further away. **e.** So as to be no longer erected or displayed: *took the decorations down.* **f.** So as to remain in the stomach: *can't keep her food down.* **2. a.** Into a lower posture. **b.** In or into a prostrate position. **3.** Out of one's grasp. **4.** Towards or in the south or in a southerly direction: *going down to London from Yorkshire.* **5. a.** Away from somewhere considered central or as a centre of activity, such as a capital city: *going down to the country from London.* **b.** Away from a town: *down in the country; down on the farm.* **c.** Away from a university. **6. a.** To the source: *tracking a rumour down.* **b.** *Informal.* Into the central part: *go down the town.* **7. a.** Towards or at a low or lower point on a scale. **b.** Lower in price, standing, or the like. **8.** To or in a quiescent or subdued state. **9. a.** To or in a low status, as of subjection or disgrace. **b.** Reduced to a specified condition: *down to begging from passers-by.* **c.** Reduced to a poor state of health: *down with measles.* **d.** Progressing through all relevant stages towards the lowest stage: *down through the ranks.* **10.** *Sports.* Being a specified number of points behind a competitor: *went two goals down in the second half.* **11.** Seriously; vigorously: *get down to work.* **12.** From earlier times or people. **13. a.** To a reduced, lessened, or diluted form: *worn down; watered down.* **b.** To a reduced but more concentrated or fine consistency: *boiling down a sauce.* **14.** In writing; on paper: *taking a statement down.* **15.** In partial payment at the time of purchase: *five pounds down.* **16.** Into a state of silence or inaudibility: *shouted her down.* **17.** In or towards a condition of lacking or falling short of an appropriate level: *£100 down on the week.* **18.** In a condition of inaction or malfunction: *The computer is down.* **19.** Scheduled or committed: *down to visit Germany in the spring.* **20.** *Informal.* Attributable: *It's all down to you now.* **21.** *Nautical.* Having the rudder to windward. **22.** *Chiefly British.* To prison: *went down for 3 years.* —**down with.** Used to express disapproval or urge the removal of someone or something.
∼*adj.* **1. a.** Moving or directed downwards: *a down escalator.* **b.** In a low position; not up. **c.** At a reduced level. **2. a.** Ill; sick. **b.** Low in spirit; depressed: *feel down.* **3.** Heading away from a relatively more important place: *the down train.* **4.** Being a deposit: *a down payment.* **5.** *Physics.* Designating a type of quark with minus one-third electronic charge, a baryon number of one-third, and no strangeness or charm. —**down on.** *Informal.* Hostile or negative towards; out of patience with. —**down to. 1.** Up to: *The decision is down to you.* **2.** Due to: *Our problems are down to you.* **3.** Reduced to: *Down to our last penny.*
∼*prep.* **1.** In a descending direction along, upon, into, or through. **2.** Along the course of. **3.** Towards the mouth of a river.
∼*n.* **1.** A downward movement; a descent. **2.** A period of ill fortune or depression; *She had her ups and downs.* —**have a down on.** *Informal.* To have a grudge against; bear ill will towards.
∼*v.* **downed, downing, downs.** —*tr.* **1.** To bring, put, strike, or throw down. **2.** To swallow hastily; gulp. —*intr.* To go or come down; descend. [Middle English *doun,* Old English *dūne,* short for *adūne,* reduced form of *ofdūne,* "from the hill" : *of,* OFF + *dūne,* dative of *dūn,* hill.]

Usage: As a general rule, *down* is used for travel in a southerly direction, and *up* for travel to the north. Clashing with this is a convention in British English that one travels *up* to a place of importance, particularly London or a university, and hence *down* to a place considered less important, such as the country.

down² *n.* **1.** Fine, soft, fluffy feathers forming the first plumage of a young bird and underlying the contour feathers in certain adult birds. **2.** *Botany.* A covering of soft, short fibres, as on some leaves. **3.** Any soft, silky, or feathery substance, such as the first growth of human beard. [Middle English *doun, downe,* from Old Norse *dúnn.*]

down³ *n.* **1.** *Usually plural.* **a.** An expanse of rolling, grassy upland, usually of chalk, especially in southern England. **b.** The temperate grasslands of New Zealand and Australia. **2.** *Often capital* **D.** Any breed of sheep having short wool, developed in the downs of England. [Middle English *doun, dun,* hill, Old English *dūn.*]

Down (down). County in Northern Ireland, stretching from the Mourne Mountains to the Irish Sea. Downpatrick is the county town.

down-and-out (dówn-ən-ówt, -owt) *n.* A destitute person, with no home or possessions. —**down-and-out** *adj.*

down-beat (dówn-beet) *n. Music.* 1. The downward stroke made by a conductor to indicate the first beat of a measure. Compare **up-beat.** 2. The first beat of a bar.
~ *adj. Informal.* 1. Depressed; pessimistic. 2. Casual; unconcerned.

down-bow (dówn-bō) *n. Music.* A stroke made by drawing a bow from nut to tip across the strings of a violin or other bowed instrument. Compare **up-bow.**

down-cast (dówn-kaast ‖ -kast) *adj.* 1. Depressed; dejected; sad. 2. Directed downwards.
~ *n.* 1. A ventilation shaft in a mine. 2. A **downthrow** *(see).* —See Synonyms at **sad.**

down-com-er (dówn-kummər) *n.* A pipe which carries water or gas downwards.

down-er (dównər) *n. Slang.* 1. A depressant or sedative drug, such as a barbiturate or tranquilliser. Compare **upper.** 2. A depressing experience.

down-fall (dówn-fawl) *n.* 1. **a.** A sudden loss of wealth, rank, reputation, or happiness; ruin. **b.** Something causing this. 2. A fall of rain or snow, especially a heavy or unexpected one.

down-grade (dówn-grayd) *n. Chiefly U.S.* A descending slope in a road. —**on the downgrade.** Declining, as in influence, reputation, or wealth; losing status.
~ *tr.v.* *(also* -gráyd) **downgraded, -grading, -grades.** 1. To lower the status or salary of. 2. To lower the importance or reputation of.

down-haul (dówn-hawl) *n. Nautical.* A rope or set of ropes for hauling down or securing a sail or spar.

down-heart-ed (dówn-hártid) *adj.* Low in spirit; depressed; discouraged. —**down-heart-ed-ly** *adv.* —**down-heart-ed-ness** *n.*

down-hill (dówn-híl) *adv.* Down the slope of a hill; in a downward direction. —**go downhill.** 1. To decline, as in quality or performance. 2. To become easier; progress more smoothly.
~ *adj. (also* -híl). 1. Sloping downwards; descending. 2. Designating a skiing race run downhill. 3. Placed lower on a slope. Said of a ski, skier's foot, or the like. 4. Leading to failure or deterioration. 5. Progressively easier.
~ *n.* 1. A downward slope. 2. A skiing event in which competitors race one at a time down a slope against the clock.

Down-ing Street (dówning) *n.* The British prime minister or government. [From the location of the prime minister's residence at No. 10 Downing Street, off Whitehall, in Westminster, London.]

down-land (dówn-lənd) *n.* Downs; grassland, especially over a chalky soil. —**down-land** *adj.*

down-load (dówn-lōd) *tr.v.* **-loaded, -loading, -loads.** *Computing.* To transmit (programs or data) from a main computer to a smaller computer or terminal. Compare **upload.** [*downline + load.*]

down-mar-ket (dówn-márkit) *adj. Chiefly British.* 1. Of, being, or intended for less well-off consumers. 2. Inferior in quality or style. Compare **up-market.**

down-pipe (dówn-pīp) *n.* A pipe which carries water from a roof or gutter down to a drain or into the ground.

down-play (dówn-pláy) *tr.v.* **-played, -playing, -plays.** To play down; minimise the importance or significance of.

down-pour (dówn-pawr ‖ -pōr) *n.* A heavy fall of rain.

down-range (dówn-ráynj) *adv.* In a direction away from the launch site and along the flight line of a missile test range.
~ *adj. (also* -raynj). Designating the area and airspace along the flight line of a missile test range.

down-right (dówn-rīt) *adj.* 1. Thoroughgoing; unequivocal. 2. Forthright; candid.
~ *adv.* Thoroughly; absolutely.

Downs, North and South (downz). Two roughly parallel ranges of chalk hills in southeast England. The North Downs run through Surrey and Kent to the white cliffs of Dover, the South Downs through Sussex to Beachy Head. Both are sheep-rearing areas.

down-side (dówn-sīd) *n.* 1. An underside. Compare **flip-side.** 2. *Informal.* A negative side; an unfortunate aspect or consequence.

down-size (dówn-sīz) *tr.v.* **-sized, -sizing, -sized.** To make smaller: *downsized staff.*

Down's syndrome (downz) *n.* A type of mental retardation caused by a chromosome abnormality, giving rise to certain characteristic physical features, notably an oblique slant of the eyes. In nontechnical usage also called "mongolism". See usage note at **mongolism.** [After John Langdon-*Down* (died 1896), English physician who classified it.] —**Down's baby** *n.*

down-stage (dówn-stáyj) *adv.* Towards or at the front of a stage.
~ *adj. (also* -stayj). Pertaining to the front part of a stage.
~ *n.* (-stayj). The front half of a stage.

down-stairs (dówn-stáirz) *adv.* 1. Down the stairs. 2. To or on a lower floor.
~ *adj. (also* -stairz). 1. Located on a lower or main floor. 2. Of or pertaining to servants' quarters in the basement of a large house. Compare **upstairs.**
~ *n.* Used with a singular verb. The lower or main floor.

down-stream (dówn-streem, -stréem) *adj.* 1. In the direction of a river's or stream's current. 2. *Finance.* Closer to the point of sale than to the point of production or manufacture. Compare **up-stream.** —**down-stream** *adv.*

down-swing (dówn-swing) *n.* 1. A swing downwards, especially in golf. 2. A declining trend, as in popularity or prosperity.

down-throw (dówn-thrō) *n. Geology.* The net downward movement of rocks on one side of a fault plane. Also used adjectively: *the downthrow side.* Also called "downcast".

down-time (dówn-tīm) *n.* The period of time when a factory, computer, piece of equipment, or operative is unable to work because of a technical malfunction.

down-to-earth (dówn-too-érth, -too- ‖ -tə-) *adj.* Realistic; sensible.

down-town (dówn-tówn) *adv. Chiefly U.S.* To, towards, or in the lower part of the business centre of a city or town.
~ *adj. (also* -town). *Chiefly U.S.* Of, pertaining to, or located in such an area.
~ *n.* (-town). *Chiefly U.S.* The business centre or lower part of a city or town. Compare **uptown.**

down-trod-den (dówn-tródd'n, -trodd'n) *adj.* 1. Oppressed; tyrannised. 2. Trampled down.

down-turn (dówn-turn) *n.* A tendency downwards, especially in business or economic activity.

down under *n. Informal.* Australia or New Zealand.
~ *adv.* In or to Australia or New Zealand.

down-ward (dówn-wərd) *adj.* 1. Descending from a higher to a lower place, point, level, character, or condition. 2. Descending from a source or origin.
~ *adv. Chiefly U.S.* Variant of **downwards.** —**down-ward-ly** *adv.*

downward mobility *n.* Movement to a lower social status.

down-wards (dówn-wərdz) *adv.* Also *chiefly U.S.* **downward.** 1. From a higher to a lower place, point, level, or condition. 2. From an earlier to a more recent time.

down-warp (dówn-wawrp) *n. Geology.* A small-scale downward movement of the earth's crust, producing no folding or faulting. —**down-warp-ing** *n.*

down-wind (dówn-wínd) *adv.* In the direction in which the wind is blowing; leeward. —**down-wind** *adj.*

down-y¹ (dówni) *adj.* **-ier, -iest.** 1. Made of, filled with, or covered with down. 2. **a.** Resembling down. **b.** Covered with something resembling down. 3. Soft, feather-like.

downy² *adj. British Slang.* Sharp-witted; astute. [From obsolete slang *down,* cunning, special use of DOWN (adverb).]

downy mildew *n.* A disease of plants caused by fungi of the order Peronosporales and characterised by grey, velvety patches of spores on the lower surfaces of leaves.

dow-ry (dówr-i) *n., pl.* **-ries.** 1. Money or property brought by a bride to her husband at marriage. Also called "dower". 2. *Archaic.* A widow's inheritance, formerly a **dower** *(see).* 3. A sum of money formerly required of a postulant when entering certain orders of nuns. 4. A natural endowment or gift. [Variant of DOWER.]

dowse¹ (dowz, *sometimes* dowss) *intr.v.* **dowsed, dowsing, dowses.** 1. To use a divining rod or pendulum to find underground water or minerals. 2. To use apparently paranormal powers to make discoveries. [17th century : origin obscure.] —**dows-er** *n.*

dowse². Variant of **douse** (to drench).

dowsing rod *n.* A divining rod *(see).*

Dowson (dówss'n), **Ernest (Christopher)** (1867–1900). English poet. Alcoholic and debt-ridden, Dowson died of tuberculosis at 32. His poems include *Non Sum Qualis.*

dox-as-tic (dok-sástik) *adj. Logic.* Of or pertaining to belief. [Greek *doxastikos,* having an opinion or belief, from *doxa,* belief.]

dox-og-ra-pher (dok-sóggrəfər) *n. Rare.* A person who collected the writings and opinions of the ancient Greek philosophers. [New Latin *doxographus,* from Greek *doxographos : doxa,* belief + -*graphos,* writer (see -**graph**).] —**dox-og-ra-phy** *n.* —**dox-o-graph-ic** (dóksə-gráffik) *adj.*

dox-ol-o-gy (dok-sólləji) *n., pl.* **-gies.** A liturgical formula of praise to God. See **Gloria in excelsis Deo, Gloria Patri.** [Medieval Latin *doxologia,* from Greek, laudation : *doxa,* opinion, judgment + -LOGY.] —**dox-o-log-i-cal** (dóksə-lójik'l) *adj.* —**dox-o-log-i-cal-ly** *adv.*

dox-y¹, dox-ie (dóksi) *n., pl.* **-ies.** *Archaic.* An opinion or a doctrine, especially on religious questions. [Abstracted from *orthodoxy, heterodoxy.*]

doxy² *n., pl.* **-ies.** *Slang.* 1. A prostitute. 2. A paramour. [16th century : (cant) origin obscure.]

doy-en (dóy-ən, dwĭ-, -en) *n. Feminine* **doy-enne** (-én). The eldest or senior member of a group, as of a diplomatic corps or literary circle. [French, from Late Latin *decānus,* chief of ten, a kind of officer, from Greek *dekanos,* from *deka,* ten.]

Doyle (doyl), **Sir Arthur Conan** (1859–1930). British writer, the creator of Sherlock Holmes. He trained as a doctor, but gave up medicine in 1890, after his first Sherlock Holmes book, *A Study in Scarlet.* He was knighted in 1902, the year he published his most celebrated piece of detective fiction, *The Hound of the Baskervilles.*

doyley, doyly. Variants of **doily.**

D'Oy-ly Carte (dóyli kárt), **Richard** (1844–1901). English theatre impresario. He presented Gilbert and Sullivan's operettas and built the Savoy Theatre (1881) for the performance of their works.

doz. dozen.

doze (dōz) *intr.v.* **dozed, dozing, dozes.** To sleep lightly and intermittently; nod sleepily; nap. —**doze off.** To fall into a light sleep.
~ *n.* A short, light sleep; a nap. [Originally transitive, to make dull, drowse, probably of Scandinavian origin; akin to Danish *døse.*]

doz-en (dúzz'n) *n., pl.* **dozen** (for sense 1) or **-ens** (for sense 2). *Abbr.* **doz., dz.** 1. A set of 12. 2. *Plural. Informal.* An indefinite number;

a great many. **—daily dozen.** Physical exercises performed regularly in the morning. **—talk nineteen to the dozen.** To chatter incessantly.
~*adj.* Twelve. [Middle English *dozeine,* from Old French, from *doze,* twelve, from Latin *duodecim : duo,* two + *decem,* ten.] **—doz·enth** *adj.*
doz·er (dṓzər) *n.* **1.** One that dozes. **2.** *British Informal.* A **bulldozer** (see).
do·zy (dṓzi) *adj.* **-zier, -ziest. 1.** Drowsy; half asleep. **2.** *British Informal.* Stupid. **—doz·i·ly** *adv.* **—do·zi·ness** *n.*
DP, D.P. displaced person.
d.p.c. damp-proof course.
D.Ph., D.Phil. Doctor of Philosophy.
DPP, D.P.P. Director of Public Prosecutions (in Britain).
dpt. 1. department. **2.** deponent.
dr dram.
dr. 1. debit. **2.** debtor. **3.** drachm. **4.** drachma. **5.** drawer.
Dr. 1. doctor. **2.** drive (in street names).
drab[1] (drab) *adj.* **drabber, drabbest. 1.** Faded and dull in appearance. **2.** Of a commonplace character; dreary. **3. a.** Of a dull light brown. **b.** Of a light olive brown or khaki colour.
~*n.* **1.** Cloth of a light dull brown, greyish brown, or unbleached natural colour; especially, a heavy woollen or cotton fabric. **2.** Moderate to greyish or light greyish yellowish brown or light olive brown. **3.** Monotony. [Variant of obsolete *drap,* cloth, from Old French. See **drape.**] **—drab·ly** *adv.* **—drab·ness** *n.*
drab[2] *n.* **1.** A slovenly woman. **2.** A prostitute.
~*intr.v.* **drabbed, drabbing, drabs.** To consort with prostitutes. [Perhaps from Low German; compare Dutch *drab,* dregs.]
drab·bet (drábbit) *n. British.* A yellowish-brown twilled linen. [From DRAB (cloth).]
drab·ble (drább'l) *v.* **-bled, -bling, -bles.** *—intr.* To draggle; become wet and muddy. *—tr.* To bedraggle. [Middle English *drabelen,* of Low German origin, akin to Low German *drabbelen,* to paddle in water or mire.]
Drab·ble, Margaret (1939–). British novelist and biographer. Novels include *The Millstone* (1966), *The Radiant Way* (1987). Biographies of Arnold Bennett (1974), Angus Wilson (1995).
dra·cae·na (drə-sēĕnə) *n.* Any of several tropical plants of the genera *Dracaena* and *Cordyline,* some species of which are cultivated as house plants for their decorative foliage. [New Latin *Dracaena,* from Late Latin, from Greek *drakaina,* feminine of *drakōn,* serpent, DRAGON.]
drachm (dram) *n. British. Abbr.* **dr. 1.** 60 grains (apothecaries' weight); one eighth of an ounce. **2.** 60 minims (apothecaries' measure); one eighth of a fluid ounce. **3.** One sixteenth of an ounce (avoirdupois weight). [Middle English, from Old French, from Late Latin *dragma,* from Greek *drakhmē,* DRACHMA.]
drach·ma (drák-mə, drākhmə) *n., pl.* **-mas** or **-mae** (-mee). *Abbr.* **d., D. dr. 1. a.** The basic monetary unit of Greece, equal to 100 lepta. **b.** A coin worth one drachma. **2.** A silver coin of ancient Greece. **3.** A unit of weight of ancient Greece. [Latin, from Greek *drakhmē.*]
Dra·co (dráykō) *n.* A constellation in the polar region of the Northern Hemisphere near Cepheus and Ursa Major. Also called "Dragon". [Latin *draco,* DRAGON.]
dra·cone (dráckōn) *n.* A large flexible container for liquids, towed by a ship. [From Latin *draco* (stem *dracōn-*), DRAGON.]
dra·co·ni·an (drə-kṓni-ən) *adj.* Also **dra·con·ic** (-kónnik, dray-). **1.** *Often capital* D. Designating an ancient Athenian law or code reputed to be of extreme severity. **2.** Harsh; rigorous: *draconian measures; a draconian penalty.* [After *Draco,* Athenian statesman and lawgiver, whose code (621 B.C.) punished even the most trivial offences by death.] **—dra·con·i·cal·ly** *adv.*
dra·con·ic[1] (drə-kónnik) *adj.* Of or pertaining to a dragon. [Latin *draco* (stem *dracōn-*), DRAGON.]
draconic[2]. Variant of **draconian.**
draff (draf, *rarely* draaf) *n.* Refuse from brewing or distilling; dregs; lees of malt. [Middle English *draf,* Old English *drœf* (unattested).]
draft (draaft ‖ draft) *n.* **1. a.** A preliminary version of a plan, document, picture, or the like. **b.** A representation of something to be constructed. **2.** A documentary instruction to transfer money. **3.** A demand, as on resources or a person's goodwill. **4. a.** The transfer of soldiers from one unit to another or to a special duty. **b.** The soldiers transferred. **5.** *U.S.* **a.** Conscription for military service. **b.** Those conscripted for military service. **6.** *Masonry.* A narrow line chiselled on a stone to guide the stonecutter in levelling its surface. **7.** An allowance made for loss of weight in merchandise. **8.** *U.S.* Variant of **draught.**
~*tr.v.* **drafted, drafting, drafts. 1. a.** To draw up a preliminary version of or plan for. **b.** To compose. **2.** *Military.* **a.** To attach or assign to a different unit. **b.** *U.S.* To conscript. **3.** To enlist the services of (a person) for a special purpose. Often used with *in.* **4.** To chisel a line on (a stone) to guide the cutter. [16th century : variant of DRAUGHT.] **—draft·er** *n.*
draft·ee (draaf-tée ‖ dráf-) *n. U.S.* One conscripted for military service.
draft·ing (draaft-ing ‖ dráft-) *n. U.S.* **Mechanical drawing** (see).
draftsman. *U.S.* Variant of **draughtsman.**
drafty. *U.S.* Variant of **draughty.**
drag (drag) *v.* **dragged, dragging, drags.** *—tr.* **1. a.** To pull or draw along the ground by force; haul. **b.** To cause to trail along the ground. **2. a.** To search or sweep the bottom of (a body of water),

as with a grappling hook or dragnet. **b.** To bring up or catch by such means. **3. a.** To take forcibly away from, to, or into. **b.** To take (a reluctant person) somewhere. **4.** To move with great reluctance, weariness, or difficulty. **5.** To break (land) with a harrow. **6.** To prolong unnecessarily or tediously. Used with *out.* **7.** To introduce gratuitously into a discussion. Used with *in.* **8.** To extract (a confession, for example) from a stubbornly reticent person. **9.** To follow (an animal or a trail). Used of hunting hounds. **10.** To bring up (a child) in a careless way. Used with *up.* **11.** *Chiefly U.S. Slang.* To bore or annoy. *—intr.* **1.** To trail along the ground. **2.** To move slowly or with effort. **3.** To lag behind. **4.** To pass or proceed slowly, tediously, or laboriously. **5.** To search or dredge the bottom of a body of water. **6.** *Slang.* To draw on a cigarette.
~*n.* **1.** The act of dragging. **2.** Something that is dragged along the ground, such as a harrow or an implement for spreading manure. **3.** A device for dragging under water, such as a grappling hook, dredge, or dragnet. **4.** A heavy sledge or cart for conveying loads. **5.** A large four-horse coach with seats inside and on top. **6.** Something that retards motion, such as a sea anchor. **7. a.** A person or thing that holds one back or hinders progress; a drawback. **b.** *Slang.* Something or someone that is obnoxiously tiresome or boring: *What a drag!* **8.** The degree of resistance involved in dragging or hauling. **9.** *Aviation.* The retarding force exerted on a moving body by a fluid medium. **10.** *Billiards.* A backspin given to the cue ball to prevent it from continuing onwards after hitting another ball. **11.** A slow, laborious motion or movement. **12.** *Hunting.* Something that provides an artificial scent. Also used adjectivally: *drag hounds.* **13.** *Slang.* A puff on a cigarette, pipe, or cigar. **14.** *Slang.* **a.** A **dragster** (see). **b.** A race for dragsters. **15.** *Slang.* Women's clothing worn by a man. Sometimes used adjectivally: *a drag show.* [Middle English *draggen,* from Old English *dragan* or Old Norse *draga.*]
drag anchor *n. Nautical.* A **sea anchor** (see).
dra·gée (dra-zháy) *n.* **1.** A tiny round, hard sweet used for decorating cakes. **2.** A small, often medicated, sweet. **3.** A sweet made of fruit and nuts and coated in hard icing. **4.** A chocolate drop. [French, "sweetmeat", from Old French *dragee*†.]
drag·gle (drágg'l) *v.* **-gled, -gling, -gles.** *—tr.* To make wet and dirty by dragging in mud. *—intr.* **1.** To become muddy by being trailed. **2.** To follow slowly; lag; straggle. [Frequentative of DRAG.]
drag·gle-tail (drágg'l-tayl) *n. Archaic.* A bedraggled or slatternly woman.
drag·gle-tailed (drágg'l-tayld) *adj.* Bedraggled.
drag·gy (drággi) *adj.* **-gier, -giest. 1.** Dull and listless. **2.** *Slang.* Obnoxiously tiresome.
drag·line (drág-līn) *n.* **1.** A line used for dragging. **2.** A kind of dredging machine.
drag link *n.* A link for transmitting rotary motion between cranks on two parallel but slightly offset shafts, such as the rod connecting the lever of the steering gear to the steering arm in a road vehicle.
drag·net (drág-net) *n.* **1. a.** A net for dragging the bottom of lakes or rivers in the search for an object. **b.** A net for catching small game. **2.** The system of interrelated police procedures used in the apprehension of criminal suspects.
drag·o·man (drág-ō-mən, -ə-, -man) *n., pl.* **-mans** or **-men** (-mən, -men). Formerly, an interpreter or guide in countries where Arabic, Turkish, or Persian was spoken. [Middle English *drogman,* from Old French *drugeman,* from Medieval Latin *dragumannus,* from Middle Greek *dragoumanos,* from Arabic *turgumān,* from Aramaic *tūrgemānā,* from Akkadian *targumānu,* "interpreter", from *ragāmu,* to call, akin to Mishnaic Hebrew *targūm,* TARGUM.]
drag·on (drággən) *n.* **1. a.** A fabulous monster, represented usually as a gigantic reptile breathing fire and having a lion's claws, the tail of a serpent, wings, and a scaly skin. **b.** A figure or other representation of this creature. **2.** *Archaic.* A large snake or serpent. **3.** A fiercely vigilant or intractable older woman. **4.** Any of various lizards, such as one of the genus *Draco,* or the **Komodo dragon** (see). **5.** A plant, the **green dragon** (see). **6.** *Capital* D. The constellation Draco (see). Preceded by *the.* **7.** *Capital* D. Satan; the Devil. Preceded by *the old.* [Middle English *drago(u)n,* from Old French *dragon,* from Latin *draco* (stem *dracōn-*), dragon, serpent, from Greek *drakōn,* serpent.]
drag·on·et (drágga-net, -nit) *n.* Any of various small, often brightly coloured marine fishes of the family Callionymidae, having a slender body and a flattened head. [Middle English, from DRAGON.]
drag·on·fly (drággən-flī) *n., pl.* **-flies.** Any of various large insects of the order Odonata, having two pairs of narrow, iridescent, net-veined wings and a long, slender body. Sometimes called "darning needle", "devil's darning needle".
drag·on·head (drággən-hed) *n.* Any of several plants of the genera *Dracocephalum* or *Physostegia,* having terminal spikes of rose-pink or purplish flowers.
drag·on·nade (drággə-náyd) *n.* **1.** *History.* An act of persecution of the Huguenots in France in the reign of Louis XIV, consisting of the quartering of dragoons on their property. **2.** Any subjection by military force.
~*tr.v.* To subject to military persecution. [French, from *dragon,* DRAGOON.]
drag·on·root (drággən-rōōt ‖ -root) *n.* A plant, the **green dragon** (see).
dragon's blood *n.* **1.** A red, resinous substance obtained from the fruit of certain palm trees, such as *Daemonorops draco,* and from the stems of various species of *Dracaena,* formerly used in the manufac-

ture of varnishes and lacquers. 2. Any of several similar resins.

dragon's teeth *pl.n. Informal.* Obstacles, such as pointed concrete stakes, placed in the ground to hinder the progress of tanks and other military vehicles.

dragon tree *n.* A tree, *Dracaena draco*, of the Canary Islands, having a thick trunk, clusters of sword-shaped leaves, and orange fruit. It yields a red resin, dragon's blood. [Its resin was once thought to be the same substance as the blood in a dragon's veins.]

dra·goon (drə-góon ‖ dra-) *n.* 1. A heavily armed trooper in some European armies of the 17th and 18th centuries. 2. A type of domestic fancy pigeon.
~*tr.v.* **dragooned, -gooning, -goons.** 1. To persecute by the use of troops. 2. To coerce; harass. [French *dragon*, carbine, "fire-breather", from Old French, DRAGON.]

drag race *n.* A race between specially modified cars to determine which can accelerate faster from a standstill.

drag rope *n.* 1. A rope used for dragging military equipment. 2. The rope which trails from a hot-air balloon and is used for braking or mooring.

drag·ster (drág-stər) *n.* A car specially modified for drag races.

drail (drayl) *n.* A fishhook weighted with lead and dragged through the water. [Probably a variant of TRAIL.]

drain (drayn) *v.* **drained, draining, drains.** —*tr.* 1. To draw off (a liquid) by a gradual process. 2. To cause liquid substance to go out from; empty; dry. 3. To drain all the contents of. 4. **a.** To consume totally; exhaust. **b.** To deplete. **c.** To fatigue or spend emotionally or physically. —*intr.* 1. To flow off or go out of. 2. To become empty or dry by the drawing off of liquid. 3. To discharge surface waters in a given tract of land or region, through natural drainage channels. —See Synonyms at **deplete.**
~*n.* 1. A pipe or channel by which liquid is drawn off, especially one carrying off rainwater, sewage, and the like. 2. *Surgery.* A device, such as a tube, inserted into the opening of a wound or cavity to facilitate discharge of fluid. 3. The action or process or an instance of depletion or exhaustion. 4. *Electronics.* The electrode in a field-effect transistor into which the majority carriers flow from the interelectrode space. —**down the drain.** *Informal.* Wasted; lost. —**laugh like a drain.** *Informal.* To laugh heartily. [Middle English *dreinen*, Old English *drēahnian*, from Germanic.] —**drain·a·ble** *adj.*

drain·age (dráynij) *n.* 1. The action or a given method of draining. 2. A natural or artificial system of drains. 3. That which is drained off. 4. *Medicine.* The draining of fluids from wounds or body cavities.

drainage basin The area drained by a river system; a catchment area.

drai·ner (dráynər) *n.* One that drains, especially a device to hold objects being drained; specifically, a wire rack to hold tableware for drying.

drain·ing board (dráyning) *n.* A grooved sloping surface on one or each side of a sink which enables wet crockery or utensils to drain.

drain·pipe (dráyn-pīp) *n.* A pipe for carrying off rainwater; a downpipe.

drain·pipes (dráyn-pīps) *pl. n.* Narrow, tight trousers, especially as worn by Teddy boys and other men in the 1950s and 1960s.

drake¹ (drayk) *n.* A male duck. [Middle English, perhaps from Low German, from West Germanic *drako* (unattested), male.]

drake² *n.* 1. A mayfly used as fishing bait. Also called "drake fly". 2. *History.* A type of small cannon. [Middle English *drake*, dragon, drake fly, Old English *draca*, from West Germanic *drako* (unattested), from Latin *dracō*, DRAGON.]

Drake (drayk), **Sir Francis** (*c.*1540–96). English admiral and navigator, the first Englishman to circumnavigate the world (1580). In 1587, when war with Spain loomed, Drake attacked Cádiz, destroying about 30 Spanish ships. He was vice-admiral of the fleet which destroyed the Spanish Armada (1588).

Dra·kens·berg Mountains (dráa-kanss-berg, -kənz-). The principal mountain range in southern Africa, extending from Eastern Transvaal through the Free State, KwaZulu-Natal and Lesotho, to Eastern Cape Province.

dram (dram) *n.* 1. A small draught of a drink, especially of whisky. 2. *Abbr.* **dr.** A drachm (*see*). [Middle English *dragme, drame*, dram, drachma, from Old French, from Medieval Latin *dragma*, from Latin *drachma*, DRACHMA.]

dram. dramatic.

dra·ma (dráa·mə ‖ drámmə) *n.* 1. A prose or verse composition written for or as if for performance by actors; a play. 2. The dramatic art or a particular dramatic repertory: *Elizabethan drama.* 3. **a.** A situation or succession of events in real life having the dramatic progression or emotional content characteristic of a play. **b.** A histrionic scene. 4. The quality or condition of being dramatic. [Late Latin *drāma*, from Greek *drama*, deed, action on the stage, drama, from *dran*, to do.]

Dram·a·mine (drámmə-meen) *n.* A trademark for dimenhydrinate, used to treat travel sickness.

dra·mat·ic (drə-máttik) *adj.* Also *rare* **dra·mat·i·cal** (-'l). *Abbr.* **dram.** 1. Of or pertaining to drama or the theatre. 2. Resembling a drama in emotional content or progression. 3. Striking in appearance or forcefully effective. [Late Latin *drāmaticus*, from Greek *dramatikos*, from *drama* (stem *dramat-*), DRAMA.] —**dra·mat·i·cal·ly** *adv.*

dramatic irony *n.* Irony occurring in a drama, when the implications of words uttered are understood by the audience but not by the characters in the play. Also called "irony".

dra·mat·ics (drə-máttiks) *n. Used with a singular or plural verb.*

1. The art of acting. 2. The study or art and practice of staging plays. 3. Dramatic or histrionic behaviour.

dramatisation (drámmə-tī-záysh'n, *rarely* draámə- ‖ *U.S.* -ti-) *n.* 1. The act of dramatising, especially of transforming a novel or similar work into a play or drama. 2. A dramatic version of something.

dramatise, dram·a·tize (drámmə-tīz, *rarely* draámə-) *v.* **-tised, -tising, -tises.** —*tr.* 1. To adapt for presentation as a drama. 2. To present or view in a dramatic or melodramatic way; exaggerate. 3. To bring home strikingly; emphasise. —*intr.* 1. To be adaptable to dramatic form. 2. To indulge in dramatic or melodramatic behaviour.

dram·a·tis per·so·nae (dráamə-tiss per-só-nī, drámmə-, -nee) *pl.n.* 1. *Used with a plural verb.* The characters in a play or story. 2. *Used with a singular verb.* A list of these characters, printed at the beginning of the text. [New Latin, "characters of the drama".]

dram·a·tist (drámmə-tist, *rarely* draámə-) *n.* A playwright.

dram·a·turge (drámmə-turj, *rarely* draámə-) *n. Formal.* Also **dram·a·turg·ist** (-túrjist, drə-mátturjist). A playwright. [French, from Greek *dramatourgos*, contriver, dramatist : *drama* (stem *dramat-*), DRAMA + *ergon*, work, deed.]

dram·a·tur·gy (drámmə-turji, *rarely* draámə-) *n.* The art of the theatre. —**dram·a·tur·gic** (-túrjik), **dram·a·tur·gi·cal** *adj.*

drank. Past tense of **drink.**

dr ap apothecaries' dram.

drape (drayp) *v.* **draped, draping, drapes.** —*tr.* 1. To dress or hang with or as if with cloth in loose folds. 2. To arrange or let fall in loose folds. 3. To hang or rest limply: *I draped my legs over the chair.* —*intr.* To fall or hang in loose folds.
~*n.* 1. A drapery. 2. *U.S.* A curtain. 3. The way in which cloth falls or hangs. [Middle English *drapen*, to weave, from Old French *draper*, from *drap*, cloth, from Late Latin *drappus*, from Celtic.]

drap·er (dráypər) *n. British.* A dealer in cloth or clothing and haberdashery. [Middle English, from Anglo-French, from Old French *drap*, DRAPE.]

drap·er·y (dráypəri) *n., pl.* **-ies.** 1. Cloth or clothing arranged in loose folds; especially, clothing draped on figures in sculpture and painting. 2. *Often plural.* Curtains, usually of heavy fabric, that drape. 3. Cloth; fabric. 4. *British.* The business or premises of a draper.

dras·tic (drástik, draástik) *adj.* 1. Violently effective. 2. Especially severe; extreme. [Greek *drastikos*, active, efficient, from *drān*, to do.] —**dras·ti·cal·ly** *adv.*

drat (drat) *tr.v.* **dratted, dratting, drats.** *Informal.* To damn. Used interjectionally to express annoyance. [Short for earlier '*od rot*, euphemism for *God rot*.]

Drau. See **Drava.**

draught (draaft ‖ draft) *n.* Also *chiefly U.S.* **draft.** 1. **a.** A current of air in an enclosed area. **b.** A current of air induced by artificial means. **c.** A device in a flue or a fireplace which controls the circulation of air. 2. **a.** The pull or traction of a load. **b.** That which is pulled or drawn. **c.** The traction power of a locomotive. 3. The depth of a loaded vessel's keel below the water line. 4. **a.** A gulp, swallow, or inhalation. **b.** The amount taken in by a single act of drinking, swallowing, or inhaling. **c.** A measured portion; a dose. 5. The drawing off of a liquid from a keg or similar container: *beer on draught.* 6. Any of the pieces used in a game of draughts. In this sense, also called "draughtsman". 7. **a.** The drawing in of a fishing net. **b.** The catch of fish in the net. —**feel the draught.** To be affected by difficult economic conditions.
~*adj.* 1. Suited for or used for drawing heavy loads: *a draught horse.* 2. Drawn from a cask or tap. Said especially of beer or wine. [Middle English, perhaps from Old Norse *drahtr*, probably also influenced by Middle Dutch *dragt*; akin to DRAW.]

draught-board (draáft-bawrd ‖ dráft-, -bōrd) *n.* A chequered board for draughts or chess. Also called "chequerboard", "chessboard".

draught excluder *n.* A strip, roll, or pad of material placed below or around a door or similar opening to prevent draughts.

draughts (draáfts ‖ drafts) *n. Used with a singular verb.* A game played on a chequered board by two people, the aim being to capture one's opponent's pieces. Also *U.S.* "checkers". [Middle English *draughtes*, plural of DRAUGHT, in obsolete sense, a chess move.]

draughts·man (draáfts-mən; *for sense 3 also* -man ‖ dráfts-) *n., pl.* **-men.** Also *U.S.* **drafts·man** (senses 1, 2). 1. A person who draws plans or designs of machinery or buildings. 2. **a.** A person who has a specified degree of skill at drawing. **b.** A person who is good at drawing. 3. *British.* Any of the 24 circular pieces used in a game of draughts. Also called "draught".

draught·y, *U.S.* **draft·y** (draáfti ‖ dráfti) *adj.* Having or exposed to draughts of air, especially cold ones.

Dra·va, Dra·ve (dráavə). German **Drau** (drów). River in east central Europe. It flows 724 kilometres (450 miles) from the Carnic Alps in northern Italy, to join the Danube near Osijek, Croatia.

dr avdp avoirdupois dram.

drave. *Archaic.* Past tense of **drive.**

Dra·vid·i·an (drə-víddi-ən) *n.* 1. A large family of languages spoken mainly in southern India and northern Ceylon, and including Tamil, Telegu, Malayalam, and Kanarese. 2. A member of any of the peoples that speak one of the Dravidian languages; especially, a member of the aboriginal population of southern India.
~*adj.* Also **Dra·vid·ic** (-víddik). Of or pertaining to Dravidian or the Dravidians. [Sanskrit *Drāviḍaḥ*, a Dravidian. See also **Tamil.**]

draw (draw) *v.* **drew** (drōō ‖ drew), **drawn, drawing, draws.** —*tr.*

1. To pull (something) towards or after one. **2.** To pull or move (something) in a given direction or to a given position. **3. a.** To remove or take out: *draw a book from the shelf.* **b.** To extract (a tooth). **c.** To take or pull out, as from a scabbard or holster. **4.** To cause to flow forth: *a pump drawing water.* **5.** To suck or take in (air or liquid). **6.** To displace (a specified depth of water) in floating: *a boat drawing 18 inches.* **7.** To cause to move, as by leading. **8.** To induce to act. **9.** To attract. **10. a.** To extract from evidence at hand; formulate: *draw conclusions.* **b.** To bring (a fact, for example) to someone's attention. **c.** To take from a source; derive. **11. a.** To earn; bring in: *draw interest.* **b.** To withdraw (money). **c.** To issue (a cheque, for example). **12.** To evoke; elicit. **13.** To force (a card) to be played. **14.** To take or accept as a chance: *draw lots.* **15.** To get or receive by chance. **16.** To end (a game) in a draw. **17.** To distort; contract. **18. a.** To stretch taut. **b.** To bend (a bow) by pulling back the string. **19.** To shape (wire or candles, for example). **20.** To eviscerate. **21. a.** To describe (a line or figure) with a pencil or similar instrument. **b.** To draft or sketch (a picture). **22.** To portray by lines, words, or imitative actions. **23.** To compose or write up (a will or contract, for example) in proper form. **24.** To close or open (a curtain). **25.** In billiards, to cause (a ball) to spin backwards after impact with another ball. **26.** To search for game in (a field, for example). —*intr.* **1.** To proceed; to move. **2.** To describe forms and figures; sketch. **3.** To be an attraction. **4.** To take in a draught of air: *The flue isn't drawing.* **5.** To use or call upon part of a fund or store. Used with *on* or *upon*. **6.** To cause suppuration. **7.** To steep in the manner of tea. **8.** To pull out a weapon for use. —**draw and quarter. 1.** To execute (a prisoner) by tying each limb to a horse and driving the horses in different directions. **2.** To disembowel and dismember after hanging. —**draw back. 1.** To step backwards. **2.** To hesitate to carry something out; withdraw from something. —**draw in. 1.** To entice or involve. **2. a.** To become shorter. Used of days. **b.** To become longer. Used of nights. **3.** To arrive at a platform. Used of a train. —**draw on.** To approach; move along. —**draw (oneself) up.** To straighten oneself up, as when provoked or annoyed. —**draw out. 1.** To cause to converse easily. **2.** To cause to behave in a relaxed or natural way. **3.** To prolong; drag out. **4.** To leave a platform. Used of a train. —**draw up. 1.** To write up in set form; draft; compose. **2.** To pull up to a halt.
~*n.* **1.** An act of drawing. **2. a.** A raffle or lottery. **b.** The random choosing of tickets, numbers, contestants, or the like in a raffle, lottery, or sporting competition. **c.** Something chosen in or as if in a lottery. **3.** A contest ending in a tie. **4.** *Informal.* A person, event, or other spectacle that attracts large numbers of people. **5.** *Chiefly U.S.* A natural drainage basin; a gully. [Draw, drew, drawn; Middle English *drawen, drow, drawen,* Old English *dragan, drōh, dragen,* to drag, draw, from Germanic.]

draw·back (dráw-bak) *n.* **1.** A disadvantage or inconvenience. **2.** A refund or remittance, such as a discount on duties or taxes for goods destined for re-export or for the manufacture of goods that are to be exported.

draw·bar (dráw-baar) *n.* **1.** A bar across the rear of a tractor to which machinery may be attached. **2.** A coupling for railway carriages or wagons.

draw·bore (dráw-bawr ‖ -bōr) *n.* A hole bored in a tenon such that a pin driven into the hole will tighten the joint.

draw·bridge (dráw-brij) *n.* A bridge that can be raised or drawn aside either to prevent access or to permit passage beneath it.

draw·ee (dráw-ée) *n.* A person or organisation, such as a bank, on whom an order for the payment of money is drawn.

draw·er (dráw-ər; dror *for sense 2;* drorz *for sense 3*) *n.* **1.** One who draws, specifically: **a.** A draughtsman. **b.** *Abbr.* **dr.** A person who draws an order for the payment of money. **2.** A boxlike compartment in furniture that can be drawn out on slides. **3.** *Plural.* Knickers, usually baggy.

draw·ing (dráw-ing ‖ dráwr-) *n.* **1.** The act or an instance of drawing. **2.** The art of depicting forms or figures on a surface by means of lines. **3.** A portrayal of a form or figure in lines on a surface.

drawing account *n. U.S.* An account recording cash payments to a partner or employee to cover expenses or as advances on commissions.

drawing board *n.* **1.** A flat rectangular board to which paper or canvas may be affixed for making drawings. **2.** *Informal.* The basic planning stages. Used chiefly in the phrase *back to the drawing board.*

drawing pin *n. British.* A small pin with a broad head, used especially for fastening paper to board or other surfaces. Also *U.S.* "thumbtack".

drawing room (dráw-ing ‖ dráwr-, dróyng) *n.* **1.** A formal reception room. **2.** Formerly, a ceremonial reception. [Originally, a room to which one retired for rest, short for *withdrawing room.*]

draw·knife (dráw-nīf) *n., pl.* **-knives** (-nīvz). A woodcutting knife with a handle at each end of the blade, used to shave a surface with a drawing motion. Also called "drawshave", "spokeshave".

drawl (drawl) *v.* **drawled, drawling, drawls.** —*intr.* **1.** To speak in a slow and lazy manner. **2.** In the speech of certain dialects, for example, to lengthen or add vowels or to make diphthongs of vowels. —*tr.* To utter with a drawl.
~*n.* The speech or manner of speaking of one who drawls: *an American drawl.* [16th century : probably cant, from Low German.] —**drawl·er** *n.*

drawn. Past participle of **draw.**

—*adj.* **1.** Pulled out of a sheath. Said of a sword. **2.** Haggard, as from fatigue or ill health. **3.** Eviscerated, as is an oven-ready chicken. **4.** Resulting in a draw. Said of a game.

drawn butter *n.* The clarified butter that separates from the salt and curds after melting, often used with herbs as a sauce.

drawn work *n.* A type of needlework done by drawing out threads from the fabric, usually linen, which is being worked, and adding other embroidery. Also called "drawn thread work".

draw·plate (dráw-playt) *n.* A die with conical holes through which wire is drawn to regulate its thickness.

draw sheet *n.* A bed sheet that can be removed easily from under an invalid.

draw·string (dráw-string) *n.* A cord or ribbon run through a hem or casing and pulled to tighten or close an opening. Also used adjectivally: *a drawstring purse.*

draw·tube (dráw-tewb ‖ -tōōb) *n.* A tube that slides within another tube to form a telescopic unit.

dray (dray) *n.* A low, heavy cart, typically without sides, used especially by brewers for haulage. [Middle English *draye,* probably Old English *dræge,* dragnet, from *dragan,* to DRAW.]

dray·age (dráy-ij) *n.* **1.** *Rare.* Transport by dray. **2.** A charge for transport by dray.

dray horse *n.* A horse for hauling heavy loads; a draught horse.

dray·man (dráy-mən, -man) *n., pl.* **-men** (-mən, -men). A driver of a dray.

dread¹ (dred) *v.* **dreaded, dreading, dreads.** —*tr.* **1.** To be in terror of; fear greatly. **2.** To anticipate with alarm, anxiety, or reluctance. **3.** *Archaic.* To hold in awe or reverence.
~*n.* **1.** Profound fear; terror. **2.** Anxious or fearful anticipation. **3.** *Archaic.* Awe; reverence. **4.** The object of fear, awe, or reverence. —See Synonyms at **fear.**
—*adj.* **1.** Terrifying; fearsome; dreadful. **2.** *Archaic.* Awesome; revered. [Middle English *drēden,* Old English *drēdan†.*]

dread² *n.* A man who wears dreadlocks; a Rastafarian. —**dread** *adj.*

dread·ful (dréd-f'l) *adj.* **1.** Extremely unpleasant; distasteful or shocking. **2.** *Informal.* Used as an intensive: *a dreadful rush.* **3.** *Archaic.* Inspiring dread; terrible. —**dread·ful·ly** *adv.* —**dread·ful·ness** *n.*

dread·locks (dréd-loks) *pl.n.* A matted, manelike hairstyle consisting of numerous twisted and waxed strands, characteristically worn by Rastafarian men. —**dread·lock** *adj.*

dread·nought (dréd-nawt) *n.* A heavily armed battleship.

dream (dreem) *n.* **1.** A series of images, ideas, and emotions occurring involuntarily to the mind in certain stages of sleep. **2.** A daydream; a reverie. **3.** A state of abstraction; a trance. **4.** A wild fancy or hope. **5.** An aspiration; an ambition. **6.** Anything extremely beautiful, fine, or pleasant. —**like a dream.** Smoothly; successfully: *The pills worked like a dream.*
~*adj.* **1.** Pertaining to dreams or experienced in a dream. **2.** Wonderful: *a dream holiday.* **3.** Ideal: *my dream lover.*
~*v.* **dreamt** (dremt) or **dreamed, dreaming, dreams.** —*intr.* **1.** To experience a dream or dreams in sleep. **2.** To daydream. **3.** To have a deep aspiration; hope for something. Used with *of.* **4.** To consider something feasible or practical; conceive even remotely. Used in the negative with *of: I wouldn't dream of going.* —*tr.* **1.** To experience an image sequence of in sleep. **2.** To conceive of; imagine. **3.** To pass idly or in reverie. Used with *away.* —**dream up.** To invent; concoct. [Middle English *drem, dreem,* Old English *drēam,* joy, gladness, music, from Germanic.]

Usage: **Dreamt** is preferred for the past tense and past participle in British English, and is uncommon in American English; *dreamed* is normal American English. See Usage note at **-t.**

dream·boat (dréem-bōt) *n. Informal.* A person who is one's romantic ideal.

dream·er (dréemər) *n.* **1.** One who dreams. **2.** A person who daydreams; an escapist. **3.** A person habitually inclined to interpret experience imaginatively without strict regard to practical concerns; a visionary.

dream·land (dréem-land) *n.* An ideal or imaginary land.

dream·scape (dréem-skayp) *n.* **1.** A dreamlike scene. **2.** A painting of such a scene. [*dream* + land*scape.*]

Dreamtime *n.* In Australian Aboriginal mythology, a golden age in which the earth received its present form. Also called "alcheringa", "alchera". [Translation of native Australian *alcheringa.*]

dream·y (dréemi) *adj.* **-ier, -iest. 1.** Resembling a dream; vague. **2.** Given to daydreams or reverie. **3.** Soothing; quiet; serene. **4.** *Informal.* Inspiring delight; wonderful. —**dream·i·ly** *adv.* —**dream·i·ness** *n.*

drear·y (dréer-i) *adj.* **-ier, -iest.** Also *literary* **drear** (dreer). **1.** Gloomy; dismal. **2.** Boring; dull. **3.** Discouraging; depressing. —See Synonyms at **boring.** [Middle English *dreri,* Old English *drēorig,* bloody, grievous, sad, from *drēor,* blood.] —**drear·i·ly** *adv.* —**drear·i·ness** *n.*

dreck, drek (drek) *n. U.S.* **1.** *Vulgar.* Excrement. **2.** *Slang.* Trash, especially inferior merchandise made to cheat the buyer. [Yiddish *drek* or German *Dreck,* from Middle High German *drëc.*]

dredge¹ (drej) *n.* **1.** Any of various machines equipped with scooping or suction devices used in deepening or clearing harbours and waterways and in underwater mining. **2.** A boat or barge equipped with such a machine. **3.** An implement consisting of a net on a frame, used for gathering shellfish.
~*v.* **dredged, dredging, dredges.** —*tr.* **1.** To clean, deepen, or

widen with a dredge. **2.** To bring up with a dredge. Used with *up.* —*intr.* To use a dredge. **—dredge up.** To come up with; unearth. [15th century (Scottish); perhaps from Low German.]

dredge² *tr.v.* **dredged, dredging, dredges.** To coat (food, for example) by sprinkling with a powder, such as flour or sugar. [From obsolete *dredge,* sweetmeat, from Old French *dragie*†, DRAGÉE.]

dredg·er¹ (dréjər) *n.* A barge or boat equipped with a dredge.

dredger² *n.* A container with a perforated lid used for coating food with a powder, such as flour.

dree (dree) *tr.v.* **dreed, dreeing, drees.** *Scottish & Archaic.* To endure. [Revived (by Sir Walter Scott) from Old English *drēogan.*]

dreep (dreep) *n. Scottish Informal.* A useless or dismal person.
~*intr.v.* **dreeped, dreeping, dreeps.** *Scottish Informal.* To hang full-length by one's arms, usually before jumping to a lower level. [From obsolete *dreep,* to drip.]

D region *n. Meteorology.* The **D layer** *(see).*

dregs (dregz) *pl.n.* **1.** The sediment of a liquid; the lees. **2.** The basest or least desirable portion. **3.** *Singular.* A small amount; a residue. **—the dregs.** *Informal.* A contemptible individual or group. [Middle English *dreg* (singular), from Old Norse *dregg.*] **—dreg·gy** (dréggi) *adj.*

Drei·bund (drī́-bo͝ont) *n.* An alliance of three powers, especially the Triple Alliance of Germany, Austria-Hungary, and Italy formed in 1882. [German, "triple bund".]

dreich (dreekh) *adj. Scottish.* Dreary; bleak. [Middle English *dreig,* enduring, Old English *drēog* (unattested), from *drēogan,* to endure.]

Drei·ser (drī́-sər, -zər), **Theodore** (1871–1945). U.S. novelist. His exposure of the seamier side of American life earned him charges of immorality, especially for his first novel, *Sister Carrie* (1900). He wrote *An American Tragedy* (1925), filmed as *A Place in the Sun.*

drench (drench) *tr.v.* **drenched, drenching, drenches.** **1.** To wet throughly; saturate. **2.** To administer a dose of liquid medicine to (an animal).
~*n.* **1.** The act of drenching. **2.** A large dose of liquid medicine. [Middle English *drenchen,* to drown, from Old English *drencan,* to give to drink, soak.] **—drench·er** *n.*

Dres·den (dréz-dən, dráyss-) City on the River Elbe in eastern Germany. It was once the capital of Saxony, and in the 17th and 18th centuries was a centre for the arts. It was badly damaged in 1760 during the Seven Years' War, and was almost completely destroyed by Allied bombing in 1945. The famous Dresden china industry was moved to Meissen in 1710. The city now manufactures machine tools, electronics, and chemicals.

Dresden china *n.* **Meissen ware** *(see).* [From DRESDEN.]

dress (dress) *v.* **dressed, dressing, dresses.** —*tr.* **1.** To put clothes on; clothe. **2.** To trim; adorn. Sometimes used with *up.* **3.** To arrange a display in: *dress a shop window.* **4.** To arrange (troops) in ranks; align. **5.** To apply bandages or other therapeutic materials to (a wound). **6.** To arrange (the hair or a hairpiece); comb and set in a style. **7.** To groom (an animal); curry. **8.** To improve (land) by adding fertiliser, lime, or the like. **9.** To protect (seeds) with a fungicide. **10.** To clean (fish or fowl) for cooking or sale. **11.** To put a finish on (stone, fabric, or other material). **12.** To prepare (hides) in leather-making. —*intr.* **1.** To put on clothes. **2.** To wear clothes. **3.** To wear formal clothes. **4.** To get into proper alignment. **—dress down. 1.** To scold; reprimand. **2.** To wear less elegant clothes than usual. **—dressed to kill.** *Informal.* Dressed with conspicuous elegance. **—dress up. 1.** To wear formal clothes, or clothing more formal than usual, as for a special occasion. **2.** To wear fancy dress. **3.** To arrange in ranks.
~*n.* **1.** Clothing; apparel. **2.** A one-piece, skirted outer garment for women and children. **3.** An outer covering or appearance. **4.** *Obsolete.* A setting right; redress.
~*adj.* **1.** For or pertaining to a dress. **2. a.** Suitable for a formal occasion: *a dress coat; dress uniform.* **b.** Requiring formal clothing: *a dress dinner.* [Middle English *dressen,* to place, put, prepare, from Old French *drecier, dresser,* from Vulgar Latin *dīrectiāre* (unattested), from Latin *dīrigere* (past participle *dīrectus*), to DIRECT.]

dres·sage (dre-saázh, dréssij) *n.* **1.** The guiding of a horse through a series of complex manoeuvres by slight movements of the hands, legs, and body weight. **2.** The training of a horse in deportment and obedience. **3.** A part of an equestrian competition in which such skills are tested. [French, preparation, from *dresser,* to DRESS.]

dress circle *n.* A section of seats in a theatre or opera house, usually the first tier above the stalls or ground floor. [Originally reserved for persons in formal dress.]

dress·er¹ (dréssər) *n.* **1.** One that dresses. **2.** A wardrobe assistant, as in a theatre; a valet. **3.** One who dresses well or in some specified way. **4.** A surgeon's assistant. **5.** A tool used for dressing stone, leather, or other materials.

dresser² *n.* **1.** A cupboard or set of shelves for the open display of dishes or kitchen utensils. **2.** A chest of drawers with a mirror. [Middle English *dressour,* kitchen sideboard on which food was prepared, from Old French *dreceur,* from *drecier,* to prepare, DRESS.]

dress·ing (dréssing) *n.* **1.** The act of one that dresses. **2.** A therapeutic material, such as gauze or lint, applied to a wound. **3.** A sauce for certain dishes, such as salads. **4.** Manure, lime, or the like, used to dress soil. **5.** Stiffening used in the finishing of fabrics. **6.** The various processes collectively by which hides are turned into leather. **7.** *U.S.* Stuffing for poultry, fish, or the like. **9.** Fungicide used to coat seeds. **9.** *Plural.* Dressed or carved stonework, used, for example, on sills or keystones.

dress·ing-down (dréssing-dówn) *n.* A severe scolding.

dressing gown *n.* A light coatlike garment, usually worn before dressing after rising or bathing.

dressing room *n.* A room in which one may change clothes or apply make-up, as in a theatre, or attached to a bedroom.

dressing station *n. Military.* A place near a battle area where emergency treatment may be given to the wounded.

dressing table *n.* A piece of bedroom furniture, usually consisting of a low chest of drawers with a mirror.

dress·mak·er (dréss-maykər) *n.* One who makes women's clothes and household articles, such as curtains, made of fabric. **—dress·mak·ing** *n.*

dress parade *n.* A military parade in dress uniform.

dress rehearsal *n.* A final, uninterrupted run-through, as of a play complete with costumes and stage properties.

dress shield *n.* A piece of waterproof material worn under the armpit to prevent sweat from staining the clothing. Also called "dress preserver".

dress suit *n.* A suit worn by a man at formal occasions in the evening and usually including a tailcoat.

dress·y (dréssi) *adj.* **-ier, -iest.** **1.** Having a penchant for smart clothing. **2.** Smart; stylish. **3.** Suitable for more formal occasions: *too dressy to wear to the office.* **—dress·i·ly** *adv.* **—dress·i·ness** *n.*

drew. Past tense of **draw.**

drey (dray) *n.* A squirrel's nest. [17th century : origin obscure.]

Drey·fus (dráy-fəss, drī́-; *French* dre-fü̈ss), **Alfred** (1859–1935). Jewish captain in the French Army. He was convicted of treason (that is, of passing secrets to the Germans) by a secret court martial (1894) and sentenced to solitary confinement for life on Devil's Island. Émile Zola and other friends of Dreyfus who suspected that anti-Semites had victimised him, campaigned on his behalf, and in 1898 it was disclosed that the evidence against him had been forged. In 1906 Dreyfus was officially cleared, reinstated as a major, and awarded the Legion of Honour.

drib·ble (dríbb'l) *v.* **-bled, -bling, -bles.** —*intr.* **1.** To flow or fall in drops or an unsteady stream; trickle. **2.** To drool; slobber. **3.** *Sports.* To dribble a ball. —*tr.* **1.** To let flow or fall in drops or an unsteady stream. **2.** *Sports.* To move (a ball) by repeated light hits or kicks, as in hockey or soccer.
~*n.* **1.** A trickle; a drip. **2.** A small quantity; a bit. **3.** *Sports.* The act of moving a ball by dribbling. [Frequentative of obsolete *drib,* variant of DRIP.] **—drib·bler** *n.*

drib·let (dríbblit) *n.* **1.** A tiny falling drop of liquid. **2.** A small amount or portion. [From obsolete *drib,* drop, from *drib,* to dribble, variant of DRIP.]

dribs and drabs (dríbz ən drábz) *pl.n.* Small and sporadic amounts. [From obsolete *drib,* a drop (see **driblet**) + *drab,* reduplication of *drib.*]

dri·er¹ (drī́-ər) *n.* **1.** One that dries. **2.** Variant of **dryer.**

drier². Alternative comparative of **dry.**

drift (drift) *v.* **drifted, drifting, drifts.** —*intr.* **1.** To be carried along by or as if by currents of air or water. **2.** To proceed without resistance; move unhurriedly and smoothly. **3. a.** To move through life with no particular goal. **b.** To progress without a set aim. **4. a.** To wander from a set course or point of attention; stray. **b.** To vary from or oscillate randomly about a fixed setting, position, or mode of operation. **5.** To be piled up in banks or heaps by the force of a current of wind or water. Used especially of snow. **6.** To execute a controlled skid. **7.** To continue in motion for a while after a switching off of power. —*tr.* To carry along by or as if by a current; cause to drift.
~*n.* **1.** The act or condition of drifting. **2.** Something moving along on a current of air or water. **3. a.** A bank or pile, as of sand or snow, heaped up by currents of air or water. **b.** Any bank or mass, as of flowers. **4.** *Geology.* **a.** Rock debris transported and deposited by or from ice, especially by or from a glacier or ice sheet. **b.** *British.* Any superficial, unconsolidated deposit above a solid rock layer. **5. a.** A trend or general bearing; a direction. **b.** General meaning or purport; tenor. **6. a.** Lateral displacement or deviation of a ship, aircraft, projectile, or the like from a planned course, especially as a result of wind, ocean current, or other disturbance in the medium of travel. **b.** Variation or random oscillation about a fixed setting, position, or mode of behaviour. **7.** The rate of flow of a water current. **8. a.** A tool for ramming or driving something down. **b.** A tapered steel pin for enlarging and aligning holes. **9.** *Mining.* **a.** A horizontal or nearly horizontal passageway running through or parallel to a vein. **b.** A secondary passageway between two main shafts or tunnels. **10.** In motor racing, a controlled skid at a bend. **11.** A driving or herding, especially of horses or cattle on a particular day to determine ownership. **12.** *Linguistics.* Gradual change in a language or group of languages. **13.** *South African.* A ford. —See Synonyms at **tendency.** [Middle English, a driving, snowdrift, a drove, both from Old Norse *drift,* snowdrift, and from Middle Dutch *drift,* herd, course.] **—drift·y** *adj.*

drift·age (dríftij) *n.* **1.** Deviation from a set course caused by drifting. **2.** Anything that has been carried along or deposited by air or water currents.

drift anchor *n.* A **sea anchor** *(see).*

drift·er (dríftər) *n.* **1.** One that drifts, especially: **a.** One who moves from place to place or from job to job. **b.** A vagabond. **c.** One who is passive and makes no attempt to control the course of his life. **2.** A fishing boat with a net that drifts with the current. **3.** A large sail on a ship used when there is little wind.

drift ice *n.* Loose pieces of ice floating on the sea, that drift with the

current or wind and so cause no danger to passing ships.
drift net *n.* A type of large fishing net with weights at the bottom and floats at the top, that drifts with the tide.
drift transistor *n.* A transistor with a good high-frequency response in which the impurity concentration in the base region varies smoothly from a high level at the emitter-base junction to a low level at the base-collector junction.
drift tube *n. Physics.* A hollow tube formerly used as an electrode in a linear accelerator, inside which electrons, accelerated between electrodes by a radio-frequency field, drift (move at a constant velocity) towards the next electrode.
drift velocity *n. Physics.* The average velocity of a carrier moving in an applied electric field, especially in a semiconductor.
drift·wood (drift-wŏŏd) *n.* **1.** Wood floating in or washed up by a tide. **2.** A collection of worthless or trivial elements.
drill¹ (dril) *n.* **1. a.** An implement with cutting edges or a pointed end for boring holes in hard materials, usually by a rotating abrasion or by repeated blows. Also called "drill bit". **b.** A hand-held tool, electrically or manually powered, for rotating such an implement. **c.** A **drill press** *(see).* **d.** A **pneumatic** drill *(see).* **2.** Disciplined, repetitious exercise as a means of teaching and perfecting a skill or procedure, especially as part of military training. **3.** A specific task or exercise designed to develop a skill or familiarity with a procedure. **4.** *Informal.* An appropriate procedure. **5.** Any of several marine gastropod molluscs of the genera *Urosalpinx, Ocenebra,* and related genera, that drill holes into the shells of bivalve molluscs; especially, *U. cinerea,* a species destructive to oysters.
∼v. **drilled, drilling, drills.** *—tr.* **1.** To make a hole in (a hard material) with a drill. **2. a.** To instruct thoroughly and by repetition in a skill or procedure. **b.** To infuse knowledge of or skill in by repetitious instruction. **3.** *Slang.* To riddle with bullets. *—intr.* **1.** To make a hole with a drill. **2.** To sink a shaft, as when searching for oil. **3.** To perform an exercise; complete a drill. —See Synonyms at **teach.** [Probably Dutch *dril* (noun), from Middle Dutch, from *drillen*† (verb).]
drill² *n.* **1.** A trench or furrow in which seeds are planted. **2.** A row of planted seeds. **3.** A machine or implement for planting seeds in holes or furrows.
∼tr.v. **drilled, drilling, drills.** **1.** To sow (seeds) in rows. **2.** To plant (a field) in drills. [18th century : perhaps special use of obsolete *drill,*† rivulet.]
drill³ *n.* Strong cotton or linen twill of varying weights, generally used for work clothes. Also called "drilling". [Shortening of *drilling,* variant of German *drillich,* from Old High German *drilīch,* from Latin *trilīx,* triple-twilled : *tri-,* three + *līcium,* thread (see **trellis**).]
drill⁴ *n.* A monkey, *Mandrillus leucophaeus,* of western Africa, related to and resembling the mandrill. [West African name.]
drill·mas·ter (dríl-maastər || -master) *n.* **1.** A military drill instructor. **2.** An instructor given to severely rigorous training. Also called "drill sergeant".
drill press *n.* A powered vertical drilling machine, used mainly on metals, in which the drill is pressed to the metal by a hand lever or automatically. Also called "drill".
drill·stock (dríl-stok) *n.* The part of a drilling tool or machine that holds the shank of a drill or bit.
drink (dringk) *v.* **drank** (drangk) or *archaic* **drunk** (drungk), **drunk** or *obsolete* **drunken** (drúngkən), **drinking, drinks.** *—tr.* **1. a.** To take into the mouth and swallow (a liquid). **b.** To swallow the liquid contents of (a vessel). **2.** To soak up (liquid or moisture); absorb; imbibe. **3.** To take in eagerly through the senses or intellect; receive with pleasure. Often used with *in.* **4.** To spend on alcoholic drink. Often used with *away: drank her wages away.* **5.** To drink something in response to (a toast) or in honour of (someone's health). *—intr.* **1.** To swallow liquid. **2.** To imbibe alcoholic liquids, especially excessively or habitually. **3.** To salute a person or occasion with a toast. Used with *to.* **—drink off.** To swallow in a single draught. **—drink up.** To finish off the contents of one's glass.
∼n. **1.** Any liquid that is fit for drinking; a beverage. **2.** An alcoholic beverage, such as a cocktail. **3. a.** An amount of liquid swallowed, such as a cupful or glassful. **b.** A liquid that is absorbed, as for example, by a plant. **4.** Alcoholic drinks collectively. **5.** Excessive or habitual indulgence in alcoholic drink. **6.** *Slang.* A body of water; the sea. Preceded by *the.* [Drink, drank or drunk, drunk or drunken; Middle English *drinken, drank* or *dronk, drunke* or *drunken,* Old English *drincan, dranc* or *druncon* (plural), *druncen,* from Germanic.]
Usage: Standard English recognises only *drank* for the past tense form of this verb, and *drunk* for the past participle. Sentences such as *I drunk it* are common in some dialects, but are nonstandard. The adjectival form *drunk* is generally used after a verb *(I was drunk),* whereas *drunken* is generally used before a noun *(a drunken driver). Drunk* is sometimes heard before a noun, but it is generally avoided in writing.
drink·a·ble (dríngkəb'l) *adj.* Suitable for drinking; potable.
∼n. A beverage. Usually used in the plural.
drink·er (dríngkər) *n.* **1.** One who drinks. **2.** One who enjoys alcoholic drinks; especially, one who drinks to excess: *a hard drinker.*
drink·ing-up time (dríngking-úp) *n.* The time allowed for finishing drinks at the end of licensed drinking hours in British public houses.
dri·og·ra·phy (drī-óggrəfi) *n.* A lithographic printing process using special inks which eliminate the need for water on nonprinting areas of the plate. [DRY + -GRAPHY.] **—dri·o·graph·ic** (drī́-ə-gráf-fik) *adj.*
drip (drip) *v.* **dripped** or *rare* **dript** (dript), **dripping, drips.** *—intr.* **1.** To fall in drops. **2.** To shed drops. *—tr.* To let fall in or as if in drops.
∼n. **1.** The process of forming and falling in drops; trickling. **2.** Liquid or moisture that falls in drops. **3.** The sound made by dripping liquid. **4.** A projection on a cornice or sill that protects the area below from rainwater. **5.** *Slang.* **a.** A cowardly or timid person. **b.** An insipid or tiresomely dull person. **6.** A drip feed. [Middle English *drippen,* perhaps from Middle Danish *drippe,* from Germanic.]
drip-dry (dríp-drī́) *adj.* Made of a fabric that, when wet, will dry to a smooth finish without having to be ironed, merely by hanging.
∼intr.v. **drip-dried, -drying, -dried.** To dry without excessive wrinkling.
drip feed *n. Medicine.* **1.** The administration of blood, plasma, saline, or sugar solutions, usually intravenously, a drop at a time. **2. a.** The machine or tubes by which these substances are administered. **b.** The substance administered. Also called "drip", "intravenous drip". **—drip-feed** (dríp-feéd) *tr.v.*
drip irrigation *n.* A form of irrigation in which water is applied to plants in small amounts at regular intervals.
drip pan *n.* Also **dripping pan.** A pan for catching the dripping from roasting meat.
drip·ping (drípping) *n.* **1.** The fat exuded from roasting meat, separated from the other juices, and solidified. **2.** *Usually plural.* Any liquid that falls in drips.
∼adj. Very wet.
∼adv. Completely; thoroughly. Used in the phrase *dripping wet.*
drip·py (dríppi) *adj.* **-pier, -piest.** **1.** *Slang.* Mawkishly sentimental; insipid. **2.** Tending to drip.
drip·stone (dríp-stōn) *n.* **1.** A drip made of stone, as on a cornice over a door or window. Also called "hood mould". **2.** Calcium carbonate in the form of stalactites or stalagmites.
drive (drīv) *v.* **drove** (drōv) or *archaic* **drave** (drayv), **driven** (drívv'n), **driving, drives.** *—tr.* **1.** To push, propel, or press onward forcibly; urge forward. **2.** To force to work, usually excessively; overwork. **3.** To force or thrust into or from a particular act or state. **4.** *Sports.* To throw, strike, or cast (a ball, for example) hard or rapidly. **5.** To force to go through or penetrate. **6.** To create or produce (a hole) by penetrating forcibly. **7. a.** To guide, control, or direct (a vehicle). **b.** To lead or control (a draught animal, for example). **8.** To convey or transport in a vehicle. **9.** To supply the motive force to and cause to function. **10.** To carry through vigorously to a conclusion. **11. a.** To chase (game or an enemy) into the open or into a trap. **b.** To search (an area) for game or an enemy in this manner. **12.** To excavate (a mine or tunnel) horizontally. *—intr.* **1.** To move along or advance quickly as if pushed by an impelling force. **2.** To rush, dash, or advance violently against an obstruction. **3.** To hit, throw, or impel a ball or other missile forcibly. **4. a.** To operate a motor vehicle. **b.** To be able or licensed to drive a motor vehicle. **5.** To go or be transported in a car or other vehicle. **6.** To make an effort to reach or achieve a particular objective; aim. **—drive at.** To mean to do or say; imply. **—drive home.** **1.** To force in completely. **2.** To cause to be evident or obvious through force or emphasis. **—let drive.** To aim or hurl forth.
∼n. **1.** The act of driving. **2. a.** *Abbr.* **Dr.** A road, usually short and residential. **b.** A private road connecting a house, garage, or other building with the street. Also called "driveway". **3.** A trip or journey in a vehicle. **4. a.** The means or apparatus for transmitting motion to a machine or machine part. **b.** The means by which power in a motor vehicle is used to propel it: *four-wheel drive.* **c.** The means or apparatus for controlling and directing a motor vehicle: *right-hand drive.* **5.** An organised effort to accomplish some purpose, such as raising money; a campaign. **6.** Energy; push; aggressiveness; initiative. **7.** *Psychology.* A strong motivating tendency or instinct, especially of sexual or aggressive origin, that prompts activity towards a particular end. **8.** A massive and sustained military offensive. **9.** *Sports.* **a.** The hitting, knocking, or thrusting of a ball very swiftly. **b.** A stroke or thrust by which a ball is driven. **10.** *British.* A gathering of people for the purpose of playing a game such as whist. **11. a.** A rounding-up and driving of cattle to new pastures or to market. **b.** A similar gathering and driving of logs down a river. **c.** The cattle or logs thus driven. **12.** The rounding up and chasing of game or enemies so that they may be captured or killed. [Drive, drove or drave, driven; Middle English *driven, drof* or *draf, driven,* Old English *drīfan, drāf, drifon,* from Germanic.] **—driv·a·ble** *adj.* **—driv·a·bil·i·ty** (-ə-billəti) *n.*
drive-in (drīv-in) *n. Chiefly U.S.* A retail establishment, such as a restaurant or cinema, designed to permit customers to remain in their cars. Also used adjectivally: *a drive-in bank.*
driv·el (drívv'l) *v.* **-elled** or *U.S.* **-eled, -elling** or *U.S.* **-eled, -els.** *—intr.* **1.** To slobber; drool. **2.** To flow like spittle or saliva. **3.** To talk stupidly or childishly. *—tr.* **1.** To allow to flow from the mouth. **2.** To say (something) stupidly.
∼n. **1.** Stupid, childish, or senseless talk; twaddle. **2.** Saliva flowing from the mouth; slaver. [Middle English *drivelen, drevelen,* Old English *dreflian.*] **—driv·ell·er** *n.*
driv·en (drívv'n) *adj.* **1. a.** Motivated by or as if by some inner compulsion. **b.** Using (whatever is specified) as a basis: *data-driven.* **2.** Carried along and piled into drifts by the wind.

drive-on (drĩv-ón) *adj.* Designating a ship, ferry, or the like onto which motor vehicles can be driven.

driv·er (drĩvər) *n.* **1.** One who drives, especially: **a.** A chauffeur. **b.** A coachman. **c.** *British.* The operator of a train or bus. **d.** A drover on a cattle drive. **2.** An employer who demands hard work of subordinates. **3.** A tool or device used for driving, such as a hammer or mallet. **4.** Any machine part that transmits motion or force to another part. **5.** A wooden-headed golf club with a long shaft, used for making long shots from the tee. **6.** *Nautical.* A spanker *(see).* —**driv·er·less** *adj.*

driver ant *n.* Any of various rapacious tropical Old World ants of the subfamily Dorylinae, that move about in huge groups.

driver's seat *n.* **1.** The seat occupied by the driver of a vehicle. **2.** *Informal.* Any position of control, authority, or superiority.

drive shaft *n.* A rotating shaft that transmits mechanical power to a point or region of application.

drive·way (drĩv-way) *n.* A private road, a **drive** *(see).*

driv·ing (drĩving) *adj.* **1. a.** Violent, intense, or forceful. **b.** Rhythmic: *a driving beat.* **2.** Capable of eliciting work or participation from others; energetic; dynamic: *a driving force.*

driving licence *n.* An official document that authorises the holder to drive a motor vehicle on public roads.

driving test *n.* A practical and theoretical test of competence which all drivers of motor vehicles must pass before being allowed to drive unaccompanied on public roads.

driving wheel *n.* **1.** A wheel, especially a gear wheel, that communicates motive power in machinery. **2.** The large wheel in a steam locomotive.

driz·zle (drizz'l) *v.* **-zled, -zling, -zles.** —*intr.* To rain gently in fine, mistlike drops. —*tr.* **1.** To let fall in fine drops or particles. **2.** To moisten with fine drops.

~*n.* A fine, gentle, continuous rain. [Perhaps a frequentative of Middle English *dresen*, to fall, Old English *drēosan.*] —**driz·zly** *adj.*

Drogh·e·da (dróy-ədə, dráw-, -hədə, -idə). *Irish* **Droichead Atha.** Port on the River Boyne in County Louth, Republic of Ireland.

drogue (drōg) *n.* **1. A sea anchor** *(see).* **2.** A drogue parachute. **3.** A funnel- or cone-shaped device towed behind an aircraft as a target. **4.** A funnel-shaped device at the end of the hose of a tanker aircraft, used as a stabiliser and receptacle for the probe of a receiving aircraft. **5.** A device for indicating wind direction, a **windsock** *(see).* [18th century : origin obscure.]

drogue parachute *n.* **1.** A parachute used in decelerating a fast-moving object, especially a small parachute used to slow down a re-entering spacecraft or satellite prior to deployment of the main parachute. **2.** A small parachute used to pull a main parachute from its storage pack.

droit (droyt; *French* drwaa) *n.* **1.** A legal right. **2.** That to which one has legal right. [Old French, from Late Latin *dīrectum,* from *dīrectus,* right, correct, from Latin, past participle of *dīregere,* to DIRECT.]

droit de sei·gneur (drwaʾa də sayn-yér, -yōr) *n., pl.* **droits de seigneur** *(pronounced as singular).* Also **droit du seigneur** (dü). **1.** The supposed right of a feudal lord to have sexual intercourse with the bride of a vassal on her wedding night. **2.** Any excessive proprietary claim. [French, "right of the lord".]

droits of Admiralty (droyts) *pl.n.* Certain privileges formerly belonging to the Lord High Admiral, especially the right to enemy property and to wrecks.

droll (drōl) *adj.* Amusingly odd; whimsically comical.

~*n. Archaic.* A buffoon. [French *drôle,* from noun, buffoon, from Middle Dutch *drol†,* "little man".] —**droll·ly** *adv.* —**droll·ness** *n.*

droll·er·y (drōləri) *n., pl.* **-ies. 1.** A droll quality; quaint comedy. **2.** A droll way of acting, talking, or behaving. **3. a.** The act of joking; clowning. **b.** Something droll, such as a story.

-drome *n. comb. form.* Indicates: **1.** A racecourse or a place for running; for example, **velodrome. 2.** A large field or arena; for example, **aerodrome.** [Old French, from Latin *-dromos,* from Greek *dromos,* race, course.]

drom·e·dar·y (drómmə-dri, drúmmə-, -dəri ‖ -derri) *n., pl.* **-ies.** An Arabian camel with one hump, of a type bred especially for racing and riding. Compare **Bactrian camel.** [Middle English *dromedarie,* from Old French *dromedaire,* from Late Latin *dromedārius,* from Greek *dromas* (stem *dromad-*), dromedary, runner.]

drom·ond (dróm-ənd, drúm-) *n.* Also **drom·on** (-ən). A large medieval sailing galley. [Middle English *dromon(d),* from Old French *dromon,* from Late Latin *dromō* (stem *dromōn-*), a kind of fast ship, from Late Greek *dromōn,* from *dromos,* a running, race, course.]

-dromous *adj. comb. form.* Indicates running or moving; for example, **catadromous.** [New Latin *-dromus,* from Greek *-dromos,* from *dromos,* a running, race, course.]

drone[1] (drōn) *n.* **1.** A male bee, especially a honeybee, characteristically stingless, performing no work, and producing no honey. Its only function is to mate with the queen bee. **2.** A person, especially male, who lives off the efforts of others; a sponger or parasite. **3.** A pilotless aircraft operated by remote control. [Middle English *drane,* Old English *drān, drǽn.*]

drone[2] *v.* **droned, droning, drones.** —*intr.* **1.** To make a continuous low, dull, humming sound. **2.** To speak in a monotonous tone. —*tr.* To utter in a monotonous low tone: *"the mosquitoes droned their angry chant"* (Somerset Maugham). —**drone on.** To talk boringly and at length.

~*n.* **1.** A continuous low humming or buzzing sound. **2.** Any of the pipes of a bagpipe tuned to produce a single note. Also called

"drone pipe". **3.** *Music.* A single sustained note. [From DRONE (bee), imitative.]

dron·go (dróng-gō) *n., pl.* **-gos** or **goes. 1.** Any of various tropical Old World birds of the family Dicruridae, characteristically having glossy black plumage and a forked tail. **2.** *Australian & N.Z. Informal.* A dull-witted person. [Malagasy.]

droob (drōōb) *n. Australian Slang.* A feeble or pathetic person. [20th century : origin obscure.] —**droob·y** *adj.*

drool (drōōl) *v.* **drooled, drooling, drools.** —*intr.* **1.** To let saliva run from the mouth; dribble. **2.** *Informal.* To make an extravagant show of appreciation. **3.** *Informal.* To talk nonsense. —*tr.* To let run from the mouth.

~*n.* **1.** Saliva; drivel. **2.** *Informal.* Silly talk; nonsense. [Variant of DRIVEL.]

droop (drōōp) *v.* **drooped, drooping, droops.** —*intr.* **1.** To bend or hang downwards; sag. **2.** To sag in dejection, exhaustion, or lifelessness —*tr.* To let bend or hang down.

~*n.* The act or condition of drooping. [Middle English *droupen,* from Old Norse *drūpa,* from Germanic.] —**droop·i·ly, droop·ing·ly** *adv.* —**droop·y** *adj.*

droop nose *n.* An aircraft nose that can be inclined downwards to increase runway visibility on takeoff and landing. Also called "droop snoot".

drop (drop) *n.* **1.** The smallest quantity of liquid heavy enough to fall in a spherical or pear-shaped mass; a globule. **2.** A minute quantity of any substance. **3.** *Plural.* Liquid medicine administered in such quantity. **4.** A trace or hint of something abstract. **5. a.** Anything shaped or hanging like a drop. **b.** A small globular sweet. **6. a.** An act of dropping or allowing to fall. **b.** An act of falling or being dropped; a rapid descent. **7.** A swift decline or decrease, as in quality, quantity, or intensity. **8. a.** The vertical distance from a higher to a lower level. **b.** The distance through which something falls or drops. **9.** A sheer incline, such as the face of a cliff; a steep slope. **10. a.** A delivery of goods, as by a carrier or parachute. **b.** A parachute jump. **11.** Something arranged to fall or be lowered, specifically: **a.** An unframed curtain that forms part of the scenery on a stage. **b.** A theatre curtain that can be lowered or raised. Also called "drop curtain". **c.** A trapdoor on a gallows. **12.** *U.S.* A slot through which something is deposited in a receptacle. **13.** A place where secret letters, illicit goods, or the like are deposited for someone else to collect. —**a drop in the bucket** or **ocean.** A tiny amount in relation to what is available or required. —**at the drop of a hat.** Immediately and willingly. —**get** or **have the drop on.** To get or have a distinct advantage over.

~*v.* **dropped** or *archaic* **dropt, dropping, drops.** —*intr.* **1.** To fall in drops. **2.** To fall from a higher to a lower place or position. **3.** To become less in number, intensity, volume, or other measure; decrease; decline. **4.** To descend from one level to another. **5.** To fall or sink into a state of exhaustion or death. **6.** To pass or slip into some specified state or condition. **7.** To cease; come to an end. **8.** To crouch. Used of a hunting dog. —*tr.* **1.** To let fall by releasing hold of. **2.** To let fall in drops. **3.** To cause to become less; decrease; reduce. **4.** To cause to fall, as by hitting or shooting. **5.** To give birth to. Used of animals. **6.** To say or offer casually. **7.** To write and send off (a note, for example) at leisure. **8.** To cease consideration or treatment of; have done with. **9.** To terminate an association or relationship with. **10. a.** To leave out (a letter, for example) in speaking or writing. **b.** In knitting, to let (a stitch) fall accidentally from the needle before it has been worked. **11.** To leave out of a team. **12.** To leave or set down at a particular place. Often used with *off.* **13.** To parachute. **14.** To lower the level of (the voice). **15.** To lose (a game or contest, for example). **16.** To lower (the hem of a garment). **17.** *Slang.* To take orally (a drug, such as LSD). —**drop behind.** To fall behind or back. —**drop by** or **in.** To stop in for a short visit. [Middle English *drop(e),* Old English *dropa,* from Germanic.] —**drop·let** *n.*

drop-dead (dróp-ded) *adv. Informal.* Stunningly: *drop-dead gorgeous* —**drop-dead** *adj.*

drop·forge (dróp-fórj ‖ -fōrj) *tr.v.* **-forged, -forging, -forges.** To forge (a metal) between dies by the force of a drop hammer.

drop goal *n.* In Rugby football, a goal scored with a drop kick.

drop hammer *n.* A machine used to forge or stamp metal, consisting of an anvil or base aligned with a hammer that is forced down upon the molten metal. Also called "drop forge", "drop press".

drop·head (dróp-hed) *n. & adj.* The fabric roof of a car, which can be folded back.

drop kick *n.* **1.** In Rugby and American football, a kick made by dropping the ball to the ground and kicking it just as it starts to rebound. **2.** In wrestling, a kick in the opponent's face or body, made with both feet together. —**drop-kick** (dróp-kik) *v.*

drop leaf *n.* A wing on a table, hinged for folding down when not in use. —**drop-leaf** (dróp-leef) *adj.*

drop·light (dróp-līt) *n.* A hanging lamp that can be lowered and raised on its cord.

drop off *intr. v.* **1.** To decrease; lessen in quantity, volume, or the like. **2.** *Informal.* To fall asleep. —**drop-off** (dróp-off, -awf) *n.*

drop out *intr. v.* **1.** To withdraw from participation in a group or organisation, such as a game, club, or school. **2.** To refuse to participate in conventional society, by deliberately avoiding employment, for example.

drop·out (dróp-owt) *n.* **1.** A person who leaves school or university before completing a course of instruction. **2.** One who has withdrawn from a given social group. **3.** In Rugby football, a drop kick played after a touchdown by a defender.

drop·per (drópper) *n.* **1.** One that drops. **2.** A small tube with a suction bulb at one end for drawing in a liquid and releasing it in drops. In this sense, also called "eyedropper".

drop·ping (drópping) *n.* **1.** That which has fallen in drops. **2.** *Plural.* The dung of certain animals, such as sheep or mice.

drop scone *n.* A small, thick pancake made by dropping a spoonful of batter onto a hot cooking surface, such as a griddle. Also called "girdle cake", "griddle cake", "Scotch pancake".

drop shipment *n.* Goods shipped by a manufacturer or seller directly to a retailer or customer but invoiced to the wholesaler.

drop shot *n.* **1.** In games such as tennis or squash, a shot that causes the ball to drop immediately after clearing the net or hitting the front wall. **2.** Shot made by percolating molten metal through a sieve and then dropping it in water.

drop·sonde (dróp-sond) *n.* A **radiosonde** *(see)* that is dropped by parachute.

drop·sy (drópsi) *n.* Pathological accumulation of diluted lymph in body tissues and cavities. [Middle English, shortened from *hydropsy,* from earlier *ydropesie,* from Old French, from Latin *hydrōpisis,* from Greek *hudrōpisis,* from *hudrōps,* from *hudōr,* water.] —**drop·si·cal** *adj.* —**drop·si·cal·ly** *adv.*

dropt. *Archaic.* Past tense and past participle of **drop.**

drop tank *n.* A fuel tank, carried externally by an aircraft, that can be jettisoned in flight.

drop·wort (dróp-wurt) *n.* **1.** A plant, *Filipendula vulgaris* (or *F. hexapetala*), native to Eurasia, having finely divided leaflets and clusters of small white flowers. **2.** Any of various water plants of the genus *Oenanthe,* having white flowers borne in an umbel.

drosh·ky (drósh-ki) *n., pl.* **-kies.** Also **dros·ky** (dróss-). An open, four-wheeled, horse-drawn carriage formerly common in Russia. [Russian *drozhki,* diminutive of *drogi,* wagon, plural formation from *droga,* beam of the wagon.]

dro·soph·i·la (dro-sóffi-lə, drə-, drō-) *n., pl.* **-las** or **-lae** (-lee). A small fly of the genus *Drosophila;* especially, the fruit fly *D. melanogaster,* used extensively in genetic studies. [New Latin : Greek *drosos†,* dew + *-philos,* loving, -PHILOUS.]

dross (dross ‖ drawss) *n.* **1.** Waste product or impurities formed on the surface of molten metal during smelting. **2. a.** Worthless or waste material. **b.** Stultifying rubbish: *reading the dross in the tabloids.* [Middle English *dros,* Old English *drōs,* dregs.] —**dross·i·ness** *n.* —**dross·y** *adj.*

drought (drowt) *n.* **1. a.** A long period with no rain, especially during a planting season. **b.** In Britain, 15 or more consecutive days having less than 0.25 millimetres (0.01 inch) of rain. **2.** A dearth of anything; a scarcity. **3.** *Archaic.* A thirst. [Middle English *drought,* Old English *drūgath,* from *drȳge,* DRY.] —**drought·y** *adj.*

drouth (drowth) *n. Archaic & Regional.* **1.** A drought. **2.** A thirst. —**drouth·y** *adj.*

drove¹. Past tense of **drive.**

drove² (drōv) *n.* **1.** A flock or herd being driven in a body. **2.** A large mass of people moving or acting as a body. **3.** A stonemason's broad-edged chisel used for rough-hewing. Also called "drove chisel". **4.** A stone surface dressed with a drove. —*tr.v.* **droved, droving, droves.** **1.** *British.* To herd (animals). **2.** To dress (stone) with a drove. [Middle English *drove,* Old English *drāf,* from *drīfan,* to DRIVE.]

drov·er (drōvər) *n.* **1.** A driver of cattle or sheep. **2.** A cattle dealer.

drove road *n. Chiefly Scottish.* An unsurfaced road along which cattle were formerly driven to market.

drown (drown ‖ *West Indies also* drung) *v.* **drowned, drowning, drowns.** —*intr.* To die by suffocating in water or other liquid. —*tr.* **1.** To kill by submerging and suffocating in water or other liquid. **2.** To drench thoroughly or cover with a liquid. **3.** To deaden one's awareness of, as by immersion: *drowned her troubles in drink.* **4.** To overwhelm and blur (a sound) by a louder sound. Often used with *out.* [Middle English *dr(o)unen,* perhaps from Scandinavian; akin to Old Norse *drukna,* to be drowned.]

drown-proof·ing (drówn-proof-ing ‖ -proof-) *n.* A technique for staying afloat for a long period by making use of controlled breathing and one's natural buoyancy.

drowse (drowz) *v.* **drowsed, drowsing, drowses.** —*intr.* To be half-asleep; doze. —*tr.* **1.** To make drowsy: *"On a half-reaped furrow sound asleep, / drowsed with the fume of poppies"* (John Keats). **2.** To pass (time) drowsing. Used with *away.* —*n.* A sleepy condition. [Back-formation from DROWSY.]

drow·sy (drówzi) *adj.* **-sier, -siest.** **1.** Dull with sleepiness. **2.** Produced or characterised by sleepiness. **3.** Inducing sleepiness; soporific. **4.** Lethargic; lazy. [Perhaps akin to Old English *drūsian,* to be sluggish, and *drēosan,* to fall.] —**drow·si·ly** *adv.* —**drow·si·ness** *n.*

drub (drub) *v.* **drubbed, drubbing, drubs.** —*tr.* **1.** To thrash with a stick. **2.** To force or drive (an idea, for example). Used with *into* or *out of.* **3.** To defeat emphatically. **4.** To stamp (the feet). —*intr.* **1.** To beat the ground; stamp. **2.** To pound; throb. —*n.* A blow with a stick. [Arabic *ḍáraba,* to beat.] —**drub·ber** *n.*

drub·bing (drúbbing) *n.* **1.** A severe thrashing. **2.** A total defeat.

drudge (druj) *n.* Also **drudg·er** (drúj ər). A person who does tedious, menial, or unpleasant work. —*intr.v.* **drudged, drudging, drudges.** To do the work of a drudge. [Perhaps akin to DRAG.] —**drudg·ing·ly** *adv.*

drudg·er·y (drújəri) *n., pl.* **-ies.** Tedious, menial, or unpleasant work. See Synonyms at **work.**

drug (drug) *n.* **1.** A substance used as medicine in the treatment of disease. **2.** A narcotic, especially one that is addictive. **3.** *Obsolete.* A chemical or dye. —*tr.v.* **drugged, drugging, drugs.** **1.** To administer a drug to. **2.** To poison or mix (food or drink, for example) with drugs. **3.** To stupefy or dull with or as if with a drug. [Middle English *drogge,* from Old French *droguet,* chemical material.]

drug addict *n.* A person addicted to a narcotic drug such as heroin.

drug·get (drúggit) *n.* **1.** A heavy felted fabric of wool or wool and cotton, having characteristic coloured designs, used for floor covering. **2.** A coarse rug made of this fabric, made in India. **3.** A fabric woven wholly or partly of wool, formerly used for clothing. [16th century : from French *droguett.*]

drug·gist (drúggist) *n. Chiefly U.S.* **1.** A pharmacist. **2.** One who sells drugs.

drug·store (drúg-stawr ‖ -stōr) *n. Chiefly U.S.* A shop where prescriptions are made up and toiletries and other articles, such as confectionery, are sold.

dru·id (drōō-id ‖ dréw-) *n. Often capital* D. **1.** A member of an order of priests in ancient Britain and Gaul, who appear in Welsh and Irish legend as prophets and mystics. **2.** A member of any of several modern mystical movements believing in one universal source of wisdom emanating from the sun. **3.** An officer of a Welsh Gorsedd. [Latin *druides,* druids, from Gaulish, perhaps "soothsayers", from Celtic *derwos* (unattested), true, or from Celtic *dru-* (unattested), tree (their rites being associated with the oak).] —**dru·id·ic** (drōō-iddik ‖ drew-), **dru·id·i·cal** *adj.* —**dru·id·ism** *n.*

drum¹ (drum) *n.* **1.** A percussion instrument consisting of a hollow cylinder or hemisphere with a membrane stretched tightly over one or both ends, played by beating with the hands or sticks. **2.** A sound produced by such an instrument. **3.** Something resembling a drum in shape or structure, especially: **a.** A metal cylinder or spool, wound with cable, wire, or heavy rope. **b.** A cylindrical or barrel-like metal container. **4.** A cylindrical device in a computer on which data is stored. Also called "magnetic drum". **5.** *Anatomy.* The **eardrum** *(see).* **6.** *Architecture.* **a.** A cylindrical block or section forming the shaft of a stone pillar. **b.** A circular or polygonal wall or other structure, such as that supporting a dome. **7.** Any of various marine and freshwater fishes of the family Sciaenidae, that make a drumming sound. Also called "drumfish". **8.** A drumlin. **9.** *Australian Slang.* A brothel. **10.** *Australian Slang.* Information; a tip: *give someone the drum.* —*v.* **drummed, drumming, drums.** —*intr.* **1.** To play the drum. **2.** To thump or tap rhythmically or continually. **3.** To produce a booming, reverberating sound as certain birds do, by beating the wings. —*tr.* **1.** To perform (a piece or tune) on or as if on a drum. **2.** To summon by or as if by beating a drum. **3.** To force (knowledge, information, or instructions) upon a person by constant repetition. Used with *into.* —**drum out.** To expel or dismiss in disgrace, originally to the beat of a drum. —**drum up.** To obtain, create or work up (business or support, for example) by canvassing, soliciting, or advertising. [Shortened from obsolete *dromslade,* drum, drummer, from Low German *trommelslag,* drumbeat : *trommel,* drum (akin to TRUMP) + *slag,* beat (akin to SLAY).]

drum² *n. Scottish & Irish.* A long, narrow ridge or hill.

drum·beat (drúm-beet) *n.* The sound produced by beating a drum.

drum brake *n.* A type of brake consisting of two shoes that are forced against the inside of the brake drum of a vehicle when the brake is applied.

drum·fire (drúm-fīr) *n.* **1.** Heavy, continuous gunfire. **2.** A sound suggestive of this.

drum·fish (drúm-fish) *n.* A fish, the **drum** *(see).*

drum·head (drúm-hed) *n.* **1.** The membrane stretched over the open end of a drum. **2.** *Nautical.* The circular top part of a capstan, used to hold bars for turning. **3.** The **eardrum** *(see).*

drumhead court-martial *n.* A court-martial held for the summary trial of an offence committed during military operations. [So called because it was sometimes held around a drumhead.]

drum·lin (drúmlin) *n.* A streamlined hill or ridge composed of glacial drift. Also called "drum". [Irish Gaelic *druim†* + -LIN(G).]

drum major *n.* A person who leads a marching band or a corps of drums, often twirling a baton.

drum majorette *n.* **1.** A female drum major. **2.** A costumed girl who twirls a baton at the head of a marching band.

drum·mer (drúmmer) *n.* **1.** One who plays a drum, as in a band. **2.** *Chiefly U.S.* A travelling salesman. **3.** *Australian.* The slowest person in a team of sheep shearers.

drum·roll (drúm-rōl) *n.* **1.** A roll on a drum. **2.** The sound of a drumroll.

drum·stick (drúm-stik) *n.* **1.** A stick for beating a drum. **2.** The lower part of the leg of a cooking fowl.

drunk (drungk) *n.* Past participle and *archaic* past tense of **drink.** —*adj.* **1.** Intoxicated with alcoholic drink to the point of impairment of physical and mental faculties; inebriated. **2.** Overcome by strong feeling: *drunk with power.* —See Usage note at **drink.** —*n.* **1.** A drunken person; especially, a drunkard. **2.** A bout of drinking; a spree; a binge.

drunk·ard (drúngkərd) *n.* One who is habitually drunk.

drunk·en (drúngkən) *n. Obsolete.* Alternative past participle of **drink.** —*adj.* **1.** Delirious with or as with strong drink; intoxicated. **2.** Habitually intoxicated; chronically drunk: *a drunken wastrel.* **3.** Per-

taining to or occurring during intoxication: *drunken driving.*
—**drunk·en·ly** *adv.* —**drunk·en·ness** *n.*
drunk·o·me·ter (drúngkə-meetər, drung-kómmitər) *n. U.S.* A
breathalyser *(see).*
dru·pa·ceous (drōō-páyshəss ‖ drew-) *adj. Botany.* 1. Pertaining to
or consisting of a drupe: *drupaceous fruit.* 2. Producing drupes: *a
drupaceous tree.*
drupe (drōōp ‖ drewp) *n. Botany.* A fleshy fruit, such as the peach,
plum, or cherry, having a single hard stone that encloses a seed.
Also called "stone fruit". [New Latin *drupa,* from Latin *drūpa,
druppa,* overripe olive, from Greek *druppa,* from *drupepēs,* "ripened
on a tree", overripe : *drus,* tree + *peptein,* to cook, to ripen.]
dru·pel (drōōp'l ‖ drewp'l) *n.* A collection of small drupes forming
an aggregate fruit in plants such as the raspberry.
drupe·let (drōōp-lət, -lit ‖ drewp-) *n. Botany.* A small drupe, such
as any of the many subdivisions of the raspberry or the blackberry.
druse (drōōz ‖ drewz) *n.* A small rock cavity lined with tiny, perfectly formed crystals of the minerals making up the rock. Compare
geode. [German *Druse,* "weathered ore", from Old High German
druos†, bump, gland.] —**drus·y** *adj.*
Druse (drōōz) *n.* Also **Druze.** A member of a sect in Syria, Israel, and
Lebanon, whose primarily Muslim region contains some elements of
Christianity. [Arabic *Durūz,* plural of *darazi,* a Druse, after Ismail al-
Darazi (died 1019), Muslim religious leader.] —**Druse, Dru·si·an,
Dru·se·an** *adj.*
dry (drī) *adj.* **drier** or **dryer, driest** or **dryest.** 1. Free from liquid or
moisture; not wet, damp, or moistened. 2. Having or characterised
by little or no rain: *a dry climate.* 3. Marked by the absence of
natural or normal moisture: *a dry month.* 4. Not under water: *dry
land.* 5. Having all or almost all the water or liquid drained away,
evaporated, or exhausted: *a dry river.* 6. No longer yielding liquid,
especially milk: *a dry cow.* 7. Lacking a mucous or watery discharge: *a dry cough.* 8. Needing or desiring drink; thirsty. 9. a. Of
or pertaining to solid rather than liquid substances or commodities.
b. Not requiring water for use: *a dry shampoo.* c. Eaten without
butter or other accompaniment: *dry toast.* 10. Not sweet, as a result
of the decomposition of sugar during fermentation. Said of wines.
11. Having a large proportion of spirits to other ingredients. Said of
a cocktail, such as a martini. 12 a. Plain; bare; bald; unadorned.
b. Lacking interest or stimulation: *a dry book.* 13. Matter-of-fact;
cold. 14. Humorous or sarcastic in a shrewd, impersonal way: *dry
wit.* 15. *Informal.* a. Prohibiting or opposed to the sale or consumption of alcoholic beverages. b. *British.* Prohibiting the sale of
alcoholic drinks on Sunday: *a dry county.* 16. *British Informal.* Uncompromisingly conservative.
~*v.* **dried, drying, dries.** —*tr.* 1. To make dry; free from moisture.
2. To preserve (meat or other foods, for example) by extracting the
moisture. —*intr.* To become dry or lose moisture. —**dry out.**
1. To dry completely. 2. *Informal.* To treat for alcoholism or drug
addiction. 3. To undergo such treatment. —**dry up.** 1. a. To become intellectually unproductive. b. To forget one's lines in a dramatic performance. 2. *Slang.* To stop talking; shut up. Often used
in the imperative.
~*n., pl.* **drys, dries.** 1. *British Informal.* An uncompromisingly conservative person. 2. *U.S. Informal.* A prohibitionist. —**the dry.**
Australian Informal. The dry season. [Middle English *dry, drye,* Old
English *drȳge.*] —**dri·ly, dry·ly** *adv.* —**dry·ness** *n.*
dry·ad (drī-əd, -ad) *n., pl.* **-ads** or **-ades** (-ədeez) *Sometimes capital
D. Greek Mythology.* A nature divinity inhabiting or presiding over
forests and trees; a wood nymph. [Latin *dryas* (stem *dryad-*), from
Greek *druas,* from *drus,* tree.] —**dry·ad·ic** (drī-áddik) *adj.*
dryad's saddle *n.* A large, edible bracket fungus, *Polyporus squa-
mosus,* that has a yellowish upper surface covered in brown scales,
found growing on deciduous trees. Also called "scaly polypore".
dry·as·dust (drī-əz-dust) *n.* A dull, pedantic speaker or writer. [Af-
ter Dr. Jonas *Dryasdust,* a fictitious character to whom Sir Walter
Scott dedicated some of his novels.] —**dry-as-dust** *adj.*
dry battery *n.* An electric battery consisting of two or more dry
cells.
dry-blow (drī-blō) *intr. v.* **-blowed, -blowing, -blows.** *Australian.* To
separate gold particles from ore by winnowing. —**dry-blow·er** *n.*
dry-bone ore (drī-bōn) *n. Mining.* **Smithsonite** *(see).*
dry-bulb thermometer (drī-bulb) *n.* An ordinary thermometer used
with a wet-bulb thermometer in a psychrometer to measure the
relative humidity of the atmosphere.
dry cell *n.* A primary cell having an electrolyte in the form of moist
paste. Compare **wet cell.** [Its contents are not spillable.]
dry-clean (drī-kleén) *tr.v.* **-cleaned, -cleaning, -cleans.** To clean
(clothing or fabrics) with chemical solvents such as trichlorethylene.
—**dry-clean·er** *n.* —**dry-clean·ing** *n.*
dry-cure (drī-kéwr) *tr.v.* **-cured, -curing, -cures.** To preserve (meat)
by salting and drying.
Dry·den (drī'd'n), **John** (1631–1700). English poet, dramatist, and
critic, and the first poet laureate (1668). He commemorated Oliver
Cromwell in *Heroic Stanzas* (1659), then on the restoration of
Charles II in 1660 hailed the return of the monarchy in *Astraea
Redux.* In the 1680s he wrote satirical and didactic poems on which
his reputation rests, the most notable being *Absalom and Achitophel*
(1681). Dryden was converted to Roman Catholicism (1686) and
refused to take the oaths when William and Mary took the throne;
as a result the poet laureateship was taken away from him.
dry distillation *n.* **Destructive distillation** *(see).*
dry dock *n.* A large floating or stationary dock in the form of a

basin from which the water can be emptied, used for maintaining,
repairing, and altering a ship below the water line.
dry-dock (drī-dók, -dok) *v.* **-docked, -docking, -docks.** —*tr.* To
place in a dry dock. —*intr.* To go into a dry dock. Used of a ship.
dry·er¹ (drī-ər) *n.* 1. Any apparatus used to reduce the moisture
content of a substance: *a grain dryer.* 2. A chemical such as a naphthene, added to a drying oil to reduce its drying time. 3. A **hair
dryer** *(see).* 4. A machine for drying clothes, such as a spin-dryer or
tumble dryer.
dryer². Alternative comparative of **dry.**
dry·est. Alternative superlative of **dry.**
dry-eyed (drī-īd) *adj.* Not weeping: *dry-eyed mourners.*
dry farming *n.* A type of farming practised in arid areas without
irrigation by maintaining a fine surface tilth or mulch which protects the natural moisture of the soil from evaporation. —**dry farm**
n. —**dry-farm** *v.* —**dry farm·er** *n.*
dry fly *n.* An artificial fly used in fishing that floats on the water's
surface when cast. Compare **wet fly.**
dry goods *pl.n.* 1. Goods not containing liquid, such as flour, grain,
or the like. 2. *U.S.* **Soft goods** *(see).*
dry ice *n.* Solid carbon dioxide, which evaporates directly to gas at
–78.5°C (–110°F) at normal atmospheric pressure and is used primarily as a refrigerant.
drying oil *n.* Any of various oily organic liquids, such as linseed oil,
soyabean oil, or dehydrated castor oil, that form a tough plastic
layer on exposure to air in thin films and are used as binders in
paints and varnishes.
dry kiln *n.* A heated chamber in which cut timber is dried and
seasoned.
dry law *n. Chiefly U.S.* A law prohibiting the sale of alcoholic beverages.
dry measure *n.* A system of units for measuring dry quantities such
as grains, fruits, and vegetables.
dry nurse *n.* A nurse employed to care for an infant without breast-
feeding it. —**dry-nurse** *tr.v.*
dry·o·pith·e·cine (drī-ō-píthə-seen) *n.* An extinct ape of the genus
Dryopithecus, known from Old World fossil remains of the Miocene
and Pliocene epochs, and believed to be an ancestor of the chimpanzees, gorillas, and man. [From New Latin *Dryopithecus* : Greek
drus, tree + *pithēkos,* ape.] —**dry·o·pith·e·cine** *adj.*
dry point *n.* 1. A technique of intaglio engraving in which a hard
steel needle is used to incise lines in the metal plate, with the burr at
the side of the furrows retained. 2. An engraving or print made
with this technique.
dry riser *n.* A metal pipe running vertically up a building, usually
just on the inside of an outer wall, having an outlet on each floor
and an inlet at the base accessible to the street. In the event of fire,
water can be pumped through the pipe from street level to any of
the upper storeys.
dry rot *n.* 1. A fungal disease of timber that causes it to become
brittle and crumble into powder. 2. Any plant disease in which the
plant tissue remains relatively dry while fungi invade and ultimately
decay bulbs, fruit, or woody tissue. Compare **soft rot.** 3. A basidiomycete fungus *Serpula* (or *Merulius*) *lacrymans* that causes dry rot.
4. Any deterioration that has gone undetected.
dry run *n.* 1. *Military.* A test exercise in bombing, attacking, or
other combat skills without the use of live ammunition. 2. A trial
run; a rehearsal.
dry-salt (drī-sawlt ‖ -solt) *tr.v.* **-salted, -salting, -salts.** To preserve
(meat or hides, for example) by salting and drying. —**dry-salt·er**
(ər) *n.*
dry-shod (drī-shod) *adv.* Without wetting the shoes or feet. —**dry-
shod** *adj.*
dry steam *n.* Steam that does not contain drops of water.
dry-stone (drī-stōn) *adj.* Made with stones piled on top of each
other without mortar: *a dry-stone wall.*
d.s. 1. *Music.* dal segno. 2. *Commerce.* days after sight. 3. document signed.
D.S. *Music.* dal segno.
DSC, D.S.C. Distinguished Service Cross.
D.Sc. Doctor of Science.
DSM, D.S.M. Distinguished Service Medal.
D.S.O. Distinguished Service Order.
d.s.p. died without issue [Latin *decessit sine prole.*]
DST, D.S.T. daylight-saving time.
d.t. double time.
DTL *Electronics.* diode transistor logic.
D.T.'s (dee-téez) *pl.n. Informal.* **Delirium tremens** *(see).*
Du. 1. duke (title). 2. Dutch.
du·ad (déw-ad ‖ dōō-) *n. Rare.* A unit of two objects; a pair.
[Greek *duas* (stem *duad-*), the number two, from *duo,* two.]
du·al (déw-əl ‖ dōō-, dewl) *adj.* 1. Composed of two parts; double;
twofold: *dual controls on a car.* 2. Pertaining or relating to two.
3. *Grammar.* Designating or pertaining to a number category that
indicates two persons or things, as in Greek, Sanskrit, or Old English. Compare **plural.**
~*n. Grammar.* 1. The dual number. 2. A word or expression in the
dual number. [Latin *duālis,* from *duo,* two.] —**du·al·ly** *adv.*
Duala. See **Douala.**
dual carriageway *n.* A road having a barrier such as a strip of land
separating the traffic travelling in opposite directions. Also *U.S.*
"divided highway", *Australian* "divided road".
dual-control *adj.* Having an auxiliary set of foot-operated controls.

Said of a motor vehicle.

du·al·ism (déw-əl-iz'm ‖ dŏŏ-, déwl-) *n.* **1.** The condition of being twofold; duality. **2.** *Philosophy.* The view that the world consists of or is explicable as two fundamental types of substance, such as mind and matter. Compare **monism, pluralism. 3.** *Psychology.* The view that there is a phenomenal distinction between mental and physical processes. **4.** *Theology.* **a.** The concept that the world is ruled by the antagonistic forces of good and evil. **b.** The concept that humankind has two basic natures, the physical and the spiritual. **c.** The concept that there are two personalities in Christ, the human and the divine. —**du·al·ist** *n.*

du·al·is·tic (déw-ə-lístik ‖ dŏŏ-) *adj.* **1.** Pertaining to or having the nature of dualism. **2.** Dual. —**du·al·is·ti·cal·ly** *adv.*

du·al·i·ty (dew-ál-əti ‖ dŏŏ-) *n.* The quality or character of being twofold; dichotomy.

du·al-pur·pose (déw-əl-púrpəss ‖ dŏŏ-, déwl-) *adj.* Having two functions or designed to serve two purposes.

dub¹ (dub) *tr.v.* **dubbed, dubbing, dubs. 1.** To tap lightly on the shoulder with a sword by way of conferring knighthood. **2.** To honour with a new title or description; style. **3.** To name facetiously or playfully; nickname. **4.** To strike, cut, or rub (timber or leather, for example) so as to make even or smooth. **5.** To dress (a fowl). **6.** To dress a fishing fly. [Late Old English *dubbian* (unattested), from Anglo-French *(a)dubert*, provide with armour, equip, arrange.]

dub² *v.* **dubbed, dubbing, dubs.** —*tr.* **1.** To thrust at; poke. **2.** To beat (a drum). —*intr.* **1.** To make a thrust. **2.** To beat on a drum. ~*n.* **1.** The act of dubbing. **2.** A drumbeat. **3.** *Music.* **a.** The basic Jamaican reggae backing rhythm, as played on bass and drums, with little or no melodic line. **b.** The purest form of instrumental reggae based on this, relying on studio effects over a heavy drum and bass. [Perhaps from Low German *dubben*, to hit, strike.]

dub³ *tr.v.* **dubbed, dubbing, dubs. 1.** To make a new recording from the original of (a record or tape) in order to make changes, cuts, or additions. **2.** To insert a new sound track, often a synchronised translation of the original dialogue, into (a film). **3.** To insert (sound) into a film or tape. Often used with *in.* ~*n.* The new sounds so added. [Short for DOUBLE.]

dub⁴ *n. British Regional.* A muddy, stagnant pool; a puddle. [Middle English (Scottish and northern) : perhaps from Scandinavian.]

Du·bai (doo-bî′). *Arabic* **Du·bayy.** The second largest of the United Arab Emirates. Its capital, Dubai, containing most of the population, is situated on the Persian Gulf, and its Port Rashid, is the chief seaport of the Emirates. The traditional occupations of smuggling and fishing have declined since the discovery of oil both onshore and offshore in the 1960s, and oil is now the major export.

du Bar·ry (dew bárri; *French* dü-ba-rée), **Jeanne Bécu, Comtesse** (1743–93). Mistress of Louis XV of France. She made a marriage of convenience with the Comte du Barry, in 1769. She remained Louis' lover until his death (1774).

dub·bin (dúbbin) *n.* Also **dub·bing** (dúbbing). An application of tallow and oil for dressing leather. [From DUB (to dress, trim).]

Dub·ček (dŏŏp-chek, dŏŏp-), **Alexander** (1921–92). Czech politician and first secretary of the Czechoslovak Communist Party in 1968. He introduced liberal reforms, relaxing censorship and pursuing an independent foreign policy. He called his policy "socialism with a human face". Soviet authorities sent tanks into Prague (August, 1968) and arrested Dubček, who was forced to resign. In 1989 a popular revolution forced the hardliners, now without Soviet support, to abandon their leading role, and Dubček was elected chairman of the national assembly.

du Bel·lay (dü bel-áy), **Joachim** (1522–60). French poet. Member of Pleiad with Ronsard.

du·bi·e·ty (dew-bî-əti ‖ dŏŏ-) *n., pl.* **-ties. 1.** The quality of being dubious. **2.** A matter of doubt; an uncertainty. —See Synonyms at **uncertainty.** [Late Latin *dubietās* (stem *dubietat*-), from Latin *dubius*, DUBIOUS.]

du·bi·ous (déw-bi-əss ‖ dŏŏ) *adj.* **1.** Fraught with uncertainty or doubt; not yet determined; undecided. **2.** Arousing doubt as to validity, quality, or propriety; questionable: *a remark in dubious taste.* **3.** Reluctant to concur; sceptical; doubtful. —See Synonyms at **doubtful.** [Latin *dubius*, dubious, fluctuating, moving in two directions, from *duo*, two.] —**du·bi·os·i·ty** (déw-bi-óssəti ‖ dŏŏ-) *n.* —**du·bi·ous·ly** *adv.* —**du·bi·ous·ness** *n.*

du·bi·ta·ble (déw-bitəb'l ‖ dŏŏ-) *adj.* Subject to doubt or question; uncertain. [Latin *dubitābilis*, from *dubitāre*, to DOUBT.] —**du·bi·ta·bly** *adv.*

du·bi·ta·tion (déw-bi-táysh'n ‖ dŏŏ-) *n. Archaic.* Doubt.

du·bi·ta·tive (déw-bi-tətiv, -taytiv ‖ dŏŏ-) *adj.* Feeling or expressing doubt or hesitancy; doubting. —**du·bi·ta·tive·ly** *adv.*

Dub·lin¹ (dúbblin). *Irish* **Baile Átha Cliath** (blaw klée-ə). Seaport and capital city of the Republic of Ireland, situated on the river Liffey. Danes settled there in the ninth century. They were driven out by the Anglo-Normans in 1170, and a year later Henry II established English rule, which was to last for more than 700 years. Dublin prospered in the 18th century as the second largest city of the British Empire. Violence and disorder in the 19th century led in 1905 to the formation of the Sinn Fein movement, which urged home rule. Despite the failure of the Easter rising of 1916, the first Sinn Fein parliament was convened in 1919 under the presidency of Eamon De Valera. St. Patrick's, the principal cathedral of the Church of Ireland, was founded in 1190. Jonathan Swift was dean from 1713 to 1745 and is buried there. The city's industries include

engineering, flour milling, glass, and brewing. —**Dub·lin·er** *n.*

Dublin². A county in Leinster, Republic of Ireland. More than 70 per cent of the population is concentrated in the city of Dublin, the county town and commercial centre.

Dublin Bay prawn *n.* A large prawn, often served as scampi. Also called "Norway lobster", "langoustine".

Dub·na (dŏŏb-naá). A town in Russia. 200 kilometres (124 miles) south of Moscow. Founded in 1956, it is the site of the Joint Institute for Nuclear Research.

Du·bon·net (dew-bónnay, déw-bo-náy ‖ dŏŏ) *n.* A trademark for a fortified French sweet wine, often used as an apéritif.

Du·brov·nik (dŏŏ-bróvnik). *Italian* **Ragusa.** A seaport on the Dalmatian coast of Croatia, founded in the 7th century by Greek refugees. Later settled by Slavs, it flourished as a virtually independent trading republic. It was ceded to Austria in 1815, and passed to Yugoslavia in 1918.

du·cal (déwk'l ‖ dŏŏk'l) *adj.* Of or pertaining to a duke, duchy, or dukedom. [French, from Late Latin *ducālis*, from Latin *dux* (stem *duc*-), leader, DUKE.] —**du·cal·ly** *adv.*

duc·at (dúckət) *n.* Any of various gold coins formerly used in European countries. [Middle English, from Old French, from Old Italian *ducato*, from Medieval Latin *ducātūs*, DUCHY (word used on one of the early ducats).]

du·ce (dŏŏch-i, -ay) *n. Italian.* **1.** A leader or commander; a chief. **2.** *Capital* D. The title of Benito Mussolini as the leader of Fascist Italy.

Du·champ (dew-shón, dü-), **Marcel** (1887–1968). French painter. He became leader, with Picabia, of the Dada movement in New York, and was the first to exhibit "ready-made" objects, such as a urinal (entitled *Fountain*) to show that all things were art, or that all art is junk. His major work was *The Bride Stripped Bare by Her Bachelors, Even* (1923), a painting and construction on glass.

duch·ess (dúch-iss, -ess) *n. Abbr.* **D. 1.** The wife or widow of a duke. **2.** A woman holding title to a duchy in her own right. **3.** *Slang.* A wife or woman. Also used as a term of address. [Middle English *duchesse*, from Old French, from Medieval Latin *ducissa*, from Latin *dux* (stem *duc*-), leader, DUKE.]

du·chesse lace (dew-shéss, dü-) *n.* A type of Brussels pillow-lace.

du·chesse potatoes (dew-shéss, dúch-iss, -ess ‖ dŏŏ-) *pl.n.* Potatoes mashed with egg, formed into small cakes, and baked.

duch·y (dúchi) *n., pl.* **-ies.** A territory formerly ruled by a duke or duchess; a dukedom. [Middle English *duchie*, from Old French *duche*, from Medieval Latin *ducātūs*, from Latin *dux* (stem *duc*-), leader, DUKE.]

duck¹ (duk) *n., pl.* **ducks** or (for wild ducks) **duck. 1.** Any of various wild or domesticated aquatic birds of the family Anatidae, characteristically having a broad, flat bill, short legs, and webbed feet. **2.** The female of one of these birds, as distinguished from a drake. **3.** The flesh of this bird used as food. **4.** *Slang.* A person, especially a peculiar one. **5.** *British Informal.* Dear. Used as a familiar term of address. In this sense, also "ducks", "ducky". **6.** In cricket, a score of zero by a batsman. —**break (one's) duck.** To score one's first run in an innings in cricket. [Middle English *doke*, Old English *dūce*, from *dūcan* (unattested), to dive, DUCK.]

duck² *v.* **ducked, ducking, ducks.** —*tr.* **1.** To lower quickly, especially so as to avoid something: *He ducked his head as he went below deck.* **2.** To evade; dodge. **3.** To push suddenly under water. —*intr.* **1.** To lower the head or body. **2.** To move swiftly, especially so as to escape being seen. **3.** To submerge the head or body briefly in water. **4.** In bridge, to lose a trick deliberately. ~*n.* **1.** A quick lowering of the head or body. **2.** A plunge into water; a dip. [Middle English *douken*, Old English *dūcan* (unattested), to dive, from West Germanic *dukjan* (unattested).] —**duck·er** *n.*

duck³ *n.* **1.** A very durable, closely woven heavy cotton or linen fabric. **2.** *Plural.* Clothing made of this fabric; especially, white trousers. [Dutch *doek*, from Middle Dutch *doek, doec,* akin to Old Norse *dūkr*†.]

duck⁴ *n.* An amphibious military vehicle used during World War II. [Variant of DUKW, its code designation.]

duck-billed platypus (dúk-bild) *n.* An aquatic, egg-laying mammal, *Ornithorhynchus anatimus,* native to Tasmania and southeastern Australia, that has webbed feet and a large, ducklike bill. Also called "duck bill", "platypus", "ornithorhyncus", and in Australia "water mole".

duck·board (dúk-bawrd ‖ -bōrd) *n.* A board or set of wooden slats laid across wet or muddy ground or flooring.

duck decoy *n.* A large pond with a number of curved channels leading off it that is used to catch ducks. They are enticed along a channel by the intermittent sight of a trained dog, which they follow to drive it away from the water's edge.

duck-dive (dúk-dīv) *intr.v.* **-dived, -diving, -dives.** To slide oneself gradually into the water from a prone position at the edge or bank. ~*n.* A slide performed in this way.

duck-egg blue (dúk-eg) *n.* A pale, greenish blue.

ducking stool *n.* A device formerly used in Europe and New England for punishment, consisting of a chair in which an offender was tied and ducked into water. Compare **cucking stool.**

duck·ling (dúckling) *n.* A young duck.

duck·pin (dúk-pin) *n. U.S.* A bowling pin, shorter and squatter than a tenpin. [From its squat appearance.]

duck·pins (dúk-pinz) *n. Used with a singular verb. U.S.* A game similar to tenpin bowling, played with duckpins.

ducks and drakes *n.* The game of skimming flat stones along the surface of water so they bounce. **—make ducks and drakes of** or **play ducks and drakes with.** To squander; waste.

duck soup *n. U.S. Slang.* Something easy to accomplish.

duck·tail (dúk-tayl) *n.* A boy's or man's hairstyle in which the hair is swept back at the sides with a large quiff at the front, turning up at the back like a duck's tail. Also called "duck's arse", "D.A."

duck·weed (dúk-weed) *n.* Any of various small, free-floating, stem-less aquatic plants of the genera *Lemna* or *Wolffia*, having a rounded, lanceolate, or oval thallus that may be a modified leaf or stem.

duck·y (dúcki) *adj.* **-ier, -iest. 1.** *Slang.* Excellent; fine. Often used ironically. **2.** *Informal.* Sweet; adorable; bijou.
~*n., pl.* **duckies.** Dear. Used as a familiar term of address. [From DUCK (darling).]

duct (dukt) *n.* **1.** Any tubular passage through which a substance, especially a fluid, is conveyed. **2.** A bodily passage, especially one for secretion. **3.** A passage in plants into which substances such as resins are secreted. **4.** Any channel through which pipes or cables pass.
~*tr.v.* **ducted, ducting, ducts.** To convey through a duct. [Latin *ductus*, a leading, a conducting, from the past participle of *dūcere*, to lead.]

duc·tile (dúk-tīl ‖ *U.S.* -til) *adj.* **1.** Capable of being drawn into wire or hammered thin. Said of metal. **2.** Capable of being easily moulded or shaped; plastic. **3.** Readily persuaded or influenced; tractable. **—See Synonyms at flexible.** [Middle English, from Old French, from Latin *ductilis*, from *ductus*, DUCT.] **—duc·til·i·ty** (duk-tíllǝti) *n.*

duct·less gland (dúkt-lǝss, -liss). An **endocrine gland** *(see).*

dud (dud) *n. Informal.* **1.** A bomb, shell, or cartridge that fails to explode when it should. **2.** Someone or something disappointingly ineffective or unsuccessful. **3.** *Plural.* Clothes; clothing. **4.** Personal belongings.
~*adj.* Useless; worthless. [Middle English *dudde†*, article of clothing, thing.]

dude (dewd ‖ dōōd) *n. U.S.* **1.** *Informal.* A city-dweller, especially one from the east of the United States, who holidays on a Western ranch. **2.** *Informal.* A conspicuously overdressed man; a dandy. **3.** *Slang.* A fellow; a chap. **4.** *Plural.* Clothes. [19th century : probably from dialect German *Dude*, fool.]

du·deen, du·dheen (dōō-déen) *n. Irish.* A short-stemmed clay pipe. [Irish *dūidīn*, diminutive of *dūd*, pipe.]

dude ranch *n.* A resort modelled on a Western ranch, featuring camping, horse-riding, and other outdoor activities.

dudg·eon[1] (dújǝn) *n.* A sullen, angry, or indignant mood: *"Slamming the door in Meg's face, Aunt March drove off in high dudgeon".* (Louisa May Alcott). [16th century : origin obscure.]

dudgeon[2] *n.* **1.** *Obsolete.* A kind of wood used in making knife handles. **2.** *Archaic.* **a.** A dagger having a hilt made from this wood. **b.** The hilt of a dagger. [Middle English *dogeon*, from Anglo-French *digeon†*.]

Dudley, Robert. See **Leicester,** Robert Dudley, 1st Earl of.

due (dew ‖ dōō) *adj.* **1.** Payable immediately or on demand. **2.** Owed as a debt; owing: *the sum still due.* **3.** Owed by right, convention, or courtesy; fitting or appropriate: *due esteem.* **4.** Meeting special requirements; sufficient; adequate: *due cause to honour him.* **5.** Expected or scheduled; especially, appointed to arrive. **—due to. 1.** Attributable to; caused by. **2.** Because of.
~*n.* **1.** Something that is owed or deserved. **2.** *Plural. Chiefly U.S.* A charge or fee, as for membership of a club or organisation.
~*adv.* **1.** Straight; directly: *due west.* **2.** *Archaic.* Duly. [Middle English, from Old French *deu*, from Vulgar Latin *dēbūtus* (unattested), "owed", from Latin *dēbitus*, past participle of *dēbēre*, to owe.]

Usage: The traditional view is that, as *due* is an adjective, it can be used only after a linking verb (*His hesitation was due to fear*) or after a noun when the construction is used adjectivally (*His hesitation, due to fear, made him late*). Criticism focuses on the use of *due to* to introduce an adverbial phrase in sentences where *owing to, because of, on account of,* or *through* are more appropriate: *He hesitated due to fear; Due to his bad leg, he didn't come downstairs.* Stylists have attacked this usage as illiterate for over 100 years. Nevertheless, it is widely employed in informal speech and writing, and is increasingly to be encountered in formal contexts (as in *Due to circumstances beyond our control*).

du·el (déw-ǝl ‖ dōō-, dewl) *n.* **1.** A prearranged combat between two persons, fought according to formal procedure with deadly weapons, typically to settle a point of honour. **2.** Any struggle for ascendancy between two contending persons, animals, groups, or ideas.
~*intr. v.* **duelled** or *U.S.* **dueled, -elling** or *U.S.* **-eling, -els.** To fight a duel. [Medieval Latin *duellum*, from Latin, archaic form of *bellum*, war.] **—du·el·ler, du·el·list** *n.*

du·el·lo (dew-éllō ‖ dōō-) *n.* **1.** The art of the duel. **2.** The code of rules by which duels were fought. [Italian, from Latin *duellum*, war. See **duel.**]

du·en·de (dōō-énd-i, -ay) *n. Spanish.* **1.** Powerful or magical attraction; magnetism. **2.** A demon or ghost.

du·en·na (dew-énnǝ ‖ dōō-) *n.* **1.** An elderly woman retained by a Spanish or Portuguese family to act as governess and companion to the daughters. **2.** Any chaperone. [Spanish *dueña,* from Latin *domina,* lady, feminine of *dominus,* lord, master.]

Duero. See **Douro.**

du·et (dew-ét ‖ dōō-) *n.* **1.** A musical composition written for two voices or two instruments. **2.** The two performers presenting such a composition. **3.** Any verbal exchange between two people. **4.** Any closely related pair of individuals. [Italian *duetto,* diminutive of *duo,* duet, from Latin, two.] **—duet·tist** *n.*

duff[1] (duf) *n.* A pudding, usually containing dried fruit, boiled in a cloth bag or steamed: *plum duff.* **—up the duff.** *Australian Slang.* **1.** Pregnant. **2.** Broken; out of order. [Northern English dialectal variant of DOUGH.]

duff[2] *n. Chiefly U.S.* **1.** Decaying leaves and branches covering a forest floor. **2.** Fine coal; coal dust; slack. [Perhaps from DUFF (dough).]

duff[3] *tr. v.* **duffed, duffing, duffs.** *Slang.* **1.** *Chiefly Australian.* To steal and change the appearance of (cattle, for example). **2.** *British.* To bungle a golf shot by hitting the ground instead of the ball. **—duff up.** *British Slang.* To beat up; thrash.
~*adj. British Slang.* Useless; dud; not performing adequately. [Perhaps back-formation from DUFFER (slow-witted or worthless person).]

duff[4] *n. Chiefly U.S. Slang.* The buttocks. [Perhaps from DUFF[1] (pudding).]

Duf·fel (dúff'l) *n.* A trademark for a blanket fabric made of low-grade woollen cloth with a nap on both sides.

duf·fer[1] (dúffǝr) *n.* **1.** *Informal.* An incompetent or slow-witted person. **2.** Something worthless or useless. **3.** *Australian.* A mine, shaft, claim, or the like that fails to yield any valuable ore. [Probably from Scottish *Duffart, doofart,* stupid fellow, worthless person.]

duffer[2] *n.* **1.** *British Informal.* A pedlar of cheap or trashy goods. **2.** *Australian.* A person who steals cattle or sheep. [From DUFF (verb).]

duf·fle, duf·fel (dúff'l) *n. Chiefly U.S.* Clothing and other personal gear carried by a camper. [Dutch, from *Duffel,* town near Antwerp, Belgium.]

duffle bag *n.* A large cloth bag of canvas or duck for carrying personal belongings, originally used by soldiers and sailors.

duffle coat *n.* A short woollen coat, usually having a hood and fastened with toggles.

Du·fy (dew-fée, dü-), **Raoul** (1877–1953). French painter and textile designer. He produced many brightly coloured racing and seaside scenes and the vast panel *La Fée Electricité* for the Paris Exhibition of 1938.

dug[1] (dug) *n.* **1.** An udder, breast, or teat of a female mammal. **2.** A human breast, especially an old woman's. [16th century : origin obscure.]

dug[2]. Past tense and past participle of **dig.**

du·gong (dōō-gong, déw-) *n.* A herbivorous marine mammal, *Dugong dugon,* of tropical coastal waters of the Old World, having flipper-like forelimbs and a deeply notched tail fin. [Variant of Malay *dūyong.*]

dug·out (dúg-owt) *n.* **1.** A boat or canoe made by hollowing out a log. **2.** *Military.* A pit dug into the ground or on a hillside and used as a shelter. **3.** A long sunken shelter at the side of a baseball field where the players stay while not on the field.

Du·ha·mel (déw-a-mél, dü-), **Georges** (1884–1966). French novelist and dramatist. From his experience as a surgeon in World War I he wrote *Civilisation* (1918), which won the Goncourt prize. His most successful play was *In the Shadow of Statues* (1914).

dui. Alternative plural of **duo.**

dui·ker, duy·ker (dáykǝr) *n.* **1.** Any of various small African antelopes, chiefly of the genus *Cephalophus,* having short, backward-pointing horns. Also called "duikerbok". **2.** *South African.* Any of several cormorants of the genus *Phalacrocorax.* [Afrikaans, "diver", from Dutch *duiken,* to dive, from Middle Dutch *dūken,* from West Germanic *dukjan* (unattested), to DUCK.]

Duis·burg (déwss-burg, *German* düss-boork). A river port in North Rhine-Westphalia, western Germany. It stands at the junction of the Rhine and the Ruhr.

dū jūn. Variant of **tuchun.**

Du·kas (dew-ka'a, dü-), **Paul** (1865–1935). French composer. Before he died he burned many of his compositions, leaving little work. He is best remembered for the symphonic scherzo, *The Sorcerer's Apprentice* (1897).

duke (dewk ‖ dōōk) *n. Abbr.* **D., Du. 1.** A nobleman with the highest hereditary rank; especially, in Britain, a man of the highest grade of the peerage. **2.** A prince who rules an independent duchy. **3.** A type of cherry intermediate between a sweet and a sour cherry. [Middle English, from Old French *duc,* from Latin *dux* (stem *duc-*), leader, from *dūcere,* to lead.]

duke·dom (déwk-dǝm ‖ dōōk-) *n.* **1.** The state or territory ruled by a duke; a duchy. **2.** The office, rank, or title of a duke.

dukes (dewks ‖ dōōks) *pl.n. Slang.* The fists: *Put up your dukes!* [From *Duke of Yorks,* rhyming slang for *forks* (fingers).]

Du·kho·bors, Dou·kho·bors (dōōk-ǝ-bawrz, dōōkh-, -ō-) *pl.n.* The members of a Christian religious sect of Russia, many of whom migrated to Canada in the 1890s to escape persecution. [Russian *dukhoborets,* "spirit-wrestlers" : *dukh,* spirit + *borets,* wrestler, from *borot',* to struggle.]

dul·cet (dúl-sit) *adj.* **1.** Pleasing to the ear; gently melodious; soothing. **2.** *Archaic.* Sweet to the taste.
~*n.* An organ stop pitched an octave higher than the dulciana. [Learned respelling of Middle English *doucet,* from Old French, from *doux* (feminine *douce*), sweet, from Latin *dulcis.*]

dul·ci·an·a (dúl-si-a'anǝ ‖ *chiefly U.S.* -ánnǝ) *n.* An organ stop with a sweet, somewhat thin tone suggestive of a stringed instrument. [New Latin, from Medieval Latin, bassoon, perhaps from Latin *dulcis*, sweet.]

dul·ci·fy (dúl-si-fī) *tr.v.* **-fied, -fying, -fies.** *Rare.* **1.** To make agreeable or gentle; mollify. **2.** To sweeten. [Late Latin *dulcificāre*, to sweeten: Latin *dulcis*, sweet + *facere*, to do.] **—dul·ci·fi·ca·tion** *n.*

dul·ci·mer (dúl-simər) *n.* **1.** A musical instrument with wire strings of graduated lengths stretched over a sound box, played with two padded hammers or by plucking. **2.** An instrument used in folk music consisting of a long, fretted fingerboard and three strings. It is usually laid across the knees and plucked. [Middle English *dowcemere*, from Old French *doulcemer, doulcemele* : probably Latin *dulcis*, sweet + *melos*, song, from Greek.]

Dul·ci·ne·a (dúl-si-néer, -née-ə, dul-sínni-ə) *n. Sometimes small* d. **1.** An idealised woman. **2.** A female sweetheart. [After *Dulcinea del Toboso*, Don Quixote's idealised sweetheart in Cervantes' *Don Quixote*.]

du·li·a (déw-li-ə ‖ dōō-) *n. Theology.* Special reverence accorded to saints in the Roman Catholic and Eastern Orthodox Churches. Compare **hyperdulia, latria.**

dull (dul) *adj.* **duller, dullest. 1.** Lacking mental agility; slow to learn; stupid. **2.** Lacking responsiveness or alertness; insensitive. **3.** Dispirited; depressed. **4.** Not brisk or rapid; sluggish. **5.** Not sharp or keen; blunt. **6.** Not intensely or keenly felt: *a dull ache.* **7.** Arousing no interest or curiosity; unexciting; boring. **8.** Not bright or vivid; dim: *a dull brown.* **9.** Cloudy; gloomy. **10.** Muffled; indistinct. **—See Synonyms at stupid.**
~*v.* **dulled, dulling, dulls.** *—tr.* **1.** To make less sharp; blunt. **2.** To make less bright or distinct. **3.** To make (the senses, for example) less keen or receptive. *—intr.* To become dull. [Middle English *dul, dulle,* from Middle Low German *dul.*] **—dul·ly** (-i, -li) *adv.* **—dull·ness, dul·ness** *n.*

dull·ard (dúllərd) *n.* A mentally dull person; a dolt.

Dul·les (dúl-iss, -əss), **John Foster** (1888–1959). U.S. politician. In 1953, he became secretary of state under President Eisenhower, and pursued a policy of active opposition to the U.S.S.R.

dull-wit·ted (dúl-wittid) *adj.* Slow to comprehend; stupid. **—dull-wit·ted·ness** *n.*

du·lo·sis (dew-lṓ-siss ‖ dōō-) *n.* A practice of certain ants in which members of one species make those of another species perform the work of the colony. Also called "helotism". **—du·lot·ic** (-lóttik) *adj.*

dulse (dulss) *n.* A coarse, reddish-brown seaweed, *Rhodymenia palmata,* sometimes eaten as a vegetable. [Irish Gaelic *duileasg,* from Old Irish *duilesc,* "seaweed".]

Dul·wich (dúl-ij, -ich). A residential suburb in Southwark, Greater London.

du·ly (déw-li ‖ dōō-) *adv.* **1.** In a proper manner; rightfully; fittingly: *duly consecrate a church.* **2.** At the expected time; punctually. [Middle English, from DUE.]

Du·ma, Dou·ma (dōō-mə, déw-) *n.* A Russian national parliament, convened and dissolved four times between 1905 and 1917, now revived. [Russian *duma,* thought, council, from Gothic *dōms,* judgment.]

Du·mas (dew-maʹa ‖ dōō-; *French* dü-), **Alexandre,** also called Dumas père (1802–70). French novelist and dramatist, father of Alexandre, *Dumas fils.* Among his most famous works are *The Three Musketeers* (1844) and *The Count of Monte Cristo* (1845).

Dumas, Alexandre, also called Dumas fils (1824–95). French novelist and dramatist. His first play, *La Dame aux Camélias* (1852), a frank treatment of the love-affair of a courtesan, caused a sensation. Verdi used the story for *La Traviata.*

Du Mau·ri·er, Daphne (dew mórri-ay, dōō, máwri-), (1907–89). British novelist. Her works include *Jamaica Inn* (1936), *Rebecca* (1938), and *The Birds,* all made into successful films.

Du Maurier, George (Louis Palmella Busson) (1834–86). British novelist and illustrator, born in France of a French father and English mother. He was an illustrator for *Punch* magazine, and wrote the novel *Trilby* (1894). Daphne's father.

dumb (dum) *adj. Sometimes* **dumber, dumbest. 1.** Lacking the power or faculty of speech; mute. **2.** Temporarily speechless with shock or fear. **3.** Unwilling to speak. **4.** Not producing or accompanied by speech or sound. **5.** Inarticulate; unable to express opinions. **6.** *Informal.* Ignorant or stupid. **7.** *Nautical.* Not self-propelling. [Middle English *dumb,* Old English *dumb†.*] **—dumb·ly** *adv.* **—dumb·ness** *n.*

Synonyms: dumb, mute, speechless, voiceless.

Dum·bar·ton (dum-bárt'n). Town in Scotland. *Gaelic* **Dun Breatann.** It is an engineering and shipbuilding centre at the confluence of the Leven and Clyde. Its Gaelic name means "Fort of the Britons".

dumb·bell (dúm-bel) *n.* **1.** A weight lifted for muscular exercise, consisting of a short bar with a metal ball at each end. **2.** *Chiefly U.S. Slang.* A dull, stupid person; a dolt. [Sense 1 : originally the weight resembled the device used for ringing a church bell, but without the bell.]

dumb blonde *n.* A physically attractive, but supposedly stupid, blonde woman.

dumb cane *n.* A tropical plant, *Dieffenbachia,* with an acrid juice that temporarily inhibits speech when a part of the plant is chewed.

dumb-cluck, dumb cluck (dúm-kluk) *n. Informal.* A fool; an idiot. [DUMB ("stupid") + CLUCK, the sound made by a hen.]

dumb down *tr.v.* **dumbed down, dumbing down, dumbs down.** *Informal.* To simplify to the lowest common denominator.

dumb·found, dum·found (dum-fównd) *tr.v.* **-founded, -founding,**

-founds. To strike dumb with astonishment or amazement; stun; nonplus. See Synonyms at **surprise.** [DUMB + (CON)FOUND.]

dum·bo (dúm-bō) *n., pl.* **dumbos.** *British Informal.* A fool; an idiot. [From DUMB.]

dumb show *n.* **1.** A part of a dramatic performance unaccompanied by speech; a pantomime. **2.** Communication by means of gestures.

dumb·struck (dúm-struk) *adj.* Temporarily unable to speak through shock or surprise.

dumb·wait·er (dúm-wáytər ‖ *U.S. also* -waytər) *n.* **1.** A small lift used to convey food or other goods from one floor to another. **2.** *Chiefly British.* A portable serving table. **3.** *Chiefly British.* A revolving tray in the middle of the table.

dum·dum bullet (dúm-dum) *n.* A small-arms bullet with a soft nose designed to expand upon contact, inflicting a gaping wound. Also called "spread-on-impact bullet". [After *Dum Dum,* military arsenal near Calcutta, where it was first made (c. 1897).]

Dum·fries (dum-freéss, dəm-). Market town in Dumfries and Galloway, Scotland. It was the county town of the former county of Dumfriesshire (or Dumfries).

Dumfries and Galloway. Unitary Authority area, bordering the Solway Firth, southwest Scotland. It is chiefly agricultural, the main crops being cereals and root vegetables.

dum·my (dúmmi) *n., pl.* **-mies. 1.** An imitation of a real or original object, intended to be used as a practical substitute. **2.** A figure imitating the human form, especially: **a.** A model used in designing and displaying clothes. **b.** A stuffed or pasteboard figure used as a target. **c.** A figure of a person or animal manipulated by a ventriloquist. **3.** *Military.* A blank round. **4.** *Informal.* A mute person. Usually considered offensive. **b.** A blockhead; a dolt. **5.** *Informal.* Someone who does not take part or contribute actively. **6.** A person or agency secretly in the service of another; a front. **7.** *Printing.* **a.** A model of a work being published, indicating its general appearance and dimensions. **b.** A model page with text and illustrations pasted into place to direct the printer; a layout. **8. a.** In the game of bridge, the partner who exposes his hand to be played by the declarer. **b.** The hand thus exposed. **c.** In the game of whist, an imaginary fourth hand. **9.** In football, a feigned pass or swerve to defeat an opponent. **10.** *Chiefly British.* A rubber or plastic imitation nipple for a baby to suck.
~*adj.* **1.** Simulating something but lacking its function; artificial: *a dummy pocket.* **2.** Silent; mute. **3.** Secretly serving another. **4.** Played with a dummy. Said of a card game.
~*tr.v.* **dummied, -mying, -mies.** *Printing.* To make a dummy of (a publication or page). Often used with *up.* [Earlier *dummie, dumbie,* dumb person, from DUMB.]

dummy run *n.* A practice or rehearsal.

du·mor·ti·er·ite (dew-mórti-ə-rīt ‖ dōō-) *n.* A greenish-blue aluminium borosilicate mineral, used in sparking-plug porcelain and in special refractories. [French, after Eugène *Dumortier,* 19th-century French palaeontologist who discovered it.]

dump (dump) *v.* **dumped, dumping, dumps.** *—tr.* **1.** To release or throw down in a large mass; drop heavily. **2.** To empty (material) out of a container or vehicle. **3.** To empty out (a container or vehicle), as by overturning or tilting. **4.** To get rid of (rubbish, for example); dispose of. **5.** To discard or reject (a burden or a problem, for example) unceremoniously. **6.** To place (goods) on the market, especially in a foreign country, in large quantities and at a lower price than in the country of origin, especially below cost price. **7.** To reproduce (data stored internally in a computer) onto an external storage medium, such as a printout. **8.** To put into temporary storage. *—intr.* **1.** To fall or drop abruptly, especially in a mass. **2.** To discharge cargo or contents; unload.
~*n.* **1.** A place where refuse is dumped. **2.** A storage place for goods or supplies; a depot. **3.** An unordered accumulation; a pile. **4.** An instance or the result of dumping data stored in a computer. **5.** *Slang.* A poorly maintained or disreputable place. [Middle English *dompen, dumpen,* to drop, fall, plunge, probably of Scandinavian origin; akin to Norwegian *dumpa,* to fall suddenly.] **—dump·er** *n.*

dump bin *n.* A freestanding container in a retail store, used to display goods that are being specially promoted.

dump·ling (dúmpling) *n.* **1.** A small ball of dough cooked with stew or soup. **2.** Sweetened dough wrapped around an apple or other fruit, baked and served as a dessert. **3.** *Informal.* A short, chubby person. [16th century : origin obscure.]

dumps (dumps) *pl.n. Informal.* A gloomy, melancholy state of mind: *down in the dumps.* [Dutch *domp,* haze, exhalation, "hazy or gloomy state of mind", from Middle Dutch *domp, damp.* See **damp.**]

dump truck *n.* Also **dumper truck.** A **tipper truck** *(see).*

dump·y¹ (dúmpi) *adj.* **-ier, -iest.** Short and stout; squat. [From archaic *dump,* a shapeless mass, lump, perhaps a back-formation from DUMPLING.] **—dump·i·ly** *adv.* **—dump·i·ness** *n.*

dumpy² *adj.* **-ier, -iest.** *Rare.* Depressed or discontented.

dumpy level *n.* A surveyor's instrument having a short telescope fixed rigidly to a horizontally rotating table.

dun¹ (dun) *tr.v.* **dunned, dunning, duns.** To importune (a debtor) persistently for payment.
~*n.* **1.** One who importunes debtors for payment; a debt collector. **2.** An importunate demand for payment. [Shortened from obsolete *dunkirk,* privateer, originally, ship from DUNKIRK, France.]

dun² *n.* **1.** A colour ranging from almost neutral brownish grey to dull greyish brown. **2.** A dun-coloured fishing fly. **3.** A dun-

coloured horse.   **4.** The dun-coloured subimaginal stages of a mayfly.
~ *adj.* **dunner, dunnest. 1.** Dull; gloomy. **2.** Greyish brown. [Middle English *dun,* Old English *dunn.*]

Duna. See **Danube.**

Dunaj. See **Danube.**

Dunărea. See **Danube.**

Dunav. See **Danube.**

Dun·bar (dun-bár). A Scottish fishing port in East Lothian. Cromwell's forces defeated the Scots at the Battle of Dunbar in 1650.

Dunbar, William (*c.*1460–*c.*1520). Scottish poet. He was probably a Franciscan who became attached to the court of James IV of Scotland. Most of his poems were allegories, such as *The Thistle and the Rose* (1503) and *The Dance of the Seven Deadly Sins* (*c.*1508).

Dun·bar·ton (dun-bárt'n, dum-). Also **Dun·bar·ton·shire** (-shər, -sheer, -shīr). Former county in western Scotland.

dun·bird (dún-burd) *n.* A diving duck, the **pochard** *(see).*

Dun·can I (dúngkən) (died 1040). King of Scotland (1034–40). He succeeded his grandfather, Malcolm II Mackenneth, in 1034. According to the legend used by Shakespeare in *Macbeth,* Duncan was slain by Macbeth at Pitgavenny, near Elgin, on August 14, 1040.

Duncan, Isadora (1878–1927). U.S. dancer. She met the choreographer, Michel Fokine, in Russia in 1905 and abandoned the traditional ballet costume for bare feet and Greek draperies. She danced to symphonic music not composed for dance, such as that of Wagner, Schubert, and Beethoven. Her championship of free movement made her a forerunner of modern dance. She was killed when her long scarf caught in the wheel of her car and strangled her.

dunce (dunss) *n.* A stupid person; a numskull. [Originally *Duns men,* a contemptuous reference to the disciples of John DUNS SCOTUS, used by their philosophical opponents.]

dunce's cap *n.* Also **dunce cap.** A cone-shaped paper cap, formerly placed upon the head of a slow or lazy pupil.

Dun·dalk (dun-dáwk ‖ -dáwlk). *Irish* **Dún Dealgan.** County town of County Louth, Republic of Ireland. It was here, in 1315, that Edward Bruce declared himself King of Ireland. He was killed nearby three years later. Its port exports beef, cattle, and grain.

Dun·dee (dun-dée, dún-). A city on the Firth of Tay, Scotland. It has been a royal burgh since 1190, and is linked with the south by rail over the Tay bridge, rebuilt in 1888, and by a road bridge, opened in 1966. Dundee manufactures linen, canvas, jute, and confectionery, and serves the North Sea oilfields. —**Dun·don·i·an** (dun-dṓn-i-ən) *n. & adj.*

Dundee cake *n.* A rich fruit cake decorated with almonds.

dun·der·head (dúndər-hed) *n.* A numskull; a dunce. [Perhaps "one stunned by a thunderstroke" : Dutch *donder,* thunder, from Middle Dutch + HEAD.] —**dun·der·head·ed** *adj.*

dun diver *n.* A young male or a female goosander.

dun·drear·ies (dun-dréer-iz) *pl.n.* Long side whiskers with a clean-shaven chin. Also called "Dundreary whiskers". [After Lord *Dundreary,* a character in the play *Our American Cousin* (1855) by Tom Taylor (1817–80), British dramatist.]

dune (dewn ‖ dōōn) *n.* A hill or ridge of wind-blown sand, especially one barren of vegetation. Also called "sand dune". [French, from Old French, from Middle Dutch *dūne.*]

dune buggy *n.* A small, light motor vehicle, generally having a rear-engine chassis and a moulded fibre-glass frame without doors and roof, and usually equipped with a modified engine and oversize tyres for driving on sand dunes.

Dun·e·din (dun-éedin ‖ *locally* -éed'n). Seaport on South Island, New Zealand. It was founded in 1848 by Scottish Presbyterian settlers and expanded when gold was discovered in Otago in 1861. Its main industries include woollen goods, clothing, footwear, and agricultural machinery.

Dun·ferm·line (dun-férm-lin). A town in Fife, East Scotland. Its 11th-century abbey was the burial place of many of Scotland's rulers, including Robert Bruce. It manufactures damask and linen.

dung (dung) *n.* **1.** The excrement of animals. **2.** Manure. **3.** Anything foul or abhorrent.
~ *v.* **dunged, dunging, dungs.** —*tr.* To fertilise with manure. —*intr.* To excrete dung. [Middle English *d(o)ung,* from Old English *dung,* akin to Old Norse *dyngja,* heap, from Germanic *dung-* (unattested).] —**dung·y** *adj.*

dun·ga·ree (dúng-gə-rée) *n.* **1.** A sturdy, usually blue denim fabric. **2.** *Plural.* Overalls or trousers, especially with a bib front, made from this fabric. [Hindi *dungrī,* from *Dungrī,* name of a district of Bombay where it originated.]

dung beetle *n.* Any of various beetles of the family Scarabaeidae, that form balls of dung on which they feed and in which they lay their eggs.

Dun·ge·ness (dúnji-néss, dúnj-). Headland in Kent, extending into the English Channel. Its old lighthouse was the first to be lit by electricity. It is now the site of two nuclear power stations.

dun·geon (dúnjən) *n.* **1.** A dark, often underground chamber or cell used to confine prisoners. **2.** A **donjon** *(see).* [Middle English *donjon,* from Old French, "keep of the lord's castle", from Medieval Latin *dominiō,* lordship, from Latin *dominus,* lord, master.]

dung fly *n.* Any of various flies of the genus *Scatophaga* whose larvae feed in dung.

dung·hill (dúng-hil) *n.* **1.** A heap of animal excrement or manure. **2.** A foul, degraded place or condition.

dun·ite (dún-īt, déwn- ‖ dōōn-) *n.* An igneous rock consisting mainly of olivine.

du·ni·was·sal (dōōni-waass'l) *n.* A member of the minor Scottish gentry.

dunk (dungk) *v.* **dunked, dunking, dunks.** —*tr.* **1.** To plunge into liquid; immerse. **2.** To dip (a biscuit, for example) into tea or other liquid before eating it. —*intr.* To go under water; submerge oneself briefly. [Pennsylvania Dutch *dunke,* from Middle High German *dunken, tunken,* from Old High German *dunkōn.*] —**dunk·er** *n.*

Dun·ker (dúng-kər) *n.* Also **Dun·kard** (-kərd). A member of the German Baptist Brethren, a sect of German-American Baptists opposed to military service and the taking of legal oaths. [Pennsylvania Dutch, from *dunke,* DUNK (referring to their baptismal rite by triple immersion).]

Dun·kirk (dun-kérk, dún-). *French* **Dunkerque.** Port in the Nord département, France. It grew around a seventh-century church built on the Dunes of St. Eloi giving it its name—"Church in the Dunes". It was ceded to Cromwell in 1658 and sold to Louis XIV by Charles II in 1662. In 1940, during World War II, 330,000 Allied troops were evacuated from the town's beaches in the face of enemy fire. Industries include oil refining, shipbuilding, and sugar refining.

Dunkirk spirit *n.* A refusal to give up in time of crisis.

Dún Laoghai·re (dun leér-i, ái-ə). A seaport in County Dublin, Republic of Ireland. It serves as Dublin's passenger port with a steamer service to Liverpool and to Holyhead in Anglesey, Wales.

dun·lin (dúnlin) *n., pl.* **-lins** or collectively **dunlin.** A brown and white sandpiper, *Erolia* (or *Calidris*) *alpina,* of northern regions. Also formerly called "stint". [DUN (colour) + -LIN(G), diminutive suffix.]

Dun·lop (dúnlop, *Scottish* dunlóp) *n.* A Scottish cheese, similar in flavour to Cheddar but paler in colour.

Dunlop (dúnlop, *Scottish* dunlóp), **John Boyd** (1840–1921). Scottish inventor of the pneumatic rubber tyre. He settled in Belfast as a veterinary surgeon and made the first pneumatic tyre for his son's tricycle in 1887. The Dunlop Company began commercial production in 1890.

dun·nage (dúnnij) *n.* **1.** Loose packing material protecting a ship's cargo from damage during transport. **2.** *Informal.* Personal belongings or baggage. [Middle English *dennage, donage,* perhaps from Middle Low German *dünne,* thin, hence "loose, light stuff".]

Dun·net Head (dúnnit). Promontory in Highland Unity Authority area, the most northerly point on the mainland of Scotland.

dun·no (də-nṓ, du-, d'n-ṓ) *Informal.* Contraction of *don't know.*

dun·nock (dúnnək) *n.* The **hedge sparrow** *(see).*

dun·ny (dúnni) *n., pl.* **-nies. 1.** *Scottish.* A cellar or underground passage. **2.** *Australian & N.Z.* An outside lavatory. [20th century : origin obscure.]

Du·nois (dew-nwáä, dü-) **Jean, Comte de,** also known as the Bastard of Orléans (*c.*1403–68). French general, the illegitimate son of the Duke of Orléans. He was in command of the defence of Orléans when it was relieved by Joan of Arc in 1429. He subsequently joined her campaign.

Dun·oon (dun-ōṓn, dən-). A resort on the Firth of Clyde, in Scotland. U.S. nuclear ballistic missile Polaris submarines are based at nearby Holy Loch.

Duns Sco·tus (dúnz skṓtəss), **Joannes,** also known as the Subtle Doctor (*c.*1265–*c.*1308). Scottish Franciscan monk and theologian, who wrote *On the First Principle.* He disputed Aquinas's harmony of faith and reason and formed a school of scholasticism, known as Scotism.

Dun·sta·ble (dún-stəb'l). A town in Bedfordshire, England, built at the intersection of the Roman Watling Street and the ancient Icknield Way. Whipsnade Wildlife Park is approximately 6 kilometres (4 miles) south of the town. Its main industries are vehicle assembly and papermaking.

Dun·stan (dún-stən), **Saint** (*c.* 910–988). English monk and archbishop of Canterbury (960–988). He was born near Glastonbury and became abbot of the monastery there in 943. He was exiled to Flanders by King Edwy, but King Eadgar recalled him as bishop of Winchester in 957, and two years later made him archbishop of Canterbury. He developed a coronation rite from which the present English one derives. His feast day is May 19.

du·o (déw-ṓ ‖ dṓō-) *n., pl.* **-os** (-ṓz) or **dui** (-ee) (for senses 1, 2). **1.** *Music.* A duet. **2.** *Music.* Two performers singing or playing together. **3.** Two people in close association; a pair. —See Synonyms at **couple.** [Italian, "two", from Latin.]

duo– *comb. form.* Indicates two; for example, **duodecimal** [Latin, from *duo,* two.]

du·o·dec·i·mal (déw-ō-déssim'l ‖ dṓō-) *adj.* **1.** Of, pertaining to, or based on the number 12: *the duodecimal system.* **2.** Of or pertaining to twelfths.
~ *n.* A twelfth. [From Latin *duodecimus,* twelfth, from *duodecim,* twelve : DUO- + *decem,* ten.] —**du·o·dec·i·mal·ly** *adv.*

du·o·dec·i·mo (déw-ō-déssi-mō ‖ dṓō-) *n., pl.* **-mos. 1.** The page size of a book, formed by folding a single printer's sheet into 12 leaves. **2.** A book composed of pages of this size. Also called "twelvemo". Also written *12mo., 12°.*
~ *adj.* Having pages of this size. [Latin, ablative of *duodecimus,* twelfth, from *duodecim,* twelve. See **duodecimal.**]

du·o·de·na·ry (déw-ō-déen-əri, -ə- ‖ dṓō-, -dén-) *adj.* Of or pertaining to the number 12; duodecimal.

du·o·de·ni·tis (déw-ō-di-nītiss ‖ dṓō-) *n.* Inflammation of the duodenum. [New Latin : DUODEN(UM) + -ITIS.]

du·o·de·num (déw-ō-déen-əm, -ə- ‖ dṓō-, *U.S. also* -ódd'n-) *n., pl.*

-na (-ə) or **-nums**. The portion of the small intestine starting at the lower end of the stomach and extending to the jejunum. [Middle English, from Medieval Latin, short for *intestinum duodenum digitō-rum,* "intestine of twelve digits" (translation of the Greek *dodeka-daktulon,* "twelve fingers long", the duodenum), from Latin *duodēni,* twelve each, from *duodecim,* twelve. See **duodecimal**.]
 —**du·o·de·nal** (-'l) *adj.*

du·o·logue (déw-ə-log, -ō- ‖ dŏŏ-) *n.* Also *chiefly U.S.* **duolog**. A play, or part of a play, in which only two actors have speaking roles.

du·op·so·ny (dew-ópsəni ‖ dŏŏ-) *n., pl.* **-nies**. *Economics.* A stock-market condition wherein two rival buyers exert a controlling influence on numerous sellers. [DUO- + Greek *opsōnia,* purchasing of victuals, catering, from *opsōnes,* victualler, caterer : *opson,* food, relish, delicacy (see **opsonin**) + *ōnē,* buying.]

du·o·tone (déw-ō-tōn, -ə- ‖ dŏŏ-) *n. Printing.* **1.** A process for printing halftone illustrations in two tones of the same colour or black and one colour. **2.** A picture in duotone.
 ~*adj. Printing.* Having a two-toned effect or appearance.

dup. duplicate.

du·pat·ta (dŏŏ-púttə) *n.* A long scarf worn by Indian women. [Hindi.]

dupe (dewp ‖ dŏŏp) *n.* **1.** A person who is easily deceived or used. **2.** A person who mainly acts as the tool of another person or a power: *a dupe of Communism.*
 ~*tr.v.* **duped, duping, dupes**. To deceive easily; fool. See Synonyms at **deceive**. [French, from dialect French *dupe,* dupe, probably jocular use of *dupe,* hoopoe (from the supposed stupid appearance of the bird), contraction of *de huppe* : *de,* of + *huppe,* HOOPOE.] —**dup·a·bil·i·ty** (-ə-bílləti) *n.* —**dup·a·ble** *adj.* —**dup·er** *n.*

dup·er·y (déwp-əri ‖ dŏŏp-) *n., pl.* **-ies**. **1.** The action of duping. **2.** The state of being duped: *"we must think so as to avoid dupery"* (William James). [French *duperie,* from *dupe,* DUPE.]

du·pi·on (déwpi-ən, dew-pée-, -on ‖ dŏŏpi-, dŏŏ-) *n.* **1.** A double cocoon formed by silkworms. **2.** A rough silk fabric made from threads from these cocoons. [French *doupion,* from Italian *doppione,* from *doppio,* DOUBLE.]

du·ple (déwp'l ‖ dŏŏp'l) *adj.* **1.** Double; consisting of two. **2.** Having two beats in a bar. Said of music. [Latin *duplus,* twofold, double.]

du·plet (déwp-lət, -lit ‖ dŏŏp-) *n.* **1.** *Music.* A pair of notes having equal time value, played in the time of three. **2.** *Electronics.* A pair of electrons shared by two atoms, forming a valence bond.

du·plex (déw-pleks ‖ dŏŏ-) *adj.* **1.** Twofold. **2.** *Engineering.* Having two identical units operating in a single frame, each capable of operating independently. **3.** *Electronics.* Able to transmit two messages simultaneously in the same or opposite directions over a single wire. Compare **multiplex, simplex**.
 ~*n.* **1.** *Chiefly U.S.* A duplex apartment or house. **2.** A DNA or RNA molecule having a double strand. [Latin, twofold, double.] —**du·plex·i·ty** (-pléksəti) *n.*

duplex apartment *n. Chiefly U.S.* A flat having rooms on two adjoining floors connected by an inner staircase.

duplex house *n. Chiefly U.S.* A house divided into two living units.

du·pli·cate (déw-pli-kət, -kit ‖ dŏŏ-) *adj. Abbr.* **dup. 1.** Identically copied from an original. **2.** Existing or growing in two corresponding parts; double. **3.** *Card Games.* Designating a manner of play in which all partnerships play the same hands and compare scores at the end.
 ~*n. Abbr.* **dup. 1.** An identical copy; a facsimile. **2.** Anything that corresponds exactly to something else, especially an original; a double. **3.** A duplicate card game.
 ~*tr.v.* (-kayt) **duplicated, -cating, -cates**. **1.** To make an identical copy of; reproduce; imitate. **2.** To double; make twofold. **3.** To do or effect again or similarly, possibly without real need: *duplicating the process.* [Middle English, from Latin *duplicātus,* past participle of *duplicāre,* to make twofold, from *duplex,* twofold, DUPLEX.] —**du·pli·cate·ly** *adv.*

du·pli·ca·tion (déw-pli-káysh'n ‖ dŏŏ-) *n.* **1. a.** The act or procedure of duplicating. **b.** The condition of being duplicated. **2.** A duplicate; a replica. —**du·pli·ca·tive** (-kətiv, -kaytiv) *adj.*

du·pli·ca·tor (déw-pli-kaytər ‖ dŏŏ-) *n.* A machine that reproduces printed or written material, especially one designed for large-quantity reproduction using ink and a master plate or stencil.

du·plic·i·ty (dew-plíssəti ‖ dŏŏ-) *n., pl.* **-ties**. Deliberate deceptiveness in behaviour or speech; double-dealing. [Middle English *duplicite,* from Old French, from Late Latin *duplicitās* (stem *duplicitat-*), from Latin *duplex* (stem *duplic-*), twofold, DUPLEX.]

dup·py (dúppi) *n., pl.* **-pies**. *West Indian* A ghost or spirit.

Du Pré (dew práy), **Jacqueline** (1945–87). British cellist. She made her professional début at London in 1961. She was forced by multiple sclerosis to abandon her performing career in 1973, but was later active as a teacher.

Du·puy·tren's contracture (dew-pwée-trenz) *n.* A contracture of one or more fingers caused by thickening and shortening of the fibrous tissue under the palm. [After G. Dupuytren (1777–1835), French surgical pathologist.]

Dur. Durham.

du·ra·ble (déwr-əb'l ‖ dŏŏr-) *adj.* Able to withstand the effects of time, especially wear and tear or decay; lasting.
 ~*n.* A manufactured product that does not require frequent replacing, such as a domestic appliance or item of furniture: *consumer durables.* [Middle English, from Old French, from Latin *dūrābilis,*

from *dūrāre,* to last, endure.] —**du·ra·bil·i·ty** (-ə-bílləti), **du·ra·ble·ness** *n.*

durable goods *pl.n.* Durables. Compare **perishable goods**.

du·ral (déwr-əl ‖ dŏŏr-) *adj.* Pertaining to the dura mater.

Du·ral·u·min (dewr-ál-yŏŏ-min ‖ dŏŏr-) *n.* A trademark for an alloy of aluminium containing copper, manganese, magnesium, iron, and silicon. It is resistant to corrosion by acids and sea water.

du·ra ma·ter (déwr-ə máytər ‖ dŏŏr-). *n* A tough fibrous membrane that covers the brain and the spinal cord. [Middle English, from Medieval Latin *dūra mater (cerebrī),* "hard mother (of the brain)" (translation from Arabic *umm al-dimāgh aṣ-ṣafīqah*) : Latin *dūra,* feminine of *dūrus,* hard + *mater,* mother.]

du·ra·men (dewr-áy-men ‖ dŏŏr-, -mən) *n. Botany.* **Heartwood** *(see).* [New Latin, from Latin, hardness, from *dūrāre,* to harden, from *dūrus,* hard.]

dur·ance (déwr-ənss ‖ dŏŏr-) *n.* Forced confinement; imprisonment. [Middle English *duraunce,* duration, "prison term", from Old French *durance,* from *durer,* to last, from Latin *dūrāre.*]

Du·ras (dewr-aa, dü-raà), **Marguerite** (1914–96). French novelist, playwright, and film-maker. She was associated with the new novel school in France and wrote the screenplay for the film *Hiroshima Mon Amour* (1959). Novels include *L'Amant* (1984). Several of her novels were filmed, some under her own direction.

du·ra·tion (dewr-áysh'n ‖ dŏŏr-) *n.* **1.** Continuance or persistence in time. **2.** The period of time during which something exists or persists. —**for the duration**. For an indefinite period. [Medieval Latin *dūrātiō* (stem *dūrātiōn-*), from Latin *dūrāre,* to last.]

durative (déwr-ətiv ‖ dŏŏr-) *adj. Grammar.* Designating a verb aspect that expresses continuing action, as in Russian.

Durazzo. See **Durrës**.

Dur·ban (dúrbən). The largest city and main seaport of KwaZulu-Natal, South Africa. Its harbour handles more foreign trade than Cape Town, exporting coal, manganese and chrome ore, sugar, oranges, pineapple, and maize, and importing machinery for the Rand Goldfields. Durban is also a major resort.

dur·bar (dúrbaar) *n.* **1. a.** A state reception, often accompanied by a military display, given formerly by an Indian prince or by a British governor in India. **b.** The reception hall. **2.** The court of an Indian prince or ruler. [Hindi *darbār,* from Persian "court" : *dar,* door + *bār,* admission, audience, time.]

Dü·rer (déwr-ər, dûr-), **Albrecht** (1471–1528). German painter and engraver. He began as an apprentice to his goldsmith father in Nuremberg. He carried the classicism of the Italian Renaissance into northern European painting.

du·ress (dewr-éss, déwr-ess, -iss ‖ dŏŏr-) *n.* **1.** Constraint by threat; coercion: *confessed under duress.* **2.** *Law.* **a.** Coercion illegally applied. **b.** Forcible confinement. [Middle English *duresse,* hardness, restraint, confinement, from Old French *dure(s)ce,* hardness, from Latin *dūritia,* from *dūrus,* hard.]

Du·rex (dewr-eks ‖ dŏŏr-) *n.* **1.** *British.* A trademark for a contraceptive sheath. **2.** *Australian.* A trademark for adhesive tape.

Dur·ga (dóorgə) *n. Hinduism.* The goddess Devi considered as a fierce though benevolent protectress of heroes and an upholder of virtue.

Dur·ham[1] (dúrrəm). **1.** County in northeast England stretching from the Pennines to the North Sea. Coalmining, though in decline, dominates the coastal plain. Other industries include light engineering and chemicals.

Dur·ham[2] (dúrrəm). Principal city and administrative centre of County Durham, England. The city is dominated by its magnificent Norman cathedral; its castle, founded by William the Conqueror in 1072, is now part of the University of Durham, established in 1832.

Dur·ham[3] (dúrrəm ‖ dúr-əm, dóor-). City in North Carolina, in the United States. It is in the heart of a tobacco region and produces a fifth of all the United States' cigarettes.

Dur·ham[4] (dúrrəm) *n.* Any of a breed of beef cattle, a **shorthorn** *(see).* [Originally bred in DURHAM (county).]

Dur·ham (dúrrəm), **John George Lambton, 1st Earl of** (1792–1840). British politician. His estates and coal mines made him one of England's richest men but his support for popular causes earned him the nickname "Radical Jack". He was sent to Canada (1838) to investigate the colonial rebellion, and published the Durham Report (1839), advocating responsible government for the colonies, a landmark in the evolution of the Commonwealth.

du·ri·an (déwr-i-ən ‖ dŏŏr-) *n.* **1.** A tree, *Durio zibethinus,* of southeastern Asia, bearing edible fruit. **2.** The fruit of this tree, having a hard, prickly rind and soft pulp with an offensive odour but a pleasant taste. [Malay.]

dur·ing (déwr-ing, jéwr-, jór- ‖ dŏŏr-) *prep.* **1.** Throughout the course or duration of. **2.** Within the time of; at some time in. [Middle English (after Old French *durant,* "lasting"), from *duren,* to last, from Old French *durer,* from Latin *dūrāre.*]

Durk·heim (dúrk-hìm; *French* dür-kém), **Emile** (1858–1917). French social scientist, a founder of modern sociology. He applied anthropological information and statistics to the study of society. He wrote *The Division of Labour in Society* (1893) and *The Rules of Sociological Method* (1895).

dur·mast (dúr-maast ‖ -mast) *n.* A European oak, *Quercus petrea,* having tough, elastic wood and sessile acorns. Also called "sessile oak". [Probably alteration of *dun mast* : DUN (greyish brown) + MAST (nut, acorn).]

du·ro (déwr-ō, dóor-) *n., pl.* **-ros**. The silver dollar of Spain and

Spanish America. [Spanish *(peso) duro,* "hard (peso)", from Latin *dūrus,* hard.]

du·roc, Du·roc (déwr-ok ‖ dŏŏr-) *n.* A large red pig of a breed developed during the 19th century in the United States. [After *Duroc,* a horse owned by the developer of the breed.]

dur·ra, dou·ra, dou·rah (dúrrə, dŏŏrrə) *n.* A cereal grain, *Sorghum vulgare durra,* of Asia and northern Africa, much cultivated in dry regions. Also called "Guinea corn", "Indian millet". [Arabic *dhurah,* grain.]

Dur·rell (dúrrəl), **Gerald** (1925–95). British naturalist and writer, born in India, the brother of Lawrence. In 1958 he founded the Jersey Wildlife Preservation Fund, which runs a zoo on the island for endangered species. His stories include *The Overloaded Ark* (1953) and *My Family and Other Animals* (1956).

Durrell, Lawrence (George) (1912–90). British writer, born in India of Irish parents. His best-known work is the Alexandria Quartet: *Justine* (1957), *Balthazar* (1958), *Mountolive* (1958), and *Clea* (1960).

Dür·ren·matt (déwr-ən-mat, dú-), **Friedrich** (1921–90). Swiss novelist and dramatist. His plays include *The Visit* (1956), *Romulus* (1949), and *The Physicists* (1962). His novels include *The Judge and his Hangman* (1952) and *The Quarry* (1953).

Dur·rës (dŏŏr-əss). *Italian* **Durazzo;** *Serbo-Croat* **Drac.** Chief seaport of Albania and its former capital. A Greek city of the seventh century B.C. and important Roman port and bishopric (449), it was later held by Normans, Byzantines, Sicilians, Greeks, Serbs, and Turks until Albanian independence in 1913. A tourist centre, Durrës also produces foodstuffs, tobacco, clothing, and ships.

durst. *Archaic.* Past tense of **dare.**

du·rum (déwr-əm ‖ dŏŏr-) *n.* A hardy wheat, *Triticum durum,* grown mainly in the Mediterranean region and used chiefly in making macaroni, spaghetti, and similar products. Also called "durum wheat". [New Latin, from Latin, neuter of *dūrus,* hard.]

durzi (dúrzi) *n.* An Indian tailor. [Hindi, from Persian *darzi,* from *darz,* sewing.]

dusk (dusk) *n.* The darker stage of evening twilight.
~*adj.* Tending to darkness.
~*v.* **dusked, dusking, dusks.** *Poetic.* —*intr.* To become dark or dusky. —*tr.* To darken. [Middle English *dosc, dusk,* dusky, from Old English *dox,* dark, dusky.]

dusk·y (dúski) *adj.* **-ier, -iest.** **1.** Dark; shadowy. **2.** Rather dark in colour, especially in skin colour. **3.** Gloomy. —See Synonyms at **dark.** —**dusk·i·ly** *adv.* —**dusk·i·ness** *n.*

dusky grouse *n.* A bird, the **blue grouse** *(see).*

Düs·sel·dorf (dŏŏss'l-dawrf, düss'l-). City in North Rhine-Westphalia, western Germany. It is a port on the river Rhine serving the Ruhr and the Wupper industrial areas. Its industries include iron, steel, car assembly, and chemicals.

dust (dust) *n.* **1. a.** Matter composed of fine particles, such as earth or pollen. **b.** Small particles of matter that are fine enough to be carried by the wind, having diameters less than 0.6 millimetre (0.02 inch). **2. a.** Clouds of such matter. **b.** A state of confusion. Used in such phrases as *let the dust settle.* **3.** Such matter regarded as the result of disintegration. **4. a.** Earth, especially when regarded as the substance of the grave: *"Dust thou art, and shalt to dust return".* (Milton). **b.** The remains of a dead person. **5.** The surface of the ground. Preceded by *the.* **6.** A debased or despised condition. Used especially in the phrase *in the dust.* **7.** Something of no worth. **8.** *British.* Ashes, household dirt, or rubbish. **9.** Disturbance; fuss. **10.** *Informal.* A lung condition caused by dust, **pneumoconiosis** *(see).* —**bite the dust. 1.** To fail or be defeated. **2.** To fall dead. —**lick the dust.** To be forced to grovel; be humiliated. —**raise** or **kick up a dust.** To create a disturbance. —**shake the dust off (one's) feet.** To leave a place angrily or indignantly. —**throw dust in (someone's) eyes.** To mislead by deliberate misrepresentation or by diverting attention.
~*v.* **dusted, dusting, dusts.** —*tr.* **1.** To remove dust from by wiping, brushing, or beating. **2.** To sprinkle with a powdery substance. **3.** To strew like dust: *Freckles dusted her nose.* **4.** To remove as dust: *dusted the crumbs off.* **5.** To restore to use. Used with *off.* **6.** *Archaic.* To cover with dust. —*intr.* **1.** To clean by removing dust. **2.** To cover itself with dust. Used of a bird. —**dust down.** *Informal.* To reprimand. [Middle English *dust, doust,* Old English *dúst.*]

dust·bath (dúst-baath ‖ -bath) *n.* The action of a bird of working dust into its feathers so as to clean them or possibly help rid itself of parasites.

dust·bin (dúst-bin) *n.* *British.* A large cylindrical container for household rubbish. Also *U.S.* "trash can".

dust bowl *n.* In semiarid regions, a barren area produced by excessive wind erosion of the soil, especially after the removal of vegetation by overgrazing or badly managed cultivation. The topsoil is removed, and the area swept by severe dust storms. —**the Dust Bowl.** Such an area that developed in the 1930s in the United States, stretching through west Kansas, Oklahoma, Texas, Colorado, and into New Mexico.

dust·cart (dúst-kaart) *n.* *British.* A motor vehicle that collects household rubbish.

dust devil *n.* A small transient whirlwind that swirls dust, debris, and sand up into the air.

dust·er (dústər) *n.* **1.** One that dusts. **2.** A cloth used to remove dust. **3.** A device for sifting or scattering a powdered substance.

4. A smock worn to protect one's clothing from dust. **5.** A woman's loose coat.

dust·ing-down (dústing-dówn) *n.* *Informal.* A reprimand.

dusting powder (dústing) *n.* A fine powder, such as talcum powder, used for dusting the body.

dust jacket *n.* **dj** A removable paper cover used to protect the binding of a book. Also called "book jacket", "dust cover".

dust·man (dúst-mən) *n., pl.* **-men** (-mən). *British.* A man employed to remove rubbish in a dustcart. Also called "dustbinman".

dust·pan (dúst-pan) *n.* A short-handled, shovel-like pan into which dust is swept.

dust·sheet (dúst-sheet) *n.* A large cloth for protecting furniture from dust, especially furniture not in use. Also called "dust cover".

dust shot *n.* The smallest-sized firing shot.

dust storm *n.* In a semiarid or arid region, a severe windstorm that sweeps clouds of dust across an extensive area.

dust·up (dúst-up) *n.* *Informal.* An argument, especially one involving violence; a scuffle.

dust·y (dústi) *adj.* **-ier, -iest.** **1.** Covered or filled with dust. **2.** Consisting of or resembling dust; powdery. **3.** Tinged with grey; subdued; dull. **4.** Dry; uninteresting. **5.** Not satisfactory or helpful: *a dusty answer.* —**not so dusty.** *Informal.* Quite good; quite satisfactory. —**dust·i·ly** *adv.* —**dust·i·ness** *n.*

dusty miller *n.* **1.** A densely hairy plant, *Cerastium tomentosum,* related to and resembling the mouse-ears. **2.** A plant, the **beach sagewort** *(see).* **3.** Any of various other plants covered with dustlike down.

dutch (duch) *n.* *British Slang.* A wife. [Short for *duchess.*]

Dutch (duch) *adj. Abbr.* **D., Du. 1.** Of or pertaining to the Netherlands, its inhabitants, or their language. **2.** *Archaic.* German.
~*n. Abbr.* **D., Du. 1.** *Used with a plural verb.* The people of the Netherlands. Preceded by *the.* **b.** *Archaic.* The Germans. **2. a.** The West Germanic language of the Netherlands and Belgium. Sometimes called "Low Dutch". **b.** The German language. Now used only in the term *High Dutch.* **3. Pennsylvania Dutch** *(see).* —**in Dutch.** *Informal.* In trouble; in disfavour.
~*adv.* So that each person pays his own way: *go Dutch for lunch.*

Dutch auction *n. Informal.* An auction in which the auctioneer opens with a high price and lowers it until a buyer is found.

Dutch bargain *n. Informal.* A transaction settled while both parties are drinking.

Dutch barn *n.* A barn with open sides and a curved roof.

Dutch cap *n.* **1.** A woman's lace cap with turned-back triangular flaps on each side. **2.** A type of contraceptive, a **diaphragm** *(see).*

Dutch courage *n. Informal.* Courage obtained from drinking alcohol.

Dutch doll *n.* A jointed wooden doll.

Dutch door *n. Chiefly U.S.* A **stable door** *(see).*

Dutch East Indies. See **Indonesia.**

Dutch elm disease *n.* A disease of elm trees caused by a fungus, *Ceratocystis ulmi,* and resulting in eventual death of the tree due to the water-conducting vessels becoming clogged up with gums produced by the fungus.

Dutch Guiana. See **Surinam.**

Dutch hoe *n.* A hoe having a crosspiece attached to two prongs, used with a pushing motion.

dutch·man (dúch-mən) *n., pl.* **-men** (-mən). Something used to conceal faulty construction. [Playful use of DUTCHMAN.]

Dutch·man *n., pl.* **-men 1.** A native or inhabitant of the Netherlands. **2.** A person of Dutch descent. **3.** *South African.* An Afrikaner. Used derogatorily.

Dutch·man's-breech·es (dúchmənz-bríchiz) *n. Used with a singular or plural verb.* A woodland plant, *Dicentra cucullaria,* of eastern North America, having finely divided leaves and yellowish-white flowers with two spurs. [From its breeches-shaped blossoms.]

Dutch metal *n.* An alloy of copper and zinc used in thin sheets as a cheap imitation of gold leaf. Also called "Dutch foil", "Dutch gold", "Dutch leaf". [Originally imported from Holland.]

Dutch New Guinea. See **West Irian.**

Dutch oven *n.* **1.** A large, heavy pot or kettle, usually of cast iron and with a tight lid, used for slow cooking. **2.** A metal utensil open on one side and equipped with shelves, that is placed before an open fire for baking or roasting food. **3.** A wall oven in which food is baked by means of preheated brick walls.

Dutch Republic. See **United Provinces of the Netherlands.**

Dutch rush *n.* A horsetail, *Equisetum hyemale,* with unbranched overwintering stems.

Dutch treat *n. Informal.* An outing, as for dinner or a film, for which each person pays his own expenses.

Dutch uncle *n. Informal.* A stern and candid critic or adviser.

Dutch West Indies. See **Netherlands Antilles.**

du·te·ous (déwti-əss ‖ dŏŏti-) *adj. Formal.* Obedient; dutiful. [From DUTY.] —**du·te·ous·ly** *adv.* —**du·te·ous·ness** *n.*

du·ti·a·ble (déwti-əb'l ‖ dŏŏti-) *adj.* Subject to import tax.

du·ti·ful (déwtif'l ‖ dŏŏtif'l) *adj.* **1.** Filled with or motivated by a sense of duty. **2.** Showing or proceeding from a sense of duty. —See Synonyms at **obedient.** —**du·ti·ful·ly** *adv.* —**du·ti·ful·ness** *n.*

du·ty (déwti ‖ dŏŏti) *n., pl.* **-ties. 1.** An act or a course of action that is exacted of one by law or social custom, or by one's position or religion. **2.** a. Moral obligation. **b.** The compulsion felt to meet such obligation. **3. a.** A service assigned to or demanded of one, especially in the armed forces. **b.** A function; an allocated task. **4.** A tax charged by a government, on imports, transactions, trans-

ference of estates, or the like. **5.** *Engineering.* **a.** The work capability of a machine under specified conditions. **b.** A measure of efficiency expressed as work per unit energy input. **6.** *Agriculture.* The amount of water required to irrigate a given area for the cultivation of some crop. **—off duty.** Not engaged in one's assigned work; not at work. **—on duty.** At one's post or work; engaged in one's work.
~*adj.* On duty; especially, available for service or consultation: *duty officer; duty chemist.* [Middle English *duete,* from Anglo-French, from Old French *deu,* DUE.]

duty-bound (déwti-bównd ‖ dŏoti-) *adj.* Obliged by a moral, legal, or other duty.

du·ty-free (déwti-frée ‖ dŏoti-) *adj.* Exempt from customs duties. ~*n. Informal.* A duty-free item of merchandise. **—du·ty·free** *adv.*

duty-free shop *n.* A shop, especially one at an airport or port, that sells duty-free goods such as tobacco, spirits, or perfume.

du·um·vir (dew-úm-vər, dŏo-, -ŏom-) *n., pl.* **-virs** or **-viri** (-vi-ree, -və-, -rī). A member of a duumvirate. [Latin, variant of *duovir* : *duo,* two + *vir,* man.]

du·um·vi·rate (dew-úm-vi-rət, dŏo-) *n.* **1.** Any of various two-man governments in the Roman Republic. **2.** Any government or authority consisting of two men.

Du·va·li·er (dew-vál-i-ay, dü-, -áy). **François** (1907-1971). Also known as Papa Doc. Haitian dictator. He was elected president of Haiti in 1957, and in 1964 he declared himself president for life. Duvalier executed opponents without trial and deprived the population of civil rights and education. His practice of voodooism led some uneducated Haitians to believe that he possessed supernatural powers.

Duvalier, Jean-Claude. (1951-). Also known as Baby Doc. Dictator of Haiti, son of François. He succeeded his father as president for life in 1971, but was deposed in 1986.

du·vet (dŏo-vay, déw-) *n.* A soft, light quilt filled with down, feathers, or a similar synthetic material and used in place of a sheet and blankets. Also called "continental quilt". [French, down, from Old French *duvet,* alteration of *dumet,* diminutive of *dum,* alteration (probably influenced by PLUME) of *dun,* from Old Norse *dūnn.*]

du·ve·tyn, du·ve·tine, du·ve·tyne (déwvə-teen, dŏovə-, -téen) *n.* A soft, napped fabric with a twill weave, made of wool, cotton, rayon, or silk. [French *duvetine,* from DUVET.]

D.V. 1. Deo volente. **2.** Douay Version (of the Bible).

dux (duks) *n.* In Scotland and some other countries, the top pupil in a class of school children. [Latin, leader.]

dvan·dva (dvaán-dvaa) *n.* A compound expression consisting of two elements typically belonging to the same part of speech and being of equal importance in determining the meaning of the compound; for example, a **fighter-bomber** is both a fighter and a bomber. Compare **bahuvrihi.** [Sanskrit, repeated nominative (exemplifying this compound) of *dva,* couple, pair.]

Dvi·na, Northern (dvee-naá). *Russian* **Severnaya Dvina** (syévir-nyəyə). River in northern Russia. It flows 750 kilometres (466 miles) northwest to Dvina Bay on the White Sea.

Dvina, Western. *Russian* **Zapadnaya Dvina** (zaápədnəyə). A river in northwestern Russia, Belarus and Latvia. It flows 1 030 kilometres (640 miles) from the Valdai Hills into the Gulf of Riga.

D.V.M. Doctor of Veterinary Medicine.

Dvo·řák (dvór-zhak, -zhaak), **Antonin** (1841-1904). Czech composer. He incorporated folk tunes into his music, especially in the *Slavonic Dances.* His last symphony, the Ninth, "From the New World" (1893), was composed in the United States where he was director of the National Conservatory in New York (1892-95).

D/W dock warrant.

dwarf (dwawrf) *n., pl.* **dwarfs** or **dwarves** (dwawrvz). **1. a.** A very small person, especially, a person afflicted with dwarfism. Compare **midget.** **b.** An atypically small animal or plant. **2.** A diminutive, often ugly, manlike creature of fairy tales and legend. **3.** A dwarf star.
~*v.* **dwarfed, dwarfing, dwarfs.** —*tr.* **1.** To check the natural growth or development of; stunt: *"the oaks were dwarfed from lack of moisture"* (John Steinbeck). **2.** To cause to appear small by comparison: *an old church dwarfed by the new office blocks.* —*intr.* To become stunted or grow smaller.
~*adj.* **1.** Diminutive; undersized; stunted. **2.** *Biology.* Much smaller than the usual type of a particular kind: *dwarf gourami; dwarf zinnias.* [Middle English *dwerf, dwergh,* Old English *dweorg, dweorh,* from Germanic *dwerg-* (unattested).]

dwarf bean *n.* A variety of **French bean** *(see).*

dwarf·ism (dwáwrfiz'm) *n.* A condition of arrested growth having various causes; especially: **1. Achondroplasia** *(see).* **2.** A deficiency of or failure to respond to growth hormone.

dwarf star *n.* A main-sequence star having relatively high density, small mass, and average or below average luminosity. Also called "dwarf". Compare **giant star.** See **white dwarf.**

dwell (dwel) *intr.v.* **dwelt** (dwelt) or **dwelled, dwelling, dwells. 1.** *Formal.* To live as a resident; reside. **2.** To exist in some place or state. **3 a.** To fasten one's attention; reflect on at length or in detail, especially in speech or writing. Used with *on* or *upon.* **b.** To emphasise or stress something: *dwelt on the importance of health care.* **c.** *Music.* To hold or sustain a note or phrase: *dwell on high C.*
~*n.* A short regular pause in the motion of a mechanical part of the constant-radius portion of a cam that causes it. [Middle English *dwellen,* to delay, linger, remain, reside, Old English *dwellan,* de-

ceive, hinder, delay (meaning influenced by Old Norse *dvelja,* "sojourn", "dwell").]

dwell·er (dwéllər) *n.* A person or animal that lives in a specified place. Used in combination: *cave-dweller, city-dweller.*

dwell·ing (dwélling) *n. Formal.* A place of residence; a house; an abode.

dwelling house *n.* A building intended for occupation; a residence.

dwel·ling-place (dwélling-playss) *n.* A dwelling.

dwin·dle (dwind'l) *v.* **-dled, -dling, -dles.** —*intr.* To become gradually less until little remains; waste away; diminish. —*tr.* To make smaller or less; cause to shrink. —See Synonyms at **decrease.** [Frequentative of obsolete *dwine,* to waste away, diminish, languish, Middle English *dwinen,* Old English *dwīnan.*]

d.w.t. deadweight tonnage.

Dy The symbol for the element dysprosium.

dy·ad (dī-ad) *n.* **1.** Two units regarded as a pair. **2.** *Chemistry.* A divalent atom or radical. **3.** A mathematical operator represented as a pair of vectors juxtaposed without multiplication.
~*adj.* Made up of two units. [From Greek *duas* (stem *duad-*), pair, from *duo,* two.]

dy·ad·ic (dī-áddik) *adj.* **1.** Twofold. **2.** Of or relating to a dyad. ~*n. Mathematics.* The direct product *(B·C) AD* of two dyads *AB* and *CD.*

Dy·ak, Day·ak (dī-ak) *n.* A member of any of various Indonesian peoples of Borneo and the Sulu Sea islands.

dyarchy. Variant of **diarchy.**

dyb·buk (díbbək, dee-bŏok) *n.* In Jewish folklore, a malevolent spirit that enters the body of a person and controls his actions. [Yiddish, devil, from Hebrew *dibbūg,* from *dābhaq,* to cling.]

dye (dī) *n.* **1. a.** Any substance used to colour materials; often permanently. **b.** A liquid containing such a substance: *a vat of dye.* **2.** A colour imparted by or as if by dyeing.
~*v.* **dyed, dyeing, dyes.** —*tr.* **1.** To colour (a material) with or as if with a dye, especially by soaking in a colouring solution. **2.** To add (colour) with a dye. —*intr.* To take on or impart colour. [Middle English *deie,* Old English *dēah, dēag†,* hue, tinge.] **—dye·r** *n.*

dyed-in-the-wool (dīd-in-thə-wŏol) *adj.* **1.** Dyed before being woven into cloth. **2.** Inflexible, especially in opinions, views, or the like; out-and-out: *a dyed-in-the wool racist.*

dyer's green·weed (green-weed) *n.* A small broomlike shrub, *Genista tinctoria,* native to Eurasia, having clusters of yellow flowers. Also called "dyer's broom", "woadwaxen", "woodwaxen". [So called because it yields a green dye.]

dyer's rocket *n.* A plant, *Reseda luteola,* native to Europe, having long spikes of small, yellowish-green flowers and yielding a yellow dye. Also called "weld".

dy·er's-weed (dī-ərz-weed) *n.* Any of various plants yielding colouring matter used as dye.

dye-stuff (dī-stuf) *n.* Any substance used as or yielding a dye. [Probably translation of German *Farbstoff.*]

dye·wood (dī-wŏod) *n.* Any wood from which dyestuffs are obtained.

Dyf·ed (dúv-ed, -id). Former county in southwest Wales, bordering the Irish Sea. It is now subdivided into Ceredigion, Carmarthenshire, and Pembrokeshire. Milford Haven refines oil.

dy·ing (dī-ing) *adj.* **1.** About to die. **2.** Drawing to an end; declining. **3.** Done or uttered just before death. **4.** Of or pertaining to death: *one's dying day.*

dyke¹, dike (dīk) *n.* **1.** An embankment of earth and rock, especially one built to prevent floods. **2.** *Scottish.* A low wall dividing or enclosing land. **3.** A barrier blocking a passage, especially for protection. **4.** A ditch; especially, one with a bank alongside made from the earth dug out. **5.** *Geology.* A sheetlike mass of igneous rock that cuts across the structure of adjacent rock. **6.** *Australian Slang.* A lavatory.
~*tr.v.* **dyked, dyking, dykes.** Also **dike. 1.** To protect, enclose, or provide with a dyke. **2.** To drain with dykes or ditches. [Middle English *dyke,* from Old English *dic,* ditch; akin to Old Norse *dik* or Middle Low German *dīk,* dam.]

dyke², dike *n. Slang.* A lesbian. Used derogatorily. [20th century : origin obscure.] **—dyk·ey** *adj.*

Dyl·an (dillən), **Bob,** born Robert Allen Zimmerman (1941-). U.S. singer and songwriter. His protest songs with their plaintive surrealism made him a notable figure in popular music in the 1960s.

dy·nam·ic (dī-námmik, *rarely* di-) *adj.* Also **dy·nam·i·cal** (-'l). **1.** Of or pertaining to energy, force, or motion in relation to force. **2.** Characterised by or tending to produce continuous change or advance. **3.** Energetic and enterprising; forceful. **4.** Of or pertaining to variation of intensity or volume, as in musical sound. **5.** Designating a computer memory that needs periodic updates. Compare **static. —See Synonyms at active.**
~*n.* A social or psychological system or drive that underlies any relationship between individuals: *the parent-child dynamic.* [French *dynamique,* from Greek *dunamikos,* powerful, from *dunamis,* power, from *dunasthai,* to be able.] **—dy·nam·i·cal·ly** *adv.*

dynamical geology *n.* **Geodynamics** *(see).*

dynamic psychology *n.* A method in psychology that emphasises the fluidity and energy of mental life and the motives of the individual that condition it.

dy·nam·ics (dī-námmiks, *rarely* di-) *n.* **1.** *Used with a singular verb. Physics.* A branch of mechanics comprising the study of the relationship between motion and the forces affecting the motion of physical systems. Also called "kinetics". Compare **kinematics, stat-**

ics. **2.** *Used with a plural verb.* The forces that produce motion and change in any field or system. **3.** *Used with a plural verb.* Variation in volume, force, or intensity, especially in musical sound. **4.** *Psychology.* **a.** *Used with a singular verb.* The action, fluidity, and energy of mental life. **b.** *Used with a plural verb.* The motives, needs, and drives of an individual or group.

dy·na·mism (dínəmiz'm) *n.* **1.** Any of various theories or philosophical systems that explain the universe in terms of an immanent force or in terms of natural forces and their interplay. **2.** A process or mechanism responsible for the development or motion of a system. **3.** The quality of being dynamic. [French *dynamisme* : DYNAM(O)- + -ISM.] **—dy·na·mist** (dínəmist) *n.* **—dy·na·mis·tic** (dínə-místik) *adj.*

dy·na·mite (dínə-mīt) *n.* **1.** A powerful explosive composed of nitroglycerin or ammonium nitrate dispersed in an absorbent material such as wood pulp and an antacid such as calcium carbonate. **2.** *Informal.* **a.** Someone or something that is potentially dangerous or violent. **b.** Someone or something outstandingly fine. **3.** *Slang.* Heroin.
~*tr.v.* **dynamited, -miting, -mites. 1.** To blow up, shatter, or destroy with or as with dynamite. **2.** To charge with dynamite. [Swedish *dynamit* : DYNAM(O)- + -ITE.] **—dy·na·mit·er** *n.*

dy·na·mo (dínə-mō) *n., pl.* **-mos. 1.** A generator, especially one for producing direct current. **2.** *Informal.* An extremely energetic and forceful person. [Short for *dynamo(electric) machine,* translation of German *dynamoelektrische Maschine.*]

dynamo– *comb. form.* Indicates power; for example, **dynamoelectric.** [Greek *dunamo-,* from *dunamis,* power, from *dunasthai,* to be able.]

dy·na·mo·e·lec·tric (dínə-mō-i-léktrik) *adj.* Also **dy·na·mo·e·lec·tri·cal** (-'l). Relating to the conversion of mechanical energy into electrical energy, or vice versa.

dy·na·mom·e·ter (dínə-mómmitər) *n.* Any of several instruments used to measure force or power. [French *dynamomètre* : DYNAMO- + -METER.]

dy·na·mom·e·try (dínə-mómmətri) *n.* Measurement by means of a dynamometer. **—dy·na·mo·met·ric** (-mō-métrik, -mə-), **dy·na·mo·met·ri·cal** *adj.*

dy·na·mo·tor (dínə-mōtər) *n.* A rotating electric machine with two armatures, used to convert alternating to direct current. [DYNA(MO)- + MOTOR.]

dy·nast (dín-əst, -ast || *Chiefly U.S.* dín-) *n.* A lord or ruler; especially, a hereditary ruler. [Latin *dynastēs,* from Greek *dunastēs,* lord, master, from *dunasthai,* to be able.]

dy·nas·ty (dín-əsti || *Chiefly U.S.* dín-) *n., pl.* **-ties. 1.** A succession of rulers from the same family or line. **2.** A family or group that maintains power or supremacy in a particular field for a considerable length of time. [French *dynastie,* from Greek *dunasteia,* domination, lordship, from *dunastēs,* ruler, DYNAST.] **—dy·nas·tic** (di-nástik || *Chiefly U.S.* dī-) *adj.* **—dy·nas·ti·cal·ly** *adv.*

dy·na·tron (dínə-tron) *n. Electronics.* A tetrode with grid and anode potentials so arranged that anode current decreases when the anode potential increases. [DYNA(MO)- + -TRON.]

dyne (dīn) *n. Physics.* A centimetre-gram-second unit of force, equal to the force required to impart an acceleration of one centimetre per second per second to a mass of one gram. [French, from Greek *dunamis,* power. See **dynamic.**]

dy·node (dín-ōd) *n.* An electrode used in certain electron tubes to provide secondary emission. [DYN(AMO)- + -ODE.]

dys– *prefix.* Indicates diseased, painful, difficult, faulty, or bad; for example, **dysentery, dyslexia.** [Middle English *dis-,* from Old French, from Latin *dys-,* from Greek *dus-.*]

dys·cra·si·a (diss-krάyzi-ə || -krάyzhə) *n. Rare.* Loosely, a morbid state or condition resulting from the presence of abnormal material in the blood. [New Latin, from Medieval Latin, disease, distemper, "disproportionate mixture of the humours," from Greek *duskrasia* : DYS- + *krasis,* mixing.]

dys·en·ter·y (díss'n-tri, -təri || -terri) *n.* An infection of the lower intestinal tract producing pain, fever, and severe diarrhoea, often with blood and mucus. [Middle English *dissenterie,* from Latin *dysenteria,* from Greek *dusenteria* : DYS- + *enteron,* intestine.] **—dys·en·ter·ic** (-térrik) *adj.*

dys·func·tion (diss-fúngksh'n) *n.* Disordered or impaired functioning. **—dys·func·tion·al** *adj.*

dys·gen·ic (diss-jénnik) *adj.* Pertaining to or causing the deterioration of hereditary qualities. [DYS- + -GENIC.]

dys·gen·ics (diss-jénniks) *n. Used with a singular verb.* The biological study of the factors producing racial degeneration. Also called "cacogenics."

dys·lex·i·a (diss-léksi-ə) *n.* A learning disorder causing impairment of the ability to read; incomplete alexia. Also called "word blindness". [New Latin : DYS- + Greek *lexis,* speech, from *legein,* to speak.] **—dys·lec·tic** (-léktik) *adj. & n.* **—dys·lex·ic** (-léksik) *adj. & n.*

dys·lo·gis·tic (diss-lə-jístik) *adj.* Conveying censure; disapproving. [DYS- + (EU)LOGISTIC.] **—dys·lo·gis·ti·cal·ly** *adv.*

dys·men·or·rhoe·a, dys·men·or·rhe·a (diss-mennə-rée-ə, diss-ménnə-, -reér) *n.* Difficult or painful menstruation. [New Latin : DYS- + Greek *mēn* (stem *mēno-*), month + -RRHEA.]

dys·pa·reu·ni·a (dispə-rōōni-ə) *n.* Pain or difficulty experienced during sexual intercourse.

dys·pep·sia (diss-pép-si-ə || -shə) *n.* Disturbed digestion; indigestion. [Latin, from Greek *duspepsia* : DYS- + *-pepsia,* digestion.]

dys·pep·tic (diss-péptik) *adj.* Also **dys·pep·ti·cal** (-'l). **1.** Pertaining to or having dyspepsia. **2.** Morose; irritable.
~*n.* One who suffers from dyspepsia. **—dys·pep·ti·cal·ly** *adv.*

dys·pha·gi·a (diss-fáyji-ə) *n.* Difficulty in swallowing. [New Latin : DYS- + -PHAGIA.] **—dys·phag·ic** (-fájik) *adj.*

dys·pha·sia (diss-fáyzi-ə, -fáyzhə) *n.* Impairment of speech and verbal comprehension, especially when associated with brain injury. [New Latin : DYS- + -PHASIA.] **—dys·pha·sic** (-fáyzik) *adj.*

dys·phe·mism (díss-fə-miz'm) *n.* **1.** The substitution of an unpleasant or derogatory term for an inoffensive one. **2.** The term thus substituted. [DYS- + EUPHEMISM.]

dys·pho·ni·a (diss-fóni-ə) *n.* Difficulty in speaking, usually resulting in hoarseness. [New Latin : DYS- + Greek *-phōnia,* -PHONY.] **—dys·phon·ic** (-fónnik) *adj.*

dys·pho·ri·a (diss-fáwri-ə || -fóri-) *n.* An emotional state characterised by anxiety, depression, and restlessness. [New Latin, from Greek *dusphoria,* distress, from *dusphoros,* hard to bear : DYS- + -PHOROUS.] **—dys·phor·ic** (-fórrik || -fáwrik) *adj.*

dys·pla·sia (diss-pláyzi-ə, -pláyzhə) *n.* Abnormal development of tissues, organs, or cells. [New Latin : DYS- + Greek *plasis,* formation, from *plassein,* to mould.] **—dys·plas·tic** (-plástik, *rarely* -pláastik) *adj.*

dysp·noe·a (disp-née-ə, diss-, -néer) *n.* Also *chiefly U.S.* **dysp·ne·a.** A sense of difficulty in breathing, often associated with lung or heart disease. [New Latin, from Greek *duspnoia,* from *duspnoos,* short of breath : DYS- + *-pnoos,* from *pnoē,* breathing, from *pnein,* to breathe.] **—dysp·noe·al, dysp·ne·ic** *adj.*

dys·pro·si·um (diss-prōzi-əm) *n. Symbol* **Dy** A soft, silvery rare-earth metal used in nuclear research. Atomic number 66, atomic weight 162.50, melting point 1,407°C, boiling point 2,335°C, relative density 8.536, valency 3. [New Latin, from Greek *dusprositos,* difficult to approach : DYS- + *prositos,* approachable, from *prosienai,* to approach : *pros-,* towards + *ienai,* to go.]

dys·thy·mi·a (diss-thími-ə) *n. Psychiatry.* **1.** A form of neurosis characterised by depression, anxiety, obsessions, and compulsive behaviour. **2.** Any condition caused by malfunction of the thymus during childhood. [New Latin, from Greek: DYS- + *thumos,* mind.]

dys·toc·ia (diss-tōk-yə) *n.* Difficult birth. [New Latin : DYS- + *-tocia,* from Greek *tokos,* offspring.]

dys·to·pi·a (diss-tópi-ə) *n.* An imaginary place where everything is as bad as it could possibly be. Compare **utopia.** [DYS- + UTOPIA (coined by J.S. Mill).]

dys·tro·phy (dístrəfi) *n.* Also **dys·tro·phi·a** (diss-trōfi-ə). **1.** Defective nutrition characterised by wasting of the tissues. **2.** Any disorder caused by defective nutrition. See **muscular dystrophy.** [New Latin *dystrophia* : DYS- + -TROPHY.] **—dys·troph·ic** (-tróffik, -trōfik) *adj.*

dys·u·ri·a (diss-yoór-i-ə) *n.* Painful or difficult urination. [New Latin, from Greek *dusouria* : DYS- + -URIA.] **—dys·u·ric** *adj.*

dz. dozen.

dzo, zo (zō) *n., pl.* **dzos, zos** or collectively **dzo, zo.** Any of a cross between a Tibetan yak and a cow, or between a bull and a female yak. [Tibetan.]

Dzon·kha (zóngkə) *n.* A language, **Bhutanese** (*see*).

e, E (ee) *n., pl.* **e's** or *rare* **es, Es** or **E's. 1.** The fifth letter of the modern English alphabet. **2.** Any of the speech sounds represented by this letter.

e, E, e., E. *Note:* As an abbreviation or symbol, *e* may be a small or a capital letter, with or without a full stop. Established forms or those generally preferred precede the definition. When no form is given, all four forms are in general use in that sense. **1.** E. earl. **2.** E Earth. **3.** east; eastern. **4.** e electron. **5.** E energy. **6.** e., E. engineer; engineering. **7.** E, E. English. **8.** E exa-. **9.** E excellent. **10.** E. illuminance. **11.** E irradiance. **12.** e *Mathematics.* The base of the natural system of logarithms, having a numerical value of approximately 2.718.... **13.** E EEC-permitted. Used as part of a numbering system for food additives. **14.** E The drug Ecstasy. **15.** The fifth in a series.

E *n., pl.* **Es** or **E's.** *Music.* **1.** The third note in the scale of C major. **2.** The key or scale in which E is the tonic. **3.** A written or printed note representing E. **4.** A string, key, or pipe tuned to E.

each (eech) *adj. Abbr.* **ea.** Every single person or thing considered individually: *Each man cast a vote.*
~*pron.* Every one of a group of objects, persons, or things considered individually; each one. Usually regarded as singular: *Each presented his gift.*
~*adv.* For or to each one; apiece: *ten pounds each.* [Middle English *ech, ælc,* Old English *ǣlc;* akin to Old High German *eogilih,* from West Germanic *aiwō galikaz* (unattested), "ever alike".]
Usage: *Each* normally takes a singular verb or pronoun in Standard English: *Each has his job to do; Each person wants an answer; Each of the boys has an apple.* In informal usage, especially in speech, the nearness of the noun to the verb in this last type of example often means that *each* is treated as if it were plural: *Each of the boys have their own food.* This sort of construction offends purists. Even without the plural noun, the "multiple" meaning of *each* is enough to encourage the use of the plural verb informally (*Each have their own food*), but that is less common. Plural agreement is normal in all styles whenever *each* follows a plural subject (*the children each have their own tickets*). There is some uncertainty as to whether to use a singular or plural verb following a compound subject, but formal styles tend to prefer the plural (*Jones and Smith each have their own ticket*). Another reason for the development of plural agreement in recent years, especially in informal speech, is the conflict between the "neutral" gender of *each* and the explicit male/female reference of accompanying singular pronouns, in sentences such as *Each person looked for his coat.* The masculine pronoun is the traditional one to use when a neutral meaning is intended, but this is sometimes ambiguous, and recently has attracted feminist criticism. To spell out the alternatives is grammatically possible, but often very awkward (*Each person looked for his or her coat*), and this has motivated the use of the plural form (*Each person looked for their coat*), which is often heard, even in formal contexts.

each other *pron.* **1.** Each the other. Used as a compound reciprocal pronoun: *They met each other* (each met the other). **2.** One another.
Usage: Traditionally *each other* refers to only two persons or things; *one another* to more than two. There is certainly a tendency for modern usage to follow this principle, but the distinction is by no means rigidly observed, and examples may be found in all styles: *The three men looked at each other; Husband and wife should confide in one another.* The phrase *each other* carries the meaning of a reciprocal relationship between people or things, and where this meaning is not intended, the use of *each other* attracts criticism, though it is often heard: *The three cars in the funeral procession followed each other down the street.* Formal usage would recommend *one another,* on the grounds that the meaning "each car is following each other car" is either unintended or impossible. But real ambiguity rarely if ever exists, with the consequence that in informal speech or writing the distinction is not rigidly observed.

each-way (eech-wáy) *adj. British.* Designating a bet on a racing animal made on its winning or coming second or third, or sometimes fourth, in a race. —**each way** *adv.*

Eads (eedz), **John Buchanan** (1820–87). U.S. engineer. He built the triple-arch steel bridge (opened 1874) which spans the Mississippi river at St. Louis.

ea-ger¹ (éegər) *adj.* **1.** Intensely desirous of something; impatiently expectant. **2.** Showing intense desire or expectancy: *an eager search for a familiar face in the crowd.* **3.** Very willing. [Middle English *egre,* sharp, keen, eager, from Old French *aigre,* from Latin *ācer* (stem *acr-*), keen, sharp.] —**ea-ger-ly** *adv.* —**ea-ger-ness** *n.*
Synonyms: *eager, avid, keen, anxious, earnest, fervid, zealous.*

ea-ger². Variant of *eagre.*

eager beaver *n. Informal.* An industrious, overzealous person.

ea-gle (éeg'l) *n.* **1.** Any of various large birds of prey of the family Accipitridae, including members of the genera *Aquila, Haliaeetus,* and other genera, characterised by a powerful hooked bill, long broad wings, and strong, soaring flight. See **golden eagle, harpy eagle. 2.** A representation of an eagle used as an emblem, insignia, seal, or the like. **3.** A former gold coin of the United States having a face value of ten dollars. **4.** A score in golf of two below par on any hole. [Middle English *egle,* from Old French *egle, aigle,* from Latin *aquila†.*]

ea-gle-eyed (éeg'l-íd) *adj.* **1.** Having keen eyesight. **2.** Highly observant.

eagle owl *n.* A large Eurasian owl, *Bubo bubo,* having brownish plumage and prominent ear tufts.

ea-glet (éeglit) *n.* A young eagle.

ea-gle-wood (éeg'l-woŏd) *n.* Aloes wood. See **aloes.**

ea-gre, eag-er (áy-gər ‖ ée-) *n.* A tidal flood, a **bore** *(see).* [Perhaps ultimately from Old English *éagor,* flood tide.]

eal-dor-man (áwldərmən) *n., pl.* **-men** (-mən). The chief official or governor of a shire in Anglo-Saxon England. [Old English *ealdormann,* prince. See **alderman.**]

Eal-ing (éeling). Borough of Greater London, in west London.

-ean. Variant of **-an.**

ear¹ (eer) *n.* **1.** *Anatomy.* **a.** The vertebrate organ of hearing, responsible, in general, for maintaining equilibrium as well as sensing sound, and divided in humans into the **external ear,** the **middle ear,** and the **internal ear** *(all of which see).* **b.** The part of this organ that is externally visible. **2.** An analogous organ in some invertebrates, such as insects. **3.** The sense of hearing. **4.** Aural sensitivity, as to differences in musical pitch or to speech sounds: *a good ear for foreign languages.* **5.** Attention; especially, favourable attention; heed: *"I shall beg your patient ear a little longer"* (Izaak Walton). **6.** Anything resembling or suggestive of the shape or position of the external ear, such as a tuft of feathers on the head of some owls or a projecting handle on a vase. **7.** A small box appearing in either of the upper corners of the front page of a newspaper, usually containing an advertisement. —**all ears.** Acutely attentive: *If you want to tell your story, we're all ears.* —**by the ears.** Involved in a quarrel; at odds. —**fall on deaf ears.** To be ignored: *His advice fell on deaf ears.* —**have** or **keep an ear to the ground.** To give attention to or watch the trend of events and opinions. —**have the ear of.** To have one's advice or requests heeded by; be able to influence. —**in one ear and out the other.** Heard but without influence or effect. —**play by ear.** To perform music without reference to or memorisation of a score. —**play it by ear.** *Informal.* To act without plan; improvise. —**turn a deaf ear.** To be unwilling to listen or pay heed. —**up to (one's)** or **the ears.** Deeply involved or committed: *up to one's ears in debt.* —**wet behind the ears.** Inexperienced or immature. [Middle English *ere,* Old English *ēare,* from Germanic; akin to Latin *auris,* Greek *ous.*] —**ear-less** *adj.*

ear² (eer) *n.* The seed-bearing spike of a cereal plant such as wheat.
~*intr.v.* **eared, earing, ears.** To form or grow ears. Used of cereal plants. [Middle English *ere, er,* Old English *ēar,* from Germanic.]

ear-ache (éer-ayk) *n.* Pain in the ear.

ear-bash (éer-bash) *v.* **-bashed, -bashing, -bashes.** *Australian Slang.* —*tr.* To talk incessantly to. —*intr.* To talk incessantly.

ear-drop (éer-drop) *n.* **1.** A pendent earring. **2.** *Plural.* Medicinal drops for inserting in the ear.

ear-drum (éer-drum) *n. Anatomy.* The **tympanic membrane** *(see).*

eared (eerd) *adj.* **1.** Having ears or earlike projections. **2.** Having a specified kind or number of ears. Often used in combination: *a crop-eared puppy.*

eared seal *n.* Any of various seals of the family Otariidae, which includes the sea lions and fur seals, characterised by external ears, earlike front flippers, and hind flippers that can be turned forwards for walking on land. Compare **earless seal.**

ear-flap (éer-flap) *n.* **1.** Either of two cloth or fur appendages to a cap that may be turned down over the ears. Also called "earlap". **2.** A flap of skin forming part of the external ear of such animals as eared seals.

ear-ful (éer-fool) *n. Informal.* **1.** A quantity of information or gossip. **2.** A severe reprimand.

Ear-hart (áirhaart), **Amelia** (1898–1937). U.S. aviator. In May 1932, she became the first woman to fly solo across the Atlantic and in January, 1935, the first to make a solo flight from Hawaii to California. Two years later she tried to fly round the world, but the plane crashed in the Pacific and she and her navigator were never found.

ear-ing (éer-ing) *n. Nautical.* A short line attaching an upper corner of a sail to the yard. [Perhaps from EAR (part of body).]

earl (erl) *n. Abbr.* **E.** A British peer next in rank above a viscount and below a marquis. [Middle English *erl,* Old English *eorl,* warrior, chief, nobleman; akin to Old Saxon *erl,* Old Norse *jarl†.*]

ear-lap (éerlap) *n.* **1. a.** The lobe of the external ear. **b.** The external ear. **2.** An earflap.

earl-dom (érldəm) *n.* **1.** The rank or title of an earl. **2.** The territory under the jurisdiction of an earl.

earless seal *n.* Any of various seals of the family Phocidae, which includes the typical seals, having rudimentary hind limbs and no external ears. Compare **eared seal.**

ear lobe *n.* The soft, fleshy tissue at the lowest portion of the external ear.

ear·ly (érli) *adj.* **-lier, -liest. 1.** Near the beginning of a given series, period of time, or course of events: *in the early evening.* **2.** In or belonging to a distant or remote period or stage of development; primitive: *Early man discovered fire.* **3.** Occurring, developing, or appearing before the expected or usual time. **4.** Occurring in the near future: *Experts are hoping for an early settlement of the dispute.* *~adv.* **1.** Near the beginning of a given series, period of time, or course of events. **2.** Before the expected or arranged time: *They left early.* **—early on.** Near the beginning of a given period or course of events. [Middle English *erly, erliche,* Old English *ǣrlīce,* from *ǣr,* ERE.] **—ear·li·ness** *n.*

Usage: The phrase *earlier on* is criticised on the grounds that the *on* is neither necessary nor compatible in meaning with *earlier* (which is backwards in time, not onwards).

early bird *n.* A person who habitually arises early or arrives before others.

Early Bird *n.* Any of a number of communication satellites that provide telephone channels between Europe and the United States. The first was launched into stationary orbit in 1965.

ear·ly-clos·ing day *n. British.* A day, usually Wednesday or Thursday, on which many shops close after lunchtime to satisfy legal requirements.

Early English *n.* A style of architecture prevalent in England from the late 12th to the late 13th centuries, characterised by pointed arches, lancet windows, and simple tracery.

ear·ly-warn·ing system *n.* A system designed to give warning of some forthcoming danger, such as an enemy attack or an earthquake.

ear·mark (éer-maark) *n.* **1.** An identifying mark on the ear of a domestic animal. **2.** Any identifying feature or characteristic. *~tr.v.* **earmarked, -marking, -marks. 1.** To mark the ear of (a domestic animal) for identification. **2.** To place an identifying or distinctive mark on. **3.** To reserve or set aside for some purpose: *earmark goods for special customers.*

ear·muff (éer-muff) *n.* Either of a pair of fur or warm cloth ear coverings often attached to an adjustable headband and worn to protect the ears against cold.

earn (ern) *tr.v.* **earned, earning, earns. 1.** To gain or deserve (a salary, wages, or other reward) for one's service, labour, or performance. **2. a.** To acquire or deserve as a result of one's behaviour: *He has earned the disapproval of his peers.* **b.** To make liable to: *His incompetence earned him a ticking-off.* **3.** To produce (interest or return) as profit. [Middle English *ernen,* Old English *earnian,* to earn, merit, akin to *esne,* labourer.]

earn·er (érnər) *n.* **1.** One that earns. **2.** *British Informal.* A profitable job, hobby, investment, or the like, bringing in money fairly effortlessly and sometimes illegally; used especially in the phrase *a nice little earner.*

ear·nest[1] (érnist) *adj.* **1.** Seriously determined; eager; zealous: *an earnest attempt.* **2.** Showing deep sincerity or feeling; serious: *an earnest gesture of goodwill.* **3.** Of an important or vital nature; not trivial or petty: *an earnest conference affecting world peace.* **—See** Synonyms at **eager, serious. —in earnest.** With a purposeful or serious intent. [Middle English *ernest,* Old English *eornost,* zeal, seriousness.] **—ear·nest·ly** *adv.* **—ear·nest·ness** *n.*

earnest[2] *n.* **1.** Money paid in advance as part payment to bind a contract or bargain. Also called "earnest money". **2.** A token of something to come; a promise or assurance. [Middle English *ernest, ernes,* from Old French *erres,* plural of *erre,* pledge, earnest money, from Latin *arra, arrha,* short for *arrabō, arrhabō,* pledge, from Greek *arrabon,* from Hebrew *'ērābhōn,* security, pledge, from *'ārabh,* he pledged.]

earn·ings (érningz) *pl.n.* Something earned, especially: **1.** The salary or wages of a person. **2.** The profits of a business enterprise. **3.** Gains from investment.

Earp (erp), **Wyatt (Berry Stapp)** (1848–1929). U.S. frontier figure, buffalo hunter, and gambler. In Tombstone, Arizona, he came into conflict with Ike Clanton and his gang, which led to the gunfight at the O.K. Corral on October 26, 1881.

ear·phone (éer-fōn) *n.* A device that converts electric signals, as from a telephone or radio receiver, to audible sound and that is worn or held in contact with the ear.

ear·piece (éer-péess) *n.* The part of a telephone handset held next to the ear.

ear·pierc·ing (éer-peer-sing) *adj.* Loud and shrill enough to hurt the ears; deafening.

ear·plug (éer-plug) *n.* A small wad, as of cotton wool or wax, placed in the ear to exclude noise or water.

ear·ring (éer-ing, -ring) *n.* An ornament or jewel worn on or hanging from the ear lobe.

ear shell *n.* A mollusc, the **abalone** (see).

ear·shot (éer-shot) *n.* The range within which sound can be heard; hearing distance.

ear·split·ting (éer-splitting) *adj.* Loud and shrill enough to hurt the ears; deafening.

earth (erth) *n.* **1.** *Often capital* **E. a.** *Abbr.* **E.** The third planet from the Sun, having a sidereal period of revolution about the Sun of 365.26 days at a mean distance of 149.6 million kilometres (92.96 million miles), an axial rotation period of 23 hours 56.07 minutes, an average radius of 6 378 kilometres (3963 miles), and a mass of 5.974×10^{24} kilograms (13.17×10^{24} pounds). **b.** The land surface of the world, as distinguished from the oceans and air. **2.** The softer, friable part of land; soil; especially, productive soil. **3.** The dwelling place of mortal men, as distinguished from heaven and hell; the temporal world. **4.** All of the human inhabitants of the world: *The earth received the news with joy.* **5.** Worldly affairs; temporal matters, as distinguished from spiritual concerns: *the temptations of the earth.* **6.** The material body of the human being considered as made of dust or clay. **7.** In ancient thought, one of the four **elements** *(see).* **8.** The lair of a burrowing animal. **9.** *Informal.* A large or excessive amount of money. Preceded by *the:* *charged us the earth.* **10.** *Electricity.* A connection between an electrical device or circuit and the earth. Also *chiefly U.S.* "ground". **11.** *Chemistry.* Any of several metallic oxides that are difficult to reduce, such as alumina or zirconia, formerly regarded as elements. **12.** *Geology.* A loose, fine-grained amorphous deposit such as fuller's earth or diatomaceous earth. See **alkaline earth, rare earth. —on earth.** Used as an intensive: *Where on earth have you been?* **—run to earth. 1.** To pursue (a fox, for example) to its lair; hunt down. **2.** *Informal.* To find; track down. *~v.* **earthed, earthing, earths. 1.** To cover or heap up (plants, seeds, or roots) with soil for protection. **2.** To chase (an animal) into an underground lair. **3.** To connect (a device or circuit) to earth. *—intr.* To burrow or hide in the ground, as a fox does. [Middle English *erthe,* Old English *eorthe,* from Germanic.]

earth·born (érth-born) *adj.* **1.** Springing from or born on the earth. **2.** Human; mortal.

earth·bound, earth-bound (érth-bownd) *adj.* **1. a.** Attached or confined to or by the earth and earthly interests. **b.** Unimaginative; ordinary. **2.** Heading for the earth: *an earthbound meteor.*

earth closet *n.* A lavatory in which excreted matter is covered with earth.

earth·en (érth'n, érth'n) *adj.* **1.** Made of dirt, soil, or earth: *an earthen fortification.* **2.** Made of baked clay: *an earthen vase.*

earth·en·ware (érth'n-wair, érth'n-) *n.* **1.** A variety of coarse, porous baked clay. **2.** Ware made from clay, such as dishes, pots, and tableware. *~adj.* Made of earthenware.

earth·light (érth-līt) *n.* **Earthshine** *(see).*

earth·ling (érthling) *n.* **1.** One who inhabits the Earth; a human being, especially as opposed to an extraterrestrial being. **2.** A person devoted to worldly things.

earth·ly (érthli) *adj.* **1.** Of the planet Earth, specifically: **a.** Not heavenly or divine; secular. **b.** Terrestrial. **2.** Conceivable; feasible; possible: *no earthly meaning whatever.* *~n. Informal.* **1.** The least idea. Used in the negative: *It's no good asking him directions: he doesn't have an earthly.* **2.** The least chance. Used in the negative: *You're backing that grey horse to win! It doesn't stand an earthly.* **—earth·li·ness** *n.*

earth·man (érth-man) *n., pl.* **-men** (-men, -mən). An inhabitant of the Earth; an earthling. Used chiefly in science fiction.

earth mother *n. Often capital* **E,** *capital* **M. 1.** A mother goddess considered as the giver of fruitfulness. **2.** A woman combining maternal and sensual qualities.

earth mover *n.* A vehicle with a mechanical shovel for excavating soil, dirt, rock, or the like.

earth·nut (érth-nut) *n.* **1. a.** An Old World plant, *Conopodium majus,* having edible, nutlike tubers. **b.** The tuber of this plant. Also called "pignut". **2.** Any of various other plants having similar edible tubers or underground parts.

earth pig *n.* Also **earth hog.** *Archaic.* An aardvark.

earth·quake (érth-kwayk) *n.* A series of shock waves in the Earth's crust or upper mantle, caused by sudden release of strains accumulated along geological faults and by volcanic action, and resulting in movements in the Earth's surface.

earth·rise (érth-rīz) *n.* The rise of the Earth above the Moon's horizon, as seen from the lunar surface or from a satellite.

earth satellite *n.* A satellite that orbits the Earth.

earth science *n.* Any of several essentially geological sciences concerned with the origin, structure, and physical phenomena of the earth.

earth·shak·ing (érth-shayking) *adj.* Of enormous consequence or fundamental importance.

earth·shat·ter·ing (érth-shattəring) *adj.* Earthshaking.

earth·shine (érth-shīn) *n.* The sunlight reflected from the Earth's surface that illuminates part of the Moon not directly lit by the Sun. Also called "earthlight".

earth·star (érth-staar) *n.* A fungus of the genus *Geastrum,* related to the puffballs and having an outer covering that splits open in a starlike form.

earth·ward (érthwərd) *adj.* Heading towards the Earth; earthbound. *~adv. Chiefly U.S.* Variant of **earthwards.**

earth·wards (érthwərdz) *adv.* Also *chiefly U.S.* **earthward.** To or towards the Earth.

earth wax *n.* **Ozocerite** *(see).*

earth wolf *n. Archaic.* An aardwolf.

earth·work (érth-wurk) *n. Often plural.* **1.** An earthen embankment, especially when used as a military fortification. **2.** Excavation and embankment of earth. **—See** Synonyms at **bulwark.**

earth·worm (érth-wurm) *n.* Any of various terrestrial annelid worms of the class Oligochaeta and especially of the family Lumbricidae, that burrow into and help aerate and enrich soil.

earth·y (érthi) *adj.* **-ier, -iest. 1.** Consisting of or resembling earth or soil. **2.** Pertaining to or characteristic of this world; worldly. **3.** Crude or coarse; unrefined: *earthy humour.* **4.** Uninhibited; hearty. —**earth·i·ness** *n.*

ear trumpet *n.* A horn-shaped instrument formerly used to direct sound into the ear of a partially deaf person.

ear·wax (éer-waks) *n.* The waxlike secretion of certain glands lining the canal of the outer ear; cerumen.

ear·wig (éer-wig) *n.* Any of various insects of the order Dermaptera, such as the European species *Forficula auricularia,* having pincerlike appendages protruding from the rear of the abdomen. ~*tr.v.* **earwigged, -wigging, -wigs.** To attempt to influence by insinuation or subterfuge. [Middle English *erwigge,* Old English *ēarwicga,* "ear insect" (thought to be able to penetrate a person's head through the ear) : EAR + *wicga,* insect.]

ear·wit·ness (éer-wít-niss, -wit-, -nəss) *n.* A person who has heard a conversation, accident, or the like, and is able to give an account of it, as in court.

ease (eez) *n.* **1.** The condition of being without discomfort; freedom from pain, worry, or agitation. **2.** Freedom from constraint, embarrassment, or awkwardness; poise; naturalness: *the ease of his approach to a stranger.* **3.** Freedom from difficulty, hard work, or great effort; readiness; facility: *play tennis with ease.* **4.** A state of rest or relaxation. **5.** Freedom from financial difficulty; affluence. —**at ease.** *Military.* In a position of rest, with the feet apart. —See Synonyms at **rest.** ~*v.* **eased, easing, eases.** —*tr.* **1.** To free from pain, worry, agitation, or trouble; soothe; comfort. **2.** To alleviate or lighten (discomfort); mitigate; lessen. **3.** To slacken the strain, pressure, tension, or stress of; loosen. Often used with *away, down, up,* or *off: ease off a cable.* **4.** To reduce the difficulty of. **5.** To move or fit into place or position slowly and carefully: *ease the patient onto the stretcher.* —*intr.* To lessen in discomfort, effort, difficulty, pressure, or the like. Often used with *up* or *off.* [Middle English *ese,* from Old French *aise,* comfort, convenience, from Latin *adjacēns,* nearby, adjacent, from *adjacēre,* to lie near : *ad-,* near to + *jacēre,* to lie, from *jacere,* to throw.]

ease·ful (éez-f'l) *adj.* Affording or characterised by comfort and peace; restful. —**ease·ful·ly** *adv.* —**ease·ful·ness** *n.*

ea·sel (éez'l) *n.* A frame, usually in the form of an upright tripod, upon which something may be displayed or which may support an artist's canvas. [Dutch *ezel,* "ass", from Middle Dutch *esel,* from Common Germanic *asiluz* (unattested), from Latin *asinus.*]

ease·ment (éezmənt) *n.* **1.** The act of easing or the condition of being eased. **2.** Something that affords ease or comfort. **3.** *Law.* A right afforded a person to make limited use of another's land, such as the right of way.

eas·i·ly (éezili) *adv.* **1.** Without difficulty or stress: *a problem easily solved.* **2.** Without doubt or question; certainly: *easily the best buy this season.* **3.** Perhaps; possibly: *That may easily have been a mistake.*

eas·i·ness (éeziniss) *n.* **1.** The condition or quality of being easy to accomplish, acquire, or the like. **2.** Ease of manner; nonchalance; poise.

east (eest) *n. Abbr.* **e, E, e., E. 1. a.** The direction of the earth's axial rotation. **b.** The cardinal point on the mariner's compass 90° clockwise from north and directly opposite west. **2.** Any area or region lying in this direction. **3.** *Often capital* **E.** The eastern part of any country or region. **4. a.** One of the four positions occupied by players in a game of bridge. **b.** The player occupying this position. —**the East. 1.** The eastern part of the earth, especially Asia and its neighbouring islands; the Orient. **2.** The former Communist countries of eastern Europe. ~*adj.* **1.** To, towards, of, facing, or in the east. **2.** Coming from or originating in the east. Said of a wind. **3.** *Capital* **E.** Officially or conventionally designating the eastern part of a country, continent, or other geographical area: *East Anglia.* ~*adv.* In, from, or towards the east. [Middle English *e(a)st,* Old English *ēast,* from Germanic.]

East An·gli·a (áng-gli-ə). Region in the east of England consisting of Norfolk, Suffolk, and parts of Cambridgeshire and Essex. It was once an Anglo-Saxon kingdom. Its main crops are wheat, barley, and sugar beet. Some of the best agricultural land in England is to be found in the flat fenland. In the Middle Ages, wool made it an area of great wealth. —**East An·gli·an** *n. & adj.*

East Asia. See **Far East, the.**

east·bound (éest-bownd) *adj.* Going towards the east.

east by north *n.* The direction or point on the mariner's compass halfway between due east and east-northeast. It is 78° 45′ east of due north. —**east-by-north** *adj. & adv.*

east by south *n.* The direction or point on the mariner's compass halfway between due east and east-southeast. It is 101° 15′ east of due north. —**east-by-south** *adj. & adv.*

East Cape. Most easterly point of New Zealand on North Island.

East China Sea. *Chinese* **Dong Hai** (dóng hî) or **Tung Hai.** Shallow section of the west Pacific Ocean. Bounded by China, South Korea, Taiwan, and the Ryukyu Islands, it is a rich fishing ground.

East End *n.* A densely populated working-class and immigrant area of London containing industrial and, formerly, dock areas. —**East End** *adj.,* **East End·er** *n.*

Eastern European Mutual Assistance Treaty *n.* The **Warsaw Pact** *(see).*

East·er (éestər) *n.* **1.** A festival in the Christian Church commemorating the Resurrection of Christ, celebrated on the first Sunday following the full moon that occurs on or just after March 21. **2.** The Sunday on which this festival is held. Also called "Easter Day", "Easter Sunday". **3.** The time leading up to or following this festival. [Middle English *ester, estre,* Old English *ēastre* (usually in plural *ēastron*); probably from *Eostre,* Germanic goddess whose festival occurred in the spring.]

Easter bunny *n. Chiefly U.S.* A rabbit, in popular folklore, that supposedly brings Easter eggs as presents for children at Easter.

Easter egg *n.* A chocolate egg, decorated hen's egg, or egg-shaped ornament offered as a gift at Easter.

Easter Island. Volcanic island in the South Pacific Ocean, 3 700 kilometres (2,300 miles) west of Chile of which it is part, discovered on Easter Day, 1722, by the Dutchman Roggeveen. It is famous for its colossal heads (up to 9 metres; 30 feet high) carved from tufa from the Rano Roraku volcano, and its wooden tablets with their ideographic scripts, which may be the work of the ancestors of the island's Polynesian inhabitants.

Easter lily *n.* Any of various white-flowered lilies that bloom around Easter, especially *Lilium longiflorum.* This species is also called "Bermuda lily".

east·er·ly (éestərli) *adj.* **1.** Situated in or towards the east. **2.** From the east. Said of wind. ~*n., pl.* **easterlies.** A storm or wind from the east. —**east·er·ly** *adv.*

Easter Monday *n.* The Monday following Easter Sunday.

Easter week *n.* The week beginning on Easter Sunday.

east·ern (éestərn) *adj. Abbr.* **e, E, e., E. 1.** Situated towards, in, or facing the east. **2.** Coming from the east. Said of wind. **3.** Native to or growing in the east. **4.** *Often capital* **E.** Of, pertaining to, or characteristic of eastern regions or the East. **5.** *Capital* **E.** Of, pertaining to, or characteristic of the eastern part of the earth, especially Asia and its neighbouring islands; Oriental: *Eastern philosophy.* **6.** *Capital* **E.** Of or pertaining to the Eastern Churches, especially the Eastern Orthodox Church, as distinguished from the Roman Catholic. [Middle English *esterne,* Old English *ēasterne.*]

East·ern Bloc *n.* The countries of the **Warsaw Pact** *(see).*

Eastern Cape New province of South Africa, created in 1994, including the southeastern part of the former Cape Province and the former homelands of Transkei and Ciskei. Capital: Bisho.

Eastern Church *n.* **1.** The Church of the Roman Empire in the east, as distinguished from the Western Church, and including the patriarchates of Constantinople, Antioch, Alexandria, and Jerusalem. Also called "Greek Church". **2.** Any of the churches which have developed from this, especially: **a.** The Eastern Orthodox Church. **b.** Any of the Uniat Churches following the rites of the Eastern Orthodox Church.

Eastern Empire *n.* See **Byzantine Empire.**

east·ern·er (ée-stərnər) *n. Often capital* **E.** A native or inhabitant of the East or the eastern part of a country.

Eastern Europe. Formerly political, now geographical region of **Europe** comprising Albania, Bulgaria, Hungary, Poland, Romania, parts of the former U.S.S.R., and the former East Germany, Yugoslavia and Czechoslovakia. After World War II, Communist regimes friendly to the U.S.S.R. were set up in all the other countries. The U.S.S.R. refused **Marshall Aid,** forced its satellites to do the same, and founded **COMECON** (1949) to coordinate economic planning for the region. The U.S.S.R. also set up the **Warsaw Pact** (signed 1955). After Mikhail Gorbachev came to power in the U.S.S.R., his reforms encouraged change away from Communism throughout the region; the Warsaw Pact was disbanded, and Comecon was replaced by a new body, the Council for Mutual Economic Assistance, itself abolished in 1991.

Eastern Europe is a transitional area between the temperate Atlantic lands and the central Eurasian landmass with its climatic extremes. It generally has less than 750 millimetres (30 inches) of rain a year.

Some 45 per cent of Eastern Europe is cultivated, and a further 20 per cent is grazing land. Potatoes, sugar beet, rye, oats, wheat, and maize are grown on the best land. Bohemia is noted for hops, the Balkan basins for cotton and tobacco, the Adriatic coast for citrus and olives, and parts of the south for grapes and wines. Eastern Europe outside the former U.S.S.R. has few natural resources and relies on imported raw materials. The Czech Republic, Poland, and, to a lesser extent, Hungary are the most industrialised countries of the region. See map, next page.

Eastern Hemisphere *n.* The part of the earth, approximately half, east of the Greenwich meridian including the continents of Europe, Africa, Asia, and Australia.

east·ern·most (ée-stərn-mōst) *adj.* Farthest east.

Eastern Orthodox Church *n.* The body of modern churches, including the Greek and Russian Orthodox, derived from the Church of the Byzantine Empire and acknowledging the primacy of the patriarch of Constantinople. Also called "Eastern Church", "Orthodox Church".

Eastern Roman Empire *n.* See **Byzantine Empire.**

Eastern Standard Time *n. Abbr.* **EST, E.S.T.** One of the four standard time zones of North America, based on the local time at the 75th meridian west of Greenwich, five hours behind Greenwich Mean Time.

EASTERN EUROPE

Easter Sunday *n.* The Sunday on which the festival of Easter is held. Also called "Easter", "Easter Day".

East·er·tide (ée-stər-tīd) *n.* **1.** The Easter season, extending in different churches from Easter to Ascension Day, Whitsunday, or Trinity Sunday. **2.** The week following Easter Sunday. In this sense, also called "Easter week".

East Germany. The unofficial name for the former German Democratic Republic. See **Germany**.

East India Company *n.* Any of several European companies organised in the 17th and 18th centuries to trade with the East Indies; especially, the company chartered to do so by the British government in 1600.

East Indiaman *n.* Formerly, a large, full-rigged merchant ship used in trade with the East Indies.

East In·dies (ín-diz ǁ -deez). Name formerly applied to India, the Malay Peninsula, and the Malay Archipelago. Subsequently it included only the Malay Archipelago or only the Dutch East Indies (the islands of the Malay Archipelago which became the Republic of Indonesia after World War II).

east·ing (éesting) *n.* **1.** *Nautical.* **a.** The distance sailed by a ship on an easterly course. **b.** The longitudinal distance from a given meridian on an easterly course. **2.** An easterly direction.

East London. Important seaport in the Eastern Cape Province of South Africa, at the mouth of the Buffalo river on the Indian Ocean.

East Lothian. Administrative Unitary Authority area in southeast Scotland.

East·man (éestmən), **George** (1854–1932). U.S. businessman and inventor. He invented a dry-plate process of film development, the roll of film, the Kodak camera, and a process for colour photography. In 1892 he founded the Eastman Kodak company in Rochester, New York.

east-north-east (éest-nawrth-éest; *nautical* -nawr-éest) *n. Abbr.* **ENE** The direction or point on the mariner's compass halfway between due east and northeast. It is 67° 30′ east of due north.

~*adj.* Situated towards, facing, or in this direction.

~*adv.* In, from, or towards this direction.

East Riding. See **Yorkshire**.

east-south-east (éest-sowth-éest) *n. Abbr.* **ESE** The direction or point on the mariner's compass halfway between due east and southeast. It is 112° 30′ east of due north.

~*adj.* Situated towards, facing, or in this direction.

~*adv.* In, from, or towards this direction.

East Sussex. County in southeast England: the eastern parts of the former county of Sussex on the English Channel.

east·ward (éestwərd) *adj.* Also **east·ward·ly** (-li). Towards, facing, or in the east.

~*n.* An eastward direction, point, or region.

~*adv.* Chiefly U.S. Variant of **eastwards**.

east·wards (éestwərdz) *adv.* Also *chiefly U.S.* **eastward**. Towards the east.

eas·y (éezi) *adj.* **-ier, -iest. 1.** Capable of being accomplished or acquired with ease; posing no difficulty: *"How easy is success to*

those who will only be true to themselves" (Anthony Trollope). **2.** Free from worry, anxiety, trouble, or pain: *"Now as I was young and easy under the apple boughs"* (Dylan Thomas). **3.** Conducive to rest or comfort; pleasant and relaxing. **4.** Relaxed; easy-going; informal: *an easy, sociable manner.* **5.** Not strict or severe; lenient: *an easy rule.* **6. a.** Readily persuaded or influenced; compliant. **b.** *Informal.* Ready to accept others' decisions; not having strong personal preferences: *I'm easy.* **7.** Not strained, hurried, or forced; moderate: *an easy walk.* **8.** *Economics.* **a.** Small in demand and therefore readily obtainable: *Commodities are easier.* **b.** Plentiful and therefore obtainable at low interest rates: *easy credit.* **9.** *Informal.* Easily, often dishonestly, obtained: *easy money.*
~*adv. Informal.* **1.** In a relaxed manner: *breathe easy.* **2.** Carefully; cautiously: *Go easy round these bends.* —**go easy on.** *Informal.* To exercise moderation in one's approach to: *Go easy on the new recruits.* —**take it easy.** *Informal.* **1.** To refrain from exertion; relax. **2.** To refrain from anger or violence; stay calm. [Middle English *esy*, from Old French *aisie*, past participle of *aisier*, to put at ease, from *aise*, EASE.]
Usage: *Easy* is used in Standard English as an adverb in only a few idiomatic or informal constructions, such as *easy come easy go*, *easier said than done*, and *take things easy*. The usual adverbial form is *easily*, as in *The handle turns easily*.

eas·y·care (ēézi-kaír) *adj.* Referring to fabrics, usually artificial or specially treated, that are easy to clean and maintain, and resistant to creasing.

easy chair *n.* A large, comfortable, well-upholstered chair.

eas·y·go·ing, eas·y·go·ing (ēézi-gō-ing, -gō-) *adj.* **1. a.** Living without intense worry; placid. **b.** Lazy and careless. **c.** Lax in moral attitudes. **2.** Undemanding: *an easy-going life.* **3.** Having or moving at an even gait. Said of a horse.

easy meat *n. Chiefly British Slang.* A person who is easily persuaded or taken advantage of.

easy street *n. Informal.* A condition of financial security or independence: *A substantial inheritance put them on easy street.*

eat (ēet) *v.* **ate** (et, ayt), **eaten** (ēét'n), **eating, eats.** —*tr.* **1. a.** To take into the mouth, chew, and swallow (food). **b.** To consume the edible parts of: *eat a chop.* **c.** To take regularly as food. **2.** To consume, ravage, or destroy by or as if by eating. Usually used with *away* or *up.* **3.** To erode or corrode. **4.** *Informal.* To vex; worry. —*intr.* **1.** To consume food; have or take a meal or meals. **2.** To exercise a gradual consuming or eroding effect. Used with *into: eating into our resources.* —**eat (one's) words.** To retract something that one has said. —**eat out.** To eat in a restaurant or public place. —**eat up.** *Informal.* **1.** To absorb enthusiastically or avidly. **2.** To cover (a distance) rapidly. [Eat, ate, eaten; Middle English *eten, et, eten*, Old English *etan, ǣt, eten*.]
Usage: The past tense form *ate* is pronounced both as (et) and (ayt) in British English, the former being the more common. In American English, however, (ayt) is the standard form, with (et) being heard only in a few regional dialects, especially in the southern United States.

eat·a·ble (ēétab'l) *adj.* Fit to be eaten; edible.
~*n. Usually plural.* Something fit to be eaten; food.
Usage: *Eatable* and *edible* are sometimes interchangeable in the sense of "fit to be eaten", but usually there is a difference. *Eatable* refers to the extent to which food has been well prepared, and is palatable. *Edible* refers to the extent to which it is possible to treat a substance as food. Food which is edible may on occasion be uneatable, because of its condition. The colloquial use of *inedible*, as a synonym for *uneatable* in such contexts, is often heard.

eat·er (ēétər) *n.* **1.** One that eats. **2.** An eating apple.

eat·er·y (ēétəri) *n., pl.* **-ies.** *U.S. Informal.* A place for eating, such as a cafeteria.

eat·ing (ēéting) *n.* Food with respect to its flavour or quality: *The peaches were not only beautiful, they were good eating.*
~*adj.* Suitable for eating raw: *eating apples.*

eating disorder *n.* Anorexia, bulimia, or the like. —**eating-disordered** *adj.*

eating house *n.* A restaurant, especially in former times; a cook's house.

eats (ēets) *pl.n. Informal.* Food.

eau de cologne (ṓ də kə-lōn) *n., pl.* **eaux de cologne** (ṓ, ōz). A toilet water, **cologne** *(see).*

eau de nil (ṓ də néel) *n.* A pale green. [French, "water of (the) Nile".]

eau de vie (ṓ də vée) *n., pl.* **eaux de vie** (ṓ, ōz). Brandy. [French, "water of life".]

eaves (ēevz) *pl.n.* The projecting overhang at the lower edge of a roof. [Middle English *eves*, Old English *yfes, efes*, eaves, edge, border; probably akin to OVER.]

eaves·drop (ēévz-drop) *intr.v.* **-dropped, -dropping, -drops.** To listen secretly to the private conversation of others. Used with *on.* [Back-formation from *eavesdropper*, Middle English *evesdropper*, from *evesdrop*, water from the eaves, probably from Old English *yfesdrype*.] —**eaves·drop·per** *n.*

ebb (eb) *n.* **1. a.** The drawing back of the tide from the shore. **b.** An ebb tide. **2.** A fading away or diminishing; a decline: *the ebb and flow of a nation's prosperity.*
~*intr.v.* **ebbed, ebbing, ebbs.** **1.** To draw back from the shore. Used of a tide. **2.** To fade or diminish. Often used with *away.* [Old English *ebbian* (verb); *ebba* (noun), from West Germanic *abhigo* (unattested); akin to Gothic *ibuks*, moving backwards.]

ebb tide *n.* **1.** The receding tide between high water and a succeeding low water. Also called "ebb". **2.** The period during which the tide is receding. Compare **flood tide.**

Ebbw Vale (ébbōō váyl). Town in South Wales. Situated on the river Ebbw, it has declining coal, steel and tinplate industries.

Eb·lis (ébbliss). Also **Ib·lis** (ib-leess). The principal evil spirit or devil of Islamic mythology. [Arabic *Iblīs*, from Greek *diabolos*, slanderer. See **devil.**]

E-boat (ēé-bōt) *n.* A German torpedo boat in World War II. [From enemy *boat.*]

eb·on (ébbən) *adj. Poetic.* **1.** Made of ebony. **2.** Black. [Middle English *eban, ebenus*, from Old French, from Medieval Latin *ebanus*, from Greek *ebenos* (the tree), from Semitic.]

eb·on·ise, eb·on·ize (ébbə-nīz) *tr.v.* **-ised, -ising, -ises.** To finish with an ebony stain.

eb·on·ite (ébbə-nīt) *n.* A hard rubber, **vulcanite** *(see).* [EBON + -ITE.]

eb·on·y (ébbəni) *n., pl.* **-ies.** **1.** Any of several chiefly tropical trees of the genus *Diospyros*; especially, *D. ebenum*, of southern Asia, having hard, dark-coloured heartwood. **2.** The wood of such a tree, used in cabinetmaking and for piano keys. **3.** Black.
~*adj.* Made of or suggesting ebony. [Middle English, from Late Latin *ebeninus*, (made) of ebony, from Greek *ebeninos*, from *ebenos*, ebony tree, EBON.]

Eboracum, Eburacum. See **York.**

e·brac·te·ate (ee-brákti-ayt, -ət, -it) *adj. Botany.* Without bracts. [New Latin *ebracteatus* : EX- (out, without) + BRACTEATE.]

E·bro (ēébrō). Longest river completely in Spain. It rises in the Cantabrian Mountains in Santander province and flows 925 kilometres (575 miles) southeast to the Mediterranean Sea. It is navigable by seagoing vessels to Tortosa, 32 kilometres (20 miles) inland.

e·bul·li·ent (i-búl-iənt, -yənt, -bōōl-) *adj.* **1.** Overflowing with excitement, enthusiasm, or exuberance. **2.** Boiling. Said of a liquid. [Latin *ēbulliēns*, (stem *ēbullient-*) present participle of *ēbullīre*, to boil over : *ex-*, completely + *bullīre*, to boil.] —**e·bul·li·ence, e·bul·li·en·cy** *n.* —**e·bul·lient·ly** *adv.*

e·bul·li·os·co·py (i-búlli-óskəpi) *n.* A method of determining the molecular weight of a substance, based on measurements of the extent to which the boiling point of a solvent is altered by its presence in solution. [Latin *ēbullīre*, to boil over (see **ebullient**) + -SCOPY.] —**e·bul·li·o·scop·ic** (-ə-skóppik) *adj.*

eb·ul·li·tion (ébbə-lísh'n) *n.* **1.** The bubbling or effervescence of a liquid; a boiling. **2.** A sudden, violent outpouring, as of emotion or unrest: *"did not . . . give way to any ebullitions of private grief"* (W.M. Thackeray). [Late Latin *ēbullītīo* (stem *ēbullītīon-*), from Latin *ēbullīre*, to boil over. See **ebullient.**]

eb·ur·na·tion (ēéb-ər-náysh'n, éb-) *n. Pathology.* The degeneration of bone into a hard, ivory-like mass, such as occurs at the articulating surfaces of bones in osteoarthritis. [Latin *eburnus*, (made) of ivory, from *ebur*, IVORY.]

EC 1. European Community. **2.** Established Church.

e·cad (ēékad) *n. Biology.* An organism or group of organisms that differs from other members of its species as a result of environmental conditions. [EC(OLOGY) + -AD.]

é·car·té (ay-kártay) *n.* **1.** A card game for two players. **2.** In ballet, a position with an arm and a leg extended on the same side of the body. [French, past participle of *écarter*, to discard.]

ec·bol·ic (ek-bóllik) *adj.* Stimulating childbirth or abortion.
~*n.* A drug or other agent that stimulates childbirth or abortion. [Greek *ekbolē*, a throwing out, ejection, from *ekballein* : *ek-*, out + *ballein*, to throw.]

Ec·ce Ho·mo (éckay hómō, écki, éksi) *n.* A picture depicting Christ wearing the crown of thorns. [Latin, "Behold the Man", words used by Pontius Pilate to present Christ crowned with thorns to his accusers. John 19:5.]

ec·cen·tric (ik-séntrik ‖ ek-) *adj.* **1.** Departing or deviating from the conventional norm, especially in an odd or amusing way: *an eccentric recluse.* **2.** Deviating from a circular form, as in an elliptical orbit. **3.** Not situated at or in the centre. **4.** Not having the same centre. Said of figures such as circles, cylinders, and spheres. Compare **concentric.** —See Synonyms at **strange.**
~*n.* **1.** One that deviates markedly from a normal, conventional, or expected course or pattern; an odd or erratic person or thing. **2.** *Machinery.* A disc or wheel having its axis of revolution displaced from its centre so that it is capable of imparting reciprocating motion. [Middle English *excentryke*, not having the same centre (said of planets), from Late Latin *eccentricus*, from Greek *ekkentros* : *ex-*, out + *kentron*, point, centre, from *kentein*, to prick.] —**ec·cen·tri·cal·ly** *adv.*

ec·cen·tric·i·ty (ék-sen-tríssət-i, -s'n-) *n., pl.* **-ties.** **1. a.** Deviation from the normal, conventional, or expected. **b.** An instance of such deviation. **2. a.** The quality of being eccentric. **b.** The degree of being off-centre or not concentric. **3.** *Machinery.* The distance between the centre of an eccentric and its axis; the throw. **4.** *Mathematics.* The ratio of the distance of any point on a conic section from a focus to its distance from the corresponding directrix.
Synonyms: eccentricity, idiosyncrasy, quirk.

ec·chy·mo·sis (écki-mō-siss) *n.* **1.** The passage of blood from ruptured blood vessels into subcutaneous tissue as a result of bruising, marked by a purple discoloration of the skin. **2.** The resultant skin discoloration. [New Latin, from Greek *ekkhumōsis*, from *ekkhum-*

487

ousthai, to pour out : *ex-*, out of + *khumos*, juice, from *khein*, to pour.] —ec·chy·mot·ic (-móttik) *adj.*

Ec·cles (éck'lz). Town west of Manchester, England, on the river Irwell and the Manchester Ship Canal.

Eccles, Sir John Carew (1903–97). Australian neurophysiologist. He was awarded the Nobel prize (1963) for physiology or medicine, with A.L. Hodgkin (1914–) and A.F. Huxley (1917–), for his work on the transmission of signals from nerve cells.

Eccles cake *n.* A round or oval cake with a case of sugared flaky pastry and a currant filling. [After ECCLES in Greater Manchester.]

ec·cle·si·a (i-klée-zi-ə, -zhi-ə) *n., pl.* **-siae** (-zi-ee, -zhi-ee). **1.** The political assembly of citizens of an ancient Greek state. **2.** A church or congregation. [Latin *ecclēsia*, from Greek *ekklēsia*, duly summoned assembly, from *ekkalein*, to call out, summon : *ex-*, out + *kalein*, to call.] —ec·cle·sial *adj.*

Ec·cle·si·as·tes (i-kléezi-ásteez) *n. Abbr.* **Eccles.** A book of the Old Testament traditionally attributed to Solomon. [Latin *Ecclēsiastēs*, from Greek *ekklēsiastēs*, member of the assembly of citizens, from *ekklēsia*, ECCLESIA.]

ec·cle·si·as·tic (i-kléezi-ástik) *adj.* Ecclesiastical.
~*n.* A clergyman; a priest.

ec·cle·si·as·ti·cal (i-kléezi-ástik'l) *adj. Abbr.* **eccl., eccles.** Of or pertaining to a church, especially as an organised institution; clerical. —ec·cle·si·as·ti·cal·ly *adv.*

ecclesiastical calendar *n.* The calendar of feasts celebrated by the Christian Church, in which the year begins on the first Sunday of Advent.

ec·cle·si·as·ti·cism (i-kléezi-ásti-siz'm) *n.* **1.** Ecclesiastical principles, practices, and activities. **2.** Excessive adherence to ecclesiastical principles and forms.

Ec·cle·si·as·ti·cus (i-kléezi-ástikəss) *n.* A book of the Apocrypha. Also called "Wisdom of Jesus, the Son of Sirach".

ec·cle·si·ol·a·try (i-kléezi-óllətri) *n.* Worship of the church, especially extreme devotion to its principles or traditions. [From ECCLĒSI(A) + -LATRY.] —ec·cle·si·ol·a·ter *n.*

ec·cle·si·ol·o·gy (i-kléezi-óllэji) *n.* **1.** The study of the Christian Church as an institution. **2.** The study of ecclesiastical art, especially in relation to the architecture and decoration of churches. —ec·cle·si·o·log·i·cal (-ə-lójik'l) *adj.* —ec·cle·si·ol·o·gist *n.*

ec·crine (éck-rin, -reen || -rīn) *adj.* **1.** Secreting externally; especially, pertaining to an eccrine gland or its secretion. **2.** Merocrine. [Greek *ekkrinein*, to exude, secrete : *ex-*, out + *krinein*, to separate.]

eccrine gland *n.* Any of the small sweat glands distributed over the body's surface.

ec·crin·ol·o·gy (éckri-nólləji) *n.* The study of eccrine secretions and secretory organs. [ECCRINE + -LOGY.]

ec·dem·ic (ek-démmik) *adj.* Designating diseases that do not normally occur in a given population but which have been brought in by immigrants, travellers, and the like; not endemic. [Greek *ek-*, out, outside + *dēmos*, people (by analogy with *epidemic*).]

ec·dys·i·ast (ek-dízzi-ast || -əst) *n.* A striptease artist. Used humorously. [From ECDYSIS; coined by H.L. MENCKEN.]

ec·dy·sis (ékdi-siss) *n., pl.* **-ses** (-seez). The shedding of an outer integument or layer of skin, as by insects, crustaceans, and snakes. [New Latin, from Greek *ekdusis*, a stripping, from *ekduein*, to take off : *ex-* (reversal) + *duein*, to get into, put on, enter.]

ec·dy·sone (ek-dī-sōn || *U.S.* ékdi-sōn) *n.* A hormone secreted by insects and crustaceans that stimulates growth and moulting. [ECDYS(IS) + -ONE.]

e·ce·sis (i-sée-siss) *n.* The successful establishment of a plant in a new environment. [Greek *oikēsis*, habitation, from *oikein*, to dwell, from *oikos*, house.]

ECG **1.** electrocardiogram. **2.** electrocardiograph.

ec·hard (ék-aard, -haard) *n. Ecology.* Soil water not available for absorption by plants. [Greek *ekhein*, to hold, hold back + *ardein†*, to water, irrigate.]

ech·e·lon (ésha-lon) *n.* **1. a.** A steplike formation of troops in which units are parallel but unaligned. **b.** A similar formation of groups, units, or individuals. **c.** A similar formation or arrangement of vessels or aircraft. **2.** A subdivision of a military or naval force: *command echelon.* **3.** A level of responsibility or authority in a hierarchy. **4.** *Optics.* A specialised form of diffraction grating consisting of parallel glass plates of equal sizes, used to determine wavelengths, especially of spectral fine structures.
~*v.* **echeloned, -loning, -lons.** —*tr.* To arrange in echelon. —*intr.* To form, march, or move in echelon. [French *échelon*, "rung of a ladder", from Old French *eschelon*, from *eschile*, ladder, from Latin *scālae*, ladder, stairs.]

ech·e·ve·ri·a (échi-véer-i-ə, -və-rée-ə) *n.* Any of various tropical American plants of the genus *Echeveria*, having thick, succulent leaves often clustered in a rosette and commonly cultivated as house plants. [New Latin *Echeveria*, after M. *Echeveri*, 19th-century Mexican botanical illustrator.]

e·chid·na (i-kíd-nə) *n., pl.* **-nas** or **-nae** (-nee). Any of several burrowing, egg-laying mammals of the genera *Tachyglossus* and *Zaglossus*, of Australia, Tasmania, and New Guinea, having a spiny coat, slender snout, and a sticky tongue used for catching ants and termites. Also called "spiny anteater". [New Latin, from Latin, viper, from Greek *ekhidna*.]

ech·i·nate (écki-nayt) *adj. Biology.* Bearing or covered with spines; prickly; spiny. [Latin *echinātus*, from *echinus*, hedgehog. See **echino-**.]

echino-, echin- *comb. form.* Indicates prickly or covered with spines; for example, **echinoderm, echinoid.** [New Latin, from Latin *echinus*, hedgehog, sea urchin, from Greek *ekhinos*.]

e·chin·o·coc·ci·a·sis (i-kīnō-ko-ki-ə-siss) *n., pl.* **-ses** (-seez). Also **e·chin·o·coc·co·sis** (-kō-siss). **Hydatid disease** *(see).*

e·chi·no·coc·cus (i-kīnə-kóckəss) *n., pl.* **-cocci** (-kóks-ee, -kók-, -ī). Any of several parasitic tapeworms of the genus *Echinococcus*, the larvae of which infect mammals and form large, spherical cysts, causing serious or fatal disease. [New Latin *Echinococcus* : ECHINO- + COCCUS.]

e·chi·no·derm (i-kīn-ō-derm, -ə-) *n.* Any of numerous marine invertebrates of the phylum Echinodermata, which includes the starfishes, sea urchins, and sea cucumbers, having a calcareous skeleton just beneath the skin, and often covered with spines. [ECHINO- + -DERM.] —e·chi·no·der·mal (-dérm'l), e·chi·no·der·ma·tous (-dérmətəss) *adj.*

e·chi·noid (i-kī-noyd, écki-) *n.* Any echinoderm of the class Echinoidea, which includes the sand dollars and sea urchins. [ECHIN(O)- + -OID.]

e·chi·nus (i-kī-nəss) *n., pl.* **-ni** (-nī). *Architecture.* A curved moulding just below the abacus of a Doric capital. [Latin, "hedgehog", "sea urchin" (from the shape). See **echino-**.]

ech·o (éckō) *n., pl.* **-oes.** **1. a.** Repetition of a sound by reflection of sound waves from a surface. **b.** The sound produced in this manner. **c.** An electronic sound effect repeating a recorded sound. **2.** Any repetition or imitation of something, as of the opinions, speech, or dress of another: *The dress is an echo of Edwardian fashion.* **3.** One who imitates another, as in opinions, speech, or dress. **4.** A sympathetic response. **5.** A consequence or repercussion: *the echoes of her assassination.* **6.** The repetition of certain sounds or syllables in poetry. **7.** *Music.* The repetition of a note or phrase in a softer tone. **8.** A signal to a partner at bridge or whist that the same suit is to be continued. **9.** *Electronics.* A reflected wave received by a radio or radar.
~*v.* **echoed, -oing, -oes.** —*tr.* **1.** To repeat by or as by an echo; send back the sound of: *The canyon echoed her cry.* **2.** To repeat or imitate: *followers echoing the thoughts of the leader.* **3.** To be reminiscent of; resemble: *events echoing those of a century ago.* —*intr.* **1.** To be repeated by or as if by an echo. **2.** To resound with or emit an echo; reverberate: *woods echoing with hunting cries.* [Middle English *ecco, ecko*, from Old French *echo*, from Latin *ēchō*, from Greek *ēkhō*.] —ech·o·er *n.* —ech·o·ey *adj.*

Ech·o (éckō). *Greek Mythology.* A nymph whose unrequited love for Narcissus caused her to pine away until nothing but her voice remained.

ech·o·car·di·o·graph·y (éckō-kárdi-ógrəfi) *n. Medicine.* A diagnostic technique that uses ultrasound waves to investigate the action of the beating heart and to depict this on a screen. —ech·o·car·di·o·graph (-kárdi-ə-graaf, -graff) *n.* —ech·o·card·i·o·graph·ic (-ə-gráffik) *adj.*

echo chamber *n.* **1.** A room fitted with wall panels that reflect sound, used for making acoustic measurements and recordings requiring echo effects. **2.** Any electronic device that produces an echo effect.

ech·og·ra·phy (ek-óggrəfi) *n.* Investigation of the internal organs of the body using ultrasound waves, which are reflected from the tissues.

e·cho·ic (e-kó-ik) *adj.* **1.** Being or resembling an echo. **2.** Imitative of sounds; onomatopoeic. —e·cho·i·cal·ly *adv.*

ech·o·ism (éckō-iz'm) *n.* The formation of words in imitation of sounds; onomatopoeia.

ech·o·la·li·a (éckō-láyli-ə) *n. Psychology.* Involuntary repetition of words or phrases just spoken by others, occurring in some mental and language disorders. [ECHO + Greek *lalia*, talk, from *lalos*, talkative.] —ech·o·la·lic (-láylik) *adj.*

ech·o·lo·ca·tion (éckō-lō-káysh'n, -lə-) *n.* **1.** The ability of an animal that emits high-frequency sounds, such as a bat or dolphin, to orientate itself by means of the reflected sound waves. **2.** *Electronics.* Ranging by acoustical echo analysis.

ech·o·prax·i·a (éckō-práksi-ə) *n. Psychology.* Pathological imitation of the actions of another person, occurring as a symptom of certain mental disorders. —ech·o·prac·tic (-práktik) *adj.*

echo sounder *n.* A device for measuring the depth of water by sending a high-frequency pulse to the bottom and measuring the time taken for the echo to return. Also called "sonar", "asdic". —echo sounding *n.*

ech·o·vi·rus (éckō-vīr-əss) *n.* Any virus of a group originally isolated from the intestinal tract and thought to cause nonspecific meningitis, many illnesses causing symptoms of the common cold, and various gastrointestinal and respiratory-tract infections. [*En*teric *C*ytopathic *H*uman *O*rphan + VIRUS.]

echt (ekt || *German* ekht) *adj.* Genuine or typical. [German.]

Eck (ek), **Johann Maier von** (1486–1543). German theologian. When Luther published his 95 theses in 1517, Eck became his principal opponent and went to Rome to bring back the papal bull condemning him in 1520.

Eck·hart (éckaart), **Johannes,** also known as Meister Eckhart (*c.* 1260– *c.* 1328). German theologian of the Dominican order. He was considered the most accomplished scholar and preacher of his day, but in 1326 was accused of heresy.

é·clair (ay-kláir, i-) *n.* A light, tubular cake made of choux pastry with cream or custard filling and usually iced with chocolate. [French, "lightning", from Old French *esclair*, from *esclairier*, to light, flash, from Vulgar Latin *exclārāre* (unattested), variant of Latin *exclārāre* : *ex-*, completely + *clārāre*, to brighten, clarify, from *clārus*, bright, clear.]

ec·lamp·si·a (i-klámpsi-ə) *n. Pathology.* Coma and convulsions arising from any of several conditions during or immediately after pregnancy. [New Latin, from Greek *eklampsis*, a shining forth, brightness, from *eklampein*, to shine forth : *ex-*, out + *lampein*, to shine.] —**ec·lamp·tic** *adj.*

é·clat (ay-klá'a) *n.* **1.** Great brilliance, as of performance or achievement. **2.** Conspicuous success or acclaim. [French, explosion, from *éclater*, to burst, explode, from Old French *esclater*, from Germanic *slītan* (unattested), to tear, SLIT.]

ec·lec·tic (i-klέktik) *adj.* **1.** Choosing what appears to be the best from diverse sources, systems, or styles. **2.** Consisting of that which has been selected from diverse sources.
~*n.* One who follows an eclectic method. [Greek *eklektikos*, from *eklektos*, selected, from *eklegein*, to single out : *ex-*, out + *legein*, to choose.] —**ec·lec·ti·cal·ly** *adv.*

ec·lec·ti·cism (i-klέkti-siz'm) *n.* **1.** An eclectic system or method. **2.** Free selection, as of ideas, from diverse sources.

e·clipse (i-klíps) *n.* **1. a.** The partial or complete obscuring, relative to a designated observer, of one celestial body by another. **b.** The period of time during which such an obscuring occurs. **2.** Any temporary or permanent dimming or cutting off of light. **3.** Any falling into obscurity; an overshadowing or decline.
~*tr.v.* **eclipsed, eclipsing, eclipses. 1.** To cause an eclipse or obscuring of; darken. **2.** To obscure or overshadow the importance, fame, or reputation of; reduce in importance by comparison. [Middle English *eclipse*, from Old French, from Latin *eclīpsis*, from Greek *ekleipsis*, cessation, abandonment, from *ekleipein*, to leave out, abandon : *ek-, ex-*, out + *leipein*, to leave.]

e·clips·ing binary *n. Astronomy.* A binary star, one component of which is regularly eclipsed by the other as a result of its orbital plane lying in or near to the line of sight. Also called "eclipsing variable".

e·clip·tic (i-klíptik) *n. Astronomy.* **1.** The apparent path of the Sun relative to the stars; the intersection plane of the Earth's solar orbit with the celestial sphere. **2.** A great circle on a terrestrial globe inclined at an approximate angle of 23° 27' to the equator. [Middle English *ecliptik*, from Late Latin *eclīpticus*, from Latin, of an eclipse, from Greek *ekleiptikos*, from *ekleipein*, to abandon. See **eclipse.**] —**e·clip·tic** *adj.*

ec·lo·gite (éckla-jīt) *n.* A coarse-grained basic rock consisting of a greenish mixture of pyroxene, quartz, and feldspar with large red garnet inclusions. [Greek *eklogē*, selection (see **eclectic**) + -ITE.]

ec·logue (éck-log ‖ -lawg) *n.* A bucolic poem, typically a pastoral dialogue. [French *éclogue*, from Old French *eglogue*, from Latin *ecloga*, "selection", from Greek *eklogē*, from *eklegein*, to single out. See **eclectic.**]

e·clo·sion (i-klōzh'n) *n.* The emergence of an adult insect from a pupal case or of an insect larva from an egg. [French *éclosion*, from *éclore*, to open, be hatched, from Vulgar Latin *exclaudere* (unattested), variant of Latin *exclūdere*, to shut out : EX- + *claudere*, to shut, close.]

eco- *comb. form.* Indicates: **1.** Ecology or the natural environment, for example **ecosystem. 2.** Ecologically sound or beneficial; for example, **eco-tourism.**

ec·o·cide (éekō-sīd, éckō-) *n.* Deliberate or avoidable destruction of the natural environment, as by pollutants. [ECO- + -CIDE.]

E. coli (ee-kṓlī) *n.* A bacillus, *Escherichia coli*, normally found in the human gastrointestinal tract and existing as numerous strains, some of which are responsible for diarrhoeal disorders. [New Latin *Escherichia coli* : After Theodore Escherich (1857–1911), German doctor + *coli*, genitive of *colon*, COLON².]

e·col·o·gy (i-kóllaji) *n. Abbr.* **ecol. 1. a.** The science of the relationships between organisms and their environments. Also called "bionomics". **b.** The relationship between organisms and their environment. **2. a.** The study of the relationships between people and their environment. **b.** The relationship between a human group and its environment. In this sense, also called "human ecology". [German *Ökologie* : Greek *oikos*, house + -LOGY.] —**e·co·log·i·cal** (éeka-lójik'l, écka-) *adj.* —**e·co·log·i·cal·ly** *adv.* —**e·col·o·gist** (i-kóllajist) *n.*

e·con·o·met·rics (i-kónna-méttriks) *n. Used with a singular verb.* The application of statistical techniques to economics in the study of problems, the analysis of data, and the development of theory. [ECONO(MICS) + -METRIC.] —**e·con·o·met·ric, e·con·o·met·ri·cal** *adj.* —**e·con·o·me·tri·cian** (-ma-trísh'n), **e·con·o·met·rist** (-méttrist) *n.*

ec·o·nom·ic (éeka-nómmik, écka-) *adj.* **1.** Of or pertaining to the production, development, and management of material wealth, as of a country, household, or business enterprise. **2.** Of or pertaining to economics. **3.** Of or pertaining to matters of finance. **4.** *Chiefly British.* Financially self-sustaining or self-justifying. **5.** Economical. **6.** Of or pertaining to the necessities of life; utilitarian. —See Usage note at **economical.**

ec·o·nom·i·cal (éeka-nómmik'l, écka-) *adj.* **1.** Not wasteful or extravagant; prudent in management of resources. **2.** Operating or designed in a way that avoids waste or excessive costs. —See Synonyms at **sparing.** —**ec·o·nom·i·cal·ly** *adv.*

Usage: Economical can be used only in the context of "saving", "not being wasteful": *an economical way of life. Economic* is the only form to use when referring to the field of economics (*economic*

issues, economic growth). On the other hand, *economic* is also sometimes found as an alternative to *economical* in the sense of "saving" (as in *It's not economic to have a home freezer unless you buy in bulk*). If one considers such pairs as *economic prices* and *economical prices*, the former is the more likely to mean "prices that do not lose money" (for the producer), the latter the more likely to mean "prices that save money" (for the consumer).

economic geography *n.* The study of the distribution and use of economic resources throughout the world.

ec·o·nom·ics (éeka-nómmiks, écka-) *n.* **1.** *Used with a singular verb. Abbr.* **econ.** The social science that deals with the production, distribution, and consumption of commodities and the theory and operation of financial systems. **2.** *Used with a plural verb.* **a.** An economic basis. **b.** Relevant financial considerations.

e·con·o·mise, e·con·o·mize (i-kónna-mīz) *v.* **-mised, -mising, -mises.** —*intr.* To be frugal; reduce expenses. —*tr.* To save by being economical. —**e·con·o·mis·a·tion** (-mī-záysh'n) *n.*

e·con·o·mis·er (i-kónna-mīzər) *n.* **1.** One that economises. **2.** A device used in power stations, steam engines, or the like, that uses some of the waste heat from a boiler flue to preheat the feed water.

e·con·o·mist (i-kónna-mist) *n.* A specialist in economics.

e·con·o·my (i-kónnami) *n., pl.* **-mies.** *Abbr.* **econ. 1.** The careful or thrifty use or management of resources, as of income, materials, or labour. **2.** An example of this; a saving. **3.** The management of the resources of a country, community, or business. **4. a.** A system for the management and development of such resources: *a monetarist economy.* **b.** The economic system of a country or area: *Floods disrupted the economy of the region.* **5.** Artistic restraint or avoidance of ornamentation. **6.** The functional arrangement of elements within a structure or system: *the economy of an organism.* **7.** *Theology.* The divine plan or system for the world or for a specific period or nation. **8.** Economy class.
~*adj.* Allowing a saving to be made, as through bulk purchase: *economy size.* [Old French *economie*, management of a household, from Latin *oeconomia*, from Greek *oikonomia*, manager of a household : *oikos*, house + *-nomos*, managing (see **-nomy**).]

economy class *n.* The least expensive and least luxurious category of airline seating and service.

é·cor·ché (áy-kor-sháy) *n.* A picture of the body or part of the body with the skin removed so as to show the appearance of the muscles. [French, "skinned".]

ec·o·spe·cies (éekō-speesh-eez, éckō-, -spees-) *n.* A taxonomic species considered in terms of its ecological characteristics and usually including several ecotypes. [ECO- + SPECIES.]

e·co·sphere (éekō-sfeer, éckō-) *n.* The regions of the universe, particularly on the Earth, that are capable of supporting life.

é·coss·aise (áykoss-áyz) *n. Music.* **1.** A piece of music with a dancelike rhythm in 2/4 time. **2.** A lively dance to such music. [French, "Scottish (dance)".]

ec·o·sys·tem (éekō-sistəm, éckō-) *n.* An ecological community together with its physical environment, considered as a unit. [ECO- + SYSTEM.]

e·co·tone (éekō-tōn, éckō-) *n.* An ecological community of mixed vegetation formed by the overlapping of adjoining communities. [ECO- + Greek *tonos*, tension, TONE.]

e·co·type (éekō-tīp, éckō-) *n.* The smallest taxonomic subdivision of an ecospecies, consisting of subspecies or varieties adapted to a particular set of environmental conditions. [ECO- + TYPE.]

ec·ru (éck-rōō, áykrōō) *n.* Greyish to pale yellow or light greyish yellowish brown. [French *écru* : *é-* (intensive) + *cru*, crude, raw.] —**ec·ru** *adj.*

ec·sta·sy (éksta-si) *n., pl.* **-sies. 1.** A state of exalted delight. **2.** A state of any emotion experienced very intensely: *an ecstasy of anger.* **3. a.** The trance, frenzy, or rapture associated with mystic or prophetic exaltation. **b.** *Psychology.* An emotional state, associated with religious or sexual experience or with drug-taking, characterised by exuberant behaviour and loss of self-control. **4.** *Capital* E. *Abbr.* **E.** A drug, $C_{11}H_{15}NO_2$, that is a mood-elevating amphetamine derivative. [Middle English *extasie*, from Old French, from Late Latin *extasis, ecstasis*, from Greek *ekstasis*, from *existanai*, to displace, drive out of one's senses : *ex-*, out + *histanai*, to place.]
Synonyms: ecstasy, rapture, transport, exaltation, euphoria, bliss, delight.

ec·stat·ic (ik-státtik, ek-) *adj.* **1.** Of, relating to, induced by, or inducing ecstasy. **2.** In a state of ecstasy; enraptured.
~*n.* One subject to ecstasies. —**ec·stat·i·cal·ly** *adv.*

ECT, E.C.T. electroconvulsive therapy.

ec·thy·ma (ékthima) *n.* An inflammatory skin disease characterised by ulcerating pustules that penetrate to the lower layer of the skin and cause scarring when they heal. [New Latin, from Greek *ekthuma*, pustule, from *ekthuein*, to break out : *ek-*, out + *thuein*, to seethe.]

ecto- *comb. form.* Indicates outside or external part or surface; for example, **ectoderm, ectoplasm.** [Greek *ekto-*, from *ektos*, outside (after *entos*, inside), from *ek, ex*, out.]

ec·to·derm (éktō-derm) *n.* The outermost of the three primary germ layers of an embryo, developing into the epidermis, nervous tissue, and, in vertebrates, sense organs. Also called "exoderm". Compare **endoderm, mesoderm.** [ECTO- + -DERM.]

ec·tog·e·nous (ék-tójanəss) *adj.* Also **ec·to·gen·ic** (ékta-jénnik). Able to live and develop outside a host. Said of certain pathogenic microorganisms. [ECTO- + -GENOUS.]

ec·to·mere (ĕktō-meer) *n. Biology.* A blastomere that develops into ectoderm. [ECTO- + -MERE.]

ec·to·morph (ĕktō-mawrf) *n.* A lean, slightly muscular human build with a large surface area of skin in relation to body weight. Compare **endomorph, mesomorph.** [ECTO- + -MORPH.] —**ec·to·mor·phic** (-máwrfik) *adj.* —**ec·to·mor·phy** (-mawrfi) *n.*

–ectomy *n. comb. form.* Indicates removal of a part by surgery; for example, **tonsillectomy.** [New Latin *-ectomia* : Greek *ek-, ex-,* out + -TOMY.]

ec·to·par·a·site (ĕktō-párrə-sīt) *n.* A parasite, such as a flea, that lives on the exterior of another organism.

ec·to·pi·a (ĕk-tōpi-ə, ek-) *n. Pathology.* **1.** Misplacement of an organ or part, which may be congenital or due to injury. **2.** The occurrence of something in an unusual position. [New Latin, from Greek *ektopos,* away from a place : *ex-,* out of + *topos,* place (see **topic**).] —**ec·top·ic** (-tóppik) *adj.*

ectopic pregnancy *n. Pathology.* Gestation outside the uterus, often in a Fallopian tube.

ec·to·plasm (ĕktō-plaz'm) *n.* **1.** *Biology.* A portion of the cytoplasm distinguishable in some cells as a relatively rigidly gelled outer layer just beneath the cell membrane. Compare **endoplasm. 2.** The spectre or emanation allegedly conjured up by a spiritualistic medium. [ECTO- + -PLASM.] —**ec·to·plas·mic** (-plázmik) *adj.*

ec·to·proct (ĕktō-prokt) *n.* A colonial invertebrate animal, a **polyzoan.** [ECTO- + Greek *prōktos,* rectum.]

ec·to·sarc (ĕktō-saark) *n. Rare.* The relatively clear outermost layer of protoplasm of certain protozoans, such as the amoeba. [ECTO- + Greek *sarx* (stem *sark-*), flesh.]

E·CU (ay-kōo) *n., pl.* **ECUs.** *Sometimes small* **e.** A notional unit used for pricing goods within the European Economic Community independently of the currencies of individual member countries. See **euro.** [From *European Currency Unit.*]

é·cu (ay-kéw) *n., pl.* **écus** (ay-kéw). Any of various French gold or silver coins. [French, from Old French *escu,* from Latin *scūtum,* shield (from the shield stamped on the coin).]

Ec·ua·dor, Republic of (ĕkwə-dawr, -dór). Country in northwest South America. The Spanish occupied Quito, part of the Inca empire, in 1534, and the region became part of the viceroyalty of Peru and later of New Granada. By 1830 Ecuador had become an independent republic. Ecuador consists of a coastal plain in the west separated from Oriente in the Amazon Basin by the Andes. The Galápagos Islands 1 000 kilometres (600 miles) offshore in the Pacific, belong to Ecuador. The country is South America's second largest oil producer, an important member of OPEC, and the world's largest producer of balsawood. Area, 272 045 square kilometres (105,037 square miles). Population, 11,700,000. Capital, Quito. —**E·cua·do·ri·an, E·cua·do·re·an** *n. & adj.*

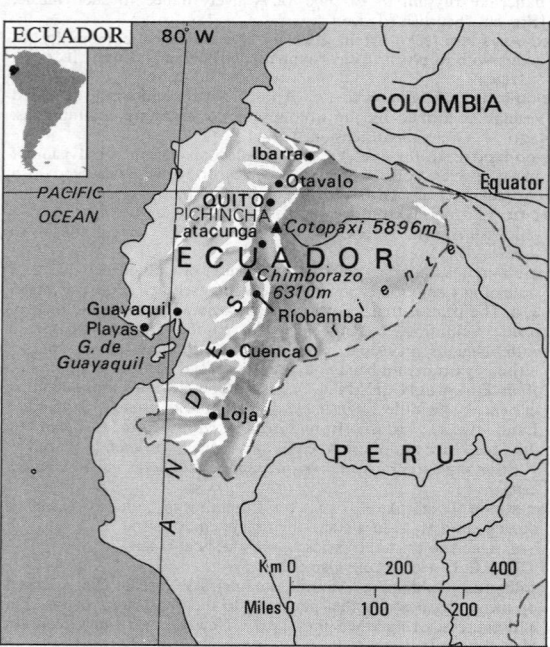

ec·u·men·i·cal (ēekew-ménnik'l, ĕckew-) *adj.* Also **ec·u·men·ic** (-ménnik). **1.** Universal; worldwide. **2.** Of or pertaining to the worldwide Christian church. **3.** Concerned with promoting unity between the churches. [Late Latin *oecūmenicus,* from Greek *oikoumenikos,* of the whole world, from *oikoumenē,* the inhabited world, from *oikein,* to inhabit, from *oikos,* house.] —**ec·u·men·i·cal·ism** *n.* —**ec·u·men·i·cal·ly** *adv.*

ecumenical council *n.* **1.** Any of several councils of the early Christian church. **2.** *Roman Catholic Church.* A general council of bishops.

ecumenical patriarch *n.* A **patriarch** *(see)* of the Eastern Orthodox Church.

ec·u·men·ism (i-kéw-mə-niz'm ‖ ĕc-kew-ménniz'm) *n.* **1.** A movement or doctrine promoting unity among the Christian churches. Also called "ecumenicalism". **2.** A movement or doctrine promoting worldwide unity among religions through greater cooperation and improved understanding.

ec·ze·ma (ĕk-simə, -smə ‖ ĕg-, ig-zée-) *n.* A noncontagious inflammation of the skin, marked mainly by redness, itching, and the outbreak of lesions that discharge serous matter and become encrusted and scaly. [New Latin, from Greek *ekzema,* eruption : *ex-,* out + *zema,* fermentation, boiling, from *zeein,* boil.] —**ec·zem·a·tous** (ek-sém-ətəss, ig-, -zéem-) *adj.*

–ed[1] *v. suffix.* Used to form the past tense of most verbs; for example, **removed.** [Middle English *-ede,* Old English *-ode, -ede, -ade.*]

–ed[2] *v. suffix.* Used to form past participles of most verbs; for example, **hoped.** [Middle English *-ed,* Old English *-od, -ed, -ad.*]

–ed[3] *adj. suffix.* Possessing, characterised by, or provided with; for example, **forked, grey-haired.** [Middle English *-ede, -de,* Old English *-ede.*]

ed. 1. edited; edited by; edition; editor. **2.** education.

e·da·cious (i-dáyshəss) *adj.* Gluttonous; voracious. Used humorously. [Latin *edax,* (stem *edāc-*) gluttonous, from *edere,* to eat.] —**e·dac·i·ty** (i-dáss-əti), **e·da·cious·ness** *n.*

Edam (ée-dam) *n.* A mild, yellow Dutch cheese, pressed into balls and usually covered with red wax. [After *Edam,* northwest Netherlands, town in which it is made.]

e·daph·ic (i-dáffik) *adj.* Of or pertaining to soil, especially as it affects living organisms. [Greek *edaphos,* ground, foundation, floor.] —**e·daph·ic·al·ly** *adv.*

Ed·da (éddə) *n.* **1.** A collection of Old Norse poems called the *Elder* or *Poetic Edda,* assembled in the 12th or early 13th century. **2.** A manual of Icelandic poetry, called the *Younger* or *Prose Edda,* compiled later. [Old Norse *edda;* perhaps from *óthr,* poetry.]

Ed·ding·ton (éddingtən), **Sir Arthur Stanley** (1882–1944). British astronomer and physicist. He was one of the earliest exponents of the theory of relativity (his *Mathematical Theory of Relativity* appeared in 1923).

ed·dy (éddi) *n., pl.* **-dies. 1.** A current, as of water or air, moving contrary to the direction of the main current, especially in a circular motion. **2.** A current that runs contrary to the main current or tradition, as of life, art, or philosophy; a byway.

~*v.* **eddied, -dying, -dies.** —*intr.* To move against the main current, as in an eddy. —*tr.* To cause to move against the main current, as in an eddy. —See Synonyms at **turn.** [Middle English *ydy,* probably from Old English *ed-,* back, again; akin to Old Norse *idha,* "that which flows back", whirlpool, from *idh-,* again.]

Ed·dy (éddi), **Mary Baker** (1821–1910). U.S. founder of the Christian Science movement (1876) and the newspaper, *Christian Science Monitor* (1908).

eddy current *n. Electricity.* An induced electric current in the iron core of an electromagnet, transformer, or the like, causing a loss of energy. Also called "Foucault current".

Ed·dy·stone Rocks (éddistən). Group of rocks dangerous to shipping, in the English Channel, 23 kilometres (14 miles) southwest of Plymouth. It has been the site of a lighthouse since 1698.

e·del·weiss (áyd'l-vīss ‖ *popularly* íd'l-) *n.* A plant, *Leontopodium alpinum,* of mountainous regions, especially the Alps, having leaves covered with whitish down and small flowers surrounded by conspicuous whitish bracts. [German *Edelweiss,* "noble white".]

E·den (ée'd'n) *n.* **1.** In the Bible, the first home of Adam and Eve; the earthly Paradise. Also called "Garden of Eden". **2.** Any delightful place or dwelling; a paradise. **3.** A state of bliss or ultimate happiness. [Middle English, from Late Latin *Ēden,* from Greek *Ēdēn,* from Hebrew *'ēdhen,* "(the place of) delight".]

Eden, (Robert) Anthony, Earl of Avon (1897–1977). British Conservative politician; Foreign Secretary 1935–8, 1940–5 and 1951–5; Prime Minister 1955–7. He entered Parliament in 1923, and in the 1930s was a determined opponent of Hitler and Mussolini. Convinced that Egypt's leader Nasser was a threat to world peace, he supported the 1956 Anglo-French invasion of Egypt in collusion with Israel; but international hostility to his policy forced a ceasefire. Domestic criticism and ill-health caused his resignation.

e·den·tate (ee-dén-tayt) *adj. Biology.* **1.** Lacking teeth. **2.** Of or belonging to the order Edentata, which includes mammals such as anteaters, armadillos, and sloths, having few or no teeth.

~*n.* A member of the Edentata. [Latin *edentātus,* toothless, from the past participle of *edentāre,* to take out the teeth : *ex-,* out + *dēns* (stem *dent-*), tooth.]

e·den·tu·lous (ee-déntewləss) *adj.* Lacking teeth. [See **edentate,** -ulous.]

É·des·sa (i-déssə). Town in central Macedonia, northern Greece. In ancient times it was Macedonia's capital, known as Aegea. It is a commercial and industrial centre known for the wine, fruit, and tobacco grown in the district.

Ed·gar or **Ead·gar** (édgər), also known as Edgar the Peaceful (*c.* 943–975). King of the English, son of Edmund I. After a revolt against his brother, Edwy, king of the English, he became king of the Mercians and Northumbrians and king of the English when Edwy died in 959.

Edgar the Aeth·e·ling (átholing) (*c.*1050–*c.*1130). English prince, grandson of Edmund Ironside. He was chosen king of the English when Harold was slain in the Battle of Hastings (1066), but submitted to the rule of William the Conqueror. After unsuccessful attempts to regain his kingdom he led the English expedition which deposed Donald III of Scotland and placed his nephew, also called Edgar, on the Scottish throne.

edge (ej) *n.* **1. a.** The usually thin, sharpened side of the blade of a cutting instrument, weapon, or tool. **b.** The degree of sharpness of a cutting blade. **c.** A penetrating or incisive quality: *"His simplicity sets off the satire, and gives it a finer edge"* (William Hazlitt). **2.** Keenness, as of desire or enjoyment; zest. **3.** A rim, brink, or crest, as of a cliff or ridge of hills. **4. a.** The line at the outside of a surface. **b.** The part of a surface nearest this line: *lying at the edge of the road.* **c.** A point close to an action or state: *on the edge of divorce.* **5.** The line of intersection of two surfaces of a solid: *the edge of a cube.* **6.** A margin of superiority; an advantage: *a slight edge over the opposition.* —See Synonyms at **border.** **—on edge. 1.** Highly tense or nervous; irritable. **2.** Eagerly anticipatory; impatient. **—set (one's) teeth on edge.** *Informal.* **1.** To give one an unpleasant nervous reaction or sensation, as of tingling. **2.** To provoke strong feelings of irritation or annoyance. **—take the edge off.** To soften or dull, as the pleasure, excitement, pain, or force of. *~v.* **edged, edging, edges.** *—tr.* **1.** To give an edge to; sharpen. **2.** To put a border or edging on. **3.** To advance or push gradually. **4. a.** To be the edge of. **b.** To be at the edge of. **5.** To cut the edge of (a lawn, for example). **6.** To hit (a cricket ball) with the edge of the bat. **7.** To dig the edge of (a ski) into the snow surface. *—intr.* To move gradually or hesitantly: *She edged towards the door.* [Middle English *egge,* Old English *ecg,* edge, point, sword; akin to Latin *acer,* sharp.]

Edge·hill (éj-híl). A ridge in the South Midlands of England on Warwickshire's southern border with Oxfordshire. It was here that the first battle in the English Civil War was fought, in 1642.

edge tool *n.* A tool, such as a chisel, having a cutting edge.

edge·ways (éj-wayz) *adv.* Also **edge·wise** (-wīz). **1.** With the edge foremost. **2.** On, by, with, or towards the edge. **—get a word in edgeways.** To manage to interrupt a talkative speaker.

Edge·worth (éj-wurth), **Maria** (1767–1849). Irish writer, born in England. Her most famous novel, *Castle Rackrent* (1800), a tale of ordinary Irish life, broke away from the romantic tradition of the 18th-century Gothic novel and helped to establish a realist tradition in English literature.

edg·ing (éjing) *n.* Something that forms or serves as an edge; a trimming; a border.

edg·y (éji) *adj.* **-ier, -iest. 1.** On edge; tense; nervous. **2.** With a sharp edge. **—edg·i·ly** *adv.* **—edg·i·ness** *n.*

edh, eth (eth) *n.* **1.** An old Germanic runic letter ð appearing in Old (and Middle) English, Old Saxon, Old Norse, and modern Icelandic. In the Scandinavian languages, it represents the interdental voiced fricative (transliterated as *dh* in the etymologies), and is distinguished from the voiceless **thorn.** In Old English, this distinction between edh and thorn (both transliterated as *th*) was not observed. **2.** The letter in the International Phonetic Alphabet representing the interdental voiced fricative, as in *the, other.*

ed·i·ble (éddi-b'l) *adj.* **1. a.** Capable of being eaten. **b.** Fit to eat; nonpoisonous. **2.** Ready to be eaten.
~n. Usually plural. Something fit to be eaten; food. —See Usage note at **eatable.** [Late Latin *edibilis,* from Latin *edere,* to eat.] **—ed·i·bil·i·ty** (-bílləti), **ed·i·ble·ness** *n.*

e·dict (éedikt) *n.* **1.** An official decree or proclamation issued by an authority. **2.** Any authoritative command or decree. [Latin *ēdictum,* from *ēdīcere,* to speak out, proclaim : *ex-,* out + *dīcere,* speak.]

ed·i·fi·ca·tion (éddifi-káysh'n) *n.* Intellectual, moral, or spiritual improvement; enlightenment: *"I am now writing this book for the edification of the world"* (Laurence Sterne). **—e·dif·i·ca·to·ry** (-káytəri) *adj.*

ed·i·fice (éddifiss) *n.* **1.** A building, especially one of imposing appearance or size. **2.** Something with an elaborate structure: *an edifice of regulations.* —See Synonyms at **building.** [Middle English, from Old French, from Latin *aedificium,* from *aedificāre,* to build : *aedēs,* building, house + *fac(e)re,* to make.]

ed·i·fy (éddi-fī) *tr.v.* **-fied, -fying, -fies.** To instruct or enlighten so as to encourage moral or spiritual improvement. [Middle English *edifien,* from Old French *edifier,* from Latin *aedificāre,* to build, instruct. See **edifice.**] **—ed·i·fi·er** *n.*

Ed·in·burgh (éddin-bərə, -brə ‖ -burrə, -burrō). Capital of Scotland. The city, once known as Auld Reekie because of the cloud of smoke that hung over low-lying areas, includes printing, publishing, brewing, whisky distilling, confectionery, and chemicals among its industries. Edinburgh is the home of an international festival of the arts, held annually. It takes its name from Edwin, king of Northumbria in the seventh century.

E·dir·ne (e-deer-ne), Formerly **A·dri·a·no·ple** (áydreeə-nṓp'l). Capital of Edirne province in European Turkey. It was expanded in the second century A.D. by the Roman emperor Hadrian, and was taken by the Goths in 378 and later by the Bulgarians before becoming the residence of the Turkish Sultans from 1365 to 1453. Ceded to Greece after World War I, it was returned to Turkey once more in 1923.

Ed·i·son (éddi-s'n), **Thomas Alva** (1847–1931). U.S. inventor. He held more than 1,300 U.S. and foreign patents for his inventions, most of them concerned with electricity. Among his first inventions were the carbon telephone transmitter (1877), the phonograph (1878), and the incandescent lamp with a carbon filament (1879). In New York (1880), he installed an experimental electric railway and (1881–2) the first central electric power plant in the world.

ed·it (éddit) *tr.v.* **-ited, -iting, -its. 1. a.** To make (written material) suitable for publication or presentation. **b.** To prepare an edition of for publication: *edit a collection of short stories.* **2.** To supervise the publication of (a newspaper or magazine, for example). **3.** To omit or eliminate; delete. Usually used with *out.* **4.** To integrate the component parts of (film, electronic tape, or sound track) by cutting, combining, and splicing.
~n. Informal. An instance of editing: *I gave his article a preliminary edit.* [Back-formation from EDITOR.]

e·di·tion (i-dísh'n) *n. Abbr.* **ed., edit. 1.** *Printing.* **a.** The entire number of copies of a publication printed from a single typesetting or other form of reproduction. Compare **printing. b.** A single copy from this group. **c.** A version of an earlier publication having substantial changes or additions. **2. a.** Any of the various forms in which something is issued or produced, as publications, music, or stamps. **b.** Any of the forms in which a publication is produced: *a leather-bound edition.* **c.** One closely similar to an original; a version: *The boy was a smaller edition of his father.* **3.** An issue of a work identified by its editor or publisher: *the Oxford edition of Shakespeare.* **4.** All the copies of a single print run of a newspaper: *the morning edition.* [Old French, from Latin *ēditiō* (stem *ēditiōn-*), a bringing forth, publication, from *ēdere* (past participle *ēdictus*), to bring forth, publish : *ex-,* out + *dāre,* to give.]

e·di·ti·o prin·ceps (i-díshi-ō prín-seps). *n., pl.* **editiones principes** (i-díshi-ōneez prín-si-peez). A first printed edition of a work. [Latin, "first edition".]

ed·i·tor (édditər) *n. Abbr.* **ed., edit. 1.** A person who edits a written work or musical composition for publication or public presentation. **2.** A person who supervises the policies or production of a publication or broadcast. **3.** A person in charge of a department of a publication: *a sports editor.* **4.** One who writes editorials. **5. a.** A person responsible for the editing of a film, sound track, or the like. **b.** A device for editing film, consisting basically of a splicer and viewer. [Late Latin, publisher, from Latin *ēdere,* to bring forth, publish. See **edition.**] **—ed·i·tor·ship** *n.*

ed·i·to·ri·al (éddi-táw-ri-əl ‖ -tṓ-) *n.* An article in a newspaper or magazine expressing the opinion of its editors or publishers.
~adj. **1.** Of, concerning, or prepared by an editor or editors. **2.** Having the nature of an editorial in expressing opinion: *editorial comments.* **—ed·i·to·ri·al·ly** *adv.*

ed·i·to·ri·al·ise, ed·i·to·ri·al·ize (éddi-táw-ri-ə-līz ‖ -tṓ-) *v.* **-ised, -ising, -ises.** *—intr.* **1.** To express an opinion in or as if in an editorial. **2.** To present a supposedly objective report in a way intended to implant an opinion. *—tr.* To state in an editorial. **—ed·i·to·ri·al·i·sa·tion** (-záysh'n) *n.* **—ed·i·to·ri·al·i·ser** *n.*

editor in chief *n., pl.* **editors in chief.** The editor having final responsibility for the operations and policies of a publication.

Ed·mon·ton (édməntən). Provincial capital of Alberta, western Canada, situated on the North Saskatchewan River. It is an industrial centre in an agricultural, and oil, coal, and gas producing region.

Ed·mund I (édmənd) (*c.* 921–946). King of the English. He succeeded his half-brother, Athelstan, in 939. He expelled the Danish rulers, Olaf and Ragnald, from Northumbria in 944 and in the following year received the homage of the king of Scotland in return for Cumbria.

Edmund I·ron·side (írn-sīd) (*c.* 981–1016). King of the English, succeeding his father, Ethelred the Unready (1016). He led the resistance against Canute's invasion (1015), but when he became king most of the nobles supported Canute and he was forced to partition the country.

Edmund, Saint (*c.*840–*c.*870). King of East Anglia. He was born in Germany and adopted by Offa, king of East Anglia, as his heir. He was killed, either during a battle against the Danes at Hoxne or shortly afterwards. He is buried at the town named after him, Bury St. Edmunds, Suffolk. His emblem is an arrow and his feast day is November 20.

Edo. See **Tokyo.**

E·dom (éedəm). Ancient country between the Dead Sea and the Gulf of Aqaba, now forming parts of Jordan and Israel. According to the Old Testament, the original inhabitants, the Edomites, were descended from Esau. **—E·dom·ite** *n.* **—E·dom·it·ish** *adj.*

EDP electronic data processing.

EDTA *n. Chemistry.* A colourless crystalline compound, $[(HOOCCH_2)_2NCH_2]_2$, used as a chelating agent in inorganic chemistry and biochemistry and as an antidote to metal poisoning. [From *e*thylene *d*iamine*t*etra-*a*cetic acid.]

ed·u·ca·ble (éddewkəb'l) *adj.* Capable of being educated. [EDUC(ATE) + -ABLE.]

ed·u·cate (éddew-kayt) *v.* **-cated, -cating, -cates.** *—tr.* **1. a.** To provide with knowledge or training, especially through formal teaching. **b.** To have (a child, for example) taught: *He educated his sons privately.* **2.** To provide with specialised training for some particular purpose: *educate someone for the priesthood.* **3.** To enlighten. Sometimes used humorously. **4.** To discipline, train, or develop (a taste or skill, for example). *—intr.* To teach or instruct a person or group: *Their purpose is to educate through the use of visual aids.* —See Synonyms at **teach.** [Middle English *educaten,* from Latin *ēducāre,* to bring up, educate. See **educe.**]

ed·u·cat·ed (éddew-kaytid) *adj.* **1.** Having an education, especially one above the average. **2.** Showing evidence of having been taught or instructed; cultivated; cultured. **3.** Based primarily on experience and some factual knowledge: *an educated guess.*

ed·u·ca·tion (éddew-káysh'n) *n. Abbr.* **ed.,** *Abbr.* **ed., educ. 1.** The act or process of imparting knowledge or skill; systematic instruction; teaching. **2.** The obtaining of knowledge or skill through such a process; learning. **3. a.** The knowledge or skill obtained or developed by such a process. **b.** A programme of instruction of a specified kind or level: *a classical education.* **4.** The field of study that is concerned with teaching and learning; the theory of teaching; pedagogy. **5.** *Informal.* An enlightening experience: *His visit to India was an education.*

ed·u·ca·tion·al (éddew-káysh'n'l) *adj. Abbr.* **educ. 1.** Of or pertaining to education: *educational psychology.* **2.** Serving to impart knowledge or skill: *an educational television programme.* **—ed·u·ca·tion·al·ly** *adv.*

ed·u·ca·tion·al·ist (éddew-káysh'n'l-ist) *n.* Also **ed·u·ca·tion·ist.** An educational theorist.

ed·u·ca·tive (éddew-kətiv ‖ -kaytiv) *adj.* Serving to educate or instruct.

ed·u·ca·tor (éddew-kaytər) *n.* **1.** One trained in teaching; a teacher. **2.** A specialist in the theory and practice of education.

e·duce (i-déwss ‖ -dōoss) *tr.v.* **educed, educing, educes. 1.** To draw or bring out; elicit; evoke. **2.** To infer or work out from given facts; deduce. [Latin *ēdūcere* : *ex-,* out + *dūcere,* to lead.] **—e·duc·i·ble** *adj.*

e·duct (éedukt) *n.* A substance that has been separated from another substance without chemical change. Compare **product.** [Latin *ēductus,* "drawn out", past participle of *ēdūcere.* See **educe.**]

e·duc·tion (i-dúksh'n) *n.* **1.** An act or the process of educing. **2.** The result of an educing; an inference. **3.** The exhaust phase of an internal-combustion engine. [Middle English *educcion,* from Late Latin *ēductiō,* from Latin *ēdūcere.* See **EDUCE.**]

Ed·ward I (édwərd) (1239–1307). King of England (1272–1307). Son of Henry III. His reign was marked by successful military campaigns against Wales and victory against the Scots at Falkirk (1298). His Model Parliament of 1295 is sometimes looked upon as the first full English parliament.

Edward II (1284–1327). King of England (1307–27). Son of Edward I. The Scots defeated Edward's army at Bannockburn (1314). In 1326 the rebellion of the Earl of March led to Edward's capture and deposition (1327). He was imprisoned in Berkeley Castle and almost certainly murdered there.

Edward III (1312–77). King of England (1327–77). Son of Edward II. During the Hundred Years' War with France, his armies won victories at Crécy (1346) and Poitiers (1356). Edward created the Round Table (1344) and the Order of the Garter (1349).

Edward IV (1442–83). King of England (1461–70, 1471–83). Son of Richard, Duke of York. As leader of the Yorkist faction in the Wars of the Roses, Edward defeated the Lancastrians at Mortimer's Cross (1461), and was proclaimed king. In 1470 the Earl of Warwick raised a rebellion against him and Edward fled to France. Henry VI, whom he had deposed, was restored to the throne, but a year later Edward returned, defeated the Lancastrians at Tewkesbury, and regained the throne. Henry VI was put to death, possibly on Edward's orders.

Edward V (1470–83). King of England (1483). Son of Edward IV. On Edward's accession to the throne at the age of 13, he was confined to the Tower of London with his younger brother Richard, Duke of York. There they were murdered, possibly on the orders of their uncle the Duke of Gloucester (later Richard III), or possibly by Henry Stafford or by Henry VII. Skeletons of boys aged about 13 and 10 were unearthed in the Tower in 1674.

Edward VI (1537–53). King of England (1547–53). Son of Henry VIII and Jane Seymour. He came to the throne at the age of 9 and died of tuberculosis at the age of 15.

Edward VII (1841–1910). King of Great Britain and Ireland (1901–10). Son of Queen Victoria, he became a popular figure as Prince of Wales. His personal popularity in France helped to create the conditions for the *Entente Cordiale* (1904).

Edward VIII (1894–1972). King of Great Britain and Ireland (1936). Son of George V. On succeeding to the throne he precipitated a constitutional crisis by his determination to marry Mrs. Wallis Warfield Simpson (1896–1986), an American divorcee. Opposition from Church and government caused him to abdicate after a reign of 325 days. Thereafter, as the Duke of Windsor, he lived with his wife in France, except for the years 1940 to 1945, when he was the governor of the Bahamas. He died in Paris but was buried in Windsor, in England.

Edward, Prince of Wales (1330–76). Eldest son of Edward III, he played a valiant part in the Hundred Years' War, especially at Crécy (1346) and Poitiers (1356), where he led the English forces which captured John II of France. He was named the Black Prince by the French, presumably because of his black armour.

Ed·ward·i·an (ed-wáwrdi-ən, -wa'ar-) *adj.* **1.** Of, pertaining to, or characteristic of the reign or person of any of several kings of England named Edward. **2.** Of, pertaining to, or characteristic of the reign or person of King Edward VII, especially in respect of the lighthearted elegance considered typical of his reign.
—n. A person living during the reign of one of these kings.

Edward the Confessor (died 1066). King of the English (1042–66). Son of Ethelred the Unready, and later stepson of Canute. Edward devoted much of his time to religious work, including the rebuilding of Westminster Abbey. Before his death he named Harold, son of

Godwin, his successor. He was canonised in the 12th century and his feast day is October 13.

Edward the Elder (died 924). King of Wessex (899–924). Son of Alfred the Great. He fought the Danes and the Viking invaders and by 918 ruled all of England south of the Humber.

–ee¹ *n. suffix.* Indicates: **1.** The recipient or object of a specified action; for example, **addressee, endorsee. 2.** One who is in a specified condition; for example, **refugee. 3.** One who is carrying out or has carried out a specified act; for example, **escapee.** [Middle English *-e,* from Old French *-e,* from past participial ending *-e,* from Latin *-ātus,* -ATE.]

–ee² *n. suffix.* Indicates: **1.** A particular type of, especially when small; for example, **bootee. 2.** Something resembling or suggestive of; for example, **goatee.** [Originally *-ie,* variant of -Y.]

e.e. errors excepted.

E.E. 1. Early English. **2.** electrical engineer; electrical engineering.

E.E. & M.P. Envoy Extraordinary and Minister Plenipotentiary.

EEC *n.* The **European Economic Community** *(see).*

EEG electroencephalogram; electroencephalograph.

eel (eel) *n., pl.* **eels** or collectively **eel. 1.** Any of various long, snakelike marine or freshwater fishes of the order Anguilliformes (or Apodes); especially, *Anguilla anguilla,* of Europe, characteristically migrating from fresh water to the Sargasso Sea to spawn. **2.** Any of several similar or related fishes. **3.** Any of several animals having an elongated body, such as the conger eel. [Middle English *ele,* Old English *ǽl,* from Common Germanic *ǽlaz*† (unattested).]

eel-grass (éel-graass ‖ -grass) *n.* **1.** Any of several submerged aquatic plants of the genus *Zostera,* of coastal areas, having narrow, grasslike leaves and growing in dense masses. **2.** Any of several similar or related plants, such as **tape grass** *(see).*

eel-pout (éel-powt) *n., pl.* **-pouts** or collectively **eelpout.** Any of various marine fishes of the family Zoarcidae, having an elongated body and a large head. The European species *Zoarces viviparus* produces live young. [Middle English *elepout* (unattested), Old English *ǽlepūte* : EEL + POUT (fish).]

eel-worm (éel-wurm) *n.* Any of various often parasitic nematode worms, such as the **vinegar eel** *(see).*

–een *n. suffix. Irish.* Indicates a diminutive; for example, **poteen, colleen.** [From Irish *-ín,* diminutive suffix.]

e'en¹ (een) *n. Poetic.* Evening.

e'en² *adv. Poetic.* Even.

–eer¹ *n. suffix.* Indicates: **1.** One who works with or is concerned with; for example, **auctioneer, volunteer.** Sometimes used derogatorily: **profiteer, racketeer. 2.** One who makes or composes; for example, **balladeer.** [Old French *-ier,* from Latin *-ārius,* -ARY.]

–eer² *v. suffix.* Indicates involvement with; for example, **profiteer, volunteer.**

e'er (air) *adv. Poetic.* Ever.

ee-rie (éer-i) *adj.* **-rier, -riest. 1.** Inspiring fear or dread without being openly threatening; peculiarly unsettling; weird. **2.** Supernatural in aspect or character; uncanny; mysterious. —See Synonyms at **weird.** [Middle English *eri,* fearful, cowardly, Old English *earg,* cowardly, timid, from Common Germanic *arg-* (unattested).]

EEZ Economic Exclusion Zone.

ef-. Variant of **ex-¹** (prefix).

eff. efficiency.

ef-fa-ble (éffəb'l) *adj. Archaic.* Capable of being expressed in words. [Latin *effābilis,* from *effārī,* to speak out : *ex-,* out + *fārī,* to speak.]

ef-face (i-fáyss) *tr.v.* **-faced, -facing, -faces. 1.** To rub or wipe out; obliterate; erase. **2.** To make faded or indistinct as if by rubbing out. **3.** To conduct (oneself) inconspicuously or humbly: *"When the two women went out together, Anna deliberately effaced herself and played to the dramatic Molly."* (Doris Lessing). —See Synonyms at **erase.** [Old French *effacer,* "to remove the face" : *ef-,* out, from Latin *ex-* + *face,* FACE.] **—ef-face-a-ble** *adj.* **—ef-face-ment** *n.* **—ef-fac-er** *n.*

ef-fect (i-fékt) *n.* **1.** Something brought about by a cause or agent; a result: *"Fortunately in England, at any rate, education produces no effect whatsoever"* (Oscar Wilde). **2.** The way in which something acts upon or influences an object: *the effect of a drug on the nervous system.* **3.** The final or comprehensive result; an outcome. **4.** The power or capacity to achieve the desired result; efficacy; influence. **5.** The condition of being in full force or execution; being; realisation: *The law will come into effect tomorrow.* **6.** An impression produced by an artifice or manner of presentation: *an effect of spaciousness.* **7.** The basic meaning or tendency of something said or written; purport: *He said he approved, or something to that effect.* **8.** A scientific law, hypothesis, or phenomenon: *the Faraday effect; photovoltaic effect.* **9.** *Plural.* Physical belongings; goods. Also called "personal effects". **10.** *Plural.* **a. Sound effects** *(see).* **b. Special effects** *(see).* —See Synonyms at **assets. —for effect.** In order to impress or influence. **—in effect. 1.** In fact; actually. **2.** In essence; virtually. **—take effect.** To become operative; gain active force.

—tr.v. **effected, -fecting, -fects.** To produce as a result; cause to occur; bring about. See Synonyms at **perform.** See Usage note at **affect.** [Middle English, from Old French, from Latin *effectus,* past participle of *efficere,* to accomplish, perform, work out : *ex-,* out + *facere,* to do.] **—ef-fect-er** *n.* **—ef-fect-i-ble** *adj.*

Synonyms: *effect, consequence, result, outcome, upshot, sequel.*

ef-fec-tive (i-féktiv) *adj.* **1.** Having the intended or expected effect; serving the purpose. **2.** Producing or adapted to produce the desired impression or response; striking: *an effective speech.* **3.** Opera-

tive; in effect: *The law is effective immediately.* **4.** Real and actual rather than supposed. **5.** Prepared for use or action in warfare: *We have eight effective troop divisions.* **6.** *Electricity.* Designating an alternating quantity, such as current, having a value equal to the square root of the mean of the squares of the instantaneous values over one cycle.
~*n.* **1.** A member of a military force or a piece of equipment that is ready for action. **2.** The total number of men prepared and available for military action. **—ef·fec·tive·ness** *n.*
Usage: The adjectives *effective, efficacious, effectual,* and *efficient* overlap in meaning, but are to be distinguished: *effective* and *effectual* may imply proven capacity for doing the job in question and *efficacious* may suggest having the potential to do it. *Efficient* implies proven capability based on productiveness in operation, and especially stresses ability to perform well and economically.
ef·fec·tive·ly (i-féktivli) *adv.* **1.** In an effective way. **2.** In effect; for all practical purposes.
ef·fec·tor (i-féktər) *n.* **1.** A nerve ending that activates either gland secretion or muscular contraction. **2.** A cell or organ, such as a muscle or gland, specialised to respond to nervous stimulation.
ef·fec·tu·al (i-féktew-əl) *adj.* **1.** Producing, or sufficient to produce, a desired effect; fully adequate. **2.** Valid or legally binding. —See Usage note at **effective.** **—ef·fec·tu·al·i·ty** (-ál-əti), **ef·fec·tu·al·ness** *n.* **—ef·fec·tu·al·ly** *adv.*
ef·fec·tu·ate (i-féktew-ayt) *tr.v.* **-ated, -ating, -ates.** To cause; bring about; effect. [Medieval Latin *effectuāre,* from Latin *efficere,* to accomplish, EFFECT.] **—ef·fec·tu·a·tion** (-áysh'n) *n.*
ef·fem·i·nate (i-fémmi-nət, -nit) *adj.* **1.** Having qualities associated with women rather than those regarded as befitting a man; unmanly. Said of a man. **2.** Characterised by weakness or lack of force; not dynamic or vigorous. [Middle English *effeminat,* from Latin *effēminātus,* past participle of *effēmināre,* "to make a woman out of", to make effeminate : *ex-,* out of + *fēmina,* woman.] **—ef·fem·i·na·cy** (-nə-si) *n.* **—ef·fem·i·nate·ly** *adv.* **—ef·fem·i·nate·ness** *n.*
ef·fen·di (e-féndi) *n.* **1.** Used in Turkey and the Middle East as a term of respectful address, equivalent to *Sir.* **2.** An educated or respected man in the Ottoman Empire. [Turkish *efendi,* "master", from Medieval Greek *aphentē,* vocative of *aphentēs,* lord, master, from Greek *authentēs.* See **authentic.**]
ef·fer·ent (éffərənt) *adj.* Directed or conducting away from an organ or section; especially, designating nerves that carry impulses from the central nervous system to an effector. Compare **afferent.**
~*n.* An efferent organ or part. [French *efférent,* from Latin *efferēns* (stem *efferent-*), present participle of *efferre,* to carry away : *ex-,* away from + *ferre,* to carry.]
ef·fer·vesce (éffər-véss) *intr.v.* **-vesced, -vescing, -vesces.** **1.** To emit small bubbles of gas, as a carbonated or fermenting liquid does. **2.** To appear and come out of a liquid in bubbles; bubble forth. **3.** To show high spirits; be lively or vivacious. [Latin *effervēscere,* to boil over : *ex-* (intensive) + *fervēscere,* to start to boil, from *fervēre,* to be hot, boil.]
ef·fer·ves·cent (éffər-véss'nt) *adj.* **1.** Emitting a profusion of small bubbles of gas; bubbling. **2.** Produced by bubbles of gas: *an effervescent hiss.* **3.** High-spirited; vivacious. **—ef·fer·ves·cence** *n.*
ef·fete (i-féet) *adj.* **1.** Exhausted of vitality, force, or effectiveness; having lost one's original power: *effete romanticism.* **2.** Characterised by unproductive self-indulgence, self-absorption, or decadence: *effete manners.* **3.** Unable to produce further offspring or fruit; barren. Said of animals or plants. [Latin *effētus,* worn out by childbearing : *ex-,* out + *fētus,* childbearing, offspring.] **—ef·fete·ly** *adv.* **—ef·fete·ness** *n.*
ef·fi·ca·cious (éffi-káyshəss) *adj.* Capable of producing the desired effect. See Usage note at **effective.** [Latin *efficāx* (stem *efficāc-*), effective, from *efficere,* to EFFECT.] **—ef·fi·ca·cious·ly** *adv.* **—ef·fi·ca·cious·ness** *n.*
ef·fi·ca·cy (éffikə-si) *n.* Power or capacity to produce the desired effect; ability to achieve results; effectiveness: *"he was a firm believer in the efficacy of prayer"* (Samuel Butler). [Latin *efficācia,* from *efficāx,* EFFICACIOUS.]
ef·fi·cien·cy (i-físh'n-si) *n., pl.* **-cies.** **1. a.** The quality or property of being efficient. **b.** The degree to which this quality is exercised. **2.** *Abbr.* **eff.** The ratio of the effective or useful output to the total input in any system; especially, the ratio of the energy delivered by a machine to the energy supplied for its operation, often expressed as a percentage. **3.** *U.S. Informal.* A **bedsitter** *(see).* In this sense, also called "efficiency apartment".
efficiency bar *n.* A point on a salary scale beyond which no further progress is possible unless employees reach satisfactory professional standards.
ef·fi·cient (i-físh'nt) *adj.* **1.** Having a direct effect; causative. **2. a.** Acting or producing effectively with a minimum of waste, expense, or unnecessary effort. **b.** Exhibiting a high ratio of output to input. —See Usage note at **effective.** [Middle English, from Old French, from Latin *efficiēns* (stem *efficient-*), present participle of *efficere,* to EFFECT.] **—ef·fi·cient·ly** *adv.*
efficient cause *n.* That which renders a thing what it is; that which causes an effect. [Translation of Latin *causa efficiens.*]
ef·fi·gy (éffiji) *n., pl.* **-gies.** **1.** A painted or sculptured representation of a person, as on a stone wall or monument. **2.** A crude image or dummy fashioned in the likeness of a person, often as an expression of mockery or hatred. [Middle English *effigie,* from Latin *effigiēs,* likeness, image, from *effingere,* to form, portray : *ex-,* out of + *fingere,* fashion, shape.]
ef·flo·resce (éff-law-réss, -lo-, -lə-) *intr. v.* **-resced, -rescing, -resces.** **1.** To blossom; flower; bloom. **2.** *Chemistry.* **a.** To become a powder by losing water crystallisation. **b.** To become covered with a powdery deposit, as by evaporation. [Latin *efflōrēscere,* to blossom out : *ex-,* out + *flōrēscere,* inceptive of *flōrēre,* to blossom, from *flōs* (stem *flōr-*), flower.]
ef·flo·res·cence (éff-law-réss'nss, -lo-, -lə-) *n.* **1.** A flowering or blooming forth. **2.** The culmination or blossoming of an artistic career or movement, for example. **3.** *Chemistry.* **a.** The process of efflorescing. **b.** The deposit that results from this process. **c.** A growth of salt crystals on surfaces, such as those of wells, due to evaporation of salt-laden water. **—ef·flo·res·cent** *adj.*
ef·flu·ence (éffloo-ənss) *n.* **1.** The act or an instance of flowing out. **2.** Something that flows out or forth; an emanation.
ef·flu·ent (éffloo-ənt) *adj.* Flowing out or forth.
~*n.* **1.** Something that flows out or forth. **2.** A stream flowing out of a lake or other body of water. **3.** An outflow of a sewer, storage tank, irrigation canal, or other channel. **4.** Liquid waste resulting from an industrial process. **5.** Radioactive waste from a nuclear power station. [Middle English, from Latin *effluēns* (stem *effluent-*), present participle of *effluere,* to flow out : *ex-,* out + *fluere,* to flow.]
ef·flu·vi·um (i-flóo-vi-əm) *n., pl.* **-via** (-viə) or **-ums.** **1.** An outflow or rising vapour of invisible or barely visible gas or particles. **2.** Foul-smelling vapour or fumes emanating from decaying matter. **3.** An imaginary outflow of imponderable radiation or invisible vapour; an aura. [Latin, from *effluere,* to flow out. See **effluent.**] **—ef·flu·vi·al** *adj.*
ef·flux (éff-lukss) *n.* Also **ef·flux·ion** (i-flúksh'n). **1.** An outward flowing; an emanating. **2.** Something that flows out or forth; an emanation. [Latin *effluxus,* past participle of *effluere,* to flow out. See **effluent.**]
ef·fort (éffərt) *n.* **1.** The use of physical or mental energy to do something; exertion. **2.** A difficult or tiring exertion of the strength or will: *It was an effort to get up.* **3.** An attempt; especially, an earnest attempt. **4.** Something done or produced through exertion; an achievement or creation. **5.** *Physics.* A force applied against inertia. [Old French *effort, esfort,* from *esforcier,* to force (reflexive *s'esforcier,* to exert oneself), from Vulgar Latin *exfortiāre* (unattested), to show strength : Latin *ex-,* out + *fortis,* strong.] **—ef·fort·ful** *adj.*
Synonyms: *effort, exertion, endeavour, strain.*
ef·fort·less (éffərt-ləss, -liss) *adj.* Calling for, requiring, or showing little or no effort. **—ef·fort·less·ly** *adv.* **—ef·fort·less·ness** *n.*
ef·front·er·y (i-frúntəri) *n., pl.* **-ies.** Impudent and insulting boldness; presumptuous self-assertion; audacity. See Synonyms at **temerity.** [French *effronterie,* from *effronté,* shameless, from Vulgar Latin *exfrontātus* (unattested), from Late Latin *effrōns* (stem *effront-*), shameless, "barefaced" : *ex-,* out of + *frōns,* forehead (see **front**).]
ef·ful·gent (i-fúljənt) *adj.* Shining forth brilliantly; resplendent. [Latin *effulgēns* (stem *effulgent-*), present participle of *effulgēre,* to shine out : *ex-,* out + *fulgēre,* to shine.] **—ef·ful·gence** *n.*
ef·fuse (i-féwss) *adj. Botany.* Spreading out loosely on a surface. Said especially of flower inflorescences.
~*v.* (i-féwz) **effused, -fusing, -fuses.** *—tr.* To pour or spread out; disseminate. *—intr.* **1.** To spread out. **2.** To exude. **3.** To flow out. [Latin *effūsus,* past participle of *effundere,* to pour out : *ex-,* out + *fundere,* to pour.]
ef·fu·si·om·e·ter (i-féwzi-ómmitər) *n.* An apparatus for determining molecular weights by measuring the rate of effusion of gases.
ef·fu·sion (i-féwzh'n) *n.* **1. a.** The act or an instance of pouring forth. **b.** Something that is poured forth. **2.** An unrestrained outpouring of feeling, as in speech or writing: *"The devout effusions of sacred eloquence"* (Edmund Burke). **3.** *Pathology.* **a.** The seeping of serous, purulent, or bloody fluid into a body cavity. **b.** The effused fluid. **4.** *Physics.* The flow of gas through an aperture under pressure in circumstances in which the diameter of the aperture is small compared to the mean distance between the gas molecules.
ef·fu·sive (i-féw-siv || -ziv) *adj.* **1.** Irrepressibly demonstrative. **2.** Unrestrained in emotional expression; gushing. See Synonyms at **talkative.** **3.** *Geology.* Poured out in a molten state and then solidified. Said of igneous rock. **—ef·fu·sive·ly** *adv.* **—ef·fu·sive·ness** *n.*
Ef·ik (éffik) *n., pl.* **-iks** or collectively **Efik.** **1.** A member of a people of southeastern Nigeria. **2.** The Ibibio language of this people. **—Ef·ik** *adj.*
eft (eft) *n.* A newt; especially, the reddish-orange immature terrestrial form of a North American species, *Diemictylus viridescens.* [Middle English *evete,* Old English *efeta*†, lizard.]
E.F.T.A. European Free Trade Association.
eft·soons (eft-sóonz) *adv.* Also **eft·soon** (-sóon). *Archaic.* **1.** Soon afterwards. **2.** Once again. [Middle English *eftsōne,* Old English *eftsōna* : *eft,* again + *sōna,* SOON.]
e.g. for example [*Latin* exempli gratia.]
Eg. Egypt; Egyptian.
e·gad (i-gád, ee-) *interj. Archaic.* Used as a mild oath expressing surprise or enthusiasm. [Euphemism for *oh God* or *ah God.*]
e·gal·i·tar·i·an (i-gál-i-táir-i-ən) *adj.* **1.** Advocating the doctrine of equal political, economic, and legal rights for all citizens. **2.** Pertaining to or arising from this doctrine.
~*n.* One who holds or advances egalitarian opinions. [French

égalitaire, from égalité, equality, from Latin aequalitās, from aequalis, EQUAL.] —**e·gal·i·tar·i·an·ism** n.

e·gest (ee-jést) tr.v. **egested, egesting, egests.** To discharge or excrete from the body. [Latin ēgerere (past participle ēgestus), to carry out, expel : ex-, out + gerere, to carry.] —**e·ges·tion** n. —**e·ges·tive** adj.

e·ges·ta (ee-jéstə) pl.n. Egested matter, especially excrement. [Latin ēgesta, neuter plural of Latin ēgestus. See **egest**.]

egg¹ (eg) n. **1.** Any of the female reproductive cells of various animals, consisting usually of an embryo surrounded by nutrient material with a protective covering, and often deposited externally. **2.** Any female gamete; an ovum. Also called "egg cell". **3.** The oval, thin-shelled ovum laid by a bird, especially a domestic fowl, used as food. **4.** Something having the characteristic shape of a hen's egg. **5.** Informal. A fellow; a person: a good egg. —**have egg on (one's) face.** To be humiliated or embarrassed. —**put** or **have all (one's) eggs in one basket.** To risk everything on a single venture, method, or act.

~tr.v. **egged, egging, eggs.** To mix or cover with beaten egg, as in cooking. [Middle English egge, from Old Norse egg.]

egg² tr.v. **egged, egging, eggs.** To encourage or incite with taunts, dares, or similar verbal appeals; urge; spur. Used with on. [Middle English eggen, Old English eggian, from Old Norse eggja.]

egg-and-dart (égən-dárt) n. A decorative moulding common in classical architecture and in cabinetwork consisting of a series of egg-shaped figures alternating with dart-, anchor-, or tongue-shaped figures. Also called "egg-and-anchor", "egg-and-tongue".

egg-and-spoon race (ég-ən-spōōn) n. A running race in which competitors must carry an egg in a spoon without dropping it.

egg-beat·er (ég-beetər) n. A kitchen utensil with rotating blades for beating eggs, whipping cream, or mixing cooking ingredients.

egg cup n. A small cup-shaped holder for a boiled egg.

eg·ger, eg·gar (éggər) n. Any of various moths of the family Lasiocampidae, of which the larvae often construct tentlike webs. [From EGG, from its egg-shaped cocoon.]

egg·head (ég-hed) n. Informal. An intellectual; a highbrow. Often used derogatorily. [Said to be originally applied to an intellectual who supported (1952) the U.S. presidential candidate Adlai Stevenson, with reference to Stevenson's baldness.]

egg·nog (ég-nóg) n. A drink consisting of milk and beaten eggs, commonly mixed with rum, brandy, or wine. Also called "egg flip", "egg noggin", "nog". [EGG + NOG (original sense "ale").]

egg·plant (ég-plaant || -plant) n. Chiefly U.S. A plant, the **aubergine** (see) or its fruit.

egg roll n. U.S. A **spring roll** (see).

egg·shell (ég-shel) n. **1.** The thin, brittle, exterior covering of a bird's egg. **2.** Pale yellow to yellowish white.

~adj. **1.** Designating a paint surface that has a matt rather than a glossy sheen. **2.** Designating a type of thin translucent china. **3.** Pale yellow to yellowish white.

egg timer n. A small device, usually in the shape of an hourglass, for timing the boiling of an egg.

egg tooth n. A structure in embryo birds and reptiles that is used to pierce the eggshell. In birds it is a projection on the beak and in reptiles a temporary tooth.

egg white n. The albumen of an egg.

egis. Variant of **aegis.**

eg·lan·tine (égglon-tīn || -tin, -teen) n. A rose, the **sweetbrier** (see). [Middle English eglentyn, from Old French aiglantine, from aiglent, from Vulgar Latin aquilentum (unattested), "prickly", irregularly from Latin aculeus, diminutive of acus, needle.]

Eg·mont (ég-mont), **Lamoraal, Graaf van** (1522–68). Flemish general and statesman, who served with Charles V and Philip II of Spain. He is the Egmont of Goethe's tragedy of the same name and also of Beethoven's Egmont overture.

e·go (éegō, éggō) n. **1.** The conscious subject, as designated by the first person singular pronoun; the self. **2.** In Freudian psychology, the personality component that is conscious, most immediately controls behaviour, and is most in touch with external reality. See **id**, **superego**. **3.** Informal. **a.** A sense of self-esteem. **b.** Conceit; egotism. [New Latin, from Latin, I.]

e·go·cen·tric (éegō-séntrik, éggō-) adj. **1.** Thinking or acting with the view that one's self is the centre, object, and norm of all experience. **2.** Self-centred; selfish. **3.** Philosophy. Real or valid only as perceived or conceived by the individual mind.

~n. An egocentric person. —**e·go·cen·tric·i·ty** (-triss-iti) n.

ego ideal n. **1.** Psychology. An individual's conception of the person he would wish to be, based on identification with persons admired during his development. **2.** Self-idealisation.

e·go·ism (éegō-iz'm, éggō-) n. **1.** The quality of thinking or acting with only oneself and one's own interests in mind; preoccupation with one's own welfare and advancement. **2.** Ethics. **a.** The doctrine that morality has its foundations in self-interest. **b.** The belief that self-interest is the just and proper motive for all human conduct. **3.** Conceit; egotism.

e·go·ist (éegō-ist, éggō-) n. **1.** One devoted to his own interests and advancement; an egocentric person. **2.** Ethics. An adherent of egoism; one who acts according to self-interest on principle. **3.** An egotist. —See Usage note at **egotist**. [French égoiste, from EGO.] —**e·go·is·tic** (-ístik), **e·go·is·ti·cal** adj. —**e·go·is·ti·cal·ly** adv.

e·go·ma·ni·a (éegō-máyni-ə, éggō-) n. Obsessive or pathological preoccupation with the self; extreme egotism. [New Latin : EGO + -MANIA.] —**e·go·ma·ni·ac** n.

e·go·tism (éegə-tiz'm, éggə-) n. **1.** An inordinately large sense of self-importance; egoism. **2.** The tendency to speak or write of oneself excessively and boastfully. [EGO + -ISM (by analogy with nouns such as NEPOTISM).]

e·go·tist (éegə-tist, éggə-) n. **1.** A conceited, boastful person. **2.** A person who acts selfishly; an egoist. —**e·go·tis·tic** (-tístik), **e·go·tis·ti·cal** adj. —**e·go·tis·ti·cal·ly** adv.

Usage: Egoist and egotist (and the associated nouns egoism and egotism) are sometimes interchangeable, but usually the words have different implications. Egotists are boastful people, full of their own importance; egoists put their own interests first in everything they do. One may be an egoist without boasting about oneself.

ego trip n. Slang. **1.** An experience that boosts or gratifies the ego. **2.** An act of self-aggrandisement or self-indulgence.

e·go-trip (éegō-trip, éggō-) intr.v. **-tripped, -tripping, -trips.** Slang. To seek personal gratification, as by self-aggrandisement or self-indulgence.

e·gre·gious (i-grée-jəss, -ji-əss) adj. Outstandingly bad; blatant; outrageous. [Latin ēgregius, "standing out from the herd" : ex-, out of + grex (stem greg-), herd, flock.] —**e·gre·gious·ly** adv. —**e·gre·gious·ness** n.

e·gress (éegress) n. **1.** The act of going out; emergence. **2.** The path or opening by means of which one goes out; an exit. **3.** The right of going out: deny egress. **4.** Astronomy. **Emersion** (see). [Latin ēgressus, from the past participle of ēgredī, to go out : ex-, out + gradī, to go, step.]

e·gret (ée-grit, -gret || U.S. also éggrit, i-grét) n. Any of several usually white wading birds of the genera Bubulcus, Casmerodius, Leucophoyx, and related genera, characteristically having long, showy, drooping plumes during the breeding season. [Middle English egrete, from Old French aigrette, from Old Provençal aigreta, from aigron, heron, from Germanic.]

E·gypt, Arab Republic of (éejipt). Arabic **Misr.** A country of north-eastern Africa, bordering the Mediterranean. It is mainly desert, and includes the Sinai peninsula, the upland Eastern desert, and the low-lying Western Desert, with its population concentrated along the fertile Nile Valley. Early Egyptian history is generally divided into 31 dynasties. The Old Kingdom, the third to the sixth dynasties, from c. 2700 to c. 2200 B.C., reached its peak when the great pyramids of Giza were built. Under a succession of vigorous rulers of the early New Kingdom (c. 1570 to c. 1200 B.C.), notably Thutmosis I and Thutmosis II, the kingdom extended her frontiers into Syria and Mesopotamia, and built the temples of Luxor and Karnak and the famous tomb of Tutankhamun. By the end of the 20th dynasty, decline set in and the Egyptian empire was conquered by the Assyrians in the seventh century B.C., and twice by the Persians. Liberated from Persian rule by Alexander the Great, the kingdom passed at his death to his general, Ptolemy, whose descendants ruled until the suicide of Cleopatra VII in 30 B.C. After Egypt was conquered by the Romans, communications were improved and irrigation of the land gave the country a century of renewed wealth. In A.D. 642 it fell to the Arabs and was absorbed into the Islamic world. It was under Turkish rule from 1517 to 1798, when Napoleon made it a French protectorate until 1801. By the mid-19th century, British and French interests in Egypt intensified and the opening of the Suez Canal in 1869 gave Egypt international prominence. Britain dominated Egyptian politics, despite nominal Ottoman sovereignty, and made Egypt a protectorate at the outbreak of World War I. It became a sovereign state in 1922. Corruption brought an end to its monarchy with the coup and abdication of King Farouk in 1952. Egypt became a republic in 1953. Under Colonel Nasser the Suez Canal was nationalised in 1956, precipitat-

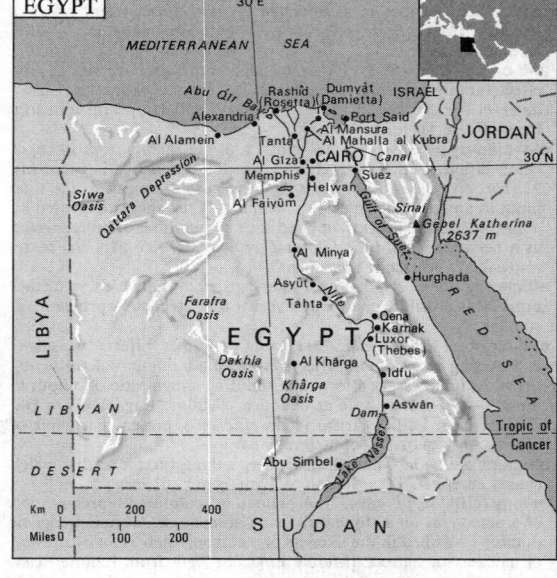

ing the "Suez Crisis" and invasion by Israeli and Anglo-French forces, who later withdrew on orders from the United Nations. From 1958 to 1961, Egypt combined with Syria as the United Arab Republic. In 1967 Egypt fought the Six-Day War against Israel and lost the Sinai peninsula till the Camp David treaty. Under President Sadat the country fought another Arab-Israeli war (1973), and signed the Camp David peace treaty with Israel (1979). Sadat was assassinated by Muslim fanatics (1981), and Vice-President Mubarak succeeded him. In the 1990s violent Islamic fundamentalism continued to threaten stability, and to damage the tourist industry. Despite the lack of water, the Aswân High Dam and other modern irrigation systems greatly increased the production of cotton (the chief cash crop), rice, millet, maize, sugar cane, fruit, and vegetables. Since the 1950s, heavy industries (iron, steel, and engineering) have been introduced, and are supplied with power from the Aswân High Dam. Area, 997 738 square kilometres (385,229 square miles). Population, 60,600,000. Capital, Cairo.

E·gyp·tian (i-jípsh'n) *adj. Abbr.* **Eg. 1.** Of or pertaining to Egypt, its people, or its culture. **2.** *Archaic.* Of or pertaining to Gypsies. ~*n.* **1.** A native or citizen of Egypt. **2.** The extinct Hamitic language spoken by the ancient Egyptians. **3.** *Archaic.* A Gypsy.

Egyptian clover *n.* A plant, **berseem** *(see).*

Egyptian cotton *n.* A long-staple, fine cotton grown chiefly in northern Africa.

E·gyp·tol·o·gy (éejip-tólləji) *n.* The study of the language, culture, and artefacts of the ancient Egyptian civilisation. —**E·gyp·to·log·i·cal** (i-jíptə-lójik'l) *adj.* —**E·gyp·tol·o·gist** *n.*

eh (ay, e) *interj.* **1.** Used interrogatively: *Eh? What was that?* **2.** Used in asking for confirmation: *He is a shrewd one, eh?*

EHF extremely high frequency.

Eh·ren·burg (áírən-burg), **Ilya Gregorievich** (1891–1967). Russian writer who was awarded the Stalin prize twice, for *The Fall of Paris* (1941) and *The Storm* (1948). In the West he is best known for his novel *The Thaw* (1954), which described repression under Stalin's regime.

Ehr·lich (áírlikh), **Paul** (1854–1915). Geman bacteriologist who discovered salvarsan and neosalvarsan, used to treat syphilis before the discovery of antibiotics. He shared the Nobel prize for physiology or medicine with Ilya Metchnikoff in 1908.

EHV extra high voltage.

E.I. East Indian; East Indies.

EIB European Investment Bank.

Eich·mann (íkhman), **Adolf** (1906–62). German official of the Nazi S.S. As head of the Gestapo's Jewish section after 1939, he was chiefly responsible for the murder of millions of Jews in occupied Europe. Arrested by the Allies in 1945, he escaped and fled to South America. He was captured by the Israeli secret service in Argentina (1960), taken to Jerusalem, tried, and executed (1962).

ei·der (ídər) *n.* Any of several sea ducks of the genus *Somateria* and related genera, especially *S. mollissima,* of northern regions, the females of which are the source of eiderdown. The males have a predominantly black and white plumage. [Icelandic *ædhur* (genitive *ædhar*), from Old Norse *ædhr.*]

ei·der·down (ídər-down) *n.* **1.** The downy breast feathers of the female eider duck, used as stuffing for quilts and pillows. **2.** A quilt, originally one stuffed with this down. **3.** *Chiefly U.S.* A warm cotton fabric with a woollen nap. [Probably from German *Eiderdaune,* from Icelandic *ædhardúnn* : *ædhar,* genitive of *ædhar,* EIDER + *dúnn,* DOWN.]

ei·det·ic (ī-déttik) *adj.* **1.** Especially vivid but unreal. Said of images experienced especially in childhood. **2.** Of or pertaining to vivid mental images: *an eidetic memory.* ~*n.* One who experiences vivid mental images. [German *eidetisch,* from Greek *eidētikos,* relating to images or knowledge, from *eidēsis,* knowledge, from *eidos,* form, shape.] —**ei·det·i·cal·ly** *adv.*

ei·do·lon (i-dō-lon, -lon) *n., pl.* **-lons** or **-la** (-lə). **1.** A phantom; an apparition. **2.** An image or an ideal. [Greek *eidōlon,* from *eidos,* form, shape.]

Eif·fel Tower (íf'l; *French* ay-fél) *n.* An iron tower on the left bank of the Seine in Paris, now standing 300 metres (984 feet) high, designed by the French engineer A.G. Eiffel (1832-1923) and originally erected for the Paris Exhibition of 1889.

eigen- *comb.form.* Indicates proper or characteristic; for example **eigenvalue.** [German, "own".]

ei·gen·func·tion (ígən-fungksh'n) *n. Physics.* An allowed function for a system as determined by wave mechanics, which enables a meaningful solution to be obtained from Schrödinger's wave equation.

ei·gen·val·ue (ígən-val-yoo) *n. Physics.* Any of a set of allowed energies of a particle in a system as determined by wave mechanics.

Ei·ger (ígər). Mountain in the Bernese Oberland, central Switzerland (3 970 metres; 13,025 feet). Its steep north face was not conquered until 1938.

eight (ayt) *n.* **1. a.** The cardinal number that is one more than seven. **b.** A symbol representing this, such as 8, VIII, or viii. **2.** A set made up of eight persons or things. **3. a.** The eighth in a series. **b.** A playing card marked with eight pips. **4.** Eight parts: *cut in eight.* **5.** A size, as in clothing, designated as eight. **6. a.** An eight-oared racing shell. **b.** A rowing crew of eight people. **7.** Eight hours after midnight or midday. **8.** A **figure of eight** *(see).* —**have had one over the eight.** *Slang.* To be drunk. [Middle English *eighte, eihte,* Old English *eahta.*] —**eight** *adj.* —**eight·fold** (áyt-fóld) *adj. & adv.*

eight·een (áy-téen ‖ áyt-) *n.* **1. a.** The cardinal number that is one more than 17. **b.** A symbol representing this, such as 18, XVIII, or xviii. **2.** A set made up of 18 persons or things. **3.** The eighteenth in a series. **4.** A team of 18 players in Australian Rules football. **5.** A size, as in clothing, designated as eighteen. [Middle English *eightetene, eihtene,* Old English *eahtatíene* : EIGHT + -TEEN.] —**eight·een** *adj.*

eight·een·mo (áy-téen-mō) *n., pl.* **-mos.** A size of a page or a book, **octodecimo** *(see).* [EIGHTEEN + -MO.] —**eight·een·mo** *adj.*

eight·eenth (áy-téenth ‖ áyt-) *n.* **1.** The ordinal number 18 in a series. **2.** One of 18 equal parts. —**eight·eenth** *adj. & adv.*

eighth (aytth ‖ ayth) *n.* **1.** The ordinal number eight in a series. **2.** One of eight equal parts. —**eighth** *adj. & adv.*

eighth note *n. Music. U.S.* A quaver *(see).*

eight·i·eth (áy-ti-əth ‖ áyt-) *n.* **1.** The ordinal number 80 in a series. **2.** One of 80 equal parts. —**eight·i·eth** *adj. & adv.*

eights (aytss) *pl.n.* Boat races at certain universities and elsewhere between crews of eight people.

eight·some reel (áyt-səm) *n.* A Scottish dance in which eight people take part.

eight·vo (áyt-vō) *n., pl.* **-vos.** A size of a page or a book, **octavo** *(see).* [EIGHT + (OCTA)VO.] —**eight·vo** *adj.*

eight·y (áy-ti ‖ áyt-) *n.* **1. a.** The cardinal number that is ten more than seventy. **b.** A symbol representing this, such as 80 or LXXX. **2.** The eightieth in a series. **3.** A set made up of 80 persons or things. **4.** A size, as in clothing, designated as 80. **5.** *Plural.* **a.** The range of numbers from 80 to 89, considered as a range of age, price, temperature, or the like. **b.** *Sometimes capital* **E.** The years numbered 80-89 in a century. Also used adjectivally: *an eighties fashion.* [Middle English *eigh(te)ty,* Old English *eahtatig* : *eahta,* EIGHT + -*tig,* -TY (ten).] —**eight·y** *adj.*

Eijkman (áykman), **Christiaan** (1858–1930). Dutch physician. He was awarded the Nobel prize for physiology or medicine with F.G. Hopkins (1929) for his work on the causes of beriberi.

eikon. Variant of **icon.**

Eilat. See **Elat.**

-ein. Variant of **-in.**

ei·na (áy-naa) *interj. South African.* Ouch. Used to express distress at sudden pain. [Hottentot.]

Eind·ho·ven (ínt-hōv'n, índ-). Industrial town of North Brabant in the Netherlands. It manufactures electrical goods, and also motor vehicles, textiles, plastics, and cigars.

ein·korn (ín-korn) *n.* A one-seeded wheat, *Triticum monococcum,* grown in arid regions. [German *Einkorn* : *ein,* one, from Old High German *ein* + *Korn,* corn, grain, from Old High German *korn.*]

Ein·stein (ín-stīn; *German* -shtīn), **Albert** (1879–1955). U.S. physicist, born in Germany. His Special and General theories of relativity revolutionised man's thinking about the nature of space and time. Einstein showed that the mass of a body is a measure of its energy content. He expressed his findings in the equation known as **Einstein's law** *(see).* Einstein was awarded the Nobel prize in physics (1921) for his work in explaining the photoelectric effect. —**Ein·stein·i·an** (-stīn-i-ən) *adj.*

ein·stein·i·um (ín-stīni-əm) *n. Symbol* **Es** A synthetic transuranic element first produced by neutron irradiation of uranium in a thermonuclear explosion. It has 12 known isotopes with half-lives ranging between 1.2 minutes and 270 days and mass numbers from 245 to 256. Atomic number 99. [New Latin, after Albert EINSTEIN.]

Einstein shift *n. Astronomy.* A small displacement towards the red in a star's spectrum, predicted by Einstein's General theory of relativity and caused by the interaction between the radiation and a gravitational field.

Einstein's law *n.* **1.** The law that $E = mc^2$, where E is the energy associated with a mass m and c is the speed of light. Also called "Einstein's equation". **2.** The law that the energy of an electron emitted in the photoelectric effect is $h\nu - \Phi$, where ν is the frequency of the incident radiation, Φ is the work function of the electron emitter, and h is the Planck constant.

Eire. The Gaelic name for the island of **Ireland.** [Irish Gaelic *Ēire,* from Old Irish *Ēriu.* See **Erin.**]

eirenic, eirenical. Variants of **irenic.**

ei·ren·i·con, i·ren·i·con (īr-réeni-kon) *n.* A proposal that attempts to create harmony between conflicting viewpoints. [Greek, from *eirēnikos,* relating to peace, from *eirēnē,* peace.]

eis·e·ge·sis (í-si-jée-siss) *n., pl.* **-ses** (-seez). An explanation or analysis, especially of a Biblical text, using one's own ideas. Compare **exegesis.** [19th century : from Greek *eis,* into + -*egesis,* as in EXEGESIS (with which the term was coined to contrast).]

Ei·sen·how·er (íz'n-howr), **Dwight David** (1890-1969). U.S. general and 34th president of the United States (1953 – 61). In 1943 he was made Supreme Commander of the Allied Expeditionary Forces and he launched the D-Day invasion of Europe in 1944. In 1950 he was made Supreme Commander of NATO, but resigned when he won the Republican presidential nomination in 1952.

Ei·sen·stein (íz'n-stīn), **Sergei Mikhailovich** (1898-1948). Russian film director, whose work included *Strike* (1924), *Battleship Potemkin* (1925), and *October* (1927), a film about the Bolshevik revolution. His first sound film was *Alexander Nevsky* (1938). His last film, *Ivan the Terrible* (1945), was intended to be a trilogy, but he died after completing only the first two parts.

ei·stedd·fod (ī-stéd-fəd, -steth-, -vod, ay-) *n., pl.* **-fods** or **eisteddfodau** (áy-steth-vód-ī, í-). **1.** Any of various annual assemblies of, or competitions between, Welsh poets and musicians. **2.** Any of various competitions in music, elocution, or the like, held in other countries. [Welsh, "session", "a sitting" : *eistedd,* to sit, from *sedd,* seat + *-fod,* from *bod,* to be.]

ei·ther (īthər, eethər) *pron.* One or the other: *Choose either.* —*conj.* Used before the first of two or more stated alternatives, the following alternatives being signalled by *or*: *Either we go now, or we remain here forever.* —*adj.* **1.** One or the other; any one (of two): *Wear either coat.* **2.** One and the other; each: *She wore rings on either hand.* —*adv.* Likewise; any more so; also. Used as an intensive following negative statements: *If you don't order a dessert, I won't either.* [Middle English *aither, either,* Old English *ǣgther, ǣghwæther.*]

Usage: In formal usage, *either* takes a singular verb or pronoun: *Either is capable of doing his job.* Informally, the plural is often heard *(Either are capable of doing their job),* and this is especially likely whenever *either* is followed by *of* and a plural noun or pronoun *(Are either of them coming? Are either of the books what you want?)* Either is usually limited to constructions involving two persons or things: *Choose either* implies a choice of two, as does *Either book is suitable.* The use of *either* to refer to more than two entities attracts strong criticism. Grammarians recommend the use of *any* (or *any one*) instead. Similarly, *either . . . or* is restricted in formal usage to two alternatives: *He said he would either fight or resign.* Informal usage, however, often employs *either . . . or* for more than two alternatives *(He would either fight or resign or leave the country),* and this may even be encountered in formal contexts. The *either . . . or* construction has other problems. It is generally recommended that the two conjunctions introduce elements that are grammatically parallel: *He either obeys or leaves,* or *Either he obeys or he leaves,* which is sometimes heard informally. Of the two pronunciations shown, the first (īthər) is generally preferred in British English, although the second (eethər) is also very widespread. In American English, eethər predominates, while īthər may even be considered somewhat affected. See also **neither, none.**

ei·ther–or (īthər-ór ‖ eethər-) *adj.* Requiring a choice between two exclusive alternatives: *an either-or situation.*

e·jac·u·late (i-jáckew-layt) *v.* **-lated, -lating, -lates.** —*tr.* **1.** To eject or discharge abruptly; especially, to discharge (semen). **2.** To utter suddenly and passionately; exclaim. —*intr.* To emit semen. —*n.* (i-jáckew-lət, -lit). Semen ejaculated. [Latin *ējaculārī* (past participle, *ējaculātus*) : *ex-,* out + *jaculārī,* to throw, shoot, from *jaculum,* dart, from *jacere,* to throw.] —**e·jac·u·la·tor** *n.*

e·jac·u·la·tion (i-jáckew-láysh'n) *n.* **1.** The act of ejaculating. **2.** An abrupt discharge of fluid; especially, an emission of seminal fluid. **3. a.** A sudden, emphatic utterance; an exclamation. **b.** A brief, pious utterance or prayer.

e·jac·u·la·to·ry (i-jáckew-lə-tri, -təri, -laytəri, -láytəri) *adj.* Also **e·jac·u·la·tive** (-lətiv, -laytiv). **1.** Of or pertaining to ejaculation. **2.** Pertaining to or constituting a sudden, brief utterance; exclamatory.

e·ject (i-jékt) *v.* **ejected, ejecting, ejects.** —*tr.* **1.** To throw out forcefully; expel. **2.** To compel to leave; evict. **3.** To emit. —*intr.* To make an emergency exit by ejection capsule or seat. [Middle English *ejecten,* from Latin *ēicere* (past participle *ējectus*) : *ex-,* out + *jacere,* to throw.]

Synonyms: eject, expel, evict, throw out.

e·jec·ta (i-jéktə) *pl.n.* Ejected matter, as that from an erupting volcano. [New Latin, from Latin *ējectus,* ejected. See **eject.**]

e·jec·tion (i-jéksh'n) *n.* **1.** The act of ejecting or the condition of being ejected. **2.** Ejected matter.

ejection seat *n.* Also **ejector seat.** A seat designed to eject the pilot clear of an aircraft and enable him to parachute to the ground in an emergency.

e·ject·ment (i-jéktmənt) *n.* **1.** The act of ejecting; eviction; dispossession. **2.** *Law.* Formerly, an action to regain possession of land held by another.

e·jec·tor (i-jéktər) *n.* **1.** A person or thing that ejects. **2.** A device in a gun that ejects the empty shell after each firing.

Ekaterinburg. See **Yekaterinburg.**

eke[1] (eek) *tr.v.* **eked, eking, ekes. 1.** To supplement with great effort; strain to fill out. Used with *out: He eked out his income by working at night.* **2.** To make (a living, for example) with great effort or strain. Used with *out: eke out a living.* **3.** To cause (a limited resource) to last longer, through economical use. Used with *out: They eked out their emergency rations for a whole week.* [Middle English *eken,* Old English *ēacan,* to increase.]

eke[2] *adv. Archaic.* Also. [Middle English *ec, eke,* Old English *ēac.*]

e·kis·tics (i-kísstiks) *n. Used with a singular verb.* The science of human settlements, including town or community planning and design. [Greek *oikistikē,* feminine of *oikistikos,* of settlements, from *oikizein,* to settle, from *oikos,* house. See **ecumenical.**] —**e·kis·tic, e·kis·ti·cal** *adj.* —**ek·is·ti·cian** (écki-stísh'n) *n.*

ek·ka (éckə) *n.* A small, one-horse vehicle in India. [Hindi *ekkā,* unit.]

el. elevation.

e·lab·o·rate (i-lábbə-rət, -rit) *adj.* **1.** Planned or executed with painstaking attention to numerous parts or details. **2.** Rich in detail; complicated; ornate. —*v.* (-rayt) **elaborated, -rating, -rates.** —*tr.* **1.** To work out with care and detail; develop thoroughly. **2.** To produce by effort; create. **3.** To add more detail to; make more complex; enrich. **4.** *Physiology.* To convert (food, for example) into a more complex chemical state for use by the body. —*intr.* To express oneself at

greater length or in greater detail; provide further information. Often used with *on* or *upon.* [Latin *ēlabōrātus,* past participle of *ēlabōrāre,* "to work out" : *ex-,* out + *labōrāre,* to work, from *labor,* work.] —**e·lab·o·rate·ly** *adv.* —**e·lab·o·rate·ness** *n.* —**e·lab·o·ra·tion** (-ráysh'n) *n.* —**e·lab·o·ra·tor** *n.*

El A·la·mein (ál-ə-mayn). Railway junction on the coast road of northern Egypt. It gave its name to a decisive battle (1942) of World War II, when the Eighth Army defeated Rommel's Afrika Corps.

E·lam (eélam). Also **Su·si·a·na** (soozi-aánə, -áynə). Ancient country now in Iran. It was established east of the Tigris *c.* 3000 B.C., and Susa, its capital, later became a capital of the Persian Achaemenid Empire. The Elamites were thought to be descended from Shem, the son of Noah.

E·lam·ite (eélə-mīt) *n.* Also **E·lam·i·tic** (-míttik) (for sense 2). **1.** A native or inhabitant of Elam. **2.** An unclassified language spoken by the ancient Elamites. In this sense, also called "Susian". —**E·lam·ite, E·lam·i·tic, E·lam·it·ish** (-mītish) *adj.*

é·lan (ay-lón, ay-lán) *n.* **1.** Enthusiasm; vigour; dash. **2.** Style; flair. [French *élan,* from Old French *eslan,* a rush, dash, from *eslancer,* to throw out : *es-,* out, from Latin *ex-* + *lancer,* to throw, from Late Latin *lanceāre,* to throw a lance, from Latin *lancea,* lance.]

e·land (eéland) *n.* Either of two large African antelopes, *Taurotragus oryx* or *T. derbianus,* having a light-brown or greyish coat, a shoulder hump, and spirally twisted horns. [Afrikaans, from Dutch *eland,* elk, from late Middle Dutch *elen, elant,* from (obsolete) German *elen, elend,* from (Old) Lithuanian *ellenis,* stag.]

élan vi·tal (vee-tál, -taál) *n.* The vital force hypothesised by Henri Bergson as a source of causation and evolution in nature. See **Bergsonism.** [French, "vital ardour".]

el·a·pid (éllapid) *n.* Any of various venomous snakes of the family Elapidae, which includes the cobras and coral snakes. —*adj.* Of or belonging to the Elapidae. [New Latin *Elapidae,* from Medieval Greek *elaps* (stem *elapid-*), variant of Greek *elops,* a fish.]

e·lapse (i-lápss) *intr.v.* **elapsed, elapsing, elapses.** To pass; slip by. Used of time. [Latin *ēlābī* (past participle *ēlapsus*) : *ex-,* away + *lābī,* to slip, glide.]

e·lapsed time (i-lápst) *n.* The measured duration of an event; especially, the actual time spent in transit, as in flight, by a moving body.

e·las·mo·branch (i-láz-mə-brangk, i-láss-) *n.* Any of numerous fishes of the subclass Elasmobranchii within the class Chondrichthyes, characterised by a cartilaginous skeleton, and including the sharks, rays, and skates. [New Latin *Elasmobranchii,* "plate-gilled ones" : Greek *elasmos,* metal plate, from *elaunein,* to drive, beat + -BRANCH.]

e·las·mo·saur (i-lázmə-sawr) *n.* Also **e·las·mo·sau·rus** (-sáwrəss). An extinct marine reptile that had a very long neck. [New Latin *elasmosaurus,* from Greek *elasmos,* metal plate (see **elasmobranch**) + *sauros,* lizard.]

e·las·tance (i-láss-tənss, -laáss-) *n. Electricity.* The reciprocal of capacitance, measured in reciprocal farads (darafs).

e·las·tic (i-láss-tik, -laáss-) *adj.* **1.** *Physics.* **a.** Returning or capable of returning to an initial form or state after deformation. **b.** Conserving total kinetic energy of translation. Said of certain collisions. **2.** Capable of adapting to change or a variety of circumstances; flexible: *an elastic schedule.* **3.** Quick to recover or revive: *an elastic spirit.* **4.** Springy; firm: *an elastic turf.* **5.** Made of or containing elastic. —*n.* **1.** A flexible stretchable fabric made with interwoven strands of rubber or an imitative synthetic fibre. **2.** *Chiefly U.S.* Something made of this fabric, as a garter or rubber band. [New Latin *elasticus,* from Late Greek *elastikos,* from Greek *elastos, elatos,* beaten, from *elaunein,* to drive.] —**e·las·ti·cal·ly** *adv.*

e·las·ti·cate (i-láss-ti-kayt, -laáss-) *tr.v.* **-cated, -cating, -cates.** To make (a fabric or garment) stretchable by the insertion of elastic.

elastic band *n.* A rubber band *(see).*

e·las·ti·cise (i-láss-ti-sīz, -laáss-) *tr.v.* **-cised, -cising, -cises. 1.** To make (a metal strip, for example) elastic. **2.** To elasticate.

e·las·tic·i·ty (í-lass-tíssəti, ée-, -laass-) *n., pl.* **-ties. 1.** The condition or property of being elastic; resilience; flexibility. **2.** *Physics.* **a.** The property of returning to an initial form or state following deformation. **b.** The degree to which this property is exhibited.

elastic limit *n.* The maximum stress that can be applied to a body or substance without causing a permanent deformation.

elastic modulus *n.* The **modulus of elasticity** *(see).*

e·las·tin (i-láss-tin, -laáss-) *n. Biochemistry.* A protein that is the principal component of *elastic tissue,* found in the walls of arteries, the dermis of the skin, and other elastic structures. [ELAST(IC) + -IN.]

e·las·to·mer (i-láss-təmər, -laáss-) *n.* Any of various polymers having the elastic properties of natural rubber. [Greek *elastos,* ELASTIC + -MER(E).]

E·las·to·plast (i-láss-tə-plaast, -laáss- ‖ -plast) *n.* A trademark for an adhesive surgical dressing.

E·lat, Ei·lat (ay-lát). Israeli port on the Gulf of Aqaba, the country's only outlet to the Red Sea.

e·late (i-láyt) *tr.v.* **elated, elating, elates.** To raise the spirits of; excite feelings of pride or optimism in; encourage. —*adj. Archaic.* Elated; joyful; lively. [Latin *ēlātus* (past participle of *effere,* to carry out, lift up) : *ex-,* out + *-lātus,* "carried".]

e·lat·ed (i-láytid) *adj.* In high spirits; lively and joyful. **—e·lat·ed·ly** *adv.* **—e·lat·ed·ness** *n.*

el·a·ter (éllətər) *n.* **1.** An elaterid beetle. **2.** *Botany.* An elongated, often spirally thickened filament occurring in the spore-bearing structures of liverworts and other bryophytes, thought to aid spore dispersal. [New Latin, from Greek *elatēr,* driver, from *elaunein,* to drive.]

e·lat·er·id (i-láttərid) *n.* Any of numerous beetles of the family Elateridae, which includes the click beetles. [New Latin *Elateridae,* from *elater,* elongated filament, ELATER.] **—e·lat·er·id** *adj.*

el·a·te·ri·um (éllə-téer-i-əm) *n.* A sediment produced from the squirting cucumber and containing the crystalline substance *elaterin,* used as a purgative. [Latin, from Greek *elatērion,* squirting cucumber, from *elatērios,* purgative, from *elaunein,* to drive.]

e·la·tion (i-láysh'n) *n.* An exalted feeling arising typically from a sense of triumph, achievement, or relief.

E layer *n.* A region, or any of various layers in the region, of the ionosphere, occurring between about 90 kilometres (55 miles) and 150 kilometres (95 miles) above the earth and influencing long-distance communications by strongly reflecting radio waves in the range from one to three megahertz. Also called "E region", "Heaviside layer", "Kennelly-Heaviside layer". [*E* (arbitrary designation) + LAYER.]

El·ba (élbə). Largest island (223 square kilometres; 86 square miles) in the Tuscan archipelago, part of Italy's Livorno province. Napoleon I spent a year in exile on Elba (1814–15).

El·be (elb ‖ *German* élbə). *Czech* **La·be** (lá-be). A river in central Europe. It rises on the south side of the Riesengebirge in northeast Bohemia, Czech Republic, flows 1 167 kilometres (725 miles) into Germany and passes Dresden and Magdeburg before flowing through Hamburg and into the North Sea at Cuxhaven.

Elberfeld. See **Wuppertal.**

el·bow (élbō) *n.* **1. a.** The joint or bend of the arm between the forearm and the upper arm. **b.** The bony outer projection of this joint. **c.** That point of a garment which covers this joint. **2.** A joint, as of a bird or quadruped, corresponding to the human elbow. **3.** Something having a bend or angle similar to an elbow, especially: **a.** A length of pipe with a sharp bend in it. **b.** A sharp bend in a river or a road. **—at (one's) elbow.** Close at hand; nearby. **—bend (one's) elbow.** *Informal.* To drink alcohol; especially, to drink too much. **—up to the elbows in** or **with.** Busily occupied with; engrossed in.

~v. elbowed, -bowing, -bows. *—tr.* **1.** To push, jostle, or shove with or as with the elbows. **2.** To make (one's way) by such pushing, jostling, or shoving. **3.** To knock or hit with one's elbow. *—intr.* To push, jostle, or shove one's way. [Middle English *elbowe,* Old English *elnboga,* "bow of the forearm" : ELL + BOW.]

elbow grease *n. Informal.* Strenuous physical effort, especially rubbing or polishing.

el·bow·room (élbō-rōōm, -rŏŏm) *n.* **1.** Room enough to move around or function; ample space. **2.** Adequate scope or leeway; freedom from limitations.

El·brus or **El·bruz, Mount** (il-brŏŏss). Highest mountain in Europe, lying in the Caucasus on the border of Russia and Georgia. It consists of two extinct volcanic peaks, the one to the west rising to 5 642 metres (18,510 feet).

El Cid (el síd ‖ *Spanish* théed), born Rodrigo (or Ruy) Díaz de Vivar (*c.* 1060–99). Spanish soldier and national hero. He fought against the Moors in the service of Ferdinand I and Sancho II of Castile, but was banished from Castile in 1081 by Alfonso VI, who feared him as a rival. He then fought for the Moorish rulers of Saragossa against Christians and Moors, and in 1094 conquered the kingdom of Valencia which he ruled until his death. His exploits were recounted in the anonymous 12th-century epic, *The Song of the Cid,* and elsewhere.

eld·er¹ (éldər) *n.* **1.** An older person. **2.** An ancestor; a predecessor; a forefather. **3.** An older, influential man of a family, tribe, or community. **4.** Any of the governing officers of a church.

~adj. Born before; older; especially, being the older of two members of a family. [Middle English *eldre,* Old English *ieldra, eldra.*] **—el·der·ship** *n.*

Usage: Elder and *eldest* refer only to people; *older* and *oldest* apply also to things. There is also a difference in construction: *elder* is not followed by *than,* and neither *elder* nor *eldest* can be used without *the* when following a verb, as in *John is the elder* (but *John is older/John is older than Mary*).

elder² *n.* **1.** Any of various shrubs or small trees of the genus *Sambucus,* having clusters of small white flowers and red or blackish berry-like fruits. Also called "elderberry". **2.** Any of several similar trees or shrubs. [Middle English *eller, eldre,* Old English *ellaern, ellen.*]

el·der·ber·ry (éldər-bri, -bəri, -berri) *n., pl.* **-ries. 1.** The small, edible fruit of an elder, used to make wine or preserves. **2.** A shrub or tree producing such fruit; an elder.

elder hand *n.* In certain card games, the first player to receive cards from the dealer and to make a play.

eld·er·ly (éldərli) *adj.* Rather old. See Synonyms at **old. —el·der·li·ness** *n.*

elder statesman *n.* An elderly person, usually a retired statesman, who acts as an unofficial adviser on national problems.

eld·est (éldist). Oldest. Said of a person. See Usage note at **elder.** [Middle English *eldest,* Old English *ieldesta, eldesta.*]

ELDO European Launcher Development Organisation.

El Do·ra·do (éldə-raádō ‖ *Spanish* el doraátho) *n.* **1.** A legendary kingdom or city in Spanish America rich in precious metals and jewels, sought after by 16th-century explorers. **2.** Any place of fabulous wealth or opportunity. [Spanish, "the gilded (one)" : *el,* the, from Latin *ille,* that + *dorado,* past participle of *dorar,* to gild, from Latin *deaurāre : de-,* thoroughly + *aurum,* gold.]

E·le·a (i-lée-ə, ee-). Ancient Greek colony in southern Italy, site of the founding of the Eleatic school of philosophy.

El·ea·nor of Aquitaine (éllinər ‖ -nawr), (*c.* 1122–1204). Queen consort of Louis VII of France and subsequently of Henry II of England. Her marriage to Louis VII was annulled in 1152. She then married Henry, adding to his lands of Normandy and Anjou her vast possessions in Aquitaine. She bore him three daughters and five sons, including the future English kings, Richard I and John.

Eleanor of Castile (died 1290). Queen consort of Edward I of England, daughter of Ferdinand III of Castile. She died in 1290, and in her memory Edward had crosses erected at 12 stages of her funeral procession from Nottinghamshire to London.

El·e·at·ic (éli-áttik) *adj.* Of or characteristic of Elea or the school of philosophy founded there in the sixth and fifth centuries B.C. by Xenophanes and Parmenides.

~n. An adherent of the Eleatic school, which held immutable being to be the only knowable reality and change and sensory perceptions to be illusory. **—El·e·at·i·cism** (-áttisiz'm) *n.*

elec. electric; electrical; electrician; electricity.

el·e·cam·pane (élli-kam-páyn) *n.* A tall, coarse plant, *Inula helenium,* native to Eurasia, having rayed yellow flowers. [Middle English *elycampane,* from Old French *enule campane,* from Medieval Latin *enula campāna : enula,* from Latin *inula,* elecampane, from Greek *helenion* + *campāna,* variant of Latin *campānea,* feminine of *campāneus,* of the field, from *campus,* field (see **camp**).]

e·lect (i-lékt) *v.* **elected, electing, elects.** *—tr.* **1.** To select by vote for an office, usually by a majority over other candidates. **2.** To choose; decide in favour of: *elect to pursue an arts course.* **3.** *Theology.* To predestine for salvation. Used in the passive. *—intr.* To make a choice, especially with deliberation; decide. **—See** Synonyms at **choose.**

~adj. 1. Chosen deliberately; singled out. **2.** Elected but not yet installed in office. Used in combination: *the governor-elect.* **3.** *Theology.* Selected by the divine will for salvation. [Middle English *electen,* from Latin *ēligere* (past participle *ēlectus*), to pick out, select : *ex-,* out + *legere,* to gather, choose.]

e·lec·tion (i-léksh'n) *n.* **1.** The act or power of choosing. **2. a.** The act or process of choosing by vote among candidates to fill an office or position, especially a political one. **b.** The fact of being so chosen. **3.** *Theology.* Predestined salvation.

e·lec·tion·eer (i-léksh'n-éer) *intr.v.* **-eered, -eering, -eers.** To work actively for a particular candidate or political party, as by canvassing.

~n. One who electioneers. **—e·lec·tion·eer·ing** *n. & adj.*

e·lec·tive (i-léktiv) *adj.* **1.** Of or pertaining to a selection by vote. **2.** Filled or obtained by election: *elective office.* **3.** Having the power or authority to elect; electoral. **4.** Capable of being chosen; optional. **5.** Tending to be concerned with certain things rather than others: *elective affinity.* **—e·lec·tive·ly** *adv.*

e·lec·tor (i-léktər) *n.* **1.** A person who elects; a qualified voter. **2.** A member of the Electoral College of the United States. **3.** *Usually capital* **E.** Any of the German princes in the Holy Roman Empire who were entitled to elect the emperor.

e·lec·tor·al (i-léktərəl ‖ -táwrəl) *adj.* **1.** Of, pertaining to, or composed of electors. **2.** Having the power or duty to elect.

electoral college *n.* **1.** A body of electors. **2.** *Capital* **E,** *Capital* **C.** A popularly elected body of electors chosen by the States to elect the president and vice-president of the United States.

e·lec·tor·ate (i-léktər-ət, -it) *n.* **1.** The body of qualified voters. **2.** In certain countries, a district or division of voters. **3.** The dignity or territory of an Elector of the Holy Roman Empire.

E·lec·tra¹, E·lek·tra (i-léktrə). In Greek legend, the daughter of Clytemnestra and Agamemnon. She avenged the murder of Agamemnon with the help of her brother Orestes, who killed their mother and her lover, Aegisthus.

Electra² *n.* A star in the constellation Pleiades. [After *Electra,* daughter of Atlas.]

Electra complex *n. Psychology.* Unconscious sexual desire of a daughter for her father generally manifesting itself first in girls between the ages of three and five. Compare **Oedipus complex.**

e·lec·tret (i-léktrit) *n.* A solid dielectric that exhibits persistent dielectric polarisation. [ELECTR(ICITY) + (MAGN)ET.]

e·lec·tric (i-léktrik) *adj.* Also **e·lec·tri·cal** (-'l). *Abbr.* **elec., elect. 1.** Of, pertaining to, producing, derived from, produced, powered, or operated by electricity. **2. a.** Emotionally exciting; thrilling. **b.** Exceptionally tense; charged with emotion.

~n. 1. *British Informal.* Electricity. Usually preceded by *the.* **2.** *Plural.* Electrical equipment. [New Latin *electricus,* "like amber", because amber produces sparks when rubbed, from Latin *ēlectrum,* amber, from Greek *ēlektron†.*] **—e·lec·tri·cal·ly** *adv.*

Usage: Electric is used of anything producing or powered by electricity: *electric chair; electric light. Electrical* has a looser connection with the physical power of electricity, being mainly used to characterise general concepts associated with the subject, or the people and activities involved in its study: *electrical engineer, electrical design.*

electrical engineering *n. Abbr.* **E.E.** The study of the design and application of circuitry and equipment for power generation and distribution, machine control, and communications. **—electrical engineer** *n.*

electric blanket *n.* A blanket heated by means of internal wiring that can be connected to the electrical mains.

electric blue *n.* Metallic light blue.

electric chair *n.* **1.** A chairlike device used in parts of the United States to restrain and electrocute a person sentenced to death. **2.** The punishment of death by electrocution.

electric charge *n.* *Electricity.* **Charge** *(see).*

electric constant *n.* *Symbol* ϵ_0 The permittivity of free space, having the value 8.854×10^{-12} farad per metre. Also called "absolute permittivity".

electric current *n.* *Electricity.* **Current** *(see).*

electric displacement *n.* The product of the electric field strength and the absolute permittivity. Also called "electric flux density".

electric eel *n.* A long, eel-like freshwater fish, *Electrophorus electricus,* of northern South America, having organs capable of producing a powerful electric discharge.

electric eye *n.* A **photoelectric cell** *(see),* especially when used as a sensor for an automatic switch.

electric fence *n.* A fence, usually consisting of a single strand of wire, that is charged with electricity.

electric field *n.* A region of space characterised by the existence of a force that is experienced by a stationary charged particle placed at any point within it.

electric field strength *n.* *Symbol* **E** The strength of an electric field equal to the force experienced by a stationary charge within the field divided by the charge. It is measured in volts per metre.

electric flux *n.* The integral over a designated surface of the component of electric displacement normal to the surface.

electric furnace *n.* An industrial or laboratory furnace heated by an electric arc, electric induction, or electric resistance.

electric guitar *n.* A guitar that transmits sounds to an amplifier by means of an electronic pick-up placed under the strings.

electric hare *n.* A dummy hare, mounted on an electric rail, which greyhounds chase when racing.

e·lec·tri·cian (i-lék-trísh'n, éllek-, éelek-, éllik-) *n. Abbr.* **elec., elect.** A person whose occupation is the installation, repair, or operation of electrical equipment and circuitry.

e·lec·tric·i·ty (i-lék-tríss-əti, éllek-, éelek-, éllik- ‖ -tríz-) *n. Abbr.* **elec., elect. 1.** The class of physical phenomena arising from the existence and interactions of positively and negatively charged particles. **2.** The physical science of such phenomena. **3.** Electric current used or regarded as a source of power. **4.** Intense emotional excitement.

electric moment *n.* The **dipole moment** *(see)* of an electric dipole.

electric motor *n.* A device for converting electrical energy directly into mechanical energy by electromagnetic induction, having a fixed part (the stator), which produces a magnetic field, and a rotating coil or conductor (the rotor), which moves under the influence of an induced force. See **induction motor, synchronous motor, linear motor.**

electric needle *n.* A cutting instrument used in surgery and powered by a high-frequency current.

electric organ *n.* **1.** *Music.* An organ operated by electricity. **2.** A group of cells in some fishes, such as the electric eel and electric ray, that generate electric shocks capable of stunning prey.

electric ray *n.* Any of various fishes of the family Torpedinidae, having a rounded body and a pair of electric organs capable of producing a fairly strong electric discharge. Also called "numbfish".

e·lec·tri·fy (i-léktri-fî) *tr.v.* **-fied, -fying, -fies. 1.** To produce electric charge on or in (a conductor). **2. a.** To wire or otherwise equip a building, for example) for the use of electric power. **b.** To convert (a railway system, for example) to enable it to operate by electricity. **c.** To provide with electric power. **3.** To thrill, startle greatly, or shock. [ELECTRI(C) + -FY.] **—e·lec·tri·fi·a·ble** *adj.* **—e·lec·tri·fi·ca·tion** (-fi-káysh'n) *n.* **—e·lec·tri·fi·er** *n.*

e·lec·tro (i-léktrõ) *n., pl.* **-tros. 1. Electroplate** *(see).* **2. Electrotype** *(see).*

electro-, electr- *comb. form.* Indicates: **1.** Electric; for example, **electromagnet, electrode. 2.** Electrically; for example, **electrocute, electrograph. 3.** Electrolysis; for example, **electrolyte.** [New Latin, from Latin *ēlectrum,* amber, from Greek *ēlektron.* See **electric.**]

e·lec·tro·a·cous·tics (i-léktrõ-ə-kŏ́ostiks) *n. Used with a singular verb.* The science of the interaction or interconversion of electric and acoustic phenomena. **—e·lec·tro·a·cous·tic** *adj.* **—e·lec·tro·a·cous·tic·al·ly** *adv.*

e·lec·tro·a·nal·y·sis (i-léktrõ-ə-nál-ə-siss) *n., pl.* **-ses** (-seez). Chemical analysis using electrolytic techniques. **—e·lec·tro·an·a·lyt·ic** (-ánnə-líttik), **e·lec·tro·an·a·lyt·i·cal** *adj.*

e·lec·tro·car·di·o·gram (i-léktrõ-kárdi-ə-gram) *n. Abbr.* **ECG** The curve traced by an electrocardiograph, used to diagnose heart disease.

e·lec·tro·car·di·o·graph (i-léktrõ-kárdi-ə-graaf, -graf) *n. Abbr.* **ECG** An instrument used to record electric potentials associated with the electric currents that initiate the heartbeat. **—e·lec·tro·car·di·o·gra·phic** (-gráffik) *adj.* **—e·lec·tro·car·di·og·ra·phy** (-óggrəfi) *n.*

e·lec·tro·chem·i·cal series *n.* The **electromotive series** *(see).*

e·lec·tro·chem·is·try (i-léktrõ-kémmistri) *n.* The science of the interaction or interconversion of electric and chemical phenomena. **—e·lec·tro·chem·i·cal** *adj.* **—e·lec·tro·chem·i·cal·ly** *adv.* **—e·lec·tro·chem·ist** *n.*

e·lec·tro·co·ag·u·la·tion (i-léktrõ-kõ-ággew-láysh'n) *n. Medicine.* The use of a high-frequency electric current to coagulate tissue so that bloodless incisions can be made during operations.

e·lec·tro·con·vul·sive therapy *n. Abbr.* **ECT** Treatment of certain mental disorders in which an electric current is passed through the brain to cause a convulsion.

e·lec·tro·cute (i-léktrə-kewt) *tr.v.* **-cuted, -cuting, -cutes.** To kill with electricity; especially, to execute by passing a high-voltage electric current through the body of. [ELECTRO- + (EXE)CUTE.] **—e·lec·tro·cu·tion** (-kéwsh'n) *n.*

e·lec·trode (i-lék-trõd) *n.* **1.** A solid electric conductor through which an electric current enters or leaves a medium such as an electrolyte, a nonmetallic solid, a molten metal, a gas, or a vacuum. **2.** A collector or emitter of electric charge or electric-charge carriers, as in a semiconducting device. [ELECTR(O)- + -ODE.]

e·lec·tro·de·pos·it (i-léktrõ-di-pózzit) *tr.v.* **-ited, -iting, -its.** To deposit (a dissolved or suspended substance) on an electrode by electrolysis.
~*n.* The substance so deposited. **—e·lec·tro·dep·o·si·tion** (-déppə-zish'n, -déepə-) *n.*

e·lec·tro·di·al·y·sis (i-léktrõ-dī-ál-ə-siss) *n., pl.* **-ses** (-seez). Dialysis at a rate speeded by the application of an electric potential across the dialysis membrane, used especially to remove electrolytes from a colloidal suspension.

e·lec·tro·dy·nam·ics (i-léktrõ-dī-námmiks) *n. Used with a singular verb.* The physics of the relationship between electric, magnetic, and mechanical phenomena. **—e·lec·tro·dy·nam·ic** *adj.*

e·lec·tro·dy·na·mom·e·ter (i-léktrõ-dīnə-mŏmmitər) *n.* An instrument that uses the interaction of the magnetic fields of fixed and moving sets of coils to measure current, voltage, or power.

e·lec·tro·en·ceph·a·lo·gram (i-léktrõ-en-séff'l-ə-gram) *n. Abbr.* **EEG** A graphic record of the electrical activity of the brain as recorded by an electroencephalograph. Also called "encephalogram".

e·lec·tro·en·ceph·a·lo·graph (i-léktrõ-en-séff'l-ə-graaf, -graf) *n.* An instrument that records the electrical activity of the brain. **—e·lec·tro·en·ceph·a·lo·graph·ic** (-gráffik) *adj.* **—e·lec·tro·en·ceph·a·log·ra·phy** (-óggrəfi) *n.*

e·lec·tro·form (i-lék-trə-fawrm, -trõ-) *tr.v.* **-formed, -forming, -forms.** To produce or reproduce by electrodeposition in a mould. [ELECTRO- + -FORM.]

e·lec·tro·gen·e·sis (i-léktrõ-jénnə-siss) *n.* The production of electrical activity; especially, that produced in living tissue. **—e·lec·tro·gen·ic** *adj.*

e·lec·tro·graph (i-lék-trə-graaf, -trõ-, -graf) *n.* **1.** Any electrically produced graph or tracing. **2.** Equipment used to produce such graphs or tracings in facsimile transmission. **3.** A visual record of the composition of a metal surface obtained by placing the surface on a paper soaked in an electrolyte and passing a current from the surface through the paper to an electrode placed on the other side of the paper. [ELECTRO- + -GRAPH.]

e·lec·tro·kin·et·ics (i-léktrõ-ki-néttiks) *n. Used with a singular verb.* The electrodynamics of heating effects and of current distribution in electric networks. **—e·lec·tro·kin·et·ic** *adj.*

e·lec·tro·lu·mi·nes·cence (i-léktrõ-lŏomi-néss'nss ‖ -léwmi-) *n.* **1.** The direct conversion of electric energy to light by a solid phosphor subjected to an alternating electric field. **2.** The emission of light caused by electric discharge in a gas. **—e·lec·tro·lu·mi·nes·cent** *adj.*

e·lec·tro·lyse, e·lec·tro·lyze (i-lék-trə-līz, -trõ-) *tr.v.* **-lysed, -lysing, -lyses.** To decompose by electrolysis. [Back-formation from ELECTROLYSIS.]

e·lec·trol·y·sis (i-lék-tróllə-siss, éllek-, éelek-) *n.* **1.** Chemical change, especially decomposition, produced in an electrolyte by an electric current. **2.** Destruction of living tissue, as of hair roots, by an electric current. [ELECTRO- + -LYSIS.]

e·lec·tro·lyte (i-lék-trə-līt, -trõ-) *n.* A substance that dissociates into ions in solution or when fused, thereby becoming electrically conducting. [ELECTRO- + -LYTE.]

e·lec·tro·lyt·ic (i-lék-trə-líttik, -trõ-) *adj.* **1. a.** Of or pertaining to electrolysis. **b.** Produced by electrolysis. **2.** Of or pertaining to an electrolyte.

electrolytic cell *n.* **1.** A cell containing an electrolyte through which an externally generated electric current is passed by a system of electrodes in order to produce an electrochemical reaction. **2.** A cell containing an electrolyte in which an electrochemical reaction produces an electromotive force.

electrolytic gas *n.* A gas formed by the electrolysis of water, consisting of two parts of hydrogen and one part of water.

e·lec·tro·mag·net (i-léktrõ-mágnit) *n.* A magnet consisting essentially of a soft-iron core wound with a current-carrying coil of insulated wire, the current in which produces the magnetisation of the core.

e·lec·tro·mag·net·ic (i-lék-trõ-mag-néttik, -trə-, -məg-) *adj.* Of or exhibiting electromagnetism. **—e·lec·tro·mag·net·i·cal·ly** *adv.*

electromagnetic field *n.* The field of force associated with an accelerating electric charge, having both electric and magnetic components and containing a definite amount of electromagnetic energy.

electromagnetic interaction *n.* A form of interaction between particles that are charged as a result of their electric or magnetic fields or the exchange of virtual photons between them. Compare **strong interaction, weak interaction, gravitational interaction.**

electromagnetic pump *n.* A pump for moving liquid metals in which the pipe holding the liquid metal is put between the poles of an electromagnet and a current is passed through the liquid metal.

electromagnetic radiation *n.* Radiation consisting of an electric field and a magnetic field perpendicular to each other and to the direction of propagation. The speed of propagation in a vacuum is 2.9979×10^8 metres per second.

electromagnetic spectrum *n.* The entire range of radiation extending in frequency approximately from 10^{21} hertz to 0 hertz (or, in corresponding wavelengths, from 10^{-13} metre to infinity) and including, in order of decreasing frequency, gamma rays, X-rays, ultraviolet radiation, visible light, infrared radiation, microwaves, and radio waves.

electromagnetic unit *n. Abbr.* **emu** Any of a system of units for electricity and magnetism based on a system of equations in which the magnetic constant is taken as unity and by means of which the **abampere** *(see)* is defined as the fundamental unit of current.

electromagnetic wave *n.* A wave propagating as a periodic disturbance of the electromagnetic field and having a frequency in the electromagnetic spectrum.

e·lec·tro·mag·net·ism (i-léktrõ-mágni-tiz'm) *n.* **1.** Magnetism arising from an accelerating electric charge. **2.** The physics of electricity and magnetism.

e·lec·tro·me·chan·i·cal (i-léktrõ-mi-kánnik'l) *adj.* Of or designating a mechanical device that is operated by electricity.

e·lec·tro·mer·ism (i-léktrõ-mérriz'm) *n. Chemistry.* A form of tautomerism in which the isomers, called *electromers,* differ in the way in which electric charge is distributed in their molecules. [ELECTRO- + (ISO)MERISM.]

e·lec·tro·met·al·lur·gy (i-léktrõ-mi-tál-ərji, -méttə-lurji) *n.* The use of electricity to purify metals or to reduce metallic compounds to metals. **—e·lec·tro·met·al·lur·gi·cal** (-méttə-lúrjik'l) *adj.*

e·lec·trom·e·ter (i-lék-trómmitər, éllek-, éelek-) *n.* An instrument for detecting or measuring potential differences, electric charge, or, indirectly, electric current by means of mechanical forces exerted between electrically charged bodies. [ELECTRO- + -METER.]

e·lec·tro·mo·tive (i-léktrõ-mõtiv) *adj.* Of, pertaining to, or producing electric current.

electromotive force *n. Abbr.* **emf, EMF** The energy per unit charge that is converted reversibly from chemical, mechanical, or other forms of energy into electrical energy in a conversion device such as a battery or dynamo. It is measured in volts.

electromotive series *n.* A series of metals, with hydrogen included, arranged in order of their electrode potentials. The series represents the order in which metals replace one another from their salts, those high in the series replacing those lower down. The series of the commoner metals is: Na, Mg, Al, Zn, Fe, Co, Ni, Sn, Pb, H, Cu, Hg, Ag, Au. Also called "electrochemical series".

e·lec·tro·my·o·gram (i-léktrõ-mí-ə-gram, -õ-) *n.* A record of the electrical activity of a muscle obtained using an electromyograph.

e·lec·tro·my·o·graph (i-léktrõ-mí-ə-graaf, -õ-, -graf) *n.* An instrument that records the electrical activity of a muscle by means of electrodes inserted into the muscle fibre. **—e·lec·tro·my·og·ra·phy** (-óggrəfi) *n.*

e·lec·tron (i-lék-tron) *n. Symbol* **e** A subatomic particle in the lepton family having a rest mass of 9.1096×10^{-31} kilogram and a unit negative electric charge of approximately 1.602×10^{-19} coulomb. [ELECTR(O)- + -ON.]

electron camera *n.* A device forming part of a television camera in which an optical image is converted into an electrical signal.

e·lec·tro·neg·a·tive (i-léktrõ-néggətiv) *adj.* **1.** Having a negative electric charge. **2.** Tending to attract electrons to form a chemical bond. **—e·lec·tro·neg·a·tiv·i·ty** (-tívvəti) *n.*

electron gun *n.* An electron-emitting electrode and associated elements, especially in a cathode-ray tube, that produce a beam of accelerated electrons.

e·lec·tron·ic (i-lék-trónnik, éllek-, éelek-) *adj.* **1.** Of or pertaining to electrons. **2.** Of, pertaining to, based on, operated by, or otherwise involving the controlled conduction of electrons or other charge carriers, especially in a vacuum, gas, or semiconducting material. **3.** Pertaining to electronics. **4.** Pertaining to computers; computerised or computer-assisted: *machine-readable electronic dictionaries.* **—e·lec·tron·i·cal·ly** *adv.*

electronic data processing *n. Abbr.* **EDP** Data processing in which electronic computers are used to manipulate the information.

electronic music *n.* **1.** Music produced entirely or in part by manipulating natural or artificial sounds with tape recorders or other electronic devices. **2.** Music consisting of sounds produced by oscillating electronic signals.

e·lec·tron·ics (i-lék-trónniks, éllek-, éelek-) *n. Used with a singular verb.* **1.** The science and technology of electronic phenomena. **2.** The commercial industry of electronic devices and systems.

electron lens *n.* Any of various devices that use an electric or a magnetic field to focus a beam of electrons.

electron micrograph *n.* A micrograph made by an electron microscope.

electron microscope *n.* Any of a class of microscopes that use a beam of electrons rather than visible light to produce magnified images, especially of objects having dimensions smaller than the wavelengths of visible light, with linear magnification up to or exceeding a million (10^6). See **scanning electron microscope.**

electron multiplier *n.* A vacuum tube in which a single electron produces a large number of secondary electrons by collision with an anode, the process generally being repeated through a number of stages to achieve great amplification.

electron optics *n.* The science of the control of electron motion by electron lenses, in systems or under conditions analogous to those involving or affecting visible light.

electron pair *n.* **1.** Any two electrons functioning or regarded as functioning in concert; especially, two electrons shared by two atoms joined by a covalent chemical bond. **2.** The combination of an electron and a positron as produced by a high-energy photon. Also called "pair". See **pair production.**

electron probe microanalysis *n. Chemistry.* A method of analysing tiny quantities (as little as 10^{-13} gram) of material by bombarding the specimen with a finely focused beam of electrons and examining the resulting X-ray emission spectrum.

electron spin resonance *n. Chemistry. Abbr.* **ESR** A method of examining the molecular structure of paramagnetic substances by subjecting them to high-frequency radiation in a strong magnetic field. Changes in the spin of unpaired electrons in the molecules cause radiation to be absorbed at certain characteristic frequencies.

electron telescope *n.* An astronomical telescope that converts infrared radiation emitted by the planets into an optical image.

electron tube *n. Chiefly U.S.* An electronic **valve** *(see).*

e·lec·tron-volt (i-lék-tron-võlt) *n. Abbr.* **eV** A unit of energy equal to the energy acquired by an electron falling through a potential difference of one volt, approximately 1.602×10^{-19} joule.

e·lec·tro·phil·ic (i-léktrõ-fillik) *n. Chemistry.* Designating an atom, molecule, or ion that behaves as an electron acceptor. [ELECTRO- + -PHILE + -IC.]

e·lec·tro·pho·re·sis (i-léktrõ-fə-rée-siss) *n.* The motion of charged particles, especially colloidal particles, through a relatively stationary liquid under the influence of an applied electric field provided, in general, by immersed electrodes. Also called "cataphoresis". [ELECTRO- + -PHORESIS.]

e·lec·troph·o·rus (i-lék-tróffə-rəss, éllek-, éelek-) *n., pl.* **-ri** (-rī). An apparatus for generating static electricity, consisting of a disc that is given a negative charge by friction and a metal plate that is charged by induction when in contact with the disc. [ELECTRO- + -PHOROUS.]

e·lec·tro·plate (i-lék-trə-playt, -trõ-, -pláyt) *tr.v.* **-plated, -plating, -plates.** To coat or cover with a thin layer of metal by electrodeposition.
~*n.* **1.** An article that has been electroplated. **2.** Electroplated articles collectively. Also called "electro".

e·lec·tro·pos·i·tive (i-léktrõ-pózzitiv) *adj.* **1.** Having a positive electric charge. **2.** Tending to release electrons to form a chemical bond.

e·lec·tro·scope (i-léktrə-skõp) *n.* An instrument used to detect the presence, sign, and in some configurations the magnitude of an electric charge by the mutual attraction or repulsion of metal foils. [ELECTRO- + -SCOPE.] **—e·lec·tro·scop·ic** (-skóppik) *adj.*

e·lec·tro·stat·ic (i-léktrõ-státtik) *adj.* **1. a.** Of or pertaining to stationary electric charges. **b.** Produced or caused by such charges. **2.** Of or pertaining to electrostatics. **—e·lec·tro·stat·i·cal·ly** *adv.*

electrostatic generator *n.* Any of various devices, including the electrophorus, the Wimshurst machine, and especially the **Van de Graaff generator** *(see),* that generate high voltages by accumulating large quantities of electric charge.

electrostatic precipitation *n.* The removal of particles suspended in a gas by electrostatic charging and subsequent precipitation onto a collector in a strong electric field.

e·lec·tro·stat·ics (i-léktrõ-státtiks) *n. Used with a singular verb.* The branch of physics dealing with electrostatic phenomena.

electrostatic unit *n. Abbr.* **esu** Any of a system of units for electricity and magnetism based on a system of equations in which the electric constant is defined as unity and by means of which a fundamental unit of charge is defined.

e·lec·tro·stric·tion (i-léktrõ-stríksh'n) *n.* A change in the dimensions of a dielectric as the result of an applied electric field.

e·lec·tro·sur·ger·y (i-léktrõ-súrjəri) *n.* Surgery using electrical methods, as in cauterisation.

e·lec·tro·ther·a·peu·tics (i-léktrõ-thérrə-péwtiks) *n. Used with a singular verb.* The branch of medicine concerned with the use of electrotherapy. **—e·lec·tro·ther·a·peu·tic** *adj.*

e·lec·tro·ther·a·py (i-léktrõ-thérrəpi) *n.* Medical therapy using electric currents, especially for stimulating muscles and nerves. **—e·lec·tro·ther·a·pist** *n.*

e·lec·tro·ther·mal (i-léktrõ-thérmal) *adj.* Of or involving both electricity and heat; especially, producing heat electrically.

e·lec·trot·o·nus (i-lék-trótt'n-əss, éllek-, éelek-) *n.* Alteration in excitability and conductivity of a nerve caused by the passage of an electric current. **—e·lec·tro·ton·ic** (-trə-tónnik, -trõ-) *adj.*

e·lec·tro·type (i-lék-trə-tĩp, -trõ-) *n.* **1.** A duplicate metal plate used in letterpress printing, made by electroplating a lead or plastic mould of the original plate. Also called "electro". **2.** The process of making such a plate.
~*tr.v.* **electrotyped, -typing, -types.** To make an electrotype of. **—e·lec·tro·typ·er** *n.* (-típpik) *adj.*

e·lec·tro·va·lency (i-léktrõ-váy-lən-si) *n.* Also *chiefly U.S.* **e·lec·tro·va·len·ce** (-lənss). **1.** Valency characterised by the transfer of electrons from atoms of one element to atoms of another. **2.** The number of electric charges lost or gained by an atom in such a transfer. **—e·lec·tro·va·lent** *adj.*

electrovalent bond *n. Chemistry.* An **ionic bond** *(see).*

e·lec·trum (i-léktrəm) *n.* An alloy of varying proportions of silver and gold, especially one used in ancient metallurgy. [Middle English *electrum,* from Latin *ēlectrum,* amber, from Greek.]

e·lec·tu·ar·y (i-léktew-əri || -erri) *n., pl.* **-ies.** A drug mixed with sugar and water or honey into a pasty mass suitable for oral administration. [Middle English *electuarie,* from Late Latin *ēlectuārium,* something that melts in the mouth.]

el·ee·mos·y·nar·y (élli-ee-mόssin-əri, él-, -mόzzi- || -erri) *adj.* **1.** Of or pertaining to alms or the giving of alms; charitable. **2.** Dependent upon or supported by alms. **3.** Contributed as alms or charity. [Medieval Latin *eleēmosynārius,* from Late Latin *eleēmosyna,* ALMS.]

el·e·gance (élli-gənss) *n.* **1. a.** Refinement and grace in movement, appearance, or manners. **b.** Tasteful opulence in form, decoration, or presentation. **2.** Something that is elegant.

el·e·gant (élligənt) *adj.* **1.** Characterised by or exhibiting elegance; refined; graceful. **2.** Ingenious and effective: *an elegant mathematical proof.* [Old French, from Latin *ēlegāns* (stem *ēlegant-*), choice, fine, from *ēligere,* to choose out, select : *ex-,* out + *legere,* to choose.] **—el·e·gant·ly** *adv.*

el·e·gi·ac (élli-jī-ak, -ək || *U.S. also* i-lée̍ji-ak) *adj.* **1. a.** Pertaining to an elegy or elegies. **b.** Expressing sorrow; mournful. **2.** Composed in classical distichs, having the first line a dactylic hexameter and the second a pentameter: *an elegiac couplet.*
~n. **1.** A distich in elegiac form. **2.** *Usually plural.* Poetry written in elegiac form. [French *élégiaque,* from Late Latin *elegīacus,* from Greek *elegeiakos,* from *elegeia,* ELEGY.]

elegiac stanza *n.* A stanza in the form of four iambic pentameters that rhyme *a b a b.*

el·e·gise, el·e·gize (élli-jīz) *v.* **-gised, -gising, -gises.** *—intr.* To compose an elegy. *—tr.* To compose an elegy upon or for.

el·e·gist (éllijist) *n.* The composer of an elegy or elegies.

e·le·git (i-lée̍jit) *n. Law.* A writ of execution against a debtor by which the plaintiff may enter the debtor's land until the debtor can settle his debt. [Latin *ēlēgit,* "he has chosen" (the first word in a phrase often used in such writs), from *ēligere,* to choose out. See **elegant.**]

el·e·gy (élliji) *n., pl.* **-gies. 1.** A poem composed in elegiac distichs. **2.** A mournful poem; especially, a poem composed to lament one who is dead. **3.** A mournful musical composition. [French *élégie,* from Latin *elegīa,* from Greek *elegeia,* from *elegos,* lament, probably from Phrygian.]

Elektra. Variant of **Electra** (daughter of Agamemnon).

el·e·ment (éllimənt) *n. Abbr.* **elem. 1. a.** A fundamental, essential, or irreducible constituent of a composite entity. **b.** A part of a larger unit, especially one with special characteristics, such as a military or social grouping. **c.** A factor affecting a decision, condition, or the like: *a stubborn element in his personality.* **2. a.** A basic assumption or proposition. **b.** *Plural.* The first principles of a subject: *elements of geometry.* **3.** *Mathematics.* **a.** A member of a set. **b.** A point, line, or plane. **c.** A part of a geometric configuration, such as an angle in a triangle. **d.** The generatrix of a geometric figure. **e.** Any of the terms in the rectangular array of terms that constitute a matrix or determinant. **4.** *Chemistry & Physics.* A substance composed of atoms having an identical number of protons in each nucleus. **5.** *Astronomy.* A numerical quantity used in describing the orbit of a planet or satellite. **6.** Earth, air, fire, or water regarded as a fundamental constituent of the universe in ancient and medieval cosmologies. **7.** *Plural.* The forces that collectively constitute the weather; especially, cold, wind, rain, or other harsh conditions. **8.** An environment naturally occupied, preferred, or regarded as being preferred by an individual. **9.** A very small amount; a hint: *an element of doubt as to his success.* **10.** The resistance wire in an electrical appliance such as a cooker, heater, or kettle. **11.** *Plural.* The bread and wine of the Eucharist. [Middle English, from Old French, from Latin *elementum,* rudiment, first principle, perhaps from Etruscan.]

el·e·men·tal (élli-mént'l) *adj.* **1.** Of, pertaining to, or being an element. **2.** Fundamental or essential; basic. **3.** Resembling a force of nature in power or effect. **—el·e·men·tal·ly** *adv.*

el·e·men·ta·ry (élli-mén-təri, -tri) *adj. Abbr.* **elem. 1.** Fundamental, essential, or irreducible. **2. a.** Rudimentary; simple. **b.** Of, involving, or introducing the fundamental or simplest aspects of a subject: *an elementary text.* **—el·e·men·ta·ri·ly** (-trəli || -térrəli) *adv.* **—el·e·men·ta·ri·ness** *n.*

elementary particle *n.* **1.** Any of the four stable particles, the photon, the electron, the neutrino, and the proton, regarded as indivisible. **2.** Any member of the lepton, meson, or baryon family which may decay into a stable particle or particles. Also called "fundamental particle".

elementary school *n.* **1.** *British.* Formerly, a primary school. **2.** *U.S.* A school attended for the first six to eight years of a child's school career. Also called "grade school", "grammar school".

el·e·mi (éllimi) *n., pl.* **-mis.** Any of various oily resins derived from certain tropical trees, especially *Canarium luzonicum,* of the Philippines, used in making varnishes and inks. [Spanish *elemí,* from Arabic *elemī,* dialectal variant of *al-lāmī,* the elemi.]

e·len·chus (i-léng-kəss) *n., pl.* **-chi** (-kī, -kee). **1.** *Logic.* A refutation that disproves an opponent's conclusion or establishes a proposition contrary to his. **2.** A syllogistic refutation. [Latin, from Greek *elenkhos,* refutation, from *elenkhein,* to refute.]

e·lenc·tic (i-léngktik) *adj. Logic.* Refuting by proving the opposite. Compare **deictic.** [Greek *elenktikos,* from *elenkhein,* to refute. See **elenchus.**]

el·e·phant (élli-fənt) *n.* **1.** Either of two very large herbivorous mammals, *Elephas maximus* of south-central Asia, or *Loxodonta africana* of Africa, having thick, almost hairless skin, a long, flexible, prehensile trunk, upper incisors forming long, curved tusks, and, in the African species, large, fan-shaped ears. **2.** Any of several animals related to the elephant, including some species now extinct. **3.** A size of paper, 711 by 584 millimetres (28 by 23 inches). [Middle English *elifaunt, elephan,* from Old French *olifant, elifant,* from Vulgar Latin *olifantus* (unattested), from Latin *elephantus,* from Greek *elephas* (stem *elephant-*), ivory, elephant, probably of non-Indo-European origin.] **—el·e·phan·toid** (-fán-toyd) *adj.*

elephant bird *n.* A large, extinct, flightless bird of the genus *Aepyornis,* remains of which have been found in Madagascar.

el·e·phan·ti·a·sis (élli-fən-tī-ə-siss) *n.* A chronic, often extreme enlargement and hardening of the cutaneous and subcutaneous tissue, especially of the legs and the scrotum, resulting from lymphatic obstruction, and usually caused by a nematode worm, *Wuchereria bancrofti.* [Latin *elephantiāsis* : Greek *elephas,* ELEPHANT (so called because the skin affected by the disease resembles an elephant's hide) + -IASIS.]

el·e·phan·tine (élli-fán-tīn || -teen, -tin) *adj.* **1.** Of or pertaining to an elephant. **2.** Oversized and unwieldy.

elephant seal *n.* Either of two large seals, *Mirounga angustirostris* or *M. leonina,* of Pacific coastal waters of North and South America, having a trunklike proboscis. Also called "sea elephant".

el·e·phant's-ear (éllifənts-eer) *n.* Also **el·e·phant-ear** (éllifənt-) **1.** A plant, *Colocasia antiquorum,* native to the East Indies, having edible tubers and large leaves resembling an elephant's ears. **2.** A similar or related plant, such as the taro.

elephant shrew *n.* Any insectivorous African mammal of the family Macroscelididae, having a long pointed nose and large ears.

El·eu·sin·i·an mysteries (éllew-sínni-ən) *pl.n.* The ancient religious rites of spring celebrated at Eleusis in Greece in honour of the goddess Demeter.

el·e·vate (élli-vayt) *tr.v.* **-vated, -vating, -vates. 1.** To raise to a higher place or position; lift up. **2.** To increase the amplitude, intensity, or volume of. **3.** To promote to a higher rank. **4.** To raise to a higher moral, cultural, or intellectual level. **5.** To lift the spirits of; elate. **6.** To raise the axis of (a gun). **7.** *Roman Catholic Church.* To raise (the host or chalice) after the consecration at Mass. —See Synonyms at **lift.** [Middle English *elevaten,* from Latin *ēlevāre* : *ex-,* up + *levāre,* to lighten, raise.] **—el·e·va·to·ry** (-vay-təri, -váy-, -tri) *adj.*

el·e·vat·ed (élli-vaytid) *adj.* **1.** Raised above a given level. **2.** Exalted; high; lofty: *an elevated tone.* —See Synonyms at **high.**

elevated railway *n.* A railway that operates on a raised structure in order to permit passage of vehicles or pedestrians beneath it.

el·e·va·tion (élli-váysh'n) *n. Abbr.* **el., elev. 1.** The act of elevating or the condition of being elevated. **2.** An elevated place or position. **3.** The height to which something is elevated above a reference point, especially above the ground. **4.** Loftiness of thought or feeling. **5.** A scale drawing of the side, front, or rear of a given structure. **6.** *Geography & Astronomy.* **Altitude** *(see).* **7.** *Surveying.* The angular distance between the plane through a point and an object above it. **8.** *Linguistics.* **Amelioration** *(see).* **9.** The technique by which a ballet dancer remains in midair during the execution of a movement.

el·e·va·tor (élli-vaytər) *n.* **1.** A mechanism used to hoist grain or other material, usually consisting of buckets or scoops attached to a conveyor. **2.** *Aeronautics.* A movable control surface, usually attached to the tailplane, and used to make an aircraft go up or down. **3.** A surgical instrument used to raise a part. **4.** *U.S.* A **lift** (sense 11).

e·lev·en (i-lévv'n) *n.* **1. a.** The cardinal number that is one more than ten. **b.** A symbol representing this, such as 11, XI, or xi. **2.** A set made up of eleven persons or things. **3.** The eleventh in a series. **4.** A size, as in clothing, designated as eleven. **5.** Eleven hours after midnight or midday. **6.** In sports, especially soccer, cricket, and hockey, a team of eleven players. [Middle English *ellevene, enlevene,* Old English *endleofan,* from Germanic : *aninaz* (unattested), ONE + *-lif* (unattested), probably "left" (that is, one left over after ten).] **—e·lev·en** *adj.*

e·lev·en-plus (i-lévv'n-plúss) *n.* Formerly, an examination taken by children around the age of 11 in British state schools to select candidates for grammar schools.

e·lev·ens·es (i-lévv'nziz) *n. Used with a singular verb. British.* A snack, often accompanied by coffee or tea, taken at about 11 o'clock in the morning.

e·lev·enth (i-lévv'nth) *n.* **1.** The ordinal number 11 in a series. **2.** Any one of 11 equal parts. **3.** *Music.* An interval of an octave plus a fourth. **—e·lev·enth** *adj. & adv.*

eleventh hour *n.* The latest possible time. [By allusion to the parable (Matthew 20:1–16) in which the workers hired at the eleventh hour received the same wages as those hired earlier.]

el·e·von (élli-von) *n.* An aircraft control surface combining the functions of an elevator and an aileron. [*Elevator* + *aileron.*]

elf (elf) *n., pl.* **elves** (elvz). **1.** In folklore, a small, manlike creature, usually represented as mischievous and having magical powers. **2.** A mischievous child, or childish person. **3.** A dwarf. [Middle English *elf,* Old English *ælf,* from Germanic.]

elf·in (élfin) *adj.* **1.** Pertaining to or of the nature of an elf; elfish. **2.** Having physical characteristics associated with elves, especially smallness, delicacy, and slightly pointed features. [Probably from Middle English *elvene,* genitive plural of ELF.]

elf·ish (élfish) *adj.* Also **elv·ish** (élvish). **1.** Of or pertaining to elves; elfin. **2.** Supernatural; weird. **3.** Mischievous.
~n. The language supposedly spoken by elves. **—elf·ish·ly** *adv.* **—elf·ish·ness** *n.*
elf·lock (élf-lok) *n.* A tangled lock of hair.
El·gar (élgaar), **Sir Edward (William)** (1857–1934). English composer. His works include the *Enigma Variations* (1899), three symphonies (1908, 1911, 1997: completed), a violin concerto (1910), and a cello concerto (1919). The song *Land of Hope and Glory* is set to the first of his five *Pomp and Circumstance* marches (1901–30).
El·gin (élgin). Town in Moray area, Scotland, situated on the river Lossie, formerly the county town of Morayshire. Gordonstoun, the famous public school founded in 1934, is nearby.
Elgin Marbles *pl.n.* Ancient Greek sculptures from the frieze of the Parthenon and other buildings on the Acropolis in Athens, brought to England by the 7th Earl of Elgin and now in the British Museum.
El Giza. See **Giza, El.**
El Gre·co (el grékkō), born Domenicos Theotocopoulos and called in Spanish "the Greek" (*c.* 1541–1614). Spanish painter born in Greece. He excelled chiefly at religious subjects, such as the masterpieces *Christ stripped of his Garments* (1579) and the *Assumption* (1613).
Elias. See **Elijah.**
e·lic·it (i-líssit) *tr.v.* **-ited, -iting, -its. 1.** To bring or draw out (something latent). **2.** To evoke; call forth. [Latin *ēlicere* (past participle *ēlicitus*) : *ex-*, out + *lacere*, to allure, deceive (see **delight**).] **—e·lic·i·ta·tion** (-áysh'n) *n.* **—e·lic·i·tor** *n.*
e·lide (i-līd) *v.* **elided, eliding, elides.** *—tr.* **1.** To omit or slur over (a vowel or syllable) in pronunciation. **2.** To run together; confuse; blur. *—intr.* To be omitted or slurred over. [Latin *ēlīdere*, to strike out : *ex-*, out + *laedere*, to strike, hurt (see **lesion**).]
el·i·gi·ble (éllij-əb'l) *adj.* **1.** Qualified for an office, position, or other function. **2.** Worthy of choice, acceptance, adoption, or the like. **3.** Qualified and desirable, especially for marriage: *an eligible bachelor.* [Middle English, from Old French, from Late Latin *ēligibilis*, from Latin *ēligere*, to choose, ELECT.] **—el·i·gi·bil·i·ty** (-ə-bílləti) *n.* **—el·i·gi·bly** *adv.*
E·li·jah (i-lījə). Also **E·li·as** (i-lī-əss). Hebrew prophet of the ninth century B.C.
e·lim·i·nate (i-límmi-nayt) *tr.v.* **-nated, -nating, -nates. 1.** To get rid of; remove. **2. a.** To leave out or omit from consideration; reject. **b.** To exclude from a contest by defeating; knock out. **3.** *Mathematics.* To remove (an unknown quantity) by combining equations. **4.** *Physiology.* To excrete (waste products). **5.** To murder. Used euphemistically. [Latin *ēlīmināre*, "to drive outside the threshold" : *ex-*, out + *līmen* (stem *līmin-*), threshold (see **limen**).] **—e·lim·i·na·tion** (-náysh'n) *n.* **—e·lim·i·na·tive** (-nətiv, -naytiv), **e·lim·i·na·to·ry** (-nətəri, -nətri, -náytəri) *adj.* **—e·lim·i·na·tor** *n.*
El·i·ot (élli-ət), **George,** pen name of Mary (or Marian) Ann Evans (1819–80). English novelist of the 19th-century realist tradition. Her writings include *Adam Bede* (1859), *The Mill on the Floss* (1860), *Silas Marner* (1861), and *Romola* (1862–1863). Most critics consider *Middlemarch* (1871–72) to be her masterpiece.
Eliot, T(homas) S(tearns) (1888–1965). English poet, playwright, and critic, born in the United States. He came to London in 1914 and became a British citizen in 1927. His early poems, *Prufrock and Other Observations* (1917) and *The Wasteland* (1922), depicted the spiritual desolation of the postwar world. In 1927 he was converted to Anglo-Catholicism, and his new faith found expression in his later poetry, notably *Ash Wednesday* (1930) and *The Four Quartets* (1935–1942). His most famous verse dramas are *Murder in the Cathedral* (1935), *The Family Reunion* (1939), and *The Cocktail Party* (1950). He won the Nobel prize for literature in 1948.
e·li·sion (i-lízh'n) *n.* **1.** The action of eliding. **2.** The omission of an unstressed vowel or syllable, as to make a line of verse scan. [Latin *ēlīsiō* (stem *ēlīsiōn-*), from *ēlīdere* (past participle *ēlīsus*), ELIDE.]
e·lite, é·lite (i-léet, ay-) *n.* **1. a.** The best, most skilled, or most privileged members of a given social group. **b.** A narrow and powerful clique. **2.** A size of type on a typewriter, allowing 12 characters to an inch. [French *élite*, from Old French *eslite*, feminine past participle of *eslire*, to choose, from Vulgar Latin *exlegere* (unattested), variant of Latin *ēligere*, ELECT.] **—e·lite** *adj.*
e·lit·ism (i-lée-tiz'm, ay-) *n.* (ay-lée-tiz'm) **1. a.** Belief in the right to power of an elite. **b.** Rule or domination by an elite. **2.** A sense of being part of a superior or privileged group: *intellectual elitism.* **—e·lit·ist** *adj. & n.*
e·lix·ir (i-líksər) *n.* **1.** A sweetened aromatic preparation of alcohol or glycerine, containing or serving as a vehicle for medicine. **2.** Any medicinal potion thought to have generalised curative or restorative powers. **3.** *Alchemy.* **a.** A substance believed to have the power to transmute base metals to gold. Also called "philosopher's stone". **b.** A substance believed to have the power to cure all human disorders. Also called "panacea". **c.** A substance believed to maintain life indefinitely. Also called "elixir of life". The three substances were often regarded as one. **4.** The quintessence or underlying principle of anything. [Middle English *elixir*, from Medieval Latin, from Arabic *al-iksīr*, "the elixir" : *al-*, the + *iksīr*, probably from Greek *xērion*, dry powder medicine, from *xēros*, dry.]
E·liz·a·beth¹ (i-lízzəbəth). The mother of John the Baptist and wife of Zacharias, and a kinswoman of Mary. Luke 1.
Elizabeth², born Elizabeth Bowes-Lyon, known as the Queen Mother (1900–). Queen consort of King George VI, and the mother of Elizabeth II. She was the daughter of the 14th Earl of Strathmore and Kinghorne and is sometimes called Elizabeth of Glamis. She married the future king in April, 1923, when he was Albert George, Duke of York.
Elizabeth I (1533–1603). Queen of England (1558–1603), daughter of Henry VIII and Anne Boleyn. In 1558 she succeeded the Catholic Mary I on the throne and re-established the Protestant religion in England. She survived several plots to murder her and place the Catholic Mary, Queen of Scots, on the throne. Elizabeth, who never married, kept Mary imprisoned from 1568 until her execution in 1587. In 1588, Philip of Spain began a Catholic crusade against Protestant England. The defeat of the Spanish Armada in that year was a mark of England's rising status.
Elizabeth II (1926–). Queen of Great Britain and Northern Ireland (1952–), daughter of George VI. In 1947 she married Philip Mountbatten, Duke of Edinburgh. While she was in Kenya, on a Commonwealth tour, George VI died, on February 6, 1952. Her coronation took place on June 2, 1953. National celebrations marked her silver jubilee in 1977.
E·liz·a·be·than (i-lízzə-béeth'n || -béth'n) *adj.* Pertaining to or characteristic of the reign of Elizabeth I or sometimes Elizabeth II.
~n. One living during the reigns of Elizabeth I or Elizabeth II.
Elizabethan sonnet *n.* A **Shakespearean sonnet** *(see).*
Elizabethville. See **Lubumbashi.**
elk (elk) *n., pl.* **elks** or collectively **elk. 1.** A large deer, *Alces alces*, of northern regions, having large, palmate antlers, and called "moose" in North America. **2.** A North American deer, the **wapiti** *(see).* **3.** A light, pliant leather of horsehide or calfskin, tanned and finished to resemble elk hide. [Middle English *elke*, from Old Norse *elgr.*]
elk·hound (élk-hownd) *n.* A hunting dog of a breed developed in Scandinavia, having a greyish coat and a tail curled up over the back. Also called "Norwegian elkhound".
ell¹ (el) *n.* **1.** A wing of a building at right angles to the main structure. **2.** A pipe or tube with a right-angle bend.
ell² *n. Abbr.* **L.** An English linear measure equal to 45 inches (114 centimetres), formerly used in measuring cloth. [Middle English *elle, eln*, Old English *eln*, forearm, ell (originally about the length from the elbow to tip of the middle finger).]
Ellas. See **Greece.**
Elles·mere Island (élzmeer). Most northerly part of Canada. An island in Northwest Territories, it is separated from Greenland by a narrow passage. There is a small Eskimo population and a number of scientific stations.
Ellesmere Port. English port in Cheshire, on the south bank of the Manchester Ship Canal. Motor vehicle manufacturing, chemicals, engineering, and petroleum products are its main industries.
Ellice Islands. See **Tuvalu.**
El·ling·ton (éllingtən), **"Duke" (Edward Kennedy)** (1899–1974). U.S. jazz musician and composer. He began his career in Washington D.C. as a jazz pianist and in 1918 formed his own dance band. His best-loved compositions include *Mood Indigo* (1930), *Sophisticated Lady* (1933), and *Don't Get Around Much Anymore* (1942). He also wrote a number of longer "suites" for concert performances, among them *Black, Brown, and Beige* (1943) and *Liberian Suite* (1947).
el·lipse (i-líps) *n.* **1.** A plane curve formed by: **a.** A conic section taken neither parallel to an element nor parallel to the axis of the intersected cone. **b.** The locus of points the sum of the distances of each of which from two fixed points is the same constant. **2.** An ellipsis. [Back-formation from ELLIPSIS; when an ellipse is formed from a conic section the angle made by the base of the cone and the intersecting plane is less than, or "falls short of", the angle made by the intersecting plane which forms a parabola.]
el·lip·sis (i-líp-siss) *n., pl.* **-ses** (-seez). Also **el·lipse** (i-líps). **1.** *Grammar.* The omission of a word or words necessary for the complete syntactical construction of a sentence but not necessary for understanding it; for example, *Coming!* for *I am coming.* **2.** The omission of words in a sentence which are left for the reader or hearer to imagine, practised for example as a literary device. **3.** A mark or series of marks (. . . or ***) used in writing or printing to indicate an omission of a word, part of a word, or words. [Latin *ellīpsis*, from Greek *elleipsis*, a falling short, defect, from *elleipein*, to leave in or behind, leave out : *en-*, in + *leipein*, to leave.]
el·lip·soid (i-líp-soyd) *n.* A geometric surface whose plane sections are all either ellipses or circles. [ELLIPS(E) + -OID.] **—el·lip·soi·dal** (éllip-sóyd'l) *adj.*
el·lip·tical (i-líp-tik'l) *adj.* Also **el·lip·ti·c** (-tik). **1. a.** Of, pertaining to, or having the shape of an ellipse. **b.** Resembling or having the shape of a flattened circle. **2.** *Grammar.* Containing or characterised by ellipsis; having a word or words omitted. **3.** Expressing ideas in a compressed way that leaves much to be supplied by the understanding of the reader or hearer: *an elliptical style.* [Greek *elleiptikos*, defective, from *elleipein*, to fall short. See **ellipsis.**] **—el·lip·ti·cal·ly** *adv.*
elliptical polarisation *n. Physics.* A type of polarisation in which the radiation is composed of two plane-polarised waves at right angles, having different amplitudes, and having a phase difference of 90°. The end of the electric or magnetic vector describes an ellipse as the wave progresses.
elliptic geometry *n.* A form of non-Euclidean geometry, **Riemannian geometry** *(see).*
el·lip·tic·i·ty (i-lip-tíssəti, éllip-) *n.* **1.** Deviation from perfect circular or spherical form towards elliptic or ellipsoidal form. **2.** The degree

of such deviation, expressed as the ratio of the length of the major axis to that of the minor axis.

El·lis (élliss), **(Henry) Havelock** (1859–1939). English writer and psychologist. His monumental *Studies in the Psychology of Sex* was published in seven volumes (1897–1928).

Ellis Island. Small island in Upper New York Bay, the reception centre for immigrants to the United States from 1892 to 1954.

Ells·worth Land (élzwərth). Situated at the base of the Antarctic peninsula, it contains the Ellsworth Mountains with Vinson Massif, at 4 897 metres (16,066 feet), the highest peak in the continent.

Ellul. Variant of **Elul**.

elm (elm) *n.* **1.** Any of various deciduous trees of the genus *Ulmus*, widely planted as shade trees, characteristically having coarsely toothed leaves with one side longer than the other. **2.** The wood of any of these trees. [Middle English *elm*, Old English *elm*.]

El Ni·ño (el Néen-yō). Phenomenon which occurs sporadically along the western coast of South America when a warm ocean current replaces the normal cool current. Its appearance is often around Christmas time; hence the name, which in Spanish means "The (Christ) Child". This occurrence brings about dramatic changes to weather patterns over large areas of the globe.

el·o·cu·tion (élla-kéwsh'n) *n.* **1.** The art of public speaking, emphasising gesture and vocal production and delivery. **2.** Style or manner of speaking, especially in public. [Middle English *elocucion*, from Latin *ēlocūtiō* (stem *ēlocūtiōn-*), from *ēloquī* (past participle *ēlocūtus*), to speak out : *ex-*, out + *loquī*, to speak.] —**el·o·cu·tion·ar·y** (-əri, -ri ‖ -erri) *adj.* —**el·o·cu·tion·ist** *n.*

E·lo·him (e-lō-him, éllō-héem). The Hebrew name for God most frequently encountered in the Old Testament. Compare **Yahweh**. [Hebrew *'Elōhīm*, plural of *'Elōah*, God, perhaps enlarged from *'Ēl*, God.] —**E·lo·hism** *n.*

E·lo·hist (e-lō-hist) *n.* The author of the passages of the Hexateuch in which the name *Elohim* is used to designate God rather than the name *Yahweh*. —**El·o·his·tic** (éllō-hístik) *adj.*

e·lon·gate (éelong-gayt ‖ *chiefly U.S.* i-lóng-, -láwng-) *v.* **-gated, -gating, -gates.** —*tr.* To lengthen or extend. —*intr.* To grow in length.
~*adj.* **1.** Lengthened; extended. **2.** Slender; tapered. [Late Latin *ēlongāre* : Latin *ex-*, out + *longus*, long.]

e·lon·ga·tion (éelong-gáysh'n ‖ i-lóng-, -láwng-) *n.* **1.** The act of elongating or the condition of being elongated. **2.** Something that elongates; an extension. **3.** *Physics.* The amount of elongation, usually expressed as a percentage of original length. **4.** *Astronomy.* The difference in celestial longitude between the Sun and the Moon or a planet.

e·lope (i-lōp) *intr.v.* **eloped, eloping, elopes. 1.** To run away with a lover, especially with the intention of getting married, usually without parental consent. **2.** To run away; abscond. [Anglo-French *aloper*, legal term applied to a wife who ran away with her lover, from Middle English *alopen* (unattested), past participle of *alepen* (unattested), to run away : *a-* (away) + *lepen*, to run, leap, Old English *hlēopan*.] —**e·lope·ment** *n.* —**e·lop·er** *n.*

el·o·quence (éllakwanss) *n.* **1.** Persuasive and fluent language. **2.** The ability or power to use such language.

el·o·quent (éllakwant) *adj.* **1.** Persuasive, fluent, and graceful in speech or writing. **2.** Vividly or movingly expressive, as of an emotion: *"Each face eloquent of polite misgiving"* (Evelyn Waugh). [Middle English, from Old French, from Latin *ēloquēns* (stem *ēloquent-*), present participle of *ēloquī*, to speak out. See **elocution**.] —**el·o·quent·ly** *adv.* —**el·o·quent·ness** *n.*

El Pas·o (el pássō). West Texas town in the United States situated on the Rio Grande, just across the Mexican border.

El Sal·va·dor, Republic of (el sál-və-dawr, -dór). The smallest and most densely populated state in mainland Latin America. Its early colonisers, the Aztecs, were conquered by Spain in *c.* 1526. From 1979 to 1992 there was civil war between left-wing guerrillas and government. The country is chiefly agricultural, producing coffee, cotton, and hardwoods. The predominantly Roman Catholic population is of mixed European and Indian descent. Area, 21 041 square kilometres (8,122 square miles). Population, 5,800,000. Capital, San Salvador. See map at **Central America.**

El·san (él-san) *n.* A trademark for a type of chemical lavatory.

else (elss) *adj.* **1.** Other; different: *somebody else.* **2.** In addition; additional; more: *Would you like anything else?*
~*adv.* **1.** In a different time, place, or manner; differently: *How else could it be done?* **2.** If not; otherwise: *Be careful, or else you will make a mistake.* —**or else.** Or there will be unpleasant consequences. Used as a threat: *Behave yourself or else!* [Middle English *elles*, Old English *elles*, otherwise; else; akin to Latin *alius*, Greek *allos*.]

Usage: The possessive forms of constructions using this word are written *anyone else's, someone else's,* and so on. *Who else's,* whether used singly or in combination with a noun *(who else's car was stolen?),* is felt to be an awkward construction, and stylists try to avoid it by using some phrase such as *who else had a car stolen? Whose else* is often heard, especially governed by the verb *to be: Whose else should it have been?* The use of *else* as a coordinating conjunction is common in informal speech *(Run, else you'll be late!),* but *or else* is recommended as the general rule.

else·where (élss-waír, -hwaír) *adv.* Somewhere or anywhere else.

Elsinore. See **Helsingør.**

ELT English Language Teaching.

e·lu·ci·date (i-lóo-si-dayt ‖ -léw-) *v.* **-dated, -dating, -dates.** —*tr.*

To make clear or plain; clarify. —*intr.* To clarify something. —See Synonyms at **explain.** [Late Latin *ēlūcidāre* : Latin *ex-*, completely + *lūcidus*, bright, clear, from *lūcēre*, to shine.] —**e·lu·ci·da·tion** (-dáysh'n) *n.* —**e·lu·ci·da·tive** (-daytiv, -dətiv) *adj.* —**e·lu·ci·da·tor** *n.*

e·lude (i-lóod, -léwd) *tr.v.* **eluded, eluding, eludes. 1.** To avoid or escape from, as by cunning, daring, or artifice; evade: *elude capture.* **2.** To escape understanding or detection by; baffle: *The meaning of her glance eluded him.* —See Synonyms at **escape.** [Latin *ēlūdere*, "to take away from (someone) at play", to cheat, deceive : *ex-*, away + *lūdere*, to play, from *lūdus*, play.] —**e·lu·sion** (-lóozh'n) *n.*

el·u·ent, el·u·ant (éllew-ant) *n. Chemistry.* A solvent used to elute a mixture in chromatography. [Latin *ēluere*, to wash out : *ē-*, *ex-*, out + *luere*, to wash.]

E·lul, El·lul (e-lóol, éllōol) *n.* The 12th month of the year in the Hebrew calendar. [Hebrew *'Elūl*, from Akkadian *ulūlu, elūlu,* "(time when harvest is) brought in".]

e·lu·sive (i-lóo-siv, -léw-) *adj.* Tending to elude grasp, perception, achievement, or mental retention: *an elusive goal.* —**e·lu·sive·ly** *adv.* —**e·lu·sive·ness** *n.*

e·lute (i-lóot, -léwt) *tr.v.* **eluted, eluting, elutes.** *Chemistry.* To separate (a mixture or a component from a mixture) by washing through a chromatography column. [Latin *ēluere* (past participle *ēlutus*), to wash out. See **eluent.**] —**e·lu·tion** *n.*

e·lu·tri·ate (i-lóo-tri-ayt, -léw-) *tr.v.* **-ated, -ating, -ates.** To purify, separate, or remove (ore, for example) by washing, settling, and decanting. [Latin *ēlūtriāre*, from *ēluere*, to wash out. See **eluvium.**] —**e·lu·tri·a·tion** (-áysh'n) *n.*

e·lu·vi·a·tion (i-lóo-vi-áysh'n, -léw-) *n.* Removal of substances in solution or in suspension from the upper and middle layers of soil by water percolating downward or horizontally. Leaching is a form of eluviation. [ELUVI(UM) + -ATION.]

e·lu·vi·um (i-lóo-vi-əm, -léw-) *n., pl.* **-via** (-vi-ə). Residue of eluviation. [New Latin, from Latin *ēluere*, to wash out : *ex-*, out + *luere*, to wash.]

el·ver (élvər) *n.* A young or immature eel. [Variant of *eelfare*, originally "the passage of young eels up a river" : EEL + FARE.]

elves. Plural of **elf.**

elvish. Variant of **elfish.**

E·ly (éeli). English city on the river Ouse, in Cambridgeshire. The scene of Hereward the Wake's last stand against William the Conqueror, Ely grew round a seventh-century nunnery. The city is dominated by its cathedral dating back to the 11th century and housing many Saxon relics. The Isle of Ely was so named because of its slightly elevated position in a landscape of low-lying fens.

E·ly·sée (e-lée-zay, áylee-záy) *n.* **1.** The residence of the president of France, in Paris on the Champs Elysées. **2.** The French government or president.

E·ly·sian (i-lízzi-ən ‖ -lízh'n) *adj.* **1.** Pertaining to or suggestive of Elysium. **2.** Blissful; delightful.

E·ly·si·um (i-lízzi-əm ‖ -lizhi-) *n.* **1.** *Greek Mythology.* The abode of the blessed after death. Also called "Elysian Fields". **2.** A place or condition of ideal happiness. [Latin *Ēlysium*, from Greek *Ēlusion†* (*pedion*), Elysian (fields).]

E·ly·tis (i-léetiss), **Odysseus,** born Odysseus Alepoudelis (1911–96). Greek poet educated at Athens and Paris. His *Axion Esti* (1959) has been partly set to music by the composer Theodorakis. Other works include *Orientations* (1940), *The Light Tree* (1971), and *West of Sorrow* (1995). In 1979 he received the Nobel prize for literature.

el·y·tron (élli-trən, -tron) *n., pl.* **-tra** (-trə). Either of the leathery or chitinous forewings of a beetle or related insect, serving to encase the thin, membranous hind wings used in flight. [New Latin, from Greek *elutron*, covering, sheath.] —**el·y·troid** *adj.*

em (em) *n.* **1.** The letter *m.* **2.** *Printing. Abbr.* **m, M** The square of the body size of any type, used as a unit of measure; especially, that of a pica M. Originally, an em was equivalent to the space occupied by the letter M in any given font.
~*adj. Printing.* Designating a dash or space equal to the width of an em.

'em (əm) *pron. Informal.* Them. [Originally from Middle English *hem*, Old English *him, heom,* dative and accusative plural of *hē*, HE; but now felt as a shortened form of *them.*]

em-[1]. Variant of **en-** (put into).

em-[2]. Variant of **en-** (into).

e·ma·ci·ate (i-máy-si-ayt, -shi-) *tr.v.* **-ated, -ating, -ates.** To make abnormally thin, as by starvation or illness. [Latin *ēmaciāre* : *ex-*, completely + *maciāre*, to make thin, from *macer*, thin.] —**e·ma·ci·a·tion** (-áysh'n) *n.*

e-mail (ee-mayl) *n.* Also *chiefly U.S.* **E·mail. 1.** Electronic mail; messages sent and received via computer. **2.** An e-mail message: *get an e-mail.*
~ *tr.v.* Also *chiefly U.S.* **E·mail. e-mailed, e-mailing, e-mails. 1.** To send e-mail or an e-mail: *e-mail a person.* **2.** To send by e-mail: *e-mail a document.*

emalangeni. Plural of **lilangeni.**

em·a·nate (émmə-nayt) *v.* **-nated, -nating, -nates.** —*intr.* To come forth or proceed, as from a source or origin; issue; originate. —*tr.* To send forth; emit. [Latin *ēmānāre*, flow out : *ex-*, out + *mānāre*, to flow.] —**em·a·na·tive** (-nətiv, -naytiv) *adj.*

em·a·na·tion (émmə-náysh'n) *n.* **1.** An act or instance of emanating; a coming or flowing forth. **2. a.** Something that emanates or issues from a source; an effluence. **b.** *Chemistry.* A gaseous product of radioactive disintegration.

e·man·ci·pate (i-mán-si-payt) *tr.v.* **-pated, -pating, -pates. 1.** To free from oppression, bondage, or authority; liberate. **2.** To free from constraints imposed by social or moral conventions. Often used in the passive. **3.** In Roman law, to release (a child) from the control of his parents. [Latin *ēmancipāre,* "to release from slavery or tutelage" : *e-,* out of, EX- + *mancipium,* ownership, purchase, from *manceps* (stem *mancip-*), purchaser.] —**e·man·ci·pa·tive** *adj.* —**e·man·ci·pa·tor** *n.*

e·man·ci·pat·ed (i-mán-si-paytid) *adj.* **1.** No longer subject to official authority or control. **2.** No longer subscribing to accepted moral and social conventions: *an emancipated woman.*

e·man·ci·pa·tion (i-mán-si-páysh'n) *n.* **1.** The act of emancipating. **2.** The condition of being emancipated; freedom; liberation.

e·mar·gi·nate (i-márji-nayt, -nit, -nət) *adj.* Having a notched tip. Said of a leaf or petal. [Latin *ēmarginātus,* past participle of *ēmargināre,* to take the edge away : *ex-,* away + *margō* (stem *margin-*), MARGIN.]

e·mas·cu·late (i-más-kew-layt) *tr.v.* **-lated, -lating, -lates. 1.** To remove the male organs of. **2.** To deprive of vigour or character; make weak or ineffectual. ~*adj.* (-lət, -lit, -layt). **1.** Emasculated. **2.** Weak; ineffectual. [Latin *ēmasculāre : ex-* (removal) + *masculus,* male, manly.] —**e·mas·cu·la·tion** (-láysh'n) *n.* —**e·mas·cu·la·tive** (-lətiv, -laytiv), **e·mas·cu·la·to·ry** (-lə-tri, -láytəri) *adj.* —**e·mas·cu·la·tor** *n.*

em·balm (im-báam, em-, -ba'alm) *tr.v.* **-balmed, -balming, -balms. 1.** To prevent the decay of (a corpse) by treatment with preservatives. **2.** To save from oblivion; preserve the memory of. [Middle English *embaumen, embalmen,* from Old French *embaumer, embasmer : en-,* to put on + *basme,* BALM.] —**em·balm·er** *n.* —**em·balm·ment** *n.*

em·bank (im-bángk) *tr.v.* **-banked, -banking, -banks.** To confine, support, or protect with a bank or embankment.

em·bank·ment (im-bángkmənt ‖ em-) *n.* **1.** The act of embanking. **2.** A mound of earth or stone built to hold back water or to support a road or railway.

em·bar·go (em-bárgō, im-) *n., pl.* **-goes. 1.** An order by a government prohibiting the movement of merchant ships into or out of its ports. **2.** A governmental suspension of foreign trade or of foreign trade in a particular commodity. **3.** An injunction forbidding the acceptance of particular freight for shipment. **4.** Any prohibition. ~*tr.v.* **embargoed, -going, -goes. 1.** To impose an embargo upon. **2.** To commandeer for state use. [Spanish, from *embargar,* to impede, restrain, from Vulgar Latin *imbarricāre* (unattested), "to place behind bars" : Latin *in-,* in + *barra* (unattested), BAR.]

em·bark (im-bárk, em-) *v.* **-barked, -barking, -barks.** —*tr.* **1.** To cause to board a vessel or aircraft. **2.** *Archaic.* To enlist (a person) or invest (money) in an enterprise. —*intr.* **1.** To go aboard a vessel or aircraft, especially at the start of a journey. **2.** To set out on a venture; commence. Used with *on* or *upon.* [Old French *embarquer,* from Late Latin *imbarcāre : in,* in + *barca,* BARK.] —**em·bar·ka·tion** (émbaar-káysh'n), **em·bark·ment** *n.*

em·bar·ras de rich·esses (ọnbará də ree-shéss) *n.* An abundance of possible choices, so great as to perplex the chooser. [Alteration of French *embarras des richesses* "embarrassment of riches".]

em·bar·rass (im-bárrəss, em-) *tr.v.* **-rassed, -rassing, -rasses. 1.** To cause to feel self-conscious or ill-at-ease; disconcert. **2.** To involve in or hamper with financial difficulties. Usually used in the passive. **3.** *Archaic.* To beset with difficulties; impede. **4.** *Archaic.* To complicate. [French *embarrasser,* from Spanish *embarazar,* from Italian *imbarazzare,* from *imbarrare,* "to put in bars", impede : *in-,* in, from Latin + *barra* (unattested), BAR.] —**em·bar·rass·ed·ly** *adv.* —**em·bar·rass·ing·ly** *adv.*

em·bar·rass·ment (im-bárrəssmənt, em-) *n.* **1.** The state of being embarrassed. **2.** Something that embarrasses. **3.** A state of financial difficulty. **4.** An overabundance. Used chiefly in the phrase *an embarrassment of riches.*

em·bas·sy (émbə-si) *n., pl.* **-sies. 1.** The position, function, or duties of an ambassador. **2.** A mission to a foreign government headed by an ambassador. **3.** An ambassador and his staff. **4.** The official headquarters of an ambassador and his staff. [Middle English, from Old French *ambassee,* from Old Italian *ambasciata,* from Old Provençal *ambaissada,* from *ambaissa* (unattested), service, from Medieval Latin *ambactia.* See ambassador.]

em·bat·tle¹ (im-bátt'l, em-) *tr.v.* **-tled, -tling, -tles. 1.** To prepare or array for battle. **2.** To fortify. [Middle English *embatailen,* from Old French *embataillier : en-,* in + *bataillier,* to battle, from *bataille,* BATTLE.]

embattle² *tr.v.* **-tled, -tling, -tles.** To furnish with battlements for defence. [Middle English *embatailen : en-,* in + *batailen,* to fortify, from Old French *bataillier,* from *bataille,* battlement, BATTLE.]

em·bat·tled (im-bátt'ld, em-) *adj.* Involved in an argument, contest, or struggle.

em·bay (im-báy, em-) *tr.v.* **-bayed, -baying, -bays. 1.** To put or force (a vessel) into a bay; shelter or detain in a bay. **2.** To enclose in or as if in a bay. **3.** To form into a bay.

em·bay·ment (im-báymənt, em-) *n.* **1.** A bay or baylike indentation in a coastline. **2.** The formation of a bay.

em·bed (im-béd, em-) *v.* **-bedded, -bedding, -beds.** Also **im·bed** (im-). —*tr.* **1.** To fix firmly in a surrounding mass. **2.** To enclose firmly. **3.** To fix in the memory. **4.** To include (a subordinate clause, for example) in a sentence. —*intr.* To become embedded.

em·bel·lish (im-béllish, em-) *tr.v.* **-lished, -lishing, -lishes. 1.** To make more beautiful, as by ornamentation; adorn. **2.** To add fanci-

ful or fictitious details to (a statement or narrative). **3.** To provide with a musical embellishment. [Middle English *embelisshen,* from Old French *embellir* (present stem *embelliss-*) : *en-* (causative) + *bel,* beautiful, from Latin *bellus.*]

em·bel·lish·ment (im-béllishmənt, em-) *n.* **1.** The act of embellishing. **2.** The state of being embellished. **3.** Something that serves to embellish; ornamentation. **4.** A decoration, such as a trill, added to a piece of music, often one improvised by the performer.

em·ber (émbər) *n.* **1.** A small piece of live coal or wood, as in a dying fire. **2.** *Plural.* The smouldering coal or ash of a dying fire. **3.** *Plural.* What is left of a once intense feeling. [Middle English *embre, emere,* Old English *ǣmerge,* embers, ashes.]

Ember day *n.* Any of three days out of each calendar season observed by special prayer and formerly by fasting in some Christian churches, falling on the Wednesday, Friday, and Saturday after the first Sunday of Lent, after Whitsunday, after September 14, and after December 13. [Middle English *Ymber Daye,* Old English *Ymbrendǣg,* "recurring day" : *ymbryne,* "a running around", circuit : *ymbe,* around + *ryne,* a running + *dǣg,* DAY.]

Ember week *n.* A week in which Ember days fall.

em·bez·zle (im-bézz'l, em-) *v.* **-zled, -zling, -zles.** —*tr.* To take (money or property) for one's own use in violation of a trust. —*intr.* To embezzle money or property. [Middle English *embesilen,* from Anglo-French *enbesiler :* Old French *en-* (intensive) + *besillert,* to do away with, destroy.] —**em·bez·zle·ment** *n.* —**em·bez·zler** *n.*

em·bit·ter (im-bíttər, em-) *tr.v.* **-tered, -tering, -ters. 1.** To arouse bitter feelings in; make resentful or hostile. **2.** To make (a trouble or quarrel, for example) more distressing; aggravate. —**em·bit·ter·ment** *n.*

em·blaze (im-bláyz, em-) *tr.v.* **-blazed, -blazing, -blazes.** *Literary.* **1.** To set on fire. **2.** To cause to glow or glitter.

em·bla·zon (im-bláyz'n, em-) *tr.v.* **-zoned, -zoning, -zons. 1.** To ornament with heraldic devices or armorial bearings. **2.** To depict according to heraldic convention. **3.** To make resplendent with brilliant colours or other ornamentation. **4.** To proclaim or display conspicuously; celebrate. [EM- + BLAZON.] —**em·bla·zon·er** *n.* —**em·bla·zon·ment** *n.*

em·bla·zon·ry (im-bláyz'nri, em-) *n.* **1.** The art of emblazoning according to heraldic convention. **2.** Heraldic devices collectively.

em·blem (émbləm) *n.* **1.** An object or a depiction of an object that comes to represent something else, usually by suggesting its nature or history; a pictorial symbol. **2.** A distinctive badge, design, or device. **3.** A typical representation or embodiment; a personification. [Middle English *emblem,* from Latin *emblēma,* inlaid work, from Greek, insertion, from *emballein,* to throw in, insert : *en-,* in + *ballein,* to throw.]

em·blem·at·ic (émblə-máttik) *adj.* Also **em·blem·at·i·cal** (-'l). **1.** Of, pertaining to, or serving as an emblem. **2.** Symbolic. —**em·blem·at·i·cal·ly** *adv.*

em·blem·a·tise, em·blem·a·tize (em-blémmə-tīz) *tr.v.* **-tised, -tising, -tises.** Also **em·blem·ise** (émblə-mīz). To express emblematically; symbolise.

em·ble·ments (émbləmənts) *pl.n. Law.* The annual crops or profits of land cultivated by a tenant farmer. [Middle English *emblayment,* from Old French *emblaement,* land sown with wheat, from *blé,* wheat, corn.]

em·bod·i·ment (im-bóddimənt, em-) *n.* **1.** The act of embodying or the condition of being embodied. **2.** The concrete representation or expression of something: *Parliament is the embodiment of our history.*

em·bod·y (im-bóddi, em-) *tr.v.* **-bodied, -bodying, -bodies. 1.** To express (a feeling or concept, for example) in tangible or concrete form: *"Guernica" embodies Picasso's horror of war.* **2.** To be a typical and concrete example or manifestation of; personify: *dedicated men who embodied the tradition of public service.* **3.** To include in a larger whole; incorporate. **4.** To invest with or as if with bodily form; make corporeal; incarnate.

em·bold·en (im-bōldən, em-) *tr.v.* **-ened, -ening, -ens.** To foster boldness in; encourage.

em·bo·lec·to·my (émbə-léktəmi) *n., pl.* **-mies.** The surgical removal of an embolus. [EMBOL(US) + -ECTOMY.]

em·bol·ic (em-bóllik) *adj. Pathology.* Of or pertaining to an embolus or an embolism.

em·bo·lism (émbə-liz'm) *n.* **1.** An obstruction or occlusion of a blood vessel by an embolus. **2.** The insertion of a period of time into a calendar; an intercalation. [Middle English *embolisme,* from Medieval Latin *embolismus,* from Late Latin, insertion, from Greek *embolismos,* from *emballein,* "to throw in", insert. See emblem.] —**em·bo·lis·mic** (-lízmik) *adj.*

em·bo·lus (émbə-ləss) *n., pl.* **-li** (-lī). An air bubble, detached clot, mass of bacteria, or other foreign body that obstructs a blood vessel. [New Latin, from Latin, piston, from Greek *embolos,* "something inserted", stopper, from *emballein,* to throw in, insert. See emblem.]

em·bo·ly (émbəli) *n. Embryology.* The development of a gastrula from a blastula by invagination. [Greek *embolē,* insertion, entrance, from *emballein,* to insert. See emblem.]

em·bon·point (ọn-bôn-pwán) *n. French.* A well-fed appearance; plumpness. [From *en bon point,* in good condition.]

em·bos·om (im-bŏoz'm, em-) *tr.v.* **-omed, -oming, -oms.** *Archaic.* **1.** To clasp to or hold in the bosom; embrace. **2.** To envelop or enclose protectively; shelter.

em·boss (im-bóss, em- ‖ -bawss) *tr.v.* **-bossed, -bossing, -bosses.** 1. To represent, mould, or carve (a design) in relief. 2. To raise (an inscription, for example) in relief on paper, metal, or the like. 3. To make raised marks or inscriptions on (paper or metal, for example.) 4. To cover with or as if with bosses: *"The whole buoy was embossed with barnacles"* (Herman Melville). 5. To cause to protrude; make prominent. [Middle English *embosen,* from Old French *embocer* (unattested), "to put a knob in" : *en-,* in + *boce,* BOSS (knob).] —**em·boss·er** *n.* —**em·boss·ment** *n.*

em·bou·chure (ómbŏŏ-shóor, -shoor ‖ -shéwr) *n.* 1. a. The mouth of a river. b. The opening out of a valley into a plain. 2. a. The mouthpiece of a wind instrument. b. The manner in which the lips and tongue are applied to such a mouthpiece. [French, from Old French *emboucher,* "to put in one's mouth" : *en-,* in + *bouche,* mouth, from Latin *bucca,* puffed-out cheek.]

em·bowed (im-bŏd, em-) *adj.* 1. Bent or curved like a bow. 2. *Architecture.* a. Arched. b. Protruding in an outward curve so as to form a recess.

em·bow·el (im-bów-əl, em-) *tr.v.* **-elled** or *U.S.* **-eled, -elling** or *U.S.* **-eling, -els.** To disembowel.

em·bow·er (im-bów-ər, em-) *tr.v.* **-ered, -ering, -ers.** *Literary.* To enclose in a bower; surround, as with sheltering foliage.

em·brace¹ (im-bráyss, em-) *v.* **-braced, -bracing, -braces.** —*tr.* 1. To clasp or hold to one with the arms, usually as a display of affection. 2. a. To encircle or surround. b. To twine around. 3. To include within its scope; encompass. 4. To take up; adopt (a cause or doctrine, for example). 5. To avail oneself of; accept eagerly: *embrace an opportunity.* 6. To take in with the eyes or mind. 7. To submit with dignity or fortitude: *embrace misfortune.* —*intr.* To clasp each other with the arms; join in an embrace. —See Synonyms at **include.**
~*n.* 1. An act of embracing; an affectionate hug. 2. *Plural.* Sexual intercourse. Used euphemistically. [Middle English *embracen,* from Old French *embracer,* from Vulgar Latin *imbracchiāre* (unattested) : Latin *in-* + *bracchium,* arm, from Greek *brakhiōn.*] —**em·brace·a·ble** *adj.* —**em·brace·ment** *n.* —**em·brac·er** *n.*

em·brace² *tr.v.* **-braced, -bracing, -braces.** *Law.* To try to influence (a judge or jury) by corrupt means. [Back-formation from EM-BRACER.] —**em·brac·er·y** *n.*

em·brac·er, em·brace·or (im-bráy-sər, em-) *n. Law.* One guilty of attempting to influence a court illegally. [Middle English *embracer,* from Old French *embraseor,* instigator, from *embraser,* "to set on fire", instigate : *en-,* in + *brese,* embers.]

em·branch·ment (im-brắanch-mənt, em- ‖ -bránch-) *n.* 1. A branching out or off, as of a mountain range or river. 2. A subdivision; a ramification.

em·bra·sure (im-bráyzhər, em-) *n.* 1. *Architecture.* An opening in a wall for a door or window, slanted so that its interior dimensions are larger than those of its exterior. 2. An opening for a gun in a wall or parapet. [French, from *embraser,* to set on fire, fire a gun. See embracer.]

em·bro·cate (émbrə-kayt) *tr.v.* **-cated, -cating, -cates.** To moisten and rub (a painful part of the body) with a lotion. [Medieval Latin *embrocāre,* from Late Latin *embrocha,* lotion, from Greek *embrokhē,* from *embrekhein,* to moisten with a lotion : *en-,* in + *brekhein,* to wet.]

em·bro·ca·tion (émbrə-káysh'n) *n.* A liniment.

em·broi·der (im-bróydər, em-) *v.* **-dered, -dering, -ders.** —*tr.* 1. To ornament (fabric) with needlework. 2. To work (a design) into fabric with a needle and thread. 3. To embellish (a narrative, for example) with fictitious details or exaggerations. —*intr.* To make embroidery. [Middle English *embroderen,* from Anglo-French *enbrouder* : Old French *en-,* in + *brouder, brosder,* to embroider, from (unattested) Frankish *brusdan.*] —**em·broi·der·er** *n.*

em·broi·der·y (im-bróydəri, em-) *n., pl.* **-ies.** 1. The art, act, or practice of embroidering. 2. Ornamentation on fabric done in needlework. 3. Fictitious or exaggerated detail added to a narrative.

em·broil (im-bróyl, em-) *tr.v.* **-broiled, -broiling, -broils.** 1. To involve in argument, conflict, or difficulties: *embroiled in a diplomatic scandal.* 2. To throw (a situation, for example) into confusion or disorder; entangle. [French *embrouiller* : Old French *en-,* in + *brouiller,* to mix, confuse, probably from *breu,* broth, from Germanic.] —**em·broil·ment** *n.*

em·brown (im-brówn, em-) *tr.v.* **-browned, -browning, -browns.** To make brown or dusky; darken.

embrue. Variant of **imbrue.**

em·bry·ec·to·my (émbri-éktəmi) *n., pl.* **-mies.** The surgical removal of an extrauterine embryo. [EMBRY(O) + -ECTOMY.]

em·bry·o (émbri-ō) *n., pl.* **-os.** 1. *Biology.* a. An organism in its early stages of development, especially before it has reached a distinctively recognisable form. b. Such an organism at any time before full development, birth, or hatching. 2. a. The fertilised egg of a vertebrate animal following cleavage. b. In man, the prefoetal product of conception up to the beginning of the third month of pregnancy. 3. *Botany.* The minute, rudimentary plant contained within a seed or archegonium. 4. a. A rudimentary or initial stage. b. Anything at a rudimentary or undeveloped stage: *the embryo of an idea.*
~*adj.* Incipient; rudimentary. [Medieval Latin *embryo* (stem *embryon-*), from Greek *embruon,* "something that grows in the body" : *en-,* in + *bruein,* to grow.]

em·bry·o·gen·e·sis (émbri-ō-jénnə-siss) *n.* Also **em·bry·og·e·ny** (-ójəni). The development and growth of an embryo. —**em·bry·o·**

gen·ic (-ō-jénnik), **em·bry·o·ge·net·ic** (-ō-jə-néttik) *adj.*

em·bry·ol·o·gy (émbri-óllaji) *n.* 1. The science dealing with the formation, early growth, and development of living organisms. 2. The embryonic structure and development of a particular organism. —**em·bry·o·log·ic** (-ə-lójik), **em·bry·o·log·i·cal** *adj.* —**em·bry·o·log·i·cal·ly** *adv.* —**em·bry·ol·o·gist** (-ólləjist) *n.*

em·bry·on·ic (émbri-ónnik) *adj.* Also **em·bry·on·al** (-ən'l, em-brí-) (for sense 1). 1. Of, pertaining to, or in the state of being an embryo. 2. Still at an early stage of development; rudimentary.

embryo sac *n.* The large oval cell in which the embryo develops in seed plants.

em·bus (im-búss, em-) *Military. v.* **-bused** or **-bussed** or **-bussing, -buses** or **-busses** —*tr.* To transport (troops, for example) by bus. —*intr.* To board a bus or other military transport.

em·cee (ém-sée) *n. Informal.* A master of ceremonies (see).
~*v.* **emceed, -ceeing, -cees.** *Informal.* —*tr.* To serve as master of ceremonies of. —*intr.* To act as master of ceremonies. [From *Master of Ceremonies.*]

-eme *n. suffix.* Indicates an irreducible linguistic unit; for example, **semanteme, morpheme.** [French *-ème,* abstracted from *phonème,* PHONEME.]

e·mend (i-ménd) *tr.v.* **emended, emending, emends.** 1. To correct and improve (a text) by critical editing. 2. *Rare.* To free from faults. [Middle English *emenden,* from Latin *ēmendāre* : *ex-* (removal) + *mendum,* fault.]

e·men·date (ée-men-dayt ‖ émmən-) *tr.v.* **-dated, -dating, -dates.** To emend (a text). —**e·men·da·tor** *n.*

e·men·da·tion (ée-men-dáysh'n ‖ émmən-) *n.* 1. The act of emending. 2. An alteration that improves something; especially, a correction in a literary work. —**e·men·da·to·ry** (i-méndə-təri, ee-, -tri ‖ ée-men-dáytəri) *adj.*

em·er·ald (émmərəld, émrəld) *n.* 1. A brilliant, transparent green beryl used as a gemstone. 2. A colour, brilliant green.
~*adj.* 1. Of, pertaining to, or similar to an emerald. 2. Of a brilliant green colour. [Middle English *emeraude,* from Old French *esmeraude,* from Vulgar Latin *smaralda* (unattested), variant of Latin *smaragdus,* SMARAGDITE.]

Emerald Isle *n.* The island of Ireland. Used chiefly in poetic or humorous contexts.

e·merge (i-mérj) *intr.v.* **emerged, emerging, emerges.** 1. To rise up from beneath the surface or come out from concealment; come into sight. 2. To become evident or known. 3. To issue, as from obscurity or difficulties: *They emerged from the war changed men.* [Latin *ēmergere* : *ex-,* out of + *mergere,* to dip, immerse.]

e·mer·gence (i-mérjəns) *n.* 1. The act or process of emerging. 2. *Botany.* A superficial outgrowth of plant tissue, such as a thorn, containing no conducting tissues. 3. *Philosophy.* The unpredicted appearance of new characteristics or phenomena in the course of biological or social evolution.

e·mer·gen·cy (i-mérjən-si) *n., pl.* **-cies.** 1. A situation or occurrence of a serious and often dangerous nature, developing suddenly and unexpectedly, and demanding immediate action. 2. A case requiring urgent medical attention. 3. A **state of emergency** (see).

e·mer·gent (i-mérjənt) *adj.* 1. Coming into existence, view, or attention; issuing forth. 2. Newly independent. Said of a state.
~*n. Botany.* An emersed plant.

emergent evolution *n. Philosophy.* A theory holding that completely new types of organisms, modes of behaviour, and consciousness appear at certain stages of the evolutionary process, usually as a result of an unpredictable rearrangement of the pre-existing elements.

e·mer·i·tus (i-mérri-təss) *adj.* Retired but retaining an honorary title corresponding to that held immediately before retirement: *a professor emeritus.*
~*n., pl.* **emeriti** (-tī). One who is emeritus. [Latin *ēmerītus,* past participle of *ēmerēri,* to earn by service : *ex-,* out of + *merērī, merēre,* to earn, deserve.]

e·mersed (ee-mérst, i-) *adj. Botany.* Rising above the surface of the water. Said of the leaves or stems of aquatic plants.

e·mer·sion (ee-mérsh'n, i-, -mérzh'n) *n.* 1. The act of emerging; emergence. 2. *Astronomy.* The appearance of a celestial object following its occultation or eclipse. In this sense, also called "egress". [Latin *ēmergere* (past participle *ēmersus*), EMERGE.]

Em·er·son (émmər-s'n), **Ralph Waldo** (1803-82). U.S. poet and essayist. A Unitarian pastor from 1829 to 1832, he subsequently became a writer and lecturer. *Nature* (1836) was an early manifesto of Transcendentalist belief in the mystical unity of nature. His essays are regarded as landmarks in the development of American thought and literary expression. —**Em·er·son·i·an** (-sŏn-i-ən) *n. & adj.*

em·er·y (émm-əri, -ri) *n.* A fine-grained impure form of corundum used for grinding and polishing. [Middle English *emery,* from Old French *emeri, esmeril,* from Vulgar Latin *smericulum* (unattested), from Medieval Greek *smēri,* variant of Greek *smuris†,* emery powder.]

emery board *n.* A small, flat strip of cardboard or thin wood coated with powdered emery, used to file the nails.

emery paper *n.* Paper coated with powdered emery, used as a fine abrasive.

emery wheel *n.* An abrasive wheel containing emery powder in a resinous binder, rotated by a motor, and used for smoothing or grinding.

em·e·sis (émmi-siss) *n.* Vomiting. [New Latin, from Greek, from *emein,* to vomit.]

e·met·ic (i-méttik) *adj.* Causing vomiting.
~*n.* An emetic agent or medicine. [Latin *emeticus,* from Greek *emetikos,* inclined to vomit, from *emetos,* vomiting, from *emein,* to vomit.] —**e·met·i·cal·ly** *adv.*

em·e·tine (émmə-teen, -tin) *n.* A bitter-tasting, crystalline alkaloid, $C_{29}H_{40}O_4N_2$, derived from ipecac root, and used as an emetic. [French *émétine* : *émétique,* causing vomiting, from Latin *emeticus* (see emetic) + -INE.]

emf, EMF electromotive force.

–emia. *U.S.* Variant of **-aemia.**

em·i·grant (émmigrənt) *n.* One who emigrates. —**em·i·grant** *adj.*

em·i·grate (émmi-grayt) *intr.v.* **-grated, -grating, -grates.** To leave one country or region, especially one's native country or region, to settle in another. [Latin *ēmigrāre,* to move away from : *ex-,* away + *migrāre,* to move.] —**em·i·gra·tion** (-gráysh'n) *n.*

e·mi·gré (émmi-gray) *n.* An emigrant, especially one who has fled his country during a political upheaval. [French, past participle of *émigrer,* to emigrate, from Latin *ēmigrāre.* See **emigrate.**]

E·mi·li·a-Ro·ma·gna (i-méel-yə rō-mán-yə). Formerly **Emilia.** Region in north Italy comprising the fertile lowlands of the river Po and part of the Apennines in the south.

em·i·nence (émminənss) *n.* Also **em·i·nen·cy** (-nən-si) *pl.* **-cies.** 1. A position of great distinction or superiority in achievement, rank, or character. 2. A rise of ground; a hill. 3. *Capital* E. A title of or form of address for a cardinal of the Roman Catholic Church. Used with *His* or *Your.* —See Synonyms at **fame.**

é·mi·nence grise (áy-mi-noNss gréez) *n., pl.* **éminences grises.** A person who exercises power behind the scenes through his influence with prominent people. Also called "grey eminence". [French, "grey eminence (that is, cardinal)", after the French monk Père Joseph (François le Clerc du Tremblay, died 1638), who served as Cardinal Richelieu's secretary.]

em·i·nent (émminənt) *adj.* 1. **a.** Outstanding in performance or character; distinguished: *an eminent historian.* **b.** Of high rank or station. 2. *Literary.* Towering above others; projecting; prominent. 3. Remarkable or noteworthy: *a man esteemed for his eminent achievements.* [Middle English, from Old French, from Latin *ēminēns* (stem *ēminent-*), present participle of *ēminēre,* to stand out : *ex-,* out + *-minēre,* to stand, project.]
Usage: Similarity in sound often leads to a confusion in spelling between *eminent* and *imminent,* but there is no overlap of meaning. *Eminent* means "prominent, outstanding"; *imminent* means "impending, about to occur".

eminent domain *n. Law.* The right of a government to appropriate private property for public use, usually with compensation to the owner.

em·i·nent·ly (émmi-nənt-li ‖ -nent-) *adv.* Extremely; especially. Used as an intensive: *eminently suitable.*

e·mir, a·mir, a·meer (e-méer) *n.* 1. A Muslim prince, chieftain, or governor in the Middle East and parts of Africa. 2. An honorary title given to the descendants of Muhammad. [French *émir,* from Spanish *emir,* from Arabic *'amīr,* commander, from *amara,* he commanded.]

e·mir·ate (émmeer-ayt, e-méer-, -ət, -it) *n.* 1. The office or jurisdiction of an emir. 2. A country ruled over by an emir.

Em·i·scan·ner (émmi-skannər) *n.* A trademark for an X-ray device that produces computer-assisted images of cross sections of the body.

em·is·sar·y (émmi-səri, -sri ‖ -serri) *n., pl.* **-ies.** 1. A messenger or agent sent to represent or advance the interests of a person or state. 2. An agent with a secret or underhand mission. [Latin *ēmissārius,* from *ēmittere* (past participle *ēmissus*), to send out, EMIT.]

e·mis·sion (i-mísh'n) *n.* 1. The action of emitting. 2. Something that is emitted, such as the exhaust gases from a car engine. 3. *Physics.* The amount of electrons, radiation, or the like emitted, or the rate of this emission. 4. An issue, as of paper money or shares. [Latin *ēmittere* (past participle *ēmissus*), EMIT.]

emission nebula *n. Astronomy.* See **nebula.**

emission spectrum *n.* The spectrum of bright lines, bands, or continuous radiation characteristic of and determined by a specific emitting substance subjected to a specific kind of excitation. Compare **absorption spectrum.**

e·mis·sive (i-míssiv) *adj.* 1. Sending forth; emitting. 2. Sent forth; emitted.

em·is·siv·i·ty (éemi-sívvəti, émmi-) *n.* The ratio of the radiation intensity emitted from a surface to the radiation intensity at the same wavelength emitted from a black body at the same temperature. Also called "emissive power".

e·mit (i-mít) *tr.v.* **emitted, emitting, emits.** 1. To give off or send out (liquid, gas, or radiation, for example). 2. To utter: *"she emitted her small strange laugh"* (Edith Wharton). 3. To issue with authority; especially, to put into circulation (paper currency or shares in a company, for example). [Latin *ēmittere,* to send out : *ex-,* out + *mittere,* to send.]

e·mit·ter (i-míttər) *n.* 1. An object that emits something. 2. *Electronics.* The region in a transistor from which charge carriers flow into the base.

Emmanuel. Variant of **Immanuel.**

em·men·a·gogue (i-ménnə-gog, -méenə-) *n.* A medicine that induces or hastens the menstrual flow. [Greek *emmēna,* the menses, from *emmēnos,* monthly : *en-,* in + *mēnē, mēn,* month + -AGOGUE.]

Em·men·thal¹, Em·men·tal (émmən-taal). Valley of the upper Emme river in the Bern canton, Switzerland, famous for its cheese. —**Em·men·thal·er** (-taaler) *n. & adj.*

Emmenthal² *n.* A hard cheese with holes, similar to Gruyère, that comes from Emmenthal.

em·mer (émmər) *n.* A primitive, slender-eared wheat, *Triticum dicoccum,* cultivated in a few areas for grain and livestock feed. [German *Emmer,* from Old High German *amaro.* See **yellowhammer.**]

Em·met (émmit), **Robert** (1778-1803). Irish revolutionary nationalist, who in July 1803 took part in a bungled uprising against British rule. A few weeks later he was captured in Dublin and hanged.

em·me·tro·pi·a (émmi-trṓpi-ə) *n.* The condition of the normal eye when parallel rays are focused exactly on the retina and vision is perfect. [New Latin : Greek *emmetros,* in measure : *en-,* in + *metron,* measure + -OPIA.] —**em·me·trop·ic** (-tróppik) *adj.*

Em·my (émmi) *n., pl.* **-mys** or **-mies.** One of the statuettes presented annually by the U.S. Academy of Television Arts and Sciences for outstanding television performances and productions. [Variation of *Immy,* short for *im(age orthicon tube).*]

e·mol·lient (i-mólli-ənt) *adj.* Having softening and soothing qualities, especially for the skin.
~*n.* 1. An agent that softens or soothes the skin. 2. Anything that assuages or mollifies. [Latin *ēmolliēns* (stem *ēmollient-*), present participle of *ēmollīre,* to soften, soothe : *ex-,* completely + *mollīre,* to soften, from *mollis,* soft.]

e·mol·u·ment (i-móllewmənt) *n.* Profit derived from one's office or employment; payment for services rendered. [Middle English, from Latin *ēmolumentum,* originally "miller's fee for grinding grain", from *ēmolere,* to grind out : *ex-,* out + *molere,* to grind.]

e·mote (i-mṓt) *intr.v.* **emoted, emoting, emotes.** *Informal.* To express emotion or sentiment, especially in an effusive and theatrical manner. [Back-formation from EMOTION.] —**e·mot·er** *n.*

e·mo·tion (i-mṓsh'n) *n.* 1. Agitation of the passions or sensibilities often involving physiological changes. 2. Any strong feeling, as of joy, sorrow, reverence, hate, or love, arising subjectively rather than through conscious mental effort. —See Synonyms at **feeling.** [French *émotion,* earlier *esmocion,* from Old French *esmovoir,* to excite, from Vulgar Latin *exmovēre* (unattested), variant of Latin *ēmovēre,* to move out, stir up, excite : *ex-,* out + *movēre,* to move.]

e·mo·tion·al (i-mṓsh'n'l) *adj.* 1. Of or pertaining to emotion. 2. Readily affected with or stirred by emotion. 3. Capable of stirring the emotions: *an emotional appeal.* 4. Revealing emotion; agitated; excited. —**e·mo·tion·al·i·ty** (-ál-əti) *n.* —**e·mo·tion·al·ly** *adv.*

e·mo·tion·al·ise, e·mo·tion·al·ize (i-mṓsh'n'l-īz) *tr.v.* **-ised, -ising, -ises.** To impart an emotional character to.

e·mo·tion·al·ism (i-mṓsh'n'l-iz'm) *n.* 1. An inclination to encourage or yield to emotion: *the emotionalism of adolescents.* 2. Undue display of emotion. 3. An ethical or aesthetic attitude basing conduct or value on emotion. —**e·mo·tion·al·ist** *n.* —**e·mo·tion·al·is·tic** (-ístik) *adj.*

e·mo·tion·less (i-mṓsh'n-ləss, -liss) *adj.* Devoid of apparent emotion.

e·mo·tive (i-mṓtiv) *adj.* Pertaining to, expressing, or tending to excite emotion; especially, likely to arouse an ill-considered or irrational response. —**e·mo·tive·ly** *adv.* —**e·mo·tive·ness, e·mo·tiv·i·ty** (éemō-tívvəti) *n.*

e·mo·ti·vism (i-mṓti-viz'm) *n. Philosophy.* The doctrine that ethical propositions are neither true nor false statements, but expressions of emotion. Compare **descriptivism, prescriptivism.** —**e·mo·ti·vist** *n. & adj.*

Emp. 1. emperor; empress. 2. empire.

empale. Variant of **impale.**

em·pan·el (im-pánn'l, en-) *tr.v.* **-elled** or *U.S.* **-eled, -elling** or *U.S.* **-eling, -els.** Also **im·pan·el** (in-). *Law.* 1. To list (a person's name) for possible jury service. 2. To select (a jury) from the names thus listed. —**em·pan·el·ment** *n.*

em·pa·thet·ic (émpə-théttik) *adj.* Also **em·path·ic** (em-páthik). Of, pertaining to, or characterised by empathy. —**em·pa·thet·i·cal·ly** *adv.*

em·pa·thise, em·pa·thize (émpə-thīz) *intr.v.* **-thised, -thising, -thises.** To feel or experience empathy. Often used with *with.*

em·pa·thy (émpəthi) *n.* 1. Understanding so intimate that the feelings, thoughts, and motives of one are readily comprehended by another. 2. The attribution of feelings aroused by an object in nature or art to the object itself, as when one speaks of "a painting full of love". [EN- (in) + -PATHY (translation of German *Einfühlung,* "a feeling in"), after Greek *empatheia,* passion.]

Em·ped·o·cles (em-péddə-kleez) (*fl.c.* 490-430 B.C.). Greek philosopher, poet, physician, and statesman, born in Sicily. He taught that all matter is composed of particles of fire, water, earth, and air. More important for the future of physics was his belief that all change is caused by motion.

em·pen·nage (em-pénnij, ómpə-naázh) *n. Aeronautics.* The **tail** *(see).* [French, originally "the feathers on an arrow", from *empenner,* to put feathers on an arrow : *en-,* in + *penne,* feather, from Latin *pinna.*]

em·per·or (ém-pərər, -prər) *n.* 1. *Abbr.* **Emp.** The ruler of an empire, having power either absolute or subject to constitutional restrictions. 2. **a.** Any of several brightly coloured butterflies of the family Nymphalidae, such as *Apatura iris,* the purple emperor, having a purple sheen on the upper side of the wings in the male. Also called "emperor butterfly". **b.** Any of several moths of the family Saturniidae; especially, an Old World species, *Saturnia pavonia,* having distinctively patterned wings. Also called "emperor moth". [Middle

English *emperour,* from Old French *empereor,* from Latin *imperātor,* emperor, commander, from *imperāre* (past participle *imperātus*), "to prepare against (an occasion)", hence to command : *in-,* against + *parāre,* to prepare.] —**em·per·or·ship** *n.*

emperor penguin *n.* A large penguin, *Aptenodytes forsteri,* of Antarctic regions, having yellow-orange patches on the neck.

em·per·y (émpəri) *n., pl.* **-ies.** *Archaic.* Empire; dominion. [Middle English *emperie,* from Old French, EMPIRE.]

em·pha·sis (émfə-siss) *n., pl.* **-ses** (-seez). **1.** Special importance or significance placed upon or imparted to something. **2.** Stress applied to a syllable, word, or passage by the use of vocal expression, gesture, italics, or other indication. **3.** Force or intensity of expression, feeling, or action. **4.** Sharpness or vividness of outline; prominence. [Latin, from Greek, reflection, meaning, significance, from *emphainein,* to exhibit, indicate : *en-,* in + *phainein,* to show.]

em·pha·sise, em·pha·size (émfə-sīz) *tr.v.* **-sised, -sising, -sises.** To impart emphasis to; stress.

em·phat·ic (im-fáttik, em-) *adj.* **1.** Expressed or performed with emphasis. **2.** Bold and definite in expression or action; positive. **3.** Striking; definite: *an emphatic victory.* **4.** Designating an English verb form using the auxiliary verb *do* to make a strong assertion. **5.** *Phonetics.* Having a hard constrictive velarised quality, as certain Arabic consonants do.

~*n. Phonetics.* An emphatic Arabic consonant. [Late Latin *emphaticus,* from Greek *emphatikos,* exhibited, hence emphatic, from *emphainein,* to exhibit. See **emphasis.**] —**em·phat·i·cal·ly** *adv.*

em·phy·se·ma (émfi-séemə) *n.* **1.** An abnormal condition of the lungs in which there is dilation of the air sacs, resulting in laboured breathing. **2.** Any distension of connective tissues due to retention of air. [New Latin, from Greek *emphusēma,* swelling, inflation, from *emphusan,* to blow in : *en-,* in + *phusan,* to blow, from *phusai,* bellows.] —**em·phy·sem·a·tous** (-sémmə-təss, -séemə-) *adj.*

em·pire (ém-pīr) *n. Abbr.* **Emp.** **1.** A political unit, usually larger than a kingdom and often comprising a number of territories or nations, ruled by a single supreme authority. **2.** The territory included in such a unit. **3. a.** Imperial dominion. **b.** The period during which such dominion exists. **4.** An extensive enterprise maintained by a unified authority: *a publishing empire.* **5.** *Capital* **E.** The **British Empire** *(see).* [Middle English *empire,* from Old French *empire, emperie,* from Latin *imperium,* dominion, empire, from *imperāre,* to command. See **emperor.**]

Em·pire (ém-pīr) *adj.* **1.** Of or characteristic of: **a.** The British Empire. **b.** The first Empire of France (1804–15). **c.** The second Empire of France (1852–70). **2.** Designating a style of dress with a high waistline and straight loose skirt as originally worn during the first French Empire. **3.** Designating a neoclassical style of art, architecture, and decor, and especially a style of solid, heavy furniture in hardwoods, with Egyptian motifs and gilded ornamentation.

em·pire-build·er (émpīr-bildər) *n. Informal.* A power-loving person who seeks to increase his influence or control by constantly acquiring new operations or staff. —**em·pire-build·ing** *n.* & *adj.*

em·pir·ic (em-pírrik, im-) *n.* One who believes that practical experience is the sole source of knowledge. [Latin *empiricus,* from Greek *empeirikos,* from *empeirā,* experience, from *empeiros,* experienced in : *en-,* in + *peira,* experiment, trial.]

em·pir·i·cal (em-pírrik'l, im-) *adj.* **1.** Relying upon or derived from observation or experiment: *empirical methods; an empirical conclusion.* **2.** Guided by practical experience and not theory, especially in medicine. —**em·pir·i·cal·ly** *adv.*

empirical formula *n.* A type of chemical formula that indicates the ratio of the elements rather than the total number of atoms in a molecule. Compare **molecular formula, structural formula.**

em·pir·i·cism (em-pírri-siz'm, im-) *n.* **1. a.** The view that experience, especially of the senses, is the only source of knowledge. **b.** *Philosophy.* The doctrine based on this view. Compare **rationalism.** **2.** The employment of empirical methods, as in an art or science. **3.** *Archaic.* The practice of medicine without scientific knowledge. —**em·pir·i·cist** *n.*

em·place·ment (im-pláyss-mənt, em-) *n.* **1.** A prepared position, such as a mounting or platform, for guns within a fortification. **2.** A setting in position; a placement. **3.** *Rare.* Position; location. [French, *place,* situation from (obsolete) *emplacer,* to place in (a position) : *em-,* in + *placer,* to PLACE.] —**em·place** *tr.v.*

emplane. Variant of **enplane.**

em·ploy (im-plóy, em-) *tr.v.* **-ployed, -ploying, -ploys.** **1.** To use in some process or effort; put to service. **2.** To devote or apply (one's time or energies, for example) to some activity. **3. a.** To engage the services of; put to work. **b.** To provide with a job and livelihood. —See Synonyms at **use.**

~*n.* **1.** The state of being employed. **2.** *Archaic.* Occupation. [Middle English *emploien,* from Old French *employer, emplier,* from Latin *implicāre,* to infold, involve : *in-,* in + *plicāre,* to fold.] —**em·ploy·a·bil·i·ty** (-ə-bíllati) *n.* —**em·ploy·a·ble** *adj.*

em·ploy·ee (em-plóy-ee, émploy-ée, im-) *n.* A person who works for another in return for financial or other compensation.

em·ploy·er (im-plóy-ər, em-) *n.* A person or concern that employs persons for wages or a salary.

em·ploy·ment (em-plóymənt, im-) *n.* **1. a.** The act of employing; a putting to use or work. **b.** The state of being employed. **2.** The work in which one is engaged; a business; a profession. **3.** The purpose of something that is used.

em·po·ri·um (em-páw-ri-əm, im- ‖ -pô-) *n., pl.* **-riums** or **-ria** (-ri-ə). **1.** A large retail shop, such as a department store, carrying a wide

variety of merchandise. **2.** A place, town, or city that is an important trade centre; a marketplace. [Latin, from Greek *emporion,* market, from *emporos,* merchant, traveller : *en-,* in + *poros,* path, journey.]

em·pow·er (im-pów-ər, em-, -pówr) *tr.v.* **-ered, -ering, -ers.** **1.** To invest with legal power; authorise. **2.** To enable or permit. **3.** To increase the self-confidence and autonomy of : *empower the oppressed.* —**em·pow·er·ment** *n.*

em·press (ém-priss, -prəss) *n. Abbr.* **Emp. 1.** A female sovereign of an empire. **2.** The wife or widow of an emperor. [Middle English *emperesse,* from Old French, feminine of *empereor,* EMPEROR.]

em·prise (em-príz) *n.* Chivalrous daring or prowess. [Middle English *emprise,* from Old French, from the feminine past participle of *emprendre,* to undertake, from Vulgar Latin *imprendere* (unattested) : Latin *in-,* in + *prendere, prehendere,* to take, seize.]

emp·ty (émpti) *adj.* **-tier, -tiest.** **1.** Void of content; containing nothing: *an empty bottle.* **2.** Having no occupants or inhabitants; vacant; unoccupied: *an empty chair.* **3.** Having no load or cargo: *an empty lorry.* **4.** Lacking purpose or substance; meaningless: *an empty life.* **5.** Idle: *empty hours.* **6.** Vacuous; inane: *an empty mind.* **7.** Needing nourishment; hungry. **8.** Devoid; destitute. Used with *of: empty of pity.*

~*v.* **emptied, -tying, -ties.** —*tr.* **1.** To remove the contents of; make empty: *empty one's pockets.* **2.** To transfer or pour off: *empty the ashes into the bin.* **3.** To unburden; relieve. Used with *of: empty oneself of doubt.* —*intr.* **4.** To become empty. **2.** To discharge or flow. Used with *into: The river empties into a bay.*

~*n., pl.* **empties.** *Informal.* An empty container, carrier, or the like. [Middle English *empty, emptie,* Old English *ǣmettig, ǣmtig,* empty, unoccupied, from *ǣmetta,* rest, leisure.] —**emp·ti·ly** *adv.* —**emp·ti·ness** *n.*

Synonyms: *empty, vacant, blank, void, vacuous, bare, barren.*

emp·ty-hand·ed (émpti-hándid) *adj.* **1.** Bearing no gift, possessions, or the like: *They arrived empty-handed.* **2.** Having received or gained nothing.

emp·ty-head·ed (émpti-héddid) *adj.* Lacking sense or discretion; foolish; scatterbrained.

empty nes·ter *n.* A parent whose grown children have left home.

Empty Quarter. See **Saudi Arabia.**

empty set *n. Mathematics.* A set that has no members. Also called "null set".

em·pur·ple (im-púrp'l, em-) *tr.v.* **-pled, -pling, -ples.** To colour or tinge with purple.

em·py·e·ma (émpī-ée-mə) *n., pl.* **-mata** (-mətə). Pus in a body cavity, especially the pleural cavity. [Medieval Latin, from Greek *empuēma,* from *empuein,* to suppurate.] —**em·py·e·mic** *adj.*

em·py·re·al (ém-pī-rée-əl, -pi-, -réerl, em-pírri- ‖ -pī-ri-) *adj.* **1.** Empyrean. **2.** Of or pertaining to the sky; celestial. **3.** Formed of pure fire or light; fiery. **4.** Heavenly; sublime. [Middle English *imperyale,* from Late Latin *empyrius, empyreus,* from Greek *empurios, empuros,* fiery : *en-,* in + *pur,* fire.]

em·py·re·an (ém-pī-rée-ən, -pi-, -réern, em-pírri- ‖ -pī-ri-) *n.* **1.** The highest reaches of heaven, believed by the ancients to be a realm of pure fire and by early Christians to be the abode of God and the angels. **2.** The sky; space.

~*adj.* Of or pertaining to the empyrean of ancient belief. [Late Latin *empyreus,* EMPYREAL.]

EMU European Monetary Union; Economic and Monetary Union.

e·mu (éemew) *n., pl.* **emus.** A large, flightless Australian bird, *Dromaius novaehollandiae,* related to and resembling the cassowary. [Portuguese *ema,* perhaps from Moluccan *eme.*]

emu electromagnetic unit.

em·u·late (émmew-layt) *tr.v.* **-lated, -lating, -lates.** **1.** To strive to equal or excel, especially through imitation. **2.** To compete with or rival successfully: *Korea emulates Japan in its single-minded productivity.* —See Synonyms at **rival.** [Latin *aemulārī,* from *aemulus,* EMULOUS.] —**em·u·la·tive** (-lə-tiv, -lay-) *adj.* —**em·u·la·tive·ly** *adv.* —**em·u·la·tor** (-laytər) *n.*

em·u·la·tion (émmew-láysh'n) *n.* **1.** Effort or ambition to equal or surpass another. **2.** Imitation of another.

em·u·lous (émmewləss) *adj.* **1.** Eager or ambitious to equal or surpass another. **2.** Characterised or prompted by a spirit of rivalry. [Latin *aemulus,* imitating, probably related to *imitārī,* IMITATE.] —**em·u·lous·ly** *adv.* —**em·u·lous·ness** *n.*

e·mul·si·fy (i-múl-si-fī) *tr.v.* **-fied, -fying, -fies.** To make into an emulsion. [EMULSI(ON) + -FY.] —**e·mul·si·fi·ca·tion** (i-múl-si-fi-káysh'n) *n.* —**e·mul·si·fi·er** *n.*

e·mul·sion (i-múl-sh'n) *n.* **1. a.** A suspension of small globules of one liquid in a second liquid with which the first will not mix, such as milk fats in milk. **b.** Any milklike liquid. **2.** A light-sensitive coating, usually of silver halide grains in a thin gelatine layer, on photographic film, paper, or glass. **3.** Emulsion paint. [New Latin, from Latin *ēmulgēre* (past participle *ēmulsus*), to drain out, milk out : *ex-,* out + *mulgēre,* to milk.] —**e·mul·sive** (-siv) *adj.*

emulsion paint *n.* A type of paint in which the pigment is dispersed in an oil which forms an emulsion with water.

e·mul·soid (i-múl-soyd) *n. Chemistry.* A type of colloid in which small droplets of a liquid are dispersed throughout a solid continuous phase. [*Emulsion* + *colloid.*]

e·munc·to·ry (i-múngktəri) *adj.* Serving to carry waste matter out of the body; excretory.

~*n., pl.* **emunctories.** An emunctory organ or passage. [Middle

English *emunctorie,* from Medieval Latin *ēmunctōrius,* from Latin *ēmungere* (past participle *ēmunctus*), to blow the nose : *ex-,* completely + *mungere,* to blow the nose.]

en (en) *n. Printing.* **1.** *Abbr.* **n, N** A space equal to half the width of an em *(see).* Also called "nut". **2.** A letter or character considered as a unit for calculating space, quantity, or the like. ~*adj. Printing.* Designating a dash or space that is equal to the width of an en.

en–[1] *v. prefix.* Also **em-** before *b, p,* and sometimes *m.* Indicates: **1.** To put into or on; for example, **encompass, enthrone. 2.** To go into or on; for example, **entrain. 3.** To cover, surround, or imbue with; for example, **enrobe, empurple. 4.** To provide with; for example, **empower. 5.** To cause to be in a specified state or condition; for example, **endanger, enslave.** [Middle English, from Old French *en-, im-.*]

en–[2] *prefix.* Also **em-** before *b, m, p,* or *ph.* Indicates in, into, or within; for example, **enzootic, empathy.** [Middle English *en-,* from Latin, from Greek. In borrowed Greek compounds, *en-* also becomes *el-* before *l,* as in **ellipsis.**]

–en[1] *v. suffix.* Indicates: **1.** To be, become, or cause to be; for example, **cheapen, redden. 2.** To cause to have or gain; for example, **lengthen, hearten.** [Middle English *-nen, -nien,* Old English *-nian.*]

–en[2] *adj. suffix.* Made of, composed of, or resembling; for example, **wooden, earthen, ashen.** [Middle English *-en,* Old English *-en.*]

en·a·ble (in-áyb'l, en-) *tr.v.* **-bled, -bling, -bles. 1. a.** To supply with the means, knowledge, or opportunity to be or do something. **b.** To make feasible or possible. **2.** To give legal power, capacity, or sanction to; permit.

en·a·bling act (in-áybling, en-) *n. British.* A law passed to give certain powers to a person or organisation, usually a minister or government department.

en·act (in-ákt, en-) *tr.v.* **-acted, -acting, -acts. 1.** To give effect to (legislation); decree by legislative process; pass. **2.** To act out as on a stage; represent. **—en·act·a·ble** *adj.* **—en·ac·tor** *n.*

en·ac·tive (in-áktiv, en-) *adj.* Having the capacity or force to enact.

en·act·ment (in-áktmənt) *n.* **1.** The act of enacting. **2.** The state of being enacted. **3.** A law or statute.

en·am·el (i-námm'l) *n.* **1.** A smooth, glassy, usually opaque, protective or decorative coating baked on metal, glass, or ceramic ware. **2.** An object with an enamelled surface, such as a piece of cloisonné. **3.** A paint that dries to a hard, glossy surface. **4.** Any glossy, hard coating resembling enamel: *nail enamel.* **5.** *Anatomy.* The hard, calcium-containing substance covering the exposed portion of a tooth. ~*tr.v.* **enamelled** or *U.S.* **enameled, -elling** or *U.S.* **-eling, -els. 1.** To coat, inlay, or decorate with enamel. **2.** To give a glossy or brilliant surface to. **3.** To adorn, as with bright colours. [Middle English *enamelen,* from Anglo-French *enameller, enamailler* : *en-,* in + *amail,* enamel, from Old French *esmail,* from Germanic.] **—en·am·el·ler, en·am·el·list** *n.*

en·am·el·ling (i-námm'l-ing) *n.* **1.** The art, craft, or occupation of a person who enamels. **2.** A coating or decoration of enamel.

en·am·el·ware (i-námm'l-wair) *n.* Articles coated with enamel.

en·am·our, *U.S.* **en·am·or** (in-ámmər, en-) *tr.v.* **-oured** or *U.S.* **-ored, -ouring** or *U.S.* **-oring, -ours** or *U.S.* **-ors.** To inspire with love; charm; captivate. Usually used in the passive with *of* or *with: enamoured of his surroundings.* [Middle English *enamouren,* from Old French *enamourer* : *en-,* in + *amour,* love, from Latin *amor,* from *amāre,* to love.]

en·an·ti·o·morph (en-ánti-ə-mawrf, in-, -ō-) *n. Chemistry.* **1.** Either of a pair of crystals that are similar in form but cannot be superimposed, one being the mirror image of the other. **2.** Either of a pair of molecules that are mirror images of each other, an **optical isomer** *(see).* Also called "enantiomer". [Greek *enantios,* opposite : *en-,* in + *antios,* opposite, from *anti,* over against + -MORPH.] **—en·an·ti·o·morph·ism** (en-ánti-ə-mórf-iz'm, in-) *n.* **—en·an·ti·o·mor·phous** (-mórfəss), **en·an·ti·o·mor·phic** (-mórfik) *adj.*

en·ar·thro·sis (énnaar-thrō-siss) *n., pl.* **-ses** (-seez). *Anatomy.* A ball-and-socket joint. [New Latin, from Greek *enarthrōsis,* from *enarthros,* jointed : *en-,* in + *arthron,* joint.]

e·nate (ée-nayt) *adj.* Also **e·nat·ic** (ee-náttik, i-) (for sense 2). **1.** Growing outwards. **2.** Related on the mother's side. ~*n.* A relative on one's mother's side. [Latin *ēnātus,* past participle of *ēnāscī,* to be born from : *ex-,* out of + *nāscī,* to be born.]

en bloc (ON blók) *adv.* All together; collectively; as a whole or single unit. [French, "in a block".]

en bro·chette (ON bro-shét) *adj.* Grilled or roasted on a skewer. [French, "on a skewer".] **—en broch·ette** *adv.*

en brosse (ON bróss) *adj.* Standing stiffly upright as a result of being cut very short. Said of hair. [French, "in a brush".] **—en brosse** *adv.*

en·cae·ni·a (en-síni-ə) *n.* An annual commemoration held at universities honouring founders and benefactors. [Latin, feast of dedication, from Greek *enkainia* (plural) : *en-,* in + *kainos,* new.]

en·cage (in-káyj, en-) *tr.v.* **-caged, -caging, -cages.** To confine in or as if in a cage.

en·camp (in-kámp, en-) *v.* **-camped, -camping, -camps. —intr.** To set up or live in a camp. **—tr.** To provide quarters for in a camp.

en·camp·ment (in-kámpmənt, en-) *n.* **1.** The act of setting up a camp. **2.** A camp or campsite.

en·cap·su·late (in-káp-sew-layt, en- ‖ -sə-) *v.* **-lated, -lating, -lates.** Also **in·cap·su·late** (in-). **—tr. 1.** To encase in or as if in a capsule.

2. To summarise very concisely. **—intr.** To become encapsulated. **—en·cap·su·la·tion** (-láysh'n, en- ‖ -sə-) *n.*

en·case (in-káyss, en-) *tr.v.* **-cased, -casing, -cases.** Also **in·case** (in-). To enclose in or as if in a case. **—en·case·ment** *n.*

en·cash (in-kásh, en-) *tr.v.* **-cashed, -cashing, -cashes.** *British.* To turn (a cheque) into cash. **—en·cash·a·ble** *adj.* **—en·cash·ment** *n.*

en·caus·tic (en-káw-stik, in-, -kó-) *adj.* Pertaining to a painting process in which coloured wax is applied and fixed with heat. ~*n.* **1.** The art of painting in this way. **2.** An encaustic painting. [Latin *encausticus,* from Greek *enkaustikos,* from *enkaiein,* to burn in : *en-,* in + *kaiein,* to burn.]

–ence, –ency *n. suffix.* Indicates action, state, quality, or condition; for example, **competence, patience.** [Middle English *-ence,* from Old French, from Latin *-entia,* from *-ēns,* present participial suffix.]

en·ceinte[1] (on-sánt ‖ en-sáynt; *French* ON-SÁNT) *adj.* Being with child; pregnant. [French, from Late Latin *incinta,* without a girdle : Latin *in-,* without + *cinta,* feminine past participle of *cingere,* to gird.]

en·ceinte[2] *n.* **1.** An encircling fortification round a fort, castle, or town. **2.** The structures or area protected by such a fortification. [French, from Latin *incincta,* feminine past participle of *incingere,* to gird in : *in-,* in + *cingere,* to gird.]

en·ce·phal·ic (en-si-fál-ik, -ki-) *adj.* **1.** Of or pertaining to the brain. **2.** Located within the cranial cavity.

en·ceph·a·lin (en-séffə-lin, -kéffə-) *n.* Also **en·keph·a·lin** (-kéffə-). A chemical occurring naturally in the brain and having effects similar to those of morphine. [ENCEPHALO- + -IN.]

en·ceph·a·li·tis (en-séffə-lítiss, -keffə-, en-séffə-, in-) *n.* Inflammation of the brain. Also called "brain fever". **—en·ceph·a·lit·ic** (-líttik) *adj.*

encephalitis le·thar·gi·ca (li-thárjikə) *n.* A viral epidemic encephalitis often held to be associated with some forms of influenza and marked by apathy, double vision, and extreme muscular weakness. Also called "lethargic encephalitis", "sleeping sickness".

encephalo–, encephal– *comb. form.* Indicates the brain; for example, **encephalogram, encephalitis.** [New Latin, from Greek *(muelos) enkephalos,* "(marrow) in the head", the brain : *en-,* in + *kephalē,* head.]

en·ceph·a·lo·gram (én-séffələ-gram, in-, -kéffələ-) *n.* **1.** An X-ray picture of the brain taken by encephalography. **2.** An **electroencephalogram** *(see).*

en·ceph·a·log·ra·phy (én-seffə-lóggrəfi, -keffə-, en-séffə-, in-) *n.* A technique for recording the structure of the brain by tracing electrical activity, detecting ultrasonic pulses, or introducing air to provide a contrast medium for X-rays. **—en·ceph·a·lo·graph** (en-séffələ-graaf, in-, -kéffələ-, -graf) *n.* **—en·ceph·a·lo·graph·ic** (-lə-gráffik) *adj.* **—en·ceph·a·lo·graph·i·cal·ly** *adv.*

en·ceph·a·lo·ma (én-seffə-lōmə, -keffə-, en-séffə-, in-) *n., pl.* **-mas** or **-mata** (-mə-tə). A tumour of the brain. [ENCEPHAL(O)- + -OMA.]

en·ceph·a·lo·my·e·li·tis (en-séffələ-mí-ə-lítiss, in-, -kéffələ-) *n.* Acute inflammation of the brain and the spinal cord.

en·ceph·a·lon (en-séffə-lon, in-, -kéffə-, -lən) *n., pl.* **-la** (-lə). The brain of a vertebrate. [New Latin, from Greek *enkephalon, enkephalos.* See encephalo-.] **—en·ceph·a·lous** *adj.*

en·ceph·a·lop·a·thy (én-seffə-lóppəthi, -keffə-, en-séffə-, in-) *n., pl.* **-thies.** Any of various diseases that affect the brain. [ENCEPHALO- + -PATHY.]

en·chain (in-cháyn, en-) *tr.v.* **-chained, -chaining, -chains. 1.** To bind with or as with chains; fetter: *Superstition enchains the mind.* **2.** To hold fast; rivet (the attention, for example). [Middle English *encheynen,* from Old French *enchaeiner* : *en-,* in + *chaeine,* CHAIN.] **—en·chain·ment** *n.*

en·chant (in-cháant, en- ‖ -chánt) *tr.v.* **-chanted, -chanting, -chants. 1.** To cast under a spell; bewitch. **2.** To delight completely; charm; enrapture. [Middle English *enchanten,* Old French *enchanter,* from Latin *incantāre,* to chant (magic words) : *in-* (intensive) + *cantāre,* frequentative of *canēre,* to sing.]

en·chant·er (in-cháant-ər, en- ‖ -chánt-) *n.* One that enchants; especially, a sorcerer or magician.

enchanter's nightshade *n.* Any of several plants of the genus *Circaea,* especially *C. lutetiana,* having small white flowers and bristly, clinging fruit.

en·chant·ing (in-cháant-ing, en- ‖ -chánt-) *adj.* Charming; delightful. **—en·chant·ing·ly** *adv.*

en·chant·ment (en-cháant-mənt, en- ‖ -chánt-) *n.* **1. a.** An act of enchanting. **b.** The state of being enchanted. **2.** Something that enchants; an irresistible charm or allure. **3.** A magic spell.

en·chant·ress (in-cháant-riss, en- ‖ -chánt-) *n.* **1.** A woman of unusual allure or fascination. **2.** A sorceress.

en·chase (in-cháyss, en-) *tr.v.* **-chased, -chasing, -chases. 1.** To set (a gem, for example) in some material. **2.** To set with or as if with gems. **3.** To decorate or ornament (a surface) by inlaying, engraving, or chasing. [Middle English *enchasen,* from Old French *enchasser* : *en-,* in + *chasse,* case, from Latin *capsa,* box.]

en·chi·la·da (énchi-laádə) *n.* A Mexican dish consisting of a fried tortilla, rolled and stuffed usually with a mixture containing meat or cheese, and served with a sauce spiced with chilli. [American Spanish, feminine past participle of *enchilar,* to put chilli in : *en-,* in, from Latin *in-* + *chile,* CHILLI.]

en·chi·rid·i·on (énkī-ríddi-ən) *n., pl.* **-ons** or **-ridia** (-ríddi-ə). *Rare.* A handbook; a manual. [Late Latin, from Greek *enkheiridion* : *en-,* in + *-kheiridion,* diminutive of *kheir,* hand.]

en·chon·dro·ma (én-kən-drŏ-mə, -kon-) *n., pl.* **-mas** or **-mata** (-tə). A benign cartilaginous tumour that occurs at the growing zone of a bone, between the end and the shaft. [EN- + CHONDR(O)- + -OMA.]

en·cho·ri·al (en-káwri-əl, in- || -kŏri-) *adj.* Also **en·chor·ic** (-káwrik, -kórrik). Belonging or native to a particular region or people. Said especially of demotic writing. [Greek *enkhōrios*, indigenous, native : *en-*, in + *khōra*, country, place.]

-enchyma *n. comb. form.* Indicates cellular tissue; for example, **collenchyma**. [New Latin, from (PAR)ENCHYMA.]

en·ci·pher (en-sīfər, en-) *tr.v.* **-phered, -phering, -phers.** To put (a message) into cipher. **—en·ci·pher·er** *n.* **—en·ci·pher·ment** *n.*

en·cir·cle (in-súrk'l, en-) *tr.v.* **-cled, -cling, -cles.** 1. To form a circle round; surround. 2. To move or go round; make a circuit of. **—en·cir·cle·ment** *n.*

Encke's comet (éngkəz) *n.* A comet with a period of 3.3 years, decreasing by 2½ hours each revolution. First observed in 1786, it is the most studied of all comets. [After Johann *Encke* (1791–1865), German astronomer.]

encl. enclosed; enclosure.

en clair (ON kláir) *adj. French.* In ordinary, uncoded language. [Literally, "in clear".] **—en clair** *adv.*

en·clasp (in-klảasp, en- || -klásp) *tr.v.* **-clasped, -clasping, -clasps.** To hold in or as if in a clasp; embrace.

en·clave (én-klayv, ón-) *n.* 1. A country or part of a country lying wholly within the boundaries of another. Compare **exclave.** 2. Any distinctly bounded area enclosed within a larger area. 3. A minority group or community: *an artistic enclave .* 4. Loosely, any quiet, unspoilt, isolated place. [French, from Old French *enclaver*, to enclose, from Vulgar Latin *inclāvāre* (unattested), to lock in with a key : Latin *in-*, in + *clāvis*, key.]

en·clit·ic (in-klíttik, en-) *adj. Linguistics.* Having no independent accent in a sentence and forming an accentual and sometimes also graphemic unit with the preceding word. Said of a word or particle; for example, *'em* in informal English: *Give 'em the works;* or *-que* in Latin: *Senatus populusque Romanus* ("The senate and people of Rome"). Compare **proclitic.** ~*n.* An enclitic word or particle. [Late Latin *encliticus*, from Greek *enklitikos*, "leaning (on the preceding word for accent)", from *enklinein*, to lean on : *en-*, in + *klinein*, to lean.]

en·close (in-klōz, en-) *tr.v.* **-closed, -closing, -closes.** Also **in·close** (in-). 1. To surround on all sides; fence in; close in. 2. **a.** To place within a container. **b.** To insert in the same envelope or package with the main letter. 3. To contain, especially so as to shelter or hide: *"every one of those darkly clustered houses encloses its own secret"* (Charles Dickens). [Middle English *enclosen*, from Old French *enclore* (past participle *enclose*), from Vulgar Latin *inclaudere* (unattested), variant of Latin *inclūdere*, INCLUDE.]

enclosed order *n.* A Christian religious order whose members are not permitted to go into the outside world.

en·clo·sure (in-klōzhər, en-) *n. Abbr.* **enc., encl.** 1. The act of enclosing. 2. The state of being enclosed. 3. An area that is enclosed. 4. Something that encloses, such as a wall or fence. 5. A letter, item, or supporting document enclosed, usually with an explanatory letter, in an envelope or package. 6. The appropriation of unclaimed or common land by fencing it in. 7. *British.* A part of a racetrack or sports ground set aside for special visitors.

en·code (in-kŏd, en-) *tr.v.* **-coded, -coding, -codes.** To put (a message) into code. **—en·cod·er** *n.*

en·co·mi·ast (en-kŏmi-ast || -əst) *n.* A person who delivers or writes encomiums; a eulogist. [Greek *enkōmiastēs*, from *enkōmiazein*, to praise, from *enkōmion*, ENCOMIUM.]

en·co·mi·as·tic (en-kŏmi-ástik) *adj.* Also **en·co·mi·as·ti·cal** (-k'l). Pertaining to, containing, or being an encomium. **—en·co·mi·as·ti·cal·ly** *adv.*

en·co·mi·um (en-kŏ-mi-əm) *n., pl.* **-ums** or **-mia** (-mi-ə). A formal expression of lofty praise; a tribute; a eulogy. [Latin *encōmium*, from Greek *enkōmion (epos)*, "(speech) in praise of a conqueror", from *enkōmios*, belonging to revels : *en-*, in + *kōmos*, celebration, revel (see **comedy**).]

en·com·pass (in-kúmpəss, en-) *tr.v.* **-passed, -passing, -passes.** 1. To form a circle or ring about; surround. 2. To enclose; envelop. 3. To comprise; include. 4. To cause to happen; devise: *encompass his rival's downfall.* **—en·com·pass·ment** *n.*

en·core (óng-kawr, -kór || -kōr) *n.* 1. A demand by an audience for an additional performance. 2. An additional performance in response to such a demand. ~*tr.v.* **encored, -coring, -cores.** 1. To demand an encore of (a performer). 2. To demand as an encore. ~*interj.* Used to demand an additional performance. [French, still, yet, again, probably from Latin *hinc ad hōram*, from that to this hour : *hinc*, from here, from *hic*, this + *ad*, to + *hōram*, accusative of *hōra*, hour, from Greek *hōra*.]

en·coun·ter (in-kówntər, en-) *n.* 1. A meeting, especially when casual and unplanned. 2. A hostile confrontation; a contest. ~*v.* **encountered, -tering, -ters.** *—tr.* 1. To meet or come upon, especially casually or unexpectedly. 2. To confront in battle or contention. 3. To come up against; be faced with or exposed to: *encounter numerous obstacles. —intr.* To meet, especially in conflict. [Middle English *encountre*, from Old French *encontre*, from *encontrer*, to meet, from Vulgar Latin *incontrāre* (unattested) : Latin *in-*, in + *contrā*, opposite, against.]

encounter group *n.* A deliberately unstructured therapy group in which individuals seek to increase their sensitivity and responsiveness to others.

en·cour·age (in-kúrrij, en-) *tr.v.* **-aged, -aging, -ages.** 1. To inspire to continue on a chosen course; impart courage or confidence to; embolden; hearten. 2. To give support to; foster. **—See Synonyms at urge.** [Middle English *encoragen*, from Old French *encorager* : *en-* (causative) + *corage*, COURAGE.] **—en·cour·age·ment** *n.*

en·cour·ag·ing (in-kúrrijing, en-) *adj.* Permitting one to be confident or hopeful. **—en·cour·ag·ing·ly** *adv.*

en·croach (in-krŏch, en-) *intr.v.* **-croached, -croaching, -croaches.** 1. To intrude gradually or insidiously upon the domain, possessions, or rights of another; trespass. Used with *on* or *upon.* 2. To advance beyond proper or prescribed limits. [Middle English *encroachen*, from Old French *encrochier*, "to catch in a hook", seize : *en-*, in + *croc*, hook, from (unattested) Frankish *krōk*.]

en·croach·ment (in-krŏch-mənt, en-) *n.* The act or an instance of encroaching. See Synonyms at **breach.**

en·crust (in-krúst, en-) *tr.v.* **-crusted, -crusting, -crusts.** Also **in·crust** (in-). 1. To cover or surmount with a crust or crustlike layer. 2. To adorn, as with jewels. [Probably from French *incruster*, from Latin *incrustāre* : *in-* (causative) + *crusta*, CRUST.] **—en·crust·a·tion** (ín-kruss-táysh'n, én-) *n.*

en·cum·ber (in-kúmbər, en-) *tr.v.* **-bered, -bering, -bers.** Also **in·cum·ber** (in-). 1. To weigh down unduly; lay too much upon. 2. To hinder, impede, or clutter, as with useless articles or unwanted additions. 3. To handicap or burden, as with obligations or legal claims. **—See Synonyms at hinder.** [Middle English *encombren*, from Old French *encombrer*, to block up : *en-*, in + *combre*, hindrance, from Gaulish *comboros†* (unattested).]

en·cum·brance (in-kúmbrənss, en-) *n.* Also **in·cum·brance** (in-). 1. One that encumbers; a burden, impediment, or obstacle. 2. *Law.* A lien or claim upon property, such as a mortgage. **—See Synonyms at obstacle.**

en·cum·branc·er (in-kúmbrən-sər, en-) *n. Law.* A person who holds an encumbrance on another's property.

ency., encyc., encycl. encyclopedia.

-ency. Variant of **-ence.**

en·cyc·li·cal (en-síklik'l, in-) *adj.* Intended for general or wide circulation. Said of letters. ~*n. Roman Catholic Church.* A papal letter on a specific subject addressed officially to the clergy or to the hierarchy of a particular country. [Late Latin *encyclicus*, from Greek *enkuklios*, in a circle, circular : *en-*, in + *kuklos*, circle.]

en·cy·clo·pe·di·a, en·cy·clo·pae·di·a (en-síklə-pẽedi-ə, in-) *n. Abbr.* **ency., encyc., encycl.** A comprehensive, often multivolume, reference work containing articles on a wide range of subjects or on numerous aspects of a particular field, usually arranged alphabetically. [Medieval Latin *encyclopaedia*, general education course, from Greek *enkuklopaideiā*, a mistaken transcription of *enkuklios paideia*, general education : *enkuklios*, circular, general (see **encyclical**) + *paideia*, education, training, from *pais* (stem *paid-*), child.]

en·cy·clo·pe·dic (en-síklə-pẽedik, in-) *adj.* 1. Of, pertaining to, or characteristic of an encyclopedia. 2. Embracing many subjects; comprehensive. **—en·cy·clo·pe·di·cal·ly** *adv.*

en·cy·clo·pe·dism (en-síklə-pẽediz'm, in-) *n.* Encyclopedic learning.

en·cy·clo·pe·dist (en-síklə-pẽedist, in-) *n.* 1. A person who writes for or compiles an encyclopedia. 2. *Capital* E. Any of the writers of the French *Encyclopédie* (1751–72), including its editors, Diderot and d'Alembert. Their ideas are considered to represent those of the **Age of Reason** *(see).*

en·cyst (en-síst, in-) *v.* **-cysted, -cysting, -cysts.** *—tr.* To enclose in a cyst. *—intr.* To take the form of or become enclosed in a cyst. **—en·cyst·ment, en·cys·ta·tion** (én-siss-táysh'n) *n.*

end (end) *n.* 1. Either extremity of something that has length. 2. The outside or extreme edge or limit of a space, form, or area; a boundary. 3. The point in time at which an action, event, or phenomenon ceases or is completed; a conclusion: *the end of a day.* 4. A result; an outcome. 5. The termination of life or existence; death. 6. An ultimate extent; a limit: *the end of one's patience.* 7. **a.** That towards which one strives; a goal: *"The end of Poetry is to produce excitement in coexistence with an overbalance of pleasure"* (William Wordsworth). **b.** The reason or object by virtue of which something exists or takes place. 8. *Usually plural.* A remainder or remnant. Used chiefly in the phrase *odds and ends.* 9. *Informal.* **a.** A share of a responsibility or obligation; a duty; a part: *your end of the bargain.* **b.** A particular area or phase of an enterprise or undertaking: *the packaging end of a business.* 10. *Sports.* **a.** Either of the defended areas of a playing field or pitch. **b.** In American football, either of the players in the outermost position at the line of scrimmage; a wing. **c.** In bowling, a period of play at one end of the green. **—See Synonyms at boundary, intention. —at a loose end.** Aimless; unoccupied. **—come to a bad or sticky end.** *Informal.* To finish disastrously or die unpleasantly. **—make (both) ends meet.** To manage to live within one's means. **—no end of.** *Informal.* A great deal of: *no end of stories to tell.* **—the end.** *Informal.* An extremely exasperating person or situation. ~*v.* **ended, ending, ends.** *—tr.* 1. To bring to an end; finish; conclude. 2. To form the end or concluding part of. 3. To bring about the extinction of; destroy. 4. To be the finest of (a kind); surpass: *a prize to end all prizes. —intr.* 1. To come to an end; cease. 2. To die. **—See Synonyms at complete. —end it all.** *Informal.* To commit suicide. **—end up.** 1. To conclude. 2. To find or put oneself in

a specified state, position, or the like: *We ended up laughing.*
~*adj.* At a position on the end; final; concluding: *end man; end point.* [Middle English *ende*, Old English *ende*, from Germanic.]
END European Nuclear Disarmament.
endamoeba. Variant of **entamoeba.**
en·dan·ger (in-dáynjər, en-) *tr.v.* **-gered, -gering, -gers.** To expose to danger or harm; imperil. —**en·dan·ger·ment** *n.*
endangered species *n.* A species in danger of extinction.
end·ar·ter·ec·to·my (en-dártə-réktəmi) *n., pl.* **-mies.** *Medicine.* The reboring of an artery that has become blocked by atheroma, by removing the inner wall and any clot that is present. [END(O)- + ARTER(Y) + -ECTOMY.]
end-brain (énd-brayn) *n. Anatomy.* The **telencephalon** (*see*).
en·dear (in-déer, en-) *tr.v.* **-deared, -dearing, -dears.** To cause to inspire affection or warm sympathy. —**en·dear·ing·ly** *adv.*
en·dear·ment (in-déermənt, en-) *n.* **1.** The act of endearing. **2.** An expression of affection; a loving word or caress.
en·deav·our, *U.S.* **en·deav·or** (in-dévvər) *n.* **1.** A conscientious or concerted effort towards a given end; an earnest attempt. **2.** *Often plural.* Earnest striving. —See Synonyms at **effort.**
~*intr.v.* **endeavoured** or *U.S.* **endeavored, -ouring** or *U.S.* **-oring, -ours** or *U.S.* **-ors.** To make an earnest attempt; strive. Usually used with an infinitive: *endeavour to stay solvent.* [Middle English *endevour,* from *endeveren,* to exert oneself, from the phrase *putten in dever,* to put in duty, make it one's duty : IN + *dever,* duty, from Old French *devoir,* DEVOIR.] —**en·deav·our·er** *n.*
en·dem·ic (en-démmik, in-) *adj.* Also **en·de·mi·al** (-démmi-əl, -déemi-), **en·dem·i·cal** (-démmik'l). **1. a.** Prevalent or deeply-rooted, especially within a particular group or locality: *troubles endemic in a class-ridden society.* **b.** Prevalent or frequently occurring in a particular context, area, or subject. **2.** *Ecology.* Native or confined to a certain region; having a comparatively restricted distribution. **3.** *Medicine.* Peculiar to and recurring in a particular locality. Said of a disease.
~*n. Ecology.* An endemic plant or animal. [French *endémique,* from Greek *endēmios, endēmos,* dwelling in a place, indigenous : *en-,* in + *dēmos,* people.] —**en·dem·i·cal·ly** *adv.* —**en·dem·ism** (éndə-miz'm) *n.*
En·der·by Land (éndərbi). Area in Antarctica, on the Indian Ocean. Discovered in 1831, it is claimed by Australia.
en·der·mic (en-dérmik) *adj. Medicine.* Acting by absorption through the skin. Said of lotions and similar preparations. [EN- + -DERM + -IC.]
Enders (éndərz), **John Franklin** (1897–1985). U.S. bacteriologist. In 1954 he was awarded the Nobel prize for physiology or medicine, with T.H. Weller (1915–) and F.C. Robbins (1916–), for successful experiments in growing polio viruses in cultures of a variety of tissues.
end-game (énd-gaym) *n.* **1.** In chess, the final stage of the game, when only a few pieces survive. **2.** The final stage of any of various other games, especially board games. **3.** Loosely, the final stage or culmination of anything, such as a battle.
end·ing (énding) *n.* **1.** A conclusion or termination. **2.** The concluding part, especially of a book, play, or film; a finale: *a happy ending.* **3.** The letter, letters, sound, or sounds added to a word or word part, especially to make a derivative or inflectional form.
en·dive (én-dīv, -div, ón-deev) *n.* A plant, *Cichorium endivia,* cultivated for its crown of crisp, succulent leaves, used in salads. Also known as **chicory.** [Middle English, from Old French, from Medieval Latin *endiva,* variant of Latin *entubus, entibus,* chicory, from Greek *entubioi,* perhaps from Egyptian *tybi,* January, because the plant grows in this month.]
end leaf *n.* An **endpaper** (*see*).
end·less (énd-ləss, -liss) *adj.* **1.** Being or seeming to be without an end; infinite; boundless. **2.** Incessant; interminable: *an endless conversation.* **3.** Formed with the ends joined; continuous: *an endless chain.* —**end·less·ly** *adv.* —**end·less·ness** *n.*
end matter *n.* Material, often including an index, appendix, bibliography, or notes, that follows the main part of a book. Also called "back matter". Compare **front matter.**
end·most (énd-mōst) *adj.* Being at or closest to the end; last.
endo-, end- *comb. form.* Indicates inside or within; for example, **endocarp, endomorph.** [Greek, from *endon,* within.]
en·do·blast (én-dō-blast, -də-, -blaast) *n.* Also **en·to·blast** (én-tō-, -tə-). In embryology, the inner layer of the blastoderm that becomes the endoderm at gastrulation. Also called "hypoblast". [ENDO- + -BLAST.] —**en·do·blas·tic** (én-dō-blástik, -də-) *adj.*
en·do·car·di·tis (éndō-kaar-dítiss) *n.* Inflammation of the endocardium. [ENDOCARD(IUM) + -ITIS.] —**en·do·car·dit·ic** (-díttik) *adj.*
en·do·car·di·um (éndō-kár-di-əm) *n., pl.* **-dia** (-di-ə). The thin, endothelial, serous membrane that lines the interior of the heart. [New Latin : ENDO- + Greek *kardia,* heart.] —**en·do·car·di·al** *adj.*
en·do·carp (éndō-kaarp, éndə-) *n. Botany.* The often hard or leathery inner layer of the pericarp of many fruits. [ENDO- + -CARP.]
en·do·cen·tric (éndō-séntrik) *adj. Grammar.* Designating a construction with the same grammatical function in combination as at least one of its constituents; for example, *five gold rings* is an endocentric construction since the entire noun phrase functions grammatically in the same way as its head noun *rings.* Compare **exocentric.** [ENDO- + -CENTRIC.]
en·do·cra·ni·um (én-dō-kráy-ni-əm, -də-) *n., pl.* **-nia** (-ni-ə). The outermost layer of the dura mater.
en·do·crine (én-dō-krīn, -də-, -krin ‖ -kreen) *adj.* Also **en·do·cri·nal**

(-krī'n'l ‖ -krée'n'l), **en·do·crin·ic** (-krínnik), **en·doc·ri·nous** (en-dóckrinəss). **1.** Secreting internally. **2.** Of or pertaining to any of the ductless or endocrine glands.
~*n.* An endocrine gland. [ENDO- + Greek *krīnein,* to separate, "secrete".]
endocrine gland *n.* Any of the ductless glands, such as the thyroid or adrenal, the secretions of which pass directly into the blood stream from the cells of the gland. Also called "ductless gland". See **hormone.**
en·do·cri·nol·o·gy (én-dō-krī-nólləji, -də-, -kri-) *n.* The study of the endocrine glands, their secretions, and their diseases. —**en·do·cri·no·log·ic** (-krínnə-lójik), **en·do·cri·no·log·ic·al** *adj.* —**en·do·cri·nol·o·gist** (-krī-nólləjist, -kri-) *n.*
en·do·derm (én-dō-derm, -də-) *n.* Also **en·to·derm** (én-tō-, -tə-). The innermost of the three primary germ layers of an embryo, developing into the lining of the intestinal tract and its derivatives. [ENDO- + -DERM.] —**en·do·der·mal** (-dérm'l) *adj.*
en·do·der·mis (én-dō-dérmiss, -də-) *n. Botany.* The innermost layer of the cortex, found in all roots and in the stems of certain plants, which controls the passage of water. [ENDO- + Greek *derma,* skin, DERMA.]
en·do·don·tics (én-dō-dón-tikss, -də-) *n. Used with a singular verb.* Also **en·do·don·ti·a** (-shə, -shi-ə). The branch of dentistry dealing with diseases of the tooth pulp. [ENDO- + -ODONT + -ICS.] —**en·do·don·tic** *adj.* —**en·do·don·tist** *n.*
en·do·en·zyme (éndō-énzim) *n.* **1.** An enzyme that acts upon inner chemical bonds in a chain molecule. **2.** An enzyme that acts inside the cell that produces it.
en·do·er·gic (éndō-érjik) *adj. Physics.* Of or involving absorption of energy. Said of nuclear reactions. [ENDO- + -ergic, from Greek *ergon,* work.]
en·dog·a·my (en-dóggəmi) *n.* **1.** *Anthropology.* Marriage within a particular group, caste, class, or tribe in accordance with set custom or law. Compare **exogamy. 2.** *Biology.* **a.** The fusion of gametes from closely related parents. **b.** Pollination between two flowers of the same plant. [ENDO- + -GAMY.] —**en·dog·a·mous** *adj.*
en·dog·e·nous (en-dójinəss) *adj.* **1.** Produced from within. **2.** *Biology.* Originating within an organ or part. [ENDO- + -GENOUS.] —**en·dog·e·nous·ly** *adv.* —**en·dog·e·ny** *n.*
en·do·lymph (én-dō-limf, -də-) *n.* The fluid in the cochlear duct of the labyrinth of the ear.
en·do·me·tri·o·sis (éndō-méetri-ō-siss) *n.* The presence of endometrium, normally confined to the uterus, in other parts of the pelvic cavity such as the ovaries, resulting in localised monthly pain.
en·do·me·tri·um (éndō-mée-tri-əm) *n., pl.* **-tria** (-tri-ə). The mucous membrane lining the uterus. [ENDO- + METR(O)- (uterus) + -IUM.]
en·do·morph (én-dō-mawrf, -də-) *n.* **1.** *Mineralogy.* A mineral found as an inclusion in another, as rutile or tourmaline may be found in quartz. Compare **perimorph. 2.** *Physiology.* A person of a type having a relatively fat body with prominent abdominal parts and weak muscular and skeletal development. Compare **ectomorph, mesomorph.** [ENDO- + -MORPH.]
en·do·mor·phic (én-dō-mórfik, -də-) *adj.* **1.** *Mineralogy.* **a.** Of or pertaining to an endomorph. **b.** Created through endomorphism. **2.** *Physiology.* Of or pertaining to an endomorphic individual. —**en·do·mor·phy** (-mawrfi) *n.*
en·do·mor·phism (én-dō-mórfiz'm, -də-) *n. Geology.* The metamorphism of igneous rock as it cools, resulting from contact with and assimilation of the wall rock.
en·do·par·a·site (éndō-párrə-sīt) *n.* An organism, such as a tapeworm, that lives parasitically within another organism.
en·do·phyte (én-dō-fīt, -də-) *n.* A plant, such as any of certain fungi, growing within another plant. [ENDO- + -PHYTE.] —**en·do·phyt·ic** (-fíttik) *adj.*
en·do·plasm (én-dō-plaz'm, -də-) *n.* The inner, less viscous portion of the cytoplasm distinguishable within some cells. Compare **ectoplasm.** [ENDO- + -PLASM.] —**en·do·plas·mic** (-plázmik) *adj.*
endoplasmic reticulum *n. Abbr.* **ER** A system of membrane-bounded sacs in the cytoplasm of cells that functions in intracellular transport.
end organ *n. Anatomy.* The expanded functional termination of a sensory or motor nerve.
en·dor·phin (en-dórfin) *n.* Any of a group of hormone-like substances with pain-killing and tranquillising properties that are secreted by the brain. [ENDO- + -orphin, as in *morphine.*]
en·dorse (in-dórss, en-) *tr.v.* **-dorsed, -dorsing, -dorses.** Also **in·dorse** (in-). **1.** To write one's signature on the back of (a cheque, money order, or the like) as evidence of the legal transfer of its ownership, especially in return for the cash or credit indicated on its face. **2. a.** To place (one's signature) on a contract or other document to indicate approval of its contents or terms. **b.** To allow one's name and reputation to be used to publicise (a product) in return for payment. **3.** To acknowledge (receipt of payment) by signing the bill, draft, or other document. **4.** To give approval of or support to; sanction. **5.** To qualify (a driving licence) by entering on it a record of a motoring offence. —**endorse out.** *South African.* Formerly, to require (a black South African) to leave an urban area in which he lacks official permission to reside. Usually used in the passive. —See Synonyms at **approve.** [Middle English *endosen,* from Old French *endosser,* "to put on the back of" : *en-,* to put on + *dos,* back, from Latin *dorsum.*] —**en·dors·a·ble** *adj.* —**en·dors·er, en·dor·sor** (-dór-sər) *n.*
en·dor·see (in-dór-sée, en-, én-dawr-) *n.* One to whom ownership

509

of a negotiable document is transferred by endorsement.

en·dorse·ment (in-dórss-mənt, en-) n. 1. An act of endorsing. 2. Something that endorses or validates, such as a signature or voucher. 3. Approbation; sanction; support. 4. An amendment to a contract, such as an insurance policy, permitting a change in the original terms. 5. *British.* A record of a driving offence on a driving licence.

en·do·scope (én-dō-skōp, -də-) n. An instrument for examining the interior of a bodily canal or hollow organ. [ENDO- + -SCOPE.] —**en·do·scop·ic** (-skóppik) adj. —**en·do·scop·i·cal·ly** adv. —**en·dos·cop·ist** (en-dóskə-pist) n. —**en·dos·co·py** n.

en·do·skel·e·ton (éndō-skéllit'n) n. An internal supporting skeleton characteristic of vertebrates. Compare **exoskeleton**. —**en·do·skel·e·tal** adj.

en·dos·mo·sis (én-doss-mṓ-siss, -doz-) n. The flow of a solvent through a semipermeable membrane from a surrounding fluid; especially, the flow of water through a cell membrane into a cell or organism. Compare **exosmosis**. [END(O)- + OSMOSIS.] —**en·dos·mot·ic** (-móttik) adj. —**en·dos·mot·i·cal·ly** adv.

en·do·some (én-dō-sōm, -də-) n. A discrete, darker area within a nucleus, especially the nucleolus.

en·do·sperm (én-dō-sperm, -də-) n. *Botany.* The nutritive tissue surrounding and absorbed by the embryo in flowering plants. [ENDO- + -SPERM.] —**en·do·sper·mic** (-spérmik) adj.

en·do·spore (én-dō-spawr, -də- ‖ -spōr) n. An asexual spore formed within the cells of certain bacteria and acting as a resting stage. —**en·dos·por·ous** (en-dóspərəss, éndō-spáw-rəss) adj.

en·do·spor·i·um (én-dō-spáwri-əm, -də- ‖ -spōri-) n. The intine (see). [New Latin, from ENDO- + SPORE.]

en·dos·te·um (en-dóss-ti-əm) n., pl. **-tea** (-ti-ə). The membrane that lines the marrow cavity of a long bone. [New Latin : END(O)- + Greek osteon, bone.] —**en·dos·te·al** adj.

en·do·the·ci·um (éndō-thée-shi-əm, -si-) n., pl. **-cia** (-ə). *Botany.* The inner tissue of an anther or a moss capsule. [New Latin : ENDO- + Greek thēkion, diminutive of thēkē, chest.]

en·do·the·li·o·ma (éndō-théeli-ō-mə) n., pl. **-mata** (-mətə) or **-mas**. Any of various tumours derived from endothelial tissue. [ENDOTHELI(UM) + -OMA.]

en·do·the·li·um (éndō-thée-li-əm) n., pl. **-lia** (-li-ə). A thin layer of flat cells that lines serous cavities, lymph vessels, and blood vessels. [New Latin : ENDO- + Greek thēlē, nipple.] —**en·do·the·li·al**, **en·do·the·li·oid** adj.

en·do·ther·mic (én-dō-thérmik, -də-) adj. Also **en·do·ther·mal** (-m'l). Characterised by or causing the absorption of heat. Said especially of chemical reactions. Compare **exothermic**. [ENDO- + THERM + -IC.] —**en·do·ther·mi·cal·ly** adv.

en·do·tox·in (éndō-tóksin) n. A toxin produced within a microorganism and released upon destruction of the cell in which it is produced. [ENDO- + TOXIN.] —**en·do·tox·ic** adj.

en·dow (in-dów, en-) tr.v. **-dowed, -dowing, -dows**. 1. To invest with property, income, or a source of income. 2. To invest with specified qualities or characteristics. Used with *with*. [Middle English endowen, from Anglo-French endouer : Old French en- (intensive) + douer, to provide with a dowry, from Latin dōtāre, from dōs (stem dōt-), dowry.]

en·dow·ment (in-dówmənt, en-) n. 1. An act of endowing. 2. Funds or property donated to an institution, individual, or group as a source of income. 3. A natural gift or quality; an attribute, such as beauty or talent.
~adj. Designating or involving a form of life insurance in which the policy matures within a specific period after issuance and becomes a claim payable to the insured at that time, or to his beneficiary upon the death of the insured before that time.

end·pa·per (énd-paypər) n. Either of two folded sheets of heavy paper having one half pasted to the inside front or back cover of a book and the other half pasted to the base of the first or last page. Also called "end leaf".

end·plate (énd-playt) n. *Physiology.* A flattened motor nerve terminal that transmits nerve impulses to muscle.

end·play (énd-play) tr.v. **-played, -playing, -plays**. In bridge, to force (an opponent) to play a particular card during a late trick. —**end·play** n.

end point n. 1. *Chemistry.* The point at which a titration is complete, with neither reactant in excess. 2. Any completion point.

end product n. The final conclusion of a series or process; specifically, the finished product of a manufacturing or similar process.

end·stopped (énd-stopt) adj. Having a punctuation mark or distinct pause at the end of a line. Said of verse. Compare **enjambement**.

en·due (in-déw, en- ‖ -dṓo) tr.v. **-dued, -duing, -dues**. Also **in·due** (in-). 1. To provide with some specified quality or trait. Used with *with*. 2. *Rare.* **a.** To put on; dress in. **b.** To clothe. [Sense 1, Middle English enduen, endeuen, from Old French enduire, to lead in, induct (meaning influenced by Middle English endowen, endow), from Latin indūcere, INDUCE. Sense 2, Middle English induen, from Latin induere, to don.]

en·dur·ance (in-déwr-ənss, en- ‖ -dóor-) n. 1. The act, quality, or power of withstanding hardship or stress. 2. The state or fact of persevering; continuing survival.

en·dure (in-déwr, en- ‖ -dóor) v. **-dured, -during, -dures**. —*tr.* 1. To carry on through, despite hardships; undergo: *endure an Arctic winter.* 2. To bear with tolerance; put up with: *endure insults.* —*intr.* 1. To continue in existence; remain; last: *buildings that en-*

dure for centuries. 2. To suffer patiently without yielding; persevere; hold out. —See Synonyms at **bear**. [Middle English enduren, from Old French endurer, from Late Latin indūrāre, "to harden one's heart against", bear, from Latin, to harden : in- (intensive) + dūrāre, to harden, from dūrus, hard.] —**en·dur·a·bil·i·ty** (-ə-bílləti) n. —**en·dur·a·ble** adj. —**en·dur·a·bly** adv.

en·dur·ing (in-déwr-ing, en-) ‖ -dóor-) adj. 1. Lasting; durable. 2. Chronic; unresolved: *an enduring problem.* 3. Long-suffering. —**en·dur·ing·ly** adv. —**en·dur·ing·ness** n.

end·ways (énd-wayz) adv. Also chiefly U.S. **end·wise** (-wīz). 1. On end. 2. With the end foremost. 3. Lengthways. 4. End to end. —**end·ways** adj.

En·dym·i·on (en-dímmi-ən). *Greek Mythology.* A handsome young man who was loved by the moon goddess Selene and whose youth was preserved by eternal sleep. [Latin, from Greek Endumiōn, "diver" (so called perhaps because Endymion was originally a sun god), from enduein, to dive into : en-, into + duein†, to dive, sink, set (as the sun).]

ENE east-northeast.

–ene n. suffix. *Chemistry.* Indicates unsaturation of an organic compound, especially one having a double bond; for example, **ethylene**. [Greek -ēnē, feminine patronymic suffix.]

en·e·ma (énnimə) n., pl. **-mas** or **-mata** (-mətə). 1. The injection of liquid into the rectum for cleansing, laxative, or other therapeutic purposes; an anal douche. 2. The fluid so injected. [Late Latin, from Greek, from enienai, to throw in, inject : en-, in + hienai, to send, throw.]

en·e·my (énnəmi) n., pl. **-mies**. 1. **a.** One who shows malice or hostility towards another; a foe. **b.** One who opposes the purposes or interests of another; an opponent. 2. **a.** A hostile, usually armed power or force, such as a nation. **b.** A member or unit of such a force. 3. Something destructive or injurious in its effects: *Fear is our chief enemy.*
~adj. Of or pertaining to a hostile power or force. [Middle English enemi, from Old French, from Latin inimīcus : in-, not + amīcus, friend.]

en·er·get·ic (énnər-jéttik) adj. Possessing, exerting, or displaying energy; vigorous. See Synonyms at **active**. [Greek energētikos, active, from energein, to be active, from energos, active. See **energy**.] —**en·er·get·i·cal·ly** adv.

en·er·get·ics (énnər-jéttiks) n. 1. Used with a plural verb. The energy changes in a particular physical system: *the energetics of a chemical reaction.* 2. Used with a singular verb. The physics of energy and of transformations of energy.

en·er·gid (énnər-jid) n. *Biology.* A unit that consists of a nucleus surrounded by cytoplasm but that does not constitute a cell. [ENERG(Y) + -ID.]

en·er·gise, en·er·gize (énnər-jīz) v. **-gised, -gising, -gises**. —*tr.* 1. To give energy to; activate; charge. 2. To power (a device, such as the field winding of an electric motor) with electricity. —*intr.* To release or put out energy. —**en·er·gis·er** n.

en·er·gu·men (énnər-géw-men, -mən) n. 1. One believed to be possessed by an evil spirit; a demoniac. 2. A zealot; a fanatic. [Late Latin energūmenus, from Greek energoumenos, worked on, "possessed", from energein, to be active, effect, from energos, active. See **energy**.]

en·er·gy (énnərji) n., pl. **-gies**. 1. **a.** Vigour or power as shown in action, exertion, or performance. **b.** Vitality and intensity of expression. 2. The capacity for action or accomplishment: *lacked energy to finish the job.* 3. Usually plural. Power exercised with vigour and determination: *devote one's energies to a worthy cause.* 4. **a.** *Physics.* Symbol **E**. The work that a physical system is capable of doing in changing from its actual state to a specific reference state, the total including, in general, contributions of **potential energy, kinetic energy**, and **rest energy** (all of which see). **b.** The capacity to make machines and other physical systems go, or to generate light and heat: *solar energy.* **c.** Energy-generating fuels or sources collectively. Also used adjectivally: *energy crisis.* —See Synonyms at **strength**. [Late Latin energīa, from Greek energeia, coined by Aristotle from energēs, energos, active, at work : en-, at + ergon, work.]

energy band n. *Physics.* A range of allowed energies of electrons in a solid.

energy density n. The energy per unit area or volume of a surface or region of space.

energy gap n. The discrepancy between the amount of fuel needed to satisfy current levels of energy consumption and the actual quantities likely to be available in the future.

energy level n. *Physics.* 1. The energy characteristic of a stationary state of any quantum mechanical system. 2. Loosely, the state characterised by such an energy.

en·er·vate (énnər-vayt) tr.v. **-vated, -vating, -vates**. To deprive of strength or vitality; debilitate; weaken. See Synonyms at **deplete**. ~adj. (i-nérv-ət, -it). Deprived of strength; devitalised. [Latin ēnervāre, "to remove the sinews from" : ex- (removal) + nervus, sinew, nerve.] —**en·er·va·tion** (énnər-váysh'n) n. —**en·er·va·tor** (-vaytər) n.

en·face (in-fáyss, en-) tr.v. **-faced, -facing, -faces**. To write, stamp or print on the face of (a cheque or other document). —**en·face·ment** n.

en fa·mille (ON fa-mée) adv. French. 1. In or with the family; at home. 2. Casually; without ceremony.

en·fant ter·ri·ble (ON-fóN te-réebl) n., pl. **enfants terribles** (pronounced as singular). **1.** A child who habitually causes embarrassment by his conduct or remarks. **2.** A person whose startlingly unconventional behaviour and ideas are a source of consternation or dismay to a cause, group, or profession. [French, "terrible child".]

en·fee·ble (in-fée'b'l, en-) *tr.v.* **-bled, -bling, -bles.** To make feeble; deprive of strength. [Middle English *enfeblen,* from Old French *enfebler* : *en-* (causative) + *feble,* FEEBLE.] **—en·fee·ble·ment** *n.* **—en·fee·bler** *n.*

en·fet·ter (in-féttər, en-) *tr.v.* **-tered, -tering, -ters.** To bind in fetters; enchain; enslave.

En·field (ěnfeeld). Borough of Greater London. Once a market town, it is an important residential and industrial suburb. The famous Enfield rifle was first made here.

Enfield rifle *n.* Any of several rifles of varying calibres used formerly by British and American troops, especially the .30 or .303 bolt-action, breech-loading model. Also called "Enfield". [After ENFIELD.]

en·fi·lade (ěnfi-láyd ‖ -lá'ad) *n.* **1.** The firing of a gun or guns so as to sweep the length of a target such as a column of troops. **2.** A position or emplacement under enfilade. ~*tr.v.* **enfiladed, -lading, -lades.** To rake with gunfire. [French, "series", from *enfiler,* to thread, from Old French : *en-,* in + *fil,* thread, from Latin *fīlum.*]

en·fleu·rage (ŏn-flur-ráazh, ŏN-flö'-) *n.* A process used in perfumery to extract essential oils from plant material, such as leaves or petals, by placing the material in contact with an odourless fat which absorbs the essential oil. The essential oil is subsequently extracted from the fat by a solvent. [French, from *enfleurer,* to cause to take in the fragrance of flowers : Old French *en-,* in + *fleur, flor,* flower, from Latin *flōs* (stem *flōr-*).]

en·fold (in-fóld, en-) *tr.v.* **-folded, -folding, -folds. 1.** To cover with or as if with folds; wrap up. **2.** To hold within limits; enclose. **3.** To embrace. **4.** To form or shape into folds. **—en·fold·er** *n.*

en·force (in-fórss, en- ‖ -fórss) *tr.v.* **-forced, -forcing, -forces. 1.** To compel observance of or obedience to: *enforce a regulation.* **2.** To impose (specified action or behaviour); compel. **3.** To give force to; stress; underline; reinforce. [Middle English *enforcen,* from Old French *enforcier,* from Vulgar Latin *infortiāre* (unattested), to make strong : Latin *in-* (causative) + *fortis,* strong.] **—en·force·a·ble** *adj.* **—en·force·ment** *n.* **—en·forc·er** *n.*

en·fran·chise (in-fránchīz, en-) *tr.v.* **-chised, -chising, -chises. 1.** To endow with the rights of citizenship, especially the right to vote. **2.** To give (a town, for example) the right to be represented in a parliament. **3.** To free, as from slavery. [Middle English *enfraunchisen,* from Old French *enfranchir* (present stem *enfranchiss-*) : *en-* (causative) + *franche, franc,* free (see **franchise**).]

eng (eng) *n.* A phonetic symbol (ŋ) representing in some pronunciation alphabets the velar nasal consonantal sound of *ng,* as in bri*ng* or lo*ng,* or of *n,* as in li*n*k. Also called "agma".

eng. 1. engine. **2.** engineer; engineering.

Eng. England; English.

En·ga·din (ěng-gə-deen, -děen). *French* **En·ga·dine** (ŏN-gà-déen). Swiss part of the upper Inn Valley, in the Grisons (or Graubünden) canton. It has several winter sports centres, including St. Moritz.

en·gage (in-gáyj, en-) *v.* **-gaged, -gaging, -gages.** —*tr.* **1.** To obtain or contract for the services of; employ: *engage a carpenter.* **2.** To contract for the use of; reserve: *engage a room.* **3.** To obtain and hold the attention of; engross: *The project engaged her interest for months.* **4.** To require the use of; occupy: *Studying engages most of a student's time.* **5.** To pledge; especially, to promise to marry; betroth. Usually used in the passive: *She is engaged to Harry.* **6.** To meet in or bring into conflict: *We have engaged the enemy.* **7.** To cause to interlock or mesh. **8.** To please or attract; win. **9.** To occupy or involve. Often used with *in: engage someone in idle chatter.* **10.** *Archaic.* To give or take as security; attach. —*intr.* **1.** To involve oneself or become occupied; participate. Usually used with *in: engage in conversation.* **2.** To assume an obligation; pledge; agree. **3.** To enter into conflict or battle. **4.** To become meshed or interlocked. [Middle English *engagen,* from Old French *engager,* from Vulgar Latin *inwadiāre* : *in-,* in + *wadiāre* (unattested), pledge, GAGE.] **—en·gag·er** *n.*

en·ga·gé (ŏN-ga-zháy) *adj.* Actively, morally, or politically committed, as to a political ideology. [French, "committed".]

en·gaged (in-gáyjd, en-) *adj.* **1. a.** Employed, occupied, or busy. **b.** *British.* In use. Said of a telephone line. **2.** Contracted for; pledged. **3.** Bound by a promise to marry; betrothed: *an engaged couple.* **4.** *Architecture.* Partly sunk, built into, or attached to another part, as are columns on a wall.

en·gage·ment (in-gáyjmənt, en-) *n.* **1.** An act of engaging or the state or period of being engaged. **2.** A promise of marriage; a betrothal. **3.** A person or thing that engages. **4.** A promise, pledge, or obligation; especially, a commitment to appear at a certain time, as for business or social activity; an appointment. **5. a.** Employment, especially for a specific time. **b.** The period of employment. **6.** A battle or encounter. **7.** *Usually plural.* Financial obligations or commitments.

en·gag·ing (in-gáyging, en-) *adj.* Tending to attract; charming; pleasing. **—en·gag·ing·ly** *adv.*

en garde (ŏN gárd) *interj.* Used to warn a fencer to assume the first position preparatory to a match. [French, "on guard".]

Eng·els (ěng-g'lz; *German* -'lss), **Friedrich** (1820–95). German political theorist and socialist revolutionary. He met Karl Marx in

Paris in 1844 and published *The Condition of the Working Classes in England.* He encouraged the growth of revolutionary movements in Europe, and with Marx published *The Communist Manifesto* (1848). He settled in England in 1850 and played an important part in the founding of the First and Second Internationals. *Anti-Dühring* (1878) and *The Origin of the Family, Private Property, and the State* (1884) were major contributions to the development of Communist theory.

en·gen·der (in-jéndər, en-) *v.* **-dered, -dering, -ders.** —*tr.* **1.** To bring into existence; give rise to; produce. **2.** To procreate; propagate. —*intr.* To come into existence; be born; be produced. [Middle English *engenderen,* from Old French *engenderer,* from Latin *ingenerāre* : *in-,* in + *generāre,* GENERATE.]

engin. engineering.

en·gine (énjin ‖ ínjin) *n. Abbr.* **eng. 1. a.** A machine that converts some form of energy into mechanical motion. **b.** Such a machine distinguished from an electric, spring-driven, or hydraulic motor by its consumption of a fuel. **c.** Any mechanical appliance, instrument, or tool. **2.** A locomotive. **3.** *Archaic.* Any of various large weapons of war. [Middle English *engin,* from Old French, skill, invention, from Latin *ingenium,* inborn talent, skill.]

engine block *n.* The metal block containing the cylinders of an internal-combustion engine. Also called "block".

engine driver *n.* A person who drives a locomotive; a train driver. Also *U.S.* "engineer".

en·gi·neer (ěnji-néer) *n. Abbr.* **E., e., eng. 1.** A person trained in, skilled at, or professionally engaged in a branch of engineering: *a mining engineer.* **2.** A person who skilfully or shrewdly manages an enterprise. **3. a.** A person who operates an engine. **b.** *U.S.* An engine driver. **4.** A person who oversees, services, or repairs: **a.** Engines, motors, and the like. **b.** Systems or appliances run by engines, and the like: *a central-heating engineer.* **5.** A soldier employed or trained in engineering as applied to military purposes. ~*tr.v.* **engineered, -neering, -neers. 1.** To plan, construct, and manage as an engineer; act as engineer. **2.** To plan, manage, and put through by skilful acts or contrivance; manoeuvre: *"Claudius's murder was engineered by his wife Agrippina"* (Robert Graves). [Middle English *enginer,* from Old French *engineor,* from Medieval Latin *ingeniātor,* contriver, from *ingeniāre,* to contrive, from Latin *ingenium,* talent. See **engine.**]

en·gi·neer·ing (ěnji-néering) *n. Abbr.* **E., e., eng., engin. 1.** The application of scientific principles to such practical ends as the design, construction, and operation of efficient and economical structures, equipment, and systems. **2.** The profession of or the work performed by an engineer. **3.** Skilful management; manoeuvring; contrivance. See **social engineering.**

en·gine·ry (énjinri) *n.* **1.** Machines and tools; machinery. **2.** Engines or instruments of war.

en·gird (in-gúrd, en-) *tr.v.* **-girt** (-gúrt) or **-girded, -girding, -girds.** *Literary.* Also **en·gird·le** (-gúrd'l). To encircle; surround, as with a girdle.

en·gla·ci·al (in-gláy-si-əl, en-, -sh'l) *adj.* Located or occurring within a glacier: *an englacial stream.* **—en·gla·ci·al·ly** *adv.*

Eng·land (íng-glənd ‖ ěng, *U.S. also* ing-lənd). Largest political division of the United Kingdom, settled by the Celts, subsequently conquered by the Romans, Angles, Saxons, Jutes, Danes, and finally the Normans. A major trading nation, its main ports are London, Liverpool, and Southampton. Though heavily agricultural, England became a leading manufacturing nation after the Industrial Revolution of the mid-18th century. Foreign competition and the loss of cheap imports from her former Empire have contributed to a decline in the 20th century. England's chief industries today include motor vehicle production, iron and steel, electronics, aircraft building, petroleum, chemicals, financial services, and tourism. Area, 130 357 square kilometres (50,331 square miles). Capital, London. See **Great Britain.**

Eng·lish (íng-glish ‖ ěng, *U.S. also* ing-lish). *adj.* **1. a.** Of, pertaining to, or characteristic of England and its inhabitants. **b.** Of a type or style predominant in England: *English breakfast.* **2.** Of, belonging to, or spoken or written in the English language. **3.** Loosely, British. ~*n. Abbr.* **E, E., Eng. 1.** *Used with a plural verb.* **a.** The people of England collectively. Preceded by *the.* **b.** Loosely, the British. Preceded by *the.* **c.** In other countries, the English or English-speaking people collectively. **2.** The West Germanic language of the English, divided historically into Old English, Middle English, and Modern English and now spoken in the British Isles, the United States, and numerous other countries. **3.** The English language as spoken or written at a specified time, in a specified region, or by a specified person or group of people: *Australian English; Shakespeare's English.* **4.** A course or individual class in the study of English literature, language, or composition. **5.** *Printing.* Formerly, a size of type, 14-point.

English bond *n.* A common masonry bond consisting of alternate rows of headers and stretchers.

English Channel. *French* **La Manche** (la mŏNsh). One of the world's busiest shipping lanes, lying between England and France. It is 560 kilometres (350 miles) long, 160 kilometres (100 miles) wide at the west end between Ushant and the Scilly Isles, and 34 kilometres (21 miles) wide at the Strait of Dover at the east end.

English flute *n.* A musical instrument, the **recorder** *(see).*

English horn *n.* A cor anglais *(see).*

Eng·lish·man (íng-glish-mən) *n., pl.* **-men** (-mən). **1.** A native or inhabitant of England. **2.** Loosely, a British man.

Englishman's tie *n. Nautical.* A **fisherman's knot** *(see).* Also called "Englishman's knot".

English setter *n.* A dog of a breed developed in England, having a silky white coat usually with black or brownish markings.

English Springer spaniel *n.* See **Springer spaniel.**

Eng·lish·wom·an (ĭng-glĭsh-wŏŏm'ən) *n., pl.* **-women** (-wĭmmin). **1.** A woman who is a native or inhabitant of England. **2.** Loosely, a British woman.

Eng. lit. *n. Informal.* English literature, especially when considered a subject for study.

en·gorge (ĭn-gôrj', ĕn-) *tr.v.* **-gorged, -gorging, -gorges. 1.** To devour greedily. **2.** To gorge; glut. **3.** To congest or fill to excess, as with blood or other fluid. Usually used in the passive. [French *engorger : en-,* in + *gorge,* throat, GORGE.] **—en·gorge·ment** *n.*

en·graft (ĭn-grăaft, ĕn-ǁ-grăft) *tr.v.* **-grafted, -grafting, -grafts.** Also **in·graft** (ĭn-). **1.** To graft (a shoot or bud) onto or into another plant. **2.** To implant firmly; incorporate. **—en·graft·ment** *n.*

en·grail (ĭn-grāyl', ĕn-) *tr.v.* **-grailed, -grailing, -grails. 1.** To indent (the edge of something) with small curves. **2.** To decorate the edge of by adding a series of curved indentations. [Middle English *engrelen,* from Old French *engresler : en-,* in + *gresle,* hail (the indentations were imagined to resemble hailstones).]

en·grain (ĭn-grāyn', ĕn-) *tr.v.* **-grained, -graining, -grains. 1.** To treat, dye, or colour so as to suggest the grain of wood. **2.** Variant of **ingrain.** [Middle English *engreinen,* from Old French *engrainer,* to dye in grain, from *en graine,* in grain : *en-,* in + *graine,* cochineal dye, kermes, from Latin *grāna,* plural of *grānum,* GRAIN.]

en·gram, en·gramme (ĕn-grăm) *n.* A persistent protoplasmic alteration hypothesised to occur on stimulation of living neural tissue and to account for memory. Also called "neurogram". [EN- + -GRAM.] **—en·gram·mat·ic** (ĕn-grə-măttĭk), **en·gram·mic** (en-grămmĭk) *adj.*

en·grave (ĭn-grāyv', ĕn-) *tr.v.* **-graved, -graving, -graves. 1.** To carve, cut, or etch (a design or letters) into a material. **2. a.** To carve, cut, or etch (a design or letters) into a block or surface used for printing. **b.** To carve a design on (a printing block or plate). **c.** To print from a block or plate made by such a process. **3.** To impress deeply; fix permanently. [EN- + GRAVE (to carve).] **—en·grav·er** *n.*

en·grav·ing (ĭn-grāyvĭng, ĕn-) *n.* **1.** The art or technique of one that engraves. **2.** An engraved surface for printing. **3.** A print made from an engraved plate or block.

en·gross (ĭn-grōss', ĕn-) *tr.v.* **-grossed, -grossing, -grosses. 1.** To occupy the complete attention of; absorb wholly. **2.** To acquire most or all of a commodity; monopolise a market. Compare **fore·stall. 3. a.** To write or transcribe in a large, clear hand. **b.** To prepare the text of (an official document) by an officially prescribed process, such as handwriting or printing. [Senses 1 and 2, Middle English *engrossen,* from Anglo-French *engrosser,* from *en gros,* in large quantity, wholesale. Sense 3, Middle English, from Anglo-French *engrosser,* from *en grosse,* in large handwriting.] **—en·gross·er** *n.*

en·grossed (ĭn-grōst', ĕn-) *adj.* Having one's attention completely occupied; totally absorbed. See Synonyms at **abstracted.**

en·gross·ing (ĭn-grō'sĭng, ĕn-) *adj.* Occupying one's complete attention; wholly absorbing. **—en·gross·ing·ly** *adv.*

en·gross·ment (ĭn-grōss-mənt, ĕn-) *n.* **1.** The state of being completely absorbed, occupied, or monopolised. **2.** A document, such as a deed or will, that has been engrossed.

en·gulf (ĭn-gŭlf', ĕn-) *tr.v.* **-gulfed, -gulfing, -gulfs.** Also **in·gulf** (ĭn-). **1.** To surround completely. **2.** To swallow up or overwhelm by or as if by flowing over and enclosing: *engulfed by bad luck.* **—en·gulf·ment** *n.*

en·hance (ĭn-hăanss, ĕn-, -hănss) *tr.v.* **-hanced, -hancing, -hances. 1.** To increase or make greater, as in value, cost, beauty, or reputation; augment. See Synonyms at **improve. 2.** To increase the clarity of (a photograph, especially one taken from space or the air), by using a computer to improve contrast. [Middle English *enhauncen,* from Anglo-French *enhauncer,* variant of Old French *enhaucer,* from Vulgar Latin *inaltiāre* (unattested), to raise : Latin *in-* (intensive) + *altus,* high.] **—en·hance·ment** *n.* **—en·hanc·er** *n.* **—en·hanc·ive** *adj.*

enhanced radiation *n.* Radiation released by certain nuclear devices in the form of neutrons and gamma rays, able to destroy life but having a reduced nuclear blast and thus causing limited damage to the nonliving environment.

enhanced radiation bomb *n.* A **neutron bomb** *(see).*

en·har·mon·ic (ĕn-haar-mónnĭk) *adj. Music.* **1.** Of, pertaining to, or involving a tiny interval of pitch, smaller than a semitone, such as that between C♯ and D♭. **2.** Of, pertaining to, or involving a note played on an instrument such as a piano whose written representation is altered, as from C♯ to D♭, as a conventional means of visually preparing for a new key. [Late Latin *enharmonicus,* from Greek *enarmonikos,* "in harmony" : *en-,* in + *harmonia,* HARMONY.] **—en·har·mon·i·cal·ly** *adv.*

e·nig·ma (ĭ-nĭgmə, ĕ-) *n.* **1.** Someone or something that is puzzling, ambiguous, or inexplicable. **2.** An obscure riddle. **3.** An obscure piece of speech or writing. [Latin *aenigma,* from Greek *ainigma,* from *ainissesthai,* to speak in riddles, hint, from *ainos,* tale, story.]

en·ig·mat·ic (ĕnnĭg-máttĭk) *adj.* Also **en·ig·mat·i·cal** (-'l). Of or resembling an enigma; puzzling: *an enigmatic smile.* **—See Synonyms at ambiguous. —en·ig·mat·i·cal·ly** *adv.*

en·isle (ĭn-īl', ĕn-) *tr.v.* **-isled, -isling, -isles. 1.** To make into an island. **2.** To set apart from others; isolate.

en·jamb·ment, en·jambe·ment (ĭn-jám-mənt, ĕn-, -jámb-, ʘN-zhónb-món) *n.* The continuation of a sentence or idea from one line or couplet of a poem to the next. Compare **end-stopped.** [French, from Old French *enjamber,* to straddle : *en-,* in + *jambe,* leg (see jamb).] **—en·jambed** *adj.*

en·join (ĭn-jóyn, ĕn-) *tr.v.* **-joined, -joining, -joins. 1.** To require or direct with authority and emphasis; command; impose. **2.** To urge or order (a person) to do something. **3.** To prohibit or forbid, especially by legal action: *The court enjoined him from visiting his children.* **—See Synonyms at command.** [Middle English *enjoinen,* from Old French *enjoindre,* from Latin *injungere,* to join to, impose : *in-,* in, to + *jungere,* join.] **—en·join·er** *n.* **—en·join·ment** *n.*

en·joy (ĭn-jóy, ĕn-) *tr.v.* **-joyed, -joying, -joys. 1.** To experience joy in; receive pleasure from; relish: *enjoy good food.* See Synonyms at **like. 2.** To have the use of; benefit from. **3.** To experience; have as one's lot: *enjoy prestige.* **4.** *Archaic.* To have sexual intercourse with. **—enjoy (oneself).** To have a pleasant time. [Middle English *enjoien,* from Old French *enjoïr : en-,* in + *joïr,* to rejoice, from Latin *gaudēre.*] **—en·joy·er** *n.*

en·joy·a·ble (ĭn-jóy-əb'l, ĕn-) *adj.* Giving or capable of giving enjoyment; pleasurable; agreeable. **—en·joy·a·ble·ness** *n.* **—en·joy·a·bly** *adv.*

en·joy·ment (ĭn-jóymənt, ĕn-) *n.* **1.** The act or state of experiencing joy or pleasure in something. **2.** The use or possession of: **a.** Something beneficial or pleasurable. **b.** A legal right: *enjoyment of the right to vote.* **3.** Something that is enjoyed. **4.** Pleasure; joy. **—**See Synonyms at **pleasure.**

enkephalin. Variant of **encephalin.**

en·kin·dle (ĭn-kĭnd'l, ĕn-) *tr.v.* **-dled, -dling, -dles. 1.** To set on fire; light; kindle. **2.** To incite; arouse. **3.** To make luminous and glowing. **—en·kin·dler** *n.*

enl. 1. enlarged. **2.** enlisted.

en·lace (ĭn-láyss, ĕn-) *tr.v.* **-laced, -lacing, -laces.** Also **in·lace** (ĭn-). **1.** To wrap or wind about with or as if with a lace or laces; encircle. **2.** To interlace; entangle; entwine. **—en·lace·ment** *n.*

en·large (ĭn-lárj, ĕn-) *v.* **-larged, -larging, -larges.** *—tr.* **1. a.** To make larger; add to; magnify. **b.** To make (a photographic print) larger than the original print or larger than the standard size. **2.** To give greater scope to; expand: *to enlarge a child's imagination.* **3.** *Archaic.* To set free; liberate. *—intr.* **1.** To become larger; grow. **2.** To speak or write at greater length or in greater detail. Used with *on* or *upon.* **—See** Synonyms at **increase.** [Middle English *enlargen,* from Old French *enlargier : en-,* in + *large,* LARGE.] **—en·larg·er** *n.*

en·large·ment (ĭn-lárjmənt, ĕn-) *n.* **1.** An act of enlarging or the state of being enlarged. **2.** Something, such as an addition, expansion, or increase, that enlarges something else. **3.** A reproduction or copy larger than the original; especially, an optically magnified print of a photographic negative.

en·larg·er (ĭn-lárjər, ĕn-) *n.* An optical instrument for producing enlarged photographic prints by projecting an image of the negative onto sensitive paper.

en·light·en (ĭn-lĭt'n, ĕn-) *tr.v.* **-ened, -ening, -ens. 1. a.** To give knowledge or truth to. **b.** To endow with spiritual understanding. **2.** To acquaint (someone) with information; inform. **3.** To free (someone) from prejudice or false belief. **—en·light·en·er** *n.*

en·light·en·ment (ĭn-lĭt'n-mənt, ĕn-) *n.* **1.** An act or means of enlightening. **2.** The state of being enlightened. **3.** *Buddhism.* A state marked by spiritual insight and freedom from illusory appearances. **—See** Synonyms at **knowledge. —the Enlightenment.** A philosophical movement of the 18th century, concerned with the critical examination of previously accepted doctrines and institutions from the point of view of rationalism. Compare **Age of Reason.**

en·list (ĭn-lĭst, ĕn-) *v.* **-listed, -listing, -lists.** *—tr.* **1.** To persuade to enter the armed forces. **2.** To engage the assistance or cooperation of; secure on one's behalf. *—intr.* **1.** To enter the armed forces voluntarily. **2.** To participate actively in some cause or enterprise. [EN- + LIST (roster).] **—en·list·ment** *n.*

enlisted man *n. Abbr.* **EM** A man enlisted in the U.S. armed forces without an officer's commission or warrant.

en·liv·en (ĭn-lĭv'n, ĕn-) *tr.v.* **-vened, -vening, -vens. 1.** To make lively or spirited; animate; invigorate. **2.** To brighten; cheer. [EN- + LIVE (adjective).] **—en·liv·en·er** *n.* **—en·liv·en·ment** *n.*

en masse (ON máss) *adv.* In one group or body; all together. [French : Old French *en,* in + *masse,* MASS (body).]

en·mesh (ĭn-mésh, ĕn-) *tr.v.* **-meshed, -meshing, -meshes.** Also **in·mesh** (ĭn-), **im·mesh** (ĭ-mésh). **1.** To entangle, involve, or catch in or as if in a net. **2.** To cover with net or mesh.

en·mi·ty (ĕn-məti) *n., pl.* **-ties.** Deep-seated hatred, as between rivals or opponents; antagonism. [Middle English *enemite,* from Old French *enemiste,* from Vulgar Latin *inimīcītās* (unattested), from Latin *inimīcus,* ENEMY.]

Synonyms: enmity, hostility, antagonism, animosity, rancour, antipathy, animus.

en·ne·ad (ĕnni-ad) *n.* Any group or set of nine. [Greek *enneas* (stem *ennead-*), from *ennea,* nine.]

en·ne·a·he·dron (ĕnni-ə-hée-drən) *n., pl.* **-drons** or **-dra** (-drə). *Mathematics.* A solid that has nine faces. [Greek *ennea,* nine + -HEDRON.]

En·nis·kil·len (ĕnnĭss-kĭllən). County town of Fermanagh in Northern Ireland, situated on an island in the river Erne. William of

Orange, the newly proclaimed King of England, defeated the forces of James II here in 1689.

en·no·ble (i-nṓb'l, e-) *tr.v.* **-bled, -bling, -bles. 1.** To invest with nobility; bring honour or glory to. **2.** To raise to the rank of nobleman; confer nobility upon. [Middle English *ennoblen,* from Old French *ennoblir* : *en-,* in + NOBLE.] —**en·no·ble·ment** *n.*

en·nui (ón-nweé) *n.* Listlessness and dissatisfaction resulting from lack of interest; boredom: *gossiping to relieve their ennui.* [French, from Old French *enui,* from Latin *in odiō,* "in hate", odious : *in,* in + *odium,* hate.]

E·noch¹ (ée-nok ‖ -nək). The eldest son of Cain. Genesis 4:17. [Late Latin, from Greek *Enōkh,* from Hebrew *Ḥanōkh,* "consecrated", "initiated", from *hānakh,* he initiated.]

E·noch². The father of Methuselah. Genesis 5:21.

e·nol (ée-nol ‖ -nōl) *n.* An organic compound containing a hydroxyl group bonded to a carbon atom which in turn is doubly bonded to another carbon atom. See **keto-enol tautomerism.** [-ENE + -OL.] —**e·nol·ic** (ee-nóll-ik ‖ -nōl-) *adj.*

enology. *U.S.* Variant of **oenology.**

e·nor·mi·ty (i-nórməti) *n., pl.* **-ties. 1.** The quality of passing all moral bounds; excessive wickedness; outrageousness. **2.** A monstrous offence or evil; an outrage.

e·nor·mous (i-nórməss) *adj.* Very great in size, extent, number, or degree; immense; vast. [Middle English *enorme,* from Latin *ēnormis,* unusual, immense : *ex-,* out of + *norma,* pattern, rule.] —**e·nor·mous·ly** *adv.* —**e·nor·mous·ness** *n.*

Synonyms: *enormous, immense, huge, gigantic, colossal, mammoth, gargantuan, vast.*

E·nos (ée-noss ‖ -nəss). A son of Seth. Genesis 4:26. [Greek *Enōs,* from Hebrew *Enōsh,* "man".]

e·nough (i-núf, ə-) *adj.* **1.** Sufficient to meet a need or satisfy a desire; adequate: *enough food for two.* **2.** Used in requests to stop: *That's enough, now!*
~*pron.* An adequate quantity or number: *He ate enough for two.*
~*adv.* **1.** To a satisfactory amount or degree; sufficiently. **2.** Very; fully; quite: *We were glad enough to leave.* **3.** Tolerably; rather: *She sang well enough, but the show was a failure.* **4.** Used as an intensive following certain adverbs: *funnily enough; sure enough; oddly enough.* [Middle English *ynough, inough,* Old English *genōg,* from Germanic.]

e·nounce (i-nównss) *tr.v.* **enounced, enouncing, enounces. 1.** To declare publicly or formally; state; announce. **2.** To pronounce; enunciate. [French *énoncer,* from Latin *ēnuntiāre,* ENUNCIATE.] —**e·nounce·ment** *n.*

e·now (i-nów) *adj. Archaic.* Enough. —**e·now** *adv.*

en pas·sant (ON pa-són, pá-SON) *adv.* In passing; by the way.
—**take en passant.** In chess, to capture (an opponent's pawn that has made an initial move of two squares) with a pawn of one's own that occupies the adjacent forward diagonal square.

en·phy·tot·ic (énfī-tóttik) *adj.* Designating or characterising a plant disease that causes a relatively constant amount of damage each year. [EN- + -PHYT(E) + -OTIC.]

en·plane (en-pláyn, in-) *intr.v.* **-planed, -planing, -planes.** Also **em·plane** (em-). To board a plane.

en·quire (in-kwír, en-, -kwí-ər) *v.* **-quired, -quiring, -quires.** Also **inquire** (in-). —*intr.* **1. a.** To request information. Used with *about* or *after*: *enquire after another's health.* **b.** *Chiefly U.S.* To put a question. **2.** To make an enquiry; look into; investigate. Used with *into.* —*tr.* To ask: *She enquired how it worked.* —See Synonyms at **ask.** [Middle English *enquiren, enqueren,* from Old French *enquerrer,* from Vulgar Latin *inquaerere* (unattested), variant of Latin *inquīrere* : *in-* (intensive) + *quaerere,* to seek, ask.] —**en·quir·er** *n.*

en·qui·ring (in-kwír-ing, en-, -kwí-ər-) *adj.* Seeking knowledge or information, especially habitually: *an enquiring mind.* —**en·qui·ring·ly** *adv.*

en·quir·y (in-kwír-i, en-, -kwí-ər- ‖ *U.S. also* ingkwəri) *n., pl.* **-ies.** Also **in·quir·y** (in-). **1.** The act of enquiring. **2.** A question; a query. **3.** A close examination of some matter in a quest for information or truth.

Usage: *Enquiry,* and the corresponding verb *enquire,* have variant forms in *inquiry* and *inquire. Enquiry* and *enquire* are more common in British English, *inquiry* and *inquire* in American English. In both British and American, however, there is a tendency for *enquiry / enquire* to be used in general contexts of seeking information, especially in the plural (*I'm making some enquiries about a lost parrot*), and for *inquiry / inquire* to be used in contexts of serious study or investigation (*an inquiry into the causes of the riot*).

en·rage (in-ráyj, en-) *tr.v.* **-raged, -raging, -rages.** To put in a rage; infuriate; anger.

en·rap·ture (in-rápchər, en-) *tr.v.* **-tured, -turing, -tures.** To move to rapture; overwhelm with delight.

en·rich (in-rích, en-) *tr.v.* **-riched, -riching, -riches. 1.** To make rich or richer. **2. a.** To add to in quality or quantity; improve. **b.** To make fuller, more meaningful, or more rewarding: *to enrich one's vocabulary.* **3.** To add fertiliser to (soil) to increase its productivity. **4.** To add nutrients to (foodstuffs) during processing. **5.** To add to the beauty or character of; embellish or adorn. **6.** *Physics.* To increase the ratio of radioactive isotopes in (a sample); especially, to increase ratio of amount of fissile uranium-235 in (natural uranium) so that it can be used as a nuclear fuel. **7.** *Chemistry.* To increase the amount of a particular substance in (a mixture or solution). [Middle English *enrichen,* from Old French *enricher* : *en-* (causative) + *riche,* RICH.] —**en·rich·er** *n.* —**en·rich·ment** *n.*

en·robe (in-rṓb, en-) *tr.v.* **-robed, -robing, -robes. 1.** To put a robe on. **2.** To dress richly in or as if in a robe.

en·rol, *U.S.* **en·roll** (in-rṓl, en-) *v.* **-rolled, -rolling, -rols** or *U.S.* **-rolls.** —*tr.* **1.** To enter the name of in a register, record, or roll. **2.** To put on record; record. **3.** To roll or wrap up. **4.** To cause (a person) to become a member. —*intr.* **1.** To place one's name on a roll or register. **2.** To become a member. [Middle English *enrollen,* from Old French *enroller* : *en-,* in + *rolle,* ROLL.]

en·rol·ment (in-rṓlmənt, en-) *n.* **1. a.** The action of enrolling. **b.** The state or process of being enrolled. **2.** *U.S.* The number enrolled.

en·root (in-rṓot, en- ‖ *U.S. also* -rŏot) *tr.v.* **-rooted, -rooting, -roots.** To establish firmly by or as if by roots; implant.

en route (ón rṓot; *French* ON rṓot) *adv.* On the route; on or along the way. [French.]

ens (enz) *n., pl.* **entia** (én-shi-ə, -ti-). *Philosophy.* **1.** Existence or being as an abstract concept. **2.** An entity as opposed to an attribute. [Medieval Latin, from Latin, irregular present participle of *esse,* to be.]

Ens. Ensign.

ENSA (énsa) *n.* Entertainments National Services Association.

en·san·guine (in-sáng-gwin, en-) *tr.v.* **-guined, -guining, -guines.** *Literary.* To cover or stain with or as if with blood.

en·sconce (in-skónss, en-) *tr.v.* **-sconced, -sconcing, -sconces. 1.** To settle (oneself) securely or comfortably: *ensconced in an armchair.* **2.** To place, fix, or conceal in a secure place. [EN- + SCONCE (fortification), originally meaning to take shelter, as behind a fortification.]

en·sem·ble (on-sómb'l; *French* ON-sónbl) *n.* **1.** A unit or group of complementary parts that contribute to a single effect. **2.** A coordinated outfit or costume. **3.** A set, as of furniture. **4.** A group of musicians, singers, dancers, or a troupe of players who perform together. **5.** Music for two or more vocalists or instrumentalists. **6.** The quality of performance by a group of actors or musicians, especially as judged in regard to their success in achieving a unity and balance of style and technique. Also used adjectively: *ensemble playing.* **7.** *Physics.* A large collection of atoms, or a collection of assemblies of atoms, used in statistical mechanics to calculate the thermodynamic properties of a system. [French, "together", from Vulgar Latin *insemul* (unattested), from Latin *insimul,* at the same time : *in-,* in + *simul, semul,* at the same time.]

en·shrine (in-shrín, en-) *tr.v.* **-shrined, -shrining, -shrines.** Also **in·shrine** (in-). **1.** To enclose in or as if in a shrine: *a book enshrining their ideals.* **2.** To cherish as sacred. —**en·shrine·ment** *n.*

en·shroud (in-shrówd, en-) *tr.v.* **-shrouded, -shrouding, -shrouds.** To shroud or cover; veil or conceal.

en·si·form (én-si-fawrm) *adj.* Sword-shaped, as the leaf of an iris or gladiolus. [French *ensiforme* : from Latin *ēnsis,* sword + -FORM.]

en·sign (én-sĭn, *Nautical* énss'n) *n. Abbr.* **Ens. 1. a.** A national flag displayed on ships and aircraft, often with the special insignia of a branch or unit of the armed forces: *the naval ensign.* **b.** *British.* A flag, usually on a ship, incorporating the Union Jack in the top left-hand corner. **2.** Any standard or banner, as of a military unit. **3.** A standard-bearer. **4. a.** A commissioned officer of the lowest rank in the U.S. Navy or Coast Guard. **b.** Formerly, a commissioned officer of the lowest rank in the British infantry. **5. a.** A badge; an emblem. **b.** A sign; a token. [Middle English *ensigne,* from Old French *enseigne,* from Latin *insignia,* INSIGNIA.]

en·si·lage (én-si-lij) *n.* **1.** The process of storing and fermenting green fodder in a silo. **2.** Fodder thus preserved; silage.
~*tr.v.* **ensilaged, -laging, -lages.** To ensile.

en·sile (en-sīl, in-, én-sīl) *tr.v.* **-siled, -siling, -siles. 1.** To store (fodder) in a silo for preservation. **2.** To convert (green fodder) into silage.

en·slave (in-sláyv, en-) *tr.v.* **-slaved, -slaving, -slaves.** To make a slave of; reduce to slavery, bondage, or dependence. —**en·slave·ment** *n.* —**en·slav·er** *n.*

en·snare (in-snaír, en-) *tr.v.* **-snared, -snaring, -snares.** To catch in or as if in a snare; trap. —**en·snare·ment** *n.* —**en·snar·er** *n.*

en·sphere (in-sféer, en-) *tr.v.* **-sphered, -sphering, -spheres.** Also **in·sphere** (in-). **1.** To enclose in or as if in a sphere. **2.** To give spherical form to.

en·sta·tite (én-stə-tīt) *n.* A variety of orthorhombic pyroxene having a magnesium silicate base, mainly $Mg_2Si_2O_6$, usually found embedded in igneous rocks. [German *Enstatit* : Greek *enstatēs,* adversary (from its refractory nature) : *en-,* in, at, near + *-statēs,* standing + -ITE.]

en·sue (in-séw, en-, -sōo ‖ -shṓo) *intr.v.* **-sued, -suing, -sues. 1.** To follow immediately afterwards; take place subsequently. **2.** To follow as a consequence; result. —See Synonyms at **follow.** [Middle English *ensuen,* from Old French *ensuivre* (stem *ensu-*), from Vulgar Latin *insequere* (unattested), variant of Latin *insequī,* to follow after or on : *in-,* in, onwards + *sequī,* to follow.]

en suite (ON sweét) *adv.* As part of a unit; forming a set of rooms.
~*adj.* Forming part of or attached to a larger room: *an en suite bathroom.* [French, "in sequence".]

en·sure (in-shóor, en-, -shór ‖ -shéwr) *tr.v.* **-sured, -suring, -sures.** To make sure or certain; make secure; guarantee.

–ent *adj. suffix.* Indicates performing the specified action; for example, **effervescent, absorbent.**
~*n. suffix.* Indicates agency; for example, **referent.** [Middle English *-ent,* from Old French, from Latin *-ens* (stem *-ent-*). Compare **-ant.**]

E.N.T. *Medicine.* ear, nose, and throat.
en·tab·la·ture (en-tábblə-chər, in-, -choor, -tewr) *n. Architecture.* **1.** The upper section of a classical order, resting on the capital and including the architrave, frieze, and cornice. **2.** Any raised, horizontal architectural feature. [Obsolete French, from Italian *intavolatura,* from *intavolare,* to put on the table : *in-*, in, from Latin + *tavola,* table, from Latin *tabula,* board, TABLE.]
en·ta·ble·ment (in-táyb'lmənt, en-) *n.* The platform supporting a statue, above the base and the dado. [French, from Old French : *en-*, in + TABLE.]
en·tail (in-táyl, en-) *tr.v.* **-tailed, -tailing, -tails. 1.** To have as a necessary accompaniment or consequence. **2.** To limit the inheritance of (property) to a specific, unalterable succession of heirs. **3.** To impose (a duty, expense, or the like) upon a person.
~*n.* **1. a.** The act of entailing, especially property. **b.** The state of being entailed. **2.** An entailed estate. **3.** A predetermined order of succession, as to an estate or to an office. **4.** Anything transmitted as if by unalterable inheritance. [Middle English *entaillen, entailen* : EN- + *taille,* TAIL (limitation).] **—en·tail·ment** *n.*
en·ta·moe·ba (éntə-meé-bə) *n., pl.* **-bas** or **-bae** (-bee). Also **en·da·moe·ba** (éndə-). Any of several parasitic amoebas of the genus *Entamoeba;* especially, *E. histolytica,* causing dysentery and ulceration of the colon and liver. [New Latin *Entamoeba* : ENT(O)- + AMOEBA.]
en·tan·gle (in-táng-g'l, en-) *tr.v.* **-gled, -gling, -gles. 1.** To twist together so that disengagement is difficult; make tangled; snarl. **2.** To complicate; confuse. **3.** To involve inextricably, as in complications or difficulties. **—en·tan·gler** *n.*
en·tan·gle·ment (in-táng-g'lmənt, en-) *n.* **1. a.** The act of entangling. **b.** The state of being entangled. **2.** A dangerous or compromising relationship, especially a sexual one. **3.** A military barrier of barbed wire.
en·ta·sis (éntə-siss) *n., pl.* **-ses** (-seez). *Architecture.* A slight bulge in a column, introduced to avoid the illusion of concavity that a straight column would give. [New Latin, from Greek, from *enteinein,* to stretch tight : *en-* (intensive) + *teinein,* to stretch.]
En·teb·be (en-tébbi || -tébbə). Town in Uganda, situated on Lake Victoria, south of Kampala. At its airport in 1976 an Israeli airborne commando force rescued all but three of 110 hostages after the hijacking of an Air France plane by Palestinian guerrillas.
en·tel·e·chy (en-télliki, in-) *n., pl.* **-chies. 1.** In the philosophy of Aristotle, the condition of a thing whose essence is fully realised; actuality as distinguished from potentiality. **2.** In various philosophical systems, a vital force urging an organism towards self-fulfilment: *"Courage is the affirmation of one's essential nature, one's inner aim or entelechy."* (Paul Tillich). [Late Latin *entelechia,* from Greek *entelekheia,* complete reality : *entelēs,* complete, full : *en-*, in + *telos,* perfection, end + *ekhein,* to have.]
en·tente (on-tónt, ON-TÓNT) *n.* **1.** An agreement, usually unformalised, between two or more governments or powers, for cooperative action or policy. Also called "entente cordiale". **2.** The coalition resulting from such an agreement. [French, "understanding", from Old French *entendre,* to understand, INTEND.]
en·ter (éntər) *v.* **-tered, -tering, -ters.** *—tr.* **1.** To come or go into. **2.** To penetrate; pierce. **3.** To introduce; insert. **4.** To become an element in or a part of. **5.** To begin (an age or phase); embark upon: *he was entering a period of crisis.* **6. a.** To obtain admission to (a school, for example). **b.** To secure the admission of. **c.** To enrol. **7. a.** To submit or register as an entry in an exhibition or competition: *enter dahlias in a flower show.* **b.** To become a participant or a contestant in. **8.** To take up; embrace (a profession or career): *Their son entered the priesthood.* **9.** *Law.* **a.** To place formally before a court or upon the records: *enter a plea.* **b.** To go upon or into (real property) as a trespasser or with felonious intent. See **breaking and entering. c.** To go upon in order to take possession of (real property, especially land). **10.** To record in a register or on a list, for example. **11.** To make known; register: *enter a protest.* *—intr.* **1.** To come or go in; make an entry. **2.** To gain entry; penetrate. **3.** To become a member. **4.** To come on stage in the theatre: *Enter stage left.* **—enter into. 1.** To participate in; take an active interest in. **2.** To be a component of; form a part of. **3.** To consider; delve into. **4.** To become party to (a contract). **5.** To empathise with; be in sympathy with. **—enter on** or **upon. 1.** To set out upon; embark upon. **2.** To take legal possession of (real property, especially land). **3.** To begin to consider or deal with (a subject). [Middle English *entren,* from Old French *entrer,* from Latin *intrāre,* from *intrā,* within.]
en·ter·ic (en-térrik, in-) *adj.* Also **en·ter·al** (-əl). Of, pertaining to, or affecting the intestine. [Greek *enterikos,* from *enteron,* ENTERON.]
enteric fever *n. Pathology.* **Typhoid** *(see).*
en·ter·i·tis (éntə-rítiss) *n.* Inflammation of the intestinal tract. [New Latin : ENTER(O)- + -ITIS.]
entero–, enter– *comb. form.* Indicates the intestine; for example, **enterostomy, enteritis.** [New Latin, from Greek *enteron,* intestines.]
en·ter·o·bi·a·sis (éntərō-bí-ə-siss) *n.* Infestation of the intestine with pinworms. Also called "oxyuriasis". [New Latin *enterobius (vermicularis),* pinworm (see **entero-**) + -IASIS.]
en·ter·o·gas·trone (éntərō-gáss-trōn) *n.* A hormone liberated by the small intestine (duodenum) that inhibits secretion of gastric juice by the stomach. [ENTERO- + GASTR(O)- + (HORM)ONE.]
en·ter·o·ki·nase (éntərō-kí-nayz, -nayss) *n.* An enzyme found in intestinal juice that converts trypsinogen to trypsin. Also called "enteropeptidase". [ENTERO- + KINASE.]
en·ter·on (éntə-ron, -rən) *n.* The intestine, especially that of an embryo or coelenterate. [New Latin, from Greek, intestine, entrails.]
en·ter·os·to·my (éntə-róstəmi) *n., pl.* **-mies.** Surgical formation of an opening into the intestine through the abdominal wall. [ENTERO- + -STOMY.] **—en·ter·os·to·mal** *adj.*
en·ter·ot·o·my (éntə-róttəmi) *n., pl.* **-mies.** Surgical incision into the intestine. [ENTERO- + -TOMY.]
en·ter·o·vir·us (éntərō-vír-əss) *n.* Any virus, such as the polio virus, that enters the body through and multiplies in the gastrointestinal tract, and then usually invades the central nervous system.
en·ter·prise (éntər-prīz) *n.* **1.** An undertaking, especially of some scope, complication, and risk. **2. a.** Commercial or economic activity; business: *private enterprise.* **b.** A business or company. **3.** Industrious effort, especially when directed towards making money. **4.** Readiness to venture; boldness; initiative. [Middle English, from Old French *entreprise,* from the feminine past participle of *entreprendre,* to undertake : *entre-*, between, from Latin *inter-* + *prendre,* to take, from Latin *prendere, prehendere.*] **—en·ter·pris·er** *n.*
en·ter·pris·ing (éntər-prīzing) *adj.* Showing imagination, initiative, and readiness to undertake new ventures. **—en·ter·pris·ing·ly** *adv.*
en·ter·tain (éntər-táyn) *v.* **-tained, -taining, -tains.** *—tr.* **1.** To hold the attention of; especially, to perform for the pleasure of; amuse. **2.** To extend hospitality towards: *entertain friends to dinner.* **3. a.** To mull over; contemplate: *entertain an idea.* **b.** To hold in mind; harbour: *entertain illusions.* **4.** *Sports.* To play at home against (an opposing team, for example). *—intr.* **1.** To have guests, as for dinner or a party. **2.** To provide entertainment. [Middle English *entertinen,* to maintain, from Old French *entretenir,* from Vulgar Latin *intertenēre* (unattested), "to hold between": Latin *inter-*, between + *tenēre,* to hold.]
en·ter·tain·er (éntər-táynər) *n.* **1.** A person who sings, dances, tells jokes, or the like as a profession. **2.** Someone who entertains.
en·ter·tain·ing (éntər-táyning) *adj.* Serving to entertain; agreeably diverting; amusing. **—en·ter·tain·ing·ly** *adv.*
en·ter·tain·ment (éntər-táynmənt) *n.* **1.** The act of entertaining. **2.** The art, profession, or field of entertaining. **3.** Something that entertains; especially, a performance or show designed to amuse or divert. **4.** The pleasure afforded by being entertained; amusement. **5.** Hospitality extended towards guests.
en·thal·py (én-thəl-pi, -thal-, en-thál-) *n. Symbol* **H** A thermodynamic function of a system, equivalent to the internal energy plus the product of the pressure and the volume. [Greek *enthalpein,* to heat in : *en-*, in + *thalpein*†, to warm, heat.]
en·thral, *U.S.* **en·thrall** (in-thráwl, en-) *tr.v.* **-thralled, -thralling, -thrals** or *U.S.* **-thralls. 1.** To hold spellbound; captivate; charm. **2.** *Archaic.* To reduce to thraldom; enslave. [Middle English *enthrallen* : EN- + THRALL.] **—en·thral·ment** *n.*
en·throne (in-thrṓn, en-) *tr.v.* **-throned, -throning, -thrones. 1.** To seat on a throne. **2.** To invest with sovereign power or with the authority of high office. **3.** To raise to a lofty position; revere; exalt. **—en·throne·ment** *n.*
en·thuse (in-théwz, en-, -thóoz) *v.* **-thused, -thusing, -thuses.** *Informal.* *—tr.* To stimulate enthusiasm in. *—intr.* To show enthusiasm. [Back-formation from ENTHUSIASM.]
en·thu·si·asm (in-théwzi-az'm, en-, -thóozi-) *n.* **1. a.** Keen interest or excitement. **b.** Eagerness; zeal. **c.** Ardent fondness. **2.** A subject or activity that inspires a lively interest. **3.** *Archaic.* **a.** Ecstasy arising from supposed possession by a god. **b.** A fanatical religious ardour. —See Synonyms at **passion.** [Late Latin *enthūsiasmus,* from Greek *enthousiasmos,* inspiration, from *enthousiazein,* to be inspired by a god, from *enthous, entheos,* possessed, inspired : *en-*, in + *theos,* god.]
en·thu·si·ast (in-théwzi-ast, en-, -thóozi-) *n.* **1.** A person filled with enthusiasm; especially, one ardently preoccupied with a particular subject: *a cricket enthusiast.* **2.** *Archaic.* A religious zealot, fanatic, or visionary. —See Synonyms at **fanatic. —en·thu·si·as·tic** *adj.* **—en·thu·si·as·ti·cal·ly** *adv.*
en·thy·meme (énthi-meem) *n. Logic.* A syllogism with one of the premises implicit or unexpressed because thought to be self-evident. [Latin *enthymēma,* from Greek *enthumēma,* from *enthumeisthai,* "to have in mind", consider : *en-*, in + *thūmos,* mind.]
en·ti·a. Plural of **ens.**
en·tice (in-tíss, en-) *tr.v.* **-ticed, -ticing, -tices.** To attract by arousing hope or desire; lure. See Synonyms at **lure.** [Middle English *enticen,* from Old French *enticier,* from Vulgar Latin *intītiāre* (unattested), to set on fire : Latin *in-*, in + *tītiō*†, firebrand.] **—en·tice·ment** *n.* **—en·tic·er** *n.* **—en·tic·ing·ly** *adv.*
en·tire (in-tír, en-, -tí-ər) *adj.* **1.** Having no part missing or excepted; whole: *an entire set of the encyclopedia; the entire country.* **2.** Without reservation or limitation; total; complete: *entire freedom; my entire approval; his entire attention.* **3.** All in one piece; unbroken; intact: *The ship was still entire after the typhoon.* **4.** Of one piece; continuous. **5.** Not castrated. **6.** *Botany.* Not indented or toothed, as the margin of a leaf.
~*n.* **1.** The whole of something; entirety. **2.** An uncastrated horse. [Middle English *entier,* from Old French, from Latin *integrum,* accusative of *integer,* intact.] **—en·tire·ness** *n.*
en·tire·ly (in-tír-li, en-, -tí-ər-) *adv.* **1.** Wholly; completely. **2.** Solely or exclusively.
en·ti·re·ty (in-tír-ə-ti, en-, -tí-ərti) *n., pl.* **-ties. 1.** The state or condition of being entire or complete; completeness. **2.** Something that is entire; a whole. **3.** The entire amount or extent; the sum total.
en·ti·tle (in-tít'l, en-) *tr.v.* **-tled, -tling, -tles. 1.** To give a name or

title to; designate: *a novel entitled "Summer".* **2. a.** To afford or prove the right of (a person) to do or have something; qualify. **b.** To afford or prove a legal right or claim of (a person) to something. [Middle English *entitlen,* from Old French *entiteler,* from Late Latin *intitulāre* : *in-,* in + *titulus,* TITLE.] **—en·ti·tle·ment** *n.*

en·ti·ty (éntəti) *n., pl.* **-ties. 1.** The fact of existence; being. **2.** Something that exists independently, not relative to other things. **3.** A particular and discrete unit: *Persons and corporations are equivalent entities under the law.* [Medieval Latin *entitās,* from Latin *ēns* (stem *ent-*), irregular present participle of *esse,* to be.]

ento- *comb. form.* Indicates within, inside; for example, **entozoa.** [New Latin, from Greek *entos,* within.]

entoblast. Variant of **endoblast.**

entoderm. Variant of **endoderm.**

entom. entomological; entomology.

en·tomb (in-tóōm, en-) *tr.v.* **-tombed, -tombing, -tombs. 1.** To place in or as if in a tomb or grave; bury. **2.** To serve as a tomb for. [Middle English *entoumben,* from Old French *entomber* : *en-,* in + *tombe,* tomb, from Late Latin *tumba,* TOMB.] **—en·tomb·ment** *n.*

entomo- *comb. form.* Indicates insect; for example, **entomology, entomophagous.** [French, from Greek *entomon,* insect, "one whose body is cut into segments", from *entomos,* cut up, from *entemnein,* to cut in, cut up : *en-,* in + *temnein,* to cut.]

entomol. entomology.

en·to·mol·o·gise, en·to·mol·o·gize (éntə-móllə-jīz) *intr.v.* **-gised, -gising, -gises.** To study or collect insects.

en·to·mol·o·gy (éntə-mólləji) *n. Abbr.* **entom., entomol.** The scientific study of insects. [ENTOMO- + -LOGY.] **—en·to·mo·log·i·cal** (-mə-lójik'l) *adj.* **—en·to·mo·log·i·cal·ly** *adv.* **—en·to·mol·o·gist** (-mólləjist) *n.*

en·to·moph·a·gous (éntə-móffəgəss) *adj. Rare.* Feeding on insects; insectivorous. [ENTOMO- + -PHAGOUS.]

en·to·moph·i·lous (éntə-móffiləss) *adj.* Pollinated by insects. [ENTOMO- + -PHILOUS.] **—en·to·moph·i·ly** *n.*

en·tou·rage (óntoor-aázh, -aazh) *n.* **1.** A group of attendants, followers, or associates. **2.** *Rare.* One's environment or surroundings. [French, from *entourer,* to surround, from Old French *entour,* surroundings : *en-,* in + *tour,* circuit, TOUR.]

en·to·zo·a (én-tō-zṓ-ə, -tə-) *pl.n. Singular* **-zoan** (-zṓ-ən) or **-zoon** (-zṓ-on). Various animals, such as tapeworms, that live within other animals, usually as parasites. [New Latin : ENTO- + -ZOA.] **—en·to·zo·ic** *adj.*

en·tr'acte (ón-trakt, -trákt) *n.* **1.** The interval between two successive acts of a theatrical performance. **2.** An entertainment, especially a piece of music, provided during this interval. [French, "between-act".]

en·trails (én-traylz || -trəlz) *pl.n.* **1.** The internal organs, especially the intestines; viscera. **2.** The inner parts of something. [Middle English *entrailles,* from Old French, from Medieval Latin *intrālia,* variant of Latin *interānea,* from the neuter plural of *interāneus,* internal, from *inter,* within.]

en·train¹ (in-tráyn, en-) *tr.v.* **-trained, -training, -trains.** To pull or draw along after itself. [Old French *entrainer* : *en-,* in + *trainer,* to draw (see **train**).]

en·train² (in-tráyn, en-) *v.* **-trained, -training, -trains.** *—tr.* To put on a train. *—intr.* To board a train. **—en·train·ment** *n.*

en·trance¹ (éntrənss) *n.* **1.** The act or an instance of entering; especially, the entry of an actor into the performing area. **2.** Any passage, opening, doorway, or the like where one can enter. **3.** The permission, power, or liberty to enter; admission. Also used adjectivally: *entrance money.* **4.** The point in a script or musical score at which a performer is to begin. [Middle English *entraunce,* from Old French *entrance,* from *entrer,* ENTER.]

en·trance² (in-traánss, en- || -tránss) *tr.v.* **-tranced, -trancing, -trances. 1.** To fill with great pleasure, wonder, or enchantment; fascinate: *a child entranced by his own reflection.* **2.** To put into a trance. **—en·trance·ment** *n.* **—en·tranc·ing·ly** *adv.*

en·trant (éntrənt) *n.* **1.** One who enters; especially, one who enters a competition: *There were ten entrants in the beauty contest.* **2.** A new member, as of a profession, organisation, university, or the like. [French, from the present participle of *entrer,* ENTER.]

en·trap (in-tráp, en-) *tr.v.* **-trapped, -trapping, -traps. 1.** To catch in or as if in a trap. **2.** To lure into danger, difficulty, or self-incrimination. [Old French *entraper* : *en-,* in + *trape,* trap.] **—en·trap·ment** *n.*

en·treat (in-tréet, en-) *v.* **-treated, -treating, -treats.** Also **in·treat** (in-). *—tr.* **1.** To ask (someone) earnestly; beseech; implore; beg. **2.** To ask for (something) earnestly; petition for. *—intr.* To make an earnest request or petition; plead. —See Synonyms at **beg.** [Middle English *entreten,* to deal with, plead with, from Old French *entraitier* : *en-,* in + *traitier, traiter,* to TREAT.] **—en·treat·ing·ly** *adv.* **—en·treat·ment** *n.*

en·treat·y (in-tréeti, en-) *n., pl.* **-ies.** An earnest request; a plea.

en·tre·chat (óN-trə-shaa, -shaá) *n.* A leap in ballet during which the dancer crosses his feet a number of times, often beating them together. [French, earlier *entrecha(se),* by folk etymology (influenced by *chasse,* chase) from Italian *(capriola) intrecciata,* "interlaced (caper)", from the feminine past participle of *intrecciare,* to interlace, entwine : *in-,* in, from Latin + *treccia,* tress, akin to Old French *tresse,* TRESS.]

en·tre·côte (ón-trə-kōt, óN-) *n.* A cut of steak taken from between the ribs. [French, "between the ribs".]

en·trée, en·tree (ón-tray, óN-) *n.* **1. a.** The power, permission, or liberty to enter; admittance. **b.** Access by special privilege to a place normally inaccessible. **2. a.** A dish served between the fish course and the main meat course, or immediately before the main course, especially in an elaborate or formal dinner. **b.** The main course, especially in an ordinary or simple meal. [French, ENTRY.]

en·tre·mets (ón-trə-may; *French* oN-trə-mé) *n., pl.* **-mets** (-mayz; *French* -mé). A side dish or dishes; especially, a dish served between principal courses or as a dessert. [French, earlier *entremes* : Old French *entre-,* between, + *mes,* dish, MESS.]

en·trench (in-trénch, en-) *v.* **-trenched, -trenching, -trenches.** Also **in·trench** (in-). *—tr.* **1.** *Military.* **a.** To provide with a trench or trenches for the purpose of draining, fortifying, defending, or supporting. **b.** To set up (a base, for example) in a defensible position. **2.** To establish firmly so as to be irremovable: *entrenched prejudices.* *—intr.* **1.** To dig a trench or trenches. **2.** To adopt a safe or strongly defended position. **3.** *Rare.* To encroach or trespass.

en·trench·ment (in-trénchmənt, en-) *n.* **1.** The act of entrenching or the condition of being entrenched. **2.** A fortification; especially, a series of banked trenches.

en·tre nous (ón-trə nóō, oN-) *adv.* Between ourselves; confidentially. [French.]

en·tre·pôt (ón-trə-pō, oN-) *n.* **1.** A place where goods are stored or deposited and from which they are distributed. **2.** A trading or market centre. [French, from *entreposer,* to put in, to store : Old French *entre-,* in, between, from Latin *inter-* + *poser,* to put, POSE.]

en·tre·pre·neur (óntrə-prə-núr, -nőr || -néwr, -nóor) *n.* A person who organises, operates, and assumes the risk for business ventures. [French, from Old French, from *entreprendre,* to undertake. See **enterprise.**] **—en·tre·pre·neur·i·al** (-i-əl) *adj.*

en·tre·sol (óntrə-sol; *French* oNtrə-sól) *n.* A floor just above the ground floor and below the first floor; a mezzanine. [French, "between floors".]

en·tro·py (éntrəpi) *n.* **1.** A measure of the capacity of a system to undergo spontaneous change, thermodynamically specified by the relationship $dS = dQ/T$, where dS is an infinitesimal change in the measure for a system absorbing an infinitesimal quantity of heat dQ at thermodynamic temperature T. **2.** The tendency of the energy of a closed system, including that of the universe itself, to become less available to do work with the passage of time. **3.** A measure of the randomness, disorder, or chaos in a system specified in statistical mechanics by the relationship $S = k\ln P + c$, where S is the value of the measure for a system in a given state, P is the probability of occurrence of that state, k is the Boltzmann constant, and c is an arbitrary constant. [German *Entropie* : Greek *en-,* in + *tropē,* a turning, change.]

en·trust (in-trúst, en-) *tr.v.* **-trusted, -trusting, -trusts.** Also **in·trust** (in-). **1.** To give over to another for care, protection, or performance: *entrusted the task to his aides.* **2.** To commit something trustfully to; place a trust upon: *entrusted his aides with the task.* —See Synonyms at **commit.**

en·try (éntri) *n., pl.* **-tries. 1.** The act or an instance of entering. **2.** The right to enter. **3. a.** The inclusion or insertion of an item in a diary, register, list, or other record. **b.** An item thus entered. **4.** An item in a reference book, such as an article in an encyclopedia or a word, term, or phrase defined or identified in a dictionary together with the text related to it. **5. a.** One registered as a participant in a competition. **b.** All such participants, considered collectively. **6.** The entrance on stage or manner of entering of an actor. **7.** The point in a piece of music at which a performer is to begin or restart. **8.** *Law.* The act of taking possession of land or property by entering. **9. a.** A passage between buildings. **b.** *Chiefly Northern English.* A passage between the backs of two rows of back-to-back terraced houses. **10.** *Chiefly U.S.* A passage or opening where one can enter. [Middle English *entre,* from Old French *entree,* from Vulgar Latin *intrāta* (unattested), from the feminine past participle of Latin *intrāre,* ENTER.]

en·try·ism (éntri-iz'm) *n.* The infiltration of a body, such as a political party, whereby new members gradually take over its organisation and seek to change its character to suit their own usually extreme views. **—en·try·ist** *n. & adj.*

en·twine (in-twīn, en-) *v.* **-twined, -twining, -twines.** Also **in·twine** (in-). *—tr.* To twine or twist around or about: *Ivy entwined the pillar.* *—intr.* To twine or twist together.

e·nu·cle·ate (i-néw-kli-ayt || -nóō-) *tr.v.* **-ated, -ating, -ates. 1.** In surgery, to remove (a tumour or eyeball, for example) from its enveloping cover or sac. **2.** *Biology.* To remove the nucleus of (a cell). ~*adj.* (-ət, -it, -ayt). Lacking a nucleus. [Latin *ēnucleāre,* to take out the kernel : *ex-,* out + *nucleus,* kernel, NUCLEUS.] **—e·nu·cle·a·tion** (-áysh'n) *n.* **—e·nu·cle·a·tor** (-aytər) *n.*

e·nu·mer·ate (i-néw-mə-rayt || -nóō-) *tr.v.* **-ated, -ating, -ates. 1.** To count off or name one by one; list. **2.** To determine the number of; count. [Latin *ēnumerāre,* to count out : *ex-,* out + *numerus,* number.] **—e·nu·mer·a·tive** (-rətiv, -raytiv) *adj.*

e·nu·mer·a·tion (i-néw-mə-ráysh'n || -nóō-) *n.* **1.** The act of enumerating. **2.** A detailed list of items.

e·nu·mer·a·tor (i-néw-mə-raytər || -nóō-) *n.* **1.** One that enumerates. **2.** *British.* A person involved in the distribution and collection of census forms.

e·nun·ci·ate (i-nún-si-ayt, -shi-) *v.* **-ated, -ating, -ates.** *—tr.* **1.** To pronounce or articulate (speech sounds); especially, to pronounce with clarity or in another specified manner. **2.** To state or set forth precisely or systematically: *enunciate a doctrine.* **3.** To announce; proclaim. *—intr.* To pronounce words, especially distinctly. [Latin ēnuntiāre, ēnunciāre : ex-, out + nuntiāre, to announce, from nuncius, nuntius, message, messenger.] —**e·nun·ci·a·ble** (-əb'l), **e·nun·ci·a·tive** (-ətiv, -aytiv), **e·nun·ci·a·to·ry** (-ətri, -ətəri, -áytəri) adj. —**e·nun·ci·a·tive·ly** adv. —**e·nun·ci·a·tor** (-aytər) n.

e·nun·ci·a·tion (i-nún-si-áysh'n, -shi-) n. 1. The act or manner of enunciating; especially, the manner in which a speaker articulates words or speech sounds. 2. An announcement, declaration, or similar official statement. —See Synonyms at **diction**.

enure. Variant of **inure**.

en·u·re·sis (énnewr-ée-siss) n. Involuntary urination. [New Latin, from Greek enourein, to urinate in : en-, in + ourein, to urinate, from ouron, urine.] —**en·u·re·tic** (-rétik) n. & adj.

env. envelope.

en·vel·op (in-vélləp, en-) tr.v. **-oped, -oping, -ops.** 1. To enclose, cover, or obscure with or as if with a covering or wrapping. 2. To serve as a covering or wrapping for. 3. To surround or enfold: enveloped in the cheerful atmosphere. [Middle English enveloupen, from Old French enveloper : en-, in + veloper, to wrap up (see **develop**).] —**en·vel·op·er** n. —**en·vel·op·ment** n.

en·ve·lope (én-və-lōp, ón-) n. Abbr. **env.** 1. Something that envelops; an enclosing or surrounding cover, coat, or wrapping. 2. A flat, folded paper container for a letter or similar object, usually rectangular and having a gummed sealing flap. 3. Biology. Any enclosing covering, membrane, or structure. 4. The bag containing the gas in a balloon. 5. Mathematics. a. A curve that is a tangent to all the curves of a family of curves. b. A surface that is a tangent to a family of surfaces. 6. The glass or metal casing of an electronic valve or similar device. [French enveloppe, from Old French envelope, from enveloper, **ENVELOP**.]

en·ven·om (in-vénnəm, en-) tr.v. **-omed, -oming, -oms.** 1. To put venom into or on; make poisonous or noxious. 2. To fill with malice; embitter. [Middle English envenimen, from Old French envenimer : **IN** + **VENOM**.]

en·vi·a·ble (énvi-əb'l) adj. 1. Arousing strong envy. 2. Highly desirable but rare: "the enviable English quality of being able to be mute without unrest" (Henry James). —**en·vi·a·bly** adv.

en·vi·ous (énvi-əss) adj. Feeling, expressing, or characterised by envy. Used with of. —**en·vi·ous·ly** adv. —**en·vi·ous·ness** n.

en·vi·ron (in-vír-ən, en-, ∥ -ví-ərn) tr.v. **-roned, -roning, -rons.** To encircle; surround. [Middle English environen, from Old French environer, from environ, around : en-, in + viron, circle, from virer, to turn, **VEER**.]

en·vi·ron·ment (in-vír-ən-mənt, en-, ∥ -ví-ərn-) n. 1. Something that surrounds; surroundings. 2. The aggregate of circumstances surrounding an organism or group of organisms, specifically: a. The combination of external or extrinsic physical conditions that affect and influence the growth and development of organisms. b. The complex of social and cultural conditions affecting the nature of an individual or community. Compare **heredity**. —**en·vi·ron·men·tal** (-mént'l) adj. —**en·vi·ron·men·tal·ly** adv.

en·vi·ron·men·tal·ist (in-vír-ən-mént'l-ist, en-, ∥ -ví-ərnz) n. 1. A person who seeks to protect the natural environment, as from air and water pollution, wasteful use of resources, and excessive human encroachment. 2. A person who believes that environment is more important than heredity in influencing intellectual growth and cultural development. In this sense, compare **hereditist**. —**en·vi·ron·men·tal·ism** n.

en·vi·rons (in-vír-ənz, en-, ∥ -ví-ərnz) pl.n. 1. The surrounding area, especially of a city; the suburbs; the outskirts. 2. Surroundings; environment.

en·vis·age (in-vízzij, en-) tr.v. **-aged, -aging, -ages.** To conceive of, especially as a future possibility. [French envisager : **IN** + **VISAGE**.]

en·vi·sion (in-vízh'n, en-) tr.v. **-sioned, -sioning, -sions.** To picture in the mind; foresee.

en·voi, en·voy (én-voy ∥ U.S. also ón-) n. A short concluding stanza of certain French verse forms, such as the ballade, originally serving as a postscript dedicating the poem to a patron and later as a pithy summation of the poem. [Middle English envoie, from Old French envoy, "a sending away", conclusion, from envoier, to send. See **envoy.**]

en·voy¹ (én-voy ∥ U.S. also ón-) n. 1. A messenger or other agent sent on a mission. 2. A representative of a government or faction sent on a special diplomatic mission. [French envoyé, one who is sent, from past participle of envoyer, to send, from Old French envoier, enveier, from Late Latin inviāre, to put on the way : Latin in-, in + via, way.]

envoy². Variant of **envoi.**

en·vy (énvi) n., pl. **-vies.** 1. a. A feeling of discontent and resentment aroused by contemplation of another's possessions, qualities, or achievements with a strong wish that they were one's own. b. A more moderate feeling aroused by admiration rather than resentment. 2. a. A possession of another that is strongly desired. b. One who possesses what another strongly desires: She was the envy of her friends. 3. Obsolete. Malevolence.
~v. **envied, -vying, -vies.** —tr. To feel envy for; regard with envy. —intr. Archaic. To be filled with envy. [Middle English envie, from Old French, from Latin invidia, from invidēre, to look at with malice : in-, in, upon + vidēre, to see.] —**en·vi·er** n. —**en·vy·ing·ly** adv.

en·wind (in-wínd, en-) tr.v. **-wound** (-wównd), **-winding, -winds.** To wind round or about; encircle.

en·wrap (in-ráp, en-) tr.v. **-wrapped, -wrapping, -wraps.** 1. To wrap up; enclose; enfold. 2. To engross.

Enzed (én-zéd) n. Australian & N. Z. Informal. 1. New Zealand.

2. A New Zealander. [From the initials N, Z.]

en·zo·ot·ic (énzō-óttik) adj. Affecting or peculiar to animals of a specific area or limited district. Said of diseases.
~n. An enzootic disease. [**EN**- (within) + **ZO**(o)- + **-OTIC**.]

en·zyme (énzīm) n. Any of numerous proteins or conjugated proteins produced by living organisms and functioning as biochemical catalysts. [German Enzym, from Medieval Greek enzumos, leavened : Greek en-, in + zumē, leaven.] —**en·zy·mat·ic** (én-zī-máttik, -zi-) adj. —**en·zy·mic** (en-zī-mik, -zi-) adj.

en·zy·mol·o·gy (én-zī-mólləji, -zi-) n. The biochemistry of enzymes. —**en·zy·mol·o·gist** n.

eo- comb. form. Indicates: 1. An early period of time; for example, **Eocene**. 2. An early form or representative; for example, **eohippus**. [Greek ēo-, from ēōs, dawn.]

e.o. ex officio.

EO Executive Officer.

EOC Equal Opportunities Commission.

E·o·cene (ée-ō-seen, -ə-) adj. Of, pertaining to, or designating the geological time, rock system, and fossils of the second oldest of the five epochs of the Tertiary period of the Cenozoic era, extending from the end of the Palaeocene to the beginning of the Oligocene, and characterised by the rise of mammals.
~n. Geology. The Eocene epoch. Preceded by the. [**EO**- + **-CENE**.]

e·o·hip·pus (ée-ō-híppəss) n. An extinct, small, herbivorous mammal of the genus Hyracotherium (or Eohippus), of the Eocene epoch, having four-toed front feet and three-toed hind feet, and related ancestrally to the horse. [New Latin : **EO**- + Greek hippos, horse.]

EOKA (ay-ōkə). See **Cyprus, Republic of.**

e·o·lith (ée-ō-lith, -ə-) n. Archaeology. Any of the alleged stone artefacts characterising the Eolithic. [**EO**- + **-LITH**.]

E·o·lith·ic (ée-ō-líthik, -ə-) adj. Archaeology. Of or pertaining to the postulated earliest period of human culture preceding the Lower Palaeolithic.
~n. The Eolithic period. Preceded by the. [**EO**- + **-LITHIC**.]

e.o.m. end of month.

eon. Chiefly U.S. Variant of **aeon**.

E·o·nism (ée-ə-niz'm) n. **Transvestism** (see) when practised by a man. [After Charles Éon de Beaumont (1728–1810), French diplomat and transvestite.]

E·os (ée-oss). Greek Mythology. The goddess of the dawn, identified with the Roman goddess Aurora. [Greek Ēōs, from ēōs, dawn.]

e·o·sin (ée-ō-sin, -ə-) n. Also **e·o·sine** (-sin, -sīn). A red crystalline powder, $C_{20}H_8Br_4O_5$, used in textile dyeing, histology, and the manufacture of inks. [Greek ēōs, dawn + -**IN**.]

e·o·sin·o·phil (ée-ō-sínnə-fil) n. Also **e·o·sin·o·phile** (-fīl). Physiology. A type of leucocyte with a lobed nucleus that stains with an eosin dye. —**e·o·sin·o·phil·ic** (-fillik), **e·o·si·noph·i·lous** (ée-ō-si-nóffiləss) adj.

-eous adj. suffix. Having the nature of or akin to; for example, **gaseous, beauteous**. [Latin -eus.]

EP n. A gramophone record of the same size as a single, but having a longer playing time. [From extended play.]

e·pact (ée-pakt ∥ ép-akt) n. 1. The excess of silver time, about 11 days, of the solar year over the lunar year. 2. The age of the moon at the beginning of the calendar year. 3. The excess of time of a calendar month over a lunar month. [Old French epacte, from Late Latin epacta, from Greek epaktai (hēmerai), "(days) brought in", from epaktos, brought in from abroad, from epagein, to lead on, bring in : from epi-, on + agein, to lead.]

ep·arch (ép-aark) n. 1. The chief administrator of an eparchy. 2. Greek Orthodox Church. A bishop or metropolitan. [Greek eparkhos, commander, governor : epi-, on, over + -**ARCH**.] —**e·par·chi·al** (e-párki-əl) adj.

ep·ar·chy (ép-aarki) n., pl. **-chies.** 1. An administrative subdivision of modern Greece. 2. Greek Orthodox Church. An ecclesiastical district; a diocese.

ep·au·lette (ép-ə-let, -aw-, -ō-, -lét) n. Also chiefly U.S. **ep·au·let.** A shoulder ornament; especially, either of two fringed straps on certain dress uniforms. [French épaulette, diminutive of épaule, shoulder, from Old French espaule, from Latin spatula. See **spatula**.]

é·pée, e·pee (ép-ay, e-páy, ay-) n. 1. A fencing sword with a bowl-shaped guard and a long, narrow, fluted blade that has no cutting edge and tapers to a blunted point. 2. The art of fencing with the épée. [French, from Latin spatha, sword, blade. See **spatula**.] —**é·pée·ist** n.

ep·ei·rog·e·ny (éppīr-ójəni) n. Also **ep·ei·ro·gen·e·sis** (-ə-jénnəsiss). The deformation of the crust of the earth by which continents and oceanic basins, or parts of these, are formed. [Greek ēpeiros, continent + -**GENY**.] —**e·pei·ro·gen·ic** (i-pīr-ō-jénnik, -ə-) adj.

ep·en·the·sis (e-pénthə-siss, i-) n., pl. **-ses** (-seez). Linguistics. The insertion of an extra sound into the pronunciation of a word, especially before an l or r sound, either as a process of phonetic development or as a feature of nonstandard speech; for example, the nonstandard pronunciation of umbrella as (úmb-ə-réllə). [Late Latin, from Greek, from epentithenai, to insert : epi-, in addition to + entithenai, to put in : en-, in + tithenai, to place.] —**ep·en·thet·ic** (ép-en-théttik) adj.

e·pergne (i-pérn, e-, -páúrn) n. A large silver or glass centrepiece for a table, usually compartmented or branched and decorated with flowers, fruit, or the like. [Probably from French épargne, saving, from épargner, to save, from Old French espargnier, from Germanic sparōjan (unattested), to **SPARE**.]

E·per·nay (ay-pair-náy). Town in northeast France, on the river Marne. After Rheims it is the most important centre for the production of champagne.

ep·ex·e·ge·sis (e-pék-si-jée-siss, ép-ek-) n. 1. The addition of explanatory material to clarify something immediately preceding it. 2. The additional material itself. [Greek *epexēgēsis,* from *epexēgeisthai,* to explain in detail : *epi-,* in addition to + *exēgeisthai,* to explain (see **exegesis**).] —**ep·ex·e·get·ic** (-jéttik), **ep·ex·e·get·i·cal** adj.

Eph. Ephesians (New Testament).

e·phah, e·pha (éefə ‖ éffə) n. A unit of dry measure equal to slightly more than a bushel, used by the ancient Hebrews. [Hebrew *'ephāh,* probably from Egyptian *'pt.*]

e·phebe (i-féeb, éffeeb) n. In ancient Greece, a youth between eighteen and twenty years of age in military training. [Latin *ephēbus,* from Greek *ephēbos* : *epi-,* at + *hēbē,* youth.] —**e·phe·bic** adj.

e·phed·ra (i-féddrə ‖ éffidrə) n. Any gymnosperm shrub of the genus *Ephedra,* found in Eurasia and the United States. [New Latin, from Greek, from *ephedros,* "a sitting upon" : *ep-,* EPI- + *hedra,* seat.]

e·phed·rine (i-féddrin, éffi-dreen, -drin) n. A white, odourless, powdered or crystalline alkaloid, $C_{10}H_{15}NO$, isolated from shrubs of the genus *Ephedra* or made synthetically, used to treat allergies and asthma and as a vasoconstrictor. [New Latin *Ephedra,* genus name of mahuang, from Latin *ephedra,* horsetail, from Greek *ephedros,* sitting upon : *epi-,* upon + *hedra,* seat + -INE.]

e·phem·er·a (i-fém-ərə, -féem-) n., pl. **-as** or **-erae** (-ə-ree) or **ephemera** (for sense 2). 1. Something short-lived or transitory. 2. Plural. Printed matter such as old periodicals, handbills, and topical pamphlets, reflecting contemporary concerns. [From the plural of EPHEMERON.]

e·phem·er·al (i-fém-ərəl, -féem-) adj. 1. Lasting for a brief time; short-lived; transitory. 2. Living or lasting only one day, as certain flowers or adult insects do. —See Synonyms at **transient**. ~n. An ephemeral thing or organism. [Greek *ephēmeros* : *epi-,* on + *hēmera,* day.] —**e·phem·er·al·i·ty** (-ə-rál-əti) n. —**e·phem·er·al·ly** adv.

e·phem·er·id (i-fémmərid) n. An insect of the order Ephemeroptera, which comprises the mayflies. [New Latin *Ephemeridae,* former name of the order, from Greek *ephēmeros,* EPHEMERAL.]

e·phem·er·is (i-fém-əriss, -féem-) n., pl. **ephemerides** (éffi-mérri-deez) 1. A table giving the coordinates of one or a number of celestial bodies at a number of specific times during a given period. 2. A publication that presents a collection of such tables; an astronomical almanac. [Late Latin *ephēmeris,* diary, from Greek, from *ephēmeros,* EPHEMERAL.]

ephemeris time n. A highly accurate astronomical sytem for the measurement of time based on the period of the earth's orbit, but in practice relying on lunar observations and an accurate lunar ephemeris to calculate corrections to be applied to clocks. The unit is the ephemeris second equal to 1/31,556,925.9747 of the tropical year for epoch 1900 January 0.

e·phem·er·on (i-fémmə-ron, -féemə-, -rən) n., pl. **-era** (-rə) or **-ons**. A short-lived thing or organism. [New Latin, from Greek *ephemēron,* mayfly, from the neuter of *ephēmeros,* EPHEMERAL.]

E·phe·sian (i-féezh'n, -féezi-ən) adj. Of or pertaining to Ephesus or its people. ~n. A native or inhabitant of Ephesus.

E·phe·sians (i-féezh'nz, -féezi-ənz) n. Used with a singular verb. Abbr. **Eph.** A book of the New Testament consisting of the Apostle Paul's epistle to the Christians of Ephesus.

Eph·e·sus (éffi-səss). Ancient Greek city of Asia Minor, in what is now western Turkey, lying near the mouth of the river Küçük Menderes. Its great Temple of Diana, one of the Seven Wonders of the World, was destroyed by the Goths (A.D. 262).

eph·od (éefod ‖ éffod) n. An embroidered vestment worn by ancient Hebrew priests. [Hebrew *ephōdh.*]

eph·or (éf-awr, -ər) n., pl. **-ors** or **-ori** (-ə-rī) Any of a body of five elected officials exercising a supervisory power over the kings of ancient Sparta. [Latin *ephorus,* from Greek *ephoros,* from *ephoran,* to oversee : *epi-,* over + *horan,* to see.]

E·phra·im[1] (ée-fray-im, ée-frəm). The younger son of Joseph. Genesis 41:52. [Hebrew, perhaps "meadows".]

E·phra·im[2] (ée-fray-im, ée-frəm) n. A tribe of Israel descended from the younger son of Joseph.

E·phra·im·ite (ée-fray-i-mīt, ée-frə-mīt) n. A member of the tribe of Ephraim. —**E·phra·im·ite** adj.

epi– prefix. Indicates: 1. On, upon; for example, **epiphyte.** 2. Over, above; for example, **epicentre.** 3. Around, covering; for example, **epicardium.** 4. To, towards, close to, next to; for example, **epicalyx.** 5. Besides, in addition; for example, **epiphenomenon.** 6. After; for example, **epigenesis.** 7. Among; for example, **epizootic.** [Greek *epi–* (before a vowel, *ep-*), from *epi,* upon, over, at, after.]

ep·i·blast (éppi-blast) n. The outer layer of a gastrula. —**ep·i·blas·tic** (-blástik) adj.

e·pib·o·ly (i-píbbəli) n. Zoology. A process in the development of the embryo in which the part of the blastula that was nearest the nucleus of the ovum grows over and encloses the part furthest from the nucleus, and eventually forms the ectoderm. [Greek *epibolē,* a throwing on, from *epiballein,* to throw on : *epi-,* on + *ballein,* to throw.] —**ep·i·bol·ic** (éppi-bóllik) adj.

ep·ic (éppik) n. 1. An extended narrative poem, such as *Beowulf* or the *Iliad,* celebrating episodes of a people's heroic tradition, typi-

cally developed by oral composition within a standard formulaic diction and set of metrical and narrative conventions, a final version being transcribed after the introduction of writing. 2. The genre represented by such poems; epos. 3. A formal poem, such as the *Aeneid,* composed in literary imitation of these conventions. 4. A story, film, or the like thought to embody the qualities characteristic of epic poetry. 5. An event or series of events regarded as a fit subject for an epic: *the epic of man's first journey to the moon.* ~adj. 1. Of or designating an epic: *an epic poem.* 2. Occurring in or characteristic of epics: *an epic simile.* 3. a. Suitable for or typical of an epic. b. Large-scale in grandeur, scope, or theme; heroic. [Latin *epicus,* from Greek *epikos,* from *epos,* song, word.]

ep·i·ca·lyx (éppi-káyl-ikss, -kál-) n., pl. **-lyxes** or **-lyces** (-li-seez). Botany. A set of bracts close to and resembling a calyx. Also called "calycle".

ep·i·can·thic fold (éppi-kánthik) n. A fold of skin of the upper eyelid that tends to cover the inner corner of the eye, characteristic of many Mongolian peoples and found in certain congenital conditions, such as Down's syndrome. Also called "epicanthus".

ep·i·car·di·um (éppi-kár-di-əm) n., pl. **-dia** (-di-ə). The inner layer of the pericardium that is in actual contact with the heart. [New Latin : EPI- + Greek *kardia,* heart.]

ep·i·carp (éppi-kaarp) n. Botany. An **exocarp** (see). [French *épicarpe* : EPI- + -CARP.]

ep·i·ce·di·um (éppi-sée-di-əm) n., pl. **-dia** (-di-ə). A funeral hymn or dirge. [Latin *epicēdium,* from Greek *epikēdeion,* from the neuter of *epikēdeios,* of a funeral : *epi-,* at + *kēdos,* sorrow, grief.]

ep·i·cene (éppi-seen) adj. 1. a. Belonging to or having the characteristics of both the male and the female: *an epicene statue; an epicene angel.* b. Effeminate; effete. c. Sexless; neuter. 2. Linguistics. Designating a noun that may be applied to both the male and the female without a change in form, such as the Greek *pais,* child (*ho pais,* the boy; *hē pais,* the girl). ~n. 1. Linguistics. An epicene noun. 2. An epicene person or object. [Middle English *epicene,* from Latin *epicoenus,* from Greek *epikoinos,* common to many, promiscuous : *epi-,* to + *koinos,* common.]

ep·i·cen·tre (éppi-sentər) n. 1. The part of the earth's surface directly above the focus of an earthquake. 2. A focal point. [New Latin *epicentrum* : EPI- + Latin *centrum,* CENTRE.]

ep·i·cle·sis (éppi-klée-siss) n. A prayer in the Mass calling on the Holy Spirit to turn the bread and wine into the body and blood of Christ. [Greek, invocation : *epi-,* EPI- + *klēsis,* prayer, from *kalein,* to call.]

ep·i·cot·yl (éppi-kottil, -kott'l) n. Botany. The part of the stem of a seedling or embryonic plant that is above the cotyledons and below the first true leaves. [EPI- + COTYL(EDON).]

ep·i·cri·sis (éppi-krī-siss) n., pl. **-ses** (-seez). Pathology. A crisis that occurs after the primary crisis of a disease.

ep·i·crit·ic (éppi-kríttik) adj. Pertaining to or designating sensory nerve fibres that make possible acute sensitivity to temperature and touch. Compare **protopathic.** [Greek *epikritikos,* decisive, from *epikritos,* decided on, from *epikrinein,* to decide.]

ep·i·cure (éppi-kewr) n. 1. A person with refined taste in food and wine. 2. Archaic. A person devoted to sensuous pleasure and luxurious living. [After EPICURUS, who supposedly advocated sensuous pleasure as the highest good.]

Ep·i·cu·re·an (éppi-kewr-ée-ən ‖ -kéwri-ən) adj. 1. Of or associated with the philosophy of Epicurus. 2. Small e. Devoted to the pursuit of pleasure; fond of good food, comfort, and ease; hedonistic. 3. Small e. Suited to the tastes of an epicure: *an epicurean repast.* —See Synonyms at **sensuous**. ~n. 1. A follower of Epicurus. 2. Small e. An epicure.

Ep·i·cu·re·an·ism (éppi-kewr-ée-ən-iz'm ‖ -kéwri-ən-) n. Also **Ep·i·cur·ism** (-kewr-iz'm). 1. The philosophy advanced by Epicurus. 2. Small e. The beliefs, tastes, or way of life of an epicure.

E·pi·cu·rus (éppi-kéwr-əss) (341–270 B.C.). Greek philosopher, born at Samos. From his philosophy the word "Epicurean" was derived to describe a life of indulgent pleasure-seeking, but his hedonism exalted the avoidance of pain rather than the satisfying of desires and was governed by a strict code of social behaviour.

ep·i·cy·cle (éppi-sīk'l) n. 1. In Ptolemaic cosmology, a small circle, the centre of which moves on the circumference of a larger circle at whose centre moves the Earth, and the circumference of which describes the orbit of a planet around the Earth. 2. A small circle that moves around the circumference of a larger circle, either on the inside or outside. [Middle English, from Old French or Late Latin, from Greek : *epi-,* EPI- + *kuklos,* circle.] —**ep·i·cy·clic** (-sîklik, -síklik) adj.

epicyclic train n. A system of gears in which at least one wheel axis revolves about another. It usually consists of a large annulus wheel with internal teeth, a small coaxial sunwheel with external teeth, and one or more planetary gears engaging with both of them.

ep·i·cy·cloid (éppi-sík-loyd) n. The curve described by a point fixed on the circumference of a circle as it rolls on the outside of the circumference of a fixed coplanar circle. [EPICYCL(E) + -OID.] —**ep·i·cy·cloid·al** (-sī-klóyd'l) adj.

epicycloidal wheel n. A planetary wheel in an epicyclic train.

Ep·i·dau·rus (éppi-dáwrəss). Modern Greek **Epidavros** or **Epidhavros** (e-péethav-ross). Ancient town of Greece, near the eastern shore of the Peloponnese, the site of the best-preserved ancient Greek theatre.

ep·i·deic·tic (éppi-dík-tik) adj. Intended for rhetorical effect or display. [Greek, from *epideiknunai*, to display; show off : *epi-* EPI- + *deiknunai*, to show.]

ep·i·dem·ic (éppi-démmik) *adj.* **1.** Spreading rapidly and extensively among many individuals in an area. Said especially of contagious diseases. **2.** Resembling or characteristic of a rapidly spreading disease: *Street crime has reached epidemic proportions.* ～*n.* **1.** An outbreak of a contagious disease that spreads rapidly and widely. **2.** A temporary, widespread popularity, as of a fashion or a fad. **3.** A rapid spread, growth, or development. [French *épidémique*, from *épidémie*, from Old French *espydymie*, from Late Latin *epidēmia*, from Greek *epidēmia (nosos)*, "(illness) prevalent among people", from *epidēmos*, prevalent, common : *epi-*, on, "among" + *dēmos*, people.] —**ep·i·dem·i·cal·ly** *adv.*

ep·i·de·mi·ol·o·gy (éppi-dèemi-óllǝji, -dèmmi-) *n.* The study of epidemics and the causes and distribution of diseases affecting populations. [Late Latin *epidēmia*, an EPIDEM(IC) + -LOGY.] —**ep·i·de·mi·o·log·i·cal** (-ǝ-lójik'l) *adj.* —**ep·i·de·mi·ol·o·gist** (-óllǝjist) *n.*

ep·i·der·mis (éppi-dérmiss) *n.* **1.** *Zoology.* **a.** The outer, protective layer of the skin in vertebrates. **b.** A single outer layer of cells in invertebrates. **2.** *Botany.* The outermost layer of cells or protective covering of a plant or plant part. [Late Latin, from Greek : *epi-*, over + *derma*, skin.] —**ep·i·der·mal, ep·i·der·mic, ep·i·der·moid** *adj.*

ep·i·di·a·scope (éppi-dí-ǝ-skōp) *n.* An optical device for projecting onto a screen the images of opaque objects or transparencies. Compare **diascope, episcope.** [EPI- + DIA- + -SCOPE.]

ep·i·did·y·mis (éppi-díddi-miss) *n., pl.* **-didymides** (-di-dímmi-deez). A long, narrow, flattened convoluted tube that is part of the spermatic duct system, connecting the testicle to the vas deferens. [New Latin, from Greek : *epi-*, at, near + *didumos*, testicle.] —**ep·i·did·y·mal** *adj.*

ep·i·dote (éppi-dōt) *n.* A natural, yellow, green, or black mineral consisting mainly of a silicate of calcium, aluminium, and iron, commonly found in metamorphic rock. [French *épidote*, from Greek *epididonai*, to give additionally, increase (so called because two sides of the mineral's base are longer than the other two) : *epi-*, in addition + *didonai*, to give.] —**ep·i·dot·ic** (-dóttik) *adj.*

ep·i·dur·al (éppi-déwr-ǝl ‖ -dóor-) *adj.* On or administered outside the dura mater. ～*n.* **1.** An injection of anaesthetic into the outer lining of the spinal cord. **2.** Anaesthesia resulting from such an injection. Also called "epidural anaesthesia". [EPI- + DURA (MATER) + -AL.]

ep·i·fo·cal (éppi-fōk'l) *adj. Geology.* Of, occurring at, or pertaining to an epicentre.

ep·i·gas·tri·um (éppi-gáss-tri-ǝm) *n., pl.* **-tria** (-tri-ǝ). The upper middle region of the abdomen. [New Latin, from Greek *epigastrion* : *epi-*, above + *gastrium*, diminutive of *gastēr*, stomach.] —**ep·i·gas·tric** *adj.*

ep·i·ge·al (éppi-jée-ǝl) *adj.* Also **e·pi·ge·an** (-ǝn), **e·pi·ge·ous** (-ǝss). **1.** *Botany.* Characterised by germination in which the cotyledons appear above the surface of the ground. Compare **hypogeal.** **2.** *Biology.* Living or occurring on or near the surface of the ground. [Greek *epigaios*, on the earth : *epi-*, on + *gaia, gē*, earth.]

ep·i·gene (éppi-jeen) *adj.* **1.** Formed, originating, or occurring on or just below the surface of the earth. **2.** Foreign; not natural to the material in which found. Said of crystals. [French *épigène*, from Greek *epigenēs*, arising after, from *epigignesthai*, to be born after : *epi-*, after + *gignesthai*, to be born.]

ep·i·gen·e·sis (éppi-jènnǝ-siss) *n.* **1.** *Biology.* The generally accepted theory that the individual is developed by structural elaboration of the unstructured egg rather than by a simple enlarging of a preformed entity. Compare **preformation.** **2.** *Geology.* Change in the mineral characteristics of a rock due to outside influence. [EPI- + -GENESIS.] —**ep·i·ge·net·ic** (-jǝ-néttik) *adj.*

e·pig·e·nous (i-píjǝnǝss) *adj. Botany.* Developing or growing on an upper surface, as fungi develop on leaves. [EPI- + -GENOUS.]

ep·i·glot·tis (éppi-glóttiss) *n., pl.* **-tises** or **-glottides** (-glótti-deez). An elastic cartilage, located at the root of the tongue, that folds over the glottis to prevent food from entering the windpipe during the act of swallowing. [New Latin, from Greek *epiglōttis* : *epi-*, over + *glōttis*, GLOTTIS.]

ep·i·gone (éppi-gōn) *n.* Also **ep·i·gon** (éppi-gon). A second-rate imitator or follower, as of an artist or philosopher. [Greek *Epigonoi*, sons of the Seven against Thebes who imitated their fathers by attacking Thebes, from the plural of *epigonos*, born after : EPI- + *gonos*, child.] —**ep·i·gon·ic** (-gónnik) *adj.*

ep·i·gram (éppi-gram) *n.* **1.** A concisely and cleverly worded statement, making a pointed observation and often concluding with a satirical twist. **2.** A short poem expressing a single thought or observation with terseness and wit. **3.** Discourse or expression by means of such statements. —See Synonyms at **saying.** [Old French *epigramme*, from Latin *epigramma*, from Greek, inscription, from *epigraphein*, to write on : *epi-*, on + *graphein*, to write.]

ep·i·gram·mat·ic (éppi-grǝ-máttik) *adj.* **1.** Of or having the nature of an epigram. **2.** Full of or given to the use of epigrams. —See Synonyms at **concise.** —**ep·i·gram·mat·i·cal·ly** *adv.*

ep·i·gram·ma·tize, ep·i·gram·ma·tise (éppi-grámmǝ-tīz) *v.* **-tised, -tising, -tises.** —*tr.* To express (a thought or sentiment) in an epigram or epigrams. —*intr.* To speak or write in epigrams. —**ep·i·gram·ma·tist** *n.*

ep·i·graph (éppi-graaf, -graf) *n.* **1.** An inscription, as on a statue or building. **2.** A motto or quotation at the beginning of a book or chapter, usually intended to give an idea of its theme. [Greek *epigraphē*, from *epigraphos*, written on, from *epigraphein*, to write on. See **epigram.**] —**ep·i·graph·ic** (-gráffik), **ep·i·graph·i·cal** *adj.* —**ep·i·graph·i·cal·ly** *adv.*

e·pig·ra·phy (i-píggrǝfi) *n.* **1.** Inscriptions collectively. **2. a.** The study of inscriptions. **b.** The interpretation of ancient inscriptions. Compare **palaeography.** —**e·pig·ra·pher, e·pig·ra·phist** *n.*

e·pig·y·ny (i-píjini) *n. Botany.* The condition in flowers when the petals, sepals, and male organs are above the female organs so that the ovary is enclosed by and fused with the tip of the flower stalk. [EPI- + -GYNY.] —**e·pig·y·nous** *adj.*

ep·i·lep·sy (éppi-lep-si) *n.* Any of various brain disorders characterised by sudden recurring attacks of motor, sensory, or psychic malfunction with or without unconsciousness or convulsive movements. See **grand mal, petit mal.** [Old French *epilepsie*, from Late Latin *epilēpsia*, from Greek, from *epilambanein* (stem *epilab-*), to seize upon : *epi-*, upon + *lambanein*, to take hold of.] —**ep·i·lep·tic** (-léptik) *n. & adj.*

ep·i·lep·toid (éppi-lép-toyd) *adj.* Resembling epilepsy or any of its symptoms. [*epilept*(ic) + -OID.]

ep·i·logue (éppi-log ‖ *U.S.* also -lawg) *n.* **1. a.** A short poem or speech spoken directly to the audience following the conclusion of a play. **b.** The performer or performers who speak this. **2.** A short addition or concluding section at the end of any literary work, often dealing with the future of its characters. **3.** *British.* A short religious programme at the end of a day's broadcasting. [Middle English *epiloge*, from Old French *epilogue*, from Latin *epilogus*, from Greek *epilogos*, from *epilegein*, to say more, to add : *epi-*, in addition + *legein*, to say.]

e·pim·er·ism (i-pímmǝr-iz'm) *n. Chemistry.* A form of optical isomerism in which isomers, called *epimers*, can form about asymmetric atoms. [EPI- + (ISO)MERISM.] —**ep·i·mer·ic** (éppi-mérrik) *adj.*

e·pi·my·si·um (éppi-mízzi-ǝm ‖ -mízhi-) *n., pl.* **-sia** (-ǝ). The fibrous sheath enclosing a muscle. [New Latin : EPI- + Greek *mus*, muscle.]

e·pi·nas·ty (éppi-nasti) *n., pl.* **-ties.** A downward bending of leaves or other plant parts, resulting from greater growth of the upper side compared with the lower side. [EPI- + -NASTY.] —**e·pi·nas·tic** (-nástik) *adj.*

ep·i·neph·rine (éppi-néf-rin, -reen) *n.* Also **ep·i·neph·rin** (-rin). *U.S.* **Adrenaline** *(see).* [EPI- + NEPHR(O)- + -INE.]

ep·i·neu·ri·um (éppi-néwr-i-ǝm ‖ -nóor-) *n., pl.* **-neuria** (-néwri-ǝ ‖ -nóori-ǝ). The connective tissue sheath surrounding the bundles of fibres that make up a nerve. [EPI- + NEUR(O)- + -IUM.] —**ep·i·neu·ri·al** *adj.*

e·piph·a·ny (i-píffǝni) *n., pl.* **-nies. 1.** A revelatory manifestation of a divine being. **2.** A spiritual event in which the essential nature of something appears to the subject, as in a sudden flash of recognition. **3.** A revelation or experience of insight. [Greek *epiphaneia*, manifestation; appearance, from *epiphanēs*, appearing, manifest, from *epiphainein*, to manifest : *epi-*, to + *phainein*, to show.]

E·piph·a·ny (i-píffǝni) *n.* A Christian festival held on January 6 in celebration of the manifestation of the divine nature of Christ to the Gentiles as represented by the Magi. Also called "Twelfth Night".

ep·i·phe·nom·e·nal·ism (éppifi-nómminǝ-liz'm) *n. Philosophy.* The doctrine that mental activities are simply epiphenomena of the neural processes of the brain and have no causal influence.

ep·i·phe·nom·e·non (éppifi-nómmi-nǝn, -non) *n., pl.* **-na** (-nǝ). **1.** A secondary phenomenon accompanying and resulting from another. **2.** *Pathology.* An unusual additional condition in the course of a disease, not necessarily connected with the disease. —**ep·i·phe·nom·e·nal** *adj.*

e·piph·y·sis (i-píffǝ-siss) *n., pl.* **-ses** (-seez). *Anatomy.* **1.** The end of a long bone, that is separated from the shaft by cartilage until growth is complete. **2.** The **pineal body** *(see).* [New Latin, from Greek *epiphusis*, a growth upon : *epi-*, upon + *phusis*, growth, from *phuein*, to grow.] —**ep·i·phys·i·al, ep·i·phys·e·al** (éppi-fízziǝl) *adj.*

ep·i·phyte (éppi-fīt) *n.* A plant, such as any of certain orchids or ferns, that grows on another plant or object upon which it depends for mechanical support but not as a source of nutrients. Also called "air plant", "aerophyte". [EPI- + -PHYTE.] —**ep·i·phyt·ic** (-fíttik), **ep·i·phyt·i·cal** *adj.*

e·pi·phy·tot·ic (éppi-fī-tóttik) *adj.* Of, pertaining to, or designating a sudden or abnormally destructive outbreak of a plant disease, usually over an extended geographical area. ～*n.* An outbreak of such a disease. [EPI- + PHYT(O)- + -OTIC.]

Epis. **1.** Episcopal; Episcopalian. **2.** Epistle.

Episc. Episcopal; Episcopalian.

e·pis·co·pa·cy (i-pískǝpǝ-si) *n., pl.* **-cies. 1.** An episcopate. **2.** The system of church government in which bishops are the chief ministers. [From EPISCOPATE.]

e·pis·co·pal (i-pískǝp'l) *adj.* **1.** Of or pertaining to a bishop or bishops. **2.** Of, having, or advocating church government by bishops. **3.** *Capital* E. *Abbr.* **Epis., Episc.** Designating or pertaining to the Anglican Communion, or a branch of it. [Middle English, from Old French, from Late Latin *episcopālis*, from *episcopus*, bishop, from Greek *episkopos*, overseer : *epi-*, over + *skopos*, watcher, seer.] —**e·pis·co·pal·ly** *adv.*

Episcopal Church *n.* Any of the branches of the Anglican Communion outside England, especially that in Scotland or, in the United States, the **Protestant Episcopal Church** *(see).*

e·pis·co·pa·li·an (i-pískǝ-páyli-ǝn) *adj.* **1.** Of or advocating church government by bishops; episcopal. **2.** *Capital* E. *Abbr.* **Epis., Episc.**

Of, pertaining to, or belonging to an Episcopal Church.
~*n.* **1.** An advocate of church government by bishops. **2.** *Capital* **E.** *Abbr.* **Epis., Episc.** A member or adherent of an Episcopal Church. **—e·pis·co·pa·li·an·ism** *n.*

e·pis·co·pal·ism (i-pískəpəl-iz'm) *n.* The belief that the power to govern the church should rest with bishops rather than laymen, elders, or a pope.

e·pis·co·pate (i-pískə-pət, -pit, -payt) *n.* **1.** The position or term of office of a bishop. **2.** The area of jurisdiction of a bishop; a diocese. **3.** Bishops collectively. [Late Latin *episcopātus,* from *episcopus,* bishop. See **episcopal.**]

ep·i·scope (éppi-skōp) *n.* An optical device for projecting onto a screen an enlarged image of an opaque object. Compare **epidiascope.** [EPI- + -SCOPE.]

ep·i·si·ot·o·my (i-pízzi-óttəmi) *n., pl.* **-mies.** A surgical incision into the tissues around the vagina during childbirth to enlarge the opening and make delivery easier. [Greek *epision,* pubic area + -TOMY.]

ep·i·sode (éppi-sōd) *n.* **1.** An incident or series of related events in the course of a continuous experience: *an episode from her childhood.* **2.** A portion of a narrative that relates an event or series of connected events and forms a coherent story in itself; an incident: *an episode of a picaresque novel.* **3.** A separately presented portion of a serialised novel, play, radio or television drama, or the like; an instalment. **4.** A section of a classical Greek tragedy that occurs between two choric songs. **5.** *Music.* A passage between statements of a main subject or theme, as in a rondo or fugue. —See Synonyms at **occurrence.** [Greek *epeisodion,* "addition", from *epeisodios,* coming in besides : *epi-,* besides + *eisodios,* coming in : *eis,* into + *hodos,* way, road.]

ep·i·sod·ic (éppi-sóddik) *adj.* Also **ep·i·sod·i·cal** (-'l). **1.** Pertaining to or resembling an episode; incidental. **2.** Proceeding by a series of episodes: *an episodic narrative.* **3.** Disjointed; not in a continuous sequence. **4.** Occasional, sporadic, or unpredictable. **—ep·i·sod·i·cal·ly** *adv.*

ep·i·spas·tic (éppi-spástik) *adj.* Causing blisters.
~*n.* A blistering agent; a vesicatory. [Greek *epispastikos,* drawing after (because blisters were thought to be humours drawn towards the skin), from *epispatos,* drawn, from *epispan,* to draw after one, attract : *epi-,* after + *span,* to draw (see **spasm**).]

Epist. Epistle.

e·pis·ta·sis (i-pístə-siss) *n., pl.* **-ses** (-seez). **1.** *Genetics.* A nonreciprocal interaction between non-allelic forms of gene in which one gene suppresses the expression of another affecting the same part of an organism. **2.** *Medicine.* The suppression of a secretion or discharge. **3.** The scum on the surface of a liquid such as stale urine. [New Latin, from Greek, stoppage, stopping, from *ephistanai,* to place upon, stop : *epi-,* upon + *histanai,* to place, set.] **—ep·i·stat·ic** (éppi-státtik) *adj.*

ep·i·stax·is (éppi-sták-siss) *n. Pathology.* A **nosebleed** *(see).* [New Latin, from Greek, "dropping", from *epistazein,* to let fall in drops upon : *epi-,* upon + *stazein,* to drip.]

e·pis·te·mol·o·gy (e-piss-tee-móllәji, i-, -tə-) *n., pl.* **-gies.** **1.** The division of philosophy that investigates the nature and origin of knowledge. **2.** A theory of the nature of knowledge. [Greek *epistēmē,* knowledge, understanding, from *epistanai,* "to stand upon", understand : *epi-,* upon + *histanai,* to stand, place + -LOGY.] **—e·pis·te·mo·log·i·cal** (-mə-lójik'l) *adj.* **—e·pis·te·mo·log·i·cal·ly** *adv.* **—e·pis·te·mol·o·gist** (-mólləjist) *n.*

e·pis·tle (i-píss'l) *n.* **1.** A letter, especially a formal one. Often used humorously. **2.** *Usually capital* **E.** *Abbr.* **Epis., Epist. a.** Any of the letters written by any of various Apostles or their helpers to early Christians and included in the New Testament. **b.** An excerpt from any of these letters, read as part of a religious service. **3.** A verse letter of the genre invented by Horace and imitated by poets of the 17th and 18th centuries. **4.** A prefatory dedication in the form of a letter. [Middle English, from Old French, from Latin *epistola,* from Greek *epistolē,* from *epistellein,* to send to : *epi-,* to + *stellein,* to send.]

e·pis·tler (i-pisslər, -pistlər) *n.* Also **e·pis·to·ler** (i-pístələr). **1.** A writer of epistles. **2.** *Usually capital* **E.** The person who reads the Epistle in a religious service.

Epistles General *pl.n.* The **Catholic Epistles** *(see).*

e·pis·to·lar·y (i-pístə-ləri || -lerri) *adj.* **1.** Of or associated with letters or letter writing. **2.** In the form of a letter or series of letters. Said of a literary work. **3.** Carried on by or made up of letters: *an epistolary friendship.* [Latin *epistolāris,* from *epistola,* EPISTLE.]

ep·i·style (éppi-stīl) *n. Architecture.* An **architrave** *(see).* [Latin *epistylium,* from Greek *epistulion* : *epi-,* upon + *stulos,* pillar.]

ep·i·taph (éppi-taaf, -taf) *n.* **1.** An inscription on a tombstone or monument in memory of the one or ones buried there. **2.** A brief literary piece summarising or epitomising a deceased person. **3.** A view expressed on someone or something considered as if dead: *an epitaph on her ex-husband.* [Middle English *epitaphe,* from Old French, from Latin *epitaphium,* funeral oration, from Greek *epitaphion,* neuter of *epitaphios,* "over a tomb" : *epi-,* over + *taphos,* tomb.] **—ep·i·taph·ic** (-táffik) *adj.*

e·pit·a·sis (i-píttə-siss) *n., pl.* **-ses** (-seez). The part of a play, especially in classical Greek drama, in which the plot develops towards its dénouement. [Greek, a stretching over, intensification, from *epiteinein,* to stretch over : *epi-,* over + *teinein,* to stretch.]

ep·i·tax·i·al (éppi-ták-si-əl) *adj.* **1.** Designating a thin layer on the surface of a crystal, especially one that has the same structure as the underlying crystal. **2.** Designating a transistor made by depositing such a layer of semiconductor on a crystal support. [EPI- + -TAXY + -AL.] **—ep·i·tax·y** (éppi-taksi), **ep·i·tax·is** *n.*

ep·i·tha·la·mi·um (éppi-thə-láy-mi-əm) *n., pl.* **-ums** or **-mia** (-mi-ə). A lyric ode in honour of a marriage. [Latin, from Greek *epithalamion,* from the neuter of *epithalamios,* belonging to a wedding : *epi-,* at + *thalamos,* bridal chamber (see **thalamus**).]

ep·i·the·li·o·ma (éppi-theéli-ṓ-mə) *n., pl.* **-mata** (-mətə) or **-mas.** A benign or malignant tumour derived from the epithelium. [New Latin : EPITHEL(IUM) + -OMA.] **—ep·i·the·li·om·a·tous** (-ómmə-təss, -ṓmə-) *adj.*

ep·i·the·li·um (éppi-theé-li-əm) *n., pl.* **-ums** or **-lia** (-li-ə). Membranous tissue, usually in a single layer, composed of closely arranged cells separated by very little intercellular substance and forming the covering of most internal surfaces and organs and the outer surface of an animal body. [New Latin : EPI- + Greek *thēlē,* nipple.] **—ep·i·the·li·al, ep·i·the·li·oid** *adj.*

ep·i·thet (éppi-thet) *n.* **1.** A term used to characterise the nature of a person or thing: *"Moderate" is a much misused epithet in politics.* **2.** An adjective or descriptive phrase that comes to form part of or to substitute for a person's name or title: *"The Lionheart" is an epithet for Richard I.* **3.** *Biology.* See **specific epithet.** **4.** An abusive or contemptuous word or phrase used to describe a person. [Latin *epitheton,* from Greek, "an addition", from *epitithenai,* to put on, add : *epi-,* on + *tithenai,* to place, put.] **—ep·i·thet·ic** (-théttik), **ep·i·thet·i·cal** *adj.*

e·pit·o·me (i-píttəmi) *n.* **1.** One that is perfectly and strikingly representative or expressive of an entire class or type; an embodiment: *Keats was the epitome of the Romantic poet.* **2.** A summary of a book, article, event, or the like; an abridgment; an abstract. [Latin *epitomē,* from Greek, from *epitemnein,* to cut upon the surface, cut short : *epi-,* upon + *temnein,* to cut.]

e·pit·o·mise, e·pit·o·mize (i-píttə-mīz) *tr.v.* **-mised, -mising, -mises.** **1.** To typify (an entire class, type, or quality); capture the essence of: *A baby epitomises innocence.* **2.** To make an epitome of; sum up.

ep·i·zo·ic (éppi-zṓ-ik) *adj.* Living or growing on the exterior of a living animal: *epizoic fungi.* [EPI- + -ZOIC.]

ep·i·zo·ot·ic (éppi-zō-óttik) *adj.* Attacking a large number of animals within a short time. Said of a disease.
~*n.* An epizootic disease. [EPI- + ZO(O)- + -OTIC.]

e plu·ri·bus u·num (ay-plóor-ibəss-yóo-nəm, ee-, -óo-). *Latin.* One out of many. The motto of the United States.

E.P.N.S. electroplated nickel silver.

ep·och (eé-pok || *Scottish* -pokh, *U.S. also* éppək) *n.* **1.** A period of history; especially, one characterised by particular remarkable events or by the predominance of a particular person, group, or state of affairs; an era. **2.** A point in time or progress that marks the beginning of such a period; a milestone; a breakthrough: *The addition of sound marked an epoch in film history.* **3.** *Geology.* A unit of geological time that is a division of a period. **4.** *Astronomy.* An instant in time that is arbitrarily selected as a reference point. [New Latin *epocha,* from Greek *epokhē,* pause.] **—ep·och·al** (ép-ok'l) *adj.*

ep·och-mak·ing (eépok-máyking) *adj.* Highly significant or important; momentous.

ep·ode (ép-ōd) *n.* **1.** The last strophe of the triad (strophe, antistrophe, and epode) that forms the basic compositional unit of the lyric ode. **2.** A lyric composition of a type invented by Archilochus and used by Horace, characterised by couplets of a long line followed by a shorter one. [Latin *epōdos,* from Greek *epōidos,* "a singing after", from *epaidein,* to sing after : *epi-,* after + *aidein,* to sing.]

ep·o·nym (éppə-nim) *n.* A real or mythical person whose name is or is thought to be the source of the name of a city, country, era, institution, or the like: *"Romulus" is the eponym of Rome.* [Greek *epōnumos,* EPONYMOUS.] **—ep·o·nym·ic** (-nimmik) *adj.*

e·pon·y·mous (i-pónniməss) *adj.* Of, pertaining to, or designating a person after whom something, such as a city, era, book, or play, is named or thought to be named: *In the film "Ben Hur", the eponymous hero was played by Charlton Heston.* [Greek *epōnumos* : *epi-,* to + *onoma,* name.]

e·pon·y·my (i-pónnimi) *n.* The derivation of the name of a city, country, era, institution, or the like, from that of a person.

ep·o·pee (ép-ə-pee, -ō-) *n.* **1.** Epic poetry, especially as a literary genre. **2.** An epic poem. [French *épopée,* from Greek *epopoiia,* from *epopoios,* epic poet : *epos,* word, EPIC + *poïein,* to make (see **poet**).]

ep·os (épposs) *n.* **1.** Oral epic poetry. **2.** An epic poem. [Latin, from Greek, word, poem.]

ep·ox·y (i-pók-si, éppok-) *adj.* Of, composed of, or containing a substance with a molecular structure in which an oxygen atom is joined to two different groups that are themselves joined to other groups.
~*n.* Any of various, usually thermosetting, resins capable of forming tough surface films and adhesives based on this structure. Also called "epoxy resin", "epoxide". [EP(I)- + OXY-.]

Ep·ping (épping). Town in Essex, now virtually a northeast suburb of London. It is famous for Epping Forest (2 270 hectares; 5,600 acres), formerly a royal hunting park.

ep·si·lon (ép-si-lon, ep-sī́lən) *n.* The fifth letter in the Greek alphabet, written Ε, ε. Transliterated in English as *E, e.* [Greek *e psilon,* "simple *e*", from *psilos,* mere, simple.]

Ep·som (épss'm). Town in Surrey, England, now part of the municipal borough of Epsom and Ewell. Its fame now rests with its racecourse, where the Derby is run annually.

Epsom salts *pl.n.* Hydrated **magnesium sulphate** *(see)* used for example as a cathartic and to reduce swellings. [After EPSOM, where it was originally obtained from a mineral spring.]

Ep·stein (ép-stīn), **Sir Jacob** (1880–1959). British sculptor, born in New York of Russian-Polish parents. He studied in Paris with Rodin before settling in England (1905). He became famous for his massive subjects in bronze and stone, among them the marble *Venus* (1917), a bronze *Christ* (1919), and the alabaster *Adam* (1939).

Ep·stein-Barr vi·rus (ép-stīn-bár) *n.* The virus that is believed to cause glandular fever. [After M.A. *Epstein* (1921–) and Y.M. *Barr* (1932–), British pathologists who discovered it.]

eq. 1. equal. 2. equation. 3. equivalent.

eq·ua·ble (ék-wə-b'l ‖ éek-) *adj.* 1. Unvarying; uniform: *an equable climate.* 2. Tranquil; serene; even-tempered. —See Synonyms at **steady.** [Latin *aequābilis,* from *aequāre,* to make even, from *aequus,* level, even, EQUAL.] —**eq·ua·bil·i·ty** (-billəti), **eq·ua·ble·ness** *n.* —**eq·ua·bly** *adv.*

e·qual (éekwəl) *adj. Abbr.* **eq.** 1. Having the same capability, quantity, or effect as another: *equal strength.* 2. *Mathematics.* Related by a reflexive, symmetrical, and transitive relationship; broadly, alike or in agreement in a specific sense with respect to specific properties. 3. Having the same privileges, status, or rights: *equal before the law.* 4. Fairly and evenly available or granted: *equal rights.* 5. Fairly and evenly balanced: *an equal contest.* 6. **a.** Having the requisite strength, ability, determination, or the like: *"Elizabeth found herself quite equal to the scene"* (Jane Austen). **b.** Adequate in extent, amount, or degree: *money equal to their needs.* 7. *Literary.* Impartial; just; equitable: *equal laws.* 8. *Archaic.* Tranquil; calm; equable. —See Synonyms at **same.**

~*n.* A person or thing that is equal to another, especially: 1. One who is equal in rank or status. 2. A worthy substitute or rival: *I am his equal in every respect.*

~*tr.v.* **equalled** or *U.S.* **equaled, equalling** or *U.S.* **equaling, equals.** 1. To be equal to, especially in amount or value. 2. To do, make, or produce something equal to: *He equalled the world record for the mile.* —**equal out.** To reach a point of equilibrium; become equal. [Latin *aequālis,* from *aequus†,* even, level.]

Usage: The main problem is whether *equal* can be used along with *more* and *most.* Purists point out that if two things are equal then one cannot be more equal than the other. But sentences such as *There is a more equal balance of marks/a more equal distribution of wealth* are possible, with *equal* having the sense "more equitable" or "more nearly equal." *Most* is less often encountered, but is still possible in such sentences as *That's the most equal division of opinion I have ever seen.*

Equally gives rise to two problems. It is often used with *as: Equally as interesting is his new book* would be reduced in careful usage to either *Equally interesting . . .* or *As interesting . . .* It is usual to use *as* when a comparison is explicit, and *equally* when it is not: *His new book is equally interesting, His new book is as interesting as his earlier books,* but not *His new book is equally interesting as his earlier books.* When comparisons are made like those in the sentence *The device is equally useful inside and outside the house, equally . . .* demonstrates more respect for careful usage than the informal *equally . . . or.*

e·qual-a·re·a projection (éekwəl-áir-i-ə) *n.* A map projection reproducing the same area ratios as exist on the earth's surface. Also called "homolographic projection".

e·qual·ise, e·qual·ize (éekwə-līz) *v.* **-ised, -ising, -ises.** —*tr.* 1. To make equal. 2. To make uniform. —*intr. Sports.* To even the score, as by scoring a goal.

e·qual·is·er (éekwə-līzər) *n.* 1. One that equalises, especially: **a.** A device for equalising pressure or strain. **b.** In sport, a goal, try, or the like that makes the score even. 2. *Electronics.* A network in a transmission system, used to reduce distortion. 3. *U.S. Slang.* A weapon; especially, a revolver.

e·qual·i·ty (i-kwólləti) *n., pl.* **-ties.** 1. The state or an instance of being equal; especially, the state of enjoying equal rights in political, economic, and social affairs. 2. A mathematical statement, usually an equation, that one thing equals another. [Middle English *equalite,* from Old French, from Latin *aequālitās,* from *aequālis,* EQUAL.]

e·qual·ly (éekwə-li) *adv.* 1. In an equal or even manner. 2. To an equal degree: *applies equally to children and adults; could equally have been an accident.* 3. On the other hand; as an alternative possibility: *Solitude is welcome: equally, I enjoy good company.*

Equal Opportunities Employer *n.* An employer that does not discriminate against job applicants, especially on the grounds of race, religion or sex. Also, *chiefly U.S.,* "Equal Opportunity Employer".

Equal Rights Amendment *n. Abbr.* **ERA** A proposed amendment to the U.S. constitution to guarantee equal rights in law to both sexes.

equal sign *n.* Also **equals sign.** The symbol (=) used, especially in an equation, to indicate that one thing is logically or mathematically equal to another.

equal temperament *n. Music.* The tuning of keyboard instruments to produce octaves of 12 equal semitones and permit the modulation of harmony. Also called "temperament".

e·qua·nim·i·ty (éekwə-nímməti, ékwə-) *n.* The quality or characteristic of being calm and even-tempered; composure. [Latin *aequanimitās,* from *aequanimis,* even-tempered : *aequus,* even, EQUAL + *animus,* mind.] —**e·quan·i·mous** (i-kwán-iməss, -kwón-) *adj.*

Synonyms: equanimity, composure, sang-froid, serenity.

e·quate (i-kwáyt) *v.* **equated, equating, equates.** —*tr.* 1. To make,

treat, or regard as equal or equivalent: *Many people equate wisdom with old age.* 2. To reduce to a standard or average; equalise or stabilise; balance: *equate profit and loss.* 3. To show or state the equality of; express in or as if in an equation. —*intr.* To be or seem to be equal; correspond; accord: *She equates easily with our conception of classic beauty.* [Middle English *equaten,* from Latin *aequāre,* from *aequus,* EQUAL.]

e·qua·tion (i-kwáy-zh'n, -sh'n) *n. Abbr.* **eq.** 1. The process or act of equating or of being equated. 2. The state of being equal; a balanced state; equilibrium. 3. *Mathematics.* A linear array of mathematical symbols separated into left and right sides that are designated at least conditionally equal by an equal sign. 4. Broadly, a concept of equivalence or balance between a variety of factors: *Salaries have risen dramatically, but on the other side of the equation there has been a comparable rise in output.* 5. *Chemistry.* A symbolic representation of a chemical reaction as a linear array of symbols for the reacting atomic and molecular species, separated into left and right sides by an equal sign, arrow, or opposing arrows. 6. A factor or consideration that must be taken into account, especially a **personal equation** or a **human equation** (*both of which see*). —**e·qua·tion·al** *adj.* —**e·qua·tion·al·ly** *adv.*

e·qua·tor (i-kwáytər) *n.* 1. *Sometimes capital* **E.** The great circle circumscribing the earth's surface, the reckoning datum of latitudes and the dividing boundary of Northern and Southern Hemispheres, formed by the intersection of a plane passing through the earth's centre perpendicular to its axis of rotation. 2. Any similar great circle drawn on the surface of a celestial body at right angles to the axis of rotation. 3. The **magnetic equator** (*see*). 4. *Astronomy.* The **celestial equator** (*see*). [Middle English, from Medieval Latin (*circulus*) *aequator (diei et noctis),* (circle) equalising (day and night), from Latin *aequāre,* EQUATE.]

e·qua·to·ri·al (ék-wə-táwri-əl, éek- ‖ -tōri-) *adj.* 1. Of or pertaining to the equator. 2. Characteristic of or existing at or near the earth's equator: *equatorial climate; equatorial rain forests.* 3. Lying in the same plane on the equator: *an equatorial orbit.* 4. Having a support with two perpendicular axes, one of which is parallel to the earth's rotational axis. Said of a telescope.

~*n. Astronomy.* An equatorial telescope. —**e·qua·to·ri·al·ly** *adv.*

Equatorial Guinea, Republic of. Formerly **Spanish Guinea.** Country of West Africa. Most of the people are subsistence farmers, but cocoa, coffee and hardwoods are exported. The country gained independence from Spain in 1968, but relied on Spanish, Soviet, and Chinese aid. Area, 28 051 square kilometres (10,828 square miles). Population, 410,000. Capital, Malabo.

eq·uer·ry (i-kwérri, ékwəri) *n., pl.* **-ries.** 1. An attendant to the British royal household. 2. Formerly, an officer charged with supervision of the horses belonging to a royal or noble household. [Earlier *escurie,* from obsolete French *escuirie†,* stable, mistakenly associated with Latin *equus,* horse.]

e·ques·tri·an (i-kwéstri-ən) *adj.* 1. Of or pertaining to horsemanship. 2. Depicting or representing the subject on horseback: *the equestrian statue of Charles I.* 3. Of, pertaining to, or composed of knights, horsemen, cavalry, or the like: *equestrian troops.*

~*n.* One who rides a horse or performs on horseback. [Latin *equester,* from *equus,* horse.]

e·ques·tri·enne (i-kwéstri-én) *n.* A female equestrian.

equi– *comb. form.* Indicates equality; for example, **equiangular.** [Middle English *equi-,* from Latin *aequi-,* from *aequus,* EQUAL.]

e·qui·an·gu·lar (éekwi-áng-gewlər ‖ ékwi-) *adj.* Having all angles equal.

e·qui·dis·tant (éekwi-distənt ‖ ékwi-) *adj.* Equally distant. —**e·qui·dis·tance** *n.* —**e·qui·dis·tant·ly** *adv.*

e·qui·lat·er·al (éekwi-láttrəl, -láttərəl ‖ ékwi-) *adj.* Having all sides or faces equal.

~*n.* 1. A side exactly equal to others. 2. A geometrical figure having equal sides. —**e·qui·lat·er·al·ly** *adv.*

e·qui·li·brant (i-kwíllibrənt) *n.* A force capable of balancing a system of forces to produce equilibrium. [EQUILIBR(ATE) + -ANT.]

e·qui·li·brate (éekwi-lī-brayt, i-kwilli-) *v.* **-brated, -brating, -brates.** —*intr.* To be in or bring about equilibrium. —*tr.* To maintain in or bring into equilibrium. [Latin *aequilibrāre,* to balance, from *aequilībris,* in perfect balance, from *aequilibrium,* EQUILIBRIUM.] —**e·qui·li·bra·tion** (-bráysh'n) *n.*

e·qui·li·bra·tor (i-kwilli-braytər, éekwi-lī-) *n.* A device that brings about and helps maintain equilibrium.

e·qui·li·brist (i-kwilli-brist) *n.* A person who performs feats of balance, such as tightrope walking. [French *équilibriste,* from Latin *aequilibrium,* EQUILIBRIUM.] —**e·qui·li·bris·tic** (-brístik) *adj.*

e·qui·lib·ri·um (éekwi-líbbri-əm ‖ ékwi-) *n.* 1. Any condition in which all acting influences are cancelled by others resulting in a stable, balanced, or unchanging state. 2. *Physics.* The condition of a system in which the resultant of all acting forces is zero and the sum of all torques about any axis is zero. 3. *Chemistry.* The state of a reaction in which its forward and reverse reactions occur at equal rates so that the concentration of the reactants does not change with time. 4. Mental or emotional balance; psychological stability. [Latin *aequilibrium,* even balance : EQUI- + *libra,* balance.]

e·qui·mo·lec·u·lar (éekwi-mə-léckewlər ‖ ékwi-) *adj.* Designating solutions, substances, or the like that contain equal numbers of molecules.

e·quine (ék-wīn, éek-) *adj.* 1. Of, pertaining to, or characteristic of a horse. 2. Of or belonging to the family Equidae, which includes the horses, asses, and zebras.

~n. A member of the Equidae. [Latin *equīnus,* from *equus,* horse.]

e·qui·noc·tial (éekwi-nóksh'l, ékwi-) *adj.* **1.** Pertaining to or occurring at an equinox. **2.** Pertaining to the celestial equator. **3.** *Botany.* Having or characterising flowers that open and close at specific times.

~n. **1.** *Meteorology.* A violent storm of wind and rain reputed to occur at or near the time of the equinox. **2.** The equinoctial circle. [Middle English *equinoxial,* from Old French, from Latin *aequinoctiālis,* from *aequinoctium,* EQUINOX.]

equinoctial circle *n.* The **celestial equator** *(see).* Also called "equinoctial", "equinoctial line".

e·qui·nox (éekwi-noks, ékwi-) *n.* **1.** Either of two points on the celestial sphere at which the ecliptic intersects the celestial equator. **2.** Either of the two times during a year when the sun crosses the celestial equator, and when the length of day and night are approximately equal all over the Earth: the **vernal equinox** and the **autumnal equinox** *(both of which see).* [Middle English *equinox,* from Old French, from Medieval Latin *aequinoxium,* variant of Latin *aequinoctium* : EQUI- + *nox* (stem *noct-*), night.]

e·quip (i-kwíp) *tr.v.* **equipped, equipping, equips.** **1.** To supply with material necessities such as tools, gear, provisions, or furnishings. **2.** To prepare in an intellectual, emotional, or spiritual way: *His training equipped him for such problems.* **3.** To dress or array. [Old French *eschiper, e(s)quiper,* to put to sea, embark, from Germanic.]

eq·ui·page (ékwipij) *n.* **1.** Equipment or furnishings, especially of a military unit or ship; accoutrements. **2.** A carriage that is elegantly equipped, as with caparisoned horses and liveried footmen. **3.** Any carriage. **4.** *Archaic.* A retinue, as of a person of royalty or nobility. **5.** *Archaic.* A set of articles, such as a dinner service or collection of jewellery.

e·quip·ment (i-kwípmənt) *n.* **1.** The act of equipping or the state of being equipped. **2.** Something material with which a person, organisation, or thing is equipped; especially, the tools, apparatus, or the like required for a particular job or purpose: *camping equipment.* **3.** A person's intellectual or emotional resources.

e·qui·poise (ékwi-poyz, éekwi-) *n.* **1.** Equality in distribution, as of weight, relationship, or emotional forces; balance; equilibrium. **2.** A counterpoise; a counterbalance.

~tr.v. **equipoised, -poising, -poises.** To counterbalance.

e·qui·pol·lence (éekwi-póllənss, ékwi-) *n.* Also **e·qui·pol·len·cy** (-póllən-si). Equality, as in effectiveness or validity; equivalence.

e·qui·pol·lent (éekwi-póllənt, ékwi-) *adj.* **1.** Equal in power, effectiveness, significance, or the like. **2.** *Logic.* Expressing the same thing; validly derived from each other. Said of two propositions. **3.** Equivalent.

~n. An equivalent. [Middle English *equipollent,* from Old French, from Latin *aequipollēns* (stem *aequipollent-*) : EQUI- + *pollēns,* present participle of *pollēre*†, to be powerful.]

e·qui·pon·der·ate (éekwi-póndə-rayt || ékwi-) *tr.v.* **-ated, -ating, -ates.** **1.** To counterbalance. **2.** To give equal balance or weight to. [Medieval Latin *aequiponderāre* : EQUI- + Latin *ponderāre,* to weigh.]

e·qui·po·ten·tial (éekwi-pə-ténsh'l, éckwi-, -pō-) *adj.* **1.** Having equal potential. **2.** *Physics.* Having the same potential at every point: *an equipotential surface.*

eq·ui·se·tum (ékwi-séetəm) *n.* Any pteridophyte plant of the genus *Equisetum,* comprising the horsetails. [New Latin, from Latin *equisaetum,* the horsetail : *equus,* horse + *saeta,* bristle, SETA.]

eq·ui·ta·ble (ékwitəb'l) *adj.* **1.** Exhibiting or characterised by equity; impartial or reasonable in judgment or treatment; fair; just. **2.** *Law.* Concerned with or valid in equity, as distinguished from statute and common law. —See Synonyms at **fair.** [French *équitable,* from Old French, from *equite,* EQUITY.] —**eq·ui·ta·ble·ness** *n.* —**eq·ui·ta·bly** *adv.*

eq·ui·tant (ékwit'nt) *adj. Botany.* Overlapping at the base to form a flat, fanlike arrangement, as the leaves of some irises do. [Latin *equitāns* (stem *equitant-*), present participle of *equitāre,* to ride, from *eques* (stem *equit-*), horseman, from *equus,* horse.]

eq·ui·ta·tion (ékwi-táysh'n) *n.* The art or practice of riding a horse; horsemanship. [Old French, from Latin *equitātiō* (stem *equitātiōn-*), riding, from *equitāre,* to ride. See **equitant.**]

eq·ui·ty (ékwəti) *n., pl.* **-ties.** **1.** The state, ideal, or quality of being just, impartial, and fair. **2.** Something that is just, impartial, and fair. **3.** The residual value of a business or property beyond any mortgage thereon and liability therein. **4.** *Plural.* Ordinary shares in a company. **5.** *Law.* **a.** An organised body of legal rules based ultimately on principles of natural justice, and applied either to cover cases not foreseen by common or statute law or to modify the rigour of common or statute law. **b.** An equitable right or claim. **6.** *Law.* Equity of redemption. **7.** *Capital* **E.** *British.* The actors' trade union. [Middle English *equite,* from Old French, from Latin *aequitās* (stem *aequitāt-*), from *aequus,* EQUAL.]

equity of redemption *n. Law.* The right of one who has mortgaged his property to redeem that property upon payment of the sum due within a reasonable amount of time after the due date. Also called "equity".

equity stock *n. U.S.* **Ordinary shares** *(see).*

equiv. equivalent.

e·quiv·a·lence (i-kwívvə-lənss) *n.* Also **e·quiv·a·len·cy** (-lən-si) *pl.* **-cies.** **1.** The state or condition of being equivalent; equality. **2.** *Mathematics.* A reflexive, symmetric, and transitive relation between elements of a set that establishes any two elements in the set as equivalent or non-equivalent. In this sense, also called "equivalence relationship". **3.** *Logic.* **a.** The relationship between two propositions having the same truth-value. **b.** The relationship between two propositions such that for one to be true and the other false gives rise to a contradiction. Compare **biconditional.**

e·quiv·a·lent (i-kwívvələnt; éekwi-váylənt *for sense 4 only*) *adj. Abbr.* **eq., equiv.** **1. a.** Equal in substance, degree, value, force, or meaning. **b.** Having similar or identical effects. **2.** Virtually the same; tantamount. Used with *to* : *This request was equivalent to an order.* **3.** *Mathematics.* **a.** Capable of being put into a one-to-one relationship. Said of two sets. **b.** Broadly, having identical corresponding parts. **c.** Equal. **4.** *Chemistry.* Having the same ability to combine. **5.** *Logic.* Exhibiting equivalence. Said of propositions. —See Synonyms at **same.**

~n. Abbr. **eq., equiv.** **1.** That which is equivalent. **2.** *Chemistry.* Equivalent weight. [Middle English, from Old French, from Late Latin *aequivalēns* (stem *aequivalent-*), present participle of *aequivalēre,* to be equal in value : EQUI- + *valēre,* to be strong, be worth.] —**e·quiv·a·lent·ly** *adv.*

equivalent weight *n.* The number of parts by weight of any element combining with or replacing the equivalent of half the atomic weight of oxygen or one atomic weight of hydrogen. Also called "combining weight", "equivalent".

e·quiv·o·cal (i-kwívvək'l) *adj.* **1.** Capable of two interpretations; ambiguous: *an equivocal statement.* **2.** Of uncertain nature; indeterminate: *an equivocal result.* **3.** Misleading; evasive. **4.** Of questionable integrity: *an equivocal sort of man.* —See Synonyms at **ambiguous.** [Late Latin *aequivocus* : EQUI- + Latin *vōx* (stem *vōc-*), voice.] —**e·quiv·o·cal·ly** *adv.* —**e·quiv·o·cal·ness** *n.*

e·quiv·o·cate (i-kwívvə-kayt) *intr.v.* **-cated, -cating, -cates.** To use equivocal language intentionally; hedge. [Middle English *equivocaten,* from Medieval Latin *aequivocāre,* from Late Latin *aequivocus,* EQUIVOCAL.] —**e·quiv·o·ca·tion** (-káysh'n) *n.*

eq·ui·voque, eq·ui·voke (ékwi-vōk) *n.* **1.** A play on words; a pun. **2.** Double meaning. [French *équivoque,* from adjective, EQUIVOCAL.]

E·quu·le·us (i-kwóō-li-əss, -kwóō-) *n.* A constellation in the equatorial region of the Northern Hemisphere near Delphinus and Pegasus. [Latin, diminutive of *equus,* horse.]

Er The symbol for the element erbium.

ER endoplasmic reticulum.

-er[1] *n. suffix.* **1.** Indicates: **a.** Someone who or something that performs the specified action; for example, **helper, blender. b.** Someone performing or involved with a specified occupation or function; for example, **photographer, bookkeeper. c.** Geographical origin or residence; for example, **New Zealander, northerner. d.** Nature or appearance; for example, **two-seater, no-hoper. 2.** Used to form informal versions of certain words; for example, **rugger** instead of **rugby.** [Middle English *-ere, -er,* Old English *-ere,* from Common Germanic *-ārjaz* (unattested), from Latin *-ārius.* See **-ary.**]

-er[2], **-r** *adj. & adv. suffix.* Used to form the comparative degree of adjectives and adverbs; for example, **whiter, slower.** [Middle English *-ere, -re,* Old English *-re, -ra.*]

-er[3] *v. suffix.* Used to form verbs indicating frequent or recurrent action or sound; for example, **quaver, twitter.** [Middle English *-rien, -ren,* Old English *-rian, -erian.*]

e·ra (éer-ə || *U.S. also* érrə) *n.* **1.** A period of time that utilises a specific point in history as the basis of its chronology: *After 1492, a new era in the history of mankind began.* **2.** A period of time that is distinctive or notable because of its new or different aspects, events, or personages: *the era of the computer.* **3.** The beginning or onset of such a period of time; a turning point or milestone; an epoch. **4.** *Geology.* The longest division of geological time comprising one or more periods. [Late Latin *aera,* era, from Latin, "counters for calculating", a number as a basis for calculating, an era from which time is reckoned, from *aes* (stem *aer-*), brass, copper, money.]

ERA Equal Rights Amendment.

e·ra·di·ate (i-ráydi-ayt, ee-) *v.* **-ated, -ating, -ates.** *—tr.* To send out (radiation); radiate. *—intr.* To emanate. [EX- + RADIATE.] —**e·ra·di·a·tion** (-áysh'n) *n.*

e·rad·i·cate (i-ráddi-kayt) *tr.v.* **-cated, -cating, -cates.** **1.** To remove all traces of; totally remove: *eradicate corruption.* **2.** To pull or tear up by the roots; uproot. —See Synonyms at **abolish.** [Latin *ērādicāre,* to pluck up by the roots, to root out : *ē-,* out, from *ex-* + *rādix* (stem *rādic-*), root.] —**e·rad·i·ca·ble** *adj.* —**e·rad·i·ca·tion** (-káysh'n) *n.* —**e·rad·i·ca·tive** (-kətiv, -kaytiv) *adj.* —**e·rad·i·ca·tor** (-kaytər) *n.*

e·rase (i-ráyz || *chiefly U.S.* i-ráyss) *tr.v.* **erased, erasing, erases.** **1.** To remove; rub, wipe, scrape, or blot out; efface. **2. a.** To remove (a sound recording) from magnetic tape. **b.** To remove a sound recording from (magnetic tape). **3.** To remove (information) from a computer memory. **4.** To destroy all traces of: *a civilisation erased by time.* [Latin *ērādere* (past participle *ērāsus*), to scrape out, scrape off : *ex-,* out + *rādere,* to scrape.] —**e·ras·a·ble** *adj.*

Synonyms: *erase, expunge, efface, delete, cancel, blot out.*

e·ras·er (i-ráyzər || i-ráy-sər) *n.* Something used for erasing writing, especially a rubber.

e·ra·sion (i-ráyzh'n) *n.* **1.** An act of erasing. **2.** *Surgery.* The removal of diseased tissue, especially bone, by scraping.

Er·a·sis·tra·tus of Ce·os (érrə-sístrətəss; sée-oss). (*fl.* third century B.C.). Greek physician who described with great accuracy (derived from surgery and post-mortem examinations) many vital organs, especially the heart and liver. He also correctly distinguished between motor and sensory nerves.

E·ras·mus (i-rázməss), **Desiderius** (c.1466–1536). Dutch scholar and humanist who worked to revive classical texts from antiquity and to restore simple Christian faith by the study of the Scriptures. His books *In Praise of Folly* (1509) and *The Handbook of a Christian Knight* (1503) exposed the worldliness of the medieval church. —**E·ras·mi·an** *n. & adj.*

E·ras·ti·an·ism (i-rásti-ə-niz'm) *n.* A doctrine attributed to the Swiss theologian Thomas Erastus (1524–83) of the submission of the church to civil authority in all matters. —**E·ras·ti·an** *adj. & n.*

e·ra·sure (i-ráyzhər || i-ráyshər) *n.* 1. An act of erasing. 2. Something that has been erased; a deletion.

Er·a·to (érrə-tō). *Greek Mythology.* The Muse of lyric poetry. [Latin *Eratō*, from Greek, from *eratos*, loved, from *eran*, to love, akin to *erōs†*, love.]

E·ra·tos·the·nes of Cyrene (érrə-tósthi-neez). (c. 276–c. 194 B.C.). Greek astronomer. He was the first man known to have measured the circumference of the Earth, by measuring the Sun's position at the summer solstice at different places.

er·bi·um (érbi-əm) *n. Symbol* **Er** A soft, malleable, silvery rare-earth element, used in metallurgy, nuclear research, and to colour glass and porcelain. [New Latin, after *Ytterby*, Sweden, where it was discovered.]

ere (air) *prep. Archaic.* Previous to; before.
~*conj. Archaic.* 1. Before. 2. Sooner than; rather than. [Middle English *ar, er,* Old English *ær,* before.]

Er·e·bus¹ (érribəss). *Greek Mythology.* The dark region beneath the earth through which the dead must pass before they reach Hades. [Latin, from Greek *Erebos.*]

Erebus². Volcanic mountain (3 743 metres; 12,280 feet) on Ross Island, in the Ross Sea, east Antarctica. It was discovered in 1841 by the British explorer, James Ross.

e·rect (i-rékt) *adj.* 1. Directed or pointing upwards; standing upright; vertical: *erect posture.* 2. Being in a stiff, rigid condition: *every hair erect.* 3. *Physiology.* In erection. Said of parts of the body. 4. *Archaic.* Wide-awake; alert.
~*v.* **erected, erecting, erects.** —*tr.* 1. To raise (a building, for example); construct: *erect a skyscraper.* 2. To raise upright; set on end; lift up: *erect a Christmas tree for decorating.* 3. To put together; fashion; assemble: *erect a child's model airport; erect a theory.* 4. To set up; establish: *erect a dynasty.* 5. To transform and exalt: *He erected the editorial into an art form.* 6. *Geometry.* To construct (an altitude, for example) from or upon a given base. —*intr. Physiology.* To become rigid and upright by filling with blood. [Middle English, from Latin *ērectus,* past participle of *ērigere,* to raise up, set erect : *ē-,* out, up, from *ex-* + *regere,* to direct, to set.] —**e·rect·ly** *adv.* —**e·rect·ness** *n.*

e·rec·tile (i-rék-tīl || U.S. -t'l) *adj.* 1. Able to be erected or raised upright. 2. *Physiology.* Of or pertaining to vascular tissue, such as that of the penis and the clitoris, that is capable of filling with blood and becoming rigid. —**e·rec·til·i·ty** (-tílliti) *n.*

e·rec·tion (i-réksh'n) *n.* 1. The act of erecting. 2. The state of being erected. 3. Something erected; especially, a construction or edifice. 4. *Physiology.* **a.** The firm and enlarged condition of erectile tissue when filled with blood. **b.** The process of filling with blood. **c.** An erect penis.

e·rec·tor (i-réktər) *n.* 1. One that erects. 2. *Anatomy.* Any muscle that holds up or causes the erection of a body part.

E region *n.* A layer of the ionosphere; the **E layer** *(see).*

er·e·mite (érri-mīt) *n.* A person who isolates himself from society, especially as a religious recluse. [Middle English *(h)ermite,* HERMIT.] —**er·e·mit·ic** (-míttik), **er·e·mit·i·cal, er·e·mit·ish** (-mítish) *adj.*

e·rep·sin (i-rép-sin) *n.* A mixture of peptidases in the small intestine that breaks down proteins into amino acids. [Probably Latin *ēr(ipere),* to snatch away : *ē-,* away, from *ex-* + *rapere,* to snatch.]

er·e·thism (érri-thiz'm) *n.* Abnormal irritability and sensitivity to stimulation in any part of the body. [French *éréthisme,* from Greek *erethismos,* irritation, annoyance, from *erethizein, erethein†,* to irritate, stir.] —**er·e·this·mic** (-thízmik) *adj.*

erf (erf, airf) *n., pl.* **erven** (-'n, erv'n, airv'n). *South African.* An urban building plot. [Afrikaans, from Dutch, "inheritance".]

erg¹ (erg) *n.* A centimetre-gram-second unit of energy or work equal to the work done by a force of one dyne acting over a distance of one centimetre. [Greek *ergon,* work.]

erg² *n.* An area of shifting sand dunes in the Sahara desert. [Arabic *'irj.*]

er·go (érgō) *conj.* Consequently; therefore.
~*adv.* Consequently; hence. [Latin *ergō,* therefore.]

er·go·cal·cif·er·ol (ergō-kal-síffə-rol || -rōl) *n.* Any of the forms in which **vitamin D** *(see)* occurs. [*Ergot* + *calciferol.*]

er·go·graph (érg-ə-graaf, -ō-, -graf) *n.* A device for determining the work performed by muscles and their rate of fatigue, used especially in athletics training. [Greek *ergon,* work (see **erg**) + -GRAPH.]

er·gom·e·ter (er-gómmitər) *n.* A **dynamometer** *(see).* [Greek *ergon,* work (see **erg**) + -METER.]

er·go·nom·ics (erg-ə-nómmiks, -ō-) *n.* The study of the application of biology and engineering to the relationship between workers and their environment. Also *U.S.* "biotechnology".

er·gos·ter·ol (er-gósta-rol || -rōl) *n.* A plant sterol, $C_{28}H_{44}O$, converted by ultraviolet radiation to vitamin D_2. [*Ergot* + *sterol.*]

er·got (ér-gət, -got) *n.* 1. Any fungus of the genus *Claviceps,* especially *C. purpurea,* infecting various cereal plants, and forming black sclerotia, or compact masses of branching filaments, that replace many of the seeds of the host plant. 2. The disease caused by such a fungus. 3. The dried sclerotia of such a fungus, usually obtained from rye seed, and used as a source of several medicinally important alkaloids and as the basic source of lysergic acid. [French, "cock's spur", which the fungus resembles, from Old French *argor, argot†.*]

er·got·ism (érgə-tiz'm) *n.* Poisoning by ergot-infected grain, notably rye, characterised by gangrene and in some cases convulsions and mental disturbance. Also called "St. Anthony's fire".

Er·hard (áir-haart), **Ludwig** (1897–1977). Chancellor of the Federal Republic of Germany (1963–66). As minister for economic affairs (1949–63), he was the chief architect of the so-called "German economic miracle".

er·i·ca (érrikə) *n.* Any shrub of the genus *Erica,* which includes the heathers and heaths. [Latin, from Greek *ereikē,* heath.]

Er·ic the Red (érrik) (*fl.* tenth century). Norse chieftain who in c.982 sailed west and discovered Greenland. Four years later he established a small colony of about 500 people there.

E·rid·a·nus (e-rídd'n-əss) *n.* A constellation located in the Southern Hemisphere near Orion and Fornax and containing the star Achernar. [Greek *Ēridanos,* a mythical river associated with the myth of Phaethon.]

E·rie (éer-i). The fourth largest of the Great Lakes between central Canada and the United States.

Er·in (érrin). *Poetic.* The island of Ireland. [Middle English *Erin,* from Old Irish *Ērinn,* dative of *Ēriu,* Ireland.]

E·rin·y·es (i-rínni-eez) *pl.n. Greek Mythology.* The Furies. [Latin *Erīnyes,* from Greek *Erinues,* plural of *Erinust†,* a Fury.]

e·ris·tic (e-rístik, i-) *adj.* 1. Of or relating to argument, controversy, or discord. 2. Given to argument or dispute, especially when specious; disputatious.
~*n.* 1. One given to or expert in argument or dispute. 2. The art or practice of debate. [Greek *eristikos,* eager for strife, from *erizein,* to strive, wrangle, from *eris,* strife, discord.]

Er·i·tre·a (érri-tráy-ə, -tree-ə). Republic, former province of Ethiopia, mainly desert, bordering the Red Sea. In 1890 it was proclaimed an Italian colony and was used as the stepping-off point for Italy's conquest of Ethiopia in 1935–36. From 1941 to 1952 it was administered by Britain. It then federated with Ethiopia, and by 1962 it had become an integral part of Ethiopia. Eritrean rebels fought to win their independence, gaining it in 1993. Area, 121 144 square kilometres (46,774 square miles). Population, 3,280,000. Capital, Asmara. See map at **Ethiopia.** —**Er·i·tre·an** *n. & adj.*

erk (erk) *n. British Slang.* 1. A rating in the navy or an aircraftman in the Royal Air Force. 2. A person one dislikes. [20th century : perhaps a corruption of *A.C.* (aircraftman).]

Er·len·mey·er flask (érlən-mīər) *n.* A conical laboratory flask with a narrow neck and flat, broad bottom. [Originated by Emil *Erlenmeyer* (1825–1909), German chemist.]

erl·king (érl-king) *n.* An evil spirit of Germanic mythology and folklore, typically represented as abducting children to the land of death. [Partial translation of German *Erlkönig,* "king of alders", coined by the 18th century German writer J.G. von Herder in a misunderstanding of Danish *ellerkonge,* variant of *elverkonge,* elf-king : *elver,* elf + *konge,* king.]

ERM *n.* The **European Exchange Rate Mechanism** *(see).*

er·mine (érmin) *n.* 1. The stoat, *Mustela erminea,* of northern regions, having brownish fur that in winter turns to white with a black tail tip. 2. The valuable white fur of this animal, used especially in the robes of peers or judges. 3. A stylised representation of ermine fur in heraldry. —**the ermine.** The office or dignity of a judge or peer. [Middle English *ermine,* from Old French, from Medieval Latin *(mūs) Armenius,* "Armenian (mouse)".]

Er·mine Street (érmin). An ancient, partially excavated Roman road in England, between London and Lincoln.

erne, ern (ern) *n.* A **sea eagle** *(see).* [Middle English *ern,* eagle, Old English *earn.*]

Er·nie (érni) *n.* In Britain, a computer used to select the winning numbers in a Premium Bond draw. [From *Electronic Random Number Indicator Equipment.*]

Ernst (airnst), **Max** (1891–1976). German painter and sculptor. In 1922 he moved to Paris and became a leading figure in the Surrealist movement and an exponent of collage and photomontage.

e·rode (i-rōd) *v.* **eroded, eroding, erodes.** —*tr.* 1. To wear down or wear away by or as if by the action of water, ice, wind, or the like. 2. To destroy gradually; undermine: *His status has been eroded.* 3. To eat away; corrode. 4. To make or form by wearing away. —*intr.* To become eroded or worn. [Latin *ērōdere,* to gnaw off, eat away : *ē-,* off, from *ex-* + *rōdere,* to gnaw.]

e·rog·e·nous (i-rójənəss) *adj.* Also **e·ro·gen·ic** (érrə-jénnik). Arousing sexual desire; especially, indicating or pertaining to parts of the body sensitive to sexual stimulation: *erogenous zones.* [Greek *erōs†,* desire, sexual love + -GENOUS.]

Er·os¹ (éer-oss, érross). *Greek Mythology.* The god of love, son of Aphrodite. [Latin *Erōs,* from Greek *erōs†,* love, desire.]

Eros² *n. Psychology.* 1. The sum of all self-preservative, as contrasted with self-destructive, instincts. 2. Sexual drive; libido. —Compare **Thanatos.** [From EROS.]

e·rose (i-rōss, -rōz) *adj.* Irregularly notched, toothed, or indented, as if gnawed; jagged: *erose leaves.* [Latin *ērōsus,* past participle of *ērōdere,* to ERODE.]

e·ro·sion (i-rōzh'n) *n.* 1. The state of being eroded or the process of eroding. 2. *Geology.* The group of natural processes including solution, abrasion, corrasion, all involving transport of material, by

which earthy or rock material is removed from any part of the earth's surface. **—e·ro·sive** *adj.*
e·rot·ic (i-róttik) *adj.* **1.** Of, concerning, or tending to arouse sexual love or desire: *erotic literature.* **2.** Dominated by sexual love or desire. [Greek *erōtikos,* of or caused by love, from *erōs*† (stem *erōt-*), love, desire.] **—e·rot·i·cal·ly** *adv.*
e·rot·i·ca (i-róttikə) *pl.n.* Literature or art concerning sex or intended to arouse sexual desire. [New Latin, from Greek *erōtika,* plural of *erōtikos,* EROTIC.]
e·rot·i·cism (i-rótti-siz'm) *n.* Also **er·o·tism** (érrə-tiz'm). **1.** Erotic quality or character. **2. a.** Sexual excitement. **b.** Abnormally persistent sexual excitement. **3.** The use of erotic themes in literature and art, especially to a degree that amounts to preoccupation.
er·o·tol·o·gy (érrə-tólləji) *n.* **1.** The study of sexual phenomena. **2.** Erotic art and literature; erotica.
e·ro·to·ma·ni·a (i-róttə-máyni-ə, -rṓtə-) *n.* Abnormally strong sexual desire. [New Latin : Greek *erōs*† (stem *erōt-*), love + -MANIA.] **—e·ro·to·ma·ni·ac** (-ak) *n.*
err (er || air) *intr.v.* **erred, erring** (ér-ing || érring), **errs. 1.** To make an error or mistake; be incorrect. **2.** To violate accepted moral standards; sin. **3.** To act with a specified bias: *to err on the side of caution.* [Middle English *erren,* to wander about, from Old French *errer,* from Latin *errāre.*] **—err·ing·ly** *adv.*
er·ran·cy (érrən-si) *n., pl.* **-cies.** A state or instance of erring; especially, the condition of being in doctrinal error.
er·rand (érrənd) *n.* **1.** A short trip taken to convey a message or perform a particular task. **2.** The purpose or object of such a trip: *His errand was to post a letter.* [Middle English *erend,* business, message, Old English *ǣrende,* message, from Germanic *arundjam* (unattested).]
er·rant (érrənt) *adj.* **1.** Roving, especially in search of adventure: *knight errant.* **2.** Straying from the proper course or standards; erring. [Middle English *erraunt,* from Old French *errant,* present participle of both *errer,* to travel, to look for an adventure, from Vulgar Latin *iterāre* (unattested), from Late Latin *itinerārī,* to ITINERATE, and *errer,* to ERR.] **—er·rant·ly** *adv.*
er·rant·ry (érrəntri) *n.* The condition of being errant; especially, the conduct or attitudes characteristic of a knight errant.
er·rat·ic (i-ráttik) *adj.* **1.** Without a fixed or regular course; straying; wandering: *an erratic route to the capital.* **2.** Deviating from the customary course in conduct or opinion; unconventional; eccentric: *erratic behaviour.* **3.** Lacking consistency, regularity, or uniformity. *~n. Geology.* A piece of rock differing from surrounding rocks, having been moved to its position by, for example, glacial action. [Middle English *erratik,* from Old French *erratique,* from Latin *errāticus,* wandering, from *errāre,* to wander.] **—er·rat·i·cal·ly** *adv.*
er·ra·tum (i-raá-təm, -ráy-) *n., pl.* **-ta** (-tə). An error in printing or writing noted in a list of corrections appended to a book; a corrigendum. [Latin *errātum,* neuter past participle of *errāre,* to wander, ERR.]
Usage: The use of *errata* as if it were singular is considered unacceptable in standard English: *An errata . . . The errata is . . . .* This rule applies even when *errata* is being used in the collective sense of "a list of errors".
er·rhine (érrīn, érrin) *adj.* Promoting nasal discharge. *~n.* An errhine medicine. [Greek *errhinos* : *en-,* in + *rhis* (stem *rhin-*), nose.]
er·ro·ne·ous (i-rṓni-əss) *adj.* Containing or derived from error; mistaken; false. [Middle English, from Old French *erroneus,* or Latin *errōneus,* wandering, from *errāre,* to wander, ERR.] **—er·ro·ne·ous·ly** *adv.* **—er·ro·ne·ous·ness** *n.*
er·ror (érrər) *n.* **1.** An act, assertion, or belief that unintentionally deviates from what is correct, right, or true. **2.** The condition of having mistaken beliefs or false knowledge. **3.** The act or an instance of deviation from the accepted code of behaviour; a transgression; a wrongdoing. **4.** A mistake: *a clerical error.* **5.** The difference between a computed or measured value and a correct value. **6.** In tennis, a failure to return the ball to one's opponent resulting in the loss of a point: *an unforced error.* [Middle English *errour,* from Old French, from Latin *error,* from *errāre,* to ERR.]
Synonyms: *error, mistake, oversight, blunder, slip.*
-ers *n. & adj. suffix. British.* Used to form humorous versions of certain nouns and adjectives, sometimes distorting the stem of the original word; for example, **brekkers** instead of **breakfast,** or **preggers** instead of **pregnant.** [Probably extended use of -ER (agent), originally in public school and university slang words.]
er·satz (aír-zats, ér-, -saats) *adj.* **1.** Substitute; artificial: *ersatz mink.* **2.** Being an inferior imitator or imitation of a specified person or thing: *an ersatz Dickens.* See Synonyms at **artificial.** *~n.* A substitute; especially, an inferior imitation. [German, from *Ersatz,* compensation, replacement, from *ersetzen,* to replace, from Old High German *irsezzen* : *ir-* (perfective prefix) + *sezzen,* to set.]
Erse (erss) *n.* The Gaelic language, especially **Irish Gaelic** *(see).* *~adj.* Of or pertaining to the Scottish or Irish Celts or their language. [Middle English (Scottish) *Erisch,* variant of IRISH.]
erst·while (érst-wīl, -hwīl) *adj.* Former. *~adv. Archaic.* Formerly.
er·u·bes·cence (érroo-béss'nss) *n.* A reddening of the skin; a flushing; a blush. [Latin *ērubēscentia,* from *ērubēscēns* (stem *ērubēscent-*), present participle of *ērubēscere,* to blush, to grow red : *ē-,* out, "completely", from *ex-* + *rubēscere,* to grow red, from *rubēre,* to be red.] **—er·u·bes·cent** *adj.*
e·ruct (i-rúkt) *v.* **eructed, eructing, eructs.** *—intr.* To belch. *—tr.* **1.** To belch (gas from the stomach). **2.** To emit (fumes) violently. Used of a volcano. [Latin *ēructāre* : *ē-,* out, from *ex-* + *ructāre,* to belch.]
e·ruc·ta·tion (i-rúk-táysh'n, éeruk-) *n.* **1.** The act or an instance of eructing or belching. **2.** Matter belched forth.
er·u·dite (érroo-dīt, érrew-) *adj.* **1.** Deeply learned. **2.** Characterised by erudition. [Middle English *erudit,* from Latin *ērudītus,* past participle of *ērudīre,* "to take the roughness out of", polish, teach : *ē-,* out of, from *ex-* + *rudis,* rough, RUDE.] **—er·u·dite·ly** *adv.* **—er·u·dite·ness** *n.*
er·u·di·tion (érroo-dísh'n, érrew-) *n.* Deep and extensive knowledge, especially when derived from books; profound learning. See Synonyms at **knowledge.**
e·rum·pent (i-rúmpənt) *adj.* Bursting through or as if through a surface or covering. [Latin *ērumpens* (stem *ērumpent-*), present participle of *ērumpere,* to ERUPT.]
e·rupt (i-rúpt, e-) *v.* **erupted, erupting, erupts.** *—intr.* **1.** To emerge violently from limits or restraint; explode. **2.** To become violently active and discharge lava. Used of a volcano. **3.** To force out or suddenly release something enclosed or pent up: *The geyser erupts periodically.* **4.** To give sudden and forceful expression to an emotion: *The crowd erupted in fury.* **5. a.** To pierce the gum. Used of a tooth. **b.** To appear on the skin. Used of a skin blemish. *—tr.* To eject violently (steam, lava, or other confined matter). [Latin *ērumpere* (past participle *ēruptus*), to erupt, to break out, to burst : *ē-,* out, from *ex-* + *rumpere,* to break.]
e·rup·tion (i-rúpsh'n, e-) *n.* **1.** An act, process, or instance of erupting; especially, the discharge of lava from a volcano, or of water or mud from a geyser. **2.** A sudden, often violent outburst. **3. a.** Redness, spotting, or other blemishing of the skin, especially as a local manifestation of a general disease. **b.** The passage of a tooth through the gum. **—e·rup·tive** *adj.* **—e·rup·tive·ly** *adv.*
-ery, -ry *n. suffix.* Used to form nouns from verbs or other nouns to indicate: **1.** A place for a specified business or activity; for example, **bakery, hatchery. 2.** A specified class of persons; for example, **Jewry. 3.** A collection or class of objects of the specified type; for example, **jewellery, cutlery. 4.** A specified craft, study, or practice; for example, **cookery, husbandry. 5. a.** Certain specified characteristics; for example, **snobbery. b.** A specified kind of behaviour; for example, **knavery. 6.** A specified condition or status; for example, **slavery.** [Middle English *-erie,* from Old French : *-er, -ier,* from Latin *-ārius* (see **-ary**) + *-ie,* from Latin *-ia* (see **-ia**).]
e·ryn·go (i-ríng-gō) *n., pl.* **-goes.** Any of several plants of the genus *Eryngium,* such as the sea holly, having spiny leaves and dense clusters of small bluish flowers. [Latin *ēryngion,* from Greek *ērungion,* diminutive of *ērungos,* eryngo, sea holly, possibly from *ēr, ear,* spring, in the sense of "spring flower".]
er·y·sip·e·las (érri-síppiləss || éer-i-) *n.* An acute disease of the skin and subcutaneous tissue caused by a streptococcus and marked by spreading inflammation, particularly on the face and scalp. Also called "St. Anthony's fire". [Middle English *erisipila, herisipila,* from Latin *erysipelas,* from Greek *erusipelas,* "red skin" : *eruthros,* red + *-pelas,* skin.] **—er·y·si·pel·a·tous** (-si-péllətəss) *adj.*
er·y·sip·e·loid (érri-síppi-loyd || éer-i-) *n.* An infectious disease of the hands characterised by red lesions, and caused by the bacterium *Erysipelothrix rhusiopathiae,* found in infected meat or fish. [ERYSIPEL(AS) + -OID.]
er·y·the·ma (érri-theémə) *n.* A redness of the skin, due to dilation of the blood capillaries, that may be caused by toxins in the blood, heat, infection, or injury. [New Latin, from Greek *eruthēma,* from *eruthainein,* to be red, from *eruthros,* red.] **—er·y·them·a·tous** (-theémə-təss, -thémmə-), **er·y·the·mat·ic** (-thi-máttik), **er·y·the·mic** (-theémik) *adj.*
e·ryth·rism (i-ríthriz'm) *n.* Unusual redness of pigmentation, as of hair or plumage. [ERYTHR(O)- + -ISM.] **—er·y·thris·mal** (érri-thrízm'l) *adj.*
e·ryth·rite (i-ríth-rīt) *n.* A reddish mineral, the hydrated arsenate of cobalt, used in colouring glass. [ERYTHR(O)- + -ITE.]
erythro-, erythr- *comb. form.* Indicates red; for example, **erythrocyte, erythrite.** [Greek *eruthros,* red.]
e·ryth·ro·blast (i-ríthrō-blast, -blaast) *n.* Any of the nucleated cells in bone marrow that develop into erythrocytes. [ERYTHRO- + -BLAST.] **—e·ryth·ro·blas·tic** (-blástik) *adj.*
e·ryth·ro·cyte (i-ríthrō-sīt) *n.* A non-nucleated, disc-shaped blood cell containing the red pigment haemoglobin, which transports oxygen and carbon dioxide around the body. It is responsible for the colour of the blood. Also called "red blood cell". [ERYTHRO- + -CYTE.] **—e·ryth·ro·cyt·ic** (-síttik) *adj.*
e·ryth·ro·cy·tom·e·ter (i-ríthrō-sī-tómmitər) *n.* An apparatus for counting the number of erythrocytes in a blood sample. [ERYTHROCYT(E) + -METER.]
e·ryth·ro·my·cin (i-ríthrō-mī́-sin) *n.* An antibiotic agent from cultures of the bacterium *Streptomyces erythreus,* effective especially against Gram-positive bacteria. [ERYTHRO- + -MYCIN.]
Es The symbol for the element einsteinium.
-es¹ *pl. n. suffix.* Indicates the plural form, for which it is used in nouns ending in a sibilant or an affricate and in some nouns ending in a vowel or a postconsonantal *y;* for example, **trusses, switches, cargoes, ladies.** Compare **-s** (in nouns). [Middle English *-es, -s,* -s (plural).]
-es² *v. suffix.* Indicates the third person singular form of the present indicative, for which it is used in most verbs ending in a sibilant, an affricate, a vowel, or a postconsonantal *y;* for example, **guesses,**

rushes, does, defies. Compare **-s** (in verbs). [Middle English *-es, -s, -s* (third person singular indicative suffix).]

ESA European Space Agency. Compare **ESRO.**

E·sa·ki (i-saáki), **Leo** (1925–). Japanese physicist. As a research physicist with IBM (1960–92) he worked on the **tunnel effect** *(see)*. He received a Nobel prize for physics (1973).

Esaki diode *n. Electronics.* A **tunnel diode** *(see).*

E·sau (eé-saw). The son of Isaac and Rebecca, who sold his birthright to his brother Jacob. Genesis 25:25. [Late Latin *Ēsau*, from Greek, from Hebrew *Ēsāw*, "hairy".]

ESCA *n. Electron spectroscopy for chemical analysis:* a technique for analysing or investigating chemical compounds by irradiating them with X-rays and monitoring the characteristic energy spectrum of electrons emitted.

es·ca·lade (éska-láyd) *n.* The act of scaling a fortified wall or rampart by means of ladders, especially during an assault. [French, from Italian *scalata*, from *scalare*, to climb, from *scala*, ladder, from Late Latin *scāla*, from Latin *scālae*, steps.] —**es·ca·lade** *tr.v.*

es·ca·late (éska-layt) *v.* **-lated, -lating, -lates.** —*tr.* To increase, enlarge, or intensify; especially, to increase the scale or intensity of (a conflict). —*intr.* To increase in scale, intensity, or extent. [Backformation from ESCALATOR.] —**es·ca·la·tion** (-láysh'n) *n.*

es·ca·la·tor (éska-laytər) *n.* A moving stairway consisting of steps attached to a continuously circulating belt, for moving passengers up and down between floors. Also called "moving staircase". [Originally a trademark: perhaps *escalade* + *elevator*.]

escalator clause *n.* A provision in a contract stipulating an increase or decrease, as in wages, benefits, or prices, under certain conditions, such as changes in the cost of living or in production costs. Also called "escalator".

es·cal·lo·ni·a (éska-lóni-ə) *n.* Any evergreen shrub of the South American genus *Escallonia*, cultivated for its red or white flowers. [After *Escallon*, 18th-century Spanish traveller who discovered it.]

es·ca·lope (éska-lóp, -lop) *n.* A thin, boneless slice of meat, such as veal, usually fried in breadcrumbs. [French, slice of meat, shell, from Old French, shell-shaped pan in which escalopes were cooked, from Old French, shell. See scallop.]

es·ca·pade (éska-payd, -páyd) *n.* **1.** An act of breaking loose from restraint; a flight from confining rules. **2.** A carefree or reckless adventure; a fling; a caper. [French, from Old French, from Old Italian *scappata*, from the feminine past participle of *scappare*, to escape, from Vulgar Latin *excappāre* (unattested), to ESCAPE.]

es·cape (i-skáyp ‖ e-) *v.* **-caped, -caping, -capes.** Also *archaic* **scape** (skayp). —*intr.* **1.** To break loose from confinement; get free. **2.** To issue from confinement or an enclosure; leak or seep out. **3.** To succeed in avoiding capture, danger, or harm. **4.** To grow beyond a cultivated area or a condition of cultivation. Used of plants. —*tr.* **1.** To get away from; succeed in avoiding (capture, danger, or harm). **2. a.** To be unnoticed by or not recallable or obvious to: *The meaning of this cryptic note escapes me.* **b.** To elude (attention or detection): *The mistake escaped my notice.* **3.** To issue involuntarily from: *A regretful sigh escaped her lips.*
~*n.* **1.** The act or an instance of escaping. **2.** A means of escaping. **3. a.** Temporary freedom from worry, care, or unpleasantness. **b.** A means of obtaining this: *Television is his escape from worry.* **4.** A gradual and accidental pouring out or leaking from a container or the like: *an escape of gas.* **5.** A cultivated plant that has become established away from cultivation. Also called "garden escape".
~*adj.* **1.** Affording a means of escape, especially in an emergency: *an escape hatch.* **2.** Providing a legal basis for avoiding liability or responsibility: *an escape clause.* [Middle English *escapen*, from Old North French *escaper*, "to take off one's cloak", to emerge from restraint, escape, from Vulgar Latin *excappāre* (unattested) : *ex-*, out, off + Late Latin *cappa*, cloak, hood (see **cape**).] —**es·cap·a·ble** *adj.* —**es·cap·er** *n.*

Synonyms: escape, avoid, shun, eschew, evade, elude.

es·cap·ee (i-skáy-peé, -pee ‖ e-) *n.* One that has escaped; especially, an escaped prisoner.

es·cape·ment (i-skáypmənt ‖ e-) *n.* **1.** A mechanism consisting in general of an escape wheel and anchor, used especially in timepieces to control the wheel movement and to provide periodic energy impulses to a pendulum or balance. **2.** The mechanism in a typewriter that controls the lateral movement of the carriage.

escape road *n.* A subsidiary road, leading to a sandbank, provided alongside a steep decline to enable drivers who have lost control of their vehicles to avoid an accident.

escape velocity *n.* The minimum velocity that a body, such as a space rocket, must attain to overcome the gravitational attraction of another body, such as the Earth.

escape wheel *n.* The rotating notched wheel periodically engaged and disengaged by the anchor in the escapement of a timepiece.

es·cap·ism (i-skáy-piz'm ‖ e-) *n.* The habit or tendency of seeking escape from unpleasant realities in self-deceiving fantasy or entertainment. —**es·cap·ist** *adj. & n.*

es·ca·pol·o·gist (éska-póllajist) *n.* A person who breaks free after being tied or locked up, usually as a form of public entertainment. —**es·ca·pol·o·gy** *n.*

es·car·got (éskaar-gó) *n., pl.* **-gots** (-gó). An edible snail, especially when cooked. [French, a snail, from Old French, from Old Provençal *escaragol†*.]

es·carp (i-skárp ‖ e-) *n.* **1.** A steep slope or cliff; an escarpment. **2.** The inner wall of a ditch or trench dug around a fortification. ~*tr.v.* **escarped, -carping, -carps.** To cut or erode so as to form a

steep slope. [French *escarpe*, from Old French, from Italian *scarpa*, SCARP.]

es·carp·ment (i-skárpmənt ‖ e-) *n.* **1.** A steep slope or long cliff resulting from erosion or faulting and separating two relatively level areas of differing elevations. **2.** The steeper slope of an asymmetrical ridge, especially one formed when gently dipping rock strata are denuded differentially. **3.** A steep slope in front of a fortification.

Escaut. See **Scheldt.**

–escence *n. suffix.* Indicates a beginning or continuing state; for example, **opalescence, luminescence.** [Old French, from Latin *-ēscentia*, from *-ēscēns* (stem *-ēscent-*), -ESCENT.]

–escent *adj. suffix.* Indicates beginning to be or exhibit; for example, **luminescent, phosphorescent.** [Old French, from Latin *-ēscēns* (stem *-ēscent-*), present participial suffix of *-ēscere*, chiefly inceptives of verbs in *-ēre*. See **-ent.**]

es·char (éss-kaar) *n.* A dry scab or slough formed on the skin as a result of a burn or by the action of a corrosive or caustic substance. [Middle English *escare*, scab, SCAR.]

es·cha·rot·ic (éska-róttik) *adj.* Producing or capable of producing an eschar; caustic; corrosive. **es·cha·rot·ic** *n.*

es·cha·tol·o·gy (éska-tóllaji) *n.* The branch of theology that is concerned with the ultimate or last things, such as death, judgment, heaven, and hell. [Greek *eskhatos*, last, extreme + -LOGY.] —**es·cha·to·log·i·cal** (-tə-lójik'l) *adj.* —**es·cha·tol·o·gist** *n.*

es·cheat (iss-cheét, ess-) *n.* **1.** The reversion of land held under feudal tenure to the manor in the absence of legal heirs or claimants. **2.** In some countries, the reversion of property to the state in the absence of legal heirs or claimants. **3.** Land or property reverting in this way.
~*v.* **escheated, -cheating, -cheats.** —*intr.* To revert to the state by escheat. —*tr.* To cause (property) to revert to the state by escheat. [Middle English *eschete*, from Old French *eschete, escheoite*, from *escheoit*, past participle of *escheoir*, to fall out, from Vulgar Latin *excadēre* (unattested) : Latin *ex-*, out + *cadere*, to fall.] —**escheat·a·ble** *adj.*

es·chew (iss-chooo, ess-) *tr.v.* **-chewed, -chewing, -chews. 1.** To take care to avoid; shun. **2.** To abstain from. —See Synonyms at **escape.** [Middle English *escheuen, eschiuen*, from Old French *eschiver, eschiuver*, to shun, to avoid, from Vulgar Latin *scivāre* (unattested), from Germanic *skiuhwan* (unattested), from *skiuhwaz* (unattested), SHY.] —**es·chew·al** *n.*

Es·cof·fier (ess-kóffi-ay, -áy), **Auguste** (1846–1935). French chef, with a reputation as "the king of chefs and the chef of kings" made chiefly in England (Savoy and Carlton hotels).

es·co·lar (éska-lár) *n., pl.* **-lars** or collectively **escolar.** Any of several slender carnivorous fishes of the family Gempylidae of warm marine waters. Also called "snake mackerel". [Spanish, "scholar" (from the spectacle-like rings around its eyes), from Late Latin *scholāris*, SCHOLAR.]

Es·co·ri·al, El (éss-korri-aál). Granite palace and monastery near Madrid in Spain, one of the world's great architectural monuments. It was begun by Juan Bautista de Toledo in 1563 and completed by Juan de Herrera in 1584.

es·cort (éss-kawrt) *n.* **1.** One or more persons accompanying another to give guidance or protection or as a mark of honour. **2.** One or more guards, often armed, travelling with important persons or goods. **3.** A man who acts as the companion of a woman in public. **4. a.** A person, usually a young woman, hired by the evening to act as a companion for social activities. **b.** A prostitute or call girl. Used euphemistically. **5.** One or more vehicles accompanying another vehicle to guide, protect, or honour its passengers.
~*tr.v.* (i-skórt, e-) **escorted, -corting, -corts.** To accompany as an escort. See Synonyms at **accompany.** [French *escorte*, from Old French *(e)scorte*, from Old Italian *scorta*, guide, an escorting, from the feminine past participle of *scorgere*, to show, to guide, from Vulgar Latin *excorrigere* (unattested), to conduct, guide, escort : Latin *ex-*, out + *corrigere*, to set right, CORRECT.]

escort agency *n.* An agency that provides male or female partners for social outings.

e·scribe (i-skríb, ee-) *tr.v.* **escribed, escribing, escribes.** To draw (a circle or other curve) touching one side of a triangle or other plane figure and the extensions of the two adjacent sides. [EX- (out) + Latin *scribere*, to write.]

es·cri·toire (éskri-twaár) *n.* A writing desk, especially one consisting of a stand or chest of drawers surmounted by smaller drawers or compartments that are concealed by a hinged lid which, when opened, provides a writing surface. [French, from Old French *escriptoire*, a study, from Medieval Latin *scriptorium*, SCRIPTORIUM.]

es·crow (éskrō, ess-krō) *n.* **1. a.** A written agreement, such as a deed or bond, put into the custody of a third party and not in effect until certain conditions are fulfilled by the grantee. **b.** *U.S.* Money or goods kept in this way. **2.** *U.S.* The condition of being ineffective until certain conditions are fulfilled: *a deed held in escrow.* [Old French *escroe*, strip of parchment, scroll, from Frankish *scrōda* (unattested), piece.]

es·cu·do (esh-kōōdō, *Portuguese* ish-kōothoo) *n., pl.* **-dos. 1. a.** The basic monetary unit of Portugal, equal to 100 centavos. **b.** The basic monetary unit of Cape Verde, equal to 100 centavos. **2.** A coin worth one escudo. [Portuguese and Spanish, "shield", from Latin *scūtum*, shield.]

es·cu·lent (éskewlənt) *adj.* Suitable for eating; edible.
~*n.* Something edible, as a vegetable. [Latin *esculentus*, from *esca*, food, from *edere*, to eat.]

es·cutch·eon (i-skúchən, e-) *n.* Also **scutch·eon** (skúchən). **1.** A shield or shield-shaped emblem bearing a coat of arms. **2.** Any ornamental shield-shaped object; especially, a movable plate covering the keyhole of a door, or a plate on which the door knocker is mounted. **3.** *Nautical.* The ornamented plate in the middle of a ship's stern inscribed with the ship's name and home port. [Middle English *escochon*, from Old French *escuchon, escusson*, from Vulgar Latin *scūtiō* (stem *scūtiōn*-) (unattested), from Latin *scūtum*, shield.] —**es·cutch·eoned** *adj.*

Es·dra·e·lon (éssdray-éelon). One of the most fertile plains in Israel. It stretches about 40 kilometres (25 miles) from the coastal lowland near Mount Carmel to the Jordan valley.

Es·dras (éz-drass, -dráss) *n. Abbr.* **Esd. 1.** Either of the first two books of the Apocrypha, I Esdras and II Esdras, called in the Douay Bible III Esdras and IV Esdras. **2.** Either of two books of the Douay Bible Old Testament, I Esdras and II Esdras, corresponding to the books Ezra and Nehemiah in the King James Bible and other versions.

–ese *n. & adj. suffix.* Indicates: **1.** A native or inhabitant; for example, **Sudanese. 2.** A language or dialect; for example, **Japanese. 3.** A literary style or diction; for example, **journalese**. In this sense, usually used derogatorily. [Old French *-eis* and Italian *-ese*, from Latin *-ēnsis*, "originating in".]

ESE east-southeast.

es·er·ine (éssə-reen, -rin) *n. Biochemistry.* **Physostigmine** (see). [*Eser-*, native African name + -INE.]

Esfahan. See **Isfahan**.

es·ker (éskər) *n.* Also **es·kar** (éss-kaar, -kər) A long, narrow ridge of sand and gravel deposited by a stream flowing between a valley glacier and the valley wall, or in a tunnel under a retreating glacial ice sheet. Also called "os". [Irish *eiscir*, ridge, from Old Irish *escir*†.]

Es·ki·mo (éski-mō) *n., pl.* **-mos** or collectively **Eskimo**. Also **Es·qui·mau** (éski-mō) *pl.* **-maux** (-mōz). *Abbr.* **Esk. 1.** A member of a people native to the Arctic coastal regions of North America and to parts of Greenland and northeastern Siberia. **2.** The language spoken by this people.

~*adj.* Also **Es·qui·mau**. *Abbr.* **Esk.** Of, pertaining to, or concerning the Eskimos or their language. [Earlier *Esquimawes*, perhaps from Micmac *eskameege*, to eat raw fish : Proto-Algonquian *ašk-* (unattested), "raw" + *-amekw-* (unattested), "fish".]

Es·ki·mo-Al·e·ut (éski-mō-ə-lōōt, -lḗwt) *n.* A family of languages spoken chiefly among peoples native to the Arctic coastal regions of North America, Greenland, the Aleutian Islands, and the northeastern tip of Siberia.

Eskimo dog *n.* A large dog of a breed used in Arctic regions as a sledge dog, having a thick coat and a plumed tail.

Es·ky (éski) *n., pl.* **-kies**. *Australian.* A trademark for a portable icebox for keeping food and drink cool.

esophagus. *U.S.* Variant of **oesophagus**.

es·o·ter·ic (éss-ə-térrik, éess-, -ō-) *adj.* **1.** Intended for, limited to, or understood by only a small group: *To the esoteric Hellenic mystery cults, Christianity opposed an exoteric religion.* See **exoteric. 2.** Difficult to understand; abstruse: *The theory remained esoteric despite efforts to popularise it.* **3.** Not publicly disclosed; confidential. **4.** Out of the ordinary; unusual: *an esoteric choice.* [Late Latin *esōtericus*, from Greek *esōterikos*, from *esōterō*, comparative of *esō*, within.] —**es·o·ter·i·cal·ly** *adv.*

ESP extrasensory perception.

esp. especially.

es·pa·drille (éspə-dríl) *n.* A light shoe having a rope or fibre sole and a canvas upper part. [French, variant of *espardille*, from Provençal *espardilho*, diminutive of *espart*, esparto, from Latin *spartum*, ESPARTO.]

es·pal·i·er (i-spál-iər, -yər, e-, -yay) *n.* **1.** A fruit tree or ornamental shrub that is trained to grow in a flat plane against a wall, often in a symmetrical pattern. **2.** A trellis or other framework upon which such a plant is grown.

~*tr.v.* **espaliered, -iering, -iers.** To train (a plant) on an espalier. [French, from Italian *spalliera*, applied to shoulder supports, hence stakes of that height, from *spalla*, shoulder, from Latin *spatula*, broad piece, flat piece. See **spatula**.]

es·par·to (e-spártō, i-) *n.* A tough, wiry grass, *Stipa tenacissima*, of Spain and northern Africa, yielding a fibre used in making paper and as cordage. Also called "esparto grass". [Spanish, from Latin *spartum*, from Greek *sparton*, rope, cable, esparto.]

es·pe·cial (i-spésh'l ‖ e-) *adj.* **1.** Outstanding; exceptional: *of especial value.* **2.** Pertaining uniquely to one person, group, or thing; particular: *her own especial quality.* —See Usage note at **special**. [Middle English, from Old French, from Latin *speciālis*, from *speciēs*, a view, appearance.]

es·pe·cial·ly (i-spésh'l-i ‖ e-) *adv. Abbr.* **esp.** To an extent or degree deserving of special emphasis; particularly.

Es·pe·ran·to (éspə-rán-tō, -ráan-) *n.* An artificial international language invented in 1887, characterised by a vocabulary based on word roots common to many European languages, a single, unvarying ending for each principal part of speech, and a regularised system of conjugation and inflection. [After Dr. *Esperanto* ("one who hopes"), pen name of Dr. L.L. Zamenhof (1859–1917), Polish philologist, who devised the language.]

es·pi·al (i-spí-əl, e-) *n.* **1.** The act of catching sight of something. **2.** The act of watching, especially in secret. **3.** The fact of being seen or noticed. [Middle English *espiaille*, from Old French, from *espier*, to watch, to SPY.]

es·pi·o·nage (éspi-ə-naazh, -náazh, -nij) *n.* The practice of spying or using spies to obtain secret information about the activities and plans of another government or rival group. [French *espionnage*, from Old French, from *espionner*, to spy, from *espion*, spy, from Old Italian *spione*, from *spia*, from Germanic.]

es·pla·nade (éspla-náyd, -náad) *n.* **1.** A flat, open, often paved stretch of ground used as a promenade; especially, such a promenade along the shore. **2.** A level area in front of a fortification. [French, from Italian *spianala*, from *spianare*, to level, from Latin *explānāre*, to flatten, EXPLAIN.]

es·pou·sal (i-spówz'l, e-) *n.* **1.** An espousing or adoption, as of an idea or cause. **2.** *Usually plural. Archaic.* A betrothal or wedding.

es·pouse (i-spówz, e-) *tr.v.* **-poused, -pousing, -pouses. 1.** To adopt and support (a cause, belief, or the like). **2.** To take in marriage; marry. **3.** To give (a woman) in marriage. [Middle English *espousen*, from Old French *espouser*, from Late Latin *spōnsāre*, from Latin *spondēre* (past participle *spōnsus*), to promise solemnly.]

es·pres·so (e-spréssō) *n., pl.* **-sos.** Also **ex·pres·so** (ik-). A strong coffee brewed by forcing steam or hot water under pressure through long-roasted, powdered beans. [Italian *(caffè) espresso*, "pressed out (coffee)", from the past participle of *esprimere*, to press out, express, from Latin *exprimere* : *ex-*, out + *premere*, to PRESS.]

es·prit (e-sprée) *n.* **1.** Spirit. **2.** Liveliness of mind and expression; wit. [French, from Latin *spīritus*, SPIRIT.]

esprit de corps (də kór ‖ kôr) *n.* A spirit of devotion and enthusiasm among members of a group for one another, their group, and its purposes. [French, "spirit of (the) body".]

esprit d'es·cal·i·er (dess-kal-yáy) *n.* Tardy wit, which keeps one from thinking of the right remark until after the event. [Alteration of French *esprit d(e l)'escalier*, "staircase wit", which starts working only as you are going down the stairs to leave.]

es·py (i-spí ‖ e-) *tr.v.* **-pied, -pying, -pies.** To catch sight of; glimpse (something distant or partly obscured): *"Through one of the rents of his gown, you espied a fat capon hung round the monk's waist"* (Henry James). See Synonyms at **see**. [Middle English *(e)spien*, from Old French *espier*, to SPY.]

Esq. Esquire (title).

-esque *adj. suffix.* Indicates possession of a specified manner or quality; for example, **statuesque, Kafkaesque**. [French, from Italian *-esco*, from Germanic *-iskaz* (unattested). See also **-ish**.]

Es·qui·line (éskwə-līn) *n.* One of the seven hills of Rome.

Esquimau. Variant of **Eskimo**.

es·quire (i-skwîr, e-) *n.* **1.** A candidate for knighthood in medieval times, serving a knight as attendant and shield-bearer; a squire. **2.** Formerly, a member of the English gentry ranking just below a knight. **3.** *Capital E. Abbr.* **Esq.** Used as a title of courtesy after a man's full name: *Martin Chuzzlewit, Esq.* [Middle English *esquier, esquire*, from Old French *esquier, escuier*, squire, "shield-carrier", from Late Latin *scūtārius*, from Latin *scūtum*, shield.]

ESR electron spin resonance.

ESRO European Space Research Organisation. Compare **ESA**.

-ess *n. suffix.* Indicates a female; for example, **heiress, lioness**. [Middle English *-esse*, from Old French *-esse*, from Late Latin *-issa*, from Greek.]

Usage: The use of this suffix is changing, in the wake of changing attitudes to feminine roles in society. Originally, the suffix simply indicated female gender, and had no additional overtones: a *poetess* was simply a female poet. These days, several *-ess* forms are considered pejorative. Strongly disliked, especially in American English, are *Negress* and *Jewess*; less pejorative are *authoress, poetess, sculptress*, and the like. A *manageress* is a female *manager* only in the case of a fairly small enterprise such as a retail shop: a woman executive of a large company would be its *manager*, not its *manageress*. Several words remain relatively unaffected, such as *waitress, actress, heiress*, but even these can become a focus of contention on occasion. See also **person**.

Ess. Essex.

es·say (e-sáy) *tr.v.* **-sayed, -saying, -says. 1.** To make an attempt at; try, especially in a tentative manner. **2.** To subject to a test; try out.

~*n.* (éssay, e-sáy *for senses 1, 3*; éssay *for sense 2*). **1.** An attempt; an endeavour. **2. a.** A short literary composition on a single subject, usually presenting the personal views of the author. **b.** An academic composition by a student on a set subject. **3.** *Archaic.* A testing or trial. [Middle English, from Old French *essaier, assaier*, from *essai, assai*, a trial, from Vulgar Latin *exagiāre* (unattested), to weigh out, from Late Latin *exagium*, a weighing, from Latin *exigere*, to weigh out, examine. See **exact**.] —**es·say·er** *n.*

es·say·ist (éssay-ist) *n.* A writer of essays.

Es·sen (éss'n). Industrial city on the river Ruhr, North Rhine-Westphalia, Germany. In the second half of the 19th century it became one of Germany's leading manufacturing towns.

es·sence (éss'nss) *n.* **1.** The quality or qualities of a thing that give it its identity; the intrinsic or indispensable properties of a thing: *"Government and Law, in their very essence, consist of restrictions on freedom"* (Bertrand Russell). **2.** The most important ingredient; the crucial element. **3.** *Philosophy.* The inherent, unchanging nature of a thing or class of things, as distinguished from its attributes or its existence. **4. a.** An extract of a substance that retains its fundamental or most desirable properties in concentrated form. **b.** Such an extract in a solution of alcohol. **c.** A perfume or scent. **d.** A flavouring. **5.** An embodiment or personification: *the essence of kindness.* **6.** A spiritual or incorporeal entity. **—of the essence.** Of supreme importance: *Speed is of the essence if we are to finish the job on time.* [Middle English *essence, essencia,* from Old French *essence,* from Latin *essentia,* from *esse,* to be.]

Es·sene (ésseen, e-séen) *n.* A member of an ascetic Jewish sect whose communities existed in ancient Palestine from the second century B.C. to the first century A.D. **—Es·se·ni·an** (e-séeni-ən), **Es·sen·ic** (e-sénnik) *adj.*

es·sen·tial (i-sén-sh'l) *adj.* **1.** Constituting or part of the essence of something: *the essential simplicity of the idea.* **2.** Of basic importance; indispensable. **3.** Of the fullest degree or extent; absolute; perfect: *the essential beauty of a sunrise.* **4.** Constituting or containing an essence of a plant, liquid, or other substance. **—See** Synonyms at **necessary.**

~n. A fundamental, necessary, or indispensable part, item, or principle. [Middle English, from Late Latin *essentiālis.* See **essence, -ial.**] **—es·sen·ti·al·i·ty** (-shi-ál-ə-ti), **es·sen·tial·ness** *n.* **—es·sen·tial·ly** *adv.*

essential amino acid *n.* Any of eight amino acids that must be included in the human diet since they cannot be synthesised by the body.

essential oil *n.* A volatile oil, usually having the characteristic odour or flavour of the plant from which it is obtained, used to make perfumes and flavourings.

Es·sex (éssiks). Originally an early kingdom of Anglo-Saxon England, settled by Saxons probably early in the 6th century. It is now a county in southeast England.

Essex, Robert Devereux, 2nd Earl of (1566-1601). English courtier and man of arms. He was a favourite at the court of Elizabeth I, but imperilled his position by marrying Sir Philip Sidney's widow in 1590 and scheming to overthrow the Queen's principal adviser, Lord Burghley. His part in a rising of the people of London led to his arrest and execution for treason.

Essex man *n.* An upwardly mobile lower-middle-class lad who aspires to be a classless hooray Henry. [Perhaps because *Essex* is a first step up from the adjacent parts of East London.]

es·so·nite (éssə-nīt) *n.* Also **hes·son·ite** (héssə-nīt). A reddish-brown variety of garnet. Also called "cinnamon stone". [French, from Greek *hēssōn,* inferior to, less than (it is less hard than true hyacinth), from *hēka,* a little, slightly.]

est (est) *n.* A form of psychological training held to develop the individual's personality and potential. [*Erhard Seminar Training.*]

EST, E.S.T. Eastern Standard Time (in the United States).

est. 1. established. **2.** *Law.* estate. **3.** estimate, estimated.

-est[1] *adj. & adv. suffix.* Indicates the superlative degree of adjectives and adverbs; for example, **greatest, earliest.** [Middle English *-est,* Old English *-est, -ost,* from Common Germanic *-istaz* (unattested).]

-est[2]**, -st** *v. suffix.* Indicates the archaic second person singular form of the present and past indicative tenses, with the pronoun *thou;* for example, **comest, didst.** [Middle English *-est,* Old English *-est, -ast.*]

es·tab·lish (i-stáblish, e-) *tr.v.* **-lished, -lishing, -lishes. 1.** To settle (a person) permanently or securely in a position or condition; install. **2.** To found or set up on a lasting basis: *establish a business.* **3.** To bring about; create: *establish order.* **4.** To introduce or institute (laws, for example). **5.** To turn (a church or religion) into a national institution. **6. a.** To gain recognition for or acceptance of: *The book established his reputation.* **b.** To make familiar to a reader or audience: *establish a character.* **7.** To prove the validity or truth of: *establish the facts.* **8.** In card games, to gain control of (a suit) so that all remaining tricks can be won. **—See** Synonyms at **confirm.** [Middle English *establissen,* from Old French *establir* (stem *establiss-*), from Latin *stabilīre,* to make firm, from *stabilis,* firm.] **—es·tab·lish·er** *n.*

es·tab·lished church (i-stáblisht, e-) *n.* A church that is officially recognised and given support as a national institution by a government.

es·tab·lish·ment (i-stáblishmənt, e-) *n.* **1.** The act of establishing. **2.** The condition or fact of being established. **3. a.** An institution, such as a business, club, or hotel. **b.** The premises of such an institution. **c.** The permanent staff of such an institution. **d.** Any organised group, such as a government, political party, or military force. **4. a.** A place of residence. **b.** Those living and working in it. **5.** *Capital E.* An established church. **—the Establishment. 1.** The people and institutions, such as prominent politicians, financiers, the armed forces, and the civil service, that collectively constitute the power structure of a given society and are regarded as exerting a strongly conservative influence. **2.** A powerful group that tacitly controls a specified field of activity, usually in a conservative manner: *the literary Establishment.*

es·tab·lish·men·tar·i·an (i-stáblishmən-taíri-ən) *adj.* Concerning an established church. **2.** Advocating the introduction or continuance of an established church. **—es·tab·lish·men·tar·i·an** *n.* **—es·tab·lish·men·tar·i·an·ism** *n.*

es·ta·mi·net (ess-támmi-nay, -náy) *n. French.* A small café.

es·tan·cia (iss-tán-si-ə, ess-) *n.* A large estate or cattle ranch in Latin America. [American Spanish, from Spanish, room, enclosure, from Vulgar Latin *stantia* (unattested), a standing (thing), from Latin *stāns* (stem *stant-*), present participle of *stāre,* to stand.]

es·tate (i-stáyt ‖ e-) *n.* **1. a.** A sizable piece of rural land, usually with a large house. **b.** Such a piece of land used for the cultivation of tobacco, rubber, or the like. **2.** An area developed for a specific use, such as housing or factories: *an industrial estate.* **3.** The whole of one's possessions; especially, all of the property and debts left by a deceased or bankrupt person. **4.** *Abbr.* **est.** *Law.* The nature and extent of an owner's rights with respect to his property and its use. **5.** A stage in one's development or maturation: *"When that I reached a man's estate"* (Shakespeare). **6. a.** *Literary.* A condition of life, wealth, or status; a rank. **b.** High rank or status: *gentlemen of estate.* **7.** A class of citizens within a nation with distinct political rights. Also called "Estate of the Realm". [Middle English *estat,* state, condition, from Old French, STATE.]

estate agent *n.* **1.** *British.* One who handles the advertising and sale of buildings and land. **2.** One who manages a rural estate.

estate car *n. British.* A large car with a combined passenger and luggage compartment, the latter being a large area at the rear, usually with access by a tailgate. Also *chiefly U.S.* "station wagon".

estate duty *n.* In Britain before 1975, a tax payable on inherited property, now replaced by **capital transfer tax** *(see).*

Es·tates-Gen·e·ral (i-stáyts jén-rəl, e-, jénnə-) *n.* The **States-General** *(see).* [Translation of French *états généraux.*]

es·teem (i-stéem ‖ e-) *tr.v.* **-teemed, -teeming, -teems. 1.** To regard as of a high order; think of with respect; prize: *Oysters were much esteemed as a delicacy.* **2.** To judge to be; regard as; consider. **—See** Synonyms at **appreciate.**

~n. 1. Favourable regard; respect: *He is held in high esteem.* **2.** *Archaic.* Judgment; opinion. **—See** Synonyms at **regard.** [Middle English *estemen,* from Old French *estimer,* from Latin *aestimāre,* to ESTIMATE.]

es·ter (éstər) *n.* Any of a class of organic compounds derived from an acid by the replacement of hydrogen by an alkyl radical. Esters, which are analogous to inorganic salts, are formed by reaction of acids with alcohols. [German *Ester,* short for *Essigäther,* "vinegar ether" : *Essig,* vinegar, from Middle High German *ezzich,* from Old High German *ezzîh,* from Latin *acêtum* + *Äther,* from Latin *aethêr,* ETHER.]

es·ter·ase (éstə-rayz, -rayss) *n.* Any enzyme that catalyses the hydrolysis of an ester.

es·ter·i·fy (e-stérrif-ī, i-) *v.* **-fied, -fying, -fies.** *Chemistry.* **—intr.** To change to an ester. **—tr.** To change (a compound) into an ester. **—es·ter·i·fi·cation** (-káysh'n) *n.*

Es·ther (éstər) *n.* A book of the Old Testament recounting the story of Esther, the Jewish queen of Persia who saved her people from massacre.

esthetics. *U.S.* Variant of **aesthetics. —esthete** *n.* **—esthetic** *adj.* **—esthetician** *n.* **—estheticism** *n.*

Esthonia. See Estonia.

es·ti·ma·ble (éstiməb'l) *adj.* **1.** Capable of being estimated or evaluated; calculable. **2.** Deserving of esteem; admirable. **—es·ti·ma·ble·ness** *n.* **—es·ti·ma·bly** *adv.*

es·ti·mate (ésti-mayt) *tr.v.* **-mated, -mating, -mates. 1.** To make a judgment or submit a statement as to (the likely or approximate cost, quantity, or extent) of something; calculate approximately. **2.** To form a tentative opinion about; evaluate: *"While an author is yet living we estimate his powers by his worst performance"* (Samuel Johnson). **—See** Synonyms at **calculate.**

~n. (-mət, -mit). *Abbr.* **est. 1.** A tentative evaluation or rough calculation. **2. a.** A preliminary calculation submitted by a contractor or workman of the cost of work to be undertaken. **b.** The written statement of such a calculation. **3.** A judgment based upon one's impressions; an opinion. [Latin *aestimāre†.*] **—es·ti·ma·tive** (-mətiv, -maytiv) *adj.* **—es·ti·ma·tor** *n.*

Synonyms: estimate, appraise, assess, assay, evaluate, rate.

es·ti·ma·tion (ésti-máysh'n) *n.* **1.** The act or an instance of estimating. **2.** An opinion reached by estimating; a judgment. **3.** Favourable regard; esteem.

estival. *U.S.* Variant of **aestival.**

estivate. *U.S.* Variant of **aestivate. —estivation** *n.*

Estonia, Republic of. Also **Es·tho·ni·a** (-thôn-, -tōn-). Formerly a constituent republic of the U.S.S.R., lying on the Baltic Sea. After World War I, it gained independence from Russia but was taken over by the U.S.S.R. in 1940. In 1991, despite a Soviet crackdown, it obtained its independence. About 65 per cent of the population is Estonian, with the rest mainly Russian. Area, 45 227 square kilometres (17,462 square miles). Population 1,470,000. Capital, Tallinn. See map at **Baltic States.**

Es·to·ni·an (ess-tôni-ən) *n.* Also **Es·tho·ni·an** (-thôni-, -tôni-). **1.** A native or inhabitant of Estonia. **2.** The Finno-Ugric language of Estonia. **—Es·to·ni·an** *adj.*

es·top (iss-tóp ‖ ess-) *tr.v.* **-topped, -topping, -tops 1.** *Law.* To prohibit, preclude, or impede, especially by estoppel. **2.** *Archaic.* To stop up. [Middle English *estoppen,* from Old French *estoper, estouper,* from Late Latin *stuppāre,* to stop up. See **stop.**] **— es·top·page** (-ij) *n.*

es·top·pel (iss-tópp'l) *n. Law.* A restraint on a person to prevent him from contradicting his own previous assertion. Also called "conclusion". [Old French *estoupail, estouppail,* from *estouper,* to ESTOP.]

es·to·vers (e-stóvərz) *pl.n. Law.* Necessaries, such as wood found by a tenant on his landlord's land, which the law allows him to take. [Middle English, from Anglo-French *estover,* from Old French *estoveir,* to be necessary, from Latin *est opus,* it is necessary : *est,* (it) is, from *esse,* to be + *opus,* need, necessity.]

es·trade (iss-traád) *n.* A raised platform or dais. [French, from Spanish *estrado,* carpeted floor, from Latin *stratum.* See **stratum.**]

es·trange (i-stráynj ‖ e-) *tr.v.* **-tranged, -tranging, -tranges. 1.** To remove from an accustomed place or relation; put at a distance, especially a psychological distance. **2.** To alienate the affections of; make hostile or unsympathetic. [Old French *estranger, estrangier,* from Medieval Latin *extrāneāre,* from Latin *extrāneus,* STRANGE.] —**es·trange·ment** *n.* —**es·trang·er** *n.*

es·tray (i-stráy ‖ e-) *n.* **1.** *Law.* A stray domestic animal. **2.** *Archaic.* A stray person, animal, or thing.
~*intr.v.* **estrayed, -traying, -trays.** *Archaic.* To stray. [Anglo-French *estray,* from Old French *estraie,* stray, wandering, from *estraier,* to STRAY.]

Es·trem·a·du·ra¹ (éstrimə-dóor-ə, *Portuguese* ĺshtrəmə-). Former province of central Portugal, comprising the lower Tagus valley, one of the country's richest farming areas. Lisbon, the national capital, is the chief town. —**Es·trem·a·du·ran** *n. & adj.*

Estremadura². See **Extremadura.**

estro-, estr-. *U.S.* Variants of **oestro-.**

es·tu·a·rine (éss-tew-ə-rīn, -choo-, -rin) *adj.* Of, pertaining to, or found in an estuary.

es·tu·ar·y (éss-tew-əri, -choo-, -tewr-i, -choor-i ‖ -erri) *n., pl.* **-ies. 1.** The part of the wide lower course of a river where its current is met and influenced by the sea tides. **2.** An arm of the sea that extends inland to meet the mouth of a river. [Latin *aestuārium,* estuary, tidal channel, from *aestus,* heat, swell, surge, tide.] —**es·tu·ar·i·al** (-áiri-əl) *adj.*

Estuary English *n.* A British accent that is near RP but includes non-RP features from South-East England and that is affected by upwardly mobile people (such as Essex men) who want to sound classless. [From the Thames *Estuary* as the probable origin of this accent.]

esu electrostatic unit.

e·su·ri·ent (i-séwr-i-ənt, -sóor- ‖ -zóor-) *adj. Rare.* Hungry; greedy. [Latin *ēsuriēns* (stem *ēsurient-*), present participle of *ēsurīre,* to want food, to be hungry, desiderative of *edere* (past participle *ēsus*) to eat.] —**e·su·ri·ence, e·su·ri·en·cy** *n.* —**e·su·ri·ent·ly** *adv.*

-et *suffix.* Indicates smallness or lesser status; for example, **bar·onet, pullet.** [Middle English *-et,* from Old French *-et,* from Common Romance *-itta, -ĕtto* (both unattested).]

e·ta (éetə ‖ *chiefly U.S.* áytə) *n.* The seventh letter in the Greek alphabet, written H, η. Transliterated in English as *e.* [Late Latin *ēta,* from Greek, from a Phoenician source, akin to Hebrew *hēth,* HETH.]

e.t.a. estimated time of arrival.

e·taer·i·o (e-téer-i-ō) *n.* An aggregate fruit, developed from a single flower, that may be composed of many drupes as the blackberry, achenes, as the buttercup, or follicles, as the larkspur. [French *etairion,* from Greek *hetaireia,* association.]

é·ta·gère, e·ta·gere (áy-tə-zháir, -ta-) *n.* A piece of furniture with open shelves for ornaments or bric-a-brac. [French, from Old French *estagiere, estage,* floor of a building, position. See **stage.**]

et al. and others [Latin *et alii.*]

e·ta·lon (éttə-lon) *n. Physics.* An arrangement of semireflecting glass or quartz plates used to produce interference fringes, especially for the accurate measurement of wavelength in spectroscopy. [French *étalon,* a standard of weights and measures, from Old French *estalon,* from Germanic *stall-* (unattested), STALL.]

eta meson *n.* A type of meson having zero spin and charge. [Greek *ēta* (arbitrary designation).]

etc. et cetera.
Usage: This form is principally appropriate to informal writing, or to special areas such as technical reporting or business correspondence. It is not appropriate to formal writing in general, where such phrases as *and so forth, and so on,* or *and the like* are preferred. The form *and etc.* is never acceptable. Some people use the full form, *et cetera,* in informal speech, but this tends to suggest a bureaucratic attitude.

et cet·er·a, et·cet·er·a (it-séttrə, et-, -séttərə. *Note: often mistakenly* ik-, ek-) *adv. Abbr.* **etc.** And further things not already mentioned; and so forth. [Latin, "and other (things)" : *et,* and + *cētera,* the rest, from the neuter plural of *cēterus,* remaining.]

et·cet·er·as (it-sét-rəz, et-, -ərəz) *pl.n.* Extras; other incidental items not worth mentioning individually.

etch (ech) *v.* **etched, etching, etches.** —*tr.* **1.** To wear away (metal or glass, for example) with or as if with acid. **2.** To make (a pattern) on a metal plate or other surface with acid. **3.** To cut or engrave. **4.** To impress or imprint (an event, for example) clearly in the mind. —*intr.* To practise etching. [Dutch *etsen,* from German *ätzen,* to etch, to bite, to feed, from Old High German *ezzen,* to feed.] —**etch·er** *n.*

etch·ant (échənt) *n.* An acid or other substance used for etching.

etch·ing (éching) *n.* **1.** A design etched on a plate. **2.** An impression made from an etched plate.

e·ter·nal (ee-térn'l, i-) *adj.* **1.** Without beginning or end; existing outside time: *eternal God.* **2.** Having a beginning but without interruption or end: *an eternal flame.* **3.** Unaffected by time; lasting; timeless. **4.** *Informal.* Seemingly endless; interminable: *tired of your eternal complaining.* **5.** Of or relating to existence after death: *one's eternal rest.* —See Synonyms at **continual, infinite.**
~*n.* Something eternal. —**the Eternal.** God. [Middle English, from Old French, from Late Latin *aeternālis,* from Latin *aeternus,* eternal.] —**e·ter·nal·i·ty** (ée-ter-nál-əti) **e·ter·nal·ness** *n.* —**e·ter·nal·ly** *adj.*

Eternal City. See **Rome.**

e·ter·na·lise, e·ter·na·lize (ee-térn'l-īz, i-) *tr.v.* **-lised, -lising, -lises.** Also **e·ter·nise** (-térn-). **1.** To make eternal. **2.** To make perpetually famous; immortalise. [Old French *eterniser,* from ETERNE.]

eternal triangle *n.* A complex emotional conflict arising from the romantic or sexual involvement of one person with two others. Also called "triangle".

e·ter·ni·ty (ee-térnəti, i-) *n., pl.* **-ties. 1.** The totality of time without beginning or end; infinite time. **2.** The state or quality of being eternal; everlastingness. **3. a.** The endless period of time following death. **b.** The afterlife; immortality. **4.** *Informal.* A very long or seemingly very long time. [Middle English *eternite,* from Old French, from Latin *aeternitās* (stem *aeternitāt-*), from *aeternus,* ETERNAL.]

eternity ring *n.* A ring studded all round with gemstones, offered to a woman as a sign of undying affection.

e·te·sian (i-téezh-'n, -i-ən) *adj.* Recurring annually. Said of prevailing northerly summer winds of the Mediterranean. [Latin *etēsius,* from Greek *etēsios,* from *etos,* year.]

eth-, etho- *comb. form.* Indicates the presence of an ethyl group or derivation from ethane; for example, **ethoxide.**

-eth¹, -th *v. suffix.* Indicates the archaic third person singular form of the present indicative tense; for example, *leadeth, praiseth.* [Middle English *-eth,* Old English *-eth, -th.*]

-eth². Variant of **-th** (in ordinal numbers).

eth·a·nal (éethən'l) *n.* An aldehyde, **acetaldehyde** *(see).*

e·tha·na·mide (eth-ánnə-mīd) *n.* **Acetamide** *(see).*

eth·ane (éethayn, éth-) *n.* A colourless, odourless gas, C_2H_6, occurring as a constituent of natural gas and used as a fuel and refrigerant. Also called "dimethyl". [ETH(YL) + -ANE.]

e·thane·di·o·ic acid (éeth-ayn-dī-ō-ik, éth-) *n.* An organic acid, **oxalic acid** *(see).*

e·thane·di·ol (éeth-ayn-dí-ol, éth- ‖ -ōl) *n.* An alcohol, **ethylene glycol** *(see).*

e·than·o·ate *n.* **Acetate** *(see).*

e·than·o·ic anhydride *n.* **Acetic anhydride** *(see).*

eth·a·nol (éth-ə-nol, éeth- ‖ -nōl) *n. Chemistry.* **Alcohol** *(see).* [ETHAN(E) + -OL.]

Eth·el·red or **Aeth·el·red** (éth'l-red), also known as Ethelred the Unready (*c.* 968-1016). King of the English (978-1016). Most of his reign was spent unsuccessfully resisting Danish invasions. He was driven from London (1013) and fled to Normandy, but returned a year later to be restored to the throne.

eth·ene (étheen) *n. Chemistry.* **Ethylene** *(see).* [ETH(YL) + -ENE.]

e·ther (éethər) *n.* Also **ae·ther** (for sense 3). **1.** Any of a class of organic compounds in which two hydrocarbon groups are linked by an oxygen atom. **2.** A volatile, highly flammable liquid, $C_4H_{10}O$, derived from the distillation of ethanol with sulphuric acid, and widely used in industry and as an anaesthetic. Also called "diethyl ether", "ethyl ether", "ethoxyethane". **3.** *Literary.* The regions of space beyond the Earth's atmosphere; the clear sky; the heavens. **4.** *Physics.* An all-pervading, infinitely elastic, massless medium formerly postulated as the medium of propagation of electromagnetic waves. [Middle English, from Latin *aethēr,* the upper or bright air, ether, from Greek *aithēr.*] —**e·ther·ic** (ee-thérrik) *adj.*

e·the·re·al (i-théer-i-əl) *adj.* **1.** Resembling ether in lightness; impalpable; intangible. **2.** Highly refined; delicate; exquisite. **3. a.** Of the celestial spheres; heavenly: *"Him the almighty power/Hurl'd headlong flaming from th' Ethereal Sky"* (Milton). **b.** Unearthly; spiritual. **4.** *Chemistry.* Of, pertaining to, or dissolved in ether. [Latin *aetherius, aethereus,* from Greek *aitherios,* from *aithēr,* ETHER.] —**e·the·re·al·i·ty** (-ál-əti), **e·the·re·al·ness** *n.* —**e·the·re·al·ly** *adv.*

e·the·re·al·ise, e·the·re·al·ize (i-théer-i-ə-līz) *v.* **-ised, -ising, -ises.** —*tr.* To make, or treat as being, ethereal; spiritualise. —*intr.* To become ethereal. —**e·the·re·al·i·sa·tion** (-lī-záysh'n ‖ *U.S.* -li-) *n.*

e·ther·i·fy (éethəri-fī, ee-thérri-) *tr.v.* **-fied, -fying, -fies.** To convert (an alcohol) into an ether. —**e·ther·i·fi·ca·tion** (-fi-káysh'n) *n.*

e·ther·ise, ether·ize (éethə-rīz) *tr.v.* **-ised, -ising, -ises. 1.** To subject to the fumes of ether; anaesthetise. **2.** *Chemistry.* To etherify. —**e·ther·i·sa·tion** (-rī-záysh'n ‖ *U.S.* -ri-) *n.* —**e·ther·is·er** *n.*

eth·ic (éthik) *n.* A principle of right or good conduct, or a body of such principles: *the work ethic.* [Middle English *et(h)ik,* the science of ethics, from Old French *ethique,* from Late Latin *ēthica* and Latin *ēthicē,* from Greek *ēthikē,* from *ēthikos,* ethical, from *ēthos,* moral custom.]

eth·i·cal (éthik'l) *adj.* **1.** Of, pertaining to, or dealing with ethics: *an ethical dilemma.* **2.** In accordance with the accepted principles of right and wrong governing the conduct of a group; specifically, dealing only with investments that are morally, politically, and ecologically sound: *a leading unit trust in the ethical sector.* **3.** Designating a medicinal preparation dispensed solely on a doctor's prescription. —See Synonyms at **moral.** —**eth·i·cal·ly** *adv.* —**eth·i·cal·ness, eth·i·cal·i·ty** (éthi-kál-əti) *n.*

eth·ics (éthiks) *pl.n.* **1.** *Used with a singular verb.* **a.** The study of the general nature of morals and of the specific moral choices to be made by the individual in his relationship with others; the philosophy of morals. Also called "moral philosophy". **b.** The moral sciences as a whole, including moral philosophy and customary, civil, and religious law. **2.** The rules or standards governing the conduct of the members of a profession: *medical ethics.* **3.** Any set of moral principles or values. **4.** The moral quality of a course of action; fitness; propriety: *I question the ethics of his decision.*

E·thi·op (éethi-op) *n.* Also **E·thi·ope** (-ōp). *Archaic.* A darᵏ

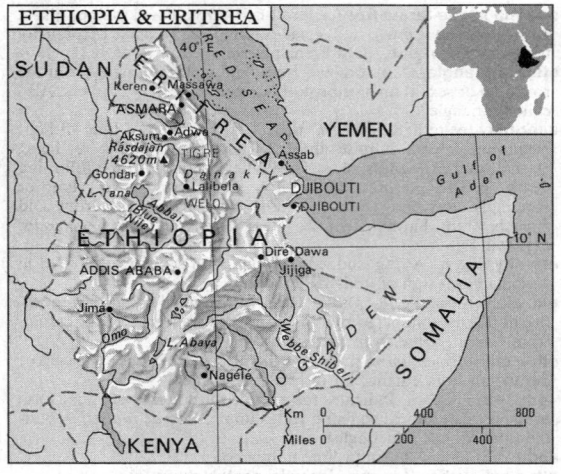

ETHIOPIA & ERITREA

African. [Latin *Aethiops,* from Greek *Aithiops,* "burnt face" : *ai-thein,* to burn + *ōps,* face.]

E·thi·o·pi·a (éethi-ṓpi-ə). A poor, largely mountainous country in northeast Africa, formerly called Abyssinia. An ancient Christian kingdom, Ethiopia was run by a Communist military junta from 1974 to 1991. Already, in the 1960s, secessionist wars had begun in Muslim Eritrea (independent since 1993), and the Somali-peopled Ogaden. Area, 1 133 380 square kilometres (437,600 square miles). Population, 58,510,000. Capital, Addis Ababa.

E·thi·o·pi·an (éethi-ṓpi-ən) *adj.* **1.** Of or pertaining to Ethiopia, its languages, or its people. **2.** *Ecology.* Of or designating the zoogeographical region that includes Africa south of the Sahara and most of Arabia. **3.** *Archaic.* Black African; Negro.
~*n.* **1.** A native or inhabitant of Ethiopia. **2.** *Archaic.* A member of the ancient Greek classification of dark-skinned Africans from the lands beyond Egypt; a Negro.

E·thi·op·ic (éethi-ṓppik, -ṓpik) *n.* **1.** The Semitic language of ancient Ethiopia, having a Christian literature, and still used for liturgical purposes in Ethiopia. Also called "Geez". **2.** A group of Semitic languages, descended from this language, currently spoken in Ethiopia. They include Amharic and Tigre. —**E·thi·op·ic** *adj.*

eth·moid (éth-moyd) *adj.* Also **eth·moi·dal** (eth-móyd'l). Of or designating a light spongy bone located between the eye sockets, that forms part of the walls of the superior nasal cavity.
~*n.* The ethmoid bone. [French *ethmoïde,* from Old French, from Greek *ēthmoeidēs,* perforated (the bone contains many perforations) : *ēthmos,* strainer, from *ēthein,* to strain, to sift + -OID.]

eth·nic (éthnik) *adj.* Also **eth·ni·cal** (-'l). **1. a.** Of, pertaining to, or designating a social group within a cultural and social system that claims or is accorded special status on the basis of complex, often variable traits including religious, linguistic, ancestral, or physical characteristics. **b.** Pertaining to the study and classification of such groups. **2. a.** Broadly, characteristic of a religious, racial, national, or cultural group. **b.** Characteristic of traditional folk styles of food, dress, or other customs. **c.** *Informal.* Quaint; picturesque. **3.** *Rare.* Pertaining to a people not Christian or Jewish; heathen; pagan: *ancient ethnic revels.*
~*n.* *U.S. Informal.* A member of a particular ethnic group. [Late Latin *ethnicus,* heathen, foreign, from Greek *ethnikos,* of a national group, foreign, from *ethnos,* people, nation.] —**eth·ni·cal·ly** *adv.*

Usage: Ethnic is generally used to refer to the characteristics of a racial, tribal, or national group. In recent years, however, especially in American English, it has developed a special sense, where it refers to objects or activities which are unusual or distinctive because of their association with such a group. *Ethnic cooking,* for example, might refer to cooking characteristic of an ethnic minority group. The adjective *ethnic* is also beginning to be used in a way that might be paraphrased as "ethnically", as in *ethnic Chinese resident in Vietnam.* Such a person is Chinese ethnically (by "ethnic origin") but Vietnamese by citizenship. *Ethnic* has also come to be used as a noun, especially in American English, meaning "an immigrant, or the descendant of an immigrant, especially from Eastern or Southern Europe". So *ethnic Canadians* can be ethnically Canadian or Canadian ethnics.

ethnic cleansing *n.* Euphemism for the forcible expulsion or elimination of an ethnic group, usually a minority, by members of another, usually the majority. [Translation of a Serbo-Croat term.]

eth·nic·i·ty (eth-níssəti) *n.* **1.** The condition of belonging to a particular ethnic group. **2.** Ethnic pride.

ethnic minority *n.* An ethnic group living in a society where members of a different race or culture predominate.

ethno-, ethn– *comb. form.* Indicates race, culture, or people; for example, **ethnocentrism.** [French, from Late Greek, from Greek *ethnos,* people.]

eth·no·bot·a·ny (éthnō-bótt'n-i) *n.* The branch of botany relating to the use of plants in religion, folk medicine, and the like. —**eth·no·bot·a·nist** *n.*

eth·no·cen·trism (éthnō-séntriz'm) *n.* **1.** Belief in the superiority of one's own ethnic group. **2.** Overriding concern with race. [ETHNO- + CENTR(O)- + -ISM.] —**eth·no·cen·tric** *adj.*

eth·nog·ra·phy (eth-nóggrəfi) *n., pl.* **-phies. 1.** The descriptive anthropology of ethnic groups, especially technologically primitive societies. **2.** Ethnology. [French *ethnographie* : ETHNO- + -GRAPHY.] —**eth·nog·ra·pher** *n.* —**eth·no·graph·ic** (éth-nə-gráffik, -nō-), **eth·no·graph·i·cal** *adj.* —**eth·no·graph·i·cal·ly** *adv.*

eth·nol·o·gy (eth-nólləji) *n.* The anthropological study of socioeconomic systems and cultural heritage, especially of cultural origins and of factors influencing cultural growth and change, usually in technologically primitive societies. [ETHNO- + -LOGY.] —**eth·no·log·ic** (éthnə-lójik), **eth·no·log·i·cal** *adj.* —**eth·no·log·i·cal·ly** *adv.* —**eth·nol·o·gist** *n.*

eth·no·mu·si·col·o·gy (éthnō-méwzi-kólləji) *n.* The study of the music and musical traditions of ethnic groups.

e·thol·o·gy (ee-thólləji, i-, e-) *n.* The scientific study of animal behaviour in the natural environment. [Latin *ēthologia,* the art of depicting character, from Greek *ēthologia* : *ēthos,* ETHOS + -LOGY.] —**eth·o·log·i·cal** (éethə-lójikˈl, éthə-) *adj.* —**e·thol·o·gist** *n.*

e·thos (éethoss) *n.* **1.** The disposition, character, or attitude peculiar to a specific people, culture, or group that distinguishes it from other peoples or groups; fundamental values or spirit; mores. **2.** The essential character of a period, movement, work of art, mode of expression, or the like: *the ethos of self-help.* [New Latin, from Greek *ēthos,* custom, usage, trait.]

eth·ox·ide (eeth-ók-sīd) *n. Chemistry.* A salt formed by the reaction of a metal with alcohol, HOC_2H_5. Also called "ethylate".

eth·ox·y·e·thane (eth-óksi-éethayn) *n.* An organic compound, **ether** (*see*).

eth·yl (ée-thīl, éthil, éth'l) *n.* A univalent organic radical, C_2H_5. [ETH(ER) + -YL.] —**eth·yl·ic** (i-thíllik, e-) *adj.*

ethyl acetate *n.* A colourless, volatile, flammable liquid, $CH_3COOC_2H_5$, used in perfumes, flavourings, lacquers, pharmaceuticals, and rayon, and as a general solvent.

ethyl alcohol *n.* **Alcohol** (*see*).

eth·yl·a·mine (éthilə-méen) *n.* A colourless, volatile liquid, $C_2H_5NH_2$, used in petroleum refining, detergents, and organic synthesis.

eth·yl·ate (éthi-layt) *tr.v.* **-lated, -lating, -lates.** *Chemistry.* To introduce the ethyl group into (a compound).
~*n.* An ethoxide. [ETHYL + -ATE.] —**eth·yl·a·tion** (-láysh'n) *n.*

ethyl carbamate *n.* A chemical compound, **urethane** (*see*).

ethyl chloride *n.* A chemical compound, C_2H_5Cl, a gas at ordinary temperatures and a colourless, volatile, flammable liquid when compressed, used as a solvent, refrigerant, and in the manufacture of tetraethyl lead.

eth·yl·ene (éthi-leen) *n.* **1.** A colourless, flammable gas, C_2H_4, derived from natural gas and petroleum and used as a source of many organic compounds, in welding and cutting metals, to colour citrus fruits, and as an anaesthetic. **2.** The bivalent organic radical C_2H_4. Also called "ethene". [ETHYL + -ENE.]

ethylene glycol *n.* A colourless, syrupy alcohol, $C_2H_6O_2$, used as an antifreeze in cooling and heating systems. Also called "ethanediol".

ethyl ether *n. Chemistry.* **Ether** (*see*).

ethyl mercaptan *n. Chemistry.* See **mercaptan**.

e·thyne (éeth-īn, éth-) *n.* A gaseous hydrocarbon, **acetylene** (*see*).

ethyne series *n.* The **acetylene series** (*see*).

e·ti·o·late (éeti-ə-layt, -ō-) *v.* **-lated, -lating, -lates.** —*tr.* **1.** To cause (a plant) to develop without normal green colouring by preventing exposure to sunlight; blanch; whiten. **2.** To cause (a person) to lose a healthy colouring and become weak. **3.** To cause to lose vigour, body, force, or the like. —*intr.* **1.** To become blanched or whitened and abnormally elongated, as when grown without sunlight. **2.** To lose a healthy colouring and become weak. [French *étioler,* from *eteule,* a stalk, from Old French *estuble,* from Latin *stipula,* stalk, straw, stubble.] —**e·ti·o·la·tion** (-láysh'n) *n.*

etiology. *U.S.* Variant of **aetiology.** —**etiological** *adj.*

et·i·quette (étti-ket, -kət, -két) *n.* A code of behaviour prescribed or conventionally accepted as correct or polite, as at court, among a profession, or in society at large. [French *etiquette,* prescribed routine, label, ticket, from Old French *estiqu(i)er,* to attach, from Middle Dutch *steken.*]

Synonyms: etiquette, propriety, decorum, protocol.

Et·na (ét-nə). Europe's highest active volcano (3 340 metres; 10,958 feet), situated near the east coast of Sicily. It is first known to have erupted in 475 B.C..

E·ton (éet'n). Town near Windsor on the river Thames. It is the home of Britain's most famous public school, Eton College, founded by King Henry VI in 1440.

Eton collar *n.* A broad, stiff, white collar worn overlapping the lapels of an Eton jacket.

Eton crop *n.* A woman's hairstyle popular in the 1920s in which the hair was cut short like a man's.

Eton fives *n.* See **fives**.

E·to·ni·an (ee-tṓni-ən, i-) *adj.* Of or pertaining to Eton College.
~*n.* A boy or man who is or has been a student at Eton College.

Eton jacket *n.* **1.** A waist-length jacket with wide lapels and cut square at the hips, worn by pupils of Eton College. **2.** A similar short jacket worn by women and girls.

E·tosh·a Game Park (ee-tósha). Largest game reserve in southern Africa. Lying in northwest Namibia, it covers 22 270 square kilometres (8,600 square miles), and includes Etosha Pan, a dried-up salt lake.

é·tri·er (éttri-ay, -áy) *n.* A short rope ladder used in mountaineering. [French, "stirrup".]

E·tru·ri·a (i-trŏŏr-i-ə). Ancient country in Italy, now Tuscany and part of Umbria. It was the centre of the civilisation of the Etruscans, but by the end of the fifth century B.C. it succumbed to Rome.

E·trus·can (i-trúskən) *adj.* Also **E·tru·ri·an** (i-trŏŏr-i-ən). Of or pertaining to Etruria, its inhabitants, or their language or culture. —*n.* Also **E·tru·ri·an.** 1. A person who lived in ancient Etruria. 2. The pre-Roman, now extinct language of the Etruscans, of undetermined linguistic affiliation.

et seq. and the following. [Latin *et sequens, et sequentia.*]

-ette *n. suffix.* Indicates: 1. Small or diminutive; for example, **kitchenette.** 2. An imitation of or a substitute for; for example, **leatherette.** 3. Female or feminine; for example, **usherette.** [Middle English *-ette,* from Old French, feminine of -ET.]

e·tude (ay-téwd ‖ -tŏŏd; *French* -tûd) *n.* 1. A piece of music composed as an exercise for the development of a given point of technique. 2. A composition embodying some point of technique but intended for performance. [French *étude,* study, from Old French *estudie,* study.]

é·tui (e-twée, ay-) *n., pl.* **étuis** (e-twéez). A case for holding small articles, such as needles or toiletries. [French, from Old French *estui,* container, prison, from *estuier,* to shut up, guard, probably from Vulgar Latin *estudiāre* (unattested), to take care of, from Latin *studium,* STUDY.]

et·y·mo·log·i·cal (éttimə-lójik'l) *adj.* Also **et·y·mo·log·ic** (-lójik). *Abbr.* **etym., etymol.** Of or pertaining to etymology, or based upon the principles of etymology. —**et·y·mo·log·i·cal·ly** *adv.*

et·y·mol·o·gise, et·y·mol·o·gize (étti-móllə-jīz) *v.* **-gised, -gising, -gises.** —*tr.* To trace and state the etymology of (a word or words). —*intr.* To give or suggest the etymology of a word or words.

et·y·mol·o·gist (étti-móllə-jist) *n.* A specialist in the principles of etymology and their application.

et·y·mol·o·gy (étti-móllə-ji) *n., pl.* **-gies.** *Abbr.* **etym., etymol.** 1. The origin and historical development of a word or word part, as evidenced by study of its basic elements, earliest known use, and changes in form and meaning; semantic derivation and evolution. 2. An account of the history of a specific word. 3. The branch of linguistics that studies the derivation of words. [Learned respelling of Middle English *ethimologie,* from Old French, from Medieval Latin *ethimologia,* from Latin *etymologia,* from Greek *etumologiā* : *etumon,* ETYMON + -LOGY.]

et·y·mon (étti-mon, -mən) *n., pl.* **-mons** or **-ma** (-mə). The earliest form of a word or word part that can be discovered, from which its modifications are derived. [Latin, origin of a word, from Greek *etumon,* true sense of a word, etymology, from *etumos,* true, real.]

Eu The symbol for the element europium.

eu- *comb. form.* Indicates: 1. Well, pleasant, or beneficial; for example, **euphony.** 2. Derivative of a specified substance: for example, **eucaine.** 3. True; truly so; for example, **eubacteria.** [Middle English *eu-,* from Greek, from *eus,* good.]

eu·bac·te·ri·a (yŏŏbak-téer-i-ə) *pl.n.* A large and diverse group of bacteria, characterised by their rigid cell walls; the true bacteria.

Eu·boe·a (yŏŏ-bée-ə). *Modern Greek* Év·voi·a (évvi-ə). Island in the Aegean Sea. The largest of the Greek islands after Crete, it produces sheep, goats, cattle, grapes, olives, and wheat.

eu·caine (yŏŏ-káyn) *n.* A crystalline substance, $C_{15}H_{21}NO_2$, formerly used as a local anaesthetic. [EU- + -CAINE.]

eu·ca·lyp·tol (yŏŏkə-líp-tol ‖ -tōl) *n.* Also **eu·ca·lyp·tole** (-tōl). A colourless oily liquid, $C_{10}H_{18}O$, derived from eucalyptus oil and used in pharmaceuticals, flavouring, and perfumery. Also called "cineol". [EUCALYPT(US) + -OL.]

eu·ca·lyp·tus (yŏŏkə-líp-təss) *n., pl.* **-tuses** or **-ti** (-tī). Also **eu·ca·lypt** (yŏŏkə-lipt). Any of numerous tall trees of the genus *Eucalyptus,* mostly native to Australia, cultivated for their aromatic leaves that yield eucalyptus oil, their timber, and for ornament. [New Latin : EU- + Greek *kaluptos,* covered (from the flower, which is covered before it opens), from *kaluptein,* to cover, hide.]

eucalyptus oil *n.* An oil derived from the leaves of the eucalyptus, used as a flavouring and as an expectorant and antiseptic.

eucaryote. Variant of **eukaryote.**

Eu·cha·rist (yŏŏkə-rist) *n.* 1. The Christian sacrament instituted at the Last Supper in which bread and wine are consecrated and then eaten and drunk as a memorial of Christ. In some churches, also called "Communion", "Holy Communion". 2. The consecrated elements of bread and wine used in this sacrament. [Middle English *eukarist,* from Old French *eucariste,* from Late Latin *eucharistia,* from Greek *eukharistia,* gratitude, from *eukharistos,* grateful : *eu-,* well, good + *kharizesthai,* to show favour, from *kharis,* favour, grace.] —**Eu·cha·ris·tic** (-rístik), **Eu·cha·ris·ti·cal** *adj.*

eucharistic prayer *n. Roman Catholic Church.* In the revised rite of Mass, that part which contains the consecration, following the Sanctus and concluding with the Lord's Prayer. Compare **canon.**

eu·chre (yŏŏkər) *n.* 1. A U.S. card game played with the 32 highest cards of the pack in which each player is dealt 5 cards; the player making the trump is required to take at least 3 tricks to win. 2. The act of euchring an opponent. —*tr.v.* **euchred, -chring, -chres.** 1. To prevent (an opponent) from taking 3 tricks in euchre. 2. *U.S. Informal.* To outwit. Often used with *out.* [19th century : origin obscure.]

eu·chro·ma·tin (yŏŏ-krómə-tin) *n.* The chromosome material that stains most deeply with basic dyes when the cell is dividing and represents the major genes involved in protein synthesis. Compare **heterochromatin.**

Eu·cken (óykən), **Rudolf Christoph** (1846-1926). German philosopher, known for works such as *The Truth of Religion* (1901) and *The Life of the Spirit* (1909). He was awarded the Nobel prize for literature (1908).

Euc·lid (yŏŏklid) (*fl.* 300 B.C.). Greek mathematician. His most important contribution to mathematics was the use of the deductive principles of logic as the basis of his geometry, deriving statements from clearly defined axioms.

Eu·clid·e·an, Eu·clid·i·an (yŏŏ-klíddi-ən) *adj.* Of or pertaining to Euclid's geometrical principles.

Euclidean algorithm *n.* A method of finding the greatest common divisor of two numbers by dividing one by the other, the second by the remainder, the remainder by the second remainder, and so on until an exact division is reached, when the last divisor is the greatest common divisor of the two numbers.

Euclidean geometry *n.* Geometry based on the postulates of Euclid; especially, the parallel postulate that, for a point outside a line, only one other line can be drawn through the point parallel to the first line.

eu·de·mon, eu·dae·mon (yŏŏ-déemən) *n.* A benevolent spirit.

eu·de·mo·ni·a (yŏŏdi-móni-ə) *n.* Happiness or well-being; especially, in Aristotelian philosophy, happiness resulting from an active, rational life. [Greek *eudaimonia,* from *eudaimōn,* lucky, with a good spirit : *eu-,* good + *daimōn,* spirit.]

eu·de·mon·ism (yŏŏ-déemə-niz'm) *n.* A system of ethics that evaluates the morality of actions in terms of their capacity to produce happiness. —**eu·de·mon·ist** *n.* —**eu·de·mon·is·tic** (-nístik), **eu·de·mon·is·ti·cal** *adj.*

eu·di·om·e·ter (yŏŏdi-ómmitər) *n. Chemistry.* A graduated glass apparatus used to study gas reactions by volume changes. [From Greek *eudios,* "clear-skied" : EU- + *dios,* genitive of *Zeus,* god of the heavens + METER; the apparatus was originally used to measure the amount of oxygen present in the air, which was believed to be greater in clear weather.] —**eu·di·o·met·ric** (-ə-méttrik), **eu·di·o·met·ri·cal** *adj.* —**eu·di·o·me·try** (-ómmətri) *n.*

eu·gen·ics (yŏŏ-jénniks) *n. Used with a singular verb.* The study of the hereditary improvement of the human race by controlled selective breeding. Compare **euthenics.** [Greek *eugenēs,* well-born : EU- + -GEN.] —**eu·gen·ic** *adj.* —**eu·geni·cal·ly** *adv.* —**eu·geni·cist** *n.*

Eu·gé·nie (yoo-zháy-nee, *French* ŏzhe-neé), née Eugénia de Montijo (1826-1920). French empress, born in Spain and the consort of Napoleon III from her marriage to him in 1853 until his overthrow in 1870. She acted as regent during his absences from France and is believed to have had much influence on events that led to the Franco-Prussian war of 1870. She fled to England after his capture at Sedan in September 1870, and died at Farnborough.

eu·ge·nol (yŏŏji-nol ‖ -nōl) *n.* A colourless aromatic oil, $C_{10}H_{12}O_2$, the chief constituent of oil of cloves. [New Latin *Eugenia,* genus of the clove, after *Eugene,* Prince of Savoy (died 1736) + -OL.]

eu·gle·na (yŏŏ-gléenə) *n.* Any of various minute unicellular freshwater organisms of the genus *Euglena,* characterised by the presence of chlorophyll, a reddish eyespot, and a single anterior flagellum. [New Latin : EU- + Greek *glēnē,* eyeball.]

eu·he·mer·ise, eu·he·mer·ize (yŏŏ-héemə-rīz, -hemmə-) *tr.v.* **-ised, -ising, -ises.** To explain or interpret (myths) euhemeristically.

eu·he·mer·ism (yŏŏ-héemə-riz'm, -hémmə-) *n.* 1. A theory attributing the origin of the gods to the deification of historical heroes. 2. Any similar theory linking mythology or folklore with real persons or events. [After *Euhemerus* (*c.* 300 B.C.), Greek philosopher, who developed the theory.] —**eu·he·mer·ist** *n.* —**eu·he·mer·is·tic** (-rístik) *adj.* —**eu·he·mer·is·ti·cal·ly** *adv.*

eu·kary·ote, eu·cary·ote (yŏŏ-kárri-ōt, -ət) *n. Biology.* Any organism in which the genetic material is enclosed by a membrane to form a nucleus. Eukaryotes include all organisms except bacteria, blue-green algae, and viruses. Compare **prokaryote.** [EU- + -*karyote,* irregularly from Greek *karuon,* kernel, nucleus. See KARYO-.] —**eu·kar·y·ot·ic** (-óttik) *adj.*

eu·la·chon (yŏŏlə-kon) *n., pl.* **-chons** or collectively **eulachon.** The candlefish (*see*). [Chinook *ulâkân.*]

Eu·ler (óylər), **Leonhard** (1707-83). Swiss mathematician. His fame rests mainly on his pioneering development of the methods of calculus and on the differential equation named after him.

Euler's formula *n. Mathematics.* 1. The formula $v + f - e = 2$ relating the numbers of vertices (*v*), faces (*f*), and edges (*e*) of a polyhedron. 2. The formula $e^{i\theta} = cos\theta + i\,sin\theta$ for complex numbers.

eu·lo·gi·a (yŏŏ-lóji-ə) *n.* Blessed bread distributed to the congregation after the liturgy in the Greek Orthodox Church. [Greek, "blessing".]

eu·lo·gise, eu·lo·gize (yŏŏlə-jīz) *tr.v.* **-gised, -gising, -gises.** 1. To write or deliver a eulogy about or for. 2. To praise highly; extol. —**eu·lo·gist, eu·lo·gis·er** *n.*

eu·lo·gy (yŏŏlə-ji) *n., pl.* **-gies.** 1. A public speech or written tribute extolling the virtues or achievements of a person or thing; especially, an oration honouring one recently deceased. 2. Great praise or commendation. [Middle English *euloge,* from Medieval Latin *eulogium,* probably variant of *eulogia,* from Greek, praise, eulogy : EU- + -LOGY.] —**eu·lo·gis·tic** (-jísstik) *adj.*

Eu·men·i·des (yŏŏ-ménni-deez) *pl.n. Greek Mythology.* The **Furies**

(see). [Latin, from Greek, "well-minded (ones)", euphemism for the Furies, from *eumenēs*, kindly, well-disposed : *eu-*, well + *menos*, spirit.]

eu·nuch (yōonək) *n.* **1.** A castrated man; especially, one of those who were employed as harem attendants or functionaries in certain Oriental courts and under the Roman emperors. **2.** *Informal.* An ineffectual or powerless man: *an artistic eunuch.* [Middle English *eunuke*, from Latin *eunūchus*, from Greek *eunoukhos*, "bed-watcher", eunuch : *eunē†*, bed + *ekhein*, to have, to hold.]

eu·on·y·mus (yōō-ónnimass) *n.* Any of various trees, shrubs, or vines of the genus *Euonymus*, many of which are cultivated for their decorative foliage or fruits. [New Latin, from Latin *euōnymus*, spindle, tree, from Greek *euōnumos*, of good name : *eu-*, good + *onoma*, name.]

eu·pat·rid (yōō-pátt-rid) *n., pl.* **-ridae** (-ridee) or **-rids.** A member of the hereditary aristocracy of ancient Athens. [Greek *eupatridēs*, of noble family : *eu-*, well + *patēr* (stem *patr-*), father + *-idēs*, patronymic suffix.] **—eu·pat·rid** *adj.*

eu·pep·si·a (yōō-pépsi-ə) *n.* Good digestion. [New Latin, from Greek, from *eupeptos*, EUPEPTIC.]

eu·pep·tic (yōō-péptik) *adj.* **1.** Pertaining to or having good digestion. **2.** Conducive to digestion. **3.** Cheerful. [Greek *eupeptos*, having good digestion : *eu-*, well + *peptein*, to digest, cook.]

eu·phau·si·id (yōō-fáwzi-id) *n.* Any small, shrimplike crustacean of the order Euphausiacea. See **krill.**

eu·phe·mise, eu·phe·mize (yōōfə-mīz) *v.* **-mised, -mising, -mises.** *—tr.* To speak of or refer to euphemistically. *—intr.* To speak with euphemisms.

eu·phe·mism (yōōfə-miz'm) *n.* **1.** The substitution of an inoffensive term for one considered offensively explicit. **2.** The term thus substituted: *"Euphemisms such as 'slumber room' . . . abound in the funeral business"* (Jessica Mitford). [Greek *euphēmismos*, from *euphēmizein*, to speak with good words, from *euphēmia*, use of good words : *eu-*, good + *phēmē*, speech, saying.] **—eu·phe·mist** *n.* **—eu·phe·mis·tic** (-místik) *adj.* **—eu·phe·mis·ti·cal·ly** *adv.*

eu·pho·ni·ous (yōō-fōni-əss) *adj.* Characterised by euphony; agreeable to the ear. **—eu·pho·ni·ous·ly** *adv.*

eu·pho·ni·um (yōō-fōni-əm) *n.* A brass musical instrument, similar to the tuba, but having a somewhat higher pitch and a mellower sound. [Greek *euphōnos*, sweet-voiced. See **euphony.**]

eu·pho·ny (yōōfəni) *n., pl.* **-nies. 1.** Agreeable sound, especially in the phonetic quality of words. **2.** *Phonetics.* The tendency to change speech sounds for the sake of easier pronunciation. [French *euphonie*, from Late Latin *euphōnia*, from Greek, from *euphōnos*, sweet-voiced, euphonious : *eu-*, good + *phōnē*, sound.] **—eu·phon·ic** (yōō-fónnik) *adj.*

eu·phor·bi·a (yōō-fórbi-ə) *n.* Any plant of the genus *Euphorbia*, which includes the spurges and poinsettia. [New Latin, from Latin *euphorbea*, from *Euphorbus*, Greek physician of the first century A.D.]

eu·pho·ri·a (yōō-fáwri-ə ‖ -fóri-) *n.* **1.** A feeling of great happiness or well-being; bliss. **2.** *Psychology.* An exaggerated sense of well-being in pathological cases involving sympathetic delusions. —See Synonyms at **ecstasy.** [New Latin, from Greek, from *euphoros*, easy to bear, well-borne : *eu-*, well + *pherein*, to bear] **—eu·phor·ic** (-fórrik ‖ -fáwrik) *adj.*

eu·pho·ri·ant (yōō-fáwri-ənt ‖ -fóri-) *adj.* Tending to produce euphoria.
~n. An agent that produces euphoria.

eu·phot·ic (yōō-fōtik, -fóttik) *adj.* Pertaining to, designating, or characterising the uppermost layer of a body of water, receiving sufficient light for photosynthesis and the growth of green plants. [EU- + PHOTIC.]

eu·phra·sy (yōōfrə-si, -zi) *n. Archaic.* A plant of the genus *Euphrasia;* eyebright. [Middle English *eufrasie*, from Medieval Latin *eufrasia*, from Greek *euphrasia*, good cheer, from *euphrainein*, to cheer, gladden : *eu-*, good + *phrēn*, mind.]

Eu·phra·tes (yōō-fráyteez). *Turkish* **Frat** (frat); *Arabic* **Al Fu·rāt** (al fərát). River in southwestern Asia, formed by the confluence of the Murad and Kara rivers and flowing for 2 740 kilometres (1,700 miles) from central Turkey through Syria into Iraq, where it joins with the river Tigris to form the Shatt al Arab.

eu·phroe, u·phroe (yōō-frō, -vrō) *n.* **1.** *Nautical.* A perforated batten through which the lines of a crowfoot are passed to suspend an awning. **2.** A piece of wood having holes through which a tent rope, for example, is passed, and by means of which tension on the rope can be adjusted. [Dutch *juffrouw*, maiden, euphroe, from Middle Dutch *joncfrouwe*.]

Eu·phros·y·ne (yōō-frózzi-nee). *Greek Mythology.* One of the three **Graces** *(see.)* [Latin *Euphrosynē*, from Greek *Euphrosunē*, "mirth", from *euphrōn*, of good mind, cheerful : *eu-*, good + *phrēn*, mind.]

eu·phu·ism (yōōfew-iz'm) *n.* **1.** An affectedly elegant style of speech or writing used by imitators of John Lyly in the late 16th and early 17th centuries, characterised by elaborate alliteration, antitheses, and similes. **2.** Broadly, affected elegance of language: *"Among his contemporaries, Willie's euphuisms only raised a laugh"* (Aldous Huxley). [After *Euphues*, a character in two works by John Lyly, from Greek *euphuēs*, shapely, well-grown : *eu-*, well + *phuein*, to grow, to bring forth.] **—eu·phu·ist** *n.* **—eu·phu·is·tic** (-ístik) *adj.* **—eu·phu·is·ti·cal·ly** *adv.*

eu·plas·tic (yōō-plástik) *adj.* Healing readily.

eu·ploid (yōōployd) *n.* An organism or cell whose chromosome number is an exact multiple of the haploid number characteristic of the species. [EU- + (HA)PLOID.] **—eu·ploid** *adj.* **—eu·ploi·dy** (-dee) *n.*

eup·noe·a, *U.S.* **eup·ne·a** (yōōp-née-ə ‖ yóōpni-ə) *n.* Normal, unlaboured breathing. [New Latin, from Greek *eupnoia*, from *eupnoos*, breathing well : *eu-*, good + *pnoē, pnoiē*, a breathing, from *pnein*, to breathe.]

—eur *n. suffix.* **—er**[1] *(1) (see).* Used in words of French origin; for example, **entrepreneur, restaurateur.** Compare **—euse.** [French.]

—euse *n. suffix.* **—er**[1] *(1) (see).* Used in words of French origin as the feminine equivalent of **—eur;** for example, **chanteuse.** [French.]

Eur·a·sia (yoor-áysha, -áyzhə). The landmass that comprises the continents of Europe and Asia.

Eur·a·sian (yoor-áysh'n, -áyzh'n) *adj.* **1.** Of, pertaining to, or originating in Eurasia. **2.** Of mixed European and Asian ancestry.
~n. A person of mixed European and Asian ancestry.

Eur·at·om (yoor-áttəm) *n.* European Atomic Energy Commission.

eu·re·ka (yoor-éeka) *interj.* Used to express triumph upon finding or discovering something. [Greek *heurēka*, "I have found (it)" (see **Archimedes),** perfect indicative of *heuriskein*, to find.]

eu·rhyth·mic (yōō-ríthmik, yoor-) *adj.* **1.** Harmonious in rhythm or proportions. **2.** Of or pertaining to eurhythmics.

eu·rhyth·mics (yōō-ríthmiks, yoor-) *n. Used with a singular verb.* The choreographic art of interpreting music through rhythmical, free-style, graceful movement of the body.

eu·rhyth·my, *U.S.* **eu·ryth·my** (yōō-ríthmi, yoor-) *n.* **1.** Harmony of proportions in architecture. **2.** Rhythmical or graceful movements. **3.** A system of rhythmical body movements in harmony with the rhythm of the spoken word, used in a form of dance training.

Eu·rip·i·des (yoor-íppi-deez) *(c.* 480-406 B.C.). Greek dramatist who ranks with Sophocles and Aeschylus as one of the great writers of classical tragedy. He wrote over 90 plays; among those that survive are *Alcestis, Hippolytus, The Trojan Women, Electra, Medea,* and *Iphigenia in Tauris.*

eu·ri·pus (yoor-í-pəss) *n., pl.* **-pi** (-pī). A sea channel characterised by turbulent and unpredictable currents in either direction. [Latin, from Greek *euripos*, strait, place where the current is violent : *eu-*, well (euphemistic) + *ripē*, rush, force, from *rīptein*, to throw.]

Eu·ro (yoor-ō) *n., pl.* **Euros. 1.** The monetary unit of the European Union. **2.** A coin or note worth one Euro. [From EURO-.]

Euro- *comb.form.* Indicates: **1.** Europe, especially Western Europe or European; for example, **Eurodollar. 2.** The European Community or Union; for example, **Eurocrat.**

Eu·ro·cen·tric (yoor-ō-séntrik) *adj.* Centring on Europe or European values, especially to the exclusion of non-European cultures. Often derogatory. **—Eu·ro·cen·trism** (-séntriz'm) *n.*

Eu·ro·cheque (yoor-ō-chek) *n. British.* **1.** An integrated banking system operating in most West European countries. **2.** A cheque drawn under this system and acceptable in a European country other than that in which it originated.

Eu·ro·crat (yoor-ō-krat, -ə-) *n. Informal.* A senior official in the administration of the European Community. Sometimes used derogatorily. [EURO- + (BUREAU)CRAT.]

Eu·ro·cur·ren·cy (yoor-ō-kurrən-si) *n., pl.* **-cies. 1.** Any of various national currencies used for trade and exchange dealings in Europe and elsewhere. **2.** A proposed common currency for the member states of the European Community. See **ECU, Euro.**

Eu·ro·dol·lar (yoor-ō-dollər, -ə-) *n.* A U.S. dollar on deposit with a bank in Europe and often used as an exchange currency.

Eu·ro·M.P. (yoor-ō-ém-pée) *n.* A member of the European Parliament; an M.E.P.

Eu·ro·pa (yoor-rōpə). *Greek Mythology.* A Phoenician princess abducted to Crete by Zeus, in the guise of a white bull.

Eu·rope (yoor-əp). The world's second smallest major land area, after Oceania. It has only 7 per cent of the globe's land, but with 15 per cent of the world's people it is the second most populous continent after Asia. Europe includes part of the world's largest country, Russia, and also its smallest sovereign state, the Vatican City. After World War II, the U.S.S.R. dominated **Eastern Europe,** also known as the Eastern or Communist Bloc, where the countries had centrally planned economies. The nations of **Western Europe,** with capitalist or mixed economies, largely looked to the United States for military alliance. From the end of the 1980s, divisions blurred as Eastern Europe moved away from communism. Area, 10 498 000 square kilometres (4,053,000 square miles), including Russia west of the Ural Mountains.

Eu·ro·pe·an (yoor-ə-pée-ən, -péern) *adj. Abbr.* **Eur. 1.** Of, pertaining to, or derived from the continent of Europe, its peoples, cultures, or languages. **2.** Indigenous to or native to Europe. **3.** Of or pertaining to the European Community.
~n. **1.** A native or inhabitant of Europe. **2.** One of European ancestry. **3.** A citizen of a country belonging to the European Community, especially with reference to the extent of the person's support for the Community: *good Europeans.* **4.** *South African.* A white native of South Africa.

European Communities *pl.n.* A union of three communities which share a common administrative organisation: the European Coal and Steel Community, the European Community, and the European Atomic Energy Commission (Euratom).

European Community *n. Abbr.* **EC.** See European Economic Community.

European Court of Justice *n.* A court in Luxembourg which deals with cases involving the laws of the European Community.

European Economic Community *n. Abbr.* **EEC.** Formerly, an association of twelve member countries (Belgium, France, West

Germany, Luxembourg, the Netherlands, and Italy, founder members; subsequently joined by the United Kingdom, the Republic of Ireland, Denmark, Greece, Spain, and Portugal), founded by the Treaty of Rome (1957) as a customs union and to promote economic and political cooperation between the member countries. Also called "Common Market". Now called "European Community", "European Union".

European Exchange Rate Mechanism *n.* A system for linking the currencies of European Community countries that allows for fluctuation in exchange rates.

Eu·ro·pe·an·ise, Eu·ro·pe·an·ize (yoŏr-ə-pée-ə-nīz) *tr.v.* **-ised, -ising, -ises.** **1.** To make European in culture, political institutions, or the like. **2.** To introduce the institutions and regulations of the European Union into (a country). —**Eu·ro·pe·an·i·sa·tion** (nī-záysh'n ‖ *U.S.* -ni-) *n.*

Eu·ro·pe·an·ism (yoŏr-ə-pée-ə-niz'm) *n.* **1.** A political movement promoting a policy of unity among European countries, especially the European Union. **2.** Support for such a policy; a favourable attitude towards the European Union. —**Eu·ro·pe·an·ist** *n.*

European Parliament *n.* The legislative assembly of the European Union.

European plan *n.* *U.S.* A system of hotel tariffs in which a guest pays for his room and services separately from his payment for meals. Compare **American plan.**

European Recovery Program *n.* A U.S. economic aid programme to European nations following World War II, initiated by George C. Marshall. Also called "Marshall Plan".

European Union *n. Abbr.* **EU.** Concept created by the 1992 Maastricht Treaty, embracing the European Community and certain other international bodies, and conferring EU citizenship on all citizens of member countries of the European Community. Its membership includes the 12 states of the former European Economic Community and Austria, Finland, and Sweden, which joined in 1995.

eu·ro·pi·um (yoŏr-ópi-əm) *n. Symbol* **Eu** A silvery-white, soft, rare-earth element occurring in monazite and bastnaesite. It is used as a laser dopant, phosphor, and in research to absorb neutrons. Atomic number 63, atomic weight 151.96, melting point 826°C, boiling point 1439°C, relative density 5.259, valencies 2, 3. [New Latin, from EUROPE.]

Europoort. See **Rotterdam.**

Eu·ro·vis·ion (yoŏr-ə-vizh'n) *n.* The television network of the European Broadcasting Union, through which news and programmes are exchanged or relayed.

eury- *comb. form.* Indicates wide or broad; for example, **eurypterid.** [New Latin, from Greek *euru-,* from *eurus,* wide.]

Eu·ry·a·le (yoŏ-rí-əli, yoor-). *Greek Mythology.* One of the three Gorgons.

Eu·ryd·i·ce (yoŏ-ríddəsi, yoor-). *Greek Mythology.* The wife of Orpheus, who was permitted by Pluto to follow her husband out of Hades, provided that he refrain from looking back at her; Orpheus did look back, and Eurydice was doomed to return to the dead. [Latin, from Greek *Eurudikē,* "wide justice" : *euru-,* EURY- + *dikē,* justice, custom, law.]

eu·ry·hal·ine (yoor-í-həlin) *adj.* Able to tolerate wide variations in salt concentration. Said of aquatic animals such as eels. Compare **stenohaline.**

eu·ryp·ter·id (yoŏ-ríptər-id, yoor-) *n.* Any of various large, extinct, aquatic arthropods of the order Eurypterida, existing from the Ordovician to the Permian period. [New Latin *Eurypterida,* from *Eurypterus* (genus) : EURY- + -PTEROUS.]

eu·ry·ther·mal (yoŏri-thér-m'l) *adj.* Also **eu·ry·ther·mic** (-mik), **eu·ry·ther·mous** (-məss). Adaptable to a wide range of temperatures. Said of an organism.

eu·ryth·my. *U.S.* Variant of **eurhythmy.** —**eurythmic** *adj.*

eu·ry·trop·ic (yoŏr-i-tróppik) *adj.* Also **eu·ry·top·ic** (-tóppik). Capable of existing in a wide range of environmental conditions. Said of plant and animal species. Compare **stenotropic.**

eu·spo·ran·gi·ate (yoŏ-spo-ránji-ayt, -spaw-, -ət, -it ‖ -spō-) *adj.* Of or designating ferns in which the sporangium develops from a group of cells. Compare **leptosporangiate.**

Eu·sta·chian tube (yoŏ-stáysh'n, -stáyki-ən) *n.* A bony and cartilaginous tube that connects the tympanic cavity with the nasal part of the pharynx and equalises air pressure on either side of the eardrum. [After Bartolommeo *Eustachio* (died 1574), Italian anatomist.]

eu·stat·ic (yoŏ-státtik) *adj.* Of or pertaining to overall changes in sea level, as produced by large-scale geological changes such as movement of the ocean floor or melting of ice caps.

eu·tec·tic (yoŏ-téktik) *adj.* **1.** Of, pertaining to, or formed at the lowest possible temperature of solidification for any mixture of specific constituents. Said especially of alloys. **2.** Exhibiting the constitution or properties of a solid so formed.
~*n.* **1.** A eutectic mixture, solution, or alloy. **2.** The temperature at which a eutectic forms. [Greek *eutēktos,* easily melted : *eu-,* well + *tēktos,* melted, from *tēkein,* to melt.]

Eu·ter·pe (yoŏ-térpi). *Greek Mythology.* The Muse of lyric poetry and music.

eu·tha·na·si·a (yoŏthə-náyzi-ə, náy-zhə) *n.* The action of inducing the painless death of a person from motives of compassion. Also called "mercy killing". [Greek : *eu-,* good + *thanatos,* death.]

eu·then·ics (yoŏ-thénniks) *n. Used with a singular verb.* The study of the improvement of human functioning and well-being by adjust-

ment of environment. Compare **eugenics.** [Greek *euthenein,* to flourish, thrive.]

eu·the·ri·an (yoŏ-théer-i-ən) *adj.* Of, pertaining to, or designating mammals of the subclass Eutheria, characterised by the formation of a placenta and including all mammals except the monotremes and marsupials. [New Latin *Eutheria* : Greek *eu-,* well + *thēria,* plural of *thērion,* beast.] —**eu·the·ri·an** *n.*

eu·troph·ic (yoŏ-tróffik, yoŏ-, -trófik) *adj.* Designating a body of water in which the increase of mineral and organic nutrients has reduced the dissolved oxygen, producing an environment that favours plant life over animal life. [Probably from German *Eutroph,* from Greek *eutrophos,* well-nourished, from *eutrophein,* to thrive : *eu-,* well + *trephein,* to nourish.] —**eu·troph·i·ca·tion** (-áysh'n) *n.*

eux·e·nite (yoŏk-si-nīt) *n.* A lustrous blackish-brown mineral consisting of cerium, erbium, niobium, titanium, uranium, and yttrium. [German *Euxenit,* from Greek *euxenos,* kind to strangers (it contains many rare or "strange" elements) : *eu-,* good + *xenos,* stranger.]

eV electronvolt.

EVA extravehicular activity.

e·vac·u·ant (i-váckew-ənt) *adj.* Causing evacuation of an organ, especially of the bowels.
~*n.* An evacuant medicine or agent; a purgative or emetic.

e·vac·u·ate (i-váckew-ayt) *v.* **-ated, -ating, -ates.** —*tr.* **1. a.** To cause to be empty by removing the contents of. **b.** To create a vacuum in. **2.** To excrete or discharge (waste matter), especially from the bowels. **3.** *Military.* **a.** To relinquish possession or occupation of (a town, fortress, or encampment, for example). **b.** To withdraw or send away (troops or inhabitants) from a threatened area. **4.** To withdraw or depart from; vacate. —*intr.* **1.** To withdraw from or vacate any place or area, especially a threatened area. **2.** To discharge waste matter from the body. [Latin *ēvacuāre,* to empty out, to evacuate : *ē-,* out, from *ex-* + *vacuus,* empty.] —**e·vac·u·a·tion** (-áysh'n) *n.* —**e·vac·u·a·tor** *n.*

e·vac·u·ee (i-váckew-ée) *n.* A person withdrawn or sent away from a threatened or dangerous area.

e·vade (i-váyd) *v.* **evaded, evading, evades.** —*tr.* **1.** To escape or avoid by cleverness or deceit: *evade arrest.* **2.** To avoid fulfilling, answering, or performing: *evade responsibility.* **3.** To baffle or elude: *The accident evades explanation.* —*intr.* To use cleverness or deceit in avoiding or escaping. —See Synonyms at **escape.** [Old French *evader,* from Latin *ēvādere,* to evade, go out, escape : *ē-,* out, from *ex-* + *vādere,* to go.] —**e·vad·a·ble** *adj.* —**e·vad·er** *n.*

e·val·u·ate (i-vál-yoo-ayt) *tr.v.* **-ated, -ating, -ates.** **1.** To ascertain or fix the value or worth of. **2.** To examine and judge; appraise; estimate. **3.** *Mathematics.* To calculate or set down the numerical value of; express numerically. —See Synonyms at **estimate.** [Back-formation from *evaluation,* from French *évaluation,* from Old French, from *evaluer,* to evaluate : *e-,* out, from Latin *ex-* + VALUE.] —**e·val·u·a·tion** (-áysh'n) *n.*

ev·a·nesce (éevə-néss, évvə-) *intr.v.* **-nesced, -nescing, -nesces.** To dissipate like vapour; disappear gradually; fade away; vanish. [Latin *ēvānēscere,* to vanish : *ē-,* completely, from *ex-* + *vānēscere,* to pass away, from *vānus,* empty, vain.] —**ev·a·nes·cence** *n.*

ev·a·nes·cent (éevə-néss'nt, évvə-) *adj.* Vanishing or likely to vanish; transitory; fleeting: *"Seeking permanence in the midst of what was only perpetually evanescent"* (Malcolm Lowry). See Synonyms at **transient.** —**ev·a·nes·cent·ly** *adv.*

e·van·gel (i-vánjəl) *n.* **1.** *Usually capital* **E.** The Christian gospel; especially, any of the four Gospels of the New Testament. **2.** Any glad tidings. **3.** *Rare.* An evangelist. [Middle English *evangelie,* from Old French *evangile,* from Late Latin *evangelium,* from Greek *euangelion,* good news, reward for bringing good news, from *euangelos,* bringing good news : *eu-,* good + *angelos,* messenger.]

e·van·gel·i·cal (éevan-jéllik'l) *adj.* Also **e·van·gel·ic** (-jéllik). **1.** Of, pertaining to, or in accordance with the Christian gospel, especially the four Gospels of the New Testament. **2.** *Often capital* **E.** Protestant. **3.** Of, pertaining to, or being a Protestant group emphasising the authority of the Gospel and the importance of personal conversion and faith in Christ as one's own saviour. **4.** Pertaining or belonging to the Evangelical Church in Germany. **5.** Pertaining or belonging to the Low Church party in the Church of England. **6.** Characterised by evangelism; zealous.
~*n.* A member of an evangelical church or party. —**e·van·gel·i·cal·ly** *adv.*

e·van·gel·i·cal·ism (éevan-jéllik'l-iz'm) *n.* **1.** Evangelical beliefs or doctrines. **2.** Adherence to a church or party professing such beliefs or doctrines.

e·van·gel·ise, e·van·gel·ize (i-vánjə-līz) *v.* **-ised, -ising, -ises.** —*tr.* **1.** To preach the gospel to. **2.** To convert to Christianity. —*intr.* To preach the gospel; be an evangelist. —**e·van·gel·i·sa·tion** (-lī-záysh'n ‖ *U.S.* -li-) *n.* —**e·van·gel·is·er** *n.*

e·van·gel·ism (i-vánjə-liz'm) *n.* **1.** The zealous preaching and dissemination of the gospel, as through missionary work. **2.** Militant zeal for any cause.

e·van·gel·ist (i-vánjə-list) *n.* **1.** *Usually capital* **E.** Any of the authors of the four New Testament Gospels: Matthew, Mark, Luke, or John. **2.** One who practises evangelism; especially, a Protestant preacher or missionary. **3.** In the Mormon Church, a **patriarch** (see). —**e·van·gel·is·tic** (-lístik) *adj.* —**e·van·gel·is·ti·cal·ly** *adv.*

Ev·ans (évv'nz), **Sir Arthur John** (1851–1941). British archaeologist and Keeper of the Ashmolean Museum, Oxford. His excavations in Crete, mostly at Knossos, from 1899, unearthed a Bronze Age civilisation which he named Minoan, after the legendary King Minos.

Evans, Dame Edith (1888–1976). English actress. After winning acclaim for her performance as Cressida in 1912, she joined the Old Vic company and thereafter played a wide variety of roles, of which her most famous was Lady Bracknell in *The Importance of Being Earnest.* Her films include *Look Back in Anger* (1959).

Evans, Sir Geraint (Llewellyn) (1922–92). Welsh baritone. He was a principal baritone of the Royal Opera, Covent Garden, from 1948. He was best known for his comic roles. He retired in 1982.

Evans, Mary Ann. See George **Eliot.**

Evans, Mostyn, known as **Moss** (1925–). British trade unionist. He was elected general secretary of the Transport and General Workers' Union in 1978.

e·vap·o·ra·ble (i-váppər-əb'l) *adj.* Capable of being evaporated. **—e·vap·o·ra·bil·i·ty** (-əbílləti) *n.*

e·vap·o·rate (i-váppə-rayt) *v.* **-rated, -rating, -rates.** *—tr.* **1. a.** To convert or change into a vapour, especially at a temperature below the boiling point. **b.** To draw off in the form of vapour. **2.** To draw moisture from, leaving only the dry solid portion. **3.** To deposit (a metal) on a substrate by vacuum sublimation. *—intr.* **1. a.** To change into vapour. **b.** To pass off in or as vapour. **2.** To produce vapour. **3.** To disappear; vanish: *His fears evaporated.* [Middle English *evaporaten,* from Latin *ēvapōrāre* (past participle *ēvapōrātus*), "to go out in vapour", evaporate : *ē-,* out of, from *ex-* + *vapor,* steam, vapour.] **—e·vap·o·ra·tion** (-ráysh'n) *n.* **—e·vap·o·ra·tive** (-rətiv, -raytiv) *adj.* **—e·vap·o·ra·tor** *n.*

e·vap·o·rat·ed milk (i-váppə-raytid) *n.* Concentrated, unsweetened milk processed by evaporating some of the water from whole milk. Compare **condensed milk.**

e·vap·o·rite (i-váppə-rīt) *n.* A sedimentary rock or mineral, such as rock salt or gypsum, that has been formed by evaporation of salt water.

e·va·sion (i-váy-zh'n || -sh'n) *n.* **1.** The act of avoiding, evading, or escaping. **2.** See **tax evasion. 3.** A means of evading; a subterfuge. **4.** An excuse or equivocal answer. [Middle English *evasioun,* from Old French *evasion,* from Late Latin *ēvāsiō* (stem *ēvāsiōn-*), from Latin *ēvāsus,* past participle of *ēvādere,* to EVADE.]

e·va·sive (i-váy-siv || -ziv) *adj.* **1.** Characterised by or exhibiting evasion. **2.** Intentionally vague or ambiguous; equivocal: *an evasive statement.* **—e·va·sive·ly** *adv.* **—e·va·sive·ness** *n.*

eve (eev) *n.* **1.** *Often capital* **E.** The evening or day preceding a special day, such as a saint's day or holiday: *Saint Agnes' Eve; New Year's Eve.* **2.** The period immediately preceding a certain event: *the eve of war.* **3.** *Poetic.* Evening. [Middle English *eve,* variant of EVEN (evening).]

Eve (eev). In the Bible, the first woman and companion of Adam. Genesis 3:20.

e·vec·tion (i-véksh'n) *n. Astronomy.* Solar perturbation of the lunar orbit. [Latin *ēvectiō* (stem *ēvectiōn-*), a going up, from *ēvectus,* past participle of *ēvehere,* to carry out : *ē-,* out, upwards, from *ex-* + *vehere,* to carry.] **—e·vec·tion·al** *adj.*

Eve·lyn (éevlin), **John** (1620–1706). Writer and one of the founders of the Royal Society. He is best known for his *Diary* (discovered 1817, published 1878), which covers most of his life and is rich in information about 17th-century England.

e·ven¹ (éev'n) *adj.* **1. a.** Having a horizontal surface; flat: *an even floor.* **b.** Having no irregularities, roughness, or indentations; smooth. **2.** Having the same plane or line; at the same height or depth; parallel; level: *The picture is even with the window.* **3.** Having no variations or fluctuations; uniform; steady; regular: *an even rate of speed.* **4.** Of uniform thickness; uniformly distributed: *an even application of varnish.* **5.** Tranquil; calm; placid: *an even temper.* **6.** Equally matched or balanced: *an even contest.* **7.** Equal or identical in degree, extent, or amount: *even amounts of wine and water.* **8.** Having equal probability. Said of alternatives, possibilities, or events: *an even chance of winning or losing.* **9. a.** Having an equal score: *The teams are even.* **b.** Being equal for each opponent. Said of a score. **10.** Neither owing nor being owed; having nothing due: *Give him five pence, and you will be even.* **11.** Having exacted full revenge. **12. a.** *Mathematics.* Exactly divisible by 2. **b.** Characterised or indicated by a number exactly divisible by 2. Compare **odd. 13. a.** Having an even number in a series. **b.** Having an even number of members. **14.** Having an exact amount, extent, or number: *an even pound.* —See Synonyms at **steady, level.**

~adv. **1.** Used to stress something that might not be expected: *even the children went; he even drove us home.* **2.** At the same time as; just: *Even as we watched, the building collapsed.* **3.** In spite of; notwithstanding: *Even with his head start, I soon overtook him.* **4. a.** To a higher degree or extent; yet; still. Used as an intensive: *an even worse condition.* **b.** Indeed; in fact; moreover. Used as an intensive: *unhappy, even weeping.* **5.** *Archaic.* To a degree that extends as specified: *loyal even unto death.* **6.** *Archaic.* The same as; identical with: *It is I, even I.* **—break even.** *Informal.* To have neither losses nor gains. **—get even.** To exact one's full measure of revenge.

~v. **evened, evening, evens.** *—tr.* **1.** To make even, smooth, or level. **2.** To settle or balance (accounts, debts, or the like); square. Often used with *off* or *up.* *—intr.* To become even or smooth. Used with *off, out,* or *up.* [Middle English *even,* Old English *ef(e)n,* even, level, from Common Germanic *ibnaz* (unattested).] **—e·ven·ly** *adv.* **—e·ven·ness** *n.*

even² *n. Archaic.* Evening. [Middle English *eve, even,* Old English *ǣfen.*]

e·ven·fall (éev'n-fawl) *n. Poetic.* The beginning of evening; twilight.

e·ven·hand·ed (éev'n-hándid) *adj.* Dealing equitably with all; impartial. **—e·ven·hand·ed·ly** *adv.* **—e·ven·hand·ed·ness** *n.*

eve·ning (éevning) *n. Abbr.* **evg. 1.** The period of decreasing daylight during the decline and setting of the sun between afternoon and night. **2. a.** The period between the termination of one's daily activities and bedtime. **b.** This period occupied in a given manner: *an evening at home.* **3.** Any latter period or time of decline: *in the evening of his life.* [Middle English *evening,* Old English *ǣfnung,* evening, from *ǣfnian,* to become evening, from *ǣfen,* evening.]

evening class *n.* A class, usually held in the evenings in a school or college, providing instruction for adults in recreational or vocational activities.

evening dress *n.* **1.** Clothing, especially formal clothing, such as a man's dinner jacket, worn for evening social events. **2.** A woman's formal dress, usually long, and worn especially in the evening. In this sense, also called "evening gown".

Evening Prayer *n.* An evening prayer service which is read or sung, especially evensong in the Anglican Church or vespers in the Roman Catholic Church.

evening primrose *n.* Any of various North American plants of the genus *Oenothera,* characteristically having four-petalled yellow flowers that open in the evening and containing an oil with a high concentration of essential fatty acids.

eve·nings (éevningz) *adj. Chiefly U.S. Informal.* Regularly or habitually each evening.

evening star *n.* Any planet that crosses the local meridian before midnight, especially Mercury or Venus when either is prominent in the west shortly after sunset. Also called "morning star" and formerly, especially referring to Venus, "Vesper".

e·vens (éev'nz) *adj.* **1.** Standing to win exactly the sum staked. Said of a bet. **2.** Being offered at these odds. Said of a horse or other racing animal. **—e·vens** *adv.*

e·ven·song (éev'n-song || *U.S.* -sawng) *n.* **1.** The service of Evening Prayer in the Anglican Church, often a choral service. **2.** A vesper service. **3.** A song sung in the evening. **4.** *Archaic.* Evening.

e·vent (i-vént) *n.* **1.** An occurrence, incident, or experience, especially one of some significance. **2.** The actual outcome or final result. **3.** One of the items in a calendar or programme of sports. **4.** An important social occasion. **5.** *Physics.* A coincidence of two or more points at a particular position in space at a particular instant of time, regarded as the fundamental observational entity in relativity theory. —See Synonyms at **occurrence. —at all events** or **in any event.** In any case; whatever the circumstances. **—in the event. 1.** If a specified condition is fulfilled: *what to do in the event of an accident.* **2.** As it turned out; as things happened: *In the event I'd had nothing to fear after all.* [Latin *ēventus,* a coming out, event, from the past participle of *ēvenīre,* to come out, happen : *ē-,* out, from *ex-* + *venīre,* to come.]

even-tempered (éev'n-témpərd) *adj.* Tranquil; difficult to anger.

e·vent·ful (i-véntf'l) *adj.* **1.** Full of or rich in events: *an eventful week.* **2.** Important; momentous: *an eventful decision.* **—e·vent·ful·ly** *adv.* **—e·vent·ful·ness** *n.*

event horizon *n. Astronomy.* The spherical surface marking the boundary of a black hole, being the place at which the escape velocity is equal to the speed of light, so that no electromagnetic radiation or information can leave the black hole.

e·ven·tide (éev'n-tīd) *n. Poetic.* Evening. [Middle English *eventide,* Old English *ǣfentīd* : *ǣfen,* EVEN (evening) + *tīd,* time, season.]

e·vent·ing (i-vénting) *n.* The practice of entering or attending **three-day events** *(see).*

e·ven·tu·al (i-vén-choo-əl, -tew-, -chōōl) *adj.* **1.** Occurring at an unspecified time in the future; ultimate: *his eventual death.* **2.** Occurring or having occurred after some time has elapsed. **3.** *Archaic.* Dependent on circumstance; possible; contingent. —See Synonyms at **last.** [From EVENT.]

e·ven·tu·al·i·ty (i-vén-choo-ál-əti, -tew-) *n., pl.* **-ties.** Something that may occur; a contingency; a possibility.

e·ven·tu·al·ly (i-vén-choo-əli, -tew-, -chōōli) *adv.* **1.** Finally; as the last step in a process. **2.** After a long delay.

e·ven·tu·ate (i-vén-choo-ayt, -tew-) *intr.v.* **-ated, -ating, -ates.** To result ultimately: *Their debate eventuated in an agreement.*

ev·er (évvər) *adv.* **1. a.** At all times; always; constantly. Sometimes used in combination: *his ever-patient sister.* **b.** Repeatedly: *ever complaining.* **2.** At any time: *Have you ever seen a circus?* **3.** Used to add emphasis, especially in questions: *How could you ever treat him so?* **4.** *Chiefly British Informal.* To a great degree; very much. Used as an intensive: *I'm ever so relieved.* **5.** *Chiefly U.S. Informal.* Certainly; without doubt: *Happy? Is she ever!* **—for ever and a day.** Always; for ever. [Middle English *ever,* Old English *ǣfre.*]

Usage: In combination with *who, which, what, when,* and *how, ever* has two distinct meanings, which are reflected by a conventional difference in writing. When written as a single word, a generalised meaning is intended: *whatever else; wherever he went.* When written as two words, *ever* acts to give emphasis: *Where ever did you go? How ever did you do that?* The intensifying phrase *ever so* may sometimes be heard without an adjective following *(I enjoyed the chocolate ever so).* See also **forever.**

Ev·er·est (évvərist, évvrist) *n.* The ultimate or highest point of achievement or ambition: *a sportsman's Everest.*

Everest, Mount. The world's highest mountain (8 848 metres; 29,028 feet) in the central Himalayas, on the border of Nepal and Tibet. In Tibet it is called Chomolungma ("Mother Goddess of the World"); it takes its English name from the surveyor-general of

India, Sir George Everest (1790–1866). The summit was first reached by Sir Edmund Hillary and Tenzing Norgay on May 28, 1953.

ev·er·glade (évvər-glayd) *n. U.S.* A tract of marshland, usually under water and covered in places with tall grass; a swamp. [Perhaps EVER ("interminable") + GLADE (open space).]

Ev·er·glades (évvər-glaydz). Swampy region of 13 000 square kilometres (5,000 square miles) at the southern tip of Florida, in the United States. It is abundant in crocodiles, alligators, egrets, and bald eagles.

ev·er·green (évvər-green) *adj.* **1. a.** Having foliage that persists and remains green throughout the year: *evergreen trees.* **b.** Persisting and remaining green throughout the year: *evergreen foliage.* Compare **deciduous.** **2.** Retaining freshness and popularity over a long period: *an evergreen musical.*
~*n.* An evergreen tree or shrub.

ev·er·last·ing (évvər-láast-ing ‖ -lást-) *adj.* **1.** Lasting forever; eternal. **2.** Continuing indefinitely or for a long period of time; perpetual. **3.** Lasting too long; incessant: *his everlasting grumbles.* **4.** Retaining colour and form for a long time when cut or dried, as certain plants do.
~*n.* **1.** Capital E. God. Preceded by *the.* **2.** Eternal duration; eternity. **3.** Any of various everlasting plants, such as *Helichrysum bracteatum.* Also called "everlasting flower", "immortelle".

ev·er·more (évvər-mór ‖ -mór) *adv.* **1.** Forever. Obsolete except in the phrase *for evermore.* **2.** Constantly; always.

e·vert (i-vért, ee-) *tr.v.* **everted, everting, everts.** To turn (the cervix, intestines, or other part of the body) inside out or outwards. [Latin *ēvertere,* to turn out, overturn : *ē-,* out, from *ex-* + *vertere,* to turn.]
—**e·ver·sion** (-vér-sh'n, -zh'n) *n.* —**e·ver·si·ble** (-vér-sib'l) *adj.*

Ev·ert (ev-ərt), **Chris(tine) Marie** (1954–). U.S. tennis player. She was U.S. women's singles champion (1975–8, 1980, 1982) and won the Wimbledon title in 1974, 1976 and 1981.

e·vert·or (i-vértər, ee-) *n.* Any muscle that acts to turn a part outwards or inside out.

eve·ry (évvri, évvəri) *adj.* **1.** Each and all single members of an aggregate; each without exception: *every student in the class.* **2.** Each particular member of a series. Used where a qualification is involved: *every third seat; every two hours.* **3.** Each thing or all possible things without exception; no matter which or when: *arrive late at every party.* **4.** The utmost, most earnest, or most extensive: *gave him every care.*
~*adv.* More or less; periodically. Used as an intensive with idioms indicating indefinite or occasional recurrence: *every once in a while; every so often.* —**every bit.** *Informal.* In all ways; quite; equally: *He is every bit as mean as she is.* —**every other. 1.** Each alternate; each second: *Leave every other door unmarked.* **2.** *Informal.* Almost each: *every other cup is chipped.* —**every which way. 1.** *U.S. Informal.* In complete disorder; chaotic. **2.** In any way or sequence. [Middle English *every, everich, everulch,* Old English *ǣfre ǣlc,* "ever each", every, each one : *ǣfre,* EVER + *ǣlc,* EACH.]
Usage: Every takes a singular verb: *Every person has to get what he wants.* There is rarely a problem over agreement with the verb, but there is some variability over agreement with a pronoun later in the sentence, especially when the speaker does not wish to select a pronoun such as *he* or *she. Every person knows what they have to do* may therefore be heard, alongside the more careful (but also more awkward) *Every person knows what he or she has to do,* and the simpler (but, to some, sexist) use of *he,* as above. See also **each.**
The phrase *each and every* has attracted occasional criticism as a redundant expression, *each and every day* being felt to be equivalent to *each day* or *every day.* But the extra emphasis conveyed by this phrase seems sufficient to explain its continued use in both formal and informal styles.

eve·ry·bod·y (évvri-boddi) *pron.* Every person; everyone. See Usage note at **everyone.**

eve·ry·day (évvri-day, -dáy) *adj.* **1.** Suitable for ordinary days or routine occasions: *an everyday suit.* **2.** Commonplace; usual; ordinary: *everyday worries.*
Usage: This is written as a single word only when it is used as an adjective, as in *an everyday happening.* In other circumstances, it is written as two words: *I go there every day.* In speech, the stress pattern is usually different, with *day* being more strongly stressed in the latter sense.

Eve·ry·man (évvri-man) *n.* An imaginary representation of the common man, with all his weaknesses, often in a Christian context. [After the character in the medieval morality play, *Everyman.*]

eve·ry·one (évvri-wun ‖ *Northern England also* -won) *pron.* Every person; everybody.
Usage: Everyone and *everybody* take singular verbs and singular pronouns in formal style: *Everyone has to look his best.* In informal contexts, and occasionally in formal contexts, a plural pronoun is used, especially where one wishes to avoid the masculine implications of the use of *his: Everyone has to look their best.* Using *his or her* in such examples is generally considered awkward. In certain kinds of questions, the plural pronoun is generally preferred: *Everyone left the room, didn't they?* The use of a singular form here would be jocular: *Everyone left the room, didn't she!*
Everyone is written as a single word when it has the general, indefinite sense of "the group as a whole"; it may refer only to persons, and is not followed by *of. Every one* refers to both persons and things, seen as a set of separate entities; it may be followed by *of.* In the latter case, *one* carries a stronger stress in speech.

eve·ry·place (évvri-playss) *adv. Chiefly U.S. Informal.* Everywhere.

eve·ry·thing (évvri-thing) *pron.* **1.** All things or factors that exist or pertain to a given instance; the entirety or totality: *everything in this room.* **2.** All relevant items or factors: *Tell him everything.* **3.** The most important fact or consideration, especially for success or happiness; the principal concern: *Her children mean everything to her.* **4.** All aspects of something; life in general: *Everything went wrong.* —**have everything.** *Informal.* To have every desirable quality or possession.

eve·ry·where (évvri-wair, -hwair) *adv.* In or to any or every place; in all places.

Eve·sham (éevsh'm). Market town for the Vale of Evesham in Worcestershire, in west central England, situated on the river Avon. In 1265, Simon de Montfort, leader of the revolt against King Henry III, was slain at the battle of Evesham.

Eve's pudding *n.* A baked sponge pudding with a base of apples or other fruit.

evg. evening.

e·vict (i-víkt) *tr.v.* **evicted, evicting, evicts. 1.** To expel (a tenant, for example) by legal process; put out. **2.** To force out; eject; dispossess: *"We have allowed the Communists to evict us from our rightful estate"* (John F. Kennedy). **3.** To recover (property, for example) by a superior claim or legal process. —See Synonyms at **eject.** [Middle English *evicten,* from Latin *ēvincere* (past participle *ēvictus*), to conquer, overcome : *ē-,* completely, from *ex-* + *vincere,* to conquer.] —**e·vic·tion** *n.* —**e·vic·tor** *n.*

ev·i·dence (évvidənss) *n.* **1.** The data on which a judgment or conclusion may be based, or by which proof or probability may be established: *fossilised evidence of climatic change.* **2.** That which serves to indicate or suggest: *His reaction was evidence of guilt.* **3.** *Law.* The documentary or verbal statements and the material objects admissible as testimony in a court of law. —**in evidence. 1.** Easily noticeable; conspicuous. **2.** Present; at hand.
~*tr.v.* **evidenced, -dencing, -dences. 1.** To indicate clearly; exemplify or prove. **2.** To support by testimony; attest. [Middle English, from Old French, from Late Latin *ēvidentia,* from Latin *ēvidēns,* EVIDENT.]

ev·i·dent (évvidənt) *adj.* Easily recognisable or perceived; clear; obvious. [Middle English, from Old French, from Latin *ēvidēns* (stem *ēvident-*), evident, clear : *ē-,* completely, from *ex-* + *vidēns,* present participle of *vidēre,* to see.]
Synonyms: evident, apparent, obvious, plain, distinct, manifest.

ev·i·den·tial (évvi-dénsh'l) *adj.* Pertaining to, providing, or having the nature of evidence. —**ev·i·den·tial·ly** *adv.*

ev·i·dent·ly (évvi-dəntli ‖ -déntli, -dentli) *adv.* **1.** Obviously; perceptibly; clearly: *He was quite evidently dead.* **2.** Apparently or seemingly; probably: *She's evidently going to be late.*

e·vil (éev'l) *adj.* **1.** Morally bad or wrong; wicked; malevolent: *an evil tyrant.* **2.** Causing an undesirable condition, such as ruin, injury, or pain; harmful; injurious: *an evil suggestion.* **3.** Characterised by or boding misfortune; foreboding; ominous: *evil omens.* **4.** Unfavourable; infamous: *an evil reputation.* **5.** Characterised by anger or spite; malicious: *an evil temper.* **6.** Objectionable; very unpleasant: *an evil smell.*
~*n.* **1.** *Sometimes capital* E. That which is destructive, corruptive, or injurious, whether from natural circumstances or by human ignorance, error, or design: *"The evil that men do lives after them"* (Shakespeare). **2.** *Sometimes capital* E. **a.** That which is morally bad or wrong; wickedness; sin. **b.** That which causes or constitutes misfortune, suffering, difficulty, or the like; woe. **3.** *Often plural.* Anything that is undesirable because of its injurious nature or effect: *the evils of war; the lesser of two evils.* **4.** *Archaic.* A disease. ~*adv.* In an evil manner. Used in combination: *evil-tasting beer.* [Middle English *evel, ivel,* Old English *yfel.*] —**e·vil·ly** *adv.* —**e·vil·ness** *n.*

e·vil·do·er (éev'l-dōō-ər) *n.* One who does evil. —**e·vil·do·ing** *n.*

evil eye *n.* **1.** A look or a stare superstitiously believed to cause injury or misfortune to others. **2.** The power supposedly possessed by certain people to bring misfortune to others with such looks. **3.** The power of evil personified as an all-watching eye and warded off since ancient times by symbols, amulets, and beads, themselves representing an eye.

e·vil·mind·ed (éev'l-míndid) *adj.* Having evil thoughts, opinions, or intentions. —**e·vil·mind·ed·ly** *adv.* —**e·vil·mind·ed·ness** *n.*

Evil One *n.* The Devil. Preceded by *the.*

e·vince (i-vínss) *tr.v.* **evinced, evincing, evinces.** To show or demonstrate clearly or convincingly; manifest; exhibit: *evince surprise.* [Latin *ēvincere,* to conquer, to prove. See **evict.**] —**e·vin·ci·ble** *adj.*

e·vis·cer·ate (i-víssə-rayt) *v.* **-ated, -ating, -ates.** —*tr.* **1.** To remove the entrails of; disembowel. **2.** To take away a vital or essential part of. **3.** *Surgery.* To remove the contents of (an eyeball). —*intr. Surgery.* To protrude through an incision of a part after an operation. ~*adj.* Disembowelled. [Latin *ēviscerāre,* "to remove the viscera from", to disembowel : *ē-,* indicating removal, from *ex-* + VISCERA.] —**e·vis·cer·a·tion** (-ráysh'n) *n.*

ev·i·ta·ble (évvitəb'l) *adj. Rare.* Avoidable. [Latin *ēvītābilis,* from *ēvītāre,* to avoid : *ē-,* away, from *ex-* + *vītāre†,* to shun.]

ev·o·ca·tion (év-ō-káysh'n, éev-, -ə-) *n.* The act of calling forth or conjuring up: *an evocation of childhood memories.*

e·voc·a·tive (i-vóckətiv) *adj.* Tending or having the power to evoke. —**e·voc·a·tive·ly** *adv.*

ev·o·ca·tor (év-ō-káytər, -ə-) *n.* **1.** One that evokes. **2.** A naturally occurring substance that induces undifferentiated embryonic tissue to develop in a particular way.

e·voke (i-vṓk, ee-) *tr.v.* **evoked, evoking, evokes.** **1.** To summon or call forth (memories, for example); reawaken; inspire. **2.** To produce or elicit (a reaction, emotion, or response): *evoke curiosity.* **3.** To cause (a spirit, for example) to appear; call up; conjure up. [Latin *ēvocāre,* to call forth, to call out, summon : *ē-,* out, from *ex-* + *vocāre,* to call.] **—ev·o·ca·ble** (évvəkə-b'l, i-vṓkə-) *adj.*

ev·o·lute (évvə-lo͞ot, -lewt) *n.* The locus of the centres of curvature of a given curve. [Back-formation from EVOLUTION.]

ev·o·lu·tion (éevə-lo͞o-sh'n, évvə-, -léw-) *n.* **1.** A gradual process in which something changes into a significantly different, especially more complex or more sophisticated, form. **2.** *Biology.* **a.** The theory that groups of organisms may change with the passage of time so that new species differing morphologically and physiologically from their ancestors are formed. See **natural selection. b.** The historical development of a related group of organisms; phylogeny. **3.** The developmental or historical process of something, as of a social institution, geographical division, or system of thought. **4.** *Often plural.* A turning movement which is part of a larger pattern, as: **a.** A wheeling motion in a dance. **b.** A tactical or parade-ground manoeuvre. **5.** A yielding or throwing off of gas, vapour, or heat, for example. **6.** *Mathematics.* The extraction of a root of a quantity. In this sense, compare **involution.** [Latin *ēvolūtiō,* an opening, an unrolling, from *ēvolūtus,* past participle of *ēvolvere,* to roll out, to open, EVOLVE.]

ev·o·lu·tion·ar·y (éevə-lo͞o-sh'n-əri, évvə-, -léw-, -ri || *U.S.* -shə-nerri) *adj.* Also **ev·o·lu·tion·al** (-sh'n'l). **1.** Of, pertaining to, or resulting from evolution: *a continuous evolutionary process.* **2.** In accord with the theory of biological evolution. **3.** Developing or evolving as a slow or historical process; gradually changing or progressing.

ev·o·lu·tion·ism (éevə-lo͞osh'n-iz'm, évvə-, -léw-) *n.* **1.** A theory of biological evolution, especially as formulated by Charles Darwin. Compare **creationism. 2.** Any belief in an evolutionary process. **—ev·o·lu·tion·ist** *n.*

e·volve (i-vólv || *Southern England also* -vṓlv) *v.* **evolved, evolving, evolves.** *—tr.* **1.** To develop or achieve gradually; devise; formulate. **2.** *Biology.* To develop by evolutionary processes. **3.** To yield, give, or throw off (gas, vapour, or heat, for example); set free. *—intr.* **1.** To be part of or subject to the process of natural, temporal, or biological evolution, as in an organism or rock stratum. **2.** To be developed, disclosed, or unfolded: *The plot evolves in many subtle ways.* **3.** To undergo change or transformation; develop. [Latin *ēvolvere,* to roll out, unfold : *ē-,* out, from *ex-* + *volvere,* to roll.] **—e·volv·a·ble** *adj.* **—e·volve·ment** *n.*

e·vul·sion (i-vúlsh'n) *n.* A pulling out; a forcible extraction. [Latin *ēvulsiō* (stem *ēvulsiōn-*), a pulling out, from *ēvulsus,* past participle of *ēvellere,* to pull out : *ē-,* out, from *ex-* + *vellere,* to pull.]

ev·zone (év-zōn) *n.* An infantryman of a special corps of the Greek army. [Modern Greek *euzōnos,* from Greek, well-girdled, active : *eu-,* well + *zōnē,* girdle.]

ewe (yo͞o || yō) *n.* A female sheep, especially when full-grown. [Middle English *ewe,* Old English *ēowu.*]

E·we (évvay, é-way) *n.* **1.** A member of a Negroid people of Togo, Ghana, and parts of Benin. **2.** The language of this people, belonging to the Niger-Congo family of languages.

ewe-neck (yo͞o-nek) *n.* A horse's neck that is thin and curved downwards rather than arched. **—ewe-necked** *adj.*

ew·er (yo͞o-ər) *n.* A large, wide-mouthed pitcher or jug. [Middle English, from Anglo-French, from Old North French *eviere,* from Vulgar Latin *aquāria* (unattested), from Latin *āquārius,* relating to water, from *aqua,* water.]

ex[1] (eks) *prep. Abbr.* **x.** **1.** *Finance.* Without; not including; not participating in: *ex dividend; ex rights.* **2.** *Commerce.* At the specified place. Used to indicate prices: *The price ex works does not include delivery.* [Latin *ex,* out of, from.]

ex[2] *n. Informal.* A former wife, husband, or lover.

ex-[1] *prefix.* Indicates: **1.** Removal out of or from; for example, **explant. 2.** Former; for example, *ex-president.* [Middle English, from Old French, from Latin. In borrowed Latin compounds *ex-* indicates: 1. out or out of, as in **expire.** 2. away from or removed away from, as in **expropriate.** 3. up; as in **elevate.** 4. completely or intensively, as in **execute.** *Ex-* becomes *e-* (when forming verbs) before consonants except *c, f, h, p, q, s;* (when forming adjectives) when it means "lacking". Latin *ex-,* from *ex,* out, out of.]

ex-[2] *prefix.* Indicates out of; for example, **exergue.** [In borrowed Greek compounds *ex-* indicates: 1. out of, as in **exegesis.** 2. away from, as in **exorcise.** Greek *ex-,* from *ex,* out of.]

ex. **1.** examination. **2.** example. **3.** except; excepted; exception. **4.** exchange. **5.** executive. **6.** exempt. **7.** exercise. **8.** express. **9.** extra.

Ex. Exodus (Old Testament).

exa- *prefix. Abbr.* **E** Indicates one-million-million-million (10^{18}); for example, *exametre.*

ex·ac·er·bate (ig-zássər-bayt, ik-sássər-, eg-, ek-) *tr.v.* **-bated, -bating, -bates. 1.** To increase the severity of (a pain, emotion, disease, problem, or the like). **2.** To embitter or irritate (a person). [Latin *exacerbāre,* aggravate, make harsh : *ex-,* completely + *acerbus,* bitter, harsh.] **—ex·ac·er·ba·tion** (-báysh'n) *n.*

ex·act (ig-zákt || eg-, ik-) *adj.* **1. a.** Accurate in every respect: *an exact copy.* **b.** Specific in its detail: *exact instructions.* **2.** Precise in quantity, weight, or the like, as opposed to approximate: *the exact amount.* **3.** Precise in technique or movement: *an exact measuring device.* **4.** Designating a science based on verifiable facts. **5.** Identical; very same: *the exact place.* **6.** Meticulously observing or adhering to a standard.
~tr.v. **exacted, -acting, -acts. 1.** To demand and enforce (payment or performance of something, for example); extort. **2.** To call for; require. [Latin *exactus,* past participle of *exigere,* "to drive out", require, examine : *ex-,* out + *agere,* to lead, drive.] **—ex·act·a·ble** *adj.* **—ex·act·ness** *n.* **—ex·ac·tor, ex·act·er** *n.*

ex·act·ing (ig-zákting || eg-, ik-) *adj.* **1.** Making severe or unremitting demands: *an exacting taskmaster.* **2.** Requiring great care, effort, or attention: *an exacting task.* —See Synonyms at **burdensome, severe. —ex·act·ing·ly** *adv.* **—ex·act·ing·ness** *n.*

ex·ac·tion (ig-záksh'n || eg-, ik-) *n.* **1.** The act of exacting. **2.** Something that is exacted, such as a sum of money or act of obedience.

ex·act·i·tude (ig-zákti-tewd || eg-, ik-) *n.* The state or quality of being exact.

ex·act·ly (ig-záktli || eg-, ik-) *adv.* **1.** In an exact manner; accurately. **2.** In all respects; just: *Do exactly as you please.*
~interj. Precisely! Just so! Used to express agreement.

ex·ag·ger·ate (ig-zájə-rayt || eg-, ik-) *v.* **-ated, -ating, -ates.** *—tr.* **1.** To enlarge (something) disproportionately; increase to an abnormal degree. **2.** To make (something) appear greater than is actually the case; magnify beyond the truth. *—intr.* To distort through emphasis; overstate. [Latin *exaggerāre,* to pile up, exaggerate : *ex-,* completely + *aggerāre,* to pile up, from *agger*†, pile, heap.] **—ex·ag·ger·a·tive** (-rətiv, -raytiv), **ex·ag·ger·a·to·ry** (-rə-təri, -tri) *adj.* **—ex·ag·ger·a·tor** *n.*

ex·ag·ger·at·ed (ig-zájə-raytid || eg-, ik-) *adj.* **1.** Unduly emphasised or magnified; going beyond truth, fact, or reality; overstated. **2.** Physically enlarged; abnormally or disproportionately developed. **—ex·ag·ger·at·ed·ly** *adv.*

ex·ag·ger·a·tion (ig-zájə-ráysh'n || eg-, ik-) *n.* **1.** The act of exaggerating. **2.** An instance of exaggerating; an overstatement.

ex·alt (ig-záwlt || eg-, ik-, -zólt) *tr.v.* **-alted, -alting, -alts. 1.** To raise in position, character, status, or the like; elevate: *"Do away with masters, exalt the will of the people"* (D.H. Lawrence). **2.** To glorify; praise; honour; extol. **3.** To increase the effect or intensity of; heighten. [Middle English *exalten,* from Old French *exalter,* from Latin *exaltāre,* to lift up, exalt : *ex-,* up + *altus,* high.] **—ex·alt·er** *n.*

ex·al·ta·tion (ég-zawl-táysh'n, ék-sawl- || -zol-, -sol-) *n.* **1.** The act of exalting. **2.** The state of being exalted; elevation. **3.** The state or feeling of intense, often excessive exhilaration and well-being; rapture; elation. See Synonyms at **ecstasy. 4.** *British.* A group of larks in flight.

ex·alt·ed (ig-záwl-tid || eg-, ik-, -zól-) *adj.* **1.** Elevated in rank, character, position, or the like. **2.** Lofty; sublime; noble: *"That provision should be made for continuing the race of . . . so exalted . . . a Being as man — I am far from denying"* (Laurence Sterne). **3.** Extremely excited; elated. **—ex·alt·ed·ly** *adv.* **—ex·alt·ed·ness** *n.*

ex·am (ig-zám || eg-, ég-zam) *n. Informal.* An examination.

ex·a·men (ig-záy-men, -mən || eg-, ik-) *n. Roman Catholic Church.* A usually daily examination of one's conscience. [Latin *exāmen,* consideration, examination, from *exigere,* to EXAMINE.]

ex·am·i·nant (ig-zámminənt || eg-, ik-) *n.* One who examines.

ex·am·i·na·tion (ig-zámmi-náysh'n || eg-, ik-) *n. Abbr.* **ex., exam. 1.** The act of examining or the state or result of being examined. **2.** An instance of examining; a thorough inspection or scrutiny. **3.** A set of questions or exercises testing knowledge or skills; a written, practical, or oral test. **4.** Formal interrogation; official inquiry. **—ex·am·i·na·tion·al** *adj.*

ex·am·ine (ig-zámmin || eg-, ik-) *tr.v.* **-ined, -ining, -ines. 1.** To inspect or scrutinise (a person, thing, or situation) in detail; observe or analyse carefully. **2.** To study the state of health of. **3.** To test the qualifications, aptitude, or knowledge of (a candidate) by means of an examination. **4.** To interrogate or question formally to elicit facts, information, or the like. **5.** To consider or test introspectively; reflect upon: *"The time has come, God knows, for us to examine ourselves"* (James Baldwin). —See Synonyms at **ask.** [Middle English *examinen,* from Old French *examiner,* from Latin *exāmināre,* to weigh accurately, examine, from *exāmen,* a weighing, consideration, from *exigere,* to examine, to lead out : *ex-,* out + *agere,* to lead.] **—ex·am·in·a·ble** *adj.* **—ex·am·in·er** *n.*

ex·am·in·ee (ig-zámmi-née || eg-, ik-) *n.* One who is examined.

ex·am·ple (ig-za'am-p'l || eg-, ik-, -zám-) *n. Abbr.* **ex. 1.** One that is representative of a group as a whole; a sample; a specimen. **2.** Someone or something that serves as a model or pattern for imitation or duplication; an exemplar. **3.** A previous case or situation that is the same as or similar to one at hand; a precedent. **4.** One that serves as a warning, such as a punishment or a punished person. **5.** An illustrative problem or exercise with its solution. **—for example.** Serving as an illustration, a model, or an instance. [Middle English *exaumple,* from Old French *example, essample,* from Latin *exemplum,* "(something) taken out", example, sample, from *eximere,* to take out : *ex-,* out + *emere,* to take.]
Synonyms: *example, instance, case, illustration, sample, specimen.*

ex·an·i·mate (ig-zánni-mət, eg-, -mit, -mayt || ik-, ek-sánni-) *adj. Formal.* Lifeless; dead.

ex·an·the·ma (ék-san-théemə || égzan-) *n., pl.* **-mata** (-mətə) or **-mas.** Also **ex·an·them** (ek-sánthəm || eg-zán-). **1.** A skin eruption accompanying a disease or fever. **2.** A disease, such as measles or scarlet fever, accompanied by a skin eruption. [New Latin, from

Late Latin *exanthēma,* from Greek, "a blooming out", eruption, from *exanthein,* to bloom out, burst forth : *ex-,* out + *anthein,* to bloom, from *anthos,* flower.] —**ex·an·the·mat·ic** (-thi-máttik), **ex·an·them·a·tous** (-thémətəss) *adj.*

ex·ar·ate (ék-sə-rayt) *adj. Zoology.* Designating pupae whose wings and legs are free and able to make limited movements. [Latin *exarātus,* "ploughed up" (apparently referring to the pupa's method of shedding its larval skin), past participle of *exarāre* : EX- + *arāre,* plough.]

ex·arch[1] (ék-saark) *n.* **1.** The ruler of a province in the Byzantine Empire. **2.** *Eastern Orthodox Church.* **a.** The deputy of a patriarch. **b.** A bishop ranking immediately below a patriarch. **c.** The head of certain Eastern churches, such as the Bulgarian. [Late Latin *exarchus,* from Greek *exarkhos,* leader, from *exarkhein,* to initiate, lead out : *ex-,* out + *arkhein,* rule, lead.]

ex·arch[2] *adj. Botany.* Having vascular tissue in which the first-formed xylem is external to that formed later. [EX- (outside) + Greek *arkhē,* beginning, origin.]

ex·ar·chate (ék-saar-kayt, ek-sár-). *n.* Also **ex·ar·chy** (ék-saarki) The office, rank, jurisdiction, or province of an exarch.

ex·as·per·ate (ig-záss-pə-rayt, -zaáss- ‖ eg-, ik-) *tr.v.* **-ated, -ating, -ates. 1.** To make very angry or irritated; tax the patience of; provoke; irk. **2.** To increase the gravity or intensity of (a passion or pain, for example). [Latin *exasperāre,* to exasperate, irritate, make rough : *ex-,* entirely + *asperāre,* to make rough, from *asper,* rough.] —**ex·as·per·at·ed·ly** *adv.* —**ex·as·per·at·ing·ly** *adv.*

ex·as·per·a·tion (ig-záss-pə-ráysh'n, -zaáss- ‖ eg-, ik-) *n.* **1.** An act or instance of exasperating. **2.** The state of being exasperated; extreme annoyance or irritation.

exc. 1. excellent. **2.** except; excepted; exception.

Exc. Excellency.

Ex·cal·i·bur (ek-skál-ibər). King Arthur's sword. [Middle English *Excalibur,* from Old French *Escalibor,* from Medieval Latin *Caliburnus,* from Welsh *Caledvwlch,* from Celtic *kaleto-* (unattested), hard.]

ex ca·the·dra (éks kə-theédrə) *adj.* With authority; from the seat of authority. Said especially of official or solemn papal pronouncements. —**ex ca·the·dra** *adv.*

ex·cau·date (eks-káwdayt) *adj. Zoology.* Tailless; without a tail.

ex·ca·vate (ékskə-vayt) *v.* **-vated, -vating, -vates.** —*tr.* **1.** To make a cavity or hole in; dig out; hollow out. **2.** To form (a tunnel, for example) by such hollowing out; dig. **3.** To remove (soil) by digging or scooping out. **4.** To expose or uncover by digging, especially in search of historical or archaeological information. —*intr.* To engage in digging, hollowing out, or removing. [Latin *excavāre,* to hollow out : *ex-,* out + *cavāre,* to hollow, from *cavus,* hollow.]

ex·ca·va·tion (éksə-váysh'n) *n.* **1.** The act or condition of excavating. **2.** A cavity formed by excavating. **3.** Something revealed by excavating, such as ruins. —See Synonyms at **hole.**

ex·ca·va·tor (éksə-vaytər) *n.* **1.** One that excavates. **2.** A power-operated digging machine; especially, a caterpillar tractor with digging attachments.

ex·ceed (ik-seéd, ek-) *tr.v.* **-ceeded, -ceeding, -ceeds. 1.** To be greater than; surpass. **2.** To go beyond the prior or proper limits of. —See Synonyms at **excel.** [Middle English *exceden,* from Old French *exceder,* from Latin *excēdere,* to depart, to go out, surpass : *ex-,* out + *cēdere,* to go.]

ex·ceed·ing (ik-seéding, ek-) *adj.* Extreme; extraordinary. —*adv. Archaic.* Exceedingly.

ex·ceed·ing·ly (ik-seédingli, ek-) *adv.* To an advanced or unusual degree; extremely.

ex·cel (ik-sél, ek-) *v.* **-celled, -celling, -cels.** —*tr.* To be better than; surpass; outdo: *excels his class in English.* —*intr.* **1.** To surpass others; be better or do better than others. **2.** To be extremely good or competent. Used with *at* or *in.* [Middle English *excellen,* from Latin *excellere,* to excel, raise up.]

Synonyms: excel, surpass, exceed, transcend, outdo, outstrip.

ex·cel·lence (éksələnss) *n.* Also *archaic* **ex·cel·len·cy** (-lən-si) *pl.* **-cies. 1.** The state, quality, or condition of excelling; superiority; pre-eminence. **2.** Something in which a person or thing excels; a surpassing feature or virtue. **3.** *Capital E.* Variant of **Excellency.** [From EXCEL.]

Ex·cel·len·cy (éksələn-si) *n., pl.* **-cies.** Also **Ex·cel·lence** (éksələnss). **1.** *Abbr.* **Exc.** A title of or form of address for certain high officials, such as ambassadors, bishops, or governors. Usually used with *His, Her,* or *Your.* **2.** *Small e. Archaic.* Variant of **excellence.**

ex·cel·lent (éksələnt) *adj.* **1.** *Abbr.* **E, exc.** Being of the highest or finest quality; exceptionally good; superb. **2.** *Archaic.* Surpassing; superior. [Middle English, from Old French, from Latin *excellēns* (stem *excellent-*), present participle of *excellere,* to EXCEL.] —**ex·cel·lent·ly** *adv.*

ex·cel·si·or (ek-sél-si-awr, ik-, -ər ‖ -ōr) *interj.* Higher! Upwards! Used to express striving for greater attainment. —*n. Chiefly U.S.* Slender, curved wood shavings used for packing, stuffing, or the like. [Latin, comparative of *excelsus,* high, from the past participle of *excellere,* to EXCEL.]

ex·cept (ik-sépt ‖ ek-) *prep. Abbr.* **ex., exc.** With the exclusion of; other than; but. Sometimes used with *for: All the eggs, except for one, broke.* —*conj.* **1.** If it were not for the fact that; only. Often used with *that: He would buy the suit, except that it costs too much.* **2.** Otherwise than; with any purpose or manner other than. Usually used with an

adverb, a clause, or a phrase: *He would not open his mouth except to yell.* **3.** *Archaic.* Unless. —*v.* **excepted, -cepting, -cepts.** —*tr.* To leave out; exclude; excuse. —*intr.* To object. Usually used with *to* or *against.* [Middle English, from Latin *exceptus,* past participle of *excipere,* to take out, except : *ex-,* out + *capere,* to take.]

Usage: In the sense of "excluding", *except* is the normal prepositional form in standard English, though *excepting* is sometimes heard in informal speech: *We all went except her;* . . .*excepting her* would be informal. *Excepting* is a standard prepositional usage only when it is preceded by a negative word or *always* (*not excepting the mayor; always excepting that kind of problem*).

ex·cept·ing (ik-sépting ‖ ek-) *prep.* Excluding; except. See Usage note at **except.** —*conj. Archaic.* Except; unless.

ex·cep·tion (ik-sépsh'n ‖ ek-) *n. Abbr.* **ex., exc. 1.** The act of excepting or state of being excepted; exclusion. **2.** One that is excepted; a case which does not conform to normal rules, general principles, or the like: *We all want to be liked — and I am no exception.* **3.** An objection or criticism; opposition: *open to exception.* **4.** *Law.* **a.** A formal objection taken in the course of an action or proceeding. **b.** A restricting clause or provision in a contract or similar document. —**take exception.** To object or take offence; take issue. Usually used with *to: I take exception to your remarks.*

ex·cep·tion·a·ble (ik-sépsh'n-əb'l ‖ ek-) *adj.* Open or liable to objection or exception. See Usage note at **exceptional.** —**ex·cep·tion·a·bly** *adv.*

ex·cep·tion·al (ik-sépsh'n'l ‖ ek-) *adj.* **1.** Being an exception; uncommon; extraordinary. **2.** Unusually skilful, accomplished, or intelligent; gifted. —**ex·cep·tion·al·ly** *adv.*

Usage: Exceptional and *exceptionable* are not interchangeable. *Exceptionable* has the meaning of "objectionable" or "debatable" — something to which exception can be taken. *Exceptional* has the meaning of "uncommon" or "extraordinary".

ex·cep·tive (ik-séptiv ‖ ek-) *adj. Rare.* **1.** Of, being, or containing an exception. **2.** Tending to object or criticise; captious; faultfinding.

ex·cerpt (ék-serpt, ég-zerpt; *or as the verb*) *n.* A passage or scene selected from a speech, book, film, or play; an extract. —*tr.v.* (ek-sérpt, ik-, eg-zérpt, ig-) **excerpted, -cerpting, -cerpts.** To select, quote, or take out (a passage or scene) from a book, speech, play, film, or the like. [Latin *excerptum,* "something picked out", excerpt, from the neuter past participle of *excerpere,* to pick out, excerpt : *ex-,* out + *carpere,* to pick, pluck.]

ex·cess (ik-séss, ek-) *n.* **1.** The state of exceeding what is normal or sufficient. **2.** An amount or quantity beyond what is requisite; a superfluity. **3. a.** The amount or degree by which one quantity exceeds another; the remainder. **b.** A proportion of a sum claimed against an insurance policy which the policyholder is required to pay. **4.** Intemperance; overindulgence: *youthful excess.* **5.** *Chemistry.* An amount of a reagent that is present in a greater quantity than that necessary to complete a given reaction. —**in excess of.** Greater than; more than. —**to excess.** To an extreme degree or extent; too much. —*adj.* (*also* ék-sess). **1.** Being more than is required, usual, or permitted. **2.** Due; not having previously been paid in full: *excess postage.* [Middle English, from Old French *exces,* from Latin *excessus,* past participle of *excēdere,* to EXCEED.]

excess baggage *n.* **1.** Baggage, as on aeroplanes, in excess of the amount carried free, and for which the passenger pays an extra charge. **2.** Anything useless or hampering; something unnecessary.

ex·ces·sive (ik-séssiv ‖ ek-) *adj.* Exceeding a reasonable degree of propriety, necessity, or the like; extreme; inordinate: *excessive charges.* —**ex·ces·sive·ly** *adv.*

Synonyms: excessive, exorbitant, extravagant, immoderate, inordinate, extreme, unreasonable.

exch. 1. exchange. **2.** exchequer.

ex·change (iks-cháynj ‖ eks-) *v.* **-changed, -changing, -changes.** —*tr.* **1.** To give and receive in a reciprocal manner; interchange: *exchange ideas.* **2.** To relinquish (one thing) for another; give over. **3.** To replace (something unsatisfactory) with something else: *exchange defective goods.* **4.** To provide or transfer (goods or services, for example) in return for something of equal value. **5.** In chess, to capture (an opponent's piece) immediately after sacrificing a piece, usually of similar value. —*intr.* To transfer something and receive something equivalent in return; reciprocate; swap. —*n. Abbr.* **ex., exch. 1.** An act or instance of exchanging. **2.** One that is exchanged. **3.** A clash of opinions; an argument: *a noisy exchange.* **4.** A **telephone exchange** *(see).* **5.** A place where things are exchanged; especially, a centre where securities and commodities are bought and sold: *a stock exchange.* **6.** A system of payments using negotiable drafts, bills of exchange, or the like, instead of money. **7.** The fee or percentage charged for participating in such a system of payment. **8.** A **rate of exchange** *(see).* **9.** The amount of difference in the actual value of two or more currencies, or between values of the same currency at two or more places. **10.** *Usually plural.* The cheques, bills, drafts, or the like, presented to a clearing house for settlement or exchange. **11.** In chess, the capture in successive moves of pieces, usually equivalent in value, by each of the two players. **12.** *Medicine.* A blood transfusion for newborn babies suffering from haemolytic disease. **13.** *Physics.* The transfer of a real or virtual particle between two other particles, such as the transfer of a meson between two nucleons. [Middle English *eschaungen,* from Anglo-French *eschaunge,* from Old French *eschan-*

gier, from Vulgar Latin *excambiāre* (unattested) : Late Latin *ex-,* showing change + *cambiāre,* to exchange.] **—ex•chang•er** *n.*
ex•change•a•ble (iks-cháynj-əb'l || eks-) *adj.* Able to be exchanged; remittable. **—ex•change•a•bil•i•ty** (-ə-bílləti) *n.*
exchange force *n. Physics.* **1.** A force between two elementary particles, such as nucleons, caused by an exchange of real or virtual particles between them. **2.** A force that aligns the magnetic dipole moments of atoms in a ferromagnetic material.
exchange rate *n.* A **rate of exchange** *(see).*
ex•cheq•uer (iks-chéckər, eks- || éks-checkər) *n.* **1.** *Capital* **E.** The department of the British and some other governments in charge of the collection and care of the national revenue. **2.** *Abbr.* **exch.** A treasury, as of a nation or an organisation. **3.** *Informal.* The total of one's financial resources; funds. [Middle English *escheker,* from Anglo-French, from Old French *eschequier,* chessboard, a counting table usually covered with a chequered cloth, from *eschec,* CHECK (at chess).]
ex•cim•er (ik-sīmər, ek-) *n. Chemistry.* A dimer formed by the association of excited and unexcited molecules, which in the ground state would remain dissociated; an excited dimer. [*Excited dimer.*]
ex•cip•i•ent (ik-síppi-ənt, eks-) *n.* Any inert substance used to dilute or bulk up a drug. [Latin *excipiēns* (stem *excipient-*), present participle of *excipere,* to EXCEPT.]
ex•cis•a•ble (ek-sīzəb'l, ik-) *adj.* **1.** Subject to an excise tax. **2.** Subject to being excised.
ex•cise¹ (ék-sīz, ek-sīz) *n.* **1.** An indirect tax levied on the production, sale, or consumption of certain commodities, such as tobacco or alcohol, within a country. Also called "excise tax". **2.** A licence fee paid to allow a person to pursue certain types of employment or amusement, such as operating a gambling casino. **3.** In Britain, the branch of the civil service that is responsible for the collection of excise tax. Also officially called "Board of Customs and Excise". [Obsolete Dutch *excijs,* from Middle Dutch, probably from Old French *acceis,* from Vulgar Latin *accēnsum* (unattested) : Latin *ad-,* against, to + *cēnsus,* tax, CENSUS.]
ex•cise² (ek-sīz, ik-) *tr.v.* **-cised, -cising, -cises.** **1.** To delete (a passage of text). **2.** To remove by or as if by cutting; especially, to remove surgically (an organ or part). [Latin *excīdere* (past participle *excīsus*), to cut out : *ex-,* out + *caedere,* to cut.] **—ex•ci•sion** (ek-sízh'n) *n.*
ex•cise•man (ék-sīz-man) *n., pl.* **-men** (-men). *British.* An officer who collects excise taxes or enforces excise laws.
ex•cit•a•ble (ik-sīt-əb'l || ek-) *adj.* **1. a.** Capable of being excited. **b.** Easily excited; sensitive or volatile. **2.** Capable of responding to stimuli. Said especially of nerves. **—ex•cit•a•bil•i•ty** (-ə-bílləti), **ex•cit•a•ble•ness** *n.* **—ex•cit•a•bly** *adv.*
ex•ci•tant (éksitənt, ik-sītənt, ek-) *adj.* Also **ex•ci•ta•tive** (ik-sītətiv, ek-), **ex•ci•ta•to•ry** (ek-sītə-təri, ik-, -tri). Capable of exciting or stimulating. **—ex•ci•tant** *n.*
ex•ci•ta•tion (ék-si-táysh'n || -sī-) *n.* **1.** The act or process of exciting something. **2.** An agent or means used to excite or stimulate. **3.** The state or condition of being excited. **4.** The stimulus-induced response of an organ or tissue, especially that of a nerve cell. **5.** The electric current producing a magnetic field in an electromagnetic device, as in a motor, generator, or transformer.
ex•cite (ik-sīt || ek-) *tr.v.* **-cited, -citing, -cites.** **1.** To stir to activity; put into motion. **2.** To elicit (a reaction or emotion, for example); induce: *excite a response.* **3. a.** To affect with a feeling of agitated elation. **b.** To arouse strong feeling in; provoke: *She excited him to anger.* **c.** To stir the sexual passions of; arouse. **4.** *Biology.* To produce increased activity in (an organism or part); stimulate. **5.** *Physics.* **a.** To increase the energy of. **b.** To raise (an atom, molecule, nucleus, or electron) to a higher energy level than the ground state. **c.** To supply current to (the coils of a motor or generator) to create a magnetic field. **d.** To supply a signal to (a transistor circuit). —See Synonyms at **provoke.** [Middle English *exciten,* from Old French *exciter,* from Latin *excitāre,* to excite, arouse, frequentative of *excière* (past participle *excitus*), to call or bring out : *ex-,* out + *ciēre, cīre,* to call, put in motion.]
ex•cit•ed (ik-sītid || ek-) *adj.* **1.** In a state of agitated elation or sexual arousal. **2.** Caused by or characterised by excitement: *an excited hush.* **3.** *Physics.* At an energy level higher than the ground state. **—ex•cit•ed•ly** *adv.*
ex•cite•ment (ik-sītmənt || ek-) *n.* **1.** The state or condition of being excited; agitation. **2.** Something that excites.
ex•cit•er (ik-sītər || ek-) *n.* **1.** One that excites. **2.** An auxiliary generator used to provide field current for a larger generator or alternator. **3.** *Electronics.* An oscillator for generating the carrier frequency of a transmitter.
ex•cit•ing (ik-sīting || ek-) *adj.* Creating excitement or agitation; rousing. **—ex•cit•ing•ly** *adv.*
ex•ci•ton (ék-sīton) *n.* An electrically neutral excited state of a crystal, often regarded as a bound state of an electron and a hole. [EXCIT(ATION) + -ON.]
ex•ci•tor (ik-sītər || ek-) *n.* Any nervous or chemical agent that induces activity in an organism.
excl. excluding; exclusive.
ex•claim (iks-kláym || eks-) *v.* **-claimed, -claiming, -claims.** *—intr.* To cry out or utter suddenly or vehemently, as from surprise or emotion. *—tr.* To cry out or utter suddenly or vehemently. [Old French *exclamer,* from Latin *exclāmāre,* to call out, exclaim : *ex-,* out + *clāmāre,* to call.] **—ex•claim•er** *n.*
ex•cla•ma•tion (éks-klə-máysh'n) *n.* **1.** An abrupt, forceful utterance; a cry. **2.** An interjection.
exclamation mark *n.* **1.** A punctuation mark (!) used after an exclamation. **2.** This sign used as a symbol in mathematics, logic, road signs, or the like. Also *U.S.* "exclamation point".
ex•clam•a•to•ry (eks-klámmə-təri, iks-, -tri) *adj.* Constituting, containing, relating to, or using exclamation. **—ex•clam•a•to•ri•ly** *adv.*
ex•claus•tra•tion (éks-klaw-stráysh'n) *n.* The release from vows and return to the outside world of a monk or nun. [Medieval Latin *exclaustrātiō* (stem *exclaustrātiōn-*), a putting outside the cloister. See **ex-, cloister.**]
ex•clave (éks-klayv) *n.* A portion of a country that is isolated in alien territory: *Cabinda, in Zaire, is an exclave of Angola.* Compare **enclave.** [EX- + (EN)CLAVE.]
ex•clo•sure (iks-klṓzhər || eks-) *n.* An area, as in a forest, fenced off to prevent intrusion.
ex•clude (iks-klṓōd, eks- || -kléwd) *tr.v.* **-cluded, -cluding, -cludes.** **1.** To prevent or keep from entering a place, group, or the like; bar; reject. **2.** To avoid noticing or considering; leave out; disregard. **3.** To eject; expel. [Middle English *excluden,* from Latin *exclūdere* : *ex-,* out + *claudere,* shut.] **—ex•clud•a•bil•i•ty** (-ə-bílləti) *n.* **—ex•clud•a•ble, ex•clud•i•ble** *adj.* **—ex•clud•er** *n.*
ex•clu•sion (iks-klṓō-zh'n, eks- || -kléw-) *n.* **1.** The act of excluding; rejection. **2.** The state of being excluded. [Latin *exclūsiō* (stem *exclūsiōn-*), from *exclūsus,* past participle of *exclūdere,* to EXCLUDE.] **—ex•clu•sion•ar•y** *adj.*
ex•clu•sion•ist (iks-klṓō-zh'n-ist, eks- || -kléw-) *n.* One who favours or practises excluding others from rights or privileges. **—ex•clu•sion•ism** *n.* **—ex•clu•sion•ist** *adj.*
exclusion principle *n.* The principle that no two particles of a given type, such as electrons, protons, or neutrons, can occupy a particular quantum state. Also called "Pauli exclusion principle".
ex•clu•sive (iks-klṓō-siv, eks- || -kléw-) *adj. Abbr.* **excl.** **1.** Pertaining to, characterised by, or requiring exclusion. **2. a.** Not divided or shared with others: *exclusive publishing rights.* **b.** Available through only one retail outlet. **3.** Single or independent; sole: *your exclusive function.* **4.** Regarded as unrelated or autonomous; separate; incompatible: *mutually exclusive roles in life.* **5.** Concentrated on the matter at hand; undivided; undistracted. **6.** Not including the specified limits or items: *paragraphs 8 to 17 exclusive.* **7. a.** Admitting only certain people to membership, participation, or the like; select. **b.** Catering to a wealthy clientele; expensive; chic: *exclusive shops.* **8.** *Logic.* Designating a disjunction that is valid if one but not both of its elements is true. **—exclusive of.** Not including or considering: *exclusive of other factors.*
~n. A news item granted to or obtained by only one person or source. **—ex•clu•sive•ly** *adv.* **—ex•clu•sive•ness** *n.*
Exclusive Brethren *pl.n.* One of the two main branches of the Plymouth Brethren, favouring strict adherence to the sect's doctrines and beliefs.
ex•cog•i•tate (eks-kóji-tayt, iks-) *tr.v.* **-tated, -tating, -tates.** *Formal.* **1.** To think out in great detail. **2.** To devise; contrive. [Latin *excōgitāre,* to find out by thinking : *ex-,* out + *cōgitāre,* to COGITATE.] **—ex•cog•i•ta•tion** (-táysh'n) *n.* **—ex•cog•i•ta•tive** (-tətiv, -taytiv) *adj.*
ex•com•mu•ni•ca•ble (ékskə-méwnikəb'l) *adj.* Liable to, meriting, or punishable by excommunication.
ex•com•mu•ni•cate (ékskə-méwni-kayt) *tr.v.* **-cated, -cating, -cates.** To cut off from the rites, privileges, or fellowship of a church by ecclesiastical authority; exclude from religious membership.
~n. (-kət, -kit, -kayt). A person who has been excommunicated.
~adj. (-kət, -kit, -kayt). Excommunicated. [Middle English *excommunicaten,* from Late Latin *excommūnicāre* (past participle *excommūnicātus*), to put out of the (church) community : Latin *ex-,* out + *commūnicāre,* to COMMUNICATE.] **—ex•com•mu•ni•ca•tive** (-kətiv, -kaytiv), **ex•com•mu•ni•ca•tory** (-kə-tri, -kay-təri, -káy-təri || *U.S.* -tawri) *adj.* **—ex•com•mu•ni•ca•tor** (-kaytər) *n.*
ex•com•mu•ni•ca•tion (ékskə-méwni-káysh'n) *n.* **1.** The act of excommunicating. **2.** The state of being excommunicated; exclusion. **3.** The formal ecclesiastical censure or motion by which one is excommunicated.
ex•co•ri•ate (ik-skáwri-ayt, ek-, -skórri- || -skṓri-) *tr.v.* **-ated, -ating, -ates.** **1.** To censure strongly; denounce severely; upbraid. **2.** To tear or wear off the skin of; abrade; chafe. [Middle English *excoriaten,* from Latin *excoriāre* (past participle *excoriātus*), to strip of its skin : *ex-,* removal from + *corium,* skin, hide, leather.]
ex•co•ri•a•tion (ik-skáwri-áysh'n, ek-, skórri- || -skṓri-) *n.* **1. a.** The act of excoriating. **b.** The state of being excoriated. **2.** The raw skin surface resulting from abrasion or scraping; a sore.
ex•cre•ment (ékskrimənt) *n.* Waste material expelled from the body; especially, faecal matter. [Latin *excrēmentum,* from *excrētus,* past participle of *excernere,* to sift out : *ex-,* out + *cernere,* to sift.] **—ex•cre•ment•al** (ékskri-mént'l) *adj.*
ex•cres•cence (ik-skréss'nss, ek-) *n.* **1.** An abnormal, disfiguring outgrowth or enlargement: *"a weird horny excrescence that had detached itself from the ceremonious big toe"* (John Cowper Powys). **2.** A normal outgrowth or appendage, such as a beard or toenail. [Middle English, from Latin *excrēscentia,* from *excrēscēns,* present participle of *excrēscere,* to grow out : *ex-,* out + *crēscere,* to grow.]
ex•cres•cen•cy (ik-skréss'n-si, ek-) *n., pl.* **-cies.** **1.** The state of being excrescent. **2.** An excrescence.
ex•cres•cent (ik-skréss'nt, ek-) *adj.* **1.** Growing out abnormally, excessively, or superfluously. **2.** *Linguistics.* Designating a speech

sound added without any grammatical or etymological basis; intrusive; epenthetic. **—ex·cres·cent·ly** *adv.*

ex·cre·ta (ik-skréetə, ek-) *pl.n.* Waste matter, such as sweat, urine, or faeces, excreted from the body. [New Latin, from Latin *excrēta*, from the neuter plural past participle of *excernere*, to sift out. See **excrement.**] **—ex·cre·tal** *adj.*

ex·crete (ik-skréet, ek-) *tr.v.* **-creted, -creting, -cretes.** To eliminate (waste matter) from the blood, tissues, or organs. [Latin *excernere* (past participle *excrētus*), to sift out. See **excrement.**]

ex·cre·tion (ik-skréesh'n, ek-) *n.* **1.** The process or act of excreting undigested food residues or metabolic wastes. **2.** The matter so excreted.

ex·cre·to·ry (iks-krée-təri, eks-) *adj.* Also **ex·cre·tive** (-tiv). **1.** Of or pertaining to excretion. **2.** Having the function of excreting: *excretory organs.*

ex·cru·ci·ate (ik-skróō-shi-ayt, ek- || -skréw-) *tr.v.* **-ated, -ating, -ates.** To afflict with severe pain, especially mental pain; torture; torment. [Latin *excruciāre*, to torment : *ex-*, completely + *cruciāre*, to torment, crucify, from *crux* (stem *cruc-*), CROSS.] **—ex·cru·ci·a·tion** (-áysh'n) *n.*

ex·cru·ci·at·ing (ik-skróō-shi-ayting, ek- || -skréw-) *adj.* **1.** Intensely painful; agonising: *an excruciating headache.* **2.** *Informal.* Very bad of its kind. **—ex·cru·ci·at·ing·ly** *adv.*

ex·cul·pate (ék-skul-payt, ik-skúl-, ek-) *tr.v.* **-pated, -pating, -pates.** To clear of a charge; prove guiltless or blameless; exonerate. [Medieval Latin *exculpāre* : Latin *ex-* (removal away from) + *culpa*, guilt, blame (see **culpa**).] **—ex·cul·pa·ble** *adj.* **—ex·cul·pa·tion** (-páysh'n) *n.*

ex·cul·pa·to·ry (ek-skúlpə-təri, -tri, ék-skul-paytəri, -páytəri) *adj.* Proving or tending to prove guiltless; exculpating.

ex·cur·rent (ek-skúrrənt) *adj.* **1. a.** Running or flowing in an outward direction. **b.** Having an outward flow. Said of a duct, tube, or anatomical passage. **2.** *Botany.* **a.** Having a single, undivided trunk with lateral branches, as have many coniferous trees. **b.** Extending beyond the apex of a leaf, as a midrib or vein does. [Latin *excurrens* (stem *excurrent-*), present participle of *excurrere*, to run out. See **excursion.**]

ex·cur·sion (ik-skúr-sh'n, -zh'n || ek-) *n.* **1.** A short journey made with the intention of returning to the starting point; an outing. **2. a.** A pleasure tour in a coach, train, or the like, especially one of limited duration and at a special low fare. **b.** The people on such a tour. **3.** A rambling from the main topic; a digression. **4.** *Obsolete.* A military raid; a sortie. **5. a.** A movement from a mean position or axis in an oscillating or alternating motion. **b.** The distance traversed in such a movement. **6.** An explosion of fissile material in a nuclear reactor, caused by an uncontrollable chain reaction of neutrons. [Latin *excursiō* (stem *excursiōn*), from *excursus*, past participle of *excurrere*, to run out : *ex-*, out + *currere*, to run.]

ex·cur·sion·ist (ik-skúr-sh'n-ist, -zh'n-, || ek-) *n.* A person who goes on an excursion.

ex·cur·sive (ek-skúr-siv, ik- || -ziv) *adj.* **1.** Given to digression; rambling: *an excursive lecturer.* **2.** Unmethodical; desultory: *excursive reading habits.* [Latin *excursus.* See **excursion.**] **—ex·cur·sive·ly** *adv.* **—ex·cur·sive·ness** *n.*

ex·cur·sus (ek-skúr-səss, ik-) *n., pl.* **-suses** or **excursus. 1.** A lengthy, appended exposition of some point raised in a text. **2.** A digression. [Latin, from the past participle of *excurrere*, to run out. See **excursion.**]

ex·cus·a·to·ry (ik-skéwzə-təri, -tri || ek-, ékskew-zaytəri) *adj.* Tending or serving to excuse; apologetic.

ex·cuse (ik-skéwz || ek-) *tr.v.* **-cused, -cusing, -cuses. 1.** To grant pardon to; forgive: *She excused him for his clumsiness.* **2.** To make allowance for (a shortcoming); overlook; condone. **3.** To serve as apology for; justify; vindicate: *Her brilliance does not excuse her rudeness.* **4.** To free, as from an obligation or duty; exempt. **5.** To give (someone) permission to leave; dismiss or release. **6.** To refrain from exacting; remit: *excuse taxes.* —See Synonyms at **forgive. —be excused.** To leave a room or gathering in order to go to the lavatory. **—excuse me. 1.** Used, sometimes ironically, as an apology. **2.** Used to request someone to move out of the way. **3.** *U.S.* Used to request someone to repeat what he has just said. **—excuse (oneself). 1.** To request forgiveness; seek indulgence; apologise. **2.** To request exemption, as from an obligation or duty. **3.** To request permission to leave.

~n. (ik-skéwss || ek-) **1.** A plea or explanation offered to elicit pardon. **2.** The reason or ground for excusing. **3.** An act of excusing; forgiveness; pardon; indulgence. **4.** *Informal.* One that falls short of certain standards or expectations: *He is a poor excuse for a poet.* [Middle English *excusen*, from Old French *excuser*, from Latin *excūsāre* : *ex-*, removal from + *causa*, accusation, CAUSE.] **—ex·cus·a·ble** *adj.* **—ex·cus·a·ble·ness** *n.* **—ex·cus·a·bly** *adv.* **—ex·cus·er** *n.*

ex·cuse-me (ik-skéwz-mi, -mee || ek-) *n. British.* A dance during which someone may interrupt another couple and take one of the partners.

ex-di·rec·to·ry (éks-dī-réktəri, -di-) *adj.* Purposely left unlisted in the telephone directory, and not procurable by enquiry.

ex dividend *adj. Abbr.* **ex div.** *Finance.* Without claim on the current dividend. Compare **cum dividend.**

ex·e·at (éksi-at) *n. British.* **1.** Official permission to be absent from classes or from residence in an institution. **2.** Official permission from a bishop for a clergyman to leave the diocese. [Latin, "let him go out".]

ex·e·cra·ble (éksi-krəb'l) *adj.* **1.** Detestable; abominable; abhorrent. **2.** Extremely inferior; very bad. [Middle English, from Old French, from Latin *ex(s)ecrābilis*, from *ex(s)ecrārī*, to EXECRATE.] **—ex·e·cra·bly** *adv.*

ex·e·crate (éksi-krayt) *tr.v.* **-crated, -crating, -crates. 1.** To inveigh against; denounce. **2.** To abominate; abhor. **3.** *Archaic.* To invoke a curse upon; curse. [Latin *ex(s)ecrārī*, to curse, execrate : *ex-*, opposing + *sacrāre*, to be sacred, from *sacer*, sacred.] **—ex·e·cra·tive** (-kraytiv) *adj.* **—ex·e·cra·tor** *n.* **—ex·e·cra·to·ry** (éksi-kray-təri || *U.S.* -krə-tawri) *adj.*

ex·e·cra·tion (éksi-kráysh'n) *n.* **1.** The act of execrating. **2.** A curse. **3.** Detestation; abhorrence. **4.** That which is execrated; something that is loathed.

ex·ec·u·tant (ig-zéckewtənt || eg-) *n.* One who performs or carries out; especially, a musical performer.

ex·e·cute (éksi-kewt) *tr.v.* **-cuted, -cuting, -cutes. 1.** To carry out; put into effect: *execute a law.* **2.** To perform; do. **3.** To produce (a work of art, for example) in accordance with a prescribed design. **4.** To make valid; legalise, as by signing and sealing: *execute a deed.* **5.** To perform or carry out what is required by: *execute a will.* **6.** To subject to capital punishment. —See Synonyms at **perform.** [Middle English *executen*, from Old French *executer*, from Medieval Latin *executāre*, from Latin *ex(s)equī* (past participle *ex(s)ecūtus*), execute, follow to the end : *ex-*, completely + *sequī*, to follow.] **—ex·e·cut·a·ble** *adj.* **—ex·e·cut·er** *n.*

ex·e·cu·tion (éksi-kéwsh'n) *n.* **1.** The act of executing. **2.** The state of being executed. **3.** The manner, style, or result of performance. **4.** A putting or being put to death as a legal penalty. **5.** *Law.* **a.** The carrying into effect of a court judgment. **b.** A writ empowering an officer to enforce a judgment. **6.** *Law.* The validating of a legal document by the performance of certain formalities, such as signing or sealing. **7.** Military destruction: *every weapon did execution among the enemy.*

ex·e·cu·tion·er (éksi-kéwsh'n-ər) *n.* **1.** One who administers capital punishment. **2.** One who puts another to death.

ex·ec·u·tive (ig-zéckewtiv || eg-, ik-) *n. Abbr.* **ex., exec. 1.** A person or group having administrative or managerial authority in an organisation. **2.** The branch of government charged with putting into effect the country's laws.

~adj. Abbr. **ex., exec. 1.** Of, pertaining to, capable of, or suited for carrying out plans, duties, or the like. **2.** Of or pertaining to the branch of government charged with the execution and administration of the nation's laws. Compare **legislative, judicial. 3.** Suitable for an executive, as in being very large, luxurious, or exclusive: *executive jet, executive desk.*

executive officer *n.* **1.** A person holding executive power in an organisation. **2.** *Capital* **E,** *capital* **O.** The lowest grade in the administrative group of British government service and below that of Higher Executive Officer. **3.** *U.S.* The officer second in command of any of various naval or military units.

executive routine *n. Computing.* A set of coded instructions given to a computer in order to use it to develop or control other routines.

executive session *n. U.S.* A legislative session, usually one closed to the public.

executive toy *n.* Any of various small puzzles or mobile ornaments, usually of metal, designed for office desktops.

ex·ec·u·tor (ig-zéckewtər || eg-, ik-; *also* éksi-kewtər *for sense 1*) *n.* **1.** A person who carries out or performs something. **2.** *Law.* A person who is appointed by a testator to execute his will. **—ex·ec·u·tor·i·al** (-táwri-əl || -tōri-əl) *adj.* **—ex·ec·u·tor·ship** *n.*

ex·ec·u·to·ry (ig-zéckew-təri, -tri || eg-, ik-) *adj.* **1.** Administrative. **2.** Operative; in effect. **3.** *Law.* Intended to go into effect, or having the potential of becoming effective at some future time; contingent.

ex·ec·u·trix (ig-zéckyew-trikss || eg-, ik-) *n., pl.* **-trixes** or **-trices** (-trī́-seez). *Law.* A woman acting as executor.

ex·e·dra (éksi-drə, ek-sée-drə) *n., pl.* **-drae** (-dree). **1.** In classical architecture, a portico with a curved continuous bench where discussions were held. **2.** A usually curved outdoor bench of masonry with a high back. **3.** *Rare.* A bishop's throne. [Latin, from Greek *exedra*, out(doors) seat, bench : *ex-*, out + *hedra*, seat.]

ex·e·ge·sis (éksi-jée-siss) *n., pl.* **-ses** (-seez). Critical explanation or analysis; especially, exposition of the Scriptures. Compare **eisegesis.** [New Latin, from Greek *exēgēsis*, from *exēgeisthai*, to show the way, expound : *ex-*, out of + *hēgeisthai*, lead.]

ex·e·gete (éksi-jeet) *n.* Also **ex·e·ge·tist** (éksi-jéetist, -jéttist). A person skilled in exegesis. [Greek *exēgētes*, from *exēgeisthai*, to expound. See **exegesis.**]

ex·e·get·ic (éksi-jéttik) *adj.* Also **ex·e·get·i·cal** (-'l). Of or pertaining to exegesis; analytical. **—ex·e·get·i·cal·ly** *adv.*

ex·e·get·ics (éksi-jéttiks) *n. Used with a singular verb.* The science of exegesis. Compare **hermeneutics.**

ex·em·plar (ig-zém-plər, -plaar || eg-, ik-) *n.* **1.** One that is worthy of being copied; a model. **2.** One considered typical or representative; an example; a specimen. **3.** An original, whether real or ideal; an archetype. **4.** A copy, as of a book, which provides the basis for later printings. —See Synonyms at **ideal.** [Middle English, from Old French *exemplaire*, from Late Latin *exemplārium*, from Latin *exemplum*, EXAMPLE.]

ex·em·pla·ry (ig-zém-pləri || eg-, ik-) *adj.* **1.** Worthy of being imitated; commendable: *exemplary behaviour.* **2.** Serving as a model or archetype. **3.** Serving as an illustration; typical. **4.** Serving as a warning: *exemplary punishment.* **—ex·em·plar·i·ly** (-plərili || *U.S.* ég-zem-plérrəli) *adv.* **—ex·em·pla·ri·ness** *n.*

exemplary damages *pl.n. Law.* An award of damages to a plaintiff that is greater in value than the loss suffered, and that is made for the purpose of punishing the defendant and deterring others.
ex·em·pli·fi·ca·tion (ig-zémplifi-káysh'n || eg-, ik-) *n.* **1.** The act of exemplifying. **2.** One that exemplifies; an example. **3.** *Law.* An official and certified copy of a document from public records.
ex·em·pli·fi·ca·tive (ig-zémplifi-kaytiv || eg-, ik-) *adj.* Serving to exemplify; providing an example.
ex·em·pli·fy (ig-zémpli-fī || eg-, ik-) *tr.v.* **-fied, -fying, -fies.** **1. a.** To illustrate by example. **b.** To serve as an example of. **2.** *Law.* To make a certified copy of (a document from public records). [Middle English *exemplifien,* from Old French *exemplifier,* from Medieval Latin *exemplificāre* : Latin *exemplum,* EXAMPLE + *facere,* to make.] **—ex·em·pli·fi·a·ble** *adj.* **—ex·em·pli·fi·er** *n.*
ex·em·pli gra·ti·a (ig-zém-plī graáti-aa, eg-, -plee, gráyshi-, -ə) *adv. Abbr.* **e.g.** *Latin.* For the sake of example; for example.
ex·em·plum (ig-zém-pləm || eg-, ik-) *n., pl.* **-pla** (-plə). **1.** A short moral story or fable used to illustrate an argument, especially in medieval sermons. **2.** Any illustrative example. [Latin, example.]
ex·empt (ig-zémpt || eg-, ik-) *tr.v.* **-empted, -empting, -empts.** To free from an obligation, duty, tax or the like; excuse; release.
~*adj.* Freed from or not liable to something to which others are subject: *No-one is exempt from blame.* Often used in combination: *a tax-exempt benefit.*
~*n.* One who is exempted from an obligation. [Middle English *exempten,* from Latin *eximere* (past participle *exemptus*), to take out, exempt. See **example.**] **—ex·empt·i·ble** *adj.*
ex·emp·tion (ig-zémpsh'n || eg-, ik-) *n.* **1.** The act of exempting or the state of being exempt. **2. a.** Something that exempts. **b.** Something that is exempt.
ex·en·ter·ate (ig-zéntə-rayt || eg-, ek-séntə-) *tr.v.* **-ated, -ating, -ates.** **1.** To disembowel; eviscerate. **2.** *Surgery.* To remove the contents of (an organ). [Latin *exenterāre* (past participle *exenterātus*), to disembowel : *ex,* from, out of + Greek *enteron,* insides, intestines.]
ex·e·qua·tur (éksi-kwáytər) *n.* **1.** An official document recognising a consul or commercial agent, granted by the country to which he is assigned. **2.** Authorisation by a secular authority for the publication of ecclesiastical documents, or for the performance by a bishop of his duties. [Latin, "let him perform", third person singular present subjunctive of *exequī,* to EXECUTE.]
ex·e·quies (éksikwiz) *pl.n.* Funeral rites. [Middle English *exequies,* from Old French, from Latin *exsequiae,* funeral ceremonies, from *ex(s)equī,* to follow, EXECUTE.]
ex·er·cise (éksər-sīz) *n.* **1.** An act of employing or putting into play; use: *"the demand for orthodoxy is stifling to any free exercise of intellect"* (Bertrand Russell). **2.** The discharge of a duty, function, or office. **3.** Activity that requires physical or mental exertion, especially when performed to develop or maintain fitness. **4. a.** A lesson, composition, problem, or the like, designed to increase one's skill, discipline, or fitness in some capacity: *a piano exercise.* **b.** A written task assigned to school pupils. **5. a.** *Military.* A programme of practice manoeuvres undertaken as part of military training. **b.** An activity whose real nature is as specified, regardless of how it may be presented officially or publicly: "*Sometimes the marketing exercise will wrap a product in the mysterious glamour of the new . . .*" (Michael Ignatieff, *The Independent*). **6.** Any of the various events in gymnastics. **7.** *Usually plural. U.S.* A ceremony, either religious or secular, including speeches, awards, and other traditional rites: *graduation exercises.*
~*v.* **exercised, -cising, -cises.** *—tr.* **1.** To put into play or operation; employ. **2.** To bring to bear; exert: *"the desire to be re-elected exercises a strong brake on independent courage"* (John F. Kennedy). **3.** To subject to forms of practice or exertion in order to train, strengthen, or condition; put through exercises: *exercise the memory; exercise a platoon.* **4.** To carry out the functions of; execute; perform: *exercise the role of disciplinarian.* **5.** To absorb the attentions of; especially, to worry, upset, or make anxious: *He was greatly exercised by his wife's illness.* *—intr.* To take exercise or do exercises. [Middle English, from Old French *exercice,* from Latin *exercitium,* exercise, from *exercitus,* past participle of *exercēre,* to drive on, drill, practise : *ex-,* out of, from + *arcēre,* enclose, restrain.] **—ex·er·cis·a·ble** *adj.*
ex·er·cis·er (éksər-sīzər) *n.* **1.** A person who exercises or performs exercises. **2.** A device for exercising the body.
ex·er·ci·ta·tion (ig-zér-si-táysh'n, eg-) *n. Formal.* **1.** *Often plural.* Exercises, as of some particular faculty or powers: *intellectual exercitations.* **2.** Practice, as of an art, with a view to improvement: *rhetorical exercitation.* **3.** A display of oratorical skill: *the exercitations of Demosthenes.* [Middle English *exercitacioun,* from Latin *exercitātiō* (stem *exercitātiōn-*), from *exercitāre,* to exercise often, frequentative of *exercēre* (past participle *exercitus*), to EXERCISE.]
ex·ergue (ek-sérg, ék-serg, eg-zérg) *n.* **1.** The space on the reverse of a coin or medal, below the central design. **2.** The inscription in this space, often showing the date and place of engraving. [French, from New Latin *exergum* : Greek *ex-,* out of + *ergon,* work.] **—ex·ergu·al** (ek-sérg'l) *adj.*
ex·ert (ig-zért || eg-, ik-) *tr.v.* **-erted, -erting, -erts.** **1.** To put into vigorous action; put forth (strength, ability, or the like). **2.** To bring to bear; exercise: *exert influence.* **3.** To cause (oneself) to make strenuous efforts. [Latin *ex(s)erere* (past participle *ex(s)ertus*), to stretch out : *ex-,* out + *serere,* to join, put in a row, unite.]
ex·er·tion (ig-zérsh'n || eg-, ik-) *n.* **1.** An act or instance of exerting. **2.** *Often plural.* Strenuous effort. See Synonyms at **effort.**

Ex·e·ter (éksitər). County town of Devon, in southwest England, on the river Exe. It was a Roman fortress town, Isca Dumnoniorum. Exeter cathedral is in the Decorated style of Gothic architecture.
ex·e·unt (éksi-unt, -ŏont). Used as a stage direction to indicate that two or more actors leave the stage. [Latin, "they go out".]
exeunt om·nes (óm-nayz). Used as a stage direction to indicate that all actors leave the stage. [Latin, "they all go out".]
ex·fo·li·ate (eks-fṓli-ayt) *v.* **-ated, -ating, -ates.** *—tr.* **1.** To remove (skin or bark, for example) in flakes or scales; peel. **2.** To cast off in scales, flakes, or the like. *—intr.* To come off or separate in scales, flakes, sheets, or layers. [Latin *exfoliāre,* to strip of leaves : *ex-,* removal from + *folium,* leaf.] **—ex·fo·li·a·tion** (-áysh'n) *n.* **—ex·fo·li·a·tive** (-ətiv, -aytiv) *adj.*
ex gra·ti·a (eks gráy-shi-ə, -shə) *adj.* Given without legal obligation; given as a favour: *an ex gratia payment.* [Latin, "from favour".]
ex·ha·lant (eks-háy-lənt, eg-záy-) *adj.* Performing or functioning in exhalation.
ex·ha·la·tion (éks-hə-láysh'n, -ə-, égzə-) *n.* **1.** An act of exhaling. **2.** That which is exhaled, such as air or vapour.
ex·hale (eks-háyl, ig-záyl, eg-) *v.* **-haled, -haling, -hales.** *—intr.* **1. a.** To breathe out. **b.** To emit air or vapour. **2.** To be given off or emitted. *—tr.* **1.** To blow forth or breathe out (vapour, smoke, or the like). **2.** To give off; emit. **3.** To draw out or off; evaporate. [Middle English *exalen,* from Old French *exhaler,* from Latin *exhālāre,* to breathe out : *ex-,* out + *hālāre,* to breathe.] **—ex·hal·a·ble** *adj.*
ex·haust (ig-záwst || eg-) *v.* **-hausted, -hausting, -hausts.** *—tr.* **1.** To let out or draw off (air or fumes). **2. a.** To draw out the contents of; drain. **b.** To draw off; drain: *exhaust the oil from a storage tank.* **3.** To create a vacuum or partial vacuum in (a container). **4.** To use up; expend; consume: *exhaust one's money.* **5.** To wear out completely; tire. **6.** To drain of resources or properties; deplete. **7.** To study or deal with comprehensively: *exhaust a topic.* *—intr.* To escape or pass out, as steam. —See Synonyms at **deplete.**
~*n.* **1.** The escape or release of gas or vapour, as from an engine. **2.** The fumes or gases released. **3.** A device or part, such as a pipe, through which such waste material escapes. Also "exhaust pipe".
~*adj.* **1.** Designating a part of an engine through which expanded steam or the products of combustion pass: *exhaust valve; exhaust manifold.* **2.** Of, pertaining to, or designating the expanded steam or products of combustion of an engine or any phase of the engine's cycle relating to their extraction: *exhaust gas; exhaust stroke.* [Latin *exhaurīre* (past participle *exhaustus*), to draw out, exhaust : *ex-,* out + *haurīre,* to draw up.] **—ex·haust·er** *n.* **—ex·haust·i·bil·i·ty** (-ə-bíllǝti) *n.* **—ex·haust·i·ble** *adj.* **—ex·haust·ing·ly** *adv.*
ex·haus·tion (ig-záwss-chən || eg-) *n.* **1.** The act or an instance of exhausting. **2.** The state of being exhausted. **3.** A state of great weariness; extreme fatigue.
ex·haus·tive (ig-záwstiv || eg-) *adj.* **1.** Dealing with or taking account of all aspects; comprehensive; thorough. **2.** Tending to exhaust. **—ex·haus·tive·ly** *adv.* **—ex·haus·tive·ness** *n.*
ex·hib·it (ig-zíbbit || eg-) *v.* **-ited, -iting, -its.** *—tr.* **1.** To show; display. **2. a.** To present for the public to view. **b.** To enter or show in an exhibition or contest. **3.** To give an instance or evidence of; demonstrate: *The specimen exhibits a cancerous condition.* **4.** *Law.* To submit (objects or documents) as evidence in a court; introduce officially. *—intr.* To put something on display; have an exhibition. —See Synonyms at **show.**
~*n.* (*rarely also* égzibit). **1.** An act of exhibiting. **2.** That which is exhibited. **3.** *Law.* Something, such as a document, formally introduced as evidence in court. [Middle English *exhibiten,* from Latin *exhibēre* (past participle *exhibitus*), to hold forth, exhibit : *ex-,* out + *habēre,* to hold.] **—ex·hib·i·tive** *adj.* **—ex·hib·i·tive·ly** *adv.*
ex·hi·bi·tion (éksi-bísh'n || égzi-) *n.* **1.** An act of exhibiting. **2.** Something exhibited. **3.** A display for the public, as of art objects, industrial achievements, or agricultural products. **4.** *British.* A scholarship given to a student by a public school or university. **—make an exhibition of (oneself).** To engage publicly in foolish behaviour.
ex·hi·bi·tion·er (éksi-bísh'nər || égzi-) *n. British.* A student who receives an exhibition.
ex·hi·bi·tion·ism (éksi-bísh'n-iz'm || égzi-) *n.* **1.** The act or practice of behaving in an ostentatious way in order to attract attention. **2.** *Psychology.* Compulsive exposure of the sexual organs in public. **—ex·hi·bi·tion·ist** *n. & adj.* **—ex·hi·bi·tion·is·tic** (-ístik) *adj.*
ex·hib·i·tor (ig-zíbbitər || eg-, ik-) *n.* One that exhibits; especially, a person or group exhibiting articles in a show.
ex·hil·a·rant (ig-zíllərənt || eg-, ik-) *adj.* Exhilarating.
~*n.* A stimulant or euphoriant.
ex·hil·a·rate (ig-zíllə-rayt || eg-, ik-) *tr.v.* **-rated, -rating, -rates.** **1.** To make cheerful; elate. **2.** To invigorate; stimulate. [Latin *exhilarāre* : *ex-,* completely + *hilarāre,* to make happy, from *hilaris,* cheerful, happy, from Greek *hilaros.*] **—ex·hil·a·ra·tion** (-raysh'n) *n.* **—ex·hil·a·ra·tive** (-rətiv, -raytiv) *adj.* **—ex·hil·a·ra·tor** *n.*
ex·hil·a·rat·ing (ig-zíllə-rayting || eg-, ik-) *adj.* **1.** Cheering; gladdening. **2.** Invigorating; stimulating. **—ex·hil·a·rat·ing·ly** *adv.*
ex·hort (ig-zórt || eg-, ik-) *v.* **-horted, -horting, -horts.** *—tr.* To urge or incite by strong argument, advice, or appeal; admonish earnestly. *—intr.* To make urgent appeal. —See Synonyms at **urge.** [Middle English *exhorten,* from Old French *exhorter,* from Latin *exhortārī* : *ex-,* completely + *hortārī,* to encourage.] **—ex·hor·ta·tive** (-ətiv), **ex·hor·ta·tory** (-ə-təri, -tri) *adj.* **—ex·hort·er** *n.*

ex·hor·ta·tion (ég-zawr-táysh'n, ék-sawr-) *n.* **1.** An act of exhorting. **2.** The practice of exhorting. **3.** A speech or discourse intended to advise, incite, or encourage.

ex·hume (eks-héwm, ig-zéwm ‖ -zóōm, zhóōm) *tr.v.* **-humed, -huming, -humes. 1.** To remove (a dead body) from a grave; disinter. **2.** To bring to light; uncover: *exhume ancient superstitions.* [French *exhumer*, from Medieval Latin *exhumāre* : Latin *ex-*, out of + *humus*, earth.] **—ex·hu·ma·tion** (éks-hew-máysh'n, éksew- ‖ ékshōō-) *n.* **—ex·hum·er** *n.*

ex hy·poth·e·si (éks hī-póthə-sī) *adv.* Following from the premise of the argument; in accordance with the stated hypothesis. [New Latin, "according to the hypothesis".]

ex·i·gen·cy (ék-sijən-si, ig-zíjən-) *n., pl.* **-cies.** Also **ex·i·gence** (éksijənss). **1.** The state or quality of being exigent. **2.** A situation demanding swift attention; a pressing state; an emergency. **3.** *Usually plural.* Urgent requirement; pressing need.

ex·i·gent (éksijənt) *adj.* **1.** Requiring immediate attention or remedy; urgent. **2.** Excessively demanding; exacting. [Latin *exigēns* (stem *exigent-*), present participle of *exigere*, to demand.] **—ex·i·gent·ly** *adv.*

ex·i·gi·ble (éksijəb'l) *adj.* Able to be exacted; demandable; requirable. [French, from *exiger*, to demand, from Latin *exigere*.]

ex·ig·u·ous (eg-zíggew-əss, ig-, ek-síggew-) *adj.* Scanty; meagre. [Latin *exiguus*, from *exigere*, to weigh exactly, demand. See *exact.*] **—ex·i·gu·i·ty** (éksi-géw-əti), **ex·ig·u·ous·ness** *n.* **—ex·ig·u·ous·ly** *adv.*

ex·ile (ég-zīl, ék-sīl ‖ *U.S. also* égz'l) *n.* **1. a.** Enforced removal from one's native country by authoritative decree; banishment. **b.** Self-imposed separation from one's country. **2. a.** The state or circumstance of being exiled. **b.** The period of time in exile. **3.** One who is or has been separated from his country. **~***tr.v.* **exiled, -iling, -iles.** To send (a person) into exile; banish. [Middle English *exil*, from Old French, from Latin *exilium*, from *exul*, one who is exiled.] **—ex·il·ic** (eg-zíllik, ek-síllik), **ex·il·i·an** (eg-zilli-ən, ek-sílli-) *adj.*

ex in. *Finance.* Without interest. [Latin *ex*, without + *interest.*]

ex·ine (ék-sin, -sīn) *n.* The outer wall of a spore or pollen grain. Also called "exosporium". [Latin *ex(timus)*, outermost + -INE.]

ex·ist (ig-zíst ‖ eg-, ik-) *intr.v.* **-isted, -isting, -ists. 1.** To have being or actuality; be. **2. a.** To have life; live. **b.** To continue to live; survive, especially in difficult or reduced circumstances. **3.** To be present under certain circumstances or in a specified place; occur: *Tapeworms exist in human intestines.* [Latin *ex(s)istere*, to exist, come forth : *ex-*, out + *sistere*, to take a position, stand firm.]

ex·is·tence (ig-zísstənss ‖ eg-, ik-) *n.* **1.** The fact or state of existing; being. **2.** The fact or state of continued being; life; survival. **3. a.** All that exists. **b.** A thing that exists; an entity. **4.** A mode or manner of existing: *a meagre existence.* **5.** Occurrence; specific presence: *the existence of life on other planets.*

ex·is·tent (ig-zístənt ‖ eg-, ik-) *adj.* **1.** Having life or being; existing. **2.** Occurring or present at the moment; current. **—See Synonyms at real.** **~***n.* One that exists.

ex·is·ten·tial (égzi-sténsh'l ‖ éksi-) *adj.* **1.** Of, pertaining to, or dealing with existence. **2.** Based on experience; empirical. **3.** *Philosophy.* Pertaining to existentialism. **4.** *Logic.* Of, pertaining to, or designating a proposition which implies or specifies the existence of at least one of its elements. **—ex·is·ten·tial·ly** *adv.*

ex·is·ten·tial·ism (égzi-sténsh'l-iz'm ‖ éksi-) *n.* A body of ethical thought, current in the 20th century, centring on the uniqueness and isolation of individual experience in a universe indifferent or even hostile to man, regarding human existence as unexplainable, and emphasising man's freedom of choice and responsibility for the consequences of his acts. **—ex·is·ten·tial·ist** *adj. & n.*

ex·it¹ (égzit, éksit). Used as a stage direction for a specified actor to leave the stage. [Latin, "He (or she) goes out".]

exit² *n.* **1.** The departure of a performer from the stage. **2. a.** The act of going away or out. **b.** Death; demise. **3.** A way out; a door or passage through which one can leave. **~** *intr.v.* **exited, -iting, -its.** To go away or out. [Latin *exitus*, exit, from the past participle of *exīre*, to go out : *ex-*, out + *īre*, to go.]

EXIT *n.* A society founded in Britain in 1935 with the purpose of changing the law on voluntary euthanasia and of advising those of its members with terminal or serious chronic illnesses on methods of suicide.

ex·i·tance (éksitənss) *n.* A measure of the ability of a surface to emit radiation. See **luminous exitance, radiant exitance.** [Latin *exitus*, departure, emission + -ANCE.]

exit permit *n.* In South Africa formerly, a permit to emigrate without the right to return.

exit poll *n.* A straw poll of voters leaving a polling station, from which the pollsters try to forecast the vote's result.

ex libris (eks lée-briss, lī-, lí-). *Abbr.* **ex lib.** *Latin.* From the library of. Used on bookplates before the owner's name.

ex·li·brist (ekss-lée-brist, -lī-, -lí-) *n.* One who collects bookplates. **—ex·li·brism** *n.*

Ex·moor (ékss-moor, -mawr). A thinly populated moorland in southwest England forming much of the Exmoor National Park. The moor contains a number of prehistoric earthworks.

Exmoor pony *n.* A pony of a hardy, sure-footed breed originating in the Exmoor region, having short ears, large eyes, and a bay, brown, or dun coat.

exo- *comb. form.* Indicates outside, external, or beyond; for example, **exocarp, exoskeleton.** [Greek *exō*, outside, from *ex*, out of.]

ex·o·bi·ol·o·gy (ék-sō-bī-óllə̄ji) *n.* **1.** A branch of biology that deals with the search for and study of extraterrestrial living organisms. Also called "astrobiology". **2.** A branch of biology that deals with the effects of extraterrestrial space on living organisms. In this sense, also called "space biology".

ex·o·carp (ék-sō-kaarp) *n. Botany.* The outermost layer of the pericarp of fruit. Also called "epicarp". [EXO- + -CARP.]

ex·o·cen·tric (ék-sō-séntrik) *adj. Grammar.* Designating a construction that serves a grammatical function different from that of any of its constituents; for example, *towards the icy summit* is an exocentric construction since it functions adverbially, whereas none of the constituent words does. Compare **endocentric.**

Ex·o·cet (éksō-set) *n.* A trademark for a versatile guided missile steered by a preset guidance system until it is near the target, after which it is guided by radar signals. [French, from New Latin *exocoeta (volans)*, the (flying) fish, from Greek *exōkoitos*, name of a fish believed to sleep out of the water at night : *exō*, out of + *koitos*, bed.]

ex·o·crine (ék-sə-krīn, -sō-, -krin, -kreen) *adj.* **1.** Having or secreting through a duct. Said of a gland. **2.** Of or pertaining to the secretion of such a gland. [EXO- + Greek *krinein*, to separate.]

Exod. Exodus (Old Testament).

ex·o·derm (ék-sō-derm) *n.* An embryonic germ layer, the **ectoderm** *(see).* [EXO- + -DERM.]

ex·o·der·mis (ék-sō-dérmiss) *n. Botany.* A layer of protective cells in roots, lying just beneath the epidermis.

ex·o·don·tics (ék-sō-dóntikss) *n.* Dentistry involving the extraction of teeth. [New Latin : EX- + -ODONT + -ICS.] **—ex·o·don·tist** *n.*

ex·o·dus (éksədəss) *n.* **1.** A movement away; a departure, usually of a large number of people. **2.** *Capital* **E.** The departure of the Israelites from Egypt. Preceded by *the.* [Late Latin, from Greek *exodos*, a going out, a way out : *ex-*, out + *hodos*, way.]

Exodus *n. Abbr.* **Ex., Exod.** The second book of the Old Testament, which recounts the Exodus of the Israelites.

ex·o·en·zyme (ék-sō-én-zīm) *n.* **1.** An enzyme that acts on the terminal chemical bonds in a chain molecule. **2.** An enzyme, such as a digestive enzyme, that functions outside a cell.

ex·o·er·gic (ék-sō-érjik) *adj. Physics.* Exergonic.

ex of·fi·ci·o (éks ə-físhi-ō, -físsi-ō) *adj. Abbr.* **e.o., ex off.** By virtue of office or position. **—ex of·fi·ci·o** *adv.*

ex·og·a·my (ek-sóggəmi) *n.* **1.** The custom of marrying outside the tribe, family, clan, or other social unit. Compare **endogamy. 2.** *Biology.* Reproduction by the fusion of gametes that are not closely related. [EXO- + -GAMY.] **—ex·o·gam·ic** (ék-sō-gámmik), **ex·og·a·mous** (ek-sóggəməss) *adj.*

ex·og·e·nous (ek-sójinəss) *adj.* **1.** *Biology.* Derived or developed from outside the body, as are substances derived from diet rather than metabolism. **2.** *Botany.* Characterised by the addition of layers of woody tissue. **3.** Having a cause external to the body. Said of diseases. **4.** Having an outside origin: *exogenous political unrest.* [French *exogène*, having additional layers : EXO- + -GEN.] **—ex·o·gen·ic** (ék-sō-jénnik) *adj.* **—ex·og·e·nous·ly** *adv.*

exo·in·tine (ék-sō-ín-tin, -teen, -tīn) *n.* The middle layer of a spore or pollen grain, between the intine and the exine. Also called "mesosporium".

ex·on (ék-son) *n.* An officer in the Yeoman of the Guard. [Pronunciation spelling of French *exempt*, EXEMPT.]

ex·on·er·ate (ig-zónnə-rayt ‖ eg-) *tr.v.* **-ated, -ating, -ates. 1.** To free from a charge; declare blameless; exculpate. **2.** To free from a responsibility, obligation, or task; exempt. [Middle English *exoneraten*, from Latin *exonerāre* (past participle *exonerātus*), to free from a burden : *ex-*, removal from + *onus* (stem *oner-*), load, burden.] **—ex·on·er·a·tion** (-ráysh'n) *n.*

ex·o·nu·mi·a (ék-sō-néw-mi-ə ‖ -nōō-) *n.* The study and collection of small items, such as tickets or labels, that are not traditionally classified as numismatic objects. [EXO- (outside, beyond) + *-numia*, from Latin *nummus*, coin.]

ex·o·nym (ék-sə-nim, -sō-) *n.* Any of the names of a city, river, or the like, used in languages other than the language of the region or country in which that place or geographical feature is located; for example, *Douvres* is an exonym of *Dover.* [EX(O)- + -ONYM.]

exophthalmic goitre *n.* A disease caused by the excessive production of thyroid hormone and characterised by an enlarged thyroid gland, protrusion of the eyeballs, a rapid heart beat, weight loss, and nervous excitability. Also called "Graves' disease". [From EX-OPHTHALMOS.]

ex·oph·thal·mos (ék-sof-thál-moss) *n.* Also **ex·oph·thal·mi·a** (-mi-ə), **ex·oph·thal·mus** (-məss). Abnormal protrusion of the eyeball. [New Latin, from Greek, with prominent eyes : *ex-*, out of + *ophthalmos*, eye.] **—ex·oph·thal·mic** (-mik) *adj.*

ex·or·bi·tant (ig-zórbitənt ‖ eg-) .*adj.* Beyond reasonable bounds; excessive; immoderate. See Synonyms at **excessive.** [Middle English, from Old French, from Late Latin *exorbitāns*, present participle of *exorbitāre*, to deviate : Latin *ex-*, out of + *orbita*, route, ORBIT.] **—ex·or·bi·tance** *n.* **—ex·or·bi·tant·ly** *adv.*

ex·or·cise, ex·or·cize (ék-sawr-sīz, -sər-, ég-zawr-) *tr.v.* **-cised, -cising, -cises. 1. a.** To expel (an evil spirit) by or as if by incantation, prayer, ceremonies, or the like. **b.** To get rid of (fear, anxiety, or the like) as if by exorcising evil spirits. **2.** To free from evil spirits. [Middle English *exorcisen*, from Old French *exorciser*, from Late Latin *exorcīzāre*, from Greek *exorkizein*, to exorcise (an evil spirit) with an oath : *ex-*, away + *horkos†*, oath.] **—ex·or·cis·er** *n.*

539

ex·or·cism (ék-sawr-siz'm, -sər-, ég-zawr-) *n.* **1.** The act of exorcising. **2.** A formula used in exorcising. **—ex·or·cist** *n.*

ex·or·di·um (ek-sór-di-əm, eg-zór-) *n., pl.* **-ums** or **-dia** (-di-ə). An introductory part, especially of a speech, treatise, or the like. [Latin, from *exōrdīrī*, to begin : *ex-*, completely + *ōrdīrī*, to begin.] **—ex·or·di·al** *adj.*

ex·o·skel·e·ton (ék-sō-skéllitən) *n.* The external protective or supporting structure of many invertebrates, such as insects and crustaceans. Compare **endoskeleton.**

ex·os·mo·sis (ék-soz-mō-siss) *n.* The flow of a solvent through a semipermeable membrane into a surrounding fluid; especially, the flow of water through a cell membrane into the external medium. Compare **endosmosis.** [EX(O)- + OSMOSIS.] **—ex·os·mot·ic** (-mót-tik) *adj.*

ex·o·sphere (ék-sō-sfeer) *n.* The outermost portion of the atmosphere, estimated to begin 450 to 900 kilometres (300 to 600 miles) above the Earth, and characterised by the ability of constituent molecules with appropriate velocities to escape from the Earth without colliding with other molecules. [EXO- + -SPHERE.]

ex·o·spore (ék-sō-spawr ‖ -spōr) *n. Botany.* The outermost layer of a spore in some algae and fungi. [EXO- + SPORE.]

ex·o·spor·i·um (ek-sō-spáwri-əm ‖ -spóri-) *n.* The **exine** (*see*).

ex·os·to·sis (ék-so-stō-siss) *n., pl.* **-ses** (-seez). A bony tumour on the surface of a bone. [New Latin, from Greek *exostōsis* : *ex-*, out of + *osteon*, bone.]

ex·o·ter·ic (ék-sə-térrik, -sō-) *adj.* **1.** Belonging to more than just an inner circle of disciples or initiates. **2.** Comprehensible to or suited to the general public; popular. Compare **esoteric. 3.** Pertaining to the outside; external. [Latin *exōtericus*, external, from Greek *exōterikos*, from *exōterō*, comparative of *exō*, outside, from *ex*, out.] **—ex·o·ter·i·cal·ly** *adv.*

ex·o·ther·mic (ék-sō-thérmik) *adj.* Also **ex·o·ther·mal** (-thérm'l). Characterised by or causing the release of heat. Compare **endothermic.** [EXO- + THERM(O)- + -IC.]

ex·ot·ic (ig-zóttik ‖ eg-, ek-sóttik) *adj.* **1.** From another part of the world; not indigenous; foreign. **2.** Having the charm of the unfamiliar; strikingly and intriguingly unusual, different, or beautiful. ~*n.* Something that is exotic, such as an alien plant, animal, or disease. [Latin *exōticus*, from Greek *exōtikos*, from *exō*, outside, from *ex*, out.] **—ex·ot·i·cal·ly** *adv.* **—ex·ot·i·cism** (-zótti-siz'm ‖ -sotti-), **ex·ot·ic·ness** *n.*

ex·ot·i·ca (ig-zóttikə ‖ eg-) *pl.n.* Exotic things, as in a collection. [Latin, neuter plural of *exōticus*, EXOTIC.]

ex·o·tox·in (ék-sō-tóksin) *n.* A toxin excreted by a microorganism into a surrounding medium and recoverable from a culture without destruction of the producing agent. See **toxin.**

exp exponential.

ex·pand (ik-spánd, ek-) *v.* **-panded, -panding, -pands.** —*tr.* **1.** To open up or out; spread out; unfold. **2.** To increase the dimensions of; cause to swell; distend. **3.** To increase the scope of; extend; develop. **4.** *Mathematics.* To write (a quantity) as a sum of terms, as a continued product, or as another extended form. —*intr.* **1.** To open up; unfold. **2.** To become larger or wider. **3.** To speak or write at length; expatiate. **4.** To become expansive. —See Synonyms at **increase.** [Middle English *expanden*, from Latin *expandere* : *ex-*, out + *pandere*, to spread.]

ex·pand·ed (ik-spándid ‖ ek-) *adj.* **1.** *Printing.* Wider than normal in proportion to its height; extended. Said of type. Compare **condensed. 2.** Puffed into a foamlike texture by the addition of gas during solidification. Said of a plastic or similar material used in packaging or insulating.

expanded metal *n.* An open metal mesh used for reinforcing brittle materials and in fencing.

ex·pand·er, ex·pand·or (ik-spándər, ek-) *n.* **1.** *Electronics.* A device for expanding the range of output voltages for a given range of input voltages according to a specific law. **2.** A device, usually spring-loaded, for exercising and developing body muscles: *a chest expander.*

expanding universe *n.* **1.** A theory that interprets the shifts of the lines in the spectra of galaxies as resulting from a Doppler effect, with the result that all galaxies are assumed to be retreating from each other at speeds proportional to the distance separating them and that the universe is expanding. **2.** The cosmological theory in which violent eruption from a point source leads to the formation of elementary particles, the subsequent formation of hydrogen and helium, and the dispersion of the galaxies that develop from this matter. Compare **steady-state theory.** See **big-bang theory.**

ex·panse (ik-spánss, ek-) *n.* **1.** A wide and open extent, as of land, sky, or water. **2.** Expansion. [Latin *expansum*, from the neuter participle of *expandere*, to EXPAND.]

ex·pan·si·ble (ik-spán-səb'l, ek-) *adj.* Capable of expanding or of being expanded. **—ex·pan·si·bil·i·ty** (-sə-bílləti) *n.*

ex·pan·sile (ik-spán-sīl, ek- ‖ *U.S. also* -spánss'l) *adj.* Of, pertaining to, or adapted for expansion.

ex·pan·sion (ik-spánsh'n, ek-) *n.* **1.** The act or process of expanding. **2.** The state of being expanded. **3.** A part or form produced by expanding. **4.** The extent or amount by which something has expanded. **5.** An enlargement, increase, or extension, as of business, currency, or territory. **6.** Increase in the dimensions of a body. **7.** *Mathematics.* **a.** A quantity written in an extended form, such as a series. **b.** The process of obtaining this form. **8.** An expanse. **—ex·pan·sion·ar·y** (-əri, -ri ‖ -erri) *adj.*

expansion bolt *n.* A bolt having an attachment that expands as the bolt is driven into a surface.

ex·pan·sion·ism (ik-spánsh'n-iz'm, ek-) *n.* The practice or policy of territorial or economic expansion, as by a nation. **—ex·pan·sion·ist** *n. & adj.* **—ex·pan·sion·is·tic** (-ístik) *adj.*

ex·pan·sive (ik-spán-siv, ek-) *adj.* **1.** Capable of expanding or tending to expand. **2.** Wide; sweeping; comprehensive. **3.** Disposed to be open and outgoing. **4.** *Psychology.* Marked by euphoria and delusions of grandeur. **5.** Grand in scale: *expansive living.* **—ex·pan·sive·ly** *adv.* **—ex·pan·sive·ness** *n.*

ex par·te (eks párti) *adj. Latin.* **1.** *Law.* From or on one side only. Said of a court application. **2.** One-sided; partisan.

ex·pa·ti·ate (ek-spáyshi-ayt, ik-) *intr.v.* **-ated, -ating, -ates. 1.** To speak or write at length on a subject; dilate. Often used with *on* or *upon.* **2.** *Rare.* To wander freely. [Latin *ex(s)patiārī*, to spread out, digress, expatiate : *ex-*, out + *spatiārī*, to walk, to spread, from *spatium,* SPACE.] **—ex·pa·ti·a·tion** (-áysh'n) *n.* **—ex·pa·ti·a·tory** (-ə-təri, -tri) *adj.*

ex·pa·tri·ate (eks-páttri-ayt, -páytri-) *v.* **-ated, -ating, -ates.** —*tr.* **1.** To banish (a person) from his native land; exile. **2.** To banish (oneself) from one's native land. —*intr.* To leave one's homeland, and often renounce one's citizenship, to reside in another country. ~*n.* (-ət, -it, -ayt). An expatriated person; an exile. ~*adj.* (-ət, -it, -ayt). Expatriated. [Medieval Latin *expatriāre* : Latin *ex-*, out of + *patria*, native land, from *pater* (stem *patr-*), father.] **—ex·pa·tri·a·tion** (-áysh'n) *n.*

ex·pect (ik-spékt ‖ ek-) *tr.v.* **-pected, -pecting, -pects. 1.** To look ahead to the probable occurrence or appearance of. **2.** To consider likely or certain. **3.** To consider reasonable or due: *I expect an apology.* **4.** To consider obligatory; require. **5.** *Informal.* To presume; suppose. **—be expecting.** To be pregnant. [Latin *ex(s)pectāre*, to look out (for), expect : *ex-*, out + *spectāre*, look at, frequentative of *specere*, to see, look at.]

Synonyms: expect, anticipate, hope, await, foresee.

ex·pec·tan·cy (ik-spék-tən-si) *n., pl.* **-cies.** Also **ex·pec·tance** (-tənss). **1.** The act or state of expecting; expectation. **2.** The state of being expected. **3. a.** Something expected. **b.** That which one can look forward to having; a prospect: *a life expectancy of seventy years.*

ex·pec·tant (ik-spéktənt) *adj.* **1.** Having or marked by expectation: *an expectant pause.* **2.** Awaiting the birth of a child: *an expectant mother.* **3.** Waiting in confident expectation. Used with *of: expectant of praise.* ~*n.* A person who is expecting something. **—ex·pec·tant·ly** *adv.*

ex·pec·ta·tion (ik-spek-táysh'n) *n.* **1. a.** The act or state of expecting. **b.** Eager anticipation. **2.** The state of being expected. **3.** *Plural.* Prospects, especially of inheritance. **4.** *Usually plural.* Something expected or hoped for. **5.** The expected value of a random variable, especially the **mean** (*see*). —See Synonyms at **prospect. —ex·pec·ta·tive** (ik-spéktətiv ‖ ek-) *adj.*

ex·pect·ing (ik-spékting ‖ ek-) *adj. Informal.* Awaiting the birth of a child; pregnant: *she's expecting.*

ex·pec·to·rant (ik-spéktərənt ‖ ek-) *adj.* Promoting or facilitating the secretion or expulsion of phlegm or other matter from the mucous membrane of the air passages. ~*n.* An expectorant medicine.

ex·pec·to·rate (ik-spéktə-rayt ‖ ek-) *v.* **-rated, -rating, -rates.** —*tr.* **1.** To eject from the mouth; spit. **2.** To cough up and eject by spitting. —*intr.* **1.** To spit. **2.** To clear out the chest and lungs by coughing up and spitting out matter. [Latin *expectorāre*, to drive from the breast : *ex-*, from, out of + *pectus* (stem *pector-*), breast.] **—ex·pec·to·ra·tion** (-ráysh'n) *n.*

ex·pe·di·en·cy (ik-spéedi-ən-si ‖ ek-) *n., pl.* **-cies.** Also **ex·pe·di·ence** (di-ənss). **1.** Appropriateness to the purpose at hand. **2.** Adherence to what is personally advantageous; self-interest. **3.** An expedient.

ex·pe·di·ent (ik-spéedi-ənt ‖ ek-) *adj.* **1.** Appropriate to the purpose at hand. **2.** Serving to promote one's interests; politic though perhaps unprincipled. ~*n.* **1.** That which answers the immediate purpose; a means to an end. **2.** A contrivance adopted to meet an urgent need. [Middle English, from Old French, from Latin *expediēns* (stem *expedient-*), present participle of *expedīre*, to free, make ready. See **expedite.**] **—ex·pe·di·ent·ly** *adv.*

ex·pe·di·en·tial (ik-speedi-énsh'l ‖ ek-) *adj.* Of, pertaining to, or concerned with what is expedient. **—ex·pe·di·en·tial·ly** *adv.*

ex·pe·dite (ék-spi-dīt, -spə-, -spe-) *tr.v.* **-dited, -diting, -dites. 1.** To speed up the progress of; help along; assist; facilitate. **2.** To perform quickly and efficiently. **3.** *Rare.* To issue officially; dispatch. —See Synonyms at **speed.** [Latin *expedīre* (past participle *expedītus*), to free the feet, to extricate.] **—ex·pe·dit·er, ex·pe·di·tor** *n.*

ex·pe·di·tion (ék-spi-dísh'n) *n.* **1.** A journey undertaken by an organised group of people with a definite objective, such as exploration. **2. a.** A long march or voyage made by military forces to a scene of battle. **b.** The force sent out, with vehicles and equipment. **3.** Speed in performance; dispatch; promptness. [Middle English *expedicioun*, from Old French *expedition*, from Latin *expedītiō* (stem *expedītiōn-*), from *expedītus*, past participle of *expedīre*, to extricate. See **expedite.**]

ex·pe·di·tion·ar·y (ék-spi-dísh'n-əri, -ri ‖ -erri) *adj.* Pertaining to or constituting an expedition, especially military.

ex·pe·di·tious (ék-spi-díshəss) *adj.* Acting or done with speed and efficiency. See Synonyms at **fast.** —**ex·pe·di·tious·ly** adv. —**ex·pe·di·tious·ness** n.

ex·pel (ik-spél, ek-) tr.v. **-pelled, -pelling, -pels. 1.** To force or drive out; eject forcefully. **2.** To discharge, as from the body or some receptacle. **3.** To dismiss from a school or membership of a society by official decision; turn out. —See Synonyms at **eject.** [Middle English *expellen,* from Latin *expellere : ex-,* out + *pellere,* to drive.] —**ex·pel·la·ble** adj. —**ex·pel·lee** (ék-spel-ée) n.

ex·pel·lant, ex·pel·lent (ik-spéllənt, ek-) adj. Expelling or tending to expel; expulsive.

~n. A medicine used to expel substances or organisms from the body, especially worms from the intestines.

ex·pel·lers (ik-spéllərz, ek-) pl.n. The residue left after an oilseed has had the oil extracted from it by crushing, used as an animal feed: *groundnut expellers.* Compare **extractions.**

ex·pend (ik-spénd) tr.v. **-pended, -pending, -pends. 1.** To put out or lay out; spend. **2.** To use up; consume. [Middle English *expenden,* from Latin *expendere,* to pay out : *ex,* out + *pendere,* weigh, pay.]

ex·pend·a·ble (ik-spénd-əb'l || ek-) adj. **1.** Subject to use or consumption. **2.** Suitable for sacrifice in the interests of gaining an objective, especially a military one.

~n. That which is expendable. —**ex·pend·a·bil·i·ty** (-ə-billəti) n.

ex·pen·di·ture (ik-spéndichər || ek-) n. **1.** The act or process of expending; outlay. **2. a.** The amount expended. **b.** An expense. —See Synonyms at **price.**

ex·pense (ik-spénss || ek-) n. **1. a.** Cost; charge. **b.** Outlay of money: *he was put to considerable expense.* **c.** A sacrifice; a price: *"Every attempt at a system is made at the expense of facts"* (Bernard Berenson). **2.** *Plural.* **a.** Charges incurred while performing one's job. **b.** *Informal.* Money allotted for payment of such charges: *claim it on expenses.* **3.** Something requiring the expenditure of money. **4.** *Archaic.* An act of expending; expenditure. —See Synonyms at **price.** [Middle English, from Old French *espense,* from Late Latin *expensa,* from the feminine past participle of Latin *expendere,* to EXPEND.]

expense account n. An account of expenses for travel, entertainment, or the like incurred by an employee in the course of his work and reimbursed by his employer.

ex·pen·sive (ik-spén-siv || ek-) adj. **1.** Involving a large expenditure; high-priced; costly. **2.** Involving considerable loss or sacrifice: *an expensive mistake.* —See Synonyms at **costly.** —**ex·pen·sive·ly** adv. —**ex·pen·sive·ness** n.

ex·pe·ri·ence (ik-spéer-i-ənss || ek-) n. **1.** The apprehension of an object, thought, or emotion through the senses or mind: *the experience of art.* **2.** Active participation in events or activities, leading to the accumulation of knowledge or skill. **3.** The knowledge or skill so derived. **4.** An event or series of events participated in or lived through, especially one that makes a powerful impression on the mind or senses. **5.** The totality of such events in the past of an individual or group.

~tr.v. **experienced, -encing, -ences.** To participate in or partake of personally; undergo: *experience a feeling of loneliness.* [Middle English, from Old French, from Latin *experientia,* from *experiens,* present participle of *experīrī,* to try, test.]

ex·pe·ri·enced (ik-spéer-i-ənst || ek-) adj. **1.** Skilled through frequent use or practice. **2.** Knowledgeable from long or wide experience: *an experienced teacher.*

experience table n. *Insurance.* A table compiled from life-insurance statistics to indicate expectation of life.

ex·pe·ri·en·tial (ik-spéer-i-énsh'l || ek-) adj. Pertaining to or derived from experience. —**ex·pe·ri·en·tial·ly** adv.

ex·pe·ri·en·tial·ism (ik-spéer-i-énsh'l-iz'm || ek-) n. *Philosophy.* The doctrine that knowledge is derived only from experience.

ex·per·i·ment (ik-spérri-mənt || ek-, -ment, *U.S. also* -spéer-i-) n. **1.** A test made to demonstrate a known truth, to examine the validity of a hypothesis, or to determine the efficacy of something previously untried: *a laboratory experiment.* **2.** The conducting of such a test. **3.** An act or approach that is original or unusual: *a theatrical experiment.*

~intr.v. (-ment) **experimented, -menting, -ments.** To conduct an experiment or experiments; try or test. [Middle English, from Old French, from Latin *experimentum,* from *experīrī,* to try, test. See **experience.**] —**ex·per·i·ment·er** n. —**ex·per·i·men·ta·tion** (-táysh'n) n.

ex·per·i·men·tal (ik-spérri-mént'l || ek-, *U.S. also* -spéer-i-) adj. **1. a.** Pertaining to or based upon experiment. **b.** Given to experimenting. **2.** Provisional; tentative. **3.** Founded upon experience; empirical. —**ex·per·i·men·tal·ly** adv.

ex·per·i·men·tal·ism (ik-spérri-mént'l-izm || ek-, *U.S. also* -spéeri-) n. The use of or reliance upon experimentation. —**ex·per·i·men·tal·ise** (-īz) intr.v. —**ex·per·i·men·tal·ist** n.

ex·pert (ék-spert) n. A person with a high degree of skill in or knowledge of a certain subject.

~adj. (ék-spert, *also* ek-spért, ik-). Having or demonstrating impressive skill, dexterity, or knowledge. [Middle English, from Old French, from Latin *expertus,* past participle of *experīrī,* to try.] —**ex·pert·ly** adv. —**ex·pert·ness** n.

ex·per·tise (ék-sper-téez || -téess) n. **1.** Expert advice or opinion. **2.** Specialised knowledge; expertness. [French, survey, evaluation, from Old French, expertness, from EXPERT.]

ex·pi·a·ble (ékspi-əb'l) adj. Capable of being expiated.

ex·pi·ate (ékspi-ayt) v. **-ated, -ating, -ates.** —tr. To make atone-

ment for; redress. —intr. To make expiation. [Latin *expiāre : ex-,* completely + *piāre,* appease, atone, from *pius,* devout.] —**ex·pi·a·tor** n.

ex·pi·a·tion (ékspi-áysh'n) n. **1.** The act of expiating; an atonement. **2.** The means of redress or atonement; amends. —**ex·pi·a·to·ry** (-ətəri, -aytəri, -áytəri) adj.

ex·pi·ra·tion (ék-spi-ráysh'n, -spīr-) n. **1.** A coming to a close; a termination; an ending. **2.** The act or sound of breathing out.

ex·pir·a·to·ry (ik-spīr-ə-təri, ek-, -spírrə-, -tri; *also* ékspərə-) adj. Of, pertaining to, or involving the expiration of air from the lungs.

ex·pire (ik-spīr || ek-) v. **-pired, -piring, -pires.** —intr. **1.** To come to an end; terminate; cease to be effective: *His membership expired.* **2.** To breathe one's last breath; die. **3.** To exhale; breathe out. —tr. **1.** To breathe out. **2.** *Archaic.* To give off, as moisture; exude. [Middle English *expiren,* from Old French *exspirer,* from Latin *ex(-s)pīrāre,* to breathe out, to expire : *ex-,* out + *spīrāre,* to breathe.]

ex·pir·ee (ék-spīr-ée) n. Formerly, a British convict who had been transported to Australia and whose sentence had expired.

ex·pir·y (ik-spīr-i || ek-) n., pl. **-ries.** An expiration, especially of a contract or agreement. [From EXPIRE.]

ex·plain (ik-spláyn || ek-) v. **-plained, -plaining, -plains.** —tr. **1.** To make plain or comprehensible; remove obscurity from; elucidate: *explain a puzzle.* **2.** To define; explicate; expound: *He explained his plan.* **3.** To offer reasons for or a cause of; answer for; justify: *explain an error.* —intr. To give an explanation. —**explain away.** To minimise, excuse, or nullify by explanation. —**explain (oneself).** To justify or excuse (oneself). [Middle English *explanen,* from Latin *explānāre,* to explain, to spread out : *ex-,* completely + *plānus,* plain, flat.] —**ex·plain·a·ble** adj.

Synonyms: explain, elucidate, expound, explicate, interpret.

ex·pla·na·tion (ék-splə-náysh'n) n. **1.** The act or process of making plain or comprehensible; elucidation; clarification: *His plan requires explanation.* **2.** That which serves to explain or to account for something: *He always has a ready explanation.* **3.** A mutual clarification of misunderstandings; a reconciliation.

ex·plan·a·to·ry (ik-splánnə-təri, -tri || ek-) adj. Serving or intended to explain. —**ex·plan·a·to·ri·ly** adv.

ex·plant (eks-pláant || -plánt) tr.v. **-planted, -planting, -plants.** To take (living tissue) from the natural site of growth and place in a medium or culture.

~n. The material explanted. Also called "tissue explant". —**ex·plan·ta·tion** (-plan-táysh'n, -plaan-) n.

ex·ple·tive (iks-pléetiv, eks- || *U.S.* éksplətiv) n. **1.** An exclamation or oath, especially one that is profane or obscene. **2.** *Grammar.* A word or phrase added to a line of verse or a sentence in order to ease syntax or rhythm but not to add any meaning; for example, the word *it* is an expletive in the sentence *It is nice to see you.*

~adj. Also **ex·ple·to·ry** (iks-plée-təri, -tri). Added or inserted merely in order to fill out something; especially, added to a line of verse or a sentence. [Late Latin *explētīvus,* from Latin *explētus,* past participle of *explēre,* to fill out : *ex-,* out + *plēre,* fill.]

ex·pli·ca·ble (éksplika-b'l, ik-splícka- || ek-splícka-) adj. Capable of being explained; explainable.

ex·pli·cate (éks-pli-kayt) tr.v. **-cated, -cating, -cates. 1.** To make clear the meaning of; explain. **2.** To devise or elaborate (a theory). —See Synonyms at **explain.** [Latin *explicāre,* to unfold, explicate : *ex-* (reversal) + *plicāre,* to fold.] —**ex·pli·ca·tor** n.

ex·pli·ca·tion (éks-pli-káysh'n) n. **1.** An explanation. **2.** Exhaustive exposition and elucidation. **3.** Critical exposition and interpretation, as of literary texts.

ex·pli·ca·tive (ik-splíckətiv, ek-, éks-pli-kaytiv) adj. Also **ex·pli·ca·to·ry** (ik-splícka-təri, ek-, -tri, ékspli-kaytəri, -káytəri || *also* éksplikə-). Serving to explain; explanatory.

ex·plic·it[1] (ik-splíssit, ek-) adj. **1.** Expressed fully and with precision; clearly defined; specific. **2. a.** Forthright in expression; unreserved; outspoken. **b.** Describing sexual acts in detail. Used euphemistically. **3.** Designating a function having an equation $y = f(x)$, in which y can be expressed directly in terms of x. Compare **implicit.** [French *explicite,* from Latin *explicitus,* past participle of *explicāre,* to EXPLICATE.] —**ex·plic·it·ly** adv. —**ex·plic·it·ness** n.

ex·plic·it[2] (ékspli-sit, -kit). A word formerly used to indicate the close of a manuscript or book. [Late Latin, short for *explicitus (est liber),* "(the book is) unrolled", from Latin *explicitus,* EXPLICIT.]

ex·plode (ik-splód || ek-) v. **-ploded, -ploding, -plodes.** —intr. **1.** To release mechanical, chemical, or nuclear energy in an explosion. **2.** To burst and be destroyed by explosion. **3.** To burst forth or break out suddenly: *explode into action.* **4.** To fly into a sudden rage. **5.** To increase suddenly, sharply, and without control. —tr. **1.** To cause to explode or burst violently and noisily; detonate. **2.** To expose as false, unreliable, or irrelevant; confute: *explode a hypothesis.* **3.** *Phonetics.* To pronounce with plosion. [Latin *explōdere,* drive out by clapping : *ex-,* out + *plaudere†,* to clap.] —**ex·plod·er** n.

exploded view n. An illustration or diagram of a construction, showing its parts separately, but in positions indicating their proper relationships to the whole.

ex·ploit (éks-ployt) n. An act or deed, especially a brilliant or heroic feat.

~tr.v. (ik-splóyt || ek-) **exploited, -ploiting, -ploits. 1. a.** To employ to the greatest possible advantage; utilise: *exploit an advantage.* **b.** To turn to maximum commercial advantage. **2.** To make use of selfishly or unethically; take advantage of: *exploit peasant labour.* [Middle English *esploit, expleit,* from Old French *exploit, esplait,* achievement, from Gallo-Romance *explictum* (unattested), from Latin *explicitus,* EXPLICIT.] **—ex·ploit·a·ble** *adj.* **—ex·ploit·a·tive** (-ətiv), **ex·ploit·ive** *adj.* **—ex·ploit·er** *n.*

ex·ploi·ta·tion (éksploy-táysh'n) *n.* **1.** The act of exploiting. **2.** The utilisation of another person for selfish purposes.

ex·plo·ra·tion (ék-splə-ráysh'n, -splaw-) *n.* **1.** The act or an instance of exploring a region. **2.** *Medicine.* An investigative operation to determine the cause of symptoms. **3.** An investigation or search. **—ex·plor·a·to·ry** (ek-splórrə-təri, ik-, -spláwrə-, -tri, -splṓrə-) *adj.*

ex·plore (ik-splór || ek-, -splṓr) *v.* **-plored, -ploring, -plores.** *—tr.* **1.** To investigate systematically; examine; study: *explore the possibility of a just peace.* **2.** To search into or range over (a country) for the purpose of scientific or economic discovery. **3.** *Medicine.* To examine for diagnostic purposes. *—intr.* **1.** To make an examination; study. **2.** To travel through an unfamiliar region, with a view to learning about it. [Latin *explōrāre,* to search out, explore : *ex-,* out + *plōrāre,* cry aloud (see **deplore**).]

ex·plor·er (ik-spláwrər || ek-, -splṓrər) *n.* **1.** One who explores; especially, one who explores a geographical area. **2.** An implement or tool used for exploring; a probe. **3.** *Capital* **E.** *Aerospace.* Any of a large series of U.S. satellites, the first of which confirmed the existance of the Van Allen belts, others being used for scientific study of the atmosphere, the Earth's magnetic field, solar radiation, X-rays from space, and the like.

ex·plo·sion (ik-splṓzh'n || ek-) *n.* **1.** A sudden rapid violent release of mechanical, chemical, or nuclear energy from a confined region; especially, such a release that generates a radially propagating shock wave accompanied by a loud, sharp report, flying debris, heat, light, and fire. **2.** The loud, sharp sound accompanying such a release. **3.** Anything regarded as having the characteristics or destructive potential of such a release. **4.** A sudden vehement expression, activity or the like: *an abrupt explosion of speech.* **5.** A sudden and great increase: *the population explosion.* **6.** *Phonetics.* A **plosion** *(see).* [Latin *explōsiō* (stem *explōsiōn-*), from *explōsus,* past participle of *explōdere,* to EXPLODE.]

ex·plo·sive (ik-splṓ-siv || ek-, -ziv) *adj.* **1.** Pertaining to or involving an explosion. **2.** Tending or liable to explode. **3.** Liable to give rise to conflict or argument: *an explosive topic.* **4.** *Phonetics.* Pertaining to a plosion; plosive.

~n. **1.** A substance, especially a prepared chemical, that explodes or causes explosion. **2.** *Phonetics.* A **plosive** *(see).* [Old French *explosif,* from Latin *explōsus.* See **explosion.**] **—ex·plo·sive·ly** *adv.* **—ex·plo·sive·ness** *n.*

ex·po (ék-spō) *n. Informal.* An exhibition, usually of industrial products. [Short for EXPOSITION.]

ex·po·nent (ik-spṓnənt || ek-) *n.* **1.** One that defines, expounds, or interprets. **2.** One that speaks for, represents, or advocates: *an exponent of international cooperation.* **3.** A performing artist, especially one highly skilled in a particular instrument or technique. **4.** *Mathematics.* Any number or symbol, as *3* in $(x+y)^3$, placed to the right of and above another number, symbol, or expression, denoting the number of times the number, symbol, or expression is to be multiplied by itself. In this sense, also called "index", "power".

~adj. Giving an explanation or analysis; explanatory. [Latin *expōnēns* (stem *expōnent-*), present participle of *expōnere,* to EXPOUND.]

ex·po·nen·tial (ék-spə-nénsh'l, -spō-) *adj.* **1.** *Mathematics.* **a.** Containing, involving, or expressed as an exponent. **b.** *Symbol* **exp** Expressed in terms of a designated exponent of e, the base of natural logarithms. **2.** Of or pertaining to an exponent.

~n. An exponential function. **—ex·po·nen·tial·ly** *adv.*

exponential growth *n. Ecology.* Optimal growth of numbers in a population, where the rate of increase is proportional to the number of individuals and thus becomes increasingly fast until some factor, such as lack of food, limits further increase.

exponential series *n. Mathematics.* The series $e^x = 1 + x + x^2/2! + x^3/3! \ldots + x^n/n!$ When $x = 1$, $e = 2.718$.

ex·po·ni·ble (ik-spṓnəb'l || ek-) *adj.* Requiring or admitting of explanation. Said especially of an obscure logical proposition. [Medieval Latin *expōnibilis,* from Latin *expōnere,* to EXPOUND.]

ex·port (eks-pórt, iks-, éks-pawrt || -pōrt) *v.* **-ported, -porting, -ports.** *—tr.* **1.** To sell (goods or services) to a foreign country, or send or carry (goods) abroad, especially for sale or trade. Compare **import. 2.** To encourage or propagate (an idea, for example) abroad: *export revolution.* *—intr.* To send or carry goods abroad, especially for sale or trade.

~n. (éks-pawrt || -pōrt). Also *chiefly U.S.* **ex·por·ta·tion** (-áysh'n) (for sense 2). **1.** The act of exporting. **2.** *Often plural.* That which is exported. [Latin *exportāre,* to carry out or away : *ex-,* out + *portāre,* to carry.] **—ex·port** *adj.* (éks-) **—ex·port·a·bil·i·ty** (-ə-bílləti) *n.* **—ex·port·a·ble** *adj.* **—ex·port·er** *n.*

ex·por·ta·tion (éks-pawr-táysh'n || -pōr-) *n.* **1.** The act, process, or business of exporting. **2.** *Chiefly U.S.* Variant of **export.**

ex·pose (ik-spṓz, ek-) *tr.v.* **-posed, -posing, -poses. 1. a.** To lay open to something undesirable or injurious; make vulnerable: *expose a child to an unnecessary risk.* **b.** To lay open or introduce to something beneficial or positive: *She was exposed to music before she had even learnt to talk.* **2.** To subject (a photographic film or plate) to the action of light. **3.** To make visible or known; make manifest: *Cleaning exposed the grain of the wood.* **4.** To disclose or unmask (a crime or criminal, for example); lay bare; make known. **5.** *Roman Catholic Church.* To leave (the Host) displayed on the altar for veneration. **6.** To abandon (an infant, for example) without food or shelter. —See Synonyms at **reveal, show. —expose (oneself).** To exhibit one's genitals in public. Used of a man. [Middle English *exposen,* from Old French *exposer,* from Latin *expōnere,* to expose, EXPOUND.] **—ex·pos·er** *n.*

ex·po·sé (ek-spṓ-zay || *U.S.* ék-spō-záy, -spə-) *n.* **1.** An exposure or revelation of something discreditable or scandalous. **2.** A book, report, or the like that contains such an exposure. **3.** A detailed account or statement of the facts; an exposition. [French, from the past participle of *exposer,* to EXPOSE.]

ex·posed (ik-spṓzd, ek-) *adj.* **1.** Open to view; not hidden. **2.** Unsheltered or uncovered: *an exposed layer of rock.* **3.** Open to attack, criticism, or danger; vulnerable; susceptible.

ex·po·si·tion (ék-spə-zísh'n) *n.* **1.** A setting forth of meaning or intent. **2.** A precise statement or definition; an explication; an elucidation. **3.** *Music.* The first part of a sonata or fugue that introduces the themes. **4.** The part of a play or story that introduces the theme and chief characters. **5.** The act of exposing or the condition of being exposed. **6.** A public exhibition or show, as of artistic or industrial products. **7.** *Roman Catholic Church.* The displaying of the Host on the altar for public veneration. **8.** *Archaic.* Exposure. [Middle English *exposicioun,* from Old French *exposition,* from Latin *expositiō* (stem *expositiōn-*), from *expositus,* past participle of *expōnere,* to EXPOUND.] **—ex·pos·i·tive** (ik-spózzitiv, ek-), **ex·pos·i·to·ry** (ik-spózzi-təri, -tri) *adj.* **—ex·pos·i·tor** *n.*

ex post fac·to (éks pṓst fáktō) *adj. Latin.* Formulated, enacted, or operating retroactively. Said especially of a law. **—ex post facto** *adv.*

ex·pos·tu·late (ik-spóstew-layt || ek-) *intr.v.* **-lated, -lating, -lates.** To reason earnestly with someone in an effort to dissuade or correct; remonstrate. Often used with *with.* See Synonyms at **object.** [Latin *expostulāre,* to demand strongly : *ex-,* entirely + *postulāre,* to demand.] **—ex·pos·tu·la·tor** *n.* **—ex·pos·tu·la·to·ry** (-lə-təri, -tri, -laytəri), **ex·pos·tu·la·tive** (-lətiv || *U.S.* -laytiv) *adj.*

ex·pos·tu·la·tion (ik-spóstew-láysh'n || ek-) *n.* The act or an instance of expostulating; remonstrance.

ex·po·sure (ik-spṓzhər, ek-) *n.* **1.** The act or an instance of exposing. **2. a.** The condition of being exposed, as to influences, danger, or the like. **b.** Lack of protection from harsh weather conditions, especially cold: *die of exposure.* **3.** The fact or state of being in public view; especially, appearing before an audience: *The election candidates sought maximum TV exposure.* **4.** A position in relation to climatic or weather conditions or points of the compass: *a room with a southern exposure.* **5. a.** The act of exposing sensitised photographic film or plate. **b.** A film or plate so exposed. **c.** The amount of radiant energy needed to expose a photographic film. **d.** A part of a film for individual pictures: *A 35-millimetre film often has 36 exposures.* **e.** The time, shutter speed, or aperture, or a combination of two or all three, that is used in exposing film. **6.** *Law.* **Indecent exposure** *(see).*

exposure meter *n.* A photoelectric instrument that measures light intensity in a given area and, in photographic use, indicates the proper exposure for a particular shutter speed and type of film. Also called "light meter".

ex·pound (ik-spównd, ek- || *West Indies also* -spúngd) *v.* **-pounded, -pounding, -pounds.** *—tr.* **1.** To give a detailed statement of; set forth. **2.** To elucidate or explain; interpret. *—intr.* To make a detailed statement; explain a point of view. Usually used with *on*: *He was expounding on his favourite sport.* —See Synonyms at **explain.** [Middle English *expoun(d)en,* from Old French *espondre,* from Latin *expōnere,* to put forth, expose : *ex-,* out + *pōnere,* place, put.] **—ex·pound·er** *n.*

ex·press (ik-spréss, ek-) *tr.v.* **-pressed, -pressing, -presses. 1.** To make known or set forth in words; state; utter: *express one's wishes.* **2.** To manifest or communicate, as by a gesture; show; exhibit: *His posture expressed his exhaustion.* **3.** To make (one's feelings or opinions) known. **4.** To convey or represent through words or other artistic means: *His poems express a sense of wonder.* **5.** To represent by a sign or symbol; symbolise: *The ∞ sign expresses infinity.* **6.** To squeeze or press out (juice from a fruit, for example). **7.** To send by special courier or rapid transport. —See Synonyms at **vent. —express (oneself).** To communicate one's thoughts or feelings through words, gestures, or artistic activity.

~adj. (*also* ék-spress). **1.** Definitely and unmistakably stated; explicit: *an express wish.* **2. a.** Sent out with or moving at high speed. **b.** Direct, rapid, and usually nonstop: *express post.* **3.** Pertaining to or handling that which is express: *an express depot.*

~adv. By express delivery or transport.

~n. **1. a.** A train that is rapid and has few stops. **b.** A coach or other means of transport that travels fast with a minimum of stops. **c.** *Chiefly U.S.* A company that deals in such transport. **2. a.** A special courier. **b.** A message delivered by special courier. **3. a.** A rapid, efficient system for the delivery of goods and mail. **b.** Goods and mail conveyed by such a system. **4.** An express rifle. **5.** *Capital* **E.** Used as part of the title of certain newspapers: *the Salisbury Express.* [Middle English *expressen,* from Old French *expresser,* from Vulgar Latin *expressāre* (unattested), to press out, express : Latin *ex-,* out + *pressāre,* to press, from *premere* (past participle *pressus*), press.] **—ex·press·er** *n.* **—ex·press·i·ble** *adj.*

ex·press·age (ik-spréssij, ek-) *n.* **1.** The conveyance of goods by express. **2.** The amount charged for such conveyance.

ex·pres·sion (ik-sprésh'n, ek-) *n.* **1.** The act of expressing, conveying, or representing in words, art, music, or movement; a manifestation: *the expression of an idea.* **2.** That which communicates, indicates, embodies, or symbolises something; a symbol; a sign; a token. **3.** *Mathematics.* Any symbolic mathematical form, such as an equation. **4. a.** The means by which something is expressed: *expression through music.* **b.** The quality of expressing feelings, attitudes, or the like through means such as tone or gesture: *His playing lacked expression.* **5.** The manner in which one expresses oneself, especially in speaking, depicting, or performing. **6.** A particular word or phrase: *a slang expression.* **7.** The outward manifestation of an inner mood or disposition: *Her tears were an expression of her grief.* **8.** A facial aspect or look that conveys a special feeling: *an expression of scorn in his eyes.* **9.** *Genetics.* The extent to which a gene affects the appearance of an organism. Also called "penetrance". **10.** The act of removing a liquid from a solid by squeezing.

ex·pres·sion·ism (ik-sprésh'n-izm, ek-) *n. Often capital* **E.** A movement in the fine arts during the first half of the 20th century that originated in Europe and aimed at conveying the quality of emotional experience rather than representing the physical world. In painting, this was achieved by the use of exaggeration and distortion, strong colours, and simplified outlines. **—ex·pres·sion·ist** *n. & adj.* **—ex·pres·sion·is·tic** (-nísstik) *adj.*

ex·pres·sion·less (ik-sprésh'n-ləss, -liss) *adj.* **1.** Lacking expression. **2.** Having a fixed expression on one's face that shows or reveals no emotion.

ex·pres·sive (ik-spréssiv, ek-) *adj.* **1.** Pertaining to, related to, or characterised by expression: *expressive hands.* **2.** Serving to express or indicate: *His actions are expressive of frustration.* **3.** Containing forceful expression; significant: *an expressive glance.* **—ex·pres·sive·ly** *adv.* **—ex·pres·sive·ness** *n.* **—ex·pres·siv·i·ty** (ék-spre-sívvəti) *n.*

ex·press·ly (ik-spréssli, ek-) *adv.* **1.** In an express or definite manner; explicitly: *I expressly order you to leave.* **2.** Especially; particularly: *These chocolates are expressly for you.*

expresso Variant of **espresso.**

express rifle *n.* A hunting rifle having low trajectory, high velocity, and a long point-blank range.

express train *n.* A passenger or goods train that travels at high speed and makes a minimum of stops.

ex·press·way (ik-spréss-way, ek-) *n. Chiefly U.S.* A major road intended for fast travel; a motorway.

ex·pro·pri·ate (iks-prṓpri-ayt, eks-) *tr.v.* **-ated, -ating, -ates. 1.** To deprive (a person) of ownership or property. **2.** To take away or transfer (ownership or property, for example) from an owner; especially, to acquire for public use. [Medieval Latin *expropriāre* : Latin *ex-* (removal away from) + *proprius,* one's own.] **—ex·pro·pri·a·tion** (-áysh'n) *n.* **—ex·pro·pri·a·tor** *n.* **—ex·pro·pri·a·to·ry** (-ə-təri, -tri, -áytəri) *adj.*

ex·pug·na·ble (ik-spéwnəb'l, ek-) *adj.* Capable of being defeated or taken by force.

ex·pul·sion (ik-spúl-sh'n, ek-) *n.* The act of expelling or the state of being expelled. **—ex·pul·sive** (-siv) *adj.*

ex·punc·tion (ik-spúngksh'n, ek-) *n.* The act of expunging, or the condition of being expunged; a deletion, erasure, or cancellation. [Latin *expunctus,* past participle of *expungere,* to EXPUNGE + -ION.]

ex·punge (ik-spúnj, ek-) *tr.v.* **-punged, -punging, -punges. 1.** To omit, erase, strike out, or obliterate (a word or sentence, for example). **2.** To eliminate physically; annihilate. —See Synonyms at **erase.** [Latin *expungere,* to prick out, erase : *ex-,* out + *pungere,* to prick.] **—ex·punge·a·ble** *adj.* **—ex·pung·er** *n.*

ex·pur·gate (éks-pər-gayt, -pur-) *tr.v.* **-gated, -gating, -gates. 1.** To amend (a published work) by removing obscene or objectionable passages from the text. **2.** To cleanse; purge. [Latin *expurgāre,* to purge out, purify : *ex-,* out + *purgāre,* to purge.] **—ex·pur·ga·tion** (-gáysh'n) *n.* **—ex·pur·ga·tor** *n.* **—ex·pur·ga·to·ry** (ek-spúrgə-təri, -tri, éks-pur-gáytəri), **ex·pur·ga·to·ri·al** (-táwri-əl || -tṓri-əl) *adj.*

ex·qui·site (iks-kwízzit, eks-, ékskwizit) *adj.* **1.** Beautifully made or designed: *an exquisite chalice.* **2.** Of such beauty or delicacy as to arouse delight: *an exquisite sunset.* **3.** Acutely perceptive or discriminating: *an exquisite sense of colour.* **4.** Intense; keen: *an exquisite pain.*

~n. Rare. One who is extremely sensitive and fastidious in dress, manners, or taste; a dandy; a fop. [Middle English *exquisit,* from Latin *exquīsītus,* chosen, exquisite, from the past participle of *exquīrere,* to search out : *ex-,* out + *quaerere,* to seek.] **—ex·qui·site·ly** *adv.* **—ex·qui·site·ness** *n.*

ex·san·gui·nate (ik-sáng-gwi-nayt, ek-) *tr.v.* **-nated, -nating, -nates.** To drain of blood. [Latin *exsanguinātus,* bloodless : *ex-,* without + *sanguis* (stem *sanguin-*), blood (see **sanguine**).] **—ex·san·gui·na·tion** (-náysh'n) *n.*

ex·san·guine (ik-sáng-gwin, ek-) *adj.* Also **ex·san·gui·nous** (-gwinəss). Lacking blood; anaemic. [Latin *exsanguis,* deprived of blood : *ex-,* without + *sanguis* (stem *sanguin-*), blood (see **sanguine**).]

ex·scind (ek-sínd) *tr.v.* **-scinded, -scinding, -scinds.** To excise or cut out; extirpate. [Latin *exscindere* : *ex-,* out + *scindere,* to cut.]

ex·sect (ek-sékt) *tr.v.* **-sected, -secting, -sects.** To cut out. [Latin *exsecāre* (past participle *exsectus*) : *ex-,* out + *secāre,* to cut.] **—ex·sec·tion** *n.*

ex·sert (ek-sért) *tr.v.* **-serted, -serting, -serts.** To thrust out or forth; cause to protrude.

~adj. Also **ex·sert·ed** (-sértid). *Biology.* Thrust outwards; protruding. Said of stamens protruding beyond the petals, for example. [Latin *ex(s)erere* (past participle *ex(s)ertus*), to EXERT.] **—ex·ser·tion** *n.*

ex·ser·vice (éks-sérviss) *adj.* **1.** Having formerly served in the armed forces. **2.** Formerly belonging to the armed forces.

ex·ser·vice·man (éks-sérviss-mən) *n., pl.* **-men** (-mən). One who has served in the armed forces. **—ex·ser·vice·wom·an** *n.*

ex·sic·cate (ék-si-kayt) *v.* **-cated, -cating, -cates.** *—tr.* To make dry; remove the moisture from; dehydrate. *—intr.* To dry up. [Latin *exsiccāre,* to dry out : *ex-,* out + *siccāre,* to dry, from *siccus,* dry.] **—ex·sic·ca·tion** (-káysh'n) *n.* **—ex·sic·ca·tive** (-kətiv, -kaytiv) *adj.* **—ex·sic·ca·tor** *n.*

ex·stip·u·late (ek-stíppew-lət, -lit, -layt) *adj. Botany.* Having no stipules. [From EX- + STIPULE.]

ext. 1. extension. **2.** exterior. **3.** external.

ex·tant (ek-stánt, ékstənt) *adj.* Still in existence; not destroyed, lost, or extinct: *extant manuscripts; extant species of mammals.* See Synonyms at **living.** [Latin *ex(s)tāns* (stem *ex(s)tant-*), present participle of *ex(s)tāre,* to stand out, exist, be prominent : *ex-,* out + *stāre,* to stand.]

ex·tem·po·ra·ne·ous (ik-stémpə-ráyni-əss, ek-) *adj.* **1.** Done, made, spoken, or otherwise performed with little or no preparation or practice; impromptu: *an extemporaneous recital.* **2.** Delivered without notes or text: *an extemporaneous sermon.* **3.** Provided, made, or adapted as an expedient; improvised; makeshift. [Late Latin *extemporāneus,* from Latin *ex tempore,* EXTEMPORE.] **—ex·tem·po·ra·ne·ous·ly** *adv.* **—ex·tem·po·ra·ne·ous·ness** *n.*

Synonyms: *extemporaneous, impromptu, improvised, unrehearsed, unpremeditated, ad lib.*

ex·tem·po·rar·y (ik-stémpə-rəri, ek-, -stémprəri || -rerri) *adj.* Extemporaneous. [Latin *ex tempore,* EXTEMPORE.] **—ex·tem·po·rar·i·ly** (-rərəli || -rérrəli) *adv.*

ex·tem·po·re (ik-stémpəri, ek-) *adv.* **1.** Impromptu; done without preparation. **2.** Without notes or text: *speak extempore.* **3.** By improvising. [Latin *ex tempore* : *ex-,* out of + *tempore,* ablative of *tempus,* time (see **temporal**).] **—ex·tem·po·re** *adj.*

ex·tem·po·rise, ex·tem·po·rize (ik-stémpə-rīz, ek-) *v.* **-rised, -rising, -rises.** *—tr.* To perform, utter, or do extempore. *—intr.* To perform or make something extempore; improvise. **—ex·tem·po·ri·sa·tion** (-rī-záysh'n || *U.S.* -ri-) *n.* **—ex·tem·po·ris·er** *n.*

ex·tend (ik-sténd, ek-) *v.* **-tended, -tending, -tends.** *—tr.* **1.** To open or straighten out to full length; unbend: *extend the leg.* Compare **flex. 2.** To stretch out or spread to fullest length: *The ladder was fully extended.* **3. a.** To exert (oneself) vigorously or to full capacity. **b.** To cause (a horse, for example) to move at full gallop. **4. a.** To enlarge the area or scope of; expand: *extend our boundaries.* **b.** To expand the influence, range, or meaning of; make more comprehensive or inclusive: *extend his responsibilities.* **5.** To offer to give or grant; afford: *extend one's greetings.* **6.** *Finance.* To cause to be longer; especially, to prolong the time of payment of (a debt, for example). *—intr.* **1.** To be or become extended. **2.** To stretch or reach, as in a certain direction, or for a certain time: *His influence extended to other continents.* —See Synonyms at **prolong, increase.** [Middle English *extenden,* from Latin *extendere* : *ex-,* out + *tendere,* to stretch.] **—ex·tend·i·bil·i·ty** (-i-bílləti) *n.* **—ex·tend·i·ble** *adj.*

ex·tend·ed (ik-sténdid, ek-) *adj.* **1.** Stretched or pulled out. **2.** Continued for a long period of time. **3.** Enlarged or extensive; widespread: *extended television coverage.* **4.** *Printing.* Expanded. **—ex·tend·ed·ly** *adv.*

extended family *n.* A family unit consisting of parents, children, and other close relatives, such as grandparents or aunts and uncles, who live together. Compare **nuclear family.**

ex·ten·der (ik-sténdər, ek-) *n.* A substance added to another substance to modify, dilute, or adulterate.

ex·ten·si·ble (ik-stén-sib'l, ek-) *adj.* **1.** Capable of being extended or protruded. **2.** Extensile. [Latin *extensus,* past participle of *extendere,* to EXTEND.] **—ex·ten·si·bil·i·ty** (-si-bílləti) *n.*

ex·ten·sile (ik-stén-sīl, ek-, *U.S.* -sténss'l) *adj.* Capable of being stretched out or protruded, especially without breaking; extensible.

ex·ten·sion (ik-sténsh'n, ek-) *n. Abbr.* **ext. 1. a.** The act of extending or the condition of being extended. **b.** That which is extended. **2.** The amount, degree, or range to which something extends or can extend; compass. **3. a.** The act of straightening or extending a limb. **b.** The position assumed by an extended limb. **4.** *Surgery.* Application of traction to a fractured or dislocated limb to restore the normal position. **5.** Any part added to or extended from a main structure to form an addition: *an extension to a hospital.* **6. a.** An additional telephone connected to the main line. **b.** The number assigned to this line. **7. a.** A granting of extra time, especially to allow payment of a debt or compliance with a legal formality. **b.** The period of this extra time. **8.** That property of something by which it occupies space; spatial magnitude. **9.** *Logic.* The class of objects designated by a specific term or concept; denotation. Compare **intension. 10.** Instruction offered by a university, college, or the like to outside or part-time students. Also used adjectivally: *an extension course.* [Middle English *extensioun,* from Old French *extension,* from Late Latin *extensiō* (stem *extensiōn-*), from Latin *extensus,* past participle of *extendere,* to EXTEND.]

ex·ten·si·ty (ik-stén-siti, ek-) *n.* **1.** The attribute of sensation that enables one to perceive space or size. **2.** *Rare.* The quality of having extension or being extensive.

ex·ten·sive (ik-stén-siv, ek-) *adj.* **1.** Having a great extent; vast; broad: *an extensive meadow.* **2.** Having a wide range; inclusive; comprehensive: *an extensive library.* **3.** Considerable in amount: *Extensive capital was invested.* **4.** Pertaining to or characterised by extension. **5.** Designating or pertaining to the agricultural cultivation of vast areas of land with a minimum of labour or expense. Compare **intensive.** **6.** *Physics.* **a.** Having a value that is the sum of the values for subdivisions of a thermodynamic system. Said of volume, for example. **b.** Designating a property or measurement that is dependent on mass. In this sense, compare **intensive.** —**ex·ten·sive·ly** *adv.* —**ex·ten·sive·ness** *n.*

ex·ten·som·e·ter (ék-sten-sómmitər) *n.* An instrument used to measure minute deformations in a test specimen of a material. [EXTENS(ION) + -O- + -METER.]

ex·ten·sor (ik-stén-sər, ek-, -sawr) *n.* Any muscle that extends or stretches a limb. [New Latin, from Latin *extensus,* past participle of *extendere,* EXTEND.]

ex·tent (ik-stént, ek-) *n.* **1.** The range over which something extends; scope; comprehensiveness. **2. a.** The dimensions to which something is extended; magnitude; spread. **b.** The distance over which a thing extends or the space it occupies. **3.** Any extensive space or area: *an extent of desert.* **4.** A certain degree, usually specified: *to a great extent; to some extent.* [Middle English *extente,* from Anglo-French, from Medieval Latin *extenta,* from Latin, feminine past participle of *extendere,* to EXTEND.]

ex·ten·u·ate (ik-sténnew-ayt, ek-) *tr.v.* **-ated, -ating, -ates. 1.** To lessen or attempt to lessen the magnitude of (an offence or guilt) by providing partial excuses. **2.** To cause to appear less serious or blameworthy: *circumstances extenuating the error.* [Latin *extenuāre,* to thin out, lessen : *ex-,* out + *tenuāre,* to make thin, from *tenuis,* thin.] —**ex·ten·u·a·tor** *n.*

ex·ten·u·at·ing (ik-sténnew-ayting, ek-) *adj.* Serving to lessen, excuse, or qualify guilt or blame: *extenuating circumstances.*

ex·ten·u·a·tion (ik-sténnew-áysh'n, ek-) *n.* **1.** The act of extenuating or the condition of being extenuated; partial justification. **2.** That which serves to extenuate; a partial excuse. —**ex·ten·u·a·tive** (-ətiv, -áytiv) *adj. & n.* —**ex·ten·u·a·to·ry** (-ə-təri, -tri, -aytəri) *adj.*

ex·te·ri·or (ek-stéer-i-ər, ik-) *adj.* **Abbr. ext. 1.** Outer; external. **2.** Originating or acting from the outside. **3.** Suitable for use outside: *an exterior paint.* **4.** Not situated or placed inside a building; out-of-doors. **5.** Outwardly apparent: *an exterior affability.*
~*n.* **Abbr. ext. 1.** A part or surface that is outside. **2.** An external or outward appearance; an aspect: *a friendly exterior.* **3. a.** A picture or photograph of an outdoor scene. **b.** A scene, as in a film, that is shot outdoors. [Latin, comparative of *exterus,* outward, outside.] —**ex·te·ri·or·i·ty** (-órrəti) *n.* —**ex·te·ri·or·ly** *adv.*

exterior angle *n.* **1.** The angle between any side of a polygon and an extended adjacent side. **2.** Any of the four angles that do not include a region of the space between two lines intersected by a transversal.

ex·te·ri·or·ise, ex·te·ri·or·ize (ek-stéeri-ər-īz, ik-) *tr.v.* **-ised, -ising, -ises. 1.** To externalise. **2.** *Surgery.* To bring (an organ or part) to the body's surface. —**ex·te·ri·or·i·sa·tion** (-ī-záysh'n || *U.S.* -i-) *n.*

ex·ter·mi·nate (ik-stérmi-nayt, ek-) *tr.v.* **-nated, -nating, -nates.** To get rid of by destroying completely; extirpate: *a spray to exterminate insects.* [Latin *extermināre,* to drive out : *ex-,* out of + *termināre,* to limit, end.] —**ex·ter·mi·na·tion** (-náysh'n) *n.* —**ex·ter·mi·na·tive** (-nətiv, -naytiv), **ex·ter·mi·na·to·ry** (-nə-təri, -tri, -naytəri) *adj.*

extermination camp *n.* In World War II, a Nazi concentration camp in which large numbers of people, especially Jews, were executed. Also called "death camp".

ex·ter·mi·na·tor (ik-stérmi-naytər, ek-) *n.* One that exterminates; especially, one whose occupation is the extermination of rodents, cockroaches, or other vermin.

ex·ter·nal (ek-stérn'l, ik-, ék-) *adj.* **Abbr. ext. 1. a.** Pertaining to, existing or visible on, or connected with the outside or an outer part; exterior. **b.** Pertaining to the outside of the body: *for external use only.* **2.** Affecting or capable of affecting the outside: *an external application.* **3.** *Philosophy.* Existing independently of the mind; objective; phenomenal: *external objects.* **4.** Acting or coming from the outside: *external pressures.* **5.** Of or pertaining to the outward appearance; superficial. **6.** Of or pertaining to foreign affairs or foreign countries; international. **7.** Pertaining to studies or courses set by a university or college but not involving attendance at the particular educational establishment: *an external degree.*
~*n.* **1.** An exterior part or surface. **2.** *Plural.* External circumstances; appearances. [Middle English, from Latin *externus,* from *exterus,* outward.] —**ex·ter·nal·ly** *adv.*

ex·ter·nal-com·bus·tion engine (ek-stérn'l-kəm-búss-chən, ik-, ék- || -kom-) *n.* An engine, such as a steam engine, in which the fuel is burned outside the engine cylinder.

external ear *n.* The portion of the ear including the auricle (or pinna) and the passage leading to the eardrums.

ex·ter·nal·ise, ex·ter·nal·ize (ek-stérn'l-īz, ik-) *tr.v.* **-ised, -ising, -ises. 1.** To make external; give external existence to. **2.** To project (a feeling or opinion) onto others or one's environment: *tending to externalise his insecurity.* **3.** To express freely (personal feelings or problems, for example), especially in words. —**ex·ter·nal·i·sa·tion** (-ī-záysh'n || *U.S.* -i-) *n.*

ex·ter·nal·ism (ek-stérn'l-iz'm, ik-) *n.* **1.** *Philosophy.* The doctrine that only objects perceived by the senses are capable of being judged real; phenomenalism. **2.** Devotion to externals or to matters of form or procedure, as in religion. —**ex·ter·nal·ist** *n.*

ex·ter·nal·i·ty (ék-ster-nál-əti) *n., pl.* **-ties. 1.** The condition or quality of being external or externalised. **2.** *Philosophy.* The quality of being external to the perceiving subject.

ex·ter·o·cep·tor (ékstər-ō-séptər) *n.* A sense organ receiving and responding to external stimuli. [New Latin : Latin *exter, exterus,* EXTER(IOR) + -O- + (RE)CEPTOR.] —**ex·ter·o·cep·tive** (-séptiv) *adj.*

ex·ter·ri·to·ri·al (éks-térri-táwri-əl || -tőri-) *adj.* Beyond the territorial limits; extraterritorial. —**ex·ter·ri·to·ri·al·i·ty** (-ál-əti) *n.* —**ex·ter·ri·to·ri·al·ly** *adv.*

ex·tinct (ik-stíngkt, ek-) *adj.* **1.** Extinguished or inactive, as a fire or volcano might be. **2.** No longer existing in living form; having died out: *extinct birds such as the dodo and moa.* **3.** Lacking a claimant; void: *an extinct title.* **4.** No longer in use; superseded: *an extinct custom.* [Middle English, from Latin *ex(s)tinctus,* past participle of *ex(s)tinguere,* to EXTINGUISH.]

ex·tinc·tion (ik-stíngksh'n, ek-) *n.* **1.** The act of extinguishing or making extinct. **2.** The fact or condition of being extinguished or extinct. **3.** *Physics.* A reduction in the intensity of light or other radiation passing through a medium, caused by absorption or scattering. **4.** The absorption of light from a planet or star by the earth's atmosphere. **5.** Complete destruction; annihilation. —**ex·tinc·tive** *adj.*

ex·tin·guish (ik-stíng-gwish, ek-) *tr.v.* **-guished, -guishing, -guishes. 1.** To put out (a fire or light); quench. **2.** To put an end to (hope, for example); destroy. **3.** *Law.* **a.** To settle or discharge (a debt). **b.** To nullify. [Latin *ex(s)tinguere* : *ex-,* out + *stinguere,* to quench.] —**ex·tin·guish·a·ble** *adj.* —**ex·tin·guish·ment** *n.*

ex·tin·guish·er (ik-stíng-gwishər, ek-) *n.* One that extinguishes; specifically, a **fire-extinguisher** *(see).*

ex·tir·pate (ék-stur-payt, -stər- || ek-stúr-) *tr.v.* **-pated, -pating, -pates. 1.** To pull up by the roots; root up or out. **2.** To destroy the whole of; exterminate. **3.** To remove by surgery. —See Synonyms at **abolish.** [Latin *ex(s)tirpāre,* to pluck up by the roots : *ex-,* out + *stirps,* root, stem (see **stirps**).] —**ex·tir·pa·tion** (-páysh'n) *n.* —**ex·tir·pa·tive** (-páytiv) *adj.* —**ex·tir·pa·tor** *n.*

ex·tol, *U.S.* **ex·toll** (ik-stől, ek-, -stól) *tr.v.* **-tolled, -tolling, -tols.** or *U.S.* **-tolls.** To praise lavishly; laud; eulogise. See Synonyms at **praise.** [Middle English *extollen,* to lift up, praise, from Latin *extollere* : *ex-,* up + *tollere,* to lift, raise.] —**ex·tol·ler** *n.* —**ex·tol·ment** *n.*

ex·tort (ik-stórt, ek-) *tr.v.* **-torted, -torting, -torts. 1.** To obtain (money or information, for example) from another by coercion, intimidation, or the wrong use of an official position. **2.** To exact; wring. [Latin *extorquēre* (past participle *extortus*), to twist out : *ex-,* out + *torquēre,* to twist.] —**ex·tort·er** *n.* —**ex·tor·tive** *adj.*

ex·tor·tion (ik-stórsh'n, ek-) *n.* **1.** The act or an instance of extorting. **2.** The criminal offence of using one's official position or power to obtain property, funds, or patronage to which one is not entitled. **3.** The exaction of an exorbitant price. **4.** Something extorted. —**ex·tor·tion·ar·y** (-əri, -ri || -erri) *adj.* —**ex·tor·tion·ist, ex·tor·tion·er** *n.*

ex·tor·tion·ate (ik-stórsh'n-ət, ek-, -it) *adj.* **1.** Exorbitant; excessive: *extortionate charges.* **2.** Using extortion. —**ex·tor·tion·ate·ly** *adv.*

ex·tra (ékstrə) *adj.* More or beyond what is usual, normal, expected, or necessary; additional; supplementary.
~*n.* **1.** Something more than what is usual or necessary. **2. a.** *Often plural.* Something, such as an accessory on a car, for which an additional charge is made. **b.** The charge made. **3.** A special edition of a newspaper. **4.** In cricket, a run not actually scored by the batsman, but awarded to his team as a result of no-balls or overthrows, for example. **5.** An actor hired to play a minor part, as in a crowd scene.
~*adv.* Exceptionally; unusually: *extra dry.* [Probably short for EXTRAORDINARY, by analogy with similar French and German shortenings.]

extra- *prefix.* Indicates outside a boundary or scope; for example, **extragalactic.** ***Note:*** Many compounds other than those entered here may be formed with *extra-.* In forming compounds, *extra-* is often joined with the following element without a space or hyphen: *extracurricular.* However, if the second element begins with a capital letter or with the letter *a,* it is separated with a hyphen: *extra-Biblical, extra-alimentary.* [Middle English, from Latin *extrā,* outside, above, beyond, without, short for *extera,* ablative feminine of *exterus,* outward.]

ex·tra·ca·non·i·cal (ékstrə-kə-nónnik'l) *adj.* Not included in any ecclesiastical canon of Scripture; noncanonical.

ex·tra·cel·lu·lar (ékstrə-séllewlər) *adj.* Located or occurring outside a cell. —**ex·tra·cel·lu·lar·ly** *adv.*

extra cover *n.* In cricket: **1.** A fielding position between cover point and mid-off. **2.** A fielder in this position.

ex·tract (ik-strákt, ek-) *tr.v.* **-tracted, -tracting, -tracts. 1.** To draw out or forth forcibly; pull out: *extract a tooth.* **2.** To obtain despite resistance, as by contrivance or extortion: *extract a promise.* **3.** To obtain from a substance by chemical or mechanical action, as by pressure, distillation, or evaporation: *extract juice from an orange.* **4. a.** To remove (a literary passage, for example) for separate consideration or publication. **b.** To remove and separate. **5.** *Mathematics.* To determine or calculate (the root of a number). **6.** To derive.
~*n.* (ék-strakt). **1.** Something drawn or pulled out. **2.** A passage from a literary work; an excerpt. **3.** A concentrated preparation of the essential constituents of a food, flavouring, or other substance: *vanilla extract.* [Middle English *extracten,* from Latin *extrahere* (past participle *extractus*), to draw out : *ex-,* out + *trahere,* to draw.] —**ex·tract·a·ble, ex·tract·i·ble** *adj.*

ex·trac·tion (ik-stráksh'n, ek-) *n.* **1.** The act of extracting or the condition of being extracted. **2.** Something obtained by extracting; an extract. **3.** Origin; descent; lineage: *of Asian extraction; of noble* *extraction.* **4.** *Plural.* The residue remaining after an oilseed has had the oil extracted from it by means of a solvent, often used as animal feed: *groundnut extractions.* In this sense, compare **expellers.**

ex·trac·tive (ik-stráktiv, ek-) *adj.* **1.** Used in or obtained by extraction. **2.** Capable of being extracted.
~*n.* **1.** Something that may be extracted. **2.** The insoluble portion of an extract.

ex·trac·tor (ik-stráktər, ek-) *n.* **1.** One that extracts; specifically, a device such as a forceps used for extracting teeth or for delivering a baby. **2.** A device, usually fitted in a window or outside wall, that extracts stale air or unwanted gases from a room. Also called "extractor fan".

ex·tra·cur·ric·u·lar (ékstrə-kə-ríckewlər) *adj.* **1.** Carried on outside the curriculum or regular course of study in school or college life. **2.** Outside the usual duties of a job or profession.

ex·tra·dit·a·ble (ékstrə-dītəb'l) *adj.* Subject to or making one liable to extradition: *an extraditable crime.*

ex·tra·dite (ékstrə-dīt) *tr.v.* **-dited, -diting, -dites. 1.** To surrender (an alleged criminal) to another authority, such as the government of a foreign country, for trial. **2.** To obtain (an alleged criminal held elsewhere) for trial. [Back-formation from EXTRADITION.]

ex·tra·di·tion (ékstrə-dísh'n) *n.* The legal surrender of an alleged criminal to the jurisdiction of another state, country, or government for trial. [French : Latin *ex-*, out + *trāditiō* (stem *trāditiōn-*), a surrendering (see **tradition**).]

ex·tra·dos (ek-stráy-doss || *U.S.* ékstrə-doss, -dōss) *n., pl.* **extrados** (-dōz) or **-doses.** *Architecture.* The upper or exterior curve of an arch. [French : Latin *extrā*, outside (see **extra-**) + French *dos*, back, from Latin *dorsum.*]

ex·tra·ga·lac·tic (ékstrə-gə-láktik) *adj.* Located or originating beyond the Galaxy.

ex·tra·ju·di·cial (ékstrə-jōō-dísh'l) *adj.* **1.** Outside the authority of a court. **2.** Outside usual judicial proceedings. **—ex·tra·ju·di·cial·ly** *adv.*

ex·tra·mar·i·tal (ékstrə-márrit'l) *adj.* Of or pertaining to a spouse's relationships, usually sexual, outside marriage; adulterous.

ex·tra·mun·dane (ékstrə-mún-dayn, -mun-dáyn, -mən-) *adj.* Occurring or existing outside the physical world or universe.

ex·tra·mu·ral (ékstrə-méwr-əl) *adj.* **1.** Connected with a university or college but taking place outside. Said especially of nonresident students or their studies. **2.** Occurring or situated outside the walls or boundaries, as of a fortress or city: *extramural skirmishes.*

ex·tra·ne·ous (ik-stráyni-əss, ek-) *adj.* **1.** Coming from outside; foreign: *extraneous interference.* **2.** Present but not essential or vital; accidental. **3.** Irrelevant. —See Synonyms at **extrinsic.** [Latin *extrāneus*, strange, from *extrā*, outward.] **—ex·tra·ne·ous·ly** *adv.* **—ex·tra·ne·ous·ness** *n.*

ex·tra·nu·cle·ar (ékstrə-néw-kli-ər || -nōō-) *adj. Biology.* Located or occurring outside the nucleus.

ex·traor·di·nar·y (ik-strórd'n-ri, ek-, ék-strə-órd'n-, -əri || -erri) *adj.* **1.** Beyond what is ordinary, usual, or commonplace: *extraordinary authority.* **2.** Exceeding the ordinary degree, amount, or extent; exceptional; remarkable: *an extraordinary feat.* **3.** Used, held, or appointed for a special service or occasion: *an extraordinary general meeting; an ambassador extraordinary.* **—ex·traor·di·nar·i·ly** (|| *also* -érrəli) *adv.*

extraordinary ray *n.* The plane-polarised ray of light that is produced by a doubly refracting crystal and does not obey the laws of refraction. Compare **ordinary ray.**

ex·trap·o·late (ik-stráppə-layt, ek-) *v.* **-lated, -lating, -lates.** —*tr.* **1.** *Mathematics.* To estimate (a value or values of a function) for values of the argument not used in the process of estimation; broadly, to infer (a value or values) from known values. **2.** To infer or estimate (unknown information) from known information. —*intr.* To engage in the process of extrapolation. [EXTRA- + (INTER)POLATE.] **—ex·trap·o·la·tion** (-láysh'n) *n.* **—ex·trap·o·la·tive** (-lətiv, -laytiv) *adj.*

ex·tra·sen·so·ry (ékstrə-sén-səri) *adj.* **1.** Not perceptible by the five normal senses. **2.** Perceptible by supernatural means. **3.** Supernatural.

extrasensory perception *n. Abbr.* **ESP** Perception other than by the five normal senses. See **clairvoyance, precognition, telepathy.**

ex·tra·sys·to·le (ékstrə-sístəli) *n. Medicine.* A generally premature heartbeat caused by a heart impulse generated outside the sinoatrial node. Also called "ectopic beat".

ex·tra·ter·res·tri·al (ékstrə-ti-réstri-əl, -te-) *n. & adj.* (A being) Originating, located, or occurring outside the Earth or its atmosphere.

ex·tra·ter·ri·to·ri·al (ékstrə-térri-táwri-əl || -tōri-) *adj.* **1.** Located outside territorial boundaries. **2.** Of or pertaining to persons exempt from the legal jurisdiction of the country in which they reside. **—ex·tra·ter·ri·to·ri·al·ly** *adv.*

ex·tra·ter·ri·to·ri·al·i·ty (ékstrə-térri-táwri-ál-əti || -tōri-) *n.* **1.** Exemption from local legal jurisdiction, as granted to foreign diplomats. **2.** The jurisdiction of a country over its nationals abroad.

ex·tra·u·ter·ine (ékstrə-yōōtə-rīn || -reen, -rin) *adj.* Located or occurring outside the uterus: *extrauterine pregnancy.*

ex·trav·a·gance (ik-strávvəgənss, ek-) *n.* Also **ex·trav·a·gan·cy** (-gən-si) *pl.* **-cies. 1.** The quality of being extravagant; immoderation, especially in expenditure. **2.** An immoderate expense or display. **3.** Something costly and self-indulgent. **4.** A gesture, claim, or the like which is unreasonable or wild.

ex·trav·a·gant (ik-strávvəgənt, ek-) *adj.* **1.** Given to lavish or imprudent expenditure; prodigal. **2.** Exceeding reasonable bounds; excessive: *extravagant demands.* **3.** Extremely abundant; profuse: *extravagant vegetation.* **4.** Unreasonably high; exorbitant. Said of a price, for example. —See Synonyms at **excessive.** [Middle English *extravagaunt*, from Old French *extravagant*, from Medieval Latin *extrāvagāns* (stem *extrāvagant-*), present participle of *extrāvagārī*, to wander beyond : Latin *extrā*, beyond + *vagārī*, to wander, akin to *vagus*, VAGUE.] **—ex·trav·a·gant·ly** *adv.* **—ex·trav·a·gant·ness** *n.*

ex·trav·a·gan·za (ik-strávvə-gánzə, ek-, ék-stravvə-) *n.* **1.** A light orchestral composition marked by freedom and diversity of form, often with burlesque elements. **2.** Any elaborate, spectacular entertainment. **3.** An instance of extravagant behaviour or activity. [Italian *(e)stravaganza*, from *(e)stravagant*, extravagant, from Medieval Latin *extrāvagāns*, EXTRAVAGANT.]

ex·trav·a·sate (ek-strávvə-sayt, ik-) *v.* **-sated, -sating, -sates.** —*tr. Pathology.* To force the flow of (blood or lymph) out into surrounding tissue. —*intr. Pathology.* To exude into the surrounding tissues. Used of blood or lymph. [EXTRA- + VAS + -ATE.] **—ex·trav·a·sa·tion** (-sáysh'n) *n.*

ex·tra·vas·cu·lar (ékstrə-váskewlər) *adj.* Located or occurring outside a blood vessel or the vascular system.

ex·tra·ve·hic·u·lar activity (ékstrə-vi-híckewlər) *n. Abbr.* **EVA** Activity or manoeuvres performed by an astronaut outside a spacecraft in space.

extraversion. Variant of **extroversion.**

extravert. Variant of **extrovert.**

ex·tra·vir·gin (ékstrə-vúrjin) *adj.* Designating what is claimed to be the best kind of virgin olive oil.

Ex·trem·a·du·ra or **Es·trem·a·du·ra** (ess-trémma-dóor-ə). Region of west central Spain comprising the Badajoz and Cáceres provinces. Long a generally poor farming area, it is being developed with irrigation, and is also noted for its cork-oak forests and pigs. **—Ex·trem·a·du·ran** *n. & adj.*

ex·treme (ik-stréem, ek- || ék-) *adj.* **1.** Outermost or farthest; most remote in any direction: *the extreme edge of the field.* **2.** Final; last. **3.** Being in or attaining the greatest or highest degree; very intense: *extreme pleasure; extreme degradation.* **4.** Extending far beyond the norm; radical: *an extreme conservative.* **5.** Of the greatest severity; drastic: *extreme measures.* —See Synonyms at **excessive.**
~*n.* **1.** The greatest or utmost degree or point: *eager in the extreme.* **2.** Either of the two ends of a state or condition considered as a measurable or approximately measurable continuum: *the extremes of boiling and freezing; the extremes of wealth and poverty.* **3.** An extreme condition. **4.** *Plural.* A drastic or immoderate expedient: *driven to extremes.* **5.** *Mathematics.* The first or last term of a ratio or series. **6.** *Logic.* The major or minor term of a syllogism. [Middle English, from Old French, from Latin *extrēmus.*] **—ex·treme·ly** *adv.* **—ex·treme·ness** *n.*

extremely high frequency *n. Abbr.* **EHF** A radio-frequency band with a range of 30 000 to 300 000 megahertz.

extreme unction *n.* The **Sacrament of the Sick** *(see).*

ex·trem·ist (ik-stréemist, ek-) *n.* A person who advocates or resorts to extreme measures, especially in politics; a radical. See Synonyms at **fanatic.**
~*adj.* Belonging or pertaining to extremists. **—ex·trem·ism** *n.*

ex·trem·i·ty (ik-strémmiti, ek-) *n., pl.* **-ties. 1.** The outermost or farthest point or portion; an end; an edge. **2.** The greatest or utmost degree: *the extremity of despair.* **3.** Grave danger, necessity, or distress. **4.** The moment at which the end, as of life, is imminent. **5.** A bodily limb or appendage. **6.** *Plural.* The hands or feet.

ex·tri·cate (ék-stri-kayt) *tr.v.* **-cated, -cating, -cates. 1.** To release from an entanglement or difficulty; disengage. **2.** To cause to be liberated or emitted: *extricate gas from a solution.* [Latin *extrīcāre* : *ex-*, out + *trīcae*†, perplexities.] **—ex·tri·ca·ble** *adj.* **—ex·tri·ca·tion** (-káysh'n) *n.*

ex·trin·sic (ek-strín-sik, -zik) *adj.* **1.** Not forming an essential part of a thing; extraneous; inessential. **2.** Not inherent; accessory; accidental. **3.** Originating from the outside; external. [Late Latin *extrinsecus*, outer, from Latin, outwardly : *exterus*, EXTERIOR + *secus*, alongside.] **—ex·trin·si·cal·ly** *adv.*

Synonyms: *extrinsic, extraneous, foreign, alien.*

ex·trorse (ek-strórss, ék-strawrss) *adj. Botany.* Facing outwards; turned away from the axis. Said especially of anthers. [Late Latin *extrōrsus*, outward : *extrā*, outside + *introrsus*, INTRORSE.]

ex·tro·ver·sion, ex·tra·ver·sion (ék-strə-vér-sh'n, -zh'n) *n.* **1. a.** *Psychology.* Interest in and aptitude for dealing with the external world and other people as opposed to, or to the neglect of, oneself or one's inner feelings. **b.** Loosely, outgoing, friendly, or lively behaviour. Compare **introversion. 2.** A turning inside out, as of an organ or part. [From *extro-*, variant of EXTRA- + Latin *versus*, past participle of *vertere*, to turn.] **—ex·tro·ver·sive** (-siv || -ziv) *adj.* **—ex·tro·ver·sive·ly** *adv.*

ex·tro·vert, ex·tra·vert (ék-strə-vert) *n. & adj.* **1.** *Psychology.* One whose behaviour is characterised by extroversion. **2.** Loosely, an outgoing, gregarious, lively person. Compare **introvert.** [From *extro-*, variant of EXTRA- + Latin *vertere*, to turn.] **—ex·tro·vert·ed** (-id, -vértid) *adj.*

ex·trude (ik-strōōd, ek- || -stréwd) *v.* **-truded, -truding, -trudes.** —*tr.* **1.** To push or thrust out. **2.** To shape (metal or plastic, for example) by forcing through a die. —*intr.* To protrude or project. [Latin *extrūdere*, thrust out : *ex-*, out + *trūdere*, to thrust.]

ex·tru·sion (ik-strōō-zh'n, ek- || -stréw-) *n.* **1.** The act or process of extruding. **2.** Material that has been extruded. **3.** *Geology.* **a.** The movement of magma through volcanic craters and fissures in the earth's crust, forming igneous rocks. **b.** The igneous rocks so formed. [Medieval Latin *extrūsiō* (stem *extrūsiōn-*), from Latin *extrūsus*, past participle of *extrūdere*, EXTRUDE.]

ex·tru·sive (ik-strōo-siv, ek- ‖ -strĕw-, -ziv) *adj.* **1.** Tending to extrude. **2.** *Geology.* Derived from magma which has cooled and solidified on the earth's surface. Said of rock.

ex·u·ber·ant (ig-zĕw-bərənt, eg-, -zōō-) *adj.* **1.** Full of unrestrained high spirits; abandonedly joyous. **2.** Lavish; effusive; overflowing. **3.** Growing or producing abundantly; luxuriant. [Middle English, from Old French, from Latin *exūberāns* (stem *exūberant-*), present participle of *exūberāre*, to EXUBERATE.] **—ex·u·ber·ance** *n.* **—ex·u·ber·ant·ly** *adv.*

ex·u·ber·ate (ig-zĕw-bə-rayt, eg-, -zōō-) *intr.v.* **-ated, -ating, -ates. 1.** To be exuberant. **2.** *Archaic.* To abound or overflow. [Latin *exūberāre* : *ex-*, completely + *ūberāre*, to be fruitful, from *ūber*, fertile.]

ex·u·date (éks-yōō-dayt) *n.* An exuded substance; an exudation. [From EXUDE.]

ex·u·da·tion (éks-yōō-dáysh'n) *n.* **1.** The act or an instance of exuding. **2.** Something that is exuded; exudate: *an exudation of sweat.* **—ex·u·da·tive** (ig-zĕw-dətiv, éks-yōō-daytiv) *adj.*

ex·ude (ig-zĕwd, eg-, -zōod, ek-séwd, -sōōd) *v.* **-uded, -uding, -udes.** *—intr.* To ooze forth; come gradually through an opening: *sap exudes from the pine bark.* *—tr.* **1.** To discharge or emit gradually. **2.** To give off copiously; make (a quality) felt: *"he exuded about as much menace as boiled haddock"* (S.J. Perelman). [Latin *ex(s)ūdāre*, to sweat out, exude : *ex-*, out + *sudāre*, to sweat, ooze.]

ex·ult (ig-zúlt, eg-) *intr.v.* **-ulted, -ulting, -ults.** To rejoice greatly; be jubilant or triumphant, especially at another's defeat: *exult over one's rivals.* [Latin *ex(s)ultāre*, frequentative of *exsilīre*, to leap up, rejoice : *ex-*, up + *salīre*, to leap.] **—ex·ul·ta·tion** (ég-zul-táysh'n, ék-sul-), **ex·ul·tan·cy** (ig-zúl-tən-si, eg-) *n.* **—ex·ult·ing·ly** *adv.*

ex·ul·tant (ig-zúltənt, eg-) *adj.* Joyful; jubilant; triumphant. **—ex·ul·tant·ly** *adv.*

ex·ur·ban·ite (eks-úrbən-īt, egz-) *n.* *Chiefly U.S.* A regular commuter living in a small community, usually a well-to-do town, beyond the suburbs of a major city. [EX- + (SUB)URBANITE.]

ex·ur·bi·a (eks-úrbi-ə, egz-) *n.* *Chiefly U.S.* A semirural residential area situated beyond the suburbs of a city. Also called "exurbs". [EX- + (SUB)URBIA.]

ex·u·vi·ae (ig-zĕw-vi-ee, eg-, -zōō-) *pl.n.* The cast-off skins or coverings of various animals, especially the larvae and nymphs of insects. [Latin, stripped-off clothing, spoils, from *exuere*, to take off.] **—ex·u·vi·al** *adj.*

ex·u·vi·ate (ig-zĕw-vi-ayt, eg-, -zōō-) *v.* **-ated, -ating, -ates.** *—tr.* To shed (a covering, such as a skin). *—intr.* To shed or cast off exuviae. [From EXUVIAE.] **—ex·u·vi·a·tion** (-áysh'n) *n.*

-ey¹. Variant of **-y** (existence or possession).

-ey². Variant of **-y** (smallness).

ey·as (ī-əss) *n.* A nestling hawk or falcon, especially one to be trained for falconry. [Middle English, variant (by incorrect division of *an ias* for *a nias*) of *niyas*, from Old French *niais*, bird taken from the nest, from Vulgar Latin *nidax* (unattested), from Latin *nīdus*, nest.]

eye (ī) *n.* **1. a.** An organ of vision or of light sensitivity. **b.** The vertebrate organ of vision, either of a pair of hollow structures located in fixed bony sockets of the skull, functioning together or independently, each having a lens capable of focusing incident light on an internal photosensitive retina from which nerve impulses are sent to the brain. **2.** The external, visible portion of this organ together with its associated structures, such as the eyelids, eyelashes, and eyebrows. **3.** The pigmented iris of this organ. **4.** The faculty of seeing; sight; vision. **5.** The ability to discriminate or appreciate; discernment: *a good eye for fashion.* **6. a.** A look; a gaze. **b.** A way of regarding something; a point of view. **7.** Anything suggestive of an eye in appearance, such as an opening in a needle, a marking on a peacock feather, or a hole in cheese. **8.** A loop, such as one for attaching a hook. **9.** *Botany.* **a.** A bud on a twig or tuber: *the eye of a potato.* **b.** The often differently coloured centre of the corolla of some flowers. **10.** *Meteorology.* The circular area of relative calm at the centre of a cyclone. **11.** Anything construed as a centre or focal point. **12.** Keen observation; attention: *keep an eye on someone.* **13.** A photosensitive device, such as a photoelectric cell. **14.** A nye *(see).* **—all eyes.** Alert; observant. **—(all) my eye.** *Informal.* Nonsense. Used to express disagreement. **—an eye for an eye.** Punishment requiring that the offender suffer what he has caused another to suffer. [A Biblical phrase: ". . . life shall go for life, eye for eye, tooth for tooth, hand for hand, foot for foot" (Deuteronomy 19:21; also Exodus 21:2).] **—catch (someone's) eye.** *Informal.* To attract someone's attention. **—give (someone) the eye.** *Informal.* To look at admiringly or invitingly. **—have an eye to.** To be on the lookout for; be careful of. **—have eyes for.** To be attentive to; be interested in: *She has eyes only for you.* **—in (one's) mind's eye.** Pictured or clearly imagined in the mind. **—in the eye of the wind.** *Nautical.* In the direction opposite to that of the wind; close to the wind. **—in the public eye.** Famous; exposed to constant publicity or interest. **—keep (one's) eyes peeled** or **skinned.** To be constantly vigilant and observant. **—make eyes at.** To glance or gaze at flirtatiously. **—one in the eye for.** *Informal.* A humiliation or embarrassment for. **—see eye to eye.** To be in agreement. **—turn a blind eye to.** To ignore deliberately (some prohibited action which one witnesses, for example). **—up to (one's) eyes.** Fully

occupied; overwhelmed, as with work. **—with an eye to.** With a view to.

~*tr.v.* **eyed, eyeing** or **eying, eyes. 1.** To concentrate the eyes on; stare at. **2.** To appraise; especially, to appraise sexually. [Middle English *eie, eighe,* Old English *ēage.*]

eye·ball (ī-bawl) *n.* **1.** The ball-shaped portion of the eye enclosed by the socket and eyelids. **2.** The eye itself. **—eyeball to eyeball.** *Informal.* Confronting each other.

~*tr.v.* **eyeballed, -balling, -balls.** *Informal.* **1.** To stare steadily at, especially in a menacing way. **2.** To confront (a rival, for example) in an uncompromising way.

eye bank *n.* A place at which corneas taken from human bodies immediately after death are stored and preserved for subsequent transplantation to individuals with corneal defects.

eye bath *n.* A small cup with a rim contoured to fit the outside of the eye, used for applying a liquid medicine or wash to the eye.

eye·bolt (ī-bōlt ‖ -bolt) *n.* A bolt having a looped head designed to receive a hook or rope.

eye·bright (ī-brīt) *n.* Any of several plants of the genus *Euphrasia;* especially, *E. officinalis,* native to the Old World, having small white and purplish flowers and formerly used in the preparation of eye lotions.

eye·brow (ī-brow) *n.* **1.** The bony ridge extending over the eye. **2.** The arch of short hairs covering this ridge.

eyebrow pencil *n.* A cosmetic in pencil form used for extending, redrawing, or darkening the eyebrows.

eye-catching (ī-kaching) *adj.* Striking; compelling attention.

eye contact *n.* **1.** Personal contact established through a direct look. **2.** The ability to meet other people's eyes in conversation.

eyed (īd) *adj.* **1.** Having an eye or eyes, as a snail might. **2.** Having eyes of a specified number or kind. Used in combination: *one-eyed; blue-eyed.* **3.** Having markings that resemble eyes.

eye-drop·per (ī-droppər) *n.* A **dropper** *(see)* for administering liquid eye medicines.

eye·ful (ī-fōōl) *n.* **1.** An amount of something that covers the eye: *an eyeful of salt water.* **2.** *Informal.* All that the eye can encompass at one time; a good look. **3.** *Informal.* A sight to please the eyes; especially, a good-looking person.

eye·glass (ī-glaass ‖ -glass) *n.* **1.** *Plural.* **a.** A pair of lenses used to correct faulty vision, held in place by hand, by a spring, or by balancing the frame. **b.** *Chiefly U.S.* **Glasses** *(see).* **2.** A monocle. **3.** An eyepiece. **4.** An eye bath.

eye·hole (ī-hōl) *n.* **1.** The socket of the eye. **2.** A peephole. **3.** An eye for the insertion of a rope, pin, hook, or the like.

eye·hook (ī-hōōk ‖ -hŏŏk) *n.* A hook attached to a ring at the end of a rope or chain.

eye·lash (ī-lash) *n.* **1.** Any of a row of short hairs fringing the edge of the eyelid. **2.** A row of these hairs.

eye·let (ī-lit, -lət) *n.* **1. a.** A small hole or perforation, usually rimmed with metal, cord, fabric, or leather, used for fastening with a cord or hook. **b.** A metal ring designed to reinforce such a hole; a grommet. **2. a.** A small hole edged with fine embroidered stitches as part of a design. **b.** A piece of embroidery so worked. Also called "eyelet embroidery". **c.** Cloth that is ornamented with machine-produced eyelet embroidery. **d.** A small hole created in knitted or crocheted material and lace by combining and separating different stitches. **3.** An aperture or peephole. **4.** A small eye.

~*tr.v.* **eyeletted, -letting, -lets.** To make eyelets in. [Middle English *oilet,* from Old French *oillet,* diminutive of *oil,* eye, from Latin *oculus,* eye.]

eye·let·eer (īlə-téer) *n.* A pointed instrument for piercing eyelets in cloth; a bodkin; a stiletto.

eye·lid (ī-lid) *n.* Either of two folds of skin and muscle that can be closed over the exposed portion of the eyeball.

eye-lin·er (ī-līnər) *n.* A cosmetic preparation that is applied close to the eyelashes to accentuate the eyes.

eye-opener *n.* A revelation, usually startling or shocking.

eye·piece (ī-peess) *n.* The lens or lens group closest to the eye in a microscope, telescope, or other optical instrument; an ocular.

eye rhyme *n.* A false rhyme consisting of words with similar spellings but different sounds; for example, *lint* and *pint.*

eye-shade (ī-shayd) *n.* A visor made of tinted plastic or a similar opaque material, worn to protect the eyes from glare.

eye shadow *n.* A cosmetic available in various colours or tints and applied to the eyelids to enhance the eyes.

eye-shot (ī-shot) *n.* The range of vision; view; sight.

eye·sight (ī-sīt) *n.* **1.** The faculty of sight; vision. **2.** The range of vision; view.

eyes-only *adj.* Designating or relating to something (such as a top-secret document) that is to be looked at or read only by a specified person.

eye·sore (ī-sawr ‖ -sōr) *n.* Something ugly or offensive to look at.

eye splice *n.* *Nautical.* A loop formed at the end of a rope by turning it back and splicing in the end strands.

eye·spot (ī-spot) *n.* **1.** A light-sensitive, pigmented area in certain algae, protozoans, and other primitive animals; a stigma. **2.** A rounded, eyelike marking, as on the tail of a peacock.

eye·stalk (ī-stawk) *n.* A movable, stalklike structure bearing at its tip one of the eyes of a crab, shrimp, or similar crustacean.

eye·strain (ī-strayn) *n.* Aching and fatigue of the eyes, often accompanied by headache, resulting from prolonged close work, uncorrected errors of vision, or an imbalance of the eye muscles.

eye·tooth (í-tōoth) *n., pl.* **-teeth** (teeth). A canine *(see)* of the upper jaw. **—give (one's) eyeteeth for.** To be willing to give up a great deal to acquire (something much desired). [So called because it lies immediately under the eye.]

eye·wash (í-wosh ‖ *U.S. also* -wawsh) *n.* **1.** A medicated solution applied as a wash for the eyes. **2.** *Informal.* Speech or writing intended to mislead or conceal.

eye·wit·ness (í-wít-niss, -wit-, -nəss) *n.* A person who has seen a particular event or act and can describe it, for example in court or to the press.

eyot (ayt, áy-ət) *n.* Also **ait** (ayt). *British.* A small island, especially in a river. [Middle English *eigt, eyt, eit*, Old English *iggath, ȳgett*, from *īeg, ȳg*, ISLAND + *-ett, -ath*, diminutive suffix.]

Eyre, Lake (air). Largest lake in Australia, lying in central South Australia. It is salty, shallow, and in the hot, arid summers of the Australian interior can dry up. At 16 metres (52 feet) below sea level it is Australia's lowest point.

eyr·ie (éer-i, áir-, ír-) *n.* Also *chiefly U.S.* **aer·ie. 1.** The nest of an eagle or other predatory bird, built on a crag or other high place.

2. A house or stronghold built on a height. [Medieval Latin *aeria*, probably from Old French *aire*, lair, from Latin *ager* (stem *agr-*), field, native ground.]

ey·rir (áy-reer) *n., pl.* **aurar** (ŏ-raar). A coin equal to ¹/₁₀₀ of the krona of Iceland. [Icelandic, from Old Norse, an ounce, probably from Latin *aureus*, gold coin, from *aurum*, gold.]

Ey·senck (í-zengk), **Hans Jürgen** (1916–97). Professor of psychology at the University of London. His *Race, Intelligence, and Education* (1971), argues that I.Q. may be linked to race.

Ezek. Ezekiel (Old Testament).

E·ze·ki·el¹ (i-zéeki-əl) A major Hebrew prophet of the sixth century B.C., author of the Old Testament Book of Ezekiel. [Greek *Iezekiel*, from Hebrew *Y'hezkēl*, "may God strengthen".]

Ezekiel² *n. Abbr.* **Ezek.** The Old Testament book bearing the name of the prophet Ezekiel.

Ez·ra¹ (ézzrə). A Hebrew high priest of the fifth century B.C. [Hebrew, "help".]

Ezra² *n.* A book of the Old Testament bearing the name of the priest Ezra. Also called "Esdras" in the Douay Bible.

F

f, F (ef) *n., pl.* **f's** or *rare* **fs, Fs** or **F's. 1.** The sixth letter of the modern English alphabet. **2.** Any of the speech sounds represented by this letter.

f, F, f., F. *Note:* As an abbreviation or symbol, *f* may be a small or a capital letter, with or without a full stop. Established forms or those generally preferred precede the definition. When no form is given, all four forms are in general use in that sense. **1.** F Fahrenheit. **2.** F farad. **3.** f. farthing. **4.** F February. **5.** F, F. fellow (of a university or other institution). **6.** female. **7.** f., F. *Grammar.* feminine. **8.** f *Physics.* femto-. **9.** f., F. *Metallurgy.* fine. **10.** F The symbol for the element fluorine. **11.** f., F. folio. **12.** f. following. **13.** F *Physics.* force. **14.** f, F *Music.* forte. **15.** f. *Sports.* foul. **16.** f. franc. **17.** F. French. **18.** F. Friday. **19.** The sixth in a series. **20.** F An academic mark equivalent to a fail. **21.** *Genetics.* A filial generation, F_1 being the first generation resulting from a given cross, F_2 the second generation resulting from crossing within the F_1 generation, and so on.

F (ef) *n., pl.* **Fs** or **F's 1. a.** The fourth note in the scale of C major. **b.** The key or a scale in which F is the tonic. **c.** A written or printed note representing F. **d.** A string, key, or pipe tuned to the pitch of F. **2.** Something shaped like the letter F.

fa (faa). *Music.* Variant of **fah.**

FA 1. field artillery. **2.** Football Association.

F.A. 1. Football Association. **2.** Fanny Adams.

fab (fab) *adj.* Also **fab·by** (fábbi). *Chiefly British Informal.* Fabulous; splendid.

Fab·er·gé (fábbər-zhay ‖ -zháy), **Peter Carl** (1846–1920). Russian goldsmith who made ornate decorative objects for European royalty. He is famous for his jewelled eggs containing surprise gifts.

Fa·bi·an (fáybi-ən) *adj.* **1.** Using or characterised by a cautious strategy of gradual social progress and avoidance of direct confrontation with the state. **2.** Of or relating to the Fabian Society. **~n.** A member or supporter of the Fabian Society. [Latin *Fabiānus*, after Quintus *Fabius* Maximus (died 203 B.C.), known as *Cunctator* ("Delayer"), Roman general who defeated Hannibal by avoiding direct conflict.] **—Fa·bi·an·ism** *n.* **—Fa·bi·an·ist** *n.* & *adj.*

Fabian Society *n.* An organisation founded in Britain in 1883 to promote the gradual spread of democratic socialism.

fa·ble (fáyb'l) *n.* **1.** A concise narrative making an edifying, moral, or cautionary point and often employing as characters animals that speak and act like human beings. **2. a.** A story or myth about legendary persons and exploits. **b.** Such stories and myths collectively. **c.** A literary genre consisting of such stories. **3.** A falsehood; a lie. **~v. fabled, -bling, -bles. —tr.** To recount as if true. **—intr.** *Archaic.* To compose fables. [Middle English, from Old French, from Latin *fābula*, narration, account, story, from *fārī*, to speak.] **—fabler** *n.*

fa·bled (fáyb'ld) *adj.* **1.** Made known or famous by fable; legendary. **2.** Existing only in fable; fictitious.

fab·li·au (fáb-li-ŏ) *n., pl.* **-liaux** (-li-ŏ). A medieval verse tale characterised by comic and ribald treatment of themes drawn from life, such as, for example, Chaucer's "Miller's Tale". [French, from Old French (Picardy dialect) *fabliaux*, plural of *fablel*, diminutive of *fable*, FABLE.]

fab·ric (fábbrik) *n.* **1.** Any material structure consisting of connected parts; a framework. **2.** A structure consisting of human relations or of relations between ideas, expressions, emotions, or the like: *"the pattern of her mind, the whole fabric of her nature"* (James Thurber). **3.** A method or style of construction. **4. a.** Any cloth produced by joining fibres as by knitting, weaving, or felting. **b.** The texture or quality of such cloth. **5.** The walls, roof, and floor

of a building. [Middle English, from Old French *fabrique*, from Latin *fabrica*, workshop, a trade, from *faber*, workman, artisan.]

fab·ri·cate (fábbri-kayt) *tr.v.* **-cated, -cating, -cates. 1.** To prepare, make, or fashion. **2.** To construct by putting together finished parts; assemble. **3.** To invent (a story); devise (a deception). [Middle English *fabricaten*, from Latin *fabricārī* (past participle *fabricātus*), fabricate, build, from *fabrica*, workshop. See **fabric.**] **—fab·ri·ca·tor** (-kaytər) *n.*

fab·ri·ca·tion (fábbri-káysh'n) *n.* **1. a.** Something, such as a deliberately false statement, that is made up or fabricated. **b.** The action of inventing a false statement or of forging a document. **2.** *Rare.* The process of fabricating; manufacture.

fab·u·list (fábbew-list) *n.* **1.** A composer of fables, especially of moral tales. **2.** An inventor or teller of falsehoods. [French *fabuliste*, from Latin *fābula*, FABLE.]

fab·u·lous (fábbew-ləss) *adj.* **1.** Of the nature of a fable or myth; legendary. **2.** Told of or celebrated in fables or legends. **3.** Barely credible; astonishing: *fabulous riches.* **4.** *Informal.* Extremely pleasing or successful: *We had a fabulous time on holiday.* [Middle English, from Latin *fābulōsus*, from *fābula*, FABLE.] **—fab·u·lous·ly** *adv.* **—fab·u·lous·ness** *n.*

fac. facsimile.

fa·çade, fa·cade (fə-saád, fa-) *n.* **1.** *Architecture.* A face of a building; especially, a front face that is given distinguishing treatment. **2.** The face or front part of anything; especially, an artificial or false appearance or aspect. [French, from Italian *facciata*, from *faccia*, face, from Vulgar Latin *facia* (unattested), FACE.]

face (fayss) *n.* **1.** The surface of the front of the head from the top of the forehead to the base of the chin and from ear to ear. Also used adjectively: *face cream.* **2.** The arrangement or expression of the features of this part of the head; the countenance. **3.** An exaggerated facial expression; a grimace. **4. a.** The outward appearance, aspect, or look: *The face of the city has changed.* **b.** An assumed bearing; a front: *we must put a good face on things.* **5.** Value or standing in the eyes of others; dignity; prestige: *The country feared it would lose face.* **6.** *Informal.* Effrontery; impudence. **7.** The most significant or prominent surface of any object, especially: **a.** The surface presented to view; the front: *the face of a building.* **b.** The outer surface: *the face of the earth.* **c.** A steep side of a hill or mountain. **d.** The upper or marked side; the most meaningful surface: *the face of a clock.* **e.** The side of an instrument or device that is applied or makes contact: *the face of a golf club.* **f.** Either side of a coin; especially a side bearing the representation of a head. **8.** *Geometry.* A planar surface bounding a solid. **9.** Any of the surfaces of a rock or crystal. **10.** *Military.* Any of the sides of a formation of men or of a fortified position. **11.** The appearance and geological surface features of an area of land; topography. **12.** The exposed working surface of coal, ore, or the like, in a mine. **13. Typeface** *(see).* **—face to face. 1.** In each other's presence; in direct communication: *We finally spoke, face to face.* **2.** Directly confronting. Used with *with: His illness brought him face to face with death.* **—fly in the face of.** To defy openly. **—in the face of. 1.** Despite the opposition of; notwithstanding. **2.** Considering the fact of; in view of. **—laugh in (someone's) face.** To be openly disrespectful or contemptuous towards someone. **—on the face of it.** From its appearance alone; apparently. **—pull a face** or **faces.** To grimace. **—put (one's) face on.** *Informal.* To put on make-up. **—set (one's) face against.** To oppose resolutely. **—show (one's) face.** To make an appearance. **—to (someone's) face.** Confronting someone in the flesh; directly and boldly: *She accused the offender to his face.* **~v. faced, facing, faces. —tr. 1.** To turn or be turned or situated in the direction of. **2.** To be opposite; have the front directly opposite to; front: *a window facing the south.* **3. a.** To realise; be cognisant of: *facing facts.* **b.** To confront or deal with boldly or bravely: *"What this generation must do is face its problems"* (John F. Kennedy). **4.** To be certain to encounter; have in store: *The unskilled youth faces a difficult life.* **5.** To cause (a soldier or formation of troops) to change direction sharply by giving a command. **6.** To turn (a playing card) so that the face is up. **7.** To furnish with a surface or cover of a different material: *bronze faced with gold foil.* **8.** To provide the edge or edges of (a cloth or garment) with finishing or trimming. **9.** To treat or dress the surface of (a material); smooth. —*intr.* **1.** To be turned or placed with the front towards a specified direction. **2.** To turn the face in a specified direction. **—face down.** To overcome or prevail over by a stare or a resolute manner. **—face off.** To start play in hockey, lacrosse, and other games by releasing the puck or ball between two opposing players. **—face out.** **1.** To endure to the end. **2.** To overcome or get through (a difficult situation) by boldness or impudence. **—face up to.** **1.** To recognise the existence or importance of. **2.** To confront bravely. [Middle English, from Old French, from Vulgar Latin *facia* (unattested), from Latin *faciēs,* form, shape, face, from *facere,* to make, form.] **—face·a·ble** *adj.*

face-ache (fáyss-ayk) *n. British.* **1.** Neuralgia of a cranial nerve; specifically, trigeminal neuralgia. **2.** *Slang.* A miserable-looking or depressing person.

face card *n. Chiefly U.S.* A **court card** *(see).*

face-centred (fáyss-sentərd, -séntərd) *adj.* Designating a crystal or crystal lattice in which there is a lattice point at the centre of each face of each unit cell. Compare **body-centred.**

facecloth (fáyss-kloth || -klawth) *n.* A cloth, usually made of towelling, used for washing the face. Also *British* "face flannel".

faced (fayst) *adj.* **1.** Having a face or faces. **2.** Having a specified number or kind of faces. Used in combination: *two-faced; red-faced.*

face-hard·en (fáyss-haard'n) *tr.v.* **-ened, -ening, -ens.** To harden the surface of (a metal).

face·less (fáyss-ləss, -liss) *adj.* **1.** Without a face. **2.** Anonymous; hard to identify: *faceless bureaucrats.*

face-lift (fáyss-lift) *n.* **1.** A cosmetic plastic-surgery operation for tightening facial tissues and improving the appearance of facial skin. **2.** A restyling or modernising of an outward appearance.

face pack *n.* A cosmetic preparation used for cleansing and toning the complexion, usually consisting of a thick paste that is washed or peeled off when dry. Also called "face mask".

face·plate (fáyss-playt) *n.* **1.** A disc attached to the headstock of a lathe to hold flat or irregularly shaped work. **2.** A flat machined plate used to test the flatness of a component or part. Also called "surface plate".

fac·er (fáyssər) *n.* **1.** A person or thing that faces; especially, a device used in smoothing or dressing metal, stone, or other material. **2.** *Chiefly British Archaic.* An unexpected blow or defeat.

face-sav·ing (fáyss-sayving) *adj.* Preserving prestige or respect in the face of potential embarrassment or humiliation. **—face-sav·er** (fáyss-sayvər) *n.*

fac·et (fáss-it, -et) *n.* **1.** Any of the flat polished surfaces cut on a gemstone. **2.** A small planar or rounded smooth surface on a bone or tooth. **3.** Any of the lenslike divisions of a compound eye, as of an insect. **4.** An aspect or phase: *The four principal characters are facets of the author's personality.*

~*tr.v.* **faceted** or **facetted, -eting** or **-etting, -ets.** To cut facets in (a gemstone). [French *facette,* diminutive of FACE.]

fa·ce·ti·ae (fə-séeshi-ee) *pl.n.* Witty or coarsely humorous writings and sayings; pleasantries. [Latin *facētiae,* plural of *facētia,* a jest, from *facētus,* FACETIOUS.]

fa·ce·tious (fə-séeshəss) *adj.* Unsuitably jocular; flippant: *a facetious remark.* [Old French *facetieux,* from *facetie,* a jest, from Latin *facētia,* from *facētus*†, elegant, fine, facetious.] **—fa·ce·tious·ly** *adv.* **—fa·ce·tious·ness** *n.*

face value *n.* **1.** The value printed or written on a note, bond, coin, or the like. **2.** The apparent value or significance: *He accepted their professed loyalty at face value.*

facia. Variant of **fascia.**

fa·cial (fáysh'l) *adj.* Of or concerning the face.

~*n.* A treatment for the face, usually consisting of a massage and the application of cosmetic creams. [Medieval Latin *faciālis.* See **face, -al.**] **—fa·cial·ly** *adv.*

facial nerve *n.* The seventh cranial nerve, which supplies motor fibres to the muscles of the face and carries sensory fibres from the tastebuds and salivary glands.

-facient *n. & adj. comb. form.* Indicates a bringing about or causing to become; for example, **absorbefacient, abortifacient.** [Latin *faciēns* (stem *facient-*), present participle of *facere,* to do.]

fa·ci·es (fáyshi-eez) *n., pl.* **facies.** **1.** The general aspect or outward appearance, as of a given growth of flora. **2.** *Medicine.* A patient's facial expression, especially when typical of a certain disorder or disease. **3.** *Geology.* The total characteristics of a rock, including appearance, composition, and fossil content, as used to distinguish rocks of the same age, according to the lateral differences. [New Latin, from Latin *faciēs,* shape, form, FACE.]

fac·ile (fáss-īl, -il) *adj.* **1.** Arrived at without due care, effort, or examination; superficial; glib. **2.** Easy and relaxed in manner. **3.** Done or achieved with little effort or difficulty; easy. **4.** Working, acting, or speaking effortlessly; fluent: *a facile speaker.* **5.** *Archaic.* Yielding; compliant. [French, from Latin *facilis,* from *facere,* to do.] **—fac·ile·ly** *adv.* **—fac·ile·ness** *n.*

fa·cil·i·tate (fə-sílli-tayt) *tr.v.* **-tated, -tating, -tates.** To free from difficulties or obstacles; make easier; aid; assist. [French *faciliter,* from Italian *facilitare,* from *facile,* easy, from Latin *facilis,* FACILE.] **—fa·cil·i·ta·tion** (-táysh'n) *n.*

fa·cil·i·ty (fə-sílləti) *n., pl.* **-ties.** **1.** Ease in moving, acting, or doing; aptitude. **2.** Ready skill derived from practice or familiarity; fluency. **3.** *Often plural.* The means or equipment to facilitate an action or process; provision: *the facilities of a library; sports facilities.* **4.** *Archaic.* An agreeable, pliable disposition. **5.** *Plural. Informal.* The available toilet arrangements. [French *facilité.* See **facile, -ity.**]

fac·ing (fáyssing) *n.* **1. a.** A piece of material sewn to the edge of a dress, coat, or other garment as lining or decoration. **b.** Fabric used for this. **c.** *Plural.* Fabric of contrasting colour used to trim the collar, cuffs, or similar parts of the jacket of a military uniform. **2.** An outer layer or coating of different material applied to a surface for protection or decoration: *a stone wall with wood facing.*

fac·sim·i·le (fak-símmili) *n. Abbr.* **fac., facsim.** **1.** An exact copy or reproduction, as of a document. **2. a.** A method of transmitting images by converting the information into an electronic signal for transmission by cable or radio. **b.** An image so transmitted.

~*adj.* **1.** Of or used to produce facsimiles. **2.** Exactly reproduced; duplicate.

~*tr.v.* **facsimiled, -leing** (-li-ing), **-les.** To make a facsimile of. [Latin *fac simile,* make (it) similar : *fac,* imperative of *facere,* to make, do + *simile,* neuter of *similis,* SIMILAR.]

fact (fakt) *n.* **1.** Something known with certainty. **2.** Something asserted as certain. **3.** Something that has been objectively verified. **4.** Something having real, demonstrable existence. **5.** *Law.* **a.** An act considered with regard to its legality. Used chiefly in the phrases *before* or *after the fact.* **b.** The aspect of a case at law comprising events determined by evidence as distinguished from interpretation of law: *The jury made a finding of fact.* **—as a matter of fact.** Actually; interestingly enough. **—in (point of) fact.** In reality; in truth; actually. [Latin *factum,* a deed, from *factus,* past participle of *facere,* to do.]

fact-find·ing (fákt-fīnding) *n.* The discovery or determination of facts or accurate information.

~*adj.* Engaged in or designed to ascertain facts: *a fact-finding committee.* **—fact-find·er** *n.*

fac·tion[1] (fáksh'n) *n.* **1.** A group of persons forming a cohesive, usually contentious, minority within a larger group. **2.** Internal dissension; conflict within an organisation or nation: *a country afflicted with faction and civil war.* [Old French, from Latin *factiō* (stem *factiōn-*), an acting (together), a making, from *factus,* past participle of *facere,* to do, make.]

fac·tion[2] *n.* A film, book, television programme, or the like whose content is a deliberate mixture of fact and fiction, usually presented in a popular style. [*fact* + *fic*tion.]

fac·tion·al (fákshən'l) *adj.* Of, characterised by, or causing a contentious faction or factions; partisan. **—fac·tion·al·ism** *n.*

fac·tious (fákshəss) *adj.* **1.** Produced or characterised by contentious faction. **2.** Creating or promoting faction; divisive. —See Synonyms at **insubordinate.** **—fac·tious·ly** *adv.* **—fac·tious·ness** *n.*

fac·ti·tious (fak-tíshəss) *adj.* **1.** Produced artificially rather than by natural process; contrived: *speculators responsible for the factitious value of some stocks.* **2.** Lacking authenticity or genuineness; sham: *a factitious smile.* [Latin *factīcius,* made by art, from *facere,* to make, do.] **—fac·ti·tious·ly** *adv.* **—fac·ti·tious·ness** *n.*

fac·ti·tive (fáktitiv) *adj. Grammar.* Of or constituting a transitive verb that in some constructions takes an objective complement to modify its direct object; for example, *They elected him chairman.* [New Latin *factitivus,* from Latin *factus,* done. See **fact.**] **—fac·ti·tive·ly** *adv.*

fact of life *n.* **1.** A fact or situation that must be faced in a realistic manner. **2.** *Plural. Informal.* The facts about human reproduction and sexuality.

fact·oid (fák-toyd) *adj.* Having the spurious appearance of fact; plausible enough to be a fact, but lacking substantiation. **—fact·oid** *n.* **—fact·oid·al** (fak-tóyd'l) *adj.*

fac·tor (fáktər) *n.* **1.** An element that actively contributes to an accomplishment, result, or process; a cause. **2. a.** One who acts for someone else; especially, one who buys and sells on commission; an agent. **b.** *Scottish.* An estate manager; a steward. **c.** A person or company that accepts trade debts as security for short-term loans. **3.** *Mathematics.* One of two or more quantities having a designated product: *2 and 3 are factors of 6.* **4.** A gene. No longer in technical usage.

~ *v.* **factored, -toring, -tors.** —*tr.* To separate into factors or components. —*intr.* To act as a factor; do business as a factor. **—factor in.** To consider as a factor: *factor in the effects of inflation.* [Middle English *factour,* from Old French *facteur,* from Latin *factor,* maker, doer, from *factus,* FACT.] **—fac·tor·age** *n.* **—fac·tor·ship** *n.*

fac·tor·a·ble (fáktər-əb'l) *adj.* Capable of being expressed as a product of factors. Said especially of mathematical expressions.

fac·to·ri·al (fak-táwri-əl || -tōri-) *n.* The product of all the positive integers from 1 to a given number. For example, 4 factorial, usually written 4!, is the product 1·2·3·4 = 24.

~*adj.* Of or relating to a factor or factorial.

fac·tor·ise, fac·tor·ize (fáktə-rīz) *tr.v.* **-ised, -ising, -ises.** To resolve (a mathematical expression) into factors. **—fac·tor·i·sa·tion** (-rī-záysh'n || *U.S.* -ri-) *n.*

factor of safety *n.* The ratio of the stress required to break a material, part, or structure to the calculated maximum working stress to which it will be subjected in use. Also called "safety factor".

fac·to·ry (fák-təri, -tri) *n., pl.* **-ries.** A building or group of buildings in which goods are manufactured; a plant. [Medieval Latin *factōria*, establishment for factors, from Latin *factor*, FACTOR.]

factory farming *n.* A method of farming employing industrial methods, such as the automated feeding of livestock, to increase production and reduce labour costs. —**factory farm** *n.*

factory ship *n.* 1. A whaling ship that has equipment for processing its catch on board. 2. Any fishing vessel that processes its catch on board.

fac·to·tum (fak-tótəm) *n., pl.* **-tums.** An employee or assistant who serves in a wide range of capacities. [Medieval Latin *factōtum,* from Latin *fac tōtum,* do everything : *fac,* imperative of *facere,* to do + *tōtum,* everything, the whole, from *tōtus,* all.]

fac·tu·al (fák-choo-əl, -tew-) *adj.* 1. Of the nature of fact; actual; real. 2. Of or containing facts. —**fac·tu·al·ly** *adv.*

fac·ture (fákchər) *n.* 1. The process or manner of making something. 2. That which is made.

fac·u·la (fáckew-lə) *n., pl.* **-lae** (-lee). Any of various large bright spots or streaks on the sun's photosphere, most conspicuous at the solar edge or near sunspots. [Latin, diminutive of *fax†* (stem *fac-*), flame, torch.]

fac·ul·ta·tive (fáck'l-tə-tiv, -tay-) *adj.* 1. Of or associated with a mental faculty or faculties. 2. Capable of occurring or not occurring; contingent. 3. Granting permission or authority. 4. Not obligatory; optional. 5. *Biology.* Capable of existing in very different environmental conditions, as certain microorganisms that can live with or without oxygen. Compare **obligate.** —**fac·ul·ta·tive·ly** *adv.*

fac·ul·ty (fáck'lti) *n., pl.* **-ties.** 1. An inherent power or ability. 2. Any of the powers or capacities possessed by the human mind. 3. The ability to perform well in a given activity; skill. 4. *Archaic.* An occupation; a trade. 5. **a.** Any of the divisions or comprehensive branches of learning at a college or university: *the faculty of law.* **b.** The instructors within such a division. 6. All of the members of a learned profession: *the medical faculty.* 7. Authorisation granted by authority; conferred power. [Middle English *faculte,* from Old French, from Latin *facultās* (stem *facultāt-*), power, capability, from Old Latin *facul,* easy.]

F.A. Cup, FA Cup *n.* 1. An annual knockout competition played for a silver cup and involving all teams that are members of the Football Association. 2. The cup itself.

fad (fad) *n.* 1. A fashion in dress, behaviour, or speech that enjoys brief popularity. 2. The object of this fashion. [19th century : originally dialect, perhaps from *fidfad,* shortening of FIDDLE-FADDLE.] —**fad·dish, fad·dy** *adj.* —**fad·dist** *n.*

FAD *n. Biochemistry.* Flavin adenine dinucleotide: a derivative of riboflavin that is a coenzyme in many oxidation-reduction reactions.

Fad·den (fádd'n), **Sir Arthur William** (1895–1973). Australian statesman. He was prime minister in 1941.

fade (fayd) *v.* **faded, fading, fades.** —*intr.* 1. To lose brightness, loudness, or brilliance gradually; dim. 2. To lose freshness; wither. 3. To lose strength or vitality; decline in energy; wane. 4. To disappear slowly or gradually; die out; vanish. Often used with *out* or *away: All hope of reaching the camp by nightfall soon faded away.* 5. To lose power. Used of brakes. 6. To fluctuate. Used of a radio signal. 7. To deviate from a straight line or the intended path. Used typically of a golf ball. —*tr.* To cause to fade.

~*n.* 1. An act or instance of fading. 2. A dissolve in films or television. [Middle English *faden,* from Old French *fader,* from *fade,* faded, vapid, from Vulgar Latin *fatidus* (unattested), probably a blend of Latin *fatuus,* insipid, foolish, FATUOUS, and *vapidus,* VAPID.] —**fade·less** *adj.* —**fade·less·ly** *adv.*

fade in *v.* Also **fade up.** —*intr.* To appear gradually. Used of a film or television image or of a sound. —*tr.* To make (an image or sound) appear gradually.

fade-in (fáyd-in) *n.* 1. The gradual coming or bringing into full visibility of an image in film or television. 2. The gradual coming or bringing into audibility of a sound, as in broadcasting.

fade out *intr.v.* To disappear gradually. Used of a film or television image or of a sound. —*tr.v.* To make (an image or sound) disappear gradually.

fade-out (fáyd-owt) *n.* 1. The gradual disappearance of a film or television image or of a sound. 2. A reduction in strength in or temporary loss of a radio or television signal. 3. A gradual decline or disappearance.

fad·ing (fáyding) *n.* 1. A waning; a decline. 2. Fluctuation in the strength of received radio signals because of variations in the transmission medium.

fa·do (fáa-dŏŏ, -thŏŏ, -dŏ) *n., pl.* **-dos.** A plaintive, usually sentimental Portuguese folk song. [Portuguese, *fado,* "fate", from Latin *fātum,* FATE.]

fae·ces, *U.S.* **fe·ces** (fée-seez) *pl.n.* Waste excreted from the bowels; excrement. [Middle English, from Latin, plural of *faex†* (stem *faec-*), dregs.] —**fae·cal** (fée'k'l) *adj.*

Fa·en·za (faa-ént-saa, -en-zə, -zaa). Town in the Emilia-Romagna district of northern Italy, situated on the River Lamone. Since the 12th century the pottery faience has been made there.

fa·er·ie (fáy-əri, fáiri) *n.* Also **fa·er·y** *pl.* **-ies.** *Archaic.* 1. A fairy. 2. The land or realm of the fairies.

~*adj.* Also **fa·er·y.** 1. *Archaic.* Of or like a fairy or fairies. 2. Enchanted; visionary; fanciful. [Variant (in Spenser's *The Faerie Queen,* 1590–96) of FAIRY.]

Fae·roe or **Fa·roe Islands** (fáirō). *Danish* **Fær·ø·er·ne** (fáir-ur-nə, -ör-). Group of twenty-two volcanic islands belonging to Denmark, lying in the north Atlantic Ocean between Iceland and the Shetland Islands. Seventeen are inhabited; on the largest of them, Streymoy, is the islands' capital, Torshavn. The economy is based on fish and wool. See map at **Western Europe.**

Fae·ro·ese, Fa·ro·ese (fáirō-éez) *n., pl.* **Faeroese.** 1. A member of a Germanic people inhabiting the Faeroe Islands. 2. Their North Germanic language.

~*adj.* Of or pertaining to the Faeroe Islands, their inhabitants, or their language.

fag¹ (fag) *n.* 1. *Informal.* **a.** Fatiguing or tedious work; drudgery. **b.** A drudge. 2. *British.* A schoolboy at some public schools who is required to perform menial tasks for a pupil in a higher class.

~*v.* **fagged, fagging, fags.** —*intr.* 1. *Informal.* To work to exhaustion; become weary from toil. 2. *British.* To serve as the fag of another pupil. —*tr.* 1. *Informal.* To exhaust from long work; weary; fatigue. Often used with *out.* 2. *British.* To use (a boy) as a fag. [16th century (to droop, hang down, flag) : origin obscure.]

fag² *n. Slang.* A cigarette. [Short for FAG END.]

fag³ *n. Chiefly U.S. Slang.* A male homosexual. Usually used derogatorily. [Short for FAGGOT.] —**fag·gy** *adj.*

fag end *n.* 1. The frayed end of a length of cloth or rope. 2. An inferior remnant or last part of anything; that which remains of something exhausted of its quality or utility. 3. *Slang.* A cigarette stub. [Middle English *fagge†.*]

fag·got *U.S.* **fag·ot** (fággət) *n.* 1. A bundle of twigs, sticks, or branches bound together. 2. A bundle of pieces of iron or steel to be welded or hammered into bars. 3. A ball or cube of chopped meat, usually pig's offal, bread, and herbs, served baked or fried. 4. *Slang.* A male homosexual. Usually used derogatorily. 5. A disagreeable person.

~*tr.v.* **faggoted, -goting, -gots.** 1. To collect or bind into a faggot or faggots; bundle. 2. To decorate with faggoting. [Middle English, from Old French, from Italian *fagotto,* from Vulgar Latin *facus* (unattested), back-formation from Greek *phakelos†.* Sense 4, originally U.S., from earlier derogatory sense applied abusively to women (compare **baggage**).]

fag·got·ing (fággəting) *n.* 1. A method of decorating cloth by pulling out horizontal threads and tying the remaining vertical threads into hourglass-shaped bunches. 2. A method of joining hemmed edges by crisscrossing thread over an open seam.

Fa·gin (fáygin) *n.* A man who trains children to steal. [After *Fagin,* an old man in Dickens' *Oliver Twist* who trains children to be pickpockets.]

fah, fa (faa) *n. Music.* In tonic sol-fa, a syllable representing the fourth note of a diatonic scale. [Middle English, from Medieval Latin, short for *famuli,* servants, word sung to this note in a hymn to Saint John the Baptist (see **gamut**), plural of Latin *famulus,* servant. See **family.**]

fah-fee, fa-fi (fáa-fée) *n.* In South Africa, an illegal gambling game popular among black city-dwellers. It is a form of roulette in which a bet is placed on any number 1 to 36, often chosen on the basis of dreams. [20th century : origin obscure.]

Fahr Fahrenheit.

Fahr·en·heit (fárrən-hīt; *German* fáarən-hīt) *adj. Abbr.* **F** or **Fahr** Of or pertaining to a temperature scale that registers the freezing point of water as 32° and the boiling point as 212° under standard atmospheric pressure. Fahrenheit temperatures are related to Celsius temperatures by the equation $F = 1.8C + 32$. [After Gabriel FAHRENHEIT.]

Fahrenheit, Gabriel Daniel (1686–1736). German physicist resident in Holland. He developed the use of mercury in thermometry and devised the temperature scale that bears his name.

fa·ience (fī-áanss, fay-; *French* fa-yónss) *n.* A kind of fine, glazed pottery, usually decorated with colourful glazes. [French, short for *(vaisselle de) Faïence,* "(vessel of) Faenza".]

fail (fayl) *v.* **failed, failing, fails.** —*intr.* 1. To prove deficient or lacking; perform ineffectively or inadequately. 2. To be unsuccessful in attempting to do or become something. 3. **a.** To receive a mark or grade, usually an academic grade, below the acceptable minimum. **b.** To fall below an acceptable standard. 4. To prove insufficient in quantity or duration; give out. 5. To decline in strength or effectiveness; wane; fade away. 6. To cease functioning properly. 7. To become bankrupt or insolvent. —*tr.* 1. To disappoint or prove undependable to: *Our sentries failed us.* 2. To abandon; forsake: *His strength failed him.* 3. To omit or neglect. Used with an infinitive: *The defendant failed to appear in court.* 4. **a.** To receive a mark or grade below the acceptable minimum in (a course, examination, or the like). **b.** To fall below an acceptable standard in (a test, for example). 5. **a.** To give a mark or grade of failure to (a student). **b.** To decide that (a candidate or student) has not reached an acceptable standard.

~*n.* A failure to reach an acceptable standard. —**without fail.** Certainly; definitely. [Middle English *failen, faillen,* from Old French *faillir,* from Vulgar Latin *fallīre* (unattested), from Latin *fallere†,* to deceive, disappoint, fail.]

fail·ing (fáyling) *n.* 1. The act of a person or thing that fails; a

failure. **2.** A minor fault or weakness; a shortcoming; a defect. —See Synonyms at **fault.**
~*prep.* In the absence of; unless there is: *Failing a rainstorm, the game will be played this afternoon.*
faille (fayl, fīl) *n.* A slightly ribbed, woven fabric of silk, cotton, or rayon. [French, from Old French *faille*†.]
fail-safe (fáyl-sayf) *adj.* **1.** Capable of compensating automatically for a failure. Said of a mechanical device. **2.** Capable of returning to a safe condition in the event of a malfunction. **3.** Acting to stop a military attack on the occurrence of any of a variety of predetermined conditions.
~*n.* A fail-safe mechanism.
fail·ure (fáyl-yər) *n.* **1.** The condition or fact of not achieving the desired end or ends: *the failure of an experiment.* **2. a.** One that fails. **b.** *Informal.* An unsuccessful or generally ineffectual person. **3.** The condition or fact of being insufficient or lacking; a falling short: *the failure of the sugar-cane harvest.* **4.** A cessation of proper functioning or performance: *an electric power failure.* **5.** Nonperformance of what is requested or expected; omission: *failure to report a change of address.* **6.** The act or fact of failing to pass a course, examination, or test, or to reach an acceptable standard. **7.** A decline in strength or effectiveness; a weakening. **8.** The act or fact of becoming bankrupt or insolvent. [Variant of earlier *failer,* from Anglo-French *failer,* from Old French *faillir,* to FAIL.]
fain (fayn) *adv. Archaic.* Preferably; gladly.
~*adj. Archaic.* **1.** Ready; willing. **2.** Obliged or required. [Middle English, from *fain,* joyful, happy, Old English *fægen.*]
fai·né·ant (fáy-ni-ənt, -nay-ON; *French* fennay-áaN) *adj.* Given to doing nothing; idle; lazy.
~*n.* An irresponsible idler. [French, folk etymological variant (influenced by *fait,* does + *néant,* nothing) of Old French *faignant,* idler, present participle of *faindre,* to be idle, FEIGN.]
fains (faynz) *interj.* Also **vains** (vaynz), **fai·nites** (fáy-nīts). *British Slang.* Used by children to claim exemption from doing something unpleasant, especially in the expression *fains* or *fains I,* which, if said before others can say it, is enough to exempt the speaker. [From FEND (in obsolete sense, "forbid".]
faint (faynt) *adj.* **fainter, faintest. 1.** Lacking strength or vigour; feeble. **2.** Lacking conviction, boldness, or courage; timid. **3.** Barely perceptible; indistinct; dim. **4.** Ready to fall into a faint; suddenly dizzy and weak.
~*n.* An abrupt, usually brief loss of consciousness, generally associated with failure of normal blood circulation.
~*intr.v.* **fainted, fainting, faints. 1.** To fall into a faint; swoon. **2.** *Archaic.* To weaken in purpose or spirit; languish. [Middle English *feint, faint,* faint, feigned, from Old French, past participles of *feindre, faindre,* FEIGN.] **—faint·er** *n.* **—faint·ly** *adv.* **—faint·ness** *n.*
faint·est (fáyntist) *n. Informal.* The least idea: *I haven't the faintest.*
faint·heart (fáynt-haart) *n.* A faint-hearted person; a coward. [Back-formation from FAINT-HEARTED.]
faint-heart·ed (fáynt-hártid) *adj.* Deficient in conviction or courage; cowardly; timid. **—faint·heart·ed·ly** *adv.* **—faint·heart·ed·ness** *n.*
faints. Variant of **feints.**
fair[1] (fair) *adj.* **fairer, fairest. 1.** Visually beautiful or admirable; lovely: *a fair maiden.* **2.** Of light colour, as: **a.** Blond: *fair hair.* **b.** Pale or white; not ruddy: *fair skin.* **3.** Clear and sunny; free of clouds or storms: *fair skies.* **4.** Free of blemishes; unstained; clean: *one's fair name.* **5.** Regular and even: *a fair edge.* **6.** Free of obstacles; open: *fair sailing.* **7.** Promising; likely; propitious: *in a fair way to succeed.* **8.** Free of favouritism or bias; impartial: *a fair judge.* **9.** Just to all parties; equitable: *a fair compromise.* **10.** Consistent with rules, standards, logic, or ethics: *a fair tactic.* **11.** Moderately good; mildly satisfying: *a fair job of redecorating.* **12.** Courteous; agreeable: *fair manners.* **13.** Superficially true or good; specious: *They coaxed us with fair words.* **14.** Favourable: *a fair wind for sailing.* **15.** *Informal.* **a.** Considerable: *a fair distance.* **b.** Real; out-and-out: *a fair old row.* **—fair do's.** Used as an interjection: **1.** To express acquiescence in a plan. **2.** To agree that some outcome or event is well deserved. **3.** Especially in indignation, to advocate fair play or equal shares. **—fair go.** *Australian & N.Z. Informal.* Used as an interjection: **1.** To express incredulity or surprise. **2.** To appeal for fair play. —See Synonyms at **average, beautiful.**
~*adv.* **1.** In a fair manner; correctly; properly: *playing fair.* **2.** Directly; squarely; straight: *a blow caught fair in the stomach.* **—fair and square.** Justly and honestly. **—look fair to.** To be likely to.
~*n. Archaic.* **1.** Loveliness; beauty. **2.** A person or thing that is fair; especially, a beautiful or beloved woman.
~*v.* **faired, fairing, fairs.** *—tr.* To make (timber, a surface, or a joint) smooth, even, or regular. *—intr. Regional.* To become cloudless or mild: *The weather should fair by morning.* [Middle English *fair, fager,* Old English *fæger,* from Germanic.] **—fair·ness** *n.*
Synonyms: *fair, just, equitable, impartial, unprejudiced, unbiased, straightforward, objective, dispassionate.*
fair[2] (fair) *n.* **1.** *Chiefly British.* An entertainment consisting of sideshows, roundabouts, dodgems, and the like, often travelling seasonally from place to place. Also called "funfair". **2.** A gathering held at a specified time and place for the buying and selling of goods; a market. **3. a.** An exhibition presented by representatives of a particular trade, in order to facilitate business. **b.** A large exhibition presented jointly by a number of nations, each of which maintains a public building containing educational, artistic, and trade exhibits: *a world fair.* **4.** An event, usually for the benefit of a charity or public institution, including entertainment and the sale of goods; a bazaar: *a church fair.* [Middle English *feire,* from Old French, from Late Latin *fēria,* from Latin *fēriæ,* holiday.]
Fair·banks (fáir-bangks). Town in central Alaska, on the River Chena. Once the scene of a gold rush in 1902, its mining now has little commercial value.
Fairbanks, Douglas, born Douglas Elton Ullman (1883–1939). U.S. silent screen actor doing swashbuckling heroics in romantic adventures. His films include *The Mark of Zorro* (1920), *The Three Musketeers* (1921), and *Robin Hood* (1922). His son, **Douglas Fairbanks Jnr.** (1909–), also a swashbuckling film adventurer, added a debonair quality to the Fairbanks tradition, as in *The Prisoner of Zenda* (1937) and *Sinbad the Sailor* (1947). Two autobiographical vols. (1988, 1993).
fair copy *n.* A copy of a document made after all corrections and revisions have been completed.
Fair·fax (fáir-faks), **Thomas, 3rd Baron Fairfax of Cameron** (1612–71). English general. He captured Leeds and Wakefield in 1643, and held a command at Marston Moor (1644). As commander in chief of Cromwell's New Model Army, he defeated Charles I at the Battle of Naseby (1645). Fairfax opposed the king's execution and resigned his command in 1650.
fair game *n.* **1.** Game, such as deer or pheasant, that it is lawful to pursue and kill. **2.** Something deserving criticism or ridicule; something that it is legitimate to attack.
fair·ground (fáir-grownd) *n.* An open space where fairs are held.
fair·ing[1] (fáir-ing) *n.* An auxiliary structure or the external surface of an aircraft, car, or vessel serving to reduce drag. [From FAIR (to make smooth).]
fairing[2] *n. British.* A gift, especially one bought or given at a fair.
fair·ish (fáir-ish) *adj.* **1.** Moderately fair. **2.** Of moderately good size or quality.
fair isle *n.* **1.** A knitting technique of working yarns of many different colours in stocking stitch to produce complicated geometrical designs, such as those that originated in Fair Isle in the Shetlands. **2. a.** The multicoloured pattern formed by this technique. **b.** Material or garments worked in fair isle. **—fair-isle** *adj.*
Fair Isle (fáir īl). The southernmost of the Shetland Islands, Scotland. It is known for its knitted woollen garments with distinctive coloured patterns and for its bird sanctuary.
fair-lead (fáir-leed) *n.* Also **fair-lead·er** (-leedər). *Nautical.* A device such as a ring or block of wood with a hole in it, through which rigging is passed to hold it in place or prevent it from snagging or chafing.
fair·ly (fáirli) *adv.* **1. a.** In a fair or just manner; equitably. **b.** Legitimately; suitably. **2.** Actually; completely; fully: *The walls fairly shook with his bellowing.* **3.** Moderately; rather: *a fairly good dinner.* **4.** *Archaic.* Clearly; distinctly.
fair-mind·ed (fáir-mīndid, -mīndid) *adj.* Just and impartial in judgment; unprejudiced. **—fair-mind·ed·ness** *n.*
fair play *n.* Conformance to the established rules or ethics of a sport, business, or other activity.
fair sex *n.* Women collectively. Preceded by *the.*
fair-spo·ken (fáir-spṓkən, -spōkən) *adj.* Civil, courteous, and gentle in speech.
fair·way (fáir-way) *n.* **1.** A stretch of ground free of obstacles to movement. **2.** The part of a golf course covered with short grass and extending from the tee to the putting green. **3.** *Nautical.* **a.** A navigable deep-water channel in a river, harbour, or along a coastline. **b.** The usual course taken by vessels through a harbour or coastal waters.
fair-weath·er (fáir-wethər) *adj.* **1.** Suitable or used only during fair weather. **2.** Only engaging in an activity during good weather. Used derogatorily: *fair-weather cyclists.* **3.** Present and dependable only in good times; failing in times of trouble: *fair-weather friends.*
fair·y (fáir-i) *n., pl.* **-ies. 1.** A tiny supernatural being in human form, typically female and depicted as clever, mischievous, and capable of assisting or harassing humans. **2.** *Slang.* A male homosexual. Used derogatorily: *fair-weather cyclists.* **3.** Present and dependable only in good times; failing in times of trouble: *fair-weather friends.*
~*adj.* **1.** Of or associated with fairies. **2.** Resembling a fairy; fanciful, graceful, or delicate. [Middle English *fairie,* from Old French *faerie, faierie,* enchantment, from *fae,* fairy, from Latin *fāta,* the Fates, plural of *fātum,* FATE.]
fairy cycle *n. British.* A child's bicycle with very small wheels, usually with two outriders attached to the back wheel for support.
fair·y·floss (fáir-i-floss) *n. Australian.* **Candyfloss** *(see).*
fairy godmother *n.* A benefactress, or sometimes benefactor; especially, one who appears unexpectedly to help in a crisis. [After such characters in well-known tales like *Cinderella.*]
fairy gold *n.* **1.** In fairy tales, a gift or theft of gold from fairyland, which turns to dust before the eyes or overnight. **2.** Anything likened to this in elusiveness; a disappointing illusion.
fair·y·land (fáir-i-land) *n.* **1.** The imaginary land of the fairies. **2.** Any charming, enchanting place; a wonderland.
fairy lights *pl.n. Chiefly British.* Small coloured lights used for decoration, as on Christmas trees or in window displays.
fairy ring *n.* A circle of darker luxuriant grass corresponding to an area of underground mycelial growth, the periphery of which is seasonally marked by an overground growth of mushrooms. [The circle is superstitiously believed to be produced by dancing fairies.]
fairy shrimp *n.* Any of various transparent freshwater crustaceans

of the order Anostraca that characteristically swim on their backs.
fairy tale *n.* **1.** A story about fairies. **2.** A fanciful tale of legendary deeds and romance, usually intended to please children. **3.** A fictitious, highly fanciful story or explanation.
fair·y-tale (fáir-i-tayl) *adj.* Suitable for or like a fairy tale; especially, so delightful as to be like a fantasy: *a fairy-tale wedding.*
Fai·sal (fī́-səl || fáy-), **Ibn Abdul Aziz al Saud** (1905–75). King of Saudi Arabia. He succeeded to the throne on the abdication of his brother King Saud in 1964. During his reign, government oil profits were used to increase industrialisation, education, and health in Saudi Arabia. He was assassinated by his nephew.
fait ac·com·pli (fáytə-kóm-plee, féttə-, -kóɴ-, -plée) *n., pl.* **faits accomplis** (*pronounced as singular*). An accomplished and presumably irreversible deed or fact. [French, "accomplished fact".]
faith (fayth) *n.* **1. a.** A confident belief in the truth, value, or trustworthiness of a person, idea, or thing. **b.** Reliance; trust. **2.** Belief that does not rest on logical proof or material evidence: *faith in miracles.* **3.** Loyalty to a person or thing; allegiance: *keeping faith with one's supporters.* **4.** Belief and trust in God and in the doctrines expressed in the Scriptures or other sacred works; religious conviction. **5.** A system of religious beliefs: *the Muslim faith.* **6.** Any set of principles or beliefs. —See Synonyms at **trust.** [Middle English *feith, feth,* from Old French *feid, feit,* from Latin *fidēs.*]
faith cure *n.* A cure of an ailment held to be accomplished through religious faith.
faith·ful (fáyth-f'l) *adj.* **1.** Adhering strictly to the person, cause, or idea to which one is bound; dutiful and loyal. **2.** Worthy of trust or credence; consistently reliable: *a faithful guide.* **3.** Consistent with truth or actuality; accurate; exact: *a faithful reproduction.* **4.** Not having sexual relations with anyone other than one's spouse or lover. **—the faithful. 1.** The practising members of a religious faith, especially of Christianity or Islam. **2.** The steadfast adherents of any faith or cause. **—faith·ful·ly** *adv.* **—faith·ful·ness** *n.*
Synonyms: *faithful, loyal, true, constant, steadfast, staunch, devoted, dependable.*
faith healer *n.* One who attempts to effect faith cures; one who tries to heal by prayer and religious faith.
faith·less (fáyth-liss) *adj.* **1.** Untrue to duty or obligation; breaking faith; disloyal. **2.** Lacking confidence or trust in a given person or cause. **3. a.** Without religious faith. **b.** Without faith in Christianity; heathen. **4.** Unworthy of faith or trust; unreliable. **—faith·less·ly** *adv.* **—faith·less·ness** *n.*
Synonyms: *faithless, unfaithful, false, disloyal, traitorous, perfidious, inconstant, fickle, undependable.*
fake[1] (fayk) *adj.* **1.** Having a false or misleading appearance; fraudulent. **2.** Counterfeit: *a fake Rubens.*
∼*n.* A person, act, or thing that is not genuine or authentic; a sham; a counterfeit.
∼*v.* **faked, faking, fakes.** *—tr.* **1.** To contrive and present as genuine; counterfeit. **2.** To simulate; pretend; feign. *—intr.* To engage in faking. —See Synonyms at **pretend.** [19th century (thieves' slang) : from obsolete *feak,* to beat, from German *fezen,* to polish, beat, rebuke.]
fake[2] (fayk) *n. Nautical.* One loop of a coiled rope or cable.
∼*tr.v.* **faked, faking, fakes.** *Nautical.* To coil (a rope or cable). [Middle English *faken*†.]
fak·er (fáykər) *n.* **1.** A person who fakes or who produces fakes. **2.** *Chiefly U.S.* One who practises fraud; a swindler. **—fak·er·y** *n.*
fa·kir (fáy-keer, faá-, fáckeer, fə-kéer, fáykər) *n.* Also **fa·keer** (fə-kéer). **1.** A Muslim religious mendicant. **2.** A Hindu ascetic or religious mendicant; especially, one who performs feats of magic or endurance. [Arabic *faqīr,* from *faqura,* he was poor.]
falafel. Variant of **felafel.**
Fa·laise (fa-láyz, fə-, -léz). Market town in Normandy, northern France, and birthplace of William the Conqueror. In the Normandy campaign of 1944 the British captured Falaise, thus opening the way for the Allied armies to liberate northern France.
Fa·lange (fál-anj, fə-lánj || fáy-; *Spanish* fa-lánkhay) *n.* A fascist organisation constituting the official ruling party of Spain under General Franco. [Spanish, from *falange,* phalanx, from Latin *phalanx* (stem *phalang-*), PHALANX.] **—Fa·lan·gist** (fə-lánjist) *n.*
fal·ba·la (fál-bələ) *n.* A flounce, frill, or ruffle. [18th century : French, from dialectal *ferbelà*†, akin to FURBELOW.]
fal·cate (fál-kayt || fáwl-) *adj.* Also **fal·ca·ted** (-kaytid, fal-káytid). *Biology.* Curved and tapering to a point at either end; sickle-shaped. [Latin *falcātus,* from *falx*† (stem *falc-*), sickle.]
fal·chion (fáwl-chən, -shən) *n.* **1.** A short, broad sword with a convex cutting edge and a sharp point, used in medieval times. **2.** *Archaic.* Any sword. [Middle English *fauchoun,* from Old French *fauchon,* from Vulgar Latin *falciō* (stem *falciōn-*) (unattested), from Latin *falx* (stem *falc-*), sickle.]
fal·ci·form (fál-si-fawrm) *adj.* Curved or sickle-shaped; falcate. [Latin *falx* (stem *falc-*), sickle (see **falcate**) + -FORM.]
fal·con (fáwl-kən, fáw-, fól- || fál-) *n.* **1. a.** Any of various birds of prey of the family Falconidae, and especially of the genus *Falco,* having long, pointed, powerful wings adapted for swift flight. **b.** Any of several species of these birds or related birds such as hawks, trained to hunt small game. **c.** In falconry, a female bird of this type. **2.** A small cannon of the 15th to 17th century. [Middle English *faucoun,* from Old French *faucon,* from Late Latin *falcō* (stem *falcōn-*).]
fal·con·er (fáwl-kə-nər, fáw-, fól- || fál-) *n.* **1.** A person who breeds and trains falcons. **2.** One who hunts with falcons.
fal·co·net (fáwl-kə-net, fáw-, fól- || fál-) *n.* **1.** A small or young falcon. **2.** Any of several small falcons of the genus *Microhierax,* chiefly of tropical Asia.
fal·con·gen·tle (fáwl-kən-jént'l, fáw-, fól- || fál-) *n.* A female falcon, especially a peregrine falcon. [Middle English *faucoun gentil,* from Old French *faucon gentil,* "noble falcon" : *faucon,* FALCON + *gentil,* noble (see **gentle**).]
fal·con·ry (fáwl-kənri, fáw-, fól- || fál-) *n.* **1.** The sport of hunting with falcons. **2.** The art of training falcons for hunting.
falderal, falderol. Variants of **folderol.**
Fal·do (fál-dō), **Nicholas (Alexander),** known as Nick Faldo (1957–). English golfer. He won the British Open in 1987, 1990, and 1992 and the U.S. Masters in 1989, 1990, and 1996.
fald·stool (fáwld-stōōl, fōld-) *n.* **1.** A small, usually cushioned stool at which worshippers kneel to pray; especially, one on which the British sovereign kneels at the coronation. **2.** A portable, backless chair or stool used by a bishop when not occupying his throne or when presiding away from his own cathedral. **3.** *Anglican Church.* A desk at which the litany is recited. [Partial translation of Medieval Latin *faldistolium,* folding stool, from Germanic.]
Falk·land Islands (fáwl-klənd, fáw-, fól-). *Spanish* **Is·las Mal·vi·nas** (éezlass malvéenass). Group of 202 small islands about 480 kilometres (300 miles) east of the Strait of Magellan in the South Atlantic Ocean. The two largest islands are East Falkland and West Falkland. The capital is Stanley (also called Port Stanley). The islands have been a British crown colony since 1833, but are claimed by Argentina, and in 1982 Argentine forces seized the islands, only to be expelled by British forces. Until 1985 the colony included the dependencies of South Georgia, 1 290 kilometres (800 miles) southeast of East Falkland, and the South Sandwich Islands, 760 kilometres (470 miles) southeast of South Georgia. They now form a separate British Overseas Territory. See map at **Argentina.**
Falkland Islands Dependencies. See **Falkland Islands.**
fall (fawl) *v.* **fell** (fel), **fallen** (fáwlən), **falling, falls.** *—intr.* **1.** To move under the influence of gravity; especially, to drop without restraint. **2.** To drop oneself from an erect to a less erect position: *He stumbled and fell.* **3.** To be severely wounded or to be killed in battle. **4.** To collapse from lack of structural support: *Several buildings fell during the earthquake.* **5.** To come to rest; strike bottom; land: *The aircraft fell in an uninhabited region.* **6.** To hang down: *Her hair fell in ringlets.* **7.** To be cast down; be averted: *Her eyes fell.* **8.** To assume an expression of disappointment: *Her face fell when she heard the report.* **9.** To be conquered or seized: *The city fell after a long siege.* **10.** To lose power; be defeated or overthrown: *During periods of crisis, governments may fall.* **11.** To follow a downward direction; slope: *The plain falls gently towards the coast.* **12.** To undergo a reduction in amount, degree, or value; diminish: *The air pressure is falling.* **13.** To diminish in pitch or volume: *His voice fell to a whisper.* **14.** To decline in rank, status, or importance. **15.** To yield to temptation; err or sin. **16.** To pass into a specified condition: *the crowd fell silent.* **17.** To arrive and pervade: *A hush fell on the crowd.* **18.** To occur at a specified time: *Christmas falls on a Tuesday this year.* **19.** To occur at a specified place: *The stress falls on the last syllable.* **20.** To come or be allotted, by chance or distribution: *The greatest task fell to him.* **21.** To be given, by right or stipulation: *The estate fell to the eldest surviving son.* **22.** To divide naturally. Used with *into: The specimens fall into three categories.* **23.** To be directed; come to rest: *His gaze fell on a small book in the corner.* **24.** To be uttered as if involuntarily; slip out: *A murmur of impatience fell from his lips.* **25.** To be born. Used chiefly of lambs. **26.** *British Regional.* To become pregnant. **27.** In cricket: **a.** To be dismissed. Used of a batsman or team. **b.** To be taken. Said of a wicket. *—tr.* To cut down (a tree); fell. **—fall about. 1.** To move around uncontrollably. **2.** *Informal.* To lose control of oneself with laughing. **—fall among.** To come casually into the company of. **—fall away. 1.** To decline; languish; weaken. **2.** To withdraw friendship or support; part company. **3.** To slope downwards. **—fall back. 1.** To give ground; recede; retreat. **2.** To move backwards. **—fall back on** or **upon. 1.** To retreat to. **2.** To resort to. **—fall behind. 1.** To lag behind; fail to keep up with. **2.** To be in arrears. **3.** To move behind. **—fall down.** *Informal.* To prove unsuccessful; fail or lag in performance. **—fall flat.** *Informal.* To fail completely to achieve the intended effect. **—fall for.** *Informal.* **1.** To become infatuated with; fall suddenly in love with. **2.** To be tricked or deceived by. **—fall foul** or **afoul.** *Nautical.* **1.** To collide. Used of vessels. **2.** *Nautical.* To become entangled. Used of rigging. **—fall foul of.** To incur the displeasure of; come into conflict with. **—fall in.** *Military.* To take one's place in a formation; form ranks. **—fall in with. 1.** To agree. **2.** To meet by chance; join. **—fall on** or **upon.** To attack suddenly; ambush. **—fall over backwards.** To put oneself to great trouble. **—fall short. 1.** To fail to attain a specified amount, level, or degree. **2.** To prove inadequate or lacking. **—fall through. 1.** To fail; collapse; miscarry. **2.** To fail to occur. **—fall to. 1.** To begin (a physical activity) energetically. **2.** To shut or move into place unaided. **—fall under. 1.** To occur in the class of; be listed or located within. **2.** To succumb to; come under the influence or power of.
∼*n.* **1.** The act or an instance of falling; a dropping down; a free descent. **2.** A sudden drop from a relatively erect to a less erect position: *He had a bad fall.* **3.** That which has fallen: *The field was covered with a fall of hail.* **4. a.** The amount of what has fallen: *a fall of two inches of rain.* **b.** The distance that something falls: *a fall of three storeys.* **5.** *Often capital* **F.** *U.S.* Autumn. **6.** *Often plural.* A

waterfall; a cascade. **7.** A downward movement or slope: *the fall of a river towards its mouth.* **8.** Any of several hanging articles of dress, especially: **a.** A veil hung from a woman's hat and down her back. **b.** An ornamental cascade of lace or trimming attached to a dress, usually at the collar. **c.** A woman's hairpiece with long, free-hanging hair. **9.** A capture, overthrow, or collapse: *the fall of a government.* **10.** A reduction in value, amount, or degree. **11.** A decline in status, rank, or importance. **12.** A loss of virtue or moral innocence; a yielding to sin. **13.** *Capital* F. *Theology.* Adam's sin of disobeying God by eating the forbidden fruit in the Garden of Eden, and the consequent loss of innocence and grace of all his descendants. Preceded by *the.* **14.** In wrestling: **a.** The act of throwing or forcing an opponent down on his back. **b.** Any of various manoeuvres used for this. **15.** *Nautical.* A break or rise in the level of a deck. **16.** *Plural. Nautical.* The apparatus used to hoist and transfer cargo or lifeboats. **17.** The end of a cable, rope, or chain that is pulled by the power source in hoisting. **18. a.** The birth of an animal; especially, the birth of a lamb. **b.** All of the animals born at one birth; a litter. —**ride for a fall.** To court danger or disaster. [Fall, fell, fallen; Middle English *fallen, fell, fallen,* Old English *feallan, fēol, feallan,* from Germanic *fallan* (unattested).]

Fal·la (fál-yə, fáa-, -yaa), **Manuel de** (1876–1946). Spanish composer and pianist. He was influenced by Debussy and Ravel and blended elements of their music with his own ebullient style, as in *Nights in the Gardens of Spain* (1916). His music later became starker, as in the ballet for Diaghilev, *The Three-Cornered Hat* (1919).

fal·la·cious (fə-láyshəss) *adj.* **1.** Containing or based on a fallacy: *a fallacious syllogism.* **2.** Deceptive in appearance or meaning; misleading: *fallacious evidence.* **3.** Not real or sound; delusive: *fallacious signs of a change in the weather.* —**fal·la·cious·ly** *adv.* —**fal·la·cious·ness** *n.*

fal·la·cy (fál-ə-si) *n., pl.* **-cies. 1.** An idea or opinion founded on mistaken logic or perception; a false notion. **2.** An argument or thesis that is inconsistent with logic or fact and thus renders the conclusion invalid. **3.** The quality of being in error; incorrectness of reasoning or belief. **4.** The quality of being deceptive. [Latin *fallācia,* deceit, trick, from *fallāx* (stem *fallāc-*), deceitful, from *fallere,* to deceive. See **fail.**]

fal·lal (fa-lál, fal-) *n. Usually plural.* A trifling, showy article of dress; a piece of finery; frippery.

~*adj. Archaic.* Affected; foppish. [18th century : perhaps akin to FALBALA.]

fallen arch *n.* A collapse of the normally arch-shaped instep of the foot that results in a flat foot.

fallen woman *n. Chiefly Archaic.* **1.** A woman considered as sexually impure or degraded. **2.** A prostitute. Used euphemistically.

fall guy *n. Chiefly U.S. Slang.* **1.** One who takes the responsibility or blame, as for another's dereliction or delinquency; a scapegoat. **2.** An easy victim, as of a confidence trick.

fal·li·ble (fál-ib'l) *adj.* **1.** Capable of erring. **2.** Tending or likely to err. [Middle English, from Medieval Latin *fallibilis,* from Latin *fallere,* to deceive. See **fail.**] —**fal·li·bil·i·ty** (-i-bíllǝti), **fal·li·ble·ness** *n.* —**fal·li·bly** *adv.*

falling band *n.* A wide collar of linen or lace turned down over the shoulders, worn during the 17th century.

fall·ing-out (fáwling-ówt) *n., pl.* **fallings-out** or **falling-outs.** A personal disagreement that has resulted in a broken or more distant relationship; an estrangement; a breach.

falling sickness *n.* **Epilepsy** (*see*). Not in technical usage.

falling star *n.* Any object, such as a meteoroid, rendered visible as a bright streak in the sky by falling and being ignited by atmospheric friction.

fall line *n.* **1.** *Geography.* An imaginary line marking a drop in land level or height, formulated by connecting the waterfalls of nearly parallel rivers. **2.** *Capital* F, *capital* L. In the United States, the line between the Piedmont Plateau and the Atlantic coastal plain. **3.** In skiing, the natural line of descent between two points on a slope.

fall off *intr.v.* **1.** To lessen in intensity, volume, number, or the like: *ticket sales are falling off.* **2.** *Nautical.* To change course to leeward.

fall-off (fáwl-off, -awf) *n.* A decline or decrease: *a falloff in sales.*

Fal·lo·pi·an tube (fə-lṓpi-ən, fa-) *n.* Either of a pair of slender ducts, along which eggs pass from the ovaries to the womb in the female reproductive system of humans and other mammals. Also called "oviduct". [After Gabriel FALLOPIUS.]

Fal·lo·pi·us (fə-lṓpi-əss, fa-), **Gabriel** (1523–62). Also **Fal·lo·pi·o** (fə-lṓpi-ō). Italian anatomist who discovered the tubes that connect the ovaries with the uterus in females, the Fallopian tubes.

fall out *intr.v.* **1.** *Military.* To leave ranks; withdraw from formation. **2.** To quarrel; become estranged. **3.** To happen; occur.

fall·out (fáwl-owt) *n.* **1. a.** The slow descent of minute particles of radioactive debris in the atmosphere following a nuclear explosion or accident in which radioactive material escapes into the atmosphere. **b.** The particles so descending. **c.** Such particles collectively. **2.** Any incidental results or side effects: *the technological fallout of the space programme; political fallout.*

fal·low¹ (fál-ō) *adj.* **1. a.** Ploughed and tilled but left unseeded during a growing season: *a fallow field.* **b.** Loosely, uncultivated. Said of land. **2. a.** Not pregnant: *a fallow mare.* **b.** Marked by the absence of pregnancy. —**lie fallow.** To go unexercised or unrealised.

~*n.* **1.** Land that has been ploughed but left unseeded during a growing season. **2.** The process of leaving ploughed land unseeded during a growing season.

~*tr.v.* **fallowed, -lowing, -lows. 1.** To make (land) fallow by ploughing. **2.** To plough (land) by way of preparing it for sowing. [Middle English *falow, falwe,* Old English *fealh†,* arable land.] —**fal·low·ness** *n.*

fal·low² *adj.* Light reddish-yellow or yellowish-brown in colour. [Middle English, from Old English *fealu,* from Germanic; akin to Latin *pallidus,* PALE.]

fallow crop *n.* A crop which tends to nourish soil and is rotated with a more demanding crop to maintain productivity of the soil.

fallow deer *n.* Either of two Eurasian deer, *Dama dama* or *D. mesopotamica,* having a yellowish-red coat spotted with white in summer, and broad, flattened antlers in the male. [From obsolete *fallow,* reddish-yellow, from Middle English *falwe,* sallow, Old English *fealu.*]

false (fawlss, folss) *adj.* **falser, falsest. 1.** Contrary to fact or truth; without grounds; incorrect. **2.** Fallacious; specious: *false logic.* **3.** Untruthful. **4. a.** Without meaning or sincerity; deceiving; sham: *false promises.* **b.** Misplaced and unjustified: *false modesty.* **c.** Deceptive; belying appearances: *a false start.* **5.** Not keeping faith; treacherous: *a false lover.* **6.** Not real or natural; artificial; synthetic: *false fur.* **7.** Supplementary to or temporarily substitute for. **8.** Resembling but not accurately or properly designated as such. Often used in plant names: *false helleborine.* **9.** *Music.* Of incorrect pitch. —See Synonyms at **faithless.** —**play (someone) false.** To betray. [Middle English *fals,* from Old French, from Latin *falsus,* past participle of *fallere,* to deceive. See **fail.**] —**false·ly** *adv.* —**false·ness** *n.*

false acacia *n.* A North American tree, *Robinia pseudoacacia,* having compound leaves, drooping clusters of fragrant white flowers, and hard, durable wood. Also called "robinia", *U.S.* "locust".

false alarm *n.* **1.** A spurious emergency alarm, whether accidental or intentional; especially, a fire alarm where no fire exists. **2.** *Informal.* Any seeming crisis, signal, or warning that is groundless or abortive.

false arrest *n. Law.* An unlawful or unjustifiable arrest.

false bottom *n.* **1.** A partition that seems to be the bottom of a trunk, case, chest, or other receptacle but under which is another compartment. **2.** A base, as of a glass or bowl, which by its shape gives a false idea of the capacity of the vessel.

false brome *n.* Either of two grasses, *Brachypodium sylvaticum* or *B. pinnatum,* having long awns like the true brome grasses.

false colours *pl.n.* **1.** The flag or symbol of another country when used for deception, as by pirates on the high seas. **2.** Misleading representation; pretence.

false dawn *n.* **1.** Faint light observed low in the sky before dawn, caused by **zodiacal light** (*see*). **2.** An apparent arrival or advent that turns out to be short-lived and premature.

false friend *n.* A word in another language that is identical or almost identical to a word in one's own, but which has a quite different meaning; for example, the French word *trombone,* meaning a paperclip as well as a trombone.

false fruit *n.* A **pseudocarp** (*see*).

false-heart·ed (fáwlss-hártid, fólss-) *adj.* Having a deceitful nature; disloyal; treacherous.

false·hood (fáwlss-hood, fólss-, -ŏŏd) *n.* **1.** Contradiction to or disparity with truth or fact; that which is groundless or specious; an inaccuracy. **2.** The act of deceiving; lying. **3.** An untrue statement; a deception; a lie.

false imprisonment *n. Law.* Unlawful arrest or detention of a person, such as that enforced without a warrant or with an illegal one.

false keel *n.* A protective strip fixed below a ship's main keel.

false position *n.* **1.** A situation in which a person's action or motives, however good or well-intentioned, will be misconstrued or seen as wrong. **2.** A situation in which a person will be forced to act against his principles.

false pretences *pl.n.* Any misrepresentation of fact or deception for an ulterior motive.

false rib *n.* In human beings, any of the ten lower ribs that do not unite directly with the sternum.

false step *n.* **1.** A slip; a stumble. **2.** A social blunder; a faux pas.

false teeth *pl.n.* Artificial teeth for one or both jaws.

fal·set·to (fawl-séttō, fol-) *n., pl.* **-tos.** A singing voice, typically male, when artificially producing notes in an upper register beyond its normal range.

~*adj.* Having the quality of falsetto: *a falsetto tone.*

~*adv.* In falsetto. [Italian, diminutive of *falso,* false, from Latin *falsus,* FALSE.]

false·work (fáwlss-wurk, fólss-) *n.* A temporary supporting framework for a structure during construction or demolition.

fals·ies (fáwl-siz, fól-) *pl.n. Informal.* **1.** Pads or padding worn inside, or as part of, a brassiere to exaggerate the dimensions of the breasts. **2.** False breasts.

fal·si·fy (fáwl-si-fī, fól-) *v.* **-fied, -fying, -fies.** —*tr.* **1.** To state untruthfully; misrepresent. **2.** To alter (a document) in order to deceive. **3.** To counterfeit; forge. **4.** *Philosophy.* To show to be false. —*intr.* To make untrue statements; lie. [Middle English *falsifien,* from Old French *falsifier,* from Medieval Latin *falsificāre* : Latin *falsus,* FALSE + *facere,* to make.] —**fal·si·fi·a·ble** (-fī-əb'l, -fī-) *adj.* —**fal·si·fi·ca·tion** (-fi-káysh'n) *n.* —**fal·si·fi·er** *n.*

fal·si·ty (fáwl-səti, fól-) *n., pl.* **-ties. 1.** The condition of being false. **2.** Something false; an untruth; a lie or falsehood.

Fal·staff·i·an (fawl-stáafi-ən, fol-, -stáffi-) *adj.* Resembling or characteristic of Falstaff, a fat, merry, ribald, and boastful knight in Shakespeare's *Henry IV*: *Parts I and II*, *Henry V*, and *The Merry Wives of Windsor*.

falt·boat (fált-bōt, fáalt-, fáwlt-) *n.* A small boat consisting of canvas stretched over a collapsible frame and resembling a kayak. Also called "foldboat". [Partial translation of German *Faltboot*, folding boat, from *falten*, to fold, from Old High German *falden*.]

fal·ter (fáwl-tər || fól-) *intr.v.* **-tered, -tering, -ters.** **1.** To waver in confidence; hesitate. **2.** To speak hesitatingly; stammer. **3.** To move ineptly or haltingly; stumble; stagger. **b.** To operate uncertainly; fail mechanically. —See Synonyms at **hesitate.**
~*n.* **1.** An unsteadiness in speech or action. **2.** A faltering sound. [Middle English *falteren*†.] **—fal·ter·ing·ly** *adv.*

fam. **1.** familiar. **2.** family.

F.A.M. Free and Accepted Masons.

Fa·ma·gus·ta (fámmə-gŏostə, fáamə-). Port on Famagusta Bay on the eastern coast of Cyprus. It is an ancient fishing and trading town, with remains of medieval walls.

fame (faym) *n.* **1.** Great reputation and recognition, usually favourable; public esteem; renown. **2.** Reputation. **3.** *Archaic.* Rumour.
~*tr.v.* **famed, faming, fames.** *Archaic.* To make famous by talking of. [Middle English, from Old French, from Latin *fāma*, talk, reputation.]
Synonyms: *fame, renown, glory, eminence, repute, notoriety.*

famed (faymd) *adj.* Having great fame; publicly acclaimed; celebrated; famous.

fa·mil·ial (fə-mílli-əl, -míl-yəl) *adj.* **1.** Of or pertaining to a family. **2.** *Genetics.* Passed on in a family; hereditary: *a familial trait.*

fa·mil·iar (fə-mílli-ər, -míl-yər) *adj. Abbr.* **fam.** **1.** Of frequent instance or occurrence; often encountered; common: *a familiar sight.* **2.** Having fair knowledge of something; acquainted. Used with *with*: *familiar with those roads.* **3.** Of established friendship; close; intimate: *be on familiar terms.* **4.** Natural and unstudied; informal: *He lectured in a familiar style.* **5.** Presuming upon acquaintance; taking liberties. **6.** *Archaic.* Familial. —See Synonyms at **common.**
~*n.* **1.** A close friend or associate. **2.** A spirit, often taking animal form, thought to attend a witch or wizard. **3.** *Roman Catholic Church.* One who performs domestic service in the household of a bishop. [Middle English, familial, from Old French *familier*, from Latin *familiāris*, from *familia*, FAMILY.] **—fa·mil·iar·ly** *adv.*
Synonyms: *familiar, close, intimate, fraternal, matey, chummy.*

fa·mil·iar·ise, fa·mil·iar·ize (fə-míl-yə-rīz) *tr.v.* **-ised, -ising, -ises.** **1.** To make generally known, recognised, or familiar; popularise. **2.** To make (oneself or another) acquainted with. **—fa·mil·iar·i·sa·tion** (-rī-záysh'n || *U.S.* -ri-) *n.* **—fa·mil·iar·is·er** *n.*

fa·mil·i·ar·i·ty (fə-mílli-árrəti) *n., pl.* **-ties.** **1.** Substantial or reasonable acquaintance with something; moderate understanding; knowledge. Used with *with*. **2.** Established friendship; candour; intimacy. **3.** Presumption; undue liberty; boldness. **4.** *Often plural.* Actions or behaviour presuming intimacy, especially sexual advances; liberties.

fam·i·ly (fámili, fámmli) *n., pl.* **-lies.** *Abbr.* **fam.** **1. a.** The most instinctive, fundamental social or mating group in man and animal. **b.** The union of man and woman, especially through marriage, and their offspring; parents and their children. **2. a.** One's spouse and children. **b.** One's children. **c.** One's parents and siblings. **3.** Persons related by blood or marriage; relatives; kin. **4.** Lineage; especially, upper-class lineage. **5.** All the members of a household; those who share one's domestic home. **6. a.** A group of like things; a class. **b.** A special or particular world of something; a kingdom; a fellowship: *the family of man.* **7.** *Biology.* A taxonomic category ranking below an order and above a genus. **8.** *Linguistics.* A language group derived from the same parent language. **9.** *Chiefly U.S.* A locally independent unit of the Mafia. **10.** A set of related curves or surfaces that are given by different values of a constant in a single equation. For example, different values of r in the equation $x^2 + y^2 = r^2$ generate a family of concentric circles.
~*adj.* **1.** Pertaining to family: *a family reunion.* **2.** Suitable for children and their parents: *a family show.* **—in the family way.** *Informal.* Pregnant. [Middle English *familie*, from Latin *familia*, family, household, servants of a household, from *famulus*†, servant.]

family allowance *n.* **Child benefit** *(see).*

family butcher *n. British.* A retail butcher's shop that either is run by the members of a single family, or sells to local families, or both.

Family Division *n. British law.* The High Court division that deals with divorce, custody and access to children, adoption, and the like.

family doctor *n.* A **general practitioner** *(see).*

family man *n.* **1.** A man who is devoted to his family, especially his wife and children, and who enjoys domestic life. **2.** A man who has a wife and children.

family name *n.* **1. a.** A surname. **b.** A surname considered as standing for the whole family and its honour. **2.** A first or middle name, often a former surname, given to many members of a family.

family planning *n.* **1.** The regulation of the number of children conceived and the intervals between them by some means of contraception. **2.** Contraception. **—family-planning** *adj.*

family tree *n.* **1.** A genealogical diagram of a family. **2.** The ancestors and descendants collectively of a family.

fam·ine (fámmin) *n.* **1.** A drastic and wide-reaching shortage of food. **2.** A drastic shortage of anything; a dearth. **3.** *Archaic.* Severe hunger; starvation. **4.** Extreme appetite, as of a starving person. [Middle English *famine*, from Old French, from Vulgar Latin *famina* (unattested), from Latin *fames*†, hunger.]

fam·ish (fámmish) *v.* **-ished, -ishing, -ishes.** *Archaic.* —*tr.* **1.** To cause to endure severe hunger; starve. **2.** To cause to die from hunger; starve to death. —*intr.* **1.** To endure severe hunger; starve. **2.** To die from hunger; starve to death. [Middle English *famishen*, extended form of *famen*, from Old French *afamer*, from Vulgar Latin *affamāre* (unattested) : Latin *ad-*, towards + *fames*†, hunger.] **—fam·ish·ment** *n.*

fam·ished (fámmisht) *adj.* Extremely hungry; starving.

fa·mous (fáyməss) *adj.* **1.** Generally recorded in history or currently renowned; publicly acclaimed; celebrated. **2.** *Informal.* First-rate; excellent. **3.** *Archaic.* Infamous; notorious. [Middle English, from Old French *fameus*, from Latin *famōsus*, from *fāma*, FAME.] **—fa·mous·ly** *adv.* **—fa·mous·ness** *n.*

fam·u·lus (fámmew-ləss) *n., pl.* **-li** (-lī, -lee). An attendant or servant, especially of a medieval magician or scholar. [German *Famulus*, from Latin *famulus*†, servant.]

fan¹ (fan) *n.* **1.** A hand-waved implement for creating a current of air or a breeze; especially, one in the form of a flat, fixed or collapsible device, usually round or approximately semicircular, and made of a light material such as silk, paper, or fine ivory. **2.** Anything resembling a fan, especially in being shaped like a semicircle or segment of a circle, such as an arrangement of seats in an auditorium. **3.** Any device for creating air movement, such as: **a.** An array of thin, rigid blades attached to a central hub. **b.** A machine that rotates one or more such arrays on electrically powered shafts in order to move air, as for cooling or to exhaust an enclosure. **4.** A machine that throws grain and chaff into the air so that the latter will be blown away. **5.** A small rudder-like vane which keeps the sails of a windmill at right angles to the wind.
~*v.* **fanned, fanning, fans.** —*tr.* **1.** To cause a current of or move (air) with or as if with a fan. **2.** To direct a current of air or a breeze upon, especially in order to cool: *fan one's face.* **3.** To stir up; activate: *fan resentment.* **4.** To open out (a hand of cards, for example) to a fan shape. **5. a.** To fire (an automatic gun) in a continuous sweep while keeping one's finger on the trigger. **b.** To fire (a nonautomatic gun) rapidly by chopping the hammer with the palm. **6.** To winnow; separate (grain) from chaff by air or wind. —*intr.* To spread like a fan. Used with *out.* [Middle English *fan(ne)*, Old English *fann*, from Latin *vannus*.]

fan² (fan) *n. Informal.* An ardent devotee or admirer, as of a sport, athletic team, or famous person. [Short for FANATIC.]

Fan·a·ga·lo, Fan·a·ka·lo (fánnəgə-lō) *n.* In South Africa, a pidgin language containing elements of Zulu, English, and Afrikaans. [From *fana ga lo*, "like this" (a common phrase in the language) : Zulu *fana*, be like + *ka*, "of" (possessive prefix) + *lo*, this.]

fa·nat·ic (fə-náttik) *n.* A person possessed by an excessive and irrational zeal, especially for a religious or political cause. Sometimes used humorously: *an opera fanatic.*
~*adj.* Variant of **fanatical.** [Latin *fānāticus*, of a temple, inspired by a god, mad, from *fānum*, temple.]
Synonyms: *fanatic, extremist, zealot, enthusiast.*

fa·nat·i·cal (fə-náttik'l) *adj.* Also **fa·nat·ic** (-náttik). **1.** Possessed or driven by excessive or irrational zeal. **2.** Pertaining to or characteristic of a fanatic. **—fa·nat·i·cal·ly** *adv.*

fa·nat·i·cism (fə-nátti-siz'm) *n.* Excessive, irrational zeal; extreme or unscrupulous dedication; monomania.

fan belt *n.* A belt that transfers torque from the crankshaft of an internal-combustion engine to the shaft of the cooling fan and the dynamo or alternator.

fan·cied (fán-sid) *adj.* **1.** Produced by the fancy; imaginary; unreal. **2.** Supposed: *this fancied insult.* **3.** Expected to do well or to win.

fan·ci·er (fán-si-ər) *n.* **1.** A person who has a special enthusiasm for something and who makes a hobby of his interest: *a fancier of antiques.* **2.** A person who breeds plants or animals: *a pigeon fancier.* **3.** A person given to reverie or whimsy; a dreamer.

fan·ci·ful (fán-si-f'l) *adj.* **1.** Created in the fancy; unreal; wishful; dubious: *a fanciful story.* **2.** Showing invention or whimsy in design; imaginative; curious: *a fanciful pattern.* **3.** Indulging in imagination and fancy: *a fanciful novelist.* —See Synonyms at **fantastic.** **—fan·ci·ful·ly** *adv.* **—fan·ci·ful·ness** *n.*

fan·cy (fán-si) *n., pl.* **-cies.** **1. a.** The light invention or play of the mind through which whims, visions, fantasies, or the like are summoned up; imagination, especially in a conscious or direct sense; caprice. **b.** In the literary theory of Coleridge, an aspect of the faculty of memory that merely combines images in contrast with true creative imagination. **2.** An associative image; fantastical invention. **3.** A notion not derived from evidence; an unfounded opinion; a delusion. **4.** A capricious idea; a whim; an impulse. **5.** *Informal.* A capricious or sudden liking; a frivolous inclination. **6.** Taste or preference; critical sensibility. **7.** The art, hobby, or profession of breeding fancy animals. **8.** A fancy cake. —See Synonyms at **caprice.** **—the fancy.** **1.** *Archaic.* **a.** The sport of boxing. **b.** The followers and patrons of this sport. **2. a.** Any sport or hobby. **b.** The followers and patrons of a sport or hobby.
~*adj.* **fancier, -ciest.** **1.** Decorative and ornamental rather than plain: *fancy socks.* **2.** Fanciful; illusory or vain. **3.** Characterised by skill or some other quality that is felt to be more ostentatious than worthwhile: *fancy speeches.* Used derogatorily. **4.** Out of the ordinary; superior; fine. **5.** Excessive or exorbitant; inordinate: *a fancy bid.* **6.** Bred for unusual qualities or special points. Said of birds and other animals.
~*tr.v.* **fancied, -cying, -cies.** **1.** To visualise; imagine; picture. **2.** To suppose; surmise. **3.** To take to or like; be fond of. **4.** *Infor-*

mal. **a.** To desire; want. **b.** To desire sexually; be physically attracted to. **5.** *Informal.* To have an unduly good or inflated opinion of (oneself): *He fancies himself as a musician.* **6. a.** To consider (a racehorse, for example) as likely to win. **b.** To consider (the chances of success of a person or team, for example) as good. **7.** To breed (pigeons or rabbits, for example) for unusual qualities or special points. —See Synonyms at **like.**
~*interj.* Used to express surprise. Often used with *that.* [Middle English *fantsy,* short for *fantasie,* fancy, FANTASY.] **—fan·ci·ly** *adv.* **—fan·ci·ness** *n.*

fancy cake *n.* A piece of sponge cake, normally cut into a diamond shape, decorated with icing. Also called "fancy".

fancy dress *n.* Special clothes, such as uniform or historical costume, worn for a party or similar entertainment. **—fan·cy-dress** (fán-si-dress) *adj.*

fan·cy-free (fán-si-frée, -free) *adj.* Carefree; without commitment or restriction; unattached.

fancy goods *pl.n.* Ornamental items; small decorative goods.

fancy man *n.* **1.** A boyfriend; a lover. **2.** A pimp. In both senses, used derogatorily.

fancy woman *n.* **1.** A girlfriend; a mistress. **2.** A prostitute. In both senses, used derogatorily.

fan·cy·work (fán-si-wurk) *n.* Any decorative needlework, such as crochet, embroidery, or needlepoint.

fan·dan·gle (fan-dáng-g'l) *n.* **1.** Elaborate ornamentation. **2.** Nonsense; foolishness. [Perhaps alteration (influenced by *newfangle*) of FANDANGO.]

fan·dan·go (fan-dáng-gō) *n., pl.* **-gos. 1.** An animated Spanish or Latin-American dance in triple time. **2.** A piece of music for such a dance. [Spanish *fandango*†.]

fan·fare (fán-fair) *n.* **1.** A loud flourish or ceremonial sounding of trumpets or other brass instruments. **2.** *Informal.* A clamorous or spectacular public display, ceremony, or reaction; a stir. [French (imitative).]

fan·fa·ron·ade (fán-farrə-náyd, -fərə- || -naád) *n.* **1.** Any vaunting or blustering manner or behaviour. **2.** A fanfare. [French *fanfaronade,* from Spanish *fanfarronada* from *fanfarrón* (imitative).]

fang (fang) *n.* **1.** A long, pointed tooth, especially: **a.** Any of the hollow, grooved teeth with which a venomous snake injects its venom. **b.** Any of the teeth of a carnivorous animal, with which it seizes and tears its prey. **c.** Either of the sharp upper incisors of the true vampire bats. **2.** A similar structure, such as a chelicera of a venomous spider. **3.** *Plural. Informal.* The teeth. [Middle English *fang,* prey, spoils, Old English *fang,* plunder, from Germanic *fang-* (unattested), to catch.] **—fanged** *adj.*

Fan·gi·o (fán-ji-ō, -khi-), **Juan Manuel** (1911–95). Argentinian racing driver. He won 24 Grand Prix races and won the world driver's championship a record five times, 1951 and from 1954 to 1957.

fan heater *n.* A **convector heater** *(see)* in which a fan blowing air over heated wires causes heat to be transferred by forced convection.

fan·kle (fáng-k'l) *tr.v.* **fan·kled, -kling, -kles.** *Scottish.* To entangle.
~*n. Scottish.* A muddle. [From *fank,* coil of rope, variant of *fang,* obsolete variant of VANG.]

fan·light (fán-līt) *n.* **1.** *Architecture.* A half-circle window, often with sash bars arranged like the ribs of a fan. Also called "fan window". **2.** A rectangular window over a door, often serving to admit light to a passage or hall. In this sense, also *U.S.* "transom".

fan mail *n.* Letters, usually of praise, to a public figure from his devotees or admirers.

fan·ny (fánni) *n., pl.* **-nies. 1.** *Vulgar Slang.* The female genitals. **2.** *U.S. Informal.* The buttocks. [20th century : origin obscure.]

Fanny Adams *n.* **1.** Nothing at all. Used chiefly in the phrase *sweet Fanny Adams.* **2.** *Archaic & Nautical.* Tinned meat. [19th century : from the name of a murder victim whose body was chopped up.]

fan·on (fánnən) *n. Ecclesiastical.* **1.** A capelike garment formerly worn only by a pope when celebrating Solemn High Mass. **2.** Formerly, any of various embroidered cloths, such as a maniple, a piece of silk attached to a bishop's crosier, or a cover for the offerings brought by worshippers. [Middle English *fanoun,* from Old French *fanon,* from Frankish *fanon* (unattested).]

fan palm *n.* Any palm tree having leaves with a short axis and consequently fanlike. Compare **feather palm.**

fan·tail (fán-tayl) *n.* **1.** Any of a breed of domestic pigeons having a rounded, fan-shaped tail. **2.** Any of several birds of the genus *Rhipidura,* of eastern Asia and Australia, having a long, fan-shaped tail. **3.** A tail, end, or part having a fanlike shape. **4.** The stern overhang of a ship. **5.** Something shaped like a fantail; for example, a flat jet of flame in certain types of burners. **—fan·tailed** *adj.*

fan-tan (fán-tan) *n.* **1.** A Chinese betting game in which the players lay wagers on the number of beans, coins, or other counters that will remain when a hidden pile of them has been divided by four. **2.** A card game in which sevens and their equivalent are played in sequence and the first to discard all his cards is the winner. [Cantonese *fan t'an,* "repeated division" : *fan,* times, division + *t'an,* distribution, division.]

fan·ta·sia (fan-táy-zi-ə, fán-tə-zée-ə || fan-táy-zhə, -zhi-ə) *n. Music.* **1.** An improvised composition, structured according to the composer's fancy. **2.** A medley of familiar themes, with variations and interludes. [Italian, fantasy, from Latin *phantasia,* FANTASY.]

fan·ta·sise, fan·ta·size (fántə-sīz) *v.* **-sised, -sising, -sises.** *—tr.* To portray in the mind; imagine; picture; fancy. *—intr.* To indulge in fantasies.

fan·tast (fán-tast) *n.* A visionary; a dreamer. [German *Fantast, Phantast,* from Medieval Latin *phantasta,* from Greek *phantastēs,* a boaster, one who is ostentatious, from *phantazein,* to make visible. See **fantasy.**]

fan·tas·tic (fan-táss-tik, fən-) *adj.* Also **fan·tas·ti·cal** (-tik'l) (for senses 1, 2, 3, 4). **1.** Bizarre in form, conception, or appearance; strange; wondrous; fanciful. **2. a.** Unbelievable; preposterous. **b.** Existing in the fancy; unreal; illusory. **3.** Unrestrainedly fanciful; extravagant: *fantastic hopes.* **4.** Capricious or fitful. Said of a person or mood. **5.** *Informal.* **a.** Wonderful or remarkable. **b.** Very large; great.
~*n. Archaic.* A person who is unrestrainedly fanciful or eccentric in behaviour or appearance. [Middle English *fantastik,* from Old French *fantastique,* from Medieval Latin *fantasticus,* from Late Latin *phantasticus,* imaginary, from Greek *phantastikos,* able to produce the appearance of, from *phantazein,* to make visible. See **fantasy.**] **—fan·tas·ti·cal·i·ty** (-ti-kál-əti), **fan·tas·ti·cal·ness** *n.* **—fan·tas·ti·cal·ly** *adv.*

Synonyms: *fantastic, bizarre, grotesque, fanciful, exotic.*

fan·ta·sy, phan·ta·sy (fántə-si, -zi) *n., pl.* **-sies. 1.** The realm of vivid imagination, reverie, depiction, illusion, and the like; the natural conjurings of mental invention and association; the visionary world; make-believe. **2.** A mental image, especially a disordered and weird image; an illusion; a phantasm. **3.** A capricious or whimsical idea or notion; a conceit. **4. a.** Literary or dramatic fiction characterised by highly fanciful or supernatural elements. **b.** An example of such fiction. **5.** *Psychology.* An imagined event or condition fulfilling a wish. Also used adjectivally: *a fantasy world.* **6.** *Music.* A fantasia. **7.** A coin, such as a commemorative coin, that is not issued as legal tender.
~*tr.v.* **fantasied, -sying, -sies.** To imagine; visualise. [Middle English *fantasie,* fancy, fantasy, from Old French, from Latin *phantasia,* from Greek, appearance, perception, faculty of imagination, from *phantazein,* to make visible, from *phainein,* to show.]

Fan·tin-La·tour (foN-taN-la-tōōr), **(Ignace) Henri (Joseph Théodore)** (1836–1904). French painter, noted for his meticulous still-life paintings of flowers and portrait groups.

fan·toc·ci·ni (fántə-chéeni || faántə-) *pl.n.* **1.** Puppets animated by moving wires; marionettes. **2.** Plays with marionettes; puppet shows. [Italian, plural of *fantoccino,* diminutive of *fantoccio,* puppet, doll, augmentative of *fante,* child, servant, short for *infante,* from Latin *infāns* (stem *infant-*), INFANT.]

fan·tod (fán-tod, -təd) *n.* **1.** Irritable behaviour. **2.** *Plural.* A state of restlessness. [19th century : origin obscure.]

fan vaulting *n. Architecture.* An intricate style of traceried vaulting, common in late English Gothic, in which ribs arch out like a fan from a single point such as a capital or corbel.

fan window *n. Architecture.* A **fanlight** *(see).*

fan worm *n.* Any bristle worm of the family Sarbellidae, living in tubes of mud on the sea shore and having fans of feathery tentacles that protrude from the tube when covered by the tide.

fan·zine (fán-zeen) *n.* A magazine for fans of a particular person, hobby, or interest, such as science fiction. [*fan* + *magazine.*]

FAO Food and Agriculture Organisation.

FAQ 1. fair average quality. **2.** frequently asked questions.

far (far) *adv.* **farther** (fárthər) or **further** (fúrthər), **farthest** (fárthist) or **furthest** (fúrthist). **1.** To, from, or at considerable distance, time, degree, or position. **2.** To or at a specific distance, time, degree, or position: *Just how far are you taking this argument?* **3.** To a considerable degree; much. Used chiefly in comparisons: *"It is a far, far better thing I do"* (Charles Dickens). **—as far as.** To the distance, extent, or degree that: *as far as I know.* **—by far.** To a considerable or evident degree. **—far and away.** By a considerable margin: *He's far and away the better skier.* **—far and wide.** All over; everywhere. **—far be it from me.** May I never; I neither hope nor dare: *Far be it from me to insult you.* **—far from.** Not at all; by no means: *Far from being annoyed about it, she was very glad.* **—far gone. 1.** In a very poor state; much deteriorated. **2.** So advanced as to be irreversible. **3.** Drunk. Used humorously. **—from far.** From a great distance. **—go far. 1.** To be successful; accomplish a great deal: *That boy will go far.* **2.** To provide for much or many; last a long time. **—so far. 1.** Up to the present moment. **2.** To a limited extent: *You can only go so far on 25 pence.* **—so far as.** To the extent that: *so far as I can tell.* **—so far so good.** Used to express satisfaction with current progress, while anticipating further difficulties.
~*adj.* **farther** or **further, farthest** or **furthest. 1.** At a considerable distance: *a far country.* **2.** More distant; opposite: *the far corner.* **3.** Extensive or lengthy: *a far trek.* **4.** Politically extreme: *the far right.* —See Synonyms at **distant.** [Middle English *fer,* Old English *feor(r),* far, distant, remote.]

fa·rad (fárrəd, fá-rad) *n. Abbr.* **F** A unit of capacitance, equal to the capacitance of a capacitor having a charge of 1 coulomb on each plate and a potential difference of 1 volt between the plates. [After Michael FARADAY.]

far·a·day (fárrə-day) *n.* The quantity of electricity that is equivalent to unit amount of substance of electrons and has the value 9.6487 $\times 10^4$ coulombs per mole. [After Michael FARADAY.]

Far·a·day (fárrə-day, -di), **Michael** (1791–1867). British chemist and physicist, discoverer of electromagnetism. In 1831 he discovered the connection between electricity and magnetism, producing an electric current by rotating a copper disc between the poles of a magnet. He also investigated the process of electrolysis.

fa·rad·ic (fə-ráddik, fa-) *adj.* Also **far·a·da·ic** (fárrə-dáy-ik). Of, pertaining to, or using an intermittent asymmetric alternating electric current produced by an induction coil. [After Michael FARADAY.]

far·a·di·sa·tion (fárrə-dĭ-záysh'n ‖ *U.S.* -di-) *n.* Also **far·a·dism** (fárrə-diz'm). Medical therapy by application of faradic currents to stimulate nerve and muscle activity.

far·a·dise, far·a·dize (fárrə-dīz) *tr.v.* **-dised, -dising, -dises.** *Medicine.* To treat (an organ or part) with faradic currents.

far·an·dole (fárrən-dōl) *n.* **1.** A spirited circle dance of Provençal derivation. **2.** The music for this dance. [French, from Provençal *farandoulo†*.]

far·a·way (faár-ə-way) *adj.* **1.** Very distant; beyond immediate contact; remote: *faraway lands.* **2.** Bemused or abstracted; dreamy: *a faraway smile.* —See Synonyms at **distant.**

farce (farss) *n.* **1.** A theatrical composition in which broad improbabilities of plot and characterisation are used for humorous effect. **2.** Something ludicrous; an empty show; a mockery: *"childish family portraits, with their farce of sentiment and smiling lies"* (Thackeray).
~*tr.v.* **farced, farcing, farces.** *Archaic.* **1.** To intersperse or fill out (one's speech or a play) with jokes or witticisms. **2.** *Obsolete.* To stuff (a bird, for example) for roasting. [Middle English *farse,* stuffing, from Old French *farce,* stuffing, farce, from *farcir,* from Latin *farcīre,* to stuff, hence to pad out with interludes.]

far·ceur (faar-súr, -sôr) *n.* Also **farc·er** (fár-sər). **1.** An actor in a farce. **2.** A writer of farces. **3.** A comic; a joker. [French, from Old French, author or actor of farce, from *farce,* FARCE.]

far·ci (faar-sée) *adj.* Stuffed. Said of food. [French, past participle of *farcir.*]

far·ci·cal (fár-sik'l) *adj.* **1.** Pertaining to farce. **2.** Resembling farce; ludicrous; absurd. —**far·ci·cal·i·ty** (-si-kál-əti), **far·ci·cal·ness** *n.* —**far·ci·cal·ly** *adv.*

far·cy (fár-si) *n. Veterinary Medicine.* Chronic, cutaneous glanders (*see*). [Middle English *farsi(n),* from Old French *farcin,* from Late Latin *farcīmen,* farcy, from Latin, sausage, from *farcīre,* to stuff. See **farce.**]

farcy bud *n. Veterinary Medicine.* A crater-like ulcer characteristic of farcy.

fard·ed (fárdid) *adj.* Painted with cosmetics. [Past participle of obsolete *fard,* from Old French *farder,* to paint (the face) with cosmetics, from Germanic.]

far·del (fárd'l) *n. Archaic.* A pack; a load; a burden. [Middle English, from Old French, diminutive of *farde,* package, from Vulgar Latin *fardum* (unattested), from Arabic *fardah, farde,* load.]

fare (fair) *intr.v.* **fared, faring, fares.** **1.** To get along: *How did he fare with his project?* **2.** To turn out; go. Used impersonally: *How does it fare with you?* **3.** *Rare.* To be entertained with food and drink. **4.** *Archaic.* To travel; wander.
~*n.* **1.** A transportation charge, as for a bus or taxi. **2.** A passenger transported for a fee. **3.** Food and drink: *modest fare.* **4.** *Archaic.* The state or condition of things. [Middle English *faren,* to travel, go, fare, Old English *faran,* from Germanic.] —**far·er** *n.*

Far East, the. Also **East Asia.** The countries of China, Japan, North and South Korea, and Mongolia and, sometimes, the countries of Indochina, Malaysia, and Indonesia as well. —**Far East·ern** *adj.*

fare·well (faír-wél) *interj.* May you fare well; Godspeed; good-bye.
~*n.* **1.** An acknowledgment at parting; a good-bye. **2.** A leave-taking; a departure.
~*adj.* (faír-wel). Pertaining to parting or leave-taking: *a farewell party.* [Middle English *fare well!* : *fare,* go, fare, imperative of *faren,* to FARE + WELL.]

far-fetched (fár-fécht) *adj.* Strained or improbable in nature or relevance: *a far-fetched alibi.*

far-flung (fár-flúng) *adj.* **1.** Widely distributed; wide-ranging: *far-flung reporters.* **2.** Remote; distant.

fa·ri·na (fə-réenə) *n.* **1.** Fine meal prepared from cereal grain and various other plant products, and often used as a cooked cereal or in puddings. **2.** Starch, especially that prepared from potato flour. [Latin *farīna,* ground corn, meal, from *far,* a kind of grain.]

far·i·na·ceous (fárri-náyshəss) *adj.* **1.** Made from, rich in, or consisting of starch. **2.** Having a mealy or powdery texture. **3.** Made from or with pasta. [Late Latin *farīnāceus,* mealy : Latin *farīna,* FARINA + -ACEOUS.]

far·i·nose (fárri-nōss, -nōz) *adj.* **1.** Similar to or yielding farina. **2.** *Biology.* Covered with short hairs resembling mealy dust or powder. [Late Latin *farīnōsus,* mealy, from Latin *farīna,* FARINA.]

farl (farl) *n.* A thin oatmeal cake. [Variant of obsolete *fardel,* a fourth part (the usually triangular cake being a quarter of a large round) : *far-,* from Old English *fēortha,* fourth + *del,* part, DEAL.]

farm (farm) *n.* **1.** A tract of agricultural land on which livestock or crops are raised. **2.** Any land or water area devoted to the raising, breeding, or production of a specified type of animal or vegetable life: *a trout farm.* **3.** A place where something is stored or treated: *a sewage farm.* **4.** In West Africa, a garden, especially a vegetable garden. **5.** *Obsolete.* **a.** The system of leasing out the rights of collecting and retaining taxes in a certain district. **b.** A district so leased. **c.** A rent, tax, or toll so collected.
~*v.* **farmed, farming, farms.** —*tr.* **1. a.** To cultivate or produce a crop or raise livestock on (land). **b.** To cultivate or produce (a crop). **c.** To breed (livestock). **2.** To have the right to operate or supervise and retain profits from (a business or tax district, for example). **3.** To let to a concessionaire the rights to operate or supervise and retain profits from (a business or tax district, for

example). Used with *out.* **4.** To offer the services of (a worker) for a fee or rent. **5.** To send (work) from a central point to be done elsewhere. Used with *out: farm out typing.* **6. a.** Formerly, to entrust (a child) to the care of a person or institution for a fixed sum. **b.** Formerly, to undertake to maintain (a child) on this basis. —*intr.* To engage in farming; be a farmer. [Middle English *ferme,* lease, rent, from Old French, from Medieval Latin *firma,* fixed payment, from Latin *firmāre,* to fortify, fix, confirm, from *firmus,* firm.]

farm·er (fármər) *n.* **1.** One who owns or operates a farm. **2.** *Archaic.* One who has paid for and holds a concession on the rights of collecting and retaining taxes.

farm·er-gen·er·al (fármər-jénrəl, -jénnərəl) *n., pl.* **farmers-general.** One who farmed certain taxes in prerevolutionary France.

farmer's lung *n.* An occupational lung disease characterised by chronic breathlessness and caused by an allergic reaction to fungal spores in hay that has not been properly dried.

farm hand *n.* A farm labourer.

farm·house (fárm-howss) *n., pl.* **-houses** (-howziz). **1.** The farmer's dwelling on a farm. **2.** A type of large white loaf.

farm·stead (fárm-sted) *n.* **1.** A farm, including its land and buildings. **2.** That part of a farm including and surrounding the farmhouse. Compare **homestead.**

farm·yard (fárm-yaard) *n.* An area surrounded by or adjacent to farm buildings.

Farn·bor·ough (fárn-bərə, -brə ‖ -burrə, -burrō). Town in Hampshire, England, site of the Royal Aircraft Establishment.

Farne Islands (farn). Group of islets of dolerite rock in the North Sea off Northumberland. The islands are preserved by the National Trust as a bird sanctuary.

Far·ne·se (faar-náy-si, -zi, -say, -zay), **Alessandro, Duke of Parma** (1545–92). Italian general, nephew of King Philip II of Spain. He fought the Turks at the naval battle of Lepanto (1571) in which the Holy League under John of Austria shattered the Ottoman navy.

far·ne·sol (fárni-sol ‖ -sōl) *n.* A compound, $C_{15}H_{26}O$, extracted from the flowers and essential oils of various plants, and used in perfumery. [New Latin *farnesiana* (an in *Acacia farnesiana*), after Odoardo *Farnese,* 17th-century Italian cardinal + -OL.]

Farn·ham (fárnəm). Market town of Surrey, southeast England. Situated on the river Wey, it is the seat of the 12th-century Farnham Castle, once the palace of the Bishops of Winchester.

far·o (faír-ō) *n.* A card game in which the players lay bets on the top card of the dealer's pack. [Variant of PHARAOH, perhaps the name originally applied to the king of hearts.]

Fa·ro (faár-ō). Atlantic port and southernmost town of Portugal, and capital of the Algarve.

Faroe. See **Faeroe Islands.**

far-off (faár-óff, -áwf) *adj.* Remote in space or time; distant; faraway. See Synonyms at **distant.**

fa·rouche (fa-rōosh, fə-) *adj. French.* **1.** Sullenly shy. **2.** Wild. [Old French *faroche,* from Medieval Latin *forasticus,* from Latin *foras,* out of doors.]

Fa·rouk I (fə-rōok) (1920–65). The last king of Egypt (1936–52). The defeat of the Egyptian army in the first Arab-Israeli war (1948–49) and Farouk's extravagant lifestyle alienated the people. In July 1952, his administration was overthrown by the Free Officers led by General Muhammad Neguib and a junior officer, Gamal Abdul Nasser. Farouk was forced to abdicate.

far-out (fár-ówt) *adj. Slang.* **1.** Extremely unconventional. **2.** Excellent; marvellous.

far point *n.* The farthest point at which an object can be seen distinctly by the eye at rest.

far·ra·go (fə-ráa-gō, -ráy-) *n., pl.* **-gos.** A medley; a conglomeration; a mixture: *"This is a farrago of absurdity"* (Virginia Woolf). [Latin *farrāgo,* mixed fodder for cattle, from *far* (stem *farr-*), a grain.] —**far·rag·i·nous** (-rájinəss) *adj.*

far-reach·ing (fár-réeching) *adj.* Having a wide range, influence, or effect; extending far.

far·ri·er (fárri-ər) *n. Chiefly British.* One who shoes horses or treats them medically. [Old French *ferrier,* blacksmith, from Latin *ferrārius,* from *ferrum,* iron.] —**far·ri·er·y** (-əri) *n.*

far·row[1] (fárrō) *n.* **1.** A litter of pigs. **2.** The act of giving birth to a litter of pigs.
~*v.* **farrowed, -rowing, -rows.** —*tr.* To give birth to (a litter of pigs). —*intr.* To produce a farrow. [Perhaps Middle English *faren* (plural), Old English *fearh,* little pig.]

far·row[2] (fárrō) *adj.* Not pregnant; barren. Said of a cow. [Middle English (Scottish dialect) *fer(r)ow,* from Middle Dutch *verwe-* (unattested), cow past the age of bearing.]

far·ru·ca (fə-rōo-kə, fa-) *n.* A kind of flamenco dance. [Spanish.]

far·see·ing (fár-sée-ing) *adj.* **1.** Prudent; foresighted. **2.** Able to see far; keen-sighted.

far·sight·ed (fár-sítid) *adj.* **1. a.** Able to see objects better from a distance than from short range; long-sighted. **b.** Hyperopic. See **hyperopia.** **2.** Planning prudently for the future; foresighted. —**far·sight·ed·ly** *adv.* —**far·sight·ed·ness** *n.*

fart (fart) *n.* **1.** *Vulgar.* The emission of wind from the anus. **2.** *Vulgar Slang.* A contemptible person.
~*intr.v.* **farted, farting, farts.** *Vulgar.* To expel wind from the anus. —**fart about** or **around.** *Vulgar Slang.* To behave in a silly manner; waste time. [Middle English, Old English *feortan* (unattested), from Germanic; akin to Sanskrit *pardatē,* he breaks wind.]

far·ther (fárthər) *adv.* **1.** To or at a more distant or more remote point in space or time. **2.** *Archaic.* In addition.

~*adj.* **1.** Remoter; more distant. **2.** *Archaic.* Additional. [Middle English *ferther,* variant of *further,* FURTHER.]

Usage: Does a man travel *further* than he intended or *farther?* When it is a question of literal distance or direction, *farther* is preferred in careful usage: *It's farther away than I thought. Further* is commoner, however, in the expression of figurative distance: *We are now further from the truth. Farther* in such a sentence seems somewhat old-fashioned. In superlative forms, *farthest* is still used figuratively: *Of all possible interpretations, this one is farthest from the truth.* In the general sense of "additional", whether referring to time, quantity, or manner, *further* is standard: *further reasons, further debts, further education, consider further.*

far·ther·most (fárthər-mōst) *adj.* Farthest.

far·thest (fárthist) *adj.* Most remote or distant. See Usage note at **farther.**

~*adv.* To or at the most distant or remote point in space or time. See Usage note at **farther.** [Middle English *ferthest,* from *ferther,* FARTHER.]

far·thing (fárthing) *n. Abbr.* **f. 1.** A former British bronze coin worth one quarter of an old penny. It was abolished as legal tender in 1961. **2.** The sum of one quarter of an old penny. **3.** Something of little value. [Middle English *ferthing,* Old English *fēorthing* : *fēortha,* FOURTH + -ING.]

far·thin·gale (fárthing-gayl) *n.* **1.** A hoop or series of hoops extending horizontally from the waist, worn beneath a woman's skirts in the 16th and 17th centuries. **2.** The skirt worn over this device. [Variant of Old French *verdugale, vertugalle,* from Spanish *verdugado,* from *verdugo,* rod, stick, shoot of a tree, from *verde,* green, from Latin *viridis,* from *virēre,* to be green.]

farthingale chair *n.* A type of chair, used in the 16th and 17th centuries in England, having no arms, a straight, low back, and a high seat.

Fas. See **Fès.**

f.a.s., F.A.S. free alongside ship.

fas·ces (fásseez) *pl.n.* **1.** A bundle of rods bound together around an axe with the blade projecting, carried before magistrates of ancient Rome as an emblem of authority. **2.** This emblem used as a symbol of the Fascists in modern Italy. [Latin, plural of *fascis,* bundle.]

fas·ci·a (fáy-shə, -shi-ə, fáshi-ə; *for sense 3 also* fáy-si-ə) *n., pl.* **-ciae** (-shi-ee, -si-ee). Also **fa·ci·a** (for sense 4). **1.** *Anatomy.* A sheet of fibrous tissue beneath the surface of the skin, enveloping the body, enclosing muscles or muscular groups, and separating muscular layers. **2.** A broad and distinct band of colour, especially that on an insect or plant. **3.** *Architecture.* A flat horizontal band or member between mouldings; especially, such a member in a classical entablature. **4. a.** The board above a shop or other business on which the name or nature of the business is displayed. **b.** A panel inside a motor vehicle on which controls and instruments are mounted. [New Latin, from Latin, band, bandage, fillet.] **—fas·ci·al** *adj.*

fas·ci·ate (fáshi-ayt) *adj.* Also **fas·ci·at·ed** (-aytid). **1.** *Botany.* Abnormally flattened or compressed, as certain stems are. **2.** *Zoology.* Marked by broad bands of colour, as certain insects. [New Latin *fasciatus* : FASCI(A) + -ATE.]

fas·ci·a·tion (fáshi-áysh'n) *n.* **1.** The act of binding up or fastening, as with bandages or bands. **2.** The manner in which something is bound up or fastened. **3.** *Botany.* An abnormal flattening or compression of stems or leaf stalks.

fas·ci·cle (fássi-k'l) *n.* Also **fas·ci·cule** (-kewl) (for sense 2). *Abbr.* **fasc. 1.** A small bundle. **2.** One of the separately published parts or instalments of a book. **3.** *Botany.* A bundle-like cluster, especially of leaves, branches, roots and fibres. **4.** *Anatomy.* A fasciculus. [Latin *fasciculus,* diminutive of *fascis,* a bundle.] **—fas·ci·cled** *adj.*

fas·cic·u·late (fə-síckew-lət, fa-, -lit, -layt) *adj.* Also **fas·cic·u·lar** (-lər), **fas·cic·u·lat·ed** (-laytid). Of, pertaining to or resembling a fascicle. **—fas·cic·u·late·ly** *adv.* **—fas·cic·u·la·tion** (-láysh'n) *n.*

fas·cic·u·lus (fə-síckew-ləss, fa-) *n., pl.* **-li** (-lī). A bundle of anatomical fibres; especially, a bundle of nerve fibres having common functions and connections. [New Latin, from Latin, FASCICLE.]

fas·ci·nate (fássi-nayt) *tr.v.* **-nated, -nating, -nates. 1.** To be an object of intense interest to; attract irresistibly. **2.** To hold motionless; spellbind or mesmerise. **3.** *Obsolete.* To bewitch; cast under a spell. [Latin *fascināre,* to enchant, bewitch, from *fascinus,* a bewitching amulet in the shape of a phallus.]

fas·ci·nat·ing (fássi-nayting) *adj.* Arousing unflagging interest, as by charm or beauty; captivating. **—fas·ci·nat·ing·ly** *adv.*

fas·ci·na·tion (fássi-náysh'n) *n.* **1.** The power of fascinating. **2.** The condition of being fascinated. **3.** A fascinating quality.

fas·ci·na·tor (fássi-naytər) *n.* **1.** One that fascinates. **2.** *Rare.* A woman's headscarf made of net, lace, or the like.

fas·cine (fa-séen, fə-) *n.* A bundle of sticks bound together used for various engineering purposes, especially the construction of fortresses, earthworks, or reinforced trenches. [French, from Latin *fascīna,* from *fascis,* bundle.]

fas·ci·o·li·a·sis (fə-sée-ə-lī-ə-siss, -sī-) *n.* Infestation with parasitic flukes of the family Fasciolidae; especially, infestation of the liver and bile ducts with the liver fluke *Fasciola hepatica.* [New Latin *Fasciolidae* (family name), from Latin *fasciola,* augmentative of *fascia,* band, fillet (see **fascia**) + -IASIS.]

fas·cism (fásh-iz'm || fáss-) *n.* **1.** A philosophy or system of government that advocates or exercises a dictatorship of the extreme right, typically through the merging of state and business leadership, together with an ideology of belligerent nationalism. **2.** *Capital* **F.** The governmental system of Italy under Benito Mussolini from 1922 to 1943. [Italian *fascismo,* from *fascio,* bundle, group, assemblage, from Latin *fascis,* bundle.]

fas·cist (fáshist || fássist) *n.* **1.** A person who advocates or practises fascism. **2.** *Often capital* **F.** A person who belongs to a fascist organisation. **3.** *Informal.* Any right-wing or authoritarian person. [Italian *fascista,* from *fascio,* bundle, group. See **fascism.**] **—fas·cist, fa·scis·tic** (fə-shiss-tik, fa-) *adj.*

Fa·scis·ti (fə-shíss-ti; *Italian* fa-shée-stee) *pl.n.* The members of the Italian political organisation led by Benito Mussolini. [Italian, plural of *fascista,* FASCIST.]

fash (fash) *n. Scottish.* Trouble; worry; inconvenience.

~*tr.v.* **fashed, fashing, fashes.** *Scottish.* To trouble; annoy. [Obsolete French *fascher,* to annoy, from Vulgar Latin *fastidicare* (unattested), from Latin *fastidium,* aversion, disdain, from *fastus,* disdain.]

fash·ion (fásh'n) *n.* **1.** The current style or custom, as in dress or behaviour; the mode for the present: *out of fashion.* **2.** Something that is in the current mode. **3.** Fashionable or style-conscious people in general; the social elite. **4.** The way in which something is formed; a configuration; an aspect: *"as he prayed, the fashion of his countenance was altered"* (Luke 9:29). **5.** A kind or variety; a sort. **6.** A manner of performing; a way: *Do it in this fashion.* —See Synonyms at **habit. —after** or **in a fashion.** In some way or other; not very well: *She sings after a fashion.*

~*tr.v.* **fashioned, -ioning, -ions. 1. a.** To make into a particular shape or form: *"And wilt thou have me fashion into speech/The love I bear thee"* (Elizabeth Barrett Browning). **b.** To train or influence into a particular state or character. **2.** To make suitable; adapt, as to a purpose or occasion. **3.** *Obsolete.* To contrive. [Middle English *facioun,* from Old French *facon,* from Latin *factiō* (stem *factiōn-*), "a making", from *factus,* past participle of *facere,* to make, do.]

Synonyms: *fashion, style, mode, vogue.*

fash·ion·a·ble (fásh-nəb'l, fásh'n-əb'l) *adj.* **1.** Conforming to the current style; in fashion. **2.** Frequented by or associated with persons of fashion. **—fash·ion·a·ble·ness** *n.* **—fash·ion·a·bly** *adv.*

fashion plate *n.* **1.** An illustration of current styles in dress. **2.** A person who consistently wears the latest fashions.

Fass·bin·der (fáss-bindər), **Rainer Werner** (1946–82). German film director. His films, both realistic and despairing, include *Fear Eats the Soul* (1974), *Fox* (1975), and *Despair* (1978).

fast[1] (faast || fast) *adj.* **faster, fastest. 1.** Acting, moving, or capable of moving quickly; swift; rapid. **2.** Accomplished in relatively little time: *a fast visit.* **3.** Indicating a time somewhat ahead of the actual time: *my wristwatch is fast.* **4. a.** Adapted to or suitable for rapid movement: *a fast road.* **b.** Showing rapidity of movement: *a fast game.* **5.** Disposed to flout conventional or moral standards; especially, sexually active: *a fast life.* **6.** Resistant. Often used in combination: *acid-fast.* **7.** Firmly fixed or fastened; not readily moved, removed, or loosened. **8.** Fixed firmly in place; secure. **9.** Loyal; constant; firm. **10.** Permanent; resisting fading: *fast dyes.* **11.** *Archaic.* Deep; sound: *a fast sleep.* **12.** *Photography.* **a.** Compatible with a high shutter speed: *a fast lens.* **b.** Designed for short exposure; highly sensitive: *fast film.* **13.** *Sports.* Delivering the ball very rapidly to the batsman. Said of a bowler in cricket.

~*adv.* **1.** Firmly; securely; tightly. **2.** Deeply; soundly: *fast asleep.* **3.** Quickly; rapidly. **4.** In a dissipated, immoderate way: *living fast.* **5.** *Archaic.* Close by; near. **—play fast and loose.** To behave without integrity or consideration. [Middle English *fast,* Old English *fæst,* from Germanic.]

Synonyms: *fast, rapid, swift, fleet, speedy, quick, hasty, expeditious, accelerated.*

fast[2] (faast || fast) *intr.v.* **fasted, fasting, fasts.** To abstain from eating all or certain foods, especially as a religious discipline or as a means of protest.

~*n.* The act or a period of fasting. [Middle English *fasten,* Old English *fæstan,* to hold fast, to observe, to abstain from food, from Germanic.]

fast·back (faást-bak || fást-) *n.* A car having a straight or slightly curved sloping back.

fast breeder reactor *n.* A fast nuclear reactor that produces more fissionable material than it consumes.

fast buck *n. Informal.* Money easily made: *earn a fast buck.*

fast day *n.* A day reserved for fasting; especially, a day thus reserved by ecclesiastical authority.

fas·ten (faáss'n || fáss'n) *v.* **-tened, -tening, -tens.** —*tr.* **1.** To attach; join; connect: *fasten the button to the skirt.* **2. a.** To make fast or secure. **b.** To close, as by shutting or fixing firmly in place. **3.** To fix or direct (the gaze, attention, or the like) steadily. **4.** To place; attribute: *Don't fasten the blame on him.* —*intr.* **1.** To become attached, fixed, or joined. **2.** To take firm hold; cling fast. Usually used with *on* or *upon.* [Middle English *fastnen,* Old English *fastnian,* to settle, establish, make fast.] **—fas·ten·er** *n.*

fast·en·ing (faáss'n-ing, faáss-ning || fáss'n-ing, fáss-ning) *n.* **1.** The act or a method of making something fast. **2.** Something used to fasten, such as a lock or hook.

fast-food (faást-fŏŏd || fást-) *adj.* Specialising in foods prepared and served quickly: *a fast-food restaurant.*

fas·tid·i·ous (fə-stíddi-əss, fa-) *adj.* **1.** Careful in all details; exacting; meticulous. **2.** Difficult to please; overcritical. **3.** Easily disgusted; squeamish. —See Synonyms at **meticulous.** [Middle English, disdainful, distasteful, loathsome, from Latin *fastīdiōsus,* from *fastīdium,* a loathing, from *fastus,* disdain.] **—fas·tid·i·ous·ly**

adv. **—fas·tid·i·ous·ness** *n.*

fas·tig·i·ate (fa-stíji-ət, fə-, -it, -ayt) *adj.* Also **fas·tig·i·at·ed** (-aytid). **1.** Tapering to a point; forming a cone or similar shape. **2.** *Botany.* Erect and almost parallel, as certain branches are. [Medieval Latin *fastīgiātus,* high, lofty, from Latin *fastīgium,* top, summit, height.]

fast lane *n.* **1.** The outside lane on a motorway or main road reserved for overtaking. **2.** *Informal.* A state of exciting but perhaps risky fast forward movement towards success or gratification: *life in the fast lane.*

fast·ness (faást-nəss, -niss || fást-) *n.* **1. a.** A fortified place; a stronghold or fortress. **b.** A remote and secret place. **2.** The condition or quality of being fast, especially: **a.** Firmness; security. **b.** *Archaic.* Rapidity; swiftness. **c.** Colourfastness.

fast neutron *n.* A neutron produced during nuclear fission that has kinetic energy in excess of O.l MeV, having lost little energy in collisions.

fast one *n. Slang.* A deceptive or unfair action done to gain advantage. Used chiefly in the phrase *pull a fast one.*

fast reactor *n.* A nuclear reactor that uses little or no moderator, the fission resulting from fast neutrons.

fast talk *n. Informal.* Rapid deceptive patter, especially when aimed at persuading someone to buy something he does not really want. **—fast-talk** *v.* **—fast-talker** *n.*

fast worker *n.* One who makes quick progress, especially in relations with the opposite sex.

fat (fat) *n.* **1. a.** The glyceride ester of a **fatty acid** *(see).* **b.** Any of various soft solid or semisolid organic compounds comprising the glyceride esters of fatty acids and associated phosphatides, sterols, alcohols, hydrocarbons, ketones, and related compounds. **c.** A mixture of such compounds occurring widely in organic tissue, especially in the subcutaneous connective tissue of animals and in the seeds, nuts, and fruits of plants. **d.** Loosely, organic tissue containing such substances. **e.** A solidified animal or vegetable oil. See **oil. 2.** Plumpness; obesity. **3.** The best or most desirable part. **—chew the fat.** *U.S. Slang.* To have a leisurely conversation.
~*adj.* **fatter, fattest. 1.** Having much or too much fat or flesh; plump or obese. **2.** Full of fat or oil; oily; greasy. **3.** Abounding in desirable elements: *Fat pine yields much resin.* **4.** Fertile or productive; rich: *"It was a fine, green, fat landscape"* (R.L. Stevenson). **5.** Having an abundance or amplitude; well-stocked: *a fat larder.* **6.** Yielding profit or plenty; lucrative: *a fat promotion.* **7.** Thick; broad; large: *a fat plank.* **8.** *Slang.* Small; meagre: *a fat chance.*
~*v.* **fatted, fatting, fats.** *—tr.* To make fat. *—intr.* To become fat. [Middle English, Old English *fǣtt,* from Germanic.] **—fat·ly** *adv.* **—fat·ness** *n.*
Synonyms: *fat, obese, corpulent, fleshy, stout, portly, podgy, rotund, plump, chubby.*

Fa·tah (fáttaa) *n.* Also **Al Fa·tah.** A Palestinian nationalist organisation, founded in 1956, the largest grouping in the PLO. [Arabic, "opening".]

fa·tal (fáyt'l) *adj.* **1.** Causing or capable of causing death; mortal. **2.** Causing ruin or destruction; disastrous: *"Such doctrines, if true, would be absolutely fatal to my theory"* (Charles Darwin). **3.** Of decisive importance; fateful. **4.** Controlling destiny. **5.** *Archaic.* Destined; inevitable. [Middle English, fated, fatal, from Old French, from Latin *fātālis,* from *fātum,* FATE.]
Synonyms: *fatal, deadly, mortal, lethal.*

fa·tal·ism (fáyt'l-iz'm) *n.* **1.** The doctrine that all events are predetermined by fate and therefore unalterable by man. **2.** The acceptance of this doctrine; submission to fate. **—fa·tal·ist** *n.* **—fa·tal·is·tic** (-ístik) *adj.* **—fa·tal·is·ti·cal·ly** *adv.*

fa·tal·i·ty (fə-tál-əti, fay-) *n., pl.* **-ties. 1. a.** A death that results from an unexpected occurrence: *fatalities from road accidents.* **b.** One who is killed as a result of such an occurrence. **c.** An occurrence or accident that results in a death. **2.** The ability to cause death or disaster; a lethal quality. **3.** The condition or quality of being governed or determined by fate. **4.** A dictate or determination by fate. **5.** A liability to disaster: *the fatality of his decision.*

fatality rate *n.* **Death rate** *(see).*

fa·tal·ly (fáyt'l-i) *adv.* **1.** So as to cause death, ruin, or disaster; mortally. **2.** According to the decree of fate; inevitably.

Fatal Sisters *pl.n.* The Fates. Preceded by *the.*

fa·ta mor·ga·na (faáta mawr-gaánə || -gánnə) *n.* A **mirage** *(see).* [Italian, Morgan le Fay (the mirage was attributed to her witchcraft).]

fat·back (fát-bak) *n.* The strip of fat taken from the upper part of a side of pork and usually dried and salt-cured.

fat cat *n. Chiefly U.S. Slang.* A wealthy and highly privileged person; especially, a heavy contributor to a political party.

fate (fayt) *n.* **1.** The supposed force, principle, or power that predetermines events. **2.** The inevitable event or events predestined by this force. **3.** A final result or consequence; an outcome. **4.** An unfavourable destiny; doom. [Middle English, from Old French, from Latin *fātum,* from the neuter past participle of *fārī,* to speak.]

fat·ed (fáytid) *adj.* **1.** Governed by fate; predetermined: *his fated lot.* **2.** Condemned to death or destruction; doomed.

fate·ful (fáyt-f'l) *adj.* **1.** Affecting one's destiny or future; crucially important: *the fateful final examination.* **2.** Controlled by or as if by fate; predetermined. **3.** Bringing death or disaster; fatal. **4.** Portentous; ominous: *a fateful sign.* **—fate·ful·ly** *adv.* **—fate·ful·ness** *n.*

Fat·eh·pur Sik·ri (fáttay-poor síckri). City in the state of Uttar Pradesh in northern India. It was the capital of the Mogul Empire, under Akbar, from its foundation in 1569 until 1584, but in the 17th century it was deserted because a water supply was lacking. It is now carefully preserved as a virtually unaltered Mogul city.

Fates (fayts) *Greek & Roman Mythology.* The three goddesses who govern human destiny. Preceded by *the.* See **Atropos, Clotho,** and **Lachesis** Also called the "Fatal Sisters", "Moirae", "Parcae".

fath, fath. fathom.

fat·head (fát-hed) *n. Slang.* A stupid person; a dolt.

fat hen *n.* A common plant, *Chenopodium album,* with clusters of small green flowers and dark green leaves covered by thick white hairs. Also *U.S.* "pigweed". See **goosefoot.**

fa·ther (faáthər) *n.* **1.** A male parent. **2.** A male who functions in a paternal capacity with regard to another; especially, a man who adopts a child. **3.** Any male ancestor; especially, the founder of a line of descent; a forefather. **4.** A man who creates, founds, or originates something: *Chaucer is considered by many to be the father of English poetry.* **5.** *Capital* **F. a.** God. **b.** The first member of the Trinity. **6.** Any elderly or venerable man. Used as a title of respect. **7.** A member of the senate in ancient Rome. **8.** *Sometimes capital* **F.** Any of the authoritative early writers in the Christian Church who formulated doctrines and codified religious observances. **9.** *Often capital* **F.** *Abbr.* **Fr.** A priest or other clergyman or dignitary in the Roman Catholic or Anglican churches. Often used as a title of respect with or without the clergyman's name. **10.** *British.* The member holding the longest tenure in a profession, society, or similar organisation; especially, the longest-serving elected Member of Parliament: *the father of the House.* **11.** A leader of a council, branch of a union, or similar organisation: *the city fathers; father of the chapel.*
~*tr.v.* **fathered, -thering, -thers. 1.** To beget. **2.** To act or serve as a father to. **3.** To create, found, or originate. **4.** To acknowledge as one's work; accept responsibility for. **5. a.** To attribute the paternity, creation, or origin of. Used with *on* or *upon.* **b.** To assign falsely or unjustly; foist. Used with *on* or *upon: You father undue significance upon my words.* [Middle English *fader,* Old English *fæder,* from Germanic *fadēr* (unattested).]

Father Christmas *n. Chiefly British.* **Santa Claus** *(see).*

father confessor *n.* **1.** A priest who hears confessions. **2.** Any person in whom one confides.

father figure *n.* **1.** A man to whom a younger woman is romantically attracted because of his stable fatherly qualities, and often because he resembles her own father. **2.** Any older person who acts in a fatherly way or is looked up to as stable and dependable.

fa·ther·hood (faáthər-hōōd) *n.* The condition of being a father; paternity.

fa·ther-in-law (faáthər-in-law) *n., pl.* **fathers-in-law.** The father of one's husband or wife.

fa·ther·land (faáthər-land) *n.* **1.** A person's native country. **2.** The land of one's forebears.

fa·ther·ly (faáthər-li) *adj.* **1.** Pertaining to, characteristic of, or appropriate to a father. **2.** Showing the affection of a father.
~*adv.* In a fatherly manner. **—fa·ther·li·ness** *n.*

Father's Day *n.* An annual day of commemoration of fathers and fatherhood observed, in Britain, on the third Sunday in June.

Father Time *n.* Time personified as an old man with a long beard carrying a scythe and an hourglass.

fath·om (fáthəm) *n., pl.* **fathoms** or **fathom.** *Abbr.* **fath, fath., fm. 1.** A unit of length equal to 1.829 metres (6 feet), and used principally in the measurement and specification of marine depths. **2.** A unit of volume equal to 0.17 cubic metres (6 cubic feet).
~*tr.v.* **fathomed, -oming, -oms. 1.** To determine the depth of; sound. **2.** To get to the bottom of; penetrate to the meaning of: *"Her simplicity fathomed what clever people falsified"* (Virginia Woolf). [Middle English *fadme,* Old English *fæthm,* a measure of length equal to two arms; akin to Old Norse *fathmr,* embrace.] **—fath·om·a·ble** *adj.*

Fa·thom·e·ter (fa-thómmitər, fə- || *U.S. also* fáthə-meetər) *n.* A trademark for a sonic depth finder.

fath·om·less (fáthəm-ləss, -liss) *adj.* **1.** Too deep to be fathomed or measured; unfathomable. **2.** Too abstruse or complicated to be understood.

fa·tid·ic (fay-tídik, fə-) *adj.* Also **fa·tid·i·cal** (-ik'l). Pertaining to or characterised by prophecy; prophetic. [Latin *fātidicus* : *fātum,* FATE + *dīcere,* to say.]

fat·i·ga·ble (fátti-gəb'l || *U.S. also* fə-teé-) *adj.* Subject to weariness; easily tired. [Late Latin *fatīgābilis,* from Latin *fatīgāre,* to FATIGUE.]

fa·tigue (fə-teég) *n.* **1.** Physical or mental weariness or exhaustion resulting from exertion. **2.** Tiring effort or activity; labour. **3.** *Physiology.* The decreased capacity or complete inability of an organism, organ, or part to function normally because of excessive stimulation or prolonged exertion. **4.** Weakness in metal, wood, or other material resulting from prolonged stress. **5.** *Military.* Manual or menial labour, such as barracks cleaning assigned to soldiers, often as a punishment: *a weekend on fatigue.* Also called "fatigue duty". **6.** *Plural.* **a.** *Military.* Clothing worn for manual or menial work. **b.** Military-style, fashionable clothing.
~*v.* **fatigued, -tiguing, -tigues.** *—tr.* **1.** To tire out; exhaust. **2.** To weaken (a metal, for example) by prolonged stress. *—intr.* **1.** To be or become exhausted or tired out. **2.** To become weakened as a result of stress. Used of metals and other materials. [French, from Old French, from *fatiguer,* to fatigue, from Latin *fatīgāre*†.]

fa·tigued (fə-teégd) *adj.* Exhausted. See Synonyms at **tired.**

Fat·i·ha, Fat·i·hah (fátti-haa) *n. Islam.* The first sura of the Koran, used as a prayer. [From Arabic, "opening".]

Fát·i·ma (fáttimə). Small hamlet in west central Portugal and site of the national shrine for Our Lady of the Rosary of Fátima. Apparitions of the Virgin Mary were reputedly seen there in 1917.

Fat·i·mah (fátti-mə, -maa) (died A.D. 632). The daughter of the prophet, Muhammad, she married Ali, one of the first to embrace Islam. She is considered by Muslims to be one of the Four Perfect Women.

Fat·i·mid¹ (fátti-mid) n. A member of a Muslim dynasty that ruled over parts of north Africa and Egypt between A.D. 909 and 1171. **—Fat·i·mid, Fat·i·mite** (-mīt) adj.

Fat·i·mid² (fátti-mid) n. A person descended from Fatima, the daughter of Muhammad. **—Fat·i·mid, Fat·i·mite** (-mīt) adj.

fat·ling (fát-ling) n. A young animal, such as a lamb or calf, fattened for slaughter.

fat mouse n. Any of various African mice of the genus *Steatomys,* eaten as a delicacy in Africa because of their high content of fat.

fat·so (fát-sō) n., pl. **-soes** or **-sos.** Slang. A fat person. Used humorously or derogatorily, often as a form of address. [FAT + -S (plural suffix) + -o.]

fat·sol·u·ble (fát-sollew-b'l) adj. Soluble in fats or fat solvents, such as ether; lipid-soluble. Said of certain vitamins.

fat·stock (fát-stok) n. Used with a singular or plural verb. Livestock that have been fattened up for market.

fat·ten (fátt'n) v. **-tened, -tening, -tens.** —tr. 1. To make plump or fat. Often used with *up.* 2. To fertilise (land). 3. To increase the amount or substance of; swell. —intr. To grow fat or fatter. **—fat·ten·er** n.

fat·tish (fáttish) adj. Somewhat fat; chubby. **—fat·tish·ness** n.

fat·ty (fátti) adj. **-tier, -tiest.** 1. a. Containing fat. b. Containing excessive amounts of fat. 2. Characteristic of fat; especially, greasy. 3. Derived from or chemically related to fat.
~n., pl. **-ties.** Informal. A fat person. Often used in direct address. **—fat·ti·ly** adv. **—fat·ti·ness** n.

fatty acid n. Any of a large group of monobasic acids having the general formula $C_nH_{2n+1}COOH$; especially, any of a commercially important subgroup obtained from animals and plants, characteristically saturated or unsaturated aliphatic compounds with an even number of carbon atoms, the most abundant of which contain 16 or 18 carbon atoms and include palmitic, stearic, and oleic acids.

fatty degeneration n. Deterioration in the functioning of a tissue or organ, such as the liver or heart, due to the abnormal deposition within it of large amounts of fat.

fa·tu·i·ty (fə-téw-əti, fa- ‖ -tōo-) n., pl. **-ties.** 1. Stupidity accompanied by an air of pride or self-satisfaction. 2. A fatuous act, remark, or sentiment. 3. Futility; vanity. [Old French *fatuite,* from Latin *fatuitās* (stem *fatuitāt-*), from *fatuus,* FATUOUS.]

fat·u·ous (fáttew-əss) adj. 1. Complacently or unconsciously stupid; asinine; inane. 2. Delusive; self-deceiving: *fatuous hopes.* —See Synonyms at **foolish.** [Latin *fatuus†,* silly, fatuous, absurd.] **—fat·u·ous·ly** adv. **—fat·u·ous·ness** n.

fat·wa, fat·wah (fát-waa, -wə) n. An authoritative decree or decision by an Islamic religious leader. [Arabic.]

fau·bourg (fō-boorg; French fō-bóor) n. A suburb, district or quarter of a town, especially in a French-speaking country. [Middle English *fabour,* from Old French *faubourg,* variant (influenced by *faux,* false) of *forsbo(u)rc,* "(something) outside the city": *fors,* outside of, from Latin *forīs,* out, outside + *borc,* fortified place, town, from Late Latin *burgus,* from Germanic.]

fau·cal (fáwk'l) adj. Also **fau·cial** (fáwsh'l). 1. Anatomy. Of or relating to the fauces. 2. Phonetics. Produced in or near the fauces. Said of a sound.

fau·ces (fáw-seez) pl.n. Anatomy. The space between the mouth and pharynx bounded by the soft palate, the base of the tongue, and the palatine arches. [Latin *faucēs†,* throat.]

fau·cet (fáw-sit) n. 1. A tap for drawing off the contents of a barrel. 2. U.S. A tap. [Middle English *faucet,* from Old French *fausset,* plug, from *fausser,* damage, break into, make false, from Late Latin *falsāre,* falsify, from Latin *falsus,* FALSE.]

faugh (faw) interj. Used to express contempt, disgust, or dismissal. [Imitative.]

fauld (fawld) n. A skirt-shaped piece of armour protecting the area between the waist and the top of the thighs.

Faulk·ner (fáwk-nər), **William** (1897–1962). U.S. novelist. Born in Mississippi, he drew on the history, legends, and social problems of his native South. His work included *Sartoris, The Sound and the Fury* (both 1929), *As I Lay Dying* (1930), *Sanctuary* (1931), *Absalom, Absalom!* (1936). Nobel prize for literature (1949).

fault (fawlt, folt) n. 1. Something that prevents perfection, as: a. A flaw, blemish, or defect. b. A mistake; an error. c. An offence, transgression, or minor vice. 2. Responsibility for such a mistake or offence; culpability. 3. Geology. A break in the continuity of a rock formation, caused by a shifting or dislodging of the earth's crust, in which adjacent surfaces are differentially displaced parallel to the plane of fracture. 4. Electricity. A defect in a circuit or wiring caused by imperfect connections, poor insulation or earthing, or shorting. 5. Sports. a. An invalid serve, as in tennis. b. A penalty incurred in showjumping when a horse hits or refuses to jump a fence. c. A device for recording such bad jumps. 6. In hunting, the loss of the scent by a dog or dogs. 7. Archaic. A lack or deficiency. —See Synonyms at **blemish. —at fault.** 1. Deserving of blame; guilty. 2. Confused and puzzled. 3. In hunting, unable to recapture the scent of the game. **—find fault.** To seek, find, and complain about faults; carp. **—to a fault.** Excessively.

—v. **faulted, faulting, faults.** —tr. 1. To find a fault in; criticise or blame. 2. Geology. To produce a fault in; fracture. —intr. 1. To commit a fault or error. 2. Geology. To shift so as to produce a fault. [Middle English *faute,* from Old French, from Vulgar Latin *fallita* (unattested), feminine past participle of Latin *fallere,* to fail, deceive. See **fail.**] **—fault·less** adj. **—fault·less·ly** adv. **—fault·less·ness** n.
Synonyms: fault, failing, weakness, frailty, foible, vice.

fault·find·er (fáwlt-fīndər, fólt-) n. One who seeks out faults; a chronic complainer.

fault·find·ing (fáwlt-fīnding, fólt-) n. Petty criticism; carping.
~adj. Disposed to find trivial faults; captious.

fault plane n. Geology. The plane along which the break or shear of a geological fault occurs.

fault·y (fáwl-ti, fól-) adj. **-ier, -iest.** 1. Containing a fault or faults; imperfect or defective. 2. Obsolete. Deserving of blame; guilty. **—fault·i·ly** adv. **—fault·i·ness** n.

faun (fawn ‖ U.S. also faan) n. Roman Mythology. Any of a group of rural deities represented as having the body of a man and the horns, ears, tail, and sometimes legs of a goat. [Middle English *faun,* from Latin *Faunus,* FAUNUS.]

fau·na (fáw-nə ‖ U.S. also fáa) n., pl. **-nas** or **-nae** (-nee). 1. Animals collectively; especially, the animals of a particular region or time. 2. A descriptive list of animals. [New Latin, from Latin *Fauna,* sister of FAUNUS.]

Fau·nus (fáw-nəss ‖ U.S. also fáa-). Roman Mythology. A god of nature and fertility, worshipped by shepherds and farmers, and identified with the Greek Pan. [Latin *Faunus†.*]

Fau·ré (fórray, fō-ráy), **Gabriel (Urbain)** (1845 – 1924). French composer and organist. He composed his *Requiem* (1888), the song cycle *La Bonne Chanson* (1891 – 1892), and the opera *Pénélope* (1913).

Faust (fowst). Also **Faust·us** (-əss). A magician and alchemist, hero of several poetic and dramatic works, who sells his soul to the devil for power and knowledge. [German, after Johann *Faust,* 16th-century magician and astrologer.] **—Faust·i·an** (-i-ən) adj.

faute de mieux (fōt-dəm-yúr, -yō) adv. French. For want of anything better.
~adj. Accepted or undertaken for want of anything better.

fau·teuil (fō-tō-i, -turl, French fō-tō-i) n. 1. A stall in a theatre. 2. An armchair. [French, from Old French *faudestuel, faldestoel,* folding stool, from Germanic.]

fauv·ism (fō-viz'm) n. Often capital F. An art movement originating in Paris in 1905 as a revolt against impressionism, characterised by simplified form and the use of vivid colours. Its members included Dufy, Derain, Matisse, and Rouault. [From French *fauve,* wild beast (term applied to Matisse, Vlaminck, and other members of the group because of their use of violent colours).] **—fauve** (fōv) n. & adj. **—fauv·ist** n. & adj.

faux-na·if (fō-naa-éef, -nī-) adj. Seeming or pretending to be ingenuous and unsophisticated.
~n. One who pretends to be ingenuous and unsophisticated. [French, "false naïve".]

faux pas (fō páa) n., pl. **faux pas** (fō páaz; French fō páa). A social blunder; a breach of etiquette. [French, "false step".]

fa·va bean (fáavə) n. A broad bean (*see*). [Italian *fava,* from Latin *faba,* bean + BEAN.]

fa·ve·o·late (fávvi-ə-layt) adj. Pitted with cavities or cells; honeycombed. [New Latin *faveolus,* diminutive of Latin *favus†,* honeycomb.]

fa·vo·ni·an (fə-vōni-ən) adj. 1. Of the west wind. 2. Mild; benign. [Latin *Favōniānus,* from *Favōnius†,* west wind.]

fa·vour, U.S. **fa·vor** (fáyvər) n. 1. a. A gracious, kind, or friendly attitude. b. An act that reveals such an attitude; an act of kindness: *Will you do me a favour?* c. Often plural. An act requiring sacrifice or special generosity; an indulgence. 2. a. Friendly regard shown by a group or a superior. b. The state of being held in such regard. 3. Approval or support; sanction. 4. Partiality; favouritism. 5. Usually plural. Sexual privileges, as granted by a woman. 6. a. Something given as a token of love, loyalty, affection, or remembrance. b. A small, decorative gift given to each guest at a party or ball. 7. Advantage; benefit: *a balance in our favour.* 8. Archaic. A communication, especially a letter. 9. Archaic. a. The aspect or appearance. b. A countenance; a visage; a face. c. Any part of the face; a feature. **—in favour of.** 1. In support of; approving. 2. To the advantage of. 3. Inscribed or made out to, as a cheque. 4. Preferring: *She turned down my suggestion in favour of yours.*
~tr.v. **favoured, -vouring, -vours.** 1. To perform a kindness for; oblige. 2. To regard with approval; like. 3. To be partial to; indulge a liking for: *He favours garish ties.* 4. To be or tend to be in support of. 5. To support through partiality; treat with favouritism. 6. To make easier or more possible; facilitate. 7. Informal. To resemble in appearance. 8. To treat with care; be gentle with: *The soldier favoured his wounded leg.* [Middle English *favour,* from Old French, from Latin *favor,* from *favēre,* to favour, be favourable.] **—fa·vour·er** n. **—fa·vour·ing·ly** adv.

fa·vour·a·ble (fáy-vərə-b'l, -vrə-) adj. 1. Advantageous; helpful. 2. Propitious; encouraging. 3. Manifesting approval; commendatory. 4. Embodying or conceding that which was desired or requested: *a favourable reply.* 5. Indulgent or partial. **—fa·vour·a·ble·ness** n. **—fa·vour·a·bly** adv.
Synonyms: favourable, propitious, auspicious, benign, conducive.

fa·voured (fáyvərd) adj. 1. Treated or thought of with kindness or liking; indulged; privileged. 2. Having special talents, gifts, or beauty. **3.** Having a physical appearance of a specified kind. Used chiefly in the combinations *well-favoured* and *ill-favoured.*

fa·vour·ite (fáy-və-rit, -vrit) *n.* **1. a.** A person or thing liked or preferred above all others. **b.** A person especially indulged by a superior. **2.** *Sports.* A competitor regarded as most likely to win.
~*adj.* Liked or preferred above all others; regarded with special favour. [Obsolete French *favorit,* from Italian *favorito,* past participle of *favorire,* to favour, from *favore,* favour, from Latin *favor,* FAVOUR.]

favourite son *n. U.S.* **1.** A man nominated as a presidential candidate, often merely as an honorary gesture, by the delegates from his own constituency at a national political convention. **2.** Any politician well-known in his own constituency but not elsewhere.

fa·vour·it·ism (fáy-vəri-tiz'm, -vri-) *n.* **1.** A display of privileged treatment or partiality, especially when unjust, towards a favoured person or group. **2.** The state of being held in special favour.

fav·rile glass (fəv-réel) *n.* Stained or iridescent glass of a kind popular in the early 1900s for decorative objects or lamps. Also called "Tiffany glass". [Former trade name (1894) of glass manufactured by L.C. Tiffany (1848–1933), based on *fabrile,* "of a craftsman", from Old French, from Latin *fabrīlis,* from *faber,* artificer.]

fa·vus (fáyvəss) *n.* A chronic fungous infection of the scalp and nails. [New Latin, from Latin, honeycomb. See **faveolate.**]

Faw·cett (fáw-sit, fóssit), **Dame Millicent,** born Millicent Garrett. (1847–1929). Pioneering women's leader. She was president of the British National Union of Women's Suffrage Societies (1897–1919).

Fawkes (fawks), **Guy** (1570–1606). English conspirator in the Gunpowder Plot. Fawkes, a Roman Catholic, took part in a plot to blow up King James I and the English Parliament on November 5, 1605, to avenge the persecution of Roman Catholics in England. He was found in a cellar with the gunpowder, was tortured, and disclosed his accomplices. He was hanged in 1606. Guy Fawkes Night is widely celebrated each November 5 by burning effigies of Fawkes on bonfires.

fawn[1] (fawn || *U.S. also* faan) *intr.v.* **fawned, fawning, fawns. 1.** To attempt to please or exhibit affection, as in the manner of a dog wagging its tail and whining. Used with *on* or *upon.* **2.** To seek favour or attention by flattery and obsequious behaviour. Often used with *on* or *upon.* [Middle English *faunen,* Old English *fagnian, fægnian,* to rejoice, from *fægen,* FAIN.] **—fawn·er** *n.* **—fawn·ing·ly** *adv.*

fawn[2] *n.* **1.** A young deer, especially one less than a year old. **2.** Light yellowish brown to light greyish brown. [Middle English *foun, fawn,* from Old French *foun, feon,* offspring of an animal, from Vulgar Latin *fētō,* from Latin *fētus,* offspring, a giving birth.] **—fawn** *adj.*

fax (faks) *n.* **1.** A system of long-distance document transmission using telephone lines to deliver a photocopied facsimile of a document. **2.** A faxed document: *get a fax.* **3.** A faxing machine: *use a fax.*
~ *tr.v.* **faxed, faxing, faxes. 1.** To transmit (a document) using this system. **2.** To fax a document to (a person). [Perhaps shortened from *Photofax* (proprietary name).]

fay[1] (fay) *v.* **fayed, faying, fays.** *—tr.* To join (beams, for example) closely or tightly. *—intr.* To be fitted or joined tightly. [Middle English *feien,* Old English *fēgan.*]

fay[2] *n.* A fairy, sprite, or elf.
~*adj.* **1.** Pertaining to or resembling a fairy. **2.** *Informal.* Pretentiously sweet or charming; arch. [Middle English *faie,* one possessing magical powers, from Old French *faie, fae,* from Latin *fāta,* the Fates, plural of *fātum,* FATE.]

fay·al·ite (fáy-ə-līt, fī-áa-) *n.* A yellowish to black mineral, mostly Fe_2SiO_4, of the olivine group. [German *Fayalit* : *Fayal,* German form for *Faial* (island in the Azores where it was first found) + -ITE.]

faze (fayz) *tr.v.* **fazed, fazing, fazes.** *Chiefly U.S. Informal.* To disrupt the composure of; bother; disconcert. [Variant of FEEZE.]

fa·zen·da (fə-zéndə) *n., pl.* **-das.** In Brazil, a hacienda, estate, or plantation, especially a coffee plantation. [Portuguese, from Latin *facienda,* things to be done, neuter plural gerundive of *facere,* to do.]

F.B.A. Fellow of the British Academy.

FBI, F.B.I. Federal Bureau of Investigation (in the United States).

f.c. *Printing.* follow copy.

F.C. Football Club.

fcap., fcp. foolscap.

F clef *n. Music.* A **bass clef** *(see).*

F.C.O. Foreign and Commonwealth Office.

F.D. 1. Fidei Defensor. **2.** fire department.

FDA Food and Drug Administration (in the United States).

FDR, F.D.R. Franklin Delano Roosevelt.

F.E. Further education.

Fe The symbol for the element iron [Latin *ferrum*].

fe·al·ty (fée-əl-ti) *n., pl.* **-ties. 1.** The obligation of loyalty owed by a vassal to his feudal lord. **2.** Faithfulness; allegiance. —See Synonyms at **fidelity.** [Middle English *fealtye, feute,* from Old French *fealte, feau(l)te,* from Latin *fidēlitās* (stem *fidēlitāt-*), faithfulness, from *fidēlis,* faithful, from *fidēs,* faith.]

fear (feer) *n.* **1.** A feeling of alarm or disquiet caused by the expectation of danger, pain, disaster, or the like; terror; dread; apprehension. **2.** An instance or manifestation of such a feeling. **3.** A state or condition of alarm or dread: *The prisoners spent the night in fear.* **4.** Extreme reverence or awe, as towards a supreme power. **5.** A ground for dread or apprehension; a possibility of danger. **—for fear of.** So as to prevent or avoid: *She tiptoed for fear of waking the children.* **—for fear that.** Lest; in case: *He hurried home for fear that he might miss his guests.* **—no fear.** Not likely; certainly not. **—no fear of.** No chance or possibility of: *There's no fear of that happening.* **—without fear or favour.** Impartially; without bias.
~*v.* **feared, fearing, fears.** *—tr.* **1.** To be afraid or frightened of. **2.** To be anxious or apprehensive about. **3.** To be in awe of; revere. **4. a.** To suspect: *I fear you are wrong.* **b.** To be sorry: *I fear I have some bad news for you.* *—intr.* **1.** To be afraid, frightened, or terrified. **2.** To feel anxious or apprehensive. Used with *for.* [Middle English *fer,* Old English *fǣr,* danger, sudden calamity, from Germanic.] **—fear·er** *n.*
Synonyms: *fear, fright, dread, terror, panic, alarm, trepidation.*

fear·ful (féer-f'l) *adj.* **1.** Causing or capable of causing fear; frightening; terrifying. **2.** Experiencing fear; frightened. **3.** Feeling anxious or apprehensive. **4.** Feeling reverence, dread, or awe. **5.** *Informal.* Very bad; dreadful: *a fearful blunder.* **—fear·ful·ness** *n.*

fear·ful·ly (féer-f'l-i, -fli) *adv.* **1.** In a fearful manner. **2.** *Informal.* Extremely; very: *I'm fearfully sorry.*

fear·less (féer-ləss, -liss) *adj.* Having no fear; unafraid; brave. See Synonyms at **brave. —fear·less·ly** *adv.* **—fear·less·ness** *n.*

fear·nought, fear·naught (féer-nawt) *n.* **1.** A heavy, thick, often rough, woollen material used in making overcoats. **2.** A garment made of this cloth.

fear·some (féer-s'm) *adj.* **1.** Causing or capable of causing fear; frightening; awesome. **2.** Afraid; frightened; fearful; timid. **—fear·some·ly** *adv.* **—fear·some·ness** *n.*

fea·sance (féez'nss) *n. Law.* The execution of an obligation or duty. [Anglo-French *fesance,* from *faire,* to do, from Latin *facere.*]

fea·si·ble (féezə-b'l) *adj.* **1.** Capable of being accomplished or brought about; practicable; possible: *a feasible outline for the project.* **2.** Capable of being utilised or dealt with successfully; suitable. **3.** Logical; likely: *He gave a feasible excuse for his absence.* —See Synonyms at **possible.** [Middle English *faisible, fesable,* from Old French *faisible,* from *faire* (present stem *fais-*), to do, from Latin *facere.*] **—fea·si·bil·i·ty** (-bíllәti), **fea·si·ble·ness** *n.* **—fea·si·bly** *adv.*

feast (feest) *n.* **1. a.** A large, elaborately prepared meal, usually for many persons and often with entertainment; a banquet. **b.** Any large, sumptuous, or delicious meal. **2.** A periodic religious festival in commemoration of an event or in honour of a god or saint. **3.** Something giving great pleasure or satisfaction: *a feast for the mind.*
~*v.* **feasted, feasting, feasts.** *—tr.* **1.** To give a feast for; entertain or feed sumptuously. **2.** To provide with pleasure; delight; gratify: *"Augustus too feasted his eyes on the same plate of fruit"* (Virginia Woolf). *—intr.* **1.** To partake of a feast. **2.** To eat with great enjoyment. Used with *on: The boys feasted on the stolen fruit.* **3.** To experience with gratification or delight. [Middle English *feste,* from Old French, from Latin *fēsta,* neuter plural (taken as feminine singular) of *fēstus,* joyous, festal.] **—feast·er** *n.*

Feast of Dedication *n.* A Jewish holiday, **Chanukkah** *(see).*

Feast of Lanterns *n.* **1.** A Chinese festival, held at the first full moon of the new year, at which coloured lanterns are displayed. **2.** A Japanese festival, **Bon** *(see).* **3.** A Hindu festival in October or November, lasting five days and dedicated to the goddess of wealth.

Feast of Tabernacles *n.* A Jewish holiday, **Succoth** *(see).*

Feast of Weeks *n.* A Jewish holiday, **Shavuot** *(see).*

feat[1] (feet) *n.* **1.** Any act or deed; especially, an act of courage. **2.** Any act or product of skill, endurance, imagination, or strength; an achievement. [Middle English *fete,* from Old French *fait, fet,* from Latin *factum,* something done, from the neuter past participle of *facere,* to do.]

feat[2] *adj.* **feater, featest.** *Archaic.* **1.** Adroit; dexterous; skilful. **2.** Neat; trim. [Middle English *fete,* adroit, skilful, from Old French *fait,* from Latin *factum,* something done. See **feat**[1].] **—feat·ly** *adv.*

feath·er (féth̲ər) *n.* **1.** Any of the light, flat structures constituting the plumage of birds, consisting of numerous slender, closely arranged parallel barbs forming a vane on either side of a tapering hollow shaft. **2.** *Plural.* Plumage. **3.** *Plural. Informal.* Clothing; attire. **4.** *Usually plural.* A tuft or fringe of hair resembling a feather, as on the legs or tail of some dogs. **5.** Character, kind, or nature: *Birds of a feather flock together.* **6.** Something small, trivial, or inconsequential. **7. a.** A strip, wedge, or flange, used as a strengthening part. **b.** A wedge or key that fits into a groove to make a joint. **8.** The vane of an arrow, made of real or imitation feathers. **9.** A feather-shaped flaw, as in a gem or precious stone. **10.** The wake made by a submarine periscope. **11.** The act of feathering the blade of an oar in rowing. **—a feather in (one's) cap.** A distinctive achievement; an act or deed to one's credit. **—in fine** or **good feather.** In excellent form, health, or humour. **—in full feather. 1.** Having plenty of money. **2.** Completely equipped; elaborately dressed. **—make the feathers fly.** To cause a commotion by directing an insult or provoking a fight. **—show the white feather to.** To accuse of cowardice; despise for being a coward. [White feathers in a fighting cock were formerly believed to be a sign of weakness and bad breeding.]
~*v.* **feathered, -ering, -ers.** *—tr.* **1.** To cover, dress, or decorate with or as if with feathers. **2.** To fit (an arrow) with a feather; fletch. **3. a.** To thin, reduce, or fringe the edge of by cutting, shaving, or wearing away. **b.** To shorten and taper (hair) by cutting and thinning. **4.** To connect with a tongue-and-groove joint. **5.** To turn (an oar blade) horizontal between strokes. **6.** *Aeronautics.* To alter the pitch of (a propeller) so that the blade chords are parallel with

the line of flight. —*intr.* **1.** To grow feathers or become feathered. **2.** To move, spread, or grow in a manner suggestive of feathers. **3.** To feather an oar. **4.** *Aeronautics.* To feather a propeller. **5.** To quiver through the whole body. Used of a hound when hunting. **—feather (one's) nest.** To grow wealthy, by using property or funds left in one's trust. [Old English *fether*.] **—feath·er·less** *adj.*

feather bed *n.* A mattress stuffed with feathers or down.

feath·er·bed (féthər-bed, -béd) *v.* **-bedded, -bedding, -beds.** —*intr.* **1.** To employ more workers than are actually needed for a given purpose. **2.** To be so employed. —*tr.* To pamper or spoil.

feath·er·brain (féthər-brayn) *n. Informal.* A silly, flighty, or empty-headed person. Also called "featherhead", "featherpate". **—feath·er·brained** *adj.*

feather duster *n.* A brush consisting of a bunch of feathers fastened to the end of a stick, used for dusting delicate objects or clearing away cobwebs.

feath·ered (féthərd) *adj.* **1.** Having feathers; covered or adorned with feathers. **2.** *Aeronautics.* Having the propeller blade chords parallel to the line of flight.

feathered friend *n.* A bird.

feath·er·edge (féthər-ej, -éj) *n.* **1.** A thin fragile edge; a tapering edge of a board. **2.** A deckle edge *(see).* **—feath·er·edged** *adj.*

feather grass *n.* Any of various grasses of the genus *Stipa,* having clusters of feather-like spikelets.

feath·er·ing (féthəring) *n.* **1.** Plumage. **2.** The feathers fitted to an arrow. **3.** A fringe of long hair on an animal's coat, especially that on a dog's leg. **4.** *Architecture.* The cusps in Gothic tracery.

feather palm *n.* Any palm tree having pinnate leaves forming feather-like fronds. Compare **fan palm.**

feather star *n.* Any of numerous crinoids of the genus *Antedon* and related genera, having a free-moving, stalkless adult stage with branched, feathery arms.

feath·er·stitch (féthər-stich) *n.* An embroidery stitch that produces a decorative zigzag line. **—feath·er·stitch** *v.*

feath·er·veined (féthər-vaynd) *adj.* Having veins branching from either side of a midrib. Said of leaves.

feath·er·weight (féthər-wayt) *n.* **1. a.** An amateur boxer weighing between 54 and 57 kilograms (119 and 125 pounds). **b.** A professional boxer weighing between 8 stone 6 pounds and 9 stone (55.53 and 57.15 kilograms). **2.** A wrestler in an equivalent weight category, or slightly heavier. **3.** Any person or thing of little weight or size. **4.** An insignificant person or thing. ~*adj.* **1.** Of or pertaining to featherweights: *a featherweight match.* **2.** Unimportant; trivial; superficial.

feath·er·y (féthəri) *adj.* **1.** Covered with or consisting of feathers. **2.** Resembling or suggestive of a feather or feathers, as in form or lightness. **—feath·er·i·ness** *n.*

fea·ture (féechər) *n.* **1.** *Plural.* The make-up or appearance of the face or its parts. **2.** Any of the distinct parts of the face, such as the nose, mouth, or eyes. **3.** Any prominent or distinctive aspect, quality, or characteristic. **4. a.** The main film in a programme presented at a cinema. **b.** A full-length fictional film, especially as opposed to a documentary. **5.** A prominent or extra article or story in a newspaper or periodical. **6.** Anything advertised as especially attractive or as an inducement, such as an item on sale at a discount in a department store. **7.** *Archaic.* Form; shape; appearance. ~*v.* **featured, -turing, -tures.** —*tr.* **1.** To give special attention to; make prominent, display, or publicise. **2.** To have or include as a prominent part or characteristic: *The film featured many well-known actors.* **3.** To draw or otherwise portray the features of. —*intr.* **1.** To be a feature. **2.** To be a prominent or distinct part or characteristic. [Middle English *feture,* from Old French *feture, faiture,* form, from Latin *factūra,* a making, formation, from *factus,* past participle of *facere,* to do, make.]

fea·tured (féechərd) *adj.* **1.** Given special attention or publicity; made prominent. **2.** Having a specified kind of facial features. Often used in combination: *small-featured; sharp-featured.*

fea·ture-length (féechər-léng-th, -lénk- ‖ -lén-) *adj.* Of normal or full length: *a feature-length film.*

fea·ture·less (féechər-lass, -liss) *adj.* With no distinguishing characteristics; unremarkable.

Feb. February.

febri– *comb. form.* Indicates fever; for example, **febrifuge.** [Latin *febris,* FEVER.]

fe·bric·i·ty (fi-bríssəti) *n.* The condition of having a fever. [Medieval Latin *febricitās* (stem *febricitāt-*), from Latin *febris,* FEVER.]

feb·ri·fa·cient (fébbri-fáyshənt) *n.* A substance that causes a fever. ~*adj.* Causing fever. [Latin *febris,* FEVER + -FACIENT.]

fe·brif·ic (fi-bríffik) *adj.* **1.** Causing fever. **2.** Having a fever; feverish. [Latin *febris,* FEVER + -FIC.]

feb·ri·fuge (fébbri-fewj) *n.* Any agent that reduces fever. ~*adj.* Fever-reducing. [French *fébrifuge,* from New Latin *febrifugus* : Latin *febris,* FEVER + *fugāre,* to drive away, from *fugere,* to flee.]

feb·rile (fée-brīl ‖ *U.S. also* féb-rəl, -ríl) *adj.* Of, or pertaining to fever; feverish. [French *fébrile,* from Latin *febris,* FEVER.]

Feb·ru·ar·y (fébbrōō-əri, fébbew- ‖ *U.S.* -erri) *n., pl.* **-ies** or **-ys.** *Abbr.* **Feb.** The second month of the year according to the Gregorian calendar. February has 28 days, 29 in leap years. [Middle English *feveryer,* from Old French *feverier,* from Late Latin *febrārius,* from Latin *februārius,* from *februa,* festival of purification held on February 15, of Sabine origin.]

feces. *U.S.* Variant of **faeces.**

fe·cit (fáykit, fée-sit) *n. Abbr.* **fec.** *Latin.* He (or she) made (or did) it. Used before or after an artist's name on a work of art.

feck·less (féck-ləss, -liss) *adj.* **1.** Lacking purpose or vitality; feeble; ineffective. **2.** Careless; irresponsible. [Scottish *feck,* efficacy, short for EFFECT + -LESS.] **—feck·less·ly** *adv.* **—feck·less·ness** *n.*

fec·u·lent (féckew-lənt) *adj.* Full of foul matter, dregs, or sediment; foul; fetid. [Middle English *feculent,* from Latin *faeculentus,* from *faex* (stem *faec-*), FAECES.] **—fec·u·lence** *n.*

fe·cund (féek-ənd, fék-, -un-) *adj.* **1.** Capable of producing offspring or vegetation; fertile; productive; fruitful. **2.** Marked by intellectual productivity. [Middle English *fecound,* from Old French *fecond,* from Latin *fēcundus,* perhaps akin to *fēlix,* happy.]

fe·cun·date (féek-ən-dayt, fék-, -un-) *tr.v.* **-dated, -dating, -dates. 1.** To make fecund or fruitful. **2.** To impregnate; fertilise. [Latin *fēcundāre,* from *fēcundus,* FECUND.]

fe·cun·di·ty (fi-kúndəti) *n.* **1.** The quality or power of producing abundantly; fertility. **2.** The capacity for or power of producing young, especially in abundance; productiveness. **3.** Productive or creative power: *the fecundity of his mind.*

fed. Past tense and past participle of **feed.**

Fed (fed) *n. U.S. Informal.* A member of the Federal Bureau of Investigation.

Fe·da·yee (fə-dáa-yee, féd-ī-ée) *n., pl.* **-yeen** (-yeen; -éen). An Arab commando, especially one operating against Israel. [Arabic *fedā'yūn,* commandos, from *fidā'ī,* one who sacrifices himself for his country, from *fidā',* redemption.]

fed·er·al (féddrəl, féddərəl) *adj. Abbr.* **Fed., fed. 1.** Of, pertaining to, or designating a form of government in which political units recognise the sovereignty of a central authority while retaining certain residual powers of government. **2.** Of or pertaining to the central government of a federation, as distinct from the governments of its constituent political units. **3.** Of, pertaining to, or formed by a treaty or compact between constituent political units: "*Our connection had been federal only, and was now dissolved by the commencement of hostilities.*" (Thomas Jefferson). **4.** *Capital* **F. a.** Of, pertaining to, or designating the central government of the United States or Canada. **b.** Of, pertaining to, or characterising the U.S. Federalist Party or Federalism. **c.** Of, pertaining to, or supporting the Federal government during the U.S. Civil War; pro-Union. ~*n.* **1.** A supporter of federation or federal government. **2.** *Capital* **F. a.** A Federalist. **b.** A supporter of the Union during the U.S. Civil War; especially, a Union soldier. [Latin *foedus* (stem *foeder-*), league, treaty, compact.] **—fed·er·al·ly** *adv.*

Federal Bureau of Investigation *n. Abbr.* **FBI, F.B.I.** An agency of the U.S. Justice Department responsible for investigating violations of Federal law.

Federal Capital Territory. See **Australian Capital Territory.**

Federal District *n.* An area in certain federal countries that is reserved as the site of the national capital, such as the District of Columbia. Also called "Federal Territory".

fed·er·al·ise, fed·er·al·ize (féddrə-līz, féddərə-) —*tr.v.* **-ised, -ising, -ises. 1.** To unite in a federal union. **2.** To subject to the authority of a federal government; put under federal control. **—fed·er·al·i·sa·tion** (-lī-záysh'n ‖ *U.S.* -li-) *n.*

fed·er·al·ism (féddrə-liz'm, féddərə-) *n.* **1. a.** The doctrine or system of federal government. **b.** The advocacy of such a government. **2.** *Capital* **F.** The doctrine of the Federalist Party.

fed·er·al·ist (féddrə-list, féddərə-) *n.* **1.** An advocate of federalism. **2.** *Capital* **F.** A member or supporter of the Federalist Party. **—fed·er·al·ist, fed·er·al·is·tic** (-lístik) *adj.*

Federalist Party *n.* Also **Federal Party.** A U.S. political party founded in 1787 that favoured strong central government.

Federal Republic of Germany. See **Germany.**

Federal Reserve System *n. Abbr.* **FRS** A U.S. banking system consisting of 12 *Federal Reserve Banks* each serving member banks in a *Federal Reserve District* and supervised by the *Federal Reserve Board,* appointed by the President.

fed·er·ate (fédda-rayt) *v.* **-ated, -ating, -ates.** —*tr.* To join or bring together in a league, federal union, or similar association. —*intr.* To unite in a federal union. ~*adj.* (fédda-rət, -rit). United under a central government; federated. [Latin *foederāre,* from *foedus* (stem *foeder-*), league, treaty.] **—fed·er·a·tive** (-rətiv, -raytiv) *adj.*

fed·er·a·tion (fédda-ráysh'n) *n. Abbr.* **fed. 1.** The act of federating; especially, a joining together of states in a league or federal union. **2.** A league or association formed by federating, especially a political unit or country so formed, in which the central government is relatively powerful. Compare **confederation.**

Fé·dé·ra·tion In·ter·na·tion·ale des É·checs (fay-day-rass-yón aN-tair-nass-yo-nál dayz ay-shék) *n. Abbr.* **F.I.D.E.** The World Chess Federation.

fe·do·ra (fi-dáwrə ‖ -dórə) *n.* A soft felt hat with a brim that can be turned up or down and a fairly low crown creased lengthways. [From *Fédora* (1882), play by Victorien Sardou (1831–1908), French playwright.]

fed up *adj.* **1.** Out of patience; irritated: *I'm fed up with your nagging.* **2.** Bored; having had too much.

fee (fee) *n.* **1. a.** A charge fixed by an institution or by law: *tuition fees; the fee for a fishing licence.* **b.** Any fixed charge. **2.** A payment for professional or special service: *a tax consultant's fee.* **3.** *Archaic.* A tip; a gratuity. **4.** *Law.* An inherited or heritable estate in land. See **fee simple, fee tail. 5. a.** In feudal law, an estate in land granted by a lord to his vassal on condition of homage and service.

In this sense, also called "feud", "feudality", "fief". **b.** The land so held. —See Synonyms at **price.** —**hold in fee.** To have absolute and legal possession of.
~*tr.v.* **feed, feeing, fees.** **1.** To give a fee to. **2.** *Chiefly Scottish.* To hire for a fee. [Middle English *fe,* inherited estate, payment, from Old French *fe, fief,* from Frankish *fehu-ōd* (unattested), cattle, property; akin to FIEF, FEUD (estate).]

fee·ble (fée'b'l) *adj.* **-bler, -blest.** **1. a.** Lacking strength; weak; especially, frail or infirm: *a feeble old woman.* **b.** Indicating weakness: *a feeble walk.* **2.** Lacking vigour or force; inadequate; ineffective: *a feeble attempt.* **3.** Barely discernible; faint; slight: *a feeble cry.* —See Synonyms at **weak.** [Middle English *feble,* from Old French *feble, fieble, fleible,* from Latin *flēbilis,* to be wept over, lamentable, from *flēre,* to weep.] —**fee·ble·ness** *n.* —**fee·bly** *adv.*

fee·ble-mind·ed (fée'b'l-mīndid) *adj.* **1.** Mentally deficient; subnormal in intelligence. **2.** Dull-witted; stupid; foolish. **3.** Irresolute; indecisive. —**fee·ble-mind·ed·ly** *adv.* —**fee·ble-mind·ed·ness** *n.*

feed (feed) *v.* **fed** (fed), **feeding, feeds.** —*tr.* **1. a.** To give food to; supply with nourishment: *feed the children.* **b.** To provide as food or nourishment: *feed fish to a cat.* **2. a.** To serve as food for: *The turkey is large enough to feed a dozen.* **b.** To produce food for: *The valley feeds an entire county.* **3. a.** To supply or maintain a flow of (a material to be consumed, utilised, or worked upon): *feed ammunition to a gun crew.* **b.** To supply with fuel: *Leaking oil fed the flames.* **4. a.** To minister to; gratify: *The story fed their appetite for the morbid.* **b.** To support or promote: *feed suspicions.* **5.** *Informal.* In the performing arts, to supply as a cue: *feed lines to a comedian.* **6.** *Sports.* To pass the ball or puck to (a teammate), especially in order to score. **7.** *Electricity.* To introduce (a current) into a circuit. —*intr.* To eat. Used chiefly of animals. —**feed on** or **upon.** **1.** To consume as food. **2.** To draw support or satisfaction from: *His ego feeds on flattery.*
~*n.* **1.** An act or instance of feeding, especially animals or babies. **2. a.** Food for animals or birds; fodder. **b.** The allowance of fodder given at one time. **3.** *Informal.* A meal. **4. a.** Material, or an amount of material, supplied to a machine. **b.** The act of supplying this material. **5. a.** The apparatus that supplies material to a machine. **b.** The aperture through which such material enters a machine. **6.** *Informal.* A performer who supplies cues to another, especially in a comic dialogue. [Feed, fed, fed; Middle English *feden, fed, fedde,* Old English *fēdan, fēdde, fēdd,* from Germanic.]

feed back *tr.v.* To return by feedback. —*intr.v.* To return as feedback.

feed·back (féed-bak) *n.* **1. a.** The return of a portion of the output of any process or system, such as microphone noise, to the input, especially when used to maintain the output within predetermined limits. See **positive feedback, negative feedback.** **b.** The portion of the output so returned. **c.** Control of a system or process by such means: *"When feedback is possible and stable, its advantage . . . is to make performance less dependent on the load."* (Norbert Wiener). **d.** The high-pitched whistle produced in a public-address system that occurs when sound from the loudspeaker is picked up by the microphone. **2.** Broadly, any information about the result of a process, experiment, or enquiry; a response.

feedback inhibition *n.* A biological control mechanism that causes excessive accumulation of the end product of a biochemical pathway to inhibit an enzyme near the beginning of the pathway.

feed·er (féedər) *n.* **1. a.** One that supplies food. **b.** One that is fed, especially an animal that is being fattened. **2.** One that feeds materials into a machine for further processing. **3. a.** A baby's bib. **b.** A baby's bottle. **4.** Anything that contributes to the operation, maintenance, or supply of something else, as: **a.** A tributary. **b.** A secondary bus, road, or railway line linking a small community with a main bus, road, or railway line. **5.** *Electricity.* Any of the medium-voltage lines used to distribute electric power from a substation to consumers or smaller substations.
~*adj.* Being or functioning as a feeder: *a feeder airline.*

feeding frenzy *n.* **1.** Frenzied feeding by a group of predators such as piranhas. **2.** *Informal.* Frenzied pursuit of a goal by a group, as of paparazzi.

feed·lot (féed-lot) *n.* An area where animals are fattened up for market.

feed·pipe (féed-pīp) *n.* A pipe through which water or some other fluid is introduced into a system, such as the pipe through which feedwater is fed into a boiler.

feed·stock (féed-stok) *n.* Raw materials fed into a machine or chemical plant for processing.

feed·water (féed-wawtər || *U.S. also* -wottər) *n.* The clean, air-free water that is fed into a boiler or some other equipment or system.

feel (feel) *v.* **felt** (felt), **feeling, feels.** —*tr.* **1. a.** To perceive through the sense of touch. **b.** To perceive as a localised physical sensation: *feel a sharp pain.* **c.** To perceive as a nonlocalised physical sensation: *feel the cold.* **2. a.** To touch. **b.** To examine by touching. **c.** To test carefully; explore with caution: *feel one's way in a new job.* **3. a.** To experience (an emotion): *I felt great shame.* **b.** To be aware of; sense: *She felt his annoyance; feel that all is well.* **c.** To suffer from; experience the impact of: *feel the loss of someone.* **d.** To be emotionally convinced of: *feel it in one's bones.* **4.** To believe or consider: *His answer was felt to be evasive.* —*intr.* **1.** To experience sensations of touch. **2.** To give or produce sensation or feeling, especially through the sense of touch: *The sheets felt smooth.* **3. a.** To perceive oneself to be: *I feel so stupid.* **b.** To have or experience a specified physical or emotional sensation: *I feel tired; He felt very sad.* **4.** To search or be guided by or as if by the sense of touch: *feeling for the light switch in the dark.* **5.** To have compassion or sympathy. Used with *with* or *for*: *I feel for him in his troubles.* **6. a.** To be emotionally moved: *feel strongly about the election.* **b.** To be guided by sentiment or emotion: *"We all do no end of feeling and we mistake it for thinking"* (Mark Twain). —**feel like.** *Informal.* To be in the mood for; have a desire for. —**feel (oneself).** To sense oneself as being in a normal state of health or spirits: *I don't feel quite myself today.* —**feel out.** To try cautiously or indirectly to ascertain the viewpoint of (a person) or the nature of (a situation). —**feel up to.** To feel capable of or ready for.
~*n.* **1. a.** The sensation experienced by touching or feeling: *the feel of a rose petal.* **b.** The act or an instance of touching or feeling: *have a feel under the chair for the pen.* **2.** The sense of touch: *rough to the feel.* **3.** The nature, condition, or quality of something perceived: **a.** Chiefly physically: *the feel of a sports car.* **b.** Emotionally or mentally: *get the feel of one's audience.* [Feel, felt, felt; Middle English *felen, felde, feld,* Old English *fēlan, fēlde, fēld,* from West Germanic.]

Usage: *Feel* (verb) is followed by an adjective when the sense relates to a person's perception of his condition of being: *I was sick last week but now I feel different; today I feel strong.* The adjectives *different* and *strong* describe the subject in such examples. In other senses of *feel* an adverb is possible in the position following the verb, as, for example, when *feel* means to have an opinion, conviction, or the like: *She feels strongly about equal rights for women; He used to agree with her position, but he feels differently now.* Here *strongly* and *differently* modify the verb with respect to degree and condition.

feel·er (féelər) *n.* **1.** One that feels. **2.** A remark, hint, question, or the like, designed to elicit the attitude or intention of others. **3.** A sensory or tactile organ, such as an antenna, tentacle, or barbel.

feeler gauge *n.* A thin metal strip of specific thickness used to measure or set a gap between two parts.

feel·ing (féeling) *n.* **1. a.** The sensation involving perception by touch. **b.** A sensation perceived by touch. **c.** Any physical sensation. **2.** Any affective state of consciousness, such as that resulting from emotions, sentiments, or desires: *a feeling of excitement.* **3.** An awareness; an impression: *a feeling that one is being followed.* **4. a.** An emotional state or disposition; emotion: *expressed deep feeling.* **b.** A tender emotion; love; fondness. **5. a.** Refined sensibility, often approaching sentimentality: *a man of feeling.* **b.** *Plural.* Emotional responses; tendency to feel wounded, moved, offended, or the like: *hurt one's feelings.* **6.** Opinion based on emotional reaction rather than on reason. **7.** An impression produced by a person, place, thing, or event. **8. a.** An appreciative regard and understanding. Used with *for*: *a feeling for propriety.* **b.** A bent; an aptitude. Used with *for*: *a feeling for carpentry.* —See Synonyms at **opinion.**
~*adj.* **1. a.** Having the ability to react or feel emotionally; sentient; sensitive. **b.** Easily moved emotionally. **2.** Having sensibility; sympathetic. **3.** Expressive of sensibility; indicating emotion: *a feeling glance.* —**feel·ing·ly** *adv.*

Synonyms: *feeling, emotion, passion.*

fee-pay·ing (fée-pay-ing) *adj.* **1.** Designating a school or similar educational establishment that charges pupils a fee for tuition. **2.** Designating a pupil of such a school.

fee simple *n., pl.* **fees simple.** *Law.* An estate in land of which the inheritor has unqualified ownership and power of disposition.

feet. Plural of **foot.** —**fall on (one's) feet.** To be successful in the end. —**feet of clay.** A weakness or flaw in someone who is apparently faultless. [Biblical allusion to the "great image" described in Daniel (2:31–34): "a stone . . . smote the image upon his feet that were iron and clay, and brake them to pieces".] —**find (one's) feet.** To become settled or accustomed, as in a new environment. —**have** or **keep both feet on the ground.** To be or remain practical and down-to-earth. —**on (one's) feet.** **1.** Well after an illness. **2.** Progressing or thriving. Said of a project, business, or the like. —**run** or **rushed off (one's) feet.** Very busy; frantic. —**stand on (one's) own (two) feet.** To be or become independent. —**sweep (one) off (one's) feet.** **1.** To fill with enthusiasm. **2.** To cause to fall in love; enchant; enrapture. —**vote with (one's) feet.** To express one's disapproval of a regime, employer, policy, or the like by resigning, physically distancing oneself, or emigrating.

fee tail *n., pl.* **fees tail.** *Law.* An estate in land limited in inheritance to a specified individual, group, or class of heirs.

feeze (feez, fayz) *n.* **1.** *Regional.* A heavy impact. **2.** *Chiefly U.S.* A state of vexation.
~*tr.v.* **feezed, feezing, feezes.** **1.** To drive off; put to flight. **2.** *Chiefly U.S.* To faze; disconcert. [Middle English *fese,* from *fesen,* to drive off, Old English *fēsian*†.]

feign (fayn) *v.* **feigned, feigning, feigns.** —*tr.* **1. a.** To give a false appearance of; pretend; sham: *jump into bed and feign sleep.* **b.** To represent falsely; pretend to: *feign authorship of a novel.* **2.** To invent; make up; fabricate: *feign an experience.* **3.** To imitate: *feign another's handwriting.* —*intr.* To pretend; dissemble. —See Synonyms at **pretend.** [Middle English *feinen,* from Old French *faindre, feindre* (present stem *fei(g)n-*), from Latin *fingere,* to form, shape, alter.]

feigned (faynd) *adj.* **1.** Not real; simulated: *"those who, with a feigned modesty, condemn as useless what they write"* (John Locke). **2.** Made-up; fictitious. —**feign·ed·ly** (fáynid-li) *adv.*

feint[1] (faynt) *n.* **1.** A misleading movement or feigned attack designed to draw defensive action away from an intended target or

objective. **2.** Any pretence intended to mislead; a stratagem. —See Synonyms at **artifice.**
~*intr.v.* **feinted, feinting, feints.** To make a feint. [French *feinte,* from Old French, from the past participle of *feindre,* to FEIGN.]
feint² *n. Printing.* The finest line used in the printing of ruled paper. [Variant of FAINT.]
feints (faynts) *pl.n.* The impure spirits produced in the first and last stages of the distillation of spirits.
feis·ty (fīsti) *adj.* **-tier, -tiest.** *Chiefly U.S. Regional.* **1.** Touchy; excitable; quarrelsome. **2.** Spirited, tough, or frisky. **3.** Impudent; bold; overbearing. [From *feist,* small mongrel dog, shortened from *fisting dog,* from obsolete *fist,* to break wind, from Old English *fistān* (unattested).]
fel·a·fel (fel-aáfəl, fə-lúff'l) *n.* Also **fal·a·fel** (fal-). A spicy vegetable dish popular in the Middle East consisting of small, deep-fried balls of crushed chickpeas, often served in pitta bread with salad and a hot sauce. [Arabic.]
feld·spar (féld-spaar, fél-) *n.* Also **fel·spar** (fél-). Any of a group of abundant rock-forming minerals occurring in most igneous, and many sedimentary and metamorphic rocks and consisting of a silicate of aluminium with one or two of the following metals: potassium, sodium, calcium, and rarely barium. [Partial translation of obsolete German *Feldspath,* "field spar" : *Feld,* field, + *Spath,* spar.] —**feld·spath·ic** (-spáthik) *adj.*
fe·li·cif·ic (féeli-siffik) *adj.* Producing or bringing about happiness. [Latin *fēlīx* (stem *fēlīc-*), favourable, fertile + -FIC.]
fe·lic·i·tate (fə-líssi-tayt, fe-) *tr.v.* **-tated, -tating, -tates.** **1.** To wish happiness to; congratulate. **2.** *Archaic.* To make happy. [Latin *fēlīcitāre,* to make happy, from *fēlīx* (stem *fēlīc-*), happy, FELICIFIC.] —**fe·lic·i·ta·tor** (-taytər) *n.* —**fe·lic·i·ta·tions** (fə-líssi-táysh'nz, fe-) *pl., n.*
fe·lic·i·tous (fə-líssitəss, fe-) *adj.* **1. a.** Well-chosen; apt; appropriate: *a felicitous comparison.* **b.** Having an appropriate and agreeable manner or style: *a felicitous writer.* **2.** Marked by well-being or good fortune: *a felicitous life.* —See Synonyms at **fit.** —**fe·lic·i·tous·ly** *adv.* —**fe·lic·i·tous·ness** *n.*
fe·lic·i·ty (fə-líssəti, fe-) *n., pl.* **-ties.** **1. a.** Great happiness; bliss. **b.** An instance of this. **2.** Something that causes or produces happiness. **3. a.** An appropriate and pleasing manner or style: *felicity of speech.* **b.** An instance of this. [Middle English *felicite,* from Old French, from Latin *fēlīcitās* (stem *fēlīcitāt-*), from *fēlīx* (stem *fēlīc-*), happy, FELICIFIC.]
fe·line (fée-līn) *adj.* **1.** Of or belonging to the family Felidae, which includes the lions, tigers, jaguars, and wild and domestic cats. **2.** Resembling or suggestive of a cat, as in suppleness, slyness, or stealthiness.
~*n.* Also **fe·lid** (féelid). A feline animal. [Latin *fēlīnus,* from *fēlēs†,* cat.] —**fe·line·ly** *adv.* —**fe·line·ness, fe·lin·i·ty** (fi-línnəti, fee-) *n.*
fell¹ (fel) *tr.v.* **felled, felling, fells.** **1.** To cause to fall; cut or knock down: *fell a tree; fell an opponent.* **2.** To sew or finish (a seam) with the raw edges flattened, turned under, and stitched down.
~*n.* **1.** *U.S.* The timber cut down in one season. **2.** A felled seam. [Middle English *fellen,* Old English *fellan, fyllan,* strike down, fell.] —**fell·a·ble** *adj.*
fell² *adj. Chiefly Poetic.* **1.** Of an inhumanly cruel nature; fierce; unsparing: *fell hordes.* **2.** Able to destroy; lethal: *a fell blow.* **3.** Dire; sinister: *by some fell chance.* **4.** *Scottish.* Sharp and biting: *a fell word.* [Middle English *fel,* from Old French, from Medieval Latin *fellō,* wicked person, FELON.] —**fell·ness** *n.*
fell³ *n.* The hide of an animal; a skin; a pelt. [Middle English *fel,* Old English *fell.*]
fell⁴ *n. Northern British.* **1.** An upland stretch of open country; a moor. **2.** The highest point of such an upland. [Middle English, from Old Norse *fjall,* hill; probably akin to Old Saxon *felis,* rock.]
fell⁵. Past tense of **fall.**
fel·la (féllə) *n.* Also **fel·ler** (féllər). *Informal.* **1.** A man or boy. **2.** A boyfriend or lover. **3.** A husband.
fel·lah (féllə || fə-laá) *n., pl.* **-lahs** or **fellahin** or **fellaheen** (féllə-heen, -héen || fə-laá-). A peasant or agricultural labourer in Arab countries. [Arabic *fellāḥ,* dialectal variant of *fallāḥ,* from *falaḥa,* to cultivate, till.]
fel·la·ti·o (fə-láyshi-ō, fe-, -laát-) *n.* Also **fel·la·tion** (fə-láysh'n, fe-). Stimulation of the male genitals by the mouth. [New Latin, from Latin *fellāre,* to suck.] —**fel·late** (fə-láyt, fe-) *v.*
fell·er (féllər) *n.* **1.** One that fells. **2.** A sewing machine attachment for felling seams.
Fel·li·ni (fe-léeni), **Federico** (1920–93). Italian film director. His films such as *La Dolce Vita* (1960) combine social satire with elements of fantasy. *La Strada* (1954), *The Nights of Cabiria* (1957), and *Amarcord* (1974), won Oscars.
fell·mon·ger (fél-mung-gər || -mong-) *n. British.* One who sells hides or prepares hides for making leather. —**fell·mon·ger·ing, fell·mon·ger·y** *n.*
fel·low (féllō) *n.* **1. a.** A man or boy. **b.** *Informal.* A boyfriend or lover. **c.** *Informal.* A husband. **2. a.** Anybody in general; any human being. **b.** A person considered to be worthless or unimportant. **3.** A companion; a comrade; an associate. **4. a.** A person similar to oneself in rank, position, or background; an equal; a peer. **b.** Either of a pair; a counterpart; a mate. **5.** *Abbr.* **F, F.** A member of a group having common interests, such as a member of a learned society. **6.** *Abbr.* **F, F.** A graduate student appointed to a position granting financial aid for a period of research. **7.** *British.* **a.** An incorporated senior member of certain colleges and universities. **b.** A member of the governing body of certain colleges and universities.
~*adj.* Being of the same kind, group, occupation, society, or locality; having in common certain characteristics or interests: *fellow workers.* [Middle English *felawe,* Old English *fēolaga,* from Old Norse *fēlagi,* partner, fellow, one who lays down money : *fē,* cattle, money + *lag,* a laying down.]
fellow creature *n.* A kindred creature; especially, another member of the human race.
fellow feeling *n.* **1.** Sympathetic awareness of others; rapport. **2.** Common interests or opinions.
fellow man *n., pl.* **fellow men.** Also **fel·low·man** (féllō-mán) *pl.* **-men** (-mén). **1.** All humanity regarded as united in shared experience. **2.** Any person regarded as related to one through the general human experience.
fellow servant *n. Law.* Formerly, any of a group of employees working together under such circumstances that the employer cannot be expected to protect against or be liable for harm to one employee caused by the negligence of another.
fel·low·ship (féllō-ship) *n.* **1. a.** The condition of being together or of sharing similar interests or experiences, as do members of a profession, religion, or nationality; companionship. **b.** The companionship of individuals in a congenial atmosphere and on equal terms. **2. a.** A union of friends or equals sharing similar interests; a club; a brotherhood. **b.** A church association. **3. a.** Friendship; comradeship. **b.** Mutual concern and trust among Christians. **4. a.** A scholarship or grant awarded to a graduate student in a college or university. **b.** The state of having been awarded such a scholarship or grant. **c.** A foundation established for the awarding of such a scholarship or grant. **5.** A position as a member of the governing body of certain colleges and universities.
fellow traveller *n.* One who sympathises with the tenets and programmes of an organised group without actually joining it; especially, a supporter of the Communist Party.
fel·ly (félli) *n., pl.* **-lies.** Also **fel·loe** (féllō). **1.** The rim of a wheel supported by spokes. **2.** A section of such a rim. [Middle English *fely,* Old English *felg,* from West Germanic *felgam* (unattested).]
fe·lo de se, fe·lo-de-se (féelō-di-sée, féllō-, -sáy) *n., pl.* **felones de se** (fə-lṓneez) or **felos de se** (féelōz, féllōz). *Law.* **1.** The act of suicide. **2.** One who commits suicide. [Medieval Latin, "felon of himself" : *felō, fellō,* FELON + *dē,* of + *sē,* ablative of *suī,* himself, oneself, from Latin.]
fel·on¹ (féllən) *n.* **1.** *Law.* Formerly, a person who committed a felony. **2.** *Archaic.* An evil person.
~*adj. Archaic.* Evil; cruel. [Middle English *feloun,* from Old French *felon,* from Medieval Latin *fellō* (stem *fellōn-*), from Vulgar Latin *fellō†* (unattested).]
fel·on² (féllən) *n.* A purulent infection at the end of a finger near or around the nail or the bone. [Middle English *feloun,* from Old French, possibly from Latin *fel,* bile, venom.]
fe·lo·ni·ous (fə-lṓni-əss, fe-) *adj.* **1.** *Law.* **a.** Of or pertaining to a felony. **b.** Characterised by or of the nature of a felony: *felonious intent.* **2.** *Archaic.* Evil; wicked. —**fe·lo·ni·ous·ly** *adv.* —**fe·lo·ni·ous·ness** *n.*
fel·on·ry (féllənri) *n.* **1.** Felons collectively. **2.** *Australian.* Formerly, the convict population of a penal settlement.
fel·o·ny (félləni) *n., pl.* **-nies.** *Law.* **1.** Formerly, any of several crimes, such as murder, rape, or burglary, considered more serious than a misdemeanour and punishable by a more stringent sentence. Compare **misdemeanour.** **2.** Any of several crimes in early English law that were punishable by forfeiture of land or goods and by possible loss of life or a bodily part.
fel·site (fél-sīt) *n.* A fine-grained igneous rock, chiefly feldspar and quartz. [FELS(PAR) + -ITE.] —**fel·sit·ic** (-síttik) *adj.*
felspar. Variant of **feldspar.**
felt¹ (felt) *n.* **1.** A fabric of matted, compressed animal fibres, such as wool or fur, sometimes mixed with vegetable or synthetic fibres. **2.** Any fabric or material resembling this. **3.** Something made of felt or a similar material.
~*adj.* **1.** Made of felt. **2.** Pertaining or similar to felt.
~*v.* **felted, felting, felts.** —*tr.* **1.** To make into felt. **2.** To cover with felt. —*intr.* To become like felt; mat together. [Middle English *felt,* Old English *felt,* from West Germanic.]
felt². Past tense and past participle of **feel.**
felt·ing (félting) *n.* **1.** The practice or process of making felt. **2.** The materials from which felt is made. **3.** Felted fabric.
fe·luc·ca (fe-lúckə || -lŏŏkə) *n.* A narrow, swift vessel, chiefly of the Mediterranean, propelled by lateen sails or oars or both. [Italian *feluc(c)a,* from obsolete Spanish *faluca,* from Arabic *fulk,* ship.]
fel·wort (fél-wurt || -wawrt) *n.* Any of several plants of the genera *Gentianella* or *Swertia*; especially, *G. amarella,* having small, purplish flowers. [Middle English *feldwort,* Old English *feldwyrt* : *feld,* FIELD + *wyrt,* WORT.]
FEM **1.** field-emission microscope. **2.** field-emission microscopy.
fe·male (fée-mayl) *adj. Abbr.* **f, F, f., F., fem.** **1.** Of, pertaining to, or designating the sex that produces ova. **2.** Characteristic of or appropriate to this sex; feminine. **3.** Consisting of members of this sex. **4.** *Botany.* **a.** Pertaining to or designating an organ, such as a pistil or ovary, that functions in producing seeds or spores after fertilisation. **b.** Bearing pistils but not stamens: *female flowers.* **5.** Designating or having a part, such as a slot or receptacle, designed to receive a complementary male part, such as a plug or prongs.
~*n. Abbr.* **f, F, f., F., fem.** **1.** A member of the sex that produces

ova. **2.** Anything or anyone female. **3.** A woman or girl, as distinguished from a man or boy. **4.** *Botany.* A plant having only pistillate flowers. [Middle English, variant (influenced by *male*) of *femelle,* from Old French, from Latin *fēmella,* diminutive of *fēmina,* woman, female.] **—fe·male·ness** *n.*
female impersonator *n.* A male comedian who dresses up as a woman.
feme (fem, feem) *n.* **1.** *Law.* A wife. **2.** *Obsolete.* A woman. [Anglo-French, from Latin *fēmina,* woman, FEMALE.]
feme cov·ert (fém-kúvvərt, féem-) *n. Law.* A married woman.
feme sole (fém-sōl, féem-) *n. Law.* A single woman, whether divorced, widowed, or never married.
fem·i·ne·i·ty (fémmi-née-əti, -áy-) *n.* Womanliness; femininity.
fem·i·nie (fémmini) *n. Archaic.* Women collectively; womankind. [Middle English, from Old French, from Latin *fēmina,* FEMALE.]
fem·i·nine (fémminin) *adj. Abbr.* **f., F., fem. 1.** Of or belonging to the female sex. Said especially of members of the human species. **2.** Characterised by or possessing qualities generally attributed to or considered appropriate to a woman; womanly: *feminine tenderness.* **3.** Effeminate; womanish. **4.** *Grammar.* Indicating or belonging to the gender of words or grammatical forms that are classified as female: *a feminine noun.* Compare **masculine, neuter.**
∼*n. Abbr.* **f., F., fem.** *Grammar.* **1.** The feminine gender. **2.** A word or form belonging to that gender. [Middle English, from Old French, from Latin *fēminīnus,* from *fēmina,* FEMALE.] **—fem·i·nine·ly** *adv.* **—fem·i·nine·ness** *n.*
feminine ending *n.* **1.** The termination of a line or verse in an unaccented syllable. **2.** *Grammar.* A final syllable or ending that marks or forms words in the feminine gender; for example, the ending *-ess* added to *lion* to form *lioness.*
feminine rhyme *n.* **1.** A rhyme of two syllables in which the second syllable is unstressed; for example, *follow* and *hollow; brightly* and *nightly.* **2.** A rhyme of three syllables in which only the first syllable is stressed; for example, *edible* and *incredible.* Compare **masculine rhyme.**
fem·i·nin·i·ty (fémmi-nínnəti) *n., pl.* **-ties. 1.** The quality or condition of being feminine; womanhood; womanliness. **2.** Women collectively.
fem·i·nise, fem·i·nize (fémmi-nīz) *v.* **-nised, -nising, -nises.** *—tr.* To make feminine. *—intr.* To become feminine. **—fem·i·ni·sa·tion** (fémmi-nī-záysh'n || *U.S.* -ni-) *n.*
fem·i·nism (fémmi-niz'm) *n.* **1.** A social movement that seeks to change the traditional role and image of women, to eliminate sexism, and to heighten appreciation of the experiences and qualities unique to the female sex. See **Women's Movement. 2.** The doctrine of this movement. **—fem·i·nist** *n. & adj.*
femme (fem) *adj.* Adopting a particularly feminine role or appearance. Said of lesbians. Compare **butch.**
femme fa·tale (fám-fə-taál || fém-, -tál) *n., pl.* **femmes fatales** (*pronounced as singular*). A woman whose sexual attractiveness leads a man into compromising or dangerous situations. [French.]
fem·o·ral (fémmərəl) *adj.* Of or pertaining to the thigh or the femur: *femoral artery.* [Latin *femur* (stem *femor-*), FEMUR.]
femto- *comb. form. Symbol* **f** Indicates 10^{-15}; for example, **femtometre.** [Danish or Norwegian *femten,* fifteen, from Old Norse *fimmtān.*]
fem·to·joule (fém-tō-jōōl, -tə-, -jowl) *n. Abbr.* **fJ** 10^{-15} joule.
fem·tom·e·tre (fém-tō-meetər, -tə-) *n. Abbr.* **fm** 10^{-15} metre.
fe·mur (féemər) *n., pl.* **-murs** or **femora** (féemərə, fémmərə). **1. a.** The proximal bone of the lower or hind limb in vertebrates, situated between the pelvis and knee in humans. Also called "thighbone". **b.** The thigh. **2.** The usually stout third segment of an insect's leg. [Latin *femur*†, thigh.]
fen[1] (fen) *n.* Low, flat, swampy land; a bog; a marsh. [Middle English *fen,* Old English *fenn,* from Germanic.] **—fen·ny** *adj.*
fen[2] *n., pl.* **fen.** A coin equal to $^1/_{100}$ of the yuan of China. [Mandarin Chinese *fēn,* division, part.]
fence (fenss) *n.* **1.** A structure serving as an enclosure, barrier, or boundary, usually made of posts or stakes joined together by boards, wire, or rails. **2.** *Archaic.* Something intended as a means of defence; a protection. **3.** *Archaic.* The art or practice of swordplay; fencing. **4.** A jump for a horse, as in show-jumping. **5. a.** One who receives and sells stolen goods. **b.** A place where such goods are received and sold. **6.** An attachment on a machine or tool that directs, regulates, and limits its action. **—be** or **sit on the fence.** *Informal.* To be undecided as to which of two sides to support, especially in order to protect one's own interests. **—mend (one's) fences.** To restore good relations.
∼*v.* **fenced, fencing, fences.** *—tr.* **1.** To surround or close in by means of a fence. **2.** To separate or close off by means of a fence. **3.** *Archaic.* To defend or ward off. **4.** To sell (stolen goods) to a fence. *—intr.* **1.** To practise or demonstrate the art of fencing. **2.** To engage in the art of skilful conversation or debate. **3.** To avoid giving direct answers; be evasive. **4.** To act as a fence for stolen goods. [Middle English *fens,* short for *defens,* DEFENCE.]
fenc·er (fén-sər) *n.* **1.** A person who fences, as with a foil; a swordsman. **2.** *Chiefly Australian & N.Z.* A person who erects or repairs fences.
fen·ci·ble (fén-səb'l) *n.* Formerly, a soldier enlisted for home service only. [Middle English, aphetic variant of DEFENSIBLE.]
fenc·ing (fén-sing) *n.* **1.** The art, practice, or sport of using a foil, épée, or sabre; swordplay. **2.** The art or practice of skilful conversation or debate; repartee. **3.** Evasiveness in answering questions or giving information. **4. a.** Material, such as wire, stakes, rails, and the like, used in the construction of fences. **b.** Fences collectively. **c.** *Chiefly Australian & N.Z.* The work, skill, or business of erecting or repairing fences.
fend (fend) *v.* **fended, fending, fends.** *—tr. Archaic.* To defend. *—intr.* To resist. **—fend for (oneself).** To provide for oneself; survive without help; manage alone. **—fend off.** To turn aside; deflect; parry. [Middle English *fenden,* shortening of *defenden.* to DEFEND.]
fend·er (féndər) *n.* **1.** One that fends or wards off. **2.** A device at the front end of a locomotive or train designed to push aside obstructions. **3.** A metal device placed in front of a fireplace to keep hot coals and debris from falling out; a fireguard. **4.** *Nautical.* A device, such as a bundle of rope, a piece of timber, or a car tyre used on the side of a vessel or dock to absorb impact or friction. **5.** *U.S.* **a.** A car **wing** *(see).* **b.** A **mudguard** *(see).*
fen·es·tel·la (fénni-stél-ə) *n., pl.* **-lae** (-lee). **1.** A small niche in the wall of a church containing the piscina. **2.** *Architecture.* A small window. [Latin, diminutive of *fenestra,* window.]
fe·nes·tra (fi-néss-trə) *n., pl.* **-trae** (-tree). **1.** *Anatomy.* A small opening; especially, either of two apertures in the medial wall of the middle ear. **2.** A window-like opening. **3.** *Biology.* A transparent spot or marking, as on the wing of an insect. [New Latin, from Latin *fenestra*†, opening in the wall, window.]
fe·nes·trat·ed (fi-néss-traytid, fénni-straytid) *adj.* Also **fe·nes·trate** (fi-néss-trayt, fénni-strayt) (especially for sense 2). **1.** Having windows or window-like openings. **2.** *Biology.* Having fenestrae. [Latin *fenestrātus,* past participle of *fenestrāre,* to provide with windows or openings, from *fenestra,* window, FENESTRA.]
fen·es·tra·tion (fénni-stráysh'n) *n.* **1.** *Architecture.* The design and placement of windows in a building. **2.** An opening in a structure. **3.** In surgery, the cutting of an opening from the external auditory canal to the labyrinth of the internal ear to restore hearing.
feng shui (fúng-shweé, féng-, -shwáy) *n.* A Chinese practice combining geomancy with advice on the best siting of objects, places, and buildings. [Chinese, from *fēng,* wind + *shǔ,* water.]
Fe·ni·an (féeni-ən, fén-yən) *n.* **1. a.** *Plural.* A legendary group of heroic Irish warriors of the second and third centuries A.D. Also called "Fianna". **b.** A member of this group. **2.** A member of a secret organisation in the United States and Ireland in the mid-19th century, whose goal was the overthrow of British rule in Ireland. **3.** *Sometimes small* **f.** Loosely, a supporter of the republican cause in Northern Ireland. [Sense 2 : from Old Irish *féne,* an ancient Irish people, confused with *fíann,* legendary group of warriors, after *Fíann,* legendary hero.] **—Fe·ni·an** *adj.* **—Fe·ni·an·ism** *n.*
fen·nec (fénn-ek, -ik) *n.* A nocturnal small fox, *Fennecus zerda,* of desert regions of northern Africa, having fawn-coloured fur and large, pointed ears. [Arabic *fanak, fenek,* fox, small furry animal.]
fen·nel (fénn'l) *n.* **1. a.** A plant, *Foeniculum vulgare,* native to Eurasia, having finely dissected leaves, clusters of small yellow flowers, and aromatic seeds. **b.** The seeds or leaves of this plant, used for flavouring. **2.** A variety of this plant, **finochio** *(see).* **3.** Any of several similar or related plants. [Middle English *fenel,* Old English *fenol, finugle,* from Vulgar Latin *fēnoclum* (unattested), from Latin *fēniculum,* diminutive of *fēnum, faenum,* hay.]
Fen·ton (fen-tón), **James (Martin)** (1949–). British poet. His collections include *The Memory of War* (1982), *Children in Exile* (1985), and *Out of Danger* (1993). He was appointed professor of poetry at Oxford University in 1994.
fen·u·greek (fénnew-greek) *n.* **1.** A clover-like Eurasian plant, *Trigonella foenum-graecum,* having white flowers and pungent, aromatic seeds used as flavouring. **2.** The seeds of this plant. [Middle English *fenigrek,* from Old French *fenugrec,* from Latin *fēnugraecum,* from *fēnum graecum,* "Greek hay" (from the use of the dried plant as fodder).]
fen·ur·on (fénnewr-on) *n.* A white compound, $C_9H_{12}N_2O$, used as a herbicide.
feoff (fef, feef) *tr.v.* **feoffed, feoffing, feoffs.** To grant a feudal estate or fee to; enfeoff.
∼*n.* A feudal estate, a **fee** *(see).* [Middle English *feoffen, feffen,* from Anglo-French *feoffer,* from Old French *fieffer,* from *fief,* FIEF.]
feoff·ee (fe-fée, fee-) *n.* A person to whom a feoffment is granted.
feof·fer, feof·for (féffər, féefər) *n.* A person who grants a feoffment.
feoff·ment (féf-mənt, féef-) *n.* A grant of lands as a fee.
-fer *n. comb. form.* Indicates agency, bearing, or production; for example, **aquifer, conifer.** [Latin, from *ferre,* to carry, bear.]
fe·ral (féerəl, férrəl) *adj.* **1.** Existing in a wild or untamed state; especially, having reverted to such a state from domestication. **2.** Of or characteristic of a wild animal; savage. [Latin *fera,* wild animal, from *ferus,* wild.]
fer·bam (fér-bam) *n.* A black iron compound, $C_9H_{18}FeN_3S_6$, used as an agricultural fungicide. [*Fer*ric dimethyl-dithiocar*bam*ate.]
fer-de-lance (fairdə-laánss || -lánss) *n.* A venomous tropical American snake, *Bothrops atrox,* having brown and greyish markings. [French, iron (head) of a lance.]
Fer·di·nand V, II, and III (férdi-nand, -férd'n-and), also known as Ferdinand the Catholic (1452–1516). King of Castile as Ferdinand V (1474–1504), King of Aragon as Ferdinand II (1479–1516), and King of Naples as Ferdinand III (1504–16), joint ruler with his wife, Isabella I of Castile. He and Isabella sent Columbus to America in 1492.
fere (feer) *n. Archaic.* **1.** A companion. **2.** A spouse. [Middle English *fere,* Old English *gefēra.*]
fer·e·to·ry (férri-təri, -tri) *n., pl.* **-ries. 1.** A shrine to hold the relics of saints. **2.** An area of a church in which such shrines are kept.

[Middle English *fertre, feretory,* from Old French *fiertre,* from Latin *feretrum,* bier, from Greek *pheretron,* from *pherein,* to bear, carry.]

fe·ri·a (féeri-ə, férri-, -aa) *n., pl.* **-as** or **-riae** (-ri-ee) *Ecclesiastical.* A day of the week on which no feast is observed. [From Medieval Latin *fēria,* from Late Latin, day of the week, from Latin *fēriae,* days of rest, holidays, festivals.] —**fe·ri·al** (-əl) *adj.*

fe·rine (féer-īn) *adj.* Untamed; feral. [Latin *ferīnus,* from *fera,* wild animal. See **feral.**]

fer·i·ty (férrəti) *n.* **1.** The condition of being feral; existence in a wild state. **2.** The condition of being savage; ferocity. [Latin *feritās* (stem *feritāt-*), from *ferus,* wild. See **feral.**]

Fer·lin·ghet·ti (fér-ling-gétti, faír-), **Lawrence** (1920–). U.S. poet. He was a leader of the 1950s beat movement that opposed social, moral, and literary conventions. His collections include *Pictures of the Gone World* (1955), and *Tyrannus Nix?* (1969).

Fer·man·agh (fər-mánnə). Former county in Northern Ireland, a district since 1973. Its chief products are potatoes, cattle, and sandstone and limestone .

Fer·mat (fər-mát, fair-máa), **Pierre de** (1601–65). French mathematician. He formulated the least-time law, **Fermat's principle,** to explain the diffraction of light, and **Fermat's theorem.**

fer·ma·ta (fər-máatə, fair-) *n. Music.* **1.** The holding or sustaining of a tone, chord, or rest for an unspecified length of time. **2.** The sign that indicates such a prolongation. [Italian, pause, stop, from the feminine past participle of *fermare,* to pause, stop, from Latin *firmāre,* to make firm, from *firmus,* firm.]

Fermat's principle *n. Physics.* The principle that the path taken by a ray of light through any system is always the one that takes the shortest possible time.

Fermat's theorem *n.* The theorem, postulated by Pierre Fermat but proved only recently, that the equation $x^n + y^n = z^n$, where *n* is an integer, has no integral solutions for *x, y,* and *z* for any value of *n* greater than 2. Also called "Fermat's last theorem".

fer·ment (fér-ment) *n.* **1.** Anything that causes fermentation, such as a yeast, bacterium, mould, or enzyme. **2.** Fermentation. **3.** A state of agitation; unrest; turbulence.

~*v.* (fər-mént) **fermented, -menting, -ments.** —*tr.* **1.** To produce by or as if by fermentation. **2.** To cause to undergo fermentation. **3.** To generate or stir up (trouble, for example). —*intr.* **1.** To undergo fermentation. **2.** To be turbulent; seethe. [Middle English, leaven, yeast, from Old French, from Latin *fermentum.*] —**fer·ment·a·bil·i·ty** (fər-méntə-bílləti) *n.* —**fer·ment·a·ble** (-mént-əb'l) *adj.* —**fer·ment·er** (-méntər) *n.*

fer·men·ta·tion (fér-men-táysh'n, -mən-) *n.* **1.** Any of a group of chemical reactions induced by living or nonliving ferments that split complex organic compounds into relatively simple substances; especially, the anaerobic conversion of sugar to carbon dioxide and ethanol by yeast, as in the making of alcoholic beverages. **2.** Unrest; commotion; agitation.

fer·men·ta·tive (fər-méntə-tiv) *adj.* **1. a.** Causing fermentation. **b.** Capable of causing or undergoing fermentation. **2.** Pertaining to or of the nature of fermentation.

fer·mi (fér-mi ‖ faír-) *n.* A unit of length equal to one femtometre (10^{-15} metre), used in nuclear and particle physics. [After Enrico FERMI.]

Fer·mi (fér-mi, faír-), **Enrico** (1901–54). Italian-born physicist. He left Italy in 1938 to settle in the United States, and was awarded the 1938 Nobel prize for physics for his work on artificial radioactivity caused by neutron bombardment. In 1942 Fermi produced the first controlled nuclear chain reaction at Chicago University. He helped to develop the atom bomb at Los Alamos.

Fer·mi-Dir·ac statistics (fér-mi-di-rák, faír-) *n. Physics.* A type of quantum statistics used for elementary particles that obey the exclusion principle (only two particles can occupy a given energy level). Compare **Bose-Einstein statistics.** [After Enrico FERMI and Paul DIRAC.]

fer·mi·on (férmi-on) *n.* A particle, such as an electron, proton, or neutron, having half-integral spin and obeying statistical rules requiring that not more than one in a set of identical particles may occupy a particular quantum state. Compare **boson.** [After Enrico FERMI.]

fer·mi·um (férmi-əm) *n. Symbol* **Fm** A synthetic transuranic metallic element having 10 isotopes with mass numbers ranging from 248 to 257 and corresponding half-lives ranging from 0.6 minute to approximately 100 days. Atomic number 100. [New Latin, after Enrico FERMI.]

fern (fern) *n.* Any of numerous flowerless, seedless pteridophyte plants of the class Filicinae, characteristically having fronds with divided leaflets, and reproducing by means of spores produced on the undersurface of the fronds. [Middle English *fern,* Old English *fearn.*]

Fer·nan·del (fair-noN-dél), born Fernand Joseph Désiré Contandin (1903–71). French comedian with a toothy grin. He starred in the 1950s *Don Camillo* film series. Other films include *Fric Frac* (1939), *The Red Inn* (1951), and *The Sheep has Five Legs* (1954).

fern·er·y (férnəri) *n., pl.* **-ies. 1.** A place or container in which ferns are grown. **2.** A bed or collection of ferns.

fern seed *pl.n.* The minute spores of ferns, formerly believed to be seeds, and supposed to have the power of making one invisible.

fern·y (férni) *adj.* **-ier, -iest. 1.** Abounding in ferns. **2.** Of, pertaining to, or characteristic of ferns.

fe·ro·cious (fə-rṓshəss) *adj.* **1.** Extremely savage; fierce. **2.** Extreme; intense: *a ferocious blizzard.* —See Synonyms at **cruel.**

[Latin *ferōx* (stem *ferōc-*), wild, fierce.] —**fe·ro·cious·ly** *adv.* —**fe·ro·cious·ness** *n.*

fe·roc·i·ty (fə-róssəti) *n., pl.* **-ties.** The condition or quality of being ferocious.

-ferous *adj. comb. form.* Indicates bearing, producing, or containing; for example, **crystalliferous, umbelliferous.** [Middle English : -FER + -OUS.]

Fer·ra·ra (fə-raárə). Capital city of the province of the same name in the Emilia-Romagna region of north Italy.

fer·rate (férrayt) *n.* A **ferrite** *(see).* [FERR(O)- + -ATE.]

fer·re·dox·in (férri-dók-sin) *n.* Any of a group of red-brown iron-containing proteins that are strong reducing agents and function in electron transport in many organisms, for example in photosynthetic plants. [Latin *ferrum,* iron + REDOX + -IN.]

fer·ret[1] (férrit) *n.* **1.** A domesticated form of the polecat, often trained to hunt rats or rabbits. **2.** A **black-footed ferret** *(see).*

~*v.* **ferreted, -reting, -rets.** —*tr.* **1.** To hunt (rats, for example) with a ferret. **2.** To drive out; expel: *ferret the troublemakers out of the team.* —*intr.* **1.** To hunt with a ferret or ferrets. **2.** To search about; rummage. **3.** To uncover and bring to light by intensive investigation. Used with *out: "piqued by the failure of all his endeavours to ferret out the assassins" (Edgar Allan Poe).* [Middle English *feret, firette,* from Old French *fuiret, furet,* from Vulgar Latin *fūrittus* (unattested), little thief, from Latin *fūr,* thief. See **furtive.**] —**fer·ret·er** *n.* —**fer·ret·y** *adj.*

ferret[2] *n.* Also **fer·ret·ing** (-ing). A narrow piece of tape used to bind or edge fabric. [Probably from Italian *fioretti,* floss silk, plural of *fioretto,* diminutive of *fiore,* flower, from Latin *flōs* (stem *flōr-*), flower.]

ferri– *comb. form. Chemistry.* Indicates iron, especially with a valency of 3; for example, **ferricyanide.** [Latin *ferrum,* iron.]

fer·ri·age (férri-ij) *n.* **1.** The act or business of ferrying. **2.** The toll charged for ferrying.

fer·ric (férrik) *adj.* Of, pertaining to, or containing iron; especially, containing iron with a valency of 3 or with a valency higher than in a corresponding ferrous compound. [FERR(O)- + -IC.]

ferric oxide *n.* A dark compound, Fe_2O_3, occurring naturally as haematite ore and rust, and used in pigments, metallurgy, polishing compounds, and magnetic tapes.

fer·ri·cy·an·ic acid (férri-sī-ánnik ‖ férrī-) *n.* A reddish-brown solid compound, $H_3[Fe(CN)_6]$.

fer·ri·cy·a·nide (férri-sī-ə-nīd ‖ férrī-) *n.* Any of various salts derived from ferricyanic acid and used in making blue pigments.

Fer·ri·er (férri-ər), **Kathleen** (1912–53). British contralto. She worked as a telephonist until she won a music festival prize. Her last appearance was in Gluck's opera *Orfeo,* at Covent Garden in 1953, the year she was made a C.B.E.

fer·rif·er·ous (fe-rífərəss, férri-) *adj.* Containing or yielding iron: *ferriferous rock.* [FERRI- +-FEROUS.]

fer·ri·mag·net·ic (férri-mag-néttik) *adj.* Pertaining to or characteristic of substances, such as certain ferrites and garnets, that have magnetic properties similar to ferromagnetic materials. Ferrimagnetic substances have weaker magnetism than ferromagnetic substances; their properties arise because the different types of atom in the crystal have unequal antiparallel magnetic moments.

~*n.* A ferrimagnetic substance. —**fer·ri·mag·net·ism** *n.*

Fer·ris wheel (férriss) *n. Often small* **f.** *Chiefly U.S.* A **big wheel** *(see).* [Designed for the Chicago World's Fair in 1893 by George W.G. *Ferris* (1859–1896), U.S. engineer.]

fer·rite (férrīt) *n.* **1.** Any of a group of nonmetallic, ceramic-like, usually ferromagnetic compounds of ferric oxide with other oxides; especially, such a compound with spinel crystalline structure, characterised by extremely high electrical resistivity and used in computer memory elements, permanent magnets, and various solid-state devices. Also called "ferrate". **2.** Iron having a body-centred cubic crystalline form, occurring commonly in steel, cast iron, and pig iron below 910°C. [FERR(O)- + -ITE.]

fer·ri·tin (férri-tin) *n.* An iron-containing protein complex that is one of the forms in which iron is stored in the tissues. [FERRITE + -IN.]

ferro–, ferr– *comb. form.* Indicates: **1.** Iron; for example, **ferromagnetic, ferrite. 2.** Iron in alloy; for example, **ferromanganese. 3.** Iron in its ferrous valency; for example, **ferrocyanide.** [Latin *ferrum,* iron.]

fer·ro·al·loy (férrō-ál-oy ‖ -ə-lóy) *n.* Any of various alloys of iron and one or more other elements, such as manganese or silicon, used in the production of steel.

fer·ro·cene (férrə-seen, férrō-) *n.* A reddish crystalline compound, $Fe(C_5H_5)$, the first known sandwich compound.

fer·ro·chro·mi·um (férrō-krṓmi-əm) *n.* An alloy of iron and chromium (50–70%) used in making chromium alloy steels.

fer·ro·con·crete (férrō-kóng-kreet ‖ -kong-kréet) *n.* **Reinforced concrete** *(see).*

fer·ro·cy·an·ic acid (férrō-sī-ánnik) *n.* A solid, white compound, $H_4Fe(CN)_6$.

fer·ro·cy·a·nide (férrō-sí-ə-nīd) *n.* A salt derived from ferrocyanic acid, the sodium and potassium salts being used in making blue pigments, blueprint paper, and ferricyanide.

fer·ro·e·lec·tric (férrō-i-léktrik) *adj.* Of or pertaining to a crystalline dielectric that can be given a permanent electric polarisation by application of an electric field.

~*n.* A ferroelectric substance. —**fer·ro·e·lec·tric·i·ty** (-lek-tríssiti) *n.*

fer·ro·mag·ne·sian (férrō-mag-née-<u>zh</u>ən, -zi-ən ‖ -shən) *adj.* Containing iron and magnesium. Said especially of certain minerals.

fer·ro·mag·net (férrō-mág-nit) *n.* **1.** A ferromagnetic substance; broadly, a substance with magnetic properties resembling those of iron. **2. A permanent magnet** *(see).*

fer·ro·mag·net·ism (férrō-mág-nə-tiz'm) *n.* A type of magnetism occurring in substances, such as iron, nickel, and cobalt, that exhibit extremely high magnetic permeability, the ability to acquire high magnetisation and saturation in relatively weak magnetic fields, a large positive magnetic susceptibility, and magnetic hysteresis. —**fer·ro·mag·net·ic** (-mag-nettik) *n.*

fer·ro·man·ga·nese (férrō-máng-gə-neez ‖ -neess) *n.* An alloy of iron and manganese (70–80%).

fer·ro·sil·i·con (férro-sílli-kən, -kon) *n.* An alloy of iron and silicon (up to 15%) used in making alloy steels.

fer·ro·type (férrō-tīp, férrə-) *n.* **1.** A positive photograph made directly on an iron plate varnished with a sensitised film. Also called "tintype". **2.** The process by which such photographs are made.

fer·rous (férrəss) *adj.* Of, pertaining to, or containing iron, especially with a valency of 2. [New Latin *ferrosus* : Latin *ferrum,* iron + -OUS.]

ferrous oxide *n.* A black powdery compound, FeO, used in the manufacture of steel, green heat-absorbing glass, and enamels.

ferrous sulphate *n.* A greenish crystalline compound, $FeSO_4 \cdot 7H_2O$, used as a pigment, fertiliser, feed additive, and in the medical treatment of iron-deficiency anaemia.

ferrous sulphide *n.* A black to brown sulphide of iron, FeS, used in making hydrogen sulphide.

fer·ru·gi·nous (fe-rōojinəss, fə-) *adj.* **1.** Of, containing, or similar to iron. **2.** Having the colour of iron rust. [Latin *ferrūginus,* from *ferrūgō* (stem *ferrūgin-*), iron rust, from *ferrum,* iron.]

fer·rule, fer·ule (férrōol, férrəl ‖ férrewl) *n.* **1.** A metal ring or cap attached to or near the end of a pole, cane, wooden handle, or the like, for reinforcement or to prevent splitting. **2.** A bushing used to secure a pipe joint.
~*tr.v.* **ferruled, -ruling, -rules.** To furnish with a ferrule. [Variant (influenced by Latin *ferrum,* iron) of earlier *verrel, virl,* from Middle English *verelle, virol,* from Old French *virelle, virole,* from Latin *viriola,* little bracelet, diminutive of *viriae,* bracelets.]

fer·ry (férri) *n., pl.* **-ries. 1.** A commercial service for transporting people, vehicles, goods, or the like, across a body of water. **2.** A boat used in such transportation. **3.** The place of embarkation of a ferryboat. **4.** A franchise or legal right to operate such a service for a fee. **5.** The transporting of a vehicle, especially an aircraft, under its own power to its eventual user. **6.** A module for transporting astronauts from a spacecraft to the surface of a planet. Also used adjectivally: *a ferry rocket.*
~*v.* **ferried, -rying, -ries.** —*tr.* **1.** To transport (a person or thing) across a body of water. **2.** To cross (a body of water) on or as if on a ferry. **3.** To deliver (a vehicle, especially an aircraft) under its own power to its eventual user. **4.** To transport (people or goods), especially to and fro over short distances. —*intr.* To cross a body of water on or as if on a ferry. [Middle English *fery, ferie,* probably from Old Norse *ferja.*]

fer·ry·boat (férri-bōt) *n.* A boat used to ferry passengers or goods.

fer·ry·man (férri-mən) *n., pl.* **-men** (-mən). A person who owns, administers, or operates a ferry.

fer·tile (fér-tīl ‖ *U.S.* fért'l) *adj.* **1.** *Biology.* **a.** Capable of reproducing. **b.** Capable of growing and developing; able to mature: *fertile seeds.* **2.** *Botany.* Capable of producing spores, pollen, seeds, or fruit. **3.** Rich in material needed to sustain plant growth: *fertile soil.* **4.** Producing many offspring. **5.** Highly or continuously productive; prolific: *a fertile imagination.* **6.** *Physics.* Capable of being converted into fissile material. [Middle English, from Old French, from Latin *fertilis,* from *ferre,* to bear, carry, produce.] —**fer·tile·ly** *adv.* —**fer·tile·ness** *n.*

Fertile Crescent. The crescent-shaped area of relatively fertile land in the Middle East in ancient times. The area extended from Mesopotamia to Assyria, then westwards to the Mediterranean and south through Palestine to the Nile Valley.

fer·til·i·sa·tion (férti-lī-záysh'n ‖ *U.S.* fért'l-i-) *n.* **1.** The act or process of initiating biological reproduction. **2.** The process in which two gametes unite to form a zygote. **3.** The act or process of rendering fertile, especially by use of fertiliser.

fer·til·ise, fer·til·ize (férti-līz, fért'l-īz) *v.* **-ised, -ising, -ises.** —*tr.* **1.** To cause fertilisation of (an ovum, animal, or plant) by providing with sperm or pollen. **2.** To render fertile, especially by spreading fertiliser. —*intr.* To spread fertiliser. —**fer·til·is·a·ble** *adj.*

fer·til·is·er (férti-līzər, fért'l-īzər) *n.* **1.** A person or agent that causes fertilisation of an animal or plant. **2.** Any of a large number of natural and synthetic materials, including manure and nitrogen, phosphorus, and potassium compounds, spread on or worked into soil to increase its fertility.

fer·til·i·ty (far-tílləti, fer-) *n.* The state or quality of being fertile.

fertility cult *n.* The celebration of various ceremonies or magical rites, usually in primitive agricultural communities, with the aim of increasing crops, bringing rain, or the like.

fertility drug *n.* Any of various drugs, such as a **gonadotrophin** *(see),* taken by infertile women to stimulate the release of an egg cell from the ovary and therefore increase the chances of a pregnancy.

fertility rate *n.* The number of live births that occur in a year per thousand women of childbearing age.

fertility symbol *n.* A symbol, usually phallic, used in the ceremonies of fertility cults.

fer·u·la (férrōo-lə, férrew-) *n., pl.* **-las** or **-lae** (-lee). *Rare.* **1.** A flat piece of wood, such as a stick; a ferule. **2.** Any plant of the genus *Ferula,* of Mediterranean regions, containing resins for which it is cultivated. [New Latin, from Latin, giant fennel. See **ferule.**]

fer·ule¹ (férrōol, férrəl ‖ férrewl) *n.* A baton, cane, strap, or stick used in punishing children.
~*tr.v.* **feruled, -uling, -ules.** To punish or discipline with a ferule. [Latin *ferula†,* giant fennel, rod used to punish.]

ferule². Variant of **ferrule.**

fer·ven·cy (férvən-si) *n., pl.* **-cies.** The condition or quality of being fervent.

fer·vent (férvənt) *adj.* **1.** Having or showing great emotion or warmth; passionate; ardent. **2.** *Poetic.* Extremely hot; glowing. [Middle English, from Old French, from Latin *fervēns* (stem *fervent-*), present participle of *fervēre,* to boil, glow.] —**fer·vent·ly** *adv.* —**fer·vent·ness** *n.*

fer·vid (férvid) *adj.* **1.** Intensely fervent or zealous; impassioned. **2.** *Poetic.* Extremely hot; burning. —See Synonyms at **eager.** [Latin *fervidus,* glowing, from *fervēre,* to glow, boil.] —**fer·vid·ly** *adv.* —**fer·vid·ness** *n.*

fer·vour, *U.S.* **fer·vor** (férvər) *n.* **1.** Intensity of emotion; fervency; zeal. **2.** Intense heat. —See Synonyms at **passion.** [Middle English *fervour,* from Old French, from Latin *fervor,* a boiling, from *fervēre,* to boil.]

Fès (fess) or **Fez** (fez). *Arabic* **Fas** (fuss). City in northern Morocco, consisting of the old city (A.D. 808) and the new city (1276).

Fes·cen·nine (féssi-nīn ‖ -neen) *adj. Literary.* Licentious; obscene. [Latin *Fescennīnus,* of the town *Fescennia* in Etruria, noted for licentious festivals and verses.]

fes·cue (féskew) *n.* **1.** Any of various grasses of the genus *Festuca,* often cultivated as pasturage and for lawns. **2.** A small stick or wand used as a pointer. [Middle English *festu,* from Old French, from Vulgar Latin *festūcum* (unattested), from Latin *festūca†,* stalk, stem.]

fesse, fess (fess) *n. Heraldry.* A wide horizontal band forming the middle section of an escutcheon. [Middle English *fesse,* from Old French, from Latin *fascia,* band, fillet.]

fesse point *n. Heraldry.* The centre point of an escutcheon.

fes·tal (fést'l) *adj.* Of, pertaining to, or of the nature of a feast or festival; festive; joyous. [Old French, from Latin *fēsta,* FEAST.] —**fes·tal·ly** *adv.*

fes·ter (féstər) *v.* **-tered, -tering, -ters.** —*intr.* **1.** To generate pus; suppurate. **2.** To form an ulcer. **3.** To decay; rot. **4.** To be or become a source of irritation; rankle. —*tr.* To infect, inflame, or corrupt.
~*n.* A small, festering sore or ulcer. [Middle English *festre,* from Old French, from Latin *fistula,* FISTULA.]

fes·ti·na len·te (fess-tee-naa lén-tay). *Latin* Make haste slowly; "more haste, less speed".

fes·ti·val (féstiv'l) *n.* **1.** An occasion for feasting or celebration; especially, a day or time of religious significance that recurs at regular intervals: *Harvest festival; the festival of Chanukkah.* **2.** A series of related performances, exhibitions, competitions, or the like; especially, such a series that recurs at regular intervals: *a film festival; the Edinburgh festival.* **3.** *Archaic.* Conviviality; revelry.
~*adj.* Festive. [Middle English, from Old French, from Medieval Latin *fēstivālis,* from *fēstivus,* FESTIVE.]

fes·tive (féstiv) *adj.* **1.** Of, pertaining to, or appropriate to a feast or festival. **2.** Merry; joyous: *a festive occasion.* [Latin *fēstivus,* from *fēstus,* joyous.] —**fes·tive·ly** *adv.* —**fes·tive·ness** *n.*

fes·tiv·i·ty (fess-tívvəti) *n., pl.* **-ties. 1.** A joyous feast, holiday, or celebration; a festival. **2.** The pleasure, joy, and gaiety of a festival or celebration. **3.** *Plural.* The proceedings or events of a festival or celebration; festive activity.

fes·toon (fess-tōon) *n.* **1.** A string or garland of leaves, flowers, ribbon, or the like, suspended in a loop or curve between two points. **2.** A representation of this, as in sculpture or architecture.
~*tr.v.* **festooned, -tooning, -toons. 1.** To decorate with or as if with a festoon or festoons. **2.** To form or make into a festoon or festoons. **3.** To join together by festoons. [French *feston,* from Italian *festone,* festal ornament, from *fēsta,* feast, festival, from Latin, plural of *fēstus,* joyous, festal.]

fes·toon·er·y (fess-tōonəri) *n., pl.* **-ies. 1.** An arrangement of or into festoons. **2.** Festoons collectively.

fest·schrift (fést-shrift) *n., pl.* **-schriften** (-shriftən) or **-schrifts.** A volume of learned essays, and the like, contributed by colleagues and admirers as a tribute to a scholar. [German, "festival writing".]

FET field-effect transistor.

feta. Variant of **fetta.**

fetch¹ (fech) *v.* **fetched, fetching, fetches.** —*tr.* **1.** To go after and return with; get; bring. **2.** To cause to come or be drawn forth: *A bell fetched the receptionist.* **3. a.** To draw in (breath); inhale. **b.** To bring forth (a sigh, for example). **4.** *Informal.* To bring in (a price); sell for. **5.** To interest; attract: *How does this idea fetch you?* **6.** *Archaic.* To perform or make (a movement, step, or the like). **7.** *Informal.* To strike or deal (a blow, punch, or the like). **8.** *Nautical.* To arrive at; come to; reach. —*intr.* **1.** To go after and return with things. **2.** In hunting, to retrieve game. Often used as a command to a dog. **3.** *Nautical.* **a.** To hold a course. **b.** To turn about; veer.
—**fetch and carry.** To do minor tasks; especially, to run to and fro

at another's bidding. **—fetch up. 1.** To reach a place and halt there; end up. **2.** *Slang.* To vomit.

~n. 1. An act or instance of fetching. **2.** A stratagem or trick. **3.** The extent of an unbroken expanse of water: *the fetch of a bay.* [Middle English *fecchen,* Old English *feccan, fetian.*] **—fetch·er** *n.*

fetch² *n. Chiefly British.* An apparition of a living person; a Doppelgänger. [18th century : origin obscure.]

fetch·ing (féching) *adj. Informal.* Very attractive; charming; captivating. **—fetch·ing·ly** *adv.*

fête, fete (fayt; *French* fet) *n.* **1.** A festival or elaborate feast. **2.** A bazaar or fair, usually held outdoors, to raise money for charity. **3.** Especially in Roman Catholic countries, the feast day of a saint, observed as a festival by those bearing the name of the saint.

~tr.v. fêted, fêting, fêtes. 1. To celebrate with a fête. **2.** To pay honour to, especially by entertaining. [French *fête,* from Old French *feste,* FEAST.]

fête cham·pê·tre (shoN-péttr) *n., pl.* **fêtes champêtres** (*pronounced as singular*). *French.* An outdoor dinner, party, or similar entertainment.

fet·e·ri·ta (fétta-réeta) *n.* A variety of sorghum, *Sorghum vulgare caudatum,* grown in warm regions for its grain and as forage. [Arabic (Sudanese dialect).]

fet·id, foe·tid (féttid, féetid) *adj.* Having an offensive odour; foul-smelling; stinking: *fetid air swarming with mosquitoes.* [Middle English, from Latin *fētidus, foetidus,* from *fētēre, foetēret,* to stink.] **—fet·id·ly** *adv.* **—fet·id·ness** *n.*

fet·ish, fet·ich (féttish, féetish) *n.* **1. a.** A material object believed among primitive cultures to have magical power. **b.** Belief in the power of such objects. **2.** An object, principle, activity, or the like that receives unreasonably excessive attention or reverence. **3.** *Psychology.* **a.** An abnormal sexual attraction to some object or part of the body not normally considered erogenous: *a foot fetish.* **b.** The object of this attraction. [French *fétiche,* from Portuguese *feitiço,* charm, sorcery, from Latin *factītius,* made by art, from *facere,* to make, do.]

fet·ish·ism (fétti-shiz'm, féeti-) *n.* **1.** The worship of or belief in fetishes. **2.** Excessive attention to or attachment for something. **3.** *Psychology.* A condition involving a fetish. **—fet·ish·ist** *n.* **—fet·ish·is·tic** (-shístik) *adj.*

fet·lock (fét-lok) *n.* **1. a.** A projection on the lower part of the leg of a horse or related animal, above and behind the hoof. **b.** A tuft of hair on such a projection. **2.** The joint marked by this projection. In this sense, also called "fetlock joint". [Middle English *fitlok,* from Germanic; akin to Middle High German *vizzelach.*]

fe·tor (fée-tər, -tawr) *n.* Also **foe·tor.** An exceptionally offensive odour; a strong stench. [Middle English *fetour,* from Latin *fētor, foetor,* from *fētēre, foetēret,* to stink.]

fet·ta, fet·a (fétt-ə, -aa) *n.* A white, crumbly cheese made usually from ewe's milk and eaten especially in Greece. [Modern Greek, short for *turi pheta,* "cheese slice" : *turi,* cheese + *pheta,* from Italian *fetta,* slice.]

fet·ter (féttər) *n.* **1.** A chain or shackle attached to the ankle to restrain movement. **2.** *Usually plural.* Anything that serves to restrict; a restraint.

~tr.v. fettered, -tering, -ters. 1. To put fetters on; shackle. **2.** To restrict the freedom of movement or thought of; confine; impede. [Middle English *feter,* Old English *feter, fetor,* from Germanic.]

fet·tle (fétt'l) *tr.v.* **-tled, -tling, -tles.** *Metallurgy.* **1.** To line (the hearth of a reverberatory furnace) with loose sand or ore preparatory to pouring molten metal. **2.** To remove excess material from a casting or moulding. **3.** *British Regional.* To repair or restore to good condition.

~n. 1. The material used to line a furnace in fettling. **2.** Proper or sound condition; good spirits: *in fine fettle.* [Middle English *fetlen,* to shape, make ready, probably from Old English *fetel,* girdle, belt, from Germanic.]

fet·tling (fét-ling) *n.* The material, such as loose ore and sand, used to line a reverberatory furnace.

fet·tu·ci·ni, fet·tu·ci·ne (féttōō-chéeni, fétta-) *n. Used with a singular or plural verb.* Italian pasta in the form of narrow strips. [Italian *fettucine* (plural), diminutive of *fetta,* slice.]

fetus. *Chiefly U.S.* Variant of **foetus.** **—fet·al** *adj.*

feu (few) *n. Scottish.* **1.** Formerly, the tenure of land for payment of grain or money instead of military service. **2.** A lease held in perpetuity in return for a fixed annual rent. **3.** Land held by either of these methods.

~tr.v. feued, feuing, feus. *Scottish.* To grant (land) on the basis of a feu. [Old French. See **fee.**]

Feucht·wang·er (fóykht-vang-ər), **Lion** (1884–1958). German novelist and dramatist. He wrote *The Ugly Duchess* (1923) and *Jew Süss* (1925). He was exiled by the Nazis in 1933, and settled in California in 1940.

feud¹ (fewd) *n.* **1.** A bitter, prolonged hostility between two families, individuals, or clans; a vendetta. **2.** A quarrel; strife.

~intr.v. feuded, feuding, feuds. To carry on a feud. [Middle English *fede, feide,* from Old French, from Old High German *fēhida;* akin to Old English *fǣhthu,* enmity (see FOE, -TH).]

feud² (fewd) *n.* A feudal estate, a **fee** (*see*). [Medieval Latin *feudum,* probably from Germanic.]

feu·dal (féwd'l) *adj.* **1.** Of, pertaining to, or characteristic of feudalism. **2.** Of or pertaining to lands held in fee or to the holding of such lands. [Medieval Latin *feudālis,* from *feudum,* FEUD (estate).] **—feu·dal·ly** *adv.*

feu·dal·ise, feu·dal·ize (féwd'l-īz) *tr.v.* **-ised, -ising, -ises.** To organise into a feudal system; make feudal. **—feu·dal·i·sa·tion** (-ī-záysh'n || *U.S.* -i-) *n.*

feu·dal·ism (féwd'l-iz'm) *n.* A political and economic system of medieval Europe, based on the relation of lord to vassal, in which land was held on condition of homage and service. **—feu·dal·ist** *n.* **—feu·dal·is·tic** (-ístik) *adj.*

feu·dal·i·ty (few-dál-əti) *n., pl.* **-ties. 1.** The state or quality of being feudal. **2.** A feudal estate, a **fee** (*see*).

feu·da·to·ry (féwdə-təri, -tri) *n., pl.* **-ries. 1.** A person who holds a feudal fee; a vassal. **2.** A feudal fee.

~adj. 1. Of, pertaining to, or characteristic of the feudal relationship between vassal and lord. **2.** Owing feudal homage or allegiance. [Medieval Latin *feudātōrius,* from *feudātus,* past participle of *feudāre,* to enfeoff, from *feudum,* FEUD (estate).]

feud·ist (féwdist) *n. U.S.* A person who feuds with another.

feu duty *n.* In Scotland, an annual fee payable on a feu. See **ground rent.**

Feu·er·bach (fóyər-bakh), **Ludwig (Andreas)** (1804–72). German philosopher. He explained history in materialist terms, claiming that "Man is what he eats". In *The Essence of Christianity* (1841), he argued that God was a projection of man's inner self.

feuil·le·ton (fö-i-tón, fōl-, -yə-) *n.* **1.** The part of a French or other European newspaper devoted to light fiction, reviews, and similar articles. **2.** An article appearing in a feuilleton, such as an instalment of a serialised novel. [French, from *feuillet,* diminutive of *feuille,* leaf, from Old French *fueille, foille,* from Latin *folia,* plural of *folium,* leaf.] **—feuil·le·ton·ism** (fö-i-tə-niz'm, fōl-, -yə-) *n.* **—feuil·le·ton·ist** *n.*

Feul·gen reaction (fóyl-gən) *n.* A staining reaction in which the presence of DNA is demonstrated by the appearance of purple colour upon contact with a reagent containing fuchsine and sulphuric acid. [After R.J. *Feulgen* (1884–1955), German biochemist.]

fe·ver (féevər) *n.* **1.** Abnormally high body temperature, usually associated with shivering and a fast pulse. **2.** Any disease characterised by abnormally high body temperatures. **3.** A condition of heightened activity or excitement; a ferment; agitation: *a fever of anticipation.* **4.** A contagious, usually short-lived enthusiasm or eagerness.

~tr.v. fevered, -vering, -vers. To put into a fever. [Middle English *fever,* Old English *fēfor, fēfer,* from Latin *febrist.*]

fe·ver·few (féevər-few) *n.* An aromatic plant, *Chrysanthemum parthenium,* native to Eurasia, having clusters of button-like, white-rayed flowers. [Middle English *feverfu,* from Anglo-French *fevrefue* (unattested), from Latin *febrifugia : febris,* FEVER + *fugāre,* to drive away, from *fugere,* to run away (from its former use as a febrifuge).]

fe·ver·ish (féevər-ish) *adj.* Also **fe·ver·ous** (-əss) (for sense 1). **1. a.** Having a fever, especially a slight fever. **b.** Of, pertaining to, or resembling a fever. **c.** Causing or tending to cause fever. **2.** In an agitated or restless state; intensely emotional or active. **—fe·ver·ish·ly** *adv.* **—fe·ver·ish·ness** *n.*

fever pitch *n.* An intense degree of excitement or agitation.

fever therapy *n.* Formerly, treatment of disease involving artificially induced fever.

fever tree *n.* Any of several trees, such as certain species of eucalyptus, or *Pinckneya pubens,* of the southeastern United States, having leaves or bark capable of reducing fever.

fe·ver·wort (féevər-wurt || -wawrt) *n.* Any of several plants considered to have medicinal properties, such as the **horse gentian** and **boneset** (*both of which see*).

few (few) *adj.* **fewer, fewest.** Amounting to or consisting of a small number. **—few and far between.** Scarce; in short supply.

~n. Used with a plural verb. 1. An indefinitely small number of persons or things; not many: *Bring me a few of your books.* **2.** A limited number of people; the select. Usually preceded by *the: the discerning few.* **—a good few.** Several or many. **—have a few too many.** *Informal.* To consume too many alcoholic drinks. **—quite a few.** A lot; many.

~pron. Used with a plural verb. A small number of persons or things: *"many are called, but few are chosen."* (Matthew 22:14). [Middle English *fewe,* Old English *fēa, fēawe.*] **—few·ness** *n.*

Usage: *Fewer* and *less* sometimes overlap in usage. *Fewer* is the preferred word when the reference is to numbers, or to entities considered as individuals which can be counted or listed. *Less* is preferred when the reference is to collective quantity or to something abstract. Contrast *fewer workers, less production,* and *fewer opportunities, less opportunity.* Informally, there is a tendency for *less* to be used in place of *fewer,* especially when there is an implicit contrast with *more: No less than 15 people telephoned; There are 15 less trains on the line today than there were last year;* here formal English prefers *fewer.* However, even formal English will accept *less* when the contrast is explicit: *we want a few more cars and a few less buses* (where *a few fewer* would be unacceptable); or in expressions of measurement, even when plural: *less than 60 years old; less than 50 feet.*

fey (fay) *adj.* **1.** *Scottish.* **a.** Fated to die soon. **b.** Full of the sense of approaching death. **2.** Having visionary power; clairvoyant. **3.** Appearing as if under a spell; enchanted; touched. **4.** Whimsical or fanciful. [Middle English *feie,* Old English *fǣge.*]

Fey·deau (fáy-dō || fay-dó), **Georges** (1862–1921). He wrote many farcical comedies, including *The Lady from Maxim's* (1899) and *A Flea in Her Ear* (1907).

Feyn·man (fīn-mən), **Richard Phillips** (1918–88). U.S. physicist. He is best-known for his work in quantum electrodynamics, especially the Feynman diagrams, which illustrate interactions between charged particles as an exchange of virtual photons. He shared the Nobel prize in 1965.

fez (fez) *n., pl.* **fezzes.** A man's felt cap in the shape of a truncated cone, usually red with a black tassel hanging from the crown, worn chiefly in the eastern Mediterranean region. [French, from Turkish, perhaps after **Fès.**]

Fez. See **Fès.**

ff *Music.* fortissimo.

ff. 1. folios. **2.** following.

FH fire hydrant.

f.h.p. friction horsepower.

fi·a·cre (fi-a′ákrə) *n.* A small hackney coach. [French, first hired out from Hôtel de St. *Fiacre,* Paris.]

fi·an·cé (fi-ón-say, -ón- ‖ fée-on-sáy, -ON-) *n.* A man engaged to be married. [French, past participle of *fiancer,* to betroth, from Old French *fiancier,* from *fier,* to trust, from Vulgar Latin *fidāre* (unattested), from Latin *fīdere.*]

    Usage: In formal writing, the accent is always preserved in *fiancé* and *fiancée.* Newspapers, however, to simplify typesetting, generally omit the accent: *fiance, fiancee.*

fi·an·cée (fi-ón-say, -ón- ‖ fée-on-sáy, -ON-) *n.* A woman engaged to be married. See Usage note at **fiancé.** [French, feminine of **FIANCÉ.**]

Fi·an·na (fée-ənə) *n.* **Fenian** *(see).*

Fi·an·na Fáil (fée-ənə fóyl) *n.* A major Irish political party founded in 1926 by de Valera with the aim of removing all British influence from Ireland. [Irish, "Fenians of the land" : *Fianna* (see **Fenian**) + *Fáil,* from *fál,* earth, sod.]

fi·as·co (fi-áskō) *n., pl.* **-coes** or **-cos.** A complete failure, especially a very embarrassing one. [French, from Italian *(far) fiasco,* "(to make) a bottle", an unexplained allusion, perhaps from Late Latin *flascō,* **FLASK.**]

fi·at (fī-ət, fée-, -at, -aat) *n.* **1.** An arbitrary order or decree. **2.** Authorisation; sanction. [Latin *fīat,* "let it be done", third person singular present subjunctive of *fierī,* to become, representing the passive of *facere,* to do.]

fiat money *n. U.S.* Paper money decreed legal tender, not backed by gold or silver, and not necessarily redeemable in coin.

fib (fib) *n.* An inconsequential lie.
   ~*intr.v.* **fibbed, fibbing, fibs.** To tell a fib. [17th century : perhaps shortened from obsolete *fible-fable,* nonsense, reduplication of **FABLE.**] —**fib·ber** *n.*

Fi·bo·nac·ci (fíbbə-naáchi), **Leonardo** (*c.*1170–*c.*1240). Italian mathematician. In North Africa he learnt the decimal system of numerals, which he published in his *Liber abaci* (*The Book of Calculation*) (1202). From 1960 interest developed in his **Fibonacci sequence.**

Fibonacci sequence *n.* A sequence of numbers (*Fibonacci numbers*) each of which is the sum of the two preceding numbers: 1, 1, 2, 3, 5, 8, 13, 21 . . . . . .

fi·bre, *U.S.* **fi·ber** (fíbər) *n.* **1.** Any slender, elongated structure; a thread or strand. **2.** Any of the elongated, thick-walled cells that give strength and support to plant tissue. **3.** Any of the filaments constituting the intracellular matrix of connective tissue. **4.** *Anatomy.* Any of various threadlike structures; especially, a **muscle fibre** or a **nerve fibre** *(both of which see).* **5.** A natural or synthetic thread, as of cotton or nylon, capable of being spun into yarn. **6. a.** Material made of such spun filaments. **b.** The grain or structure of any material made from or as if made from fibres. **7.** The essential substance. **8.** Internal strength; character: *lacking in moral fibre.* [Middle English, from Old French *fibre,* from Latin *fibra†.*]

fi·bre·board (fíbər-bawrd ‖ -bōrd) *n.* **1.** A building material composed of wood or other plant fibres bonded together and compressed into rigid sheets. **2.** A sheet of this material.

fi·bre·fill (fíbər-fil) *n.* Synthetic fibre for stuffing cushions, quilting, or the like.

Fi·bre·glass (fíbər-glaass ‖ -glass) *n.* A trademark for **glass fibre** *(see).*

fibre optics *n. Used with a singular verb.* The optics of light transmission through very fine, flexible glass fibres by internal reflection. —**fi·bre·op·tic** (fíbər-óptik) *adj.*

fi·bre·scope (fíbər-skōp) *n.* A flexible fibre-optic instrument used to view objects that would otherwise be inaccessible, especially tissues and organs in inaccessible parts of the body.

fi·bri·form (fī-bri-fawrm, fíbbri-) *adj.* Similar in form or structure to a fibre.

fi·bril (fī-bril ‖ fíbbril) *n.* Also **fi·bril·la** (fī-bríllə, fi- ‖ fíbbri-lə) *pl.* **-brillae** (-bríl-ee, fíbbri-lee). A small, slender fibre, such as a root hair or a constituent thread of a muscle fibre. [New Latin *fibrilla,* diminutive of Latin *fibra,* **FIBRE.**] —**fi·bril·lar** (fī-bri-lər, fíbbri-, fi-bríllər), **fi·bril·lar·y** (-ləri ‖ -lerri) *adj.*

fib·ril·la·tion (fī-bri-láysh′n, fíbbri-) *n.* **1.** The forming of fibres. **2.** Uncoordinated twitching of individual muscle fibres with little or no movement of the muscle as a whole. **3.** *Pathology.* Fine, rapid fibrillar movements that replace the normal contraction of the heart muscle. [New Latin *fibrilla,* **FIBRIL.**]

fi·bril·li·form (fī-bríllí-fawrm, fi-) *adj.* Having the form of a fibril.

fi·bril·lose (fī-bri-lōss, fíbbri-, -lōz) *adj.* Having or consisting of fibrils.

fi·brin (fī-brin, fíbbrin) *n.* An elastic, insoluble protein derived from the interaction of fibrinogen with thrombin and forming a fibrous network in the coagulation of blood. [FIBR(O)- + -IN.]

fi·brin·o·gen (fī-brínnə-jən, fi-) *n.* A protein in the blood plasma that is converted to fibrin by the action of thrombin in the presence of ionised calcium, in blood coagulation. [FIBRIN + -GEN.]

fi·bri·nol·y·sin (fī-bri-nólli-sin, fíbbri-, -nə-lī-sin) *n.* An enzyme, **plasmin** *(see).* [FIBRIN + -O- + LYSIN.]

fi·brin·ol·y·sis (fī-bri-nólli-siss, fíbbri-, -nə-lī-siss) *n.* The breakdown of blood clots, which involves the dissolution of fibrin by the enzyme plasmin. [FIBRIN + -LYSIS.]

fi·brin·ous (fī-brinəss, fí-) *adj.* Of, pertaining to, or having the nature of fibrin.

fi·bro (fíbrō) *n., pl.* **-bros.** *Australian Informal.* A house made of fibrocement.

fibro-, fibr- *comb.form.* Indicates: **1.** Fibrous tissue; for example, **fibrovascular, fibrosis. 2.** Fibre; for example, **fibrocement.** [Latin *fibra,* **FIBRE.**]

fi·bro·blast (fī-brō-blast ‖ *U.S. also* fíbrō-) *n.* A cell in connective tissue that is responsible for producing fibres. [FIBRO- + -BLAST.]

fi·bro·car·ti·lage (fíbrō-kártilij) *n.* A type of cartilage containing many fibres and found, for example, in the intervertebral discs.

fi·bro·ce·ment (fíbrō-si-mént) *n.* A building material made out of cement and asbestos mixed together and formed into sheets.

fi·broid (fī-broyd ‖ *U.S. also* fíbbroyd) *adj.* Resembling or composed of fibrous tissue.
   ~*n.* A benign tumour of smooth muscle, especially in the uterine wall. [FIBR(O)- + -OID.]

fi·bro·in (fī-brō-in ‖ *U.S. also* fíbbrō-) *n.* A white protein that is the essential component of raw silk and spider-web filaments. [French *fibroïne* : FIBRO- + -IN.]

fi·bro·ma (fī-brō-mə) *n., pl.* **-mas** or **-mata** (-mətə). Any benign tumour derived from fibrous tissue, such as a fibroid. [New Latin : FIBR(O)- + -OMA.] —**fi·brom·a·tous** (-brómmə-təss, -brōmə-) *adj.*

fi·bro·sis (fī-brō-siss) *n.* The formation of excess fibrous tissue in an organ, such as the lung, usually as a result of inflammation or injury. See **cystic fibrosis.** [New Latin : FIBR(O)- + -OSIS.]

fi·bro·si·tis (fī-brə-sītiss ‖ *U.S. also* fíbbrə-) *n.* Inflammation of fibrous connective tissue, especially in the muscles and muscle sheaths of the back. [New Latin *fibrosus,* FIBROUS + -ITIS.]

fi·brous (fī-brəss) *adj.* Having, consisting of, or resembling fibres.

fi·bro·vas·cu·lar (fī-brō-váskew-lər ‖ *U.S. also* fíbbrō-) *adj. Botany.* Having fibrous tissue and vascular tissue. Said of the vascular bundles in woody tissue.

fib·u·la (fíbbew-lə) *n., pl.* **-lae** (-lee) or **-las. 1.** The outer and smaller of two bones of the human leg or the hind leg of an animal, in humans between the knee and ankle. **2.** A broochlike clasp used in the ancient world. [Latin *fibula,* perhaps from the root of *fīgere,* to fix.] —**fib·u·lar** *adj.*

-fic *adj. suffix.* Indicates making, causing, or creating; for example, **morbific.** [New Latin *-ficus,* from Latin, from *facere,* to do, make.]

fiche (feesh ‖ *U.S. also* fish) *n.* A **microfiche** *(see).*

fi·chu (fée-shoo, físhoo; *French* fee-shǘ) *n.* A woman's triangular scarf of lightweight fabric, worn over the shoulders and crossed or tied in a loose knot at the breast. [French, from the past participle of *ficher,* to fix, attach, from Vulgar Latin *fīgicāre* (unattested), from Latin *fīgere,* to FIX.]

fick·le (fick′l) *adj.* Changeable, especially with regard to affections or attachments; inconstant; capricious. See Synonyms at **faithless.** [Middle English *fikel,* false, treacherous, Old English *ficol.*] —**fick·le·ness** *n.*

fic·tile (fík-tīl ‖ *U.S. also* fíkt′l) *adj.* **1.** Able to be moulded; plastic. **2.** Formed of a mouldable substance, such as clay or earth. **3.** Of or pertaining to earthenware or pottery. [Latin *fictilis,* from *fictus,* past participle of *fingere,* to touch, form, mould, shape.]

fic·tion (fíksh′n) *n.* **1.** An event, statement, or occurrence that has been invented or feigned rather than having actually taken place. **2.** The act of producing such inventions; a feigning. **3.** A lie. **4. a.** A literary work whose content is produced by the imagination and is not necessarily based on fact. **b.** The category of literature comprising works of this kind, including novels and short stories. **5.** Something accepted as fact without any real justification, but merely for the sake of convenience: *a legal fiction.* [Middle English *ficcioun,* invention, from Old French *fiction,* from Latin *fictiō* (stem *fictiōn-*), a making, fashioning, from *fictus,* past participle of *fingere,* to touch, form, mould.] —**fic·tion·al** *adj.* —**fic·tion·al·ly** *adv.*

fic·tion·al·ise, fic·tion·al·ize (fíksh′n-ə-līz) *tr.v.* **-ised, -ising, -ises.** To make (a true story, for example), into fiction by changing details such as names and locations. —**fic·tion·al·i·sa·tion** (-lī-záysh′n ‖ *U.S.* -li-) *n.*

fic·ti·tious (fik-tíshəss) *adj.* **1.** Of, pertaining to, or characterised by fiction; non-existent; imaginary; unreal: *a fictitious event.* **2.** Purposefully deceptive; false; untrue: *a fictitious name.* —**fic·ti·tious·ly** *adv.* —**fic·ti·tious·ness** *n.*

fictitious force *n. Physics.* A force, such as centrifugal or Coriolis force, that arises because of the frame of reference of the observer and disappears on transformation to a more suitable frame.

fic·tive (fíktiv) *adj.* **1.** Of or pertaining to the creation of fiction. **2.** Pertaining to or characterised by fiction; fictitious; imaginary. **3.** Feigned; sham. —**fic·tive·ly** *adv.*

fid (fid) *n. Nautical.* **1.** A square bar used as a support for a topmast. **2.** A large, tapering pin used to open the strands of a rope prior to splicing. [17th century : origin obscure.]

-fid *adj. comb.form.* Indicates a division or separation into parts or lobes; for example, **pinnatifid.** [Latin *-fidus,* from *findere,* to split.]

Fid. Def. Fidei Defensor.

fid·dle (fídd'l) *n.* **1. a.** *Informal.* A **violin** *(see).* **b.** Any member of the violin family, including similarly designed medieval and Oriental instruments. **2.** *Nautical.* A guard rail used on a table during rough weather to prevent things from slipping off. **3.** *Informal.* Nonsensical trifling; stupidity. **4.** *British Informal.* An illegal or underhand practice or act: *a tax fiddle.* **—fit as a fiddle.** Very healthy. **—play second fiddle.** *Informal.* To be subordinate.
~*v.* **fiddled, -dling, -dles.** *—intr.* **1. a.** To move one's fingers or hands in a restless fashion; fidget. **b.** To tamper; touch. Used with *with: Don't fiddle with my belongings.* **2.** To waste time. Usually used with *about* or *around.* **3.** *Informal.* To play a violin. *—tr. Informal.* **1.** To arrange or contrive, especially by slightly underhand methods. **2.** To prepare (accounts) to one's own advantage. **3.** To cheat or swindle. **4.** To play (a tune) on a violin. [Middle English *fithele, fidle,* Old English *fithele,* from West Germanic *fithula* (unattested), from Medieval Latin *vītula,* from Latin *vītulārī,* to celebrate a victory, from *Vītula,* goddess of joy and victory, probably of Sabine origin.]
fid·dle-back (fídd'l-bak) *adj.* Shaped like the body of a violin: *a fiddle-back chair.*
fid·dle-de-dee (fídd'l-di-dée) *interj.* Used to express mild annoyance or impatience. [Nonsensical formation from FIDDLE.]
fid·dle-fad·dle (fídd'l-fadd'l) *interj.* Used to express mild annoyance or impatience.
~*n.* Nonsense or petty matters.
~*intr.v.* **fiddle-faddled, -dling, -dles.** To fritter away one's time; dally. [Reduplication of FIDDLE.] **—fid·dle-fad·dler** *n.*
fid·dle-head (fídd'l-hed) *n.* A curved, scroll-like ornamentation at the top of a ship's bow that resembles the neck of a violin.
fiddle pattern *n.* A flatware pattern for the handles of forks, spoons, or the like in the shape of a fiddle.
fid·dler (fíddlər) *n. Informal.* A person who plays the violin.
fiddler crab *n.* Any of various burrowing crabs of the genus *Uca* having one of the anterior claws much enlarged in the male. [So called from its large claw which it seems to hold like a fiddle.]
fid·dle·sticks (fídd'l-stiks) *interj.* Used to express mild annoyance or impatience.
fid·dling (fíddling) *adj.* Unimportant; trifling; silly.
fid·dly (fíddli) *adj.* **-lier, -liest.** Awkward or difficult to do, use, or handle, especially because of smallness of size or extreme detail.
F.I.D.E. *F*édération *I*nternationale *d*es *É*checs : the international governing body of chess.
Fi·de·i De·fen·sor (fī-di-ī di-fén-sawr, fée-day-ée, fi-dáy-i, -day- || -sōr) *n. Abbr.* **F.D., Fid. Def.** *Latin.* Defender of the Faith. Used as one of the titles of the British sovereign.
fi·de·ism (fée-day-iz'm, fī-di-) *n.* The belief or doctrine that knowledge of religious matters can be obtained only through revelation or faith and cannot be established by rational means. [Latin *fidēs,* faith + -ISM.]
fi·del·i·ty (fi-délləti, fī-) *n., pl.* **-ties. 1.** Faithfulness to obligations, duties, or observances; loyalty. **2.** Faithfulness or loyalty, as to a friend or cause; specifically, faithfulness to a spouse or lover. **3.** Correspondence with fact or a given quality, condition, or event; verity; truthfulness; accuracy. **4.** *Abbr.* **fid.** The degree to which an electronic system, such as a radio or record player, accurately reproduces at its output the essential characteristics of its input signal. [Middle English *fidelite,* from Old French, from Latin *fidēlitās* (stem *fidēlitāt-*), from *fidēlis,* faithful, from *fidēs,* faith.]
Synonyms: *fidelity, allegiance, fealty, loyalty, devotion.*
fidg·et (fíjit) *v.* **-eted, -eting, -ets.** *—intr.* **1.** To keep some part of one's body in continuous motion, as by shifting one's hands or feet; move nervously or restlessly. **2.** To play with or finger something nervously. Used with *with: The lecturer fidgeted with his notes.* *—tr.* To cause (someone) to fidget; make restless or nervous.
~*n.* **1.** *Usually plural.* A condition of restlessness. **2.** One who fidgets. [Frequentative of obsolete *fidge,* variant of *fitch, fike,* from Middle English *fiken,* probably from Old Norse *fīkjast,* akin to Old English *fācian†,* to try to obtain.]
fidg·et·y (fíjiti) *adj.* **1.** Habitually fidgeting; nervous; restless. **2.** Unnecessarily fussy. **—fidg·et·i·ness** *n.*
FIDO *n.* *F*og *I*nvestigation *D*ispersal *O*peration : a method of dispersing fog over an airport using petrol burners.
fi·du·cial (fi-déw-shi-əl, -si-, -sh'l || fī-, -dōō-) *adj.* **1.** Based on or pertaining to faith or trust. **2.** Pertaining to a legal trust; fiduciary. **3.** Regarded or employed as a standard of reference, as in measurement. [Late Latin *fīdūciālis,* from Latin *fīdūcia,* trust, from *fīdere,* to trust.] **—fi·du·cial·ly** *adv.*
fi·du·ci·ar·y (fi-déw-shi-əri, -si-, -shəri || fī-, -dōō-, -shəri, -erri) *adj.* **1.** Of, pertaining to, or involving one who holds something in trust for another: *a fiduciary heir; a fiduciary contract.* **2. a.** Of, pertaining to, or designating a trustee or trusteeship. **b.** Held in trust. **3.** Of, pertaining to, or consisting of paper currency that is issued without being backed by gold.
~*n., pl.* **fiduciaries.** A person who stands in a special relation of trust, confidence, or responsibility in his obligations to others, such as a company director or an agent of a principal. [Latin *fīdūciārius,* from *fīdūcia,* trust. See **fiducial.**]
fie (fī) *interj.* **1.** *Archaic.* Used to express distaste or shock. **2.** Used humorously to express pretended shock. [Middle English *fi,* from Old French, from Latin *fī,* expression of disgust at a bad smell.]
fief (feef) *n.* **1.** A feudal estate, a **fee** *(see).* **2.** A sphere of authority or influence. [French, from Old French *fie(f),* FEE.]
fief·dom (féef-dəm) *n.* **1.** A fief. **2.** A person's sphere of influence or control.
field (feeld) *n. Abbr.* **fld. 1.** A broad, level, open expanse of land; a meadow: *a field of buttercups.* **2.** An expanse of land, usually enclosed grassland, used for pasturage. **3.** A cultivated expanse of land, especially one devoted to a particular crop. **4.** A portion of land or a geological formation containing a specified natural resource: *an oil field.* **5.** A large, flat surface used by aircraft for landing and taking off; an airfield. **6.** A background area, as on a flag, painting, or coin: *a blue insignia on a field of red.* **7.** *Heraldry.* The background area of a shield, or one of the divisions of the background. **8.** *Sports.* **a.** A delineated area on which a sports event, such as a soccer game or a cricket match, takes place. **b.** The portion of a playing field having specific dimensions on which the action of a game takes place: *The spectators were ordered to stay off the field.* **c.** All the contestants or participants in an event. **d.** In horse-racing, all the contestants except the favourite. **e.** In sports such as cricket, the team that is fielding. **f.** The body of horsemen following a pack of hounds. **9.** A group of rival candidates for selection: *chosen from a talented field of applicants.* **10. a.** An area of human activity or interest: *a field of endeavour.* **b.** A topic, subject, or area of academic interest or specialisation. **c.** Profession, employment, or business: *data processing is definitely not his field.* **11.** An area or setting of practical activity or application, especially as distinguished from one of academic study or theoretical research: *out in the field selling encyclopedias.* **12. a.** The scene of a battle. **b.** A battle while it is in progress. **c.** The land, especially when considered topographically, where a battle has been fought; a battlefield. **13.** *Mathematics.* A set with two binary operations, *addition* and *multiplication,* satisfying the conditions that the set is a commutative group with respect to addition, that the set with the zero omitted is a commutative group with respect to multiplication, and that multiplication is distributive over addition for all elements in the set. **14.** *Physics.* A region of space characterised by a physical property, such as gravitational or electromagnetic force or fluid pressure, having a determinable value at every point in the region. **15.** *Optics.* The usually circular area in which the image is rendered by the lens system of an optical instrument. **16.** *Computing.* **a.** A group of characters treated as a unit of information. **b.** The characters recorded in a vertical column on a punched card. **—keep** or **hold the field.** To continue in one's position in the face of adversity. **—leave the field.** *Informal.* To concede one's interest to another or others. **—play the field.** *Informal.* To maintain a broad range of options in personal or business matters, rather than making a specific commitment. **—take the field.** To begin or resume activity, as in military operations or in a sport.
~*v.* **fielded, fielding, fields.** *—tr.* **1.** *Sports.* **a.** To retrieve, catch, or stop (a ball). **b.** To place (a team or player) in playing position, or be able to put (a team, for example) into a contest: *England fielded a strong side.* **2.** To handle adequately and be able to return in kind; cope with: *The Home Secretary fielded the question very clumsily.* *—intr. Sports.* **1.** To retrieve, catch, or stop a ball. **2.** To play or take a turn as a fielder.
~*adj.* **1.** Of, pertaining or appropriate to, or carried out in a field or fields: *field work.* **2.** Growing or living in a field or fields. [Middle English *feld, field,* Old English *feld,* from West Germanic.]
field artillery *n. Abbr.* **FA** Artillery, with the exception of antiaircraft artillery, light enough to be mounted for use in the field.
field battery *n.* A tactical artillery unit usually consisting of four or six field guns.
field boot *n.* A knee-length, tight-fitting boot.
field coil *n.* An electric coil used to generate a magnetic field, as in a motor or direct-current generator.
field·craft (féeld-kraaft || -kraft) *n.* **1.** The skills appropriate to soldiers fighting in the field, such as camouflage and knowledge of the terrain. **2.** Knowledge of the countryside.
field-day (féeld-day) *n.* **1.** A day spent outdoors engaged in a planned activity such as an athletic competition or nature study. **2.** *Military.* An exercise or a public demonstration. **3.** *Informal.* An opportunity for expressing or asserting oneself with the fullest pleasure or triumph.
field-ef·fect transistor (féeld-i-fekt) *n. Abbr.* **FET** A transistor device in which a current flowing in a narrow channel between two regions (the source and the drain) is controlled by an electric field applied to a third region (the gate).
field emission *n.* The emission of electrons from the surface of a conductor, caused by a strong electric field at the surface distorting the potential barrier.
field-e·mis·sion microscope (féeld-i-mísh'n) *n. Abbr.* **FEM.** An instrument for investigating metal surfaces, consisting of a sharply pointed piece of metal to which a high electric field is applied in a vacuum, so that electrons escaping by field emission are accelerated to a fluorescent screen where they produce a highly magnified image of the tip of the sample. **—field-e·mis·sion microscopy** *n.*
field·er (féeldər) *n.* *Sports.* **1.** A person who fields a ball. **2.** In sports such as cricket, a member of the team that is not batting.
field events *pl.n.* The throwing and jumping events of an athletics meeting, as distinguished from the running events.
field·fare (féeld-fair) *n.* A European thrush, *Turdus pilaris,* having grey and brown plumage. [Middle English *feldefare,* probably late Old English *feldefare,* "field-goer" : FIELD + *faran,* to go.]
field glasses *pl.n.* A portable binocular instrument used for magnifying and viewing distant objects.

field gun *n.* A mobile piece of field artillery.

field hand *n. U.S.* A hired labourer or worker on a farm.

field hockey *n. U.S.* **Hockey** *(see)* played on a field.

field hospital *n.* A hospital set up on a temporary basis for soldiers serving in a remote area.

Field·ing (féelding), **Henry** (1705–54). English novelist and dramatist. He wrote numerous plays and novels, many of them satirical, and topical comedies. His most successful novel was *Tom Jones* (1749); his other works include *Joseph Andrews* (1742).

field intensity *n.* The effectiveness of a field of force at any point as measured by the force exerted on a unit entity, for example a unit charge or unit magnetic pole, subjected to the field at that point. Also called "field strength".

field-i·on microscope (féeld-í-ən, -í-on) *n. Abbr.* **FIM** An instrument for investigating metal surfaces, consisting of a sharply pointed piece of metal to which a high electric field is applied in a low pressure of helium gas. Helium ions formed at the surface by field ionisation are accelerated to a fluorescent screen, where they produce a highly magnified image of the tip of the sample. —**field-i·on microscopy** *n.*

field lens *n.* The lens that is farthest from the eye in a compound eyepiece.

field magnet *n.* A magnet used to provide a magnetic field in an electrical device such as a generator or motor.

field-marshal *n. Abbr.* **F.M.** **1.** The highest-ranking officer in the British and Australian armies. **2.** An officer in some European armies, usually ranking just below the commander in chief.

field mouse *n.* Any of various small, nocturnal, long-tailed mice of the genus *Apodemus*, inhabiting meadows and fields and often causing damage to crops.

field mushroom *n.* A common edible fungus, *Agaricus campestris*, having a white cap and pink or brown gills. Also called "meadow mushroom".

field officer *n. Abbr.* **F.O.** *Military.* An officer, such as a major, lieutenant-colonel, or colonel, ranking above a captain and below a brigadier.

field of force *n.* A region of space throughout which the force produced by a single agent, such as an electric current, is operative. Also called "force field".

field of honour *n.* **1.** The scene of a duel involving a matter of personal honour. **2.** A battlefield.

field·piece (féeld-peess) *n.* A field gun.

Fields (feeldz), **Gracie,** also called Dame Grace Stansfield (1898–1979). British singer and comedienne. She made her debut as a singer in a cinema in Rochdale, Lancashire, in 1906. Her Lancashire humour and inimitable voice won her great popularity, especially in the depression of the 1930s. Her most notable films include *Sally in our Alley* (1931) and *Sing As We Go* (1934).

Fields, W.C., born William Claude Dukenfield (1879–1946). U.S. screen actor and comedian. He began making films in the early 1920s, and quickly found fame as an off-beat misogynist, a screen character he based on his own genuine eccentricity.

fields·man (féeldz-mən) *n., pl.* **-men** (-mən). *Cricket.* A fielder.

field spaniel *n.* A dog of a breed developed by crossing the cocker spaniel with the Sussex spaniel.

field sports *pl.n. Chiefly British.* Sports engaged in in the country, especially hunting, shooting, and fishing.

field·stone (féeld-stōn) *n.* A stone naturally occurring in fields, often used as a building material.

field strength *n.* **Field intensity** *(see).*

field theory *n.* The theory concerned with algebraic fields.

field trial *n.* **1.** A test for young, untried hunting dogs to determine their competence in pointing and retrieving. **2.** *Often plural.* **a.** The testing of a new fungicide, insecticide, or plant variety under normal field conditions, often in many different localities, before putting it on the market. **b.** Testing to observe efficiency, durability, or performance, as of a special vehicle or invention.

field trip *n.* An excursion or expedition for the purpose of first-hand observation, as to an area of geological or historical interest.

field winding *n.* The electrically conducting winding of a field magnet that produces electrical excitation, especially of a motor or generator.

field work *n.* Work done or observations made in the field, as at a site of archaeological or geological study, rather than in a library, laboratory, or other place of academic study. —**field worker** *n.*

field·work (féeld-wurk) *n. Military.* Any temporary fortification erected in the field.

fiend (feend) *n.* **1.** An evil spirit; a demon. **2.** *Usually capital* F. Satan; the Devil. **3. a.** A diabolically evil or wicked person. **b.** Any annoying person, especially a child. Used humorously. **4.** *Informal.* **a.** One who is addicted to a specified vice: *a dope fiend.* **b.** A person completely absorbed in or obsessed with a specified job or pastime: *a crossword-puzzle fiend.* [Middle English *fe(o)nd,* enemy, devil, fiend, Old English *fēond, fīond.*]

fiend·ish (féendish) *adj.* **1.** Pertaining to, similar to, or suggestive of a fiend; diabolical. **2.** *Informal.* **a.** Extremely difficult or gruelling. **b.** Extremely clever but slightly devious: *a fiendish manoeuvre.* —**fiend·ish·ly** *adv.* —**fiend·ish·ness** *n.*

fierce (feerss) *adj.* **fiercer, fiercest.** **1.** Having a savage and violent nature; ferocious. **2.** Extremely severe or violent; terrible: *fierce thunders.* **3.** Intense or ardent; extreme: *fierce loyalty.* **4.** *Informal.* Very difficult or unpleasant: *a fierce exam.* [Middle English *f(i)ers,*

from Old French, from Latin *ferus,* wild.] —**fierce·ly** *adv.* —**fierce·ness** *n.*

fi·e·ri fa·ci·as (fí-ə-rīfáy-shi-əss, fi-áir-i fácki-ass) *n. Law.* A writ of execution commanding a sheriff to lay a claim to and seize the goods and chattels of a debtor to fulfil a judgment against him. [Latin, "cause (it) to be done" (words used in such a writ).]

fier·y (fīr-i, fī-əri) *adj.* **-ier, -iest.** **1.** Consisting of or containing fire: *a fiery furnace.* **2.** Of, pertaining to, or resembling a fire: *a fiery sunset.* **3.** Torridly hot: *a fiery gust of the sirocco.* **4.** Flammable; liable to explode. Said of gas, a mine, or the like. **5.** Causing a hot, burning sensation; strong or highly spiced. Said of food or drink: *a fiery curry.* **6.** Emitting or appearing to emit sparks; glowing. **7. a.** Easily excited or emotionally volatile; tempestuous: *a fiery temper.* **b.** Showing passion or strong feeling: *a fiery outburst.* **8.** Inflamed. Said of the skin. [Middle English *fiery, firi,* from FIRE.] —**fier·i·ly** *adv.* —**fier·i·ness** *n.*

fiery cross *n.* **1.** Formerly, a wooden cross with charred or bloody ends used by the Scottish clans to summon forth men into battle. **2.** *U.S.* A burning cross, used by the Ku Klux Klan as a symbol.

Fi·e·so·le (fi-áy-zō-lay). Ancient town founded by the Etruscans, near to present-day Florence in Tuscany, Italy. It is a tourist spot because of its Etruscan and Roman museum.

fi·es·ta (fi-éstə) *n.* **1.** A religious feast or holiday; especially, a saint's day celebrated in Spanish-speaking countries. **2.** A celebration or festival. [Spanish, from Latin *fēsta,* neuter plural of *fēstus,* joyous, festive.]

FI·FA (féefə) *n. Fédération Internationale de Football Association* : the international governing body of soccer.

fife (fīf) *n.* A musical instrument similar to a flute but higher in range, used primarily to accompany drums in military music. ~*v.* **fifed, fifing, fifes.** —*tr.* To play (a tune) on a fife. —*intr.* To play a fife. [German *Pfeife,* from Old High German *pfīffa,* from West Germanic *pīpa* (unattested), from Vulgar Latin *pīpa* (unattested), from Latin *pīpāre,* to chirp.]

Fife. Unitary Authority area in east central Scotland, formerly Fife Region and before that the county of Fife. It borders on the North Sea between the Firth of Tay and the Firth of Forth. Fishing, arable farming, and coalmining make it one of the most prosperous regions in Scotland.

fife-rail (fīf-rayl) *n.* A rail around the lower part of a ship's mast to which the belaying pins for the rigging are secured.

fif·teen (fif-téen) *n.* **1. a.** The cardinal number that is one more than fourteen. **b.** A symbol representing this, such as 15 or XV. **2.** A set made up of fifteen persons or things. **3.** The fifteenth in a series. **4.** A size, as in clothing, designated as fifteen. **5.** In Rugby football, a team of fifteen players: *He was in the first fifteen at university.* [Middle English *fiftene,* Old English *fīftȳne, fīftēne.*] —**fif·teen** *adj.*

Fifteen In British history, the **Jacobite Rebellion** *(see)* of 1715. Preceded by *the.*

fif·teenth (fif-téenth) *n.* **1.** The ordinal number 15 in a series. **2.** One of 15 equal parts. **3.** *Music.* **a.** An interval of two octaves. **b.** An organ stop pitched two octaves above the normal pitch. —**fif·teenth** *adj. & adv.*

fifth (fifth ‖ fifth) *n.* **1.** The ordinal number five in a series. **2.** Any of five equal parts. **3. a.** A musical interval encompassing five diatonic notes, such as C, D, E, F, and G. **b.** Either of the two notes constituting the extremities of such an interval. **4.** An additional fifth gear on some motor vehicles, higher than fourth and designed for driving at speed. —**the Fifth.** The **Fifth Amendment** : *take the Fifth.* [Middle English *fifthe, fifte,* Old English *fīfta.*] —**fifth** *adj. & adv.* —**fifth·ly** *adv.*

Fifth Amendment *n.* An amendment to the Constitution of the United States, ratified in 1791, that deals with the rights of accused persons by providing that no person may be forced to testify as a witness against himself.

fifth column *n.* **1.** A clandestine subversive organisation working within a given country to further an invading enemy's military and political aims. **2.** Any subversive element working within an organisation or institution. [First applied in 1936 to the Franco supporters in Madrid by General Emilio Mola who was leading four rebel columns of troops against that city.] —**fifth columnist** *n.*

fifth wheel *n.* **1.** A wheel or portion of a wheel placed horizontally over the forward axle of a carriage to provide support and stability during turns. **2.** An additional wheel carried on a four-wheeled vehicle as a spare. **3.** Any extra or unnecessary person or thing.

fif·ti·eth (fífti-ith) *n.* **1.** The ordinal number 50 in a series. **2.** Any of 50 equal parts. —**fif·ti·eth** *adj. & adv.*

fif·ty (fífti) *n.* **1. a.** The cardinal number that is ten more than forty. **b.** A symbol representing this, such as 50 or L. **2.** A set made up of fifty persons or things. **3.** The fiftieth in a series. **4.** A size, as in clothing, designated as fifty. **5.** A banknote or coin having a denomination of fifty: *I'll have the money in fifties.* **6.** *Plural.* **a.** The numbers from 50 to 59, considered as a range of age, price, temperature, or the like. **b.** *Sometimes capital* F. The years numbered 50 to 59 in a century. [Middle English *fifti,* Old English *fīftig.*] —**fif·ty** *adj.*

fif·ty-fif·ty (fifti-fifti) *adj. Informal.* **1.** Divided or shared in two equal portions: *a fifty-fifty deal.* **2.** Even: *a fifty-fifty chance.* —**fif·ty-fif·ty** *adv.*

fig¹ (fig) *n.* **1.** Any of several trees or shrubs of the genus *Ficus*; especially, *F. carica,* native to the Middle East and western Asia and widely cultivated for its edible fruit. Also called "fig tree". **2.** The sweet, pear-shaped, many-seeded fruit of this tree. **3. a.** Any of several plants bearing similar edible fruit, such as the Hottentot fig, *Mesembryanthemum edule,* of southern Africa. See **fig marigold. b.** The fruit of such a plant. **4.** A trivial or contemptible amount; a jot; a whit: *"None of them . . would have cared a fig the more for me"* (Nathaniel Hawthorne). [Middle English *fig(e),* from Old French *figue,* from Old Provençal *figa,* from Vulgar Latin *fīca* (unattested), from Latin *fīcus,* from the same Mediterranean source as Greek *sukon.* See also **syconium.**]

fig² *tr.v.* **figged, figging, figs.** *Informal.* **1.** To dress or furnish with; array; furbish. Used with *out: all figged out.* **2.** To make (a horse) appear lively, usually by means of drugs. Used with *up* or *out.*
~n. Informal. **1.** Dress; array: *in full fig.* **2.** Physical condition; shape: *in poor fig.* [Variant of obsolete *feague,* from German *fegen,* to polish, furbish. See **fake.**]

fig³ *n. Archaic.* An obscene gesture of contempt made by brandishing a fist with the thumb held between the first and second fingers. [French *(faire la) figue,* to make this gesture, from Italian *fica,* vulva, fig, from Vulgar Latin *fīca* (unattested), FIG.]

fig. **1.** figurative; figuratively. **2.** figure.

fig-bird (fíg-burd) *n.* An Australian oriole of the genus *Sphecotheres,* that feeds on figs and other fruits.

fight (fīt) *v.* **fought** (fawt), **fighting, fights.** *—intr.* **1.** To participate in combat or battle. **2.** To struggle in any way: *fight for freedom and against oppression.* **3.** To quarrel; argue. **4.** To stand up against something or assert oneself; be aggressive. *—tr.* **1.** To contend with physically or in battle. **2.** To box or wrestle against in a ring. **3.** To contend with or struggle against in any manner: *fight prejudice.* **4.** To strive to stop the development or prevent the occurrence of: *fight a fire.* **5. a.** To wage (a battle or war, for example). **b.** To engage in (a lawsuit, election or other contest) against another. **6.** To do battle for; contend for: *"I now resolved that Calais should be fought to the death"* (Winston Churchill). **7.** To make (one's way), as by fighting: *He fought his way to the top of his profession.* **8. a.** To make (dogs or fighting cocks, for example) fight each other. **b.** To deploy (troops or ships, for example) in battle. **—fight off.** **1.** To defend against or drive back (a hostile force). **2.** To struggle to get rid of or avoid: *fight off temptation.* **—fight out.** To fight until settled or until one side is clearly the victor: *fight it out in public.* **—fight shy of.** To avoid; be reluctant to confront.
~n. **1.** A battle waged between opposing groups; a combat. **2.** A struggle, quarrel, or conflict. **3. a.** A physical conflict between two or more individuals; a brawl. **b.** A boxing or wrestling match; a bout. **4.** The power or inclination to fight; pugnacity. **—put up a fight.** Make a determined show of resistance. —See Synonyms at **conflict.** [Fight, fought, fought; Middle English *fighten, fa(u)ght, fo(u)ghten,* Old English *feohtan, feaht, fohten,* from Germanic.]

fight·er (fītər) *n.* **1.** One engaged in fighting. **2.** One employed to fight; a boxer. **3.** A pugnacious, unyielding, or determined person. **4.** *Military.* A fast, manoeuvrable combat aircraft used to engage enemy aircraft and to escort and defend bombers.

fight·er-bomb·er (fītər-bómmər) *n.* An aeroplane capable of functioning both as a fighter and bomber.

fight·ing (fīting) *adj.* **1.** Ready to fight; equipped, prepared, or inclined to oppose. **2.** Liable to provoke: *fighting words.* **—fighting fit.** Very fit; in peak condition.

fighting chance *n.* A reasonable chance of winning.

fighting cock *n.* **1.** A cock bred for fighting. **2.** *Informal.* A quarrelsome person.

fighting fish *n.* Any of various small freshwater fishes of the genus *Betta,* of tropical Asia; especially, the **Siamese fighting fish** *(see).*

fighting fund *n.* A fund set up to finance a campaign.

fig leaf *n.* **1.** A stylised representation of the leaf of a fig, used especially to conceal the genitalia on statues. **2.** A usually unsuccessful device or ploy intended to conceal something offensive or disguise something discreditable.

fig marigold *n.* Any of various plants of the genus *Mesembryanthemum,* native to southern Africa, having thick, fleshy leaves and variously coloured flowers.

fig·ment (fíg-mənt) *n.* **1.** Something imaginary; a fabrication. **2.** An arbitrary notion. [Middle English, from Latin *figmentum,* a formation, from *fingere,* to mould, fashion.]

fig tree *n.* A tree, the **fig** *(see).*

fig·ur·al (fíggərəl, fíggewr-əl) *adj.* Consisting of or forming a pictorial composition or design of human or animal figures.

fig·u·rant (fíggewr-ənt; *French* fee-gü-róɴ) *n.* **1.** A member of a corps de ballet who does not perform solos. **2.** A stage performer without a speaking part. [French, from the present participle of *figurer,* to figure, represent, from Old French, from Latin *figūrāre,* to form, from *figūra,* FIGURE.]

fig·ur·ate (fíggewr-ət, -it) *adj.* **1.** Having a definite or particular shape or form; figured. **2.** *Music.* Florid or exhibiting figuration. [Latin *figūrātus,* past participle of *figūrāre,* to shape, from *figūra,* form, FIGURE.]

fig·ur·a·tion (fíggewr-áysh'n, fíggər-) *n.* **1.** The act of forming something into a particular shape. **2.** A shape, form, or outline. **3.** The act of representing with figures. **4.** A figurative representation, often symbolic or emblematic. **5.** *Music.* **a.** The continuous repetition of a pattern of notes or musical figures for decorative purposes. **b.** Ornamentation. **6.** The ornamentation of something with small designs.

fig·ur·a·tive (fíggewr-ətiv, fíggər-) *adj. Abbr.* **fig. 1. a.** Based on or making use of figures of speech, especially metaphor; not literal; metaphorical: *figurative language.* **b.** Containing many figures of speech; ornate. **2.** Represented by a figure or figures; symbolic or emblematic. **3.** *Art.* **a.** Of or relating to representation by means of animal or human figures; figural. **b.** Representational rather than abstract. **c.** Designating a style of painting in which the subjects are recognisable but not conventionally depicted. **—fig·ur·a·tive·ly** *adv.* **—fig·ur·a·tive·ness** *n.*

fig·ure (fíggər || *U.S.* fíg-yər) *n. Abbr.* **fig. 1.** A written symbol representing anything other than a letter; especially, a number. **2.** *Plural.* Mathematical calculation involving the use of such symbols: *She is good at figures.* **3. a.** An amount represented in numbers: *a large figure.* **b.** An estimate: *Can you give me a figure?* **4.** The outline, form, or silhouette of a thing. **5. a.** The shape or form of a human body, especially as regards weight and proportion: *a pear-shaped figure.* **b.** A slim, attractive body: *still hasn't lost her figure at 52.* **6.** An individual, especially a well-known personage. **7.** The impression an individual makes through his behaviour or appearance: *He cuts a dashing figure.* **8.** A person, animal, or object that symbolises something: *she'll always be a mother figure to me.* **9.** A pictorial or sculptural representation, especially of the human body. **10. a.** A diagram. **b.** A design or pattern. **11.** An illustration printed from an engraved plate or block. **12.** A configuration or distinct group of steps in skating or a dance. **13.** *Music.* A brief melodic or harmonic unit often constituting the base for a larger musical phrase or structure. **14.** *Logic.* Any one of the forms that a syllogism can take, depending on the position of the middle term. **15.** A **figure of speech** *(see).* **16.** *Mathematics.* A geometric shape formed by lines, curves, or surfaces, either a **plane figure** *(see)* in two dimensions or a **solid figure** *(see)* in three. —See Synonyms at **form.**
~v. **figured, -uring, -ures.** *—tr.* **1.** To calculate with numbers; tally or work out mathematically. **2. a.** To make a likeness of; depict. **b.** To symbolise; represent. **3.** To adorn with a design or figures. **4.** *Music.* To indicate the chordal structure of (a bass line of single notes) with a sequence of conventionalised numbers. **5.** *Chiefly U.S. Informal.* To conclude, believe, or predict: *What do you figure will happen?* *—intr.* **1.** To calculate; compute. **2.** To be an element; have mention, pertinence, or importance: *Your name didn't even figure in the conversation.* **3.** *Informal.* To make sense; add up: *That figures!* **—figure on** or **upon.** *Chiefly U.S. Informal.* **1.** To count on. **2.** To take into consideration; expect. **—figure out.** *Informal.* To solve; comprehend; work out. [Middle English, from Old French, from Latin *figūra,* form, shape, figure.]

fig·ured (fíggərd) *adj.* **1.** Decorated with a design; patterned: *a richly figured carpet.* **2.** Represented, as in graphic art or sculpture.

figured bass *n. Music.* A **continuo** *(see).*

fig·ure-ground (fíggər-grownd) *n. Psychology.* The organisation of visual perception into a unified object standing out from a background. The organisation of a visual field can change depending on the individual and the familiarity or regularity of parts of the field, or those parts of the field being attended to, and is used as the basis for many types of optical illusion.

fig·ure·head (fíggər-hed) *n.* **1.** A person given a position of nominal leadership but having no actual authority or responsibility. **2.** *Nautical.* A carved, decorative figure placed on the prow of a ship.

figure of eight *n.* **1.** *Aeronautics.* The manoeuvre in which an aircraft flies a path tracing the outline of the number 8. **2.** The outline made by skating or dancing a continuous path shaped like the number 8. **3.** Any of various forms or representations having the shape of the number 8, such as a knot.

figure of speech *n.* An expression in which words are used, not in their literal sense, but to create a more forceful or dramatic image, such as a **metaphor, simile,** or **hyperbole** *(all of which see).*

fig·u·rine (fíggewr-éen, fíggər-, -een) *n.* A small ornamental figure, as one carved or formed from wood, porcelain, glass, or metal; a statuette. [French, from Italian *figurina,* diminutive of *figura,* figure, from Latin *figūra,* FIGURE.]

fig wasp *n.* A small wasp of the genus *Blastophaga,* which is the agent for caprification in figs.

fig·wort (fíg-wurt || -wawrt) *n.* Any of various plants of the genus *Scrophularia,* having loose, branching clusters of small greenish or purple flowers. [From FIG, alluding to swellings, as in scrofula, for which the plant was believed to be a remedy.]

Fi·ji¹ (fée-jee, fee-jée). Independent republic consisting of more than 330 islands and islets in the southern Pacific Ocean. The capital, Suva, is on the largest island, Viti Levu. They were discovered by Abel Tasman in 1643 and explored by Captain Bligh after he was set adrift by the *Bounty* mutineers (1789). Annexed by Great Britain in 1874, they remained a crown colony until 1970. Fiji withdrew from the Commonwealth in 1987, but rejoined in 1997. Sugar is the most important crop. Area, 18 376 square kilometres (7,095 square miles). Population, 803,500.

Fi·ji² *n.* **1.** A Fijian. **2.** The language of the Fijians.

Fi·ji·an (fi-jée-ən, fée-ji-) *adj.* Of Fiji or the Fiji Islands, or the people or language of these places.
~n. **1.** A native of Fiji or the Fiji Islands, being of predominantly Melanesian stock with an admixture of Polynesian. **2.** The Oceanic language of Fiji or the Fiji Islands.

fi·la. Plural of **filum.**

filagree. Variant of **filigree.**

fil·a·ment (fíllə-mənt) *n.* **1.** A fine or thinly spun thread, fibre, wire, or the like. **2.** *Biology.* A slender, threadlike appendage, part, or structure, especially: **a.** The slender stalk of a stamen on which the anther is borne. **b.** A chainlike series of cells, as in some algae and

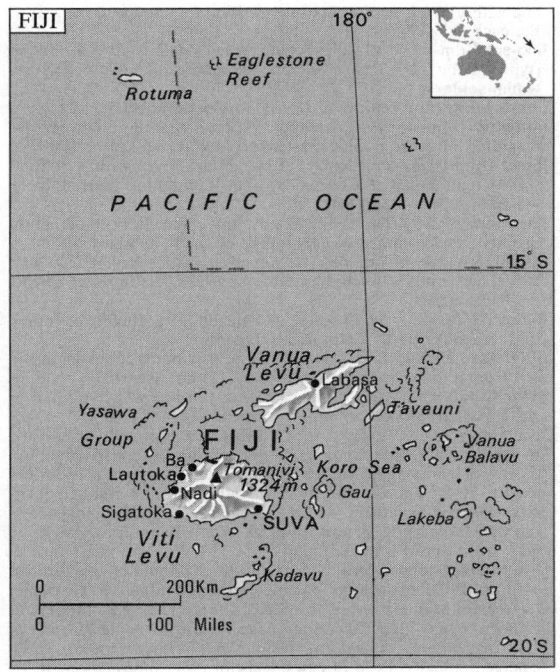

FIJI

Eaglestone Reef

Rotuma

180°

PACIFIC OCEAN

15° S

Vanua Levu

Labasa

Yasawa Group

Taveuni

FIJI

Vanua Balava

Ba

Tomanivi

Koro Sea

Lautoka

1324 m

Gau

Nadi

Sigatoka

SUVA

Lakeba

Viti Levu

Kadavu

0   200 Km
0   100 Miles

20° S

---

bacteria. **c.** The free barb of a down feather. **3. a.** *Electricity.* A fine wire heated electrically to incandescence in an electric lamp. **b.** *Electronics.* A high-resistance wire or ribbon forming the cathode in some thermionic valves. [Old French, from Medieval Latin *filamentum,* from Late Latin *filāre,* to wind threads, spin, from Latin *filum,* thread.] **—fil·a·men·tous** (-méntəss), **fil·a·men·ta·ry** (-méntəri, -tri) *adj.*

fi·lar (fílər) *adj.* **1.** Of or pertaining to a thread or threads. **2.** Having fine threads across the field of view for measuring small distances, as in a microscope or telescope eyepiece. [Latin *filum,* thread.]

fil·a·ree (fíllə-ré·e) *n.* A plant, the **alfilaria** *(see).* [Variant of American Spanish *alfilerillo,* ALFILARIA.]

fi·lar·i·a (fi-láir-i-ə) *n., pl.* **-iae** (-i-ee). Any of various parasitic nematode worms of the superfamily Filarioidea, that infest man and other vertebrates. [New Latin *Filaria* (former genus name), "threadworm", from Latin *filum,* thread.] **—fi·lar·i·al, fi·lar·i·an** *adj.*

fil·a·ri·a·sis (fillə-rí-ə-siss, fi-láir-i-áy-) *n.* Infestation of the lymph glands with the filariae *Wuchereria bancrofti* or *Brugia malayi,* resulting in inflammation and **elephantiasis** *(see).* [New Latin : FI-LAR(IA) + -IASIS.]

fil·a·ture (fillə-chər, -choor, -tewr) *n.* **1.** The act or process of spinning, drawing, or twisting into threads. **2.** The act or process of reeling raw silk from cocoons. **3.** A reel used in this process. **4.** An establishment where this process is performed. [French, from Late Latin *filātus,* past participle of *filāre,* to draw out thread, spin. See **filament.**]

fil·bert (fílbərt) *n.* . **1.** A Eurasian shrub or tree, *Corylus maxima,* a species of hazel, cultivated for its edible nuts. **2.** The rounded, smooth-shelled nut of this shrub. **3.** Any hazelnut. [Middle English *filbert, philliberd,* from Anglo-French *(noix de) filbert,* "nut of St. Philibert"* (died A.D. 684), Frankish abbot whose feast day on August 22 marks the ripening season of the nut.]

filch (filch) *tr.v.* **filched, filching, filches.** To steal (something) in a furtive manner; pilfer. See Synonyms at **rob.** [Middle English *filchen†.*] **—filch·er** *n.*

file¹ (fíl) *n.* **1.** A receptacle, such as a folder or box, that keeps loose objects, such as papers, cards, or any collection of small items, in useful order. **2.** A collection of objects kept thus; especially, a set of documents related to one subject, such as a particular client or case. **3. a.** A line of persons, animals, or things positioned one behind another. **b.** *Military.* A line of soldiers or vehicles so positioned. **4.** Any of the rows of squares which run vertically on a chessboard. **5.** A set of data with an identifying label held in a computer storage device. **—on file.** Catalogued or recorded in a file; entered; on hand.

~v. filed, filing, files. —tr. 1. To put or keep (papers or cards, for example) in useful order; catalogue. **2. a.** To enter (a legal document, for example) on public record or official record. **b.** To submit (a complaint or legal petition, for example) to a relevant authority. **3.** To send or submit (copy) to a newspaper or other news agency. **—intr. 1.** To march or walk in a line or lines. **2.** To submit a formal application, as for divorce. [Noun, sense 1: Old French *fil,* "thread", wire or string on which documents are strung, from Latin *filum,* thread. Noun, sense 3: Old French *file,* from *filer,* "to draw out thread", march in a line, from Late Latin *filāre,* to spin, from Latin *filum,* thread.] **—fil·er** *n.*

file² *n.* **1.** Any of several steel tools with hardened ridged surfaces, used in smoothing, polishing, grinding down, or boring. **2.** *Archaic British Slang.* A deceitful, cunning person.

~tr.v. filed, filing, files. To smooth, polish, grind, bore, or remove with or as if with a file. [Middle English *file, fyle,* Old English *fēol, fíl.*] **—fil·er** *n.*

file·fish (fíl-fish) *n., pl.* **-fishes** or collectively **filefish.** Any of various chiefly tropical marine fishes of the family Balistidae, related to and resembling the triggerfishes. [Referring to the rough scales of some species.]

fi·let¹ (fillit, fíllay ‖ fi-láy) *n.* A net or lace with a simple pattern of squares. [French, from Old French *filé,* from Old Provençal *filat,* "made of threads", from *fil,* thread, from Latin *filum.*]

fi·let². *Cookery. Chiefly U.S.* Variant of **fillet.**

fi·let mi·gnon (fíllay meen-yón, fi-láy; *French* fee-láy meen-yón) *n.* A small, round, very choice cut of beef from the centre of the fillet. [French, "dainty fillet".]

fil·i·al (fílli-əl) *adj.* **1.** Of, pertaining to, or befitting a son or daughter. **2.** *Genetics.* Designating any of the generations resulting from a particular cross that follow the parental generation. F_1 is the first filial generation, F_2 is the second filial generation, obtained by crossing the F_1 generation and so on. In this sense, compare **parental.** [Middle English, from Late Latin *filiālis,* from Latin *filius,* son.] **—fil·i·al·ly** *adv.* **—fil·i·al·ness** *n.*

fil·i·ate (fílli-ayt) *tr.v.* **-ated, -ating, -ates. 1.** *Rare.* To affiliate. **2.** *Law.* To assign paternity to (an illegitimate child, for example). [Medieval Latin *filiāre,* to acknowledge as a son, from Latin *filius,* son.]

fil·i·a·tion (filli-áysh'n) *n.* **1.** The condition or fact of being the child of a certain parent. **2.** A line of descent; derivation; lineage. **3. a.** The act or fact of forming a new branch, as of a society or language group; expansion or division. **b.** The branch thus formed; an offshoot. **4.** *Law. Chiefly U.S.* Affiliation.

fil·i·beg (filli-beg) *n.* A kilt. [Scottish Gaelic *féileadhbheag* : *féileadh†,* fold, kilt + *beag,* small, little, akin to Old Irish *becc,* small, from Common Celtic *biggo-* (unattested).]

fil·i·bus·ter (filli-bustər) *n.* **1. a.** The use of obstructionist tactics, such as the making of prolonged speeches or the introduction of irrelevant material, for the purpose of delaying legislative action. **b.** An instance of the use of such tactics in a legislative body. **c.** A filibusterer. **2.** An adventurer who engages in a private military action in a foreign country.

~v. filibustered, -tering, -ters. —intr. 1. To use obstructionist tactics, especially overlong speeches, in a legislative body. **2.** To engage in a private military action in a foreign country. **—tr.** To obstruct (legislation, for example). [Originally "freebooter", from Spanish *filibustero,* from French *flibustier,* from Dutch *vrijbuiter,* pirate, "one who plunders freely" : *vrij,* free + *-buiter,* plunderer, from *buit,* BOOTY.] **—fil·i·bus·ter·er** *n.*

fil·i·cide (filli-síd) *n. Rare.* **1.** The act of killing one's child. **2.** One who kills his child. [Latin *filius,* son, or its derivative *filia,* daughter + -i- + -CIDE.] **—fil·i·cid·al** (-síd'l) *adj.*

fil·i·form (filli-fawrm, fí-li-) *adj. Biology.* Resembling or having the form of a thread; threadlike. [Latin *filum,* thread + -i- + -FORM.]

fil·i·gree, fil·a·gree, fil·la·gree (filli-gree) *n.* **1.** Delicate and intricate ornamental work made from gold, silver, or other fine twisted wire. **2.** Any intricate, delicate, or fanciful ornamentation.

~adj. Resembling or made of filigree.

~tr.v. filigreed, -greeing, -grees. To decorate with or as if with filigree. [Earlier *filigreen,* from French *filigrane,* from Italian *filigrana* : *fili-,* from Latin *filum,* thread + *grana,* grain, from Latin *grānum.*]

filing cabinet *n.* A cabinet with drawers used for holding documents, files, or the like.

filing clerk *n.* A person employed to maintain the files and records of an office.

fil·ings (fílingz) *pl.n.* Particles or shavings removed by a file.

Fil·i·pi·no (filli-péenō) *n., pl.* **-nos.** A native, citizen, or inhabitant of the Philippines.

~adj. Of or pertaining to the Philippines or Filipinos. [Spanish, from *(Islas) Filipinas,* the PHILIPPINE(S).]

fill (fil) *v.* **filled, filling, fills. —tr. 1.** To put into as much as can be held; load completely; make full. **2.** To close or plug up (an opening, for example). **3.** To stop up a cavity in (a tooth). **4.** To produce a sensation of fullness in (the stomach, for example). **5.** To supply (an empty space) with material, such as writing, an inscription, or an illustration. **6.** To put someone into or elect to (an office or position); furnish with a holder or occupant. **7.** To occupy or hold (an office or position). **8. a.** To occupy the whole of: *fill one's time.* **b.** To pervade: *cries filled the air.* **9.** To affect profoundly (the mind or thoughts, for example): *filled with dread.* **10.** To add an inferior substance or substances to (a product) to increase bulk. **11. a.** To cause (a sail) to swell. **b.** To adjust (a yard) so that wind will cause a sail to swell. **—intr.** To become full. **—fill out. 1.** To make or become fuller, rounder, broader, or shapelier. **2.** *Chiefly U.S.* To complete (a form, for example) by adding the necessary information.

~n. 1. That which is needed to make full, complete, or satisfied: *eat one's fill.* **2. a.** A built-up piece of land; an embankment. **b.** The material, such as earth, gravel, or sand, used for this. **—have (one's) fill.** To be thoroughly sated or weary. [Middle English *fillen,* Old English *fyllan.*]

fille de joie (fée də zhwáa) *n., pl.* **filles de joie** *(pronounced as singular).* French. A prostitute. [Literally, "daughter of joy".]

filled gold *n. U.S.* **Rolled gold** *(see).*

fill·er (fíllər) *n.* **1.** One who fills. **2.** Something added in order to augment weight or size or to fill space. **3.** A composition, especially a semisolid that hardens on drying, used to fill pores, cracks, or holes in a wood, plaster, or other construction surface prior to finishing. **4.** Tobacco used in a plug or to form the body of a cigar. **5.** A short item used to fill space in a newspaper, magazine, or other publication. **6.** Something, such as a news item or piece of music, used to fill time in a radio, television, or theatrical presentation. **7.** A device, such as a funnel, used to fill something. **8.** *Architecture.* Any element, such as a plate, used to fill the space between two supporting members.

fil·lér (fíll-air) *n., pl.* **-lérs** or collectively **fillér.** A coin equal to 1/100 of the forint of Hungary. [Hungarian.]

filler cap *n.* A device that closes the fuel inlet on a car.

fil·let (fíllit || *U.S.* fíllay, *or for sense 2* fi-láy) *n.* Also *chiefly U.S.* **fi·let** (for sense 2). **1.** A narrow strip of ribbon or similar material or a thin band of metal, often worn in the hair or round the head. **2. a.** A strip or compact piece of boneless meat or fish. **b.** A cut of beef taken from the underside of the loin. **c.** A cut of pork, veal, or lamb taken from the top of the hind leg. **3.** *Architecture.* **a.** A thin, flat moulding used as separation between or ornamentation for larger mouldings. **b.** A ridge between the indentations of a fluted column. **4. a.** A narrow decorative line impressed upon the cover of a book. **b.** A hand tool or wheel used in making such a line. **5.** *Heraldry.* A narrow horizontal band placed in the lower fourth area of the chief. **6.** *Anatomy.* A loop-shaped band of fibres, such as the lemniscus. **7.** A raised band or rim on a surface. **8.** A structure added to round off an angle; a fairing.
~*tr.v.* **filleted** (*U.S. usually* fi-láyed *for sense 2*), **-leting** (*U.S. usually* -láy-ing *for sense 2*), **-lets** (*U.S. usually* -láyz *for sense 2*). **1.** To bind or decorate with or as with a fillet. **2.** To slice, bone, or make into a fillet or fillets. [Middle English *filet,* from Old French, diminutive of *fil,* thread, from Latin *fīlum.*]

fill in *tr.v.* **1.** To place material in (a hole or space, for example) so as to occupy completely. **2.** To complete (a form, for example) by adding the necessary information. **3.** To occupy (time). **4.** To set down (information), as on a form: *Fill in your name and address.* **5.** *Informal.* To inform. Used with *on*: *Fill me in on what's happening.* **6.** *British Slang.* To assault. —*intr.v.* To act as a substitute.

fill-in (fíllin) *n. Informal.* **1.** One that fills a vacancy, gap, or temporary need. **2.** *U.S.* A summary of necessary or important information; a briefing.

fill·ing (fílling) *n.* **1.** Something used to fill a space or container: *a custard filling in a pie.* **2.** Any of various substances, such as amalgam or cement, used to fill a cavity drilled in a decayed tooth. **3.** A filled tooth. **4.** The horizontal threads that cross the warp in weaving; weft.
~*adj.* Tending to fill; especially, tending to cause a sensation of fullness in the stomach.

filling station *n.* An establishment which sells petrol, oil, and the like to motorists, but which does not usually carry out car repairs. Also called "petrol station".

fil·lip (fíllip) *n.* **1.** A light blow or flick made by pressing a fingertip against the thumb and suddenly releasing it. **2.** A slight goad or incentive; a stimulus.
~*v.* **filliped, -liping, -lips.** —*tr.* **1.** To strike or propel with a fillip. **2.** To excite, arouse, or stimulate. —*intr.* To make a fillip. [15th century : imitative.]

fill up *tr.v.* **1. a.** To fill completely. **b.** To fill (the petrol tank of a motor vehicle). **2.** To fill in (a form, for example). —*intr.v.* To become full.

fill-up (fíll-up) *n.* An act or instance of filling up.

fil·ly (fílli) *n., pl.* **-lies.** **1.** A young female horse; a young mare. **2.** *Informal.* A lively and high-spirited girl. [Middle English *filli,* from Old Norse *fylja,* from Germanic *ful-* (unattested), FOAL.]

film (film) *n.* **1.** A thin sheet or strip of flexible cellulose material coated with a photosensitive emulsion, used to make photographic negatives or transparencies. **2. a.** A series of connected photographic images to be projected consecutively onto a screen, thus creating the impression of a continuously moving subject, usually accompanied by a soundtrack. **b.** The story, event, or the like shown in such a series of images. **c.** *Plural.* Such films collectively as an industry, entertainment, or art form. **3. a.** Any thin covering or coating. **b.** A thin, generally flexible, transparent sheet, as of plastic or rubber, used in wrapping or packaging. **4.** A thin skin or membranous coating. **5.** An abnormal, thin, opaque coating on the cornea in certain eye diseases. **6.** A haze or mist.
~*v.* **filmed, filming, films.** —*tr.* **1.** To cover with or as if with a film. **2.** To photograph (an event, scene, or person, for example) in the making of a cinematic film. **3.** To turn (a novel, for example) into a cinematic film. —*intr.* **1.** To become coated or obscured with or as if with a film. **2.** To make a cinematic film. **3.** To be reproduced in a cinematic film. [Middle English *film,* Old English *filmen,* from Germanic.] —**film·ic** *adj.*

film·go·er (fílm-gō-ər) *n.* One who regularly goes to the cinema.

film·mak·ing (fílm-mayking) *n.* The production of cinematic films. —**film·mak·er** *n.*

fil·mog·ra·phy (fil-móggrə-fi) *n., pl.* **-phies.** A list of the films that a given actor or director, for example, has made, or that have a similar subject.

film pack *n.* A pack of sheet films that can be exposed in succession and withdrawn from the exposure position for storage at the rear of the pack.

film·set (fílm-set) *tr.v.* **-set, -setting, sets.** *Printing. British.* To set (type matter) by means of photocomposition; photocompose. —**film·set·ter** *n.*

film·set·ting (fílm-setting) *n. British.* **Photocomposition** *(see).*

film·strip (fílm-strip) *n.* A length of film containing photographs, diagrams, or other graphic matter prepared for still projection.

film·y (fílmi) *adj.* **-ier, -iest.** **1.** Resembling or consisting of film; transparent; gauzy. **2.** Covered by or as if by a film; blurred; hazy. —**film·i·ly** *adv.* —**film·i·ness** *n.*

filmy fern *n.* Any fern having fronds only one cell thick and consequently usually limited to very humid or shady habitats.

fil·o·plume (fíllə-ploom, fílə-) *n.* A hairlike feather having few or no barbs, occurring between the contour feathers. [Latin *fīlum,* thread + -O- + PLUME.]

fi·lose (fī-lōss, -lōz) *adj. Biology.* **1.** Threadlike. **2.** Having or ending in a threadlike part. [Latin *fīlum,* thread.]

fils (feess). *French.* Son. Used after a proper name to distinguish a son from a father with the same name. Compare **père.**

fil·ter (fíltər) *n.* **1.** Any porous substance through which a liquid or gas is passed in order to remove suspended matter. **2. a.** A device containing or consisting of such a substance, especially when used to extract impurities from air, water, or the like. **b.** A filter tip. **3.** Any of various electric, electronic, acoustic, or optical devices used to reject signals, vibrations, or radiations of certain frequencies while passing others. **4.** A system at a set of traffic lights allowing vehicles wishing to turn to do so, even while traffic wishing to go straight ahead is halted.
~*v.* **filtered, -tering, -ters.** —*tr.* **1.** To pass (a liquid or gas) through a filter. **2.** To remove by passing through a filter. **3.** To obtain (coffee, for example) by using a filter. —*intr.* **1.** To pass through or as if through a filter: *"The chapel was flooded by the dull scarlet of light that filtered through the lower blinds"* (James Joyce). **2.** To emerge gradually. Used of news, facts, or other information. **3.** To flow or proceed gradually: *people filtered into the room.* **4.** To move forward at a traffic filter. [Middle English *filtre,* a piece of felt (used to strain liquid), from Old French, from Medieval Latin *filtrum,* from Frankish *filtir* (unattested).] —**fil·ter·er** *n.*

fil·ter·a·ble (fíl-tərə-b'l, -trə-) *adj.* Also **fil·tra·ble** (-trə-). **1.** Capable of being filtered; especially, capable of being removed by filtering. **2.** Sufficiently minute to pass through a fine filter, thereby maintaining the infectivity of the filtrate. Said of certain viruses. —**fil·ter·a·bil·i·ty** (-bílləti) *n.*

filter bed *n.* A layer of sand or gravel on the bottom of a reservoir or tank used to filter water or sewage.

filter feeder *n.* Any aquatic animal that uses a filtering mechanism to ingest minute food particles from the water. —**filter feeding** *n.*

filter paper *n.* Porous paper suitable for use as a filter.

filter pump *n.* A simple vacuum pump by which air is removed from a system by carrying it away in a narrow, fast jet of water.

filter tip *n.* **1.** A small tube of porous material attached to the end of a cigarette to remove part of the harmful substances from the smoke. **2.** A cigarette with such an attachment.

filth (filth) *n.* **1. a.** Foul or dirty matter. **b.** Refuse. **2.** A dirty or corrupt condition; foulness. **3.** Material or language considered obscene, prurient, or immoral. **4.** *British Slang.* The police. Used derogatorily, preceded by *the.* [Middle English *filth, fulth,* Old English *fȳlth,* putrid matter.]

filth·y (fílthi) *adj.* **-ier, -iest.** **1.** Heavily soiled; very dirty. **2.** Obscene; scatological. **3.** Highly objectionable; vile; nasty. **4.** *Informal.* Very bad; unpleasant: *filthy weather.* —See Synonyms at **dirty.** —**filth·i·ly** *adv.* —**filth·i·ness** *n.*

fil·trate (fíl-trayt) *v.* **-trated, -trating, -trates.** —*tr.* To put through a filter. —*intr.* To go through a filter.
~*n.* The portion of filtered material that passes through the filter. [Medieval Latin *filtrāre,* from *filtrum,* FILTER.]

fil·tra·tion (fil-tráysh'n) *n.* The act or process of filtering.

fi·lum (fī-ləm) *n., pl.* **-la** (-lə). Any threadlike anatomical structure; a filament. [Latin *fīlum,* thread.]

FIM field-ion microscope; field-ion microscopy.

fim·bri·a (fím-bri-ə) *n., pl.* **-briae** (-bri-ee). A fringelike structure, as at the opening of the Fallopian tube in mammals. [Late Latin, fibre, fringe, from Latin *fimbriae*†, fibres, threads. See also **fringe.**]

fim·bri·ate (fím-bri-ət, -it, -ayt) *adj.* Also **fim·bri·at·ed** (-aytid). Fringed, as the edge of a petal or the opening of a duct may be. [Late Latin *fimbriātus,* fringed, from FIMBRIA.] —**fim·bri·a·tion** *n.*

fin (fin) *n.* **1.** A membranous appendage extending from the body of a fish or other aquatic animal, used for propelling, steering, or maintaining balance. **2.** Something resembling a fin in shape or function, such as a diver's flipper. **3.** A fixed or movable vane or aerofoil used to stabilise an aircraft or missile in flight. **4.** An appendage on a boat, such as a submarine; especially, a **fin keel** *(see).* **5.** A projecting vane used for cooling, as on a radiator or engine cylinder. **6.** An ornamental projection, as on the rear wing of a car.
~*v.* **finned, finning, fins.** —*tr.* **1.** To equip with fins. **2.** To cut the fins from. —*intr.* To emerge with the fins above water. [Middle English *finne,* Old English *finn,* akin to Middle Low German *finne*†.]

fin. **1.** finance; financial. **2.** finish.

Fin. Finland; Finnish.

fin·a·ble, fine·a·ble (fīnə-b'l) *adj.* Liable to a fine or fines.

fi·na·gle (fi-náyg'l) *v.* **-gled, -gling, -gles.** *Informal.* —*tr.* **1.** To achieve by dubious or crafty methods; wangle. **2.** To trick or delude; deceive. —*intr.* To use crafty, deceitful methods. [20th century : perhaps variant of dialect *fainaigue*†, cheat.] **—fi·na·gler** *n.*

fi·nal (fín'l) *adj.* **1. a.** Forming or occurring at the end; concluding; last. **b.** *Phonetics.* Occurring at the end of a word or syllable. **2.** Pertaining to or constituting the end result of a process or procedure; ultimate: *the final purpose.* **3.** Decisive; conclusive; unalterable: *The judges' decision is final.* **4.** *Grammar.* Indicating purpose: *a final clause.* —See Synonyms at **last.**
~*n.* Something that comes at or forms the end, especially: **1.** The last or one of the last of a series of sports contests or other competitions. **2.** *Plural.* The last series of examinations of an academic course. **3.** The edition of a newspaper published last in the day. [Middle English, from Old French, from Latin *fīnālis,* from *fīnis*†, end.]

final cause *n. Philosophy.* The ultimate purpose of something.

fi·na·le (fi-naá-li || -nál-i) *n.* The concluding part of an entertainment or work, especially a musical composition. [Italian, "final", from Latin *fīnālis,* FINAL.]

fi·nal·ise, fi·nal·ize (fínə-līz) *tr.v.* **-ised, -ising, -ises. 1.** To put into final form. **2.** To complete arrangements for. **—fi·na·li·sa·tion** (-lī-záysh'n, *U.S.* -li-) *n.*
Usage: This verb is widely used in official communications. Because of its bureaucratic associations, many people avoid using it, preferring *complete, conclude,* or *put in final form.*

fi·nal·ist (fínə-list) *n.* A contestant in the final session of a competition.

fi·nal·i·ty (fī-nál-əti || fi-) *n., pl.* **-ties. 1.** The condition or fact of being final; conclusiveness. **2.** A final, conclusive, or decisive act or utterance. **3.** The principle of final causes operating in the world.

fi·nal·ly (fínə-li, fín'l-i) *adv.* **1.** At the final point; at the end; last. **2.** Decisively; irrevocably. **3.** After a considerable delay; eventually; at last. **4.** Ultimately; in the end. **5.** Used to introduce a concluding point of discussion: *Finally, we must consider . . .*

Final Solution *n.* **1.** The Nazi plan in World War II for the mass killing of European Jews. **2.** *Small* **f,** *small* **s.** Any attempt at mass destruction of a people.

fi·nance (fī-nánss, fi-, fí-nanss) *n.* **1.** *Abbr.* **fin. a.** The science of the management of money and other assets. **b.** The disposition of public revenues by a government. **2.** *Plural.* **a.** Monetary resources or funds, especially of a government or corporate body. **b.** The monetary affairs or arrangements of a person, company, or the like. **3.** Money available to support a purchase, business venture, or the like.
~*v.* **financed, -nancing, -nances.** —*tr.* To supply the funds or capital for. —*intr.* To manage finances. [Middle English *finaunce,* end, settlement, payment, from Old French *finance,* from *finer,* to end, settle, from *fin,* end, from Latin *fīnis*†.]

finance bill *n.* A legislative act designed to raise public revenues.

finance company *n.* A company offering loans for the purchase of goods or property. Also called "finance house".

fi·nan·cial (fī-nánshəl, fi-) *adj. Abbr.* **fin.** Of or pertaining to finances or those who deal with finances. **—fi·nan·cial·ly** *adv.*
Synonyms: *financial, pecuniary, fiscal, monetary.*

Financial Times Industrial Ordinary Share Index *n.* The **FT Index** *(see).*

financial year *n.* Any period of twelve months at the end of which a company or institution balances its accounts. Also *chiefly U.S.* "fiscal year". See **tax year.**

fin·an·cier (fi-nán-si-ər, fī- || *U.S. also* finnən-séer) *n.* One who is occupied with or expert in large-scale financial affairs. [French, from FINANCE.]

fin·back (fín-bak) *n.* A whale, the **rorqual** *(see).*

finch (finch) *n.* Any of various relatively small birds of the family Fringillidae, such as a goldfinch, bullfinch, chaffinch, or canary, having a short, stout bill adapted for cracking seeds. [Middle English *finch,* Old English *finc,* from Germanic.]

find (fínd) *v.* **found** (fownd, *West Indian also* fungd), **finding, finds.** —*tr.* **1.** To come upon by accident; discover by chance. **2.** To come upon after a search: *find the cause of the trouble.* **3.** To come upon through experience or effort; obtain knowledge of; attain: *found contentment at last.* **4.** To succeed in reaching; arrive at: *The dart found the mark.* **5. a.** To learn by inquiry or research; determine; ascertain. **b.** To learn accidentally. **6.** To consider; regard: *I find her charm irresistible.* **7.** To recover (something lost). **8.** To recover the use of; regain. **9.** To manage to obtain: *find money for food.* **10.** To declare as a verdict or conclusion. **11.** To furnish; supply. Often used with *in*: *find someone in clothes.* —*intr.* To come to a legal decision or verdict: *The jury found for the defendant.* **—find (oneself). 1.** To discover what one truly wishes to be and do in life. **2.** To become aware of being in a condition or place. **—find out. 1.** To learn by accident or through enquiry. **2.** To discover the dishonesty, bad reputation, or deceit of (a person).
~*n.* **1.** An act of finding. **2.** That which is found; especially, a rare or valuable discovery. [Find, found, found; Middle English *finden, found, founden,* Old English *findan, fand* (plural *fundon*), *funden,* from Germanic.]

find·er (fíndər) *n.* **1.** One that finds. **2.** A **viewfinder** *(see).* **3.** *Astronomy.* A small telescope attached to the body of a larger one for locating an object to be observed with the larger telescope.

fin-de-siè·cle (fáN də si-ékl) *adj.* Of or characteristic of the last part of the 19th century, especially with reference to its artistic climate of effete sophistication. [French, "end of the century".]

find·ing (fínding) *n.* **1.** Something that has been found. **2.** *Usually plural.* A conclusion reached after examination or investigation. **3.** *Plural.* The tools and materials used by an artisan or workman.

fine[1] (fín) *adj.* **finer, finest. 1.** Of superior quality, skill, or appearance; admirable. **2.** Most enjoyable; pleasant. **3.** Free from impurities: *fine copper.* **4.** *Abbr.* **f., F.** Containing pure metal in a specified proportion or amount: *gold 21 carats fine.* **5.** Cut or honed to great sharpness: *a blade with a fine edge.* **6. a.** Thin; slender. **b.** Not coarse in texture: *fine hair.* **7.** Showing workmanship of great care and delicacy: *fine china.* **8.** Consisting of extremely small particles; not coarse: *fine dust.* **9.** Subtle or precise: *a fine shade of meaning.* **10.** Able to make or detect subtle or precise effects; sensitive: *a fine eye for colour.* **11.** Trained to the highest degree of physical efficiency; superbly conditioned: *a fine racehorse.* **12.** Of refined manners; elegant. **13.** Grand or elevated in a somewhat pompous way: *fine speeches.* **14.** Awful; terrible. Used ironically: *That's a fine position to be in.* **15.** Thoroughly satisfactory or acceptable: *A cup of tea would be fine.* **16.** Having no clouds; clear; sunny: *a fine day.* **17.** *Informal.* Quite well; in satisfactory health: *I'm fine, and you?* **18.** In cricket, designating an area or a fielding position behind the batsman's wicket that deviates only slightly from an imaginary line drawn between the two wickets and extending as far as the boundary: *fine leg.*
~*adv.* **1.** Finely. **2.** *Informal.* Very well: *doing fine.* **3.** In or towards a fine position in cricket.
~*v.* **fined, fining, fines.** —*tr.* **1.** To make finer; refine. **2.** To taper or make smaller or thinner. **3.** To clarify (wine, for example). —*intr.* To become finer, purer, or cleaner. **—fine up.** *Australian.* To become fine. Said of weather. [Middle English *fin,* from Old French, from Latin *fīnis*†, the end (as in *fīnis honorum,* the height of honour).]

fine[2] (fín) *n.* **1.** A sum of money imposed as a penalty for an offence. **2.** *Law.* Formerly, a fee paid to a feudal lord by his tenant. **3.** *Obsolete.* Finish; end; termination. **—in fine. 1.** In conclusion; finally. **2.** In summation; in brief.
~*tr.v.* **fined, fining, fines.** To require the payment of a fine from; impose a fine on. [Middle English *fin,* a fine, a payment for completion, an end, from Old French, from Latin *fīnis*†, limit, end.]

fi·ne[3] (fée-nay) *n. Music.* The end. Used to indicate the end of a passage that is to be repeated. [Italian, from Latin *fīnis*†, end.]

fine[4] (feen) *n.* A cognac, fine champagne.

fineable. Variant of **finable.**

fine art *n.* **1.** Art produced or intended primarily for beauty alone rather than utility. **2.** *Often plural.* Any of the forms such art takes, including sculpture, painting, drawing, and often architecture, literature, drama, music, and the dance. **3.** *Informal.* An activity requiring considerable skill. [Translation of French *beaux arts* (plural).]

fine champagne (feen) *n. French.* A cognac made from grapes from the Grande Champagne and Petite Champagne districts in southwest France. Also called "fine". [Contraction of *eau-de-vie de la Champagne,* "fine brandy from Champagne".]

fine-cut (fín-kút) *adj.* Finely and evenly shredded, as tobacco.

fine-draw (fín-dráw) *tr.v.* **-drew** (-droo || -dréw), **-drawn** (-dráwn), **-drawing, -draws. 1.** To mend or sew (a seam or tear) in such a way that the joint is invisible. **2.** To draw out (wire, for example) to a slender, threadlike state.

fine-drawn (fín-dráwn) *adj.* **1.** Subtly or precisely fashioned, as an argument or theory may be. **2.** Delicately formed; suggestive of refinement: *fine-drawn features.*

fine-grained (fín-gráynd) *adj.* Having a fine, smooth, even grain, as may have leather or wood.

fine·ly (fínli) *adv.* **1.** In a fine manner; excellently; splendidly. **2.** To a fine point; discriminatingly. **3.** Delicately or subtly. **4.** In small pieces or parts: *finely chopped nuts.*

fine·ness (fín-nəss, -niss) *n.* **1.** The condition or quality of being fine. **2.** The proportion of pure metal, such as gold, in an alloy.

fine print *n.* **Small print** *(see).*

fin·er·y[1] (fínəri) *n.* Elaborate adornment; fine clothing and accessories. [From FINE (excellent).]

finery[2] *n., pl.* **-ies.** A furnace or hearth where cast iron is made malleable. [French *finerie,* from *finer,* to REFINE.]

fines herbes (féen zairb, airb) *pl.n. French.* Finely chopped herbs, such as parsley, chives, tarragon, and thyme, used as a seasoning.

fine-spun (fín-spún) *adj.* **1.** Spun or drawn out to extreme fineness or subtlety; elaborate and delicate. **2.** Developed to excessive fineness; oversubtle.

fi·nesse (fi-néss) *n.* **1.** Restraint and delicacy of performance or behaviour. **2.** Subtlety or tact in manoeuvring; craftiness. **3.** In bridge and whist, the playing of a card in a suit in which one holds a nonsequential higher card, either to induce an opponent to play an intermediate card that one's partner can then top, or to win the trick economically. **4.** Any stratagem in which one appears to decline an advantage. —See Synonyms at **artifice, tact.**
~*v.* **finessed, -nessing, -nesses.** —*tr.* **1.** To accomplish with finesse. **2.** To handle with a deceptive or evasive strategy. **3.** To play (a card) as a finesse. —*intr.* **1.** To employ finesse. **2.** To make a finesse in a card game. [Old French, delicacy, fineness, from *fin,* FINE.]

fine structure *n.* **1.** *Physics.* Structure in spectral lines caused by the magnetic moments of orbiting electrons. Under high resolution certain lines can be resolved into two or more closely spaced lines. See **hyperfine structure. 2.** *Biology.* **Ultrastructure** *(see).*

fine-tooth comb (fīn-tōōth kōm || -tōōth; *also* fīn-tōōth-kōm) *n.* Also **fine-toothed comb** (-tōōtht- || -tōōtht). A comb with thin, closely spaced teeth. **—go over with a fine-tooth comb.** To examine in exhaustive detail.

fine-tune (fīn-téwn || -tōōn) *tr.v.* **-tuned, -tuning, -tunes.** **1.** To make small adjustments to the tuning of (a radio receiver, car engine, or the like) to obtain efficient or improved operation. **2.** Broadly, to make small adjustments or changes to. **—fine-tun·er** (-téwnər || -tōōnər) *n.*

fin·foot (fín-fōōt) *n.* Any of various aquatic, tropical, or subtropical cranelike birds of the family Heliornithidae, having lobed toes and pale brown plumage. Also called "sungrebe".

fin·ger (fíng-gər) *n.* **1.** Any of the five digits of the hand; especially, any one other than the thumb. **2.** The part of a glove designed to cover such a digit. **3.** Something resembling a finger, such as a peninsula. **4.** The length or width of a finger. **5.** *Informal.* A measure of spirits, a quantity approximately one fingerbreadth deep in a glass. **6.** *Machinery.* Any small projecting machine part. **—burn (one's) fingers.** To suffer as a result of meddlesome, inquisitive, or incautious behaviour. **—have a finger in the pie.** To be involved, especially in a meddlesome way, in some matter. **—pull (one's) finger out.** *British Slang.* To make an effort or show signs of activity after a period of slackness. **—put (one's) finger on.** To identify or point out with precision. **—snap (one's) fingers at.** **1.** To treat contemptuously. **2.** To disobey or ignore defiantly. **—twist round (one's) little finger.** *Informal.* To dominate utterly and effortlessly.

~v. **fingered, -gering, -gers.** *—tr.* **1.** To touch with the fingers; handle. **2.** *Music.* To mark (a score) with indications of which fingers are to play the notes. **3.** *Music.* To play (an instrument) by using the fingers in a particular way. **4.** *Chiefly U.S. Slang.* **a.** To inform on. **b.** To designate as an intended victim. *—intr.* **1.** To handle something with the fingers. **2.** To use the fingers, especially in playing an instrument. **3.** To be played by using the fingers in a specified way: *His clarinet fingers like yours.* [Middle English *finger,* Old English *finger,* from Germanic.] **—fin·ger·er** *n.*

fin·ger·board (fíng-gər-bawrd || -bōrd) *n.* A strip of wood on the neck of a stringed instrument against which the strings are pressed in playing.

finger bowl *n.* A small bowl or basin to hold water for rinsing the fingers at table.

fin·ger·breadth (fíng-gər-bredth, -bretth) *n.* Also **finger's breadth.** The breadth of one finger; approximately $^{3}/_{4}$ of an inch.

fin·gered (fíng-gərd) *adj.* **1.** Having a finger or fingers. **2.** Having a specified number or kind of fingers. Used in combination: *light-fingered; rosy-fingered.*

fin·ger·ing[1] (fíng-gəring) *n.* **1.** The technique used in playing a musical instrument with the fingers. **2.** The indication on a score of which fingers are to be used in playing.

fin·ger·ing[2] *n.* Fine knitting wool.

finger lake *n.* A long, narrow lake formed when glacial debris impedes drainage of a U-shaped glaciated valley.

fin·ger·ling (fíng-gər-ling) *n.* **1.** A young or small fish; especially, a young salmon or trout. **2.** Any small object or creature.

fin·ger·mark (fíng-gər-maark) *n.* A mark left on a surface by a dirty or greasy finger.

fin·ger·nail (fíng-gər-nayl) *n.* A thin, horny, transparent plate covering the upper surface of the tip of each finger.

fin·ger-paint (fíng-gər-paynt) *v.* **-painted, -painting, -paints.** *—intr.* To engage in finger painting. *—tr.* To make by finger painting.

finger painting *n.* **1.** The technique of painting by applying colours to moistened paper with the fingers. **2.** A painting so made.

fin·ger·plate (fíng-gər-playt) *n.* A plate of metal, plastic, or the like fixed to a door near the handle to protect it from fingermarks.

finger post *n.* A signpost resembling a pointing finger.

fin·ger·print (fíng-gər-print) *n.* **1.** An impression of the curves formed by the system of ridges on the skin surface of the ball of a finger; especially, such an impression made in ink for purposes of identification. **2.** Any identifying characteristic; a hallmark.

~tr.v. **fingerprinted, -printing, -prints.** To take an ink impression of a fingerprint or the fingerprints of.

fin·ger·stall (fíng-gər-stawl) *n.* A protective covering worn on an injured finger. Also called "stall".

fin·ger·tip (fíng-gər-tip) *n.* The extreme end or tip of a finger. **—have at (one's) fingertips.** **1.** To have readily or instantly available. **2.** To have a thorough knowledge of.

finger wave *n.* A wave set into damp hair using only the fingers.

fi·ni·al (fíni-əl, fínni-) *n. Architecture.* **1.** An ornament fixed to the peak of a gable, arched structure, or the like. **2.** Any ornamental terminating part, such as the screw on top of a piece of furniture. [Middle English *finial,* from adjective, "final", variant of FINAL.]

fin·i·cal (fínnik'l) *adj.* Fastidious; finicky. [Probably originally university slang, irregularly from FINE (delicate).] **—fin·i·cal·i·ty** (fínni-kál-iti), **fin·i·cal·ness** *n.* **—fin·i·cal·ly** *adv.*

fin·ick·y (fínniki) *adj.* Also **fin·ick·ing** (fínniking). Highly fastidious in tastes or standards; hard to please; fussy. [From FINICAL.]

fin·ing (fí-ning) *n.* **1.** The process of clarifying wines or other liquids. **2.** *Plural.* A substance, such as isinglass, used in this process.

fi·nis (fínniss, fée-niss, fí-) *n.* The end. Formerly used to indicate the end of a book or film. [Middle English, from Latin *fīnis.*]

fin·ish (fínnish) *v.* **-ished, -ishing, -ishes.** *—tr.* **1.** To arrive at or attain the end of: *finish a race.* **2.** To bring to an end; terminate; accomplish: *finish a task.* **3.** To consume all of; use up: *finish a pie.* **4.** To put the final touches to; bring to a desired or required state; perfect: *finish a painting.* **5.** To give (wood or cloth, for example) a desired surface texture. **6.** To complete the education of. **7.** To vanquish; destroy; kill: *finish an enemy.* **8.** *Informal.* To bring about the ruin of; overcome: *The stock-market crash finished him.* *—intr.* **1.** To come to a conclusion; end; stop. **2.** To reach the end of a task, course, or relationship. **—finish off.** **1.** To bring to a final conclusion. **2.** To kill (a wounded person, for example). **3.** To ruin completely (a failing venture, for example). **—finish up.** To end. Often used with *by* or a participle: *I finished up paying the whole bill.* **—finish with.** **1.** To have no further use for. **2.** To end a relationship with (someone). —See Synonyms at **complete.**

~n. Abbr. **fin.** **1. a.** The final part or conclusion of something; end: *a close finish in the race.* **b.** The reason for one's ruin; downfall. **2.** Something that completes, concludes, or perfects. **3. a.** The last treatment or coating of a surface. **b.** The surface texture thus produced. **4.** The material used in surfacing or finishing something: *a wax finish.* **5.** Completeness, thoroughness, or smoothness of execution; perfection. **6.** Polish or refinement in speech, manners, and the like. **7.** *Sports.* The ability to perform well at the end of a contest. [Middle English *finishen,* from Old French *fenir, finir* (stems *feniss-, finiss-*), from Latin *fīnīre,* to limit, complete, from *fīnis,* end.] **—fin·ish·er** *n.*

fin·ished (fínnisht) *adj.* **1.** Skilled; accomplished; perfected. **2.** Having all hopes of further progress destroyed.

finishing school *n.* A private school that trains girls in the social graces for life in polite society.

finishing touch *n. Often plural.* A final act, decorative addition, or the like that achieves the desired total effect.

Fin·is·tère (fínni-stáir). A département in Brittany, occupying the most westerly tip of France.

Fin·is·terre, Cape. Rugged, steep promontory at the tip of an Atlantic peninsula forming the westernmost point of Spain. It takes its name from the Latin, *finis terrae,* "land's end".

fi·nite (fí-nīt) *adj.* **1. a.** Having boundaries; limited. **b.** Capable of being bounded, enclosed, or encompassed. **2.** Being neither infinite nor infinitesimal. **3.** *Mathematics.* **a.** Bounded in an interval. Said of a quantity defined in an interval. **b.** Incapable of being put into one-to-one correspondence with a part of itself. Said of a set. **c.** Real or complex, as distinguished from ideal. Said of a number. **4.** Existing, persisting, or enduring for a limited time only; impermanent; transient. **5.** *Grammar.* Limited by person, number, tense, and mood; not an infinitive, gerund, or participle. Said of verbs.

~n. Finite entities collectively. Preceded by *the.* [Middle English *finit,* from Latin *fīnītus,* past participle of *fīnīre,* to limit, FINISH.] **—fi·nite·ly** *adv.* **—fi·nite·ness** *n.*

fin·i·tude (fí-ni-tewd, fínni- || -tōōd) *n.* The quality or condition of being finite.

fink (fingk) *n. Chiefly U.S. Slang.* **1.** A hired strikebreaker. **2.** One who informs against another. **3.** A person who is despised or disliked.

~intr.v. **finked, finking, finks.** *Chiefly U.S. Slang.* **1.** To inform. Used with *on.* **2.** To withhold support or participation. Used with *out: He finked out on me.* [20th century : origin obscure.]

fin keel *n.* A short keel usually made of metal, with ballast on the lower edge, used chiefly on racing yachts.

Fin·land (fín-lənd). *Finnish* **Su·o·mi** (soo-ōmi). Republic of north Europe, in EU since 1995. It has been independent since 1919, when it gained its freedom from the neighbouring U.S.S.R., having been a Grand Duchy of Russia since the early 19th century. After World War II Finland was forced to cede part of the Karelian isthmus and other land totalling 12 per cent of its area to the U.S.S.R. Finland is largely a barren, ice-scoured "shield", covered by more than 70,000 lakes and vast forests. Its forest-based industries account for more than half its exports. The chief port is Helsinki. Area, 337 009 square kilometres (130,085 square miles). Population, 5,120,000. Capital, Helsinki.

Finland, Gulf of. Eastern arm of the Baltic Sea. About 460 kilometres (285 miles) long, with a maximum width of 120 kilometres (75 miles), it separates Finland's southern coast from Estonia and Russia. It is an important shipping lane, whose chief ports are St Petersburg and Helsinki, but it is frozen from December to March.

Fin·land·i·sa·tion, Fin·land·i·za·tion (fín-lənd-ī-záysh'n || *U.S.* -i-) *n.* Formerly, the adoption of a neutral or conciliatory policy in relations with the U.S.S.R., as practised by Finland.

Finn (fin) *n.* **1.** A native or inhabitant of Finland. Also called "Finlander". **2.** One who speaks Finnish or a Finnic language. [Swedish *Finne* (superseding Old English *Finnas,* Finns), from Germanic *Finnar* (unattested).]

fin·nan haddock (fínnən) *n.* Also **finnan had·die** (háddi). Smoked haddock. [Earlier *findon haddock,* from earlier *findhorn haddock,* after the river *Findhorn* in Scotland.]

finned (find) *adj.* Having a fin, fins, or finlike parts.

fin·ner (fínnər) *n.* A **rorqual** *(see).* [FIN + -ER.]

Fin·ney (fínni), **Albert** (1936–). British actor. Following his early successes in the theatre, he made a number of films, including *Saturday Night and Sunday Morning* (1960), *Tom Jones* (1963), and *Charlie Bubbles* (1968). He has since returned to the stage in such classic roles as Tamburlaine and Hamlet.

Finn·ic (fínnik) *adj.* Of or pertaining to Finland, the Finns, or Finnic.

~n. A branch of Finno-Ugric.

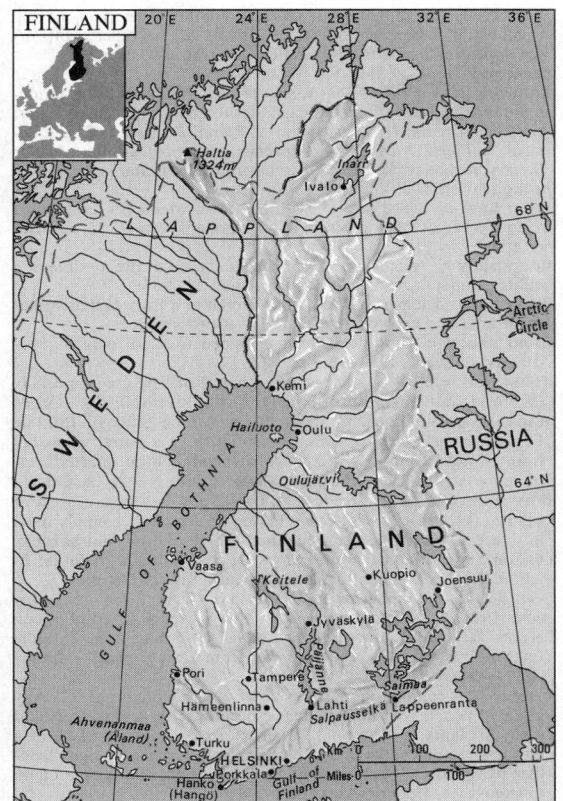

FINLAND

Haltia 1324m

Inari

Ivalo

Arctic Circle

68°N

Kemi

Hailuoto Oulu

Oulujärvi

64°N

FINLAND

Vaasa

Keitele

Kuopio

Joensuu

Jyväskylä

Pori

Tampere

Saimaa

Ahvenanmaa (Åland)

Hämeenlinna

Lahti

Salpausselkä

Lappeenranta

Turku

HELSINKI

Porkkala Gulf of Finland

Hanko (Hangö)

Miles

100   200   300

100

Finn·ish (fínnish) *adj. Abbr.* **Fin.** Of or pertaining to Finland, its language, or its people.
~*n.* The Uralic language spoken by the Finns.

Fin·no-U·gric (fínnō-ōō-grik, -yōō-) *n.* Also **Fin·no-U·gri·an** (-ōō-gri-ən, -yōō-). A subfamily of the Uralic language group, including Finnish and Hungarian.
~*adj.* **1.** Pertaining to the Finns and the Ugrians. **2.** Pertaining to the languages of the Finns and the Ugrians.

fin·ny (fínni) *adj.* **-nier, -niest. 1.** Having a fin or fins. **2.** Resembling a fin; finlike. **3.** Of, pertaining to, or full of fish.

fi·no (feènō) *n., pl.* **-nos.** The driest sherry. [Spanish, "fine".]

fi·noch·i·o, fi·noc·chi·o (fi-nócki-ō || *U.S.* -nóki-ō) *n.* A variety of fennel, *Foeniculum vulgare dulce,* whose thickened leafstalks are eaten as a vegetable. Also called "Florence fennel", "sweet fennel". [Italian *finocchio,* from Vulgar Latin *fēnuculum* (unattested), fennel, from Latin *fēniculum,* diminutive of *fēnum,* hay.]

fiord, fjord (fyord, fi-órd) *n.* A long, narrow, deep inlet from the sea bordered by steep hills, having a bar or threshold near its mouth. Fiords are submerged U-shaped glaciated valleys, found especially around the coasts of Norway and Alaska. [Norwegian, from Old Norse *fjörthr,* from Germanic; akin to FIRTH, FORD.]

fi·or·in (fi-ə-rin) *n.* **Creeping bent grass** *(see).* [Irish Gaelic *fiorthann.*]

fip·ple (fípp'l) *n.* **1.** A wooden block that forms a flue at the mouth end of certain musical wind instruments. **2.** A similar object in an organ pipe. [17th century : origin obscure.]

fipple flute *n.* A flute with a fipple, such as a recorder.

fir (fur) *n.* **1.** Any of various evergreen coniferous trees of the genus *Abies,* having flat needles and erect cones. **2.** Any of several similar or related trees, such as the **Douglas fir** *(see).* **3.** The wood of any of these trees. [Middle English *fir(re),* Old English *furh,* probably from Old Norse *fyri-,* from Germanic.] —**fir·ry** *adj.*

Fir·bank (fúr-bangk), **(Arthur Annesley) Ronald** (1886–1926). British novelist. His work, set in the Edwardian period, reflects his eccentricity and has a witty and impressionistic style. It includes the novels *Caprice* (1916), *Valmouth* (1919), and the posthumous *Artificial Princess* (1934).

fire (fir) *n.* **1.** A rapid, persistent chemical reaction that releases heat and light; especially, the exothermic combination of a combustible substance with oxygen. **2. a.** A quantity of combustible material such as wood or coal, undergoing this reaction and used for heating, cooking, or the like. **b.** Combustible material intended to undergo this reaction: *lay a fire.* **c.** A destroying or consuming of an object by fire. **3.** A heating appliance powered by gas or electricity. **4.** *a.* Intensity, as of feeling; ardour, especially in love or rage. **b.** Enthusiasm or energy. **5.** Luminosity or brilliance, as of a cut and polished gemstone. **6.** The result of inspiration; vividness; brilliance: *the fire of his verse.* **7.** A sensation of heat or burning, such as that produced by fever or by drinking alcoholic spirits. **8.** A torment, trial, or tribulation. **9. a.** The discharge of firearms; firing. **b.** The bullets, shells, or similar projectiles discharged. **10.** A rapid succession of questions, criticisms, or the like. **11.** In ancient thought, one of the four **elements** *(see).* —**between two fires.** Being attacked from two sources or sides simultaneously. —**catch** or **take fire. 1.** To become ignited. **2.** To become excited or enthusiastic. —**hang fire. 1.** To fail to fire or to delay firing, as a gun. **2.** To be delayed, as an event or decision. —**on fire. 1.** Ignited; burning; ablaze. **2.** Filled with enthusiasm or excitement. —**open fire. 1.** To commence shooting. **2.** To commence asking questions or making criticisms. —**play with fire.** To take part in a dangerous or risky situation; be foolhardy. —**set fire to** or **set on fire. 1.** To ignite. **2.** To make excited; inflame. —**under fire. 1.** Exposed or subjected to armed attack. **2.** Exposed or subjected to criticism or censure.
~*v.* **fired, firing, fires.** —*tr.* **1.** To cause to burn; ignite. **2. a.** To add fuel to (something burning). **b.** To maintain or intensify a fire in (a boiler, for example). **c.** To be the fuel for (a central heating system, for example). **3.** To bake in a kiln; *fire a flowerpot.* **4.** To dry or cure by heat: *fire tobacco.* **5. a.** To arouse the emotions of; make enthusiastic or ardent: *He was fired by patriotism.* **b.** To stimulate (enthusiasm, for example). **6.** To cause to glow. **7.** To detonate or discharge (a firearm, explosives, or a projectile): *fire a rifle; fire a rocket.* **8.** To cauterise (an animal's wound). **9.** *Informal.* To project or hurl suddenly and forcefully: *fire a shot at goal; fire questions at a witness.* **10.** *Informal.* To discharge from a position; dismiss: *fire an employee.* —*intr.* **1. a.** To become ignited; flame up. **b.** To allow internal combustion to occur. Said of the cylinders in an engine. **2.** To become excited or ardent; feel deeply. **3.** To tend a fire. **4.** To have a specified reaction to being fired in a kiln: *This bowl will fire beautifully.* **5.** To become yellowed, brown, or blotchy before reaching maturity. Said of grain. **6.** To discharge; go off: *The mortar fired towards the enemy.* **7.** To detonate or shoot a weapon: *He fired at the enemy.* **8.** *Informal.* To project or hurl a missile. —**fire away.** To bombard someone, as with projectiles or questions. [Middle English *fir, fur, feir, fire,* Old English *fȳr,* from West Germanic *fūir* (unattested).]

fire alarm *n.* **1.** A warning of the outbreak of a fire. **2.** A device, such as a bell or siren, used in announcing the outbreak of a fire.

fire-and-brim·stone (fir-ən-brím-stōn) *adj.* **1.** Characteristic or suggestive of hellfire. **2.** Extremely zealous in warning of divine punishment awaiting sinners. [From the Biblical *fire and brimstone,* which God often used to destroy sinners. Revelation 20:10.]

fire ant *n.* Any of several ants of the genus *Solenopsis;* especially, *S. geminata* or *S. saevissima,* of the southern United States and tropical America, that can inflict a painful bite.

fire-arm (fir-aarm, fi-ə-) *n.* Any weapon capable of firing a missile; especially, a pistol or rifle using an explosive charge as a propellant.

fireback *n.* **1.** An iron plate, usually ornamental, at the back of a fireplace. **2.** A pheasant of the genus *Lophura,* of Southeast Asia.

fire-ball (fir-bawl, fi-ər-bawl) *n.* **1.** Any brilliantly burning sphere; especially, a flash of **ball lightning** *(see).* **2.** An exceptionally bright meteor. **3.** A highly luminous, intensely hot, spherical cloud of dust, gas, and vapour generated by a nuclear explosion. **4.** *Slang.* A highly energetic person.

fire-bird (fir-burd, fi-ər-) *n.* Broadly, any bird having bright scarlet or orange plumage.

fire blight *n.* A destructive disease of apples, pears, and related plants, caused by a bacterium, *Erwinia amylovora.* [From the scorched appearance it produces.]

fire bomb *n.* An **incendiary bomb** *(see).* —**fire-bomb** *tr.v.*

fire-box (fir-bokss, fi-ər-) *n.* A chamber in which fuel is burned; especially, the furnace of a steam locomotive.

fire-brand (fir-brand, fi-ər-) *n.* **1.** A piece of burning wood. **2.** A person who stirs up trouble or kindles a revolt.

fire-brat (fir-brat, fi-ər-) *n.* A small, wingless insect, *Thermobia domestica,* frequenting warm areas of buildings.

fire-break (fir-brayk, fi-ər-) *n.* A strip of cleared or ploughed land used to stop the spread of a fire. Also called "fireguard", "fire line".

fire-brick (fir-brik, fi-ər-) *n.* A refractory brick, especially of fire clay, used for lining furnaces, fireboxes, chimneys, or fireplaces.

fire brigade *n.* **1.** *British.* An organised body of people trained to fight fires. **2.** A military unit designed to deal with a sudden outbreak of violence. **3.** Broadly, any body of reinforcements or helpers called in to help in an emergency.
~*adj.* Responding to an emergency once it has arisen rather than aiming at prevention.

fire-bug (fir-bug, fi-ər-) *n. Informal.* A person who deliberately sets fire to property; an arsonist.

fire clay *n.* A type of heat-resistant clay used to make firebricks, crucibles, and other objects exposed to high temperatures.

fire company *n.* **1.** A business firm that sells fire insurance. **2.** *U.S.* A fire brigade.

fire control *n. Abbr.* **FC** The control of the delivery of gunfire on military targets.

fire-crack·er (fir-krackər, fi-ər-) *n. Chiefly U.S.* A small explosive charge in a cylinder of heavy paper, used to make noise.

fire-crest (fir-krest, fi-ər-) *n.* A small European warbler, *Regulus ignicapillus,* having a crown with yellow, black, and white stripes.

fire-cure (fir-kewr, fi-ər-) *tr.v.* **-cured, -curing, -cures.** To cure (tobacco, for example) by exposing it to the heat and smoke of a wood fire.

fire-damp (fir-damp, fi-ər-) *n.* **1.** A combustible gas, chiefly methane, occurring naturally in coal mines and forming explosive mixtures with air. **2.** The explosive mixture itself. Compare **damp.**

fire department *n. Chiefly U.S. Abbr.* **F.D.** A department, especially of a municipal authority, whose purpose is to fight fires.

fire-dog (fīr-dog, fĭ-ər || -dawg) *n.* An **andiron** *(see).*

fire door *n.* An internal door in a building with a strong spring that makes it self-closing, designed to stop the spread of fire by eliminating through draughts.

fire-drake (fīr-drayk, fĭ-ər-) *n.* A fiery dragon of Germanic mythology. [Middle English *firdrake,* Old English *fȳr-draca* : *fȳr,* FIRE + *draca,* dragon, DRAKE.]

fire drill *n.* A practice exercise in the use of fire-fighting equipment or the exit procedure to be followed in case of a fire.

fire-eat-er (fīr-eetər, fĭ-ər-) *n.* **1.** A performer who pretends to swallow fire. **2.** A vigorous or pugnacious person.

fire engine *n.* Any of various large motor vehicles that carry firemen and equipment to a fire, and that support extinguishing operations, as by pumping water or raising telescopic ladders.

fire escape *n.* Any structure or device, as a metal ladder or an outside stairway attached to a building, erected for emergency exit in the event of fire.

fire extinguisher *n.* A portable apparatus containing water or chemicals that can be discharged in a jet to extinguish a small fire.

fire-fight-er (fīr-fītər, fĭ-ər-) *n.* One engaged in extinguishing a fire, usually as a member of a fire brigade. **—fire-fight-ing** *n.*

fire-fly (fīr-flī, fĭ-ər-) *n., pl.* **-flies.** Any of various nocturnal beetles of the family Lampyridae, characteristically having luminous abdominal organs that produce a flashing light.

fire-guard (fīr-gaard, fĭ-ər-) *n.* **1.** A metal screen placed in front of an open fireplace to catch sparks. Also called "fire screen". **2.** A **firebreak** *(see).*

fire hall *n. Chiefly Canadian.* A fire station.

fire hydrant *n.* A **hydrant** *(see).*

fire insurance *n.* Insurance against the damage or loss of property as a result of fire or lightning.

fire irons *pl.n.* The equipment used to tend a fireplace, including tongs, a shovel, and a poker.

fire-less cooker (fīr-ləss, -liss, fĭ-ər-) *n.* An insulated container which when preheated retains sufficient heat to cook food.

fire-light (fīr-līt, fĭ-ər-) *n.* The light from a fire, as in a fireplace or at a campsite.

fire-lighter (fīr-lītər, fĭ-ər-) *n. British.* A block of easily ignited material, used to help to light solid fuel.

fire line *n.* A strip of cleared land, a **firebreak** *(see).*

fire-lock (fīr-lok, fĭ-ər-) *n.* A **flintlock** *(see).*

fire-man (fīr-mən, fĭ-ər-) *n., pl.* **-men** (-mən, -men). **1.** A member of a fire brigade. **2.** A man who tends a boiler or furnace; a stoker. **3. a.** A man who tends the boiler of a steam train. **b.** A train driver's assistant. **4.** *Informal.* A person responsible for conciliating parties in dispute.

Firenze. See **Florence.**

fire opal *n.* An opal with brilliant flamelike yellow, orange, and red colours. Also called "girasol".

fire-pan (fīr-pan, fĭ-ər-) *n.* A metal grate or brazier for holding or carrying fire.

fire-place (fīr-playss, fĭ-ər-) *n.* **1.** An open recess for holding a fire at the base of a chimney; a hearth. **2.** A structure, usually of stone or brick, for holding an outdoor fire.

fire-plug (fīr-plug, fĭ-ər-) *n. U.S.* A **hydrant** *(see).*

fire-pow-er (fīr-powr, -pow-ər, fĭ-ər-) *n.* The capacity, as of a weapon, military unit, or ship, for discharging ammunition.

fire-proof (fīr-prōōf || -prōōf, fĭ-ər-) *adj.* Capable of withstanding or resisting damage by fire.

~ *tr.v.* **fireproofed, -proofing, -proofs.** To make fireproof.

fir-er (fīr-ər, fĭ-ər-) *n.* **1.** One that fires. **2.** A firearm, considered with respect to the speed or technique of its firing. Often used in combination: *rapid-firer.*

fire-rais-er (fīr-rayzər, fĭ-ər-) *n.* An arsonist. **—fire-raising** *n.*

fire screen *n.* **1.** An ornamental screen placed in front of a fireplace that is not in use. **2.** A **fireguard** *(see).*

fire ship *n.* A vessel loaded with explosives and combustible material and set adrift among enemy ships to destroy them.

fire-side (fīr-sīd, fĭ-ər-) *n.* **1.** The area immediately surrounding a fireplace or hearth. **2.** Home.

fire station *n.* The headquarters of a fire brigade.

fire-stone (fīr-stōn, fĭ-ər-) *n.* **1.** A flint or other stone used to strike a spark of fire. **2.** A fire-resistant stone, for example any of certain sandstones, used as a construction material.

fire-storm (fīr-storm) *n.* A violent storm caused by hot air rising from an area on fire, typically following nuclear or other heavy bombing, with very high winds rushing in to replace the rising air.

fire-thorn (fīr-thorn) *n.* Any of various thorny shrubs of the genus *Pyracantha,* native to Asia, and often cultivated for their evergreen foliage and showy reddish or orange berries.

fire-trap (fīr-trap, fĭ-ər-) *n.* A building susceptible to catching fire easily or difficult to escape from in the event of fire.

fire wall *n.* A fireproof wall used to prevent the spread of a fire.

fire warden *n. U.S.* An official responsible for the prevention or putting out of fires, especially in forested areas.

fire-watch-er (fīr-wochər) *n.* One who keeps a lookout for fires started by bombs. **—fire-watch-ing** *n.*

fire-wa-ter (fīr-wawtər, fĭ-ər- || *U.S. also* -wottər) *n. Slang.* Strong alcoholic spirits, especially when of poor quality. [Translation of some Algonquian term such as Ojibwa *iškotēwābō.*]

fire-weed (fīr-weed, fĭ-ər-) *n.* **1.** A plant, **rosebay willowherb** *(see).*

2. A weedy North American plant, *Erechtites hieracifolia,* having small white or greenish flowers. **3.** Any of various other plants often appearing as the first vegetation in burnt-over areas.

fire-wood (fīr-wōōd, fĭ-ər-) *n.* Wood used as fuel.

fire-work (fīr-wurk, fĭ-ər-) *n.* **1.** Any of various devices using combinations of explosives and combustibles to generate coloured lights, smoke, and noise for amusement. **2.** *Plural.* A display of such devices. **3.** *Plural.* An exciting or spectacular display, as of musical or literary virtuosity. **4.** *Plural.* A temperamental outburst.

fir-ing (fīr-ing, fĭ-ər-) *n.* Fuel for fires.

firing line *n.* **1.** The line of positions from which fire is directed against a target. **2.** A position in which one is exposed to criticism or attack.

firing party *n.* A detachment of soldiers chosen to fire a salute at a military funeral. Also called "firing squad".

firing pin *n.* The part of the bolt or breech of a firearm that strikes the primer and explodes the charge of the projectile.

firing squad *n.* **1.** A detachment assigned to shoot persons condemned to death. **2.** A firing party.

fir-kin (fúrkin) *n.* **1.** A small wooden barrel or keg, used especially for storing butter, cheese, or lard. **2.** Any of several British units of capacity, usually equal to about 41 litres (nine gallons). [Middle English *ferdekin, ferken,* a cask, one-fourth of a barrel, probably from Middle Dutch *vierdelkijn* (unattested), "little quarter", diminutive of *vierdel,* fourth part : *vierde,* fourth + *deel,* part, deal.]

firm[1] (furm) *adj.* **firmer, firmest. 1.** Unyielding to pressure; rigid or solid to the touch. **2.** Not easily moved or detached; securely fixed in place. **3.** Showing determination or resolution; unshakable. **4.** Constant; steadfast: *a firm ally.* **5.** Fixed formally; definite; final: *a firm offer.* **6.** Unfluctuating; steady. Said of prices.

~ *v.* **firmed, firming, firms.** —*tr.* To make firm. —*intr.* **1.** To become firm. **2.** To begin to rise again after a decline. Used of prices. ~*adv.* Resolutely; unwaveringly: *stand firm; hold firm.* [Middle English *ferm,* from Old French *ferme,* from Latin *firmus.*] **—firm-ly** *adv.* **—firm-ness** *n.*

firm[2] *n.* **1.** A commercial partnership of two or more people. **2.** Any group of people working together; especially, a team of doctors and their assistants in a hospital. [Italian *firma,* signature, name of a business establishment or partnership, from *firmare,* to sign, "confirm by signature", from Late Latin *firmāre,* to confirm, from Latin, to strengthen, from *firmus,* FIRM.]

fir-ma-ment (fúrmə-mənt) *n. Literary.* The vault or expanse of the heavens; the sky. [Middle English, from Old French, from Late Latin *firmāmentum* (translation of Greek *stereōma,* heavenly vault, translation of Hebrew *rāqī'a*), from Latin, a strengthening, support, from *firmāre,* to make firm, from *firmus,* FIRM.] **—fir-ma-men-tal** (-mént'l) *adj.*

fir-mer chisel (fúrmər) *n.* A chisel or gouge with a thin blade, used to shape and finish wood. Also called "firmer". [French *fermoir,* variant (influenced by *fermer,* to make firm) of Old French *formoir,* from *former,* to form, shape, from Latin *fōrmāre,* from *fōrma,* FORM.]

firm-ware 1. A computer program that is stored in a read-only memory so that it cannot be accidentally overwritten or erased. **2.** An electronic device incorporating such programs. Compare **soft-ware, hardware.**

firn (feern) *n.* Snow that has been partially consolidated by thawing and freezing but not yet converted to glacial ice. [German *Firn,* "last year's (snow)", from (Swiss dialect) *firn,* of last year, from Old High German *firni,* old.]

first (furst) *adj.* **1.** Coming, counted, or located before all others. **2.** Occurring or acting prior to all others; earliest. **3.** Ranking above all others; foremost in position, quality, or importance: *the First Secretary of the Treasury.* **4.** *Music.* Highest in pitch or foremost in carrying melody: *first soprano; first trumpet.* **5.** Of or pertaining to the transmission gear, or corresponding gear ratio, used to produce the range of lowest drive speeds in a motor vehicle.

~*adv.* **1.** Before anything else. **2.** Before or above all others in time or rank. **3.** For the first time: *since you first came.* **4.** Preferably; rather: *I'd die first.*

~*n.* **1.** The ordinal number one in a series. **2.** The one coming, counted, occurring, or ranking before or above all others. **3.** The beginning; the outset: *from the first; at first.* **4.** *Music.* The voice or instrument highest in pitch or foremost in carrying melody. **5.** The transmission gear or corresponding gear ratio used to produce the range of lowest drive speeds in a motor vehicle. **6.** The winner or winning position in a contest. **7.** *British.* A first-class honours degree. **8.** An innovation or breakthrough: *a first for British technology.* **9.** *Plural.* The best grade or quality of merchandise. [Middle English *first,* Old English *fyrst,* from Germanic *furistaz* (unattested), superlative of *fur-, for-* (unattested).]

Usage: First and *last* usually precede a numeral in a collective expression such as *the first two chapters, the last four chapters. The two first chapters* means the first chapters of two different books.

In listing a set of points, there is some variation in usage over whether to use *first* or *firstly.* Formal tradition prefers *first,* but analogy with *secondly, thirdly,* and so on has led to an increasing use of *firstly,* even in formal contexts.

first aid *n.* Emergency treatment administered to injured or sick persons before professional medical care is available.

first base *n.* In baseball, the first of the bases in the infield. **—not to make** or **get to first base.** *Informal.* To achieve no success.

first-born (fúrst-bawrn) *adj.* First in order of birth; born first. ~*n.* A first-born child.

first cause *n.* **1.** A primary cause; an origin. **2.** *Capital* **F**, *capital* **C**. God considered as creator.

first class *n.* **1.** The first, highest, or best group of a particular category. **2.** The most luxurious and most expensive class of accommodation on a train or other means of transport. **3.** A class of mail given priority for handling and delivery.

first-class, first class (fúrst-kláss ‖ -kláss) *adj.* **1.** Indicating the first, highest, or best group of a particular category. **2.** Of the foremost excellence or highest quality; first-rate: *a first-class mind.* ~*adv.* **1.** In first-class accommodation. **2.** By first-class mail.

first cousin *n.* See **cousin.**

first-day cover (fúrst-day) *n.* An envelope bearing stamps postmarked on their day of issue.

first-de-gree burn (fúrst-di-grée) *n.* A burn affecting the outer layer of the skin. No longer in technical usage.

first floor *n.* **1.** *British.* The floor immediately above the ground floor. **2.** *U.S.* The ground floor of a building.

first-foot (fúrst-fŏŏt) *n.* The first person to enter a house at New Year, who by tradition should be tall and dark-haired. ~*intr.v.* **first-footed, -footing, -foots.** To be the first person to enter a house at New Year.

first fruit *n.* Also **first fruits. 1.** The first product of a season's harvest. **2.** The first result or profit of an undertaking.

first-gen-e-ra-tion (fúrst-jenna-ráysh'n) *adj.* Belonging to a group of contemporaries that is as specified for the first time, their parents not having been so: *first-generation Australians.*

first-hand, firsthand (fúrst-hánd) *adj.* Received from the original source: *first-hand information.* ~*adv.* From the original source; directly. [Originally, *at (the) first hand.*]

First International *n.* See **International.**

first lady, First Lady *n.* **1.** The wife of the mayor or similar official. **2.** In the United States, the wife of the president. **3.** The foremost woman of a specified profession or art: *the first lady of the ballet.*

first lieutenant *n.* *Chiefly U.S.* A **lieutenant** *(see).*

first-ling (fúrst-ling) *n.* **1.** The first of a kind or category. **2.** The first-born offspring.

first-ly (fúrst-li) *adv.* **1.** Before anything else. **2.** Before all others. **3.** In the first place; to begin with. —See Usage note at **first.**

first mate *n.* An officer on a merchant ship ranking immediately below the captain. Also called "first officer".

first name *n.* A person's given, personal, or Christian name. —**on first-name terms.** Friendly enough to use first names.

first night *n.* The official opening performance of a play, opera, or the like.

first-night-er (fúrst-nítər) *n.* One attending a first night.

first offender *n.* One found guilty of an offence who has no previous convictions.

first-past-the-post (fúrst-paast-thə-pŏst ‖ -past-) *adj.* Designating a voting system in which the candidate for whom the most votes have been cast secures election, even without an absolute majority. Compare **proportional representation.**

first person *n.* **1.** A category of linguistic forms, such as verbs or pronouns, designating the speaker or writer of the sentence in which they appear, and in the plural, those with whom he associates himself. **2.** Any of these forms; for example, *I, we.* **3.** A discourse or literary style in which the narrator recounts his own experiences and impressions using such forms: *a novel written in the first person.*

first post *n.* *Military.* The first of two bugle calls signalling the time to retire for the night.

first principles *pl.n.* The basic premises from which any intellectual argument proceeds.

first-rate (fúrst-ráyt) *adj.* Foremost in quality or rank.

first refusal *n.* The right to be the first to be offered the opportunity to do something, especially to purchase something.

first strike *n.* An aggressive rather than retaliatory attack with nuclear weapons, intended to reduce or destroy an enemy's ability to strike back. Also used adjectivally: *first-strike missiles.*

first string *n.* **1.** A regular team member rather than a reserve. **2.** The leading member of a team playing an individual sport. ~*adj.* Also **first-string. 1.** Being a regular team member. **2.** Being the leading member of a team playing an individual sport. **3.** First-rate; of high importance or quality.

first thing *adv.* At the earliest possible moment.

first water *n.* **1.** The highest degree of quality or value in gems or pearls. **2.** The foremost rank or quality: *a pianist of the first water.*

First World *n.* The industrialised nations of the world, including Western Europe, North America, Australia and New Zealand, and Japan, and sometimes thought to include the former Soviet bloc.

First World War *n.* **World War I** *(see).*

firth (furth) *n.* In Scotland, a long, narrow inlet of the sea; a fiord. [Middle English *ford, furth,* from Old Norse *fjörthr,* FIORD.]

Firth of Forth. See **Forth.**

fisc (fisk) *n.* The treasury of a state. [Old French, from Latin *fiscus†,* woven basket, money basket used by tax collectors, treasury.]

fis-cal (fisk'l) *adj.* **1.** Of or pertaining to the treasury or finances of a nation or branch of government, and especially matters of taxation. **2.** Of or pertaining to finances in general: *a fiscal agent.* —See Synonyms at **financial.** ~*n.* A **procurator fiscal** *(see).* [Old French, from Latin *fiscālis,* from *fiscus†,* treasury, basket.] —**fis-cal-ly** *adv.*

fiscal drag *n.* The limitation of economic growth caused by taxation affecting a higher proportion of taxpayers as inflation reduces the real value of money but seems to raise incomes.

fiscal year *n.* *U.S.* A **financial year** *(see).*

Fisch-er (físhər), **Bobby,** born Robert James Fischer (1943–). U.S. chess player. An International Grandmaster at fifteen, he was world champion (1972–75). He became a recluse, but returned to beat Boris Spassky for a $5 million purse in 1992.

Fisch-er-Die-skau (físhər-dée-skow), **Dietrich** (1925–). German baritone. He is famous for his interpretations of Schubert's songs.

fish¹ (fish) *n., pl.* **fishes** or collectively **fish. 1.** Any of numerous cold-blooded aquatic vertebrates of the superclass Pisces, characteristically having fins, gills, and a streamlined body, and including: **a.** Any of the class Osteichthyes, having a bony skeleton. **b.** Any of the class Chondrichthyes, having a cartilaginous skeleton, and including the sharks, rays, and skates. **c.** The flesh of such animals for use in cooking. **2.** Any aquatic vertebrate of the class Agnatha, lacking jaws, and including the lampreys and hagfishes. **3.** Loosely, any of various unrelated aquatic animals, such as a jellyfish, cuttlefish, or crayfish. **4.** *Informal.* A person likened to a fish for lacking some human attribute or advantage: *a cold fish.* ~*v.* **fished, fishing, fishes.** —*intr.* **1.** To catch or try to catch fish. **2.** To search or hunt for something in or under water: *fish for sponges.* **3.** To look for something by feeling around. **4.** To seek to elicit information, compliments, or the like. —*tr.* **1.** To catch or try to catch fish in: *fish a lake.* **2.** To pull out or up in the manner of one who fishes. Used with *out* or *from.* [Middle English *fish, fisk,* Old English *fisc,* from Germanic.]

Usage: This word has two plural forms: *fish* and *fishes. Fish* is the more widely used, referring to fish viewed collectively (*the fish in the sea, those fish are bad*). *Fishes* is used in technical writing, usually to emphasise individual fish or species of fish: *the fishes pass through the hole one at a time.* See also **fruit.**

fish² *n., pl.* **fishes.** A piece of wood or an iron plate used to join or strengthen a beam, bar, or the like. ~*tr.v.* **fished, fishing, fishes.** To join, reinforce, or mend with a fish. [French *ficher,* to fix, from Vulgar Latin *figicare* (unattested), from Latin *figere.*]

fish-and-chip shop (fish-ən-chíp) *n.* In Britain, a shop selling fried fish and chips, usually to be eaten off the premises.

fish-bowl (fish-bōl) *n.* **1.** A transparent bowl in which live fish are kept. **2.** Something that can be seen through at all sides or at all points.

fish cake *n.* A fried cake, patty, or ball of chopped fish, often mixed with potato or rice.

fish eagle *n.* The **osprey** *(see).*

fish-er (físhər) *n.* **1. a.** One that fishes. **b.** A fisherman. **2. a.** A carnivorous mammal, *Martes pennanti,* of northern North America, having thick, dark brown fur. Also called "pekan". **b.** The fur of this animal.

Fish-er (físhər), **Andrew** (1862–1928). Australian statesman. Born in Scotland, he went to Queensland in 1885. In 1901 he entered the Commonwealth Parliament and subsequently served three terms as Labor prime minister: 1908–09, 1910–13, and 1914–15.

Fisher, John Arbuthnot, 1st Baron (1841–1920). British admiral. As First Sea Lord (1904–10, 1914–15) he was responsible for the introduction of Dreadnought battleships and Invincible cruisers.

fish-er-man (físhər-mən) *n., pl.* **-men** (-mən, -men). **1.** One who fishes as an occupation or sport. **2.** A commercial fishing vessel.

fisherman's bend *n.* A knot used to secure the end of a line to a ring or spar, made by two turns with the end passing back under both.

fisherman's tale *n.* An implausible and boastful story.

fish-er-y (físhəri) *n., pl.* **-ies. 1. a.** The industry or occupation of catching, processing, or selling fish and fish products. **b.** A place where fish are processed and sold. **2.** An area where commercial fishing is carried on; a fishing ground. **3.** A hatchery for fish. **4.** The legal right to fish in specific waters or areas.

Fish-es (físhiz) *pl.n.* The constellation and sign of the zodiac, **Pisces** *(see).* Usually preceded by *the.*

fish-eye lens (fish-ī) *n. Photography.* A lens with a large curvature used to take pictures over a very wide field of view but producing a somewhat distorted image of the sides.

fish farm *n.* A place in which food fish are bred commercially in tanks or ponds.

fish finger *n.* Fish fillet made into an oblong stick and covered in breadcrumbs.

fish-gig (fish-gig) *n.* Also **fiz-gig** (fíz-). A pronged instrument for spearing fish. Also called "gig". [Variant (influenced by FISH) of earlier *fisgig,* from Spanish *fisga†.*]

fish hawk *n.* The **osprey** *(see).*

fish-hook (fish-hŏŏk, -ōŏk) *n.* A barbed metal hook used for catching fish.

fish-ing (físhing) *n.* The sport or occupation of catching fish.

fishing rod *n.* A rod of wood, steel, or glass fibre used with a line for catching fish.

fish joint *n.* A joint formed by bolting fishplates to either side of two rails or beams.

fish kettle *n.* A long, oval-shaped saucepan with a lid and usually a detachable grid that fits inside, for poaching or steaming whole fish.

fish ladder *n.* A set of pools one above the other that enables fish to pass over a dam or similar obstacle when swimming upstream.

fish louse *n.* Any of various small, rounded parasitic crustaceans of the subclass Branchiura that live attached to fish.

fish·meal (fish-meel) *n.* A nutritive mealy substance produced from fish and used as animal feed and fertiliser.

fish·mon·ger (fish-mung-gər ‖ -mong-) *n. Chiefly British.* One who sells fish.

fish·net (fish-net) *n.* 1. A meshed openwork fabric resembling netting used for catching fish. 2. *Chiefly U.S.* A net for catching fish. ~*adj.* Meshed or woven together like a fishing net: *fishnet tights.*

fish·plate (fish-playt) *n.* Any of the connecting metal plates bolted along the side of two rails or beams placed end to end, used especially in the laying of railway track.

fish·pond (fish-pond) *n.* A small body of water stocked with fish.

Fish River Canyon. A spectacular canyon formed by the Fish river in southern Namibia (Southwest Africa), second in size only to the Grand Canyon of the Colorado river in Arizona. Maximum depth approximately 600 metres (2,000 feet).

fish·tail (fish-tayl) *adj.* Resembling or suggestive of the tail of a fish in shape or movement.
~*intr.v.* **fishtailed, -tailing, -tails.** To swing the rear end of a motor vehicle or aircraft from side to side while moving forwards.
~*n.* 1. A fishtailing manoeuvre. 2. An attachment for a bunsen burner that produces a thin, broad flame.

fish·wife (fish-wīf) *n., pl.* **-wives** (-wīvz). 1. A woman who sells fish. 2. A coarse, abusive woman.

fish·y (fishi) *adj.* **-i·er, -i·est.** 1. Resembling or suggestive of fish, as in taste or smell. 2. Cold or expressionless: *a fishy stare.* 3. *Informal.* a. Unlikely; questionable. b. Giving rise to suspicion; dubious. —**fish·i·ly** *adv.* —**fish·i·ness** *n.*

fissi- *comb. form.* Indicates a split or cleft shape; for example, **fissipalmate.** [Latin *fissus,* past participle of *findere,* to cleave, split.]

fis·sile (fissīl ‖ *U.S. also* fiss'l) *adj.* 1. Capable of being split. 2. *Physics.* Fissionable, especially by neutrons of all energies. [Latin *fissilis,* from *fissus,* split. See **fissi-**.] —**fis·sil·i·ty** (fi-silliti) *n.*

fis·sion (fish'n) *n.* 1. The act or process of splitting into parts. 2. *Physics.* A nuclear reaction in which any of certain heavy atomic nuclei split into fragments, usually two fragments of comparable mass, releasing a large amount of energy. Also called "nuclear fission". Compare **fusion.** 3. *Biology.* An asexual reproductive process in which a unicellular organism splits into two or more independently maturing daughter cells. [Latin *fissiō* (stem *fissiōn-*), from *fissus,* past participle of *findere,* to split.]

fis·sion·a·ble (fish'n-əb'l) *adj.* Capable of undergoing fission; especially, capable of being induced to undergo nuclear fission by slow neutrons. Said of isotopes.

fission bomb *n.* A bomb in which the explosion is produced by nuclear fission; an atomic bomb.

fission reactor *n.* A nuclear reactor that produces energy by controlled nuclear fission of a radioactive fuel.

fis·si·pal·mate (fissi-pál-mayt) *adj.* Having lobed or partially webbed, separated toes. Said of the feet of certain birds.

fis·sip·a·rous (fi-síppərəss) *adj.* 1. Reproducing by biological fission. 2. Tending to split; faction-prone. [FISSI- + -PAROUS.]

fis·si·ped (fissi-ped) *adj.* Having the toes separated from one another, as certain carnivorous mammals.
~*n.* A carnivorous mammal having such toes, such as a dog or cat. [Late Latin *fissipēs* : FISSI- + -PED.]

fis·sure (fish-ər, -oor) *n.* 1. A narrow crack or cleft, as in a rock face. 2. A schism; a split. 3. *Anatomy.* A groove or furrow, as in the liver or brain, that divides an organ into lobes or separates it into areas. 4. *Pathology.* A cleft in the skin or mucous membrane resulting from disease. 5. A crack in the surface of a tooth.
~*v.* **fissured, -suring, -sures.** —*tr.* To cause a fissure in; split. —*intr.* To form fissures; become cleft; crack. [Middle English, fracture, opening, from Old French, from Latin *fissūra,* from *fissus.* See **fission.**]

fist (fist) *n.* 1. The hand closed tightly, with the fingers bent against the palm. 2. *Informal.* A grasping hand; a clutch: *Don't let him get his fists on this.* 3. A printer's mark, an **index** (see). 4. *Informal.* An attempt: *made a good fist of it.*
~*tr.v.* **fisted, fisting, fists.** 1. To hit with the fist. 2. *Nautical.* To grasp or handle: *fisting a slippery anchor chain.* [Middle English *fist, fust,* Old English *fȳst,* from Germanic.]

fist·ful (fist-fool) *n., pl.* **-fuls.** A handful.

fist·ic (fistik) *adj.* Of or pertaining to fighting with the fists; pugilistic. Used humorously.

fist·i·cuffs (fisti-kufs) *pl.n.* A fist fight. [Earlier *fisty cuff : fisty,* from FIST + CUFF (a blow).] —**fist·i·cuff·er** *n.*

fis·tu·la (fiss-tew-lə) *n., pl.* **-las** or **-lae** (-lee). An abnormal duct or passage from an abscess, cavity, or hollow organ to the body surface or to another hollow organ. [Middle English, from Latin *fistula†,* pipe, tube, fistula.]

fis·tu·lous (fiss-tew-ləss) *adj.* 1. Of or resembling a fistula. 2. Tubular and hollow; reedlike. 3. Made of or containing tubular parts.

fit¹ (fit) *v.* **fitted** or *U.S. also* **fit, fitted, fitting, fits.** —*tr.* 1. To be the proper size and shape for. 2. To be appropriate or suitable to; be in keeping with. 3. To modify or adapt so as to be of the desired size or type. 4. To be in conformity with; correspond to; suit: *Let the punishment fit the crime.* 5. To render competent or qualified; prepare. 6. To equip or furnish. Used with *up* or *out.* 7. To provide a place or time for. Used with *in* or *into.* 8. To insert so as to be properly in place; install: *fit a new gearbox.* —*intr.* 1. To conform as to size and shape. 2. To be appropriate or suitable. 3. To correspond to or agree with, as with the circumstances of a given situation.

Often used with *in* or *into.* —**fit up.** *British Slang.* To incriminate (a person) falsely; frame.
~*adj.* **fitter, fittest.** 1. Suited, adapted, or adequate to a given circumstance, end, or design. 2. Appropriate; proper; fitting. 3. Rightly deserving or entitled: *not fit to live.* 4. Ready; disposed: *fit to drop from exhaustion.* 5. Physically sound, especially as a result of regular exercise.
~*n.* 1. Adjustment or alteration to a given pattern or standard. 2. The manner in which clothing fits. 3. The degree of precision with which surfaces or parts are adjusted or adapted to each other at a joint or edge.
~*adv. Informal.* In a manner likely to lead to a specified outcome: *They were laughing fit to burst.* [Middle English, probably from the past participle of *fitten†,* to marshal troops, (hence) to arrange.] —**fit·ly** *adv.* —**fit·ness** *n.*
   Synonyms: fit, suitable, proper, appropriate, apt, fitting, happy.
   Usage: In some uses of this verb in the past tense and past participle, American English prefers *fit*: *My shoes fit me last year.* British English prefers *fitted*: *My shoes fitted me last year.*

fit² *n.* 1. *Medicine.* a. A seizure or convulsion, especially one due to epilepsy. b. A sudden attack, as of coughing. 2. A sudden outburst or display of some specified emotion: *a fit of pique.* 3. A sudden period of vigorous activity. —**by** or **in fits and starts.** With irregular intervals of action and inaction; intermittently; spasmodically. [Middle English *fit,* hardship, painful experience, Old English *fitt†,* conflict.]

fit³ *n. Archaic.* A section of a poem or ballad; a canto. [Middle English *fit,* Old English *fit(t)†.*]

fitch (fich) *n.* The polecat or its fur. [Middle Dutch *fisse†.*]

fit·ful (fit-f'l) *adj.* Occurring in or characterised by intermittent periods; spasmodic; irregular. See Synonyms at **periodic.** —**fit·ful·ly** *adv.* —**fit·ful·ness** *n.*

fit·ment (fit-mənt) *n.* 1. A mechanical attachment or part. 2. *Chiefly British.* A movable item of furniture or the like; a fitting.

fit·ted (fittid) *adj.* 1. Cut for a close fit: *a fitted shirt.* 2. Cut and laid so as to fit a floor area exactly: *a fitted carpet.* 3. Forming a fixed, integral part of a structure: *fitted wardrobes.* 4. Built so that all parts harmonise with each other and fit a specified room or space.

fit·ter (fittər) *n.* 1. One who alters or adjusts garments. 2. One who installs or adjusts parts of machines or other equipment.

fit·ting (fitting) *adj.* Suitable; appropriate. See Synonyms at **fit.**
~*n.* 1. A trying-on for fit, as of clothes. 2. A small, detachable part for a machine or an apparatus. 3. *Plural.* Movable furnishings or accessories. Compare **fixture.** 4. The work of a fitter. 5. *Chiefly British.* A size of clothing or footwear. —**fit·ting·ly** *adv.* —**fit·ting·ness** *n.*

Fit·ti·pal·di (fitti-pál-di), **Emerson** (1946–). Brazilian motor-racing driver. He was twice world champion (1972 and 1974), and won the Indianapolis 500 in 1989 and 1993.

Fitz·Ger·ald (fits-jérrəld), **Edward** (1809–83). British poet and translator. His English version of the *Rubáiyát of Omar Khayyám* (1859) is by far the best known.

Fitz·ger·ald (fits-jérrəld), **Ella** (1918–96). U.S. jazz and popular singer. Her first worldwide hit came in 1938 with *A-tisket, A-tasket.* She is highly regarded as a female jazz singer.

Fitzgerald, F(rancis) Scott (Key) (1896–1940). U.S. novelist and short-story writer. After the success of his first novel, the autobiographical *This Side of Paradise* (1920), he married Zelda Sayre (1900–47). For a time he lived on the French Riviera where he wrote his best-known novel, *The Great Gatsby* (1925).

Fitzgerald, Garret (1926–). Irish politician, born in Dublin. A member of the Fine Gael Party, he was Prime Minister (1981-82) and again (1982-87).

Fitz·sim·mons (fit-símmənz, fits-), **Bob** (1862–1917). British-born New Zealand boxer. He was world middleweight champion (1891–97), world heavyweight champion (1897–99), and world light-heavyweight champion (1903–05).

Fiume. See **Rijeka.**

five (fīv) *n.* 1. a. The cardinal number that is one more than four. b. A symbol representing this, such as 5, V, or v. 2. A set made up of five persons or things. 3. a. The fifth in a series. b. A playing card marked with five pips. 4. Five parts: *cut in five.* 5. A size, as in clothing, designated as five. 6. A banknote or coin having a denomination of five. 7. Five hours after midnight or midday. [Middle English *fif, five,* Old English *fīf.*] —**five** *adj.* —**five·fold** *adj. & adv.*

five-eighth (fīv-áytth) *n. Australian & N.Z.* A rugby player positioned between the halfbacks and the three-quarters.

five-fin·ger (fīv-fing-gər) *n.* Any of several plants having compound leaves with five leaflets, such as the **cinquefoil** (see).

five-finger exercise *n.* 1. A piano exercise to develop fingering technique. 2. A simple task.

Five Nations *n.* See **Iroquois.**

five-o'clock shadow (fīv-ə-klok) *n.* The beard stubble visible on the face of a clean-shaven man by early evening.

five-pins (fīv-pinz) *n. Used with a singular verb.* An indoor bowling game common in Canada, using five pins. Also called "fivepin bowling".

fiv·er (fīvər) *n. Informal.* 1. *British.* A five-pound note. 2. *U.S.* A five-dollar bill.

fives (fīvz) *n. Used with a singular verb.* A British ball game played with the gloved hand: in Eton fives, only doubles may be played and the court is irregular with a buttress protruding from the left-hand wall. In Rugby fives, singles or doubles may be played in a four-walled court. [17th century : plural of FIVE (perhaps originally played by two teams of five each).]

five stones *n. Used with a singular verb.* Jacks played with five stones.

Five-Year Plan (fív-yéer, -yér) *n.* A programme for national economic development over a five-year period, administered by a socialist government. [Translation of Russian *pyatilyetnii plan, pyatilyetka.*]

fix (fiks) *v.* **fixed, fixing, fixes.** —*tr.* **1. a.** To place or fasten securely; attach: *fix the notice to the wall.* **b.** To set or implant permanently: *fix something in one's memory.* **2.** To put into a stable or unalterable form, as: **a.** *Chemistry.* To make (a substance) nonvolatile or solid. **b.** *Biology.* To convert (nitrogen) into stable, biologically assimilable compounds. **c.** To kill, harden, and preserve (a specimen) for microscopic study. **d.** To prevent discoloration of (a photographic image) by washing or coating with a chemical preservative. **3.** To set (one's jaw, for example) firmly. **4.** To immobilise; rivet: *fixed to the spot.* **5. a.** To direct (the gaze, for example) steadily; concentrate. **b.** To give (a person, for example) a penetrating look. **6.** To establish definitely; specify: *fix a time.* **7.** To ascribe; allot: *fixing the blame.* **8.** To restore to proper condition or functioning; set right; repair. **9.** *Chiefly U.S.* To arrange; adjust: *fix one's hair.* **10.** *Chiefly U.S. Informal.* To make ready (a meal, for example); put together; prepare. **11.** To spay or castrate (an animal). **12.** *Informal.* **a.** To take revenge upon; get even with. **b.** To deal with (a troublesome person). **c.** To put a stop to (something troublesome). **13.** To determine (a location, for example). **14.** *Informal.* To arrange the outcome of (a contest, for example) by deceitful means. —*intr.* **1.** To become fixed, firm, or secure. **2.** *U.S. Informal.* To make plans or preparations; get ready. —**be fixed for.** *Informal.* To be in a specified position with regard to: *How are we fixed for time?* —**fix on** or **upon.** To decide or agree on. —**fix up.** *Informal.* **1.** To set right; repair. **2.** To provide; equip. **3.** To assemble or prepare. **4.** To arrange: *fix up accommodation.*

~*n.* **1.** A difficult or embarrassing position; a predicament; a dilemma. **2.** The position, as of a ship or aircraft, as determined by observations or radio. **3.** *Informal.* A contest whose outcome has been fraudulently fixed: *Everyone knows the election was a fix.* **4.** *Slang.* An intravenous injection of heroin or a similar drug. **5.** *Informal.* A dose of something considered addictive: *An Englishman desperate for his fix of tea.* [Middle English *fixen,* partly from Medieval Latin *fixāre,* to fix, from Latin *fīgere* (past participle *fīxus*), to fasten, partly from Old French *fix,* fixed, from Latin *fīxus,* past participle of *fīgere.*] —**fix·a·ble** *adj.* —**fix·er** *n.*

fix·ate (fík-sayt, fik-sáyt) *v.* **-ated, -ating, -ates.** —*tr.* **1.** To make fixed, stable, or stationary. **2.** To focus one's eyes or concentrate one's attention on. **3.** *Psychology.* **a.** To cause (the libido) to be arrested at an immature stage of psychosexual development. **b.** To cause (a person) to become attached to someone or something in an immature or neurotic fashion. —*intr.* **1.** To focus or concentrate one's attention. **2.** *Psychology.* To become fixated; form a fixation.

fix·a·tion (fik-sáysh'n) *n.* **1.** The act or process of fixing or fixating. **2.** *Psychology.* A strong attachment to a person or thing; especially, such an attachment formed in childhood or infancy and persisting in immature or neurotic behaviour.

fix·a·tive (fíksətiv) *adj.* Acting to fix; tending to make permanent, firm, or stable.

~*n.* Something that fixes, protects, or preserves, especially: **1.** A liquid preservative applied to works of art, such as watercolour paintings or charcoal drawings. **2.** A fluid, such as alcohol, used to preserve and harden fresh tissue for microscopic examination. **3.** A substance mixed with perfume to prevent rapid evaporation.

fixed (fikst) *adj.* **1.** Firmly in position; stationary; unmovable. **2.** *Chemistry.* **a.** Nonvolatile: *fixed oils.* **b.** In a stable combined form: *fixed nitrogen.* **3.** Not subject to change or variation; constant: *a fixed routine.* **4.** Officially established; unchangeable: *fixed prices.* **5.** No longer developing: *The language became fixed in the 17th century.* **6.** Firmly, often dogmatically, held to: *a fixed notion.* **7.** *Informal.* Illegally prearranged as to outcome. —**fix·ed·ly** (fík-sidli) *adv.* —**fix·ed·ness** *n.*

fixed assets *pl.n.* The capital assets of a commercial enterprise, such as property or plant.

fixed head *n.* A fixed device for reading or imprinting information on a single track of magnetic tape, as in a tape recorder.

fixed idea *n.* An idea, especially an incorrect idea, held persistently and essentially unmodified despite contrary evidence or rational refutation; an idée fixe.

fixed oil *n.* A nonvolatile oil; especially, a fatty oil from a plant as distinguished from an essential oil.

fixed point *n.* **1.** *Physics.* A reference temperature used in defining a practical temperature scale at standard pressure, usually a boiling, melting, or triple point of some pure substance, such as water, helium, or gold. **2.** *Mathematics.* A point that is not changed by a given transformation.

fixed-point (fíkst-póynt) *adj. Mathematics.* Designating or pertaining to a system of representing numbers by a single string of digits, with the position of a digit in the string determining the power of the base of the number system. Compare **floating-point.**

fixed-point theorem *n. Mathematics.* The principle that for all points within a closed cell, for example a circle, polygon, sphere, polyhedron, or the like, any transformation that takes all points of the set into points of the same set will leave at least one point fixed.

fixed star *n.* A star so distant from the Earth that its movements can be measured only over long periods of time. The term was used originally to distinguish such stars from wandering stars (planets).

fix·er (fíksər) *n.* **1.** A fixative agent used in developing photographic prints. **2.** *Informal.* One who arranges; especially, one who makes fraudulent arrangements in an attempt to change the normal outcome of a contest, political process, or the like.

fix·ings (fíksingz) *pl.n. U.S. Informal.* Accessories; trimmings.

fix·i·ty (fíksəti) *n., pl.* **-ties.** **1.** The quality or condition of being fixed; immutability; stability. **2.** Something that is fixed.

fix·ture (fíks-chər) *n.* **1.** Something securely fixed in place. **2.** Something attached as a permanent appendage, apparatus, or appliance: *plumbing fixtures.* **3.** *Law.* A chattel considered to belong to or be part of a property. Compare **fitting. 4.** A person or thing long associated with or established in a position or function. **5.** *Chiefly British.* **a.** A sporting or social event. **b.** The date appointed for such an event. [Variant of obsolete *fixure* (influenced by MIXTURE), Late Latin *fixūra,* from Latin *fīxus.* See **fix.**]

fiz·gig[1] (fíz-gig) *n.* **1.** A frivolous, giddy woman. **2.** A firework that produces a hissing or sputtering sound. [Earlier *fisgigg* : probably obsolete *fise,* breaking wind, fart, probably from Scandinavian + GIG (carriage, original sense, "frivolous woman").]

fiz·gig[2]. Variant of **fishgig.**

fizz (fiz) *intr.v.* **fizzed, fizzing, fizzes.** **1.** To make a hissing or bubbling sound. **2.** To effervesce. Used of drinks.

~*n.* **1.** A hissing or bubbling sound. **2.** Effervescence. **3.** Effervescent drink, especially lemonade or champagne. [Imitative.]

fiz·zle (fízz'l) *intr.v.* **-zled, -zling, -zles.** **1.** To make a hissing or sputtering sound. **2.** *Informal.* To fail or die out, especially after a hopeful beginning. Usually used with *out.*

~*n.* **1.** A fizzling sound. **2.** *Informal.* A failure; a fiasco. [Probably frequentative of obsolete *fist,* to break wind. See **feist.**]

fjeld (fyeld) *n.* A high, barren plateau in the Scandinavian countries. [Danish, from Old Norse *fjall,* mountain.]

fjord. Variant of **fiord.**

fl fluid.

fL foot-lambert.

fl. **1.** floor. **2.** floruit. **3.** fluid.

Fla. Florida.

flab (flab) *n.* Loose, unwanted fatty tissue on the body. [Back-formation from FLABBY.]

flab·ber·gast (flábbər-gaast || -gast) *tr.v.* **-gasted, -gasting, -gasts.** To confound or overwhelm with astonishment; astound. See Synonyms at **surprise.** [18th century (slang) : perhaps humorous blend of FLABBY + AGHAST.]

flab·by (flábbi) *adj.* **-bier, -biest.** **1.** Lacking firmness; loose and yielding to the touch; flaccid: *flabby skin.* **2.** Obese. **3.** Lacking force or vitality; feeble; ineffectual. [Variant of *flappy,* from FLAP.] —**flab·bi·ly** *adv.* —**flab·bi·ness** *n.*

fla·bel·late (flə-bél-ət, -it, -ayt) *adj.* Also **fla·bel·li·form** (-i-fawrm) *Biology.* Fan-shaped. [Latin *flābellum,* fan. See **flabellum.**]

fla·bel·lum (flə-béllәm) *n., pl.* **-bella** (-béllə). **1.** A fan-shaped biological structure. **2.** A fan used in certain religious ceremonies. [Latin *flābellum,* small fan, diminutive of *flābrum* (usually in plural *flābra*), gust of wind, from *flāre,* to blow.]

flac·cid (flássid, flák-sid) *adj.* Lacking firmness; soft and limp; flabby: *"His mouth, pink and flaccid, trembled sometimes like the underlip of a cow."* (H.E. Bates). [French *flaccide,* from Latin *flaccidus,* from *flaccus*†, hanging, flabby.] —**flac·cid·i·ty** (flə-siddəti, flak-), **flac·cid·ness** *n.* —**flac·cid·ly** *adv.*

flack. Variant of **flak.**

fla·con (flák-ən, -on, fla-kóɴ) *n.* A small stoppered bottle, as for perfume. [French, from Old French *fla(s)con,* FLAGON.]

flag[1] (flag) *n.* **1.** A piece of cloth or bunting varying in size, colour, and design, used as a symbol, standard, signal, and especially as a national emblem. **2.** A small paper badge, often resembling a flag, sold on a flag day. **3.** A ship carrying the flag of an admiral; a flagship. **4.** The masthead of a newspaper. **5.** A distinctively shaped or marked tail, as of a dog or deer. **6.** *British.* A metal plate on the lever of a taximeter raised or lowered to show when a taxi has been hired. —**fly the flag.** *Informal.* To represent one's country in a particular field or activity with exuberance and pride.

~*tr.v.* **flagged, flagging, flags.** **1.** To decorate with a flag or flags. **2.** To signal or communicate (a message) with or as if with a flag. **3.** To mark with a symbol for purposes of identification. —**flag down.** To signal (a vehicle) to stop. [16th century : perhaps from obsolete adjective *flag*†, hanging limp, drooping.] —**flag·ger** *n.*

flag[2] *n.* Any of various plants having long bladelike leaves, especially the sweet flag (*Acorus calamus*). [Middle English *flagge*†, rush, reed.]

flag[3] *intr.v.* **flagged, flagging, flags.** **1.** To hang limply; droop. **2.** To become tired; decline in vigour. **3.** To decline in interest; grow dull. [16th century : akin to obsolete adjective *flag*†, drooping.]

flag[4] *n.* **1.** A slab of flagstone used for paving. **2.** *Geology.* **Flagstone** *(see).*

~*tr.v.* **flagged, flagging, flags.** To pave with flags. [Middle English *flagge,* piece of turf, sod, probably from Old Norse *flaga,* slab of stone.]

flag captain *n.* The captain of a flagship.

flag day *n.* A day on which collections in aid of charity are held and badges given to contributors. Also *Australian* "button day".

Flag Day *n.* In the United States, an annual holiday on June 14 celebrating the adoption in 1777 of the national flag.

flag·el·lant (flájələnt, flə-jéllənt) *n.* One who whips; especially, one who scourges himself by way of religious discipline or for sexual stimulation. [Latin *flagellāns* (stem *flagellant-*), present participle of *flagellāre,* to FLAGELLATE.] **—flag·el·lant** *adj.*

flag·el·late (flájə-layt) *tr.v.* **-lated, -lating, -lates.** To whip or flog; scourge.
~*adj.* **1.** Having a flagellum or flagella, as do unicellular animals of the class Flagellata (or Mastigophora). **2.** Resembling or having the form of a flagellum; whiplike.
~*n.* A flagellate organism. [Latin *flagellāre,* to whip, scourge, from *flagellum,* diminutive of *flagrum,* whip.] **—flag·el·la·tion** (flájə-láysh'n) *n.*

fla·gel·li·form (flə-jélli-fawrm) *adj.* Long, thin, and tapering; whip-shaped: *flagelliform appendages.* [Latin *flagellum,* small whip (see **flagellate**) + -FORM.]

flag·el·lin (flə-jéllin) *n.* A protein that is a constituent of flagella. [FLAGELLA + -IN.]

fla·gel·lum (flə-jélləm, fla-) *n., pl.* **-gella** (-jéllə). *Biology.* A long, threadlike appendage; especially, one of the whiplike extensions of certain cells or unicellular organisms, usually functioning in locomotion. [New Latin, from Latin, small whip. See **flagellate.**] **—fla·gel·lar** *adj.*

flag·eo·let (flájə-lét, -lay) *n.* **1.** A small flutelike instrument having a cylindrical mouthpiece, four fingerholes, and two thumbholes. **2.** A haricot bean. [French, diminutive of Old French *flajol,* from Vulgar Latin *flabeolum* (unattested), flute, from Latin *flāre,* to blow.]

flag·ging[1] (flágging) *adj.* **1.** Drooping; languid. **2.** Declining; weakening. **—flag·ging·ly** *adv.*

flag·ging[2] *n.* A pavement laid with flagstones.

fla·gi·tious (flə-jishəs) *adj.* **1.** Guilty of or addicted to extremely brutal or cruel crimes; vicious. **2.** Shockingly evil; infamous; scandalous; heinous. [Middle English *flagicious,* from Latin *flāgitiōsus,* from *flāgitium,* noisy protest against one's conduct, scandal, shameful act, from *flāgitāre,* to demand fiercely.] **—fla·gi·tious·ly** *adv.* **—fla·gi·tious·ness** *n.*

flag·man (flág-mən) *n., pl.* **-men** (-mən). One who signals with or carries a flag.

flag of convenience *n.* A flag of a country that offers ship owners financial, and in some cases legal, advantages to register their ships in that country.

flag officer *n.* A naval officer holding the rank of rear-admiral, vice-admiral, or admiral.

flag of truce *n.* A white flag brought or displayed to an enemy as an invitation to a conference or a signal of surrender.

flag·on (flággən) *n.* **1.** A vessel for holding wine or the like, usually made of metal or pottery and having a handle and spout. **2.** The quantity of liquid contained in such a vessel. **3.** A large bottle, especially of cider. [Middle English *flagon, flakon,* from Old French *fla(s)con,* from Late Latin *flascō* (stem *flascōn-*), bottle, FLASK.]

flag·pole (flág-pōl) *n.* A pole on which a flag is hoisted; a flagstaff.

flag rank *n.* The rank of a flag officer.

fla·grant (fláy-grənt || flá-) *adj.* **1.** Outstanding or conspicuous in being wrong or evil; notorious; shocking: *a flagrant miscarriage of justice.* **2.** *Obsolete.* Flaming; blazing. **—See Synonyms at outrageous. —See Usage note at blatant.** [Latin *flagrāns* (stem *flagrant-*), present participle of *flagrāre,* to burn, blaze.] **—fla·gran·cy, fla·grance** *n.* **—fla·grant·ly** *adv.*

Synonyms: *flagrant, glaring, gross, rank.*

flag·ship (flág-ship) *n.* **1.** A ship bearing the flag of a fleet or squadron commander. **2.** The best or largest ship or aeroplane operated by a passenger line. **3.** A company's most prestigious product.

Flag·stad (flág-stad, -staa; *Norwegian* flák-staa), **Kirsten (Malfrid)** (1895–1962). Norwegian soprano, celebrated for her performances of Wagner's heroines, such as Brünnhilde in *Der Ring des Nibelungen* and Kundry in *Parsifal.*

flag·staff (flág-staaf || -staf) *n., pl.* **-staffs** or **-staves** (-stayvz). A flagpole.

flag·stone (flág-stōn) *n.* **1.** A flat, natural or artificial stone used in paving. **2.** *Geology.* Hard, fine-grained sedimentary rock easily split into layers or large slabs, usually a sandstone or sandy limestone. In both senses, also called "flag". [FLAG + STONE.]

flag·wav·ing (flág-wayving) *n.* A display of patriotic fervour.

Fla·her·ty (fláir-ti, fláa-hə-ti, flá-hə-), **Robert (Joseph)** (1884–1951). U.S. film director and explorer. His films, including *Nanook of the North* (1921) and *Moana* (1926), were the first major documentaries. They greatly influenced documentary film-making.

flail (flayl) *n.* A manual threshing device, consisting of a long wooden handle or staff and a shorter, free-swinging stick attached to its end.
~*v.* **flailed, flailing, flails.** **—***tr.* **1.** To thresh using a flail. **2.** To beat, thrash, or strike with or as with a flail. **—***intr.* To move about erratically; thresh about: *arms flailing.* [Middle English *fleil, flail,* from Old English *flegil* (unattested) and Old French *flaiel,* both from Latin *flagellum,* diminutive of *flagrum,* whip.]

flair (flair) *n.* **1.** A natural talent or aptitude; a bent; a knack: *a flair for interior decorating.* **2.** Instinctive discernment; keenness. **3.** A natural and exuberant sense of style. [French, "sense of smell", from Old French, from *flairer,* to scent, smell, from Vulgar Latin *flāgrāre* (unattested), from Latin *frāgrāre,* to emit a smell.]

flak, flack (flak) *n.* **1.** Antiaircraft artillery. **2.** The bursting shells fired from such artillery. **3.** *Slang.* Excessive criticism; abuse. [German *Flak,* short for *Fl(ieger)a(bwehr)k(anone),* "aircraft defence gun".]

flake[1] (flayk) *n.* **1.** A flat, thin piece or layer; a chip. **2.** A small piece of something that has been peeled, rubbed, or sliced off: *flakes of fish.* **3.** A small, crystalline particle of snow. **4.** *Archaeology.* A piece of stone that has been chipped off for use as a tool.
~*v.* **flaked, flaking, flakes.** **—***tr.* **1.** To break flakes from; take off in flakes; chip. **2.** To cover, mark, or overlay with or as if with flakes; fleck. **3.** To form into flakes: *flaked almonds.* **—***intr.* To come off in flakes; chip off. **—flake out.** *Informal.* To fall asleep or become unconscious; collapse from fatigue or exhaustion. [Middle English, perhaps from Scandinavian, akin to Norwegian *flak.*] **—flak·er** *n.*

flake[2] *n.* A frame or platform for drying fish or other produce. [Middle English *fleke,* from Old Norse *fleki, flaki.*]

flake white *n.* A pigment made of flakes of white lead.

flak jacket *n.* A bulletproof waistcoat.

flak·y (fláyki) *adj.* **-ier, -iest.** **1.** Made of or resembling flakes. **2.** Forming or tending to form flakes or thin, crisp fragments. **3.** *Chiefly U.S. Informal.* Offbeat; off-the-wall. **—flak·i·ly** *adv.* **—flak·i·ness** *n.*

flaky pastry *n.* A type of pastry resembling puff pastry but less rich and firm in texture.

flam[1] (flam) *n. Chiefly Regional & Informal.* **1.** A lie or hoax; a deception. **2.** Nonsense; drivel. [Short for FLIMFLAM.]

flam[2] *n.* A drumbeat produced by two almost simultaneous strokes. [Perhaps imitative.]

flam·bé (fla'ám-bay, flóm-, flám-; *French* floN-báy) *adj.* Served covered in flaming brandy or other spirit. Said of food. [French, flamed.]

flam·beau (flám-bō) *n., pl.* **-beaux** or **-beaus** (-bōz, -bō). A flaming torch. [French, from Old French, from *flambe, flamble,* "small flame", from Latin *flammula,* diminutive of *flamma,* FLAME.]

Flam·bor·ough Head (flám-bərə, -brə). Rugged promontory on the coast of Humberside, northeastern England. The high cliffs at its tip are a notable breeding-ground for sea birds.

flam·boy·ant (flam-bóy-ənt) *adj.* **1.** Given to or characterised by elaborate ostentation; showy: *a flamboyant dresser.* **2.** Richly coloured; vivid; resplendent. **3.** *Architecture.* Pertaining to or designating the style of 15th- and 16th-century French Gothic architecture characterised by waving lines and flamelike forms. **—See Synonyms at ornate.**
~*n.* A tree, the royal poinciana *(see).* [French, from Old French, present participle of *flamboyer, flambeiier,* to blaze, from *flambe, flamble,* small flame. See **flambeau.**] **—flam·boy·ance, flam·boy·an·cy** *n.* **—flam·boy·ant·ly** *adv.*

flame (flaym) *n.* **1. a.** The zone of burning gases and fine suspended matter associated with the combustion of a substance. **b.** Broadly, a hot, luminous mass of burning gas or vapour, typically tongue-shaped and flickering. **2.** *Often plural.* The condition of active, blazing combustion: *burst into flames.* **3.** Something flamelike in motion, brilliance, intensity, or shape. **4.** A violent or intense passion; a burning emotion. **5.** A reddish orange. **6.** *Informal.* A sweetheart: *an old flame.* **—See Synonyms at flame.**
~*v.* **flamed, flaming, flames.** **—***intr.* **1.** To burn brightly; give off flames or a flame; blaze. Often used with *up.* **2.** To colour or glow suddenly. **3. a.** To display a violent or intense emotion: *flaming with indignation.* **b.** To burst out with violent and intense expression: *The people's anger flamed up.* **—***tr.* **1.** To burn, ignite, or scorch. **2.** *Obsolete.* To inflame. [Middle English *flaume, flam(m)e,* from Old French *flam(m)e,* from Latin *flamma.*] **—flam·y** *adj.*

flame cell *n.* A hollow cell in flatworms and certain other invertebrates that contains cilia and functions as an organ of excretion.

flame gun *n.* A portable gas or oil burner used to destroy weeds.

fla·men (fláy-men, -mən) *n., pl.* **-mens** or **flamines** (fláy-mi-neez, flámmi-) A priest or servant of a Roman deity. [Latin *flāmen;* akin to Sanskrit *Brahmán,* BRAHMA.]

fla·men·co (flə-méng-kō) *n., pl.* **-cos.** **1.** A dance style of the Andalusian Gypsies characterised by forceful, often impassioned rhythms. **2.** The guitar music that usually accompanies this dance style.
~*adj.* Of or pertaining to such dancing or music: *a flamenco guitar.* [Spanish *flamenco,* Gypsy living in Andalusia, resembling a Gypsy, Flemish, from Middle Dutch *Vlāming,* FLEMING.]

flame-out (fláym-owt) *n.* Failure of a jet aircraft engine in flight.

flame-proof (fláym-prōof || -prōof) *adj.* **1.** Able to withstand direct contact with flame; specifically, able to be used over a gas flame. Compare **ovenproof.** **2.** Insulated to prevent sparks igniting any surrounding gas. Said of electrical apparatus.

flame test *n. Chemistry.* A simple qualitative test for the presence of certain metals by holding the sample in a flame and observing characteristic colours produced. A blue flame, for example, indicates the presence of copper.

flamethrower (fláym-thrō-ər) *n.* A weapon that projects ignited incendiary fuel, such as napalm, in a steady stream.

flame tree *n.* Any of several trees with red or orange flowers, such as *Butea frondosa,* of India and Burma, or *Brachychiton acerifolium,* of Australia.

flam·ing (fláyming) *adj.* **1.** On fire; in flames; ablaze. **2.** Brilliant; splendid; flamelike. **3.** Intense; passionate: *a flaming row.* **4.** *Informal.* Used as an intensive to express annoyance: *a flaming nuisance.*
~*adv. Informal.* Used as an intensive to express annoyance: *It's flaming stupid!* **—flam·ing·ly** *adv.*

fla·min·go (flə-míng-gō, fla-) *n., pl.* **-gos** or **-goes.** **1.** Any of several large, gregarious wading birds of the family Phoenicopteridae, of tropical regions, having reddish or pinkish plumage, long legs, a long, flexible neck, and a bill turned downwards at the tip. **2.** Moderate pinkish orange. [Perhaps Portuguese *flamengo,* from Provençal *flamenc,* probably "fire bird" (from its bright plumage) : *flama,* flame, from Latin *flamma* + *-enc,* from Germanic *-ing,* suffix denoting "belonging to".]

Fla·min·i·an Way (flə-mínni-ən). Great Roman road, the chief transport route between Rome and the Adriatic. Construction was begun by Caius Flaminius in *c.* 220 B.C. and the original road ran to Ariminum (Rimini), a distance of about 335 kilometres (208 miles).

flam·ma·ble (flámmə-b'l) *adj.* Easily ignitable and capable of burning with rapidity; inflammable. [Latin *flammāre,* to blaze, from *flamma,* FLAME.] **—flam·ma·bil·i·ty** (-bílləti) *n.* **—flam·ma·ble** *n.*

Usage: *Flammable* and *inflammable* have the same meaning of "highly combustible". The prefix *in-* is an intensive here, and not an expression of negation, so that *inflammable* really means *inflame* + *able.* Something that cannot be burned is *nonflammable.* Because of the widespread use of the prefix *in-* with a negative meaning, however (*invisible, incapacity*), *inflammable* is open to be interpreted as if it were negative. For this reason, *flammable* is the preferred term in technical writing, and in contexts where people are being warned. In figurative usage, only *inflammable* is used: *an inflammable nature* or *temper.*

Flam·steed (flám-steed), **John** (1646–1719). English astronomer. Under the patronage of Charles II, he established the Royal Observatory at Greenwich, and in 1675 became the first astronomer royal.

flan (flan || flon) *n.* **1.** An open tart with a sweet or savoury filling, often containing eggs, cheese, or cream. **2.** A metal disc to be stamped as a coin; a blank. [French, from Old French *fla(o)n,* from Germanic.]

flanch[1] (flanch) *n.* Also **flaunch** (flawnch). A slope of cement or similar material surrounding a structure such as a chimney top to drain off rainwater.
~v. **flanched, flanching, flanches.** Also **flaunch, flaunched, flaunching, flaunches.** *—tr.* To provide with a flanch. *—intr.* To have a flanch. [18th century : perhaps from Old French *flanchir,* from *flanche,* variant of *flanc,* FLANK.]

flanch[2] *n.* Either of two inward-curving segments at each side of a heraldic field.

Flan·ders (flaán-dərz || flán-). Former county of the Low Countries, lying west of the river Schelde. It included the present East and West Flanders provinces of Belgium, the Nord and Pas-de-Calais départements of France (where it is known as French Flanders), and a small part of Zeeland province in the Netherlands. During the Middle Ages the county was the centre of the rich Flemish cloth industry. The area saw heavy fighting in both World Wars.

Flanders poppy *n.* The **corn poppy** *(see).*

flâ·neur (flaan-ör) *n. French.* An aimless idler.

flange (flanj) *n.* **1.** A protruding rim, edge, rib, or collar, as on a wheel or a pipe shaft, used to strengthen an object, hold it in place, or attach it to another object. **2.** The flat face of an I- or H-girder.
~tr.v. **flanged, flanging, flanges.** To furnish with a flange. [17th century : perhaps from obsolete *flange,* to widen, from Old French *flangir,* variant of *flanchir.* See **flanch, flank.**]

flank (flangk) *n.* **1. a.** The section of flesh between the last rib and the hip; a side. **b.** A cut of meat from this section of an animal. **2.** The side of the thigh. **3.** A side or lateral part: *the flank of a mountain.* **4. a.** The right or left side of a military formation: *attack on both flanks.* **b.** The right or left side of a bastion.
~tr.v. **flanked, flanking, flanks. 1.** To protect or guard the flank of. **2.** To menace, attack, or manoeuvre around the flank of. **3.** To be placed or situated at the flank or side of. [Middle English *fla(u)nke,* from Old French *flanc,* from Frankish *hlanca* (unattested), side.]

flank·er (fláng-kər) *n.* **1.** One that flanks. **2.** A division of soldiers guarding the flank of a marching column. **3.** A fortification attached to the side or flank of another part. **4.** *Informal.* An unscrupulous trick.

flan·nel (flánn'l) *n.* **1.** A soft woven cloth of wool or of a blend of wool and cotton or synthetics. **2.** Flannelette. **3.** *Plural.* Clothing, especially trousers, made of flannel. **4.** *British.* A facecloth. **5.** *British Informal.* Insincere talk intended to deceive; flattery or bluff.
~tr.v. **flannelled** or *U.S.* **-neled, -nelling** or *U.S.* **-neling, -nels. 1.** To wash, clean, or rub with flannel. **2.** To wrap in flannel. **3.** *British Informal.* To deceive by insincere flattery or evasive talk. [Middle English, probably from *flanen,* sackcloth, from Welsh *gwlanen,* "woollen cloth", from *gwlān,* wool. Informal senses (insincere talk), probably with reference to the Welsh, with whom the cloth was associated (as in Shakespeare's *Merry Wives of Windsor,* Act V, scene 5.] **—flan·nel·ly** *adj.*

flan·nel·board (flánn'l-bawrd || -bōrd) *n.* A piece of board covered in flannel or similar material to which paper or cloth cutouts may be attached, as in making a collage or as a visual aid in teaching.

flan·nel·ette (flánn'l-ét) *n.* A cotton cloth processed to resemble flannel.

flannel flower *n.* An Australian plant of the genus *Actinotus,* having white, flannel-like bracts.

flap (flap) *v.* **flapped, flapping, flaps.** *—tr.* **1.** To wave (wings or arms, for example) up and down; beat. **2.** To cause to wave or undulate; agitate. **3.** To hit with something broad and flat; slap. **4.** *Phonetics.* To produce (an r sound) while bringing the tongue rapidly in contact with the alveolar ridge or uvula. *—intr.* **1.** To wave about while fixed at one edge or corner to something stationary; flutter. **2.** To wave arms or wings up and down; beat the air. **3.** To fly by beating the air with the wings. **4.** *Informal.* To become agitated or nervous.
~n. **1.** A flat covering piece usually intended to double over and protect or seal something, as on an envelope, pocket, or hat. **2.** The action of waving or fluttering; flapping. **3.** The sound of flapping. **4.** A blow given with something flat; a slap. **5.** *Aeronautics.* A variable control surface on the trailing edge of an aircraft wing, used primarily to increase lift or drag. **6.** *Surgery.* Tissue that has been partially detached and used in plastic surgery to fill an adjacent defect or to cover the cut end of a bone after amputation. **7.** *Phonetics.* A flapped (r) sound. **8.** *Informal.* A condition of agitated distress. [Middle English *flappen* (probably imitative).]

flap·doo·dle (fláp-dōōd'l) *n. Slang.* Foolish talk; nonsense. [Origin obscure.]

flap·jack (fláp-jak) *n.* **1.** A sweet, crunchy biscuit made from rolled oats, syrup, and butter. **2.** *Chiefly U.S.* A pancake. [FLAP (to toss) + *Jack* (name).]

flap·per (fláppər) *n.* **1.** One that flaps, such as a device for swatting flies. **2.** A flipper or similar broad, flexible part. **3.** *Informal.* A young woman, especially one in the 1920s who flaunted her disdain for conventional dress and behaviour.

flare (flair) *v.* **flared, flaring, flares.** *—intr.* **1.** To flame up with a bright, wavering light; blaze unsteadily. **2.** To burst into intense, short-lived flame. Often used with *up.* **3.** To widen gradually, as a skirt or vase might. **4.** *Metallurgy.* To give off burning gas. Used of a molten metal. *—tr.* **1.** To cause (something) to flare. **2.** To signal with flares. **3.** To burn off (gas given off at a wellhead). Used with *off.*
~n. **1.** A brief, wavering blaze of light. **2.** A device that can be fired into the sky to produce a bright light for signalling, illumination, or identification. **3.** An outbreak, as of emotion or activity. **4.** A gradual widening: *trousers with a slight flare.* **5.** *Photography.* A lens reflection or the resultant film fogging. **6.** Reddening of the skin due to infection, irritation, or an allergic reaction. **7.** *Astronomy.* A localised outburst of radiation from the surface of the Sun. —See Synonyms at **blaze.** [Origin unknown.]

flare·back (flaír-bak) *n.* A flame produced in the breech of a gun by ignition of residual gases.

flare star *n. Astronomy.* A star that shows sudden, short-lived increases in brightness. Flares can increase the luminosity of a star by several magnitudes for a few minutes.

flare up *intr.v.* **1.** To display sudden intense emotion or passion. **2. a.** To break out suddenly or undergo a sudden increase in intensity. Used of wars, quarrels, or the like. **b.** To become active suddenly, causing reddening of the skin: *her rash has flared up again.*

flare-up (flaír-up) *n.* **1.** A sudden outbreak of flame or light. **2.** An outburst or eruption: *a flare-up of anger.* **3.** An intensification of something hitherto mild or dormant: *a flare-up of old antagonisms.*

flash (flash) *v.* **flashed, flashing, flashes.** *—intr.* **1.** To appear or emerge suddenly in, or as if in, bright flame. **2.** To appear or be perceived for an instant only. **3.** To be lighted intermittently; sparkle; scintillate. **4.** To move rapidly. **5.** To be suddenly perceived by the mind or sight. **6.** To flow rapidly; rush. Used of water. **7.** *Informal.* To expose oneself indecently. *—tr.* **1. a.** To cause (light) to appear suddenly or in intermittent bursts. **b.** To cause to shine or reflect light briefly: *flashed his torch at the intruders.* **c.** To cause to burst into flame. **d.** To reflect (light). **e.** To reflect light from (a surface). **2. a.** To expose to a flash or flashes of light. **b.** To expose to a flash of radiation. **3.** To display as if by a flash of light: *Her eyes flashed hatred at me.* **4. a.** To send (a message) with light signals. **b.** To signal to (another driver) with a flash of one's car headlights. **5. a.** To communicate (information) at great speed. **b.** To display (a picture, for example) rapidly on a screen. **6.** To reveal (something concealed) briefly. **7.** *Informal.* To display ostentatiously; flaunt. **8. a.** To fill suddenly with a rush of water. **b.** To sweep away (a boat, for example) on a rush of water. **9.** To cover (glass) with a thin layer of metal or different coloured glass, for example. **10.** To cause (a liquid) to boil and evaporate through direct contact with a hot surface. **11.** To provide (a roof, for example) with flashing.
~n. **1.** A sudden, brief, intense display of light. **2.** A sudden manifestation of a quality, such as insight or wit. **3.** A split second; an instant: *in a flash.* **4.** A brief, important news dispatch or transmission. Also called "newsflash". **5. a.** Instantaneous illumination for photography. **b.** Any equipment or device, such as a flashbulb, flashgun, or flash lamp, used to produce such illumination. **6.** In a film, a brief display of a scene. **7.** *Informal.* A sudden brief display: *He gave me a flash of his wallet.* **8.** *Chiefly British.* A patch of coloured cloth on a military uniform for identification. **9.** A patch of colouring on an animal's coat. **10.** A sudden heavy onrush of water, deliberately released to take a boat over a shallow stretch of water. —See Synonyms at **blaze, moment.** **—flash in the pan. 1.** An explosion of the gunpowder in the pan of a flintlock rifle that does not set off the charge. **2.** Someone or something that has merely transitory interest, success, or appeal.
~adj. **1.** Happening suddenly or very quickly: *flash freezing.* **2.** *Informal.* Ostentatious or showy: *a flash car.* **3.** Counterfeit; bogus. **4.** Of or pertaining to gamblers and followers of racing and boxing. **5.** Of or pertaining to thieves, confidence men, and underworld figures. [Middle English *flashen,* to splash, flame up (imitative).]

Synonyms: *flash, gleam, glance, glint, sparkle, glitter, glisten, shimmer, glimmer, twinkle, spark, scintillate.*

flash back *intr.v.* To interrupt a story in order to portray or recount an incident or scene from the past; cut back.

flash·back (flásh-bak) *n.* In a film, novel, or the like, a depiction of events belonging to an earlier part of the story, or a reversion to previously depicted events.

flash·board (flásh-bawrd ‖ -bôrd) *n.* Boarding that extends above a dam to increase the depth of water held.

flash·bulb (flásh-bulb) *n.* A glass bulb filled with finely shredded aluminium or magnesium foil that is ignited by electricity to produce a short-duration, high-intensity light flash for taking photographs. Also called "photoflash".

flash burn *n.* A burn resulting from brief exposure to intense radiation.

flash·card (flásh-kaard) *n.* Any of a set or integrated series of cards used for brief, usually successive, display; especially, such a card used by a teacher as a visual aid in spelling or other exercises.

flash·cube (flásh-kewb) *n.* A small cube that contains four flash bulbs and that rotates automatically when a picture is taken with a camera to which it is attached.

flash·er (flásher) *n.* 1. One that flashes. 2. A device that automatically switches an electric lamp off and on, such as a car's direction indicator. 3. *Informal.* A man who indecently exposes himself.

flash flood *n.* A sudden, violent flood in a normally dry valley after a heavy rain.

flash·gun (flásh-gun) *n.* A photographic apparatus that holds and electrically triggers a flash bulb.

flash·ing (fláshing) *n.* Sheet metal or weather stripping used to reinforce and weatherproof the joints and angles of a roof.

flash lamp *n.* An electric lamp for producing a high-intensity light of very short duration for use in photography.

flash·light (flásh-līt) *n.* 1. *Chiefly U.S.* A **torch** (sense 2). 2. A brief, brilliant flood of light from a photographic lamp. 3. A bright, flashing beam or light, as of a beacon or signal lamp.

flash·o·ver (flásh-ōvər) *n.* An unintended electric arc, as between two pieces of apparatus.

flash photolysis *n.* A technique for studying the spectra and reactions of short-lived free radicals by subjecting a sample, usually a gas in a glass or quartz tube, to a brief intense pulse of light and recording an absorption spectrum using a separate continuous light source.

flashpoint *n.* 1. The lowest temperature at which the vapour of a combustible liquid can be made to ignite momentarily in air. 2. The point at which a contained situation erupts or may erupt.

flash tube *n.* A gas discharge tube used in an electronic flash to produce a brief, intense pulse of light.

flash unit *n.* 1. An electronic flash system containing both power supply and flash tube in a single compact unit. 2. **a.** A flash gun. **b.** A flash gun and reflector.

flash·y (fláshi) *adj.* **-i·er, -i·est.** 1. Giving a momentary or superficial impression of brilliance. 2. Cheap-looking and showy; tastelessly ostentatious. —**flash·i·ly** *adv.* —**flash·i·ness** *n.*

flask (flaask ‖ flask) *n.* 1. A small bottle or other container with a narrow neck and usually a cap, especially: **a.** A **hip flask** (see). **b.** A **vacuum flask** (see). **c.** A container or case for carrying gunpowder or shot. **d.** A vial or round long-necked bottle for laboratory use. 2. A frame for holding a sand mould in a foundry. [Old French *flasque, flaske,* from Late Latin *flascō, flasca,* probably from Germanic *flaska-* (unattested).]

flas·ket (fláaskit, flá-) *n.* 1. A long, shallow basket. 2. *Rare.* A small flask. [Old North French *flasquet,* diminutive of Old French *flasque,* FLASK.]

flat[1] (flat) *adj.* **flatter, flattest.** 1. Having no curves; of zero curvature. 2. Extending or lying completely in a plane, especially a horizontal plane; planar. 3. **a.** Having a smooth, even, level surface. **b.** Not hilly; generally level: *a flat landscape.* **c.** Lying closely against another surface: *clasped it flat against his chest.* **d.** Extended or levelled, after being rolled up, folded, or the like. 4. Not deep or high; shallow; low: *a flat box.* 5. Lying prone; prostrate. 6. Unequivocal; unqualified; absolute: *a flat refusal.* 7. Fixed; unvarying: *a flat rate.* 8. Neither more nor less; to the exact measure: *ten minutes flat.* 9. Uninteresting; dull: *the party was rather flat.* 10. **a.** Lacking zest or animation. **b.** Having lost a characteristic effervescence; dead; stale. Said of beverages. 11. **a.** Deflated. Said of a tyre. **b.** Electrically discharged. Said of a battery or accumulator. 12. Commercially inactive; sluggish: *a flat market.* 13. Unmodulated; monotonous: *a flat voice.* 14. **a.** Executed with an even thickness of paint; lacking relief. **b.** Lacking contrast in tint or shading; uniform. Said of a painting or photograph. 15. Matt; not glossy. Said of a paint. 16. *Music.* **a.** Below the intended pitch. **b.** Designating a key with one or more flats in the signature. **c.** Being half a step lower than the corresponding natural key: *the key of B flat.* Compare **sharp.** 17. Designating the vowel *a* as pronounced in *bad* or *cat.* 18. With low heels. Said of shoes. 19. Having little or no arch. Said of a foot. 20. *Chiefly British.* **a.** Designating horse races run over level ground without obstacles. **b.** Concerning such races or their organisation: *the flat season.* —See Synonyms at **level.**
~*adv.* 1. **a.** Horizontally; level with the ground. **b.** Prostrate. 2. So as to be flat. 3. Directly; completely: *He went flat against the rules.* 4. *Music.* Below the intended pitch: *sing flat.* —**fall flat.** To fail:

Our plans fell flat. —**flat out.** *Informal.* 1. With the utmost effort or vigour. 2. Prostrate. 3. Exhausted.
~*n.* 1. A flat surface or part. 2. **a.** *Often plural.* A stretch of level ground: *the salt flats.* **b.** Low-lying, partly flooded ground such as tideland. **c.** A shallow; a shoal. 3. Stage scenery on a movable wooden frame. 4. The inner side of the extended hand. 5. *Chiefly U.S.* A deflated tyre. 6. *Music.* **a.** A sign (♭) affixed to a note to indicate that it is to be lowered by half a tone below its natural pitch. **b.** A note that is lowered in this way: *B flat.* In this sense, compare **sharp.** 7. *Chiefly British. Often capital* F. Flat racing or the flat racing season. Preceded by *the.*
~*tr.v.* **flatted, flatting, flats.** 1. To make flat; flatten. 2. *Music. U.S.* To lower (a note) by a semitone. [Middle English, from Old Norse *flatr,* from Germanic.] —**flat·ly** *adv.* —**flat·ness** *n.*

flat[2] *n. Chiefly British.* A self-contained place of residence, usually on a single floor of a building.
~*v.* **flatted, flatting, flats.** —*tr.* To divide (a building) into separate flats. —*intr. Australian & N.Z.* To live in a flat. [Variant (influenced by the adjective) of obsolete *flet,* interior of a house, Middle English *flet,* Old English *flett,* floor, ground, hall.]

flat-bed press (flát-bed) *n.* A printing press in which the type is supported by a flat surface (bed) and the paper is applied to the type either by a flat platen (in older models) or by a cylinder against which the bed moves.

flat·boat (flát-bōt) *n.* A boat with a flat bottom and square ends, used for transporting goods on inland waterways.

flat·fish (flát-fish) *n., pl.* **-fishes** or collectively **flatfish.** Any of numerous chiefly marine fishes of the order Pleuronectiformes (or Heterosomata), which includes the sole, halibut, and turbot.

flat·foot (flát-fŏot) *n., pl.* **-feet** (-feet) (for sense 1) or **-foots** (for sense 2). 1. A condition in which the arch of the foot is absent so that the entire sole makes contact with the ground. 2. **a.** *Informal.* A person with flat feet. **b.** *Slang.* A policeman. Used derogatorily.

flat-footed (flát-fŏottid) *adj.* 1. Of or suffering from flatfoot. 2. *Informal.* Without reservation; forthright; uncompromising: *a flat-footed denial.* 3. *Informal.* Clumsy; graceless. 4. *Informal.* Uninspired; tedious. 5. *Informal.* Unprepared; unable to react quickly: *caught him flat-footed.* —**flat·foot·ed·ly** *adv.* —**flat·foot·ed·ness** *n.*

flat·head (flát-hed) *n.* A food fish of the family Platycephalidae, of Pacific waters, having a tapering body and a large, flat head covered with spines and ridges.

flat·i·ron (flát-īrn, -ī-ərn) *n.* An externally heated iron for pressing clothes.

flat knot *n.* A reef knot (see).

flat·let (flát-lit, -lət) *n. Chiefly British.* A small flat (living accommodation).

flat spin *n.* 1. *Aeronautics.* A spin round a nearly horizontal axis. 2. *Informal.* A state of great agitation.

flat·ten (flátt'n) *v.* **-tened, -tening, -tens.** —*tr.* 1. To make flat or flatter. 2. To knock down; lay low. 3. *Informal.* To humiliate or subdue. 4. *Music.* To lower (a note) by a semitone. —*intr.* 1. To become flat or more nearly flat. 2. To make or become flat, horizontal, or prostrate. Used with *out.* 3. *Aeronautics.* To bring (an aircraft) into a horizontal position. Used with *out.* —**flat·ten·er** *n.*

flat·ter[1] (flátter) *v.* **-tered, -tering, -ters.** —*tr.* 1. To compliment excessively and often insincerely, especially in order to win the favour of; court; blandish. 2. To please or gratify; feed the vanity of: *"What really flatters a man is that you think him worth flattering"* (G.B. Shaw). 3. **a.** To portray favourably. **b.** To show off becomingly or advantageously. 4. To persuade (oneself) that something one wants to believe is the case: *"many flattered themselves that I had turned out a failure"* (John Stuart Mill). —*intr.* To practise flattery. [Middle English *flateren,* from Old French *flat(t)er,* "to caress with the hand", smooth, flatter, from Frankish *flat* (unattested), flat, flat part of a person's hand.] —**flat·ter·er** *n.* —**flat·ter·ing·ly** *adv.*

flat·ter[2] *n.* 1. A flat-faced swage or hammer used by blacksmiths. 2. A die plate for flattening metal into strips, as in the manufacture of watch springs.

flat·ter·y (flátteri) *n., pl.* **-ies.** 1. The act or practice of flattering. 2. Excessive, false, or sycophantic praise.

flat·tie *n. Informal.* A flat-heeled women's shoe.

flat·ting (flátting) *n.* The process of rolling sheet metal.

flat·tish (fláttish) *adj.* Somewhat flat.

flat·u·lence (fláttew-lənss) *n.* Also **flat·u·len·cy** (-lən-si). 1. The presence of excessive gas in the digestive tract, causing breaking of wind. 2. Windy, high-flown speech; pomposity.

flat·u·lent (fláttew-lənt) *adj.* 1. **a.** Of, suffering from, or caused by flatulence. **b.** Inducing flatulence. 2. Inflated with self-importance; pompous and pretentious: *flatulent oratory.* [French, from New Latin *flatulentus,* from Latin *flātus,* a breaking of wind. See **flatus.**] —**flat·u·lent·ly** *adv.*

fla·tus (fláytəss) *n.* Gas generated in the stomach or intestines. [Latin *flātus,* a breaking of wind, a blowing, from the past participle of *flāre,* to blow.]

flat·ware (flát-wair) *n.* Tableware that is fairly flat and fashioned usually of a single piece, especially: 1. *British.* Plates, saucers, and the like. 2. *U.S.* Cutlery. Compare **hollow-ware.**

flat·ways (flát-wayz) *adv.* Also *U.S.* **flat·wise** (-wīz). With the flat side down or in a horizontal position; with a surface uppermost.

flat·worm (flát-wurm) *n.* Any wormlike animal of the phylum Platyhelminthes; a **platyhelminth** (see).

Flau·bert (flō-báir, flố-bair), **Gustave** (1821–80). French novelist.

His novels include *Madame Bovary* (1856), *Salammbô* (1862), and *La Tentation de Saint Antoine* (1874). *Trois contes* (1877) established him as a master of the short story. **—Flau·bert·i·an** (-báir-ti-ən, -bérsh'n) *adj.*

flaunch. Variant of **flanch.**

flaunt (flawnt || *U.S. also* flaant) *v.* **flaunted, flaunting, flaunts.** *—tr.* **1.** To exhibit ostentatiously; show off: *she flaunted her engagement ring.* **2.** *Nonstandard.* To flout. *—intr.* **1.** To parade oneself ostentatiously or pertly; show oneself off. **2.** To be gaudily in evidence. **3.** To wave proudly, as a flag does. **—**See Synonyms at **show.** [16th century : origin obscure.] **—flaunt·er** *n.* **—flaunt·ing·ly** *adv.*

Usage: The similarity in form between *flaunt* and *flout* has led to the former term being used in place of the latter in the general sense of "treat with contempt", and this usage has often appeared in print. But there is a clear distinction between *flaunt,* meaning "show off", and *flout.* A soldier who *flaunts* his new uniform is proud of it, and is not likely to *flout* the regulations ordering him to wear it.

flau·tist (fláw-tist || *U.S. also* flów-) *n.* Also *chiefly U.S.* **flu·tist.** (flóō-tist). One who plays the flute. [Italian *flautista,* from *flauto,* FLUTE.]

fla·ves·cent (flə-véss'nt) *adj.* Turning yellow; yellowish. [Latin *flāvēscens,* present participle of *flāvēscere,* to turn yellow, inceptive of *flāvēre,* to be yellow, from *flāvus,* yellow.]

fla·vin, fla·vine (fláyvin) *n.* **1.** Any of various water-soluble yellow pigments derived from riboflavin, including **FAD** and **FMN** *(both of which see),* found in plant and animal tissue as prosthetic groups of flavoprotein. **2.** A compound, $C_{10}H_6N_4O_2$, that is the nucleus of various natural yellow pigments. [Latin *flāvus,* yellow + -IN.]

flavin adenine dinucleotide *n.* **FAD** *(see).*

fla·vine (fláy-veen, -vin) *n.* **1.** A brownish-red crystalline powder, $C_{14}H_{15}N_3Cl_2$, used as an antiseptic. **2.** Variant of **flavin.**

flavin mononucleotide *n.* **FMN** *(see).*

fla·vone (fláy-vōn) *n.* A crystalline compound, $C_{15}H_{10}O_2$, the parent substance of a number of important yellow pigments. [Latin *flāvus,* yellow + -ONE.]

fla·von·oid (fláyvə-noyd) *n.* Any of a large group of plant pigments, including the anthocyanins. [FLAVONE + -OID.]

fla·vo·pro·tein (fláyvō-prō-teen, -tee-in) *n.* Any of a class of enzymes containing flavin bound to protein and acting as dehydrogenation catalysts in biological reactions. [Latin *flāvus,* yellow + PROTEIN.]

fla·vour, *U.S.* **fla·vor** (fláyvər) *n.* **1.** Distinctive taste; savour: *a flavour of smoke in bacon.* **2.** An ineffable quality felt to be characteristic of a specified thing: *the flavour of the Orient.* **3.** A seasoning; a flavouring. **4.** *Archaic.* Aroma. **5.** *Physics.* Any of various types of quark. Symmetry between quarks and leptons requires at least six flavours, these quarks being designated as up, down, charmed, strange, top, and bottom.

~tr.v. **flavoured** or *U.S.* **flavored, -vouring** or *U.S.* **-voring, -vours** or *U.S.* **-vors.** To give flavour to. [Middle English *flavour,* aroma, variant (influenced by *savour*) of Old French *flaor,* from Vulgar Latin *flātor* (unattested), from Latin *flātus,* blowing, breeze, from the past participle of *flāre,* to blow.] **—fla·vour·er** *n.* **—fla·vour·ful, fla·vour·ous, fla·vour·some** (-səm) *adj.* **—fla·vour·less** *adj.*

fla·vour·ing (fláyvər-ing) *n.* A substance that imparts flavour, such as an extract or spice.

flavour of the month *n. Informal.* Something or someone currently popular or fashionable. [Suggestive of an advertising campaign to promote a different flavour of ice-cream every month.]

flaw[1] (flaw) *n.* **1.** An imperfection; a blemish or defect. **2.** *Law.* A defect in a legal document, proceeding, or piece of evidence, that renders it invalid. **3.** A small fissure; a crack. **—**See Synonyms at **blemish.**

~v. **flawed, flawing, flaws.** *—tr.* To make defective; mar. *—intr.* To become defective. [Middle English *flawe, flai,* flake, fragment, from Old Norse *flaga,* slab or layer of stone.] **—flaw·less** *adj.* **—flaw·less·ly** *adv.* **—flaw·less·ness** *n.*

flaw[2] *n.* **1.** A brief gust or blast of wind; a squall. **2.** A brief spell of stormy weather. [Probably from Middle Low German *vlāge* or Middle Dutch *vlāghe,* a push, attack, storm.] **—flaw·y** *adj.*

flax (flaks) *n.* **1.** Any of several plants of the genus *Linum;* especially, a widely cultivated species, *L. usitatissimum,* having blue flowers, seeds that yield linseed oil, and slender stems from which a fine, light-coloured textile fibre is obtained. **2.** The textile fibre obtained from this plant, from which linen is made. **3.** Any of several plants resembling flax. **4.** Greyish yellow. [Middle English *flax, flex,* Old English *fleax, flæx.*] **—flax·y** *adj.*

flax·en (fláks'n) *adj.* **1.** Made of or resembling flax. **2.** Having the colour of flax fibre; pale yellow.

Flax·man (fláksmən), **John (Henry)** (1755–1826). British sculptor and book illustrator. A designer of friezes and portrait medallions for Wedgwood, he also established a reputation as a neoclassical artist with illustrations for the *Odyssey* and *Iliad* (1793).

flax·seed (fláks-seed) *n.* The seed of flax, the source of linseed oil and of emollient medicinal preparations.

flay (flay) *tr.v.* **flayed, flaying, flays. 1. a.** To skin (an animal). **b.** To strip off the skin of (a person), as by whipping. **2.** To strip of money or goods, especially by fraud; fleece. **3.** To assail with stinging criticism. [Middle English *flen,* Old English *flēan.*] **—flay·er** *n.*

F layer *n.* **1.** The highest zone of the ionosphere, extending continuously at night from approximately 195 to 400 kilometres (120 to 250 miles). **2.** Either of two layers into which this zone is divided during the day, especially in summer, usually designated F_1 and F_2, and extending respectively from 145 to 240 kilometres (90 to 150 miles) and from 240 kilometres (150 miles) upwards. Also called "F region", "Appleton layer". [*F* (arbitrary designation) + LAYER.]

fld. field.

flea (flee) *n.* **1.** Any of various small, wingless, bloodsucking insects of the order Siphonaptera, that have legs adapted for jumping and are parasitic on warm-blooded animals. **2.** Any of various small crustaceans that resemble or move like fleas, such as the **water flea** *(see).* **—a flea in (one's) ear.** *Informal.* A sharp, stinging rebuke or pointed, annoying hint. [Middle English *fle,* Old English *flēa(h),* from Germanic.]

flea·bag (flée-bag) *n. Slang.* **1.** A bed or sleeping bag. **2.** *British.* A dirty or disreputable person, especially an old woman; a hag.

flea·bane (flée-bayn) *n.* Any of various plants of the genus *Erigeron,* having variously coloured, daisy-like flowers, such as Canadian fleabane, *E.* (or *Conyza*) *canadensis,* having white flowers. [From its supposed ability to drive away fleas.]

flea beetle *n.* Any of various small beetles of the family Chrysomelidae that have hind legs enlarged for jumping.

flea·bite (flée-bīt) *n.* **1. a.** The bite of a flea. **b.** The little red mark caused by a flea's bite. **2.** A trifling loss, inconvenience, or annoyance.

flea-bit·ten (flée-bitt'n) *adj.* **1.** Covered with fleas or fleabites. **2.** *Informal.* Shabby; mean; wretched. **3.** Having a pale coat with reddish-brown flecks. Said of horses.

flea collar *n.* A collar containing an insecticide, worn by dogs and cats to kill fleas and ticks.

flea market *n.* A shop or open market selling antiques, second-hand household goods, curios, and the like.

flea·pit (flée-pit) *n. British Informal.* A cheap or squalid cinema or theatre.

flea·wort (flée-wurt || -wawrt) *n.* **1.** Any of various plants reputed to repel fleas, such as *Senecio integrifolius,* which has yellow, daisy-like flowers, and a species of plantain, *Plantago psyllium.* **2. Ploughman's spikenard** *(see).*

flèche (flaysh, flesh) *n.* **1.** *Architecture.* A slender spire, especially one on a church above the intersection of the nave and transepts. Also called "spirelet". **2.** *Architecture.* An outward-pointing parapet on a fortified wall. **3.** Any of the points on a backgammon board. **4.** In fencing, a lunging attack. [French, "arrow", from Old French, from Frankish *fliugika* (unattested).]

flé·chette (flay-shét, fle-) *n.* A steel missile or dart dropped from an aeroplane, as used in World War I. [French, from FLÈCHE.]

fleck (flek) *n.* **1.** A tiny mark or spot, such as a freckle. **2.** A small bit or flake. **3.** A small patch of colour or light.

~tr.v. **flecked, flecking, flecks.** To spot or streak. [Probably from Middle English *flecked,* spotted, dappled, from Old Norse *flekkōttr,* from *flekkr,* spot, stain.]

Fleck·er (fléckər), **(Herman) James Elroy** (1884–1915). British poet and dramatist. He used Eastern life as a background to many of his works, including his best-known poem, *The Golden Journey to Samarkand* (1913), and his play, *Hassan* (1922).

flec·tion, flex·ion (fléksh'n) *n.* **1.** The act or process of bending or flexing. **2.** A bent part; a curve; a bend. **3.** *Grammar.* Inflection. [Latin *flexiō* (stem *flexiōn-*), a bending, from *flexus,* past participle of *flectere,* to bend, FLEX.] **—flec·tion·al** *adj.*

fled. Past tense of **flee.**

fledge (flej) *v.* **fledged, fledging, fledges.** *—tr.* **1.** To take care of (a young bird) until it is ready to fly. **2.** To cover with or as if with feathers. **3.** To provide with feathers; feather (an arrow); fletch. *—intr.* To grow the plumage necessary for flight. [Probably from obsolete *fledge,* feathered, from Middle English *flegge,* Old English *-flycge.*]

fledg·ling, fledge·ling (fléj-ling) *n.* **1.** A young bird that has recently acquired its flight feathers. **2.** One that is young and inexperienced. Also used adjectivally: *a fledgling republic.*

fledg·y (fléji) *adj.* **-ier, -iest.** *Poetic.* Covered with feathers; feathery.

flee (flee) *v.* **fled** (fled), **fleeing, flees.** *—intr.* **1.** To run away, as from trouble or danger. **2.** To withdraw abruptly; rush off: *flees to her bedroom.* **3.** To pass swiftly away; vanish: *time fleeing too soon.* *—tr.* To run away from; shun. [Middle English *flen, fleon,* Old English *flēon,* from Germanic. (The past tense *fled* and past participle *fled* are from Middle English *fledde* and *fledd,* which superseded the strong forms inherited from Old English.)] **—fle·er** *n.*

fleece (fleess) *n.* **1.** The coat of wool of a sheep or similar animal. **2.** The yield of wool shorn from a sheep at one time. **3.** Any soft, woolly covering or mass. **4.** Any fabric with a soft deep pile.

~tr.v. **fleeced, fleecing, fleeces. 1.** To shear the fleece from. **2.** To defraud of money or property; swindle. **3.** To cover with or as if with fleece. [Middle English *flees, fles,* Old English *flēos,* from Germanic.] **—fleec·er** *n.*

fleec·y (flées-si) *adj.* **-ier, -iest.** Of, like, or covered with fleece: *fleecy clouds.* **—fleec·i·ly** *adv.* **—fleec·i·ness** *n.*

fleer (fleer) *v.* **fleered, fleering, fleers.** *—tr.* To sneer at; scoff; scorn. *—intr.* To smirk or laugh in contempt or derision.

~n. A scoffing or taunting look or gibe. [Middle English *flerien,* to laugh mockingly, jeer, from Scandinavian; akin to Norwegian and Swedish dialectal *flira,* to laugh, Danish dialectal *flire,* to giggle. See **flimflam.**] **—fleer·ing·ly** *adv.*

fleet[1] (fleet) *n.* **1. a.** A number of warships operating together under one command. **b.** The entire navy of a state. **2.** Any group of craft or vehicles, such as taxis or fishing boats, owned or operated as a unit. [Middle English *flete,* Old English *flēot,* from *flēotan,* to float.]

fleet² *adj.* **fleeter, fleetest. 1.** Moving swiftly; rapid or nimble. **2.** *Poetic.* Passing swiftly; evanescent. —See Synonyms at **fast.** —*v.* **fleeted, fleeting, fleets.** —*intr.* **1.** To move or pass swiftly. **2.** *Archaic.* To glide imperceptibly away; fade; vanish. **3.** *British Regional.* To float. —*tr.* **1.** *Archaic.* To pass (time) quickly. **2.** *Nautical.* To alter the position of (tackle, rope, or the like). [Probably from Middle English *fleten,* to flow, glide swiftly, Old English *flēotan,* to float, drift.] —**fleet·ly** *adv.* —**fleet·ness** *n.*

fleet³ *n. British Regional.* A small inlet or creek. [Middle English *flete,* Old English *flēot.*]

Fleet Admiral *n.* The officer having the highest rank in the U.S. and some other navies. See **Admiral of the Fleet.**

fleet·ing (flēeting) *adj.* Passing quickly; very brief. See Synonyms at **transient.** —**fleet·ing·ly** *adv.* —**fleet·ing·ness** *n.*

Fleet Street. Ancient London road, running from Ludgate Circus to Temple Bar. Celebrated for its taverns in the 17th and 18th centuries, it was associated with the press from the early 18th century to the 1980s. The first regular newspaper to be published there was the *Daily Courant,* established in 1702.

Flem. Flemish.

Flem·ing (flémming) *n.* **1.** A native of Flanders. **2.** A Belgian who speaks Flemish. Compare **Walloon.** [Middle English, from Old Norse *Flǣmingi,* from Middle Dutch *Vlāming,* from *Vlām-,* FLAN-DERS.]

Flem·ing (flémming), **Sir Alexander** (1881–1955). British bacteriologist, discoverer of penicillin. Fleming was unable to isolate or identify the antibiotic, but this was later achieved by Florey and Chain, with whom he shared the Nobel prize for physiology or medicine in 1945.

Fleming, Ian (Lancaster) (1908–64). British writer. His most famous character, the often-filmed super-spy, 007 James Bond, first appeared in the book *Casino Royale* (1953).

Fleming's rules *pl.n. Physics.* Two rules used for electromagnetic induction to determine the relative directions of field, current, and motion. The hand is held with the first and second fingers and the thumb mutually at right angles: the first finger points in the field direction, the second finger in the current direction, and the thumb in the direction of motion. The *left-hand rule* is used when current and field produce motion, as in an electric motor. The *right-hand rule* is used when a current produces motion, as in an electric generator. [After Sir John Ambrose *Fleming* (1849–1945), British electrical engineer.]

Flem·ish (flémmish) *adj. Abbr.* **Flem.** Of or pertaining to Flanders, the Flemings, or their language.
—*n. Abbr.* **Flem. 1.** The West Germanic language, very similar to Dutch, that is one of Belgium's two official languages. Officially called Dutch since 1973. **2.** *Used with a plural verb.* The Flemings. Preceded by *the.* [Middle English, from Old Norse *Flǣmskr,* from Middle Dutch *Vlāmish,* from *Vlām-,* FLANDERS.]

Flemish bond *n.* In masonry, a bond consisting of alternate headers and stretchers in each course.

flench (flench) *tr.v.* **flenched, flenching, flenches.** To flense.

flense (flenss, flenz) *tr.v.* **flensed, flensing, flenses.** To strip the blubber or skin from (a whale or seal, for example). [Danish *flense.*] —**flens·er** *n.*

flesh (flesh) *n.* **1.** The soft tissue of the body; especially, skeletal muscle as opposed to bone and viscera. **2.** The meat of animals, as distinguished from the edible tissue of fish or, sometimes, poultry. **3.** The pulpy, usually edible part of a fruit or vegetable. **4.** Excess tissue; fat; plumpness. **5.** The surface or skin of the human body. **6. a.** The body as distinguished from the mind or soul. **b.** Man's physical or carnal nature. **c.** Sensual appetites. **7. a.** Mankind: *"The glory of the Lord shall be revealed, and all flesh shall see it together."* (Isaiah 40:3). **b.** All living animals **8.** Yellowish pink to pale greyish brown. —**in the flesh. 1.** Alive. **2.** In person; present. —*v.* **fleshed, fleshing, fleshes.** —*tr.* **1.** To encourage (a hunting dog or falcon) by feeding it flesh; blood. **2.** To inure to battle or bloodshed. **3.** To fill out or give substance to (a framework or plan, for example). Used with *out.* **4.** To plunge or thrust (a weapon) into flesh. **5.** To clean (a hide) of adhering flesh. —*intr.* To gain weight; become plump or fleshy. Used with *out.* [Middle English *flesh, fleish,* Old English *flǣsc,* from Germanic.]

flesh and blood *n.* **1.** Human nature or physical existence, together with its weaknesses. **2.** One's blood relatives; kin.

flesh·er (fléshər) *n. Scottish.* A butcher.

flesh fly *n.* Any of various flies of the genus *Sarcophaga,* the larvae of which are parasitic in animal tissue or feed on carrion.

flesh·ings (fléshingz) *pl.n.* Flesh-coloured tights, as formerly worn by actors.

fleshy fruit *n.* A fruit, such as a drupe or berry, whose pericarp is soft and pulpy as opposed to hard and dry.

flesh·ly (fléshli) *adj.* **-lier, -liest. 1.** Of or pertaining to the body; corporeal. **2.** Inclined to or concerned with carnality; sensual. **3.** Not spiritual; worldly. **4.** Tending to plumpness; fleshy. —**flesh·li·ness** *n.*

flesh·pots (flésh-pots) *pl.n.* **1.** Material and physical self-indulgence; sensual gratification. **2.** Where such gratification is obtained.

flesh wound *n.* A wound that penetrates the flesh but does not damage bones or vital organs.

flesh·y (fléshi) *adj.* **-ier, -iest. 1.** Pertaining to, consisting of, or resembling flesh. **2.** Having much flesh; corpulent; plump. **3.** Not

fibrous; firm and pulpy. Said of fruit, leaves, or the like. —See Synonyms at **fat.** —**flesh·i·ness** *n.*

fletch (flech) *tr.v.* **fletched, fletching, fletches.** To feather (an arrow); fledge. [Perhaps from FLETCHER.]

fletch·er (fléchər) *n.* One who makes arrows. [Middle English *flecher,* from Old French *flech(i)er,* from *fleche,* arrow, from Frankish *fliugika* (unattested).]

Fletch·er (fléchər), **John** (1579–1625). English dramatist and poet, plague victim. With Sir Frances Beaumont he wrote romantic tragicomedies, e.g. *Philaster* (1610) and *The Maid's Tragedy* (1611).

Flet·ton (flétt'n) *n.* A common type of brick made by compressing ground clay, mixed with the minimum of water, in a steel mould before firing. [After *Fletton,* Cambridgeshire, near the source of the clay originally used for this brick.]

fleur de coin (flör-də-kwáN) *adj.* In mint condition. Said of a coin. [French, "flower of the minting-die".]

fleur-de-lis, fleur-de-lys (flör-də-lée, -léess ‖ floor-) *n., pl.* **fleurs-de-lis, fleurs-de-lys** (flör-də-léez ‖ floor-) Also *archaic* **flow·er-de-luce** (flówr-də-lōoss, flów-ər-) *pl.* **flowers-de-luce. 1.** *Heraldry.* A device consisting of a stylised three-petalled iris flower, used as the armorial emblem of the kings of France. **2.** An iris; especially, a white-flowered form of *Iris germanica.* [Middle English, from Old French *flor de lis,* lily flower : *flo(u)r,* FLOWER + *de,* of + *lis,* LILY.]

fleur·on (flér-on; *French* flöroN) *n.* A crescent-shaped piece of puff pastry, used as a garnish in cookery.

flew¹. Past tense of **fly.**

flew². Variant of **flue** (fishing net).

flews (flōoz ‖ flewz) *pl.n.* The pendulous corners of the upper lip of certain dogs, such as the bloodhound. [16th century : origin obscure.]

flex (fleks) *v.* **flexed, flexing, flexes.** —*tr.* **1. a.** To bend (something pliant or elastic). **b.** To bend (a joint). **c.** To bend (a joint) repeatedly. **2.** To contract (a muscle). Compare **extend.** —*tr.* To bend: *"his hands flexed nervously as he spoke"* (Mary McCarthy). —*n.* Flexible insulated electric wire. [Latin *flectere†* (past participle *flexus*), to bend.]

flex·a·gon (flék-sə-gən) *n.* A folded paper construction capable of being flexed along its folds to reveal different combinations of faces. [FLEX + -GON.]

flexi- *comb. form.* Indicates flexible; for example, **flexitime.**

flex·i·ble (flék-si-b'l) *adj.* Also **flex·ile** (flék-sīl ‖ *U.S. also* -səl). **1.** Capable of being bent or flexed; pliable. **2.** Susceptible to influence or persuasion; tractable. **3.** Responsive to change; adaptable. **4.** Capable of variation or modification. —**flex·i·bil·i·ty** (-si-bílləti), **flex·i·ble·ness** *n.* —**flex·i·bly** *adv.*
   Synonyms: *flexible, ductile, plastic, pliable, pliant, supple, adaptable.*

flexible sandstone *n.* **Itacolumite** *(see).*

flex·ion (fléksh'n) *n.* **1.** *Anatomy.* **a.** The act of bending a limb or joint. **b.** The condition of being bent. **2.** Variant of **flection.** [Variant of FLECTION.] —**flex·ion·al** *adj.* —**flex·ion·less** *adj.*

flex·i·time (fléksi-tīm) *n.* An arrangement by which employees may vary their own starting and finishing hours within agreed limits, while maintaining a fixed average number of hours per working day.

flex·og·ra·phy (flek-sóggrəfi) *n. Printing.* **1.** A system of rotary printing, used especially for printing on metal or plastic sheets. **2.** Anything printed by this method. —**flex·o·graph·ic** (fléksə-gráf-fik) *adj.* —**flex·o·graph·i·cal·ly** *adv.*

flex·or (fléksər) *n.* A muscle that acts to bend a joint. Compare **extensor.** [New Latin, from Latin *flexus,* past participle of *flectere,* to FLEX.]

flex·u·ous (fléksew-əss) *adj.* Also **flex·u·ose** (-ōss, -ōz). Bending or winding alternately from side to side; sinuous. [Latin *flexuōsus,* from *flexus.* See **flex.**] —**flex·u·ous·ly** *adv.*

flex·ure (flékshər) *n.* **1.** A bend, curve, or turn, such as a bend in a tubular organ: *the hepatic flexure of the colon.* **2.** A bending or flexing; flexion. —**flex·ur·al** *adj.*

fley (flay) *v.* **fleyed, fleying, fleys.** *Chiefly Scottish.* —*tr.v.* **1.** To frighten. **2.** To cause to run away in fright; scare off. —*intr.* To be frightened; take fright. [Middle English *flayen, fleien,* to put to flight, frighten, Old English *-flȳgan.*]

flib·ber·ti·gib·bet (flíbbərti-jíbbit, -jíbbit) *n.* A silly, scatterbrained, or garrulous person, especially a young girl. [Earlier *flibbergib, flipergebet†* (imitative of foolish talk).]

flick¹ (flik) *n.* **1.** A light, quick blow, jerk, or touch, as with a whip or fingernail. **2.** The sound accompanying such a movement; a snap. **3.** A light splash, dash, or streak.
—*v.* **flicked, flicking, flicks.** —*tr.* **1.** To touch or hit with a light, quick movement. **2.** To cause to move with a light movement, usually of the hand or finger; snap. **3.** To remove with such a light, quick movement.
—*intr.* **1.** To look through (a book, for example) inattentively or very quickly. Used with *through.* **2.** To twitch or flutter. [Middle English (imitative).]

flick² *n. Slang.* **1.** A cinematic film. **2.** *Plural.* The cinema. Preceded by *the.* Not in current usage. [Back-formation from FLICKER.]

flick·book (flík-book) *n.* A small booklet containing a series of similar but gradually changing images. On flicking its pages in quick succession, the illusion of continuous movement is achieved.

flick·er¹ (flíckər) *v.* **-ered, -ering, -ers.** —*intr.* **1.** To give off inconstant, fitful light; burn unsteadily. **2.** To shine or blaze momentarily, as lightning does. **3.** To move waveringly; flutter. *—tr.* To cause to flicker.

~n. **1.** An inconstant or wavering light: *"a flicker like green fire in his eyes"* (J.R.R. Tolkien). **2.** A brief or slight sensation, as of an emotion: *a flicker of hope.* **3.** A tremor or flutter. [Middle English *flikeren, flekeren,* to flutter, flicker, Old English *flicorian*†, to flutter, hover.]

flick·er[2] *n.* Any of several large North American woodpeckers of the genus *Colaptes.* [Imitative of its call.]

flick knife *n.* A knife with a retractable blade that springs out at the press of a switch. Also *U.S.* "switchblade".

fli·er, fly·er (flīr, flī-ər) *n.* **1. a.** One that flies. **b.** An aircraft pilot; an aviator. **2.** A step in a straight as opposed to winding staircase. Compare **winder.** **3.** In athletics, a flying start. **4.** *Informal.* A daring financial venture. **5.** *Informal.* A pamphlet or circular.

flight[1] (flīt) *n.* **1. a.** The motion of an object in or through a medium, especially through the Earth's atmosphere or through space, that is characterised by lack of contact with any other object, especially with the Earth. **b.** An instance of such motion, as of a ball, dart, spacecraft, or the like. **c.** The duration or manner of an instance of such motion. **d.** The ability to engage in such motion. **2.** The act or process of flying; locomotion through the air by means of wings. **3.** Any swift passage or movement. **4. a.** A journey in an aircraft, especially a scheduled airline trip. **b.** The aircraft making such a trip: *Your flight leaves in 15 minutes.* **5.** A group, especially of birds or aircraft, flying together. **6.** A number of military aircraft forming a subdivision of a squadron. **7.** An effort that transcends the usual restraints; a soaring: *a flight of fancy.* **8.** A flight feather. **9.** A series of stairs from one landing to another. **10.** A series or line of hurdles, gates, canal locks, or the like. **11.** The flared tail of an arrow or dart, usually made of feathers or plastic, and designed to give stability. **12.** In archery, a thin, light arrow designed for long-range shooting. Also called "flight arrow". **13.** In angling, a device that whirls the bait rapidly in trolling.

~v. **flighted, flighting, flights.** *—intr.* To migrate or fly in flocks. *—tr. Sports.* To cause (a ball or dart, for example) to float in an unpredictable trajectory: *a flighted delivery.* [Middle English *flight,* Old English *flyht*; akin to FLY (verb).]

flight[2] *n.* A running away; an escape. **—put to flight.** To drive or frighten away; repel; rout. **—take (to) flight.** To run or fly away; withdraw rapidly; flee. [Middle English *flight,* Old English *flyht* (unattested); akin to FLEE.]

flight check *n.* A proficiency check in an airborne aircraft of the pilot, crew members, or a piece of equipment.

flight deck *n.* **1.** The upper deck of an aircraft carrier, used as a runway. **2.** The forward compartment in a large aircraft, used by the pilot, copilot, and flight engineer.

flight engineer *n.* The crew member responsible for the mechanical performance of an aircraft flight.

flight feather *n.* Any of the comparatively large, stiff feathers of a bird's wing or tail, that are necessary for flight. Also called "flight".

flight·less (flīt-ləss, -liss) *adj.* Incapable of flying. Said of certain birds and insects.

flight lieutenant *n.* An officer in the British and certain other air forces ranking between a squadron leader and a flying officer, and equivalent in rank to a captain in the army and a lieutenant in the navy.

flight path *n.* The precise route taken or due to be taken through the air by an aircraft, spacecraft, or the like.

flight plan *n.* A detailed statement of an aircraft's expected departure time, route, and so on.

flight recorder *n.* An electronic device that records details of an aeroplane's performance during flight. Also called "black box".

flight·y (flīti) *adj.* **-ier, -iest.** **1.** Given to capricious behaviour; fickle or unstable. **2.** Given to flirting. **3.** Easily excited; skittish. Said of a horse. [Originally "swift", from FLIGHT.] **—flight·i·ly** *adv.* **—flight·i·ness** *n.*

flim·flam (flím-flam) *n. Informal.* **1.** Nonsense; humbug. **2.** A deception; a swindle.

~tr.v. **flimflammed, -flamming, -flams.** *Informal.* To swindle or dupe. [Reduplication (imitative) of an unknown Scandinavian word akin to Old Norse *flīm,* mockery, Danish dialectal *flire,* to giggle, from Germanic *fli-* (unattested).] **—flim·flam·mer** *n.* **—flim·flam·mer·y** *n.*

flim·sy (flímzi) *adj.* **-sier, -siest.** **1.** Light, thin, and insubstantial. **2.** Lacking solidity or strength: *a flimsy building.* **3.** Lacking plausibility; unconvincing: *a flimsy theory.*

~n., pl. **flimsies.** **1.** Thin paper usually used to make multiple copies. **2.** Something written on such paper. [17th century : origin obscure.] **—flim·si·ly** *adv.* **—flim·si·ness** *n.*

flinch (flinch) *intr.v.* **flinched, flinching, flinches.** **1.** To betray fear, pain, or surprise with an involuntary gesture such as a start; wince. **2.** To draw away; retreat. —See Synonyms at **recoil.**

~n. An act or instance of flinching. [Old French *flenchir, flainchir,* from Germanic.] **—flinch·er** *n.* **—flinch·ing·ly** *adv.*

flin·ders (flíndərz) *pl.n.* Bits; fragments; splinters. [Middle English *flenderis,* from Scandinavian; akin to Norwegian *flindra,* splinter.]

Flin·ders (flíndərz), **Matthew** (1774–1814). British navigator and hydrographer. In 1795 he sailed to New South Wales and subsequently made a thorough study of the Australian coast. Among his scientific works is *A Voyage to Terra Australis* (1814). Flinders Island, Flinders Range, and Flinders River are named after him.

Flinders Range. Mountain chain between Lake Torrens and Lake Frome, in South Australia. About 420 kilometres (260 miles) long, it has valuable deposits of uranium and copper, which are mined.

fling (fling) *v.* **flung** (flung), **flinging, flings.** *—tr.* **1.** To throw violently or carelessly; hurl. **2.** To put or send suddenly or unexpectedly: *The army was flung into battle.* **3.** To throw (oneself) into some activity with abandon and energy. **4.** To throw (an opponent or rider, for example) to the ground. **5.** To toss aside; discard: *fling propriety away.* **6.** To speak or shout (words) in a passionate way. *—intr.* To move quickly, violently, or impulsively: *she flung out of the room in a temper.* —See Synonyms at **throw.**

~n. **1.** An act of flinging or hurling; a throw. **2.** A brief period of indulging one's impulses; a spree. **3.** A dance in which the arms and legs are flung about; especially, the **Highland fling** *(see).* **4.** *Informal.* A brief attempt: *Have a fling at it.* [Fling, flung, flung; Middle English *flingen, flung* (more often *flang*), *flungen,* from Scandinavian; akin to Old Norse *flengja,* to flog.]

flin·kite (fling-kīt) *n.* A brownish-green mineral form of magnesium arsenate. [German *Flinkit,* after Gustav *Flink* (1849–1931), Swedish mineralogist.]

flint (flint) *n.* **1.** A very hard, fine-grained quartz that sparks when struck with steel. **2.** A piece of flint fashioned into a tool by prehistoric man. **3. a.** A piece of flint used formerly to produce a spark. **b.** A small solid cylinder of a spark-producing alloy, used in lighters to ignite the fuel. **4.** Anything likened to flint in hardness: *a jaw of flint.* [Middle English *flint,* Old English *flint,* from Germanic.]

flint glass *n.* A soft, fusible, lustrous, brilliant lead-oxide optical glass with high refraction and low dispersion. Also called "lead glass". Compare **crown glass.**

flint·lock (flínt-lok) *n.* **1.** An obsolete gunlock in which a flint embedded in the hammer produces a spark that ignites the charge. **2.** A firearm having such a gunlock. Also called "firelock".

Flint·shire (flínt-shər, -sheer). A Unitary Authority area and former county in Wales in the northeast of the principality on the Dee estuary. The county town was Mold. Its former heavy industries based on the North Wales coalfield have declined in recent years.

flint·y (flínti) *adj.* **-ier, -iest.** **1.** Containing or composed of flint. **2.** Unyielding or unfeeling; stony. **—flint·i·ly** *adv.* **—flint·i·ness** *n.*

flip (flip) *v.* **flipped, flipping, flips.** *—tr.* **1.** To throw or flick with a brisk motion, especially of the finger and thumb; toss. **2.** To toss (a coin, for example) in the air, imparting a spin. **3.** To reverse or turn over quickly and effortlessly. *—intr.* **1.** To strike at something quickly or lightly, as with a fillip. **2.** To move suddenly or jerkily. **3.** *Slang.* **a.** To be overwhelmed by excitement or enthusiasm: *They flipped when they saw the new car.* **b.** To fly into a rage. **c.** To lose one's mind; go mad. Often used with *out.* **4.** To look through (a book, for example) quickly or inattentively. Used with *through.*

~n. **1.** An act of flipping, especially: **a.** A fillip or tap. **b.** A quick, jerky movement. **c.** A somersault. **2.** A mixed drink made with any of various alcoholic beverages, usually including beaten eggs.

~adj. Informal. Disrespectful; impertinent: *a flip attitude.* [Perhaps from FILLIP.]

flip-flop (flíp-flop) *n.* **1.** *Informal.* The movement or sound of repeated flapping: *the flip-flop of sandals on a tile floor.* **2.** A simple rubber sandal held on the foot by a forked strap meeting between the first and second toes. **3.** *Electronics.* An electronic circuit having two stable states, either of which can be assumed depending on the input signal. Flip-flops are used in computers to store a single bit of information. **4.** *U.S. Informal.* A backward somersault. [Reduplication of FLIP.] **—flip-flop** *intr.v. & adv.*

flip·pant (flíppənt) *adj.* **1. a.** Marked by disrespectful and insensitive levity; pert. **b.** Clever in a shallow or superficial way. **2.** *Archaic.* Talkative; voluble. [Probably FLIP + -ANT.] **—flip·pan·cy** *n.* **—flip·pant·ly** *adv.*

flip·per (flíppər) *n.* **1.** One that flips. **2.** A wide, flat limb, as of a seal, whale, or other aquatic animal, adapted especially for swimming. **3.** A foot-covering with a flat, widening surface beyond the toes to increase propulsion in swimming. **4.** *Slang.* A hand.

flip·ping (flípping) *adj. British Informal.* Used as an intensive to express annoyance: *a flipping nuisance.* **—flip·ping** *adv.*

flip side *n. Informal.* **1.** The reverse side, as of a gramophone record. **2.** The less obvious and typically less nice concomitant of something.

flirt (flurt) *v.* **flirted, flirting, flirts.** *—intr.* **1.** To amuse oneself in playful amorousness; play lightly or teasingly at courtship. **2.** To deal playfully, triflingly, or coyly; toy. **3.** To move abruptly or jerkily; dart; flit.

~tr. **1.** To toss or flip suddenly; flick. **2.** To move quickly; jerk or wave briskly.

~n. **1.** One given to flirting. **2.** An abrupt, jerking movement. [16th century ("sudden pull or twist", brisk movement (as of a bird's tail, a fan), flighty woman, hence current senses) : imitative.]

flir·ta·tion (flur-táysh'n) *n.* **1.** The practice of flirting; coquetry. **2.** A casual, playful romance. **3.** Any brief involvement.

flir·ta·tious (flur-táyshəss) *adj.* **1.** Given to flirting. **2.** Full of playful allure: *a flirtatious glance.* **—flir·ta·tious·ly** *adv.* **—flir·ta·tious·ness** *n.*

flit (flit) *intr.v.* **flitted, flitting, flits.** **1.** To move about rapidly and nimbly; dart or fly. **2.** To move quickly from one location to another. **3.** *British Informal.* To move house; change one's address.

~n. **1.** A fluttering or darting movement. **2.** A hasty escape or departure, as to avoid payment of rent. Used especially in the phrase *do a moonlight flit.* [Middle English *flitten,* to transport, convey, from Old Norse *flytja,* to convey.] **—flit·ter** *n.*

flitch (flich) *n.* 1. A salted and cured side of bacon. 2. A longitudinal cut from the trunk of a tree. 3. Any of several planks secured together to form a single beam. [Middle English *fliche*, side of animal salted and cured, Old English *flicce*, from Germanic.]

flit·ter (flittər) *intr.v.* **-tered, -tering, -ters.** To flit about; flutter. [Frequentative of FLIT.]

flit·ter·mouse (flittər-mowss) *n.* A bat *(see)*. [Translation of German *Fledermaus*.]

float (flōt) *v.* **floated, floating, floats.** *—intr.* 1. a. To remain suspended within or on the surface of a fluid without sinking. b. To be suspended unsupported in space without falling. 2. To move from position to position, especially at random; drift. 3. To move easily and lightly as if suspended: *"Miss Golightly . . . floated round in their arms light as a scarf"* (Truman Capote). 4. *Finance.* To find a level in relation to other currencies solely in response to the law of supply and demand: *The dollar should be allowed to float.* *—tr.* 1. To cause to remain suspended without sinking or falling. 2. To flood (land), as for irrigation. 3. a. To launch or establish (a business enterprise, for example). b. To set (an idea, rumour, or the like) in circulation. 4. To offer (shares, bonds, or the like) for sale. 5. To make the surface of (plaster, for example) level or smooth. 6. To seek support for (a scheme or idea). 7. *Finance.* To allow (the exchange value of a currency) to find its real level freely in relation to other currencies.

~n. 1. Something that floats, as: a. A raft. b. A buoy. c. A life belt. d. A cork or other floating object on a fishing line. e. A pontoon for amphibious aircraft. f. A hollow ball attached to a lever to regulate the water level in a tank. g. An air-filled or gas-filled organ or sac that enables an organism to remain suspended in water. 2. a. An exhibit carried through the streets in a parade. b. A large, flat vehicle bearing such an exhibit. 3. A tool for smoothing the surface of plaster or cement. 4. A soft drink with ice cream floating in it. 5. Any of the blades on a paddle wheel. 6. A small motor vehicle, usually battery-powered and used for deliveries: *a milk float.* 7. *Australian.* A horsebox. 8. A sum of money used for providing change to shoppers at the start of a day's business. 9. *Finance. Chiefly U.S.* The amount of money representing debts still outstanding. 10. *Plural.* Footlights in a theatre. [Middle English *floten*, Old English *flotian*.] **—float·a·ble** *adj.* **—float·y** *adj.*

floatage. Variant of **flotage.**

floatation. Variant of **flotation.**

float·er (flōtər) *n.* 1. One that floats. 2. *Finance.* A government stock certificate or the like recognised as security. 3. *Chiefly U.S.* One who wanders from place to place or job to job; a drifter. 4. *Chiefly U.S.* A floating voter. 5. *Plural.* **Muscae volitantes.**

float glass *n.* Flat plate glass made by floating molten glass on molten lead or some other liquid, and allowing the glass to harden.

float·ing (flōting) *adj.* 1. Buoyed on or suspended in or as if in a fluid. 2. Not secured in place; unattached. 3. Inclined to move about; drifting; errant. 4. *Finance.* a. Available for use; in circulation. Said of capital. b. Short-term and usually unfunded. Said of a debt. c. Freed to rise and fall in value in relation to other currencies. Said of a currency.

floating dock *n.* A structure that can be submerged to permit the entry and docking of a ship and then raised to lift the ship from the water for repairs. Also called "floating dry dock".

floating island *n.* 1. A solid mass of soil and vegetation floating in water. 2. A dessert of soft custard with beaten egg whites or whipped cream floating on its surface.

floating kidney *n. Medicine.* 1. An abnormal condition in which one or both kidneys are mobile and descend into the pelvis. 2. Such a kidney.

float·ing-point (flōting-póynt) *adj. Mathematics.* Designating or pertaining to a system of expressing numbers by two separate numbers, one giving the value of the digits and the other the power of the number base. For example, 2,3 is 2×10^3 (or 2,000) in base 10. Compare **fixed-point.**

floating rib *n.* Any of the four lower ribs of man that, unlike the other ribs, are not attached at the front to the breastbone.

floating voter *n.* An uncommitted voter who may vote for different parties or candidates at successive elections.

floc (flok) *n.* A flocculent mass as formed in certain serological precipitin tests. [Latin *floccus*, tuft of wool.]

floc·cu·late (flóckew-layt) *v.* **-lated, -lating, -lates.** *—tr.* 1. To cause (soil or chemical precipitates, for example) to form lumps or masses. 2. To cause (clouds) to form fluffy masses. *—intr.* To turn into lumpy or fluffy masses. [From FLOCCULE.] **—floc·cu·la·tion** (-láysh'n) *n.*

floc·cule (flóckewl) *n.* Any small, loosely held mass or aggregate of fine particles suspended in or precipitated from a solution. [From FLOCCULUS.]

floc·cu·lent (flóckewlənt) *adj.* 1. Having a fluffy or woolly appearance. 2. *Chemistry.* Made up of or containing woolly masses. 3. *Biology.* Flaky, waxy, and wool-like, as is the secretion covering some insects. [Latin *floccus*, tuft + -ULENT.] **—floc·cu·lence** *n.* **—floc·cu·lent·ly** *adv.*

floc·cu·lus (flóckew-ləss) *n., pl.* **-li** (-lī). 1. A small, fluffy mass. 2. *Anatomy.* Either of two small lobes on the lower posterior border of each lobe of the cerebellum. 3. *Astronomy.* Any of various masses of gases appearing as bright or dark patches on the Sun's surface. Also called "plage". [New Latin, diminutive of Latin *floccus*, tuft of wool.]

floc·cus (flóckəss) *n., pl.* **-ci** (flók-sī). 1. The downy or woolly covering of the young of certain birds. 2. A woolly tuft of hairs or filaments. [Latin, FLOCK.]

flock¹ (flok) *n.* 1. A group of animals, such as birds or sheep, that live, travel, or feed together. 2. A group of people under the leadership of one person; especially, the members of a church or congregation. 3. A large crowd or number.

~intr.v. **flocked, flocking, flocks.** To congregate or travel in a flock or crowd: *flock to the January sales.* [Middle English *flok*, Old English *flocc*, from Germanic *flugnaz* (unattested).]

Synonyms: flock, flight, herd, drove, pack, gang, gaggle, bevy, brood.

flock² *n.* 1. A tuft, as of fibre or hair. 2. Waste wool or cotton used for stuffing furniture and mattresses. 3. An inferior grade of wool added to cloth for extra weight. 4. Pulverised wool applied to paper, cloth, or metal to produce a texture or pattern. 5. A floccule.

~tr.v. **flocked, flocking, flocks.** 1. To stuff with flock. 2. To texture or pattern with flock. [Middle English *flok*, probably from Old French *floc*, from Latin *floccus*.]

Flod·den (flódd'n). Hillside near Branxton, Northumberland, England, where on September 9, 1513, the English routed the Scots. James IV and more than 10,000 men were slain.

floe (flō) *n.* 1. A large, flat mass of ice formed on the surface of a body of water. 2. A segment separated from such an ice mass. 3. An **ice field** *(see).* [Probably from Norwegian *flo*, layer, slab, from Old Norse *flō*, stratum, coating.]

flog (flog) *v.* **flogged, flogging, flogs.** *—tr.* 1. To beat harshly with a whip or rod. 2. *Chiefly British Slang.* To sell. 3. *Slang.* To exert (oneself) strenuously. [Perhaps shortened from Latin *flagellāre*, to whip, from *flagellum*, diminutive of *flagrum*, whip.] **—flog·ger** *n.*

flong (flong) *n. Printing.* Papier maché or a paper-like substance used in making a stereotype mould.

flood (flud) *n.* 1. An overflowing of water onto land that is normally dry; a deluge. 2. Flood tide. 3. Any abundant flow or outpouring: *choke back a flood of tears.* 4. *Archaic.* A sea. 5. *Informal.* A floodlight. **—in flood.** At an abnormally high level. Said of a river. **—the Flood.** The universal deluge recorded in the Bible as having occurred during the life of Noah. Genesis 7.

~v. **flooded, flooding, floods.** *—tr.* 1. To cover or submerge with a flood; inundate. 2. To fill with an abundance or an excess. *—intr.* 1. To become inundated or submerged. 2. To pour or flow in or as if in a flood: *Applications flooded in.* 3. *Medicine.* a. To have a haemorrhage of the uterus, as after childbirth. b. To have an unusually heavy menstrual flow. [Middle English *flod*, *flud*, Old English *flōd*, from Germanic.]

flood-gate (flúd-gayt) *n.* 1. A gate used to control the flow of a body of water. Also called "water gate". 2. *Often plural.* Anything that restrains a flood or onrush.

flood·light (flúd-līt) *n.* 1. Artificial light in an intensely bright and broad beam, as used to illuminate a sports field, for example. 2. A lamp or lighting unit that produces such a beam.

~tr.v. **floodlighted** or **-lit** (-lit), **-lighting, -lights.** To illuminate with a floodlight.

flood plain *n.* A plain bordering a river, subject to flooding.

flood tide *n.* The incoming or rising tide. Compare **ebb tide.**

floor (flor ‖ flōr) *n. Abbr.* **fl.** 1. The surface of a room on which one stands. 2. The lower or supporting surface of any structure. 3. A minimum or base; a lower limit, especially of wages or prices. 4. The ground or lowermost surface, together with accumulated layers of detritus, as of a forest or ocean. 5. A level area on which a specified activity takes place: *a dance floor; a factory floor; a threshing floor.* 6. The lower part of a room, such as a legislative chamber or stock exchange, where business is conducted. 7. a. The right to address an assembly, as granted under parliamentary procedure: *be given the floor.* b. The body of assembly members: *a motion from the floor.* 8. A storey or level of a building. **—take the floor.** To start dancing on a dance floor.

~tr.v. **floored, flooring, floors.** 1. To provide with a floor. 2. To knock or press to the floor or ground. 3. *Informal.* To stun; overwhelm. [Middle English *flor*, Old English *flōr*, from Germanic.] **—floor·er** *n.*

floor·age (flór-ij ‖ flōr-) *n.* A stretch of floor; floor space.

floor·board (flór-bawrd ‖ flōr-bōrd) *n.* Any of the boards forming a floor.

floor·ing (flór-ing ‖ flōr-) *n.* 1. a. Floors collectively. b. A floor. 2. Material, such as wood or tiles, used in making floors.

flooring saw *n.* A saw with a curved toothed edge, used for cutting through floorboards.

floor manager *n.* 1. The supervisor of a floor of departments in a large department store or shop. 2. The supervisor or stage manager present on the set during a television production.

floor plan *n.* A scale diagram of a room or building drawn as if seen from above.

floor show *n.* A series of entertainments presented in a nightclub, hotel, or the like.

floor·walk·er (flór-wawkər ‖ flōr-) *n. U.S.* A **shopwalker** *(see).*

floo·zy, floo·zie (flóozi) *n., pl.* **-zies.** *Slang.* A slovenly or vulgar woman; especially, a cheap prostitute. [Origin unknown.]

flop (flop) *v.* **flopped, flopping, flops.** *—intr.* 1. To move or fall heavily and clumsily. 2. To swing or move about in a loose, noisy way; flap. 3. *Informal.* To fail. 4. *Slang.* To go to bed. Often used with *out.* *—tr.* To cause to fall down suddenly and noisily.

~n. 1. The action of flopping. 2. The sound of flopping; a dull thud. 3. *Informal.* An utter failure. [Variant of FLAP.] **—flop·per** *n.*

flop·house (flóp-howss) *n., pl.* **-houses** (-howziz). *U.S.* A **doss-house** *(see).*
flop·py (flóppi) *adj.* **-pier, -piest.** Tending to flop; loose and flexible. *~n. Computing.* A floppy disk.
floppy disk *n. Computing.* A thin flexible plastic disk with a magnetic coating, used as a storage device. Also called "magnetic disk", "floppy", "diskette".
flo·ra (fláw-rə || flṓ-) *n., pl.* **-ras** or **-rae** (-ree). **1.** Plants collectively; especially, the plants of a particular region or time. **2.** A systematic compilation describing plants. **3. Intestinal flora** *(see).* [From FLORA.]
Flo·ra. *Roman Mythology.* The goddess of flowers. [Latin *Flōra,* from *flōs* (stem *flōr-*), flower.]
flo·ral (fláwrəl, flórrəl || flṓrəl) *adj.* Of, pertaining to, consisting of, or suggestive of a flower or flowers. **—flo·ral·ly** *adv.*
floral envelope *n.* The perianth of a flower, which surrounds the stamens and pistil; the sepals and petals collectively.
flo·re·at (flórri-at, fláwri- || flṓri-). *Latin.* May it flourish. Used as a motto or slogan with the name of a place or institution: *Floreat Aula.* In the plural, it takes the form *floreant.*
Flor·ence (flórrəns). *Italian* **Fi·ren·ze** (fee-rént-say). City in the Tuscany region of northern central Italy, lying on the Arno river at the foot of the Apennines. Originally an Etruscan settlement, Florence was one of the most powerful and artistically brilliant city-states of the Italian Renaissance, when it was under the rule of the Medici family. Giotto, Michelangelo, Leonardo, Raphael, Dante, and Donatello were all active there.
Florence fennel *n.* A variety of fennel, **finochio** *(see).*
Flor·en·tine (flórrən-tīn, -teen || fláwrən-) *adj.* **1.** Of or pertaining to the city of Florence. **2.** Of or pertaining to the style of art and architecture that flourished in Renaissance Florence. **3.** *Often small* **f.** Cooked or served with spinach. Said of eggs and other dishes. *~n.* **1.** A native or inhabitant of Florence. **2.** A large rich biscuit containing nuts and preserved fruit and coated with chocolate on one side. [Latin *Flōrentīnus,* from *Flōrentia,* FLORENCE.]
flo·res·cence (flaw-réssənss, flo-, flə-) *n.* The condition, time, or period of blossoming. [New Latin *florescentia,* from Latin *flōrēscens,* present participle of *flōrēscere,* to begin to bloom, inceptive of *flōrēre,* to bloom, from *flōs* (stem *flōr-*), FLOWER] **—flo·res·cent** *adj.*
flo·ret (flórr-it, -et || fláwr-) *n.* A small flower, usually part of a dense cluster; especially, one of the disc or ray flowers of a composite plant, such as a daisy. [Middle English *flouret,* from Old French *florete,* diminutive of *flo(u)r,* FLOWER.]
Flo·rey (fláwri), **Howard Walter, Baron** (1898–1968). Australian pathologist. Working with E. Chain, he isolated and purified the antibiotic penicillin, discovered by A. Fleming in 1928. They and Fleming shared the Nobel prize for physiology or medicine in 1945.
flo·ri·at·ed, flo·re·at·ed (fláwri-aytid) *adj.* Decorated with floral designs; flowery or flower-like. [Latin *flōs* (stem *flōr-*), flower.]
flo·ri·bun·da (fláwri-búndə, flórri-) *n.* Any of several hybrid roses bearing numerous single or double flowers. [New Latin, feminine of *floribundus,* blossoming freely, from Latin *flōs* (stem *flōr-*), FLOWER.]
flo·ri·cul·ture (fláwri-kulchər, flórri-) *n.* The cultivation of flowering plants. [Latin *flōs* (stem *flōr-*), FLOWER + CULTURE.] **—flo·ri·cul·tur·al** (-kúlchərəl) *adj.* **—flo·ri·cul·tur·ist** (-kúlchərist) *n.*
flor·id (flórrid || fláwrid) *adj.* **1.** Flushed with rosy colour; ruddy. **2.** Heavily adorned or embellished; flowery: *"their style is clear, masculine, and smooth, but not florid"* (Jonathan Swift). **3.** *Archaic.* Healthy; blooming. —See Synonyms at **ornate.** [French *floride,* from Latin *flōridus,* from *flōrēre,* to bloom, from *flōs* (stem *flōr-*), FLOWER.] **—flo·rid·i·ty** (flə-ríddit), **flor·id·ness** *n.* **—flor·id·ly** *adv.*
Flor·i·da (flórri-də || fláwri-). State of the United States occupying a long peninsula between the Atlantic Ocean and the Gulf of Mexico. It was admitted to the Union in 1845. Florida's wide, sandy beaches and hot climate make it one of the country's leading tourist regions, and its southern swamps form the Everglades National Park. Florida is the leading producer of citrus fruits in the United States. Tallahassee is the state capital. **—Flo·rid·i·an** (flo-ríddi-ən, flə-), **Flor·i·dan** *adj. & n.*
Florida Keys. Chain of small, sandy, coral and limestone islands and reefs stretching about 240 kilometres (150 miles) off southern Florida, in the United States. The subtropical keys, from the Spanish *cayos* (islands), are popular tourist resorts. The world's longest overwater motorway links the islands with 42 bridges.
flo·rif·er·ous (flaw-ríffərəss, flo-) *adj.* Bearing flowers; especially, flowering abundantly. [Latin *flōrifer* : *flōs* (stem *flōr-*), FLOWER + -FEROUS.]
flo·ri·gen (flórri-jən || fláwri-) *n.* A hypothetical plant hormone thought to be produced in the leaves and transmitted to the growing points where it causes the initiation of flower buds. [Latin *flōs* (stem *flōr-*), flower + -GEN.]
flor·in (flórrin || flṓ-rin, fláw-) *n. Abbr.* **fl. 1. a.** A former British coin worth two shillings (ten pence). **b.** The sum of two shillings (ten pence). **2.** A monetary unit, the **guilder** *(see).* **3. a.** A gold coin first issued in Florence in 1252. **b.** Any of several obsolete European gold coins similar to the Florentine florin. [Middle English *flore(i)n,* from Old French *florin,* from Italian *fiorino,* from *fiore,* flower (the original coins bore the figure of a lily), from Latin *flōs* (stem *flōr-*), FLOWER.]
flo·rist (flórrist || flṓ-rist, fláw-) *n.* A person whose business is the growing or selling of flowers and ornamental plants. [Latin *flōs* (stem *flōr-*), FLOWER + -IST.]
flo·ris·tics (flo-rístiks || flaw-) *n. Used with a singular verb.* The study of the types and numerical distribution of the plant species in a particular area. [*Flora* + *statistics.*] **—flo·ris·tic** *adj.*
-florous *adj. comb. form.* Indicates number or kind of flowers; for example, **tubuliflorous.** [Late Latin *-flōrus,* from Latin *flōs* (stem *flōr-*), FLOWER.]
flo·ru·it (fláw-rōō-it, fló- || -rew-) *n. Abbr.* **fl.** The period during which a person, or sometimes a group, movement, or the like, was most active or flourishing. [Latin, he (or she) flourished, from *flōrēre,* to bloom, FLOURISH.]
floss (floss || flawss) *n.* **1. a.** Short fibres or waste silk from the cocoon of a silkworm. **b.** The fluffy mass of fibres from cotton or similar plants. **2.** A soft, loosely twisted thread used in embroidery. **3.** Any soft, silky, fibrous substance, such as the styles and stigmas of maize. **4. Dental floss** *(see).* [Possibly from French *floche,* from Old French *flosche*†, down.]
floss·y (flóssi || fláwssi) *adj.* **-ier, -iest. 1.** Made of or resembling floss; downy; silky. **2.** *U.S. Slang.* Ostentatiously stylish; flashy.
flo·tage, float·age (flṓtij) *n.* **1.** Flotation. **2.** Floating material.
flo·ta·tion, float·a·tion (flō-táysh'n, flə-) *n.* **1.** The act, process, or condition of floating or launching. **2.** *Finance.* **a.** An act or instance of launching or financing a business venture by selling an issue of shares or bonds. **b.** The raising of a loan by such an issue. **3.** Any of several processes in which different materials, notably minerals, are separated by agitation of a pulverised mixture of the material with water, oil, and chemicals that cause differential wetting of the suspended particles, the unwetted particles being carried by air bubbles to the surface for collection. [Alteration of earlier *floatation* (FLOAT + -ATION), after *rotation.*]
flo·til·la (flə-tíllə, flō-) *n.* **1. a.** A fleet of small ships. **b.** A small fleet of ships. **2.** Any group resembling a small fleet: *a flotilla of taxis.* [Spanish, diminutive of *flota,* fleet, from Old French *flote,* from Old Norse *floti,* raft, fleet.]
flot·sam (flótsəm) *n.* **1.** Any wreckage or cargo that remains afloat after a ship has sunk. Compare **jetsam. 2.** Any discarded odds and ends. **3.** Unemployed and vagrant people; tramps. **4.** Miscellaneous articles. [Earlier *flotsen, flotson,* from Anglo-French *floteson,* from *floter,* to float, from Vulgar Latin *flottāre* (unattested), from Germanic.]
flounce[1] (flownss) *n.* A strip of gathered or pleated material secured on its upper edge to another surface, such as a garment or curtain. *~tr.v.* **flounced, flouncing, flounces.** To trim with a flounce or flounces. [Variant of obsolete *frounce,* Middle English *frounce,* a wrinkle, crease, from Old French *fronce,* from *froncir,* to wrinkle, from Frankish *hrunkjan* (unattested).]
flounce[2] *intr.v.* **flounced, flouncing, flounces.** To move with exaggerated motions expressive of displeasure or impatience.
~n. The act of flouncing. [16th century : perhaps imitative.]
floun·der[1] (flówndər) *intr.v.* **-dered, -dering, -ders. 1.** To move clumsily and with difficulty, as if trying to regain balance. **2.** To proceed clumsily and in confusion.
~n. The act of floundering. [Probably blend of FOUNDER and BLUNDER (and influenced by FLOUNCE, to move jerkily).]
floun·der[2] *n., pl.* **-ders** or collectively **flounder. 1.** A European flatfish, *Platichthys flesus,* that has a greyish-brown mottled body and is an important food fish. **2.** Any other flatfish of the families Bothidae and Pleuronectidae. [Middle English, from Anglo-French *floundre,* probably from Scandinavian.]
flour (flowr) *n.* **1.** A soft, fine, powdery substance obtained by grinding and sifting the meal of a grain, especially wheat. **2.** Any similar soft, fine powder.
~tr.v. **floured, flouring, flours. 1.** To cover or coat with flour. **2.** *Chiefly U.S.* To make into flour. [Middle English *flour, flur,* finer meal, farina, FLOWER.] **—flour·y** *adj.*
flour·ish (flúrrish) *v.* **-ished, -ishing, -ishes.** *—intr.* **1.** To grow well or luxuriantly: *Most flowers flourish in full sunlight.* **2.** To fare well; thrive; prosper. **3.** To be active; especially, to be at the peak of one's activity, fame, or the like. See **floruit. 4.** To make bold, sweeping movements; wave vigorously: *The flag flourished in the wind.* *~tr.* To wield, wave, brandish, or exhibit dramatically: *flourish a baton.*
~n. **1.** An act or instance of ostentatiously waving or brandishing: *The swordsman made a flourish.* **2.** An embellishment or ornamentation, as in handwriting or literary composition. **3.** A dramatic action or gesture. **4.** A musical fanfare or similar passage. **5.** *Archaic.* A period or state of thriving or of being in flower. [Middle English *florishen,* from Old French *florir* (stem *floriss-*), to bloom, from Vulgar Latin *flōrīre* (unattested), from Latin *flōrēre,* from *flōs* (stem *flōr-*), flower.] **—flour·ish·er** *n.*
flout (flowt) *v.* **flouted, flouting, flouts.** *—tr.* To show contempt for, especially in one's actions; scorn: *flout convention.* *—intr.* To be scornful; jeer. **—**See Usage note at **flaunt.**
~n. Rare. A contemptuous action or remark; an insult. [Probably extended use of Middle English *flouten,* to play the flute, from Old French *flauter,* from *flaute,* FLUTE.] **—flout·er** *n.* **—flout·ing·ly** *adv.*
flow (flō) *v.* **flowed, flowing, flows.** *—intr.* **1.** To move or run freely in the manner characteristic of a fluid. **2.** To circulate, as the blood in the body does. **3.** To discharge in a stream; pour forth. **4.** To move or proceed smoothly and steadily, as if in an uninterrupted stream: *The traffic flowed across the bridge.* **5.** To proceed with ease: *The conversation flowed.* **6.** To appear smooth, harmonious, or graceful: *the building's flowing lines.* **7.** To rise. Used of the tide.

8. To arise; derive: *Several conclusions flow from this hypothesis.* **9.** To abound or be plentiful. **10.** To hang loosely and gracefully: *The cape flowed from his shoulders.* **11.** To undergo plastic deformation without cleavage or breaking, as slate might. —*tr.* **1.** To release as a flow. **2.** To cause to flow. **3.** To flood.

~*n.* **1. a.** The smooth motion characteristic of fluids. **b.** The act of flowing. **2.** A stream. **3. a.** A continuous output or outpouring; a flood: *a flow of ideas.* **b.** A continuous movement or circulation: *the flow of traffic.* **4.** The amount that flows in a given period of time. **5.** The incoming or rise of the tide. **6.** Continuity and smoothness of appearance. **7.** Menstrual discharge. [Middle English *flouen,* Old English *flōwan,* from Germanic.] —**flow·ing·ly** *adv.*

flow·age (flṓ-ij) *n.* **1.** The act of flowing or overflowing. **2.** The state of being flooded. **3.** A liquid that flows or overflows. **4.** The gradual plastic deformation of a solid body, as by stress.

flow chart *n.* A schematic representation of a sequence of operations, as in a manufacturing process or a computer program. Also called "flow diagram", "flow sheet".

flow·er (flowr, flṓw-ər) *n.* **1. a.** The reproductive structure of an angiosperm plant, characteristically having specialised male and female organs (stamens and a pistil) enclosed in an outer envelope of petals and sepals, all borne on a receptacle. **b.** Any such structure having showy or colourful parts; a blossom. **2.** Any similar reproductive organ of other plants, as gymnosperms and mosses. **3. a.** A plant cultivated or conspicuous for its blossoms. **b.** The condition of being in blossom: *in flower.* **4.** That which is produced by any natural process; an outgrowth: *"His attitude was simply a flower of his general good-nature"* (Henry James). **5.** The period of highest development; the peak. **6.** The highest or brightest example; the best representative of something: *the flower of our generation.* **7.** An embellishment. **8.** *Usually plural. Chemistry.* A fine powder, produced by condensation or sublimation.

~*v.* **flowered, -ering, -ers.** —*intr.* **1.** To produce a flower or flowers; blossom; bloom. **2.** To develop fully; reach a peak. —*tr.* To decorate with flowers or with a floral pattern. [Middle English *flo(u)r,* from Old French *flo(u)r,* from Latin *flōs* (stem *flōr-*).] —**flow·er·less** *adj.*

flow·er·age (flṓwr-ij, flṓw-ər-) *n.* **1.** Flowers collectively. **2.** The process or state of flowering.

flow·er·bed (flṓwr-bed, flṓw-ər-) *n.* A plot of earth, as in a garden or park, in which flowers are grown.

flow·ered (flowrd, flṓw-ərd) *adj.* **1.** Having flowers. **2.** Decorated with flowers or a floral pattern: *flowered wallpaper.*

flow·er·er (flṓwr-ər, flṓw-ər-) *n.* A plant that flowers in a specified way or at a specified time: *a late flowerer.*

flow·er·et (flṓwr-it, flṓw-ər-, -et) *n.* A small flower. [Middle English *flourette,* from Old French *flo(u)rete,* diminutive of *flo(u)r,* FLOWER.]

flower girl *n.* **1.** A girl or woman who sells flowers in the street. **2.** A girl who carries flowers in a procession, especially at a wedding.

flower head *n.* A dense cluster of very small flowers at the tip of the plant stem.

flow·er·ing (flṓwr-ing, flṓw-ər-) *adj.* Capable of producing decorative flowers. Said of plants, especially trees.

flowering currant *n.* An ornamental shrub, *Ribes sanguineum,* native to North America but widely cultivated for its drooping clusters of small pink flowers, which appear before the leaves.

flowering maple *n.* Any of several tropical shrubs of the genus *Abutilon;* especially, *A. hybridum,* having lobed leaves resembling those of the maple and variously coloured flowers.

flowering plant *n.* An **angiosperm** (see).

flowering quince *n.* A shrub, **japonica** (see).

flow·er·peck·er (flṓwr-pek·ər, flṓw-ər-) *n.* Any small bird of the family Dicaeidae, of Australia and southeast Asia.

flow·er·pot (flṓwr-pot, flṓw-ər-) *n.* A pot in which plants are grown.

flower power *n. Informal.* **1.** The goal or ethos of a youth cult prevalent in the 1960s, advocating peace and love. A flower was used to symbolise the ideals of the *flower children* or *flower people* involved. **2.** The cult itself.

flow·er·y (flṓwri, flṓw-əri) *adj.* **-ier, -iest. 1.** Abounding in or bedecked with flowers. **2.** Suggestive of flowers: *a flowery perfume.* **3.** Having a floral pattern. **4.** Full of figurative and ornate expressions; highly embellished. —**flow·er·i·ly** *adv.* —**flow·er·i·ness** *n.*

flow meter *n.* An apparatus for monitoring, measuring, or recording fluid flow, especially of a gaseous fuel.

flown. Past participle of **fly.**

flow sheet *n.* A **flow chart** (see).

fl. oz. fluid ounce.

flu (flṓ ‖ flew) *n. Informal.* Influenza.
   Usage: Because of the widespread informal use of this word it is now readily recognised, and thus generally used without an apostrophe when it occurs in writing.

fluc·tu·ant (flúktew-ənt) *adj.* Varying; fluctuating; unstable. [Latin *fluctuāns* (stem *fluctuant-*), present participle of *fluctuāre,* FLUCTUATE.]

fluc·tu·ate (flúktew-ayt) *v.* **-ated, -ating, -ates.** —*intr.* **1.** To vary irregularly. **2.** To waver; vacillate. **3.** To rise and fall like waves; undulate. —*tr.* To cause to fluctuate. —See Synonyms at **swing.** [Latin *fluctuāre,* from *fluctus,* a flowing, from the past participle of *fluere,* to flow.] —**fluc·tu·a·tion** (-áysh'n) *n.*

flue¹ (flṓ ‖ flew) *n.* A pipe, tube, or channel through which hot air, gas, steam, or smoke may pass, as in a boiler or a chimney.

2. a. A flue pipe. **b.** The air passage in such a pipe. [16th century; origin obscure.]

flue² *n.* The fluffy waste from textile, fur, or the like. [Flemish *vluwe,* from French *velu,* velvety, from Old French, shaggy. See **velvet.**]

flue³, flew *n.* Any of several kinds of fishing net. [Middle English *flue,* from Middle Dutch *vluwe.*]

flu·ent (flṓ-ənt ‖ fléw-) *adj.* **1. a.** Expressing oneself readily and effortlessly: *a fluent speaker.* **b.** Effortless; flowing; polished: *speak fluent French.* **2.** Flowing smoothly and easily; graceful: *fluent curves.* **3.** *Rare.* Flowing or capable of flowing; fluid; liquid. [Latin *fluēns* (stem *fluent-*), present participle of *fluere,* to flow.] —**flu·en·cy** *n.* —**flu·ent·ly** *adv.*

flue pipe *n.* An organ pipe sounded by means of a current of air striking a lip in the side of the pipe and causing the air within to vibrate. Also called "flue". Compare **reed pipe.**

flue stop *n.* An organ stop controlling a set of flue pipes. Compare **reed stop.**

fluff (fluf) *n.* **1.** Light, feathery down or nap. **2.** Something having a light, soft, or frothy consistency or appearance. **3.** Something of little consequence; a trifle. **4.** *Informal.* A young woman. Used especially in the phrase *a bit of fluff.* **5.** *Informal.* An error or lapse of memory in the reading, recitation, or delivery of lines, as by an actor or announcer.

~*v.* **fluffed, fluffing, fluffs.** —*tr.* **1.** To make light and puffy by shaking or patting into a soft, loose mass: *fluff a pillow.* **2.** *Informal.* To misread or forget (one's lines). **3.** *Informal.* To make a mistake or blunder. —*intr.* **1.** To become soft and puffy or feathery. **2.** *Informal.* To forget or botch one's lines. [Probably variant of FLUE (down).]

fluff·y (flúffi) *adj.* **-ier, -iest. 1.** Of, like, or covered with fluff or down. **2.** Light and airy; soft: *fluffy curls.* —**fluff·i·ly** *adv.* —**fluff·i·ness** *n.*

flü·gel·horn (flṓṓg'l-hawrn; German flügal-) *n.* A bugle with valves, similar to the cornet but having a wider bore. [German : *Flügel,* wing, flank (formerly used to summon flanks during a battle), from Middle High German *vlügel* + *Horn,* horn.]

flu·id (flṓ-id ‖ fléw-) *n. Abbr.* **fl, fl.** A substance that has a low resistance to flow and the tendency to assume the shape of its container; a liquid or a gas.

~*adj. Abbr.* **fl, fl. 1.** Characteristic of a fluid; especially, flowing easily. **2.** Used in the measurement of fluids. **3.** Readily reshaped; pliable. **4.** Characterised by smoothness and grace; flowing. **5.** Likely or tending to change; not stable: *The political situation remains fluid and uncertain.* **6.** Convertible into cash: *fluid assets.* [Middle English, from Old French *fluide,* from Latin *fluidus,* from *fluere,* to flow.] —**flu·id·i·ty** (floo-íddəti ‖ flew-), **flu·id·ness** *n.* —**flu·id·ly** *adv.*

fluid drachm *n.* One-eighth of a **fluid ounce** (see).

fluid extract *n.* A concentrated alcohol solution of a vegetable drug containing the equivalent of one gram in powdered form of the active principle in each millilitre.

flu·id·ic (flṓṓ-íddik ‖ flew-) *adj.* Of, pertaining to, or operated by fluids.

flu·id·ics (flṓṓ-íddiks ‖ flew-) *n. Used with a singular verb.* The technology of fluids used as nonmoving, non-electrical components of control and sensing systems.

flu·id·ise, flu·id·ize (flṓṓ-i-dīz ‖ flew-) *tr.v.* **-ised, -ising, -ises.** To convert (a solid) into fine, flowing powder that can be conveyed in a stream of gas. —**flu·id·is·a·tion** (-dī-záysh'n ‖ U.S. -di-) *n.*

fluid mechanics *n. Used with a singular verb.* The branch of engineering concerned with the study and applications of fluid flow.

fluid ounce *n. Abbr.* **fl. oz. 1.** A unit of volume or capacity in the British Imperial System, used in liquid and dry measure, equal to 28.41 cubic centimetres (1.734 cubic inches). **2.** A unit of volume or capacity in the U.S. Customary System, used in liquid measure, equal to 29.6 cubic centimetres (1.804 cubic inches).

fluke¹ (flṓṓk ‖ flewk) *n., pl.* **fluke** (for sense 2) or **flukes. 1.** A flatworm, a **trematode** (see); especially, of various parasitic species. See **liver fluke. 2.** Any of various flatfishes; especially, a **flounder** (see). [Middle English *fluke, flok,* Old English *flōc,* from Germanic.]

fluke² *n.* **1.** The triangular blade at the end of either arm of an anchor, designed to catch in the ground. **2.** A barb or barbed head, as on an arrow or harpoon. **3.** Either of the two horizontally flattened divisions of the tail of a whale or related animal. [Probably from FLUKE (fish or worm, from its shape).]

fluke³ *n.* **1.** An accidental stroke of good luck. **2.** Any chance occurrence. **3.** *Sports.* An accidentally lucky or successful stroke.

~*v.* **fluked, fluking, flukes.** —*tr.* To get, make, or do by chance. —*intr.* To produce a fluke. [19th century : origin obscure.]

fluk·y (flṓṓki ‖ flẃki) *adj.* **-ier, -iest.** Also **fluk·ey.** *Informal.* **1.** Resulting from mere chance. **2.** Constantly shifting; uncertain; variable: *a fluky wind.* [From FLUKE (chance shot).]

flume (flṓṓm ‖ flewm) *n.* **1.** A narrow defile or gorge, usually with a stream flowing through it. **2.** An artificial channel or chute for a stream of water, as for furnishing power or conveying logs.

~*tr.v.* **flumed, fluming, flumes. 1.** To divert (water) by means of a flume. **2.** To transport (logs, for example) by the use of a flume. [Earlier, "river", from Middle English *flum,* from Old French, from Latin *flūmen,* from *fluere,* to flow.]

flum·mer·y (flúmməri) *n., pl.* **-ies. 1. a.** Any of several soft, light, bland foods, such as a custard or blancmange. **b.** Originally, a soft gelatinous food made by straining boiled oatmeal, to which fruit, honey, or the like, could be added. **2.** Meaningless flattery; mere nonsense; humbug. [Welsh *llymru†*.]

flum·mox (flúmməks) *tr.v.* **-moxed, -moxing, -moxes.** *Informal.* To confuse; perplex. [Of dialect origin (imitative).]

flung. Past tense and past participle of **fling.**

flunk (flungk) *v.* **flunked, flunking, flunks.** *Chiefly U.S. Informal.* —*intr.* To fail an examination or course of study. —*tr.* **1.** To fail (an examination or course). **2.** To give (someone) a failing mark. **—flunk out.** *Chiefly U.S.* To be expelled from an educational institution or course because of failure to meet required standards. [19th century : origin obscure.]

flun·ky (flúng-ki) *n., pl.* **-kies.** Also **flun·key** *pl.* **-keys. 1.** A liveried manservant or valet; a lackey. **2.** An obsequious or fawning person; a toady. **3.** A person who does menial or trivial work. [Originally Scottish (dialectal) *flunky†*.] **—flun·ky·ism** *n.*

flu·or (flóō-awr, -ər, floor || fléw-ər) *n.* Fluorspar. [New Latin, from Latin, a flowing, fluid (from its use as a flux in smelting), from *fluere,* to flow.]

flu·o·resce (floor-éss, flóō-ər- || flōr-, flawr-) *v.* **-resced, -rescing, -resces.** —*intr.* To undergo, produce, or show fluorescence. —*tr.* To cause to produce fluorescence. [Back-formation from FLUORESCENCE.]

flu·o·res·ce·in (floor-éssi-in, flóō-ər- || flōr-, flawr-) *n.* An orange-red compound, $C_{20}H_{12}O_5$, that exhibits intense fluorescence in alkaline solution. It is used to dye sea water for spotting or tracing operations and as a chemical indicator.

flu·o·res·cence (floor-éss'nss, flóō-ər- || flōr-, flawr-) *n.* **1.** The emission of electromagnetic radiation, especially of light, resulting from irradiation with other electromagnetic radiation or with particles, and persisting only as long as the stimulating radiation is continued. **2.** The radiation so emitted. Compare **phosphorescence.** [FLUOR + -ESCENCE.] **—flu·o·res·cent** *adj.*

fluorescent lamp *n.* A lamp that produces light by fluorescence; especially, a glass tube, the inner wall of which is coated with a material that fluoresces when bombarded by a gaseous discharge within the tube.

flu·o·ri·date (flóor-i-dayt, flóō-ər-, fláwr- || flṓr-) *tr.v.* **-dated, -dating, -dates.** To add a fluorine compound to (a water supply, for example) for the purpose of preventing tooth decay. [Back-formation from *fluoridation* : FLUORID(E) + -ATION.] **—flu·o·ri·da·tion** (-dáysh'n) *n.*

flu·o·ride (flóor-īd, flóō-ər-, fláwr-) *n.* Any binary compound of fluorine with another element. [FLUOR(O)- + -IDE.]

flu·o·rine (flóor-een, flóō-ər-, -in || fléw-) *n.* *Symbol* **F** A pale yellow, highly corrosive, highly poisonous, gaseous halogen element, the most electronegative and most reactive of all the elements. It is used in a wide variety of industrially important compounds. Atomic number 9, atomic weight 18.9984, freezing point –219.62°C, boiling point –188.14°C, relative density of liquid 1.108, valency 1. [French, from New Latin *fluor,* generic name for a group of minerals used as fluxes, FLUOR.] **—flu·o·ri·nate** (-i-nayt) *tr.v.* **—flu·o·ri·na·tion** (-i-náysh'n) *n.*

flu·o·rite (flóor-īt, flóō-ər-) *n.* A white or colourless mineral, CaF_2, often tinged green, blue, violet, yellow, or brown by impurities. The coloured varieties are fluorescent in ultraviolet radiation. Also called "fluorspar".

fluoro–, fluor– *comb. form.* Indicates: **1.** *Chemistry.* Fluorine in compound; for example, **fluorosis. 2.** Fluorescence; for example, **fluoroscope.** [From FLUORINE and FLUORESCENCE.]

flu·o·ro·car·bon (flóor-ō-kárbən, flóō-ər-) *n.* Any of various inert organic compounds derived from hydrocarbons with fluorine replacing all or part of the hydrogen, used as aerosol propellants, refrigerants, solvents, lubricants, and in making plastics and resins.

flu·o·rom·e·ter (floor-ómmitər, flóō-ər-) *n.* Any instrument for detecting and measuring fluorescence. [FLUORO- + -METER.] **—flu·o·rom·e·try** (-ómmətri) *n.*

flu·o·ro·scope (flóor-ə-skōp, flóō-ər-) *n.* A suitably mounted fluorescent screen on which the contents or internal structure of an object, the human body, or the like, may be continuously viewed as shadows formed by differential transmission of X-rays through the object. Also called "radioscope".

~*tr.v.* **fluoroscoped, -scoping, -scopes.** To examine the interior of (an object) with a fluoroscope. [FLUORO- + -SCOPE.] **—flu·o·ro·scop·ic** (-skóppik) *adj.* **—flu·o·ro·scop·i·cal·ly** *adv.*

flu·o·ros·co·py (floor-óskəpi, flóō-ər-) *n.* Examination with the use of a fluoroscope.

flu·o·ro·sis (floor-ṓ-siss, flóō-ər-) *n.* An abnormal condition caused by excessive intake of fluorides, as in drinking water, characterised chiefly by mottling of the teeth. [New Latin : FLUOR(O)- + -OSIS.]

flu·or·o·u·ra·cil (flóor-ō-yóor-ə-sil) *n.* A drug, $C_4H_3FN_2O_2$, used in the treatment of cancer of the breast and digestive system.

flu·or·spar (flóor-spaar, flóō-ər-) *n.* Fluorite. [FLUOR(O)- + SPAR.]

flu·ox·e·tine hydrochloride (flōō-óksə-teen) *n.* An SSRI antidepressant, **Prozac** *(see).*

flur·ry (flúrri) *n., pl.* **-ries. 1.** A sudden gust of wind. **2.** A sudden burst of confusion, excitement, or bustling activity; a stir. **3.** A light shower of snow or rain.

~*v.* **flurried, -rying, -ries.** —*tr.* To agitate, confuse, or make nervous; fluster. —*intr.* To become agitated or confused. [From obsolete *flurr,* to whirl up, scatter, probably an expressive formation on analogy with HURRY.]

flush[1] (flush) *v.* **flushed, flushing, flushes.** —*intr.* **1.** To turn red in the face from fever, embarrassment, or strong emotion; colour; blush. **2.** To flow suddenly and abundantly; spread out quickly; flood. **3.** To glow, especially with a reddish colour. **4. a.** To be cleaned by a rapid, brief gush of water. **b.** To function by means of a flushing mechanism. Used of a lavatory. —*tr.* **1.** To cause to redden or glow. **2.** To excite or elate, as with a feeling of pride or accomplishment. Usually used in the passive: *flushed with victory.* **3. a.** To wash, empty, or purify with a sudden, rapid flow of water or other liquid. **b.** To remove or dispose of by flushing.

~*n.* **1.** A blush or glow: *a flush of red on a cloud.* **2.** A brief but copious flow or gushing, as of water. **3.** Redness of the skin, as with fever. See **hot flush. 4.** A feeling of animation or exhilaration; a rush of emotion. **5.** A freshness, development, or growth.

~*adj.* **flusher, flushest. 1. a.** Having surfaces in the same plane; even; level. **b.** Arranged with adjacent sides, surfaces, or edges touching. **2.** Abundant; plentiful. **3.** *Informal.* Having an abundant supply of money; prosperous; affluent. **4.** Lively; vigorous; lusty. **5.** Having a healthy reddish colour; blushing; glowing. **6.** *Printing.* Having the copy lined up evenly at the margins with no indentations. —See Synonyms at **level.**

~*adv.* **1.** So as to be even, in one plane, or aligned with a margin. **2.** Squarely; solidly: *The ball hit him flush on the face.* [Probably from FLUSH (to take flight, dart out).] **—flush·ness** *n.*

flush[2] *n.* In poker or similar games, a hand in which all the cards are of the same suit, rated above a straight and below a full house. See **royal flush, straight flush.** [Probably from Old French *flus, flux,* from Latin *fluxus,* a flow, FLUX.]

flush[3] *v.* **flushed, flushing, flushes.** —*tr.* **1.** To frighten (a game bird, for example) from cover. **2.** To cause to leave a place of concealment. Used with *out*: *used tear gas to flush out the terrorists.* —*intr.* To dart out or fly from cover; take flight. [Middle English *flusshen,* perhaps from (unattested) Old English *flyscan* (imitative).]

flus·ter (flústər) *v.* **-tered, -tering, -ters.** —*tr.* To make nervous, confused, or agitated. —*intr.* To become nervous or excited, as from confusion or bewilderment.

~*n.* A state of agitation, confusion, or excitement; a flurry; a flap. [Middle English *flostren,* possibly from Scandinavian, akin to Icelandic *flaustra,* to bustle.]

flute (flōōt || flewt) *n. Abbr.* **fl. 1.** A high-pitched instrument of the woodwind family, tubular in shape and with fingerholes and keys on the side and a reedless mouthpiece either at the end, as in the recorder, or on the side, as in the transverse flute. **2.** An organ stop whose flue pipe produces a flutelike tone. **3.** *Architecture.* Any of the long parallel grooves, usually with rounded inner surfaces, incised on the shaft of a column as a decorative motif. **4.** A similar groove in some other material, such as a pleated ruffle.

~*v.* **fluted, fluting, flutes.** —*tr.* **1.** To play (a tune) on a flute. **2.** To sing, whistle, or otherwise produce (a flutelike sound). **3.** To make flutes in (a column or piece of cloth, for example). —*intr.* **1.** To play a flute. **2.** To sing, whistle, or utter with a flutelike sound. [Middle English *floute, floite,* from Old French *flaute, fleute* (probably imitative); the initial consonant cluster was probably influenced by FLAGEOLET and Latin *flāre,* to blow.] **—flut·y** *adj.*

flut·ed (flóōtid || fléwtid) *adj.* **1.** Decorated with parallel grooves, as a column or ruffle. **2.** Having a sound like that of a flute; high-pitched and clear.

flut·er (flóōtər || fléwtər) *n.* **1. a.** One who makes flutings. **b.** A device used in making flutings. **2.** *Rare.* A flautist.

flut·ing (flóōting || fléwting) *n.* **1.** A decorative motif consisting of a series of long, rounded, parallel grooves, such as those incised in the surface of a column. **2.** The grooves formed by narrow pleats in cloth, as in a ruffle.

flut·ist (flóōtist || fléwtist) *n. Chiefly U.S.* A **flautist** *(see).*

flut·ter (flúttər) *v.* **-tered, -tering, -ters.** —*intr.* **1.** To wave or flap lightly and rapidly in an irregular manner: *The curtains fluttered in the breeze.* **2. a.** To fly by a quick, light flapping of the wings. **b.** To flap the wings without flying. **3.** To move or fall in a manner suggestive of tremulous flight: *"Her arms rose, fell, and fluttered with the rhythm of the song"* (Evelyn Waugh). **4.** To vibrate or beat rapidly or erratically: *His heart fluttered wildly.* **5.** To move quickly in a nervous, restless, or excited fashion; flit. **6.** To be excited, flustered, or nervous. —*tr.* **1.** To cause to flutter; wave; flap: *fluttering her eyelashes.* **2.** To make excited or nervous; confuse; fluster.

~*n.* **1.** An act of fluttering; a quick flapping. **2.** A condition of nervous excitement or agitation. **3.** A brief state of excitement, surprise, or bewilderment; a commotion; a flurry. **4.** *Medicine.* Abnormally rapid beating of the heart. **5.** *Electronics.* A distortion in reproduced sound due to frequency deviations created by faulty recording or reproduction techniques. **6.** *British Informal.* A small bet. [Middle English *floteren,* to flutter, be tossed by waves, Old English *floterian.*] **—flut·ter·er** *n.* **—flut·ter·y** *adj.*

flutter kick *n.* A swimming kick in which the legs are held horizontally and alternately moved up and down in rapid strokes without bending the knees.

flutter tonguing *n.* The trill-like playing of a wind instrument, achieved by means of a rapid vibration of the tongue.

flu·vi·al (flóōvi-əl || fléwvi-) *adj.* **1.** Of, pertaining to, or inhabiting a river or stream. **2.** Formed or produced by the action of flowing water. [Middle English, from Latin *fluviālis,* from *fluvius,* river, from *fluere,* to flow.]

flu·vi·o·ma·rine (flóōvi-ō-mə-réen) *adj. Geology.* Designating a series of deposits, some of which were laid down by rivers and some in the sea. [Latin *fluvius,* river, from *fluere,* to flow + MARINE.]

flux (flúks) *n.* **1. a.** A flow or flowing. **b.** A continued flow or flood.

2. *Physics.* **a.** The rate of flow across a unit area of a fluid, electromagnetic energy, or particles such as neutrons. **b.** Flux density. **3.** *Medicine.* The discharge of large quantities of fluid material from the body, such as watery faeces in diarrhoea. **4.** Continuous change: *a state of flux.* **5.** *Chemistry & Metallurgy.* A substance that aids, induces, or otherwise actively participates in a flowing, as: **a.** A mineral added to a furnace charge to promote fusing of metals or to prevent the formation of oxides. **b.** A substance applied in soldering and brazing to portions of a surface to be joined, acting on application of heat to prevent oxide formation and to facilitate the flowing of solder. **c.** Any readily fusible glass or enamel used as a base in ceramic work.
~*v.* **fluxed, fluxing, fluxes.** —*tr.* **1.** To melt; fuse. **2.** To apply a flux to. —*intr.* **1.** To become fluid. **2.** To flow; stream. [Middle English, from Old French, from Latin *fluxus,* from the past participle of *fluere,* to flow.]
flux density *n. Physics.* The strength of a magnetic or electric field or the like per unit area.
flux·ion (flúksh'n) *n.* **1.** *Rare.* Continual change. **2.** Something that flows; a discharge or issue. **3.** *Mathematics.* **a.** A derivative. **b.** *Plural.* Differential calculus. No longer in technical usage. [Old French, from Latin *fluxiō* (stem *fluxiōn-*), from *fluxus,* FLUX.] **—flux·ion·al, flux·ion·ar·y** (-əri || -erri) *adj.* **—flux·ion·al·ly** *adv.*
fly¹ (flī) *v.* **flew** (floō || flew), **flown** (flōn || flō-ən), **flying, flies.** —*intr.* **1.** To engage in flight, especially: **a.** To move through the air with the aid of wings. **b.** To travel by air. **c.** To pilot an aircraft. **2.** To glide through the air sustained by winglike parts. **3. a.** To rise in the air or be carried through the air by the wind. **b.** To float or flutter in the air. **4.** To be sent or driven through the air with great speed or force. **5. a.** To rush; run. **b.** To flee; escape or try to escape. **c.** To hasten; spring: *He flew to my defence.* **6.** To pass by swiftly, as time or youth might. **7.** To be dissipated rapidly; vanish unaccountably, as money might. **8.** To react explosively; burst: *He flew into a rage.* **9.** To shoot forth: *Sparks flew in all directions from the torch.* —*tr.* **1. a.** To cause to fly, hover, or float in the air. **b.** To keep (a flag) aloft. **2. a.** To pilot (an aircraft). **b.** To transport or dispatch in an aircraft. **c.** To pass over in an aircraft: *fly the ocean.* **d.** To travel by air using (a particular airline). **3.** To shun; run away from; flee from. **—fly at.** To attack suddenly, either physically or verbally. **—fly blind.** To fly an aircraft relying wholly on instruments, as in bad visibility. **—fly high. 1.** To be in the clouds; be elated. **2.** To prosper; be successful. **—let fly. 1.** To emit, send forth, or direct with force or violence. **2.** To release pent-up feelings of anger. Used with *at.*
~*n., pl.* **flies. 1. a.** An overlapping fold of cloth that hides a zip, buttons, or other fastening, as in a pair of trousers. **b.** *Plural. Informal.* The zip on the front of a pair of trousers. **2.** A cloth flap that covers an entrance, or forms a roof extension for a tent or wagon. **3.** A flyleaf. **4.** The length of a flag from the staff to the outer edge. **5.** The outer edge of a flag. **6.** A flywheel or similar mechanism. **7.** *Printing.* A person or device that carries the printed sheets from the press and places them in a flat pile. **8.** *Plural.* The area directly over the stage of a theatre and behind the proscenium, containing the overhead lights, drop curtains, and equipment for raising and lowering sets. **9.** *British.* A one-horse carriage, formerly hired out. **—on the fly.** In flight; on the run; in a hurry. [Fly, flew, flown; Middle English *flien, flew, flowen,* Old English *flēogan, flēah* (plural *flugon*), *flogen,* from Germanic.]
fly² *n., pl.* **flies. 1.** Any of numerous two-winged insects of the order Diptera; especially, any of the family Muscidae, which includes the **housefly** *(see).* **2.** Any of various other flying insects, such as the caddis fly. **3.** A fishing lure simulating a fly. **—drink with the flies.** *Australian.* To drink on one's own. **—fly in the ointment.** *Informal.* Something that detracts from the pleasure, value, or effectiveness of something; a jarring or negative factor. [Biblical allusion: "Dead flies cause the ointment of the apothecary to send forth a stinking savour. . ." (Ecclesiastes 10:1).] **—fly on the wall.** One who is in a position to observe others while not being seen himself. **—there are no flies on (someone).** *Informal.* Used of an astute or shrewd person. [Middle English *flie,* Old English *flēoge,* from Germanic.]
fly³ *adj. British Informal.* Alert; clever; sharp. [Probably from FLY (to go swiftly).]
fly agaric *n.* A poisonous mushroom, *Amanita muscaria,* usually having a red or orange cap with white patches. Also called "fly amanita". [From its use as a fly poison.]
fly ash *n.* Fine ash carried into the air during combustion.
fly·a·way (flī-ə-way) *adj.* **1.** Blown or appearing to be blown by the wind; fluttering or streaming. **2.** Flighty; frivolous; giddy.
fly·blow (flī-blō) *n.* The egg or larva of a blowfly, usually deposited on food.
~*tr.v.* **flyblew** (-bloō || -blew), **-blown** (-blōn), **-blowing, -blows. 1.** To deposit (the eggs of a blowfly) in. **2.** To taint; contaminate.
fly·blown (flī-blōn) *adj.* **1.** Contaminated with flyblows. **2. a.** Spoiled; tainted; corrupt. **b.** Seedy; shabby.
fly·book (flī-bŏok) *n.* A case for artificial flies for fishing.
fly·by (flī-bī) *n., pl.* **-bys.** A flight passing close to a specific target or position; especially, a manoeuvre in which a spacecraft passes sufficiently close to a planet to make relatively detailed observations without landing.
fly-by-night (flī-bī-nīt || -bi-, -bə-) *adj. Informal.* **1.** Unreliable with regard to business dealings; shady. **2.** Dubious and temporary.
~*n.* **1.** One who cheats his creditors, as by absconding in the night. **2.** Something of a dubiously transitory nature.
fly·catch·er (flī-kachər) *n.* **1.** Any of various birds of the Old World family Muscicapidae that feed on insects, usually catching them in flight. **2.** Any similar bird of the American family Tyrannidae. In this sense, also called "tyrant flycatcher".
fly-drive (flī-drīv) *n.* An organised holiday providing air travel to a destination and a rented car on arrival. **—fly-drive** *adj. & adv.*
flyer. Variant of **flier.**
fly-fishing (flī-fishing) *n.* Angling using artificial flies for bait. **—fly-fish** (flī-fish) *intr.v.* **—fly-fish·er** *n.*
fly front *n.* A garment front that has a fly concealing the fastenings.
fly half *n.* In Rugby football, a **stand-off half** *(see).*
fly·ing (flī-ing) *adj.* **1.** Moving through the air with or as if with wings. **2.** Brief; hurried: *a flying visit.* **3.** Concerned with or used in aviation: *a flying jacket.* **4.** *Nautical.* Not secured by spars or stays. Said of sails.
~*n.* **1.** Flight in an aircraft. **2.** The piloting of an aircraft.
flying boat *n.* A large seaplane that is kept afloat by its hull rather than by pontoons.
flying bomb *n.* A small, explosive-carrying, gyroscopically guided winged missile powered by a pulse jet. It was used by the Germans in World War II. Also called "V-1", "buzz bomb", "robot bomb".
flying buttress *n. Architecture.* An arched masonry prop that springs from a pier or other support and abuts against another part of the structure to take thrust away. Also called "arc-boutant".
flying circus *n.* **1.** A squadron of fighter planes in World War I. **2.** An exhibition of stunt flying; an aerobatic display. **3.** The aircraft and team of men involved in such an exhibition.
flying colours *pl.n.* Triumph; outstanding success: *pass an exam with flying colours.*
flying doctor *n.* A doctor, usually in a sparsely populated area, who uses an aircraft to visit patients.
flying dragon *n.* The flying lizard.
Flying Dutchman *n.* **1.** A legendary mariner condemned to sail the seas against the wind until Judgment Day. **2.** His spectral ship, said to appear in storms near the Cape of Good Hope.
flying field *n.* An airfield.
flying fish *n.* Any of various marine fishes of the family Exocoetidae, having enlarged pectoral or pelvic fins capable of sustaining them in brief, gliding flight over the water.
flying fox *n.* **1.** Any of various fruit bats of the genus *Pteropus,* chiefly of tropical Africa, Asia, and Australia, having a foxlike muzzle and ears. **2.** Any of several similar or related mammals.
flying frog *n.* A tree-dwelling frog, *Rhacophorus reinwardtii,* of southeast Asia, having toes connected by broad webbing and capable of gliding considerable distances.
flying gurnard *n.* Any of various chiefly tropical marine fishes of the family Dactylopteridae, having winglike, much enlarged pectoral fins, and capable of gliding flight over the water.
flying jib *n. Nautical.* A light sail that extends beyond the jib and is attached to an extension of the jib boom.
flying lemur *n.* Either of two mammals, *Cynocephalus volans* or *C. variegatus,* of tropical Asia, that are sustained in gliding leaps by a wide, fur-covered membrane extending from each side of the body. Also called "gliding lemur", "colugo".
flying lizard *n.* Any of various small tropical Asian lizards of the genus *Draco,* capable of gliding by spreading the winglike membranes on each side of the body. Also called "flying dragon".
flying machine *n.* A machine designed for flight; especially, any of the early experimental types of aircraft.
flying mare *n.* In wrestling, a throw in which one grabs the opponent's wrist or head, turns round quickly, and flips him over one's shoulder onto the ground.
flying officer *n.* An officer in the British and certain other air forces, ranking between a flight lieutenant and pilot officer, and equivalent in rank to a lieutenant in the army and a sublieutenant in the navy.
flying picket *n.* A picket from elsewhere that reinforces or replaces local pickets during a strike.
flying possum *n.* The **gliding possum** *(see).* Also called "flying phalanger".
flying saucer *n.* Any of various unidentified flying objects typically described as discs and alleged to have come from outer space.
flying snake *n.* A tree-dwelling snake of the genus *Chrysopelea,* of south Asia and the East Indies, that can glide for short distances by flattening its belly scales.
flying squad *n.* A small mobile group, especially of policemen equipped with motor vehicles, capable of moving very swiftly into action when summoned or alerted.
flying squirrel *n.* Any of various nocturnal squirrels of the genera *Pteromys, Glaucomys,* and related genera, having membranes between the forelegs and hind legs that enable them to glide.
flying start *n.* **1.** The crossing of the starting line of a race at full speed. **2.** Any quick or promising start. **3.** An advantage over one's rivals at the outset.
flying wing *n.* An aircraft in which a single large streamlined wing incorporating the fuselage constitutes the principal portion of the airframe.
fly·leaf (flī-leef) *n., pl.* **-leaves** (-leevz). A blank leaf at the beginning or end of a book, between the lining paper and the first or last signature. See **endpaper.**
fly net *n.* A net covering used to keep flies off or out.
Flynn (flin), **Errol** (1909–59). Australian actor, noted for his swashbuckling roles in such films as *Captain Blood* (1935), and *The*

Adventures of Robin Hood (1938).

fly·o·ver (flī′-ōvər) *n.* **1.** *British.* **a.** An intersection of two roads or railways or a road and a railway, where one passes over the other on an elevated section. **b.** The elevated part of such an intersection. **2.** *U.S.* A fly-past.

fly·pa·per (flī′-paypər) *n.* A ribbon of paper coated with a sticky, sometimes poisonous substance, and used to catch flies.

fly-past (flī′-paast ‖ -past) *n.* A flight of aircraft at low altitude over a particular area, usually as a military or ceremonial display.

fly-pitch (flī′-pich) *intr.v.* **-pitched, -pitching, -pitches.** *British.* To set up a stall, tray or the like without being licensed to do so, and attempt to sell goods to the public. **—fly-pitch·er** *n.*

fly-post (flī′-post) *tr.v.* To stick posters up in (a wall or district, for example) in places where they are illegal or discouraged.

fly-swatter *n.* A swatter *(see).*

fly-trap (flī′-trap) *n.* **1.** A trap for catching flies. **2.** A plant that traps insects, such as the **Venus's flytrap** *(see).*

fly-ty·ing (flī′-tī-ing) *n.* The art or hobby of making artificial fishing flies out of materials such as coloured feathers or tinsel.

fly·weight (flī′-wayt) *n.* **1.** In professional boxing, a boxer of the lightest weight class, weighing 112 pounds (51 kilograms) or less. **2.** In amateur boxing, a boxer weighing 48 to 51 kilograms (106 to 112 pounds).

fly·wheel (flī′-weel, -hweel) *n.* A heavy rotating wheel used to minimise speed variation in a machine subject to fluctuation in drive and load.

fm frequency modulation.

Fm The symbol for the element fermium.

FM frequency modulation.

fm. fathom.

F.M. field-marshal.

FMN *n.* Flavin *mononucleotide:* a derivative of riboflavin that functions, like **FAD** *(see),* as a coenzyme in many oxidation-reduction reactions.

fn. footnote.

f-num·ber (ĕf-numbər) *n.* The ratio of focal length to the effective aperture diameter in a lens or lens system. Also called "f-stop". [*F*, symbol for *focal length.*]

F.O. **1.** field officer. **2.** Flying Officer. **3.** Foreign Office.

foal (fōl) *n.* The young offspring of a horse or other equine animal, especially when under a year old. **~***v.* **foaled, foaling, foals.** *—tr.* To give birth to (a foal). *—intr.* To give birth to a foal. [Middle English *fole,* Old English *fola,* from Germanic.]

foam (fōm) *n.* **1.** A mass of gas bubbles; especially, a light, bubbly, gas-and-liquid mass formed by agitating a liquid containing certain soaps or detergents. **2. a.** Frothy saliva from the mouth. **b.** The frothy sweat of a horse or other equine animal. **3.** *Poetic.* The sea. **4.** Any of various light, bulky materials used as thermal or mechanical insulators in packaging, furniture, and the like, made by injecting a gas into a material such as latex or polystyrene. Also used adjectively: *foam plastic; foam rubber.* **5.** Any of various chemical substances used in fire extinguishers. **~***v.* **foamed, foaming, foams.** *—intr.* **1.** To produce or come forth in foam; froth. **2.** *Informal.* To be extremely angry. *—tr.* To cause to foam. [Middle English *fom,* saliva, foam, Old English *fām.*] **—foam·ing·ly** *adv.*

foam·y (fōmi) *adj.* **-ier, -iest.** **1.** Pertaining to or resembling foam. **2.** Consisting of or covered with foam. **—foam·i·ly** *adv.* **—foam·i·ness** *n.*

fob[1] (fob) *n.* **1.** A small pocket in the front of a waistcoat, used to hold a watch or coins. **2.** A short chain or ribbon attached to a pocket watch and worn hanging in front of the waistcoat. **3.** An ornament or seal attached to a watch chain. [17th century (originally cant) : probably akin to German (dialectal) *Fuppe*†, pocket.]

fob[2] *tr.v.* **fobbed, fobbing, fobs.** **1.** To put off or appease by deceitful or evasive means. Used with *off.* **2.** To dispose of (goods) by fraud or deception; palm off. Used with *off.* **3.** *Archaic.* To deceive; cheat. [Middle English *fobben*†.]

f.o.b., F.O.B. free on board.

F.O.C. *British. n.* Father of the chapel: the male leader of the members of a trade union in a particular newspaper office, printing firm, or the like. Compare **M.O.C..**

fo·cal (fōk′l) *adj.* **1.** Of or pertaining to a focus. **2.** Placed at or measured from the focus. **—fo·cal·ly** *adv.*

focal infection *n.* An infection localised in a specific part of the body.

fo·cal·ise, fo·cal·ize (fōkə-līz) *v.* **-ised, -ising, -ises.** *—tr.* To adjust or bring to a focus. *—intr.* To come or be brought to a focus. **—fo·cal·i·sa·tion** (-lī-záysh'n ‖ *U.S.* -li-) *n.*

focal length *n.* *Physics.* The distance of the focal point from the surface of a mirror or from the centre of a lens. Also called "focal distance", "focus".

focal plane *n.* A plane in which the image from a lens, mirror, or optical instrument is in focus.

focal point *n.* **1.** A point on the axis of symmetry of an optical system, as of a mirror or lens, to which parallel incident rays converge or from which they appear to diverge after reflection or transmission. Also called "principal focus". **2.** A centre of activity or interest; a focus.

Foch (fosh ‖ fawsh), **Ferdinand** (1851–1929). French marshal who in World War I was largely responsible for halting the German advance at the Marne (1914) and for the Allied victory at Ypres

(1915). In 1918, as Allied commander, he launched the July advance that pushed the Germans back to the Rhine and ended the war.

fo'c's'le. Variant of **forecastle.**

fo·cus (fō′-kəss) *n., pl.* **-cuses** or **-ci** (-sī, -kī). **1.** A point to which something converges or from which something diverges. **2.** *Physics.* **a.** A point in an optical system to which rays converge or from which they appear to diverge; a focal point. **b.** Focal length. **c.** The distinctness or clarity with which an optical system renders an image. **d.** Adjustment for distinctness or clarity. **3.** A place, person, issue, or the like on which attention converges or around which activity centres. **4.** *Medicine.* The region of a localised bodily infection. **5.** *Geology.* The point of origin of an earthquake. **6.** *Geometry.* A point that together with a directrix determines a conic section. **—in focus.** Sharply or clearly defined; distinct. **—out of focus.** Not distinct; blurred; cloudy. **~***v.* **focused** or **focussed, -cusing** or **-cussing, -cuses** or **-cusses.** *—tr.* **1. a.** To produce a clear image of (photographed material, for example) by adjustment of a projection lens or other optical equipment. **b.** To adjust the setting of (a lens, for example) to produce a clear image. **2.** To direct (attention or effort, for example) towards a particular point or purpose. *—intr.* **1.** To converge at a point of focus; be focused. **2.** To bring objects into focus. [Latin *focus,* fireplace, hearth (the centre of the home).]

fod·der (fóddər) *n.* **1.** Feed for livestock, especially hay, straw, and other plants. **2.** Raw material, as for artistic creation. **3.** People viewed as raw material for the achievement of a specified commercial, political, or military end: *cannon fodder.* **~***tr.v.* **foddered, -dering, -ders.** To feed (animals) with fodder. [Middle English *fodder,* Old English *fōdor,* from Germanic.]

foe (fō) *n.* **1.** A personal enemy. **2.** An enemy in war. **3.** An adversary; an opponent. **4.** Something that serves to oppose, injure, or impede. [Middle English, Old English *gefā,* from *gefāh,* at feud with, hostile, from Germanic.]

foe·man (fō′-mən) *n., pl.* **-men** (-mən, -men). *Archaic.* A foe in battle; an enemy.

foe·tal (féet′l) *adj.* Of, pertaining to, or resembling a foetus.

foetal alcohol syndrome *n.* A group of congenital defects, including stunted growth and heart abnormalities, present in infants born to alcoholic mothers.

foetal diagnosis *n.* **Prenatal diagnosis** *(see).*

foe·ta·tion (fee-táysh'n) *n.* **1.** The state of pregnancy. **2.** The development of a foetus.

foe·ti·cide (féeti-sīd) *n.* The intentional destruction of a human foetus in the uterus. **—foe·ti·cid·al** (-síd′l) *adj.*

foetid. Variant of **fetid.**

foe·to·lo·gy (fee-tólləji) *n.* The branch of medicine concerned with the study of foetuses. **—foe·to·lo·gist** *n.*

foetor. Variant of **fetor.**

foe·tos·co·py (fee-tóskəpi) *n.* **1.** The examination of a foetus in the uterus by the insertion of a fibre-optic device *(foetoscope)* equipped with a lens into the amniotic cavity. **2.** A technique in which foetal blood is withdrawn by means of a hollow needle inserted into the womb of a pregnant woman and examined for abnormalities.

foe·tus, fe·tus (féetəss) *n.* **1.** A human embryo from the end of the second month of pregnancy until birth. **2.** The embryo of any other mammal in the later stages of development. [Middle English, from Latin *fētus,* pregnancy, offspring.]

fog[1] (fog ‖ fawg) *n.* **1.** Condensed water vapour droplets with particles of dust and smoke in suspension, occurring in cloudlike masses close to the ground and limiting visibility to less than one kilometre (0.6 mile). **2.** Any mass of floating material, such as dust or smoke, that forms an obscuring haze. **3.** A state of bewilderment. **4.** In photography, a dark blur on a developed negative. **~***v.* **fogged, fogging, fogs.** *—tr.* **1.** To cover or envelop with fog. **2.** To cause to be clouded or obscured; blur. **3.** To make uncertain or unclear; bewilder. **4.** In photography, to obscure or dim (a negative) with a dark blur. *—intr.* **1.** To be covered or enveloped with fog. Often used with *up* or *over.* **2.** To be blurred or obscured. **3.** In photography, to be dimmed or obscured with a dark blur. Used of a print or negative. [Perhaps a back-formation from earlier *foggy,* murky, moist, boggy, from FOG (rank grass).]

fog[2] *n.* **1.** A second growth of grass on a field that has been mown or grazed. **2.** Tall, thick grass left standing after cutting or grazing. [Middle English *fogge, fog,* perhaps from Scandinavian.]

fog bank *n.* An opaque mass of fog sharply defined in contrast to surrounding, clearer air; especially, such a fog occurring at sea.

fog-bound (fóg-bownd ‖ fáwg-) *adj.* **1.** Immobilised by heavy fog. **2.** Clouded or obscured by fog.

fog-bow (fóg-bō ‖ fáwg-) *n.* A faint white or yellowish arc-shaped light, similar to a rainbow, often seen opposite the sun in a fog bank. Also called "seadog".

fog-dog (fóg-dog ‖ fáwg-dawg) *n.* A bright spot in a fog bank.

fo·gey (fógi) *n., pl.* **-geys.** Also **fo·gy** *pl.* **-gies.** A person of old-fashioned habits and outmoded attitudes: *an old fogey.* [Origin obscure.] **—fo·gy·ish** *adj.*

fog·gy (fóggi ‖ fáwgi) *adj.* **-gier, -giest.** **1.** Full of, surrounded by, or suggestive of fog. **2.** Clouded; obscure; indistinct. **3.** In photography, obscured or dimmed by a fog or dark blur. **—not have the foggiest (idea).** *Informal.* Not to know at all; have no idea. **—fog·gi·ly** *adv.* **—fog·gi·ness** *n.*

fog-horn (fóg-hawrn ‖ fáwg-) *n.* **1.** A horn used by ships and coastal installations to sound warning signals, typically of long, deep tones,

in fog or darkness. **2.** *Informal.* A loud, booming voice.
föhn, foehn (fern, fön) *n.* A warm dry wind coming off the leeward side of a mountain range, especially off the northern slopes of the Alps. [German, from Old High German *phōnno,* from Latin *Favōnius*†, the west wind. See **favonian.**]
foi·ble (fóyb'l) *n.* **1.** A minor weakness or failing of character; a small personal fault. **2.** The weaker section of a sword blade, from the middle to the tip. In this sense, compare **forte.** —See Synonyms at **fault.** [Obsolete French, variant of *faible,* weak, FEEBLE.]
foie gras (fwáa gráa) *n.* **Pâté de foie gras** *(see).*
foil¹ (foyl) *tr.v.* **foiled, foiling, foils.** **1.** To prevent from being successful; thwart. **2.** To obscure or confuse (a trail or scent) so as to evade pursuers. —See Synonyms at **frustrate.**
~n. **1.** *Archaic.* A foiling; a repulse; a setback. **2.** The trail or scent of a hunted animal, especially one that confuses its pursuer. [Originally to trample, tread upon, Middle English *foilen,* perhaps from Anglo-French *fuler* (unattested), variant of Old French *fouler,* to FULL (cloth).]
foil² *n.* **1.** A thin, flexible leaf or sheet of a metal. **2.** A thin layer of bright metal placed under a displayed gem or piece of jewellery to lend it brilliance. **3.** Any person or thing that, by strong contrast, underlines or enhances the distinctive characteristics of another. **4.** The metal coating applied to the back of a plate of glass to form a mirror. **5.** *Architecture.* A leaflike design or space worked in stone or glass, found especially in Gothic window tracery. **6.** An **aerofoil** *(see).* **7.** A **hydrofoil** *(see).* **8.** **Aluminium foil** *(see).*
~tr.v. **foiled, foiling, foils.** *Rare.* **1.** To back or cover with a thin, pliant sheet of metal. **2.** To serve as a foil to; set off by contrast. **3.** *Architecture.* To ornament (windows or walls) with foils. [Middle English *foil(le), foile,* thin sheet of metal, leaf, from Old French, from Latin *folium.*]
foil³ *n.* **1.** A fencing sword with a flat guard for the hand and a thin blade, with a blunt point to prevent injury. **2.** *Plural.* The art or act of fencing with such swords. [16th century : origin obscure.]
foin (foyn) *intr.v.* **foined, foining, foins.** *Archaic.* To thrust with a pointed weapon.
~n. *Archaic.* A lunge or thrust with a pointed weapon. [Middle English *foinen,* from *foin,* a thrust, a three-pronged fork for spearing fish, from Old French *foin, foisne,* from Latin *fuscina*†, trident.]
Fo·ism (fṓ-iz'm) *n.* Chinese Buddhism. [Mandarin Chinese *fó,* Buddha, from Sanskrit *Buddha,* BUDDHA.] —**Fo·ist** *n. & adj.*
foi·son (fóyz'n) *n.* *Archaic.* **1.** A plentiful harvest; a good crop. **2.** Abundance; plenty. [Middle English *foisoun,* from Old French *foison,* power, abundance, from Vulgar Latin *fusiō* (unattested), from Latin *fūsiō* (stem *fūsiōn-*), an outpouring, effusion, from *fūsus,* past participle of *fundere,* to pour.]
foist (foyst) *tr.v.* **foisted, foisting, foists.** **1.** To pass off as genuine, valuable, or worthy; palm off. **2.** To impose (someone or something unwanted) upon another by coercion or trickery. **3.** To insert fraudulently or deceitfully. [Original sense, to introduce a palmed dice surreptitiously, from Dutch (dialectal) *vuisten,* from *vuist,* fist.]
Fo·kine (fóckeen, fo-kéen, fō-), **Michel,** born Mikhail Fokine (1880–1942). Russian dancer and choreographer. Working with Diaghilev's Ballets Russes in Paris from 1909, he was partly responsible for revitalising the ballet through his choreography for such revolutionary works as Stravinsky's *The Firebird* (1910) and *Petrushka* (1912). From 1923 he worked in the United States.
Fok·ker (fóckər), **Anthony Hermann Gerard** (1890–1939). Dutch aircraft engineer. In 1912 he opened an aircraft factory in Germany that supplied the Germans with some of the most advanced planes of World War I. He revolutionised aerial warfare in 1915, by synchronising a machine gun to fire through the propeller of a plane.
fol. folio.
fo·late (fṓ-layt) *n.* **Folic acid** *(see).* [*Folic* acid + -ATE.]
fold¹ (fōld) *v.* **folded, folding, folds.** *—tr.* **1.** To bend over or double up so that one part lies on another part: *fold a newspaper.* **2.** To make compact by successively bending over parts. Sometimes used with *up.* **3.** To bring from an extended to a closed position: *On alighting, the hawk folded its wings.* **4.** To place together and intertwine: *fold one's arms.* **5.** To bend, clasp, or entwine. **6.** To surround with the arms; enfold; embrace. **7.** To wrap; envelop. **8.** In cooking, to mix in (an ingredient) by slowly and gently turning one part over another. **9.** *Geology.* To form (rock) into folds. *—intr.* **1.** To become folded, or to be capable of being folded: *a folding bed.* **2.** *Informal.* To close for lack of funds; fail financially. **3.** *Informal.* To weaken or collapse, as from exertion or laughter. Usually used with *up.* **4.** *Geology.* To form folds. Used of stratified rocks.
~n. **1.** The act or an instance of folding. **2.** A part or section that has been folded over another. **3.** The space or hollow at the junction of two folded parts. **4.** A hollow or dale in hilly country. **5.** *Geology.* A bend in rock strata. **6.** A coil, as of rope or a snake. **7.** *Anatomy.* A crease apparently formed by folding, as of a membrane; a plica. [Middle English *folden, falden,* Old English *faldan, fealdan,* from Germanic.]
fold² *n.* **1.** A fenced enclosure for domestic animals, especially sheep. **2.** The sheep enclosed in such a pen. **3.** A flock of sheep. **4.** Any group of people bound together by common beliefs and aims, or by mutual loyalty; especially, the members of a church.
~tr.v. **folded, folding, folds.** To place or keep (sheep) in a fold. [Middle English *fold,* Old English *fald, falod,* akin to Middle Low German *valt*†.]
-fold *adj. & adv. suffix.* Indicates: **1.** Division into a specified number of parts; for example, **fivefold.** **2.** Multiplication by a specified number; for example, **tenfold.** [Middle English *-fold, -fald,* Old English *-f(e)ald.*]
fold·a·way (fṓld-ə-way) *adj.* Designating a piece of furniture, especially a bed, that can be folded up and stored when not in use.
fold·boat (fṓld-bōt) *n.* A **faltboat** *(see).* [Translation of German *Faltboot.*]
fold·er (fṓldər) *n.* **1.** One that folds. **2.** A sheet of cardboard or thick paper folded in the centre and used as a holder for loose paper. **3.** *Chiefly U.S.* A folded sheet of printed matter.
fol·de·rol (fóldə-rol) *n.* Also **fal·de·ral** (fál-də-ral), **fal·de·rol** (fál-də-rol). **1.** Foolish talk or procedure; nonsense. **2.** A worthless trifle; a gewgaw. [From *fol-de-rol* and *fal-deral,* a meaningless refrain in some old songs.]
fold-out (fṓld-owt) *n.* *Printing.* A **gatefold** *(see).*
fo·li·a. Plural of **folium.**
fo·li·a·ceous (fṓli-áyshəss) *adj.* **1.** Of, relating to, or resembling the leaf of a plant. **2.** Having leaves or leaflike structures. **3.** Consisting of thin laminated layers, as do certain rocks. [Latin *foliāceus,* from *folium,* leaf, FOLIUM.]
fo·li·age (fṓli-ij) *n.* **1.** The leaves of growing plants; plant leaves collectively. **2.** An ornamental representation of leaves, branches, or flowers. [Middle English *foilage,* from Old French *feuillage, foillage,* from *feuille, foille,* leaf, from Latin *folium.*] —**fo·li·aged** *adj.*
foliage plant *n.* A plant cultivated chiefly for its ornamental leaves.
fo·li·ar (fṓli-ər) *adj.* Of or pertaining to a leaf or leaves. [French *foliaire,* from Latin *folium,* leaf, FOLIUM.]
fo·li·ate (fṓli-ət, -it, -ayt) *adj.* **1.** Of or pertaining to leaves. **2.** Having a specified number or kind of leaves or layers. Used in combination: *trifoliate, perfoliate.*
~v. (fṓli-ayt) **foliated, -ating, -ates.** *—tr.* **1.** To hammer or cut (metal) into thin plates, leaf, or foil. **2. a.** To coat (glass) with metal foil. **b.** To furnish or adorn with metal foil. **3.** *Architecture.* To decorate (an arch, for example) with foils. **4.** To number the leaves of (a book). In this sense, compare **paginate.** *—intr.* **1.** To produce foliage; put forth leaves. **2.** To become split into thin layers. [Latin *foliātus,* bearing leaves, from *folium,* leaf, FOLIUM.]
fo·li·a·tion (fṓli-áysh'n) *n.* **1.** *Botany.* The state of being in leaf or putting forth leaves. **2.** Decoration with foliage. **3.** *Architecture.* The decoration of an archway, window, or other opening with cusps and foils, as in Gothic tracery. **4. a.** The act or process of foliating metal. **b.** The foliating of glass. **5.** The process of numbering consecutively the leaves of a book. [Latin *folium,* leaf, FOLIUM.]
fo·lic acid (fṓlik, fóllik) *n.* A yellowish-orange compound, $C_{19}H_{19}N_7O_6$, a member of the vitamin B complex, occurring in green plants, fresh fruit, liver, and yeast, and used medicinally to treat pernicious anaemia. Also called "folate", "pteroylglutamic acid", "vitamin B_c". [Latin *fol(ium),* leaf, FOLIUM + -IC.]
fo·lie à deux (fólli-a-dṓ) *n.* *French.* The simultaneous presence of symptoms of mental illness in two closely attached people, usually a married couple or siblings. [French, "madness of two".]
fo·lie de gran·deur (fólli də groN-dốr) *n.* *French.* Delusions of grandeur.
fo·li·o (fṓli-ō) *n., pl.* **-os.** *Abbr.* **f., F., fol.** **1.** A large sheet of paper, folded once in the middle, making two leaves or four pages of a book or manuscript. **2. a.** The largest common size of book or manuscript, usually about 38 centimetres (15 inches) in height and made up of such folded sheets. **b.** A book or manuscript of this size. **3.** A leaf of a book numbered only on the front side. **4.** A page number in a book; especially, one assigned to a page during the printing process. **5.** *Accounting.* A page in a ledger, or two facing pages assigned a single number. **6.** *Law.* A specific number of words used as a unit for measuring the length of the text of a document.
~adj. **1.** Of or pertaining to a folio: *folio pages.* **2.** Presented in the form of a folio: *a folio edition.*
~tr.v. **folioed, -oing, -os.** To number consecutively the pages of (a book). [Medieval Latin, ablative (used for page references, "at leaf *x*") of Latin *folium,* leaf, FOLIUM.]
fo·li·o·late (fṓli-ə-layt, fō-lée-ə-layt, -lit, -lət) *adj.* *Botany.* Having or consisting of leaflets. Usually used in combination: *bifoliolate.* [From earlier *foliole,* leaflet, from French, from New Latin *foliolum,* diminutive of Latin *folium,* leaf, FOLIUM.]
fo·li·ose (fṓli-ōss, -ōz) *adj.* **1.** *Botany.* Bearing numerous leaves or leaflets; leafy. **2.** Of, pertaining to, or resembling a leaf or leaves. [Latin *foliōsus,* from *folium,* leaf, FOLIUM.]
fo·li·ot (fṓli-ət) *n.* A clock escapement of the earliest type, consisting of a bar adjusted by weights placed along its length. [French, from Old French, probably from *folier,* to play the fool, from *fol,* foolish. See **fool.**]
fo·li·um (fṓ-li-əm) *n., pl.* **-lia** (-li-ə). **1.** *Geology.* A thin layer or stratum occurring especially in metamorphic rock. **2.** *Geometry.* A plane cubic curve having a single loop, a node, and two ends asymptotic to the same line. In this sense, also called "folium of Descartes". [New Latin, from Latin, leaf.]
folk (fōk ‖ fōlk) *n., pl.* **folk** or *informal* **folks.** **1.** *Usually plural.* People of a specified group or kind: *city folk.* **2.** *Plural. Informal.* **a.** The members of one's family or childhood household; one's relatives. **b.** One's parents. **3.** *Often plural. Informal.* People in general: *Folks will talk.* **4.** *Used with a singular or plural verb. Archaic.* A people; an ethnic group; a race. **5.** *Informal.* Folk music.
~adj. Of, occurring in, or originating among the common people; especially, untutored or unrefined: *folk painting.* [Middle English

folk, Old English *folc,* the people, nation, tribe, from Germanic *folkam* (unattested).]

folk dance *n.* **1.** A traditional dance originating among the rural areas of a nation or region. **2.** The music accompanying such a dance. **3.** A social gathering at which such dances are performed. **—folk dancing** *n.*

Folke·stone (fŏ́k-stən || -stōn). Residential town and resort in Kent, southeastern England. Its harbour is a leading departure point for cross-Channel ferry services to France.

Fol·ke·ting, Fol·ke·thing (fōlkə-ting) *n.* The parliament of Denmark consisting of a single chamber. [Danish : *folk,* the people, FOLK + *ting,* assembly, from Old Norse *thing.*]

folk etymology *n.* **1.** A change in form of a word or phrase, resulting from an incorrect popular notion of the origin or meaning of the term or from the influence of more familiar terms mistakenly taken to be analogous. **2.** A word or phrase that is a product of this modification, as *sparrowgrass* from *asparagus.* **3.** A popular but mistaken view of the origin of a word; for example, *hybrid* may be taken to derive from *high-bred.* **—folk-et·y·mo·log·i·cal** (fŏ́k-ét-timə-lójik'l) *adj.*

folk·lore (fŏ́k-lawr || -lōr) *n.* **1.** The traditional orally transmitted beliefs, practices, and tales of people. **2.** The comparative study of folk knowledge and culture. **3.** A body of widely accepted but specious notions about a place, group, or institution: *the folklore of Hollywood.* **—folk·lor·ic** (-lórrik, -láw-rik || -lṓ-) *adj.* **—folk·lor·ist** *n.*

folk medicine *n.* Medicine as practised among primitive peoples, which relies on the use of herbal and other traditional remedies.

folk·moot (fŏ́k-mōōt) *n.* Also **folk·mote** (-mōt). A general assembly of the people of a town, district, or shire in medieval England. [Old English *folcmōt* : *folc,* FOLK + *mōt,* meeting, assembly.]

folk music *n.* **1.** Music and song originating among the common people of a nation or region and characterised by a tradition of oral transmission and usually anonymous authorship. **2.** Contemporary music and song using elements of the style of traditional folk music.

folk rock *n.* A variety of popular music that combines elements of rock 'n' roll and folk music.

folk singer *n.* A singer of folk songs. **—folk singing** *n.*

folk song *n.* **1.** A song belonging to the folk music of a people or area, characterised chiefly by directness and simplicity of expression and often sung or performed in several versions. **2.** A song of known authorship composed in imitation of such songs.

folk·sy (fŏ́ksi) *adj.* **-sier, -siest.** *Informal.* **1.** Simple and unpretentious in social behaviour. **2.** Affectedly rustic or simple. **3.** *U.S.* Characterised by congeniality and affability. **—folk·si·ness** *n.*

folk tale *n.* A story or legend forming part of an oral tradition and passed on from generation to generation.

folk·way (fŏ́k-way) *n.* A way of thinking or acting adopted unreflectively by the members of a group as part of their shared culture.

folk weave *n.* A type of cloth with a loose or rough weave.

fol·li·cle (fóllik'l) *n.* **1.** *Anatomy.* An approximately spherical group of cells containing a cavity, such as a sac from which a hair grows or any of the cavities in the ovary containing ova. **2.** *Botany.* A single-chambered fruit, such as that of larkspur, that splits along only one seam to release its seeds. [Latin *folliculus,* little bag, diminutive of *follis,* bellows.] **—fol·lic·u·lar** (fo-líckew-lər, fə-), **fol·lic·u·late** (-layt), **fol·lic·u·lat·ed** *adj.*

fol·li·cle-stim·u·lat·ing hormone (fóllik'l-stímmew-layting) *n. Abbr.* **FSH** A gonadotrophic hormone of the anterior pituitary gland that stimulates the growth of follicles in the ovary and induces the formation of sperm in the testis.

fol·li·cu·li·tis (fo-líckew-lītiss, fə-, fóllikew-) *n.* Inflammation of the hair follicles in the skin. [Latin *folliculus,* FOLLICLE + -ITIS.]

fol·lies (fólliz || fólleez) *n. Used with a singular verb.* An elaborate, richly costumed theatrical revue consisting of a series of musical or dance skits. [Plural of FOLLY.]

fol·low (fóllō) *v.* **-lowed, -lowing, -lows.** *—tr.* **1.** To come or go after; move behind and in the same direction as. **2.** To go after with or as if with the intention of overtaking; pursue. **3.** To come or go with; accompany; attend. **4.** To move along the course of; take (a course or direction): *We followed a path to the shore.* **5.** To accept the guidance or leadership of; have as a model; emulate. **6.** To adhere to the cause or principles of; advocate: *follow outdated doctrines.* **7.** To be governed by; obey; comply with: *We follow the rules.* **8. a.** To occur after (a specified event) in a temporal sequence. **b.** To occupy a position that occurs after (a specified position) in a hierarchy, list, or other ordering: *Captain follows major in rank.* **9.** To succeed to the place or position of: *Elizabeth II followed George VI.* **10.** To engage in; work at (a trade or occupation): *to follow the law.* **11.** To occur or be evident as a consequence of: *Your conclusion does not follow your premise.* **12.** To be attentive to; listen to or watch closely: *I was too sleepy to follow the sermon.* **13.** To grasp the meaning or logic of; keep up with the reasoning of: *Do you follow my argument?* **14.** To inform oneself of the course or progress of: *follow the stock market.* **15.** To be a keen and knowledgeable fan of (a sport, team, or the like): *follow Arsenal.* *—intr.* **1.** To come, move, or take place after some other person or thing in order or time. **2.** To occur or be evident as a consequence; result; ensue: *If you ignore your diet, trouble will follow.* **3.** To grasp the meaning or reasoning of what is said; understand. **—as follows.** As is now to be given or explained; as listed or explained below. **—follow out.** To comply with fully; carry out.

∼n. A billiards shot in which the cue ball is struck in such a way that it follows the path of the object ball after impact. [Middle English *fol(o)wen,* Old English *folgian* and *fylgan,* from Germanic *fulg-* (unattested).]

Synonyms: *follow, succeed, ensue, result, supervene.*

Usage: *As follows* is a fixed phrase in standard English, and does not change along with the number of the noun that precedes it. *His reply was as follows* is found alongside *His replies were as follows. As follow* in this last example would be unacceptable.

fol·low·er (fóllō-ər) *n.* **1.** One that comes or occurs after another. **2.** One who is keenly interested in a sport, team, fashion, or the like; a devotee. **3.** An attendant, servant, or subordinate. **4.** One who subscribes to the teachings or methods of another; an adherent. **5.** A machine element moved by another machine element. **6.** *Archaic.* A male admirer of a woman.

fol·low·ing (fóllō-ing) *adj.* **1.** *Abbr.* **f., ff., foll.** Coming next in time or order: *in the following chapter.* **2.** Now to be enumerated: *The following men will report for duty.* **3.** Blowing in the same direction as the course of a ship or aircraft. Said of a wind.

∼n. A group or gathering of admirers, adherents, or disciples: *a lecturer with a large following.* **—the following. 1.** What is to be mentioned or listed next: *Please buy the following.* **2.** What is now to be said or specified: *Listen closely to the following.*

fol·low-my-lead·er (fóllō-mī-leédər, -mi-) *n.* A children's game in which players have to imitate the actions of a selected member of the group. Also *chiefly U.S.* "follow-the-leader".

∼adj. Copying or obeying in an unthinking or uncritical way.

follow on *intr.v.* In cricket, to have to play a second innings immediately after the first as a result of failing to score a minimum of a given number of runs less than the opposing team's score.

fol·low-on (fóllō-on, -ón) *n.* In cricket, a second innings immediately following the first, enforced on a team that has failed to score a minimum of a given number of runs less than the opposing team.

follow through *tr.v.* **1.** *Sports.* To continue (a stroke or shot) to natural completion after hitting the ball. **2.** To carry (an act, project, or train of thought) to completion; pursue fully. *—intr.v.* To follow a stroke or shot through.

fol·low-through (fóllō-thrōō, -thrṓō) *n.* **1.** The carrying of a stroke to natural completion after the ball has been hit, as in tennis, golf, or cricket. **2.** The concluding part of a stroke, after the ball has been hit. **3.** The completion of a sequence of acts or processes after the main one.

follow up *tr.v.* **1.** To carry to completion; follow through. **2.** To increase the effectiveness of by repetition or further action.

fol·low-up (fóllō-up) *n.* **1.** The act or an instance of repeating or adding to previous action, so as to increase effectiveness. **2.** The means, such as a letter, procedure, or visit, used to increase or reinforce the effectiveness of previous action. Also used adjectivally: *a follow-up letter.* **3.** A newspaper article giving further information on a previously published item of news.

fol·ly (fólli) *n., pl.* **-lies. 1.** The condition or quality of being foolish; a lack of good sense, understanding, or foresight. **2. a.** Any act or instance of foolishness. **b.** A costly undertaking having an absurd or ruinous outcome. **3.** *Archaic.* Action or behaviour considered immoral or criminal. **4.** An ornamental building or structure built purely for decoration. [Middle English *folie,* from Old French, from *fol,* foolish, from Latin *follis,* bellows. See **fool.**]

Fo·mal·haut (fṓ-mə-lōt, -məl-hawt) *n.* The brightest star in the constellation Piscis Austrinus, 24 light-years from earth. [Arabic *fum'l-ḥūt,* "mouth of the fish".]

fo·ment (fə-mént, fō-) *tr.v.* **-mented, -menting, -ments. 1.** To promote the growth or arousal of (discontent or strife); stir up; instigate. **2.** To treat (the skin) by fomentation. [Middle English *fomenten,* from Old French *fomenter,* from Late Latin *fōmentāre,* from Latin *fōmentum,* warm application, short for *fovementum* (unattested), from *fovēre,* to warm, cherish.] **—fo·ment·er** *n.*

fo·men·ta·tion (fō-men-táysh'n, -mən-) *n.* **1.** The act or an instance of promoting discontent, rebellion, or strife; instigation. **2. a.** A warm, moist, medicinal compress; a poultice. **b.** The therapeutic application of warmth and moisture.

fo·mes (fṓ-miz) *n., pl.* **fo·mi·tes** (-mətiz). Any object or substance that has been used by an infected person and serves to transfer the infection to others. Also called "fomite". [New Latin, from Latin *fomēs,* tinder; akin to *fovēre,* to warm.]

fond[1] (fond) *adj.* **fonder, fondest. 1.** Affectionate; tender: *a fond embrace.* **2.** Having a tender interest or affection or great liking. Used with *of*: *"He was fond of the fine arts, fond of long words, and fond of me"* (Mary McCarthy). **3.** Immoderately or irrationally affectionate; infatuated; doting. **4.** Cherished; dear: *my fondest hopes.* **5.** *Archaic.* Naively credulous; foolish. [Middle English *fonned,* foolish, probably from *fon*†, a fool.] **—fond·ly** *adv.*

fond[2] (fond; *French* FOɴ) *n.* The background of a design in lace. [French, from Latin *fundus,* bottom.]

Fon·da (fóndə), **Henry (Jaynes)** (1905–82). U.S. actor. He became a Hollywood star with such films as *Young Mr. Lincoln* (1939), *The Grapes of Wrath* (1940), and *Twelve Angry Men* (1957). He received an Oscar in 1982 for *On Golden Pond.* His daughter Jane (1937–) made her first major film appearance in *Barbarella* (1968). Later films include *Klute* (1971) and *Coming Home* (1978). Her brother Peter (1939–) starred in *Easy Rider* (1969) and *Ulee's Gold* (1997).

fon·dant (fóndənt; *French* FOɴ-DÓɴ *n.* **1.** A sweet, creamy sugar paste eaten as a sweet or used in icings or as a filling for other sweets. **2.** A sweet made of or containing fondant. [French, from the present participle of *fondre,* to melt (it melts quickly in the mouth), from Latin *fundere,* to pour, melt.]

fon·dle (fónd'l) *v.* **-dled, -dling, -dles.** *—tr.* To handle or stroke with affection; caress lovingly with the hands. *—intr. Rare.* To show fondness or affection by caressing. [Back-formation from earlier *fondling* : FOND + -LING.]

fond·ness (fónd-nəss, -niss) *n.* **1.** Warm affection; tender liking. **2.** Strong preference; inclination; relish. **3.** *Archaic.* Naive trustfulness; credulity. —See Synonyms at **love.**

fon·due (fón-dew, fon-déw || -dōō, -dṓō, *French* foN-dǘ) *n.* **1.** A hot dish made of melted cheese and wine into which pieces of bread or meat are dipped. **2.** A dish made with pieces of beef that are cooked individually on skewers in hot oil at table and eaten with a variety of sauces. Also called "fondue bourguignonne". **3.** A similar dish made with pieces of fruit or vegetable that are dipped in a hot sauce and eaten. [French, feminine past participle of *fondre,* to melt.]

font (font) *n.* **1.** A basin, usually mounted on a stone pedestal, holding baptismal water in a church. **2.** A receptacle for holy water; a stoup. **3.** The oil reservoir in an oil-burning lamp. **4.** *Archaic.* A fountain or spring. **5.** *Archaic.* Any source of abundance; a fount: *a font of knowledge.* [Middle English, Old English *font, fant,* from Latin *fōns* (stem *font-*), spring, fountain.] **—font·al** *adj.*

Fon·taine·bleau (fóntin-blō; *French* foN-ten-blṓ). Town in France, 59 kilometres (37 miles) southeast of Paris. From the 10th century it was a residence of the French kings, chiefly because of the good hunting ground offered by the Forest of Fontainebleau. Its magnificent palace, an outstanding example of French Renaissance architecture, was built by Francis I in the 16th century and decorated by Il Rosso, Francesco Primaticcio, and other members of the so-called Fontainebleau school.

fon·ta·nelle, fon·ta·nel (fóntə-nél || *U.S. also* -nel) *n.* Any of the soft membranous gaps between the incompletely formed cranial bones of foetuses and infants. Also called "soft spot". [Middle English *fontinel,* a hollow, from Old French *fontenele,* diminutive of *fontaine,* FOUNTAIN.]

Fon·teyn (fon-táyn || fón-tayn), **Dame Margot,** born Hookham (1919–91). British ballerina. She joined the Sadler's Wells Company (subsequently the Royal Ballet Company) in 1934. The beauty of her line, her musicality, and her dramatic interpretation of roles made her famous, especially in partnership with the Russian dancer Rudolf Nureyev (from 1962).

Foochow. See **Fuzhou.**

food (fōōd) *n.* **1.** Any material, usually of plant or animal origin, containing or consisting of essential nutrients, such as carbohydrates, fats, proteins, vitamins, or minerals, that is taken in and assimilated by an organism to maintain life and growth. **2.** A specified kind of nourishment: *breakfast food; plant food.* **3.** Nourishment eaten in solid form, as distinguished from liquid nourishment: *good food and wine.* **4.** Anything that nourishes or sustains in a way suggestive of physical nourishment: *food for thought.* [Middle English *fode,* Old English *fōda,* from Germanic.]

food chain *n.* A succession of organisms in an ecological community, each of which feeds on a lower member and is in turn eaten by a higher member.

food fish *n.* Any edible fish, such as a cod, plaice, or herring, that is used commercially as a source of human food.

food·ie (foodi) *n. Informal.* A person with an obsessive and trendy interest in food. [FOOD + –IE.]

food poisoning *n.* **1.** Poisoning caused by eating food contaminated by bacteria, especially bacteria of the genus *Salmonella,* and characterised, with varying severity, by vomiting, diarrhoea, prostration, and sometimes shock. See **salmonellosis. 2.** Poisoning caused by eating foods containing natural toxins.

food processor *n.* An appliance consisting of a container with interchangeable blades that processes food, as by mincing, shredding, slicing, or mixing, at very high speed.

food·stuff (fōōd-stuf) *n.* **1.** Any substance suitable for food; especially, a crude product suitable for food after processing. **2.** Any substance, such as protein or fat, that forms part of a food.

food web *n.* A group of organisms in an ecological community that forms a complex of interconnected food chains.

fool¹ (fōōl) *n.* **1.** One who shows himself, by words or actions, to be deficient in judgment, sense, or understanding; a stupid or thoughtless person. **2.** One who acts unwisely on a given occasion: *I was a fool to have refused the job.* **3.** Formerly, a member of a royal or noble household who entertained the court with jests, mimicry, and the like; a jester; a buffoon. **4.** One who has been or can be easily deceived or imposed upon; a dupe: *They made a fool of me.* **5.** *Archaic.* A feeble-minded person; an idiot. **6.** *Informal.* A person with extreme fondness or enthusiasm for a specified activity or person: *a fool for stamp-collecting.* **—no** or **nobody's fool.** A shrewd or wise person. **—play** or **act the fool. 1.** To act in an irresponsible or foolish manner. **2.** To behave in a playful or comical manner.

~v. **fooled, fooling, fools.** *—tr.* To deceive or misinform, especially for amusement or to gain an advantage; trick; dupe. See Synonyms at **deceive.** *—intr.* **1.** To act or speak in jest; play; joke; be amusing. **2.** To act, speak, argue, or contend without, but as if with, serious or harmful intent: *They thought he might shoot, but he was only fooling.* **—fool about** or **around.** *Informal.* **1.** To engage in or amuse oneself with useless or trifling activity. **2.** To trifle; not treat seriously. Used with *with.* **3.** To behave irresponsibly. [Middle English *fol(e),* a fool, foolish, from Old French *fol,* from Latin *follis,* bellows, windbag.]

fool² *n. Chiefly British.* A dessert made of crushed, stewed, or puréed fruit, mixed with cream or custard and served cold. [Perhaps a specialised use of FOOL.]

fool·er·y (fōōləri) *n., pl.* **-ies. 1.** Foolish behaviour or speech; playfulness or facetiousness. **2.** An instance of this; a jest, or trick.

fool·har·dy (fōōl-haardi) *adj.* **-dier, -diest.** Unwisely bold or adventurous; rash. See Synonyms at **reckless.** [Middle English *fol-hardi,* from Old French *folhardi* : *fol,* foolish (see **fool**) + *hardi,* HARDY.] **—fool·har·di·ly** *adv.* **—fool·har·di·ness** *n.*

fool·ish (fōōlish) *adj.* **1.** Lacking good sense or judgment; silly: *foolish remarks.* **2.** Resulting from stupidity or misinformation; ill-advised; unwise: *a foolish decision.* **3.** Ridiculous; inane: *a foolish grin.* **4.** Abashed; embarrassed: *I feel foolish telling you this.* **5.** *Archaic.* Insignificant; worthless: *"We have a trifling foolish banquet"* (Shakespeare). **—fool·ish·ly** *adv.* **—fool·ish·ness** *n.*

Synonyms: *foolish, silly, fatuous, absurd, preposterous, ridiculous, ludicrous, inane.*

fool·proof (fōōl-prōōf || -prōōf) *adj.* **1.** Designed so as to be proof against or resistant to human incompetence, error, or misuse: *a foolproof detonator.* **2.** Always effective; completely dependable; infallible: *a foolproof scheme.*

fools·cap (fōōlz-kap) *n. Abbr.* **fcp., fcap.** *British.* A sheet of writing or printing paper approximately 34x43 centimetres (13½x17 inches). [From the watermark of a fool's cap with bells originally marking this type of paper.]

fool's errand *n.* A fruitless errand or undertaking.

fool's gold *n.* **Pyrite** *(see)* sometimes mistaken for gold.

fool's paradise *n.* A state of delusive contentment or false hope.

fool's-pars·ley (fōōlz-paar-sli) *n.* A poisonous plant, *Aethusa cynapium,* native to Eurasia, having finely divided leaves, clusters of small white flowers, and an unpleasant smell.

foot (fōōt) *n., pl.* **feet** (feet) or **foot** (for sense 8). **1.** The lower extremity of the vertebrate leg that is in direct contact with the ground in standing or walking. **2.** A structure used for locomotion or attachment in an invertebrate animal, such as the muscular organ extending from the ventral side of a mollusc. **3.** *Botany.* The lower part of some plants or plant structures. **4.** Something resembling or suggestive of a foot in position or function, especially: **a.** The bottom or lowest part of anything standing vertically, or considered in its vertical dimension: *the foot of a mountain; the foot of a page.* **b.** The termination of the leg on a table or chair. **c.** The end or final section of an order or series; rear: *the foot of a queue.* **d.** The inferior part or rank: *the foot of the class.* **5.** The lower end of an object, or the end opposite the head, as of a bed or table. **6.** The part of a stocking, sock, boot, or the like that encloses the foot. **7.** A manner of moving; a step: *He walks with a light foot.* **8.** Foot soldiers; infantry. **9.** The attachment on a sewing machine that clamps down and guides the cloth. **10.** *Prosody.* A metric unit consisting of a stressed or unstressed syllable or syllables. **11.** *Symbol* ′ *Abbr.* **ft** A unit of length in the U.S. Customary and British Imperial systems, equal to $^1/_3$ yard or 12 inches, and equivalent to 0.3048 metre. **—have one foot in the grave.** To be very old or very ill and so be unlikely to live for much longer. **—my foot.** Used to express contemptuous disbelief. **—on foot. 1.** Walking or standing; not riding or travelling in a vehicle. **2.** In motion; progressing; underway. **—on the wrong** (or **right**) **foot.** In a disadvantageous (or advantageous) position. **—not put a foot wrong.** To avoid making a mistake. **—put (one's) best foot forward.** *Informal.* To make a good beginning or favourable first impression. **—put (one's) foot down.** *Informal.* **1.** To assert one's will emphatically. **2.** To accelerate. **—put (one's) foot in it.** *Informal.* To make an embarrassing or tactless blunder. **—under foot. 1.** At one's feet; on the ground or floor. **2.** Obstructing free movement; in the way.

~v. **footed, footing, foots.** *—intr.* **1.** To go on foot; walk. Often used with *it.* **2.** To dance. Often used with *it.* *—tr.* **1.** To go by foot on or through; pace; tread. **2.** To provide (a stocking, for example) with a foot. **3.** To add (a column of numbers) and write the total at the bottom; total. Used with *up: Foot up the bill.* **4.** *Informal.* To pay: *Can you foot the bill?* [Foot, feet; Middle English *fot, fet,* Old English *fōt, fēt,* from Germanic.]

Usage: This word has alternative plural forms when it is used as a unit of measurement. In precise measurements, *feet* is formal, *foot* is informal: *three feet long, three foot long.* When the term *inches* is added it is usual, even informally, to retain *feet*: *three feet two inches,* but *three foot two.* In compound adjectives *foot* is standard: *a six-foot ruler, a six-foot-wide table.* But after the verb, usage reverts to *feet*: *the table was six feet wide.*

Foot (fōōt), **Michael (Mackintosh)** (1913–). British Labour politician. After entering Parliament in 1945, he became leader of the House of Commons (1976–79), then leader of the Labour Party (1980–83). Among his works are a two-volume biography of Aneurin Bevan (1962, 1973) and one of H.G. Wells (1995).

foot·age (fōōtij) *n.* **1.** The length or extent of something as expressed in feet. **2.** A portion of cinematic film; especially, an amount of film depicting a specified event or kind of action: *news footage.* **3.** *Mining.* **a.** Payment calculated on the number of feet mined. **b.** The amount of payment thus calculated.

foot-and-mouth disease (fōōt-ən-mówth) *n.* An acute, highly contagious, usually nonfatal, viral disease of cattle and other cloven-hoofed animals such as pigs, sheep, and goats, characterised by fever and the eruption of vesicles around the mouth and hoofs.

foot·ball (fŏŏt-bawl) *n.* **1.** Any of various typically outdoor team games in which a ball is kicked, carried, or sometimes thrown; especially: **a. Soccer** *(see).* Also used adjectivally: *football supporter; Football League.* **b. Rugby football** *(see).* **c. Australian Rules** *(see).* **2.** The ball used in such games. **3.** Any problem or issue that is passed about among groups or persons without being settled: *unemployment has become a political football.* **—foot·baller** *n.*

football pools *pl.n. British.* A gambling pool in which people pay to bet on the results of forthcoming football matches.

foot·bath (fŏŏt-baath || -bath) *n., pl.* **-baths. 1.** A small bath used for washing or disinfecting the feet. **2.** An act of washing the feet.

foot·board (fŏŏt-bawrd || -bōrd) *n.* **1.** A board or small raised platform on which to support or rest the feet, as in a carriage. **2.** An upright board across the foot of a bedstead.

foot·boy (fŏŏt-boy) *n.* A youth employed as a servant or page.

foot brake *n.* A brake operated by pressure of the foot on a pedal, as in a car.

foot·bridge (fŏŏt-brij) *n.* A narrow bridge designed to carry only pedestrians.

foot-can·dle (fŏŏt-kand'l) *n. Abbr.* **fc** *Physics.* A former unit of illumination equal to one lumen per square foot. Also called "candle-foot".

foot·ed (fŏŏttid) *adj.* **1.** Having a foot or feet. **2.** Having a specified kind or number of feet. Used in combination: *web-footed.*

foot·er[1] (fŏŏttər) *n.* A person or thing measuring a specified number of feet in height or length. Used in combination: *a six-footer.*

footer[2] *n. Slang.* **1.** Soccer. **2.** Rugby football.

foot·fall (fŏŏt-fawl) *n.* **1.** A footstep. **2.** The sound of a footstep.

foot·fault (fŏŏt-fawlt) *n. Tennis.* A fault against the server called for failure to keep both feet behind the base line when serving.
~*intr.v.* **foot-faulted, -faulting, -faults.** To commit a foot-fault.

foot·gear (fŏŏt-geer) *n.* Sturdy footwear, such as shoes or boots.

foot·hill (fŏŏt-hil) *n. Often plural.* A low hill near the base of a mountain or mountain range, usually as part of a parallel range.

foot·hold (fŏŏt-hōld) *n.* **1.** A place affording support for the foot in climbing or standing. **2.** A firm or secure position enabling one to proceed with confidence.

foot·ie (fŏŏtti). *Sports.* Variant of **footy.**

foot·ing (fŏŏtting) *n.* **1.** A secure placement of the feet in standing or moving. **2.** A place on which one can stand or move securely. **3.** A surface or the condition of a surface with respect to the ease with which one may walk or run on it: *poor footing on the track.* **4.** *Architecture.* The supporting base or groundwork of a structure, as for a monument or wall. **5.** A basis; a foundation: *a business on a good footing.* **6.** A social or business relationship; standing.

foot-lam·bert (fŏŏt-lámbərt) *n. Abbr.* **fL** *Physics.* A former unit of luminance equal to $1/\pi$ candela per square foot.

foot·le (fŏŏt'l) *intr.v.* **-led, -ling, -les.** *Informal.* **1.** To waste time; trifle. Used with *around* or *about.* **2.** To talk nonsense.
~*n. Informal.* Foolishness; nonsense; twaddle. [Probably a variant of dialectal *footer,* probably from French *foutre,* to copulate with, from Old French, from Latin *futuere.*]

foot·lights (fŏŏt-līts) *pl.n.* **1.** Lights placed in a row along the front of a stage floor. **2.** The theatre as a profession; the stage.

foot·ling (fŏŏt-ling) *adj. Informal.* **1.** Foolish; trifling; insignificant. **2.** Stupid; inept. [Present participle of FOOTLE.]

foot·loose (fŏŏt-lŏŏss) *adj.* Having no attachments or ties; free to do as one pleases.

foot·man (fŏŏt-mən) *n., pl.* **-men** (-mən). **1.** A male servant employed in the house to wait at table, attend to the door, and run various errands. **2.** A metal stand or trivet used in a fireplace for keeping things hot. **3.** *Archaic.* A foot soldier; an infantryman.

foot·mark (fŏŏt-maark) *n.* A footprint.

foot·note (fŏŏt-nōt) *n.* **1.** *Abbr.* **fn.** A note placed at the bottom of a page of a book or manuscript or at the end of a chapter that comments on or cites a reference for a designated part of the text. **2.** Something said or done after the more important work has been completed; an afterthought.
~*tr.v.* **footnoted, -noting, -notes.** To furnish with footnotes.

foot·pace (fŏŏt-payss) *n.* **1.** A walking pace. **2.** A raised platform in a room, as for a lecturer; a dais.

foot·pad (fŏŏt-pad) *n. Archaic.* A highwayman or street robber who goes about on foot. [FOOT + earlier *pad,* path, probably from Middle Dutch, path.]

foot·path (fŏŏt-paath || -path) *n., pl.* **-paths** (-paath͟z, -paaths || -pat͟hz, -paths). A narrow path for persons on foot; especially, one along the side of a road.

foot·plate (fŏŏt-playt) *n.* A metal plate or platform in a steam locomotive on which the crew stand.

foot·plate·man (fŏŏt-playt-mən, -man) *n., pl.* **-men** (-mən, -men). *British.* A railway engine driver or fireman.

foot-pound (fŏŏt-pównd) *n. Abbr.* **ft-lb** A unit of work equal to the work done by a force of one pound weight acting through a distance of one foot in the direction of the force.

foot-pound·al (fŏŏt-pównd'l) *n.* A unit of work equal to the work done by a force of one poundal acting through a distance of one foot in the direction of the force.

foot-pound-sec·ond (fŏŏt-pównd-séckənd) *adj. Abbr.* **fps** Of, designating, or characteristic of a system of units based on the foot, the pound, and the second as the fundamental units of length, mass, and time.

foot·print (fŏŏt-print) *n.* **1.** An outline or indentation left by a foot on a surface. **2.** In telecommunications, the area of the Earth's surface where adequate reception of a signal from a communications satellite in a geostationary orbit may be obtained. Also called "groundprint".

foot·rest (fŏŏt-rest) *n.* A low stool, metal bar, or other support on which to rest the feet.

foot·rope (fŏŏt-rōp) *n. Nautical.* **1.** A rope attached to the lower border of a sail. **2.** A rope, rigged beneath a yard, for men to stand on during the reefing or furling of sail.

foot-rot (fŏŏt-rot) *n.* **1.** An inflammatory infection of the feet in certain hoofed animals, especially cattle or sheep, often resulting in loss of the hoof. **2.** Any of various plant diseases caused by fungi that attack the base of the stem or trunk and bring about the eventual death of the plant. **3.** *Informal.* **Athlete's foot** *(see).*

foot rule *n.* A rigid measure one foot (304 millimetres) long.

foots (fŏŏts) *pl.n.* The sediment that forms during the refining of oils and other liquids; dregs. [A plural of FOOT.]

foot·sie, foot·sy (fŏŏt-si) *n. Informal.* Also **footy.** A flirting game in which a couple touch feet or legs, usually in secret, as under a table. Used especially in the phrase *play footsie.* [From FOOT.]

foot·slog (fŏŏt-slog) *intr.v.* **-slogged, -slogging, -slogs.** *Informal.* To walk, tramp, or march, especially over a long distance. **—foot·slog·ger** *n.* **—foot·slog·ging** *n.*

foot soldier *n.* A soldier who fights on foot; an infantryman.

foot·sore (fŏŏt-sawr || -sōr) *adj.* Having sore or tired feet from much walking. **—foot·sore·ness** *n.*

foot·stalk (fŏŏt-stawk) *n. Biology.* A supporting stalk, such as a peduncle or pedicel.

foot·stall (fŏŏt-stawl) *n.* **1.** The pedestal or plinth of a pillar. **2.** The stirrup on a sidesaddle.

foot·step (fŏŏt-step) *n.* **1.** A step with the foot. **2.** The distance covered by one step: *a footstep away.* **3.** The sound of a foot stepping. **4.** A footprint. **5.** A step up or down: *the footsteps of a stairway.* **—follow in (someone's) footsteps.** To carry on the work or tradition of a predecessor.

foot·stool (fŏŏt-stōōl) *n.* A low stool for supporting or resting feet.

foot·wall (fŏŏt-wawl) *n.* The mass of rock underlying the mineral deposit in a mine.

foot·way (fŏŏt-way) *n.* A walk or path for pedestrians.

foot·wear (fŏŏt-wair) *n.* Anything worn on the feet, such as shoes or slippers, with the exception of hosiery.

foot·work (fŏŏt-wurk) *n.* **1.** The manner in which the feet are employed, as in dancing, boxing, fencing, or tennis. **2.** Skilful manoeuvring to attain one's ends: *fancy footwork.*

foot·worn (fŏŏt-wawrn || -wōrn) *adj.* **1.** Footsore. **2.** Having been worn down by feet, as a path or carpet.

foot·y (fŏŏtti) *n. Informal.* Also **foot·ie** (for sense 1). **1.** Football. **2.** Variant of **footsie.**

foo yong (fōō yúng, yóng) *n.* In Chinese cooking, an omelette made with green peppers, bean sprouts, and onion. [Cantonese *foo yong (dan),* Mandarin *fú róng (dàn),* hibiscus (egg) (from the fancied resemblance between the omelette and the large showy flower).]

fop (fop) *n.* A vain, affected man who is preoccupied with his clothes and manners; a dandy. [Middle English *fop, foppe,* a fool, perhaps akin to *fobben,* to cheat, FOB.]

fop·per·y (fóppəri) *n., pl.* **-ies.** The dress or manner of a fop.

fop·pish (fóppish) *adj.* Of, pertaining to, or characteristic of a fop; dandified. **—fop·pish·ly** *adv.* **—fop·pish·ness** *n.*

for (for; *weak form* fər) *prep.* **1.** Directed or sent to: *a letter for me.* **2.** Directed or inclined towards: *an eye for pretty girls.* **3.** As a result of; out of: *crying for joy.* **4.** To the extent of: *The road is paved for one mile.* **5.** Through the length or duration of: *sit still for an hour.* **6.** In order to go to: *leave for Scotland.* **7.** With an aim or view to: *We swim for fun.* **8.** In order to have or find: *look for a bargain.* **9.** In order to serve in or as: *train for the ministry.* **10.** In or to the amount of: *a bill for three pounds.* **11.** At the price of: *buy a dog for ten pounds.* **12.** In response to; as requital of: *tit for tat.* **13.** Considering the nature or usual character of: *very warm for May.* **14.** Appropriate or suitable to: *a time for dying.* **15.** At or on (an appointed time or occasion): *an appointment for three o'clock.* **16.** Notwithstanding; despite: *For all her experience, she is inefficient.* **17.** Intended to be used as: *Books are for reading.* **18.** With a desire or longing towards: *The puppy whimpered for his supper.* **19.** So as to obtain: *work for a salary.* **20.** In honour of: *a dinner for the ambassador.* **21.** In place of: *use artificial flowers for real ones.* **22.** In its effect on: *Fresh air is good for you.* **23.** In favour, defence, or support of: *vote for the candidate of one's choice.* **24.** Accompanying; paired with: *one rotten apple for every good one.* **25.** As against; as measured or compared with: *pound for pound.* **26.** As being: *We mistook her for the waitress.* **27.** In order to retain, conserve, or save: *Run for your life!* **28.** As the duty or task of; up to: *It is for the judge to rule.* **29. a.** To the advantage of: *I built up the business for my daughter.* **b.** As a help or remedy: *pills for his headache.* **30.** Explaining; resulting in: *motives for action.* **31.** Because of the fact or existence of; on account of: *If it wasn't for you, I could be free.* **32.** Allocated to: *one for you, two for me.* **—for it.** *British Informal.* In trouble. **—nothing for it.** No alternative. **—for to.** *Archaic & Regional.* In order to.
~*conj.* Because; since. [Middle English *for,* Old English *for* (the conjunction develops from Old English phrases such as *for thon the,* "for the (reason) that").]

Usage: In the following types of construction, standard British English prefers *for,* whereas American English prefers *in*: *the first time for/in months, that's the worst rain for/in years.*

for- *prefix.* Indicates: **1.** Completely; to exhaustion; excessively; for example, **forspent, forlorn. 2.** Prohibition; abstention; for example, **forswear, forbid.** [Old English *for-, fær-*; akin to Latin *per-*, Greek *peri-*.]

fo·ra. Alternative plural of **forum.**

for·age (fórrij || fáwrij) *n.* **1.** Food for domestic animals, such as horses, cows, and sheep; fodder. Also used adjectivally: *forage crop.* **2.** The act of looking or searching for such food. **3.** The act of looking or searching for supplies of any kind.
~*v.* **foraged, -aging, -ages.** —*intr.* **1.** To search for food or provisions. **2.** To make a raid, as for food, supplies, or anything needed or desired. **3.** To hunt or search about. —*tr.* **1.** To wander or rummage through, especially in search of provisions. **2.** To raid; plunder. **3.** To provide with fodder; feed. **4.** To secure by searching about. [Middle English, from Old French *fo(ur)rage,* from *feurre,* fodder, from Germanic.] **—for·ag·er** *n.*

forage cap *n.* A brimless, close-fitting, military cap with a central dent running lengthways.

fo·ra·men (fo-ráy-men, fə-, -mən) *n., pl.* **-ramina** (-rámminə) or **-mens.** An opening or perforation in a bone or through a membranous anatomical structure. [New Latin, from Latin *forāmen,* an opening, from *forāre,* to bore.] **—fo·ram·i·nal** *adj.*

foramen magnum *n.* The large orifice in the base of the skull through which the spinal cord passes and becomes continuous with the medulla oblongata. [New Latin, "large orifice".]

for·a·min·if·er·an (fórrə-mínnifər-ən, fáwrə-, -mi-nífferən) *n.* Also **for·am** (fáwr-əm || fōr-), **for·a·min·i·fer** (fórrə-mínnifər, fáwrə-). Any of the unicellular microorganisms of the order Foraminifera, characteristically having a calcareous shell with perforations through which numerous pseudopodia protrude. [New Latin *Foraminifera* : *forāmen,* opening, FORAMEN + -FER.] **—fo·ram·i·nif·er·ous, fo·ram·i·nif·er·al** *adj.*

for·as·much as (fər-əz-múch, fáwr-) *conj. Archaic.* Inasmuch as; since.

for·ay (fórray || fáwr-ay) *n.* **1.** A sudden raid or military advance. **2.** A venture or initial attempt in some field. **3.** An outing or expedition with the object of finding certain animals or plants in their natural surroundings: *a fungus foray.*
~*v.* **forayed, -aying, -ays.** —*intr.* To make a raid. —*tr.* To make a raid against; plunder. [Middle English *forrai,* from *forraien,* to foray, back-formation from *forreour,* raider, plunderer, from Old French *forrier,* from Vulgar Latin *fodrārius* (unattested), from Germanic.]

forb (forb) *n.* Any herbaceous plant other than a grass, especially one growing in a field or meadow. [Greek *phorbē,* fodder, from *pherbein*†, to feed, graze.]

for·bear[1] (fawr-báir, fər-) *v.* **-bore** (-bór || -bṓr), **-borne** (-bórn || -bṓrn), **-bearing, -bears.** —*tr.* **1.** To refrain from; keep oneself from: *forbear replying.* **2.** To desist from; cease. **3.** *Archaic.* To endure; tolerate. —*intr.* **1.** To hold back; refrain. **2.** To be tolerant or patient. [Middle English *forberen,* Old English *forberan,* to bear, endure, from Germanic.] **—for·bear·er** *n.*
Usage: *Forbear* is a verb meaning "to refrain from"; *forebear* is a noun meaning "ancestor", occasionally spelt *forbear.*

for·bear[2]. Variant of **forebear.**

for·bear·ance (fawr-báir-ənss, fər-) *n.* **1.** The act of refraining from something; abstinence. **2.** Tolerance and restraint in the face of provocation; patience. **3.** *Law.* The act of a creditor who refrains from enforcing a debt when it falls due. —See Synonyms at **mercy, patience.**

for·bear·ing (fawr-báiring, fər-) *adj.* Tolerant; patient.

for·bid (fər-bíd, fawr-) *tr.v.* **-bade** (-bád, -báyd) or **-bad** (-bád), **-bidden** (-bídd'n) or **-bid, -bidding, -bids. 1.** To command (someone) not to do something: *I forbid you to go.* **2.** To prohibit; interdict: *Smoking is forbidden.* **3.** To have the effect of preventing; preclude. **—God forbid.** Let it not happen; I do not wish it to happen. [Middle English *forbidden, forbeden,* Old English *forbēodan,* from Germanic.] **—for·bid·dance** *n.* **—for·bid·der** *n.*
Usage: The standard English constructions with this verb are the infinitive (*I forbid you to go*) and the *-ing* form of the verb (*I forbid your going*), which is a little more formal. The use of a preposition (*I forbid you from going*) is not standard. See also **prevent, prohibit.**

for·bid·den (fər-bídd'n, fawr-) *adj. Physics.* Of or pertaining to secondary quantum effects: *forbidden spectral lines.*

Forbidden City. Name given to the ancient imperial residence and seat of central government within the Inner or Tatar city, Beijing (Peking), China. Now a vast museum, it comprises two sets of three imperial palaces and some smaller palaces, in a walled enclosure.

forbidden fruit *n.* Anything desirable but forbidden; especially, illicit sexual pleasure. [Alluding to the fruit forbidden to Adam in the garden of Eden (Genesis 2:17).]

for·bid·ding (fər-bídding, fawr-) *adj.* **1.** Tending or threatening to impede progress. **2.** Unfriendly; disagreeable. **3.** Grim; ominous.

for·bye, for·by (fawr-bí) *prep. Scottish.* Besides.
~*adv.* In addition. [Middle English : FOR- + BY.]

force (forss || fōrss) *n.* **1.** Capacity to do work or cause physical change; strength; power. **2.** *Northern English.* A waterfall. [Middle English *fors, force,* from Old Norse *fors.*] **3.** Power made operative against resistance; exertion: *use force in driving a nail.* **4.** Violence or the threat of violence used against a person or thing. **5.** Intellectual power or vigour, as of a statement. **6.** A capacity for influencing the mind or behaviour; efficacy. **7.** Anything or anyone possessing such capacity: *forces of evil.* **8.** A body of persons or other resources organised or available for a specified purpose: *a work force.* **9. a.** A group organised for military, police, or hostile purposes: *an armed force.* **b.** *Plural. Often capital* **F.** The armed forces of a country; the navy, army, and air force. **10.** *Law.* Legal validity; efficacy. **11.** *Symbol* **F** *Physics.* A vector quantity that tends to produce an acceleration of a body in the direction of its application. **—in force. 1.** In full strength. **2.** In effect; operative: *a rule no longer in force.* **—join forces.** To unite; combine efforts. **—the force.** *Often capital* **F.** *Informal.* The police.
~*tr.v.* **forced, forcing, forces. 1.** To compel to perform an action; coerce. **2.** To obtain by the use of force or coercion: *force a confession.* **3.** To produce by effort: *force a tear from one's eye.* **4.** To move (something) against resistance; push: *force open the barricaded door.* **5.** To move, open, or clear by force: *force one's way through a crowd.* **6.** To break down or open by force: *force a lock.* **7.** To rape. **8.** To inflict or impose: *force one's will on someone.* **9.** To place undue strain upon; push beyond normal capacity or use: *force one's voice.* **10.** To cause to grow or mature by artificially accelerating the normal processes: *force flowers in a greenhouse.* **—force down.** To force (an aeroplane) to land. [Middle English, from Old French, from Vulgar Latin *fortia* (unattested), from Latin *fortis,* strong.] **—force·a·ble** *adj.* **—forc·er** *n.*
Synonyms: *force, compel, coerce, constrain, necessitate, oblige.*

forced (forst || fōrst) *adj.* **1.** Enforced, compulsory; involuntary: *forced labour.* **2.** Produced under strain; not spontaneous: *forced laughter.* **3.** Effected in an emergency: *a forced landing.* **—forc·ed·ly** (fórs-id-li, fṓrs-) *adv.* **—forc·ed·ness** *n.*

forced march *n.* A long march made at a rigorously fast pace over a longer distance than normal.

force feed *n.* A system that supplies lubricants under pressure, as to a car engine.

force-feed (fórss-féed || fṓrss-) *tr.v.* **-fed** (-féd), **-feeding, -feeds. 1.** To force to ingest food; feed forcibly. **2.** To force to assimilate ideas, information, or the like. **—forced feeding, force-feeding** *n.*

force field *n.* A **field of force** *(see).*

force·ful (fórss-f'l || fōrss) *adj.* Characterised by or full of force; effective; persuasive. **—force·ful·ly** *adv.* **—force·ful·ness** *n.*

force ma·jeure (ma-zhōr, -jóor) *n.* An unexpected or uncontrollable event that upsets one's plans or releases one from obligations, especially legal obligations. [French, "superior force".]

force·meat (fórss-meet || fṓrss-) *n.* Finely chopped spiced meat or poultry, used in stuffing or as a garnish. [From *force,* variant of FARCE (to stuff).]

for·ceps (fór-seps, -sips) *n., pl.* **forceps. 1.** An instrument resembling a pair of pincers or tongs, used for grasping, manipulation, or extracting; especially, as used by surgeons or dentists. **2.** A pincer-like clasping organ at the posterior end of the abdomen in certain insects, such as earwigs. [Latin *forceps,* fire tongs, pincers.]

force pump *n.* A pump with a solid piston and valves used to raise a liquid or expel it under pressure.

for·ci·ble (fór-səb'l || fṓr-) *adj.* **1.** Effected through the use of force: *a forcible entry.* **2.** Characterised by force; forceful; persuasive. **—for·ci·ble·ness** *n.* **—for·ci·bly** *adv.*

forc·ing house (fór-sing || fṓr-) *n.* A place where living things, such as flowers, fruit, or animals, are artificially matured, or where growth is accelerated.

ford (ford || fōrd) *n.* A shallow place in a body of water, such as a river, where a crossing can be made on foot, or in a vehicle.
~*tr.v.* **forded, fording, fords.** To cross (a body of water) at a ford. [Middle English *ford,* Old English *ford.*] **—ford·a·ble** *adj.*

Ford (ford || fōrd), **Ford Madox,** born F. Hermann Hueffer (1873–1939). British novelist and editor. He collaborated with Conrad on *The Inheritors* (1901) and *Romance* (1903), and wrote novels, e.g. *The Good Soldier* (1915), *Parade's End* (1924–28), verse, and criticism. He founded the *English Review* (1908), and the *Transatlantic Review* (1924).

Ford, Gerald R(udolph), born King (1913–). Thirty-eighth president of the United States. He entered politics as a Republican, and was elected to the House of Representatives in 1949. In 1973 he became vice-president to Richard Nixon, and a year later after Nixon's resignation over the Watergate scandal became president. He was defeated by Jimmy Carter (1976).

Ford, Henry (1863–1947). U.S. motor-car manufacturer. He founded the Ford Motor Company in 1903 and produced the first of the legendary model Ts in 1908. With assembly-line production he was turning out two million cars a year by 1924, at prices that made them accessible to the general public.

Ford, John[1] (1586–*c.*1640). English dramatist. He collaborated with other dramatists, notably Dekker and Webster, and wrote works of his own which include *'Tis Pity She's a Whore* (1633) and *Perkin Warbeck* (1634).

Ford, John[2], born Sean Aloysius O'Feeney (1895–1973). U.S. director of 125 feature films. Starring John Wayne, his films include *Stagecoach* (1939), *The Searchers* (1956), and *The Man Who Shot Liberty Valance* (1962). Other films include *The Informer* (1935) and *The Grapes of Wrath* (1940), which both won Oscars.

for·do, fore·do (fawr-dóo || fōr-) *tr.v.* **-did** (-díd), **-done** (-dún), **-doing, -does** (-dúz). *Archaic.* **1.** To kill. **2.** To bring to ruin. **3.** To exhaust utterly. [Middle English *fordon,* Old English *fordōn* : FOR- (indicating destruction) + *dōn,* to DO.]

fore (for || fōr) *adj.* Located at or towards the front; anterior.
~*n.* **1.** Something at or towards the front. **2.** The front part.

3. The bow of a ship. **—to the fore.** In, into, or towards a position of prominence.

~adv. Towards or at the bow of a ship; forward.

~prep. Also **'fore.** *Archaic.* Before. Frequently used in oaths: *Fore God, Sir, you are mistaken!*

~interj. *Golf.* Used to warn those ahead that a ball is about to be driven in their direction. [Middle English *fore*, probably from adverb, "beforehand", Old English *for(e).*]

fore– *prefix.* Indicates: **1.** Before in time; for example, **forebode, foresight. 2.** The front or first part; for example, **foredeck, foreskin.** [Middle English *for-, fore-,* Old English *fore-,* from *fore* (adverb), in front, beforehand.]

fore and aft *adv.* **1.** From the bow to the stern of a ship; lengthways of a ship. **2.** In, at, or towards both ends of a ship.

fore-and-aft (fáwr-ən-aáft || fór-, -áft) *adj.* Parallel with the keel of a ship.

fore-and-aft-er (fáwr-ən-aáftər || fór-, -áftər) *n.* A sailing ship, such as a ketch or schooner, carrying a fore-and-aft rig.

fore-and-aft rig *n.* A ship rig with quadrilateral and triangular fore-and-aft sails. Compare **square rig. —fore-and-aft-rigged** *adj.*

fore-and-aft sail *n.* A sail set parallel with the keel of a vessel, as opposed to being hung from a horizontal bar (yard) across the mast as in a **square rig** (*see*).

fore·arm[1] (fawr-árm || fór-) *tr.v.* **-armed, -arming, -arms.** To prepare or arm in advance of some confrontation.

fore·arm[2] (fór-aarm || fór-) *n.* The part of the arm between the wrist and elbow.

fore·bear, for·bear (fór-bair || fór-) *n.* A forefather; an ancestor. See Usage note at **forbear.** [Middle English (Scottish dialect) *forebear* : FORE- + *bear*, "be-er", from *been*, to BE.]

fore·bode (fawr-bṓd || fór-) *v.* **-boded, -boding, -bodes. —tr. 1.** To indicate the threatening likelihood of; give warning of; portend. **2.** To have a premonition of (a future misfortune). —See Synonyms at **foretell.**

fore·bod·ing (fawr-bṓding || fór-) *n.* **1.** A dark sense of impending evil; premonition. **2.** An evil omen; a portent. —See Synonyms at **apprehension.**

~adj. Ominous. **—fore·bod·ing·ly** *adv.*

fore·brain (fór-brayn || fór-) *n.* **1.** The anterior region of the embryonic brain from which the telencephalon and diencephalon develop. Also called "prosencephalon". **2.** Cerebrum (*see*).

fore·cast (fór-kaast || fór-, -kast) *v.* **-cast** *or* **-casted, -casting, -casts. —tr. 1.** To estimate or calculate in advance, especially; **a.** To predict (weather conditions) by analysis of meteorological data. **b.** To predict (the behaviour of the economy, financial markets, or the like) by the analysis of economic and financial data. **2.** To serve as an advance indication of; foreshadow. **—intr.** To make an estimation in advance. —See Synonyms at **foretell.**

~n. A prediction, as of the weather. **2.** A conjecture concerning the future. [Middle English *forecasten,* to devise beforehand : FORE- + CAST.] **—fore·cast·er** *n.*

forecast bet *n.* A bet that is staked on the winners of the first two, three, or four places in a race. Compare **reverse forecast.**

fore·cas·tle, fo'c's'le (fṓk-səl || fór-kass'l, fór-, -kaa-s'l) *n.* **1.** The section of the upper deck of a ship located at the bow, in front of the foremast. **2.** A raised deck at the bow of a merchant ship, where the crew was formerly housed.

fore·close (fawr-klṓz || fór-) *v.* **-closed, -closing, -closes. —tr. 1.** *Law.* **a.** To deprive (a mortgagor) of the right to redeem mortgaged property, as when he has failed in his payments; repossess the mortgaged property of. **b.** To bar the right to redeem (a mortgage). **2.** To shut out; bar. **3.** To settle or resolve beforehand. **4.** To hinder; deter; thwart. **—intr.** To foreclose a mortgage. Often used with *on.* [Middle English *forclosen,* to shut out, preclude, from Old French *forclore* (past participle *forclos*) : *fors,* outside, from Latin *forīs* + *clore,* from Latin *claudere,* to CLOSE.] **—fore·clos·a·ble** *adj.*

fore·clo·sure (fawr-klṓzhər || fór-) *n.* The act of foreclosing; especially, a legal proceeding by which a mortgage is foreclosed.

fore·course (fór-kawrss || fór-kōrss) *n.* A foresail.

fore·court (fór-kawrt || fór-kōrt) *n.* **1.** A courtyard in front of a building. **2.** *British.* An area in front of a filling station, next to the petrol pumps. **3.** The part of a playing court nearest the net or wall, as in tennis or handball.

fore·date (fawr-dáyt || fór-) *tr.v.* **-dated, -dating, -dates.** To antedate.

fore·deck (fór-deck || fór-) *n.* The forward part of a deck, usually the main deck.

foredo. Variant of **fordo.**

fore·doom (fawr-dṓom || fór-) *tr.v.* **-doomed, -dooming, -dooms.** To doom or condemn beforehand. **—fore·doom** (fór-doom || fór-) *n.*

fore·fa·ther (fór-faathər || fór-) *n.* An ancestor.

forefend. Variant of **forfend.**

fore·fin·ger (fór-fing-gər || fór-) *n.* The **index finger** (*see*).

fore·foot (fór-foŏt || fór-) *n., pl.* **-feet** (-feet). **1.** Either of the front feet of a quadruped. **2.** *Nautical.* The part of a ship at which the prow joins the keel.

fore·front (fór-frunt || fór-) *n.* **1.** The foremost part or area of something. **2.** The position of most importance or prominence.

foregather. Variant of **forgather.**

fore·go[1] (fawr-gṓ || fór-) *tr.v.* **-went** (-wént), **-gone** (-gón || U.S. also -gáwn) **-going, -goes** (-gṓz). To precede or go before, as in time or place. **—fore·go·er** *n.*

forego[2]. Variant of **forgo.**

fore·go·ing (fawr-gṓ-ing, fór-gṓ- || fōr-gṓ-, fór-gṓ-) *adj.* Just past; preceding; previously said or written.

fore·gone (fór-gón || fór-, -gaán, -gáwn) *adj.* Having gone or been completed previously; departed; past. [Past participle of FOREGO.]

foregone conclusion *n.* An end or result regarded as inevitable.

fore·ground (fór-grownd || fór-) *n.* **1.** The part of a view or sight that is nearest to the viewer. **2.** The part of a picture, as in a painting or photograph, that is represented as nearest to the viewer. **3.** The most important or prominent position.

fore·gut (fór-gut || fór-) *n.* The anterior part of the digestive tract, which in vertebrates extends from the buccal cavity to the bile duct and in arthropods comprises the buccal cavity, oesophagus, crop, and gizzard.

fore·hand (fór-hand || fór-) *adj.* **1. a.** Made with the hand moving palm forwards: *a forehand tennis stroke.* **b.** Pertaining to the side of the body on which a forehand stroke is played. **2.** Foremost; leading. **3.** Taking place beforehand; prior.

~n. 1. a. A forehand stroke, as in tennis. **b.** The side of the body on which a forehand stroke is played. **2.** The part of a horse in front of the rider. **3.** A position of advantage; upper hand.

fore·hand·ed (fór-hánded || fór-) *adj.* **1.** Forehand, as in tennis. **2.** *U.S.* Looking or planning ahead. **3.** *U.S.* Having ample financial resources; well-off. **—fore·hand·ed·ness** *n.*

fore·head (fórrid, fór-hed || fáwrid, fór-hed) *n.* The part of the head or face between the eyebrows, the normal hairline, and the temples.

for·eign (fórrən, fórrin || fáwrən) *adj.* **1.** Located away from one's native country: *foreign parts.* **2.** Of, characteristic of, or from a country other than one's own: *a foreign custom.* **3.** Conducted or involved with other nations or governments; not domestic: *foreign trade.* **4.** Situated in an abnormal or improper place: *a foreign body.* **5.** Outside of a scope, range, or essential nature; alien: *lying is quite foreign to her nature.* **6.** Not to the point; extraneous; irrelevant. **7.** *Law.* Subject to the jurisdiction of another political unit. —See Synonyms at **extrinsic.** [Middle English *forein,* from Old French *forein, forain,* from Late Latin *forānus,* from Latin *forās,* out of doors, abroad.] **—for·eign·ness** *n.*

foreign affairs *pl.n.* **1.** A country's relationships and dealings with other countries. **2.** Events that take place in another country.

foreign aid *n.* Financial and practical assistance given by one country to another, especially by a technologically advanced country to a less developed one. Also called "aid".

Foreign and Commonwealth Office *n. Abbr.* **F.C.O.** In the United Kingdom, the government department in charge of foreign affairs.

foreign bill *n.* A draft for a sum of money to be paid in another country. Also called "foreign bill of exchange", "foreign draft".

foreign correspondent *n.* A journalist or reporter situated in a foreign country who sends news of that country to his own.

for·eign·er (fórrə-nər, fórri- || fáwrə-) *n.* A person from a foreign country.

foreign exchange *n.* **1.** The transaction of international monetary business, as between governments or businessmen of different countries. **2.** Negotiable bills drawn in one country to be paid in another country.

Foreign Legion *n.* A French military unit composed of volunteers of any nationality.

foreign minister, Foreign Minister *n.* The government minister in charge of dealings between his own government and those of foreign countries. Also *chiefly British* "Foreign Secretary".

foreign mission *n.* **1.** A group sent to a foreign country for missionary service, as in religion or medicine. **2.** A group sent to a foreign country for diplomatic service.

Foreign Office *n. Abbr.* **F.O.** The official government department, in several countries, that is in charge of foreign affairs.

fore·judge, for·judge (fawr-júj || fór-) *v.* **-judged, -judging, -judges. —tr.** To judge beforehand; prejudge. **—intr.** To judge something or someone beforehand.

fore·knowl·edge (fór-nóllij || fór-) *n.* Knowledge or awareness of something prior to its existence or occurrence; prescience.

fore·land (fór-lənd || fór-) *n.* **1.** A projecting land mass; a promontory; a cape. **2.** Land or territory lying to the fore, as borderland or land at the edge of a body of water.

fore·leg (fór-leg || fór-) *n.* Either of the front legs of a quadruped.

fore·limb (fór-lim || fór-) *n.* An anterior appendage, such as a leg, wing, or flipper in a vertebrate.

fore·lock[1] (fór-lok || fór-) *n.* A lock of hair that grows or falls on the forehead; especially, the part of a horse's mane that falls forwards between the ears. **—to pull** *or* **tug one's forelock:** to express deference by, or as if, touching or pulling one's forelock.

fore·lock[2] *n.* A cotter pin; a linchpin.

fore·man (fór-mən || fór-) *n., pl.* **-men** (-mən). **1.** A man who has charge of a group of workers, as at a factory. **2.** The chairman and spokesman for a jury. **—fore·man·ship** *n.*

fore·mast (fór-məst, -maast || fór-, -mast) *n.* The forward mast on any sailing vessel with two or more masts, with the exception of the ketch and the yawl.

fore·most (fór-mṓst || fór-) *adj.* Ahead of all others, especially in position or rank; paramount. See Synonyms at **chief.**

~adv. In the front or first position. [Variant (influenced by FORE-) of Middle English *formest, formost,* Old English *formest,* superlative of *forma,* first.]

fore·name (fór-naym || fór-) *n.* A first name; a Christian name.

fore·named (fór-náymd || fór-) *adj.* Named earlier; aforesaid.

fore·noon (fór-nōn, fawr-nōon || fór-, fōr-nōon) *n.* **1.** The period of time between sunrise and noon; daylight morning hours. **2.** The latter part of the morning.

fo·ren·sic (fə-rĕn-sĭk, fo-, -zĭk) *adj.* **1.** Pertaining to or employed in legal proceedings or argumentation. **2.** Pertaining to a forensic science, such as pathology: *a forensic laboratory.* **3.** Of or employed in debate or argument; rhetorical. [Latin *forēnsis,* of a market or forum, public, from *forum,* forum.] —**fo·ren·si·cal·ly** *adv.*

forensic medicine *n.* The application of medical science to interpret or establish the facts in civil or criminal law cases. Also called "medical jurisprudence".

fo·ren·sics (fə-rĕn-sĭks, fo-, -zĭks) *n. Used with a singular verb.* The study or practice of formal debate; argumentation.

fore·or·dain (fôr-awr-dáyn ‖ fŏr-) *tr.v.* **-dained, -daining, -dains.** To appoint, determine, or ordain beforehand; predestine. —**fore·or·dain·ment** *n.* —**fore·or·di·na·tion** (-di-náysh'n) *n.*

fore·part (fôr-paart ‖ fŏr-) *n.* The first or foremost part.

fore·paw (fôr-paw ‖ fŏr-) *n.* Either of the front feet of a land mammal that does not have hoofs.

fore·peak (fôr-peek ‖ fŏr-) *n.* The section of the hold of a ship that is within the angle made by the bow.

fore·person (fôr-perss'n ‖ fŏr-) *n.* A foreman or forewoman.

fore·play (fôr-play ‖ fŏr-) *n.* Sexual stimulation that precedes sexual intercourse.

fore·quar·ter (fôr-kwawrtər, -kawrtər ‖ fŏr-) *n.* **1.** The front section of a side of meat. **2.** *Plural.* The forelegs, shoulders, and adjacent parts of an animal, especially a horse.

fore·reach (fawr-réech ‖ fŏr-) *v.* **-reached, -reaching, -reaches.** —*tr.* **1.** To get ahead of; pass, especially in a sailing vessel. **2.** To get the advantage over; excel. —*intr.* To move up; gain ground, especially upon a sailing vessel.

fore·run (fawr-rún ‖ fŏr-) *tr.v.* **-ran** (-rán), **-run, -running, -runs. 1.** To run in advance or in front of. **2.** To be the precursor of; foreshadow. **3.** To forestall; prevent.

fore·run·ner (fôr-runnər ‖ fŏr-) *n.* **1.** Someone who or something that precedes, as in time; a predecessor. **2.** An ancestor; a forebear. **3.** Someone who or something that provides advance notice of the coming of others; a harbinger; a precursor.

fore·said (fôr-sed ‖ fŏr-) *adj.* Previously named or said; aforesaid.

fore·sail (fôr-səl, -sayl ‖ fŏr-) *n. Nautical.* **1.** The principal square sail hung to the foremast of a square-rigged vessel. Also called "forecourse". **2.** The principal triangular sail hung to the mast of a fore-and-aft-rigged vessel. **3.** The triangular sail hung to the forestay of a cutter or sloop. **4.** *Plural.* The sails on the foremast or before the mast.

fore·see (fawr-seé ‖ fŏr-) *tr.v.* **-saw** (-sáw), **-seen** (-séen), **-seeing, -sees.** To see or know beforehand; anticipate; envision. See Synonyms at **expect.** —**fore·see·a·ble** *adj.* —**fore·se·er** *n.*

fore·shad·ow (fawr-sháddō ‖ fŏr-) *tr.v.* **-owed, -owing, -ows.** To present an often ominous indication or suggestion of beforehand; portend.

fore·sheet (fôr-sheet ‖ fŏr-) *n.* **1.** A rope used in trimming a foresail. **2.** *Plural.* The space near the bow of an open boat.

fore·shock (fôr-shok ‖ fŏr-) *n.* A minor tremor that precedes an earthquake.

fore·shore (fôr-shawr ‖ fŏr-shōr) *n.* **1.** The part of a shore covered at high tide. **2.** The part of a shore between the water and occupied or cultivated land. **3.** *Law.* That part of the shore between high tide and low tide, that is considered as part of the adjoining parish.

fore·short·en (fawr-shórt'n ‖ fŏr-) *tr.v.* **-ened, -ening, -ens. 1.** In drawing or painting, to represent the long axis of (an object or form) by contracting its lines so as to produce an illusion of depth or distance. **2.** To shorten beforehand; curtail.

fore·side (fôr-sīd ‖ fŏr-) *n.* The front or upper side.

fore·sight (fôr-sīt ‖ fŏr-) *n.* **1.** The ability to foresee. **2.** The act of looking forward. **3.** Concern or prudence with respect to the future. —**fore·sight·ed** *adj.* —**fore·sight·ed·ly** (fawr-sítid-li) *adv.* —**fore·sight·ed·ness** *n.*

fore·skin (fôr-skin ‖ fŏr-) *n.* The loose fold of skin that covers the glans of the penis. Also called "prepuce".

fore·speak (fawr-speék ‖ fŏr-) *tr.v.* **-spoken** (-spókən), **-speaking, -speaks.** *Rare.* **1.** To speak of in advance; predict. **2.** To arrange for or engage in advance.

forespent. Variant of **forspent.**

for·est (fórrist ‖ fawrəst) *n.* **1. a.** A large area covered by a dense growth of trees, together with other plants. **b.** The trees themselves. **2.** Something that resembles a forest in density, quantity, or profusion: *a forest of skyscrapers.* **3.** *Law.* A defined area of land formerly set aside in England as a royal hunting ground. —*tr.v.* **forested, -esting, -ests.** To plant trees on; transform into a forest. [Middle English, from Old French, from Late Latin expression *forestis (silva),* outside (forest), referring originally to the royal forest or game preserve of Charlemagne, probably from Latin *forīs,* outside, outdoors.] —**for·est·al, fo·res·ti·al** (fə-résti-əl) *adj.* —**for·es·ta·tion** (fórri-stáysh'n ‖ fáwrə-) *n.*

fore·stall (fawr-stáwl ‖ fŏr-) *tr.v.* **-stalled, -stalling, -stalls. 1.** To prevent, delay, or take precautionary measures against beforehand. **2.** To deal with or think of beforehand; anticipate. **3.** To prevent or hinder normal sales by buying up merchandise, discouraging others from bringing their goods to market, or encouraging an increase in prices of goods already on the market. Compare **engross.** —See Synonyms at **prevent.** [Middle English *forestallen,* to forestall, obstruct, from *forestal,* the crime of waylaying or ambushing on the highway, Old English *foresteall,* waylaying, interception : *fore-,* in

front of + *steall,* position, place.] —**fore·stall·er** *n.* —**fore·stall·ment** *n.*

fore·stay (fôr-stāy ‖ fŏr-) *n.* A stay extending from the head of the foremast to the bowsprit of a ship.

fore·stay·sail (fawr-stáy-səl, -sayl ‖ fŏr-) *n.* A triangular sail set on the forestay.

for·est·er (fórri-stər ‖ fáwrə-) *n.* **1.** A person trained in forestry. **2.** One that inhabits a forest. **3.** Any of various chiefly tropical moths of the genus *Ino,* many of which are a brilliant green.

For·est·er (fórri-stər ‖ fáwrə-), **C(ecil) S(cott)** (1899-1966). British novelist. He is best known for his *Captain Hornblower* series, sea adventures set in Napoleonic times. His other books include *Payment Deferred* (1926) and *The African Queen* (1935).

for·est·ry (fórri-stri ‖ fáwrə-) *n.* **1.** The science and art of cultivating, maintaining, and developing forests. **2.** The management of a forest land. **3.** Forest land.

foreswear. Variant of **forswear.**

fore·taste (fôr-tayst ‖ fŏr-) *n.* An advance taste, experience, or realisation: *a foretaste of doom.* —*tr.v.* **foretasted, -tasting, -tastes.** To have an advance realisation of; anticipate.

fore·tell (fawr-tél ‖ fŏr-) *v.* **-told** (-tóld), **-telling, -tells.** —*tr.* To tell of or indicate beforehand; prophesy; predict. —*intr.* To tell beforehand. Often used with *of: foretell of disaster.* —**fore·tell·er** *n.*
Synonyms: *foretell, predict, forecast, prophesy, divine, augur, portend, forebode, presage, bode, betoken, foretoken.*

fore·thought (fôr-thawt ‖ fŏr-) *n.* **1.** Deliberation, consideration, or planning beforehand. **2.** Preparation or thought for the future; prudent anticipation. —**fore·thought·ful** *adj.* —**fore·thought·ful·ly** *adv.* —**fore·thought·ful·ness** *n.*

fore·time (fôr-tīm ‖ fŏr-) *n. Archaic.* Former time; the past.

fore·to·ken (fawr-tókən ‖ fŏr-) *tr.v.* **-kened, -kening, -kens.** To foreshow; foreshadow; presage. —See Synonyms at **foretell.** —*n.* (fôr-tókən ‖ fŏr-). An advance warning.

fore·top (fôr-təp, -top ‖ fŏr-) *n.* **1.** A platform at the top of a ship's foremast. **2.** A forelock, especially of a horse.

fore·top·gal·lant (fôr-tə-gál-ənt, -top- ‖ fŏr-) *adj. Nautical.* Of or relating to the mast directly above the foremast.

fore·top·gal·lant·mast (fôr-tə-gál-ənt-məst, -top-, -maast ‖ fŏr-, -mast) *n.* The mast above the fore-topmast.

fore·top·mast (fawr-tóp-məst, -maast ‖ fŏr-, -mast) *n.* The mast that is above the foretop.

fore·top·sail (fawr-tóp-səl, -sayl ‖ fŏr-) *n.* The sail hung from the fore-topmast.

for ever, for·ev·er (fə-révvər, faw-) *adv.* **1.** For everlasting time; eternally. **2.** At all times; incessantly. —*interj.* Used to express enthusiastic support for a team, country, or the like: *Ireland for ever!*
Usage: In the literal sense "for eternity", *for ever* is more acceptable than *forever.* In the more everyday sense of "constantly", it is usual to write a single word: *he's forever complaining.*

for evermore, for·ev·er·more (fə-révvər-mór, faw- ‖ -mŏr) *adv.* For ever.

fore·warn (fawr-wáwrn ‖ fŏr-) *tr.v.* **-warned, -warning, -warns.** To warn clearly in advance. See Synonyms at **warn.**

fore·went. Past tense of **forego** (to go before).

fore·wing (fôr-wing ‖ fŏr-) *n.* Either of a pair of anterior wings, as in certain insects.

fore·wom·an (fôr-wŏŏmmən ‖ fŏr-) *n., pl.* **-women** (-wimmin). A woman who acts as a foreman.

fore·word (fôr-wurd, -wərd ‖ fŏr-) *n.* A preface or introductory note, especially at the beginning of a book. [Translation of German *Vorwort.*]

foreworn. Variant of **forworn.**

fore·yard (fôr-yaard ‖ fŏr-) *n. Nautical.* The lowest yard on a foremast.

For·far (fôr-fər, -faar). Royal burgh and town in Angus, Scotland. It lies in the rich farmlands of Strathmore. Its castle was the site of a Scottish parliament in 1057.

For·far·shire (fôr-fər-sheer, -faar-, -shər). Until 1928 the name of the Scottish county of Angus.

for·feit (fôr-fit) *n.* **1.** Something surrendered as punishment for a crime, offence, error, or breach of contract; a penalty or fine. **2.** Something given up or surrendered for a breach of rules or a mistake in a game. **3.** A forfeiture. **4.** *Often plural.* A game in which forfeits are required. —*adj.* Surrendered or alienated for a crime, offence, error, or breach of contract. —*tr.v.* **forfeited, -feiting, -feits. 1.** To surrender or be forced to surrender as a forfeit. **2.** To subject to forfeiture. [Middle English *forfet,* forfeit, transgression, from Old French *forfet,* from *for(s)faire,* to commit a crime : *fors-,* beyond (here, beyond what is permitted), from Latin *forīs,* outside + *faire,* to do, act, from Latin *facere.*] —**for·feit·a·ble** *adj.* —**for·feit·er** *n.*

for·fei·ture (fôr-fi-chər ‖ -choor) *n.* **1.** The act of surrendering something as a forfeit. **2.** Something that is forfeited.

for·fend, fore·fend (fawr-fénd ‖ fŏr-) *tr.v.* **-fended, -fending, -fends. 1.** To keep or ward off; avert. **2.** *U.S.* To defend or protect. [Middle English *forfenden,* to forbid, prevent : FOR- (prohibition) + FEND.]

for·fi·cate (fôrfi-kət, -kit, -kayt) *adj.* Deeply forked, as is the tail of certain birds. [Latin *forfex* (stem *forfic-*), a pair of scissors.]

for·gat. Archaic past tense of **forget.**

for·gath·er, fore·gather (fawr-gáthər || fōr-) *intr.v.* **-ered, -ering, -ers. 1.** To gather together; assemble. **2.** *Rare.* To have a chance encounter; meet by accident. **3.** To keep company or consort. Used with *with.* [Originally Scottish : FOR- + GATHER.]

for·gave. Past tense of **forgive.**

forge[1] (forj || fōrj) *n.* **1.** A furnace or hearth where metals are heated or wrought; a smithy. **2.** A workshop where pig iron is transformed into wrought iron.
~v. **forged, forging, forges.** *—tr.* **1.** To form (metal) by heating in a forge and beating or hammering into shape. **2.** To give form or shape to; bring about, especially by dint of effort or application: *forge a friendship.* **3.** To fashion or reproduce for fraudulent purposes; fake; counterfeit. *—intr.* **1.** To work at a forge or smithy. **2.** To make a forgery or counterfeit. [Middle English, from Old French, from Vulgar Latin *faurga* (unattested), from Latin *fabrica,* smithy, artisan's workshop, from *faber,* smith.] **—forg·er** *n.*

forge[2] *intr.v.* **forged, forging, forges. 1.** To advance gradually but steadily. Often used with *ahead.* **2.** To advance with an abrupt increase of speed. Often used with *ahead.* [Perhaps a variant of FORCE, which has been used in the same senses.]

for·ger·y (fórjəri || fṓr-) *n., pl.* **-ies. 1.** The crime of producing something counterfeit or forged. **2.** Something counterfeit, forged, or fraudulent.

for·get (fər-gét || fawr-) *v.* **-got** (-gót) or *archaic* **-gat** (-gát), **-gotten** (-gótt'n) or **-got, -getting, -gets.** *—tr.* **1.** To be unable to remember or call to mind. **2.** To lack concern for; treat with inattention; neglect: *forget one's family.* **3.** To leave behind unintentionally. **4.** To fail to mention; pass over. **5.** To banish from one's thoughts: *forget a disgrace.* *—intr.* **1.** To cease remembering. **2.** To fail or neglect to become aware at the proper moment: *forget about paying one's taxes.* **—forget (oneself).** To lose one's proper sense of decorum or self-restraint. [Middle English *forgeten,* Old English *forgietan,* from Germanic.] **—for·get·ta·ble** *adj.* **—for·get·ter** *n.*

for·get·ful (fər-gét-f'l || fawr-) *adj.* **1.** Tending or likely to forget. **2.** Neglectful; thoughtless; careless: *forgetful of one's duties.* **—for·get·ful·ly** *adv.* **—for·get·ful·ness** *n.*
Synonyms: *forgetful, unmindful, oblivious, heedless, abstracted, absent-minded, distracted.*

for·get-me-not (fər-gét-mi-not || fawr-) *n.* Any of various plants of the genus *Myosotis,* having small blue flowers. Also called "scorpion grass". [Translation of Old French *ne m'oubliez mie.*]

forg·ing (fórjing || fṓr-) *n.* Something that is forged.

for·give (fər-gív || fawr-) *v.* **-gave** (-gáyv), **-given** (-gívv'n), **-giving, -gives.** *—tr.* **1.** To excuse for a fault or offence; pardon. **2.** To renounce anger or resentment against; cease to blame. **3.** To absolve from payment of. *—intr.* To grant forgiveness. [Middle English *foryeven, forgiven,* Old English *forgiefan* (translation of Medieval Latin *perdōnāre,* to pardon).] **—for·giv·a·ble** *adj.* **—for·giv·er** *n.*
Synonyms: *forgive, pardon, excuse, condone.*

for·give·ness (fər-gív-nəss, -niss || fawr-) *n.* **1.** The act of forgiving. **2.** The willingness to forgive. **3.** Pardon.

for·go, fore·go (fawr-gṓ || fōr-) *tr.v.* **-went** (-wént), **-gone** (-gón || -gáwn) **-going, -goes. 1.** To relinquish; give up; forsake. **2.** To abstain from; do without. See Synonyms at **relinquish.** [Middle English *forgon, forgan,* Old English *forgān,* originally to pass on, pass away : FOR- (exclusion) + *gān,* to go.] **—for·go·er** *n.*
Usage: The usual spelling is *forgo,* but *forego* is increasingly being used. There is nowadays little chance of confusion with the verb *forego* ("to go before"), as only the participial forms are in modern use, as in a *foregone conclusion, the foregoing views.*

for·got. Past tense and alternative past participle of **forget.**

for·got·ten. Past participle of **forget.**

for·int (fórrint, fáwrint) *n.* **1.** The basic monetary unit of Hungary, equal to 100 fillér. **2.** A coin worth one forint. [Hungarian, from Italian *fiorino,* FLORIN.]

forjudge. Variant of **forejudge.**

fork (fork) *n.* **1.** An implement or piece of equipment with two or more prongs used for raising, carrying, piercing, or digging. **2.** A utensil with prongs for serving or eating food. **3.** Any device, piece of machinery, or the like with two or more prongs. **4. a.** A bifurcation or separation into two or more branches or parts. **b.** The point at which such a bifurcation or separation occurs: *a fork in a road.* **c.** Either of the branches of such a bifurcation or separation: *take the right fork.* **5.** A simultaneous attack on two chessmen by one.
~v. **forked, forking, forks.** *—tr.* **1.** To raise, carry, pitch, or pierce with a fork. **2.** To give the shape of a fork to. **3.** To launch an attack on (two chessmen) with one chessman. *—intr.* **1.** To make a fork; divide into two or more branches. **2.** To take one branch at a fork in a road, river, or the like. **3.** *Informal.* To hand over; pay. Used with *out, over,* or *up*: *forked out their savings to buy a T.V.*
~adj. Intended to be eaten using only a fork; buffet-like: *a fork lunch.* [Middle English *forke,* Old English *force, forca,* fork (for digging), from Latin *furca*†, two-pronged fork, fork-shaped prop.]

forked (forkt, fórkid) *adj.* **1.** Containing or characterised by a fork: *a forked river.* **2.** Shaped like or similar to a fork: *forked lightning; a forked tail.* **3.** Ambiguous; equivocal; deceitful: *a forked tongue.*

fork·ful (fórk-fŏŏl) *n., pl.* **forkfuls** or **forksful.** As much as a fork will hold or lift.

fork-lift truck *n.* A small industrial vehicle with a power-operated pronged platform that can be raised and lowered for insertion under a load to be lifted and carried.

for·lorn (fər-lórn || fawr-) *adj.* **1.** Wretched or pitiful in appearance or condition. **2.** Suffering extreme want; destitute. **3.** Deserted; abandoned. **4.** Nearly hopeless; desperate. **5.** Very unhappy; miserable. **6.** *Literary.* Bereft: *forlorn of hope.* [Middle English *forloren,* past participle of *forlēsen,* to forfeit, lose, abandon, Old English *forlēosan.*] **—for·lorn·ly** *adv.* **—for·lorn·ness** *n.*

forlorn hope *n.* **1.** A hopeless or arduous undertaking. **2.** A misguided or vain hope. **3.** *Archaic.* An advance guard of men sent on a hazardous mission. [Variant by folk etymology of Dutch *verloren hoop,* "lost troop" : *verloren,* past participle of *verliezen,* to lose + *hoop,* "heap", band, troop.]

form (form) *n.* **1. a.** Shape or outward appearance. **b.** The contour, structure, or pattern of something as distinguished from its substance or content. **2.** The body or outward appearance of a person or animal, especially considered separately from the face or head. **3.** *Philosophy.* The essence of something as distinguished from its matter. **4. a.** The way or mode in which a thing exists, acts, or manifests itself: *Help appeared in the form of a lifeboat.* **b.** Kind; type; variety: *Ice is a form of water.* **c.** A group of organisms that differ in colour, size, or some other aspect from other members of the same species. **5.** Procedure as determined or governed by regulation or custom: *know the form.* **6.** Manners as governed by etiquette, decorum, or custom: *good form.* **7. a.** Performance or condition considered with regard to acknowledged criteria: *true to form.* **b.** Mental or physical state, expecially when good: *Jeremy was really on form at the party.* **8. a.** Fitness, as of an athlete or animal, with regard to health or training. **b.** The record (as of a racehorse or greyhound) of training and races run; details of previous performances. **9.** A fixed order of words or procedures, as used in a ceremony or other regulated social situation. Also used adjectivally: *a form letter.* **10.** A document with blanks for the insertion of details or information: *an entry form.* **11.** Style or manner of presenting ideas or concepts in literary or musical composition or in organised discourse. **12.** The design, structure, or pattern of a work of art. **13.** A model for making a mould. **14.** A copy of the human figure used for modelling clothes. **15.** *U.S.* Variant of **forme** (see). **16.** In Britain and some other countries, a class, or all the children in the same year in a school: *sixth form.* **17. a.** A **linguistic form** *(see).* **b.** The external aspect of words, with regard to their inflections, pronunciation, or spelling: *verb forms.* **18.** *Chiefly British.* A backless bench. **19.** The resting place of a hare. **20.** *Slang.* A criminal record; previous convictions.
~v. **formed, forming, forms.** *—tr.* **1.** To give form to; shape; mould. **2. a.** To shape or mould into a particular form. **b.** To make; bring into being. **3.** To fashion, train, or develop by instruction or precept: *form the mind.* **4.** To come to have; develop; acquire: *form a habit.* **5.** To constitute or compose an element, part, or characteristic of. **6.** To develop in the mind; conceive: *form an opinion.* **7.** To produce (a tense, for example) by assuming an inflection: *form the pluperfect.* **8.** To make (a word) by derivation or composition. **9.** To put in order; draw up; arrange. *—intr.* **1.** To become formed or shaped. **2.** To be created; come into being; arise. **3.** To assume a specified form, shape, or pattern. Often used with *up.* [Middle English *forme, fourme,* from Old French, from Latin *fōrma,* form, contour, shape.]
Synonyms: *form, figure, outline, shape, contour, profile.*

-form *adj. comb. form.* Indicates having the form of; for example, **cuneiform, cruciform.** [New Latin *-formis,* from Latin *-fōrmis,* from *fōrma,* FORM.]

for·mal (fórm'l) *adj.* **1. a.** Pertaining to the external, non-essential, extrinsic aspect of something as distinguished from its substance or material. **b.** Pertaining to structure rather than content: *formal logic.* **2.** *Philosophy.* Being or pertaining to the essential form or constitution of something. **3.** Following or adhering to accepted forms, conventions, or regulations: *a formal requirement.* **4.** Done in proper, regular, or official form: *a formal reprimand.* **5.** Characterised by strict or meticulous observation of forms; ceremonial; proper. **6.** Stiff or cold; ceremonious: *a formal manner.* **7.** Done for the sake of form only; having the outward appearance but wanting in substance: *a purely formal greeting.* [Middle English, from Old French, from Latin *fōrmālis,* of or for form, from *fōrma,* FORM.] **—for·mal·ly** *adv.*

for·mal·de·hyde (fawr-máldi-hīd, fər-) *n.* A colourless, gaseous compound, HCHO, used in aqueous solution to manufacture melamine and phenolic resins, fertilisers, dyes, and as a preservative and disinfectant. [German *Formaldehyd* : FORM(IC ACID) + ALDEHYDE.]

for·ma·lin (fórmə-lin || *U.S. also* -leen) *n.* A 37 per cent by weight solution of formaldehyde in water with some methanol, used especially for preserving biological specimens.

for·mal·ise, for·mal·ize (fórmə-līz) *tr.v.* **-ised, -ising, -ises. 1.** To give a definite form or shape to. **2. a.** To render formal. **b.** *Logic.* To translate into logical symbolism. **3.** To give formal endorsement to. **—for·mal·i·sa·tion** (fórmə-lī-záysh'n || *U.S.* -li-) *n.*

for·mal·ism (fórmə-liz'm) *n.* **1.** Rigorous or excessive adherence to recognised forms, especially as opposed to content. **2.** The mathematical or logical structure of a scientific argument, especially as distinguished from its content. **3.** In the philosophy of mathematics, the doctrine that mathematics has no subject matter or content, and is purely the study of symbols and their rule-governed configurations and manipulation. **4.** A deliberately stylised presentation, as in the theatre. **—for·mal·ist** *n.* **—for·mal·is·tic** (-lístik) *adj.*

for·mal·i·ty (fawr-mál-əti) *n., pl.* **-ties. 1.** The quality or condition of being formal. **2.** Rigorous or ceremonious adherence to established

forms, rules, or customs. **3.** An established form, rule, or custom. **4.** Something done for the sake of form, custom, or decorum.
formal logic *n.* The study of the properties of propositions by abstraction and analysis of their form rather than content, especially by the use of rules and symbols. See **symbolic logic.**
For·man (fórmən), **Miloš** (1932–). Czech-born film director, known for his use of comedy and disturbing realism. His films include *One Flew Over the Cuckoo's Nest* (1975) and *Amadeus* (1984).
for·mant (fórmənt) *n.* Any of several frequency regions of relatively great intensity in a sound spectrum, which together determine the characteristic quality of a vowel sound, musical instrument, or other sound source. [German *Formant,* from Latin *fōrmāns* (stem *fōrmant-*), present participle of *fōrmāre,* to form, from *fōrma,* FORM.]
for·mat (fór-mat) *n.* **1.** A plan for the organisation and arrangement of a production, such as a television programme. **2.** The material form or layout of a publication. **3.** The way in which data is arranged in a computer storage device.
~*tr.v.* **-matted, -matting, -mats.** To put into a particular format; especially, to arrange (data) in a suitable format for use in a computer. [French, from German *Format,* from Latin *fōrmātus,* past participle of *fōrmāre,* to form, from *fōrma,* FORM.]
for·mate (fór-mayt) *n.* A salt or ester of formic acid. [FORM(IC ACID) + -ATE.]
for·ma·tion (fawr-máysh'n) *n.* **1.** The process of forming or producing. **2.** Something that is formed. **3.** The manner or style in which something is formed. **4.** A specific arrangement, configuration, or deployment, as of troops, aircraft in flight, dancers, or the like. Also used adjectivally: *formation dancing.* **5.** *Geology.* The primary unit of lithostratigraphy, consisting of a succession of strata useful for mapping or description. **6.** *Ecology.* A plant community, such as savannah, that extends over a large area. **—for·ma·tion·al** *adj.*
for·ma·tive (fórmə-tiv) *adj.* **1.** Forming or capable of forming. **2.** Susceptible of transformation by growth and development. **3.** Pertaining to formation, growth, or development: *a formative stage.* **4.** Pertaining to the formation or inflection of words.
~*n.* The element of a word that is not contained in the base and that gives the word a suitable form.
form class *n.* A set of linguistic forms that share one or more morphological or syntactical features, such as a plural or past tense form.
form drag *n.* A component of the drag on a body moving through a fluid that is dependent on the shape of the body.
forme, *U.S.* **form** (form) *n. Printing.* **1.** Type that has been assembled and locked up in a chase, and is ready for printing. **2.** A large sheet, usually film, prepared for printing in four multiples of four pages; a signature. [Variant of FORM.]
form·er¹ (fórmər) *n.* **1.** One that forms. **2.** A tool or device that gives something a particular shape or form.
for·mer² (fórmər) *adj.* **1.** Occurring earlier in time; pertaining to a period previous to the one specified. **2.** Coming before in place or order. **3.** Being the first mentioned of two.
~*n.* The first mentioned of two. Used with *the.* [Middle English, earlier, from *forme,* first, Old English *forma.*]
-former *comb. form.* Indicates a pupil in a specified year at school; for example, **sixth-former.**
for·mer·ly (fórmər-li) *adv.* At a former time; previously.
Former Yugoslav Republic of Macedonia. See **Macedonia, Former Yugoslav Republic of.**
form·fit·ting (fórm-fitting) *adj.* Closely fitted to the body.
for·mic (fórmik) *adj.* **1.** Of or pertaining to ants. **2.** Of, derived from, or containing formic acid. [Latin *formīca,* ant.]
For·mi·ca (fawr-míkə, fər-) *n.* A trademark for any of various high-pressure laminated plastic sheets of melamine and phenolic materials, used especially for chemical and heat-resistant surfaces.
formic acid *n.* A colourless caustic fuming liquid, HCOOH, used in dyeing and finishing textiles and paper and in the manufacture of fumigants, insecticides, and refrigerants. [From FORMIC (from its natural occurrence in ants).]
for·mi·car·y (fórmi-kəri || *U.S.* -kerri) *n., pl.* **-ies.** Also **for·mi·car·i·um** (-kaír-i-əm) *pl.* **-iums** or **-ria** (-i-ə). **1.** A nest of ants; an anthill. **2.** A glass-sided box containing a colony of ants, kept for observation. [Medieval Latin *formīcārium,* from Latin *formīca,* ant.]
for·mi·cate (fórmi-kayt) *intr.v.* **-cated, -cating, -cates. 1.** To swarm with or as if with ants. **2.** To crawl like ants. [Latin *formīcāre,* to swarm like ants, from *formīca,* ant. See **formic.**]
for·mi·ca·tion (fórmi-káysh'n) *n.* A spontaneous abnormal sensation of ants or other insects running over the skin.
for·mi·da·ble (fórmi-dəb'l, fawr-míddəb'l, fər-) *adj.* **1.** Arousing fear, dread, or alarm. **2.** Admirable or awe-inspiring. **3.** Difficult to surmount, defeat, or undertake; awesome. [Middle English, from Old French, from Latin *formīdābilis,* from *formīdāre,* to dread, from *formīdō,* fright, fear.] **—for·mi·da·bil·i·ty** (fórmi-də-bílləti), **for·mi·da·ble·ness** *n.* **—for·mi·da·bly** *adv.*
form·less (fórm-ləss, -liss) *adj.* Having no specified form; shapeless.
Formosa. See **Taiwan.**
for·mu·la (fórmew-lə) *n., pl.* **-las** or **-lae** (-lee, -lī). **1.** An established form of words or symbols for use in a ceremony or procedure. **2.** An utterance of conventional notions or beliefs; a hackneyed expression; a cliché. **3.** *Chemistry.* **a.** A symbolic representation of the composition, or of the composition and structure, of a chemical compound. **b.** The chemical compound so represented. **4.** A prescription of ingredients in fixed proportion; a recipe. **5.** A mathematical statement, especially an equation, of a rule, principle, answer, or other logical relation. **6.** A method, procedure, specified combination of actions, or the like, tending towards some end or result: *a formula for success; a peace formula.* **7.** In motor racing, a category of car defined by its engine size, weight, and fuel capacity. **8.** *U.S.* A specially prepared liquid infant food. [Latin *fōrmula,* diminutive of *fōrma,* FORM.] **—for·mu·la·ic** (-láy-ik) *adj.*
for·mu·lar·ise, for·mu·lar·ize (fórmew-lə-rīz) *tr.v.* **-ised, -ising, -ises.** To formulate. **—for·mu·lar·i·sa·tion** (-rī-záysh'n || *U.S.* -ri-) *n.*
for·mu·lar·y (fórmew-ləri || -lerri) *n., pl.* **-ies. 1.** A book or other collection of formulas. **2.** A statement expressed in formulas. **3.** A formula. **4.** A book containing the names of pharmaceutical substances, their uses, and means of preparation.
~*adj.* **1.** Using or containing formulas. **2.** Pertaining to formulas.
for·mu·late (fórmew-layt) *tr.v.* **-lated, -lating, -lates. 1.** To state as a formula. **2.** To express in systematic terms or concepts. **3.** To devise; invent. **4.** To prepare according to a specific formula. **—for·mu·la·tion** (-láysh'n) *n.* **—for·mu·la·tor** (-laytər) *n.*
formula weight *n.* **Molecular weight** *(see).*
for·mu·lise, for·mu·lize (fórmew-līz) *tr.v.* **-lised, -lising, -lises.** To formulate. **—for·mu·li·sa·tion** *n.* **—for·mu·lis·er** *n.*
for·mu·lism (fórmew-liz'm) *n.* Adherence to or dependency upon formulas. **—for·mu·lis·tic** (-lístik) *adj.*
form word *n.* A **function word** *(see).*
for·myl (fór-mīl, -mil) *n.* The univalent radical CHO. [FORM(IC ACID) + -YL.]
For·nax (fór-naks) *n.* A constellation in the Southern Hemisphere near Sculptor and Eridanus. [Latin *fornāx,* furnace, oven.]
for·ni·cate¹ (fórni-kət, -kit, -kayt) *adj.* Also **for·ni·cat·ed** (-kaytid). *Biology.* Arched or vaulted. [Latin *fornicātus,* from *fornix* (stem *fornic-*), vault, arch.]
for·ni·cate² (fórni-kayt) *intr.v.* **-cated, -cating, -cates.** To commit fornication. [Late Latin *fornicārī,* from *fornix* (stem *fornic-*), vault, arch, in the late republican period a vaulted underground dwelling in Rome where poor people and prostitutes lived, hence (especially in early Christian writings) a brothel.] **—for·ni·ca·tor** (-kaytər) *n.*
for·ni·ca·tion (fórni-káysh'n) *n.* **1.** *Law.* Voluntary sexual intercourse between two unmarried persons who are not closely related. **2.** Loosely, voluntary sexual intercourse.
for·nix (fór-niks) *n., pl.* **-nices** (-ni-seez). **1.** *Anatomy.* Any vaultlike structure; especially the *fornix cerebri,* an arched band of white matter in the brain between the hippocampus and hypothalamus. **2.** A vaulted space. [New Latin, from Latin, vault, arch.]
for·rad·er, for·rard·er (fór-ərdər) *adv. British Informal.* Farther forward.
For·res (fórriss). Ancient royal burgh of Scotland, in the Moray area. Its castle was a residence of the kings Duncan and Macbeth, and is mentioned in Shakespeare's *Macbeth.*
for·sake (fər-sáyk, fawr-) *tr.v.* **-sook** (-so͝ok), **-saken** (-sáykən), **-saking, -sakes. 1.** To give up; renounce. **2.** To desert; abandon. [Forsake, forsook, forsaken; Middle English *forsaken, forsok, forsaken,* to object to. Old English *forsacan, forsōc, forsacen.*]
for·sooth (fər-so͞oth, fawr-) *adv. Archaic.* In truth; indeed. Sometimes used humorously. [Middle English *for soth,* Old English *forsōth* : FOR + SOOTH.]
for·spent, fore·spent (fawr-spént, fər-) *adj. Archaic.* Worn out with exertion; exhausted.
For·ster (fór-stər), **E(dward) M(organ)** (1879–1970). British novelist and essayist. Following his first novel, *Where Angels Fear to Tread* (1905), he wrote such classics as *A Room With a View* (1908), *Howards End* (1910), and his masterpiece, *A Passage to India* (1924), in which he examines the cultural and human conflicts between Indians and their rulers, the British.
for·ster·ite (fórstə-rīt) *n.* A white or yellow olivine mineral, Mg_2SiO_4. [After Johann *Forster* (1729–98), Prussian naturalist.]
for·swear, fore·swear (fawr-swaír || fōr-) *v.* **-swore** (-swáwr || -swṓr), **-sworn** (-swáwrn || -swōrn), **-swearing, -swears.** —*tr.* **1.** To renounce or forsake unalterably. **2.** To disavow or repudiate unalterably. **3.** To perjure (oneself). —*intr.* To swear falsely; commit perjury. [Middle English *forsweren,* from Old English *forswerian,* to swear falsely : *for-,* wrongly + *swerian,* to SWEAR.]
for·syth·i·a (fawr-sīthi-ə, fər-, -síthi-ə) *n.* Any shrub of the genus *Forsythia,* native to Asia, cultivated for its early-blooming yellow flowers. [After William *Forsyth* (1737–1804), English botanist.]
fort (fort || fōrt) *n. Abbr.* **ft.** A fortified place or position stationed with troops; a fortification; a bastion. **—hold the fort.** To manage or cope, especially in a difficult situation, while acting as a substitute for someone else. [Middle English, from Old French *fort,* from *fort(e),* strong, from Latin *fortis.*]
for·ta·lice (fórtə-liss) *n.* A minor defensive structure or position; a small fort. [Middle English, from Medieval Latin *fortalitia,* from Latin *fortis,* strong.]
Fort-de-France (fór-də-fróɴss). Capital of Martinique. It is a tourist resort and also exports sugar, bananas, and rum.
forte¹ (fór-tay, -ti, fort || fōrt) *n.* **1.** Something in which a person excels; a strong point. **2.** The strong part of a sword blade, between the middle and the hilt. Compare **foible.** [Old French *fort,* from adjective, "strong". See **fort.**]
for·te² (fór-tay, -ti) *adv. Abbr.* **f, F** *Music.* Loudly; forcefully. Used as a direction.
~*n. Music.* A note, passage, or chord played forte.
~*adj. Music.* Loud; forceful. [Italian, "strongly", from adjective, "strong", from Latin *fortis.*]
forth (forth || fōrth) *adv.* **1.** Forwards in time, place, or order; on;

onwards. **2.** Out into view, as from confinement or concealment. **3.** Away from a specified place; abroad. **—and so forth.** Etcetera; and the like.
~prep. *Archaic.* Out of; forth from. [Middle English *forth,* Old English *forth.*]
Forth, Firth of. The estuary of the river Forth, Scotland, forming an arm of the North Sea. It is about 80 kilometres (50 miles) long, and some 30 kilometres (18 miles) wide at its entrance, marked by the Isle of May. It is a major seaway with several ports, including Edinburgh's port, Leith, and the Rosyth naval base. Three bridges span the firth: The Kincardine Bridge (1936), the Forth Road Bridge (1964), one of the longest suspension bridges in Europe, and the Forth Railway Bridge (1890), the world's first cantilever bridge.
forth·com·ing (fórth-kúmming ‖ fôrth-) *adj.* **1.** About to appear; approaching; coming: *the forthcoming elections.* **2.** Available when required or as promised. **3.** Responsive; open; informative. **—forth·com·ing·ness** *n.*
forth·right (fórth-rīt, -rīt ‖ fôrth-) *adj.* Straightforward; frank; candid: *a forthright appraisal.*
~adv. **1.** Unhesitatingly; frankly. **2.** *Archaic.* At once; directly; immediately. **—forth·right·ly** *adv.* **—forth·right·ness** *n.*
forth·with (fórth-with, -with ‖ fôrth-) *adv.* At once; immediately; without delay. See Synonyms at **immediately.**
for·ti·eth (fórti-ith) *n.* **1.** The ordinal number 40 in a series. **2.** Any of 40 equal parts. **—for·ti·eth** *adj. & adv.*
for·ti·fi·ca·tion (fórti-fi-káysh'n) *n. Abbr.* **ft. 1.** The act, science, or art of fortifying. **2.** *Often plural.* Something that serves to defend, strengthen, or fortify; especially, a military defensive work.
fortified wine *n.* An alcoholic drink, such as sherry or port, made from wine to which extra alcohol, usually in the form of brandy, has been added.
for·ti·fy (fórti-fī) *v.* **-fied, -fying, -fies. —tr. 1.** To strengthen and secure (a position) with fortifications. **2.** To add strength to (a structure) by reinforcement; reinforce: *fortify a fence with props.* **3.** To impart physical strength to; invigorate: *The coffee fortified him.* **4.** To give moral or mental strength to; encourage: *He fortified his troubled spirit by praying.* **5.** To corroborate; confirm; support. **6.** To strengthen or increase the content of (a substance), as by adding extra alcohol to wine or vitamins to food: *cereal fortified with vitamin D.* **—intr.** To prepare defensive works; build fortifications. [Middle English *fortifien,* from Old French *fortifier,* from Late Latin *fortificāre,* from Latin *fortis,* strong.] **—for·ti·fi·a·ble** *adj.* **—for·ti·fi·er** *n.*
for·tis (fórtiss) *adj. Phonetics.* Pronounced with tension and strong articulation. Said of certain consonants such as *f* and *p.* Compare **lenis.**
~n. *Phonetics.* A fortis consonant. [New Latin, from Latin *fortis,* strong.]
for·tis·si·mo (fawr-tíssimō) *adv. Abbr.* **ff** *Music.* Very loudly. Used as a direction.
~n., pl. fortissimos. *Music.* A fortissimo note, passage, or chord. [Italian, from Latin *fortissimus,* superlative of *fortis,* strong.] **—for·tis·si·mo** *adj.*
for·ti·tude (fórti-tewd ‖ -tōōd) *n.* Strength of mind that allows one to endure pain or adversity with courage. See Synonyms at **courage.** [Middle English, from Old French, from Latin *fortitūdō,* from *fortis,* strong.] **—for·ti·tu·di·nous** (-téwdi-nəss ‖ -tōōdi-) *n.*
Fort Knox (noks). U.S. military reservation, occupying 44 550 hectares (110,000 acres) of northern Kentucky. Most of the country's reserves of gold bullion are stored in the steel and concrete vaults of the depository built there in 1936-37.
Fort Lamy. See **N'djamena.**
Fort Lau·der·dale (láwdər-dayl). City and resort on the Atlantic coast of southeastern Florida, in the United States. It is built on the site of a fort established in 1837 during the Seminole War.
fort·night (fórt-nīt ‖ fôrt-) *n.* **1.** A period of 14 days and nights; two weeks. **2.** A fortnight from a specified day: *Friday fortnight.* [Middle English *fourtenight,* Old English *fēowertīene niht* : FOURTEEN + NIGHT.]
fort·night·ly (fórt-nītli ‖ fôrt-) *adj.* Happening or appearing once in or every two weeks.
~adv. Once in two weeks; every fortnight.
~n., pl. fortnightlies. A publication issued every two weeks.
FORTRAN, For·tran (fór-tran) *n.* A computer programming language for problems that can be expressed in algebraic terms. [*For*mula *tran*slation.]
for·tress (fórtriss) *n.* A fortified place, especially a large and permanent military stronghold, often including a town; a fort.
~tr.v. fortressed, -tressing, -tresses. *Archaic.* To strengthen or fortify with or as if with a fortress. [Middle English *forteresse,* from Old French, from Vulgar Latin *fortaritia* (unattested), from Latin *fortis,* strong.]
Fort Sumter. Site in Charleston, South Carolina, of the first conflict of the American Civil War (1861–65).
for·tu·i·tous (fawr-téw-i-təss, fər- ‖ tōō) *adj.* **1.** Happening by accident or chance; unplanned. **2.** Happening by fortunate accident; lucky. **—See Synonyms at accidental.** [Latin *fortuitus,* from *forte,* by chance, ablative of *fors,* chance.] **—for·tu·i·tous·ly** *adv.* **—for·tu·i·tous·ness** *n.*
for·tu·i·ty (fawr-téw-əti, fər- ‖ -tōō-) *n., pl.* **-ties. 1.** An accidental occurrence. **2.** The quality or condition of being fortuitous.
For·tu·na (fawr-téw-nə ‖ -tōō-). The Roman goddess of fortune. [Latin *Fortūna,* from *fortūna,* FORTUNE.]

for·tu·nate (fórchə-nət, -nit) *adj.* **1.** Occurring by good fortune or favourable chance; bringing something that is good and unforeseen; auspicious. **2.** Having unusual good fortune; lucky. **—for·tu·nate·ly** *adv.*
for·tune (fór-chōōn, -chən, -tewn) *n.* **1.** A hypothetical, often personified force or power that favourably or unfavourably governs the events of one's life: *Fortune is on our side.* **2.** The good or bad luck that is to befall someone; destiny; fate: *It is my fortune to be a failure.* **3.** Luck, especially when good; success: *Fortune accompanied his endeavours.* **4. a.** A person's condition or standing in life determined by material possessions or money. **b.** Extensive amounts of material possessions or money. **c.** A large amount of money. **5.** Material or financial success; prosperity. [Middle English *fortune,* chance, luck, from Old French, from Latin *fortūna,* chance, fate, (good or bad) luck, from *forst†,* chance, luck.]
fortune cookie *n. U.S.* A small Oriental cake made from a thin layer of dough folded and baked around a slip of paper bearing a prediction of fortune or a maxim.
fortune hunter *n.* A person who seeks to become wealthy, especially through marriage.
for·tune-tell·er (fór-chōōn-tellər, -chən-, -tewn-) *n.* A person who, usually for a fee, will undertake to predict future events in a person's life. **—for·tune-tell·ing** *n. & adj.*
Fort Wil·liam (wíl-yəm). Resort at the head of Loch Linnhe in the area of Highland, Scotland. The fort, built in 1690 for William III, was pulled down in 1855.
Fort Worth (wurth). City in north Texas, in the United States. An army post was established there in 1847, and the settlement became a great railway town, a centre for meat-packing and oil refining. Since 1945 it has been dominated by the aircraft industry.
for·ty (fórti) *n. pl.* **-ties. 1. a.** The cardinal number that is ten more than thirty. **b.** A symbol representing this, such as 40 or XL. **2.** A set made up of forty persons or things. **3.** The fortieth in a series. **4.** A size, as in clothing, designated as forty. **5.** *Plural.* **a.** The range of numbers from 40 to 49, considered as a range of age, price, temperature, or the like. **b.** The years numbered 40 to 49 in a century. Also used adjectively: *a forties film.* **—for·ty** *adj.*
for·ty-five (fórti-fív) *n.* **1.** A .45-calibre pistol. **2.** A gramophone record, a **single** *(see).*
Forty-Five *n.* In British history, the later **Jacobite Rebellion** *(see)* of 1745. Preceded by *the.*
for·ty-nin·er (fórti-nínər) *n.* In U.S. history, one who took part in the 1849 California gold rush.
forty winks *n. Informal. Used with a singular verb.* A short nap.
fo·rum (fáwr-əm ‖ fór-) *n., pl.* **-rums** or **fora** (fáwrə ‖ fórə) (for sense 1). **1.** The public square or marketplace of an ancient Roman city that was the assembly place for judicial and other public activity. **2. a.** Any public meeting place for open discussion. **b.** A meeting for open discussion. **c.** Any medium for open discussion, such as a magazine or radio or television programme. **3.** A court of law; a tribunal. **4.** *Capital* F. The forum in ancient Rome. [Middle English, from Latin, *forum,* place out-of-doors.]
for·ward (fór-wərd) *adj. Nautical* (fórrərd) *adj.* **1. a.** At, near, or belonging to the front; fore: *the forward part of a train.* **b.** Towards the front of a ship: *a forward cabin.* **c.** Lying ahead or in the line of motion. **2. a.** Going, tending, or moving towards a position in front: *a forward thrust of a sword; a forward fall down a flight of stairs.* **b.** *Sports.* Going, tending, or moving towards an opponent's goal. **3. a.** *Archaic.* Ardently inclined; eager; anxious. **b.** Presumptuous; impudent; bold: *a forward manner.* **4.** Progressive, especially technologically, politically, or economically: *a forward new nation; a forward concept.* **5.** Mentally, physically, socially, or biologically advanced; precocious: *a forward child.* **6.** Prompt; eager. **7.** For the future; completed or made in advance: *My broker does not intend to bid on forward contracts for corn.* **—See Synonyms at shameless.**
~adv. **1.** Variant of **forwards. 2.** In or towards the future; at a future time; onwards: *I look forward to seeing you.* **3.** Into view or prominence; forth; out: *Neighbours came forward to help.*
~n. Abbr. fwd. *Sports.* **1.** A player in certain games, such as soccer, who is part of the front line and usually plays in an attacking position. **2.** The position itself.
~tr.v. forwarded, -warding, -wards. 1. To send on (letters, for example) to a subsequent destination or address. **2.** To advance; promote; advocate. **3.** To prepare (a book) for the finisher by supplying with a paper cover. [Middle English *for(e)ward,* Old English *foreweard* : FORE- + -WARD.]
for·ward·er (fór-wərdər) *n.* One that forwards; especially, a forwarding agent.
for·ward·ing agent (fór-wərding) *n.* An agent, agency, or other business that facilitates and assures the passage of received goods to their destination; a forwarder of goods.
for·ward-look·ing (fór-wərd-lōōking ‖ -lōōking) *adj.* **1.** Progressive; having advanced and enlightened views. **2.** Careful of and concerned with the future.
for·ward·ly (fór-wərd-li) *adv.* **1.** At or towards the front; forwards. **2.** In a bold or forward manner; presumptuously. **3.** With dispatch or eagerness; promptly.
for·ward·ness (fór-wərd-niss) *n.* **1.** The condition or state of being forward; readiness; zeal; eagerness. **2.** An advanced state of development or progress; precocity. **3.** Overeagerness to promote oneself; audacity; boldness.
forwards (fór-wərdz) *adv.* Also **for·ward. 1.** Towards or tending to

the front: *face forwards*. **2.** Towards or tending to a time or place in advance or ahead.

for·went. Past tense of **forgo.**

for·why (fawr-wǐ, -hwǐ) *adv. Archaic.* For what reason; why. *~conj. Obsolete.* Because; since. [Middle English *forwhy*, Old English *for hwȳ* : FOR + *hwȳ*, instrumental of *hwæt*, WHAT.]

for·worn, fore·worn (fawr-wórn ‖ -wôrn) *adj. Archaic.* Worn-out. [Past participle of obsolete *forwear*, from Middle English *forweren*, to hollow out : FOR (destruction) + WEAR.]

forzando. Variant of **sforzando.**

Fos·bur·y flop (fózbəri flóp) *n.* A technique in modern high-jumping whereby the jumper goes over the bar headfirst with the back towards the ground and the face up. [After Richard *Fosbury* (1947–), U.S. Olympic champion (Mexico, 1968).]

fos·sa¹ (fóssə) *n., pl.* **fossae** (fóss-ee, -ī). *Anatomy.* A hollow or depression, as in a bone. [Latin, ditch, trench, from the feminine past participle of *fodere*, to dig.]

fossa² *n.* **1.** A carnivorous Madagascan mammal, *Cryptoprocta ferox*, of the family Viverridae, having a long tail, short legs, and a pointed snout. **2.** Any animal of the genus *Fossa*, which includes the Madagascan civets. [Malagasy.]

fosse, foss (foss) *n.* A ditch; especially, a moat round a fortification. [Middle English, from Old French, from Latin *fossa*.]

Fosse Way. Modern English name for the major Roman road that ran across Britain from the mouth of the river Axe in Devon to meet Ermine Street near Newark.

fos·sick (fóssik) *v.* **-sicked, -sicking, -sicks.** *—intr.* **1.** To search for gold, especially by reworking washings or waste piles. **2.** To rummage or search, especially for a possible profit. *—tr.* To search for by or as if by rummaging. [Perhaps variant of dialectal *fussick*, to bustle about, from FUSS.] **—fos·sick·er** *n.*

fos·sil (fóss'l) *n.* **1.** A remnant or trace of an organism of a past geological age, such as a skeleton, footprint, or leaf imprint, embedded in the earth's crust. **2.** One that is outdated or antiquated; especially, a person with outmoded ideas. **3.** An obsolete word or word element used only in an idiom, as *fro* in *to and fro*. *~adj.* **1.** Of or pertaining to a fossil or fossils. **2.** Derived from fossils: *Coal is a fossil fuel.* [Latin *fossilis*, dug up, from *fossus*, past participle of *fodere*, to dig.]

fossil fuel *n.* A carbon or hydrocarbon fuel, such as coal, petroleum, or natural gas, derived from the decomposition of organisms of an earlier geological period.

fos·sil·if·er·ous (fóssi-líffərəss) *adj.* Containing fossils. [FOSSIL + -FEROUS.]

fos·sil·ise, fos·sil·ize (fóssi-līz) *v.* **-ised, -ising, -ises.** *—tr.* **1.** To convert into a fossil. **2.** To make outmoded, rigid, or fixed; antiquate; freeze. *—intr.* **1.** To become a fossil. **2.** To become outmoded, rigid, or fixed. **—fos·sil·i·sa·tion** (-lī-zásh'n ‖ U.S. -li-) *n.*

fos·so·ri·al (fo-sáwr-i-əl ‖ -sôr-) *adj. Zoology.* Adapted for or used in burrowing or digging. [Medieval Latin *fossorius*, from Latin *fossus*, past participle of *fodere*, to dig.]

fos·ter (fóstər ‖ fáwstər) *tr.v.* **-tered, -tering, -ters.** **1.** To bring up, rear, or nurture; especially, to bring up (a child that is not one's own or one's adopted child). **2.** To promote the development or growth of; encourage; cultivate: *fostered his love of music.* **3.** To nurse; cherish: *foster a secret hope.* **4.** *Chiefly British.* To place (a child) in a foster home. *~adj.* Receiving, sharing, or affording parental care and nurture although not related through legal or blood ties: *a foster home.* Often used in combination: *foster-mother.* [Middle English *fostren*, Old English *fōstrian*, to provide with food, nourish, from *fōstor*, food.] **—fos·ter·age** *n.*

Fos·ter (fóstər, fáwstər), **Stephen (Collins)** (1826–64). U.S. songwriter. Among the popular, quasi-folk songs he composed are *The Old Folks at Home, My Old Kentucky Home,* and *Swanee River.*

Foster, Sir Norman (Robert) (1935–). British architect. He has designed many major buildings throughout the world, including the Hong Kong and Shanghai Bank, Hong Kong (1979–85), the Century Tower, Tokyo (completed 1991), and the cultural centre in Nîmes, France (1984–92).

fos·ter·ling (fóstər-ling ‖ fáwstər-) *n. Rare.* A foster child.

Fou·cault (fōō-kõ), **Jean Bernard Léon** (1819–68). French physicist. In 1851 he demonstrated the rotation of the earth with the **Foucault pendulum.** He also measured the velocity of light and showed that it travels more slowly in water. He is credited with having invented the gyroscope in 1852.

Foucault, Michel (1926–84). French historian of ideas. He wrote such influential books as *Les Mots et les choses* (*The Order of Things,* 1966), *The History of Sexuality* (1976), and *The Archaeology of Knowledge* (1969). He is best known for his work on the history of attitudes to the insane, as in *Madness and Civilization* (1961).

Foucault current *n.* **Eddy current.** [After J.B.L. FOUCAULT.]

Foucault pendulum *n.* A simple pendulum suspended so that the plane of motion is not fixed, set into motion along a meridian, and appearing to turn clockwise in the Northern Hemisphere, or anticlockwise in the Southern Hemisphere, demonstrating the axial rotation of the Earth. [Demonstrated by J.B.L. FOUCAULT.]

fou·droy·ant (fōō-dróy-ənt ‖ *French* fōōdrwə-yón) *adj.* **1.** *Rare.* Dazzling; stunning. **2.** Designating a disease occurring suddenly and with great severity. [French, present participle of *foudroyer*, to strike (as with lightning), from Old French *foudroier*, from *foudre*, lightning, from Latin *fulgur*, from *fulgēre*, to shine.]

fought. Past tense and past participle of **fight.**

foul (fowl) *adj.* **fouler, foulest.** **1.** Offensive to the senses; disgusting; revolting. **2.** Having an offensive odour; fetid; rank; smelly. **3.** Spoiled; rotten; putrid. Said especially of food. **4.** Full of dirt or mud; dirty; filthy. **5.** Immoral; wicked; detestable. **6.** Vulgar; obscene; profane: *foul language.* **7.** *Archaic.* Ugly; unattractive. **8.** *Informal.* Terrible; disagreeable; displeasing: *a foul party.* **9.** Unpleasant; bad; unfavourable. Often said of weather: *a foul day.* **10.** Not according to accepted standards or rules; unfair; dishonourable: *win by foul means.* **11.** *Sports.* Contrary to the rules of a game or sport. **12.** Covered with barnacles, weed, or the like. Said of a ship's bottom. **13.** Entangled; twisted: *a foul anchor.* **14.** Clogged or obstructed by something; blocked: *a foul ventilator shaft.* **—See Synonyms at dirty.** *~n.* **1.** Anything that is dirty or foul. **2.** *Sports.* An infraction or violation of the rules of play. **3.** An entanglement or collision. **4.** A clogging or obstructing. *~adv.* In a foul manner. *~v.* **fouled, fouling, fouls.** *—tr.* **1.** To make dirty or foul; soil; pollute; sully. **2.** To bring into dishonour; disgrace; besmirch. **3.** To clog or obstruct; block. **4.** To entangle or catch. Used of a rope. **5.** To encrust (a ship's hull) with foreign matter, such as barnacles. **6.** *Sports.* To commit a foul against. **7.** To deposit excrement on. *—intr.* **1.** To become foul. **2.** *Sports.* To commit a foul. **3.** To become entangled or twisted: *The anchor fouled on a rock.* **4.** To become clogged or obstructed. [Middle English *foul*, Old English *fūl*, from Germanic.] **—foul·ly** *adv.*

fou·lard (fōō-laar, fōō-lárd, -lár) *n.* **1.** A lightweight twill or plain-woven fabric of silk, or silk and cotton, usually having a small printed design. **2.** An article, especially a handkerchief or scarf, made of this fabric. [French *foulard†*.]

foul line *n. Sports.* Any boundary limiting the playing area.

foul-mouthed (fówl-mówthd ‖ -mówtht) *adj.* Using obscene or scurrilous language.

foul·ness (fówl-nəss, -niss) *n.* **1.** The state or condition of being foul. **2.** Foul matter; filth; trash; waste. **3.** Obscenity; vulgarity; wickedness.

foul play *n.* **1.** Malicious or treacherous action, especially when involving violence. **2.** Conduct that is unsportsmanlike.

foul up *tr.v.* **1.** To make dirty; contaminate. **2.** To entangle, choke, or obstruct. **3.** To cause to go wrong because of mistakes, poor judgment, or unforeseen difficulties.

foul-up (fówl-up) *n. Informal.* **1.** A condition of confusion caused by poor judgment, mistakes, or unforeseen difficulties. **2.** Mechanical trouble.

found¹ (fownd) *v.* **founded, founding, founds.** *—tr.* **1.** To originate or establish (a business or college, for example); create; set up. **2.** To establish the foundation of (a building); lay a base for. **3.** To base (an argument or story, for example). Used with *on* or *upon.* *—intr.* To have a foundation or base. Used with *on* or *upon.* [Middle English *founden*, from Old French *fonder*, from Latin *fundāre*, to lay the foundation for, from *fundus*, bottom.]

found² *tr.v.* **founded, founding, founds.** **1.** To melt (a material, such as metal) and pour into a mould. **2.** To make (objects) in this fashion; cast. [Middle English *founden*, from Old French *fondre*, from Latin *fundere*, to pour; melt.]

found³. Past tense and past participle of **find.**

foun·da·tion (fown-dáysh'n) *n.* **1.** The act of founding or state of being founded; especially, the establishment of an institution with provision for future maintenance. **2. a.** The basis on which a thing stands, is founded, or is supported; an underlying support. **b.** *Often plural.* The part of a building or other structure that is below the ground and on which it rests or is supported. **c.** The grounds or basis for a claim, argument, story, or the like. **3.** Funds for the perpetual support of an institution, such as a school; an endowment. **4.** An institution supported by such a fund; an endowed institution. **5.** A foundation garment. **6.** A cosmetic used as a base for facial make-up. **—See Synonyms at base. —foun·da·tion·al** *adj.*

foundation garment *n.* A woman's supporting undergarment, such as a corset or girdle.

foundation stone *n.* A stone, usually bearing a commemorative inscription, laid at the beginning of a building's construction.

found·er¹ (fówndər) *n.* **1.** One who founds an institution, business, movement, or the like; one who initiates or lays the basis. **2.** One who casts metal: *a bell founder.*

foun·der² *v.* **-dered, -dering, -ders.** *—intr.* **1.** To stumble; especially, to stumble and as a consequence go lame. Used of horses. **2.** To fail utterly; collapse or break down; give way. **3.** *Nautical.* To sink below the water. **4.** To cave in; fall in; sink. Used of ground or buildings. **5.** *Veterinary Medicine.* To be afflicted with founder. Used of horses. **6.** To become ill from overeating. Used of livestock. *—tr.* To cause to founder. *~n. Veterinary Medicine.* A disease of horses, **laminitis** (*see*). [Middle English *foundren*, to fall to the ground, from Old French *fondrer*, to submerge, from Vulgar Latin *fundorāre* (unattested), from Latin *fundus*, bottom.]

founders' shares *pl.n.* Shares issued to the founders or original subscribers of a company and often carrying special privileges.

founding father *n.* **1.** *Capital* **F**, *capital* **F.** A delegate to the American Constitutional Convention of 1787. **2.** One considered as having an important role as an innovator or originator: *one of the founding fathers of socialism.*

found·ling (fówndling) *n.* A child deserted by parents whose identity is not known. [Middle English, probably from *founden,* past participle of *finden,* to FIND.]

foun·dry (fówndri) *n., pl.* **-dries.** 1. An establishment in which metal castings are made. **2. a.** The art or operation of casting metals. **b.** The castings made in a foundry.

foundry proof *n.* A proof taken from composed type for a final check before plates are made.

fount[1] (fownt) *n.* 1. A fountain. 2. Any source. Used especially in the phrase *a fount of wisdom.* 3. A reservoir for liquids; especially, one for ink in a fountain pen. [Probably a back-formation from FOUNTAIN.]

fount[2], **font** *n. Printing.* A complete set of type of one size and face. [Old French, casting, from *fondre,* to melt, cast. See **fondant.**]

foun·tain (fówn-tin, -tən) *n.* 1. A spring; especially, the source of a stream. 2. A source; a point of origin. **3. a.** An artificially created jet or stream of water. **b.** A device that produces and contains such a jet or stream: *a drinking fountain.* 4. A reservoir, tank, or chamber containing a supply of something, such as ink or oil, that can be siphoned off as needed. 5. *U.S.* A **soda fountain** (see). [Middle English *fountaine,* spring, from Old French *fontaine,* from Late Latin *fontānus,* of a spring, from *fons* (stem *font-*), spring.]

foun·tain·head (fówn-tin-hed, -tən-, -héd) *n.* 1. A spring that is the source or head of a stream. 2. A principal source or origin.

Fountain of Youth *n.* A legendary spring believed to have the power of rejuvenation, sought by Ponce de León and other explorers in Florida and the West Indies.

fountain pen *n.* A pen filled from an external source and containing an ink reservoir that automatically feeds the nib.

Foun·tains Ab·bey (fówntinz). Ruins of one of Europe's wealthiest Cistercian monasteries, 6 kilometres (4 miles) southwest of Ripon in North Yorkshire, England. It was founded in 1132.

four (for ‖ fōr) *n.* **1. a.** The cardinal number that is one more than three. **b.** A symbol representing this, such as 4, IV, or iv, or rarely IIII or iiii. 2. A set made up of four persons or things. 3. The fourth in a series. 4. Four parts: *cut in four.* 5. A size, as in clothing, designated as four. 6. Four hours after midnight or midday. **7. a.** A racing boat for four oarsmen. **b.** The crew of such a boat. 8. In cricket: **a.** Four runs scored by a batsman from a ball that is hit over the boundary and touches the ground. **b.** Such a hit. —**on all fours.** On hands and knees. —**four** *adj.* —**four·fold** *adj. & adv.*

four-ball (fór-bawl ‖ fōr-) *n.* A golf match between two pairs of players with each player having a ball, the score of the better-playing partner only being counted at the end of the game.

four·chette (foor-shét) *n.* 1. A narrow, forked strip of material joining the front and back sections of the fingers of gloves. 2. *Anatomy.* The fold of skin forming the posterior margin of the vulva. 3. *Anatomy.* A **furcula** (see). [French, "fork", from Old French *forchete,* diminutive of *forche,* fork, pitchfork, from Latin *furca,* (two-pronged) FORK.]

four-col·our (fór-kúllər ‖ fōr-) *adj.* Designating a colour printing or photographic process in which three primary colours and black (used in combination) are transferred by four different plates or filters to a surface, reproducing the colours of the subject matter.

four-di·men·sion·al (fór-di-ménsh'n'l, -dī- ‖ fōr-) *adj.* Exhibiting or being specified by four dimensions, especially the three spatial dimensions and single temporal dimension of relativity theory.

Four·drin·i·er (foor-drínni-ər) *adj.* Designating a papermaking machine used to produce paper in a continuous roll or web. [After Henry (died 1854) and Sealey (died 1847) *Fourdrinier,* English papermakers.]

four-eyed fish (fór-íd ‖ fōr-). Either of two freshwater fishes, *Anableps anableps* or *A. microlepis,* of tropical America, having bulging eyes divided longitudinally, with the upper part adapted for aerial vision, the lower part for underwater vision.

four-eyes (fór-īz ‖ fōr-) *n. Informal.* A person who wears glasses. Used humorously or derogatorily.

four flush *n.* In poker, a five-card hand with four cards in one suit. The hand need not be worth much.

four-flush (fór-flush ‖ fōr-) *intr.v.* **-flushed, -flushing, -flushes.** *U.S.* 1. To bluff in poker with a four-flush hand. 2. *Slang.* To bluff.

four-flush·er (fór-flush-ər) *n. U.S. Slang.* A person who cannot or does not substantiate his pretensions; a bluffer; a faker.

four-foot·ed (fór-fŏŏtid ‖ fōr-) *adj.* Having four feet.

Four Freedoms *pl.n.* Four basic human freedoms, freedom of speech and religion and freedom from want and fear. Preceded by *the.*

four·gon (foor-góN) *n., pl.* **-gons** (-góN). *French.* A wagon used mainly for carrying baggage.

four·hand·ed (fór-hándid ‖ fōr-) *adj.* 1. Involving or requiring four players, as some games do. 2. Designed to be played by four hands: *a four-handed waltz.* 3. Having four extremities functioning like hands; quadrumanous.

four hundred *n. Often capital* **F.** *capital* **H.** *U.S.* The wealthiest and most exclusive social set. Preceded by *the.* [Term introduced (1892) by Ward McAllister (1827–95), New York socialite, to describe members of "true" New York society.]

Fou·ri·er (fóŏrri-ay, -ər ‖ -áy), **(François Marie) Charles** (1772–1837). French utopian socialist philosopher. He believed that social harmony could be achieved through "phalanxes", small self-sustaining communal groups of people, who would live in communal "phalansteries". Work would be shared according to each person's natural abilities and preferences. —**Fou·ri·er·ism** *n.* —**Fou·ri·er·ist, Fou·ri·er·ite** *n. & adj.*

Fourier, (Jean Baptiste) Joseph, Baron (1768–1830). French mathematician and physicist. He made valuable contributions to scientific knowledge, especially in the field of heat theory.

Fourier analysis *n. Mathematics.* A method of analysing a periodic function into its harmonic components, the sum of which form a Fourier series. [After J.B.J. *Fourier.*]

Fourier series *n.* An infinite series of sine and cosine functions, capable if uniformly convergent of approximating a wide variety of mathematical functions. [Devised by J.B.J. FOURIER.]

four-in-hand (fór-in-hánd ‖ fōr-) *n.* 1. A vehicle drawn by four horses and driven by one person. 2. A team of four horses. 3. *U.S.* A tie tied in a slipknot with the ends left hanging and overlapping. —*adj.* Designating or pertaining to a four-in-hand.

four-leaved clover (-leevd) *n.* A clover leaf having four leaflets instead of the normal three, considered to be an omen of good luck.

four-let·ter word (fór-lettər ‖ fōr-) *n.* Any of several short English words generally regarded as vulgar or obscene.

four-mast·ed (fór-maást-id ‖ fōr-, -mást-) *adj. Nautical.* Having four masts. —**four-mast·er** *n.*

four-o'clock (fór-ə-klók ‖ fōr-) *n.* Any of several plants of the genus *Mirabilis;* especially, *M. jalapa,* native to tropical America, and widely cultivated for its tubular, variously coloured flowers that open in the late afternoon. Also called "marvel-of-Peru".

four·pence (fór-pənss ‖ fōr-) *n. British.* 1. A sum of money equal to four pence or four old pennies. Used chiefly before the decimalisation of British currency. 2. Formerly, a small silver coin of this value.

four·pen·ny (fór-pəni, -pni ‖ fōr-) *adj.* Costing four pence. —**fourpenny one.** *Slang.* A slap.

four-post·er (fór-pőstər ‖ fōr-) *n.* A bed having tall corner posts to support curtains or a canopy. Also called "four-poster bed".

four·ra·gère (foor-ə-zhaír) *n.* 1. An ornamental braided cord usually looped around the left shoulder. 2. Such a cord awarded to an entire military unit. [French, from the feminine of *fourrager,* of forage, from *fourrage,* forage, from Old French *forage,* FORAGE.]

four·score (fór-skór ‖ fōr-skōr) *adj.* Eighty; four times twenty.

four·some (fór-s'm ‖ fōr-) *n.* 1. Any group of four persons; especially, two couples. **2. a.** A game, such as a golf match, played by four persons, two on each side. **b.** The players in such a game. —*adj.* Consisting of or involving a group of four. [Middle English *four-sum,* from Old English *fēowra sum,* one of four : *fēowra,* genitive of *fēower,* FOUR + *sum,* one, SOME.]

four·square (fór-skwaír ‖ fōr-) *adj.* 1. Unyielding; firm. 2. Forthright; honest; frank. —*adv.* Squarely; forthrightly.

four-stroke (fór-strōk ‖ fōr-) *adj.* Designating an internal-combustion engine in which the pistons make four strokes for each explosion. Compare **two-stroke.**

four·teen (fór-téen ‖ fōr-) *n.* **1. a.** The cardinal number that is one more than 13. **b.** A symbol representing this, such as 14 or XIV. 2. A set made up of 14 persons or things. 3. The 14th in a series. 4. A size, as in clothing, designated as 14. —**four·teen** *adj.*

four·teenth (fór-téenth ‖ fōr-) *n.* 1. The ordinal number 14 in a series. 2. One of 14 equal parts. —**four·teenth** *adj. & adv.*

fourth (forth ‖ fōrth) *n.* 1. The ordinal number four in a series. 2. Any of four equal parts. 3. *Music.* **a.** In a diatonic scale, a note four degrees above or below any given note. **b.** The interval between two such notes. **c.** The harmonic combination of these notes. **d.** In a scale, the subdominant. 4. The transmission gear or corresponding gear ratio used to produce the range of highest driving speeds in most motor vehicles. [Middle English *fourthe,* earlier *ferthe, furthe,* Old English *fēortha, fēowertha.*] —**fourth** *adj. & adv.* —**fourth·ly** *adv.*

fourth dimension *n.* Time regarded as a dimension, which together with the three spatial dimensions, is required to specify completely the location of any event in a space-time continuum.

fourth estate *n. Sometimes capital* **F,** *capital* **E.** The public press; journalism or journalists generally. [Formerly used jocularly to refer to something outside the (three) Estates of the Realm.]

Fourth International *n.* See **International.**

Fourth of July *n.* Independence Day in the United States.

four-wheel drive (fór-weél, -hweél ‖ fōr-) *n. Abbr.* **f.w.d.** A motor-vehicle drive mechanism in which all four wheels are connected to the source of driving power.

fo·ve·a (fō-vi-ə) *n., pl.* **-veae** (-vi-ee). 1. A shallow cuplike depression or pit in a bone or other organ. 2. The fovea centralis. [New Latin, from Latin *fovea,* small pit, possibly from Etruscan.] —**fo·ve·al, fo·ve·ate** (-ayt) *adj.*

fovea cen·tra·lis (sen-traáliss) *n.* A small depression in the retina of the eye, constituting the area of most distinct vision. Also called "fovea".

fowl (fowl) *n., pl.* **fowls** or collectively **fowl.** 1. Any of various birds of the order Galliformes; especially, the common, widely domesticated chicken, *Gallus gallus.* 2. Any bird used as food or hunted as game. 3. The edible flesh of such a bird. 4. *Archaic.* Any bird. —*intr.v.* **fowled, fowling, fowls.** To hunt, trap, or shoot wild fowl. [Middle English *foul,* Old English *fugol.*] —**fowl·er** *n.*

fowl cholera *n.* An acute, infectious, often fatal intestinal disease of domestic poultry and wild birds, caused by a bacterium, *Pasteurella multocida,* and characterised by enteritis, submucous haemorrhage, and vascular congestion.

Fow·ler (fówlər), **H(enry) W(atson)** (1858–1933). British lexicographer. He worked with his brother Francis George Fowler

(1870–1918) on English dictionaries and edited the *Concise Oxford Dictionary* (1911). He wrote *Modern English Usage* (1926; revised by E. Gowers in 1965 and by R. Burchfield in 1996).

Fowles (fowlz), **John** (1926–). British novelist. *The Magus* (1966), his first novel, was not published until after *The Collector* (1963). Other works are *The French Lieutenant's Woman* (1969), *Daniel Martin* (1977), *Mantissa* (1982), and *Tessara* (1993).

fowl·ing (fówling) *n.* The hunting of wild fowl for food or for spoil.

fowling piece *n.* A light shotgun for shooting birds and small animals.

fowl pest *n.* A severe and often fatal viral disease of poultry characterised by high temperature, refusal to eat, and discoloration of the wattles and comb. Also called "Newcastle disease".

fowl pox *n.* A viral infection of poultry and other birds, characterised by wartlike nodules on the skin and cankers in the digestive and upper respiratory tracts.

fox (foks) *n.* **1.** Any of various carnivorous mammals of the genus *Vulpes* and related genera, related to the dogs and wolves, and characteristically having upright ears, a pointed snout, and a long, bushy tail. **2.** The fur of a fox. **3.** A crafty, sly, or clever person. **4.** *Archaic.* A sword. **5.** *Nautical.* Small cordage made by twisting together two or more strands of tarred yarn.
~*v.* **foxed, foxing, foxes.** —*tr.* **1. a.** To trick or fool by ingenuity or cunning; outwit. **b.** *Informal.* To baffle or confuse. **2.** *Archaic.* To make drunk or intoxicate. —*intr.* To act deceitfully or craftily; pretend.

Fox, Charles James (1749–1806). English Whig statesman. He entered parliament in 1768, and in 1782 was appointed Britain's first Foreign Secretary. An ardent promoter of contemporary Liberal causes, he supported American independence, parliamentary reform, and the French Revolution, but was dismissed from the Privy Council in 1798 for opposing war with France.

Fox, George (1624–91). Founder of the Society of Friends (Quakers). Originally a shoemaker's apprentice, he became a travelling preacher in 1647. His stand against the established church won him many supporters. He was frequently imprisoned for his beliefs. His *Journal* was published in 1694.

foxed (fókst) *adj.* Discoloured with yellowish-brown stains, as an old book or print may be. [From the resemblance of the stain to the colour of a fox.]

fox·fire (fóks-fīr) *n.* A phosphorescent glow, especially that produced by certain fungi found on rotting wood. [Middle English, perhaps from the silvery quality of some fox fur.]

fox·glove (fóks-gluv) *n.* **1.** Any of several plants of the genus *Digitalis;* especially, *D. purpurea,* native to Europe, having a long cluster of large, tubular, pinkish-purple flowers, and leaves that are the source of the medicinal drug digitalis. **2.** Any of several similar or related plants. [Middle English *foxes-glove,* Old English *foxes glófa,* "fox's glove" (the reason for association with the fox is not known).]

fox·hole (fóks-hōl) *n.* A shallow pit dug by a soldier for immediate individual refuge against enemy fire.

fox·hound (fóks-hownd) *n.* A dog developed for fox hunting; especially, a short-haired hound of either of two breeds, the *English foxhound* and the *American foxhound.*

fox hunt *n.* The hunting of a fox with hounds.

fox-hunting (fóks-hunting) *n.* The sport of hunting a fox with hounds, usually by people on horseback.

fox·ing (fóksing) *n.* A brownish discoloration of paper or a book, caused by damp.

fox·tail (fóks-tayl) *n.* **1.** Any of several grasses of the genus *Alopecurus,* having dense, silky or bristly flowering spikes. **2.** Any of several similar or related plants.

fox terrier *n.* A small dog having a white coat with dark markings, bred in both wire-haired and smooth-coated varieties.

fox·trot (fóks-trot) *n.* **1.** A ballroom dance in 2/4 or 4/4 time, composed of a variety of slow and fast steps. **2.** The music or a piece of music for this dance.
~*intr.v.* **fox-trotted, -trotting, -trots.** To dance a foxtrot. [From the short steps attributed to the comparatively short-legged fox.]

fox·y (fóksi) *adj.* **-ier, -iest. 1.** Suggestive of a fox; sly; cunning; clever. **2.** Having a reddish-brown colour. **3.** Discoloured as by decay; stained; foxed. **4.** *Chiefly U.S. Slang.* Sexually attractive and usually independent-minded: *a foxy lady.* —See Synonyms at **sly.** —**fox·i·ly** *adv.* —**fox·i·ness** *n.*

foy (foy) *n. Chiefly Scottish.* A farewell entertainment, feast, drink, or gift, as at the end of a harvest or on the eve of a wedding. [Dialectal Dutch *fooi,* feast given for farm labourers after harvest, from Middle Dutch *foye, voye,* "voyage", feast given at parting, from Old French *voie,* way, journey, from Latin *via.*]

foy·er (fóy-ay, -ər || *French* fwa-yáy) *n.* The entrance hall, lobby, or anteroom of a public building, such as a theatre or hotel. [French, hearth, home, foyer, from Medieval Latin *focārius,* from Latin *focus,* hearth, fireplace.]

Foyle, Lough (foyl). Sea-lough on the western border of Northern Ireland with the Republic of Ireland.

fp freezing point.

F.P.A. Family Planning Association.

F.P.C. Family Planning Clinic.

fpm, f.p.m. feet per minute.

fps foot-pound-second.

f.p.s. 1. feet per second. **2.** frames per second. **3.** foot-pound-second.

Fr The symbol for the element francium.

fr. 1. franc. **2.** from.

Fr. 1. father (clergyman). **2.** France; French. **3.** frater. **4.** Frau. **5.** friar.

Fra (fraa) *n.* Brother. Used as a title for an Italian monk or friar. [Italian, short for *frate,* "brother", from Latin *frāter.*]

frab·jous (frábjəss) *adj. Informal.* Delightful; wonderful. [Coined by Lewis Carroll, perhaps based on *fair* and *joyous.*]

fra·cas (fráckaa || *U.S.* fráyk-əss, fráck-) *n., pl.* **tracas.** A disorderly uproar; a noisy quarrel; a brawl. [French, from Italian *fracasso,* from *fracassare,* probably a blend of Latin *frangere,* to break, and *quassāre,* to shatter.]

frac·tal (trákt'l) *n.* See **chaos theory.**

frac·tion (fráksh'n) *n.* **1.** A small part of something; a scant portion: *a fraction of the populace.* **2.** A disconnected piece of something; a fragment; a scrap; a bit. **3.** *Mathematics.* An indicated quotient of two quantities. **4.** *Chemistry.* A component separated by a fractional process; a product of fractionation. **5.** The breaking of the host in the Eucharist. [Middle English *fraccioun,* from Late Latin *fractiō* (stem *fractiōn-*), act of breaking (especially bread), from Latin *fractus,* past participle of *frangere,* to break.]

frac·tion·al (fráksh'n'l) *adj.* **1.** Of, pertaining to, or constituting a fraction or fractions. **2.** Very small; insignificant; infinitesimal. **3.** Being in fractions or pieces; fragmentary. **4.** Designating a chemical process in which components of a mixture are separated according to their physical properties: *fractional crystallisation.*

fractional currency *n.* Any currency in a denomination less than the standard monetary unit.

fractional distillation *n.* **1.** Distillation in which the purity of the product is increased by bringing the vapour into contact with the condensed liquid in a countercurrent system. **2.** Distillation in which the product is collected in a series of separate fractions.

frac·tion·ate (fráksh'n-ayt) *tr.v.* **-ated, -ating, -ates.** To separate (a chemical mixture) into components by a fractional process, as by distillation or crystallisation. —**frac·tion·a·tion** (-áysh'n) *n.* —**frac·tion·a·tor** *n.*

frac·tion·ise, frac·tion·ize (fráksh'n-īz) *v.* **-ised, -ising, -ises.** —*tr.* To divide into fractions. —*intr.* To divide something into fractions. —**frac·tion·i·sa·tion** (-ī-záysh'n || *U.S.* -i-) *n.*

frac·tious (frákshəss) *adj.* **1.** Inclined to make trouble; unruly: *He was very fractious when drunk.* **2.** Having a peevish nature; irritable. [From FRACTION, in the sense of "breaking".] —**frac·tious·ly** *adv.* —**frac·tious·ness** *n.*

frac·to·cu·mu·lus cloud (fráktō-kéwmewləss) *n.* Low, ragged cumulus cloud. [Latin *fractus,* broken (past participle of *frangere*) + CUMULUS.]

frac·to·stra·tus cloud (fráktō-strǽatəss || -stráttəss) *n.* Low ragged stratus cloud. [Latin *fractus,* broken (see **fractocumulus cloud**) + STRATUS.]

frac·ture (frákchər) *n.* **1. a.** The act or process of breaking. **b.** The condition of being broken. **2.** A break, rupture, tear, or crack, as in bone or cartilage, as: *a comminuted fracture,* a fracture in which the bone is broken into several pieces; a *compound* or *open fracture,* a fracture with an open wound, often with the broken bone exposed; an *impacted fracture,* a fracture in which the broken ends have been forced into each other; a *simple* or *closed fracture,* a fracture with no break in the skin. **3.** *Mineralogy.* **a.** The characteristic manner in which a mineral breaks. **b.** The characteristic appearance of a broken mineral.
~*v.* **fractured, -turing, -tures.** —*tr.* To break; crack. —*intr.* To undergo a fracture. —See Synonyms at **break.** [Middle English, from Old French, from Latin *fractūra,* from *fractus,* broken. See **fraction.**]

frae (fray) *prep. Scottish.* From.

fraenulum. Variant of **frenulum.**

frae·num (fréenəm) *n.* Also *chiefly U.S.* **trenum.** A membranous fold that supports or restricts the movement of a part, such as the fold under the tongue. [Latin, "bridle".]

frag·ile (frájīl || *U.S.* frájəl) *adj.* **1.** Easily broken or damaged; brittle. **2.** Physically weak; frail. **3.** Suggesting fragility; delicate. **4.** Tenuous; flimsy: *a fragile claim to fame.* [Old French, from Latin *fragilis,* from *frangere,* to break.] —**frag·ile·ly** *adv.* —**fra·gil·i·ty** (frə-jílləti, fra-), **frag·ile·ness** *n.*
Synonyms: *fragile, breakable, frail, delicate, brittle.*

frag·ment (frágmənt) *n.* **1.** A part broken off or detached from a whole. **2.** Something incomplete or unconnected; an odd bit or piece: *a fragment of conversation.* **3.** An extant part of an unfinished or lost text.
~*v.* (frag-mént) **fragmented, -menting, -ments.** —*tr.* To break or separate (something) into fragments. —*intr.* To break into pieces. [Middle English, from Latin *fragmentum,* from *frangere,* to break.]

frag·men·tal (frag-mént'l) *adj.* **1.** Fragmentary. **2.** *Geology.* Consisting of broken material moved from its place of origin.

frag·men·tar·y (frágmən-təri, frag-mén-, -tri || *U.S.* -terri) *adj.* Consisting of fragments or disconnected parts; broken. —**frag·men·tar·i·ly** *adv.* —**frag·men·tar·i·ness** *n.*

frag·men·ta·tion (frág-men-táysh'n, -mən-) *n.* **1.** The act or process of breaking into fragments. **2.** The scattering of the fragments of an exploding grenade, bomb, or shell; dispersion.
~*adj.* Exploding into lethal fragments of high-velocity metal: *a fragmentation grenade.*

fragmentation bomb *n.* An aerial antipersonnel bomb that scatters shrapnel over a wide area. Also called "cluster bomb".

frag·ment·ed (frag-méntid) *adj.* Broken into fragments.

frag·ment·ise, frag·ment·ize (frágmən-tīz) v. -ised, -ising, -ises. *Chiefly U.S.* —*tr.* To break (something) into fragments. —*intr.* To fragment.

Fra·go·nard (fraggō-nár), **Jean Honoré** (1732-1806). French painter and engraver. He is best known for his rococo paintings depicting lovers in exotic settings, cupids, nymphs, and other romantic figures. Among his best-known paintings is *The Swing* (1769).

fra·grance (fráygrənss) n. 1. The state or quality of being fragrant. 2. A sweet or pleasant odour; a perfume. —See Synonyms at **smell**.

fra·grant (fráygrənt) adj. Having a pleasant odour; sweet-smelling; perfumed. [Middle English, from Old French, from Latin *fragrāns* (stem *fragrant-*), present participle of *fragrāre,* to emit an odour (good or bad), to reek.]

frail¹ (frayl) adj. **frailer, frailest. 1.** Having a delicate constitution; physically weak; not robust. **2.** Slight; weak; not strong or substantial. **3.** Easily broken or destroyed; vulnerable; fragile; uncertain. **4.** Morally weak; easily led astray or into evil. —See Synonyms at **fragile, weak.** [Middle English *frele, frail,* from Old French *frele, fraile,* from Latin *fragilis,* FRAGILE.] —**frail·ly** adv. —**frail·ness** n.

frail² n. **1.** A rush basket for holding fruit, especially dried fruit. **2.** The quantity of fruit, such as raisins or figs, contained in a frail, usually from 23 to 34 kilograms (50 to 75 pounds). [Middle English *fraiel,* from Old French *fraiel†.*]

frail·ty (fráylti) n., pl. **-ties. 1.** The condition or quality of being frail; weakness, especially of resolution. **2.** A fault arising from weakness; a failing: *human frailties.* —See Synonyms at **fault.**

fraise (frayz) n. **1.** A barrier or defence of pointed, inclined stakes or of barbed wire. **2.** A ruff for the neck, worn in the 16th century. **3.** A tool for enlarging a small circular hole. **4.** A tool for cutting teeth on a wheel, especially on a watch wheel. [French, "mesentery of a calf or lamb", originally "outer covering", "casing", from Old French *fraiser,* to remove the outer covering (used especially of beans), from Vulgar Latin *frēsāre* (unattested), from Latin *(faba) frēsa,* ground (bean), from *frēsus,* past participle of *frendere,* to grind with the teeth.]

Frak·tur (frak-tŏōr) n. A style of letter formerly used in German manuscripts and printing. [German *Fraktur,* from Latin *fractūra,* a breaking (from the curlicues which appear to break up the word), FRACTURE.]

fram·boe·si·a, *U.S.* **fram·be·si·a** (fram-béezi-ə) n. *Pathology.* **Yaws** *(see).* [New Latin, from French *framboise,* raspberry (from the appearance of the excrescences), from Old French, variant (influenced by *fraise,* strawberry) of Frankish *brām-besi* (unattested), "brambleberry".]

fram·boise (fron-bwáaz) n. A clear French brandy distilled from raspberries. [French, "raspberry". See **framboesia.**]

frame (fraym) v. **framed, framing, frames.** —*tr.* **1.** To construct by putting together the various parts of; build. **2.** To formulate or conceive; fashion; design; draw up. **3.** To arrange or adjust for a purpose; compose. **4. a.** To put into words; phrase: *frame a reply.* **b.** To form (words) silently with the lips. **5.** To provide with or as if with a surrounding or bordering frame; enclose or encircle. **6.** *Slang.* **a.** To rig evidence or events so as to incriminate (a person) falsely. **b.** *Chiefly U.S.* To fix (a contest, for example) so as to ensure a desired fraudulent outcome: *frame a prize fight.* —*intr. Archaic.* **1.** To resort; proceed. **2.** To manage or contrive to do something.

~n. **1.** Something composed of parts fitted and joined together; a structure, such as: **a.** A basic or skeletal structure designed to give shape or support: *the frame of a house.* **b.** An open structure or rim for encasing, holding, or bordering something: *a window frame; a picture frame; spectacle frames.* **c.** The human body. **d.** A **cold frame** *(see).* **e.** A climbing apparatus as used in a gymnasium or children's playground. **2.** A machine built upon or utilising a frame. **3.** The general structure of something; system; order: *the frame of government.* **4. a.** Any of the transverse ribs of a ship's hull from the gunwale to the keel or the bilge, consisting of either a *square frame,* perpendicular to the keel's vertical plane, or a *cant frame,* at an oblique angle to it. **b.** A transverse stiffening rib in the fuselage of an aircraft. **5. a.** In snooker, a rigid triangular device for arranging the balls at the beginning of a game. **b.** The balls so arranged. **6.** A round or period of play in some games, such as tenpin bowling or snooker. **7. a.** A single exposure on a roll of cinematic film. **b.** A single scene in a cartoon strip. **8.** The total area of a television picture formed by a single traverse of the scanning spot. **9.** In electronics, computing, and telecommunications, a cycle of regularly recurring pulses in a train of pulses. **10.** A slat or slats, serving as a base for building honeycombs, that is part of the structure of a man-made beehive. **11.** *Slang.* A frame-up. **12.** *Obsolete.* Shape; form. [Middle English *framen, framien,* to be advantageous, benefit, form, construct, Old English *framian,* to benefit, avail.] —**fram·er** n.

frame aerial n. A **loop aerial** *(see).*

frame house n. A house constructed with a wooden framework, and usually covered with wooden boards.

frame of mind n. Mental state or attitude; mood.

frame of reference n. **1.** *Physics.* A set of coordinate axes in terms of which position or movement may be specified, or with reference to which physical laws may be mathematically stated. **2.** A set or system of ideas, as of philosophical or religious doctrine, in terms of which other ideas are interpreted or assigned meaning.

frame-up (fráym-up) n. *Slang.* **1.** A prearranged or fraudulent scheme; a fix. **2.** A conspiracy to throw guilt on an innocent person; a scheme involving falsified charges or evidence.

frame·work (fráym-wurk) n. **1.** A structure for supporting, defining, or enclosing something; especially, skeletal erections and supports used as the basis for something being constructed. **2.** Any outlying erection or work platform that allows access to something being constructed or worked on in some way; a rig; scaffolding. **3.** A basic arrangement, form, or system; a design.

fram·ing (fráyming) n. A frame, framework, or system of frames.

franc (frangk) n. *Abbr.* **f., fr. 1.** The basic monetary unit of France, Belgium, Switzerland, and numerous other countries, especially former French colonies. It is equal to 100 centimes. **2.** A coin worth one franc. [Middle English *frank,* from Old French *franc,* from the Latin legend *Francorum rex,* "king of the Franks", on gold coins struck during the reign of Jean le Bon (1350-64).]

France (fraanss ‖ franss). Republic on the western seaboard of Europe. It is the continent's oldest state and third largest country after Russia and Ukraine. It was settled by the Franks, a Germanic people from across the Rhine, after the retreat of the Romans, who had conquered the Celtic Gauls in 57-51 B.C. The country enjoys all three European climates—maritime, continental, and Mediterranean. Its richest resource is its soil; 90 per cent of the land is productive, whether as arable land, permanent pasture, or forest. France is the world's second producer of wine after Italy, and is self-sufficient in meat and cereals. It is also heavily industrialised, and tourism is a major industry. Area, 543 965 square kilometres (210,026 square miles). Population, 58,370,000. Capital, Paris. [Middle English, *Fraunce,* from Old French *France,* from Late Latin *Francia,* country of the Franks, from *Francus,* a FRANK.] See map, next page.

France (froNSS), **Anatole** born Thibault (1844-1924). French novelist. He was a great short story writer and literary satirist. His works include *Thaïs* (1890). *l'Ile des pingouins* (1908), and *la Révolte des anges* (1914). He won the Nobel prize in 1921.

Francesca, Piero della. See **Piero della Francesca.**

fran·chise (frán-chīz) n. **1.** A privilege or right granted a person or a group by a government, state, or sovereign, especially: **a.** The constitutional or statutory right to vote; suffrage. **b.** Formerly, legal immunity from certain burdens, servitude, or other restrictions. **2.** Authorisation granted by a manufacturer to a distributor or dealer to sell his products. **3.** The territory or limits within which some privilege, right, or immunity may be exercised. —See Synonyms at **right.**

~*tr.v.* **franchised, -chising, -chises.** *Chiefly U.S.* To endow with a franchise. [Middle English *fraunchise,* freedom, privilege, from Old French *franchise,* from *franc* (feminine *franche*), free, FRANK.]

Fran·cis·can (fran-sísskən) n. A member of a religious mendicant order founded by St. Francis of Assisi in 1209 and now divided into three independent branches. Formerly called "Grey Friar".

~*adj.* Of or pertaining to St. Francis of Assisi or to the order founded by him.

Fran·cis Jo·seph (fráan-siss jó-zif ‖ frán-, -sif). *German* **Franz Josef** (1830-1916). Austrian emperor. His reign (1848-1916) began at the height of the 1848 Revolution and was marked by a succession of crises. To ease tensions within his empire, he created the Dual Monarchy (1867) with Austria and Hungary. He was defeated by the Prussians (1866) but later allied with the German Empire (1879) and with Italy (1882) to form the Triple Alliance. Following the assassination (1914) of his nephew, Archduke Francis Ferdinand, by a Serbian nationalist, he issued an ultimatum to Serbia that was to lead to World War I.

Francis of Assisi, Saint (c. 1182-1226). Founder of the Franciscan Order. Born in Assisi, the son of a cloth merchant, he served for a time as a soldier, but in 1206 devoted himself to a life of poverty. In 1210 he received papal permission to found his holy order, and he and his followers took Christ's teaching as far as North Africa and the Holy Land. His *Canticle to the Sun* (1225-26) testifies to his love of nature. He was canonised in 1228 and in 1980 was declared patron saint of ecology. His feast day is October 4.

Fran·cis Xa·vi·er (fráan-siss záyvi-ər ‖ frán-), **Saint** (1506-52). Spanish Jesuit missionary. He was co-founder, with Ignatius of Loyola, of the Jesuit order. Known as the Apostle of the Indies, he established missions in the Indies, Japan, and Ceylon.

fran·ci·um (frán-si-əm) n. *Symbol* **Fr** An extremely unstable radioactive metallic element, having 20 known isotopes, the most stable of which is Fr 223 with a half-life of 21 minutes. Atomic number 87, valency 1. [New Latin, from FRANCE.]

Franck (froNk), **César (Auguste)** (1822-90). Belgian composer and organist. He travelled to Paris in 1834 and became one of the most influential musical figures in mid-19th-century France. Though he composed mainly for the organ, his works also include an orchestral symphony and some oratorios.

Fran·co (frángkō), **Francisco** (1892-1975). Spanish dictator. As military governor of the Canary Islands, he helped to direct the uprising of July 1936 and later that year became head of the Nationalist government and rebel armed forces. Following the defeat of the Republicans in the Spanish Civil War (1939), he ruled Spain until his death, when he was succeeded by a restored Bourbon monarchy.

Franco- *comb. form.* Indicates France or French; for example, **Francophile.** [Medieval Latin *Francus,* a Frenchman, from Late Latin, a FRANK.]

fran·co·lin (frángkəlin) n. **1.** Any of various Old World birds of the

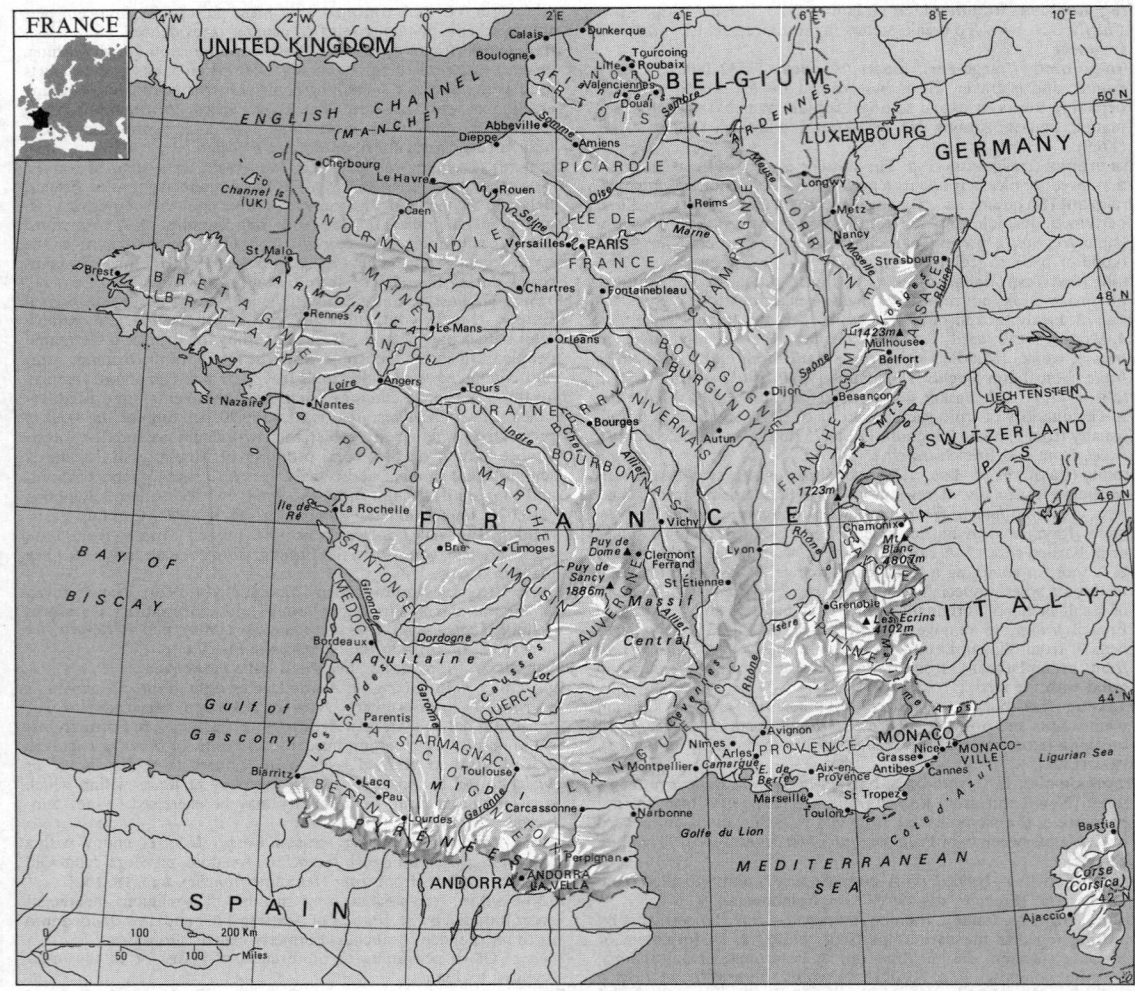

FRANCE

genus *Francolinus,* related to and resembling the quails and partridges. **2.** Any of various related birds, such as the Chinese francolin, *Excalfactoria.* [French, from Italian *francolino†.*]

Fran·co·phile (fráng-kə-fīl, -kō-) *n.* Also **Fran·co·phil** (-fil). An admirer of France, its people, and its customs. [FRANCO- + -PHILE.] —**Fran·co·phile** *adj.*

Fran·co·phobe (fráng-kə-fōb, -kō-) *n.* One who hates France, its people, or its customs. [FRANCO- + -PHOBE.] —**Fran·co·phobe** *adj.*

Fran·co·phone (fráng-kə-fōn, -kō-) *adj.* French-speaking.
~*n.* A French-speaking person. [FRANCO- + -PHONE.]

Fran·co·Prus·sian War (fráNGkō-prúsh'n) *n.* The war of 1870–71 between Prussia and France.

franc tir·eur (froN tee-rốr) *n., pl.* **francs tireurs** (*pronounced as singular*). *French.* An irregular soldier or guerrilla. [French, "free shooter".]

fran·gi·ble (fránji-b'l) *adj.* Easily broken; breakable. [Middle English, from Old French, from Medieval Latin *frangibilis,* from Latin *frangere,* to break.] —**fran·gi·bil·i·ty** (-billəti), **fran·gi·ble·ness** *n.*

fran·gi·pan·i (fránji-paáni ‖ -pánni) *n.* Also (for senses 2, 3). **fran·gi·pane** (fránji-payn). **1.** Any of various tropical American shrubs of the genus *Plumeria,* having milky juice and showy, fragrant, variously coloured flowers. **2.** A perfume derived from or similar in scent to these flowers. **3.** A creamy pastry filling flavoured with almonds. [French *frangipane,* from *(gants de) frangipane,* (gloves with) frangipani, after the Marquis *Frangipani* of Rome, who invented a perfume for scenting gloves in the 16th century.]

Fran·glais (fróng-glay) *n.* French as used with numerous English words, word-endings, and other borrowings from English. [Blend of French *Français,* French, and *Anglais,* English.]

frank (franGk) *adj.* **franker, frankest. 1.** Open and sincere in expression; straightforward. **2.** Clearly manifest; undisguised; evident: *frank enjoyment.* **3.** *Rare.* Liberal in giving; generous. **4.** *Obsolete.* Free; open.
~*tr.v.* **franked, franking, franks. 1.** Formerly, to put an official mark on (a letter, for example) to ensure free delivery through special official privilege. **2.** To place a stamp or mark on (a letter or parcel) to show the payment of postage. **3.** To place a postmark on. **4.** *Rare.* To enable (a person) to come and go easily; allow to go free of charge.
~*n.* **1.** A mark or signature placed on a letter or parcel to indicate the right to send it free of postage. **2.** A franked letter or parcel. [Middle English, free, generous, from Old French *franc,* free, from Medieval Latin *francus,* from Late Latin *Francus,* Frank (in Frankish Gaul full freedom was the right only of the conquering people or those under their protection).] —**frank·ness** *n.*

Synonyms: *frank, candid, outspoken, open, ingenuous.*

Frank (franGk) *n.* A member of one of the Germanic tribes of the Rhine region in the early Christian era; especially, one of the Salian Franks who conquered Gaul about 500 A.D. and established an extensive empire which reached its greatest power in the ninth century. [Middle English *Franc,* from Old English *Franca,* and Old French *Franc,* from Late Latin *Francus,* from Germanic.]

Frank, Anne (1929–45). A Jewish girl who fled Germany with her family in 1933 to escape Nazi persecution, she was trapped in Amsterdam by the German invasion (1941). The family hid in a sealed room from 1942 until her arrest in 1944. She died in Belsen concentration camp. The diary of her years in hiding was published (1947; fuller version 1997); the house is preserved as a museum.

Frank·en·stein monster (fránGkən-stīn) *n.* Also **Frank·en·stein's monster** (-stīnz). **1.** Any agency or creation that slips from the control of and ultimately destroys its creator. **2.** A monster having the appearance of a man; specifically, the monster created by the protagonist of Mary Shelley's novel *Frankenstein* (1818) which brought about the ruin of its creator. Also called "Frankenstein".

Frank·furt am Main (fránGk-furt am mīn, *German* -foort). Industrial city, financial centre, and river port in Hessen, central western Germany. From 1816 to 1866, the city was the virtual capital of Germany, where the Federal Diet (parliament) met. —**Frank·furt·er** *n.*

Frankfurt an der O·der (an dair ốdər). Town in eastern Germany, on the river Oder, at the Polish border. It is an industrial centre and agricultural market.

frank·furt·er (fránGk-furtər) *n.* A smoked sausage of pork, beef, or beef and pork made in long, reddish links. [From FRANKFURT (AM MAIN), where it was originally made.]

frank·in·cense (fránGkin-senss) *n.* An aromatic gum resin obtained from African and Asian trees of the genus *Boswellia,* and used chiefly as incense. Also called "olibanum". [Middle English *frank encens,* from Old French *franc encens* : *franc,* free, superior, FRANK + *encens,* INCENSE.]

Frank·ish (frángkish) *adj.* Of or pertaining to the Franks or their language.
~*n.* The West Germanic language of the Franks.

frank·lin (frángklin) *n.* In England during the late medieval period, a freeholder not of noble birth but with extensive property; a country gentleman. [Middle English *frankelein,* from Medieval Latin *francālānus,* from *francālis,* (feudal estate) held without dues, from *francus,* free, FRANK.]

Frank·lin (frángklin). District within the Northwest Territories, Canada. It comprises the islands of the Canadian Arctic and the Boothia and Melville peninsulas. It was named after the British Arctic explorer, Sir John Franklin (1786–1847).

Frank·lin (frángklin), **Benjamin** (1706–90). U.S. statesman, philosopher, physicist, and journalist. Following the success of his journal, *Poor Richard's Almanac,* he entered politics and played a major part in the War of Independence. He negotiated French support for the colonists, promoted the Declaration of Independence (1776), and signed the Treaty of Independence (1783). He is remembered for his work on the drafting of the American constitution, and his development of the lightning conductor.

frank·lin·ite (frángkli-nīt) *n.* A blackish, slightly magnetic mineral of zinc, iron, and manganese, that is a valuable source of zinc. [After *Franklin,* New Jersey, where it is mined.]

frank·ly (frángkli) *adv.* 1. In a frank manner; openly; candidly. 2. Speaking honestly; in truth: *Frankly, I don't care.*

frank·pledge (frángk-plej) *n.* 1. In old English law, a system in which units or tithings composed of ten households were formed, in each of which members were held responsible for one another's conduct. 2. A member of such a group, bound in pledge for his neighbours. 3. The tithing itself. [Middle English *fraunkiplegge,* from Anglo-French *frauncplege,* intended as a translation of Old English *frithborh* (unattested), "peace pledge", with *frith,* peace, misapprehended as meaning free : *franc,* FRANK + Old French *plege,* PLEDGE.]

fran·tic (frántik) *adj.* 1. Emotionally distraught, as from fear, pain, worry, or passion; desperate; overwrought. 2. Uncontrolled; wildly excited; frenzied. 3. *Archaic.* Mad; insane. [Middle English *frantik, frenetik,* FRENETIC.] —**fran·ti·cal·ly, fran·tic·ly** *adv.* —**fran·tic·ness** *n.*

Franz Josef. See **Francis Joseph.**

Franz Jos·ef Land (fránts yőzef). *Russian* **Zemlya Frantsa Iosifa.** Arctic archipelago to the north of Novaya Zemlya. It was claimed by the U.S.S.R. in 1926 and is Russia's most northerly territory. The 87 islands are mostly ice-covered all the year and are inhabited mainly by polar bears, arctic foxes, walrus, and seals. The only human inhabitants are scientists at Russian weather stations. The group was first explored by an Austrian expedition in 1873, and named after the Austrian emperor. The group is also called **Fridtjof Nansen Land,** after the Norwegian explorer who led an expedition there (1895–99).

frap (frap) *tr.v.* **frapped, frapping, fraps.** *Nautical.* 1. To make secure by lashing: *frap a sail.* 2. To tighten; take up the slack of. [Middle English *frapen,* to strike, from Old French *fraper,* possibly from Frankish *hrappan†* (unattested).]

frap·pé (fráppay, fra-páy) *n., pl.* **frappés.** 1. A frozen, fruit-flavoured mixture similar to a sorbet and served as a dessert or appetiser. 2. A beverage, usually a liqueur, poured over crushed ice. ~*adj.* Cooled or iced. Said of drinks, especially wine. [French, from the past participle of *frapper,* "to strike", chill, from Old French *fraper,* to strike. See **frap.**]

Fra·sca·ti (fra-scáat-i). Town in south Italy about 16 kilometres (10 miles) east of Rome. It is the site of the ruins of Cicero's villa and is also known for its dry white wine.

Fra·ser, (John) Malcolm (1930–). Australian politician. In 1975 he became prime minister, a position he held through three subsequent general elections until 1983.

Fraser, Peter (1884–1950). New Zealand politician, born in Scotland. He emigrated to New Zealand (1910) and helped to form the Labour Party (1916). Elected to parliament (1918), he became prime minister (1940) and influenced the Allies' Pacific strategy during World War II. He was defeated in the 1949 general election.

Fraser, Simon (1776–1862). Canadian fur-trader and explorer. He worked for the North West Company and explored the river named after him, in British Columbia.

frass (frass) *n.* 1. The excrement of insects or insect larvae. 2. The refuse left by hole-boring insects. 3. Fine debris; waste matter. [German *fressen,* to feed, devour.]

fratch·y (fráchi) *adj. British Regional.* Quarrelsome. [Imitative.]

fra·ter¹ (fráytər) *n. Abbr.* **Fr.** A brother, as in a religious order or a fraternity. [Medieval Latin *frāter,* from Latin.]

frater² *n.* A refectory in a medieval monastery. [Middle English, from Old French *fraitur,* aphetic variant of *refreitor,* from Medieval Latin *refectorium,* REFECTORY.]

fra·ter·nal (frə-térn'l) *adj.* 1. **a.** Of or pertaining to brothers. **b.** Brotherly. 2. Pertaining to or constituting a fraternity. 3. *Biology.* Of or pertaining to a twin or twins developed from separately fertilised ova. —See Synonyms at **familiar.** [Middle English, from Medieval Latin *frāternālis,* from Latin *frāternus,* from FRATER (brother).] —**fra·ter·nal·ism** *n.* —**fra·ter·nal·ly** *adv.*

frat·er·nise, frat·er·nize (fráttər-nīz) *intr.v.* **-nised, -nising, -nises.** 1. To associate with others in a brotherly or congenial way. 2. To mix intimately with the people of an enemy or conquered country, often in violation of military law. [French *fraterniser,* from Medi-eval Latin *frāternizāre,* from Latin *frāternus,* FRATERNAL.] —**frat·er·ni·sa·tion** (-nī-zásh'n || *U.S.* -ni-) *n.* —**frat·er·nis·er** *n.*

fra·ter·ni·ty (frə-térnəti) *n., pl.* **-ties.** 1. A body of men, such as a religious order or a guild, associated for some common purpose or interest. 2. A group of men linked together by similar backgrounds, predilections, or occupations: *the fraternity of birdwatchers.* 3. *U.S.* A chiefly social organisation of male college students, usually designated by Greek letters. Compare **sorority.** 4. The relationship of a brother or brothers; brotherhood. 5. Brotherliness. —See Synonyms at **circle.** [Middle English *fraternite,* from Old French, from Latin *frāternitās* (stem *frāternitāt-*), from *frāternus,* FRATERNAL.]

frat·ri·cide (fráttri-sīd) *n.* 1. The killing of one's brother or sister. 2. One who has killed his brother or sister. [Middle English (sense 2 only), from Old French (both senses), from Latin *frātricīda* (the person) and *frātricīdium* (the act) : *frāter,* FRATER + -CIDE.] —**frat·ri·ci·dal** (-sīd'l) *adj.*

Frau (frow) *n., pl.* **Frauen** (frów-ən). *Abbr.* **Fr.** 1. A married woman in a German-speaking country or district. Used as a title corresponding to *Mrs.* 2. *Informal.* A German woman. [German *Frau,* from Middle High German *vrouwe,* from Old High German *frouwa.*]

fraud (frawd) *n.* 1. A deception deliberately practised in order to secure unfair or unlawful gain. 2. A piece of trickery; a swindle. 3. **a.** One that defrauds; a cheat. **b.** One who assumes a false pose; an impostor. **c.** Something that is not what it appears or is claimed to be; a sham. [Middle English *fraude,* from Old French, from Latin *fraus†* (stem *fraud-*).]

fraud·u·lent (fráwdewlənt) *adj.* 1. Engaging in fraud; deceitful. 2. Characterised by, constituting, or gained by fraud: *a fraudulent contract.* [Middle English, from Old French, from Latin *fraudulentus,* from *fraus,* FRAUD.] —**fraud·u·lence** *n.* —**fraud·u·lent·ly** *adv.*

fraught (frawt) *adj.* 1. Filled or attended; charged. Used with *with: an occasion fraught with peril.* 2. *Informal.* **a.** Causing anxiety or difficulty. **b.** Anxious or harassed. 3. *Archaic.* Laden; freighted. [Middle English, past participle of *fraughten,* to load a ship, from Middle Dutch *vrachten,* from *vracht,* freight.]

Fräu·lein (fróy-līn, frów-) *n., pl.* **Fräulein.** *Abbr.* **Frl.** 1. An unmarried girl or woman in a German-speaking country or district. Used as a title corresponding to *Miss.* 2. *Chiefly British.* A German governess. [German, from Middle High German *vrouwelīn,* diminutive of *vrouwe,* wife, FRAU.]

Fraun·ho·fer (frówn-hōfər), **Joseph von** (1787–1826). German physicist. His development of optical lenses led to important discoveries in spectroscopy.

Fraunhofer lines *pl.n.* A set of several hundred dark lines appearing against the bright background of the continuous solar spectrum, produced by the absorption of light by cooler gases in the sun's outer atmosphere at frequencies corresponding to the atomic transition frequencies of these gases. [After J.v. FRAUNHOFER.]

frax·i·nel·la (frák-si-néllə) *n.* The **gas plant** *(see).* [New Latin, diminutive from Latin *fraxinus,* ash tree (from the resemblance of its leaves to those of the ash).]

fray¹ (fray) *n.* 1. A fight; a scuffle; a brawl. 2. A heated dispute or contest. [Middle English, fright, commotion, conflict, from *fraien,* to frighten, short for *afraien, affraien,* from Old French *affreer,* to AFFRAY.]

fray² *v.* **frayed, fraying, frays.** —*tr.* 1. To unravel, wear away, or tatter (the edges of fabric, for example) by rubbing. 2. To strain; chafe: *nerves frayed by noise.* —*intr.* To become tattered, unravelled, or threadbare along the edges. [Middle English *fraien,* from Old French *fraier,* from Latin *fricāre,* to rub.]

Fray Ben·tos (fráy béntoss; *Spanish* frī). River port in southwest Uruguay, on the Uruguay river. It was founded in 1859, and has long been an important meat-packing centre, noted for corned beef.

Fra·zer (fráyzər), **Sir James George** (1854–1941). British anthropologist and writer. His most famous work, *The Golden Bough* (1890), examined the development of human thought with reference to magic, religion, and science.

Fra·zier (fráy-zhər, -z-yər), **Joe,** also known as "Smokin' " Joe Frazier (1944–). U.S. boxer. Olympic heavyweight champion (1964), he later won the world professional heavyweight title (1970) but lost it to George Foreman (1973).

fra·zil (fráyzil) *n.* Ice fragments, often sharp and pointed, that occur in turbulent water in which sheets of ice cannot form. [Canadian French *frasil;* akin to French *fraisil,* cinders.]

fraz·zle (frázz'l) *v.* **-zled, -zling, -zles.** *Informal.* —*tr.* 1. To fray; chafe. 2. *Informal.* To wear out the nerves or strength of. —*intr.* To become frazzled or worn out.
~*n.* 1. A frayed or tattered condition. 2. *Informal.* A condition of nervous exhaustion. —**to a frazzle.** *Informal.* To the last remnants; so that almost nothing is left: *burnt to a frazzle.* [Probably a blend of FRAY (wear) and dialectal *fazzle,* to fray, from Middle English *faselen,* from *fasel,* fringe, frayed edge, diminutive of *fas,* fringe, Old English *fæs,* from Germanic *fas-* (unattested).]

F.R.C.M. Fellow of the Royal College of Music.

F.R.C.O. Fellow of the Royal College of Organists.

F.R.C.P. Fellow of the Royal College of Physicians.

F.R.C.S. Fellow of the Royal College of Surgeons.

freak¹ (freek) *n.* 1. A thing or occurrence that is very unusual or irregular. Also used adjectivally: *a freak wind.* 2. An abnormally formed organism; especially, a person or animal regarded as a curiosity or monstrosity. 3. A sudden capricious turn of the mind; a whim. 4. *Slang.* **a.** A drug user or addict: *a speed freak.* **b.** A per-

son with a great enthusiasm or liking for a specified interest, activity, or the like: *a Wagner freak.* **5.** *Slang.* An unconventional or intentionally bizarre person.
~*v.* **freaked, -freaking, freaks.** *Slang.* —*intr.* **1.** To become highly excited and emotional about something. **2.** To become emotionally or mentally unstable, or outlandishly uninhibited in behaviour. Often used with *out.* **3.** To undergo a hallucinatory experience, especially as a result of taking drugs. Used with *out.* —*tr.* To cause to freak or freak out. [16th century : of dialect origin.] —**freak·y** *adj.* —**freak·i·ly** *adv.*
freak² *n. Rare.* A fleck or streak of colour.
~*tr.v.* **freaked, freaking, freaks.** *Rare.* To speckle or streak with colour. [Originally *freaked,* probably formed by Milton, probably variant (influenced by STREAK) of obsolete *freckt,* from FRECKLE.]
freak·ish (frékish) *adj.* **1.** Unusual; outlandish; abnormal. **2.** Pertaining to or characteristic of a freak. **3.** Capricious. —**freak·ish·ly** *adv.* —**freak·ish·ness** *n.*
freck·le (fréck'l) *n.* A small brown mark or precipitation of pigment in the skin, often brought out by the sun.
~*v.* **freckled, -ling, -les.** —*tr.* To dot with freckles or spots of colour. —*intr.* To become dotted with freckles. [Middle English *frakles* (plural), variant of *fraknes,* from Old Norse *freknur* (plural).] —**freck·ly** *adj.*
Fred·er·ick I (frédrik ‖ fréddərik), known as Barbarossa (Redbeard) (c. 1123–90). Holy Roman Emperor (1155–90). On his accession, he asserted imperial power against the papacy in an attempt to enforce his feudal rights in Italy, but was crushingly defeated at Legnano (1176). He drowned while leading the Third Crusade.
Frederick (II) the Great (1712–86). King of Prussia (1740–86). In a brilliant military career he elevated Prussia to a position of great power in Germany. He pursued a policy of enlightened despotism, laying the foundations of the Prussian military state.
free (free) *adj.* **treer, treest.** **1.** At liberty; not bound or constrained. **2.** Discharged from arrest or detention. **3.** Not under obligation or necessity. **4. a.** Politically independent. Said of a country or nation. **b.** Governed by consent and possessing civil liberties: *a free society.* **c.** Immune to arbitrary interference by government or others: *a free press.* **5. a.** Not affected or restricted by a given condition or circumstance. Used with *from* or *of: free from need.* Often used in combination: *trouble-free.* **b.** Not subject to a given condition; exempt. Often used in combination: *duty-free.* **c.** Not containing; without. Often used in combination: *fat-free, sugar-free.* **6. a.** Not subject to external constraint: *free criticism.* **b.** Not subject to external physical restraint: *free fall.* **c.** Graceful; easy: *free gestures.* **d.** Not fixed, attached, or tied: *the free end of a rope.* **7. a.** Not strict or literal: *a free translation.* **b.** Not following formal rules or conventions: *free verse.* **c.** Not subject to any melodic or rhythmic patterns; completely improvised: *free jazz.* **8. a.** Costing nothing; gratuitous: *a free ticket.* **b.** Public; open to all: *free education.* **c.** Not paying the usual fee; without charge. **9. a.** Unoccupied; available for use: *a free shelf.* **b.** Not busy; available: *a free afternoon; free to see you now.* **c.** Unobstructed; clear: *a free lane.* **10.** Guileless; frank: *"The Moor is of a free and open nature."* (Shakespeare). **11.** Taking undue liberties; forward. **12.** Liberal or lavish: *free with his money.* **13.** Uninhibited; racy: *much free talking and flirting at the party.* **14.** Uncommitted; independent: *a free woman.* **15.** *Chemistry & Physics.* **a.** Unconstrained; unconfined: *free expansion.* **b.** Not fixed in position; capable of relatively unrestricted motion: *a free electron.* **c.** Not chemically bound; uncombined: *free oxygen.* **d.** Involving no collisions or interactions: *a free path.* **16.** *Nautical.* Favourable. Said of a wind. **17.** *Phonetics.* Designating a vowel in an open syllable, unchecked by a consonant; for example, *o* in *go* is a free vowel. **18.** *Botany.* Not joined to one another or to other organs. Said especially of petals, sepals, and other parts of a flower.
~*adv.* **1.** In a free manner; freely. **2.** Without charge. —**make free with.** To take liberties with. —**run free.** *Nautical.* To sail with the wind aft.
~*tr.v.* **freed, freeing, frees.** **1.** To set at liberty; release. **2.** To rid or release. Used with *of* or *from: a people freed from fear.* **3.** To disengage; untangle: *free a rope.* [Middle English *fre(e),* Old English *frēo,* from Germanic *frijaz* (unattested).] —**free·ly** *adv.* —**free·ness** *n.*
Usage: In its sense "unaffected, unrestricted by a given condition", *free* takes both *from* and *of. Of* is found in the context of finance (*free of charge, free of tax*) and where the general sense is one of removing a problem or restriction: *the room has been disinfected and is now free of disease. From* tends to be used where the general sense is one of actively preventing a problem from developing: *to keep the garden free from weeds.*
free agent *n.* A person unconstrained by ties of emotion, contract, or other commitments.
free alongside ship *adj. Abbr.* **f.a.s., F.A.S.** Delivered to the pier or dock at no extra charge. Said of cargo going by sea.
free-and-easy (frée-ənd-éezi) *adj.* Also **free and easy.** Informal in manner and unconcerned with strict niceties.
free association *n.* **1.** A spontaneous, logically unconstrained association of ideas and feelings. **2.** A psychoanalytic technique in which a patient's articulation of such associations is encouraged in order to elicit repressed thoughts and emotions.
free·bie (fréebi) *n. Informal.* A free gift; something provided without payment; especially, an entertainment or excursion for journal-

ists or others, usually in anticipation of publicity. [Arbitrarily formed from FREE.]
free·board (frée-bawrd ‖ -bōrd) *n. Nautical.* The distance between the water line and the uppermost full deck.
freeboard deck *n.* The uppermost deck that is officially considered completely watertight.
free·boot (frée-bōot) *intr.v.* **-booted, -booting, -boots.** To act as a freebooter; plunder.
free·boot·er (frée-bōotər) *n.* A person who pillages and plunders; especially, a pirate; a buccaneer. [Partial cognate translation of Dutch *vrijbuiter,* from *vrijbuit,* free booty : *vrij,* FREE + *buit,* BOOTY.]
free·born (frée-bawrn) *adj.* **1.** Born as a free person. **2.** Pertaining to or befitting a person born free.
free capital *n.* **1.** Capital available for investment. **2.** Capital not earmarked for a specific use.
Free Church *n. Chiefly British.* **1.** Any non-Anglican Protestant Church; a Nonconformist church. **2.** Any church that is not the established church of the state, or is free of state control. —**Free-Church** *adj.*
free city *n.* **1.** A sovereign city-state, such as those established in Germany and Italy in the Middle Ages. **2.** A city governed as an autonomous political unit under international auspices.
free companion *n.* A mercenary of the Middle Ages.
free company *n.* A company of free companions.
freed·man (fréed-mən, -man) *n., pl.* **-men** (-mən, -men). A man who has been freed from bondage; an emancipated slave.
free·dom (fréedəm) *n.* **1.** The condition of being free of restraints. **2.** The condition of not being subject to slavery, oppression, or imprisonment. **3. a.** Political independence. **b.** Possession of civil rights; immunity from the arbitrary exercise of authority. **4.** Exemption from unpleasant or onerous conditions. Used with *from: freedom from fear and want.* **5.** The capacity to exercise choice; free will. **6.** Facility or ease, as of movement. **7.** Originality of style or conception. **8.** Frankness. **9. a.** Boldness; impertinence. **b.** An instance of improper boldness; a liberty. **10.** Unrestricted use or access. **11.** The right of enjoying all the privileges of membership or citizenship: *the freedom of the city.* [Middle English *fredom,* Old English *frēodōm : frēo,* FREE + -DOM.]
free·dom fighter *n.* One who takes militant action against an established government, usually one of an authoritarian nature.
freedom of the seas *n. International Law.* **1.** The doctrine that ships of any nation may travel through international waters unhampered. **2.** The right of neutral shipping in wartime to trade at will except where blockades are established.
freed·wo·man (fréed-wōomən) *n., pl.* **-women** (-wimmin). A woman freed from bondage; an emancipated slave.
free electron *n.* An electron that is not bound to an atom, such as an electron in a conductor that is available to move in a current.
free energy *n.* **1.** A thermodynamic quantity that is the difference between the internal energy and the product of the thermodynamic temperature and entropy of a system. Also called "Helmholtz free energy". **2.** A thermodynamic quantity that is the difference between the enthalpy and the product of the thermodynamic temperature and entropy of a system. In this sense, also called "Gibbs free energy".
free enterprise *n.* The freedom of private businesses to operate competitively for profit, with minimal government regulation.
free fall *n.* **1.** The fall of a body within the atmosphere without a drag-producing device such as a parachute. **2.** The unconstrained motion of a body in a gravitational field. **3.** Unchecked decline.
free flight *n.* Flight, as of an aircraft or spacecraft, after termination of powered flight.
free-floating (frée-flóting) *adj.* **1.** Not attached or fixed to any specific base or source. **2.** Not committed to any particular viewpoint or course of action; independent.
free-for-all (frée-fər-awl) *n.* A brawl, argument, or competition in which everyone present takes part.
free form *n. Linguistics.* A morpheme capable of standing alone and retaining meaning. Compare **bound form.**
free-form (frée-fawrm) *adj.* Designating music, art, literature, or the like that is free of stylistic conventions.
free gift *n.* An object given away with, or accompanying without extra charge, a purchased object. Often used as an inducement to purchase, especially in mail-order selling.
free hand *n.* Full liberty to do or decide as one sees fit.
free-hand (frée-hand) *adj.* Drawn by hand without the aid of tracing or guiding instruments: *a freehand sketch.*
~*adv.* By hand, without mechanical aids.
free-hand·ed (frée-hándid) *adj.* Openhanded; generous; unstinting. —**free-hand·ed·ly** *adv.* —**free-hand·ed·ness** *n.*
free-heart·ed (frée-hártid) *adj.* Unreserved; open; generous; liberal. —**free-heart·ed·ly** *adv.* —**free-heart·ed·ness** *n.*
free·hold (frée-hōld) *n.* **1.** *Law.* **a.** An estate held in fee simple, fee tail, or for life. **b.** The tenure by which such an estate is held. Compare **leasehold.** **2.** Loosely, outright ownership of land. **3.** A tenure of an office or a dignity for life. [Middle English *frehold* (translation of Anglo-French *fraunc tenement,* "free or frank holding") : FREE + HOLD.] —**free·hold** *adj.* —**free·hold·er** *n.*
free house *n. Chiefly British.* A public house that can sell the beers and spirits of more than one brewer. Compare **tied house.**
free kick *n.* In types of football, an unhindered kick awarded to a team for an infringement of the rules by the opposing team.
free·lance (frée-laanss ‖ -lanss) *n.* Also **free·lanc·er** (frée-láansər).

1. A person, especially a writer or an artist, who sells his services to employers without a long-term commitment to any one of them. 2. One who remains uncommitted to a party and proceeds as an independent. 3. A medieval mercenary; a free companion. ~*v.* **freelanced, -lancing, -lances.** —*intr.* To work as a freelance. —*tr.* To produce and sell as a freelance. ~*adj.* Pertaining to or produced by a freelance. ~*adv.* On a freelance basis.

free·liv·ing (frée-lívving) *adj.* 1. Given to self-indulgence. 2. *Biology.* Living or moving independently; not part of a parasitic or symbiotic relationship.

free·load (frée-lōd, -lŏd) *intr.v.* **-loaded, -loading, -loads.** *Chiefly U.S. Informal.* To act as a freeloader; sponge.

free·load·er (frée-lōdər, -lŏdər) *n. Chiefly U.S. Informal.* One who takes advantage of the generosity, or hospitality of others; a sponger.

free love *n.* The practice of sexual relations without marriage and without formal or legal obligations.

free·man (fréemən) *n., pl.* **-men** (-mən, -men). 1. A person not in slavery or serfdom. 2. a. One who possesses the rights or privileges of a citizen. b. One who has been awarded privileged rights of citizenship as an honour: *He was made a freeman of the City of London.*

free·mar·tin (frée-maartin) *n.* A sterile or otherwise sexually deficient female calf born as the twin of a bull calf. [17th century : origin obscure.]

free·ma·son (frée-may-sən) *n.* 1. A member of a guild of skilled, itinerant masons of the Middle Ages. 2. *Capital* F. A member of the Free and Accepted Masons, an international secret society. In this sense, also called "Mason". [Originally, perhaps a mason not subject to guild control and so free to work anywhere.]

free·ma·son·ry (frée-may-sənri) *n.* 1. Tacit fellowship and sympathy among a number of people. 2. *Capital* F. a. The institutions, precepts, and rites of the Freemasons. b. The Freemasons. In this sense, also called "Masonry".

free on board *adj. Abbr.* **f.o.b., F.O.B.** 1. In international commerce, designating goods delivered and insured at the seller's expense until arriving at the port of shipment named by the buyer. 2. Delivered on board or into a carrier without charge.

free port *n.* 1. A port open on equal terms to all commercial vessels. 2. An area in which imported goods can be held or processed before re-export, free of customs duties.

fre·er¹ (frée-ər) *n.* One who frees.

freer². Comparative of **free.**

free radical *n.* An atom or group of atoms containing at least one unpaired electron and having a short lifetime before reacting to form a stable molecule.

free-range (frée-ráynj) *adj. Chiefly British.* 1. Designating hens and other poultry that are kept in farmyards and fields rather than batteries. 2. Designating eggs laid by such poultry.

free-sheet (frée-sheet) *n.* A newspaper financed solely by advertising and given away or distributed without charge.

free·si·a (frée-zi-ə, -zhi-ə, -zhə) *n.* Any of several widely cultivated plants of the genus *Freesia,* native to southern Africa, having one-sided clusters of fragrant, variously coloured flowers. [New Latin, after Friedrich H.T. *Freese* (died 1876), German physician.]

free silver *n.* The free coinage of silver, especially at a fixed ratio to gold.

free speech *n.* The right to express any opinion in public.

free-spo·ken (frée-spŏkən) *adj.* Candid in expression; outspoken; frank. **—free·spo·ken·ness** *n.*

fre·est. Superlative of **free.**

free·stand·ing (frée-stánding) *adj.* Standing independently; free of support or attachment.

Free State¹ *n.* A U.S. state prohibiting slavery, prior to the American Civil War. 2. The Irish Free State.

Free State² *n.* A province of South Africa, formerly Orange Free State, lying on the plateau of the Highveld. The economy is chiefly agricultural. Mineral resources include gold, uranium, and coal. Boer farmers settled in the territory from the 1820s but it was annexed by Britain as the Orange River Sovereignty (1848). After conflicts with the Boers, Britain granted the territory independence as the Orange Free State (1854). The British again annexed the Free State as the Orange River Colony (1900), but it was granted self-government (1907) and became a founding province in the Union of South Africa (1910). Area, 129 152 square kilometres (49,866 square miles). Capital, Bloemfontein.

free·stone (frée-stōn) *n.* 1. A stone, such as some sandstones or limestones, fine-grained and even-textured enough to be cut easily in any direction without shattering or splitting. 2. A fruit, especially a peach, having a stone that does not adhere to the pulp. In this sense, compare **clingstone.** ~*adj.* Having a stone that does not adhere to the pulp.

free-style (frée-stīl) *n.* 1. In swimming, a race in which any stroke may be used. The **crawl** *(see)* is usually chosen because of the speed achieved with this stroke. 2. In various sports, a contest or style of performing in which any movements are allowed. Used adjectively: *freestyle wrestling.* **—free-style** *adj. & adv.*

free-swim·ming (frée-swímming) *adj. Zoology.* Able to swim freely; not sessile or attached: *the free-swimming larva of the oyster.* **—free-swim·mer** *n.*

free-think·er (frée-thíngkər) *n.* One who has rejected authority and dogma, especially in his religious thinking, in favour of rational inquiry and speculation. **—free·think·ing** *adj. & n.*

free thought *n.* Freethinking; unorthodox thought.

free trade *n.* Trade between nations or states without protective customs tariffs or other restrictions.

free transfer *n.* In soccer, a transfer requiring no payment to a player's current team.

free verse *n.* Verse that does not follow a conventional metrical or stanzaic pattern and has either an irregular rhyme or no rhyme. [Translation of French *vers libre.*]

free-way (frée-way) *n. U.S.* 1. A major road having several lanes and no intersections or stoplights; an expressway. 2. A major road without tolls.

free-wheel (frée-weél, -hweél) *n.* 1. A transmission device in a motor vehicle that allows the drive shaft to continue turning when its speed is greater than that of the engine shaft. 2. A device in the rear-wheel hub of a bicycle that permits the wheel to turn without pedal action. Also used adjectively: *a freewheel bicycle.* ~*intr.v.* **freewheeled, -wheeling, -wheels.** To coast in a vehicle or on a bicycle using a freewheel.

free-wheel·ing (frée-weél-ing, -hweél-) *adj.* 1. Pertaining to or equipped with a freewheel. 2. *Informal.* a. Free of restraints or rules in organisation, methods, or procedure. b. Heedless; carefree.

free will *n.* 1. The power or discretion to choose; free choice. 2. The belief that man's choices ultimately are or can be voluntary, and are not determined by external causes. Compare **determinism.** [Translation of Late Latin *liberum arbitrium.*]

free world *n. Sometimes capital* F, *capital* W. The non-Communist countries of the world. Used especially by anti-Communists.

freeze (freez) *v.* **froze** (frōz), **frozen** (frŏz'n), **freezing, freezes.** —*intr.* 1. a. To pass from the liquid to the solid state by loss of heat. b. To acquire a surface of ice from cold. Often used with *over.* 2. To become inoperative owing to frost or the formation of ice: *The pipes froze.* 3. To become hard from cold, as laundry or the ground. 4. To undergo freezing and thawing successfully: *raspberries don't freeze well.* 5. a. To be at that degree of temperature at which ice forms. Used impersonally: *It may freeze tonight.* b. To be uncomfortably cold. Used impersonally: *It's freezing in here.* 6. To be harmed, ruined, or killed by cold or frost: *The crops froze.* 7. To feel the cold acutely: *I'm freezing.* 8. To become fixed, stuck, or attached by or as if by frost: *The bolt had frozen in place.* 9. To become motionless, as from fear, horror, or shyness. 10. To become icily silent in manner. Often used with *up: She froze up at the rebuke.* —*tr.* 1. a. To convert into ice. b. To cause ice to form upon. c. To cause to become solid, congeal, or stiffen from extreme cold. 2. To preserve by subjecting to freezing temperatures. 3. To damage, kill, or make inoperative by cold or by the formation of ice. 4. a. To make very cold; chill. b. To chill with an icy or formal manner. 5. To make rigid and inflexible. 6. To fix (prices or wages) at a given or current level. 7. To prohibit further manufacture or use of. 8. To prevent or restrict the exchange, liquidation, or granting of by law: *The banks have agreed to freeze investment loans.* 9. a. *Surgery.* To anaesthetise by freezing. b. Loosely, to apply a local anaesthetic to. 10. a. To stop (a moving film) at a particular frame. b. To repeat a frame (in a moving film) to give the impression of arrested movement. 11. To stop (a process or action) at a particular point in development. **—freeze in (one's) tracks.** To stop short and remain motionless, as with fear. **—freeze out.** *Informal.* To shut out or bar, as from a business or a social group, by boycotting, snubbing, or cold treatment. ~*n.* 1. a. An act of freezing. b. The state of being frozen. 2. A spell of cold weather; a frost. [Freeze, froze, frozen; Middle English *fresen, frose, frosen,* variant (influenced by present tense) of *froren,* Old English *frēosan, frēas, froren,* from Germanic.]

freeze-dry (frée-drī) *tr.v.* **-dried, -drying, -dries.** To preserve by freeze-drying.

freeze-dry·ing (frée-drī-ing) *n.* Preservation, as of foodstuffs or histological specimens, by rapid freezing and drying in a vacuum.

freeze-etch·ing (frée-eching) *n.* A method of preparing a specimen for examination under an electron microscope whereby the specimen is frozen and then fractured with a knife so that a shadowed replica of the surface can be made.

freeze-frame *n.* The capacity in film projection systems to stop a moving film at a particular frame. Also used adjectively: *freeze-frame capacity.*

freez·er (fréezər) *n.* 1. One that freezes. 2. A thermally insulated cabinet, compartment, or room that maintains a subfreezing temperature for the rapid freezing and storing of perishable food. Also called "deep freeze".

freeze-up (fréez-up) *n. Informal.* 1. A period of intensely cold weather. 2. *U.S.* The freezing over of lakes and rivers.

freez·ing (fréezing) *adj.* Extremely cold. ~*adv.* Used as an intensive: *freezing cold.*

freezing mixture *n.* A mixture of two substances, usually ice and salt, that gives a temperature of less than 0°C.

freezing point *n. Abbr.* **fp** 1. The temperature at which a liquid solidifies. 2. The temperature at which the liquid and solid phases of a substance are in equilibrium at atmospheric pressure.

free zone *n.* An area at a port or city where goods may be received and held without the payment of duty.

F region *n.* A region of the ionosphere, the **F layer** *(see).*

Freiburg. See **Fribourg.**

freight (frayt) *n. Abbr.* **frt.** 1. a. Goods carried by a vessel or aircraft; lading. b. Goods transported as cargo by a commercial carrier, as distinguished from luggage and mail. 2. A charge or burden.

3. The commercial transportation of goods. **4.** The charge for transporting goods by cargo carrier. **5.** *Chiefly British.* The cargo of a ship or aeroplane.

~*tr.v.* **freighted, freighting, freights. 1.** To convey commercially as cargo. **2.** To load (a ship or aeroplane) with goods to be transported. [Middle English *fraught, freight,* from Middle Dutch *vrecht, vracht,* cargo, fee for a transport vessel.]

freight·age (fráytij) *n.* **1.** The commercial transportation of goods. **2.** The charge for such transportation. **3.** Cargo.

freight·er (fráytər) *n.* **1.** A ship or aircraft for carrying freight. **2.** A shipper of cargo.

freight-liner (fráyt-līnər) *n.* A goods train made up of wagons designed to carry containers that can be transferred to road vehicles or ships.

freight train *n. U.S.* A **goods train** (see).

Fre·man·tle (frée-mant'l). Chief port of Western Australia, now part of the city of Perth. One of the oldest European settlements in Australia, it was named after the British naval officer, Sir Charles Fremantle.

frem·i·tus (frémmitəss) *n., pl.* **fremitus.** *Pathology.* A palpable vibration, as felt by the hand placed on the chest during coughing or speaking. [Latin, noise, roar, from the past participle of *fremere,* to roar.]

French (french) *adj. Abbr.* **F., Fr.** Of, pertaining to, or characteristic of France or its people, language, or culture.

~*n. Abbr.* **F., Fr. 1.** The Romance language spoken by the people of France, western Switzerland, and southern Belgium, and in various former French possessions. **2.** *Used with a plural verb.* The people of France. Preceded by *the.* **3. French vermouth** (see). **4.** *Informal.* Bad or obscene language. Used euphemistically and humorously, especially in the phrase *pardon my French.* [Middle English *french,* Old English *frencisc,* FRANKISH.]

French, John Denton Pinkstone, 1st Earl of Ypres (1852–1925). British Field Marshal. He led the British Expeditionary Force to Europe at the outbreak of World War 1, but following its near annihilation in the first two battles of Ypres he resigned his command (1915).

French and Indian War *n.* A war (1754–63) fought in North America between England and France, who had the support of Indian allies.

French bean *n.* **1.** A dwarf or climbing leguminous plant, *Phaseolus vulgaris,* bearing white or lilac flowers, and cultivated for its slender, edible pods and the beans they contain. **2.** The pod or bean of this plant. Also called "dwarf bean", "haricot", "kidney bean", or *U.S.* "string bean".

French bread *n.* Bread made with water, flour, and yeast and baked in long, crusty loaves.

French bulldog *n.* A small compact dog of a breed developed in France from toy English bulldogs and native breeds.

French Canada *n.* **1.** The region of Canada dominated by French Canadians; especially Quebec. **2.** French Canadians collectively.

French Canadian *n.* **1.** A Canadian of French descent. **2.** The French language as spoken in Canada. —**French-Ca·na·di·an** (frénch-kə-náydi-ən) *adj.*

French chalk *n.* Chalk made of a soft, white variety of talc, used by tailors for marking fabrics, and by dry cleaners for removing grease.

French Community *n.* Association of France and its territories and some former colonies, established in 1958 by the constitution of the Fifth Republic to replace the French Union. It is made up of the French Republic, comprising metropolitan France (mainland France and Corsica) and the overseas départements and territories, and several independent African republics. It is a loose association, designed to promote members' cooperation in military, economic and cultural affairs.

French Congo. See **Congo, Republic of the.**

French cricket *n.* A children's game played with a tennis ball and a tennis or cricket bat, using the batsman's legs as the wicket.

French cuff *n.* A wide cuff that is folded back to make a double cuff and fastened with a cufflink.

French curve *n.* A flat instrument with curved edges and scroll-shaped cutouts, used by draughtsmen for drawing irregular curves and as a guide in connecting a set of individual points with a smooth curve.

French dressing *n.* A seasoned oil-and-vinegar salad dressing.

French Equatorial Africa. Former French territory in west central Africa, known before 1910 as the French Congo. It consisted of: Gabon, Middle Congo (now the People's Republic of Congo), Chad, and Ubangi-Shari (now the Central African Republic); its capital was Brazzaville. When each constituent voted to become independent in 1958, the territory broke up and in 1960 the four new republics became members of the French Community.

French fries *pl.n. Chiefly U.S.* Potato **chips** (see).

French Guiana. French overseas département, on the Atlantic coast of northeast South America. It became a permanent French colony in 1817 and in 1946 was given the status of an overseas département. Devil's Island, just off the coast, was formerly the site of a penal colony. The capital is Cayenne. See map at **Guyana.**

French Guinea. See **Guinea.**

French heel *n.* A curved moderately high heel on a woman's shoe.

French horn *n.* A valved brass wind instrument with a circular shape, tapering from a narrow mouthpiece to a flaring bell at the other end, and producing a mellow tone.

french·i·fy (frénchi-fī) *v.* **-fied, -fying, -fies.** —*tr.* To give a French

character or quality to. —*intr.* To assume French ways or characteristics. Often used derogatorily in both senses.

French India. A former Overseas Territory of France in India, including the settlements of Chandernagore, Pondicherry (the capital), and Yanaon on the east coast, and Mahé on the west, with a combined area of 500 square kilometres (193 square miles). The territory was returned to India (1949–54).

French Indochina. *French* **In·do·chine** (aṅdō-sheén). Part of Southeast Asia formerly controlled by France, mostly until 1954. Set up in 1887, it included Cochin China, Annam and Tonkin (which now make up Vietnam), and Cambodia (now Kampuchea). Laos was added in 1893.

French kiss *n.* A kiss given with the tongue inserted into the partner's mouth. —**French-kiss** *v.*

French knickers *pl.n.* Wide-legged women's underpants.

French knitting *n.* A technique of braiding yarn round pins attached to the top of a cotton reel. The finished work is pulled through the centre of the reel as a knitted tube, which is then rolled up and sewn into mats.

French knot *n.* A decorative stitch made by looping the thread two or more times around the needle which is then inserted into the fabric.

French leave *n.* An unauthorised or unannounced departure or absence. [From an 18th-century French custom of leaving without bidding good-bye to the host or hostess.]

French letter *n. Chiefly British Informal.* A contraceptive **sheath** (see).

French·man (frénch-mən) *n., pl.* **-men** (-mən). **1.** A native or citizen of France. **2.** A French ship. **3.** A tool used by bricklayers for cutting off excess mortar when repointing.

French marigold *n.* A widely cultivated plant, *Tagetes patula,* native to Mexico, having divided leaves and yellow flowers with reddish markings.

French Morocco. A former French protectorate established over most of the area of present-day Morocco in 1912, and now part of the Kingdom of Morocco.

French navy *n.* Lightish navy blue.

French North Africa. A term formerly used to designate Algeria, French Morocco, and Tunisia collectively.

French pastry *n.* Any of a wide variety of rich and elaborate pastries prepared in individual portions.

French pleat *n.* A type of women's hairstyle with the hair pulled back from the face and worn in a cylindrical roll at the back of the head. Also called "French roll".

French polish *n.* **1.** A wood varnish consisting of a solution of shellac dissolved in methanol. **2.** The finish produced on a piece of furniture by this varnish.

French-pol·ish (frénch-póllish) *tr.v.* **-polished, -polishing, -polishes.** To apply French polish to (a surface).

French Polynesia. French overseas territory consisting of about 130 tropical islands strewn over some 4 million square kilometres (1.5 million square miles) of the east Pacific Ocean. The capital, Papeete, is on Tahiti. The island groups became a French colony in 1880 and in 1958 opted to become an overseas territory within the French Community. Tourism and copra export are the mainstays of the economy. See map at **Pacific Ocean.**

French Revolution *n.* A revolt in France against the monarchy and aristocracy lasting from 1789 to 1799, when Napoleon gained control.

French roof *n. Architecture.* A curb roof resembling the mansard and having nearly perpendicular slopes.

French seam *n.* A seam stitched first on the right side and then turned in and stitched on the wrong side so that the raw edges are enclosed in the seam.

French skipping *n.* A children's game played by leaping in various ways over an elastic loop stretched taut, usually around the legs, between two other people.

French Somaliland. See **Djibouti, Republic of.**

French Southern and Antarctic Territories. *French* **Terres Australes et Antarctiques Françaises.** Overseas territory of France comprising Adélie Land (Terre Adélie) in Antarctica and several islands south of 38° S. The islands are the Kerguelen and Crozet groups, and Amsterdam (formerly Nouvelle Amsterdam) and Saint-Paul Islands. The only population of the territory, administered from Paris, is the staff of the hospital and office on Amsterdam, and scientific and meteorological research workers scattered over the territory.

French stick *n.* A long, thin, almost cylindrical loaf, tapered at each end. Also called "French loaf".

French Sudan. See **Mali, Republic of.**

French toast *n.* **1.** Bread toasted on one side only, and usually buttered on the uncooked side. **2.** Sliced bread soaked in a milk and egg batter and lightly fried.

French Togoland. A former United Nations Trust Territory in western Africa, administered by France (1946–60). See **Togo, Republic of.**

French vermouth *n.* A dry, white, wine-based beverage flavoured with herbs and spices. Also called "French".

French West Africa. *French* **Afrique Occidentale Française.** Former federation of French colonies in Africa. Established in 1895, it included Senegal, French Guinea, the Ivory Coast, and French Sudan (Mali), and was administered as one colony from Dakar. Later Dahomey, Upper Senegal-Niger, Mauritania, and Upper Volta were incorporated. The federation was dissolved in 1958 and the territories, with the exception of French Guinea, became independent republics within the French Community.

French West Indies. Unofficially, the French Overseas Départements of Guadeloupe and Martinique, in the Caribbean.

French window *n.* A door with one large or several small glass panes, or a casement window extending to floor level, often hung in pairs and giving access to a garden or balcony.

French·wo·man (frénch-wŏŏmən) *n., pl.* **-women** (-wimmin). A woman who is a native or citizen of France.

French·y (frénchi) *adj.* **-ier, -iest.** *Informal.* Displaying French characteristics.
~*n., pl.* **Frenchies.** *Slang.* A French person.

fre·net·ic (frə-néttik) *adj.* Frantic; frenzied. [Middle English *frenetik,* frenzied, insane, from Old French *frenetique,* from Latin *phrenēticus,* from Greek *phrenitikos,* from *phrenitis,* brain disease, insanity, from *phrēn,* mind.] —**fre·net·i·cal·ly** *adv.*

fren·u·lum, fraen·u·lum (frénnew-ləm) *n., pl.* **-la** (-lə). 1. A bristly structure on the hind wing of certain moths and other insects that holds the forewing and hind wing together during flight. 2. A small fraenum *(see).* [New Latin, diminutive of FRAENUM.]

frenum. *U.S.* Variant of **fraenum.**

fren·zied (frénzid) *adj.* Characterized by, affected with, or filled with frenzy; frantic. —**fren·zied·ly** *adv.*

fren·zy (frénzi) *n., pl.* **-zies.** 1. A seizure of violent agitation or wild excitement, often accompanied by manic activity. 2. Temporary madness or delirium. 3. An extravagant idea; a mania; a craze. Used with *for: "man had a frenzy for getting away from any control"* (D.H. Lawrence).
~*tr.v.* **frenzied, -zying, -zies.** To drive into a frenzy. [Middle English *frenesie,* from Old French, from Medieval Latin *phrenēsia,* from Latin *phrenēsis,* from *phrēn,* mind, from Greek.]

Fre·on (frée-on) *n.* A trademark for any of various nonflammable gaseous or liquid fluorocarbons that are used mainly as working fluids in refrigeration and air conditioning and as aerosol propellants. Also called, generically, "chlorofluorocarbon", "CFC".

fre·quen·cy (frée·kwən-si) *n., pl.* **-cies.** 1. *Mathematics & Physics.* The number of times a specified phenomenon occurs within a specified interval, as: **a.** The number of repetitions of a complete sequence of values of a periodic function per unit variation of an independent variable. **b.** The number of complete cycles of a periodic process occurring per unit time. **c.** The number of repetitions per unit time of a complete waveform, as of an electric current. 2. *Statistics.* **a.** The number of measurements in an interval of a frequency distribution. **b.** The ratio of the number of times an event occurs in a series of trials of a chance experiment to the number of trials of the experiment performed. In this sense, also called "relative frequency". 3. The property or condition of occurring repeatedly at short intervals. 4. The number of times that something regularly recurs. [Latin *frequentia,* crowd, from *frequēns,* FREQUENT.]

frequency band *n.* A band of frequencies. See **band.**

frequency curve *n. Statistics.* A graphical representation of a frequency distribution obtained by plotting the variable property along the x-axis divided into intervals and the numbers of members along the y-axis. If there is a finite number of intervals of significant size and if the points are joined by straight lines, the resulting diagram is a **frequency polygon.**

frequency distribution *n. Statistics.* The way in which some property is distributed amongst members of a set, according to the numbers of members having particular values of the property. It is obtained by dividing the variable (property) into intervals and specifying the number of members of the set having a value of the property lying within each interval.

frequency modulation *n. Abbr.* **FM, fm** *Electronics.* The encoding of a carrier wave by variation of its frequency in accordance with an input signal. Compare **amplitude modulation.**

frequency polygon *n.* A graphic representation of a frequency distribution consisting of a set of points each obtained by plotting class frequency as ordinate and class mark as abscissa, together with line segments joining points of adjacent classes.

fre·quent (frée·kwənt) *adj.* Occurring or appearing quite often or at close intervals.
~*tr.v.* (fri-kwént ‖ frée·kwənt) **frequented, -quenting, -quents.** To pay frequent visits to; be often in, at, or in the company of. [Middle English, profuse, ample, from Old French, from Latin *frequēns* (stem *frequent-*), full, frequent.] —**fre·quent·er** *n.* —**fre·quent·ness** *n.*

fre·quen·ta·tion (frée-kwen-táysh'n, -kwən-) *n.* 1. The act or practice of frequenting a place. 2. A place or person frequented.

fre·quen·ta·tive (fri-kwéntə-tiv, free-) *adj. Abbr.* **freq.** *Grammar.* Expressing or denoting repeated action.
~*n. Abbr.* **freq.** A frequentative verb, such as *flicker* or *wobble.*

fre·quent·ly (frée·kwəntli) *adv. Abbr.* **fr., freq.** At frequent intervals; often.

fres·co (fréskō) *n., pl.* **-coes** or **-cos.** 1. The art of painting by applying pure pigments dissolved in water onto fresh lime plaster. 2. A painting executed on plaster.
~*tr.v.* **frescoed, -coing, -coes.** To paint on fresh plaster. [Italian, from phrases such as *(in) fresco,* (on the) fresh (plaster), from West Germanic *friskaz* (unattested), FRESH.] —**fres·co·er, fres·co·ist** *n.*

fresh (fresh) *adj.* **fresher, freshest.** 1. New to one's experience; not encountered before. 2. Novel; different; original: *a fresh slant.*

3. Recently made, produced, or harvested; not stale, spoilt, or withered: *fresh bread.* 4. Not preserved, as by canning, smoking, drying, or freezing: *fresh vegetables.* 5. Not saline or salty: *fresh water.* 6. Not yet used or soiled; clean: *a fresh sheet of paper.* 7. Additional; new: *a fresh start.* 8. Bright and clear; not dull or faded: *a fresh colour; a fresh memory.* 9. Having the glowing, unspoiled appearance of youth or health. 10. Untried; inexperienced: *fresh recruits.* 11. Having just arrived; straight: *fresh from Paris.* 12. **a.** Revived or reinvigorated; refreshed. **b.** Charged with energy; frisky. 13. Revivifying; cool and invigorating: *fresh morning air.* 14. Fairly strong; brisk: *a fresh wind.* 15. *Chiefly U.S.* Having recently calved and therefore with milk. Said of a cow. 16. *Informal.* Bold and forward, especially sexually. Said of a man. —**get fresh with.** To importune sexually.
~*adv.* Recently; newly. Usually used in combination: *fresh-baked bread.* —**fresh out.** *Chiefly U.S. Informal.* Having just run out: *fresh out of sugar.*
~*n.* 1. The early and fresh part: *the fresh of the day.* 2. A freshet. [Middle English, from Old French *freis* (feminine *fresche*), from West Germanic *friskaz* (unattested).] —**fresh·ly** *adv.* —**fresh·ness** *n.*

fresh breeze *n.* A wind whose speed is 8 to 10.7 metres per second, force 5 on the Beaufort scale.

fresh·en (frésh'n) *v.* **-ened, -ening, -ens.** —*intr.* 1. To become fresh. Often used with *up.* 2. To make oneself clean and fresh. Used with *up: freshen up after a day's work.* 3. To become brisk; increase in strength. Used of a wind. 4. To lose saltiness. Used of water. 5. *Chiefly U.S.* To calve and therefore produce milk. —*tr.* To impart a fresh quality to; make fresh. —**fresh·en·er** *n.*

fresh·er (fréshər) *n. Chiefly British.* A first-year student at a university. Also *chiefly U.S.* "freshman".

fresh·et (fréshit) *n.* 1. A sudden surge of water down a small stream resulting from a heavy rainstorm or a thaw. 2. A stream of fresh water that empties into a body of salt water. [FRESH + -ET.]

fresh·wa·ter (frésh-wawtər ‖ *U.S. also* -wottər) *adj.* 1. Pertaining to, living in, or consisting of fresh water. 2. Unaccustomed to the seas: *a freshwater sailor.*

fres·nel (fráyn'l) *n.* A unit of frequency equal to 10^{12} hertz. [After A.J. *Fresnel* (1788–1827), French physicist.]

Fresnel lens *n.* An optical lens made up of a number of smaller lenses, arranged to give a short focal length. [After A.J. *Fresnel* (see **fresnel**).]

fret¹ (fret) *v.* **fretted, fretting, frets.** —*tr.* 1. To cause to be uneasy; distress; vex. 2. **a.** To gnaw or wear away. **b.** To produce a hole or worn spot in; chafe; corrode. 3. To form (a passage or channel) by erosion. 4. To disturb the surface of (water or a stream); agitate. —*intr.* 1. To be vexed or troubled; worry. 2. To be worn or eaten away; become corroded. 3. To move agitatedly; be ruffled.
~*n.* 1. An act or instance of fretting. 2. A hole, worn spot, or path made by abrasion or erosion. 3. A state of irritation, annoyance, or worry. [Middle English *freten,* to devour, irritate, Old English *fretan,* from Germanic *fra-* (unattested), FOR- + *etan* (unattested), EAT.]

fret² *n.* Any of several guide ridges, usually of metal, set across the fingerboard of a guitar or other stringed instrument.
~*tr.v.* **fretted, fretting, frets.** To provide with frets. [15th century : origin obscure.]

fret³ *n.* 1. An ornamental design contained within a band or border, consisting of repeated, symmetrical, and often geometrical figures. 2. Such an ornamental design made in relief, often with numerous small openings.
~*tr.v.* **fretted, fretting, frets.** To provide with a fret or frets. [Middle English, from Old French *frete†,* trellis, embossed work.]

fret·ful (frétf'l) *adj.* Inclined to fret; peevish; plaintive. —**fret·ful·ly** *adv.* —**fret·ful·ness** *n.*

fret saw *n.* A narrow-bladed saw having fine teeth, used in producing ornamental work in thin wood or metal.

fret·work (frét-wurk) *n.* 1. Ornamental work consisting of three-dimensional frets; geometric openwork. 2. Such ornamental work represented graphically in monochrome or contrasting colours.

Freud (froyd; *German* froyt), **Sigmund** (1856–1939). Austrian psychiatrist. After long experience of working with hysterical and neurologically disturbed patients, he developed the theory of psychoanalysis. When first publicised in the 1880s, his ideas attracted hostility, but by 1910 they had gained general recognition, and works such as *The Interpretation of Dreams* (1900) and *The Ego and the Id* (1923) have had a profound influence on 20th-century thought. He fled to London (1938) to escape Nazi persecution.

Freu·di·an (fróydi-ən) *adj.* 1. Pertaining to or in accordance with the psychoanalytic theories of Sigmund Freud. 2. *Informal.* Psychologically telling or revealing.
~*n.* 1. One who actively applies the psychoanalytic methods or theories of Freud in conducting psychotherapy. 2. One who studies or applies the psychoanalytic theories of Freud for interpretation or explanation, as in historical or literary criticism.

Freudian slip *n.* A slip of the tongue or pen, or some other unintentional act, that seems to reveal an individual's real state of mind or character.

Frey (fray). Also **Freyr** (fráy-ər). *Norse Mythology.* The god who dispenses peace, good weather, prosperity, and bountiful crops.

Frey·a, Frey·ja (fráy-ə). *Norse Mythology.* The sister of Frey and the goddess of love and beauty.

F.R.G.S. Fellow of the Royal Geographical Society.

Fri. Friday.

fri·a·ble (frí-əb'l) *adj.* Readily crumbled. [French, from Latin *friābilis,* crumbling, from *friāre,* to crumble.] —**fri·a·bil·i·ty** (-ə-bíllət i), **fri·a·ble·ness** *n.*

fri·ar (frí-ər) *n. Abbr.* **Fr.** A member of a Roman Catholic order, such as the Dominicans or Franciscans, which was originally mendicant. [Middle English *frere,* from Old French, from Latin *frāter* (stem *frātr-*), brother.]

fri·ar·bird (frí-ər-burd) *n.* Any of various birds of the genus *Philemon,* of Australia and adjacent regions, having a partly naked head. Also called "leatherhead". [From its bare head, likened to a friar's tonsure.]

friar's balsam *n.* A preparation containing benzoin which, when mixed with hot water, is used as an inhalant to relieve colds and sore throats.

fri·ar·y (frí-əri) *n., pl.* **-ies.** A monastery of friars.

frib·ble (fríbb'l) *v.* **-bled, -bling, -bles.** —*tr.* To waste (time, for example). —*intr.* To waste time; trifle. ~*n.* **1.** A frivolity; a trifle. **2.** A frivolous person. [17th century (imitative).] —**frib·bler** *n.*

Fri·bourg (free-bóor). *German* **Frei·burg** (frí-boork). Mainly French-speaking, Roman Catholic canton of northern Switzerland. It occupies the west of the Swiss plateau, and is a rich agricultural region noted for its cheeses, including Gruyère.

fric·an·deau (fríckən-dō) *n., pl.* **-deaux** (-dōz). A cut of veal, usually rump or shoulder, that has been larded and braised or roasted with vegetables. [French, from *fricasser,* to FRICASSEE.]

fric·as·see (fríckə-sée, -see, -say) *n.* Poultry or meat cut into pieces, stewed, and served usually with a white sauce. ~*tr.v.* **fricasseed, -seeing, -sees.** To prepare as a fricassee. [French *fricassée,* from the past participle of *fricasser†,* to fry.]

fric·a·tive (fríckə-tiv) *adj. Phonetics.* Produced by the forcing of breath through a constricted passage, as are such consonantal sounds as (f) and (v), (s) and (z), (sh) and (zh), (th) and (th). ~*n. Phonetics.* A fricative consonant. Also called "spirant". [Latin *fricāre,* to rub.]

fric·tion (fríksh'n) *n.* **1.** The rubbing of one object or surface against another. **2.** Conflict, as of dissimilar ideas, persons, or interests obliged to coexist; clashing. **3.** *Physics.* A force tangential to the common boundary of two bodies in contact that resists the motion or tendency to motion of one relative to the other. **4.** A massage of the body or scalp for therapeutic purposes. [French, from Latin *frictiō* (stem *frictiōn-*), from *frictus,* past participle of *fricāre,* to rub.] —**fric·tion·al** *adj.* —**fric·tion·al·ly** *adv.*

friction clutch *n.* A clutch in which axial pressure with resultant friction between the clutch faces, rather than the interlocking of mated parts, transmits torque.

friction drive *n.* A transmission system in which motion is transmitted from one part to another by the surface friction of rolling contact rather than by toothed gears.

friction match *n.* A match that ignites when struck on an abrasive surface.

fridge (frij) *n. Informal.* A refrigerator.

Frídtjof Nansen Land. See **Franz Josef Land.**

Frie·dan (fri-dán), **Betty,** born Elizabeth Naomi Goldstein (1921–). U.S. feminist. She wrote *The Feminine Mystique* (1963), about the role of women in U.S. society. She went on to found the National Organization for Women (1966), of which she became first president, and led the U.S. Women's Strike for Equality (1970).

Fried·man (fréedmən), **Milton** (1912–). U.S. economist. He set out his philosophy of monetary control and government non-intervention in *Capitalism and Freedom* (1962). Several Western governments pursued his policies after the stagnation and inflation of the mid-1970s. Economics Nobel prize (1976)

Frie·drich (fréedrikh), **Caspar David** (1774–1840). German painter. His mysterious, frequently moonlit landscapes are characteristic of the Romantic movement. His later works symbolise man's insignificance in relation to the elements, as in *Wreck of the "Hope"* (1822).

friend (frend) *n.* **1.** A person whom one knows, likes, and trusts. **2.** Any associate or acquaintance. Often used as a form of address: *my honourable friend.* **3.** A favoured companion: *man's best friend is his dog.* **4.** One with whom one is allied in a struggle or cause; a comrade. **5.** One who supports, sympathises with, or patronises a group, cause, or movement. **6.** *Capital* **F.** A member of the Society of Friends; a Quaker. Also used by Quakers as a term of address. —**be friends with.** To be a friend of. —**make friends with.** To enter into friendship with. ~*tr.v.* **friended, friending, friends.** *Archaic.* To befriend. [Middle English *frend,* Old English *frēond,* from Germanic.]

friend at court *n.* An influential person whom one knows and who will be able to advance one's interests.

friend·less (frénd-ləss, -liss) *adj.* Without friends.

friend·ly (fréndli) *adj.* **-lier, -liest. 1.** Of, pertaining to, or befitting a friend. **2.** Favourably disposed; not antagonistic. **3.** Warm; welcoming. **4.** On terms of friendship. ~*adv.* Also **friend·li·ly** (frénd-li-li, -lə-). In the manner of a friend; amicably. ~*n., pl.* **friendlies.** *Sports.* A match played purely for its own sake or for fun, and not in a competition or for a league placing. Also called "friendly match". —**friend·li·ness** *n.*

-friendly *adj. comb. form.* Indicates: not antagonistic to; not causing problems for; for example, **ozone-friendly.** [Possibly from

German *-freundlich,* -friendly. See **user-friendly.**]

Friendly Islands. See **Tonga.**

friendly society *n.* An association that guarantees its members financial aid in times of need, as in sickness or old age, by the collection of dues or other regular payments. Also called "provident society", *U.S.* "benefit society".

friend·ship (frénd-ship, frén-) *n.* **1.** The condition or relation of being friends. **2.** Friendly feeling towards another; friendliness.

frier. Variant of **fryer.**

Friesian¹ (fréezh'n, fréezi-ən) *n.* A large black and white breed of dairy cow. Also *U.S.* "Holstein", "Holstein-Friesian".

Friesian². Variant of **Frisian.**

Fries·land (fréezlənd). *Dutch* **Vries·land.** Province in the northern Netherlands. It includes the West Frisian Islands and land reclaimed from the Ijsselmeer. The district is chiefly a beef-producing and dairying area, and the Friesian breed of cow that originated there is highly prized worldwide.

frieze¹ (freez) *n. Architecture.* **1.** A plain or decorated horizontal part of an entablature between the architrave and cornice. **2.** Any decorative horizontal band, as along the upper part of a wall in a room. [French *frise,* from Old French, from Medieval Latin *frisium, frigium,* fringe, embroidered cloth, from Latin *Phrygium,* of Phrygia, a place noted for its embroidery.]

frieze² (freez) *n.* A coarse, woollen cloth with an uncut nap. Also called "frisé". [Middle English *frise,* from Old French, from Middle Dutch *vriese,* perhaps from *Vriese,* from Latin *Frīsiī,* FRISIAN.]

frig·ate (frig-it, -ət) *n.* **1.** A high-speed, medium-sized sailing war vessel of the 17th, 18th, and 19th centuries. **2.** A British warship intermediate between a corvette and a destroyer. **3.** A U.S. warship intermediate between a cruiser and a destroyer. **4.** *Archaic.* Any fast, light vessel. [French *frégate,* from Italian *fregata†.*]

frigate bird *n.* Any of various large, tropical sea birds of the genus *Fregata,* which characteristically snatch food from other birds in flight. Also called "man-o'-war bird".

Frigg (frig). Also **Frig·ga** (fríggə). *Norse Mythology.* The consort of Odin and goddess of married love and the hearth. [Old Norse, from Germanic *frijaz* (unattested), noble, FREE.]

frig·ging (frígging) *adj. or adv. Vulgar Slang.* Used as an intensive. [From *frig,* to masturbate, copulate (originally, "to rub").]

fright (frīt) *n.* **1.** Sudden, intense fear, as of something immediately threatening; alarm. **2.** *Informal.* Something extremely unsightly, alarming, or strange. —**take fright.** To become frightened. —See Synonyms at **fear.** ~*tr.v.* **frighted, frighting, frights.** *Archaic.* To frighten. [Middle English *fright,* Old English *fryhto, fyrhto,* from Germanic *furht-* (unattested), afraid.]

fright·en (frít'n) *tr.v.* **-ened, -ening, -ens. 1.** To make suddenly afraid; alarm or startle. **2.** To drive or force by arousing fear. Used with *away, into, off,* or *out: He was frightened into confessing.* [From FRIGHT.] —**fright·en·er** *n.*

Synonyms: frighten, scare, alarm, terrify, terrorise, panic.

frightened (frít'nd) *adj.* **1.** Afraid. Often used with of. **2.** Timid.

fright·en·ing (frít'n-ing) *adj.* Causing fright or sudden alarm. —**fright·en·ing·ly** *adv.*

fright·ful (frítf'l) *adj.* **1.** Causing disgust or shock; horrifying. **2.** Causing fright; terrifying. **3.** *Informal.* **a.** Excessive; extreme: *a frightful liar.* **b.** Disagreeable; distressing: *frightful weather.* —**fright·ful·ly** *adv.* —**fright·ful·ness** *n.*

frig·id (fríjid) *adj.* **1.** Lacking warmth of feeling; stiff and formal in manner: *a frigid refusal to a request.* **2.** Disliking sexual intercourse. Usually said of women. **3.** Extremely cold. [Latin *frīgidus,* from *frīgēre,* to be cold, from *frīgus,* cold.] —**fri·gid·i·ty** (fri-jíddəti), **frig·id·ness** *n.* —**frig·id·ly** *adv.*

Frigid Zone *n.* The areas within the Arctic or Antarctic Circles.

frig·o·rif·ic (fríggə-ríffik) *adj. Archaic.* Causing coldness; chilling. [Latin *frīgorificus: frīgus* (stem *frīgor-*), FRIGID + -FIC.]

fri·jol (frée-hōl, -hól ‖ *Spanish* fri-khól) *n., pl.* **frijoles** (-hóleez, -hólz ‖ *Spanish* hólayss). Also **fri·jo·le** (-ay). A bean cultivated and used for food, especially in Mexico and in the southwestern United States. [Spanish, variant of *fresol,* from Latin *phaseolus,* diminutive of *phasēlus,* kidney bean, from Greek *phasēlos†.*]

frik·ka·del (fríckə-dél) *n. South African.* A fried patty or ball of mincemeat; a rissole. [Afrikaans, ultimately from FRICANDEAU.]

frill (fril) *n.* **1. a.** A ruffled, gathered, or pleated border or projection, such as a fabric edge used to trim clothing. **b.** A similar curled paper strip used, for example, for decorating the bone of a piece of meat. **2.** *Zoology.* A ruff of hair or feathers or a similar membranous projection about the neck of an animal or bird. **3.** *Photography.* A wrinkling of the edge of a film. **4.** *Usually plural. Informal.* Anything superfluous, pretentious, and artificial; an embellishment: *plain home-cooking with no frills; cheap, no-frills flights to the U.S.A.* ~*v.* **frilled, frilling, frills.** —*tr.* **1.** To make into a ruffle or frill. **2.** To add a ruffle or frill to. —*intr. Photography.* To become wrinkled along the edge. [16th century : origin obscure.]

frilled lizard *n.* An Australian lizard, *Chlamydosaurus kingi,* having a broad membrane extending from the neck and throat that can be extended like a ruff when the mouth is opened.

fril·ly (frílli) *adj.* **-lier, -liest. 1.** Decorated with or having a frill or frills. **2.** Similar to or suggesting a frill or frills. **3.** *Informal.* Superfluously ornamental.

fringe (frinj) *n.* **1.** A decorative border or edging of hanging threads, cords, or strips, often attached to a separate band. **2.** Hair combed

over the forehead and cut near eyebrow-level. **3.** Anything placed or growing along an edge. **4.** A marginal or peripheral part; an edge: *the fringes of the crowd.* **5.** Artistic activities that are considered to lie outside the mainstream or that are deliberately unconventional or uncommercial. Also used adjectivally: *fringe theatre.* **6.** Those members of a group or political party holding extreme views. **7.** *Optics.* Any of the light or dark bands produced by the diffraction or interference of light.
~*tr.v.* **fringed, fringing, fringes. 1.** To decorate with a fringe. **2.** To grow or occur along the edge of; border: *"deep and sullen pools fringed with tall rushes"* (H. Rider Haggard). [Middle English *frenge,* from Old French, from Vulgar Latin *frimbia* (unattested), from Late Latin *fimbria.* See fimbria.] —**fring·y** *adj.*

fringe benefit *n.* An employment benefit given in addition to one's wages or salary.

fringed orchis *n.* Any of various orchids of the genus *Habenaria,* having variously coloured flowers with a fringed lip.

frin·gil·lid (frin-jíllid) *adj.* Also **frin·gil·line** (frin-jíll-īn, -in). Of or belonging to the family Fringillidae, which includes relatively small birds, such as the finches, sparrows, and buntings.
~*n.* A member of the Fringillidae. [New Latin *Fringillidae : Fringilla* (type genus), from Latin *fringilla*†, finch + -ID.]

fringing reef *n.* A coral reef along a coast.

Frink (fringk), **Dame Elisabeth** (1930–93). British sculptor. She held her first one-woman exhibition in 1955, and afterwards won worldwide distinction for her bronze sculptures of monumental human heads, and stylised animal figures.

frip·per·y (fríppəri) *n., pl.* **-ies. 1.** Pretentious finery; excessively ornamented dress. **2.** Pretentious elegance; ostentation. **3.** Trivia.
~*adj.* Pretentious and trivial. [French *friperie,* from Old French *freperie,* from *frepe, felpe,* frill, from Medieval Latin *faluppa*†, fibre.]

Fris. Frisian.

Fris·bee (fríz-bi, -bee) *n.* A trademark for a concave disc made of light plastic that is thrown in the air with a spinning motion as a game. Also written "Frisby", "frisbee".

Frisch (frish), **Karl von** (1886–1982). Austrian zoologist. He is best known for his discovery of the "dance" of the bees, by which the location of flowers is communicated. In 1973 he shared the Nobel prize for physiology or medicine with Konrad Lorenz (1903–89) and Nikolaas Tinbergen (1907–88).

Frisch (frish), **Otto Robert** (1904–79). Austrian-born British physicist. He worked on nuclear fission in Copenhagen and at Los Alamos during World War II, and contributed to the development of the atomic bomb.

Frisch (frish), **Ragnar A.K.** (1895–1973). Norwegian economist. In 1969 he shared the first Nobel prize for economics with Jan Tinbergen (1903–94) for his contribution in econometrics.

Fris·co (frískō). A nickname for San Francisco, California.

fri·sé (frée-zay) *n.* A fabric, **frieze** (see). [French, from the past participle of *friser,* to curl, FRIZZ.]

frisette. Variant of **frizette.**

Fri·si·a (frízi-ə). Ancient country of the Frisians. In the 8th century, it included what is now northern Belgium, the Netherlands, and West Germany west of the river Weser.

Fri·sian (frízh'n) *adj.* Also **Frie·sian** (frée-zh'n). *Abbr.* **Fris., Frs.** Of the Frisian Islands, Friesland, or Frisia.
~*n.* Also **Frie·sian.** *Abbr.* **Fris., Frs. 1.** A native or inhabitant of the Frisian Islands or Friesland. **2.** The Germanic language spoken by the Frisian people.

Frisian Islands. Group of about 30 low, sandy islands in the North Sea, off northwest Europe. The West Frisians (the Wadden Islands) belong to the Netherlands, the East Frisians to Germany, and the North Frisians are divided between Germany and Denmark. There are few permanent inhabitants, although there are numerous holiday homes. See also **Friesland.**

frisk (frisk) *v.* **frisked, frisking, frisks.** —*intr.* To move about briskly and playfully, as a puppy does; gambol; frolic. —*tr.* To search (a person) for something concealed, especially weapons, by passing the hands quickly over clothes or through pockets.
~*n.* **1.** An energetic, playful movement; a gambol; a caper. **2.** An act of frisking, as for concealed weapons. [From obsolete *frisk,* lively, from Old French *frisque,* from Common Germanic *friskaz* (unattested), FRESH.] —**frisk·er** *n.*

fris·ket (frískit) *n.* A light frame with a windowed sheet of parchment that protects areas of the paper not to be printed in a hand printing press. [French *frisquette*†.]

frisk·y (fríski) *adj.* **-ier, -iest.** Energetic, lively, and playful: *"Their quiet ponies were almost frisky, sniffing and moving restlessly"* (J.R.R. Tolkien). [From obsolete *frisk,* lively. See **frisk.**] —**frisk·i·ly** *adv.* —**frisk·i·ness** *n.*

fris·son (frée-SON, fri-, -SÓN) *n.* A pleasurable shiver caused by excitement or thrilling danger. [French, shiver.]

frit (frit) *n.* **1.** The fused or partially fused materials used in making glass. **2.** A vitreous substance used in making porcelain or glazes.
~*tr.v.* **fritted, fritting, frits.** To make into frit. [Italian *fritta,* from the feminine past participle of *friggere,* to fry, from Latin *frīgere,* to FRY.]

frit fly *n.* Any of several small flies of the family Chloropidae; especially, *Oscinella frit,* having larvae that are destructive to cereal plants, particularly oats. [19th century : origin obscure.]

frith (frith) *n. Scottish.* An estuary. [Variant of FIRTH.]

frit·il·lar·y (fri-tílləri ‖ *U.S.* fritt'l-erri) *n., pl.* **-ies. 1.** Any of various bulbous plants of the genus *Fritillaria,* having nodding, variously coloured, often spotted or chequered bell-shaped flowers. In this sense, also called "snakeshead". **2.** Any of various butterflies of the family Nymphalidae having brownish wings marked with black or silvery spots. [New Latin *Fritillaria,* from Latin *fritillus*†, dice box, a reference to the chequered markings.]

frit·ter¹ (fríttər) *tr.v.* **-tered, -tering, -ters. 1.** To reduce wastefully or squander little by little. Usually used with *away: He frittered his money away on expensive cars.* **2.** *Rare.* To break, tear, or cut into bits; shred. [Probably from obsolete *fritter,* to break in pieces, perhaps related to Middle High German *vetze,* rags.]

frit·ter² *n.* A small piece of batter, often containing fruit, vegetables, meat, or fish, sautéed or fried in deep fat. [Middle English *friture,* from Old French, from Vulgar Latin *frīctūra* (unattested), from Latin *frīctus,* past participle of *frīgere* to FRY.]

Fri·u·li (free-ōōli). A historic region and former duchy of northeastern Italy, part of which now extends into Slovenia. [Latin *Forojulium,* from *Forum Julii,* "Forum of Julius", supposedly founded by Julius Caesar.]

Fri·u·li·an (free-ōōli-ən) *n.* **1.** A member of a people inhabiting Friuli in northeastern Italy. **2.** The Rhaeto-Romanic dialect spoken by these people.

triv·ol (frívv'l) *v.* **-olled** or *U.S.* **-oled, -olling** or *U.S.* **-oling, -ols.** *Informal.* —*tr.* To squander. Used with *away.* —*intr.* To behave frivolously. [Back-formation from FRIVOLOUS.] —**triv·ol·er** *n.*

fri·vol·i·ty (fri-vólləti) *n., pl.* **-ies. 1.** The condition or quality of being frivolous. **2.** A frivolous act or thing.

friv·o·lous (frívv'l-əss) *adj.* **1.** Unworthy of serious attention; insignificant; trivial. **2.** Marked by flippancy; silly. —See Synonyms at **playful.** [Middle English, from Latin *frīvolus*†.] —**friv·o·lous·ly** *adv.* —**friv·o·lous·ness** *n.*

fri·zette, fri·sette (fri-zét) *n.* A curled fringe of hair, usually worn on the forehead by a woman. [French *frisette,* "little curl", from *friser,* to curl, FRIZZ.]

frizz¹, friz (friz) *v.* **frizzed, frizzing, frizzes.** —*tr.* To form (nap or hair, for example) into small, tight curls or tufts. —*intr.* To be formed into small, tight curls or tufts.
~*n.* **1.** The condition of being frizzed. **2.** A tight curl or tight curls of hair or fabric. **3.** A hairstyle consisting of small, tight curls. [French *friser,* to curl, to shrivel up (as when fried), perhaps from *frire* (stem *fris-*), to FRY.] —**friz·zer** *n.*

frizz², friz *v.* **frizzed, frizzing, frizzes.** —*tr.* To fry or burn with a sizzling noise. —*intr.* To be fried or burnt with a sizzling noise. [Perhaps from FRIZZLE (to fry).]

friz·zle¹ (frízz'l) *v.* **-zled, -zling, -zles.** —*tr.* **1.** To fry until crisp and curled: *frizzled the bacon.* **2.** To scorch or sear with heat. —*intr.* **1.** To fry or sear with a sizzling noise. **2.** To scorch. [Perhaps blend of FRY and SIZZLE.]

frizzle² *v.* **-zled, -zling, -zles.** —*tr.* To frizz (hair). —*intr.* To form tight curls.
~*n.* A small, tight curl. [16th century : origin uncertain, earlier than FRIZZ (to form curls).]

friz·zly (frízzli) *adj.* **-zlier, -zliest.** Tightly curled.

friz·zy (frízzi) *adj.* **-zier, -ziest.** Tightly curled; frizzly. —**friz·zi·ly** *adv.* —**friz·zi·ness** *n.*

Frl. Fräulein.

fro (frō) *adv.* Away; back again. Used in the phrase *to and fro.*
~*prep. Scottish.* From. [Middle English *fra, fro,* adverb and preposition, from Old Norse *frā.*]

Fro·bish·er (frōbishər), **Sir Martin** (*c.* 1535–94). English explorer. He made three voyages to the Canadian Arctic in 1576, 1577, and 1578, seeking a northwest passage to Cathay.

Frobisher Bay or **Kimmirut** (*Inuit*). Arm of the North Atlantic Ocean, cutting deeply into Baffin Island, Canada. It is about 240 kilometres (150 miles) long and 65 kilometres (40 miles) at its widest. The bay was discovered by sir Martin Frobisher in 1576.

frock (frok) *n.* **1.** A long, loose outer garment, such as that worn by artists and craftsmen; a smock. **2.** A woollen garment formerly worn by sailors; a jersey. **3.** A frock coat. **4.** A robe worn by monks, friars, and other clerics; a habit. **5.** The state of being a priest or clergyman. **6.** A woman's or girl's dress.
~*tr.v.* **frocked, frocking, frocks. 1.** To clothe in a frock. **2.** *Rare.* To invest with clerical office. [Middle English *frok,* from Old French *froc,* from Germanic *hrok-* (unattested).]

frock coat *n.* A man's dress overcoat with knee-length skirts, worn chiefly in the 19th century.

Froe·bel (frōb'l), **Friedrich Wilhelm August** (1782–1852). German educationist who believed that school should be happy. His book *Education of Man* (1826) was profoundly influential. In 1837 he opened the first kindergarten, at Blankenburg.

frog¹ (frog ‖ frawg) *n.* **1.** Any of numerous tailless, chiefly aquatic amphibians of the order Anura, and especially of the family Ranidae, characteristically having a smooth, moist skin, webbed feet, and long hind legs adapted for leaping. **2.** A spiked or perforated object placed in a container and used to support stems in a decorative floral arrangement. **3.** *Slang. Sometimes capital* **F.** A Frenchman or Frenchwoman. Used humorously or derogatorily. **4.** A recess or groove in one side, or on opposite sides, of a brick. —**a frog in (one's) throat.** Mucus on the vocal cords that causes a croak in one's speech. [Middle English *frogge,* Old English *frogga,* a pet form of *forse, frosc,* from Germanic.]

frog² *n.* A grooved iron or steel plate that guides the wheels of a train over an intersection in the track. [19th century : origin obscure.]

frog³ *n.* **1.** A loop fastened to a belt to hold a tool or weapon. **2.** An ornamental looped braid or cord with a button or knot for fastening the front of a garment. [18th century : origin obscure.]
frog⁴ *n.* A wedge-shaped, horny material in the sole of a horse's hoof. [17th century : perhaps from FROG (animal), influenced by synonymous French *fourchette* and Italian *forchetta* (diminutives of *fourche, forca,* FORK, referring to the shape of the material).]
frog·bit (fróg-bit) *n.* An aquatic perennial plant, *Hydrocharis morsusranae,* with heart-shaped bronzy-green leaves, and three-petalled white flowers with a yellow centre.
frog·fish (fróg-fish) *n., pl.* **-fishes** or collectively **frogfish.** Any of various anglerfishes of the family Antennariidae, of tropical and temperate seas.
frogged (frogd) *adj.* Decorated with ornamental frogs; covered with frogging. Said of a coat, uniform, or the like.
frog·ging (frógging) *n.* The ornamental loops of braid or cord on a garment; decorative frogs collectively.
frog·gy (fróggi) *adj.* **-gier, -giest. 1.** Of, resembling, or characteristic of a frog. **2.** Full of frogs.
~n., pl. **froggies.** *Sometimes capital* **F.** A Frenchman or Frenchwoman. Used humorously or derogatorily.
frog·hop·per (fróg-hoppər) *n.* Any of various jumping bugs of the insect family Ceropidae, the nymphs of which secrete a protective spittle-like substance (cuckoo spit) around themselves. Also called "spittle insect", "spittle bug".
frog kick *n.* A swimming kick in which the legs are drawn up close beneath one, then thrust outwards and together vigorously.
frog·man (fróg-mən) *n., pl.* **-men** (-mən). A swimmer provided with breathing apparatus and other equipment, such as a rubber suit and flippers, to execute underwater operations.
frog-march (fróg-maarch) *n. Chiefly British.* **1.** A method of carrying a resisting prisoner, for example face downwards and horizontally, in which four people each carry a limb. **2.** Any method of forcing an unwilling person to move, especially by pinning his arms behind his back and pushing him forwards.
~tr.v. **frog-marched, -marching, -marches.** Also **frog·march.** To force (a person) forwards using a frog-march.
frog·mouth (fróg-mowth) *n.* Any of various brown or grey nocturnal insectivorous birds of the genera *Podargus* and *Batrachostomus,* of southeastern Asia and Australia, having a wide mouth.
frog·spawn (fróg-spawn) *n.* A transparent gelatinous mass interspersed with black dots, comprising many fertilised frogs' eggs or developing tadpoles, each surrounded by nutrient jelly.
frog spit *n.* Also **frog spittle. 1.** An insect secretion, **cuckoo spit** *(see).* **2.** A foamlike aggregation of small aquatic plants, such as green algae, on the surface of a pond.
frol·ic (fróllik) *n.* **1.** Gaiety; merriment. **2.** A gay, carefree time. **3.** A prank, trick, or antic.
~intr.v. **frolicked, -icking, -ics. 1.** To behave playfully and uninhibitedly; romp. **2.** To engage in merrymaking, joking, or teasing.
~adj. Archaic. Merry; frisky; prankish. [Dutch *vrolijk,* from Middle Dutch *vrolijc* : *vro,* gay, happy + *-lijc,* -ly.] **—frol·ick·er** *n.*
frol·ic·some (frólliks'm) *adj.* Full of high-spirited fun; playful.
from (from, *weak form* frəm || frum) *prep. Abbr.* **fr. 1.** Beginning at a specified place or time: *walked home from the station; from six o'clock on.* **2. a.** With a specified time or point as the first of two limits: *from age four to age eight.* **b.** With a specified lowest limit: *real leather shoes from £12.* **3.** With a person, place, or thing as the source, cause, or instrument: *a note from the teacher.* **4.** Out of: *take a book from the shelf.* **5.** Out of the jurisdiction, control, restraint, or possession of: *escape from the gallows; free from pain.* **6.** So as not to be engaged in: *keep someone from making a mistake.* **7.** Measured by or with reference to: *far away from home.* **8.** As opposed to: *know right from wrong.* **9.** Because of: *faint from hunger; crying from desperation.* **10.** Beginning with or in a specified state: *from rags to riches; from annoyance to fury.* **11.** Belonging to: *memories from childhood.* **12.** Using as evidence: *judging from appearances.* [Middle English *from, fram,* Old English *from, fram.*]
Fromm (from), **Erich** (1900–1980). German-born U.S. psychoanalyst and philosopher. Challenging the theories of Sigmund Freud, he argued the importance of sociological and cultural influences in causing psychological disturbances.
frond (frond) *n.* **1.** The usually compound leaf of a fern. **2.** A large compound leaf of certain other plants, such as a palm. **3.** A leaflike thallus, as of a seaweed or lichen. [Latin *frōns*† (stem *frond-*), branch, leaf.] **—frond·ed** *adj.*
Fronde (frond || *French* froNd) *n.* The French political movement that opposed Cardinal Mazarin and the court during the minority of Louis XIV in the mid-17th century. [French, "sling" (a derogatory comparison to schoolboys who use slings only behind a teacher's back), from Old French, from Vulgar Latin *fundula* (unattested), from Latin *funda,* probably akin to Greek *sphendonē*†.]
fron·des·cent (fron-déss'nt) *adj.* Bearing, resembling, or having a profusion of leaves or fronds; leafy. [Latin *frondescens* (stem *frondescent-*), present participle of *frondescere,* to become leafy, from *frondēre,* to put forth leaves, from *frōns* (stem *frond-*), leaf, FROND.] **—fron·des·cence** *n.*
fron·dose (frón-dōss, -dōz) *adj.* **1.** Bearing fronds. **2.** Resembling a frond or fronds; frondlike. [Latin *frondōsus* : *frōns* (stem *frond-*), FROND + -OSE.] **—fron·dose·ly** *adv.*
front (frunt) *n.* **1.** The forward part or surface, as of a building. **2.** The area, location, or position directly before or ahead. **3.** The position of leadership or superiority; the forefront. **4.** The first part; the beginning; the opening. **5.** The forehead, especially of an animal or bird. **6.** *Archaic.* The entire face; the countenance. **7.** Demeanour or bearing, when faced with a particular situation: *maintain a brave front.* **8.** An outward or feigned aspect; a false appearance or manner. **9.** Land bordering a lake, river, or street: *a house on the lake front.* **10.** A promenade along a beach. **11.** The top forward part of a garment: *spilt gravy down his front.* **12.** A detachable part of a man's dress shirt covering the chest; a dickey. **13.** *Military.* **a.** The most forward line of a military combat force. **b.** An area of contact between opposing combat forces. **14.** *Meteorology.* The interface between air masses at different temperatures. Also called "discontinuity". **15.** A group or movement uniting various individuals or organisations for the achievement of a common purpose; a coalition. **16.** An apparently respectable person, group, or business acting as cover for secret or illegal activities.
~adj. **1.** Of, pertaining to, aimed at, or located in the front. **2.** *Phonetics.* Produced with the front of the tongue in a forward position. Said of vowel sounds.
~v. **fronted, fronting, fronts.** *—tr.* **1.** To face; look out upon. **2.** To meet in opposition; confront. **3.** To provide a front for. **4.** To serve as a front for; head. *—intr.* **1.** To have a front; face. Usually used with *on: Her property fronts on the main road.* **2.** To act as a front. Used with *for.* **3.** *Australian Informal.* To arrive; appear. Usually used with *up.* [Middle English, from Old French, from Latin *frōns*† (stem *front-*), front, forehead.]
front·age (frúntij) *n.* **1.** The front part of a piece of property, such as a lot or building. **2.** The length of such a part. **3.** The land between a building and the street. **4.** The direction in which something faces. **5.** Land adjacent to something such as a street, or body of water.
fron·tal¹ (frúnt'l) *adj.* **1.** Of, pertaining to, directed towards, or situated at the front. **2.** Of or pertaining to a meteorological front. **3.** Of or pertaining to the forehead. **—fron·tal·ly** *adv.*
frontal² *n.* **1.** An ornamental drapery covering the front of an altar. **2.** The façade of a building. [Middle English *frontel,* from Medieval Latin *frontellum,* from Latin *frōns* (stem *front-*), FRONT.]
frontal bone *n.* A cranial bone consisting of a vertical portion corresponding to the forehead and a horizontal portion that forms the roofs of the orbital and nasal cavities.
frontal lobe *n.* The anterior portion of each cerebral hemisphere, extending back to the central sulcus.
frontal plane *n. Anatomy.* A plane parallel to the long axis of the body that is perpendicular to the sagittal plane.
front bench *n.* The front row of seats on either side of the House of Commons or a similar legislative body, traditionally reserved for government ministers and leading members of the opposition. **—front-bench** *adj.* **—front-bench·er** *n.*
front door *n.* **1.** The main entrance at the front of a building. **2.** A point of access to country, region, or the like. **3.** A proper or fair means of approach to achieving an objective.
front-end (frúnt-énd) *Computing.* Designating or pertaining to a computer that is attached to another computer to relieve it of some of its basic tasks.
front end *n. Computing.* A piece of software designed to make another piece of software easier to operate or understand.
Fronte·nac (froNt-nák), **Louis de Buade, comte de Palluau et de** (1620–98). French soldier and governor of New France (1672–82 and 1689–98).
fron·tier (frún-teer, frón- || frun-téer) *n.* **1.** An international border, or the area along it. **2.** *U.S.* A region just beyond or at the edge of a settled area. **3.** The limit of what is known in a science or other branch of knowledge. —See Synonyms at **boundary.**
~adj. Of, pertaining to, or situated at a frontier. [Middle English *frountier,* from Old French *frontiere,* from *front,* FRONT.]
fron·tiers·man (frun-téerz-mən) *n., pl.* **-men** (-mən). *Chiefly U.S.* A man who lives on the frontier.
fron·tis·piece (frúntiss-peess) *n.* **1.** *Abbr.* **front.** An illustration that faces or immediately precedes the title page of a book, book section, or magazine. **2.** *Architecture.* A façade; especially, an ornamental façade. **3.** *Architecture.* A small ornamental pediment, as on top of a door or window. [Variant (influenced by PIECE) of earlier *frontispice,* from Old French, from Late Latin *frontispicium,* "examination of the front", building exterior : Latin *frōns* (stem *front-*), FRONT + *specere,* to look at.]
front·let (frúntlit) *n.* **1.** An ornament or band worn on the forehead. **2.** The forehead of an animal or bird, especially when distinctively marked. **3.** *Ecclesiastical.* The ornamental border of a frontal. **4.** A **phylactery** *(see)* worn on the forehead. [Middle English, from Old French *frontelet,* diminutive of *frontel,* from Latin *frontāle,* from *frōns* (stem *front-*), FRONT.]
front line *n.* A front or boundary, especially between military, political, or ideological positions, or between old and new.
front man *n.* **1.** A person who publicly represents an organisation, project, or the like. **2.** A person who acts as a front for groups or organisations carrying on secret or illegal activities. **3.** A presenter of a radio or television programme.
front matter *n.* The material, such as the preface, frontispiece, and title page, preceding the text in a book. Compare **end matter.**
front office *n. Chiefly U.S.* The policy-making members of an organisation, based at its head office.
front of house *n.* Those parts of a theatre to which the audience have access, as opposed to the stage and backstage areas. **—front-of-house** *adj.*

fron·to·gen·e·sis (frúntō-jénni-siss) *n.* Development or intensification of a meteorological front. [New Latin : FRONT + -GENESIS.]
fron·tol·y·sis (frun-tólli-siss) *n.* The disintegration of a meteorological front. [New Latin : FRONT + -LYSIS.]
front-page (frúnt-páyj) *adj.* Receiving or worthy of coverage on the front page of a newspaper.
Front Range. Line of mountains running some 480 kilometres (300 miles) through Wyoming and Colorado. The loftiest part of the U.S. Rocky Mountains, its highest elevation is Mount Elbert (4 399 metres; 14,432 feet).
front-runner (frúnt-runnər, -rúnnər) *n.* A leading contender in a contest, election, or the like.
front·wards (frúnt-wərds) *adv.* Also *chiefly U.S.* **front·ward** (-wərd). Towards the front.
front-wheel drive (frúnt-weel, -hweel) *n. Abbr.* **f.w.d.** A motor vehicle drive mechanism in which the drive is applied only to the front wheels.
frost (frost || frawst) *n.* **1.** A deposit or covering of minute ice crystals formed from frozen water vapour. **2.** The atmospheric conditions when the temperature is at or below the freezing point of water. **3.** The process of freezing. **4.** A cold or icy manner; aloofness. **5.** *Informal.* Something given a cold reception; a fiasco; a failure. **6.** *Chiefly British Informal.* A fraud; a swindle.
~*v.* **frosted, frosting, frosts.** —*tr.* **1.** To cover with frost. **2.** To damage or kill by frost. **3.** To cover (glass or metal) with a roughened or speckled decorative surface. **4. a.** To dust the surface of (a cake) with icing or caster sugar. **b.** *Chiefly U.S.* To decorate (a cake) with icing. —*intr.* To become covered with or as if with frost. [Middle English *frost,* Old English *frost, forst,* from Germanic.]
Frost (frost), **Robert (Lee)** (1874–1963). U.S. poet. From the age of 10, he spent much of his life in rural New England, and his work frequently uses aspects of this experience to explore man's relationship with nature. His collections include *A Boy's Will* (1913) and *In the Clearing* (1962); *Selected Letters* (1965).
frost·bite (fróst-bīt) *n.* Tissue destruction resulting from ice forming in the tissues, especially of the nose, fingers, toes, and ears.
frost·bit·ten (fróst-bitt'n) *adj.* Affected by frostbite.
frost·ed (fróstid) *adj.* **1.** Covered by frost. **2.** Frostbitten. **3.** Dusted with icing or caster sugar. **4.** *Chiefly U.S.* Covered or decorated with icing. **5.** Decorated with a frostlike surface, as metal or glass. **6.** Treated with bleach at the tips. Said of hair.
frost heave *n.* An uplifting of soil, a pavement, or a similar surface as a result of freezing below the surface.
frost hollow *n.* A low-lying area which may experience frost while surrounding higher areas are frost-free, or which may have more severe frost than surrounding areas. Also called "frost pocket".
frost·ing (fróst-ing) *n.* **1. a.** A light covering of caster or icing sugar. **b.** *Chiefly U.S.* An icing made of sugar, butter, water, and egg whites. **2.** A roughened or speckled surface imparted to glass or metal.
frost-resistant (fróst-ri-zistənt) *adj.* Designating plants that are able to survive the period of winter frost. —**frost resistance** *n.*
frost·work (fróst-wurk) *n.* **1.** The intricate patterns produced by frost, as on a windowpane. **2.** Similar ornamental patterns produced artificially, as on metal or glass.
frost·y (frósti) *adj.* **-ier, -iest. 1.** Producing or characterised by frost; freezing. **2.** Covered with or as if with frost. **3.** Silvery white; hoary. **4.** Cold in manner; haughty; distant. —**frost·i·ly** *adv.* —**frost·i·ness** *n.*
froth (froth || frawth) *n.* **1.** A mass of bubbles in or on a liquid; foam. **2.** A salivary foam released as a result of disease or exhaustion. **3.** Anything unsubstantial or trivial.
~*v.* (*U.S. also* fro<u>th</u>) **frothed, frothing, froths.** —*tr.* **1.** To exude or expel in the form of foam. **2.** To cover with foam. **3.** To cause to foam. —*intr.* To exude or expel froth; foam. [Middle English, from Old Norse *frodha,* from Germanic *frudh-* (unattested).]
froth flotation *n.* A method of separating the valuable constituent of a low-grade ore, in which the ore is ground and mixed with water containing surface-active agents so that the valuable constituent floats up to the froth and can be skimmed off.
froth·y (fróthi || fráwthi, fro<u>th</u>i) *adj.* **-ier, -iest. 1.** Made of, covered with, or resembling froth; foamy. **2.** Playfully frivolous in character or content. —**froth·i·ly** *adv.* —**froth·i·ness** *n.*
frot·tage (fróttaa<u>zh</u>, fro-taá<u>zh</u>) *n.* **1.** *Art.* The technique of taking a rubbing to obtain a design. **2.** The practice of deriving sexual satisfaction from rubbing against another's body while clothed. [French, rubbing, from *frotter,* to rub.]
frou-frou (fro͞o-fro͞o) *n.* **1.** A rustling sound, as of silk. **2.** Fussy or showy dress or ornamentation. [French (imitative).]
fro·ward (frṓ-wərd, -ərd) *adj.* Stubbornly contrary and disobedient; obstinate. [Middle English *froward* : FRO + -WARD.] —**fro·ward·ly** *adv.* —**fro·ward·ness** *n.*
frown (frown) *v.* **frowned, frowning, frowns.** —*intr.* **1.** To wrinkle the brow, as in thought, worry, or displeasure. **2.** To regard with disapproval or distaste. Used with *on* or *upon*: *"The English frown on the use of tea bags"* (Craig Claiborne). —*tr.* **1.** To express (disapproval or distaste, for example) by wrinkling the brow. **2.** To wrinkle the brow so as to dismiss (a person or statement, for example): *frown objections away.*
~*n.* A wrinkling of the brow in thought, worry, or displeasure. [Middle English *frounen,* from Old French *froigner,* from Celtic, akin to Welsh *ffroen*†, nose.] —**frown·er** *n.* —**frown·ing·ly** *adv.*
frowst (frowst) *n. Chiefly British.* A hot and stuffy atmosphere.
~*intr.v.* **frowsted, frowsting, frowsts.** To lounge in a hot and stuffy atmosphere. [Back-formation from FROWSTY.] —**frowst·er** *n.*
frowst·y (frów-sti) *adj.* **-ier, -iest.** *Chiefly British.* Having a hot and stuffy atmosphere. [Perhaps a variant of FROWZY.]
frow·zy, frow·sy (frów-zi) *adj.* **-zier, -ziest. 1.** Unkempt in appearance; slovenly; shabby. **2.** Having an unpleasant smell; musty. —See Synonyms at **sloppy.** [17th century : origin obscure.] —**frow·zi·ness** *n.*
froze. Past tense of **freeze.**
fro·zen (frṓz'n). Past participle of **freeze.**
~*adj.* **1.** Made into, covered with, or surrounded by ice. **2.** Affected or killed by extreme cold. **3.** Preserved by freezing. **4.** Rendered immobile. **5.** Expressive of cold unfriendliness or disdain: *a frozen stare.* **6. a.** Fixed at an arbitrary level. Said of wages, profits, or the like. **b.** Incapable of being withdrawn, sold, or liquidated. Said of investments, assets, or the like. —**fro·zen·ness** *n.*
F.R.S. Fellow of the Royal Society.
fruc·tif·er·ous (fruk-tiffərəss, fro͝ok-) *adj.* Bearing fruit. [Latin *frūctifer* : *frūctus,* FRUIT + -FEROUS.]
fruc·ti·fi·ca·tion (frúk-tifi-káysh'n, fro͝ok-) *n.* **1.** The producing of fruit. **2.** The fruit of a seed-bearing plant. **3.** A spore-bearing structure.
fruc·ti·fy (frúk-ti-fī, fro͝ok-) *v.* **-fied, -fying, -fies.** —*tr.* To cause to produce fruit; make fruitful or productive. —*intr.* To bear fruit. [Middle English *fructifien,* from Old French *fructifier,* from Latin *frūctificāre* : *frūctus,* FRUIT + *facere,* to make, do.]
fruc·tose (frúk-tōss, fro͝ok-, -tōz) *n.* A very sweet sugar, $C_6H_{12}O_6$, occurring in many fruits and honey and used as a preservative for foodstuffs and as an intravenous nutrient. Also called "fruit sugar", "laevulose". [Latin *frūctus,* FRUIT + -OSE.]
fruc·tu·ous (frúk-choo-əss, fro͝ok-, -tew-) *adj.* Fruitful; productive. [Middle English, from Old French, from Latin *frūctuōsus,* from *frūctus,* FRUIT.]
fru·gal (fro͞og'l) *adj.* **1.** Avoiding unnecessary expenditure of money; thrifty. **2.** Not plentiful and costing little. —See Synonyms at **sparing.** [Latin *frūgālis,* back-formation from *frūgālior,* comparative of *frūgī,* useful, worthy, dative of *frūx* (stem *frūg-*), fruit.] —**fru·gal·i·ty** (fro͞o-gál-əti), **fru·gal·ness** *n.* —**fru·gal·ly** *adv.*
fru·giv·o·rous (fro͞o-jívvərəss) *adj.* Feeding on fruit; fruit-eating. [Latin *frūx* (stem *frūg-*), fruit + -VOROUS.]
fruit (fro͞ot || frewt) *n., pl.* **fruit** or **fruits. 1. a.** The ripened ovary or ovaries of a seed-bearing plant, containing the seeds and occurring in a wide variety of forms. **b.** Any other edible fleshy part of a plant that contains seeds, but consists of other tissue, such as the receptacle, in addition to the ripened ovary; a pseudocarp or false fruit. **2. a.** Such parts collectively, considered as a type of food. **b.** A vegetable fruit, such as rhubarb. **c.** A part or amount of such a plant product, served as food. **3.** The spore-bearing structure of a nonseed-bearing plant. **4.** A plant crop or product. **5.** *Often plural.* Result; issue; outcome: *the fruits of their labour.* **6.** *Literary.* Offspring; progeny. **7.** *British Informal.* A person; a fellow. Used, especially formerly, in the phrase *old fruit.* **8.** *Chiefly U.S. Slang.* A male homosexual. Used derogatorily.
~*v.* **fruited, fruiting, fruits.** —*intr.* To produce fruit. —*tr.* To cause to produce fruit. [Middle English, from Old French, from Latin *frūctus,* enjoyment, use, produce, fruit, from the past participle of *fruī,* to enjoy, to eat fruit.]
Usage: When referring to apples, oranges, or the like, this word has two plural forms: *fruit* and *fruits.* The former is the more widely used when the fruit is viewed collectively: *A lot of fruit in the garden. Fruits* is used when there is an emphasis on the individual items in a group, especially when the items are of different kinds (*a basket of succulent fruits: apples, grapes, and pears*), although *fruit* would be acceptable.
fruit·age (fro͞o-tij || fréw-) *n.* **1.** The process, time, or condition of bearing fruit. **2.** Fruit collectively.
frui·ta·ri·an (fro͞o-táiri-ən) *n.* One who lives entirely on fruit. [Formed by analogy with *vegetarian.*] —**frui·ta·ri·an** *adj.* —**frui·ta·ri·an·ism** *n.*
fruit bat *n.* Any of various fruit-eating bats of the family Pteropodidae, of tropical and subtropical regions of the Old World.
fruit-cake, fruit·cake (fro͞ot-kayk || fréwt-) *n.* **1.** A heavy, spiced cake containing citron, nuts, raisins, and preserved fruits. **2.** *Informal.* A person whose behaviour is considered strange or eccentric.
fruit cocktail *n.* A fruit salad made with pieces of various fruits.
fruit cup *n.* A non-alcoholic drink made from mixed fruit juices, often with pieces of fruit added.
fruit·er (fro͞o-tər || fréw-) *n.* **1.** A tree that produces fruit. **2.** One who grows fruit. **3.** A ship that transports fruit.
fruit·er·er (fro͞ot-ərər || fréwt-) *n.* A fruit retailer. [Middle English, from FRUITER (grower).]
fruit fly *n.* **1.** Any of various small flies of the family Drosophilidae, having larvae that feed on ripening or fermenting fruit; especially, a common species, *Drosophila melanogaster,* also called "vinegar fly". **2.** Any of various flies of the family Trypetidae (or Tephritidae), having larvae that hatch in and damage plant tissue.
fruit·ful (fro͞ot-f'l || fréwt-) *adj.* **1.** Producing fruit. **2.** Producing fruit or offspring in abundance; prolific. **3.** Conducive to productivity; leading to abundant crops: *a fruitful climate.* **4.** Producing results; profitable. —**fruit·ful·ly** *adv.* —**fruit·ful·ness** *n.*
fruit gum *n.* A chewy sweet containing gelatine and fruit flavouring.
fruiting body *n.* A specialised spore-producing structure, especially of a fungus.

fru·i·tion (frōō-ísh'n ‖ frew-) *n.* **1.** Enjoyment derived from use or possession; pleasure. **2.** The achievement of something desired or worked for; accomplishment; realisation. **3.** The condition of bearing fruit. [Middle English *fruicioun*, from Old French *fruition*, from Late Latin *fruitiō* (stem *fruitiōn-*), from *fruī*, to enjoy, eat fruit.]

fruit knife *n.* A small knife with a stainless-steel blade, used for cutting or peeling fruit.

fruit·less (frōōt-ləss, -liss ‖ frewt-) *adj.* **1.** Producing no fruit. **2.** Having negligible or no results; unproductive: *"In these fruitless searches he spent ten months"* (Samuel Johnson). —**fruit·less·ly** *adv.* —**fruit·less·ness** *n.*

fruit machine *n. British.* A coin-operated gambling machine, typically with drums bearing pictures of fruit which spin independently, money being paid out if the pictures are aligned in certain combinations when the drums come to rest.

fruit salad *n.* A dish of assorted fresh or preserved fruits, served in their juice.

fruit salts *pl.n.* Mineral salts.

fruit sugar *n.* Fructose *(see).*

fruit tree *n.* Any tree that produces fruit.

fruit·y (frōōti ‖ fréwti) *adj.* **-ier, -iest. 1.** Of, containing, or relating to fruit. **2. a.** Tasting and smelling richly of fruit. **b.** Tasting of the grape. Said of a wine. **3.** Mellow; rich: *a fruity voice.* **4.** Exuding sentiment or unctuousness. **5.** *Slang.* Salacious in tone or character; suggestive. —**fruit·i·ness** *n.*

fru·men·ta·ceous (frōō-men-táyshəss, -mən- ‖ frèw-) *adj.* Resembling or consisting of grain, especially wheat. [Late Latin *frūmentāceus* : Latin *frūmentum*, grain, perhaps from *fruī*, to enjoy, eat fruit + -ACEOUS.]

fru·men·ty (frōō-mənti ‖ frèw-) *n.* Also **fur·men·ty** (fúr-), **fro·men·ty** (frō-). *British.* Hulled wheat boiled in milk and flavoured with sugar and spices. [Middle English *frumente*, from Old French *frumentee*, from *frument*, grain, from Latin *frūmentum*. See frumentaceous.]

frump (frump) *n.* A dull, plain, unfashionably dressed girl or woman. [Perhaps short for dialectal *frumple*, to wrinkle, from Middle English *fromplen*, from Middle Dutch *verrompelen* : *ver-*, for- + *rompelen*, to RUMPLE.] —**frump·ish, frump·y** *adj.* —**frump·ish·ly, frump·i·ly** *adv.* —**frump·ish·ness, frump·i·ness** *n.*

frus·trate (fru-stráyt ‖ *chiefly U.S.* frúss-trayt) *tr.v.* **-trated, -trating, -trates. 1. a.** To prevent from accomplishing a purpose or fulfilling a desire; thwart. **b.** To cause feelings of discouragement or dissatisfaction in. **c.** To hinder from finding an outlet for sexual desires. **2.** To prevent the accomplishment or development of; nullify. ~*adj. Archaic.* Baffled or thwarted. [Middle English *frustraten*, from Latin *frūstrāre* (past participle *frūstrātus*), to disappoint, frustrate, from *frūstrā*, in error, uselessly.] —**frus·trat·er** *n.* —**frus·trat·ing** *adj.* —**frus·trat·ing·ly** *adv.*

  Synonyms: frustrate, thwart, foil, baulk.

frus·tra·ted (fru-stráytid ‖ *chiefly U.S.* frúss-traytid) *adj.* **1.** Suffering from feelings of annoyance or dissatisfaction, especially sexual dissatisfaction, through the frustration of one's aims or desires. **2.** Unsuccessful in some activity; unfulfilled.

frus·tra·tion (fru-stráysh'n) *n.* **1.** The condition or an instance of being frustrated. **2.** One that frustrates. **3.** *Psychology.* **a.** Feelings of dissatisfaction caused by an inability to achieve personal or sexual fulfilment. **b.** Something that gives rise to such feelings.

frus·tule (frústewl) *n. Botany.* The hard, siliceous shell of a diatom. [French, from Latin *frustulum*, diminutive of *frustum*, piece.]

frus·tum (frúss-təm) *n., pl.* **-tums** or **-ta** (-tə). A part of a solid, such as a cone or pyramid, between two parallel planes cutting the solid, especially the section between the base and a plane parallel to it. [Latin, piece, piece cut off.]

fru·tes·cent (frōō-téss'nt ‖ frew-) *adj.* Pertaining to, resembling, or assuming the form of a shrub; shrubby. [Latin *frutex*, bush (see **fruticose**) + -ESCENT.] —**fru·tes·cence** *n.*

fru·ti·cose (frōō-ti-kōss, -kōz ‖ frèw-) *adj.* Shrublike, especially in form. [Latin *fruticōsus*, from *frutex†* (stem *frutic-*), shrub, bush.]

fry¹ (frī) *v.* **fried, frying, fries.** —*tr.* To cook over direct heat in hot oil or fat. —*intr.* **1.** To undergo frying. **2.** *Informal.* To swelter. **3.** *U.S. Slang.* To undergo execution in an electric chair. ~*n., pl.* **fries. 1.** A dish of any fried food. **2.** Offal from certain animals, fried for eating. **3.** *U.S.* A social gathering featuring fried food: *a fish fry.* [Middle English *frien*, from Old French *frire*, from Latin *frigere*.]

fry² *n., pl.* **fry. 1.** A small fish; especially, a young, recently hatched fish. **2.** The similar young of certain other animals. **3.** *Informal.* Young people: *Plan to invite the young fry to a party. See* **small fry.** [Middle English, young offspring, perhaps from Anglo-French *frie*, from Old French *freier*, to spawn, rub, from Latin *fricāre*, to rub.]

Fry (frī), **Christopher,** born Christopher Harris (1907–). British playwright. He became a major figure in postwar drama with his verse plays, especially *A Phoenix Too Frequent* (1946) and *The Lady's Not for Burning* (1948).

Fry, Elizabeth, née Gurney (1780–1845). British preacher and philanthropist. A Quaker, she visited Newgate prison in 1813 and was moved to campaign for penal reform; she achieved major improvements in the conditions of women's prisons, and later, of people transported to Australia.

Fry, Roger (Eliot) (1866–1934). British painter and critic. His exhibitions (1910–12) did much to promote recognition of the post-impressionist movement in Britain, while his study of Paul Cézanne (1927), and works like *Vision and Design* (1920) led to his appointment as Slade professor of Fine Arts at Cambridge (1933).

Frye (frī), **H(erman) Northrop** (1912–91). Canadian literary critic, made chancellor of Victoria College, University of Toronto in 1978. He wrote *Fearful Symmetry* (1947), a study of William Blake, and *Anatomy of Criticism* (1957).

fry·er, fri·er (frí-ər) *n.* **1.** One that fries, especially, a pan or vessel suitable for frying. **2.** *U.S.* A small, young chicken suitable for frying.

frying pan *n.* A shallow, long-handled pan used for frying food.

fry-up (frí-up) *n.* **1.** A meal consisting of a variety of foods, such as eggs and sausages, cooked in a frying pan. **2.** The preparation of such a meal.

F.S.A. Fellow of the Society of Antiquaries.

FSH follicle-stimulating hormone.

f-stop (éf-stop) *n.* **1.** A camera lens aperture setting calibrated to a corresponding f-number. **2.** An **f-number** *(see).* [Focal length *stop.*]

f-sys·tem (éf-sistəm) *n.* A method of indicating the relative aperture of a camera lens, based on the f-number.

ft foot.

ft-c foot-candle.

FT Index *n.* The daily index of prices on the London stock exchange, based on the average price of 30 selected shares. Called in full "Financial Times Industrial Ordinary Share Index".

ft-lb foot-pound.

fub·sy (fúbzi) *adj.* **-sier, -siest.** *British Regional.* Somewhat fat and squat. [From obsolete *fubs†*, a chubby person.]

Fu-chien. See Fujian.

Fu-chou. See Fuzhou.

Fuchs (fōōks), **Klaus Emil Julius** (1911–88). German-born physicist. He worked on atomic research in Britain during and after World War II, and was imprisoned (1950–59) for passing secret information to the Soviet government.

Fuchs (fōōks), **Sir Vivian (Ernest)** (1908–). British geologist and explorer. He led the Commonwealth Trans-Antarctic Expedition (1957–58), for which he was knighted.

fuch·sia (féwshə) *n.* **1.** Any of various chiefly tropical shrubs of the genus *Fuchsia,* widely cultivated for their showy, drooping, purplish, reddish, pink, or white flowers. **2.** The hardy or common fuchsia, *F. magellanica,* having flowers with scarlet sepals and purple-blue petals forming a bell. **3.** Strong, vivid purplish red. [New Latin, after Leonard *Fuchs* (1501–66), German botanist.]

fuch·sine (fōōk-sin, -seen ‖ féwk-) *n.* Also **fuch·sin** (-sin). A dark-green synthetic aniline dyestuff, the hydrochloride of rosaniline, used to make a purple-red dye used to colour textiles and leather and as a bacterial stain. Also called "magenta". [FUCHS(IA) + -IN.]

fuck (fuk) *v.* **fucked, fucking, fucks.** *Vulgar.* —*tr.* To have sexual intercourse with. —*intr.* To have sexual intercourse. —**fuck off.** *Vulgar Slang.* **1.** To go away. Used in the imperative. **2.** To stop speaking or behaving stupidly. Used in the imperative. ~*n. Vulgar.* **1.** An act of sexual intercourse. **2.** A person considered as a partner in sexual intercourse. —**not give a fuck.** *Vulgar Slang.* Not to care in the least. [16th century : probably of Germanic origin; akin to Middle Dutch *fokken,* to strike.]

fuck·ing (fúcking) *adj. Vulgar Slang.* Used as an intensive to express annoyance. —**fuck·ing** *adv.*

fuck up *tr.v.* **Vulgar Slang. 1.** To mess up; bungle. **2.** To cause difficulties for. —**fuck-up** *n.*

fu·coid (féw-koyd) *adj.* Of or belonging to the order Fucales, which includes brown algae such as wracks, kelps, and similar seaweeds. ~*n.* A member of the Fucales. [Perhaps FUC(US) + -OID.]

fu·cus (féwkəss) *n.* Any of various brown algae of the genus *Fucus,* which includes many of the larger seaweeds found between high and low tide mark. [New Latin *Fucus,* from Latin *fūcus,* red dye, orchil, from Greek *phukos.* See **phyco-**.]

fud·dle (fúdd'l) *v.* **-dled, -dling, -dles.** —*tr.* To muddle with or as if with strong drink; intoxicate. —*intr.* To drink; tipple. ~*n.* A state of intoxication or confusion. [16th century : origin obscure.]

fud·dy-dud·dy (fúddi-duddi) *n., pl.* **-dies.** One who is old-fashioned and fussy. [20th century : origin obscure.] —**fud·dy-dud·dy** *adj.*

fudge¹ (fuj) *n.* A soft, rich sweet made of sugar, butter, milk, and flavouring. [19th century : perhaps from FUDGE (to bodge).]

fudge² *n.* Nonsense; humbug. ~*interj.* Used to express disbelief, disappointment, or annoyance.

fudge³ *n.* A small section of a newspaper page in which last-minute copy may be inserted after the plate or type is on the printing press. **2.** The news item so inserted. **3.** An instance of fudging. ~*v.* **fudged, fudging, fudges.** —*tr.* To make or repair in a clumsy way; bodge. **2.** To evade (an issue, for example); dodge. —*intr.* To act or talk in an evasive or indecisive manner. [Perhaps from obsolete *fadge†,* to adjust, fit, fake, deceive.]

Fue·gi·an (fwáy-ji-ən, few-áy-, few-ée-) *adj.* Of or relating to Tierra del Fuego, its inhabitants, or its culture. ~*n.* An inhabitant of Tierra del Fuego.

fuehrer. Variant of **führer.**

fu·el (féw-əl, fewl) *n.* **1.** Anything consumed to produce energy, especially: **a.** A material such as coal, gas, or oil burned to produce heat. **b.** Fissionable material used in a nuclear reactor. **c.** Nutritive material metabolised by a living organism. **2.** Anything that maintains or heightens an activity or an emotion. ~*v.* **fuelled** or *U.S.* **fueled, -elling** or *U.S.* **-eling, -els.** —*tr.* To provide with fuel. —*intr.* To take in fuel. [Middle English *feuel,* from Old French *fouaille,* from Vulgar Latin *focālia* (unattested), from Latin *focus†,* fire, hearth.] —**fu·el·ler** *n.*

fuel cell *n.* An electrochemical cell in which the energy of a reaction between a fuel such as liquid hydrogen and an oxidant such as liquid oxygen is converted directly and continuously into the energy of direct electric current.
fuel element *n.* A can that contains the nuclear fuel in a nuclear reactor.
fuel injection *n.* Any of several methods or mechanical systems by which a fuel is vaporised and sprayed into the cylinders of an internal-combustion engine without the use of a carburettor.
fuel oil *n.* Any liquid or liquefiable petroleum product that ignites spontaneously at a temperature above 100°F, used to generate heat or power.
fug (fug) *n.* A hot, stuffy and usually smoke-laden atmosphere. [19th century : origin obscure.] **—fug·gy** *adj.*
fu·ga·cious (fyo͞o-gáyshəss) *adj.* **1.** Passing away quickly; evanescent. **2.** *Botany.* Withering or dropping off early: *fugacious petals.* [Latin *fugāx* (stem *fugāc-*), swift, fleeting, from *fugere,* to flee.] **—fu·ga·cious·ly** *adv.* **—fu·ga·cious·ness** *n.*
fu·gac·i·ty (few-gássəti) *n.* **1.** The state of being fugacious. **2.** *Symbol* **f** (usually italic *f*). A property of a gas that is a measure of its ability to escape or expand, given by d $(\log_e f) = d\mu/RT$, where μ is the chemical potential, R is the gas constant, and T is the thermodynamic temperature.
Fu·gard (fo͞ogaard), **Athol** (1932–). South African playwright, actor, director. His plays, including *The Blood Knot* (1963), *Boesman and Lena* (1969), and *A Lesson from Aloes* (1981), examine the treatment of society's misfits and outcasts. Novel: *Tsotsi* (1980).
-fuge *n. comb. form.* Indicates an expulsion or driving away; for example, **vermifuge.** [Latin *fugāre,* to put to flight, expel, from *fuga,* flight.]
fu·gi·tive (fyo͞ojitiv) *adj.* **1.** Running or having run away; fleeing, as from justice or the law. **2. a.** Passing quickly; fleeting: *fugitive hours.* **b.** Difficult to comprehend or retain; elusive. **c.** Given to change or disappearance; perishable. **3.** Having to do with topics of temporary interest; ephemeral. —See Synonyms at **transient.**
∼*n.* **1.** One who flees; a runaway; a refugee. **2.** Anything fleeting or ephemeral. [Middle English *fugitif,* from Old French, from Latin *fugitīvus,* from adjective, "fleeing", from *fugitus,* past participle of *fugere,* to flee.] **—fu·gi·tive·ly** *adv.* **—fu·gi·tive·ness** *n.*
fu·gle (fyo͞og'l) *intr.v.* **-gled, -gling, -gles.** *Archaic.* To act as a fugleman. [Back-formation from FUGLEMAN.]
fu·gle·man (féwg'l-man, -mən) *n., pl.* **-men** (-men, -mən). **1.** *Archaic.* A soldier who serves as a guide and model for his company. **2.** A leader; especially, a political leader. [German *Flügelmann,* soldier, "man on the wing" : *Flügel,* wing, + *Mann,* man.]
fugue (fewg) *n.* **1.** A polyphonic musical style or form in which a theme or themes stated sequentially and in imitation are developed contrapuntally. **2.** A pathological amnesiac condition during which the patient leaves his usual surroundings to begin a new life somewhere else. He is apparently conscious of his actions but on return to normal has no recollection of them. [French *fugue,* or Italian *fuga,* flight, from Latin, flight.] **—fu·gal** *adj.* **—fu·gal·ly** *adv.*
füh·rer, fueh·rer (féwr-ər || *German* fü-rər) *n.* **1.** A leader; especially, one exercising the powers of a dictator. **2.** *Capital* **F.** The title of Adolf Hitler as the leader of the German Nazis. [German *Führer,* from Middle High German *vüerer,* bearer, from *vüeren,* to lead, bear, from Old High German *fuoren,* to lead.]
Fu·jian or **Fu·chien** (fo͞o-jén). Also **Fukien** (fo͞o-jyen). Province in southeast China. It has some of Asia's finest scenery, with wooded mountains such as the Wuyi Shan, terraced rice paddies, orchards, and tea gardens. [Chinese, "happy establishment".]
Fu·ji·ya·ma (fo͞oji-yaámə). Also **Fuji-san** or **Mount Fuji.** Active volcano, on the island of Honshu, and the highest mountain (3 776 metres; 12,388 feet) in Japan. Its summit is a place of pilgrimage, and its snow-capped, strikingly symmetrical cone has long been a favourite subject of Japanese painters. The last major eruption took place in 1707.
Fukien. See **Fujian.**
-ful *suffix.* Indicates: **1.** Having the characteristics of; for example, **masterful. 2.** Tendency or ability; for example, **useful. 3.** The amount or number that will fill; for example, **armful.** [Middle English *-ful,* Old English *-ful, -full,* from *full,* FULL.]
Usage: Usage now generally favours a final *-s* as the plural of nouns ending in *-ful,* such as *bucketfuls, spoonfuls. Bucketsful* or *spoonsful* are now considered to be somewhat old-fashioned.
Fu·la (fo͞olə) *n., pl.* **-las** or collectively **Fula.** Also **Fu·lah** (fo͞olaa). A mostly Muslim people of the western Sudan region of Africa, of mixed Hamitic and Negroid stock.
Fu·la·ni (fo͞o-laáni, fo͞oləni) *n., pl.* **-nis** or collectively **Fulani. 1.** A member of the Fula. **2.** The language of the Fula.
ful·crum (fo͞ol-krəm, fúl-) *n., pl.* **-crums** or **-cra** (-krə). **1.** The point or support on which a lever turns. **2.** A factor critically affecting an outcome, reaction, or the like: *Cost was the fulcrum of their decision.* [Latin, bedpost, support, from *fulcīre,* to prop up, support.]
ful·fil, *U.S.* **ful·fill** (fo͞ol-fíl) *tr.v.* **-filled, -filling, -fils** or *U.S.* **-fills. 1.** To realise (expectations or promise, for example); achieve. **2.** To carry out (an order or duty, for example). **3.** To measure up to; satisfy. **4.** To go to the end of (a period of time); finish or complete. **—fulfil (oneself).** To achieve personal fulfilment. —See Synonyms at **perform.** [Middle English *fulfillen,* Old English *fullfyllan,* to fill full : FULL + *fyllan,* to FILL.] **—ful·fill·er** *n.*
ful·fil·ment (fo͞ol-fílmənt) *n.* **1.** The act or process of fulfilling. **2.** The state or quality of being fulfilled; completion. **3.** Satisfaction gained from fully realising one's personal aims or potential. **4.** The processing of orders in a direct mail operation, as for magazine subscriptions.
ful·gent (fúljənt) *adj. Literary.* Shining brilliantly. [Middle English, from Latin *fulgēns* (stem *fulgent-*), present participle of *fulgēre,* to flash, shine.] **—ful·gent·ly** *adv.*
ful·gu·rant (fúl-gewr-ənt || fo͞ol-) *adj.* **1.** *Rare.* Flashing like lightning. **2.** *Medicine.* Fulminant. [Latin *fulgurāns* (stem *fulgurant-*), present participle of *fulgurāre,* to FULGURATE.]
ful·gu·rate (fúl-gewrayt || fo͞ol-) *v.* **-rated, -rating, -rates.** *—intr.* To give off or seem to give off flashes of lightning. *—tr. Medicine.* To destroy (tissue) by fulguration. [Latin *fulgurāre,* to flash, glow like lightning, from *fulgur,* lightning, from *fulgēre,* to flash, shine.]
ful·gu·ra·tion (fúl-gewr-áysh'n || fo͞ol-) *n.* **1.** The act of flashing like lightning or flashing with light. **2.** The destruction of unwanted tissue, such as warts, with electric current.
ful·gu·rite (fúl-gewr-īt || fo͞ol-) *n.* A tubular body of glassy rock produced by lightning striking loose unconsolidated sand or more solid rock. [Latin *fulgur,* lightning (see **fulgurate**) + -ITE.]
ful·gu·rous (fúl-gewr-əss || fo͞ol-) *adj. Rare.* **1.** Emitting flashes of lightning. **2.** Appearing or acting like lightning. [Latin *fulgur,* lightning. See **fulgurate.**]
fu·lig·i·nous (few-líjinəss) *adj.* **1.** Sooty. **2.** Coloured by or as if by soot. [Late Latin *fūlīginōsus,* from Latin *fūlīgō* (stem *fūlīgin-*), soot.] **—fu·lig·i·nous·ly** *adv.*
full¹ (fo͞ol) *adj.* **fuller, fullest. 1.** Containing all that is normal or possible; filled: *a full bottle.* **2. a.** Not deficient or partial: *a full view of the stage.* **b.** Complete; no less than: *a full half hour.* **c.** Maximum: *its full length.* **d.** Whole; entire: *He realised the full implications of his act.* **e.** At the highest degree or at the greatest extent: *at full speed; in full colour.* **3. a.** Having a great deal or many of. Used with *of*: *A room full of people.* **b.** Abounding in. Used with *of*: *full of enthusiasm.* **4. a.** Profoundly affected by an emotion. **b.** Deeply engrossed or preoccupied by; talking and thinking of nothing else. Used with *of*: *They were all full of the idea.* **5. a.** Very busy: *a full day:* **b.** Satisfying; fulfilling: *a full life.* **6. a.** Having all appropriate rights and responsibilities: *a full member.* **b.** Designating a relation or relationship based on descent from the same parents: *a full cousin.* **7. a.** Rounded in shape; plump: *a full figure.* **b.** Of ample cut or generous proportions; wide: *full draperies.* **8. a.** Satiated, especially with food or drink; abundantly fed. **b.** *Slang.* Drunk. **9. a.** Having depth and body; rich: *a full colour.* **b.** Resonant: *the full tone of the cellos.* **10.** Full-bodied. Said of wines. **11.** Thoroughly documented and presented; detailed: *a full report.* **12.** Having the observable surface completely illuminated. Said of the moon. **13.** At the flood; high. Said of the tide. **14.** Extended by the wind. Said of sails.
∼*adv.* **1.** To a complete extent; entirely. Often used in combination: *full-grown.* **2.** Exactly; directly: *full in the path of the ball.* **3.** Quite; equally: *full wicked as I am.* **—full well.** Very well: *I know full well how you feel.*
∼*v.* **fulled, fulling, fulls.** *—tr.* To make (a garment) full, as by pleating or gathering. *—intr.* To become full. Used of the moon.
∼*n. Rare.* The maximum or complete size, amount, or development. **—at the full.** At the state or period of fullness. **—in full. 1.** To, for, or with the entire amount. **2.** Completely; with nothing left out. **—to the full.** To the utmost extent; completely. [Middle English *ful(l),* Old English *full.*]
full² *v.* **fulled, fulling, fulls.** *—tr.* To clean and increase the weight and bulk of (cloth) by washing, shrinking, and beating or pressing. *—intr.* To become heavier and more compact. Used of cloth. [Middle English *fullen,* from Old French *fouler,* from Vulgar Latin *fullāre* (unattested), from Latin *fullō*†, a fuller.]
full·back (fo͞ol-bak) *n.* **1.** In Rugby football, soccer, and other games, a defensive player positioned near the goal. **2.** The position played by a fullback.
full blood *n.* **1.** Relationship established through having the same parents. **2.** A person or animal of unmixed race or breed; a purebred.
full-blood·ed (fo͞ol-blúddid) *adj.* Also **full-blood** (fo͞ol-blud) (for sense 1). **1. a.** Of unmixed ancestry; purebred. **b.** Related through having the same parents. **2.** Vigorous; forceful. **3.** Thoroughgoing: *a full-blooded communist.*
full·blown (fo͞ol-blṓn) *adj.* **1.** In full blossom; fully open: *a full-blown tulip.* **2.** Fully developed or matured: *a full-blown beauty; full-blown AIDS.*
full board *n.* The provision of all meals at a hotel, boarding house, or the like.
full-bod·ied (fo͞ol-bóddid) *adj.* Having richness and intensity of flavour. Said of wines.
full-bot·tomed (fo͞ol-bóttəmd) *adj.* Long at the back. Said of a wig.
full brother *n.* See **brother.**
full cousin *n.* See **cousin.**
full-cream (fo͞ol-kréem) *adj.* Designating or made with milk that has had none of the cream skimmed away.
full dress *n.* The attire appropriate for formal or ceremonial events.
full-dress (fo͞ol-dréss) *adj.* **1.** Requiring or consisting of full dress; formal: *a full-dress banquet.* **2.** Full-scale: *a full-dress investigation.*
full·er¹ (fo͞ollər) *n.* A person who fulls cloth. [Middle English *fullere,* Old English *fullere,* from Latin *fullō.* See **full** (verb).]
fuller² *n.* **1.** A hammer used by a blacksmith for grooving or spreading iron. **2.** A groove made with this tool.

~*tr.v.* **fullered, -ering, -ered.** To make (a groove) with a fuller. [Perhaps from the name *Fuller*.]

Ful·ler (fŏŏllər), **(Richard) Buckminster** (1895–1983). U.S. designer and architect. His high-efficiency, low-pollution, prefabricated "Geodesic Domes" are popular in the United States, and his book, *Operating Manual for Spaceship Earth* (1969), was influential in the environmentalist movement of the 1970s.

Fuller, Roy (Broadbent) (1912–91). British poet and novelist. A practising solicitor, he published his first collection of poetry in 1939; Oxford professor of poetry (1968–73). His later works include *New Poems* (1968), and the novel, *My Child, My Sister* (1965).

ful·ler·ene (fŏŏllə-rēen) *n.* Any of a class of carbon molecules with pentagonal and hexagonal faces. Compare **buckminsterfullerene, buckyball.** [After FULLER, *(Richard) Buckminster* (because the shape can resemble that of his "Geodesic Domes") + -ENE.]

fuller's earth *n.* A highly absorbent clay used in fulling woollen cloth from which it absorbs fat, as a decoloriser, as a filter, and as a catalyst.

fuller's teasel *n.* A European plant, *Dipsacus fullonum,* having bristly flower heads used by fullers to raise the nap on cloth. See **teasel.**

full face *adv.* Face on to an observer or a specified object.

full-fron·tal (fŏŏl-frúnt'l) *adj.* **1.** Directed or situated at the front: *a full-frontal attack.* **2.** *Informal.* Designating or giving a front view of a naked person.

~*n. Informal.* A full-frontal picture or photograph.

full house *n.* **1.** In poker, a hand containing three of a kind and a pair. **2.** A theatre, cinema, or the like in which every seat for a performance is taken. **3.** A winning set of numbers at bingo.

full-length (fŏŏl-léngth, -léngkth ‖ -lénth) *adj.* **1.** Showing, covering, or fitted to the entire length of someone or something: *a full-length mirror.* **2.** Of a normal length; unabridged: *a full-length novel.*

full monty (món-ti) *n. Informal.* The (full) works, with nothing withheld. Used with *the.* [Perhaps from MONTE or by alteration of *amount.*]

full moon *n.* **1.** The phase of the moon when it is visible as a fully illuminated disc. **2.** The period of the month when this occurs. **3.** The fully illuminated moon.

full-mouthed (fŏŏl-mówthd, -mówtht) *adj.* **1.** Having a complete set of teeth. Said of cattle and other livestock. **2.** Uttered loudly or noisily: *a full-mouthed oath.*

full nelson *n.* A wrestling hold in which both hands are first thrust under the opponent's arms from behind and then pressed against the back of his neck. Compare **half nelson.**

full·ness, *U.S.* **ful·ness** (fŏŏl-nəss, -niss) *n.* The quality or state of being full. —**in the fullness of time.** At the proper, appointed time.

full out *adj.* Written out in full; not abbreviated. **2.** *Printing.* Not indented; aligned with the margin. —**full out** *adv.*

full radiator *n. Physics.* A **black body** (see).

full-rig·ged (fŏŏl-rígd) *adj.* Having three or more masts all square-rigged.

full rhyme *n.* A **perfect rhyme** (see).

full-scale (fŏŏl-skáyl) *adj.* **1.** Of the actual or full size; not reduced: *a full-scale model.* **2.** Carried out in a thoroughgoing manner and with a total commitment of effort: *a full-scale campaign.* **3.** Occurring on a large scale: *a full-scale disaster.*

full sister *n.* See **sister.**

full stop *n. Chiefly British.* A dot indicating the end of a sentence or an abbreviation. Also called "full point".

full time *n.* In sports such as soccer and Rugby football, the end of a match.

full-time (fŏŏl-tím) *adj.* **1.** Of, pertaining to, or designating work requiring attendance throughout the working week. Compare **part-time. 2.** Performing an activity or job for the normal or required amount of time: *a full-time student.* **3.** Of or pertaining to an activity that requires a person's full attention. —**full-time** *adv.*

full toss *n.* In cricket, a ball bowled so as to reach the batsman without bouncing. Also call "full pitch".

ful·ly (fŏŏlli) *adv.* **1.** Totally or completely. **2.** Adequately; sufficiently. **3.** At a conservative estimate; at least.

fully fashioned *adj.* Shaped so as to follow the line of the body. Said of knitted garments, stockings, or the like.

fully fledged *adj.* **1.** Having fully developed adult plumage. **2.** Having reached full development; mature. **3.** Having reached full professional status: *a fully fledged doctor.*

ful·mar (fŏŏl-mər, -maar) *n.* **1.** A gull-like bird, *Fulmarus glacialis,* of Arctic regions, having smoky grey plumage. Also called "fulmar petrel". **2.** Any of several similar, related birds. [Perhaps from Old Norse *fúlmár,* "foul gull" (probably referring to its smell) : *fúll,* foul + *már,* gull, from Germanic *maiwa-* (unattested), gull, MEW.]

ful·mi·nant (fúl-minənt, fŏŏl-) *adj.* **1.** Fulminating. **2.** *Pathology.* Occurring suddenly, rapidly, and with great intensity. Said of symptoms, especially of pain. [Latin *fulmināns* (stem *fulminant-*), present participle of *fulmināre,* to strike with lightning, FULMINATE.]

ful·mi·nate (fúl-mi-nayt, fŏŏl-) *v.* **-nated, -nating, -nates.** —*intr.* **1.** To issue a thunderous verbal attack or denunciation; inveigh: *fulminate against political chicanery.* **2.** To explode or detonate with sudden violence. —*tr.* **1.** To thunder out or issue (a decree or denunciation, for example). **2.** To cause to explode.

~*n.* An explosive salt or ester of fulminic acid; especially, fulminate of mercury. [Middle English *fulminaten,* from Medieval Latin *fulmināre* (past participle *fulminātus*), to censure (in ecclesiastical decrees), from Latin, to strike with lightning, from *fulmen* (stem *fulmin-*), lightning.] —**ful·mi·na·tor** *n.* —**ful·mi·na·to·ry** (-nətri, náytəri) *adj.*

fulminate of mercury *n.* A grey crystalline powder, $Hg(CNO)_2$, that explodes on impact when dry and is used as a high explosive.

fulminating powder *n.* An explosive powder that can be detonated by impact.

ful·mi·na·tion (fúl-mi-náysh'n, fŏŏl-) *n.* **1.** The act of fulminating. **2.** A thunderous denunciation or censure. **3.** A violent explosion.

ful·min·ic acid (ful-mínnik, fŏŏl-) *n.* An unstable acid, HONC, that forms highly explosive salts and esters. [Latin *fulmen* (stem *fulmin-*), lightning. See **fulminate.**]

ful·some (fŏŏl-səm) *adj.* **1.** Lavish; abundant: *fulsome praise.* **2.** Offensively excessive or insincere. **3.** *Archaic.* Offensive to the senses; loathsome; disgusting. [Middle English *fulsom,* abundant : FULL + -SOME.] —**ful·some·ly** *adv.* —**ful·some·ness** *n.*

ful·vous (fúl-vəss, fŏŏl-) *adj.* Tawny, yellowish-brown. [Latin *fulvus;* akin to *fulgēre,* to shine.]

fu·mar·ic acid (few-márrik) *n.* An acid, $C_4H_4O_4$, found in various plants and produced synthetically, used mainly in resins, paints, and varnishes. [New Latin *Fumaria,* genus of fumitory, from Late Latin *fūmāria,* fumitory, from Latin *fūmus,* smoke.]

fu·ma·role (féwma-rōl) *n.* A vent or small hole in a volcanic area from which hot water vapours, smoke and gases arise. [Italian *fumarola,* from Late Latin *fūmāriolum,* smoke hole, from Latin *fūmārium,* smoke chamber, from *fūmus,* smoke.]

fu·ma·to·ri·um (féwmə-táwri-əm ‖ -tôri-) *n., pl.* **-ums** or **-toria** (táwri-ə ‖ tôri-). Also **fumatory.** An airtight fumigation chamber in which chemical vapours are used to destroy insects and fungi on plants. [New Latin, from Latin *fūmātus,* past participle of *fūmāre,* to smoke, from *fūmus,* smoke.]

fu·ma·to·ry (féwmə-təri, -tri) *adj.* Of or pertaining to smoke or fumigating.

~*n., pl.* **fumatories.** A fumatorium. [New Latin *fumatorius,* from FUMATORIUM.]

fum·ble (fúmb'l) *v.* **-bled, -bling, -bles.** —*intr.* **1.** To touch or handle nervously or idly: *fumble with a necktie.* **2.** To grope awkwardly to find or to accomplish: *fumble for a key.* **3.** To proceed awkwardly and uncertainly; blunder: *fumble through a speech.* —*tr.* **1.** To catch, touch, or handle clumsily or idly. **2.** To feel or make (one's way) awkwardly.

~*n.* **1.** The act of fumbling. **2.** An instance of fumbling. [Low German *fummeln†.*] —**tum·bler** *n.*

fume (fewm) *n.* **1.** *Often plural.* An exhalation of smoke, vapour, or gas; especially, an irritating or disagreeable exhalation. **2.** A strong or acrid odour. **3.** A state of irritation or anger.

~*v.* **fumed, fuming, fumes.** —*tr.* **1.** To subject to or treat with fumes. **2.** To give off in or as if in fumes. —*intr.* **1.** To emit fumes. **2.** To rise or dissipate in vapour. **3.** To feel or show agitation and anger. [Middle English, from Old French *fum,* from Latin *fūmus,* smoke, steam.]

fume cupboard *n.* A cupboard or glass chamber in a laboratory within which operations involving chemicals that emit harmful vapours are performed, or where such chemicals are stored.

fumed (fewmd) *adj.* Coloured or darkened as a result of exposure to ammonia fumes: *fumed oak.*

fu·mi·gate (féwmi-gayt) *tr.v.* **-gated, -gating, -gates.** To subject to smoke or fumes, usually in order to exterminate vermin or insects. [Latin *fūmigāre* : *fūmus,* smoke, FUME + *agere,* to make, do.] —**fu·mi·gant** *n.* —**fu·mi·ga·tion** (-gáysh'n) *n.* —**fu·mi·ga·tor** *n.*

fuming sulphuric acid *n.* A mixture of sulphuric acids made by dissolving sulphur trioxide in concentrated sulphuric acid. It is principally pyrosulphuric acid, $H_2S_2O_7$. Also called "oleum", "Nordhausen acid".

fu·mi·to·ry (féwmi-təri, -tri) *n., pl.* **-ries. 1.** A scrambling annual plant, *Fumaria officinalis,* native to Europe, having finely divided leaves and spurred purplish flowers. **2.** Any other plants of the genus *Fumaria.* [Middle English *fumetere,* from Old French *fumeterre,* from Medieval Latin *fūmus terrae,* "smoke of the earth" (its growth resembles a cloud of smoke over the ground) : Latin *fūmus,* smoke, FUME + *terrae,* genitive of *terra,* earth.]

fun (fun) *n.* **1.** A source of enjoyment or pleasure; amusing diversion: *Clowns are fun.* **2.** Enjoyment; pleasure: *have fun at the beach.* **3.** Excited, playful activity or altercation. —**for** or **in fun.** As a joke; playfully. —**make fun of** or **poke fun at.** To ridicule.

~*intr.v.* **funned, funning, funs.** To behave playfully; joke.

~*adj. Informal.* Providing fun; amusing: *a fun group of people.* [Perhaps from obsolete *fun,* to trick, from Middle English *fonnen,* to make fun of, from *fon, fonne,* a fool. See **fond.**]

fu·nam·bu·list (few-námbew-list) *n.* One who performs on a tightrope or a slack rope. [Probably from Latin *fūnambulus,* rope dancer : *fūnis†,* rope + *ambulāre,* to walk around.] —**fu·nam·bu·lism** *n.*

func·tion (fúngksh'n) *n.* **1.** The natural or proper action for which a person, office, thing, or organ is fitted or employed. **2. a.** Assigned duty or activity: *His functions include maintaining office records.* **b.** Specific occupation or role: *in his function as mayor.* **3.** An official ceremony or elaborate social occasion. **4.** Something closely related to another thing and dependent upon it for its existence, value, or significance. **5.** *Grammar.* The role or position of a linguistic element in a construction. **6.** *Mathematics.* **a.** A variable so related to another that for each value assumed by one there is a value determined for the other. **b.** A rule of correspondence between two sets such that there is a unique element in one set assigned to each element in the other.

~*intr.v.* **functioned, -tioning, -tions.** To have or perform a function; operate. [Latin *functiō* (stem *functiōn-*), activity, performance, from *functus*, past participle of *fungī*, to perform.]

func·tion·al (fúngksh'n'l) *adj.* **1.** Of or pertaining to a function or functions. **2. a.** Designed for or adapted to a particular practical need or activity: *functional clothing for infants*. **b.** Stressing practical usefulness and function other than extraneous embellishment: *functional architecture*. **3.** Capable of performing; operative. **4.** *Pathology*. Pertaining to a disease having no apparent physiological or structural cause. **5.** *Mathematics*. Of, relating to, or indicating a function or functions. **—func·tion·al·ly** *adv.*

functional disease *n.* Any disease having no apparent physiological or structural cause. Compare **organic disease**.

functional group *n. Chemistry*. The group of atoms in a molecule that determines its chemical behaviour; for example, -CHO is the functional group in aldehydes.

func·tion·al·ism (fúngksh'n'l-iz'm) *n.* **1.** The doctrine or the application of the doctrine that the function of an object should determine its design and materials. **2.** Any doctrine or its application stressing purpose, practicality, and utility.

functional shift *n. Linguistics*. A shift in the syntactic function of a word without a change in its form, as when a noun serves as a verb.

func·tion·ar·y (fúngksh'n-əri || -erri) *n., pl.* **-ies**. A person who holds an office or a trust; an official.

function word *n. Linguistics*. A word used to show a grammatical, logical or textual relationship in a sentence or phrase, such as a pronoun, conjunction, or article. Also called "form word".

fund (fund) *n.* **1.** A source of supply; a stock: *a fund of good will*. **2. a.** A sum of money or other resources set aside for a specific purpose: *the rebuilding fund*. **b.** *Plural*. Available money; finances. **3.** *Plural. British*. The permanent national debt, considered as securities. Preceded by *the*. **4.** An organisation established to administer a fund.
~tr.v. **funded, funding, funds**. **1.** To provide money for paying off the interest or principal of (a debt). **2.** To convert (a debt) into a long-term or floating debt with fixed interest payments. **3.** To place in a fund or accumulate. **4.** To furnish a fund or finance for: *fund cancer research*. [Blend of French *fond*, bottom, and *fonds*, stock, both from Latin *fundus*, bottom, landed property.]

fun·da·ment (fúndəmənt) *n.* **1. a.** The buttocks. **b.** The anus. In both senses, used humorously. **2.** The natural features of a land surface unaltered by human beings. **3.** A foundation. **4.** A theoretical basis; an underlying principle. [Middle English *foundement*, foundation, lower part, from Old French *fondement*, from Latin *fundāmentum*, from *fundāre*, to lay the bottom for, from *fundus*, bottom.]

fun·da·men·tal (fúndə-mént'l) *adj.* **1. a.** Having to do with the foundation; elemental; basic. **b.** Critical or central: *of fundamental importance*. **2.** Having to do with the origin; generative; primary: *fundamental research*. **3.** *Physics*. **a.** Of or pertaining to the component of lowest frequency of a periodic wave or quantity. **b.** Of or pertaining to the lowest possible frequency at which a system or element will vibrate naturally.
~n. **1.** Something that is an elemental part of a system, such as a principle or law; an essential. **2.** *Physics*. The lowest frequency of a periodically varying quantity or of a vibrating system. **3.** *Music*. The lowest or bass note of a chord, considered as the root of the chord. **—fun·da·men·tal·ly** *adv.*

fundamental constant *n. Physics*. The value of a physical quantity, such as the speed of light in a vacuum or the electronic charge, that is regarded as basic and constant under all circumstances. Also called "universal constant".

fun·da·men·tal·ism (fúndə-mént'l-iz'm) *n.* **1.** Belief in the Bible as factual historical record and incontrovertible prophecy, including such doctrines as the Creation, the Virgin Birth, and the Second Coming. **2. a.** *Often capital* F. A movement among Protestants based upon this belief. **b.** Adherence to this belief. **3.** Unswerving belief in a set of basic and unalterable principles of a religious or philosophical nature: *Muslim fundamentalism*. **—fun·da·men·tal·ist** *n. & adj.* **—fun·da·men·tal·ist·ic** (-ístik) *adj.*

fundamental particle *n. Physics*. An **elementary particle** *(see)*.

fundamental unit *n.* Any of a set of unrelated units used to measure different quantities, such as length, mass, and time, that form the basis of a system of units.

fun·di (fŏondi) *n.* **1.** *East African*. A maintenance man or mechanic; a mechanical expert. **2.** *South African*. An expert or authority in any field; a pundit. [Swahili.]

fund·rais·er (fúnd-rayzər) *n.* **1.** One who raises funds. **2.** A party or other activity to raise funds; benefit. **—fund·rais·ing** *adj. & n.*

fun·dus (fún-dəss) *n., pl.* **-di** (-dī). *Anatomy*. The inner basal surface of an organ farthest away from the opening, as in the eye or uterus. [New Latin, from Latin, bottom.]

Fun·dy, Bay of (fúndi). Arm of the Atlantic Ocean between the provinces of Nova Scotia and New Brunswick in eastern Canada. It is some 270 kilometres (168 miles) long, with a maximum width of 80 kilometres (50 miles). The bay's tidal range, which can be as much as 21 metres (68 feet), is the greatest in the world.

fu·ner·al (féwnərəl) *n.* **1.** The ceremonies held in connection with the burial or cremation of the dead. **2.** A party accompanying a body to the grave; a funeral procession. **3.** *Informal*. A problem; a source of trouble or worry: *that's his funeral!*
~adj. Of or relating to a funeral. [Middle English *funerelles*, rites for a dead person, from Old French *funerailles*, from Medieval Latin *fūnerālia*, from Late Latin, neuter plural of *fūnerālis*, funereal,

from Latin *fūnus†* (stem *fūner-*), funeral, death.]

funeral director *n.* An undertaker.

funeral honours *pl.n.* Last honours *(see)*.

fu·ner·ar·y (féwnə-rəri || -rerri) *adj.* Of or suitable for a funeral or burial. [Latin *fūnerārius*, from *fūnus* (stem *fūner-*), FUNERAL.]

fu·ne·re·al (few-néer-i-əl) *adj.* **1.** Of or suitable for a funeral: *a funereal wreath*. **2.** Suggesting gloom; mournful. [From Latin *fūnereus*, from *fūnus* (stem *fūner-*), FUNERAL]. **—fu·ne·re·al·ly** *adv.*

fun·fair (fún-fair) *n. British*. A **fair** *(see)* (sense 1).

fun·gal (fúng-g'l) *adj.* Of, pertaining to, or caused by a fungus; fungous.

fun·gi·ble (fúnjib'l) *adj. Law*. Being of such a nature or kind that one unit or part may be exchanged or substituted for another equivalent unit or part in the discharging of an obligation.
~n. Something fungible, such as money or grain. [Medieval Latin *fungibilis*, serving a function, from *fungī*, to perform.]

fun·gi·cide (fúnji-sīd, fúng-gi-) *n.* A substance that kills or is capable of killing fungi. [FUNG(US) + -I- + -CIDE]. **—fun·gi·cid·al** *adj.*

fun·gi·form (fúnji-fawrm, fúng-gi-) *adj.* Shaped like a mushroom. [FUNG(US) + -I- + -FORM.]

fun·gi·stat (fúnji-stat, fúng-gi-) *n.* A substance that stops or is capable of stopping the growth of fungi. **—fun·gi·stat·ic** (-státtik) *adj.*

fun·goid (fúng-goyd) *adj.* Resembling a fungus.

fun·gous (fúng-gəss) *adj.* **1.** Of, pertaining to, resembling, or characteristic of a fungus; fungal. **2.** Caused by a fungus. [Middle English, from Latin *fungōsus*, from *fungus*, FUNGUS.]

fun·gus (fúng-gəss) *n., pl.* **-gi** (-gī, -gee, fúnjī) or **-guses**. **1.** Any of numerous mainly terrestrial organisms of the divisions Eumycophyta (true fungi) or Myxomycophyta (slime fungi), which lack chlorophyll and are therefore generally parasitic or saprophytic. They range from single cells to masses of filamentous hyphae that often produce specialised fruiting bodies, and include the yeasts, moulds, mildews, and toadstools. **2.** Loosely, any soft, spongy growth. [Latin, probably from Greek *sp(h)ongos*, SPONGE.]

fu·ni·cle (féwnik'l) *n. Botany*. The stalk connecting the ovule with the placenta in angiosperm ovaries. [Latin *fūniculus*, diminutive of *fūnis*, rope.]

fu·nic·u·lar (few-níckewlər, fə-) *adj.* **1.** Of, pertaining to, or resembling a rope or cord. **2.** Operated or moved by a cable. **3.** Of, pertaining to, or constituting a funiculus.
~n. A cable railway on a steep incline; especially, such a railway with simultaneously ascending and descending cars counterbalancing one another. Also called "funicular railway".

fu·nic·u·lus (few-níckew-ləss, fə-) *n., pl.* **-li** (-lī). Also **fu·ni·cle** (féwnik'l). **1.** *Anatomy*. A slender cordlike strand or band; especially: **a.** A bundle of nerve fibres in the nerve trunk; a fasciculus. **b.** One of the three major columns of white matter in each lateral half of the spinal cord. **c.** *Obsolete*. The umbilical cord or spermatic cord. **2.** *Botany*. A funicle. [New Latin, from Latin *fūniculus*, diminutive of *fūnis*, rope.]

funk¹ (fungk) *n. Chiefly British Informal*. **1. a.** A state of cowardly fright; panic. **b.** A state of extreme depression. **2.** A cowardly, fearful person.
~v. **funked, funking, funks**. *Chiefly British Informal*. *—tr.* **1.** To try to avoid out of fright; shrink from. **2.** To frighten. *—intr.* To shrink in fright; cower. [18th century (Oxford University slang) : perhaps special use of obsolete *funk*, tobacco smoke.] **—funk·er** *n.*

funk² *n. Slang*. Funky music.

funk hole *n. Chiefly British Informal*. **1.** A dugout. **2.** A job allowing the holder to avoid conscription. [From FUNK (panic).]

funk·y¹ (fúngki) *adj.* **-ier, -iest**. Frightened; panicky.

funky² *adj.* **-ier, -iest**. **1.** Designating a type of popular music, combining elements from jazz and blues, and characterised by a slow, syncopated rhythm and a heavily repetitive bass line. **2.** Characterised by self-expression, originality, and modishness; trendy and unconventional: *funky clothes*. [Originally "smelly", from obsolete *funk*, tobacco smoke. See **funk** (panic).] **—funk·i·ness** *n.*

fun·nel (fún'l) *n.* **1.** A conical utensil with a small hole or narrow tube at the apex used to channel a substance into a small-mouthed container or to support a filter paper in filtration. **2.** Something having such a conical form. **3.** A shaft, flue, or chimney for the passage of smoke or fumes; especially, the smokestack of a ship or locomotive.
~v. **funnelled** or *U.S.* **funneled, -nelling** or *U.S.* **-neling, -nels**. *—intr.* **1.** To assume the shape of a funnel. **2.** To move through or as if through a funnel: *Tourists funnel slowly through customs*. *—tr.* To cause to funnel. [Middle English *fonel*, from Provençal *fonilh*, from Latin *infundibulum*, from *infundere*, to pour in : *in-*, in + *fundere*, to pour.]

fun·nel-web spider (fún'l-web) *n.* Any large, black, poisonous spider of the family Agelemidae, constructing funnel-shaped webs.

fun·ny (fúnni) *adj.* **-nier, -niest**. **1.** Causing laughter or amusement; humorous or witty. **2.** Strange; odd; curious. **3.** *Informal*. Dizzy or unwell.
~n., pl. **funnies**. *Chiefly U.S. Informal*. **1.** A joke or witticism. **2.** *Plural*. Comic strips. [From FUN.] **—fun·ni·ly** *adv.* **—fun·ni·ness** *n.*

funny bone *n. Informal*. **1.** The point near the elbow where the ulnar nerve runs close to the surface and if accidentally knocked against the bone produces a tingling sensation; the **olecranon** *(see)*. Also *U.S.* "crazy bone". **2.** A sense of humour.

funny business *n. Informal.* Dishonest or underhand activity.

funny farm *n. Slang.* A mental hospital. Used facetiously.

fur (fur) *n.* **1.** The thick coat of hair covering the body of any of various animals, such as a fox, beaver, or cat. **2. a.** A dressed animal pelt, or part of one, used in the making of garments, trimmings, or decoration. **b.** Such pelts collectively. **c.** A synthetic fabric resembling dressed animal pelts. **3.** Any garment made of or lined with such pelts. **4.** Any coating of furlike material. **5.** A coating of whitish cellular debris on the tongue caused by stomach upset or smoking, for example. **6.** A greyish deposit, consisting mainly of calcium carbonate, deposited from hard water onto the internal surfaces of pipes, boilers, kettles, and the like. **—make the fur fly.** *Slang.* To cause or engage in a dispute or brawl.
~*adj.* Made of or lined with fur.
~*v.* **furred, furring, furs.** *—tr.v.* **1.** To cover or line with fur. **2.** To provide fur garments for. **3.** To cover with a furlike deposit: *intestinal disorders that fur the tongue.* **4.** To line (a wall or floor) with furring.
~*intr.* To become coated with calcium fur. Often used with *up.* [Middle English *furre,* from *furren,* to line with fur, from Old French *forrer,* from *forre,* lining, from Germanic.]

fur. furlong.

fu·ran (fewr-ən, fewr-án) *n.* Also **fur·fur·an** (fúr-fər-an, -fewr-). A colourless, volatile, liquid heterocyclic compound, C_4H_4O, derived from the dehydration of certain carbohydrates, used in the synthesis of organic compounds, especially nylon. [FUR(FURAL) + -AN.]

fur·be·low (fúrbi-lō) *n.* **1.** A ruffle or flounce on a garment. **2.** Any small piece of showy ornamentation.
~*tr.v.* **furbelowed, -lowing, -lows.** To decorate with furbelows. [Variant of FALBALA.]

fur·bish (fúrbish) *tr.v.* **-bished, -bishing, -bishes. 1.** To brighten by cleaning or rubbing; burnish. **2.** To restore to attractive or serviceable condition; renovate. [Middle English *furbishen,* from Old French *fo(u)rbir* (stem *fo(u)rbiss-*), from Germanic.] **—fur·bish·er** *n.*

fur·cate (fúr-kayt, fur-káyt) *intr.v.* **-cated, -cating, -cates.** To divide into branches; fork.
~*adj.* (fúr-kayt, -kit, -kət). Forked. [Late Latin *furcātus,* from Latin *furca,* FORK.]

fur·cu·la (fúrkew-lə) *n., pl.* **-lae** (-lee). Also **fur·cu·lum** (-ləm) *pl.* **-la** (-lə). A forked part or bone; especially, the wishbone of a bird. [New Latin, from Latin, diminutive of *furca,* FORK.]

fur·fur (fúrfər) *n., pl.* **-fures** (-fə-reez). *Sometimes plural.* A skin scale, as in dandruff. [Latin *furfur†,* bran, scales.]

fur·fur·a·ceous (fúr-fər-áyshəs, -fewr-) *adj.* **1.** Made of or covered with scaly particles, such as dandruff. **2.** Pertaining to or resembling bran. [Late Latin *furfurāceus* : FURFUR + -ACEOUS.]

fur·fur·al (fúr-fər-al, -fewr-) *n.* A colourless mobile liquid, C_4H_3OCHO, used as a solvent for cellulose nitrate and in the manufacture of dyes and plastics. Also called "fufuraldehyde". [*furfur* + *al*dehyde.]

Fu·ries (féwr-iz) *pl.n. Greek & Roman Mythology.* The three terrible, winged goddesses with serpents for hair, Alecto, Megaera, and Tisiphone, who pursue and punish doers of unavenged crimes. [Latin *Furiae,* plural of *furia,* FURY.]

fu·ri·o·so (féwr-i-ō-sō, -zō) *adv. Music.* In a tempestuous and headlong manner. Used as a direction. [Italian, from Latin *furiōsus,* FURIOUS.] **—fu·ri·o·so** *adj.*

fu·ri·ous (féwr-i-əss) *adj.* **1.** Full of or characterised by extreme anger; raging. **2.** Wild or frenetic in action or appearance: *the furious sea.* [Middle English, from Old French *furieus,* from Latin *furiōsus,* from *furia,* FURY.] **—fu·ri·ous·ly** *adv.* **—fu·ri·ous·ness** *n.*

furl (furl) *v.* **furled, furling, furls.** *—tr.* **1.** To take in and secure (a sail) to a yard, or mast. **2.** To roll up (an umbrella, flag, or the like). *—intr.* **1.** To be rolled up. **2.** To disappear as if furled: *the clouds furled away.*
~*n.* **1.** The act of furling. **2.** A single roll or rolled section of something furled. [Old French *ferler, ferlier* : *fer(m),* firm, from Latin *firmus,* FIRM + *lier,* to bind, from Latin *ligāre.*]

fur·long (fúr-long) *n. Abbr.* **fur.** A unit for measuring distance, equal to 201 metres, being $1/8$ mile or 220 yards. [Middle English *furlong,* Old English *furlang* : *furh,* FURROW + *lang,* LONG. Originally the length of the furrow made on a square field of 10 acres.]

fur·lough (fúrlō) *n. Chiefly U.S.* A leave of absence; especially leave of absence from duty granted to enlisted personnel of the armed services.
~*tr.v.* *Chiefly U.S.* **furloughed, -loughing, -loughs.** To grant a furlough to. [Dutch *verlof,* leave, permission, from Middle Dutch.]

furmenty. Variant of **frumenty.**

furn. furnished.

fur·nace (fúrniss) *n.* **1.** An enclosure in which energy in a non-thermal form is converted to heat; especially, such an enclosure in which heat is generated by the combustion of a suitable fuel to raise steam, smelt ores or burn refuse. **2.** Any intensely hot, enclosed place. **—tried in the furnace.** Severely tested. [Middle English *furna(i)s,* from Old French *fornais,* from Latin *fornāx* (stem *fornāc-*).]

Fur·ness (fúrniss). Low-lying peninsula on the coast of Cumbria in northwest England, between the Duddon estuary and Morecambe Bay.

fur·nish (fúrnish) *tr.v.* **-nished, -nishing, -nishes. 1.** To equip with what is needed. **2.** To provide furniture and other accessories for. **3.** To provide; supply: *The dictionary furnished an apt quotation.* [Middle English *furnisshen,* from Old French *furnir* (stem *furniss-*),

fornir, from Common Romance *fornir* (unattested), to supply, from Germanic.] **—fur·nish·er** *n.*

fur·nish·ings (fúrnishingz) *pl.n.* The furniture, curtains, carpets, and similar articles used to decorate and furnish a home or office.

fur·ni·ture (fúrnichər) *n.* **1. a.** The functional portable articles, such as beds, chairs or cupboards, as distinct from household equipment, with which a living area is provided. **b.** Fittings or accessories: *door furniture.* **2.** The necessary equipment for a factory, ship, or the like. **3.** *Printing.* Blank strips of wood or metal, placed between and around type on a page to hold it in place. [Old French *fourniture,* from *fournir, furnir,* to FURNISH.]

fu·ro·re (fewr-ráw-ri || -rō-) *n.* Also *chiefly U.S.* **fu·ror** (féwr-awr, -ōr). **1.** Violent anger; frenzy. **2.** A general commotion; public disorder or uproar. **3.** A fashion adopted enthusiastically by the public; a fad. [Latin, from *furere,* to rage. See **fury.**]

fur·phy (fúrfi) *n. Australian Slang.* A rumour or untrue story. [From *Furphy carts,* used in World War I for moving water and sewage (made at a foundry established by the Furphy family).]

furred (furd) *adj.* **1.** Bearing fur. **2.** Made, covered, or trimmed with fur. **3.** Wearing fur garments. **4.** Covered with a furlike deposit. **5.** Provided with furring, as a wall, ceiling, or floor.

fur·ri·er (fúrri-ər) *n.* One whose occupation is the dressing, designing, selling, or repairing of furs. [Middle English *furrer,* from Old French *forreor,* from *forrer,* to line with fur. See **fur.**]

fur·ri·er·y (fúrri-əri) *n., pl.* **-ies. 1.** Fur garments and trimmings collectively. **2.** The business of a furrier.

fur·ring (fúr-ing) *n.* **1. a.** A trimming or lining made of fur. **b.** Fur trimmings and linings, collectively. **2.** A furlike coating, as on the tongue or in a pipe. **3. a.** The act of preparing a wall, ceiling, or floor with strips of wood or metal to provide a level surface for the fixing of floorboards, plasterboard, or the like. **b.** Strips of material used for this. Also used adjectivally: *a furring strip.*

fur·row (fúrrō) *n.* **1.** A long, narrow, shallow trench made in the ground by a plough or other implement. **2.** Any rut, groove, or narrow depression similar to this. **3.** A deep wrinkle in the skin, as on the forehead. **—plough a lonely furrow.** To pursue one's objectives alone and unaided.
~*v.* **furrowed, -rowing, -rows.** *—tr.* **1.** To make furrows in; plough. **2.** To form deep wrinkles in. *—intr.* To become furrowed or deeply wrinkled. [Middle English *for(o)we, furgh,* Old English *furh.*]

fur·ry (fúr-i) *adj.* **-rier, -riest. 1.** Consisting of or decorated with fur. **2.** Covered with fur or a furlike coating. **3.** Resembling fur in thickness or softness. **—fur·ri·ness** *n.*

fur seal *n.* Any of several eared seals of the genera *Callorhinus* or *Arctocephalus,* having thick, soft underfur that is valued commercially.

fur·ther (fúrthər) *adj.* **1.** More distant in time or degree. **2.** Additional. **3.** More distant in space. **—See Usage note at farther.**
~*adv.* **1.** To a greater extent; more. **2.** In addition; furthermore; also. **3.** At or to a more distant point in space or time. **—See Usage note at farther.**
~*tr.v.* **furthered, -thering, -thers.** To help the progress of; advance. See Synonyms at **advance.** [Middle English *further,* Old English *furthor, furthra, fyrthrian,* (verb).] **—fur·ther·er** *n.*

fur·ther·ance (fúrthərənss) *n.* **1.** The act of furthering, advancing, or helping forward. **2.** One that furthers or assists.

further education *n.* Full- or part-time education provided for those who have left secondary school and wish to pursue vocational courses, as in engineering, commerce, or art.

fur·ther·more (fúrthər-mór || -mór) *adv.* Moreover; in addition.

fur·ther·most (fúrthər-mōst) *adj.* Most distant or remote.

fur·thest (fúrthist) *adj.* **1.** Most distant in time or degree. **2.** Most distant in space. **—See Usage note at farther.**
~*adv.* **1.** To the greatest extent or degree. **2.** At or to the most distant point in space or time. **—See Usage note at farthest.** [Middle English, from FURTHER.]

fur·tive (fúrtiv) *adj.* **1.** Characterised by stealth; surreptitious. **2.** Suggesting hidden motives or purposes; shifty. **—See Synonyms at secret.** [French *furtif,* from Old French, from Latin *furtīvus,* from *furtum,* theft, from *fūr†,* thief.] **—fur·tive·ly** *adv.* **—fur·tive·ness** *n.*

Furt·wäng·ler (fóort-veng-glər), **(Gustav Heinrich Ernst Martin) Wilhelm** (1886–1954). German orchestral and operatic conductor. The conductor of the Berlin Philharmonic Orchestra from 1922 until his death except for a short interval in 1934, he was the leading interpreter of 19th-century Romantic composers.

fu·run·cle (féwr-ungk'l) *n. Pathology.* A boil (*see*). [Latin *fūrunculus;* petty thief, vine knob that "steals" the sap from the main branches, boil, diminutive of *fūr,* thief. See **furtive.**] **—fu·run·cu·lar** (fewr-rúngkewlər) *adj.*

fu·run·cu·lo·sis (fewr-rúngkew-lō-siss) *n.* A skin complaint characterised by the simultaneous occurrence or continuing recurrence of furuncles. [Latin *fūrunculus,* FURUNCLE + -OSIS.]

fu·ry (féwr-i) *n., pl.* **-ries. 1.** Violent anger; rage. **2.** An outburst of violent rage. **3.** Violent, uncontrolled action; turbulence. **4.** One given to fits of violent anger. **5.** *Capital F.* Any of the Furies (*see*). **—See Synonyms at anger.** [Middle English *furie,* from Old French, from Latin *furia,* from *furere†,* to rage.]

furze (furz) *n.* A spiny shrub, **gorse** (*see*). [Middle English *furse, firse,* Old English *fyrs.*]

fu·sain (few-záyn || *French* fü-záN) *n.* **1.** Fine charcoal in stick form, made from the wood of a spindle tree. **2.** A sketch or drawing made with this. [French, from Vulgar Latin *fūsāgō* (unattested), spindle (formerly made from the wood of the spindle tree), from Latin *fūsus*, spindle. See **fuse**.]

fuse¹ (fewz) *n.* Also *U.S.* **fuze** (for sense 1). **1.** A length of readily combustible material that is lighted at one end to carry a flame to and detonate an explosive at the other. **2.** Any mechanical or electrical mechanism used to detonate an explosive charge or device, such as a bomb or a grenade. —*tr.v.* **fused, fusing, fuses.** To provide or equip with a fuse. [Italian *fuso*, from Latin *fūsus*†, spindle.]

fuse² *v.* **fused, fusing, fuses.** —*tr.* **1.** To liquefy or reduce to a plastic state by heating; melt. **2.** To mix together by or as if by melting; blend. **3.** To fit a fuse to (an electric plug, for example). **4.** To stop (an electrical appliance, for example) from functioning by overloading the fuse. —*intr.* **1.** To become liquefied from heat. **2.** To become mixed or united by or as if by melting together: *joy and sorrow fused into one.* **3.** To stop functioning when an electrical fuse has been overloaded. —*n.* **1.** A device containing an element that protects an electric circuit by melting when overloaded, thereby opening the circuit. **2.** A circuit-breaker fulfilling the same function. —See Synonyms at **mix**. [Latin *fundere* (past participle *fūsus*), to pour, melt.]

fuse box *n.* A box in which the fuses protecting a number of electrical circuits are housed.

fu·see, fu·zee (few-zée) *n.* **1.** A friction match with a large head capable of burning in a wind. **2.** A grooved, cone-shaped pulley in old-style clocks. **3.** A fuse for detonating explosives. [French *fusée*, spindle-shaped figure, from Old French *fusee*, from *fus*, spindle, from Latin *fūsus*. See **fuse**.]

fu·se·lage (féw-zi-laazh ‖ -sə-, -laaj) *n.* The central body of an aircraft that accommodates passengers, cargo, and crew, and to which the wings and tail assembly are attached. [French, from *fuseler*, to shape like a spindle, from *fuseau*, spindle, from Old French *fusel*, spindle, diminutive of *fus*, spindle, from Latin *fūsus*. See **fuse**.]

Fu·se·li (few-zélli), **Henry,** earlier Johann Heinrich Füssli (1741–1825). Swiss-born British artist. His works, including *The Nightmare* (1782), and his illustrations of the works of Shakespeare and Milton, display a fantastic, macabre quality which was to influence the Surrealists of the 1920s and 1930s.

fu·sel oil (féwz'l) *n.* A clear, colourless, poisonous, liquid mixture of amyl alcohols, obtained as a by-product of the fermentation of starch-containing and sugar-containing plant materials, and used as a solvent for fats, oils, resins, and waxes, and in the manufacture of explosives and pure amyl alcohols. [German *Fusel*†, bad liquor.]

fuse wire *n.* Thin metal wire, used in electrical fuses, that melts when a current passed through it exceeds a specific safe limit.

fu·si·ble (féwzi-b'l) *adj.* Capable of being fused or melted by heating. —**fu·si·bil·i·ty** (-billáti) *n.* —**fu·si·ble·ness** *n.*

fusible metal *n.* A metal alloy having a melting point below 300°F, used as solder and for safety plugs and fuses. Also called "fusible alloy".

fu·si·form (féwzi-fawrm) *adj.* Tapering at each end; spindle-shaped. [Latin *fūsus*, spindle (see **fuse**) + -i- + -FORM.]

fu·sil (féw-zil, -z'l) *n.* A light, flintlock musket. [French, musket, from Old French *fuisil*, fusil, steel for a tinderbox, from Vulgar Latin *focīle* (unattested), from Latin *focus*, fireplace. See **fuel**.]

fu·sile, fu·sil (few-sīl, -zīl ‖ *U.S. also* -z'l) *adj.* **1.** Formed by melting or casting. **2.** Capable of being fused. [Latin *fūsilis*, from *fūsus*, past participle of *fundere*, to melt, pour.]

fu·si·lier (féwzi-léer) *n.* Also **fu·si·leer** (for sense 2). **1.** A soldier armed with a fusil. **2.** *Capital F. Plural.* Soldiers belonging to certain British army regiments. [French, from FUSIL.]

fu·sil·lade (féw-zi-láyd ‖ -si-, -láad) *n.* **1.** A discharge of many firearms, simultaneously or in rapid succession. **2.** Any rapid outburst or barrage: *a fusillade of insults.* —*tr.v.* **fusilladed, -lading, -lades.** To attack or shoot down with a fusillade. [French, from *fusiller*, to shoot, from FUSIL.]

fu·sion (féwzh'n) *n.* **1.** The act or procedure of liquefying or melting together by heat. **2.** The liquid or melted state induced by heat. **3.** A union resulting from fusing. **4.** The merging of different elements into a union. **5.** *Physics.* A nuclear reaction in which any of certain light atomic nuclei combine to form more massive nuclei with the simultaneous release of energy. In this sense, also called "nuclear fusion". Compare **fission**. [Latin *fūsiō* (stem *fūsiōn-*), from *fūsus*, past participle of *fundere*, to pour, melt.]

fusion bomb *n.* An atomic bomb that derives its energy output principally from fusion reactions among light nuclei; especially, a **hydrogen bomb** (*see*). Also called "thermonuclear bomb".

fu·sion·ism (féwzh'n-iz'm) *n.* The theory, practice, or advocacy of forming coalitions of political groups or factions. —**fu·sion·ist** *n.*

fuss (fuss) *n.* **1.** Needless or useless excited activity; commotion; bustle. **2. a.** A state of excessive and unwarranted concern over an unimportant matter; needless worry. **b.** Objections; protests. **3.** A quarrel. —**make a fuss of.** To treat with exaggerated care and attention.
—*v.* **fussed, fussing, fusses.** —*intr.* **1.** To trouble or worry over trifles. **2.** To be excessively careful or solicitous. —*tr. Informal.* To disturb or vex with unimportant matters. [18th century (Anglo-Irish) : origin obscure.] —**fuss·er** *n.*

fuss·pot (fúss-pot) *n. Informal.* A person who fusses over trifles. Also *U.S.* "fussbudget".

fuss·y (fússi) *adj.* **-ier, -iest. 1.** Given to fussing; easily upset: *"The bridegroom, fussy as a poodle, pops his eyes"* (Kenneth Tynan). **2.** Insistent upon petty matters or details; fastidious. **3.** Calling for or requiring great attention to trivial details; meticulous. **4.** Full of superfluous details or trimmings; ornate. —**fuss·i·ly** *adv.* —**fuss·i·ness** *n.*

fus·ta·nel·la (fústə-néllə) *n.* A short, stiff skirt of white cloth worn by men in modern Greece. [Italian, from Modern Greek *phoustanella*, diminutive of *phoustani*, from Italian *fustagno*, coarse cloth, from Medieval Latin *fustāneus*, FUSTIAN.]

fus·ti·an (fústi-ən) *n.* **1.** Any of several thick, twilled cotton fabrics with a short nap. **2.** Pretentious speech or writing; pompous language.
—*adj.* **1.** Made of fustian. **2.** Pompous; ranting; bombastic. [Middle English, from Old French *fustai(g)ne,* from Medieval Latin *fustāneus*, cloth, perhaps of *Fostat,* suburb of Cairo.]

fus·tic (fústik) *n.* **1.** A tropical American tree, *Chlorophora tinctoria,* having wood yielding a yellow dyestuff. **2.** The wood of this tree. **3.** The dyestuff obtained from such wood. **4.** Any of various trees, such as sumacs, that yield a similar dye. [Middle English *fustik,* from Old French *fustoc,* from Arabic *fustuq,* from Greek *pistakē,* PISTACHIO.]

fus·ti·gate (fústi-gayt) *tr.v.* **-gated, -gating, -gates.** To beat with a club; cudgel. [Late Latin *fūstigāre* : Latin *fūstis*†, club + *agere,* to do.]

fus·ty (fústi) *adj.* **-tier, -tiest. 1.** Smelling of mildew or decay; musty; mouldy. **2.** Old-fashioned; antiquated. [Middle English, from Old French *fuste,* barrel, stale odour of a barrel, from *fust,* barrel, tree trunk, club, from Latin *fūstis*†, club.] —**fus·ti·ly** *adv.* —**fus·ti·ness** *n.*

fut. *Grammar.* future.

fu·thark, fu·tharc (fóo-thaark) *n.* Also **fu·thork, fu·thorc** (-thawrk) The runic alphabet. [From the first six letters of the alphabet: *f, u, th* (thorn), *a* or *o, r, k.*]

fu·tile (féwtīl ‖ *U.S.* -t'l) *adj.* **1.** Having no useful result; ineffectual; useless; vain. **2.** Unproductive; frivolous; idle: *futile talk.* [Latin *futtilis, fūtilis,* untrustworthy, useless.] —**fu·tile·ly** *adv.* —**fu·tile·ness** *n.*

fu·til·i·tar·i·an (few-tilli-taír-i-ən) *adj.* Holding or based on the view that human endeavour is futile.
—*n.* One who holds such a view. [Blend of FUTILE and UTILITARIAN.]

fu·til·i·ty (few-tílləti) *n., pl.* **-ties. 1.** The quality of being futile; uselessness; ineffectiveness. **2.** Lack of importance or purpose. **3.** Anything that is futile.

fu·ton (fóo-tón) *n.* A Japanese mattress for sleeping on. [Japanese.]

fut·tock (fúttək) *n. Nautical.* Any of the curved timbers that form a rib in the frame of a wooden ship. [Middle English *fottek,* perhaps variant of *fothok* (unattested) : FOOT + HOOK.]

futtock plate *n. Nautical.* Any of the iron plates attached to a top on a mast to hold the ends of the futtock shrouds.

futtock shroud *n. Nautical.* Any of the iron rods extending from the futtock plate, used to brace a top on a mast.

fu·ture (féwchər) *n.* **1.** The indefinite period of time yet to be; time that is to come. **2.** That which will happen in time to come. **3.** The prospective or foreseen condition of a person or thing: *a man's future.* **4.** Prospects of advancement; chances of success: *a business with no future.* **5.** *Plural.* Commodities or shares bought or sold at an agreed price for delivery in time to come. **6.** *Abbr.* **fut.** *Grammar.* **a.** The future tense. **b.** A verb in the future tense. —**in future.** **1.** As from now. **2.** On subsequent occasions.
—*adj.* **1.** That is to be or come in the future. **2.** Of or relating to time to come. **3.** That will be as specified at a later time: *a future politician.* [Middle English, from Old French *futur,* from Latin *futūrus,* future participle of *esse,* to be.]

future life *n.* An existence posited for human beings after death.

future perfect *n. Grammar.* **1.** A verb tense expressing action completed by a specified time in the future. This tense is formed in English by combining *will have* or *shall have* with a past participle; for example, *They will have counted all the votes by midnight.* **2.** A verb in this tense.

future shock *n.* The disorientation suffered by people bewildered by rapid changes in the social structure or technology of modern society. [After the book *Future Shock* (1970) by Alvin Toffler (born 1928), U.S. author.]

future tense *n.* A verb tense used to express action in the future; for example, *I will see you tomorrow.*

fu·tur·ism (féwchə-riz'm) *n.* An artistic movement originating in Italy in about 1909 and marked by an attempt to depict vividly the energetic and dynamic quality of contemporary life, as influenced by the motion and force of modern machinery. —**fu·tur·ist** *n. & adj.*

fu·tu·ris·tic (féwchə-rístik) *adj.* **1.** Of or pertaining to futurism. **2.** Suggesting the future; indicating advanced thinking: *futuristic design.*

fu·tu·ri·ty (few-téwr-əti) *n., pl.* **-ties. 1.** The future. **2.** The condition or quality of being in or of the future. **3.** A future event or possibility.

fu·tu·ro·lo·gy (féwchə-róllə ji) *n.* The study or prediction of the likely future state of the world and its inhabitants.

fuze *U.S.* Variant of **fuse**.

fuzee. Variant of **fusee**.

Fu·zhou, Fu-chou or **Foochow** (fóo-jó). Capital city of the southeastern province of Fujian in China, situated on the estuary of the Min Jiang. It is an ancient walled city, dating from at least the 2nd century B.C., and has been the capital of Fujian province since the 10th century. Since the mid-19th century it has been one of China's major naval stations and international trading ports.

fuzz¹ (fuz) *n.* **1.** A mass of fine, light particles, fibres, or hairs; down: *the fuzz on a peach.* **2.** A blur.
~*v.* **fuzzed, fuzzing, fuzzes.** —*tr.* To cover with fuzz. —*intr.* To become blurred. [Perhaps back-formation from FUZZY.]

fuzz² *n. Slang.* The police; policemen collectively. Preceded by *the.* [20th century : origin obscure.]

fuzz·y (fúzzi) *adj.* **-ier, -iest. 1.** Covered with fuzz. **2.** Of or resembling fuzz. **3.** Not sharply delineated or focused; indistinct; blurred. **4.** Not clearly reasoned or expressed; confused. **5.** Frizzy or very tightly curled. Said of hair. [Perhaps from Low German *fussig,* spongy.] —**fuzz·i·ly** *adv.* —**fuzz·i·ness** *n.*

fuz·zy-wuz·zy (fúzzi-wuzzi) *n., pl.* **-zies. 1.** *Slang.* A black or coloured person. Usually considered offensive. **2.** *Informal.* Formerly, a Sudanese soldier. [Reduplication of FUZZY (with reference to the hair).]

fwd. forward.

f.w.d. 1. four-wheel drive. **2.** front-wheel drive.

FX *pl.n.* In radio, films, or television, special visual effects or sound effects. Compare SFX. [Pronunciation spelling of *effects*.]

-fy *v. suffix.* Indicates a making or forming into; for example, **reify, nitrify.** [Middle English *-fien,* from Old French *-fier,* from Latin *-ficāre,* from *-ficus,* -FIC.]

fyl·fot (fíl-fot) *n.* An ornamental figure identified with the swastika. [Middle English, device for filling the foot of a painted window : *fillen,* to FILL + FOOT.]

Fy·ling·dales Moor (fíling-daylz). Bleak stretch of the North York Moors in England. It is dominated by the huge golfball-like radar spheres of the Fylingdales Early Warning Stations, a part of NATO's defence system against enemy missiles.

FYROM *Former Yugoslav Republic of Macedonia.*

F.Z.S. Fellow of the Zoological Society.

G

g, G (jee) *n., pl.* **g's** or *rare* **gs, Gs** or **G's. 1.** The seventh letter of the modern English alphabet. **2.** Any of the speech sounds represented by this letter.

g, G, g., G. *Note:* As an abbreviation or symbol, *g* may be a small or a capital letter, with or without a full stop. Established forms or those generally preferred precede the definition. When no form is given, all four forms are in general use in that sense. **1. g.** acceleration of free fall. **2. g.** gallon. **3. g., G.** gauge. **4. G.** *Physics.* gauss. **5. g.** gelding. **6. g.** gender. **7. g.** genitive. **8. G** German. **9. G.** giga-. **10. g., G.** good. **11. g., G.** gourde. **12. g.** gram. **13. G.** *Physics.* gravitational constant. **14. g.** guide. **15. g., G.** guinea. **16. G.** gulf (ocean area). **17.** The seventh in a series.

G *n., pl.* **Gs** or **G's. 1.** *Music.* **a.** The fifth note in the scale of C major. **b.** The key or a scale in which G is the tonic. **c.** A written or printed note representing G. **d.** A string, key, or pipe tuned to the pitch of G. **2.** Something shaped like the letter G. **3.** *Slang.* A grand (one thousand pounds, dollars, or the like).

Ga The symbol for the element gallium.

Ga. Georgia.

G.A. 1. general assembly. **2.** general average.

gab (gab) *intr.v.* **gabbed, gabbing, gabs.** *Informal.* To talk easily or excessively about trivial matters; chatter.
~*n. Informal.* Chatter; prattle. [Perhaps from Scottish *gab,* mouthful, lump, mouth, variant of GOB (lump).] —**gab·ber** (gábbər) *n.*

gab·bart (gább-ərt) *n.* Also **gab·bard** (-ərd). *Scottish.* A flat-bottomed barge used to load and unload cargo offshore or to transport goods on inland waterways. [Modification of Old French *gab(-b)arre,* from Old Provençal *gabarra,* probably from Late Latin *carabus,* a small, rawhide-covered boat, from Greek *karabos†,* horned beetle, crayfish, light ship.]

gab·ble (gább'l) *v.* **-bled, -bling, -bles.** —*intr.* **1.** To speak rapidly or incoherently; jabber. **2.** To make rapid, repeated cackling noises. Used especially of geese. —*tr.* To utter quickly or unintelligibly. ~*n.* **1.** Rapid, incoherent, or meaningless speech. **2.** A jumble of cackling noises or meaningless utterances. [Middle Dutch *gabbelen* (imitative).]

gab·bro (gábbrō) *n., pl.* **-bros.** Coarse-grained, intrusive igneous rock composed chiefly of plagioclase feldspar and pyroxene, sometimes with other minerals. There are several types, including norite. [Italian, from Latin *glaber,* smooth, bald.]

gab·by (gábbi) *adj.* **-bier, -biest.** *Informal.* Tending to talk excessively.

gab·er·dine (gábbər-deen, -dèen) *n.* Also **ga·bar·dine** (for sense 1). **1.** A worsted cotton, wool, or rayon twill, used in making dresses, suits, and coats. **2.** A raincoat made of this material. **3.** A long, coarse garment, such as a cloak or frock, worn during the Middle Ages. [Earlier *gawbardine,* from Old French *gauvardine, gallevardine,* "pilgrim's frock", from Middle High German *wallevart,* pilgrimage : *wallen,* to roam, from Old High German *wallōn + vart,* journey, way, from *faran,* to go.] —**gab·er·dine** *adj.*

Ga·bin (ga-bán), **Jean,** born Jean Alexis Moncorgé (1904–76). French film actor. He starred in *La Grande Illusion* (1937), and played Simenon's detective, Inspector Maigret.

ga·bi·on (gáybi-ən ‖ gábbi-) *n.* **1.** A cylindrical wicker basket filled with earth and stones, formerly used in building fortifications. **2.** A similar cylinder, often of metal, used in constructing dams, foundations, and the like. [Old French *gabion,* from Old Italian *gabbione,* augmentative of *gabbia,* cage, from Latin *cavea,* a hollow, enclosure, from *cavus,* hollow.]

ga·bi·on·ade (gáybi-ə-náyd ‖ gábbi-) *n.* A fortification or defensive embankment or wall built with gabions. [French *gabionnade,* from Old Italian *gabbionata,* from *gabbione,* GABION.]

ga·ble (gáyb'l) *n. Architecture.* **1.** The triangular wall section at the ends of a pitched roof, bounded by the two roof slopes and the ridge. **2.** That end of a building having a gable in the roof section. Also called "gable end". **3.** Any triangular architectural section, usually ornamental, as over a door or window. [Middle English *gable, gabyl,* from Old French *gable,* probably from Old Norse *gafl.*] —**ga·bled** *adj.*

Ga·ble (gáyb'l), **Clark** (1901–60). U.S. actor. He became known as the King of Hollywood after his success in *Gone With the Wind* (1939). He died shortly after making *The Misfits* (released 1961), in which he did his own stunt-work.

gable roof *n.* A pitched roof that ends in a gable.

Ga·bo (gaábō), **Naum,** born Naum Neemia Pevsner (1890–1977). Russian-born U.S. sculptor. He left Russia in 1923 after his work in the constructivist movement fell into disfavour. He settled in the United States (1946).

Ga·bon, Republic of (gə-bón; *French* ga-bón). *French* **République Gabonaise.** Country in equatorial Africa. European slavers reached the area in about 1470. The French dominated it in the 19th century, settling freed slaves at Libreville ("free town"), and in 1910 it became part of French Equatorial Africa. Dr. Albert Schweitzer founded the region's first hospital in 1913, at Lambaréné. It became independent in 1960. French remains the official language. Area, 267 667 square kilometres (103,319 square miles). Population, 1,110,000. Capital and chief port, Libreville. —**Gab·o·nese** (gábbə-neéz) *n. & adj.*

Ga·bor (gə-bór, gaá-bawr), **Dennis** (1900–79). Hungarian-born British electrical engineer. He won the Nobel prize in physics (1971) for his work on holography.

Gab·o·ro·ne (gábbə-rōni, khábbə-). Capital of Botswana.

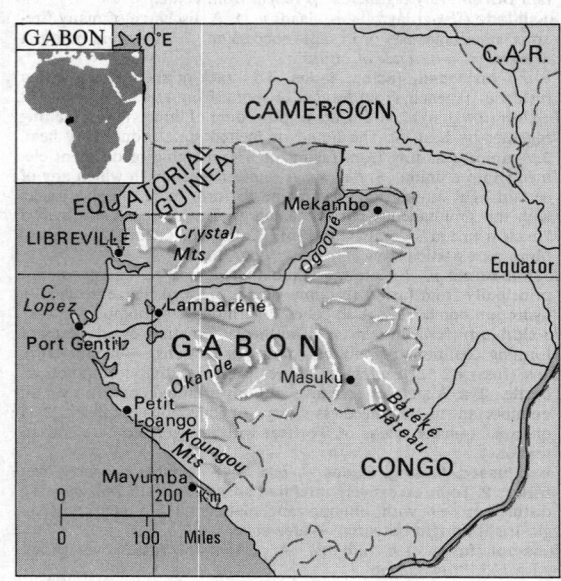

Ga·bri·el (gáybri-əl). An archangel who acts as the messenger of God in the Bible.

ga·by (gáybi) *n. Archaic & British Regional.* A simpleton. [18th century : origin obscure.]

gad¹ (gad) *interj.* Used to express surprise or as a mild oath. Often preceded by *by.* Now used only humorously. [Euphemistic for *God.*]

gad² *intr.v.* **gadded, gadding, gads. 1.** To roam about aimlessly or restlessly. **2.** To go about in search of pleasure or entertainment. Used with *about* or *around.* See Synonyms at **wander.** ~*n.* The action of gadding. Used only in the phrase *on the gad.* [Middle English *gadden,* probably back-formation from *gadeling,* companion, (hence) wanderer, Old English *gædeling.*] **—gad·der** *n.*

gad³ *n.* **1.** *Mining.* A spike or other pointed tool for working or breaking rock or ore. **2.** A goad, as for prodding cattle. ~*tr.v.* **gadded, gadding, gads. 1.** *Mining.* To break up (rock or ore, for example) with a gad. **2.** To goad (cattle). [Middle English *gad(de),* from Old Norse *gaddr,* rod, goad, spike.]

Gad (gad) *n.* The tribe of Israel descended from Gad.

gad·a·bout (gáddə-bowt) *n. Informal.* One who goes about seeking amusement or excitement.

Gad·a·rene (gáddə-reen) *adj. Sometimes small* **g.** Involving or taking part in a headlong rush; impetuous; reckless. [Late Latin, from Greek *gadarēnos,* referring to the Gadarene swine in the Bible (Matthew 8:28-33).]

Gad·daf·i or **Qad·da·fi** (gə-daáfi), **Moammar al-** (1942–). Libyan ruler. In 1969 he led an army coup which toppled the Libyan monarchy and imposed Islamic socialist policies on the country.

gad·fly (gád-flī) *n., pl.* **-flies. 1.** Any of various flies, especially horse flies and clegs, that bite or annoy livestock and other animals. **2.** A person who is persistently critical, irritating, or provocative. **3.** Something that acts as a provocative stimulus. [GAD (goad, sting) + FLY.]

gadg·et (gájit) *n.* **1.** A small specialised mechanical or electronic device; a contrivance. **2.** Any ingenious device, especially one that is labour-saving. See Synonyms at **tool.** [19th century (nautical) : origin obscure.]

gadg·et·ry (gájitri) *n.* **1.** Gadgets collectively. **2.** The designing or constructing of gadgets.

Gadhelic, Gaedhelic. Variants of **Goidelic.**

ga·did (gáydid) *adj.* Of or belonging to the family Gadidae, which includes fishes such as the cod and the hake. ~*n.* A member of the Gadidae. [New Latin *Gadus* (genus name), from Greek *gados*†, kind of fish + -OID.]

gad·o·lin·ite (gádd'l-i-nīt) *n.* A rare blackish mineral silicate of iron, beryllium, and yttrium, $2BeO.FeO.Y_2O_3.2SiO_2$. Also called "ytterbite". [After Johan *Gadolin* (1760–1852), Finnish chemist.]

gad·o·lin·i·um (gáddə-línni-əm) *n. Symbol* **Gd** A silvery-white, malleable, ductile, metallic rare-earth element obtained from monazite and bastnaesite. It has the highest neutron-absorption cross-section known and is useful in improving high-temperature characteristics of iron, chromium, and related metallic alloys. Atomic number 64, atomic weight 157.25, melting point 1,312°C, boiling point approximately 3,000°C, relative density 7.9, valency 3. [New Latin, after Johan *Gadolin* (1760–1852), Finnish chemist.]

ga·droon, go·droon (gə-drōōn) *n.* **1.** *Architecture.* A band of convex moulding ornamentally carved with beading or reeding. **2.** Any ornamental band, especially as used in silverwork, embellished with fluting, reeding, or some other pattern. [French *godron,* from Old French *goderon,* perhaps diminutive of *godet,* drinking cup, from Middle Dutch *codde*†, cylindrical piece of wood.]

gad·wall (gád-wawl) *n.* A widely distributed duck, *Anas strepera,* having greyish or brown plumage. [17th century : origin obscure.]

gad·zooks (gad-zōōks) *interj.* Used to express surprise, annoyance, or the like. Now used only humorously. [17th century : GAD (God) + *zooks*†; perhaps originally *God's hooks,* "God's hooks", that is, the nails of the Crucifixion.]

Gae·a (jée-ə). Also **Gai·a** (gáy-ə), **Ge** (jee, gee). *Greek Mythology.* The goddess of the earth, who bore and married Uranus and became the mother of the Titans and the Cyclopes. [Greek *Gaia,* personification of *gaia, gē,* earth.]

Gae·kwar (gǐ-kwaar) *n.* The hereditary title of the ruling princes of Baroda, formerly an independent state, now part of the state of Gujarat in India. [Marathi *Gaekvād,* "Protector of Cows" : Sanskrit *gauh,* ox, cow + *-vād,* "watcher", from *veda,* I have seen, I know.]

Gael (gayl) *n.* **1.** A Gaelic-speaking Celt of Scotland, Ireland, or the Isle of Man. **2.** A Scottish Highlander. [Scottish Gaelic *Gaidheal,* probably from Old Irish *goidel,* a Celt, from Old Welsh *Gwyddel,* Irishman, probably from *gwydd,* wild.]

Gael·ic (gáylik, gál-ik ‖ gaálik) *adj. Abbr.* **Gael.** Of or relating to the Gaels or their languages. ~*n. Abbr.* **Gael. 1.** The Goidelic family of the Celtic languages. **2.** Any of the languages of the Gaels; Irish, Manx, or the language of the Scottish Highlanders. [Scottish Gaelic *Gaidhealach,* of the Gaels, and *Gaidhlig,* the Gaelic language, from *Gaidheal,* GAEL.]

Gaelic coffee *n.* **Irish coffee** (*see*).

Gaelic football *n.* A type of football played in Eire and by Irish people elsewhere. It is similar to Rugby football, with teams of 15, but the ball is spherical and the lower half of the goal is netted.

Gael·tacht (gáyl-takht) *n.* Any region in Ireland where the vernacular speech is Irish Gaelic.

gaff¹ (gaf) *n.* **1.** An iron hook attached to a pole and used to land and manoeuvre large fish. **2.** *Nautical.* A spar used to extend the top edge of a fore-and-aft sail. **3.** A metal spur attached to the leg of a gamecock for a cockfight. **—blow the gaff.** *British Slang.* To give away a secret. [From 19th-century slang sense of *gaff*†, secret.] ~*tr.v.* **gaffed, gaffing, gaffs. 1.** To hook or land (a fish) using a gaff. **2.** *Slang.* To alter or fix (dice, for example) in order to cheat. [Middle English *gaffe,* from Old French, from Old Provençal *gaf*†.]

gaff² *n. British Slang.* **1.** A public place of entertainment; especially, a cheap or disreputable music hall or theatre. **2.** Someone's place of work or residence. [18th century : origin obscure.]

gaffe (gaf) *n.* A clumsy social error; a faux pas. [French, from *gaffer,* to hook, hence in seaman's slang, to blunder, from *gaffe,* hook, GAFF.]

gaf·fer (gáffər) *n.* **1.** An old man or rustic. **2.** *British Informal.* A boss or foreman. **3.** The electrician in charge of lighting on a film or television set. [Contraction of GODFATHER.]

gaff rig *n. Nautical.* A rig with a fore-and-aft sail that has its upper edge supported by a gaff. **—gaff-rig·ged** *adj.*

gaff-top·sail (gáf-tóp-sayl, -səl) *n. Nautical.* A light, triangular or quadrilateral sail set over a gaff.

gag (gag) *n.* **1.** Something forced into or put over the mouth to prevent the utterance of sound. **2.** Any obstacle to or censoring of free expression. **3.** A device placed in the mouth to keep it open, as in dentistry or surgery. **4.** *Informal.* **a.** A practical joke; a hoax. **b.** A comic effect or remark; a joke. **5.** In Parliament, a **closure** (*see*). —See Synonyms at **joke.** ~*v.* **gagged, gagging, gags.** —*tr.* **1.** To prevent from uttering any sounds by using a gag. **2.** To repress or censor (free speech, the press, and the like). **3.** To keep (the mouth) open by using a gag. **4.** To block off or stop up (a pipe or valve, for example). **5.** To cause to choke or retch. —*intr.* **1.** To choke or retch from nausea. **2.** *Informal.* To make jokes or quips. [Middle English *gaggen,* to suffocate (probably imitative).]

ga·ga (gaá-gaa) *adj. Informal.* **1.** Senseless; crazy. **2.** Senile. [French, from *gaga,* foolish old man (imitative of stammering).]

Ga·ga·rin (gə-gaár-in, gaa-), **Yuri Alexeevich** (1934–68). Russian cosmonaut. In 1961 he became the first man to travel in space. His home town of Gzhatsk was renamed Gagarin after he died in a flying accident.

gage¹ (gayj) *n.* **1.** Something deposited or given as security against an obligation; a pledge. **2.** Something, such as a glove, offered or thrown down as a pledge or challenge to fight. **3.** Any test or challenge. ~*tr.v.* **gaged, gaging, gages.** *Archaic.* **1.** To pledge as security. **2.** To offer as a stake in a bet; wager. [Middle English, from Old French, from Germanic *wadhjam* (unattested).]

gage² *n.* A greengage.

gage³ *n. U.S.* Variant of **gauge.**

gag·ger (gággər) *n.* **1.** One that gags. **2.** A piece of iron used to keep the core in position in a foundry mould.

gag·gle (gágg'l) *intr.v.* **-gled, -gling, -gles.** To make gabbling sounds; cackle. Used of geese. ~*n.* **1.** A flock of geese. **2.** A disorderly crowd, especially of women or girls. [Middle English *gagelen*†.]

gag·man (gág-man) *n., pl.* **-men** (-men). A person who writes jokes or comedy routines for plays, films, or performers. Also "gagster".

gag rein *n.* A horse's rein adjusted to make the bit more powerful.

gahn·ite (gaá-nīt) *n.* A grey mineral, $ZnO.Al_2O_3$. Also called "zinc spinel". [German *Gahnit,* after Johan G. *Gahn* (1745–1818), Swedish chemist.]

Gaia. Variant of **Gaea.**

Gaia hypothesis *n.* The hypothesis that the Earth functions as a self-regulating organism rather than just as the passive subject of external forces.

gai·e·ty (gáy-əti) *n., pl.* **-ties.** Also *chiefly U.S.* **gay·e·ty. 1.** A state of being cheerful or merry. **2.** Activity brought about by or inspiring joyousness; festivity; merriment. **3.** Gay colour or showiness, as of dress; finery. [French *gaieté,* from Old French *gai,* GAY.]

gail·lar·di·a (gay-lárdi-ə) *n.* Any of several plants of the genus *Gaillardia,* of western North America, having yellow or reddish rayed flowers. [New Latin *Gaillardia,* after *Gaillard* de Marentonneau, 18th-century French botanist.]

gai·ly (gáyli) *adv.* Also *chiefly U.S.* **gay·ly. 1.** In a cheerful manner; merrily. **2.** With brightness; colourfully; showily: *gaily dressed.*

gain¹ (gayn) *v.* **gained, gaining, gains.** —*tr.* **1.** To become the owner of; obtain; get. **2.** To acquire in competition or battle; win. **3.** To achieve through one's efforts or merits, or as a natural development: *gained recognition; gained widespread support.* **4.** To secure as a profit or through labour. **5.** To build up an increase of (weight or momentum, for example). **6.** To come to; arrive at; reach. **7.** To become fast by (the specified amount of time). Used of a timepiece: *my watch gains two minutes a day.* —*intr.* **1.** To become better or more; benefit; advance or progress. **2.** To come nearer; get closer. Used with *on* or *upon.* **3.** To increase a lead. Used with *on, upon,* or *over.* **4.** To go fast. Used of a timepiece. —See Synonyms at **reach.** ~*n.* **1.** Something earned, won, or otherwise acquired; a profit; an advantage; an increase. **2.** The act of acquiring something; attainment. **3.** *Electronics.* **a.** An increase in signal power. **b.** The ratio of output to input, as of output power to input power in an aerial or of output voltage to input voltage in an amplifier. [Old French *gaaignier, gaigner,* from Germanic *waithanjan* (unattested).]

gain² *n.* A notch or mortise cut on a board to receive another part. [17th century : origin obscure.]

gain·er (gáynər) *n.* **1.** One that gains. **2.** A dive in which the diver leaves the board facing forwards, does a backward somersault, and enters the water feet first.

gain·ful (gáynf'l) *adj.* Earning a profit; profitable; lucrative. —**gain·ful·ly** *adv.* —**gain·ful·ness** *n.*

gain·ings (gáy-ningz) *pl.n.* The amount of money earned; profits.

gain·say (gayn-sáy) *tr.v.* -**said** (-séd), -**saying**, -**says**. **1.** To declare false; deny. **2.** To be contrary to; oppose; contradict. [Middle English *gaynsayen*, "to say against" : *gayn-*, against, Old English *gegn-* + SAY.] —**gain·say·er** *n.*

Gains·bor·ough (gáynz-bərə, -brə), **Thomas** (1727–88). English landscape and portrait painter. His masterpieces include *The Blue Boy* (early 1770s) and *The Harvest Wagon* (1767). He was a founder member of the Royal Academy (1768).

'gainst, gainst (genst, gaynst) *prep. Poetic.* Against.

gait (gayt) *n.* **1.** A way of moving on foot; a particular fashion of walking or running. **2.** Any of the ways a horse or other four-legged animal may move by lifting the feet in different order or rhythm, as in a canter, trot, or walk. [Middle English *gate, gait,* way, passage from Old Norse *gata,* path, street.]

gait·ed (gáytid) *adj.* Having a specified gait or number of gaits. Usually used in combination: *fast-gaited; a three-gaited mare.*

gai·ter (gáytər) *n.* **1.** A leather or heavy cloth covering for the legs extending from the knee to the instep; a legging. **2.** A smaller covering worn over a shoe and extending from the ankle to the instep; a spat. [French *guêtre,* from Old French *guestre, guietre,* probably from Frankish *wrist* (unattested), instep.]

Gait·skell (gáyt-skəl), **Hugh (Todd Naylor)** (1906–63). British politician. He became an M.P. (1945), Labour Chancellor of the Exchequer (1950–51), and leader of the Labour Party (1955–63). He persuaded the party to abandon unilateral disarmament (1961).

gal[1] (gal) *n. Informal.* A girl.

gal[2] *n.* A unit of acceleration in the cgs system equal to one centimetre per second per second. [After GALILEO.]

gal. gallon.

Gal. Galatians (New Testament).

ga·la (gaálə, gáylə ‖ gál-ə) *n.* **1.** A festive occasion or celebration; a festival. Also used adjectivally: *a gala occasion.* **2.** *British.* A competitive sports meeting, especially a swimming competition. **3.** An annual festivity held by miners in Durham and other parts of Northern England. [Italian, from Spanish, from Old French *gale,* pleasure, merrymaking, from *galer,* to make merry, live a gay life, from Gallo-Roman *walare* (unattested), from Frankish *wala* (unattested), well.]

ga·lac·ta·gogue (gə-láktə-gog) *n.* A substance that induces a flow of milk.
~*adj.* Inducing a flow of milk. [GALACT(O)- + -AGOGUE.]

ga·lac·tic (gə-láktik) *adj.* **1.** Of or pertaining to a galaxy or galaxies. **2.** *Sometimes capital* **G.** Of, pertaining to, occurring, or originating in the Milky Way. [Late Latin *galacticus,* from Greek *galaktikos,* from *gala* (stem *galakt-*), milk. See **galaxy.**]

galactic equator *n.* The great circle of the celestial sphere that lies in the plane bisecting the band of the Milky Way, inclined at an angle of approximately 62° to the celestial equator.

galactic nebula *n.* A nebula lying within the Milky Way Galaxy. Also called "nebula".

galactic noise *n.* Radio-frequency radiation originating within the Milky Way.

galactic year *n.* The **cosmic year** *(see).*

galacto-, galact– *comb. form.* Indicates milk or milky; for example, **galactopoiesis, galactose.** [Greek *gala* (stem *galakt-*), milk.]

ga·lac·to·poi·e·sis (gə-lák-tō-poy-ée-siss, -tə-) *n.* The secretion and continued production of milk. [GALACTO- + -POIESIS.] —**ga·lac·to·poi·et·ic** (-éttik) *adj.*

ga·lac·to·sae·mia (gə-lák-tō-séemi-ə, -tə-) *n.* A congenital disease characterised by the inability to metabolise galactose, which consequently accumulates in the blood and if untreated causes mental retardation and stunted growth. [GALACTOSE + -AEMIA.]

ga·lac·tose (gə-lák-tōss, -tōz) *n.* A simple sugar, $C_6H_{12}O_6$, commonly occurring in **lactose** *(see).* [French : GALACT(O)- + -OSE.]

gal·a·go (gə-laá-gō, -láy-) *n., pl.* -**gos.** A small primate, the **bush baby** *(see).* [New Latin *Galago,* perhaps from an African word *goigkh,* monkey.]

ga·lah (gə-laá) *n.* **1.** An Australian cockatoo, *Cacatua* (or *Kakatoe*) *roseicapilla,* having pale, blue-grey plumage and a pink breast. **2.** *Australian Slang.* A fool; an idiot. [From a native Australian language.]

Gal·a·had (gál-ə-had) *n.* Any man considered to be noble, pure, or chivalrous. [After *Galahad,* a knight of Arthur's Round Table known for his purity and who alone succeeded in the quest for the Holy Grail.]

ga·lan·gal (gə-láng-g'l) *n.* **1.** A plant, *Alpinia officinarum,* of eastern Asia, having pungent, aromatic roots used medicinally and as seasoning. **2.** The dried roots of this plant. **3.** The **galingale** *(see).* [Originally a variant of GALINGALE.]

gal·an·tine (gál-ən-teen) *n.* A dish of boned, stuffed, usually white meat or fish, cooked and served cold coated with aspic or its own jelly. [Middle English *galauntyne,* a sauce for fish and poultry, from Old French *galantine, galatine,* from Medieval Latin *galatina, gelatina,* probably from Latin *gelāre,* to freeze.]

ga·lan·ty show (gə-lánti) *n.* A play performed by casting the shadows of miniature figures on a screen or wall. [Perhaps from Italian *galanti,* plural of *galante,* a gallant, from Old French *galant* (from the stories of gallantry portrayed in the show).]

Ga·lá·pa·gos Islands (gə-láppə-gəss,-goss). *Spanish* **Archipiélago de Colón.** An Ecuadorian archipelago in the Pacific Ocean. The 15 large and many small volcanic islands lie some 970 kilometres (600 miles) west of Ecuador, and the population is concentrated on Isabela (Albemarle), the largest island, and San Cristóbal (Chatham). Most of the reptile life and over half the flora are peculiar to the islands, now a nature reserve. In 1835, Darwin collected a wealth of scientific data there, which led to his theory of evolution. Giant tortoises once abounded on the islands, which take their name from the Spanish *galpágo,* "tortoise". Area (including sea), 7 844 square kilometres (3,028 square miles). See map at **Pacific Ocean.**

gal·a·te·a (gál-ə-tée-ə, -téer) *n.* A durable cotton fabric, often striped, used in making clothing. [Originally used for children's sailor suits, after the *Galatea,* 19th-century British warship.]

Gal·a·te·a (gál-ə-tée-ə). *Greek Mythology.* An ivory statue of a maiden, brought to life by Aphrodite in answer to the pleas of the sculptor, Pygmalion, who had fallen in love with his creation.

Ga·la·tia (gə-láyshə). Ancient country forming part of central Asia Minor. Chief city, Ancyra (modern Ankara, Turkey). —**Ga·la·tian** *adj. & n.*

Ga·la·tians (gə-láysh'nz) *n. Abbr.* **Gal.** A book of the New Testament consisting of an Epistle written to the Christians of Galatia by the apostle Paul in about A.D. 58. Called in full "Epistle to the Galatians".

galavant. Variant of **gallivant.**

gal·ax·y (gál-ək-si) *n., pl.* -**ies.** **1.** *Astronomy.* **a.** Any of numerous large-scale aggregates of stars, gas, and dust, having one of several more or less definite overall structures, containing an average of 100 billion (10^{11}) solar masses, and ranging in diameter from 1,500 to 300,000 light-years. **b.** *Usually capital* **G.** The galaxy of which the Earth's sun is a part, the **Milky Way** *(see).* Usually preceded by *the.* **2.** An assembly of brilliant, beautiful, or distinguished persons or things. [Middle English *galaxie,* the Milky Way, from Old French, from Latin *galaxiās,* from Greek *galaxias (kuklos),* "milky (circle)", from *gala,* milk.]

gal·ba·num (gál-bənəm ‖ *U.S. also* gáwl-) *n.* A bitter, aromatic gum resin extracted from an Asiatic plant, *Ferula galbaniflua,* or any of several related plants, and used in incense and medicinally as a counterirritant. [Middle English, from Latin, from Greek *khalbanē,* from Hebrew *helbānāh.*]

Gal·braith (gál-brayth, gal-bráyth), **John Kenneth** (1908–). Canadian-born U.S. economist. He has opposed monetarist economic philosophy, in books such as *The Affluent Society* (1958). He was U.S. ambassador to India (1961–63), and professor of economics at Harvard (1949–75).

gale[1] (gayl) *n.* **1. a.** A very strong wind. **b.** *Meteorology.* A wind whose speed is 17.2 to 20.7 metres per second (39 to 46 miles per hour), force 8 on the Beaufort scale. See **near gale, strong gale.** **2.** *Poetic.* A breeze. **3.** A forceful outburst, as of laughter. —See Synonyms at **wind.** [Probably short for *gale wind,* "bad wind", perhaps from Norwegian *galen,* bad, probably from Old Norse *galinn,* bewitched, enchanted, from *gala,* to sing, enchant, bewitch.]

gale[2] *n.* A plant, the **bog myrtle** *(see).* [Middle English, *gale, gayl,* Old English *gagel,* akin to Middle Dutch *gaghel†.*]

ga·le·a (gáy-li-ə) *n., pl.* -**leae** (-li-ee). *Biology.* A helmet-shaped part, such as the upper petal of certain plants or part of the maxilla of an insect. [Latin, leather helmet, originally "cap made of weasel skin", from Greek *galeē,* weasel.]

ga·le·ate (gáyli-ayt) *adj.* Also **ga·le·at·ed** (-aytid). *Biology.* **1.** Having a galea. **2.** Helmet-shaped. [Latin *galeātus,* from *galea,* GALEA.]

ga·le·i·form (gáyli-i-fawrm, gə-lée-, gə-láy-) *adj.* Helmet-shaped. [French *galéiforme* : Latin *galea,* GALEA + -i- + -FORM.]

Ga·len (gáylən), **(Claudius Galenus).** (*c.*A.D. 130–*c.*200). Greek physician. He compiled Greek medical knowledge into treatises which formed the basis of European medicine until the Renaissance.

ga·le·na (gə-léenə) *n.* A grey mineral, essentially PbS, the principal ore of lead. Also called "lead glance". [Latin *galēna†,* lead ore.]

ga·len·ic (gay-lénnik, gə-) *adj.* Also **ga·len·i·cal.** Designating a drug preparation of plant or animal origin. —**ga·len·ic, ga·len·i·cal** *n.* [After GALEN.]

Ga·len·ism (gáylən-iz'm) *n.* The medical system based on Galen's surviving treatises, including the notion of the four bodily humours. —**Ga·len·ic** (gay-lénnik, gə-), **Ga·len·i·cal** *adj.* —**Ga·len·ist** *adj. & n.*

ga·lère (ga-láir) *n. French.* A group or coterie, especially of undesirable people. [Literally, "galley".]

Ga·li·bi (gaa-léebi, gə- ‖ gál-əbi) *n., pl.* -**bis** or collectively **Galibi.** **1.** A member of the Carib people of French Guiana. **2.** The language of this people. [Carib *galibi,* "strong man", akin to Cariban *caribe,* brave, CARIB.]

Ga·li·ci·a[1] (gə-líssi-ə, -lísh-ə). Region and former kingdom in northwest Spain. It comprises the provinces of Coruña (Corunna), Lugo, Orense, and Pontevedra. Colonised by the Goths in the 6th century, it became a subject of Castile in the 11th century. The chief towns are Vigo, La Coruña, and Santiago de Compostela.

Galicia[2]. *Polish* **Halicz;** *Russian* **Galich** or **Galitsiya.** Province in Central Europe. It became an independent principality in 1087, but was conquered by the Russians in the 12th century. Absorbed by Poland in the 14th century, it became Austrian four centuries later. Following World War I, it was returned to Poland, but after World War II, East Galicia was ceded to the U.S.S.R. Krakow and L'viv are the major towns.

Ga·li·ci·an (gə-líshi-ən, -lísh-, lissi-) *adj.* **1.** Of or pertaining to

Spanish Galicia, its people, or their language. 2. Of or pertaining to Polish Galicia or its people.

~*n.* 1. A native or inhabitant of Spanish or Polish Galicia. 2. The Portuguese dialect spoken in Spanish Galicia.

Gal·i·le·an¹ (gál-i-lée-ən) *adj.* Of or pertaining to Galilee or its people.

~*n.* 1. A native or inhabitant of Galilee. 2. A Christian. —**the Galilean.** Jesus.

Gal·i·le·an² (gál-i-láy-ən) *adj.* Of, pertaining to, or in accordance with the work of Galileo.

gal·i·lee (gál-i-lee) *n.* A small chapel or porch at the western end of some medieval English churches and cathedrals. Also called "galilee porch". [Middle English *galile,* from Old French *galilee,* from Medieval Latin *galilaea,* from Latin *Galilaea,* GALILEE.]

Gal·i·lee (gál-i-lee). *Hebrew* **Hagalil.** A region in northern Israel. The northernmost region of Palestine and of the ancient Jewish kingdom of Israel, Galilee was the province where Jesus Christ began his ministry. It became part of the newly founded state of Israel in 1949.

Galilee, Sea of. *Hebrew* **Yam Kinneret;** *Arabic* **Buhayrat Tchariyā.** Biblical names **Sea of Ti·be·ri·as** (tī-béer-i-ass, -əss) or **Lake of Gen·nes·a·ret** (gi-nézzə-rit, ge-, -ret) or **Sea of Chin·ne·reth** (chínnə-reth). Lake in north Israel. It is 21 kilometres (13 miles) long and lies in the Great Rift Valley, its surface being 209 metres (686 feet) below sea level.

Gal·i·le·o Gal·i·le·i (gál-i-láy-ō gál-i-láy-i) (1564–1642). Italian astronomer and mathematician. He developed his own telescope (1609), and discovered four satellites of Jupiter and the nature of lunar illumination. His belief that Copernicus was right to claim that the Sun was the centre of our universe led to his persecution by the Inquisition (1633). He recanted, but is said to have muttered under his breath "But it (the Earth) does move."

gal·i·ma·ti·as (gál-i-máyshi-əss, -mátti-) *n.* Nonsensical talk; gibberish. [French, perhaps originally students' jargon : Latin *gallus,* "cock", student who takes part in a discussion + Greek *-mathia,* knowledge, from *manthanein,* to learn.]

gal·in·gale (gál-ing-gayl) *n.* Any of various sedges of the genus *Cyperus;* especially, *C. longus,* of Europe, having rough-edged leaves, reddish spikelets, and aromatic roots. Also called "galangal". [Middle English, from Old French *galingal,* from Arabic *khalanjān,* from Chinese *gāo liáng jiāng,* good ginger from Gaozhou (present-day Maoming in Guangdong province).]

galiot. Variant of **galliot.**

gal·i·pot (gál-i-pot ‖ -pō) *n.* A resin obtained from various pine species, especially the cluster pine *Pinus pinaster,* and often seen as a hardened mass on the bark. [18th century : from French, of obscure origin.]

gall¹ (gawl) *n.* 1. a. Bile *(see).* b. The gall bladder. No longer in technical usage. 2. Rancour; bitterness. 3. Something bitter to endure: *the gall of disappointment.* 4. Impudence; effrontery: *He had the gall to try to borrow money.* —See Synonyms at **temerity.** [Middle English *gall(e),* Old English *gealla,* from Germanic.]

gall² *n.* 1. A skin sore caused by friction and abrasion: *a saddle gall.* 2. a. Exasperation; irritation; vexation. b. The cause of such vexation.

~*v.* **galled, galling, galls.** —*tr.* 1. To make (the skin) sore by abrasion; chafe. 2. To damage or break the surface of by or as if by friction or abrasion; abrade: *the bark of saplings galled by improper staking.* 3. To exasperate; vex. —*intr.* To become irritated, chafed, or sore. [Middle English *galle,* from Middle Low German; akin to Old English *gealla,* sore place, Old Norse *galli,* fault.]

gall³ *n.* An abnormal swelling of plant tissue, caused by insects, microorganisms, or external injury. [Middle English *galle,* from Old French, from Latin *galla†.*]

gall. gallon.

Gal·la (gál-ə) *n., pl.* **-las** or collectively **Galla.** 1. A member of a pastoral Hamitic people of southern Ethiopia and Somalia. 2. The language of this people, belonging to the Ethiopian or Cushitic group of the Afro-Asiatic languages.

~*adj.* Of or pertaining to this people or their language. [Perhaps from Arabic *ghalīz,* rough.]

gal·lant (gál-ənt *for senses 1, 3, 4;* gál-ənt, gə-lánt ‖ -laánt *for sense 2*) *adj.* 1. Courageous; daring; valorous: *gallant soldiers.* 2. a. Attentive to women; chivalrous; courteous. b. Amorous. 3. Stately; majestic; noble: *"On my word, master, this is a gallant trout"* (Isaak Walton). 4. Showy and gay in appearance, dress, or bearing; dashing. —See Synonyms at **brave.**

~*n.* (gál-ənt, gə-lánt ‖ -laánt). 1. A fashionable young man. 2. A man courteously attentive to women; a ladies' man. b. A woman's lover; a paramour.

~*v.* (gə-lánt ‖ -laánt) **gallanted, -lanting, -lants.** *Rare.* —*tr.* To woo, attend, or escort (a lady); pay court to. —*intr.* To play the gallant. [Middle English *galaunt,* from Old French *galant,* gorgeous, showy, brave, from the present participle of *galer,* to rejoice, from Gallo-Roman *walāre* (unattested), from Frankish *wala* (unattested), well.] —**gal·lant·ly** *adv.*

gal·lant·ry (gál-əntri) *n., pl.* **-ries.** 1. Nobility of spirit or action; great courage. 2. a. Chivalrous attention towards women; courtliness; courteousness. b. Sexual intrigue. 3. An act or instance of gallantry in speech or behaviour. 4. *Archaic.* A bold or colourful display or appearance.

gall bladder *n.* A small, pear-shaped, muscular sac located under the right lobe of the liver, in which bile secreted by the liver is stored.

Gal·le (gaálə). Formerly **Point de Galle.** Seaport and commercial centre of Sri Lanka. It was the country's main port under the Arabs and Portuguese, and the capital under the Dutch until 1656.

gal·le·ass, gal·li·ass (gál-i-ass, -əss) *n.* A large, heavily armed, three-masted Mediterranean galley of the 16th and 17th centuries. [Old French *galeasse,* from Old Italian *galeaza,* augmentative of *galea,* galley, from Medieval Latin, GALLEY.]

gal·le·on (gál-i-ən) *n.* A large, three-masted sailing ship generally having two or more decks, used during the 15th and 16th centuries by Spain and other countries as a merchantman or warship. [Spanish *galeon,* from Old French *galion,* from *galie,* GALLEY.]

gal·ler·y (gál-əri) *n., pl.* **-ies.** 1. A roofed promenade, especially one extending along the wall of a building, with its roof supported by pillars on the outer side; a colonnade. 2. An elevated covered platform along the outer wall of a building; a long balcony. 3. a. An enclosed narrow passageway, such as a hall or corridor. b. A long room or passage resembling such a corridor and used for a specified purpose: *a shooting gallery.* 4. a. An upper floor projecting over the main floor of a theatre, and usually providing cheaper seats than those in the stalls. b. The seats in such a section. c. The audience occupying these seats. d. Any similar projecting upper floor in a large building, as in a church, law court, or legislative assembly. 5. Any large audience or group of spectators, as in a stadium, grandstand, or legislative assembly. 6. a. A building or hall in which sculpture, paintings, photographs, or other works of art are exhibited. b. A private institution that exhibits and sells works of art. 7. An underground tunnel or other passageway, such as one dug for military or mining purposes, or found in animal burrows, insects' nests, and so on. 8. *Nautical.* A platform or balcony at the stern or quarters of certain early sailing ships. 9. A decorative upright trimming or moulding along the edge of a table top, tray, or shelf. —**play to the gallery.** 1. To perform a play, scene, or role in a manner calculated to please the less sophisticated members of an audience who, in former times, were mainly congregated in the gallery. 2. To try to gain the favour or applause of the general public, especially by crude or obvious means.

~*tr.v.* **galleried, -lerying, -leries.** To provide with a gallery. [Middle English *galerie,* from Old French, portico, from Italian *galleria,* from Medieval Latin *galeria,* perhaps variant of *galilaea,* porch of a church, GALILEE.]

gallery forest *n.* A stretch of forest bordering a river and backed by open country.

gal·ley (gál-i) *n., pl.* **-leys.** 1. A large medieval ship of shallow draught and with a single deck, propelled by sails and oars, and used as a merchantman or warship in the Mediterranean. 2. An ancient seagoing vessel propelled by oars. 3. A large rowing boat, such as one formerly used on the river Thames by customs officers. 4. The kitchen of a ship, boat, or airliner. 5. *Printing.* a. A long tray, usually of metal, used for holding composed type. b. A galley proof. [Middle English *galeie, galy,* from Old French *galie, galee,* from Medieval Latin *galea,* from Medieval Greek *galea†.*]

galley proof *n. Printing.* A printer's proof taken from composed type before page composition to allow for the detection and correction of errors. Also called "galley".

galley slave *n.* 1. A slave or convict forced to man an oar of a galley. 2. A person forced to perform tedious or menial tasks; a drudge.

galley west *adv. U.S. Informal.* Out of shape; out of commission. Used in the phrase *to knock galley west.* [Perhaps alteration of dialectal *collywest,* askew, perhaps from *Collyweston,* village in Northamptonshire.]

gall·fly (gáwl-flī) *n., pl.* **-flies.** Any of various small insects, such as the gall midge or gall wasp, that deposit their eggs on plant stems or in the bark of trees, causing the formation of galls in which their larvae grow.

Gallia. See **Gaul.**

gal·li·am·bic (gál-i-ámbik) *adj.* Designating or characteristic of a verse metre formed by two iambic dimeters. [Latin *galliambus,* song of the *Gallī* (priests of Cybele); see **iamb.**]

gal·liard (gál-i-aard, -ərd) *adj. Archaic.* Spirited; lively; gay.

~*n.* 1. A spirited dance popular in the 16th and 17th centuries. 2. The music for this dance. [Middle English *galiard, gaillard,* valiant, lively, from Old French *gaillard,* from Gallo-Roman *galia* (unattested), strength, power.]

galliass. Variant of **galleass.**

gal·lic (gál-ik) *adj. Chemistry.* Of or pertaining to gallium. Used especially of chemical compounds that contain gallium with a valency of 3.

Gal·lic (gál-ik) *adj.* Of or pertaining to ancient Gaul or to modern France; French. [Latin *Gallicus,* Gaulish, from *Galli,* Gauls.]

gallic acid *n.* A colourless crystalline compound, $C_7H_6O_5 \cdot H_2O$, derived from tannin and used in photography, as a tanning agent, and in ink and paper manufacture.

Gal·li·can (gál-i-kən) *adj.* Pertaining to or characteristic of Gallicanism.

~*n.* A supporter of Gallicanism. [Middle English, from Old French, from Medieval Latin *Gallicānus,* French, from Latin, Gaulish, from *Gallicus,* GALLIC.]

Gal·li·can·ism (gál-i-kən-iz'm) *n.* A movement originating among the French Roman Catholic clergy, favouring the restriction of papal control and the achievement by each nation of individual administrative autonomy. Compare **Ultramontanism.**

Gal·li·cise, Gal·li·cize (gál-i-sīz) v. **-cised, -cising, -cises.** —intr. To become like the French in speech, character, or custom. —tr. To make French in any of these ways.

Gal·li·cism (gál-i-siz′m) n. **1.** A French phrase or idiom appearing in another language. **2.** A characteristic French trait.

gal·li·gas·kins (gál-i-gáss-kinz) pl.n. **1.** Full-length, loosely fitting hose or breeches worn in the 16th and 17th centuries. **2.** Any loose breeches. Used humorously. **3.** Regional. Leggings. [Earlier gallogascaine, garragascoyne, perhaps from Old French garguesque, greguesque, from Old Italian grechesca, "Grecian breeches", from the feminine of grechesco, Grecian, from greco, Greek, from Latin Graecus, GREEK.]

gal·li·mau·fry (gál-i-máwfri) n., pl. **-fries.** A jumble; a hotchpotch. [French galimafrée, from Old French calimafree : probably galer, to live a gay life (see **gallant**) + Picard mafrer, to eat voraciously, from Middle Dutch maffelen†.]

gal·li·na·ceous (gál-i-náyshəss) adj. **1.** Of, belonging to, or characteristic of the order Galliformes, which includes the common domestic fowl as well as the pheasants, turkeys, and grouse. **2.** Relating to or resembling the domestic fowl. [Latin gallīnāceus, of poultry, from gallīna, hen, feminine of gallus, cock.] —**gal·li·na·cean** n.

gall·ing (gáwling) adj. Causing acute irritation, humiliation, exasperation, or discomfort. —**gall·ing·ly** adv.

gal·li·nule (gál-i-newl ‖ -nōōl) n. Any of various wading birds of the genera Porphyrio or Porphyrula, frequenting swampy regions and characteristically having dark, iridescent plumage. [New Latin Gallinula, from Latin gallīnula, chicken, pullet, diminutive of gallīna, hen, feminine of gallus, cock.]

gal·li·ot, gal·i·ot (gál-i-ət) n. **1.** A light, swift galley propelled by sails and oars, formerly used on the Mediterranean. **2.** A light, single-masted, flat-bottomed Dutch merchant ship or seagoing barge. [Middle English, from Old French galiote, from Italian galeotta, from Medieval Latin galiote.]

Gal·lip·o·li (gə-líppəli). Turkish Gelibolu. Seaport of European Turkey. It lies on the Gallipoli peninsula in the Dardanelles, and in 1356 was the Ottoman Turks' first European conquest. From April 1915 to January 1916, the peninsula was the scene of unsuccessful and costly landings by Australian, New Zealand, French, and British troops in an attempt to clear the Dardanelles and thus the sea route to Russia. The devastated town was ceded to Greece in 1920, but returned to Turkey in 1923.

gal·li·pot (gál-i-pot) n. A small, glazed earthenware jar formerly used by pharmacists for medicaments. [Middle English galy pott : probably GALLEY + POT (originally imported from the Mediterranean by galleys).]

gal·li·um (gál-i-əm) n. Symbol **Ga** A rare metallic element that is liquid near room temperature, expands on solidifying, and is found as a trace element in coal, bauxite, and other minerals. It is used in semiconductor technology and as a component of various low-melting alloys. Atomic number 31, atomic weight 69.72, melting point 29.78°C, boiling point 2,403°C, relative density 5.907 (20°C), valencies 2, 3. [New Latin, from Latin gallus, cock (playful translation of the name of its discoverer, Lecoq de Boisbaudran, 1838–1912, French chemist). See **gallinaceous.**]

gallium arsenide n. A dark grey crystalline compound, GaAs, used in transistors, solar cells, and semiconducting lasers.

gal·li·vant, gal·a·vant (gál-i-vant, -vánt) intr.v. **-vanted, -vanting, -vants. 1.** To roam about aimlessly or frivolously; gad about. **2.** To consort frivolously with members of the opposite sex; flirt. [Perhaps alteration of GALLANT.]

gal·li·wasp (gál-i-wosp ‖ -wawsp) n. Any of several long-bodied lizards of the genera Diploglossus or Celestus, of Central America and the West Indies. [18th century : origin obscure.]

gall midge n. Any of various small, mosquito-like flies making up the family Cecidomyidae, the larvae of which produce galls in plants.

gall mite n. Any of various mites of the family Eriophyina that produce galls in plants.

gall·nut (gáwl-nut) n. A plant gall having a rounded form suggestive of a nut.

Gallo– comb. form. Indicates Gaul or France; for example, **Gallo-Roman.** [Latin Gallus, a Gaul.]

galloglass. Variant of **gallowglass.**

gal·lon (gál-ən) n. Abbr. **gal., gall. 1.** A unit of volume in the British Imperial system, used in liquid and dry measure, equal to 4.55 litres (277.420 cubic inches). **2.** A unit of volume or capacity in the U.S. Customary System, used in liquid measure, equal to 3.79 litres (231 cubic inches, or 0.83 of a British gallon). [Middle English gallun, gallon, from Old North French, from Medieval Latin gallēta, jug, measure for wine, perhaps from Celtic.]

gal·lon·age (gál-ə-nij) n. The amount of something measured in gallons.

gal·loon (gə-lōōn) n. A narrow band or braid used as trimming, and commonly made of lace, metallic thread, or embroidery. [French galon, from Old French galonner, to decorate with ribbons, perhaps from Frankish wōlōn, to tie up with cord.]

gal·lop (gál-əp) n. **1.** The fastest gait of a horse or other quadruped, in which all four legs are off the ground at the same time. **2.** A ride taken at the gallop.

~v. **galloped, -loping, -lops.** —tr. **1.** To cause to gallop. **2.** To transport at or as if at a gallop. —intr. **1.** To go at a gallop. Used of a horse or its rider. **2.** To move or progress rapidly: galloped through the agenda. [Middle English galopen, from Old French galoper, variant of Old North French waloper, from Frankish walahlaupan (unattested), "to run well" : wala (unattested), well + hlaupan (unattested), to jump, run.] —**gal·lop·er** n.

gallopade. Variant of **galop.**

gal·lop·ing (gál-əping) adj. **1.** Of or resembling a gallop, especially in rhythm or rapidity. **2. a.** Developing at an accelerated rate and leading to death. Said of certain diseases, principally in nontechnical contexts. **b.** Increasing rapidly or uncontrollably: galloping inflation.

Gal·lo-Ro·man (gál-ō-rṓmən) n. **1.** A native or inhabitant of Roman Gaul. **2.** The Vulgar Latin spoken by the Romanised inhabitants of Gaul. —**Gal·lo-Ro·man** adj.

Gal·lo-Ro·mance (gál-ō-ro-mánss) n. A hypothetical language that is supposed to have developed out of Gallo-Roman and been spoken in Gaul after the end of Roman rule and before the development of Old French. —**Gal·lo-Ro·mance** adj.

gal·lo·way (gál-ə-way) n. Often capital **G. 1.** Any of a breed of hornless black cattle. **2.** Any of a breed of small hardy horses. [After GALLOWAY in Scotland, where they were originally bred.]

Galloway. Area in southwest Scotland, mainly in Dumfries and Galloway. Unitary Authority area.

gal·low·glass, gal·lo·glass (gál-ō-glaass, -glass) n. Formerly, an armed retainer or mercenary in the service of an Irish chieftain. [Irish Gaelic galloglach, "foreign youth" : gall, foreigner + oglach, youth : og, young, from Old Irish ōac + -lach, abstract suffix.]

gal·lows (gál-ōz) n., pl. **gallows. 1.** A device usually consisting of two upright beams supporting a crossbeam from which a noose is suspended, and used for execution by hanging. Also called "gallows tree". **2.** Any similar structure used for supporting or suspending; especially, in Australia, a frame on which slaughtered cattle are hoisted. **3.** Execution on a gallows or by hanging. Preceded by the. [Middle English galwes, galawis, plural of galwe, gallows, cross, from Old English gealga.]

gallows bird n. Informal. One who deserves to be hanged.

gallows humour n. Macabre humour.

gall·stone (gáwl-stōn) n. A small, hard, pathological concretion of cholesterol, calcium salts, and bile pigments, formed in the gall bladder or in a bile duct.

Gal·lup (gál-əp), **George Horace** (1901–84). U.S. statistician. Through his techniques of polling the public, he accurately predicted the result of the 1936 presidential election. Gallup polls have been used regularly since.

Gallup poll (gál-əp) n. A sampling of the views of a representative section of the population on a particular issue; especially, one taken to assess the relative popularity of different political parties or to forecast the outcome of an election.

gal·lus·es (gál-ə-siz) pl.n. Regional. Braces for trousers. [Plural of gallus, variant of GALLOWS (obsolete sense "braces").]

gall wasp n. Any of various wasps of the family Cynipidae that produce distinctively shaped galls on oaks and other plants.

ga·loot (gə-lōōt) n. Slang. A clumsy, uncouth, or stupid person. [19th century (nautical slang) : origin obscure.]

gal·op (gál-əp, ga-lóp, -lō̃) n. Also **gal·o·pade** (-ə-páyd, -ə-paád), **gal·lo·pade. 1.** A lively dance in duple rhythm, popular in the 19th century. **2.** The music for this dance. [French, gallop, from Old French galoper, to GALLOP.]

ga·lore (gə-lór ‖ -lṓr) adj. Informal. In great numbers; in abundance. Used after the noun: dresses galore; opportunities galore. [Irish Gaelic go leór : go, to, from Old Irish co, cu† + leór, sufficiency, enough, from Old Irish lour.]

ga·losh, go·losh (gə-lósh) n. **1.** A waterproof overshoe. **2.** Archaic. A sturdy heavy-soled boot or shoe. [Middle English galoche, from Old French, probably from Late Latin gallicula, diminutive of Latin gallica (solea), "Gaulish (sandal)", from the feminine of gallicus, Gaulish, Gaelic, from Galli, Gauls.]

Gals·wor·thy (gáwlz-wurthi), **John** (1867–1933). British novelist and playwright. He wrote the sequence The Forsyte Saga (1906–21) and many other Forsyte novels and stories, and was awarded the Nobel prize for literature (1932).

Galt (gawlt ‖ golt), **John** (1779–1839). Scottish novelist. He described country life in novels such as The Annals of the Parish (1821). He also wrote a life of Byron (1830).

Gal·ton (gáwl-tən ‖ gól-), **Sir Francis** (1822–1911). British biologist; a cousin of Charles Darwin. He showed that mental characteristics could be inherited, and developed identification by fingerprints.

ga·lumph (gə-lúmf, -lúmpf) intr.v. **-lumphed, -lumphing, -lumphs.** Informal. To move or jump about in a clumsy way. [19th century (coined by Lewis Carroll) : probably a blend of GALLOP + TRIUMPH.]

galv. galvanised.

Gal·va·ni (gal-vaáni), **Luigi** (1737–98). Italian physician. His experiments making frogs' legs twitch led him to believe, erroneously, that electricity was a fluid in nerve tissue. He gave his name to galvanism, electricity generated by chemical means.

gal·van·ic (gal-vánnik) adj. **1.** Of or pertaining to direct-current electricity, especially when produced chemically. **2.** Having the effect of or produced as if by an electric shock. [French galvanique, from galvanisme, GALVANISM.] —**gal·van·i·cal·ly** adv.

galvanic cell n. Electricity. A primary cell (see).

galvanic couple n. Electricity. A voltaic couple (see).

galvanic pile *n. Electricity.* A **voltaic pile** *(see).*

gal·va·nise, gal·va·nize (gálvə-nīz) *tr.v.* **-nised, -nising, -nises.** 1. To stimulate or shock with an electric current. 2. To arouse to awareness or action; spur. 3. To coat (iron or steel) with rust-resistant zinc, by spraying, immersion, or electrolytic deposition. —**gal·va·ni·sa·tion** (-nīz-áysh'n || *U.S.* -niz-) *n.* —**gal·va·nis·er** *n.*

gal·va·nism (gálvə-niz'm) *n.* 1. Direct-current electricity, especially when produced chemically. Also called "voltaism". 2. Formerly, any form of medical treatment using electricity. [French *galvanisme*, from Italian *galvanismo*, first described by Luigi GALVANI.]

gal·va·nom·e·ter (gálvə-nómmitər) *n.* A device for detecting or measuring small electric currents by means of mechanical effects produced by the current to be measured. [GALVAN(ISM) + -METER.] —**gal·va·no·met·ric** (-nō-méttrik, gal-vánnō-), **gal·va·no·met·ri·cal** (-méttrik'l) *adj.* —**gal·va·nom·e·try** (-nómmitri) *n.*

gal·va·no·scope (gálvənə-skōp, gal-vánnə-) *n.* A galvanometer used to detect the presence and direction of electric currents by the deflection of a magnetic needle. [GALVAN(ISM) + -SCOPE.] —**gal·va·no·scop·ic** (-skóppik) *adj.* —**gal·va·no·scop·y** (gálvə-nóskəpi) *n.*

Gal·way[1] (gáwlway). *Irish* **Contae na Gaillmhe.** County in Connacht in the west of the Republic of Ireland. The main towns are Galway, Ballinasloe, and Tuam. Area, 5 936 square kilometres (2,292 square miles).

Galway[2]. *Irish* **Gaillimh.** Fishing port and the county town of County Galway in the Republic of Ireland. Situated at the mouth of the river Corrib, it is a well-known salmon-fishing centre.

gal·yak (gál-yak, -yák) *n.* A flat, glossy fur made from the pelt of a stillborn lamb or kid. [Russian dialectal *galyak*, perhaps from Russian *golyĭ*, bald, naked.]

gam[1] (gam) *n.* 1. A school or herd of whales. 2. A social meeting, especially between whalers at sea. ~*v.* **gammed, gamming, gams.** —*intr.* To come together socially, especially while at sea. —*tr. U.S.* To socialise with. [Perhaps short for GAMMON (deceptive talk).]

gam[2] *n. Slang.* A person's leg. [Probably from obsolete *gamb*, leg of an animal, from Old North French *gambe*, Late Latin *gamba*, hook, leg, from Greek *kampē*, a bend.]

Ga·ma (gaámə || gámmə), **Vasco da**, also known as Count of Vidigueria (*c.* 1469–1524). Portuguese navigator. He discovered the sea route from Europe to India via the Cape of Good Hope (1498–99).

ga·ma grass (gaámə, gámmə) *n.* A perennial grass, *Tripsacum dactyloides,* of southern North America, that is grown for fodder. [*Gama*, probably alteration of Spanish *grama*, from Latin *grāmen*, grass.]

ga·may (gám-ay, ga-máy) *n.* A variety of red grape used for making red wines, especially Beaujolais. [French, after *Gamay,* a hamlet in the wine-growing area of Beaune.]

gam·ba (gámbə) *n.* 1. A **viola da gamba** *(see).* 2. An organ stop with a violin-like tone. [Italian, leg (both senses, shortened from **viola da gamba**).]

gam·ba·do[1] (gam-báydō) *n., pl.* **-does** or **-dos.** Also **gam·bade** (-báyd, -baád). 1. In dressage, a low leap of a horse in which all four feet are off the ground. 2. A leaping or gambolling movement; a flourish. 3. An escapade; an antic. [Spanish *gambada,* from Italian *gambata,* GAMBOL.]

gam·ba·do[2] *n., pl.* **-does** or **-dos.** 1. Either of a pair of leather gaiters attached to a saddle. 2. A rider's legging or gaiter. [Italian *gamba,* leg (perhaps influenced by BASTINADO). See **gambol.**]

gam·be·son (gámbi-sən) *n.* A sleeveless garment of leather or quilted material worn under armour in the Middle Ages. [Middle English *gambisoun,* from Old French *gambe(i)son,* from *gambais, wambais,* probably from Frankish *wamba* (unattested), belly, from Common Germanic *wambō* (unattested), WOMB.]

Gam·bet·ta (gam-béttə; *French* goN-be-tá), **Léon** (1838–82). French politician. After the defeat of Napoleon III at the Battle of Sedan (1870), Gambetta helped to set up the Third Republic, escaping from the siege of Paris by balloon. He virtually ruled France until its defeat by Germany (1871). He was prime minister (1881–82).

Gam·bi·a (gámbi-ə). River in West Africa. Rising in the Fouta Djallon Plateau of Guinea, it flows 1 126 kilometres (700 miles) through Senegambia to the Atlantic Ocean, and can take ocean-going vessels almost 320 kilometres (199 miles) inland.

Gambia, Republic of The. Africa's smallest independent state. Lying in West Africa, it comprises the lower valley of the river Gambia. It is primarily agricultural, groundnuts and tourism being the mainstay of the economy. The Portuguese reached The Gambia in 1456, and British merchants were granted trading rights in 1588. The area became a British protectorate in 1894, and an independent republic within the Commonwealth in 1970. The Gambia joined Senegal in the Confederation of **Senegambia** (1981–89), which involved economic integration and cooperation in foreign policy. Area, 11 295 square kilometres (4,360 square miles). Population, 1,140,000. Capital, Banjul (formerly Bathurst). —**Gam·bi·an** *adj. & n.*

gam·bier, gam·bir (gám-beer) *n.* A resinous, astringent extract obtained from a woody vine, *Uncaria gambier* (or *gambir*), of south-central Asia, used medicinally and in tanning and dyeing. [Malay *gambir.*]

gam·bit (gámbit) *n.* 1. A chess opening in which one or more pawns are offered in exchange for a favourable position. 2. An opening remark or manoeuvre, as in a conversation or series of negotiations. [Earlier *gamet,* from Italian *gambetto,* "a tripping up", from *gamba,* leg. See **gambol.**]

gam·ble (gámb'l) *v.* **-bled, -bling, -bles.** —*intr.* 1. **a.** To bet money on the outcome of a game, contest, or other event. **b.** To play a game of chance for money or other stakes. 2. To take a risk in the hope of gaining an advantage; speculate. Often used with *on.* —*tr.* 1. To risk by gambling; expose to hazard. 2. To lose by gambling. Used with *away.* ~*n.* 1. A bet, wager, or other gambling venture. 2. An act or undertaking of uncertain outcome; a risk. [Probably from earlier *gamel,* from *gamner,* gambler, from *gamene,* to gamble, Middle English *gamenen,* Old English *gamenian,* to sport, play, from *gamen,* amusement. See **game.**] —**gam·bler** (-blər) *n.*

gam·boge (gam-bōj, -boōzh) *n.* 1. A brownish or orange resin obtained from any of several trees of the genus *Garcinia,* of south-central Asia, and yielding a golden-yellow pigment. Also called "camboga". 2. Strong yellow. [New Latin *gambogium, cambugium,* obtained from CAMBODIA.] —**gam·boge** *adj.*

gam·bol (gámb'l) *intr.v.* **-bolled** or *U.S.* **-boled, -bolling** or *U.S.* **-boling, -bols.** To leap about playfully; frolic; skip. ~*n.* A skipping or frolicking about. [Earlier *gamba(u)de,* from Old French *gambade,* from Italian *gambata,* from *gamba,* leg, from Late Latin *gamba,* hoof, leg, from Greek *kampē,* bend.]

gam·brel (gámbrəl) *n.* 1. The hock of a horse or other animal. 2. A wooden or metal frame used by butchers for hanging carcasses by the legs. [Old North French *gamberel,* diminutive of *gambier,* gambrel, from *gambe,* leg, from Late Latin *gamba,* hoof, leg.]

gambrel roof *n.* 1. *British.* A hipped roof that is topped by a small gable with vertical ends. 2. *U.S.* A **mansard roof** *(see).*

game[1] (gaym) *n.* 1. A way of amusing oneself; a pastime; a diversion. 2. A sport or other competitive activity governed by specific rules: *the game of tennis.* 3. **a.** A single instance of such an activity: *We lost the first game.* **b.** *Plural.* A gathering of competitors for athletics and other sporting events: *the Olympic Games.* **c.** *Plural.* A period in the school curriculum in which sports are taught: *She decided to miss games.* 4. **a.** The total number of points required to win a game: *One hundred points is game in bridge.* **b.** The score accumulated at any given time in a game: *At half-time, the game was 14 to 12.* 5. The equipment needed for playing certain games: *Pack the children's games in the car.* 6. A particular style or manner of playing a game: *His bridge game is only adequate.* 7. A calculated action or approach; a scheme; a plan: *You'll never see through his game.* 8. **a.** Wild animals, birds, or fish hunted for food or sport. Also used adjectively: *game birds.* **b.** The flesh of game, eaten as food. 9. **a.** Anything hunted or fit to be hunted; quarry; prey. **b.** An object of ridicule, teasing, or scorn: *His arrogance makes him fair game.* 10. *Mathematics.* A set of rules defining an abstract model of a strategic competition. See **game theory.** 11. *Informal.* A vocation or business, especially a competitive one: *the publishing game.* 12. Something undertaken lightly: *School work was just a game to most of the boys.* 13. *Chiefly British Slang.* Prostitution. Used chiefly in the phrase *on the game.* —**give the game away.** To reveal a secret. —**play the game.** To abide by the rules; behave as expected. ~*v.* **gamed, gaming, games.** —*tr. Archaic.* To waste or lose by gambling. —*intr.* To play for money or other stakes. ~*adj.* **gamer, gamest.** 1. Plucky and unyielding in manner; resolute; brave. 2. *Informal.* Ready and willing: *Are you game for a swim?* —See Synonyms at **brave.** [Middle English *game(n),* Old English *gamen,* amusement, sport, from Common Germanic *gam-* (unattested), to enjoy.]

game[2] *adj.* **gamer, gamest.** Lame. [Perhaps from French *gambi†,* crooked.]

game chips *pl.n.* Chips made of thin slices of potato, deep fried, and served with game.

game·cock (gáym-kok) *n.* A cock trained for cockfighting. Also called "fighting cock".

game fowl *n.* 1. A bird sought after as game. 2. Any of several breeds of domestic fowl bred especially for cockfighting.

game·keep·er (gáym-keepər) *n.* A person employed to protect and maintain game birds and animals, especially on an estate or game preserve.

gam·e·lan (gámmi-lan) *n.* A type of orchestra common in the East Indies, consisting mainly of tuned metal or wooden chimes and other percussion instruments. [Javanese.]

game laws *pl.n.* Regulations for the protection of game animals, including birds and fish, that define the hunting season for each species and place restrictions on the method of capture and on the number of animals that may be taken.

game·ly (gáymli) *adv.* With pluck; courageously.

game·ness (gáym-nəss, -niss) *n.* Courage; pluck.

game plan *n. U.S.* 1. A strategy devised for winning a game, as in American football. 2. Any strategy for reaching an objective.

game point *n.* The state of play reached in a game, especially in tennis, when one side or player will win after gaining the next point.

game show *n.* A popular entertainment in which contestants compete for prizes before an audience; especially, a game show broadcast on television or radio.

games·man·ship (gáymz-mən-ship) *n.* The art or practice of winning a game or contest by methods which may be unsportsmanlike or devious but which do not actually break the rules.

game·some (gáym-səm) *adj. Literary.* Frolicsome; playful; merry. —**game·some·ly** *adv.* —**game·some·ness** *n.*

game·ster (gáym-stər) *n.* A habitual gambler.

games theory *n.* The mathematical analysis of abstract models of situations involving a conflict of interest with the object of determining the best strategy and anticipating the reactions of opponents. It has applications in linear programming, statistical decision-making, operations research, and military and economic planning. Also called "theory of games". See **game**.

gam·e·tan·gi·um (gămmi-tán-ji-əm) *n., pl.* **-gia** (-ji-ə). *Botany.* An organ or cell in which gametes are produced, especially in primitive plant forms. [GAMET(O)- + Greek *angeion*, vessel.] **—gam·e·tan·gi·al** *adj.*

gam·ete (gămmeet, gə-méet) *n.* A germ cell possessing the haploid number of chromosomes (half the number of chromosomes possessed by the somatic or body cells); especially, a mature sperm or egg, capable of participating in fertilisation. See **fertilisation**. [New Latin *gameta*, from Greek *gametē*, wife, and *gametēs*, husband, both from *gamos*, marriage.]

gameto– *comb. form.* Indicates gamete; for example, **gametophyte**, **gametophore**. [New Latin *gameta*, GAMETE.]

ga·me·to·cyte (gə-mée-tō-sīt, -tə-) *n.* A cell from which gametes develop by meiotic division; a spermatocyte or an oocyte. [GAMETO- + -CYTE.]

ga·me·to·gen·e·sis (gămmitō-jénnə-siss, gə-méetō-) *n.* Also **gam·e·tog·e·ny** (gămmi-tójəni). The production of gametes. [GAMETO- + -GENESIS.] **—ga·me·to·gen·ic** (-jénnik), **gam·e·tog·e·nous** (-tójənəss) *adj.*

ga·me·to·phore (gə-mée-tō-fawr, -tə- ‖ -fōr) *n. Botany.* A structure, as in mosses, on which gametangia are borne. [GAMETO- + -PHORE.] **—ga·me·to·phor·ic** (-fórrik ‖ -fáwrik) *adj.*

ga·me·to·phyte (gə-mée-tō-fīt, -tə-) *n. Botany.* The generation or form that reproduces sexually in a plant characterised by alternation of generations. Compare **sporophyte**. [GAMETO- + -PHYTE.] **—gam·e·to·phyt·ic** (gămmi-tō-fíttik, gə-mée-tō-, -tə-) *adj.*

game warden *n.* One who looks after game, especially in a reserve or safari park.

gamey. Variant of **gamy**.

gam·ic (gámmik) *adj.* Of or requiring fertilisation in reproduction; sexual. [Greek *gamos*, marriage. See **gamete**.]

gam·in (gámmin) *French* ga-máN) *n.* A boy who roams about the streets; a street urchin; a waif. [French, perhaps from German *Gammel*, loud rejoicing, (hence) ungainly young man, good-for-nothing, from Old High German *gaman*, amusement, game, from Common Germanic *gam-* (unattested), to enjoy.]

gam·ine (gámmeen, ga-méen) *n.* **1.** A female urchin. **2.** An attractively boyish girl or young woman. [French, feminine of GAMIN.]

gam·ing (gáyming) *n.* The playing of games of chance; gambling. Also used adjectivally: *the gaming laws; a gaming house.*

gam·ma (gámmə) *n.* **1.** The third letter in the Greek alphabet, written γ. Transliterated in English as *g*, or as *n* before *g*, *k*, or *kh*. **2.** A gamma ray. **3.** The third highest mark or grade award for school work or in an examination. [Greek *gamma*, from Semitic, akin to Hebrew *gīmel*, probably "camel".]

gam·ma·di·on (ga-máydi-ən, gə-) *n.* A cross composed of four capital Greek gammas, especially so as to form a swastika; a fylfot. [Medieval Greek, from Greek, from GAMMA.]

gamma globulin *n.* Any of several globulin fractions of blood plasma, most of which are immunoglobulins.

gamma iron *n.* An allotropic form of iron that exists between 910°C and 1400°C, and is nonmagnetic.

gamma radiation *n.* **1.** Electromagnetic radiation emitted by radioactive decay and having energies in a range overlapping that of the highest energy X-rays, extending up to several hundred thousand electronvolts. **2.** Any electromagnetic radiation with energy greater than several hundred thousand electronvolts. **3.** A **ray** (*see*) of such radiation.

gam·mer (gámmər) *n. Regional & Archaic.* An elderly woman. [Probably contraction of GODMOTHER.]

gam·mon¹ (gámmən) *n.* A victory in backgammon occurring before the loser has removed a single man.
~ *tr.v.* **gammoned, -moning, -mons.** To defeat in backgammon by scoring a gammon. [Probably from Middle English *gamen*, GAME.]

gam·mon² *n. British Informal.* Misleading or nonsensical talk.
~ *v.* **gammoned, -moning, -mons.** *British Informal.* —*tr.* To mislead by deceptive talk. —*intr.* To talk gammon. [Perhaps from thieves' slang expressions *to give gammon, to keep in gammon,* to talk to and divert the attention of (someone) while another thief is robbing him, perhaps slang use of GAMMON (backgammon term).] **—gam·mon·er** *n.*

gam·mon³ *n.* **1.** A ham that has been cured or smoked. **2.** The lower or bottom part of a side of bacon. [Old North French *gambon*, from *gambe*, leg, from Late Latin *gamba*, hoof, leg, from Greek *kampē*, a bend.]

gam·mon⁴ *tr.v.* **-moned, -moning, -mons.** *Nautical.* To fasten (a bowsprit) to the stem of a ship. [Perhaps from GAMMON (cured ham, hence, "the tying up of a ham").]

gam·my (gámmi) *adj. British Slang.* Lame; injured. Said of a leg. [Dialect variant of GAME (lame).]

gamo– *comb. form.* Indicates: **1.** Sexual union; for example, **gamogenesis**. **2.** Union or fusion; for example, **gamopetalous.** [Greek *gamos*, marriage.]

gam·o·gen·e·sis (gămmō-jénni-siss, gámmə-) *n.* Sexual reproduction. [GAMO- + -GENESIS.] **—gam·o·ge·net·ic** (-jə-néttik) *adj.* **—gam·o·ge·net·i·cal·ly** *adv.*

gam·o·pet·al·ous (gămmō-péttələss, gámmə-) *adj. Botany.* Having or designating a corolla with the petals fused or partially fused;

sympetalous. [New Latin *gamopetalus* : GAMO- + PETALOUS.]

gam·o·phyl·lous (gámmō-fílləss, gámmə-) *adj. Botany.* Having or designating united leaves or leaflike parts. [GAMO- + -PHYLLOUS.]

gam·o·sep·al·ous (gámmō-séppələss, gámmə-) *adj. Botany.* Having the sepals united or partly united; synsepalous. [GAMO- + -SEPALOUS.]

–gamous *adj. comb. form.* Indicates marriage or sexual union; for example, **bigamous, dichogamous.** [Greek *gamos,* marriage.]

gamp (gamp) *n. British Informal.* A large, baggy umbrella. Used humorously. [After Mrs. Sarah *Gamp,* nurse in Charles Dickens' *Martin Chuzzlewit* (1844), who owns an umbrella.]

gam·ut (gámmət) *n.* **1.** The complete range of anything; the extent. **2.** The entire series of recognised musical notes. [Middle English, contracted from Medieval Latin *gamma ut* : *gamma,* note one tone lower than the first note in Guido d'Arezzo's scale, from Greek letter GAMMA + *ut* (now *doh*), lowest note in Guido's scale. (The notes of the scale are named after syllables in a Latin hymn to St. John: *Ut* queant laxis *resonāre fibris* Mira gestorum *famuli tuorum,* Solve polluti *labii reatum,* Sancte Iohannes.)]

gam·y, gam·ey (gáymi) *adj.* **-ier, -iest. 1.** Having the flavour or odour of game, especially of game that has been hung too long. **2.** Showing an unyielding spirit; plucky; hardy: *a gamy little mare.* **3.** *U.S.* Scandalous; risqué. **—gam·i·ness** *n.*

–gamy *n. comb. form.* Indicates marriage or sexual union; for example, **allogamy.** [Greek *-gamia,* from *gamos,* marriage.]

gan (gan) *intr.v.* **ganned, ganning, gans.** *British Regional.* To go. [Old English *gangan*; see **gang** (group).]

Gand. See **Ghent.**

gan·der (gándər) *n.* **1.** A male goose. **2.** *Informal.* A simpleton; a halfwit. **3.** *Slang.* A quick look; a glance. [Middle English *gander,* Old English *gandra, ganra.*]

Gan·dhi (gán-di, gaán-), **Indira** (1917–84). Indian politician. She followed her father Jawaharlal Nehru, India's first prime minister, into politics and became prime minister in 1966. In 1975 she declared a state of emergency following allegations of repression and corruption, and was defeated in the 1977 election. She was re-elected in 1980, but was assassinated in 1984.

Gandhi, Mohandas Karamchand, known as **Mahatma** (1869–1948). Indian politician. He went to South Africa in 1893 to defend the Asian community there and developed his policy of "satyagraha", passive resistance. He returned to India in 1914 and became leader of the home rule movement. The British frequently imprisoned him for acts of civil disobedience. Independence was achieved in 1947, and Gandhi won worldwide respect for the bloodless way this aim had been achieved. He was murdered for his commitment to Hindu-Muslim reconciliation. **—Gan·dhi·an** *adj.*

Gandhi, Rajiv (1944–91). Indian politician, prime minister (1984–89). The son of Indira Gandhi, he played no part in politics until the death of his brother Sanjay in 1981. He became General Secretary of the Congress (I) Party in 1983, and on Mrs Gandhi's assassination the following year was sworn in as prime minister. He subsequently won a general election, but lost power in 1989. In 1991 he was assassinated by a bomb during an election campaign.

ga·nef (gaánəf) *n. U.S. slang.* A thief, scoundrel, or rascal. [Yiddish *ganef, gannef,* from Hebrew *gannābh,* from *gānnabh,* he stole.]

gang¹ (gang) *n.* **1.** A group of people, especially: **a.** A group, especially of young people, who associate regularly on a social basis. **b.** A group of criminals, juvenile delinquents, or the like who band together. **c.** A group of labourers organised together on one job or under one foreman: *a railway gang.* **d.** A number of slaves or prisoners. **2.** A set, especially of matched tools: *a gang of chisels.* **3.** *U.S.* A herd, especially of buffalo or elk.
~ *v.* **ganged, ganging, gangs.** —*intr.* To band together as a group or gang. —*tr.* **1.** To group together into a gang. **2.** *Electronics.* To arrange (two or more components) so that they can be varied by a single control. **—gang up on.** *Informal.* To band together against (someone). [Originally "a going", "journey", "way", Middle English *gang,* Old English *gang,* from Germanic.]

gang² *intr.v. Scottish.* To go. [Old English *gangan*; see **gang** (group).]

gang-bang (gáng-bang) *n. Slang.* Sexual intercourse by several men one after the other with the same woman, usually against her will.
~ *tr.v.* **gangbanged, -banging, -bangs.** To subject (a woman) to a gangbang.

gang·er (gáng-ər) *n. Chiefly British.* A gang foreman.

Gan·ges (gánjeez). *Hindi* **Gan·ga** (gáng-gə). River of India and Bangladesh. It flows 2 505 kilometres (1,557 miles) from the Himalayas to the Bay of Bengal and has the largest delta in the world. It is the Hindus' most sacred river.

gang hook *n.* A multiple fishhook consisting of two or more hooks joined shank to shank. [From GANG (set of tools).]

gang·land (gáng-land, -lənd) *n. Informal.* The criminal underworld.

gan·gli·at·ed (gáng-gli-aytid) *adj.* Also **gan·gli·on·at·ed** (-ə-naytid) Having ganglia.

gan·gling (gáng-gling) *adj.* Also **gang·ly** (-gli), **-lier, -liest.** Tall, thin, and ungraceful; awkwardly built; lanky. [Irregularly from dialectal *gang,* to go, straggle, Middle English *gangen.* See **gangrel**.]

gan·gli·on (gáng-gli-ən) *n., pl.* **-ions** or **-glia** (-gli-ə). **1.** *Anatomy.* A group of nerve cell bodies, such as one located outside the brain or spinal cord. **2.** Any centre of power, activity, or energy. **3.** *Pathology.* A harmless cystic lesion resembling a tumour, occurring in a tendon sheath or joint capsule. [Greek *ganglion,* cystlike tumour, hence nerve bundle, ganglion.] **—gan·gli·on·ic** (-ónnik) *adj.*

Gang of Four *n.* **1.** A radical faction within the Chinese Communist Party that made an unsuccessful attempt to seize power after the death of Mao Ze-dong (Mao Tse-tung) in 1976. Its members were Mao's widow Jiang Qing, Zhang Chun-zhao, Wang Hong-wen and Yao Wen-yuan. **2.** Loosely, any four-person faction that emerges as a significant force.

gang·plank (gáng-plangk) *n.* A board or ramp used as a removable footway between a ship and a pier, or across a building site or any other wet or muddy place; a gangway. [GANG (in obsolete sense "passage") + PLANK.]

gan·grene (gáng-green ‖ -gréen) *n.* **1.** Death and decay of tissue in a part of the body, usually a limb, due to failure of blood supply, injury, or disease. Compare **necrobiosis. 2. a.** Moral decay. **b.** Something causing or symptomatic of moral decay.
—*v.* **gangrened, -grening, -grenes.** —*tr.* To affect with gangrene. —*intr.* To become affected with gangrene. [Old French *gangrine,* from Latin *gangraena,* from Greek *gangraina.*] —**gan·gre·nous** (-grinəss) *adj.*

gang saw *n.* A saw in which a group of blades fitted in a frame make parallel simultaneous cuts.

gang·sta (gáng-stə) *adj.* Of, pertaining to, or designating rap music with lyrics with attitude that glorify violence and badmouth women. [Alteration of *gangster* to suggest its non-rhotic pronunciation. In U.S. black ghettos.]

gang·ster (gáng-stər) *n.* A member of an organised group of criminals; a racketeer. [GANG + -STER.]

gangue (gang) *n.* The worthless rock or other material in which valuable minerals are found. [French, from German *Gang,* course, lode, vein, from Old High German, a going.]

gang·way (gáng-way) *n.* **1.** *Nautical.* **a.** A passage along either side of a ship's upper deck. **b.** A gangplank. **c.** An opening in the bulwark of a ship through which passengers may board. **2.** *British.* **a.** The aisle that runs lengthways and divides the seating sections of the House of Commons, separating the front and back benches. **b.** Any aisle between seating sections, as in a theatre. **3.** *Mining.* The main level of a mine.
—*interj.* Used to clear a passage through a crowd or obstructed area. [GANG (in obsolete sense "passage") + WAY.]

gan·is·ter, gan·nis·ter (gánni-stər) *n.* **1.** A silicon-rich sedimentary rock used for refractory furnace linings. **2.** A mixture of fire clay and ground quartz, used to line furnaces.

gan·ja (gán-jə, gaán-) *n.* Marijuana. [Hindi *gā̃njhā,* from Sanskrit *grñja.*]

gan·net (gánnit) *n.* Any of several large sea birds of the genus *Morus;* especially, *M. bassanus,* of northern coastal regions, having white plumage with black wing tips and a yellow crown. [Middle English *ganat, ganett,* Old English *ganot.*]

gan·oid (gánn-oyd) *adj.* Of, pertaining to, or characteristic of certain bony fishes, such as the sturgeon and the gar, having armour-like scales consisting of bony plates covered with layers of dentine and enamel.
—*n.* A ganoid fish. [New Latin *Ganoidei* (former designation), from French *ganoïde,* having a shiny surface : Greek *ganos,* brightness, joy, from *ganusthai,* to rejoice.]

Gan·su, Kan·su (gán-sóo). Province in north central China. Much of its population is Muslim. Area, 530 000 square kilometres (204,580 square miles). Capital, Lanzhou (Lanchow).

gant·let¹, gaunt·let (gánt-lit, gáwnt-) ‖ *U.S. also* gaánt-) *n.* A section of double railway tracks where the two tracks are overlapped, in order to allow trains to pass one another at a narrow place without switching.
—*tr.v.* **gantleted, -leting, -lets.** To overlap (railway tracks) to form a gantlet. [Alteration (influenced by GAUNTLET) of earlier *gant(e)-lope,* from Swedish *gatlopp,* from Old Swedish *gatulop,* "passage-way" : *gata,* road, way + *lop,* course.]

gant·let². *U.S.* Variant of **gauntlet** (glove) and **gauntlet** (ordeal).

gant·line (gánt-lin, -lin) *n.* A rope passed through a single block at the top of a mast or stackpole and used for hoisting. [Perhaps alteration of *girtline* : GIRT (girdle) + LINE.]

gan·try (gántri) *n., pl.* **-tries.** Also **gaun·try** (for sense 4). **1.** A bridge-like frame over which a travelling crane moves. **2.** A similar spanning frame supporting a group of railway signals over several tracks. **3.** *Aerospace.* A massive vertical structure used in assembling or servicing rockets. **4.** A support for a barrel lying on its side. [Probably dialect variant of *gallon-tree.*]

Gan·y·mede¹ (gánni-meed). *Greek Mythology.* A Trojan prince of great beauty whom Zeus carried away to be cupbearer to the gods.

Gan·y·mede² *n. Astronomy.* The third moon of Jupiter, one of the largest planetary satellites in the Solar System. [After GANYMEDE.]

gaol. *Chiefly British.* Variant of **jail.**
Usage: Gaol is the standard spelling in British usage, but *jail* is the more widely used spelling in informal writing and is the only form in American English.

gap (gap) *n.* **1.** An opening, as in a partition or wall; a break; a cleft. **2.** A break in a mountain range; a pass or gorge. **3.** A suspension of continuity; an interval; a hiatus: *a gap in his report.* **4.** A conspicuous difference; a disparity: *a gap between expenses and receipts.* **5.** *Electricity.* A space traversed by an electric spark; a spark gap. [Middle English *gap(pe),* from Old Norse *gap,* chasm.]

gape (gayp ‖ gap) *intr.v.* **gaped, gaping, gapes. 1.** To open the mouth wide; yawn. **2.** To stare wonderingly, as with the mouth open. **3.** To become widely open or separated: *The curtains gaped when the wind blew.* —See Synonyms at **gaze.**

—*n.* **1.** An act or instance of gaping. **2.** A large opening. **3.** *Zoology.* The width of the space between the open jaws or mandibles of a vertebrate. [Middle English *gapen,* Old Norse *gapa,* to open the mouth.]

ga·per (gáypər) *n.* Any of various marine bivalve molluscs of the genera *Lutraria* and *Mya,* having oval shells that gape at both ends; especially, the sand gaper, *M. arenaria.* Also U.S. "soft-shell clam" (for this species).

gapes (gayps) *n.* **1.** *Used with a singular verb.* A disease of birds, especially young domesticated poultry caused by gapeworms and resulting in obstructed breathing. **2.** *Used with a plural verb.* A fit of yawning. Preceded by *the: "another hour of music was to give pleasure or the gapes"* (Jane Austen).

gape·worm (gáyp-wurm) *n.* Any of several nematode worms of the genus *Syngamus;* especially, *S. trachea,* infecting the trachea of certain birds and causing gapes.

gap·ing (gáyping) *adj.* Deep and wide open; cavernous: *a gaping wound.* —**gap·ing·ly** *adv.*

gap-toothed (gáp-tootht ‖ -tóotht) *adj.* Having wide gaps between the front teeth.

gar¹ (gar) *n.* **1.** Any of several ganoid fishes of the genus *Lepisosteus,* of fresh and brackish waters of North and Central America, having an elongated body and a long snout. **2.** A similar or related fish, such as the needlefish. Also called "garfish", "garpike". [Short for GARFISH.]

gar² *tr.v.* **garred, garring, gars.** *Northern British.* To cause or compel. [Middle English *gere,* from Old Norse *gera,* to make, do.]

ga·rage (gárr-aazh, -ij ‖ *U.S.* gə-ráazh, -ráaj) *n.* **1.** A building or wing of a building, as of a house, in which to park a car or cars. **2.** A commercial establishment that sells motor fuels and buys, sells, repairs, and services motor vehicles.
—*tr.v.* **garaged, -raging, -rages.** To put in or bring to a garage. [French, from *garer,* to dock (ships), store in a garage, from Old French, to warn, protect, guard, from Frankish *warōn* (unattested).]

ga·ram ma·sa·la (gáarəm maa-saálə) *n.* A mixture of spices used in Indian cooking.

garb (garb) *n.* **1. a.** Clothing, especially if distinctive or unusual. Often used humorously. **b.** The clothing worn by people in a specified profession or job: *clerical garb.* **2.** An appearance or outward show.
—*tr.v.* **garbed, garbing, garbs.** To cover with or as if with clothing; dress; array. [Obsolete French *garbe,* graceful appearance, from Italian *garbo,* grace, elegance of dress, from Germanic.]

gar·bage (gárbij) *n.* **1.** *Chiefly U.S.* Household waste; refuse. **2.** Worthless writing or speech; trash; rubbish: *rhetorical garbage.* [Middle English, probably from Anglo-French *garbelage,* removal of discarded matter.]

gar·ban·zo (gaar-bánzō) *n., pl.* **-zos.** A plant, the **chickpea** (*see*), or its edible seed. [Spanish *garbanzo,* alteration (influenced by *garroba,* carob) of Old Spanish *arvanço,* from Germanic, akin to Old High German *araweiz,* pea, Latin *ervum,* bitter vetch, probably of Asiatic origin.]

gar·ble (gárb'l) *tr.v.* **-bled, -bling, -bles. 1.** To distort unintentionally or confuse (an account or message) so that it becomes unintelligible. **2.** To deliberately distort (an account or message), especially by the selective omission of relevant data. **3.** *Archaic.* To sort out; sift; cull.
—*n.* The act or an instance of garbling. [Middle English *garbelen,* to sift, select, from Italian *garbellare,* from Arabic *gharbala,* from *ghirbāl,* sieve, from Late Latin *crībellāre,* to sift, from *crībellum,* diminutive of *crībrum,* sieve.] —**gar·bler** *n.*

gar·bo (gár-bō) *n., pl.* **-bos.** *Australian Informal.* A dustman. [From *garbage.*]

Gar·bo (gár-bō), **Greta,** born Greta Louisa Gustavson (1905–90). Swedish-born U.S. actress. She became a Hollywood star in 1926, but kept herself aloof and mysterious, retiring suddenly in 1941. Her films include *Queen Christina* (1933) and *Camille* (1936). She received a special Academy Award (1954).

gar·board (gár-bawrd ‖ -bôrd) *n. Nautical.* The first range or strake of planks laid next to the ship's keel. [Obsolete Dutch *gaarboord* : perhaps *garen,* to gather, contraction of Middle Dutch *gaderen* + Dutch *boord,* border, ship's side, from Middle Dutch *bort,* board.]

gar·boil (gár-boyl) *n. Archaic.* Confusion; uproar. [Old French *garbouil(le),* from Old Italian *garbuglio,* reduplicative formation (with *gar-* for *bar-*) from Latin *bullīre,* to boil, bubble.]

García Lorca. See **Lorca.**

García Márquez. See **Márquez.**

gar·çon (gaar-sóN, -sóN, gár-son) *n., pl.* **-çons** (-sóN). A waiter, especially if French.

gar·da (gárdə) *n., pl.* **gardai** (gárdi). A member of the Irish police force. —**the Garda.** The Irish police force. [Irish.]

Gar·da, Lake (gárdə). Lake in northern Italy, the largest in the country. The sheltering Alps to the north and the mitigating effects of the lake give its shores an unusually temperate climate.

gar·den (gárd'n) *n.* **1.** A plot of land adjoining a house, used for the cultivation of grass, flowers, vegetables, or fruit, and for recreation. **2.** *Often plural.* Grounds adorned with flowers, shrubs, and trees for public enjoyment. **3.** An open-air place where refreshments are served: *a tea garden.* **4.** A fertile, well-cultivated region: *Kent is the garden of England.* —**lead (someone) up the garden path.** *Informal.* To mislead.
—*v.* **gardened, -dening, -dens.** —*tr.* To cultivate (a plot of

ground) as a garden. —*intr.* **1.** To tend a garden. **2.** To work as a gardener.
~*adj.* **1.** Of, pertaining to, intended for, or found in a garden. **2.** Surrounded by gardens; provided with open areas and greenery: *a garden city.* **3.** *British.* Designating a flat situated on the ground floor or in the basement of a building, usually having access to a garden. [Middle English *gardyn,* from Old North French *gardin,* from Vulgar Latin *(hortus) gardīnus* (unattested), "enclosed (garden)", from *gardo* (unattested), fence, enclosure, from Frankish *gardo* (unattested).]

garden centre *n.* A place where trees, plants, gardening tools, garden furniture, and similar items are sold.

garden city *n.* A town of limited size planned so as to provide a pleasant non-urban environment, with low-density housing and plenty of trees, open spaces, and the like. One of the first garden cities, Letchworth in England, was designed (1903) by Sir Ebenezer Howard (1850–1928).

garden cress *n.* A pungent-tasting plant, *Lepidium sativum,* with fragrant white or pinkish flowers, cultivated for use in salads.

gar·den·er (gárd-nər, gárd'n-ər) *n.* A person who works in or tends a garden for pleasure or profit.

garden escape *n.* A garden plant growing wild, an escape *(see).*

gar·de·ni·a (gaar-deeni-ə) *n.* **1.** Any of various shrubs and trees of the genus *Gardenia;* especially, *G. jasminoides,* native to China, having glossy, evergreen leaves and large, fragrant, usually white waxy flowers. This species is also called "Cape jasmine". **2.** The flower of this shrub. [New Latin *Gardenia,* after Dr. Alexander *Garden* (1731–91), American-born Scottish naturalist and vice-president of the Royal Society.]

Garden of Eden *n.* **Eden** *(see).*

garden party *n.* A social gathering held on a lawn, at which refreshments are served.

garden suburb *n.* A planned, low-density residential suburb with gardens and community facilities.

garde-robe (gárd-rōb) *n.* *Archaic.* **1. a.** A chamber for storing clothes; a wardrobe. **b.** The contents of a wardrobe. **2.** Any private chamber. [Middle English, from Old French : *garder, guarder,* to GUARD + *robe,* ROBE.]

gar·fish (gar-fish) *n., pl.* **-fishes** or collectively **garfish.** Either of two fishes, the **gar** or **garpike** *(both of which see).* [Middle English *garfyssh,* probably "spear fish" : *gare, gore,* spear, Old English *gār* + FISH.]

gar·ga·ney (gárgəni) *n., pl.* **-neys.** An Old World duck, *Anas querquedula,* having a conspicuous white stripe running over each eye and down the back of the head in the male. Also called "garganey teal". [Italian dialectal *gargenei* (imitative).]

Gar·gan·tu·a (gaar-gán-tew-ə). A giant king noted for his enormous physical and intellectual appetites, the hero of Rabelais' satires *Gargantua* and *Pantagruel.*

gar·gan·tu·an (gaar-gán-tew-ən) *adj.* *Often capital* **G.** Of immense size or volume; gigantic; colossal; huge. See Synonyms at **enormous.**

gar·get (gárgit) *n.* Mastitis of domestic animals, especially cattle. [Perhaps specialised use of Middle English *garget, gargat,* throat; from Old French *garguette, gargate,* from Old Provençal *gargata,* probably from Latin *gurges,* throat.]

gar·gle (gárg'l) *v.* **-gled, -gling, -gles.** —*intr.* **1.** To force exhaled air through a liquid held in the back of the mouth, with the head tilted back, in order to cleanse or medicate the mouth or throat. **2.** To produce the characteristic sound of gargling. —*tr.* **1.** To rinse or medicate (the mouth or throat) by gargling. **2.** To circulate or apply (a solution or medicine) by gargling. **3.** To utter with a gargling sound.
~*n.* **1.** A medicated solution for gargling. **2.** An act of gargling. **3.** A gargling sound. [Old French *gargouiller,* from *gargouille, garoule,* throat, GARGOYLE.]

gar·goyle (gár-goyl) *n.* **1.** A roof spout carved to represent a grotesque human or animal figure, and projecting from a gutter to carry rainwater clear of the wall. **2.** Any grotesque ornamental figure or projection. **3.** A person of grotesque appearance. [Middle English *gargoyl,* from Old French *gargouille, gargoul,* "throat", from Latin *gurguliō,* windpipe.]

gar·i·bal·di (gárri-báwldi) *n.* **1.** A loose high-necked blouse styled after the red shirts of Garibaldi and his soldiers, fashionable among women in the mid-19th century. **2.** *British.* A type of biscuit containing a layer of currants.

Ga·ri·bal·di (gárri-báwldi), **Giuseppe** (1807–82). Italian soldier and nationalist leader. He and his 1,000 volunteers, the redshirts, captured Sicily and Naples (1860) to add to the kingdom of Italy.

gar·ish (gáir-ish, gárr-) *adj.* **1. a.** Marred by strident colour or excessive ornamentation; gaudy; tawdry. **b.** Loud and flashy: *garish make-up.* **2.** Glaring; dazzling: *"Hide me from Day's garish eye"* (Milton). [Formerly also *gaurish,* perhaps from obsolete *gaur,* to stare, Middle English *gauren†.*] —**gar·ish·ly** *adv.* —**gar·ish·ness** *n.*

gar·land (gárland) *n.* **1.** A wreath, circlet, or festoon of flowers, leaves, or other material worn as a crown or collar, or hung as an ornament. **2.** A representation of a garland in metal or other material, for ornamentation or as a heraldic device. **3.** Something resembling a garland. **4.** A mark of victory or distinction; a prize. **5.** *Nautical.* A ring or collar of rope or wire used to hoist spars or prevent rubbing or fraying. **6.** An anthology, as of ballads or poems.
~*tr.v.* **garlanded, -landing, -lands. 1.** To embellish or deck with a garland. **2.** To serve as a garland for. [Middle English *gerlond, garland,* from Old French *gerlande, garlande,* "ornament made with gold threads", from Frankish *wiara, weara* (unattested), wire, thread.]

Gar·land (gár-lənd), **Judy,** born Frances Ethel Gumm (1922–69). U.S. singer and actress. She made her stage debut at five and starred in *The Wizard of Oz* (1939) and *A Star is Born* (1954). She received a special Academy Award (1939).

gar·lic (gárlik) *n.* **1.** A plant, *Allium sativum,* related to the onion, having a bulb with a strong, distinctive odour and flavour. **2.** The bulb of this plant, divisible into separate cloves, and used as a flavouring. [Middle English *garlec, garly,* Old English *gārlēac,* "spear leek" (from its spear-shaped leaves) : *gār,* spear + *lēac,* leek.]

gar·lick·y (gárliki) *adj.* Containing, tasting of, or smelling of garlic.

garlic mustard *n.* A weedy plant, *Alliaria officinalis* (or *petiolata*), native to Europe, having small white flowers and an odour of garlic. Also called "jack-by-the-hedge".

gar·ment (gármənt) *n.* Any article of clothing.
~*tr.v.* **garmented, -menting, -ments.** *Literary.* To clothe; to dress. Usually used in the passive. [Middle English *gar(ne)ment,* from Old French *garnement,* "equipment", from *g(u)arnir,* to furnish, equip.]

garn (garn) *interj.* *Informal.* Used to express derision or disbelief. [Pronunciation spelling (Cockney) *go on.*]

gar·ner (gárnər) *tr.v.* **-nered, -nering, -ners. 1.** To gather and store in or as if in a granary. **2.** To amass; acquire.
~*n.* *Archaic.* A granary; a storehouse. [Middle English *gerner, garner,* granary, from Old French *gernier, grenier,* from Latin *grānārium,* from *grānum,* grain.]

gar·net (gárnit) *n.* **1.** Any of several widespread silicate minerals, often embedded in igneous and metamorphic rocks, coloured red, brown, black, green, yellow, or white, and used both as gemstones and as abrasives. **2.** Dark to very dark red. [Middle English *gernet, granate,* from Old French *grenat,* dark red, garnet, pomegranate-coloured, from *pome grenate,* POMEGRANATE.]

gar·ni·er·ite (gárni-ə-rīt) *n.* A mineral, $(Ni,Mg)_6(OH)_8Si_4O_8 \cdot H_2O$, apple-green in colour and an important nickel ore. [Discovered by Jules *Garnier* (died 1904), French geologist.]

gar·nish (gárnish) *tr.v.* **-nished, -nishing, -nishes. 1.** To enhance the appearance of by adding decorative touches; especially, to embellish (food) by decorating it, usually with something savoury such as a sprig of parsley or slice of lemon. **2.** *Law.* To garnishee.
~*n.* **1. a.** Ornamentation; embellishment. **b.** Something used to garnish food. **2.** *Slang.* An unwarranted fee, as one formerly extorted from a new prisoner by a jailer. [Middle English *garnysshen,* to equip, adorn, from Old French *guarnir, garnir* (present stem *garniss-*), from Germanic.] —**gar·nish·er** *n.*

gar·nish·ee (gár-ni-shée) *n.* *Law.* **1.** A debtor against whom a plaintiff has instituted process of garnishment. **2.** A third party who has been warned that money or property in his control, but due or belonging to the defendant, has been arrested and is to be paid to the plaintiff.
~*tr.v.* **garnisheed, -eeing, -ees.** *Law.* **1.** To attach (a debtor's pay, for example) by garnishment. **2.** To serve with a garnishment.

gar·nish·ment (gár-nish-mənt) *n.* **1.** Ornamentation; embellishment. **2.** *Law.* **a.** A legal proceeding whereby money or property due or belonging to a debtor but currently in the possession of a third party, such as a trustee, is applied to the payment of the debt to the plaintiff. **b.** A court order directing a third party who owes the defendant money, or holds property belonging to him, to withhold such money or property.

gar·ni·ture (gárni-chər) *n.* Something that garnishes or decorates; embellishment. [Old French *garniture, garneture,* from *garnir,* to GARNISH.]

Ga·ronne (ga-rón). River of southwest France. It rises in the Spanish Pyrenees and flows 503 kilometres (312 miles) through Toulouse and Bordeaux to the Gironde estuary. Its main tributaries are the Lot, Tarn, and Ariège.

gar·pike (gár-pīk) *n.* **1.** A fish, the **gar** *(see).* **2.** A marine fish, *Belone belone,* of European waters, having long toothed jaws and green bones. Also called "garfish".

gar·ret (gárrit) *n.* A room on the top floor of a house, typically immediately under a pitched roof; an attic. [Middle English *garet(te),* turret, watchtower, from Old French *garite,* from *g(u)arir,* to defend, protect, from Germanic.]

gar·ri (gárri) *n.* A staple food in West Africa made from cassava.

Gar·rick (gárrik), **David** (1717–79). English actor and theatre manager. He was considered the foremost interpreter of Shakespeare of his time.

gar·ri·son (gárriss'n) *n.* **1.** A military post, especially one permanently established. **2.** The troops stationed at such a post.
~*tr.v.* **garrisoned, -soning, -sons. 1.** To assign (troops) to a military post. **2.** To supply (a post) with troops. **3.** To occupy as or convert into a garrison. [Middle English *gariso(u)n,* protection, fortress, from Old French *garison,* from *g(u)arir,* to protect, from Germanic.]

gar·rotte, ga·rotte, gar·rote (gə-rót ‖ -rŏt) *n.* **1. a.** A former Spanish method of execution by strangulation or by breaking the neck with an iron collar screwed tight with a knoblike device. **b.** A collar used for this. **2.** Strangulation, especially in order to rob.
~*tr.v.* **garrotted** or **garroted, -rotting** or **-roting, -rottes** or **rotes. 1.** To execute by garrotte. **2.** To strangle or throttle, especially in order to rob. [Spanish, cudgel, probably from Old French *garrot,*

earlier *guaroc*, club, turning rod, from *garokier†*, to bend down, strangle.] **—gar·rot·ter** *n.*

gar·ru·lous (gárrə-ləss, gárrew-) *adj.* **1.** Habitually talkative; loquacious. **2.** Wordy; prolix. —See Synonyms at **talkative.** [Latin *garrulus*, from *garrīre*, to chatter.] **—gar·ru·lous·ly** *adv.* **—gar·ru·lous·ness, gar·ru·li·ty** (gə-ró͞oləti, gə-) *n.*

gar·ry·a (gárri-ə) *n.* Any evergreen shrub of the American genus *Garrya*, some species of which have long catkins and are grown for ornament. [New Latin, after Nicholas *Garry*, 19th-century English official of Hudson's Bay Company.]

gar·ter (gártər) *n.* **1. a.** An elasticised band worn round the leg to support a sock or stocking. **b.** *U.S.* A suspender. **c.** An elasticised band worn round the arm to keep the sleeve pushed up. **2.** *Capital* **G. a.** The **Order of the Garter** (*see*). **b.** The badge of this order. **c.** Membership of this order.
~*tr.v.* **gartered, -tering, -ters. 1.** To fasten and hold with a garter. **2.** To put a garter upon. [Middle English *garter, garder*, from Old North French *gartier*, from *garet*, bend of the knee, from Gaulish *garr-* (unattested), leg.]

garter belt *n. U.S.* A **suspender belt** (*see*).

garter snake *n.* **1.** Any of various nonvenomous North American snakes of the genus *Thamnophis*, having longitudinal stripes. **2.** Any of several African snakes of the genus *Elaps*, marked with black and white bands.

garter stitch *n.* **1.** A knitting stitch formed by working each row in plain stitch only. **2. a.** The raised pattern formed by this technique. **b.** Material worked in garter stitch.

garth (garth) *n.* **1.** A grassy quadrangle surrounded by cloisters. **2.** *Archaic.* A yard, garden, or paddock. [Middle English, from Old Norse *garthr*, yard.]

ga·ru·da (gáar-ōōdə; *also* gə-rōōdə) *n.* **1.** A partly human bird of Hindu myth, often depicted with the god Vishnu on its shoulders. **2.** This bird as the national emblem of Indonesia.

gas (gass) *n., pl.* **gases** or **gasses. 1. a.** The state of matter distinguished from the solid and liquid states by very low density and viscosity, relatively great expansion and contraction with changes in pressure and temperature, the ability to diffuse readily, and the spontaneous tendency to become distributed uniformly throughout any container. **b.** A substance in this state. **c.** A substance in this state at room temperature and atmospheric pressure. **2.** A gaseous fuel such as **natural gas** (*see*). **3.** *Mining.* An explosive mixture of firedamp (methane) and air. **4.** A gaseous asphyxiant, irritant, or poison. **5.** A gaseous anaesthetic. **6.** *Chiefly U.S. Informal.* Petrol; gasoline. **7.** *Slang.* Idle or boastful talk. **8.** *Chiefly U.S. Slang.* Something providing great fun and excitement: *The party was a real gas.* **—step on the gas. 1.** *Informal.* To accelerate in a motor vehicle. **2.** To go faster; hurry up.
~*v.* **gassed, gassing, gasses** or **gasses.** —*tr.* **1.** To treat chemically with gas. **2.** To disable or kill with gas. —*intr.v.* **1.** To give off gas. **2.** *Informal.* To talk excessively. **3.** *U.S.* To fill a tank with petrol. Often used with *up.* [Dutch *gas*, an occult principle supposed to be present in all bodies, coined (by J.B. van *Helmont*, (1577–1644), Belgian chemist) from Greek *khaos*, CHAOS.]

gas·bag (gáss-bag) *n.* **1.** An expandable bag for holding gas. **2.** *Slang.* One given to empty chatter.

gas burner *n.* **1.** A nozzle or jet on a fitting through which combustible gas is released to burn. **2.** A device consisting of a set of such jets, as on a gas cooker.

gas chamber *n.* A sealed enclosure in which people or animals are killed by means of a poisonous gas. Also called "gas oven".

gas chromatography *n.* Chromatography in which the substance to be analysed is vaporised and diffused along with a carrier gas through a liquid or solid adsorbent for differential adsorption. See **gas-liquid chromatography.**

gas coal *n.* Coal containing a large amount of volatile hydrocarbons, suitable for converting into fuel gas.

gas·con (gáss-kən) *n.* A boastful person; a braggart. [French, from Old French *gascon*, GASCON (from the traditional garrulity of the Gascons).]

Gas·con (gáss-kən) *n.* **1.** A native of Gascony. **2.** The French dialect of the Gascons.
~*adj.* Of or pertaining to Gascony or the Gascons.

gas·con·ade (gásskə-náyd) *n.* Boastfulness; bravado; swagger.
~*intr.v.* **gasconaded, -ading, -ades.** *Rare.* To boast or swagger.

gas constant *n. Symbol* **R.** The constant in the ideal gas law, equal to 8.3143 joules per kelvin per mole. Also called "universal gas constant".

Gas·co·ny (gáskəni). *French* **Gas·cogne** (ga-skón-yə). Ancient province in southwest France. It is bounded by the Garonne, Pyrenees, and Atlantic. In the sixth century it was settled by the Vascones (Basques) who later set up the duchy of Vasconia (Gascony). This was united with neighbouring Aquitaine in 1052.

gas-cooled reactor (gáss-kō͞old) *n.* A nuclear reactor in which heat is removed from the core by a gaseous coolant, usually carbon dioxide. See **advanced gas-cooled reactor.**

gas-e-lier (gássə-léer) *n.* A chandelier having tubular branches with gas jets. [*gas* +chande*lier*.]

gas·e·ous (gássi-əss, gáysi-, gáyzi-) *adj.* **1.** Of, pertaining to, or existing as a gas. **2.** Lacking concreteness; tenuous.

gas equation *n.* An equation applying to ideal gases: $pV = nRT$, where p is the pressure, V the volume, n the amount of substance (number of moles), R the gas constant, and T the thermodynamic temperature. The equation approximately describes the behaviour of real gases. Also called "ideal gas law", "gas law".

gas fitter *n.* A workman who installs or repairs gas pipes, fixtures, or appliances.

gas gangrene *n.* Gangrene occurring in a wound infected with bacteria of the genus *Clostridium*, especially with *C. welchii* or *C. oedematiens*, and characterised by the presence of gas in the affected tissue and constitutional septic symptoms.

gash (gash) *tr.v.* **gashed, gashing, gashes.** To make a long, deep cut in; slash deeply.
~*n.* **1.** A long, deep cut. **2.** A deep flesh wound. [Earlier *garsh, garse*, Middle English *garsen*, to cut, slash, from Old North French *garser*, probably from Late Latin *charaxāre*, from Greek *kharassein*, to carve, cut.]

gas·hold·er (gáss-hōldər) *n.* A storage container for fuel gas, especially a large, telescoping, cylindrical tank. Also called "gasometer".

gas·i·form (gássi-fawrm) *adj.* In the form of gas; gaseous.

gas·i·fy (gássi-fī) *v.* **-fied, -fying, -fies.** —*tr.* **1.** To convert into gas. **2.** To produce gas from (wood or coal, for example). —*intr.* To become gas. **—gas·i·fi·a·ble** *adj.* **—gas·i·fi·ca·tion** (-fi-káysh'n) *n.*

Gas·kell (gáss-k'l), **Elizabeth (Cleghorn),** born Elizabeth Cleghorn Stevenson (1810–65). English novelist. She wrote *Cranford* (1853), *North and South* (1855), and a life of her friend Charlotte Brontë (1857).

gas·ket (gáskit) *n.* **1.** Any of a wide variety of seals or packings used between matched machine parts or around pipe joints to prevent the escape of a gas or fluid. **2.** *Nautical.* A cord or canvas strap used to secure a furled sail to a yard boom or gaff. **—blow a gasket.** *Slang.* To explode with anger. [Perhaps variant of obsolete *gassit*, from French *garcette*, "little girl", rope, diminutive of *garce*, girl, from *gars*, boy.]

gas·kin (gásskin) *n.* **1.** The part of the hind leg of a horse or related animal between the stifle and the hock. **2.** *Plural. Obsolete.* Breeches; galligaskins. [Probably shortened from GALLIGASKINS.]

gas laws *pl.n.* Laws relating to the pressure, volume, and temperature of gases, especially Boyle's law and Charles' law. See **gas equation.**

gas·light (gáss-līt) *n.* **1.** Light produced by burning illuminating gas. **2.** A gas burner or lamp.

gas lighter *n.* **1.** A device for igniting gas on a gas cooker and similar applicances. **2.** A cigarette lighter fuelled by gas.

gas-liq·uid chromatography (gáss-likwid) *n. Abbr.* **GLC** A form of gas chromatography in which the adsorbent medium is an inert solid coated with a liquid.

gas main *n.* A major pipeline or conduit conveying gas to smaller pipes for distribution to consumers.

gas·man (gáss-man) *n., pl.* **-men** (-men). **1.** A person employed to read gas meters for the billing of consumers. **2.** A gas fitter.

gas mantle *n.* An incandescent mantle used in a gaslight.

gas mask *n.* A respirator covering the face and having a chemical air filter to protect against poisonous gases.

gas meter *n.* A device for measuring the rate of flow of a gas; especially, a device for measuring and recording the amount of fuel gas used by a domestic consumer.

gas oil *n.* A mixture of hydrocarbons intermediate between paraffin and lubricating oil, obtained by distilling petroleum and used as fuel.

gas·o·line (gáss-ə-leen ‖ *U.S. also* -léen) *n. Chiefly U.S.* Petrol.

gas·om·e·ter (gass-ómmitər) *n.* **1.** A gasholder. **2.** An apparatus for measuring the volume of gases. [French *gazomètre* : *gaz*, from GAS + -METER.]

gas oven *n.* **1.** A domestic oven fuelled by gas. **2.** A cremation chamber fuelled by gas. **3.** A **gas chamber** (*see*).

gasp (gaasp ‖ gasp) *v.* **gasped, gasping, gasps.** —*intr.* **1.** To draw in or catch the breath sharply, as from shock. **2.** To breathe convulsively or laboriously. **3.** *Informal.* To long; crave. Used with *for*: *gasping for a drink.* —*tr.* To utter between gasps. Often used with *out.*
~*n.* A short convulsive intake or catching of the breath. **—at the last gasp.** At the final extremity; at the moment of death. [Middle English *ga(y)spen*, from Old Norse *geispa*.]

Gaspar. See **Caspar.**

gasp·er (gáaspər ‖ gáspər) *n.* **1.** One who gasps. **2.** *British Slang.* A cigarette.

gas plant *n.* A plant, *Dictamnus albus*, native to Eurasia, having aromatic foliage and white flowers, and emitting a vapour capable of being ignited. Also called "burning bush", "dittany", "fraxinella".

gas poker *n.* A device resembling a hollow poker, fitted with a gas jet and, when ignited, used to kindle a fire.

gas ring *n.* A device consisting of a set of gas jets arranged in a circle, as on a gas cooker.

gas·ser (gássər) *n.* **1.** A well or drilling that yields natural gas. **2.** *U.S. Slang.* Something unusually entertaining; a gas.

gas station *n. U.S.* A **filling station** (*see*).

gas·sy (gássi) *adj.* **-sier, -siest. 1.** Containing, full of, or resembling gas. **2.** *Slang.* Bombastic; boastful.

gast·ar·bei·ter (gást-aar-bītər) *n., pl.* **gastarbeiter.** *Often capital* **G.** An immigrant worker; especially a worker in West Germany of Italian, Yugoslav, or Turkish origin. [German, "guest worker".]

gasteropod. *Rare.* Variant of **gastropod.**

gas thermometer *n.* An apparatus for measuring temperature by determining the volume of a gas at constant pressure (*constant-pres-*

sure *gas thermometer*) or by the pressure at constant volume (*constant-volume gas thermometer*).

gas·tight (gáss-tīt) *adj.* Not permitting the escape or entry of gas.

gas·trec·to·my (gass-tréktəmi) *n., pl.* **-mies.** Surgical excision of part or all of the stomach. [GASTR(O)- + -ECTOMY.]

gas·tric (gáss-trik) *adj.* Of, pertaining to, or near the stomach. [French *gastrique,* from New Latin *gastricus,* from Greek *gastēr,* (stem *gastr-*), belly, womb.]

gastric glands *pl.n.* Tubular glands in the mucous membrane lining the stomach that secrete gastric juice.

gastric juice *n. Often plural.* The colourless, watery, acidic digestive fluid secreted by the gastric glands of the stomach and containing hydrochloric acid, pepsin, rennin, and mucin.

gastric ulcer *n.* An ulcer in the mucous membrane lining the stomach.

gas·trin (gáss-trin) *n.* A hormone secreted by the gastric mucosa that stimulates production of gastric juice. [GASTR(O)- + -IN.]

gas·tri·tis (gass-trítiss) *n.* Chronic or acute inflammation of the stomach. [New Latin : GASTR(O)- + -ITIS.]

gastro-, gastr– *comb. form.* Indicates stomach; for example, **gastroscope, gastritis.** [Greek *gastēr* (stem *gastr-*), belly, womb.]

gas·troc·nem·i·us (gáss-trok-néemi-əss, -trək-) *n.* The muscle that forms the major part of the calf of the leg. [New Latin, from Greek *gastroknēmē,* calf of the leg : GASTRO- (belly) + *knēmē,* shin, leg.]

gas·tro·en·ter·ic (gáss-trō-en-térrik) *adj.* Gastrointestinal.

gas·tro·en·ter·i·tis (gáss-trō-éntə-rítiss) *n.* Inflammation of the mucous membrane of the stomach and intestine.

gas·tro·en·ter·ol·o·gy (gáss-trō-éntə-róllǝji) *n.* The medical study of diseases of the stomach and the intestines. **—gas·tro·en·ter·o·lo·gi·cal** (-rǝ-lójik'l) *adj.* **—gas·tro·en·ter·ol·o·gist** *n.*

gas·tro·en·ter·os·to·my (gáss-trō-éntə-róstəmi) *n., pl.* **-mies.** The surgical formation of a passage between the stomach and the small intestine.

gas·tro·in·tes·ti·nal (gáss-trō-in-téstin'l, -tess-tín'l) *adj.* Of or pertaining to the stomach and intestines; gastroenteric.

gas·tro·lith (gáss-trǝ-lith) *n.* A pathological, small, stony mass formed in the stomach; a gastric calculus. [GASTRO- + -LITH.]

gas·trol·o·gy (gass-tróllǝji) *n.* The medical study of the stomach and its diseases. [Greek *Gastrologia* (title of a poem) : GASTRO- + -LOGY.] **—gas·tro·log·i·cal** (-trǝ-lójik'l) *adj.* **—gas·trol·o·gist** *n.*

gas·tro·nome (gáss-trǝ-nōm) *n.* Also **gas·tron·o·mist** (gass-trónnǝmist). A connoisseur of good food and drink; a gourmet. [From GASTRONOMY.]

gas·tro·nom·ic (gáss-trǝ-nómm-ik) *adj.* Also **gas·tro·nom·i·cal** (-ik'l). Of or pertaining to gastronomes or gastronomy. **—gas·tro·nom·i·cal·ly** *adv.*

gas·tron·o·my (gass-trónnǝmi) *n.* **1.** The art or science of good eating. **2.** Cooking, as of a particular region or country. [French *gastronomie,* from Greek *gastronomia* : GASTRO- + -NOMY.]

gas·tro·pod (gáss-trǝ-pod) *n.* Also *rare* **gas·ter·o·pod** (-tǝ-rǝ-). Any mollusc of the class Gastropoda, such as a snail, slug, cowry, or limpet, characteristically having a single, usually coiled shell and a ventral muscular foot serving as an organ of locomotion. *~adj.* Of or belonging to the Gastropoda. [New Latin *Gastropoda,* "belly-footed creatures" (from their ventral discs used as feet) : GASTRO- + -POD.] **—gas·trop·o·dan** (gass-tróppǝ-dǝn) *n.* **gas·trop·o·dous** (-tróppǝ-dǝss) *adj.*

gas·tro·scope (gáss-trǝ-skōp) *n.* An instrument used for examining the interior of the stomach. [GASTRO- + -SCOPE.] **—gas·tro·scop·ic** (-skóppik) *adj.* **—gas·tros·co·pist** (-tróskǝ-pist) *n.* **—gas·tros·co·py** (-tróskǝpi) *n.*

gas·tros·to·my (gass-tróss-təmi) *n., pl.* **-mies.** The surgical construction of a permanent opening from the external surface of the body into the stomach, usually for inserting a feeding tube. [GASTRO- + -STOMY.]

gas·trot·o·my (gass-tróttǝmi) *n., pl.* **-mies.** A surgical incision into the stomach. [GASTRO- + -TOMY.]

gas·tro·trich (gáss-trǝ-trik) *n.* Any minute aquatic animal of the phylum Gastrotricha, having a wormlike, ciliated body. [GASTRO- + -TRICH.]

gas·tro·vas·cu·lar (gáss-trō-váss-kewlǝr) *adj.* Having both a digestive and circulatory function. Said especially of the body cavity of a coelenterate.

gas·tru·la (gáss-trōō-lǝ, -trǝ-) *n., pl.* **-las** or **-lae** (-lee). An embryo at the stage following the blastula, consisting of a layer of cells differentiated into ectoderm, endoderm, and mesoderm, and enclosing a cavity, the archenteron, which opens to the exterior by the blastopore. [New Latin, "small stomach" (from its shape), diminutive of Greek *gastēr,* (stem *gastr-*), belly, womb.] **—gas·tru·lar** *adj.*

gas·tru·late (gáss-trōō-layt, -trǝ-) *intr.v.* **-lated, -lating, -lates.** To form or become a gastrula. **—gas·tru·la·tion** (-láysh'n) *n.*

gas turbine *n.* An internal-combustion engine consisting essentially of an air compressor, a combustion chamber, and a turbine wheel, used especially for propulsion rather than fixed power generation.

gas well *n.* A well that yields natural gas.

gas·works (gáss-wurks) *n., pl.* **gasworks.** An industrial plant in which gas for heating and lighting is produced.

gat¹ (gat) *n.* **1.** A narrow passage extending inland from a shore. **2.** A tidal channel between offshore islands or shoals. [Probably from Dutch *gat,* "opening", from Middle Dutch, from Germanic *gatam* (unattested). See **gate¹.**]

gat² *n.* Chiefly *U.S. Slang.* A pistol. [Short for GAT(LING GUN).]

gat³. *Archaic.* Past tense of **get.**

gate¹ (gayt) *n.* **1.** A structure that may be swung, drawn, or lowered to block an entrance or passageway. **2. a.** An opening in a wall or fence for entrance or exit; a gateway. **b.** The structure surrounding such an opening, as the monumental or fortified entrance to a palace or walled town. **3. a.** Something that gives access: *the gate to fortune.* **b.** A place giving access to another region or country; especially, a mountain pass. **4.** A device for controlling the passage of water or gas through a dam, lock, or pipe. **5. a.** The number of spectators attending an event such as a football match: *the problem of falling gates.* **b.** The total admission receipts at such an event. In this sense, also called "gate money". **6.** Any of the numbered exits, as in an airport terminal, through which passengers proceed for embarkation. **7.** *Metallurgy.* The channel through which molten metal flows into the shaped cavity of a mould. **8.** *Electronics.* **a.** A circuit extensively used in computers that has an output dependent on some function of its input. **b.** Such a circuit having an output when any or all of a designated set of inputs are received within a given time interval. In this sense, also called "coincidence gate". **c.** A circuit designed to cut out part of a signal. **d.** The region or electrode that controls the current in a field-effect transistor. **9.** In photography, a device that holds a frame of cine film in place behind the lens. **10.** A slotted frame enabling the gear lever of a motor vehicle to be moved into different positions when engaging gears. *~tr.v.* **gated, gating, gates. 1.** *British.* To punish (a student) by confining within the school or college gates after a certain hour or for a certain period of time. **2.** *Electronics.* To connect (one or more inputs) to a gate. [Middle English *gat, g(e)ate,* Old English *geat,* from Common Germanic *gatam* (unattested).]

gate² *n.* **1.** *Archaic & Regional.* A path or road; a way. **2.** *Regional.* A particular way of acting or doing; a manner. [Middle English, from Old Norse *gata,* path, passage.]

–gate *n. Comb. form. Informal.* Indicates scandalous behaviour or corruption chiefly involving the person or place bearing the name specified in combination; for example, **Irangate.** [Abstracted from *Watergate,* building in Washington, D.C., Democratic Party headquarters in 1972, site of burglary and origin of the scandal that subsequently forced President Nixon's resignation.]

gâ·teau, ga·teau (gáttō) *n. pl.* **-teaux** or **-teaus.** A large, elaborate cream cake. [French, "cake".]

gate-crash·er (gáyt-krashǝr) *n. Informal.* A person who gains admittance, as to a party or concert, without being invited or without paying. **—gate-crash** *v.*

gate-fold (gáyt-fōld) *n.* A folded insert in a book or magazine whose full size exceeds that of the regular page. Also called "fold-out".

gate-house (gáyt-howss) *n.* **1.** A lodge at the entrance to the drive of a country house or estate. **2.** A fortified room built over a gateway to a city or castle, often used as a prison. **3.** A building that houses the controls of a dam or lock.

gate-keep·er (gáyt-keepǝr) *n.* A person in charge of a gate. Also called "gateman".

gate-leg table (gáyt-leg). A drop-leaf table with movable legs arranged in pairs.

gate-post (gáyt-pōst) *n.* An upright post on which a gate is hung or against which a gate is closed. **—between you, me, and the gatepost.** *Informal.* In strict confidence.

Gates (gayts), **Bill,** born William Henry Gates (1955–). U.S. businessman, computer scientist, and software manufacturer. At the age of nineteen, with Paul Allen, he founded the Microsoft Corporation (1975). They licensed their MS-DOS operating system to IBM in 1980 for use in the rapidly expanding personal computer market. Microsoft are now one of the world's largest producers of microcomputer software.

gate-way (gáyt-way) *n.* **1.** A structure, such as an arch, framing an entrance or passage that may be closed by a gate. **2.** A place or a thing that serves as an entrance or means of access: *a gateway to success.* **3.** *Computing.* A link that enables information to be exchanged between one computer network and another.

gath·er (gáthǝr) *v.* **-ered, -ering, -ers.** *—tr.* **1.** To cause to come together; convene. **2. a.** To accumulate gradually; amass. **b.** To harvest or pick: *gather flowers; gather in the crops.* **c.** To gain by a process of gradual increase: *The ship began to gather speed as it left the quayside.* **3. a.** To collect into one place; assemble. **b.** In bookbinding, to arrange (signatures) in sequence. **4.** To pick up and embrace. Used with *in* or *into: gathered the child into his arms.* **5. a.** To pull (cloth) along a thread so as to create small folds or puckers. **b.** To contract (the brow) so as to form wrinkles. **6.** To draw (a garment, for example) about or closer to something. **7.** To conclude or apprehend; infer: *I gather that a decision has not been reached.* **8. a.** To summon up; muster: *gather courage.* **b.** To collect (one's wits or powers). Often used with *together.* **9.** To attract or be a centre of attraction for: *a movement that is gathering support; books gathering dust.* *—intr.* **1.** To come together or assemble. **2.** To accumulate. **3.** To grow or increase by degrees. **4.** *Informal.* To come to a head, as a boil does; fester. *~n.* **1.** An act of gathering or something that is gathered. **2.** A small tuck or pucker in cloth. **3.** In bookbinding, a **signature** *(see).* [Middle English *gad(e)ren,* Old English *gad(e)rian,* to put together, come together, from Germanic.] **—gath·er·er** *n.*

Synonyms: gather, collect, assemble, accumulate, amass, marshal, rally.

gath·er·ing (gáthǝr-ing) *n.* **1.** Something gathered or amassed; a collection; an accumulation. **2.** An assembly of persons; a meeting. **3.** A gather in cloth. **4.** *Informal.* A suppurated swelling; a boil or abscess. **5.** A signature *(see)* of a book during binding.

Gat·ling gun (gátling) *n.* A machine gun having a cluster of barrels each of which is fired as the cluster is turned. [Designed by Richard J. *Gatling* (1818–1903), U.S. inventor.]

GATT General Agreement on Tariffs and Trade.

gauche (gōsh) *adj.* **1.** Awkward in manner; lacking social grace; tactless; clumsy. See Synonyms at **awkward. 2.** *Chemistry.* Of or designating a conformation of a chemical compound in which two groups or atoms attached to two adjacent atoms are on the same side of the bond but one is displaced rotationally with respect to the other. [French, "left", originally "bent", "askew", from Old French *gauchir,* to turn aside, detour, probably altered from earlier *guenchir,* from Frankish *wenkjan* (unattested).] —**gauche·ly** *adv.* —**gauche·ness** *n.*

gau·che·rie (gōshə-ri) *n.* **1.** An awkward or tactless action, manner, or expression. **2.** Tactlessness; awkwardness. [French, from *gauche,* left, GAUCHE.]

gau·cho (gówchō) *n., pl.* **-chos.** A cowboy of the South American pampas. [American Spanish, probably from Quechua *wáhcha,* poor person, vagabond.]

gaud (gawd ‖ *U.S. also* gaad) *n.* Something gaudy or showy. [Middle English *gaude, gawde,* jest, plaything, toy, from Old French *gaudir,* to rejoice, from Latin *gaudēre,* to delight in.]

gaud·er·y (gáw-dəri) *n., pl.* **-ies.** Showy things; finery.

Gau·dier-Brzes·ka (gōd-yáy bzhess-kaá), **Henri,** born Henri Gaudier (1891–1915). French sculptor and draughtsman. He was a member of the Vorticist movement. He died in World War I.

gaud·y¹ (gáwdi) *adj.* **-ier, -iest. 1.** Characterised by tasteless or showy colours; garish. **2.** Crude and showy. —See Synonyms at **showy.** [From GAUD.] —**gaud·i·ly** *adv.* —**gaud·i·ness** *n.*

gaudy² *n., pl.* **-ies.** *British.* A feast; especially, an annual university dinner. [Latin *gaudium,* joy, from *gaudēre,* to rejoice.]

gauffer. Variant of **goffer.**

gauge (gayj) *n.* Also *U.S. & nautical* **gage. 1. a.** A standard or scale of measurement. **b.** A standard dimension, quantity, or capacity. **2.** An instrument for measuring or testing. **3.** A means of estimating or evaluating; a test: *a gauge of character.* **4.** *Nautical.* The position of a vessel in relation to another vessel and the wind. **5. a.** The distance between the two rails of a railway. **b.** The distance between two wheels on an axle. **6.** The diameter of a shotgun barrel as determined by the number of lead balls in a pound that exactly fit the barrel. **7.** The amount of plaster of Paris mixed with common plaster to speed its setting. **8.** Thickness or diameter, as of sheet metal or wire. **9.** The fineness of knitted cloth as determined by the number of stitches used per inch. **10.** The distance between nails securing tiles or slates to a roof.

~*tr.v.* **gauged, gauging, gauges. 1.** To measure precisely. **2.** To determine the capacity, volume, or contents of. **3.** To evaluate or judge: *gauge ability.* **4.** To adapt to a specified measurement. **5.** To mix (plaster) in specific proportions. **6.** To chip or rub (bricks or stones) to size.

~*adj. Physics.* Measured above or below atmospheric pressure as the zero reference. Used after the noun: *7 bar gauge.* Compare **absolute** (pressure). [Middle English, from Old North French *gauge†.*]

gaug·er (gáyjər) *n.* **1.** One that gauges. **2.** *Chiefly British.* **a.** A revenue officer who inspects bulk goods subject to duty. **b.** A collector of excise duties.

Gau·guin (gō-gaN; *French* gō-gáN), **Paul** (1848–1903). French ex-stockbroker post-impressionist painter, settled in Tahiti (1891). His influential paintings there show the influence of primitive art.

Gaul¹ (gawl). Latin name **Gal·li·a** (gál-i-ə). The name given in antiquity to the region in Europe south and west of the Rhine, west of the Alps, and north of the Pyrenees, comprising approximately the territory of modern France and Belgium. [French *Gaule,* from Latin *Gallia,* from *Galli,* the Gauls.]

Gaul² *n.* **1.** A Celt of ancient Gaul. **2.** A Frenchman.

Gau·lei·ter (gów-lītər) *n.* **1.** A governor of a district in Germany during the Nazi regime. **2.** *Small* **g.** A petty tyrant. [German *Gau,* administrative district + *Leiter,* leader.]

Gaul·ish (gáwlish) *n.* The Celtic language of ancient Gaul.

~*adj.* Of or pertaining to ancient Gaul, or to its people, language, and culture.

Gaull·ism (gō-líz'm, gáw-) *n.* **1.** The political movement supporting Charles de Gaulle as leader of the French government in exile during World War II. **2.** The body of political theory and practice characterising General de Gaulle's exercise of the presidency in France and by his followers thereafter. —**Gaull·ist** *adj. & n.*

gault (gawlt) *n. Geology.* **1.** *Often capital* **G.** A formation of Cretaceous origin in Britain, consisting of clay and marl and occurring between the Greensand formations. **2.** The clay and marl comprising this formation. **3.** A brick made from this type of clay. [16th century : origin obscure.]

gaul·the·ri·a (gawl-théer·i-ə) *n.* Any shrub of the genus *Gaultheria,* having aromatic evergreen foliage; especially, the **wintergreen** *(see).* [New Latin, after Jean-François *Gaultier,* 18th-century Canadian botanist.]

gaunt (gawnt ‖ gaant) *adj.* **gaunter, gauntest. 1.** Thin and bony; angular; lank. **2.** Emaciated and haggard; drawn. **3.** Bleak and desolate; barren. —See Synonyms at **lean.** [Middle English *gawnt,*

gaunt, slim, lean, perhaps from Scandinavian; akin to Norwegian dialectal *gand†,* thin stick, lanky person.] —**gaunt·ly** *adv.* —**gaunt·ness** *n.*

gaunt·let¹ (gáwnt-lit ‖ gaánt-) *n.* Also *chiefly U.S.* **gant·let. 1. A** protective glove worn as a part of medieval armour. **2.** A protective glove with a flaring cuff, used in manual labour, for driving, and in some sports. **3.** A challenge. Used chiefly in the phrases *fling* or *throw down the gauntlet.* [Middle English *gaunt(e)let,* from Old French *gantelet,* diminutive of *gant,* glove, from Frankish *want†* (unattested), mitten.]

gauntlet² *n.* Also *chiefly U.S.* **gantlet.** Two lines of men facing each other and armed with sticks or other weapons with which they beat a person forced to run between them. —**run the gauntlet.** To be subjected to criticism or disgrace. [Earlier *gantlope.* See **gantlet** (railway track).]

gauntlet³. Variant of **gantlet** (railway track).

gauntry. Variant of **gantry.**

gaur (gowr, gów-ər) *n.* A large, dark-coated bovine mammal, *Bos gaurus,* of hilly areas of southeastern Asia. [Hindi *gaur,* from Sanskrit *gaura.*]

gauss (gowss) *n. Symbol* **G** The centimetre-gram-second electromagnetic unit of magnetic flux density, equal to one maxwell per square centimetre (10^{-4} tesla.) [After Karl F. GAUSS.]

Gauss (gowss), **(Johann) Karl Friedrich** (1777–1855). German mathematician. His contributions to algebra, differential geometry, probability theory, and number theory were of vital importance. He also worked in astronomy and contributed to the invention of the telegraph.

Gauss·i·an distribution (gów-si-ən) *n.* **Normal distribution** *(see).*

gauss·me·ter (gówss-meetər) *n. Physics.* Any of various instruments used to measure magnetic flux density. [After Karl Friedrich GAUSS.]

gau·teng (hów-téng). New province of South Africa created from part of the former Transvaal and centred around the Johannesburg conurbation. The provincial capital is Johannesburg.

gauze (gawz) *n.* **1. a.** A thin, transparent fabric with a loose open weave, used for curtains or clothing. **b.** A thin, open-woven cotton surgical dressing. **c.** A thin plastic or metal woven mesh. **2.** A mist or haze. [French *gaze,* probably after GAZA, where it was supposed to be made.] —**gauz·i·ly** *adv.* —**gauz·i·ness** *n.* —**gauz·y** *adj.*

ga·vage (gávv-aazh ‖ gə-vá'azh, gaa-) *n.* The introduction of usually nutritive material into the stomach by means of a tube; force-feeding. [French, from *gaver,* to force down the throat, stuff, from Picard, from Old Latin *gaba†* (unattested), throat.]

gave. Past tense of **give.**

gav·el¹ (gávv'l) *n.* **1.** The mallet or hammer used by a chairman, judge, or auctioneer. **2.** A maul used by masons in fitting stones. [19th century : origin obscure.]

gavel² *n.* Tribute or rent in ancient and medieval England. [Middle English *gavel,* Old English *gafol,* tribute.]

gav·el·kind (gávv'l-kīnd) *n.* A system of tenure, prevalent especially in Kent from Anglo-Saxon times until 1926, whereby land was held in exchange for rent rather than services, and could be inherited by all qualified heirs rather than by primogeniture. [Middle English *gavelkynde,* Old English *gafolgecynd* (unattested), "tenure by payment of rent" : *gafol,* GAVEL (rent) + *cynd, gecynd,* KIND.]

ga·vi·al (gáyvi-əl) *n.* A large reptile, *Gavialis gangeticus,* of southern Asia, resembling the crocodiles, and having a long, slender snout. Also called "gharial". [French, from Hindi *ghariyāl†.*]

ga·votte (gə-vót) *n.* **1.** A French dance resembling the minuet. **2.** Music for this dance, or in a similar style, in moderately quick $^4/_4$ time. [French, from Provençal *gavoto,* from *Gavot,* "mountaineer", "rustic", inhabitant of the Alps (where the dance originated), perhaps from *gava,* crop of a bird, frill, goitre, from Old Latin *gaba†* (unattested), throat.]

Ga·wain (gá-wayn, gaá-). A nephew of King Arthur and a knight of the Round Table.

Gawd (gawd) *interj. Slang.* Used as an expression of annoyance, surprise, or the like. [Pronunciation spelling (Cockney) of *God.*]

gawk (gawk) *n.* An awkward or self-conscious person.

~*intr.v.* **gawked, gawking, gawks.** *Informal.* To stare like a gawk; gape stupidly. [Perhaps alteration of obsolete *gaw,* to stare, gape, Middle English *gawen,* from Old Norse *gā,* to heed.]

gawk·y (gáwki) *adj.* **-ier, -iest.** Awkward; ill-at-ease. —**gawk·i·ly** *adv.* —**gawk·i·ness** *n.*

gawp (gawp) *intr.v.* **gawped, gawping, gawps.** To gawk; gape. [Variant of earlier *gaup, galp,* Middle English *galpen,* to yawn, YELP.]

gay (gay) *adj.* **gayer, gayest. 1.** Showing or characterised by cheerfulness and light-hearted excitement; merry. **2.** Bright or brilliant, especially in colour. **3. a.** Homosexual. **b.** Of, pertaining to, or for homosexuals. **4.** Full of or given to social or other pleasures. **5.** *Rare.* Dissolute; licentious.

~ *n. Informal.* A homosexual, typically male. [Middle English *gay, gai,* from Old French *gai,* from Old Provençal, probably from Gothic *gaheis* (unattested), akin to Old High German *gāhi†,* sudden, impetuous.] —**gay·ness** *n.*

Gay (gay), **John** (1685–1732). English poet and dramatist. A friend and protégé of Pope, he is best remembered for *The Beggars' Opera* (1728), a colourful satire which shocked many of his contemporaries by its candid portrayal of low life.

ga·yal (gə-yaál) *n.* A domesticated bovine mammal, *Bos frontalis,* of India and Burma, having thick, pointed horns, a dark coat, and a tufted tail. [Bengali *gayāl*, probably from Sanskrit *gauḥ,* cow.]

gayety. *Chiefly U.S.* Variant of **gaiety.**

Gay Gordons *n.* *Used with a singular verb.* A lively Scottish dance. [After the *Gordon Highlanders* (2nd Battalion, 92nd Highlanders).]

Gay-Lus·sac (gáy-lōo-sak, -lü-sák), **Joseph Louis** (1778–1850). French chemist and physicist. His experiments added considerably to knowledge of the way in which elements combine to form compounds. He discovered **Gay-Lussac's law** and isolated the element boron.

Gay-Lussac's law *n.* **1.** The principle that gases react in volumes that have a simple ratio to each other and to the volumes of gaseous products. **2. Charles's law** *(see).* [After J.L. GAY-LUSSAC.]

Ga·za (gäzə ‖ *U.S. also* gázzə, gáyzə). *Arabic* **Ghazzah.** City in the Gaza Strip. Inhabited for more than 3,000 years, it was a major city of the Philistines, where Samson killed himself and his jailers by bringing down its temple as described in Judges 16.

gaz·a·ni·a (gə-záyni-ə) *n.* Any South African plant of the genus *Gazania,* some species of which are grown for their ornamental yellow or orange flowers. [New Latin, irregularly from Teodoro *Gaza,* 15th-century Greek scholar.]

Gaza Strip. Territory between southwest Israel and the Mediterranean Sea. It was part of the British League of Nations mandate for Palestine (1920–48), but following the Arab–Israeli war of 1948–9, it came under Egyptian military rule. Apart from a brief Israeli occupation (November 1956–March 1957) it remained under Egyptian rule until taken in 1967 by the Israelis, who set up a military regime. A Palestine independence movement led to violent unrest, and under an agreement made in 1993 between Israel and the PLO, the Israelis have handed over law and order responsibility to Palestinian authority. The strip has several huge Arab refugee camps.

gaze (gayz) *intr.v.* **gazed, gazing, gazes.** To look or stare steadily for some length of time, often in an absorbed or abstracted way. —*n.* A steady look. [Middle English *gazen,* probably from Scandinavian, akin to Swedish dialectal *gasa†.*] —**gaz·er** *n.*
  Synonyms: gaze, stare, gape, glare, peer, ogle.

ga·ze·bo (gə-zée-bō ‖ -záy-) *n.,* pl. **-bos** or **-boes.** A pavilion, summerhouse, or belvedere, especially one having a view. [Probably mock Latin formation from GAZE (with Latin future suffix -*ēbō,* as in *vidēbō,* I shall see).]

gaze·hound (gáyz-hownd) *n.* A dog that hunts its prey by sight rather than scent.

ga·zelle (gə-zél) *n.* Any of various small antelopes of the genus *Gazella* and related genera, of Africa and Asia, characteristically having a slender neck, and ringed, lyrate horns. [Old French, probably from Spanish *gacela,* from Arabic *ghazāl.*]

ga·zette (gə-zét) *n.* *Abbr.* **gaz. 1. a.** A newspaper. **b.** *Capital G.* Used as part of the title of certain newspapers: *The Western Gazette.* **2.** An official journal, especially one recording public appointments and printing other general announcements. **3.** Formerly, a newsheet.
—*tr.v.* **gazetted, -zetting, -zettes.** *British.* To announce or publish in a gazette. "*Sham colonels gazetted*" (W.S. Gilbert). [French, from Italian *gazzetta,* from Venetian *gazeta (de la novita)* (newspaper sold for) a small copper coin, from *gazeta,* a small copper coin, probably diminutive of *gaz(z)a,* magpie, from Latin *gaia,* from *gaius,* jay (perhaps imitative).]

gaz·et·teer (gázzə-téer) *n.* *Abbr.* **gaz.** A dictionary or index of places.

gaz·pa·cho (gaz-pa′achō, gass-) *n.,* pl. **-chos.** A Spanish soup made from salad ingredients, such as tomatoes, peppers, garlic, and olive oil, and served chilled. [Spanish.]

ga·zump (gə-zúmp) *v.* **-zumped, -zumping, -zumps.** —*tr.* **1.** To go back on an agreement with (a prospective purchaser of a property) by raising a previously agreed price. **2.** To swindle. —*intr.* To raise the previously agreed price of a property. [20th century : origin obscure.] —**ga·zump·er** *n.*

G.B., GB Great Britain.

G.B.E. Grand Cross of the British Empire (in Britain).

G.B.H. grievous bodily harm.

G.C. George Cross (in Britain).

G.C.B. Grand Cross of the Bath (in Britain).

GCE, G.C.E. *n.,* pl. **GCE's, G.C.E.'s.** In Britain, the General Certificate of Education: either of two sets of public examinations at secondary level which were formerly taken in a variety of subjects either at **O** level or **A** level (*both of which see*). **2.** A certificate awarded for passing such an examination.

G clef *n.* The **treble clef** (*see*).

G.C.M.G. Grand Cross of St. Michael and St. George (in Britain).

GCSE General Certificate of Secondary Education: used in reference to a system of educational evaluation introduced in 1988 in England, Wales, and Northern Ireland, intended to replace O-levels and CSEs.

G.C.V.O Grand Cross of the Royal Victorian Order (in Britain).

Gd The symbol for the element gadolinium.

Gdańsk (gdansk; *Polish* gdīNsk). *German* **Dan·zig** (dánsig; *German* dántsikh). Polish port and industrial centre on the Baltic Sea. A rich Hanseatic town from the 13th century, it was a free city 1466-1793 (under Polish sovereignty), 1807-14, and 1919-39. Hitler's claim to Danzig in 1939 led to the German invasion of Poland and World War II. Returned to Poland in 1945, the city was rebuilt with shipyards among the world's largest. Riots by shipworkers in 1970 led to government changes and in 1980, Solidarity,

Communist Poland's first independent trade union, was founded there.

gde. gourde.

gdns. gardens.

GDP Gross Domestic Product.

G.D.R. German Democratic Republic (East Germany).

gds. goods.

Gdy·nia (gdín-yə). *German* **Gding·en** (gdíng-ən). A Polish port and rail centre on the Baltic Sea, 19 kilometres (12 miles) from Gdańsk.

Ge The symbol for the element germanium.

Ge. Variant of **Gaea.**

gean (geen) *n.* A wild cherry tree, *Prunus avium,* of Eurasia and North Africa, from which cultivated trees bearing dessert cherries have been derived. Also called "wild cherry". See **sweet cherry.** [French *guinet†.*]

ge·an·ti·cline (jee-ánti-klīn) *n.* A large upward fold of the earth's crust. [Greek *gē,* earth + ANTICLINE.] —**ge·an·ti·cli·nal** (-klĭn′l) *adj.*

gear (geer) *n.* **1. a.** A toothed wheel, cylinder, or other machine element that meshes with another toothed element to transmit motion or to change speed or direction. **b.** A complete assembly that performs a specific function in a larger machine. **c.** A transmission configuration for a specific ratio of engine to axle torque in a motor vehicle. **2. a.** Equipment, apparatus, or clothing required for a particular activity or purpose; tackle: *a plumber's gear.* **b.** *Informal.* Clothes and accessories, especially as worn by young people following fashion. **c.** *Slang.* Stolen goods. **3.** The harness for a draught animal. **4.** The rigging of a ship. **5. a.** A sailor's personal effects. **b.** *Informal.* Personal belongings. —**in** (or **out of**) **gear. 1.** Having a gear engaged (or not engaged). **2.** Performing (or not performing) well.
—*v.* **geared, gearing, gears.** —*tr.* **1. a.** To provide with gears. **b.** To connect by gears. **c.** To put into gear. **2.** To adjust or adapt. Sometimes used with *up, down,* or *to: geared up to summer demand.* **3.** To provide with gear. —*intr.* **1.** To be or become in gear. **2.** To adjust so as to fit or blend. [Middle English *gere,* from Old Norse *gervi,* equipment, gear.]

gear·box (geer-boks) *n.* The assembly of gears in a motor vehicle.

gear·ing (geer-ing) *n.* **1.** A system of gears and associated elements by which motion is transferred within a machine. **2.** The act or technique of providing with gears. **3.** *British.* The ratio of a company's fixed-interest debt to its equity capital.

gear·le·ver (geer-leevər ‖ *U.S. also* -levvər) *n.* A lever used for changing from one gear to another in a motor vehicle. Also *U.S.* "gearshift".

gear train *n.* A system of two or more intermeshing gear wheels transmitting motion.

gear·wheel (geer-weel, -hweel) *n.* A wheel with a toothed rim.

geck·o (géckō) *n.,* pl. **-os** or **-oes.** Any of various usually small lizards of the family Gekkonidae, of warm regions, having toes with adhesive pads that enable them to climb on vertical surfaces. [Malay *ge'kok* (imitative of its cry).]

gee¹ (jee) *interj.* Gee whiz. [Euphemistic shortening of JESUS.]

gee² *n.* The gravitational acceleration at the Earth's surface. [From the symbol "g" for gravitational acceleration.]

gee³ *intr.v.* **geed, geeing, gees.** *U.S. Informal.* To fit or go with; agree with.

gee⁴ *n.* *U.S. Slang.* A thousand dollars. [Short for GRAND.]

gee⁵ *interj.* Also **gee up.** Used to encourage a horse or similar animal to start moving or to move more quickly.
—*tr.v.* **geed, geeing, gees. 1.** To urge (a horse, for example) forwards. Used with *up.* **2.** To hurry (a person, for example). Used with *along* or *up.* **3.** *Informal.* To arouse feelings of anger, excitement, or anxiety in (someone), usually deliberately. Used with *up.* [17th century : origin obscure.]

gee-gee (jée-jee) *n.* *Informal.* A horse. [Child's word for horse, from GEE (interjection).]

geek (geek) *n.* *Slang.* **1.** A carnival performer whose act consists of biting the head off a live animal, such as a chicken or snake. **2.** Broadly, any person whose behaviour is considered to be eccentric or freakish. **3. a.** A freak: *a computer geek.* **b.** A nerd. [Perhaps variant of Scottish *geck,* fool, from Middle Low German.]

Gee·long (jə-lóng). Port in Victoria, Australia. It was founded in 1837 on the western shore of Corio Bay, 68 kilometres (42 miles) southwest of Melbourne.

gee·pound (jée-pownd) *n.* A unit of mass, the **slug** (*see*). [GEE (gravitational acceleration) + POUND (weight).]

geese. Plural of **goose.**

gee whiz, gee whizz *interj.* *Chiefly U.S.* Used to express mild surprise or delight.

Ge'ez (gée-ez) *n.* **Ethiopic** (*see*).

gee·zer (géezər) *n.* *Slang.* A man; especially, an eccentric old man. [Probably dialectal pronunciation of *guiser,* one in disguise, masquerader, from GUISE.]

ge·fil·te fish, ge·füll·te fish (gə-filtə) *n.* Chopped fish mixed with crumbs, eggs, and seasonings, cooked in stock, and usually served chilled in the form of balls or oval-shaped cakes. [Yiddish, "filled fish" : this mixture served as stuffing for fish.]

ge·gen·schein (gáygən-shīn) *n.* A faint, glowing spot in the sky, opposite the position of the sun. Also called "counterglow". [German *Gegenschein,* "opposite light" : *gegen,* against, + *Schein,* light.]

Ge·hen·na (gi-hénnə) *n.* **1.** A place or state of burning, torment, or suffering. **2.** Hell. [Late Latin, from Greek *Geenna,* from Hebrew

Gê' Hinnōm, Valley of Hinnom, a ravine outside ancient Jerusalem where refuse was dumped, (hence figuratively) hell.]

Gei·ger (gī'-gər), **Hans** (1882–1945). German physicist. He is best known for his work with Rutherford at Manchester, which resulted in the invention of the **Geiger counter.**

Geiger counter *n. Abbr.* **GM counter.** An instrument consisting of a Geiger tube and associated electronic equipment, used to detect, measure, and record ionising radiation and charged particles. Also called "Geiger-Müller counter". [After Hans GEIGER.]

Geiger tube *n. Abbr.* **GM tube.** A gas-filled tube containing a fine wire electrode inside a coaxial cylindrical electrode, between which a potential difference slightly below the breakdown voltage is maintained, so that production of a pair of ions in the gas by the passage of a charged particle or by ionising radiation causes a breakdown throughout the volume of the tube. Also called "Geiger-Müller tube". [After Hans GEIGER.]

gei·sha (gáy-shə ‖ gée-) *n., pl.* **geisha** or **-shas.** A Japanese girl trained to provide entertainment, such as singing, dancing, or amusing talk, especially for men. [Japanese, "artist" : *gei,* art + *sha,* person.]

Geis·sler tube (gī'-slər) *n. Physics.* An electrical discharge tube having two electrodes separated by a narrow capillary, used as a source of visible or ultraviolet radiation. [After Heinrich *Geissler* (1815–79), German mechanic.]

geist (gīst) *n.* **1.** Reason or intelligence; especially, that of an individual. **2.** A prevailing intellectual character. [German, "spirit".]

gel (jel) *n.* **1.** A colloid in which the disperse phase has combined with the continuous phase to produce a semisolid material, such as a jelly. **2.** *Informal.* A gelatine used in theatrical lighting. ~*v.* **gelled, gelling, gels.** —*intr.* **1.** To form into a gel. **2.** Variant of **jell.** —*tr.* To cause (a colloid) to become a gel. [Short for GELATINE.]

gel·a·ble (jéll'əb'l) *adj.* Capable of gelling.

gel·a·da (jéll'-ədə, géll'-, jə-laádə, gə-) *n.* A baboon, *Theropithecus gelada,* of Ethiopia, having a dark coat with a bare reddish area on the chest, and a mane covering the shoulders. Also called "gelada baboon". [Perhaps from Arabic *qilādah,* mane.]

ge·län·de·sprung (gə-lénde-sprŏŏng, -shprŏŏng) *n.* A jump in skiing made from a crouching position with the use of both poles. [German : *Gelände,* level land + *Sprung,* a jump.]

gel·a·tine, gel·a·tin (jéllə-tin, -teen) *n.* **1.** A colourless or slightly yellow, transparent, brittle protein formed by boiling the specially prepared skin, bones, and connective tissue of animals, and used in foods, drugs, and photographic film. **2.** Any of various similar substances. **3.** A jelly made with gelatine, used as a dessert or salad base. **4.** A thin, transparent, coloured membrane, used in theatrical lighting. [French *gélatine,* from Italian *gelatina,* diminutive of *gelata,* jelly, from Vulgar Latin *gelāta* (unattested), from Latin, feminine past participle of *gelāre,* to freeze, congeal.]

ge·lat·i·nise, ge·lat·i·nize (jə-látti-nīz, je-) *v.* **-nised, -nising, -nises.** —*tr.* **1.** To convert to gelatine or jelly. **2.** To coat with gelatine. —*intr.* To become gelatinous. —**ge·lat·i·ni·sa·tion** (-nī-záysh'n ‖ U.S. -ni-) *n.*

ge·lat·i·nous (jə-láttinəss) *adj.* **1.** Thick and viscous; resembling jelly. **2.** Of, pertaining to, containing, or similar to gelatine. —**ge·lat·i·nous·ly** *adv.* —**ge·lat·i·nous·ness** *n.*

ge·la·tion (jə-láysh'n, je-) *n.* **1.** Solidification by cooling or freezing. **2.** The process of forming a gel. [Latin *gelātiō* (stem *gelātiōn-*), from *gelāre,* to freeze, congeal.]

geld¹ (geld) *tr.v.* **gelded** or **gelt** (gelt), **gelding, gelds.** **1.** To castrate (a horse or other animal). **2.** To emasculate; weaken. [Middle English *gelden,* from Old Norse *gelda.*]

geld² *n.* A tax paid to the crown by English landholders under Anglo-Saxon and Norman kings. [Medieval Latin (Domesday Book) *geldum,* from Old English *g(i)eld,* payment, tribute.]

geld·ing (gélding) *n.* A castrated animal; especially, a castrated male horse. [Middle English, from Old Norse *geldingr,* from *gelda,* GELD (to castrate).]

Gel·dof (gél-dof ‖ -dorf), **Robert Frederick Zenon (Bob)** (1954–). Irish rock singer and charity organiser. In 1984 he was the moving spirit behind Band Aid, a musical charity that raised £8 million for African famine relief, and in 1985 organised the Live Aid concert at Wembley, London, which raised a further £48 million. In 1986 he was awarded an honorary knighthood (KBE).

gel·id (jéllid) *adj.* Very cold; icy. [Latin *gelidus,* from *gelū,* cold, frost.] —**ge·lid·i·ty** (jə-lídditi), **gel·id·ness** *n.* —**gel·id·ly** *adv.*

gel·ig·nite (jéllig-nīt) *n.* A high explosive made by combining nitroglycerin with wood pulp and sodium or potassium nitrate. [From GELATINE + Latin *ign(is),* fire + -ITE.]

Gell-Mann (gél-mán), **Murray** (1929–). U.S. physicist. In 1954 he introduced the concept of "strangeness" to explain the slow decay of certain particles, and in 1961 postulated the existence of elementary particles he called "quarks". He was awarded the Nobel prize for physics in 1969. Author: *The Quark and the Jaguar* (1994).

gel·se·mi·um (jel-seémi-əm) *n.* **1.** Any shrub of the genus *Gelsemium,* such as G. *sempervirens,* yellow jasmine, of the southeastern United States. **2.** The powdered root of the yellow jasmine, which has sedative properties. [New Latin, from Italian *gelsomino,* JASMINE.]

gelt¹ (gelt) *n. Chiefly U.S. Slang.* Money. [Yiddish *gelt* and German *Geld,* from Old High German *gelt,* recompense, reward.]

gelt². Alternative past tense and past participle of **geld.**

gem¹ (jem) *n.* **1.** A precious or semiprecious stone that has been cut and polished. **2. a.** Something that is valued for its beauty or perfection. **b.** A beloved or highly prized person: *a real gem.* **3.** In printing, a size of type approximately equal to four point. ~*tr.v.* **gemmed, gemming, gems.** To adorn with or as if with gems. [Middle English *gemme,* from Old French, from Latin *gemma,* bud, precious stone.]

gem² (jəm) *adj. Chemistry.* Designating or pertaining to a chemical compound that has two identical atoms or groups attached to the same atom. Compare **vicinal.** [Shortened from GEMINATE.]

Ge·ma·ra (ge-maárə) *n.* The second part of the Talmud, consisting chiefly of commentary on the Mishnah. [Aramaic *gemārā,* completion, from *gemār,* to complete.] —**Ge·mar·ic** *adj.* —**Ge·mar·ist** *n.*

gem·i·nate (jémmi-nayt) *v.* **-nated, -nating, -nates.** —*tr.* To arrange in pairs or to double. —*intr.* To occur in pairs. ~*adj.* (-nət, -nit, -nayt). Also **gem·i·na·ted** (-naytid). Forming a pair; doubled. [Latin *gemināre,* from *geminus,* twin.] —**gem·i·na·tion** (náysh'n) *n.*

Gem·i·ni (jémmi-nī, -nee, -née) *n.* **1.** *Astronomy.* A constellation in the Northern Hemisphere containing the stars Castor and Pollux. **2. a.** The third sign of the **zodiac** (*see*). Also called the "Twins". **b.** One born under this sign. **3.** Any of a series of U.S. space probes designed to gain experience of manual flight and practise docking methods. There were 12 Gemini flights (1964–66), the first two being unmanned, and the others each carrying a pair of astronauts. [Latin, plural of *geminus,* twin.] —**Gem·i·ni·an** (jemmin-í-ən) *adj. & n.*

gem·ma (jémmə) *n., pl.* **-mae** (-mee). An asexual reproductive structure, as in liverworts and mosses, consisting of a cell or group of cells capable of developing into a new individual; a bud. [Latin, bud, precious stone.]

gem·mate (jémmayt) *adj.* Having or reproducing by gemmae. ~*intr.v.* **gemmated, -mating, -mates.** To produce gemmae or reproduce by means of gemmae. [Latin *gemmāre,* to bud, from *gemma,* bud, GEMMA.] —**gem·ma·tion** (je-máysh'n) *n.*

gem·mip·a·rous (je-míppərəss) *adj.* Reproducing by buds or gemmae. [New Latin *gemmiparus* : Latin *gemma,* bud, GEMMA + -PAROUS.]

gem·mol·o·gy, gem·ol·o·gy (je-móllǝji) *n.* The study of gemstones. —**gem·mo·log·i·cal** (jémmə-lójik'l) *adj.* —**gem·mol·o·gist** *n.*

gem·mu·la·tion (jémmew-láysh'n) *n.* Production of or reproduction by gemmules.

gem·mule (jémmewl) *n.* **1.** A small gemma or similar structure; especially, a reproductive structure in some sponges that remains dormant through the winter and later develops into a new individual. **2.** A hypothetical particle of heredity postulated in the theory of **pangenesis** (*see*). [French, from Latin *gemmula,* diminutive of *gemma,* GEMMA.]

ge·mot, ge·mote (gi-mōt) *n.* A public meeting or local judicial assembly in England prior to the Norman Conquest. [Old English *gemōt* : *ge-,* perfective prefix + *mōt,* assembly, council.]

gems·bok (gémz-bok) *n.* An antelope, *Oryx gazella,* of arid regions of southern Africa, having long, sharp, straight horns and a black band along each flank. [Afrikaans, from Dutch *gemsbok,* "male chamois", from German *Gemsbock* : *Gemse,* chamois + *Bock,* he-goat, buck.]

gem·stone (jém-stōn) *n.* A precious or semiprecious stone that may be used as a gem when cut and polished.

ge·müt·lich (gə-mút-likh, -mŏŏt-lik) *adj. German.* Having a feeling of warmth or congeniality; cheerful; cosy.

Ge·müt·lich·keit (gə-mút-likh-kīt, -mŏŏt-lik-) *n. German.* Congeniality; a cosy atmosphere.

–gen, –gene *n. comb. form.* Indicates: **1.** That which produces; producing; for example, **antigen. 2.** Something produced; for example, **phosgene.** [French *-gène,* from Greek *-genēs,* born.]

gen (jen) *n. British Informal.* Relevant information. ~*tr.v.* **genned, genning, gens.** *Informal.* To give (a person) relevant information on a subject. Used with *up.* —**gen up on.** To inform oneself intensively about (a subject). [Probably from general information.]

gen. 1. gender. **2.** generally; generally. **3.** generator. **4.** generic. **5.** genitive. **6.** genus.

Gen. 1. general (military rank). **2.** Genesis (Old Testament).

ge·nappe (jə-náp) *n.* An exceptionally smooth worsted yarn used in the manufacture of fringes and braids. [After *Genappe,* Belgium, where it was originally made.]

gen·darme (zhón-daarm; *French* ZHoN-dárm) *n., pl.* **-darmes** (-daarmz; *French* -dárm). **1.** A member of a national police organisation in France and some countries formerly controlled by France, constituting a branch of the armed forces with responsibilities for internal defence, frontier and customs guard, traffic control, and general law enforcement in rural districts. **2.** A cavalryman belonging to any of various units organised under royal authority in France from the 15th century until 1789. **3.** *Informal.* A French policeman. **4.** *Slang.* Any policeman. **5.** An isolated pinnacle on a mountain ridge forming an obstacle to climbers. [French, from *gens d'armes,* "men of arms".]

gen·darm·e·rie (zhon-dármǝri; *French* ZHoN-daarma-reé) *n.* Also **gen·dar·me·ry** (for sense 2). **1.** A military police organisation having general responsibility for public security and law enforcement in France and some countries formerly controlled by France. **2.** A headquarters of a body of gendarmes. **3.** A French royal cavalry corps, as variously organised at different times between the 15th century and 1789. [French, from GENDARME.]

gen·der (jéndər) *n. Abbr.* **g., gen.** **1.** *Grammar.* **a.** Any set of two or more categories, such as masculine, feminine, and neuter, into which words are divided according to sex, animation, psychological associations, or some other characteristic, and that determine agreement with or the selection of modifiers, referents, or grammatical forms. **b.** One category of such a set. See **common gender, grammatical gender, natural gender.** **c.** The classification of a word or grammatical form in such a category. **d.** The distinguishing form or forms used. **2. a.** Classification of sex. **b.** The sex of a person. **c.** Sexual identity as influenced by, or evaluated according to, social norms. ~*tr.v.* **gendered, -dering, -ders.** *Archaic.* To engender. [Middle English *gendre*, from Old French *gen(d)re*, kind, sort, from Latin *genus* (stem *gener-*), race, kind.]

gender bender *n. Informal.* A person, especially a male, who adopts the dress and mannerisms of the opposite sex for amusement or publicity rather than sexual gratification.

gene (jeen) *n.* A hereditary unit located on a chromosome that determines a specific characteristic or function in the organism. Genes are capable of replication and recombination, exist in a number of different forms, called **alleles** *(see),* and can mutate.

–gene. Variant of **-gen.**

ge·ne·al·o·gy (jéeni-ál-əji, jénni- ǁ -ólləji) *n., pl.* **-gies.** *Abbr.* **geneal.** **1.** A record or table of the descent of a family, group, or person from an ancestor or ancestors; a family tree. **2.** Direct descent from an ancestor; lineage; pedigree. **3.** The study or investigation of ancestry and family histories. **4.** The study of the development of plants and animals from their earlier forms. [Middle English *genealogie*, from Old French, from Late Latin *genealogia*, from Greek : *genea*, race, generation + -LOGY.] —**ge·ne·a·log·i·cal** (-ə-lójik'l) *adj.* —**ge·ne·a·log·i·cal·ly** *adv.* —**ge·ne·al·o·gist** *n.*

gen·e·col·o·gy (jéeni-kólləji) *n.* The study of the genetics of populations in relation to their environment. [GENE(TICS) + ECOLOGY.]

gene flow *n.* The introduction and movement of new allelic forms of genes in populations due to immigration and subsequent interbreeding.

gene frequency *n.* The frequency of occurrence of an allelic form of a gene in relation to that of other alleles of the same gene.

gene pool *n.* The total number of genes in an interbreeding population at a given time.

gen·e·ra. Plural of **genus.**

gen·er·a·ble (jénnərəb'l) *adj.* Capable of being generated. [Middle English *generabill*, from Latin *generābilis*, from *generāre*, GENERATE.]

gen·er·al (jénrəl, jénnerəl) *adj. Abbr.* **gen., genl.** **1. a.** Relating to, concerned with, or applicable to the whole, or every member of a class or category: *a programme to improve general welfare.* **b.** *Medicine.* Pertaining to or involving the whole body. **2.** Widespread; prevalent: *a general discontent.* **3.** Being usually the case; true or applicable in most instances but not all: *the general correctness of his decisions.* **4. a.** Not limited in scope, area, or application; not restricted: *a general rule to follow.* **b.** Not limited to or dealing with one class of things; diversified; miscellaneous: *general studies; a general store.* **5.** Involving only the main or more obvious features of something; lacking detail or precision: *a general grasp of a subject.* **6.** Highest or superior in rank; chief within a particular sphere: *the general manager; secretary general.* **7.** Ordinary. Said of an academic degree. ~*n.* **1.** *Abbr.* **Gen.** **a.** An officer of the British and Australian armies ranking between a field-marshal and a lieutenant-general and equivalent in rank to an admiral in the Navy and an air chief marshal in the Air Force. **b.** An officer of the highest rank in the Royal Marines. **c.** An officer in the U.S. Army, Air Force, or Marine Corps holding a rank above colonel; especially, an officer of the second-highest rank in the U.S. Army or Air Force and the highest rank in the Marine Corps. **2.** A tactician or organiser. **3. a.** The head of certain Roman Catholic religious orders. **b.** The head of the Salvation Army. **4.** Something, such as a condition, principle, or fact, that embraces or is applicable to the whole. **5.** *Archaic.* The public: " *'twas caviare to the general"* (Shakespeare). **—in general.** Generally speaking. [Middle English, from Old French, from Latin *generālis*, belonging to a kind or species, relating to all, from *genus* (stem *gener-*), birth, race, kind.] —**gen·er·al·ness** *n.*

General Agreement on Tariffs and Trade. *n. Abbr.* **GATT.** Trade liberalisation treaty signed at Geneva in 1993 by 117 countries after seven years of negotiation.

general anaesthetic *n.* An anaesthetic that causes loss of sensation in the entire body and induces unconsciousness. Compare **local anaesthetic.**

General Assembly *n. Abbr.* **GA, G.A.** **1.** The principal deliberative body of the United Nations in which each member nation is represented and has one vote. **2.** The supreme governing body of some religious denominations, especially that of the Church of Scotland and other Presbyterian churches. **3.** Any of various legislative bodies, especially that of a U.S. state.

General Certificate of Education *n.* See **G.C.E.**

general confession *n.* **1.** In the services of the Anglican Church, a prayer of confession recited by the whole congregation. **2.** In the Roman Catholic Church, a confession in which the penitent considers his life in general rather than his recent past.

general delivery *n. U.S.* **Poste restante** *(see).*

general election *n.* An election at which all constituencies return a representative to a parliament or similar body.

general hospital *n.* A district hospital that provides basic services for its patients without specialising in particular diseases.

gen·er·al·i·sa·tion (jénnərə-lī-záysh'n, jénnrə- ǁ *U.S.* -li-) *n.* **1.** An act or instance of generalising. **2.** A general principle, statement, or idea, especially one based on incomplete consideration of facts. **3.** *Psychology.* A process by which behaviour prompted by a particular stimulus can also be prompted by a similar stimulus.

gen·er·al·ise, gen·er·al·ize (jénnərə-līz, jénnrə-) *v.* **-ised, -ising, -ises.** —*tr.* **1. a.** To reduce to a general form, class, or law. **b.** To render indefinite or unspecific. **2. a.** To infer from many particulars. **b.** To draw inferences or a general conclusion from. **3. a.** To make generally or universally applicable. **b.** To popularise. —*intr.* **1. a.** To form a concept inductively. **b.** To form general notions or conclusions, especially after incomplete consideration of the facts. **2.** To speak or think in generalities; speak vaguely. **3.** *Medicine.* To spread through the body. Used of a usually localised disease.

gen·er·al·ised (jénnərə-līzd, jénnrə-) *adj.* **1.** Generally prevalent. **2. a.** General; unspecific. **b.** Not well-adapted to a specific environment or function; undifferentiated.

generalised order *n. Psychology.* An organised group whose group identity allows an individual to establish a personal identity by reference to it.

gen·er·al·is·si·mo (jénnərə-líssimō, jénnrə-) *n., pl.* **-mos.** The commander in chief of all the armed forces in certain countries, or, occasionally, of the armed forces of allied countries in a joint campaign. [Italian, superlative of *generale*, general, from Latin *generālis*, belonging to a kind, GENERAL.]

gen·er·al·ist (jénnərə-list, jénnrə-) *n.* A person with broad general knowledge and skills in several disciplines, fields, or areas.

gen·er·al·i·ty (jénnə-rál-əti) *n., pl.* **-ties.** **1.** The condition or quality of being general. **2.** An observation or principle having general application; a generalisation. **3.** A statement or idea that is imprecise or vague. **4.** The greater portion or number; the majority.

general knowledge *n.* Knowledge of a wide variety of facts from many fields.

gen·er·al·ly (jénnərə-li, jénnrə-) *adv. Abbr.* **gen.** **1.** For the most part; widely: *generally known.* **2.** As a rule; usually. **3.** Viewing circumstances overall; not specifically: *generally speaking.*

general paralysis of the insane *n. Abbr.* **GPI** A brain disease occurring as a late consequence of syphilis, characterised by mental deterioration, speech disturbances, and progressive muscular weakness. Also called "general paresis", "paresis".

General Post Office *n. Abbr.* **G.P.O.** **1.** Formerly in Britain, the central government department providing postal and telecommunications services. **2.** The main post office in a district.

general practitioner *n. Abbr.* **G.P.** A doctor in general practice, treating most cases of illness, but sending patients requiring more specialised treatment to a hospital or a consultant.

gen·er·al·pur·pose *adj.* Able to be used or applied in many circumstances.

general relativity *n. Physics.* The later part of the theory of **relativity** *(see),* dealing with accelerated motion.

general semantics *n.* Used with a singular verb. A doctrine proposed by Alfred Korzybski (1879–1950) that presents a method of improving human behaviour through a more critical use of words and symbols.

gen·er·al·ship (jénnərəl-ship, jénnrəl-) *n.* **1.** The rank, office, or tenure of a general. **2.** Leadership or skill in the conduct of a war. **3.** Any skilful management or leadership.

general staff *n. Abbr.* **GS, G.S.** *Military.* A group of officers, usually of the rank of major and above, who are charged with assisting senior officers in planning and supervising operations.

general strike *n.* **1.** A concerted strike involving workers throughout the industries of a nation or area. **2.** *Capital* G, *capital* S. The strike by workers in British industries in 1926.

General Synod *n.* The governing body of the Church of England, composed of the diocesan bishops and elected clerical and lay representatives.

gen·er·ate (jénnə-rayt) *tr.v.* **-ated, -ating, -ates.** **1. a.** To bring into existence; give rise to: *generate discussion.* **b.** To produce (electricity or heat, for example) as a result of a chemical or physical process. **2.** To engender (offspring); beget. **3.** To form (a geometric figure) by describing a curve or surface. **4.** *Linguistics.* To specify (a sentence, for example) as grammatical by following certain rules. [Latin *generāre,* from *genus* (stem *gener-*), birth, race, kind.] —**gen·er·a·tive** (-rətiv, -raytiv) *adj.*

gen·er·a·tion (jénnə-ráysh'n) *n.* **1.** The act or process of generating; especially, origination, production, or procreation. **2.** Offspring having a common parent or parents and constituting a single stage of descent. **3.** *Biology.* All the individuals produced during a particular phase of the life cycle that have the same method of reproduction: *the sporophyte generation.* **4.** A class of objects derived from a preceding class: *the new generation of minicomputers.* **5. a.** A group of contemporaneous individuals. **b.** A group of individuals, usually contemporaneous, regarded as having a common cultural or social attribute: *the beat generation.* **6.** The average time interval between the birth of parents and the birth of their offspring: *spanning three generations.*

generation gap *n.* The differences in outlook and attitude between people of different generations, especially between young people and their parents.

generative grammar *n. Linguistics.* A system of rules intended to produce all and only the well-formed sentences of a language; specifically, **transformational-generative grammar** *(see)*.

generative semantics *n. Used with a singular verb.* A theory based on the belief that syntactic and semantic structures are of the same nature and that the mind relates surface structure to meaning.

gen·er·a·tor (jénnə-raytər) *n. Abbr.* **gen.** **1.** One that generates. **2.** A machine that converts mechanical energy into electrical energy, especially: **a.** A large dynamo in a power station. **b.** A small apparatus for producing static electricity. **3.** An apparatus that generates a vapour or gas. **4.** A generatrix.

gen·er·a·trix (jénnə-ray-trikss, -ráy-) *n., pl.* **generatrices** (-tri-seez, *also* -rə-trí-seez). A point, line, or plane that generates a geometric figure; especially, a straight line that generates a surface by moving in a given fashion.

ge·ner·ic (jə-nérrik, je-) *adj. Abbr.* **gen.** **1.** Relating to or descriptive of an entire group or class; general. **2.** *Biology.* Of or relating to a genus. **3.** Commonly available; not protected by trademark; nonproprietary. **4.** Designating a drug sold or prescribed under its chemical name rather than under a brand name.
~*n.* An unbranded product sold at low cost by a supermarket or chain store with plain packaging. [French *générique,* from Latin *genus* (stem *gener*-), race, species, kind.] —**ge·ner·i·cal·ly** *adv.*

gen·er·os·i·ty (jénnə-róssəti) *n., pl.* **-ties.** **1.** The quality of being generous; liberality or willingness in giving. **2.** Nobility of thought or behaviour; magnanimity. **3.** Amplitude; abundance. **4.** A generous act.

gen·er·ous (jénnərəss, jénnrəss) *adj.* **1.** Willing to give or share; unselfish. **2.** Lacking pettiness or meanness in thought or behaviour; magnanimous. **3.** Characterised by abundance; bountiful; ample. **4.** Having a rich bouquet and flavour. Said of wine. **5.** Fertile. Said of soil. [Old French *genereux,* from Latin *generōsus,* of noble birth, excellent, magnanimous, from *genus* (stem *gener*-), birth, race, kind.] —**gen·er·ous·ly** *adv.* —**gen·er·ous·ness** *n.*

gen·e·sis (jénni-siss) *n., pl.* **-ses** (-seez). The coming into being of anything; an origin; a creation. [Latin, from Greek, generation, birth, origin.]

Gen·e·sis (jénni-siss) *n. Abbr.* **Gen.** The first book of the Old Testament, recounting the creation of the world and the establishment and early history of Israel.

–genesis *n. comb. form.* Indicates generation; for example, **biogenesis, paragenesis.** [New Latin, from Latin *genesis,* birth, GENESIS.]

gen·et¹ (jénnit, jə-nét) *n.* Any of several Old World carnivorous mammals of the genus *Genetta,* having greyish or yellowish fur with dark spots, and a long, ringed tail. [Middle English *genete,* from Old French, from Arabic *jarnayṭ.*]

genet². Variant of **jennet.**

Ge·net (zhə-náy), **Jean** (1910–86). French novelist and playwright. After many convictions for theft and homosexuality, he was released from a life sentence when many of France's leading intellectuals, led by Jean Cocteau, petitioned the President. His early works such as *The Miracle of the Rose* (1946) and *A Thief's Journal* (1949) draw on his prison experiences. His later works tend towards the nihilistic and the absurd.

ge·net·ic (jə-néttik) *adj.* Also **ge·net·i·cal** (-'l). **1.** Of or pertaining to the origin or development of something. **2. a.** Of or pertaining to genetics or genes. **b.** Affecting genes: *a genetic disorder.* [From GENESIS.] —**ge·net·i·cal·ly** *adv.*

genetic code *n.* The information carried by DNA, which determines the nature of all the proteins made in the cell. The code is expressed by the sequence of nitrogenous bases in the DNA molecule, three consecutive bases (a codon) coding for a particular amino acid in the protein.

genetic drift *n.* The tendency for a genetic variant to become fixed in or lost from a population by chance, rather than by natural selection. It most commonly occurs in small, isolated populations. Also called "Sewall-Wright effect".

genetic engineering *n.* The modification of the structure of the chromosomes of living organisms, especially bacteria and viruses, in such a way as to benefit man. It has been employed in agriculture and medicine. —**genetic engineer** *n.*

genetic fingerprinting *n.* A forensic test for blood relationships between people, made by comparing the genetic information contained in body cells.

ge·net·i·cist (jə-nétti-sist) *n.* One who specialises in genetics.

ge·net·ics (jə-néttiks) *n.* **1.** *Used with a singular verb.* The biology of heredity; especially, the study of the mechanisms of hereditary transmission and the variation of heritable characteristics. **2.** *Used with a singular or plural verb.* The genetic constitution of an individual, group, or class.

Ge·ne·va (jə-néevə). *French* **Ge·nève** (zhə-név); *German* **Genf** (genf). A city in Switzerland, situated on the southwest corner of Lake Geneva. It is the country's third largest city and capital of the Geneva canton. Many international organisations, such as the Red Cross, and agencies of the United Nations, including the World Health Organisation, have their headquarters there. The population is mainly French-speaking and Protestant.

Geneva, Lake. *French* **Lac Lé·man** (lak lay-món); *German* **Gen·fer·see** (génfər-zay). Lake of Switzerland and France. Approximately 72 kilometres (45 miles) long and 13 kilometres (8 miles) at its widest point, it lies between southwest Switzerland and the Haute-Savoie département of France. The surface is subject to changes of

level (seiches) caused by variations in atmospheric pressure and wind direction.

Geneva bands *pl.n.* Two strips of white cloth hanging from the collar of some clerical and academic robes. [Originally worn by Calvinist clergymen in Geneva.]

Geneva Convention *n.* Any of several agreements, the first of which was formulated at an international convention held in Geneva, Switzerland, in 1864, establishing rules for the wartime treatment of prisoners and the sick or wounded.

Geneva cross *n.* A red Greek or St. George's cross on a white ground, used as a symbol by the Red Cross and as a sign of neutrality.

Geneva gown *n.* A loose, black, academic or clerical gown with wide sleeves. [Originally worn by Calvinist clergymen in Geneva.]

Ge·ne·van (jə-néev'n) *adj.* Also **Gen·e·vese** (jénni-véez). **1.** Of or relating to Geneva, Switzerland. **2.** Of or relating to Geneva during the time of Calvin; Calvinist.
~*n.* Also **Gen·e·vese.** **1.** A native or inhabitant of Geneva, Switzerland. **2.** A follower of Calvin; a Calvinist.

Geneva Protocol *n.* A document drafted in 1925 that sought to ban the use of poison gas in warfare and to enforce sanctions against the aggressors in wars.

Gen·ghis Khan, Chingiz Khan, or **Jenghiz Khan** (jéng-giss ká·an, géng-), born Temujin (*c.* 1162–1227). Mongolian emperor. The son of a Mongol chieftain, he united the Mongolian tribes by conquest, and in 1206 took the title Genghis Khan (supreme ruler). By brilliant use of light cavalry, he annexed north China, central Asia, Iran, and southern Russia. Though capable of horrific cruelty in battle, he was a far-sighted administrator and lawmaker.

gen·ial¹ (jéeni-əl) *adj.* **1.** Having a pleasant or friendly disposition or manner; cordial; kindly. **2.** Conducive to life or growth; giving warmth; mild. **3.** *Rare.* Characteristic of or relating to genius. [Latin *geniālis,* of generation or birth, nuptial, hence festive, joyous, from *genius,* deity of generation and birth.] —**gen·ial·ly** *adv.* —**ge·ni·al·i·ty** (jéeni-ál-iti), **gen·ial·ness** *n.*

ge·ni·al² (jée-ní-əl) *n. Anatomy.* Of or pertaining to the chin. [Greek *geneion,* chin, from *genus,* jaw.]

gen·ic (jénnik, jéenik) *adj.* Of, relating to, produced by, or being a gene or genes; genetic.

–genic *adj. comb. form.* Indicates: **1.** Generation or production; for example, **antigenic.** **2.** Suitability for; for example, **photogenic.** [From -GEN.]

ge·nic·u·late (jə-níckew-lət, -lit, -layt) *adj.* Also **ge·nic·u·lat·ed** (-laytid). **1.** *Biology.* Bent at an abrupt angle like that of a bent knee. **2.** Jointed so as to be capable of bending at an abrupt angle. [Latin *geniculātus,* with bent knee, curved, from *geniculum,* diminutive of *genu,* knee.] —**ge·nic·u·late·ly** *adv.* —**ge·nic·u·la·tion** (-láysh'n) *n.*

ge·nie (jéeni ‖ jénni) *n.* A supernatural creature who does one's bidding. [French *génie,* spirit, from Latin *genius,* guardian spirit, GENIUS.]

ge·ni·i. Alternative plural of **genius.**

genip. Variant of **guinep.**

gen·i·pap (génni-pap) *n.* **1.** An evergreen tree, *Genipa americana,* of the West Indies, having yellowish-white flowers and edible fruit. **2.** The reddish-brown fruit of this tree. Also called "guinep", "marmalade box". [Portuguese *genipapo,* from Tupi.]

gen·is·ta (ji-nísstə) *n.* Any shrub of the European genus *Genista,* similar and related to the broom; especially, **dyer's greenweed** *(see).* [New Latin *Genista* (genus), from Latin, broom.]

genit. genitive.

gen·i·tal (jénnit'l) *adj.* **1.** Of or relating to biological reproduction. **2.** Of or pertaining to the genitals. **3.** *Psychoanalysis.* Pertaining to or designating a stage at which a child's anal and oral impulses give way to more mature personal relationships. Compare **anal, oral.** [Middle English *genytal,* from Old French *genital,* from Latin *genitālis,* from *gignere* (past participle *genitus*), to beget, produce.]

genital herpes *n.* A recurrent viral infection of the genital region which may cause painful eruptions of the skin or be symptomless. See **herpes.**

gen·i·ta·li·a (jénni-táyli-ə) *pl.n.* The reproductive organs; especially, the external sex organs. [Latin *genitālia (membra),* genital (members), neuter plural of *genitālis,* GENITAL.]

gen·i·tals (jénnit'lz) *pl.n.* Genitalia.

gen·i·ti·val (jénni-tív'l) *adj. Grammar.* Of, pertaining to, or in the genitive case. —**gen·i·ti·val·ly** *adv.*

gen·i·tive (jénnitiv) *n. Abbr.* **g., gen., genit. 1.** The grammatical case in certain languages, usually expressed in English by a prepositional phrase with *of,* that denotes possession, measurement, or source. **2.** A form or construction in this case.
~*adj. Abbr.* **g., gen., genit.** *Grammar.* Designating, pertaining to, or inflected in the genitive. [Middle English *genitif (case),* from Latin *(casus) genitīvus,* "case of production or origin" (translation of Greek *genikē ptōsis,* "case of race"), from *gignere* (past participle *genitus*), to beget, produce.]

gen·i·tor (jénni-tər, -tawr) *n.* **1.** One who begets or creates. **2.** *Anthropology.* A natural father as distinguished from the socially responsible foster father in certain cultures. [Middle English *genytur,* from Latin *genitor,* from *gignere* (past participle *genitus*), to beget.]

gen·i·to·u·ri·nar·y (jénnitō-yóor-in-əri, -ri ‖ *U.S.* -erri) *adj. Abbr.* **GU, G.U.** Of or pertaining to the genital and urinary organs or their functions. [GENIT(AL) + URINARY.]

ge·ni·us (jéeni-əss) *n., pl.* **-iuses** or **genii** (jéeni-ī) (for senses 4, 6).

1. a. Exceptional or transcendent intellectual and creative power. **b.** One who possesses such power. **2. a.** A natural talent or inclination. Used with *to* or *for*: *She has a genius for acting.* **b.** One who has such a talent or inclination: *He is a genius at diplomacy.* **3.** The prevailing spirit or character, as of a place, person, time, or group: *the genius of the Elizabethan poets.* **4.** *Roman Mythology.* **a.** A tutelary deity or guardian spirit allotted to a person from birth. **b.** Any guiding spirit of a person or place. **5.** A person who has great influence over another. **6.** In Muslim legend, a jinni or demon. [Latin *genius*, deity of generation and birth, guardian spirit.]

ge·ni·us lo·ci (jēeni-əss lō´-sī, lō-kī, lóckee) *n. Latin.* **1.** A guardian deity of a particular locality. **2.** The distinctive atmosphere or particular character of a place.

ge·ni·zah (je-néezə) *n.* A room adjacent to a synagogue where discarded books and sacred relics are stored. [Hebrew, "hiding place", from *gānaz*, to hide.]

genl., Genl. general; General.

Gennesaret, Lake of. See **Galilee, Sea of.**

Gen·o·a (jénnō-ə). *Italian* **Gen·o·va** (jénnova). Port on the Gulf of Genoa, Italy. The capital of Liguria and of Genoa province, it is Italy's chief seaport, handling over one-third of the country's foreign trade. **—Gen·o·ese** (-éez) *adj. & n.*

Genoa cake *n.* A rich sponge cake, sometimes made with cherries. [After GENOA, Italy.]

Genoa jib *n. Nautical.* A large jib used on a racing yacht. [After GENOA, Italy.]

gen·o·cide (jénnə-sīd, jénnō-) *n.* The systematic, planned annihilation of a racial, political, or cultural group. [Greek *genos*, race + -CIDE.] **—gen·o·ci·dal** (-sīd'l) *adj.*

ge·nome (jée-nōm) *n.* Also **ge·nom** (jée-nom). *Biology.* A complete haploid set of chromosomes. [German *Genom* : *Gen*, GENE + (CHROMOS)OME.]

gen·o·type (jénnō-tīp, jénnə-, jéenə-) *n.* **1.** The genetic constitution of an organism, especially as distinguished from its physical appearance. Compare **phenotype.** **2.** A group or class of organisms having the same genetic constitution. [Greek *genos*, race + TYPE.] **—gen·o·typ·ic** (-típpik), **gen·o·typ·i·cal** *adj.* **—gen·o·typ·i·cal·ly** *adv.* **—gen·o·ty·pic·i·ty** (-ti-píssiti, -tī-) *n.*

–genous *adj. comb. form.* Indicates: **1.** Generating or producing; for example, **androgenous.** **2.** Generated by, produced by, or arising from; for example, **endogenous.** [From -GEN.]

gen·re (zhónrə) *n.* **1.** Type; class; variety. **2.** A category of art, literature, or films distinguished by a definite style, form, or content. **3.** Genre painting. **~***adj.* Of or relating to genre. [French, kind, from Old French *gen(d)re*, from Latin *genus* (stem *gener*-), race, kind.]

genre painting *n.* A style of painting concerned with depicting scenes and subjects of common everyday life. Also called "genre".

gen·ro (génn-rō) *n., pl.* **-ros.** **1.** In Japan, a group of elder statesmen, formerly advisers to the emperor. **2.** Any of these elder statesmen. [Japanese *genrō.*]

gens (jenz, genz) *n., pl.* **gentes** (jén-teez, gén-tayz). **1.** The patrilinear clan forming the basic unit of the Roman tribe and having originally a common name, land, cult, and burial ground. **2.** *Anthropology.* An exogamous patrilineal clan. [Latin *gēns*, clan.]

gent (jent) *n. Informal.* A gentleman; a man. [Shortened from GENTLEMAN.]

Gent. See **Ghent.**

gen·ta·mi·cin (jéntə-mí-sin) *n.* An antibiotic used to treat a wide variety of infections and applied by injection or in the form of a cream or drops. [Variant of earlier *gentamycin* : *genta-* (probably irregularly formed from *gentian violet*, referring to the colour of the organism from which it is derived) + -*mycin*, as in STREPTOMYCIN.]

gen·teel (jen-téel) *adj.* **1. a.** Striving to convey a manner or appearance of refinement and respectability. **b.** Marked by affected and somewhat prudish refinement. **2.** Refined in manner; well-bred; polite. **3.** Free from vulgarity or rudeness. **3.** Fashionable; elegant: *"It was a genteel old-fashioned house, very quiet and orderly"* (Charles Dickens). **—See Synonyms at polite.** [Old French *gentil*, GENTLE.] **—gen·teel·ly** *adv.* **—gen·teel·ness** *n.*

gen·teel·ism (jen-téel-iz'm) *n.* A word or expression thought by its user to be genteel.

gen·tian (jénsh'n, -shi-ən) *n.* **1.** Any of numerous plants of the genus *Gentiana*, characteristically having showy blue, yellow, or red flowers. **2.** The dried rhizome and roots of a yellow-flowered European gentian, *G. lutea*, sometimes used as a tonic. [Middle English *gencian*, from Old French *genciane*, from Latin *gentiāna*, probably after *Gentius*, king of Illyria (second century B.C.), supposed discoverer of the medicinal properties of the plant.]

gen·tian·el·la (jénti-shə-néllə, -shi-ə-) *n.* **1.** An alpine plant, *Gentiana acaulis*, with ornamental blue flowers. **2.** Any of several similar and related plants. [New Latin, diminutive of GENTIAN.]

gentian violet *n.* **Crystal violet** (see).

gen·tile (jén-tīl) *adj.* **1.** Of or pertaining to the gens or to the tribal society based on it. **2.** Of or relating to Gentiles. **3.** *Grammar.* Of or pertaining to a noun or adjective designating a nation, place, or people: *American* and *Italian* are gentile nouns. **~***n.* **1.** A member of a gens. **2.** A gentile noun or adjective. [Latin *gentīlis*, from *gēns*, clan, GENS.]

Gen·tile (jén-tīl) *n. Sometimes small* **g.** **1.** Anyone who is not of the Jewish faith or is of a non-Jewish nation. **2.** A Christian as distinguished from a Jew. **3.** A pagan or heathen. **4.** Among Mormons, a person who is not a Mormon.

~*adj. Sometimes small* **g.** Of or pertaining to a Gentile. [Middle English *gentil, gentyle*, from Late Latin *gentīles*, pagans, heathens, from *gentīlis*, pagan, from Latin, of the same clan, from *gēns*, clan, GENS.]

Gen·ti·le (jen-tée-le), **Giovanni** (1875–1944). Italian philosopher and politician in Mussolini's Fascist government. He was executed by partisans.

gen·ti·lesse (jént'l-ess, -éss) *n. Archaic.* Refinement; courtesy; good breeding. [Middle English *gentilete*, from Old French, from *gentil*, GENTLE.]

gen·til·i·ty (jen-tílləti) *n.* **1.** The condition of being genteel. **2.** Gentle birth. **3.** Persons of gentle birth collectively; the gentry. [Middle English *gentilete*, from Old French, from Latin *gentīlitās* (stem *gentīlitāt*-), clanship, from *gentīlis*, belonging to a clan, GENTILE.]

gen·tle (jént'l) *adj.* **-tler, -tlest.** **1.** Considerate or kindly in disposition; tender and patient: *a gentle mother.* **2.** Not harsh, severe, or violent; mild: *a gentle scolding.* **3.** Easily managed or handled; docile; tame: *a gentle horse.* **4.** Gradual; not steep or sudden: *a gentle incline.* **5.** Moderate. **6.** Of good family; well-born. **7.** *Archaic.* Noble; chivalrous: *a gentle knight.*
~*n.* **1.** *Archaic.* One of gentle birth or station. **2.** The larva of a bluebottle.
~*tr.v.* **gentled, -tling, -tles.** **1.** To make gentle; pacify; mollify. **2.** To tame (a horse, for example). [Middle English *gentil*, well-born, noble, graceful, from Old French, from Latin *gentīlis*, of the same clan, of noble birth, from *gēns*, clan.] **—gent·ly** *adv.*

gentle breeze *n.* A wind whose speed is 3.4 to 5.4 metres per second, force 3 on the Beaufort scale.

gen·tle·folk (jént'l-fōk) *pl.n.* Also **gen·tle·folks** (-fōks). Persons of good family and breeding.

gen·tle·man (jént'l-mən) *n., pl.* **-men** (-mən, -men). **1.** A polite, gracious, or considerate man with high standards of propriety or correct behaviour. **2.** A man of gentle or noble birth or superior social position. **3. a.** Any man. **b.** *Plural.* A form of address for a group of men. Used both in speech and writing. **4.** Formerly, a nonprofessional cricketer. **5.** *British.* Formerly, a man higher than a yeoman in social position. **6.** Formerly, a smuggler. Used euphemistically. [GENTLE + MAN (after French *gentilhomme*).] **—gen·tle·man·ly** *adj.*
Usage: *Gentleman* is used instead of *man* only in restricted contexts, and usually carries a nuance: *He's no gentleman* (meaning that he does not act in a well-mannered considerate way). The form is used neutrally in direct address: *Ladies and gentlemen; We must now turn, gentlemen, to the second point on the agenda.* It is also preferred when referring to a person in his presence: *You had better ask this gentleman to wait outside* (where *man* would sound abrupt and rude). See also **lady.**

gen·tle·man-at-arms (jént'l-mən-ət-ármz) *n., pl.* **gentlemen-at-arms** (-mən-, -men-). Any of a corps of about 35 senior retired army officers who attend the British sovereign as a ceremonial guard on state occasions.

gentleman farmer *n., pl.* **gentlemen farmers.** A man who farms chiefly for pleasure rather than income or whose means permit him to be an absentee proprietor of his farming interests.

gentleman's agreement *n.* An agreement guaranteed only by the honour of the participants and not legally binding; an understanding.

gentleman's gentleman *n.* A manservant; a valet.

gen·tle·ness (jént'l-nəss, -niss) *n.* **1.** The quality of being gentle. **2.** *Physics.* A property or quantum number of elementary particles, similar to charm. It is conserved in strong interactions.

gentle sex *n.* Women collectively. Usually used facetiously or in literary contexts, preceded by *the.*

gen·tle·wom·an (jént'l-wōōmən) *n., pl.* **-women** (-wimmin). **1.** A woman of gentle birth or superior social position. **2.** A polite, gracious, or considerate woman. **3.** A woman acting as a personal attendant to a lady of rank.

Gen·too (jén-tōō) *n., pl.* **-toos.** *Archaic.* A Hindu. [Portuguese *gentio*, "a pagan", from Late Latin *gentīlis*, pagan, GENTILE.]

gen·tri·fy (jéntri-fī) *tr.v.* **-fied, -fying, -fies.** *British.* To change the character of (a previously working-class area) by an influx of middle-class residents. **—gen·tri·fi·ca·tion** (-fi-káysh'n) *n.* [GENTRY + -FY.]

gen·try (jéntri) *n.* **1.** People of gentle birth, good breeding, or high social position. **2.** In Britain, the upper middle classes. **3.** People of a particular class or group. [Middle English *gentri(se)*, gentle birth, from Old French *genterise, gentelise*, from *gentil*, GENTLE.]

gents (jents) *n., pl.* **gents.** *British Informal.* A public lavatory for men.

gen·u (jénnew) *n., pl.* **genua** (jénnew-ə). *Anatomy.* **1.** The knee. **2.** Any structure resembling the knee or having a kneelike bend. [New Latin, from Latin.]

gen·u·flect (jénnew-flekt) *intr.v.* **-flected, -flecting, -flects.** **1.** To bend the knee in a kneeling or half-kneeling position, as in reverence. **2.** To exhibit a deferential or obsequious attitude or manner. [Late Latin *genuflectere* : Latin *genu*, knee + *flectere*, to bend.]

gen·u·flec·tion (jénnew-fléksh'n) *n.* Also *chiefly British* **gen·u·flex·ion.** The act of kneeling briefly by bending one knee, as in reverence.

gen·u·ine (jénnew-in) *adj.* **1.** Actually being as stated; corresponding faithfully to the description given: *genuine sorrow; genuine leather.* **2.** Not spurious or counterfeit; authentic: *a genuine claim.* **3.** Free from hypocrisy or dishonesty; sincere: *genuine admiration.* **4.** Being of pure or original stock. **—See Synonyms at real.** [Latin *genuīnus*, perhaps originally "placed on the knees" (from the ancient custom that a father acknowledges a child by placing him or her on his knees), from *genu*, knee.] **—gen·u·ine·ly** *adv.* **—gen·u·ine·ness** *n.*

ge·nus (jéenəss, jénnəss) *n., pl.* **genera** (jénnərə). *Abbr.* **gen.** **1.** *Biology.* A taxonomic category ranking below a family and above a species, used in taxonomic nomenclature followed by a Latin adjective or epithet to form the name of a species. **2.** *Logic.* A class of objects divided into subordinate species having certain common attributes. **3.** Any class, group, or kind with common attributes. **4.** *Mathematics.* A number denoting the topological complexity of a surface. A sphere has a genus of 0; a torus has a genus of 1. [Latin *genus*, birth, race, kind.]

-geny *n. comb. form.* Indicates manner of origin or development; for example, **ontogeny**. [Greek *-geneia*, from *-genēs*, born.]

geo- *comb. form.* Indicates the Earth; for example, **geotropism**, **geology**. [Greek *geō-*, from *gē*, Earth.]

ge·o·cen·tric (jée-ō-séntrik) *adj.* **1.** Pertaining to, measured from, or observed from the centre of the Earth. **2.** Having the Earth as a centre. **—ge·o·cen·tri·cal·ly** *adv.*

geocentric parallax *n. Astronomy.* **Diurnal parallax** (see).

ge·o·chem·is·try (jée-ō-kémmi-stri) *n.* The science and study of the composition and chemical processes that take place in the Earth's crust. **—ge·o·chem·i·cal** *adj.* **—ge·o·chem·ist** *n.*

ge·o·chro·nol·o·gy (jée-ō-krə-nóllǝji) *n.* The chronology of the Earth's history as determined by geological events.

geod. **1.** geodesy. **2.** geodesic. **3.** geodetic.

ge·ode (jée-ōd) *n.* A small hollow, usually spheroidal, often with crystals lining the inside wall. [Latin *geōdēs*, from Greek, Earthlike : *gē*, Earth + *-ODE* (resembling).]

ge·o·des·ic (jée-ō-déss-ik, -ə-, -déess- ‖ -dézz-, -déez-) *adj.* Also **geo·des·i·cal** (-ik'l). *Abbr.* **geod.** *Mathematics.* Of or pertaining to the geometry of geodesics.

~*n. Mathematics.* In three-dimensional Euclidean space, a curve whose principal normal at any point is the normal to the surface on which the curve occurs; the shortest line between two points on any mathematically derived surface.

geodesic dome *n.* A domed or vaulted structure of lightweight straight elements that form interlocking polygons.

ge·od·e·sy (jee-óddə-si) *n. Abbr.* **geod.** The branch of mathematics concerned with the size and shape of the Earth, including the techniques of measuring distance on the Earth's surface and of determining exact geographical location. [French *geodesie*, from New Latin *geodaesia*, from Greek *geōdaisia*, "division of the Earth" : GEO + *daiesthai*, to divide.] **—ge·od·e·sist** *n.*

ge·o·det·ic (jée-ō-déttik, -ə-) *adj. Abbr.* **geod.** **1.** Of or pertaining to geodesy. **2.** Geodesic. **—ge·o·det·i·cal·ly** *adv.*

ge·o·dy·nam·ics (jée-ō-di-námmiks) *n. Used with a singular verb.* The study of the forces acting inside the Earth's crust and the way in which they affect its formation, alteration, and disturbance. **—ge·o·dy·nam·ic** *n.* **—ge·o·dy·nam·i·cal** *adj.*

Geof·frey of Monmouth (jéffri) (c. 1100–54). English writer. His *History of the Kings of Britain*, tracing an almost entirely fictitious line of descent from the Trojans to King Arthur, recorded much of British folk history and inspired the Arthurian writers and Shakespear's *King Lear* and *Cymbeline*.

geog. **1.** geographer. **2.** geographical. **3.** geography.

ge·o·graph·i·cal (jée-ə-gráff-ik'l) *adj.* Also **ge·o·graph·ic** (-ik). *Abbr.* **geog.** **1.** Pertaining to geography. **2.** Concerning the topography of a specific region. **—ge·o·graph·i·cal·ly** *adv.*

geographical mile *n.* A nautical mile.

ge·og·ra·phy (jee-óggrəfi) *n., pl.* **-phies.** *Abbr.* **geog.** **1. a.** The study of the Earth and its surface features, how they influence human distribution and activity, and how they in turn are affected by human activity. **b.** Broadly, the science of the distribution of all the components of the physical world. **2.** The geographical characteristics of an area. **3.** A book on geography. **4.** An ordered arrangement of constituent elements. [Latin *geōgraphia*, from Greek : GEO + -GRAPHY.] **—ge·og·ra·pher** *n.*

ge·oid (jée-oyd) *n.* **1.** The hypothetical surface of the Earth formed from mean sea level and its continuation through the continents. **2.** A geometrical figure similar to this surface. [German *Geoid*, from Greek *geoidēs*, earthlike : GE(O)- + -OID.]

geol. **1.** geologic. **2.** geologist. **3.** geology.

geological time scale *n.* The division of geological time into chronological units. The last 570–600 million years are divided into the units, **era**, **period**, **epoch**, and **age** (*all of which see*). The time before this is the **Precambrian** (see).

ge·ol·o·gise, ge·ol·o·gize (jee-óllə-jīz) *intr.v.* **-gised, -gising, -gises.** To study geology or make geological investigations.

ge·ol·o·gy (jee-óllǝji) *n., pl.* **-gies.** *Abbr.* **geol.** **1.** The scientific study of the origin, history, structure, and processes of the Earth. **2.** The structure of a specific region of the Earth's surface: *the geology of the Pennines.* [New Latin *geologia* : GEO- + -LOGY.] **—ge·o·log·ic** (jée-ə-lójik), **ge·o·log·i·cal** *adj.* **—ge·o·log·i·cal·ly** *adv.* **—ge·ol·o·gist** (jee-óllǝjist), **ge·ol·o·ger** *n.*

geom. **1.** geometric. **2.** geometry.

geomagnetic equator *n.* The great circle on the Earth's surface formed by the intersection of a plane passing through the Earth's centre perpendicular to the axis connecting the north and south magnetic poles. It is the geometric rationalisation of the empirically defined **magnetic equator** (see).

ge·o·mag·ne·tism (jée-ō-mág-nə-tiz'm) *n.* **1.** The magnetism of the Earth. **2.** The study of the Earth's magnetic field. **—ge·o·mag·net·ic**

(-mag-néttik) *adj.* **—ge·o·mag·net·i·cal·ly** (-mag-néttikli) *adv.*

ge·o·man·cy (jée-ō-man-si, -ə-) *n.* Divination by means of dust patterns, lines and figures, or geographical features. [Middle English, from Old French *geomancie*, from Medieval Latin *geōmantia*, from Late Greek *geōmanteia*, divination from signs obtained from the Earth : GEO- + -MANCY.] **—ge·o·man·cer** *n.* **—ge·o·man·tic** (-mántik) *adj.*

ge·o·me·chan·ics (jée-ō-mi-kánniks) *n. Used with a singular verb.* The study of the mechanics of rock and soil and its application in civil engineering.

ge·om·e·ter (jée-ómmitər) *n.* **1.** A geometrician. **2.** A geometrid.

ge·o·met·ric (jée-ə-métt-rik) *adj.* Also **ge·o·met·ri·cal** (-rik'l). *Abbr.* **geom.** **1.** Of or pertaining to geometry, its methods and principles. **2.** Using simple geometric forms in design and decoration. **—ge·o·met·ri·cal·ly** *adv.* **—ge·o·met·ri·cian** (jée-ómmə-trísh'n, jée-əmə-) *n.*

geometrical isomerism *n.* **Cis-trans isomerism** (*see*).

geometrical optics *n.* The study of reflection, refraction, and other optical phenomena using rays to represent the paths of light without reference to the wave properties of the light.

geometric mean *n.* The *n*th root, usually the positive *n*th root, of a product of *n* factors; for example, the geometric mean of 1, 3, and 9 is the cubic root of $1 \times 3 \times 9$.

geometric progression *n.* A sequence of terms, such as 1, 3, 9, 27, 81, each of which is a constant multiple of the immediately preceding term. Also called "geometric sequence".

geometric series *n.* A sum in which the terms are members of a geometric progression, as in the series $1 + 3 + 9 + 27 + 81 + \ldots$.

ge·om·e·trid (jee-ómmə-trid, jée-ə-méttrid) *n.* Any of various moths of the family Geometridae, having caterpillars that move by looping the body in alternate contractions and expansions and are commonly called "measuring worms", "loopers", or "inchworms".

~*adj.* Of or belonging to the Geometridae. [New Latin *Geometridae*, "land measurers" (from the movement of the caterpillars), from Latin *geōmetrēs*, geometrician, from Greek, from *geōmetrein*, to measure land. See **geometry**.]

ge·om·e·trise, ge·om·e·trize (jee-ómmə-trīz) *v.* **-trised, -trising, -trises.** —*intr.* To study geometry. —*tr.* To apply the methods of geometry to (a physical theory, for example).

ge·om·e·try (jee-ómmətri) *n., pl.* **-tries.** *Abbr.* **geom.** **1. a.** The mathematics of the properties, measurement, and relationships of points, lines, angles, surfaces, and solids. **b.** A system of geometry: *Euclidean geometry.* **c.** A geometry restricted to a class of problems or objects: *solid geometry.* **2.** Configuration; arrangement. **3.** A surface shape. **4.** Any physical arrangement suggesting geometric forms or lines. [Middle English, from Old French *geometrie*, from Latin *geōmetria*, from Greek, from *geōmetrein*, to measure land : GEO- + *metrein*, to measure, from *metron*, measure.] **—ge·om·e·tri·cian** (jee-ómmə-trísh'n, jée-ə-mə-) *n.*

ge·o·mor·phic (jée-ō-mórfik, -ə-) *adj.* Of or like the Earth, its shape, or surface configuration. [GEO- + -MORPHIC.]

ge·o·mor·phol·o·gy (jée-ō-mawr-fóllǝji, -ə-) *n.* The scientific study of the configuration and evolution of land forms. **—ge·o·mor·pho·log·ic** (-mórfǝ-lójik), **ge·o·mor·pho·log·i·cal** *adj.* **—ge·o·mor·pho·log·i·cal·ly** *adv.*

ge·oph·a·gy (jee-óffǝji) *n.* Also **ge·o·phag·ia** (jée-ə-fáy-jə, -ji-ə), **ge·oph·a·gism** (jee-óffə-jiz'm). The practice of eating earthy substances, such as clay. [GEO- + -PHAGY.] **—ge·oph·a·gist** *n.*

ge·o·phys·ics (jée-ō-fízzikss, -ə-) *n. Used with a singular verb.* The physics of the Earth, and of the processes that take place on and within it, sometimes including of fields such as meteorology and climatology and also the physics of the Moon and planets. **—ge·o·phys·i·cal** (-ik'l) *adj.* **—ge·o·phys·i·cist** (-i-sist) *n.*

ge·o·phyte (jée-ō-fīt, -ə-) *n. Botany.* A perennial plant propagated by underground buds. [GEO- + -PHYTE.] **—ge·o·phyt·ic** *adj.*

ge·o·pol·i·tics (jée-ō-póllitikss) *n. Used with a singular verb.* **1.** The study of the relationship between politics and geography. **2.** A Nazi doctrine of expansion that concentrated on the reallocation of geographical, economic, and political boundaries. **—ge·o·po·lit·i·cal** (-pə-líttik'l) *adj.*

ge·o·pon·ic (jée-ō-pónnik, -ə-) *adj.* **1.** Of or relating to agriculture or farming. **2.** Rustic; bucolic. [Greek *geōponikos*, from *geōponia*, tillage, from *geōponein*, to till land : GEO- + *ponein*, to toil, labour.]

ge·o·pon·ics (jée-ō-pónnikss, -ə-) *n. Used with a singular verb.* The study or science of agriculture.

Geor·die (jórdi) *n.* **1.** A person who lives on Tyneside, or comes from that region. **2.** The distinctive accent or dialect of people from Tyneside.

~*adj.* Of or pertaining to Tyneside, its people, or their accent or dialect.

George (jorj) *n. British Informal.* The automatic pilot system in an aeroplane.

George I (1660–1727). Elector of Hanover (1698–1727), and king of Great Britain and Ireland (1714–27). As a Protestant, he was offered the British throne in 1714, the Roman Catholic James Stuart having been excluded by Parliament. He left the running of the country to his Whig ministers, the chief of whom, Sir Robert Walpole, is regarded as Britain's first prime minister.

George II (1683–1760). King of Great Britain and Ireland and Elector of Hanover (1727–60). His victory at the Battle of Dettingen (1743) was the last time that a British monarch led his troops in the field.

George III (1738–1820). King of Great Britain and Ireland

(1760–1820), and of Hanover (Elector 1760–1815; King 1815–20). His attempts to interfere in government were instrumental in the loss of the American colonies (1776).

George IV (1762–1830). King of Great Britain and Ireland (1820–30), and of Hanover. As regent during his father's 30-year long mental and physical illness, he patronised art and fashion, but scandals brought the monarchy into disrepute.

George V (1865–1936). King of Great Britain and Ireland and the British Commonwealth, and Emperor of India (1910–36). He changed the name of the royal house to Windsor in World War I. In 1932 he made the first of the monarch's Christmas broadcasts on the radio.

George VI (1895–1952). King of the United Kingdom and the British Commonwealth (1936-52), and Emperor of India (1936–47). He acceded to the throne on the abdication of his brother, Edward VIII, and he won enormous popularity thanks to his dedication to his duties as a constitutional monarch.

George Cross *n. Abbr.* **G.C.**. A British civilian award for bravery.

George Town (jórj-town). Also **Pinang** (pi-náng) or **Penang**. City in northwest Malaysia. The capital of Pinang state, and the chief port, exporting tin, rubber, and copra. It became part of the Straits Settlements in 1867, joining the Federation of Malaya in 1948.

George·town (jórj-town ‖ *locally* -tung). Capital and chief port of Guyana, situated at the mouth of the Demerara river.

geor·gette (jawr-jét) *n.* A sheer, strong, silk or silklike crepe fabric with a dull surface, used for dresses, blouses, or trimming. Also called "georgette crepe". [Originally a trademark, after Madame *Georgette* de la Plante, a French modiste.]

Geor·gia (jór-ji-ə, -jə). State in the southeast of the United States. Named after George II, it was founded in 1732, the youngest of the thirteen original colonies. As a supporter of the Confederate cause, it suffered considerable damage in the American Civil War. In the 20th century it has experienced many of the social and economic problems of the South with the decline of the cotton industry and racial unrest. Atlanta is the state capital.

Georgia, Republic of. Former constituent republic of the U.S.S.R. on the Black Sea. An independent kingdom in the Middle Ages, it was invaded by the Mongols in 1234, divided between Persia and Turkey in 1555, and annexed by Russia in the 19th century. Independent in 1918, it joined the U.S.S.R. in 1922 as a member of the Transcaucasian S.F.S.R., becoming a separate republic in 1936. It gained full independence again in 1991, but civil war between its ethnic elements ensued. In 1993 Georgia joined the Commonwealth of Independent States. Georgia is rich in minerals, especially manganese, coal, oil, and gold. Area, 69 700 square kilometres (26,911 square miles). Population, 5,410,000. Capital, T'bilisi. See map at **Caucasus**.

Geor·gian (jór-ji-ən, -jən) *adj.* **1.** Of, pertaining to, or characteristic of any of the reigns of the four Georges who ruled Great Britain from 1714 to 1830; especially, of or pertaining to the architectural style of this period, characterised by plain, symmetrical facades including many classical features. **2.** Of, pertaining to, or characteristic of the reign of King George V of Great Britain: *Georgian poetry.* **3.** Pertaining to the U.S. state of Georgia or to its inhabitants. **4.** Pertaining to the Republic of Georgia, or to its people or their language.
~ *n.* **1.** A native or inhabitant of the U.S. state of Georgia. **2.** A native or inhabitant of the Republic of Georgia. **3.** The Caucasian language of the Republic of Georgia **4.** A person belonging to or whose style is imitative of the period of any of the reigns of the Georges in Great Britain.

Georgian Bay. Large bay of Lake Huron in Ontario, Canada. Forty islands and part of the mainland comprise the Georgian Bay Islands National Park.

geor·gic (jórjik) *adj.* Of or pertaining to agriculture or rural life.
~ *n.* **1.** *Capital G. Plural.* A poem by Virgil in four books, concerning agriculture and country life. **2.** Any poem concerning farming or rural life; a bucolic. [Latin *Georgica,* from Greek *geōrgika,* cultivated lands, from neuter plural of *geōrgikos,* agricultural, from *geōrgos,* farmer, "(one) tilling the soil" : GEO- + *ergon,* work.]

ge·o·sci·ence (jée-ō-sí-ənss) *n.* The science of the Earth, including geology, geophysics, oceanography, and applied sciences such as mining and engineering geology. Sometimes meteorology, climatology, and similar subjects are included.

ge·o·stat·ics (jée-ō-státtiks) *n. Used with a singular verb.* The study of the forces within the Earth, as, for example, the pressure exerted by rock or soil. —**ge·o·stat·ic** *adj.*

ge·o·sta·tion·ar·y (jée-ō-stáysh'n-əri, -ri ‖ -erri) *adj.* Of, pertaining to, or designating an artificial satellite that maintains a constant position above a point on the Earth's equator.

ge·o·stroph·ic (jée-ō-stróffik, -ə-) *adj.* Of or pertaining to or caused by the Earth's rotation: *a geostrophic wind.* [GEO- + Greek *strophē,* a turning, STROPHE.]

ge·o·syn·chro·nous (jée-ō-síng-krənəss) *adj.* Of or pertaining to an artificial satellite that orbits the Earth in the same direction as the Earth's rotation and with an orbital period equal to the Earth's rotation period.

ge·o·syn·cline (jée-ō-sín-klīn) *n.* An extensive, usually linear depression in the Earth's crust in which sedimentation takes place, and which subsides under the weight.

ge·o·tax·is (jée-ō-ták-siss) *n. Biology.* The movement of an organism in response to the forces of gravity. —**ge·o·tac·tic** (-ták-tik) *adj.* —**ge·o·tac·ti·cal·ly** *adv.*

ge·o·tec·ton·ic (jée-ō-tek-tónnik) *adj.* Of or relating to the mode of formation, shape, structure, and arrangement of the rock masses constituting the Earth's crust.

ge·o·ther·mal (jée-ō-thér-m'l) *adj.* Also **ge·o·ther·mic** (-mik). Pertaining to the internal heat of the Earth. —**ge·o·ther·mal·ly** *adv.*

geothermal power *n.* Heat originating in the Earth's interior, as in volcanoes or geysers, and used as a source of energy.

ge·ot·ro·pism (jee-óttrə-piz'm) *n. Biology.* The response of a plant organ to gravity, as the downward growth of plant roots (*positive geotropism*). [GEO- + -TROPISM.] —**ge·o·trop·ic** (jée-ō-tróppik, -ə-, -trópik) *adj.* —**ge·o·trop·i·cal·ly** *adv.*

ger. gerund.

Ger. **1.** German. **2.** Germany.

ge·rah (géer-ə) *n.* **1.** An ancient Hebrew coin and unit of weight; ¹⁄₂₀ of an ancient shekel. **2.** An ancient Hebrew unit of weight. [Hebrew *gērāh,* "bean".]

ge·ra·ni·al (jə-ráyni-əl, -al) *n.* A perfume and flavouring ingredient, an isomer of **citral** (*see*). [GERANI(UM) + -AL (aldehyde).]

ge·ra·ni·ol (jə-ráyni-ol, -raáni- ‖ -ōl) *n.* A fragrant pale yellow liquid, $C_{10}H_{18}O$, derived chiefly from the oils of geranium and citronella, and used in cosmetics and flavourings. [GERANI(UM) + -OL (alcohol).]

ge·ra·ni·um (jə-ráyni-əm) *n.* **1.** Any of various plants of the genus *Pelargonium,* native chiefly to southern Africa; especially, *P. domesticum,* widely cultivated for its rounded, often variegated leaves and showy clusters of red, pink, or white flowers. **2.** Any of various plants of the genus *Geranium,* having divided leaves and pink or purplish flowers. See **cranesbill**. **3.** Strong to vivid red. [Latin, from Greek *geranion,* "small crane" (because the fruit resembles a crane's bill), from *geranos,* crane.]

ger·a·tol·o·gy (jérrə-tólləji) *n.* The branch of medicine concerned with the study of the ageing process and the problems and diseases associated with it. [Greek *gēras* (stem *gērat-*), old age + -LOGY.]

ger·bil (jérbil) *n.* Any of various small, mouselike rodents of the genus *Gerbillus* and related genera, of arid regions of Africa and Asia Minor, having long hind legs and a long tail. [French *gerbille,* from New Latin *Gerbillus,* diminutive of *gerboa, jerboa,* JERBOA.]

ge·rent (jéer-ənt, jérrənt) *n. Rare.* A ruler or manager; an overseer. [Latin *gerēns* (stem *gerent-*), present participle of *gerere,* to carry, conduct, govern.]

ge·re·nuk (gérri-nōok) *n.* An African gazelle, *Litocranius walleri,* having long legs, a long, slender neck, and backward curving horns in the male. [Somali *garanug.*]

gerfalcon. Variant of **gyrfalcon**.

ger·i·at·ric (jérri-áttrik ‖ jeeri-) *adj.* Of or pertaining to the aged or to geriatrics. Sometimes used derogatorily.
~ *n.* An aged person, especially one requiring medical or social care. Sometimes used derogatorily. [Greek *gēras,* old age + -IATRIC.]

ger·i·at·rics (jérri-áttrikss ‖ jéeri-) *n. Used with a singular verb.* The branch of medicine concerned with the diagnosis and treatment of diseases of the elderly. —**ger·i·a·tri·cian** (-ə-trísh'n), **ger·i·at·rist** (-áttrist ‖ *U.S. also* jə-rí-ə-trist) *n.*

Gé·ri·cault (zherri-kō), **Théodore** (1791–1824). French painter. His most famous work, *The Raft of the Medusa* (1819), portrayed an actual maritime disaster which had caused a political scandal.

germ (jerm) *n.* **1.** A microorganism such as a bacterium or virus, especially one causing disease. **2.** *Biology.* A small organic structure or cell from which a new organism may develop. **3.** Something that may serve as the basis of further growth or development: *the germ of an idea.* [French *germe,* from Latin *germen,* offshoot, sprout, foetus.]

Usage: Germ, microbe, bacteria, bacillus, virus are nouns denoting minute organisms or agents, invisible to the unaided human eye, some of which are related to the production of disease. They are not interchangeable in careful usage except as indicated. *Germ* and *microbe* are nonscientific terms for such microorganisms; in popular usage they usually refer to disease-producing bodies. *Bacteria* (plural of *bacterium*) is the scientific term for a large group of microorganisms, only some of which produce disease. Many others are active in processes beneficial or not harmful to human, animal, and plant life. *Bacillus* is the scientific designation for a specific class of bacteria that includes some disease-producing microorganisms; only in loose popular usage is the term employed as the equivalent of any bacterium or any pathogenic bacterium. *Virus* is the technical term for any of a group of extremely small agents capable of producing certain diseases in human, animal, and plant life.

ger·man (jérmən) *adj.* **1.** Having the same parents, or having the same grandparents on one side. Obsolete except as the second element in combinations: *cousin-german.* **2.** *Rare.* Related; germane. [Middle English *germa(i)n,* from Old French *germain,* from Latin *germānus,* "from the same race", from *germen,* offshoot, foetus.]

Ger·man (jérmən) *adj. Abbr.* **Ger.** Of, pertaining to, or characteristic of Germany, its people, or their language.
~ *n. Abbr.* **Ger.** **1. a.** A native or citizen of Germany. **b.** A person of German descent. **c.** A person who speaks German as his native language. **2.** The West Germanic language spoken in Germany, Austria, and part of Switzerland. [Middle English *Germanes,* Teutons, Germans, from Latin *Germānus,* German, perhaps from Celtic, akin to Old Irish *gairt,* neighbour.]

German cockroach *n.* A small cockroach, *Blatella germanica,* that is a common household pest.

German Democratic Republic. See **Germany**.

ger·man·der (jer-mándər, jər-) *n.* Any of various usually aromatic plants of the genus *Teucrium,* having purplish or reddish two-lipped flowers. [Middle English *germandre,* from Old French *germandree,* from Medieval Latin *germandra,* alteration of *gama(n)drea,* from Latin *chamadreos,* from Greek *khamaidrus,* "ground oak" : *khamai,* on the ground + *drus,* oak.]

germander speedwell *n.* A creeping Eurasian plant, *Veronica chamaedrys,* having small blue flowers with white centres.

ger·mane (jer-máyn) *adj.* Having a bearing upon a point at issue; related; pertinent. Usually used with *to.* See Synonyms at **relevant.** [Middle English *germa(i)n,* having the same parents, GERMAN.]

ger·man·ic (jer-mánnik, jər-) *n.* Of or pertaining to germanium. Said especially of compounds that contain germanium with a valency of 4. [GERMANIUM + -IC.]

Ger·man·ic (jer-mánnik, jər-) *adj.* 1. a. Characteristic of Germany, any of the German people, or their culture. b. Of or pertaining to Teutons. c. Of or pertaining to a Germanic-speaking people. 2. Of, pertaining to, or constituting Germanic.
~*n.* 1. A branch of the Indo-European language family, divided into North, West, and East Germanic. It includes English, Dutch, German, and the Scandinavian languages. 2. The unrecorded ancestor language of this branch, **Proto-Germanic** *(see).*

Ger·man·ise, Ger·man·ize (jérmə-nīz) *v.* **-ised, -ising, -ises.** —*tr.* 1. To give a German quality or character to; make German. 2. *Archaic.* To translate into German. —*intr.* To adopt German customs or attitudes. —**Ger·man·i·sa·tion** (-nī-záysh'n ‖ *U.S.* -ni-) *n.* —**Ger·man·is·er** *n.*

Ger·man·ism (jérmə-niz'm) *n.* 1. An attitude, custom, or practice that seems characteristically German. 2. A German idiom or phrasing that is literally translated into another language. 3. Esteem for Germany and emulation of German ways.

ger·man·ite (jérmə-nīt) *n.* A mineral consisting of a complex sulphide of copper and arsenic with small amounts of germanium, gallium, and other metals. It is an ore of germanium and gallium. [GERMANIUM + -ITE.]

ger·ma·ni·um (jer-máyni-əm, jər-) *n. Symbol* **Ge** A brittle, crystalline, grey-white metalloid element, widely used as a semiconductor, as an alloying agent and catalyst, and in certain optical glasses. Atomic number 32, atomic weight 72.59, melting point 937.4°C, boiling point 2,830°C, relative density 5.323 (25°C), valencies 2, 4. [New Latin, from Latin *Germānia,* Germany, from Latin *Germānus,* GERMAN.]

German measles *n.* A mild, contagious, eruptive disease caused by a virus. It can cause early congenital defects in infants born to mothers infected during pregnancy. Also called "rubella".

Ger·man·o·phile (jer-mánnə-fīl, jər-) *n.* One who loves or admires Germany, the Germans, or German ways. [Latin *Germānus,* GERMAN + -PHILE.]

Ger·man·o·phobe (jer-mánnə-fōb, jər-) *n.* One who hates or has an obsessive fear of Germany, the Germans, or German ways. [Latin *Germānus,* GERMAN + -PHOBE.]

ger·man·ous (jer-mánnəss, -máynəss) *n.* Of or pertaining to germanium. Said especially of compounds that contain germanium with a valency of 2.

German shepherd *n.* A large breed of dog with a thick brownish coat, often used as a guard dog, a police dog, or as a guide-dog for the blind. Also called "alsatian".

German silver *n.* An alloy, **nickel silver** *(see).*

Ger·ma·ny (jérməni). German **Deutsch·land** (dóychlant). Country in central Europe. Occupied from *c.* 500 B.C. by Germanic tribes, it had become part of the kingdom of the Franks by the time of Charlemagne. After the death of Charlemagne in 814, Germany became a loose federation of principalities. This was strengthened under the Saxon dynasty. The third in this line of rulers, Otto I, was crowned Holy Roman Emperor by Pope John XII in 962. By the 14th century Germany's frontiers extended as far east as the Vistula. The 16th and 17th centuries, however, were dominated by religious strife and dynastic feuds culminating in the Thirty Years War (1618–48) which left Germany divided into a predominantly Roman Catholic south and a Protestant north. In 1806 Napoleon finally broke up the Empire and united the country. From 1815 Germany was a confederation, with Prussia being the dominant state. Under Bismarck, Prussia defeated Austria in 1866 and France in 1871, and Bismarck realised his dream of a united German Empire with the Prussian king as hereditary ruler.
Rapid industrialisation and colonial expansion took place in the late 19th and early 20th centuries; the international aspirations were a major cause of World War I (1914–18). Following defeat in 1918, the Empire was dissolved and the Weimar Republic established. By the end of the 1920s, the depressed economy facilitated Hitler's rise to power. His aggressive and expansionist foreign policy led to the outbreak of World War II in 1939, defeat by the Allies in 1945, and a subsequent split into the Federal Republic of Germany (West Germany) and the German Democratic Republic (East Germany).
West Germany, with Bonn as its capital, expanded its economy rapidly from 1948 with substantial American aid. It was a full member of NATO from 1955 and the EEC from 1958.
East Germany, with East Berlin as its capital, became an independent Communist state, and suffered economic austerity and curbs on civil liberties. The Berlin Wall was erected in 1961 to stop mass migration to West Germany.
In 1989, with Soviet control over Eastern Europe relaxing, pro-democracy demonstrations in East Germany led to free elections; and in 1990 reunification of the two Germanys took place.
Industries include iron, steel, mining, chemicals, motor vehicles, shipbuilding, textiles, and precision instruments. Area, 356 974 square kilometres (137,828 square miles). Population, 81,910,000. Capital, Berlin. Temporary seat of government, Bonn. See map, next page.

germ cell *n.* A cell having reproduction as its principal function; especially, an egg or sperm cell.

ger·mi·cide (jérmi-sīd) *n.* Any substance that kills germs. [GERM + -CIDE.] —**ger·mi·ci·dal** (-sīd'l) *adj.*

ger·mi·nal (jérmin'l) *adj.* 1. Of, pertaining to, or having the nature of a germ cell. 2. Of, in, or pertaining to the earliest stage of development; embryonic. [French, from Latin *germen* (stem *germin-*), offshoot, GERM.]

germinal disc *n. Biology.* A disclike region from which the embryo begins to develop in certain ova. Also called "blastodisc".

germinal epithelium *n.* The epithelium of the ovary or testis, containing cells that develop into ova or spermatozoa.

germinal vesicle *n. Biology.* The nucleus of an oocyte.

ger·mi·nant (jérminənt) *adj.* Germinating; sprouting.

ger·mi·nate (jérmi-nayt) *v.* **-nated, -nating, -nates.** —*intr.* 1. *Biology.* To begin to grow; sprout. 2. To develop or grow: *His hatred germinated slowly.* 3. To come into being; be born: *The conspiracy germinated in the pub one night.* —*tr.* 1. *Biology.* To cause (seeds or spores) to sprout. 2. To cause to grow; cultivate; develop. 3. To bring into existence; initiate; produce. [Latin *germināre,* to sprout, from *germen* (stem *germin-*), sprout, GERM.] —**ger·mi·na·ble** (-nəb'l), **ger·mi·na·tive** (-nətiv, -naytiv) *adj.* —**ger·mi·na·tion** (-náysh'n) *n.* —**ger·mi·na·tor** (-naytər) *n.*

Ger·mis·ton (jérmisstən). Town in the Transvaal in South Africa. It has the world's largest gold refinery.

germ layer *n.* Any of three cellular layers, the **ectoderm, endoderm,** or **mesoderm** *(all of which see),* into which most animal embryos differentiate.

germ plasm *n.* 1. The protoplasm of an egg cell, especially that part containing the hereditary material. 2. Germ cells collectively. 3. The hereditary material postulated by Weismann and other 19th-century biologists, thought to be transmitted in the germ cells and to remain unchanged from one generation to the next.

germ theory *n.* 1. The doctrine that infectious diseases are caused by the activity of microorganisms within the body. 2. The theory that living organisms can only develop from other living organisms through the fusion and subsequent differentiation of germ cells.

germ warfare *n.* **Biological warfare** *(see).*

Ger·on·i·mo (jə-rónni-mō), *Apache* Goyathlay (1829–1909). Apache chief. From 1871 to 1886 he led the Chiricahua Apaches in daring guerrilla campaigns against the U.S. and Mexican governments. His name has been adopted as the war-cry of U.S. paratroops.

geronto-, geront- *comb. form.* Indicates old people or old age; for example, **gerontology.** [French *géronto-,* from Greek *gerōn* (stem *geront-*), old man.]

ger·on·toc·ra·cy (jérr-on-tóckra-si, gérr-, -ən-) *n., pl.* **-cies.** 1. Government based on rule by old men. 2. A governing group of old men. [French *gérontocratie* : GERONTO- + -CRACY.] —**ge·ron·to·crat·ic** (jə-rónta-kráttik, gə-) *adj.*

ger·on·tol·o·gy (jérr-on-tólləji, -gérr-, -ən-) *n.* The study of the diseases and other phenomena associated with old age. [GERONTO- + -LOGY.] —**ger·on·to·log·i·cal** (jə-rónta-lójik'l, gə-) *adj.* —**ger·on·tol·o·gist** *n.*

ger·ry·man·der (jérri-mandər, -mándər) *v.* **-dered, -dering, -ders.** —*intr.* To divide a constituency, county, or city into voting districts so as to give unfair advantage to one party in elections. —*tr.* 1. To divide (a voting area) in this manner. 2. To machinate or alter to one's own advantage.
~*n.* An act or product of gerrymandering. [From Elbridge *Gerry,* 18th-century U.S. politician + (SALA)MANDER, from the shape of an election district formed (1812) in Massachusetts while Gerry was governor.]

Gersh·win (gérshwin), **George,** born Jacob Gershvin (1898–1937). U.S. composer. A master of most forms of popular music of his day, he is best known for his experiments in orchestral jazz, notably *Rhapsody in Blue* (1924), and the black American opera *Porgy and Bess* (1935), co-written (like more than 20 musicals) with his brother Ira, born Israel (1896–1983), a gifted lyricist.

ger·und (jérr-ənd, -und) *n. Abbr.* **ger.** 1. In Latin, a verbal form that can be used as a noun in all singular cases except the nominative, while conveying the meaning of the verb; for example, in the phrase *modus vivendi* (a manner of living), *vivendi* is a gerund, formed from the verb *vivere,* to live. 2. In English, the verbal form ending in -*ing* when used as a noun, while conveying the meaning of the verb; for example, in the sentences *Cooking is an art* and *I don't like cooking, cooking* is a gerund formed from the verb *cook.* 3. The analogous grammatical form in some other languages. [Late Latin *gerundium,* from Latin *gerundum, gerendum,* acting, carrying, gerund of *gerere,* to carry, act.] —**ge·run·di·al** (jə-rúndi-əl) *adj.*

Usage: When a verb form ending in -*ing* is used as a noun it raises different problems of usage from when it is used as a verb (see also **participle**). The -*ing* form used as a noun (or *gerund,* as it is known in traditional grammar) is illustrated in *The inspector objected to my going.* In formal English, the possessive form of the item preceding the gerund is standard, and this involves the use of the apostrophe when the item is a noun, as in *He objected to John's going.* Informal English, on the other hand, often uses the neutral

GERMANY

form, as in *He objected to me/John going*. Even in formal English the use of the possessive is sometimes very awkward or impossible, as in *His absence prevented anything (not anything's) being accomplished*. In such cases it is usually recommended that the construction be rephrased (for example, *prevented the accomplishment of anything*). Similarly, in cases where the addition of an *'s* would lead to ambiguity it is generally avoided: *He objected to his son leaving the room*, where *son's* might be confused with *sons*. It is also not used when there is an irregular plural noun: *the problems of mice (not mice's) damaging the wires*.

ge·run·dive (jə-rúndiv) *n.* **1.** In Latin, a verbal adjective with the construction of a future passive participle, suggesting appropriateness, necessity, or imminence; for example, in the sentence *Legibus parendum est* ("The laws must be obeyed" or "The laws are to be obeyed"), *parendum* is a gerundive. **2.** The analogous grammatical form or construction in some other languages.
~*adj.* Pertaining to or like a gerund or gerundive. [Middle English *gerundif*, from Late Latin *gerundivus*, from *gerundium*, GERUND.]

Ge·ry·on (gérri-ən). *Greek Mythology.* A monster with three heads and upper bodies who was robbed of his herd of cattle and slain by Hercules as the tenth of his labours.

ges·so (jéssō) *n.* **1.** A preparation of plaster of Paris and glue used

as a base for low relief sculpting or as a surface for painting. **2.** A surface of this preparation. [Italian, gypsum, chalk, from Latin *gypsum*, GYPSUM.]

gest, geste¹ (jest) *n. Archaic.* **1.** A feat or exploit; a notable deed. **2. a.** A verse romance or tale. **b.** A prose romance. [Middle English *geste, jeste,* from Old French, from Latin *gesta,* actions, exploits, from *gestus,* past participle of *gerere,* to act, carry.]

gest, geste² *n. Archaic.* **1.** Mien or bearing. **2.** A gesture. [Old French *geste,* from Latin *gestus.* See **gesture.**]

ge·stalt (gə-shtaált, -shtált ‖ -shtáwlt) *n., pl.* **-stalts** or **-stalten** (-shtaál-tən, -shtál- ‖ -shtáwl-). *Often capital* **G.** **1.** A unified physical, psychological, or symbolic configuration having properties that cannot be derived from its parts. **2.** *U.S. Informal.* Any complicated combination, especially of the experiences that go to constitute a relationship or personal experience. [German *Gestalt,* form, shape, from Middle High German *gestalt,* from *ungestalt,* deformity, from Old High German *ungistalt,* ugly : *un-,* not + *gistalt,* past participle of *stellen,* to set, place.]

gestalt psychology *n. Often capital* **G.** A school or doctrine of psychology holding that psychological phenomena are made up of irreducible gestalts.

Ge·sta·po (ge-staápō; *German* ge-shtaápō) *n.* The notorious German security police as organised under the Nazi regime. [German, short for *Ge(heime) Sta(ats)po(lizei),* "secret state police".]

Ges·ta Ro·ma·no·rum (jéstə rōmə-náwr-əm || -nŏr-) *n.* An anthology of popular tales in Latin, collected in England in the late 13th or early 14th century, and used as a source by preachers and by Chaucer and Shakespeare. [Latin, "deeds of the Romans".]

ges·tate (je-stáyt || jéss-tayt) *v.* **-tated, -tating, -tates.** *—tr.* **1.** To carry (unborn young) within the uterus for a period following conception. **2.** To conceive and develop (a plan or idea, for example) in the mind. *—intr.* **1.** To carry unborn young for a period following conception; be pregnant. **2.** To develop slowly in a person's mind, as an idea or plot might. [Back-formation from GESTATION.]

ges·ta·tion (je-stáysh'n) *n.* **1.** The period during which an embryo grows and develops in the uterus between conception and birth; pregnancy. **2.** The development or duration of development of a plan or idea in the mind. [Latin *gestātiō* (stem *gestatiōn-*), from *gestāre,* frequentative of *gerere* (past participle *gestus*), to carry, bear.] **—ges·ta·to·ry** (jéstə-təri, -tri, je-stáytəri) *adj.*

ges·tic·u·late (je-stíckew-layt) *v.* **-lated, -lating, -lates.** *—intr.* To make animated and vigorous motions or gestures, especially as an expression complementing or substituting for speech. *—tr.* To say or express by gestures. [Latin *gesticulārī,* from *gesticulus,* diminutive of *gestus,* action, GEST.] **—ges·tic·u·la·tive** (-lə-tiv || -laytiv) *adj.* **—ges·tic·u·la·tor** (-laytər) *n.*

ges·tic·u·la·tion (je-stíckew-láysh'n) *n.* **1.** The act of gesticulating. **2.** A deliberate and vigorous motion or gesture. **—ges·tic·u·la·to·ry** (-lə-tri, -lay-, -təri) *adj.*

ges·ture (jéss-chər) *n.* **1.** A motion of the limbs or body made to express or help express thought or to emphasise speech. **2.** The use of such motions as a means of expression. **3.** Any act or expression made as a sign, often formal, of intention or attitude: *a gesture of friendship; a mere gesture.*
~*v.* **gestured, -turing, -tures.** *—intr.* To make gestures. *—tr.* To show, express, or direct by gestures. [Medieval Latin *gestūra,* bearing, carriage, from Latin *gestus,* past participle of *gerere,* to carry, act.] **—ges·tur·er** *n.*

Ge·sund·heit (gə-zŏŏnt-hīt) *interj. German.* Used to wish good health to a person who has just sneezed. [Literally, "(good) health".]

get[1] (get; git *for intransitive sense 6*) *v.* **got** (got) or *archaic* **gat** (gat), **got** or *chiefly U.S.* **gotten** (gótt'n), **getting, gets.** *—tr.* **1.** To obtain or acquire. **2.** To procure; gain; secure. **3.** To go after; fetch; retrieve. **4.** To reach or make contact with by or as if by radio or telephone. **5.** To earn; gain: *get a reward.* **6.** To receive or come into possession of: *get a present.* **7.** To buy. **8.** To incur: *get a tongue-lashing.* **9.** *Informal.* To meet with; suffer: *He got a few knocks, but he'll recover.* **10.** To catch; contract: *They all got chicken pox at once.* **11.** To have or reach by calculation: *If you add them, you'll get 1,000.* **12.** To have obtained or received and possess. Used only in the form of the perfect, and generally equivalent to *have*: *I've got a large collection of books.* **13.** *U.S. Informal.* To possess or gain understanding or mastery of by study: *I must get this by heart.* **14.** To understand; comprehend: *Do you get his point?* **15.** *Informal.* To register or catch, as by eye or ear: *I'm sorry, I didn't get your name.* **16.** *Informal.* To understand the meaning of a remark made by (a person): *I don't quite get you.* **17.** To put: *get your hat on.* **18.** To cause to become or to be in a specified condition: *He can get the hook loose; get a friend into trouble.* **19.** To cause to move, come, or go: *Get that dog out of here!* **20. a.** To bring: *I'll get him in here, and you can talk to him.* **b.** To gather: *get a few clothes together.* **21.** To induce or persuade; prevail upon: *I'll get my friend to show you his house.* **22.** To overpower; destroy: *Frost got our tomato crop.* **23.** To capture or catch: *The police got him.* **24.** *Slang.* To cause harm to; especially, to reciprocate by causing harm to: *I'll get you for that remark.* **25.** *Informal.* To strike or hit: *That blow got him on the chin.* **26. a.** In cricket, baseball, or similar games, to dismiss or put out: *The bowler got him out with an off-spin.* **b.** In Rugby football and similar games, to tackle; touch. **27.** *Slang.* To baffle; puzzle: *you've got me on that one!* **28.** *Slang.* To elicit a strong, usually negative reaction in: *Noisy eaters really get me.* **29.** To catch (a scheduled train or plane, for example). **30.** To have the obligation; be constrained. Used only in the form of the present perfect, and equivalent to *must*: *I have got to go.* *—intr.* **1.** To become, as by: **a.** Change: *get well again; get angry.* **b.** Movement: *get out of earshot.* **c.** Endeavour: *get to be chairman; get into Parliament.* **2.** To move as specified: *get down from the ladder; get off the bus; get out.* **3.** To continue or proceed. Used with *back to, on,* or *on with*: *get back to work; get on with the job.* **4.** To arrive at or reach a particular point. Often used with *in, into,* or *to*: *The train gets in at midnight; get to the end.* **5.** *Informal.* To start: *Get going!* **6.** *Regional & Informal.* To be off; depart: *Now get!* **7.** To work for gain or profit; make money: *He spends all his time getting and spending.* **—get about** or **around. 1.** *Informal.* **a.** To be active socially; go to many social events. **b.** To have many lovers. **2.** To spread or travel. Used of a rumour or news. **—get across. 1.** To make understandable or clear: *Am I getting this across to you?* **2.** To be clear or understandable: *It's not getting across to him.* **3.** To communicate one's meaning or personality, as to an audience. **—get ahead.** To be successful; attain prosperity. **—get along. 1.** To be mutually congenial; be at harmony. **2.** To manage or fare with reasonable success: *He hasn't much money, but he gets along.* **3.** To make progress; advance; improve. **—get at. 1.** To reach; find a way to: *It's under the desk and I can't get at it.* **2.** To lead up to or imply, as a conclusion or meaning: *Do you understand what I'm getting at?* **3.** To nag or criticise persistently: *she's always getting at me.* **4.** *Informal.* To influence, especially by bribery. **—get away with.** *Informal.* To be successful in avoiding the discovery of (something done that deserves punishment). **—get back at.** *Informal.* To retaliate against or have revenge on: *He swears he'll get back at him.* **—get by.** To manage; survive; fare: *It will be a hard year, but we'll get by.* **—get down. 1.** To take cover; duck; hide. **2.** To write (something) down. **3.** To depress or demoralise: *You mustn't let a small setback get you down.* **4.** To succeed in swallowing: *The pill was too big for him to get down.* **—get down to.** To begin doing; actively engage in: *They got down to some serious thinking.* **—get in. 1.** *Slang.* To gain the favour of. Used with *with*: *He will get in with that teacher.* **2.** To become involved in or part of. Used with *with*: *She wants to get in with a different crowd.* **3.** To be elected. **—get into.** *Informal.* **1.** To cause an alteration in the behaviour of: *I don't know what's got into her today.* **2.** To develop an interest in or enthusiasm for: *I'm really getting into my new job.* **—get it. 1.** To comprehend; understand. **2.** *Informal.* To be punished or scolded. **—get nowhere.** To make no progress; have no success. **—get off. 1.** To send (a letter, for example). **2.** To escape, as from punishment or labour: *He got off scot-free.* **3.** To gain an acquittal for (a person). **4.** *Informal.* To desist from unreasonable, foolish, or irritating talk. Used in the imperative. **5.** To stop taking or using (an addictive drug, for example). **—get off on.** *Slang.* **1.** To reach a state of euphoric consciousness through; get high on: *get off on acid.* **2.** To be stimulated or excited by; enjoy greatly: *get off on Mozart.* **—get off with.** *Informal.* To begin a sexual relationship with (a person). **—get on. 1.** To succeed; fare well. **2.** To advance. Used of time or ageing: *It's getting on towards noon; He's getting on in years.* **3.** To be friendly or well-disposed towards another or each other. Often used with *with.* **—get onto. 1.** *Informal.* To make contact with or communicate with: *I'll get onto the accounts department and find out.* **2.** To discover or become aware of (especially something secret or illegal). **3.** To begin to discuss or work at. **—get out of. 1.** To derive or draw: *He gets out of it what he can.* **2.** To avoid or get round. **—get over. 1.** To recover from (a sorrow or illness, for example). **2.** To overcome or rise above (a difficulty): *He'll soon get over his unfamiliarity with our procedures.* **3.** To complete (especially something unpleasant). Often used with *with*: *Let's get the shopping over with first.* **4.** To communicate (especially something difficult); get across: *That's what I'm trying to get over to you.* **—get round.** *Informal.* **1.** To avoid or circumvent (a problem, obstacle, or the like). **2.** To persuade or convince by wheedling or flattering. **3.** To consider or deal with after an initial delay. **—get somewhere.** To make progress; achieve success. **—get there.** *Informal.* To attain one's goal. **—get through. 1.** To finish or complete. **2.** To undergo and survive: *I wonder if that tree will get through the winter.* **3.** To reach a destination, especially in the face of difficulties. **4.** To pass an examination. **5.** To succeed in making contact by telephone. Often used with *to.* **6.** To use up or spend (petrol or money, for example). **—get through to.** To make oneself or something understandable or apparent to. **—get to. 1.** To have the opportunity of or be able to: *I hope I get to go.* **2.** *Informal.* To happen to start; begin: *Then we got to remembering good times.* **3.** *Slang.* To impress or affect emotionally: *her singing really gets to me.* **—get with it.** *Slang.* To become up-to-date. **—have got.** To own or possess.
~*n. Rare.* **1.** The act of begetting. **2.** Progeny; offspring. [Get, got, got; Middle English *getten, gat, getten,* from Old Norse *geta, gat, getinn.*] **—get·a·ble, get·ta·ble** *adj.*

Usage: *Got* has attracted much criticism, especially the use of *have got* instead of *have* in spoken English. The *have got* form is usual in informal British English (*How many books have you got?*), and alternatives sound much more formal (*How many books do you have?*) and sometimes even archaic (*How many books have you?*). The *got* form sometimes allows a degree of emphasis, reinforcing the notion of obligation, which the *have* form lacks: *You've got to do it! Have you got to go?*

Gotten is a common past participle form in American English, but it is not used when the senses involved are those of obligation or possession, as in *I've got to go* and *I've got one in my hand. I've gotten a new car* means "I have just obtained" and *I've gotten to do it* means "I have succeeded in doing it". In such cases, British English would use a different verb.

get[2], **gett** *n.* A Jewish bill of divorce. [Hebrew *gēt.*]

ge·ta (gáy-tə) *n., pl.* **-ta** or **-tas.** A wooden-soled shoe worn by the Japanese. [Japanese.]

get away. *intr.v.* **1.** To escape. **2.** To start off in a race.

get·a·way (géttə-way) *n.* **1.** The act or an instance of escaping. **2.** A start, as of a race; a takeoff. **—get·a·way** *adj.*

geth·sem·a·ne (geth-sémməni) *n.* Any instance or place of great suffering.

Geth·sem·a·ne (geth-sémməni). The garden outside Jerusalem that was the scene of the agony and arrest of Jesus. Matthew 26:36–56.

get out *intr.v.* **1.** To become public or known, as news. *—tr.v.* **1.** To publish (a newspaper for example). **2.** To say with an effort: *he stammered, but managed to get the name out eventually.*

get-out (gét-owt) *n. Informal.* An escape or means of avoiding difficulty: *A feigned headache was her get-out.*

get-rich-quick (gét-rich-kwík) *adj.* Of, pertaining to, or being a plan or project designed to make money by rapid and often unscrupulous methods.

get·ter (géttər) *n.* **1.** One that gets. **2. a.** A material added in small

amounts during a chemical or metallurgical process to absorb impurities. **b.** A substance, usually a metal, used to remove residual gas from a high-vacuum enclosure.
~*v.* **gettered, -tering, -ters.** —*tr.* **1.** To remove impurities from (a metal, for example) with a getter. **2.** To remove (gas) with a getter. —*intr.* To use a getter, as in removing impurities from a substance.
get together *intr.v.* To come together; assemble, especially socially: *Let's get together for a drink.* —**get it together.** *Slang.* **1.** To achieve personal fulfilment. **2.** To function with optimum efficiency in a particular sphere.
get-to·geth·er (gĕt-tə-gĕthər) *n. Informal.* **1.** A small party. **2.** A meeting or informal conference.
Get·ty (gĕtti), **J(ean) Paul** (1892-1976). U.S. financier and art collector. A millionaire by the age of 22, he turned his father's oil business into one of the world's largest financial empires. His third son, John Paul Getty Junior (1932-), lives in Britain. He has devoted vast sums to a variety of causes, one major beneficiary being London's National Gallery. In 1986 he was awarded an honorary knighthood (KBE).
Get·tys·burg (gĕttiz-burg). Town in southern Pennsylvania in the United States. It was there that the Federal Army under Meade defeated the Confederates under Lee in July, 1863, during the American Civil War.
get up *intr.v.* **1.** To arise, as from bed or a stooping or prone position. **2.** To rise to one's feet. **3.** To increase in force or intensity: *the wind's getting up.* **4.** To engage in mischievous or underhand behaviour. Used with *to*: *I see she's getting up to her old tricks again.* —*tr.v. Informal.* **1.** To study or revise. **2.** To create or devise: *get up a party.* **3.** To dress or make up (oneself) elaborately.
get-up (gĕt-up) *Informal. n.* **1.** An outfit or costume, especially one that is remarkable or bizarre. **2.** The arrangement and production style, as of a magazine or book.
get-up-and-go (gĕttup-ən-gō) *n. Informal.* Energy and ambition; initiative and determination; drive.
ge·um (jēē-əm) *n.* Any plant of the genus *Geum,* which includes **avens** and **herb bennet** *(both of which see).* [New Latin, from Latin *gaeum,* herb bennet.]
GeV *Physics.* Giga (10⁹) electron volts. See **BeV**.
gew·gaw (gĕw-gaw, gōō-) *n.* A decorative trinket; a bauble. ~*adj.* Decorative and showy, but valueless. [Middle English : origin obscure.]
Ge·würz·tram·i·ner (gə-vûrtss-tra-meenər) *n.* A dry, white table wine with a distinctive spicy flavour, produced in Alsace.
gey (gī, gay) *adv. Scottish.* Very: *It's gey wet today.* [Variant of GAY.]
gey·ser (gī-zər, gēē- for sense 1; for sense 2 gēē-zər ‖ gī-) *n.* **1.** A natural hot spring that intermittently ejects a column of water and steam into the air. **2.** *British.* A domestic, usually gas-operated hot-water heater. [Icelandic *Geysir,* "gusher", the name of a hot spring in Iceland, from *geysa,* to gush, from Old Norse.]
gey·ser·ite (gī-zə-rīt, gēē-) *n.* An opaline, usually siliceous deposit formed around natural hot springs. It is a form of sinter.
Gha·na, Republic of (gaánə). Country in West Africa on the Gulf of Guinea. In 1472 European trading posts were established and the territory subsequently became a centre of the slave trade and the scene of bitter rivalries between British, Danish, French, and Dutch companies. In 1874 the south was established as the British Colony of the Gold Coast, and the north was added by 1901. Together with the British section of Togo, the country became independent in 1957, and in 1960 it became a republic within the Commonwealth. Agriculture is important; cocoa, of which Ghana is one of the world's principal producers, is the major export. Area, 238 537 square kilometres (92,100 square miles). Population, 17,830,000. Capital, Accra. See map at **West African States.** —**Gha·na·ian** (gaa-náy-ən), **Gha·ni·an** *adj. & n.*
gha·ri·al (gárri-əl) *n.* A reptile, the **gavial** *(see).*
ghar·ry, ghar·ri (gárri ‖ gaári) *n.* A small horse-drawn carriage in India. [Hindi *gārī.*]
ghast·ly (gaást-li ‖ gást-) *adj.* **-lier, -liest. 1.** Terrifying; dreadful. **2.** Having a deathlike pallor: *"amid the dim and ghastly glare of a snowy night"* (Washington Irving). **3.** *Informal.* Extremely unpleasant or bad: *a ghastly little book.*
~*adv.* Dreadfully; horribly. [Middle English *gastlich,* Old English *gǣstlīc,* spiritual, ghostly, ghastly, from *gǣst,* soul, ghost.] —**ghast·li·ness** *n.*
Synonyms: ghastly, grim, gruesome, grisly, macabre, lurid.
ghat, ghaut (gaat, gawt ‖ *West Indies* gut) *n.* **1.** In India: **a.** A mountain pass. **b.** A mountain chain. **c.** A flight of steps down to the bank of a river. **d.** An area beside a river, used for bathing. **2.** In the West Indies, a ravine. [Hindi *ghāt,* from Sanskrit *ghaṭṭa,* perhaps from *ghṛṣṭa,* rubbed.]
Ghats (gaats, gawts). Two coastal mountain ranges in India, forming the edges of the Deccan plateau. The Western Ghats extend approximately 1 500 kilometres (932 miles) along the west coast, and rise to 2 698 metres (8,852 feet) at Anai Mudi. The Eastern Ghats extend approximately 1 400 kilometres (880 miles) along the east coast, rising to 2 637 metres (8,651 feet) at Doda Betta.
gha·zi (gaázi) *n., pl.* **-zies. 1.** A Muslim warrior who has fought successfully against infidels. Often used as a title of honour. **2.** A high-ranking Turkish warrior. [Arabic *ghāzi,* participle of *ghazā,* he made war.]
Ghazzah. See **Gaza.**
ghee (gee) *n.* Clarified butter from the butterfat of buffalo or other milk. It is used in cooking, especially in India and neighbouring

countries. [Hindi *ghī,* from Sanskrit *ghrta,* present participle of *ghṛ,* to sprinkle.]
Ghent (gent). *Flemish* **Gent** (khent); *French* **Gand** (goN). A city and port in Belgium, the capital of East Flanders.
ghe·rao (ge-rów) *n.* In India, a coercive tactic adopted during industrial disputes whereby workers surround an employer and detain him on his own premises until he agrees to their demands. ~*tr.v.* **gheraoed, -raoing, -raoes.** To coerce (an employer) by using this technique. [Bengali, to surround, from Indic *gher-* (unattested), causative of *ghir-* (unattested), "to go around", from Dravidian.]
gher·kin (gérkin) *n.* **1.** A small cucumber, especially one used for pickling. **2.** A tropical American vine, *Cucumis anguria,* bearing prickly, edible fruit. **3.** The fruit of this vine. [Dutch *agurk(je),* from Low German *agurke,* from Lithuanian *agurkas,* from Polish *ogorek, ogurek,* from Medieval Greek *angourion,* probably from Greek *agouros,* youth, "unripe", from *aōros : a-,* not + *ōros,* time.]
ghet·to (gĕttō) *n., pl.* **-tos** or **-toes. 1.** A slum section of a city occupied predominantly by members of a minority group who live there because of social or economic pressure. **2.** A section or quarter in a European city to which Jews were formerly restricted. **3.** An area occupied by a group, institution, or the like, with a distinctive, and often exclusive, specified common trait: *a cultural ghetto; a middle-class ghetto*†.] —**ghet·to·ise, ghet·to·ize** *tr.v.*
ghetto blaster *n. Informal.* A large, powerful portable stereo. [Perhaps from its supposed use by *ghetto-*dwellers to *blast* away their cares with loud music.]
Ghib·el·line (gíbbi-līn, -leen ‖ -lin) *n.* Any of the members of the aristocratic political faction who fought during the Middle Ages for German imperial control of Italy, in opposition to the Guelphs, who favoured papal control. Compare **Guelph.** [Italian *Ghibellino,* from Middle High German *Waiblingen,* name of a Hohenstaufen estate.]
Ghi·ber·ti (gi-baírti), **Lorenzo** (c.1378-1455). Italian goldsmith and sculptor. He is best known for the series of bronze sculpted panels for the doors of the baptistery of Florence Cathedral, depicting scenes from the New and Old Testaments.
ghilgai. Variant of **gilgai.**
ghil·lie (gílli) *n., pl.* **-lies. 1.** A shoe with fringed laces, originally worn by the Scots. **2.** Variant of **gillie.** [Scottish Gaelic *gille,* boy, servant, GILLIE.]
ghost (gōst) *n.* **1.** The spirit of a dead person, supposed to haunt living persons or former habitats; a spectre; a phantom; a wraith. **2.** *Archaic.* The animus or soul, as opposed to the body. **3.** A returning or haunting memory or image. **4.** A slight trace or vestige of something; a hint; a semblance: *a ghost of a smile; a ghost of a chance.* **5.** A faint, false secondary image, such as: **a.** A displaced image in a mirror caused by reflection from the front of the glass. **b.** A displaced image in a photograph caused by the optical system of the camera. **c.** A secondary image on a television or radar screen caused by reflected waves. **d.** A false spectral line caused by imperfections in the diffraction grating. **6.** *Printing.* A variation or unevenness of colour intensity on a surface intended to be solidly tinted, as the result of irregular distribution of ink. **7.** *Obsolete.* The Holy Ghost. **8.** *Informal.* A ghostwriter. **9.** A nonexistent publication listed in bibliographies. In this sense, also called "ghost edition". **10.** A ghost word. —**give up the ghost.** To die.
~*v.* **ghosted, ghosting, ghosts.** —*intr. Informal.* To ghostwrite. —*tr.* **1.** To haunt. **2.** *Informal.* To ghostwrite (a work). [Middle English *gost, gast,* Old English *gāst,* from Germanic.]
ghost dance *n.* Either of two religious dances practised chiefly by certain North American Indians of the southwestern United States and California during the latter half of the 19th century, to invoke a return of their former condition.
ghost gum *n.* Any of various Australian eucalyptus trees with a smooth, whitish trunk and branches.
ghost·ly (gōst-li) *adj.* **-lier, -liest. 1.** Pertaining to or resembling a ghost or apparition; spectral; eerie. **2.** Pertaining to the spirit or to religion; spiritual: *"it would cure you of all evils ghostly and bodily"* (Laurence Sterne). —**ghost·li·ness** *n.*
ghost moth *n.* Any of various moths of the family Hepialidae that have large, pale wings and are active at dusk. Also called "swift moth".
ghost town *n.* A town, especially a boom town of the western United States, that has now been completely abandoned.
ghost word *n.* A word that has come into a language through the perpetuation of a misreading of a manuscript, a typographical error, or a misunderstanding. For example, in *Ye Olde Sweete Shoppe,* *Ye* is a ghost word, the *y* having been a misreading of the runic letter thorn.
ghost·write (gōst-rīt) *v.* **-wrote** (-rōt), **-written** (-rítt'n), **-writing, -writes.** —*intr.* To work as a ghostwriter. —*tr.* To write (something) as a ghostwriter.
ghost·writ·er (gōst-rītər) *n.* A person who is hired to write for another person who then takes credit of authorship. Also informally called "ghost".
ghoul (gōōl) *n.* **1.** One who delights in what is revolting, macabre, or loathsome. **2.** A grave robber. **3. a.** A malevolent spirit or demon. **b.** An evil spirit or demon in Muslim folklore supposed to plunder graves and feed on corpses. [Arabic *ghūl,* from *ghāla,* he took suddenly.] —**ghoul·ish** *adj.* —**ghoul·ish·ly** *adv.* —**ghoul·ish·ness** *n.*
GHQ, G.H.Q. general headquarters.
Ghurkha. Variant of **Gurkha.**
ghyll. Variant of **gill** (stream or ravine).

gi gill (liquid measure).

Gi gilbert (unit of magnetomotive force).

GI (jée-ī) *n., pl.* **GIs** or **GI's.** A serviceman in or ex-serviceman of any of the U.S. armed forces.
~*adj.* **1.** Pertaining to or characteristic of a GI. **2.** In conformity to or accordance with U.S. military regulations or procedures. **3.** Issued by an official U.S. military supply department. [Abbreviation of *general issue* or *government issue.*]

Gia·co·met·ti (jáckō-métti), **Alberto** (1901–66). Swiss painter and sculptor. From 1922 to 1935 he experimented with cubism, but later evolved a distinctive, elongated style of representing the human figure.

Giam·bo·log·na (jámbō-lón-yə). *Italian* **Giovanni da Bologna;** *French* **Jean de Bologne** (1529–1608). Flemish-born Italian sculptor. He is best known for the fountains, religious groups, and bronze statuettes he produced in the Mannerist style, in Florence.

gi·ant (jī-ənt) *n.* **1. a.** A person or thing of extraordinary size or strength. **b.** A person of outstanding importance or achievement: *He is a giant in his field.* **2.** *Greek Mythology.* Any of a race of manlike beings of enormous strength and stature who warred with the Olympians, by whom they were finally destroyed. **3.** Any similar being in folklore or myth. **4.** *Astronomy.* A giant star.
~*adj.* Of immense size; gigantic; huge. [Middle English *geant*, from Old French, from Vulgar Latin *gangante* (unattested), from Latin *gigās* (stem *gigant-*), from Greek *gigas†.*]

giant anteater *n.* See **anteater.**

giant chromosome *n.* A chromosome consisting of many parallel strands of chromatids that have failed to separate after duplication. Giant chromosomes, which occur in the salivary glands of *Drosophila* and other insects, are used to study gene activity.

gi·ant·ess (jī-ən-tess, -téss, -tiss) *n.* A female giant.

giant fibre *n.* *Zoology.* A nerve fibre with a very large diameter found in many invertebrate animals that is capable of rapid conduction of impulses. Also called "giant axon".

giant hogweed *n., pl.* **giant hogweeds** or collectively **giant hogweed.** A very tall plant, *Heracleum mantegazzianum*, with clusters of small white flowers, found especially on waste ground. It can produce an unpleasant rash when touched.

gi·ant·ism (jī-ən-tiz'm) *n.* **1.** The condition of being a giant. **2.** *Pathology.* Gigantism (*see*).

giant-kill·er (jī-ənt-killər) *n.* An individual, such as a sportsman, that defeats an apparently more powerful opponent against all expectations.

giant panda *n.* See **panda.**

giant planet *n.* A planet with a large mass of low density. The giant planets are **Jupiter, Saturn, Neptune,** and **Uranus.**

giant powder *n.* A high explosive consisting of trinitroglycerin absorbed in kieselguhr.

Giant's Causeway. Promontory in Northern Ireland, 11 kilometres (7 miles) east-northeast of Portrush, on the North Channel. It consists of thousands of basaltic columns formed by a flow of lava into the sea. Legend has it that it was once a bridge for giants to cross between Ireland and Scotland.

giant sequoia *n.* A very tall evergreen tree, *Sequoiadendron giganteum*, of mountainous regions of southern California, having a massive trunk and light-coloured, reddish wood. Also called "big tree", "wellingtonia". Compare **redwood.**

giant star *n.* Any of a class of highly luminous, exceptionally massive stars, having relatively low density and lying above the main sequence. Also called "giant". Compare **dwarf star.**

gia·our (jowr, jów-ər) *n.* A nonbeliever; especially, a Christian. Used derogatorily by Muslims. [Turkish *giaur*, infidel, from Persian *gaur*, variant of *gäbr†*, fire worshipper.]

gi·ar·di·a·sis (jée-aar-dī-ə-siss) *n.* A disease caused by infestations of the small intestine with the parasitic protozoan *Giardia lamblia* and characterised by diarrhoea and nausea. [New Latin *giardia*, after A.M. *Giard* (1846–1908), French biologist + -IASIS.]

gib[1] (gib) *n.* A plain or notched, often wedge-shaped, piece of wood or metal designed to hold parts of a machine or structure in place or to provide a bearing surface, usually adjusted by a screw or key.
~*tr.v.* **gibbed, gibbing, gibs.** To apply a gib to. [18th century : origin obscure.]

gib[2] (gib) *n.* A male cat, especially one that has been castrated. [Perhaps from the name *Gilbert.*]

Gib (jib). *Informal.* Gibraltar. Used as a nickname.

gib·ber[1] (jíbbər, gíbbər) *intr.v.* **-bered, -bering, -bers. 1.** To make rapid, chattering noises, as a monkey does. **2.** To prattle or chatter unintelligibly.
~*n.* Senseless talk or prate; gibberish. [Imitative.]

gib·ber[2] (gíbbər) *n.* *Australian.* A stone or rock, especially one polished by the wind. [From a native Australian language.]

gib·ber·el·lic acid (jíbbə-réllik) *n.* A substance, $C_{19}H_{22}O_6$, first isolated from a fungus, *Gibberella fujikuroi*, and occurring naturally in many plants where it promotes elongation of the cells. [From GIBBERELLIN.]

gib·ber·el·lin (jíbbə-réllin) *n.* Any of a class of natural plant growth substances, such as gibberellic acid, that promote elongation of the stems and leaves. [New Latin *Gibberella*, diminutive of Latin *gibber*, hunchbacked, akin to Latin *gibbus*, hump.]

gib·ber·ish (jíbbə-rish, gíbbə-) *n.* Nonsensical, rapid talk; prattle.

gib·bet (jíbbit) *n.* **1.** A gallows. **2.** An upright post with a crosspiece, forming a T-shaped structure from which executed criminals were hung for public viewing.
~*tr.v.* **gibbeted** or **gibbetted, -beting** or **-betting, -bets. 1.** To execute by hanging. **2.** To hang on a gibbet for public viewing. **3.** To expose to infamy or public ridicule. [Middle English *gibet*, from Old French, diminutive of *gibe*, staff, club, possibly from Frankish *gibb-†* (unattested), forked stick.]

gib·bon (gíbbən) *n.* Any of several apes of the genera *Hylobates* or *Symphalangus*, of tropical Asia, that live in trees and have a slender body and long arms. [French, perhaps from a native word in India.]

Gib·bon (gíbbən), **Edward** (1737–94). British historian. His principal work, *The History of the Decline and Fall of the Roman Empire* (1776–88), covers some 1,200 years of history and remains a monumental work of its kind.

Gib·bons (gíbbənz), **Grinling** (1648–1721). Dutch-born British sculptor. He excelled in the carving of fruit and flowers in wood, and was commissioned by Sir Christopher Wren to work on the choir stalls and organ screen of St. Paul's Cathedral.

Gib·bons, Orlando (1583–1625). English composer. Organist at the Chapel Royal from 1604, he was appointed organist of Westminster Abbey in 1623. His compositions include beautiful madrigals.

gib·bos·i·ty (gi-bóssəti ‖ ji-) *n., pl.* **-ties. 1.** The condition of being gibbous. **2.** A rounded hump or protuberance; a swelling. **3.** *Pathology.* A sharply angled curvature of the spine, formerly commonly caused by tuberculosis.

gib·bous (gíbbəss ‖ jíbbəss) *adj.* **1.** Rounded; convex; protuberant. **2.** More than half but less than fully illuminated. Said of the moon or a planet. **3.** Hunchbacked. [Middle English, from Late Latin *gebbōsus*, humpbacked, from *gibbus*, hump (expressive).] —**gib·bous·ly** *adv.* —**gib·bous·ness** *n.*

Gibbs function (gibz) *n.* *Symbol* **G.** A measure of the thermodynamic free energy of a system, used for changes at constant pressure, equal to the enthalpy minus the product of entropy and thermodynamic temperature. Also called "Gibbs free energy". [After J.W. *Gibbs* (1839–1903), U.S. physicist and mathematician.]

gibbs·ite (gíb-zīt) *n.* Hydrated aluminium oxide, $Al_2O_3 \cdot 3H_2O$, a constituent of bauxite. [After George *Gibbs* (1782–1833), U.S. mineralogist.]

gibe, jibe (jīb) *v.* **gibed, gibing, gibes.** —*intr.* To make heckling or mocking remarks; scoff. Usually used with *at.* —*tr.* To reproach by taunting; deride. —See Synonyms at **ridicule.**
~*n.* A derisive remark; a taunt. [Perhaps from Old French *gibert†*, to handle roughly.] —**gib·er** *n.* —**gib·ing·ly** *adv.*

Gib·e·on·ite (gíbbi-ə-nīt) *n.* Any of the inhabitants of Gibeon, a village of ancient Palestine, condemned by Joshua to serve as manual labourers for the Israelites. Joshua 9.

gib·lets (jib-lits, -ləts ‖ gib-) *pl.n. Sometimes singular.* The edible inside parts of a fowl, such as the heart, liver, or gizzard. [Middle English *gibelet*, from Old French, probably variant of *giberet* (unattested), diminutive of *gibier*, hunting, game, from Frankish *gabaiti* (unattested), hunting with falcons.]

Gib·ral·tar (ji-bráwl-tər ‖ -ból-). British Overseas Territory at the west entrance to the Mediterranean Sea. Linked by a sandy isthmus to the Spanish mainland, it rises to 427 metres (1,400 feet) at the Rock of Gibraltar. In ancient times it was the Calpe of the Greeks and the Romans, forming, with ancient Abyla on the African coast, the Pillars of Hercules, long thought to mark the western edge of the world. Successively ruled by the Moors and Castile, it was taken by Admiral Rooke in 1704 and has remained a British possession since. In 1967 it was granted a measure of internal self-government. Following Spanish demands for decolonisation (1967), a referendum was held; the population voted 12,138 to 44 in favour of the status quo. Gibraltar has few natural resources and relies chiefly on its strategic position as a port. Tourism is also important. Its name is derived from Jabel-al-Tarik after its Moorish conqueror of 711, Tarik. —**Gib·ral·tar·i·an** (jib-rawl-taír-i-ən ‖ -rol-) *n. & adj.*

Gibraltar, Strait of. Channel between southern Spain and Morocco in northwest Africa. Some 58 kilometres (36 miles) long and 13 kilometres (8 miles) at its narrowest point, it links the Mediterranean Sea with the Atlantic Ocean.

Gib·ran (ji-bráan), **Khalil** (1883–1931). Lebanese poet. His major work in the English language, *The Prophet* (1923), expounds his philosophy with a vivid use of metaphor.

Gib·son Desert (gíb-s'n) The central section of the desert of Western Australia, lying between the Great Sandy Desert and the Victoria Desert.

Gib·son girl *n.* The ideal American girl of the 1890s as portrayed in sketches by the U.S. illustrator Charles Dana Gibson (1867–1944), typically dressed in a tailored shirtwaister with leg-of-mutton sleeves, and a long skirt.

gid (gid) *n.* A disease of sheep caused by the presence of the larva of a tapeworm, *Taenia caenurus*, in the brain, and resulting in a staggering gait. Also called "sturdy", "waterbrain". [Back-formation from GIDDY.]

gid·dy (gíddi) *adj.* **-dier, -diest. 1. a.** Having a reeling, light-headed sensation; dizzy. **b.** Causing or capable of causing dizziness: *a giddy climb to the top of the tower.* **2.** Frivolous and lighthearted; flighty: *giddy young girls.*
~*v.* **giddied, -dying, -dies.** —*intr.* To become giddy. —*tr.* To make giddy. [Middle English *gidy*, mad, foolish, Old English *gydig*, possessed by a god, insane.] —**gid·di·ly** *adv.* —**gid·di·ness** *n.*

gid·dy-up (gíddi-úp) *interj.* Also **gid·dap** (gi-dáp). Used as a command to make an animal, especially a horse, move or go faster. [From *get up.*]

Gide (zheed), **André** (1869–1951). French novelist and diarist.

Much of his work examines the tensions between desire and duty, with particular reference to his own Christianity and homosexuality. His novels include *La Porte étroite* (1909), and *Les Faux-Monnayeurs* (1925). He was awarded the Nobel prize for literature in 1947.

Gid·e·on (gíddi-ən). A judge of Israel; conqueror of the Midianites. Judges 6–8. [Hebrew *Gidh'ōn*, "hewer", "feller", from *gādha*, he cut down.]

Gideon Bible *n.* A Bible placed in a hotel room, hospital room, or the like, by a member of the Gideons, a Christian organisation. [After GIDEON.]

gie (gee) *v.* **gied** or **gae**, **gied** or **gien**, **gieing**, **gies**. *Scottish*. To give.

Giel·gud (géel-gōōd), **Sir (Arthur) John** (1904–). British actor and director. He won popular acclaim with his performances in and productions of Shakespeare's plays. He received a knighthood in 1953 and an Oscar in 1981 for *Arthur*.

Gie·rek (géer-ek; *Polish* gyérrek), **Edward** (1913–). Polish politician. After working as a miner in France and Belgium, he returned to Poland (1948) and became a member of the Politburo (1956). He was appointed secretary of the United Workers' Party after the food riots of 1970 but was obliged to resign following industrial unrest over high food prices in 1980.

gift (gift) *n.* **1.** Something that is bestowed voluntarily and without compensation; a present. **2.** The act, right, or power of giving: *The living is in the gift of the Bishop.* **3.** A talent, endowment, aptitude, or power: *a gift for languages.* **4.** *Informal.* Something obtained very easily or cheaply. —**the gift of the gab.** A talent for speaking easily or well.
~*tr.v.* **gifted**, **gifting**, **gifts**. **1.** To present with a gift. **2.** *Chiefly British.* To bestow as a gift. **3.** To endow with; invest. [Middle English *gift*, *yift*, from Old Norse *gipt*, *gift*.]

gift·ed (gíftid) *adj.* **1.** Endowed with natural ability, talent, or other assets; especially, endowed with exceptional intelligence: *a gifted child.* **2.** Revealing talent: *a gifted rendition of a song.* —**gift·ed·ly** *adv.* —**gift·ed·ness** *n.*

gift-horse (gíft-hawrss) *n.* —**look a gift-horse in the mouth.** To be suspicious of or to find fault with a gift or lucky chance. [Alluding to the practice of examining a horse's teeth to determine its age.]

gift of tongues *n.* An ecstatic utterance that is partly or wholly unintelligible to hearers, especially as practised liturgically in certain Christian congregations. Also called "glossolalia". [By allusion to the Pentecostal miracle whereby the Apostles "were all filled with the Holy Ghost, and began to speak with other tongues, as the Spirit gave them utterance." Acts 2:4.]

gift token *n.* A voucher, intended as a present, that can be exchanged for goods to the stated value. Also called "gift voucher".

gift-wrap (gíft-rap) *tr.v.* **-wrapped**, **-wrapping**, **-wraps**. To wrap (a purchase or present) in fancy paper with elaborate trimmings.

gig¹ (gig) *n.* **1.** A light, two-wheeled vehicle drawn by one horse. **2. a.** A long, light ship's boat having oars, sails, or a motor, and usually reserved for use by the ship's captain. **b.** A fast, light rowing boat. [Middle English *gigg†*, giddy girl, something that whirls.]

gig² *n.* **1.** An arrangement of barbless hooks that is dragged through a school of fish to hook them in the bodies. **2.** A spear for fishing, a **fishgig** (*see*).
~*v.* **gigged**, **gigging**, **gigs**. —*tr.* **1.** To catch with a gig. **2.** *Regional.* To goad; prod. —*intr.* To fish with a gig. [Short for FISH-GIG.]

gig³ *n.* *Informal.* **1.** A job, engagement, or booking for musicians, especially pop or jazz musicians. **2.** A performance by pop or jazz musicians at a club, concert, or the like.
~*intr.v.* **gigged**, **gigging**, **gigs**. *Slang*. To perform at a club, concert, or the like. [20th century : origin obscure.]

giga–, **gig·a** (gigga, jigga) *prefix. Symbol* **G** Indicates one thousand million (10⁹); for example, *gigavolt*, (1,000,000,000 volts). [Greek *gigas*, GIANT.]

gi·gan·tic (jī-gántik ‖ jə-) *adj.* **1.** Pertaining to or suitable for a giant. **2. a.** Exceedingly large of its kind: *a gigantic toadstool.* **b.** Very large or extensive: *a gigantic radio network.* —See Synonyms at **enormous.** [Latin *gigās* (stem *gigant-*), GIANT.] —**gi·gan·ti·cal·ly** *adv.*

gi·gan·tism (jí-gan-tiz'm, jī-gán- ‖ jə-gán-) *n.* **1.** Excessive growth of the body or any of its parts as a result of oversecretion of the pituitary growth hormone during childhood. Also called "giantism". **2.** Abnormal size.

gi·gan·tom·a·chy (jī-gan-tómməki) *n.* Also **gi·gan·to·ma·chi·a** (jīgántō-máyki-ə). **1.** *Greek Mythology.* The war of the giants against Zeus and the other Olympian gods. **2.** Any battle or contest on a massive scale. [Greek *gigantomakhia* : *gigas* (stem *gigant-*), GIANT + -MACHY.]

gig·gle (gigg'l) *intr.v.* **-gled**, **-gling**, **-gles**. To laugh with repeated short, high-pitched, convulsive sounds, as when nervous or when attempting to suppress mirth.
~*n.* **1.** A high-pitched, spasmodic laugh. **2.** A prank or joke: *did it for a giggle; a bit of a giggle.* [Imitative.] —**gig·gler** *n.*

gig·gly (giggli, gígg'l-i) *adj.* **-glier**, **-gliest**. Inclined to giggle.

gig·o·lo (zhíggə-lō, jiggə-) *n.*, *pl.* **-los**. **1.** A young man who is kept as a lover by a woman, especially an older woman. **2.** A paid male escort or dancing partner. [French, from *gigolette*, dance-hall partner, from *giguer*, to dance, from *gigue*, leg, fiddle, from Old French, from Old High German *gīga†*.]

gig·ot (jiggət, zhée-gō) *n.* **1.** A leg of mutton or lamb for cooking. **2.** A leg-of-mutton sleeve. Also called "gigot sleeve". [Old French,

diminutive of *gigue,* leg, fiddle. See **gigolo**.]

gigue (zheeg) *n.* **1.** A dance, the **jig** (*see*). **2.** *Music.* A lively piece of music in ⁶/₈, ⁹/₈, or ¹²/₈ time, often forming the final movement of the classical suite. [French, from English JIG.]

GI Joe *n.* *U.S. Informal.* A serviceman in the U.S. Army, especially during World War II.

Gi·jón (*Spanish* khi-khón). Port in northwest Spain, situated on the Bay of Biscay, in the Oviedo province in Asturias. It is an important industrial centre.

Gi·la monster (héelə) *n.* A venomous lizard, *Heloderma suspectum*, of the southwestern United States and northern Mexico, having a stout body covered with black and orange or yellowish scales. [After the *Gila* river in New Mexico and Arizona.]

gil·bert (gílbərt) *n. Symbol* **Gi** The centimetre-gram-second electromagnetic unit of magnetomotive force, equal to ¹⁰/₄π ampere-turn. [After William GILBERT.]

Gil·bert (gílbərt), **William** (1544–1603). English physicist. His work on magnets led to his theory, broadly correct, that the Earth is a magnet with its poles at the North and South Poles. He also coined the term "electricity", and was a physician to Elizabeth I.

Gilbert, Sir W(illiam) S(chwenk) (1836–1911). English librettist and humourist. He is best known for the Savoy Operas he wrote with the composer, Sir Arthur Sullivan.

Gilbert Islands. See Kiribati, Republic of.

gild¹ (gild) *tr.v.* **gilded** or **gilt** (gilt), **gilding**, **gilds**. **1.** To cover with or as if with a thin layer of gold. **2.** To give an often deceptively attractive or improved appearance to; gloss or gloss over. **3.** *Archaic.* To smear with blood. [Middle English *gilden*, Old English *gyldan*.]

gild². Variant of **guild**.

gild·er¹ (gíldər) *n.* A person whose work is gilding.

gilder². Variant of **guilder**.

gild·ing (gílding) *n.* **1.** The art or process of applying gilt to a surface. **2.** Gilt. **3.** Something used to give a superficially attractive appearance.

Giles (jīlz), **(Carl) Ronald** (1916–95). British cartoonist. His cartoons, which appeared in the *Daily Express* and *Sunday Express* from 1943, are invaluable social documents.

gi·let (ji-láy) *n.* A woman's waistcoat. [French.]

gil·gai, ghil·gai (gil-gī) *n.* In Australia, a cracked, uneven, natural depression in the ground; a water hole. [From a native Australian language.]

gill¹ (gil) *n.* **1.** *Zoology.* The respiratory organ of fishes, larval amphibians, and numerous aquatic invertebrates, typically consisting of a membranous appendage well supplied with blood vessels for gaseous exchange. **2.** *Usually plural.* The wattle of a bird. **3.** *Usually plural. Informal.* The area around the chin and neck. **4.** *Botany.* Any of the thin, platelike, spore-producing structures on the underside of the cap of a mushroom or similar fungus. —**green about the gills.** Looking or feeling sick or nauseous.
~*tr.v.* **gilled**, **gilling**, **gills**. **1.** To catch (fish) in a gill net. **2.** To gut or clean (fish). [Middle English *gille*, probably from Old Norse *gil* (unattested).]

gill² (jil) *n. Abbr.* **gi 1.** A unit of volume or capacity in the British Imperial System, used in dry and liquid measure, equal to 5 fluid ounces (¹/₄ pint) or 9.024 cubic inches (0.148 litre). **2.** *Northern British Informal.* A half-pint. **3.** A unit of volume or capacity in the U.S. Customary System, used in liquid measure, equal to 4 fluid ounces or 7.216 cubic inches (0.118 litre). [Middle English *gille*, from Old French *gille*, *gelle*, from Late Latin *gillot†*, water pot.]

gill³, ghyll (gil) *n. British Regional.* **1.** A swift-flowing mountain stream. **2.** A ravine. [Middle English *gille*, from Old Norse *gil*.]

Gill (gil), **(Arthur) Eric (Rowton)** (1882–1940). British sculptor, wood engraver, and typographer. He began his career as a letter cutter, and after joining the Golden Cockerel Press he illustrated many books with wood engravings. His sculptures include the *Stations of the Cross* (1914–18) for Westminster Cathedral, and *Prospero and Ariel* (1931) on Broadcasting House in London. His type designs include Perpetua (1925) and Gill Sans-serif (1927).

gill bar (gil) *n.* Any of a series of skeletal structures in the pharyngeal wall of fishes that supports the tissue separating the gill slits.

gill books *pl.n.* The respiratory organs of king crabs, consisting of layers of thin vascular plates attached to the abdominal appendages.

Gil·les·pie (gi-léss-pi), **Dizzy,** born John Birks Gillespie (1917–93). U.S. jazz trumpeter. From 1944 he worked with the Billy Eckstine band and began to develop the style known as "(be)bop".

gill fungus (gil) *n.* Any fleshy fungus having a cap with gills on the underside.

gil·lie, gil·ly, ghil·lie (gílli) *n.*, *pl.* **-lies**. *Scottish*. A professional guide and servant for sportsmen, especially in fishing and deerstalking. [Scottish Gaelic *gille*, boy, servant, akin to Irish *giolla†*.]

gil·lion (jílli-ən) *n. British.* One thousand million. [Blend of GIGA- + MILLION.]

gill net (gil) *n.* A fishing-net set vertically in the water so that fish swimming into it are entangled by their gills in its mesh.

gill pouch (gil) *n.* Any of a series of paired pouches in the pharyngeal wall of chordate embryos that become the gill slits of aquatic vertebrates.

Gill·ray (gil-ray), **James** (1757–1815). British caricaturist. Largely self-taught, he published the satirical portraits of the royal family, *A New Way to Pay the National Debt* (1786), and thereafter was a much commissioned caricaturist, sometimes savage in his wit.

gill slit (gil) *n.* Any of several narrow, paired, external openings connecting with the pharynx, present in all vertebrates during embryonic development, and characteristic of adult fishes and other aquatic vertebrates.

gil·ly·flow·er, gil·li·flow·er (gílli-flowr) *n.* **1.** *Archaic.* The clove pink or a similar plant of the genus *Dianthus.* **2.** Any of several other plants having fragrant flowers, such as the stock or wallflower. [Alteration (influenced by FLOWER) of Middle English *gilofre, gelofer,* from Old French *girofre, girofle,* from Medieval Latin *caryophylum,* clove, from Greek *karuophullon* : *karuon,* nut + *phullon,* leaf.]

gil·son·ite (gíl-sə-nīt) *n.* A natural black bitumen found in Utah and Colorado, used in the manufacture of acid, alkali, and waterproof coatings. Also called "uintaite". [After S.H. *Gilson,* of Salt Lake City, Utah, who discovered it.]

gilt[1] (gilt). Alternative past tense and past participle of **gild.**
~*adj.* **1.** Gilded. **2.** Having the appearance of gold.
~*n. Abbr.* **gt. 1.** Gold leaf or a paint containing or simulating gold. **2.** Shining brilliance; glitter. **3.** *Usually plural.* A gilt-edged security: *his money is in gilts.* —**take the gilt off the gingerbread.** To remove that which makes a thing attractive; spoil.

gilt[2] *n.* A young sow that has not yet produced a litter. [Middle English *gilt,* young sow, from Old Norse *gylta,* sow.]

gilt-edged (gílt-ějd) *adj.* Also **gilt-edge** (-ěj). **1.** Having gilded edges, as the pages of a book. **2. a.** Of the highest quality or value. **b.** Of a high degree of reliability.

gilt-edged security *n.* A government-issued security having little risk as an investment. Also called "gilt".

gim·bals (jím-b'lz, gím-) *pl.n.* A device consisting of two rings mounted on axes at right angles to each other so that an object such as a ship's compass will remain suspended in a horizontal plane between them regardless of their motion. [Plural of *gimbal,* from Old French *gemel,* GIMMAL.]

gim·crack (jím-krak) *n.* A cheap and showy object of little or no use; a knick-knack.
~*adj.* Cheap and shoddy; flimsy. [Middle English *gibecrake*†, ornament, gimcrack.] —**gim·crack·er·y** *n.*

gim·el (gimm'l) *n.* The third letter of the Hebrew alphabet. [Hebrew *gīmel,* "camel" (from the ancient form of the letter), akin to *gāmāl,* CAMEL.]

gim·let (gímlit) *n.* **1.** A small hand tool for boring holes, having a spiralled shank, a screw tip, and a cross handle. **2.** A cocktail made with vodka or gin and lime juice, garnished with a slice of lime.
~*tr.v.* **gimleted, -leting, -lets.** To penetrate with or as if with a gimlet; puncture; pierce.
~*adj.* Piercing; penetrating: *gimlet eyes.* [Middle English, from Old French *guimbelet,* probably from Middle Dutch *wimmelkijn,* diminutive of *wimmel,* auger.]

gim·mal (gímm'l) *n.* A ring made of two narrower rings interlocked. [Earlier *gemel,* from Old French, from Latin *gemellus,* diminutive of *geminus,* twin.]

gim·me (gímmi). *Slang.* Contraction of *give me.*

gim·mick (gímmik) *n. Informal.* **1.** A clever device or stratagem, especially one used to promote or publicise a something: *an advertising gimmick.* **2.** Any trivial or unnecessary innovation used to attract attention or interest. [20th century (American) : origin obscure.] —**gim·mick·ry** *n.* —**gim·mick·y** *adj.*

gimp[1] (gimp) *n.* A narrow braid or cord of fabric, sometimes stiffened, used to trim or pipe clothes, curtains, or upholstered furniture. Also called "guimpe", "guipure".
~*tr.v.* **gimped, gimping, gimps.** To trim or edge with gimp. [Dutch *gimp*†.]

gimp[2] *n. Slang.* Spirit; courage. [20th century : origin obscure.]

gin[1] (jin) *n.* **1.** A strong alcoholic drink made by distilling rye, barley, or other grains and flavouring it with juniper berries. **2.** A similar spirit flavoured with some other aromatic substance, such as sloes or aniseed. [Shortened from Dutch *jenever,* from Middle Dutch *geniver, genever,* juniper, from Old French *geneivre,* from Latin *jūniperus,* JUNIPER.]

gin[2] (jin) *n.* **1.** Any of several machines or devices, as: **a.** A machine for hoisting or moving heavy objects. **b.** A **pile driver** *(see).* **c.** A snare or trap for game. **d.** A pump operated by a windmill. **2.** A **cotton gin** *(see).*
~*tr.v.* **ginned, ginning, gins. 1.** To remove the seeds from (cotton) with a cotton gin. **2.** To trap (game) in a gin. [Middle English *gin,* short for *engin,* ENGINE.]

gin[3] (jin) *n.* A card game, **gin rummy** *(see).*

gin[4] (jin) *n. Australian.* An Aboriginal woman. [From a native Australian language.]

gin[5] (gin) *prep. Scottish.* If. [Probably akin to *gif,* IF.]

gin and it (jin) *n. Chiefly British.* A cocktail made from gin and Italian vermouth. [*It,* from Italian *(vermouth).*]

gin·ger (jínjər) *n.* **1.** A plant, *Zingiber officinale,* of tropical Asia, having yellowish-green flowers and a pungent, aromatic rootstock. **2.** The rootstock of this plant, often dried and powdered and used as flavouring, or, in sugared form, as a sweet. **3.** Any of various other plants of the family Zingiberaceae, having variously coloured, often fragrant flowers. **4.** the **wild ginger** *(see).* **5.** A reddish yellow or yellowish brown. **6.** *Informal.* Liveliness; vigour.
~*tr.v.* **gingered, -gering, -gers. 1.** To spice with ginger. **2.** *Informal.* To make more lively. Often used with *up: She gingered up the party.* [Middle English *gingivere,* from Old English *gingifer* and Old French *gingivre, gingembre,* from Medieval Latin *gingiber, gingiver,* from Latin *zinziberi,* from Greek *ziggiberis,* from Prakrit *singabēra,*

from Sanskrit *śṛṅgaveram* : *śṛṅga-,* horn + *vera-*†, body (so called from its shape).]

ginger ale *n.* An effervescent soft drink, pale orange or brown in colour, and flavoured with ginger.

ginger beer *n.* An effervescent soft drink popular in England, cloudy grey in colour and flavoured with fermented ginger.

gin·ger·bread (jínjər-bred) *n.* **1. a.** A dark treacle cake flavoured with ginger. **b.** A soft treacle and ginger biscuit cut in various shapes, sometimes elaborately decorated with coloured icing and, formerly, with gilt. **2. a.** Any elaborate ornamentation. **b.** Any superfluous or tasteless embellishment, especially in architecture.
~*adj.* **1.** Made of gingerbread. **2.** Tastelessly elaborate. [Middle English *gingebred,* preserved ginger, alteration (influenced by *bred,* BREAD) of Old French *gingebras,* from Medieval Latin *gingibrātum,* from *gingiber,* GINGER.]

gingerbread tree *n.* An African tree, *Parinarium macrophyllum,* having large edible fruits and useful wood. Also called "gingerbread plum".

ginger group *n. Chiefly British.* A group of people within an association or organisation that represent a challenging, progressive, or radical viewpoint. [From GINGER (verb).]

gin·ger·ly (jínjər-li) *adv.* **1.** With great care or delicacy. **2.** Cautiously; carefully; timidly.
~*adj.* Cautious; careful; timid. [Earliest sense "daintily", perhaps from Old French *gensor, genzor,* comparative of *gent,* pretty, of noble birth, from Latin *genitus,* past participle of *gignere,* to bring forth.] —**gin·ger·li·ness** *n.*

gin·ger·snap (jíngər-snap) *n.* A flat, brittle, sweetened biscuit spiced with ginger. Also called "gingernut".

gin·ger·y (jínjəri) *adj.* **1.** Having the spicy flavour of ginger. **2.** Sharp and pungent; biting: *a gingery remark.* **3.** Reddish-yellow or yellowish-brown.

ging·ham (gíng-əm) *n.* A yarn-dyed cotton fabric woven in stripes, checks, or plaids. [Dutch *gingang,* from Malay *ginggang, gĕnggang,* "interspace".]

gin·gi·li (jínjili) *n.* **1.** Oil extracted from sesame seeds. Also called "gingili oil". **2.** The sesame plant. [Hindi *jingali.*]

gin·gi·va (jin-jiv-ə, jin-jīv-) *n. Anatomy.* The **gum** *(see).*

gin·gi·val (jin-ji-v'l, jin-jī-) *adj.* Of or having to do with the gums. [Latin *gingīva*†, gum.]

gin·gi·vi·tis (jín-ji-vītiss) *n.* Inflammation of the gums. [New Latin : Latin *gingīva*†, gum + -ITIS.]

gin·gly·mus (jing-gli-məss, ging-) *n., pl.* **-mi** (-mī). *Anatomy.* A hinge joint, such as the elbow or knee joint, allowing movement in one plane only. [New Latin, from Greek *ginglumos,* hinge.]

gink (gingk) *n. Slang.* A man or boy, especially one considered odd in some way. [19th century (American) : origin obscure.]

gink·go (gingk-gō, -ō) *n., pl.* **-goes.** A gymnosperm tree, *Ginkgo biloba,* native to China, having fan-shaped leaves and fleshy, yellowish fruit, and often planted for ornament. Also called "maidenhair tree". [Japanese *ginkyō,* from ancient Chinese *ngien hang* (Mandarin *yín xing),* "silver apricot" : *ngien,* silver + *hang,* apricot.]

gin·nel (ginn'l, jinn'l) *n. Northern British.* A narrow alleyway; a passage between buildings. [Perhaps a corruption of CHANNEL.]

gin rummy (jin) *n.* A variety of rummy for two or more persons in which a person may win by matching all his cards or may end the game by melding when his unmatched cards add up to ten points or less. Also called "gin". [GIN (alcohol) + RUMMY, suggested by a play on RUM (alcohol).]

Gins·berg (gínz-berg), **Allen** (1926–97). U.S. poet. A member of the beat generation, he became a celebrity in the 1960s for his part in campaigns on behalf of black civil rights and against the Vietnam war. His books include *Howl* (1956), *Kaddish* (1960), and *Reality Sandwiches* (1963).

gin·seng (jín-seng ‖ -sang, -sing) *n.* **1.** Any of several plants of the genus *Panax;* especially, *P. schinseng,* of eastern Asia, or *P. quinquefolium,* of North America, having small greenish flowers and a forked root believed to have medicinal properties, especially the power to promote long life. **2.** The root of either of these plants. [Mandarin Chinese *rén shēn* : *rén,* man (because the forked root resembles a human being with limbs) + *shēn,* ginseng.]

gin sling (jin) *n.* An iced, often sweetened, cocktail made from gin, lime or lemon juice, and water.

Gior·gio·ne (jawr-jō-nay, -ji-ō-, -ni), **II,** originally Giorgio Barbarelli; also known as Giorgio da Castelfranco (*c.*1477–1510). Italian painter of the Venetian school. He left not a single signed and dated painting, and was one of the first to paint small canvases for private collectors.

Gior·gi system (jórji) *n. Physics.* A system of units based on the metre, kilogram, second, and ampere in which the magnetic constant has the value $4\pi \times 10^{-7}$ henries per metre. Also called "MKSA system". [After Giovanni *Giorgi* (1871–1950), Italian physicist.]

Giot·to (jóttō, jót-tō, ji-ót-), also known as Giotto di Bondone (*c.* 1266–1337). Italian Florentine painter and architect who heralded the Renaissance. Among his most famous works is the fresco cycle, *Lives of the Virgin and Christ* which decorates the walls of the Arena chapel at Padua. Other great fresco cycles are at Assisi and in Santa Croce, Florence.

Giovanni da Bologna. See **Giambologna.**

gip. Variant of **gyp.**

gippo. Variant of **gyppo.**

gip·py tummy (jíppi) *n. British Informal.* Diarrhoea or dysentery.

[*Gippy,* from *Egyptian,* referring to the diarrhoea affecting visitors to Egypt (or other hot climates).]
Gipsy. Variant of **Gypsy.**
gipsy moth *n.* A moth, *Lymantria dispar,* native to Europe but introduced elsewhere, the caterpillars of which feed on foliage and are destructive to trees.
gip·sy·wort (jíp-si-wurt) *n.* A Eurasian plant, *Lycopus europaeus,* with hairy stems and leaves and white two-lipped flowers marked with purple dots.
gi·raffe (ji-ráaf, -ráf) *n.* An African ruminant mammal, *Giraffa camelopardis,* having a very long neck and legs, a tan coat with brown blotches, and short horns. It is the tallest living mammal. [Italian *giraffa,* from Arabic *zirāfah,* probably of African origin.]
Gi·ral·dus Cam·bren·sis (ji-ráldəss kam-brén-siss), also known as Gerald de Barri or Gerald of Wales (*c.*1146–*c.*1223). Welsh churchman and historian. His writings provide a vivid picture of early medieval life in Wales and Ireland, especially the *Topographia Hibernica,* the *Expugnatio Hibernica,* and the *Itinerarium Cambriae.*
gir·an·dole (jírrən-dōl) *n.* **1. a.** A rotating display, as of a jet of water or fireworks. **b.** A branched candlestick, sometimes backed by a mirror. **2.** A piece of jewellery, such as an earring, having a large stone surrounded by small drops. [French *girandole,* from Italian *girandola,* from *girare,* to turn, from Latin *gȳrāre,* to GYRATE.]
gir·a·sol, gir·o·sol, gir·a·sole (jírrə-sol, -sōl) *n.* A **fire opal** *(see).* [Italian *girasole* : *girare,* to turn (see **girandole**) + *sole,* sun, from Latin *sōl.*]
Gi·rau·doux (zhéerō-dōō), **Jean** (1882–1944). French novelist and playwright. His literary career began with a novel, *Suzanne et le Pacifique* (1921), but he wrote principally for the stage; his most famous play being *La Guerre de Troie n'aura pas lieu* (1935).
gird[1] (gurd) *tr.v.* **girded** or **girt** (gurt), **girding, girds. 1. a.** To encircle with a belt or band. **b.** To fasten or secure with a belt, cord, or the like. **c.** To surround: *an island girded by water.* **2. a.** To equip: *girded with the sword of knighthood.* **b.** To endow with some attribute: *girded with righteousness.* In both senses, sometimes used with *up.* **3.** To prepare for action. Used chiefly in the phrase *gird (up) one's loins.* [Middle English *girden,* Old English *gyrdan.*]
gird[2] (gurd) *v.* **girded, girding, girds.** —*tr. Archaic.* To jeer at; mock. —*intr.* To make taunting remarks; jeer.
~*n. Archaic.* A sarcastic remark. [Middle English *girden*†, to strike, cut, charge.] **—gird·er** *n.*
gird·er (gúrdər) *n.* A horizontal beam, as of steel or wood, used as a main support for a vertical load.
gir·dle[1] (gúrd'l) *n.* **1. a.** A belt, sash, or the like, worn at the waist. **b.** A band or structure that encircles like a belt. **2.** An elasticised, flexible corset worn over the waist and hips. **3.** A band made around the trunk of a tree by the removal of a strip of bark. **4.** The edge of a cut gem held by the setting. **5.** *Anatomy.* The **pelvic girdle** or **pectoral girdle** *(both of which see).*
~*tr.v.* **girdled, -dling, -dles. 1.** To encircle with or as if with a belt. **2.** To put a girdle on or around. **3.** To remove a band of bark completely from the circumference of (a tree), usually to kill it. [Middle English *girdel,* Old English *gyrdel.*]
girdle[2]. *Chiefly Scottish.* Variant of **griddle.**
girdle cake *n.* A **drop scone** *(see).*
gird·ler (gúrd-lər) *n.* **1.** One that girdles. **2.** Any of various insects that chew circular bands around twigs or stems in preparing nesting sites. **3.** *Archaic.* One who makes girdles.
girl (gurl; *also old-fashioned* gel || gal) *n.* **1.** A female who has not yet attained womanhood. **2.** A female child. **3.** A single young woman. **4.** *Informal.* Any woman. **5.** A daughter. **6.** A girlfriend. **7.** *Plural. Informal.* A group of female friends, especially ones who meet regularly. **8. a.** A female worker or employee. **b.** A female servant. **9.** Used of a female animal. [Middle English *girle, gerle, gurle*†.]
girl Friday *n. Informal.* A female employee, especially one having a great variety of responsibilities. [By analogy with MAN FRIDAY.]
girl·friend (gúrl-frend) *n.* **1.** A favourite female friend, especially one with whom a person is sexually or romantically involved. **2.** Any female friend.
Girl Guide *n. Sometimes small* **g,** *small* **g.** A member of the Girl Guides Association.
Girl Guides Association *n.* A British youth organisation founded in 1910 to promote character development and practical skills.
girl·hood (gúrl-hōōd) *n.* The state or time of being a girl.
girl·ie, girl·y (gúrli) *adj.* **1.** Containing or displaying pictures of naked or almost naked women that are intended to be sexually stimulating: *girlie magazines.* **2.** Girlish.
girl·ish (gúrlish) *adj.* Pertaining to, characteristic of, or suitable for a girl or girls.
Girl Scout *n.* A member of the Girl Scouts, a youth organisation founded in the United States in 1912 on the plan of the Girl Guides Association.
girn (gurn) *intr.v.* **girned, girning, girns.** *Scottish.* To complain in a whining voice. [Middle English *girnen,* variant of *grinnen,* to grimace, whimper, GRIN.]
gi·ro (jīr-ō) *n., pl.* **-ros. 1.** A centrally operated system of settling debts and transferring credits between different banks or post offices. **2.** *Capital* **G.** The British Post Office giro system. Also officially called "National Girobank". **3.** *Informal.* A Post Office giro cheque. [German, from Italian, "circulation".] **—gi·ro** *adj.*
Gi·ronde[1] (zhee-róNd). France's largest département, lying in the southwest of the country. It contains some of the country's finest vineyards, the districts of Médoc, Graves, and Sauternes having given their names to several famous wines. Bordeaux is the capital.
Gironde[2]. Estuary in southwest France, formed by the rivers Garonne and Dordogne. Some 70 kilometres (45 miles) long, it is the seaway to the port of Bordeaux.
Gi·rond·in (*French* zhee-roND-ÍN) *n.* Also **Gi·rond·ist** (ji-rónd-ist). A member of a moderate republican party of Revolutionary France (1791–93). See **Jacobin.** [After GIRONDE[1], because the leaders of the party were deputies of that département.] **—Gi·ron·dist** *adj.*
girosol. Variant of **girasol.**
girt[1] (gurt) *v.* **girted, girting, girts.** —*tr.* **1.** To gird; encircle or bind. **2.** To measure the girth of. —*intr.* To measure in girth. [Variant of GIRD.]
girt[2]. Alternative past tense and past participle of **gird** (to encircle).
girth (gurth) *n.* **1.** The distance around something; the circumference. **2.** The size of something; bulk. **3.** A strap encircling the body of a horse or other animal to secure a load or saddle upon its back.
~*tr.v.* **girthed, girthing, girths. 1.** To measure the circumference of. **2.** To encircle. **3.** To secure with a girth. [Middle English *gerth,* from Old Norse *györth,* girdle.]
gi·sarme (gi-zárm) *n.* A halberd with a long shaft and a two-sided blade, carried by medieval foot soldiers. [Middle English, from Old French *g(u)isarme,* from Old High German *getīsarn* : *getan*†, to weed + *īsarn,* iron, from Common Germanic *īsarna-* (unattested), IRON.]
Gis·card d'Es·taing (zhee-skaar-dess-táN), **Valéry** (1926–). French politician. He was first elected to the National Assembly at the age of 29 and twice held office as Minister of Finance (1962–66 and 1969–74). He was elected president of the Republic as leader of the Independent Republicans in 1974 and was defeated in his attempt to be reelected in 1981. He was leader of the Union for French Democracy (1978–96), and in 1989 resigned from the National Assembly to enter the European Parliament.
Gish (gish), **Lillian,** née de Guiche (1896–1993). U.S. actress. She made her film debut in 1912 and won international acclaim in 1915 for her role in *The Birth of a Nation.*
gis·mo, giz·mo (gízmō) *n., pl.* **-mos.** *Chiefly U.S. Slang.* A mechanical device or part, the name of which is forgotten or not yet designated. [20th century : origin obscure.]
Gis·sing (gíssing), **George (Robert)** (1857–1903). British novelist. His best-known works are *New Grub Street* (1891) and the semiautobiographical, imaginary journal, *The Private Papers of Henry Ryecroft* (1903).
gist (jist) *n.* **1.** The central idea of some matter, such as an argument or a speech; the essence. **2.** *Law.* The grounds for action in a suit. [Old French *(cest action) gist,* (this action) lies, from *gesir,* to lie, from Latin *jacēre,* from *jacere,* to throw.]
git (git) *n. British Slang.* A silly or contemptible person. [Variant of GET (offspring, fool).]
Giu·li·ni (jōō-léeni, jōō-), **Carlo Maria** (1914–). Italian conductor who made his debut in Rome in 1944. He was principal conductor of the London New Philharmonia Orchestra. In 1978 he was appointed the musical director of the Los Angeles Philharmonic.
Giul·io Ro·ma·no (jōōli-ō rō-máanō) (*c.*1499–1546). Italian painter and architect, the favourite pupil of Raphael and one of the founders of Mannerism. After Raphael's death in 1520 he completed a number of the master's unfinished works, including the *Sala di Constantino* frescoes in the Vatican.
give (giv) *v.* **gave** (gayv), **given** (gívv'n), **giving, gives.** —*tr.* **1. a.** To make a present of; bestow ownership of on: *gave her flowers for her birthday.* **b.** To deliver in exchange or in recompense. Used with *for: He will give you five pounds for the book.* **c.** To put temporarily at the disposal of; entrust to: *give them the cottage for a week.* **d.** To place in the hands of: *Give me the scissors.* **2. a.** To convey or offer; communicate: *Give him my best wishes.* **b.** To bestow; confer: *give authority.* **c.** To grant: *give permission.* **3.** To contribute; furnish; donate: *give one's time.* **4. a.** To be a source of; afford: *His remark gave offence.* **b.** To expose or subject to: *She gave him measles.* **5.** To produce; yield: *This cow gives three gallons of milk per day.* **6.** To provide (something required or expected): *give one's name and address.* **7.** To administer: *give a spanking.* **8. a.** To grant; concede: *I'll give you that point.* **b.** To allow: *give odds of five to one.* **c.** To relinquish; yield: *give ground.* **9.** To emit or utter: *give a sigh.* **10. a.** To allot; assign: *give her five minutes to finish.* **b.** To designate; cite: *give a departure date.* **11. a.** To award: *give first prize to.* **b.** To judge to be in a specified condition: *gave the batsman out.* **12.** To ascribe; attribute: *give him the blame.* **13.** To grant as a supposition; acknowledge: *Given their superiority, we can't expect to win.* **14. a.** To stage: *give a dinner party.* **b.** To proffer: *give a toast.* **c.** To manifest: *give promise of brilliance.* **d.** *Informal.* To offer by way of explanation: *Don't give me that old story!* **e.** To execute: *give a bow.* **f.** To engage in: *give battle.* **15.** To submit for consideration or acceptance; tender: *give an opinion.* **16.** To allow or lead: *She gave me to think she loved me.* **17.** To devote: *give oneself to one's work.* **18.** To sacrifice: *give a son to the war.* **19.** To propose as a toast to: *I give you the regiment.* —*intr.* **1.** To make gifts or donations: *Please give generously.* **2.** To be unable to hold up; yield: *give under pressure.* **3.** To afford a view of or access to something: *The French doors give onto a terrace.* **4.** *Informal.* To be happening; occur: *What gives?* **—give as good as (one) gets.** To respond to an attack with equal force. **—give forth. 1.** To report; circulate. **2.** To emit. **—give in. 1.** To cease opposition; concede. **2.** To hand in; submit: *give in an essay.* **—give off.** To discharge; send forth; emit.

—**give or take**. Adding or subtracting. *I'll be there at five, give or take ten minutes.* —**give out. 1.** To let (something) be known; broadcast. **2.** To break down; become exhausted; fail. —**give over. 1.** To hand over; relinquish the care of. **2.** To devote or assign: *A week given over to indulgence.* **3.** *Informal.* To stop; desist. —**give rise to.** To cause; occasion. —**give (someone) one.** *Slang.* To hit; strike. —**give (someone) what for.** *Slang.* To scold; punish. —**give up. 1.** To surrender: *give yourself up.* **2.** To stop: *give up smoking.* **3.** To relinquish: *give up hope.* **4.** To abandon hope for: *give her up as lost.* **5.** To admit defeat. —**give way. 1. a.** To withdraw; retreat. **b.** To make room for or wait for the passage of: *give way to an oncoming car.* **2.** To collapse; break: *The ladder gave way.* **3.** To abandon oneself: *give way to hysteria.*
~*n. Informal.* The quality of being able to yield, adapt, or stretch under pressure; flexibility: *The mattress has lots of give.* [Give, gave, given; Middle English *given, gaf, given,* Old English *giefan, geaf, giefen.*]
give and take *intr.v.* To exchange on equal or even terms.
give-and-take (gívv'n-táyk) *n.* **1.** The practice of compromise. **2.** Lively exchange of ideas or conversation.
give away *tr.v.* **1.** To make a gift of. **2.** To observe ceremonially the transfer of (a bride) from her family to her husband. **3.** To reveal or make known, often accidentally.
give·a·way (gívvə-way) *n. Informal.* **1.** Something that betrays or exposes, often accidentally. **2.** Something offered at a bargain price. **3.** *Chiefly U.S.* Something given away at no charge.
giv·en (givv'n) *adj.* **1. a.** Specific: *a given date.* **b.** Issued on a specific date. Said of legal documents. **2.** Accepted as a fact; acknowledged; assumed. **3.** Habitually inclined. Used with *to: given to shyness.* **4.** Bestowed; presented.
given name *n. Chiefly U.S.* A name given to a person at birth or at baptism; a Christian name.
Gi·za, Al (géézə). *Arabic* **Al Gi·zeh.** Town in Egypt. The capital of the Giza governate, it is situated on the west bank of the river Nile. Nearby is the Great Pyramid of Khufu (Cheops), one of the seven wonders of the ancient world.
giz·zard (gízzərd) *n.* **1.** An enlargement of the alimentary canal in birds, often having dense muscular walls and containing fine grit eaten to aid in breaking up hard food. **2.** A similar digestive organ of certain invertebrates, such as the earthworm. **3.** The **proventriculus** *(see)* of insects and crustaceans. **4.** *Informal.* The stomach. [Middle English *giser,* from Old French *giser, gezier,* from Vulgar Latin *gicerium* (unattested), from Latin *gigeria,* cooked entrails of poultry, perhaps from Persian *jigar.*]
Gjel·le·rup (géllə-rŏŏp), **Karl Adolf** (1857–1919). Danish writer. He wrote poetry but was more famous for his novels, such as *An Idealist* (1878) and *The Pilgrim Kamanita* (1906). With Henrik Pontoppidan, he was awarded the Nobel prize for literature (1917).
Gk. Greek.
gla·bel·la (glə-béllə) *n., pl.* **-bellae** (-béllee). *Anatomy.* The smooth area between the eyebrows just above the nose, formed by part of the frontal bone. [New Latin, from Latin *glabellus,* hairless, from *glaber,* hairless, bald, GLABROUS.]
gla·brous (gláy-brəss) *adj. Biology.* Having no hairs or down; smooth. [Latin *glaber,* hairless, bald.]
gla·cé (glássay, glássi ‖ gla-sáy) *adj.* **1.** Having a glazed, glossy surface. **2.** Coated with a sugar glaze or icing.
~*tr.v.* **glacéed, -céing, -cés.** To coat with sugar glaze or icing. [French, past participle of *glacer,* to ice, glaze, from *glace,* ice, from Latin *glaciês.*]
gla·ci·al (gláy-si-əl, glássi-, -shi-, -sh'l) *adj.* **1.** Of, pertaining to, or derived from a glacier or ice sheet. **2.** Characterised or dominated by the existence of glaciers or ice sheets. **3.** Extremely cold; icy. **4.** Having the appearance of ice. [Latin *glaciālis,* icy, from *glaciês,* ice.] —**gla·ci·al·ly** *adv.*
glacial acetic acid *n.* Almost pure **acetic acid** *(see).*
glacial period *n. Often capital* **G,** *capital* **P. 1.** Any of several periods during the Pleistocene epoch, up to one million years ago, when much of the earth's surface was covered by ice. Also called "ice age". **2.** The Pleistocene epoch. Also called "glacial epoch".
gla·ci·ate (gláy-si-ayt, glássi-, -shi-) *v.* **-ated, -ating, -ates.** —*tr.* **1.** To subject to the effects of glaciers. **2.** *Rare.* To freeze. —*intr.* To become covered with glaciers or ice sheets. [Latin *glaciāre,* to freeze, from *glaciês,* ice. See **glacier.**]
gla·ci·a·tion (glay-si-aysh'n, glássi-, -shi-) *n. Geology.* **1.** The formation, movement, and retreat of ice sheets and glaciers. **2.** The overall effects on a landscape produced by glacial action.
gla·ci·er (glássi-ər, gláy-si- ‖ *U.S.* gláy-shər, -zhər) *n.* **1.** A huge mass of ice, originating from compacted snow, moving slowly in a continuous stream down a valley under its own weight. **2.** An ice sheet that has spread out from a central mass and covers a large part of a continent. [French, from *glace,* ice, from Latin *glaciês.*]
gla·ci·ol·o·gy (glássi-óllǝji, gláy-si- ‖ *U.S. also* -shi-) *n.* The scientific study of glaciers. [GLACIER + -LOGY.] —**gla·ci·o·log·ic** (-ǝ-lójik), **gla·ci·o·log·i·cal** (-ǝ-lójik'l) *adj.* —**gla·ci·ol·o·gist** *n.*
gla·cis (glássiss, glássi, gláy-siss ‖ gla-sée) *n.* **1.** A gentle slope; an incline. **2.** A slope extended in front of a fortification in such a way that approaching attackers are made particularly vulnerable to the defenders' fire. [French, from Old French *glacier,* to slide, from *glace,* ice, from Latin *glaciês.*] •
glad¹ (glad) *adj.* **gladder, gladdest. 1.** Experiencing or exhibiting joy and pleasure. **2.** Providing joy and pleasure: *a glad occasion.* **3.** Willing: *glad to help.* **4.** *Archaic.* Of a cheerful disposition.
~*tr.v.* **gladded, gladding, glads.** *Archaic.* To gladden. [Middle English *glad,* joyful, happy, shining, Old English *glæd,* from Germanic.] —**glad·ly** *adv.* —**glad·ness** *n.*
Synonyms: *glad, happy, cheerful, light-hearted, joyful, joyous.*
glad² *n.* Also *chiefly Australian* **glad·die** (gláddi). *Informal.* A gladiolus.
glad·den (gládd'n) *v.* **-dened, -dening, -dens.** —*tr.* To make glad. —*intr. Archaic.* To become glad.
glade (glayd) *n.* An open space in a wood or forest. [16th century : origin obscure.]
glad eye *n. Informal.* A provocative look: *He gave her the glad eye.*
glad hand *n. Informal.* **1.** A hearty and friendly handshake. **2.** A hearty welcome or greeting.
glad-hand (glád-hand) *v.* **-handed, -handing, -hands.** *Informal.* —*tr.* To extend a glad hand to. —*intr.* To extend a glad hand. —**glad-hand·er** (-hándər) *n.*
glad·i·ate (gláddi-ət, gláydi-, -it, -ayt) *adj.* Sword-shaped, as a leaf. [New Latin *gladiatus,* from Latin *gladius,* sword.]
glad·i·a·tor (gláddi-aytər) *n.* **1.** In ancient Rome, a professional combatant, slave, captive, or condemned prisoner trained to entertain the public by engaging in combat in the arena. **2.** A contender or debater, especially one chosen to represent his faction or party in public. [Middle English, from Latin *gladiātor,* from *gladius,* sword.] —**glad·i·a·to·ri·al** (-ǝ-táwri-əl ‖ -tóri-) *adj.*
glad·i·o·lus (gláddi-ŏ-lǝss) *n., pl.* **-li** (-lī, -lee) or **-luses.** Also **glad·i·o·la** (-lǝ) (for sense 1). **1.** Any of various plants of the genus *Gladiolus,* native to tropical regions but widely cultivated elsewhere, having sword-shaped leaves and a spike of showy, variously coloured, funnel-shaped flowers. Also called "sword lily". **2.** *Anatomy.* The large middle section of the sternum. [Latin, diminutive of *gladius,* sword.]
glad rags *pl.n. Informal.* One's best or most elegant clothes.
glad·some (glád-səm) *adj. Archaic.* **1.** Glad; joyful. **2.** Causing gladness. —**glad·some·ly** *adv.* —**glad·some·ness** *n.*
Glad·stone (glád-stən, -stōn) *n.* **1.** A light four-wheeled convertible carriage with two interior seats and places outside for a driver and footman. **2.** A Gladstone bag. [After W.E. GLADSTONE.]
Gladstone, William Ewart (1809–98). British statesman. He was Liberal prime minister four times (1868–74, 1880–85, 1886, and 1892–94). His first government passed a Land Act to protect Irish tenants, established national education in England, and introduced the secret ballot in parliamentary elections. During his second term of office the Reform Act of 1884 was passed. His third and fourth terms of office were taken up with unsuccessful attempts to gain support for a Home Rule Bill for Ireland.
Gladstone bag *n.* A piece of light hand luggage consisting of two hinged compartments. [After W.E. GLADSTONE.]
Glag·o·lit·ic (glággə-líttik) *adj.* Also **Glag·o·lith·ic** (-líthik). Belonging to or written in an alphabet attributed to St. Cyril, formerly used in the writing of various Slavonic languages but now limited to the Catholic liturgical books used by some communities along the Dalmatian coast. Compare **Cyrillic alphabet.** [New Latin *glagoliticus,* from Serbo-Croatian *glagolica,* the Glagolitic alphabet, from *glagól,* word; akin to Old Church Slavonic *glagolǔ,* word.]
glaik·it, glaik·et (gláy-kit) *adj. Chiefly Scottish.* Foolish; empty-headed. [15th century : origin obscure.]
glair, glaire (glair) *n.* **1.** Raw egg white used in sizing or glazing. **2. a.** A size, glaze, or adhesive made of egg white. **b.** Any similar viscous substance.
~*tr.v.* **glaired, glairing, glairs.** To apply glair to. [Middle English *glaire,* from Old French, from Vulgar Latin *clāria ovi* (unattested), white of egg, from *clārus,* clear.]
glair·y (gláir-i) *adj.* **-ier, -iest.** Also **glair·e·ous** (gláiri-əss). **1.** Like glair. **2.** Coated with glair. —**glair·i·ness** *n.*
glaive (glayv) *n. Archaic & Poetic.* A sword; especially, a broadsword. [Middle English *glaive,* from Old French, from Latin *gladius,* sword.]
Glam. Glamorgan; Glamorganshire.
Glamis (glaamz). Village in Angus in east Scotland. Glamis Castle was the childhood home of Queen Elizabeth the Queen Mother and the brithplace of Princess Margaret. The castle is built on the site of an earlier structure which belonged to the thane of Glamis, better known as Shakespeare's Macbeth.
Gla·mor·gan (glǝ-mórgən). Also **Gla·mor·gan·shire** (glǝ-mórgən-shər, -sheer). A former county of South Wales, which, in subsequent administrative reorganisations, has been fragmented into smaller units.
glam·or·ise, glam·or·ize, glam·our·ise (glámmə-rīz) *tr.v.* **-ised, -ising, -ises. 1.** To make glamorous or add glamour to. **2.** To treat or portray in a romantic manner; make attractive; glorify. —**glam·or·i·sa·tion** (-rī-záysh'n ‖ *U.S.* -ri-) *n.* —**glam·or·is·er** *n.*
glam·or·ous, glam·our·ous (glámmərəss) *adj.* Characterised by glamour. —**glam·or·ous·ly** *adv.* —**glam·or·ous·ness** *n.*
glam·our (glámmər) *n.* Also *U.S.* **glam·or. 1.** Compelling charm, romance, and excitement especially when delusively alluring: *The glamour of a James Bond film.* **2.** Sophisticated or fashionable attractiveness, especially when aided by the use of cosmetics. Also used adjectivally: *a glamour girl.* **3.** *Archaic.* Magic; enchantment; a magic spell. [Scottish variant of GRAMARYE.]
glance¹ (glaanss ‖ glanss) *v.* **glanced, glancing, glances.** —*intr.* **1.** To strike a surface at such an angle as to be deflected: *A pebble glanced off the windscreen.* **2.** To direct the gaze briefly: *glance at the menu.* **3.** To shine briefly; glint. **4.** To refer to or touch upon

briefly. **5.** In cricket, to hit a ball with the bat held at an oblique angle. —*tr.* **1.** To strike (a surface) at an angle; graze: *The ball glanced the fence.* **2.** To cause to strike a surface at an angle: *glance a stone over the stream.* **3.** In cricket, to hit (a ball) with an angled bat. —See Synonyms at **flash.**
~*n.* **1.** An oblique movement following impact; a deflection. **2.** A brief or cursory look. **3.** A quick flash of light; a gleam. **4.** In cricket, a stroke made with the bat held obliquely so that the ball is deflected, usually towards the leg side. Also called "glide". —**at a glance.** Immediately; with only a brief look: *I could tell at a glance that he was upset.* [Alteration of Middle English *glacen* (influenced by *glenten*, to shine, GLINT), from Old French *glacier*, to slide, from *glace*, ice, from Latin *glaciēs*.]

glance² *n.* Any of various minerals, usually sulphides, that have a brilliant lustre: *silver glance.* [German *Glanz*, from Old High German *glanz*, bright.]

gland (gland) *n.* **1. a.** *Anatomy.* An organ that synthesises specific substances, such as hormones, and secretes them into the bloodstream or elsewhere. See **endocrine gland, exocrine gland. b.** Any of various nonsecretory or excretory organs that resemble such organs, such as a lymph node. **2.** *Botany.* An organ or cell that secretes a substance. **3.** *Machinery.* A part that seals a casing to prevent fluid leakage at a point where a moving shaft comes out. [French *glande,* from Old French, glandular swelling, acorn, from Latin *glāns* (stem *gland-*), acorn.]

glan-ders (glándərz) *n.* A contagious, often chronic, sometimes fatal disease of horses and other animals, caused by a bacillus, *Actinobacillus mallei,* and characterised by a nasal discharge and ulcers in the lungs, respiratory tract, and skin. [Old French *glandres,* plural of *glandre,* glandular swelling, from Latin *glandula,* diminutive of *glāns* (stem *gland-*), acorn.] —**glan-der-ous** *adj.*

glan-du-lar (glándew-lər) *adj.* **1.** Of, pertaining to, affecting, or resembling a gland or its secretion. **2.** Functioning as a gland. **3.** Having glands. **4.** Resulting from abnormal gland function. [French *glandulaire,* from *glandule,* small gland, from Latin *glandula,* glandular swelling.]

glandular fever *n. Pathology.* An infectious disease mainly affecting adolescents and young adults, causing an abnormally large number of leucocytes with single nuclei in the bloodstream and characterised by fever, headache, and loss of energy. Also called "infectious mononucleosis", "mononucleosis".

glan-dule (glán-dewl) *n.* A small gland. [Latin *glandula,* diminutive of *glāns* (stem *gland-*), gland.]

glans (glanz) *n., pl.* **glan-des** (glán-deez). *Anatomy.* **1.** The glans penis. **2.** The glans clitoridis. [Latin *glāns,* "acorn" (from its shape).]

glans cli-tor-i-dis (kli-táwri-diss, klī-) *n.* The small mass of erectile tissue at the tip of the clitoris. Also called "glans".

glans penis *n.* The head or tip of the penis. Also called "glans".

glare¹ (glair) *v.* **glared, glaring, glares.** —*intr.* **1.** To stare fixedly and angrily. **2.** To shine intensely and blindingly; dazzle. **3.** To be conspicuous; stand out obtrusively. —*tr.* To express (an emotion) by staring fixedly and angrily. —See Synonyms at **gaze.**
~*n.* **1.** A fixed, angry stare. **2.** An intense and blinding light. **3.** Unwelcome attention: *the glare of publicity.* **4.** Rare. Showy brilliance; gaudiness: *the pomp and glare of rhetoric.* —See Synonyms at **blaze.** [Middle English *glaren,* probably from Middle Low German, to gleam.] —**glar-y** *adj.*

glare² *n. Chiefly U.S.* A sheet or surface of ice.

glar-ing (glaír-ing) *adj.* Painfully conspicuous. —**glar-ing-ly** *adv.*

Glas-gow (glaáz-gō, gláz-, gláss-, glaáss-). The largest city in Scotland, a port and administrative centre, situated on the river Clyde in the west of the country. A cathedral city since the 12th century, Glasgow prospered in the 18th century through trade in sugar and tobacco with the Americas. It is a major industrial centre. —**Glas-we-gian** (glaz-weéjən, glass-) *n. & adj.*

glas-nost (gláz-nost, glaáz-) *n. Russian.* Openness in the divulging and discussion of official policy; specifically, suggested as a reform measure in the Soviet Union associated with Mikhail Gorbachev and his supporters: *"The endless repetitions of the need for glasnost . . . are only a last gigantic effort to make the system work, not to change it."* (*The Spectator*). [Russian *glasnost',* publicity: *glas,* voice, variant of *golos,* akin to CALL, from a supposed Indo-European root *gal-†* + *nost', -ness.*]

glass (glaass ‖ glass) *n.* **1.** Any of a large class of materials with highly variable mechanical and optical properties that solidify from the molten state without crystallisation and are typically based on silicon dioxide, boric oxide, aluminium oxide, or phosphorus pentoxide. They are generally transparent or translucent and are regarded physically as supercooled liquids rather than true solids. **2.** Objects made of glass collectively; glassware. **3.** Something made of glass, especially: **a.** A drinking vessel. **b.** A mirror. **c.** A barometer. **d.** A windowpane. **4.** *Usually plural.* Any device containing a lens or lenses and used as an aid to vision. **5.** *Plural.* A pair of lenses used to correct faulty vision and worn in front of the eyes supported by a light frame that passes over the nose and round the ears. Also called "spectacles", *U.S.* "eyeglasses". **6.** The quantity contained by a drinking vessel; a glassful. **7.** *Geology.* Hard, shiny rock which has no crystalline structure.
~*adj.* Of, pertaining to, or made of glass.
~*v.* **glassed, glassing, glasses.** —*tr.* **1.** To place within glass or a glass container. **2.** To provide with glass or glass parts. **3.** *Poetic.* **a.** To see reflected, as in a mirror. **b.** To mirror; reflect. **4.** *Slang.*

To attack with a broken bottle. —*intr.* To become like glass. [Middle English *glas,* Old English *glæs,* from Germanic.]

glass-blow-ing (glaáss-blō-ing ‖ gláss-) *n.* The art or process of shaping an object from molten glass by blowing air into it through a tube. —**glass-blow-er** *n.*

glass ceiling *n.* An upper limit to promotion (as of women or ethnic minorities) that is no less real for being unacknowledged. [With *glass* suggesting the invisibility of the *ceiling,* upper limit.]

glass-cut-ter (glaáss-kuttər ‖ gláss-) *n.* **1.** One who cuts or etches patterns on glass. **2.** A tool for cutting glass.

glass eel *n.* An eel in its transparent, postlarval stage.

glass electrode *n.* An instrument for measuring pH (acidity or alkalinity), consisting of a thin glass bulb containing a buffer solution with a platinum wire dipping into it. The bulb is placed in the solution to be investigated and the pH is indicated by the potential difference between the glass and the platinum.

glass eye *n.* An artificial eye made of glass.

glass fibre *n.* A composite material consisting of glass fibres in resin. Also called "spun glass". A trademark is "Fibreglass".

glass-fish (glaáss-fish ‖ gláss-) *n., pl.* **-fishes** or collectively **glass-fish.** Any of various fishes of the family Centropomidae, of warm and tropical waters, having a transparent body and a cleft dorsal fin. Also called "glassperch".

glass-ful (glaáss-fōol ‖ gláss-) *n., pl.* **-fuls.** The quantity contained in a glass.

glass harmonica *n.* An 18th-century musical instrument consisting of a set of graduated glass bowls that produce tones when a moistened finger is passed over their rims. Also called "musical glasses".

glass-house (glaáss-howss ‖ gláss-) *n.* **1.** *Chiefly British.* A greenhouse. **2.** *British Slang.* A military prison. **3.** *Chiefly U.S.* A glassworks.

glass-ine (gla-seén) *n.* A nearly transparent, resilient, glazed paper resistant to the passage of air and grease.

glass jaw *n. Informal.* A jaw, specifically a boxer's jaw, that is very vulnerable to a knockout punch.

glass-mak-er (glaáss-maykər ‖ gláss-) *n.* One who makes glass. —**glass-mak-ing** *n.*

glass-pa-per (glaáss-paypər ‖ gláss-) *n.* Strong paper embedded with small glass particles and used to rub down or smooth.
~*tr.v.* **glasspapered, -pering, -pers.** To rub down or smooth (a surface) with glasspaper.

glass snake *n.* Any of several slender, limbless, snakelike lizards of the genus *Ophisaurus,* having a tail that breaks or snaps off readily. [From the brittleness of its tail.]

glass-ware (glaáss-wair ‖ gláss-) *n.* Objects, especially vessels, made of glass.

glass wool *n.* Fine-spun fibres of glass used for insulation, air filters, and the like, and for synthetic composite materials.

glass-work (glaáss-wurk ‖ gláss-) *n.* **1. a.** The manufacture of glassware or glass. **b.** The cutting and fitting of glass panes; glaziery. **2.** Glassware.

glass-works (glaáss-wurks ‖ glás-) *n., pl.* **glassworks.** A workshop or factory where glass is made.

glass-wort (glaáss-wurt ‖ gláss-, -wawrt) *n.* **1.** Any of various plants of the genus *Salicornia,* growing in salt marshes and having fleshy stems and rudimentary, scalelike leaves. Also called "marsh samphire". **2.** A plant, **saltwort** (*see*). [Formerly used in making glass.]

glass-y (glaá-si ‖ glássi) *adj.* **-ier, -iest. 1.** Resembling or pertaining to glass. **2.** Lifeless; expressionless: *a glassy stare.* —**glass-i-ly** *adv.* —**glass-i-ness** *n.*

Glas-ton-bur-y (gláss-tən-bəri, glaáss-, -bri ‖ -berri). A market town in Somerset in the southwest of England. It is the traditional site of King Arthur's Isle of Avalon and is also associated with the legend of St. Joseph of Arimathea. Its ruined Benedictine abbey of St. Mary is built on the site of an earlier Celtic monastery (*c.* 678).

Glau-ber's salts, Glau-ber's salt (glówbərz) *n.* A hydrated sodium sulphate, $Na_2SO_4 \cdot 10H_2O$, used in paper and glass manufacturing and as a laxative. [After J.R. *Glauber* (1604–70), German alchemist.]

glau-co-ma (glaw-kṓmə ‖ glow-) *n.* A disease of the eye characterised by high intraocular pressure, damaged optic disc, hardening of the eyeball, and partial or complete loss of vision. [Latin *glaucōma,* cataract, from Greek *glaukōma,* from *glaukos,* GLAUCOUS.] —**glau-co-ma-tous** *adj.*

glau-co-nite (gláwkə-nīt) *n.* A greenish mineral, consisting essentially of a hydrous silicate of potassium and iron, found most commonly in greensand, used as a water softener and a fertiliser. [Greek *glaukon,* neuter of *glaukos,* GLAUCOUS + -ITE.] —**glau-co-nit-ic** (-níttik) *adj.*

glau-cous (gláwkəss) *adj.* **1.** Greyish green or bluish green. **2.** *Botany.* Covered with a fine, whitish, powdery coating. [Latin *glaucus,* from Greek *glaukos†,* gleaming, bluish green or grey.]

glaur (glor) *n. Scottish.* Mire. [Middle English (Scottish and northern English); perhaps akin to Old Norse *leir,* mud.] —**glaur-y** *adj.*

glaze (glayz) *n.* **1. a.** A thin, smooth, shiny coating. **b.** The substance of which this coating is made, either before or after it has solidified. **2.** A coating of coloured, opaque, or transparent material applied to ceramics to produce a glassy, waterproof surface. **3.** A coating, such as syrup or gelatine, put on food. **4.** A transparent coating applied to the surface of a painting to modify the colour tones. **5.** A glassy film, as over the eyes. **6.** *U.S.* Glaze ice.
~*v.* **glazed, glazing, glazes.** —*tr.* **1.** To fit or furnish (a window,

for example) with glass. **2.** To apply a glaze to. **3.** To give a smooth, lustrous surface to. —*intr.* **1.** To be or become glassy. Often used with *over.* **2.** To form a glaze. [Middle English *glāsen,* to provide with glass or a glassy surface, from *glas,* GLASS.] —**glaz·er** *n.*

glaze ice *n.* A thin, glassy coating of ice on the ground, on exposed objects, or on aircraft, caused by freezing weather after a partial thaw, or by the freezing of rain or fog droplets on impact with a cold or freezing surface. Also called "black ice", "glazed frost", "silver frost", "silver thaw", *U.S.* "glaze".

gla·zi·er (glá-zi-ər, -zhi-, -zhər) *n.* One who cuts and fits window glass. [Middle English *glasier,* from *glas,* GLASS.]

gla·zi·er·y (glá-zi-əri, -zhi-, -zhəri) *n.* The cutting and fitting of window glass.

glaz·ing (glá-zing) *n.* **1.** Glass set or made to be set in frames. **2.** The process of applying a glaze.

Gla·zu·nov (glázzōō-nof, *Russian* -náwf), **Alexander Konstantinovich** (1865–1936). Russian composer. He was taught by Rimsky-Korsakov, with whom he completed Borodin's opera *Prince Igor.* He wrote eight symphonies and many chamber works.

GLC 1. Greater London Council. **2.** gas-liquid chromatography.

gld. guilder.

gleam (gleem) *n.* **1.** A fleeting beam or flash of light. **2.** A steady but subdued shining; a glow. **3.** A brief or dim manifestation or indication: *a gleam of intelligence.*
~*intr.v.* **gleamed, gleaming, gleams. 1.** To emit a gleam; flash or glow. **2.** To be manifested or indicated briefly or faintly. —See Synonyms at **flash.** [Middle English *gleem, glem,* Old English *glǣm,* from Germanic.]

glean (gleen) *v.* **gleaned, gleaning, gleans.** —*intr.* To gather corn left behind in a field after the crop has been harvested. —*tr.* **1.** To gather (corn left behind in a field after harvesting). **2.** To collect (knowledge or information, for example) bit by bit: *Historians glean their knowledge from old records and documents.* [Middle English *glenen,* from Old French *glener,* from Late Latin *glennāre,* from Celtic *glend-no-* (unattested).] —**glean·er** *n.*

glean·ings (gléeningz) *pl.n.* **1.** Knowledge or information collected bit by bit. **2.** The corn left behind in a field after the crop has been harvested.

gle·ba (glée-bə) *n., pl.* **-bae** (-bee). *Botany.* The inner, spore-bearing mass of puffballs and related fungi. [New Latin, from Latin *glēba, glǣba,* clod, GLEBE.]

glebe (gleeb) *n.* **1.** *British.* A plot of land granted to a clergyman as part of his benefice during his tenure of office. **2.** *Poetic.* The soil or earth, regarded as the source of vegetation; land. [Middle English, from Latin *glēba, glǣba,* clod.]

glede (gleed, gled) *n. British Regional.* A predatory bird, the red kite, *Milvus milvus.* [Middle English *glede,* Old English *glida,* from Germanic; akin to GLIDE.]

glee (glee) *n.* **1.** Merriment; joy; delight. **2.** An unaccompanied part song scored for three or more male voices that was popular in the 18th century. —See Synonyms at **mirth.** [Middle English *glē,* Old English *glēo,* merriment, play, music, from Germanic.]

glee club *n. Chiefly U.S.* A group of singers who perform pieces of choral music.

gleed (gleed) *n. British Regional.* A glowing coal; an ember. [Middle English *glede, gleed,* Old English *glēd.*]

glee·ful (gléef'l) *adj.* Full of glee; merry. —**glee·ful·ly** *adv.* —**glee·ful·ness** *n.*

glee·man (glée-mən) *n., pl.* **-men** (-mən, -men). *Archaic.* A medieval itinerant singer; a minstrel. [Middle English *gleeman,* Old English *glēoman* : *glēo,* GLEE + *mann,* MAN.]

gleet (gleet) *n.* **1.** Inflammation of the urethra resulting from chronic gonorrhoea, characterised by discharge of mucus and pus. **2.** The discharge characterising this condition. [Middle English *glet,* slime, mucus, from Old French *glete,* from Latin *glittus,* sticky.] —**gleet·y** *adj.*

gleg (gleg) *adj. Scottish.* Alert and quick to respond. [Middle English *gleg,* clear-sighted, from Old Norse *glöggr.*]

glei. Variant of **gley.**

Gleizes (glez), **Albert (Léon)** (1881–1953). French cubist painter. He published with Jean Metzinger (1883–1956) the first manifesto of cubist principles, *Du Cubisme* (1912).

glen (glen) *n.* A narrow, flat-bottomed, steep-sided valley in Scotland and Ireland. [Middle English *glen,* from Scottish Gaelic *gle(a)nn,* from Old Irish *glend†.*]

Glen Albyn. See **Great Glen.**

Glen·coe (glen-kō). A glen in the highlands of western Scotland, issuing into Loch Leven. Ossian was allegedly buried in the glen, and the Macdonalds were massacred there by the Campbells in 1692.

Glen·dow·er (glen-dówr, -dówər), **Owen,** also known as Owain Glyndŵr (*c.*1359–*c.*1416). Welsh national leader. He led a revolt against the English in 1400 and by 1404 controlled most of Wales. In 1405 he summoned a Welsh parliament, but two defeats marked the end of his rebellion, and he ended his life in hiding.

glen·gar·ry (glen-gárri) *n., pl.* **-ries.** A brimless woollen cap originating in Scotland, that is creased lengthways and often has short ribbons at the back. Also called "glengarry bonnet". [After *Glengarry,* Scotland.]

Glen Mòr. See **Great Glen.**

gle·noid cavity (gléenoyd) *n. Anatomy.* The cavity at the top of the scapula that forms the socket of the shoulder joint, into which the

head of the humerus fits. [Greek *glēnoeidēs,* from *glēnē,* socket of a joint, eyeball.]

gley, glei (glā) *n.* A sticky, bluish-grey soil layer formed under the influence of excessive moisture. [Ukranian, CLAY.]

gli·a (glée-ə) *n.* Neuroglia (*see*).

gli·a·din (glī-ədin) *n.* Any of several simple proteins derived from rye or wheat gluten. [Italian *gliadina,* from Medieval Greek *glia, gloia,* glue.]

glib (glib) *adj.* **glibber, glibbest.** Easy and fluent in speech and writing, but superficial and insincere. [Probably from Low German *glibbrig,* from Middle Low German *glibberich,* slippery.] —**glib·ly** *adv.* —**glib·ness** *n.*

glide (glīd) *v.* **glided, gliding, glides.** —*intr.* **1.** To move in a smooth, effortless manner. **2.** To occur or pass imperceptibly. **3. a.** To fly a glider. **b.** To move in the air without engine power, wing movements, or other forms of motive power; fly without propulsion. **4.** *Music.* To blend one note into the next; slur. **5.** *Phonetics.* To articulate a glide. **6.** *Physics.* To deform so that one crystal plane slips over another. Used of solids. —*tr.* To cause to glide. ~*n.* **1.** A smooth effortless movement. **2.** *Aeronautics.* An act of flying without propulsion. **3.** The sliding section of a trombone's tubing. **4.** *Music.* A slur. **5.** *Phonetics.* **a.** The transitional sound produced by passing from the articulatory position of one speech sound to that of another. **b.** A semivowel (*see*). **6. a.** Any of various dances involving smooth, gliding dance steps. **b.** Such a dance step. **7.** In cricket, a glance (*see*). [Middle English *gliden,* Old English *glīdan,* from Germanic.]

glide path *n.* The path of an aircraft when descending to land as marked out by a radio beam.

glid·er (glīdər) *n.* **1.** One that glides. **2.** A light, engineless aircraft with specially extended wings to provide lift, designed for long periods of gliding after launch from a towing vehicle. **3.** One who flies or is trained to fly such an aircraft.

glid·ing (glīding) *n.* The practice or sport of flying gliders.

gliding lemur *n.* The **flying lemur** (*see*).

gliding possum *n.* Any of several small marsupials of the family Phalangeridae; especially, one of the genus *Petaurus,* of Australia, New Guinea, and Tasmania, capable of gliding through the air sustained by large folds of skin between the forelegs and hind legs. Also called "flying possum", "flying phalanger".

glim (glim) *n. Archaic Slang.* **1.** A source of light, such as a candle. **2.** An eye. [Perhaps shortened from GLIMMER.]

glim·mer (glímmər) *n.* **1.** A dim or intermittent light; a flicker. **2.** A faint manifestation or indication; a glimpse: *a glimmer of hope.* ~*intr.v.* **glimmered, -mering, -mers. 1.** To emit a dim or intermittent light. **2.** To appear or be indicated faintly. —See Synonyms at **flash.** [Middle English *glimeren,* probably from Scandinavian, akin to Swedish *glimra.*]

glimpse (glimps) *n.* **1.** A brief, incomplete view or look. **2.** A brief indication: *a glimpse of what she intended.* **3.** *Archaic.* A brief flash of light. ~*v.* **glimpsed, glimpsing, glimpses.** —*tr.* **1.** To obtain a brief, incomplete view of. **2.** To obtain a brief indication of. —*intr.* To obtain a brief, incomplete view. Used with *at.* [Middle English *glimsen, glymsen,* from Germanic; akin to Middle High German *glimsen,* to gleam.]

Glin·ka (glín-kə), **Mikhail Ivanovich** (1804–57). Russian composer, often called the father of Russian music. His two most famous operas, which display Russian folk influences, are *A Life for the Tsar* (1836) and *Russlan and Ludmilla* (1842).

glint (glint) *n.* **1.** A momentary flash of light; a sparkle. **2.** A faint or fleeting manifestation; a trace. **3.** *Archaic.* A glance. ~*v.* **glinted, glinting, glints.** —*intr.* **1.** To gleam or flash. **2.** *Archaic.* To move abruptly; dart. —*tr.* To cause to gleam or flash. —See Synonyms at **flash.** [Middle English *glinten, glenten,* to shine, move quickly, from Scandinavian; akin to Swedish dialectal *glänta, glinta,* to shine!]

gli·o·ma (glī-ōmə) *n.* A tumour in any part of the nervous system consisting of neuroglia cells. [New Latin : GLIA + -OMA.]

glis·sade (gli-saad, -sáyd) *n.* **1.** A gliding ballet step. **2.** A controlled slide, as: **a.** In a standing position, as when using an implement such as an ice-axe, in order to slow the descent. **b.** In a sitting position, as when descending a steep icy or snowy incline. ~*intr.v.* **glissaded, -sading, -sades.** To perform a glissade. [French, from Old French, sliding motion, from *glisser,* to slide, from *glier,* to glide, from Frankish *glīdan* (unattested).]

glis·san·do (gli-sán-dō) *n., pl.* **-di** (-dee) or **-dos.** *Music.* A blending of one note into the next in a scalelike passage, as by running a finger along a set of piano keys or harp strings. [Probably pseudo-Italian formation from GLISSADE.]

glis·ten (gliss'n) *intr.v.* **-tened, -tening, -tens.** To shine by reflection; reflect or be reflected lustrously. See Synonyms at **flash.** ~*n.* A shine or sparkle. [Middle English *glistnen,* Old English *glisnian.*]

glis·ter (glístər) *intr.v.* **-tered, -tering, -ters.** *Poetic.* To shine; glisten. ~*n. Poetic.* Glitter; brilliance. [Middle English *glistren,* probably from Middle Dutch *glisteren.*]

glitch (glich) *n.* **1.** *Astronomy.* A temporary change in the frequency of emission of a pulsar. **2.** *Slang.* A temporary breakdown or malfunction in a piece of machinery, electrical equipment, or the like. [Perhaps from German *Glitsche,* a slip, slide.]

glit·ter (glíttər) *n.* **1.** A sparkling light or brightness. **2. a.** Brilliant attractiveness. **b.** Showy splendour: *the glitter of showbusiness.*

3. Small pieces of highly reflective decorative material. ~*intr.v.* **glittered, -tering, -ters.** 1. To sparkle brilliantly; glisten. 2. To be brilliantly attractive or colourful. —See Synonyms at **flash.** [Middle English *gliteren,* from Old Norse *glitra.*] —**glit·ter·ing·ly** *adv.* —**glit·ter·y** *adj.*

glitz (glits) *n. Informal.* Specious showiness. [Back-formation from *glitzy,* flashy, showy, probably from German *glitzen,* to shine, from Old High German *glīzan.*] —**glitz·i·ness** *n.* —**glitz·y** *adj.*

gloam·ing (glōming) *n.* Also *archaic* **gloam** (glōm). *Poetic.* Twilight; dusk. [Middle English *gloming* (Scottish dialect), Old English *glōmung,* from *glōm,* dusk; akin to GLOW.]

gloat (glōt) *intr.v.* **gloated, gloating, gloats.** To regard with great, excessive, smug, or malicious pleasure or satisfaction. Often used with *over: gloat over one's possessions.* ~*n.* An act of gloating. [Perhaps from Scandinavian; akin to Old Norse *glotta,* to smile scornfully.] —**gloat·ing·ly** *adv.*

glob (glob) *n. Informal.* 1. A small drop of something; a globule. 2. A rounded, usually large, lump or mass of something: *a glob of mashed potatoes.* [Middle English *globbe,* large mass, from Latin *globus,* GLOBE.]

glob·al (glōb'l) *adj.* 1. Of, pertaining to, or involving the entire earth; worldwide: *a global disarmament treaty.* 2. Comprehensive; entire; total. —**glob·al·ly** *adv.*

glob·al·ise, glob·al·ize (glōbəliz) *tr.v.* **-ised, -ising, -ises.** To make (certain economic practices, for example) worldwide, especially through deregulation and the removal of protectionism. —**glob·al·i·sa·tion** *n.*

global village *n.* The world considered as reduced to a small community by 20th-century technological innovations in international communication. [Coined by Marshall McLuhan.]

global warming *n.* A heating of the earth forecast by some climatologists. It is suggested that increased use of fossil fuels will increase the level of carbon dioxide in the atmosphere, intensifying the **greenhouse effect.**

glo·bate (glō-bayt) *adj.* Also **glo·bat·ed** (-báytid). Having the shape of a globe; globular. [Latin *globātus,* past participle of *globāre,* to form into a globe, from *globus,* GLOBE.]

globe (glōb) *n.* 1. Any body having the shape of a sphere; especially, a representation of the earth or heavens in the form of a hollow ball. 2. **a.** The earth itself. Usually used with *the.* **b.** Any planet. 3. Any object resembling a globe; especially, a rounded container, such as a fishbowl. 4. *Chiefly Australian & South African.* A light bulb. 5. A sphere emblematic of sovereignty; an orb. ~*v.* **globed, globing, globes.** —*intr.* To assume the shape of a globe. —*tr.* To form into a globe. [Middle English from Old French, from Latin *globus.*]

globe artichoke *n.* An **artichoke** (*see*).

globe·fish (glōb-fish) *n., pl.* **-fishes** or collectively **globefish.** Any of various fishes, such as the **puffer** (*see*), having or capable of assuming a globular shape.

globe·flow·er (glōb-flowr) *n.* Any of several plants of the genus *Trollius,* having globe-shaped, usually yellow flowers.

globe thistle *n.* A tall thistle of the genus *Echinops,* native to south and central Europe and often planted in gardens for its large, spherical, usually blue flower heads.

globe·trot·ter (glōb-trottər) *n.* One who travels often and widely. —**globe·trot·ting** *n. & adj.*

glo·big·er·i·na (glō-bíjə-rīnə) *n.* Any of the small, marine protozoans of the genus *Globigerina,* having rounded spiny shells that accumulate in large numbers on the ocean floor to form a deposit (*globigerina ooze*). [New Latin : from Latin *globus,* GLOBE + *gerere,* to bear.]

glo·bin (glōbin) *n.* A simple protein that is a constituent of haemoglobin. [Latin *globus,* GLOBE + -IN.]

glo·boid (glō-boyd) *adj.* Having a globelike shape; spheroid. ~*n.* A globe-shaped object; a spheroid. [GLOB(E) + -OID.]

glo·bose (glō-bōss, glō-bōss) *adj.* Also **glo·bous** (-bəss). Spherical; globular. [Latin *globōsus,* from *globus,* GLOBE.] —**glo·bose·ly** *adv.* —**glo·bose·ness, glo·bos·i·ty** (-bóssiti) *n.*

glob·u·lar (glóbbewlər) *adj.* 1. Having the shape of a globe or globule; spherical. 2. Consisting of globules. 3. Worldwide; global. —**glob·u·lar·ly** *adv.* —**glob·u·lar·ness** *n.*

globular cluster *n. Astronomy.* A roughly spherical cluster of stars.

glob·ule (glóbbewl) *n.* A small, often minute, spherical mass; especially, a small drop of liquid. [Latin *globulus,* diminutive of *globus,* GLOBE.]

glob·u·lif·er·ous (glóbbew-liffərəss) *adj.* Composed of or producing globules. [GLOBUL(E) + -FEROUS.]

glob·u·lin (glóbbewlin) *n.* Any of a class of simple proteins that are found extensively in blood (*serum globulins*), milk, muscle, and plant seeds, and are insoluble in pure water, soluble in dilute salt solution, and coagulated by heat. [GLOBUL(E) + -IN.]

glo·chid·i·um (glō-kidi-əm) *n., pl.* **-ia** (-i-ə). Also **glo·chid** (glōkid) (for sense 2). 1. *Zoology.* A parasitic larva of certain freshwater mussels of the family Unionidae, having hooks for attaching to a host fish. 2. *Botany.* Any of the barbed hairs or bristles on certain plants, such as the prickly pear and some ferns. [New Latin, from Greek *glōkhīs,* barb of an arrow.] —**glo·chid·i·ate** (-ət, -it, -ayt) *adj.*

glock·en·spiel (glóckən-speel, -shpeel) *n.* A percussion musical instrument having a series of metal bars tuned to the chromatic scale and played with two light hammers. [German *Glockenspiel,* "play of bells" : *Glocke,* bell, from Old High German *glocka* (imitative) + *Spiel,* play.]

glogg (glog) *n.* Also **glögg** (glög). A hot punch, originally from Sweden, made of red wine and brandy and flavoured with almonds, raisins, and orange peel.

glom·er·ate (glómmə-rət, -rit, -rayt) *adj.* Formed into a compact, rounded mass; tightly clustered; conglomerate. [Latin *glomerātus,* past participle of *glomerāre,* to make into a ball, from *glomus* (stem *glomer-*), ball.]

glom·er·a·tion (glómmə-ráysh'n) *n.* A compact, rounded mass; a cluster; a conglomeration.

glom·er·ule (glómmə-rōōl ‖ -rewl) *n.* 1. *Botany.* A compact cluster of flowers borne on a single stem. 2. *Anatomy.* A glomerulus. [New Latin *glomerulus,* from Latin *glomus* (stem *glomer-*), ball.] —**glo·mer·u·late** (glō-mérrōō-lət, -mérrew-, -lit, -layt) *adj.*

glo·mer·u·lus (glo-mérrōō-ləss, -mérrew-) *n., pl.* **-li** (-lī). *Anatomy.* 1. A tuft of capillaries situated within the capsule at the end of a urine-secreting tubule in the vertebrate kidney. 2. The twisted secretory portion of a sweat gland. Also called "glomerule". [New Latin, GLOMERULE.]

glo·mus (glōməss) *n., pl.* **glomera** (-mərə). *Anatomy.* A small body that forms a connection between fine arteries and veins. [New Latin, from Latin *glomus,* ball.]

gloom (glōōm) *n.* 1. Partial or total darkness; dimness. 2. *Poetic.* A partially or totally dark place. 3. **a.** An appearance or atmosphere of melancholy or depression. **b.** A state of melancholy or depression; dejection; despondency. ~*v.* **gloomed, glooming, glooms.** *Rare.* —*intr.* 1. To be or become dark, shaded, or obscure. 2. To appear despondent, sad, or mournful. —*tr.* 1. To make dark, shaded, or obscure. 2. To make despondent; sadden. [Middle English *gloum(b)ent†,* to look glum, become dark.]

gloom·y (glōōmi) *adj.* **-ier, -iest.** 1. Dismal, dark, or dreary. 2. Showing or filled with gloom; despondent: *gloomy faces.* 3. **a.** Causing or producing gloom or dejection; depressing: *gloomy news.* **b.** Marked by hopelessness; pessimistic: *gloomy predictions.* —See Synonyms at **glum.** —**gloom·i·ly** *adv.* —**gloom·i·ness** *n.*

glo·ri·a (gláw-ri-ə ‖ glō-) *n.* 1. A halo, aureole, or nimbus. 2. A lightweight fabric chiefly of silk, wool, or cotton, used for umbrellas and dresses. [Late Latin *glōria,* from Latin, GLORY.]

Glo·ri·a (gláwr-i-ə) *n.* 1. Any of the Christian prayers of praise beginning with the word *Gloria.* 2. The music to which any of these is set. [Middle English, from Latin *glōria†,* glory.]

Gloria in ex·cel·sis De·o (ek-sél-siss dáy-ō, -chél-, -shel-) *n.* A Latin doxology forming part of the Ordinary of the Mass, beginning with the words *Gloria in excelsis Deo.* Also called the "greater doxology". [Late Latin, "Glory to God in the highest".]

Gloria Pa·tri (páatree, páttree) *n.* A short Latin prayer of praise to the Trinity, often sung or recited at the end of another, as to conclude a psalm or a decade of the rosary. Also called the "lesser doxology". [Late Latin, "Glory to the Father".]

glo·ri·fy (gláwr-i-fī ‖ glō-) *tr.v.* **-fied, -fying, -fies.** 1. To invest with glory or radiance; secure honour, worship, or praise for. 2. To bestow glory, honour, or praise upon; extol. 3. To cause to be or seem more glorious or excellent than is actually the case; exaggerate the importance of. 4. To give glory to, especially through worship. [Middle English *glorifien,* from Old French *glorifier,* from Late Latin *glōrificāre* : Latin *glōria,* GLORY + -FY.] —**glo·ri·fi·ca·tion** *n.* —**glo·ri·fi·er** *n.*

glo·ri·ole (gláwr-i-ōl ‖ glōr-) *n.* A halo, aureole, or nimbus; a gloria. [French, from Latin *glōriola,* diminutive of *glōria,* GLORY.]

glo·ri·ous (gláwr-i-əss ‖ glōr-) *adj.* 1. Having or deserving glory; famous; illustrious. 2. Conferring or advancing glory: *a glorious achievement.* 3. Characterised by great beauty and splendour; magnificent; resplendent. 4. *Informal.* Very pleasant; delightful; wonderful. —**glo·ri·ous·ly** *adv.* —**glo·ri·ous·ness** *n.*

Glorious Revolution *n.* The period in British history (1688–89) during which King James II was deposed, and his sister Mary and her husband William of Orange were invited to assume the throne as joint monarchs Mary II and William III. Also called the "Bloodless Revolution".

glo·ry (gláwri ‖ glōri) *n., pl.* **-ries.** 1. Exalted honour, praise, or distinction accorded by common consent; renown. 2. Something that brings honour or renown: *the glory of her position as president of the club.* 3. A highly praiseworthy asset: *Her hair is her crowning glory.* 4. Adoration, praise, and thanksgiving offered in worship: *We sing Thy glory.* 5. Majestic beauty and splendour; resplendence: *"And the glory of the Lord shall be revealed."* (Isaiah 40:5). 6. The splendour and bliss of heaven; a state of perfect happiness. 7. A height of achievement, enjoyment, or prosperity. 8. A halo, nimbus, or aureole. —See Synonyms at **fame.** ~*intr.v.* **gloried, -rying, -ries.** 1. To rejoice triumphantly; exult. Used with *in.* 2. *Obsolete.* To brag; boast. Used with *in.* [Middle English *glorie,* from Old French, from Latin *glōria†,* glory.]

glory box *n. Australian & N.Z.* Especially formerly, a box or other receptacle in which a young woman stores linen, clothes, and the like in preparation for marriage; a bottom drawer.

glory hole *n. Informal.* A box, drawer, small space, or room in a house or on a ship where unwanted or unsorted articles are stored.

glo·ry-of-the-snow (gláwri-əv-thə-snō ‖ U.S. also glōri-) *n.* A small bulbous plant, *Chionodoxa luciliae,* native to Asia Minor, cultivated for its early-blooming blue flowers.

Glos. Gloucestershire.

gloss¹ (gloss ‖ glawss) *n.* 1. A surface shininess or lustre. Also used adjectively: *gloss paint.* 2. A deceptive or superficially attractive

appearance. **3.** A cosmetic applied to give shine or brilliance: *lip gloss*.
~*v.* **glossed, glossing, glosses.** —*tr.* **1.** To give a bright sheen or lustre to. **2.** To apply a gloss to. **3.** To make attractive or acceptable by deception or superficial discussion. Used with *over*: *He glossed over the bad war news.* —*intr.* To become shiny or lustrous. [Perhaps from Scandinavian; akin to Icelandic *glossi*, spark.]

gloss² *n. Abbr.* **gl. 1.** A brief explanatory note or translation of a difficult or technical expression, often inserted in the margin or between lines of a text or manuscript. **2.** An expanded version of such notes; a glossary. **3.** A purposely misleading interpretation or explanation. **4.** An extensive commentary, often accompanying a text or publication.
~*v.* **glossed, glossing, glosses.** —*tr.* **1.** To provide (a word, expression, or text) with a gloss or glosses. **2.** To give a false interpretation to. —*intr.* To make a gloss or glosses. [Middle English *glose*, from Old French, from Medieval Latin *glōsa*, from Latin *glōssa*, word that needs explanation, from Greek *glōssa*, tongue, language.] —**gloss·er** *n.*

glos·sa (glóssə ‖ *U.S. also* gláwssə) *n., pl.* **-sae** (-sī) or **-sas. 1.** *Anatomy.* The tongue. **2.** *Zoology.* A paired tonguelike structure in the labium of an insect. [Greek *glōssa*, tongue.]

glos·sal (glóss'l ‖ *U.S. also* gláwss'l) *adj.* Of or pertaining to the tongue. [Greek *glōssa*, tongue. See **gloss** (explanation).]

glos·sa·ry (glóss-əri ‖ *U.S. also* gláwss-) *n., pl.* **-ries.** *Abbr.* **gloss.** A collection of glosses, such as a vocabulary of specialised terms with accompanying definitions. [Latin *glossārium*, from *glōssa*, GLOSS (explanation).] —**glos·sar·i·al** (glo-saír-i-əl) *adj.* —**glos·sar·i·al·ly** *adv.* —**glos·sa·rist** *n.*

glos·sec·to·my (glo-séktəmi ‖ *U.S. also* glaw-) *n.* The surgical removal of the tongue. [GLOSSO- + -ECTOMY.]

gloss·eme (glóss-eem ‖ *U.S. also* gláwss-) *n. Linguistics.* Any of the most basic elements of meaning in a language, such as a unit of stress or form. [Greek *glōssēma*. See **glosso-**, **-eme**.]

glos·si·tis (glo-sītiss ‖ *U.S. also* glaw-) *n.* Inflammation of the tongue. [GLOSSO- + -ITIS.]

glosso-, gloss– *comb. form.* Indicates the tongue or language; for example, **glossitis, glossology.** [Greek *glōssa*, tongue. See **gloss** (explanation).]

glos·sog·ra·phy (glo-sóggrəfi ‖ *U.S. also* glaw-) *n.* The writing and compilation of glosses or glossaries. [Greek *glōssa*, tongue, language, GLOSS (explanation) + -GRAPHY.] —**glos·sog·ra·pher** *n.*

glos·so·la·li·a (glóss-ō-láyli-ə ‖ *U.S. also* gláwss-) *n.* **1.** Incoherent or nonsensical speech, especially as associated with trance states and sleeping. **2.** The **gift of tongues** (see). [New Latin *glossolalia*, from (New Testament) Greek *glōssais lalein*, "to speak with tongues" : *glossa*, tongue + *lalein*, to talk, babble.]

glos·sol·o·gy (glo-sólləji ‖ *U.S. also* glaw-) *n. Linguistics.* Not in current technical usage. [Greek *glōssa*, tongue, language, GLOSS (explanation) + -LOGY.] —**glos·sol·o·gist** *n.*

glos·so·phar·yn·ge·al nerve (glóss-ō-fárrin-jéé-əl, -fə-rínjəl ‖ *U.S. also* gláwss-) *n.* The ninth cranial nerve, which supplies the tongue, soft palate, pharynx, and parotid salivary gland.

gloss·y (glóssi ‖ *U.S. also* gláwssi) *adj.* **-ier, -iest. 1.** Having a smooth, shiny, lustrous surface. **2.** Superficially attractive; specious.
~*n., pl.* **glossies. 1.** In photography, a print on smooth, shiny paper. Also called "glossy print". **2.** An expensively produced magazine printed on high-quality, glossy paper. Also called "glossy magazine", *U.S.* "slick". —**gloss·i·ly** *adv.* —**gloss·i·ness** *n.*

glot·tal (glótt'l) *adj.* **1.** Of or relating to the glottis. **2.** *Phonetics.* Articulated in the glottis. [From GLOTTIS.]

glottal stop *n. Phonetics.* A speech sound produced by a momentary complete closure of the glottis, followed by an explosive release.

glot·tis (glóttiss) *n., pl.* **-tises** or **glottides** (-i-deez). **1.** The space between the vocal cords at the upper part of the larynx. **2.** The vocal structures of the larynx. [New Latin, from Greek *glōttis*, from *glōtta*, *glōssa*, tongue, language.]

glot·to·chro·nol·o·gy (glóttō-krə-nólləji) *n.* The investigation, by means of statistics, of the historical relationships between various languages, including the approximate times when related languages began to diverge from one another.

Glouces·ter (glóstər). A city in the west of England, the administrative centre of Gloucestershire, situated on the river Severn. Known as Glevum to the Romans, it became the capital of Mercia in Anglo-Saxon times. Its cathedral (founded 1100) contains fine examples of Norman work with Perpendicular additions.

Glouces·ter·shire (glóstər-shər, -sheer ‖ -shīr). A county in the west of England. It encompasses much of the Cotswolds to the east, the Forest of Dean to the west, and a central region formed by the valley of the lower Severn. Agriculture is the main occupation.

glove (gluv) *n.* **1. a.** A fitted covering for the hand, usually made of leather, wool, or cloth, having a separate sheath for the thumb and, usually, for each finger. **b.** A gauntlet. **2.** Any of various oversized padded coverings for the hand, used in many sports, for example, a **boxing glove** (see). —**like a glove.** Perfectly; exactly. Used in the phrase *fit like a glove.* —**with the gloves off.** In a state of readiness or determination to fight.
~*tr.v.* **gloved, gloving, gloves. 1.** To furnish with gloves. **2.** To cover with or as if with a glove. [Middle English *glove*, Old English *glōf*, from Germanic.]

glove box *n.* **1.** An enclosure with a window and two long rubber

gloves sealed into the front, used for handling toxic, corrosive, or radioactive substances. **2.** A glove compartment.

glove compartment *n.* A small storage container in the dashboard of a car. Also called "glove box".

glove puppet *n.* A cloth figure of an animal or person that fits over the hand and is made to move by the fingers inside it.

glov·er (glúvvər) *n.* One who makes or sells gloves.

glow (glō) *intr.v.* **glowed, glowing, glows. 1. a.** To burn or shine brightly and steadily, especially without a flame. **b.** To shine as if with intense heat. **c.** To be extremely hot. **2.** To have a bright, warm colour, usually reddish. **3. a.** To have a healthy, ruddy complexion. **b.** To flush; blush. **4.** To be exuberant or radiant, as with pride.
~*n.* **1. a.** A light produced by a body heated to luminosity; incandescence. **b.** A bright, warm, steady light. **2.** Brilliance or warmth of colour, especially redness. **3.** A sensation of physical warmth. **4.** A warm feeling of passion or emotion; ardour. **5.** A glow discharge. —See Synonyms at **blaze.** [Middle English *glowen*, Old English *glōwan*, from Germanic.]

glow discharge *n.* A continuous luminous discharge of electricity through a gas at low pressure, as in neon or fluorescent lighting. Also called "glow".

glow·er (glów-ər) *intr.v.* **-ered, -ering, -ers.** To look or stare angrily or sullenly; frown.
~*n.* An angry, sullen, or threatening stare. [Middle English *glo(u)ren*, to shine, stare, probably from Scandinavian; akin to Norwegian dialectal *glora*.] —**glow·er·ing·ly** *adv.*

glow·ing (glō-ing) *adj.* **1.** Incandescent; luminous. **2.** Characterised by rich, warm coloration; especially, having a ruddy, healthy complexion. **3.** Ardently enthusiastic or favourable.

glow lamp *n.* A small electric light bulb, as in a night light, in which a glow discharge occurs between two small electrodes in a medium of neon or similar gas at low pressure.

glow plug *n.* A small heating element in a diesel-engine cylinder used to facilitate starting.

glow-worm (glō-wurm) *n.* The luminous larva or wingless, grublike female of a firefly, especially the European *Lampyris noctiluca*.

glox·in·i·a (glok-sínni-ə) *n.* Any of several tropical South American plants of the genus *Sinningia*; especially, *S. speciosa*, cultivated as a house plant for its showy, variously coloured flowers. [New Latin, after Benjamin Peter *Gloxin*, 18th-century German botanist and physician.]

gloze (glōz) *v.* **glozed, glozing, glozes.** —*tr.* **1.** To minimise or underplay; gloss. Used with *over*. **2.** To explain or comment on; gloss. —*intr. Archaic.* To use flattery or cajolery. [Middle English *glosen*, to gloss, falsify, flatter, from Old French *glosser*, from *glose*, GLOSS (explanation).]

glu·ca·gon (glōo-kə-gon, -gən ‖ glēw-) *n.* A hormone produced by the pancreas, that stimulates an increase in the amount of sugar in the blood, thus opposing the action of insulin. [GLUC(OSE) + Greek *agōn*, leading.]

Gluck (glook), **Christoph Willibald von** (1714–87). German composer. He rid opera music of baroque ornamentation of the Italian style and sought to write unified lyrical tragedy in a manner that foreshadowed Wagner. His best-known operas are *Orpheus and Eurydice* (1762) and *Alceste* (1767).

gluco-, gluc– *comb. form.* Indicates glucose; for example, **gluconeogenesis.**

glu·co·cor·ti·coid (glōo-kō-kórti-koyd ‖ glēw-) *n.* Any of a group of corticosteroids that control carbohydrate, fat, and protein metabolism and have anti-inflammatory properties.

glu·co·ne·o·gen·e·sis (glōo-kō-née-ō-jénnə-siss ‖ glēw-) *n.* The biochemical process in which glucose is formed from noncarbohydrate sources, such as amino acids.

glu·cos·am·ine (glōo-kóssə-meen, -kózə- ‖ glēw-) *n.* An amino sugar, $C_6H_{13}NO_5$, that is a constituent of heparin and other polysaccharides. [GLUCOSE + AMINE.]

glu·cose (glōo-kōz, -kōss ‖ glēw-) *n.* **1.** A white monosaccharide sugar, $C_6H_{12}O_6$, the most abundant form of which is **dextrose** (see), a major energy source for plants and animals. **2.** A colourless to yellowish syrupy mixture of dextrose, maltose, and dextrins with about 20 per cent water, used in confectionery, alcoholic fermentation, tanning, and treating tobacco. [French, from Greek *gleukos*, sweet new wine, must.]

glu·co·side (glōo-kə-sīd ‖ glēw-) *n.* A **glycoside** (see), the sugar component of which is glucose. —**glu·co·sid·ic** (-siddik) *adj.*

glue (glōo ‖ glew) *n.* **1.** An adhesive substance or solution; a viscous substance used to join or bond. **2.** An adhesive obtained by boiling animal **collagen** (see) and drying the residue. In this sense, also called "animal glue". **3.** An adhesive or solvent with a vapour inhaled to produce euphoria. See **glue-sniffing.**
~*tr.v.* **glued, gluing, glues.** To stick or fasten together with or as if with glue. [Middle English *gleu*, glue, birdlime, gum, from Old French *glu*, from Late Latin *glūs* (stem *glūt-*), from Latin *glūten*.] —**glu·er** *n.* —**glue·y** *adj.*

glue-snif·fing (glōo-sniffing) *n.* The highly dangerous practice of inhaling the vapour from synthetic adhesives, solvents, or the like to produce feelings of excitement or euphoria. —**glue-snif·fer** *n.*

glum (glum) *adj.* **glummer, glummest. 1.** In low spirits; dejected; sullen. **2.** Gloomy; dismal. [Middle English *glomen*, *glomen*, to look sullen, GLOOM.] —**glum·ly** *adv.* —**glum·ness** *n.*
Synonyms: glum, gloomy, morose, dour, mournful.

glu·ma·ceous (glōō-máyshəss) *adj.* Having or resembling a glume or glumes.

glume (glōōm ‖ glewm) *n. Botany.* A chaffy basal bract on the spikelet of a grass. [New Latin *gluma*, from Latin *glūma*, husk.]

glu·on (glōō-on ‖ gléw-) *n. Physics.* A hypothetical elementary particle postulated to be exchanged between quarks to hold them together.

glut (glut) *v.* **glutted, glutting, gluts.** —*tr.* **1.** To fill beyond capacity; satiate. **2.** To flood (a market) with an excess of goods so that supply exceeds demand. —*intr.* To eat excessively. —See Synonyms at **satiate.**
~*n.* **1.** An oversupply. **2.** The act or process of glutting. [Middle English *glotten, glouten,* probably from Old French *gloutir,* to swallow, from Latin *gluttīre.*]

glu·ta·mate (glōō-tə-mayt ‖ gléw-) *n.* Any salt of glutamic acid, especially a sodium salt, **monosodium glutamate** (see). [GLUTAMIC + -ATE.]

glu·tam·ic acid (glōō-támmik ‖ glew-) *n.* An amino acid, $C_5H_9NO_4$, present in all complete proteins, found widely in plant and animal tissue, and having an important role in nitrogen metabolism. [GLUT(EN) + AM(IDE) + -IC.]

glu·ta·mine (glōō-tə-meen, -min ‖ gléw-) *n.* A white crystalline amino acid, $C_5H_{10}N_2O_3$, occurring in plant and animal tissue and produced commercially for use in medicine and biochemical research. [GLUT(EN) + AMINE.]

glu·ta·thi·one (glōō-tə-thí-ōn ‖ gléw-) *n.* A peptide consisting of glutamic acid, cysteine, and glycine that functions as a coenzyme in various oxidation-reduction reactions. [GLUTAMIC + THI- + -ONE.]

glu·te·lin (glōō-təlin ‖ gléw-) *n.* Any of a group of simple proteins occurring in cereals and soluble only in dilute acids and bases. [Irregularly from GLUTEN + -IN.]

glu·ten (glōō-t'n, -tin ‖ gléw-) *n.* A mixture of plant proteins occurring in cereal grains, chiefly wheat, and used as an adhesive and as a flour substitute. It produces coeliac disease in children who are allergic to it. [Latin *glūten,* glue.] —**glu·te·nous** *adj.*

gluten bread *n.* Bread made from flour with a high gluten content and low starch content.

glu·te·us (glōō-tée-əss, glōóti- ‖ gléw-) *n., pl.* **-tei** (-tée-ī, -ti-ī). Any of three large muscles of the buttocks: **a.** *gluteus maximus,* which extends the thigh; **b.** *gluteus medius,* which rotates and abducts the thigh; **c.** *gluteus minimus,* which abducts the thigh. [New Latin, from Greek *gloutos,* buttock.] —**glu·te·al** *adj.*

glu·ti·nous (glōō-tin-əss ‖ gléw-) *adj.* Resembling or of the nature of glue; sticky; viscous. [Latin *glūtinōsus,* from *glūten,* glue.] —**glu·ti·nous·ly** *adv.* —**glu·ti·nous·ness, glu·ti·nos·i·ty** (-óssəti) *n.*

glut·ton[1] (glútt'n) *n.* **1.** One that eats or consumes immoderately. **2.** One that has inordinate capacity to receive or withstand something specified: *a glutton for punishment.* [Middle English *glotoun,* from Old French *gluton, gloton,* from Latin *gluttō* (stem *gluttōn-*); akin to *gluttire,* to swallow, *gluttus,* greedy.] —**glut·ton·ous** *adj.* —**glut·ton·ous·ly** *adv.*

glut·ton[2] *n.* A mammal, the **wolverine** (see). [From GLUTTON (eater), translation of German *Vielfrass,* "great eater".]

glut·ton·ise (glútt'n-īz) *intr.v. Archaic.* To indulge in overeating.

glut·ton·y (glútt'n-i) *n.* Excess in eating or drinking.

glyc·er·ic acid (gli-sérrik, glíssərik) *n.* A syrupy, colourless compound, $C_3H_6O_4$. [From GLYCERIN.]

glyc·er·ide (glíssə-rīd) *n.* An ester of glycerol and fatty acids. [GLYCER(IN) + -IDE.]

glyc·er·ine (glíssə-rin, -reen) *n.* Also **glyc·er·in** (glíssərin). Glycerol. Not in technical usage. [French, from Greek *glukeros,* sweet.]

glyc·er·ol (glíssə-rol ‖ -rōl) *n.* A syrupy, sweet, colourless or yellowish liquid, $C_3H_8O_3$, obtained from fats and oils as a by-product of the manufacture of soaps and fatty acids. It is used as a solvent, antifreeze, and antifrost fluid, plasticiser, and sweetener, and in the manufacture of dynamite, cosmetics, liquid soaps, inks, and lubricants. [GLYCER(IN) + -OL.]

glyc·er·yl (glíssəril) *n.* The trivalent radical of glycerol, CH_2CHCH_2. [GLYCER(IN) + -YL.]

gly·cin (glí-sin) *n.* Also **gly·cine** (-seen, -sin). A poisonous compound, $C_8H_9NO_3$, used as a photographic developer. [From GLYCINE.]

gly·cine (glí-seen, glī-séen) *n.* **1.** A white, very sweet crystalline amino acid, $C_2H_5NO_2$, the principal amino acid occurring in sugar cane, derived by alkaline hydrolysis of gelatine, and used in biochemical research and medicine. **2.** Variant of **glycin.** [GLYC(O)- + -INE.]

glyco-, glyc– *comb. form.* Indicates: **1.** Sugar; for example, **glycine. 2.** Glycogen; for example, **glycogenesis.** [Greek *glukus,* sweet.]

gly·co·gen (glíkə-jən, -jen) *n.* A carbohydrate, $(C_6H_{10}O_5)_n$. It is the main form in which carbohydrate is stored in animals and occurs primarily in the liver and muscles. Also called "animal starch", "liver starch". [GLYCO- + -GEN.] —**gly·co·gen·ic** (glíkō-jénnik) *adj.*

gly·co·gen·e·sis (glíkō-jénnə-siss) *n.* **1.** The formation of glycogen. **2.** The formation of sugar from glycogen. [GLYCO- + -GENESIS.]

gly·col (glí-kol ‖ -kōl) *n.* **1.** Ethylene glycol (see). **2.** Loosely, any alcohol with two hydroxyl groups. [GLYC(O)- + -OL.] —**gly·col·ic, gly·col·lic** (-kóllik) *adj.*

gly·col·ic acid *n.* A colourless, crystalline compound, $C_2H_4O_3$, found in sugar beets, cane sugar, and unripe grapes, and used in

leather dyeing and tanning, and in pharmaceuticals, pesticides, adhesives, and plasticisers.

gly·co·lip·id (glíkō-líppid) *n.* Any of a group of lipids that contain one or more sugar molecules.

gly·col·y·sis (glī-kólli-siss) *n.* The biochemical breakdown of glucose to lactic acid, with the production of energy in the form of ATP. [GLYCO- + -LYSIS.]

gly·co·pro·tein (glíkō-prō-teen, -tee-in) *n.* Any of several conjugated proteins that contain carbohydrates as prosthetic groups.

gly·co·side (glíkō-sīd) *n.* Any of a group of organic compounds, occurring abundantly in plants, that produce sugars and related substances on hydrolysis. A medically important example is digitalis. [*Glycose,* variant of GLUCOSE + -IDE.] —**gly·co·sid·ic** (-síddik) *adj.*

gly·co·su·ri·a (glíkō-séwr-i-ə ‖ -shóor-, -sóor-) *n.* The excretion of excess quantities of sugar in the urine, as occurs in diabetes. [*Glycose,* variant of GLUCOSE + -URIA.] —**gly·co·su·ric** *adj.*

Glynde·bourne (glínd-bawrn ‖ -bōrn). An estate in East Sussex in southeast England. Since 1934, it has been the site of an annual festival of opera.

gly·ox·a·line (glī-óks-səlin) *n.* A chemical compound, **imidazole** (see). [GLY(COL) + OXAL(IC ACID) + -INE.]

glyph (glif) *n.* **1.** *Architecture.* A vertical groove, especially in a Doric column or frieze. **2.** A symbolic figure, either engraved or incised; a hieroglyph. [Greek *gluphē,* carving, from *gluphein,* to carve.] —**glyph·ic** *adj.*

glyp·tal (glípt'l) *n.* A synthetic resin used for surface coatings, made by copolymerising dihydric alcohols and dibasic acids.

glyp·tic (glíptik) *adj.* Of or pertaining to engraving or carving, especially on precious stones. [Greek *gluptikos,* from *gluptēs,* carver, from *gluphein,* to carve.] —**glyp·tics** *n.*

glyp·to·dont (glíptə-dont) *n.* Any extinct South American mammal of the genus *Glyptodon* and related genera, that lived in the late Cenozoic period and resembled a giant armadillo. [New Latin : Greek *gluptos,* carved, from *gluphein,* to carve + -ODONT.]

glyp·to·graph (glíptə-graaf, -graf) *n.* An engraved inscription on a precious stone. [Greek *gluptos,* carved, from *gluphein,* to carve + -GRAPH.]

glyp·tog·ra·phy (glip-tóggrəfi) *n.* The art or process of carving or engraving on precious stones. —**glyp·tog·ra·pher** *n.* —**glyp·to·graph·ic** (-tə-gráffik) *adj.* —**glyp·to·graph·i·cal** *adj.*

gm gram.

G.M. 1. general manager. **2.** grand master. **3.** George Medal.

G-man (jée-man) *n., pl.* **-men** (-men). An agent of the U.S. Federal Bureau of Investigation. [government *man.*]

G.M.A.T. Greenwich mean astronomical time.

G.M.C. General Medical Council (in Britain).

GM counter *n.* A Geiger counter (see).

GMT, G.M.T. Greenwich Mean Time.

GM tube *n.* A Geiger tube (see).

gnarl (narl) *n.* A protruding knot on a tree.
~*tr.v.* **gnarled, gnarling, gnarls.** To make knotted; cause to be deformed; twist. See Synonyms at **distort.** [Back-formation from GNARLED.]

gnarled (narld) *adj.* **1.** Having gnarls; knotty or misshapen: *gnarled branches.* **2.** Crabbed in temperament; bad-tempered. **3.** Knotty in appearance: *gnarled hands.* [Probably variant of KNURLED.]

gnash (nash) *v.* **gnashed, gnashing, gnashes.** —*tr.* **1.** To grind or strike (the teeth) together. **2.** To bite or chew by grinding the teeth. —*intr.* To grind the teeth together.
~*n.* The grinding together of the teeth, or an action or sound resembling this. [Middle English *gnasten, gnaisten,* probably from Scandinavian, akin to Old Norse *gnast(r)an,* gnashing (probably imitative).]

gnat (nat) *n.* Any of numerous small, biting, winged insects, especially the common gnat, *Culex pipiens,* common in swarms over stagnant water. [Middle English *gnat,* Old English *gnæt.*]

gnat·catch·er (nát-kachər) *n.* Any of several small New World birds of the genus *Polioptila* and related genera, having greyish and white plumage and a long tail.

gnath·ic (náthik) *adj. Anatomy.* Of or relating to the jaw. [Greek *gnathos,* jaw.]

gna·thi·on (náythi-on, náthi-) *n. Anatomy.* The lowest point of the midline of the lower jaw. [New Latin, from Greek *gnathos,* jaw.]

gna·thite (náy-thīt, náth-īt) *n.* A jaw or jawlike appendage of an insect or other arthropod. [Greek *gnathos,* jaw + -ITE.]

–gnathous *adj. comb. form.* Indicates the jaw; for example, **prognathous.** [New Latin *-gnathus,* from Greek *gnathos,* jaw.]

gnaw (naw) *v.* **gnawed, gnawed** or **gnawn** (nawn), **gnawing, gnaws.** —*tr.* **1.** To bite, chew on, or erode with the teeth. **2.** To produce by gnawing: *gnaw a hole.* **3.** To erode or diminish gradually as if by gnawing. **4.** To afflict or irritate. —*intr.* **1.** To bite or chew persistently. Often used with *at* or *upon.* **2.** To cause erosion or gradual diminishment. **3.** To cause persistent pain or distress. Often used with *at.*
~*n.* The action or an instance of gnawing. [Middle English *gnawen,* Old English *gnagan.*]

gnaw·ing (náw-ing) *adj.* Persistently painful or worrying: *a gnawing doubt.* —**gnaw·ing·ly** *adv.*

gneiss (nīss) *n. Geology.* A coarse-grained banded or foliated metamorphic rock, in which the minerals are arranged in darker and lighter layers. [German *Gneis,* perhaps from Middle High German *gneiste,* spark (because of its sheen), from Old High German *gneisto.*] **—gneiss·ic, gneiss·oid, gneiss·ose** *adj.*

gnoc·chi (nócki, nyócki) *pl.n.* Dumplings made of flour, semolina, or potato starch, boiled, baked, or grilled and served with grated Parmesan cheese or with various sauces. [Italian, plural of *gnocco, nocchio,* "knot (of a tree)", "lump", from Germanic.]

gnome[1] (nōm) *n.* **1.** Any of a fabled race of dwarflike creatures, often portrayed as wizened old men, who live underground and guard treasure hoards. **2.** A shrivelled old man. **3.** A small statue of a gnome, often placed in a garden as a decoration. **4.** *Informal.* An influential international financier or banker. Used humorously or derogatorily, chiefly of Swiss financiers and in the phrase *the gnomes of Zurich.* [French, from New Latin *gnomus*† (coined by Paracelsus).] **—gnom·ish** *adj.*

gnome[2] *n.* A pithy saying that expresses a general truth or fundamental principle; a maxim; an aphorism. [Greek *gnōmē,* intelligence, judgment, maxim, from *gignōskein,* to know.]

gno·mic (nōmik) *adj.* Of or of the nature of pithy sayings; aphoristic: *gnomic utterances.*

gno·mon (nō-mon, -mən) *n.* **1.** An object, such as the style (projecting arm) of a sundial, that casts a shadow used as an indicator. **2.** *Mathematics.* The figure that remains after a parallelogram has been removed from a similar but larger parallelogram with which it has a common corner. [Latin *gnōmōn,* from Greek, one who knows, indicator, interpreter, from *gignōskein,* to know.] **—gno·mon·ic** (nō-mónnik), **gno·mon·i·cal** *adj.*

gno·mon·ic projection *n.* A type of azimuthal or zenithal map projection in which great circles of the earth are shown as straight lines and all straight lines are great circles.

gno·sis (nō-siss) *n.* Intuitive apprehension of spiritual truths, an esoteric form of knowledge sought by the Gnostics. [Greek *gnōsis,* knowledge, from *gignōskein,* to know.]

-gnosis *n. comb. form. Medicine.* Indicates knowledge or recognition; for example, **diagnosis, psychognosis.** [Latin, from Greek *-gnōsia,* from *gnōsis,* knowledge, GNOSIS.] **— -gnostic** *adj. comb. form.*

gnos·tic (nósstik) *adj.* Of, relating to, or possessing knowledge, especially spiritual knowledge.

Gnos·ti·cism (nóssti-siz'm) *n.* The doctrines of certain early Christian sects, considered heretical, that valued inquiry into spiritual truth above faith, thought salvation attainable only by the few whose faith enabled them to transcend matter, and viewed Christ as noncorporeal. **—Gnos·tic** *adj. & n.*

gno·to·bi·ot·ics (nōtō-bī-óttiks) *n. Used with a singular verb.* The study of organisms in relation to the effects on them of known microorganisms. [New Latin : Greek *gnōtos,* known, past participle of *gignōskein,* to know + *bios,* life.] **—gno·to·bi·ot·ic** *adj.* **—gno·to·bi·ot·i·cal·ly** *cal·ly adv.*

GNP gross national product.

gnu (noo, new) *n.* Either of two large African antelopes, *Connochaetes gnou* or *C. taurinus,* having a drooping beard, a long, tufted tail, and curved horns in both sexes. Also called "wildebeest". [Xhosa *nqu.*]

go[1] (gō) *v.* **went** (went), **gone** (gon || gawn, gaan), **going, goes.** *—intr.* **1. a.** To move along; proceed. **b.** To move as specified: *go fast; go up.* **2.** To move to a particular place. **3.** To move from a particular place; depart. **4.** To start to move away. **5.** To start an action; begin to move. **6.** To get out of sight; move out of someone's presence: *Go away!* **7.** To proceed to the performance of an activity: *went to eat.* **8.** Used in the form *be going* with the sense of *will* to indicate indefinite future intent or expectation: *He is going to learn to fly.* **9.** To engage in an activity. Used with a present participle: *go riding.* **10.** To function; operate: *The car won't go.* **11.** To make a specified sound: *The glass went ping.* **12. a.** To belong in a specified habitual place or position. **b.** To lie in a specified place or position. **c.** To lie or point in a specified direction. **13.** To extend from one place or thing to another. **14.** To spread. **15.** To pass or be given into someone's possession. **16.** To be allotted: *money to go for food.* **17.** To serve; help: *It goes to show he was wrong.* **18. a.** To be compatible; harmonise: *The rug goes well with this room.* **b.** To match or fit. **c.** To occur with or together. **19.** To proceed in a particular form or sequence: *Is this the way the song goes?* **20.** To die. **21.** To come apart or cave in; be damaged or break. **22.** To fail, as hearing or vision. **23.** To be consumed or used up. **24.** To lose effect; disappear. **25.** To be given up or abolished: *Unnecessary expenditures must go.* **26. a.** To pass, as does time or youth. **b.** To pass by; travel past. **27.** To pass in a commercial transaction; be sold or auctioned off. **28.** To enter into a specified condition; become: *go insane.* **29.** To be or continue to be in a specified condition: *go unchallenged.* **30.** To fare. **31.** To be thought of; be judged: *As cats go, this one is well-behaved.* **32.** To pursue a course: *go too far; go to a lot of trouble.* **33.** To act, especially under guidance or on advice: *go on someone's word.* **34.** To hold out; endure. **35.** To be transmitted; circulate: *measles went through the whole school; a rumour went round.* **36.** To have access or recourse; turn: *go to him for help.* **37.** To join; become a member of a profession: *go on the stage; go to sea.* **38.** To attend regularly: *does he go to school yet?* **39.** To make regular trips; journey constantly: *the Northern line goes to Edgware.* **40.** To be accepted or acceptable: *anything goes.* **41.** To be the rule; be the only acceptable thing: *What I say goes.* **42.** To turn out; happen: *did it go well?* **43.** To be contained; be part of: *5 goes into 25 five times.* **44.** To be known. Usually used with *under* or *by*: *goes by the name of Jones.* **45.** *Informal.* **a.** To be very lively: *She really goes.* **b.** To move very fast. *—tr.* **1.** To withstand; endure: *went the distance.* **2.** To wager; bid: *He went three spades.* **3.** To take part to the extent of: *go fifty-fifty on a deal.* **4.** *Chiefly U.S.* To furnish: *go bail for a client.* **—as it goes.** *British Nonstandard.* As it happens: *I used to live there, as it goes.* **—go about. 1.** To busy oneself with; get down to. **2.** To change direction in a sailing vessel; tack. **—go against. 1.** To be or act in opposition to. **2.** To be unfavourable to. **—go along.** To be in agreement; cooperate. Usually used with *with.* **—go around** or **round. 1.** To move from one place to another. **2.** To be habitually in the company of, especially in public. Used with *with.* **3.** To be engaged in: *she goes around making a nuisance of herself.* **4.** To spread; circulate: *a rumour going around.* **5.** To be sufficient: *enough to go round.* **—go at. 1.** To attack verbally or physically. **2.** To work at diligently or energetically. **—go away.** To take a holiday away from home. **—go back.** To be established or be recorded in history; have existed in an earlier time. **—go back on.** To back down on; repudiate. **—go down. 1.** To be beaten; lose. **2.** To sink. Used of ships. **3.** To decrease in size or weight. **4.** *British.* To fall ill: *He went down with measles.* **5.** *British.* To travel away or graduate from a university. **6.** *British Slang.* To go to prison. **7.** To go below the horizon: *The sun went down.* **8.** To be renowned or remembered: *This occasion will go down in history.* **9.** To be received in a specified way: *His speech went down very badly.* **—go for. 1.** To try to obtain. **2.** *Informal.* To enjoy or appreciate. **3.** To be sold for. **4.** To pass as; be thought of as. **5.** To attack. **6.** To apply to: *That goes for you too!* **7.** To be advantageous for; help. **—go hard.** To cause difficulty, trouble, or unhappiness. Used with *with* or *on.* **—go in. 1.** To be obscured by a cloud or clouds. Used of the sun, and sometimes the moon. **2.** *Informal.* To be understood or comprehended: *I heard the speech but nothing went in.* **3.** In cricket, to begin an innings; begin to bat. **—go in for.** *Informal.* **1.** To enjoy doing or participating in. **2.** To enter or participate in (a competition or contest). **—go into. 1.** To investigate; inquire about. **2.** To take up or turn to as an occupation, study, or pastime. **3.** To hit: *The lorry went into the wall.* **—go it.** *Informal.* **1.** To move very fast. **2.** To participate energetically. **—go it alone.** To be independent; act by oneself. **—go off. 1.** To happen in a specified manner: *went off according to plan.* **2.** To be fired or shot; explode: *the gun went off.* **3.** To cease functioning; cease to be available: *the heating went off.* **4.** To leave. **5.** To abscond. **6.** To cease being felt or perceived. **7.** To fall asleep. **8.** *Informal.* To become rotten or unpleasant. Used of food, drink, and the like. **9.** *Informal.* To cease to like. **—go on. 1.** To continue. **2.** To happen; occur. **3.** To have a turn or ride on: *go on the helter-skelter.* **4.** To make one's entrance on the stage of a theatre. **5.** To act; behave. **6.** To talk at length. **7.** To scold constantly; nag. Usually used with *at.* **8.** To use as evidence or a basis for further action. **9.** To approach a time, amount, or the like. Used with *for*: *going on for half-full.* **10.** In cricket, to start bowling. **11.** To start functioning: *the heating went on.* **12.** Used as an interjection to express surprise or disbelief. **—go one better.** To surpass or outdo by one degree. **—go out. 1. a.** To stop burning or casting light. **b.** To stop operating or functioning. **2.** To cease to be popular; become unfashionable. **3.** To become unconscious or asleep. **4.** To be broadcast or transmitted. **5.** To attend parties, social engagements, and the like. **6.** To associate with regularly, on a sexual or romantic basis. Used with *together* or *with.* **7.** In card games, to lay down all one's cards. **—go over. 1.** To check or examine. **2.** To be received in a specified manner: *a speech that went over well.* **3.** To clean: *go over the carpet with the vacuum.* **4.** To rehearse; repeat. **5.** To change: *I've gone over to brown bread.* **—go through. 1.** To search or examine thoroughly. **2. a.** To suffer; undergo. **b.** To experience; participate in. **3.** To use up entirely. **4.** To gain acceptance; be voted for, as a plan or law. **5.** To rehearse. **6.** To come to the end; complete. Used with *with.* **—go to (it).** *Informal.* To tackle or engage in energetically. **—go under. 1.** To sink. **2.** To be overwhelmed by difficulties. **—go up. 1.** To be erected: *new buildings going up.* **2.** To be completely destroyed. Used chiefly in the phrases *go up in flames* and *go up in smoke.* **3.** *British Informal.* To travel to or start at a university. **—go with. 1.** To be the regular romantic or sexual partner of. **2.** To regard as concluded or sufficient; make do with. **—to go. 1.** Remaining: *three minutes to go.* **2.** *U.S.* To be consumed off the premises. Said of restaurant food.

~n., pl. **goes.** *Informal.* **1.** A try; a venture. **2.** A bargain; an agreement; a deal: *no go.* **3.** An action or instance of going or occurring. **4.** A turn, as in a game. **5.** Energy; vitality. **6.** A busy or lively state of affairs: *it was all go.* **—from the word go.** *Informal.* From the very beginning. **—on the go.** *Informal.* Perpetually busy; active.

~adj. Informal. Prepared to go into action: *All planes are go.* [Go, gone; Middle English *gon, gōn(e),* Old English *gān, gegān.* Went; Middle English *wente,* past tense of *wenden,* to turn, WEND.]

go[2] *n.* A Japanese game for two, played with pebble-like counters on a board divided into 361 squares.

go·a (gō-ə) *n.* A gazelle, *Procapra picticaudata,* of eastern Asia, the male of which has backward-curving horns. [Tibetan *dgoba.*]

Go·a (gō-ə). State on the west coast of India, formerly a Portuguese possession. Annexed by India in 1961, it now forms part of the territory of Goa, Daman, and Diu. The district centres on the port of Goa which formerly controlled the spice trade with the East.

Goa, Daman, and Diu. Until 1984 a territory of India, formed from three former Portuguese possessions on the west coast. It is now a separate state of India. Goa lies south of Bombay (Mumbai), Daman to the north, while Diu is an island off Gujarat. Though separated by long stretches of coastline they share a common cultural background and were all annexed by India in 1961.

goad (gōd) *n.* **1.** A long stick with a pointed end used for prodding animals. **2.** That which prods or urges; a stimulus or irritating incentive.

~*tr.v.* **goaded, goading, goads.** To prod with or as if with a goad; give impetus to; incite. [Middle English *gode,* Old English *gād,* from Germanic.]

go ahead *intr.v.* To start or continue after an interruption; proceed.

go-a-head (gō-ə-héd, -hed) *n. Informal.* Permission to proceed. Preceded by *the.*

~*adj.* Enterprising and adventurous.

goal (gōl) *n.* **1.** The purpose towards which an endeavour is directed; an end; an objective. **2.** The finishing point or line of a race. **3.** *Sports.* **a.** A structure or area into or over which players endeavour to advance a ball or puck. **b.** A successful attempt at scoring in this way. **c.** The score awarded for such an act. —See Synonyms at **intention.** [Middle English *gol,* boundary, limit, probably from Old English *gǣl†* (unattested), obstacle.]

goal area *n.* In soccer, a rectangular area in front of the goal, 6 yards deep and 20 yards wide, in which goal kicks are taken.

goal-keep-er (gōl-keepər) *n.* A player assigned to protect the goal in various sports. Also informally called "goalie".

goal kick *n.* In soccer, a free kick taken from the goal area, awarded to the defending team when the ball has been put out of play over the goal line by an attacking player.

goal line (gōl-līn) *n. Sports.* Either of two lines running the width of the playing area at each end of the field. In games such as soccer, Rugby football, and hockey, the goals are located along it; it may mark the boundary of the playing area, as in soccer and hockey; in Rugby football and American football, the ball must be carried over the goal line to score a try or touchdown.

goal-mouth (gōl-mowth) *n. Sports.* The area between the goalposts just in front of the goal.

goal-post (gōl-pōst) *n.* Either of a pair of posts joined with a crossbar and set at each end of a playing-field, forming the goal.

go-an-na (gō-ánnə) *n.* Any of various monitor lizards of Australia. [Mispronunciation of IGUANA.]

Goa powder *n.* **Araroba** (see).

goat (gōt) *n.* **1.** Any of various horned, bearded, ruminant mammals of the genus *Capra,* originally of mountainous regions of the Old World; especially, any of the domesticated forms of *C. hircus,* kept for milk, wool, and meat. **2.** *Capital G. Astronomy.* The constellation and sign of the zodiac, *Capricornus (see).* Usually preceded by *the.* **3.** A lecherous man. **4.** A silly person; a fool. —**get (someone's) goat.** *Informal.* To make (someone) angry or annoyed. [Middle English *gote,* Old English *gāt.*]

goat antelope *n.* Any of various ruminant mammals, such as the Rocky Mountain goat or the chamois, having characteristics of both goats and antelopes.

goat-ee (gō-tée) *n.* A small chin beard trimmed to a point, and resembling that of a goat. [From GOAT + -EE.]

goat-fish (gōt-fish) *n., pl.* **-fishes** or collectively **goatfish.** *U.S.* The red mullet (see).

goat-herd (gōt-herd) *n.* A person who looks after goats.

goat-ish (gōt-ish) *adj.* **1.** Of, pertaining to, or resembling a goat. **2.** Lecherous; lustful. —**goat-ish-ly** *adv.* —**goat-ish-ness** *n.*

goat moth *n.* A European moth, *Cossus cossus,* with large, pale brownish wings.

goats-beard, goat's-beard (gōts-beerd) *n.* **1.** A plant, *Tragopogon pratensis,* native to Europe, having grasslike leaves and yellow, dandelion-like flowers. **2.** A tall American plant, *Aruncus dioicus,* having compound leaves and branching clusters of small white flowers.

goat-skin (gōt-skin) *n.* **1.** The skin of a goat. **2.** A container, as for wine, made from such a skin.

goat's-rue (gōts-rōō || -rew) *n.* **1.** A Eurasian plant, *Galega officinalis,* cultivated for its showy, variously coloured flowers. **2.** A North American plant, *Tephrosia virginiana,* having yellow and pink flowers.

goat-suck-er (gōt-suckər) *n. U.S.* A **nightjar** (see). [The bird was thought to suck goat's milk.]

go-away bird (gō-ə-wáy) *n.* Any of various touracos of the genus *Corythaixoides,* of Africa. [Imitative of its call.]

gob¹ (gob) *n.* **1.** A small piece or lump. **2.** A small mass or lump of spit or phlegm. **3.** *Plural. Chiefly U.S. Informal.* A large quantity, as of money.

~*intr.v.* **gobbed, gobbing, gobs.** *British Informal.* To spit. [Middle English *gobbe,* lump, mass, from Old French *gobe,* mouthful, lump, from *gober,* to swallow, gulp, from Gallo-Roman *gobb-* (unattested), from Celtic *gobbo-* (unattested), mouth, beak, GOB.]

gob² *n. Slang.* The mouth. [Perhaps from Scottish and Irish Gaelic *gob,* beak, mouth, from Celtic *gobbo-* (unattested).]

gob³ *n. Slang.* A sailor. [20th century : origin obscure.]

Go-bat (gō-bàa), **Charles Albert** (1843–1914). Swiss government official and writer of works on international law. He helped to establish the International Peace Bureau at Berne in 1902 and won the Nobel peace prize in the same year.

gob-bet (góbbit) *n.* **1.** An extract from a text. **2.** A piece or chunk, especially of raw meat. [Middle English *gobet,* from Old French, diminutive of *gobe,* GOB (lump).]

Gob-bi (góbbi), **Tito** (1915–84). Italian baritone. He made his debut in *La Traviata* at Rome in 1938. He was most famous for his roles in operas by Verdi and Puccini, especially as Scarpia in *Tosca.*

gob-ble¹ (góbb'l) *v.* **-bled, -bling, -bles.** —*tr.* **1.** To devour in large, greedy gulps. **2.** To snatch greedily; grab. —*intr.* To eat greedily or rapidly. [Frequentative of Middle English *gobben,* to drink greedily, probably from *gobbe,* lump, GOB.]

gob-ble² *intr.v.* **-bled, -bling, -bles.** To make the guttural, chortling sound of a male turkey. —*n.* A guttural, chortling sound made by, or as if by, a male turkey. [Imitative.]

gob-ble-de-gook, gob-ble-dy-gook (góbb'ldi-gōōk, -gōōk) *n.* Unclear, often verbose language, usually bureaucratic jargon. [From GOBBLE (to sound like a turkey), influenced by GOOK.]

gob-bler (góbblər) *n. Informal.* A male turkey.

Gob-e-lins (gōbə-lin, góbbə- || *French* gō-blán) *n.* A tapestry of a kind woven at the Gobelins works in Paris, noted for its rich pictorial design.

go-be-tween (gō-bi-tween) *n.* One who acts as an intermediary.

Go-bi (gōbi). A vast desert in northern China and southern Mongolia, encompassing an area of some 1 295 000 square kilometres (500,000 square miles). It lies on a plateau roughly 1 200 metres (4,000 feet) high and consists chiefly of sand and gravel plains, broken by low rocky ranges and saltpans. It is mostly dry but has some small lakes. Its fringe of sparse pastureland is inhabited by Mongolian nomads.

Gob-ind Singh (góbbind síng). (1666–1708). Tenth and last Sikh guru and writer. He was the founder of the Khalsa ("Pure"), the inner council of the Sikhs, in 1699. He wrote poetry, codified the Sikh law, and is said to be the author of the epic, *Dasam Granth* ("Tenth Volume").

Gob-i-neau (gobbi-nō), **Joseph Arthur, Comte de** (1816–82). French diplomat and writer. In his *Essay on the Inequality of the Human Races* (1853–55), he argued that the strength of civilisations is impaired by racial miscegenation. The theory later had a considerable influence on the Nazi movement.

gob-let (góbblit) *n.* **1.** A drinking glass or similar vessel with a stem and base. **2.** *Archaic.* A drinking bowl without handles. [Middle English *gobelet,* from Old French, diminutive of *gobel,* cup, from Gallo-Roman *gobb-* (unattested), from Celtic *gobbo-* (unattested), mouth, beak, GOB.]

goblet cell *n. Biology.* Any of the pear-shaped cells in vertebrate epithelium that secrete the chief constituents of mucus.

gob-lin (góbblin) *n.* A grotesque, elfin creature of folklore, thought to work mischief or evil. [Middle English *gobelin,* from Old French, from Middle High German *kobolt,* goblin.]

go-bo (gōbō) *n., pl.* **-bos** or **-boes.** **1.** A screen around a microphone to reduce extraneous sound. **2.** A screen around a camera lens to block unwanted light. [20th century : origin obscure.]

gobsmacked (gób-smakt) *n. British Slang.* Taken aback or overwhelmed, with surprise or delight. [Probably from GOB (mouth), alluding to a blow or kiss on the mouth.]

gob-stop-per (gób-stoppər) *n.* **1.** A large round, hard sweet with differently coloured layers. **2.** Loosely, any large sweet.

go by *intr.v.* To pass: *three minutes went by; three buses went by.* ~*tr.v.* **1.** To estimate; judge: *go by appearances.* **2.** To be guided by; follow: *go by the instructions.*

go-by (gō-bī) *n. Informal.* An intentional slight; a snub. Used chiefly in the phrase *give someone the go-by.*

go-by (gōbi) *n., pl.* **-bies** or collectively **goby.** Any of numerous usually small freshwater and marine fishes of the family Gobiidae, having the pelvic fins united to form a sucking disc. [Latin *gōbius,* variant of *cōbius,* from Greek *kōbios†,* GUDGEON.]

go-cart (gō-kaart) *n.* Also **go-kart** (for sense 4). **1.** A small wagon for children to ride in, drive, or pull. **2.** A handcart. **3.** *U.S.* A **baby-walker** (see). **4.** A miniature car with an open framework and four small wheels, used for racing on a track. Also called "kart".

god (god || gawd) *n.* **1.** A being of supernatural powers or attributes, believed in and worshipped by a people; especially, a male deity thought to control some part of nature or reality or to personify some force or activity. **2.** An image of a deity; an idol. **3.** One that is worshipped or idealised as a god. **4.** A man who is godlike in aspect or power. —**the gods.** *Informal.* The highest, cheapest seats in a theatre; the gallery. [Middle English *god,* Old English *god.*]

God *n.* **1.** A being conceived as the perfect, omnipotent, omniscient originator and ruler of the universe, the principal object of faith and worship in monotheistic religions. **2.** The force, effect, or a manifestation or aspect of this being. **3.** The single supreme agency postulated in some philosophical systems to explain the phenomena of the world, having a nature variously conceived in such terms as prime mover, an immanent vital force, or infinity.

~*interj.* Used as an oath, or to express surprise, dismay, impatience, or the like, often in phrases such as *Oh God!* and *Thank God!*

Go-dard (góddaar, go-dár), **Jean-Luc** (1930–). French film director, a leading figure of the 1960s "new wave". His films, which use experimental narrative techniques and reflect his Marxist views, include *A Married Woman* (1964), *Weekend* (1968), *Tout Va Bien* (1972), *Slow Motion* (1980), and *Hélas pour Moi* (1993).

god-aw-ful (gód-áwf'l) *adj. Slang.* Extremely trying; atrocious.

god-child (gód-chīld) *n., pl.* **-children.** A person who is sponsored at baptism by an adult.

god-damn (gód-dám) *adj.* Also **god-damned** (gód-dám'd). *Chiefly U.S. Informal.* Extreme; blatant; great. Used as an intensive: *a goddamn idiot.*

~*interj. Chiefly U.S. Informal.* Used to express surprise, frustration, and sometimes delight.

God·dard (góddaard), **Robert Hutchings** (1882–1945). U.S. physicist. He made the first liquid fuelled rocket and successfully launched it.

god·daugh·ter (gód-dawtər) n. A female godchild.

God·den (gódd'n), **Rumer** (1907–). English novelist and short-story writer. Her novels include *A Candle for St. Jude* (1948), *An Episode of Sparrows* (1955), *The Diddakoi* (1972), and *Pippa Passes* (1994).

god·dess (gód-iss, -ess) n. 1. A female deity. 2. A woman of great beauty or grace. 3. A woman adored as a deity.

Gö·del (gőd'l), **Kurt** (1906–78). U.S. mathematician and logician, born in Czechoslovakia. He settled in the United States in 1940. In 1951 he was awarded, with Julian Schwinger, the Albert Einstein award for outstanding achievement in the natural sciences.

Gödel's proof n. A mathematical proof that under a given consistency condition, any sufficiently strong formal axiomatic system must contain a proposition such that neither it nor its negation is provable and that any consistency proof for the system must use ideas and methods beyond those of the system itself. [After Kurt GÖDEL.]

go·de·tia (gə-déeshə) n. Any plant of the genus *Godetia*, some species and varieties of which are grown as garden ornamentals because of their showy flowers. [After C.H. *Godet* (died 1879), Swiss botanist.]

go·dev·il (gő-devv'l) n. *Chiefly U.S.* 1. A jointed tool for cleaning an oil pipeline and disengaging obstructions. 2. An iron dart dropped into an oil well to explode a charge of dynamite.

god·fa·ther (gód-faathər) n. 1. A man who sponsors a child at its baptism. 2. *Often capital.* **G.** *Slang.* **a.** The head of a Mafia family or similar criminal organisation. **b.** Any powerful leader.

god-fearing (gód-feer-ing) adj. Religious; devout.

god·for·sak·en (gód-fər-sáykən) adj. 1. Desolate; cheerless; forlorn. 2. Desperate; depraved.

god·head (gód-hed) n. 1. Divinity; godhood. 2. *Capital* **G.** God or the essential and divine nature of God regarded abstractly. Preceded by *the*. [Middle English *godhede* : GOD + *-hede*, variant of *-hode*, -HOOD.]

god·hood (gód-hŏŏd) n. The quality or state of being a god; divinity. [Middle English *godhād* : GOD + *-hād*, -HOOD.]

Go·di·va (gə-dívə), **Lady** (*fl. c.*1040–80). English heroine, the wife of Leofric, Earl of Mercia. She was the benefactor of several monasteries, including one at Coventry in 1043. She is famous for the episode, probably legendary, in which, to secure a promise from her husband that he would reduce taxation in Coventry, she rode naked through the town on a white horse.

god·less (gód-ləss, -liss) adj. 1. Irreverent; wicked. 2. Recognising or worshipping no god. —**god·less·ly** adv. —**god·less·ness** n.

god·like (gód-lík) adj. Resembling or of the nature of a god or God.

god·ly (góddli) adj. **-lier, -liest.** 1. Having great reverence for God; pious. 2. Divine. —**god·li·ness** n.

god·moth·er (gód-muthər) n. A woman who sponsors a child at its baptism.

Go·dol·phin (gə-dólfin), **Sidney, 1st Earl of** (1645–1712). English courtier and politician, the life-long ally of John Churchill, 1st Duke of Marlborough. He first became an M.P. in 1668 and served in the administrations of Charles II, James II, William III, and Anne.

go·down (gő-down) n. In India and east Asia, a warehouse, especially one at a dockside. [Portuguese *gudão*, from Malay *godong*, perhaps from Telugu *gidangi*, warehouse, from *kidu*, to lie.]

god·par·ent (gód-pair-ənt) n. A godfather or godmother.

godroon. Variant of **gadroon.**

God's acre n. *Poetic.* A churchyard or burial ground. [Translation of German *Gottesacker*, God's field.]

god·send (gód-send) n. An unexpected boon or stroke of luck that comes just when it is most needed; a windfall. [Middle English *goddes sand*, God's message : GOD + *sand*, message, Old English *sand*, message, messenger.]

god·son (gód-sun) n. A male godchild.

God slot n. *British Slang.* 1. A religious programme on radio or television. 2. The period of time during which such a programme is regularly broadcast.

God·speed (gód-spéed) n. Success or good fortune. Used in the phrase *wish someone Godspeed.* [From the phrase *God speed*, may God prosper (someone).]

Godthåb. See **Nuuk.**

Go·du·nov (góddə-nof ‖ *Russian* gədŏŏ-nóf), **Boris** (*c.*1550–1605). Russian statesman, Tsar of Russia (1598–1605). He was chief adviser to Ivan the Terrible, upon whose death in 1584 he became regent to Fyodor I and virtual dictator of Russia. He may have been implicated in the murder of Dimitry, Fyodor's younger brother and heir to the throne, in 1591. On Fyodor's death in 1598 he was chosen as tsar.

God·win or **Godwine** (gódwin) (died 1053). Earl of Wessex. He was the chief adviser of Canute, who made him an earl in *c.* 1018. His son Harold (died 1066) succeeded Edward the Confessor briefly as King of England, Harold II.

God·win (gódwin), **William** (1756–1836). British political theorist and novelist, husband of Mary Wollstonecraft and father-in-law of the poet Shelley. A staunch supporter of the French Revolution and an adherent of utilitarian principles in ethics, his most important work was the radical, pro-anarchist work, *Enquiry Concerning Political Justice* (1793).

Godwin-Aus·ten (gódwin-áwstin, -óstin), **Mount.** Also **K2.** The world's second highest mountain (after Mount Everest), situated in the Karakoram range of northern India. It rises to 8 611 metres (28,250 feet), and is also known as K2 because it was the second Karakoram peak to be measured for height.

god·wit (gódwit) n. Any of various wading birds of the genus *Limosa*, having a long, slender, slightly upturned bill. [16th century : origin obscure.]

Goeb·bels (gúrb'lz; *German* gőb'lss), **(Paul) Joseph** (1897–1945). German politician. After a brief career as a journalist and unsuccessful novelist, he joined the Nazi party and by 1926 was appointed district party leader, or Gauleiter, in Berlin. There he founded and edited the party's propaganda organ, *Der Angriff* ("Attack"). In 1928 he was elected to the Reichstag and when Hitler was made Chancellor (1933) he was appointed Minister of Propaganda. His venomous attacks on the Jews, his powerful oratory, and his use of radio and mass meetings made him the second most powerful man in the party. He played an important part in the "final solution" directed against the Jews, and remained loyal to Hitler until April, 1945, when he and his wife killed their children and committed suicide in Hitler's bunker.

go·er (gő-ər) n. 1. A person who goes to or attends something regularly. Usually used in combination: *a theatregoer.* 2. *Informal.* One that moves very fast. 3. *Informal.* **a.** One who is very lively. **b.** One who is sexually promiscuous. 4. *Australian & N.Z. Informal.* An idea, project, or proposal that looks likely to be successful.

Goe·ring or **Gö·ring** (gúr-ring; *German* gő-), **Hermann (Wilhelm)** (1893–1946). German politician and high-ranking official in the Nazi party. He joined the National Socialist party and took part with Hitler in the Munich putsch of 1923. In 1928 he was elected to the Reichstag, and when Hitler became Chancellor (1933) he was appointed Air Minister. During World War II, he was in command of the German air offensive, until he lost favour with Hitler (1943) and was stripped of authority. He killed himself before his death sentence at the Nuremberg trials (1946) could be carried out.

Goe·the (gúrtə; *German* gőtə), **Johann Wolfgang von** (1749–1832). German writer, scientist, and a major figure in world literature. Although trained as a lawyer, he devoted his life to his poetry, novels, and dramas. He first gained notice with the historical drama *Götz von Berlichingen* (1773), and the novel, *The Sorrows of Young Werther* (1774). In 1775 he was invited to the ducal court at Weimar, where he spent the remainder of his life. His two greatest works were the novel *Wilhelm Meister*, completed in 1829, and the poetic drama *Faust*, the first part of which appeared in 1808 and the second part after his death.

goe·thite (gő-thit, gő-) n. A brown mineral, essentially a hydrated oxide of iron, $Fe_2O_3 \cdot H_2O$, used as an iron ore. [Named in honour of Johann W. von GOETHE.]

go·fer (gőfər) n. *Chiefly U.S.* A person who runs errands and does menial or odd jobs. [From the phrase *go for* (i.e., fetch something).]

gof·fer, gauf·fer (gőfər ‖ *U.S.* gőff-ər, gáwf-) *tr.v.* **-fered, -fering, -fers.** 1. To press ridges or narrow pleats into (a frill, for example); flute; crimp. 2. To emboss (the edges of paper or a book) with a repeating pattern.
~n. 1. An iron used for goffering. 2. Ridged or pleated ornamentation, or an embossed pattern, produced by goffering. [French *gaufrer*, to crimp lace, from Old French *gaufre*, honeycomb, waffle, from Middle Low German *wāfel*.]

Gog and Ma·gog (góg ənd máygog). In Biblical prophecy, the heathen nations to be led by Satan in a war against the Kingdom of God. Revelation 20:7–8.

go-get·ter (gő-gettər) n. *Informal.* An enterprising, forceful, and ambitious person.

gog·ga (khókhə) n. *South African Informal.* Any small insect. [Hottentot *xoxon*, insects.]

gog·gle (gógg'l) v. **-gled, -gling, -gles.** —*intr.* 1. To stare with wide and bulging eyes. 2. To roll or bulge. Used of the eyes. —*tr.* To roll or bulge (the eyes).
~n. 1. A stare or leer. 2. *Plural.* A covering for the eyes consisting of glass or a pair of glasses, often tinted, with shielding sidepieces, worn as a protection against water, snow, wind, dust, or glare. 3. *Plural. Slang.* Glasses; a pair of spectacles. [Middle English *gog(e)len*, to roll the eyes, frequentive, perhaps from *gog-*, root expressive of up and down movement.] —**gog·gly** adj.

gog·gle-box (gógg'l-boks) n. *British Slang.* A television set.

gog·gle-eyed (gógg'l-íd) adj. Having prominent or rolling eyes.

Gogh. See **Van Gogh.**

go-go dancer (gő-gő) n. A girl who dances in a lively, titillating manner, often on a platform, in a discothèque or cabaret. —**go-go dancing** n.

Go·gol (gőgol; *Russian* gáwgəl), **Nikolay Vasilyevich** (1809–52). Russian writer, one of the founders of the Russian realist tradition. He was of Cossack descent, and his first literary success was the collection of tales of the Ukraine, *Evenings on a Farm near Dikanka* (1832). His most famous play, *The Inspector-General* (1836), revealed his talent for satirising Russian officialdom, a talent which reached its highest expression in the novel *Dead Souls* (1842).

Goi·del (góyd'l) n. A member of a Goidelic-speaking people. [Old Irish.]

Goi·del·ic, Goi·dhel·ic (goy-déllik) n. Also **Ga·dhel·ic, Gae·dhel·ic** (gə-déllik, -déelik). A group of Celtic languages comprising Irish Gaelic, Scottish Gaelic, and Manx.
~*adj.* Also **Ga·dhel·ic, Gae·dhel·ic.** 1. Of or pertaining to the

Gaels. **2.** Of, pertaining to, or characteristic of Goidelic. [Old Irish *Goidel*, Gael, Celt, from Old Welsh *gwyddel*, from *gwydd*, wild.]

go·ing (gō'ing) *n.* **1. a.** A departure. **b.** a demise; a death. **2.** The condition underfoot as it affects one's headway in walking or riding. **3.** *Informal.* Progress or existence considered with regard to the conditions to be coped with. **4.** The activity of attending something. Used in combination: *partygoing.*
~adj. **1.** Working; running: *in going order.* **2.** In full operation; flourishing: *a going concern.* **3.** Current; prevailing: *The going rates are low.* **4.** Available; to be found. Used after the noun: *the best products going.*

go·ing-over (gō'ing-ō'vər) *n.pl.* **goings-over.** *Informal.* **1.** An examination; an inspection. **2.** A rehearsal. **3.** A beating; a thrashing. **4.** *Chiefly U.S.* A scolding or rebuke.

go·ings-on (gō'ingz-ón') *pl.n.* *Informal.* Events or behaviour, especially when regarded as improper or mysterious.

goi·tre, *U.S.* **goi·ter** (góy'tər) *n.* *Pathology.* A chronic, noncancerous enlargement of the thyroid gland, visible as a swelling at the front of the neck, that may be due to under- or overactivity of the gland and may be associated with iodine deficiency. Also called "struma". See **exophthalmic goitre.** [French *goitre*, from Provençal *goitron*, from Vulgar Latin *gutturōnem* (unattested), from Latin *guttur†*, throat.] **—goi·trous** (-trəss) *adj.*

go-kart. Variant of **go-cart.**

Go·lan Heights (gō'lan, gō·laʹan). Range of hills to the east of the river Jordan, disputed between Syria and Israel. Marking Syria's southern border after World War II, it was used from 1948 as a base from which to shell Israeli settlements. The heights were stormed by Israel during the last hours of the 1967 Middle East War and were subsequently colonised by Jewish settlers. They remain of vital strategic importance and their administration is a key issue in Middle East peace negotiations.

Gol·con·da (gol-kón'də) *n.* A source of great riches, especially a mine. [After *Golconda,* India, city near Hyderabad, formerly noted for its diamonds.]

gold (gōld) *n.* **1.** *Symbol* **Au** A soft, yellow, corrosion-resistant element, the most malleable and ductile metal, occurring in veins and alluvial deposits, and recovered by mining or by panning or sluicing. It is a good thermal and electrical conductor, is generally alloyed to increase its strength, and is used as an international monetary standard, in jewellery, for decoration, in dentistry, and as a plated coating on a wide variety of electrical and mechanical components. Atomic number 79, atomic weight 196.967, melting point 1,063.0°C, boiling point 2,966.0°C, relative density 19.32, valencies 1, 3. Also called "yellow metal". **2. a.** Coinage made of gold. **b.** A gold standard. **3.** Money; riches. **4.** Light olive-brown to dark yellow, or moderate, strong, to vivid yellow. **5.** Something regarded as having great value or goodness: *a heart of gold.* **6.** The central circle on an archery target; a bull's eye. **7.** A gold medal.
~adj. **1.** Pertaining to or containing gold. **2.** Having the colour of gold. **3.** Redeemable or secured by gold: *gold certificate.* [Middle English *gold*, Old English *gold.*]

Gold·bach's conjecture (gōld-bakhs) *n.* *Mathematics.* The hypothesis that every even number greater than two is the sum of two prime numbers. It is generally thought to be true, but so far is unproved. [After C. *Goldbach* (1690–1764), German mathematician.]

gold basis *n.* A gold standard as a basis for determining prices.

gold·beat·er's skin (gōld-beet'ərz) *n.* Treated animal membrane used to separate sheets of gold being hammered into gold leaf.

gold·beat·ing (gōld-beet'ing) *n.* The act, art, or process of beating sheets of gold into gold leaf. **—gold·beat·er** *n.*

gold brick *n.* Also **gold·brick** (gōld-brik) (for sense **2.**). **1.** A fraudulent and worthless substitute. **2.** *U.S. Slang.* A shirker or loafer.

gold bug *n. U.S.* Any beetle of the family Chrysomelidae.

Gold Coast¹ (gōld). The name of Ghana, before the country's independence (1957). The term was first applied by European traders to its coastline on the Gulf of Guinea, where gold was brought for sale from the Akan forests inland.

Gold Coast². Coastal resort area in southern Queensland, Australia, situated to the south of Brisbane. It incorporates the towns of Southport, Coolangatta, and Burleigh Heads.

gold·crest (gōld-krest) *n.* A small Eurasian songbird, *Regulus regulus,* with yellow-green plumage and an orange or yellow crest.

gold-digger (gōld-diggər) *n.* **1.** *Informal.* A person, especially a woman, who seeks gifts and expensive pleasures from others. **2.** One that digs for gold.

gold disc *n.* An award in the form of a gold-plated gramophone record, presented to a recording artist or a group of artists when the sales of a record that they have made reach a given number. Also called "gold record".

gold dust *n.* Gold in powder form, such as that found in **placer mining** *(see).*

gold·en (gōld'ən) *adj.* **1.** Made of or containing gold. **2. a.** Having the colour of gold or a yellow colour suggestive of gold. **b.** Suggestive of gold, as in richness or splendour: *a golden voice.* **3.** Of the greatest value or importance; precious. **4.** Marked by peace, prosperity, and often creativeness: *a golden age.* **5.** Very favourable or advantageous; excellent: *a golden opportunity.* **6.** Having a promising future; seemingly assured of success. **7.** Being the fiftieth in a series. Said of anniversaries: *golden wedding.* **—gold·en·ly** *adv.* **—gold·en·ness** *n.*

golden age *n.* **1.** *Greek & Roman Mythology.* The first age of the world, an untroubled and prosperous era during which humankind lived in ideal happiness. **2.** A period when a nation or some wide field of endeavour reaches its height. Compare **iron age, silver age.**

golden anniversary *n.* A 50th anniversary, symbolised by gold.

golden calf *n.* **1.** A golden image of a sacrificial calf fashioned by Aaron and worshipped by the Israelites. Exodus 32. **2.** Wealth as an object of worship; mammon.

golden chain *n.* A shrub, the **laburnum** *(see).*

Golden Delicious *n.* A variety of eating apple having greenish-yellow skin and sweet flesh.

golden eagle *n.* An eagle, *Aquila chrysaetos,* of mountainous areas of the Northern Hemisphere, having dark plumage with yellowish feathers on the head and neck.

gol·den·eye (gōld'ən-ī) *n.* Either of two ducks, *Bucephala clangula* or *B. islandica,* of northern regions, having a short black bill, a rounded head, yellow eyes, and black and white plumage. [From their golden-yellow eyes.]

golden ferret *n.* In golf, the holing of a ball after hitting it out of a bunker.

Golden Fleece *n.* *Greek Mythology.* The magic fleece of the winged ram, stolen by Jason and the Argonauts.

Golden Gate Bridge. Suspension bridge near San Francisco on the west coast of the United States. It crosses the Golden Gate strait which links San Francisco Bay with the Pacific Ocean. The bridge was completed in 1937 and its central span of 1 280 metres (4,200 feet) was then the longest in the world.

golden handshake *n.* *Informal.* **1.** A generous payment made to an employee on redundancy, or on retirement as a reward for long or outstanding service. **2.** The act or practice of making such a payment.

Golden Horde *n.* The Mongol army that swept over eastern Europe in the 13th century and established a suzerain in Russia. [Translation of Tatar *altūn ordū,* from the colour of the tent of their commander, Batu Khan.]

Golden Horn. *Turkish* **Ha·liç** (ha-léech). Inlet of the Bosporus in northwest Turkey. It has served as the harbour for Istanbul since ancient times.

golden mean *n.* **1.** The course between extremes; moderation. **2.** The golden section.

golden pheasant *n.* A pheasant, *Chrysolophus pictus,* of China and Tibet, having a long tail and brilliantly coloured plumage.

golden retriever *n.* A dog of a breed of retriever having a dense, wavy, cream or yellow coat.

gold·en·rod (gōld'ən-ród, -rod) *n.* Any of various plants of the chiefly North American genus *Solidago,* having clusters of small yellow flowers that bloom in late summer or autumn.

golden rule *n.* **1.** The maxim or teaching that one should behave towards others as one would have others behave towards oneself. Matthew 7:12. **2.** Any basic important principle.

golden samphire *n.* A plant, the **samphire** *(see).*

gold·en·seal (gōld'ən-séel, -seel) *n.* A woodland plant, *Hydrastis canadensis,* of eastern North America, having small greenish-white flowers and a yellow root formerly used medicinally.

golden section *n.* A ratio between the two dimensions of a plane figure or the two divisions of a line such that the smaller is to the larger as the larger is to the sum of the two, roughly a ratio of three to five. The proportion, which is used in the fine arts, is considered particularly aesthetically pleasing. Also called "golden mean".

golden syrup *n.* A clear, thick golden-coloured liquid made from cane-sugar juice and used to sweeten puddings, cakes, tarts, and the like. Also called "treacle".

golden wattle *n.* Any of several yellow-flowered, Australian trees or shrubs of the genus *Acacia;* especially, *A. pycnantha.*

gold-ex·change standard (gōld-iks-chaynj, -eks-) *n.* A monetary system in which a country maintains its currency at par with the currency of another country on the gold standard.

gold-filled (gōld-fild) *adj. U.S.* Made of a hard base metal with an outer layer of gold.

gold·finch (gōld-finch) *n.* **1.** A small Eurasian bird, *Carduelis carduelis,* having brownish plumage with red, yellow, and black markings. In this sense, also called "redcap". **2.** Any of several small American birds of the genus *Spinus;* especially, *S. tristis,* of which the male has yellow and black plumage.

gold·fish (gōld-fish) *n., pl.* **-fishes** or collectively **goldfish. 1.** A freshwater fish, *Carassius auratus,* native to eastern Asia, characteristically having brassy or reddish colouring, and bred in many ornamental forms as an aquarium fish. **2.** Any of various similar aquarium fishes, especially the golden **orfe** *(see).*

goldfish bowl *n.* **1.** A **fish bowl** *(see).* **2.** A place or condition of exposure to public view.

gold foil *n.* Gold rolled or beaten into thin sheets thicker than gold leaf.

gold·i·locks (gōld'i-loks) *n.* **1.** A European plant, *Linosyrus vulgaris,* having narrow leaves and clusters of small yellow flowers. **2.** A Eurasian woodland plant, *Ranunculus auricomus,* similar and related to the buttercup. [Obsolete *goldy,* golden, from GOLD + LOCK(S).]

Gold·i·locks (gōld'i-loks) *n.* A person, especially a little girl, with curly golden hair. [*Goldy* (see **gold**) + *locks.*]

Gold·ing (gōld'ing), **Sir William (Gerald)** (1911–93). British novelist. He established his reputation with *Lord of the Flies* (1954). Later novels include *Pincher Martin* (1956), *Free Fall* (1959), and

The Scorpion God (1971). He was awarded the Booker Prize (1980) for *Rites of Passage*, and the Nobel prize for literature (1983).

gold leaf *n.* Gold beaten into extremely thin sheets, used for gilding.

Gold·man (gṓldmən), **Emma,** nicknamed Red Emma (1869–1940). U.S. anarchist agitator, born in Russia. She founded the anarchist paper *Mother Earth* with Alexander Berkman (1870–1936). In 1916 she was imprisoned for advocating birth control, in 1917 for opposing military conscription. In 1919 she was deported, with Berkman, to Russia. She went to Spain during the Civil War and died in Canada, in 1940. Her writings include *Anarchism and Other Essays* (1911) and *My Disillusionment in Russia* (1923).

gold medal *n.* A medal made of gold, or something looking like gold, awarded as a prize for coming first in a race, competition, or the like. Compare **bronze medal, silver medal.**

gold mine *n.* **1.** A mine yielding gold ore. **2.** *Informal.* A source of great wealth or profit.

gold-of-pleas·ure (gṓld-əv-pléžhər) *n.* A plant, *Camelina sativa,* native to Europe and Asia, having small yellow flowers and seeds rich in oil.

Gol·do·ni (gol-dṓni), **Carlo** (1707–93). Italian comic playwright. He wrote over 250 plays, 150 of which are comedies, including *The Mistress of the Inn* (1753), *The Fan* (1764), and *The Accomplished Maid* (1756). He lived in Paris after 1762 and died there a pauper.

gold plate *n.* **1.** Vessels, dishes, and utensils made of gold. **2.** A covering of gold, usually produced by electroplating.

gold-plate (gṓld-pláyt) *tr.v.* **-plated, -plating, -plates.** To cover with gold plate, usually by electroplating.

gold point *n.* **1.** The point in foreign-exchange rates at which it is no more expensive to import or export gold bullion in settling international accounts than to buy or sell bills of exchange. Also called "specie point". **2.** *Physics.* The melting point of gold, used as a fixed point for temperature scales.

gold reserve *n.* The reserve of gold bullion held by a government or central bank to redeem its notes.

gold rush *n.* A rush of migrants to an area where gold has been discovered, such as that to California in 1849.

Gold·schmidt process (gṓld-shmit) *n.* A process for extracting metals by reducing the oxide with aluminium. [After Hans *Goldschmidt* (died 1923), German chemist.]

gold·smith (gṓld-smith) *n.* **1.** An artisan who fashions objects in gold. **2.** A tradesman who deals in gold articles.

Gold·smith (gṓld-smith), **Oliver** (*c.* 1728–74). Irish writer. He settled in London in 1756 and published his first work, *Enquiry into the Present State of Polite Learning* (1759). The publication of the satirical essays, *The Citizen of the World* (1762), established him as a man of letters. His most famous works are his novel *The Vicar of Wakefield* (1766), the pastoral poem *The Deserted Village* (1770), and the dramatic comedy *She Stoops to Conquer* (1773).

goldsmith beetle *n.* Any of various scarabaeid beetles having metallic greenish-yellow colouring, especially the rose chafer, *Cetonia aurata.*

gold standard *n.* A monetary standard under which the basic unit of currency is equal in value to and exchangeable in principle for a given amount of gold.

Gold Stick *n. British.* **1.** A ceremonial gilt rod carried by the colonel of the Life Guards or the captain of the Gentlemen-at-arms. **2.** The officer carrying this rod.

gold·stone (gṓld-stōn) *n.* An **aventurine** *(see)* with gold-coloured inclusions.

gold-tail moth (gṓld-tayl) *n.* The **yellow-tail moth** *(see).*

Gold·wyn (gṓldwin), **Samuel,** born Schmuel Goldfish (1882–1974). Polish-born U.S. film producer. In 1916 he established his own Goldwyn Pictures Corporation, and merged with Louis Mayer in 1924 to become Metro-Goldwyn-Mayer. Goldwyn produced a number of major films, including *Guys and Dolls* (1955) and *Porgy and Bess* (1959). He won an Oscar for *The Best Years of Our Lives* (1946). He was noted for "Goldwynisms" such as "include me out".

go·lem (gṓ-lem, -ləm) *n.* In Jewish folklore, an artificially created human being endowed with life by supernatural means.

golf (golf, *old-fashioned* gof, gawf || *U.S. also* gawlf) *n.* A game played on a large outdoor obstacle course having a series of usually 9 or 18 holes spaced far apart, the object being to propel a small ball by the use of a club into each hole with as few strokes as possible.

~*intr.v.* **golfed, golfing, golfs.** To play golf. [Middle English *golf†* (Scottish dialect).] —**golf·er** *n.*

golf ball *n.* **1.** A small, hard, dimpled ball used in golf. **2.** *Informal.* A revolving metal sphere on which the type is carried in many electric typewriters. **3.** A typewriter equipped with such a sphere.

golf club *n.* **1.** Any of a set of clubs having a slender shaft and a head of wood or iron, used in golf. **2.** An organisation of golfers usually having its own golf course and premises. **3.** Such premises.

golf course *n.* A large tract of land laid out for golf.

golf links *n., pl.* **golf links.** A golf course on coastal land.

Gol·gi (gólji), **Camillo** (1844–1926). Italian physician. He established the existence of a complex of vesicles present in cells, now known as the **Golgi apparatus.** For his work on the structure of the nervous system he was awarded, with Ramón y Cajal (1852–1934), the Nobel prize for physiology or medicine (1906).

Golgi apparatus *n.* A stack of membranous vesicles present in living cells and believed to function in the formation of secretions within the cell. Also called "Golgi body", "Golgi complex". [After Camillo GOLGI.]

gol·go·tha (gólgəthə, gol-góthə) *n.* **1.** A place of burial. **2.** A place or occasion of suffering or agony. [After GOLGOTHA.]

Gol·go·tha (gólgəthə, gol-góthə). The hill of Calvary, where Jesus was crucified. [Late Latin, from Greek, from Aramaic *gulgŭltha,* skull (from the shape of the hill).]

gol·iard (gṓl-yərd, -i-aard) *n.* Any of a class of wandering students in medieval Europe, who are supposed to have led a life of conviviality and debauchery and to have composed ribald and satirical Latin songs. [Middle English *goliard,* from Old French, from *gole,* throat, from Latin *gula,* gullet.] —**gol·iar·dic** (gōl-yárdik) *adj.*

Go·li·ath (gə-lī-əth). The giant Philistine warrior who was slain by David with a stone and sling. I Samuel 17:4–51.

goliath beetle *n.* Any of several very large, herbivorous, scarabaeid beetles; especially, the African species *Goliathus giganteus,* which can reach a length of 20 centimetres (8 inches).

goliath frog *n.* The largest known frog, *Rana goliath,* which occurs in Africa and can reach a length of 35 centimetres (14 inches).

gol·li·wog, gol·li·wogg (gólli-wog) *n.* A male doll with a black face and longish hair standing out from its head, usually made from soft material. [Originally the name of a doll designed by Florence Upton (1873–1922) for a series of children's books by Bertha Upton (1849–1912); possibly after POLLIWOG.]

gol·ly[1] (gólli) *n., pl.* **-ies.** *British Informal.* A golliwog.

golly[2] *interj. Informal.* Used to express mild surprise or wonder. [Euphemism for GOD.]

golly[3] *intr.v.* **-lied, -lying, -lies.** *Australian Slang.* To spit. ~*n., pl.* **gollies.** *Australian Slang.* A lump of spit. [From obsolete *gollion,* gob of phlegm, probably of imitative origin.]

GOM, G.O.M. Grand Old Man.

golosh. Variant of **galosh.**

gombo. Variant of **gumbo.**

gom·broon (gom-brṓon) *n.* A kind of Persian pottery. [After *Gombroon,* town in Iran.]

Gó·mez (gṓ-mez; *Spanish* -mess), **Juan Vicente** (1857–1935). Venezuelan politician; President of the republic (1908–35). Once a cattle herdsman and almost illiterate, he gathered a guerrilla force around him which helped win the presidency for Cipriano Castro. Castro made him vice-president in 1899 but Gomez deposed him in 1908. He ruled by the severest methods and established a police state. He also established the foundations of Venezuela's modern industrial economy.

Go·mor·rah (gə-mórrə || -máwrə). A city of ancient Palestine near **Sodom** *(see).*

Gom·pers (gómpərz), **Samuel** (1850–1924). English-born U.S. trade union leader who took part in the founding of the Federation of Organized Trades and Labor Unions (1881). When it was reorganised as the American Federation of Labor (1886) he became its first president, an office he held until his death.

gom·pho·sis (gom-fṓ-siss) *n. Anatomy.* An immovable articulation consisting of a peg and rigid socket, such as a tooth and its bony socket. [New Latin, from Greek *gomphōsis,* from *gomphoun,* to fasten with bolts, from *gomphos,* bolt.]

Go·muł·ka (gə-mṓolkə; *Polish* go-mṓowka), **Władysław** (1905–82). Polish Communist party leader. An active trade unionist, he was secretary of the Polish Workers' Central Committee (1943–49) and played a leading part in the resistance movement against the Germans. From 1945 to 1949 he was deputy premier of Poland, but was purged for alleged "bourgeois nationalism" and sympathy with Tito. He was imprisoned without trial (1951–54), but re-admitted to the party in 1956 and elected as first secretary. He removed Stalinists from key positions, reduced the secret police terror, ended compulsory collectivisation, and reached a compromise with the Church. In 1970, he resigned as first secretary in the wake of food riots.

go·mu·ti (gə-mṓoti) *n.* **1.** A palm tree, *Arenga pinnata,* of southeast Asia, the sap of which yields sugar. Also called "sugar palm". **2.** The leaf fibres of this palm, used to make cord, rope, and the like. [Malay *gēmuti.*]

–gon *n. comb. form.* Indicates a figure having a specified number of sides and angles; for example, **nonagon.** [Greek *-gōnon,* from *-gōnos,* -angled, from *gōnia,* angle.]

go·nad (gṓnad) *n.* An organ in animals that produces gametes; especially, a testis or ovary. [New Latin, from Greek *gonos,* offspring, procreation, genitals.] —**go·nad·al** (gṓ-nadd'l, -nádd'l), **go·nad·ic** (go-náddik) *adj.*

gon·a·do·troph·ic (gṓnədō-tróffik, -trófik) *adj.* Also **gon·a·do·trop·ic** (-tróppik). Acting on or stimulating the gonads, as does a hormone.

gon·a·do·tro·phin (gṓnədō-trṓfin) *n.* Also **gon·a·do·tro·pin** (-trṓpin). Any of several hormones that are secreted by the pituitary gland and stimulate activity of the ovaries and testes, as for example the **follicle-stimulating hormone** *(see).* Also called "gonadotrophic hormone".

Gon·cha·rov (gónchə-róf; *Russian* gənchi-róf), **Ivan Alexandrovich** (1812–91). Russian novelist, famous for one novel, *Oblomov* (1858), a masterpiece of comedy.

Gon·court (goN-kṓor), **Edmond (Louis Antoine) Huot de** (1822–96) and his brother **Jules (Alfred) Huot de** (1830–70). French writers and literary critics. They are best known for their journal, published in nine volumes (1887–96). Edmond's will provided for the foundation of the Goncourt Academy, which annually awards the Goncourt Prize for literature.

Gond (gond) *n.* A member of a people of Dravidian stock of central India.

Gon·dar (góndaar). Town in northwest Ethiopia. It was a capital of Ethiopia, flourishing from *c.*1630 to *c.*1860.

Gon·di (góndi) *n.* The Dravidian language of the Gonds.

gon·do·la (góndələ ‖ gon-dṓlə) *n.* **1.** A narrow, lightweight barge having ends that curve up into a point and often a small cabin in the middle, propelled with a single oar from the stern, used on the canals of Venice. **2.** Any of various containers or vehicles suspended from a framework or larger vehicle as : **a.** A cabin or basket suspended from a balloon or airship. **b.** A car or seat suspended from cables, as on a ski lift. **c.** A movable platform or container suspended from a building and used by builders and other workmen to gain access to outside walls and windows. **3.** A set of freestanding shelves or a similar structure used for displaying goods in supermarkets and other shops. **4.** *U.S.* An open, shallow railway goods vehicle. Also called "gondola car". **5.** *U.S.* A flat-bottomed river boat. [Italian (Venetian dialect), *gondola*†, roll, rock.]

gon·do·lier (góndə-léer) *n.* The boatman of a gondola.

Gond·wa·na (gon-dwáanə). Region of north central India noted for its rock system and fossil flora. [Sanskrit *gondavana*, "Gond forest": *gonda*, fleshy navel, name applied to the GOND + *vana*, forest.]

Gond·wa·na·land (gond-wáanə-land) *n.* A hypothetical southern portion of the earth's original land mass, Pangaea. Africa, South America, India, Arabia, Australia, Madagascar, New Guinea, the Malay Peninsula, Indonesia, and Antarctica are thought to have begun drifting apart, out of Gondwanaland some 200 million years ago. Compare **Laurasia.**

gone (gón ‖ gawn, gaan). Past participle of **go.**
~*adj.* **1.** Past; bygone. **2.** Advanced beyond hope or recall. **3.** Dying or dead. **4.** Ruined; lost. **5.** *Informal.* **a.** Carried away; absorbed. **b.** Exhilarated; excited. **6.** Used up; exhausted. **7.** *Informal.* At a specified stage of a pregnancy: *four months gone.* —**gone on.** *Slang.* Infatuated with: *gone on the girl.*

gon·er (gónnər ‖ gáwnər) *n.* *Slang.* One who is ruined or doomed. [From GONE.]

gon·fa·lon (gónfələn) *n.* A banner suspended from a crosspiece, especially as a standard in an ecclesiastical procession or as the ensign of a medieval Italian republic. [Italian *gonfalone*, standard, from Germanic.]

gon·fa·lon·ier (gónfələ-néer) *n.* **1.** The bearer of a gonfalon. **2.** The chief magistrate in any of several medieval Italian republics.

gong (gong ‖ gawng) *n.* **1. a.** A hanging rimmed metal disc that produces a loud, sonorous tone when struck with a padded mallet. **b.** See **tam-tam. 2.** A usually saucer-shaped bell that is struck with a mechanically operated hammer. **3.** *British Slang.* A medal. [Malay *gong* (imitative).]

Gon·gor·ism (góng-gə-riz'm) *n.* A florid, cluttered literary style. [Popularised by Luis de *Góngora y Argote* (1561-1627), Spanish poet.] —**Gon·go·ris·tic** (-rístik) *adj.*

go·ni·a·tite (gŏni-ə-tīt) *n.* Any of various extinct cephalopod molluscs of the genus *Goniatites,* the fossil remains of which are common constituents of Devonian and Carboniferous rocks. [Greek *gōnia,* angle (referring to the angular sutures in some species).]

go·nid·i·um (gə-níddi-əm, gō-) *n., pl.* **-nidia** (-níddi-ə). **1.** An asexually produced reproductive cell that separates from the parent body, as in certain colonial algae. **2.** An algal cell in the thallus of a lichen, so called because they were once thought to be the reproductive cells of the lichen. [New Latin : GON(O)- + Greek *-idion,* diminutive suffix.]

go·ni·om·e·ter (gŏni-ómmitər) *n.* **1.** An optical instrument for measuring crystal angles. **2.** A radio receiver and directional antenna used as a system to determine the angular direction of incoming radio signals. [Greek *gōnia,* angle + -METER.] —**go·ni·o·met·ric** (-ō-méttrik, -ə-), **go·ni·o·met·ri·cal** *adj.*

go·ni·om·e·try (gŏni-ómmətri) *n.* The science of measuring angles. [Greek *gōnia,* angle + -METRY.]

go·ni·on (gŏni-ən, -on) *n., pl.* **-nia.** The point of the angle on either side of the lower jaw. [New Latin, from Greek *gōnia,* angle.]

go·ni·o·punc·ture (gŏni-ō-pungkchər) *n.* An operation for glaucoma in which fluid is drained from the eye by inserting a small knife through the cornea.

-gonium *n. comb. form.* Indicates a reproductive cell or seed; for example, **oogonium.** [New Latin *gonium,* seed, cell, from Greek *gonos,* seed, procreation.]

gonk (gongk) *n.* A soft, cuddly children's toy, representing a creature with a very large face. [20th century : origin obscure.]

gonna (gənə; *also* gúnnə, gónnə). *Slang.* Contraction of *going to.*

gono-, gon- *comb. form.* Indicates sexual, reproductive, or procreative; for example, **gonococcus, gonidium.** [New Latin *gono-,* from Greek, from *gonos,* offspring, seed, procreation.]

gon·o·coc·cus (gónnō-kóckəss) *n., pl.* **-cocci** (-kóksī). The bacterium, *Neisseria gonorrhoeae,* that causes gonorrhoea. [New Latin : GONO- + -COCCUS.]

gon·o·cyte (gónō-sīt) *n.* **1.** An embryonic cell that develops into an ovum or a spermatozoon. **2.** An oocyte or spermatocyte. [GONO- + -CYTE.]

gon·o·phore (gónnō-fawr ‖ -fōr) *n.* A structure bearing or consisting of a reproductive organ or part, such as a reproductive cell or bud in a hydroid colony. [GONO- + -PHORE.] —**gon·o·phor·ic** (gónnō-fórrik ‖ -fáwrik), **go·noph·o·rous** (gə-nóffərəss) *adj.*

gon·o·pore (gónnō-pawr ‖ -pōr) *n.* A reproductive aperture or pore, as in insects.

gon·or·rhoe·a (gónnə-rée-ə) *n.* An infectious disease of the genito-urinary tract, rectum, and cervix, caused by the gonococcus, transmitted chiefly by sexual intercourse, and characterised by acute purulent urethritis with dysuria. [Late Latin *gonorrhoea,* from Greek *gonorrhoia* : GONO- + -RRHOEA.] —**gon·or·rhoe·al, gon·or·rhoe·ic** *adj.*

-gony *n. comb. form.* Indicates the production of; for example, **sporogony.** [Latin *-gonia,* from Greek, from *-goneia,* generation, from *gonos,* offspring, seed.]

Gon·za·ga (*Italian* gon-tsáaga). Illustrious Italian princely house, whose members ruled Mantua from the 14th to the 18th century. Francesco Gonzaga (1466-1519) made Mantua into a centre of learning and the arts.

Gon·za·les (gən-záaliss), **Richard Alonzo,** known as "Pancho" (1928 – 95). U.S. tennis player. He won the U.S. lawn and clay-court championships for two years in succession (1948-49) before turning professional. He was the world professional champion every year but one between 1954 and 1961.

goo (gŏo) *n. Informal.* **1.** A sticky moist substance. **2.** Sentimental drivel. [Perhaps short for BURGOO.] —**goo·ey** *adj.* —**goo·i·ly** *adv.*

goo·ber (gŏobər) *n. U.S. Regional.* A peanut *(see).* Also called "goober pea". [Angolese *nguba.*]

Gooch, Graham (Alan) (1953-). England cricketer, captain of the side in 34 Tests. He set a Test record of 8293 runs scored in 107 matches 1975–93. Retired from cricket (1997).

good (gŏod) *adj.* **better, best. 1. a.** Having positive or desirable qualities; not bad or poor. **b.** Virtuous; morally admirable; upright: *a good man.* **2. a.** Serving the end desired; suitable; serviceable: *a good outdoor paint.* **b.** Worthy of proper treatment; not to be spoilt or wasted: *don't ruin good work.* **3. a.** Not spoilt or ruined; able to be used: *The milk is still good.* **b.** In excellent condition; whole; sound: *a good tooth.* **c.** Handsome or fine in appearance: *a good figure.* **4.** Superior to the average: *a good student.* **5. a.** Of high quality: *good books.* **b.** Discriminating: *good taste.* **c.** Well-tested or trustworthy: *a good brand of tuna.* **6.** Suitable for special or formal occasions: *his good clothes.* **7. a.** Beneficial; salutary: *a good night's rest.* **b.** Undisturbed or comfortable: *The patient had a good night.* **8.** Competent; skilled: *a good machinist; good at maths.* **9.** Complete; thorough: *a good workout.* **10. a.** Safe; sure: *a good investment.* **b.** Valid or sound: *a good reason.* **c.** Genuine; real: *a good pound note.* **d.** Applicable; relevant: *his claim to the money was good.* **11. a.** Ample; substantial; considerable: *a good income.* **b.** Bountiful: *a good table.* **12.** Full: *a good mile from here.* **13. a.** Pleasant; enjoyable: *having a good time at the party.* **b.** Propitious; favourable: *good weather; a good omen.* **14. a.** Benevolent; cheerful; kind: *a good soul.* **b.** Loyal; staunch: *a good Socialist.* **15. a.** Well-behaved; obedient: *a good child.* **b.** Socially correct; proper: *good manners.* **c.** Kindly; well-disposed: *She's good to her husband.* **16.** Fertile: *good land.* **17.** Well-established; well-bred; of a high class: *a good family.* **18.** Physically pleasurable or materially enjoyable: *the good things in life.* **19.** Large; substantial: *a good distance away.* **20.** Used to introduce meeting and leave-taking formulas: *good morning; good evening; good night.* —**as good as.** Practically; virtually; nearly: *as good as new.* —**good and.** *Informal.* Very; entirely: *good and tired.* —**good for. 1.** Able to serve or continue performing for a specified period of time: *good for another year.* **2.** Able to be counted upon for producing something specified: *good for a laugh.* **3.** Worth in exchange: *a ticket good for two trips.* —**make good. 1.** To fulfil a promise, commitment, or the like; make valid. **2.** To compensate for or replace. **3.** To prove; verify. **4.** *Informal.* To succeed; do well.
~*n.* **1. a.** That which is good. **b.** The good, valuable, or useful part or aspect: *get the good out of something.* **c.** Benefit; real advantage: *Some good may yet come of it.* **2.** Welfare; benefit; well-being: *for the common good.* **3.** Goodness; virtue; merit: *There is much good in him.* —**come to no good.** To come to a bad end; prove worthless. —**for good (and all).** For all time to come; permanently; forever: *She came home to stay for good.* —**no good.** *Informal.* **1.** Worthless. **2.** Futile; useless: *It's no good trying to coax him.* —**to the good.** To one's benefit; for the best: *ended up 5 to the good.*
~*adv.* Nonstandard. Well. [Middle English *god, gode,* Old English *gōd.*]

Usage: There is a clear distinction between the use of *good* and *well* following verbs. *Good* is an adjective that qualifies the subject of a linking verb, such as *be, feel, seem, smell, taste: It feels good; that tastes good. Well* is an adverb that qualifies the verb directly: *He dances well; he acts really well.* It is nonstandard to say or write *he dances good* or *he acts real good.*

good book *n. Often capital G,* capital B. The Bible. Often preceded by *the.*

good-bye, good-bye, *U.S.* **good-by** (gŏod-bí) *interj.* Used to express farewell on parting.
~*n., pl.* **goodbyes. 1.** An expression of farewell. **2.** *Usually plural.* An act of leave-taking: *lingering over their goodbyes.* [Contraction of *God be with you.*]

good faith *n.* Integrity; sincerity of intent: *a promise made in good faith.*

good fellow *n.* A genial, companionable person.

good-fel·low·ship (gŏod-féllōship) *n.* Pleasant sociability; comradeship.

good-for-noth·ing (good-fər-nuthing ‖ -nothing) *n.* A person of little worth or usefulness.
~*adj.* Having little worth; useless.
Good Friday *n.* The Friday before Easter, observed by Christians in commemoration of the Crucifixion of Jesus.
good-heart·ed (good-hártid) *adj.* Kind and generous. —**good-heart·ed·ly** *adv.* —**good-heart·ed·ness** *n.*
good-hu·moured (good-héwmərd) *adj.* Cheerful; amiable. —**good-hu·moured·ly** *adv.* —**good-hu·moured·ness** *n.*
goodie. Variant of **goody**[1].
good·ish (goodish) *adj.* **1.** Somewhat good. **2.** Somewhat large or big; goodly.
good-look·er (good-look ər ‖ -look ər) *n. Informal.* A good-looking person, especially a woman.
good-look·ing (good-looking ‖ -looking) *adj.* Of a pleasing appearance; attractive; handsome.
good looks *pl.n.* Attractive appearance; handsomeness.
good·ly (goodli) *adj.* **-lier, -liest. 1.** Fairly large; considerable: *a goodly sum.* **2.** Of pleasing appearance; comely. —**good·li·ness** *n.*
good·man (good-man, -mən) *n., pl.* **-men** (-men, -mən). *Archaic.*
1. a. The male head of a household; the master. **b.** A husband. **2.** A courteous title of or form of address for a man not of gentle birth.
Good·man (goodmən), **Benny,** originally Benjamin David Goodman (1909–86). U.S. clarinettist, known as the "King of Swing." In New York in 1935 he formed the Benny Goodman trio with Gene Krupa and Teddy Wilson; a year later Lionel Hampton made it a quartet. For at least 30 years Goodman was a fine jazz musician. He also became an accomplished classical clarinettist.
good nature *n.* Cheerful, obliging disposition.
good-na·tured (good-náychərd) *adj.* Having an easy-going, cheerful disposition. See Synonyms at **amiable.** —**good-na·tured·ly** *adv.* —**good-na·tured·ness** *n.*
good·ness (good-nəss, -niss) *n.* **1.** The state or quality of being good; excellence; merit; worth. **2.** Virtuousness; moral rectitude. **3.** Kindness; benevolence; generosity. **4.** The good part of something; essence; strength.
~*interj.* Used as a euphemism for "god", often in phrases such as *Thank goodness* or *My goodness,* to express relief, surprise, or the like.
good offices *pl.n.* Favourable intervention, usually unobtrusive, on a person's behalf.
good-oh, good-o (good-ō, -ó) *interj. Chiefly Australian Informal.* Used to express consent, approval, or delight.
goods (goodz) *pl.n. Abbr.* **gds. 1.** Merchandise; wares. **2.** Portable personal property. **3.** *Chiefly British.* Merchandise to be transported; freight. Also used adjectivally: *a goods train.* **4.** *Economics.* Physical commodities, usually movable, and only consumed some time after production. Compare **services. 5.** *Used with a singular or plural verb. U.S.* Fabric; material. —**deliver the goods.** *Informal.* To produce what is expected; carry out a promise. —**get or have the goods on.** *U.S. Slang.* To obtain or have incriminating information or material against. —**the goods.** *Slang.* The real or genuine thing. [Plural of GOOD.]
Good Samaritan *n.* **1.** In a New Testament parable, the only passer-by to aid a man who had been beaten and robbed. Luke 10:30–37. **2.** A compassionate person who unselfishly helps another or others.
goods and chattels *pl.n.* Personal belongings.
Good Shepherd *n.* A name for Jesus. John 10:11–12.
good-sized (good-sizd) *adj.* Of a fairly large size.
good-tem·pered (good-témpərd) *adj.* Having an even or mild temper; not easily irritated. —**good-tem·pered·ly** *adv.* —**good-tem·pered·ness** *n.*
good-time (good-tīm) *adj.* Designating a person eager to enjoy life. Used chiefly in the phrase *good-time girl.*
good turn *n.* An act or gesture that helps another person; a favour.
good·wife (good-wīf) *n., pl.* **-wives** (-wīvz). *Archaic.* **1.** The female head of a household; the mistress. **2.** A courteous title of or form of address for a woman not of gentle birth.
good·will, good will *n.* **1.** Friendly or neighbourly feeling; benevolence. Also used adjectivally: *a goodwill visit.* **2.** Cheerful acquiescence or willingness. **3.** *Accounting.* The good relationship of a business enterprise with its customers, regarded and assessed as an intangible asset.
Good·win Sands (goodwin). Group of sandbanks in the Strait of Dover, lying about 10 kilometres (6 miles) off the southeast coast of England. Shifting and partially exposed at low tide, they are extremely dangerous to shipping.
good·y[1], **good·ie** (goodi) *n., pl.* **-ies.** *Informal.* **1.** *Usually plural.* Something attractive, interesting, or delectable; especially, something sweet to eat. **2.** A goody-goody. **3.** The virtuous character, as in a cinematic film. Compare **baddy.**
~*adj. Informal.* Goody-goody.
~*interj.* Used to express childish delight.
goody[2] *n., pl.* **-ies.** *Archaic.* A polite title of or form of address for a married woman of humble rank. Often used with a surname. [Short for GOODWIFE.]
Good·year (good-yeer), **Charles** (1800–60). U.S. inventor. After experimenting for ten years to find a method of raising the melting point of rubber, he accidentally came upon vulcanisation when rubber mixed with sulphur dropped on a hot stove. The method was patented in 1844, but after failing to establish companies in Britain

and France, Goodyear was imprisoned in Paris for debt in 1855 and died a pauper.
good·y-good·y (goodi-goodi) *adj.* Affectedly sweet or good; cloyingly sanctimonious.
~*n., pl.* **goody-goodies.** One who is affectedly good or virtuous.
goof (goof) *n. Slang.* **1.** An incompetent, foolish, or stupid person. **2.** A careless mistake; a slip.
~*v.* **goofed, goofing, goofs.** *Slang.* —*intr.* **1.** To make a silly mistake; blunder. **2.** To have aimless fun; fool about. Used with *about, around,* or *off.* —*tr.* **1.** To spoil; bungle. Often used with *up.* **2.** To give drugs to (a horse, for example); dope. **3.** To take or swallow (drugs). [Variant of dialect *goff,* from Old French *goffe,* awkward, from Medieval Latin *gufus†,* coarse.]
goof·ball (goof-bawl) *n. U.S. Slang.* **1.** A barbiturate sleeping pill. **2.** An eccentric or deranged person.
goof·y (goofi) *adj.* **-ier, -iest.** *Informal.* **1.** Silly; awkward; ridiculous: *a goofy hat.* **2.** *British.* **a.** Protruding or conspicuous. Said of teeth. **b.** Toothy: *a goofy smile.* —**goof·i·ly** *adv.* —**goof·i·ness** *n.*
goog·ly (googli) *n., pl.* **-lies. 1.** In cricket, an off-break ball designed to deceive the batsman into thinking it is a leg break. **2.** A difficult or trick question. [20th century (Australian) : origin obscure.]
goo·gol (googol, -g'l) *n.* The number 10 raised to the power 100 (10^{100}); the number 1 followed by 100 zeros.
goo·gol·plex (goo-gol-pleks, -g'l-) *n.* The number 10 raised to the power of one googol; the number 1 followed by 10^{100} zeros. [*googol* + *duplex.*]
Goolagong, Evonne. See **Cawley, Evonne.**
Goole (gool). Port in Humberside in eastern England, situated at the confluence of the rivers Ouse and Don.
goo·lies (gooliz) *pl.n. Vulgar Slang.* The testicles. [Probably from Hindi *golí,* bullet, ball, pill.]
goon (goon) *n.* **1.** *Slang.* A stupid or oafish person. **2.** *U.S. Informal.* A thug hired to commit acts of intimidation or violence. [From dialectal *gooney, gony†,* fool; popularised by the comic-strip character Alice the *Goon,* created by E.C. Segar (1894–1938).]
goon·er·y (goonəri) *n. British.* Crazy and high-spirited behaviour or talk. [After *The Goon Show,* a BBC radio programme featuring this kind of humour.]
goo·ney bird (gooni) *n.* An albatross; especially, *Diomedea nigripes,* common on islands of the Pacific. [From dialectal *gooney,* fool. See **goon.**]
goos·an·der (goo-sándər) *n.* A duck, *Mergus merganser,* the male of which has a dark head and white or pinkish body. [Probably GOOS(E) + Old Norse *önd* (stem *andar-*), duck.]
goose[1] (gooss) *n., pl.* **geese** (geess) or **gooses** (for sense 5). **1.** Any of various wild or domesticated water birds of the family Anatidae, and especially of the genera *Anser* and *Branta,* characteristically having a shorter neck than that of a swan and a shorter, more pointed bill than that of a duck. **2.** The female of such a bird, as distinguished from a gander. **3.** The flesh of such a bird, used as food. **4.** *Informal.* A silly person; a simpleton. **5.** A tailor's pressing iron with a long curved handle. —**cook (someone's) goose.** *Informal.* To ruin someone's chances. [Goose, geese; Middle English *goos, gees,* Old English *gōs, gēs.*]
goose[2] *tr.v.* **goosed, goosing, gooses.** *Chiefly U.S. Slang.* To jab (someone) between the buttocks.
~*n. pl.* **gooses.** *Chiefly U.S. Slang.* An unexpected jab between the buttocks. [Perhaps after GOOSE[1], from the supposed resemblance of an upturned thumb to an outstretched goose's neck.]
goose barnacle *n.* Any of various barnacles of the genus *Lepas,* which are attached by a stalk to wood and other surfaces and have flattened shells. [So named from the belief that geese were born from barnacles.]
goose·ber·ry (gooz-bəri, -bri ‖ gooss-, gooss-, gooz-, *U.S.* -berri) *n., pl.* **-ries. 1.** A spiny shrub, *Ribes uva-crispa* (or *R. grossularia*), native to Eurasia, having lobed leaves, greenish flowers, and edible greenish or reddish berries. **2.** The fruit of this plant. **3.** Any of several plants bearing fruit similar to the gooseberry, such as the **Cape gooseberry** *(see).* **4.** *British Informal.* An unattached and unwelcome person accompanying a couple, as on a social outing. Used chiefly in the phrase *play gooseberry.* [Perhaps GOOSE + BERRY.]
goose egg *n. U.S. Slang.* Zero, especially when written as a numeral to indicate that no points have been scored.
goose·fish (gooss-fish) *n., pl.* **-fishes** or collectively **goosefish.** *U.S.* The **monkfish** *(see).*
goose flesh *n.* Momentary roughness of skin caused by erection of the papillae in response to cold or fear. Also called "goose bumps", "goose pimples".
goose·foot (gooss-foot) *n., pl.* **-foots.** Any of various usually weedy plants of the genus *Chenopodium,* having small greenish flowers. [From the shape of its leaves.]
goose-gog (gooz-gog, gooss-) *n. British Regional.* A gooseberry. [Humorous alteration.]
goose grass *n.* A plant, **cleavers** *(see).*
goose·herd (gooss-herd) *n.* One who tends a flock of geese.
goose·neck (gooss-nek) *n.* **1.** A slender, curved object or part, such as the flexible shaft of a type of desk lamp. **2.** *Nautical.* A metal fitting joining a boom to a mast. —**goose·necked** *adj.*
goose step *n.* A military parade step performed by swinging each leg alternately sharply from the hips and keeping the knees locked.
goose-step (gooss-step) *intr.v.* **-stepped, -stepping, -steps.** To execute or march in a goose step.
Goos·sens (gooss'nz), **Sir Eugene** (1893–1962). British violinist,

conductor, and composer. From 1923 he was conductor of the Rochester Philharmonic Orchestra in the United States and later, conductor of the Cincinnati Symphony Orchestra (1931–47) and the Sydney Symphony Orchestra (1947–56).

goos·y, goos·ey (goo-si) *adj.* **-ier, -iest. 1.** Pertaining to or resembling a goose. **2.** *Informal.* Foolish; scatterbrained. **3.** *Informal.* Causing or affected with goose flesh.

GOP *U.S.* Grand Old Party (the Republican Party).

go·pher (gōfər) *n.* **1.** Any of various short-tailed, burrowing mammals of the family Geomyidae, of North America, having fur-lined external cheek pouches. Also called "pocket gopher". **2.** A **ground squirrel** *(see),* especially one of the genus *Citellus.* **3.** Any of several burrowing tortoises of the genus *Gopherus;* especially, *G. polyphemus,* of the southeastern United States. In this sense, also called "gopher tortoise". [Shortening of earlier *magopher†*.]

go·pher·wood (gōfər-wŏŏd) *n.* Also **gopher wood** (for sense 1). **1.** An unidentified wood, probably a kind of cypress, used in the construction of Noah's ark. Genesis 6:14. **2.** *U.S.* A tree, the **yellow-wood** *(see).* [Hebrew *gōper.*]

go·ral (gáw-rəl ‖ gō-) *n.* Either of two goat antelopes, *Naemorhedus goral* or *N. cranbrooki,* of mountainous regions of eastern Asia, having short, ridged, backward-curving horns in both sexes. [Hindi *gūral, goral,* perhaps from Sanskrit *gaura,* gaur.]

Gor·ba·chev (górbəchoff; *Russian* gorba-chóff), **Mikhail Sergeevich** (1931–). Soviet politician and leader. The success of his pioneering agrarian reforms earned him a place on the Central Committee in 1978, as Secretary for Agriculture. In 1980 he was elected to the Politburo, where he became a protégé of Yuri Andropov and an energetic advocate of economic and administrative reform. In 1985, he was elected General Secretary of the Communist party of the U.S.S.R. In 1988 he succeeded Gromyko as President. He set the U.S.S.R. on a path of social and economic reform, and relaxed Soviet control over the countries of the former Eastern Bloc. Nobel peace prize (1990). With the break-up of the U.S.S.R. in 1991, he retired from politics.

Gor·bals (górb'lz). District of Glasgow in Scotland, situated by the Clyde in the centre of the city. Formerly notorious for its slums, the area has now mostly been cleared and redeveloped.

gor·bli·mey (gór-blĭmi) *interj.* Used to express surprise or exasperation.
~*adj. Informal.* Lower-class; plebeian. [Pronunciation spelling of the oath *God blind me.*]

gor·cock (gór-kok) *n.* Male red grouse. [From *gor†* + COCK.]

Gor·di·an knot (górdi-ən) *n.* **1.** An intricate knot tied by King Gordius of Phrygia and cut by Alexander the Great with his sword after hearing an oracle promise that whoever could undo it would be the next ruler of Asia. **2.** An exceedingly complicated problem or deadlock. **—cut the Gordian knot.** To solve a problem by resorting to prompt and bold measures.

Gor·di·mer, Nadine (1923–). South African novelist and short-story writer, noted for her sensitive portrayals of inter-race relationships. She won the Nobel Prize for Literature in 1991. Among her best-known works are *The Soft Voice of the Serpent* (1953), *A Guest of Honour* (1970) and *July's People* (1981).

Gor·don (górd'n), **Charles George** (1833–85). British soldier who took part in the British capture of Peking in 1860. His later command of the Chinese army raised to put down the Taiping rebellion earned him the name of "Chinese Gordon". As governor-general of Sudan, he died fighting the Mahdi when his garrison at Khartoum was overrun before a British relief force sent up the Nile could reach him.

Gordon setter *n.* A hunting dog of a breed originating in Scotland, having a silky black-and-tan coat. [After the 4th Duke of *Gordon* (died 1827).]

gore¹ (gor ‖ gōr) *tr.v.* **gored, goring, gores.** To pierce or stab with a horn or tusk. [Middle English *gōren,* to pierce, from *gore,* spear, Old English *gār.*]

gore² *n.* **1.** A triangular or tapering piece of cloth used as a part of a garment, such as a skirt, or in an umbrella or sail. **2.** A small triangular piece of land.
~*tr.v.* **gored, goring, gores. 1.** To make or provide with a gore or gores. **2.** To cut into a gore. [Middle English *gore,* Old English *gāra,* triangular piece of land; akin to Old English *gār,* spear (from the triangular shape of the spearhead).]

gore³ *n.* **1.** Blood, especially coagulated blood from a wound. **2.** *Informal.* Violence or killing, as in film scenes. [Middle English *gore,* Old English *gor†,* dung; dirt.]

gorge (gorj) *n.* **1.** A deep, narrow passage with precipitous rocky sides, enclosed between mountains, usually a river valley or former river valley. **2.** A narrow entrance or passageway from the rear into the bastion or other outwork of a fortification. **3. a.** The contents of a stomach. **b.** *Archaic.* The throat; the gullet. **4.** An instance of gluttonous eating; a gorging. **5.** A mass obstructing a narrow passage: *The shipping lane was blocked by an ice gorge.* **gorge rise.** To make one feel strong revulsion or violent anger.
~*v.* **gorged, gorging, gorges.** —*tr.* **1.** To stuff; satiate; glut. Usually used reflexively. **2.** To devour greedily. —*intr.* To eat gluttonously. **—See Synonyms at satiate.** [Middle English, throat, from Old French, from Vulgar Latin *gurga* (unattested), variant of Latin *gurges,* whirlpool, throat.] **—gor·er** *n.*

gor·geous (górjəss) *adj.* **1.** Dazzlingly brilliant; resplendent; magnificent. **2.** Strikingly beautiful or attractive. **3.** *Informal.* Wonderful; delightful. [Middle English *gorgeouse,* showy, splendid, from

Old French *gorgias†,* stylish, fine, elegant.] **—gor·geous·ly** *adv.* **—gor·geous·ness** *n.*

gor·ger·in (górjərin) *n. Architecture.* The necking of a column. [French, from *gorge,* throat, GORGE.]

gor·get (górjit) *n.* **1.** A piece of armour protecting the throat. **2.** An ornamental collar. **3.** The scarflike part of a wimple covering the neck and shoulders. **4.** A band or patch of distinctive colour on the throat of an animal, especially a bird. **5.** A surgical instrument used to remove stones from the bladder. [Middle English, from Old French, diminutive of *gorge,* throat, GORGE.]

Gor·gi·o (gór-ji-ə, -jō) *n.* A person who is not a Gypsy. Used by Gypsies. [Romany.] **—Gor·gi·o** *adj.*

Gor·gon (górgən) *n.* **1.** *Greek Mythology.* Any of the three sisters Stheno, Euryale, and the mortal Medusa who had terrifying teeth and claws, snakes for hair, and eyes which, if looked into, turned the beholder into stone. **2.** *Small* **g.** A repulsively ugly or terrifying woman. [Middle English, from Latin *Gorgō* (stem *Gorgōn-),* from Greek, from *gorgos†,* terrible.] **—Gor·go·ni·an** (-gŏni-ən) *adj.*

gor·go·nei·on (górgə-née-on, -ən) *n., pl.* **-neia** (-née-ə). A representation of a Gorgon's head, especially one of Medusa. [Greek, from the neuter of *gorgoneios,* of a Gorgon, from *Gorgō,* GORGON.]

gor·go·ni·an (gawr-gŏni-ən) *n.* Any of various corals of the order Gorgonacea, having a flexible, often branching skeleton of horny material.
~*adj.* Of or belonging to the Gorgonacea. [Latin *Gorgonia,* coral, from *Gorgō,* GORGON.]

gor·gon·ise, gor·gon·ize (górgəniz) *tr.v.* **-ised, -ising, -ises.** To have a paralysing effect upon; petrify, as with fear. [From GORGON.]

Gor·gon·zo·la (górgən-zōlə) *n.* A pungent, blue-veined, cream-coloured Italian cheese made of pressed cow's milk. [First made at *Gorgonzola,* village near Milan, Italy.]

go·ril·la (gə-rĭllə) *n.* **1.** A large anthropoid ape, *Gorilla gorilla,* of forests of equatorial Africa, having a stocky body and coarse, dark hair. **2.** A brutish or thuglike man. [New Latin (adopted 1847), from Greek *Gorillai†,* name of African tribe of hairy men.]

Gorky or **Gorki** (górki). See **Nizhniy Novgorod.**

Goring. See **Goering.**

Gor·ky or **Gor·ki, Maxim,** originally Alexey Maximovich Pyeshkov (1868–1936). Self-educated Russian writer, often considered the father of Soviet literature. His works include the play *The Lower Depths* (1902) and the novel *Mother* (1907).

gormand. Variant of **gourmand.**

gor·mand·ise, gor·mand·ize (górmən-dīz) *v.* **-ised, -ising, -ises.** —*intr.* To eat gluttonously; gorge. —*tr.* To devour (food) gluttonously; gorge.
~*n.* (-deez). *Rare.* Variant of **gourmandise.** [From GOURMANDISE (obsolete sense "gluttony").] **—gor·mand·is·er** *n.*

gorm·less (górm-ləss, -liss) *adj. British Informal.* Stupid; unable to deal with practical problems; blundering. [Variant of earlier *gaumless,* from dialect *gaum,* understanding, from Old English *gom, gome,* from Old Norse *gaumr,* heed.]

Gormley (górm-li), **Antony** (1950–). British sculptor. His early sculptures used moulds made from his own body, as in *Untitled (for Francis)* (1985). His later works include *Field for the British Isles* (1993), a room containing forty thousand clay figurines, and the massive *Angel of Gateshead* (1998).

gorse (gorss) *n.* Any of several spiny, thickset shrubs of the genus *Ulex;* especially, *U. europaeus,* native to Europe, having fragrant yellow flowers. Also called "furze", "whin". [Middle English *gorst, gors,* Old English *gorst, gors.*]

Gor·sedd (gór-seth) *n. Sometimes small* **g.** A committee of druids convened occasionally, as during an eisteddfod, to plan activities and award bardic titles. [Welsh, "throne".]

Gor·ton (górt'n), Sir **John Grey** (1911–). Australian politician. He was a fighter pilot in World War II and in 1949 was elected a Liberal member of the senate. He became prime minister (1968) after the death of Harold Holt. In 1971 he was ousted from office by his Liberal party colleagues.

go·ry (gáwri ‖ gōri) *adj.* **-rier, -riest. 1.** Covered or stained with gore; bloody; bloodstained. **2.** Characterised by a great effusion of blood: *a gory battle.* **3.** Full of or characterised by bloodshed, slaughter, or acts of violence: *a gory narrative.* **—gor·i·ly** *adv.* **—gor·i·ness** *n.*

gosh (gosh) *interj. Informal.* Used to express mild surprise or delight. [Euphemistic variant of GOD.]

gos·hawk (góss-hawk) *n.* **1.** A large hawk, *Accipiter gentilis,* having broad, rounded wings and grey or brownish plumage. **2.** Any of several similar or related hawks. [Middle English *goshawke,* Old English *gōshafoc* : *gōs,* GOOSE + *hafoc,* HAWK.]

Go·shen¹ (gōsh'n). Region of ancient Egypt on the eastern delta of the Nile, inhabited by the Israelites from the time of Joseph until the Exodus. Genesis 45:10.

Goshen² *n.* A land of bounty and contentment. [After the Biblical GOSHEN.]

gos·ling (góz-ling ‖ *U.S. also* gáwz-) *n.* **1.** A young goose. **2.** An inexperienced young person. [Middle English, earlier *gesling,* from Old Norse *gæslingr.* See **goose, -ling.**]

go-slow (gō-slō) *n.* A form of industrial action in which workers achieve a slower rate of production than normal by strictly following offical procedure. Also *chiefly U.S.* "slowdown". **—go slow** *intr.v.*

gos·pel (góss-p'l; *also* -pel) *n.* **1.** *Sometimes capital* **G.** The teachings of Jesus and the Apostles. **2. a.** *Capital* **G.** Any of the first four books of the New Testament describing the life, death, and resurrection of Jesus. **b.** A similar narrative. **3.** *Often capital* **G.** A reading from any of these books included as part of a religious service. **4.** A teaching or doctrine of a religious teacher. **5.** A principle that is strongly advocated: *the gospel of hard work.* **6.** The infallibly accurate account of matters; the last word; *Don't take Freud as gospel.* Also used adjectivally: *the gospel truth.* **7.** Religious music of a style originated among blacks in the southern United States, characterised by evangelical lyrics and fervent singing, and much influenced by jazz. Also used adjectivally: *a gospel song.* [Middle English *gospel*, Old English *godspell*, "good news" (translation of Late Latin *evangelium*, EVANGEL) : *gōd*, GOOD + *spel*, news.]

gos·pel·ler, gos·pel·er (góspələr) *n.* **1.** One who teaches or professes faith in a gospel. **2.** A person who reads or sings the Gospel as part of a church service. [Middle English *gospeller*, Old English *godspellere*, from *godspellian*, to teach the gospel, from *godspell*, GOSPEL.]

gos·po·din (góspə-déen; *Russian* gəspa-) *n.*, *pl.* **-da** (-dá). A courteous form of address used in Russia for non-Russians. [Russian, "master", "lord".]

Gos·port (góss-port ‖ -pōrt). Port in Hampshire on the south coast of England, situated at the mouth of Portsmouth harbour. It shared Portsmouth's development as a naval base and has important naval establishments.

gos·sa·mer (góss-əmər ‖ gózz-) *n.* **1.** A fine film of cobwebs often seen floating in the air or caught on bushes or grass. **2.** A soft, sheer, gauzy fabric. **3.** Anything delicate, light, or insubstantial. ~*adj.* Also **gos·sa·mer·y** (-əməri). Light, thin, and delicate. [Middle English *gossomer, gosesomer* : perhaps *goos, gos,* GOOSE + *somer,* SUMMER (that is, early November (St. Martin's summer), when geese are eaten and gossamer is most in evidence).]

gos·san (góss'n) *n. Geology.* An outcrop of quartz and iron oxides, often marking a sulphide ore. [Cornish *gossen,* from *gōs,* blood, from Old Cornish *guit* (referring to its russet colour).]

Gosse (goss), **Sir Edmund (William)** (1849–1928). British critic and writer. He wrote essays and criticism and was chiefly responsible for introducing modern Scandinavian literature, especially that of Ibsen, to English readers. He is best known for his autobiographical work, *Father and Son,* published anonymously (1907).

gos·sip (góssip) *n.* **1. a.** Trifling, often groundless rumour, usually of a personal, sensational, or intimate nature. **b.** A friendly conversation on unimportant matters; a chat. **c.** News of no great importance, as in a letter or article, written in a light style. **2.** A person who habitually talks about other people and their private affairs, especially in a disparaging way. **3.** *Archaic.* A close woman friend or companion. **4.** *Archaic.* A godparent. ~*intr.v.* **gossiped, -siping, -sips.** To engage in or spread gossip. See Synonyms at **speak.** [Middle English *godsib,* godparent, godchild, close friend, Old English *godsibb* : *god,* GOD + *sibb,* kinsman.] —**gos·sip·er** *n.* —**gos·sip·y** *adj.*

gossip column *n.* A newspaper column that gives news of the private lives of famous people.

gos·sip·mong·er (góssip-mungər) *n.* A person who spreads gossip. Used derogatorily.

gos·soon (go-sōōn) *n. Irish.* A boy; especially, a servant boy. [French *garçon,* GARÇON.]

got. Past tense and past participle of **get.**

Gö·te·borg (yōtə-bór). *English* **Goth·en·burg** (góth'n-burg). Chief port and second largest city in Sweden, situated at the mouth of the river Göta on the southwest coast of the country, and connected to Stockholm by the Göta canal (1832). The city has major oil refineries.

Goth (goth) *n.* **1.** A member of the Germanic people that originally occupied a region between the Baltic and the Black Sea, and that invaded the Roman Empire in the early centuries of the Christian era. See **Ostrogoth, Visigoth. 2.** An uncivilised or barbaric person. [Middle English *Gothes,* Goths, from Late Latin *Gothī* (singular *Gothus*), from Gothic *Gutans†* (unattested), tribal name.]

Goth·a (gṓthə; *German* gṓtə). Town in central Germany. It was once the residence of the dukes of Saxe-Coburg-Gotha. The *Almanach de Gotha,* published there (1761-1944), was an annual record of Europe's royal and aristocratic houses.

Got·ham (gṓtəm, góttəm ‖ gṓthəm) *n.* **1.** Village of southern Nottinghamshire in England, whose early inhabitants, the *Wise Men of Gotham,* are reputed by legend to have feigned stupidity in order to discourage King John from establishing a residence there. **2.** New York City. Used as a nickname. —**Goth·am·ite** *n.*

Gothenburg. See **Göteborg.**

Goth·ic (góthik) *adj. Abbr.* **Goth. 1. a.** Of or pertaining to the Goths or their language. **b.** Germanic; Teutonic. **2.** Of or pertaining to the Middle Ages; medieval. **3. a.** Of, pertaining to, or designating an architectural style prevalent in western Europe from the 12th to the 16th century, and characterised by pointed arches, rib vaulting, and flying buttresses. **b.** Of or pertaining to painting, sculpture, or other art forms prevalent in northern Europe from the 12th to the 16th century. **c.** Of or relating to an architectural style derived from medieval Gothic. **4.** *Sometimes small* **g.** Of, pertaining to, or reminiscent of a literary style of fiction prevalent in the late 18th and early 19th centuries which emphasised the grotesque, mysterious, and desolate: *a Gothic novel.* **5.** *Sometimes small* **g.** Barbarous; uncivilised; primitive; crude.

~*n. Abbr.* **Goth. 1.** The extinct East Germanic language of the Goths. **2.** Gothic art or architecture. **3.** *Often small* **g.** *Printing.* **a.** An old-fashioned, German, heavy typeface with broad strokes contrasted with some thin ones and ornamental serifs. Also called "black letter". **b.** A modern, heavy, black, sans-serif typeface. —**Goth·i·cal·ly** *adv.*

Gothic arch *n. Architecture.* A pointed arch, especially one with a jointed apex.

Goth·i·cise, Goth·i·cize (góthi-sīz) *tr.v.* **-cised, -cising, -cises.** To make Gothic.

Goth·i·cism (góthi-siz'm) *n.* **1.** Use of, imitation of, or an instance of Gothic style, as in architecture, art, or literature. **2.** A barbarous or crude manner or style.

Got·land or **Goth·land** or **Gott·land** (gótlənd; *Swedish* gótlant). The largest Swedish island, situated in the Baltic Sea to the east of the mainland. By tradition it is the original homeland of the Goths. The capital is Visby.

got·ta (gótta). *Chiefly U.S. Slang.* Contraction of *got to* or *have got to.*

got·ten. *Chiefly U.S.* Past participle of **get.**

Göt·ter·däm·mer·ung (götər-démmərōong) *n.* **1.** *Germanic Mythology.* The process of destruction of the ancient gods by the forces of evil. Also called "Twilight of the Gods". **2.** Any failure or slow destruction of some heroic person, magnificent enterprise, or the like.

Göt·ting·en (götingən). City in Lower Saxony in central Germany, situated on the Leine Canal. It is famous for its university (founded 1734) and its influential Society of Sciences.

gouache (gōō-áash, gwaash) *n.* **1.** A method of painting using opaque water colours mixed with a preparation of gum. **2.** An opaque pigment prepared in such a way. **3.** A painting executed with such pigments. [French, from Italian *guazzo,* "puddle", from Latin *aquātiō,* watering, from *aquārī,* to bring water to, from *aqua,* water.]

Gou·da¹ (gówdə, gốodə; *Dutch* khṓdə). Town in the South Holland province of the Netherlands, situated at the confluence of the rivers Gouwe and Ysel. It has the largest market square in Holland.

Gouda² *n.* A mild, close-textured, pale yellow cheese made from whole or partially skimmed milk and often covered with a protective coating of wax. [Originally named after GOUDA.]

gouge (gowj) *n.* **1. a.** A chisel with a rounded, troughlike blade. **b.** A surgical instrument resembling this, used to cut and remove bone. **2.** A scooping or digging action, as with a gouge. **3.** A groove, hole, or indentation scooped with or as if with a gouge. **4.** *U.S. Informal.* **a.** An act of extortion or swindling. **b.** A large amount of money extorted. **5.** *Geology.* A deposit of clay, rock particles, or the like, in a fault or vein. ~*tr.v.* **gouged, gouging, gouges. 1.** To cut or scoop out with or as if with a gouge: *gouge a pattern in the sand.* **2.** To force out: *gouged out his eyes.* **3.** *U.S. Informal.* **a.** To extort from. **b.** To swindle. [Middle English *gouge,* from Old French, from Late Latin *gubia,* perhaps from Celtic, akin to Old Irish *gulban†.*] —**goug·er** *n.*

gou·jon (*French* gōō-zhón) *n.* A strip of fish, as of filleted Dover sole, coated in breadcrumbs and deep-fried. [French.]

gou·lash (gōō-lash, -laash) *n.* A stew of beef, lamb, or veal and vegetables, highly seasoned with paprika. Also called "Hungarian goulash". [Hungarian *gulyás (hus),* "herdsman('s meat)", from *gulya,* herd.]

Gould (gōōld), **Glenn** (1932–82). Canadian pianist. He first played with the Toronto Symphony Orchestra when 14. He was acclaimed for his performances of Bach, Beethoven, and Brahms.

goun·dou (gōōndōō) *n. Medicine.* A condition occurring in the tropics as a complication of yaws, in which bony swellings occur on either side of the nose. [From a West African name.]

Gou·nod (gōōnō; *French* gōō-nō), **Charles (François)** (1818–93). French composer. He wrote symphonies, oratorios, and songs, but he is mainly remembered for the operas *Faust* (1859) and *Romeo and Juliet* (1867), and for his church music.

gou·ra·mi (gŏor-əmi, gōō-ráami) *n., pl.* **-mis** or collectively **gourami.** Any of various freshwater fishes of the family Anabantidae, of southeastern Asia, many species of which are brightly coloured and popular in home aquariums. *Osphronemus goramy* has been widely introduced and bred as a food fish. [Malay *gurāmi.*]

gourd (gŏord ‖ gord, gōrd) *n.* **1.** Any of several vines of the family Cucurbitaceae, such as the **bottle gourd** *(see),* related to the pumpkin, squash, and cucumber, and bearing fruits with a hard rind. **2.** The fruit of such a vine, such as a calabash, often of irregular and unusual shape. **3.** The dried and hollowed-out shell of one of these fruits, used as a drinking vessel or utensil. **4.** A small gourd-shaped bottle. [Middle English *gourde,* from Old French, from Latin *cucurbita,* probably of Mediterranean origin.]

gourde (gŏord) *n. Abbr.* **g., G., gde. 1.** The basic monetary unit of Haiti, equal to 100 centimes. **2.** A coin worth one gourde. [French, feminine of *gourd,* heavy, from Latin *gurdus†,* heavy, dull, stupid.]

gour·mand, gor·mand (gŏormənd; *French* gōor-món) *n.* A person who delights in eating well and heartily. [Middle English *gourmaunt,* glutton, from Old French *gourmand, gourmant†.*]

gour·mand·ise (gŏormən-déez) *n.* A taste and relish for good food. [Middle English, from Old French *gourmandise,* from GOURMAND.]

gour·met (gŏor-may ‖ goor-máy) *n.* A connoisseur of fine food and drink. Used adjectively: *gourmet foods.* [French, from Old French *gromet, gourmet†,* wine-taster.]

gout (gowt) *n.* **1.** *Pathology.* A disturbance of uric-acid metabolism, occurring predominantly in males, in which deposits of urates accumulate in the joints, especially those of the big toe, and cause arthritic attacks that may become chronic and produce deformity. **2.** A large blob or clot: *"and makes it bleed great gouts of blood"* (Oscar Wilde). [Middle English *goute,* from Old French, "drop" (from the belief that gout was caused by a flowing down of morbid humours), from Latin *gutta†,* drop.]

gout·weed (gówt-weed) *n.* A plant, **ground elder** (see).

gout·y (gówti) *adj.* **-ier, -iest. 1.** Of, relating to, or resembling gout. **2.** Suffering from or showing the effects of gout. —**gout·i·ly** *adv.* —**gout·i·ness** *n.*

gov. 1. government. **2.** governor.

Gov. Governor.

gov·ern (gúvvərn) *v.* **-erned, -erning, -erns.** —*tr.* **1.** To control the actions or behaviour of; guide; direct. **2.** To make and administer public policy for (a political unit); exercise sovereign authority in. **3.** To control the speed or magnitude of; regulate: *a valve governing fuel intake.* **4.** To keep under control; restrain. **5.** To decide; determine: *Chance usually governs the outcome of the game.* **6.** *Grammar.* **a.** To require (a noun or verb) to be in a particular case or mood. **b.** To require the use of (a specified case or mood). —*intr.* **1.** To exercise political authority. **2.** To have or exercise a predominating influence. [Middle English *governen,* from Old French *governer,* from Latin *gubernāre,* to direct, steer, from Greek *kubernan†.*] —**gov·ern·a·ble** *adj.*

gov·ern·ance (gúvvərnənss) *n.* **1.** The act, process, or power of governing; government; authority. **2.** The system of government. **3.** The state of being governed.

gov·ern·ess (gúvvərniss) *n.* **1.** A woman employed to educate and train the children of a private household. **2.** *Rare.* A female governor.

governing body *n.* A group of people responsible for the administration of a school, college, or similar institution.

gov·ern·ment (gúvvərn-mənt, gúvvə-) *n. Abbr.* **gov., govt. 1.** The act or process of governing; especially, the administration of public policy in a political unit; political jurisdiction. **2.** The office, function, or authority of one who governs or a governing body. **3.** A system or policy by which a political unit is governed. **4.** Political science. **5.** A governing body or organisation. **6.** An area within a single rule; a political unit. **7.** Influence; regulation; determination. **8.** *Grammar.* The affecting of a word's case or mood by another word. —**gov·ern·men·tal** (-mént'l) *adj.* —**gov·ern·men·tal·ly** *adv.*

Government Issue *n. Abbr.* **GI, G.I.** *U.S.* Anything issued by the government or a government agency, such as U.S. Army equipment. —**government issue** *adj.*

gov·er·nor (gúvvərnər, gúvnər) *n. Abbr.* **gov., Gov. 1.** A person who governs, especially: **a.** An official appointed to govern a colony or territory. **b.** The chief executive of a state in the United States. **2.** The manager or administrative head of an organisation, business, or institution. **3.** A military commandant. **4.** The senior administrative officer of a prison. **5.** *British Slang.* **a.** Used as a form of address, equivalent to *sir,* to a stranger, respected acquaintance, employer, or superior. **b.** One's father. **6.** *Machinery.* A feedback device on a machine or engine used to provide automatic control, as of speed, pressure, or temperature. [Middle English *governour,* from Old French *governeor,* from Latin *gubernātor,* from *gubernāre,* GOVERN.]

gov·er·nor-gen·er·al (gúvvərnər-jénrəl, gúvnər-, -jénnərəl) *n., pl.* **governors-general** or **governor-generals.** *Abbr.* **Gov. Gen. 1.** *Often capital* **G,** *capital* **G.** The highest-ranking representative of the Crown in some Commonwealth countries or formerly in a British colony. **2.** A governor who has other, subordinate governors under his jurisdiction. —**gov·er·nor-gen·er·al·ship** *n.*

gov·er·nor·ship (gúvvərnər-ship, gúvnər-) *n.* The office, term, or jurisdiction of a governor.

Gov. Gen. governor-general.

govt. government.

gow·an (gów-ən) *n. Scottish.* A yellow or white wild flower, especially the daisy. [Dialect *gollan,* from Middle English, probably from Scandinavian; akin to Old Norse *gullinn,* golden.]

Gow·er (gów-ər, gowr). Peninsula in southern Wales, situated to the west of Swansea. It has important prehistoric sites and a scenic coastline.

gowk (gowk) *n. Northern British.* A stupid person; a fool. [Middle English *gowke,* from Old Norse *gaukr,* a cuckoo, from Germanic *gaukaz* (imitative).]

gown (gown) *n.* **1.** Any of various long, loose, flowing garments, such as a dressing gown or surgeon's protective coat. **2.** A long, usually formal, woman's dress. **3.** A distinctive outer robe·worn on ceremonial occasions, as by scholars or clergymen. **4.** *British.* The academic community of a university town, as distinguished from the townspeople: *town and gown.* Compare **town.** —*tr.v.* **gowned, gowning, gowns.** To dress in or invest with a gown. [Middle English *goune,* from Old French, from Late Latin *gunna†,* robe, fur.]

Gow·on (gów-ən), **Yakubu** (1934–). Nigerian army officer and politician. Trained at the Sandhurst Military Academy in England, he took a commission in the Nigerian army (1954), becoming battalion commander (1966). After two coups (1966), he was appointed army commander in chief and head of the new military government. He led the federal forces in their successful war against the secessionist Biafran government (1967–70). He was deposed (1975).

goy (goy) *n., pl.* **goys** or **goyim** (góy-im). A person who is not a Jew;

a Gentile. Often used derogatorily. [Yiddish, from Hebrew *gōy,* nation, people.] —**goy·ish** *adj.*

Goy·a (y Lu·ci·en·tes) (góy-ə ee lōōthi-éntess), **Francisco José de** (1746–1828). Spanish painter and etcher. His best portraits, including *The Duchess of Alba,* were done mostly in the 1790s, his so-called "silver period". The war against France inspired some of his most powerful work, including 65 etchings, *The Disasters of the War* (1810–14).

Go·zo (gōzō). See **Malta.**

G.P. 1. general practitioner. **2.** graduated pension. **3.** Grand Prix.

G-par·i·ty (jée-párriti) *n. Physics.* A quantum property of elementary particles that have zero strangeness and baryon number, conserved in strong interactions.

GPI general paralysis of the insane.

g.p.m. gallons per minute.

GPO 1. general post office. **2.** Government Printing Office (in the United States).

g.p.s. gallons per second.

GPU, G.P.U. Government Political Administration (Russian *Gosudarstvennoye Politicheskoye Upravlenie*): a former administrative branch of the Soviet government functioning as a policing and security organisation in succession to the **Cheka** (see) and corresponding in broad outline to the later **KGB** (see).

gr. 1. grade. **2.** gram. **3.** gross. **4.** group.

Gr. Greece; Greek.

Graaf·i·an follicle (gráafi-ən) *n. Anatomy.* Any of the follicles in the mammalian ovary, containing a maturing ovum. [After Regnier de *Graaf* (1641–73), Dutch anatomist.]

grab¹ (grab) *v.* **grabbed, grabbing, grabs.** —*tr.* **1.** To take or grasp suddenly; snatch; seize. **2.** To capture or restrain; arrest. **3.** To obtain or appropriate unscrupulously or forcibly. **4.** To consume hurriedly: *He grabbed a bite to eat.* **5.** *Slang.* To make an impression on; affect, especially in a positive or favourable way. —*intr.* To make a snatch: *He grabbed for the gun.* —*n.* **1.** The act of grabbing; a sudden seizure. **2.** Anything grabbed. **3.** A mechanical device for gripping, for example, the jaws of an earth-moving machine. —**up for grabs.** *Informal.* Available for anyone to take. [Middle Dutch and Middle Low German *grabben.*] —**grab·ber** *n.*

grab² *n.* An Oriental coastal vessel with two or three masts. [Arabic *ghurāb,* raven, swift galley.]

grab bag *n. Chiefly U.S.* **1.** A container filled with articles, such as party gifts, to be drawn at random. **2.** Any miscellaneous collection of often valuable items.

grab·ble (gráb'l) *intr.v.* **-bled, -bling, -bles. 1.** To feel around with the hands; grope. **2.** To sprawl on the ground on all fours. [Dutch *grabbelen,* frequentative of Middle Dutch *grabben,* GRAB (to seize).]

gra·ben (gráabən) *n.* A usually elongated depression of the earth's crust between two parallel faults. [German *Graben,* trench, from Old High German *grabo,* from *graban,* to dig.]

grab rope *n.* A rope for steadying oneself, as on a gangplank or an open deck.

Grac·chus (gráckəss), **Tiberius Sempronius** (c.163–133 B.C.), and **Caius Sempronius** (c.153–121 B.C.), known as the Gracchi. Roman statesmen. Tiberius was elected tribune of the people in 133 B.C. He passed a law to redistribute land but was killed in the same year during a riot. In 123 Caius was elected tribune and when he proposed granting Roman citizenship to Latins, he too was killed in riots.

grace (grayss) *n.* **1.** Seemingly effortless beauty or charm of movement, form, or proportion. **2.** A characteristic, quality, or accomplishment pleasing for its charm or refinement: *social graces.* **3.** Skill at avoiding the inept or clumsy course; a sense of fitness or propriety. **4. a.** A disposition to be generous or helpful; goodwill. **b.** Mercy; clemency. **5. a.** A favour rendered by one who need not do so. **b.** Kindly feeling; indulgence. **6.** Temporary immunity from penalties, granted after a deadline has been passed: *a period of grace before a new law is enforced.* **7.** *Theology.* **a.** Divine love and protection bestowed freely upon mankind. **b.** The state of being protected or sanctified by the favour of God. **c.** An excellence or power granted by God; an unmerited gift from God. **8.** A short prayer of blessing or thanksgiving said before or after a meal. **9.** *Usually capital* **G.** A title of or form of address for a duke, duchess, or archbishop. Used with *His, Her,* or *Your.* **10.** *Music.* A musical embellishment, such as an appoggiatura. —**fall from grace.** To lose the esteem in which one was formerly held, usually as a result of some misconduct. —**in (someone's) good (or bad) graces.** In (or out of) favour with; well (or unfavourably) regarded by. —**with (a) good (or bad) grace.** In a willing (or grudging) manner. —*tr.v.* **graced, gracing, graces. 1.** To honour or favour. **2.** To give beauty, elegance, or charm to. **3.** *Music.* To embellish with grace notes. [Middle English, from Old French, from Latin *grātia,* pleasure, favour, thanks, from *grātus,* favourable, pleasing.]

Grace (grayss), **W(illiam) G(ilbert)** (1848–1915). English cricketer. He played for 40 years and was captain of England 13 times, scoring the first Test century in 1880, against Australia. Famous mainly as a batsman, he was a great all-rounder and established a set of aggregate first-class figures still unrivalled: 54,896 runs, 126 centuries, 2,876 wickets, and 877 catches.

grace-and-favour (gráyss-ənd-fáyvər) *adj. British.* Let or lent free of charge by the Crown: *a grace-and-favour residence.*

grace cup *n.* **1.** A cup used at the end of a meal, usually after grace, for the final toast. **2.** The final toast.

grace·ful (gráyssf'l) *adj.* Showing grace of movement, style, form, or proportion. **—grace·ful·ly** *adv.* **—grace·ful·ness** *n.*

Usage: *Graceful* and *gracious* are occasionally confused. *Graceful* refers to movement, style, or form: *a graceful pose/gesture. Gracious* refers to a state of mind, or the behaviour characteristic of a state of mind, in which kindness, compassion, or condescension feature. There is often an implicit sense of social division in the use of *gracious*: people of high rank are supposed to act graciously towards people of lower rank.

grace·less (gráyss-ləss, -liss) *adj.* **1.** Lacking grace; clumsy. **2.** Having no sense of propriety or decency. **—grace·less·ly** *adv.* **—grace·less·ness** *n.*

grace note *n. Music.* **1.** A musical note without melodic, harmonic, or time value, especially an appoggiatura, added as an embellishment. **2.** Any decorative flourish.

Grac·es (gráy-siz) *pl.n. Greek Mythology.* Three sister goddesses, Aglaia, Euphrosyne, and Thalia, who dispense charm and beauty. Also called the "Three Graces".

grac·ile (grássīl || *U.S. also* gráss'l) *adj.* **1.** Gracefully slender. **2.** *Rare.* Graceful. [Latin *gracilis*†, slim, slender.] **—gra·cil·i·ty** (grə-síllәti) *n.*

gra·ci·o·so (grássi-ṓ-sō; *Spanish* grath-yṓ-sō) *n., pl.* **-sos. 1.** A clown or buffoon in Spanish comedies. **2.** *Obsolete.* A court favourite. [Spanish, "amusing (person)", clown, from Latin *grātiōsus*, GRACIOUS.]

gra·cious (gráyshəss) *adj.* **1.** Characterised by kindness and warm courtesy. **2.** Merciful; compassionate. **3.** Condescendingly courteous; indulgent. **4.** Leisurely; elegant: *a gracious dinner.* **5.** *Obsolete.* Fortunate; prosperous. —See Synonyms at **kind.** —See Usage note at **graceful.**

~interj. Used to express surprise or wonder. [Middle English, from Old French, from Latin *grātiōsus*, favourable, pleasing, from Latin *grātia*, GRACE.] **—gra·cious·ly** *adv.* **—gra·cious·ness** *n.*

gracious speech *n.* The **Speech from the Throne** *(see).*

grack·le (gráck'l) *n.* **1.** Any of several New World birds of the family Icteridae, and especially of the genera *Quiscalus* or *Cassidix*, having iridescent blackish plumage. Also called "crow blackbird". **2.** Any of several Asian mynas of the genus *Gracula*, such as the Indian grackle, *G. religiosa.* [New Latin *Gracula*, from Latin *grāculus*, jackdaw.]

grad·a·ble (gráydəb'l) *adj.* **1.** Capable of or subject to being graded. **2.** *Linguistics.* Of, pertaining to, or designating a word such as *hot, warm,* or *cold,* which implicitly refers to a scale or standard and can be modified by *very* or *much,* for example, to indicate degree or extent.

gra·date (grə-dáyt || *U.S.* gráy-dayt) *v.* **-dated, -dating, -dates.** *—intr.* To pass imperceptibly from one degree, shade, or tone to another. *—tr.* **1.** To cause to pass imperceptibly from one degree, shade, or tone to another. **2.** To arrange according to or in grades. [Back-formation from GRADATION.]

gra·da·tion (grə-dáysh'n || gray-) *n.* **1.** A series of gradual, successive stages; a systematic progression. **2.** Any of the degrees or stages in such a progression. **3.** Advancement by successive stages, tones, or shades, as from one colour to another. **4.** The act of gradating or arranging in grades. **5.** *Geology.* **a.** The process of levelling land by filling in or wearing away existing features. **b.** *Chiefly U.S.* Degradation. **6.** *Linguistics.* An **ablaut** *(see).* [Latin *gradātiō* (stem *gradātiōn-*), from *gradus,* step, GRADE.] **—gra·da·tion·al** *adj.* **—gra·da·tion·al·ly** *adv.*

grade (grayd) *n. Abbr.* **gr., grad. 1.** A stage or degree in a process. **2.** A position in a scale of size or quality, as of eggs or meat. **3.** A group of persons or things all falling within the same limits; a class. **4.** *Chiefly U.S.* A mark indicating a student's level of accomplishment. **5.** *Chiefly U.S.* A class at an elementary school, or the pupils in it. **6.** *Chiefly U.S.* A military, naval, or civil-service rank. **7.** A domestic animal produced by crossbreeding one of purebred stock with one of ordinary stock. **8.** *Chiefly U.S.* A gradient (slope or degree of slope). **9.** *Abbr.* **grad.** A unit of angle equal to one hundredth of a right angle. It is indicated by a superscript g: $1^g = 0.9^o$. **—at grade.** *U.S.* **1.** On the same level. **2.** At the same degree of inclination. **—make the grade.** *Informal.* **1.** To succeed; reach a goal. **2.** To meet a standard.

~v. **graded, grading, grades.** *—tr.* **1.** To arrange in steps or degrees; rank; sort. **2.** To arrange in a series or according to a scale. **3. a.** *Chiefly U.S.* To determine the quality of (academic work, for example); evaluate. **b.** To give a grade to (a student, for example). **4.** To level or smooth to a desired or horizontal gradient. **5.** To gradate. **6.** To improve the quality of (livestock) by crossbreeding with purebred stock. Often used with *up.* **7.** To effect a gradual change of shading in (colours or a coloured area). *—intr.* To change or progress gradually. [French, from Latin *gradus,* step.]

-grade *adj. comb. form.* Indicates progression or movement; for example, **plantigrade, retrograde.** [French, from Latin *-gradus,* stepping, going, from *gradī,* to step, go.]

grade·ly (gráydli) *adj. Northern English.* Fine; excellent. [Middle English *greithli(c),* from Old Norse *greithligr,* from *greithr,* ready.]

grad·er (gráydər) *n.* **1.** One that grades. **2.** A machine that smooths a surface to the desired gradient and flatness, especially in road building.

grade school *n. U.S.* An **elementary school** *(see).*

gra·di·ent (gráydi-ənt) *n. Abbr.* **grad. 1.** An ascending or descending part of a road, railway, or the like; an incline. **2.** The degree of slope measured by the vertical change in height per horizontal distance travelled. **3.** *Physics.* The maximum rate at which a variable physical quantity changes in value per unit change in position. **4.** *Mathematics.* **a.** The slope of the tangent to a curve at a given point. **b.** A vector having coordinate components that are the partial derivatives of a function with respect to its variables. The gradient of a function f is written grad f. or ∇f.

~adj. Of a consistent slope. [Perhaps from GRADE.]

gra·din (gráydin) *n.* Also **gra·dine** (grə-déen). **1.** Any of a series of steps or tiered seats, as in an amphitheatre. **2.** A shelf next to an altar, for holding candles or ornaments. [French, from Italian *gradino,* diminutive of *grado,* step, GRADE.]

grad·u·al (grájoo-əl, gráddəw-əl) *adj.* **1.** Occurring in small stages or degrees or by even, continuous change. **2.** Moderate and regular: *a gradual slope.*

~n. Roman Catholic Church. **1.** A book containing liturgical antiphons. **2.** An antiphon sung between the Epistle and the Gospel of the Tridentine Mass. [Middle English, from Medieval Latin *graduālis,* step by step, from Latin *gradus,* step, GRADE.] **—grad·u·al·ly** *adv.* **—grad·u·al·ness** *n.*

grad·u·al·ism (grájoo-əl-iz'm, gráddew-) *n.* The belief in or policy of advancing towards a goal, especially a political goal, by gradual, often slow stages. **—grad·u·al·ist** *n.* & *adj.* **—grad·u·al·is·tic** (-ístik) *adj.*

grad·u·and (grájoo-ənd, gráddew-) *n. Chiefly British.* A student or former student who is on the point of receiving a degree. [Medieval Latin *graduandus,* gerundive of *graduāre,* to GRADUATE.]

grad·u·ate (grájoo-ayt, gráddew-) *v.* **-ated, -ating, -ates.** *—intr.* **1.** To be granted an academic degree or diploma. **2.** To change gradually, or by degrees. **3.** To progress to something more advanced: *From being stage manager, he graduated to directing.* *—tr.* **1.** To arrange or divide into categories, steps, or grades. **2.** To divide into marked intervals, especially for use in measurement. **3.** *Chiefly U.S.* To grant a diploma or degree to.

~n. (-ət, -it). *Abbr.* **grad.** One who has received an academic degree.

~adj. (-ət, -it). **1.** Possessing an academic degree or diploma. **2.** Of, pertaining to, or designating studies beyond a bachelor's degree: *graduate courses.* [Middle English *graduaten,* from Medieval Latin *graduāre,* from Latin *gradus,* degree, step, GRADE.] **—grad·u·a·tor** *n.*

grad·u·a·tion (grájoo-áysh'n, gráddew-) *n.* **1.** The conferring or receipt of an academic degree or diploma marking completion of studies. **2.** A ceremony at which degrees or diplomas are conferred. **3. a.** A division or interval on a graduated scale. **b.** A mark indicating the boundary of such an interval. **4.** An arrangement in or division into stages, intervals, or degrees.

grad·us (grád-əss, gráyd-) *n., pl.* **-duses. 1.** A dictionary of prosody used as an aid in writing Latin or Greek poetry. **2.** A manual for developing a student's ability, especially a book of musical exercises. [Short for *Gradus ad Parnassum,* "step to Parnassus", dictionary of prosody formerly used in English public schools, from Latin *gradus,* step, GRADE.]

Grae·ae, Grai·ae (grée-ee, grī́-ī) *pl.n. Greek Mythology.* Three female deities personifying old age, who, with only one eye and one tooth among them, guarded their sisters, the Gorgons.

Grae·cise, Grae·cize (grée-sīz) *v.* **-cised, -cising, -cises.** *—tr.* To provide with or convert into a Greek form or style; Hellenise. *—intr.* To follow or adopt Greek culture, art, or thoughts, especially that of ancient Greece. [Latin *Graecizāre,* from *Graecus,* Greek.]

Grae·cism (grée-siz'm) *n.* **1.** The style or spirit of Greek culture, art, or thought. **2.** Admiration, adoption, or imitation of such style or spirit. **3.** Any sculpture, design, or the like made in such style or spirit. **4.** An idiom of the Greek language. **5.** An idiom or turn of phrase in a foreign language that has been literally translated from a Greek idiom. [French *grécisme,* from Medieval Latin *Graecismus,* from *Graecus,* Greek.]

Grae·co-, *U.S.* **Gre·co-** *comb. form.* Indicates Greek; for example, **Graeco-Roman.** [From Latin *Graecus.*]

Grae·co-Ro·man (gréekō-rṓmən, gréckō-) *adj.* **1.** Pertaining to the history, culture, or civilisation common to Ancient Greece and Rome: *Graeco-Roman mythology.* **2.** Designating a style of wrestling, in which leverage and holds are restricted to the upper body.

Graf (graaf) *n., pl.* **Grafen** (graáfən). *Feminine* **Gräf·in** (gréf-in) *pl.* **-inen** (-inən). A count. Used as a title of German, Austrian, or Swedish nobility corresponding to the English earl. [German, from Old High German *grāvo.*]

Graf (Stefanie Maria) "Steffi" (1969–). German tennis player. In 1988 she became the first woman to win the women's singles titles at the four major tournaments in one year. She also won an Olympic gold medal in 1988. Wimbledon champion (1988–89, 1991–93), with 20 grand-slam titles (July 1996).

graf·fi·to (grə-fée-tō, gra-) *n., pl.* **-ti** (-tee). **1.** *Archaeology.* A crude drawing or inscription scratched on stone, plaster, or some other hard surface. **2.** *Usually plural.* Any scrawling written or drawn so as to be seen by the public, as on a wall or lavatory door, and often obscene or humorous. [Italian, diminutive of *graffio,* a scratching, from *graffiare,* to scratch, perhaps from *grafio,* a pencil, stylus, from Latin *graphium,* from Greek *graphion,* from *graphein,* to write.]

graft[1] (graaft || graft) *tr.v.* **grafted, grafting, grafts. 1.** In horticulture: **a.** To unite (a shoot or bud) with a growing plant by insertion or placing in close contact. **b.** To join (a plant or plants) by such union. **2.** *Medicine.* To transplant or implant (tissue, for example) into a bodily part to replace a damaged part or compensate for a defect. **3.** To attach or incorporate, especially in an artificial way. ~*n.* **1.** In horticulture: **a.** A detached shoot or bud united or to be united with a growing plant. **b.** The union or point of union of a detached shoot or bud with a growing plant by insertion or attachment. **c.** A plant produced by such union. **2.** *Medicine.* **a.** Material, especially tissue or an organ, surgically attached to or inserted into a bodily part to replace a damaged part or compensate for a defect. **b.** The procedure of transplanting such material. **c.** The configuration or condition resulting from such a procedure. **3.** Any act or product of attaching or incorporating. [Middle English *grafte, graff,* from Old French *grafe, grefe,* pencil, shoot for grafting (from its pencil-like shape), from Latin *graphium.* See **graffito.**] —**graft·er** *n.*

graft² *n.* **1.** *British Informal.* Hard work or study. **2.** *Chiefly U.S.* **a.** The unscrupulous use of one's position to derive profit or advantages; extortion. **b.** Money or an advantage gained or yielded under such circumstances. ~*v.* **grafted, grafting, grafts.** —*tr. Chiefly U.S.* To gain by graft. —*intr.* **1.** *Informal.* To work or study very hard. **2.** *Chiefly U.S.* To practise graft. [Perhaps extended use of GRAFT (insertion, hence "additional activity").] —**graft·er** *n.*

graft copolymer *n. Chemistry.* A copolymer that has main chains of one type of monomer with side chains of the other monomer.

graft hybrid *n.* A plant produced by grafting in which the tissue of the scion mingles with that of the stock. It is a type of **chimaera** *(see).*

Graf·ton (gráaft'n). A city and river port in New South Wales, Australia, situated on the Clarence river.

gra·ham (gráy-əm) *adj. Chiefly U.S.* Made from or consisting of whole-wheat flour. [After Sylvester *Graham* (1794–1851), U.S. vegetarian who urged dietary reform.]

Gra·ham (gráy-əm), **Martha** (1895–1991). U.S. ballet dancer, teacher, and choreographer. She made her debut as a dancer in 1920 in Los Angeles and in 1930 founded the Dance Repertory Theatre in New York. Her full-length works include *Appalachian Spring* (1944) and *Clytemnestra* (1958).

Graham, Thomas (1805–69). British chemist. His investigation of gases and liquids led to the formulation of **Graham's law.** His work on colloids and crystalloids led to his discovery of dialysis.

Gra·ham, William Franklin, known as Billy (1918–). U.S. evangelist. Ordained minister in the Southern Baptist Church in 1939, he conducted his first intensive evangelical campaign in Los Angeles. Since then he has been to all continents. Autobiography: *Just as I Am* (1997).

Gra·hame (gráy-əm), **Kenneth** (1859–1932). English writer. He wrote two volumes of childhood autobiography, *The Golden Age* (1895) and *Dream Days* (1898), but is best known for his children's book *The Wind in the Willows* (1908).

Graham Land. A part of the Antarctic Peninsula in Antarctica, bordering the Weddell Sea. Consisting chiefly of ice-bound rock, it was formerly a dependency of the Falkland Islands and now forms part of the British Antarctic Territory.

Graham's law *n. Physics.* The principle that the rates of diffusion of gases are inversely proportional to the square roots of their densities. Also called "Graham's law of diffusion". [Formulated by Thomas GRAHAM.]

Gra·hams·town (gráy-əmz-town). *Afrikaans* **Gra·ham·stad** (gráy-əm-staat). Town in Eastern Cape province in South Africa. Founded in 1812, it has two cathedrals and is the site of Rhodes university (established 1904).

Graiae. Variant of **Graeae.**

grail (grayl) *n. Often capital* **G. 1.** The cup or chalice in medieval legend used by Christ at the Last Supper and subsequently the object of many chivalrous quests. Also called "Holy Grail", "Sangraal". **2.** The object of a prolonged endeavour. [Middle English *graal,* from Old French, from Medieval Latin *gradális†,* dish.]

grain (grayn) *n.* **1.** A small, hard seed or fruit, especially that produced by a cereal grass such as wheat, barley, rice, or oats. **2.** The seeds of such plants collectively, especially after having been harvested. **3.** Cereal grasses collectively: *a field of grain.* **4.** A relatively small discrete particle or crystalline mass: *a grain of sand.* **5.** *Aerospace.* A mass of solid propellant formed from a number of smaller pieces. **6.** The very smallest amount; a tiny quantity: *a grain of truth.* **7. a.** A unit of weight, one seven-thousandth of a pound in the avoirdupois, Troy, and apothecaries' systems. It is equal to 0.0648 gram. **b.** A metric unit of weight equal to 50 milligrams. It is used in weighing certain precious stones. In this sense, also called "metric grain". **8. a.** The arrangement, direction, or pattern of the fibrous tissue in wood. **b.** The arrangement, direction, or pattern of muscle fibres or meat. **9. a.** The outer side of a hide or piece of leather from which the hair or fur is removed. **b.** The pattern or markings on this side of leather. **10.** The pattern or markings on the skin. **11.** The pattern produced, as in stone, by the arrangement of particulate constituents. **12.** The relative size of the particles composing a substance or pattern: *a coarse grain.* **13.** Any painted, stamped, or printed design that imitates the pattern found in wood, leather, or stone. **14.** The direction or texture of fibres in a woven fabric. **15.** *Chemistry.* **a.** A state of fine crystallisation. **b.** A small crystalline region in a polycrystalline solid. **16.** Temperament; nature; character. **17.** Any of the particles in a photographic emulsion that determine by their size the degree of the image's resolution. **18.** *Archaic.* Colour; tint; hue. **19. a.** Cochineal or kermes. **b.** Red dye made from cochineal or kermes. **c.** Any fast dye. Not in cur-

rent technical usage. —**against the grain.** In contradiction to one's natural disposition or character. ~*v.* **grained, graining, grains.** —*tr.* **1.** To form or cause to form into grains; granulate; crystallise. **2.** To paint, stamp, or print with a design imitating the grain of wood, leather, or stone. **3.** To give a granular or rough texture to. **4.** To remove the hair or fur from (hides) in preparation for tanning. —*intr.* To form into or become grains. [Middle English, from Old French, from Latin *gránum,* seed.] —**grain·er** *n.*

grain alcohol *n.* **Alcohol** *(see).*

grain elevator *n.* **1.** A building equipped with mechanical lifting devices, used for storing grain. **2.** The machine used for lifting grain, typically having an endless belt carrying a number of scoops.

Grain·ger (gráynjər), **(George) Percy (Aldridge)** (1882–1961). Australian-born composer and pianist who settled in the United States. As a pianist he was associated especially with the music of Grieg, from whom he acquired his deep interest in folk music, which inspired many of his compositions, including *Country Gardens* and *Shepherds' Hey.* Founder: Grainger Museum (Melbourne).

grain·ing (gráyning) *n.* **1.** The pattern of the grain in wood or leather. **2.** The application of an artificial grain or design to a surface, by painting, stamping, or printing. **3.** A fabric or surface patterned in this way. **4.** An artificially produced grainlike pattern.

grains (graynz) *n. Usually used with a singular verb.* An iron harpoon with two or more barbed prongs used for spearing fish. [Middle English *grein,* fork, from Old Norse *grein†,* branch, twig.]

grains of paradise *pl.n.* **1.** The pungent, aromatic seeds of either of two tropical African plants, *Aframomum melegueta* or *A. granum-paradisi,* used medicinally. **2.** The seeds of **cardamom** *(see).*

grain·y (gráyni) *adj.* **-i·er, -i·est. 1.** Made of, full of, or resembling grain; granular. **2.** Resembling the grain of wood. **3.** In photography, speckled or poor in definition, as a result of large grains in the emulsion. Said of a photograph or photographic image.

gram¹, gramme (gram) *n. Abbr.* **g, gm., gr.** A metric unit of mass and weight, equal to one thousandth (10^{-3}) of a kilogram (0.002205 pound). [French *gramme,* from Late Latin *gramma,* a small unit, from Greek, small weight, letter of the alphabet.]

gram² *n.* **1.** Any of several plants, such as a bean, *Phaseolus mungo,* or the chickpea, bearing seeds widely used as food in tropical Asia. **2.** The seeds of such a plant. [Portuguese *grão,* from Latin *gránum,* seed, GRAIN.]

-gram¹ *n. comb. form.* Indicates something written or drawn; for example, **diagram, telegram.** [Latin *-gramma,* something written, from Greek, *-gramma, -grammos,* respectively from *gramma,* letter and *grammē,* line.]

-gram² *n. comb. form.* Indicates a gram, as used in the metric system; for example, **kilogram.** [From GRAM (unit).]

gram. grammar; grammatical.

gra·ma (gráamə) *n.* Any of various grasses of the genus *Bouteloua,* of western North America and South America, forming dense tufts or mats, and often used as pasturage. Also called "grama grass". [Spanish *grama,* from Latin *grámina,* plural of *grámen,* grass.]

gram·a·doe·las (khrámmə-dóol-ass, -əz) *pl.n. South African Informal.* Remote or uninhabited parts of the country; the back of beyond. [Afrikaans, perhaps from Nguni *amaduli,* plural of *-duli,* hill.]

gram·a·rye (grámməri) *n. Archaic.* Occult learning; magic; necromancy. [Middle English *gramarie,* from Old French *gramaire,* GRAMMAR.]

gram-at·om (grám-áttəm) *n.* The mass in grams of an element numerically equal to the atomic weight.

gram calorie *n.* A **calorie** *(see).*

gra·mer·cy (grə-mér-si) *interj. Archaic.* Used to express surprise or gratitude. [Middle English *gramercye, grand mercy,* great thanks, from Old French *grand merci* : *grand,* GRAND + *merci,* thanks, MERCY.]

gram flour *n.* Flour made from gram seeds.

gram·i·cid·in (grámmi-sídin) *n.* An antibiotic produced by a bacterium, *Bacillus brevis,* and used against most Gram-positive pathogenic bacteria. [GRAM-(POSITIVE) + -CID(E) + -IN.]

gra·min·e·ous (grəmínni-əss) *adj.* Also **gra·min·a·ceous** (grámmi-náyshəss). **1.** Of, pertaining to, or characteristic of grasses. **2.** Of or belonging to the family Gramineae, which includes the grasses. [Latin *grámineus,* grassy, from *grámen* (stem *grámin-*), grass.]

gram·i·niv·or·ous (grámmi-nívvərəss) *adj.* Feeding on grasses, grain, or seeds. [Latin *grámen* (stem *grámin-*), grass + -VOROUS.]

gram·mar (grámmər) *n. Abbr.* **gram. 1.** The study of language as a systematically composed body of words that exhibit discernible regularity of structure (morphology), and their arrangement into sentences (syntax), sometimes including such aspects of language as the pronunciation of words (phonology), the meanings of words (semantics), and the history of words (etymology). **2. a.** The phenomena with which this study deals, as exhibited by a specific language at a specific time. **b.** The system of rules implicit in a language, viewed as a mechanism for generating all sentences possible in that language. **c.** A systematic description or listing of such rules. **3. a.** A normative or prescriptive system of rules setting forth the current standard or usage for teaching or reference purposes. **b.** A book containing such rules: *old-fashioned school grammars.* **4.** Writing or speech judged with regard to the rules or practice of grammar, especially syntax: *bad grammar.* **5. a.** The basic principles of any area of knowledge: *the grammar of music.* **b.** A book dealing with such principles. [Middle English, from Anglo-French *gramere,* from Old French *gramaire,* from Latin *grammatica,* from

Greek *grammatikē (tekhnē)*, "(art) of the letters", from *grammatikos*, pertaining to letters, from *gramma*, letter.]

gram·mar·i·an (grə-maír-i-ən) *n.* A specialist in grammar.

grammar school *n.* **1.** *British.* A secondary school, formerly state-assisted, with a selected intake of pupils and a curriculum emphasising academic subjects. Compare **comprehensive school, high school, public school, secondary modern school. 2.** *U.S.* An **elementary school** *(see).*

gram·mat·i·cal (grə-mátti-k'l) *adj. Abbr.* **gram. 1.** Of or relating to grammar. **2.** Conforming to the rules of grammar. [Late Latin *grammaticālis*, from Latin *grammaticus*, from Greek *grammatikos*, pertaining to letters. See **grammar.**] —**gram·mat·i·cal·i·ty** (-kál-əti) *n.* —**gram·mat·i·cal·ly** *adv.*

grammatical gender *n.* The gender assigned to a word in the grammar of a language, as distinct from natural gender or sex. Compare **common gender, natural gender.**

gram·ma·tol·o·gy (grámmə-tólləji) *n.* The study and science of systems of graphic script. [French *grammatologie* : Greek *gramma* (stem *grammat-*), written character + -LOGY.] —**gram·ma·to·log·ic** (-tə-lójik), **gram·ma·to·log·i·cal** *adj.* —**gram·ma·tol·o·gist** (-tóllə-jist) *n.*

gramme. Variant of **gram** (metric unit).

gram·mo·lec·u·lar weight (grám-mə-léckewlər) *n. Chemistry.* A **mole** *(see).* Also called "gram molecule".

Gram-neg·a·tive (grám-néggətiv) *adj. Sometimes small* **g.** Of, pertaining to, or designating a microorganism that does not retain the purple dye used in Gram's method.

gram·o·phone (grámmə-fōn) *n.* A record player. Also used adjectivally: *a gramophone record.* [Originally a trademark from earlier *graphophone*, inversion of PHONOGRAPH.]

Gram·pi·an Region (grámpi-ən). Formerly an administrative region of Scotland bordering the North Sea in the northeast of the country. It is now divided into Aberdeenshire, Moray and the City of Aberdeen. The southwest of the region is mountainous, lying in the Grampians. The terrain descends to arable lowlands in the northeast.

Gram·pi·ans[1] (grámpi-ənz). Also **Grampian Mountains.** Mountain range extending across central Scotland, bounded to the north by the Great Glen and to the south by the central Lowlands. Its highest peak is Ben Nevis 1 344 metres (4,406 feet), the highest mountain in Britain, and it also includes the peaks of the Cairngorms.

Grampians[2] (grámpi-ənz). A small range of mountains in Victoria state, southeast Australia. It forms the southwesterly extremity of the Great Dividing Range, its highest peak being Mount William 1 166 metres (3,827 feet), near Ballarat.

Gram-pos·i·tive (grám-pózzətiv) *adj. Often small* **g.** Of, pertaining to, or designating a microorganism that retains the purple dye used in Gram's method.

gram·pus (grámpəss) *n.* **1.** A marine mammal, *Grampus griseus*, related to and resembling the dolphins but lacking a beaklike snout. **2.** Any of several similar cetaceans, such as the **killer whale** *(see).* **3.** *Informal.* A person who is short-winded and breathes heavily. [Middle English *graspeis*, from Old French *graspois, craspois*, from Medieval Latin *craspiscis* : *cras*, fat, from Latin *crassus* (see **crass**) + *piscis*, fish.]

Gram·sci (grámshi), **Antonio** (1891-1937). Founder of the Italian Communist Party. The notebooks he wrote during his imprisonment following the banning of the Party by the Fascists were published posthumously in 1947.

Gram's method (gramz) *n.* A differential staining technique using the retention or lack of retention of a purple dye to classify bacteria. [After Hans Christian Joachim *Gram* (1853–1938), Danish physician.]

gran (gran) *n. Informal.* A grandmother.

Gra·na·da (grə-naádə; *Spanish* gra-naáthə). A historic city in southern Spain, the capital of Granada province. It has many fine examples of Moorish architecture, including the Alhambra. The city was the capital of the Muslim state of Granada which, under the Nasrid dynasty (1238-1492), was the last Moorish stronghold in Spain.

gran·a·dil·la (gránnə-díllə) *n.* **1.** Any of various tropical American passionflowers; especially, *Passiflora quadrangularis*, bearing edible fruit. **2.** The egg-shaped, fleshy fruit of such a plant. In this sense, also called "passion fruit". [Spanish, diminutive of *granada*, pomegranate, from Vulgar Latin *grānāta* (unattested), from Latin *grānātum*, seedy, from *grānum*, GRAIN.]

Gra·na·dos (*Spanish* gra-naáthoss) **(y Campiña), Enrique** (1867–1916). Spanish composer whose most important compositions were for the piano. Among them the set called *Goyescas* (1912–14), inspired by paintings of Goya.

gran·a·ry (gránnəri ‖ *U.S. also* gráynəri) *n., pl.* **-ries. 1.** A building for storing threshed grain. **2.** A region yielding a copious quantity of grain. [Latin *grānārium* : *grānum*, GRAIN + -ARY.]

granary meal *n.* A mixture of malted wheat and rye, and sometimes wholemeal kernels, used in making *granary bread*. Also called "granary flour".

gran cas·sa (grán kássa) *n., pl.* **gran casse** (kásse). *Music.* A bass drum. [Italian, "great drum".]

grand (grand) *adj.* **grander, grandest. 1.** Large and impressive in size, scope, or extent. **2. a.** Magnificent; splendid. **b.** *Chiefly British Regional.* Wonderful; outstanding; very good. **3.** Rich and sumptuous: *grand furnishings.* **4.** Having higher rank than others of the same specified category: *grand duke.* **5.** The most important; principal; main: *grand ballroom.* **6.** Illustrious; outstanding: *a grand*

assemblage. **7. a.** Pretentious. **b.** Calculated to impress: *a grand manner.* **8.** Dignified and admirable: *a grand old man.* **9.** Stately; regal. **10.** Lofty; noble: *a grand purpose.* **11.** *Music.* **a.** Written for a large ensemble. **b.** Complete in form; containing all the movements. **12.** Inclusive; complete: *grand total.*
~n. **1.** A **grand piano** *(see).* **2.** *Abbr.* **G** *Chiefly U.S. Slang.* A thousand dollars or pounds. [French, from Old French, from Latin *grandis*†, grand, full-grown.] —**grand·ly** *adv.* —**grand·ness** *n.*
    Synonyms: *grand, magnificent, imposing, stately, majestic, august, grandiose.*

grand- *comb. form.* Indicates a family relationship or relative one generation removed from the relative specified; for example, **grandson.** [French, rendering Latin *magnus* in kinship terms of ascent (for example, *amita magna, grand-tante*), later extended in English to terms of descent as well (for example, *grandson*, but French *petit-fils*).]

gran·dam (grán-dəm, -dam) *n.* Also **gran·dame** (-daym, -dəm). **1.** A grandmother. **2.** An old woman. [Middle English *graundam*, from Anglo-French *graund dame*. See **grand, dame.**]

grand-aunt (gránd-aant ‖ -ant) *n.* A **great-aunt** *(see).*

Grand Banks. A submerged plateau, rising from the continental shelf, off southeastern Newfoundland, Canada. It is about 480 kilometres (300 miles) long and 640 kilometres (400 miles) wide.

Grand Canyon. A vast ravine of the Colorado river in Arizona, southwestern United States. The river's course has cut a canyon 451 kilometres (280 miles) long, exposing multicoloured tiers of rock which have been spectacularly eroded by the weather. The canyon is at some points over 1.6 kilometres (1 mile) deep.

grand·child (gránd-chīld) *n., pl.* **-children** (-children). A child of a son or daughter.

Grand Cou·lee Dam (kōoli). A major dam on the Columbia river, situated in Washington state in the northwestern United States. The reservoir has a capacity of 11 600 million cubic metres (15,080 million cubic yards) and is used for irrigation, hydroelectricity, and flood control.

grand·dad (grán-dad) *n. Informal.* A grandfather.

grand·dad·dy (grán-daddi) *n., pl.* **-dies.** *Chiefly U.S. Informal.* **1.** A grandfather. **2.** An originator or pre-eminent figure: *the granddaddy of them all.*

grand·daugh·ter (grán-dawtər) *n.* The daughter of a son or daughter.

grand duchess *n. Abbr.* **G.D. 1.** The wife or widow of a grand duke. **2.** A woman who is sovereign of a grand duchy. **3.** The daughter of a tsar or of one of his male descendants.

grand duchy *n. Abbr.* **G.D.** A territory ruled by a grand duke or a grand duchess.

grand duke *n. Abbr.* **G.D. 1.** A nobleman who is below a king in rank and is sovereign of a grand duchy. **2.** A son or grandson of a tsar.

grande dame (grón dám, daám) *n., pl.* **grandes dames** (*pronounced as singular*). *French.* A woman revered as an authority or leading figure in her group or profession. Sometimes used humorously.

gran·dee (gran-deé) *n.* **1.** A nobleman of the highest rank in Spain or Portugal. **2.** A person of eminence or high rank. [Spanish and Portuguese *grande*, "great (one)", from Latin *grandis*, GRAND.]

gran·deur (grán-jər, -dewr) *n.* **1.** Greatness; splendour: *"The world is charged with the grandeur of God."* (Gerard Manley Hopkins). **2.** Personal dignity or proud bearing, often of an unwarranted, self-important kind. [Middle English, from Old French, from *grand*, GRAND.]

grand·fa·ther (gránd-faathər) *n.* **1.** The father of a mother or father. **2.** A forefather; an ancestor. **3.** Any old man. Sometimes used as a familiar form of address.

grandfather clock *n.* A pendulum clock enclosed in a tall, narrow cabinet. Also called "longcase clock".

grand·fa·ther·ly (gránd-faathərli) *adj.* **1.** Characteristic of or befitting a grandfather. **2.** Having the qualities of a grandfather; kindly; indulgent; benevolent.

Grand Gui·gnol (grón geen-yól) *n.* **1.** A short, horrifying stage play. **2.** A style typical of or resembling such a play in being sensational, violent, or macabre, often in a deliberately stylised way. [After *Le Grand Guignol*, a theatre in Montmartre, Paris, that specialised in such plays.] —**Grand-Gui·gnol** *adj.*

gran·dil·o·quence (gran-díllokwənss) *n.* Pompous or bombastic speech or expression. [Latin *grandiloquus*, speaking loftily : *grandis*, GRAND + *loquī*, to speak.] —**gran·dil·o·quent** *adj.* —**gran·dil·o·quent·ly** *adv.*

gran·di·ose (grándi-ōss, -ōz) *adj.* **1.** Characterised by greatness of scope or intent; grand. **2.** Characterised by feigned or affected grandeur; pompous. —See Synonyms at **grand.** [French, from Italian *grandioso*, from *grande*, great, grand, from Latin *grandis*, GRAND.] —**gran·di·ose·ly** *adv.* —**gran·di·os·i·ty** (-óssəti), **gran·di·ose·ness** *n.*

gran·di·o·so (grándi-ō-sō) *adv. Music.* In a grand and noble style. Used as a direction. [Italian, GRANDIOSE.] —**gran·di·o·so** *adj.*

grand jury *n. Chiefly U.S. Law.* A jury of 12 to 23 persons convened in private session to evaluate accusations against persons charged with crime and to determine whether the evidence warrants bringing an indictment. Compare **petit jury.**

Grand Lama *n.* Either of two senior lamas, the **Dalai Lama** or the **Panchen Lama** *(both of which see).*

grand larceny *n.* The theft of property of a value exceeding the amount constituting **petit larceny** *(see).*

grand·ma (gránd-maa, grán-, grám- ‖ grámmə, *U.S. also* -maw) *n.* Also **grand·ma·ma** (gránd-mə-maa, grán-). *Informal.* A grandmother.

grand mal (grón mál) *n.* A form of epilepsy characterised by severe seizures involving spasms and loss of consciousness. Compare **petit mal.** [French, "great illness" : GRAND + *mal,* illness, from Old French, bad, ill, from Latin *malus.*]

grand master *n.* Also **grand·mas·ter** (gránd-maastər ‖ -mastər) (for sense 1). **1.** In chess, an **international grand master** (*see*). **2.** *Often capital* **G,** *capital* **M.** A title of or form of address for the head of any of various private and usually secret organisations, such as the Freemasons or Templars.

grand·moth·er (gránd-muthər, grán-) *n.* **1.** The mother of a father or mother. **2.** A female ancestor. **3.** Any old woman. Sometimes used as a familiar form of address.

grandmother clock *n.* A clock of a type resembling but shorter than a grandfather clock.

grand·moth·er·ly (gránd-muthərli) *adj.* **1.** Characteristic of or befitting a grandmother. **2.** Having the qualities of a grandmother; solicitous; indulgent.

Grand National *n.* In Britain, a steeplechase horserace held every year at Aintree racetrack near Liverpool. Preceded by *the.*

grand-neph·ew (gránd-nevvew, -neffew) *n.* A **great-nephew** (*see*).

grand-niece (gránd-neess) *n.* A **great-niece** (*see*).

Grand Old Man *n. Abbr.* **G.O.M.** A man revered as a figure of long-standing eminence in his field. Sometimes used humorously.

Grand Old Party *n. Abbr.* **G.O.P.** *U.S. Informal.* The Republican Party.

grand opera *n.* A serious or melodramatic drama having the entire text set to music.

grand·pa (gránd-paa, gran-, gram- ‖ grámpə, *U.S. also* -paw) *n.* Also **grand·pa·pa** (gránd-pə-paa, grán-). *Informal.* A grandfather.

grand·par·ent (gránd-pair-ənt) *n.* A parent of a mother or father; a grandmother or grandfather.

grand piano *n.* A piano having the strings strung in a horizontal harp-shaped frame supported usually on three legs and ranging in size from the baby grand to the concert grand. Compare **upright piano.**

Grand Prix (grón prée) *n., pl.* **Grands Prix** or **Grand Prixes** (préez, prée). *Abbr.* **G.P. 1.** Any of a series of international competitive races for cars of specific engine size over an exacting course, and counting towards the award of the driver's world championship each year. **2.** Any of various other major races, as in cycling or horseracing, held annually. [French, big prize].

Grand Rapids. A city in Michigan in the northeastern United States, situated on the Grand river. Founded in 1826, it developed as a lumber centre and became famous for the manufacture of high-quality furniture, still a major industry.

grand sei·gneur (*French* gron say-nyőr) *n., pl.* **grands seigneurs** (*pronounced as singular*). *French.* A man of very dignified bearing. Often used ironically.

grand sherif *n.* A **sherif** (*see*).

grand siècle (*French* gron syékl) *n. French.* The 17th century in France with reference to the arts, especially the classical period during the reign of Louis XIV. [Literally, "great age".]

grand-sire (gránd-sər, -sīr) *n. Archaic.* **1.** A grandfather. **2.** A male ancestor; a forefather. **3.** Any old man.

grand slam *n.* **1.** In bridge and other card games, the winning of all the tricks during the play of one hand. **2.** In various sports, especially tennis and golf, the winning of all major events in a particular series or season.

grand-slam (gránd-slám) *adj.* Of, pertaining to, or designating an event that counts towards a sporting grand slam: *20 grand-slam titles; a grand-slam tournament.*

grand·son (gránd-sun, grán-) *n.* The son of a son or daughter.

grand·stand (gránd-stand, grán-) *n.* **1.** A roofed stand for spectators at a sports ground or race course, usually offering the best view and having the most expensive seats. **2.** The spectators seated in such a stand.

grandstand view *n.* An unobstructed view.

grand tour *n.* **1.** Formerly, an extended tour of continental Europe considered as a part of the education of young men of the English upper class. **2.** *Informal.* A comprehensive tour or inspection.

grand-un·cle (gránd-ungk'l) *n.* A **great-uncle** (*see*).

grange (graynj) *n.* **1.** *British.* A farm; especially, the residence and attached farm buildings of the farmer. **2.** A feudal farm building used for storing grain paid as tithes. **3.** *Archaic.* A granary. [Middle English, from Old French, from Medieval Latin *grānica,* from Latin *grānum,* GRAIN.]

grang·er·ise, grang·er·ize (gráynjər-īz) *tr.v.* **-ised, -ising, -ises.** **1.** To illustrate (a book) with drawings, prints, or engravings taken from other books. **2.** To mutilate (a book) by clipping out its illustrative material for such use. [After J. *Granger* (1723–1776), English biographer who published (1769) his *Biographical History of England* with blank pages where the reader could insert such illustrations.] —**grang·er·ism, grang·er·i·sa·tion** (-ī-záysh'n ‖ *U.S.* -i-) *n.* —**grang·er·is·er** *n.*

grani– *comb. form.* Indicates grain; for example, **granivorous, graniform.** [Latin *grāni-,* from *grānum,* GRAIN.]

gra·nif·er·ous (gra-níffərəss, grə-) *adj.* Bearing grain. [Latin *grānifer* : GRANI- + -FER.]

gran·i·form (gránni-fawrm) *adj.* Resembling a grain in form. [GRANI- + -FORM.]

gra·ni·ta (gra-néetə) *n.* A coarse-textured water ice. [Italian, "grained (ice)".]

gran·ite (gránnit) *n.* **1.** A common, coarse-grained, hard, and igneous rock consisting chiefly of quartz, orthoclase or microcline, and often mica, used in monuments and for building. **2.** Unyielding endurance; steadfastness; firmness. [Italian *granito,* "grained", from the past participle of *granire,* to impart a grained surface to, from *grano,* grain, from Latin *grānum,* GRAIN.] —**gra·nit·ic** (grə-níttik), **gran·it·oid** *adj.*

gran·ite·ware (gránnit-wair) *n.* **1.** Enamelled iron utensils. **2.** Earthenware with a speckled glaze resembling granite.

gra·niv·o·rous (gra-nívvərəss, grə-) *adj.* Feeding on grain and seeds. [GRANI- + -VOROUS.] —**gran·i·vore** (gránni-vawr ‖ -vōr) *n.*

gran·ny, gran·nie (gránni) *n., pl.* **-nies. 1.** *Informal.* A grandmother. **2.** A fussy or finicky person. [From obsolete *grannam,* variant of GRANDAM.]

granny bond *n. British.* A type of national savings certificate, formerly available only to people of retirement age.

granny flat *n.* A flat that adjoins or is part of a house, especially one used for the accommodation of an elderly parent.

granny glasses *pl.n.* A pair of small, round, glasses with gold or steel rims.

granny knot *n.* Also **granny's knot.** A knot like a reef knot but with the second tie crossed incorrectly so that it readily comes undone. [Originally a sailor's disparaging term for such a knot.]

Granny Smith *n.* A variety of apple with a green skin and hard, crisp flesh, eaten cooked or raw.

grano– *comb. form.* Indicates: **1.** Of or like granite; for example, **granolith. 2.** Granular; for example, **granophyre.** [German, from *Granit,* granite, from Italian *granito,* GRANITE.]

gran·o·di·o·rite (gránno-dĭ-ə-rīt) *n.* A coarse-grained acid igneous rock, intermediate between granite and diorite. It contains almost twice as much plagioclase as orthoclase.

gran·o·lith (gránnō-lith) *n.* A paving stone of crushed granite and cement. [GRANO- + -LITH.] —**gran·o·lith·ic** (-líthik) *adj.*

gran·o·phyre (gránnō-fīr) *n.* A grained granite porphyry having a groundmass with irregular intergrowths of quartz and feldspar. [German *Granophyr* : GRANO- + *Porphyr,* porphyry, from Medieval Latin *porphyrum,* PORPHYRY.] —**gran·o·phyr·ic** (-fírrik) *adj.*

grant (graant ‖ grant) *tr.v.* **granted, granting, grants. 1.** To allow to have; consent to the fulfilment of: *grant a wish.* **2.** To permit or accord, as a favour or privilege: *grant a kiss.* **3. a.** To bestow; confer: *grant aid.* **b.** To transfer (property) by a deed; convey. **4.** To concede; acknowledge. —**take for granted. 1.** To consider as true or proven. **2.** To accept as being likely or probable; anticipate correctly. **3.** To accept the benefit of without due acknowledgment. ~*n.* **1.** The act of granting. **2.** Something granted as: **a.** In Britain, a sum of money allocated by the government to finance students in universities and other higher institutions. **b.** A sum of money given by a government or a public fund as foreign aid. **3.** *Law.* A transfer of property by deed.—See Synonyms at **bonus.** [Middle English *graunten,* from Old French *gr(e)anter, creanter,* to insure, guarantee, from Vulgar Latin *crēdentāre* (unattested), from Latin *crēdēns* (stem *crēdent-*), present participle of *crēdere,* to believe, trust.] —**grant·a·ble** *adj.* —**grant·er** *n.*

Grant (graant ‖ grant), **Cary,** born Archibald Leach (1904–86). U.S. film actor, born in England. In 1933 he played his first important role opposite Mae West in *She Done Him Wrong* and remained in films until 1969. His most famous films include *The Philadelphia Story* (1940), *Arsenic and Old Lace* (1944), *To Catch A Thief* (1955), and *North by Northwest* (1959).

Grant, Ulysses S(impson), originally Hiram Ulysses Grant (1822–85). 18th U.S. president and military commander. With the Illinois Volunteers he captured Fort Henry and Fort Donelson (1862), the first major Unionist victories in the American Civil War, and after the victorious Vicksburg campaign (1862–63) he was made commander in chief of the Unionist army. He won the 1868 presidential election as the Republican candidate and was re-elected in 1872.

grant·ee (graan-tée ‖ gran-) *n. Law.* One to whom a grant is made.

Granth (graant) *n.* The holy scriptures of the Sikhs. [Hindi, book, from Sanskrit *grantha.*]

grant-in-aid (gráant-in-áyd ‖ gránt-) *n., pl.* **grants-in-aid.** A grant made by a government or private organisation to a lower level of government or local authority for the funding of public works, educational programmes, or the like.

grant of probate *n. Law.* Authority given by a court to an executor to deal with the estate of a deceased person as provided for by the will.

gran·tor (gráan-tər ‖ grán-) *n. Law.* One who makes a grant.

gran tur·is·mo (grán toor-ízmō) *n. Abbr.* **GT 1.** A fast touring car. **2.** Broadly, a car having sporting lines. [Italian, "great touring".]

gran·u·lar (gránnew-lər) *adj.* **1.** Composed of or appearing to be composed of granules or grains. **2.** Grainy. —**gran·u·lar·i·ty** (-lárrəti) *n.* —**gran·u·lar·ly** *adv.*

gran·u·late (gránnew-layt) *v.* **-lated, -lating, -lates.** —*tr.* **1.** To form into grains or granules. **2.** To make rough and grainy. —*intr.* **1.** To become granular or grainy. **2.** *Physiology.* To undergo granulation. —**gran·u·la·tive** (-lətiv, -laytiv) *adj.* —**gran·u·la·tor, gran·u·la·ter** *n.*

gran·u·la·tion (gránnew-láysh'n) *n.* **1. a.** The act or process of granulating. **b.** The condition or appearance of being granulated. **2.** *Physiology.* **a.** The formation of small, fleshy, beadlike protuberances on the surface of a wound while healing. **b.** Any of these protuberances. Also called "granulation tissue".

gran·ule (gránnewl) *n.* **1.** A small grain or pellet; a particle. **2.** *Astronomy.* Any of the smallest transient, brilliant markings visible in the photosphere of the sun. [Late Latin *grānulum,* diminutive of *grānum,* GRAIN.]

gran·u·lite (gránnew-līt) *n.* A granular metamorphic rock often banded in appearance and composed chiefly of feldspar, quartz, and garnet. [GRANUL(E) + -ITE.] **—gran·u·lit·ic** (-líttik) *adj.*

gran·u·lo·cyte (gránnew-lə-sīt, -lō-) *n.* Any of a group of white blood cells having granules in their cytoplasm. [From GRANULE + -CYTE.] **—gran·u·lo·cyt·ic** (-síttik) *adj.*

gran·u·lo·ma (gránnew-lṓ-mə) *n., pl.* **-mas** or **-mata** (-mətə). A mass of inflamed granulation tissue, usually associated with ulcerated infections. [New Latin : GRANUL(E) + -OMA.] **—gran·u·lom·a·tous** (-lómmətəss) *adj.*

gran·u·lose (gránnew-lōss, -lōz) *adj.* Having a surface covered with granules. [GRANUL(E) + -OSE.]

Gran·ville-Bark·er (gránvil-bárkər), **Harley** (1877–1946). British actor, producer, dramatist, and critic. He was co-manager of the Royal Court Theatre (1904–7) and producer of Shakespeare at the Savoy Theatre (1912–14). He is best remembered for his drama criticism, especially the *Prefaces to Shakespeare* (1927–47).

grape (grayp) *n.* **1.** Any of numerous woody vines of the genus *Vitis;* especially, *V. vinifera,* bearing clusters of edible fruit, and widely cultivated in many subspecies and varieties. Also called "grapevine". **2.** The fleshy, smooth-skinned, purple, red, or green fruit of such a vine, eaten raw or dried, and widely used in wine-making. **3.** Grapeshot. **—the grape.** Wine. [Middle English, from Old French, bunch of grapes, hook, from Germanic.] **—grap·ey,** **grap·y** *adj.*

grape·fruit (gráyp-frōōt ‖ -frewt) *n.* **1.** An evergreen tropical or semitropical tree, *Citrus paradisi,* cultivated for its edible fruit. **2.** The large, round fruit of this tree, typically having a yellow rind, and with a juicy, somewhat acid pulp. Also called "pomelo". [So called because the fruit grows in clusters, like grapes.]

grape hyacinth *n.* Any of various plants of the genus *Muscari,* native to Eurasia, having narrow leaves and dense, spike-shaped clusters of rounded, usually blue flowers.

grape ivy *n.* An evergreen climbing shrub, *Rhoicissus rhomboidea,* native to Africa grown as a house plant for its foliage.

grap·er·y (gráypəri) *n., pl.* **-ies.** A building or plantation where grapes are grown.

grapes *n. Used with a singular verb.* An abnormal growth resembling a bunch of grapes on the pastern or fetlock of a horse.

grape·shot (gráyp-shot) *n.* A cluster of small iron balls formerly used as a cannon charge. [From its resemblance to a cluster of grapes.]

grape sugar *n.* **Dextrose** (*see*).

grape·vine (gráyp-vīn) *n.* **1.** A vine on which grapes grow. **2.** An informal, often secret means of transmitting information, gossip, or rumour from person to person: *heard it on the grapevine.* **3.** An information source.

graph (graf, graaf) *n.* **1.** A drawing that expresses a relationship, often functional, between two sets of numbers as a set of points having coordinates that are plotted from a pair of axes and are determined by the relationship between the two sets. **2.** Any pictorial device, such as a pie chart or bar graph, used to display numerical relationships. Also called "chart". **3.** A representation of a quantity, as of a complex number, by a geometric object such as a point in a plane. **4.** A visual representation, such as a letter, of a phoneme or other speech unit.
~tr.v. **graphed, graphing, graphs.** **1.** To represent by a graph. **2.** To plot (a function) on a graph. [Short for *graphic formula;* sense 4, from Greek *graphē,* writing.]

-graph *n. comb. form.* Indicates: **1.** An apparatus that writes or records; for example, **telegraph, seismograph.** **2.** Something drawn or written; for example, **lithograph, monograph.** [French *-graphe,* from Latin *-graphum,* from Greek *-graphon,* neuter of *-graphos,* written, from *graphein,* to write.] **—graphic, -graphical** *adj. comb. form.* **—graphically** *adv. comb. form.*

graph·eme (gráffeem) *n.* **1.** A letter of an alphabet. **2.** The sum of letters and letter combinations that represent a single phoneme. [Greek *graphēma,* letter, from *graphein,* to write.] **—gra·phe·mic** (gra-féemik) *adj.* **—gra·phe·mi·cal·ly** *adv.*

-grapher *n. comb. form.* Indicates: **1.** A person who writes about or is skilled in a specified subject; for example, **geographer.** **2.** One who employs a specified means to write, draw, or record; for example, **stenographer.** [Late Latin *-graphus,* from Greek *-graphos,* from *graphein,* to write.]

graph·ic (gráffik) *adj.* Also **graph·i·cal** (-'l). **1.** Of or pertaining to written or pictorial representation. **2.** Of, pertaining to, or represented by or as if by a graph. **3.** Described in vivid detail; clearly outlined or set forth: *a graphic account.* **4.** Of or pertaining to the graphic arts. **5.** Of or pertaining to graphics. **6.** *Geology.* Having crystals resembling printed characters.
~n. **1.** A graphic device, such as a picture or map, used for illustration. **2.** *Computing.* A pictorial, as opposed to written, representation on a VDU screen or printout. [Latin *graphicus,* from Greek *graphikos,* from *graphē,* a writing, from *graphein,* to write.] **—graph·i·cal·ly** *adv.* **—graph·ic·ness** *n.*

graphic arts *pl.n.* **1.** The fine or applied visual arts that involve the application of lines and strokes to a two-dimensional surface. **2.** The reproductions made from blocks, plates, or type, such as engravings, etchings, woodcuts, and lithographs.

graphic novel *n.* A novel in comic-strip form, usually intended for young adults.

graph·ics (gráffiks) *n. Used with a singular or plural verb.* **1.** The making of drawings in accordance with the rules of mathematics, as in engineering or architecture. **2.** Calculations, as of structural stress, from such drawings. **3.** The artwork accompanying written matter. **4.** *Computing.* The processing and displaying of data in pictorial form, as on a VDU screen.

graph·ite (gráffīt) *n.* The soft, steel-grey to black, hexagonally crystallised allotrope of carbon, used in lead pencils, lubricants, paints and coatings, bricks, electrodes, crucibles, etc. [German *Graphit* : Greek *graphein,* to write + -ITE.] **—gra·phit·ic** (gra-fíttik) *adj.*

graph·i·tise, graph·i·tize (gráffi-tīz) *tr.v.* **-tised, -tising, -tises.** **1.** To convert into graphite by a heating process. **2.** To coat or impregnate with graphite. **—graph·i·ti·sa·tion** (-ĭ-záysh'n ‖ *U.S.* -ĭ-) *n.*

graph·ol·o·gy (gra-fóllǝji) *n.* **1.** The study of handwriting, especially when employed as a means of analysing the character of the writer. **2.** The study of writing systems. [Greek *graphē,* a writing (see **graphic**) + -LOGY.] **—graph·o·log·i·cal** (gráffǝ-lójik'l) *adj.* **—graph·ol·o·gist** *n.*

graph paper *n.* Paper ruled into small squares of equal size for use in drawing charts, graphs, or diagrams.

-graphy *n. comb. form.* Indicates: **1.** A specified process or method of writing, recording, or describing; for example, **cacography, photography.** **2.** A descriptive science of a specified subject or field; for example, **oceanography.** [Latin *-graphia,* from Greek, from *graphein,* to write.]

grap·nel (grápn'l) *n.* **1.** An iron shaft with claws at one end for grasping and holding; especially, one for drawing and holding an enemy ship alongside. Also called "grappling", "grappling-hook", "grappling iron". **2.** A small anchor with three or more flukes. [Middle English *grapenel,* from Anglo-French *grapenel* (unattested), diminutive of Old French *grapon,* hook, from Germanic.]

grap·pa (gráppǝ ‖ gráápǝ) *n.* An Italian brandy distilled from the residue of pressed grapes. [Italian, "grape stalk", from Germanic.]

Grap·pel·li, Stephane (1908–97). French jazz violinist. He set up the Quintette du Hot Club de France with the guitarist Django Reinhardt and others (1934), and played with Lord Menuhin.

grap·ple (grápp'l) *n.* **1.** Any instrument, such as a grapnel, used for grasping and holding. **2.** The act of grappling. **3. a.** A contest in which the participants attempt to clutch or grip each other. **b.** A grasp or grip in such a contest.
~v. **grappled, -pling, -ples.** *—tr.* **1.** To seize and hold with a grapnel. **2.** To seize firmly with the hands. *—intr.* **1.** To hold on to something with or as if with a grapnel. **2.** To attempt to resolve or overcome: *grapple with one's conscience.* [Middle English *grapel,* from Old French *grapil,* from Old Provençal, diminutive of *grapa,* hook, from Germanic.] **—grap·pler** *n.*

grap·to·lite (gráptǝ-līt) *n.* Any of numerous extinct colonial marine animals chiefly of the orders Dendroidea and Graptoloidea, of the late Cambrian to Carboniferous periods. [Greek *graptos,* written, painted, from *graphein,* to write (see **graphic**) + -LITE (so called from the fossilised impressions resembling markings on slate).]

Gras·mere (graáss-meer ‖ gráss-). A village in Cumbria in northwestern England, situated by Lake Grasmere. Set in the heart of the Lake District, it is famous for the beauty of its surroundings. Wordsworth lived there at Dove Cottage, which now houses a Wordsworth museum.

grasp (graasp ‖ grasp) *v.* **grasped, grasping, grasps.** *—tr.* **1.** To take hold of or seize firmly with or as if with the hand. **2.** To hold firmly with or as if with the hand; clutch; clasp. **3.** To take in mentally; comprehend: *"It is this distinction between freedom and licence that many parents cannot grasp"* (A.S. Neill). **—See** Synonyms at **apprehend.** *—intr.* **1.** To make a motion of seizing, snatching, or clutching. **2.** To show eager and prompt willingness or acceptance. Used with *at.*
~n. **1.** The act of grasping. **2.** A firm hold or grip. **3.** The ability or power to seize or attain; reach: *The directorship was within his grasp.* **4.** Understanding; comprehension: *an intuitive grasp of the problem.* [Middle English *graspen,* Old English *grapsan* (unattested), from Germanic.] **—grasp·er** *n.*

grasp·ing (graásp-ing ‖ grásp-) *adj.* Eager for gain; greedy; avaricious. **—grasp·ing·ly** *adv.* **—grasp·ing·ness** *n.*

grass (graass ‖ grass) *n.* **1. a.** Any of numerous plants of the family Gramineae, characteristically having narrow leaves, hollow, jointed stems, and spikes or clusters of membranous flowers borne in smaller spikelets. **b.** Such plants collectively. **2.** Any of various plants, such as knotgrass, having slender leaves like those of the true grasses. **3.** An expanse of ground, such as a meadow or lawn, covered with grass or similar plants. **4.** Grazing land; pasture. **5.** *Slang.* Cannabis. **6.** *British Slang.* A person who informs, especially on fellow-criminals, to the police. **—put out to grass.** **1.** To retire (a horse). **2.** *Informal.* To retire (a person) from active life.
~v. **grassed, grassing, grasses.** *—tr.* **1.** To cover with grass; grow grass on. **2.** To land (a fish). **3.** To shoot down (a bird). *—intr.* **1.** To become covered with grass. **2.** *British Slang.* To inform on someone to the police. [Middle English *gras,* Old English *græs,* from Germanic.]

Grass, Günter (Wilhelm) (1927–). German poet, playwright, and novelist. Most of his novels are directly concerned with the social and political life of Germany. His two early novels, *The Tin Drum* (1959) and *Dog Years* (1963), are the most widely known.

grass-box (gráass-boks ‖ gráss-) *n.* A container fitted to a lawnmower for catching the cut grass.

grass-cloth (gráass-kloth ‖ gráss-, -klawth) *n.* A material woven from rough natural plant fibres such as hemp or ramie.

grass court *n.* A tennis court with a cut grass surface.

grass-cut-ter (gráass-kuttər ‖ gráss-) *n.* A West African water rat, *Thryonomis swinderianus*, with stiff, short fur. Also called "cane rat".

Grasse (grass). A town in the Alpes-Maritimes département of southern France, situated to the north of Cannes. Surrounded by extensive fields of flowers, it is famous for the manufacture of essences for perfume.

grass-finch (gráass-finch ‖ gráss-) *n.* Any of various Australian weaver finches of the genus *Poephila* and related genera, some species of which are kept as cage birds for their colourful plumage.

grass hockey *n. Canadian.* Field hockey as opposed to ice hockey.

grass-hop-per (gráass-hoppər ‖ gráss-) *n.* **1.** Any of numerous insects of the families Locustidae (or Acrididae) (*short-horned grasshoppers*) and Tettigoniidae (*long-horned grasshoppers*), often destructive to plants and characteristically having long hind legs adapted for jumping. **2.** A cocktail consisting of crème de menthe, crème de cacao, and cream.

grass-land (gráass-land ‖ gráss-) *n.* An area, such as a prairie or meadow, of grass or grasslike vegetation.

grass-of-Par-nas-sus (gráass-əv-paar-nássəss ‖ gráss-) *n.* Any of various plants of the genus *Parnassia*; especially, *P. palustris*, having stalked basal leaves and a stem bearing a single white or yellowish flower.

grass parakeet *n.* Any of various small Australian parrots typically having a long tail and green plumage.

grass-roots (gráass-róóts ‖ gráss-, -róóts) *pl.n.* **1.** People considered from a political viewpoint as constituting the basic voting population. **2.** The foundation or source of something; the basis; the origin. ~*adj.* **1.** Originating in or emerging from the people who make up the mass of an electorate: *a grassroots policy.* **2.** Fundamental; basic.

grass-ski-ing (gráass-skee-ing) *n.* The sport of skiing down grassy slopes on specially adapted skis.

grass skirt *n.* A skirt made from lengths of flax or other grasses strung from a waistband and worn especially by the Polynesians.

grass snake *n.* Any of several greenish, nonvenomous snakes; especially, *Natrix natrix*, of Europe, which is brownish-green with darker markings.

grass tree *n.* Any of several woody-stemmed Australian plants of the genus *Xanthorrhoea*, having stiff, grasslike leaves and a spike of small white flowers. They yield a gum used in making varnishes.

grass widow *n.* **1.** A woman whose husband is habitually or temporarily absent. **2.** A woman who is divorced or separated from her husband. [Earliest sense, "unwed mother", probably with an allusion to a bed of straw or grass as a symbol of illicit sexual conduct.]

grass wren *n.* Any of various small Australian songbirds of the genus *Amytormis*, typically having a brown body and tail and a whitish breast.

grass-y (gráa-si ‖ grássi) *adj.* **-i-er, -i-est. 1.** Covered with grass. **2.** Resembling or suggestive of grass, as in colour or odour.

grate¹ (grayt) *v.* **grated, grating, grates.** —*tr.* **1.** To reduce to fragments, shreds, or powder by rubbing against an abrasive surface: *grate cabbage.* **2.** To cause to make a harsh grinding or rasping sound through friction. **3.** *Archaic.* To rub or wear away. —*intr.* **1.** To make a harsh rasping sound by or as if by scraping or grinding. **2.** To cause irritation or annoyance. Sometimes used with *on: grate on one's nerves.* ~*n.* A harsh, rasping sound made by scraping or rubbing: *the grate of a key in a lock.* [Middle English *graten*, from Old French *grater*, to scrape, from Germanic.] —**grat-ing-ly** *adv.*

grate² *n.* **1.** A framework of parallel or latticed bars used to hold the fuel in a stove, furnace, or fireplace. **2.** A similar framework used to block an opening; a grille; a grating. **3.** A fireplace. **4.** A perforated iron plate or screen for sieving and grading crushed ore. ~*tr.v.* **grated, grating, grates.** To equip with a grate. [Middle English, from Old French, grille, from Vulgar Latin *grata* (unattested), variant of Latin *crātis*, wickerwork, hurdle.]

grate-ful (gráyt-fl) *adj.* **1.** Appreciative of benefits received; thankful. **2.** Expressing gratitude. **3.** Affording pleasure or comfort; welcome: "*he left his home to enjoy the grateful air*" (Ronald Firbank). [From obsolete *grate*, agreeable, thankful, from Latin *grātus*, pleasing, favourable.] —**grate-ful-ly** *adv.* —**grate-ful-ness** *n.*

grat-er (gráytər) *n.* **1.** One that grates. **2.** An implement with rough or sharp-edged slits and perforations on which to shred or grate foods.

grat-i-cule (grátti-kewl) *n.* **1.** A grid of meridians and parallels derived from a particular projection, used in drawing a map. **2.** *Optics.* A grid or pattern used to establish scale or position, placed in the eyepiece of an optical instrument. Also called "reticle", "reticule". [French, from Latin *crāticula*, gridiron, diminutive of *crātis*, wickerwork, hurdle.]

grat-i-fi-ca-tion (grátti-fi-káysh'n) *n.* **1.** The act of gratifying. **2.** The condition of being gratified; satisfaction; pleasure. **3.** An instance or cause of gratification. **4.** *Archaic.* A reward; a gratuity; a bonus.

grat-i-fy (grátti-fī) *tr.v.* **-fied, -fying, -fies. 1.** To please or satisfy: *His achievement gratified his father.* **2.** To indulge; give in to (a desire, for example). **3.** *Archaic.* To requite; reward. [Middle English *gra-*

tifien, to favour, from Old French, from Latin *grātificārī*, to reward, do favour to, from *grātus*, favourable, pleasurable.] —**grat-i-fi-er** *n.*

grat-i-fy-ing (grátti-fī-ing) *adj.* Causing pleasure and satisfaction, as to the self-esteem: *his interest in the project is most gratifying.* —**grat-i-fy-ing-ly** *adv.*

gra-tin (gráttan ‖ *U.S. also* grátt'n, gráat'n) *n.* A rich baked crust on dishes that have been topped with grated cheese or buttered crumbs. [French, from Old French, from *grater*, to GRATE (scrape).]

grat-ing (gráyting) *n.* **1.** A grille or network of bars set in a window or door or used as a partition; a lattice; a grate. **2.** *Physics.* **Diffraction grating** (*see*).

gra-tis (gráa-tiss, gráy-, gráttiss) *adv.* Freely; for nothing; without charge. ~*adj.* Free; gratuitous. [Middle English, from Latin *grātīs*, reduced form of *grātiīs*, without reward, as a favour, from *grātia*, favour, from *grātus*, favourable.]

grat-i-tude (grátti-tewd ‖ -tood) *n.* An appreciative awareness and thankfulness, as for kindness shown or a gift received. [Middle English, from Old French, from Medieval Latin *grātitūdō*, from *grātus*, favourable.]

gra-tu-i-tous (grə-téw-i-təss ‖ -tóō-) *adj.* **1.** *Law.* Given or granted without return or recompense. **2.** Given or received without cost or obligation; free; gratis. **3.** Unnecessary or unwarranted; unjustified: *gratuitous criticism.* [Latin *grātuītus*, given as a favour, from *grātus*, favourable, pleasing.] —**gra-tu-i-tous-ly** *adv.* —**gra-tu-i-tous-ness** *n.*

gra-tu-i-ty (grə-téw-əti ‖ -tóō-) *n., pl.* **-ties. 1.** A material favour or gift, usually in the form of money, given in return for service; a tip. **2.** *British.* A sum of money given on retirement or discharge in token of long service. See Synonyms at **bonus**. [Old French *gratuite*, from Medieval Latin *grātuitās* (stem *grātuitāt-*), present, gift, from Latin *grātuītus*, given free, GRATUITOUS.]

grat-u-lant (gráttew-lənt) *adj. Archaic.* Congratulatory.

grat-u-late (gráttew-layt) *tr.v.* **-lated, -lating, -lates.** *Archaic.* **1.** To greet with pleasure; welcome. **2.** To congratulate. [Latin *grātulārī*, to greet, salute, from *grātus*, pleasing, GRATEFUL.] —**grat-u-la-tion** (-láysh'n) *n.* —**grat-u-la-to-ry** (-lə-tri, -lay-, -láy-, -təri) *adj.*

graunch (grawnch) *v.* **graunched, graunching, graunches.** *Informal.* —*intr.* To make a grinding or crunching sound. —*tr.* **1.** To cause to graunch. **2.** To damage (a mechanism). [Imitative.]

graunch-y (gráwn-chi) *adj.* **-ier, -iest.** *Chiefly N.Z. Informal.* Trying; testing.

grau-pel (grówp'l) *n.* Precipitation consisting of pellets of snow. Also called "snow pellets", "soft hail". [German *Graupel*, diminutive of *Graupe*, hulled grain, groats, probably from Serbo-Croat *krupa*.]

grav (grav) *n.* A unit of acceleration equal to the acceleration of free fall or 9.807 metres per second per second. [Shortened from *gravity*.]

gra-va-men (grə-váy-men, -mən) *n., pl.* **-vamina** (-vámminə). **1.** *Law.* **a.** The part of a charge or accusation that weighs most substantially against the accused. **b.** The essential part of a complaint. **2.** A grievance. [Late Latin *gravāmen*, grievance, from Latin *grāvāre*, to weigh down, burden, from *gravis*, heavy, GRAVE.]

grave¹ (grayv) *n.* **1. a.** A hole dug in the ground to receive a corpse. **b.** A tombstone, mound, or other marker indicating such a burial place. **2.** Any place of burial or final laying to rest: *The sea was his grave.* **3.** The sign or marker of a burial place. **4.** *Poetic.* Death or extinction. —**dig (one's) own grave.** To be the cause of one's own failure or downfall. —**turn in (one's) grave.** To feel shock or disapproval at some modern event or action that runs counter to one's beliefs or ideas. Used of a dead person. [Middle English *grave*, Old English *græf*, from Germanic.]

grave² (grayv; graav *for sense 6*) *adj.* **graver, gravest. 1.** Extremely serious; important; weighty: *a grave decision in a time of crisis.* **2.** Fraught with danger; critical: *in grave difficulties.* **3.** Grievous; dire: *a grave sin.* **4.** Dignified in conduct; sedate: *a grave procession.* **5.** Sombre or worried: *a grave expression.* **6.** *Linguistics.* **a.** Written with or modified by the mark (` `), as the *è* in *Sèvres.* **b.** Articulated towards the back of the oral cavity. —See Synonyms at **serious.** ~*n.* (graav). A grave accent, (` `), as one indicating a pronounced *e* for the sake of metre in the usually nonsyllabic ending *-ed* in English poetry. [Old French, from Latin *gravis*, heavy, weighty.] —**grave-ly** *adv.* —**grave-ness** *n.*

grave³ (grayv) *tr.v.* **graved, graven** (gráyv'n), **graving, graves. 1.** To stamp or impress deeply; fix (words or ideas, for example) permanently. **2.** *Archaic.* To sculpt or carve; engrave: "*I wish I could grave my sonnets on an ivory tablet.*" (Oscar Wilde). [Grave, graven; Middle English *graven, graven*, Old English *grafan* (dig, engrave), *grafen*, from Germanic; akin to GRAVE (place of burial).]

grave⁴ (grayv) *tr.v.* **graved, graving, graves.** To clean (the bottom of a wooden ship) by removing barnacles and other accretions, and coating with pitch. [Middle English *graven*, probably from Old French *greve, grave*, sand, GRAVEL.]

gra-ve⁵ (gráa-vay, -vi) *adv. Music.* Slowly and solemnly. Used as a direction. [Italian, from Latin *gravis*, heavy, weighty, GRAVE.] —**gra-ve** *adj.*

grave-clothes (gráyv-klōthz, -klōz) *pl.n.* The clothes or shroud in which a body is interred.

grave-dig-ger (gráyv-diggər) *n.* A person whose occupation is digging graves.

grav-el (grávv'l) *n.* **1.** Any unconsolidated mixture of rock frag-

ments or pebbles. **2.** *Pathology.* Sandlike granular material occurring in the kidneys or bladder.
~*tr.v.* **gravelled** or *U.S.* **graveled, -velling** or *U.S.* **-veling, -vels.** **1.** To apply a surface of gravel to: *gravel a drive.* **2.** *Rare.* To confuse; perplex: *His inconsistencies gravel the reader.* [Middle English, from Old French *gravele, gravelle,* diminutive of *grave, greve,* gravel, sand, pebbly shore, from Celtic.]

grav·el-blind (grávv'l-blīnd) *adj. Literary.* Having minimal vision; purblind. [GRAVEL + BLIND (by analogy with SANDBLIND).]

graven image *n.* An idol or fetish carved in wood or stone.

grav·er (gráyvər) *n.* **1.** A person who carves or engraves; a stonecarver. **2.** An engraver's cutting tool; a burin.

grave robber *n.* A person who plunders valuables from tombs or graves or who steals corpses, as for illicit dissection.

Graves (graav) *n.* A dry, usually white wine produced near Bordeaux, in southwestern France. [After *Graves,* district in southwestern France.]

Graves (grayvz), **Robert (Ranke)** (1895–1985). British poet, novelist, and critic. As a war poet, he published *Over the Brazier* (1916) and *Fairies and Fusiliers* (1917) while serving in Europe during World War I. His novels include *I, Claudius* (1934) and a semiautobiographical work on the postwar generation, *Goodbye to All That* (1929).

Graves' disease (grayvz) *n. Pathology.* **Exophthalmic goitre** (see). [After Robert James *Graves* (1796–1853), Irish physician.]

Graves·end (gráyvz-énd). A port in Kent, situated on the river Thames in southeast England.

grave·stone (gráyv-stōn) *n.* A stone placed over a grave as a marker; a tombstone.

grave·yard (gráyv-yaard) *n.* **1.** An area set aside as a burial ground, especially a small area around a church. **2.** An event or circumstance leading to the final ruin or failure of someone or something: *the graveyard of all our hopes.*

grav·id (grávvid) *adj.* **1.** Pregnant. **2.** Full of ripe eggs or distended by such fullness: *a fish gravid with roe.* [Latin *gravidus,* pregnant, from *gravis,* heavy.] **—gra·vid·i·ty** (grə-víddəti, gra-), **grav·id·ness** *n.* **—grav·id·ly** *adv.*

gra·vim·e·ter (grə-vímmitər, gra-, grávvi-meetər) *n.* **1.** Any instrument used to determine relative density. **2.** Any instrument used to measure the earth's gravitational field at a given point on its surface. [French *gravimètre* : Latin *gravis,* heavy, GRAVE + -METER.]

grav·i·met·ric (grávvi-méttrik) *adj.* Also **grav·i·met·ri·cal** (-méttrik'l). Of or pertaining to measurement by weight: *gravimetric analysis.* Compare **volumetric.** [Latin *gravis,* heavy, GRAVE + METRIC.] **—grav·i·met·ri·cal·ly** *adv.* **—gra·vim·e·try** (grə-vímmitri, gra-) *n.*

graving dock *n.* A dry dock in which ships are repaired and their bottoms are cleaned.

grav·i·tas (grávvi-tass) *n. Latin.* A solemn, grave manner or bearing.

grav·i·tate (grávvi-tayt) *intr.v.* **-tated, -tating, -tates.** **1.** To move in response to the force of gravity. **2.** To move downwards; sink; settle. **3.** To be attracted by or as if by an irresistible force. Used with *to* or *towards*: *"My excuse must be that all Celts gravitate towards each other."* (Oscar Wilde). [New Latin *gravitare,* from Latin *gravitās,* GRAVITY.] **—grav·i·tat·er** *n.*

grav·i·ta·tion (grávvi-táysh'n) *n.* **1.** *Physics.* **a.** The natural phenomenon of attraction between massive bodies. **b.** The action or process of moving under the influence of this attraction. **c.** The degree of such attraction. **2.** Any movement towards a source of attraction or place of settlement: *the gravitation of the middle classes to the suburbs.* **—grav·i·ta·tion·al** (-táysh'n'l), **grav·i·ta·tive** (-tətiv, -taytiv) *adj.* **—grav·i·ta·tion·al·ly** *adv.*

gravitational constant *n. Symbol* **G** The universal constant used in Newton's law of gravitation. It is equal to $Fd^2/m_1m_2,$ where F is the gravitational force between two masses, m_1 and $m_2,$ separated by a distance of $d.$ It has the value 6.670×10^{-11} N m^2 kg$^{-2}.$

gravitational field *n.* The region of space in which one massive body exerts a force of attraction on another massive body. The force is inversely proportional to the square of the distance between the bodies and directly proportional to the product of their masses.

gravitational interaction *n.* The interaction that occurs between bodies as a result of their mass. It is the weakest of all forms of interaction. Compare **strong interaction, weak interaction, electromagnetic interaction.**

gravitational mass *n.* The mass of a body as determined by its response to a gravitational field, especially to the force of gravity. Compare **inertial mass.**

grav·i·ton (grávvi-ton) *n.* A particle postulated to be the quantum of gravitational interaction, and presumed to have zero electric charge, zero rest mass, and spin 2. [GRAVIT(ATION) + -ON.]

grav·i·ty (grávvəti) *n.* **1.** *Physics.* **a.** The force of gravitation, being, for any two sufficiently massive bodies, directly proportional to the product of their masses and inversely proportional to the square of the distance between them; especially, the attractive gravitational force exerted by a celestial body, such as the Earth on bodies on or near its surface. **b.** Loosely, gravitation. **c.** *Rare.* Weight. **2.** Grave nature or seriousness: *the gravity of their problem.* **3.** Solemnity or dignity of manner: *"With stern and austere gravity he persevered in his task"* (Sir Walter Scott). [Old French *gravite,* from Latin *gravitās* (stem *gravitāt-*), from *gravis,* heavy, serious, GRAVE.]

gravity cell *n.* An electrolytic cell with the electrodes in two different electrolytes, which are separated into two vertical layers as a result of differences in their relative densities.

gravity feed *n.* **1.** A method of supplying a fuel, lubricant, or other liquid to an engine, boiler, or plant, that relies on gravity rather than a pump. **2.** A system for providing a continuous supply of a powder or granular solid by allowing it to trickle from the base of a container, as, for example, the system used to supply fuel to a boiler.

gra·vure (grə-véwr ‖ *U.S. also* gray-) *n.* **1.** A method of printing with etched plates or cylinders; intaglio printing. **2.** A tonal reproduction process using photomechanically prepared plates or cylinders to reproduce photographs on newsprint; photogravure. **3.** A plate or reproduction produced by gravure or used in the process. [French, from *graver,* to engrave, dig into, from Old French, from Frankish *graban* (unattested).]

gra·vy (gráyvi) *n., pl.* **-vies. 1. a.** The juices that drip from cooking meat. **b.** A sauce made by thickening and seasoning these juices. **2.** *Chiefly U.S. Slang.* Money or profit easily or unexpectedly gained; especially, money in excess of that required for necessities. [Middle English *gravey,* perhaps a misreading of Old French *grané,* "(dish) seasoned with grains (of spice)", from *grain,* spice, GRAIN.]

gravy boat *n.* An elongated vessel with a lip, used for serving gravy.

gravy train *n. Chiefly U.S. Slang.* An occupation or job that requires little effort while yielding considerable profit.

gray¹. *U.S.* Variant of **grey.**

gray² (gray) *n. Abbr.* **Gy.** The SI unit of absorbed dose of ionising radiation equal to the energy in joules absorbed by one kilogram of irradiated material. [After L.H. *Gray* (1905–65), British radiobiologist.]

Gray (gray), **Thomas** (1716–71). English poet. He was educated at Cambridge where he spent most of his life as a scholar and professor of history and modern languages. His most famous poem, *Elegy Written in a Country Churchyard* (1751), won him the offer of the poet laureateship in 1757 which he declined.

gray·ling (gráyling) *n., pl.* **-lings** or collectively **grayling,** (for sense 1). **1.** Any of several freshwater food fishes of the genus *Thymallus,* of the Northern Hemisphere, having a small mouth and a large dorsal fin. **2.** Any of several greyish or brownish butterflies of the family Satyridae, especially the European species *Eumenis semele.*

Gray's Inn (grayz) *n.* One of the four legal societies forming the **Inns of Court** (see) in England.

Graz (graats). Formerly **Gratz.** The second largest city in Austria, situated on the river Mur in the southeast of the country. It is the capital of Styria province.

graze¹ (grayz) *v.* **grazed, grazing, grazes.** *—intr.* **1.** To feed on growing grasses and herbage. **2.** To pasture livestock. *—tr.* **1.** To put (livestock) out to feed. **2.** To tend (feeding livestock) in a pasture. **3.** To feed on (pasture). [Middle English *grasen,* to feed on grass, Old English *grasian,* from *græs,* GRASS.] **—graz·er** *n.*

graze² *v.* **grazed, grazing, grazes.** *—tr.* **1.** To touch lightly in passing; skim; brush. **2.** To scrape or scratch slightly; abrade. *—intr.* To scrape or touch something lightly in passing.
~*n.* **1.** A brushing or scraping along a surface. **2.** A scratch or abrasion resulting from such contact. [Perhaps from GRAZE (remove grass close to the ground).]

gra·zi·er (gráy-zi-ər, -zhi-, -zhər) *n.* A person who grazes and fattens cattle.

graz·ing (gráyzing) *n.* Land used for feeding; pasturage.

gra·zi·o·so (gráat-si-ō-zō, -sō) *adv. Music.* Gracefully; smoothly. Used as a direction. [Italian, from Latin *grātiōsus,* GRACIOUS.] **—gra·zi·o·so** *adj.*

grease (greess) *n.* **1.** Animal fat when melted or soft. **2.** Any thick oil or viscous lubricant. **3. a.** The oily substance present in raw wool; suint. **b.** Raw wool that has not been cleansed of this. In this sense, also called "grease wool", "wool in the grease".
~*v.* (greess, greez) **greased, greasing, greases.** *—tr.* **1.** To coat, smear, lubricate, or soil with grease. **2.** To smear (a cake tin, frying pan, or the like) with cooking fat. *—intr. Chiefly British Slang.* To behave in an unctuous or ingratiating manner. **—grease up to.** *Slang.* To behave in an ingratiating manner towards: *He's always greasing up to the teacher.* [Middle English *grese,* from Old French *graisse,* from Vulgar Latin *crassia* (unattested), from Latin *crassus,* fat.]

grease cup *n.* A small cuplike container in which grease is stored and fed through a narrow tube into a bearing.

grease gun *n.* A device consisting of a cylinder fitted with a plunger and a nozzle, which forces grease from the cylinder into the grease nipple of a bearing.

grease monkey *n. Informal.* A mechanic.

grease nipple *n.* A **nipple** (see) on a bearing.

greasepaint (gréess-paynt) *n.* Theatrical make-up. Also called "paint".

grease-proof paper (gréess-prōōf ‖ -prŏŏf) *adj.* Paper that withstands grease and is used especially for wrapping food.

greas·er (grée-sər, -zər) *n. Slang.* **1.** *British.* A mechanic or engineer, especially on a ship. **2.** *British.* A member of a gang of motorcyclists. **3.** *Chiefly British.* A person who behaves in an unctuous and ingratiating manner.

grease·wood (gréess-wŏŏd) *n.* **1.** A spiny shrub, *Sarcobatus vermiculatus,* of western North America, the oil from which has been used as fuel. **2.** Any of various similar or related plants, such as the **creosote bush** (see).

greas·y (grée-si, -zi) *adj.* **-ier, -iest. 1.** Coated or soiled with grease. **2.** Containing grease, especially too much grease. **3.** Suggestive of or resembling something greased; slick; unctuous: *a greasy character.* **—greas·i·ly** *adv.* **—greas·i·ness** *n.*

greasy pole *n.* **1.** *Sports. British.* A greased pole that competitors try to climb up or walk on. **2.** A difficult or challenging route to success. Preceded by *the.*

greasy spoon *n. Informal.* A small, cheap, usually dirty restaurant that sells unappetising food.

great (grayt) *adj.* **greater, greatest.** *Abbr.* **gt. 1.** Extremely large; bulky; big. **2.** Larger than others of the same kind: *the great auk.* **3.** Large in quantity or number: *A great throng awaited him.* **4.** Of considerable duration; extensive in time or distance. **5.** Extreme in magnitude, degree, or extent: *a great mistake.* **6.** Significant; important; meaningful: *A great work of art.* **7.** Chief or principal: *the great house on the estate.* **8.** Superior in quality or character; noble; excellent. **9.** Powerful; influential: *"Seek to be good, but aim not to be great."* (George Lyttelton). **10.** Eminent; distinguished: *a great leader.* **11.** Grand; aristocratic. **12.** *Archaic.* Pregnant. Used with *with: great with child.* **13.** *Informal.* Enthusiastic: *a great boxing fan.* **14.** *Informal.* Skilful: *He's great at algebra.* **15.** *Informal.* First-rate; very good: *a great book.* **16.** Used as an intensive, especially in exclamations: *great balls of fire!* **17.** *Archaic.* Capital; upper case. Said of letters: *a great A.* **18.** Designating a relative one generation removed from the relative specified. Used in combination: *a great-grandfather.* **—be great on.** *Informal.* **1.** To be keen on. **2.** To be knowledgeable about. —See Synonyms at **large.**
~*n. Plural.* Outstanding individuals: *Many of the sport's greats were there.*
~*adv. Chiefly U.S. Informal.* Very well. [Middle English *grete,* Old English *great,* thick, coarse, from Germanic.] **—great·ness** *n.*

great ape *n.* Any large anthropoid ape, such as a gorilla or orang-utan.

Great Artesian Basin. Also **Great Australian Basin.** Largest artesian area in the world. It lies in eastern Australia, between the Great Dividing Range and Western Plateau, and stretches northwards to the Gulf of Carpentaria, an area of some 1 750 000 square kilometres (676,250 square miles). It derives its water from the Eastern Highlands.

great auk *n.* A large, flightless sea bird, *Pinguinus impennis,* formerly common on northern Atlantic coasts but extinct since the middle of the 19th century.

great-aunt (grayt-aant || -ant) *n.* A sister of one's grandparent. Also called "grand-aunt".

Great Australian Bight. A broad bay in the coast of southern Australia. It extends from West Cape in Western Australia to South West Cape in Tasmania.

Great Barrier Reef. Largest coral reef in the world, situated in the Coral Sea off the coast of northeastern Australia. It extends from the Torres Strait, along the coast of Queensland almost to southern New Guinea, a distance of some 2 012 kilometres (1,250 miles). Its banks of vividly coloured corals teem with exotic fish and crustaceans, and there are coral islets overgrown with mangroves, palms, and flowering plants.

Great Basin. Region of the western United States, lying between the Wasatch mountains and the Sierra Nevada. Covering an area of about 518 000 square kilometres (200,000 square miles), it consists of steep-sided block mountains with broad plains between. Though not entirely arid, it includes Death Valley and the Mojave and Great Salt Lake deserts.

Great Bear *n. Astronomy.* A constellation, **Ursa Major** *(see).*

Great Bear Lake. Lake in Mackenzie district in Northwest Territories, Canada. It is 31 800 square kilometres (12,275 square miles) in area, the largest lake in Canada.

Great Brit·ain (britt'n). The largest island in Europe, situated in the northwest of the continent and separated from the mainland by the English Channel. The name has been used since 1707 to denote the political union of England, Scotland, and Wales. Great Britain excludes the Isle of Man and Channel Islands, as well as the province of Northern Ireland. It is often loosely referred to as Britain. See also **United Kingdom.**

great circle *n.* A circle that is the intersection of the surface of a sphere with a plane passing through the centre of the sphere. Compare **small circle.**

great·coat (grayt-kōt) *n.* A heavy overcoat.

Great Dane *n.* A very large and powerful dog of a breed developed in Germany, having a smooth, short coat and a narrow head.

Great Divide *n.* **1.** The **Continental Divide** *(see).* **2. a.** An important dividing point or line. **b.** Death. Used euphemistically. **3.** The Great Dividing Range.

Great Dividing Range. Also **Great Divide.** Belt of highlands and plateaus in eastern Australia, extending roughly parallel to the coast, from the base of the Cape York peninsula to the Grampians. Acting as the watershed of the eastern seaboard, it is only partially mountainous, but includes the Australian Alps which rise to 2 230 metres (7,316 feet) at Mount Kosciusko.

great·en (grayt'n) *v.* **-ened, -ening, -ens.** *Archaic.* —*tr.* To make great or greater; enlarge. —*intr.* To become great or greater.

Great·er (graytər) *adj.* Designating a city and its immediate suburbs: *Greater London.*

Greater Antilles. Northern part of the chain of islands which separates the Caribbean Sea from the main body of the Atlantic Ocean. It includes Cuba, Jamaica, Hispaniola (Haiti and the Dominican Republic), and Puerto Rico, the four largest islands in the West Indies. See also **Lesser Antilles.** See map at **Latin America.**

greater doxology *n.* The **Gloria in excelsis Deo** *(see).*

Greater London. See **London.**

Greater Manchester. Former metropolitan county in northwestern England, now administratively subdivided. It included the cities Manchester and Salford, and the towns Wigan, Bolton, Bury, Rochdale, Oldham, Ashton-Under-Lyne, and Stockport.

Greater New York. See **New York.**

great·est (gráy-tist). Superlative of **great.**
~*n.* **—the greatest.** *Informal.* A wonderful or admirable person or thing.

Great Glen. Also **Glen Al·byn** (álbin) or **Glen Mòr** (mòr). Valley in northwest Scotland. It stretches for about 97 kilometres (60 miles) from the Moray Firth to Loch Linnhe. The valley was formed by a fault in the earth's crust, and the glacial lakes formed along the fault line, including Loch Ness, have a depth hundreds of feet below sea level.

great-grand·child (grayt-grán-chīld, -gránd-) *n., pl.* **-children** (-childrən). Any of the children of a grandchild.

great-grand-daugh·ter (grayt-grán-dawtər, -gránd-) *n.* Any daughter of a grandchild.

great-grand·fa·ther (grayt-grán-faathər, -gránd-) *n.* The father of any grandparent.

great-grand·moth·er (grayt-grán-muthər, -gránd-) *n.* The mother of any grandparent.

great-grand·par·ent (grayt-grán-pair-ənt, -gránd-) *n.* Either of the parents of any grandparent.

great-grand·son (grayt-grán-sun, -gránd-) *n.* Any of the sons of a grandchild.

Great Grimsby. See **Grimsby.**

great gross *n. Abbr.* **g.gr.** A dozen gross.

great-heart·ed (grayt-hártid) *adj.* **1.** Noble or courageous in spirit; stout-hearted. **2.** Great in generosity; unselfish; magnanimous. **—great-heart·ed·ly** *adv.* **—great-heart·ed·ness** *n.*

Great Lake. The largest natural freshwater lake in Australia, lying in the central uplands of Tasmania. It has a surface area of 142 square kilometres (54 square miles) but an average depth of only 13 metres (43 feet). It is used as a hydroelectric reservoir.

Great Lakes. Five freshwater lakes in central North America, forming part of the boundary between Canada and the United States. From east to west they are Lake Ontario, Lake Erie, Lake Huron, Lake Michigan, and Lake Superior, and together they form the world's largest area of fresh water. Only Lake Michigan is wholly in the United States. They were formed at the end of the last Ice Age, when their glacier-carved basins filled with meltwater. The largest of the lakes, and the largest freshwater lake in the world, is Lake Superior; the smallest is Lake Erie, which is also the only one of the five whose depth does not extend below sea level.

great·ly (grayt-li) *adv.* **1.** In a style or manner befitting greatness; nobly. **2.** To a great degree; very much; exceedingly.

great-neph·ew (grayt-névvew, -néffew) *n.* A son of a nephew or niece. Also called "grand-nephew".

great-niece (grayt-neess) *n.* A daughter of a nephew or niece. Also called "grand-niece".

great organ *n.* The principal manual, together with its pipes, of an organ that has more than one manual.

Great Ouse (ōoz). River in southern England, sometimes referred to simply as the Ouse. It rises in Northamptonshire and flows northeast for about 250 kilometres (155 miles) until it empties into The Wash near King's Lynn, Norfolk.

Great Plains. Vast area of short grassland in North America, stretching from the Mackenzie delta in the north to southern Texas. The plains slope generally eastwards from the foot of the Rocky Mountains to about 100°W, where they merge with the wetter prairies. Most of the area is given over to ranches for cattle or sheep. In the east, wheat is grown where there is sufficient water, but soil erosion can be a problem as in the Dust Bowl, produced in the 1930s. The Great Plains have vast mineral resources, including oil, gas, coal, and gold.

Great Power *n.* A nation that has great military strength and economic influence; a superpower.

great primer *n. Printing.* Formerly, a size of type, 18-point.

Great Rebellion *n.* The English **Civil War** *(see).* Preceded by *the.*

Great Red Spot *n. Astronomy.* A feature of Jupiter, the **Red Spot** *(see).*

Great Rift Valley. An extended geological fault system, stretching for about 6 400 kilometres (4,000 miles) from northern Syria, through the trough of the Red Sea and south as far as central Mozambique. For much of its length its traces have been lost by erosion, but in some parts, most spectacularly in southern Kenya, its cliffs rise thousands of feet. In Africa the valley has a western and eastern branch, with lakes and volcanoes.

Great Russian *n.* **1.** A member of the main ethnic group of Russian-speaking people, inhabiting Russia and some of the former Soviet Republics. **2.** The language of these people that is the official Russian language.
~*adj.* Of or pertaining to this people or their language.

Greats (grayts) *pl.n.* At Oxford University: **1.** The final examination sat for a B.A. in classics with philosophy. Compare **Mods. 2.** The course for this examination.

Great Salt Lake. A shallow saltwater lake lying in northeastern Utah in the United States. It is the largest saltwater lake in North America, with a surface area of about 2 600 square kilometres (1,000 square miles). Its size and depth vary from year to year, according to climatic conditions, but its average depth is about 4 metres (13 feet).

Great Sanhedrin n. The **Sanhedrin** (see).

Great Schism n. The division in the Roman Catholic Church from 1378 to 1417, when rival popes ruled at Rome and Avignon.

great seal n. Often capital **G**, capital **S**. The principal seal of a government, sovereign, or state, used to stamp very important official documents.

Great Slave Lake. Canada's second largest lake, in the Mackenzie district, Northwest Territories. It is the deepest lake in North America, reaching a depth of 615 metres (2,015 feet).

Great Spirit n. The principal deity in the religion of many North American Indian tribes.

Great St. Bernard Pass. See **St. Bernard Passes.**

great tit n. A common European bird, Parus major, the largest of the tits, having a black and white head, greenish back, and yellow and black breast.

Great Trek n. In South Africa, the migration, from the mid-1830s to the mid-1840s, of Boer farmers northwards away from the Cape in order to find lands free from British rule. Preceded by the.

great-un·cle (gráyt-úng-k'l) n. The uncle of one's father or mother. Also called "grand-uncle".

Great Wall of China. Chinese **Wan-li chang-cheng** (wán-lée cháng-chóng). A fortification, consisting of walls, watchtowers, and guard stations, running for 2 400 kilometres (1,500 miles) in a winding course across northern China from Gansu province to Hebei province. For most of its length it runs along the southern border of the Mongolian plain. It was built originally to keep out nomadic invaders from the north and the first continuous wall was built in the third century B.C. Most of the present wall was built during the Ming dynasty (1368–1644). The average height of the wall is 7.5 metres (25 feet) and the average thickness at the base is about 7 metres (23 feet), although at most points it tapers to only about 3.5 metres (11 feet) at the top.

Great War n. World War I (see). Preceded by the.

great white hope n. A person or thing in whom great expectations of success or achievement are placed. [Originally U.S.; used in boxing of a favourite white boxer challenging a black champion.]

great white shark n. A **white shark** (see).

Great Yar·mouth (yárməth). Port and tourist resort in Norfolk, England. Built on a spit at the mouth of the river Yare, its fine harbour became one of the world's largest herring ports, and is famous for Yarmouth bloaters — slightly salted and smoked herrings.

great year n. A period of 25,800 years that is one complete cycle of the equinoxes.

greave (greev) n. Leg armour worn below the knee. [Middle English, from Old French grevet, shin.]

greaves (greevz) pl.n. The unmelted residue left after animal fat or tallow has been rendered. [Low German greven.]

grebe (greeb) n. Any of various diving birds of the family Podicipedidae, that have lobed, fleshy membranes along each toe and a pointed bill. [French grèbet.]

Gre·cian (gréesh'n) adj. **1.** Conforming to the styles and tastes of classical Greece. Said especially of architecture. **2.** Greek. ~n. One who studies or specialises in Greek language and literature. [Latin Graecia, Greece, from Graecus, GREEK.]

Grecian bend n. A posture in which the upper torso is thrust forwards and the pelvis and buttocks backwards, adopted by women of fashion in the late 19th century and often emphasised by wearing a bustle.

Grecian nose n. A long, straight nose extending in an unbroken line from the forehead.

Greco-. Chiefly U.S. Variant of **Graeco-.**

grecque (grek) adj. Cooked in olive oil, lemon juice, spices, and tomato purée: mushrooms à la grecque. [French, "Greek".]

gree¹ (gree) n. Archaic. Scottish. **1.** Superiority or victory. **2.** The prize or reward for victory. [Middle English, rank, from Old French gre, from Latin gradus, GRADE.]

gree² intr.v. **greed, greeing, grees.** Northern British. To be in harmony or agreement. [Aphetic variant of AGREE.]

Greece (greess). Ancient Greek **Hel·las** (héllass); Modern Greek **El·las** (e-laáss). Independent republic, officially called the Hellenic Republic, lying at the southern tip of the Balkan peninsula. It comprises an indented, mountainous mainland whose ranges continue in numerous islands which make up a fifth of the country. Cereals, olives, and vines are the chief crops, and large numbers of sheep and goats are kept. Greece relies mainly on imported fuels but oil

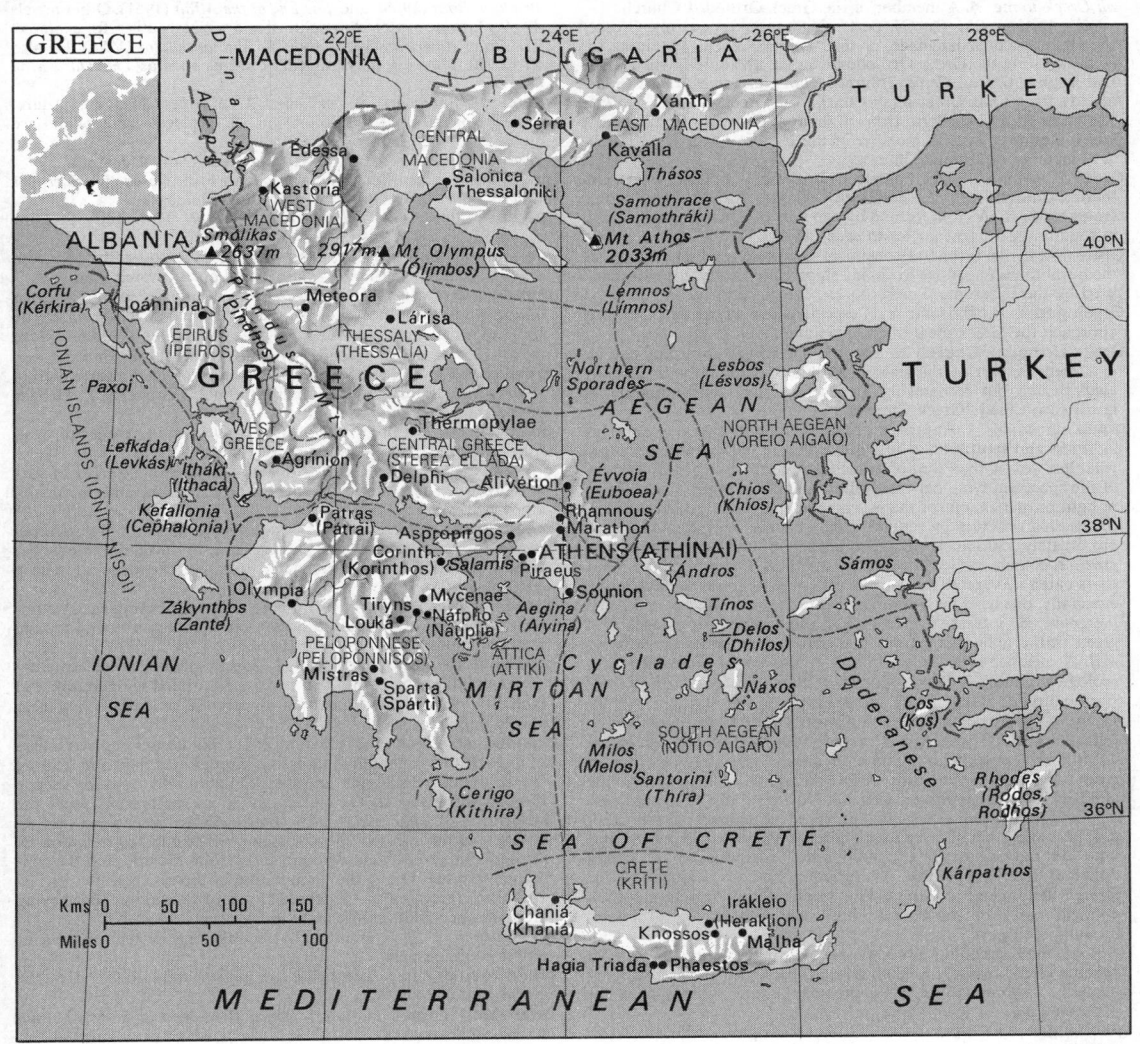

has been discovered beneath the Aegean Sea. Tourism is a major industry, and the country has large merchant and fishing fleets. Minoan civilisation, Europe's first, flourished in Crete (*c.*3000–1400 B.C.). Trade (*c.*1100 B.C.) brought prosperity and heralded the Classical age. Inter-city strife allowed Philip of Macedon to conquer most of Greece (338 B.C.), and his son Alexander (356–323 B.C.) ruled both Macedon and Greece and built a short-lived empire that was to spread Greek culture from Macedon and Egypt to India. The Romans conquered Greece (168–146 B.C.) and it was later part of the Byzantine Empire. It was conquered by the Ottoman Turks in the 15th century but finally gained independence (1832) and a king (1833), after the Greek War of Independence. The army usurped power and deposed the king (1967), but were removed in 1974 and Greece became a republic in 1975. The country became a full member of the European Economic Community (1981). It is also a strategic member of NATO, but has strained relations with fellow member Turkey over its claims in the Aegean and Cyprus. Area, 131 957 square kilometres (50,949 square miles). Population 10,470,000. Capital, Athens.

greed (greed) *n.* A rapacious desire for more than one needs or deserves, as of food, wealth, or power; avarice. [Back-formation from GREEDY.]

greed·y (gréedi) *adj.* **-ier, -iest. 1.** Excessively eager to acquire or possess something, especially in quantity; covetous; avaricious. **2.** Wanting to eat or drink more than one can reasonably consume; gluttonous; voracious. [Middle English *gredy*, Old English *grǣdig*, from Germanic *grǣdhuz* (unattested), hunger.] **—greed·i·ly** *adv.* **—greed·i·ness** *n.*

greed·y-guts (gréedi-gutss) *n. pl.* **-gutses** or **-gutsies.** *Chiefly British Informal.* A very greedy person. Often used humorously.

greegree. Variant of **grigri.**

Greek (greek) *n.* **1.** *Abbr.* **Gk., Gr.** The language of the Hellenes, constituting the Hellenic group of Indo-European, chronologically divided into **Proto-Greek, Ancient Greek** with the **Koine, Late Greek, Medieval Greek,** and **Modern Greek** (*all of which see*). *Note:* Most frequently *Greek* is used to mean *Ancient Greek* or *Classical Greek,* as in the etymologies of this dictionary. **2.** *Abbr.* **Gk., Gr.** A native or inhabitant of Greece, or a descendant of such a person. **3.** *Informal.* Something unintelligible. Used chiefly in the phrase *It's all Greek to me.* **4.** A member of the Greek Orthodox Church. *—adj.* **1.** *Abbr.* **Gk., Gr.** Of, pertaining to, or designating Greece, the Hellenes, their language, or their culture. **2.** Of, pertaining to, or designating the Greek Orthodox Church. [Middle English *Grek,* Old English *Grēcas, Crēcas* (plural), from Germanic *Krēkaz* (unattested), from Latin *Graecus* (singular), from Greek *Graikos, Graikoi,* the name of a prehistoric tribe of Epirus, probably from Illyria.]

Greek Catholic *n.* **1.** A member of the Eastern Orthodox Church. **2.** A member of a Uniat Church.

Greek Church *n.* **1.** The **Eastern Church** (*see*). **2.** The **Eastern Orthodox Church** (*see*). **3.** The Greek Orthodox Church.

Greek cross *n.* A cross formed by two bars of equal length crossing at the middle at right angles to each other.

Greek fire *n.* An incendiary chemical substance used in ancient and medieval times to set fire to enemy ships; specifically, the substance used by the Byzantine Greeks in the seventh century.

Greek god *n.* A handsome man, especially one whose looks seem to approach the Greek ideal of male beauty.

Greek Orthodox Church *n.* The established self-governing church of Greece, a part of the Eastern Orthodox Church, with its own chief bishop but recognising the Patriarch of Constantinople as head. Also called "Greek Church".

green (green) *n.* **1.** Any of a group of colours that may vary in lightness and saturation, whose hue is that of the emerald, or somewhat less yellow than that of growing grass; the hue of that portion of the spectrum lying between yellow and blue; one of the additive or light primaries; one of the psychological primary hues, evoked in the normal observer by radiant energy having a wavelength of approximately 530 nanometres. See **primary colour. 2. a.** Something green in colour. **b.** Green clothing. **3.** *Plural.* Leafy plants or plant parts eaten as vegetables or in salads. **4. a.** A grassy area or lawn; especially, one used for a specified purpose: *a putting green; a bowling green.* **b.** A grass-covered area in the middle of a village. **5.** A green traffic light that signals that drivers may proceed. **6.** *Informal.* A member of a political party or movement concerned with ecological issues. **7.** *Slang.* Money. **8.** *Slang.* Cannabis of an inferior quality. **9.** *Plural. Slang.* Sexual intercourse. *—adj.* **1.** Of the colour green. **2.** Covered with green vegetation or foliage. **3.** Made with green or leafy vegetables: *a green salad.* **4.** Mild or temperate in climate. **5.** Fresh; youthful; vigorous: *a green old age.* **6.** Not mature or ripe; young: *green bananas.* **7.** Pale and sickly in appearance; wan. **8.** Not yet fully processed, as: **a.** Not aged: *green wood.* **b.** Not cured or tanned: *green pelts.* **9.** Designating one of three quark colours, the others being red and blue. **10.** Lacking training, conditioning, or experience. **11.** Easily duped or deceived; gullible. **12.** *Informal.* Envious; jealous. **13.** *Informal.* Belonging to, supporting, designating, or relating to a political party or movement concerned with ecological issues; broadly, ecological. *—v.* **greened, greening, greens.** *—tr.* To make green. *—intr.* To become green. [Middle English *grene,* Old English *grēne,* from Germanic.] **—green·ish** *adj.* **—green·ly** *adv.* **—green·ness** *n.* **—green·y** *adj.*

green algae *pl.n.* Algae of the division Chlorophyta, which includes spirogyra, sea lettuce, and others having pronounced green colouring due to predominance of the pigment chlorophyll.

Green·a·way (gréenə-way), **Kate** (1846–1901). English watercolourist and illustrator. She excelled as an illustrator of her own children's books, such as *Under the Window* (1879), *A Day in a Child's Life* (1881), and *Kate Greenaway's Birthday Album* (1885).

green·back (gréen-bak) *n.* *U.S. Informal.* **1.** An inconvertible legal-tender note of U.S. currency. **2.** A dollar bill.

green ban *n.* *Australian.* A refusal by a trade union to do work that may harm the environment.

green bean *n.* **1.** Any bean plant, especially the **French bean** (*see*), having green pods that are eaten when unripe. **2.** Any of these pods, used as food.

green belt *n.* An area of parks, farmland, or uncultivated land surrounding a town or city.

Green Beret *n.* *Informal.* A member of a U.S. commando unit.

green·bottle (gréen-bott'l) *n.* A common insect, *Lucilia caesar,* related to the blowflies, that has a green metallic colouring and lays its eggs in decaying flesh.

green·bri·er (gréen-brīr) *n.* Any of several thorny vines of the genus *Smilax;* especially, *S. rotundifolia,* having heart-shaped leaves, small green flowers, and blackish berries. Also called "cat brier".

green card *n.* **1.** An international insurance document for motorists. **2.** A U.S. permit for foreigners, allowing unconditional residence in the U.S.A.

green corn *n.* Young, tender ears of sweet corn.

Green Cross Code *n.* *British.* A set of rules or instructions designed to teach young children road safety.

green currency *n.* Formerly, any artificial currency unit, such as the green pound, used for agricultural transactions within the European Economic Community in order to protect Community prices from the currency fluctuations of the member nations. See **ECU.**

green dragon *n.* A plant, *Arisaema dracontium,* of eastern North America, having minute flowers at the base of a long stalk projecting from a narrow green bract. Also called "dragonroot".

Greene (green), **(Henry) Graham** (1904–91). British novelist and playwright. He wrote both serious and light novels, the former being marked by questions of morality and redemption (Greene was a convert to Roman Catholicism). Among his major works are *Brighton Rock* (1938), and *The End of the Affair* (1951). Other novels display Greene's interest in political and social troubles; for example, *The Quiet American* (1955) and *The Human Factor* (1978). He also wrote short stories, plays, and film scripts such as *The Third Man* (1949).

green·er·y (gréenəri) *n., pl.* **-ies. 1. a.** Green foliage; verdure. **b.** Such foliage used for decoration. **2.** A place where plants are grown.

green-eyed (gréen-īd) *adj.* **1.** Having green eyes. **2.** Jealous.

green·finch (gréen-finch) *n.* A Eurasian bird, *Carduelis chloris* (or *Chloris chloris*), having green and yellow plumage.

green fingers *pl.n. Chiefly British Informal.* The ability to grow plants successfully. Also *U.S.* "green thumb".

green·fly (gréen-flī) *n., pl.* **-flies** or collectively **greenfly.** A green aphid commonly occurring as a parasite on cultivated plants.

green·gage (gréen-gayj) *n.* **1.** A variety of plum, *Prunus domestica italica,* whose fruit has yellowish-green skin and sweet flesh. **2.** The fruit of this tree. [GREEN + *gage,* after Sir William *Gage* (1777–1864), English botanist, who introduced it into England.]

green gland *n.* Either of a pair of excretory organs in certain crustaceans that discharges waste matter through an opening at the base of the antennae.

green·gro·cer (gréen-grō-sər) *n. Chiefly British.* A retailer of fresh fruit and vegetables. **—green·gro·cer·y** *n.*

green·head (gréen-hed) *n.* **1.** A male mallard duck. **2.** Any of various green-headed Australian ants of the genus *Chalcopnera,* having a powerful sting.

green·heart (gréen-haart) *n.* **1.** A tropical American tree, *Ocotea rodioei* (or *Nectandra rodioei*), having dark, greenish, durable wood. **2.** Any of various similar or related trees. **3.** The wood of such a tree.

green·horn (gréen-hawrn) *n. Informal.* **1.** An inexperienced or immature person. **2.** A gullible person. [Originally, a young animal with immature horns.]

green·house (gréen-howss) *n.* **1.** A usually glass-enclosed structure used for cultivating plants that require controlled temperature and humidity. **2.** *Informal.* A part of an aircraft covered with a clear plastic bubble or shell.

greenhouse effect *n.* **1.** A heating effect that occurs in greenhouses as a result of solar radiation passing through the glass and heating the contents, which emit infrared radiation that cannot escape through the glass. **2.** The analogous effect that results from the absorption of solar radiation by the Earth, its conversion and re-emission in the infrared, the absorption of the infrared radiation by atmospheric ozone, water vapour, and carbon dioxide, and the consequent gradual rise in the temperature of the atmosphere.

green·ing¹ (gréening) *n.* An apple of any of several varieties having green-skinned fruit, used chiefly in cooking.

greening² *n.* *U.S. Informal.* The reawakening or rejuvenation of public consciousness.

green·keep·er (gréen-keepər) *n.* A person who looks after the greens of golf courses.

Green·land (gréen-lənd, -land). *Danish* **Grøn·land** (grôn-laan). *Inuit* **Ka·laa-llit Nu·naat** (ka-laá-hlit noo-naát). Island belonging to Denmark, lying mostly within the Arctic Circle. It is the largest island in the world. Most of the island is permanently ice-covered and uninhabited. The bulk of the population, which is of mixed Eskimo and European descent, is concentrated on the west coast. Fishing and fish processing are the principal industries and there is some mining. Greenland was discovered by Eric the Red in *c*.960, but modern settlement of the island dates from the early 18th century, when it came under Danish control. It became an integral part of Denmark (1953) but gained internal home rule in 1979. It has great strategic importance and there are U.S. air bases on it. Area 2 175 000 square kilometres (840,000 square miles). See map at **Arctic Ocean.** —**Green·land·er** *n.*

Greenland whale *n.* An arctic whale, *Balaena mysticetus,* having a black body with a pale throat.

Greenland spar *n.* A mineral, **cryolite** *(see).*

green leek *n.* Any of various green or mostly green Australian parrots.

green·let (gréenlit) *n.* Any of various greenish birds of the genus *Hylophilus,* of Central and South America, related to the vireos.

green light *n.* **1.** The green-coloured traffic light, meaning "go". **2.** Permission to proceed with a project or course of action.

green·ling (gréenling) *n.* Any of various food fishes of the family Hexagrammidae, of the northern Pacific.

green man *n.* Especially in Britain, a pre-Christian spirit represented as a man dressed in foliage and often regarded as malevolent.

green manure *n.* A growing crop, such as a clover or grass, that is ploughed into soil to improve fertility.

green monkey *n.* Any of several African monkeys of the genus *Cercopithecus;* especially, *C. aethiops sabaeus,* having yellowish-grey fur with a greenish tinge.

green monkey disease *n.* **Marburg disease** *(see).*

Green·ock (gréen-ɔk, grínn-, grénn-). Burgh in Inverclyde, western Scotland, lying on the Firth of Clyde. It is a port, and shipping and shipbuilding are the chief industries.

green·ock·ite (gréenɔ-kīt) *n.* A yellow to brown or red mineral, essentially cadmium sulphide (CdS), used as a cadmium ore. [After Charles Cathcart, Lord *Greenock* (died 1859), British soldier.]

green paper *n.* In Britain, a government document published to allow consultation among interested parties before legislative proposals are finalised. Compare **white paper.** [From the colour of paper used (originating in the Department of Economic Affairs, 1967).]

green pepper *n.* The unripened green fruit of various pepper plants, especially the sweet pepper, eaten raw or cooked.

green plover *n.* A bird, the **lapwing** *(see).*

green pound *n.* See **green currency.**

green revolution *n.* The increased agricultural production in developing countries resulting from the introduction of new high-yielding crop varieties and modern farming techniques.

green·room (gréen-room, -room) *n.* A waiting room in a theatre, concert hall, television studio, or the like for the use of performers when off-stage. [From its being typically painted green.]

green·sand (gréen-sand) *n.* **1.** A sand or sediment given a dark greenish colour by grains of glauconite. **2.** *Often capital* **G.** Either of two formations of Cretaceous origin in Britain, the *Upper* or *Lower Greensand,* consisting of this sediment.

green·shank (gréen-shangk) *n.* An Old World wading bird, *Tringa nebularia,* having greenish legs and a long bill.

green soap *n.* A translucent, yellowish-green, soft or liquid soap made chiefly from vegetable oils, potassium hydroxide, oleic acid, glycerine, and purified water, used medicinally as a stimulant in chronic skin disorders. Also called "soft soap".

green·stick fracture (gréen-stik) *n.* A fracture in a long bone of a child or young animal in which the bone is bent and splintered but not completely broken.

green·stone (gréen-stōn) *n.* **1.** Any of various altered basic igneous rocks coloured green by chlorite, hornblende, or epidote. **2.** The most common variety of jade, found in New Zealand and used for making tikis, ornaments, tools, or the like.

green·stuff (gréen-stuf) *n.* Green vegetables.

green·sward (gréen-swawrd) *n. Poetic.* Turf or short grass.

green tea *n.* Tea made from leaves that are not fermented before being dried. Compare **black tea.**

green thumb *n. Chiefly U.S.* **Green fingers** *(see).*

green turtle *n.* A large marine turtle, *Chelonia mydas,* having greenish flesh prized as food, used especially in turtle soup.

green vitriol *n.* A chemical compound, **ferrous sulphate** *(see).*

green·weed (gréen-weed) *n.* See **dyer's greenweed.**

Green·wich (grínn-ij, grénn-, -ich). An ancient village, now a borough in Greater London in England. It is the site of the original Royal Observatory, designed by Wren, through which passes the prime meridian, or longitude 0°. The Royal Naval College and the National Maritime Museum are also in the borough.

Green·wich mean time *n. Abbr.* **G.M.T.** Mean solar time for the meridian at Greenwich, England, used as a basis for calculating time throughout most of the world. Also called "Greenwich time".

Greenwich meridian *n.* The **prime meridian** *(see)* that passes through Greenwich in England.

Greenwich Village. Village dating from colonial times, now a residential quarter of lower Manhattan in New York City. Since the early 20th century it has been famous as an artists' and writers' quarter. Is is also renowned for its cafés and jazz clubs.

green·wood (gréen-wŏod) *n. Literary.* A wood or forest when the foliage is green.

Greer (greer), **Germaine** (1939–). Australian feminist and writer. Her books include the influential *Female Eunuch* (1970), which attacked marriage and the misrepresentation of female sexuality. She was director of the Tulsa (Oklahoma) Center for the Study of Women's Literature from 1979 to 1982.

greet[1] (greet) *tr.v.* **greeted, greeting, greets. 1.** To address in a friendly and respectful way. **2.** To receive or welcome in a friendly manner. **3.** To receive with a specified reaction: *greet a joke with laughter.* **4.** To present itself to; be perceived by: *A din greeted our ears.* [Middle English *greten,* Old English *grētan,* from Germanic.] —**greet·er** *n.*

greet[2] *intr.v.* **greeted, greeting, greets.** *Archaic & Scottish.* To cry; weep.

greet·ing (gréeting) *n.* **1.** An act or instance of greeting a person. **2.** *Often plural.* A gesture or word of welcome or salutation. Also used adjectively: *a greetings card.*

greg·a·rine (gréggɔ-reen, -rin ‖ *U.S. also* -rīn) *n.* Any of various sporozoan protozoans of the order Gregarinida, that are parasitic within invertebrates such as arthropods and annelids. ~*adj.* Of or belonging to the Gregarinida. [New Latin *Gregarina* (genus name), from Latin *gregārius,* GREGARIOUS.]

gre·gar·i·ous (gri-gaír-i-ɔss ‖ *U.S. also* -gárri-) *adj.* **1.** Tending to move in or form a group with others of the same kind, in a herd, pack, or flock. **2.** Seeking and enjoying the company of others of one's kind; sociable. **3.** *Botany.* Growing in groups that are close together but not densely clustered or matted. [Latin *gregārius,* belonging to a flock, from *grex* (stem *greg-*), herd, flock.] —**gre·gar·i·ous·ly** *adv.* —**gre·gar·i·ous·ness** *n.*

grège, greige (grayzh) *n.* Light greyish-brown.

Gre·go·ri·an (gri-gáwri-ɔn ‖ -góri-) *adj.* Pertaining to, associated with, or introduced by Pope Gregory I or Pope Gregory XIII.

Gregorian calendar *n.* The calendar now in use, introduced in 1582 by Pope Gregory XIII, as a corrected form of the earlier **Julian calendar** *(see).* The Gregorian calendar stipulates that each ordinary year consists of 365 days and each leap year, or year whose number is divisible by four, of 366 days except for centenary years whose numbers are not divisible by 400.

Gregorian chant *n.* The monodic liturgical plainsong of the Roman Catholic Church, systematised during the papacy of Gregory I. Also called "plainsong".

Greg·o·ry I (gréggɔri), **Saint,** known as Gregory the Great (*c.* 540–604). Roman Doctor of the Church. As Pope Gregory I (590–604), he did much to increase papal authority and to establish the temporal independence of the papacy. He sent St. Augustine on a missionary expedition to Britain in 596.

Greig (greg), **Anthony William,** known as Tony. (1946–). English cricketer, born in Rhodesia. He played for Sussex (1966–1978) and in 58 Test matches for England, fourteen of them as captain. His Test figures were 3,695 runs (average 40.43), eight centuries, 152 wickets, and 87 catches.

grei·sen (gríz'n) *n.* A granitic rock composed chiefly of quartz and mica. [German *Greisen, Greissen,* from *greissen*†, to split.]

gre·mi·al (gréemi-ɔl) *n.* In the Roman Catholic church, a silk cloth formerly placed on the lap of a bishop during Mass. [Medieval Latin *gremiāle,* from Latin *gremium,* lap.]

grem·lin (grémlin) *n.* **1.** An imaginary gnomelike creature to whom mechanical problems in military aircraft were frequently attributed during World War II. **2.** Any source of trouble or mischief. [20th century : origin obscure, but influenced by GOBLIN.]

Gre·na·da (grɔ-náydɔ). Independent republic within the Commonwealth, lying in the southeastern Caribbean Sea. It was a British colony until 1974. After the left-wing prime minister was murdered by rival Marxists in 1983, troops from the United States and Caribbean countries invaded Grenada to restore order. It consists of the volcanic island of Grenada, the southernmost of the Windward Islands, and the smaller islands of the southern Grenadines. The economy is almost entirely agricultural. Area, 344 square kilometres (133 square miles). Population, 100,000. Capital, St. George's.

gre·nade (grɔ-náyd) *n.* **1.** A missile containing priming and bursting charges, designed to be thrown by hand or fired from a launcher-equipped rifle. **2.** A glass container filled with a volatile chemical or a liquid that is dispersed when the glass is thrown and smashed. [French, from Old French *pome grenate,* POMEGRANATE (from its shape).]

gren·a·dier (grénnɔ-déer) *n.* **1. a.** A member of the British Grenadier Guards, the first regiment of the royal household infantry. **b.** Formerly, a soldier who threw grenades. **2.** Any of various deep-sea fishes of the family Macrouridae, having a long tapering tail and lacking a tail fin. In this sense, also called "rat-tail". **3.** Any of several African weaverbirds of the genus *Estrilda,* having a brightly coloured plumage and bill. [French, "grenade thrower", from *grenade,* GRENADE.]

gren·a·dine[1] (grénnɔ-deen, -déen) *n.* A thin, openwork fabric of silk, wool, cotton, or synthetic material. [French *grenadine,* perhaps from *Granada,* in Spain.]

grenadine[2] *n.* A thick, sweet syrup made from pomegranates or redcurrants and used as flavouring, especially in drinks. [French, from Old French *pome grenate,* POMEGRANATE.]

Grenadines. Group of some 600 small islands and islets in the Windward Islands, which lie between the Caribbean Sea and the main body of the Atlantic Ocean. The southern Grenadines, including Carriacou, the largest island, are part of **Grenada**, while the northern islands are part of **St. Vincent and the Grenadines**.

Gre·no·ble (grə-nõb'l; *French* grə-nóbl). City lying in the foothills of the Alps, on the river Isère, in southeastern France. It is the capital of Isère département, and a marketing and industrial centre. Grenoble is the principal hydro-electric centre of France and an important centre for nuclear research.

Gresh·am (gréshəm), **Sir Thomas** (*c.*1519–79). English banker, merchant, and financier. He made a fortune as a banker and was one of the founders of the Royal Exchange (completed in 1570). The economic dictum **Gresham's Law** is named after him.

Gresh·am's law (gréshəmz) *n. Economics.* The theory that if two kinds of money in circulation have the same denominational value but different intrinsic value, the money with higher intrinsic value (called *good*) will be hoarded and eventually driven out of circulation by the money with lesser intrinsic value (called *bad*). [After Sir Thomas GRESHAM.]

gres·so·ri·al (gre-sáwri-əl || -sõri-) *adj. Zoology.* Adapted for walking or having legs adapted for walking. Said of the ostrich and other flightless birds. [New Latin *gressõrius*, from *gressor*, one that walks, from Latin *gradī* (past participle *gressus*), to step, go.]

Gret·na Green (grétnə gréen). Village in Dumfries and Galloway in Scotland, about 2 kilometres (1.25 miles) from the English border. It was famous as a place where eloping lovers were married without residential qualifications or the consent of parents (1754–1856). After 1856, one of the parties had to have resided in Scotland for at least 21 days before the marriage. The services were usually performed by the local blacksmith until 1940.

grey, *U.S.* **gray** (gray) *adj.* **1.** Of or pertaining to an achromatic colour of any lightness between the extremes of black and white. **2. a.** Dull or dark; as from lack of light; clouded: *a grey, rainy afternoon.* **b.** Cheerless; gloomy; dismal. **3. a.** Having grey hair. **b.** Old; venerable; ancient. **4.** Dull; lacking in vividness or animation. **5.** Intermediate in character or position; neutral. **6.** Unidentifiable; unknown: *a grey figure.* **7.** Of or designating fabric that has not been bleached or dyed: *grey goods.* ∼*n.* **1.** An achromatic colour of any lightness between the extremes of black and white. **2. a.** An object or animal of this colour. **b.** A horse that is white or whitish. **3.** Grey clothes. ∼*v.* **greyed** or *U.S.* **grayed, greying** or *U.S.* **graying, greys** or *U.S.* **grays.** ∼*intr.* To become grey. ∼*tr.* To make grey. [Middle English, from Old English *grǣg*, from Germanic *grǣwaz* (unattested).] —**grey·ish** —**grey·ly** *adv.* —**grey·ness** *n.*

Grey (gray), **Charles, 2nd Earl** (1764–1845). British politician. He became the acknowledged leader of the Whigs on the death of Fox in 1806. In 1830 he became prime minister and presided over the passing of the Great Reform Act (1832) and the abolition of slavery throughout the British Empire (1833). Resigned 1834.

Grey, Lady Jane (1537–54). Queen of England for nine days. She was great-granddaughter of Henry VII and on Edward VI's death (July 4, 1553), she was proclaimed Queen, but the country rallied to Mary Tudor (Mary I), and after nine days Lady Jane was imprisoned. She was subsequently beheaded.

grey area *n.* **1.** An area that has not been researched; something about which very little is known. **2.** An area with no clear or established limits or boundaries; an ill-defined area not clearly separate from others.

grey·beard (gráy-beerd) *n.* An old man.

grey eminence *n.* An **éminence grise** (see).

Grey Friar *n.* A **Franciscan** (see).

grey·hen (gráy-hen) *n.* The female of the **black grouse** (see).

grey·hound (gráy-hownd) *n.* **1.** A large, slender dog of an ancient breed, having a smooth coat, a narrow head, and long legs, and capable of running swiftly. [Middle English *grehound*, Old English *grīghund* : *grīeg* (unattested), bitch + *hund*, dog, HOUND.]

greyhound racing *n.* A sport in which greyhounds race round a track chasing a dummy hare.

grey iron *n.* A type of cast iron in which part of the carbon is present as uncombined graphite.

grey·lag (gráy-lag) *n.* A grey Eurasian goose, *Anser anser,* having an orange bill, a barred neck, and pink legs. Also called "greylag goose". [GREY + LAG (referring to its lagging behind other species at times of migrating).]

grey market *n. Economics.* A legal though sometimes secret trading of goods at excessive prices.

grey matter *n.* **1.** *Anatomy.* The brownish-grey nerve tissue of the brain and spinal cord, containing nerve-cell bodies and dendrites but no myelinated fibres. Compare **white matter. 2.** *Informal.* Brains; intellect.

grey mullet *n.* See **mullet.**

Grey of Fal·lo·don (fál-ədən), **Edward Grey, 1st Viscount** (1862–1933). British politician. As Foreign Secretary (1905–1916), he was directly responsible for the Anglo-Russian entente (1907) and the secret Treaty of London (1915) which brought Italy into World War I.

grey squirrel *n.* A common squirrel, *Sciurus carolinensis,* native to eastern North America but now widespread in Britain and elsewhere, having grey fur and a very bushy tail.

grey·wack·e (gráy-wackə) *n.* Any of various dark, very hard standstones, comprising angular rock particles of different sizes cemented together in a matrix of finer material. [Partial translation of German *Grauwacke.* see **wacke.**]

grey whale *n.* A whalebone whale, *Eschrichtius glaucus,* of Pacific

waters, having greyish colouring with white markings.

grey wolf *n.* The **timber wolf** (see).

grib·ble (gríbb'l) *n.* Any of several small, wood-boring marine crustaceans of the genus *Limnoria;* especially, *L. lignorum,* which often damages underwater wooden structures. [Perhaps a diminutive of GRUB.]

grid (grid) *n.* **1.** A framework of parallel or crisscrossed bars; a gridiron. **2.** A pattern of horizontal and vertical lines forming squares of uniform size on a map, chart, aerial photograph, or the like, used as a reference for locating points. **3.** *Electricity.* **a.** An interconnected system of electric cables and power stations that distributes electricity over a large area. **b.** A corrugated or perforated conducting plate in a storage battery. **c.** A network or coil of fine wires located between the anode and the cathode of a vacuum tube. Also called "control grid". **4.** *Chiefly British.* Any interconnecting system of services, especially one that extends over a wide area: *the national gas grid.* **5.** In American football, a gridiron. [Short for GRIDIRON.]

grid bias *n.* The fixed voltage applied between the cathode and the grid of a vacuum tube.

grid·dle (grídd'l) *n.* A thick, flat iron pan or other flat metal surface used for cooking by dry heat. Also *chiefly Scottish* "girdle". ∼*tr.v.* **griddled, -dling, -dles.** To cook on a griddle. [Middle English *gredil,* from Old French, from Vulgar Latin *crãticulum* (unattested), small grid, from Latin *crãticula,* diminutive of *crãtis,* wickerwork.]

grid·dle·cake (grídd'l-kayk) *n.* **1.** *British.* A **drop scone** (see). **2.** *U.S.* A thick, spongy **pancake** (see).

grid·i·ron (gríd-īrn) *n.* **1.** A flat framework of parallel metal bars used for grilling meat or fish. **2.** Any framework or network suggestive of a gridiron. **3.** In American football, a football field. **4.** A metal structure high above the stage of a theatre, from which ropes or cables are strung to scenery and lights. ∼*tr.v.* **gridironed, -ironing, -irons.** To put, arrange, or construct in crisscrossing vertical and horizontal lines: *gridiron the country with railways.* [Middle English *gredire,* variant (influenced by *iren,* IRON) of *gredile, gredil,* GRIDDLE.]

grid·lock (gríd-lok) *n.* **1.** *U.S.* A traffic jam in which no traffic can move in any direction because the vehicles have formed into intersecting crisscrossed lines. **2.** Deadlock (sense 1). —**grid·locked** *adj.*

grief (greef) *n.* **1.** Intense mental anguish; deep remorse, acute sorrow, or the like. **2.** A source of deep remorse or acute sorrow. —See Synonyms at **regret.** —**come to grief.** To meet with disaster; fail. [Middle English *gref,* from Old French *grief, gref,* from *grever,* GRIEVE.]

Grieg (greeg), **Edvard (Hagerup)** (1843–1907). Norwegian composer. He was inspired by Norwegian folk tunes and many of its idioms occur in his music. His most famous works are the incidental music for *Peer Gynt* (1875) and the Piano Concerto (1868).

Grier·son (gréer-s'n), **John** (1898–1972). British film director and producer. He was a pioneer of documentary films, including *Drifters* (1929), a study of North Sea fishermen, *Industrial Britain* (1933), and *Night Mail* (1936), with verse by W.H. Auden and music by Benjamin Britten.

griev·ance (gréevəns) *n.* **1. a.** An actual or supposed circumstance regarded as just cause for complaint or protest. **b.** A complaint or protestation based on such a circumstance. **2.** Indignation or resentment stemming from a feeling of being wronged. —See Synonyms at **injustice.** [Middle English *grievaunce,* from Old French *grevance,* from *grever,* GRIEVE.]

grieve (greev) *v.* **grieved, grieving, grieves.** ∼*tr.* **1.** To cause to be sorrowful or anguished; distress. **2.** *Archaic.* To hurt or harm. ∼*intr.* To be sorrowful; lament; mourn. [Middle English *greven,* from Old French *grever,* from Latin *gravãre,* to oppress, weigh upon, from *gravis,* heavy, weighty.] —**griev·ing·ly** *adv.*

Grieve, Christopher Murray. See **MacDiarmid, Hugh.**

griev·ous (gréevəss) *adj.* **1. a.** Causing grief, pain, or anguish. **b.** Expressing grief; mourning. **2.** Serious or dire; grave. —**griev·ous·ly** *adv.* —**griev·ous·ness** *n.*

grievous bodily harm *n. Abbr.* G.B.H. In criminal law, serious physical harm inflicted by one person on another.

griff (grif) *n. British Slang.* The information; all the facts. Preceded by *the.* [Shortened from slang *griffin†,* hint, tip in betting.]

grif·fin, gry·phon (gríffin) *n. Greek Mythology.* A fabulous beast with the head and wings of an eagle and the body of a lion. [Middle English *griffon,* from Old French *grifoun,* from Late Latin *grȳphus,* from Latin, from Greek *grups.*]

Grif·fith (gríffith), **Arthur** (1872–1922). Irish nationalist leader. In 1905 he founded the Sinn Fein movement for Irish independence and in 1918 he was elected to the British Parliament. With the other Sinn Fein members, he withdrew and established the Irish Dáil. He headed the Irish group which negotiated the 1921 treaty establishing the Irish Free State.

Griffith, D(avid) W(ark) (1875–1948). U.S. film director and producer. His film *The Birth of a Nation* (1915) used the innovative techniques for which he is famous: the fade-in and fade-out, close-ups, moving-camera shots, flashbacks, and montage effects.

Griffith-Joyner (jóynər), **Florence (Delorez),** known as Flo-Jo (1959–). American sprinter who set new women's world records for 100 and 200 metres in 1988, when she was women's Olympic champion in both events.

grif·fon (gríff'n) *n.* **1.** Any of several breeds of dog having a wiry coat; especially, a small dog of a breed originating in Belgium, having a short, bearded muzzle. 2. Any of several Old World vultures of the genus *Gyps,* especially *G. fulvus,* having black wings and a greyish body. [From *griffon,* variant of GRIFFIN.]

grig (grig) *n. Regional.* 1. A grasshopper or cricket. 2. A small eel. 3. A lively merry person. [Middle English (originally "dwarf") : origin obscure.]

Gri·gnard reagent (green-yaa, green-yár) *n. Chemistry.* Any of a group of reagents with the general formula RMgX, where R is an organic group and X is a halogen atom. They are used in the synthesis of organic compounds. [After Victor *Grignard* (1871–1935), French chemist.]

gri·gri, gree·gree, gris·gris (grée-gree) *n.* An African Negro charm, fetish, or amulet. [17th century : of African origin.]

grill (gril) *v.* **grilled, grilling, grills.** —*tr.* 1. To cook on a gridiron or under a grill. 2. To torture as if by subjecting to great heat. 3. *Informal.* To question relentlessly; cross-examine. 4. To mark or emboss with a gridiron. —*intr.* To be cooked under a grill or on a gridiron.
~*n.* 1. A part of a cooker that gives out intense downward heat, under which food may be cooked; a gridiron. 2. Food cooked by grilling. 3. A grillroom. 4. Variant of **grille.** [French *griller,* from *gril, grille,* a grating, gridiron, from Old French *grille, grail,* from Vulgar Latin *grāticula* (unattested), variant of Latin *crāticula.* See **griddle.**]

gril·lage (grillij) *n.* A network or frame of crossed timbers serving as a foundation, usually on treacherous soil. [French, from *grille,* grating, GRILL.]

grille, grill (gril) *n.* 1. A metal grating used as a screen, divider, barrier, or decorative element, as: **a.** In a window or gateway for observing callers. **b.** In a convent or prison for separating visitors. **c.** On a motor vehicle to protect the radiator. 2. A square opening at the back of the hazard side of a court used for playing real tennis. [French, grating, GRILL.]

grilled (grild) *adj.* 1. Cooked under a grill. 2. Having a grille.

grill·room (gril-rōōm, -rŏŏm) *n.* A restaurant or room in a restaurant where grilled foods are served. Also called "grill".

grilse (grilss) *n., pl.* **grilse.** A young salmon on its first return from the sea to fresh or brackish waters. [Middle English *grilles,* variant of *girsil,* perhaps from Old French *grisel,* grey. See **grizzle.**]

grim (grim) *adj.* **grimmer, grimmest.** 1. Unrelenting; rigid; stern. 2. Uninviting or unnerving in aspect. 3. **a.** Ghastly; sinister. **b.** Savagely ironic: *a grim jest.* 4. *Archaic.* Ferocious; savage. 5. *Informal.* Unpleasant; repellent: *a grim prospect.* —See Synonyms at **ghastly.** [Middle English *grim,* Old English *grim,* fierce, severe, from Germanic.] —**grim·ly** *adv.* —**grim·ness** *n.*

gri·mace (gri-máyss, grímməss) *n.* A sharp contortion of the face expressive of pain, contempt, or disgust.
~*intr.v.* **grimaced, -macing, -maces.** To contort the facial features. [French *grimace,* earlier *grimache,* from Spanish *grimazo,* caricature, from *grima,* fright, from Germanic; akin to GRIM.]

Gri·mal·di (gri-máwldi), **Joseph** (1779–1837). English clown.

gri·mal·kin (gri-mál-kin, -máwl-) *n.* 1. A cat; especially, an old female cat. 2. A shrewish old woman. [Variant of *greymalkin* : GREY + dialectal *malkin,* lewd woman, hussy, Middle English *Malkyn,* diminutive of *Mald,* pet form for *Matilda.*]

grime (grīm) *n.* Black dirt or soot; especially, such dirt clinging to or ingrained in a surface.
~*tr.v.* **grimed, griming, grimes.** To cover with dirt; begrime. [Middle English *grim(e),* from Middle Dutch *grīme.*]

Grimm (grim), **Jakob** (1785–1863) and **Wilhelm** (1786–1859). German brothers, writers and philologists. They are famous for their collections of fairy tales (1812–14).

Grimm's Law *n. Phonetics.* A formula describing the regular changes undergone by Indo-European stop consonants represented in Germanic. It states that Indo-European *p, t,* and *k* become Germanic *f, th,* and *h;* Indo-European *b, d,* and *g* become Germanic *p, t,* and *k;* and Indo-European *bh, dh,* and *gh* become Germanic *b, d,* and *g.* [After Jakob GRIMM.]

Grim·ond (grimmənd), **Jo(seph), Baron Grimond of Firth** (1913–93). British politician and Liberal M.P. for Orkney and Shetland from 1950. He was the leader of the Liberal Party (1956–67, May–July 1976).

grim reaper *n.* Death, viewed as an untimely destroyer of life, and based on the notion of Father Time wielding his scythe.

Grims·by (grímzbi). Official name **Great Grimsby.** Fishing port lying at the mouth of the river Humber.

grim·y (grimi) *adj.* **-ier, -iest.** Covered or ingrained with grime. See Synonyms at **dirty.** —**grim·i·ly** *adv.* —**grim·i·ness** *n.*

grin (grin) *v.* **grinned, grinning, grins.** —*intr.* 1. To draw back the lips and bare the teeth, especially in a wide smile. 2. To smile in a forced or supercilious manner. —*tr.* To express with a grin. —**grin and bear it.** To put up with stoically; accept one's lot.
~*n.* 1. The act of grinning. 2. The expression on the face produced by grinning. [Middle English *grinnen,* Old English *grennian,* to grimace (in pleasure or displeasure); akin to *grānian,* to GROAN.] —**grin·ner** *n.* —**grin·ning·ly** *adv.*

grind (grīnd) *v.* **ground** (grownd), **grinding, grinds.** —*tr.* 1. **a.** To crush, pulverise, or powder with friction, especially by rubbing between two hard surfaces: *grind wheat into flour.* **b.** To shape, sharpen, or refine with friction: *grind a lens.* 2. To rub (two surfaces) together; gnash: *grind the teeth.* 3. To bear down on harshly; oppress. Often used with *down.* 4. **a.** To operate by turning a crank: *grind an organ.* **b.** To produce (a tune, for example) by turning a

crank. Used with *out.* 5. To produce mechanically or without inspiration. Used with *out: publishers grinding out the same old stuff year after year.* 6. To instil or teach by persistent repetition. Used with *into: grind the truth into their heads.* —*intr.* 1. To perform the operation of grinding something. 2. To be ground. 3. To move with noisy friction; grate. 4. *Informal.* To devote oneself to study or work. 5. *Slang.* To rotate the pelvis in the manner of a striptease artist. Used chiefly in the phrase *bump and grind.*
~*n.* 1. The act of grinding. 2. A crunching or grinding noise. 3. A specific grade or degree of pulverisation, as of coffee beans: *coarse grind.* 4. *Informal.* **a.** A laborious task, routine, or study: *tired of the daily grind of work and commuting.* **b.** *Chiefly U.S.* One who works or studies excessively. [Grind, ground, ground; Middle English *grinden, grond, ygrounden;* Old English *grindan†, grond* (plural *grundon), gegrunden.*] —**grind·ing·ly** *adv.*

grin·de·li·a (grin-déeli-ə) *n.* 1. Any plant of the U.S. genus *Grindelia,* having yellow, aster-like flowers, sometimes cultivated for ornament. 2. The dried plants of certain species of grindelia, used medicinally in tonics, for example. [New Latin, after D.H. *Grindel* (1777–1836), Russian botanist.]

grind·er (grīndər) *n.* 1. One that grinds; especially, a person who sharpens cutting edges. 2. A grinding machine: *a coffee grinder.* 3. A molar.

grind·ing wheel (grínding) *n.* An abrasive wheel usually consisting of a composite of hard particles, such as emery, bonded by a resin and used for grinding and sharpening tools.

grind·stone (grīnd-stōn) *n.* 1. A stone disc turned on an axle for grinding, polishing, or sharpening tools. 2. A millstone. —**keep** or **have (one's) nose to the grindstone.** To work diligently and continuously.

grin·go (gríng-gō) *n., pl.* **-gos.** In Latin America, a foreigner; especially, an American or English person. Used derogatorily. [Spanish *gringo†,* unknown tongue, gibberish.]

griot (gri-ot) *n.* An oral historian or bard in a West African community. [French, from a West African language, perhaps Wolof.]

grip (grip) *n.* 1. A tight hold; a firm grasp. 2. The pressure or strength of such a grasp. 3. **a.** A manner of grasping and holding something, such as a racket or golf club. **b.** A part for holding or grasping. 4. A handshake. 5. Mastery; command; understanding: *he has a good grip on French grammar.* 6. A spasm or seizure, as of pain. 7. **a.** A mechanical device that grasps and holds. **b.** A part designed to be grasped and held; a handle. 8. A small bag, a **handgrip** *(see).* 9. **a.** A stagehand who helps in shifting scenery. **b.** A member of a film production crew who adjusts sets and props and sometimes assists the cameraman. 10. *British.* A hairgrip *(see).* 11. The degree of hold a tyre has on the road. —**come** or **get to grips.** 1. To fight in hand-to-hand combat. 2. To deal actively and conclusively, as with a problem. —**get a grip on (oneself).** To be mentally in control of oneself. —**lose (one's) grip.** *Informal.* To lose control or mastery, especially of oneself.
~*v.* **gripped, gripping, grips.** —*tr.* 1. To secure and maintain a tight hold on; seize firmly. 2. To take hold of the mind or emotions of: *The audience was gripped by surprise.* —*intr.* To hold securely. [Middle English *grip,* partly Old English *gripa,* grasp, and partly Old English *gripa,* handful.]

gripe (grīp) *v.* **griped, griping, gripes.** —*tr.* 1. To cause sharp pain in the bowels of. 2. *Archaic.* To grasp; seize. 3. *Archaic.* To oppress or afflict. —*intr.* 1. To have sharp pains in the bowels. 2. *Informal.* To complain naggingly or petulantly; grumble. 3. *Nautical.* To tend to turn into the wind. Used of a boat.
~*n.* 1. *Plural.* Sharp, repeated pains in the bowels. 2. *Informal.* A complaint. 3. *Rare.* A grip; a grasp. 4. *Plural.* Ropes used to tie up a boat. 5. *Archaic.* A handle. [Middle English *gripen,* Old English *grīpan,* from Germanic.] —**grip·er** *n.* —**grip·ing·ly** *adv.*

gripe-wa·ter (grīp-wawtər ‖ *U.S. also* -wottər) *n.* A liquid medicament given especially to babies to relieve wind or colic.

grippe, grip (grip, greep) *n. Pathology.* Formerly, **influenza** *(see).* [French, from *gripper,* to seize, from Old French, from Frankish *grīpan* (unattested).]

grip·ping (grípping) *adj.* Holding one's undivided attention; riveting. —**grip·ping·ly** *adv.*

Gri·qua (grée-kwə-, -kwaa) *n.* A member of a South African people of mixed racial origin, living mainly in the Griqualand areas.

Gri·qua·land (grée-kwə-land, grí-). Either of two distinct districts within the boundaries of the Republic of South Africa; Griqualand West is a relatively arid, diamond-rich region in Northern Cape province and is the traditional home of the Griqua people; Griqualand East is a region on the east coast which was settled by migrant Griquas in the 19th century.

Gris (greess), **Juan,** born José Victoriano Gonzáles (1887–1927). Spanish cubist painter. He settled in Paris in 1906. He contributed especially to the development of synthetic cubism.

gri·saille (gri-záyl, -zī, -zī̄; *French* gree-zīy) *n.* 1. A style of monochromatic painting in shades of grey. 2. A painting or design in this style. [French, from *gris,* grey, from Old French, from Frankish *gris* (unattested).]

gris·e·o·ful·vin (grízzi-ō-fŏŏlvin) *n.* An antibiotic used to treat ringworm and other fungal infections of the hair, skin, and nails. [New Latin, from *Penicillium griseofulvum dierckx,* fungus from which it was isolated : Medieval Latin *griseus,* grey + Latin *fulvus,* (reddish) yellow.]

gris·e·ous (gríssi-əss, grizzi-) *adj.* Greyish; mottled or grizzled with grey. [Medieval Latin *griseus,* from Germanic.]

gri·sette (gri-zét) *n.* A French working girl, such as a shop assistant, for example. [French, an inexpensive grey fabric for dresses, a woman wearing such a dress, from *gris,* grey. See **grisaille**.]

gris-gris. Variant of **grigri**.

gris·ly (grízzli) *adj.* **-lier, -liest.** Horrifying; repugnant; gruesome. See Synonyms at **ghastly**. [Middle English *grisly,* Old English *gris·líc.*]

gri·son (grí-s'n, grízz'n) *n.* Either of two carnivorous mammals, *Grison vittatus* or *G. cuja,* of Central and South America, having grizzled fur, a slender body, and short legs. [French, from Old French, grey animal, from *gris,* grey. See **grisaille**.]

gris·sin·i (gri-séeni) *pl.n.* Singular **grissine.** *Italian.* Long, slender, crisp sticks of bread.

grist (grist) *n.* **1.** Grain or a quantity of grain for grinding. **2.** Ground grain. **—grist for** or **to the mill.** Something that can be used or turned to one's advantage. [Middle English *grist,* Old English *grīst.*]

gris·tle (gríss'l) *n.* **Cartilage** *(see),* especially when present in meat. [Middle English *gristil,* Old English *gristle,* from Germanic *gristil-* (unattested).]

gris·tly (gríssli) *adj.* **-tlier, -tliest. 1.** Composed of or containing gristle. **2.** Resembling gristle. **—gris·tli·ness** *n.*

grist·mill (gríst-mil) *n.* A mill for grinding grain.

grit (grit) *n.* **1.** Minute rough granules, as of sand or stone. **2.** The texture or structure of stone to be used in grinding. **3.** A coarse hard sandstone, used for making grindstones and millstones. Also called "gritstone". **4.** *Informal.* Indomitable spirit; pluck. **—v. gritted, gritting, grits. —tr. 1.** To clamp (the teeth) together, especially through anger or frustration. **2.** To cover or treat with grit. **—intr.** To make a grinding noise. [Middle English *grete,* Old English *grēot,* from Germanic.]

grith (grith) *n.* **1.** Protection or sanctuary provided by Old English law in certain circumstances, as when in a church or travelling on the king's highway. **2.** *Archaic.* Mercy or protection given in battle. [Middle English *grith,* Old English *grith,* from Old Norse *gridht.*]

grits (gritss) *pl.n.* **1.** Coarsely ground grain, especially oats. **2.** *U.S.* **Hominy grits** *(see).* [Middle English *gryt,* bran, Old English *grytt,* from Germanic.]

grit·ty (grítti) *adj.* **-tier, -tiest. 1.** Containing or resembling grit. **2.** Showing resolution and fortitude; plucky. **—See** Synonyms at **brave. —grit·ti·ness** *n.*

Gri·vas (grée-vass), **Georgios** (1898–1974). Cypriot soldier and politician, one of the principal advocates of Enosis (Cypriot union with Greece). He formed a guerrilla army, EOKA (National Organisation for the Cyprus Struggle), to fight against British rule. He opposed the 1959 agreements which gave Cyprus independence and after 1964, as commander of the Cypriot National Guard, led the Greek Cypriots in the fighting against the Turkish Cypriots.

gri·vet (grívvit) *n.* A long-tailed African monkey, *Cercopithecus aethiops,* having a greenish-grey coat and tufts of white hair on the face. [French *grivet†.*]

griz·zle¹ (grízz'l) *v.* **-zled, -zling, -zles. —tr.** To make grey. **—intr.** To become grey.
—n. 1. The colour grey. **2.** *Archaic.* Grey hair. [Middle English *grisel,* grey, from Old French, diminutive of *gris,* grey, from Frankish *grīs* (unattested).]

grizzle² *intr.v.* **-zled, -zling, -zles.** *Chiefly British.* **1.** To whimper; whine. **2.** To complain; grumble. [18th century (originally, to grin) : perhaps an ironic allusion to *patient Grizel* (Griselda), character in tales who exemplified the patient and uncomplaining wife.] **—griz·zler** *n.*

griz·zled (grízz'ld) *adj.* **1.** Streaked with or partly grey. **2.** Having grey or greying hair.

griz·zly (grízzli) *adj.* **-zlier, -zliest.** Grizzled.
—n., *pl.* **grizzlies.** A grizzly bear.

grizzly bear *n.* The greyish form of the brown bear, *Ursus arctos,* of northwestern North America, sometimes considered a separate species, *U. horribilis.* Also called "grizzly".

gro. gross.

groan (grōn) *v.* **groaned, groaning, groans. —intr. 1.** To voice a deep, wordless, prolonged sound expressive of pain, grief, annoyance, or disapproval. **2.** To produce a similar sound expressive of stress or strain: *The house groaned in the wind.* **3.** *Informal.* To complain or grumble, especially continually. **4.** To suffer oppression. **—tr.** To utter or convey with groaning.
—n. The sound made in groaning; a moan. [Middle English *gronen,* Old English *grānian,* akin to *grennian,* to GRIN.] **—groan·er** *n.* **—groan·ing·ly** *adv.*

groat (grōt) *n.* A British silver fourpence piece used from the 14th to the 17th century. [Middle English *grote,* from Middle Dutch *groot,* "great" (referring to the thickness of the coin).]

groats (grōts) *pl.n.* **1.** Hulled, usually crushed grain, especially oats. **2.** Ground oat kernels boiled to a paste in water and used as food. [Middle English *grotes,* Old English *grotan.*]

gro·cer (grō-sər) *n.* A shopkeeper who sells foodstuffs and sundry household supplies. [Middle English, from Old French *grossier,* wholesale dealer, from Medieval Latin *grossārius,* from Latin *grossus,* GROSS.]

gro·cer·y (grō-səri) *n., pl.* **-ies. 1.** A shop selling foodstuffs and household supplies. **2.** The occupation of a grocer. **3.** *Plural.* Goods sold by a grocer.

grock·le *n.* *Southwest English.* A tourist.

grog (grog) *n.* **1.** *Chiefly Australian & N.Z.* Alcoholic drinks in general. **2.** Rum diluted with water. [After Admiral Edward *Vernon* (1684–1757), nicknamed Old *Grog* because of his habit of wearing a GROGRAM coat. He ordered that diluted rather than neat rum be served to his sailors.]

grog·gy (gróggi) *adj.* **-gier, -giest.** Unsteady and dazed, as from sleep or drugs; weak. [From GROG.] **—grog·gi·ly** *adv.* **—grog·gi·ness** *n.*

grog·ram (gróggrəm ‖ *U.S. also* grōgrəm) *n.* A coarse, often stiffened fabric of silk, mohair, or wool, or a blend of these. [Alteration of GROSGRAIN.]

groin (groyn) *n.* **1. a.** *Anatomy.* The crease at the junction of the thighs with the trunk, together with the adjacent region. **b.** The external genital organs. **2.** *Architecture.* The curved edge at the junction of two intersecting vaults. **3.** *Chiefly U.S.* Variant of **groyne.**
~tr.v. groined, groining, groins. To provide or build with groins. [Earlier *gryne,* Middle English *grynde,* perhaps from Old English *grynde,* abyss, depression, from Germanic *grundja-* (unattested), from Common Germanic *grunduz* (unattested), GROUND.]

grom·met (grómmit, grúmmi) *n.* **1. a.** A reinforced eyelet in cloth, leather, or the like, through which a fastener may be passed. **b.** A rubber or plastic ring set in a hole through metal, especially in the chassis of an electronic device, through which wires can be passed without chafing. **2.** *Nautical.* A rope or metal ring used for securing the edge of a sail. Also called "grummet". [Obsolete French *grom-(m)ette, gourmette,* bridle ring, from Old French *gourmel,* perhaps from Frankish *worm* (unattested), worm.]

grom·well (gróm-wəl, -wel) *n.* **1.** Any of several plants of the genus *Lithospermum,* such as *L. officinale,* having small yellow or white flowers. **2.** Any of several similar or related plants. [Middle English *gromil,* from Old French, perhaps from Vulgar Latin *gruīnum milium* (unattested), "crane's millet" : Latin *gruīnus,* of a crane, from *grūs,* crane + *milium,* MILLET.]

Gro·my·ko (grə-mée-kō; *Russian* gra-míckə), **Andrey Andreyevich** (1909–89). Soviet politician, born in Belorussia. He joined the Communist Party in 1931 and in 1939 the diplomatic service. In 1943 he was appointed ambassador to the United States and became the Soviet delegate to the United Nations (1946–48). He was Foreign Minister from 1957 to 1985, and became President of the U.S.S.R. 1985–8.

Gro·ning·en (grōning-ən; *Dutch* khrōning-ə). A province in the northeastern Netherlands. It is largely an agricultural region, but it acquired new industrial importance when vast reserves of natural gas were discovered there in 1961. The provincial capital is the city of Groningen.

Grønland. See **Greenland.**

groom (grōōm, grōōm) *n.* **1.** A man or boy employed to take care of horses. **2.** A bridegroom. **3.** Any of several officers in an English royal household. **4.** *Archaic.* **a.** A man. **b.** A manservant.
~tr.v. groomed, grooming, grooms. 1. To make (clothes, hair, or the like) neat and clean. **2.** To clean and brush (an animal). **3.** To train, as for a specified position: *groom a candidate for Parliament.* [As "bridegroom", shortening of BRIDEGROOM; as "man", "servant", Middle English *gromt†.*]

grooms·man (grōōmz-mən, grōōmz-) *n., pl.* **-men** (-mən). The best man or an usher at a wedding.

groove (grōōv) *n.* **1.** A long, narrow furrow or channel, such as the spiral cut in a gramophone record. **2. a.** A situation or activity to which one is especially well suited; a niche. **b.** A settled, humdrum routine; a rut. **3.** Something that is very pleasing or satisfying.
~v. grooved, grooving, grooves. —intr. *Slang.* **1.** To relax or let oneself move freely to the rhythm or beat of music, especially jazz. **2.** To settle easily or harmoniously into a situation, relationship, or the like. **—tr.** To cut a groove in. [Middle English *grofe,* from Middle Dutch *groeve,* ditch, from Germanic; akin to GRAVE.]

groov·er (grōōvər) *n.* *Slang.* A person who grooves or is groovy.

groov·y (grōōvi) *adj.* **-ier, -iest.** *Slang.* Pleasing; deeply satisfying. [From slang expression *in the groove,* playing (jazz) fluently, hence exciting, satisfying.]

grope (grōp) *v.* **groped, groping, gropes. —intr. 1.** To reach about uncertainly; feel one's way. **2.** To search blindly or uncertainly: *grope for an answer.* **—tr. 1.** To make (one's way) by groping. **2.** *Informal.* To touch or fondle sexually, usually in a clumsy manner.
~n. The act or an instance of groping. [Middle English *gropen,* Old English *grāpian,* from Germanic.] **—grop·er** *n.* **—grop·ing·ly** *adv.*

Gro·pi·us (grōpi-əss), **Walter** (1883–1969). German architect, a leading figure in the modern movement, founder and director of the Bauhaus (1919–28). He fled from Nazi Germany in 1934 and became professor of architecture at Harvard in 1938.

gros·beak (grōss-beek, gróss-, gróz-) *n.* Any of various finches of the genera *Hesperiphona, Pinicola,* and related genera, having a thick, rounded bill. A Eurasian species is the pine grosbeak, *P. enucleator.* [Partial translation of French *grosbec* : Old French *gros,* thick, GROSS + *bec,* beak.]

gro·schen (grōsh'n, grósh'n) *n., pl.* **groschen.** A coin equal to ¹/₁₀₀ of the schilling of Austria. [German *Groschen,* from Middle High German *gros(se), grosche,* from Czech *grosh,* from Medieval Latin *(denārius) grossus,* "thick (penny)", from Latin *grossus,* thick, GROSS.]

gros·grain (grō-grayn) *n.* **1.** A heavy silk or rayon fabric with narrow ribs. **2.** A ribbon made of this. [French *gros grain,* "coarse grain" : Old French *gros*, thick, GROSS + GRAIN.]

gros point (grō) *n.* **1.** A large needlepoint stitch covering two vertical and two horizontal threads used, for example, in upholstery. **2.** Work done in this stitch. Compare **petit point.** [French, "large point".]

gross (grōss) *adj.* **grosser, grossest. 1. a.** Exclusive of deductions; total; entire. Compare **net. b.** Unmitigated in any way; utter. **2.** Glaringly obvious; flagrant: *gross injustice.* **3. a.** Coarse; vulgar; obscene. **b.** Lacking sensitivity or discernment; unrefined. **c.** *Informal.* Offensive; distasteful. **4. a.** Overweight or corpulent, especially disgustingly so. **b.** Dense; profuse. **c.** Impenetrable; thick. Said especially of vegetation. **5.** *Pathology.* Visible to the naked eye: *a gross lesion.* —See Synonyms at **coarse, flagrant.**
~*n., pl.* **grosses** (for sense 1) or **gross** (for sense 2). **1.** The entire body or amount; a total. **2.** *Abbr.* **gr., gro. a.** Twelve dozen, used as a unit of measurement. **b.** A group of 144 or 12 dozen items. —**in the gross. 1.** Taken as a whole; in bulk. **2.** Wholesale.
~*tr.v.* **grossed, grossing, grosses.** To earn as a total income or profit before deductions. —**gross up.** To increase a net amount to its gross value before deductions. [Middle English, from Old French *gros*, thick, large, from Latin *grossus*.] —**gross·ly** *adv.* —**gross·ness** *n.*

gross domestic product *n. Abbr.* **GDP** The total market value of the goods and services produced within a country during a given period, excluding income derived from investments abroad.

Gros·smith (grō-smith), **George** (1847–1912) and **Weedon** (1854–1919). English brothers, famous as the joint authors of the comic masterpiece *The Diary of a Nobody,* published in 1892.

gross national product *n Abbr.* **GNP** The total market value of all the goods and services produced by a nation during a given period, including income derived from investments abroad. Compare **national income.**

gros·su·lar·ite (gróssew-lə-rīt) *n.* A light-green, pink, grey, or brown garnet with composition $Ca_3Al_2(SiO_4)_3$, found alone or as a constituent part of the common garnet. [German *Grossularit,* "gooseberry stone" (from the colour of certain kinds of garnet), from New Latin *Grossularia,* former genus of gooseberry, from Old French *groiselle, grosele,* gooseberry, from Middle Dutch *croesel,* "curly berry" (from its beard), diminutive of *kroes,* curled.]

grosz (grosh) *n., pl.* **groszy** (gróshi). A coin equal to ¹/₁₀₀ of the zloty of Poland. [Polish, from Czech *grosh.* See **groschen.**]

Grosz (grōss), **George** (1893–1959). German painter, illustrator, and caricaturist. A leading member of the Berlin Dada movement before World War I, his reputation rests on the biting wit of his antibourgeois and antimilitarist drawings of the 1920s, executed with grotesque distortions. He became a U.S. citizen (1938).

grot (grot) *n. Poetic.* A grotto.

gro·tesque (grō-tésk) *adj.* **1.** Characterised by ludicrous or incongruous distortion. **2.** Extravagant; outlandish; bizarre. **3.** Of or designating the grotesque in art or a work executed in this style. —See Synonyms at **fantastic.**
~*n.* **1.** Anything thought to resemble the grotesque style in art. **2. a.** An artistic and decorative style developed in 16th-century Italy, characterised by incongruous combinations of monstrous human, animal, or natural forms. **b.** A work of art executed in this style. **3.** *Printing.* The family of 19th-century sans serif typefaces. [Earlier *crotescque,* from Old French *crotesque, grotesque,* from Old Italian *(pittura) grottesca,* "grotto-like (painting)", from *grottesco,* of a grotto, from *grotta,* GROTTO.] —**gro·tesque·ly** *adv.* —**gro·tesque·ness** *n.*

gro·tes·que·rie, gro·tes·que·ry (grō-téskəri) *n., pl.* **-ries. 1.** The state of being grotesque; grotesqueness. **2.** Something grotesque.

Gro·ti·us (grōti-əss), **Hugo,** originally Huig de Groot (1583–1645). Dutch lawyer and writer. He wrote on politics, theology, and law. His *Of the Law of War and Peace* (1625), is generally considered to be the first comprehensive treatise on international law.

grot·to (gróttō) *n., pl.* **-toes** or **-tos. 1.** A small cave or cavern. **2.** An artificial structure or excavation, as in a garden, resembling a cave or cavern. [Italian *grotta, grotto,* from Old Italian, from Vulgar Latin *grupta* (unattested), variant of Latin *crypta,* vault, CRYPT.]

grot·ty (grótti) *adj.* **-tier, -tiest.** *Chiefly British Informal.* Unpleasant, grubby, or squalid. [From GROTESQUE.]

grouch (growch) *intr.v.* **grouched, grouching, grouches.** To grumble or sulk.
~*n.* **1.** A grumbling or sulky mood. **2.** A complaint; a grudge. **3.** A habitually complaining or irritable person. [Middle English *grutchen,* to GRUDGE.]

grouch·y (grówchi) *adj.* **-ier, -iest.** Inclined to grumbling and complaining; ill-humoured; peevish; grumpy. —**grouch·i·ly** *adv.* —**grouch·i·ness** *n.*

ground¹ (grownd ‖ *West Indies also* grungd) *n.* **1. a.** The solid surface of the earth. **b.** The floor of a body of water, especially the sea. **2. a.** Soil; earth: *level the ground for a lawn.* **b.** Land or earth having a specified characteristic: *high ground.* **3.** *Sometimes plural.* An area of land designated for a specified purpose: *burial grounds.* **4.** *Plural.* The land surrounding or forming part of a house or other building: *The embassy has beautiful grounds.* **5.** *Often plural.* The foundation for an argument, belief, or action; a basis; a premise. **6.** *Usually plural.* The underlying condition prompting some action; a cause; a reason. Used with *for: grounds for suspicion.* **7.** An area of reference; a subject: *on familiar ground.* **8. a.** A surrounding area; a background. **9.** The undecorated part of something. **10.** *Plural.* The preparatory coat of paint on which a picture is to be painted. **10.** *Plural.*

The sediment at the bottom of a liquid, especially coffee. **11.** *Music.* A ground bass. **12.** *Electricity. U.S.* Earth (*see*). **13.** Headway, progress, or advantage, as in a competition. **14.** In cricket, the area within which the batsman must stand. —See Synonyms at **base.**
—**break fresh** or **new ground.** To start to experiment with, research, or try out new ideas, fields, methods, or the like. —**cover the ground. 1.** To travel a considerable distance. **2. a.** To make headway; accomplish a great deal. **b.** To deal with a subject fully. —**cut the ground from under (someone's) feet.** To anticipate a person's ideas or arguments and dispose of them or refute them before they are put forward. —**down to the ground.** *Chiefly British Informal.* Completely, absolutely: *His holiday plans suit me down to the ground.* —**gain ground. 1.** To make progress. **2.** To catch up with. Used with *on.* —**get off the ground. 1.** To get properly under way; have a successful beginning. Used of a project, idea, or the like. **2.** To cause to get off the ground. —**go to ground. 1.** To run into a burrow. Used of a fox, hare, or the like. **2.** To withdraw from public attention. —**hold** or **stand (one's) ground.** To maintain one's position; not yield or retreat. —**on home ground.** In a familiar area or on a familiar subject. —**run into the ground.** To work or push until exhausted. —**thin on the ground.** Not much in evidence; scarce.
~*adj.* **1.** Of, on, or near the ground. **2.** Living or used in or on the ground.
~*v.* **grounded, grounding, grounds.** —*tr.* **1.** To place or set on the ground. **2.** To provide a basis for (an argument, theory, or the like); substantiate; justify. **3.** To supply with basic and essential information; instruct in fundamentals; school. **4.** To prevent (an aircraft or pilot) from flying. **5.** *Electricity. Chiefly U.S.* To connect (an electric circuit) to a ground; earth. **6.** *Nautical.* To run (a vessel) aground. **7.** To cover (a canvas or other surface) with a preparatory coat of paint. —*intr.* **1.** To hit or reach the ground. **2.** *Nautical.* To run aground. [Middle English *ground,* Old English *grund,* from Common Germanic *grunduz* (unattested).]

ground² Past tense and past participle of **grind.**

ground·age (grówndij) *n. British.* A fee paid when a vessel enters a port.

ground bait *n. Angling.* Bait thrown into the water to attract fish.

ground bass *n.* A short musical bass passage or motif that is continually repeated under the changing harmonies and melodies of the upper range. Also called "basso ostinato", "ground".

ground beetle *n.* **1.** Any of numerous chiefly black or brown beetles of the family Carabidae, that often crawl under stones, logs, or debris. **2.** Any of various other beetles that live near the ground, such as any member of the family Tenebrionidae.

ground cherry *n.* Any of various chiefly New World plants of the genus *Physalis,* having round, fleshy fruit enclosed in a papery, bladder-like husk. See **winter cherry.**

ground control *n.* **1.** The centre on the ground that feeds continuous messages by radio to the pilot of an aircraft making a blind landing. **2.** The centre on the ground, together with its personnel, computers, and radio equipment, that monitors the progress of an aircraft or spacecraft.

ground cover *n.* Low-growing plants that form a dense, extensive growth and tend to prevent soil erosion and discourage weeds.

ground crew *n.* A team of mechanics and technicians who maintain and service aircraft on the ground.

ground elder *n.* A perennial herbaceous Eurasian plant, *Aegopodium podagraria,* widespread as a weed and on waste ground, having clusters of small white flowers and leaves composed of three leaflets. Also called "bishop's weed", "goutweed", "herb Gerard".

ground·er (grówndər) *n.* In cricket, baseball, and soccer, a ball that is struck or kicked so that it rolls along the ground.

ground floor *n.* The floor of a building at or nearly at ground level. —**get in on the ground floor.** To work with a project or business from its inception.

ground glass *n.* Glass that has been subjected to grinding or etching to diffuse light.

ground hog *n.* A rodent, the **woodchuck** (*see*).

ground·ing (grównding) *n.* A thorough knowledge of or training in the rudiments of a subject: *has a good grounding in maths.*

ground ivy *n.* A creeping or trailing aromatic plant, *Glechoma hederacea,* native to Eurasia, having rounded, scalloped leaves and small purplish flowers.

ground·less (grównd-ləss, -liss) *adj.* Having no grounds or reasons; unjustified; unsubstantiated: *groundless optimism.* —**ground·less·ly** *adv.* —**ground·less·ness** *n.*

ground·ling (grównd-ling) *n.* **1. a.** A plant or animal living on or close to the ground. **b.** A fish that lives at the bottom of the water. **2.** A person with uncultivated tastes. **3.** A spectator in the cheapest part of a theatre. **4.** A person on the ground as opposed to one in an aeroplane.

ground loop *n.* A sharp, uncontrollable turn of an aircraft while taxiing, landing, or taking off.

ground·mass (grównd-mass) *n.* The fine-grained crystalline base of porphyritic rock, in which phenocrysts are embedded.

ground·nut (grównd-nut) *n.* **1.** *Chiefly British.* The **peanut** (*see*). **2.** A climbing vine, *Apios tuberosa,* of eastern North America, having compound leaves, clusters of fragrant brownish flowers, and small, edible tubers. **3.** Any of several other plants having underground tubers or nutlike parts. **4.** The tuber or nutlike part of such a plant.

ground pine *n.* **1.** A low-growing plant, *Ajuga chamaepitys,* native to the Old World, having narrow leaves, yellow flowers, and a resinous odour. **2.** A North American **club moss** *(see)*; especially, *Lycopodium obscurum* or any similar species.

ground pink *n.* A plant, the **moss pink** *(see)*.

ground plan *n.* **1.** A plan of a floor of a building as if seen from overhead. **2.** A preliminary or basic plan.

ground plum *n.* **1.** A plant, *Astragalus crassicarpus,* of the central and western United States, having purple or white flowers and green, plumlike, edible fruit. **2.** The fruit of this plant.

ground·print (grównd-print) *n.* In telecommunications, a **footprint** *(see)*.

ground rent *n. Chiefly British.* **1.** Rent reserved on land by a lessor, usually for a stipulated lengthy term, to be used chiefly for building. **2.** Rent paid by the lessee of a flat to the freeholder, over a specified period of time.

ground rule *n.* Any basic rule of procedure modified or amended to fit a particular situation or event.

ground·sel (grówn-s'l, grównd-) *n.* Any of various plants of the genus *Senecio,* especially the Eurasian species *S. vulgaris,* having rayed, usually yellow flowers. [Middle English *groundeswele,* Old English *grundeswylige,* variant (influenced by *grund,* GROUND) of *gundæswelgæ,* "pus-absorber" (from its use to reduce abscesses) : *gund,* pus + *swelgan,* to swallow.]

ground sheet *n.* **1.** A waterproof cover used to protect an area of ground, such as a football field. **2.** A waterproof sheet placed in a tent or under camp bedding as a protection against damp.

ground·sill (grównd-sil) *n.* The horizontal timber nearest the ground in the frame of a building. Also called "ground plate".

grounds·man (grówndz-mən) *n., pl.* **-men** (-mən, -men). A person employed to look after a cricket pitch, playing field, park, or the like.

ground·speed (grównd-speed) *n. Aeronautics.* The speed of an airborne aircraft calculated in terms of the ground distance traversed in a given period of time. Compare **airspeed.**

ground squirrel *n.* Any of various squirrel-like rodents of the genus *Citellus* (or *Spermophilus*) and related genera, which live in underground burrows. Also called "gopher".

ground state *n. Physics.* The stationary state of least energy in a physical system.

ground stroke *n.* In tennis, a stroke played to a ball that has bounced.

ground substance *n. Anatomy.* The matrix of connective tissue, containing various cells and fibres.

ground·swell (grównd-swel) *n.* **1.** An undulation of the ocean with deep rolling waves, often caused by a distant storm or earthquake. **2.** A gathering of force, as of public opinion.

ground tissues *pl.n. Botany.* Plant tissues, such as pith and cortex, that are not specialised for a particular function.

ground water *n.* **1.** Any water beneath the earth's surface. **2.** A region of subsurface water beneath the water table, including underground streams. It forms the saturation zone in which all pore spaces are filled with water.

ground wave *n.* A radio wave that travels along the earth's surface. Compare **sky wave.**

ground·work (grównd-wurk) *n.* A foundation or basis; preliminary work.

ground zero *n.* The point on the surface of the earth immediately below a nuclear explosion. Also called "hypocentre".

group (grōōp) *n. Abbr.* **gr. 1.** An assemblage of persons or objects considered together: *a group of dinner guests; a group of Chinese porcelains.* **2.** Two or more figures that make up a unit or a design, as in sculpture or painting. **3.** A number of individuals or things considered together because of certain similarities. **4.** *Linguistics.* A subdivision of a linguistic family, less inclusive than a branch. **5.** A unit of two or more squadrons in an air force, smaller than a wing. **6.** Any class or collection of related objects or entities, as: **a.** Two or more atoms behaving or regarded as behaving as a single chemical unit. Also called "radical". **b.** A vertical column in the periodic table of elements. Compare **period. c.** A geological stratigraphic unit, especially a unit consisting of two or more formations. **7.** *Mathematics.* A set together with a binary operation under which the set is closed and associative, and for which the set contains an identity element and an inverse for every element in the set. **8.** A small number of players, usually including a singer or singers, that perform popular or modern music. **9.** *British.* A number of associated companies, usually consisting of a holding company and several subsidiary companies.

~*v.* **grouped, grouping, groups.** —*tr.* To place or arrange in a group or groups. —*intr.* To form or be part of a group. [French *groupe,* from Italian *gruppo,* "knot", from Germanic.]

group captain *n.* A commissioned officer in the Royal and Australian Air Forces, ranking between an air commodore and a wing commander, equivalent in rank to a colonel in the army and a captain in the navy.

group·er (grōōpər) *n., pl.* **groupers** or collectively **grouper.** Any of various often large food and game fishes of the genera *Epinephelus, Mycteroperca,* and related genera, of warm seas. [Portuguese *garupa,* probably from a native South American name.]

group·ie (grōōpi) *n. Informal.* **1.** A fan, usually female, of a rock or pop group who follows the group around on tours, usually in the hope of having personal contact with them. **2.** A sycophant or hanger-on.

group·ing (grōōping) *n.* **1.** The act or process of arranging in

groups. **2.** A collection of objects arranged in a group.

group insurance *n.* Insurance covering members of a group under a single contract or under individual contracts, usually at reduced cost.

group·oid (grōō-poyd) *n. Algebra.* A nonempty set *G* together with a binary operation that associates with every pair of elements *x, y* in *G* a third element *z* in *G* denoted by *xy* or *x·y.*

group practice *n.* A medical practice run by several general practitioners who share premises, secretarial help, and other resources.

group therapy *n.* Psychotherapy involving more than one patient at a time, in which the changing interaction among the patients is part of the therapeutic process. Also called "group psychotherapy".

grouse[1] (growss) *n., pl.* **grouse.** Any of various game birds of the family Tetraonidae, chiefly of the Northern Hemisphere, having mottled brown or greyish plumage. See **black grouse.** [16th century : earlier *grewes,* perhaps plural of *grue* (unattested), perhaps from medieval Latin *grūtat.*]

grouse[2] *intr.v.* **groused, grousing, grouses.** *Informal.* To complain; carp; grumble.
~*n.* A complaint; a grievance. [19th century : origin obscure.] —**grous·er** *n.*

grouse[3] *adj. Australian & N.Z. Informal.* Great; marvellous. [20th century : origin obscure.]

grout (growt) *n.* **1. a.** A thin mortar used to fill cracks and crevices between masonry and around tiles. **b.** A finishing plaster. **2.** *Usually plural. Chiefly British.* Sediment; lees. **3. a.** *Plural.* Groats. **b.** Wholemeal porridge.
~*tr.v.* **grouted, grouting, grouts.** To fill or finish with grout. Often used with *in*: *grout in tiles.* [Middle English *grout,* Old English *grūt,* akin to GRITS, GROATS.] —**grout·er** *n.*

grove (grōv) *n.* A small wood or group of trees lacking dense undergrowth. [Middle English *grove,* Old English *grāf*†.]

Grove (grōv), **Sir George** (1820–1900). British civil engineer and musicologist. His *Dictionary of Music and Musicians,* now a standard work, first appeared in four volumes between 1879 and 1889.

grov·el (gróvv'l, grúvv'l) *intr.v.* **-elled, -eled, -elling** or *U.S.* **-eling, -els. 1.** To humble oneself in a servile or demeaning manner; cringe. **2.** To lie or crawl in a prostrate position, often as a token of subservience or humility. **3.** To give oneself over to base pleasures. [Back-formation from obsolete *groveling,* prone, Middle English *gruflinge,* in prostrate position, from phrase *on grufe,* on the face, from Old Norse *ā grūfu : ā,* on + *grūfu*†, proneness.] —**grov·el·ler** *n.* —**grov·el·ling·ly** *adv.*

Groves (grōvz), **Sir Charles** (1915–92). British conductor. He conducted many leading British orchestras and was musical director of the Welsh National Opera (1961–63) and the English National Opera (1978–79). He championed new works by British composers.

grow (grō) *v.* **grew** (grōō ‖ grew), **grown** (grōn ‖ grŏ-ən), **growing, grows.** —*intr.* **1. a.** To increase naturally in size or length, often in a specified direction. **b.** To increase in size by the addition of material through assimilation or accretion. **2. a.** To expand; gain: *The business grew under new management.* **b.** To increase in amount or degree: *membership is growing.* **c.** To become extended or intensified: *Her anxiety grew.* **3.** To develop and reach maturity. **4.** To be capable of growth; thrive; flourish: *plants that will grow in deep shade.* **5.** To become in a specified position in relation to something else or to each other, by or as if by the process of growth: *the edges of the wound grew together; we've grown apart recently.* **6.** To follow as a result of; originate. Usually used with *out*: *Their love grew out of friendship.* **7.** To develop by a gradual process or by degrees; become: *grow angry; grow cold; grow rich.* **8.** To come into existence; spring up: *Friendship grew between the two men.* —*tr.* **1.** To cause to grow; cultivate: *grow tulips.* **2.** To let grow: *grow a beard.* **3.** To develop; put forth: *The plant has not grown any leaves yet.* —See Synonyms at **increase.** —**grow into.** To develop in size or maturity so as to fit: *grow into a dress.* —**grow on** or **upon.** To become more pleasurable, acceptable, or essential to: *a style that grows on one.* —**grow out of.** To outgrow. —**grow over.** To cover with growth: *a path grown over with moss.* —**grow up. 1.** To reach maturity; become an adult. **2.** To come into being; develop. [Grow, grew, grown; Middle English *growen, grewe, growen,* Old English *grōwan, grēow, grōwen,* from Germanic.]

grow·er *n.* **1.** One that grows, especially at a specified rate: *a fast grower.* **2.** One who grows plants, especially on a commercial scale: *a rose grower.*

grow·ing (grō-ing) *adj.* **1.** Increasing in number or degree: *a growing desire to confess.* **2.** Of or associated with growth: *during the growing season.* —**grow·ing·ly** *adv.*

growing pains *pl.n.* **1.** Pains in the limbs and joints of children, often mistakenly attributed to rapid growth. **2.** Problems arising in the initial stages of an enterprise.

growing season *n.* The period of the year during which temperatures are high enough for the growth of a particular crop, usually regarded as the period between the last severe frost of spring and the first in the following autumn.

growl (growl) *v.* **growled, growling, growls.** —*intr.* **1.** To utter a growl. **2.** To speak in an angry or surly manner. —*tr.* To utter with a growl: *growl orders.*
~*n.* **1.** The low, guttural, menacing sound made by a dog or other animal, usually in anger. **2.** A sound suggestive of this. **3.** A gruff, surly utterance. [Perhaps imitative.]

growl·er (grówlər) *n.* **1.** One that growls. **2.** A small iceberg or area of floe ice, large enough to be a danger to ships. **3.** A four-wheeled hansom cab.

grown (grōn ‖ grṓ-ən). Past participle of **grow.**
~*adj.* **1.** Having attained full growth; mature; adult. **2.** Produced or cultivated in a specified way or place. Used in combination: *home-grown vegetables.*

grown-up (grōn-up, -úp) *adj.* **1.** Characteristic of or suitable for an adult. **2.** Being mature, fully-developed, or older than one's years in outlook, attitudes, or appearance.
~*n.* An adult.

growth (grōth) *n.* **1. a.** The process of growing. **b.** A stage in the process of growing; size. **c.** Full development; maturity. **2.** Development from a lower or simpler to a higher or more complex form; evolution. **3.** An increase, as in size, number, value, or strength; extension or expansion: *population growth.* **4.** Something that grows or has grown: *a new growth of grass.* **5.** Broadly, an abnormal tissue formation, such as a tumour. **6.** The result of growth; production; cultivation.

growth industry *n.* An industry whose rate of growth exceeds that of most other industries.

growth hormone *n.* A hormone, secreted by the pituitary gland, that stimulates tissue growth, especially of the bones. Also called "somatotrophin". Compare **growth substance.**

growth ring *n.* An **annual ring** (see).

growth stock *n. Economics.* Shares that tend to increase in capital value rather than providing a high-interest income.

growth substance *n.* A substance produced by a plant that, in very small quantities, controls growth and development; a plant hormone. Also called "phytohormone". Compare **growth hormone.**

groyne (groyn) *n.* Also *chiefly U.S.* **groin.** A low wall built out into the sea to prevent erosion of the shore. [From dialect *groin,* snout, from Old French, snout, promontory, from Late Latin *grunium,* snout, from Latin *grunīre,* to grunt.]

grub (grub) *v.* **grubbed, grubbing, grubs.** —*tr.* **1.** To clear of roots and stumps by digging. **2.** To dig up by the roots. Often used with *up* or *out.* —*intr.* **1.** To dig in the earth; dig underground. **2. a.** To search laboriously; rummage. **b.** To toil arduously; drudge. Used with *on, along,* or *away: grub away for a living.*
~*n.* **1.** The thick, wormlike larva of certain beetles and other insects. **2.** *Informal.* Food. **3.** *Chiefly British Informal.* A dirty or unkempt person, especially a child. **4.** *Archaic.* A drudge. [Middle English *grubben,* Old English *grybban* (unattested).]

grub·ber (grúbbər) *n.* **1.** A person who grubs: *"The archaeologist is the last grubber among things mortal"* (Loren Eiseley). **2.** A grub hoe. **3.** In Rugby football, a kick that sends the ball forward along the ground. Also called "grubber kick".

grub·by (grúbbi) *adj.* **-bier, -biest. 1.** Dirty; unkempt. **2.** Infested with grubs. **3.** Contemptible; beggarly. —**grub·bi·ly** *adv.* —**grub·bi·ness** *n.*

grub hoe *n.* A heavy hoe for grubbing up roots. Also called "grubbing hoe", "grubber".

grub screw *n.* A small headless screw used to secure a collar or other similar part to a shaft.

grub·stake (grúb-stayk) *n. U.S.* Supplies or funds advanced to a mining prospector or a person starting a business, in return for a promised share of the profits. Also informally called "stake".
~*tr.v.* **grubstaked, -staking, -stakes.** *U.S.* To supply with a grubstake. [GRUB (food) + STAKE (bet).] —**grub·stak·er** *n.*

Grub Street (grub) *n.* The world of impoverished writers and literary hacks. [From *Grub Street,* London, now Milton Street, formerly inhabited by such writers.]

grub-street (grúb-street) *adj.* Turned out by hacks; poor; inferior: *a shelf of grubstreet novels.*

grudge (gruj) *tr.v.* **grudged, grudging, grudges. 1.** To be reluctant to allow or grant. **2.** To show or feel reluctance about: *"His nature grudged thinking, for it crippled his speed in action"* (T.E. Lawrence).
~*n.* **1.** A deep-seated feeling of resentment or rancour provoked by some incident or situation. **2.** The grounds for such a feeling. [Middle English *gruggen,* variant of *grutchen,* from Old French *grouchier*†, to murmur.] —**grudg·er** *n.*

grudg·ing (grújing) *adj.* Not offered willingly or spontaneously: *grudging praise.* —**grudg·ing·ly** *adv.*

gru·el (grŏo-əl) *n.* **1.** A thin, watery porridge. **2.** *Archaic.* Severe punishment.
~*tr.v.* **gruelled** or *U.S.* **grueled, -elling** or *U.S.* **-eling, -els. 1.** To exhaust and wear down. **2.** *Archaic.* To punish. [Middle English *grewel,* from Old French *gruel,* diminutive of *gru,* groats, oatmeal, from Frankish *grūt* (unattested).]

gru·el·ling (grŏo-əling) *adj.* Demanding and exhausting.
~*n.* A gruelling experience, especially punishment.

grue·some (grŏo-səm) *adj.* Causing horror and repugnance; frightful and shocking: *the gruesome sight of the dismembered corpse.* See Synonyms at **ghastly.** [From obsolete Scottish *grue,* to shiver, from Scandinavian.] —**grue·some·ly** *adv.* —**grue·some·ness** *n.*

gruff (gruf) *adj.* Rough and stern in manner, voice, or appearance; harsh. [Dutch *grof,* from Middle Dutch, from Germanic.] —**gruff·ly** *adv.* —**gruff·ness** *n.*
Synonyms: gruff, brusque, blunt, bluff, curt, crusty.

grum·ble (grúmb'l) *v.* **-bled, -bling, -bles.** —*intr.* **1.** To mumble in discontent: *Bosses will always find something to grumble about.* **2.** To rumble or growl. —*tr.* To express in a grumbling, discontented manner.
~*n.* **1. a.** A grumbling utterance. **b.** Grounds for grumbling. **2.** A rumble. [Frequentative of Middle English *grummen,* to grumble,

perhaps from Middle Dutch *grommen.*] —**grum·bler** *n.* —**grum·bling·ly** *adv.* —**grum·bly** *adj.*

grumb·ling appendix (grúmbling) *n.* An appendix that causes the sufferer occasional discomfort but is not actually inflamed.

grum·met (grúmmit) *n. Nautical.* A **grommet** (see).

gru·mous (grŏo-məss) *adj.* Also **gru·mose** (-mōss). *Botany.* Formed of or consisting of granular tissue, as certain roots are. [Latin *grūmus*†, little heap of earth.]

grump (grump) *n. Informal.* **1.** *Plural.* A fit of ill temper. **2.** A surly, complaining person. [Imitative.]

grump·y (grúmpi) *adj.* **-ier, -iest.** Fretful and peevish; irritable; bad-tempered. [From dialectal *grump,* ill-tempered (imitative).] —**grump·i·ly** *adv.* —**grump·i·ness** *n.*

Grund·y·ism (grúndi-iz'm) *n.* Narrow-minded criticism of the morals of others. [After Mrs *Grundy,* character in *Speed the Plough* (1798), a play by T. Morton.]

Grü·ne·wald (grŏonə-wawld; *German* grünə-valt), **Matthias,** born Mathis Gothart Neithart (*c.*1475–1528). One of the great early German masters of northern European painting. He painted chiefly religious subjects, especially the Crucifixion of Christ.

grunge (grunj) *n. Slang.* Dirt or shabbiness. [Origin obscure : suggests blend of GRIME + GUNGE.] —**grung·y** (grún-ji) *adj.*

grun·ion (grún-yən) *n.* A small fish, *Leuresthes tenuis,* of coastal waters of California and Mexico, that spawns along beaches during high spring tides. [Perhaps from Spanish *gruñón,* grumbler, from *gruñir,* to grumble, grunt, from Latin *grunnīre.*]

grunt (grunt) *v.* **grunted, grunting, grunts.** —*intr.* **1.** To utter a grunt. **2.** To make a deep, guttural sound. —*tr.* To utter or express (a reaction, for example) with a grunt: *he grunted approval.*
~*n.* **1.** The deep, guttural sound characteristic of a pig. **2.** Any of various chiefly tropical marine fishes of the genus *Haemulon* and related genera, that produce grunting sounds. Also called "grunter". [Middle English *grunten,* Old English *grunnettan,* probably frequentative of *grunnian.*] —**grunt·ing·ly** *adv.*

grunt·er (grúntər) *n.* **1.** One that grunts. **2.** *Informal.* A pig. **3.** A fish, the grunt.

grun·tled (grúnt'ld) *adj.* Extremely pleased. Used humorously. [Back-formation from DISGRUNTLED.]

Grus (grŏoss) *n.* A constellation in the Southern Hemisphere near Indus and Phoenix. [New Latin, from Latin *grūs,* crane.]

Gru·yère (grŏo-yaír ‖ gree-; *French* grü-) *n.* A pale yellow, firm-textured cheese with holes, made from whole milk. [Originally made in *Gruyère,* a district in Switzerland.]

gryphon. Variant of **griffin.**

grys·bok (gríss-bok, khráyss-) *n.* Either of two small African antelopes, *Raphicerus melanotis* or *R. sharpei,* having small, straight horns. [Afrikaans, "grey buck".]

GS, G.S. general staff.

gsoh, GSOH good sense of humour (used in small ads).

G-string (jée-string) *n.* **1.** A narrow strip of cloth passing between the legs and supported by a waistband, worn especially by strip-tease artistes. **2.** A string tuned to G on a musical instrument.

G-suit (jée-sŏot, -sewt) *n.* A flight garment designed to counteract the effects of high acceleration by exerting pressure on parts of the body below the chest. Also called "anti-G suit". Compare **pressure suit.** [G, short for GRAVITY.]

gt. **1.** gilt. **2.** great. **3.** *Medicine.* gutta.

G.T. gran turismo.

gtd. guaranteed.

gua·ca·mo·le (gwaʹakə-mṓli) *n.* **1.** Any of a variety of Mexican or South American salads featuring avocado. **2.** A dip or spread of mashed avocado, tomato pulp, mayonnaise, and seasoning. [Mexican Spanish, from Nahuatl *ahuacamolli,* "avocado sauce" : *ahuacatl,* AVOCADO + *molli,* sauce.]

gua·cha·ro (gwaʹachə-rō) *n., pl.* **-ros.** The **oilbird** (see). [American Spanish *guácharo,* from *guacho,* orphan, little bird, from Quechua *wáhcha,* diminutive of *wah,* strange.]

gua·co (gwaʹakō) *n., pl.* **-cos.** Any of several tropical American plants used as an antidote against snakebites; especially, *Mikania guaco* or *Aristolochia serpentina.* [American Spanish, from a native word in South America.]

Gua·dal·ca·nal (gwaʹad'l-kə-nál). Largest island in the Solomon Islands in the southwest Pacific Ocean. Its origin is volcanic; its dominant peak, Mt. Popomanasiu, which rises to a height of 2 331 metres (7,647 feet), is surrounded by jungle. Most of the population works on coastal coconut plantations. See map at **Pacific Ocean.**

Gua·de·loupe (gwaʹad'l-ŏop). An overseas département of France, one of the Leeward Islands in the Caribbean. It consists of two large islands, Basse Terre and Grande Terre, and several smaller islands. The capital is Basse-Terre. It was a French colony until 1946, when it was granted département status. See map at **Latin America.**

guai·a·col (gwíʹ-ə-kol ‖ -kōl) *n.* A yellowish, oily, aromatic liquid, $C_7H_8O_2$, used chiefly as an expectorant and a local anaesthetic. [GUAIAC(UM) + -OL.]

guai·a·cum (gwíʹ-ə-kəm) *n.* **1.** A tree of the genus *Guaiacum;* especially, the **lignum vitae** (see). **2.** The wood of such a tree. **3.** A greenish-brown resin obtained from the lignum vitae, and used medicinally and in varnishes. [New Latin, from Spanish *guayacan,* from Taino.]

Guam (gwaam). Unincorporated territory of the United States, the largest and most southerly of the Marianas archipelago, lying in the north Pacific Ocean. It has a mountainous interior and is fringed by coral reefs. Since 1954 it has been the site of the Pacific headquarters of the United States. Strategic Air Command. See map at **Pacific Ocean.**

guan (gwaan) *n.* Any of several birds of the genus *Penelope* and related genera, of the jungles of tropical America, related to and resembling the curassows. [American Spanish, from a native name in South America.]

gua·na·co (gwaa-naákŏ, gwə-) *n., pl.* **-cos.** A brownish South American mammal, *Lama guanicoe,* related to and resembling the domesticated llama. [Spanish, from Quechua *huanaco.*]

gua·nase (gwaá-nayz, -nayss) *n.* An enzyme in the liver and spleen that catalyses the removal of an amino group from guanine, which is thereby converted to xanthine. [GUAN(INE) + -ASE.]

guan·eth·i·dine (gwaa-néthi-deen) *n.* A drug administered in the form of pills to reduce high blood pressure. [Blend of GUANIDINE + ETHYL.]

Guang·dong, Kuang·tung, or **Kwang·tung** (gwaáng-toŏong). Province of southeast China. It is hilly, and has more than 700 offshore islands. The province is a major producer of sugar cane, rice, silk, hemp, tea, tobacco, tropical and subtropical fruits, forest products, fish, and salt. It has reserves of tungsten, iron, uranium, and oil. Most of the people are Cantonese, and some 50 per cent of overseas Chinese originated in the province, part of China since *c.*200 B.C. Guangzhou (Canton) is the capital.

Guang·zhou, Kuang·chou, or **Kwang·chow** (gwaáng-jŏ). Also **Can·ton** (kan-tón). Port in southern China and the capital of Guangdong province. Situated on the Zhu Jiang (Pearl River) delta, it is the commercial and industrial centre of southern China. The Portuguese, in the 16th century, and the British, in the 17th century, regularly used the port. The Opium War between Britain and China resulted in Guangzhou's becoming one of the first Treaty Ports (1842).

gua·ni·dine (gwaáni-deen, gwánni-, -din) *n.* A strong crystalline base, CH_5N_3, found in plant and animal tissues and used for organic syntheses. [GUAN(INE) + -ID(E) + -INE.]

gua·nine (gwaá-neen, goŏo-ə-) *n.* A purine, $C_5H_5N_5O$, that is a constituent of the nucleic acids DNA and RNA. [From GUANO, in which it is found.]

gua·no (gwaá-nŏ, gew-aá-) *n.* **1.** A substance composed chiefly of the dung of sea birds or bats, accumulated along certain coastal areas or in caves, and used as fertiliser. **2.** A similar artificially produced substance. [Spanish, from Quechua *huanu,* dung.]

gua·no·sine (gwaáno-seen, -zeen) *n.* A nucleoside consisting of guanine and the sugar ribose. [Blend of GUANINE + RIBOSE.]

guar. guaranteed.

gua·ra·ni (gwaárə-neé, -ni) *n., pl.* **-nis** or **guarani. 1.** The basic monetary unit of Paraguay, equal to 100 centimos. **2.** A note worth one guarani. [Spanish *guaraní,* GUARANI.]

Gua·ra·ni (gwaárə-neé) *n., pl.* **-nis** or collectively **Guarani. 1.** A member of a Tupi-Guaranian group of South American Indians of Paraguay, Bolivia, and southern Brazil. **2.** The Tupian language spoken by these peoples. [Spanish *guaraní,* a native tribal name.]

guar·an·tee (gárrən-teé ‖ gaáərən-) *n.* **1.** *Law.* **a.** A contract whereby a person undertakes to answer for the debt, default, or miscarriage of another. **b.** *Rare.* A person making or receiving such an undertaking. **2.** A formal undertaking whereby something is ensured; specifically, an undertaking by a manufacturer or vendor that his goods or services meet a certain standard. **3.** Something given or held as security. **4.** That which secures or ensures something: *Their name is a guarantee of quality.*
~*tr.v.* **guaranteed, -teeing, -tees. 1.** To assume responsibility for the debt, default, or miscarriage of; vouch for. **2.** To assume responsibility for the quality or execution of. **3.** To undertake to accomplish or secure: *He guaranteed to free the captives.* **4.** To ensure (a desired outcome, for example). **5.** To furnish security for. **6.** To express or declare with conviction. [Earlier *garante,* perhaps from Spanish, warrant. See **guaranty.**]

guar·an·tor (gárrən-tór, gə-rán-tawr ‖ gaáərən-, -tər) *n.* **1.** A person who makes or gives a guarantee. **2.** A person who makes or gives a guaranty.

guar·an·ty (gárrən-ti ‖ gaáərən-) *n., pl.* **-ties. 1.** An agreement by which one person assumes the responsibility of assuring payment or fulfilment of another's debts or obligations. **2.** That which guarantees something: *His record is a guaranty of his honesty.* **3.** Anything held or provided as security for the execution, completion, or existence of something. **4.** The provision of such security. **5.** A guarantor.
~*tr.v.* **guarantied, -tying, -ties.** To guarantee. [Old French *garantie,* from *garant,* warrant, from Frankish *wārjan* (unattested), to vouch for the truth of.]

guard (gard) *v.* **guarded, guarding, guards.** —*tr.* **1.** To protect from harm; watch over; defend. **2. a.** To watch over to prevent escape or violence. **b.** To watch over to prevent mistakes, indiscretions, or the like: *guard one's words.* **3.** To keep watch at (a door or gate, for example) to supervise entries and exits. **4.** To supply with proper controls and checks; safeguard. **5.** To furnish (a device or object) with a protective piece. **6.** *Archaic.* To escort. —*intr.* To take precautions; secure. Used with *against: guard against infection.*
—See Synonyms at **defend.**
~*n.* **1.** One that guards, keeps watch over, or protects. **2.** An individual or a group that stands watch or acts as a sentinel. **3.** One who supervises prisoners. **4.** A body of persons who form an escort or perform drill exhibitions on ceremonial occasions: *a guard of*

honour. **5.** *Capital* G. *British.* A member of any of various regiments whose official duties include the ceremonial protection of the sovereign. **6.** *British.* A railway employee in charge of a train. **7.** In basketball, a player who specialises in passing and dribbling in the centre of the court. **8. a.** A defensive position or stance in certain sports such as boxing or fencing. **b.** In cricket, the defensive positioning of the bat in front of the wicket. **c.** An item of protective clothing worn by sports players. **9.** The act, condition, or duty of guarding: *"Have you had quiet guard?"* (Shakespeare). **10.** Something that gives protection; a safeguard: *a guard against tooth decay.* **11.** Any guard or apparatus that prevents injury, damage, or loss. **12.** An attachment or covering put on a machine to protect the operator. **13.** A chain or band used to help safeguard a thing, such as a watch or bracelet, from loss. **14.** A guard ring. **15.** The portion of the hilt of a sword or the handle of a knife or fork that protects the hand. **16.** The metal apparatus that encircles and guards the trigger of a firearm. —**mount guard.** To go on duty. Said of a sentinal. —**off (one's) guard.** Unprepared; not alert. —**on (one's) guard.** Alert and watchful; cautious. —**stand guard. 1.** To act as a sentinel. **2.** To keep watch over someone or something.
~*adj.* Of, relating to, or acting as a guard: *guard duty.* [As verb, Middle English *garden,* from Old French *garder, guarder,* from Germanic. As noun, Middle English, from Old French *garde,* from *garder,* to guard.] —**guard·a·ble** *adj.* —**guard·er** *n.*

guar·dant (gárd'nt) *adj. Heraldry.* Designating an animal shown with its face turned towards the viewer. [Old French *gardant,* present participle of *garder,* to GUARD.]

guard cell *n. Botany.* Either of the paired epidermal cells that control the opening and closing of a stoma in plant tissue.

guard·ed (gárdid) *adj.* Cautious; restrained; prudent: *guarded behaviour.* —**guard·ed·ly** *adv.* —**guard·ed·ness** *n.*

guard hair *n.* Any of the coarse hairs that form a layer covering the underfur of certain mammals.

guard·house (gárd-howss) *n.* **1.** A building that accommodates a military guard. **2.** A building used as a prison for military personnel guilty of minor offences.

guard·i·an (gárdi-ən) *n.* **1.** One who guards, protects, or defends. **2.** *Law.* A person who is legally responsible for the care and management of the person or property of one who is considered by law to be incompetent to manage his own affairs, such as a child during its minority. **3.** A superior in a Franciscan convent. [Middle English from Anglo-French, variant of Old French *gardien,* from *garder,* to GUARD.] —**guard·i·an·ship** *n.*

guardian angel *n.* **1.** *Roman Catholic Church.* An angel appointed to watch over a person. **2.** Someone who seems inseparable from another person and is supposedly looking after his interests. Used humorously.

guard·rail (gárd-rayl) *n.* **1.** A protective rail, as on a staircase. **2.** An inner rail placed along the main rail of a railway track at curves and crossings to prevent a train from jumping the tracks.

guard ring *n.* **1.** A ring used to prevent a more valuable ring from sliding off the finger. Also called "guard". **2.** An electrode in a computer or electron lens that counteracts distortion of the electric field at the edges of other electrodes.

guard·room (gárd-roŏom, -roŏom) *n.* **1.** A room used by guards on duty. **2.** A room in which prisoners are confined.

guards·man (gárdz-mən) *n., pl.* **-men** (-mən). **1.** One who acts as a guard. **2.** *British.* A soldier in a regiment of household guards. **3.** *U.S.* A member of the U.S. National Guard.

guard's van *n. Chiefly British.* The railway carriage in which the guard travels, generally located at the rear of the train.

Guar·neri (gwaar-neéri, -náiri). Italian family of violin-makers, whose workshops were in Cremona. The first member of the family to make violins was Andrea (*c.*1626–98). The craft was carried on by each generation down to Giuseppe (*c.*1687–1744), who is considered second only to the Stradivari family for the quality of his instruments.

Guar·ne·ri·us (gwaar-neér-i-əss, -naír-) *n.* Any of the violins of superlative tone made by members of the Guarneri family in the 17th and 18th centuries.

Gua·te·ma·la, Republic of (gwaátə-maálə, gwátti-). Independent republic of Central America. It was the home of the Mayan civilisation for 1,000 years before the Spanish conquest of 1524. It declared its independence from Spain in 1821. The country is chiefly agricultural, and coffee, cotton, beef, timber, and chicle are the chief exports. Nickel and petroleum are mined. An earthquake in 1976 killed more than 24,000 people. Area, 108 889 square kilometres (42,042 square miles). Population, 10,930,000. Capital, Guatemala City. See map at **Central American States.** —**Gua·te·ma·lan** *adj. & n.*

Guatemala City. *Spanish* **Guatemala de los Caballeros de Guatemala la Nueva.** Capital city of the republic of Guatemala, lying in a broad fertile plain in the southwestern region of the country. It is the largest city in Central America. It was founded in 1776 to replace Antigua as the capital, because its site was believed to be free of the danger of an earthquake. In 1917, however, an earthquake destroyed the city and it had to be rebuilt.

gua·va (gwaávə ‖ gwáwvə) *n.* **1.** Any of various tropical American and Asian shrubs and trees of the genus *Psidium;* especially, *P. guajava,* having white flowers and edible fruit. **2.** The pear-shaped fruit of this tree, having a yellow rind and pink flesh, and eaten fresh or preserved. [Spanish *guava, guayaba,* of South American Indian origin.]

Gua·ya·quil (gwa-ya-kíl). Official name **Santiago de Guayaquil**. City and chief port of Ecuador, and capital of Guayas province. Its industries include tanning, sugar refining, and iron founding.

gua·yu·le (gwə-yōōli, gwī-) *n.* A woody plant or shrub, *Parthenium argentatum*, of the southwestern United States and Mexico, having sap sometimes used as a source of rubber. [American Spanish, from Nahuatl *cuauhuli* : *cuahuitl*, tree + *uli*, gum.]

gub·bins (gúbbinz) *n., pl.* **gubbinses**. **1.** Something worthless. **2.** A device, utensil, or gadget. **3.** *Informal*. A foolish person. [16th century (originally, fragments) : from obsolete *gobbon*, perhaps akin to GOBBET.]

gu·ber·nac·u·lum (gōōbər-náckew-ləm) *n., pl.* **-la**. (-lə). *Anatomy*. Either of two ligaments in the foetus that are attached to the gonads. In males they guide the testes into the scrotum. [New Latin, from Latin, rudder : *gubernāre*, to steer + *-culum*, diminutive suffix.]

gu·ber·na·to·ri·al (gōō-bər-nə-táwri-əl, gēw- || -tóri-) *adj.* *Chiefly U.S.* Of or relating to a governor. [Late Latin *gubernātorius*, from Latin *gubernātor*, GOVERNOR.]

gu·ber·ni·ya (gōō-baírni-ə) *n.* **1.** An administrative subdivision of a soviet in the U.S.S.R. **2.** An administrative division equivalent to a province in Russia prior to 1917. [Russian, province, perhaps from Polish *gubernja*, from Latin *gubernāre*, GOVERN.]

guck (guk, gōōk) *n.* *Slang*. A messy substance, such as sludge. [Perhaps GOO + MUCK.]

gud·dle (gúdd'l) *v.* **-dled, -dling, -dles.** —*intr.* To catch fish with the hands by tickling with the fingers: *to guddle for trout.* —*tr.* To catch (a fish) in this manner. [19th century : origin obscure.]

gudg·eon¹ (gújən) *n.* **1.** A small Eurasian freshwater fish, *Gobio gobio*, related to the carp and used as food and bait. **2.** Any of various similar fishes. **3.** An enticement; a bait. **4.** *Slang*. Someone who is easily duped; a gullible person.

—*tr.v.* **gudgeoned, -eoning, -eons.** *Slang*. To dupe; cheat. [Middle English *gojoun*, from Old French *goujon*, from Latin *gōbiō*, *gōbius*, GOBY.]

gudgeon² *n.* **1.** A metal pivot or journal at the end of a shaft or axle, around which a wheel or other device turns. **2.** The part of a hinge into which the pin fits. **3.** *Nautical*. The socket for the pintle of a rudder. **4.** A metal pin that joins two pieces of stone. [Middle English *gudyon*, from Old French *goujon*, diminutive of *gouge*, GOUGE (chisel).]

gudgeon pin *n.* A pin that secures the little end of the connecting rod to the piston in an internal-combustion engine. Also *chiefly U.S.* "wrist pin".

Gud·run (gōōd-rōōn). Also **Guth·run** (gōōth-), **Kud·run** (kōōd-). The daughter of the king of the Nibelungs and wife of Sigurd in the *Volsunga Saga*.

guel·der rose (géldər) *n.* A shrub, *Viburnum opulus*, native to Eurasia, having clusters of white flowers and small red fruit. [Originally grown in GELDERLAND.]

Guelph, Guelf (gwelf) *n.* A member of a strong faction in medieval Italy that supported the power of the pope and the city-states in a struggle against the German emperors and the Ghibellines. —**Guelph·ic** *adj.* —**Guelph·ism** *n.*

Guenevere. Variant of **Guinevere**.

gue·non (gə-nón, -náwn, -nōn) *n.* Any of various African monkeys of the genus *Cercopithecus*, having long hind legs and a long tail. [French *guenon†*.]

guer·don (gérd'n) *n.* *Poetic*. A reward; a recompense.

—*tr.v.* **guerdoned, -doning, -dons.** *Poetic*. To reward. [Middle English, from Old French, from Medieval Latin *widerdōnum*, alteration (influenced by Latin *dōnum*, gift) of Old High German *widarlōn* : *widar*, again + *lōn*, reward, payment.]

Gue·ric·ke (gúri-kə), **Otto von** (1602–86). German physicist. His fame rests on his experiments in pneumatics, especially the invention of an air pump in *c.*1650. He also invented a primitive machine to generate electricity.

Guer·ni·ca (gérni-kə, ger-néekə, gair-). Historic town in the Basque region of northern Spain, in the province of Vizcaya. The severe air bombing of the town by German aircraft supporting the Nationalists in April, 1937, provoked Picasso to paint the famous work, *Guernica*.

guern·sey (gérnzi) *n., pl.* **-seys**. **1.** A knitted woollen sweater with a distinctive ribbed pattern across the shoulder, originally worn by seamen. **2.** *Australian*. A football jersey. [First worn by seamen on the island of GUERNSEY.]

Guern·sey¹ (gérnzi). An island and bailiwick in the English Channel. Guernsey Island itself is the second largest of the Channel Islands. The bailiwick includes all the Channel Islands except the largest, Jersey. The capital is St. Peter Port. Market gardening, dairy farming, and tourism are the chief industries.

Guernsey² *n., pl.* **-seys.** Any of a breed of brown and white dairy cattle originally developed on the Isle of Guernsey.

guer·ril·la, gue·ril·la (gə-ríllə, gyə- || ge-) *n.* A member of an irregular military unit, usually associated with a revolutionary movement, that seeks to overthrow a government or an occupying enemy by means of sudden acts of harassment.

—*adj.* Of or relating to guerrillas or their methods of fighting: *guerrilla warfare*. [Spanish *guerrilla*, diminutive of *guerra*, war, from Germanic.]

guess (gess) *v.* **guessed, guessing, guesses.** —*tr.* **1. a.** To predict (a result or event) with incomplete information. **b.** To assume, presume, or assert (a fact) without sufficient information. **2.** To esti-

mate correctly on the basis of incomplete information. **3.** *Chiefly U.S.* To suppose; judge. —*intr.* **1.** To make a conjecture. Often used with *at*: *We could only guess at his motives*. **2.** To make a correct guess. **3.** *Chiefly U.S.* To suppose. —See Synonyms at **conjecture**.

—*n.* **1.** An act or instance of guessing. **2.** A conjecture arrived at by guessing. [Middle English *gessen*, perhaps from Scandinavian; akin to Old Swedish and Danish *gisse*.] —**guess·er** *n.*

guess·ti·mate, gues·ti·mate (gésti-mət, -mit) *n.* An estimate based more on intuition than on strict calculation. [GUESS + ESTIMATE.] —**guess·ti·mate** (gésti-mayt) *v.*

guess·work (géss-wurk) *n.* **1.** The process of making guesses. **2.** An estimate or judgment made by this process.

guest (gest) *n.* **1.** One who receives hospitality at the home or table of another. **2.** One to whom some entertainment or service is offered. **3.** A visitor, such as a foreign dignitary, to whom the hospitality of an institution, municipality, or government has been extended. **4.** The patron of a restaurant, hotel, boarding house, or the like. **5.** A contestant, performer, speaker, or other person appearing in a concert, television programme, or the like. **6.** *Zoology*. A commensal organism; especially, an insect that lives in the nest or burrow of another species.

—*adj.* Of, for, or being a guest: *a guest conductor; a guest room*. —*v.* **guested, guesting, guests.** —*tr.* *Rare*. To entertain as one's guest. —*intr.* *Chiefly U.S.* To appear as a guest, especially on a television show. [Middle English *gest*, from Old Norse *gestr*.]

guest·house (gést-howss) *n.* A boarding house or small hotel.

guest rope *n.* *Nautical*. **1.** An extra line used with the towline to steady a ship being towed. **2.** A rope dropped over the side of a ship for steadying or securing a smaller boat coming alongside. Also called "guess rope".

Gue·va·ra (gə-vaár-ə, gi-), **Ernesto**, known as Che Guevara (1928–67). Latin-American revolutionary leader, born in Argentina. When Castro took power in Cuba (1959), Guevara was appointed President of the National Bank, and was Minister of Industry (1961–65). He later assisted revolutionary movements in other countries, but was captured by the Bolivian army and executed (1967). He wrote several books, among them a manual for revolutionaries, *Guerrilla Warfare* (1961).

guff (guf) *n.* *Slang*. Foolish talk; nonsense. [Originally, "puff", imitative.]

guf·faw (gu-fáw, gə- || *U.S. also* gúffaw) *n.* A hearty or coarse burst of laughter.

—*intr.v.* **guffawed, -fawing, -faws.** To laugh explosively. [Imitative.]

Gug·gen·heim (gōōggən-hīm, gōōgən-). Family of U.S. industrialists and philanthropists. Solomon (1861–1949) established the foundation which built the Guggenheim Museum of Modern Art in New York (opened 1957).

Gui·a·na or **Guy·a·na** (gī-ánə). Region on the north coast of South America, bounded by the rivers Orinoco, Amazon, and Negro. It consists of eastern Venezuela, Guyana, Surinam, French Guiana, and northern Brazil. See map at **Guyana**.

Gui·a·nas (gī-ánəz), **The**. Guyana (formerly British Guiana), Surinam (formerly Dutch Guiana), and French Guiana. See map at **Guyana**.

gui·dance (gíd'nss) *n.* **1.** An act or instance of guiding. **2.** Counselling, as on vocational, educational, or marital problems. **3.** Any of various processes or techniques by which missiles carrying sensing or information-processing equipment are guided in flight.

guide (gīd) *n. Abbr.* **g. 1.** One who shows the way by leading, directing, or advising, usually by reason of his greater experience with the course to be pursued. **2.** A person employed to guide a tour, group, or the like. **3. a.** Any sign or mark that serves to direct. **b.** An example, model, or criterion of accuracy to be followed. **4. a.** A guidebook. **b.** A book or manual that serves to instruct or to direct one's thinking. **5.** Any device, such as a ruler, line, ring, tab, or bar, that acts as an indicator or that regulates the motion of one's hand, a tool, or a machine part. **6. a.** A soldier stationed at the right or left of a column to control the alignment of the marchers, show the direction, or mark the point of pivot. **b.** A ship or vehicle on which other members of a convoy may align themselves. **7.** *Sometimes capital* **G.** A Girl Guide *(see)*.

—*v.* **guided, guiding, guides.** —*tr.* **1.** To show the way to; lead; direct. **2.** To direct the course of; steer: *guide a ship through a channel.* **3.** To manage the affairs of; govern. **4. a.** To influence the conduct or opinions of. **b.** To be a criterion for or motive of (an action, for example). —*intr.* To serve as a guide. [Middle English *g(u)ide*, from Old French, from Frankish *wītan*.] —**guid·a·ble** *adj.* —**guid·er** *n.*

guide·book (gíd-bŏŏk || -bōōk) *n.* A handbook of information for travellers, tourists, students, or the like.

guide·dog (gíd-dog || -dawg) *n.* A dog that has been specially trained to guide a blind person. Also *U.S.* "seeing eye dog".

guide·line (gíd-līn) *n.* **1.** *Printing*. A mark used to orient lettering, a drawing, or the like. **2.** *Usually plural*. A statement of policy or principles by a person or group having authority over an activity. **3.** Something serving as an example or source of instruction.

guided missile *n.* Any missile capable of being guided while it is in flight. Compare **ballistic missile**.

guide·post (gíd-pōst) *n.* A post with a sign giving directions placed at an intersection or fork in a road; a signpost.

guid·er (gī́dər) *n.* **1.** One that guides. **2.** *Capital* **G.** An adult who supervises a company of Girl Guides.

guide rope *n.* **1.** A rope fastened to another rope that is lifting a load, to guide the rope and steady the load. **2.** A rope used to steady or moor an airship or balloon.

gui·don (gī́d'n ‖ *U.S. also* gī́-don) *n. Military.* **1.** A small flag or pennant, often with a forked end, carried as a standard by a regiment or other military unit. **2.** The soldier bearing this standard. [French, from Italian *guidone,* from *guida,* GUIDE.]

guild, gild (gĭld) *n.* **1.** An association or corporation of persons of the same trade, pursuits, or interests formed for their mutual aid and protection, the maintenance of standards, or the furtherance of some purpose; especially, in medieval times, a society of merchants or artisans. **2.** *Ecology.* A group of plants having a characteristic mode of existence that involves some dependence upon other plant life, such as the lianas and epiphytes. [Middle English *gilde,* from Old Norse *gildi,* payment, fraternity, contribution.]

guil·der, gild·er (gĭldər) *n. Abbr.* **gld. 1.** The basic monetary unit of the Netherlands, Surinam, and the Netherlands Antilles, equal to 100 cents. **2.** A coin worth one guilder. Also called "gulden", "florin". [Middle English, alteration of Dutch *gulden,* GULDEN.]

guild·hall (gĭld-hawl) *n.* **1.** The meeting hall of a guild or corporation, especially in medieval times. **2. a.** A town hall. **b.** *Capital* **G.** The meeting hall of the Corporation of the City of London.

guilds·man (gĭldz-mən) *n., pl.* **-men** (-mən). A member of a guild.

guilds·wom·an (gĭldz-wŏŏmən) *n., pl.* **-women** (-wimmin). A female member of a guild.

guild socialism *n.* A type of socialism formerly advocated in England in which industry would be owned by the state but managed by a council of workers.

guile (gīl) *n.* **1.** Cunning; craftiness. **2.** *Obsolete.* A trick; a ruse. —See Synonyms at **artifice.**
~*tr.v.* **guiled, guiling, guiles.** *Archaic.* To beguile; deceive. [Middle English *gile,* from Old French *guile,* from Germanic; akin to Old English *wigle,* divination, sorcery.]

guile·ful (gīl-f'l) *adj.* Full of guile; artfully deceitful; crafty. —**guile·ful·ly** *adv.* —**guile·ful·ness** *n.*

guile·less (gīl-ləss, -liss) *adj.* Free of guile; simple; artless. See Synonyms at **naive.** —**guile·less·ly** *adv.* —**guile·less·ness** *n.*

Guil·laume (gee-yŏm), **Charles Edouard** (1861–1938). Swiss physicist. For his discovery of the steel-nickel alloy called *invar* he was awarded the Nobel prize for physics (1920).

guil·le·mot (gĭlli-mot) *n.* Any of several small sea birds of the genera *Uria* and *Cepphus,* of northern regions, having dark plumage with white markings. [French, diminutive of *Guillaume,* William.]

guil·loche (gi-lósh, -lôsh, gee-ŏsh) *n. Architecture.* An ornamental border formed of two or more bands interlaced in such a way as to repeat a design. [French *guillochis,* from *guillocher,* to decorate with guilloche, perhaps from Italian *ghiocciare,* dialectal variant of *gocciare,* to drip, trickle, from *goccia,* drop, from Latin *gutta.* See gout.]

guil·lo·tine (gĭllə-teen, -téen ‖ *U.S. also* gée-ə-) *n.* **1. a.** A machine with a heavy blade that falls freely between upright guides to behead a condemned prisoner. **b.** Any of various other machines used for execution by beheading. **c.** Execution by such a machine. Preceded by *the.* **2.** Any of various more or less similar cutting instruments, such as a surgical device used to remove tonsils. **3.** A device consisting of a long blade that is brought down onto a sheet of paper, metal, or the like to cut or trim it. **4.** *British.* A method of cutting off debate on a bill in Parliament by fixing beforehand a time for voting on successive stages. Compare **kangaroo closure.**
~*tr.v.* **guillotined, -tining, -tines. 1.** To behead with a guillotine. **2.** To cut or trim with a guillotine. [After Joseph Ignace *Guillotin* (1738–1814), French doctor who proposed its use.] —**guil·lo·tin·er** *n.*

guilt (gĭlt) *n.* **1.** The fact of being responsible for an offence or wrongdoing. **2.** *Law.* Culpability for a crime or breach of regulations that carries a legal punishment or penalty. **3. a.** Remorseful awareness of having done something wrong. **b.** Feelings of remorse arising from a sense of inadequacy or imagined wrongdoing. **4.** *Rare.* Guilty behaviour. [Middle English *gult, gilt,* Old English *gylt†.*]

guilt complex *n. Psychology.* An obsession with the idea of being to blame for something.

guilt·less (gĭlt-ləss, -liss) *adj.* **1.** Free from guilt; blameless; innocent. **2.** Without knowledge or experience of something. —**guilt·less·ly** *adv.* —**guilt·less·ness** *n.*

guilt·y (gĭlti) *adj.* **-ier, -iest. 1.** Responsible for or chargeable with some reprehensible act. Often used with *of: guilty of cheating.* **2.** *Law.* Having committed a crime or a breach of regulations or having been adjudged to have done so: *plead guilty.* **3.** At fault; culpable: *the guilty party.* **4.** Suffering from or showing a sense of guilt: *a guilty conscience.* —**guilt·i·ly** *adv.* —**guilt·i·ness** *n.*

guimpe (gimp, gamp) *n.* **1.** A short-sleeved blouse worn under a jumper. **2.** A yoke insert for a low-necked dress. **3.** A starched cloth covering the neck and shoulders as part of a nun's habit. **4.** Variant of **gimp** (trimming).

Guin. Guinea.

guin·ea (gĭnni) *n. Abbr.* **G., g. 1.** A former British gold coin worth one pound and one shilling. **2.** The sum of one pound and one shilling. [Originally made of gold from the *Guinea* coast of Africa.]

Guin·ea, Gulf of (gĭnni). Broad bay of the Atlantic Ocean formed by the large bend of the west coast of Africa. It extends, roughly, from the west coast of Ivory Coast to the Gabon estuary, and includes the bights of Benin and Biafra.

Guinea, Republic of. *French* **République populaire et révolutionnaire de Guinée.** Formerly **French Guinea.** Independent republic on the west coast of Africa. The interior consists chiefly of highlands, although in the northeast the land descends to the Niger plains. The bulk of the labour force is employed in agriculture, but the major exports are bauxite and alumina. Guinea was a French colony from 1891 until 1958, when it gained its independence. Area, 245 856 square kilometres (94,925 square miles). Population, 7,520,000. Capital, Conakry. See map at **West African States.**

Guin·ea-Bis·sau, Republic of (gĭnni-bi-sów). Formerly **Portuguese Guinea.** Independent republic on the west coast of Africa. Except for the highlands on the border with Guinea, the land is low-lying. The chief exports are peanuts and peanut products, palm products, and copra. The country was a Portuguese colony from 1879 until 1974, when it gained its independence under the African Party for the Independence of Guinea and Cape Verde. Area, 36 125 square kilometres (13,948 square miles). Population, 1,090,000. Capital, Bissau. See map at **West African States.**

Guinea corn *n.* Durra *(see).*

guinea fowl *n.* Any of several pheasant-like birds of the family Numididae, native to Africa; especially, a widely domesticated species, *Numida meleagris,* having blackish plumage marked with many small white spots. Also called "guinea hen". [From the *Guinea* coast of Africa.]

guinea hen *n.* **1.** A female guinea fowl. **2.** The guinea fowl.

Guinea pepper *n.* **1.** A variety of the plant, *Capsicum frutescens,* from which cayenne pepper is made. **2.** The spicy fruit of an African tree, *Xylopia aethiopica,* which is made into a condiment.

guinea pig *n.* **1.** A domesticated rodent descended from the Brazilian or Peruvian cavy, *Cavia procellus,* having variously coloured hair and no visible tail, and widely kept as pets and as experimental animals. **2.** A subject for experimentation. [Probably from a confusion of GUIANA with the *Guinea* coast of Africa.]

guinea worm *n.* A long, threadlike nematode worm, *Dracunculus medinensis,* of tropical Asia and Africa, that is a subcutaneous parasite of man and other animals, causing ulcers on the arms, legs, and feet. [Probably from the *Guinea* coast of Africa.]

guin·ep, gin·ep (gĭnn-ep) *n.* **1.** A tropical American tree, *Melicocca bijuga,* having small greenish-white fruit. **2.** The sweet, edible fruit of that tree. **3.** The **genipap** *(see).* [American Spanish *guenepo.*]

Guin·e·vere (gwĭnni-veer). Also **Guen·e·vere** (gwĕnni-). In Arthurian legend, the wife of King Arthur and the mistress of Lancelot. [Welsh *Gwenhwyvar,* perhaps "white phantom" : *gwyn,* white + *-hwyvar†,* phantom.]

Guin·ness (gĭnniss), **Sir Alec** (1914–). English stage and screen actor, knighted 1959. His films include *Kind Hearts and Coronets* (1949), in which he played eight parts, *The Lavender Hill Mob* (1951), *The Bridge on the River Kwai,* (1957, Oscar), and *Star Wars* (1977). His second volume of autobiography, *My Name Escapes Me,* came out in 1996.

gui·pure (gi-péwr, -póor; *French* gee-púr) *n.* A kind of coarse, large-patterned lace without a supporting net mesh. **2.** A trimming, **gimp** *(see).* [French, from Old French, from *guiper,* to cover with silk, wool, or the like, from Frankish *wīpan.*]

gui·ro (gwéer-ō, wéer-) *n.* A percussion instrument consisting of a dried gourd with parallel grooves cut across it. It produces a rattling sound when a stick is drawn across it. [Spanish, gourd.]

guise (gīz) *n.* **1.** Outward appearance; aspect. **2.** False appearance; pretence. **3.** Mode of dress; garb: *in the guise of a beggar.* **4.** *Obsolete.* Custom; habit.
~*v.* **guised, guising, guises.** —*tr. Archaic.* To costume. —*intr. Chiefly Scottish.* To go in disguise; masquerade. [Middle English, fashion, manner, from Old French, from Germanic.]

Guise (geez). A powerful French ducal line of the 16th and 17th centuries.

guis·er (gīzər) *n. Chiefly Scottish.* One who goes from door to door wearing mask and fancy dress at Hallowe'en, performing for money, sweets, or the like. [From dialectal *guise,* to masquerade, from GUISE (noun).]

gui·tar (gi-tár) *n.* A musical instrument similar to the lute, having a large flat-backed sound box generally in the shape of a violin, a long fretted neck, and usually six strings, played by strumming or plucking. [French *guitare,* from Old French, from Spanish *guitarra,* from Arabic *qītār,* from Greek *kithara,* lyre.] —**gui·tar·ist** *n.*

gui·tar·fish (gi-tár-fish) *n., pl.* **-fishes** or collectively **guitarfish.** Any of several bottom-dwelling marine fishes of the family Rhinobatidae having a guitar-shaped body.

Gui·try (gee-trée), **Sacha** (1885–1957). French playwright, actor, and film director. The best-known of the films which he directed are *The Story of a Cheat* (1935) and *Pearls of the Crown* (1937).

Gu·ja·rat (gŏŏ-jə-raat, gŏŏ-jə-). State in western India, lying on the Arabian Sea and including almost all of the Kathiawar peninsula. It was created in 1960 from the Gujarati-speaking parts of the former state of Bombay. The capital is Ahmadabad. Gujarat is the centre of India's cotton textile industry.

Gu·ja·ra·ti (gŏŏjə-raati, gŏŏjə-) *n., pl.* **Gujarati. 1.** The Indic language spoken in Gujarat. **2.** A native or inhabitant of Gujarat or speaker of Gujarati.

gu·lag (gŏŏ-lag) *n. Often capital* **G.** A forced labour camp or prison, used especially for political prisoners. [Russian *Glavnoye Uprav-*

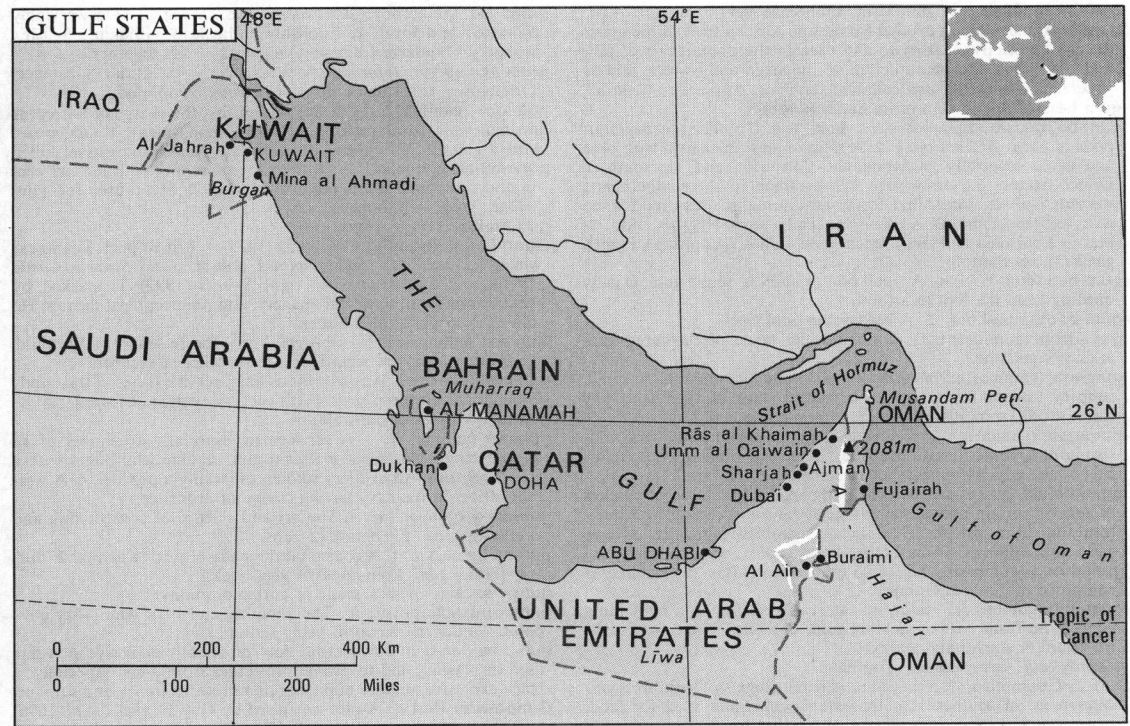

GULF STATES

IRAQ
KUWAIT
Al Jahrah • KUWAIT
Burgan • Mina al Ahmadi

SAUDI ARABIA

IRAN

THE
BAHRAIN
Muharraq
AL-MANAMAH
Strait of Hormuz
Musandam Pen.
OMAN
2081m
Dukhan
QATAR
DOHA
Rās al Khaimah
Umm al Qaiwain
Sharjah • Ajman
Dubai
Fujairah
GULF
Gulf of Oman
ABŪ DHABI
Buraimi
Al Ain
UNITED ARAB EMIRATES
Līwa
OMAN
Hajar
Tropic of Cancer

48°E   54°E   26°N

0   200   400 Km
0   100   200 Miles

---

leniye Trudovykh *Lag*erei, Main Administration for Corrective Labour Camps.]

gu·lar (gōō-lər, gēw-) *adj.* Of, pertaining to, or located on the throat. [Latin *gula,* throat.]

gulch (gulch) *n. U.S.* A small ravine, especially one cut by a torrent. [Origin obscure.]

gul·den (gōōl-dən, gōōl-) *n., pl.* **guldens** or **gulden.** A monetary unit, the **guilder** *(see).* [Dutch *gulden (florijn),* golden (florin), from Middle Dutch.]

gules (gēwlz) *n. Heraldry.* The colour red, indicated on a blazon by engraved vertical lines.
~*adj. Heraldry.* Red. Usually used after the noun: *a lion gules.* [Middle English *goules,* from Old French *go(u)les,* red, red fur neckpiece, from the plural of *gole,* throat, from Latin *gula,* throat.]

gulf (gulf) *n.* **1.** *Abbr.* **G.** A large area of a sea or ocean partially enclosed by land; especially, a long landlocked portion of sea opening through a strait. **2.** A deep, wide chasm; an abyss. **3.** A separating distance or wide gap caused especially by a lack of understanding or communication. **4.** A whirlpool; an eddy.
~*tr.v.* **gulfed, gulfing, gulfs.** To swallow; engulf. [Middle English *golf, goulf,* from Old French *golfe,* from Old Italian *golfo,* from Vulgar Latin *colp(h)us* (unattested), from Greek *kolpos, kolphos,* bosom, fold, bay.]

Gulf, The. 1. Also **Persian Gulf** or **Arabian Gulf.** Arm of the Indian Ocean, between Iran and the Arabian Peninsula. Bounded in the south by the Strait of Hormuz, it is 816 kilometres (507 miles) long. Strategically important for the Middle East because of the access it gives to its large offshore oil reserves. See map at **Gulf States.** **2.** *U.S.* The Gulf of **Mexico** *(see).*

Gulf States. The small, oil-rich Arab states on The Gulf: Bahrain, Kuwait, Qatar, and the United Arab Emirates.

Gulf Stream *n.* A warm ocean current of the North Atlantic, issuing from the Gulf of Mexico and flowing east through the Straits of Florida, northeast along the southeastern coast of the United States, then east to become the North Atlantic Drift Current.

gulf·weed (gúlf-weed) *n.* Any of several brownish seaweeds of the genus *Sargassum,* especially *S. natans,* of tropical Atlantic waters, having rounded air bladders and often forming dense, floating masses. Also called "sargassum", "sargassum weed". [After the Gulf of Mexico, where it is found.]

gull¹ (gul) *n.* Any of various chiefly coastal aquatic birds of the subfamily Larinae, having long wings, webbed feet, and usually grey and white plumage. [Middle English *gull,* probably from Welsh *gwylan,* from Celtic *voilenno-* (unattested).]

gull² *n.* A gullible person; a dupe; a simpleton.
~*tr.v.* **gulled, gulling, gulls.** To deceive; cheat; dupe. [Probably from dialectal *gull,* unfledged bird, Middle English *golle, gulle,* probably from *gul,* yellow, pale, from Old Norse *gulr.*]

Gul·lah (gúllə) *n.* **1.** Any of a group of Negroes inhabiting the Sea Islands and coastal area of South Carolina, Georgia, and northern Florida. **2.** The creolised English spoken by these people.

gul·let (gúllit) *n.* **1.** *Anatomy.* The oesophagus. **2.** The throat. **3.** A gully or ravine, especially one that serves as a water channel. **4.** A cut in the earth preliminary to mining or excavating. [Middle Eng-

lish *golet,* from Old French *goulet,* diminutive of *gole, goule,* throat, from Latin *gula.*]

gul·li·ble (gúllə-b'l) *adj.* Able to be taken in; easily deceived or duped; credulous. [From GULL (dupe).] —**gul·li·bil·i·ty** (-bíllti) *n.* —**gul·li·bly** *adv.*

Gull·strand (gúl-strand, -stran), **Allvar** (1862–1930). Swedish ophthalmologist. For his experiments on the refraction of light in the eye he was awarded the Nobel prize in 1911.

gul·ly¹ (gúlli) *n., pl.* **-lies. 1.** A deep ditch or channel cut in the earth by running water, usually after a downpour. **2.** A gutter or channel. **3.** *Australian & N.Z.* A river valley. **4.** In cricket: **a.** A fielding position between the point and slips. **b.** A fielder in this position.
~*tr.v.* **gullied, -lying, -lies.** To make a gully in. [Alteration of GULLET.]

gully² *n., pl.* **-lies.** *Chiefly Scottish.* A large knife. [Short for *gully knife* : *gully,* probably alteration of GULLET + KNIFE.]

gu·los·i·ty (gew-lóssəti) *n. Literary.* Gluttony. [Late Latin *gulōsitās* (stem *gulōsitāt-*), from Latin *gulōsus,* greedy, from *gula,* gullet.]

gulp (gulp) *v.* **gulped, gulping, gulps.** —*tr.* **1.** To swallow greedily or rapidly in large amounts. Usually used with *down: gulp down coffee.* **2.** To stifle by or as if by swallowing. —*intr.* **1.** To choke or gasp; swallow air, as in nervousness. **2.** To swallow food or drink in gulps. **3.** To make a noise in the throat when swallowing.
~*n.* **1.** The act of gulping. **2.** A large mouthful. **3.** A convulsive attempt to swallow; a catching of air in the throat. [Middle English *gulpen,* from Middle Dutch *gulpen* (imitative).] —**gulp·er** *n.* —**gulp·ing·ly** *adv.*

gulp·er eel (gúlpər) *n.* Any of various eel-like fishes of the genera *Eurypharynx* and *Saccopharynx,* which live on the sea bottom and can swallow prey much larger than themselves.

gum¹ (gum) *n.* **1. a.** Any of various viscous substances that are exuded by certain plants and trees and that dry into water-soluble, noncrystalline, brittle solids. **b.** Loosely, a similar plant exudate, such as a resin. **2.** Any of various adhesives made from such exudates or from some other sticky substance. **3. a.** Any of various trees, such as one of the genera *Eucalyptus, Liquidambar,* or *Nyssa,* that are a source of gum. Also called "gum tree". **b.** The wood of such a tree. Also called "gumwood". **4.** Chewing gum or bubble gum.
~*v.* **gummed, gumming, gums.** —*tr.* To cover, smear, seal, fill, or fix in place with gum. —*intr.* **1.** To exude or form gum. **2.** To become sticky or clogged with gum or a similar substance. —**gum up. 1.** To become clogged, as with gum. **2.** *Slang.* To ruin; bungle; spoil: *gum up the works.* [Middle English *gumme, gomme,* from Old French *gomme,* from Vulgar Latin *gumma* (unattested), from Latin *gummi, cummi,* from Greek *kommi,* from Egyptian *kemai.*]

gum² *n.* The firm connective tissue that is covered by mucous membrane and that envelops the bones of the jaw containing the tooth sockets and surrounds the bases of the teeth. Also called "gingiva". [Middle English *gome,* Old English *gōma,* palate, jaw.]

gum³ *interj. British.* Used as a mild oath: *By gum, it's cold out!* [Euphemistic for *God.*]

gum ac·croi·des (ə-króy-deez) *n.* A gum resin, **acaroid gum** *(see).* [New Latin *accroides,* from ACAROID.]

gum ammoniac *n.* A gum resin, **ammoniac** *(see).*

gum arabic *n.* A gum exuded by various African trees of the genus *Acacia,* especially *A. senegal,* and used in the preparation of pills and emulsions, the manufacture of mucilage and sweets, and in general as a thickener and colloidal stabiliser. Also called "acacia".

gum benzoin *n.* A gum resin, **benzoin** *(see).*

gum·bo, gom·bo (gúmbō) *n., pl.* **-bos. 1. a.** *U.S.* The mucilaginous pods of okra. **b.** Okra *(see).* **2.** A soup or stew thickened with okra and eaten especially in Africa, the Caribbean and the southern United States. **3.** A fine silty soil, common in the southern and western United States, that forms an unusually sticky mud when wet. **4.** Often capital **G.** A patois spoken by some Negroes and Creoles in Louisiana and the French West Indies. [Louisiana French *gombo,* from Bantu.]

gum·boil (gúm-boyl) *n.* A small boil or abscess on the gum, usually opening from the root of a tooth.

gum·boot (gúm-bōōt) *n.* A **Wellington boot** *(see).*

gum·drop (gúm-drop) *n.* A small sweet made of flavoured gum arabic or gelatine.

gum·ma (gúmmə) *n., pl.* **-mas** or **gummata** (gúmmətə). A small, rubbery tumour formed in an advanced stage of syphilis. [New Latin, from Latin *gummi,* GUM.] **—gum·ma·tous** *adj.*

gum·mite (gúmmīt) *n.* A yellow to orange amorphous mineral consisting of hydrated uranium oxides. [German *Gummi,* GUM (referring to the gummy appearance of some types) + -ITE.]

gum·mo·sis (gu-mṓ-siss) *n.* The pathological formation of patches of gum on certain plants, such as sugar cane and certain fruit trees, resulting from attack by insects, microorganisms, or adverse weather conditions. [New Latin : Latin *gummi,* GUM + -OSIS.]

gum·mous (gúmm-əss) *adj.* Also **gum·mose** (-ōss). **1.** Gumlike or composed of gum. **2.** Gummy.

gum·my[1] (gúmmi) *adj.* **-mier, -miest. 1.** Consisting of or containing gum. **2.** Suffused with or yielding gum. **3.** Sticky; viscid. **4.** Coated with gum or something gumlike.

gummy[2] *adj.* **-mier, -miest.** Toothless.
~*n., pl.* **gummies. 1.** *Australian.* A small sluggish shark, *Mustelus antarcticus,* of southern Pacific waters, sometimes used for food. **2.** *Australian & N.Z. Informal.* A sheep that has lost all its teeth. [From GUM (of the mouth).]

gump·tion (gúmpsh'n) *n. Informal.* **1.** Basic common sense; practicality. **2.** Enterprise or initiative, especially when requiring courage or nerve. [18th century (Scottish) : origin obscure.]

gum resin *n.* A mixture of gum and resin that exudes from some trees and other plants.

gum·shield (gúm-sheeld) *n.* A rubber device or plate worn to protect the mouth in playing sports.

gum·shoe (gúm-shōō) *n. U.S.* **1.** A rubber shoe or overshoe. **2.** A sneaker. **3.** *Slang.* A detective.
~*intr.v.* **gumshoed, -shoeing, -shoes.** *U.S. Slang.* To investigate stealthily; pry.

gum tree *n.* A tree, the **gum** *(see).* **—up a gum tree.** *Informal.* **1.** In difficulties. **2.** Baffled; having no clue.

gum·wood (gúm-wŏŏd) *n.* The wood of a gum tree. See **gum.**

gun (gun) *n.* **1.** A weapon consisting essentially of a metal tube from which a projectile is fired at high velocity. **2.** A cannon, as distinguished from a small firearm. **3.** A portable firearm. **4.** A device that shoots a projectile. **5.** A discharge of a gun as a signal or salute. **6.** One who carries or uses a gun, such as a member of a shooting party. **7.** A device that projects something under pressure or at great speed: *a grease gun; an electron gun.* **8.** *Australian & N.Z. Informal.* An expert. Also used adjectivally: *a gun shearer.* **—go great guns.** *Informal.* To proceed with vigour or success. **—jump the gun. 1.** To begin a race before the starting signal. **2.** *Informal.* To act before the appropriate moment. **—spike (someone's) guns.** To hinder or obstruct someone's plans. **—stick to (one's) guns.** To hold fast to an opinion or appointed course of action.
~*v.* **gunned, gunning, guns. —***tr.* **1.** To fire upon; shoot. Often used with *down.* **2.** *Chiefly U.S. Informal.* To open the throttle of so as to accelerate: *gun an engine. —intr.* To hunt or shoot with a gun. **—gun for. 1.** To seek to catch, overcome, or destroy. **2.** To go after in earnest; set out to obtain: *gun for the best deal available.* [Middle English *gunne, gonne,* probably from *Gunna* (unattested), pet form of feminine name *Gunhild* (sometimes applied to a war engine), from Old Norse *Gunnhildr* : *gunnr,* war + *hildr,* war.]

gun·boat (gún-bōt) *n.* A small armed vessel.

gunboat diplomacy *n.* Diplomacy that makes use of the threat of military intervention in order to achieve its purpose.

gun carriage *n.* A frame or structure upon which a gun is mounted for firing or manoeuvring.

gun·cot·ton (gún-kott'n) *n.* An explosive, **cellulose nitrate** *(see).*

gun dog *n.* A dog trained or bred to assist hunters, as in flushing or retrieving game.

gun·fight (gún-fīt) *n.* Also **gun·fight·ing** (-ing). *U.S.* A duel or battle with firearms. **—gun·fight·er** *n.*

gun·fire (gún-fīr) *n.* The firing of guns.

gun·flint (gún-flint) *n.* The piece of flint used to strike the igniting spark in a flintlock.

gunge (gunj) *n. Chiefly British Informal.* Any gluey, sticky, usually repulsive, substance.
~*tr.v.* **gunged, gunging, gunges.** *Chiefly British Informal.* To block or clog with gunge: *The drains are gunged up.* [Imitative (influenced by GOO and SPONGE).] **—gun·gy** (gún-ji) *adj.*

gung ho (gúng hṓ) *adj. Chiefly U.S. Slang.* **1.** Unswervingly dedicated and loyal. **2.** Foolishly enthusiastic. [Pidgin English : probably Mandarin Chinese *gōng,* work + *hé,* together.]

gunk (gungk) *n. Informal.* A filthy, slimy, or greasy substance. [Originally a trade name for a degreasing compound.]

gun·lock (gún-lok) *n.* A device for igniting the charge of a firearm.

gun·man (gún-mən, -man) *n., pl.* **-men** (-mən, -men). **1.** One armed with a gun. **2.** A desperado; an outlaw. **3.** A professional killer.

gun·met·al (gún-mett'l) *n.* **1.** An alloy of copper with ten per cent tin and sometimes a few per cent of zinc. **2.** Metal used for guns. **3.** Dark grey. **—gun·met·al** *adj.*

gun moll *n. Slang.* A **moll** *(see).*

Gunn (gun), **Thom(son William)** (1929–). British poet. His work, which includes *My Sad Captains* (1961), *Jack Straw's Castle* (1976), and *The Man with Night Sweats* (1992), is marked by strictness of form, powerful imagery, and philosophical themes. He now lives in the United States.

Gun·nar (gŏŏnnaar). *Norse Mythology.* The husband of Brynhild, the brother-in-law of Sigurd, and the brother of Gudrun.

gun·nel[1] (gúnn'l) *n.* Any of various long, eel-like fishes of the family Pholidae, of northern seas. [17th century : origin obscure.]

gunnel[2]. Variant of **gunwale.**

gun·ner (gúnnər) *n.* **1.** A serviceman, especially a member of an aircraft crew, who aims or fires a gun. **2.** One who hunts with a gun. **3.** *British.* An artillery soldier, especially a private. **4.** A warrant officer in the navy having charge of ordnance.

gun·ner·y (gúnnəri) *n.* **1.** The art and science of constructing and operating guns. **2.** The use of guns.

gun·ny (gúnni) *n.* **1.** A coarse fabric made of jute or hemp. **2.** Burlap. [Hindi *gōnī,* from Sanskrit *goṇī,* sack.]

gunny sack *n.* A sack made of burlap or gunny.

gun·point (gún-poynt) *n.* The shooting end of a gun. **—at gunpoint.** Under the threat of being shot at.

gun·pow·der (gún-powdər) *n.* Any of various explosive powders used in blasting and to propel projectiles from guns; especially, a black explosive mixture of potassium nitrate, charcoal, and sulphur.

Gunpowder Plot *n.* A plot organised by Guy Fawkes (1570–1606) to blow up Parliament and kill James I on November 5, 1605, in protest against the increasing repression of Roman Catholics in England. See **Guy Fawkes Night.**

gunpowder tea *n.* A green tea whose leaves are rolled into pellets.

gun·room (gún-rōōm, -rŏŏm) *n.* The quarters of midshipmen and junior officers on a British warship.

gun·run·ner (gún-runnər) *n.* One that smuggles firearms and ammunition. **—gun·run·ning** *n. & adj.*

gun·ship (gún-ship) *n.* An armed helicopter or other aircraft used to support troops and cover transport helicopters.

gun·shot (gún-shot) *n.* **1.** Shot fired from a gun. **2.** A shooting of a gun. **3.** The range of a gun: *within gunshot.*

gun·shy (gún-shī) *adj.* Afraid of gunfire. Said mainly of gun dogs.

gun·sling·er (gún-sling-ər) *n. U.S. Slang.* A gunman; a gunfighter. **—gun·sling·ing** *n. & adj.*

gun·smith (gún-smith) *n.* One who makes or repairs firearms.

gun·stock (gún-stok) *n.* A **stock** *(see).*

Gun·ter's chain (gúntərz) *n.* A measuring instrument; a chain. [After Edmund *Gunter* (1581–1626), English mathematician.]

Gun·ther (gŏŏntər). In the *Nibelungenlied,* a king of Burgundy whose wife Brunhild is won for him by Siegfried, who receives Kriemhild, Gunther's sister, as his wife. Identified with Gunnar.

gun·wale, gun·nel (gúnn'l) *n.* The upper edge of a ship's side. [Middle English *gonnewale* : GUN + WALE (so called because it served formerly as a prop for the ship's guns).]

gun·yah (gún-yə) *n.* An Australian Aboriginal hut made of branches and bark. [From a native Australian language.]

Guo·min·dang, Kuo·min·tang (gwṓ-mín-dáng) *n.* A political party founded by Sun Zhong Shan (Sun Yat-sen) in China in 1911, now the official ruling party in Taiwan.

Guo·yu, Kuo·yü (gwṓ-yū) *n.* **Mandarin Chinese** *(see).* [Mandarin Chinese *guó yŭ* : *guó,* nation, national + *yŭ,* language.]

gup·py (gúppi) *n., pl.* **-pies.** A small, brightly coloured freshwater fish, *Poecilia reticulata* (or *Lebistes reticulatus*), of northern South America and adjacent islands of the West Indies, that is popular in home aquariums. [After R.J.L. *Guppy,* 19th-century clergyman of Trinidad who supplied the British Museum with the first specimen.]

Gur (goor) *n.* A group of languages of the Niger-Congo family spoken chiefly in Ghana and Upper Volta.

gur·gi·ta·tion (gúrji-táysh'n) *n.* A whirling motion, as of water; ebullition. [Late Latin *gurgitāre,* to engulf, from Latin *gurges* (stem *gurgit-*), whirlpool, gulf.]

gur·gle (gúrg'l) *v.* **-gled, -gling, -gles. —***intr.* **1.** To flow in a broken, uneven current making intermittent low sounds. **2.** To make such sounds: *the baby gurgled with pleasure. —tr.* To express or pronounce with a gurgling sound.
~*n.* The act or sound of gurgling. [Probably from Medieval Latin *gurgulāre,* from Latin *gurguliō,* gullet.] **—gur·gling·ly** *adv.*

Gur·kha (gúr-kə, goór-) *n., pl.* **-khas** or collectively **Gurkha.** Also **Ghurkha. 1.** A member of a Rajput ethnic group that was driven out of India by the Muslims and is now predominant in Nepal. **2.** A soldier from Nepal serving in the British or Indian armies.

Gur·mu·khi (goór-mŏŏki) *n.* The alphabet used for the sacred writings of the Sikhs. [Sanskrit : *guru,* teacher + *mukh,* mouth.]

gur·nard (gúr-nərd) *n., pl.* **gurnards** or collectively **gurnard.** Also **gur·net** (gúr-nit). Any of various marine fishes of the family Triglidae, and especially of the Old World genus *Trigla*, having large, finger-like, pectoral fins and a large, armoured head. Compare **flying gurnard**. [Middle English, from Old French *gornart*, from Latin *grundīre, grunnīre*, to grunt (because it grunts when caught).]

gu·ru (gŏŏr-ōō, gŏŏ-rōō || *U.S. also* gə-rōō *n.* **1.** *Often capital* **G.** A spiritual teacher or leader, as in the Hindu or Sikh religions. **2.** *Informal.* A charismatic leader or guide: *a management guru.* [Hindi *gurū*, "the venerable one", from Sanskrit *guruh*, heavy, venerable.]

gush (gush) *v.* **gushed, gushing, gushes.** —*intr.* **1.** To flow forth suddenly and violently. **2.** To issue or emanate abundantly. **3.** To make an excessively demonstrative or affected display of sentiment or enthusiasm. —*tr.* To emit abundantly.
~*n.* **1.** A sudden, violent, or copious outflow: *a gush of tears.* **2.** An excessive, usually insincere, display of emotion. [Middle English *guschen, gosshen,* perhaps from Scandinavian, akin to Icelandic *gusa.*]

gush·er (gúshər) *n.* **1.** One that gushes. **2.** A gas or oil well with an abundant natural flow.

gush·y (gúshi) *adj.* **-ier, -iest.** Characterised by excessive, affected displays of sentiment or enthusiasm.

gus·set (gússit) *n.* **1.** A triangular insert, as in a garment, for strengthening or enlarging. **2.** A triangular metal bracket used to strengthen a joist. [Middle English, from Old French *gousset*, armpit, piece of armour under the armpit, diminutive of *gousse†*, pod, shell.] —**gus·set·ed** *adj.*

gus·sie (gússi) *n. Australian Informal.* A silly or effeminate man.

gus·sy (gússi) *tr.v.* **-sied, -sying, -sies.** *Slang.* To dress smartly. Used with *up: all gussied up in her Sunday best.* [Origin obscure.]

gust[1] (gust) *n.* **1.** A violent, abrupt rush of wind, smoke, or the like. **2.** An abrupt outburst of emotion, as of rage. —See Synonyms at **wind.** [Old Norse *gustr.*]

gust[2] *n. Archaic.* **1.** Relish; gusto. **2.** Personal taste or inclination; liking. [Middle English *guste*, taste, from Latin *gustus.*]

gus·ta·tion (gu-stáysh'n) *n.* The act or faculty of tasting; taste. [Latin *gustātiō* (stem *gustātiōn-*), from *gustāre*, to taste, from *gustus*, taste.]

gus·ta·to·ry (gústa-təri, -tri) *adj.* Also **gus·ta·tive** (-tiv). Of or pertaining to the sense of taste.

Gus·ta·vus II (gōō-stáavəss), known as **Gustavus Adolphus** (1594–1632). King of Sweden (1611–32). As a general he fought successfully against Denmark, Russia, and Poland. He was drawn into the Thirty Years' War by his desire to assure Swedish control of the Baltic. He met his death at the battle of Lützen (1632).

gus·to (gústō) *n.* **1.** Vigorous enjoyment; relish; zest. **2.** *Archaic.* Artistic style of execution. [Italian, from Latin *gustus*, taste.]

gus·ty (gústi) *adj.* **-tier, -tiest. 1.** Blowing in or characterised by gusts. **2.** Marked by sudden outbursts: *a gusty temperament.* —**gus·ti·ly** *adv.* —**gus·ti·ness** *n.*

gut (gut) *n.* **1.** The alimentary canal or a portion thereof; especially, the intestine or stomach. **2.** *Plural.* The bowels; the entrails; the viscera. **3.** *Plural.* The essential contents or part of something: *the guts of the engine.* **4.** The intestines of some animals prepared as strings for musical instruments or as surgical sutures; catgut. **5.** *Plural. Informal.* Courage; nerve. **6.** A narrow passage or channel. **7.** Fibrous material taken from the silk gland of a silkworm before it spins a cocoon, used for fishing tackle. **7.** *Informal.* A **beer gut** *(see).* —**hate (someone's) guts.** *Informal.* To detest or feel very hostile towards someone. —**sweat** or **work (one's) guts out.** *Informal.* To work extremely hard.
~*tr.v.* **gutted, gutting, guts. 1.** To remove the intestines or entrails of. **2.** To strip the contents or interior from: *gut a house.* **3.** To extract the essential points of (a book, article, or the like); summarise.
~*adj. Slang.* Arousing or aroused by basic emotions; visceral; instinctive: *a gut response.* [Middle English *gut*, Old English *guttas* (plural).]

gut·buck·et (gút-buckit) *n.* **1.** An early style of jazz, with a strong beat. Also called "barrelhouse". **2.** A homemade instrument, resembling a double bass, on which this music was originally played.

Gu·ten·berg (gōōt'n-berg; *German-* bairk), **Johann** (*c.*1397–1468). German printer. He was the first European to print with movable type set in moulds. His Mazarin Bible of *c.* 1455 is believed to be the first book printed with movable type.

Guth·rie test (gúthri) *n.* A blood test to determine the presence of the metabolic disease phenylketonuria in young children. [After Samuel *Guthrie* (1782–1848), U.S. chemist.]

Guthrun. Variant of **Gudrun.**

gut·less (gút-ləss, -liss) *adj. Informal.* **1.** Lacking courage or drive. **2.** Insubstantial; weak. —**gut·less·ness** *n.*

guts (gutss) *n., pl.* **gutses.** *Informal.* A person who eats far too much; a greedy person.
~*v.* **gutsed, gutsing, gutses.** *Chiefly Australian & N.Z. Informal.* —*tr.* To stuff (oneself) full of food. —*intr.* To eat greedily.

-guts *n. comb. form. Informal.* Indicates a person with a specified tendency; for example, **greedy-guts, worry-guts.**

guts·er (gút-sər) *n. Australian Informal.* A bad fall. Used chiefly in the phrase *to come a gutser.*

guts·y (gút-si) *adj.* **-ier, -iest.** *Informal.* **1.** Full of courage; daring; plucky. **2.** Earthy and uninhibited; raunchy: *a gutsy singing voice.* **3.** Greedy. —**guts·i·ness** *n.*

gut·ta (gútta || gŏótta) *n., pl.* **guttae** (gútt-ee || gŏót-, -ī) **1.** *Architecture.* One of a group of small, droplike ornaments on a Doric entab-

lature. **2.** *Abbr.* **gt.** *Medicine.* A drop. [Latin, drop.]

gut·ta-per·cha (gútta-pérchə) *n.* **1.** Any of several tropical trees of the genera *Palaquium* and *Payena*, having sap in the form of milky latex. **2.** A rubbery substance derived from the latex of these trees, used as electrical insulation and for waterproofing. [Malay *gĕtah percha* : *gĕtah*, sap + *percha*, (name of tree).]

gut·tate (gútt-ayt) *adj.* Also **gut·tat·ed** (-aytid). **1.** In the form of drops or having drops. **2.** *Biology.* Spotted as if by drops. [Latin *guttatus*, from *gutta*, drop.]

gut·ta·tion (gu-táysh'n, gə-) *n.* Loss of water from the surface of a plant in the form of liquid drops rather than vapour. [Latin *gutta*, drop.]

gut·ter (gúttər) *n.* **1.** A channel for draining off water at the edge of a street or road. **2.** A pipe or trough for draining off water, fitted to the edge of a roof. **3.** A furrow or groove formed by running water. **4.** The trough on either side of a bowling alley. **5. a.** The space left for perforation, between stamps on a sheet. **b.** *Printing.* The white space between the facing pages of a book. **6.** An environment of poverty, vulgarity, or criminal activities; a slum.
~*v.* **guttered, -tering, -ters.** —*tr.* To form gutters or furrows in. —*intr.* **1.** To flow in channels or rivulets. **2.** To melt away through the channel formed by a burning wick. Said of candles. **3.** To burn with a low flame; flicker. [Middle English *guter, goter*, sewer, trough, drain, from Anglo-French *gotere*, from Vulgar Latin *guttāria* (unattested), from Latin *gutta*, drop.]

gut·ter·ing (gúttəring) *n.* The drainpipes, gutters, and the like, fitted to the outside of a building to drain off rainwater.

gutter press *n.* The section of the popular press that seeks to reveal facts about people's personal lives in a sordid way.

gut·ter·snipe (gúttər-snīp) *n.* A street urchin.

gut·tur·al (gútt-ərəl, -rəl) *adj.* **1.** Of or pertaining to the throat. **2.** Produced in the throat. **3.** *Phonetics.* Produced in or near the throat; velar or uvular. Not in technical usage.
~*n.* A guttural sound, such as a **velar** *(see).* [Old French, from Latin *guttur*, throat.] —**gut·tur·al·ism, gut·tur·al·i·ty** (-ə-rál-əti), **gut·tur·al·ness** *n.* —**gut·tur·al·ly** *adv.*

gut·tur·al·ise, gut·tur·al·ize (gúttərə-līz) *tr.v.* **-ised, -ising, -ises.** *Phonetics.* To make guttural. —**gut·tur·al·i·sa·tion** (-lī-záysh'n || *U.S.* -li-) *n.*

guv (guv) *n. British.* Governor. Used as an informal term of address.

guv·nor, guv'nor (gúvnər) *n. British.* Governor. Used as an informal term of address.

guy[1] (gī) *n.* A rope, cord, or cable used for steadying, guiding, or holding something.
~*tr.v.* **guyed, guying, guys.** To fasten, guide, or hold with a guy. [Probably from Low German, akin to Dutch *gei†*, brail.]

guy[2] *n.* **1.** *Informal.* A man; a fellow. **2.** *British.* One who is odd or grotesque in appearance or dress. **3.** *Chiefly British.* An effigy of Guy Fawkes burned on Guy Fawkes Night. [After *Guy Fawkes.*]
~*tr.v.* **guyed, guying, guys.** To make fun of; mock.

Guy·an·a, Cooperative Republic of (gī-ánnə). Formerly **British Guiana.** Independent republic within the Commonwealth, lying in northeastern South America. It was a British colony from 1814 until 1966, when it gained its independence. It became a republic in 1970. Bauxite has now overtaken sugar and its by-products as its major export. Rice, gold, and diamonds are also exported. Some 51 per cent of the population are of Asian origin (descendants of indentured labourers), and 33 per cent are descendants of African slaves. Area, 214 969 square kilometres (83,000 square miles). Population, 840,000. Capital, Georgetown. See map, next page.

Guyane Française. See French Guiana.

Guy Fawkes Night (gī fáwks, fawks) *n.* In Britain, the night of November 5, commemorating the discovery of the **Gunpowder Plot** in 1605 and celebrated with fireworks and a bonfire on which a guy is burned. Also called "Bonfire Night".

guyot (gee-ō) *n.* A flat-topped submarine mountain. [After Arnold *Guyot*, Swiss 19th-century geographer and geologist.]

guz·zle (gúzz'l) *tr.v.* **-zled, -zling, -zles.** To eat or drink greedily or inordinately. [Perhaps from Old French *gosiller*, vomit, from *gosier†*, throat.] —**guz·zler** *n.*

Gwent (gwent). Formerly a county in southeast Wales, now administratively subdivided. It comprised the county of Monmouth excluding the Rhymney valley, plus Brynmawr, formerly part of Brecknockshire.

Gwyn (gwin), **Nell**, properly Eleanor Gwyn (1650–87). English actress, the mistress of Charles II. She bore Charles two sons, of whom the elder was made Duke of St. Albans.

Gwyn·edd (gwín-eth, -əth). From 1974 to 1976, a county of northwest Wales created by the merger of the counties of Anglesey, Caernarvon, Merioneth, and that part of the Conwy valley then in Denbighshire. Since 1996 it has been a Unitary Authority area in Wales encompassing the old counties of Caernarvonshire and Merionethshire.

gwyn·i·ad (gwínni-ad) *n.* A freshwater fish, *Coregonus pennantii,* found in Lake Bala, Wales. It is a variety of whitefish. [Welsh, from *gwyn*, white.]

gybe, jibe (jīb) *v.* **gybed** or **jibed, gybing** or **jibing, gybes** or **jibes.** —*intr.* To shift a fore-and-aft sail from one side of a vessel to the other while sailing before the wind; jib. —*tr.* To cause to gybe.
~*n.* The act of gybing. [From obsolete Dutch *gijben†.*]

gym (jim) *n.* **1.** A gymnasium. **2.** Gymnastics.

gym·kha·na (jim-káanə || -kánnə) *n. Chiefly British.* **1.** An event at

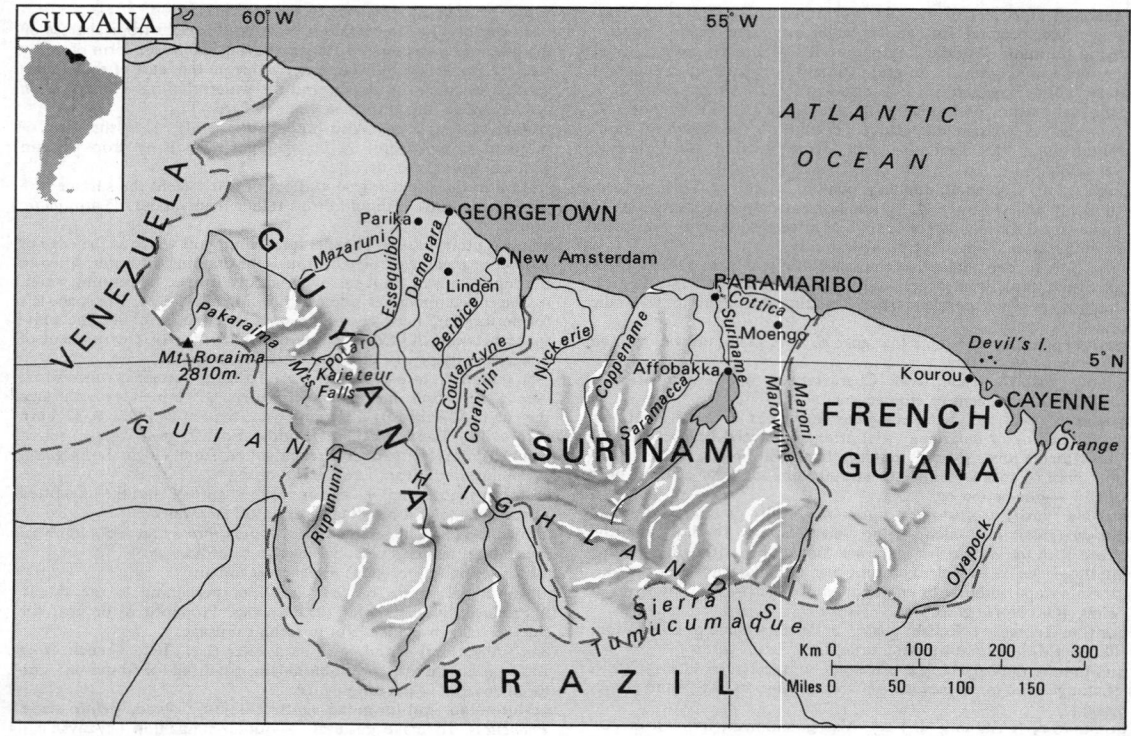

which various competitions are held to test the speed and skill of horses or ponies and their riders. **2.** An athletic competition or display. **3.** A place where such an event or competition is held. [Blend of GYM(NASIUM) + Hindi *(gend)-khānā,* "(ball) house", racket court, from *khāna,* house, from Persian *khāna*†.]

gym·na·si·um (jim-náy-zi-əm *for sense 1;* gim-ná́azi-ŏŏm *for sense 2*) *n., pl.* **-ums** or **-sia** (-zi-ə). **1.** A room or building equipped with ropes, mats, bars, and the like for gymnastics and sports. **2.** An academic high school in various central European countries, especially Germany. [Latin, *gymnasium,* school, from Greek *gumnasion,* from *gumnazein,* "to train naked", practise gymnastics, from *gumnos,* naked.]

gym·nast (jím-nast) *n.* One skilled in gymnastic exercises. [Greek *gumnastēs,* from *gumnazein,* to practise gymnastics. See **gymnasium.**]

gym·nas·tic (jim-nástik) *adj.* Of, pertaining to, or involving gymnastics. **—gym·nas·ti·cal·ly** *adv.*

gym·nas·tics (jim-nástikss) *n.* **1.** *Used with a singular verb.* The practice of performing exercises that increase strength, suppleness, or agility, especially those performed with special apparatus in a gymnasium. **2.** *Used with a plural verb.* **a.** The exercises performed. **b.** Complex intellectual or artistic exercises: *mental gymnastics.*

gymno– *comb. form.* Indicates bare or naked; for example, **gymnosperm.** [Greek *gumnos,* naked.]

gym·nos·o·phist (jim-nóssə-fist) *n.* Any of an ancient sect of Indian ascetics who went naked or nearly naked. [French *gymnosophiste,* from Latin *gymnosophistae* (plural) from Greek *gumnosophistai* : *gumnos,* naked + *sophistēs,* SOPHIST.]

gym·no·sperm (jím-nŏ-sperm, gim-) *n.* Any plant of the class Gymnospermae, which includes the coniferous trees and other plants having seeds not enclosed within an ovary. [New Latin *Gymnospermae* : Greek *gumnos,* naked + -SPERM.] **—gym·no·sperm·ous** (-spérməss) *adj.*

gym·nure (jim-newr) *n.* An insectivorous mammal of the family Erinaceidae, of southeast Asia. Also called "hairy hedgehog". [New Latin *gymnura:* GYMNO- + -URA (tail).]

gym shoe *n.* A **plimsoll** (see).

gym-slip (jím-slip) *n.* A sleeveless, often belted tunic worn by girls, usually as part of a school uniform. Also called "gym-tunic".

gy·nae·ce·um (jīni-sée-əm, jínni- *for sense 1;* jī-née-si-əm, gī-, ji- *for sense 2*) *n., pl.* **-cea** (-sée-ə *for sense 1;* -si-ə *for sense 2*). Also **gy·nae·ci·um** *pl.* **-cia** (-si-ə). **1.** The women's quarters in an ancient Greek or Roman household. **2.** Variant of **gynoecium.** [Latin, from Greek *gunaikeion,* from *gunaikeios,* of women, from *gunē* (stem *gunaik-*), woman.]

gynaeco-, *U.S.* **gyneco-** *comb. form.* Indicates woman or women; for example, **gynaecology.** [Greek, from *gunē* (stem *gunaik-*), woman.]

gy·nae·coc·ra·cy (gĭni-kóckrə-si, jīnə-) *n., pl.* **-cies.** Government by women. [GYNAECO- + -CRACY.]

gynaecol. gynaecological; gynaecology.

gy·nae·col·o·gy (gĭni-kóllji ‖ jīni-, jinni-) *n. Abbr.* **gyn., gynaecol.** The medical study of disease in females, especially those diseases affecting the female reproductive organs and adjacent organs, such as the urinary tract. [GYNAECO- + -LOGY.] **—gy·nae·co·log·i·cal** (-kə-lójik'l), **gy·nae·co·log·ic** *adj.* **—gy·nae·col·o·gist** (-kólləjist) *n.*

gy·nae·co·mas·ti·a (gĭni-kō-másti-ə) *n.* Abnormal enlargement of the breasts in a man, due to hormone imbalance or hormone therapy. [New Latin : GYNAECO- + Greek *mastis,* breast.]

gyn·ae·cop·a·thy (gĭnə-kóppəthi ‖ jĭnə-, jinnə-) *n. Pathology.* Any of various diseases peculiar to women.

gy·nan·dro·morph (ji-nán-drŏ-mawrf, gī-, jī-) *n.* An individual having male and female characteristics; especially, an insect with such characteristics resulting from an abnormality in the sex chromosomes. [GYNO- + ANDRO- + -MORPH.] **—gy·nan·dro·morph·ic** (-mórfik), **gy·nan·dro·morph·ous** *adj.* **—gy·nan·dro·morph·ism** (-mórfiz'm), **gy·nan·dro·mor·phy** *n.*

gy·nan·drous (jī-nándrəss, ji-, gī-) *adj. Botany.* Having the stamens and pistil united to form a column. Said of such flowers as the orchid. [Greek *gunandros,* of doubtful sex : *gunē,* woman + *anēr* (stem *andr-*), man.]

gyn·ar·chy (jĭ-naarki, gī-) *n., pl.* **-chies.** Gynaecocracy. [GYNO- + -ARCHY.] **—gyn·ar·chic** (jī-nárkik, gī-) *adj.*

gyn·i·at·rics (gĭni-áttrikss) *n. Used with singular verb.* The treatment of diseases peculiar to women.

gyno–, gyn– *comb. form.* Indicates: **1.** Woman or female; for example, **gynarchy, gynandromorph. 2.** Female reproductive organ; for example, **gynophore.** [Greek *guno-,* from *gunē,* woman.]

gy·no·di·oe·cious (gĭnō-dī-éeshəss, jĭnō-) *adj. Botany.* Designating a species of plant in which female and hermaphrodite flowers are borne on separate plants. [GYNO- + DIOECIOUS.]

gy·noe·ci·um (jī-née-si-əm, gī- ‖ jĭnō-) *n., pl.* **-cia** (-si-ə). Also **gy·nae·ce·um.** *Botany.* The female reproductive organs of a flower; the pistil or pistils collectively. [New Latin, alteration of GYNAECEUM.]

gy·no·mon·oe·cious (jĭnō-mon-éeshəss, gĭnō-) *adj. Botany.* Designating a species of plant on which female and hermaphrodite flowers are borne on the same plant. [GYNO- + MONOECIOUS.]

gy·no·phore (jĭnō-fawr, gĭnō- ‖ jinnə-, -fōr) *n. Botany.* A stalk in some plants that bears the pistil. [GYNO- + -PHORE.] **—gy·no·phor·ic** (-fórrik ‖ -fáwrik) *adj.*

–gynous *adj. comb. form.* Indicates: **1.** Women or females; for example, **monogynous. 2.** Female organs such as pistils; for example, **perigynous.** [New Latin *-gynus,* having pistils, from Greek *-gunos,* having a wife or wives, from *gunē,* woman.]

–gyny *n. comb. form.* Indicates: **1.** The condition of having a specified number or kind of women or females; for example, **monogyny. 2.** The condition of having female organs or pistils; for example, **epigyny.** [Greek *gunē,* woman.]

gyp¹, gip (jip) *tr.v.* **gypped** or **gipped, gypping** or **gipping, gyps** or **gips.** Also **gip.** *Informal.* To swindle, cheat, or defraud.
~*n.* **1.** The act or an instance of cheating; a swindle. **2.** One who cheats; a swindler. [Perhaps from GYP (servant).] **—gyp·per** *n.*

gyp² *n. British.* A servant who cleans students' rooms, especially at Cambridge University. [Perhaps from obsolete *gippo,* kitchen servant, short tunic, from obsolete French *jupeau;* akin to French *jupe,* skirt.]

gyp, gip³ *n. British Informal.* A severe pain or punishment. Used in the phrase *give (someone) gyp.* [Perhaps from GEE UP.]

gyp·soph·i·la (jip-sóffilə) *n.* Any of various plants of the genus *Gypsophila*, having small white or pink flowers, and including the baby's-breath. [New Latin *Gypsophila* : GYPSUM + -PHILA.]

gyp·sum (jíp-səm) *n.* A white mineral, $CaSO_4 \cdot 2H_2O$, used in the manufacture of cements and plasters, especially plaster of Paris, and also in some fertilisers. [Latin, from Greek *gupsos*, from Semitic; akin to Hebrew *gephes*, plaster.] —**gyp·se·ous** (-si-əss), **gyp·sif·er·ous** (jip-siffərəss) *adj.*

Gyp·sy, Gipsy (jíp-si) *n., pl.* -**sies**. 1. *Sometimes small* **g**. One of a nomadic Caucasoid people originally migrating from the border region between Iran and India to Europe in the 14th or 15th century and now living principally in Europe and the United States, making a living from such itinerant trades as peddling, fortune-telling, and music-making. 2. The Indic language spoken by this people; Romany. 3. *Often small* **g**. One that resembles a Gypsy in appearance or behaviour, especially in having a wandering or care-free lifestyle.
~*adj. Often small* **g**. Of, pertaining to, or resembling Gypsies. [Shortening of EGYPTIAN, because they were believed to have come from Egypt.]

gy·ral (jír-əl) *adj.* 1. Moving in a circular or spiral path; gyratory. 2. Pertaining to a gyrus. —**gy·ral·ly** *adv.*

gy·rate (jir-ráyt, jī || *U.S.* -ayt) *v.* -**rated, -rating, -rates**. —*intr.* 1. To revolve on or around a centre or axis. 2. To circle or spiral. —*tr.* To move in circles around a centre: *gyrate your hips in time with the beat.* —See Synonyms at **turn**.
~*adj. Biology.* In rings; coiled. [Latin *gȳrāre*, from *gȳrus*, circle, from Greek *guros*, GYRE.] —**gy·ra·tion** (-ráyshn) *n.* —**gy·ra·tor** *n.* —**gy·ra·tor·y** (jírə-təri, -tri, jī-ráytəri) *adj.*

gyre (jīr, jí-ər) *n.* 1. The circular flow of water that occurs in each of the great ocean basins of the world, produced by the combined effects of prevailing winds and the earth's rotation. 2. *Chiefly Poetic.* **a.** A ring or circle; a vortex; a spiral. **b.** A circular or spiral motion.
~*intr.v.* **gyred, gyring, gyres**. *Chiefly Poetic.* To gyrate. [Latin *gyrus*, from Greek *guros*, circle.]

gyr·fal·con, ger·fal·con (jér-fawl-kən, -faw- || -fal-) *n.* A large falcon, *Falco rusticolus*, of northern regions, having various colour phases ranging from black to white. [Middle English *gerfaucoun*, from Old French *gerfaucon*, from Old Norse *geirfalki*.]

gy·ro (jír-ō) *n., pl.* -**ros**. A gyroscope.
gyro- *comb. form.* Indicates: 1. Gyrating; for example, **gyroplane**. 2. Spiral; for example, **gyroscope**. 3. Gyroscope; for example, **gyrocompass**. [Latin, from Greek *guro-*, from *guros*, circle.]

gy·ro·com·pass (jír-ō-kum-pəss || -kom-) *n.* A nonmagnetic navigational device in which the interaction of a gyroscope's angular momentum with the force produced by the earth's rotation is used to maintain a north-south orientation of the gyroscopic spin axis, thereby providing a stable directional reference.

gy·ro·mag·net·ic (jír-ō-mag-néttik) *adj.* Of, pertaining to, or resulting from the magnetic properties of a spinning, electrically charged particle.

gyromagnetic ratio *n.* The ratio of the magnetic moment to the intrinsic angular momentum of a spinning particle.

gyro pilot *n.* An automatic pilot incorporating a gyroscope to maintain a preset course and altitude.

gy·ro·plane (jír-ə-playn) *n.* An aircraft such as a helicopter or autogyro with wings that rotate about a vertical axis.

gy·ro·scope (jír-ə-skōp) *n.* 1. A device consisting essentially of a spinning mass, typically a disc or wheel, the spin axis of which turns between two low-friction supports and maintains its angular orientation with respect to inertial coordinates when not subjected to external torques. 2. Broadly, any spinning mass. Also called "gyro". [French : GYRO- + -SCOPE.] —**gy·ro·scop·ic** (-skóppik) *adj.* —**gy·ro·scop·i·cal·ly** *adv.*

gy·ro·sta·bi·lis·er (jír-ō-stáybi-līzər) *n.* A device having a heavy gyroscope whose axis spins in a vertical plane to reduce the side-to-side rolling of a ship or aircraft.

gy·ro·stat·ic (jír-ō-státtik) *adj.* Of, pertaining to, or designating a gyroscope or gyrostatics. [GYRO- + -STAT + -IC.] —**gy·ro·stat·i·cal·ly** *adv.*

gy·ro·stat·ics (jír-ō-státtiks) *n. Used with a singular verb.* The study of rotating bodies.

gy·rus (jír-əss) *n., pl.* **gyri** (jír-ī). Any of the prominent, rounded, elevated convolutions on the surfaces of the cerebral hemispheres. [New Latin, from Latin, circle, GYRE.]

gyve (jīv || *U.S. also* gīv) *n. Archaic.* A shackle or fetter, especially for the leg.
~*tr.v.* **gyved, gyving, gyves**. To shackle or fetter. [Middle English *gyve*†.]

H

h, H (aych || *regional* haych) *n., pl.* **h's** or *rare* **hs, Hs** or **H's**. 1. The eighth letter of the modern English alphabet. 2. Any of the speech sounds represented by this letter.

h, H, h., H. *Note:* As an abbreviation or symbol, *h* may be a small or a capital letter, with or without a full stop. Established forms or those generally preferred precede the definition. When no form is given, all four forms are in general use in that sense. 1. H *Physics.* Hamiltonian. 2. h., H. harbour. 3. h., H. hard; hardness. 4. H hecto-. 5. h., H. height. 6. H henry. 7. h., H. high (gear). 8. h., H. *Music.* horn. 9. H hot (water). 10. h hour. 11. h. hundred. 12. h., H. husband. 13. H The symbol for the element hydrogen. 14. h The symbol for Planck's constant. 15. The eighth in a series.

H *adj.* Designating a pencil or pencil lead that is hard. A number sometimes precedes *H* to indicate the degree of hardness, the hardest pencil being 6H. See **B, HB**.
~*n.* An H pencil.

ha[1] (haa) *interj.* Also **hah**. Used to express surprise, wonder, triumph, puzzlement, or pique. [Middle English.]

ha[2]. See **hum** (sense 6).

ha hectare.

h.a. this year (Latin *hoc anno*).

Haag, den. See **Hague, the**.

Haa·kon VII (háw-kon), (1872–1957). King of Norway (1905–57).

haar (har) *n. British Regional.* A cold fog or mist off the east coast of England or Scotland. [Probably from Old Norse *hárr*, HOAR.]

Haar·lem (hárləm). City in the western Netherlands, the capital of North Holland province, lying on the river Spaarne near the North Sea. It was a major centre of the golden age of Dutch painting in the 16th and 17th centuries. It is now famous for the culture and export of flowers and bulbs, especially tulips.

Hab. Habakkuk (Old Testament).

Ha·bak·kuk[1] (hábbə-kək, -kuk, hə-báckək). Hebrew prophet of the late seventh century B.C.

Habakkuk[2] *n. Abbr.* **Hab**. A book of prophecies by Habakkuk in the Old Testament.

Habana. See **Havana**.

ha·ba·ne·ra (hábbə-naír-ə || *U.S.* áabə-) *n.* 1. A slow Cuban dance. 2. The music for this dance, in duple time, with a repetitive rhythmic pattern. [Spanish *(danza) habanera*, "Havanan (dance)", from feminine of *habanero*, HABANERO.]

Ha·ba·ne·ro (hábbə-naír-ō || *U.S.* áabə-) *n., pl.* -**ros**. A native or inhabitant of Havana. [Spanish, from *La Habana*, HAVANA.]

hab·da·lah (hav-dáalə, háav-də-láa) *n. Often capital* **H**. A Jewish religious ceremony observed at or marking the end of a Sabbath or holy day. [Hebrew *habdālāh*, separation.]

ha·be·as cor·pus (háybi-əss kórpəss) *n. Law.* 1. Any of a variety of writs that may be issued to bring a party before a court or judge, having as its function the release of a party from unlawful restraint. 2. The right to demand such a writ. [Latin, "you shall have the body".]

hab·er·dash·er (hábbər-dashər) *n.* 1. *British.* A dealer in sewing accessories and dressmaking materials. 2. *U.S.* A dealer in items of menswear, such as gloves, hats, or the like. [Middle English *haberdasher*, probably from Anglo-French *haberdasser*, *hapertasser* (both unattested), from *hapertas*†, perhaps the name of a kind of cloth.]

hab·er·dash·er·y (hábbər-dashəri) *n., pl.* -**ies**. 1. The goods sold by a haberdasher. 2. A shop or department selling these goods.

hab·er·geon (hábbər-jən) *n.* Also **hau·ber·geon** (háwbər-). 1. A short, sleeveless coat of mail. 2. A hauberk. [Middle English, from Old French *haubergeon*, from *hauberc*, HAUBERK.]

Ha·ber process (háa-bər) *n.* An industrial process, first developed in 1908, for producing ammonia from hydrogen and atmospheric nitrogen by reacting the two gases together at a temperature of about 5000°C and a pressure of 20-50 megapascals. In the later **Haber-Bosch process** a method of making the hydrogen from water gas and steam was added. [After Fritz *Haber* (1868–1934), German chemist.]

hab·ile (hábbīl || *U.S.* hábbil) *adj.* Adroit; deft. [French, from Old French, from Latin *habilis*, able, easily handled, from *habēre*, to hold, have.]

ha·bil·i·ment (hə-bíllimənt, ha-) *n.* 1. *Plural.* **a.** The dress or garb associated with an office or occasion: *"shrouded from head to foot in the habiliments of the grave"* (Edgar Allan Poe). **b.** Clothes. 2. *Rare.* Outfit; attire. [Middle English, from Old French *(h)abillement*, from *habiller*, to make fit, fit out, from HABILE.]

ha·bil·i·tate (hə-bílli-tayt, ha-) *v.* -**tated, -tating, -tates**. —*tr. Archaic.* To clothe. —*intr.* To qualify oneself for an office, especially as a teacher in a German university. [Medieval Latin *habilitāre* (past participle *habilitātus*), to qualify, from Latin *habilitās*, ability, from HABILE.] —**ha·bil·i·ta·tion** (-táysh'n) *n.*

hab·it (hábbit) *n.* **1. a.** A constant, often unconscious inclination to act in a particular way, acquired through frequent repetition over a long period. **b.** An established trend of the mind or character. **c.** *Psychology.* An automatic or mechanical reaction to a particular situation, acquired through frequently encountering it. **2.** *Often plural.* Customary manner or practice: *a man of ascetic habits.* **3.** An addiction, especially to a hard drug. **4.** *Archaic.* Physical constitution. **5.** Characteristic appearance, form, or manner of growth, especially of a plant or crystal. **6. a.** A distinctive dress or costume, especially of a religious order. **b.** A riding habit. ~*tr.v.* **habited, -iting, -its. 1.** To clothe; dress. **2.** *Archaic.* To habituate. **3.** *Archaic.* To inhabit. [Middle English *(h)abit,* from Old French, from Latin *habitus,* from the past participle of *habēre,* to hold, have.]
Synonyms: habit, practice, custom, usage, use, fashion.
hab·it·a·ble (hábbit-əb'l) *adj.* Suitable to live in; inhabitable. [Middle English *abitable,* from Old French *(h)abitable,* from Latin *habitābilis,* from *habitāre,* to inhabit, reside, from *habēre* (past participle *habitus*), to have, hold.] —**hab·it·a·bil·i·ty** (-ə-bílləti), **hab·it·a·ble·ness** *n.* —**hab·it·a·bly** *adv.*
hab·i·tant (hábbitənt; *for sense 2 also* ábbi-tón) *n.* Also **ha·bi·tan** (for sense 2). **1.** An inhabitant. **2.** An inhabitant of French descent in Canada or Louisiana. [Old French, from the present participle of *habiter,* to inhabit, from Latin *habitāre.* See **habitable.**]
hab·i·tat (hábbi-tat) *n.* **1.** The area or type of environment in which an organism or biological population normally lives or occurs. **2.** The place where a person or thing is most likely to be found. [Latin, "it dwells" (the first word in Latin descriptions of plant and animal species in old natural histories), third person singular present indicative of *habitāre,* to inhabit. See **habitable.**]
hab·i·ta·tion (hábbi-táysh'n) *n.* **1.** The act of inhabiting; occupancy: *fit for human habitation.* **2. a.** A natural environment or locality. **b.** A place of abode. [Middle English *habitacioun,* from Old French *habitation,* from Latin *habitātiō* (stem *habitātiōn-*), from *habitātus,* past participle of *habitāre,* to inhabit. See **habitable.**]
hab·it·ed (hábbitid) *adj.* **1. a.** Dressed. **b.** Attired in a habit. **2.** *Archaic.* Inhabited.
hab·it-form·ing (hábbit-fawrming) *adj.* **1.** Leading to psychological or physiological addiction: *a habit-forming drug.* **2.** Tending to become habitual.
ha·bit·u·al (hə-bíttew-əl, -bíchoo-) *adj.* **1. a.** Of the nature of a habit; done constantly or repeatedly. **b.** Being so by force of habit: *a habitual smoker.* **2.** Customary; constant; inveterate: *habitual rudeness.* **3.** Established by long use; usual. —See Synonyms at **usual.** —**ha·bit·u·al·ly** *adv.* —**ha·bit·u·al·ness** *n.*
ha·bit·u·ate (hə-bíttew-ayt, -bíchoo-) *tr.v.* **-ated, -ating, -ates. 1.** To accustom by frequent repetition or prolonged exposure. Often used reflexively. **2.** To cause to become psychologically dependent on a drug. [Late Latin *habituāre,* from Latin *habitus,* **HABIT.**] —**ha·bit·u·a·tion** (-áysh'n) *n.*
hab·i·tude (hábbi-tewd ‖ -tōōd) *n.* A customary manner or way of behaving; a habit. [Middle English *(h)abitude,* from Old French *habitude,* from Latin *habitūdo,* condition, habit, from *habitus,* **HABIT.**]
ha·bit·u·é (hə-bíttew-ay, ha-, -bíchoo- ‖ *U.S. also* -áy) *n.* A frequent visitor of a particular place, especially a place of entertainment. [French, from the past participle of *habituer,* to frequent, from Late Latin *habituāre,* **HABITUATE.**]
hab·i·tus (hábbitəss) *n., pl.* **habitus. 1.** Physical and constitutional characteristics, especially as related to susceptibility to a disease. **2.** The habit of a plant or animal. [New Latin, from Latin, appearance, **HABIT.**]
Habs·burg or **Haps·burg** (hápsburg). The dominant royal house in Europe from the late Middle Ages until the 20th century. The family name came from the castle of Habsburg, built on the river Aar, Switzerland, (1028) by Werner I, Bishop of Strasbourg. The Habsburgs reached the height of their power in the 16th century under Charles V, when Spain with her European and American territories was added to the family's possessions, creating a vast and unwieldy domain. Charles abdicated in 1558, dividing his empire between the two Habsburg lines of Spain and Austria. The Spanish branch ceased to rule after 1700. In the 19th century, the Napoleonic wars and Prussian and Italian nationalism weakened the Habsburgs' grip on central Europe. The Habsburg-ruled Austro-Hungarian Empire finally disintegrated after World War I.
ha·bu (haáboō) *n.* A large, venomous, Japanese snake, *Trimeresurus flavoviridis,* found in the Ryukyu Islands. [Japanese.]
H.A.C. Honourable Artillery Company.
há·ček (haá-chek) *n.* A diacritic mark (ˇ) placed over a letter to modify it that is used especially in Slavonic languages, as sometimes over a *c* (*č*) in Czech. [Czech.]
ha·chure (ha-shéwr, -shoór ‖ háshoor) *n.* Any of the short lines used to shade or to indicate slopes on relief maps and also to show their degree and direction. ~*tr.v.* **hachured, -churing, -chures.** To make hachures on (a map). [French, from *hacher,* to engrave lines on, chop up. See **hash.**]
ha·ci·en·da (hássi-éndə ‖ *U.S.* haá-si-) *n.* **1.** In Spanish-speaking countries or areas influenced by Spain, a large estate, plantation, or large ranch. **2.** The house of the owner of a hacienda; especially, in the southwestern United States, a low, sprawling house with a projecting roof and wide porches. [Spanish, domestic work, landed property, from Latin *facienda,* things to be done, neuter plural gerundive of *facere,* to do.]

hack¹ (hak) *v.* **hacked, hacking, hacks.** —*tr.* **1. a.** To cut (branches or undergrowth, for example) with irregular and heavy blows or in a random manner. **b.** To chip, notch, chop off, or chop up roughly with a pick, knife, axe, or other tool. **c.** To make by cutting or chopping in such a way: *hacked a hole in the wood.* **2.** To break up (earth) into clods or ridges. **3. a.** To kick the shin of (an opponent), especially in soccer. **b.** To strike the arm of (an opponent) in basketball. **4.** To destroy the quality of (a story or article, for example) by excessive cutting or bad editing. **5.** *U.S. Informal.* To deal with successfully; cope with: *She tried living on her own, but simply couldn't hack it.* —*intr.* **1.** To chop or chip away at something. **2.** To cough in short, dry-throated spasms. ~*n.* **1.** A rough irregular cut or notch made by hacking. **2.** A tool, such as a hoe or mattock, used for chopping or breaking up something. **3. a.** A kick or chopping blow, especially one on the shins in soccer. **b.** A wound from this. **4.** *Chiefly U.S. Informal.* A hacking cough. [Middle English *hacken,* Old English *haccian,* to cut to pieces, from Germanic, of imitative origin.]
hack² *n.* **1.** A horse used for riding or driving; a hackney. **2.** A broken-down horse for hire; a jade. **3.** *Chiefly Australian & N.Z.* A horse that is over 14.2 hands high; a horse as opposed to a pony. **4.** *Chiefly British.* A leisurely ride in the country on horseback. **5. a.** An undistinguished politician, concerned with narrow party considerations. **b.** A person who is involved in politics at a minor level and who is constantly badgering others to vote for him or to support the political candidate he works for. **6.** A person who makes his living by hiring himself out to do mediocre or routine work, especially writing or journalism. **7.** *U.S. Informal.* A taxi. ~*v.* **hacked, hacking, hacks.** —*tr.* **1.** To let (a horse) out for hire. **2.** *Informal.* To write as a hack or in the manner of a hack. **3.** To make banal or hackneyed with indiscriminate use. —*intr.* **1.** *Informal.* To work as a hack, especially a hack writer. **2.** To ride on horseback in the country at a leisurely pace. ~*adj.* **1.** Working as a literary or journalistic hack: *a hack writer.* **2.** Produced by or characteristic of a hack; banal; routine; commercial. [Short for **HACKNEY.**]
hack³ *n.* **1.** A drying frame or rack, as for bricks. **2.** A row of unfired bricks laid out to dry. **3.** A feeding rack, especially for hawks. —**at hack.** Not being allowed to prey for itself; having only partial liberty. Said of a hawk. ~*tr.v.* **hacked, hacking, hacks. 1.** To set out on a rack to dry. **2.** To keep (hawks) at partial liberty. [Variant (influenced by **HECK** (frame)) of **HATCH** (door).]
hack·a·more (háckə-mawr ‖ -mōr) *n.* *U.S.* A rope or rawhide halter with a wide band that can be lowered over a horse's eyes, used to break in horses. [Alteration (influenced by **HACK**) of Spanish *jaquima,* headstall of a halter, from Old Spanish *xaquima,* from Arabic *shakīmah,* bit of a bridle, restraint.]
hack·ber·ry (hák-berri, -bəri, -bri) *n., pl.* **-ries. 1.** Any of various North American trees or shrubs of the genus *Celtis,* having inconspicuous flowers and berry-like, often edible fruit. **2.** The fruit of a hackberry. **3.** The soft, yellowish wood of a hackberry. [Variant of earlier *hagberry* : *hag-,* from Scandinavian, akin to Old Norse *heggr,* hackberry + **BERRY.**]
hack·but (hák-but) *n.* Also **hag·but** (hág-). An obsolete type of gun, a harquebus *(see).* [Old French *haguebute, hacquebute,* from Middle Dutch *hakebusse,* **HARQUEBUS.**] —**hack·bu·teer** (-éer), **hack·but·ter** (-ər) *n.*
hack·er (hác-kər) *n.* **1.** A computer enthusiast who obsessively experiments with software. **2.** Such an enthusiast who gains unauthorized computer access to other people's programs. **3.** One that hacks. [From **HACK** (to work like a hack) + **-ER.**]
hack·ette (hak-ét) *n.* A female hack journalist. Often humorous.
hack·ie (hácki). *n.* *U.S. Slang.* A taxi driver. [From **HACK** (taxi).]
hack·ing (hácking) *adj.* Designating a cough or laughter that is rough, dry, and usually spasmodic.
hacking jacket *n.* A riding jacket with slits at the sides or back.
hack·le (hák'l) *n.* **1.** Any of the long, slender, often glossy feathers on the neck of a bird, especially a male domestic fowl. **2.** *Plural.* The erectile hairs at the back of the neck, especially of a dog or similar animal. **3. a.** A tuft of cock feathers trimming an artificial fishing fly. **b.** A hackle fly. **4.** A steel comb used for flax. —**get (one's) hackles up.** To make angry or ready to fight. —**make the hackles rise. 1.** To put in a fighting mood. **2.** To cause a dog to bristle belligerently. ~*tr.v.* **hackled, -ling, -les. 1.** To trim (a fly) with a hackle. **2.** To comb (flax) with a hackle. [Middle English *hakell, hekele, hechele,* **HATCHEL.**]
hackle fly *n.* An artificial fishing fly trimmed with hackles and usually without wings. Also called "hackle".
hack·ly (háckli) *adj.* Nicked or notched; jagged; rough. [From **HACKLE** (to hack).]
hack·ney (hákni) *n., pl.* **-neys. 1.** *Often capital* **H.** A horse of a trotting breed developed in England, having a gait characterised by pronounced flexion of the knee. **2.** A horse suited for routine riding or driving; a hack. **3.** A coach or carriage for hire. ~*tr.v.* **hackneyed, -neying, -neys. 1.** To overuse and cause to become banal and trite; cheapen. **2.** To hire out; let. ~*adj.* Hired: *a hackney carriage.* [Middle English, perhaps after **HACKNEY,** where there were pastures from which horses may have been taken to the market at Smithfield.]
Hack·ney (hákni). Borough in the northeast of Greater London, England.

hack·neyed (hák-nid ‖ -need) *adj.* Overused so as to become stale or meaningless; trite; banal. See Synonyms at **trite**.

hack·saw (hák-saw) *n.* A saw consisting of a tough, fine-toothed blade stretched taut in a frame, used for cutting metal.

had (had; *weak forms* həd, əd, d). Past tense and past participle of **have**.

ha·dal (háyd'l) *adj.* Of or designating the deepest parts of the oceans, especially those parts below about 6 000 metres (36,100 feet). [HADES (the nether world) + -AL.]

had·a·way (háddə-wáy) *interj. Northeastern English.* Used to encourage others to set to. [Perhaps from HOLD + AWAY.]

had·dock (háddək) *n., pl.* **-docks** or collectively **haddock.** A food fish, *Melanogrammus aeglefinus,* of northern Atlantic waters, related to and resembling the cod. [Middle English *haddok,* from Anglo-French *hadoc,* variant of Old French *(h)adot†.*]

hade (hayd) *n. Geology.* The angle of inclination from the vertical of a vein, fault, or lode.
~*intr.v.* **haded, hading, hades.** To incline from the vertical. Used of a vein, fault, or lode. [Perhaps a dialect variant of HEAD.]

Ha·des¹ (háydeez). *Greek Mythology.* The god of the nether world and dispenser of earthly riches; a brother of Zeus and husband of Persephone; identified with the Roman god Pluto.

Hades² *n.* **1.** *Greek Mythology.* The nether-world kingdom of Hades, the abode of the shades of the dead. **2.** *Often small* **n.** Hell. [Greek *Haidēs.*] **—Ha·de·an** *adj.*

Had·ith (háddith, haa-déeth) *n., pl.* **Hadith** or **-iths.** The body of traditions relating to Muhammad. [Arabic, "tradition".]

hadj, haj, hajj (haj) *n.* A pilgrimage to Mecca made during Ramadan as an objective of the religious life of a Muslim. [Arabic *ḥajj,* pilgrimage.]

hadj·i, haj·i (hájee) *n., pl.* **-is.** Also **haj·ji** *pl.* **-jis. 1. a.** A Muslim who has made a pilgrimage to Mecca. **b.** *Capital H.* A title used for the name of a Muslim who has made this pilgrimage. **2.** A Christian of the Near East or Orient who has visited the Holy Sepulchre in Jerusalem. [Arabic *ḥājjī,* from *ḥajj,* HADJ.]

had·n't (hádd'nt). Contraction of *had not.*

Ha·dri·an (háydri-ən), in full Publius Aelius Hadrianus (A.D. 76– 138). Roman emperor (117–138). As emperor, he began to end distinctions between Rome and her provinces. He visited Britain in 122, where he ordered the building of Hadrian's Wall.

Hadrian IV. See **Adrian IV.**

Hadrian's Wall. Roman wall built by the emperor Hadrian between *c.* 122 and 126, and extended by Septimius Severus a century later, to fortify the northern boundary of Roman Britain. It stretched for about 120 kilometres (75 miles) from Wallsend on the river Tyne to Bowness at the head of Solway Firth. Fragments of the wall and several stone blockhouses, or mile stations, remain.

had·ron (háddron) *n. Physics.* Any elementary particle that can take part in a strong interaction. The elementary nature of hadrons is controversial as they are believed to consist of arrangements of quarks. [Greek *hadros,* thick, heavy + -ON.] **—had·ron·ic** (ha-drónnik) *adj.*

had·ro·saur (háddrə-sawr) *n.* Any of various amphibious dinosaurs of the genus *Anatosaurus* and related genera, which had webbed feet and a ducklike bill. [Greek *hadros,* thick, heavy + –SAUR.]

hadst (hadst; *weak forms* hədst, ədst). *Archaic.* Second person singular past indicative of **have.** Used with *thou.*

hae (hay, ha) *tr.v.* **haed, haen** (hayn, han), **haeing, haes.** *Scottish.* To have.

haem, *U.S.* **heme** (heem) *n.* An iron-containing compound, $C_{34}H_{32}Fe N_4O_4$, that combines with the protein globin to form the blood pigment haemoglobin. [Probably abstracted from HAEMOGLOBIN.]

haem–. Variant of **haemo–.**

hae·mag·glu·tin·ate (héemə-glóoti-nayt ‖ hémmə-, -gléwti-) *tr.v.* **-ated, -ating, -ates.** To cause agglutination of (red blood cells). **—hae·mag·glu·ti·na·tion** (-náysh'n) *n.*

hae·mag·glu·ti·nin (héemə-glóoti-nin ‖ hémmə-, -gléwti-) *n.* An antibody that causes agglutination of red blood cells. [HAEM(O)- + AGGLUTININ.]

hae·ma·gogue (héemə-gog) *n.* A drug or other agent that promotes the flow of blood, as in menstruation. [HAEM(O)- + -AGOGUE.]

hae·mal (héem'l) *adj.* **1.** Of or pertaining to the blood or blood vessels. **2.** Relating to or designating the side of the body that contains the heart. [From Greek *haima†,* blood.]

hae·man·gi·o·ma (héem-anji-ómə) *n.* A nonmalignant tumour of blood vessels, often seen on the skin as a type of birthmark. [HAEM(O)- + ANGIOMA.]

hae·ma·te·in (héemə-tée-in, -teen ‖ hémmə-) *n.* A dark purple, crystalline compound, $C_{16}H_{12}O_6$, used as an indicator and as a biological stain. [HAEMAT(O)- + -*ein,* variant of -IN.]

hae·ma·tem·e·sis (héemə-témmə-siss ‖ hémmə-) *n.* The vomiting of blood, often due to a bleeding gastric or duodenal ulcer. [HAEMATO- + Greek *emesis,* vomiting.]

hae·mat·ic (hee-máttik) *adj.* Of, pertaining to, resembling, containing, or acting on blood.
~*n.* A haematinic drug. [Greek *haimatikos,* from *haima†* (stem *haimat-),* blood.]

hae·ma·tin (héemə-tin, hémmə-) *n.* A blue to blackish-brown powder, $C_{34}H_{32}N_4O_4.FeOH$, that is the hydroxide of haem, containing ferric iron. [HAEMAT(O)- + -IN.]

haem·a·tin·ic (héemə-tinnik, hémmə-) *adj.* Acting to increase the amount of haemoglobin in the blood.
~*n.* A haematinic drug used to treat iron-deficiency anaemia. [HAEMATIN + -IC.]

haem·a·tite (hémmə-tīt, héemə-) A blackish-red to brick-red mineral, essentially Fe_2O_3, the chief ore of iron. Also called "iron glance". [Latin *haematitēs,* from Greek *(lithos) haimatitēs,* "blood-like (stone)", red iron ore, from *haima†* (stem *haimat-),* blood.]

haemato-, haemat- *comb. form.* Indicates blood; for example, **haematology, haematin.** [Greek *haimato-,* from *haima†* (stem *haimat-),* blood.]

haem·a·to·blast (hée-mətə-blaast, hee-máttə-, -blast) *n.* **1.** A platelet of the blood. **2.** An immature blood cell. [HAEMATO- + -BLAST.] **—haem·a·to·blas·tic** (-blástik) *adj.*

haem·a·to·cele (hémmə-tə-seel, héemə-, -tō-) *n.* A haemorrhage contained within a membranous cavity, especially in the testicle. [HAEMATO- + -CELE.]

haem·a·to·crit (hémmə-tō-krit, héemə-) *n.* **1.** A centrifuge used to separate the cellular and other particulate matter of blood from the plasma. **2.** Packed cell volume *(see).* [HAEMATO- + Greek *kritēs,* judge, from *krinein,* to decide, judge.]

haem·a·to·gen·e·sis (héemə-tə-jénnə-siss, hémmə-, -tō-) *n.* Haematopoiesis. [HAEMATO- + -GENESIS.] **—haem·a·to·gen·ic** (-jénnik) *adj.* **—haem·a·to·ge·net·ic** (-jə-néttik) *adj.*

hae·ma·tog·e·nous (héemə-tójənəss, hémmə-) *adj.* **1.** Producing blood. **2.** Originating or carried in the blood. [HAEMATO- + -GENOUS.]

hae·ma·toid (héemə-toyd, hémmə-) *adj.* **1.** Bloody. **2.** Like blood. [Greek *haimatoeides :* HAEMAT(O)- + -OID.]

hae·ma·tol·o·gy (héemə-tólləji) *n.* The science encompassing the generation, anatomy, physiology, pathology, and therapeutics of blood. [HAEMATO- + -LOGY.] **—hae·ma·to·log·i·cal** (-tə-lójik'l) *adj.* **—hae·ma·to·log·i·cal·ly** *adv.* **—hae·ma·tol·o·gist** (-tólləjist) *n.*

hae·ma·tol·y·sis (héemə-tóllə-siss) *n. Biology.* **Haemolysis** *(see).* [HAEMATO- + -LYSIS.]

hae·ma·to·ma (héemə-tō'-mə, hémmə-) *n., pl.* **-mas** or **-mata** (-mətə). *Pathology.* A localised swelling filled with blood. [HAEMAT(O)- + -OMA.]

haem·a·to·poi·e·sis (héemə-tō-poy-ée-siss, hémmə-) *n.* The formation of blood in the body. Also called "haematogenesis", "haemopoiesis". [HAEMATO- + -POIESIS.] **—haem·a·to·poi·et·ic** (-éttik) *adj.*

hae·ma·to·sis (héemə-tō'-siss, hémmə-) *n.* Oxygenation of venous blood in the lungs. [HAEMAT(O)- + -OSIS.]

haem·a·tox·y·lin (héemə-tóksilin, hémmə-) *n.* A yellow or red crystalline compound, $C_{16}H_{14}O_6.3H_2O$, the colouring principle of logwood, used in dyes, inks, and stains. [HAEMATOXYL(ON) + -IN.]

haem·a·tox·y·lon (héemə-tóksilon, hémmə-) *n.* Any tree or shrub of the genus *Haematoxylon;* especially, the **logwood** *(see),* from which haematoxylin is obtained. [HAEMATO- + Greek *xulon,* wood.]

haem·a·to·zo·on (héemə-tō-zō'-on, hémmə-) *n., pl.* **-zoa** (-zō'-ə). A parasitic protozoan or similar organism that lives in the blood. [HAEMATO- + -ZOON.] **—haem·a·to·zo·ic** *adj.*

haem·a·tu·ri·a (héemə-téwr-i-ə, hémmə- ‖ -tóor-) *n.* A condition in which blood or red blood cells are present in the urine. [HAEMAT(O)- + -URIA.] **—haem·a·tu·ric** *adj.*

–haemia. Variant of **-aemia.**

hae·mic (héemik, hémmik) *adj.* Of or pertaining to blood; haematic. [From Greek *haima†,* blood.]

hae·min (héemin) *n.* A brown or blue crystalline compound $C_{34}H_{32}N_4O_4.FeCl$, that is the chloride of haem and is used in identifying bloodstains. [HAEM(O)- + -IN.]

haemo-, haem-, *U.S.* **hemo-, hem-** *comb. form.* Indicates blood; for example, **haemocyte, haemin.** [From Greek *haima†,* blood.]

hae·mo·chro·ma·to·sis (héemō-krōmə-tó-siss) *n.* A hereditary disease in which excessive amounts of iron are absorbed by and stored in the body. Symptoms include diabetes, a bronze pigmentation of the skin, and severe damage to the liver and pancreas. Also called "bronze diabetes". [HAEMO- + CHROMAT(O)- + -OSIS.]

hae·mo·coel (héemə-seel) *n.* The body cavity of arthropods and molluscs, consisting of a blood-filled expanded portion of the circulatory system. [HAEMO- + Greek *koilos,* hollow.]

hae·mo·cy·a·nin (héemō-sī-ə-nin) *n.* A bluish, oxygen-bearing, copper-containing substance similar to haemoglobin, present in the blood of certain insects, crustaceans, and other invertebrates. [HAEMO- + -CYAN(O) + -IN.]

hae·mo·cyte (héemə-sīt, -mō-, hémmə-) *n.* A cell in the blood. [HAEMO- + -CYTE.]

hae·mo·cy·tom·e·ter (héemō-sī-tómmitər, hémmə-) *n.* An apparatus for counting the number of cells in a sample of blood.

hae·mo·di·al·y·sis (héemō-dī-ál-ə-siss) *n.* A technique for removing waste products in the circulating blood of patients with kidney failure using the principle of **dialysis** *(see).* Blood is passed through a dialyser (kidney machine) and the waste products filter through a semipermeable membrane.

hae·mo·dy·nam·ics (héemō-dī-námmiks) *n.* The study of the circulation of the blood.

hae·mo·er·yth·rin (héemō-érrith-rin, -i-rith-) *n.* A red, oxygen-bearing substance, similar to haemoglobin, present in the blood of brachiopods and related invertebrates. [HAEMO- + ERYTHRO- + -IN.]

hae·mo·flag·el·late (héemō-flája-layt, hémmō-) *n.* A flagellate protozoan, such as a trypanosome, that is parasitic in the blood.

hae·mo·glo·bin (héemə-glóbin, -mō- ‖ hémmə-) *n. Abbr.* **Hb** The oxygen-bearing, iron-containing conjugated protein in vertebrate red blood cells, consisting of about 6 per cent haem and 94 per cent globin, and having as a typical formula $C_{738}H_{1166}FeN_{203}O_{208}S_{24}$. [Shortening of earlier *haematoglobulin* : HAEMATIN + GLOBULIN.]

hae·mo·glo·bin·o·pa·thy (hḗemə-glŏ́bi-nóppəthi ‖ hĕmmə-) *n., pl.* **-thies.** Any of various inherited diseases, including sickle-cell anaemia, in which haemoglobin production is abnormal. [HAEMOGLOBIN + -PATHY.]

hae·mo·glo·bi·nu·ri·a (hḗemə-glŏ́bi-nĕwr-i-ə ‖ hĕmmə-, -noor-) *n.* The presence of haemoglobin in the urine. —**hae·mo·globi·nu·ric** *adj.*

hae·mo·leu·co·cyte (hḗemō-lĕwk-ō-sīt, -lŏok-, -ə-) *n.* A leucocyte *(see).*

hae·mo·ly·sin (hḗemō-lī́-sin, hee-móllí- ‖ hĕmmə-) *n.* An agent or substance, such as an antibody or bacterial toxin, that initiates destruction of red blood cells, thereby liberating haemoglobin. [HAEMO- + LYSIN.]

hae·mo·ly·sis (hee-móllə-siss, hi-) *n.* The destruction of red blood cells, either in the body or in a blood sample. Also called "haematolysis". [HAEM(O)- + -LYSIS.] —**hae·mo·ly·t·ic** (hḗemə-líttik ‖ hĕmmə-) *adj.*

haemolytic disease of the newborn *n.* The condition in newborn babies resulting from destruction of the red blood cells of the foetus by antibodies from the mother's blood. It usually occurs due to incompatibility of maternal and foetal blood groups.

hae·mo·phil·i·a (hḗemə-fílli-ə ‖ hĕmmə-) *n.* A hereditary blood coagulation disorder, principally affecting males but transmitted by females, and characterised by excessive, sometimes spontaneous, bleeding. [HAEMO- + -PHILIA.]

hae·mo·phil·i·ac (hḗemə-fílli-ak ‖ hĕmmə-) *n.* A person who suffers from haemophilia. Also called "bleeder".

hae·mo·phil·ic (hḗemə-fíllik ‖ hĕmmə-) *adj.* **1.** Pertaining to haemophilia. **2.** Growing well in blood, or in a culture containing blood, as do certain bacteria.

hae·mo·pho·bi·a (hḗemə-fṓbi-ə ‖ hĕmmə-) *n.* A morbid fear of blood. [HAEMO- + -PHOBIA.] —**hae·mo·pho·bic** (-fṓbik) *adj.*

hae·mo·poi·e·sis (hḗemō-poy-ée-siss) *n. Physiology.* Haematopoiesis *(see).* [HAEMO- + -POIESIS.] —**hae·mo·poi·e·tic** (-éttik) *adj.*

hae·mo·pro·tein (hḗemō-prṓ-tee-in, -teen) *n.* Any protein containing haem, such as haemoglobin, myoglobin, and cytochrome.

haem·op·ty·sis (hee-móptə-siss, hi-) *n.* The spitting up of blood from the lungs or bronchial tubes. [HAEMO- + Greek *ptusis*, a spitting, from *ptuein*, to spit.]

haem·or·rhage (hĕmmə-rij) *n.* Bleeding; especially, copious discharge of blood from the vessels.
—*intr.v.* **haemorrhaged, -rhaging, -rhages.** To bleed copiously in or as if in a haemorrhage. [Earlier *haemorrhagy*, from Old French *hémorragie*, from Latin *haemorrhagia*, from Greek *haimorrhagia* : HAEMO- + -RRHAGIA.] —**haem·or·rhag·ic** (-rájik) *adj.*

haem·or·rhoid (hĕmmə-royd) *n.* **1.** An itching or painful mass of dilated veins in swollen anal tissue. **2.** *Plural.* The pathological condition in which such swollen masses occur. In this sense, also called "piles". [Middle English *emeroudis*, from Old French *emeroyde*, from Latin *haemorrhoida*, from Greek *(phlebes) haimorrhoides*, bleeding (veins), from *haimorrhoos*, flowing with blood : HAEMO- + -rrhoos, from *rhein*, to flow.]

haem·or·rhoid·al (hĕmmə-róyd'l) *adj.* **1.** Of or pertaining to haemorrhoids. **2.** *Anatomy.* Supplying the region of the rectum and anus. Said of certain arteries.

haem·or·rhoid·ec·to·my (hĕmməroyd-éktəmi) *n., pl.* **-mies.** The removal of haemorrhoids by surgery.

hae·mo·si·der·in (hḗemō-sī́dər-in, -siddər-) *n.* An iron-containing protein serving to store iron in the body. Excessive amounts are formed in certain disorders, such as haemochromatosis. [HAEMO- + Greek *sideros*, iron + -IN.]

hae·mo·sta·sis (hḗemō-stáy-siss ‖ hĕmmə-) *n.* Also **hae·mo·sta·si·a** (-zi-ə, -zhə). The stopping of the flow or circulation of blood. [HAEMO- + STASIS.]

hae·mo·stat (hḗemə-stat, hĕmmə-) *n.* **1.** Any agent, such as a chemical, that stops bleeding. **2.** A clamplike instrument in surgery to reduce or prevent bleeding. [HAEMO- + -STAT.]

hae·mo·static (hḗemə-státtik, hĕmmə-) *adj.* Acting to stop the flow of blood or profuse bleeding.
—*n.* A haemostatic agent. [Late Greek *haimostatikos* : HAEMO- + -STATIC.]

haere mai, hae·re·mai (hír-ə-mī́) *interj. N.Z.* Used to express welcome or as a greeting. [Maori, "come hither".]

Ha·erh·pin. See **Harbin.**

haet (hayt) *n. Scottish.* A minute amount; a whit; a jot. [Contraction of *hae it!*, take it!]

ha·fiz (haáfiz) *n.* **1.** A Muslim who has memorised the Koran. **2.** A title of respect used with the name of a Muslim who has accomplished this memorisation. [Persian, from Arabic *hāfiz*, guard, watch, one who knows the Koran by heart, from *hafiza*, to watch, protect, memorise.]

haf·ni·um (háfni-əm) *n. Symbol* Hf A brilliant, silvery, metallic element separated from ores of zirconium and used in nuclear reactor control rods, as a getter for oxygen and nitrogen, and in the manufacture of tungsten filaments. Atomic number 72, atomic weight 178.49, melting point 2150°C, boiling point 5400°C, relative density 13.29, valency 4. [New Latin, from *Hafnia*, Latin name for Copenhagen, from Danish *(Køben)havn.*]

haft (haaft ‖ haft) *n.* A handle or hilt; especially, a handle of a bladed instrument, such as a sword, knife, or sickle.
—*tr.v.* **hafted, hafting, hafts.** To fit or equip with a hilt or handle;

set into a handle. [Middle English *haft*, Old English *hæft.*]

Haftarah. Variant of **Haphtarah.**

hag¹ (hag) *n.* **1.** An old woman who is repulsive in appearance or manner; a crone. **2.** A witch; a sorceress. **3.** *Obsolete.* A female demon. **4.** A hagfish. [Middle English *hagge*, probably short for Old English *hægtesse†*, witch.] —**hag·gish** *adj.* —**hag·gish·ly** *adv.* —**hag·gish·ness** *n.*

hag² *n. Regional.* **1.** A boggy area on a moor. **2.** A piece of firmer ground in boggy land. **3.** A place where peat has been dug from a bog. [Middle English *hag*, gap, chasm, probably from Old Norse *högg*, gap, cutting blow.]

Ha·gar (háy-gaar, -gər). The concubine of Abraham, mother of his bastard son Ishmael, and handmaiden to his wife Sarah, who, through jealousy for her own son Isaac, turned Hagar and Ishmael out of Abraham's household. Genesis 16–19.

hagbut. Variant of **hackbut.**

Ha·gen (haágon). In the *Nibelungenlied*, the murderer of Siegfried.

Ha·gen (háygən), **Walter Charles** (1892–1969). U.S. golfer. He won the U.S. Open championship twice (1914 and 1919); the British Open four times from 1922–29, and the U.S. Professional Golfers' Association championship five times from 1921–27.

hag·fish (hág-fish) *n., pl.* **-fishes** or collectively **hagfish.** Any of various primitive, eel-shaped marine fishes of the family Myxinidae, having a jawless sucking mouth with rasping teeth with which they bore into and feed on other fishes. Also called "hag".

Hag·ga·dah, Hag·ga·da (hə-gaá-də, haágə-daá) *n., pl.* **-doth** (-dot ‖ -dáwt). **1.** Traditional Jewish literature; especially, the nonlegal part of the Talmud. Compare **Halakah. 2.** The book containing the story of the Exodus and the ritual of the Seder, read at the Passover Seder. [Hebrew *haggādāh*, narration, telling, from *hagged*, to narrate, tell, from the Semitic root *ngd*, to rise, become conspicuous.] —**hag·gad·ic, Hag·gad·ic** (-gaádik, -gáddik) *adj.*

hag·ga·dist (hə-gaádist) *n. Often capital* H. **1.** A haggadic writer. **2.** A student of haggadic literature. —**hag·ga·dis·tic** (hággə-dístik) *adj.*

Hag·ga·i¹ (hággī, hággay-ī). A Hebrew prophet of the sixth century B.C.

Haggai² *n. Abbr.* **Hag.** A book of the Old Testament attributed to Haggai.

hag·gard (hággərd) *adj.* **1. a.** Appearing worn and exhausted from or as if from suffering, anxiety, or deprivation; gaunt: "*he looked as haggard as an actor by daylight*" (Henry James). **b.** Wild and unruly; uncontrolled. **2.** Wild and intractable. Said of a hawk used in falconry.
—*n.* An adult hawk captured for training. [French *hagard*, untamed hawk, wild hawk, perhaps from Germanic.] —**hag·gard·ly** *adv.* —**hag·gard·ness** *n.*
Synonyms: haggard, wasted, worn, careworn.

Hag·gard (hággərd), **Sir Henry Rider** (1856–1925). British novelist. He served as a government official in the Transvaal (1875–81). His novels include *King Solomon's Mines* (1885), *She* (1887), and *Allan Quatermain* (1887).

hag·gis (hággiss) *n., pl.* **-gises** or **haggis.** A Scottish dish consisting of a mixture of the minced heart, lungs, and liver of a sheep or calf mixed with suet, onions, oatmeal, and seasonings, and traditionally boiled in the stomach of the animal. [Middle English *hageset†*.]

hag·gle (hágg'l) *v.* **-gled, -gling, -gles.** **1.** To bargain, as over the price of something; wrangle: "*he preferred to be overcharged than to haggle*" (Somerset Maugham). **2.** To argue in an attempt to come to terms. —*tr. Archaic.* **1.** To cut in a crude, unskilful manner; hack; mangle. **2.** To harass or worry by wrangling. —See Synonyms at **argue.**
—*n.* An instance of haggling. [Frequentative of dialectal *hag*, to cut, from Middle English *haggen*, from Old Norse *höggva*, to HEW.] —**hag·gler** *n.*

hag·i·ar·chy (hággi-aarki ‖ *U.S. also* háyji-) *n., pl.* **-chies.** Also **hag·i·oc·ra·cy** (-óckrə-si) (for sense 1). **1.** Government by holy men, such as clerics. **2.** A hierarchy of saints. [HAGI(O)- + -ARCHY.]

hagio-, hagi- *comb. form.* Indicates: **1.** A saint or body of saints; for example, **hagiology, hagiarchy. 2.** A sacred or holy place; for example, **hagioscope.** [Late Latin, from Greek, from *hagios*, holy.]

Hag·i·og·ra·pha (hággi-óggrəfə ‖ *U.S. also* háyji-) *n. Used with a singular or plural verb.* The third of the three ancient Jewish divisions of the Old Testament, containing those books not in the Law (Torah) or the Prophets, and comprising usually the Psalms, Proverbs, Job, the Song of Solomon, Ruth, Lamentations, Ecclesiastes, Esther, Daniel, Ezra, Nehemiah, and Chronicles. Also called "Writings". [Late Latin, from Greek, "sacred writings" : *hagio-*, sacred + -*grapha*, writings, plural of -*graphos*, -GRAPH.]

hag·i·og·ra·phy (hággi-óggrəfi ‖ *U.S. also* háyji-) *n., pl.* **-phies.** **1.** Biography of saints. **2.** Any idealising or worshipful biography. [HAGIO- + -GRAPHY.] —**hag·i·og·raph·er** *n.* —**hag·i·o·graph·ic** (-ə-gráffik), **hag·i·o·graph·i·cal** *adj.*

hag·i·ol·a·try (hággi-óllətri ‖ *U.S. also* háyji-) *n. Theology.* Worship of the saints in a manner appropriate only to God. [HAGIO- + -LATRY.] —**hag·i·ol·a·ter** *n.* —**hag·i·ol·a·trous** *adj.*

hag·i·ol·o·gy (hággi-ólləji ‖ *U.S. also* háyji-) *n., pl.* **-gies.** **1.** Literature dealing with the lives of saints. **2.** A history of sacred writings. **3.** An authoritative list of saints. [HAGIO- + -LOGY.] —**hag·i·o·log·ic** (-ə-lójik), **hag·i·o·log·i·cal** *adj.* —**hag·i·ol·o·gist** (-ólləjist) *n.*

hag·i·o·scope (hággi-ə-skōp ‖ *U.S. also* háyji-) *n.* A small opening provided in an interior wall of a church to enable those in the transept to have a view of the main altar. Also called "squint".

[HAGIO- + -SCOPE.] —**hag·i·o·scop·ic** (-skóppik) *adj.*

hag·rid·den (hág-ridd'n) *adj.* **1.** Harassed or pursued by or as if by a witch. **2.** Tormented or harassed, as by nightmares or unreasoning fears.

Hague, The (hayg). *Dutch* **'s Gra·ven·hage** (skhraávən-haakhə), **den Haag** (den haʹakh). City in the western Netherlands, the capital of South Holland province, lying on the North Sea. Most of the Netherlands government's administrative offices are located there, as are the national legislature, the supreme court, and foreign embassies. It is also the site of the International Court of Justice.

Hague Tribunal *n.* Officially, the Permanent Court of Arbitration. A tribunal established at The Hague in 1899 for the peaceful settlement of international disputes.

hah. Variant of **ha.**

ha-ha¹ (haa-háa, háa-) *n.* A sound made in imitation of laughter. ~*interj.* Also **haw-haw** (háw-haw, -háw). Used to express amusement or scorn. [Middle English, Old English.]

ha-ha² (háa-haa) *n.* Also **haw-haw** (háw-haw). A moat, walled ditch, or hedge sunk in the ground to serve as a fence without impairing the view. Also called "sunk fence". [French, apparently expressing surprise at finding such an unexpected obstacle.]

Hahn (haan), **Kurt** (1886–1974). German educationalist. He was forced to leave Germany after the Nazis came to power (1933). He settled in Britain and founded Gordonstoun School, where individual initiative and self-reliance are encouraged.

Hahn, Otto (1879–1968). German chemist and physicist who discovered the process of nuclear fission. In 1938, he found that uranium atoms could be split in two when bombarded with neutrons, releasing atomic energy. Hahn received the Nobel prize for chemistry (1944).

Hai·da (hídə) *n., pl.* **-das** or collectively **Haida. 1.** A member of a group of North American Indian peoples inhabiting the Queen Charlotte Islands, British Columbia, and Prince of Wales Island, Alaska. **2.** The language of these peoples, the sole survivor of the Haida family of languages. —**Hai·dan** *adj.*

Hai·fa (hífə). The chief city of northern Israel, lying on the Mediterranean Sea at the foot of Mt. Carmel. The old city was destroyed by Saladin in 1191; the prosperity of the modern city dates from the early 19th century. It is an industrial centre, one of Israel's chief ports, the world centre of Bahaism, and the site of the shrine of the Abd ol-Bahá.

Haig (hayg), **Douglas, 1st Earl** (1861–1928). British commander in chief on the Western Front (1915–18). He went to France as commander of the First Army Corps and succeeded Sir John French as commander in chief. He was responsible for the costly assault at the Somme (1916). In 1918, he directed the counterattack which broke the Hindenburg Line. President of the Royal British Legion (1921–28).

haik, haick (hīk, hayk) *n.* A large piece of cotton, silk, or wool cloth, draped over the head and about the body, worn as an outer garment by Arabs. [Arabic *ḥāʹik,* from *ḥāka,* to weave.]

hai·ku (hí-kōō) *n., pl.* **haiku.** A Japanese lyric poem of a fixed, 17-syllable form that often simply points to a thing or pairing of things in nature that has moved the poet. Also called "hokku". [Japanese : *hai,* amusement + *ku,* sentence, verse.]

hail¹ (hayl) *n.* **1. a.** Precipitation in the form of pellets of ice. **b.** A hailstone. **c.** *Archaic.* A hailstorm. **2.** Something suggestive of a shower of hail, as in force and quantity: *a hail of criticism; a hail of bullets.* ~*v.* **hailed, hailing, hails.** —*intr.* **1.** To precipitate hail: *It's hailing outside.* **2.** To fall like hail. —*tr.* To pour down or forth: *hail oaths at someone.* [Middle English *hail, hagel,* Old English *hagol, hagalian.*]

hail² *v.* **hailed, hailing, hails.** —*tr.* **1. a.** To salute or greet; welcome. **b.** To greet or acclaim enthusiastically. **2.** To call out to in order to catch the attention of: *hail a cab.* **3.** To signal or call to (a passing ship) in greeting or to identify oneself. —*intr.* To hail a passing ship. —**hail from.** To come or originate from: *He hails from Bombay.* ~*n.* **1.** The act of hailing. **2.** A shout made to greet or catch the attention of someone. **3.** The range within which a hail will be heard: *within hail.* ~*interj. Chiefly Poetic.* Used to express a greeting or tribute. [Middle English *hailen, haeilen,* from *(wæs)haeil,* "(be) healthy", hail, from Old Norse *heill,* HALE, whole, healthy.] —**hail·er** *n.*

Hai·le Se·las·sie I (hílі si-lássi), born Ras Tafari Makonnen (1892–1975). Emperor of Ethiopia (1930–36, 1941–74). After resisting the Italian invasion of his country (1935), he fled to England, returning with the Allies in 1941. His autocratic leadership brought opposition and he was deposed in a military coup of 1974. He is revered as "the Lion of Judah, the Elect of God" by the Rastafarian cult of West Indians.

hail-fel·low-well-met (háyl-fellō-wél-mét) *adj.* Heartily friendly and congenial, especially in a shallow or gushing way. Also "hail-fellow". [From the archaic greetings *Hail, fellow!* and *Hail, fellow! well met!*]

Hail Mary *n.* The **Ave Maria** *(see).*

Hail·sham (háylshəm), **Quintin (McGarel) Hogg, Baron** (1907-). British lawyer and politician. He was Lord Chancellor (1970-74, 1979-87).

hail·stone (háyl-stōn) *n.* A hard pellet of ice.

hail·storm (háyl-stawrm) *n.* A storm with hail.

Hail·wood (háylwŏŏd), **Mike,** born Stanley Michael Bailey Hail-wood (1940–81). British motorcyclist and racing driver. He won nine world motorcycle championships (1961–69) before taking up car racing. He died in a road accident.

Hai·nan (hí-nán || *U.S.* -náan). Also **Hainan Dao.** An island off the south China coast, belonging to China and administratively part of Guangdong province. After Taiwan, it is the largest island off the China coast. The largest city and chief port is Haikou. The island is rich in minerals and the site of valuable rubber plantations.

Hai·naut (háy-nawt; *French* e-nǒ). *Flemish* **Henegouwen.** Low-lying province of southern Belgium, bordering on France. The capital is Mons, and the population is predominantly French-speaking.

Hai·phong (hí-fóng). City in northeastern Vietnam, lying on the delta of the Song Hong (Red River), about 16 kilometres (10 miles) inland from the Gulf of Tonkin. One of southeast Asia's leading ports, it was severely damaged by bombing during the Vietnam war.

hair (hair) *n.* **1. a.** Any of the cylindrical, often pigmented filaments characteristically growing from the epidermis of a mammal. **b.** A growth of such filaments, such as that forming the coat of an animal or covering the scalp of a human being. **2.** Any similar filamentous projection or bristle, such as a seta of an arthropod or an epidermal process of a plant. **3.** Fabric made from the hair of certain animals: *a coat of camel's hair.* **4.** A minute distance or narrow margin: *win by a hair.* —**get in (someone's) hair.** To upset or annoy someone. —**let (one's) hair down.** To drop one's reserve or inhibitions. —**split hairs.** To make petty and fine distinctions. —**turn a hair.** To reveal discomfiture. Used in negative constructions: *accepted the challenge without turning a hair.* ~*adj.* **1.** Made of or with hair. **2.** For the hair: *a hair dryer.* [Middle English *haire, hare,* Old English *hær,* from Germanic *hǣram* (unattested).]

hair·ball (háir-bawl) *n.* A small mass of hair swallowed by an animal, often causing indigestion or convulsions.

hair·band (háir-band) *n.* A headband *(see).*

hair·breadth (háir-bredth, -bret-th) *adj.* Extremely close: *a hair-breadth escape.* ~*n.* Variant of **hair's-breadth.**

hair·brush (háir-brush) *n.* A brush for grooming the hair.

hair clip *n.* **1.** A hinged clip that snaps together, used to hold the hair in place. **2.** *British.* A hair-slide. **3.** *Australian & N.Z.* A kirby grip or a hair-grip. Also called "clip".

hair·cloth (háir-kloth || -klawth) *n.* A wiry fabric having usually a cotton or linen warp with a horsehair filler, used for upholstering and for stiffening and interlining garments.

hair·cut (háir-kut) *n.* **1.** A cutting of the hair. **2.** The style in which hair is cut.

hair·do (háir-dōō) *n., pl.* **-dos. 1.** A cutting or arranging of the hair, especially a woman's hair. **2.** The style in which the hair is thus cut or arranged.

hair·dress·er (háir-dressər) *n.* A person who cuts, perms, colours, or arranges people's hair, especially women's hair. —**hair·dress·ing** *n.*

hair dryer *n.* A machine for drying hair.

haired *adj.* Having hair, especially of a specified kind. Used chiefly in combination: *short-haired.*

hair follicle *n.* A tubular infolding of the epidermis that contains the root of a hair.

hair grass *n.* Any of various grasses having long, narrow stems and leaves, such as the tufted hair grass, *Deschampsia cespitosa.*

hair·grip (háir-grip) *n. British.* A clip or clasp used to fasten the hair, typically made of horn, plastic, or tortoiseshell. Also "grip".

hair·less (háir-ləss, -liss) *adj.* Having little or no hair.

hair·line (háir-lĩn) *n.* **1.** The outline of the growth of hair on the head, especially across the front. **2.** A very slender line. Also used adjectivally: *a hairline fracture.* **3.** *Printing.* **a.** A very fine line on a typeface. **b.** A style of type using such lines. **4. a.** A textile design having thin, threadlike stripes. **b.** A fabric, usually a worsted, with such stripes.

hair mouse *n.* A ring-shaped hairpiece inserted to fill out a woman's bun. Also called "mouse".

hair·net (háir-net) *n.* A very fine net worn to hold the hair in place.

hair·piece (háir-peess) *n.* A covering or bunch of human or artificial hair used to cover baldness or give shape to a hairstyle.

hair·pin (háir-pin) *n.* A thin, cylindrical strip of metal bent in a long U shape, used by women to secure a hairstyle or a headdress. ~*adj.* Doubled back in a deep U: *a hairpin bend in the road.*

hair·rais·ing (háir-rayzing) *adj.* Horrifying; terrifying.

hair's-breadth (háirz-bredth, -bret-th) *n.* Also **hair·breadth** (háir-). A small space or distance; a narrow margin: *win by a hair's-breadth.*

hair seal *n.* Any of various earless seals having a stiff, hairlike coat in the adult.

hair-set (háir-set) *n.* A styling or arranging of the hair at a hairdresser's, usually using rollers.

hair sheep *n.* Any sheep of a breed having hair rather than wool and yielding a fine-grained hide.

hair shirt *n.* A coarse haircloth garment worn next to the skin by religious ascetics to mortify the flesh.

hair-slide (háir-slīd) *n.* A fancy or decorative hair-grip, often fastened by a catch that slides under the hair and catches in a loop to hold it.

hair space *n. Printing.* The narrowest of the spaces used for separating words or letters.

hair-split·ting (háir-splitting) *n.* The making of unreasonably fine distinctions; quibbling.

~*adj.* Concerned with subtle but petty distinctions. —**hair·split· ter** *n.*

hair·spring (háir-spring) *n.* A fine coiled spring that regulates the movement of the balance wheel in a watch or clock.

hair·streak (háir-streek) *n.* Any of numerous butterflies of the sub-family Theclinae, having transverse streaks on the underwings and fine, hairlike projections on the hind wings.

hair stroke *n.* A very fine line in writing or printing, as a serif.

hair·style (háir-stīl) *n.* The design or style in which hair is cut, set, or arranged. —**hair·sty·list** *n.*

hair·tail (háir-tayl) *n.* Any fish of the marine family Trichiuridae, having spiny fins, a long, whiplike body, and long teeth.

hair transplant *n.* The grafting of strands of one's own hair onto a bald area of the scalp.

hair trigger *n.* A gun trigger adjusted to respond to a very slight pressure.

hair·trig·ger (háir-trigɡər) *adj.* Responding to the slightest provoca-tion: *a hair-trigger temper.*

hair·worm (háir-wurm) *n.* **1.** Any of various slender, parasitic nematode worms of the genus *Trichostrongylus,* that infest the stom-ach and small intestine of cattle, sheep, and related animals. **2.** A horsehair worm *(see).*

hair·y (háir-i) *adj.* **-ier, -iest. 1.** Covered with hair or hairlike growths; hirsute: *a hairy arm.* **2.** Of or like hair: *a hairy coat.* **3.** *Slang.* Fraught with difficulties; hazardous: *a hairy escape.* —**hair·i·ness** *n.*

hairy frog *n.* A frog, *Astylosternus robustus,* of Cameroon, the males of which grow hairlike filaments on the thighs during the breeding season.

hairy hedgehog *n.* A gymnure *(see).*

Hai·ti, Republic of (háyti). Independent republic in the Caribbean, comprising the western third of the island of Hispaniola and the two small islands of Tortuga and Gonâve. A slave rebellion against French rule won the islanders their independence in 1804. Political instability led to U.S. occupation (1915–34), and the repressive dictatorship of François Duvalier, "Papa Doc" (1957–71). His son and successor Jean-Claude ("Baby Doc") Duvalier was overthrown in 1986. Father Jean-Bertrand Aristide won free presidential elec-tions in 1990, but the military stopped him taking office. In 1994 U.S. forces landed to restore democracy. Haiti is the poorest country in Latin America. Coffee is the mainstay of the economy, and bauxite and sugar are also exported. Area, 27 750 square kilometres (10,714 square miles). Population, 7,340,000. Capital, Port-au-Prince. See map at **Dominican Republic.**

Hai·ti·an, Hay·ti·an (háysh-yən, -'n, háyti-ən) *adj.* Of or pertaining to Haiti, its people or their language.

~*n.* **1.** A native or inhabitant of Haiti. **2.** The French patois spo-ken by most Haitians. Also called "Haitian Creole".

Hai·tink (hītingk), **Bernard** (1929–). Dutch conductor. From 1978 to 1988 he was musical director of the Glyndebourne Opera, and in 1987 became musical director of the Royal Opera House, Covent Garden, and in 1994 of the E.U. Youth Orchestra.

haj, hajj. Variants of **hadj.**

haji, hajji. Variants of **hadji.**

ha·ka (háakə) *n.* N.Z. A Maori war dance accompanied by chant-ing. [Maori.]

hake[1] (hayk) *n., pl.* **hakes** or collectively **hake. 1.** Any of various marine food fishes of the genus *Merluccius,* such as *M. merluccius,* related to and resembling the cod. **2.** Any of various other fishes, such as species of the American genus *Urophycis* or the Australian barracouta, *Thyrsites atun.* [Middle English *hake,* perhaps from *hakefish,* from dialect *hake,* Old Norse *haki,* hook (from the shape of its underjaw).]

hake[2] *n.* A wooden rack or frame for drying cheese, bricks, or fish. [Variant of HECK (frame).]

ha·ke·a (háyki-ə) *n.* Any Australian tree of the genus *Hakea,* some species of which produce useful wood. [After C.L. von *Hake* (died 1818), German horticulturist.]

Ha·ken·kreuz (háakən-kroyts) *n.* The swastika used as a symbol of Nazi Germany or of anti-Semitism. [German, "hooked cross".]

ha·kim[1]**, ha·keem** (ha-kéem, haa-) *n.* A Muslim physician. [Arabic *hakīm,* wise, learned, philosopher, from *hakama,* to be wise, exercise authority.]

ha·kim[2] (háak-im, -eem) *n. pl.* **hakim** or **-kims.** A Muslim ruler, provincial governor, or judge. [Arabic *hākim,* governor, from *ha-kama,* to exercise authority.]

Hak·ka (háka) *n., pl.* **-kas. 1.** A member of a Chinese people gener-ally thought to have originated in central northern China, but now mostly scattered throughout southern China. **2.** A dialect of Chi-nese spoken by the Hakkas. [From dialect pronunciation of Man-darin *kè jiā,* guest people, more recent migrants to a settled area.]

Hak·luyt (háklōot), **Richard** (*c.* 1552–1616). English geographer. He collected accounts of English voyages of exploration, and pub-lished them in *Principal Navigations, Voyages, Traffics, and Discoveries of the English Nation* (1589, enlarged 1598–1600).

Ha·la·fi·an (hə-láafiən) *adj.* Of, pertaining to, or designating a cul-ture that flourished in parts of Syria and Iraq before 3500 B.C., characterised especially by its polychrome pottery. [After Tell *Ha-laf,* a site near the present village of Ras el 'Ain, northeast Syria near the Turkish border.]

Ha·la·kah (hə-láa-khə, hál-ə-khàa, háal-) *n., pl.* **-koth** (-khŏt, -khŏt) or **-kahs.** Also **Hal·la·cha** *pl.* **-choth** or **-chas.** *Judaism.* The legal part of Talmudic literature, an interpretation of the laws of the Scriptures. Compare **Haggadah.** [Mishnaic Hebrew *halākhāh,* rule, tradition, from *hālakh,* to go.] —**Ha·lak·ic** (hə-láckik) *adj.*

ha·la·kist, ha·la·chist (hál-ə-kist, háal-) *n. Often capital* H. A He-brew judge or scholar who has written parts of the Halakah.

ha·lal, hal·lal (haa-láal) *tr.v.* **-laled, -laling, -lals.** To slaughter (ani-mals) in the prescribed Muslim manner.

~*n.* Meat killed in this manner. Also used adjectivally: *halal meat; a halal butcher.* [Arabic, "lawful".]

ha·la·tion (hə-láysh'n, ha-, hay-) *n.* **1.** A blurring or spreading of light around bright objects or areas on a photographic negative or print. **2.** A ring of light appearing around a bright object on a television screen. [HAL(O) + -ATION.]

halavah. Variant of **halvah.**

hal·berd (hál-bərd, háwl-, -berd) *n.* Also **hal·bert** (-bərt). A weapon of the 15th and 16th centuries having an axelike blade and a steel spike mounted on the end of a long shaft. [Middle English *halberd,* from Old French *hallebarde,* from Middle High German *helmbarde,* "handle axe" : *helm,* handle + *barte,* axe, hatchet, from Old High German *barta.*]

hal·ber·dier (hál-bər-déer, háwl-) *n.* A soldier, attendant, or guard armed with a halberd.

hal·cy·on (hál-si-ən) *n.* **1.** A fabled bird, identified with the king-fisher, that was supposed to have had the power to calm the wind and the waves during the winter solstice while it nested on the sea. **2.** *Poetic.* A kingfisher.

~*adj.* **1.** Calm and peaceful; tranquil. **2.** Prosperous; golden: *hal-cyon years.* —See Synonyms at **calm.** [Middle English *alceon,* from Latin *(h)alcyon,* from Greek *(h)alkuōn*†, a mythical bird, perhaps the kingfisher.]

halcyon days *pl.n.* **1.** Days of fine weather occurring near the win-ter solstice, especially the seven days before and the seven after, attributed by legend to the magical powers of the halcyon. **2.** A happy period of peace and prosperity.

hale[1] (hayl) *adj.* **haler, halest.** Sound in health; not infirm; vigor-ous; robust. Used especially in the phrase *hale and hearty.* See Syn-onyms at **healthy.** [Middle English *hal(e),* Old English *hāl,* WHOLE.] —**hale·ness** *n.*

hale[2] *tr.v.* **haled, haling, hales. 1.** *Literary.* To compel to go; force: *hale a man into court.* **2.** *Archaic.* To pull, drag, draw, or hoist: *"The rope that haled the buckets from the well."* (Tennyson). [Middle Eng-lish *halen,* from Old French *haler,* from Old Norse *hala,* from Mid-dle Low German *halen,* to pull.]

Haleb. See **Aleppo.**

ha·ler (hál-ər, -air) *n., pl.* **-lers** or **haleru** (hál-ərōō, -airōō). A Czech and Slovak monetary unit equal to $1/100$ of the koruna. [Czech, from Middle High German *haller,* an early German silver coin, from *Hall,* town in Swabia, where they were once minted.]

half (haaf ‖ *chiefly U.S.* haf) *n., pl.* **halves** (haavz ‖ havz). **1. a.** Either of two equal parts that together constitute a whole. **b.** A part of something approximately equal to the remainder: *Half her life is spent dreaming.* **2.** *Informal.* **a.** A half pint of beer, cider, or the like. **b.** *Scottish.* A measure of whisky. **3.** In some sports, either of the two playing periods into which a game is divided. **b.** Either of two periods into which an event, such as a concert or play, may be divided. **4.** *Sports.* A half-back. **5.** A golf score equal to the opponent's score on a hole or a round. **6.** Either of the two sections of a playing field, considered as belonging to the team defending the goal in that section. **7.** Half an hour. Used in ex-pressing time: *half past one.* **8.** A ticket sold at a reduced price, especially for children on public transport. —**and a half.** *Informal.* Of an exceptional kind: *a fight and a half.* —**by half.** By a consid-erable and often excessive amount. —**by halves. 1.** Partially; im-perfectly. **2.** Reluctantly; unenthusiastically. —**go halves.** To share equally. —**in half.** Into halves.

~*adj.* **1.** Being a half, as in size, quantity, or the like: *a half-bottle.* **2.** Being approximately a half. **3.** Partial; incomplete.

~*adv.* **1.** To the extent of exactly or nearly 50 per cent: *a half-empty tank.* **2.** Not completely or sufficiently; partly: *only half pre-pared.* **3.** To some extent; somewhat: *I was half afraid she'd leave.* **4.** *Informal.* Tolerably; reasonably: *wanting a café with half-decent food.* —**not half.** *British Informal.* Used as an intensive: *He didn't half get angry.*

~*pron.* Either of the two quantities, lengths of time, or the like into which something may be divided: *Half will be given away and the rest stays here.* [Middle English *half,* Old English *healf,* from Ger-manic.]

Usage: In certain expressions, *half* can either precede or follow the indefinite article: *half a dozen, a half-dozen* or *half an hour, a half-hour.* The double use of the article (*a half an hour*) is often heard in informal speech, but is not standard.

half-a-dollar (haáf-ə-dóllər ‖ háf-) *n. British Slang.* A half-crown.

half-and-half (haáf-ən-haáf, -ənd- ‖ háf-, -háf) *adj.* Being half one thing and half another.

~*adv.* In equal portions.

~*n.* **1.** A mixture of two things in equal portions. **2.** *British.* A blend of light ale and bitter.

half-back (haáf-bak ‖ háf-) *n. Abbr.* **hb, hb. 1.** Any of several play-ers in various sports, such as some types of football and hockey, stationed behind the forward line; especially, in Rugby football, either of two players, the **stand-off half** or the **scrum half** *(both of which see).* Also called "**half**". **2.** The position played by a half-back.

half-baked (haáf-báykt ‖ háf-) *adj.* **1.** Only partly baked; not cooked through. **2.** *Informal.* Not sufficiently thought out; ill-conceived; foolish: *a half-baked scheme.* **3.** *Informal.* Lacking good judgment or common sense: *a half-baked idiot.*

half-ball (haʹaf-bawl ‖ háf-) *adj.* In billiards and snooker, designating a stroke aimed so as to make the cue ball hit the side of another ball.

half-beak (haʹaf-beek ‖ háf-) *n.* Any of various marine and freshwater fishes of the family Hemiramphidae, related to the flying fishes, and having the lower jaw extended beyond the upper jaw.

half binding *n.* A bookbinding in which the back and often the corners of the volume are bound in a material differing from the rest of the cover: *a half binding of leather.*

half blood *n.* Also **half-blood** (haʹaf-blud ‖ háf-) **1.** The relationship existing between persons having only one parent in common. **2.** A person existing in such a relationship. **3.** A half-breed. **4.** A half-blooded domestic animal.

half-blood-ed (haʹaf-blúddid ‖ háf-) *adj.* **1.** Having only one parent in common. **2.** Having parents of different ethnic types. **3.** Having one parent of pedigree stock and the other of unknown or mixed ancestry. Said of an animal.

half-blue (haʹaf-blooˊ ‖ háf-, -bléw) *n.* **1.** A student at Oxford or Cambridge university who is in a reserve or second university team for a sport such as Rugby football, soccer, or rowing or who represents the university in a minor sport, such as billiards or chess. **2.** An award, such as a scarf or jersey, given to a half-blue.

half board *n.* Accommodation in a hotel comprising bed, breakfast, and one main meal. Also called "demi-pension".

half boot *n.* A low boot extending just above the ankle.

half-bound (haʹaf-bównd ‖ háf-; *West Indian also* -bungd) *adj.* Having a half binding. Said of a book.

half-bred (haʹaf-bred ‖ háf-) *adj.* **1.** Having only one parent that is purebred; half-blooded. **2.** Having parents of different ethnic types.

half-breed (haʹaf-breed ‖ háf-) *n.* A person having parents of different ethnic types; especially, the offspring of a white person and an American Indian.
~*adj.* Half-blooded; hybrid.

half-broth-er (haʹaf-bruthər ‖ háf-) *n.* A brother related through one parent only.

half-butt (haʹaf-but ‖ háf-) *n.* In billiards and snooker, a cue that is shorter than a long butt though longer than an ordinary cue.

half-caste (haʹaf-kaast ‖ háf-, -kast) *n.* A person of mixed racial descent; especially, a Eurasian or a person of mixed white and black descent. —**half-caste** *adj.*

half cock *n.* The position of the hammer of a firearm when it is raised halfway and locked by a catch so that the trigger cannot be pulled. —**at half cock.** At a premature stage; before proper preparations are made.

half-cocked (haʹaf-kókt ‖ háf-) *adj.* **1.** At the position of half cock. **2.** *Informal.* Inadequately prepared or conceived; not fully thought out.
~*adv. Informal.* Prematurely; hastily; carelessly: *fall half-cocked into an argument.*

half-crown (haʹaf-krówn ‖ háf-) *n.* Also **half-a-crown** (-ə-krówn). **1.** A British coin worth two shillings and sixpence (12½ new pence), no longer in circulation. **2.** The sum of two shillings and sixpence.

half-cut (haʹaf-cút ‖ háf-) *adj. Chiefly British Informal.* Drunk or tipsy. [19th century : earlier *half-shaved.* Compare **half-seas-over.**]

half-dead (haʹaf-déd ‖ háf-) *adj. Chiefly British Informal.* Exhausted; very tired.

half dollar *n.* A U.S. or Canadian coin worth 50 cents.

half-forward (haʹaf-fórˊwərd ‖ háf-, -fórˊ-) *n.* In Australian Rules: **1.** A position on the line between the centre line and the full forward line. **2.** A player occupying this position.

half gainer *n.* A dive in which the diver springs from the board facing forward, rotates backward in the air in a half backward somersault, and enters the water headfirst, facing the board.

half-har-dy (haʹaf-hárdi ‖ háf-) *adj.* Designating a cultivated plant that can survive outside during winter except during a severe frost.

half-heart-ed (haʹaf-hártid ‖ háf-) *adj.* Done with or possessing little interest or enthusiasm; uninspired: *a halfhearted attempt at painting.* —**half-heart-ed-ly** *adv.* —**half-heart-ed-ness** *n.*

half hitch *n.* A hitch made by looping a rope or strap around an object, and then back around itself, bringing the end of the rope through the loop.

half-hour (haʹaf-ówr ‖ háf-) *n.* **1.** A period of 30 minutes. **2.** The point that marks 30 minutes after a given hour.
~*adj.* **1.** Lasting 30 minutes. **2.** Occurring on or indicating the half-hour: *a half-hour chime.* —**half-hour-ly** *adj. & adv.*

half-hunt-er (haʹaf-húntər ‖ háf-) *n.* A pocket watch with a metal cover over all but the centre part of the glass. Compare **hunter.**

half-in-te-gral (haʹaf-íntigrəl ‖ háf-) *adj.* Having an integer as a numerator and 2 as a denominator. Said of a fraction.

half-jack (haʹaf-jak) *n. South African Informal.* A flat half-bottle of alcohol.

half landing *n.* A landing that is halfway up a staircase.

half-length (haʹaf-length, -lengkth ‖ háf-, -lenth) *n.* A portrait that shows only the upper half and hands of a person.
~*adj.* **1.** Of or denoting such a portrait. **2.** Of half the full length.

half-life (haʹaf-lïf ‖ háf-) *n., pl.* **-lives** (-līvz). **1.** *Physics.* The time required for half the nuclei in a sample of a specific isotopic species to undergo **radioactive decay** *(see).* **2.** *Biology.* **a.** The time required by living tissue, an organ, or an organism to eliminate by

biological processes half the quantity of a radioactive substance taken in. Also called "biological half-life". **b.** The time required for the radioactivity of material taken in by a living organism to be reduced to half its initial value by a combination of biological elimination processes and radioactive decay. Also called "effective half-life".

half-light (haʹaf-lït ‖ háf-) *n.* The soft, subdued light found at dusk or dawn or in dimly lit interiors.

half-line (haʹaf-lïn ‖ háf-) *n.* A straight line extending in just one direction from a given point.

half-mast (haʹaf-maˊast ‖ háf-, -mást) *n.* The position about halfway up a mast or pole at which a flag is flown as a symbol of mourning for the dead or as a signal of distress.
~*tr.v.* **half-masted, -masting, -masts.** To place (a flag) at this position.

half measures *pl.n.* Inadequate or inappropriate procedures.

half-moon (haʹaf-moˊon ‖ háf-) *n.* **1.** The moon when only half its disc is illuminated. **2.** Something shaped like a half-moon, as the lunula of the fingernail.
~*adj.* Shaped like a half-moon: *half-moon spectacles.*

half nelson *n.* A wrestling hold in which one arm is passed under the opponent's arm from behind to the back of his neck. Compare **full nelson.**

half note *n. U.S. Music.* A **minim** *(see).*

half-pen-ny (háyp-əni, -ni, haʹaf-pénni ‖ háf-) *n., pl.* **-nies** (for senses 1, 2); **halfpence** (háypənss) (for sense 3). Also **ha'pen-ny.** **1.** A British coin worth half of a new penny, now no longer in circulation. **2.** A British coin worth half an old penny, now no longer in circulation. **3.** The sum of half of a penny. **4.** A small or negligible amount. —See Usage note at **penny.** —**half-pen-ny-worth** *n.*

half pint *n. Slang.* A small or insignificant person or animal.

half-plate (haʹaf-playt ‖ háf-) *n.* A photographic plate measuring 16.5 centimetres (6½ inches) by 10.8 centimetres (4¼ inches).

half-price (haʹaf-prïs ‖ háf-) *adv.* At a reduced price, usually half the full price. —**half-price** *adj.*

half relief *n.* **Mezzo-relievo** *(see).*

half-seas-o-ver (haʹaf-seez-ōˊvər ‖ háf-) *adj. Informal.* Moderately drunk; tipsy. [Originally *half sea's over,* halfway across the sea, hence, between one state or condition and another.]

half-sis-ter (haʹaf-sistər ‖ háf-) *n.* A sister related through one parent only.

half-slip (haʹaf-slip ‖ háf-) *n.* A woman's slip that extends from the waist to the hem of the outer garment.

half-sole (haʹaf-sōl ‖ háf-) *n.* A shoe sole extending from the shank to the toe.
~*tr.v.* **half-soled, -soling, -soles.** To fit or repair with a half-sole.

half sovereign *n.* An obsolete British gold coin worth ten shillings.

half step *n. U.S. Music.* A **semitone** *(see).*

half-tide (haʹaf-tïd ‖ háf-) *n.* **1.** The condition of the tide at a time halfway between high tide and low tide. **2.** The period during which this condition exists.

half-tim-bered (haʹaf-tímbərd ‖ háf-) *adj.* Also **half-tim-ber** (-timbər). *Architecture.* Having a wooden framework with plaster, brick, stone, or other masonry filling the spaces.

half time *n.* The interval between two halves of a game. Also used adjectivally: *the half-time score.*

half title *n.* **1.** The title of a book printed at the top of the first page of the text or on a full page preceding the main title page. **2.** The title of a section of a book, consisting of only one line and printed on the leaf preceding the text of that section.

half-tone (haʹaf-tōn ‖ háf-) *n.* **1.** *Art.* A tone or value halfway between a highlight and a dark shadow. **2.** In photogravure: **a.** A picture in which the gradations of light are obtained by the relative darkness and density of tiny dots produced by photographing the subject through a fine screen. **b.** The technique or process that produces such pictures. **c.** The metal plate obtained by such a process. **d.** A picture made from such a plate.
~*adj.* Relating to, used in, or made by halftone.

half-track (haʹaf-trak ‖ háf-) *n.* A military motor vehicle, often lightly armoured, with caterpillar treads in place of rear wheels. —**half-track, half-tracked** *adj.*

half-truth (haʹaf-trooth ‖ háf-) *n.* A statement, especially one intended to deceive, that omits some of the facts necessary for a truthful description or account.

half volley *n.* **1.** A stroke, as in tennis or cricket, in which the ball is hit immediately after it bounces off the ground. **2.** The position of the ball immediately after it bounces: *hit it on the half volley.*

half-way (haʹaf-wáy, -way ‖ háf-) *adj.* **1.** Midway between two points or conditions; in the middle. **2.** Reaching or including only half or a portion; partial: *halfway measures.* —**half-way** *adv.*

halfway house *n.* **1.** An inn or other stopping place that marks the midpoint of a journey. **2.** A rehabilitation centre where people who have left an institution, such as a mental hospital or prison, are helped to readjust to the outside world. **3.** A measure intended as a compromise.

half-wit (haʹaf-wit ‖ háf-) *n.* A stupid, foolish, or frivolous person; a simpleton. —**half-wit-ted** *adj.* —**half-wit-ted-ly** *adv.* —**half-wit-ted-ness** *n.*

hal-i-but (hál-i-bət, -but ‖ hól-) *n., pl.* **-buts** or collectively **halibut.** Any of several large, edible flatfishes of the genus *Hippoglossus* and related genera, of northern Atlantic or Pacific waters. [Middle English *halybutte* : *hali, holi,* HOLY (it was eaten on holy days) + *butte,* flatfish, from Middle Dutch.]

Haliç. See **Golden Horn.**

hal·ide (hál-īd ‖ háyl-, -id) n. A binary chemical compound of a halogen with a more electropositive element or group. Also called "haloid". [HAL(O-) + -IDE.]

hal·i·dom (hál-i-dəm) n. **1.** Obsolete. Holiness; sanctity. **2.** Archaic. A holy relic. **3.** Archaic. A sanctuary. [Middle English halidom, Old English hāligdōm : hālig, HOLY + -DOM.]

Hal·i·fax[1] (hál-i-faks). Town in Calderdale, in northern England. Since the Industrial Revolution it has been a centre for the manufacture of carpets, textiles, and, more recently, machine tools.

Hal·i·fax[2] Capital city of the province of Nova Scotia, in eastern Canada. It is Canada's leading ice-free Atlantic port and the eastern terminus of the country's railway network. It was founded in 1749 and named after the Earl of Halifax.

hal·ite (hál-īt ‖ háyl-) n. **Rock salt** (see). [New Latin halites : HAL(O)- + -ITE.]

hal·i·to·sis (hál-i-tố-siss) n. Foul-smelling breath. [New Latin : Latin hālitus, breath, from hālāre†, to breathe + -OSIS.]

hall (hawl) n. **1.** A large entrance room or vestibule in a building; a lobby; a foyer **2.** A corridor or passageway leading from an entrance in a house, hotel, or other building. **3. a.** A building for public gatherings or entertainments, as concerts, lectures, or plays. **b.** The large room in which such events are held. **4. a.** A large building belonging to a school used for assembly, entertainments, or the like. **b.** A large room in a college or university where meals are served and lectures or concerts occasionally held. **c.** British. A meal served in such a building. **d.** British. A sitting of such a meal: second hall. **e.** British. A hall of residence (see): living in hall. **5.** The main house on a landed estate; especially, the house of a nobleman. **6. a.** The house or castle of a medieval king, chieftain, or nobleman. **b.** The large principal room in such a house or castle, used for dining, entertaining, and sleeping. [Middle English hal(le), Old English h(e)all.]

Hall (hawl), **Sir Peter** (1930–). Director of Royal Shakespeare Company (1960–68) and National Theatre (1973–88); artistic director of Glyndebourne Opera (1983–90) and Old Vic (1997–).

hallah. Variant of **challah.**

hallal. Variant of **halal.**

Hal·lé (hál-ay), **Sir Charles**, born Karl Hallé (1819–95). German-born pianist and conductor, who became a British citizen. In 1857, he founded the Hallé Orchestra in Manchester.

Hall effect n. Electronics. An effect in which an electrical potential difference is produced between two faces of a conductor carrying a current when a magnetic field is applied at right angles to the current. [After E.H. Hall (1855–1938), American physicist.]

Hal·lel (ha-láyl, haa-, -lél) n. Judaism. A chant of praise consisting of Psalms 113 to 118, used during Passover and on certain other Jewish holidays. [Hebrew hallēl, song of praise, praise, from həllēl, to praise.]

hal·le·lu·jah (hál-i-lóo-yə ‖ chiefly Welsh -léw-) interj. Used, especially in religious contexts, to express praise or joy.
~n. **1.** The exclamation of "hallelujah". **2.** A musical composition expressing praise and based on the word "hallelujah". See **alleluia.** [Hebrew hallelūyāh, praise the Lord : hallelū, plural imperative of həllēl, to praise + yāh, short for YAHWEH.]

Hal·ley (hál-i, háwli), **Edmond** (1656–1742). British astronomer. He applied Newton's laws of motion to a particular comet of 1682, and in 1705 he correctly predicted its return in 1758. He was appointed Astronomer Royal in 1720.

Halley's comet n. A comet with a period of approximately 76 years, the first comet for which a return was successfully predicted. It last appeared in 1986. [After Edmond HALLEY.]

halliard. Variant of **halyard.**

hall·mark (háwl-maark) n. **1.** A mark used in the United Kingdom to stamp gold, silver, or platinum articles that meet established standards of purity. Also called "platemark". **2.** Any mark indicating quality or excellence. **3.** Any conspicuous indication of the character or quality of something: A sense of humour is the hallmark of humanity.
~tr.v. **hallmarked, -marking, -marks.** To mark with a hallmark. [After Goldsmith's Hall, London, where gold and silver articles were appraised and stamped.]

hallo. Variant of **hello.**

hall of fame n. U.S. **1.** A room or building housing busts, plaques, or the like, honouring illustrious persons. **2.** A group of persons judged to be outstanding in a sport, profession, or other category.

hall of residence n. Chiefly British. A building administered by a university, college, or the like, for housing students.

hal·loo (hə-lóo, ha-) interj. Also **hal·loa** (hə-lố, ha-). **1.** Used to gain someone's attention. **2.** Used to urge on hounds in a hunt.
~n. Also **hal·loa.** A shout or call of "halloo".
~v. **hallooed, -looing, -loos.** Also **hal·loa, -loaed, -loaing, -loas.** —intr. To shout "halloo"; call out. —tr. **1.** To urge on or pursue by calling "halloo" or shouting. **2.** To call out to. **3.** To utter with a loud shout. [Perhaps variant of earlier hallow, to shout so as to incite hounds, from Middle English halowen, from Old French halloer (imitative).]

hal·low (hál-lō) tr.v. **-lowed, -lowing, -lows. 1.** To make or set apart as holy; sanctify; consecrate. **2.** To honour as being holy; revere; adore. [Middle English halowen, Old English hālgian, from Germanic hailag- (unattested), HOLY.]

hal·lowed (hál-lōd) adj. **1.** Made or set apart as being holy; sanctified; consecrated. **2.** Highly venerated; unassailable; sacrosanct.

Hal·low·een, Hal·low·e'en (hál-ō-éen) n. The eve of All Saints' Day, falling on October 31 and celebrated by children who go in costume from door to door begging or playing pranks. [Short for All Hallows Even.]

Hal·low·mas, Hal·low·mass (hál-ō-mass, -məss) n. Archaic. The feast of All Saints' Day or Allhallowmas on November 1. [Short for ALLHALLOWMAS.]

hall porter n. A porter in the lobby of a hotel or office building who looks after keys, takes messages, arranges porters to carry luggage, and the like.

Hall process n. The electrolytic reduction process by means of which aluminium is recovered from aluminium oxide. [After Charles Martin Hall (1864–1914), American chemist, who invented it.]

Hall·statt (hál-stat, German -shtat ‖ háwl-) adj. Also **Hall·statt·i·an** (-státti-ən, -shtátti-). Of, designating, or pertaining to a dominant late Bronze Age and early Iron Age culture of central and western Europe, probably chiefly Celtic, that flourished from the ninth century B.C. to the fourth century B.C. [After Hallstatt, Austria, site of remains typical of the culture.]

hal·lu·ci·nate (hə-lóo-si-nayt, -léw-) v. **-nated, -nating, -nates.** —intr. To undergo hallucinations. —tr. Rare. To cause to have hallucinations. [Latin hallūcinārī, alūcinārī, to wander in mind, from Greek aluein, to wander, be distraught.]

hal·lu·ci·na·tion (hə-lóo-si-náysh'n, -léw-) n. **1.** False perception with a characteristically compelling sense of the reality of something not really present, as occurring in some psychological and neurological disorders, and under the influence of certain drugs. **2.** The hallucinatory material so perceived. **3.** Any false or mistaken idea; a delusion.

hal·lu·ci·na·to·ry (hə-lóo-si-nə-tri, -léw-, -təri, -náytəri) adj. **1.** Characterising or characterised by hallucination. **2.** Inducing hallucination.

hal·lu·cin·o·gen (hə-lóo-si-nə-jen, -léw-, -jən) n. Any drug, such as mescaline or LSD, that induces hallucination. [HALLUCIN(ATION) + -GEN.] —**hal·lu·cin·o·gen·ic** (-jénnik) adj.

hal·lu·ci·no·sis (hə-lóo-si-nố-siss, -léw-) n. Any abnormal condition or mental state characterised by hallucination. [New Latin : HALLUCIN(ATION) + -OSIS.]

hal·lux (hál-əks) n., pl. **halluces** (hál-yoo-seez). **1.** The inner or first digit on the hind foot of a mammal; in man, the big toe. **2.** The homologous digit of a bird, reptile, or amphibian. In birds it is often directed backwards. [New Latin, from Latin hallux, (h)allus†, big toe.]

hall·way (háwl-way) n. Chiefly U.S. **1.** A corridor, passageway, or hall leading from an entrance in a house or building. **2.** An entrance hall; a foyer; a vestibule.

halm. Variant of **haulm.**

hal·ma (hál-mə) n. A board game (like Chinese chequers) for two or four players in which the pieces are moved to the diagonally opposite corners by jumping over other pieces. [Greek halma, a leap, from hallesthai, to leap.]

ha·lo (háylō) n., pl. **-los** or **-loes. 1.** A luminous ring or disc of light surrounding the heads or bodies of sacred figures, as of saints in religious paintings; a nimbus. **2.** The aura of majesty or glory surrounding a person, thing, or event regarded with reverence, awe, or a similar sentiment. **3.** Meteorology. A circular band of light, sometimes coloured, around the Sun or Moon, caused by the refraction of light by ice particles or water drops suspended in the intervening atmosphere. **4.** A spherical band of stars that surrounds the Galaxy and other spiral galaxies. **5.** Pathology. Any of the coloured rings seen around a light source by people with glaucoma or cataract.
~v. **haloed, -loing, -los** or **-loes.** —tr. To adorn or invest with a halo. —intr. To form a halo. [Medieval Latin halō, from Latin halōs, from Greek halōs†, threshing floor, halo, disc of the Sun or Moon.]

halo-, hal– comb. form. Indicates salt or the sea; for example, **halophyte, halite.** [French, from Greek, from hals, salt, sea.]

ha·lo·bi·ont (hál-ō-bí-ont ‖ hayl-) n. An organism that lives or grows in a saline environment. [HALO- + BIONT.]

hal·o·gen (hál-ə-jen, -jən ‖ hayl-) n. Any of a group of five chemically related nonmetallic elements that consists of fluorine, chlorine, bromine, iodine, and astatine. [Swedish : HALO- + -GEN.] —**ha·log·e·nous** (hə-lójənəss) adj.

hal·o·gen·ate (hál-ə-jə-nayt ‖ hayl-) tr.v. **-ated, -ating, -ates.** To treat or cause to combine with a halogen. —**hal·o·gen·a·tion** (-náysh'n) n.

hal·oid (hál-oyd ‖ hayl-) adj. Derived from or resembling a halogen.
~n. A **halide** (see). [HALO- + -OID.]

hal·o·per·i·dol (hál-ō-pérri-dol ‖ -dōl) n. A tranquilliser used in the treatment of psychiatric disorders, including schizophrenia. [HALO- + (PI)PERID(INE) + -OL.]

hal·o·phil·ic (hál-ō-fíllik ‖ hayl-) adj. Designating organisms, especially bacteria, that grow best in a salty environment. [HALO- + -PHILIC.] —**hal·o·phile** n.

hal·o·phyte (hál-ə-fīt ‖ hayl-) n. A plant that grows in saline soil, such as that of a salt marsh. [HALO- + -PHYTE.] —**hal·o·phyt·ic** (-fíttik) adj.

hal·o·thane (hál-ō-thayn, -ə- ‖ hayl-) n. A general anaesthetic administered by inhalation for inducing and maintaining anaesthesia during surgery. [HALO- + -thane (as in METHANE).]

Hals (halss, haalss), **Frans** (c. 1580–1666). Dutch painter, noted for fine portraits, including The Laughing Cavalier (1624).

halt¹ (hawlt ‖ holt) *n.* **1.** A suspension or cessation of movement or progress, particularly of marching; a stop or pause. **2.** *British.* A stopping-place, without station facilities, used by trains on minor routes. **—call a halt to.** To put a stop to; end.
~*v.* **halted, halting, halts.** —*tr.* To cause to stop; arrest. —*intr.* To stop; pause.
~*interj.* Used as a command to stop, especially to marching troops. [German *Halt,* from Middle High German *halt,* from the imperative of *halten,* to stop, hold, from Old High German *haltan.*]
halt² *intr.v.* **halted, halting, halts.** **1.** To be defective or to proceed poorly, as in the development of an argument in logic or in the rhythmical structure of a verse. **2.** To proceed or act with uncertainty or indecision; waver. **3.** *Archaic.* To limp or hobble, as a cripple.
~*n. Archaic.* The act of limping; lameness.
~*adj. Archaic.* Having a limp; lame; crippled. [Middle English *halten,* to be lame, Old English *healtian,* from Germanic.]
hal·ter (hôltər ‖ hóltər) *n.* **1.** A device made of rope or leather straps that fits around the head or neck of an animal, particularly a horse or cow, and can be used to lead or secure it. **2.** A rope with a noose used for execution by hanging. **3.** Death or execution by hanging. **4.** A bodice for women which ties behind the neck and across the back, leaving the arms, shoulders, and back bare. Also used adjectivally or in combination: *a halter-necked dress.* **5.** Variant of **haltere.**
~*tr.v.* **haltered, -tering, -ters.** **1.** To put a halter on; tie up with a halter. **2.** To put to death by hanging. [Middle English *halter,* Old English *hælftre.*]
hal·tere (hál-teer ‖ háwl-, hól-) *n.* Also **hal·ter** (-tər) *pl.* **halteres** (-téer-eez). Either of the small, clublike balancing organs that are the rudimentary hind wings of dipterous insects such as flies or mosquitoes. Also called "balancer". [New Latin, from Latin *haltēr,* leaden weights used in leaping exercises, from Greek, from *hallesthai,* to jump.]
halt·ing (hôwlt-ing ‖ hólt-) *adj.* **1.** Limping; lame. **2.** Imperfect; defective: *a halting argument.* **3.** Hesitant or wavering; showing a lack of command: *a halting voice; a halting translation.* **4.** Uneven; jerky: *halting rhythm.* **—halt·ing·ly** *adv.*
hal·vah, hal·va (hál-və, -vaa ‖ haál-). Also **ha·la·vah** (-ə-váa). A sweetmeat of Turkish origin consisting of crushed sesame seeds and honey. [Yiddish *halva,* and from Turkish *helva,* from Arabic *ḥalwā.*]
halve (haav ‖ *chiefly U.S.* hav) *tr.v.* **halved, halving, halves.** **1.** To separate or divide into two equal portions or parts. **2.** To lessen or reduce by half; remove half of. **3.** *Informal.* To share equally; divide up. **4.** In carpentry, to join (two pieces of wood) by cutting off half of each at the joint so they will fit together smoothly. **5.** In golf, to play (a game or hole) using the same number of strokes as one's opponent. [Middle English *halven, halfen,* from *half,* HALF.]
halves. Plural of **half.**
hal·yard, hal·liard (hál-yərd) *n.* A rope used to raise or lower a sail, flag, or yard. [Variant (influenced by YARD) of Middle English *halier,* from *halen,* to pull, HALE.]
ham (ham) *n.* **1.** The thigh of the hind leg of certain animals, especially a pig. **2.** The meat of this part of a pig, often preserved by smoking or drying. **3.** The back of the knee. **4.** The back of the thigh. **5.** *Plural.* The buttocks. **6.** *Informal.* **a.** An actor who overacts or a performer who exaggerates dramatic gestures, comic effects, or the like. Sometimes used adjectivally: *a ham actress.* **b.** Any person who, liking attention or acclaim, makes himself ridiculous or obnoxious. **7.** *Informal.* A **radio ham** *(see).*
~*v.* **hammed, hamming, hams.** —*tr.* To overact. —*tr.* To exaggerate or overdo (a role, line, or the like). Often used with *up.* [Middle English *ham(me),* Old English *ham(m).*]
Ham (ham). The second of the three sons of Noah and in some traditions considered the ancestor of the Egyptians. Genesis 5:32.
ham·a·dry·ad (hámmə-drí-əd, -ad) *n., pl.* **-ads** or **-ades** (-ə-deez). **1.** *Greek & Roman Mythology.* A wood nymph living only as long as the tree of which she is the spirit and in which she lives. **2.** A snake, the **king cobra** *(see).* [Latin *Hamādryas* (stem *Hamādryad-*), from Greek *Hamadruas,* "one together with a tree" : *hama,* together with + *druas,* dryad, from *drus,* tree.]
ha·ma·dry·as (hámmə-drí-əss, -ass) *n.* A baboon, *Comopithecus* (or *Papio*) *hamadryas,* of northern Africa and Arabia, the adult male of which has a heavy mane. [New Latin, from Latin, HAMADRYAD.]
ha·mal, ham·mal (hə-maál, -máwl) *n.* A porter or bearer in certain Muslim countries. [Arabic *ḥammāl,* porter, from *ḥamala,* to carry.]
Ha·man (háy-mən, -man) *n.* A chief minister of the Persian king Ahasuerus, who was hanged from his own gallows when his plot against the Jews was revealed by Esther. Esther 8:7.
ha·mate (háymayt) *adj.* Hooked at the tip. [Latin *hāmātus,* from *hāmus†,* hook.]
hamate bone *n.* A small hook-shaped bone in the wrist. Also called "unciform bone".
ham·ba (hám-bə, húm-) *interj. South African Slang.* Used as an expletive to scare or chase away a person or animal. Often considered offensive. [Nguni, imperative of *ukuhamba,* to go.]
Ham·burg (hám-burg, *German* -boork). *Official name* **Freie und Hansestadt Hamburg.** City in northern Germany, capital of and coextensive with the state of Hamburg. Situated on the river Elbe near its mouth on the North Sea, it is the chief port and one of the largest cities in Germany.
ham·burg·er (hám-burgər) *n.* **1. a.** A cake of minced beef, cooked by frying or grilling. **b.** A sandwich consisting of such a cooked

patty inside a roll. **2.** *U.S.* Minced beef. [Short for *Hamburger steak,* after HAMBURG.]
hame (haym) *n.* Either of the two curved wooden or metal pieces of a harness which fit around the neck of a draught animal and to which the traces are attached. [Middle English, probably from Middle Dutch.]
Hame·lin (hám-lin, -i-lin). *German* **Ha·meln** (háam'ln). Town in Lower Saxony, northwestern Germany, lying on the river Weser. It is the site of the legendary tale of the Pied Piper of Hamelin.
ham-fist·ed (hám-fístid) *adj. Informal.* **1.** Clumsy; maladroit. **2.** Having very large hands.
ham-hand·ed (hám-hándid) *adj.* Ham-fisted.
Ham·il·ton¹ (hámm'ltən). A burgh in South Lanarkshire, Scotland, lying at the confluence of the rivers Avon and Clyde. It was near Hamilton that Rudolf Hess landed on his supposed peace mission flight from Germany in May, 1941.
Hamilton². Industrial city in Ontario, Canada, lying at the western end of Lake Ontario. It was originally settled by United Empire Loyalists in 1778 and has grown into one of Canada's largest cities and the country's leading producer of steel and iron.
Hamilton³. Capital of Bermuda, founded in 1790. Lying on Bermuda Island, it is a free port and tourist centre.
Hamilton, Alexander (1755–1804). U.S. statesman. As First Secretary of the Treasury (1789–95) he established the national bank and public credit system.
Hamilton, Lady Emma, born Emma Lyon (*c.* 1761–1815). Mistress of Horatio Nelson. The daughter of a Cheshire blacksmith, she became the mistress of Charles Greville (1749–1809) and later married his uncle Sir William Hamilton (1730–1803), the British envoy to Naples. She met Nelson in 1793 and bore him a daughter in 1801. After her husband's death she lived with Nelson.
Ham·il·to·ni·an (hámm'l-tōni-ən) *n. Symbol* **H** **1.** *Physics.* A mathematical function that can be used systematically and with great generality to generate the equations of motion of a dynamic system, equal for many such systems to the sum of the kinetic and potential energies of the system expressed in terms of the system's coordinates and momenta treated as independent variables. **2.** A mathematical operator that generates such a function. [After William Rowan *Hamilton* (1805–65), Irish mathematician, who formulated it.] **—Ham·il·to·ni·an** *adj.*
Ham·ite (hámmīt) *n.* **1.** One said to be descended from Ham. **2.** A member of a group of related peoples inhabiting northern and northeastern Africa, including the Berbers and the descendants of the ancient Egyptians.
Ha·mit·ic (ha-míttik, hə-) *adj.* Of or relating to Ham, the Hamites, or the language of the Hamites.
~*n.* A group of North African languages related to Semitic, including the Berber dialects, ancient Egyptian and its descendant, Coptic, and the Cushitic dialects spoken in Ethiopia.
Ham·i·to-Se·mit·ic (hámmitō-si-míttik) *n.* A family of languages, **Afro-Asiatic** *(see).* [HAMIT(IC) + SEMITIC.] **—Ham·i·to-Se·mit·ic** *adj.*
ham·let (hám-lət, -lit) *n.* A small village. [Middle English, from Old French *hamelet,* diminutive of *hamel,* diminutive of *ham,* from Germanic.]
Ham·let (hám-lət, -lit) *n.* An indecisive person. [After *Hamlet,* Prince of Denmark, hero of Shakespeare's tragedy (1604).]
hammal. Variant of **hamal.**
Ham·mar·skjöld (hámmər-shōold, -shöld), **Dag (Hjalmar Agne Carl)** (1905–61). Swedish Secretary General of the United Nations (1953–61). During the Congo crisis (1960), he was killed in a plane crash over Zambia. He was posthumously awarded the Nobel peace prize in 1961.
ham·mer (hámmər) *n.* **1.** A hand tool used to exert an impulsive force by striking; especially, such a tool consisting of a handle with a perpendicularly attached head of a relatively heavy, rigid material, such as iron or hard rubber, used to drive nails or shape construction materials. **2.** Any tool or device of analogous function or action, as: **a.** The part of a gunlock that hits the primer or firing pin or explodes the percussion cap causing the gun to go off. **b.** Any of the padded wooden pieces of a piano that strike the strings. **c.** Any part of an apparatus that strikes a gong or bell, as in a clock. **d.** A power tool that delivers blows with a weight. **3.** *Anatomy.* A bone, the **malleus** *(see).* **4.** *Sports.* **a.** A metal ball weighing 7.26 kilograms (16 pounds) and having a long wire or wooden handle by which it is thrown. **b.** The field event in which this ball is thrown. **5.** A small mallet used by auctioneers. **—go** or **come under the hammer.** To be put up for auction. **—hammer and tongs.** With tremendous energy or effort; vigorously.
~*v.* **hammered, -mering, -mers.** —*tr.* **1. a.** To hit once or repeatedly with or as if with a hammer; strike; pound. **b.** To drive by hammering. **2.** To beat into a shape or flatten with a hammer: *He hammered the metal flat.* **3.** To put together, fasten, or seal, particularly with nails, by hammering. **4.** To defeat (an opponent or enemy). **5.** To cause (ideas or information) to be absorbed by constant repetition: *She hammered the highway code into her pupils.* **6.** To subject to harsh criticism or relentless questioning. **7.** *British.* On the stock exchange, to declare (a broker) defaulted. —*intr.* **1.** To deal repeated blows with or as if with a hammer; pound; pummel: *branches hammering at the windows.* **2.** To beat in the manner of a hammer: *His pulse hammered.* **3.** To subject to repeated questioning or testing. Used with *away: hammered away at the examination candidates.* **4.** *Informal.* To work diligently; keep at

something continuously. Often used with *away: He hammered away at his homework.* —**hammer out. 1.** To remove (a dent, for example) by hammering. **2.** To make by hammering. **3.** To settle or arrive at (a policy or agreement, for example) by vigorous discussion. [Middle English *hamer,* Old English *hamor.*] —**ham·mer·er** *n.*

hammer and sickle *n. Used with a singular verb.* **1.** An emblem of the Communist movement, consisting of a crossed hammer and sickle signifying the alliance of workers and peasants. **2.** *Informal.* Communism.

Hammer, Armand (1898–1990). American industrialist. Concerned mainly with oil and banking, he was also a patron of the arts. He maintained close links with the U.S.S.R. from the 1920s, and in 1973 was appointed Director of the U.S.-U.S.S.R. Trade and Economic Council.

ham·mer·beam (hámmər-beem) *n.* A bracket projecting horizontally from the top of a wall and bearing the weight of the roof through the vertical hammerpost.

hammerbeam roof *n.* A roof whose weight is supported through a system of hammerbeams and hammerposts.

hammer drill *n.* A pneumatically operated drill for boring holes in stone in which the drilling bit is given a reciprocating motion.

ham·mered (hámmərd) *adj.* Created, shaped, or worked by hand with a metalworker's hammer or other tools and often showing the marks of these tools: *hammered gold.*

Ham·mer·fest (hámmər-fest). A town in northern Norway, on Kvaløy Island. It is the most northerly town in Europe, yet its harbour is ice-free the year round.

ham·mer·head (hámmər-hed) *n.* **1.** The head of a hammer. **2.** Any of several large, predatory sharks of the genus *Sphyrna,* having the sides of the head elongated into large, fleshy extensions with the eyes at the ends. **3.** A wading bird, *Scopus umbretta,* of Africa and southwestern Asia, having brown plumage, a large, bladelike bill, and a long, backward-pointing crest. Also called "hammerkop." **4.** An African fruit bat, *Hypsignathus monstrosus,* with a hammer-shaped nose. —**ham·mer·head·ed** *adj.*

hammer lock *n.* A wrestling hold in which the opponent's arm is pulled behind his back and twisted upward.

ham·mer·post (hámmər-pōst) *n.* A vertical post between a purlin and a hammerbeam.

ham·mer·smith (hámmər-smith) *n.* One who works metals by hand with a hammer.

Ham·mer·smith. Borough in western Greater London, England.

Ham·mer·stein II (hámmər-stīn, -steen), **Oscar** (1895–1960). U.S. songwriter who collaborated with Richard Rodgers on a series of musicals. Their successes include *Oklahoma!* (1943), *South Pacific* (1949), *The King and I* (1951), and *The Sound of Music* (1959).

ham·mer·toe (hámmər-tō, -tō) *n. Pathology.* A toe, usually the second, that is permanently bent downwards.

ham·mock¹ (hámmək) *n.* A length of canvas, netting, or the like, hung between two supports, used for relaxation and formerly as a bed for sailors. [Spanish *hamaca,* from Taino.]

hammock². Variant of **hummock.**

Ham·mond (hámmənd), **Dame Joan Hood** (1912–96). British soprano, born in New Zealand. She gave her first European performances in London and Vienna (1939). She was created a Dame in 1974.

Hammond, Walter Reginald (Wally), (1903–65). British cricketer. A fine all-rounder, he played for Gloucestershire and England, and in 140 test innings scored 7,249 runs, including 22 centuries.

Ham·mu·ra·bi (hámmoo-ráabi), (died 1750 B.C.). King of Babylon (1792–50 B.C.). He made Babylon the dominant Mesopotamian kingdom and collated the laws of his people and of the Sumerians.

ham·my (hámmi) *adj.* -mier, -miest. **1.** *Informal.* Characterised by exaggerated acting. **2.** Tasting or smelling of ham.

Hamp·den (hám-dən, hámp-), **John** (1594–1643). English parliamentarian. A cousin of Oliver Cromwell, he refused to pay a forced loan imposed by Charles I and was one of the five Members of Parliament whom Charles I tried to arrest (1642) on the eve of the Civil War. He died after a skirmish near Oxford.

ham·per¹ (hámpər) *tr.v.* -pered, -pering, -pers. To prevent the free movement, action, or progress of; impede. See Synonyms at **hinder.** ~*n. Nautical.* Necessary but encumbering equipment on a ship. [Middle English *hamperen†.*]

hamper² *n.* **1.** A large basket, typically of wickerwork, and usually having a cover. **2.** Such a basket or any other container packed with food and drink: *a Christmas hamper.* [Middle English *hampere,* variant of HANAPER.]

Hamp·shire (hámp-shər, -sh). County on the south coast of England. It is noted for sheep and dairy farming. Winchester, the ancient capital of Wessex, is the county town.

Hamp·stead (hám-sted, hámp-). Residential district of North London, noted for its heathland and intellectual community.

Hamp·ton (hámptən), **Lionel** (1913–). U.S. jazz musician. He was the first to popularise the vibraphone as a virtuoso solo instrument. He formed his own orchestra in 1940.

ham·shack·le (hám-shack'l) *tr.v.* -led, -ling, -les. **1.** To hobble (an animal) by tying a rope or strap between one of the legs and the head. **2.** To hold back; hinder. [Perhaps from HAMPER (verb) + SHACKLE.]

ham·ster (hám-stər, hámp-) *n.* Any of several Eurasian rodents of the family Cricetidae; especially, *Mesocricetus auratus,* the golden hamster, having large cheek pouches and a short tail, popular as a pet and used in laboratory research. [German *Hamster,* from Old

High German *hamustro,* from Slavic; akin to Old Slavic *choměstorŭ†.*]

ham·string (hám-string) *n.* **1.** Either of two tendons at the rear hollow of the human knee. **2.** The large sinew in the back of the hock of a quadruped, such as a horse.

~*tr.v.* **hamstrung** (-strung) **-stringing, -strings. 1.** To cut the hamstring of (an animal or person) and thereby cripple. **2.** To destroy or hinder the efficiency of (somebody or something); frustrate. [HAM (thigh) + STRING.]

Ham·sun (hám-sōon), **Knut,** pen name of Knut Pedersen (1859–1952). Norwegian novelist. He wrote of individuals facing struggles of existence in works including *Hunger* (1890) and *The Growth of the Soil* (1917). In 1920 he won the Nobel prize for literature.

ham·u·lus (hámmew-ləss) *n., pl.* -li (-lī). A small hooklike projection or process, as at the end of a bone. [New Latin, from Latin *hāmulus,* little hook, diminutive of *hāmus†,* hook.]

ham·za, ham·zah (hámzə) *n.* A sign in Arabic orthography used to represent the sound of a glottal stop, transliterated in English as an apostrophe. [Arabic *hamza,* compression (of the windpipe), from *hamaza,* to press on, spur, goad.]

Han (han || *U.S.* haan) *n.* **1.** A Chinese dynasty (206 B.C.–A.D. 220) noted for the unification and expansion of the national territory and for the promotion of literature and the arts. **2.** The Chinese as distinguished from other ethnic groups in China such as the Manchus and the Mongols. —**Han** *adj.*

han·a·per (hánnəpər) *n.* A wicker container or hamper used for storing documents. [Middle English *hanaper,* from Old French *hanapier,* case for holding goblets, from *hanap,* goblet; akin to Old English *hnæpp,* bowl, from Germanic *hnap* (unattested).]

hance (hanss, haanss) *n.* **1.** *Architecture.* **a.** The half arch that joins a lintel to a jamb. **b.** A **haunch** (see). **2.** *Nautical.* A curved rise or contour on a ship, as of the bulwarks. [Obsolete *ha(u)nce,* lintel, from *ha(u)nce,* to raise, from Middle English *hauncen,* probably short for *enhauncen,* to ENHANCE.]

Han·cock (hán-kok, háng-), **Tony** (1924–68). British comedian. He created a popular radio series, *Hancock's Half Hour* (produced from 1954), later adapted for television. His humour was characterised by the doleful, self-mocking attitude of the embittered romantic.

hand (hand) *n. Abbr.* **hd. 1.** The terminal part of the human arm below the wrist, consisting of the palm, four fingers, and an opposable thumb, used for grasping and holding. **2.** A homologous or similar part in other animals. **3.** A unit of length equal to four inches (10.16 centimetres), used especially to specify the height of a horse. **4.** Something suggesting the shape or function of the human hand. **5. a.** Any of the rotating pointers on the face of a mechanical clock. **b.** A pointer on any of various similar instruments, such as on gauges or meters; a needle. **6.** A printer's mark, **index** *(see).* **7.** Lateral direction indicated according to the way in which one is facing: *at my right hand.* **8.** A style or individual sample of writing; handwriting; penmanship. **9.** A round of applause to signify approval; clapping. **10.** An act of physical assistance; help: *Give me a hand with these trunks.* **11.** In card games: **a.** The cards held by a given player at any time: *a winning hand.* **b.** The number of cards dealt each player; a deal. **c.** A player or participant: *a fourth hand for bridge.* **d.** A portion or section of a game during which all the cards dealt out are played: *a hand of poker.* **12.** A person who performs manual labour: *a factory hand.* **13.** A person who is part of a group or crew. **14.** Any participant in an activity. **15.** A person regarded in terms of a specialised skill or trait: *a dab hand at drawing.* **16.** A source of information considered in terms of its immediacy or degree of reliability: *at first hand.* **17. a.** *Usually plural.* Possession, ownership, or keeping: *The books should be in her hands by noon.* **b.** *Often plural.* Power; jurisdiction; care: *out of my hands.* **c.** Doing or involvement; participation: *The hand of the Russians is evident here.* **d.** An influence or effect; a share: *I detect the professor's hand in your decision.* **18.** Permission or a promise, especially: **a.** A pledge to marry. **b.** A business agreement sealed by a clasp or handshake; one's word: *You have my hand on that.* **19.** Capacity for doing something that requires skill: *try one's hand at painting.* **20.** A manner or way of performing something; an emphasis; an approach: *a light hand with make-up.* **21.** The lower part of a pork shoulder. **22.** A large bunch of bananas. —**at hand. 1.** Close by; near; easily accessible. **2.** Near in time; imminent. —**at the hand or hands of.** Through the agency of. —**by hand. 1.** Using the hands as opposed to mechanical means: *sorted by hand.* **2.** Individually delivered, rather than handled by the Post Office. —**by (one's) own hand.** By one's own act or agency: *die by one's own hand.* —**change hands.** To pass into different ownership. —**come to hand.** To be or become available. —**eat out of (someone's) hand.** To accept someone's views, wishes, or orders meekly and without protest. —**force (someone's) hand.** To force someone to act prematurely or against his own wishes. —**from hand to hand.** From one person successively to another person. —**from hand to mouth. 1.** In dire poverty. **2.** On an unplanned, day-to-day basis. —**hand and foot. 1.** So as to prevent movement or escape: *tied up hand and foot.* **2.** With slavish devotion: *She waited on her master hand and foot.* —**hand in glove.** In close association or collusion. —**hand in hand. 1.** Holding each other's hand. **2.** In cooperation; jointly. —**hand over fist.** At a tremendous rate: *making money hand over fist.* —**hands down.** With no trouble; easily. —**Hands off.** Do not touch. Keep away. —**have (one's) hands full.** To be unable to take on more duties or responsibilities because one is

fully occupied. **—hold** or **stay (one's) hand.** To restrain oneself from proceeding with a planned punishment or action. **—in hand. 1.** Under control. **2.** Presently accessible. **3.** In preparation or being processed **—keep (one's) hand in.** To practise or keep in practice. **—lay hands on.** To bless, ordain, or consecrate by touching. **—on hand.** Available. **—on** or **upon (one's) hands.** In one's possession, often as an imposed responsibility or burden. **—on the one hand.** As one point of view or side of an issue; in one respect. **—on the other hand.** As another, or opposite, point of view; from another standpoint. **—out of hand. 1.** Out of control. **2.** Abruptly and without proper consideration. **—play into the hands of.** To act or behave so as to give an advantage to (an opponent). **—show (one's) hand.** To reveal something previously hidden, such as one's motives or intentions. **—take in hand. 1.** To put under control or care. **2.** To deal with; treat. **—throw up (one's) hands.** To give up in despair; concede. **—to hand. 1.** Nearby. **2.** In one's possession. **—turn** or **put (one's) hand to.** To take up as an activity; work at. **—wash (one's) hands of.** To relinquish involvement in or responsibility for. **—with a heavy hand. 1.** In a clumsy or awkward manner. **2.** With great severity or emphasis. **—with a high hand.** In a presumptuous or cavalier fashion; overbearingly.
~*adj.* **1.** Of or pertaining to the hand. **2.** Made to be transported by hand: *hand luggage.* **3.** Performed or operated by hand; manual. **4.** Created by hand.
~*tr.v.* **handed, handing, hands. 1.** To give or pass with or as if with the hands; present: *Hand me your keys.* **2.** To aid, direct, or conduct with the hands: *The usher handed the lady to her seat.* **3.** *Nautical.* To roll up and secure (a sail); furl. **—hand down. 1.** To bequeath as an inheritance to or as to one's heirs. **2.** *Chiefly U.S.* To release or pronounce a court decision or verdict. **—hand in.** To turn in; submit: *hand in one's work.* **—hand it to.** *Informal.* To give credit to. **—hand on. 1.** To give to a successor. **2.** To pass on (a tradition, heirloom, or the like). **—hand over. 1.** To release into the possession of another; relinquish. **2.** To transfer one's responsibility, task, or the like to another. [Middle English *hand,* Old English *hand, hond,* from Germanic *handuz* (unattested).]

hand·bag (hánd-bag, hán-) *n.* **1.** A bag, usually a woman's, for carrying articles such as money, keys, and personal items. Also *U.S.* "pocketbook", "purse". **2.** A piece of small hand luggage.

hand·ball (hánd-bawl, hán-) *n.* **1.** A wall game played by two or more players batting a ball against a wall with their hands, usually with a special glove. **2.** The small rubber ball used in this game. **3.** A ball game similar to soccer in which the ball is passed, intercepted, and aimed by hand rather than by foot. In the outdoor version of the game, each team has 11 players; in the indoor game, 5 or 7. **4.** The round, inflated leather ball used in this game, similar to a small football. **5.** In soccer, a foul that occurs when a player handles the ball illegally, and which is penalised by the award of a free kick to the opposing team.
~*tr.v.* **handballed, -balling, -balls.** In Australian Rules, to pass (the ball) by punching it.

hand·bar·row (hánd-barrō, hán-) *n.* A flat framework or litter having carrying poles at each end.

hand·bell (hánd-bel, hán-) *n.* A bell to be rung by hand, especially one of a set tuned to particular notes.

hand·bill (hánd-bil, hán-) *n.* A printed sheet or pamphlet distributed by hand; a leaflet; a notice or advertisement.

hand·book (hánd-bŏŏk, hán- ‖ -bŏŏk) *n. Abbr.* **hdbk.** A manual or small reference book providing specific information or instruction about a subject, activity, place, or the like; a guide; a directory.

hand·brake (hánd-brayk, hán-) *n.* **1.** A brake on a vehicle that is operated by a hand lever. **2.** The hand lever that operates such a brake.

hand·breadth (hánd-bredth, hán-, -bret-th) *n.* Also **hand's breadth, hand's-breadth** (hándz-). A linear measurement approximating the width of the palm of the hand.

h. and c. hot and cold (running water).

hand·cart (hánd-kaart, hán-) *n.* A small, usually two-wheeled, cart pulled or pushed by hand.

hand·clap (hánd-klap, hán-) *n.* A beating together of the palms of one's hands, usually repeatedly, used to indicate applause, attract attention, or provide a rhythmic accompaniment to music. See **slow handclap.**

hand·clasp (hánd-klaasp, hán- ‖ -klasp) *n.* An act of clasping the hand of another person, especially to show warmth or friendship.

hand·craft (hánd-kraaft ‖ -kraft) *n.* **Handicraft** (*see*).
~*tr.v.* (-kra̋aft ‖ -kráft) **handcrafted, -crafting, -crafts.** To make by hand.

hand·cuff (hánd-kuf, hán-, háng-) *n.* Either of a pair of strong, connected hoops which can be tightened and locked about the wrists and used as a restraining device on one or both arms of a person in custody; a manacle. Also called "cuff".
~*tr.v.* **handcuffed, -cuffing, -cuffs.** To restrain with handcuffs.

hand·ed (hándid) *adj.* **1.** Having a hand or hands. **2.** Having a specified number or kind of hands, or a specified preference as regards a hand or hands. Used in combination: *one-handed; left-handed.* **3.** Involving a specified number of people. Used in combination: *a four-handed card game.*

hand·ed·ness (hándid-nəss) *n. Chemistry.* **Chirality** (*see*).

Han·del (hánd'l), **George Frederick** (1685–1759). German-born composer (naturalised British 1726). Handel wrote many Italianate operas, including *Rinaldo* (1711). With *Saul* (1738) he moved from opera to biblical oratorio, a medium he brought to perfection in

Messiah (1742). Other works include the orchestral *Water Music* (1717). **—Han·del·i·an** (han-deéli-ən, -délli-) *adj.*

-hander *n. comb. form. Informal.* Indicates a play, sporting activity, or the like involving a specified number of people; for example, *two-hander.*

hand·fast (hánd-faast, hán- ‖ -fast) *n. Archaic.* **1.** A secure grasp or grip. **2.** A handclasp used to signify a pledge, as a contract or a marriage.
~*tr.v.* **handfasted, -fasting, -fasts.** *Archaic.* **1.** To grip securely with the hand. **2.** To betroth or marry (a man and a woman, or a person of the opposite sex) by joining the hands.

hand·feed (hánd-feéd, hán-) *tr.v.* **-fed, -feeding, -feeds. 1.** To feed (a person or animal) by hand. **2.** To feed (an animal) with regulated amounts of food at scheduled times.

hand·ful (hánd-fŏŏl, hán-) *n., pl.* **-fuls. 1.** The quantity or number that can be held in the hand. **2.** A small but undefined quantity or number: *a handful of requests.* **3.** *Informal.* A person or thing too difficult to control or handle easily.

hand glass *n.* **1.** A small magnifying glass held in the hand. **2.** A mirror with a handle. **3.** A time glass used in timing the running out of a line used with a nautical log.

hand grenade *n.* A small grenade to be thrown by hand.

hand·grip (hánd-grip, hán-) *n.* **1.** A grip by the hand or hands. **2.** Something suited to or facilitating a grip by the hand, as a handle or indentation. **3.** *Plural.* Hand-to-hand fighting. **4.** A travelling bag; a holdall. In this sense, also called "grip".

hand·gun (hánd-gun, hán-) *n. Chiefly U.S.* A firearm that can be used with one hand; a pistol.

hand·held (hánd-held) *adj.* Designating a film camera that is carried rather than mounted.

hand·hold (hánd-hōld) *n.* **1.** A grip by the hand or hands. **2.** Something that one can hold by the hand or hands for support, such as a branch or indentation on a rock surface.

hand·i·cap (hándi-kap) *n.* **1.** A race or contest in which advantages or compensations are given to different contestants, according to their varied abilities or experience, to equalise the chances of winning. **2.** Such an advantage or penalty; especially, a handicap assigned to a golfer showing the number of strokes by which he is expected to exceed par for a given course. **3. a.** A deficiency, especially an anatomical, physiological, or mental deficiency, that prevents or restricts normal living. **b.** Any disadvantage, hindrance, or disability: *I find not being able to drive a handicap.*
~*tr.v.* **handicapped, -capping, -caps. 1.** To assign a handicap or handicaps to (a contestant). **2.** To put at a disadvantage; impede. [From the phrase *hand i' cap* ("hand in cap"), originally a lottery game in which players held forfeits in a cap.] **—hand·i·cap·per** *n.*

hand·i·capped (hándi-kapt) *adj.* **1.** Physically or mentally disabled. **2.** Having or being under a handicap. Said of a contestant.

hand·i·craft (hándi-kraaft ‖ -kraft) *n.* **1.** Skill and facility with the hands; workmanship. **2.** A particular trade or craft requiring skilled use of the hands, such as basketry. **3.** The work produced by such a trade or craft. Also called "handcraft". [Middle English *handie-craft,* variant of *handcraft* : HAND + CRAFT.]

hand·i·crafts·man (hándi-kraafts-mən ‖ -krafts-) *n., pl.* **-men** (-mən). A person skilled in handicraft; a craftsman.

hand·i·ly (hándili, hánd'l-i) *adv.* **1.** In a handy or easy manner; dexterously. **2.** Conveniently.

hand·i·ness (hándi-nəss, -niss) *n.* **1.** The quality of being handy; facility; expertise. **2.** The quality of being easy to use or readily accessible; convenience.

hand·i·work (hándi-wurk) *n.* **1.** Work performed by hand or the objects produced by hand. **2.** That which is accomplished by a single person's efforts. **3.** The results of a person's actions. [Middle English *handiwork,* Old English *handgeweorc* : HAND + *geweorc,* work : *ge-,* collective prefix + *weorc,* WORK.]

hand·ker·chief (hángkər-chif, -cheef. *Note: the plural is sometimes* -cheevz.) *n.* **1.** A small square of cotton, linen, or silk, carried by a person for use in wiping the nose, mouth, or the like. **2.** A slightly larger piece of cloth worn as a decorative article; a kerchief; a scarf. [HAND + KERCHIEF.]

hand·knit (hánd-nít) *adj.* Also **hand·knit·ted** (-níttid). Knit by hand.
~*tr.v.* **hand-knitted, -knitting, -knits.** To knit by hand.

han·dle (hánd'l) *v.* **-dled, -dling, -dles. —*tr.* 1.** To touch, lift, or turn with the hands. **2.** To operate with the hands; manipulate. **3.** To specialise in or have responsibility for; take charge of: *My colleague handles financial matters.* **4. a.** To deal with; process: *handle an application.* **b.** To trade in. **5.** To manage, administer to, or represent: *handle a boxer.* **6.** To behave or act towards; treat. **7.** To confront or cope with, especially: **a.** To control or command: *handle a crowd.* **b.** To discuss or approach: *handle a problem.* **—*intr.*** To respond or react to control or manipulation; function under operation: *This bicycle handles well at high speed.*
~*n.* **1.** That by which a tool, object, door, or the like is held or manipulated with the hand. **2.** An opportunity that may serve as an advantage for someone; a means; an opening. **3.** *Slang.* A person's title or name. **—fly off the handle.** *Informal.* To fly into a rage; become very angry suddenly. [Old English *handle* (noun), *handlian* (verb), from HAND.]

Synonyms: handle, manipulate, wield, ply.

han·dle·bar (hánd'l-baar) *n. Usually plural.* A curved metal steering bar, as on a bicycle.

handlebar moustache *n.* A thick moustache that curls upwards at the side of the lips.

han·dler (hándlər) *n.* **1.** One that handles. **2. a.** A person who trains or exhibits an animal, such as a dog. **b.** A person who acts as the trainer or second of a boxer.

han·dling (hándling) *n.* **1.** A touching, feeling, or manipulating with the hands. **2.** The way in which a matter is taken care of or treated; management. **3.** The way in which a subject is approached or discussed. **4.** The process of packing and distributing merchandise. **5.** *Law.* The act of receiving or selling stolen property.

hand·made (hánd-máyd, hán-) *adj.* Made or prepared by hand rather than by machine.

hand·maid·en (hánd-mayd'n, hán-) *n.* **1.** A female servant or attendant. **2.** That which serves or assists a higher cause: *Language is the handmaiden of thought.*

hand-me-down (hánd-mi-down, hán-, -mee-) *adj.* **1.** Handed down to one person after being used and discarded by another; secondhand. **2.** Of inferior quality; shabby. ∼*n.* Something passed on from one person to another, especially an item of clothing.

hand-off (hánd-off, -awf) *n.* In Rugby football, the act of fending off an opponent with the arm extended and the hand open.

hand organ *n.* A barrel organ operated by turning a crank.

hand out *tr.v.* To distribute (food, samples, or leaflets, for example).

hand·out (hánd-owt) *n.* **1.** Food, clothing, or money donated to one in need. **2.** A folder or leaflet distributed, especially as an accompaniment to a talk or lecture. **3.** A prepared news or publicity release.

hand·pick (hánd-pík, hán-) *tr.v.* **-picked, -picking, -picks.** **1.** To gather or pick by hand. **2.** To select carefully, especially for a particular task or purpose. **—hand·picked** *adj.*

hand·rail (hánd-rayl) *n.* A rail, as along a staircase, to be grasped with the hand for support.

hand·saw (hánd-saw, hán-) *n.* A saw that can be used with one hand.

hand's breadth, hand's-breadth. Variants of **handbreadth.**

hand·sel, han·sel (hánss'l) *n.* *Regional.* A gift to express good wishes at the beginning of a new year or enterprise. ∼*tr.v.* **handselled** or *U.S.* **handseled, -selling** or *U.S.* **-seling, -sels.** *Regional.* **1.** To give a handsel to. **2.** To inaugurate or initiate. [Middle English *hansele,* Old English *handselen,* a giving into someone's hands, from Old Norse *handsal,* a giving of the hand : HAND + *sal,* a giving, payment.]

hand·set (hánd-set, hán-) *n.* That part of a telephone which is held by the hand next to the ear and mouth, with a small receiver at one end and a transmitter at the other.

hand·shake (hánd-shayk, hán-) *n.* **1.** The grasping of hands by two people as a gesture of greeting, leave-taking, congratulation, agreement, or the like. **2.** *Computing.* A dialogue between parts of a computer system in which information is exchanged regarding the transmission and reception of data.

hands-off (hándz-óff). *adj.* Designating, pertaining to, or characterised by a policy of non-intervention or of no physical contact.

hand·some (hán-səm, hánt-) *adj.* **1. a.** Having an attractive and well-proportioned appearance, especially facial features: *a handsome man.* **b.** Having an appealingly smart and gracious appearance: *a handsome woman.* **2.** Impressively well made: *a handsome building.* **3. a.** Generous or liberal: *a handsome offer.* **b.** Considerable; plentiful: *a handsome reward.* **4.** Gracious; magnanimous: *a handsome gesture.* **5.** *Chiefly U.S.* Marked by or requiring great skill or accomplishment. —See Synonyms at **beautiful.** [Middle English *handsom,* easy to handle, handy : HAND + -SOME.] **—hand·some·ly** *adv.* **—hand·some·ness** *n.*

hands-on (hándz-ón). *adj.* Designating direct experience of something, especially the manual operation of a computer system.

hand·spike (hánd-spīk, hán-) *n.* A heavy bar used as a lever.

hand·spring (hánd-spring, hán-) *n.* A gymnastic feat in which the body is flipped completely forwards or backwards from an upright position, landing first on the hands, then on the feet.

hand·stand (hánd-stand, hán-) *n.* The act of balancing on the hands with one's feet in the air.

hand-to-hand (hánd-tə-hánd, hán-) *adj.* At close quarters. **—hand to hand** *adv.*

hand-to-mouth (hánd-tə-mówth, hán-) *adj.* Characterised by constant financial difficulties. **—hand to mouth** *adv.*

hand-wash *tr.v.* **-washed, -washing, -washes.** To wash (clothing or fabrics) by hand rather than in a machine.

hand·work (hánd-wurk) *n.* Work done by hand.

hand·writ·ing (hánd-rīting) *n.* **1.** Writing done with the hand rather than typed or printed. **2.** The writing characteristic of a particular person.

hand·y (hándi) *adj.* **-ier, -iest.** **1.** Manually adroit. **2.** Readily accessible. **3.** Conveniently situated. **4.** Easy to use or handle. **5.** Supplying a need; useful: *The extra cash will come in handy.* —See Synonyms at **dexterous.** [From HAND.]

Han·dy (hándi), **William Christopher** (1873–1958). U.S. jazz composer and publisher. He wrote *St. Louis Blues* (1914, inter alia).

hand·y·man (hándi-man, -mən) *n., pl.* **-men** (-men). **1.** A do-it-yourself enthusiast. **2.** One who does odd jobs or various small tasks; especially, one employed to do them.

hang (hang) *v.* **hung** (hung) or **hanged** (for transitive sense 3 and intransitive sense 2), **hanging, hangs.** —*tr.* **1.** To fasten from above with no support from below; suspend. **2.** To suspend or fasten so as to allow free movement at or about the point of suspension: *hang a door.* **3.** To kill by putting a noose around the neck and allowing to drop, especially as a mode of execution. **4.** To fix or attach at an appropriate angle: *hang a scythe to its handle.* **5.** To alter the hem of (a garment) so as to fall evenly at an appropriate height. **6.** To furnish, decorate, or appoint by suspending objects around or about: *hang a room with tapestries.* **7.** To hold or incline downwards; let droop: *hang one's head in sorrow.* **8.** To attach to a wall: *hang wallpaper.* **9.** To deadlock (a jury) by failing to render a unanimous verdict. **10.** To leave (venison or other game) exposed to the air for some time to improve its flavour. **11. a.** To exhibit (paintings, for example). **b.** To exhibit the work of (a painter, for example). —*intr.* **1.** To be attached from above with no support from below. **2.** To suffer death by hanging. **3. a.** To remain suspended or poised over a place or object; hover. **b.** To be suspended from a pivot and able to move freely. **4.** To attach oneself as an impediment or dependent; cling. Usually used with *on.* **5.** To incline downwards; droop. **6.** To depend. **7.** To maintain close contact; pay strict or devoted attention: *hang on every word.* **8.** To remain unresolved or uncertain: *hang in the balance.* **9.** To fit or drape from the body in a specified way: *Her dress hangs awkwardly.* **10.** To loom; be likely to occur or be realised: *the threat hanging over us.* **11.** To pass very slowly: *Time hung heavily on her.* **—hang about** or **around.** *Informal.* **1.** To spend time in idleness; loiter. **2.** To remain; wait. **—hang back. 1.** To lag. **2.** To be averse; hold back. **—hang in.** *U.S. Informal.* To persevere. **—hang loose.** *Chiefly U.S. Informal.* To remain calm; relax. **—hang on. 1.** To continue persistently or resolutely; persevere. **2.** *Informal.* To wait a while; be patient. **3.** *Informal.* To keep a telephone connection open; hold the line. **—hang one on.** *U.S. Informal.* **1.** To strike (a person). **2.** To become drunk. **—hang together. 1.** To stand united; stick together. **2.** To constitute a coherent totality. ∼*n.* **1.** The way in which something hangs. **2.** A downward inclination or slope. **—get the hang of.** *Informal.* **1.** To come to understand a process, argument, or the like. **2.** To develop the correct technique for doing something. **—not to give** or **care a hang.** To be totally unconcerned or indifferent. [Hang, hung, hung; partly Middle English *hon, hong, hongen,* Old English *hōn* (transitive verb), to hang, suspend, *heng, hangen;* partly Middle English *hangen, hong, hanged,* Old English *hangian* (transitive and intransitive verb), to hang, be hung, suspend, *hangode, hanged;* partly Middle English *hingen,* from Old Norse *hanga* (transitive verb), to cause to hang.] *Usage:* The usual past tense and past participle form of this verb is *hung,* but in the context of capital punishment, the form *hanged* is preferred: *The prisoner (was) hanged at six o'clock.* The use of *hung* in such a context would generally be considered nonstandard.

hang·ar (háng-ər) *n.* A large structure for housing, constructing, or maintaining aircraft. [French, from Old French, probably from Medieval Latin *angarium†,* shed for shoeing horses.]

hang·bird (háng-burd) *n. U.S.* A bird, such as a Baltimore oriole, that builds a hanging nest. Also called "hangnest".

hang·dog (háng-dog ‖ -dawg) *adj.* **1.** Shamefaced or guilty. **2.** Downcast; intimidated. ∼*n.* A suspicious-looking or shamefaced person. [Originally, despicable person who was fit only to hang a dog.]

hang·er (háng-ər) *n.* **1.** One that hangs. **2.** A contrivance to which something hangs or by which something is hung. **3.** A coat hanger *(see).* **4.** A loop or strap by which something is hung. **5.** A bracket on a motor vehicle's spring shackle designed to hold it to the chassis. **6.** A small sword that is hung from the waist.

hang·er-on (háng-ər-ón ‖ -áwn) *n., pl.* **hangers-on** (-ərz-). A person who attaches himself to another, as from vanity or hope of gain.

hang-glide (háng-glīd) *intr.v.* To fly by means of a hang-glider. **—hang-glid·ing** *n.*

hang-glid·er (háng-glīdər) *n.* **1.** A small aircraft, normally unpowered, with a cloth wing, from which the pilot is suspended in a harness. **2.** The pilot of such a machine.

hang·ing (háng-ing) *n.* **1.** An act of killing by putting a noose around the victim's neck and allowing him to drop. **2.** A drapery hung over a wall or window. ∼*adj.* **1.** Situated on a sharp declivity. **2.** Projecting downwards; overhanging. **3.** Suited for holding something that hangs. **4. a.** Susceptible to or meriting death by hanging: *a hanging crime.* **b.** Disposed to inflict the sentence of death by hanging: *a hanging judge.*

hanging valley *n.* A tributary valley that joins a main valley where the latter has been deepened, usually by glacial erosion. There is usually a steep fall from the floor of the tributary valley to that of the main valley.

hanging wall *n.* The wall of rock on the upper side of an inclined fault plane or mineral vein.

hang·man (háng-mən) *n., pl.* **-men** (-mən). One employed to execute condemned prisoners by hanging.

hang·nail (háng-nayl) *n.* A small piece of dead skin at the side or the base of a fingernail that is partly detached from the rest of the skin. [By folk-etymology from AGNAIL.]

hang out *intr.v.* **1.** To project downwards. **2.** *Informal.* To reside or spend time. —*tr.v.* **1.** To spread out (washing, for example) to dry. **2.** To suspend for public display: *hang out a sign.* **—let it all hang out.** To be entirely uninhibited.

hang·out (háng-owt) *n. Informal.* A frequently visited place.

hang·o·ver (háng-ōvər) *n.* **1.** Unpleasant physical effects following the heavy consumption of alcohol; especially, a severe headache.

2. A vestige; a survival: *hangovers from prewar legislation.*

hang up *tr.v.* **1.** To replace (a telephone handset) on its cradle. **2.** To retard, impede, or interrupt: *hang up a project.* **3.** To halt the movement or action of. **4.** *Informal.* To be a source of anxiety or preoccupation for: *Don't let it hang you up.* See **hung up.** —*intr.v.* **1.** To end a telephone conversation by replacing the handset. **2.** To become halted or snagged. —**be hung up on.** *Informal.* To be obsessed or fixated by.

hang-up, hang·up (háng- up) *n. Informal.* **1. a.** A source of irritation or inhibition. **b.** An inhibition or fixation. **2.** An obstacle; an inconvenience.

hank (hangk) *n.* **1.** A coil or loop. **2.** *Nautical.* A ring on a stay attached to the head of a jib or staysail. **3.** A looped bundle, as of yarn. **4.** A length of yarn (768 metres; 840 yards) or fabric (512 metres; 560 yards). [Middle English, from Scandinavian; akin to Old Norse *hönk*†, hank, skein.]

han·ker (hángkər) *intr.v.* **-kered, -kering, -kers.** To have a longing; crave. Often followed by *after* or *for.* See Synonyms at **yearn.** [Akin to dialectal *hank,* probably from Dutch (dialectal) *hankeren.*] —**hank·er·er** *n.*

hank·y, hank·ie (hángki) *n., pl.* **hankies.** *Informal.* A handkerchief (sense 1).

han·ky-pan·ky (hángki-pángki) *n. Informal.* **1.** Devious or mischievous activity. **2.** Improper sexual relations. [Fanciful coinage, influenced by *hocus-pocus.*]

Han·ni·bal (hánnib'l), (247–183 B.C.). Carthaginian soldier and statesman, the son of Hamilcar Barca (died 229 B.C.). Hannibal crossed the Alps in 218 with about 35,000 men and 37 elephants, and routed Roman armies at Trasimene and Cannae. He lacked the resources to attack Rome itself and was recalled to Africa in 203 to defend Carthage against an invasion by Scipio Africanus. Hannibal was defeated at Zama (202).

Han·no·ver (*German* ha-nőfər). *English* **Han·o·ver** (hánnő-vər, hánnə-). Capital city of Lower Saxony in northern Germany, lying on the river Leine. It is an industrial and commercial centre and the site of an important annual industrial fair.

Ha·noi (ha-nóy ‖ *U.S. also* haa-, hə-). Capital city of Vietnam, situated on the right bank of the Song Hong (Red River), in northern Vietnam. It is the country's major industrial city.

Han·o·ver (hánnő-vər, hánnə-) **1.** The family name of an electoral house of Germany (1692–1814). **2.** The family name of the royal family of Britain and Ireland (1714–1917). **3. Hannover.**

Han·o·ve·ri·an (hánnő-véer-i-ən, hánnə-) *adj.* Of or pertaining to the city of Hanover, the electoral house, or the royal family of Hanover.

Han·sard (hán-saard, -sərd) *n.* **1.** The official verbatim report of the proceedings and debates of the British Parliament. **2.** A similar report of the proceedings of various other legislative bodies. [After its first printer Luke *Hansard* (1752–1828).]

hanse (hanss) *n.* **1. a.** A medieval merchant guild or trade association. **b.** The entrance fee to such a guild. **2.** *Capital* **H.** A town belonging to the Hanseatic League. Also called "Hanse town". **3.** *Capital* **H.** *Rare.* The Hanseatic League. [Middle English *hans,* from Old French *hanse,* from Middle Low German *hanse,* from Old High German *hansa,* troop, company, from Germanic *khansō* (unattested).] —**han·se·at·ic** (hán-si-áttik) *adj.*

Hanseatic League *n.* A protective and commercial association of free towns in northern Germany and neighbouring areas, formally organised in 1358 and dissolved in the 17th century.

hansel. Variant of **handsel.**

Han·sen's disease (hánss'nz) *n.* **Leprosy** (*see*). [After G.A. *Hansen* (1841–1912), Norwegian physician who discovered the bacillus that causes leprosy.]

han·som (hánss'm) *n.* A two-wheeled covered carriage with the driver's seat above and behind. Also called "hansom cab". [After Joseph A. *Hansom* (1803–82), English architect who designed it.]

Hanukah, Hanukkah. Variants of **Chanukah.**

han·u·man (hún-ŏŏ-máan, hán-) *n., pl.* **-mans.** A monkey, *Presbytis entellus,* of southern Asia, having bristly hairs on the crown and the sides of the face. Also called "entellus". [Hindi, from Sanskrit *hanumant,* "having jaws", from *hanu,* jaw.]

ha·o (haá-ō, how) *n., pl.* **hao.** Also **chao** (cháa-ō, chow). A monetary unit equal to ¹⁄₁₀ of the dong of Vietnam. [Vietnamese.]

hap (hap) *n. Archaic.* **1.** Fortune; chance. **2.** A happening; an occurrence.
~*intr.v.* **happed, happing, haps.** *Archaic.* To happen. [Middle English, from Old Norse *happ,* good luck, chance.]

ha·pax le·go·me·non (háppaks li-gómmi-nən, le-, -non) *n., pl.* **hapax legomena** (-nə). A word or form that occurs only once in the recorded corpus of a given language. Often shortened to "hapax". [Greek, "a thing said only once".]

ha'penny. Variant of **halfpenny.**.

hap·haz·ard (háp-házzərd, hap-) *adj.* **1.** Dependent upon or characterised by mere chance. **2.** Slipshod; untidy. See Synonyms at **chance.**
~*n.* Mere chance; fortuity.
~*adv.* Casually; by chance. [HAP + HAZARD.] —**hap·haz·ard·ly** *adv.* —**hap·haz·ard·ness** *n.*

Haph·ta·rah, Haf·ta·rah (haáf-táwrə, háf-, -tə-ráa) *n., pl.* **-taroth** (-táwrot, -tə-rŏt). *Judaism.* A reading selected from the Prophets, read in the synagogue service on the Sabbath. [Mishnaic Hebrew *haphṭārāh,* "conclusion", from *haphṭēr,* to conclude, discard, dismiss, from Hebrew *pāṭar,* separated, discharged.]

hap·less (háp-ləss, -liss) *adj.* Luckless; unfortunate.

haplite. Variant of **aplite.**

hap·log·ra·phy (hap-lóggrəfi) *n.* The shortening of the spelling of a word by the omission of a letter or syllable that should be repeated; for example, the spelling *deteriate* for *deteriorate.* [Greek *haplos,* single, simple (see **haploid**) + -GRAPHY.]

hap·loid (hápployd) *adj. Genetics.* Having the number of chromosomes present in the normal germ cell equal to half the number in the normal somatic cell. Compare **diploid.**
~*n.* A haploid individual or cell. [Greek *haploeidēs,* single : *ha-plo(u)s,* single, simple : *ha-,* one + *-plo(u)s,* -fold + -OID.]

hap·loi·dy (hápploydi) *n. Genetics.* The state or condition of being haploid.

hap·lol·o·gy (hap-lóllǝji) *n.* The shortening of a word by the omission of a sound or syllable in its pronunciation; for example, the pronunciation (témpərəli) for *temporarily.* [Greek *haplos,* single, simple (see **haploid**) + -LOGY.]

hap·lont (hápplont) *n. Biology.* A haploid organism representing the vegetative phase of the life cycle of certain algae in which only the zygote is diploid. [HAPL(OID) + -ONT.]

hap·lo·sis (hap-lő-siss) *n. Genetics.* Reduction of the diploid number of chromosomes by one half to the haploid number by meiosis. [New Latin : Greek *haplos,* single, simple (see **haploid**) + -OSIS.]

hap·ly (háppli) *adv. Archaic.* **1.** By chance or accident. **2.** Perhaps.

ha'porth (háypərth) *n. British.* **1.** A **halfpennyworth** (*see*). **2.** *Informal.* A creature. Used in phrases like *you daft ha'porth.*

hap·pen (háppən) *intr.v.* **-pened, -pening, -pens. 1.** To come to pass; come into being; take place. **2.** To befall or affect one. Used with *to: What happened to you?* **3. a.** To be the case by chance: *It happens that I used to live out there; I used to live there, as it happens.* **b.** To chance: *She happened to be in.* **4.** To come upon someone or something by chance. Used with *on* or *upon.* —**happen by.** *Chiefly U.S.* To appear by chance; turn up.
~*adv. Northern English.* Perhaps; maybe. [Middle English *happenen,* from HAP.]
Synonyms: happen, occur, chance, befall, betide, supervene.

hap·pen·ing (háppəning, hápning) *n.* **1.** An event. **2.** An improvised spectacle or performance. —See Synonyms at **occurrence.**

hap·pen·stance (háppən-staanss, -stanss) *n.* A chance circumstance. [HAPPEN + (CIRCUM)STANCE.]

hap·py (háppi) *adj.* **-pier, -piest. 1.** Characterised by luck or good fortune; prosperous. **2. a.** Having, taking, or demonstrating pleasure or satisfaction; glad. **b.** Giving or causing pleasure or satisfaction: *a happy day for everyone.* **3.** Well-adapted; appropriate; felicitous: *a happy turn of phrase.* **4.** *Informal.* Slightly drunk; tipsy. **5.** Characterised by a spontaneous or obsessive inclination to use something. Used in combination: *trigger-happy.* —See Synonyms at **fit, glad.** [Middle English, from HAP.] —**hap·pi·ly** *adv.* —**hap·pi·ness** *n.*

hap·py-clap·py (háppi-kláppi) *adj.* Evangelical and enthusiastic, but unsophisticated and perhaps superficial: *happy-clappy church services.* [From the *clapping* that accompanies the music of services in certain churches, perhaps influenced by the words "If you're *happy* and you know it *clap* your hands".]

hap·py-go-luck·y (háppi-gő-lúcki) *adj.* Taking things easily; trusting to luck; carefree.

happy hour *n.* A period of time, usually in the early evening, when drinks are served at reduced prices in bars or hotels.

happy hunting-ground *n.* **1.** *Sometimes plural.* In North American Indian mythology, heaven or paradise. **2.** *Informal.* Any place or situation offering a plentiful supply of a particular sought-after item or commodity: *Junk shops are a happy hunting-ground for collectors of antiques.*

Hapsburg. See **Habsburg.**

hap·ten (háp-tən, -ten) *n.* Also **hap·tene** (-teen). *Biology.* An antigen that is incomplete and cannot by itself cause antibody formation but can neutralise specific antibodies when combined with one of the body's proteins. [German *Hapten* : Greek *haptein,* to fasten + -ENE.]

hap·ter·on (háp-təron) *n., pl.* **-tera** (-tərə). The tissue in certain algae, especially the large seaweeds, that serves to attach the plant to a substrate. [From Greek *haptein,* to fasten.]

hap·tic (háptik) *adj.* Of or pertaining to the sense of touch. [Greek *haptikos,* able to touch, from *haptein,* to touch, fasten.]

hap·to·nas·ty (háptō-naasti, -nasti) *n.* Movement of a plant part in response to touch, seen particularly in the leaves of insectivorous plants. [Greek *haptein,* to touch + -NASTY.]

hap·to·trop·ism (háptō-trŏp-iz'm) *n. Biology.* **Thigmotropism** (*see*). [Greek *haptein,* to touch + TROPISM.]

ha·ra-ki·ri (hárrə-kírri, -kéer-i. *Note: popularly, but wrongly,* hár-ri-kárri, -kaári) *n.* Ritual suicide by disembowelment as formerly practised by the Japanese upper classes when disgraced or under sentence of death, and still occasionally practised today. Also called "seppuku". [Japanese, from *hara,* belly + *kiri,* cutting.]

ha·rangue (hə-ráng) *n.* **1.** A long, pompous speech, especially one delivered before a gathering. **2.** A speech characterised by strong feeling or vehement expression; a tirade.
~*v.* **harangued, -ranguing, -rangued.** —*tr.* To deliver a harangue to. —*intr.* To deliver a harangue. [Middle English *arang,* from Old French *arenge, harangue,* from Medieval Latin *harenga,* perhaps from Germanic *harihring-* (unattested), assembly : *harjaz,* crowd + *hringaz,* RING (both unattested).] —**ha·rangu·er** *n.*

Ha·rap·pa (həráppə). Archaeological site of the Indus Valley civilisation (*c*.2500–1500 B.C.) in the Punjab, Pakistan. It has the remains of a well laid out city.

Ha·ra·re (ha-ráaray, hə-). Capital and largest city of Zimbabwe, situated on the Mashonaland plateau in the northeast of the country. Founded in 1890, it was originally named Salisbury, after the prime minister of that period, Lord Salisbury. It has two cathedrals and a university (1970). Harare is an important tobacco marketing centre, and its manufactured products include processed food and tobacco, textiles and clothing, steel, chemicals, and furniture.

har·ass (hárrəss, hə-ráss. *Note: until the 1970s the only accepted pronunciation was* hárrəss.) *tr.v.* **-assed, -assing, -asses. 1.** To disturb, pester, or irritate persistently. **2.** To enervate (an enemy) by repeated attacks or raids. [French *harasser*, from Old French *harer*, to set a dog on, from *hare*, cry used to set a dog on, perhaps from Old High German *harēn*, to call.] **—har·ass·er** *n.* **—har·ass·ment** *n.*
　　Synonyms: harass, hound, badger, pester, plague, bait, torment.
Har·bin (haar-béen, -bín). Also **Ha·erh·pin** (haa-er-béen, -bín). *Russian* **Kharbin.** Capital of Heilongjiang province, northeast China. Situated on the Songhua Jiang river (Sungari) it grew with the granting of a trade concession to Russia (1896). An important port and railway junction, it is part of the Manchurian industrial region.
har·bin·ger (hárbinjər) *n.* One that signals an approach; a forerunner: *"in a few minutes would appear the train's harbinger . . . a puff of white smoke"* (Vladimir Nabokov).
　　~tr.v. **harbingered, -gering, -gers.** To signal the approach of; presage. [Middle English *harbergere*, from Anglo-French and Old French, from *herbergier*, to provide lodging for, from *herberge*, lodging, from Old Saxon *heriberga*, lodging : *heri*, army + *berg-* (unattested), to protect.]
har·bour, *U.S.* **har·bor** (hárbər) *n. Abbr.* **h., H. 1.** A sheltered part of a body of water deep enough to provide anchorage for ships; a port. **2.** Any protected place; a shelter; a refuge.
　　~v. **harboured** or *U.S.* **harbored, -bouring** or *U.S.* **-boring, -bours** or *U.S.* **-bors.** *—tr.* **1.** To give shelter to; protect; keep. **2.** To entertain or nourish (a thought or feeling). *—intr.* To shelter in or as if in a harbour. [Middle English *herberen, herber*, late Old English *hereborg*, shelter, lodging. See **harbinger.**] **—har·bour·er** *n.*
har·bour·age (hárbərij) *n.* **1.** Shelter and anchorage for ships. **2.** Shelter; refuge. **3.** A place of shelter.
har·bour·mas·ter (hárbər-maastər ‖ -mastər) *n.* An officer who oversees and enforces the regulations of a harbour.
harbour seal *n.* A hair seal, *Phoca vitulina,* of coastal waters of the Northern Hemisphere, having a spotted coat.
hard (hard) *adj.* **harder, hardest.** *Abbr.* **h., H. 1.** Resistant to pressure; not readily penetrated; firm; rigid. **2.** Physically toughened; rugged: *hard feet.* **3.** Strong-minded; not influenced by emotional considerations. **4.** Rigorous; stringent; demanding. **5.** Mentally and emotionally toughened; unfeeling. **6.** Characterised by an unwillingness to compromise or negotiate. **7.** Intense; forceful. **8.** Keen; penetrating. **9.** Assiduous; diligent; energetic: *a hard worker.* **10.** Difficult to accomplish, finish, or continue; strenuous; arduous. **11.** Difficult to understand, express, or convey; abstruse. **12.** Difficult to endure. **13.** Cruel; oppressive; unjust. **14.** Bitter; rancorous; harsh: *hard feelings.* **15.** Unpleasant because too bright, loud, or harsh: *a hard voice.* **16.** Uncompromisingly adhering to the principles of a specified political alignment: *on the hard left of the party.* **17.** Metallic, as opposed to paper. Said of money: *hard money.* **18. a.** Backed by bullion and having a stable exchange rate. Said of a currency. **b.** Being legal tender: *hard cash.* **19.** Demonstrably true: *hard facts.* **20.** *U.S.* Durable: *hard merchandise.* **21.** Consisting of rigid boards, usually covered with cloth, leather, or the like. Said of the binding of a book. **22.** Having a high alcoholic content; intoxicating. **23.** Containing dissolved substances, as salts, that interfere with the lathering action of soap. Said of water. **24.** *Phonetics.* **a.** Pronounced as a stop, as the *c* in *cake* and the *g* in *log.* **b.** Voiceless. Said of consonants. **c.** Not palatalised. Said of consonants in Slavonic languages. **25.** *Physics.* Of relatively high energy; penetrating: *hard X-rays.* **26.** High in gluten content: *hard wheat.* **—be hard on. 1.** To be unpleasant and difficult for. **2.** To deal with severely; be harsh with.
　　~adv. **1.** Energetically; vigorously: *drink hard.* **2.** Intently; earnestly; persistently: *think hard.* **3.** With intensity or force. **4.** With difficulty; strenuously: *a fight hard won.* **5.** Close; near. Used with *by* or *upon.* **6.** Reluctantly: *die hard.* **7.** Towards or into a solid condition: *The cement will set hard within a day.* **8. a.** As much as possible: *Turn hard right.* **b.** *Nautical.* Completely; fully: *hard alee.* **—be hard put.** To have a good deal of difficulty in doing. **—go hard with.** To cause pain or distress; gall: *This news will go hard with him.* **—hard at it.** Working busily. **—hard put.** Only just able: *She is hard put to make ends meet.*
　　~n. **1.** *British Slang.* Hard labour. **2.** *British.* A firm beach or foreshore. **3.** *Vulgar Slang.* An erection of the penis. Used in the phrase *have a hard on.* [Middle English *hard,* Old English *hard, heard.*]
　　Synonyms: hard, difficult, arduous, intricate, troublesome.
hard-and-fast, hard and fast (hárd-ən-fáast ‖ -fast) *adj.* Rigidly applied; inflexible; allowing of no exceptions. Said of a rule.
hard·back (hárd-bak) *adj.* Having a binding or cover of rigid boards, usually covered with cloth, leather, or the like. Said of books. Also "casebound," "hard-bound," "hardcover."
　　~n. A hardback book.
hard·bake (hárd-bayk) *n.* Almond toffee.

hard-bit·ten (hárd-bítt'n) *adj.* Toughened by experience; unsentimental.
hard·board (hárd-bawrd ‖ -bōrd) *n.* Thin wooden board manufactured from compressed wood pulp and sawdust.
hard-boiled (hárd-bóyld) *adj.* **1.** Cooked by boiling to a solid consistency. Said of an egg. **2.** *Informal.* **a.** Callous; unfeeling. **b.** Having no illusions; unromantic; cynical.
hard case *n.* **1.** A tough, unsentimental person. **2.** *British Informal.* A person who is persistently insolent or difficult to control.
hard cheese *n. British Informal.* Bad luck. Used interjectionally to express sympathy, sometimes ironically, at another's misfortune.
hard cider *n. U.S.* Fermented apple juice; cider. Compare **sweet cider.**
hard coal *n.* **Anthracite** *(see).*
hard copy *n.* Matter, such as computer printout, which may be read by the human eye, as distinguished from electronically stored material.
hard core *n.* **1.** The durable and resistant central part of a given entity; especially, the most intractable or die-hard nucleus of a group or organisation: *the hard core of the separatist movement.* **2.** A material used in constructing foundations for buildings, roads, and the like, consisting of broken bricks, stones, and other hard debris. **3.** *Informal.* Hard-core pornography.
hard-core, hard·core (hárd-kawr ‖ -kōr) *adj.* **1.** Stubbornly resistant or inveterate: *the hard-core criminal element.* **2.** Held to constitute an intractable social problem: *hard-core poverty.* **3.** Sexually very explicit, and often dealing with sexual practices regarded as deviant: *hard-core pornography.*
hard court *n.* A tennis court with a hard surface, such as asphalt or concrete, rather than grass.
hard drug *n.* A drug, such as heroin, that is considered to be physiologically addictive, and hence more damaging to the health than a soft drug.
Har·de·ca·nute or **Har·tha·ca·nute** (hárdikə-newt, hárthəkə- ‖ -nōōt) (*c.*1019–42). King of England (1040–42) and of Denmark (1035–42); the legitimate son of King Canute.
hard ecu *n.* A proposed currency which might have been issued in the form of banknotes in the **ERM** *(see).* See also **ecu.**
hard-edge (hárd-éj) *n.* A style of abstract painting characterised by the sharp delineation of brightly coloured geometric forms. **—hard-edge** *adj.*
hard·en (hárd'n) *v.* **-ened, -ening, -ens.** *—tr.* **1.** To make firm or firmer; make solid or hard. **2.** To toughen mentally or physically; make rugged; inure. **3.** To make unfeeling or emotionally barren. **4.** To strengthen: *It hardened their opposition to the plan.* *—intr.* **1.** To become hard or hardened; set; fix; firm; freeze. **2.** *Economics.* **a.** To rise. Used of prices. **b.** To become stable. **3.** To become inured: *"But poor boys either harden early or are destroyed"* (T.H. White). **—harden off. 1.** To make (a cultivated plant) able to withstand outdoor conditions by gradually increasing exposure to a cold atmosphere. **2.** To become accustomed to outdoor conditions in this way. Used of plants. [Middle English, from HARD.]
hard·en·er (hárd'n-ər) *n.* **1.** One that hardens. **2.** A substance added to varnish or paint to give a harder surface or finish. **3.** A substance added to certain glues to cause or hasten setting.
hard·en·ing (hárd'n-ing) *n.* **1.** The act or process of becoming hard or harder. **2.** Something that hardens, such as a substance added to iron to yield steel.
hardening of the arteries *n.* **Arteriosclerosis** *(see).*
hard-fea·tured (hárd-féechərd) *adj.* Having sharp or harsh features.
hard hat *n.* **1.** A bowler hat. **2.** A lightweight protective helmet, usually of metal or reinforced plastic, worn by construction workers. **3.** *Chiefly U.S. Informal.* A construction worker. **4.** *Informal.* A person with conservative or reactionary views.
hard-hat (hárd-hat) *adj.* **1.** Designating an area on a building site where hard hats must be worn. **2.** Characterised by conservative or reactionary views.
hard·head (hárd-hed) *n.* **1.** A shrewd and tough person. **2.** A stubborn, unmovable person.
hard·head·ed (hárd-héddid) *adj.* **1.** Realistic; concerned with practical matters. **2.** *Chiefly U.S.* Stubborn. **—hard·head·ed·ly** *adv.* **—hard·head·ed·ness** *n.*
hard·heads (hárd-hedz) *n. Used with a singular verb.* A European plant, *Centaurea nigra,* with reddish-purple, thistle-like flowers.
hard·heart·ed (hárd-hártid) *adj.* Lacking in feeling, compassion, or sympathy; cold; pitiless. **—hard·heart·ed·ly** *adv.* **—hard·heart·ed·ness** *n.*
hard-hit (hárd-hít) *adj.* Badly or adversely affected.
hard-hit·ting (hárd-hítting) *adj.* Uncompromising in criticism or abuse: *a hard-hitting article.*
Har·die (hárdi), **James Keir** (1856–1915). A founder of the British Parliamentary Labour Party. Born in Scotland, he was a miner from the age of 10, and became an independent Labour M.P. (1892–95, 1910–15) and leader of the Parliamentary Labour Party (1906).
har·di·hood (hárdi-hōōd) *n.* Boldness and daring; audacity. [HARDY + -HOOD.]
har·di·ly (hárdili) *adv.* In a hardy manner; boldly.
har·di·ness (hárdi-nəss, -niss) *n.* **1.** Vigour; robustness; strength. **2.** Hardihood; daring.
hard labour *n.* Compulsory physical labour imposed on convicted criminals.
hard landing *n.* The landing, by impact, of a spacecraft lacking devices such as retrorockets to slow it down.

hard line *n.* A firm, uncompromising policy, position, or stance.

hard-line (hárd-lín, -lín) *adj.* Characterised by a firm, uncompromising position or stance: *a hard-line foreign policy.* —**hard-lin-er** *n.*

hard lines *n. British Informal.* Bad luck. Used interjectionally to express sympathy at another's misfortune.

hard luck *n.* Bad luck. Used interjectionally to express sympathy at another's misfortune.

hard-ly (hárdli) *adv.* **1.** Barely; scarcely; just. **2.** To an almost negligible degree; almost not: *He could hardly make himself heard.* **3.** Probably not or almost surely not. **4.** Not in the prevailing circumstances: *I could hardly refuse.* **5.** Harshly. **6.** With difficulty. [Middle English *hardli*, boldly, hardily, Old English *h(e)ardlice* : HARD + -LY.]

   Synonyms: hardly, scarcely, barely.

   Usage: Hardly is not used with a negative word in standard English: *I could hardly see; I had hardly left.* Constructions such as *I couldn't hardly see* or *without hardly seeing* are often heard in colloquial speech, but are not acceptable in formal speech or writing. Following clauses are introduced by *when* or *before: He had hardly left when/before the fire broke out.* The use of *than* or *until* in such constructions is not acceptable in standard English.

hard-mouthed (hárd-mowtht, -mówthd) *adj.* **1.** Not easily controlled by the bit. Said of a horse. **2.** Obstinate.

hard-ness (hárd-nəss, -niss) *n. Abbr.* **h., H. 1.** The quality or condition of being hard. **2.** The relative resistance of a mineral to scratching, as measured by the **Mohs scale** *(see).* **3.** The relative resistance of a metal to denting, scratching, or bending.

hard-nosed (hárd-nōzd) *adj. Chiefly U.S. Informal.* Hard-headed; tough-minded; practical: *a hard-nosed politician.*

hard of hearing *adj.* Deaf or slightly deaf.

hard pad *n.* A form of distemper in dogs.

hard palate *n.* The relatively hard, bony front part of the **palate** *(see).*

hard-pan (hárd-pan) *n.* **1.** A layer of hard soil or clay lying at or below the surface. **2.** Hard, unbroken ground. See **caliche.**

hard paste *n.* Porcelain made from kaolin and feldspar. Compare **soft paste.**

hard-pressed (hárd-prést) **1.** Closely pursued. **2.** Constantly troubled by harassment, economic difficulties, or the like. **3.** Barely able: *We'd be hard-pressed to find the money.*

hard rock *n.* A style of rock music characterised by an insistent beat and high volume.

hard roe *n.* The egg-laden ovary of a female fish.

hard rubber *n.* A relatively inelastic rubber made by vulcanisation with 30 to 50 per cent sulphur and usually some lime or magnesia as a filler.

hards (hardz) *n. Used with a singular verb.* The coarse refuse of flax or similar fibre. [Middle English *herdes, hurdes,* Old English *heordan* (plural).]

hard sauce *n.* A creamy sauce of butter and sugar with rum, brandy, or vanilla flavouring, served chilled with sweet dishes.

hard sell *n. Informal.* Aggressive, high-pressure selling or promotion. Compare **soft sell.**

hard-shell (hárd-shel) *adj.* Also **hard-shelled** (-sheld, -shéld). **1.** Having a thick, heavy, or hardened shell. **2.** *Chiefly U.S.* Unyieldingly orthodox; uncompromising; confirmed. —*n.* A hard-shell crab.

hard-shell crab *n.* A marine crab with a fully hardened shell; especially, the edible species, *Cancer pagurus,* in this stage.

hard-ship (hárdship) *n.* **1.** Suffering or difficulty; adversity. **2.** A source or cause of privation or difficulty.

hard shoulder *n. British.* A concreted or reinforced verge at the side of a motorway on which vehicles may drive and stop only in emergencies.

hard-spun (hárd-spun) *adj.* Twisted tightly in spinning, often to the point of curling and looping. Said of yarn.

hard-stand-ing (hárd-stánding) *n.* A hard-surfaced area, usually adjacent to an airstrip, for parking aircraft or ground vehicles.

hard-tack (hárd-tak) *n.* A hard biscuit or bread made only with flour and water and formerly eaten by sailors. Also called "ship's biscuit." [HARD + TACK (food).]

hard-top (hárd-top) *n.* Also **hard top.** A car having a fixed or detachable hard roof. —**hard-top** *adj.*

hard up *adj. Informal.* **1.** Short of money. **2.** Having an inadequate supply of something needed: *hard up for reliable staff.*

hard-ware (hárd-wair) *n.* **1.** Metal goods and utensils such as locks, tools, and cutlery. **2. a.** A computer and the associated physical equipment directly involved in the performance of communications or data-processing functions. Compare **software, firmware. b.** Broadly, machines and other physical equipment directly involved in performing an industrial, technological, or military function. **3.** *Informal.* Heavy military weapons and equipment.

hard water *n.* Water containing dissolved salts of calcium and magnesium; especially, water containing more than 85.5 parts per million of calcium carbonate. Compare **soft water.**

hard-wear-ing (hárd-waír-ing) *adj.* Durable; able to withstand constant wear.

hard-wired (hard-wīrd, -wī-ərd) *adj.* **1.** *Computing.* Designating or employing permanently wired circuits or components that are capable of logical decisions: *a hard-wired terminal.* **2.** Deeply implanted and difficult to change; resembling an instinct more than a habit: *hard-wired behaviour patterns characteristic of the species.*

hard-wood (hárd-wŏŏd) *n.* **1.** The wood of a broad-leaved flowering tree, as distinguished from that of a conifer. **2.** A broad-leaved flowering tree. Compare **softwood.**

hard-work-ing (hárd-wúrking) *adj.* Industrious in carrying out one's work.

har-dy[1] (hárdi) *adj.* **-dier, -diest. 1.** Robust; rugged; strong: *"a rude and hardy race, that lived mostly out of doors"* (Henry Thoreau). **2.** Courageous; intrepid; stouthearted. **3.** Brazenly daring; audacious; hotheaded. **4.** Capable of surviving unfavourable conditions such as cold weather or lack of moisture. Said chiefly of cultivated plants. —See Synonyms at **healthy.** [Middle English *hardy, hardi,* from Old French *hardi,* from the past participle of *hardir,* to become bold, make hard, from Germanic.]

har-dy[2] *n., pl.* **-dies.** A square-shanked chisel or fuller that fits into a square hole in an anvil. [Probably from HARD.]

Hardy, Oliver. See **Laurel and Hardy.**

Har-dy (hárdi), **Thomas** (1840–1928). British novelist and poet. A builder's son, he started his career as an architect and published his first short story in 1865. His Wessex novels, set in the southwest of England, include *Far From the Madding Crowd* (1874), *The Mayor of Casterbridge* (1886), *Tess of the d'Urbervilles* (1891), and *Jude the Obscure* (1896).

hardy hole *n.* The square hole in an anvil for inserting a hardy.

hare (hair) *n.* Any of various mammals of the family Leporidae, and especially of the genus *Lepus,* related to and resembling the rabbits but having longer ears, large hind feet, and long legs adapted for jumping. —**start a hare.** Raise a subject for discussion. ~*intr.v.* **hared, haring, hares.** To run quickly: *He hared down the corridor.* [Middle English *hare,* Old English *hara,* from Germanic.]

hare and hounds *n.* A game in which one group of players leaves a trail of paper scraps for a pursuing group to follow.

hare-bell (haír-bel) *n.* A plant, *Campanula rotundifolia,* having slender stems and leaves and bell-shaped blue flowers. Also called "bluebell." [Middle English : HARE (perhaps because it grows in places frequented by hares) + BELL.]

hare-brained (haír-braynd) *adj.* Foolish; ill-considered: *harebrained schemes.*

Ha-re Krish-na (hárri kríshnə) *n. Informal.* A member of the International Society for Krishna Consciousness, a sect practising a form of Hinduism dedicated to Krishna.

hare-lip (haír-lip) *n.* A congenital fissure or pair of fissures in the upper lip, often associated with a cleft palate. —**hare-lipped** *adj.*

har-em (haír-əm, haár-, -eem, -éem) *n.* Also **har-eem** (ha-réem). **1.** A house or a section of a house reserved for women members of a Muslim household; a gynaeceum. **2.** The women occupying a harem; the wives, concubines, female relatives, and servants of a Muslim household. **3.** The wives and concubines collectively of a Muslim man, especially a wealthy one. **4.** A number of female animals, such as seals, that are the mates of a single male. [Arabic *ḥarīm,* sacred, forbidden place, from *ḥarama,* he prohibited.]

hare's-foot (haírz-fŏŏt) *n.* A Eurasian plant, *Trifolium arvense,* having white or pink, downy, clover-like flowers. Also called "hare's-foot clover."

Har-greaves (hárgreevz), **James** (died 1778). British inventor of the spinning jenny (*c.* 1764). A weaver in Blackburn, Lancashire, Hargreaves developed his device to allow one operator to spin several threads at once. It was nicknamed a "jenny" after his daughter.

har-i-cot (hárri-kō) *n.* **1.** The edible pod or seed of any of several beans, especially the French bean. **2.** The **French bean** *(see).* **3.** A highly seasoned mutton or lamb stew with vegetables. [French, perhaps from Nahuatl.]

har-i-jan (húrri-jən, hárri-) *n.* A Hindu belonging to one of the lowest castes, traditionally regarded by those of higher caste as unclean and forbidden physical contact with them. Also called "Untouchable." [Sanskrit, one devoted to Vishnu : *Hari,* Vishnu + *jana,* person. The use of the term in its present sense was introduced by Mahatma Gandhi.]

Ha-rin-gey (hárring-gay). Formerly **Har-rin-gay.** Largely residential borough in northern Greater London.

hark (hark) *v.* **harked, harking, harks.** —*intr.* To listen attentively; hearken. Often used with *to.* —*tr. Archaic.* To listen to; hear. —**hark at.** To listen to (someone who is being pompous, ridiculous, or the like). —**hark back. 1.** To recall an earlier time or point, as in narrative or reminiscence: *always harking back to his childhood.* **2.** To originate in or survive from: *This custom harks back to the Middle Ages.* [Middle English *herk(i)en,* Old English *heorcian* (unattested).]

harken. Variant of **hearken.**

harl[1] (harl) *n.* Filaments or fibres, as of hemp or flax. [Middle English *herle,* fibre, perhaps from Middle Low German *herle, harle*†.]

harl[2] *tr.v.* **harled, harling, harls.** *Scottish.* To roughcast. [Middle English, of obscure origin.]

Har-lech (hár-lekh, -lek). A town in Gwynedd, Wales. Situated on Cardigan Bay, it has a ruined 13th-century castle.

Har-lem (hárləm). A residential and business district of New York City, in upper Manhattan. Though economically depressed, it is an important social and cultural centre for black Americans.

har-le-quin (hárli-kwin ‖ *U.S. also* -kən) *n.* **1.** *Capital* H. A conventional buffoon of the commedia dell'arte, traditionally presented in a mask and parti-coloured tights. **2.** A clown; a buffoon. ~*adj.* Bright; parti-coloured; spangled; suggesting the dress of Harlequin. [Variant (influenced by obsolete French *harlequin*) of earlier *Harlicken, Harlaken,* from Old French *Herlequin, Hellequin,* leader of a troop of demon horsemen riding at night, probably from Old English *Herla cyning,* King *Herla,* a mythical figure who has been identified with Woden.]

har·le·quin·ade (hárlikwi-náyd) *n.* **1.** A comedy or pantomime in which Harlequin is the main attraction. **2.** A succession of farcical clownings; buffoonery.

harlequin bug *n.* A flat-bodied, brightly coloured insect, *Murgantia histrionica,* that has a fetid odour, and is destructive to cabbage and other plants.

Har·ley Street (hárli) *n.* The London street in or around which many medical specialists have their private consulting rooms.

har·lot (hárlət) *n.* A promiscuous woman, especially a prostitute. [Middle English *harlot, herlot,* vagabond, itinerant jester, male servant, prostitute, from Old French *(h)arlot, herlot†,* young fellow, vagabond.] —**har·lot·ry** (hárlətri) *n.*

Har·low (hárlō) *n.* A town in Essex, England, on the river Stort. Originally a small market town, since 1947 it has been developed as a light industrial centre and residential satellite of London.

Harlow, Jean, stage name of Harlean Carpentier (1911-37). U.S. film actress. She won stardom with *Hell's Angels* (1930) in which she appeared as a wise-cracking sex-symbol. Her other films include *Platinum Blonde* (1931), and *Bombshell* (1933).

harm (harm) *n.* **1.** Injury or damage, whether physical, psychological, or moral. **2.** Wrong; evil. —**in harm's way.** In danger; in a risky position. —**out of harm's reach** or **way.** Out of danger; in a safe place.
~*tr.v.* **harmed, harming, harms.** To damage; injure; impair. See Synonyms at **injure.** [Middle English *harm,* Old English *hearm,* from Germanic.]

har·mat·tan (haar-mátt'n, hármə-tán) *n.* A dry, dusty wind that blows from the Sahara across West Africa. In the humid lands along the Gulf of Guinea its dryness is refreshing, and it is called "The Doctor". [Twi *haramata,* probably from Arabic *ḥarām,* a forbidden or accursed thing, from the stem of *ḥarama,* forbid, akin to *ḥaruma,* to be forbidden. See **harem.**]

harm·ful (hármf'l) *adj.* Capable of harming or causing harm; damaging; injurious. —**harm·ful·ly** *adv.* —**harm·ful·ness** *n.*

harm·less (hárm-ləss, -liss) *adj.* **1.** Not harmful; not capable of harming. **2.** Inoffensive. —**harm·less·ly** *adv.* —**harm·less·ness** *n.*

har·mon·ic (haar-mónnik) *adj.* **1. a.** Of or pertaining to musical harmony as distinguished from melody or rhythm. **b.** Of or pertaining to harmonics. **2.** Characterised by harmony; concordant. **3. a.** *Mathematics.* Designating a function or series that can be expressed in terms of sines or cosines. **b.** Designating a function that appears in a harmonic series.
~*n.* **1.** In music and acoustics, a tone in the harmonic series of overtones produced by a fundamental tone. Also called "overtone", "partial", "partial tone". **2.** A tone produced on a stringed instrument by lightly touching an open or stopped vibrating string at a given fraction of its length so that both segments vibrate. [Latin *harmonicus,* from Greek *harmonikos,* from *harmonia,* HARMONY.] —**har·mon·i·cal·ly** *adv.*

har·mon·i·ca (haar-mónnikə) *n.* **1.** A small, rectangular musical instrument consisting of a row of free reeds set back in air holes, played by exhaling or inhaling. Also called "mouth organ". **2.** A **glass harmonica** *(see).* [Variant (influenced by HARMONIC) of earlier *armonica,* from Italian, from *armonico,* harmonious, from Latin *harmonicus,* HARMONIC.]

harmonic analysis *n.* The representation of mathematical functions by means of linear operations, such as summation or integration, on characteristic sets of functions; especially, such representation by Fourier series.

harmonic mean *n.* The reciprocal of the arithmetic mean of the reciprocals of a given set of numbers.

harmonic minor scale *n. Music.* A minor scale having the seventh note sharpened, so that it lies only a semitone below the tonic. Compare **melodic minor scale.**

harmonic motion *n. Physics.* A form of periodic motion in which the displacement is symmetrical about a central point. See **simple harmonic motion.**

harmonic progression *n.* A sequence of quantities the reciprocals of which form an arithmetic progression; for example, 1, ⅓, ⅕, ⅐, ...

har·mon·ics (haar-mónniks) *n. Used with a singular verb.* The theory or study of the physical properties and characteristics of musical sound.

harmonic series *n.* **1.** *Mathematics.* A series whose terms are in harmonic progression; for example, $1 + \frac{1}{3} + \frac{1}{5} + \frac{1}{7} + \ldots$. **2.** In acoustics, a series of tones consisting of a fundamental tone and the overtones produced by it, whose frequencies are consecutive integral multiples of the frequency of the fundamental.

har·mo·ni·ous (haar-mōni-əss) *adj.* **1.** Exhibiting accord in feeling or action; sympathetic: *a harmonious relationship.* **2.** Having component elements pleasingly or appropriately combined: *a harmonious structure.* **3.** Characterised by harmony of sound; concordant. —**har·mo·ni·ous·ly** *adv.* —**har·mo·ni·ous·ness** *n.*

har·mo·nise, har·mo·nize (hármə-nīz) *v.* **-nised, -nising, -nises.** —*tr.* **1.** To bring into agreement or harmony; make harmonious. **2.** To provide harmony for (a melody). —*intr.* **1.** To be in agreement; be harmonious. **2.** To sing or play in harmony. —See Synonyms at **agree.** —**har·mo·nis·er** *n.*

har·mo·nist (hármənist) *n.* **1.** A scholar who collates and seeks to harmonise the discrepancies in parallel passages of text, especially

of the Gospels. **2. a.** One skilled in musical harmony. **b.** *Poetic.* A maker of harmonious music: *"The Ocean is a mighty harmonist"* (William Wordsworth). **3.** One of a school of ancient Greek musical theorists whose principles were based on the subjective effects of notes rather than on the mathematical relations between them. **4.** One who brings notes into consonance or accord; a harmoniser.

har·mo·nis·tic (hármə-nístik) *adj.* **1.** Of or relating to a harmony. **2.** Of or relating to the harmonising of parallel passages of text. —**har·mo·nis·ti·cal·ly** *adv.*

har·mo·ni·um (haar-mōni-əm) *n.* An organ-like keyboard instrument that produces notes with free metal reeds vibrated by air forced from a bellows. [French, from *harmonie,* harmony, from Old French *armonie,* HARMONY.]

har·mo·ny (hárməni) *n., pl.* **-nies. 1.** Agreement in feeling, approach, action, disposition, or the like; sympathy; accord. **2.** The pleasing interaction or appropriate combination of the elements in a whole. **3.** *Music.* **a.** The study of the structure, progression, and relation of chords. **b.** The simultaneous combination of notes in a chord. **c.** Such a chord or chords added when writing or playing a melody to provide musical emphasis, background, or substance. **d.** The structure of a musical work or passage as considered from the point of view of its chordal characteristics and relationships. **4.** Pleasing sounds; music. **5.** A collation of parallel passages from a text, especially the Gospels, with a commentary demonstrating their consonance and explaining their discrepancies. —See Synonyms at **proportion.** [Middle English *armonie,* from Old French *(h)armonie,* from Latin *harmonia,* from Greek, agreement, harmony, means of joining, from *harmos,* joint.]

Harmsworth, Alfred. See **Northcliffe, 1st Viscount.**

Harmsworth, Harold. See **Rothermere, 1st Viscount.**

har·ness (hárniss) *n.* **1.** The equipment, consisting of straps and sometimes buckles, used by a draught animal to pull a vehicle or implement. **2.** Anything resembling a harness, such as the arrangement of straps used to hold a parachute to the body. **3.** A device that raises and lowers the warp threads on a loom. **4.** *Archaic.* Armour for a man or a horse. —**in harness.** On duty; at work.
~*tr.v.* **harnessed, -nessing, -nesses. 1. a.** To put a harness on (a draught animal). **b.** To attach (a draught animal) to a vehicle or implement by means of a harness. **2.** To bring under control and direct the force of: *If he can harness his energy, he will accomplish a great deal.* **3.** *Archaic.* To fit with armour; arm or equip for battle. [Middle English *harness, harnais,* baggage, equipment, trappings of a horse, from Old French *harneis,* military equipment, from Old Norse *hernest* (unattested), provisions for an army : *herr,* army + *nest,* provisions.] —**har·ness·er** *n.*

har·nessed antelope (hárnist) *n.* Any of several African antelopes with markings resembling harness straps, such as the **bushbuck** *(see).*

harness hitch *n.* A type of knot forming a fixed loop in a rope.

harness race *n.* A race between horses harnessed to sulkies.

Har·old I Harefoot (hárrəld) (d. 1040). Danish King of England (1037–40). He was the illegitimate son of King Canute and became King while Hardecanute, Canute's legitimate son, was preoccupied in Denmark. He died as Hardecanute was preparing to invade England and claim his throne.

Harold II (*c.*1022–66). King of England (1066), the last of the Anglo-Saxon monarchs. He was the son of Godwin, Earl of Essex, and brother-in-law of Edward the Confessor. Shipwrecked in France (*c.* 1064), he was forced by the Normans to swear to support William of Normandy (William the Conqueror) in any claim on the English Crown. When Edward died in 1066, Harold succeeded him. He defeated the forces of his brother Tostig and Harold III Hardraade at Stamford Bridge, Yorkshire. He then rode south to meet William's Norman invasion, and died at the Battle of Hastings (1066).

Harold III Hardraade (1015–66). King of Norway (1046–66). In 1066, Hardraade (hard ruler) invaded England, supporting Tostig against Harold II, and was killed at the Battle of Stamford Bridge.

harp (harp) *n.* **1.** A musical instrument consisting of an upright, open, triangular frame with 46 strings of graded lengths which are played by plucking with the fingers. **2.** Something similar to a harp in shape or sound. **3.** *Informal.* A harmonica, especially when played in pop music.
~*v.* **harped, harping, harps.** —*intr.* To play a harp. —*tr. Archaic.* To give expression to; utter; refer to. —**harp on** or **upon.** To talk or write about to an excessive and tedious degree; dwell upon. [Middle English *harp(e),* Old English *hearpe,* from Germanic *harpōn-* (unattested).] —**harp·er** *n.*

har·pins (hárp-inz) *pl.n.* Also **har·pings** (-ingz). **1.** *Nautical.* The wooden supports of a ship under construction. **2.** The timbers used for strengthening the bow of a ship. [Perhaps from HARP.]

harp·ist (hárpist) *n.* A person who plays the harp.

har·poon (haar-pōōn, hár-) *n.* A spearlike implement having a barbed head and attached rope that is hurled by hand or shot from a gun, and is used in hunting whales and large fish.
~*tr.v.* **harpooned, -pooning, -poons.** To strike, kill, or capture with or as if with a harpoon. [French *harpon,* from *harpe,* clamp, dog's claw, from Latin *harpē, harpa,* sickle, from Greek *harpē.*] —**har·poon·eer** (hárpōō-néer), **har·poon·er** *n.*

harpoon gun *n.* A small cannon used to fire harpoons.

harp seal *n.* An earless seal, *Pagophilus groenlandicus,* occurring in the North Atlantic and Arctic Oceans. [From the harp-shaped marking on its back.]

harp·si·chord (hárpsi-kawrd) *n.* A keyboard instrument in which the strings are sounded by means of quill or leather plectrums rather than by hammers. [Obsolete French *harpechorde*, from Italian *arpicordo* : *arpi*, harp, from Late Latin *harpa*, from Germanic *harpon-* (unattested), HARP + *corda*, string, from Latin *chorda*, from Greek *khordē*.]

har·py (hárpi) *n., pl.* **-pies**. **1.** A cruel and greedy person. **2.** A shrewish woman. [From HARPY.]

Har·py (hárpi) *n., pl.* **-pies**. *Greek Mythology.* Any of several loathsome, voracious monsters, having a woman's head and trunk and a bird's tail, wings, and talons. [French *harpie*, from Latin *harpȳia*, from Greek *harpuiai†*, "snatchers".]

harpy eagle *n.* A large eagle of South and Central America, *Harpia harpyja*, with an erectile head crest and a mottled grey plumage. [After the HARPY.]

har·que·bus (hárkwi-bəss ‖ hárkə-, -buss) *n.* Also **ar·que·bus**. A heavy, portable, matchlock gun invented during the 15th century. Also called "hackbut". [Old French *(h)arquebuse*, from Middle Dutch *hakebusse* : *hake*, hook + *busse*, gun, from Late Latin *buxis*, BOX.]

har·ri·dan (hárridən) *n.* A malicious, scolding old woman. [17th century (cant) : perhaps a variant of French *haridelle†*, worn-out horse.]

har·ri·er[1] (hárri-ər) *n.* **1.** One that harries. **2.** Any of various slender, narrow-winged hawks of the genus *Circus*, such as *C. pygargus*, Montagu's harrier, that prey on small animals.

harrier[2] *n.* **1.** A small hound of a breed originally used in hunting hares. **2.** A cross-country runner. [From HARE.]

Har·ri·man (hárrimən), **(William) Averell** (1891–1986). U.S. diplomat. He was the son of a rail magnate, and became ambassador to the Soviet Union (1943–46) and Secretary of Commerce (1946–48). He failed in 1956 to win the Democratic presidential nomination. He was Governor of New York (1955–59).

Har·ris (hárriss), **Roy (Ellsworth)** (1898–1979). U.S. composer. He was a farmer and a lorry driver before he began composing at 27. He was influenced by U.S. folk singers in the 1930s.

Har·ris·burg (hárriss-burg). Capital of Pennsylvania, in the United States. Situated on the Susquehanna river, it is an important railway junction and industrial centre.

Har·ri·son (hárriss'n), **George** (1943–). British pop musician, formerly lead guitarist with The Beatles. His best-known compositions include *Here Comes the Sun* and *My Sweet Lord.*

Harris tweed *n.* A trademark for a rough tweed fabric. [After *Harris* in the Outer Hebrides, where it is woven.]

Har·ro·gate (hárrə-gət, hárrō-, -git, -gayt). A residential town in North Yorkshire, England. It has been a spa since 1596, and is a popular holiday resort and retirement area.

Har·ro·vi·an (hə-rṓvi-ən, ha-) *n.* A person who was or is being educated at Harrow public school. [New Latin *Harrōvia*, HARROW.] **—Har·ro·vi·an** *adj.*

har·row[1] (hárrō) *n.* A farm instrument consisting of a heavy frame with teeth or upright discs, used to break up and level ploughed ground.
~tr.v. harrowed, -rowing, -rows. 1. To break up and level (soil or land) with a harrow. **2.** To inflict great distress or torment on the mind of; torment; rack. [Middle English, from Old Norse *herri*.]

har·row[2] *tr.v.* **-rowed, -rowing, -rows.** *Archaic.* To plunder or harry. [Middle English *harwen*, variant of *harien*, to HARRY.]

Har·row (hárrō). A residential borough of northwest Greater London. It is noted for one of England's most famous public schools, founded in 1571, whose former pupils include Byron, Palmerston, and Sir Winston Churchill.

har·row·ing (hárrō-ing) *adj.* Extremely distressing.

harrowing of hell *n.* The rescue by Christ, following his crucifixion, of the souls of the righteous held captive in hell since the generation of Adam.

har·rumph (hə-rúmf) *interj.* Used to express scepticism, disapproval, or discontent.
~v. -rumphed, -rumphing, -rumphs. —intr. To express scepticism, disapproval, or discontent by uttering "harrumph". **—tr.** To give vent to or express (one's scepticism or disapproval, for example) by uttering "harrumph".

har·ry (hárri) *tr.v.* **-ried, -rying, -ries. 1.** To raid, as in a war; sack; pillage. **2.** To disturb or annoy by constant attacks; harass. [Middle English *harien, herien*, Old English *hergian*, from Germanic.]

harsh (harsh) *adj.* **1.** Producing an unpleasant sensory response, as: **a.** Coarse in texture; rough. **b.** Disagreeable to the ear; grating or discordant. **c.** Having a bitter or astringent taste. **d.** Visually jarring or irritating. **2.** Extremely severe or exacting; stern. **—See** Synonyms at **burdensome**. [Middle Low German *harsch*, "hairy", rough. See **hair, -ish**.] **—harsh·ly** *adv.* **—harsh·ness** *n.*

harsh·en (hársh'n) *v.* **-ened, -ening, -ens. —tr.** To make harsh. **—intr.** To become harsh.

harslet. Variant of **haslet.**

hart (hart) *n., pl.* **harts** or collectively **hart.** A male deer; especially, a male red deer over five years old. [Middle English *hert*, Old English *heor(o)t*, from Germanic.]

Hart (hart), **Moss** (1904–61). U.S. dramatist and librettist. He wrote Broadway hit comedies with George S. Kaufman, including *Once in a Lifetime* (1930) and *The Man Who Came to Dinner* (1939).

har·tal (haar-táal) *n.* A halting of work and business in India, usually as a political protest or as a mark of respect; a strike or boycott. [Hindi *hartāl*, from *hattāl*, "locking of shops" : *hāt*, shop, from Sanskrit *hatta*, shop, perhaps from *hatika*, gold, from *hari*, yellow +

tālā, lock, bolt, from Sanskrit *tālā, tāḍā*, latch, probably from Dravidian.]

Harte (hart), **(Francis) Bret(t)** (1836–1902). U.S. author. As editor of *Overland Monthly* (1868–71) he contributed many tales about Californian mining towns. *The Luck of Roaring Camp and Other Sketches* (1870) is his best-known collection.

har·te·beest (hárti-beest ‖ hárt-) *n., pl.* **-beests** or collectively **hartebeest.** Also **hart·beest** (hárt-). Either of two African antelopes, *Alcelaphus bucelaphus* or *A. lichtensteini*, having a brownish coat and ridged, outward-curving horns. [Obsolete Afrikaans, from Dutch *hartebeest, hertebeest* : *hert*, HART + *beest*, BEAST.]

Hart·ford (hártfərd). Capital city of Connecticut, in the United States. Traditionally a centre for commerce and finance, it is of international importance in the field of insurance.

Hart·le·pool (hártli-pōōl). An industrial and fishing port in northeast England. Situated on the Tees estuary, it is the main port of the Durham coalfields; its industries include shipbuilding, heavy engineering, clothing, and tourism.

Hart·ley (hártli), **L(esley) P(oles)** (1895–1972). British novelist. His works include *The Shrimp and the Anemone* (1944), *Eustace and Hilda* (1947), and *The Go-Between* (1953).

Hart·nell (hártnəl), **Sir Norman** (1901–79). British fashion designer. He designed utility wear during World War II, and later became official dressmaker to Queen Elizabeth II. He was knighted in 1977.

har·tree (hár-tree) *n.* A unit of energy used in atomic physics equal to the ratio of the square of the charge on an electron (atomic unit of charge) to the radius of the first Bohr orbit of an atom (atomic unit of length). It has the value 4.850×10^{-18} joule. [After Douglas Rayner *Hartree* (1897–1958), British mathematician and physicist.]

harts·horn (hárts-hawrn) *n. Archaic.* **Sal volatile** (see). [Old English *heortes horn*, hart's horn (originally the chief source of ammonia).]

hart's-tongue (hárts-tung ‖ -tong) *n.* An evergreen fern, *Phyllitis scolopendrium*, having narrow, undivided fronds. [So called from the shape of its fronds.]

har·um-scar·um (haír-əm-skaír-əm) *adj.* Lacking a sense of responsibility; rash; reckless.
~adv. With abandon; recklessly.
~n. *Informal.* **1.** One who acts recklessly. **2.** Reckless behaviour. [Perhaps from HARE + SCARE.]

Ha·run ar-Ra·shid (ha-rṓōn-a-ra-sheéd) (*c.*766–809). The fifth caliph of Baghdad (786–809) of the Abbassid dynasty. He figures in many tales of the Arabian Nights, and symbolises the golden age of Islamic rulers.

ha·rus·pex (hə-rúspeks, hárrə-speks) *n., pl.* **haruspices** (hə-rúspi-seez). Also **a·rus·pex** (ə-rúspeks). A priest in ancient Rome who practised divination by the inspection of the entrails of animals. [Latin, from *haru-* (origin obscure; perhaps akin to Greek *chordé*, chord, gut + *spex*, from *specere*, to inspect).]

Har·vard (hárvərd). The oldest college in the United States, founded in 1636 at New Towne (now Cambridge), Massachusetts, and named after one of its early benefactors, the English clergyman John Harvard, in 1638. Originally a training college for Puritan ministers, it became a university under Charles W. Eliot (1834–1926), its president (1869–1909). Harvard has been the alma mater of six American presidents, including John Adams, Franklin D. Roosevelt, and John F. Kennedy. Other famous Harvard graduates include Emerson, Thoreau, Henry James, and T.S. Eliot.

Harvard classification *n.* A method of classifying stars that originally used the letters A to P to indicate the strength of the hydrogen absorption lines in their spectra but was later modified so that most stars could be classified, according to decreasing surface temperature, into seven groups known by the letters O,B,A,F,G,K,M. [After HARVARD University, where it was developed.]

har·vest (hárvist) *n.* **1.** The act or process of gathering a crop, especially a grain crop. **2.** The crop thus gathered. **3.** The amount or measure of such a crop. **4.** The time or season of such a gathering. **5.** The result or consequence of any action.
~v. harvested, -vesting, -vests. —tr. 1. To gather (a crop). **2.** To gather a crop from (a field or orchard, for example). **3.** To store; lay up. **4.** To receive (the benefits or consequences of an action). **—intr.** To gather a crop.
~adj. Of or relating to a harvest: *a harvest supper.* [Middle English *hervest*, autumn, Old English *hærfest*, from Germanic.]

har·vest·er (hárvistər) *n.* **1.** A person who harvests. **2.** A machine that harvests, especially a combine harvester. **3.** An arachnid, the harvestman.

harvest festival *n.* A service or thanksgiving on the completion of the harvest, held in a church or other building decorated inside with flowers, fruit, and vegetables.

harvest home *n.* **1.** The completion of the harvest. **2. a.** The time of completing the harvest. **b.** A festival held at this time, especially a harvest supper. **c.** A song sung at this time.

har·vest·man (hárvist-man, hárviss-, -mən) *n., pl.* **-men** (-men). **1.** One who harvests. **2.** An arachnid of the order Opiliones, having very long slender legs, and particularly common in temperate regions in the late summer. Also *chiefly U.S.* "daddy longlegs".

harvest mite *n.* Any of various mites of the genus *Trombicula*, whose red larvae are parasites of man and other vertebrates and cause intense itching of the skin. Also called "harvest bug", "harvest tick", "chigger" [So called from its being a nuisance during harvest.]

harvest moon *n.* The full moon that occurs nearest to the autumnal equinox.

harvest mouse *n.* A very small Eurasian mouse, *Micromys minutus*, with reddish-brown fur and a prehensile tail, found in cornfields and hedgerows.

Har·vey (hárvi), **William** (1578–1657). English physician and anatomist who discovered the circulation of the blood. He became physician to James I and Charles I. His treatise *On the Motion of the Heart and Blood* (1628) accurately described the circulation via heart, lungs, arteries, and veins.

Har·well (hár-wəl, -wel). A village in Oxfordshire, England. An atomic research station was established there in 1947 by the U.K. Atomic Energy Authority.

Har·wich (hárrij, hárrich). A port in Essex, eastern England. Situated on the Stour estuary, it is an important passenger and commercial sea link with Denmark and the Netherlands.

Harz Mountains (harts). A mountain range in northern Germany. Extending from the river Weser to the river Elbe, it is the northernmost range of the European mountain system. Its forested slopes and mineral springs attract tourists.

has (haz; *weak forms* həz, əz, z, s). Third person singular present indicative of **have**.

has-been (házbeen, -bin) *n. Informal.* One that is no longer famous, popular, successful, or useful.

Ha·šek (háshek), **Jaroslav** (1883–1923). Czech novelist. He is best remembered for the novel *The Good Soldier Schweik* (1920–23).

hash¹ (hash) *n.* **1.** A dish of minced or diced meat, especially meat that has been previously cooked, and sometimes vegetables, usually browned and baked in a sauce. **2.** A jumble, hotchpotch, or mess. **3.** A reworking or restatement of material already familiar. **—make a hash of.** To make a mess of; botch. **—settle (someone's) hash.** *Informal.* To silence or subdue.
~*tr.v.* **hashed, hashing, hashes. 1.** To chop into pieces; mince. Often used with *up*. **2.** To make a mess of; mangle. Often used with *up*. **3.** *U.S. Informal.* To discuss carefully; review. Often used with *over*: *hash over future plans.* [French *hachis*, from *hacher*, to chop up, from Old French *hachier*, from *hache*, axe, HATCHET.]

hash² (hash) *n. Informal.* Hashish.

Hash·i·mo·to's disease (háshi-mōtō) *n.* An autoimmune disease resulting in chronic inflammation of the thyroid gland, with partial or total suppression of thyroid-hormone secretion. [After H. *Hashimoto* (1881–1934), Japanese surgeon.]

hash·ish, hash·eesh (hásh-éesh, -ish) *n.* A purified resin prepared from the dried flowers of the hemp plant, smoked or chewed as a narcotic and hallucinogen. Also informally called "hash". [Arabic *ḥashīsh*, hemp, dried grass.]

Hasidim. Variant of **Chassidim.**

has·let (házz-lit, ház-) *n.* Also **hars·let** (hárz-, hárss-). **1.** The heart, liver, and other edible viscera of an animal, especially of a pig. **2.** A dish prepared from such viscera, compacted into a loaf and served cold. [Middle English *hastelet, hastlet,* from Old French *hastelet,* diminutive of *haste,* spit, roast meat, perhaps from Latin *hasta,* spear.]

has·n't (házz'nt). Contraction of *has not.*

hasp (haasp ‖ hasp) *n.* A metal fastener having a hinged, slotted part that fits over a staple and may be secured by a pin, bolt, or padlock.
~*tr.v.* **hasped, hasping, hasps.** To fasten or lock with a hasp. [Middle English *hasp(e),* Old English *hæsp(e), hæpse,* fastening, hinge, from Germanic *hasp-* (unattested).]

Has·san II (ha-sáan, háss'n) (1929–). King of Morocco (1961–). He succeeded his father, Muhammad V (reigned 1957–61).

Hassidim. Variant of **Chassidim.**

has·sle (háss'l) *n. Informal.* **1.** An argument or fight. **2.** Trouble; bother.
~*v.* **hassled, -sling, -sles.** *Informal.* —*intr.* To argue or fight. —*tr.* To bother or harass: *street gangs hassling passers-by.* [Perhaps a blend of HAGGLE + TUSSLE.]

has·sock (hássək) *n.* **1.** A thick cushion used as a footstool or for kneeling upon. **2.** A dense clump of grass; a tussock. [Middle English *hassok,* Old English *hassuc†,* clump of matted vegetation.]

hast (hast; *weak forms* həst, əst, st). *Archaic.* Second person singular present indicative of **have.** Used with *thou.*

has·tate (hástayt) *adj.* Shaped like the head of an arrow or spear: *a hastate leaf.* [New Latin *hastatus,* from Latin *hasta,* spear.]

haste (hayst) *n.* **1.** Swiftness; rapidity. **2.** Eagerness or necessity to move swiftly; urgency. **3.** Careless or headlong hurrying; precipitateness. **—make haste.** To move or act swiftly; hurry.
~*v.* **hasted, hasting, hastes.** *Poetic.* —*intr.* To hasten. —*tr.* To cause to hurry; hasten. [Middle English, from Old French, from West Germanic *haisti-* (unattested), violence.]

has·ten (háyss'n) *v.* **-tened, -tening, -tens.** —*intr.* **1.** To move or act swiftly. **2.** To be eager or anxious. Used with an infinitive: *I hasten to point out that I was not actually present.* —*tr.* **1.** To cause to hurry; urge on. **2.** To bring about more quickly; accelerate: *events that hastened the downfall of the government.* —See Synonyms at **speed.**

Hast·ings¹ (háystingz). A coastal town in East Sussex, England. Though no longer a port, it is the chief of the Cinque Ports with a long history of commercial and naval importance. Today, it is a popular resort and residential town. William the Conqueror's victory at the Battle of Hastings (1066), fought at nearby Battle, ended Saxon rule in England, and installed a Norman-French dynasty.

Hastings². City in New Zealand. Situated in Hawke's Bay district, on the east coast of North Island, it is the centre of a fruit-growing

region and known as the "fruit bowl of New Zealand". It was rebuilt after an earthquake in 1931.

Hastings, Warren (1732–1818). The first Governor General of India (1774–85). He carried out land and legal reforms, facing the hostility of Sir Philip Francis (1740–1818) who tried to get him impeached for corruption. At the end of a long trial (1788–95), the House of Lords found Hastings not guilty.

hast·y (háysti) *adj.* **-ier, -iest. 1.** Characterised by speed; swift; rapid. **2.** Done, made, or acting too quickly to be accurate or wise; rash; impetuous: *a hasty decision.* **3.** Easily angered; irritable. —See Synonyms at **fast, impetuous.** —**hast·i·ly** *adv.* —**hast·i·ness** *n.*

hasty pudding *n.* **1.** A sweetened milk pudding with flour, semolina, or tapioca. **2.** *U.S.* Cornmeal mush served with maple syrup, brown sugar, or other sweetening.

hat (hat) *n.* **1.** A covering for the head; especially, one having a shaped crown and brim. **2.** A capacity or office as specified: *answered the question wearing her politician's hat.* **—eat (one's) hat if.** Used to express firm conviction that a specified event will not occur: *I'll eat my hat if he marries her.* **—hat in hand.** In a servile or apologetic way. **—My hat!** Used to express surprise, disbelief, or rejection of a claim or report. **—pass the hat round.** To take up a monetary collection. **—take (one's) hat off to.** To respect, admire, or congratulate. **—talk through (one's) hat. 1.** To talk nonsense. **2.** To bluff. **—at the drop of a hat.** Without hesitation or compunction. **—throw** or **toss (one's) hat into the ring.** To enter a race or contest; especially, to run for office. **—under (one's) hat.** Confidential; secret.
~*tr.v.* **hatted, hatting, hats.** To supply or cover with a hat. [Middle English *hat,* Old English *hæt(t),* from Germanic.]

hat·band (hát-band) *n.* A band of ribbon or cloth around the crown of a hat just above the brim.

hat·box (hát-boks) *n.* A round box or case for a hat.

hatch¹ (hach) *n.* **1. a.** An opening in the deck of a ship leading to the hold; a hatchway. **b.** The cover for such an opening. **c.** A ship's compartment. **2.** Any small door or opening, as in a roof or floor. **3. a.** A Dutch door. **b.** The lower half of a Dutch door. **4.** A floodgate. **—down the hatch.** *Slang.* Down the throat; drink up. Used as a toast. **—under hatches. 1.** Below decks. **2.** Concealed. **3.** *Slang.* Dead. [Middle English *hacche, hecche,* Old English *hæc(c),* hatch, wicket, from Germanic *khak-* (unattested).]

hatch² *v.* **hatched, hatching, hatches.** —*intr.* **1.** To emerge from or break out of the egg. **2.** To crack open and release a young animal. Used of an egg. —*tr.* **1.** To produce (young) from an egg. **2.** To cause (an egg or eggs) to produce young. **3.** To originate or formulate; especially, to devise (a plot, for example) in secret.
~*n.* **1.** The act or an instance of hatching. **2.** The young hatched at one time; a brood. [Middle English *hacchen,* Old English *hæccan* (unattested).] **—hatch·er** *n.*

hatch³ *tr.v.* **hatched, hatching, hatches.** To shade by drawing or etching fine parallel or crossed lines on.
~*n.* Such a line. [Middle English *hachen,* from Old French *hach(i)er,* from *hache,* axe. See **hatchet.**]

hatch·back (hách-bak) *n.* **1.** A motor car with a steeply sloping rear consisting of a door which opens upwards. **2.** A door of this kind.

hatch·el (hách əl) *n.* A comb for separating flax fibres. Also called "heckle".
~*tr.v.* **hatchelled** or *U.S.* **hatcheled, -elling** or *U.S.* **-eling, -els.** To separate (flax fibres) with a hatchel. [Middle English *hechele,* flaxcomb. See **heckle.**]

hatch·er·y (háchəri) *n., pl.* **-ies.** A place where eggs, especially those of fish or poultry, are hatched under controlled artificial conditions.

hatch·et (háchit) *n.* **1.** A small, short-handled axe, for use in one hand. **2.** A tomahawk. **—bury the hatchet.** To stop fighting; make peace. **—dig up the hatchet.** To resume hostilities [Middle English *hachet, hatchet,* small axe, from Old French *hachette,* diminutive of *hache,* axe, from Germanic.]

hatchet face *n.* A long, gaunt face with sharp features. **—hatch·et-faced** *adj.*

hatchet job *n. Informal.* A malicious verbal attack, either spoken or written, intended to destroy the reputation of another.

hatchet man *n. Informal.* **1.** Someone who carries out unpleasant duties on behalf of another. **2.** A hired assassin. **3.** A harsh or malicious critic.

hatch·ing (háching) *n.* **1.** The fine lines used in graphic arts to show shading. **2.** The process of decorating with such lines.

hatch·ling (hách-ling) *n.* A newly hatched bird, reptile, amphibian, or fish.

hatch·ment (háchmənt) *n. Heraldry.* A panel, usually diamond-shaped, bearing the coat of arms of a dead person. Formerly also called "achievement". [Earlier *(h)achement, achiment,* perhaps short for ACHIEVEMENT.]

hatch·way (hách-way) *n.* **1. a.** An opening in the deck of a ship leading to a hold, compartment, or lower deck. **b.** A ladder or stairway within such an opening. **2. a.** Any similar opening, as in a roof or floor. **b.** Any similar ladder or stairway.

hate (hayt) *v.* **hated, hating, hates.** —*tr.* **1.** To feel hatred towards; loathe; detest. **2.** To find deeply distasteful or disagreeable; dislike: *hated having to borrow money.* —*intr.* To feel hatred.
~*n.* **1.** Strong dislike; animosity; hatred. **2.** An object of detestation or hatred: *a pet hate.* [Middle English, Old English *hatian,* (verb), from Germanic.] **—hat·a·ble, hate·a·ble** *adj.* **—hat·er** *n.*

hate·ful (háytf'l) *adj.* **1.** Inspiring hatred; detestable; despicable.

2. *Archaic.* Feeling or expressing hatred; malevolent. —**hate·ful·ly** *adv.* —**hate·ful·ness** *n.*

Synonyms: *abhorrent, hateful, detestable, odious, obnoxious, offensive, repellent.*

Hat·field (hát-feeld). A town in Hertfordshire, England. It has been expanded since 1948 and contains a massive aircraft engineering complex. The old town contains Hatfield House (1607), and part of Hatfield Palace (1497), where Elizabeth I was first told of her accession to the throne.

hath (hath; *weak forms,* həth, əth). *Archaic.* Third person singular present indicative of **have.**

Hath·a·way (hátha-way), **Anne** (*c.*1556–1623). Wife of William Shakespeare. She was born at Shottery, near Stratford, and married Shakespeare in 1582. She bore him three children: a daughter, Susanna, and the twins Hamnet and Judith. The farmhouse where she lived is preserved as a museum.

ha·tha yoga (hátha, hútta) *n.* **1. Yoga** (*see*). **2.** A yoga concentrating on postures and breathing. [Sanskrit : *hatha,* force + YOGA.]

Hath·or (háth-awr, -ər). The ancient Egyptian goddess of love, creation, happiness, and beauty, represented as having a cow's horns or head. [Greek *Hathōr,* from Egyptian *ḥt-ḥr.*]

hat·pin (hát-pin) *n.* A long thick pin, usually with a decorative head, for securing a woman's hat to her hair.

ha·tred (háytrid) *n.* Violent dislike or animosity; abhorrence. [Middle English *hatred, hatereden* : *hate, hete,* hate, Old English *hete* + *-reden,* Old English *rēden,* condition.]

hat·ter (háttər) *n.* One whose occupation is the manufacture, selling, or repair of hats. —**mad as a hatter.** Completely insane. [Referring to the symptoms, resembling insanity, caused by mercury poisoning, formerly a common disease of hatters, who used the metal in making hats.]

hat trick *n.* **1.** In cricket, the taking of three wickets by a bowler in three consecutive balls. **2.** The scoring of three goals, tries, or the like by one player in any one match. **3.** Any set of three victories or other notable achievements, especially when consecutive, in any field of endeavour. [The cricketing feat was once rewarded by the gift of a hat.]

hau·berk (háwberk) *n.* A long tunic made of chain mail. [Middle English *hauberk,* from Old French *hauberc,* from Frankish *halsberg* (unattested), "neck protector": *hals,* neck + *berg-* (unattested), to protect.]

haugh (haw ‖ haakh, haaf) *n. Northern British.* A low-lying meadow, part of a river valley. [Middle English (Scottish) *holch, hawch,* Old English *healh,* corner of land.]

Haugh·ey (háw-hi ‖ -khi), **Charles James** (1925–). Irish politician. President of the Fianna Fail Party since 1979, he was Taoiseach (Prime Minister of the Republic of Ireland) in 1979–81, 1982, and 1987–92.

haugh·ty (háwti) *adj.* **-tier, -tiest.** Proud and vain to the point of arrogance; scornful and self-satisfied. See Synonyms at **proud.** [From archaic *haught,* haughty, Middle English *haute,* from Old French *haut,* from Latin *altus,* high.] —**haugh·ti·ly** *adv.* —**haugh·ti·ness** *n.*

haul (hawl) *v.* **hauled, hauling, hauls.** —*tr.* **1.** To pull or drag forcibly; tug. **2.** To transport, as with a lorry; cart. **3.** To change the course of (a ship); especially, to sail (a ship) closer into the wind. Often used with *up.* **4.** To bring before a court or other authority, especially for a reprimand. Often used with *up*: *hauled up before the directors.* —*intr.* **1.** To pull; tug. **2.** To provide transport for heavy goods; cart. **3. a.** To change compass bearing in a clockwise direction. Used of the wind. **b.** To blow from a direction nearer the bow of a ship. Used of the wind. Compare **veer.** **4. a.** To sail, as on a certain course. **b.** To change the course of a ship. —**haul off. 1.** To steer a ship away from an object. **2.** *U.S.* To pull the arm back in order to deliver a blow.

~*n.* **1.** The act of pulling or dragging. **2.** The act of transporting or carting. **3.** The distance covered, or time taken, in travelling or transporting, or in achieving anything involving sustained effort: *the long haul to the South Pole.* **4.** Something that is pulled or transported; a load. **5.** Everything collected or acquired by a single effort; a take: *a haul of fish.* [Middle English *halen,* to pull, draw, from Old French *haler,* from Germanic.]

haul·age (háwlij) *n.* **1.** The act, process, or business of hauling. **2.** The force required to haul something. **3.** The charge made for hauling something.

haul·i·er (háwliər) *n.* Also *chiefly U.S.* **haul·er** (háwlər). **1.** One that hauls. **2.** A company dealing in the tranportation of goods by road.

haulm, halm (hawm) *n. Chiefly British.* **1.** The stems or stalks of peas, beans, potatoes, or grasses, used as litter for animals or for thatching. **2.** A single stalk of this kind. [Middle English *halm,* Old English *h(e)alm,* straw, stem.]*

haulyard. Variant of **halyard.**

haunch (hawnch ‖ haanch) *n.* **1.** The hip, buttock, and upper thigh in man and animals. **2.** The loin and leg of an animal as used for food: *a haunch of venison.* **3.** *Architecture.* Either of the sides of an arch, curving down from the apex to an impost. In this sense, also called "hance". —**sit on (one's) haunches.** To crouch down with the knees bent and buttocks resting on the heels. [Middle English *ha(u)nche,* from Old French *hanche,* from Germanic *hanka* (unattested).]

haunt (hawnt ‖ haant) *v.* **haunted, haunting, haunts.** —*tr.* **1.** To visit or appear to in the form of a ghost or other supernatural being. **2.** To visit often; frequent. **3.** To be frequently in the company of.

4. To recur to continually; obsess: *The riddle continued to haunt her.* **5.** To linger or remain in; pervade. —*intr.* To recur or visit often; especially, to appear habitually as a ghost or other supernatural being.

~*n.* (*U.S. also* hant *for sense 2*). **1. a.** A place much frequented. **b.** A place where animals usually gather to feed. **2.** *Regional.* A ghost or other supernatural being. [Middle English *haunten,* from Old French *hanter,* from Germanic.]

haunt·ing (háwnting ‖ háanting) *adj.* Continually recurring to the mind, especially in a poignant way; unforgettable. —**haunt·ing·ly** *adv.*

Hau·sa (hów-sə, -zə) *n., pl.* **Hausa. 1.** A member of a Negroid people of Niger and northern Nigeria. **2.** The language of this people, used widely as a trade language in Africa. —**Hau·sa** *adj.*

haus·frau (hówss-frow) *n. Chiefly U.S.* A housewife, especially one who is houseproud. [German *Hausfrau.*]

Hauss·mann (óss-man, hówss-, -mən), **Georges Eugène, Baron** (1809–91). French politician and town planner. He was responsible for rebuilding in Paris under Napoleon III.

haus·tel·lum (haw-stéllm) *n., pl.* **haustella** (-stéllə). The distal portion of the proboscis adapted as a sucking organ, seen in many insects, such as the bluebottle. [New Latin, from Latin *haustus,* past participle of *haurīre,* to draw, draw up.] —**haus·tel·late** (-stéllayt, háwstel-ayt) *adj.*

haus·to·ri·um (haw-stáwri-əm ‖ -stóri-) *n., pl.* **haustoria** (-ə). *Botany.* A specialised organ by which parasitic plants such as fungi obtain food from a host plant. [New Latin, from Latin *haustus,* past participle of *haurīre,* to draw, draw up.]

haut·boy (ó-boy, hó-) *n., pl.* **-boys.** Also **haut·bois** (ó-boy, hó-) *pl.* **hautboys.** *Archaic.* An oboe. [French *hautbois,* "high wood" (from its pitch) : *haut,* high, from Latin *altus* + *bois,* wood, from Germanic.]

haute cou·ture (ót kōō-téwr, kōō- ‖ -tóor) *n.* **1.** High-class dressmaking; high fashion. **2.** Leading clothes designers and dressmakers collectively. **3.** The clothes designed and made by these people. [French.]

haute cui·sine (ót kwi-zéen) *n.* High-class cooking; especially, that in the French tradition. [French.]

haute é·cole (ót ay-kól, -kól) *n.* The art, techniques, or practice of expert horsemanship. [French, "high school".]

hau·teur (ō-túr, -tôr, ō-tur ‖ hō-, -téwr) *n.* Haughtiness in bearing and attitude; arrogance. [French, from *haut,* high, pious, from Old French. See **hautboy.**]

haut monde (ó mónd) *n. French.* Fashionable society. [Literally, "high world".]

Ha·van·a (hə-vánnə). *Spanish* **Ha·ba·na** (a-báana). Capital city of Cuba. Situated on the northwest coast, it has an excellent natural harbour and is one of the largest cities in the West Indies. It was founded in 1519 by the Spanish and has been prominent since 1552 when it became the country's capital. Since the revolution (1959) it has been extensively modernised and an oil refinery has been built on the outskirts. The chief exports include tobacco (especially Havana cigars), sugar, rum, and clothing.

Havana cigar *n.* Also **Havana.** Any of several high-quality cigars made in Havana and elsewhere in Cuba, especially a very large type.

have (hav; *weak forms* həv, əv, v) *v.* **had** (had; *weak forms* həd, əd, d), **having, has** (haz; *weak forms* həz, əz, z, s). Present tense, first person **have**; second person **have** or *archaic* **hast** (for singular); third person singular **has** or *archaic* **hath**; third person plural **have.** Used as an auxiliary verb before a past participle to form the past, present, and future perfect tenses, indicating completed or virtually completed action: *We had left before dawn; They have done it; I shall have finished by then.* —*tr.* **1. a.** To be in possession of, as one's property; own: *have a big house.* **b.** To possess as a physical attribute: *have red hair.* **2. a.** To be related to: *have three aunts.* **b.** To be in a particular relationship to, as specified or implied: *has friends in high places; has a staff of 25.* **3.** To be in a position to make use of or enjoy: *have time to play.* **4.** To hold in one's mind; entertain: *have doubts.* **5.** To hold by law or entitlement. **6.** To bribe or buy off. **7.** To engage the attention of; captivate. **8.** To win a victory or advantage over: *He has you on that point.* **9.** *Informal.* To cheat, deceive, or trick. Often used in the passive: *I've been had!* **10.** To keep or put in a specified place, position, or condition: *have the carpet in the hall; had them eating out of his hand.* **11.** To accept or take: *I'll have the grey jacket.* **12.** To partake of; consume, as by eating or drinking. **13.** To obtain or receive. **14.** To be made of, consist of, or contain. **15.** To feel, as an emotion: *have great love for.* **16.** To exercise or bring into play. Used with *on*: *have mercy on me.* **17.** To allow; permit. Usually used in the negative: *I will not have the children out after dark.* **18. a.** To cause or arrange for (something to be done): *have the car fixed.* **b.** To order, invite, or compel: *have him go home; must have you over for a drink.* **19.** To perform (an action) or take part in (an activity): *have a look at this; have the next dance.* **20.** To engage in. **21.** To carry out or stage: *have a party.* **22.** To be the subject of: *have a large funeral.* **23. a.** To experience; undergo. **b.** To enjoy: *have a good summer.* **24.** To suffer from (a disease or physical disability, for example): *She has multiple sclerosis.* **25.** To give birth to; bear: *She's going to have twins.* **26.** To be compelled: *have to go now.* **27.** To be scheduled for: *have an appointment at noon.* **28.** To be able to use; be in command of or competent in: *have the necessary technique; has no Latin.* **29.** To come to know; be informed about: *have it on good* authority. **30.** To receive as a guest: *She has her mother-in-law for a fortnight.* **31.** To imply or state: *Rumour has it she's going to resign.* **32.** To be sick of. Used in the perfect tenses only: *I've had it up to here.* **—had better.** Ought to: *You had better go now.* **—had just as well.** Might as well. **—have at.** To attack. **—have done with.** To be through with; finish. **—have had it.** *Informal.* **1.** To be physically and mentally exhausted. **2.** To have lost a chance. **3.** To have become out-of-date and unfashionable. **—have it coming.** *Informal.* To deserve or be about to suffer retribution. **—have it in for.** To wish to harm. **—have it out.** To settle a dispute by a full discussion or by a fight. **—have on. 1.** To be wearing. **2.** *Informal.* To be scheduled for or committed to. **—have (someone) on.** To deceive in a teasing, lighthearted way. **—have something on (someone).** To have well-supported suspicions or incriminating evidence regarding someone. **—I have it.** I know the answer. **—let (someone) have it.** *Informal.* To attack (someone). **—not have any.** *Informal.* **1.** To refuse to tolerate. **2.** To refuse to become interested or involved. **—See Usage note at get.**

~n. **1.** A person or class enjoying material comforts, as opposed to a have-not. Used chiefly in the plural. **2.** *Slang.* A swindle. [Have, had, had, has; Middle English *haven* or *habben, hadde, had, has,* Old English *habban, hæfde, (ge)hæfd, hæbbe,* from Germanic *habbēn.*]

Ha·vel (haável), **Václav** (1936-). Czech playwright and human rights activist, and subsequently statesman. Both prize-winning dramatist and political prisoner under the former Communist government of Czechoslovakia, he became president of the country following the free elections held there in 1990. He was elected president of the Czech Republic on the break-up of Czechoslovakia in 1993.

have·lock (háv-lok, -lɔk) n. A cloth covering for a cap, having a flap to protect the back of the neck. [After Sir Henry *Havelock* (1795–1857), British general in India.]

ha·ven (háyv'n) n. **1.** A harbour or anchorage; a port. **2.** A place of refuge; a sanctuary. **—See Synonyms at shelter.** [Middle English, Old English *hæfen,* from Old Norse *höfn.*]

have-not (háv-not) n. A person or class enjoying few or no material comforts. Used chiefly in the plural.

have·n't (hávv'nt). Contraction of *have not.*

ha·ver (háyvər) *intr.v.* **-vered, -vering, -vers. 1.** *British.* To dither; vacillate. **2.** *Scottish & Northern English.* To chatter idly; babble. ~n. *Scottish & Northern English.* Foolish or inconsequential talk; chitchat or nonsense. [18th century : origin obscure.]

hav·er·sack (hávvər-sak) n. A canvas bag with straps worn over a shoulder or on the back to carry supplies on a hike or march. [French *havresac,* from German *Habersack,* originally bag for oats : *Haber,* oats + *Sack,* SACK.]

Ha·ver·sian canal (ha-vérsh'n, -vérzh'n) n. *Anatomy.* Any of the fine interconnecting channels that carry the blood and nerve supply in bones. [After C. *Havers* (1650–1702), English anatomist who discovered the channels.]

hav·er·sine (hávvər-sīn) n. *Mathematics.* Half the value of a versed sine. [Blend of *half* + *versed* + *sine.*]

hav·il·dar (hávvil-daar) n. A noncommissioned officer in the Indian army corresponding to a sergeant. [Hindi, from Persian *hawāldār,* one having charge.]

hav·oc (hávvək) n. **1.** Destruction, as caused by a natural calamity or war; devastation. **2.** Confusion; disorder; muddle. **—cry havoc.** To unleash anarchy. **—play havoc with.** To destroy, ruin, or make a mess of.
~v. havocked, -ocking, -ocs. *Poetic.* —tr. To destroy; devastate. —intr. To cause havoc. [Middle English *havok,* from Anglo-French, variant of Old French *havort†,* plunder, cry used to begin plunder.]

haw¹ (haw) n. A vocalised pause in speech.
~intr.v. hawed, hawing, haws. To pause in speaking. Used in the phrase *hem and haw.* See **hem** (short cough). [Imitative.]

haw² n. **1.** The fruit of a hawthorn. **2.** A hawthorn or similar tree or shrub. [Middle English *haw(e),* Old English *haga,* hawthorn, hedge, from Germanic.]

haw³ n. The nictitating membrane, especially of a domesticated animal. [16th century : origin obscure.]

Ha·wai·i (hə-wĬ-ee, haa-, -wáa-; *locally also* -vĬ-). A group of islands in the north Pacific; in 1959 it became the fiftieth state of the United States. Formerly the Sandwich Islands, it comprises more than 20 volcanic islands, including Maui, Kauai, Oahu (on which Honolulu, the state capital, is situated), and Hawaii, the principal and southernmost island of the group. Its economy depends on sugar-cane and pineapple cultivation, and tourism. Since Captain Cook's discovery of the islands (1778), the population and culture has become a mix of European, Oriental, and Polynesian.

Ha·wai·ian (hə-wĬ-ən, -yən ‖ haa-) n. **1.** A native or resident of Hawaii. **2.** The Polynesian language spoken by the inhabitants of Hawaii. **—Ha·wai·ian** adj.

Hawaiian Islands. See **Hawaii.**

haw·finch (háw-finch) n. A Eurasian bird, *Coccothraustes coccothraustes,* having a thick bill, brown, white, and black plumage, and a short tail. [HAW (fruit) + FINCH.]

haw-haw. Variant of **ha-ha** (laughter).

hawk¹ (hawk) n. **1.** Any of various birds of prey of the family Accipitridae, and especially of the genera *Accipiter* and *Buteo,* characteristically having a short, hooked bill and strong claws adapted for seizing. **2.** *Chiefly U.S.* Any of various similar birds. **3.** A grasping, rapacious, or ruthless person. **4. a.** One who favours an aggressive foreign policy. **b.** Broadly, one who takes a vigorous, uncompro-

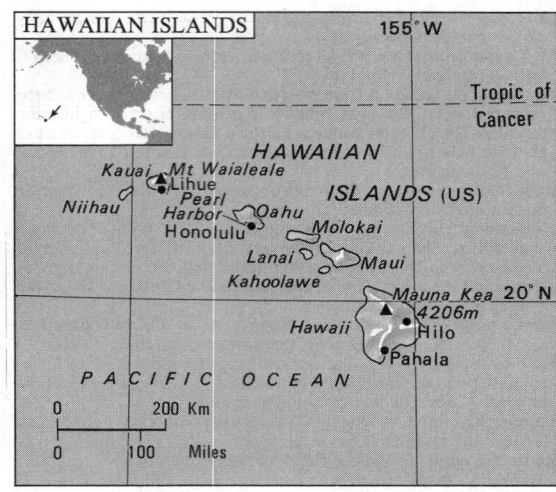

mising line on any matter of policy: *The hawks in the cabinet voted for further cuts in the education budget.* In this sense, compare **dove.**
~v. hawked, hawking, hawks. —intr. **1.** To hunt with trained hawks. **2.** To swoop and strike in the manner of a hawk. —tr. To hunt on the wing. Used of a bird. [Middle English *hauk,* Old English *h(e)afoc,* from Germanic.] **—hawk·er** n. **—hawk·ish** adj. **—hawk·ish·ness** n.

hawk² v. hawked, hawking, hawks. —intr. To peddle; especially, to peddle wares by crying them in the streets. —tr. **1.** To carry (goods) about in the streets and offer them for sale; peddle. **2.** To spread (gossip, one's opinions, and the like). [Back-formation from HAWKER.]

hawk³ v. hawked, hawking, hawks. —intr. To clear or attempt to cle⁓ ᴛhe throat by coughing up phlegm. —tr. To clear the throat by coughing up (phlegm).
~n. An audible effort to clear the throat by expelling phlegm.

hawk⁴ n. A small board with a handle on the underside, used to hold mortar or plaster. [17th century : origin obscure.]

Hawke (hawk), **Robert (James Lee)** (1929-). Australian politician. He was prime minister of a Labour government 1983-91.

haw·ker (háwkər) n. A pedlar, typically one who solicits business by calling at private houses. [Probably from Low German *höker,* from Middle Low German *hōker,* from *hōken,* to peddle, bend.]

hawk-eyed (háwk-īd) adj. Having very sharp eyesight.

hawk moth n. Any of various moths of the family Sphingidae, having a large body and long, narrow forewings. Most feed in flight on nectar from flowers. Also called "sphinx moth".

Hawks (hawks), **Howard** (1896–1977). U.S. film director. His films include the thrillers *Scarface* (1932) and *The Big Sleep* (1946), the western *Red River* (1948), war films such as *The Dawn Patrol* (1930), and comedies including *Bringing Up Baby* (1938).

hawk's-beard (háwks-beerd) n. Any of various plants of the genus *Crepis,* resembling the dandelion. [After its large bristly pappus.]

hawks·bill (háwks-bil) n. A tropical sea turtle, *Eretmochelys imbricata,* valued as a source of tortoiseshell.

Hawks·moor (háwks-moor, -mawr), **Nicholas** (1661–1736). English architect. He was a pupil of Sir Christopher Wren and worked with Vanbrugh, whose Blenheim Palace he completed.

hawk·weed (háwk-weed) n. Any of various plants of the genus *Hieracium,* having yellow or orange dandelion-like flowers.

Ha·worth (hów-ərth). Village in West Yorkshire, England. It was here that the Brontë sisters lived and wrote; some of their novels, including *Wuthering Heights,* are set in the surrounding countryside. The parsonage that was their home is now a museum.

hawse (hawz) n. *Nautical.* **1.** The part of a ship where the hawse-holes are located. **2.** A hawsehole or hawsepipe. **3.** The space between the bows of an anchored ship and her anchors. **4.** The arrangement of a ship's anchor cables when both starboard and port anchors are secured. [Middle English *halse,* probably from Old Norse *hals,* neck, ship's bow.]

hawse·hole (háwz-hōl) n. *Nautical.* An opening in the bow of a ship through which a cable or hawser is passed.

hawse·pipe (háwz-pīp) n. *Nautical.* A metal pipe running through a hawsehole, through which a cable or hawser is passed.

haw·ser (háwzər) n. *Nautical.* A cable or rope used in mooring or towing a ship. [Middle English *hauceour, hawser,* from Anglo-French *hauceour,* from Old French *haucier,* to lift, hoist, from Vulgar Latin *altiāre* (unattested), from Latin *altus,* high.]

haw·thorn (háw-thorn) n. Any of various thorny trees or shrubs of the genus *Crataegus,* especially *C. monogyna,* having white or pinkish flowers and reddish fruit. Also called "haw", "may", "may tree", "mayflower". [Middle English *haw(e)thorn,* Old English *hagathorn : haga,* HAW (fruit) + THORN.]

Haw·thorn (háw-thorn), **Mike,** born John Michael Hawthorn (1929–58). The first British world motor-racing champion. He died in a road accident only six weeks after winning the title in 1958.

Haw·thorne (háw-thorn), **Nathaniel** (1804–64). U.S. novelist and short-story writer. He was born at Salem in Massachusetts and won fame with the novels *The Scarlet Letter* (1850) and *The House of the Seven Gables* (1851). He was U.S. consul at Liverpool (1853–57).

hay (hay) *n*. 1. Grass or other plants such as clover, cut and dried for fodder. 2. *U.S. Slang*. A trifling amount of money. Used only in negative phrases, especially *that ain't hay*. —**hit the hay.** *Slang*. To go to bed. —**make hay (while the sun shines).** To take full advantage of an opportunity.
~*v*. **hayed, haying, hays.** —*intr*. To convert grass into hay. —*tr*. 1. To make (grass) into hay. 2. To feed with hay. 3. To put (land) under hay. [Middle English *hei, hay,* Old English *hīeg,* from Germanic.]

hay·box (háy-boks) *n*. A box filled with hay in which heated food can be left to continue cooking by retained heat.

hay·cock (háy-kok) *n. Chiefly British*. A conical mound of hay in a field.

Hay·dn (híd'n), **Franz Joseph** (1732–1809). Austrian composer. He wrote 104 symphonies and 84 string quartets, as well as operas and concertos. Among his works are the oratorios *The Creation* (1798) and *The Seasons* (1801). Mozart and Beethoven studied under him.

hay fever *n*. An allergic condition of the upper respiratory tract and the eyes, characterised by a running nose, watering eyes, and sneezing, due to histamine release caused by an abnormal sensitivity to certain airborne particles, notably pollen and dust.

hay·fork (háy-fawrk) *n*. 1. A long-handled pronged tool for moving hay; a pitchfork. 2. A machine-operated fork for moving hay.

hay·loft (háy-loft || -lawft) *n*. A loft for storing hay.

hay·mak·er (háy-maykər) *n*. 1. One who makes grass into hay. 2. A machine that makes hay; especially, one that processes it so that it dries evenly and quickly. 3. *Slang*. A powerful blow with the fist.

hay·mow (háy-mō) *n*. 1. A hayloft or haystack. 2. The hay stored in a hayloft or haystack.

hay·rack (háy-rak) *n*. 1. A rack from which livestock eat hay. 2. *U.S.* A rack fitted to a wagon for carrying hay.

hay·rick (háy-rik) *n*. A haystack.

hay·seed (háy-seed) *n*. 1. Grass seed shaken out of hay. 2. Pieces of chaff or straw that fall from hay. 3. *U.S. Informal*. A country bumpkin.

hay·stack (háy-stak) *n*. A large stack of hay, usually built up into a cuboid shape with a ridged top.

Haytian. Variant of **Haitian.**

hay·ward (háy-wərd, -wawrd) *n*. An officer formerly charged with the repair of fences and enclosures, and especially with the retention of cattle on the town common. [Middle English *hayward, heiward* : obsolete *heie,* hedge, fence, Old English *hege* + WARD.]

hay·wire (háy-wīr) *adj. Informal*. 1. Put together in a makeshift way. 2. Not functioning properly; broken or in a state of disorder. 3. Mentally confused or erratic; crazy. —**go haywire.** 1. To function improperly or fall into disorder. 2. To break down mentally and act erratically. [From the use of wire for hay-baling in various makeshift repair jobs.]

haz·ard (házzərd) *n*. 1. **a.** A source of potential loss or danger; a peril; a risk: *an occupational hazard.* **b.** Vulnerability to loss or danger: *at hazard.* 2. A chance or accident. 3. *Obsolete*. A gamble; a stake. 4. A dice game resembling the American game of craps. 5. Any of the openings in a real-tennis court through which the ball may be hit for points. 6. A bunker or other obstacle on a golf course. —See Synonyms at **danger.**
~*tr.v.* **hazarded, -arding, -ards.** 1. To imperil; jeopardise. 2. To run the risk of; expose oneself to. 3. To venture (something); dare: *hazard a guess.* [Middle English *hasard, hazard,* from Old French *hasard,* from Spanish *azar,* throw of the dice, accident, from Arabic *al-zahr,* luck, chance.]

haz·ard·ous (házzərdəss) *adj*. 1. Marked by danger; perilous. 2. Depending on chance; risky.

hazard warning signal *n*. The simultaneous flashing of all the direction indicators on a motor vehicle, used as a warning to other road users when the vehicle has broken down or is otherwise obstructing traffic.

HAZ·CHEM (ház-kem) *n. Haz*ardous *chem*icals. Used on warning signs.

haze[1] (hayz) *n*. 1. **a.** Atmospheric moisture, dust, smoke, or vapour causing mistiness and restricted visibility. **b.** *Meteorology*. The atmospheric condition so formed, when visibility is less than 2 kilometres (1.24 miles), but not less than 1 kilometre (0.62 miles). **c.** Indistinct visibility caused by rising heat: *a heat haze.* 2. A vague or confused state of mind.
~*v*. **hazed, hazing, hazes.** —*intr*. To become misty or hazy; blur. —*tr*. To make hazy. [Back-formation from HAZY.]

haze[2] *tr.v.* **hazed, hazing, hazes.** 1. *Nautical*. To persecute or punish with meaningless, difficult, or humiliating tasks. 2. *U.S.* To initiate, as into a college fraternity, by exacting humiliating performances from or playing rough practical jokes upon. [Perhaps akin to Old French *haser†,* to insult, harass.] —**haz·er** *n*.

ha·zel (háyz'l) *n*. 1. Any of various shrubs or small trees of the genus *Corylus;* especially, *C. avellana,* of Europe, or *C. americana,* of North America, bearing edible nuts enclosed in a leafy husk. Also called "cob". 2. The nut of such a tree or shrub, a hazelnut. 3. Light to strong brown or yellowish brown. [Middle English *hasel,* Old English *hæsel,* from Germanic.] —**ha·zel** *adj.*

hazel hen *n*. A Eurasian grouse, *Tetrastes bonasia,* having brownish-red plumage with grey and white markings. Also called "hazel grouse".

ha·zel·nut (háyz'l-nut) *n*. The edible nut of a hazel, having a smooth, hard, brown shell. Also called "cob", "cobnut", "filbert".

Haz·litt (házlit), **William** (1778–1830). British essayist and critic. He was a friend of Coleridge and Wordsworth. His works include *Characters of Shakespeare* (1817) and *The Spirit of the Age* (1825).

haz·y (háyzi) *adj*. **-ier, -iest.** 1. Marked by the presence of haze; misty. 2. Not clearly defined; vague; confused. [17th century (nautical) : origin obscure.] —**haz·i·ly** *adv*. —**haz·i·ness** *n.*

hazzan. Variant of **chazan.**

Hb haemoglobin.

HB *adj*. Designating a pencil or pencil lead that is medium hard. ~*n*. An HB pencil. [Abbreviation for *hard black.*]

H-beam (áych-beem || háych-) *n*. A steel joist or girder with an H-shaped cross section. Also called "H-girder".

H.B.M. Her (or His) Britannic Majesty ('s).

H-bomb (áych-bom || háych-) *n*. A **hydrogen bomb** *(see).*

h.c., H.C. 1. Holy Communion. 2. House of Commons.

h.c.f., H.C.F. highest common factor.

hd. 1. hand. 2. head.

hdbk. handbook.

hdqrs. headquarters.

he[1] (hee; *weak forms* ee, hi, i) *pron*. The third person singular pronoun in the nominative case, masculine gender. 1. Used to represent the male person, animal, or other being last mentioned or implied. 2. Used to represent any person whose sex is not specified: *Everyone knows he is mortal.* —See Usage note at **me.**
~*n*. 1. A male animal or person: *Is the cat a he?* 2. Often used in combination: *a he-cat.* [Middle English *he,* Old English *hē.*]

he[2] (hay) *n*. The fifth letter of the Hebrew alphabet. [Hebrew *hē,* possibly "lattice window".]

he[3] (hee) *interj*. Also **he-he.** Used to express amusement or derision.

he[4] (hee) *n*. A children's game, **tag** *(see).* [From HE (pronoun).]

He The symbol for the element helium.

HE, H.E. 1. high explosive. 2. His Eminence. 3. His (or Her) Excellency.

head (hed) *n., pl.* **heads** or **head** (for sense 7b). *Abbr.* **hd.** 1. **a.** The upper or anterior vertebrate extremity, containing the brain and the eyes, ears, nose, mouth, and jaws. **b.** The analogous part of an invertebrate. 2. The seat of the faculty of reason; intelligence, intellect, or mind. 3. **a.** A mental facility or aptitude: *a head for mathematics.* **b.** A natural ability to deal with the specified thing or situation without losing one's self-control: *no head for drink; a good head for heights.* 4. **a.** Poise; wits; composure: *Keep your head in a crisis.* **b.** Freedom to move or act without restraint. 5. A portrait or representation of a head. 6. Life: *a crime that cost him his head.* 7. **a.** An individual considered as a unit: *The cost is £5 per head; a head count.* **b.** A single animal within a herd: *20 head of cattle.* 8. The hair on the human head. 9. **a.** One who occupies the foremost position; a leader, chief, or director: *the head of a big engineering company.* **b.** A headmaster or headmistress. **c.** The foremost or leading position: *at the head of the parade.* 10. **a.** The difference in depth of a liquid at two given points. **b.** The measure of pressure at the lower point expressed in terms of this difference. **c.** Pressure, as of a liquid or vapour: *a head of steam.* 11. The foam on an effervescent liquid. 12. The breaking point or tip of a suppurating abscess, boil, or pimple. 13. A turning point; a crisis: *bring matters to a head.* 14. A projection, weight, or fixture at one end of an elongated object: *the head of a pin.* 15. The operating part of a tool, machine, or other device, such as: **a.** The working end of a hammer or axe. **b.** The operative part of a tape recorder or other device for recording and detecting stored information on magnetic tape or disks. **c.** The explosive part of a bomb, missile, or the like; a warhead. 16. A rounded, compact mass of leaves, or sometimes flower buds, as of cabbage, lettuce, or cauliflower. 17. *Botany*. A dense, compact cluster of flowers, as of composite plants or clover. 18. The end of an object whose two ends are interchangeable, such as a drum. 19. *Nautical*. **a.** The forepart of a vessel. **b.** The latrine of a vessel. **c.** The top part or upper edge of a sail. 20. The source of a stream; a headwater. 21. The upper end or extremity of something: **a.** The top of a staircase. **b.** The top of a page. **c.** The end of a bed where one's head lies. **d.** The end associated with a real or figurative head: *sitting at the head of the table.* **e.** The upper, landward end of a bay or lake. 22. A high promontory, cape, or cliff rising above a body of water. 23. A passage or gallery in a mine. 24. *Astronomy*. The coma and nucleus of a comet. 25. *Grammar*. The word in a construction that determines the grammatical character of the construction; for example, in the phrase *a lazy young boy, boy* is the head which determines that the whole structure functions as a noun. 26. A **cylinder head** *(see).* 27. **a.** A headline or heading. **b.** A distinct topic or category. 28. Headway; progress. 29. The head used as a rough unit of measure: *taller by a head; lost by a head.* 30. *Informal*. A headache. 31. *Slang*. A habitual user of drugs such as cannabis and LSD. —**bite (someone's) head off.** *Informal*. To speak angrily to someone. —**(down) by the head.** With the bow lying lower in the water than the stern. —**go to (someone's) head.** 1. To make lightheaded or drunk. 2. To increase the pride or conceit of. —**head and shoulders above.** Far superior to. —**in (one's) head.** In one's mind; internally: *did the sum in her head.* —**keep (one's) head above water.** To keep out of trouble, such as debt or poverty. —**not make head (n)or tail of.** To be completely baffled by. —**off (one's) head.** Crazy; insane. —**off the top of (one's) head.** Impromptu; without giving detailed consideration. —**on** or **upon (one's) head.** Within one's own responsibility, or at one's own risk: *"My deeds upon my head!"* (Shakespeare). **—(one's) head off.** *Informal.* Immoderately; inordinately; to extreme: *He snored his head off.* **—out of (one's) head. 1.** Delirious. **2.** High on drugs or alcohol. **—over (one's) head. 1.** Beyond one's ability to understand or deal with: *a subject that is over his head.* **2.** To one higher in command: *go over the sergeant's head.* **3.** Notwithstanding the claims of others: *promoted over the heads of several senior managers.* **—put** or **lay heads together.** To combine forces or abilities. **—take it into (one's) head.** To make a sudden decision to do something, especially something unusual or irrational. **—turn (someone's) head. 1.** To infatuate someone, especially if the passion inspired is groundless or rash. **2.** To make someone conceited. *~adj.* **1.** Foremost in rank or importance: *the head librarian.* **2.** Placed at the top or front: *the head name on the list.* **3.** Coming from ahead or the front: *head winds.*

~v. **headed, heading, heads.** *—tr.* **1.** To be director or chief of; command: *head the committee.* **2.** To assume or be placed in the first or foremost position of: *head the line of march.* **3.** To aim or direct: *head the horse for home.* **4.** To remove the top of (a plant or tree). Often used with *down.* **5.** In soccer, to drive (the ball) by hitting it with the head. **6.** To provide with a head or heading: *headed notepaper.* **—head off. 1.** To block the progress of and force to change direction; intercept. **2.** To forestall or deflect (criticism, for example). *—intr.* **1.** To proceed or set out in a specified direction: *head for town.* **2.** To proceed towards or be destined for a specified, usually undesirable, condition: *headed for bankruptcy.* **3.** To form a head, as lettuce or cabbage. **4.** To originate; rise. Used of a stream or river. [Middle English *heved, he(f)d,* Old English *hēafod,* from Germanic.]

head·ache (héd-ayk) *n.* **1.** A pain in the head caused by mental or emotional stress, fatigue, or illness. **2.** *Informal.* Someone or something that annoys or bothers. **—head·ach·y** (-ayki) *adj.*

head·band (héd-band) *n.* **1.** A band worn around the head. **2.** A cloth band attached to the top of the spine of a book.

head·bang (héd-bang) *intr.v.* **-banged, -banging, -bangs.** To shake the head in a wild, frenzied manner while dancing to heavy-metal music. **—head·bang·er** *n.* **—head·bang·ing** *n. & adj.*

head·board (héd-bawrd || -bôrd) *n.* A board, panel, or the like, that stands at the head, as of a bed.

head·case (héd-kayss) *n. British Slang.* A very stupid person; a nutcase.

head cold *n.* **Coryza** (see).

head·dress (héd-dress) *n.* Anything worn on the head, as a covering or ornament.

head·ed (héddid) *adj.* **1.** Growing or grown into a head. **2.** Having a head or heads of the specified type or number. Used in combination: *three-headed.* **3.** Having a mental make-up of the specified type. Used in combination: *level-headed.*

head·er (héddər) *n.* **1.** One that fits a head on an object. **2.** One that removes a head from an object; especially, a machine that reaps the heads of grain and passes them into a wagon or receptacle. **3.** A pipe that serves as a central connection for two or more smaller pipes. **4.** A brick laid across rather than parallel with the wall. Compare **stretcher. 5.** *Informal.* A headlong dive or fall. **6.** The action of striking the ball with the head in football. **7.** A raised tank or hopper that maintains a constant pressure or supply to some system, especially the small tank supplying water to a central-heating system. Also called "header tank".

head·fast (héd-faast || -fast) *n.* A mooring rope or chain that secures the bow of a ship to the quay.

head·first (héd-fúrst) *adv.* Also **head·fore·most** (héd-fór-mōst || -fôr-, -məst). **1.** With the head leading; headlong: *go headfirst down the stairs.* **2.** Impetuously; brashly. **—head·first** *adj.*

head gate *n.* A control gate upstream of a lock or canal.

head·gear (héd-geer) *n.* **1.** A covering, such as a hat or helmet, for the head. **2.** The part of a harness that fits about a horse's head. **3.** The rigging for hauling or lifting located at the head of a mine shaft. **4.** *Nautical.* The rigging on the forward sails.

head·hunt·ing (héd-hunting) *n.* **1.** The taking of human heads as trophies, practised for religious purposes in some primitive societies. **2.** *Informal.* The procurement of executive personnel. **3.** *U.S. Slang.* The process of eliminating or neutralising political rivals. **—head·hunt·er** *n.*

head·ing (hédding) *n.* **1. a.** A word or words at the head of a chapter, paragraph, letter, or the like. **b.** A division or category. **2.** *Navigation.* The course or direction of movement of a ship or aircraft. **3.** *Mining.* **a.** A gallery or drift. **b.** The farther end of a gallery or drift.

head·land (héd-lənd || -land) *n.* **1.** A point of land, usually high and with a sheer drop, extending out into a body of water; a promontory. **2.** The unploughed land at the end of a ploughed furrow.

head·less (héd-ləss, -liss) *adj.* **1. a.** Formed without a head. **b.** Decapitated. **2.** Without a leader or director. **3.** Witless; foolish.

head·light (héd-līt) *n.* A powerful lamp at the front of a vehicle, usually one of a pair. Also called "headlamp".

head·line (héd-līn) *n.* **1.** The title or caption of a newspaper article, set in large type, the size denoting the importance of the article. **2.** A line at the head of a page giving the title, author, page number, or the like. **3.** *Plural.* A brief resumé of the main items of interest at the beginning or end of a radio or television news bulletin.

~adj. Easy to publicise (as in headlines), especially because superficial or oversimplified: *the headline rate of inflation, different from the underlying rate.*

~tr.v. **headlined, -lining, -lines. 1.** To supply (an article or page) with a headline. **2.** *U.S.* To serve as the headliner of: *He headlines the bill.*

head·lin·er (héd-līnər) *n. U.S.* A performer who receives prominent billing; a star.

head·lock (héd-lok) *n.* A wrestling hold in which the head of one wrestler is locked under the arm of the other.

head·long (héd-long, -lóng || -láwng) *adv.* **1.** With the head leading; headfirst. **2.** Impetuously; rashly. **3.** At breakneck speed or with uncontrolled force.

~adj. **1.** Headfirst; done with the head leading: *a headlong fall.* **2.** Impetuous; rash. **3.** Uncontrollably forceful or fast. **4.** *Archaic.* Steep; sheer. **—See Synonyms at impetuous.** [Middle English *hedlong,* variant of *hedling* : *hed,* HEAD + -LING.]

head·man (héd-man, -mən) *n., pl.* **-men** (-men, -mən). A chief or leader of a tribe or village.

head·mas·ter, head master (héd-maástər, hed-, -maastər || -mástər, -mastər) *n. Abbr.* **H.M.** A male school principal.

head·mis·tress, head mistress (héd-míss-triss, hed-, -miss-, -trəss) *n.* A female school principal.

head money *n.* **1.** A reward paid for the capture and delivery of a fugitive; a bounty. **2.** *Archaic.* A poll tax.

head note *n.* A note at the beginning of a page or document; especially, one prefixed to a report of a legal case and summarising its contents.

head of state *n.* One, typically a monarch or president, who acts as the formal and ceremonial head of a nation, as opposed to the head of the government. The head of state may either be a figurehead or have executive power, depending on the constitution of the state.

head of the river *n. British.* **1.** Any of various rowing regattas; especially, one at which bumping races are held. **2.** The boat or crew holding the leading position in such a regatta.

head·on (héd-ón || -áwn) *adj.* **1.** Facing forwards; frontal. **2.** With the front end exposed and receiving the impact: *a head-on collision.* **3.** Direct and uncompromising. **—head-on** *adv.*

head over heels *adv.* **1.** Rolling, as if in a somersault. **2.** To the point of abandon; hopelessly: *head over heels in love.*

head·phone (héd-fōn) *n.* A receiver, as for a telephone, radio, or record player, held to the ears by a band that fits over the head.

head·piece (héd-peess) *n.* **1.** A helmet, hat, or other headgear. **2.** A set of headphones; a headset. **3.** *Printing.* An ornamental design at the top of a page. **4.** *Archaic.* The head as the seat of intellect.

head·quar·ter (héd-kwáwr-tər, hed-, -káwr- || -kwawr-, -kwaw-) *v.* **-tered, -tering, -ters.** *Chiefly U.S. Informal.* *—intr.* To establish headquarters. *—tr.* To provide with a headquarters. [Back-formation from HEADQUARTERS.]

head·quar·ters (héd-kwáwr-tərz, hed-, -kawr- || -kwawr-, -kwaw-) *pl.n. Abbr.* **hdqrs., h.q., HQ, H.Q.** *Sometimes used with a singular verb.* **1.** The offices of a commander, as of a military unit, from which official orders are issued. **2.** Any centre of operations: *Father makes the study his headquarters.*

head·race (héd-ráyss) *n.* A watercourse that feeds water into a mill, water wheel, or turbine. Compare **tailrace.**

head·rest (héd-rest) *n.* A support for the head, as at the back of a chair or car seat.

head·room (héd-rŏom, -rōōm) *n.* The vertical space in a room or under a bridge, doorway, or the like; clearance.

heads (hedz) *n. Used with a singular verb.* The obverse side of a coin, often carrying a representation of a head. Compare **tails.**

head·sail (héd-sayl, *nautical* -s'l) *n.* Any sail, such as a jib, set forward of a foremast.

head·scarf (héd-skaarf) *n.* A scarf worn over the head, usually folded in a triangle and tied under the chin.

head sea *n.* Waves running directly against the course of a ship.

head·set (héd-set) *n.* A pair of headphones.

head·ship (héd-ship) *n.* **1.** The position or office of the head or leader; primacy; command. **2.** *British.* The position of a headmaster or headmistress.

head shrinker *n.* **1.** *Slang.* A psychiatrist. **2.** A head-hunter who shrinks the heads of his victims.

heads·man (hédz-mən) *n., pl.* **-men** (-mən). Formerly, a public executioner who beheaded condemned prisoners.

head·spring (héd-spring) *n.* A fountainhead; a source.

head·stall (héd-stawl) *n.* The section of a bridle that fits over the horse's head.

head·stand (héd-stand) *n.* An act of balancing on the head, usually supported by the hands, with one's feet in the air.

head start *n.* A start before other contestants in a race, or any comparable advantage.

head·stock (héd-stok) *n.* A nonmoving part of a machine or powered tool that supports a revolving part, such as a lathe spindle.

head·stone (héd-stōn) *n.* **1.** A memorial stone set at the head of a grave. **2.** *Architecture.* A keystone (see).

head·strong (héd-strong || -strawng) *adj.* **1.** Inclined to insist on having one's own way; wilful; obstinate. **2.** Resulting from wilfulness or obstinacy. **—See Synonyms at obstinate, unruly.**

head waiter *n.* A waiter in charge of the other waiters in a restaurant, who often seats guests and generally serves as host. Also called "maître d'hôtel".

head·wa·ter (héd-wawtər) *n. Often plural.* The waters from which a river rises; the source.

head·way (héd-way) *n.* **1.** Forward movement or rate of forward movement, especially of a ship. **2.** Progress; advance. **3.** *Architec-*

ture. Headroom; clearance. **4.** The distance in time or space between two vehicles travelling the same route.

head wind *n.* A wind blowing directly against the course of an aeroplane or ship. Compare **tail wind**.

head·word (héd-wurd) *n.* A word placed at the beginning of a paragraph, or forming a heading; especially, a word entered and defined in a dictionary or encyclopedia.

head·work (héd-wurk) *n.* Mental activity or work.

head·y (héddi) *adj.* **-ier, -iest. 1.** Tending to upset the balance of the senses or mental faculties; intoxicating. **2.** Exciting; exhilarating. **3.** Headstrong; obstinate. **—head·i·ly** *adv.* **—head·i·ness** *n.*

heal (heel) *v.* **healed, healing, heals.** *—tr.* **1.** To restore to health; cure. **2.** To set right; amend: *healed the rift between us.* **3.** To rid of sin, anxiety, or the like; restore. *—intr.* **1.** To become whole and sound; return to health. **2.** To repair by natural processes, as by forming scar tissue. Used of cuts, wounds, and burns. [Middle English *helthe,* Old English *hælen;* akin to WHOLE.] **—heal·a·ble** *adj.*

heal-all (héel-awl) *n.* A plant, the **self-heal** *(see).*

heal·er (héelər) *n.* **1.** One that heals. **2.** A person who aims to cure by spiritual, magical, or other means not accepted by conventional Western medicine.

Hea·ley (héeli), **Denis Winston, Baron** (1917–). British Labour Party politician. He became an M.P. in 1952 and, as defence minister (1964–70), supervised British withdrawals from east of Suez. He was Chancellor of the Exchequer (1974–79), and deputy leader of the Labour Party (1980–83).

health (helth) *n.* **1.** The state of an organism with respect to functioning, disease, and abnormality at any given time. **2.** The state of an organism functioning normally without disease or abnormality. **3.** Broadly, any state of optimal functioning, well-being, or progress. **4.** A wish for someone's good health, expressed as a toast. [Middle English *helthe,* Old English *hælth.* See **whole, -th.**]

health centre *n.* A building containing the surgeries, offices, and other rooms of a group of general medical practitioners.

health farm *n.* A residential centre where people go to improve their health and fitness by following diets, taking exercise, undergoing massage, and the like.

health food *n.* Food considered to be beneficial to the health; especially, food that has been organically grown and has not been over-refined or processed. Also called "wholefood".

health·ful (hélthf'l) *adj.* **1.** Conducive to good health; salutary. **2.** *Rare.* Healthy. **—health·ful·ly** *adv.* **—health·ful·ness** *n.*

health physics *n. Used with a singular verb.* The branch of medical physics concerned with protection from radiation.

Health Service Commissioner. See **Ombudsman.**

health visitor *n.* A nurse who visits old and sick people and those with young children in their homes.

health·y (hélthi) *adj.* **-ier, -iest. 1.** Possessing good health. **2.** Conducive to good health; healthful: *healthy air.* **3.** Indicative of a rational or constructive frame of mind; sound: *a healthy attitude.* **4.** Indicative of or being in a sound and prosperous condition: *The firm's overseas operations are particularly healthy.* **5.** Sizable; considerable: *a healthy portion.* **—health·i·ly** *adv.* **—health·i·ness** *n.*

Synonyms: healthy, sound, wholesome, hale, robust, well, hardy, vigorous, well-preserved.

Heaney, Seamus (Justin) (1939–). Irish poet born in Ulster. His poetry is typified by dense, earthy imagery, and, increasingly, has shown a concern for the political crisis in Ulster. His books include *North* (1975), *Field Work* (1979), and *Spirit Level* (1996). Oxford professor of poetry (1989–94); Harvard professor of rhetoric and oratory (1985–97); Nobel prize (1995).

heap (heep) *n.* **1.** A group of things haphazardly gathered or in disorder; a pile. **2.** *Often plural. Informal.* A great deal; lots. **3.** *Slang.* An old or run-down car; a jalopy. **4.** *Slang.* A very untidy place.

~tr.v. **heaped, heaping, heaps. 1.** To put or throw in a heap; pile up. **2.** To fill to overflowing: *heap a plate with vegetables; a heaped tablespoonful.* **3.** To bestow (praise, for example) in abundance; lavish. [Middle English *heap, hep(e),* Old English *hēap,* from Germanic.]

hear (heer) *v.* **heard** (herd), **hearing, hears.** *—tr.* **1.** To perceive (sound) by the ear. **2.** To listen to attentively: *Hear me out.* **3.** To learn by the speech of others; be told; receive information. **4.** To listen to in an official, professional, or formal capacity: *The fourth witness was heard in the afternoon; hear someone's confession.* **5.** To listen to with favour; give consideration to: *Lord, hear my plea.* *—intr.* **1.** To be capable of perceiving sound. **2.** To receive communication in some form. Used with *from.* **3. a.** To be informed; learn: *I heard about your accident.* **b.** To encounter or experience. Used with *of: I've never heard of him!* **—hear tell (of).** *British Regional.* To learn or hear about something. **—not hear of.** To forbid mention or consideration of: *I won't hear of your going!* **—I hear you.** *Chiefly U.S. Informal.* I really do understand what you are saying – and the feeling behind it. **—hear hear!** Used to express agreement with a speaker. [Middle English *heren,* Old English *hīeran,* from Germanic.] **—hear·er** *n.*

hear·ing (héer-ing) *n.* **1.** The sense by which sound is perceived; the capacity to hear. **2.** The range of audibility; earshot. **3.** An opportunity to be heard. **4.** *Law.* An opportunity for a person to put forward arguments or evidence to a judge or tribunal concerning a matter under investigation; especially, a preliminary examination, a trial, or an appeal.

hearing aid *n.* A small electronic apparatus that amplifies sound

and is worn in or behind the ear to compensate for poor hearing. Also called "deaf-aid".

heark·en, hark·en (hárkən) *v.* **-ened, -ening, -ens.** *Archaic & Poetic.* *—intr.* To listen attentively; give heed. *—tr.* To listen to; hear. [Middle English *herk(n)en,* Old English *he(o)rcnian,* from *he(o)rcian,* to HARK.]

hear·say (héer-say) *n.* **1.** Information heard from another. **2.** *Law.* Evidence based on the reports of others rather than on a witness' own knowledge, and therefore generally not admissible as testimony. In this sense, also called "hearsay evidence".

hearse (herss) *n.* **1.** A vehicle for conveying a coffin. **2.** *Archaic.* A framelike structure over a coffin or tomb on which to hang epitaphs. [Middle English *herse,* harrow-shaped triangular frame for holding candles placed over a bier, from Old French, from Latin *hirpex* (stem *hirpic-*), harrow, rake, probably from Oscan (Samnite) *hirpus,* wolf (alluding to its teeth).]

Hearst (herst), **William Randolph** (1863–1951). U.S. newspaper magnate. He owned the *Morning Journal* from 1895, and pioneered popular journalism, building up the world's largest press empire.

heart (hart) *n.* **1. a.** *Anatomy.* The hollow, muscular organ in vertebrates that pumps blood through the circulatory system; it is divided vertically into two halves, each having an upper atrium and a lower ventricle. **b.** A similarly functioning structure in invertebrates. **2.** The approximate location of this organ in or on the body; the breast; the bosom. **3. a.** The heart thought of as the vital centre of one's being, emotions, and sensibilities; the seat or repository of emotions: *decided with his heart rather than his head.* **b.** The heart thought of as the repository of one's deepest and sincerest feelings and beliefs: *an appeal from the heart; a subject near to his heart.* **4. a.** Character, disposition, or emotional constitution: *a man after my own heart.* **b.** One's prevailing mood or inclination: *a heavy heart; a change of heart; My heart wasn't in it.* **c.** Capacity for sympathy or generosity; compassion: *He has no heart.* **d.** Love; affection: *The child won his heart.* **5. a.** Courage; resolution; determination: *Don't lose heart.* **b.** The firmness of will or lack of feeling required for an unpleasant task or responsibility: *didn't have the heart to tell him.* **6.** A person esteemed as lovable, loyal, or courageous: *a dear heart.* **7. a.** The central or innermost part: *the heart of the financial district.* **b.** The compact central part of a cabbage, artichoke, or the like. **c.** The essential feature; the most vital part: *get to the heart of the problem.* **8.** The condition of land with respect to fertility. Used chiefly in the phrase *in good heart.* **9.** A conventionalised two-lobed representation of the heart, usually coloured red or pink. **10. a.** The red, heart-shaped symbol appearing on one of the four suits of playing cards. **b.** A card bearing this symbol. **c.** *Plural.* The suit of cards identified by this symbol. Used with a singular or plural verb. See **hearts.** **—at heart.** Essentially; fundamentally. **—break (someone's) heart.** To cause someone disappointment, sorrow, or grief. **—by heart.** By memory or rote. **—eat (one's) heart out. 1.** To undergo bitter, hopeless anguish or longing. **2.** To be consumed with envy. **—have (one's) heart in (one's) mouth.** To be anxious or apprehensive to an extreme. **—have (one's) heart in the right place. 1.** To mean well; have good intentions. **2.** To be an admirable and worthy person. **—in (one's) heart of hearts.** In one's truest feelings. **—take to heart.** To take seriously and be affected or troubled by. **—to (one's) heart's content.** To one's entire satisfaction, without limitation. **—wear (one's) heart on (one's) sleeve.** To show one's feelings clearly by one's behaviour. [From Iago's comment, "But I will wear my heart upon my sleeve / For daws to peck at. . .", in Shakespeare's *Othello* (1604), Act 1, scene 1.]

~v. **hearted, hearting, hearts.** *—tr. Rare.* To encourage; hearten. *—intr.* To form a heart. Used of a cabbage, lettuce, or similar vegetable. [Middle English *he(o)rt, hart,* Old English *heorte.*]

heart·ache (hárt-ayk) *n.* Emotional anguish; deep sorrow. See Synonyms at **regret.**

heart attack *n.* **1.** An acute medical condition marked by a sudden severe pain in the chest, and sometimes also the arms and throat, resulting from abnormal functioning of the heart; especially, **coronary thrombosis** *(see).* See **myocardial infarction. 2.** An instance or episode of such a condition.

heart·beat (hárt-beat) *n.* A single complete pulsation of the heart.

heart·break (hárt-brayk) *n.* Intense sorrow or grief; crushing disappointment.

heart·break·ing (hárt-brayking) *adj.* Causing heartbreak; acutely saddening or pitiful. **—heart·break·ing·ly** *adv.*

heart·bro·ken (hárt-brōkən) *adj.* Suffering from crushing grief or despair; having a broken heart. **—heart·bro·ken·ly** *adv.* **—heart·bro·ken·ness** *n.*

heart·burn (hárt-burn) *n.* A burning sensation in the stomach and oesophagus, often accompanied by the eructation of small quantities of a highly acid fluid, caused by the regurgitation of stomach fluids; pyrosis. Also called "cardialgia".

heart disease *n.* Any organic or functional abnormality of the heart.

heart·ed (hártid) *adj.* Having or showing a specified kind of disposition or emotional make-up. Used in combination: *lighthearted; false-hearted.*

heart·en (hárt'n) *tr.v.* **-ened, -ening, -ens.** To give strength or hope to; encourage; cheer. **—heart·en·ing·ly** *adv.*

heart failure *n.* The partial mechanical failure of the heart as a pump, resulting in congestion of the lungs and liver, shortness and wheezing of breath, and oedema in the legs.

heart·felt (hárt-felt) *adj.* Deeply or sincerely felt; earnest. See Synonyms at **sincere**.

hearth (harth) *n.* **1.** The floor of a fireplace, usually extending into a room and paved with brick, flagstone, or the like. **2.** The hearth thought of as the centre of family life; the fireside; the home. **3.** *Metallurgy.* **a.** The lowest part of a blast furnace or cupola, from which the molten metal flows. **b.** The bottom of a reverberatory furnace where ore is exposed to the flame. **4.** The fireplace or brazier used by a blacksmith. [Middle English *herth,* Old English *heorth,* from Germanic.]

hearth-rug (hárth-rug) *n.* A rug laid on the floor in front of a fireplace.

hearth·stone (hárth-stōn) *n.* **1.** Stone used in the construction of a hearth. **2.** A soft stone or powder used for scouring and whitening a hearth, steps, or the like.

heart·i·ly (hártili, hárt'l-i) *adv.* **1.** In a hearty manner; with warmth, enthusiasm, or good appetite. **2.** Thoroughly; completely: *heartily sick of his complaining.*

heart·land (hárt-land) *n.* A central region; especially, one considered to be strategically, economically, or politically vital.

heart·less (hárt-ləss, -liss) *adj.* **1.** Without compassion; pitiless; cruel. **2.** *Archaic.* Without enthusiasm; spiritless. **—heart·less·ly** *adv.* **—heart·less·ness** *n.*

heart-lung machine (hárt-lúng) *n.* A machine used during heart surgery that bypasses the heart and lungs and circulates oxygenated blood round the body.

heart murmur *n.* A sound, audible through a stethoscope placed over the heart, produced by turbulent blood flow and typically indicating some structural abnormality. Also called "bruit", "murmur". **heart-rend·ing** (hárt-rending) *adj.* Causing anguish or deep sympathy; acutely moving.

hearts (harts) *n. Used with a singular or plural verb.* A card game in which the object is either to avoid hearts when taking tricks or to take all the hearts.

heart-search·ing (hárt-serching) *n.* An examination of one's innermost feelings.

hearts·ease, heart's-ease (hárts-eez) *n.* **1.** Peace of mind. **2.** A plant, *Viola tricolor,* native to Eurasia, having small, spurred, violet, yellow, or violet and yellow flowers. Also called "wild pansy". [Middle English *herts ease : herts,* genitive of *hert,* HEART + EASE.]

heart·sick (hárt-sik) *adj.* Sick at heart; profoundly disappointed; despondent. **—heart·sick·ness** *n.*

heart·some (hártsəm) *adj. British Regional.* **1.** Encouraging; that gives heart. **2.** Cheerful; blithe.

heart-start·er (hárt-startər) *n. Australian Slang.* The first drink of the day, especially the first alcoholic drink.

heart-strick·en (hárt-strickən) *adj.* Also **heart-struck** (-struk). Overwhelmed with grief, dismay, or remorse.

heart·strings (hárt-stringz) *pl.n.* **1.** The deepest feelings or affections. Often used facetiously: *a performance geared to tug at the heartstrings.* **2.** In notions of anatomy held before the 17th century, sinews and tendons bracing and sustaining the heart.

heart-throb (hárt-throb) *n.* **1.** A beat of the heart. **2.** An object of infatuation; an idol or sweetheart.

heart-to-heart (hárt-tə-hárt, -tōō-) *adj.* Personal and candid; frank. **~***n.* A frank and intimate conversation.

heart-warm·ing (hárt-wawrming) *adj.* **1.** Gratifying; encouraging. **2.** Moving.

heart·wood (hárt-wōod) *n.* The older, inactive, central wood of a tree or woody plant, usually darker and harder than the sapwood. Also called "duramen".

heart·worm (hárt-wurm) *n.* A nematode worm, *Dirofilaria immitis,* parasitic in the heart and bloodstream of dogs and other mammals.

heart·y (hárti) *adj.* **-ier, -iest. 1.** Expressed with warmth of feeling; exuberant and unrestrained: *a hearty welcome.* **2.** Complete or thorough; unequivocal: *hearty support.* **3. a.** Enjoying or requiring much food: *a hearty appetite.* **b.** Providing abundant nourishment; substantial: *a hearty bowl of soup.*
~*n., pl.* **hearties. 1.** A good fellow; a comrade; especially, a sailor. **2.** *British Informal.* A keen sportsman, especially at university. Often used derogatorily.

heat (heet) *n.* **1.** A form of energy associated with the motion of atoms or molecules. It is energy transferred as a result of a temperature difference, and is transmitted through solid and fluid media by conduction, through fluid media by convection, and through empty space by radiation. **2.** The perceptible, sensible, or measurable effect of such energy so transmitted; especially, a physiological sensation of being hot. **3.** An intense or pathological manifestation of such a perception or sensation; excessive warmth. **4.** The condition of being warm or hot. **5.** A hot season; hot weather. **6. a.** Intensity, as of colour, appearance, emotion, or effect. **b.** The point or moment of greatest intensity: *in the heat of the argument.* **7.** A period or condition of sexual excitement in female mammals, **oestrus** *(see).* **8. a.** A single course in a race or competition made up of several. **b.** A preliminary race or contest to determine finalists. **9.** *Slang.* **a.** Entanglement with or pursuit by the police. **b.** Loosely, pressure or harassment: *turn on the heat.*
~*v.* **heated, heating, heats.** **—***tr.* **1.** To make warm or hot. **2.** To excite the feelings of; inflame. **—***intr.* **1.** To become warm or hot. **2.** To become excited emotionally or intellectually. [Middle English *he(e)te,* Old English *hǣtu,* from Germanic.]

heat barrier *n.* **Thermal barrier** *(see).*

heat capacity *n.* The amount of heat required to raise the temper-

ature of a body by one degree, either at constant pressure or at constant volume and without inducing chemical changes or change of phase. See **specific heat capacity**.

heat content *n.* A thermodynamic function, **enthalpy** *(see).*

heat death *n.* A state of maximum entropy in a closed system; especially, the hypothetical fate of the universe when it runs down.

heat·ed (heetid) *adj.* Marked by anger and emotion; impassioned: *a heated exchange.* **—heat·ed·ly** *adv.*

heat engine *n. Physics.* A device for obtaining mechanical work from heat, as by the expansion of a gas.

heat·er (heetər) *n.* **1.** An apparatus that heats or provides heat. **2.** Someone who heats something or tends a heating apparatus. **3.** *Electronics.* An electrically heated filament that indirectly heats the cathode in a valve. **4.** *Chiefly U.S. Slang.* A pistol.

heat exchanger *n.* A device to transfer heat from fluid flowing on one side of a barrier to fluid flowing on the other.

heat exhaustion *n.* A reaction to excessive heat, marked by prostration, weakness, and collapse, resulting from dehydration. Also called "heat prostration". Compare **heat stroke.**

Heath (heeth), **Sir Edward (Richard George)** (1916–). British Conservative prime minister (1970–74). An MP since 1950, he was leader of the Conservative Party from 1965, and as prime minister took the United Kingdom into the EEC (1973).

heath (heeth) *n.* **1.** Any of various usually low-growing shrubs of the genus *Erica* and related genera, native to the Old World, having small, evergreen leaves and small, urn-shaped pink or purplish flowers. Many species are also called "heather". **2.** An extensive tract of open, uncultivated land often on sandy soil, covered with shrubby plants, especially heaths. **3.** Any of various butterflies of the genus *Coenonympha* in the family Satyridae. [Middle English *he(e)th, heath,* Old English *hǣth,* from Germanic.]

heath cock *n.* The male of the **black grouse** *(see).*

hea·then (heeth'n) *n., pl.* **heathens** or collectively **heathen. 1.** One who does not acknowledge the God of Judaism, Christianity, or Islam; especially, one who adheres to the polytheistic or animistic beliefs of a primitive people. **2.** One who is regarded as irreligious, uncivilised, or unenlightened. [Middle English *hethen,* Old English *hǣthen,* from Germanic, heath-dwelling, savage, from *haith-* (untested), HEATH; sense 1 probably influenced by Latin *pāgānus,* PAGAN.] **—hea·then** *adj.* **—hea·then·dom** (-dəm), **hea·then·ism, hea·then·ry** *n.*

hea·then·ish (heeth'n-ish) *adj.* **1.** Of or pertaining to heathens. **2.** Uncouth or barbarous in the manner ascribed to heathens. **—hea·then·ish·ly** *adv.* **—hea·then·ish·ness** *n.*

heath·er (hethər) *n.* **1.** A low-growing shrub, *Calluna vulgaris,* native to Eurasia, growing in dense masses and having small evergreen leaves and clusters of small, urn-shaped, pinkish-purple flowers. Also called "ling". **2.** Any of several similar, related plants of the genus *Erica* or other genera; heath. **3.** Greyish purple to purplish red. [Middle English (Scottish) *hadder, hathir†,* assimilated to *he(e)th, heath,* HEATH.] **—heath·er** *adj.*

heath·er·y (hethəri) *adj.* **1.** Of or like heather. **2.** Covered with heather: *heathery hills.*

heath hen *n.* **1.** The female of the **black grouse** *(see).* **2.** An extinct form of the prairie chicken, *Tympanuchus cupido.*

Heath Robinson *adj.* Ludicrously ingenious and complicated in design and construction. Said of a mechanical contrivance. [After William *Heath Robinson* (1872–1944), English cartoonist and book illustrator noted for his drawings of such contrivances.]

Heath·row (heeth-rō). Site of London Airport, 24 kilometres (15 miles) west of central London.

heat lightning *n.* Intermittent flashes of light across the horizon in summer unaccompanied by thunder and thought to be cloud reflections of distant lightning. Also called "summer lightning".

heat of fusion *n.* The quantity of heat required to melt a given mass of a solid at a given temperature. See **latent heat.**

heat of vaporisation *n.* The amount of heat required to convert a given mass of liquid into vapour at a given temperature. See **latent heat.**

heat pipe *n.* A device for conducting heat, consisting of a metal tube closed at both ends and containing volatile liquid at low pressure. Heat is carried down the tube by vaporised molecules of liquid, which returns by capillary action through a wire-mesh coating inside the tube.

heat prostration *n.* **Heat exhaustion** *(see).*

heat pump *n.* An engine that transfers heat from a relatively low-temperature reservoir to a hotter one, used for domestic heating.

heat rash *n. Pathology.* **Miliaria** *(see).*

heat-seal (heet-seel) *tr.v.* **-sealed, -sealing, -seals.** To seal by heating: *heat-sealed blood vessels.*

heat-seek·ing (heet-seeking) *adj.* Designating or pertaining to missiles that home on their target by sensing the radiant heat emitted. **—heat seek·er** *n.*

heat shield *n.* A barrier that prevents the heating of a space by absorbing, reflecting, or dissipating external heat; especially, a protective structure on a spacecraft or missile that dissipates heat on atmospheric re-entry by melting and vaporising.

heat sink *n.* **1.** An environment having a much greater heat capacity and at a lower temperature than an object with which it is in thermal contact. **2.** Any device by means of which heat is absorbed or stored in or removed from a thermal system.

heat stroke *n.* A severe illness caused by exposure to excessively high temperatures, and characterised by severe headache, high fever with a dry, hot skin, and, in serious cases, collapse and coma. Also called "sun stroke". Compare **heat exhaustion**.

heat-treat (héet-treet) *tr.v.* To subject (a material, especially a metal or alloy) to controlled changes of temperature in order to modify its properties.

heat-wave (héet-wayv) *n.* A long spell of unusually hot weather.

heave (heev) *v.* **heaved** or *chiefly nautical* **hove** (hōv), **heaving**, **heaves**. —*tr.* **1.** To raise or lift with strenuous effort; hoist. **2. a.** To throw with great effort (a heavy object, for example); hurl. **b.** To throw. **3.** To breathe or emit painfully or unhappily: *heaved a sigh.* **4.** *Nautical.* **a.** To raise (an anchor or net, for example). **b.** To pull on or haul (a rope or cable, for example). **5.** *Geology.* To cause (rock strata) to move in a horizontal direction. —*intr.* **1.** To rise up or swell, especially from turbulence; bulge; billow. **2.** *Informal.* To vomit or try to vomit. **3.** *Nautical.* **a.** To come to be in a specified position. Used of ships: *She hove alongside; hove into view.* **b.** To pull on or haul a rope, cable, or the like: *heave around on the anchor.* **c.** To push or pull, on a capstan bar or the like. —See Synonyms at **lift, throw.** —**heave to.** *Nautical.* To come to a stop, or to bring (a ship) to a stop.
~*n.* **1.** The act or strain of heaving. **2.** *Geology.* The horizontal movement of rock strata displaced by a fault. **3.** *Informal.* A throw, especially one made with considerable effort. **4.** A rising of the gorge; an attempt to vomit: *dry heaves.* **5.** Dismissal; the heave ho. Preceded by *the.* [Heave, hove, hove; Middle English *hebben* or *heven, hove, hove,* Old English *hebban, hōf, hafen,* from Germanic.]

heave ho (héev hō) *interj. Nautical.* Used as a command to give a hard push or pull together.
~*n.* Also **heave-ho.** *Slang.* Dismissal, especially from a job. Preceded by *the.* [Originally used for heaving up an anchor.]

heav-en (hévv'n) *n.* **1.** *Often plural.* The sky or universe as seen from the earth; the firmament. **2.** *Often capital* H. **a.** In the Christian tradition, the abode of God, the angels, and the souls of those who are granted salvation. **b.** In a number of other religions and mythologies, a place of bliss where the souls of the blessed go after death. **3. a.** *Capital* H. The divine Providence: *May Heaven help you.* **b.** *Often plural.* A euphemism for God, used in exclamations: *Good heavens!* **4.** *Plural.* The celestial powers; the gods: *The heavens favoured the young ruler.* **5. a.** Supreme happiness; a state of bliss. **b.** A thing or place which is wonderful or enchantingly perfect; a sheer delight: *The lake was heaven.* —**move heaven and earth.** To do everything possible to bring something about. [Middle English *heven, hefen,* Old English *heofon, hefen.*]

heav-en-ly (hévv'n-li) *adj.* **1.** Sublime; enchanting; lovely. **2.** Of or having to do with Heaven or the heavens; celestial. —**heav-en-li-ness** *n.*

heav-en-sent (hévv'n-sent) *adj.* Providential; occurring at an opportune time.

heav-en-wards (hév'n-wardz) *adv.* Also **heav-en-ward** (-wərd). Towards heaven. —**heav-en-ward** *adj.*

heav-er (héevər) *n.* **1.** One that lifts or heaves. **2.** *Nautical.* A short bar used as a lever for twisting rope.

heaves (heevz) *pl.n. Used with a singular or plural verb.* A pulmonary disease of horses, characterised by coughing and other serious respiratory irregularities. Also called "broken wind".

heav-i-er-than-air (hévvi-ər-thən-aír) *adj.* **1.** Denser than air. Said of a gas. **2.** Obtaining lift from aerodynamic forces rather than buoyancy. Said of an aircraft.

heav-i-ness (hévvi-nəss, -niss) *n.* The state or quality of being heavy.

Heav-i-side layer (hévvi-sīd) *n.* A layer of the earth's atmosphere, the **E layer** *(see).* [After Oliver *Heaviside* (1850–1925), English physicist.]

heav-y (hévvi) *adj.* **-ier, -iest. 1.** Having relatively great weight: *a heavy load.* **2.** Having relatively high density: *a heavy metal.* **3. a.** Of greater than average amount, volume, output, or the like; substantial: *heavy rainfall; a heavy turnout; heavy losses.* **b.** Of greater than average intensity, violence, or extent: *heavy fighting; a heavy frost; heavy seas.* **4.** Dense or thick: *heavy fog.* **5. a.** Indulging to a great or habitual degree; chronic: *a heavy drinker.* **b.** Involved or participating on a large scale; prodigious: *a heavy investor.* **c.** Requiring or consuming relatively large quantities: *The car is heavy on oil.* **6. a.** Of great import or seriousness; grave: *heavy matters of state.* **b.** Ponderous; requiring effort to assimilate: *The report makes heavy reading.* **c.** Sad or painful: *heavy news.* **7. a.** Laborious; arduous: *a heavy day at work.* **b.** Burdensome; oppressive: *heavy taxes.* **8. a.** Copious: *a heavy breakfast.* **b.** Not easily or quickly digested: *an unusually heavy fruitcake.* **9.** Marked by a lack of fineness or gracefulness; coarse; inelegant: *heavy features; a heavy style of architecture.* **10.** Overcast: *heavy skies.* **11.** Dull and deep, suggesting great weight. Said of a sound: *fell with a heavy thump.* **12. a.** Clayey and tending to retain water. Said of soil. **b.** Spongy and tending to retard progress. Said of the going on a racecourse. **13.** Weighed with concern or sadness; despondent: *a heavy heart.* **14.** Lumbering; clumsy. **15.** Strong and pervasive; pungent: *a heavy odour.* **16. a.** Weighed down, as from being full; laden: *trees heavy with plums.* **b.** Showing weariness; listless: *heavy eyes.* **17.** Involving the large-scale extraction of raw materials or the manufacture of large commodities such as aircraft, motor vehicles, or armaments: *heavy industry.* **18.** *Archaic.* Gravid; in an advanced state of pregnancy. **19.** *Theatre.* **a.** Of or pertaining to a serious or tragic dramatic role. **b.** Of or pertaining to the role of a villain. **20.** *Physics.* **a.** Designating an isotope with a mass greater than that of others found in the same element. **b.** Designating an atomic particle having a mass between that of pi mesons and protons. **21.** Bearing heavy arms or armour: *heavy cavalry.* **22.** *Slang.* **a.** Unpleasant or threatening: *a heavy scene.* **b.** Too intimate or demanding: *Don't get heavy with me.*
~*adv.* Heavily. —**hang heavy.** To pass slowly or tediously: *Time hung heavy on his hands.*
~*n., pl.* **heavies. 1.** A villain in a story or play. **2.** *Informal.* A ruffian; a tough: *a gang of heavies.* **3.** *Informal.* An important or influential person; a heavyweight. **4. a.** A serious or tragic role in a play. **b.** An actor playing such a role. **5.** A serious, up-market newspaper. **6.** *Scottish.* Heavy bitter beer. [Middle English *hevi,* Old English *hefig,* from Germanic.] —**heav-i-ly** *adv.*
Synonyms: heavy, weighty, hefty, massive, ponderous, cumbersome, unwieldy.

heav-y-dut-y (hévvi-déwti ‖ -dōoti) *adj.* Made for hard use or wear.

heav-y-foot-ed (hévvi-fōotid) *adj.* Having a heavy, lumbering gait.

heav-y-hand-ed (hévvi-hándid) *adj.* **1.** Clumsy. **2.** Tactless. **3.** Oppressive. —**heav-y-hand-ed-ly** *adv.* —**heav-y-hand-ed-ness** *n.*

heav-y-heart-ed (hévvi-hártid) *adj.* Melancholy; sad; depressed. —**heav-y-heart-ed-ly** *adv.* —**heav-y-heart-ed-ness** *n.*

heavy hydrogen *n.* An isotope of hydrogen with mass number greater than 1, especially **deuterium** *(see).*

heav-y-lad-en (hévvi-láyd'n) *adj.* **1.** Laden with a heavy load. **2.** Burdened with cares; troubled.

heavy metal *n.* A style of rock music characterised by a heavy bass beat and the use of powerful amplification. —**heav-y-met-al** (hévvi-métt'l) *adj.*

heav-y-set (hévvi-sét) *adj.* Having a heavy, compact build.

heavy spar *n.* A mineral, barytes *(see).*

heavy water *n.* Any of several isotopic varieties of water, especially **deuterium oxide** *(see),* consisting chiefly or exclusively of molecules containing hydrogen with mass number of 2, and used as a moderator in certain nuclear reactors.

heav-y-weight (hévvi-wayt) *n.* **1.** One of above average weight. **2.** One that competes in the heaviest class, specifically: **a.** A professional boxer of any weight, usually weighing more than 12 stone 7 pounds (79 kilograms). **b.** An amateur boxer weighing more than 81 kilograms (179 pounds). **c.** A wrestler weighing over 97 kilograms (214 pounds). **3.** *Informal.* A person of great importance or influence.

Heb. 1. Hebrew. **2.** Hebrews (New Testament).

heb-do-mad (hébdə-mad) *n. Rare.* **1.** A group of seven. **2.** A period of seven days; a week. [Latin *hebdomas* (stem *hebdomad-*), the number seven, seven days, from Greek, from *hepta,* seven.]

heb-dom-a-dal (heb-dómməd'l) *adj.* Weekly. —**heb-dom-a-dal-ly** *adv.*

Hebdomadal Council *n.* The governing board of Oxford University, which meets weekly.

he-be (héebi) *n.* Any plant of the genus *Hebe,* which contains small evergreen shrubs with spikes of variously coloured flowers, widely grown as garden ornamentals. Also called "shrubby veronica". [New Latin, after HEBE.]

He-be (héebi). *Greek Mythology.* The goddess of youth and spring, the cupbearer of Zeus. [Greek *Hēbē,* personification of *hēbē,* youth, youthful vigour.]

He-bei or **Ho-pei** or **Ho-peh** (húbbáy, hō-páy). Province of northeast China, the oldest continuously civilised area in the world. Tianjin (or Tientsin) is the capital.

he-be-phre-ni-a (héebi-fréeni-ə) *n.* A schizophrenia, typically starting at puberty, characterised by foolish mannerisms, apathy, senseless laughter, and regressive behaviour. [Greek *hēbē,* youth + -PHRENIA.] —**he-be-phren-ic** (-frénnik) *adj.*

heb-e-tate (hébbi-tayt) *tr.v.* **-tated, -tating, -tates.** *Rare.* To make blunt or dull. [Latin *hebetāre,* from *hebes†* (stem *hebet-*), blunt, dull.] —**heb-e-ta-tion** (-táysh'n) *n.* —**heb-e-ta-tive** (-tətiv, -taytiv) *adj.*

heb-e-tude (hébbi-tewd ‖ -tōod) *n.* Dullness of mind; mental lethargy. [Late Latin *hebetūdo* : Latin *hebes* (stem *hebet-*), blunt, dull + -TUDE.] —**heb-e-tu-di-nous** (-téwdi-nəss ‖ -tōodi-) *adj.*

Hebr. Hebrew.

He-bra-ic (hee-bráy-ik, hi-) *adj.* Of, pertaining to, or characteristic of the Hebrews or their language or culture. [Middle English *Ebrayke,* from Late Latin *Hebraicus,* from Greek *Hebraikos,* from *Hebraios,* HEBREW.] —**He-bra-i-cal-ly** *adv.*

He-bra-ise, He-bra-ize (hée-bray-īz) *v.* **-ised, -ising, -ises.** —*tr.* To make Hebraic in form or idiom. —*intr.* To use or adopt Hebraisms.

He-bra-ism (hée-bray-iz'm) *n.* **1.** A manner or custom characteristic of the Hebrews; especially, a Hebrew expression or idiom. **2.** The culture, spirit, or character of the Hebrew people. [From HEBRAIC.]

He-bra-ist (hée-bray-ist) *n.* A scholar of Hebrew. —**He-bra-is-tic** (-ístik), **He-bra-is-ti-cal** *adj.* —**He-bra-is-ti-cal-ly** *adv.*

He-brew (hée-brōo ‖ -brew) *n. Abbr.* **Heb., Hebr. 1.** A member of the Semitic people claiming descent from Abraham, Isaac, and Jacob; an Israelite; a Jew. **2. a.** The Semitic language of the ancient Hebrews, used in most of the Old Testament. **b.** Any of various later forms of this language, especially the form now spoken by the people of Israel. [Middle English *Ebreu, Hebrewe,* from Old French *Ebreu,* from Latin *Hebraeus,* Hebraic, from Greek *Hebraios,* from Aramaic *'ibhray, 'ebhray,* from Hebrew *'ibhrī,* "he who came from across (the river)", from *'ēbher,* region across, from *ābhar,* to pass across or over.] —**He-brew** *adj.*

Hebrew calendar *n.* The **Jewish calendar** *(see).*

He·brews (hée-brōōz ‖ -brewz) *n. Abbr.* **Heb.** *Used with a singular verb.* A book of the New Testament, the Epistle to the Hebrews.

Hebrew Scriptures *pl.n.* The Pentateuch, the Prophets, and the Hagiographa, forming the covenant between God and the Jewish people that is the foundation and Bible of Judaism, while constituting for Christians the **Old Testament** *(see).*

Heb·ri·des (hébbri-deez), **The.** Also **Western Isles, The.** An archipelago of about 500 islands off the western coast of Scotland. It is divided into the Outer Hebrides, including Lewis, Harris, and the Uists; and the Inner Hebrides, including Skye, Mull, and Islay. —**Heb·ri·de·an** (hébbri-dée-ən) *n. & adj.*

Heb·ron (héb-rən, héeb-). *Arabic* **Al Kha·lil** (al khaaléel). Town on the Israeli-occupied West Bank, Jordan. It is one of the oldest inhabited cities in the world and is the traditional site of Abraham's tomb.

Hec·a·te (héckəti; *in Shakespeare also* héckət). *Greek Mythology.* An ancient fertility goddess who later became identified with Persephone as queen of Hades and protectress of witches.

hec·a·tomb (héckə-tōōm, -tōm) *n.* **1.** In ancient Greece, a large-scale public offering to the gods, originally of 100 oxen. **2.** Any large-scale sacrifice. [Latin *hecatombē,* from Greek *hekatombē* : *hekaton,* hundred + *-bē,* from *bous,* ox.]

heck¹ (hek) *n.* Used as an intensive, as a euphemism for **hell** (sense 8): *ran like heck.* ~*interj.* Used as a euphemism for **hell.**

heck² *n. Northern British.* A frame or grating that obstructs the passage of fish in a river. [Middle English (northern dialect), variant of HATCH.]

heck·el·phone (héck'l-fōn) *n. Music.* A bass oboe having a pitch between that of the cor anglais and the bassoon. [German *Heckelphon,* after Wilhelm *Heckel* (1856–1909), German instrument-maker.]

heck·le (héck'l) *v.* **-led, -ling, -les.** —*tr.* **1.** To harass (a speaker or performer) persistently, as with questions, gibes, or objections; badger publicly. **2.** To comb (flax or hemp) with a hatchel. —*intr.* To engage in heckling a speaker or interrupting a public meeting. [Middle English *hekelen,* to comb flax, from *hekell, hechele,* flaxcomb, hatchel, Old English *hæcel* (unattested).] —**heck·ler** *n.*

hec·tare (héktair) *n. Abbr.* **ha** A metric unit of area equal to 10 000 square metres or 2.471 acres. [French : HECT(O)- + ARE.]

hec·tic (héktik) *adj.* **1.** Characterised by feverish activity, confusion, or haste. **2.** Of, relating to, or designating an undulating fever, as in diseases such as tuberculosis or septicaemia. **3.** Consumptive; feverish. **4.** Flushed. ~*n.* **1.** A hectic fever. **2.** A person suffering from a hectic fever. [Middle English *etik,* from Old French *etique,* from Late Latin *hecticus,* from Greek *hektikos,* formed by habit, consumptive, hectic, from *hexis,* condition, habit, from *ekhein,* to have, hold, be in a certain condition.]

hecto-, hect- *comb. form. Symbol* **h** Indicates 100; for example, **hectocotylus, hectare.** [French, from Greek *hekaton,* hundred.]

hec·to·cot·y·lus (héktō-kótti-ləss) *n., pl.* **-li** (-lī). A modified arm of the male of certain cephalopods, such as the octopus, containing sperm and functioning as a reproductive organ. Also called "hectocotylus arm". [New Latin *Hectocotylus,* name given by G. L. Cuvier to the detached arm which he thought was a parasitic worm : HECTO- + Greek *kotulē,* cup, hollow object (see **cotyledon**).]

hec·to·gram, hec·to·gramme (hék-tə-gram, -tō-) *n. Abbr.* **hg** A metric unit of mass equal to 100 grams or 3.527 avoirdupois ounces.

hec·to·graph (hék-tə-graaf, -tō-, -graf) *n.* A machine using a glycerine-coated layer of gelatine to make copies of typed or written material. Also called "copygraph". ~*tr.v.* **hectographed, -graphing, -graphs.** To copy by means of a hectograph. [German *Hektograph* : HECTO- + -GRAPH.] —**hec·to·graph·ic** (-gráffik) *adj.* —**hec·to·graph·i·cal·ly** *adv.*

hec·to·li·tre (hék-tə-léetər, -tō-) *n. Abbr.* **hl** *n.* A unit of volume equal to 100 litres (about 22 gallons).

hec·to·me·tre (hék-tə-méetər, -tō-) *n. Abbr.* **hm** A metric unit of length equal to 100 metres (about 328 feet).

hec·tor (héktər) *v.* **-tored, -toring, -tors.** —*tr.* To intimidate in a blustering way. —*intr.* To behave like a bully; swagger. ~*n.* A bully. [After HECTOR.]

Hec·tor (héktər). In Greek legend, a Trojan prince who led the forces of Troy in the Trojan war and was killed by Achilles. [Greek *Hektōr.*]

Hec·u·ba (héckewbə). In Greek legend, the wife of Priam and mother of Hector, Paris, and Cassandra.

he'd (heed; *weak forms* eed, hid, id). **1.** Contraction of *he had.* **2.** Contraction of *he would.*

hed·dle (héddl) *n.* One of a set of parallel cords or wires in a loom used to separate and guide the warp threads and make a path for the shuttle. [Probably altered from Middle English *helde,* heddle, Old English *hefeld,* from Germanic *hafjan* (unattested), to raise.]

heder Variant of *cheder.*

hedge (hej) *n.* **1. a.** A row of closely planted shrubs or low-growing trees forming a fence or boundary. **b.** A line of objects or people forming a barrier. **2.** A means of protection or defence, especially against financial loss. **3. a.** An intentionally noncommittal or ambiguous hedging statement. **b.** A qualifying expression such as *typically, especially, generally.* ~*v.* **hedged, hedging, hedges.** —*tr.* **1.** To enclose or bound with or as if with a hedge or hedges. **2.** To restrict; hem in; confine.

Often used with *in* or *about.* **3.** To counterbalance (a bet, for example) with other transactions, so as to limit the risk of loss. —*intr.* **1.** To plant or cultivate a hedge or hedges. **2.** To take compensatory measures against possible loss. **3.** To avoid committing oneself, as by making cautious or ambiguous statements. [Middle English *hegge,* Old English *hegg, hecg* (unattested), from Germanic.] —**hedg·er** *n.* —**hedg·y** *adj.*

hedge·hog (héj-og, -hog ‖ *U.S. also* -hawg) *n.* **1.** Any of several small Old World mammals of the family Erinaceidae, and especially of the genus *Erinaceus,* having the back covered with dense, erectile spines, and characteristically rolling into a ball for protection. **2.** *Chiefly U.S.* Any of several similar spiny animals. **3.** The spiny, burlike fruit of any of several plants. **4.** *Military.* An emplacement bristling with fortifications. [From the animal's piglike snout and its habit of frequenting hedges.]

hedge·hop (héj-hop) *intr.v.* **-hopped, -hopping, -hops.** To fly an aircraft close to the ground, rising above objects as they appear, as for spraying crops. —**hedge·hop·per** *n.*

hedge·row (héj-rō) *n.* A row of bushes, shrubs, or trees forming a hedge.

hedge sparrow *n.* A European bird, *Prunella modularis,* of the family Prunellidae, having brownish plumage streaked with black. Also called "dunnock".

he·don·ic (hee-dónnik, hi-) *adj.* **1.** Of, pertaining to, or marked by pleasure. **2.** Of hedonism or hedonics. [Greek *hēdonikos,* from *hēdonē,* pleasure.]

he·don·ics (hee-dónniks, hi-) *n. Used with a singular verb.* **1.** *Psychology.* The study of pleasant and unpleasant sensations. **2.** *Philosophy.* A branch of ethics that deals with the relation of pleasure to duty.

he·don·ism (héed'n-iz'm, héedōn-) *n.* **1.** Pursuit of or devotion to pleasure, especially the pleasures of the senses. **2.** The ethical doctrine that only that which is pleasant is intrinsically good. **3.** *Psychology.* The doctrine that behaviour is motivated by the desire for pleasure and the avoidance of pain. [Greek *hēdonē,* pleasure + -ISM.] —**he·don·ist** *n.* —**he·don·is·tic** (-ístik) *adj.* —**he·don·is·ti·cal·ly** *adv.*

-hedral *adj. comb. form.* Indicates surfaces or faces; for example, **dihedral, polyhedral.** [From -HEDRON.]

-hedron *n. comb. form, pl.* **-hedra.** Indicates a geometric figure having faces or surfaces; for example, **pentahedron, polyhedron.** [Greek *-edron,* from *hedra,* base, seat.]

hee·bie-jee·bies (héebi-jeébiz) *pl.n. Slang.* Feelings of uneasiness or nervousness; the jitters. [20th century : origin obscure.]

heed (heed) *v.* **heeded, heeding, heeds.** —*tr.* To pay attention to; listen to and consider. —*intr.* To pay attention. ~*n.* Close attention or consideration. [Middle English *heden,* Old English *hēdan,* from Germanic.]

heed·ful (héedf'l) *adj.* Paying close attention; taking heed; mindful. —**heed·ful·ly** *adv.* —**heed·ful·ness** *n.*

heed·less (héed-ləss, -liss) *adj.* Paying little or no attention; not taking heed; unmindful. See Synonyms at **careless, impetuous, forgetful.** —**heed·less·ly** *adv.* —**heed·less·ness** *n.*

hee-haw (hée-haw, -háw) *n.* **1.** The braying sound made by a donkey. **2.** A noisy laugh; a guffaw. ~*intr.v.* **heehawed, -hawing, -haws.** **1.** To bray. **2.** To laugh noisily; guffaw. [Imitative.]

heel¹ (heel) *n.* **1.** The rounded posterior portion of the human foot under and behind the ankle. **2.** A corresponding part in other vertebrates. **3.** That part of footwear, such as a sock, shoe, or stocking, that covers the heel. **4.** The built-up portion of a shoe or boot, supporting the heel. **5.** Either of the crusty ends of a loaf of bread. **6.** Something resembling the heel in position or shape; a lower, rearward surface, such as: **a.** The cushion of muscle on the palm of the hand below the thumb. **b.** The head of a golf club where it joins the shaft. **c.** The handle end of a violin bow. **d.** The lower end of a mast. **e.** The aft end of a ship's keel. **7.** *Horticulture.* The basal end of a cutting, tuber, or other plant part used in propagation. **8.** In Rugby football, the possession of the ball after a scrum. Used chiefly in the phrase *get the heel.* **9.** *Slang.* A callous or dishonourable man; a cad. —**cool** or **kick (one's) heels.** To be kept waiting for a long time, especially out of deliberate rudeness. —**dig (one's) heels in.** To refuse to compromise or change one's position. —**down at heel.** **1.** Having one's shoe heels worn down. **2.** Shabby; run-down. —**lay by the heels.** To put in fetters or shackles; imprison or confine: *"If the king blames me for 't, I'll lay ye all/By the heels."* (Shakespeare). —**on** or **upon the heels of.** **1.** Directly behind. **2.** Immediately following. —**show a clean pair of heels.** To run away. —**take to (one's) heels.** To flee; run away. —**to heel. 1.** Close behind; at one's heel. **2.** Under control; disciplined. —**under the heel of.** Dominated or subjugated by. ~*interj.* Used when ordering a dog to keep to heel. ~*v.* **heeled, heeling, heels.** —*tr.* **1.** To furnish with a heel or repair the heels of. **2.** To follow upon the heels of; follow closely behind. **3. a.** In Rugby football, to kick (the ball) backwards using the heel. **b.** In golf, to strike (the ball) with the heel of the club. —*intr.* **1.** To follow at someone's heels. **2.** To perform a dance step or movement with the heels. [Middle English *heel, he(e)le,* Old English *hēla,* from Germanic.] —**heel·less** *adj.*

heel² *v.* **heeled, heeling, heels.** —*intr.* To tip to one side; tilt; list. Used especially of ships. —*tr.* To cause (a ship) to list. ~*n.* A tilting or inclining to one side; a cant; a list. [Probably from obsolete *heeld,* to incline, Middle English *he(e)lden,* Old English *hieldan,* from Germanic.]

heel-and-toe (héel-ən-tó) *adj.* Characterised by a stride in which the heel of one foot touches ground before the toe of the other foot is lifted, as in walking races.
~*intr.v.* **heel-and-toed, -toeing, -toes.** To operate the brake and accelerator of a car with the heel and toes of the same foot.

heel ball *n.* A coloured wax used to stain and polish the edges of the soles and heels of shoes, or for taking brass rubbings.

heel bar *n.* A small shop or a counter in a large shop where shoes are repaired while the customer waits.

heel bone *n.* The calcaneus *(see).*

heeled (heeld) *adj.* **1.** Having or fitted with heels. **2.** *Slang.* Provided with money.

heel-er (héelər) *n.* **1.** One who heels shoes. **2.** *U.S. Informal.* A **ward heeler** *(see).*

heel-post (héel-pōst) *n.* The post to which a door or gate is hinged.

heel-tap (héel-tap) *n.* **1.** A layer of material added to the heel of a shoe; a lift. **2.** A small amount of alcoholic drink remaining in a container or drinking vessel.

Hee-nan (héenən), **Cardinal John Carmel** (1905–75). English Roman Catholic prelate. In 1963 he became Archbishop of Westminster, and two years later was created a cardinal.

heft (heft) *n. British Regional & U.S. Informal.* Weight; heaviness; bulk.
~*tr.v.* **hefted, hefting, hefts.** *British Regional & U.S. Informal.* **1.** To determine or estimate the weight of by lifting. **2.** To hoist up; heave. [From HEAVE (by analogy with such pairs as *cleave, cleft*).]

heft-y (héfti) *adj.* **-ier, -iest. 1.** Weighty; heavy. **2.** Large and powerful; bulky; muscular. **3.** Large in amount: *a hefty fine.* —See Synonyms at **heavy.**

He-gel (háyg'l), **Georg Wilhelm Friedrich** (1770–1831). German philosopher. His main works, including *Encyclopedia of the Philosophical Sciences* (1817) and the *Philosophy of Right* (1821), proposed that truth is reached by a continuing dialectic: an initial *thesis,* when found unsatisfactory, generates an *antithesis;* these interact to form a *synthesis,* which may itself constitute a new thesis. Marx and Engels adapted the theory.

He-ge-li-an-ism (hay-gée-li-ən-iz'm, hi-, -gáy-) *n.* The monist, idealist philosophy of Hegel and his followers; especially, Hegel's doctrine of the "phenomenology of the mind", whereby all that exists must be mental, and therefore thought is reality; history, and especially the history of thought, represents the search for truth through **dialectic** *(see).* —**He-ge-li-an** *adj. & n.*

he-gem-o-ny (hee-gémməni, hi-, héji-məni ‖ *chiefly U.S.* -jémməni, héji-mōni) *n., pl.* **-nies.** Predominance; rule; especially, the preponderant influence of one state over others. [Greek *hēgemonia,* authority, rule, from *hēgemōn,* leader, from *hēgeisthai,* to lead.] —**heg-e-mon-ic** (hégg-mónnik, héego-, héji-) *adj.*

He-gi-ra, He-ji-ra (héjirə, hi-jîr-ə) *n.* **1.** The flight of Muhammad from Mecca to Medina in A.D. 622. **2.** The Muslim era, which is reckoned from this date. **3.** *Small h.* Any flight, as from danger. [Arabic *(al)hijrah,* emigration, flight, departure, from *hajara,* to leave, depart.]

he-gu-men (hee-géw-men, hi-) *n.* The head of a religious community in the Greek Orthodox Church. [Late Latin *hēgūmenus,* from Late Greek *hēgoumenos,* from Greek, leader, from *hēgeisthai,* to lead.]

heh (hay) *interj.* **1.** Used to express surprise or inquiry, or to attract attention. **2.** Used to express malicious glee.

Hei-deg-ger (hí-deggər), **Martin** (1889–1976). German philosopher. His discussions on the "sense of being", which is the subject of *Being and Time* (1927), influenced Sartre and other existentialists.

Hei-del-berg (híd'l-berg, -bairk). A city in western Germany. Situated on the river Neckar, in the state of Baden-Württemberg, it was once the capital of the Palatinate. It has a spectacular ruined castle dating from the 13th century, and its university (1386) is the oldest in Germany.

Heidelberg man *n.* An extinct, early member of the human species, suggested as intermediate between *Homo erectus* and Neanderthal man, known primarily from a fossil jawbone found near Heidelberg, Germany, in 1907.

heif-er (héffər) *n.* A young cow, especially one that has not yet given birth to a calf. [Middle English *heyfre, hayfre,* Old English *hēahforet,* young ox.]

heigh (hay, hī) *interj. Archaic.* Used to express encouragement or to call attention.

heigh-ho (háy-hó ‖ *chiefly U.S.* hí-) *interj.* Used to express fatigue, melancholy, mild surprise, or disappointment.

height (hīt) *n.* Also *archaic* **heighth,** *obsolete* **highth** (hīt-th, hīth). *Abbr.* **h., H., hgt., ht 1. a.** The distance from the base to the top of something. **b.** The elevation of something above a given level; altitude. **2.** The condition or attribute of being sufficiently or relatively high or tall. **3.** The highest or uppermost point; the summit; the apex. **4. a.** The highest or most advanced stage or degree: *the height of stupidity; at the height of his fame.* **b.** The point of highest intensity; the climax: *the height of a storm.* **5.** *Often plural.* An eminence or area of high ground: *the Golan Heights.* **6.** *Archaic.* High rank, estate, or degree. **7. a.** *Archaic.* Loftiness of mind. **b.** *Obsolete.* Arrogance; hauteur. [Middle English *he(i)ghth,* Old English *hēhthu, hīehthu.* See **high, -th.**]

height-en (hīt'n) *v.* **-ened, -ening, -ens.** —*tr.* **1.** To increase the quantity or degree of; intensify. **2.** To make high or higher; raise. —*intr.* **1.** To rise in degree or quantity; intensify. **2.** *Archaic.* To

become high or higher. —**height-en-er** *n.*

height-to-pa-per (hīt-tə-páypər) *n. Printing.* The height of type from foot to face, standardised in Britain at 2.330 centimetres (0.9175 inch).

heil (hīl) *interj.* Hail! Used as a greeting, especially in the Nazi greeting *Heil Hitler!* [German.]

Hei-long-jiang (hay-lóong-jiáng). Northernmost province of China, formerly the northern part of Manchuria. Agriculture and forestry have been expanded since 1949, and its industries include oil-refining, coal-mining, and manufacturing. Capital, Harbin.

Hei-ne (hínə), **(Christian Johann) Heinrich** (1797–1856). German poet, a leading German Romantic. Heine lived after 1831 in Paris, where he supported a revolutionary literary movement known as "Young Germany". He published several volumes of lyric poems, including *The Book of Songs* (1827).

hei-nous (háynəss) *adj.* Grossly wicked or reprehensible; abominable; odious; vile. [Middle English *heynous,* hateful, from Old French *haïneus,* from *haïne,* hate, from *haïr,* to hate, from Frankish *hatjan* (unattested).] —**hei-nous-ly** *adv.* —**hei-nous-ness** *n.*

heir (air) *n.* **1.** *Law.* A person who inherits or is entitled by law or by the terms of a will to inherit the estate of another. **2.** A person who succeeds or is in line to succeed to a hereditary rank, title, or office. **3.** One who is entitled, or regarded as entitled, to receive a heritage, as of ideas, from a predecessor; a successor: *the natural heirs of the Whig tradition in British politics.* [Middle English *(h)eir, (h)air,* from Old French *(h)eir,* from Latin *hērēs.*] —**heir-dom.** —**heir-ship** *n.*

heir apparent *n., pl.* **heirs apparent.** *Law.* An heir whose right to inheritance is indefeasible by law, provided he survives his ancestor.

heir-ess (áir-ess, -iss, -éss) *n.* A female heir, especially one who inherits or is due to inherit great wealth.

heir-loom (áir-lōom) *n.* **1.** A valued possession passed down in a family through succeeding generations. **2.** *Law.* An article of personal property included in an inherited estate. [Middle English *heir lome :* HEIR + *lome,* utensil, tool, LOOM.]

heir of the body *n.* An heir who is a direct descendant.

heir presumptive *n., pl.* **heirs presumptive.** *Law.* An heir whose claim can be defeated by the birth of a closer relative before the death of the ancestor.

Hei-sen-berg (híz'n-berg, *German* -bairk), **Werner Karl** (1901–76). German physicist, one of the founders of quantum theory. For his **uncertainty principle** *(see),* which had a profound effect on physics, he was awarded the Nobel prize in 1932.

Heisenberg uncertainty principle *n. Physics.* The **uncertainty principle** *(see).*

heist (hīst) *tr.v.* **heisted, heisting, heists.** *Chiefly U.S. Slang.* To rob; steal.
~*n. Chiefly U.S. Slang.* A robbery; a burglary. [Dialectal variant of HOIST.]

hei-ti-ki (háy-teeki) *n. N.Z.* A neck ornament of greenstone worn by Maoris. [Maori : *hei,* to hang + TIKI, amulet.]

He-jaz or **He-djaz** (heejáz). *Arabic* **Al Hijaz.** Province of Saudi Arabia, bordering the Red Sea, and containing the Muslim holy cities of Mecca and Medina.

Hejira. Variant of **Hegira.**

Hel (hel). *Norse Mythology.* **1.** The daughter of Loki and the goddess of death. **2.** The underworld for the dead not killed in battle. [Old Norse *Hel.*]

He-La cell (héllaa) *n.* Any of the cells of the first continuously cultured human carcinoma strain, often used in the study of cellular processes. [After *Henrietta Lacks* (died 1951), patient from whose tissue the cells were first taken.]

held. Past tense and past participle of **hold.**

Hel-den-te-nor (héldən-te-nór) *n. German.* A singer with a powerful tenor voice suitable for heroic operatic parts. Also called "heroic tenor".

Hel-en (hél-ən, -in). In Greek legend, the daughter of Zeus and Leda and wife of Menelaus. Her abduction by Paris led to the Trojan War.

he-li-a-cal (hee-lí-ək'l, hi-, he-) *adj.* Of or pertaining to the Sun; especially, rising and setting with the Sun. [From Late Latin *hēliacus,* from Greek *hēlios,* from *hēlios,* the Sun.]

he-li-an-thus (héeli-ánthəss, hélli-) *n., pl.* **-thuses.** Any of various plants of the genus *Helianthus,* such as the sunflower and the Jerusalem artichoke, having large, yellow, daisy-like flowers. [New Latin, from Greek *hēlios,* the Sun + *anthos,* flower.]

hel-i-cal (héllik'l) *adj.* Having the shape of or similar to a helix. [Greek *helix* (stem *helik-*), HELIX.] —**hel-i-cal-ly** *adv.*

helical gear *n.* A gear in which the teeth are shaped in a helix about the axis.

he-li-ces. Alternative plural of **helix.**

hel-i-chry-sum (hélli-krí'z'm, héeli-) *n.* Any plant of the genus *Helichrysum,* whose papery, daisy-like flowers retain their form and colour on drying. [New Latin, from Greek *helikhrusos :* heli-, spiral, HELIX + *khrusos,* gold.]

he-lic-i-ty (hee-líssəti, hi-, he-) *n. Physics.* The component of the spin of a particle along its direction of motion. [Greek *helix* (stem *helik-*), HELIX + -ITY.]

hel-i-coid (héllikoyd) *adj.* Arranged in or having the approximate shape of a flattened spiral.
~*n. Geometry.* A surface generated by a plane curve or a twisted curve that is rotated about a linear axis and at the same time is translated in the direction of the axis so that the two rates have a constant ratio. [Greek *helikoeidēs :* HELIX + -OID (shaped).]

hel·i·con (héli-kən, -kon) *n.* A large spiral brass tuba that fits around the player's body. [After *Helicon,* mountain in Boeotia sacred to the Muses.]

hel·i·cop·ter (héli-koptər) *n.* An aircraft that derives its lift from blades that rotate about an approximately vertical central axis. [French *hélicoptère,* "spiral wing" : Greek *helix* (stem *helik-*), HELIX + -PTER.]

Hel·i·go·land (hélligō-land). *German* **Hel·go·land** (hélgō-lant). A small island belonging to Germany in the North Sea off the mouth of the river Elbe.

helio– *comb. form.* Indicates the Sun or of or by the Sun; for example, **heliograph, heliotrope.** [Greek *hēlios,* the Sun.]

he·li·o·cen·tric (héeli-ō-séntrik) *adj.* 1. Referred or relative to the Sun. 2. Having the Sun as a centre: *a heliocentric model of the universe.* **—he·li·o·cen·tric·i·ty** (-sen-tríssəti) *n.*

heliocentric parallax *n. Astronomy.* **Annual parallax** (*see*).

he·li·o·gram (héeli-ə-gram, -ō-) *n.* A message sent by heliograph. [HELIO- + -GRAM.]

he·li·o·graph (héeli-ə-graaf, -ō-, -graf) *n.* 1. An apparatus formerly used to photograph the Sun. 2. A signalling apparatus that reflects sunlight with a movable mirror to flash coded messages. 3. A print obtained by the process of photoengraving.
~*tr.v.* **heliographed, -graphing, -graphs.** To transmit (messages) by heliograph. [HELIO- + -GRAPH.] **—he·li·og·raph·er** (-óggrafər) *n.* **—he·li·o·graph·ic** (-gráffik) *adj.* **—he·li·og·raph·y** (-óggrəfi) *n.*

he·li·o·gra·vure (héeli-ə-grə-véwr, -ō-) *n. Printing.* **Photogravure** (*see*).

he·li·o·lith·ic (héeli-ə-líthik, -ō-) *adj.* Of or designating a civilisation characterised by sun-worship and the erection of megaliths. [HELIO- + -LITHIC.]

he·li·om·e·ter (héeli-ómmitər) *n.* A telescope equipped to measure small angular distances between celestial bodies. [French *héliomètre* : HELIO- + -METER.] **—he·li·o·met·ric** (-ə-métrik, -ō-), **he·li·o·met·ri·cal** *adj.* **—he·li·om·e·try** (-ómmətri) *n.*

He·li·os (héeli-oss). *Greek Mythology.* The sun god, son of Hyperion, depicted as driving his four-horse chariot across the sky from east to west daily. [Greek *Hēlios,* from *hēlios,* the Sun.]

he·li·o·stat (héeli-ə-stat, -ō-) *n.* An instrument in which a mirror is automatically moved so that it reflects sunlight in a constant direction. [New Latin *heliostata* : HELIO- + -STAT.]

he·li·o·tax·is (héeli-ə-táksiss, -ō-) *n. Biology.* The movement of an organism in response to the light of the sun. [New Latin : HELIO- + -TAXIS.] **—he·li·o·tac·tic** (-táktik) *adj.*

he·li·o·ther·a·py (héeli-ə-thérrəpi, -ō-) *n.* Medical therapy involving exposure to sunlight.

he·li·o·trope (héeli-ə-trōp, hél-yə-) *n.* 1. Any of several plants of the genus *Heliotropium*; especially, *H. arborescens,* native to South America, having small, fragrant, purplish flowers. 2. Any of various plants that turn towards the sun. 3. **Bloodstone** (*see*). 4. Moderate, light, or brilliant violet to moderate or deep reddish purple. [New Latin *Heliotropium,* from Latin *hēliotropium,* from Greek *hēliotropion,* sundial, bloodstone, heliotrope : HELIO- + *tropos,* a turning (see **trope**).] **—he·li·o·trope** *adj.*

hel·i·o·trop·in (héeli-óttrəpin, -ə-trōpin) *n. Chemistry.* **Piperonal** (*see*). [New Latin *Heliotropium,* HELIOTROPE + -IN.]

he·li·ot·ro·pism (héeli-óttrəpiz'm) *n. Biology.* Growth of a plant part towards or away from the light of the sun. [HELIO- + -TROPISM.] **—he·li·o·trop·ic** (-ə-tróppik) *adj.* **—he·li·o·trop·i·cal·ly** *adv.*

he·li·o·type (héeli-ə-tīp, -ō-) *n. Printing.* 1. A photomechanically produced plate for pictures or type made by exposing a gelatine film under a negative, hardening it with chrome alum, and printing directly from it. 2. The process of producing such a plate. **—he·li·o·typ·ic** (-típpik) *adj.*

he·li·o·zo·an (héeli-ə-zṓ-ən, -ō-) *n.* Any of various aquatic protozoans of the order Heliozoa, with many stiff, radiating pseudopodia. [New Latin *Heliozoa* : HELIO + -ZOAN.] **—he·li·o·zo·an** *adj.*

hel·i·port (hélli-pawrt ‖ -pōrt) *n.* An airport for helicopters. [HELI(COPTER) + -PORT.]

he·li·um (héeli-əm, héel-yəm) *n. Symbol* **He** A colourless, odourless, tasteless, inert gaseous element. It is used to inflate and so provide lift for balloons, as an inert component of various artificial atmospheres, in gaseous laser media, and as a superfluid in the form of helium II for low-temperature research. Atomic number 2, atomic weight 4.0026, boiling point -268.6°C, liquid density at boiling point 0.176 kilogram per cubic metre. [New Latin, from Greek *hēlios,* the Sun (the element was first discovered in an examination of the solar spectrum).]

helium I *n. Symbol* **He I** Liquid helium existing as a normal fluid between the superfluid transition point of approximately 2.178 K at 1 atmosphere pressure and its boiling point of 4.2 K.

helium II *n. Symbol* **He II** Liquid helium existing as a superfluid below the transition point of approximately 2.178 K at 1 atmosphere and having extremely low viscosity and extremely high thermal conductivity.

he·lix (héeliks) *n., pl.* **-lixes** or **helices** (hélli-seez, héeli-). 1. A three-dimensional curve that lies on a cylinder or cone and cuts the elements at a constant angle. 2. Any spiral form or structure. 3. *Anatomy.* The folded rim of skin and cartilage around the outer ear. 4. *Architecture.* A volute on a Corinthian or Ionic capital. 5. Any terrestrial mollusc of the genus *Helix,* such as the garden snail, *H. aspersa.* [Latin, from Greek, spiral, spiral object.]

hell (hel) *n.* 1. *Sometimes capital* **H.** The abode of the dead; the underworld where departed souls were believed to dwell; specifi-

cally, Sheol in the Hebrew Scriptures, and Hades in Graeco-Roman tradition. 2. *Sometimes capital* **H.** In the Christian tradition, the abode of condemned souls and devils; the place or state of eternal torture and punishment for the wicked after death, presided over by Satan, and conventionally depicted as a place of everlasting fire. 3. The infernal powers of evil and darkness. 4. **a.** A place or state of great wickedness, torment, misery, or destruction. **b.** A cause or source of great misery or agony. 5. *Archaic.* A gambling house. 6. *Archaic.* **a.** A tailor's receptacle for discarded material. **b.** A hellbox. 7. **a.** A severe punishment or reprimand: *The boss gave me hell.* **b.** Turmoil; havoc; pandemonium: *All hell was let loose. The weather played hell with the cricket season.* 8. Used to express annoyance or surprise, or as an intensive: *a hell of a good book; it hurts like hell.* **—for the hell of it.** Purely for the sake of amusement. **—from hell.** *Informal.* That which is hellishly bad or incompetent : *The cleaner from hell left everything dirty.* **—hell and** or **or high water.** *Informal.* The ultimate ordeal, suffering, or deprivation: *I followed her through hell and high water. We're staying, come hell or high water.* **—hell to pay.** Severe retribution: *If we're caught doing this, there'll be hell to pay!* **—like hell.** *Informal.* Most assuredly not; never. Used for emphasis in rejecting a possibility. **—raise** or **kick up hell.** To make a great fuss. **—the hell in.** *South African.* Extremely angry; furious. **—what the hell.** *Informal.* Used to express indifference or resignation.
~*interj. Slang.* Used to express acute anger, disgust, or impatience. [Middle English *hel(l),* Old English *hel(l),* from Germanic.]

he'll (heel). 1. Contraction of *he will.* 2. Contraction of *he shall.*

Hel·lad·ic (he-láddik, hi-) *adj.* Of or pertaining to the Bronze Age culture on the mainland of Greece prior to 1100 B.C. [Latin *Helladicus,* from Greek *Helladikos,* from *Hellas* (stem *Hellad-*), HELLAS.]

Hel·las (héllass). The Greek name for **Greece.** [Greek, from *Hellēn†,* eponymous ancestor of the Greeks.]

hell·bend·er (hél-bendər) *n.* A large aquatic salamander, *Cryptobranchus alleganiensis,* of eastern and central North America.

hell·bent (hél-bent, -bént) *adj.* Impetuously or recklessly bent on doing, reaching, or achieving something. Used with *on* or *for.*

hell·box (hél-boks) *n.* A printer's receptacle for broken or discarded type.

hell·cat (hél-kat) *n.* 1. A furious and evil woman; a witch. 2. A fiendish person.

hel·le·bore (hélli-bawr ‖ -bōr) *n.* Any of various plants of the genus *Helleborus,* native to Eurasia, most species of which are poisonous. See **Christmas rose.** [Middle English *ellebre,* from Old French, from Latin *elleborus,* from Greek *(h)elleboros,* perhaps "eaten by fawns" : *(h)ellos,* fawn + *-boros,* eaten, from *bibrōskein,* to eat, devour.]

hel·le·bor·in (hélli-báwrin ‖ -bōrin) *n.* A poisonous compound, $C_{36}H_{42}O_6$, extracted from a species of hellebore, *Helleborus niger.* [HELLEBOR(E) + -IN.]

hel·le·bo·rine (hélli-bə-rīn, -báwr-een ‖ -bōr-) *n.* 1. Any of various orchids of the genera *Epipactis* or *Cephalanthera.* 2. Any of various similar plants; especially, the false helleborine, *Veratrum album,* having broad, pleated leaves and yellow flowers arranged on a spike. [French, from Greek *helleborinē,* plant resembling hellebore.]

Hel·lene (hélleen) *n.* A Greek. [Greek *Hellēn.* See **Hellas.**]

Hel·len·ic (hi-léenik, he-, -lénnik) *adj.* Of or relating to the ancient or modern Greeks or their language; Greek.
~*n.* The Greek language in both its early and modern forms.

Hel·le·nise, Hel·le·nize (héllen-īz) *v.* **-nised, -nising, -nises.** *—intr.* To adopt Greek ways and speech; become Greek. *—tr.* To make Greek in character or culture. **—Hel·le·ni·sa·tion** (-ī-záysh'n ‖ *U.S.* -i-) *n.* **—Hel·le·nis·er** *n.*

Hel·le·nism (hélliniz'm) *n.* 1. An idiom, custom, or the like peculiar to the Greeks. 2. The civilisation and culture of ancient Greece. 3. Admiration for or adoption of Greek ideas, style, or culture. 4. The Greek nation; the Greek world as a whole.

Hel·le·nist (héllinist) *n.* 1. One in classical times who adopted the Greek language and culture, particularly a Jew of the Diaspora. 2. A devotee or student of Greek civilisation, language, or literature.

Hel·le·nis·tic (hélli-nístik) *adj.* 1. Of or relating to Greek civilisation, art, and culture from the death of Alexander the Great in 323 B.C. to the accession of Augustus (27 B.C.). 2. Of the Hellenists.

Hellespont. See **Dardanelles.**

hell·fire (hél-fīr, -fîr) *n.* The fires, torment, or punishment of hell.
~*adj.* Preaching or zealously believing in the torments of hell: *an old-fashioned hellfire preacher.*

hell-for-leath·er (hél-fər-léthər) *adv. Informal.* At breakneck speed.

hell·hole (hél-hōl) *n.* A hellish place, especially one of extreme wretchedness, squalor, or lewdness.

hell·hound (hél-hownd) *n.* 1. A hound of hell; especially, Cerberus, watchdog of Hades. 2. A devilish person; a fiend.

hel·lion (hél-yən) *n. U.S. Informal.* A mischievous, unrestrainable person, especially a young person or child. [Probably altered by assimilation to HELL from dialectal *hallion†,* scurvy person.]

hell·ish (héllish) *adj.* 1. Of, relating to, or worthy of hell; devilish. 2. *Informal.* Awful; unpleasant: *hellish weather.*
~*adv. British Informal.* Extremely; very. **—hell·ish·ly** *adv.* **—hell·ish·ness** *n.*

Hell·man (hélmən), **Lillian** (1905–84). U.S. playwright. Her first play, *The Children's Hour* (1934), treated the then taboo subject of lesbianism. She also wrote *The Little Foxes* (1939) and *Watch on the Rhine* (1941). The first volume of her autobiography, *An Unfinished Woman,* won the American National Book Award (1969).

hel·lo (hə-lố, he-) *interj.* Also **hal·lo, hul·lo** (hə-, húllố). **1.** Used to greet another informally, answer the telephone, or summon attention. **2.** Used to express surprise. ~*n., pl.* **helloes.** Also **hal·lo, hul·lo** *pl.* **-loes.** A calling or greeting of "hello". ~*v.* **helloed, -loing, -loes.** Also **hal·lo, hul·lo.** —*tr.* To say or call "hello" to. —*intr.* To call "hello". [Variant of earlier *hallo, hollo, holla,* from French *holà,* "ho there!"]

Hell's Angel (hélz áynjəl) *n.* One who belongs to a motorcycle gang of a type that originated in the United States, whose members wear denim, black leather, and Nazi regalia, and are generally believed to behave in a violent and lawless manner.

hel·lu·va (héllavə) *adv. Chiefly Informal.* Used as an intensive: *a helluva long queue.* ~*adj. Chiefly U.S. Informal.* **1.** Outstandingly bad; trying or unpleasant: *I've had a helluva day.* **2.** Outstandingly fine or impressive: *That was a helluva shot.* [Pronunciation spelling of *hell of a.*]

helm¹ (helm) *n.* **1.** *Nautical.* The tiller or wheel or the whole steering gear of a ship. **2.** A position of leadership or control: *at the helm.* —**ease the helm.** *Nautical.* To bring the helm somewhat towards midships in order to reduce strain on the rudder. ~*tr.v.* **helmed, helming, helms.** To be at the helm of; steer; guide. [Middle English *helme,* Old English *helma.*]

helm² *n. Archaic.* A helmet. ~*tr.v.* **helmed, helming, helms.** *Archaic.* To cover or furnish with a helmet. [Middle English *helm(e), healm,* Old English *helm.*]

hel·met (hélmit) *n.* **1.** A piece of ancient, medieval, or modern armour, usually of metal, designed to protect the head. **2. a.** A head covering of hard material, such as leather, metal, or plastic, worn by policemen, firemen, motorcyclists, and others to protect the head. **b.** The headgear with a glass mask worn by deep-sea divers. **c.** A pith helmet; a topi. **d.** Any hat or headgear resembling a helmet, such as a balaclava. **3.** *Botany.* The hood-shaped sepal or corolla of some flowers. [Middle English, from Old French *helme, heaume,* helmet, from Frankish *helm* (unattested).] —**hel·met·ed** *adj.*

Helm·holtz (hélm-hōlts, -holts), **Hermann Ludwig Ferdinand von** (1821–94). German physicist and physiologist. He formulated the mathematical law of the conservation of energy in 1847.

Helmholtz coils *pl.n. Physics.* Two identical flat coils carrying the same electric current in the same direction, mounted parallel at a distance apart equal to their radii. The arrangement produces a uniform magnetic field between the coils of known field strength. [Invented by H.L.F. von HELMHOLTZ.]

Helmholtz function *n. Symbol* **A** A measure of the thermodynamic free energy of a system, equal to the internal energy minus the product of thermodynamic temperature and entropy. Also called "Helmholtz free energy". [Devised by H.L.F. von HELMHOLTZ.]

hel·minth (hélminth) *n.* A worm; especially, a parasitic intestinal nematode fluke, or tapeworm. [Greek *helmi(n)s* (stem *helminth-*), parasitic worm.]

hel·min·thi·a·sis (hélmin-thí-ə-siss) *n.* A disease resulting from infestation with parasitic worms. [New Latin : HELMINTH + -IASIS.]

hel·min·thic (hel-mínthik) *adj.* **1.** Of or pertaining to worms, especially parasitic intestinal worms. **2.** Tending to expel worms; anthelmintic. ~*n.* A vermifuge or anthelmintic.

hel·min·thol·o·gy (hélmin-thóllƏji) *n.* The scientific study of worms, especially parasitic worms. [HELMINTH + -LOGY.] —**hel·min·thol·o·gist** *n.*

helms·man (hélmz-mən) *n., pl.* **-men** (-mən). One who steers a ship.

he·lo·phyte (hée-lə-fīt, -lō-) *n.* A marsh plant. [Greek *helos,* marsh + -PHYTE.]

hel·ot (héllət ‖ *chiefly U.S.* héelət) *n.* **1.** *Capital* **H.** One of a class of serfs in ancient Sparta, neither a slave nor a free citizen. **2.** A serf; a bondsman. [Latin *Hēlōtes,* serfs, helots, from Greek *Heilōtes,* plural of *Heilōs†.*]

hel·ot·ism (héllət-iz'm ‖ *chiefly U.S.* héelət-) *n.* **1.** A system under which a particular section of the community, such as a religious or racial minority, is permanently oppressed and degraded. **2.** *Zoology.* **Dulosis** *(see).*

hel·ot·ry (héllət-ri ‖ *chiefly U.S.* héelət-) *n.* **1.** The condition of serfdom. **2.** Helots as a class.

help (help) *v.* **helped** or *archaic* **holp** (hōlp, holp), **helped** or *archaic* **holpen** (hōlpən, hólpən), **helping, helps.** —*tr.* **1. a.** To do something or provide something that will be of use to (someone) in achieving a purpose; give assistance to; aid: *I helped her to find the book.* **b.** To give assistance so as to enable (someone) to carry out an action more easily. Used elliptically with a preposition or an adverb: *He helped her into her coat. Help me down—I'm stuck.* **2.** To further the advancement or promote the interests of: *The party's disunity will only help its enemies.* **3.** To give relief to (one in difficulty or distress); succour. **4.** To alleviate or cure. **5.** To improve; benefit. **6.** To prevent, change, or rectify. Used with *can* or *cannot*: *I cannot help her laziness.* **7.** To refrain from; avoid. Used with *can* or *cannot*: *He cannot help laughing.* **8.** To serve in a shop or at table. —*intr.* To be of use or service; give assistance; aid. —See Synonyms at **improve.** —**cannot (help) but.** To be compelled to; be unable to avoid or resist: *He cannot (help) but do what they ask.* —**help oneself to.** To take (something) without asking permission. —**help out.** To help with a problem or difficulty. —**so help me (God).** Used as an oath in solemn affirmation of what one has declared.

~*n.* **1.** The act of helping; aid; assistance. **2.** Someone or something that helps: *You've been a great help.* **3.** Relief; remedy. **4.** Succour. **5. a.** A person employed to assist; especially, a farm worker or a domestic servant. **b.** Such employees collectively. ~*interj.* Used to express an urgent need for assistance. [Middle English *helpen,* Old English *helpan,* from Germanic.] —**help·er** *n.*

Synonyms: help, aid, assist, succour.

Usage: The construction *I couldn't help but admire her,* and similar sentences, is common in informal speech, but is strictly a blend of two different constructions in formal English. The construction with the infinitive is illustrated by *One could not but admire her;* the construction with the -ing form is illustrated by *One couldn't help admiring her.*

An infinitive following *help* is often preceded by *to,* more often in British than in American English, and it is always possible to insert *to,* as in *She helped me (to) carry the carpet.* In both varieties, however, there is a strong tendency for the *to* form to be omitted if the subject of the clause is actively involved in the activity (*She helped me carry . . .*); when the subject is not actively involved, the *to* form is normal (*The medicine will help you to feel relaxed*).

help·ful (hélpf'l) *adj.* Providing help; useful; beneficial. —**help·ful·ly** *adv.* —**help·ful·ness** *n.*

help·ing (hélping) *n.* A portion of food for one person.

helping hand *n.* Assistance; aid.

help·less (hélp-ləss, -liss) *adj.* **1.** Unable to manage by oneself; defenceless; dependent. **2.** Lacking power or strength; impotent; ineffectual. **3.** Irremediable; hopeless: *a helpless situation.* **4.** Uncontrollable; unable to be helped: *helpless laughter.* —**help·less·ly** *adv.* —**help·less·ness** *n.*

help·line *n.* A free telephone service offering victims of emergency or abuse access to the appropriate aid organisation.

Help·mann (hélpmən), **Sir Robert (Murray)** (1909–86). Australian dancer, choreographer, actor, and director. He appeared in the films *The Red Shoes* (1948) and *The Tales of Hoffman* (1953).

help·mate (hélp-mayt) *n.* A helper or helpful companion, especially a spouse. [HELP + MATE (influenced by HELPMEET).]

help·meet (hélp-meet) *n.* A helpmate. [From *I will make an help meet for him* (Genesis 2:18, 20), "I will make a help suitable for him" : HELP + MEET (suitable).]

Hel·sing·or (hélssing-ör). *English* **El·sin·ore** (élsinor). Danish port on the island of Zealand. The 16th century Kronborg Castle was the setting for Shakespeare's play *Hamlet.*

Hel·sin·ki (hél-sin-ki, hel-sing-ki). *Swedish* **Hel·sing·fors** (hél-sing-fawrss). Capital city of Finland. Built on a promontory and several islands in the Gulf of Finland, it has two harbours. Its industries include paper, textiles, and shipbuilding.

hel·ter-skel·ter (héltər-skéltər) *adv.* **1.** In disorderly haste; pell-mell. **2.** In confusion; haphazardly. ~*adj.* **1.** Characterised by disorderly haste. **2.** Haphazard. ~*n.* **1.** *British.* A tower at a funfair supporting a spiral track down which people may slide on a mat. **2.** Chaos; confusion. [16th century : perhaps based on Middle English *skelte,* hasten.]

helve (helv) *n.* A handle of a tool, such as an axe, chisel, or hammer. [Middle English *helve, hilf,* Old English *hielf(e).*]

Hel·vel·lyn (hel-véllin). Knife-edge mountain (951 metres; 3,120 feet) in the Lake District, Cumbria, England. Eroded by ice, it lies between Ullswater to the northeast and Thirlmere to the west.

Helvetia. See **Switzerland.**

Hel·ve·tian (hel-véesh'n) *adj.* **1.** Of or relating to the Helvetii. **2.** Swiss. [Latin *Helvētius,* of the Helvetii.] —**Hel·ve·tian** *n.*

Hel·vet·ic (hel-véttik) *adj.* Helvetian; Swiss. ~*n.* A Swiss Protestant; a Zwinglian.

Hel·ve·ti·i (hel-véeshi-ī, -vétti-ee) *pl.n.* A Celtic people inhabiting Switzerland during the time of Julius Caesar.

hem¹ (hem) *n.* **1.** An edge or border of a piece of cloth; especially, a finished edge for a garment, curtain, or the like, made by folding the selvage or raw edge under twice and stitching it down. **2.** The level of a hem; a hemline. ~*tr.v.* **hemmed, hemming, hems. 1.** To fold back and stitch down the edge of. **2.** To encircle and confine; enclose or restrict. Used with *in, about,* or *around*: *hemmed in by mountains.* [Middle English *hem(m),* Old English *hem(m).*] —**hem·mer** *n.*

hem² *n.* Also **h'm** (hm). A short cough or clearing of the throat made to gain attention, warn, fill a pause in speech, hide embarrassment, or the like. Often used as an interjection. ~*intr.v.* **hemmed, hemming, hems. 1.** To utter this sound. **2.** To hesitate in speaking; hum and ha. [Imitative.]

he-man (hée-man) *n., pl.* **-men** (-men). *Informal.* A strong, muscular, virile man.

hemato-. *U.S.* Variant of **haemato-.**

hem·i·el·y·tron (hi-mélli-tron, he-) *n., pl.* **-tra** (-trə). Also **hem·i·el·y·tron** (hémmi-élli-tron). An insect forewing that is thickened at the base and membranous at the apex, characteristic of the true bugs. [HEM(I)- + ELYTRON.]

hem·er·a·lo·pi·a (hémmərə-lốpi-ə, héemərə-) *n.* A visual defect manifested as the inability to see as clearly in bright light as in dim light. Also called "day blindness". Compare **nyctalopia.** [New Latin, from Greek *hēmeralōps,* "day blind" : *hēmera,* day + *alaos†,* blind + -OPIA.]

hem·e·ro·cal·lis (hémmərō-kál-iss, héemərō-) *n.* The **day lily** *(see).* [New Latin, from Latin, from Greek *hēmerokalles,* name of a kind of lily : *hēmera,* day + *kallos,* beauty.]

hemi-, hem-. *prefix.* Indicates half; for example, **hemichordate,**

hemelytron. Compare **demi-, semi-.** [Latin *hēmi-,* from Greek.]

–hemia. *U.S.* Variant of **-aemia.**

hem·i·al·gi·a (hémmi-álj-ə, -i-ə) *n.* Pain affecting one half of the body. [New Latin : HEMI- + -ALGIA.]

hem·i·cel·lu·lose (hémmi-séllew-lŏss, -lōz) *n.* Any of several polysaccharides that are more complex than a sugar and less complex than cellulose, derived from plants and produced commercially from various seeds and other plant tissues.

hem·i·chor·date (hémmi-kórdayt) *n.* Any of various wormlike marine animals of the phylum or subphylum Hemichordata, having a primitive notochord and gill slits. ~*adj.* Of or belonging to the Hemichordata. [New Latin *Hemichordata* : HEMI- + CHORDATE.]

hem·i·cy·cle (hémmi-sīk'l) *n.* A semicircular structure or arrangement. [French *hémicycle,* from Latin *hēmicyclium,* from Greek *hēmikuklion* : HEMI- + *kuklos,* circle, CYCLE.] —**hem·i·cyc·lic** (-sícklik, -síklik) *adj.*

hem·i·dem·i·sem·i·qua·ver (hémmi-démmi-sémmi-kwayvər) *n.* *Chiefly British. Music.* A note which has the time value of one sixty-fourth of a semibreve; half a demisemiquaver. [HEMI- + DEMISEMIQUAVER.]

hem·i·he·dral (hémmi-héedrəl) *adj.* Exhibiting only half the faces required for complete symmetry. Said of a crystal. [HEMI- + -HEDRAL.]

hem·i·hy·drate (hémmi-hídrayt) *n.* A hydrate in which the molecular ratio of water molecules to anhydrous compound is 1:2. —**hem·i·hy·drat·ed** (-hī-dráytid ‖ -hídraytid) *adj.*

hem·i·mor·phic (hémmi-mórfik) *adj.* Asymmetric at the axial ends. Said of a crystal. [HEMI- + -MORPHIC.]

hem·i·mor·phite (hémmi-mórfīt) *n.* A mineral, **smithsonite.** [HEMI-MORPH(IC) + -ITE.]

Hem·ing·way (hémming-way), **Ernest (Miller)** (1899–1961). U.S. novelist. He served in World War I with the Red Cross, then was a newspaper reporter in Toronto, before settling in Paris with a group of U.S. writers, including Ezra Pound and Gertrude Stein. The novel *The Torrents of Spring* (1926) first revealed his clipped style. His major works are *The Sun Also Rises* (1926), *A Farewell to Arms* (1929), *For Whom the Bell Tolls* (1940), and *The Old Man and the Sea* (1952). He was awarded the Nobel prize for literature in 1954.

hem·i·par·a·site (hémmi-párrə-sīt) *n.* 1. An organism, such as mistletoe, that obtains some food from its host but also photosynthesizes. Also called "semiparasite". 2. An organism that can live parasitically and independently; a facultative parasite.

hem·i·ple·gi·a (hémmi-pléej-ə, -i-ə) *n.* Paralysis of one side of the body only. Compare **paraplegia, quadriplegia.** [New Latin, from Middle Greek *hēmiplēgia* : HEMI- + -PLEGIA.] —**hem·i·ple·gic** (-pléejik ‖ -pléjik) *adj. & n.*

he·mip·ter·an (hi-míptə-rən, he-) *n.* Also **he·mip·ter·on** (-ron). A hemipterous insect. ~*adj.* Of or belonging to the Hemiptera; hemipterous. [New Latin *Hemiptera* : HEMI- + -PTER.]

he·mip·ter·ous (hi-míptərəss, he-) *adj.* Of or belonging to the Hemiptera, a large group of insects characterised by piercing or sucking mouthparts in the form of a beak or rostrum. The group includes the **heteropterous** and **homopterous** bugs *(both of which see).*

hem·i·sphere (hémmi-sfeer) *n.* 1. a. A half of a sphere bounded by a great circle. b. A half of a symmetrical, approximately spherical object as divided by a plane of symmetry: *cerebral hemisphere.* 2. Either half of the celestial sphere, as divided by the ecliptic, the celestial equator, or the horizon. 3. Either the northern or southern half of the Earth as divided by the equator, or the eastern or western half as divided by a meridian. [Middle English *(h)emisper(i)e,* from Latin *hēmisphaerium,* from Greek *hēmisphairion* : HEMI- + *sphairon,* diminutive of *sphaira,* SPHERE.] —**hem·i·spher·ic** (-sférrik ‖ *U.S. also* -sféer-ik), **hem·i·spher·i·cal** *adj.* —**hem·i·spher·i·cal·ly** *adv.*

hem·i·stich (hémmi-stik) *n.* Half a line of verse, especially when separated rhythmically from the rest of the line by a caesura. [Latin *hēmistichium,* from Greek *hēmistikhion* : HEMI- + *stikhos,* line.]

hem·i·ter·pene (hémmi-térpeen) *n.* Any of a group of hydrocarbons that have the formula C_5H_8. See **terpene.**

hem·line (hém-līn) *n.* The height or level of the hem of a skirt, dress, or coat.

hem·lock (hém-lok) *n.* 1. A tall, fetid, poisonous, Eurasian plant, *Conium maculatum,* with purple-spotted stems and small white flowers. Also *U.S.* "poison hemlock". 2. The poisonous alkaloid coniine *(see),* derived from this plant. 3. A type of spruce tree of the genus *Tsuga,* native to North America, having small cones and short, flat needles. See **western hemlock.** 4. The wood of such a tree. [Old English *hymlic(e)†.*]

hemo-. *U.S.* Variant of **haemo-.**

hemp (hemp) *n.* 1. A tall plant, *Cannabis sativa,* native to Asia, having stems that yield a coarse fibre used in cordage, and small greenish flowers. Also called "cannabis", "Indian hemp", "marijuana". 2. The fibre of this plant. 3. Any of various narcotic drugs, such as hashish, derived from this plant. 4. a. Any of various similar or related plants, especially one yielding a fibre similar to that of *Cannabis sativa.* b. The fibre of such a plant. [Middle English *hemp(e),* Old English *hænep, henep,* from Germanic *hanipiz* (unattested); akin to Greek *kannabis.*]

hemp agrimony *n.* A Eurasian plant, *Eupatorium cannabinum,* having clusters of small reddish-purple flowers.

hemp·en (hémpən) *adj.* Made of or resembling hemp.

hemp nettle *n.* Any of various Eurasian plants of the genus *Galeopsis;* especially, *G. tetrahit,* having white or reddish flowers.

hem·stitch (hém-stich) *n.* 1. A decorative stitch usually bordering a hem, as on a handkerchief, made by drawing out several parallel threads and catching together the cross threads in uniform groups, thus creating an open design. 2. Needlework using this stitch. —**hem·stitch** *tr.v.* —**hem·stitch·er** *n.*

hen¹ (hen) *n.* 1. A female bird; especially, the adult female of the domestic fowl. 2. The female of certain aquatic animals, such as an octopus or a lobster. [Middle English *hen,* Old English *hen(n).*]

hen² *n. Scottish.* A woman or girl; a lass. Used as an affectionate form of address. [Perhaps akin to HINNY (honey).]

He·nan or **Ho·nan** or **Ho·nan** (hú-nán, hŏ-). Province of northeast and central China. Traversed by the rivers Huang He (Yellow River) and Huai He, which irrigate its densely populated and fertile central plain, it produces cereals and anthracite. The capital, Zhengzhou (Chengchow), lies in the northwest of the province.

hen-and-chick·ens (hén-ən-chíckinz) *n., pl.* **hens-and-chickens** (hénz-). Any of several plants having many runners or offshoots; especially, the **houseleek** *(see).*

hen·bane (hén-bayn) *n.* A poisonous plant, *Hyoscyamus niger,* native to the Mediterranean region, having an unpleasant smell, clammy leaves, and funnel-shaped yellow, purple-veined flowers, and yielding a juice used medicinally. [Middle English, from HEN (fowl) + BANE (alluding to its poison).]

hen·bit (hén-bit) *n.* A plant, *Lamium amplexicaule,* native to Europe, having toothed leaves and small purplish-pink flowers. Also called "henbit deadnettle". [HEN + BIT (morsel).]

Hen·bur·y Craters (hén-bri, -bəri ‖ -berri). A formation of meteoric craters in central Australia, near the town of Henbury in southern Northern Territory.

hence (henss) *adv.* 1. a. For this reason; as a result; therefore: *hand-made and hence expensive.* b. From this source: *She grew up in the Sudan; hence her interest in Nubian art.* 2. a. From this time; from now: *A year hence he will have forgotten.* b. *Rare.* Henceforth: *Hence I'll trust no one.* 3. a. Forth from this place; away from here. Usually used with an imperative: *Get thee hence!* b. Distant from here: *an inn two miles hence.* c. *Rare.* From this life: *depart hence.* —**from hence.** *Archaic.* From this place. ~*interj. Archaic.* Go; get out: "Hence, loathed Melancholy" (Milton). —**hence with!** Away with! [Middle English *hennes,* extended form of *henne,* hence, Old English *heonane,* from here, away.]

hence·forth (hénss-fórth, -fawrth ‖ -fórth, -fórth) *adv.* Also **hence·for·ward** (hénss-fór-wərd). From this time forth; from now on.

hench·man (hénch-mən) *n., pl.* **-men** (-mən). 1. A loyal and trusted follower or subordinate. 2. *Chiefly U.S.* A person who supports a political figure chiefly out of self-interest. 3. *Obsolete.* A page of honour to a prince or other person of high rank. [Middle English *hengestman, henx(st)man,* probably groom, squire : *hengest,* horse, stallion, Old English, from Germanic *hangista-* (unattested) + MAN.]

hen·coop (hén-kōop ‖ -kōop, -kōōb) *n.* A coop or cage for poultry.

hendeca- *comb. form.* Indicates 11; for example, **hendecahedron.** [Greek *hendeka,* eleven : *hen,* neuter of *heis,* one + *deka,* ten.]

hen·dec·a·gon (hen-déckə-gən ‖ *U.S.* -gon) *n.* A polygon with 11 sides. [HENDECA- + -GON.] —**hen·dec·a·go·nal** (héndek-ággən'l) *adj.*

hen·dec·a·he·dron (hén-deckə-héed-rən, -héd- ‖ *U.S.* hen-déckə-) *n., pl.* **-drons** or **-dra** (-rə). A polyhedron with 11 plane surfaces. [HENDECA- + -HEDRON.] —**hen·dec·a·he·dral** *adj.*

hen·dec·a·syl·lab·ic (hén-deckə-si-lábbik ‖ *U.S.* hen-déckə-) *adj.* Containing 11 syllables. ~*n.* Also **hen·dec·a·syl·la·ble** (-silləb'l, -sílləb'l). A line of verse containing 11 syllables. [Latin *hendecasyllabus,* a hendecasyllable : Greek *hendeka,* eleven : *hen,* neuter of *heis,* one + *deka,* ten + *sullabē,* SYLLABLE.]

Hen·der·son (héndər-s'n), **Arthur** (1863–1935). British Labour politician. He was an ironworker and trade union leader, and was elected to parliament in 1903. He was home secretary in the first Labour government of 1924. In the Labour government of 1929–31, he was foreign secretary and led Labour opposition to Ramsay MacDonald's decision to form a National government with the Conservatives (1931). From 1932 until his death he was president of the World Disarmament Conference. He was awarded the Nobel peace prize in 1934.

hen·di·a·dys (hen-dī-ə-diss) *n.* A figure of speech in which two distinct words connected by a conjunction are used to express a single complex notion that would normally be expressed by an adjective and a noun; for example, in *He struck with steel and sword,* the phrase *steel and sword* is a hendiadys, used instead of *a steel sword.* [Medieval Latin, from Greek *hen dia duoin,* one by means of two : *hen,* neuter of *heis,* one + *dia,* through (see **dia-**) + *duoin,* genitive of *duō,* two.]

Hen·don (héndən). District of the Greater London borough of Barnet. Its aerodrome, founded in 1909, now houses the Royal Air Force, Battle of Britain, and Bomber Command museums.

Hen·drix (héndriks), **Jimi** born James Marshall Hendrix (1942–1970). American rock musician. His innovative style of electric guitar playing changed the course of rock music. With his first major group, the Jimi Hendrix Experience, he recorded hits such as *Purple Haze* and *Foxy Lady,* which were his own compositions.

Henegouwen. See **Hainaut.**

hen·e·quen, hen·e·quin, hen·i·quen (hénni-kwin) *n.* **1.** A tropical American plant, *Agave fourcroydes,* having large, thick leaves that yield a coarse reddish fibre used in making rope and twine. **2.** The fibre obtained from this plant. [Spanish *henequén, jeniquén,* perhaps from Taino.]

henge (henj) *n.* A structure of ritual significance belonging to the Neolithic or Bronze Age, circular in form and sometimes having stone or wooden posts. [Abstracted from STONEHENGE.]

Hen·gist (hén-gist), (*d. c.*488). Germanic chieftain. With his brother **Horsa** he led (A.D. 449) the Jutes who invaded southern Britain. They landed in the Isle of Thanet, but were defeated at Aylesford, where Horsa was slain, *c.*455. Hengist then conquered Kent where he ruled *c.*455–*c.*488.

hen harrier *n.* A common harrier, *Circus cyaneus,* that nests in marshy ground. Also *U.S.* "marsh hawk."

hen·house (hén-howss) *n., pl.* **-houses.** A chicken coop.

Hen·ie (hénni), **Sonja** (1913–69). Norwegian ice-skater. She was largely responsible for making ice-skating a popular, competitive sport. She was Norwegian champion at 10, won Olympic gold medals in 1928, 1932, and 1936, and won ten consecutive world championships between 1927 and 1936. In 1936 she settled in the United States, where she starred in ice shows and films.

Hen·ley-on-Thames (hénli-on-témz). Town in Oxfordshire, in south central England. Situated on the river Thames, it is best known for its annual royal regatta, first held in 1839.

hen·na (hénnə) *n.* **1.** A tree or shrub, *Lawsonia inermis,* of Asia and northern Africa, having fragrant white or reddish flowers. **2.** A reddish powder obtained from the leaves of this plant, used as a hair colouring and for dyeing leather. **3.** Moderate or strong reddish brown to strong brown.
~*tr.v.* **hennaed, -naing, -nas.** To dye or rinse (hair) with henna. [Arabic *ḥinnā'.*] —**hen·na** *adj.*

henna wax *n.* A wax preparation derived from the henna plant and used as a non-colorant hair conditioner.

hen·ner·y (hénnəri) *n., pl.* **-ies. 1.** A poultry farm. **2.** A coop or cage for poultry.

hen·o·the·ism (hénnō-thée-iz'm, hénnə-) *n.* Belief in one god, such as a special clan or tribal god, without denying the existence of others. Compare **monotheism.** [German *Henotheismus* : Greek *heno-,* from *hen,* neuter of *heis,* one + THEISM.] —**hen·o·the·ist** *n. & adj.* —**hen·o·the·is·tic** (-thee-ístik) *adj.*

hen party *n. Informal.* A party or outing exclusively for women. Compare **stag party.**

hen·peck (hén-pek) *tr.v.* **-pecked, -pecking, -pecks.** *Informal.* To dominate or harass (one's husband) with persistent nagging. [Back-formation from *henpecked,* alluding to a hen that is imagined as attacking and dominating a cock.] —**hen·pecked** *adj.*

Hen·ri·et·ta Ma·ri·a. (hén-ri-éttə mə-rée-ə) (1609–69). Queen consort of Charles I of England, the daughter of Henry IV of France. She married Charles in 1625 and by remaining a Roman Catholic increased Charles's unpopularity with the Puritans.

hen·ry (hénri) *n., pl.* **-ries** or **-rys.** *Abbr.* **H** The unit of inductance in the SI system, equal to the inductance that has an induced electromotive force of one volt when the current is varied at the rate of one ampere per second. [After Joseph HENRY.]

Hen·ry I (hénri), also known as Henry Beauclerc (1068–1135). King of England (1100–35). He was the youngest son of William the Conqueror, and succeeded his brother, William II (Rufus).

Henry II[1] (1133–89). King of England (1154–89), son of Queen Matilda and founder of the Angevin (through his father Geoffrey, Count of Anjou), or Plantagenet, royal line. Henry appointed Thomas Becket Archbishop of Canterbury in 1162, but quarrelled with him over the issue of the Crown's authority over the Church. This led to the murder of Becket in 1170.

Henry II[2] (1519–59). King of France (1547–59), the son of Francis I. He regained Calais from the English in 1558.

Henry III (1207–72). King of England (1216–72). He succeeded his father, King John. His reign was troubled by baronial opposition, led by Simon de Montfort, whose representative parliament, called in 1265, is regarded as the first full English parliament.

Henry IV[1], also known as Henry Bolingbroke (1367–1413). King of England (1399–1413), eldest son of John of Gaunt and grandson of Edward III. He was banished from England by Richard II in 1398. The following year, John of Gaunt died and Richard confiscated his estates, to which Henry was heir. Henry returned, raised a military force, and compelled Richard to abdicate. Parliament confirmed his claim, and the Lancastrian dynasty was founded.

Henry IV[2], also known as Henry of Navarre (1553–1610). King of France (1589–1610), the son of Antoine de Bourbon and founder of the Bourbon royal line. He rid France of Spanish influence by his successful war against Spain (1595–98) and gave political rights to French Protestants in the Edict of Nantes (1598).

Henry V (1387–1422). King of England (1413–22), son of Henry IV. In the first years of his reign he suppressed the Lollards, executing their leader Sir John Oldcastle in 1417. He also reopened the Hundred Years' War, defeating the French at Agincourt (1415). By 1419 all of Normandy was once again in English hands.

Henry VI (1421–71). King of England (1422–61, 1470–71), only son of Henry V. He succeeded to the throne as a baby, and for most of his reign exercised little control over the royal administration. The Yorkist victory at Northampton in 1460 left Henry a prisoner of his enemies. The following year, Edward IV was proclaimed king. Henry, rescued from captivity, regained the throne in 1470. He was

recaptured at the battle of Barnet and murdered in the Tower of London in 1471.

Henry VII, also known as Henry Tudor (1457–1509). King of England (1485–1509), son of Edmund Tudor and founder of the Tudor line. He was head of the house of Lancaster after the death of Henry VI in 1471, and led the opposition to Richard III. In 1485 he defeated Richard at Bosworth Field and was acclaimed king. He married Elizabeth, daughter of Edward IV, and united the houses of York and Lancaster.

Henry VIII (1491–1547). King of England (1509–1547), second son and successor of Henry VII. He married the first of his six wives, Catherine of Aragon, shortly after his accession in 1509. Her failure to deliver a male heir led to the divorce which compelled Henry to break with Rome by the Act of Supremacy in 1536. That same year, he began the dissolution of the monasteries.

Henry, Joseph (1797–1878). U.S. physicist. He was the first director of the Smithsonian Institute, founded in 1846. He invented the electromagnetic telegraph and, independently of Faraday, discovered electromagnetic induction, the principle on which the transformer and the dynamo are based.

Henry, O., pen name of William Sydney Porter (1862–1910). U.S. short-story writer. He wrote about 600 stories, most with surprise endings, including *The Gift of the Magi.*

Henry's law *n. Chemistry.* The principle that at equilibrium the amount of gas dissolved in a liquid is proportional to the gas pressure. [After William *Henry* (1774–1836), English chemist.]

Henry the Navigator (1394–1460). Prince of Portugal. In 1416 he established a headquarters for overseas exploration, which laid the foundations of Portugal's overseas empire.

Hen·ze (hentsə), **Hans Werner** (1926–). German composer. He has written six symphonies, but is best known for his operas, which include *The Bassarids* (1974) and *We Come to the River* (1976), for which the libretto was written by Edward Bond.

H.E.O. Higher Executive Officer.

hep·a·rin (héppərin) *n.* A complex organic acid found especially in lung and liver tissue and having the ability in certain circumstances to prevent the clotting of blood. [New Latin *hepar,* liver, from Late Latin *hēpar,* from Greek + -IN.]

he·pat·ic (hi-páttik, he-) *adj.* **1.** Of, pertaining to, or resembling the liver. **2.** Liver-coloured. **3.** Of or belonging to the Hepaticae, a class of plants containing the liverworts.
~*n.* **1.** A drug used to treat liver diseases. **2.** A plant of the class Hepaticae, the **liverwort** *(see).* [Middle English *epatik,* from Latin *hēpaticus,* of liver, from Greek *hēpatikos,* from *hēpar* (stem *hēpat-*), liver.]

he·pat·i·ca (hi-páttikə, he-) *n.* Any of several woodland plants of the genus *Hepatica;* especially, *H. nobilis,* having three-lobed leaves and usually bluish-purple flowers. [New Latin *Hepatica,* from Medieval Latin *hēpatica,* liverwort, from Latin, feminine of *hēpaticus,* HEPATIC.]

hep·a·ti·tis (héppə-títiss) *n.* Inflammation of the liver due to infection or toxins, characterised by fever, weakness, and jaundice. [New Latin : Greek *hēpar* (stem *hēpat-*), liver + -ITIS.]

hepato-, hepat– *comb. form.* Indicates the liver; for example, **hepatogenic.** [Greek *hēpar* (stem *hēpat-*), liver.]

Hep·burn (hép-burn, -bərn), **Katharine** (1907–). U.S. actress. She made her stage debut in 1928, and became a popular Hollywood film star. She has won an Oscar as best actress four times, for *Morning Glory* (1933), *Guess Who's Coming to Dinner* (1967), *The Lion in Winter* (1968), and *On Golden Pond* (1981).

hep·cat (hép-kat) *n. Slang.* A performer or devotee of swing and jazz during the 1940s.

He·phaes·tus (hi-féess-təss, he– ‖ *chiefly U.S.* -féss-). *Greek Mythology.* The lame god of fire and metalworking; identified with the Roman god Vulcan.

Hep·ple·white (hépp'l-wīt, -hwīt) *adj.* Designating an English style of furniture of the late 18th century, noted for its light, graceful lines, its use of concave curves, and the shield or heart backs of its chairs. [After George HEPPLEWHITE.]

Hepplewhite, George (died 1786). English cabinetmaker. His elegant style, now much admired, was unfashionable in his day. His reputation rests on the designs in his *Cabinet-Maker and Upholsterer's Guide* (published in 1788).

hepta-, hept– *comb. form.* Indicates seven; for example, **heptahedron, heptane.** [Greek *hepta,* seven.]

hep·tad (hép-tad) *n.* A group or series of seven. [Greek *heptas* (stem *heptad-*), the number seven, period of seven years, from *hepta,* seven.]

hep·ta·de·ca·no·ic acid (héptə-déckə-nṓ-ik) *n.* An organic acid, **margaric acid** *(see).*

hep·ta·gon (héptə-gən ‖ *U.S.* -gon) *n.* A polygon with seven sides and seven angles. [Greek *heptagonos,* having seven angles : HEPTA- + -GON.]

hep·tag·o·nal (hep-tággən'l) *adj.* **1.** Having seven sides and seven angles. **2.** Of, pertaining to, or formed in heptagons. —**hep·tag·o·nal·ly** *adv.*

hep·ta·he·dral (héptə-héedrəl) *adj.* **1.** Having seven plane surfaces. **2.** Of, pertaining to, or formed in heptahedrons. —**hep·ta·he·dral·ly** *adv.*

hep·ta·he·dron (héptə-héed-rən, -héd-) *n., pl.* **-drons** or **-dra** (-rə) A polyhedron with seven plane surfaces. [HEPTA- + -HEDRON.]

hep·ta·hy·drate (héptə-hídrayt) *n. Chemistry.* A hydrate in which the ratio of water molecules to anhydrous compound is 7:1.

hep·tam·er·ous (hep-támmərəss) *adj.* Having seven parts or arranged in groups of seven. Said especially of plant parts. [HEPTA- + -MEROUS.]

hep·tam·e·ter (hep-támmitər) *n.* **1.** A metrical unit consisting of seven feet. **2.** A line of verse written in such meter. [HEPTA- + -METER.]

hep·tane (héptayn) *n.* A volatile, colourless, highly flammable liquid hydrocarbon, $CH_3(CH_2)_5CH_3$, obtained in the fractional distillation of petroleum, and used as a standard in determining octane ratings, as an anaesthetic, and as a solvent. [HEPT(A)- (from the number of carbon atoms it possesses) + -ANE.]

hep·tan·gu·lar (hep-táng-gew-lər) *adj.* Having seven angles.

hep·tar·chy (hép-taarki) *n., pl.* **-chies. 1. a.** Government by seven persons. **b.** A state so governed. **2.** A state divided into seven units, each with its own ruler. **3.** *Often capital* **H. a.** The informal confederation of the Anglo-Saxon kingdoms from the fifth to the ninth century, consisting of Kent, Sussex, Wessex, Essex, Northumbria, East Anglia, and Mercia. **b.** The historical period covering the existence of this confederation. [HEPT(A)- + -ARCHY.]

hep·ta·stich (héptə-stik) *n.* A poem, stanza, or strophe consisting of seven lines. [HEPTA- + Greek *stikhos,* line of verse.]

Hep·ta·teuch (héptə-tewk || -tōōk) *n.* The first seven books of the Old Testament. [Greek *heptateukhos (biblos),* "(book) in seven volumes" : HEPTA- + *teukhos,* tool, case holding writing material, volume.]

hep·ta·va·lent (héptə-váylənt) *adj. Chemistry.* Having a valency of seven; septivalent.

hep·tode (hép-tōd) *n.* A type of thermionic valve with seven electrodes: an anode, a cathode, and five grids. [HEPTA- + -ODE.]

Hep·worth (hép-wərth, -wurth), **Dame (Jocelyn) Barbara** (1903–75). English sculptor. Her works, like those of Henry Moore, explore the relationship between space and large rounded forms. She was made a dame in 1965.

her (hur; *weak forms* hər, ər) *pron.* The objective case of the third person pronoun *she.* It is used: **1.** As the direct object of a verb: *They assisted her.* **2.** As the indirect object of a verb: *They offered her a lift.* . **3.** As the object of a preposition: *This letter is addressed to her.* **4.** After *than* or *as* in comparisons in which the first term is in the objective case: *The judges praised him more than her.* **5.** *U.S. Informal.* In place of the reflexive pronoun *herself* as the indirect object of a verb: *She went to buy her a car.* **6.** In various elliptical, absolute, or interjectional phrases in which it is neither subject nor object: *Her and her fancy airs!*
~The possessive form of the pronoun *she.* Used attributively to indicate possession, agency, or reception of an action by the feminine person or entity spoken of: *her purse; pursuing her tasks; suffered her first rebuff.* —See Usage note at **me.** [Middle English *hire, her(e),* Old English *hire.*]

her. heraldry.

He·ra (héer-ə). Also **He·re** (-ee). *Greek Mythology.* The sister and consort of Zeus; identified with the Roman goddess Juno.

Heracles, Herakles. The Greek name for **Hercules.**

Heraklion, Herakleion. See **Iraklion.**

her·ald (hérrəld) *n.* **1.** A person who proclaims important news; a messenger; an envoy. **2.** A person or thing that announces or gives indication of something to come; a harbinger; a precursor. **3.** *British.* An official responsible for regulating all matters and settling all questions relating to heraldry; an officer of arms. **4. a.** An official formerly charged with making royal proclamations and with bearing messages of state between sovereigns. **b.** An official who formerly made proclamations and conveyed challenges at a tournament. **5.** *Capital* **H.** Used as part of the title of certain newspapers: *the Glasgow Herald; the Catholic Herald.*
~*tr.v.* **heralded, -alding, -alds. 1.** To proclaim; announce: *"the cocks that herald dawn all night"* (Malcolm Lowry). **2.** To usher in; inaugurate. [Middle English *herau(l)d,* from Old French *herau(l)t,* from Germanic.]

he·ral·dic (hi-rál-dik, he-, hə-) *adj.* Of or pertaining to heralds or heraldry. —**he·ral·di·cal·ly** *adv.*

heraldic achievement *n. Heraldry.* A coat of arms, or representation of a coat of arms, complete with crest, motto, and supporters.

her·ald·ist (hérrəldist) *n.* One who practises or studies heraldry.

her·ald·ry (hérrəldri) *n., pl.* **-ries. 1.** *Abbr.* **her. a.** The profession of devising, granting, and blazoning arms, of tracing pedigrees, and of ruling on questions of precedence, as practised by an officer of arms. **b.** A branch of knowledge dealing with the history and description in proper terms of armorial bearings and their accessories; armoury. **2.** Armorial ensigns or similar insignia. **3.** Pomp and ceremony, especially as attended with armorial trappings; pageantry.

Heralds' College *n.* The **College of Arms** *(see).*

herb (herb || *U.S.* erb) *n.* **1.** An angiosperm plant that has a fleshy stem as distinguished from the woody tissue of shrubs and trees, and that generally dies back at the end of each growing season; a herbaceous plant. **2.** Any of various often aromatic plants used especially in medicine or as seasoning. See Note at **plant.** [Middle English *(h)erbe,* from Old French, from Latin *herba†.*]

her·ba·ceous (her-báyshəss, hər- || *U.S. also* er-) *adj.* **1.** Pertaining to or characteristic of a herb as distinguished from a woody plant. **2.** Green and leaflike in appearance or texture. [Latin *herbāceus : herba,* HERB + -ACEOUS.]

herbaceous border *n.* A flower bed that contains herbaceous perennial plants rather than annuals or woody plants.

herb·age (hérb-ij || *U.S.* érb-) *n.* **1.** Herbaceous plant growth, especially grass or similar vegetation used for pasturage. **2.** The fleshy, often edible parts of plants. [Middle English *(h)erbage,* from Old French, from *(h)erbe,* HERB.]

herb·al (hérb'l || *U.S. also* érb'l) *adj.* Of, relating to, or containing herbs.
~*n.* A book about plants, especially those that are useful to mankind.

herb·al·ist (hérb'l-ist || *U.S. also* érb'l-) *n.* One who grows, collects, sells, or specialises in the use of herbs, especially medicinal herbs.

her·bar·i·um (her-báír-i-əm || *U.S. also* er-), *n., pl.* **-iums** or **-ia** (-i-ə). **1.** A collection of dried plants mounted and labelled for use in scientific study. **2.** A place or institution where such a collection is kept. [Late Latin *herbārium,* from Latin *herba,* HERB.]

herb bennet *n.* A hairy Eurasian plant, *Geum urbanum,* having small yellow flowers and an astringent root formerly used medicinally. [Middle English *herb beneit,* from Old French *herbe beneite* (or *benoite),* from Medieval Latin *herba benedicta,* "blessed herb" (from its medicinal properties) : Latin *herba,* HERB + *benedicta,* feminine past participle of *benedīcere,* to bless (see **benediction**).]

Her·bert (hérbərt), **George** (1593–1633). English poet, one of the Metaphysical Poets. None of his poems was published in his lifetime. They were collected in *The Temple* (1633).

herb Ge·rard (jérraard, jérrərd) *n., pl.* **herbs Gerard.** A plant, **ground elder** *(see).* [After St. *Gerard,* whose name was invoked by those suffering from gout, for which the plant was formerly prescribed.]

her·bi·cide (hérbi-sīd || *U.S. also* érbi-) *n.* A substance used to destroy plants, especially weeds. [HERB + -CIDE.] —**her·bi·ci·dal** (-sīd'l) *adj.*

her·bi·vore (hérbi-vawr || -vōr, *U.S. also* érbi-) *n.* A herbivorous animal. [New Latin *Herbivora* (former designation of herbivores), from the neuter plural of *herbivorus,* HERBIVOROUS.]

her·biv·o·rous (her-bívvərəss, hər- || *U.S. also* er-) *adj.* Feeding on plants; plant-eating. [New Latin *herbivorus :* HERB + -VOROUS.]

herb-of-grace (hérb-əv-gráyss || *U.S.* érb-) *n., pl.* **herbs-of-grace.** *Archaic.* A plant, **rue** *(see).* [Probably from the association of rue (the plant) with rue (repentance).]

herb Paris *n., pl.* **herbs Paris.** A European plant, *Paris quadrifolia,* having a whorl of four leaves and a solitary yellow or greenish flower. [Probably Medieval Latin *herba paris,* "herb of a pair" (perhaps a reference to the two pairs of leaves on the whorl), assimilated to *Paris* : Latin *herba,* HERB + *paris,* genitive of *par,* equal.]

herb Robert *n., pl.* **herbs Robert.** A low-growing plant, *Geranium robertianum,* having divided leaves and small reddish-purple flowers. [Middle English *herbe Robert,* from Medieval Latin *herba Robertī,* "herb of Robert," variously supposed to be named after *Robert* Duke of Normandy, Saint *Robert* (died 1067), French churchman, or Saint *Rupert,* seventh-century Bavarian ecclesiastic.]

Her·cu·la·ne·um (hérkew-láyni-əm). *Italian* **Er·co·la·no** (aircō-laánō). Ancient town of southern Italy. Situated 8 kilometres (5 miles) southeast of Naples, on the slopes of Vesuvius, it was completely buried in the volcano's eruption (A.D. 79) and remained undiscovered until 1709.

her·cu·le·an (hérkew-lée-ən, her-kéwli-ən) *adj.* **1.** Tremendously difficult or demanding: *a herculean task.* **2.** *Often capital* **H.** Resembling Hercules in size, power, or courage: *Herculean strength.* **3.** *Capital* **H.** Of or relating to Hercules.

Her·cu·les[1] (hérkew-leez). *Greek* **Her·a·cles, Her·a·kles** (hérrə-kleez). *Greek & Roman Mythology.* The son of Zeus and Alcmene, a hero of extraordinary strength who won immortality by performing the 12 labours demanded by Eurystheus.

Hercules[2] *n.* A man of enormous strength.

Hercules[3] *n. Astronomy.* A constellation in the Northern Hemisphere near Lyra and Corona Borealis, that contains the star Ras Algethi and the globular cluster M13.

Her·cyn·ian (her-sínni-ən) *adj.* Designating or belonging to a phase in the late Palaeozoic era (Carboniferous and Permian periods) characterised by mountain building.

herd (herd) *n.* **1. a.** A group of cattle or other domestic animals of a single kind kept together. **b.** A number of wild animals of one species that remain together as a group: *a herd of elephants.* **2.** A number of people grouped together by some common factor: *a herd of stranded passengers.* **3.** *Archaic.* One who tends a herd; a herdsman. Now used chiefly in combination: *a goatherd.* —**the herd.** The multitude of common people regarded as undistinguished and easily led or influenced.
~*v.* **herded, herding, herds.** —*intr.* **1.** To congregate in a herd or group. **2.** *Archaic.* To keep company; associate. —*tr.* **1. a.** To gather, tend, or drive (animals) in a herd. **b.** To gather or drive (people) as if in a herd. **2.** To place in a group. [Middle English *herd(e),* Old English *heord.*]

herd·er (hérdər) *n. Chiefly U.S.* A herdsman.

her·dic (hérdik) *n. U.S.* A small horse-drawn cab having two wheels, side seats, and an entrance at the back. [After Peter *Herdic* (1824–1888), American carriage-maker.]

herd instinct *n. Psychology.* An instinct that impels people to come together in groups and to conform to the prevailing modes of thought and behaviour of such groups.

herds·man (hérdz-mən) *n., pl.* **-men** (-mən). *Chiefly British.* A person who tends or breeds livestock as a profession.

here (heer) *adv.* **1.** At or in this place: *Stop here.* **2.** At this time; now: *Let's adjourn the meeting here and resume after lunch.* **3.** At or on this point, detail, or item: *There is great disagreement here.* **4.** In the present life or condition. **5.** To this place; hither: *Come here.* **6.** Used for emphasis after an imperative: *Look here! Now just you listen here.* **—here and there.** In various places. **—neither here nor there.** Of no relevance or significance.

~*adj.* **1.** *Informal.* Existing in this place. Used for emphasis after a noun or demonstrative pronoun: *I'll have this one here; this word here.* **2.** *Nonstandard.* Used for emphasis between a demonstrative pronoun and a noun: *this here word.*

~*n.* This place: *lives a mile from here; I left it near here.*

~*interj.* Used as a response to a roll call, as a command to an animal, as a way of calling attention, or as a rebuke or admonishment. **—here's to.** Used to propose a toast to a specified person or thing. [Middle English *her(e),* Old English *hēr.*]

Here. Variant of **Hera.**

here·a·bouts (héer-ə-bowts, -bówts) *adv.* Also **here·a·bout** (-bowt, -bówt). In this general vicinity; around here.

here·af·ter (heer-aáftər, héer- ‖ -áftər) *adv.* **1.** Immediately following this in time, order, or place; after this. **2.** In a world to come; in the afterlife: *win salvation hereafter.*

~*n.* **1.** The future. **2.** The world to come; life after death: *belief in a hereafter.*

here·at (heer-át, héer-) *adv. Archaic.* Because of this; at this.

here·by (heer-bī́, héer-, héerbī) *adv. Formal.* By virtue of this act, decree, bulletin, or document; by this means.

he·re·des. Plural of **heres.**

he·red·i·ta·ble (hi-réddɪtəb'l, he-, hə-) *adj. Rare.* Heritable.

her·e·dit·a·ment (hérrə-díttəmənt) *n. Law.* Any kind of property that can be inherited. [Medieval Latin *hērēditāmentum,* from Late Latin *hērēditāre,* to inherit, from Latin *hērēs* (stem *hērēd-*), heir.]

he·red·i·tar·i·an·ism (hi-réddi-taír-i-ən-iz'm, he-, hə-) *n. Psychology.* The doctrine or school that regards heredity as the major factor in determining intelligence and behaviour. Compare **environmentalism.** **—he·red·i·tar·i·an** *n. & adj.*

he·red·i·tar·y (hi-réddi-tri, he-, hə-, -təri ‖ *U.S.* -terri) *adj.* **1.** *Law.* **a.** Descending from an ancestor to a legal heir; passing down by inheritance. **b.** Having title or possession through inheritance. **2.** Genetically transmitted or transmissible. **3. a.** Appearing in or characteristic of successive generations. **b.** Derived or fostered from one's ancestors: *a hereditary prejudice.* **4.** Of or pertaining to heredity or inheritance. **—See Synonyms at innate.** [Latin *hērēditārius,* from *hērēditās,* HEREDITY.] **—he·red·i·tar·i·ly** (-trəli ‖ -térrəli) *adv.* **—he·red·i·tar·i·ness** *n.*

he·red·i·tist (hi-réddətist, he-, hə-) *n.* One who supports the theory that heredity rather than environment determines behaviour.

he·red·i·ty (hi-réddəti, he-, hə-) *n., pl.* **-ties.** **1.** The genetic transmission of characteristics from parents to offspring. **2.** The totality of characteristics and associated potentialities so transmitted to an individual organism. In this sense, compare **environment.** [Old French *heredite,* from Latin *hērēditās* (stem *hērēditāt-*), inheritance, from *hērēs* (stem *hērēd-*), heir.]

Her·e·ford[1] (hérrifərd) *n.* County town of Herefordshire, west central England, on the river Wye. Its cathedral houses the famous "Mappa Mundi" (World Map).

Her·e·ford[2] (hérri-fərd ‖ hér-) *n.* Any of a breed of beef cattle originally developed in Herefordshire and other border counties, having a reddish coat with white markings.

Hereford and Worcester. Former county (1974–1998) in west central England, bordering Wales.

Her·e·ford·shire (hérrifərd-shər, -sheer). County in west central England, bordering Wales, drained mainly by the river Wye and its tributaries. It is mostly agricultural. The county town is Hereford.

here·in (heer-ín, héer-) *adv. Formal.* In or into this; especially, in this book, document, or the like.

here·in·af·ter (héer-in-aáftər ‖ -áftər) *adv. Formal.* In a following part of this document, statement, or book; after this.

here·in·be·fore (héer-in-bi-fór ‖ -fór) *adv. Formal.* In a preceding part of this document, statement, or book; before this.

here·in·to (heer-ín-tōō, héer-, -tōō) *adv. Formal.* Into this matter, circumstance, situation, or place; into this.

here·of (heer-óv, héer- ‖ *Chiefly U.S.* -úv) *adv. Formal.* Pertaining to or concerning this.

here·on (heer-ón, héer- ‖ -áwn) *adv. Formal.* Hereupon.

He·re·ro (he-raír-ō, -réer-, haír-ə-rō, héer-) *n., pl.* **Hereros** or collectively **Herero.** **1.** A member of a Negroid people, living mainly in central Namibia. **2.** The language of this people, belonging to the Niger-Congo family of Bantu languages.

Hereroland. See **Damaraland.**

he·res (híer-eez) *n., pl.* **heredes** (hi-rée-deez, he-, hə-, -ráy-). *Law.* An heir. [Latin *hērēs.*]

he·re·si·arch (hi-réezi-aark, he-, hə- ‖ hérrə-si-) *n.* The founder or chief proponent of a heresy or heretical movement. [Late Latin *haeresiarcha,* from Late Greek *hairesiarkhēs* : Greek *hairesis,* sect (see **heresy**) + -ARCH.]

her·e·sy (hérrə-si) *n., pl.* **-sies.** **1. a.** A belief or doctrine at variance with the orthodox doctrine of a religious system; especially, a belief or opinion involving dissension from or denial of Christian dogma by a professed believer: *the Pelagian heresy.* **b.** Adherence to such dissenting belief or doctrine. **2. a.** A controversial or unorthodox opinion or doctrine in politics, philosophy, science, or other fields. **b.** Adherence to such unorthodox opinion. [Middle English *(h)eresie,* from Old French, from Late Latin *haeresis,* from Late Greek

hairesis, from Greek, "a taking", school of thought, faction, from *haireint,* to take, grasp, choose.]

her·e·tic (hérrətik) *n.* A person who holds controversial or unorthodox opinions in any area; especially, one who publicly dissents from the officially accepted dogma of a religion. [Middle English *(h)eretik,* from Old French *(h)eretique,* from Late Latin *haereticus,* from Greek *hairetikos,* able to choose, factious, from *hairetos,* from *hairein,* to take, choose. See **heresy.**] **—he·ret·i·cal** (hə-réttik'l, he-, hi-) *adj.* **—he·ret·i·cal·ly** *adv.*

here·to (heer-tōō, héer-) *adv. Formal.* To this place, document, matter, or proposition; to this: *Attached hereto is my voucher.*

here·to·fore (héer-tōō-fór, -tōō-, -tə- ‖ -fór) *adv. Formal.* Up to the present time; before this; previously. [Middle English : HERE + *tofore, toforn,* before, Old English *tōforan* : TO + *foran,* before, from *fore,* FORE (in front).]

here·un·der (heer-úndər, héer-) *adv. Formal.* **1.** In a following part of this document, statement, or book; after this. **2.** By the authority or under the powers of this decree, document, or the like.

here·un·to (heer-un-tōō ‖ -úntōō) *adv. Archaic.* Hereto.

here·up·on (héer-ə-pón ‖ -pon, -pawn) *adv.* Following instantly upon this; immediately after this; at this.

Her·e·ward the Wake (hérri-wərd), *(fl.* 1070). Anglo-Saxon folk hero. He led an English uprising against William the Conqueror in 1070, establishing himself and his followers on the Isle of Ely. William took control of the island in 1071, but Hereward escaped and is believed to have been pardoned later by William.

here·with (heer-wíth, héer-, -wíth) *adv.* **1.** *Formal.* Along with this. **2.** *Rare.* By this means; hereby.

her·i·ot (hérri-ət) *n. Law.* In feudal law, a death duty and later a tax on the expiry or abandoning of a holding, paid by a tenant to his lord. It consisted commonly of the tenant's best beast, and later of a money payment. [Middle English *heriet, heriot,* Old English *heregeatwe,* military equipment, "army-trappings" : *here,* army + *geatwa,* equipment, trappings.]

her·i·ta·ble (hérritəb'l) *adj.* **1.** Capable of being inherited; passing by inheritance. **2.** Transmitted from one generation to another; hereditary. **3.** Capable of inheriting or of taking by inheritance. [Middle English *heretable,* from Old French *heritable,* from *heriter,* to inherit. See **heritage.**]

her·i·tage (hérritij) *n.* **1.** *Law.* Property that is or can be inherited; an inheritance. **2.** Something other than property passed down from preceding generations; a legacy; a set of traditions, values, or treasured material things. **3.** A condition or lot accruing to one through the circumstances of one's birth; a birthright: *a heritage of affluence and position.* [Middle English *(h)eritage,* from Old French, from *heriter,* to inherit, from Late Latin *hērēditāre,* from Latin *hērēs* (stem *hērēd-*), heir.]

her·i·tor (hérritər) *n. Law.* An inheritor. [Middle English *heriter,* from Anglo-French, variant of Old French *heritier,* from Latin *hērēditārius,* HEREDITARY.]

her·i·tress (hérri-triss,-tress) *n.* Also **her·i·trix** (-triks). *Law.* A female inheritor.

herl (herl) *n.* **1.** The barb of a feather used in trimming an artificial fly for angling. **2.** A fishing fly made with this. [Middle English *herle,* probably from Middle Low German *herle, harlet.*]

her·ma (hér-mə) *n., pl.* **-mae** (-mee, -mī). Also **herm** (herm). In ancient Greece, a statue consisting of the head of the Greek god Hermes mounted on a square stone post. [Latin, from Greek *hermēs,* from *Hermēs,* HERMES.]

her·maph·ro·dite (her-máffrə-dīt) *n.* **1.** One having the sex organs and many of the secondary sex characteristics of both male and female. **2.** *Biology.* An organism, such as an earthworm, or a structure, such as a monoclinous flower, having both male and female reproductive organs. **3.** Anything consisting of a combination of diverse or contradictory elements. [Middle English *hermofrodite,* from Latin *hermaphrodītus,* from Greek *hermaphroditos,* after *Hermaphroditos,* Hermaphroditus, son of Hermes and Aphrodite who became united in one body with the nymph Salmacis.] **—her·maph·ro·dite, her·maph·ro·dit·ic** (-díttik) *adj.* **—her·maph·ro·dit·i·cal·ly** *adv.*

hermaphrodite brig *n. Nautical.* A two-masted vessel having a square-rigged foremast and a schooner-rigged mainmast. Also called "brigantine". [It combines the characteristics of a brig and a schooner.]

her·maph·ro·dit·ism (her-máffrə-dīt-iz'm) *n.* Also **her·maph·rod·ism** (-diz'm). The condition of being a hermaphrodite.

her·me·neu·tics (hérmi-néwtiks ‖ -nōōtiks) *n. Used with a singular verb.* The science and methodology of interpretation, especially of Scriptural text. Compare **exegetics.** [New Latin *hermeneutica,* from Greek *hermēneutikē (tekhnē),* (art) of interpretation, from the feminine of *hermēneutikos,* interpreter, from *hermēneuein,* to interpret, from *hermēneus†,* interpreter.] **—her·me·neu·tic, her·me·neu·ti·cal** *adj.* **—her·me·neu·ti·cal·ly** *adv.*

Her·mes (hér-meez) *Greek Mythology.* The god of commerce, invention, cunning, and theft, who also served as messenger and herald for the other gods, as patron of travellers and rogues, and as the conductor of the dead to Hades; identified with the Roman god Mercury.

Hermes Tris·me·gis·tus (tríss-mi-gís-təss, -jíss-). A legendary author of works on alchemy, astrology, and magic. [Latin, from Greek *Hermēs trismegistos,* "Hermes the thrice greatest".]

her·met·ic (her-méttik) *adj.* Also **her·met·i·cal** (-méttik'l). **1. a.** Completely sealed; especially, sealed against the escape or entry of air. **b.** Impervious to outside interference or influence; insulated; cloistered: *retreated to the hermetic confines of his room.* **2.** *Capital* **H.** Of or relating to Hermes Trismegistus or to the works ascribed to him. **3.** Of or pertaining to the occult sciences, especially alchemy; magical; recondite. [New Latin *hermeticus,* from Latin *Hermes* (stem *Hermet-*) *Trismegistus,* HERMES TRISMEGISTUS. He is said to have invented a magic seal to make vessels airtight.] —her·met·i·cal·ly *adv.*

her·mit (hérmit) *n.* A person who has withdrawn from society and lives a solitary existence, especially for religious reasons; a recluse. [Middle English *(h)ermite,* from Old French, from Late Latin *erēmīta,* from Greek *erēmitēs,* "(one) of the desert", from *erēmia,* desert, solitude, from *erēmos,* deserted, solitary.] —her·mit·ic (her-míttik), her·mit·i·cal *adj.* —her·mit·i·cal·ly *adv.*

her·mit·age (hérmitij) *n.* **1.** The habitation of a hermit or group of hermits. **2.** A place where one can live in seclusion; a retreat; a hideaway.

hermit crab *n.* Any of various decapod crustaceans of the section Anomura, having a soft, unarmoured abdomen, and occupying and carrying about the empty shell of a snail or other univalve mollusc.

Her·mit·i·an conjugate (her-mítti-ən, -mish- ‖ *U.S. also* -méesh-) *n. Mathematics.* A matrix formed by the transpose of the complex conjugate of a given matrix. [After Charles *Hermite* (1822–1901), French mathematician.]

Hermitian matrix *n. Mathematics.* A matrix that is identical to its Hermitian conjugate. [After Charles *Hermite.* See **Hermitian conjugate.**]

hern (hern) *n. Archaic.* A heron. [Variant of HERON.]

her·ni·a (hérni-ə) *n., pl.* **-as** *or* **herniae** (-ee). The protrusion of an organ, organic part, or any bodily structure through the wall that normally contains it. Hernia usually requires surgical treatment. Also called "rupture". [Middle English *hernia, hirnia,* from Latin *hernia.*] —her·ni·al *adj.*

her·ni·ate (hérni-ayt) *intr.v.* **-ated, -ating, -ates.** To protrude through an abnormal bodily opening. [HERNI(A) + -ATE.] —her·ni·a·tion (-áysh'n) *n.*

he·ro (héer-ō) *n., pl.* **-roes.** **1.** In mythology and legend, a man, often born of one mortal and one divine parent, who is endowed with great courage and strength, celebrated for his bold exploits, and favoured by the gods. **2.** Any man noted for feats of courage or nobility of purpose; especially, one who has risked or sacrificed his life: *heroes of forgotten wars.* **3.** A person who is greatly admired because of his special achievements or contributions in some event, field, or period: *The schoolboys discussed their football heroes.* **4.** The principal male character in a novel, poem, play, or the like. **5.** *Pl.* **-ros.** *U.S. Informal.* A very large sandwich made with a small loaf of crusty bread split lengthways, containing lettuce, condiments, and a variety of meats and cheeses. In this sense, also called "hero sandwich", "submarine". [Back-formation from Middle English *heroes* (plural), from Latin *hērōs* (plural *hērōēs*), a hero, from Greek *hērōs* (plural *hērōes*).]

He·ro (héer-ō). *Greek Mythology.* A priestess of Aphrodite loved by Leander, who nightly swam the Hellespont to visit her; upon finding him drowned, Hero drowned herself.

Her·od (hérrəd), known as Herod the Great (*c.*73 B.C.–4 B.C.). King of Judaea (37 B.C.–4 B.C.), son of Antipater II. He was named king of Judaea by the Roman senate. He is said by St. Matthew to have ordered the killing of all children under the age of two in Bethlehem (in order to destroy the infant Jesus).

Herod An·ti·pas (ánti-pass) (died *c.*A.D. 40). Tetrarch of Galilee (4 B.C.–A.D. 39). Herod's marriage to his niece Herodias brought the disapproval of John the Baptist. The aggrieved Herodias persuaded her daughter, Salome, to ask for the Baptist's head as payment for dancing at Antipas's birthday celebration. Antipas complied, and the Baptist was executed.

He·rod·o·tus (hi-róddətəss, he-, hə-) (*c.*484 B.C.–*c.*425 B.C.). Greek historian, commonly known as the "father of history". His writing, chiefly concerning the Persian Wars, is the earliest known attempt at secular, narrative history.

he·ro·ic (hi-rō-ik, hə-, he-) *adj.* Also **he·ro·i·cal** (-ik'l). **1.** Of, relating to, or resembling the heroes of legend, especially of Greek and Roman legend. **2.** Having or displaying the qualities of a hero; courageous; noble: *heroic deeds.* **3.** Bold and daring, especially in the face of insurmountable odds; gallant: *a heroic attempt to halt the enemy's advance.* **4. a.** Impressive in size or scope; grand; grandiose: *a heroic undertaking.* **b.** In fine arts, of a size somewhat larger than life: *heroic sculpture.* **5.** High-flown; ostentatious: *heroic language.* **6.** Of, pertaining to, or resembling heroic verse. —*n.* **1.** A heroic verse or poem. **2.** *Plural.* Melodramatic behaviour or language. —he·ro·i·cal·ly *adv.* —he·ro·i·cal·ness *n.*

heroic age *n.* The period in a nation's history, especially that of ancient Greece and Rome, when its legendary heroes are supposed to have lived.

heroic couplet *n.* A verse unit consisting of two rhymed lines in iambic pentameter.

heroic play *n.* A type of Restoration tragedy written in rhymed couplets and generally characterised by extravagant declamatory rhetoric.

heroic stanza *n.* An iambic pentameter quatrain rhymed *abab.* Also called "heroic quatrain".

heroic tenor *n.* A Heldentenor *(see).*

heroic verse *n.* Any of several verse forms suitable for and traditionally used in epic and dramatic poetry; typically, the dactylic

hexameter in Greek and Latin, and the iambic pentameter in English. Also called "heroic meter".

her·o·in (hérrō-in) *n.* A white, odourless, bitter, crystalline compound, $C_{17}H_{17}NO(C_2H_3O_2)_2$, that is derived from morphine and is a highly addictive narcotic. Also called "diacetylmorphine". [From a trademark.]

her·o·ine (hérrō-in) *n.* **1.** A woman having, or regarded as having, heroic characteristics. **2.** The principal female character in a novel, poem, play, or the like. [Latin *hērōīna,* Greek *hērōinē,* feminine of *hērōs,* HERO.]

her·o·ism (hérrō-iz'm) *n.* **1.** The condition or quality of being a hero. **2.** Heroic characteristics or conduct; courage; gallantry. See Synonyms at **courage.**

he·ron (hérrən) *n.* Any of various wading birds of the family Ardeidae, having a long neck, long legs, a long, pointed bill, and usually white or grey plumage. [Middle English *he(i)roun, hern(e),* from Old French *hairon,* from Frankish *haigro* (unattested).]

her·on·ry (hérrənri) *n., pl.* **-ries.** **1.** A place where herons nest and breed. **2.** A colony of herons or their nests.

hero worship *n.* **1.** Profound or excessive admiration for popular heroes or for other revered persons. **2.** Worship of the heroes of one's culture. — **he·ro-wor·ship** *tr.v.* —**he·ro-wor·ship·per** *n.*

herp. herpetology.

her·pes (hérpeez) *n.* Any of several viral diseases causing eruptions of the skin or mucous membrane; especially, herpes simplex or herpes zoster. [Latin *herpēs,* from Greek, shingles, "a creeping", from *herpein,* to creep.] —her·pet·ic (her-péttik) *adj.*

herpes sim·plex (símpleks) *n.* A viral infection causing inflammation at junctions of the skin and mucous membrane, especially on the face. Also called "cold sore". See **genital herpes.** [New Latin, "simple herpes".]

herpes zos·ter (zóstər, zóstər) *n.* A viral infection, **shingles** *(see).* [New Latin, "girdle herpes".]

her·pe·tol·o·gist (hérpi-tólləjist) *n.* A zoologist specialising in the study of reptiles and amphibians.

her·pe·tol·o·gy (hérpi-tólləji) *n. Abbr.* **herp., herpetol.** The scientific study of reptiles and amphibians as a branch of zoology. [Greek *herpeton,* "creeping thing", reptile, from *herpetos,* creeping, from *herpein,* to creep + -LOGY.] —her·pe·to·log·ic (-tə-lójik), her·pe·to·log·i·cal *adj.* —her·pe·to·log·i·cal·ly *adv.*

Herr (hair) *n., pl.* **Herren** (hérrən). *Abbr.* **Hr.** A title of courtesy prefixed to the name or professional title of a German man, equivalent to the English *Mr.* or *Sir.* [German, "Lord".]

Her·ren·volk (hérrən-folk) *n., pl.* **-völker** (-föl-kər, -föl-). The **master race** *(see).* [German, "master race".]

Her·rick (hérrik), **Robert** (1591–1674). English poet. Most of his work appeared in the collection *Hesperides* (1648).

her·ring (hérring) *n., pl.* **-rings** *or* collectively **herring.** Any of various fishes of the family Clupeidae; especially, a commercially important food fish, *Clupea harengus,* of Atlantic and Pacific waters. [Middle English *hering, heirreng,* Old English *hæring,* from West Germanic *hēringaz* (unattested).]

her·ring·bone (hérring-bōn) *n.* **1.** A pattern consisting of rows of short, slanted parallel lines, with the direction of the slant alternating row by row, used in masonry, parquetry, and weaving. Also used adjectively: *a herringbone brick pathway.* **2.** A twilled fabric woven in this pattern. Also used adjectively: *a herringbone suit.* **3.** An embroidery stitch of one row of slanted parallel lines crossing another slanted in the opposite direction, so that each line is crossed symmetrically at top and bottom only. **4.** In skiing, a method of climbing a slope with the skis pointed outwards, thus making tracks in a herringbone pattern.

~*v.* **herringboned, -boning, -bones.** —*tr.* To arrange in or decorate with a herringbone pattern. —*intr.* **1.** To produce this pattern. **2.** In skiing, to ascend a slope using the herringbone method. [From its resemblance to the skeletal structure of a herring.]

herringbone gear *n. Engineering.* A type of gearwheel in which two sets of teeth are cut on the rim, one set being at an angle to the other so that the teeth are V-shaped. Also called "double helical gear".

herring gull *n.* A common, widely distributed gull, *Larus argentatus,* having grey and white plumage with black wing tips. [From its habit of preying on herrings.]

hers (hurz). Possessive pronoun, absolute form of **her.** **1.** Belonging to her; her own. Used predicatively: *The red boots are hers.* **2.** The one or ones belonging to her. Used substantively: *If you can't find your hat, take hers.* —**of hers.** Belonging or pertaining to her: *a friend of hers.* [Middle English *hirs, hires,* a double possessive from *hire,* HER.]

Herschel, Sir John Frederick William (1792–1871). English mathematician and astronomer, son of Sir William. He extended his father's catalogue of double stars and nebulae.

Herschel, Sir William, born Friedrich Wilhelm Herschel (1738–1822). English astronomer, born in Germany. He settled in England in 1757, working as a music teacher and studying the sky in his own time. In 1781 he discovered Uranus, and was appointed astronomer to King George III. He also catalogued more than 800 double stars and about 2,500 nebulae.

her·self (hur-sélf; *also when non-initial* ur-) *pron.* A specialised form of the third person singular feminine pronoun. It is used: **1.** As a reflexive pronoun, forming the direct or indirect object of a verb or the object of a preposition: *hurt herself; gives herself time; talks to herself.* **2.** For emphasis, after *she: She herself wasn't certain.* **3.** As an emphasising substitute: *Herself in debt, she couldn't help us. It was addressed to her brother and herself.* **4.** As an indication of her real, normal, or healthy condition or identity: *She hasn't been herself lately.* **5.** *Chiefly Irish.* An important or prominent woman, such as the mistress of a household. Sometimes used humorously.

Herst·mon·ceux, Hurst·mon·ceux (hérst-mən-sew, -mon-, -soo). Village in East Sussex, southeast England. Its restored castle (1440), one of the finest medieval brick buildings, housed the Royal Observatory from its transfer from Greenwich in 1950 until 1990.

Hert·ford (hárt-fərd, hár-). Market town in southeast England. Situated on the river Lea, it is the county town of Hertfordshire.

Hert·ford·shire (hárt-fərd-shər, hár-, -sheer). County of southeast England. Mainly low-lying, but rising to the Chiltern hills in the northwest, it is largely agricultural.

Herts. (harts). Hertfordshire.

hertz (herts, hairts) *n., pl.* **hertz.** *Symbol* **Hz** A unit of frequency in the SI system, equal to one cycle per second. [After Heinrich HERTZ.]

Hertz (hairts), **Gustav Ludwig** (1887–1975). German physicist. In 1925 he was awarded, with James Franck, the Nobel prize in physics for his work on the impact of electrons on atoms.

Hertz, Heinrich Rudolf (1857–94). German physicist. He succeeded in producing the first radio waves artificially. The unit of frequency, the hertz, is named after him.

Hertz·i·an wave (hérts-i-ən, háirts-) *n.* A **radio wave** (*see*). No longer in technical usage. [After Heinrich HERTZ.]

Hertzog, (James) Barry (Munnik) (1866–1942). South African general in the Boer War (Second Anglo-Boer War) and founder of the South African National Party. In 1924 he became South Africa's first National Party prime minister in an election pact with the Labour Party. He steered South Africa to greater independence from Britain until 1939, when his policy of neutrality in World War II was defeated by J.C. Smuts's policy of fighting on the British side against Germany. Hertzog is regarded as an early advocate of racial segregation in South Africa and a champion of the Afrikaans language.

Hertz·sprung-Rus·sell diagram (hérts-sprung-rúss'l) *n.* A graph of the logarithms of the luminosities of stars plotted against the logarithms of their surface temperatures. Points on the diagram fall into groups corresponding to different types of star. Also called "Russell diagram". See **main sequence.** [Developed by Ejnar *Hertzsprung* (1873–1967), Danish astronomer, and Henry N. *Russell* (1877–1957), American astronomer.]

Her·zen (háirts'n ‖ *Russian* gyáir-tsən), **Alexander Ivanovich** (1812–70). Russian revolutionary and writer. He wrote *From the Other Shore* (1855), a series of essays on European politics, and the autobiography *My Past and Thoughts* (1855).

Her·zl (háirts'l), **Theodor** (1860–1904). Hungarian-born founder of the Zionist movement. He reported the Dreyfus affair in Paris for a Vienna newspaper, and decided that Jewish assimilation in European society was impossible. In 1896 he advocated the establishment of a Jewish national state in a pamphlet, *Der Judenstaat.* In 1897 he founded the Zionist World Congress and was its president until his death.

he's (heez; *weak forms* eez, hiz, iz). **1.** Contraction of *he is.* **2.** Contraction of *he has.*

Heshvan. Variant of **Cheshvan.**

He·si·od (hée-si-əd, hé-, -od) (*fl. c.*8th century B.C.). Greek poet. He wrote a long didactic poem on agriculture, *Works and Days,* and may have written a genealogy of the gods, the *Theogony,* and *The Shield of Heracles.*

hes·i·tan·cy (hézzitən-si) *n., pl.* **-cies. 1.** The state or quality of being hesitant; indecision. **2.** An instance of hesitating.

hes·i·tant (hézzitənt) *adj.* Inclined or tending to hesitate; irresolute. **—hes·i·tant·ly** *adv.*

hes·i·tate (hézzi-tayt) *intr.v.* **-tated, -tating, -tates. 1. a.** To be slow to act or decide; hold back in uncertainty; waver. **b.** To be reluctant, especially out of propriety, scruples, or concern for others; have qualms; demur: *"do you think she will hesitate to sacrifice you?"* (G.B. Shaw). **2.** To pause briefly as in uncertainty: *hesitate on the way upstairs.* **3.** To speak haltingly; falter. [Latin *haesitāre,* to stick fast, be undecided, hesitate, frequentative of *haerēre* (past participle *haesum*), to hold or hang fast, stick.] **—hes·i·tat·er** *n.* **—hes·i·tat·ing·ly** *adv.*

Synonyms: hesitate, vacillate, waver, falter.

hes·i·ta·tion (hézzi-táysh'n) *n.* **1.** The act or an instance of hesitating. **2.** A pause or faltering in speech. **—hes·i·ta·tive** (-tətiv, -taytiv) *adj.* **—hes·i·ta·tive·ly** *adv.*

Hes·pe·ri·a (he-spéer-i-ə). *Poetic.* The Western Land. A name applied by the Greeks to Italy and by the Romans to Spain or regions beyond. [Latin, from Greek, from *hesperos, hesperios,* of evening, western, from *hesperos,* evening.]

Hes·pe·ri·an (he-spéer-i-ən) *adj. Poetic.* **1.** Of or pertaining to Hesperia or the west. **2.** Of or relating to the Hesperides.

Hes·per·i·des (he-spérri-deez) *pl.n. Greek Mythology.* **1.** The nymphs, daughters of Atlas, who together with a dragon watched over the garden of the golden apples in the Islands of the Blessed. **2.** *Used with a singular verb.* The garden of the golden apples. **3.** The Islands of the Blessed, situated at the western end of the earth. [Latin *Hesperidēs,* from Greek *Hesperides,* plural of *Hesperis,* "western", daughter of the west, from *hesperos, hesperios,* of evening, western. See **Hesperia.**] **—Hes·per·id·i·an** (héspə-ríddi-ən), **Hes·per·id·e·an** (héss-perri-dée-ən) *adj.*

hes·per·i·din (hess-pérri-din) *n.* A white or colourless crystalline compound, $C_{28}H_{34}O_{15}$, occurring in citrus fruits. [HESPERID(IUM) + -IN.]

hes·per·id·i·um (héspər-íddi-əm) *n., pl.* **-idia** (-íddi-ə). *Botany.* A form of berry having a thickened, leathery rind and juicy pulp consisting of fluid-filled hairs, and divided into segments, such as an orange, lemon, or other citrus fruit. [New Latin, after the golden apples in the garden of HESPERIDES.]

Hes·per·us (hésпərəss) *n.* **1.** The evening star, Venus. **2.** Any of various other stars or planets prominently visible in the early evening. [Latin, from Greek *hesperos,* western.]

Hess (hess), **Dame Myra** (1890–1965). British pianist. During World War II she organised daily lunchtime concerts at the National Gallery, London. She was made a dame in 1941.

Hess, Rudolf (1894–1987). German politician, born in Egypt. He joined Hitler in 1920, took part in the Munich putsch, and was jailed. When Hitler became Chancellor in 1933, he named Hess as his deputy Führer. In 1939, Hess was named second in succession to the Nazi leadership after Goering. Hess flew to Scotland in May, 1941, apparently in a bid to start peace talks with the British government. At the Nuremberg trials of 1946 he was sentenced to life imprisonment in Spandau prison, Berlin, for war crimes.

Hess, Victor Francis (1883–1964). U.S. physicist, born in Austria. He discovered cosmic rays, and shared the Nobel prize for physics with C.D. Anderson in 1936.

Hess, Walter Rudolf (1881–1973). Swiss physiologist. He shared the Nobel prize in physiology or medicine with (António) Egas Moniz (1874–1955) in 1949, for work on the separate control over body organs of different areas of the brain.

Hesse (hess, -ə). *German* **Hes·sen** (héss'n). A state of Germany. In the west central area of the country, it consists mainly of forested uplands; there is some cattle-raising, and potatoes, beets, and wheat are grown. The capital is Wiesbaden.

Hesse, Hermann (1877–1962). German novelist and poet. He was a pacifist and, in 1914, moved to Switzerland, becoming a Swiss citizen in 1923. His novels, which explore psychological alienation, include *Steppenwolf* (1927) and *The Glass Bead Game* (1943). He was awarded the Nobel prize for literature in 1946.

hes·si·an (héssi-ən, héss-yən ‖ *U.S.* hésh'n) *n.* A coarse fabric made of jute, used for sacks, carpet-backing, and the like. [After HESSE, where it was made.]

Hes·si·an *n.* **1.** A native or inhabitant of Hesse. **2. a.** A Hessian mercenary in the British army in the War of American Independence. **b.** *U.S.* Any mercenary. **—***adj.* Of or relating to Hesse or its people.

Hessian boot *n.* A high, tasselled men's boot introduced into England from Hesse in the early 19th century.

Hessian fly *n.* A small fly, *Mayetiola destructor,* having larvae that infest and destroy wheat and other grain plants. [Supposed to have been introduced to America by Hessian troops during the War of Independence.]

hes·site (héssīt) *n.* A black or grey mineral form of silver telluride, Ag_2Te. [German *Hessit,* after Henry *Hess,* 19th-century Swiss chemist.]

hessonite. Variant of **essonite.**

Hes·ti·a (hésti-ə). *Greek Mythology.* The goddess of the hearth, daughter of Cronus and Rhea; identified with the Roman goddess Vesta.

het. See **het up.**

he·tae·ra (hi-tír-ə, he-) *n., pl.* **-ras** or **-taerae** (-tír-ee). Also **he·tai·ra** (-tír-ə) *pl.* **-ras** or **-tairai** (-tír-ī). A courtesan or concubine; especially, in ancient Greece, one of a special class of cultivated female companions. [Greek *hetaira,* feminine of *hetairos,* companion.]

he·tae·rism (hi-tír-iz'm, he-) *n.* **1.** Concubinage. **2.** *Anthropology.* The practice of communal marriage, supposed to have been characteristic of primitive societies. **—he·tae·rist** *n.* **—he·tae·ris·tic** (-ístik) *adj.*

hetero–, heter– *comb. form.* Indicates other, another, or different; for example, **heterogamy, heterosexual.** [Greek *heteros,* other.]

het·er·o·cer·cal (héttərō-sérk'l) *adj. Zoology.* Pertaining to, designating, or characterised by a tail fin having two unequal lobes, with the vertebral column extending into the upper, usually larger lobe, as in sharks. Compare **homocercal.** [HETERO- + Greek *kerkos,* tail.]

het·er·o·chro·mat·ic (héttərō-krə-máttik, -krō-) *adj.* **1.** Of or pertaining to different colours; varicoloured. **2.** Consisting of different wavelengths or frequencies. **3.** Of or pertaining to heterochromatin. **—het·er·o·chro·ma·tism** (-krómətiz'm) *n.*

het·er·o·chro·ma·tin (héttərō-krómətin) *n. Genetics.* Chromosomal material exhibiting maximal staining in the nuclear meiotic interphase and lacking specific genetic activity. Compare **euchromatin.**

het·er·o·chro·mo·some (héttərō-krómə-sōm) *n. Genetics.* **1.** An atypical chromosome, such as a sex chromosome. **2.** A chromosome composed primarily of heterochromatin.

het·er·o·clite (héttər-ə-klīt, -ō-) *n.* **1.** A word formed or inflected in an unusual way. **2.** Anything or anyone that departs from the normal or usual. [Late Latin, from Greek *heteroklitos,* irregularly inflected : HETERO- + Greek *klitos,* from *klinein,* to bend, inflect.] **—het·er·o·clite, het·er·o·clit·ic** (-klíttik) *adj.*

het·er·o·cy·clic (héttərō-síklik, -sícklik) *adj. Chemistry.* Of, pertaining to, or designating a chemical compound having a ring of atoms in its molecules that contains at least one atom of an element other than carbon.

~*n. Chemistry.* A heterocyclic compound. Compare **homocyclic**.

het·er·o·dac·tyl (héttərō-dáktil) *adj.* Designating a bird's foot on which the first and second toes point backwards and the third and fourth forwards.

~*n.* A bird having heterodactyl feet.

het·er·o·dont (héttər-ə-dont, -ō-) *adj.* Having teeth of various different kinds. Said of most mammals. [HETERO- + -ODONT.]

het·er·o·dox (héttrə-doks, héttər-ə-, -ō-) *adj.* **1.** Not in agreement with accepted beliefs; especially, departing from an established religious doctrine or dogma. Compare **orthodox**. **2.** Holding unorthodox opinions. [Late Latin *heterodoxus,* from Greek *heterodoxos,* differing in opinion : HETERO- + *doxa,* opinion, notion, from *dokein,* to expect, think.]

het·er·o·dox·y (héttrə-doksi, héttər-ə-, -ō-) *n., pl.* **-ies. 1.** The condition or quality of being heterodox. **2.** A heterodox opinion or doctrine.

het·er·o·dyne (héttər-ə-dīn, -ō-) *adj. Electronics.* Having alternating currents of two different frequencies that are combined to generate a current that has sum and difference frequencies, either of which may be used in radio or television receivers by proper tuning or filtering.

~*tr.v.* **heterodyned, -dyning, -dynes.** To combine (a radiofrequency wave) with a locally generated wave of different frequency in order to produce a new frequency equal to the sum or difference of the two.

het·er·oe·cious (héttə-réeshəss) *adj.* Spending alternate stages of a life cycle on different, unrelated hosts. Said of parasites such as rusts and tapeworms. [HETERO- + Greek *oikia,* house.] —**het·er·oe·cism** (-rée-siz'm) *n.*

het·er·o·gam·ete (héttərō-gámmeet, -ga-méet) *n.* Either of two conjugating gametes, such as the small, motile male spermatozoon and the larger, nonmotile female ovum, that differ in size, form, or behaviour.

het·er·o·ga·met·ic (héttərō-ga-méttik, -gə-) *adj.* Having a dissimilar pair of sex chromosomes, as in human males, or one unpaired sex chromosome, as in some male insects. Compare **homogametic**.

het·er·og·a·mous (héttə-róggəməss) *adj.* **1.** *Biology.* Characterised by the fusion of unlike gametes in the reproductive process. **2.** *Botany.* Bearing flowers of different kinds, especially both male and female flowers, on one plant. [HETERO- + -GAMOUS.]

het·er·og·a·my (héttə-róggəmi) *n.* **1.** Alternation of generations, one sexual, the other parthenogenetic, as in some aphids. **2.** A state in which uniting gametes are dissimilar in structure and size as well as in function. [HETERO- + -GAMY.] —**het·er·o·gam·ic** (-rō-gámmik) *adj.*

het·er·o·ge·ne·i·ty (héttər-ō-jə-née-əti, -ə-, -náy-) *n.* The quality or state of being heterogeneous; nonuniformity; dissimilarity.

het·er·o·ge·ne·ous (héttə-jéeni-əss, -ō-, -jéen-yəss) *adj.* Also **het·er·og·e·nous** (héttə-rójənəss) (for sense 1). **1.** Consisting of or involving parts that are unlike or without interrelation; having dissimilar constituents or elements; not homogeneous: *a heterogeneous collection of people.* **2.** Completely different; incongruous. **3.** *Physics & Chemistry.* Of, involving, or designating a system of two or more different phases: *a heterogeneous mixture; heterogeneous catalysis.* Compare **homogeneous**. —See Synonyms at **miscellaneous**. [Medieval Latin *heterogeneus,* from Greek *heterogenēs* : HETERO- + *genos,* kind.] —**het·er·o·ge·ne·ous·ly** *adv.* —**het·er·o·ge·ne·ous·ness** *n.*

het·er·o·gen·e·sis (héttərō-jénnə-siss) *n.* **Alternation of generations** *(see).* —**het·er·o·ge·net·ic** (-jə-néttik) *adj.*

het·er·og·e·nous¹ (héttə-rójənəss) *adj.* Also **het·er·o·gen·ic** (-rō-jénnik) Originating outside the body. [HETERO- + -GENOUS.] —**het·er·og·e·ny** *n.*

heterogenous². Variant of **heterogeneous**.

het·er·og·o·nous (héttə-róggənəss) *adj.* **1.** *Biology.* Characterised by the alternation of sexual and asexual generations. **2.** *Botany.* Designating plants in which the flowers differ from each other in the lengths of the stamens and styles. [HETERO- + -GON(Y) + -OUS.] —**het·er·og·o·ny** *n.*

het·er·o·graft (héttər-ə-graaft, -ō- || -graft) *n.* A type of tissue graft in which the donor and recipient are of different species. Also called "xenograft".

het·er·og·ra·phy (héttə-róggrəfi) *n., pl.* **-phies. 1.** Spelling that is inconsistent in respect of single sounds, as the spelling of modern English is; for example, the *-uf* sound is rendered very differently in the words *cuff* and *tough*. **2.** Spelling that departs from conventional usage. [HETERO- + -GRAPHY.]

het·er·og·y·nous (héttə-rójinəss) *adj. Zoology.* Having two types of female, one able to reproduce sexually, the other infertile, as in ants. [HETERO- + -GYNOUS.]

het·er·o·junc·tion (héttərō-jungksh'n) *n. Electronics.* A junction between two semiconductors with different types of conductivity.

het·er·o·kar·y·on (héttərō-kárri-ən, -on) *n.* A cell containing two or more nuclei of different types, or an organism made up of such cells. —**het·er·o·kar·y·ot·ic** (óttik) *adj.*

het·er·o·kar·y·o·sis (héttərə-kárri-ō-siss) *n. Biology.* The presence of more than one type of nucleus in a single cell, as occurs in certain fungi. [HETERO- + KARY(O)- + -OSIS (condition).]

het·er·o·lec·i·thal (héttərō-léssith'l) *adj.* Having nonhomogeneous distribution of yolk in an ovum. Said of birds' eggs. Compare **isolecithal**. [HETERO- + Greek *lekithos,* yolk (see **lecithin**) + -AL.]

het·er·ol·o·gous (héttə-rólləgəss) *adj.* **1.** Derived from a different species: *a heterologous graft.* **2.** Of or pertaining to cytological or histological elements not normally occurring in a designated part of the body. [HETERO- + -LOG(Y) + -OUS.]

het·er·ol·o·gy (héttə-rólləji) *n.* Lack of correspondence between bodily parts, as in structure, arrangement, or development, arising from differences in origin. [HETERO- + -LOGY.]

het·er·ol·y·sis (héttə-róllə-siss) *n., pl.* **-ses** (-seez). **1.** *Biology.* Dissolution of cells or protein components in one species by lytic agents of another. Compare **autolysis**. **2.** *Chemistry.* A reaction in which the breaking of a chemical bond leads to the formation of a pair of ions with opposite charges. Also called "heterolytic fission". Compare **homolysis**. [New Latin : HETERO- + -LYSIS.] —**het·er·o·lyt·ic** (-rō-líttik) *adj.*

het·er·om·er·ous (héttə-rómmərəss) *adj. Biology.* Having unequal or differing parts within the same structure or similar structures. [HETERO- + -MEROUS.]

het·er·o·mor·phic (héttər-ə-mórfik, -ō-) *adj.* Also **het·er·o·mor·phous** (-mórfəss). **1.** Having a different shape, size, or function from the normal; atypical. **2.** Designating homologous chromosome pairs in which one differs from the other in size or shape. **3.** *Biology.* Having differing forms, as in different stages of an insect's life cycle. In this sense, compare **polymorphic**. [HETERO- + -MORPHIC.] —**het·er·o·mor·phism** *n.*

het·er·on·o·mous (héttə-rónnəməss) *adj.* **1.** Subject to external or foreign laws or domination; not autonomous. **2.** Differing in development or manner of specialisation, as the dissimilar segments of certain arthropods. [HETERO- + Greek *nomos,* law + -OUS.] —**het·er·on·o·mous·ly** *adv.*

het·er·o·nym (héttər-ə-nim, -ō-) *n.* One of two or more words that have identical spelling but different meanings and pronunciations; for example, *row* (a line) and *row* (a fight). [Back-formation from HETERONYMOUS.]

het·er·on·y·mous (héttə-rónniməss) *adj.* **1.** Of or pertaining to a heteronym. **2.** Designating names or terms that are different but have correspondence or interrelationship; for example, *master* and *mistress*. [Late Greek *heterōnumos* : HETERO- + Greek *onoma,* name.]

Het·er·o·ou·si·an (héttərō-ṓ-si-ən, -ów-) *n.* Also **Het·er·ou·si·an** (héttə-rṓō-, -rów-). A Christian holding that the substance and nature of God the Father and God the Son are different; an Arian. Compare **Homoiousian, Homoousian**.

~*adj.* Designating or pertaining to the Heteroousians or their beliefs. [Late Greek *hetero(o)usios,* of different substance : HETERO- + Greek *ousia,* substance, essence, from *ōn* (stem *ous*-), present participle of *einai,* to be.]

het·er·oph·o·ny (héttə-róffəni) *n. Music.* The simultaneous playing or singing of a single melody, by two or more different instruments or singers. [HETERO- + -PHONY.]

het·er·o·phor·i·a (héttər-ə-fáwri-ə, -ō- || -fóri-) *n.* A tendency to squint. [HETERO- + -*phoria,* tendency, act of bearing, from Greek *pherein,* to carry, bear.]

het·er·o·phyl·lous (héttə-rō-fílləss, -róffiləss) *adj. Botany.* Having unlike leaves on one plant. [HETERO- + -PHYLLOUS.] —**het·er·o·phyl·ly** *n.*

het·er·o·phyte (héttər-ə-fīt, -ō-) *n.* A plant, such as a facultative parasite, that can obtain its nourishment from living or dead organic sources. [HETERO- + -PHYTE.]

het·er·o·plas·ty (héttərō-plasti) *n., pl.* **-ties.** The surgical grafting of tissue obtained from another person or from a lower animal. [HETERO- + -PLASTY.]

het·er·op·ter·ous (héttə-róptərəss) *adj.* Also **het·er·op·ter·an** (-róptərən). Of or belonging to the insect order Heteroptera, which includes the true bugs, characterised by forewings and hind wings that differ from one another. [New Latin *Heteroptera* : HETERO- + -PTEROUS.]

het·er·o·sce·das·tic (héttərō-ski-dástik, -ske-) *adj. Statistics.* Pertaining to or designating variables for which all possible values do not have constant variance. [HETERO- + *scedastic,* from Greek *skedasis,* dispersion, scattering.] —**het·er·o·sce·das·tic·i·ty** (-skédass-s-tíssəti) *n.*

het·er·o·sex·u·al (héttra-sék-sew-əl, héttər-ə-, -ō-, -shoo-, -shwəl) *adj.* **1.** Characterised by attraction to the opposite sex. **2.** Of or pertaining to different sexes or to sexual relations between persons of the opposite sex.

~*n.* A heterosexual person. —**het·er·o·sex·u·al·i·ty** (-ál-əti) *n.*

het·er·o·sis (héttə-rō-siss) *n. Biology.* Increased vigour or other superior qualities arising from the crossbreeding of genetically different plants or animals. Also called "hybrid vigour". [New Latin, from Greek *heter(oi)ōsis,* alteration, transformation, from *heteroioun,* to alter, from *heteroios,* different in kind, from *heteros,* one of two, the other.]

het·er·os·po·rous (héttə-róspərəss, -rō-spáwr-əss || -spór-) *adj. Botany.* Producing microspores and megaspores. Said of seed plants and some ferns. [HETERO- + -SPOROUS.] —**het·er·os·po·ry** *n.*

het·er·o·tax·is (héttərō-táksiss) *n.* Also **het·er·o·tax·y** (-táksi), **het·er·o·tax·i·a** (-táksi-ə). Abnormal structural arrangement, as of organs of the body. [HETERO- + -TAXIS.] —**het·er·o·tac·tic** (-táktik), **het·er·o·tac·tous** *adj.*

het·er·o·thal·lic (héttərō-thál-ik) *adj. Botany.* Producing male gametangia in one structure or plant, and female gametangia in a different structure or plant, so that gametangia from different individuals must meet before fusion can occur. Said of some algae and fungi. [HETERO- + Greek *thallos,* young shoot, THALLUS.] —**het·er·o·thal·lism** *n.*

het·er·o·top·i·a (hèttər-ə-tṓpi-ə, -ō-) *n.* Also **het·er·ot·o·py** (hèttə-róttəpi). *Pathology.* Displacement of an organ or other part of the body from its normal position. —**het·er·o·top·ic** (-tóppik) *adj.*

het·er·o·troph·ic (hèttə-rō-trṓffik, -trṓfik) *adj.* Obtaining nourishment from organic substances, as do all animals and some plants. Compare **autotrophic**. [HETERO- + -TROPHIC.] —**het·er·o·troph·i·cal·ly** *adv.* —**het·er·o·troph·ism, het·er·ot·ro·phy** (-róttrəfi) *n.*

het·er·o·typ·ic (hèttərō-típpik) *adj.* **1.** *Biology.* Relating to or designating the first reduction division of meiosis. **2.** Of a different type or form. Compare **homeotypic**. [HETERO- + TYPIC(AL).]

het·er·o·zy·go·sis (hèttərō-zī-gṓ-siss) *n.* **1.** Derivation from or union between genetically different gametes. **2.** The condition of being a heterozygote.

het·er·o·zy·gote (hèttərō-zī-gōt) *n.* An organism that has inherited different alleles for one or more genes; a hybrid. —**het·er·o·zy·gous** (-zígəss) *adj.*

heth. Variant of **cheth.**

het·man (hétmən) *n.* A Cossack military leader. [Polish, probably from German *Hauptmann,* captain.]

het up (hét úp) *adj. Informal.* Angry or flustered; worked up. [Dialect *het,* past participle of HEAT.]

heu·land·ite (hḗwlən-dīt) *n.* A white, red, or yellow zeolite mineral with composition $(Ca,Na,K)_6Al_{10}(Al,Si)Si_{29}O_{80} \cdot 25H_2O$. [After Henry *Heuland,* 19th-century English mineral collector.]

heu·ris·tic (hewr-rístik) *adj.* **1.** Assisting the process of learning or discovery; guiding or furthering investigation: *I propose this theory purely as a heuristic device.* **2.** Designating the educational method in which the student is allowed or encouraged to learn independently through his own investigation. **3.** *Mathematics.* Designating a method of problem-solving that relies on inductive reasoning from past experience, in the absence of a relevant algorithm: *a heuristic approach.* [From Greek *heuriskein,* to discover, find.] —**heu·ris·tic·al·ly** *adv.*

heu·ris·tics (hewr-rístiks) *n. Used with a singular verb.* The science or study of heuristic methods and practices.

Heus·ler alloy (hóyz-lər, héwz-) *n.* Any of a class of alloys of manganese, aluminium, zinc, and copper, that are ferromagnetic even though their components are not. [After Conrad *Heusler,* 19th century German chemist and mining engineer.]

Hev·e·sy (hévveshi), **Georg von** (1885–1966). Hungarian physicist and chemist. He used isotopes as tracers to investigate chemical processes and discovered the element hafnium. He was awarded the Nobel prize for chemistry in 1943.

hew (hew) *v.* **hewed, hewn** (hewn) or **hewed, hewing, hews.** —*tr.* **1. a.** To make or shape with an axe, knife, or other cutting tool. Often used with *out: hew out a small canoe.* **b.** To form (a fissure, channel, or the like) by natural means, as by the action of lightning or dripping water. **2.** To cut down with an axe; fell. Used with *away, down, from,* or *off: hew down an oak.* **3.** To strike or cut; cleave; chop: *hewed in pieces.* —*intr.* **1.** To cut by repeated blows of an axe, sword, or the like. **2.** *U.S.* To adhere or conform: *hew to the line.* [Hew, hewn; Middle English *hewen, hewen,* Old English *hēawan, hēawan,* from Germanic.] —**hew·er** *n.*

hex (heks) *n. Chiefly U.S.* **1.** An evil spell; a curse. **2.** A person or thing that exercises an evil or dominating influence. **3.** A witch. —**put the hex on.** To hex (a person). ~*tr.v.* **hexed, hexing, hexes.** *Chiefly U.S.* **1.** To work evil on; bewitch. **2.** To wish or bring bad luck to, especially through superstitious means. [Pennsylvania Dutch, from German *Hexe,* witch, from Middle High German *hecse, häxe,* probably from Old High German *hagazusa, hagzissa.*]

Hex (heks) *n.* A trademark for a game played by two people on a board made up of hexagons, the aim being to complete a chain of counters from one side of the board to the other.

hex. hexagon; hexagonal.

hexa–, hex– *comb. form.* Indicates six; for example, **hexagram, hexane.** [Greek, from *hex,* six.]

hex·a·canth (hèksə-kanth) *n. Zoology.* An **oncosphere** *(see).* [HEXA + Greek *akantha,* thorn, spine.]

hex·a·chlo·ro·cy·clo·hex·ane (hèksə-kláwrō-síklō-héksayn ‖ -klṓrō-) *n.* A white compound, $C_6H_6Cl_6$, derived from benzene and having several isomeric forms, usually used as a mixture of isomers as an insecticide. Also called "benzine hexachloride".

hex·a·chlo·ro·éth·ane (hèksə-kláwrō-éthayn, -kláwr- ‖ -klṓrō-) *n.* Also **hex·a·chlor·eth·ane** (-kláwr- ‖ -klṓr-). A colourless crystalline compound, Cl_3CCCl_3, that is used as a camphor substitute and in pyrotechnics, explosives, and veterinary medicine.

hex·a·chlo·ro·phene (hèksə-kláwrə-feen, -klórrə- ‖ -klṓrə-) *n.* A white powder, $(C_6HCl_3OH)_2CH_2$, formerly used as a bactericidal agent in soaps, cosmetics, and skin medications.

hex·a·chord (hèksə-kawrd) *n.* In medieval music, any of three diatonic sequences of six notes, the central interval being a semitone, and the others whole tones. [HEXA- + -CHORD.]

hex·ad (héks-ad) *n.* A group or series of six. [Late Latin *hexas* (stem *hexad*-), the number six, from Greek, from *hex,* six.] —**hex·ad·ic** (hek-sáddik) *adj.*

hex·a·de·ca·nol (hèksə-déckə-nol ‖ -nōl) *n.* **Cetyl alcohol** *(see).*

hex·a·dec·i·mal (hèksə-déssim'l) *adj.* Designating or pertaining to a number system with base 16, used in computing to represent groups of 4 bits. ~*n.* **1.** A hexadecimal number. **2.** A hexadecimal notation.

hex·a·gon (hèksə-gən ‖ *chiefly U.S.* -gon) *n. Abbr.* **hex.** A polygon having six sides and six angles. [Late Latin *hexagōnum,* from Greek *hexagōnon,* from *hexagōnos,* six-angled : HEXA- + -GON.]

hex·ag·o·nal (hek-sággənəl, hék-) *adj. Abbr.* **hex.** **1.** Having six sides and six angles. **2.** Of, pertaining to, or formed in hexagons. **3.** *Chemistry & Geology.* Having three equal axes intersecting at 60° in one plane, and one axis of variable length that is at right angles to the others. Said of crystals or crystal structures. —**hex·ag·o·nal·ly** *adv.*

hex·a·gram (héksə-gram) *n.* **1.** A six-pointed star, consisting of a regular hexagon with each of the sides extended to form equilateral triangles. See **Star of David**. **2.** Any figure of six lines or sides. [HEXA- + -GRAM.]

hex·a·he·dral (hèksə-heédrəl) *adj.* **1.** Having six plane surfaces. **2.** Of, pertaining to, or formed in hexahedrons. [HEXAHEDR(ON) + -AL.] —**hex·a·he·dral·ly** *adv.*

hex·a·he·dron (hèksə-heé-drən) *n., pl.* **-drons** or **-dra** (-drə) A polyhedron with six plane surfaces. [Greek *hexaedron,* from *hexaedros,* six-sided : HEXA- + -HEDRON.]

hex·a·hy·drate (hèksə-hídrayt) *n. Chemistry.* A crystalline substance that has six molecules of water of crystallisation per molecule of the compound.

hex·am·er·ous (hek-sámmərəss) *adj.* **1.** Having six similar parts or divisions. **2.** *Botany.* Having flower parts, such as petals, sepals, and stamens, in sets of six. Also written *6-merous.* [HEXA- + -MEROUS.] —**hex·am·er·ism** *n.*

hex·am·e·ter (hek-sámmitər) *n.* A line of verse consisting of six metrical feet. [Latin, from Greek *hexametron,* from *hexametros,* having six metrical feet : HEXA- + -METER.] —**hex·a·met·ric** (héksə-métrik), **hex·a·met·ri·cal** *adj.*

hex·a·mine (héksə-meen) *n.* A colourless crystalline compound, $C_6H_{12}N_7$, used in solution as an antiseptic, especially for infections of the urinary tract. Also called "hexamethylenetetramine", "methenamine". [HEXA + AMINE.]

hex·ane (héksayn) *n.* **1.** A colourless, flammable liquid, $CH_3(CH_2)_4CH_3$, derived from the fractional distillation of petroleum and used as a solvent and as the working fluid in low-temperature thermometers. **2.** Any of a group of isomeric alkane hydrocarbons with the formula C_6H_{14}. [HEX(A)- + -ANE.]

hex·an·gu·lar (hek-sáng-gew-lər) *adj.* Having six angles.

hex·a·no·ic acid (hèksə-nṓ-ik) *n.* An organic acid, **caproic acid** *(see).* [From HEXANE.]

hex·a·pla (héksəplə) *n.* An edition of the Old Testament, compiled by Origen, having six versions of the text in separate columns. [Greek, neuter plural of *hexaplous,* sixfold : HEXA- + *plous,* -fold.]

hex·a·pod (hèksə-pod) *n.* Any member of the class Insecta (or Hexapoda); an insect. ~*adj.* Also **hex·ap·o·dous** (hek-sáppədəss). **1.** Of or belonging to the Hexapoda. **2.** Having six legs or feet. [New Latin *Hexapoda* : HEXA- + -POD.]

hex·ap·o·dy (hek-sáppədi) *n.* A line of verse consisting of six metrical feet. [HEXA + *-pody,* from Greek *-podia,* condition of having a certain number of feet, from *pous* (stem *pod*-), foot.]

hex·a·stich (hèksə-stik) *n.* A poem, stanza, or strophe consisting of six lines. [HEXA- + Greek *stikhos,* line of verse.]

Hex·a·teuch (hèksə-tewk ‖ -tōōk) *n.* The first six books of the Old Testament. [HEXA- + Greek *teukhos,* tool, case holding writing material, roll of papyrus, volume.]

hex·a·va·lent (hèksə-váylənt) *adj. Chemistry.* Having a valency of 6; sexivalent.

hex·o·san (hèksə-san) *n.* Any of several polysaccharides that form a hexose on hydrolysis. [HEXOS(E) + -AN.]

hex·ose (héks-ōss, -ōz) *n.* Any of various simple sugars, such as glucose, that have six carbon atoms per molecule. [HEX(A)- + -OSE.]

hex·yl (héksil) *n.* The hydrocarbon radical C_6H_{13}, having a valency of 1, especially the radical derived from normal hexane, $CH_3(CH_2)_5$. [HEX(A)- + -YL.]

hex·yl·re·sor·ci·nol (héksil-ri-zór-si-nol, -rə- ‖ -nōl) *n.* A yellowish-white crystalline phenol, $C_{12}H_{18}O_2$, used as an antiseptic and anthelmintic.

hey (hay) *interj.* **1.** Used to express surprise, appreciation, wonder, or the like: *Hey, that's nice!* **2.** Used to attract attention: *Hey, you!* [Middle English *hei, hay.*]

hey·day (háyday) *n.* The period of greatest popularity, success, fashion, power, or the like; the prime: *The heyday of the ecology movement is over.* [Earlier *heyda,* probably an extension of HEY; akin to Low German *heida,* hurrah!]

Hey·er·dahl (hī-ər-daal, háy-), **Thor** (1914–). Norwegian anthropologist and explorer. He led the Kon Tiki expedition on a raft across the Pacific Ocean from Peru to the Tuamotu islands in 1947, to demonstrate that Polynesians might be of South American origin. In 1970 he crossed the Atlantic Ocean from Morocco to Barbados in a papyrus boat to show that the ancient Egyptians might have sailed to America. Wrote *Pyramids of Tucume* (1995).

hf high frequency.

Hf The symbol for the element hafnium.

hg hectogram.

Hg The symbol for the element mercury (Latin *hydrargyrum*).

HG, H.G. 1. High German. **2.** His (or Her) Grace. **3.** Home Guard.

H-gir·der (áych-gurdər ‖ háych-) *n.* An **H-beam** *(see).*

hgt. height.

HGV heavy goods vehicle.

H.H. 1. His (or Her) Highness. **2.** His Holiness.

H-hour (áych-owr, -ow-ər ‖ háych-) *n. Military.* **Zero hour** *(see).* [H, abbreviation for HOUR.]

hi (hī) *interj.* **1.** *Informal.* Used as a greeting. **2.** Used to attract attention. [Middle English *hy,* parallel form to HEY.]

H.I. Hawaiian Islands.

hi·a·tus (hī-áytəss) *n., pl.* **hiatuses** or **hiatus. 1.** A gap or missing section; a lacuna. **2.** Any loss or interruption in time or continuity; a break. **3.** *Phonetics.* The immediate sequence of two vowel sounds, each of which constitutes or belongs to a separate syllable. **4.** *Anatomy.* A separation, aperture, or fissure. [Latin *hiātus,* a gaping, gap, from the past participle of *hiāre,* to gape.]

hiatus hernia *n.* A hernia in which part of the stomach protrudes through the oesophagus's opening (hiatus) in the diaphragm.

Hi·a·watha (hī-ə-wóthə ‖ *U.S. also* heè-, -wáwthə), **Haionhwat'ha** (*fl.* 1570). American Indian Onondagan chief credited with the organisation of the Iroquois Confederacy. His name was given to the hero of Longfellow's poem *The Song of Hiawatha* (1855).

hi·ba·chi (hi-báachi) *n., pl.* **-chis.** A portable charcoal-burning brazier with a grill, often used for cooking at table. [Japanese : *hi,* fire + *bachi,* bowl.]

hi·ber·nac·u·lum (hī́bər-náckew-ləm) *n., pl.* **-la** (-lə). Also **hi·ber·na·cle** (-nack'l) (for sense 2). **1.** *Biology.* A case, covering, or structure in which an organism remains dormant for the winter. **2.** The shelter of a hibernating animal. [Latin *hībernāculum,* winter residence, from *hībernus,* winter.]

hi·ber·nal (hī-bérn'l) *adj.* Occurring in or pertaining to winter. [Latin *hībernālis,* from *hībernus,* winter.]

hi·ber·nate (hī́bər-nayt) *intr.v.* **-nated, -nating, -nates. 1.** *Zoology.* To pass the winter in a dormant or torpid state. **2.** To be inactive. [Latin *hībernāre,* from *hībernus,* winter.] —**hi·ber·na·tor** (-naytər) *n.*

hi·ber·na·tion (hī́bər-náysh'n) *n.* **1.** The action of hibernating. **2.** The state of torpidity or inactivity in which some organisms pass the winter. Compare **aestivation. 3.** Any state or period of inactivity likened to that of a wintering animal: *"Stirring suddenly from long hibernation I knew myself once more a poet"* (Robert Graves).

Hi·ber·ni·a (hī-bérni-ə). *Poetic.* Ireland. [Latin, variant (influenced by *hībernus,* winter) of *I(u)verna, Juberna,* from Greek *Iernē.*] —**Hi·ber·ni·an** *adj.*

Hi·ber·ni·cism (hī-bérni-siz'm) *n.* Also **Hi·ber·ni·an·ism** (-ən-iz'm). **1.** An idiom peculiar to Irish English. **2.** An Irish trait or custom.

hi·bis·cus (hī-bískəss) *n.* Any of various chiefly tropical plants, shrubs, or trees of the genus *Hibiscus,* having large, showy, variously coloured flowers. Several species are cultivated for ornament. [New Latin *Hibiscus,* Latin, from Greek *hibiskos†,* marshmallow.]

hic (hik) *n.* The sound of a hiccup.

hic·cup (híckup) *n.* Also **hic·cough** (híckup). **1.** A spasm of the diaphragm resulting in a sudden, abortive inhalation that is stopped by a spasmodic closure of the glottis. In technical usage, also called "singultus". **2.** *Plural.* An attack of hiccups. **3.** *Informal.* A slight difficulty or delay.

—*v.* **hiccupped, -cupping, -cups.** Also **hic·cough, -coughed, -coughing, -coughs.** —*intr.* **1.** To make a sound resembling that of a hiccup. **2.** To have an attack of hiccups. —*tr.* To say or express while hiccupping. [Earlier *hicket, hickop* (imitative).]

hic ja·cet (hík yácket) *Latin. Abbr.* **H.J.** Here lies. Used in epitaphs on gravestones.

hick (hik) *n. Chiefly U.S. Informal.* A gullible, provincial person; a yokel; a bumpkin.

—*adj. Chiefly U.S. Informal.* Backward or unsophisticated. Used derogatorily. [From *Hick,* pet form of *Richard* (name).]

hick·ey (hícki) *n., pl.* **-eys.** *U.S. Informal.* **1.** Any device or contrivance; a gadget. **2.** A pimple, scar, or other mark on the skin. [20th century : origin obscure.]

Hick·ok (híckok), **James Butler,** also known as Wild Bill Hickok (1837–76). U.S. marshal and gunfighter.

hick·o·ry (híckəri) *n., pl.* **-ries. 1.** Any of several chiefly North American deciduous trees of the genus *Carya,* having hard, smooth nuts with an edible kernel. **2.** The hard, tough, heavy wood of any of these trees. **3.** The nut of any of these trees. **4.** A walking stick or switch made from hickory wood. [Shortening of earlier *pohickery,* from Virginian native name *pawcohiccora,* food prepared from crushed hickory nuts.]

hid. Past tense of hide.

hi·dal·go (hi-dál-gō) *n., pl.* **-gos.** A member of the minor nobility in Spain. [Spanish, from Old Spanish *hijo dalgo,* "son of something (that is to say, property)" : *hijo,* son, + *de,* of + *algo,* something.]

hid·den (hídd'n). Past participle of **hide.**

—*adj.* Not immediately apparent; having its true nature disguised: *hidden unemployment* ; *hidden agenda.*

hid·den·ite (hídd'n-īt) *n.* A transparent emerald-green variety of spodumene, used as a gemstone. [After William E. *Hidden* (1853–1918), American mineralogist.]

hide¹ (hīd) *v.* **hid** (hid), **hidden** (hídd'n) or **hid, hiding, hides.** —*tr.* **1.** To put or keep out of sight; secrete. **2.** To prevent the disclosure or recognition of; conceal. **3.** To cut off or obstruct from sight; cover up. **4.** To avert (one's gaze) in shame or grief. —*intr.* **1.** To keep oneself out of sight. **2.** To seek refuge.

—*n. British.* A hiding place, such as a camouflaged tent, used by hunters and birdwatchers. Also *chiefly U.S.* "blind". [Hide, hid, hidden or hid; Middle English *hiden, hid, hidden* (formed by analogy with RIDE, RIDDEN) or *hidd,* Old English *hȳdan, hȳdde, hīdd.*] —**hid·er** *n.*

Synonyms: hide, conceal, secrete, cache, screen, bury, cloak.

hide² *n.* **1.** The skin of an animal; especially, the comparatively thick, tough skin or pelt of a large animal. **2.** *Informal.* The human skin.

—*tr.v.* **hided, hiding, hides.** *Informal.* To beat the hide of; flog. [Middle English *hyde, hide,* Old English *hȳd.*]

hide³ *n.* An old English measure of land, usually the amount held to be adequate for one free family and its dependents, and varying from 60 to 120 acres. [Middle English *hide, hyde,* Old English *hīgid, hīd.*]

hide-and-seek (híd'n-seék) *n.* Also *chiefly U.S.* **hide-and-go-seek** (-gō-seék). **1.** A children's game in which one player tries to find and catch others who are hiding. **2.** Any game or action involving evasion. —**hide-and-seek** *adj.*

hide·a·way (híd-ə-way) *n.* **1.** A place of concealment; a hide-out. **2.** A secluded or isolated place.

hide·bound (híd-bownd) *adj.* **1.** Having abnormally dry, stiff skin that adheres closely to the underlying flesh. Said of undernourished domestic animals such as cattle. **2.** Having the bark so contracted and unyielding as to hinder growth. Said of trees. **3.** Unduly adhering to the rules or to one's own opinions or prejudices; narrow-minded and inflexible.

hid·e·ous (híddi-əs) *adj.* **1.** Physically repulsive; revolting; ugly. **2.** Horrifying; appalling; terrifying. **3.** Repugnant to the moral sense; despicable; odious. [Middle English *hidous,* from Anglo-French, Old French *hidous, hideus,* from *hi(s)de,* fear, horror, perhaps from Latin *hispidus,* rough, shaggy.] —**hid·e·ous·ly** *adv.*

hide-out (híd-owt) *n.* A place of shelter or concealment, especially for a person on the run.

hid·ey-hole, hid·y-hole (hídi-hōl) *n. Informal.* A hiding place.

hi·ding¹ (híding) *n.* A state or place of concealment: *stayed in hiding until the coast was clear.*

hiding² *n. Informal.* **1.** A spanking or beating. **2.** A crushing defeat. —**be on a hiding to nothing.** To waste one's time.

hi·dro·sis (hī-drō-siss, hi-) *n.* Perspiration, especially in excessive or abnormal amounts. [New Latin, from Greek *hidrōsis,* sweating, from *hidrōs,* sweat.]

hi·drot·ic (hī-dróttik, hi-) *n.* Any drug or other agent that promotes sweating.

—*adj.* **1.** Stimulating sweating. **2.** Pertaining to sweating.

hie (hī) *intr.v.* **hied, hieing** or **hying, hies.** *Poetic.* To go quickly; hasten; hurry. [Middle English *hien, hyghen,* Old English *hīgian,* to strive, exert oneself, hurry.]

hi·e·mal (hī-əm'l) *adj.* Occurring in or pertaining to winter; hibernal. [Latin *hiemālis,* from *hiems,* winter.]

hi·er·arch (hír-aark, hí-ər- ‖ hí-raark) *n.* **1.** One who occupies a position of authority in an ecclesiastical hierarchy. **2.** One who occupies a high position in a hierarchy. [Old French *hierarche,* from Medieval Latin *hierarcha,* from Greek *hierarkhēs,* president of sacred rites, high priest : HIER(O)- + -ARCH.]

hi·er·ar·chism (hír-aar-kiz'm, hí-ər- ‖ hí-raar-) *n.* Hierarchical practice or principles. —**hi·er·ar·chist** *n.*

hi·er·ar·chy (hír-aarki, hí-ər- ‖ hí-raarki) *n., pl.* **-chies. 1. a.** A body of persons organised or classified according to rank, capacity, or authority. **b.** A body of things arranged in a graded series. **c.** The system or practice of organising or classifying people or things in such a series. **2. Hierocracy. 3.** The body of clergy in a country or area, especially the bishops. [Middle English *ierarchie,* from Old French, from Medieval Latin *(h)ierarchia,* rule of a priest, from Greek *hierarkhia,* from *hierarkhēs,* HIERARCH.] —**hi·er·ar·chi·cal** (-árkik'l), **hi·er·ar·chic** *adj.* —**hi·er·ar·chi·cal·ly** *adv.*

hi·er·at·ic (hír-áttik, hí-ər- ‖ hí-ráttik) *adj.* Also **hi·er·at·i·cal** (-'l) (for sense 1). **1.** Of or associated with sacred persons or offices; sacerdotal: *a hieratic gesture.* **2.** Designating or pertaining to a simplified cursive style of Egyptian hieroglyphics that was developed and chiefly used by the priestly class. Compare **demotic. 3.** Designating or pertaining to various styles of art that follow rules or conventions established by religious tradition, especially in ancient Egypt.

—*n.* The hieratic script of ancient Egypt. [Latin *hierāticus,* from Greek *hieratikos,* from *hieratos* (unattested), from *hierasthai,* to be a priest, from *hiereus,* priest, from *hieros,* sacred, supernatural.] —**hi·er·at·i·cal·ly** *adv.*

hiero-, hier- *comb. form.* Indicates sacred or holy; for example, **hierocracy, hierogram.** [Greek, from *hieros,* holy, sacred, supernatural.]

hi·er·oc·ra·cy (hír-óckrə-si, hí-ər- ‖ hí-róckrə-) *n., pl.* **-cies.** Government by the clergy; ecclesiastical rule : *"Vermont will emerge next, because least . . . under the yoke of hierocracy."* (Thomas Jefferson). [HIERO- + -CRACY.] —**hi·er·o·crat·ic** (-ə-kráttik), **hi·er·o·crat·i·cal** *adj.*

hi·er·o·dule (hír-ə-dewl, hí-ər-, -dōōl ‖ hí-rə-) *n.* A temple slave in the service of a particular deity. [Late Latin *hierodūlus,* from Greek *hierodoulos* : HIERO- + *doulos†,* slave.]

hi·er·o·glyph·ic (hír-ə-glíffik, hí-ər- ‖ hí-rə-) *adj.* Also **hi·er·o·glyph·i·cal** (-'l). **1.** Written in or pertaining to a system of writing used in ancient Egypt, in which figures or objects are used to represent words or sounds. **2.** Containing or inscribed with hieroglyphic pictures or symbols. **3.** Hard to read or decipher; illegible.

—*n.* Also **hi·er·o·glyph** (-gliff). **1.** A picture or symbol used in hieroglyphic writing. **2.** *Plural.* Hieroglyphic writing. **3.** A picture or symbol with a hidden meaning; an emblem. **4.** *Plural.* Illegible or undecipherable writing. [Old French *hieroglyphique,* from Late Latin *hieroglyphicus,* from Greek *hierogluphikos,* written in hieroglyphics : HIERO- (originally used in Egyptian sacred writings) +

gluphē, carving, engraving, from *gluphein,* to carve.] —**hi·er·o·glyph·i·cal·ly** *adv.* —**hi·er·o·glyph·ist** *n.*

hi·er·o·gram (hír-ə-gram, hí-ər- ‖ hí-rə-) *n.* A sacred symbol. [HIERO- + -GRAM.]

hi·er·ol·o·gy (hír-óllǝji, hí-ər- ‖ hí-róllǝji) *n., pl.* **-gies.** The sacred literature of a given people. [HIERO- + -LOGY.]

hi·er·o·phant (hír-ə-fant, hí-ər-, -ō- ‖ hí-rə-, -rō-) *n.* **1.** In ancient Greece, an expounder of sacred mysteries, especially of the Eleusinian mysteries. **2.** An interpreter of esoteric or arcane knowledge: *"What did even the hierophants of science know of . . . evil?"* (Malcolm Lowry). [Late Latin *hierophanta, hierophantēs,* from Greek *hierophantēs,* interpreter of sacred mysteries : HIERO- + *phainein,* to reveal, show.] —**hi·er·o·phan·tic** (-fántik) *adj.*

hifalutin. Variant of **highfalutin.**

hi-fi (hí-fí) *n.* **1.** High fidelity *(see).* **2.** An electronic system or equipment for reproducing high-fidelity sound from radio, records, or magnetic tape. [High *f*idelity.] —**hi-fi** *adj.*

hig·gle (hígg'l) *intr.v.* **-gled, -gling, -gles.** To haggle; bargain. [Variant of HAGGLE.]

hig·gle·dy-pig·gle·dy (hígg'ldi-pígg'ldi) *adv.* In utter disorder or confusion.
~*n.* A jumble; a muddle.
~*adj.* Topsy-turvy; jumbled. [Rhyming and jingling formation probably based on PIG (presumably from the manner in which pigs huddle together).]

high (hí) *adj.* **higher, highest. 1. a.** Extending, projecting, or placed far upwards; tall; elevated. **b.** Extending further upwards than is usual: *a high forehead.* **2. a.** Having a specified elevation: *ten feet high.* **b.** Being at a specified level: *waist-high.* **3.** Being at or near its peak or culmination: *high noon.* **4.** Beginning to decompose, as meat; excessively gamy. **5.** Far removed in time; remote: *high antiquity.* **6.** Designating a sound produced by a relatively great frequency of vibrations: *a high note.* **7.** Situated far from the equator: *a high latitude.* **8.** Of great moment or importance, as: **a.** Preeminent in rank or standing: *the high priest; high command.* **b.** Main; chief: *high street.* **c.** Serious; weighty; grave: *high treason.* **9.** Lofty or exalted in quality, character, or style: *high moral standards; high culture.* **10. a.** Of relatively great quantity, magnitude, value, or degree: *a high temperature; high wage demands; a high vitamin content.* **b.** Of great force or violence: *high winds.* **11.** Luxurious: *high life.* **12.** Showing pride, arrogance, or disdain. **13.** Characterised by a state of excitement or euphoria; elated: *high spirits.* **14.** *Informal.* Intoxicated by alcohol or a narcotic. **15.** At an advanced stage of development or complexity: *high finance.* **16. a.** Favourable: *high opinion.* **b.** Well-regarded: *high standing.* **17.** *Phonetics.* Pronounced with part of the tongue close to the palate: *a high vowel.* **18.** *Usually capital* H. Of or pertaining to the High Church. **19.** Designating a gear, as in a motor vehicle, that produces a relatively great output speed.
~*adv.* **1.** At or to a high level: *rise very high.* **2.** In a high manner: *riding high; sing high; priced high.* **3.** *Nautical.* With full sails, sailing close to the wind.
~*n.* **1. a.** A high place, region, or level. **b.** A highest point: *the pound reached a high of 2.4 against the dollar.* **2.** *Abbr.* **h., H.** The highest transmission gear of a motor vehicle. **3.** A centre of high atmospheric pressure; an anticyclone. **4.** *Informal.* A state of intoxication or euphoria induced by or as if by a stimulant or a narcotic. **5.** *Chiefly U.S.* A high school. —**on high. 1.** At a high level or position. **2.** In heaven. [Middle English *hei, high,* Old English *hēah,* from Germanic.]
Synonyms: *high, tall, lofty, towering, elevated.*

high altar *n.* The principal altar in a church.

high and dry *adv.* **1.** Helpless; destitute. **2.** Out of water. Said of ships.

high and low *adv.* Everywhere: *searched high and low.*

high and mighty *adj.* Arrogant; domineering; disdainful.

high·ball (hí-bawl) *n. U.S.* An iced drink consisting of alcoholic spirits and water, soda water, or the like, served in a tall glass. [Earlier *high ball,* apparently alluding to a tall glass.]

high·bind·er (hí-bíndǝr) *n. U.S.* **1.** A member of a former Chinese-American secret society of paid assassins and blackmailers. **2.** *Informal.* Any gangster. **3.** A corrupt politician. [From the *High-binders,* a New York City gang (circa 1806).]

high·born (hí-bórn) *adj.* Of noble birth.

high·boy (hí-boy) *n. U.S.* A tall chest of drawers divided into two sections and supported on four legs. Compare **tallboy.**

high·brow (hí-brow) *n. Informal.* One who has or affects superior learning or culture. Compare **middlebrow, lowbrow.** [Referring to a lofty forehead as a conventional sign of intellectual superiority.] —**high·brow, high·browed** *adj.*

high·chair (hí-cháir, -chair) *n.* A baby's feeding chair, usually with a detachable tray and mounted on tall legs.

High Church *n.* That branch of the Anglican Church which stresses the value of an episcopal hierarchy and sacramental ritual. Compare **Anglo-Catholic, Broad Church, Low Church.** —**High-Church** (hí-chúrch) *adj.* —**High-Church·man** (-mǝn) *n.*

high-class (hí-kláass ‖ -kláss) *adj.* **1.** Of superior quality; first-class; first-rate: *a high-class carpenter.* **2.** Pertaining to, belonging to, or imitating the upper social classes.

high-col·oured (hí-kúllǝrd) *adj.* Extremely pink; florid. Said of the complexion.

high commissioner *n. Often capital* H, *capital* C. **1.** The chief diplomatic representative of one Commonwealth country serving in another. **2.** Any senior commissioner, especially one heading an international commission. **3.** The chief administrative official in a colony or similar dependent region.

High Court of Justice *n. Law.* In England and Wales, the division of the Supreme Court of Judicature below the Court of Appeal, comprising the Family Division, the Chancery Division, and the Queen's Bench Division, in which serious civil cases are heard and occasionally criminal cases as when on a point of law. Also called "High Court". Compare **Crown Court, Court of Appeal.**

High Court of Justiciary *n. Law.* In Scotland, the senior criminal court, to which serious criminal cases are sent for trial and appeal.

high day *n.* A holy day; a feast day. Used chiefly in the phrase *high days and holidays.*

high-definition (hí-deffi-nísh'n) *adj.* Of or designating a televised image with a high degree of clarity.

High·er (hí-ǝr) *n.* In Scotland: **1.** An examination taken as a prerequisite for university entrance. **2.** An examination pass at this level.

higher algebra *n.* The algebra of sets, groups, propositions, vectors, matrices, tensors, or the like, as opposed to the simple algebra of numbers.

higher criticism *n.* Critical study of Biblical texts with regard to such matters as their authorship, composition, editing, and compilation. Compare **lower criticism.**

higher education *n.* Education that takes place after attendance at secondary school, as at training colleges, universities, and the like.

Higher Executive Officer *n. Abbr.* **H.E.O.** An administrative officer in the British government service who ranks between a Principal Officer and an Executive Officer.

higher mathematics *n.* Mathematics involving advanced abstract ideas, including such topics as number theory, noneuclidean geometry, topology, and analysis, as distinguished from simple arithmetic, algebra, geometry, and trigonometry.

high·er-up (hí-ǝr-úp) *n. Informal.* One who has a higher rank, position, or status.

high·est common factor (hí-ist, -ǝst) *n. Abbr.* **h.c.f., H.C.F.** The largest number that is a factor of two or more given numbers. Also called "greatest common divisor".

high explosive *n. Abbr.* **HE** A powerful, fast-acting explosive.

high·fa·lu·tin, hi·fa·lu·tin (hí-fǝ-lóō-tin, -léw- ‖ -t'n) *adj.* Also **high·fa·lu·ting** (-ting). *Informal.* Pompous or pretentious, especially in the use of language. [HIGH + *falutin,* perhaps variant of *fluting,* present participle of FLUTE.] —**high·fa·lu·tin** *n.*

high fashion *n.* **Haute couture** *(see).*

high fidelity *n.* The electronic reproduction of sound, especially from broadcast, recorded, or taped sources, with minimal distortion. Also called "hi-fi". —**high-fi·del·i·ty** *adj.*

high finance *n.* Complex financial dealings involving large sums of money.

high-fli·er, high-fly·er (hí-flí-ǝr) *n.* **1.** One that flies high. **2. a.** A person of great ambition. **b.** A person expected by his superiors to go far. **3.** A very successful person, especially one who has a high status for his age. —**high-fly·ing** *adj.*

high-flown (hí-flón) *adj.* **1.** Lofty; exalted. **2.** Pretentious.

high frequency *n. Abbr.* **hf** A **radio frequency** *(see)* in the range between 3 and 30 megahertz.

High·gate (hí-git, -gayt). A residential district of north London. In its cemetery are the graves of several famous people, including Karl Marx and George Eliot.

High German *n.* **1.** *Abbr.* **HG, H.G.** The German language as spoken and written in southern Germany. See **Low German, Old High German, Middle High German. 2.** Any of various German dialects. [Translation of German *Hochdeutsch.*]

high-grade (hí-gráyd) *adj.* Of superior quality.

high-hand·ed (hí-hándid) *adj.* Arrogant or arbitrary in manner. —**high-hand·ed·ly** *adv.* —**high-hand·ed·ness** *n.*

high-hat (hí-hát) *n. Chiefly U.S. Informal.* A snobbish or patronising person.
~*tr.v.* **high-hatted, -hatting, -hats.** To be condescending or supercilious towards. —**high-hat** *adj.*

highjack. Variant of **hijack.**

high jinks *pl.n. Informal.* Mischievous merriment; lively sport.

high jump *n.* **1.** An athletic event in which individual athletes compete to jump highest over an adjustable horizontal bar. **2.** Any of the jumps in such a competition. —**(in) for the high jump.** *British Informal.* In trouble; due for punishment. —**high-jump·er** *n.*

high-keyed (hí-kéed) *adj.* **1.** Having a high pitch; shrill. **2.** Bright in colour; intense. **3.** *U.S.* Excitable; nervous; highly strung.

high·land (hí-lǝnd) *n.* **1.** Elevated land. **2.** *Plural.* A mountainous or hilly region or part of a country.
~*adj.* **1.** Of, relating to, or characteristic of such a region. **2.** *Capital* H. Of or relating to the Highlands.

Highland cattle *n.* A breed of long-horned cattle having shaggy, usually reddish-brown hair.

high·land·er (hí-lǝndǝr) *n.* **1.** One who lives in a highland area. **2.** *Capital* H. An inhabitant of the Highlands.

Highland fling *n.* An energetic reel or folk dance of the Highlands.

Highland pony *n.* A pony of a breed originating in the Highlands, having strong legs and used for trekking and pack work.

Highland Region. Former region of northern Scotland, now a Unitary Authority area, formed from Caithness, Sutherland, Ross and Cromarty, Inverness, Nairn, and parts of Argyll.

Highlands, The. The part of Scotland lying north of a line drawn from Dumbarton in the west northeastwards to Stonehaven.

Highland Unitary Authority area. See **Highland Region.**

high-lev-el language (hī-levv'l) *n. Computing.* A programming language that uses words and common mathematical symbols. Compare **low-level language.**

high life *n.* Also **high·life** (hī-līf) (for sense 2). 1. A fashionable or luxurious style of living. 2. A style of West African music combining traditional African and American jazz elements. —**high life, high·life** *adj.*

high·light (hī-līt) *n.* 1. In painting or photography, a brilliantly lighted area of the subject appearing as a luminous spot. 2. An outstanding event or detail. 3. *Usually plural.* A bleached or light dyed streak in the hair. ~*tr.v.* **highlighted, -lighting, -lights.** 1. To give prominence to; focus attention upon. 2. To add highlights to, as in painting. 3. To dye or bleach (the hair) to produce highlights. 4. To be the highlight of.

high·light·er (hī-lītər) *n.* 1. A cosmetic in powder or cream form used to create highlights on the face. 2. A felt-tipped pen with fluorescent ink used to pick out a word or passage in a text.

high·ly (hīli) *adv.* 1. a. Extremely; very. Used as an intensive: *highly indignant.* b. To a greater than average degree: *highly paid.* 2. Approvingly; favourably: *I think highly of his results.*

highly strung *adj.* Also *U.S.* **high-strung** (hī-strúng). Constantly nervous and tense; easily excited or upset. [*Strung,* past participle of STRING in obsolete sense, to provide (the body) with nerves and sinews (this sense derived from stringing a bow, etc.).]

High Mass *n. Roman Catholic Church.* A sung Mass celebrated by a priest or prelate, sometimes assisted by a deacon and a subdeacon, and with full ceremonial.

high-mind·ed (hī-míndid) *adj.* 1. Characterised by morally lofty ideals or conduct; principled. 2. *Archaic.* Disdainfully proud; arrogant; haughty. —**high-mind·ed·ly** *adv.* —**high-mind·ed·ness** *n.*

high muckamuck *n. U.S. Informal.* A **muckamuck** *(see).*

high·ness (hī-nəss, -niss) *n.* 1. The quality of being high, especially: a. Tallness; height. b. Greatness, as of degree or amount. 2. *Capital* H. A title of or form of address for any of various members of a royal family. Used with *His, Her, Your,* or *Their: Their Highnesses the Prince and Princess.*

high-oc·tane (hī-óktayn) *adj.* Having a high octane number.

high-pass filter (hī-paass ‖ -pass) *n. Electronics.* A circuit that allows transmission of signals with frequencies above a given value, rejecting frequencies below this value.

high-pitched (hī-pícht) *adj.* 1. a. Having a high pitch to the ear. b. Tuned to a high pitch. 2. Lofty; exalted, as a sermon might be. 3. Steeply sloped, as a roof might be.

high place *n.* 1. In early Semitic religions, a place of worship on top of a hill. 2. *Plural.* Positions of power or influence, especially in public office: *corruption in high places.*

high point *n.* The single event or moment in a period of time, project, or the like, that stands out as particularly rewarding or revealing: *The high point of the concert was the oboe concerto.*

high-pow·ered (hī-pówrd, -pów-ərd) *adj.* 1. Dynamic and highly motivated: *a high-powered salesman.* 2. Intellectually demanding or impressive: *a high-powered seminar.* 3. Capable of very great magnification. Said of optical instruments: *a high-powered telescope.*

high-pres·sure (hī-préshər) *adj.* 1. Of or pertaining to pressures higher than normal; especially, much higher than atmospheric pressure. 2. Involving great psychological stress or great dedication of energy: *a high-pressure job.* 3. *Informal.* Using aggressive and persistent persuasion in selling. ~*tr.v.* **high-pressured, -suring, -sures.** *Informal.* To convince or influence by using high-pressure methods of persuasion.

high priest *n.* 1. In ancient Judaism, the senior priest serving in the temple, who alone could enter the holy of holies. 2. Any of various other senior priests in various religions or sects. 3. *Informal.* The unofficial leader or most influential figure of any fashion, theory, or movement: *the high priest of monetarism.*

high profile *n. Informal.* A conspicuous, well-publicised presence or stance. Compare **low profile.**

high relief *n.* A sculptural relief in which the modelled forms project from the background by at least half their depth. Also called "alto-relievo". [Translation of French *haut-relief.*]

high-rise (hī-rīz, -rīz) *adj.* Designating a tall building with many storeys such as a block of flats or offices. Compare **low-rise.** ~*n.* A high-rise building.

high·road (hī-rōd) *n.* 1. *Chiefly British.* A main road; a highway. 2. A simple, direct, or sure path: *the highroad to happiness.*

high school *n.* 1. *British.* Any of various senior secondary schools. Not in technical usage. 2. *U.S.* A secondary school that includes grades 9 to 12 or grades 7 to 12. —**high-school** *adj.*

high seas *pl.n.* The open waters of an ocean or sea beyond the limits of national territorial jurisdiction.

high season *n.* Any of the periods in the course of a year when attendance or demand is particularly high, as at a holiday resort.

high sheriff *n.* In England and Wales, a **sheriff** *(see).*

high-sound·ing (hī-sównd-ing ‖ *West Indies also* -súngd-) *adj.* Impressive or pompous.

high-speed (hī-speed) *adj.* 1. Moving, operating, or used at a high speed. 2. Of, pertaining to, or designating photographic film that requires only a short exposure.

high-speed steel *n.* A type of steel that remains hard when hot, used for cutting tools for lathes, milling machines, and the like.

high-spir·it·ed (hī-spírritid) *adj.* 1. Having a proud or unbroken spirit; brave. 2. Vivacious. —**high-spir·it·ed·ly** *adv.* —**high-spir·it·ed·ness** *n.*

high spot *n.* The best or most memorable part of a particular period of time: *The high spot of the holiday was a visit to Maxim's.*

high-street (hī-street) *adj.* Of, pertaining to, or designating shops or other commercial enterprises of a kind typically found in every high street: *a high-street grocer.*

high-strung *adj. U.S.* Variant of **highly strung.**

hight (hīt) *adj. Archaic.* Named; called. [Middle English *highten, hihten,* from *hehte, hight,* past tense of *hoten,* to call, be called, Old English *hātan* (past tense *heht*).]

high table *n.* The dining table, sometimes on a raised platform, in the dining hall of an institution such as a university college, at which senior members and their guests take their meals.

high·tail (hī-tayl) *intr.v.* **-tailed, -tailing, -tails.** *Chiefly U.S. Informal.* To move or depart in a great hurry; especially, to escape. —**hightail it.** To rush; hurry. [A reference to some animals who, when startled, raise their tails and flee.]

high tea *n. British.* A substantial meal that typically includes tea, a hot course, and bread and butter, served in the late afternoon or early evening.

high-tech (hī-ték) *n.* 1. A modern style of furnishings, fittings, and design in which industrial materials such as metal piping are used. 2. Up-to-date or sophisticated technology. —**high-tech** *adj.*

high-ten·sion (hī-ténsh'n) *adj. Abbr.* **H.T.** Having or carrying a high voltage: *high-tension wires.*

high-test (hī-tést) *adj.* 1. Meeting the most exacting requirements. 2. Of or pertaining to highly volatile, high-octane fuel.

high tide *n.* 1. The tide at its full, when the water reaches its highest level. 2. The time at which this occurs. 3. A point of culmination; an acme.

high-toned (hī-tónd) *adj.* 1. Intellectually or morally elevated: *a high-toned lecture.* 2. Socially superior: *a high-toned finishing school.* 3. *U.S. Informal.* Having pretensions to elegance or slickness.

high treason *n.* Treason against one's state or sovereign.

highty-tighty. Variant of **hoity-toity.**

high-up (hī-up, -úp) *adj. Informal.* Of high position or status. ~*n. Informal.* A person who has a high rank or position.

High·veld (hī-felt) *n.* In South Africa, the savannah of the African plateau above 1 500 metres (about 5,000 feet).

high water *n. Abbr.* **H.W.** 1. High tide. 2. The state of a body of water that has reached its highest level.

high-wa·ter mark (hī-wáwtər ‖ *U.S. also* -wóttər) *n.* 1. a. A mark indicating the highest level reached by a body of water. b. This level itself. 2. The highest point of achievement; an apex.

high·way (hī-way) *n.* 1. *Chiefly U.S. & Law.* A main public road connecting towns and cities. 2. Any main route, on land, over water, or in the air. 3. A direct course or path; a highroad.

Highway Code *n.* In Britain: 1. Rules and suggestions for the safe use of public roads. 2. A booklet issued by the Department of Transport, laying out these rules and suggestions. Compare **Green Cross Code.**

high·way·man (hī-way-mən ‖ -man) *n., pl.* **-men** (-mən, -men). Formerly, a robber who held up travellers.

H.I.H. His (or Her) Imperial Highness.

hi-hat (hī-hat) *n.* A pair of cymbals on a stand operated by a foot-pedal and used in jazz and rock music. [From *high hat.*]

hi·jack, high·jack (hī-jak) *tr.v.* **-jacked, -jacking, -jacks.** 1. To hold up (a vehicle, such as a train or armoured van) by stopping it in transit. 2. To steal (goods) from a vehicle by stopping it in transit. 3. To seize or commandeer (a moving vehicle, such as an aircraft, ship, or car) by force or with threats of force, especially in an attempt to enforce political or other demands. 4. To steal from (a person). 5. To take control of using coercive or underhand methods: *The meeting was hijacked by a well-organised group of militants.* ~*n.* An act or instance of hijacking. [20th century : origin obscure.] —**hi·jack·er** *n.*

hike (hīk) *v.* **hiked, hiking, hikes.** —*intr.* 1. a. To go on an extended walk, particularly for pleasure. b. To go on an extended march, especially over rough terrain; tramp. 2. *Chiefly U.S.* To go up, as prices. Often used with *up: The cost of living has hiked up again.* 3. *Chiefly U.S.* To be raised or hitched. Usually used with *up: Her coat has hiked up at the back.* —*tr. Chiefly U.S.* 1. To increase or raise in amount. Usually used with *up.* 2. To pull, move, or raise with a sudden motion; hitch. Usually used with *up: He hiked up his pants.* ~*n.* 1. A walk or march. 2. A rise, as in prices. [19th century (dialect) : origin obscure.] —**hik·er** *n.*

hi·lar·i·ous (hi-láir-i-əss ‖ *U.S. also* hī-) *adj.* Boisterously funny, gay, or merry: *a hilarious joke.* See **hilarity.** —**hi·lar·i·ous·ly** *adv.* —**hi·lar·i·ous·ness** *n.*

hi·lar·i·ty (hi-lárrəti ‖ hī-) *n.* Boisterous merriment. See Synonyms at **mirth.** [Old French *hilarite,* from Latin *hilaritās,* from *hilaris, hilarus,* cheerful, from Greek *hilaros.*]

Hil·a·ry term (hílləri) *n.* At Oxford university, the term that begins in January, the spring term.

Hil·bert (híl-bairt, -bərt), **David** (1862–1943). German mathematician. His work on integral equations laid the foundations of 20th-century functional analysis.

hill (hil) *n.* 1. A well-defined, naturally elevated area of land smaller than a mountain. 2. *Plural.* a. A range or group of such elevations. b. *Informal.* Any remote rural area located in such elevated areas.

3. A heap, pile, or mound, such as that formed by a living organism. Often used in combination: *anthill.* **4.** An incline, especially in a road; a slope. **—over the hill.** *Informal.* No longer young; past one's prime.
~*tr.v.* **hilled, hilling, hills. 1.** To form into a hill, pile, or heap. **2.** To cover (a plant or plants) with a mound of soil. [Middle English *hill,* Old English *hyll.*] **—hill·er** *n.* **—hill·y** *adj.*

Hill (hil), **Archibald Vivian** (1886-1977). British physiologist and biochemist. He investigated heat production in muscles and nerves. In 1922 he shared the Nobel prize for physiology or medicine with Otto Meyerhof.

Hill, Graham (1929-75). British motor-racing driver. He won the world championship driving for BRM in1962 and again, driving for the Lotus team, in 1968.

Hill, Octavia (1838-1912). English nature-lover and conservationist. She was leader of the open-space movement which led to the establishment of the National Trust in 1895.

Hill, Sir Rowland (1795-1879). English schoolmaster and inventor. He developed the system of prepaid penny postage, introduced into England on 10 January 1840.

Hil·la·ry (hílləri), **Sir Edmund Percival** (1919-). New Zealand mountaineer. Hillary and Tenzing Norgay became the first men to reach the summit of Mount Everest in 1953.

hill·bil·ly (híl-billi) *n., pl.* **-lies.** *Informal.* A person from a rural mountainous area, especially of the southeastern United States. Usually used disparagingly.
~*adj.* Of or characteristic of the culture of such an area: *hillbilly music.* [HILL + *Billy,* pet form of *William.*]

hill-fort (híl-fawrt ‖ -fôrt) *n. Archaeology.* A fortified hilltop, showing traces of ramparts, ditches, and the like.

Hil·li·ard (hílli-ərd, -aard, híl-yərd), **Nicholas** (1537-1619). English miniature painter. He was appointed goldsmith, carver, and limner to Queen Elizabeth.

Hil·ling·don (híllingdən). A borough in the west of Greater London. Mainly residential, it was created in 1965 from several districts of the former county of Middlesex.

hill myna *n.* A black songbird, *Gracula religiosa,* of India and the East Indies, that is kept as a cage bird for its ability to mimic human speech.

hill·ock (hillək) *n.* A small hill. [Middle English : HILL + -OCK.] **—hill·ock·y** *adj.*

hill·side (híl-sīd) *n.* The side or slope of a hill.

hill station *n.* In India and various other Asian countries, a resort or settlement at a high altitude, frequented during the summer months because of its relatively cool climate.

hill·top (híl-top) *n.* The crest or top of a hill.

hilt (hilt) *n.* The handle of a weapon or tool, especially of a sword or dagger. **—to the hilt.** Completely.
~*tr.v.* **hilted, hilting, hilts.** To provide with a hilt. [Middle English *hilt,* Old English *hilt,* from Germanic *hilt-* (unattested).]

hi·lum (hí-ləm) *n., pl.* **-la** (-lə). **1.** *Botany.* **a.** The scarlike mark on a seed, such as a bean, formed at the point where it was joined to the stalk connecting it to the placenta. **b.** The nucleus of a starch grain. **2.** *Anatomy.* Variant of **hilus.** [New Latin, from Latin *hīlum†,* trifle.]

hi·lus (hí-ləss) *n., pl.* **-li** (-lī). Also **hi·lum** *pl.* **-la.** *Anatomy.* An indentation on the surface of an organ marking the point of entrance or exit of a blood vessel, nerve, or the like. [New Latin, from Latin, "a trifle".]

him (him; *weak form* im) *pron.* The objective case of the third person pronoun *he.* It is used: **1.** As the direct object of a verb: *They assisted him.* **2.** As the indirect object of a verb: *They offered him a lift.* **3.** As the object of a preposition: *This letter is addressed to him.* **4.** After *than* or *as* in comparisons in which the first term is in the objective case: *The judges praised her more than him.* **5.** *U.S. Informal.* In place of the reflexive pronoun *himself,* as the indirect object of a verb: *He went to buy him a car.* **6.** In various elliptical, absolute, or interjectional phrases in which it is neither subject nor object: *Him and his sweet talk!* See Usage note at **me.** [Middle English *him,* Old English *him.*]

H.I.M. His (or Her) Imperial Majesty.

Him·a·la·yas (hímmə-láy-əz, *rarely* hi-maál-yəz). Also **Hi·ma·la·ya** (hi-maál-i-ə). A mountain system of central Asia. The largest and highest chain in the world, it extends 2 415 kilometres (1,500 miles) across the northern Indian subcontinent from the Karakorum range to the north-to-south section of the river Brahmaputra. Forming the southern edge of the central Asian plateau, it consists of a number of parallel ridges, and is the source of the Indus, Ganges, and Brahmaputra river systems. Its Mount Everest (8 848 metres; 29,028 feet) is the world's highest mountain. **—Him·a·la·yan** *adj.*

hi·mat·i·on (hi-mátt-i-ən, -on) *n., pl.* **-ia** (-i-ə). A long loose outer garment worn by men and women in ancient Greece. [Greek, diminutive of *hima* (stem *himat-*), garment, from *hennunai,* to clothe.]

Himm·ler (hímlər), **Heinrich** (1900-45). German Nazi leader. In 1929 he was given command of the SS, the party's elite corps and Hitler's bodyguard. In 1936 he became head of the Third Reich's police forces and of the secret police, the Gestapo. He was also the commandant of the concentration and extermination camps. He was captured by British troops in May, 1945, and committed suicide by taking poison.

him·self (him-sélf; *also when non-initial* im-) *pron.* A specialised form of the third person singular masculine pronoun. It is used: **1.** As a reflexive pronoun, forming the direct or indirect object of a verb or the object of a preposition: *hurt himself, gives himself time, talks to himself.* **2.** For emphasis, after *he*: *He himself wasn't certain.* **3.** As an emphasising substitute: *In debt himself, he cannot help you. It was addressed to Kate and himself.* **4.** As an indication of his real, normal, or healthy condition or identity: *He hasn't been himself lately.* **5.** *Chiefly Irish.* An important or prominent man, such as the head of a household. Sometimes used humorously. [Middle English *himself,* Old English *him selfum* : HIM + *selfum,* dative of *self,* SELF.]

Him·yar·ite (hím-yə-rīt) *n.* Also **Him·yar·it·ic** (-ríttik) (for sense 2). **1.** A member of an ancient people of southwestern Arabia. **2.** An Arabic dialect, closely related to Ethiopian, spoken by these people.
~*adj.* Also **Him·yar·it·ic** (-ríttik). Of, relating to, or characteristic of these people, their language, or their culture. [After *Himyar,* legendary ancient king in Yemen.]

Hi·na·ya·na (héena-yáanə) *n.* A branch of Buddhism, **Theravada** *(see).* Compare **Mahayana.** [Sanskrit *hīnayāna,* "lesser action or vehicle".] **—Hi·na·ya·nist** *n.* **—Hi·na·ya·nis·tic** (-yaa-nístik) *adj.*

Usage: Adherents of this school of Buddhism prefer the term *Theravada,* the term *Hinayana* having originally been a disparaging term coined by Mahayana Buddhists.

hind¹ (hīnd) *adj.* Also **hind·er** (hīndər). Superlative **hindmost, hindermost.** Located at or forming the back or rear; posterior: *hind legs.* [Middle English *hint,* perhaps from Old English *hinder,* behind, or *hindan,* from behind.]

hind² *n.* **1.** A female red deer. **2.** Any of several fishes of the genus *Epinephelus,* of Atlantic waters, related to and resembling the groupers. [Middle English *hinde,* Old English *hind.*]

hind³ *n. Archaic.* **1.** A peasant or farm labourer. **2.** A steward or bailiff. [Middle English, Old English *hīne* (plural), perhaps from *hīgen,* member of a family

hind·brain (hīnd-brayn) *n.* The **rhombencephalon** *(see).*

Hin·de·mith (híndəmit), **Paul** (1895-1963). German composer. He composed chamber music, instrumental works, and operas.

Hin·den·burg (híndən-burg, *German* -boork), **Paul Ludwig Hans Anton von** (1847-1934). German field-marshal and politician, President of the Weimar republic (1925-1934). He appointed Hitler Chancellor in January, 1933.

hin·der¹ (híndər) *v.* **-dered, -dering, -ders.** —*tr.* **1.** To hold back; be in the way of; hamper; delay. **2.** To obstruct or delay the progress of; prevent; stop. —*intr.* To be an obstacle or encumbrance. [Middle English *hindren,* Old English *hindrian,* from Germanic.] **—hin·der·er** *n.*

Synonyms: hinder, hamper, impede, retard, encumber, obstruct, block, dam, bar, baulk.

hinder². Variant of **hind** (rear).

hind·gut (hīnd-gut) *n.* **1.** The posterior portion of the colon in vertebrates. **2.** The posterior portion of the alimentary canal in arthropods. Compare **foregut.**

Hin·di (hínd-i, -ee) *n.* **1.** A group of vernacular Indic dialects spoken in northern India. **2.** A literary language based upon these dialects, now an official language and usually written in the Devanagari alphabet. **3.** A member of a cultural group of northern India speaking a Hindi dialect. [Hindi *Hindi,* from *Hind,* India, from Persian, from Old Persian *Hindu,* the river Indus. See **India.**] **—Hin·di** *adj.*

hind·most (hīnd-mōst) *adj.* Also **hin·der·most** (hīndər-). Farthest to the rear; most remote; last.

hind·quar·ter (hīnd-kwáwr-tər, -káwr-, -kwawr-, -kawr-) *n.* **1.** The posterior portion of a side of beef, lamb, or the like, including a hind leg and one or two ribs. **2.** *Usually plural.* The posterior part of a quadruped, adjacent to the hind legs; the rump.

hin·drance (híndrənss) *n.* **1.** The act of hindering. **2.** One that hinders; an impediment; an obstruction. —See Synonyms at **obstacle.** [Middle English *hind(e)raunce,* from *hindren,* to HINDER.]

hind·sight (hīnd-sīt) *n.* **1.** Perception or understanding of events after they have occurred. **2.** The rear sight of a firearm.

Hin·du (hín-dōō, -dōō) *n.* Also *archaic* **Hin·doo. 1.** A believer in Hinduism. **2.** A native of India, especially northern India.
~*adj.* Also *archaic* **Hin·doo.** Of or pertaining to the Hindus or Hinduism. [Urdu, from Persian *Hindū,* from *Hind,* India. See **Hindi.**]

Hindu calendar *n.* The lunisolar calendar of the Hindus. The solar year is divided into 12 months in accordance with the successive entrances of the sun into the signs of the Zodiac, the months varying in length from 29 to 32 days.

Hin·du·ism (híndōō-iz'm) *n.* Also *archaic* **Hin·doo·ism.** A diverse body of religion, philosophy, and cultural practices native to and predominant in India, characterised broadly by beliefs in reincarnation and a supreme being of many forms and natures, by the view that opposing theories are aspects of one eternal truth, by a system of **caste** *(see),* and by the view that killing animals is wrong.

Hindu Kush (kōōsh). Mountain range principally in northeast Afghanistan. A western extension of the Himalayas, it runs 800 kilometres (500 miles) southwest from the Pamirs in Tajikstan to include the Koh i Baba range in Afghanistan. The highest peak is Tirich Mir (7 692 metres; 25,236 feet) in Chitral, Pakistan.

Hin·du·stan (híndōō-staán, -stan). Also **Hin·do·stan** (híndō-). **1.** A historical region roughly occupying the part of the Indian subcontinent that lies to the north of the Deccan plateau, characterised by the prevalence of Indic languages. **2.** The Indian subcontinent.

Hin·du·sta·ni (híndōō-staáni ‖ *U.S.* also -stánni) *n.* **1.** A subdivision of the Indic branch of languages, including Urdu, Hindi, and other languages of northern India. **2.** A native of Hindustan.
~*adj.* Of or pertaining to Hindustani or Hindustan.

hinge (hinj) *n.* **1.** A jointed or flexible device permitting turning or pivoting of a part, such as a door, lid, or flap, on a stationary frame. **2.** A structure or part similar to a hinge, especially: **a.** An anatomical joint between bones, such as the elbow. **b.** A joint that enables the valves of a bivalve mollusc to open and close. **3.** A small folded paper rectangle gummed on one side, used to fasten stamps, photographs, or the like in an album. **4.** A point, quality, or circumstance upon which subsequent situations or events depend. —*v.* **hinged, hinging, hinges.** —*tr.* To attach by or equip with a hinge or hinges. —*intr.* **1.** To turn or hang, as on a hinge. **2.** To depend; be contingent. Usually used with *on* or *upon.* [Middle English *he(e)ng.*]

hin·ny[1] (hínni) *n., pl.* **-nies.** The hybrid offspring of a male horse and a female ass. Compare **mule.** [Latin *hinnus,* variant (influenced by *hinnīre,* to HINNY) of Greek *innos, ginnos†.*]

hinny[2] *intr.v.* **-nied, -nying, -nies.** *Rare.* To whinny; neigh. [Earlier *henny,* from Old French *hennir,* from Latin *hinnīre* (imitative).]

hinny[3] *n. Chiefly Northeastern English.* Used as an affectionate form of address, as to a woman or child. [Variant of HONEY.]

hint (hint) *n.* **1.** A subtle suggestion or slight indication; an intimation. **2.** A statement or gesture conveying veiled information; a clue. **3.** A piece of useful advice, as on how to proceed with a task. **4.** A barely perceptible amount: *gin with a hint of vermouth.* **5.** *Archaic.* An occasion; an opportunity. —*v.* **hinted, hinting, hints.** —*tr.* To make known by a hint; intimate. —*intr.* To give a hint or hints. Often used with *at: He hinted at the true purpose of his visit.* —See Synonyms at **suggest.** [Perhaps from obsolete *hent,* to grasp, seize, from Old English *hentan,* from Germanic.] —**hint·er** *n.*

hin·ter·land (híntər-land) *n.* **1.** The land lying inland from a coast. **2.** A region served by a port city and its facilities. **3.** A region remote from urban areas; back country. **4.** Any region, period, or situation that is remote or undefined. [German : *hinter,* behind, rear, German *hintar* + *Land,* land.]

hip[1] (hip) *n.* **1.** The laterally projecting prominence of the pelvis or pelvic region from the waist to the thigh. **2.** The corresponding posterior part in quadrupeds. **3.** The hip joint. **4.** *Architecture.* The external angle formed by the meeting of two adjacent, sloping sides of a roof. —**shoot from the hip.** *Slang.* To act or react impulsively and without proper thought. [Middle English *hip, hupe,* Old English *hype,* from Germanic.]

hip[2] *adj.* **hipper, hippest.** *Chiefly U.S. Slang.* **1.** Aware of or in accordance with fashionable tastes and attitudes. **2.** Cognizant; aware. Used with *to: hip to the plan.* [Variant of earlier *hept†.*] —**hip·ness** *n.*

hip[3] *n.* The fleshy, berry-like fruit of a rose, consisting of an enlarged receptacle containing several small, hairy achenes. Also called "rosehip". [Middle English *hepe, hipe,* Old English *hēope.*]

hip[4] *interj.* Used as a cheer or a signal for a cheer: *Hip, hip, hurrah!* [19th century : origin obscure.]

hip-bath (híp-baath ‖ -bàth) *n.* A bath in which one can sit down but not lie down.

hip·bone (híp-bōn) *n.* The **innominate bone** (see).

hip-flask (híp-flaask ‖ -flàsk) *n.* A flask, usually containing spirits, designed to fit into a hip pocket.

hip girdle *n.* The **pelvic girdle** (see).

hip joint *n.* The ball-and-socket joint between the innominate bone of the pelvis and the femur.

hip·parch (híppaark) *n.* An ancient Greek cavalry commander. [Greek *hipparkhos,* "horse leader" : *hippos,* horse + -ARCH.]

Hip·par·chus (hi-párkəss) (*fl.* 2nd century B.C.). Greek astronomer, the first of whom there is any record. Ptolemy constructed his geocentric view of the universe from observations made by Hipparchus, chiefly on Rhodes. His chart of the skies, in which 850 stars are placed, is the first known in history.

hip·pe·as·trum (híppi-ástrəm) *n.* Any plant of the South American genus *Hippeastrum,* some species of which are cultivated for their large, red, funnel-shaped flowers. [New Latin, from Greek *hippeus,* horseman (referring to the appearance of the leaves, which seem to ride one another) + *astron,* star (referring to shape of the flower).]

hipped[1] (hipt) *adj.* **1.** Having hips of a specified kind. Used in combination: *swivel-hipped, broad-hipped.* **2.** *Archaic.* Having the hip dislocated. **3.** *Architecture.* Having a hip or hips. Said of a roof.

hipped[2] *adj.* Also **hip·pish** (híppish). *Archaic.* Melancholy; sad; depressed. [Shortened variant of HYPOCHONDRIAC.]

hipped[3] *adj. U.S. Informal.* Obsessively absorbed. Used with *on: hipped on meditation.* [From HIP (aware).]

hip·pie, hip·py (híppi) *n.* **1.** A member of a loosely knit, nonconformist group generally characterised by emphasis on nonviolence and universal love, and a general rejection of the mores of conventional society, especially regarding dress, personal appearance, and living habits. **2.** Loosely, any young person who is exaggeratedly casual in dress, appearance, and behaviour. [From HIP (aware).] —**hip·pie, hip·py** *adj.*

hip·po (híppō) *n., pl.* **-pos.** *Informal.* A hippopotamus.

hip·po·cam·pus (hípə-kám-pəss) *n., pl.* **-pi** (-pī). **1.** *Anatomy.* Either of two ridges along each lateral ventricle of the brain that form part of the limbic system. **2.** *Greek & Roman Mythology.* A sea horse having the forelegs of a horse and the tail of a fish or dolphin. [Late Latin, from Greek *hippokampos* : *hippos,* horse + *kampos†,* sea monster.]

hip·po·cras (híppə-krass) *n.* A cordial that was made from wine and flavoured with spices, and formerly used as a medicine. [Middle English *ypocras,* from Old French, from Medieval Latin *(vinum) Hippocraticum,* (wine) of Hippocrates (it was strained through a filter called Hippocrates' bag).]

Hip·poc·ra·tes (hi-póckrə-teez) (*c.*460–*c.*370 B.C.). Greek physician, recognised as the father of medicine. He played an important part in laying the foundations of scientific medicine and separating it from philosophical speculation and superstition. The Hippocratic oath, although it represented his ethical position, cannot be confidently attributed directly to him.

Hip·po·crat·ic oath (híp-ə-kráttik, -ō-) *n.* An oath of ethical professional behaviour formerly taken by newly qualified doctors, attributed to Hippocrates.

Hip·po·crene (híp-ə-kréeni, -ō-, -kreen). *Greek Mythology.* A fountain on Mount Helicon, Greece, held sacred to the Muses and regarded as a source of poetic inspiration. [Latin *Hippocrēnē,* from Greek *Hippokrēnē* : *hippos,* horse (supposedly created by a stroke of Pegasus' hoof) + *krēnē†,* fountain.]

hip·po·drome (híppə-drōm) *n.* **1.** An open-air stadium with an oval course for horse and chariot races in ancient Greece and Rome. **2.** An arena for horse and circus shows or similar entertainments. [Old French, from Latin *hippodromus,* from Greek *hippodromos* : *hippos,* horse + -DROME.]

hip·po·griff, hip·po·gryph (híppə-griff) *n.* A mythological monster having the wings, claws, and head of a griffin and the body and hindquarters of a horse. [French *hippogriffe,* from Italian *ippogrifo* : *ippo-,* horse, from Latin *hippos,* from Greek + *grifo,* griffin, from Late Latin *grýphus,* GRIFFIN.]

Hip·pol·y·ta (hi-póllitə). *Greek Mythology.* A queen of the Amazons, variously said to have been killed by Hercules in completion of one of his 12 labours, or to have been conquered by him and given in marriage to Theseus of Athens.

Hip·pol·y·tus (hi-póllitəss). *Greek Mythology.* A son of Theseus who spurned the advances of his stepmother, Phaedra, and was killed by Poseidon.

hip·po·pot·a·mus (híppə-póttə-məss) *n., pl.* **-muses** or **-mi** (-mī). **1.** A large, chiefly aquatic African mammal, *Hippopotamus amphibius,* having dark, thick, almost hairless skin, short legs, and a broad, wide-mouthed muzzle. Also called "river horse". **2.** A similar but smaller animal, *Choeropsis liberiensis.* Also called "pygmy hippopotamus". [Latin, from Late Greek *hippopotamos,* from Greek *hippos ho potamios,* "horse of the river" : *hippos,* horse + *potamos,* river.]

hip·py[1] (híppi) *adj.* Having broad or prominent hips.

hippy[2]. Variant of **hippie.**

hip roof *n.* A roof having sloping edges and sides.

hip·ster[1] (hípstər) *n. Slang.* One who is in touch with contemporary ideas and fashions, especially when unconventional. [HIP + -STER.]

hipster[2] *adj.* Worn so as to hang from the hips and not the waist. Said of skirts, trousers, or the like.

hip·sters (hípstərz) *pl.n.* Trousers or briefs worn from the hips rather than the waist.

hi·ra·ga·na (héer-ə-gáanə) *n.* One of two sets of Japanese syllabaries (written characters) of the kana system, having a cursive form. Also called "kana". See **katakana.** [Japanese, "flat kana".]

hir·cine (húr-sīn ‖ -sin) *adj.* Of or characteristic of a goat, especially in having a strong odour or being lustful. [Latin *hircīnus,* from *hircus†,* he-goat.]

hire (hīr) *tr.v.* **hired, hiring, hires. 1. a.** To engage the services of (a person) on a temporary basis and for a fee. **b.** *Chiefly U.S.* To employ. **2.** To arrange to use (a car, for example) on a temporary basis and for a fee; rent. **3.** To grant the services or allow the use of for remuneration; rent out. Often used with *out: I hire out my caravan for the summer; he hired himself out as a labourer.* —*n.* **1.** The payment for services or use of something. **2.** The act of hiring. **3.** The condition or fact of being hired. —**for** or **on hire.** Available for use or services in exchange for payment. [Middle English *hiren,* Old English *hȳr(i)an,* from Germanic (Low German area) *khūrjan* (unattested), from *khūrjō* (unattested), payment.] —**hir·a·ble, hire·a·ble** *adj.* —**hir·er** *n.*

hire·ling (hīr-ling) *n.* One who offers his services solely for payment; especially, a person willing to perform odious or offensive tasks for a fee; a mercenary. Often used derogatorily.

hire-pur·chase (hīr-púr-chiss, -chəss) *n. British. Abbr.* **H.P.** A system of purchasing goods whereby the customer takes possession of the purchase after paying an initial deposit, and acquires legal ownership after paying a predetermined number of regular instalments that usually include an interest charge. Also *U.S.* "instalment plan".

Hi·ro·hi·to (hírrə-héetō) (1901–89). Emperor of Japan (1926–89). He had little political power, but in 1945 he influenced the Japanese government to accept unconditional surrender. In 1946 he renounced his divine status.

Hi·ro·shi·ma (hírrə-shéemə, hírro-, hi-róshimə). A city in southern Japan, on the coast of Honshu. On August 6, 1945, it was almost entirely destroyed by an atomic bomb, the first city to become such a target. It has since been rebuilt as an industrial centre and seaport, manufacturing textiles, rubber goods, and machinery.

hir·sute (húr-sewt ‖ -sōōt, -sŏŏt) *adj.* **1.** Covered or coated with hair; hairy. **2.** Of, pertaining to, or consisting of hair. **3.** *Botany.* Covered with long, soft hairs: *hirsute stems.* [Latin *hirsūtus.*] —**hir·sute·ness** *n.*

hir·u·din (hi-rōō-din ‖ hírrə-, hírrew-) *n.* A substance extracted from the salivary glands of leeches and used as an anticoagulant.

[Originally a trademark, from New Latin *hirudo*, a leech, from Latin *hirūdo*†.]

hi·run·dine (hi-rún-dīn || -din) *adj.* Of, pertaining to, or characteristic of a swallow or the swallow family, Hirundinidae. [Latin *hirundo*†, a swallow + -INE.]

his (hiz, *weak form* iz). The possessive form of the pronoun *he.* Used to indicate possession, agency, or reception of an action by the masculine being or person spoken of or unspecified person considered to be male: **1.** Used attributively: *his wallet; pursuing his tasks; suffered his first rebuff; each child should be accompanied by his mother.* **2.** Used absolutely: **a.** As a predicate adjective: *The white boots are his.* **b.** As a substantive: *If you can't find your hat, take his.* **—of his.** Belonging or pertaining to him: *a friend of his.* [Middle English *his,* Old English *his.*]

His·pan·ic (hi-spánnik) *adj.* **1.** Of, pertaining to, or characteristic of the language, people, and culture of Spain or Spain and Portugal. **2.** *Chiefly U.S.* Of or pertaining to Latin America.
~*n. U.S.* A Latin American, especially one who has emigrated to the United States. [Latin *Hispānicus,* from *Hispānia,* SPAIN.]

his·pan·i·cise, his·pan·i·cize (hi-spánni-sīz) *tr.v.* **-cised, -cising, -cised.** To give a Spanish character to.

his·pan·i·cist (hi-spánni-sist) *n.* A student of, or specialist in the language, culture, or literature of Spain.

His·pan·i·ola (híss-panni-ṓlə, hi-spánni-, híspən-yṓlə). Second largest island of the West Indies. Lying between Cuba and Puerto Rico, it is divided into French-speaking Haiti to the west, and the Spanish-speaking Dominican Republic to the east.

Hispano- *comb.form.* Indicates: **1.** Spanish: for example, **Hispano-Arabian. 2.** *U.S.* Latin American : for example, **Hispano-American.** [From Latin *Hispānus,* Spanish.]

his·pid (híspid) *adj.* Covered with stiff or rough hairs; bristly: *hispid stems.* [Latin *hispidus.*]

hiss (hiss) *n.* **1.** A sharp, sibilant sound similar to a sustained *s,* such as that produced by breathing out through closed teeth or by gas escaping through a small gap. **2.** An expression of disapproval, contempt, or dissatisfaction by making this sound. **3.** Continuous unwanted noise from a loudspeaker, with a wide frequency range.
~*v.* **hissed, hissing, hisses.** —*intr.* To make a hiss, especially as an expression of disapproval. —*tr.* **1.** To utter (words or sounds) with a hissing sound. **2.** To express disapproval, derision, or hatred for by hissing. [Middle English *hissen* (imitative).] **—hiss·er** *n.*

hist (hist) *interj.* Used to attract attention, enjoin silence, or the like.

hist. 1. histology. **2.** historian; historical; history.

his·tam·i·nase (hi-stámmin-ayz, hístəmin-, -ayss) *n.* An enzyme that occurs in the digestive system and is responsible for the inactivation of histamine. [HISTAMIN(E) + -ASE.]

his·ta·mine (hístə-meen, -min) *n.* A white crystalline compound, $C_5H_9N_3$, found in plant and animal tissue, formed from histidine by the action of putrefactive bacteria. It stimulates gastric secretion, contracts smooth muscle, and is released during allergic reactions. [HIST(O)- + -AMINE.] **—his·ta·min·ic** (-mínnik) *adj.*

his·ti·dine (hísti-deen, -din) *n.* A colourless, crystalline amino acid, $C_6H_9N_3O_2$, used as a feed additive and dietary supplement. [HIST(O)- + -ID(E) + -INE.]

his·ti·o·cyte (hísti-ō-sīt) *n.* A **macrophage** *(see)* found in connective tissue. [Greek *histion,* diminutive of *histos,* web + -CYTE.]

histo–, hist– *comb. form.* Indicates bodily tissue; for example, **histamine, histolysis.** [Greek *histos,* web, beam, mast.]

his·to·chem·is·try (hístō-kémmistri) *n.* The chemistry of cells and tissues. **—his·to·chem·i·cal** *adj.*

his·to·com·pat·i·bil·i·ty (hístō-kəm-páttə-bílləti || -kom-) *n.* Compatibility between the various components of tissues, especially components of cell membranes, required for survival of tissue or organ transplants.

his·to·gen (hístə-jen, -jən) *n.* Any of the parts of a plant that give rise to the epidermis, cortex, and vascular tissue. [HISTO- + -GEN.]

his·to·gen·e·sis (hístō-jénnə-siss, -ə-) *n.* The formation and development of bodily tissues. [New Latin : HISTO- + -GENESIS.] **—his·to·ge·net·ic** (-jə-néttik), **his·to·gen·ic** (-jénnik) *adj.* **—his·to·ge·net·i·cal·ly, his·to·gen·i·cal·ly** *adv.*

his·to·gram (hístə-gram) *n. Statistics.* A graphic representation of a frequency distribution in which the widths of contiguous vertical bars are proportional to the class widths of the variable and the heights of the bars are proportional to the class frequencies. [HISTO(RY) + -GRAM.]

his·toid (hístoyd) *adj.* **1.** Resembling normal tissue. Said of some tumours. **2.** Consisting of one particular kind of tissue. [HISTO- + -OID.]

his·tol·o·gy (hi-stólləji) *n. Abbr.* **hist. 1.** The anatomical study of the microscopic structure of animal and plant tissues. **2.** The microscopic structure of tissue. [French *histologie* : HISTO- + -LOGY.] **—his·to·log·i·cal** (hístə-lójik'l) *adj.* **—his·to·log·i·cal·ly** *adv.* **—his·tol·o·gist** *n.*

his·tol·y·sis (hi-stóllə-siss) *n.* The breakdown and disintegration of organic tissue. [New Latin : HISTO- + -LYSIS.] **—his·to·lyt·ic** (hístə-líttik) *adj.* **—his·to·lyt·i·cal·ly** *adv.*

his·tone (hístōn) *n.* Any of several simple, water-soluble proteins, found especially in cell nuclei associated with nucleic acids, that can release on hydrolysis a high proportion of basic amino acids. [HIST(O)- + -ONE.]

his·to·pa·thol·o·gy (hístō-pə-thólləji) *n.* The histology of diseased tissue. **—his·to·path·o·log·i·cal** (-páthə-lójik'l) *adj.*

his·to·phys·i·ol·o·gy (hístō-fízzi-ólləji) *n.* The physiology of the microscopic functioning of bodily tissues. **—his·to·phys·i·o·log·i·cal** (-ə-lójik'l) *adj.*

his·to·plas·mo·sis (hístō-plaz-mṓ-siss) *n.* A disease affecting the lungs caused by inhalation of spores of the fungus *Histoplasma capsulatum.*

his·to·ri·an (hi-stáwri-ən, i- || -stṓri-) *n. Abbr.* **hist.** A writer or student of history; especially, one who is an authority on history.

his·to·ri·at·ed (hi-stáwri-aytid) *adj.* Decorated with artistic designs: *a historiated initial.* [Medieval Latin *historiāre* (past participle *historiātus*), to tell a story (by pictures), from *historia,* story, HISTORY.]

his·tor·ic (hi-stórrik, i- || -stáwrik) *adj.* **1. a.** Having importance in or influence on history; renowned. **b.** Likely to become important in history; having considerable contemporary significance: *a historic meeting.* **2. a.** Historical. **b.** Associated with events in history: *historic cities.* **3.** Of or designating tenses of verbs, especially in Latin or Greek, that refer to past time.

Usage: *Historic* and *historical* have similar meanings, but they are rarely interchangeable. *Historic* is largely restricted to what is important in history, or to what has a long history attached to it: *a historic first voyage, a historic meeting, a historic city. Historical* refers more broadly to what is concerned with history or has an actual existence in history: *a historical account, a historical pageant. A historic novel* is an extremely important one, which may or may not be concerned with history; *a historical novel,* by contrast, must be concerned with the events of history, and may or may not be important. *Historic,* then, refers to being or becoming *part of* history; *historical,* to being *about* history.

his·tor·i·cal (hi-stórri-k'l, i- || -stáwri-) *adj. Abbr.* **hist. 1.** Of, relating to, or of the nature of history as opposed to fiction or legend. **2. a.** Based on or concerned with events in history: *historical novel.* **b.** Caused by events in history. **3.** Having considerable importance or influence in history; historic. **4.** *Linguistics.* **Diachronic** *(see).* —See Usage note at **historic. —his·tor·i·cal·ly** *adv.* **—his·tor·i·cal·ness** *n.*

historical geology *n.* Geological study of the earth and its atmosphere from the time of its formation to the present day.

historical linguistics *pl.n.* The study of language development, especially that of a single variety, with emphasis on chronological change. Compare **comparative linguistics.**

historical materialism *n.* The Marxist theory, part of **dialectical materialism** *(see),* which states that society arises fundamentally from an economic base, and that it is characterised by a conflict of classes that will eventually result in a classless society.

historical method *n.* A method of analysis or exposition whereby a subject is considered in its origin and subsequent historical development.

historical present *n.* The present tense used as a literary device in the narration of events set in the past.

historical school *n.* A school of theorists, as in law or economics, stressing the influence of historical conditions.

his·tor·i·cism (hi-stórri-siz'm, i- || -stáwri-) *n.* **1.** The belief that inevitable processes are at work in history. **2.** The relativistic theory that all social and cultural phenomena are historically determined and that particular past events, cultures, or the like should be judged only in relation to other periods of history, rather than in relation to one's own values. **3.** Veneration of the past or of tradition. **—his·tor·i·cist** *adj.* & *n.*

his·to·ric·i·ty (histə-ríssəti) *n.* Historical authenticity: *the historicity of an event.*

his·to·ri·og·ra·pher (hi-stórri-óggrəfər, i-, -stáwri- || -stṓri-) *n.* **1.** One trained in or practising historiography. **2.** A historian; especially, one officially appointed by a group or public institution.

his·to·ri·og·ra·phy (hi-stórri-óggrəfi, i-, -stáwri- || -stṓri-) *n.* **1.** The principles or methodology of historical study. **2.** The writing of history. **3.** Historical literature. [Old French *historiographie,* from Greek *historiographia* : HISTORY + -GRAPHY.]

his·to·ry (hístri, hístəri) *n., pl.* **-ries. 1.** *Abbr.* **hist.** The branch of knowledge that records and analyses past events. Sometimes used adjectivally: *a history book.* **2.** A chronological record of events, as of the life or development of a people, country, or institution. **3.** *Abbr.* **hist.** A narrative of events; a story; a chronicle. **4.** The events forming the subject matter of history. **5.** An interesting past: *a house with a history.* **6.** That which is not of current concern: *My youth is now history.* **7.** A drama based on historical events. **8. a.** A study or record of what has happened to a person or thing, especially from a particular point of view: *a patient's medical history.* **b.** A past or record marked by a particular characteristic: *has a history of violence.* **—make history.** To be of historic importance, especially by being the first of one's kind. [Latin *historia,* from Greek, inquiry, observation, from *histōr,* learned man.]

his·tri·on·ic (hístri-ónnik) *adj.* Also **his·tri·on·i·cal** (-ónnik'l). **1.** Overemotional or dramatic; theatrical; affected. **2.** *Archaic.* Of or pertaining to actors or acting. [Late Latin *histriōnicus,* theatrical, from *histriō*†, actor.] **—his·tri·on·i·cal·ly** *adv.*

his·tri·on·ics (hístri-ónniks) *n.* **1.** Exaggerated emotional behaviour calculated for effect. Used with a plural verb. **2.** *Archaic.* Theatrical arts. Used with a singular verb.

hit (hit) *v.* **hit, hitting, hits.** —*tr.* **1.** To come in contact with forcefully; strike. **2.** To cause to make sudden and forceful contact; knock; bump: *hit her hand against the wall.* **3.** To deal a blow to. **4.** To strike with a missile: *He fired and hit the target.* **5.** To reach and affect adversely: *hit hard by the depression.* **6.** To come upon; arrive at; reach: *hit an all-time low.* **7.** To accord with; appeal to;

suit: *The idea hit his fancy*. **8.** To propel with a blow. **9. a.** To make (a shot or stroke) when striking a ball in a game: *hit a volley*. **b.** To score (runs) in cricket. **10.** *Informal*. To set out on or towards: *hit the road; hit town*. **11.** *Informal*. To resort to excessively: *hit the bottle*. **12.** *Chiefly U.S. Informal*. To request or obtain money from: *The vagrant hit me for a dime*. **13.** *Chiefly U.S. Slang*. To kill. —*intr*. **1. a.** To strike or deal a blow. Often used with *out*. **b.** *Informal*. To criticise or condemn. Used with *at* or *out at*. **2.** To come in contact; bump. **3.** To achieve or find something desired or sought, often by chance. Used with *on* or *upon*. —**hit it off**. *Informal*. To get along well together. —**hit off**. *Informal*. To mimic or imitate. —*n*. **1.** A collision or impact. **2.** A successfully executed shot, blow, thrust, or throw. **3.** A show, song, performer, or the like that has popular success. Also used adjectivally: *a hit musical*. **4.** A bit of luck. **5.** An apt or effective jest, remark, or witticism. **6.** *Chiefly U.S. Slang*. **a.** A killing by a hit man. **b.** The target of such a killing. [Hit (infinitive, past tense, and past participle); Middle English *hitten, hitte, hit*, from Old Norse *hitta†*, to hit.] —**hit·ter** *n*.

Hi·ta·chi (hi-tá́achi). City in east Japan, on the coast of Honshu. Japan's major producer of electrical equipment.

hit-and-run (hítt'n-rún) *adj*. **1.** Designating or involving the driver of a motor vehicle who, after striking a pedestrian or another vehicle, fails to stop. **2.** Of or designating warfare tactics typically conducted on a basis of quick attacks and swift withdrawals from the scene of the action.

hitch (hich) *v*. **hitched, hitching, hitches**. —*tr*. **1.** To fasten or catch temporarily with a loop, hook, or noose; tie. **2.** To connect or attach, as to a vehicle. Often used with *up*. **3.** To move with jerks: *hitched his chair closer*. **4.** To raise by pulling or jerking. Often used with *up*: *hitch up one's trousers*. **5.** *Informal*. To obtain (a lift) by hitchhiking. **6.** *Slang*. To unite in marriage. Used chiefly in the phrase *get hitched*. —*intr*. **1.** To become entangled, snarled, or fastened. **2.** *Informal*. To hitchhike. **3.** To move haltingly, as with a limp. —*n*. **1.** Any of various knots used for attaching a rope to a fixed object, such as a **harness hitch** or **half hitch** *(both of which see)*. **2.** A short jerking motion; a tug. **3.** A hobble or limp. **4.** An impediment or delay: *a hitch in our plans for the party*. **5.** *Informal*. A lift obtained by hitchhiking: *a hitch down to London*. [Middle English *hytchen†*, to move or lift with a jerk.]

Hitch·cock (hích-kok), **Sir Alfred** (1899–1980). U.S. suspense-film director, born in London. His films include *The 39 Steps* (1935), *The Lady Vanishes* (1938), *Rebecca* (1940), *North by Northwest* (1959), *Vertigo* (1958), *Psycho* (1960), and *The Birds* (1964).

hitch·hike (hích-hīk) *v*. **-hiked, -hiking, -hikes**. —*intr*. To travel by soliciting free lifts along a road. —*tr*. To solicit or get (a free lift) along a road. —**hitch·hik·er** *n*.

hitch·ing post (híching) *n*. A post for temporarily tying up a horse or other animal.

hi-tech *adj. & n*. Variant of **high-tech**.

hith·er (híthər ǁ híthər) *adv. Formal*. To or towards this place: *come hither*. —*adj. Archaic*. Located towards this side; nearer. [Middle English *hither*, Old English *hider*.]

hither and thither *adv*. Towards one place and then another, as in a state of turmoil; in all directions. Also "hither and yon."

hith·er·to (híthər-tóo, -tōo) *adv. Formal*. **1.** Until this time; up to now. **2.** *Archaic*. To this place; thus far.

hith·er·ward (híthər-wərd) *adv*. Also **hith·er·wards** (-wərdz). *Archaic*. Hither.

Hit·ler¹ (hítlər), **Adolf**, born Adolf Schicklgrüber (1889–1945). Austrian-born founder of the German Nazi party and Chancellor of the Third Reich (1933–45). Hitler served in the German Army in World War I. He joined the German Workers' Party and by 1921 had gained the leadership of it, re-founding it as the National Socialist German Workers' Party. He was arrested after the "beer hall putsch" in Munich in 1923, and spent some months in prison where he wrote the major part of *Mein Kampf*. By 1930 he had built the Nazi party into the second largest party in Germany. He lost the 1932 presidential election to Hindenburg, but a few months later the Nazis won most seats at a general election and in January, 1933, Hitler was appointed Chancellor. He brought every German institution under the totalitarian control of the Nazi party. In September, 1939, Hitler's troops invaded Poland, causing the outbreak of World War II. By the spring of 1945 Germany faced defeat. On April 29, Hitler married his mistress, Eva Braun, and the next day they committed suicide. —**Hit·le·ri·an** (hit-leér-i-ən) *adj*.

Hitler² *n*. A petty tyrant. Used derogatorily: *a little Hitler*. [After Adolf HITLER.]

hit list *n. Informal*. **1.** A list of people who are to be murdered. **2.** A list of people or organisations against which some punitive action is to be taken. **3.** A list of projects, enterprises, or the like, from which support is to be withdrawn.

hit man *n. Chiefly U.S. Informal*. One employed to commit murder; a hired assassin.

hit parade *n*. A list of the best-selling recorded songs over a given period.

hit-or-miss (hít-awr-míss ǁ -ər-) *adj*. Also **hit-and-miss** (-ən-). Random; haphazard; only occasionally effective.

Hit·tite (híttīt) *n*. **1.** A member of an ancient people living in Asia Minor and northern Syria about 2000–1200 B.C. **2.** An extinct Indo-European language spoken by these people. [Hebrew *Ḥittī*, from Hittite *Hatti*.] —**Hit·tite** *adj*.

HIV *n*. *H*uman *I*mmunodeficiency *V*irus: the virus that probably causes **AIDS** *(see)*.

hive (hīv) *n*. **1.** A natural or artificial structure for housing bees, especially honeybees. **2.** A colony of bees living in a hive. **3.** A place swarming with active, industrious people: *a hive of activity*. —*v*. **hived, hiving, hives**. —*tr*. **1.** To collect (bees) into a hive. **2.** To store (honey) in a hive. **3.** To store up; accumulate. Used with *up* or *away*. —*intr*. **1.** To enter a hive. **2.** To live together in close association. —**hive off**. **1.** To leave in a large group, like bees forming a new hive. **2.** To assign or transfer (work or responsibilities, for example) elsewhere. **3.** *Chiefly British*. To dispose of (part of a nationalised company, for example) on the open market. [Middle English *hive*, Old English *hӯf*.]

hives (hīvz) *n. Pathology*. **Urticaria** *(see)*. [16th century (Scottish): origin obscure.]

H.J. hic jacet.

hl hectolitre.

H.L. House of Lords.

Hluhluwe (hlōohlóoway). Town in Zululand (Kwazulu), northeast Natal, South Africa. To the west lies Hluhluwe Game Reserve, established in 1951, and noted for its rare white rhinos.

hm hectometre.

H.M. **1.** headmaster. **2.** headmistress. **3.** Her (or His) Majesty.

h'm. Variant of **hem**.

H.M.A.S. Her (or His) Majesty's Australian Ship.

H.M.C.S. Her (or His) Majesty's Canadian Ship.

H.M.I. Her (or His) Majesty's Inspector (of schools).

H.M.N.Z.S. Her (or His) Majesty's New Zealand Ship.

H.M.S. **1.** Her (or His) Majesty's Service. **2.** Her (or His) Majesty's Ship.

H.M.S.O. Her (or His) Majesty's Stationery Office.

H.N.C. *n*. Higher National Certificate: a British qualification in technical subjects, similar in standard to a Higher National Diploma, and recognised as a higher technical qualification.

H.N.D. *n*. Higher National Diploma: a British qualification in technical subjects, especially engineering and applied sciences, that is sometimes recognised as equivalent to an ordinary degree.

ho (hō) *interj*. Used to express surprise or joy or to attract attention to something sighted or to urge onward: *Land ho! Westward ho!* [Middle English, partly from Old Norse *hō!* and partly from Old French *ho!, halt!*]

Ho The symbol for the element holmium.

HO, H.O. **1.** Head Office. **2.** Home Office (in Britain).

ho. house.

hoactzin. Variant of **hoatzin**.

Hoad (hōd), **Lew(is) Alan** (1934–). Australian tennis player. He won the Wimbledon singles championship twice, in 1956 and 1957.

hoar (hor ǁ hōr) *adj. Chiefly Poetic*. Hoary. —*n*. **1.** Hoariness. **2.** Hoarfrost. [Middle English *ho(o)r*, Old English *hār*.]

hoard (hord ǁ hōrd) *n*. **1.** A hidden or stored fund or supply guarded for future use. **2.** A cache of ancient coins, jewels, or the like; a treasure. **3.** An accumulated store, as of facts, ideas, or the like. **4.** *Plural*. A very large amount: *hoards of time*. —*v*. **hoarded, hoarding, hoards**. —*intr*. **1.** To gather or accumulate a hoard. **2.** To buy in an unnecessarily large stock, as of groceries, for example, as a precaution against shortages. —*tr*. **1.** To accumulate or gather by saving or hiding. **2.** To keep an unnecessarily large stock of (goods) as a precaution against shortages. [Middle English *hord*, Old English *hord*.]

hoard·er (hórd-ər ǁ hôrd-) *n*. One that hoards; especially, a person who never throws anything away.

hoard·ing (hord-ing ǁ hôrd-) *n*. **1.** A temporary wooden fence around a building or structure under construction or repair. **2.** *Chiefly British*. A structure for the display of advertisements in public places or alongside roads. [Earlier *hoard*, a fence, from earlier *hourd*, from Anglo-French *hurdis*, from Old French *hourd*, scaffold, from Germanic.]

hoar·frost (hór-frost ǁ hôr-, -frawst) *n*. Frozen dew that forms a white coating on a surface. Also called "hoar", "white frost".

hoarhound. Variant of **horehound**.

hoarse (horss ǁ hôrss) *adj*. **hoarser, hoarsest**. **1.** Low and grating in sound; husky; croaking. **2.** Having a husky, grating voice, often as a result of shouting or illness. [Middle English *hors*, from Old Norse *hārs* (unattested), variant of *hās*, from Germanic *hai(r)sa-* (unattested).] —**hoarse·ly** *adv*. —**hoarse·ness** *n*.

hoars·en (hórss'n ǁ hôrss'n) *v*. **-ened, -ening, -ens**. —*tr*. To cause to be hoarse. —*intr*. To become hoarse.

hoar·y (háwri ǁ hôri) *adj*. **-ier, -iest**. **1.** Grey or white with or as if with age. **2.** Covered with greyish hair or down: *hoary leaves*. **3.** Very old; ancient. —**hoar·i·ness** *n*.

hoary cress *n*. A white-flowered perennial plant, *Cardaria* (or *Lepidium*) *draba*, native to the Mediterranean but widespread as a weed.

ho·at·zin (hō-át-sin; wat-séen ǁ *U.S. also* waat-) *n*. Also **ho·act·zin** (-ákt-; wakt-). A brownish, crested bird, *Opisthocomus hoazin*, of tropical South America, having claws on the wings in the young. [American Spanish, from Nahuatl *uatzin*, pheasant.]

hoax (hōks) *n*. An act intended to deceive or trick, either as a practical joke or as a serious fraud. —*tr.v*. **hoaxed, hoaxing, hoaxes**. To deceive or trick with a hoax. [Perhaps shortened variant of HOCUS.] —**hoax·er** *n*.

hob¹ (hob) *n*. **1.** A shelf or projection at the back or side of the inside of a fireplace, for keeping things warm. **2.** A flat plate on top of a cooker fitting over the cooking rings. **3.** A rotating tool used for cutting gears. [16th century : perhaps a variant of HUB (in the sense projection, lump).]

hob² *n.* A hobgoblin, sprite, or elf. **—play** (or **raise**) **hob.** To make mischief or trouble. Often used with *with.* [Middle English *hob,* from *Hobbe,* pet form of *Robert* or *Robin.*]

Ho·ba meteorite (hṓbə) *n.* The world's largest meteorite (weighing 60 tonnes) discovered in 1920 near Grootfontein, Namibia.

Ho·bart (hṓ-baart). Capital city and chief seaport of Tasmania, Australia. Built on a bight approximately 19 kilometres (12 miles) from the sea, it has an excellent natural harbour. Included among its exports are agricultural produce, timber, and wool; principal industries are zinc refining, flour milling, and chemicals.

Hobbes (hobz), **Thomas** (1588–1679). English political philosopher. He wrote *Leviathan* (1651), outlining his philosophy that individuals are essentially selfish.

Hobb·ism (hóbbiz'm) *n.* A theory promulgated by Thomas Hobbes, advocating powerful, especially monarchical, government as the only means of adequately controlling the problems created by competing individual needs and interests.

hob·bit (hóbbit) *n.* Any of a race of fictional creatures, half the size of human beings. [After the characters in J.R.R. Tolkien's *The Hobbit* (1937) and *The Lord of the Rings* (1954–55).]

hob·ble (hóbb'l) *v.* **-bled, -bling, -bles.** Also **hop·ple** (hópp'l). **—intr. 1.** To walk or move awkwardly or with difficulty; limp. **2.** To proceed haltingly or unsteadily. **—tr. 1. a.** To put a hobble on (an animal). **b.** To put a hobble on (the legs of an animal). **2.** To cause to limp. **3.** To hamper the action or progress of; restrain; impede. **~n.** Also **hop·ple. 1.** An awkward, clumsy, or irregular walk or gait. **2.** A device, such as a rope or strap, used to tie the legs of an animal together in order to restrict its movement. **3.** *Archaic.* An unfortunate or awkward situation. [Middle English *hoblen,* of Low German origin, akin to Middle Dutch *hobbelen†,* to roll.] **—hob·bler** *n.*

hob·ble·de·hoy (hóbb'l-di-hóy, -hoy) *n., pl.* **-hoys.** A gawky adolescent boy or girl. [16th century : origin obscure.]

hobble skirt *n.* A type of long skirt, popular between 1910 and 1914, that was so narrow below the knees that it restricted normal stride.

Hobbs (hobz), **Sir Jack,** born John Berry Hobbs (1882–1963). English cricketer, widely regarded as the finest English batsman of this century. Playing for Surrey and England, Hobbs scored a record 197 centuries. The first professional cricketer to be knighted (1953).

hob·by¹ (hóbbi) *n., pl.* **-bies. 1.** An occupation, activity, or interest, such as stamp-collecting or gardening, engaged in primarily for pleasure; a pastime. **2.** *Archaic.* A little horse; a nag. **3.** A hobbyhorse. **4.** An early kind of velocipede without pedals. [Middle English *hoby,* a hobbyhorse, something one pursues, perhaps from *Hobbin,* pet form of *Robin.*] **—hob·by·ist** *n.*

hobby² *n., pl.* **-bies.** Any of several small falcons of the genus *Falco;* especially, an Old World species, *F. subbuteo,* formerly used for hawking. [Middle English *hoby,* from Old French *hobé, hobet,* diminutive of *hobet†,* a small bird of prey.]

hob·by·horse (hóbbi-hawrss) *n.* **1.** A child's toy consisting of a long stick with an imitation horse's head on one end. **2.** A rocking horse. **3. a.** A figure of a horse worn around the waist of a morris dancer or other performer pretending to ride a horse. **b.** A person wearing such a costume. **4.** An early form of bicycle, a hobby. **5.** A pet topic or idea about which one constantly talks; a subject that obsesses one.

hob·gob·lin (hób-gobblin, -góbblin) *n.* **1.** A goblin variously represented as being mischievous or as ugly and evil. **2.** A bugbear. [HOB (elf) + GOBLIN.]

hob·nail (hób-nayl) *n.* A short nail with a thick head used to protect the soles of shoes or boots. [HOB (projection, archaic sense peg) + NAIL.]

hob·nob (hób-nob, -nób) *intr.v.* **-nobbed, -nobbing, -nobs.** To associate familiarly; socialise. Used with *with: He hobnobs with the rich.* [Originally *hob* or *nob,* (drink) to one another, from earlier *hab or nab,* hit or miss : perhaps Middle English *habbe,* present subjunctive of *habben,* to HAVE + *nabbe,* from *ne habbe,* not to have.]

ho·bo (hṓbō) *n., pl.* **-boes** or **-bos.** *Chiefly U.S.* **1.** A tramp; a vagrant. **2.** A migratory, usually unskilled worker. [19th century : origin obscure.] **—ho·bo·ism** *n.*

Hob·son-Job·son (hób-s'n-jób-s'n) *n.* Folk-etymological alteration of a word borrowed from another language. An example of Hobson-Jobson is the word **compound²** *(see)* which is from Malay *kampong.* [Anglo-Indian, coinage, itself a Hobson-Jobson alteration (influenced by *Hobson* and *Jobson,* English surnames) of Arabic *yā Ḥasan, yā Ḥusayn!* 'O Hasan, O Husain! (ritual cry of mourning for Hasan and Husain, Muhammad's grandsons who were killed in battle).]

Hob·son's choice (hób-s'nz) *n.* The option of accepting that which is offered or nothing; a choice with no real alternative. [After Thomas *Hobson* (c. 1544–1631), Cambridge liveryman, who required his customers to take the next available horse rather than give them a choice.]

Hoch·huth (hókh-hōōt), **Rolf** (1931–). Swiss dramatist. He specialised in the documentary treatment of recent historical events. *The Soldiers* (1966) caused dispute by suggesting that Churchill was implicated in the death of the Polish general, Sikorski.

Ho Chi Minh (hṓ chée mín), born Nguyen That Tanh (1890–1969). Founder and first president of North Vietnam (1954–69). After studying in Moscow, he founded the Indochinese Communist Party (1930), and returned to Vietnam to establish the Vietminh as a force struggling for independence against French rule. In 1945, after Japan's surrender in World War II, he and his followers seized Hanoi, declaring independence. Forced to withdraw (1946), he led a jungle war which culminated in victory at Dien Bien Phu (1954). The Geneva Agreement that year established the new state of North Vietnam. Ho Chi Minh supported Vietcong guerrillas in the South, but died before the reunification of Vietnam.

Ho Chi Minh City. Formerly (until 1975) **Sai·gon** (sī-gón). A port in south Vietnam. On the river Saigon, near the Mekong Delta, it was successively the capital of Cochin China, French Indochina, and the republic of South Vietnam. The presence of U.S. forces during the Vietnamese War (1961–75) between the North and the South caused much social decay, exacerbated by their withdrawal and the republic's subsequent defeat.

hock¹ (hok) *n.* **1.** The tarsal joint of the hind leg of a horse or similar animal, corresponding to the human ankle. Also called "hough". **2.** A similar joint in the leg of a domestic fowl. **~tr.v.** **hocked, hocking, hocks.** To disable by cutting the tendons of the hock; hamstring. [Middle English *hoch,* Old English *hōh,* heel.]

hock² *n. Chiefly British.* **1.** Any of several white wines from the German Rhine. **2.** Any of various white wines similar to German hock. [Short for obsolete *hockamore,* from German *Hochheimer (Wein),* wine of *Hochheim,* district in Germany.]

hock³ *tr.v.* **hocked, hocking, hocks.** *Informal.* **1.** *Chiefly U.S.* To pawn. **2.** *Chiefly Australian & N.Z.* To sell, especially for a low price. **~n.** *Chiefly U.S. Informal.* The state of being pawned. **—in hock.** *Chiefly U.S. Informal.* **1.** In pawn. **2.** Held in jail. **3.** In debt. [From Dutch *hok†,* prison.]

hock·ey (hócki) *n.* **1.** A game played on a field in which two opposing teams of 11 players, using curved sticks, try to drive a ball into the opponents' goal. Also *U.S.* "field hockey". **2. Ice hockey** *(see).* [16th century : origin obscure.]

hockey stick *n.* A stick with one curved end, used in hockey.

Hock·ney (hók-ni), **David** (1937–). British artist. He developed a distinct style of fine figure drawing. He has also done stage designs. Autobiography: *That's the Way I See It* (1993).

hock·shop (hók-shop) *n. Chiefly U.S. Informal.* A pawnshop.

ho·cus (hṓkəss) *tr.v.* **-cussed** or *U.S.* **-cused, -cussing** or *U.S.* **-cusing, -cusses** or *U.S.* **-cuses. 1.** To fool or deceive; hoax; cheat. **2.** To stupefy, as with a drug. **3.** To adulterate (food or drink) with a drug. [Short for HOCUS-POCUS.]

ho·cus-po·cus (hṓkəss-pṓkəss) *n.* **1.** Nonsense words or phrases used as a formula by conjurers. **2.** A trick performed by a magician or juggler; sleight of hand. **3.** Any deception or chicanery. **4.** Any words or jargon used to mystify. **~v.** **hocus-pocussed** or *U.S.* **hocus-pocused, -cussing** or *U.S.* **-cusing, -cusses** or *U.S.* **-cuses. —tr.** To deceive; fool; cheat. **—intr.** To be deceptive. [17th century : mock Latin.]

hod (hod) *n.* **1.** An open container carried on a pole over the shoulder for transporting loads, such as bricks or mortar. **2.** A coal scuttle. [Perhaps variant of earlier dialectal *hot,* from Old French *hotte,* from Germanic.]

hod·den (hódd'n) *n. Scottish.* Coarse, woollen, homespun cloth. [16th century : origin obscure.]

hodden grey *n.* Hodden made from a mixture of black and white wools.

hodge (hoj) *n. British.* A farm labourer or rustic.

hodgepodge *n. Chiefly U.S.* Variant of **hotchpotch.**

Hodg·kin (hój-kin), **Dorothy Mary Crowfoot** (1910–94). British biochemist. She helped to pioneer the analysis of pepsin and penicillin through X-ray diffraction. She also studied the molecular structure of vitamin B_{12} and got the Nobel chemistry prize in 1964.

Hodgkin, Thomas (1798–1866). British doctor. In 1832 he identified the disease of lymphatic tissues since called Hodgkin's disease.

Hodgkin's disease *n.* A usually chronic, progressive, malignant disease marked by enlargement of the lymph nodes, spleen, and often of the liver and kidneys and occurring approximately twice as often in adult males as females. [After Thomas HODGKIN.]

hod·man (hód-mən) *n., pl.* **-men** (-mən). A person who carries loads in a hod for a builder or bricklayer.

hod·o·scope *n. Physics.* Any of various devices for indicating the paths of high-energy particles, used especially for investigating cosmic rays. [From Greek *hodos,* path, road + -SCOPE.]

hoe (hṓ) *n.* **1.** A tool with a flat blade attached at an angle to a long handle, used for weeding and breaking up the soil. **2.** *West African.* A short-handled farming tool with a blade set at right angles, used with a hacking action for digging. **~v.** **hoed, hoeing, hoes. —tr.** To weed, cultivate, or dig up with a hoe. **—intr.** To work with a hoe. **—hoe in** or **into.** *Chiefly Australian Informal.* To eat with enthusiasm. [Middle English *howe,* from Old French *houe,* from Frankish *hauwa* (unattested).] **—ho·er** *n.*

hoe·cake (hṓ-kayk) *n. U.S.* A thin cake made of cornmeal. [It was sometimes baked on the blade of a hoe.]

hoe·down (hṓ-down) *n.* **1.** A boisterous dance; especially, a square dance. **2.** The music for a hoe-down. **3.** A party at which hoe-downs are danced. [HOE + DOWN.]

Hoff·man (hóf-mən), **Dustin** (1937–). U.S. film actor, star of *The*

Graduate (1967), *Midnight Cowboy* (1969) and *Straw Dogs* (1971). His performances in *Kramer vs Kramer* (1979) and *Rain Man* (1989) won him Academy Awards.

hog (hog || hawg) *n.* Also **hogg** (for sense 4). **1.** A domesticated pig; especially, a castrated male pig weighing over 54 kilogrammes (120 pounds). **2.** *U.S.* Any of various mammals of the family Suidae; any species of pig. **3.** A self-indulgent, gluttonous, or vulgar person. **4.** *British.* A young sheep before its first shearing. Also called "hogget". **—go the whole hog.** To do something thoroughly.
~*v.* **hogged, hogging, hogs.** —*tr.* **1.** To keep or take more than one's share of. **2.** To cause (the back) to arch. **3.** To cut off (a horse's mane). —*intr.* To arch upwards in the middle. Used of a ship's keel. [Middle English *hogge,* Old English *hogg,* from Celtic.]

ho·gan (hṓ-gaan, -gən) *n.* An earth-covered Navaho dwelling. [Navaho *hogan.*]

Ho·gan (hṓgən) **(William Benjamin) "Ben"** (1912–97). U.S. golfer. He won the U.S. Open and Professional championships in 1948; and the U.S. Open in 1950, 1951, and 1953. He won the British Open in 1953.

Ho·garth (hṓ-gaarth), **William** (1697–1764). British painter and engraver. In 1729 he started on *A Harlot's Progress,* a series of allegorical paintings. Other series included *A Rake's Progress* (1733) and *Marriage-à-la-Mode* (1745). His satirical paintings attacked the contradiction of luxury and squalor in society.

hog·back (hóg-bak || háwg-) *n.* Also **hog's back.** A sharp ridge with steeply sloping sides, produced by the erosion of the broken edges of highly tilted strata. [From a fancied resemblance to a hog's back.]

hog badger *n.* A badger, *Arctonyx collaris,* of southeast Asia, having a mobile, piglike nose.

hog cholera *n. U.S.* **Swine fever** *(see).*

hog·fish (hóg-fish || háwg-) *n., pl.* **-fishes** or collectively **hogfish. 1.** A colourful fish, *Lachnolaimus maximus,* of warm Atlantic waters, having a long snout in the adult male. **2.** Any of several similar or related fishes, such as the **pigfish** *(see).*

Hogg (hog || hawg), **James,** called the Ettrick Shepherd (1770–1835). Scottish poet. Originally a shepherd, he was discovered by Sir Walter Scott. His verse included *The Queen's Wake* (1813).

hog·gish (hóg-ish || háwg-) *adj.* **1.** Coarsely self-indulgent or gluttonous. **2.** Filthy. **—hog·gish·ly** *adv.* **—hog·gish·ness** *n.*

Hog·ma·nay (hóg-mə-náy, -nay) *n. Chiefly Scottish.* New Year's Eve. [17th century (Scottish) : perhaps from Norman French *Hoguinané,* Old French *aguillanneuf*†.]

hog's fennel *n.* Any of various Eurasian plants of the genus *Peucedanum*; especially, *P. officinale,* growing in marshes and having clusters of small white flowers.

hogs·head (hógz-hed || háwgz-) *n. Abbr.* **hhd 1.** Any of various units of volume or capacity differing in size depending on the liquid; for example 52.5 imperial gallons for wine and 54 imperial gallons for beer. **2.** A large barrel or cask with such capacity. [Middle English, "hog's head" (the reason for the name is obscure).]

hog-tie, hog·tie (hóg-tī || háwg-) *tr.v.* **-tied, -tying** or **-tieing, -ties.** *U.S.* **1.** To tie together the legs of. **2.** To impede or disrupt in movement or action.

hog·wash (hóg-wosh || háwg-, -wawsh) *n.* **1.** Worthless, false, or ridiculous speech or writing. **2. Pigswill** *(see).*

hog·weed (hóg-weed || háwg-) *n.* **1.** A tall, coarse, weedy plant, *Heracleum sphondylium,* having flattened clusters of small white flowers. Also called "cow parsnip". See **giant hogweed. 2.** Any of various other coarse, weedy plants.

Hoh·en·zol·lern (hṓ-ən-zóllərn, *German* -tsóllərn). A German royal family. It supplied the Electors of Brandenburg from 1415, later extending control to Prussia (1618). Under Frederick I (reigned 1701–13), the Hohenzollerns' possessions were unified as the kingdom of Prussia. From 1871 to 1918, Hohenzollern monarchs ruled the German empire.

ho-ho (hō-hṓ, hṓ-) *interj.* Used as an imitation of laughter or to express contempt.

ho-hum (hṓ-húm) *interj.* Used as a sigh to express a feeling of weariness, boredom, or dissatisfaction.

hoick (hoyk) *v.* **hoicked, hoicking, hoicks.** *British.* —*tr.* To lift or bring up with a jerk. —*intr.* To bring up phlegm from the throat; hawk. [Perhaps a variant of HIKE.]

hoi pol·loi (hóy po-lóy, pə-, pólloy) *n. Used with a plural verb.* The common people viewed from a position of social, economic, or intellectual advantage or privilege; the masses. Preceded frequently but redundantly by *the.* [Greek *hoi polloi,* the many, the masses : *hoi,* plural of *ho,* the + *polloi,* plural of *polus,* many.]

hoist (hoyst) *tr.v.* **hoisted, hoisting, hoists.** To raise or haul up, particularly with the help of mechanical apparatus. See Synonyms at **lift.**
~*n.* **1.** An apparatus for lifting heavy or cumbersome objects. **2.** An act of hoisting. **3.** *Nautical.* **a.** The height or vertical dimension of a flag or of any square sail other than a course. **b.** A group of flags raised together as a signal. **c.** The inner edge of a flag, nearest to the pole. [Variant of dialectal *hoise,* from earlier *heise;* akin to Dutch *hijsen,* Low German *hissen*†.] **—hoist·er** *n.*

hoi·ty-toi·ty (hóyti-tóyti) *adj.* Also **high·ty-tigh·ty** (hī́ti-tī́ti). **1. a.** Haughtily petulant. **b.** Pretentiously snobbish. **2.** *Archaic.* Lightheaded; flighty.
~*n.,* Also **high·ty-tigh·ty.** *Archaic.* Flightiness; giddy behaviour. [Reduplication of *hoity,* from dialectal *hoit*†, to romp.]

hoke (hōk) —*tr.v.* **hoked, hoking, hokes.** To act (a part) in a melodramatic or insincere way; overplay. Usually used with *up.* [From HOKUM.]

ho·key-co·key (hṓki-kṓki) *n.* A lively group dance performed while singing a song and doing the movements specified by the words of the song. [Perhaps influenced by HOKEY-POKEY.]

ho·key-po·key (hṓki-pṓki) *n.* **1.** Hocus-pocus. **2.** Inferior or cheap ice cream sold by street vendors. **3.** *Chiefly N.Z.* **a.** A crunchy bar of golden coloured toffee. **b.** Ice cream flavoured with small chips of this. [Senses 2,3 : origin obscure.]

Hok·kai·do (ho-kī́-dō). Northernmost of the four major islands which constitute Japan. It is the second largest of the islands, but the least populated. It was called Yezo until the Meiji restoration of 1868, when it was given its present name, which means "land of the northern sea". The interior of the island is largely mountainous and heavily forested and is rich in coal and iron. The northern part of the island is virtually uninhabited; the major cities, Sapporo, Hakodate, and Otaru are all on the island's southwestern peninsula.

Hok·ki·en (hokyén) *n.* A dialect of Chinese spoken in Fujian province, and also widely spoken in Taiwan and by people of Chinese origin in Southeast Asia.

hok·ku (hóckōō) *n.* A Japanese verse form, a **haiku** *(see).*

ho·kum (hṓ'kəm) *n.* **1.** Nonsense; bunk. **2.** Sentimental or clichéd material used in a play or film as a means of obtaining a predictable audience response. [20th century : origin obscure.]

Hol·arc·tic (hol-árk-tik, hōl-, -ár-) *adj.* Of or designating the zoogeographical region that includes the northern areas of the earth and is divided into Nearctic and Palaearctic regions. [HOL(O)- + ARCTIC.]

Hol·bein (hól-bīn || hṓl-), **Hans,** also known as Holbein the Younger (*c.*1497–1543). German painter. The son and pupil of Hans Holbein the Elder (*c.*1465–1524), he worked in Basel and visited England in 1526. From about 1536 he was court painter to Henry VIII. Holbein is noted for his portraits.

hold¹ (hōld) *v.* **held** (held), **held** or *archaic* **holden** (hṓldən), **holding, holds.** —*tr.* **1.** To have and keep, as in the hands, arms, or teeth; grasp; clasp. **2.** To support; keep up; bear: *This nail is too small to hold that mirror.* **3. a.** To maintain in a certain position or relationship; keep: *held his assailant at arm's length.* **b.** To maintain (oneself) in a specified posture or condition: *hold oneself erect.* **c.** To maintain in a steady or unchanged state: *hold prices down.* **4. a.** To contain; be filled by. **b.** To accommodate; seat: *The church holds 500.* **5.** To keep or have in one's possession (property, assets, or the like); own. **6. a.** To have or maintain for use; wield: *hold an advantage.* **b.** To have gained: *hold a certificate.* **7.** To maintain control over; restrain: *The dam held the flood waters; Hold your tongue!* **8. a.** To retain the attention or interest of: *she held the audience with her eyes.* **b.** To retain (a person's attention). **9. a.** To defend from attack; preserve: *hold the fort.* **b.** To keep despite a challenge: *held her seat at the last election.* **10. a.** To keep under restraint or in confinement: *held in custody.* **b.** To detain or delay: *Try to hold him until the police arrive.* **c.** To prevent from making further gains: *held to a draw.* **11.** To have the position of; occupy: *He holds the office of commander.* **12.** *Law.* **a.** To be the legal possessor of. **b.** To make (a person) fulfil the terms of a contract. Used with *to.* **c.** To adjudge or decree. **13.** To cause to fulfil an agreement or promise; bind: *They held him to his promise.* **14. a.** To keep in one's mind or heart; harbour: *hold a grudge.* **b.** To regard in a specified manner: *hold her in contempt.* **15. a.** To have as (an opinion, belief, view, or the like). **b.** To assert; affirm: *hold that his hypotheses are incorrect.* **16.** To cause to take place; put on: *The race was held in Liverpool; Let's hold a party.* **17.** To assemble; convene: *Court was held in the morning.* **18.** To set aside; not sell or allocate: *The shop is holding the shoes until tomorrow.* **19.** To be able to consume (alcohol) without noticeable effects: *He can't hold his drink.* **20.** *Music.* To sustain (a note). **21.** *Computing.* To keep (data) on a storage device although it has been copied onto another location or another storage device. **22.** To keep (a telephone line) open. —*intr.* **1.** To maintain a grasp, clutch, or grip. **2. a.** To maintain a desired or accustomed position or condition: *Hold still!* **b.** To last; remain unchanged: *This weather won't hold.* **3.** To adhere closely; keep: *They held to a southwesterly course.* **4.** To stand up under stress, pressure, or opposition; last: *will never hold under your weight.* **5.** To be valid, applicable, or true: *His theory still holds. The rule holds for all of us.* **6.** To wait while on the telephone; not hang up. —See Synonyms at **contain. —hold down. 1.** To keep in check; restrain; suppress. **2.** To work at and keep (a job). **—hold forth.** To talk at length; lecture. **—hold in.** To keep back, check, or suppress (an impulse or emotion, for example). **—hold it. 1.** To stop or wait. Usually used in the imperative. **2.** To maintain a position or pose; freeze. Used in the imperative, by a photographer. **—hold off. 1.** To prevent from reaching; keep at some distance: *hold off the enemy.* **2.** To defer or delay doing something; put off: *hold off buying a car until the spring.* **—hold on. 1.** To maintain one's grip; cling. **2.** To keep at; continue. **3.** To stop or wait for someone or something. **—hold (one's) own. 1.** To maintain one's ground or position; not falter. **2.** To prove oneself adequate or competent; be good enough. **—hold out. 1.** To present; offer. **2.** To last; stand up; endure. **3.** To refuse to surrender or give up; continue resisting. **—hold out for.** To insist upon or wait for, accepting no compromises. **—hold out on.** *Informal.* To refuse to give or divulge something expected or deserved. **—hold to.** To keep true or steadfast to; remain loyal or faithful to. **—hold together. 1.** To remain or cause to remain coherent or in one piece. **2.** To wear well or last a long time: *the old bike has held* *together well.* —**hold water.** To stand up under examination; be believable, valid, or tenable. —**hold with. 1.** To agree with. **2.** To be on the side of; support. **3.** To approve of; subscribe to. ~*n.* **1.** The act or a means of grasping; a grip; a clasp. **2.** A means of obtaining, retaining, or controlling something. **3.** Something held onto, as for support. **4.** A device that grips something so as to keep it in place. **5.** A strong psychological influence or power: *he seems to have a hold over her.* **6.** A means of influencing the behaviour of a person, as through knowing discreditable information: *he has a hold on me with that letter.* **7.** A prison cell. **8.** *Archaic.* A fortified place; a stronghold. **9.** *Music.* **a.** The sustaining of a note longer than its indicated time value. **b.** The symbol designating this pause; a fermata. **10.** A temporary halt of pause: *put on hold.* **11.** A manner of gripping an opponent in wrestling: *a neck hold.* —**get hold of. 1.** To obtain. **2.** To establish contact with. —**no holds barred.** Without any restrictions; all methods allowed, regardless of fairness. [Hold, held, held, holden; Middle English *holden, heold, haldan, holden,* Old English *healdan, hēold, healden.*]

hold² *n. Nautical.* **1.** The interior of a ship below decks where cargo is stored. **2.** The place in an aeroplane where the cargo is put. [Variant (influenced by HOLD) of Middle English *hole,* HOLE.]

hold·all (hṓld-awl) *n.* A case or bag for carrying miscellaneous items, as when travelling.

hold back *tr.v.* **1.** To curb; restrain. **2.** To save for future use; keep apart or aside; retain. —*intr.v.* To refrain.

hold·back (hṓld-bak) *n.* A strap or iron placed between the shaft and the harness on a drawn wagon, allowing the horse to stop or back up.

hold·en. *Archaic.* Past participle of **hold.**

hold·er (hṓldər) *n.* **1.** A person who holds, possesses, or occupies something. Often used in combination: *a landholder; a shareholder.* **2.** A device for holding something. **3.** *Law.* One who legally possesses and is entitled to the payment of a cheque, bill, or promissory note.

hold·fast (hṓld-faast ‖ -fast) *n.* **1.** Any of various devices used to fasten something securely. **2.** *Biology.* An organ or structure of attachment; especially, the **hapteron** *(see)* of certain seaweeds.

hold·ing (hṓlding) *n.* **1.** Land rented or leased from another. **2.** Often *plural.* Legally possessed property, such as land, capital, or stocks.

holding company *n.* A company having partial or complete control of other companies.

holding operation *n.* A procedure intended only to keep a situation under control and prevent any deterioration.

holding pattern *n.* A fixed route on which an aeroplane is put if unable to land immediately.

hold over *tr.v.* **1.** To delay taking action or making a decision on. **2.** To postpone. **3.** To continue longer than expected: *hold over a film for another week.* **4.** To use as a threat or for blackmail: *You can't hold my past over me like that.*

hold·o·ver (hṓld-ōvər) *n. Chiefly U.S.* Someone or something kept on longer than originally intended, such as an elected official after his term is over or an entertainer or entertainment beyond the original engagement.

hold up *tr.v.* **1.** To present; show: *hold my work up as an example to all.* **2.** To hinder or interrupt; delay. **3.** To rob using the threat of weapons. —*intr.v.* To last; stand up; endure.

hold·up (hṓld-up) *n.* **1.** A suspension of activity; a delay; an interruption. **2.** A robbery; especially, an armed robbery.

hole (hōl) *n.* **1.** A cavity in a solid. **2.** An opening or perforation through something; a gap; an aperture: *a hole in the clouds.* **3. a.** A deep place in water. **b.** A small, deep pond. **c.** *U.S.* A small bay; a cove. **4.** An animal's hollowed-out habitation, such as a burrow: *a rabbit hole.* **5.** *Informal.* An ugly, squalid, or depressing place or dwelling. **6.** A deep or isolated place of confinement; a dungeon. **7.** A fault or flaw; an error: *picked holes in the prosecution's argument.* **8.** *Informal.* A bad situation from which it seems difficult to extract oneself; a predicament. **9.** *Golf.* **a.** The small pit lined with a cup into which the ball must be hit. **b.** One of the 9 or 18 divisions of a golf course, from tee to cup. **10.** *Electronics.* A vacant electron energy state that is manifested as a charge defect in a crystalline solid, the defect behaving as a positive charge carrier with charge magnitude equal to that of the electron. —**hole in one.** *Golf.* The driving of the ball from the tee into the hole in only one stroke. —**in the hole.** *U.S. Informal.* In debt. —**make a hole in.** To use up a substantial amount of: *made a real hole in my bank balance.* ~*v.* **holed, holing, holes.** —*tr.* **1.** To put a hole or holes in; puncture; perforate. **2.** To put, propel, or drive into a hole. —*intr.* To make a hole or holes. —**hole out.** *Golf.* To put the ball into a hole. —**hole up.** To shut oneself up, especially in cramped quarters: *They were all holed up in that tiny flat.* [Middle English *hol(e),* hole, ship's hold, Old English *hol,* hollow place.] —**hol·ey** *adj.*

Synonyms: hole, hollow, cavity, excavation, pit, pocket.

hole-and-cor·ner (hōl-ən-kórnər) *adj.* Also **hole-in-the-corner** *Informal.* Underhand; furtive.

hole in the heart *n.* A congenital defect in which there is an opening between the right and left sides of the heart so that a proportion of the blood is not pumped to the lungs.

hole in the wall *n.* A small, squalid, or out-of-the-way place. —**hole-in-the-wall** *adj.*

-holic, -aholic, -oholic *n. & adj. suffix.* Indicates addiction to or compulsive need or desire for; for example, **workaholic.** [Abstracted from *alcoholic.*]

hol·i·day (hṓllə-di, hólli-, -day) *n.* **1.** A day on which custom or the law dictates a halting of general business activity to commemorate or celebrate a particular event. **2.** A religious feast day; a holy day. **3.** A day free from work which one may spend at leisure; a day off. **4.** *Chiefly British.* **a.** *Often plural.* A period of time during which one is free from work, studies, or one's usual activities and which one may devote to rest, amusement, or travel. **b.** *Usually plural.* A fixed period during which a school or other institution suspends its normal activities. **5.** A period of time spent away from home for recreation, as in a resort. ~*adj.* Of, suitable for, or characteristic of a holiday: *a holiday mood.* ~*intr.v.* **holidayed, -daying, -days.** *Chiefly British.* To take a holiday: *holidaying in the Bahamas.* [Middle English *holiday,* Old English *hāligdæg : hālig,* HOLY + *dæg,* DAY.]

holiday camp *n.* An establishment that provides comprehensive holiday facilities, such as accommodation, sports facilities, swimming pools, and entertainment.

hol·i·day·maker (hóllə-di-maykər, hólli-, -day-) *n. Chiefly British.* A person who is or is about to be on holiday.

ho·li·er-than-thou (hṓli-ər-thən-thów) *adj.* Showing an attitude of superior virtue; self-righteously pious.

ho·li·ness (hṓli-nəss, -niss) *n.* **1.** The state or quality of being holy; sanctity. **2.** *Capital H.* A title of or form of address for various high ecclesiastical dignitaries and especially for the Pope. Preceded by *His* or *Your.*

Hol·in·shed (hóllin-shed), **Raphael** (died *c.*1580). English chronicler. His *Chronicles* (1578), a history of England, Scotland and Ireland, form a valuable source of historical information, which was extensively used by Shakespeare and other Elizabethan dramatists.

ho·lism (hól-iz'm, hól-) *n.* The theory that reality is made up of organic or unified wholes that are greater than the simple sum of their parts. [HOL(O)- + -ISM.] —**ho·list** *n.*

ho·lis·tic (hō-lístik, ho-, hə-) *adj.* **1.** Of or pertaining to holism. **2. a.** Emphasising the importance of the whole and the interdependence of its parts. **b.** Designating or relating to an approach to medicine that claims to take account of the patient as a whole person—body, mind, and spirit—rather than just of his symptoms. —**ho·lis·ti·cal·ly** *adv.*

hol·land (hólland) *n.* A hard-wearing linen fabric used especially for upholstery. [After HOLLAND, where it was made.]

Holland. See **Netherlands, Kingdom of the.**

Hol·land (hólland), **Henry** (1745–1806). British neoclassical architect. Originally a partner of Capability Brown, he designed Brooks's Club, London (1776) and much of Carlton House (1783).

Holland, Parts of. Formerly a division of **Lincolnshire.**

hol·lan·daise sauce (hóllən-dáyz, -déz, -dayz) *n.* A creamy sauce of butter, egg yolks, and lemon or vinegar, served especially with fish or vegetables. [Translation of French *sauce Hollandaise,* Dutch sauce, from *Hollandaise,* feminine of *Hollandais,* Dutch, from *Hollande,* HOLLAND.]

Hol·land·er (hólləndər) *n.* A Dutchman.

Holland's gin *n.* A type of Dutch gin that is not so thoroughly distilled as London gin and is usually sold in stone jars or crocks and drunk neat. Also called "geneva", "Hollands".

hol·ler (hóllər) *v.* **-lered, -lering, -lers.** *Chiefly U.S.* —*intr.* To yell or shout; cry out; call. —*tr.* To yell or shout (an utterance). ~*n. Chiefly U.S.* A yell or shout; a call. [Originally dialect variant of HOLLO.]

hol·lo, hol·la (hóllō, hóllə) *interj.* Used as a shout to catch a person's attention. ~*n., pl.* **hollos, hollas.** A cry for attention. ~*intr.v.* To shout; call out. [French *holà,* "ho there!"]

hol·low (hóllō) *adj.* **1.** Having a cavity, gap, or space within; not solid: *a hollow wall.* **2.** Being deeply indented or concave; having depth or inclines; depressed. **3.** Deeply recessed; sunken; fallen: *hollow cheeks.* **4.** Without substance or character; empty; superficial: *a hollow person.* **5.** Not genuine or real; specious: *hollow victories.* **6.** Having a reverberating, sepulchral sound; booming; echoing: *hollow footsteps.* **7.** Cynical; false: *hollow laughter.* **8.** Hungry or unsatisfied. ~*n.* **1.** A cavity, gap, or space within something: *the hollow behind a wall.* **2.** An indented or concave surface or area; a shallow pocket: *the hollow of one's hand.* **3.** A valley or depression. —See Synonyms at **hole.** ~*adv.* Outright; thoroughly: *I was beaten hollow at chess.* ~*v.* **hollowed, -lowing, -lows.** —*tr.* **1.** To make hollow. Used with *out: hollow out a pumpkin.* **2.** To scoop or form by making concave. Used with *out: hollow out a nest in the sand.* —*intr.* To become hollow. [Middle English *hol(e)we,* from *holh,* hole, Old English *holh,* hole, hollow place.] —**hol·low·ly** *adv.* —**hol·low·ness** *n.*

hol·low·ware (hóllō-wair) *n.* Serving pieces, especially of silver, such as bowls, jugs, and the like. Compare **flatware.**

hol·ly (hólli) *n., pl.* **-lies. 1. a.** Any of numerous trees or shrubs of the genus *Ilex,* such as *I. aquifolium,* of Eurasia, often having bright-red berries and glossy, evergreen leaves with spiny margins. **b.** Branches or leaves of holly, traditionally used for Christmas decoration. **2.** Any of various similar or related plants. [Middle English *holi(n),* Old English *holen,* probably of Germanic origin.]

hol·ly·hock (hólli-hok) *n.* A tall plant, *Althaea rosea,* native to China and widely cultivated for its showy spikes of large, variously coloured flowers. [Middle English *holihoc* : *holi,* HOLY + *hoc,* a mallow, Old English *hoc†.*]

Hol·ly·wood¹ (hŏlli-wŏŏd). District of the city of Los Angeles, California. It has been the centre of the U.S. film industry since before World War I. The Hollywood Bowl, a vast outdoor theatre, is located in the foothills of the Santa Monica mountains.

Hollywood² *n.* The U.S. film industry or the somewhat meretriciously glamorous atmosphere often attributed to it.

holm (hōm ‖ holm, hōlm) *n. British.* **1.** An island in a river. **2.** Low land near a stream. [Middle English *holm,* from Old Norse *holmr,* islet, meadow.]

Holmes (hōmz ‖ hōlmz), **Oliver Wendell** (1809–94). U.S. author. A professor of anatomy and physiology at Harvard (1847–82), he wrote humorous conversational pieces, including *The Autocrat of the Breakfast-Table* (1858).

hol·mic (hŏl-mik, hŏl-) *adj.* Pertaining to or containing holmium.

hol·mi·um (hŏl-mi-əm, hŏl-) *n.* Symbol **Ho** A relatively soft, malleable, stable rare-earth element occurring in gadolinite, monazite, and other rare-earth minerals. Atomic number 67, atomic weight 164.930, melting point 1,461°C, boiling point 2,600°C, relative density 8.803, valency 3. [From New Latin *holmia,* Latinised form of Stock*holm,* Sweden.]

holm oak *n.* A tree, *Quercus ilex,* native to the Mediterranean region, having prickly evergreen leaves. Also called "holly oak", "ilex". [Middle English, variant of *holin,* HOLLY.]

holo-, hol- *comb. form.* Indicates whole or a whole, or entirely; for example, **Holarctic, holoblastic.** [Greek *holos,* whole, entire.]

hol·o·blas·tic (hŏl-ō-blástik, -ə- ‖ hŏl-) *adj.* Exhibiting or denoting cleavage in which the entire egg separates into individual blastomeres. Compare **meroblastic.** [HOLO- + -BLAST + IC.]

hol·o·caust (hŏl-ə-kawst ‖ hŏl-) *n.* **1.** Great or total destruction by fire; a conflagration. **2. a.** Any widespread, horrific destruction of human life. **b.** *Often capital* **H.** The mass killings of Jews by the Nazi regime during World War II. **3.** *Archaic.* A sacrificial offering that is consumed entirely by flames; a burnt offering. —See Synonyms at **disaster.** [Middle English, from Old French *holocauste,* from Latin *holocaustum,* from Greek *holokauston,* from *holokaustos,* burnt whole : *holo-,* whole + *kaustos,* variant of *kautos,* burnt, from *kaein,* to burn.] —**hol·o·caus·tal** (-káwst'l), **hol·o·caus·tic** (-káwstik) *adj.*

Hol·o·cene (hŏl-ə-seen ‖ hŏl-) *adj. Geology.* Of, belonging to, or designating the geological time or the rock system of the more recent of the two epochs of the Quaternary period, extending from the end of the Pleistocene to the present.

~*n. Geology.* The Holocene epoch or system of deposits. Preceded by *the.* Also called "Recent". [HOLO- + -CENE.]

hol·o·crine (hŏl-ə-krin, -kreen ‖ hŏl-, -krīn) *adj.* Pertaining to or designating a gland whose secretion is formed by the degeneration of the gland's cells, as sebaceous glands. Compare **merocrine.** [HOLO- + Greek *krinein,* to separate, divide.]

hol·o·en·zyme (hŏl-ō-én-zīm ‖ hŏl-) *n.* An enzyme in its active form, consisting of an apoenzyme and a coenzyme.

hol·o·gram (hŏl-ə-gram ‖ hŏl-) *n.* **1.** The pattern produced on a photosensitive medium that has been exposed by holography and then photographically developed. **2.** The photosensitive medium so exposed and so developed. Also called "holograph". [HOLO- + -GRAM.]

hol·o·graph¹ (hŏl-ə-graaf, -ō-, -graf ‖ hŏl-) *n.* **1.** A document written wholly in the handwriting of the person whose signature it bears. **2.** A hologram. [Late Latin *holographus,* entirely written by the signer, from Greek *holographos,* written in full : *holo-,* whole + -GRAPH.] —**hol·o·graph·ic** (-gráffik), **hol·o·graph·i·cal** *adj.* —**hol·o·graph·i·cal·ly** *adv.*

ho·lo·graph² *tr.v.* **-graphed, -graphing, -graphs. 1.** To produce an image of (a physical object) by holography. **2.** To form a hologram of (a physical object). [HOLO- + -GRAPH.]

ho·log·raph·y (ho-lóggrəfi, hə-, hō-) *n.* The technique of producing a three-dimensional image of an object, a hologram, by recording the wave pattern of light reflected from the object, especially by using lasers to record on a photographic plate the diffraction pattern from which a three-dimensional image can be projected. [HOLO- + -GRAPHY.] —**hol·o·graph·ic, hol·o·graph·i·cal** *adj.* —**hol·o·graph·i·cal·ly** *adv.*

hol·o·he·dral (hŏl-ə-héedrəl, -ō- ‖ hŏl-) *adj.* Having as many planes as required for complete symmetry in a given crystal system. [HOLO- + -HEDRAL.]

hol·o·mor·phic (hŏl-ə-mórfik, -ō- ‖ hŏl-) *adj. Mathematics.* **Analytic** *(see).*

hol·o·phras·tic (hŏl-ə-frástik, -ō- ‖ hŏl-) *adj. Linguistics.* Expressing a whole phrase or set of ideas by means of a single word. [HOLO- + Greek *phrastikos,* indicative, expressive, from *phrazein,* to show.]

hol·o·phytic (hŏl-ə-fíttik, -ō- ‖ hŏl-) *adj.* Designating organisms, such as green plants, that manufacture their food by photosynthesis; autotrophic. [HOLO- + -PHYTIC.]

hol·o·plank·ton (hŏl-ə-plángktən, -ō- ‖ hŏl-) *n.* Microorganisms that are constituents of plankton for all stages of their life cycle.

hol·o·thu·ri·an (hŏl-ə-théwr-i-ən, -ō- ‖ hŏl-) *n.* Any of various echinoderms of the class Holothuroidea, which includes the sea cucumbers. [New Latin *Holothuria* (genus), from *holothūria,* water polyp, from Greek *holothourion†.*] —**hol·o·thu·ri·an** *adj.*

hol·o·type (hŏl-ə-tīp, -ō- ‖ hŏl-) *n.* The single specimen used as the basis of the original published description of a taxonomic species.

Also called "type specimen". [HOLO- + TYPE.] —**hol·o·typ·ic** (-típpik) *adj.*

hol·o·zo·ic (hŏl-ə-zṓ-ik, -ō- ‖ hŏl-) *adj.* Obtaining nourishment by the ingestion of organic material, as do animals. [HOLO- + -ZOIC.]

holp. *Archaic.* Past tense of **help.**

holp·en. *Archaic.* Past participle of **help.**

hols (holz) *pl.n. British Informal.* Holidays.

Holst (hŏlst ‖ holst), **Gustav (Theodore)** (1874–1934). British composer, of part-Swedish descent. His best-known work is the orchestral suite *The Planets* (1914–16).

Hol·stein (hŏl-stīn ‖ hŏl-) *n. U.S.* A breed of cattle, **Friesian** *(see).* Also called "Holstein-Friesian".

hol·ster (hṓl-stər ‖ hŏl-) *n.* A leather case shaped to hold a pistol and usually designed to be attached to a belt. [Dutch.] —**holstered** *adj.*

holt (hōlt ‖ holt) *n. Archaic.* **1.** A wood or grove; a copse. Often used in place names. **2.** A wooded hill. [Middle English *holt,* wood, Old English *holt.*]

Holt (hōlt ‖ holt), **Harold (Edward)** (1908–67). Australian Prime Minister (1966–67). Holt, a Liberal, relaxed immigration laws. He died, apparently by drowning, in Port Phillip Bay.

ho·lus-bo·lus (hṓləss-bṓləss) *adv. Informal.* All together; all in a lump. [Probably pseudo-Latin, perhaps based on *whole* and *bolus.*]

ho·ly (hṓli) *adj.* **-lier, -liest. 1.** Belonging to, associated with, or consecrated to God or a divine power; sacred. **2.** Worthy of worship or high esteem; revered: *a holy book.* **3. a.** Living according to a religious or spiritual system; devout. **b.** Having great spiritual insight or wisdom; godly: *a holy man.* **c.** Morally blameless; saintly. **4.** Intended or set apart for a religious purpose: *a holy hour.* **5.** Solemnly undertaken; sacrosanct: *a holy pledge.* **6. a.** Formally associated with or pertaining to an established or organised religion. **b.** Religious in theme, depiction, or subject: *holy paintings.* **7.** Used as an intensive, especially in exclamations: *holy mackerel!* [Middle English *holy, holi, hali,* Old English *hālig,* from Germanic; akin to WHOLE.] —**ho·li·ly** *adv.* —**ho·li·ness** *n.*

Holy Alliance *n.* An agreement that was made between Russia, Prussia, and Austria in 1815, to govern by Christian principles.

Holy Ark *n.* The cabinet in a synagogue in which the scrolls of the Torah are kept.

Holy Bible *n.* The Bible.

Holy City *n.* **1.** Any city that is held to be sacred by a particular religion, such as Jerusalem by the religions of Judaism, Christianity, and Islam. Preceded by *the.* **2.** Heaven. Preceded by *the.*

Holy Communion *n. Abbr.* **H.C.** The **Eucharist** *(see).*

holy day *n.* A day set aside for a religious observance.

holy day of obligation *n. Roman Catholic Church.* A day other than a Sunday on which believers are required to attend Mass, such as Christmas Day.

Holy Family *n.* The child Jesus together with Mary and Joseph. Preceded by *the.*

Holy Father *n.* One of the titles of the pope.

Holy Ghost *n.* The third person of the Christian Trinity. Also called "Holy Spirit".

Holy Grail *n.* The **Grail** *(see).*

Hol·y·head (hŏlli-héd, -hed). *Welsh* **Caer-gybi** (kīr-gúbbi). Resort town and port on Holy Island, Wales, off the northwest coast of Anglesey.

Holy Innocents' Day *n.* December 28, a day commemorating the massacre of male infants by Herod after the birth of Jesus.

Holy Island. 1. Island off the coast of Northumberland, in northeastern England, also known as Lindisfarne. At low tide it is connected to the mainland. Celtic Christianity found its first home in England at the church and monastery built there by St. Aidan in 635. The Lindisfarne Gospels, also known as the Book of Durham, is a 7th-century illuminated manuscript made here. **2.** See **Holyhead.**

Holy Joe *n. Informal.* **1.** A pious or self-righteous person. **2.** A clergyman. [From nautical slang.]

Holy Land. See **Palestine.**

Holy Loch. See **Dunoon.**

Ho·ly·oake (hŏli-ōk), **Sir Keith (Jacka)** (1904–83). New Zealand Prime Minister (1957, 1960–72). He was knighted in 1970.

Holy Office *n.* Official name, Congregation of the Holy Office. A congregation of the Roman Catholic Church that deals with such matters as the protection of the faith and morals.

holy of holies *n.* **1.** The innermost shrine of a Jewish tabernacle and temple where the Ark of the Covenant was located. **2.** Any place held to be especially sacrosanct. Also called "sanctum sanctorum".

holy orders *pl.n. Ecclesiastical.* **1.** *Used with a singular verb.* The sacrament or rite of ordination; the ceremony of admission into the priesthood or ministry. **2.** *Used with a plural verb.* The rank or status of an ordained Christian minister; clerical status. **3.** *Used with a plural verb.* Any of the grades of the ordained ministry of the Christian church, especially the priesthood and the diaconate, comprising the **major orders** and **minor orders.**

holy place *n.* **1.** The outer chamber of the sanctuary in a Jewish temple. **2.** A place to which a pilgrimage is made.

Holy Roller *n.* A member of any of various fundamentalist Christian sects in which spiritual fervour is expressed by shouts and boisterous bodily movements. Often used derogatorily.

Holy Roman Empire. The loosely federated political entity of European Christendom, from the coronation of Otto I as Holy Roman Emperor by the Pope in 962 to the dissolution of the Empire by Napoleon in 1806. The last Emperor was Francis II (*r.* 1792–1806).

The term itself did not come into use until several centuries after Otto's accession. From the outset the rule of the Emperor was bedevilled by rivalry between the papal and the secular authority and, after the 13th century, by the rising ambitions of the nascent nation states of Europe. After the election of Rudolf of Habsburg as Emperor in 1273, the imperial crown remained in Habsburg hands, and the Empire came to mean little more than the Habsburg domains, chiefly Austria and Spain.

holy rood *n.* **1.** A cross or crucifix; especially, one placed over a rood screen. **2.** *Often capital* **H,** *capital* **R.** The cross upon which Jesus was crucified.

Holy Saturday *n.* The Saturday before Easter Sunday.

Holy Scripture *n.* The Old and New Testaments of the Bible. Also called "Holy Writ", "Scripture", "Scriptures".

Holy See *n. Roman Catholic Church.* **1.** The See of Rome; the office or jurisdiction of the pope. **2.** The administrative officials of the Vatican.

Holy Sepulchre *n.* The tomb thought to be that of Jesus outside Jerusalem, regarded as a Christian shrine.

Holy Spirit *n.* The **Holy Ghost** *(see).*

ho·ly·stone (hóli-stōn) *n.* A piece of soft sandstone used for scouring the wooden decks of a ship. **~**tr.v. **holystoned, -stoning, -stones.** To scrub or scour with a holystone. [From its use while in a kneeling position.]

Holy Synod *n.* The administrative or governing body of any of the Eastern Orthodox churches.

Holy Thursday *n.* **1.** *Roman Catholic Church.* **Maundy Thursday** *(see).* **2.** *Anglican Church.* **Ascension Day** *(see).*

holy water *n.* Water blessed by a priest and used in various ceremonies.

Holy Week *n.* The week before Easter Sunday.

Holy Writ *n.* **1.** Holy Scripture. **2.** Any writing or pronouncement regarded as sacrosanct or unquestionable.

hom·age (hómmij ‖ *U.S. also* ómmij) *n.* **1.** Ceremonial acknowledgment under feudal law by a vassal or tenant of allegiance to his lord. **2.** Honour or respect publicly expressed to a person or idea: *pay homage to our forefathers with this hymn.* **—See Synonyms at honour.** [Middle English, acknowledgment of a man's allegiance, from Old French, from Medieval Latin *hominăticum,* from Latin *homō* (stem *homin-*), man.]

hom·bre (óm-bray, -bri) *n. Western U.S. Slang.* A man; a fellow. [Spanish, from Latin *homō.*]

hom·burg (hóm-burg) *n.* A man's felt hat having a dented crown and a shallow, slightly rolled brim. [First manufactured in *Homburg,* town near Wiesbaden, West Germany.]

home (hōm) *n.* **1.** A place where one lives; a residence; a habitation. **2.** The physical structure or the portion of it within which one lives, such as a house or flat. **3.** One's immediate family and its place of residence, considered as an environment to which one belongs: *house and home; didn't leave home till he was 21.* **4.** Any environment or haven of shelter, happiness, and love. **5.** Any place or condition valued as a refuge or place of origin. **6.** The place where one was born or spent one's early childhood, as a town, county, or country. **7.** The native habitat of a plant, animal, or the like. **8.** The place where something is discovered, founded, developed, or promoted; the source: *Scotland, the home of haggis.* **9.** A place where a body, such as a company or a sports team, is based or established. **10.** A goal or place of safety towards which players of a game, such as rounders, backgammon, or tag, progress. **11.** An institution providing temporary or permanent residential care, as for old people or those convalescing from illness: *a nursing home.* **12.** *Informal.* A mental institution. **—a home from home.** A place which seems as familiar or pleasant as one's own home. **—at home. 1.** In one's own house, environment, or city; not away or absent. **2.** Available to receive visitors: *If anyone calls I'm not at home.* **3.** Giving a small party in one's house. **4.** At ease or comfortable, as if in one's own home: *Make yourself at home.* **5.** Having facility in a field or skill; feeling an easy competence and familiarity: *at home in French.* **—close to home.** Alluding to something about which a person is very sensitive.

~adj. **1.** Of or pertaining to a home, especially to one's household or house: *home furnishings, home cooking.* **2.** Of or pertaining to one's country, place of birth, or nation, rather than to that which is foreign; domestic. **3.** Of or pertaining to a base of operations or headquarters: *the home office of a worldwide company.* **4.** Going straight to the point; reaching its mark directly and accurately: *a home thrust.* **5.** Taking place or based at one's own headquarters: *a home game; the home team.*

~adv. **1.** At, to, or towards the direction of home. **2.** To the point at which something is directed; on target: *The arrow struck home.* **3. a.** To the furthest possible point or extent. **b.** To the centre or heart of something; deeply. **4.** *Nautical.* Towards a vessel. **—bring home to.** To make clear to; cause to be understood: *cannot seem to bring it home to him how careful one must be.* **—come home to.** To be brought home; become clear: *The real truth finally came home to him.* **—nothing to write home about.** *Informal.* Of no great value or interest; nothing special.

~v. **homed, homing, homes.** **—**intr. **1.** To go or return home, especially from a distance. Used especially of birds such as pigeons. **2.** To be guided to a target automatically, as by inertial guidance or heat sensing. **—**tr. To guide (a missile or aircraft) to a target automatically. **—home in.** To arrive directly; aim straight. Used with

on: *home straight in on the correct answer.* [Middle English *hom(e),* Old English *hām,* from Germanic.]

Usage: British and American English exhibit different tendencies in their use of this word. In the sense of "in one's house", British English prefers *at home,* in such examples as: *I was at home all day, Is John at home?, I stayed at home.* American English, especially informally, prefers *I was home/stayed home,* and so on. *Home* also has a wide use in American English, being used in places where British English would use *house*—for example, in selling houses or remarking on the quality of a house, American English tends to use *home: New homes for sale, They've bought a lovely home.* Note, however, that with verbs of motion, such as *go, home* is always used in both varieties: *I went home* (where *home* means "to one's house").

home and dry *adj. British Informal.* Having safely accomplished one's objective.

home-bod·y (hŏm-boddi) *n. pl.* **-ies.** One who likes to stay or work at home; a domestic person.

home-bred (hŏm-bréd) *adj.* **1.** Produced, bred, or reared at home; domestic; indigenous. **2.** Not cultivated or sophisticated.

home-brew (hŏm-brōō ‖ -brew) *n.* An alcoholic beverage, especially beer, that is made at home. **—home-brewed** *adj.*

home·com·ing (hŏm-kumming) *n.* A return to one's home, or to a place where one formerly lived, worked, or studied.

Home Counties *pl.n.* The counties of England nearest to London. Formerly the term covered Kent, Surrey, Middlesex, and Essex, but is now often used to include Buckinghamshire, Berkshire, Hertfordshire, and Sussex.

home economics *pl.n. Used with a singular verb.* The science or study of home management, including household budgets, purchase of food and clothing, child care, cooking, nutrition, and the like.

home farm *n. British.* A farm that is part of an estate which it is supposed to supply with food.

home front *n.* The civilian population of a country at war regarded as part of the front line of battle.

home-grown (hŏm-grōn, -grōn) *adj.* **1.** Grown or produced at home, as in one's own garden, district, or country. Said especially of fruit and vegetables. **2.** Produced or originating in one's own country: *The TV station shows few home-grown programmes.*

Home Guard *n.* **1.** A volunteer force formed to defend a homeland while the regular army is fighting elsewhere; especially, the force organised to defend Great Britain in the event of a German invasion in World War II. **2.** A member of such a force.

home help *n.* A person who does housework; especially, in Britain, a person provided by the social services to help elderly or very ill people.

home·land (hŏm-land, -lənd) *n.* **1.** The land of one's allegiance; one's native land. **2.** The place of origin of a people. **3.** Formerly, any of the nine regions designated by the government of South Africa for the black population, in accordance with the policy of apartheid. Four of the homelands were granted self-governing status, namely Transkei (1976), Bophuthatswana (1977), Venda (1979), and Ciskei (1981), but they were not internationally recognised as independent states. In this sense, also called "Bantustan".

home·less (hŏm-ləss, -liss) *adj.* Without a home; as: **1.** Deliberately homeless through abandonment or renunciation of home: *go forth into the homeless life in search of enlightenment.* **2.** Involuntarily homeless through loss of one's home: *homeless and sleeping rough.* **—home·less·ness** *n.*

home·ly (hŏm-li) *adj.* **-lier, -liest. 1.** Of a nature associated with or suited to the home; domestic; familiar: *homely relaxed atmosphere.* **2.** Of a simple or unassuming nature; uncomplicated or unsophisticated; plain. **3.** *Chiefly U.S.* Not attractive or good-looking; plain. Said of a person. **—home·li·ness** *n.*

home·made (hŏm-máyd) *adj.* **1. a.** Made or prepared in the home; not bought: *homemade pie; a homemade dress.* **b.** Made with care, using wholesome ingredients and usually sold on the premises. **2.** Made or assembled by oneself; crude or simple: *a homemade bomb.*

home·mak·er (hŏm-maykər) *n.* A person who manages a household or who creates a homely environment.

home movie *n.* A film shown at home; especially, a film made by oneself of one's own activities.

home nurse *n.* A nurse who cares for patients in their own homes. Also called "district nurse".

homeo-, homoeo-, homoio- *comb. form.* Indicates like or similar; for example, **homeostasis, homoiotherm.** [Latin *homoeo-,* from Greek *homoio-,* from *homoios,* similar, from *homos,* same.]

Home Office *n.* A department of the British government that deals with home affairs, especially law and order and immigration.

Home of the Hir·sel (hewm; húrss'l), **Alec Douglas-Home, Baron,** born Alexander Frederick Douglas-Home (1903–). British prime minister (1963–64). See **Douglas-Home.**

ho·me·o·mor·phism, ho·moe·o·mor·phism (hŏm-i-ō-mórf-iz'm, hóm-, -ə-) *n.* **1.** *Chemistry.* A close similarity in the crystal forms of unlike chemical compounds. **2.** *Mathematics.* A one-to-one correspondence between the points of two geometric figures that is continuous in both directions. [Greek *homoiomorph(os),* of similar form : HOMEO- + -MORPH(OUS) + -ISM.] **—ho·me·o·mor·phous, ho·me·o·mor·phic** *adj.*

ho·me·op·a·thy, ho·moe·op·a·thy (hŏm-i-óppəthi, hóm-) *n.* A system of medical treatment based on the use of minute quantities of remedies that in large doses produce effects similar to those of the disease being treated. Compare **allopathy.** [German *Homöopathie* :

HOMEO- + -PATHY.] —**ho·me·o·path** (-ə-path, -ō-) *n.* —**ho·me·o·path·ic** (-ə-páthik, -ō-) *adj.* —**ho·me·o·path·i·cal·ly** *adv.*

ho·me·o·sta·sis, ho·moe·o·sta·sis (hŏm-i-ō-stáy-siss, hóm-, -ə-) *n.* A state of physiological equilibrium produced by a balance of functions and of chemical composition within an organism. [New Latin : HOMEO- + -STASIS.] —**ho·me·o·stat·ic** (-státtik) *adj.*

ho·me·o·typ·ic, ho·moe·o·typ·ic (hŏm-i-ō-típpik, hóm-, -ə-) *adj.* Relating to or designating the second nuclear division of **meiosis** *(see)*. Compare **heterotypic**. [HOMEO- + TYPIC(AL).]

home plate *n.* In baseball, the **plate** *(see).*

hom·er¹ (hōmər) *n.* **1.** A homing pigeon. **2.** *U.S. Informal.* A home run. [From HOME.]

homer² *n.* An ancient Hebrew measure of capacity containing 10 ephahs (about 10 or 11 bushels) in dry measure, or 10 baths (about 100 gallons) in liquid measure. [Hebrew *ḥomer.*]

Ho·mer (hōmər) (8th century B.C.). Greek poet, supposed author of the epics *The Iliad* and *The Odyssey*. Both poems clearly derive from an orally transmitted tradition, describing the events of the Trojan War (*c.*1200) and its aftermath. The epics mix fact with fantasy, and embody the myths of ancient Greece.

Ho·mer·ic (hō-mérrik) *adj.* **1.** Of, pertaining to, or characteristic of the poet Homer, his works, or the legends and age of which he wrote. **2.** Heroic in proportion, degree, or character. —**Ho·mer·i·cal·ly** *adv.*

Homeric laughter *n.* Unchecked, natural, loud laughter, as that of the gods.

home rule *n. Abbr.* **H.R.** **1.** The principle or practice of self-government in domestic matters in a dependent country or province. **2.** *Capital* H, *capital* R. The movement in Ireland from 1870 until the 1920s to obtain self-government, the goal of the Irish Nationalists.

home run *n.* In baseball or rounders, a hit that allows the batter to make a complete circuit and score a run.

Home Secretary *n.* In Britain, the Secretary of State for the Home Department, the political head of the Home Office.

home·sick (hŏm-sik) *adj.* Depressed by separation from one's family and home; longing for home. —**home·sick·ness** *n.*

home·spun (hŏm-spun) *adj.* **1.** Spun or woven in the home. **2. a.** Made of a homespun fabric. **b.** Homemade. **3.** Simple and homely in character; unpretentious.
~*n.* **1.** A plain coarse woollen cloth made of homespun yarn. **2.** A similar sturdy fabric made on a power loom.

home·stead (hŏm-sted, -stid) *n.* **1.** A house, especially a farmhouse, with adjoining buildings and land. **2.** *Australian & N.Z.* The house of the owner or manager of a sheep or cattle station. **3.** *U.S. Law.* Property designated by a householder as his home and protected by law from forced sale to meet debts. **4.** *U.S.* Land claimed by a settler or a squatter, especially under the Homestead Act of 1862.
~*v.* **homesteaded, -steading, -steads.** —*intr.* To settle and farm land, especially under the Homestead Act. —*tr.* To claim and settle (land) as a homestead. —**home·stead·er** *n.*

Homestead Act *n.* An act passed by the U.S. Congress in 1862, promising ownership of a 160-acre tract of public land to a head of a family after he had cleared and improved the land and lived on it for five years.

home straight *n. British.* The part of a racecourse from the last turn to the finish.

home stretch *n.* **1.** *Chiefly U.S.* The home straight. **2.** The final stages of an undertaking or journey.

home truth *n.* A fact about a person that is true but unpleasant for that person to know. [From the adverbial sense of HOME, a truth that strikes home.]

home·ward (hŏm-wərd) *adj.* Directed towards home.

home·wards (hŏm-wərdz) *adv.* Also *chiefly U.S.* **home·ward** (-wərd). Towards home.

home·work (hŏm-wurk) *n.* **1.** Schoolwork that is to be done outside school hours, especially at home. **2.** Any work of a preparatory or preliminary nature.

homey *Chiefly U.S.* Variant of **homy**.

hom·i·ci·dal (hómmi-sǐd'l ‖ hómi-) *adj.* **1.** Of or pertaining to homicide. **2.** Likely to commit homicide. —**hom·i·ci·dal·ly** *adv.*

hom·i·cide (hómmi-sīd ‖ hómi-) *n.* **1.** The killing of one person by another. Compare **murder. 2.** A person who kills another person. [Middle English, from Old French, from Latin *homicīda*, killer, and *homicīdium*, killing : *homō*, man + *-cīda*, *-cīdium*, -CIDE (killer and killing).]

hom·i·let·ic (hómmi-léttik) *adj.* Also **hom·i·let·i·cal** (-'l). **1.** Pertaining to or of the nature of a homily. **2.** Pertaining to homiletics. —**hom·i·let·i·cal·ly** *adv.*

hom·i·let·ics (hómmi-léttiks) *n.* *Used with a singular verb.* The art of preaching or writing sermons as a subject of theological study. [Greek *homilētikē*, art of conversing, from *homilētikos*, social, affable, from *homilētos*, conversation, from *homilein*, to consort with, from *homilos*, crowd. See **homily**.]

hom·i·ly (hómmili, hómm'l-i) *n., pl.* **-lies. 1.** A sermon, especially one intended to edify in a practical way rather than to expound religious doctrine. **2.** A tedious moralising lecture or admonition. [Learned respelling of Middle English *omelie*, from Old French, from Late Latin *homīlia*, from Greek *homilia*, discourse, intercourse, association, from *homilos*, crowd : *homou*, together + *ilē*†, crowd.] —**hom·i·list** *n.*

hom·ing (hōming) *adj.* **1.** Of or pertaining to the ability, as of certain birds and fishes, to return home, especially from a great distance: *the homing instinct.* **2.** Assisting in guiding a missile or aeroplane towards a target: *a homing guidance system.*

homing missile *n.* A missile that steers itself towards a target by means of an internal mechanism, such as a device that senses the target's heat radiation.

homing pigeon *n.* A domestic pigeon, such as one used for racing or for carrying messages, trained to return to its home roost. Also called "homer".

hom·i·nid (hómminid) *n.* Any primate of the family Hominidae, of which modern man, *Homo sapiens,* is the only extant species.
~*adj.* Of the Hominidae. [New Latin *Hominidae* : *Homo* (stem *homin-*), HOMO + -ID.]

hom·in·i·sa·tion (hómmin-ī-záysh'n ‖ *U.S.* -i-) *n.* The evolutionary development in man and his forebears of characteristics regarded as distinguishing man from animals. [Latin *homo* (stem *homin-*), man + -IS(E) + -ATION.] —**hom·in·ised** (-īzd) *adj.*

hom·i·noid (hómminoyd) *adj.* **1.** Of or belonging to the superfamily Hominoidea, which includes the apes and man. **2.** Resembling a human being; manlike. [New Latin *Hominoidea* : *Homo* (stem *homin-*), HOMO + *-oidea*, from -OID.] —**hom·i·noid** *n.*

hom·i·ny (hómməni) *n.* Hulled and dried kernels of maize, prepared as food by boiling. [Perhaps of Algonquian origin.]

hominy grits *pl.n.* *U.S.* Hominy ground into a coarse white meal. Also called "grits".

ho·mo¹ (hōmō) *n.* Any member of the genus *Homo*, which includes the extinct and extant species of man. [New Latin *Homo*, from Latin *homō*, man.]

ho·mo² *n., pl.* **-mos.** *Slang.* A homosexual.

homo-, hom– *comb. form.* Indicates same or like; for example, **homogamous, homodont.** [Latin, from Greek, from *homos,* same.]

ho·mo·cen·tric (hŏm-ō-séntrik, hóm-) *adj.* Having the same centre. [New Latin *homocentricus,* from Greek *homokentros* : *homo-,* same + *kentron,* CENTRE.]

ho·mo·cer·cal (hŏm-ō-sérk'l, hóm-) *adj.* Pertaining to, designating, or characterised by a tail fin having two symmetrical lobes extending from the end of the vertebral column, as in most bony fishes. Compare **heterocercal.** [HOMO- + *-cercal,* from Greek *kerkos,* tail.]

ho·mo·chro·mat·ic (hŏm-ō-krə-máttik, hóm-, -ə-) *adj.* Of or characterised by one colour; monochromatic. —**ho·mo·chro·ma·tism** (-krōmətiz'm) *n.*

ho·mo·cy·clic (hŏm-ə-sī-klik, hóm-, -ō-, -sícklik) *adj. Chemistry.* Of, pertaining to, or designating a chemical compound having rings in its molecules formed of only one type of atom.
~*n.* A homocyclic compound. Compare **heterocyclic.**

ho·mo·dont (hŏm-ə-dont, hóm-, -ō-) *adj.* Having teeth that are all of the same kind. Said of most vertebrates except mammals. [HOM(O)- + -ODONT.]

homoeo–. Variant of **homeo–.**

ho·mo·e·rot·i·cism (hŏm-ō-i-rótti-siz'm, hóm-) *n.* Also **ho·mo·er·o·tism** (-érrətiz'm). Sexual attraction for one's own sex; homosexuality. —**ho·mo·e·rot·ic** (-i-róttik) *adj.*

ho·mo·ga·met·ic (hŏm-ō-ga-méttik, hóm-, -ə-, -gə-) *adj.* Having a similar pair of sex chromosomes, as in human females. Compare **heterogametic.**

ho·mog·a·mous (ho-móggəməss, hə-) *adj. Botany.* **1.** Having flowers that are sexually alike in the same plant or inflorescence. **2.** Having stamens and pistils that mature simultaneously. [HOMO- + -GAMOUS.] —**ho·mog·a·my** *n.*

ho·mo·ge·ne·i·ty (hŏm-ō-ji-née-əti, hóm-, -ə-, -náy-) *n.* The state or quality of being homogeneous.

ho·mo·ge·ne·ous (hŏm-ə-jéeni-əss, hóm-, -ō-) *adj.* Also **ho·mo·ge·nous** (ho-mójənəss, hə-, hō-) (for senses 1, 2). **1.** Like in nature or kind; similar; congruous. **2.** Uniform in structure or composition throughout. **3.** *Mathematics.* Consisting of terms of the same degree or elements of the same dimension. **4.** *Chemistry.* Having or involving only one phase. [Medieval Latin *homogeneus,* from Greek *homogenēs* : *homo-,* same + *-genēs,* born (see **-gen**) + -OUS.] —**ho·mo·ge·ne·ous·ly** *adv.* —**ho·mo·ge·ne·ous·ness** *n.*

ho·mog·en·ise, ho·mog·en·ize (hə-mója-nīz, ho- ‖ hō-) *tr.v.* **-ised, -ising, -ises. 1.** To make homogeneous. **2. a.** To reduce to particles and disperse throughout a fluid. **b.** To make uniform in consistency; especially, to render (milk) uniform in consistency by emulsifying the fat content. —**ho·mog·en·i·sa·tion** (-nī-záysh'n ‖ *U.S.* -ni-) *n.* —**ho·mog·en·is·er** *n.*

ho·mog·e·nous (hə-mójənəss, ho- ‖ hō-) *adj.* **1.** *Biology.* Of or exhibiting homogeny. **2. Homogeneous** (senses 1,2). [Medieval Latin *homogen(e)us,* HOMOGENEOUS.]

ho·mog·e·ny (hə-mójəni, ho- ‖ hō-) *n. Biology.* Correspondence between organs or parts of different species, possibly of dissimilar function, due to common descent; homology. [Greek *homogeneia,* from *homogenēs,* HOMOGENEOUS.]

ho·mog·o·nous (hə-móggənəss, ho-, hō-) *adj.* Designating plants in which the stamens and styles are of the same length in all the flowers. [HOMO- + -GON(Y) + -OUS.] —**ho·mog·o·ny** *n.*

ho·mo·graft (hóm-ə-graaft, -ō- ‖ hŏm-, -graft) *n.* A graft of tissue obtained from a member of the same species as the individual receiving it.

hom·o·graph (hóm-ə-graaf, -ō-, -graf ‖ hŏm-) *n.* A word that is spelt in the same way as another word but differs in meaning and origin and may differ in pronunciation. [HOMO- + -GRAPH.] —**hom·o·graph·ic** (-gráffik) *adj.*

homoio–. Variant of **homeo–.**

ho·moi·o·therm (hə-móy-ə-therm, ho-, hō-, -ō-) *n.* Also **ho·me·o·therm, ho·moe·o·therm** (hómmi-, hōmi-). A homoiothermic organism, such as a bird or mammal. [HOMOIO- + -THERM.]

ho·moi·o·ther·mic (hə-móy-ə-ther-mik, ho-, hō-, -ō-) *adj.* Also **ho·moi·o·ther·mal** (-məl), **ho·me·o·ther·mic** (hómmi-, hōmi-). Maintaining a relatively constant and warm body temperature that is independent of environmental temperature; warm-blooded. Compare **poikilothermic.**

Ho·moi·ou·si·an (hóm-oy-ō͞o-si-ən, hōm-, -ów-) *n.* In the fourth century, a Christian holding a modified version of the Arian view, to the effect that God the Father and Jesus the Son were of similar but not of the same substance. Compare **Heteroousian, Homoousian.** [Greek *homoiousios,* of similar substance : HOMOIO- + *ousia,* substance, from *ōn* (stem *ous-*), present participle of *einai,* to be.]

ho·mol·o·gate (hə-mólla-gayt, ho-, hō-) *tr.v.* **-gated, -gating, -gates.** *Chiefly Scottish Law.* To ratify, assent to, or approve (a contract, deed, legal proceeding, or the like). [Medieval Latin *homologāre,* from Greek *homologein,* to concur, agree, from *homologos,* HOMOLOGOUS.]

ho·mo·log·i·cal (hə-mə-lójik'l, hōm-) *adj.* Also **ho·mo·log·ic** (-lójik). Homologous. —**ho·mo·log·i·cal·ly** *adv.*

ho·mol·o·gise (hə-mólla-jīz, ho-, hō-) *tr.v.* **-gised, -gising, -gises.** 1. To make homologous. 2. To show to be homologous. —**ho·mol·o·gis·er** *n.*

ho·mol·o·gous (hə-mólləgəss, ho-, hō-) *adj.* 1. Corresponding or similar in position, value, structure, or function. 2. *Biology.* Corresponding in structure and evolutionary origin, as the flippers of a seal and the arms of a human being. Compare **analogous.** 3. *Genetics.* Designating two chromosomes that are similar in appearance, have the same linear sequence of genes, and pair during meiosis. One is derived from the male gamete and the other from the female gamete. 4. *Chemistry.* Belonging to or being a series of organic compounds, each successive member of which differs from the preceding member by a constant increment, especially by an added CH_2 group. 5. *Mathematics.* Having the same effect or role in different functions or figures. [Greek *homologos,* agreeing : HOMO- + *logos,* word, proportion, from *legein,* to speak.]

hom·o·lo·graph·ic (hə-mólla-gráffik, hō-, hómmalō-) *adj.* Maintaining the ratio of parts. [Irregularly from Greek *homalos,* even, level + GRAPHIC.]

homolographic projection *n.* An equal-area projection (see).

hom·o·logue (hóm-ə-log ‖ hōm-, -lawg) *n.* Also *U.S.* **hom·o·log.** Something homologous; a homologous organ or part.

ho·mol·o·gy (hə-mólləji, ho-, hō-) *n., pl.* **-gies.** 1. The quality or condition of being homologous. 2. A homologous relationship or correspondence. 3. *Mathematics.* A topological classification of configurations into distinct types that imposes an algebraic structure or hierarchy on families of geometric figures. [Greek *homologia,* agreement, from *homologos,* HOMOLOGOUS.]

Ho·mol·o·sine projection (hə-mólla-sīn, ho-, hō-) *n.* Also **Goode's Interrupted Homolosine projection.** An equal-area map projection in which the sinusoidal projection is used for latitudes between 40°N and 40°S, and the Mollweide Projection for higher latitudes. It is interrupted over ocean areas so that the continents appear with minimal distortion, and was invented by the British cartographer, J.P. Goode (1923). [Irregularly from Greek *homalos,* even, flat + -INE.]

ho·mol·y·sis (hə-mólla-siss, hə-, hō-) *n. Chemistry.* A chemical reaction in which a bond breaks to give two electrically neutral free radicals. Also called "homolytic fission". Compare **heterolysis.** [HOMO- + -LYSIS.] —**ho·mo·ly·tic** (hōm-ə-líttik, hóm-, -ə-) *adj.*

ho·mo·mor·phism (hōm-ə-mórf-iz'm, hóm-, -ō-) *n.* Similarity of external form, appearance, or size. [HOMO- + MORPH(O)- + -ISM.] —**ho·mo·mor·phic, ho·mo·mor·phous** *adj.*

hom·o·nym (hóm-ə-nim, -ō- ‖ hōm-) *n.* 1. One of two or more words that have the same sound and often the same spelling but differ in meaning. Compare **homophone.** 2. a. A word that is used to designate several different things. b. A namesake. 3. *Biology.* One of two or more identical but conflicting taxonomic designations independently proposed for members of different categories. [Latin *homōnymum,* from Greek *homōnumon,* from *homōnumos,* HOMONYMOUS.] —**hom·o·nym·ic** (-nímmik) *adj.*

ho·mon·y·mous (hə-mónniməss, ho-, hō-) *adj.* 1. Having the same name. 2. Of the nature of a homonym; homonymic. [Latin *homōnymus,* from Greek *homōnumos* : HOMO- + *onuma,* name.] —**ho·mon·y·mous·ly** *adv.*

ho·mon·y·my (hə-mónnimi, ho-, hō-) *n.* The quality or condition of being homonymous.

Ho·mo·ou·si·an (hōm-ō-ō͞o-si-ən, hóm-, -ów-) *n.* Also **Ho·mou·si·an** (ho-mōo-). A Christian supporting the Council of Nicaea's Trinitarian definition of Jesus the Son of God as consubstantial with God the Father. Compare **Heteroousian, Homoiousian.** [Late Latin *homousiānus,* from *homousius,* consubstantial, from Greek *homoousios,* of identical substance : HOMO- + *ousia,* being (see **Homoiousian**).]

ho·mo·pho·bi·a (hō-mə-fób-i-ə, hóm-, -ō-) *n.* Prejudice against homosexuals. [HOMO(SEXUAL)+-PHOBIA.] **-ho·mo·pho·bic** (-ik) *adj.*

hom·o·phone (hóm-ə-fōn, -ō- ‖ hōm-) *n.* 1. A word having the same sound as another word but differing from it in spelling, origin, and meaning; for example, English *sum* and *some* are homophones. Compare **homonym.** 2. A symbol, such as a letter or a group of letters, that represents the same sound as another; for example,

English *kn* and *n* are homophones. [HOMO- + -PHONE.]

hom·o·phon·ic (hóm-ə-fónnik, -ō- ‖ hōm-) *adj.* Also **ho·mo·pho·nous** (hə-móffənəss, ho-, hō-). 1. Having the same sound. 2. *Music.* Having or characterised by parts that move in unison to a single melodic line. [Greek *homophōnos,* having the same sound : HOMO- + *phōnē,* sound (see **-phone**).]

ho·moph·o·ny (hə-móffəni, ho-, hō-) *n.* 1. The quality or condition of being homophonic. 2. Homophonic music. Compare **polyphony, monophony.**

ho·moph·y·ly (hə-móffili, ho-, hō-, hóm-ō-fīli, hóm-, -ə-) *n.* Resemblance arising from common ancestry. [HOMO- + Greek *phulē,* tribe, PHYLE.] —**ho·mo·phyl·ic** (hóm-ō-fíllik, hóm-, -ə-) *adj.*

ho·mo·plas·tic (hóm-ə-plástik, hóm-, -ō-) *adj.* 1. *Biology.* Of, pertaining to, or exhibiting superficial structural similarity arising from **convergence** (see). 2. Of, pertaining to, or derived from a different individual of the same species: *a homoplastic graft.* [HOMO- + -PLASTIC.] —**ho·mo·plas·ti·cal·ly** *adv.* —**ho·mo·plas·ty, ho·mo·pla·sy** (-pláy-zi, -si) *n.*

ho·mo·po·lar (hóm-ə-pṓlər, hóm-, -ō-) *adj. Chemistry.* Not ionic or polar; having uniform charge distribution. Said of covalent bonds.

ho·mop·ter·ous (ho-móptər-əss, hə-, hō-) *adj.* Also **ho·mop·ter·an** (-ən). Of or belonging to the order Homoptera, which includes insects such as the cicadas, aphids, and scale insects. [New Latin *Homoptera* : HOMO- + -PTEROUS.]

hom·or·gan·ic (hóm-awr-gánnik, hóm-) *adj. Phonetics.* Designating two or more speech sounds, such as the alveolar consonants *t, d,* and *n,* formed in the same area or with the same organs of articulation. [HOM(O)- + ORGANIC.]

Ho·mo sa·pi·ens (hōmō sáp-i-enz, sáyp- ‖ -ənz) 1. The taxonomic designation for modern man, the only extant species of the genus *Homo.* 2. Man as a thinking creature as distinguished from other organisms. [New Latin : HOMO + Latin *sapiēns,* SAPIENT.]

ho·mo·sce·das·tic (hóm-ō-ski-dástik, hóm-, -ə-) *adj. Statistics.* Of or designating variables for which all possible values have constant variance. [HOMO- + *scedastic,* from Greek *skedasis,* dispersion, scattering.] —**ho·mo·sce·das·tic·i·ty** (-dastíssəti) *n.*

ho·mo·sex·u·al (hóm-ə-sék-sew-əl, hóm-, -ō-, -shoo-, -shwəl) *adj.* 1. Characterised by attraction to the same sex. 2. Of or pertaining to sexual relations between persons of the same sex.

~*n.* A homosexual person. —**ho·mo·sex·u·al·i·ty** (-ál-əti) *n.*

ho·mos·po·rous (ho-móspərəss, hō-, hə-, hóm-ə-spáwr-əss, hóm-, -ō- ‖ -spáwr-) *adj. Botany.* Producing spores of one kind only. Said of certain ferns. [HOMO- + -SPOROUS.] —**ho·mos·po·ry** *n.*

ho·mo·tax·is (hóm-ō-táksiss, hóm-, -ə-) *n.* Similarity of arrangement and fossils in noncontemporaneous or widely separated geological deposits. [New Latin : HOMO- + -TAXIS.] —**ho·mo·tax·ic, ho·mo·tax·i·al** *adj.*

ho·mo·thal·lic (hóm-ō-thál-ik, hóm-, -ə-) *adj. Botany.* Having male and female reproductive structures in the same thallus, as in some fungi and algae. —**ho·mo·thal·lism** *n.*

ho·mo·zy·go·sis (hóm-ō-zī-gṓ-siss, hóm-, -ə-) *n.* The union of genetically identical gametes, resulting in the formation of a homozygote. —**ho·mo·zy·got·ic** (-góttik) *adj.*

ho·mo·zy·gote (hóm-ō-zī́g-ōt, hóm-, -ə-, -zíg-) *n.* An organism derived from the union of genetically identical gametes and having identical alleles for one or more genes. —**ho·mo·zy·gous** (-əss) *adj.*

ho·mun·cu·lus (hə-múngkew-ləss, ho-, hō-) *n., pl.* **-li** (-lī) 1. A diminutive man; a pygmy; a manikin. 2. A fully formed individual believed by adherents of the early biological theory of preformation to be present in a sperm cell. [Latin, diminutive of *homō,* man.]

hom·y (hōmi) *adj.* **-ier, -iest.** Also *Chiefly U.S.* **home·y.** *Informal.* Having a pleasant, homelike quality; cosy.

Hon. 1. honorary. 2. Honourable (title).

Honan. See **Henan** (province), **Luoyang** (city).

Hondo. See **Honshu.**

Hon·du·ras, Republic of (hon-déwr-əss, -ass ‖ -dóor-). Independent republic of the Central American mainland. It gained its independence from Spain in 1821. The economy is predominantly agricultural, and the main exports are bananas, coffee, timber, and silver. Area, 112 088 square kilometres (43,266 square miles). Population, 6,140,000. Capital, Tegucigalpa. See map at **Central American States.** —**Hon·du·ran** *adj. & n.*

hone¹ (hōn) *n.* 1. A fine-grained whetstone for giving a keen edge to razors and tools. 2. A tool with a rotating abrasive tip for enlarging holes to precise dimensions.

~*tr.v.* **honed, honing, hones.** To sharpen on or as if on a hone; give an edge to. [Middle English *hone,* Old English *hān,* stone, from Germanic.]

hone² *intr.v.* **honed, honing, hones.** *Regional & Archaic.* 1. To whine or moan. 2. To hanker; yearn. Often used with *for* or *after.* [Old French *hoigner†*.]

hon·est (ónnist) *adj.* 1. Not given to lying, cheating, stealing, or taking unfair advantage; truthful; trustworthy. 2. a. Not characterised by deception or fraud; genuine. b. Not calculated or constructed to defraud: *honest dice.* 3. Equitable; fair: *honest wages for an honest day's work.* 4. a. Having or manifesting integrity and truth; not false: *honest reporting.* b. Sincere; candid; frank: *Give me your honest opinion.* 5. a. Of guileless or ingenuous appearance; open: *"Flushed with purple grace/He shows his honest face."* (John Dryden). b. Unfeigned; undisguised: *honest pleasure.* 6. a. Of good repute; respectable; decent. b. Unpretentious; unaffected: *honest country folk.* 7. *Archaic.* Free from moral stain; virtuous; chaste. Usually said of a woman. —**make an honest woman of.** To marry

(a woman) after having had a sexual relationship with her. Used humorously. [Middle English, from Old French *honeste,* from Latin *honestus,* honourable, from *honōs,* HONOUR.]
honest broker *n.* A neutral mediator between parties involved in a dispute, especially at international level.
hon·est·ly (ónnist-li, ónniss-) *adv.* **1.** In an honest manner. **2.** Really; truly. Used as an intensifier: *I honestly don't know.*
~interj. Used to express disbelief, amazement, disgust, or the like.
hon·est-to-good·ness (ónnist-tə-gŏŏdnəss) *adj.* Authentic; straightforward; unaffected: *honest-to-goodness English cooking.*
hon·es·ty (ónnisti) *n.* **1.** The capacity or condition of being honest; integrity; trustworthiness. **2.** Truthfulness; sincerity: *in all honesty.* **3.** *Obsolete.* Chastity. **4.** A plant, *Lunaria annua,* native to Eurasia, cultivated for its fragrant purplish flowers and round, flat, papery, silver-white seed pods. In this sense, also called "satinpod."
hone·wort (hōn-wurt || -wawrt) *n.* **1.** A European plant, *Trinia glauca,* having clusters of small whitish flowers. **2.** Any of several similar and related plants. [*Hone-*† + WORT.]
hon·ey (húnni) *n., pl.* **-eys. 1.** A sweet, yellowish or brownish, viscid fluid produced by various bees from the nectar of flowers and used as food. **2.** A similar substance made by certain other insects. **3.** A sweet substance, such as the nectar of flowers. **4.** Sweetness. **5.** *Chiefly U.S. Informal.* Sweet one; dear. Used as a term of endearment. **6.** *Chiefly U.S. Informal.* A remarkably fine example: *a honey of a dress.*
~tr.v. **honeyed** or **honied, -eying, -eys.** To sweeten with or as if with honey. [Middle English *hony,* Old English *hunig,* from Germanic.]
honey agaric *n.* The **honey fungus** *(see).*
honey ant *n.* Any of various ants, such as one of the genus *Myrmecocystus,* that collect and store honeydew in the distensible abdomens of specialised workers.
honey badger *n.* A carnivorous mammal, *Mellivora capensis,* of Africa and Asia, having short legs and a thick coat. It feeds on honey and small animals. Also called "ratel".
honey bear *n.* A mammal, the **kinkajou** *(see).*
hon·ey·bee (húnni-bee) *n.* Any of several social bees of the genus *Apis* that produce honey; especially, *A. mellifera,* widely domesticated as a source of honey and beeswax.
honey buzzard *n.* A bird of prey of Africa, Europe, and Asia, *Pernis apivorus,* having a brown plumage with white streaks on the underparts. It feeds mainly on wasps and wild bees and their honey.
hon·ey·comb (húnni-kōm) *n.* **1.** A structure of hexagonal, thin-walled cells constructed from beeswax by honeybees to hold honey and eggs. **2.** Something suggesting this in structure or pattern.
~tr.v. **honeycombed, -combing, -combs. 1.** To fill with cavities like a honeycomb: *castle walls honeycombed with little windows.* **2.** To penetrate thoroughly, so as to weaken or undermine: *His story was honeycombed with lies.* **3.** To form in or cover with a honeycomb pattern.
hon·ey·creep·er (húnni-kreepər) *n.* **1.** Any of various small, often brightly coloured tropical American birds of the subfamily Dacninae, having a curved bill adapted for sucking nectar from flowers. **2.** Any of several birds of the family Drepanididae, of Hawaii.
hon·ey·dew (húnni-dew || -dōō) *n.* **1.** A sweet, sticky substance excreted by various insects, especially aphids, on the leaves of plants. **2.** Any similar sweet exudate on the leaves of plants.
honeydew melon *n.* A melon, a variety of *Cucumis melo,* having a smooth, yellow rind and greenish white flesh.
hon·ey·eat·er (húnni-eetər) *n.* Any of various birds of the family Meliphagidae, of Australia and adjacent regions, having a curved bill and a long tongue adapted for sucking nectar from flowers.
hon·eyed, hon·ied (húnnid || húnneed) *adj.* **1.** Containing, full of, or sweetened with honey. **2.** Ingratiating; sugary: *honeyed words.* **3.** Sweet; dulcet: *a honeyed voice.*
honey fungus *n.* A honey-coloured mushroom, *Armillaria mellea,* that grows on tree stumps and is a serious pest of trees. Also called "honey agaric", "bootlace fungus".
honey guide *n.* Any of various tropical Old World birds of the family Indicatoridae, some species of which lead animals or people to the nests of wild honeybees, where they eat the wax that remains after the honey has been removed.
honey locust *n.* **1.** A thorny tree, *Gleditsia triacanthos,* of eastern North America, bearing long pods containing a sweet pulp. **2.** A similar tree, the **mesquite** *(see).*
hon·ey·moon (húnni-mōōn) *n.* **1.** A holiday taken by a newly married couple. Also used adjectivally: *the honeymoon suite.* **2.** A usually short-lived period of harmony and cooperation at the beginning of any joint undertaking or working relationship: *After a brief honeymoon, relations between the union and the paper's new proprietor quickly deteriorated.*
~intr.v. **honeymooned, -mooning, -moons.** To have a honeymoon. Used with *in* or *at.* [HONEY + MOON (month), the first month of marriage being thought of as the sweetest.] **—hon·ey·moon·er** *n.*
honey mouse *n.* A small Australian marsupial, *Tarsipes spenserae,* having a long snout and tongue and prehensile tail. It climbs shrubs to feed on nectar. Also called "honey phalanger", "honeysucker".
hon·ey·suck·er (húnni-suckər) *n.* Any of various animals that feed on nectar, especially the honeyeater and the honey mouse.
hon·ey·suck·le (húnni-suck'l) *n.* **1.** Any of various shrubs or vines of the genus *Lonicera,* having tubular, often very fragrant yellowish, white, or pink flowers. **2.** Any of various similar or related plants, such as any of certain Australian trees or shrubs of the genus *Banksia,* having dense spikes of flowers. **3.** A New Zealand tree, the **rewarewa** *(see).* [Middle English *honysoukel,* variant of *honysouke,* Old English *hunigsūce* : *hunig,* HONEY + *sūcan,* to SUCK.]
hong (hong || hawng) *n.* Formerly, a warehouse, factory, or foreign trading house in China. [Cantonese *hong,* corresponding to Mandarin Chinese *hang²,* profession, business establishment.]
Hong Kong (hóng kóng). Also **Xingang** (Pinyin Chinese). Formerly a British Crown Colony in southern China, it was returned to, and became an integral part of, China at the end of June 1997. The territory embraces Hong Kong Island at the mouth of the Zhujiang and about 230 islets in the South China Sea, Kowloon Peninsula, and the New Territories on the Chinese mainland. The island was ceded to Great Britain in the Treaty of Nanking (1842); part of the Kowloon Peninsula was acquired (1860); and the New Territories were leased to Great Britain for 99 years in 1898. In 1984 Britain and China agreed that at the end of the lease in 1997 Hong Kong would be returned to China as a Special Administrative Region, with social and economic systems to continue unchanged for 50 years. Hong Kong remains a free port and a major commercial, banking, and manufacturing centre. Area, 1 045 square kilometres (403 square miles). See map at **China.**
ho·ni soit qui mal y pense (ónni swáa kee mál ee póNSS) *French.* Shamed be he who thinks evil of it. Used as the motto of the Order of the Garter.
Hon·i·ton lace (hónnitən, húnnitən) *n.* A type of bobbin lace consisting of floral sprigs sewn on net or joined by other lace. [After *Honiton,* Devon, where it was originally made.]
honk (hongk || *U.S. also* hawngk) *n.* **1.** The raucous, resonant sound characteristically uttered by a wild goose. **2.** A similar sound, such as that made by a motor car horn.
~v. **honked, honking, honks.** *—intr.* To emit a honk. *—tr.* To cause (a horn) to produce a honk. [Imitative.] **—honk·er** *n.*
hon·ky, hon·kie (hóng-ki || háwng-) *n., pl.* **-kies.** *Chiefly U.S. Slang.* A white man. Used derogatorily. [20th century : origin obscure.]
hon·ky-tonk (hóngki-tongk || *U.S. also* háwngki-tawngk) *n. U.S. Slang.* A cheap, noisy saloon or dance hall.
~adj. Designating a type of ragtime usually played on a tinny old piano. [20th century : origin obscure.]
Hon·o·lu·lu (hónnə-lōōlōō). Capital of the U.S. state of Hawaii, situated on the island of Oahu. It is a crossroads of transport across the Pacific Ocean, as well as the economic centre and leading port of Hawaii.
honor. *U.S.* Variant of **honour.**
hon·o·ra·ri·um (ónnə-ráir-i-əm) *n., pl.* **-ums** or **-ia** (-i-ə). A voluntary fee paid, often by tradition, to a person for professional services that carry no legal fee. [Latin, neuter of *honorārius,* HONORARY.]
hon·or·ar·y (ónnə-rəri, ón- || -rerri) *adj. Abbr.* **hon., Hon. 1.** Held, given, or conferred as a mark of honour without the usual prerequisites or privileges: *an honorary degree.* **2. a.** Holding an office or title given as an honour, without payment: *the honorary secretary of the association.* **b.** Voluntary; unpaid. **3.** Relying upon honour; not legally enforceable. Said of a duty or obligation.
hon·o·rif·ic (ónnə-riffik) *adj.* Conferring or showing respect or honour.
~n. A title, phrase, or grammatical form conveying respect, used especially when addressing a social superior. [Latin *honorificus.* See **honour, -fic.**] **—hon·o·rif·i·cal·ly** *adv.*
ho·no·ris cau·sa (o-náwr-iss ków-zaa, ho-, -saa || -nōr-) *adv. Latin.* Conferred as a mark of honour. Said of an honorary degree.
hon·our, *U.S.* **hon·or** (ónnər) *n.* **1.** Esteem; respect; reverence: *the honour shown to him.* **2. a.** Reputation; good name. **b.** Credit: *It was to his honour that he refused the award.* **3. a.** Glory; fame; distinction. **b.** A mark, token, or gesture of respect or distinction: *buried with full military honours.* **c.** A decoration or title conferred in respect of distinguished conduct or achievement. **4.** Nobility of mind; probity; personal integrity. **5.** High rank; exalted position. **6.** One that imparts distinction by association: *He is an honour to our organisation.* **7.** Great privilege: *I have the honour to present the managing director.* **8.** *Capital* **H. a.** A title of respect used to or of certain judges. Preceded by *Your, His,* or *Her.* **b.** *Irish.* A form of address used to any person of rank. Used chiefly humorously as a supposed characteristic of Irish speech. **9. a.** A code of principally male dignity, integrity, and pride, maintained in some societies, as it was in feudal Europe, by force of arms. **b.** A woman's chastity or her reputation for chastity. **10.** *Plural.* **a.** Special recognition for unusual academic achievement: *graduate with honours.* **b.** A course for a degree that is of a higher standard or more specialised than for an ordinary pass. Also used adjectivally: *an honours degree.* **11.** In golf, the right of teeing off first. **12.** *Plural.* In card games, the four or five highest cards in the trump suit or in all suits. —See Synonyms at **honesty. —do the honours. 1.** To perform the social courtesies required of a host or hostess. **2.** To perform a particular social act such as filling up glasses or carving meat. **—(in) honour bound.** Constrained or obliged by one's moral or social standards. **—in honour of. 1.** As a sign of respect for. **2.** As a celebration of. **—on** or **upon (one's) honour.** With one's good name as a pledge.
~tr.v. **honoured, -ouring, -ours. 1. a.** To esteem; hold in respect. **b.** To show respect for. **2.** To confer distinction upon: *The ambassador honoured us with his presence.* **3.** To accept or pay as valid (a credit card or cheque, for example). **4.** To abide by (an agreement) or fulfil (an obligation): *Both parties claim to have honoured their side of the bargain.* [Middle English *hono(u)r,* from Old French *hon-*

our, from Latin *honour, honōs*† (stem *honōr-*).] **—hon·our·er** *n.*
Synonyms: *honour, homage, reverence, veneration, deference.*
hon·our·a·ble (ónrəb'l, ónnərəb'l) *adj.* **1.** Deserving or winning honour and respect; creditable: *an honourable deed.* **2.** Bestowing honour; bringing distinction or recognition: *an honourable burial.* **3.** Possessing and characterised by honour: *"for Brutus is an honourable man"* (Shakespeare). **4.** Consistent with honour or good name: *the only honourable course.* **5.** Capital **H.** *Abbr.* **Hon. a.** Used with *the* as a title of respect for certain high officials. **b.** *British.* Used with *the* as a courtesy title for the children of barons and viscounts and the younger sons of earls. **c.** *British.* Used in the House of Commons as a title of respect when speaking of another member. **—hon·our·a·ble·ness** *n.* **—hon·our·a·bly** *adv.*
honourable discharge *n.* A discharge from the armed forces with a clean record.
honourable mention *n.* A written or spoken mention, as in a list, of one who has performed well in a competition but has not been awarded a prize.
hon·ours list (ónnərz) *n. British.* A list of persons on whom an honour, such as a peerage or membership of a certain order, is to be conferred.
honours of war *pl.n.* Certain courtesies granted a surrendering foe, such as the privilege of marching out bearing arms and colours.
Hon. Sec. (ón sék). Honorary Secretary.
Hon·shu (hón-shōō). Also **Hon·do** (hón-dō). The largest and economically most important of the four main islands which constitute Japan. It is predominantly mountainous and is the site of Japan's highest peak, Fujiyama (3 776 metres; 12,389 feet). Most of Japan's tea and silk comes from Honshu and the island is also the industrial heartland of the country, with the Tokyo-Yokohama and Osaka-Kobe urban agglomerations.
hooch (hōōch) *n. Chiefly U.S. Slang.* Alcoholic spirits, especially when inferior or illicit. [Short for Alaskan *Hoochinoo,* a tribe that made a kind of distilled liquor.]
hood[1] (hōōd) *n.* **1.** A loose covering for the head and neck, either attached to a cloak or jacket or separate. **2.** A draping of cloth hung from the shoulders of an academic gown that indicates the wearer's degree. **3.** A sack used to cover a falcon's head to keep it quiet. **4.** Something resembling a hood in shape or function, as: **a.** A metal cover or cowl for a hearth or stove. **b.** A folding waterproof top for a pram or sportscar. **c.** An expanded part, crest, or marking on or near the head of an animal. **5.** *U.S.* The bonnet of a motor vehicle.
~*tr.v.* **hooded, hooding, hoods.** To supply or cover with a hood. [Middle English *ho(o)d,* Old English *hōd,* from Germanic.]
hood[2] (hōōd || hōōd)) *n. Chiefly U.S. Slang.* A hoodlum; a thug. [Short for HOODLUM.]
–hood *n. suffix.* Indicates: **1.** The state, condition, or quality of being; for example, **manhood. 2.** All the members of a grouping of a specified nature; for example, **neighbourhood.** [Middle English *-hod(e),* Old English *-hād,* originally an independent noun (condition, quality,) from Germanic.]
Hood (hōōd), **Thomas** (1799–1845). British poet. He is best known for his comic and topical verse, including *The Dream of Eugene Aram* (1831). *The Song of the Shirt* (1843) exposed the miseries of industrial work.
hood·ed (hōōdid) *adj.* **1.** Covered with or having a hood. **2.** Shaped like a hood, cowl, or similar covering. **3.** *Zoology.* Having a crest, coloration, or skin formation suggesting a hood.
hooded crow *n.* A variety of the carrion crow that has a grey back and underparts, and black head, wings, and tail.
hooded seal *n.* A seal, *Cystophora cristata,* of northern seas, having a greyish, spotted coat and an inflatable hoodlike or bladder-like pouch in the region of the nose. Also called "bladdernose".
hood·lum (hōōd-ləm || hōōd-) *n.* **1.** A gangster; a thug. **2.** A tough, destructive youth. [19th century : origin obscure.]
hood·man-blind (hōōd-mən-blīnd) *n. British Archaic.* Blindman's buff.
hood mould *n. Architecture.* A **dripstone** (see).
hoo·doo (hōōdōō) *n., pl.* **-doos.** *Chiefly U.S. Informal.* **1.** Voodoo. **2. a.** Bad luck. **b.** One that brings bad luck.
~*tr.v.* **hoodooed, -dooing, -doos.** *Chiefly U.S. Informal.* To bring bad luck to. [Perhaps variant of VOODOO.] **—hoo·doo·ism** *n.*
hood·wink (hōōd-wingk) *tr.v.* **-winked, -winking, -winks. 1.** To deceive; trick; take in. **2.** *Archaic.* To blindfold. **3.** *Obsolete.* To conceal. —See Synonyms at **deceive.** [HOOD + WINK.]
hoo·ey (hōō-i) *n. Slang.* Nonsense.
~*interj.* Used as an exclamation of impatience or disbelief. [20th century : origin obscure.]
hoof (hōōf || hōōf) *n., pl.* **hoofs** or **hooves** (hōōvz || hōōvz). **1.** The horny sheath covering the toes or lower part of the foot of a mammal of the orders Perissodactyla and Artiodactyla, such as a horse, ox, or deer. **2.** The foot of such an animal, especially a horse. **3.** *Informal.* The human foot. Used humorously. **—on the hoof.** Alive; not yet slaughtered. Said especially of cattle.
~*v.* **hoofed, hoofing, hoofs.** —*tr.* To trample or kick with the hoofs. —*intr. Informal.* **1.** To dance. **2.** To go on foot; walk. Often used with *it: Let's hoof it instead of taking the bus.* [Middle English *hoof,* Old English *hōf,* from Germanic.]
hoof·bound (hōōf-bownd || hōōf-) *adj.* Afflicted with drying and contraction of the hoof, resulting in lameness. Said of a horse.
hoofed (hōōft || hōōft) *adj.* Having hoofs; ungulate.

hoof·er (hōōf-ər || hōōf-) *n. Slang.* A professional dancer; especially, a tap dancer.
Hoogh·ly or **Hu·gli** (hōōgli). River of northeast India. It is the most westerly arm of the Ganges delta. Leaving the mainstream near the Bangladesh border, it flows 233 kilometres (145 miles) south to the Bay of Bengal. Constantly dredged to prevent silting, the Hooghly connects Calcutta to the sea.
hoo·ha (hōō-haa) *n. Informal.* A noisy fuss or uproar, especially one about nothing of importance. [Imitative.]
hook (hōōk || hōōk) *n.* **1.** A curved or sharply bent device, usually of metal, used to catch, drag, suspend, or fasten something. **2.** A fishhook. **3.** A means of catching or ensnaring; a trap. **4.** Anything shaped like a hook, as: **a.** A curved or barbed plant or animal part. **b.** A short angled or curved line on a letter. **c.** *Music.* A short stroke attached to the stem of a crotchet to indicate notes of a shorter time value. **d.** The lip of a breaking wave. **e.** A sickle. **5. a.** A sharp bend or curve, as in a river. **b.** A spit of land with a sharply curved end. **6.** *Cricket.* A shot by which the ball is hit from the off side round to the on side by means of an upward stroke. **7.** *Boxing.* A short, swinging blow delivered with a crooked arm. **8.** *Golf.* A stroke which sends the ball to the left of a right-hand player or vice-versa. **9.** *Nautical.* An anchor. **10.** The part of a telephone on which the receiver sits or from which it is hung. **—by hook or (by) crook.** By whatever means possible, fair or unfair. **—hook, line, and sinker.** *Informal.* Without reservation; entirely; completely. **—off the hook. 1.** *Informal.* Freed as from blame or a vexatious obligation. **2.** Left off its rest. Said of a telephone receiver. **—sling (one's) hook.** *British Slang.* To leave quickly.
~*v.* **hooked, hooking, hooks.** —*tr.* **1. a.** To get hold of or catch with or as if with a hook. **b.** *Informal.* To snare. **c.** *Slang.* To steal; snatch. **2.** To fasten or hold up with or as if with a hook. Often used with *up.* **3.** To pierce or gore with the horns. Used especially of a bull. **4.** In cricket, to hit (a ball) with a hook. **5.** In boxing, to hit with a hook. **6.** In golf, to drive (a ball) with a hook. **7.** In Rugby football, to secure and pass (a ball) backwards out of a scrum, using the feet. **8.** *U.S.* To make (a rug) by looping yarn through canvas with a type of crochet hook. —*intr.* **1.** To bend like a hook. **2.** To be fastened by means of a hook or a hook and eye. Used with *on, up,* and other adverbs. **3.** *Slang.* To make a getaway; escape. [Middle English *ho(o)k,* Old English *hōc.*]
hook·ah (hōōk-ə, -aa) *n.* An Eastern smoking pipe designed with a long tube passing through an urn of water which cools the smoke as it is drawn through. Also called "narghile", "hubble-bubble", "water pipe". [Urdu, from Arabic *huqqah,* small box, casket.]
hook and eye *n.* A clothes fastener consisting of a small blunt metal hook with a corresponding loop.
Hooke (hōōk || hōōk), **Robert** (1635–1703). English physicist, mathematician, and inventor. He was curator of experiments to the Royal Society (1662–1703) and defined **Hooke's law.** He invented the wheel barometer, improved astronomical instruments, and formulated the theory of planetary movement.
hooked (hōōkt || hōōkt) *adj.* **1.** Bent or angled like a hook. **2.** Having a hook or hooks. **3.** Made by hooking yarn. **4.** *Informal.* **a.** Addicted to a narcotic. **b.** Enjoying or liking something very much; captivated. Often used with *on: He was hooked on the place and went back every year.* **5.** *Informal.* Married. **—hook·ed·ness** (hōōk-id-nəss, -niss || hōōk-, hōōkt-nəss) *n.*
hook·er[1] (hōōk-ər || hōōk-) *n.* **1.** A single-masted fishing smack used off southwest England and Ireland. **2.** Any old worn-out or clumsy ship, especially one that uses hooks and lines rather than nets. [Dutch *hoeker,* from *hoek,* hook, fishhook (as in *hoekboot, hookboat*), from Middle Dutch *hoec.*]
hook·er[2] *n.* **1.** One that hooks. **2.** The player in a rugby team who hooks the ball out of the scrum. **3.** *Chiefly U.S. Slang.* A prostitute.
Hook·er (hōōkər), **Sir Joseph Dalton** (1817–1911). British botanist, the son of Sir William. He wrote *Genera Plantarum* (1862–83), a global study of the distribution of plants, and succeeded his father as director of Kew Gardens (1865–85).
Hooker, Richard (1554?–1600). English churchman and theologian. His great work, *Laws of Ecclesiastical Polity* (1594) helped to formulate the tone and direction of Anglican theology.
Hooker, Sir William Jackson (1785–1865). British botanist. He was the first director of the Royal Botanical Gardens at Kew (1841–65).
Hooke's law *n.* The principle that the stress applied to a solid body produces a strain proportional to it, provided that the elastic limit is not reached. [After Robert HOOKE.]
hook·nose (hōōk-nōz || hōōk-) *n.* An aquiline nose. **—hook·nosed** *adj.*
Hook of Holland (hōōk || hōōk). *Dutch* **Hoek van Holland** (hōōk fan hólant). Outer port of Rotterdam, in the Netherlands. It is on the Hook of Holland cape, and is connected by canal to Rotterdam.
hook up *tr.v.* **1.** To assemble or wire (a mechanism). **2.** To connect or link (a mechanism) to another mechanism or a source of power. Often used with *to: hooked up to the big central computer.* **3.** To fasten together with a hook or hooks. —*intr.v. Informal.* To marry. Often used with *with.*
hook·up (hōōk-up || hōōk-) *n.* **1.** A system of electric circuits and electrically powered equipment designed to operate together as, for example, the linking of television or radio stations so that they can broadcast a special programme together. **2.** A plan or schematic drawing of such a system. **3.** *Informal.* A connection, often between unlikely associates or factors.

hook·worm (hŏŏk-wurm ‖ hŏŏk-) n. Any of numerous small, parasitic nematode worms of the family Ancylostomatidae, having hooked mouth parts with which they fasten themselves to the intestinal walls of various hosts, including man, causing the disease ancylostomiasis.

hookworm disease n. **Ancylostomiasis** (see).

hook·y, hook·ey[1] (hŏŏki ‖ hŏŏki) n. Chiefly U.S. Informal. Absence without leave; truancy. Used in the phrase play hooky. [Perhaps from HOOK (to escape).]

hooky[2] adj. British Slang. 1. Stolen. 2. Dishonest, corrupt. [Perhaps by analogy with bent, stolen, corrupt.]

hoo·li·gan (hŏŏligan) n. Informal. A young ruffian; a thug. [19th century : perhaps variant of the Irish surname Houlihan.] —**hoo·li·gan·ism** n.

hoop (hŏŏp ‖ hŏŏp) n. 1. A circular band of metal or wood put around a cask or barrel to bind the staves together. 2. Something resembling a hoop, as: **a.** A large wooden, plastic, or metal ring used as a toy or for circus animals to jump through. **b.** One of the lightweight circular supports for a hoop skirt. **c.** One of a pair of circular wooden or metal frames used to hold material taut for embroidery or similar needlework. 3. In croquet, one of the metal arches through which the ball is driven. Also U.S. "wicket". 4. In netball and basketball, the metal ring to which the net is attached to form the basket. —**go** or **be put through the hoop.** To undergo or be forced to undergo an ordeal or test. ~tr.v. **hooped, hooping, hoops.** To hold together or support with or as if with a hoop or hoops. [Middle English hoop, Old English hōp, from Germanic hōpaz (unattested).]

hoop·la (hŏŏp-laa, hŏŏp-) n. 1. A game in which small rings are thrown in an attempt to encircle an object and so win it. 2. Chiefly U.S. Informal. Talk or publicity intended to mislead or confuse; ballyhoo. Compare **hype**. [French houp-là†.]

hoo·poe (hŏŏ-pŏŏ ‖ -pō) n. An Old World bird, Upupa epops, having distinctively patterned pinkish-brown plumage, a fanlike crest, and a slender, downward-curving bill. [Variant of obsolete hoop, from Old French huppe, from Latin upupa (imitative).]

hoop pine n. An Australian tree, Araucaria cunninghamii, having rough bark with hooplike cracks around its trunk and branches.

hoop skirt n. A long full skirt belled out with a series of connected hoops.

hoop snake n. Any of several American snakes, such as the mud snake, Farancia abacura, that supposedly grasp the tail in the mouth and move with a rolling, hooplike motion.

hoo·ray, hur·ray (hŏŏ-ráy, hə-) interj. Also **hur·rah** (-ra'a). Used as an exclamation of pleasure, approval, elation, or victory. ~n. A shout of "hooray". [Variant of HUZZA.] —**hoo·ray** intr.v.

hoo·ray Hen·ry (hŏŏ-ray hénri) n. British Informal. A young man of upper-class or upper-middle-class background, chiefly characterised by a brash, extrovert, and self-confident manner, often combined with deeply conservative and anti-intellectual attitudes.

hoose·gow (hŏŏss-gow) n. U.S. Slang. A jail. [Spanish juzgado, courtroom, from the past participle of juzgar, to judge, from Latin jūdicāre, to JUDGE.]

hoot[1] (hŏŏt) v. **hooted, hooting, hoots.** —intr. 1. To utter the characteristic cry of an owl. 2. To make a loud derisive or contemptuous cry; jeer. 3. To sound a motor car horn. —tr. 1. To shout down or drive off with jeering cries. Used especially with down or off: hoot a speaker off a platform. 2. To express or convey by hooting: hoot one's disgust. 3. To cause (a motor car horn) to sound. ~n. 1. **a.** The characteristic cry of an owl. **b.** A sound suggesting an owl's cry; especially, the sound of a motor car horn. 2. An inarticulate cry of contempt or derision. 3. The least amount; a jot. Used chiefly in the phrase not give a hoot. 4. British Informal. An exceptionally amusing person or thing. [Middle English h(o)uten (imitative).]

hoot[2] n. Also **hoo·too** (hŏŏtōō). Australian & N.Z. Informal. A payment of money, especially as recompense. [Maori utu, price.]

hoot·en·an·ny (hŏŏt'n-anni) n., pl. **-nies.** U.S. 1. A gathering of folk singers, typically with participation by the audience. 2. Informal. An unidentified or unidentifiable gadget. [20th century (dialect) : originally, "gadget", origin obscure.]

hoot·er (hŏŏtər) n. Chiefly British. 1. The horn of a motor vehicle or a device that makes a similar noise. 2. Slang. The nose.

hoot owl n. Any of various owls having a hooting cry. Compare **screech owl**.

hoots (hŏŏts, ōōts) interj. Chiefly Scottish. Used to express annoyance or objection. It is used only humorously, as a supposed characteristic of Scottish speakers.

hoo·ver (hŏŏvər) n. 1. Capital H. A trade mark for a vacuum cleaner. 2. Loosely, any vacuum cleaner. ~v. **hoovered, -vering, -vers.** —tr. To clean with a vacuum cleaner. —intr. To use a vacuum cleaner.

Hoo·ver (hŏŏvər), **Herbert (Clark)** (1874–1964). Republican 31st president of the United States (1929–33). He was orphaned at ten, but became a millionaire through mining. After the Wall Street crash, Hoover was unwilling to finance employment through federal intervention, and lost the presidency to the Democrat Franklin D. Roosevelt in 1932.

Hoover, J(ohn) Edgar (1895–1972). U.S. lawyer, director of the F.B.I. (1924–1972). He led the fight against gangsterism during the Prohibition era (1919–33). In his later years, Hoover was criticised for his obsession with anticommunism.

Hoover Dam. Formerly **Boulder Dam.** Dam on the Colorado River

between Nevada and Arizona, in the United States. Built (1931–36) for hydroelectric power, flood control, and irrigation, it is 221 metres (726 feet) high, and forms Lake Mead, one of the world's largest reservoirs. [After Herbert (Clark) HOOVER.]

hooves. Alternative plural of **hoof**.

hop[1] (hop) v. **hopped, hopping, hops.** —intr. 1. To move with light bounding skips or leaps, using one foot or both or all four feet. Used especially of animals. 2. To jump, either up and down or along, on one foot. 3. Informal. To move quickly, as: **a.** To board, get in, or mount a vehicle, bicycle, or the like. Used with in, into, or on. **b.** To alight from, get out of, or dismount from a vehicle, bicycle, or the like. Used with out, out of, or off. —tr. 1. To skip or jump over: hop the fence. 2. Informal. To jump aboard; get on (a vehicle): hopped the train to Edinburgh. 3. Chiefly U.S. Informal. To cross (a stretch of water) in an aeroplane: hop the English Channel. —**hop into.** Australian Informal. To begin (a task, job, or the like) briskly and enthusiastically. —**hop it.** British Slang. To go away; clear out. ~n. 1. A light springy jump or leap, especially on one foot. 2. Informal. An informal dance. 3. A short aeroplane trip. —**on the hop.** Informal. 1. Very busy; active. 2. Unprepared; without any warning: caught on the hop by the unexpected snowfall. [Middle English hoppen, Old English hoppian.]

hop[2] n. 1. Any of several twining vines of the genus Humulus; especially, H. lupulus, having lobed leaves and green, conelike female flowers. 2. Plural. The dried, ripe female flowers of this plant, containing a bitter, aromatic oil and used as flavouring in brewing beer. 3. Plural. Australian & N.Z. Informal. Beer. ~v. **hopped, hopping, hops.** —tr. To flavour with hops. —intr. To gather hops. —**hop up.** Chiefly U.S. Slang. 1. To increase the power or energy of. 2. To stimulate with a narcotic. [Middle English hoppe, from Middle Dutch.]

hop·cal·ite (hóp-kə-līt) n. A granular mixture of the oxides of copper, cobalt, manganese, and silver, used in gas masks to convert carbon monoxide to carbon dioxide. [(Johns) Hop(kins University + University of) Cal(ifornia) + -ITE.]

hope (hōp) v. **hoped, hoping, hopes.** —intr. To entertain a wish for something with some expectation: hoping for a favourable reply. —tr. 1. To wish for with some confidence of fulfilment: We hope to get there by Friday, but it depends on the weather. 2. To expect with confidence; trust: I hope that this apology will satisfy your client. —See Synonyms at **expect**. —**hope against hope.** To persist in hoping for something against the odds. ~n. 1. A wish or desire supported by some confidence of its fulfilment. 2. A ground for expectation, optimism, or trust. 3. That which is desired or anticipated. 4. That in which one places one's confidence; one on whom hopes are centred: She was our main hope for a gold medal of the games. [Middle English hopen, Old English hopian, akin to Old Frisian hopia†.]

Hope (hōp), **Sir Anthony**, born Anthony Hope Hawkins (1863–1933). British novelist. The most successful of his adventure stories was The Prisoner of Zenda (1894). He was knighted in 1918.

Hope, Bob, born Leslie Townes Hope (1903–). U.S. comedian, born in Britain. He co-starred with Bing Crosby in the popular Road films, begining with the Road to Singapore (1940).

hope chest n. U.S. A **bottom drawer** (see).

hope·ful (hōpf'l) adj. 1. Having or manifesting hope. 2. Inspiring hope; promising. ~n. A person who aspires to success or who shows promise of succeeding. —**hope·ful·ness** n.

hope·ful·ly (hōp-fəli, -fōōli) adv. 1. With hope; in a hopeful manner. 2. It is to be hoped; let us hope: Hopefully, your attitude will improve in the future.

Usage: In the sense "let us hope" or "it is to be hoped", this word is very common, especially at the beginning of a sentence. It has however attracted a great deal of criticism from stylists, who would like the word to be used only in a literal sense to mean "in a hopeful way" or "with a feeling of hope". It is interesting that other similar words (such as naturally and thankfully) do not attract criticism when used analogously. But whereas Naturally/Thankfully your attitude improved implies that it did improve, Hopefully your attitude improved does not imply either that it did or that it did not.

Hopeh, Ho-pei. See **Hebei**.

hope·less (hóp-ləss, -liss) adj. 1. Having no hope; despairing. 2. Offering no hope; bleak. 3. Incurable: a hopeless case of cancer. 4. Insoluble; impossible: a hopeless problem. 5. Informal. Totally lacking in competence or effectiveness; useless: a hopeless shot at goal. —**hope·less·ly** adv. —**hope·less·ness** n.

hop garden n. A field in which hops are cultivated. Also called "hop yard".

hop·head (hóp-hed) n. 1. Australian & N.Z. Informal. A person who drinks an excessive amount of alcohol. 2. U.S. Slang. A drug addict. [From obsolete slang hop, opium, probably from HOP (plant).]

hop hornbeam n. Any of several trees of the genus Ostrya; especially, O. carpinifolia, of Eurasia, similar to the hornbeam but having fruit resembling hops. Also called "ironwood".

Ho·pi (hō-pi, -pee) n., pl. **Hopi** or **-pis.** 1. A member of a Uto-Aztecan-speaking North American Indian people now inhabiting a reservation in northeastern Arizona. 2. The language of these people. [Hopi hópi, peaceful.]

Hopkins, Gerard Manley (1844–89). British poet. He converted to

Roman Catholicism (1866) and became a Jesuit priest. None of his poems was published during his lifetime, but a posthumous collection (1918) influenced the interwar poets. Among his works are "The Windhover", and the long poem "The Wreck of the Deutschland".

hop·lite (hópplīt) n. A heavily armed foot soldier of ancient Greece. [French, from Greek *hoplitēs,* from *hoplon*†, weapon.] **—hop·lit·ic** (hop-líttik) adj.

hop·per (hóppər) n. **1.** One that hops; especially, a hopping insect. **2. a.** A large funnel from which materials, such as grain or fuel, are dispensed for use. **b.** A railway truck that is designed to discharge its load through the floor. **c.** A barge that transports mud, silt, or the like away from a dredging-machine, and discharges it. **d.** A device for holding a stack of punched cards and feeding them into a computer.

hop·ping (hópping) adv. Very; extremely. Used in the phrase *hopping mad.*

hop·sack (hóp-sack) n. Also **hop·sack·ing** (-sacking). **1.** A loosely woven, coarse fabric of cotton or wool used in clothing. **2.** A coarse fabric of hemp, jute, or the like used to make sacks. [Used by hop growers for bags.]

hop·scotch (hóp-skoch) n. A children's game in which players toss an object into succeeding sections of a figure such as a series of squares on the ground, then hop through the figure and back on one foot as they retrieve the object. [HOP + SCOTCH (line).]

hop, step, and jump n. **1.** An athletic event, the **triple jump** *(see).* **2.** A short distance. Also called "hop, skip, and jump".

hop trefoil n. A Eurasian clover plant, *Trifolium campestre,* having yellow flower heads that when withered resemble the female flowers of the hop.

ho·ra, ho·rah (háwrə ‖ hṍrə) n. **1.** A traditional round dance of Romania and Israel. **2.** The music to which this dance is performed. [Modern Hebrew *hōrāh,* from Romanian *horā,* from Turkish *hora.*]

Hor·ace (hórriss, hórrəss), born Quintus Horatius Flaccus (65–8 B.C.). Roman poet. His *Odes* and *Satires* express a humane philosophy.

ho·ra·ry (hórrəri, háwr-əri ‖ hṍr-) adj. **1.** Of an hour or the hours. **2.** Occurring once an hour. [Medieval Latin *hōrārius,* from Latin *hōra,* HOUR.]

Ho·ra·tian (hə-ráy-shi-ən, ho-, -sh'n) adj. Of, relating to, or characteristic of the poet Horace, as in formal rigour, succinctness, or elegance.

Horatian ode n. An ode in which a fixed strophic pattern is followed. [After HORACE.]

Ho·ra·tius Co·cles (hə-ráy-shi-əss kók-leez, ho-, -shəss, kók-). A legendary Roman hero of the sixth century B.C. who held off an army of Etruscans at a bridge on the Tiber.

horde (hord ‖ hõrd) n. **1.** A throng or swarm, as of people, animals, or insects. **2.** A nomadic Mongol tribe. **3.** Any nomadic group. [Old French, from German *Horde,* from Polish *horda,* from Turkish *ordū,* camp. See also **Urdu.**]

Ho·reb (háw-reb ‖ hṍ-). A mountain generally identified in the Old Testament with Mount **Sinai** *(see).*

hore·hound, hoar·hound (hór-hownd ‖ hõr-) n. **1.** An aromatic plant, *Marrubium vulgare,* native to Eurasia, having leaves covered with soft whitish hairs and yielding a bitter extract formerly used as flavouring and as a cough remedy. Also called "white horehound". **2.** Any of several similar or related plants, such as the black **horehound** (see). [Middle English *horhoune,* Old English *hārhūne* : *hār,* HOAR + *hūne*†, horehound.]

ho·ri·zon (hə-rīz'n, hoō-, ə-) n. **1.** The apparent intersection of the earth and sky as seen by an observer. Also called "apparent horizon", "visible horizon". **2.** *Astronomy.* **a.** The circular intersection of a plane tangent to the Earth at the observer's station with the celestial sphere. Also called "sensible horizon". **b.** The intersection with the celestial sphere of a plane through the centre of the Earth and perpendicular to the line connecting the zenith and the nadir. Also called "rational horizon". **c.** The great circle of the celestial sphere at the intersection of the sensible and rational horizons at infinity, its plane passing through the centre of the Earth. Also called "celestial horizon". **3.** *Often plural.* The range or limits of knowledge, experience, observation, or interest: *broaden one's horizons.* **4.** *Geology.* **a.** A specific position in a stratigraphic column, as the location of one or more fossils, that serves to identify the stratum with a particular period. **b.** A specific layer of soil in a cross-section of land. **—on the horizon.** Emerging as a possibility; become apparent. [Middle English *orizon(te),* from Old French, from Late Latin *horizōn,* from Greek *horizōn,* from the present participle of *horizein,* to divide, separate, from *horos*†, boundary, limit.]

hor·i·zon·tal (hórri-zónt'l ‖ háwri-) adj. **1.** Of, relating to, or near the horizon. **2.** Parallel to or in the plane of the horizon; level. Compare **vertical. 3.** Of, pertaining to, or involving those at the same rank, stage in a process, or the like: *a horizontal study of sixth-formers throughout Britain; horizontal mergers for economic integration.* Compare **vertical. 4.** Flat.
—n. Anything, such as a line, plane, or object, that is horizontal or assumed to be parallel with the horizon. [From Late Latin *horizōn* (stem *horizont-*), HORIZON.] **—hor·i·zon·tal·ly** adv.

hor·mone (hór-mōn) n. **1.** A substance formed in an endocrine gland and conveyed by the bloodstream to a specific organ or tissue, whose function it modifies by means of its chemical activity. **2.** A compound produced by a plant that affects growth; a growth substance. **3.** Any of various synthetic compounds having effects similar to either of these substances. [Greek *hormōn,* from the present participle of *horman,* to urge on, from *hormē*†, impulse, onrush.] **—hor·mo·nal** (-mōn'l), **hor·mon·ic** (-món-ic) adj.

hormone replacement therapy n. *Abbr.* **H.R.T.** A medical treatment for women, designed to relieve symptoms of menopause and osteoporosis by supplying the body with the hormone oestrogen.

Hor·muz (hór-mõoz, -mõoz, -muz). Also **Or·muz** (ór-). An island, 44 square kilometres (17 square miles) in area, off the southern coast of Iran in the Strait of Hormuz.

horn (horn) n. **1.** Any of the hard, usually permanent structures projecting from the head of certain mammals, such as cattle, sheep, goats, or antelopes, consisting of a bony core covered with a sheath of keratinous material. **2.** A similar hard protuberance, such as an antler or a projection on the head of a giraffe or rhinoceros. **3.** A projecting structure or growth suggestive of a horn, such as the eyestalk of a snail. **4. a.** The hard, smooth, keratinous material forming the outer covering of the horns of cattle or related animals. **b.** A substance resembling this. **5.** A container made from a horn: *a powder horn.* **6.** *Archaic.* A symbol or source of strength. **7.** *Archaic.* A symbol of the cuckold. **8.** Anything resembling a horn in appearance, especially: **a.** A cornucopia. **b.** Either of the ends of a crescent moon. **c.** The point of an anvil. **d.** The pommel of a saddle. **e.** An ear trumpet. **f.** A device for projecting sound waves, as in a loudspeaker. **g.** A hollow, metallic, electromagnetic transmission aerial with a characteristically rectangular cross-section. Also called "horn antenna". **9.** *Abbr.* **h., H.** *Music.* **a.** A wind instrument made of an animal horn. **b.** A wind instrument made of brass. **c.** A French horn. **d.** *Slang.* In jazz, any wind instrument, especially the saxophone or trumpet. **10.** A signalling device, usually electrical, that produces a sound similar to that of a sounded animal horn: *a car horn.* **11.** *Aviation.* A short lever projecting from a control surface on an aircraft, to which is attached the cable, line, or rod by which the surface is operated. **12.** *Vulgar Slang.* An erect penis. **—lock horns.** To become embroiled, as in an argument. **—on the horns of a dilemma.** Forced to choose between equally undesirable alternatives. **—pull** or **draw in (one's) horns. 1.** To restrain oneself; draw back. **2.** To take back a previous statement; recant. **3.** To economise. **—the Horn.** Cape Horn *(see).*
~*tr.v.* **horned, horning, horns. 1.** To gore or wound with a horn. **2.** *Archaic.* To cuckold. **—horn in.** *Slang.* To join without being invited; intrude. [Middle English *horn,* Old English *horn,* from Germanic.] **—horn** adj. **—horn·less** adj. **—horn·like** adj.

horn·beam (hórn-beem) n. **1.** Any of various trees of the genus *Carpinus;* especially, the Eurasian species *C. betulus,* having smooth, greyish bark and hard, whitish wood. **2.** The wood of such a tree. Also called "ironwood".

horn·bill (hórn-bil) n. Any of various tropical Old World birds of the family Bucerotidae, having a very large bill, often surmounted by an enlarged protuberance at the base.

horn·blende (hórn-blend) n. A common, greenish black to black amphibole mineral, essentially calcium magnesium iron sodium aluminium aluminosilicate, found in igneous and metamorphic rocks. [German *Hornblende* : HORN + BLENDE.]

horn·book (hórn-bõok ‖ -bõok) n. **1.** A primer used formerly in teaching children to read, consisting of a single page protected by a transparent sheet of horn. **2.** Any book treating the rudiments of a subject.

horned (hórnd; *poetically also* hórnid) adj. **1.** Having a horn or horns. **2.** Having hornlike projections such as ear tufts: *a horned owl.*

horned owl n. Any of various owls of the genus *Bubo* that have prominent ear tufts.

horn·ed poppy (hórnid, hornd) n. Any of various Eurasian poppies of the genera *Glaucium* and *Roemeria,* having variously coloured flowers and long, curved seed capsules.

horned toad n. Any of several lizards of the genus *Phrynosoma,* of western North America and Central America, having hornlike projections on the head, a flattened, spiny body, and a short tail. Also called "horned lizard".

horned viper n. **1.** A venomous African snake, *Cerastes cornutus,* having a hornlike projection above each eye. Also called "sand viper". **2.** Any of various similar snakes of the genera *Cerastes* and *Pseudocerastes.*

hor·net (hórnit) n. Any of various large stinging wasps, especially *Vespa crabro,* characteristically building a large papery nest. [Middle English *hernet,* Old English *hyrnet.*]

hornet's nest n. A vehement or antagonistic response: *a provocative speech that stirred up a hornet's nest.*

horn·fels (hórn-felz) n. A hard, compact, metamorphic rock formed by the action of heat on clay rocks. Also called "hornstone". [German, "horn rock".]

horn·mad (hórn-mád) adj. *Archaic.* Extremely angry; furious; enraged. [Originally "enraged enough to horn someone".]

horn of plenty n. A **cornucopia** *(see).*

horn·pipe (hórn-pīp) n. **1.** An obsolete musical instrument with a single reed, finger holes, and a bell and mouthpiece made of horn. **2.** A spirited dance, usually performed by one person and originally accompanied by a hornpipe. **3.** The music for such a dance.

horn·rimmed (hórn-rímd, -rimd) n. Having rims or frames made of horn, tortoiseshell, or a material such as hard plastic made to resemble these. Said of spectacles.

horn silver n. Cerargyrite (see).

horn·swog·gle (hórn-swogg'l) tr.v. **-gled, -gling, -gles.** Slang. To deceive; bamboozle. [19th century : origin obscure.]

horn·tail (hórn-tayl) n. Any of various sawflies of the family Siricidae, the female of which has a long, stout ovipositor with which it inserts its eggs into the wood of trees.

horn·wort (hórn-wurt) n. 1. Any of several aquatic plants of the genus Ceratophyllum, forming submerged branching masses in quiet water. 2. Any of various plants of the genus Anthoceros.

horn·y (hórni) adj. **-ier, -iest.** 1. Having horns or similar projections. 2. Made of horn. 3. Resembling horn in hardness. 4. Slang. Sexually aroused; in a state of sexual excitement. —**horn·i·ness** n.

hor·o·loge (hórra-loj, háwra-, -lōj) n. Archaic. A timepiece. [Middle English horologe, orloge, from Old French orloge, from Latin horologium, from Greek hōrologion, from hōrologos, "hour-teller" : hōra, HOUR + legein, to speak.]

Hor·o·lo·gi·um (hórra-lōji-am, háwra-) n. A constellation in the Southern Hemisphere near Hydrus, Eridanus, and Reticulum. [Latin hōrologium, HOROLOGE.]

ho·rol·o·gy (ho-rólla-ji, haw-) n. 1. The science of measuring time. 2. The art of making clocks and watches. [Middle English horologie, from Latin hōrologium, HOROLOGE.] —**ho·rol·o·gist** (-jist), **ho·rol·o·ger** (-jer) n. —**hor·o·log·ic** (hórra-lójik, háwra-), **hor·o·log·i·cal** adj.

hor·o·scope (hórra-skōp || háwra-) n. Astrology. 1. The configuration of the planets and stars at a given moment, such as the moment of a person's birth. 2. A diagram of the signs of the zodiac based on such a configuration. 3. A forecast of a person's future based on such a diagram. [Old French, from Latin hōroscopus, from Greek hōroskopos, astrologer : hōra, HOUR + skopos, observer.]

ho·ros·co·py (ho-róskapi, ha- || haw-) n., pl. **-pies.** The casting and reading of horoscopes.

Hor·o·witz (hórra-vits || háwra-), **Vladimir** (1904–89). U.S. pianist, of Russian birth. He settled in the United States in 1940. Horowitz was noted for the speed and dynamism of his playing.

hor·ren·dous (ho-réndass, ha- || haw-) adj. 1. Hideous; horrifying; dreadful. 2. Informal. Disagreeable; unpleasant. [Latin horrendus, from the gerundive of horrēre, to tremble.] —**hor·ren·dous·ly** adv.

hor·rent (hórrant || háwrant) adj. Archaic. 1. Bristling. 2. Terrified; shuddering. [Latin horrēns (stem horrent-), present participle of horrēre, to tremble.]

hor·ri·ble (hórrab'l, hórrib'l) adj. 1. Causing horror; dreadful: "War is beyond all words horrible" (Winston Churchill). 2. Unpleasant; disagreeable; offensive. [Middle English, from Old French, from Latin horrībilis, from horrēre, to tremble.] —**hor·ri·ble·ness** n. —**hor·ri·bly** adv.

hor·rid (hórrid || U.S. also háwrid) adj. 1. Unpleasant; disagreeable. 2. Unkind; nasty: What a horrid thing to say! 3. Causing horror. 4. Archaic. Bristling; rough: "horrid with fern and intricate with thorn" (John Dryden). [Latin horridus, from horrēre, to tremble.] —**hor·rid·ly** adv. —**hor·rid·ness** n.

hor·rif·ic (ho-ríffik, ha- || haw-) adj. 1. Causing horror; terrifying. 2. Informal. Disagreeable; unpleasant. [Old French horrifique, from Latin horrificus : horrēre, to tremble.] —**hor·ri·fi·cal·ly** adv.

hor·ri·fy (hórri-fī || U.S. also háwra-) tr.v. **-fied, -fying, -fies.** 1. To fill with horror; terrify. 2. To cause unpleasant surprise; shock. [Latin horrificāre, from horrificus, HORRIFIC.] —**hor·ri·fi·ca·tion** (-fi-káysh'n) n.

hor·rip·i·la·tion (hórripi-láysh'n, ho-ríppi- || haw-) n. The bristling of the body hair, as from fear or cold; goose flesh. [Late Latin horripilātiō, from Latin horripilātus, past participle of horripilāre, to bristle with hairs : horrēre, to bristle + pilus, hair.]

hor·ror (hórrar || U.S. also háwrar) n. 1. An intense and painful feeling of repugnance and fear; terror. 2. Intense dislike; abhorrence; loathing: has a horror of snakes. 3. a. The quality of causing horror. b. One that excites horror; a horrifying person or thing: the horrors of war. 4. An unpleasant or irritating person, especially a child: a little horror. 5. Obsolete. A bristling or shuddering condition.
~adj. Calculated to terrify the reader, listener, or watcher: a horror story. [Middle English (h)orrour, from Old French, from Latin horror, from horrēre, to tremble, bristle, be in horror.]

hor·rors (hórrarz || U.S. also háwrerz) pl.n. Informal. Intense, nervous depression or anxiety, especially as a symptom of delirium tremens. Preceded by the.
~interj. Used to express dismay, often humorously.

hor·ror-strick·en (hórrar-strickan || háwrar-) adj. Also **hor·ror-struck** (-struk). Horrified; filled with sudden fear or repugnance.

Hor·sa (hór-sa), (d. c.455). See Hengist.

hors de com·bat (ór da kón-baa, kóm-bat || U.S. kon-báa) adj. French. Out of action; injured or disabled. —**hors de com·bat** adv.

hors d'oeuvre (awr-dérv, ór-, French -dŏvr) n., pl. **hors d'oeuvres** (-z) or **hors d'oeuvre.** 1. An appetiser served with drinks or before a meal. 2. Any of various small dishes, such as spiced meat or specially garnished vegetables, served as a first course. [French, outside of the ordinary meal, side dish, "outside of work" : hors, outside, from Latin forīs + de + oeuvre, work, from Latin opera, from opus (stem oper-), work, OPUS.]

horse (horss) n., pl. **horses** or **horse** (for senses 4,9). 1. a. A large, hoofed mammal, Equus caballus, having a short-haired coat, a long mane, and a long tail, and domesticated since ancient times for riding and to pull vehicles or carry loads. b. An adult male of this species. 2. A horse over a certain size, usually over 14½ hands high, as opposed to a pony. 3. Any of various other equine mammals, such as the wild Asian species, **Przewalski's horse** (see), or certain extinct forms related ancestrally to the modern horse. 4. Plural. Mounted soldiers; cavalry: a squadron of horse. 5. A supportive frame or device, such as a clothes horse or sawhorse. 6. A gymnastic device having four legs and a padded body used for vaulting and other exercises. 7. Slang. Heroin. 8. Plural Informal. Horse-racing or horse-races. Preceded by the: lost a fortune on the horses. 9. Horsepower. 10. Geology. a. A block of rock interrupting a vein and containing no minerals. b. A large block of displaced rock that is caught along a fault. —**a horse of another** or **a different colour.** Another matter entirely; something else. —**be** or **get on (one's) high horse.** To be or become disdainful, superior, or conceited. —**flog a dead horse.** 1. To continue to pursue some enterprise that has no hope of success. 2. To dwell on or attempt to arouse interest in a subject that has long bored everyone else. —**hold (one's) horses.** To check or rein one's eagerness; restrain oneself. —**the horse's mouth.** Any source of information regarded as original or unimpeachable.
~v. **horsed, horsing, horses.** —tr. To provide with or place upon a horse. —intr. 1. To mount or ride upon a horse. 2. Informal. To indulge in horseplay. Usually used with around or about.
~adj. 1. Of or pertaining to a horse. 2. Mounted on a horse or horses. 3. Drawn or operated by a horse or horses. [Middle English hors, Old English hors, from Germanic hors- (unattested).]

horse·back (hórss-bak) n. The back of a horse. Used in the phrase on horseback.
~ adj. & adv. U.S. On horseback: horseback riding; ride horseback.

horse bean n. The broad bean (see).

horse-box (hórss-boks) n. A large van, or a trailer that can be pulled by a motor vehicle, used for transporting horses.

horse-brass, horse brass (hórss-braass || -brass) n. A flat ornament made of brass and originally worn on a horse's harness to frighten away evil spirits.

horse chestnut n. 1. Any of several trees of the genus Aesculus; especially, A. hippocastanum, native to Eurasia, having palmate leaves, erect clusters of pink or white flowers tinged with red, and brown, shiny nuts enclosed in a spiny bur. 2. The nut of such a tree. In this sense, also called "conker". [Formerly used in treating ailments of horses.]

horse·flesh (hórss-flesh) n. 1. Horses collectively; especially, race-horses considered in terms of their racing potential. 2. The flesh of a horse; especially, edible horse meat.

horse·fly (hórss-flī) n., pl. **-flies.** Any of numerous large flies of the family Tabanidae, the females of which suck the blood of various mammals, including man, inflicting painful bites.

horse gentian n. Any of various plants of the genus Triosteum, having small purplish-brown flowers and leathery orange-yellow fruit. Also called "feverwort".

Horse Guards n. 1. A cavalry brigade of the household troops of the British royal family, especially the Blues and Royals. 2. The headquarters of the Horse Guards, in Whitehall, London.

horse·hair (hórss-hair) n. 1. The hair of a horse, especially from the mane or tail. 2. Cloth made of horsehair, used chiefly in upholstery.
~adj. 1. Made of horsehair. 2. Covered or stuffed with horsehair.

horsehair worm n. Any of various slender aquatic worms of the phylum Nematomorpha, the larvae of which are parasitic within insects. Also called "hairworm". [These hairlike worms were once thought to have formed from horsehairs that dropped into drinking troughs.]

horse·hide (hórss-hīd) n. 1. The hide of a horse. 2. Leather made from this hide.

horse latitudes pl.n. Either of two belts of latitudes located mostly over the oceans at about 30° to 35° north and south, having high barometric pressure, calms, light changeable winds, and fine weather. [18th century : perhaps alluding to the old nautical practice of throwing overboard horses that were being transported to the Americas when the ship's passage was unduly lengthened by calms.]

horse·laugh (hórss-laaf || -laf) n. A loud, coarse, often mocking laugh; a guffaw.

horse·leech (hórss-leech) n. Any of several large leeches of the genus Haemopis.

horse·less carriage (hórss-lass, -liss) n. Archaic. A motor car. Often used humorously.

horse mackerel n. 1. Any of several large, mackerel-like, marine fishes of the genus Trachurus; especially, T. trachurus. Also called "scad". 2. Any of several tunas or related fishes.

horse·man (hórss-man) n., pl. **-men** (-man, -men). 1. A man who rides a horse. 2. One skilled at horsemanship.

horse·man·ship (hórssman-ship) n. The art and skill of riding a horse; equitation.

horse marine n. 1. a. A marine assigned to the cavalry. b. A cavalryman assigned to a ship. 2. One who is out of his element; a misfit.

horse·mint (hórss-mint) n. Any of several coarse, aromatic plants, such as Mentha longifolia, a European species of mint.

horse mushroom n. A large, edible mushroom, Agaricus arvensis, having a white cap with a greyish undersurface.

horse opera n. Chiefly U.S. A film or other theatrical work about the Wild West; a Western. Used derogatorily and humorously.

horse·play (hórss-play) n. Rowdy, rough play.

horse·pow·er (hórss-powr, -pow-ar) n. Abbr. **hp** 1. A unit of power in the fps system, equal to 745.7 watts or 550 foot-pounds per second. **2.** The power exerted by a horse in pulling.

horse·pow·er-hour (hórss-powr-ówr, -ów-ər) *n.* A unit of work or energy equal to the work done by working at 1 horsepower for 1 hour, which is equivalent to 2.686×10^6 joules.

horse·rad·ish (hórss-raddish) *n.* **1.** A coarse plant, *Armoracia rusticana* (or *A. lapathifolia*), native to Eurasia, having a thick, whitish, pungent root. **2.** The grated root of this plant, often combined with vinegar or other ingredients, and used as a condiment.

horse sense *n. Informal.* Common sense.

horse·shoe (hórss-shoo, hórsh-) *n.* **1.** A narrow U-shaped iron plate fitted and nailed to a horse's hoof. **2.** Something having a similar shape. Also used adjectively: *a horseshoe magnet.* ~*tr.v.* **horseshoed, -shoeing, -shoes.** To shoe (a horse).

horseshoe bat *n.* Any of various Old World insectivorous bats of the genus *Rhinolophus* and related genera, having a fleshy, horseshoe-shaped outgrowth around the nostrils that is used in echolocation.

horseshoe crab *n.* Any of various marine arthropods of the class Merostomata; especially, *Limulus polyphemus* (or *Xiphosura polyphemus*), of eastern North America, having a large, rounded body and a stiff, pointed tail. Also called "king crab".

horse·tail (hórss-tayl) *n.* Any of various nonflowering, pteridophyte plants of the genus *Equisetum*, having a jointed, hollow stem and narrow, sometimes much reduced leaves.

horse-trad·ing (hórss-trayding) *n.* Negotiation characterised by shrewd and vigorous bargaining.

horse·weed (hórss-weed) *n. U.S.* Canadian **fleabone** (*see*).

horse·whip (hórss-wip, -hwip) *n.* A whip used to control a horse. ~*tr.v.* **horsewhipped, -whipping, -whips.** To flog with a horsewhip.

horse·wom·an (hórss-woomən) *n., pl.* **-women** (-wimmin). **1.** A woman who rides a horse. **2.** A woman skilled at horsemanship.

horst (horst) *n.* A massive block of the earth's crust that lies between two parallel faults and is higher than the surrounding land. [German *Horst*, heap.]

hors·y, hors·ey (hórssi) *adj.* **-ier, -iest. 1. a.** Of, pertaining to, or characteristic of a horse. **b.** Suggestive of a horse in appearance. **2. a.** Devoted to horses and horsemanship: *the horsy set.* **b.** *British.* Having a hearty, almost ingenuous enthusiasm for outdoor pursuits such as riding and foxhunting. Said of a woman, typically one belonging to the upper middle class.

hort. horticultural; horticulture.

hor·ta·tive (hórtətiv, hawr-táytiv) *adj.* Giving exhortation; encouraging. [Late Latin *hortātīvus*, from Latin *hortātus*, past participle of *hortārī*, to exhort.] **—hor·ta·tive·ly** *adv.*

hor·ta·to·ry (hórtə-tri, haw-táytəri) *adj.* Hortative; encouraging. [Late Latin *hortātōrius*, from *hortātus*. See **hortative**.]

hor·ti·cul·ture (hórti-kulchər) *n. Abbr.* **hort. 1.** The science or art of cultivating plants, especially those for ornamental use, or fruit and vegetables for food. **2.** The cultivation of a garden. [Latin *hortus*, garden + (AGRI)CULTURE.] **—hor·ti·cul·tur·al** (-kúlchərəl) *adj.* **—hor·ti·cul·tur·al·ly** *adv.* **—hor·ti·cul·tur·ist** (-kúlchərist) *n.*

hor·tus sic·cus (hórtəss síckəss) *n.* A collection of dried plants; a herbarium. [Latin, "dry garden".]

Ho·rus (háw-rəss ‖ hō-). The ancient Egyptian god of the sun and the sky, represented as having the head of a hawk.

Hos. Hosea (Old Testament).

ho·san·na (hō-zánnə, ho-) *interj.* Used to express praise or adoration to God or the Messiah. ~*n.* **1.** A cry of "hosanna". **2.** Any shout of fervent and worshipful praise. [Middle English, from Late Latin *(h)ōsanna*, from Greek, from Hebrew *hosha'nā*, "save us!"]

hose (hōz) *n., pl.* **hose** or *archaic* **hosen** (hóz'n) (for senses 1, 2); **hoses** (for sense 3). **1.** Stockings, socks, or tights. **2.** Formerly: **a.** A man's garment covering legs and hips and fastening to a doublet by points; tights. **b.** Short full breeches meeting the stockings at the knees. **3.** A flexible tube for conveying liquids or gases under pressure. In this sense, also called "hosepipe". ~*tr.v.* **hosed, hosing, hoses.** To water, drench, or wash with a hose. Often used with *down.* [Middle English *hose*, a stocking, Old English *hosa*, leg covering.]

Ho·se·a¹ (hō-zéer, -zée-ə ‖ -záy-ə). Hebrew Minor Prophet of the eighth century B.C.

Hosea² *n. Abbr.* **Hos.** A prophetic book of the Old Testament, attributed to Hosea.

ho·si·er (hóz-i-ər, hózh-, -yər ‖ hózhər) *n.* A maker of or dealer in hose and knitted underclothing. [Middle English *hosyer*, from *hose*, HOSE.]

ho·sier·y (hóz-yəri, hózh- ‖ hózhəri) *n.* **1. a.** Hose. **b.** *British.* Stockings, socks, tights, and underclothing. **2.** The business of a hosier.

hosp. hospital.

hos·pice (hóspiss) *n.* **1.** A shelter or lodging for travellers, children, or the destitute, often maintained by a monastic order. **2.** An institution that specialises in the care of the terminally ill, especially by the controlled use of strong, painkilling drugs. [French, from Old French, from Latin *hospitium*, hospitality, from *hospes* (stem *hospit-*), HOST (receiver of guests).]

hos·pi·ta·ble (hóspit-əb'l, ho-spít-, hə-) *adj.* **1. a.** Welcoming guests with warmth and generosity. **b.** Well-disposed towards strangers. **2.** Having an open and generous mind; receptive. **3.** Promoting well-being; agreeable: *a hospitable climate.* [New Latin *hospitabilis*, from Latin *hospitārī*, to be hospitable to, from *hospes* (stem *hospit-*), HOST (receiver of guests).] **—hos·pi·ta·bly** *adv.*

hos·pi·tal (hóspit'l) *n. Abbr.* **hosp. 1.** An institution providing medical or surgical care and treatment for people who are ill or injured, obstetric treatment for pregnant women, psychiatric treatment for the mentally ill, and the like. See **day hospital, general hospital. 2.** *Archaic.* **a.** A hospice for travellers or pilgrims. **b.** A home, often charitable, for old people, the infirm, or foundlings. **3.** A repair shop for specified items: *a dolls' hospital.* [Middle English, hospice, from Old French, from Medieval Latin *hospitāle,* from Latin *hospitālis,* of a guest, from *hospes* (stem *hospit-*), HOST.]

hospital corner *n.* **1.** A method of folding sheets and blankets securely at each corner of the foot of a bed, commonly used in making up hospital beds. **2.** The sheet and blankets so folded.

hos·pi·tal·ise, hos·pi·tal·ize (hóspit'l-īz) *tr.v.* **-ised, -ising, -ises.** To put (a patient) into hospital. **—hos·pi·tal·i·sa·tion** (-ī-záysh'n ‖ *U.S.* -i-) *n.*

hos·pi·tal·i·ty (hóspi-tál-əti) *n., pl.* **-ties. 1.** The act of being hospitable or a tendency towards being hospitable; welcoming and generous behaviour towards guests or strangers. **2.** An instance of being hospitable. [Middle English *hospitalite,* from Old French, from Latin *hospitālitās* (stem *hospitālitāt-*), from *hospitālis,* of a guest. See **hospital.**]

Hos·pi·tal·ler, *U.S.* **Hos·pi·tal·er** (hóspit'l-ər) *n.* **1.** A member of a military religious order founded among European crusaders in 11th-century Palestine. **2.** A member of any of several religious orders dedicated to the care of hospital patients. [Middle English *Hospitalier,* from Old French, from Medieval Latin *hospitāble,* hospice. See **hospital.**]

host¹ (hōst) *n.* **1.** One who recieves or entertains guests in a social or business capacity. **2.** *Biology.* **a.** An organism that harbours and provides nourishment for a parasite. **b.** Any organism that supports another organism, for example a commensal, or that supports part of another organism, for example a tissue graft. **3.** The presenter of a show, television programme, or the like; a compere. **4.** A place or institution providing the venue for an organised event: *The city has been designated as host for the next Olympic Games.* **5.** *Archaic.* The landlord of an inn: *mine host.* ~*tr.v.* **hosted, hosting, hosts.** To serve as host for (a party, television programme, function, or the like). [Middle English *(h)oste,* from Old French, host, guest, from Latin *hospes* (stem *hospit-*), guest, host, stranger.]

host² *n.* **1.** A great number: *"a host of golden daffodils"* (William Wordsworth). **2.** *Archaic.* An army. **—See Synonyms at multitude.** [Middle English, from Old French, from Medieval Latin *hostis,* army, from Latin, stranger, enemy.]

host³ *n. Often capital* **H.** *Ecclesiastical.* The consecrated bread or wafer of the Eucharist. [Middle English *oste,* from Old French *oiste,* from Latin *hostia†,* sacrifice, victim.]

hos·ta (hóstə) *n. Botany.* The **plantain lily** (*see*).

hos·tage (hóstij) *n.* **1.** A person taken, often by force, and held as a security for the fulfilment of certain terms. **2.** Anything held as a security. **—a hostage to fortune.** Something one has acquired and may lose. [Middle English *(h)ostage,* from Old French, either from *oste, hoste,* guest, HOST, or from Vulgar Latin *obsidāticum* (unattested), from Late Latin *obsidātus,* hostage (sense 2), from Latin *obses* (stem *obsid-*), a hostage : *ob-,* in the way of, in front of + *sedēre,* to sit.]

hos·tel (hóst'l) *n.* **1. a.** Any of various types of supervised, inexpensive lodging-houses or residences for groups of people such as students, the homeless, or young travellers. **b.** A **youth hostel** (*see*). **2.** *Archaic.* An inn. [Middle English *(h)ostel,* from Old French, from Medieval Latin *hospitāle,* hospice. See **hospital.**]

hos·tel·ler, *U.S.* **hos·tel·er** (hóst'l-ər) *n.* **1.** A traveller who stays at youth hostels. **2.** *Archaic.* An innkeeper.

hos·tel·ry (hóst'l-ri) *n., pl.* **-ries.** *Archaic.* An inn or public house. Often used humorously.

host·ess (hós-tiss, -tess, -téss) *n.* **1.** A woman who acts as a host. **2.** A woman whose occupation is greeting and entertainment patrons, as in a night club. **3.** An **air hostess** (*see*).

hos·tile (hóst-īl ‖ *U.S.* -'l) *adj.* **1.** Of or pertaining to an enemy. **2.** Feeling or showing enmity or hatred; antagonistic. **3.** Inhospitable; unwelcoming: *a hostile environment.* [Old French, from Latin *hostīlis,* from *hostis,* HOST (enemy).] **—hos·tile·ly** *adv.*

hostile witness *n.* A witness called to give evidence for a party, whose evidence is unfavourable or unfairly biased against that party.

hos·til·i·ty (ho-stílləti) *n., pl.* **-ties. 1.** The state of being hostile; antagonism; enmity. **2. a.** A hostile act or incident. **b.** *Plural.* Overt warfare. **—See Synonyms at enmity.**

hostler. Variant of **ostler.**

hot (hot) *adj.* **hotter, hottest. 1. a.** Possessing great heat. **b.** Yielding much heat. **c.** Being at a high temperature. **2.** Warmer than is normal or desirable: *a hot forehead.* **3. a.** Causing a burning sensation because highly spiced: *a hot curry.* **b.** Heated and not having cooled down: *a hot drink.* **4. a.** *Informal.* Charged or as if charged with electricity: *a hot wire.* **b.** Radioactive. **5.** Explosive; fiery: *a hot dispute; hot-tempered.* **6.** Eager; excited; ardent: *in hot pursuit.* **7.** *Slang.* **a.** Recently stolen: *hot goods.* **b.** Wanted for criminal activity. **8.** Close to success or achievement: *hot on the trail.* **9.** *Informal.* Highly sensitive; dangerously controversial: *The issue proved too hot for the government to handle.* **10.** *Informal.* A new; fresh: *hot off the press.* **b.** Currently popular: *one of the hottest young talents around.* **c.** Confidently expected to win: *the hot favourite.* **11.** *Slang.* Good or impressive. Usually used in the negative: *not so* *hot.* **12.** *Slang.* **a.** Skilful; clever: *hot at maths.* **b.** Keen: *hot on football.* **c.** Vigilant; strict: *hot about rule-breaking.* **13.** *Slang.* Producing exciting emotional and physical reactions by means of strong rhythms and inspired improvisation. Said of jazz. **14.** Feeling or expressing strong emotion, passion, or the like. **15.** Strong; striking; bright. Said of a colour. **16.** *Metallurgy.* At a temperature sufficiently high for metal to become soft enough to work or cast. Said of a process or a metal. **17.** *Physics.* **a.** Highly radioactive: *a hot material.* **b.** In an excited energy state: *a hot storm.* —**make it hot for.** *Informal.* To make things uncomfortable or dangerous for. ~*v.* **hotted, hotting, hots.** —*intr.* To become more intense, exciting, or dangerous. Used with *up: The race was hotting up.* —*tr.* **1.** To cause to hot up. **2.** To make (an engine or vehicle) more powerful; soup up. Used with *up.* [Middle English *hot,* Old English *hāt,* from Germanic.] —**hot·ly** *adv.*

hot air *n. Informal.* Empty talk; boastful nonsense.

hot-air balloon (hŏt-âír) *n.* A balloon consisting of a large fabric or plastic bag containing air, which is heated by a naked flame, and a passenger-carrying basket or gondola.

hot·bed (hŏt-bĕd) *n.* **1.** A glass-covered bed of soil heated with fermenting manure or by electricity, used for the germination of seeds or for protecting tender plants. **2.** An environment conducive to rapid, excessively vigorous growth, especially of something bad: *a hotbed of intrigue.*

hot-blood·ed (hŏt-blŭddid) *adj.* **1.** Easily excited or angered. **2.** Passionate. **3.** Rash or reckless. —**hot-blood·ed·ness** *n.*

hotch (hoch) *v.* **hotched, hotching, hotches.** *Scottish.* —*tr.* To shake; jog. —*intr.* To fidget. [Perhaps from Old French *hocher, hochier,* perhaps from Frankish *hottisôn*† (unattested).]

hotch·pot (hŏch-pot) *n. Law.* The gathering together of properties to secure an equal division of the total for distribution, as among the heirs of an intestate parent. [Middle English *hochepot,* from Old French : *hocher, hochier,* HOTCH + *pot,* pot, from (unattested) Vulgar Latin *pottus.*]

hotch·potch (hŏch-poch) *n.* **1.** A mixture of dissimilar ingredients. Also *chiefly U.S.* "hodgepodge". **2.** A stew made from many different ingredients. **3.** *Law.* A hotchpot. [Variant of HOTCHPOT.]

hot cross bun *n.* A sweet bun made with raisins and having a cross of pastry on top, traditionally eaten on Good Friday.

hot dipping *n.* The process of dipping metal objects in a second molten metal to give them a thin protective or decorative coating.

hot dog *n.* A long, thin hot sausage, usually a frankfurter, usually served in a long, soft roll. [Perhaps from its fancied resemblance to a dachshund.]

hot-dog (hŏt-dog ‖ *U.S.* -dawg) *intr.v.* **-dogged, -dogging, -dogs.** *U.S. Slang.* To do stunts or acrobatic feats while skiing or surfing.

ho·tel (hō-tĕl, hə-, ō-, ə-) *n.* **1.** An establishment that provides accommodation and usually meals and other services for the public. **2.** *Australian & N.Z.* A public house. [French *hôtel,* from Old French *hostel,* HOSTEL.]

ho·tel·i·er (hō-tĕlli-ay, hə-, ō-, ə-, -ər) *n.* A person who owns or manages a hotel or hotels. [French *hôtelier,* from Old French *hostelier,* innkeeper : *(h)ostel,* HOSTEL + *-ier,* -ER.]

hot flush *n.* A transient vasomotor symptom of the menopause, resulting from hormone imbalance, that involves the whole body in a flush of heat.

hot·foot (hŏt-fŏot, -fŏt) *intr.v.* **-footed, -footing, -foots.** To go in haste. Used with *it.* ~*adv.* In haste. [Middle English (adverb), "with eager feet".]

hot-gos·pel·ler (hŏt-gŏsp'l-ər) *n.* A zealous, evangelising Christian, especially a revivalist preacher.

hot·head (hŏt-hĕd) *n.* One who is hotheaded.

hot·head·ed (hŏt-hĕddid) *adj.* **1.** Having a fiery temper. **2.** Impetuous; rash. —**hot·head·ed·ly** *adv.* —**hot·head·ed·ness** *n.*

hot·house (hŏt-howss) *n., pl.* **-houses** (-howziz) *.* A heated greenhouse or conservatory for plants requiring an even, relatively warm temperature. ~*adj.* **1.** Grown in a hothouse. **2.** Like or characteristic of a plant grown in a hothouse; delicate; sensitive.

hot line *n.* A direct communications link, as a telephone line, especially one between heads of government for use in time of crisis, as to prevent an accidental outbreak of war.

hot-met·al printing (hŏt-mĕtt'l) *n.* A method of printing using metallic type that is cast into shape in the molten state.

hot money *n.* Capital transferred from place to place at frequent intervals in order to achieve the maximum possible return, for example by exploiting fluctuating interest rates.

HOTOL Horizontal take off and landing. Used specifically in reference to a British design for an aerospace vehicle that can function as either spacecraft or aeroplane.

hot pants *pl.n.* **1.** Brief, close-fitting shorts worn by young women, especially in the early 1970s. **2.** *Slang.* Sexual desire.

hot pepper *n.* **1.** The pungent fruit of any of several varieties of *Capsicum frutescens.* **2.** A condiment made from such fruit.

hot plate *n.* **1.** An electrically heated plate for cooking or warming food, especially one that forms part of an electric cooker. **2.** A table-top cooking device having one or two burners.

hot·pot (hŏt-pot) *n. British.* A stew of meat, especially lamb, with layers of potatoes, usually baked in a tight-lidded pot.

hot potato *n. Informal.* A highly controversial or sensitive issue: *The question of police accountability has become a political hot potato.*

hot-press (hŏt-prĕss) *tr.v.* **-pressed, -pressing, -presses.** To subject (paper or cloth) to heat and pressure in order to extract oil.

~*n.* (-press). A machine for hot-pressing.

hot property *n. Informal.* A person or thing regarded as having great promise or potential.

hot rod, hot·rod (hŏt-rod) *n.* A car rebuilt or remodelled for increased speed and acceleration. —**hot rod·der** *n.*

hot seat *n.* **1.** *Informal.* A difficult or exposed position. **2.** *U.S. Slang.* The electric chair.

hot·shot (hŏt-shot) *n. Slang.* An ostentatiously skilful person.

hot spot *n.* **1.** An area of high temperature in an engine or machine, either one that results from a malfunction or one that is used to vaporise fuel. **2.** A place full of danger, violence, or unrest. **3.** An area on the surface of the earth, away from a tectonic plate margin, that has a higher than average heat flow, and that often gives rise to a volcano. **4.** An exciting, lively place, such as a nightclub.

hot spring *n.* A natural spring continuously discharging water that is above body temperature, or over 37°C (98°F).

hot stuff *n.* Someone or something considered outstanding or sexually exciting.

Hot·ten·tot (hŏtt'n-tot) *n., pl.* **-tots** or collectively **Hottentot. 1.** A southern African people, held to be related to the Bantu and Bushmen. **2.** The language of this people. [Afrikaans.]

hot toddy *n.* A beverage, a **toddy** *(see).*

hot water *n. Informal.* Trouble; disgrace.

hot-wa·ter bottle (hŏt-wáwtər) *n.* A container made of rubber or sometimes earthenware, designed to be filled with hot water and used to warm a part of the body or a bed, for example.

hot-water crust *n.* A type of pastry made from flour and melted fat and water, used in making raised pies.

Hou·dan (hōo-dăn) *n.* A domesticated fowl having black and white plumage and a V-shaped comb. [French, developed in *Houdan,* a village near Paris.]

Hou·di·ni (hōo-deeni), **Harry,** born Erich Weiss (1874–1926). U.S. showman and escapologist. He was adept at escaping from chains, handcuffs, straitjackets, and padlocked containers.

hough (hok) *n. British.* **1.** A hock *(see).* **2.** A joint of meat, such as beef, from the hock or the part of the leg above it. ~*tr.v.* **houghed, houghing, houghs.** To hock or hamstring. [Middle English, Old English *hōh,* heel, attested in *hōhsinu,* "hock-shin", hamstring.]

hound¹ (hownd) *n.* **1.** A dog of any of various breeds used for hunting, characteristically having drooping ears, a short coat, and a deep, resonant voice. Also used in combination: *bloodhound; foxhound.* **2.** Any dog. **3.** A runner who pursues in the game of hare and hounds. **4.** A contemptible person; a scoundrel: *You lying hound!* **5.** One who eagerly pursues something: *a news hound.* —**ride to hounds.** To take part in a fox hunt. ~*tr.v.* **hounded, hounding, hounds. 1.** To pursue or harrass relentlessly and tenaciously: *hounded by the press.* **2.** To incite to give chase; urge on. —See Synonyms at **harass.** [Middle English *h(o)und,* Old English *hund,* from Germanic.]

hound² *n.* **1.** Either of two projections at the side of a masthead that supports the trestletrees of large vessels or the rigging of smaller ones. **2.** Either of a pair of horizontal braces for reinforcing the running gear of a horse-drawn vehicle. [Middle English *hune, hownde,* probably from Old Norse *hūnn,* knob, knob at the top of a masthead.]

hound shark *n.* Any of various harmless edible sharks of the genus *Mustelus,* having flat teeth and well-developed spiracles. Also called "smoothhound", "soft-mouthed shark". [From its resemblance to a dog or hound.]

hound's-tongue (hówndz-tung, hównz- ‖ -tong) *n.* Any of several plants of the genus *Cynoglossum;* especially, *C. officinale,* native to Eurasia, having hairy leaves, small reddish-purple flowers, and prickly, clinging fruit. [From the shape of its leaves.]

hound's-tooth check (hówndz-tōoth, hównz- ‖ -tōoth) *n.* A patterned textile design, consisting of small, broken checks. Also called "dog's tooth check", "dogtooth check".

hour (owr, ów-ər) *n. Abbr.* **h, hr 1.** The 24th part of a day. **2. a.** One of the points on a timepiece marking off 12 or 24 successive intervals of 60 minutes, from midnight to noon and noon to midnight, or from midnight to midnight. **b.** The time of day indicated by a 12-hour clock. **c.** *Plural.* The time of day determined on a 24-hour basis: *1700 hours.* **3. a.** A customary time allotted for something: *dinner hour.* **b.** *Plural.* A period in which a particular or specified activity takes place or is allowed to take place: *banking hours; drinking after hours.* **4. a.** The work that can be accomplished in an hour. **b.** The distance that can be travelled in an hour. **5.** *Plural.* **a.** A time for daily liturgical devotion, as the canonical hours. **b.** The prayers recited during the canonical hours. **6. a.** A time of significance: *His hour had come.* **b.** The present time. Preceded by *the: the hero of the hour.* **7.** A time that is an exact number of hours, as one o'clock or six o'clock. Preceded by *the: I'll leave on the hour; the clock struck the hour.* **8.** *Plural.* Times of rising and going to bed, working, and the like: *keeps late hours; works long hours.* **9.** An angle of 15° (a 24th part of the celestial equator), used as a measure of right ascension. —**till** or **until all hours.** Until very late at night. [Middle English *hour, (o)ure,* from Old French *(h)ore,* from Latin *hōra,* from Greek, time, season.]

hour angle *n.* The angle measured westwards along the celestial equator from the celestial meridian of the observer to the hour circle passing through a celestial body.

hour circle *n.* A great circle passing through the poles of the celestial sphere and intersecting the celestial equator at right angles.

hour·glass (ówr-glaass || -glass) n. An instrument for measuring time consisting of two glass chambers with a narrow connecting channel, and containing sand or mercury requiring an exact period of time, usually one hour, to trickle from one chamber to the other. ~adj. Shaped like an hourglass; narrow-waisted.

hour hand n. The indicator on a timepiece that shows the hour.

hou·ri (hóor-i || hówr-i) n., pl. **-ris. 1.** A voluptuous woman. **2.** One of the beautiful virgins of the Koranic paradise. [French, from Persian ḥūrī, from Arabic ḥur, plural of haura', gazelle-like (dark-eyed).]

hour·ly (ówrli) adj. **1. a.** Occurring every hour. **b.** Frequent; continual. **2.** By the hour as a unit: hourly pay. **—hour·ly** adv.

house (howss) n., pl. **houses** (hówziz || hów-siz). Abbr. **ho. 1. a.** A structure serving as a dwelling for one or several families. **b.** A place of abode; a residence. **c.** Something that serves as an abode. **2.** A building used for shelter or storage. Often used in combination: a warehouse; a henhouse. **3.** A building having a particular function or providing a particular service to the public. Often used in combination: a schoolhouse; a coffee-house. **4.** A dwelling for a religious community. **5.** A household. **6.** Often capital H. A family line, including ancestors and descendants; especially, a royal or noble family: House of Orange. **7.** A commercial firm: banking house. Also used adjectivally: house style; house magazine. **8. a.** A residential building for pupils at a boarding school. **b.** A division in some schools that groups together children of all ages, especially to facilitate administration and for competitive activities. Also used adjectivally: a house prefect. **9. a.** A place of entertainment, such as a cinema or theatre. **b.** A performance at a theatre, cinema, or the like: We'll be late for the second house. **c.** A theatre or cinema audience. **10.** A hotel, restaurant, public house, club, or the like: a drink on the house; speciality of the house. Also used adjectivally: the house wine. **11. a.** A legislative or deliberative assembly. **b.** The hall where such an assembly meets. **c.** A quorum of an assembly. **12.** The people attending and voting in a formal debate: spoke for the motion "This house would restore capital punishment". **13.** Astrology. **a.** One of the 12 parts into which the heavens are divided. **b.** The sign of the zodiac indicating the seat or station of a planet in the heavens. Also called "mansion". **—bring the house down.** To cause wild and general applause; be an enormous popular success. **—keep house.** To look after a house and the people in it. **—like a house on fire.** With great speed and effectiveness; very well; superbly. **—put** or **set (one's) house in order.** To organise one's disordered affairs. **—the House.** The House of Commons, or sometimes the House of Lords. **—See Usage note at home.**
~v. (howz) **housed, housing, houses. —tr. 1.** To provide with a house or houses; furnish living quarters for: The cottage housed ten boys. **2.** To cover with or as with a roof; shelter. **3.** To store. **4.** To contain; harbour. **5.** To fit into a socket or mortise. **6.** Nautical. To secure or stow safely. **—intr.** To lodge; dwell. [Middle English h(o)us, house, Old English hūs, from Germanic hūsam (unattested).]

House n. Pop music heavily dependent upon sound-mixing and the creation and modification of sounds by electronic means. [Probably from (The Ware)house in Chicago, a club where this style is said to have originated.] **—House** adj.

house agent n. An **estate agent** (see).

house arrest n. Confinement to one's home enforced by administrative or judicial order.

house·boat (hówss-bōt) n. A barge or boat equipped for use as a home.

house·bound (hówss-bownd) n. Unable to leave one's house, especially because of illness.

house·boy (hówss-boy) n. A male servant in a house.

house·break·ing (hówss-brayking) n. **1.** Burglary. **2.** English Law. Burglary during the daytime, between 6 a.m. and 9 p.m., abolished as a distinct offence in 1968. **—house·break·er** n.

house·bro·ken (hówss-brōkən) adj. Chiefly U.S. House-trained. Said of a pet.

house·carl (hówss-kaarl) n. A member of the bodyguard or household troops of a Danish or early English king or noble.

house·coat (hówss-kōt) n. A woman's garment resembling a dressing gown, used for informal wear at home.

house·dust mite (hówss-dust) n. A mite, Dermatophagoides farinae, that lives on shed scales of human skin and is extremely common in the dust of mattresses and pillows. It can induce asthma or inflammation of the mucous membranes of the nose in people who are allergic to it.

house·fa·ther (hówss-faathər) n. A male houseparent.

house·fly (hówss-flī) n., pl. **-flies.** A common, widely distributed fly, Musca domestica, that frequents human dwellings, and is a transmitter of a wide variety of diseases.

house·hold (hówss-hōld) n. A domestic establishment including the members of a family and others living under the same roof.
~adj. **1.** Of or pertaining to a household; domestic. **2.** Well-known; familiar: has become a household name since his record-breaking run. [Middle English HOUSE + hold, possession, property (from the verb).]

house·hold·er (hówss-hōldər) n. One who owns or rents and occupies a house or flat.

household troops n. The regiments of cavalry and infantry that escort and, nominally, guard the sovereign and royal family.

house·hus·band (hówss-huzbənd) n. A man who stays at home and looks after the house, and often the children, usually while his wife or partner goes out to work.

house·keep·er (hówss-keepər) n. One who has charge of domestic tasks in a household.

house·keep·ing (hówss-keeping) n. **1.** The management of a house and its occupants. **2.** Money used to run the house, buy food and clothes, pay bills, and the like. Also called "housekeeping money".

hou·sel (hówz'l) n. Archaic. The Eucharist.
~tr.v. **houselled** or U.S. **houseled, -selling** or U.S. **-seling, -sels.** Archaic. To administer the Eucharist to. [Middle English housel, Old English hūsl.]

house·leek (hówss-leek) n. Any of various plants of the genus Sempervivum, native to the Old World; especially, S. tectorum, having a basal rosette of fleshy leaves and a branching cluster of pinkish or purplish flowers. Also called "hen-and-chickens".

house lights pl. n. The lights in a cinema or theatre that light the auditorium as opposed to those that illuminate stage or screen.

house·line (hówss-līn) n. Nautical. A small line formed of three strands, used for seizings. [From its use in housing larger ropes.]

house·maid (hówss-mayd) n. A woman employed to do housework.

housemaid's knee n. A chronic, inflammatory swelling of the bursa of the knee anterior to the kneecap, caused by prolonged kneeling on hard floors.

house·man (hówss-mən, -man) n., pl. **-men** (-mən). British. A male house officer working in a hospital. **—house·man·ship** n.

house martin n. A Eurasian bird, Delichon urbica, having blue-black plumage with white markings and a forked tail.

house·mas·ter (hówss-maastər || -mastər) n. A male teacher in charge of a house at a school.

house·mis·tress (hówss-miss-triss, -trəss) n. A female teacher in charge of a house at a school.

house·moth·er (hówss-muthər) n. A female houseparent.

house mouse n. Any of various Old World mice of the genus Mus, especially M. musculus, that have greyish fur and are widely distributed household pests.

house name n. An assumed name used by a journalist, as when writing several different articles in the same newspaper.

house of cards n. A flimsy, insubstantial enterprise, theory, etc.

House of Commons n. Abbr. **H.C. 1. a.** The lower house of Parliament in the United Kingdom, having the main legislative powers and an elected membership. **b.** The members of the House of Commons collectively. In both senses, also called the "Commons", the "House". **2.** The lower house of the Canadian parliament.

house of correction n. Formerly, an institution housing persons convicted of minor criminal offences.

house officer n. British. A junior doctor working in a hospital. Also called U.S. "intern".

house of God n. A church or chapel.

house of ill repute n. A brothel. Used euphemistically. Also called "house of ill fame".

House of Lords n. Abbr. **H.L. 1.** The upper house of Parliament in the United Kingdom, a nonelected chamber with limited powers. **2.** The members of the House of Lords collectively. Also "the Lords".

House of Representatives n. Abbr. **H.R. 1.** The lower house of the U.S. Congress and of most state legislatures in the United States. **2.** In Australia, the lower house of Parliament. **3.** In New Zealand, the legislative assembly.

house·par·ent (hówss-pair-ənt) n. A person in charge of a group of children living in a residential institution, and usually in charge of running the institution.

house party n. **1.** A party at which guests stay overnight or for several days in a private home or other residence. **2.** The guests at a house party.

house physician n. A resident physician in a hospital.

house plant n. A plant that is grown indoors for ornament.

house·proud (hówss-prowd) adj. Extremely fastidious about the cleaning, tidiness, and general appearance of a house.

house·room (hówss-room, -room) n. Room for lodging or storage in a house. **—not give (something) house room.** To refuse to have or accept something.

Houses of Parliament pl.n. In Britain: **1.** The House of Commons and House of Lords collectively. **2.** The building where they meet.

house sparrow n. A small bird, Passer domesticus, native to the Old World but widely naturalised elsewhere, having brown and grey plumage, and a black throat in the male.

house·top (hówss-top) n. The cover of a house; a roof. **—shout** or **proclaim from the housetops.** Make something known publicly.

house·train (hówss-trayn) tr.v. **-trained, -training, -trains. 1.** To teach (a pet) to excrete outside or in a particular place. **2. Domesticate** (sense 3). Used humorously: My husband's housetrained!

house·warm·ing (hówss-wawrming) n. A party to celebrate the occupancy of a new home. Also called "housewarming party".

house·wife (hówss-wīf for sense 1; húzzif for sense 2) n., pl. **-wives** (-wīvz) (for sense 1); **housewifes** (húzzifs) or **housewives** (húzzivz) (for sense 2). **1.** A married woman who supervises the affairs of a household, especially one who has no outside employment. **2.** A pocket container for sewing equipment.

house·wife·ly (hówss-wīf-li) adj. Of, pertaining to, or characteristic of a housewife; domestic. **—house·wife·li·ness** n.

house·wif·er·y (hówss-wiffəri, húzzifri || -wīf-ri) n. The function or duties of a housewife; housekeeping.

house·work (hówss-wurk) n. The tasks performed in housekeeping.

hou·sey-hou·sey (hówzi-hówzi) n. A form of bingo or lotto. [From HOUSE (military slang sense, a gambling form of lotto).]

hous·ing¹ (hówzing) n. **1.** Buildings or other shelters in which people live, considered collectively. **2.** The provision of houses or dwellings. Also used adjectivally: *housing policy.* **3. a.** Something that covers, protects, or guards. **b.** A frame, bracket, or box for holding or protecting a mechanical part: *a wheel housing.* **c.** An enclosing frame in which a shaft revolves. **4.** A hole, groove, or slot in a piece of wood for the insertion of another piece. **5.** A niche for a statue. **6.** The part of a mast that is below deck or of a bowsprit that is inside the hull.

housing² *n.* **1.** An ornamental or protective covering for a saddle. **2.** *Usually plural.* Trappings. [Middle English, from *house,* covering, from Old French *houce,* from Medieval Latin *hultia,* from Germanic.]

housing association *n.* A non-profit-making association that rehabilitates old housing or builds new, for rent.

housing estate *n.* A residential area, sometimes having shops and other amenities, planned and built as a unit and usually in a uniform style.

Hous·man (hówss-mən), **A(lfred) E(dward)** (1859–1936). British poet. He was professor of Latin at Cambridge, and published two volumes of poetry, *A Shropshire Lad* (1896) and *Last Poems* (1922), and an essay, *The Name and Nature of Poetry* (1933).

Hous·ton (héwss-tən ‖ yōōss-). A city in southeastern Texas, in the United States, a deep-water port lying on the Houston Ship Canal. It is the largest city of the south and southeast regions of the United States, one of the world's leading oil centres, and the third busiest port, after New York and New Orleans, in the country. It is also an important centre for space research.

hout·ing (hówting) *n.* A European food fish, *Coregonus oxyrhynchus,* a species of white fish that lives in the sea but spawns in rivers and lakes. [Dutch, from Middle Dutch *houtic†.*]

hove. *Chiefly Nautical.* Past tense and past participle of **heave.**

hov·el (hóvv'l, húvv'l) *n.* **1.** A small, miserable dwelling. **2.** An open, low shed. **3.** A cone-shaped building housing a kiln. [Middle English *hovel†.*]

hov·er (hóvvər, húvvər) *intr.v.* **-ered, -ering, -ers. 1.** To fly, soar, or float, remaining roughly in one place, as if suspended: *gulls hovering over the waves.* **2.** To remain or linger in close proximity; move back and forth in or near a place. **3.** To be in a state of uncertainty; waver; vacillate: *hover between scepticism and belief.* —*n.* **1.** The condition of hovering. **2.** An act or instance of hovering. [Middle English *hoveren,* frequentative of *hovent†,* to hover, linger.] —**hov·er·er** *n.* —**hov·er·ing·ly** *adv.*

hov·er·craft (hóvvər-kraaft, húvvər- ‖ -kraft) *n.* A vehicle capable of low-level flight over land or water on a cushion of air formed by the action of downward-directed fans. Also called "air-cushion vehicle".

hover fly *n.* Any fly of the family Syrphidae, having a hovering flight and typically having colourings that mimic wasps or bees.

hov·er·port (hóvvər-pawrt, húvvər- ‖ -pōrt) *n.* A port that caters only for hovercraft.

how¹ (how) *adv.* **1.** In what manner or way: *He showed us how to work the machine; How did he react?* **2.** By what means; with what cause or explanation: *I don't know how you can afford it; How is it possible?* **3.** In what state or condition: *How do I look in this jacket?* **4.** To what extent, amount, or degree: *How do you like that? How much did it cost?* **5.** With what meaning: *How should I interpret this?* **6.** In what state of health or general well-being: *How are you? How is your mother?* **7.** Of what kind or quality: *How was the party?* **8.** To a very great degree: *How we laughed!* —**and how!** *Informal.* Very much so. —**how about?** What is your feeling or thought regarding? —**how come?** Why is it that...? —**how comes?** *British Nonstandard.* **how come?** —**how is that?** or **how's that? 1.** What? Usually used in requesting that something said be repeated: *How is that again?* **2.** Used by the fielding side in cricket to appeal to an umpire to declare a batsman out. —**how so?** Why is it so? —*conj.* **1.** Of the manner or style in which: *Be careful how you address the ambassador.* **2.** The fact that: *Remember how we used to go out drinking every night.* **3.** However; in whatever way: *As long as it gets done you can do it how you like.* —*n.* A manner or method of doing or performing: *learn the how of a procedure.* [Middle English *hou, how,* Old English *hū,* from Germanic.]

how² *interj.* Used to express greeting in presumed imitation of North American Indian speech. [From Sioux; akin to Dakota *háo,* and Omaha *hau.*]

How·ard, Catherine (*c.*1520–42). English Catholic noblewoman who became the fifth wife of Henry VIII (1540). Her love affairs brought charges of treason from the Protestant faction at court, and she was executed.

Howard, John (*c.*1726–90). English Quaker and campaigner for prison reform. His plan that jailers should be paid wages, rather than fees extracted from prisoners, became law in 1774.

Howard, Leslie, born L.H. Stainer (1890–1943). British stage and screen actor. He played the lead in the film *The Scarlet Pimpernel* (1935) and Ashley Wilkes in *Gone with the Wind* (1939).

Howard, Trevor (Wallace) (1916–88). British actor. He made his screen debut in 1944. He starred in *Brief Encounter* (1945), and played Captain Bligh in *Mutiny on the Bounty* (1962).

how·be·it (how-bée-it, hów-) *adv. Archaic.* Be that as it may; nevertheless.

—*conj. Obsolete.* Although.

how·dah (hówdə) *n.* A seat, usually fitted with a canopy and rail-

ing, placed on the back of an elephant or camel. [Urdu, from Persian *haudah,* from Arabic *haudaj,* litter.]

how do you do *interj.* Used in greeting a person formally, especially when being introduced for the first time.

how-do-you-do (hów-dew-dōō, -jōō-, -jə-) *n.* Also **how-d'ye-do** (-dyi-, -ji-). *Informal.* A difficult or embarrassing predicament. Usually used with *pretty, fine,* or *nice.*

how·dy (hówdi) *interj. Chiefly U.S. Regional.* Used to express greeting. [From *how do you* (or *d'ye*) *do?*]

Howe (how), **(Richard Edward) Geoffrey, Baron** (1926–). British Conservative politician, Chancellor of the Exchequer (1979–83), Foreign Secretary (1983–89).

how·e'er (how-áir) *Poetic.* Contraction of *however.*

Howel Dda. See **Hywel the Good.**

how·ev·er (how-évvər, hów-) *adv.* **1. a.** By contrast; on the other hand: *The first part was easy; the second stage, however, was considerably harder.* **b.** Nevertheless; in spite of that: *The tickets are expensive; however, I still think we should go.* **2.** By whatever manner or means: *However you come, come early.* **3.** To whatever degree or extent: *"I never am bored, however familiar the scene."* (Theodore Roethke). **4.** *Informal.* How. Used to add emphasis or show surprise: *However did he manage it?* —See Usage note at **ever.** —*conj.* **1.** In whatever way: *Dress however you like.* **2.** *Archaic.* Although; notwithstanding that. —See Usage note at **but.**

howf, howff (howf, hōf) *n. Scottish.* A popular meeting place. [16th century : origin obscure.]

how·it·zer (hów-itsər) *n.* A cannon with a barrel longer than a mortar that delivers shells with medium velocities, either by a low or, more usually, by a high trajectory against targets that cannot be reached by flat trajectories. [Dutch *houwitser,* from German *Haubitze,* earlier *haufenitz,* from Czech *houfnice,* catapult.]

howl (howl) *v.* **howled, howling, howls.** —*intr.* **1.** To utter or emit a long, mournful, plaintive sound characteristic of wolves or dogs. **2.** To cry or wail loudly and uncontrollably in pain, sorrow, or anger. **3.** *Slang.* To make a wailing sound indicative of laughter or derision. —*tr.* To express or utter with a howl or howls. —**howl down.** To drown the sound of or silence (a speaker) by loud derisive calls and howls.

—*n.* **1.** The sound of one that howls. **2.** A high-pitched whine produced in a sound system by electronic feedback. **3.** *Slang.* Something uproariously funny or absurd. [Middle English *houlen, howlen,* perhaps from Middle Dutch *hūlen.*]

howl·er (hówlər) *n.* **1.** One that howls. **2.** Any of several monkeys of the genus *Alouatta,* of tropical America, having a long, prehensile tail and a loud, howling call. Also called "howler monkey". **3.** A device that produces a loud noise in a telephone receiver to attract attention when the receiver has not been correctly replaced. **4.** *Informal.* An amusing or ridiculous blunder.

how·let (hówlit) *n. Archaic.* An owl or owlet. [Middle English *howlat,* diminutive of *(h)owle,* OWL.]

howl·ing (hówling) *adj. Informal.* Very great; tremendous: *a howling success.*

how·so·ev·er (hów-sō-évvər) *adv.* **1.** To whatever degree or extent. **2.** By whatever means.

how·zat (how-zát) *interj. Cricket.* Used when appealing to the umpire to declare a batsman out. ["How's that?"]

Hox·ha (hójə), **Enver** (1908–85). Albanian statesman, the dominant figure in Albanian politics since World War II (1946). He led his country's resistance forces in World War II, and became prime minister (1946–54). In 1954 he became first secretary of the newly named (communist) Party of Labour.

hoy¹ (hoy) *n., pl.* **hoys. 1.** A small sloop-rigged coasting ship formerly used for transporting passengers or as a tender to a larger vessel. **2.** A heavy barge used for cargo. [Middle English, from Middle Dutch *hoei, hoede†.*]

hoy² *interj.* Used to attract attention or to drive or direct animals. [Middle English (expressive).]

hoy·a (hóy-ə) *n.* Any plant of the genus *Hoya*; especially, the **waxplant** *(see).* [After Thomas Hoy, 19th-century English gardener.]

hoy·den (hóyd'n) *n.* A high-spirited, often impudent girl or woman. —*adj.* High-spirited; boisterous. [Originally, a rude youth, probably from Middle Dutch *heiden,* "heathen".]

Hoyle (hoyl), **Edmond** (1672–1769). British author of a *Short Treatise on the Game of Whist* (1742), which defined the laws of the game and remained the standard authority until 1864. The expression "according to Hoyle" is used to mean "according to the rules".

Hoyle, Sir Fred (1915–). British astronomer. In 1948, he helped to formulate the "steady-state" theory, which holds that the universe is expanding, while the density of matter remains constant.

hp horsepower.

H.P. 1. hire purchase. **2.** Houses of Parliament.

HQ, h.q., H.Q. headquarters.

hr hour.

Hr. Herr.

H.R.E. Holy Roman Emperor; Holy Roman Empire.

H.R.H. His (or Her) Royal Highness.

hrs hours.

H.R.T. Hormone replacement therapy (see).

Hrvatska. See **Croatia.**

H.S.H. His (or Her) Serene Highness.

Hsiamen. See **Xiamen.**

Hsi-an. See **Xi'an.**

Hsiang Chiang. See **Xiang Jiang.**

Hsi Chiang. See **Xi Jiang.**

Hsinking. See **Changchun.**

H.S.M. His (or Her) Serene Majesty.

ht height.

H.T. high tension.

Hts. heights (in place names).

Hua Guo-feng (hwáa gwō-féng), also known as **Hua Kuo-feng** (1920–). Chinese prime minister (1976–80). In 1976, he succeeded Zhou En-lai as prime minister, and Mao as chairman of the Communist party. With Deng Xiao-ping, he initiated a programme of modernisation, increasing contacts with the West. He resigned in 1980.

Huam·bo (hwámbō). *(1951–75)* **Nova Lisboa.** City lying on the high plateau of Angola. Founded in 1912, it is the chief city and communications and trade centre of central Angola.

Huang He (hwáang hö). Also **Hwang Ho** (hö) or **Yellow River.** Major river of northern China, some 4 670 kilometres (2,900 miles) long. Its lower valley, a vast fertile alluvial plain, was the cradle of Chinese civilisation. Since the communists came to power (1949), the river has been much regulated, and the devastating floods that gave it the name of "China's Sorrow" rarely occur.

hua·ra·che (wə-ráa-chi, hōō-, -chay) *n.* A flat-heeled sandal with an upper of woven leather strips. [Mexican Spanish *guarache, huarache†.*]

hub (hub) *n.* **1.** The centre portion of a wheel, fan, or propeller. **2.** A centre of activity or interest; a focal point. [16th century : probably a variant of HOB (in the sense, lump, projection).]

Hub·ble (húbb'l), **Edwin Powell** (1889-1953). U.S. astronomer. In 1929, he published his discovery that the velocities of nebulae increased with distance. The **Hubble constant** is named after him.

hub·ble-bub·ble (húbb'l-bubb'l) *n.* **1.** A water pipe, the **hookah** *(see).* **2. a.** A bubbling sound. **b.** A confused sound, as of people talking; a hum. [Reduplication of BUBBLE.]

Hubble constant *n.* The ratio of the velocity at which a distant galaxy is receding from the Earth to its distance from the Earth, approximately equal to about 50 to 100 kilometres per second per million parsecs. [After E.P. HUBBLE.]

hub·bub (húbbub) *n.* **1.** A confused babble of loud sounds and voices; a din; an uproar. **2.** Confusion; upheaval; tumult. —See Synonyms at **noise.** [Irish *hooboobbes,* akin to Old Irish *abú,* a war cry, from Old Irish *buide,* "victory", from Celtic *bod-io-†* (untested).]

hub·by (húbbi) *n., pl.* **-bies.** *Informal.* A husband.

hub·cap (húb-kap) *n.* A round metal covering clamped over the hub of the wheel of a road vehicle.

Hu·bei or **Hu·peh** or **Hu·pei** (hōō-báy, -páy). Province in east central China, consisting chiefly of an alluvial plain drained by the Chiang Jiang (Yangtze) and Han Shui. The capital is Wuhan.

hu·bris (héw-briss) *n.* Also **hy·bris** (hí-). **1.** Overbearing pride or presumption; arrogance. **2.** In Greek tragedy, overbearing pride and insolence shown especially towards the gods that leads to personal downfall and ruin. [Greek *hubris* insolence.] —**hu·bris·tic** (hew-brístik) *adj.*

huck·a·back (húckə-bak) *n.* A coarse absorbent cotton or linen fabric used especially for towelling. Also called "huck". [17th century : origin obscure.]

huck·le (húck'l) *n.* The hip or haunch. [Diminutive of earlier *huck,* hip, haunch, from Middle English *huck-, huke-,* perhaps from Germanic; akin to Middle Low German *hūken,* to sit bent.]

huck·le·ber·ry (húck'l-bəri, -berri) *n., pl.* **-ries. 1.** Any of various American shrubs of the genus *Gaylussacia,* related to the blueberries and bearing edible fruit. **2.** The glossy, blackish, many-seeded berry of such a bush. **3.** Any of various similar or related shrubs, such as the blueberry or whortleberry. [Probably variant of dialectal *hurtle-berry,* WHORTLEBERRY.]

huck·ster (húkstər) *n.* **1.** A person who sells wares in the street; a pedlar; a hawker. **2.** A salesman whose techniques are dubious or aggressive.
~*v.* **huckstered, -stering, -sters.** —*tr.* **1.** To sell; peddle. **2.** To haggle or bargain over. —*intr.* To haggle. [Middle English *huccstere,* perhaps from Middle Dutch *hokester.* See **hawker, -ster.**]

Hud·ders·field (húddərz-feeld). Industrial town in Kirklees, north central England. It is the chief woollen textile-manufacturing centre of the region.

hud·dle (húdd'l) *n.* **1.** A densely packed group or crowd, as of people or animals. **2.** A confused array; a jumble. **3.** *Informal.* A small private conference or meeting.
~*v.* **huddled, -dling, -dles.** —*intr.* **1.** To crowd together, as from cold or fear; nestle; snuggle. **2.** To draw oneself together; curl or hunch up; crouch. Often used with *up.* **3.** *Informal.* To gather in order to confer secretly; meet privately. —*tr.* **1.** To crowd together. **2.** To draw (oneself) together; hunch; crouch. Often used with *up.* **3.** *British.* To bring or throw together hastily or carelessly. [16th century : perhaps from Low German; akin to HIDE (to conceal).]

Hud·dles·ton (húdd'l-stən), **(Ernest Urban) Trevor** (1913–98). British missionary and bishop. His *Naught for your Comfort* (1956) exposed moral problems raised by apartheid in South Africa. He was Archbishop of the Indian Ocean 1978–83.

Hu·di·bras·tic (héwdi-brástik) *adj.* In the mock-heroic style of Samuel Butler's satire *Hudibras* (1663-78). [From *Hudibras,* by analogy with such words as *bombastic.*]

Hud·son (húd-s'n), **Henry** (died 1611). English navigator. In 1609, he tried to find a northwest passage, and discovered the river which now bears his name. While he was returning from a second attempt in which he discovered the Hudson Bay (1610–11), his crew mutinied. Hudson and his son were cast adrift in a boat and never seen again.

Hudson Bay. Large inland sea in north central Canada, connected to the Atlantic Ocean by the Hudson Strait. It covers an area of about 1 230 000 square kilometres (475,000 square miles).

Hudson River. River in New York State, in the United States, rising in the Adirondack mountains and flowing south for about 510 kilometres (315 miles) to Upper New York Bay at New York City.

Hudson's Bay Company *n.* A British company chartered in 1670 to participate in fur trading with the North American Indians in competition with the French in Canada.

Hudson seal *n.* Muskrat fur that is dyed, plucked, and sheared in imitation of sealskin.

hue (hew) *n.* **1.** The dimension of colour that is referred to a scale of perceptions ranging from red to yellow, green, and blue, and (circularly) back to red. **2.** A particular gradation of colour; a tint; a shade. **3.** Colour: *all the hues of the rainbow.* **4.** Character; aspect: *the weird hue of the deserted house.* [Middle English *hewe,* complexion, appearance, Old English *hēo, hīw,* appearance, form, colour, beauty.]

hue and cry *n.* **1.** Formerly: **a.** The pursuit of a criminal announced by loud shouts to alert others then legally obliged to aid in the chase. **b.** The loud shout used to arouse the pursuers. **2.** Any public clamour or stir, as of protest or demand; an outcry: *a big hue and cry over the latest spending cuts.* [Middle English *hew, heu,* from Old French *heu, hu,* an outcry, from *huer,* to cry out (imitative).]

Hu·é (hōō-áy, hew-, hü-). City in central Vietnam, lying on the Hué River. It is one of the most ancient towns of Vietnam, dating from the 3rd century B.C., and is a former capital of Annam. It was the seat of the Nguyen dynasty from the early 19th century, but lost its historic status as the capital in 1887, when Saigon became the capital of Indochina.

hued (hewd) *adj.* Having a given hue, aspect, or character. Used in combination: *rosy-hued dawn.*

huff (huf) *n.* **1.** A fit of anger or annoyance; pique: *he stormed off in a huff.* **2.** In draughts, an act of huffing. Also called "blow".
~*v.* **huffed, huffing, huffs.** —*intr.* **1.** *Archaic.* To puff; blow. **2.** To speak or act with noisy, empty threats; bluster. Now used chiefly in the phrase *huff and puff.* **3.** To act or react indignantly; take offence. —*tr.* **1.** To puff or blow up; inflate. **2.** *Archaic.* To treat with insolence; bully; tease. **3.** To put in a huff; anger; annoy. **4.** In draughts, to penalise (an opponent) by removing from the board a draught that has failed to make a capture, when in a position to do so. [Imitative of puffing or blowing. Sense 4, from the custom of blowing on the piece before removing it.]

huff·ish (húffish) *adj.* **1.** Peevish; sulky; in a huff. **2.** Arrogant; insolent. —**huff·ish·ly** *adv.* —**huff·ish·ness** *n.*

huff·y (húffi) *adj.* **-ier, -iest. 1.** Easily offended; sensitive; touchy. **2.** Irritated or annoyed; indignant. **3.** *Archaic.* Arrogant; disdainful; haughty. —**huff·i·ly** *adv.* —**huff·i·ness** *n.*

hug (hug) *v.* **hugged, hugging, hugs.** —*tr.* **1.** To clasp or hold closely, especially in one's arms; embrace or enfold, as in affection. **2.** To ascribe steadfastly to (a belief or opinion, for example); cherish. **3.** To keep, remain, or be situated close to: *The old footpath winds inland, hugging the foot of the hill.* **4.** To be very pleased with (oneself); congratulate (oneself). —*intr.* To embrace or be in physical contact with; cling together closely; snuggle.
~*n.* **1.** An affectionate, close embrace. **2.** A crushing embrace. [Scandinavian, akin to Old Norse *hugga,* to comfort, console, from Germanic *hugjan* (unattested).] —**hug·ga·ble** *adj.* —**hug·ger** *n.*

huge (hewj ‖ yōōj) *adj.* **huger, hugest.** Of exceedingly great size, extent, degree, or quantity; tremendous. See Synonyms at **enormous.** [Middle English *huge, hoge,* shortened from Old French *ahuge, ahoge†.*] —**huge·ly** *adv.* —**huge·ness** *n.*

huge·ous (héwjəss) *adj. Archaic.* Huge. Used chiefly for humorous effect. —**huge·ous·ly** *adv.* —**huge·ous·ness** *n.*

hug·ger-mug·ger (húggər-muggər) *n.* **1.** Disorder; confusion; muddle. **2.** Concealment; secrecy.
~*adj.* **1.** Disordered; jumbled: *"worry out her financial problems in her own hugger-mugger way"* (Samuel Butler). **2.** Secret; surreptitious; clandestine: *hugger-mugger political deals.*
~*v.* **hugger-muggered, -gering, -gers.** —*tr.* To keep concealed or secret. —*intr.* To act in a surreptitious manner. [16th century : also *hucker mucker,* and earlier *hoder moder,* all perhaps akin to Middle English *hoder,* huddle, and *mokere,* to hide.] —**hug·ger-mug·ger** *adv.*

Hughes (hewz), **Howard (Robard)** (1905-76). U.S. film producer, aviator, and multimillionaire magnate. Among his films was *Hell's Angels* (1930). He founded the Hughes Aircraft Corporation, broke the aeroplane speed record (1935), and flew around the world in record time (1938). From 1950 he lived as a recluse.

Hughes, Richard (Arthur Warren) (1900–76). British novelist. His books include *A High Wind in Jamaica* (1929), *The Fox in the Attic* (1961), and *The Wooden Shepherdess* (1973).

Hughes, Ted (Edward James) (1930–). British poet. His works, which include *A Hawk in the Rain* (1957), *Lupercal* (1960), *Crow* (1970) and *Gaudete* (1977) emphasise the dynamic vitality of nature as against the relatively enervating existence of human beings. He was appointed Poet Laureate in 1984. 1997 saw his *Tales from Ovid* and 1998, *Birthday Letters.*

Hughes, Thomas (1822–96). British lawyer and author. His *Tom Brown's Schooldays* (1857) describes public-school life at Rugby, under its famous headmaster Dr. Thomas Arnold. Hughes was a Liberal M.P. (1865–74).

Hugli. See **Hooghly**.

hug-me-tight (húg-mi-tīt) *n.* A woman's close-fitting, usually knitted jacket, with or without sleeves.

Hu-go (héwgō; *French* ü-gṓ), **Victor (Marie)** (1802–85). French poet, novelist, and dramatist. Shortly after Napoleon III seized power (1852), he went into exile in the Channel Islands, returning to France in 1870. His novels include *The Hunchback of Notre Dame* (1831), *Les Misérables* (1862), and *Toilers of the Sea* (1866).

Hu-gue-not (héwgə-nŏ, -not) *n.* A French Protestant of the 16th and 17th centuries. [French *huguenot*, assimilation (to *Hugues*, burgomaster of Geneva) of earlier (Genevan) French *eyguenot*, referring to those who opposed annexation by the Duke of Savoy, from Swiss German *Eidgenosse(n)*, confederate(s), from Middle High German *eitgenōz* : *eit*, oath, from Old High German *eid* + *genōz*, companion, from Old High German *ginōz*.] —**Hu-gue-not, Hu-gue-not-ic** (-nóttik) *adj.* —**Hu-gue-not-ism** *n.*

huh (hu, hə) *interj.* Used in asking a question or to express surprise, contempt, or indifference.

hu-ia (hōo-yə) *n.* An extinct New Zealand songbird, *Heteralocha acutirostris*, that had a beak that was strong and straight in the male and slender and curved in the female. [Maori.]

hu-la (hōōlə) *n.* Also **hu-la-hu-la** (hōōlə-hōōlə) 1. A Polynesian ethnic dance performed by men or women alone or together and characterised by undulating movements of the hips, arms, and hands, pantomiming a story. 2. The music for this dance, composed typically of rhythmic drumbeats and chants. [Hawaiian.]

Hula Hoop *n.* A large, light hoop, often made of plastic, that is whirled round the body by the movement of the hips.

hulk (hulk) *n.* 1. A heavy, unwieldy ship. 2. a. The hull of an old, unseaworthy, or wrecked ship. b. An old or unseaworthy ship formerly used as a prison or warehouse. 3. a. A clumsy, awkward, or overweight person. b. A clumsy or bulky object. —*intr.v.* **hulked, hulking, hulks.** 1. To loom or rise in a towering or impressive fashion: *The big lorry hulked out of the fog in front of our car.* 2. *British Regional.* To move about in a lazy or clumsy manner. [Middle English *hulke*, Old English *hulc*, ship, from Medieval Latin *hulcus*, from Greek *holkas*, "ship that is towed", merchant vessel, from *helkein*, to pull, tow.]

hulk-ing (húlking) *adj.* Also **hulk-y** (húlki) Unwieldy, clumsy, or bulky; towering: *a hulking great elephant.*

hull (hul) *n.* 1. a. The enlarged calyx of a strawberry or similar fruit, usually green and easily detached. b. The dry outer covering of a fruit, seed, or nut; husk. 2. *Nautical.* The main body of a ship, exclusive of masts, sails, yards, and rigging. 3. The main body or frame of any of various other large vehicles, such as a tank, an airship, or a flying boat. 4. The outer casing of a rocket, guided missile, or spaceship. —*tr.v.* **hulled, hulling, hulls.** 1. To remove the hull or hulls of (fruit or seeds). 2. To pierce or break through the hull of (a ship, tank, or the like). [Middle English *hull, hole*, husk, Old English *hulu*; akin to *helan*, to cover.]

Hull (hul). Full name **Kingston upon Hull.** City in northeast England. It stands on the north shore of the Humber estuary on the river Hull. It is a port with a busy North Sea traffic.

hul-la-ba-loo, hul-la-bal-loo (húllə-bə-lōō) *n., pl.* **-loos.** A great confused noise or din; an uproar. See Synonyms at **noise.** [Earlier *hollo-ballo*, akin to the interjection HALLOO.]

hull down *adj.* 1. So far away that the hull is below the horizon. Said of a ship. 2. Concealed apart from the turret. Said of a tank.

hullo. Variant of **hello.**

hum[1] (hum) *v.* **hummed, humming, hums.** —*intr.* 1. To utter a continuous low droning sound like that of the speech sound (m) when prolonged. 2. a. To emit the continuous droning sound of an insect on the wing, or a similar sound. b. To move with such a sound. 3. a. To give out a low, continuous drone blended of many sounds: *The avenue hummed with traffic.* b. To be full of activity. 4. To produce a tune without opening the lips or forming words. 5. *British Slang.* To give off an unpleasant smell. 6. To hesitate while speaking; vacillate. Used chiefly in the phrase *hum and ha.* —*tr.* To sing (a tune) without opening the lips or forming words.

—*n.* 1. A noise or tune produced by humming. 2. A low-frequency continuous noise produced by an amplifier, usually as result of interference from the mains frequency. 3. *British Slang.* An unpleasant smell.

—*interj.* 1. Uttered as a pause in speech or to indicate thought. 2. Used to express surprise or displeasure. [Middle English *hummen* (imitative).] —**hum-mer** *n.*

hum[2] *tr.v.* **hummed, humming, hums.** *Australian.* To borrow; cadge. [Shortened from HUMBUG, to trick, deceive.]

hu-man (héw-mən ‖ yōo-) *adj.* 1. Of, relating to, or characteristic of man or mankind: *the course of human events.* 2. Having or manifesting the form, nature, or qualities characteristic of man, especially: a. Showing qualities characteristic of man as distinguished from machines, such as sympathy or fallibility: *human kindness; his mistake was only human.* b. Pertaining to or being a man as distinguished from a lower animal; reasoning; moral. c. Pertaining to or being a man as distinguished from a divine entity or infinite intelligence; mortal; earthly. 3. Made up of people: *They formed a human bridge across the river.*

—*n.* A human being; a person. [Middle English *humain(e), humayn(e)*, from Old French *humain* (feminine *humaine*), from Latin *hūmānus*, akin to *homo* (stem *homin-*), man.] —**hu-man-ness** *n.*

human being *n.* A member of the genus *Homo,* and especially of the species *Homo sapiens;* a person.

hu-mane (hew-máyn ‖ yōo-) *adj.* 1. Characterised by qualities of kindness, mercy, or compassion: *a humane judge.* 2. Tending to evoke or promote these qualities; refining; civilising: *a humane education.* 3. Painless. Said especially of an agent or instrument for killing animals: *humane killer; a humane killing.* [Middle English *humaine*, HUMAN.] —**hu-mane-ly** *adv.* —**hu-mane-ness** *n.*

human ecology *n.* **Ecology** (sense 2) (*see*).

human engineering *n.* 1. The industrial management of labour. 2. The technology of efficient use of machines by human beings.

human interest *n.* The often sentimental preoccupation with the affairs or feelings of individuals, as in popular journalism. Also used adjectivally: *a human-interest story.*

hu-man-ise, hu-man-ize (héw-mən-īz ‖ yōo-) *v.* **-ised, -ising, -ises.** —*tr.* 1. To make human; cause to have human characteristics or attributes. 2. To make humane; imbue with human sympathy; civilise. —*intr.* 1. To become human. 2. To become humane. —**hu-man-i-sa-tion** (-ī-záysh'n ‖ *U.S.* -i-) *n.* —**hu-man-is-er** *n.*

hu-man-ism (héw-mən-iz'm ‖ yōo-) *n.* 1. Concern with the interests and needs of human beings. 2. A philosophy or attitude that addresses itself exclusively to human as opposed to divine or supernatural concerns, often coupled with the belief that man is capable of reaching self-fulfilment without divine aid. 3. The study of the humanities; cultured learning. 4. *Often capital* H. A cultural and intellectual movement of a secular character that occurred during the Renaissance following the rediscovery of the literature, art, and civilisation of ancient Greece and Rome.

hu-man-ist (héw-mən-ist ‖ yōo-) *n.* 1. A follower of the philosophy of humanism. 2. One who is concerned with the study and welfare of human beings. 3. One who studies the humanities; especially, a student of classical learning. 4. *Often capital* H. A Renaissance student or follower of Humanism.

—*adj.* Also **hu-man-is-tic** (-istik). Of or relating to humanism or the humanities. —**hu-man-is-ti-cal-ly** *adv.*

hu-man-i-tar-i-an (hew-mánni-taír-i-ən, héw-manni- ‖ yōo-) *adj.* 1. Concerned with the well-being of mankind and the alleviation of human suffering. 2. Of or relating to humanitarianism.

—*n.* One devoted to the promotion of human welfare and the advancement of social reforms; a philanthropist.

hu-man-i-tar-i-an-ism (hew-mánni-taír-i-ən-iz'm, héw-manni- ‖ yōo-) *n.* 1. The ideas, principles, or methods of humanitarians; philanthropy. 2. *Ethics.* The belief that man's sole moral obligation is to work for the improved welfare of humanity. 3. *Theology.* The belief or doctrine that Jesus was only human and not divine.

hu-man-i-ty (hew-mánnəti ‖ yōo-) *n., pl.* **-ties.** 1. Human beings collectively; the human race; mankind. 2. The condition, quality, or fact of being human; human nature; humanness. 3. The quality of being humane; benevolence; kindness; mercy. 4. A humane attribute or action. 5. *Plural.* a. The study of the classical languages and literature of ancient Greece and Rome. b. Those branches of knowledge concerned with man and his culture, as philosophy, literature, and the fine arts, as distinguished from the sciences. [Middle English *humanite*, from Old French, from Latin *hūmānitās* (stem *hūmānitāt-*), from *hūmānus*, HUMAN.]

hu-man-kind (héw-mən-kīnd ‖ yōo-) *n.* The human race; mankind.

hu-man-ly (héw-mən-li ‖ yōo-) *adv.* 1. In a human way. 2. By human means, capabilities, or powers. 3. According to human experience or knowledge.

hu-man-oid (héw-mən-oyd ‖ yōo-) *adj.* Having human characteristics; being evolutionarily closer to man rather than the apes.

—*n.* 1. A humanoid being. 2. A synthetic man, an **android** (*see*).

Hum-ber (húmbər). A river in northeast England, consisting of the estuary of the rivers Trent and Ouse and extending from their confluence for about 60 kilometres (40 miles) to the North Sea. The fishing ports of Hull and Grimsby stand on its northern and southern shores respectively.

Hum-ber-side (húmbər-sīd). From 1974 to 1996, a county in northeast England, now administratively subdivided.

hum-ble (húmb'l ‖ úmb'l) *adj.* **-bler, -blest.** 1. Having or showing feelings of humility rather than of pride; aware of one's shortcomings; modest; meek. 2. Showing deferential respect. 3. a. Lacking high social status. b. Lowly; unpretentious.

—*tr.v.* **humbled, -bling, -bles.** 1. To curtail or destroy the pride of; humiliate. 2. To give a lower condition or station to; abase. —See Synonyms at **degrade.** [Middle English *(h)umble*, from Old French *(h)umble*, from Latin *humilis*, low, lowly, base, from *humus*, ground, soil.] —**hum-ble-ness** *n.* —**hum-bly** *adv.*

Synonyms: humble, meek, modest, reserved, retiring.

hum-ble-bee (húmb'l-bee) *n.* A bumblebee (*see*). [Middle English *humbylbee*, perhaps from Middle Low German *hummelbē* : *hummel*, bumblebee + *bē*, bee.]

humble pie *n.* Formerly, a pie made from the edible organs of a deer. —**eat humble pie.** To be made to apologise for or admit one's faults; be humiliated. [*Humble*, from earlier *humbles*, unexplained variant of *umbles*; see **numbles.** Phrase (influenced by HUMBLE, to humiliate) originally referred to eating the offal or least desirable part of a deer.]

Hum-boldt (húm-bŏlt, hōom-), **(Friedrich Wilhelm Karl Heinrich) Alexander von** (1769–1859). German explorer and geographer.

Younger brother of Wilhelm. He originated the study of the environment, ecology. The Humboldt Current (now called the Peru Current), off Peru's Pacific coast, was named after him.

Humboldt, (Karl) Wilhelm von (1767–1835). German statesman and philologist. He explored the relationship between language and culture.

hum·bug (húm-bug) *n.* **1.** Something intended to deceive; a hoax; a fraud. **2.** One who tries to trick or deceive others; an impostor; a charlatan. **3. a.** Nonsense; rubbish. **b.** Pretence or hypocrisy. **4.** *British.* A boiled sweet, usually peppermint-flavoured.
~*v.* **humbugged, -bugging, -bugs.** —*tr.* To deceive; trick; cheat. —*intr.* To practice trickery. [18th century : origin obscure.] —**hum·bug·ger** *n.* —**hum·bug·ger·y** (húm-buggəri) *n.*

hum·ding·er (húm-ding-ər) *n. Informal.* Someone or something extraordinary or superior; a marvel. [20th century : origin obscure.]

hum·drum (húm-drum) *adj.* Without change, variety, or excitement; monotonous; ordinary. See Synonyms at **boring.**
~*n.* Something or someone dull or unexciting. [Originally also *humtrum,* probably reduplication of HUM.]

Hume (hewm), **Cardinal (George) Basil** (1923–). Roman Catholic Archbishop of Westminster from 1976.

Hume, David (1711–76). Scottish philosopher and historian. He argued that the perceptions of the mind were essentially impressions from sensations, emotions, and ideas.

Hume, John (1937–). Northern Irish politician. Leader of the Social Democratic and Labour Party (1979–) and an M.P. and M.E.P. He has worked towards peace and reconciliation in Northern Ireland over many years particularly in his meetings with Gerry Adams, and by his participation in the 1996–98 peace talks chaired by U.S. senator George Mitchell (1933–).

hu·mec·tant (hew-méktənt) *n.* A moistening agent.
~*adj.* Promoting moisture retention. [Latin *hūmectāns* (stem *hūmectant-*), present participle of *(h)ūmectāre,* to moisten, from *(h)ūmectus,* moist, from *(h)ūmēre,* to be moist.]

hu·mer·al (héwmərəl) *adj.* **1.** Pertaining to or located in the region of the humerus or the shoulder. **2.** Pertaining to or designating a body part analogous to the humerus. —**hu·mer·al** *n.*

humeral veil *n. Roman Catholic Church.* A shawl-like vestment worn over the shoulders by a priest when carrying the Blessed Sacrament at benediction or in procession.

hu·mer·us (héw-mərəss) *n., pl.* **-meri** (-mə-rī). **1.** The long bone of the upper part of the arm, extending from the shoulder to the elbow. **2.** The corresponding bone in vertebrate animals. [New Latin, from Latin *umerus, humerus,* upper arm, shoulder.]

hu·mic (héwmik ‖ yōomik) *adj.* Of, pertaining to, or derived from humus.

hu·mid (héwmid ‖ yōomid) *adj.* Containing or marked by a high amount of moisture; oppressively damp: *humid weather.* See Synonyms at **wet.** [Old French *humide,* from Latin *(h)ūmidus,* from *(h)ūmēre,* to be moist.] —**hu·mid·ly** *adv.*

hu·mid·i·fi·er (hew-míddi-fī-ər ‖ yōo-) *n.* An apparatus for increasing the humidity in a room, greenhouse, or other enclosed area.

hu·mid·i·fy (hew-míddi-fī ‖ yōo-) *tr.v.* **-fied, -fying, -fies.** To make more humid; especially, to increase the amount of water vapour in (the air). —**hu·mid·i·fi·ca·tion** (-fi-káysh'n) *n.*

hu·mid·i·stat (hew-míddi-stat ‖ yōo-) *n.* An instrument designed to indicate or control the relative humidity of the air. Also called "hygrostat". [HUMIDI(TY) + -STAT.]

hu·mid·i·ty (hew-míddəti ‖ yōo-) *n.* **1.** Dampness, especially of the air. **2.** A measure of the amount of water vapour in the air. See **absolute humidity, relative humidity.** [Middle English *humidite,* from Old French, from Latin *hūmiditās* (stem *humiditāt-*), from *hūmidus,* HUMID.]

hu·mi·dor (héwmi-dawr ‖ yōomi-) *n.* A case for the storage of cigars and other tobacco products, containing a device for keeping the humidity level constant. [From HUMID.]

hu·mil·i·ate (hew-mílli-ayt ‖ yōo-) *tr.v.* **-ated, -ating, -ates.** To lower the pride, dignity, or status of; humble or disgrace; degrade. —See Synonyms at **degrade.** [Late Latin *humiliāre,* from *humilis,* HUMBLE.] —**hu·mil·i·a·to·ry** (-ətri, -áytəri) *adj.*

hu·mil·i·a·tion (hew-mílli-áysh'n, héw-milli- ‖ yōo-) *n.* **1.** The act of humiliating; degradation. **2.** The state or condition of being humiliated; disgrace; shame.

hu·mil·i·ty (hew-mílləti ‖ yōo-) *n.* The quality or condition of being humble; lack of pride; modesty. [Middle English *humilite,* from Old French *humilite,* from Latin *humilitās* (stem *humilitāt-*), from *humilis,* HUMBLE.]

hum·ming·bird (húmming-burd) *n.* Any of numerous chiefly tropical New World birds of the family Trochilidae, usually very small in size, and having a long, slender bill, wings capable of beating very rapidly, and often brilliantly coloured plumage. [From the humming sound produced by the rapidly vibrating wings.]

hummingbird hawk moth *n.* A European hawk moth, *Macroglossum stellatarum,* that resembles a hummingbird when hovering over and feeding from flowers.

hum·mock (húmmək) *n.* Also **ham·mock** (hámmək) (for sense 2). **1.** A low mound or ridge of earth; a knoll. **2.** In the southern United States, a tract of forested land elevated above the level of an adjacent marsh. **3.** A ridge or hill of ice in an ice field. [16th century : origin obscure.] —**hum·mock·y** *adj.*

hum·mous, hum·mus (hōōmmōoss) *n.* A puree of chickpeas and oil, often flavoured with garlic, sesame seed, and lemon, and eaten as a dip or appetiser. [Arabic.]

hu·mor·al (héw-mərəl, yōo-) *adj.* Pertaining to or arising from any of the bodily humours.

hu·mor·esque (héwmə-résk, yōo-) *n.* A whimsical or playful musical composition. [German *Humoreske,* from *Humour,* humour, from English HUMOUR.]

hu·mor·ist (héw-mərist, yōo-) *n.* **1.** A person with a sharp sense of humour. **2.** A performer or writer of comedy.

hu·mor·ous (héw-mərəss, yōo-) *adj.* **1.** Appealing to the sense of humour; funny; laughable; comical: *a humorous sight.* **2.** Characterised by or expressing humour; comic; witty; droll: *a humorous speaker.* **3.** *Archaic.* Capricious. **4.** *Obsolete.* Damp; moist. —**hu·mor·ous·ly** *adv.* —**hu·mor·ous·ness** *n.*

hu·mour, U.S. **hu·mor** (héwmər, yōomər) *n.* **1.** The quality of being laughable or comical; funniness: *He saw the humour of the situation.* **2.** Something designed to induce laughter or amusement: *a story full of humour.* **3.** The ability to perceive, enjoy, or express what is comical or funny: *a sense of humour.* **4.** In medieval physiology, any of the four fluids of the body, blood, phlegm, choler (or yellow bile), and black bile, the dominance of which was thought to determine a person's character and general health. Accordingly, one's disposition might be **sanguine, phlegmatic, choleric,** or **melancholy** *(all of which see).* In this sense also called "cardinal humour". **5.** A state of mind; a mood: *in a bad humour.* **6.** Disposition; character; temperament: *a girl of a most sullen humour.* **7. a.** A sudden, unanticipated whim. **b.** Capricious or peculiar behaviour or action. **8.** *Physiology.* Any of various body fluids; especially, the **aqueous humour** or **vitreous humour** *(both of which see).* —See Synonyms at **mood, wit.** —**out of humour.** In a bad mood; irritable.
~*tr.v.* **humoured, -mouring, -mours. 1.** To comply with the whims or ideas of (another); go along with; indulge. **2.** To adapt or accommodate oneself to. [Middle English *(h)umour,* fluid from an animal or plant, one of the four principal body fluids that affected mental disposition, from Anglo-French, from Latin *(h)ūmor,* liquid, fluid.]

hu·mour·less (héwmər-ləss, yōomər-, -liss) *adj.* **1.** Devoid of a sense of humour. **2.** Said or done without humour: *a humourless laugh.* —**hu·mour·less·ly** *adv.* —**hu·mour·less·ness** *n.*

hump (hump) *n.* **1.** A rounded mass or protuberance, such as the fleshy structure on the back of a camel or over the shoulders of some cattle. **2.** A deformity of the back, due in human beings to an abnormal curvature of the spine. **3.** A low mound of earth; a hummock. **4.** *British Slang.* A feeling of depression or extreme annoyance. Often preceded by *the.* —**over the hump.** Past the worst or most difficult part of something.
~*v.* **humped, humping, humps.** —*tr.* **1.** To make into a hump; arch; round. **2.** *Informal.* To carry (something large or heavy). **3.** *Vulgar Slang.* To have sexual intercourse with. —*intr.* To bend or arch so as to become a hump. [Shortened from earlier *humpback(ed),* possibly a blend of earlier *crumpbacked* and HUNCHBACK(ED).]

hump·back (húmp-bak) *n.* **1.** An individual afflicted with an abnormally curved or humped back; a hunchback. **2.** An abnormally curved or humped back. **3.** The pathological condition, **kyphosis** *(see),* causing this. **4.** A whalebone whale, *Megaptera novaeangliae,* having a rounded back and long, knobby flippers. **5.** A salmon, *Oncorhynchus gorbuscha,* of the Pacific Ocean, the male of which has a humped back and hooked jaws. —**hump·backed** *adj.*

humpback bridge *n.* Also **humpbacked bridge.** A narrow bridge forming part of a road, having a steep incline and decline.

humped (humpt) *adj.* Having a hump: *humped cattle.*

Hum·per·dinck (hōōmpər-dingk), **Engelbert** (1854–1921). German composer. He wrote the fairy-tale opera, *Hänsel and Gretel* (1893).

humph (humf) *interj.* Used to express doubt, displeasure, or contempt.

Hum·phrey (húmfri), **Hubert Horatio** (1911–78). U.S. Democratic politician. He was vice-president (1965–69) under Lyndon Johnson. He was defeated for the presidency in 1968 by Richard Nixon, and failed to win the Democratic nomination in 1972.

hump·ty (húmpti) *n. British.* A small, low, padded seat. [From *humpty* (adjective), hunchbacked; perhaps influenced by HUMPTY DUMPTY.]

Humpty Dumpty (húmpti dúmpti) *n.* **1.** An egg-shaped character in a nursery rhyme who fell off a wall and broke into pieces. **2.** *Small* **h,** *small* **d.** *Informal.* A short, fat person.

hump·y¹ (húmpi) *adj.* **-ier, -iest. 1.** Covered with or containing humps. **2.** *British Slang.* Depressed or annoyed.

hump·y² *n., pl.* **-pies.** *Australian.* A primitive, temporary shelter or hut, often in the bush. [From a native Australian language.]

hu·mus (héw-məss ‖ yōo-) *n.* A brown or black organic substance consisting of decayed vegetable and animal matter that provides nutrients for plants and increases the ability of soil to retain water. [Latin *humus,* earth, ground, soil.]

Hun (hun) *n.* **1.** Any of a fierce barbaric race of Asiatic nomads who invaded Europe in the late fourth century A.D. and, led by Attila, overran large parts of it in the mid-fifth century. **2.** Any savage, uncivilised, or destructive person. [Old English *Hūne* and *Hūnas* (both plural), from Late Latin *Hūnī,* from Turki *Hun-yü.*]

Hu·nan or **Hu-nan** (hōō-nán). Province in south central China. Rich in mineral resources and forests, the province is especially famous for its cedar. Capital, Changsha.

hunch (hunch) *n.* **1.** An intuitive feeling or guess about something; a premonition. **2.** A hump. **3.** A lump or chunk.
~*v.* **hunched, hunching, hunches.** —*tr.* To bend, arch, or draw

up into a hump: *hunched his shoulders against the wind.* —*intr. Chiefly U.S.* To draw oneself up closely into a crouched or cramped posture: *The scared child hunched in a corner.* [16th century *(hunchbacked)* : origin unknown.]

hunch·back (húnch-bak) *n.* An individual afflicted with an abnormally curved or hunched back. See **humpback.** —**hunch·backed** *adj.*

hun·dred (hún-drəd, -drid ‖ -dərd) *n., pl.* **hundred** or **-dreds** (for senses 2, 4, and 5). *Abbr.* **h.** 1. **a.** The cardinal number that is ten more than ninety. **b.** A symbol representing this, such as 100 or C. 2. A coin or banknote worth a hundred of any unit of currency: *I've only got hundreds.* 3. The number in the third position left of the decimal point in an Arabic numeral. 4. *Plural.* **a.** An unspecified large number: *I've been there hundreds of times.* **b.** The numbers between 100 and 999: *The dress was valued in the hundreds.* 5. *Plural.* A specified era of a hundred years: *the nineteen-hundreds.* 6. Formerly an administrative division of some English and American counties. [Middle English *hundred,* Old English *hundred, hund,* from Germanic.] —**hun·dred** *adj.* —**hun·dred·fold** (-fōld) *adj. & adv.*

hundreds and thousands *pl.n.* Very small pieces of variously and brightly coloured sugar, used for covering and decorating sweets and cakes.

hun·dredth (hún-drəd-th, -drid- ‖ -dərd-) *n.* 1. The ordinal number 100 in a series. Also written 100th. 2. One of 100 equal parts. —**hun·dredth** *adj. & adv.*

hun·dred·weight (hún-drəd-wayt, -drid- ‖ -dərd-) *n., pl.* **hundredweight** or **-weights.** *Abbr.* **cwt.** 1. A unit of weight in the British Imperial System equal to 112 pounds. 2. A unit of weight in the U.S. Customary System equal to 100 pounds. Also called "short hundredweight".

Hundred Years' War *n.* A series of wars between England and France lasting from 1337 until 1453.

hung (hung). Past tense and past participle of **hang.** See Usage note at **hang.**
~*adj.* 1. With no party having a working majority. Said of a legislative assembly: *a hung parliament.* 2. So divided in opinion as to be unable to reach a verdict: *a hung jury.*

Hun·gar·i·an (hung-gaír-i-ən) *adj. Abbr.* **Hun., Hung.** Of or relating to Hungary, its people, language, or culture.
~*n.* 1. A citizen or native of Hungary; Magyar. 2. The Finno-Ugric language spoken in Hungary; Magyar.

Hungarian goulash *n.* **Goulash** (*see*).

Hungarian puli *n.* A dog, the **puli** (*see*).

Hun·ga·ry (húng-gəri), **Republic of.** Independent republic of central Europe. The country consists for the most part of plains, broken by the rivers Danube and Tisza. Hungary was part of the dual monarchy of Austria-Hungary from 1867 until 1918, when a Hungarian republic was proclaimed. After World War II the Communist party seized power and a new constitution, on the Soviet model, was established (1949). An uprising in Budapest (1956) was put down by Soviet troops. In the 1980s reform gained ground, and in 1989 a new multi-party system was announced. Free elections were held in 1990. Area, 90 030 square kilometres (35,910 square miles). Population, 10,190,000. Capital, Budapest.

hun·ger (húng-gər) *n.* 1. **a.** The weakness, debilitation, or pain caused by a prolonged lack of food; starvation. **b.** Mild discomfort or an uneasy sensation caused by a lack of food. **c.** A strong desire for food. 2. A strong desire or craving for anything: *a hunger for affection.* —*v.* **hungered, -gering, -gers.** —*intr.* 1. To have a need or desire for food. 2. To have a strong desire or craving for anything. Used with *after* or *for: Reduced to poverty, he hungered for his old life.*
~*tr.* 1. To cause to experience hunger; make hungry: *The thought of food hungered him even more.* 2. To bring or reduce to the specified state because of hunger: *hungered the terrorists into submission.* —See Synonyms at **yearn.** [Middle English *hunger,* Old English *hungor, hungur,* from Germanic.]

hunger march *n.* A procession or demonstration by the unemployed and poor to protest about their condition.

hunger strike *n.* A refusal to eat or a voluntary fast undertaken as a method of protest. —**hunger striker** *n.*

hung over *adj.* Suffering from a hangover.

hun·gry (húng-gri) *adj.* **-grier, -griest.** 1. Experiencing weakness, pain, or other discomfort from lack of food. 2. Desiring or craving food. 3. **a.** Strongly desiring or craving anything: *hungry for recognition.* **b.** Using or requiring large quantities of something: *a fuel-hungry heating system.* 4. Characterised by or expressing hunger, greed, or craving: *a hungry look.* 5. Lacking richness or fertility: *hungry soil.* [Middle English *hungri,* Old English *hungri(g),* from *hungor,* HUNGER.] —**hun·gri·ly** *adv.* —**hun·gri·ness** *n.*

hung up *adj. Slang.* 1. Emotionally or psychologically disturbed or upset. 2. Overinterested in or obsessed by something or someone. Used with *on.*

hunk (hungk) *n.* 1. *Informal.* A large piece; a chunk. 2. *Chiefly U.S. Slang.* A sexually appealing man, especially one with a powerful physique. [Probably akin to West Flemish *hunke†,* hunk of food.] —**hunk·y** *adj.*

hun·kers (húng-kərz) *pl.n.* The haunches. [Scottish, from *hunker,* to squat, perhaps from Scandinavian; akin to Old Norse *hokra,* to crouch.]

hunks (hungks) *n., pl.* **hunks.** 1. An irritable or disagreeable old person. 2. A stingy, covetous man; a miser. [17th century : origin obscure.]

hun·ky-do·ry (húng-ki-dáwri ‖ -dóri) *adj. Informal.* Perfectly all right; quite satisfactory; fine. [19th century : origin obscure.]

Hun·nish (húnnish) *adj.* 1. Of or pertaining to the Huns or their language. 2. *Sometimes small* **h.** Barbarous.
~*n.* The language of the Huns, variously classified as Turkic or Mongolian. —**Hun·nish·ness** *n.*

hunt (hunt) *v.* **hunted, hunting, hunts.** —*tr.* 1. **a.** To pursue (game or other wild animals) for food or sport. See **hunting.** **b.** To seek out; track; search for. **c.** To search for (something deliberately hidden), as in a children's game: *hunt the thimble; hunt the slipper.* 2. To search through (an area), as for game or prey. 3. To make use of (hounds or horses, for example) in hunting. 4. To drive out forcibly; chase away, especially by harassing. 5. To harass persistently; persecute. —*intr.* 1. To pursue game or other wild animals in order to capture or kill them. 2. To conduct a diligent search; seek. Often used with *for.* 3. *Aerospace.* **a.** To yaw back and forth about a flight path, as if seeking a new direction or another angle of attack. Used of aircraft, rockets, and space vehicles. **b.** To rotate up and down or back and forth without being deflected by the pilot. Used of a control surface or a rocket motor in gimbals. 4. **a.** To oscillate about a selected value or setting. Used of a control system, electric motor, engine, carburettor, or the like. **b.** To swing back and forth or to oscillate. Used of an indicator on a display or measuring instrument. —**hunt down.** To search for and locate. —**hunt out.** To search for and find. —**hunt up.** To find after searching.
~*n.* 1. The act or sport of hunting game; the chase. 2. **a.** A hunting expedition or outing. **b.** Those taking part in a hunt with horses and hounds. **c.** An organisation or group that regularly takes part in a hunt in a particular district or area. **d.** A district used regularly for hunting. 3. A diligent search or pursuit. [Middle English *hunten,* Old English *huntian,* from Germanic *huntjan* (unattested), akin to *hanthatjan* (unattested), to HENT.]

Hunt (hunt), **(Henry Cecil) John, Baron Hunt of Llanfairwaterdine** (1910–). British mountaineer. He led the 1952–53 British Everest expedition in which Sir Edmund Hillary and Tenzing Norgay became the first men to reach the summit. He wrote *The Ascent of Everest* (1953).

Hunt, (James Henry) Leigh (1784–1859). British radical essayist and journalist. He edited *The Examiner* with his brother from 1808 and they were both jailed (1813–15) for a libel on the Prince Regent.

Hunt, James (Simon Wallis) (1947–93). British racing driver. He became World Champion (1976), and won 10 Grand Prix races. He retired in mid-season, in 1979.

Hunt, (William) Holman (1827–1910). British artist, who with Rossetti and Millais formed the Pre-Raphaelite Brotherhood. His works include *The Light of the World* (1854), *The Scapegoat* (1856), and *The Miracle of the Sacred Fire* (1898).

hunt·a·way (húntə-way) *n.* A sheepdog of a breed of New Zealand origin: *"Huntaways, a New Zealand breed compounded from labradors, retrievers, cattle dogs and 'possibly sort of Kiwi dingoes' "* (Sunday Times).

hunt·er (húntər) *n.* 1. One that hunts; especially, a person who hunts game for food or sport, or who captures wild animals. 2. A horse bred or trained for use in hunting, typically a fast, strong jumper. 3. A dog bred or trained for use in hunting. 4. A person who searches for or seeks something. Usually used in combination: *a house-hunter.* 5. A watch with a hinged metal covering or case protecting the face and its glass covering. Compare **half-hunter.**

hunt·er-gath·er·er *n.* A member of a group of primitive people, such as the Bushmen of the Kalahari, whose subsistence is based on hunting and collecting fruit and other plant foods.

hunt·er-kill·er (húntər-kíllər) *adj.* Designating any of a class of submarines designed to locate, chase, and destroy enemy submarines.

hunter's moon *n.* The full moon following the harvest moon.

hunt·ing (húnting) *n.* 1. The pursuit of animals as a sport, especially: **a.** *British.* The hunting of foxes or other vermin using packs of hounds but not guns. **b.** *U.S.* The hunting of wild animals, game birds, and the like using guns. 2. The act of conducting a serious

HUNGARY

search for something. Often used in combination: *job-hunting; house-hunting.*
~*adj.* Pertaining to or used in the sport of hunting: *a hunting horn; hunting dogs.*

Hun·ting·don and Pe·ter·bor·ough (húnting-dən; péetər-brə, -bərə ‖ -burrə, -burrō). Former county in east central England, created in 1965 by the merger of the counties of Huntingdonshire and the Soke of Peterborough. In 1974 it was absorbed into Cambridgeshire and in 1998 Peterborough became a separate Unitary Authority area.

hunt·ing-ground (hunting-grownd) *n.* **1.** The location of a hunt. **2.** An area regarded as a potential source of some sought-after object.

hunting leopard *n.* The **cheetah** (*see*).

hunting lodge *n.* A small house or lodge located in a hunting district and occupied by hunters. Also called "**hunting box**".

hunting pink *n. Chiefly British.* **1.** The scarlet coat worn by foxhunters. **2.** The colour of such coats.

hunting spider *n.* The **wolf spider** (*see*).

hunt·ress (hún-triss, -trəss, -tress) *n.* **1.** A woman or female that hunts. **2.** *Rare.* A mare used for hunting.

hunts·man (húnts-mən) *n., pl.* **-men** (-mən, -men). **1.** A person who hunts; a hunter. **2.** One who manages a pack of foxhounds, harriers, beagles, or the like, and handles them when they are hunting.

Hu·on pine (héw-on) *n.* A coniferous tree, *Lagarostrobus franklinii,* of Southeast Asia, Australia, and Chile, having scalelike leaves and berry-like fruits. [After the River *Huon,* Tasmania.]

Hupeh or **Hupei.** See **Hubei.**

hur·dies (húrdiz) *pl.n. Scottish.* The buttocks or haunches.

hur·dle (húrd'l) *n.* **1.** A light, portable barrier, usually consisting of two uprights between which a horizontal bar may be hung at varying heights and which must be jumped by competitors in certain races. **2.** *Plural.* A race for horses or men in which a series of such hurdles are used. **3.** Any obstacle or problem that must be overcome. **4.** *Chiefly British.* A portable section of fencing made of intertwined branches or wattle and used chiefly for fencing in sheep. **5.** *British.* A frame or sledge formerly used to carry condemned traitors to their executions.
~*v.* **hurdled, -dling, -dles.** —*tr.* **1.** To jump over (a barrier) in or as if in a race. **2.** To enclose with hurdles. **3.** To overcome or successfully deal with (an obstacle or problem). —*intr.* To jump over barriers in or as if in a race. [Middle English *hurdel, hirdle,* Old English *hyrdel,* from Germanic.] —**hur·dler** *n.*

hur·dy-gur·dy (húrdi-gurdi, -gúrdi) *n., pl.* **-dies.** **1.** A medieval instrument shaped like a lute, played by street musicians with a crank that causes a resin-covered wheel to scrape across the strings. **2.** *Informal.* Any musical instrument played by turning a crank, such as a barrel organ. [Probably imitative.]

hurl (hurl) *v.* **hurled, hurling, hurls.** —*tr.* **1.** To throw with great force; fling; pitch. **2.** To move or impel vigorously; thrust. **3.** To exclaim vehemently; shout out: *hurl abuse.* —*intr.* **1.** To play the game of hurling. **2.** *Archaic.* To move with great speed, force, or violence; hurtle. —See Synonyms at **throw.**
~*n.* A forceful pitch or throw. [Middle English *h(o)urlen†,* to be driven with great force, throw, rush on.] —**hurl·er** *n.*

hur·ley (húrli) *n.* **1.** The stick used in the game of hurling. Also called "eaman". **2.** The game of hurling. [From HURL.]

hurl·ing (húrling) *n.* Also **hur·ley** (húrli). A fast Irish game resembling lacrosse and hockey, played between teams of 15 with broadbladed sticks and a hard ball. [From HURL.]

hur·ly-bur·ly (húrli-burli, -búrli) *n., pl.* **-lies.** Turbulence; commotion; disorder.
~*adj.* Full of noise or commotion. [Earlier *hurling and burling,* reduplication of *hurling,* tumult, from Middle English, gerund of HURL.]

Hu·ron (héwr-ən, -on ‖ yoór-) *n., pl.* **-rons** or collectively **Huron.** **1.** A member of a confederation of four tribes of Iroquoianspeaking North American Indians formerly inhabiting the region east of Lake Huron and the St. Lawrence Valley. **2.** The Iroquoian language spoken among these tribes. [French, "one who has dishevelled hair", boor, from *hure,* dishevelled head, from Old French *hure†.*] —**Hu·ron** *adj.*

Huron, Lake. One of the five Great Lakes, on the border between the United States and Canada. It is the second largest of the group of lakes. It forms part of the Great Lakes-St. Lawrence seaway system and is navigated by ocean-going vessels.

hurray, hurrah. Variants of **hooray.**

hur·ri·cane (húrri-kən ‖ *chiefly U.S. and West Indies* -kayn) *n.* **1. a.** A violent tropical cyclone originating in the Gulf of Mexico or Caribbean Sea, travelling north, northwest, or northeast from its point of origin, and usually involving heavy rains and thunder. **b.** A similar cyclone off the north of Australia. **2.** Wind exceeding 32.7 metres per second, force 12 on the Beaufort scale. See Synonyms at **wind.** [Spanish *huracán* and Portuguese *furacão,* both from Carib *huracan, furacan.*]

hurricane deck *n.* The upper deck on a ship such as a passenger steamer.

hurricane lamp *n.* A lamp consisting of a candle or electric bulb covered by a glass chimney.

hur·ried (húrrid ‖ húrreed) *adj.* **1.** Obliged to move or act rapidly; rushed. **2.** Done in great haste: *a hurried tour.* —**hur·ried·ly** *adv.* —**hur·ried·ness** *n.*

hur·ry (húrri) *v.* **-ried, -rying, -ries.** —*intr.* To move or act with

haste. Often used with *up.* —*tr.* **1.** To cause to move or act rapidly or more rapidly; hasten: *hurry the children.* **2.** To cause to move or act too quickly; rush: *hurried them into marriage.* **3.** To hasten to completion; expedite: *This should hurry things along.* —See Synonyms at **speed.**
~*n., pl.* **hurries.** **1.** The act of hurrying; hastened progress. **2. a.** The need or wish to hurry: *There's no hurry.* **b.** A condition or state of urgency or eagerness: *Are you in a great hurry to leave?* —**in a hurry.** *Informal.* **1.** Eagerly; willingly. **2.** With no difficulty; with ease. [16th century (Shakespeare) : perhaps of dialectal origin, imitative of agitation and commotion.]

hurt (hurt) *v.* **hurt, hurting, hurts.** —*tr.* **1. a.** To cause physical damage or pain to; injure; wound. **b.** To produce a feeling of pain in (a person or living creature): *The tight collar hurt his neck.* **2.** To cause to suffer mental or emotional anguish; distress or offend. **3.** To harm; be prejudicial to; impair: *hurt his chances.* —*intr.* **1. a.** To have a feeling of pain or discomfort: *His leg hurts.* **b.** To produce a feeling of pain: *That collar hurts.* **2.** To cause distress, hardship, or damage: *The tax bill hurts.* —See Synonyms at **injure.**
~*n.* **1.** Something that hurts; a pain, injury, or wound. **2.** Mental suffering; anguish. **3.** A wrong; damage; harm. [Middle English *hurten, hirten,* to strike, harm, from Old French *hurter,* from Gallo-Roman *hūrtare†* (unattested).] —**hurt·er** *n.*

hurt·er (húrt-ər) *n.* A concrete, stone, or iron block or post placed at the corner of a building to protect it from damage by passing traffic. [Middle English, shoulder of an axle against which the nave strikes, from Old French *hurtoir,* from *herter,* to strike, knock against, HURT.]

hurt·ful (húrtf'l) *adj.* Causing hurt or injury; painful; damaging. —**hurt·ful·ly** *adv.* —**hurt·ful·ness** *n.*

hur·tle (húrt'l) *v.* **-tled, -tling, -tles.** —*intr.* **1.** To move with or as if with great speed and often with a rushing or crashing noise: *The river hurtles over the waterfall.* **2.** To collide violently; crash. —*tr.* To throw or send forcibly or violently; hurl. [Middle English *hurtlen,* dash one thing against another, collide, frequentative of *hurten,* to strike, HURT.]

Hus, Jan. See **John Huss.**

Hu·sák (hŏŏ-saak, hŏŏ-), **Gustáv** (1913–91). Czechoslovak communist leader. In April 1954, in a party purge, Husák was sentenced to life imprisonment. He was later released and, under Alexander Dubček, became a vice-premier. After Russian intervention to halt the Dubček reforms in 1968, Husák emerged as leader of the proSoviet faction. He became First Secretary of the Czech Communist Party (1969), Secretary-General (1971) and President of Czechoslovakia (1975). He was ousted from his positions in 1988.

hus·band (húzbənd) *n.* **1.** *Abbr.* **h., H.** A man joined to a woman in marriage; a woman's spouse. **2.** *Archaic.* **a.** A manager or steward. **b.** One who manages his affairs in the specified way.
~*tr.v.* **husbanded, -banding, -bands.** **1.** To spend or use economically; budget; conserve: *husband one's energy.* **2.** *Archaic.* **a.** To marry. **b.** *Archaic.* To find a husband for. **3.** *Archaic.* To till (land). [Middle English *housbonde, hus(e)bonde,* husband, husbandman, Old English *hūsbonda,* master of a household, husband, from Old Norse *hūsbōndi* : *hūs,* house, from Germanic *hūsam* (unattested), HOUSE + *bōndi,* earlier *bōandi, būandi,* present participle of *bōa, būa,* to dwell.]

hus·band·man (húzbənd-mən) *n., pl.* **-men** (-mən, -men). One whose occupation is husbandry; a farmer. [Middle English *housbondeman* : *housbonde,* husbandman, HUSBAND + MAN.]

hus·band·ry (húzbəndri) *n.* **1. a.** The cultivation of plants or the raising of livestock; farming; agriculture. **b.** The application of scientific principles to a branch of farming, especially animal breeding: *animal husbandry.* **2.** The careful management of resources; conservation. [Middle English *housbondrie* : *housbonde,* husbandman, HUSBAND + -(E)RY.]

hush (hush) *v.* **hushed, hushing, hushes.** —*tr.* **1.** To cause to be silent; quieten. **2.** To quell or still; calm; soothe. —*intr.* To be or become silent or still. —**hush up.** To prevent from becoming publicly known; suppress; conceal.
~*n.* A silence; stillness; quiet.
~*interj.* Used to demand quiet or to calm a child. [Back-formation from earlier *husht* (interjection), from Middle English *huissht.*]

hush·a·bye (húshə-bī) *interj.* Used to soothe a child or lull him to sleep. [HUSH + *-bye* (as in *goodbye*).]

hush-hush (húsh-húsh) *adj. Informal.* Secret; confidential.

hush money *n. Informal.* A bribe or payment made to keep something secret.

husk (husk) *n.* **1.** The membranous or green outer envelope of many fruits and seeds. **2.** The shell or outer covering of anything, especially when worthless.
~*tr.v.* **husked, husking, husks.** To remove the husk or husks from. [Middle English *husk(e),* probably from Middle Dutch *hūskijn,* diminutive of *hūs,* house, from Germanic *hūsam* (unattested), HOUSE.] —**husk·er** *n.*

husk·y¹ (húski) *adj.* **-ier, -iest.** **1.** Having a hoarse, often breathy quality, either naturally or from overuse or emotion. Said of a voice or vocal sounds. **2.** Like or resembling a husk. **3.** Full of or containing husks. **4.** *Informal.* Rugged, strong, and burly.
~*n., pl.* **huskies.** A husky person. [Originally, "dry as a husk".] —**husk·i·ly** *adv.* —**husk·i·ness** *n.*

hus·ky² *n., pl.* **-kies.** **1.** *Sometimes capital* H. A dog of a breed developed in Siberia for pulling sledges, having a dense, variously coloured coat, small erect ears, and a bushy tail curled over the back.

Also called "Siberian husky". **2.** A dog of any of several similar breeds of Arctic origin. [Probably a shortened variant of ESKIMO.]

huss (huss) *n.* A type of dogfish, *Scyliorhinus stellaris,* that is used as food. Also called "nurse hound".

Huss, (huss, *German and Czech* hŏŏss), **John** also known as Jan Hus (1369?–1415). Czech religious reformer. Huss attacked the corruption of the clergy and was excommunicated in 1412, when he denounced the bulls of the antipope John XXII. In exile he wrote *De Ecclesia,* which accorded the state the right to supervise the church. His death by burning made him a national hero.

hus·sar (hŏŏ-zár) *n.* **1.** A member of a light cavalry regiment, having dress uniforms, typically with much frogging. **2.** A horseman of the Hungarian light cavalry that was organised during the 15th century. [Hungarian *huszár,* "freebooter", hussar, from Old Serbian *husar, gusar,* from Old Italian *corsaro,* CORSAIR.]

Hus·sein (hŏŏ-sáyn) **(Ibn Talal)** (1935–). King of Jordan from 1953. Hussein has used diplomacy and a fiercely loyal militia to retain his throne. He suffered military defeat by Israel in 1967, but he has since quelled Arab guerrilla attacks.

Hussein, Saddam (1937–). Iraqi politician, president from 1979. He has ruled through a revolutionary council, repressing opponents including Shia Muslims and Kurdish separatists. In 1980 he launched a long and inconclusive war against Iran, and in 1990 provoked the Gulf War by invading Kuwait. In 1995 he was confirmed as president for seven years more.

Huss·ite (húss-īt, hŏŏss-) *n.* A follower of John Huss.
~*adj.* Of or pertaining to John Huss or his religious theories.
—**Huss·it·ism** (-iz'm) *n.*

hus·sy (hússi, húzzi) *n., pl.* **-sies. 1.** A saucy or flippant girl. **2.** A lewd or sexually promiscuous woman. [Variant of HOUSEWIFE.]

hust·ings (hústingz) *pl.n. Sometimes used with a singular verb.* **1.** *British.* A court formerly held in London. **2.** *British.* A platform from which (prior to the Ballot Act of 1872) candidates for Parliament addressed the electors. **3.** Political campaigning, especially in connection with an election: *a veteran of the hustings.* [Middle English *husting,* an assembly, Old English *hústing,* from Old Norse *hus-thing,* "house assembly" : *hūs,* house, from Germanic *hūsam* (unattested), HOUSE + *thing,* assembly.]

hus·tle (húss'l) *v.* **-tled, -tling, -tles.** —*tr.* **1.** To jostle or shove roughly. **2.** To usher hurriedly or urgently: *hustle the prisoner onto a plane.* **3.** To hurry along; cause or urge to proceed hurriedly: *hustled the board into a quick decision.* **4.** *Slang.* To obtain (money) in questionable ways: *He hustles a living somehow.* **b.** To sell by high-pressure means. —*intr.* **1.** To jostle and push. **2.** *Informal.* To work busily and quickly. **3.** *Slang.* To use vigorous, aggressive, or questionable means in order to make money. **4.** *Chiefly U.S. Slang.* To solicit customers for or as a prostitute.
~*n.* **1.** The act or an instance of hustling. **2.** *Informal.* A source of income; a job or business, especially one of questionable legality. **3.** *Informal.* Hurried activity. Often used in the phrase *hustle and bustle.* [Originally to shake back and forth, from Middle Dutch *husselen,* frequentative of *hutsen,* to shake, from (unattested) Germanic *khut-* (probably imitative).] —**hus·tler** *n.*

Hus·ton (héwstən), **John (Marcellus),** (1906–87). U.S. film director. He began his film career as a scriptwriter (1938), but later made successful action films, including *The Maltese Falcon* (1941), *The African Queen* (1951), and *The Man Who would be King* (1975).

hut (hut) *n.* **1.** A makeshift or crudely constructed dwelling or shelter. **2.** *Military.* A temporary structure for sheltering troops or arms. **3.** *Australian.* A building housing employees on a cattle or sheep station.
~*v.* **hutted, hutting, huts.** —*tr.* To shelter or store in a hut. —*intr.* To live or take shelter in a hut. [Old French *hutte,* from Middle High German *hütte,* or Old High German *hutt(e)a.*]

hutch (huch) *n.* **1.** A box, pen, or coop, usually having a wire-mesh side, for small animals, especially rabbits. **2.** A small house or hut. Used derogatorily. [Middle English *huche,* chest, from Old French *huche, huge,* from Medieval Latin *hutica†.*]

hutch·ie (hŏŏchi) *n. Australian.* A waterproof sheet draped over a small tree, an upright stick, or the like to make a temporary shelter. [From HUTCH.]

hut·cir·cle (hút-súrk'l) *n. Archaeology.* A ring or partial ring of stones or earth indicating the site of a simple prehistoric dwelling.

hut·ment (hútmənt) *n.* An encampment of huts.

Hut·ter·ite (húttər-īt, hŏŏtər-) *n.* A member of an **Anabaptist** *(see)* sect, originating in Moravia and now living in parts of Canada and the United States. Hutterites are mainly farmers, and hold property in common. [After J. *Hutter,* 16th-century Moravian Anabaptist.]

Hut·ton (hútt'n), **James** (1726–97). Scottish geologist and farmer. His principle of **uniformitarianism** (1785), describing the igneous origins of rocks and minerals, forms the basis of modern geology.

Hutton, Sir Leonard, also known as Len Hutton (1916–90). English cricketer. Hutton played for Yorkshire and England, and made a record Test score of 364 against the Australians in 1938.

Hux·ley (húksli), **Aldous (Leonard)** (1894–1963). British novelist and essayist. In *Brave New World* (1932), he painted a grim picture of a future utopia, a scientifically organised society in which conventional human suffering had been eliminated. His fascination with mysticism shows in *Eyeless in Gaza* (1936).

Huxley, Sir Julian (Sorell) (1887–1975). British biologist and brother of Aldous. He was professor of zoology at King's College, London (1925–27); secretary of the Zoological Society of London (1935–42); and the first director-general of U.N.E.S.C.O. (1946–48).

He was knighted in 1958. Huxley advocated the application of scientific principles to moral, social, and political issues.

Huxley, Thomas Henry (1825–95). British biologist, who championed Darwin's theory of evolution. He was the grandfather of Aldous and Julian Huxley. His works include *Zoological Evidences as to Man's Place in Nature* (1863) and *Science and Culture* (1881).

Huy·gens (hígənz), **Christiaan** (1629–95). Dutch mathematician, astronomer, and physicist. He invented the micrometer (1655), discovered Saturn's rings (1655), pioneered the use of the pendulum in clocks (about 1656), and formulated **Huygens' principle**.

Huygens' principle *n. Physics.* The principle that any point on a wave front may be regarded as the source of a secondary wave and that the position of the wave front at any time is determined by the envelope at that time of the secondary waves arising from a previous wavefront. [After Christiaan HUYGENS.]

huz·za, huz·zah (hŏŏ-záa, hu-) *n. Archaic.* A shout of encouragement or triumph; a cheer.
~*interj. Archaic.* Used to express joy, encouragement, appreciation, or the like.
~*v.* **huzzaed, huzzaing, huzzas.** *Archaic.* —*intr.* To shout "huzza"; cheer. —*tr.* To cheer or encourage with shouts of huzza. [16th century : perhaps of nautical origin.]

H.V. high voltage.

H.W., h.w. 1. high water. **2.** *Cricket.* hit wicket.

Hwang Ho. See **Huang He.**

hwyl (hŏŏ-il) *n. Welsh.* Passionate, poetic fervour; emotional eloquence.

hy·a·cinth (hí-ə-sinth) *n.* **1.** Any of several bulbous plants of the genus *Hyacinthus,* native to the Mediterranean region, having narrow leaves and a terminal cluster of variously coloured, usually very fragrant flowers; especially, the widely cultivated species *H. orientalis.* **2.** Any of several similar or related plants, such as the **grape hyacinth** *(see).* **3.** A plant, perhaps a lily, gladiolus, or iris, that, according to Greek mythology, sprang from the blood of the slain Hyacinthus. **4.** Deep purplish blue to vivid violet. **5.** A reddish or cinnamon-coloured variety of transparent zircon, used as a gemstone. Also called "jacinth". [Latin *hyacinthus,* from Greek *huakinthos,* wild hyacinth (connected by folk etymology with HYACINTHUS), of Mediterranean origin.] —**hy·a·cin·thine** (-sín-thīn ‖ -thin) *adj.*

hyacinth bean *n.* A twining vine, *Dolichos lablab,* of the Old World tropics, having purple or white flowers and edible pods and seeds.

Hy·a·cin·thus (hí-ə-sínthəss). *Greek Mythology.* A beautiful youth loved but accidentally killed by Apollo, from whose blood Apollo caused the hyacinth to grow.

Hy·a·des (hí-ə-deez) *pl.n.* **1.** *Greek Mythology.* The five daughters of Atlas and sisters of the Pleiades, placed by Zeus in the heavens. **2.** *Astronomy.* A cluster of five stars in the constellation Taurus, supposed by ancient astronomers to indicate rain when they rose with the Sun.

hyaena. Variant of **hyena.**

hy·a·lin (hí-ə-lin) *n.* Also **hy·a·line** (-lin, -leen, -līn). **1.** *Physiology.* The uniform matrix of hyaline cartilage. **2.** *Pathology.* A transparent substance occurring in certain degenerative skin conditions. [Greek *hualos†,* glass + -IN.]

hy·a·line (hí-ə-lin, -leen, -līn) *adj.* Resembling glass; glassy; translucent or transparent.
~*n.* **1.** *Archaic & Poetic.* Something having a glassy or transparent appearance, such as a clear sky or a calm lake. **2.** Variant of **hyalin.** [Late Latin *hyalinus,* from Greek *hualinos,* of crystal or glass, from *hualos, huelos†,* crystalline stone, glass.]

hyaline cartilage *n.* A common type of cartilage that has a glassy, translucent appearance and a bluish colour, which in the adult is composed of cells in a seemingly homogeneous, translucent matrix, as in joints, and which in the foetus forms most of the skeleton.

hyaline membrane disease *n.* **Respiratory distress syndrome.**

hy·a·lite (hí-ə-līt) *n.* A clear, colourless opal. [German *Hyalit,* from Greek *hualos†,* glass, crystal.]

hyalo-, hyal- *comb. form.* Indicates glass or glassy material; for example, **hyaloplasm.** [Greek *hualos,* glass.]

hy·a·loid (hí-ə-loyd) *adj.* Glassy or transparent in appearance; hyaline. [Greek *hualoeidēs :* *hualos,* glass (see **hyaline**) + -OID.]

hyaloid membrane *n.* The transparent membrane that separates the vitreous humour of the eye from the retina.

hy·a·lo·plasm (hí-ə-lō-plaz'm) *n.* The clear, fluid portion of cytoplasm, as distinguished from included granular and netlike components. [German *Hyaloplasma :* Greek *hualos†,* crystal + PLASM.] —**hy·a·lo·plas·mic** (-plázmik) *adj.*

hy·al·ur·on·ic acid (hí-əl-yoor-ónnik, -oor-) *n.* A mucopolysaccharide that is present in connective tissue and in the synovial fluid around joints. [HYAL(O)- + Greek *ouron,* urine.]

hy·al·ur·on·i·dase (hí-əl-yoor-ónni-dayz, -oor-, -dayss) *n.* An enzyme that breaks down hyaluronic acid, thereby making the fluid in which it is found less viscous. [HYAL(O)- + Greek *ouron,* urine + -ID + -ASE.]

hy·brid (híbrid) *n. Abbr.* **hyb. 1.** *Genetics.* The offspring of genetically dissimilar parents or stock; especially, the offspring produced by breeding plants or animals of different varieties, species, or races. **2.** Something of mixed origin or composition. **3.** A word whose elements are derived from different languages. [Latin *hybrida, hibrida†,* hybrid, mongrel.] —**hy·brid** *adj.* —**hy·brid·ism** *n.* —**hy·brid·i·ty** (hī-bríddəti) *n.*

hybrid circuit *n.* An integrated electronic circuit formed from a number of distinct integrated circuits interconnected on a substrate. Compare **monolithic circuit.**

hybrid computer *n.* A computer that combines elements of both a digital and an analog computer; especially, one in which an analog input is converted to digital form for fast processing.

hy·brid·ise, hy·brid·ize (hī́brid-īz) *v.* **-ised, -ising, -ises.** —*tr.* To cause to produce hybrids; crossbreed. —*intr.* To produce hybrids. —**hy·brid·i·sa·tion** (-ī-záysh'n ‖ *U.S.* -i-) *n.* —**hy·brid·is·er** *n.*

hybrid vigour *n.* **Heterosis** *(see).*

hybris. Variant of **hubris.**

hy·da·thode (hī́də-thōd) *n.* The structure in plants through which **guttation** *(see)* occurs, most commonly on the leaves. [Greek *hudōr* (stem *hudat-*), water + *hodos,* way.]

hy·da·tid (hī́də-tid) *n.* **1.** A cyst formed as a result of infestation by a tapeworm, *Echinococcus granulosus,* in a larval stage. **2.** The encysted larva of *E. granulosus.* Also called "hydatid cyst". [Greek *hudatis* (stem *hudatid-*), watery vesicle, hydatid, from *hudōr* (stem *hudat-*), water.] —**hyda·tid** *adj.*

hydatid disease *n.* The disease caused by the presence of hydatids in the liver, lungs, or brain, characterised by malignant tumours or tissue damage. Also called "echinococciasis", "echinococcosis".

Hyde. See **Jekyll and Hyde.**

Hyde Park (hīd). Ancient park in central London, occupying 146 hectares (360 acres) west of Park Lane. It became a royal deer park under Henry VIII. Charles I opened it to the public in 1635.

Hy·der·a·bad¹ (hí-drə-bad, -dərə-, -bád). Former state in south central India, since 1956 partitioned among the states of Karnataka, Maharashtra, and Andhra Pradesh. It is an almost entirely agricultural region, lying within the Deccan plateau. The city of Hyderabad, formerly the capital of the state of the same name, is now the capital of Andhra Pradesh.

Hyderabad². Capital city of the province of Sind, in southern Pakistan. It is a manufacturing centre and the third largest city in Pakistan.

hy·dra¹ (hí-drə) *n., pl.* **-dras** or **-drae** (-dree). Any of various small, freshwater polyps of the genus *Hydra* and related genera, having a naked, cylindrical body and an oral opening surrounded by tentacles. [New Latin *Hydra,* HYDRA (so called because polyps may reproduce themselves from parts cut off).]

hydra² *n.* A multifarious source of evil, trouble, or destruction that cannot be eradicated by a single attempt. [After HYDRA.]

Hy·dra¹ (hí-drə). *Greek Mythology.* A many-headed monster that sprouted two heads for each one cut off, but was finally slain by Hercules who cauterised each neck after severing its head. [Middle English *Ydre,* from Old French, from Latin *Hydra,* from Greek *Hudra,* from *hudra,* water serpent.]

Hydra² *n.* A constellation in the equatorial region of the southern sky near Cancer, Libra, and Centaurus. Also called the "Snake". [After HYDRA.]

hy·drac·id (hī-drássid) *n.* An acid, such as hydrocyanic acid, that contains no oxygen. [HYDR(O)- + ACID.]

hy·dran·ge·a (hī-dráyn-jə, -ji-ə) *n.* Any of various shrubs or trees of the genus *Hydrangea,* cultivated for their large, flat-topped or rounded clusters of white, pink, or blue flowers. [New Latin, "water vessel" (from the cuplike shape of the seed pod): HYDR(O)- + Greek *angos,* vessel, pitcher (see **angiology**).]

hy·drant (hí-drənt) *n.* An outlet from a water main consisting of an upright pipe with one or more nozzles or spouts. See also **fire hydrant.** [HYDR(O)- + -ANT.]

hy·dranth (hí-dranth) *n. Zoology.* A polyp in a hydroid colony that is specialised for feeding. [HYDRO- + Greek *anthos,* flower.]

hy·drar·gy·rism (hī-drárji-riz'm) *n.* Also **hy·drar·gy·ri·a** (hídraar-jírri-ə, -jéeri-). *Pathology.* **Mercurialism** *(see).* [From New Latin *hydrargyrum,* from Latin *hydrargyrus,* from Greek *hudrarguros,* "silver water" : HYDR(O)- + *aguros,* silver.]

hy·dras·tine (hī-dráss-teen, -tin) *n.* A poisonous white alkaloid, $C_{21}H_{21}NO_6$, obtained from the root of the goldenseal, *Hydrastis canadensis,* and formerly used to treat uterine haemorrhage. [From HYDRASTIS.]

hy·dras·tis (hī-drástiss) *n.* Any plant of the genus *Hydrastis,* having ornamental foliage and fruits, including the **goldenseal** *(see).* [New Latin *Hydrastis* (genus) : hydro- + -astis†.]

hy·drate (hí-drayt) *n.* A compound containing water combined in a definite ratio, the water being retained or regarded as being retained in its molecular state.
~*v.* (hī-dráyt ‖ hí-drayt). **hydrated, -drating, -drates.** —*tr.* To combine with water; especially, to cause to form a hydrate. —*intr.* To become a hydrate. [HYDR(O)- + -ATE.] —**hy·dra·tion** (-dráysh'n) *n.* —**hy·dra·tor** (-ər) *n.*

hy·drat·ed (hí-dráytid ‖ hí-draytid) *adj.* Chemically combined with water; especially, existing in the form of a hydrate.

hy·drau·lic (hī-dráwlik, -dróllik) *adj.* **1.** Of, involving, moved, or operated by a fluid, especially water, under pressure. **2.** Of or pertaining to hydraulics. [Latin *hydraulicus,* from Greek *hudraulis,* a water organ invented by Ctesibius in the second century B.C. : HYDR(O)- + *aulos,* tube, pipe.] —**hy·drau·li·cal·ly** *adv.*

hydraulic brake *n.* A brake in which the braking force is transmitted to the braking surface by a compressed fluid.

hydraulic cement *n.* A cement capable of solidifying under water. See **Portland cement.**

hydraulic press *n.* A machine in which a large force is exerted on the larger of two pistons in a pair of hydraulically coupled cylinders by means of a relatively small force applied to the smaller piston.

hydraulic ram *n.* **1.** A water pump in which the downward flow of naturally running water is intermittently halted by a valve so that the flow is forced upward through an open pipe into a reservoir. **2.** The large output piston of a hydraulic press.

hy·drau·lics (hī-dráwliks, -drólliks) *n. Used with a singular verb.* The physical science and technology of the static and dynamic behaviour of fluids. Also called "fluid mechanics".

hydraulic suspension *n.* A form of motor-vehicle suspension in which springs are replaced by hydraulic devices consisting of a piston moving in a cylinder filled with fluid. See **hydroelastic suspension.**

hy·dra·zine (hí-drə-zeen, -zin) *n.* A colourless, fuming, corrosive, hygroscopic liquid, H_2NNH_2, used in jet and rocket fuels. [HYDR(O)- + AZ(O)- + -INE.]

hy·dra·zo·ic acid (hí-drə-zṓ-ik) *n.* A colourless, highly explosive liquid, HN_3, that forms explosive salts, called azides, when combined with heavy metals. [HYDR(O)- + AZO- + -IC.]

hy·dric (hí́drik) *adj.* **1.** Of, containing, or pertaining to hydrogen. **2.** Pertaining to, characterised by, or requiring considerable moisture. [HYDR(O)- + -IC.]

hy·dride (hí́drīd) *n.* A compound of hydrogen with another, more electropositive element or group. [HYDR(O)- + -IDE.]

hy·dri·od·ic acid (hí́dri-óddik) *n.* A clear, colourless or pale-yellow aqueous solution of hydrogen iodide, HI, that is a strong acid and reducing agent. [HYDR(O)- + IODIC ACID.]

hy·dro (hí́drō) *n., pl.* **hydros. 1.** A hotel or similar establishment, especially at a spa resort, providing hydropathic treatment. **2.** *Canadian.* **a.** A power station. **b.** Electricity.
~*adj. Informal.* Hydroelectric.

hydro-, hydr– *comb. form.* Indicates: **1.** Water; for example, **hydrous, hydroelectric. 2.** Liquid; for example, **hydrometallurgy, hydrostatic. 3.** Composed of or combined with hydrogen; for example, **hydrochloride, hydrosulphide. 4.** Hydroid; for example, **hydrozoan.** [Greek *hudōr,* water.]

hy·dro·bro·mic acid (hí́drə-brṓmik) *n.* A clear, colourless or faintly yellow, highly acidic and corrosive aqueous solution of hydrogen bromide, HBr, used in the manufacture of bromides.

hy·dro·car·bon (hí́drə-kárbən) *n.* Any of numerous organic compounds, such as benzene and methane, that contain only carbon and hydrogen.

hy·dro·cele (hí́drō-seel, hí́drə-) *n.* A pathological accumulation of serous fluid in a bodily cavity, especially in the testicles. [Latin *hydrocēlē,* from Greek *hudrokēlē* : HYDRO- + -CELE.]

hy·dro·cel·lu·lose (hí́drō-sél/lew-lōz, -lōss) *n.* A gelatinous form of hydrated cellulose, made by treating cellulose with acid, alkali, or water and used in making rayon, mercerised cotton, and paper.

hy·dro·ceph·a·lus (hí́drō-séffə-ləss, hí́drə-, -kéffə-) *n.* Also **hy·dro·ceph·a·ly** (-li). A usually congenital condition in which an abnormal accumulation of cerebrospinal fluid in the cerebral ventricles causes enlargement of the skull and compression of the brain. In nontechnical usage, also called "water on the brain". [Late Latin, from Greek *hudrokephalon : hudōr* + *kephalē,* head.] —**hy·dro·ce·phal·ic** (-si-fál-ik, -ki-), **hy·dro·ceph·a·loid** (-séffə-loyd, -kéffə-), **hy·dro·ceph·a·lous** *adj.*

hy·dro·chlo·ric acid (hí́drə-kláwrik, -klórrik ‖ -klórik) *n.* A clear, colourless, fuming, poisonous, highly acidic, aqueous solution of hydrogen chloride, HCl, used in petroleum production, as a chemical intermediate, in ore reduction, food processing, pickling, and metal cleaning. Formerly called "spirits of salt".

hy·dro·chlo·ride (hí́drə-kláwrīd ‖ -klōr-) *n.* A compound resulting or regarded as resulting from the reaction of hydrochloric acid with an organic base.

hy·dro·cor·al (hí́drō-kórrəl ‖ *U.S. also* -káwrəl) *n.* Any of various colonial marine hydrozoans of the order Hydrocorallinae, having a limestone skeleton and resembling the corals. See **millepore.**

hy·dro·cor·ti·sone (hí́drō-kórti-zōn, hí́drə-, -sōn) *n.* A bitter, crystalline hormone, $C_{21}H_{30}O_5$, derived from the adrenal cortex, and having activity and medical uses similar to those of **cortisone** *(see).* Also called "cortisol".

hy·dro·cy·an·ic acid (hí́drō-sī-ánnik) *n.* A colourless, volatile, extremely toxic, flammable, aqueous solution of hydrogen cyanide, HCN, used in the manufacture of dyes, fumigants, and plastics. Also called "prussic acid", "hydrogen cyanide".

hy·dro·dy·nam·ic (hí́drō-dī-námmik) *adj.* **1.** Of or pertaining to hydrodynamics. **2.** Of, pertaining to, or operated by the force of liquid in motion. —**hy·dro·dy·nam·i·cal·ly** *adv.*

hy·dro·dy·nam·ics (hí́drō-dī-námmiks) *n. Used with a singular verb.* The dynamics of fluids, especially incompressible fluids, in motion. Also called "hydromechanics".

hy·dro·e·lec·tric (hí́drō-i-léktrik) *adj.* **1.** Generating electricity by conversion of the energy of running water. **2.** Using or involving electricity so generated. —**hy·dro·e·lec·tric·i·ty** (-i-lék-tríssəti, -íl-lek-, -éllek-, -eelek-, -trízzəti) *n.*

hy·dro·flu·or·ic acid (hí́drō-flṓo-órrik ‖ -floor-ik, -flew-, -áwrik) *n.* A colourless, fuming, corrosive, dangerously poisonous aqueous solution of hydrogen fluoride, HF, used to etch or polish glass, pickle certain metals, and clean masonry.

hy·dro·foil (hí́drə-foyl, hí́drō-) *n.* **1.** Any of a set of blades attached to the hull of a boat and aligned in the water at a small angle to the horizontal so that when the boat is in motion the fluid striking each blade's underside creates a high-pressure region below the blade, low pressure above it, and a resultant lift that raises the craft out of the water for efficient high-speed operation. **2.** A boat equipped with hydrofoils. In this sense, also called "hydroplane".

hy·dro·gen (hídrəjən) n. Symbol **H** A colourless, highly flammable gaseous element, the lightest of all gases and the most abundant element in the universe, used in the production of synthetic ammonia and methanol, in petroleum refining, hydrogenation of organic materials, as a reducing atmosphere, in oxyhydrogen torches, and in rocket fuels. Atomic number 1, atomic weight 1.00797, melting point $-259.14°C$, boiling point $-252.5°C$, density 0.08988 kilogram per cubic metre, valency 1. [French hydrogène, "water generating" (it forms water when oxidised) : HYDRO- + -GEN.] —**hy·drog·e·nous** (hī-drójənəss) adj.

hy·dro·gen·ase (hī-drójən-ayz, hídrəjən-, -ayss) n. Any enzyme that catalyses reduction reactions by causing the addition of hydrogen to a compound.

hy·dro·gen·ate (hī-drójən-ayt, hídrəjən-) tr.v. **-ated, -ating, -ates.** To combine with or subject to the action of hydrogen; especially, to combine (an unsaturated compound) with hydrogen. —**hy·dro·gen·a·tion** (-áysh'n) n. —**hy·dro·gen·a·tor** (-ər) n.

hydrogen bomb n. An explosive weapon of far greater destructive power than the atomic bomb, derived from the fusion of nuclei of various hydrogen isotopes in the formation of helium nuclei. Also called "H-bomb", "fusion bomb", "thermonuclear bomb".

hydrogen bond n. An essentially ionic weak chemical bond between a strongly electronegative atom and a hydrogen atom already bonded to another strongly electronegative atom.

hydrogen bromide n. An irritating colourless gas, HBr, used in the manufacture of barbiturates and synthetic hormones.

hydrogen carbonate n. **Bicarbonate** (see).

hydrogen chloride n. A colourless, fuming, corrosive, suffocating gas, HCl, used in the manufacture of plastics.

hydrogen cyanide n. **Hydrocyanic acid** (see).

hydrogen fluoride n. A colourless, fuming, mobile, corrosive liquid, or a highly soluble corrosive gas, HF, used in the manufacture of hydrofluoric acid, as a reagent, catalyst, and fluorinating agent, and in the refining of uranium and the preparation of many fluorine compounds.

hydrogen iodide n. A corrosive, colourless, suffocating gas, HI, used to manufacture hydriodic acid.

hydrogen ion n. **1.** The positively charged ion of hydrogen, H^+, formed by removal of the electron from atomic hydrogen. **2.** An ionised hydrogen molecule, $H^+{}_2$.

hy·dro·gen·ise, hy·dro·gen·ize (hī-drójən-īz, hídrəjən-) tr.v. **-ised, -ising, -ises.** To hydrogenate. —**hy·dro·gen·is·a·tion** (-ī-záysh'n || U.S. -i-) n.

hy·dro·gen·ol·y·sis (hī-drə-jə-nóllə-siss, -drō-, -je-) n. The breaking of a chemical bond in an organic molecule with the simultaneous addition of a hydrogen atom to each of the resulting molecular fragments. [HYDROGEN + -LYSIS.]

hydrogen peroxide n. A colourless, heavy, strongly oxidising liquid, H_2O_2, an essentially unstable compound, capable of reacting explosively with combustibles, and used principally in aqueous solution as an antiseptic, bleaching agent, oxidising agent, oxidiser in rocket fuels, and laboratory reagent.

hydrogen sulphide n. A colourless, flammable, poisonous compound, H_2S, having a characteristic rotten-egg odour, and used as a precipitant, purifier, and reagent.

hy·dro·ge·o·lo·gy (hídrō-jee-óllaji) n. The scientific study of waters below the earth's surface, and the geological aspects of the surface waters and their interaction with the solid structure of the earth.

hy·dro·graph (hídrə-graaf, -graf) n. A graph showing seasonal variations of level, flow, or velocity in a body of water. [HYDRO- + GRAPH.]

hy·dro·gra·phy (hī-dróggrəfi) n., pl. **-phies. 1.** The scientific study, description, and analysis of the physical conditions, boundaries, flow, and related characteristics of oceans, seas, and coastlines, and their winds. **2. a.** The mapping of such bodies of water. **b.** Maps or charts of such bodies of water. [Old French hydrographie : HYDRO- + -GRAPHY.] —**hy·drog·ra·pher** n. —**hy·dro·graph·ic** (hídrə-gráffik) adj. —**hy·dro·graph·i·cal·ly** adv.

hy·droid (hídroyd) n. **1.** Any of numerous characteristically colonial hydrozoan coelenterates of the order Hydroida, having a polyp rather than a medusoid form as the dominant stage of the life cycle. The order includes the hydra, one of the few solitary hydroids. **2.** The asexual, hydra-like polyp in the life cycle of any hydrozoan. ~adj. Of, pertaining to, or characteristic of a hydroid. [HYDR(A) (genus name) + -OID.]

hy·dro·ki·net·ic (hídrō-kī-néttik, -ki-) adj. **1.** Of or pertaining to hydrokinetics. **2.** Of or pertaining to the kinetic energy and motion of fluids.

hy·dro·ki·net·ics (hídrō-kī-néttiks, -ki-) n. Used with a singular verb. The kinetics of fluids, especially incompressible fluids, in motion.

hy·dro·lase (hídrə-layz, -layss) n. Any of a group of enzymes that catalyse hydrolysis reactions by causing the addition or removal of a molecule of water. [HYDROL(YSIS) + -ASE.]

hy·dro·las·tic suspension (hídrō-lástik, -láastik) n. A form of hydraulic motor-vehicle suspension in which there is hydraulic compensation between the front and the rear systems.

hydrologic cycle n. A **water cycle** (see).

hy·drol·o·gy (hī-dróllaji) n. The scientific study of the properties, distribution, and effects of water and ice on the earth's land surface, in the soil and underlying rocks, and in the atmosphere. [New Latin hydrologia : HYDRO- + -LOGY.] —**hy·dro·log·ic** (hídrə-lójik),

hy·dro·log·i·cal adj. —**hy·dro·log·i·cal·ly** adv. —**hy·drol·o·gist** (-dróllajist) n.

hy·drol·y·sate (hī-drólli-sayt) n. A product of hydrolysis. [HYDROLYS(IS) + -ATE.]

hy·dro·lyse, U.S. **hy·dro·lyze** (hídrə-līz) v. **-lysed, -lysing, -lyses.** —tr. To subject to hydrolysis. —intr. To undergo hydrolysis. [From HYDROLYSIS.] —**hy·dro·lis·a·ble** adj. —**hy·dro·ly·sa·tion** (-lī-záysh'n || U.S. -li-) n.

hy·drol·y·sis (hī-drólla-siss) n. Decomposition of a chemical compound by reaction with water, such as the dissociation of a dissolved salt or the catalytic conversion of glucose to starch. [HYDRO- + -LYSIS.] —**hy·dro·ly·tic** (hídrə-líttik, hídrō-) adj. —**hy·dro·ly·tic·al·ly** adv.

hy·dro·lyte (hídrə-līt) n. A substance that is hydrolysed. [HYDRO- + -LYTE.]

hy·dro·man·cy (hídrō-man-si, hídrə-) n. Divination by means of signs appearing in water. [Middle English ydromancy, from Old French hydromancie, from Latin hydromantía, from Greek hydromanteia (unattested) : HYDRO- + -MANCY.] —**hy·dro·manc·er** n. —**hy·dro·man·tic** (-mántik) adj.

hy·dro·mag·net·ics (hídrō-mag-néttiks) n. Used with a singular verb. **Magnetohydrodynamics** (see).

hy·dro·me·chan·ics (hídrō-mi-kánniks) n. Used with a singular verb. **Hydrodynamics** (see).

hy·dro·me·du·sa (hídrō-mi-déw-zə, -me-, -sə || -dóo-) n., pl. **-sas** or **-sae** (-zee, -see). A hydrozoan in its medusoid stage. See **medusa.** —**hy·dro·me·du·san** adj.

hy·dro·mel (hídrō-mel, hídrə-) n. A liquid composed of honey and water that, after fermentation, is called mead. [Middle English ydromel, from Old French, from Late Latin hydromel, from Latin hydromeli, from Greek hudromeli : HYDRO- + meli, honey.]

hy·dro·met·al·lur·gy (hídrō-mi-tál-ərji, -me-, -métt'l-urji) n. The separation of metal from ores and concentrates by chemical reactions in aqueous solution, such as leaching, extraction, and precipitation. —**hy·dro·met·al·lur·gi·cal** (-métt'l-úrjik'l) adj.

hy·dro·me·te·or (hídrō-méeti-ər) n. A precipitation body, such as rain, snow, sleet, or hail, derived from the condensation of water in the atmosphere.

hy·dro·me·te·or·ol·o·gy (hídrō-méeti-ə-róllaji) n. The meteorology of the occurrence, motion, and changes of state of atmospheric water.

hy·drom·e·ter (hī-drómmitər) n. An instrument used to determine relative density; especially, a sealed, graduated tube, weighted at one end, that sinks in a fluid to a depth related to the fluid's density. —**hy·dro·met·ric** (hídrə-méttrik, hídrō-), **hy·dro·met·ri·cal** adj. —**hy·dro·met·ri·cal·ly** adv. —**hy·drom·e·try** (hī-drómmətri) n.

hy·dro·ni·um (hī-dróni-əm) n. A hydrated hydrogen ion, H_3O^+. Also called "hydronium ion," "hydroxonium ion". [HYDR(O)- + (AMM)ONIUM.]

hy·drop·a·thy (hī-dróppəthi) n. The therapeutic use of water, both internally and externally. Also called "water cure". [HYDRO- + -PATHY.] —**hy·dro·path·ic** (hídrə-páthik, hídrō-), **hy·dro·path·i·cal** adj. —**hy·drop·a·thist** (hī-dróppəthist), **hy·dro·path** (hídrə-path, hídrō-) n.

hy·dro·per·i·car·di·um (hídrō-pérri-kárdi-əm) n. Excessive serous fluid within the pericardium, which surrounds the heart.

hy·dro·phane (hídrə-fayn, hídrə-) n. An opal that is almost opaque when dry, but transparent when wet. [HYDRO- + -PHANE.] —**hy·droph·a·nous** (hī-dróffənəss) adj.

hy·dro·phil·ic (hídrə-fíllik, hídrō-) adj. Having an affinity for water; absorbing, tending to combine with, or capable of dissolving in or being wetted by water. [New Latin hydrophilus, HYDROPHILOUS.] —**hy·dro·phile** (-fīl) n.

hy·droph·i·lous (hī-dróffiləss) adj. Botany. **1.** Growing or thriving in water; hydrophytic. **2.** Having water as a pollinating agent. [New Latin hydrophilus : HYDRO- + -PHILOUS.]

hy·droph·i·ly (hī-dróffili) n. Botany. Pollination by water. [HYDRO- + -PHILY.]

hy·dro·pho·bi·a (hídrə-fóbi-ə, hídrō-, -fób-yə) n. **1.** Fear of water; especially, an abnormal aversion to drinking. **2. Rabies** (see). [Late Latin, from Greek hudrophobia : HYDRO- + -PHOBIA.]

hy·dro·phob·ic (hídrə-fóbik, hídrō-, -fóbbik) adj. **1.** Antagonistic to, shedding, tending not to combine with, or incapable of dissolving in water. **2.** Of or exhibiting hydrophobia.

hy·dro·phone (hídrə-fōn) n. An electrical instrument for detecting or monitoring sound under water. [HYDRO- + -PHONE.]

hy·dro·phyte (hídrə-fīt, hídrō-) n. A plant that grows in an aquatic or very wet environment. Compare **mesophyte, xerophyte.** [HYDRO- + -PHYTE.] —**hy·dro·phyt·ic** (-fíttik) adj.

hy·dro·plane (hídrə-playn, hídrō-) n. **1.** A seaplane. **2.** A motorboat designed so that the prow and much of the hull lift out of the water and skim the surface at high speeds. **3.** A **hydrofoil** (see). **4.** A horizontal rudder on a submarine. ~intr.v. **hydroplaned, -planing, -planes. 1.** To rise out of and skim along on the surface of the water in, or as if in, a hydroplane.

hy·dro·pon·ics (hídrə-pónniks, hídrō-) n. Used with a singular verb. The cultivation of plants in gravel or other soilless substances through which water containing dissolved inorganic nutrients is pumped. Also called "aquiculture". [HYDRO- + (GEO)PONICS.] —**hy·dro·pon·ic** adj. —**hy·dro·pon·i·cal·ly** adv.

hy·dro·qui·none (hídrō-kwi-nōn, hídrə-, -kwínōn, hī-drókwi-nōn) n. Also **hy·dro·qui·nol** (-kwín-ol, -drókwin || -ōl). A white, crystalline compound, $C_6H_4(OH)_2$, used as a photographic developer, antioxidant, stabiliser, and reagent.

hy·dro·scope (hídrə-skōp) *n.* An optical device used for viewing objects much below the surface of water. [HYDRO- + -SCOPE.] —**hy·dro·scop·ic** (-skóppik) *adj.*

hy·dro·ski (hídrō-skee, hídrə-) *n.* A form of hydrofoil on some seaplanes, used to provide extra lift to assist in taking off.

hy·dro·sol (hídrə-sol ‖ -sŏl) *n.* A sol with water as the dispersing medium. [HYDRO- + SOL(UTION).]

hy·dro·sphere (hídrə-sfeer, hídrō-) *n.* The waters of the earth distinguished from the lithosphere and the atmosphere.

hy·dro·stat (hídrə-stat, hídrō-) *n.* A device that detects the presence or absence of water, used especially in steam boilers to prevent them boiling dry. [HYDRO- + -STAT.]

hy·dro·stat·ic (hídrə-státtik, hídrō-) *adj.* Also **hy·dro·stat·i·cal** (-'l). Of or pertaining to hydrostatics. —**hy·dro·stat·i·cal·ly** *adv.*

hy·dro·stat·ics (hídrə-státtiks, hídrō-) *n. Used with a singular verb.* The statics of fluids, especially incompressible fluids.

hy·dro·sul·phate (hídrō-súlfayt, hídrə-) *n.* A salt formed by the union of sulphuric acid with an alkaloid or other organic base.

hy·dro·sul·phide (hídrō-súlfīd, hídrə-) *n.* A chemical compound derived from hydrogen sulphide by replacement of one of the hydrogen atoms with a basic radical or base.

hy·dro·sul·phite (hídrō-súlfīt, hídrə-) *n.* **1.** A salt of hyposulphurous acid. **2.** A bleaching agent, **sodium hydrosulphite** (see).

hy·dro·sul·phu·rous acid (hídrō-súlfərəss, -sul-féwr-əss) *n.* **Hyposulphurous acid** (see).

hy·dro·tax·is (hídrō-táksiss) *n. Biology.* Movement of an organism or cell in response to moisture. [New Latin : HYDRO- + -TAXIS.] —**hy·dro·tac·tic** (-táktik) *adj.*

hy·dro·ther·a·peu·tics (hídrō-thérrə-péwtiks) *n. Used with a singular verb.* Hydrotherapy. —**hy·dro·ther·a·peu·tic** *adj.*

hy·dro·ther·a·py (hídrō-thérrəpi) *n., pl.* **-pies.** The medical use of water in the treatment of certain diseases; especially, the exercising of diseased joints and muscles in remedial swimming pools. —**hy·dro·ther·a·pist** *n.*

hy·dro·ther·mal (hídrō-thérm'l) *adj.* **1.** Of or pertaining to hot water. **2.** *Geology.* **a.** Of or pertaining to hot magmatic emanations that are rich in water. **b.** Of or pertaining to the rocks, ore deposits, and springs produced by such emanations. —**hy·dro·ther·mal·ly** *adv.*

hy·dro·tho·rax (hídrō-tháw-raks, hídrə- ‖ -thô-) *n.* The presence of serous fluid from the blood in one or both pleural cavities, often associated with cardiac failure.

hy·drot·ro·pism (hī-dróttrəpiz'm) *n. Botany.* Growth of a plant or part of a plant towards or away from water. [HYDRO- + -TROPISM.] —**hy·dro·trop·ic** (hídrə-tróppik, hídrō-) *adj.* —**hy·dro·trop·i·cal·ly** *adv.*

hy·drous (hídrəss) *adj.* Containing water, especially that of crystallisation or hydration. [HYDR(O)- + -OUS.]

hy·drox·ide (hī-dróksīd) *n.* A chemical compound containing the hydroxyl group. [HYDR(O)- + OXIDE.]

hydroxide ion *n.* The ion OH⁻, characteristic of basic hydroxides. Also called "hydroxyl ion".

hy·drox·o·ni·um ion (hī-drok-sṓni-əm) *n.* **Hydronium** *(see).* [HYDROX(Y)- + ONIUM (ION).]

hy·drox·y (hī-dróksi) *adj.* Containing the hydroxyl group. Often used in combination: *hydroxyproline.* [From HYDROXYL.]

hy·drox·yl (hī-dróksil) *n.* The univalent radical or group, OH, characteristic of bases, certain acids, phenols, alcohols, carboxylic and sulphonic acids, and amphoteric compounds. [HYDR(O)- + OX(YGEN) + -YL.] —**hy·drox·y·lic** (hī-drok-síllik) *adj.*

hy·drox·yl·a·mine (hī-dróksil-ə-méen, -ámmin, hídrok-síllə-meen, -sílə-) *n.* A colourless, crystalline compound, NH_2OH, explosive when heated above 130°C, that is used as a reducing agent and in organic synthesis.

hy·drox·y·pro·line (hī-dróksi-prṓ-leen, -lin) *n.* An amino acid, $C_5H_9NO_3$, occurring in proteins, particularly collagen.

hy·drox·y·tryp·ta·mine (hī-dróksi-tríptə-meen, -min) *n.* **Serotonin** *(see).*

hy·dro·zo·an (hídrə-zṓ-ən, hídrō-) *n.* Any of numerous coelenterates of the class Hydrozoa, which includes the hydras, polyps, and Portuguese men-of-war. —*adj.* Of, pertaining to, or belonging to the class Hydrozoa. [New Latin *Hydrozoa* : HYDRO- + -ZOAN.]

Hy·drus (hídrəss) *n.* A southern constellation near Tucana and Mensa. [Latin, "water serpent", from Greek *hudros.*]

hy·e·na, hy·ae·na (hī-éenə) *n.* Any of several carnivorous mammals of the genera *Hyaena* or *Crocuta* of Africa and Asia, having powerful jaws and relatively short hind limbs. [Middle English *hyene,* from Latin *hyaena,* from Greek *huaina,* from *hus,* swine.]

hy·e·tal (hí-it'l) *adj.* Of or relating to rain or to rainy regions. [Greek *huetos,* rain, a heavy shower.]

hy·et·o·graph (hí-ə-tə-graaf, -graf) *n.* **1.** A self-recording device for measuring rainfall. **2.** A chart showing the rainfall in a certain area, usually over a period of a year. [Greek *huetos,* rain + -GRAPH.] —**hy·e·to·graph·ic** (-gráffik) *adj.* —**hy·e·to·graph·y** (-tógrəfi) *n.*

Hy·gie·ia (hī-jée-ə). *Greek Mythology.* The goddess of health. [Greek *Hugieia,* from *hugieia,* health, from *hugiēs,* healthy.]

hy·giene (hí-jeen) *n.* **1.** The science of health and the prevention of disease. Also called "hygienics". **2.** The practice of maintaining health, especially by cleanliness. [French *hygiène,* earlier *hygiaine,* from New Latin *hygieina,* feminine of *hygiei-*

nos, healthful, from *hugiēs,* healthy.] —**hy·gien·ist** (-ist, hī-jéen-) *n.*

hy·gi·en·ic (hī-jéenik ‖ *U.S.* híji-énnik) *adj.* **1.** Of or pertaining to hygiene. **2.** Sanitary. **3.** Tending to promote or preserve health. —**hy·gi·en·i·cal·ly** *adv.*

hygienist *n.* A **dental hygienist** *(see).*

hygro– *comb. form.* Indicates wet, moist, or moisture; for example, **hygrograph.** [Greek *hugros,* wet, moist.]

hy·gro·graph (hígrō-graaf, hígrə-, -graf) *n.* An automatic hygrometer that records variations in atmospheric humidity. [HYGRO- + -GRAPH.]

hy·grom·e·ter (hī-grómmitər) *n.* Any of several instruments that measure atmospheric humidity. [HYGRO- + -METER.] —**hy·gro·met·ric** (hígrə-méttrik) *adj.* —**hy·grom·e·try** (-grómmətri) *n.*

hy·gro·phi·lous (hī-gróffiləss) *adj.* Growing in moist places. Said of certain plants. —**hy·gro·phile** (hí-grə-fīl, -grō-) *n.*

hy·gro·scope (hígrə-skōp) *n.* An instrument that measures changes in atmospheric moisture. [HYGRO- + -SCOPE.]

hy·gro·scop·ic (hígrə-skóppik) *adj.* Readily absorbing moisture, as from the atmosphere. [HYGROSCOP(E) + -IC.] —**hy·gro·scop·i·cal·ly** *adv.* —**hy·gro·scop·ic·i·ty** (-skō-píssəti, -sko-) *n.*

hy·gro·stat (hí-grə-stat, -grō-) *n.* A **humidistat** *(see).* [HYGRO- + -STAT.]

hy·la (hílə) *n.* Any tropical American tree frog of the genus *Hyla.* [New Latin *Hyla* (genus), from Greek *hulē,* wood, forest.]

hy·lic (hílik) *adj. Rare.* Of or pertaining to matter. [Late Latin *hylicus,* from Greek *hulikos,* from *hulē,* matter.]

hylo– *comb. form.* Indicates matter; for example, **hylotheism.** [Greek *hulē,* matter, wood.]

hy·lo·morph·ism (hī-lə-mórfiz'm, -lō-) *n.* The philosophical doctrine that matter as opposed to spirit, for example, is the first cause of the universe. [HYLO- + -MORPHISM.]

hy·lo·the·ism (hī-lə-thée-iz'm, -lō-) *n.* The philosophical doctrine that matter and God are identical.

hy·lo·zo·ism (hī-lə-zṓ-iz'm, -lō-) *n.* The philosophical doctrine that life is a property or derivative of matter, or that life and matter are inseparable. [Greek *hulē,* wood + ZO(O)- + -ISM.] —**hy·lo·zo·ic** *adj.* —**hy·lo·zo·ist** *n.* —**hy·lo·zo·is·tic** (-zṓ-ístik) *adj.*

hy·men (hí-men ‖ *chiefly U.S.* -mən) *n.* A membranous fold of tissue partly or completely blocking the vaginal external orifice at birth. It usually ruptures spontaneously before puberty. [Latin *hymēn,* from Greek *humēn,* membrane.] —**hy·men·al** *adj.*

Hy·men (hí-men). *Greek Mythology.* The god of marriage. [Latin, from Greek *Humēn†.*]

hy·me·ne·al (hí-me-née-əl, -mə-) *adj. Archaic & Poetic.* Of or pertaining to a wedding or marriage. —*n.* A wedding song or poem. [Latin *hymenaeus,* from Greek *humēnaios,* bridal song, wedding, from *Humēn,* HYMEN.]

hy·me·ni·um (hī-méeni-əm) *n., pl.* **-nia** (-ə) or **-ums.** The spore-bearing layer of the fruiting body of certain fungi, containing basidia. [New Latin, from HYMEN.]

hy·men·op·ter·an (hí-mi-nóptər-ən, -me-) *n., pl.* **-tera** (-ə) or **-terans.** Also **hy·men·op·ter·on** (-on) *pl.* **-tera** or **-terons.** Any insect of the order Hymenoptera, characteristically having two pairs of membranous wings, an ovipositor modified as a sting or drill, and including the bees, wasps, and ants. —*adj.* Also **hy·men·op·ter·ous** (-əss). Of or belonging to the Hymenoptera. [New Latin *Hymenoptera,* from Greek *humenopteros,* "membrane-wing" : *humēn,* membrane, HYMEN + -PTEROUS.]

hymn (him) *n.* **1.** A song of praise or thanksgiving to God. **2.** Any song of praise or joy; a paean. —*v.* **hymned, hymning, hymns.** —*tr.* **1.** To praise, glorify, or worship in a hymn. **2.** To express in a hymn. —*intr.* To sing hymns. [Middle English *ymne, imne,* from Old French *ymne,* from Latin *hymnus,* from Greek *humnos†,* hymn, ode of praise of gods or heroes.]

hym·nal (hím-nəl) *n.* A book or collection of church hymns. Also called "hymnbook". —*adj.* Of or pertaining to a hymn or hymns. [Middle English *hymnale,* from Medieval Latin *hymnāle,* from Latin *hymnus,* HYMN.]

hym·nist (hím-nist) *n.* Also **hym·no·dist** (-nə-dist). A composer of hymns.

hym·no·dy (hím-nədi) *n., pl.* **-dies.** **1.** The singing of hymns. **2.** The composing of hymns. **3.** The hymns of a particular period or church. [Medieval Latin *hymnōdia,* from Greek *humnōidia* : *humnos,* HYMN + *ōidē,* song.]

hym·nol·o·gy (him-nólləji) *n.* **1.** The composition of hymns. **2.** The study of hymns. [Greek *humnologia,* "hymn-singing" : *humnōs,* HYMN + -LOGY.] —**hym·no·log·ic** (hím-nə-lójik), **hym·no·log·i·cal** *adj.* —**hym·nol·o·gist** (-nólləjist) *n.*

hy·oid bone (hí-oyd) *n.* A U-shaped bone between the mandible and the larynx at the base of the tongue. Also called "hyoid". [French *hyoïde,* from New Latin *hyoides,* from Greek *huoeides,* "in the form of an upsilon" : *hu,* name of the letter upsilon + -OID.] —**hy·oid, hy·oid·e·an** (-óydi-ən) *adj.*

hy·o·man·dib·u·lar (hī-ō-man-díbbewlər) *n.* A u-shaped bone in fishes that attaches the jaw to the skull. [*Hyo-,* from Greek *hu,* upsilon (referring to the shape of the bone) + MANDIBULAR.]

hy·os·cine (hí-ə-seen, -ō-) *n.* A drug, **scopolamine** *(see).* [German *Hyoscin,* from New Latin *Hyoscyamus,* genus of henbane from which it is obtained, from Greek *huoskuamus* : *huos,* genitive of *hus,* pig + *kuamos†,* bean.]

hy·os·cy·a·mine (hí-ə-sí-ə-meen, hí-ō-, -min) *n.* A poisonous, white, crystalline alkaloid, $C_{17}H_{23}NO_3$, isomeric with atropine, and used as an antispasmodic, analgesic, and sedative. [New Latin *Hyoscyamus.* See **hyoscine**.]

hyp·a·bys·sal (híppə-bíss'l, hípə-) *adj.* Solidifying chiefly as a minor intrusion, especially as a dyke or sill, before reaching the earth's surface. Said of rocks. [HYP(O)- + ABYSSAL.]

hy·pae·thral (hī-péethrəl, hi-) *adj.* Open to the sky; roofless: *an ancient hypaethral temple.* [Latin *hypaethrus,* from Greek *hupaithros* : *hupo-,* beneath + *aithēr,* sky.]

hypaesthesia. Variant of **hypoaesthesia.**

hy·pan·thi·um (hī-pánthi-əm, hi-) *n., pl.* **-thia** (-ə). The cup-shaped or flattened floral receptacle of various plants, having the gynoecium at the centre and the other flower parts round the rim. [New Latin : HYP(O)- + ANTH(O)- + -IUM.] **—hy·pan·thi·al** *adj.*

hype¹ (hīp) *n. Slang.* **1.** Deception. **2.** Deceptively inflated advertising or promotion. **3.** A promotional gimmick or campaign.
~*tr.v.* **hyped, hyping, hypes.** *Slang.* To publicise, promote, or exploit by touting and often overrating: *hyping a new film.* [20th century (U.S.), originally, to short-change, swindle) : origin obscure.]

hype² *n. Slang.* **1.** A hypodermic injection, syringe, or needle. **2.** A drug addict.
~*tr.v.* **hyped, hyping, hypes.** *Slang.* To stimulate with or as if with an injection of a drug. Sometimes used with *up: hype up emotions.* [Short for HYPODERMIC.]

hy·per (hípər) *adj. Slang.* Hyperactive ; manic.

hyper- *prefix.* Indicates: **1.** Over, above, or in great amount; for example, **hypersonic. 2.** In abnormal excess; for example, **hyperacid. 3.** To an excessive degree; for example, **hypercritical.** [Greek *huper,* over, above, beyond, exceeding.]

hy·per·a·cid·i·ty (hípər-ə-síddəti, -a-) *n.* Excessive acidity, especially of the gastric juices in the stomach. **—hy·per·ac·id** (-ássid) *adj.*

hy·per·ac·tive (hípər-áktiv) *adj.* Excessively or abnormally active. **—hy·per·ac·tiv·i·ty** *n.*

hy·per·ae·mi·a (hípər-éemi-ə) *n.* The presence of an excessive amount of blood in the vessels supplying a particular organ of the body. [HYPER- + -AEMIA.] **—hy·per·ae·mic** *adj.*

hy·per·aes·the·si·a (hípər-eess-théezi-ə, -théezhə || U.S. -ess-) *n. Pathology.* Abnormally high sensitivity, especially of the skin, to touch, heat, cold, and pain. **—hy·per·aes·the·tic** (-théttik) *adj.*

hy·per·bar·ic (hípər-bárrik) *adj.* Of, pertaining to, producing, operating, or occurring at pressures higher than normal atmospheric pressure: *a hyperbaric chamber; hyperbaric therapy.* [HYPER- + BAR(O)- + -IC.]

hy·per·bo·la (hī-pérbə-lə) *n., pl.* **-las** or **-lae** (-lee). *Geometry.* A plane curve having two branches, formed by: **1.** A conic section intersecting both halves of a right circular cone. **2.** The locus of points related to two given points such that the difference in the distances of each point from the two given points is a constant. [New Latin, from Greek *huperbolē,* "a throwing beyond", excess (when a hyperbola is formed from a conic section, the angle made by the base of the cone and the intersecting plane is greater than the angle formed by a parabola), from *huperballein,* "to throw beyond", exceed : *huper-,* beyond + *ballein,* to throw.]

hy·per·bo·le (hī-pérbəli) *n.* Exaggeration or extravagant statement used as a figure of speech; for example, *I could sleep for a year; This book weighs a ton.* [Earlier *yperbole,* from Latin *hyperbolē,* from Greek *huperbolē,* excess. See **hyperbola**.]

hy·per·bol·ic (hípər-bóllik) *adj.* Also **hy·per·bol·i·cal** (-'l). **1.** Of, pertaining to, or employing hyperbole. **2.** *Mathematics.* **a.** Of, pertaining to, or having the form of a hyperbola. **b.** Based on or having a metric that is a hyperbola: *hyperbolic geometry.* **c.** Of or pertaining to a hyperbolic function: *hyperbolic cosine.* **—hy·per·bol·i·cal·ly** *adv.*

hyperbolic function *n. Mathematics.* Any of a set of six functions related, for a real variable z, to the hyperbola in a manner analogous to the relationship of the trigonometric functions to a circle, including: **1.** *Symbol* **sinh** The *hyperbolic sine,* defined by the equation $\sinh z = 1/2(e^z - e^{-z})$. **2.** *Symbol* **cosh** The *hyperbolic cosine,* defined by the equation $\cosh z = 1/2(e^z + e^{-z})$. **3.** *Symbol* **tanh** The *hyperbolic tangent,* defined by the equation $\tanh z = \sinh z/\cosh z$. **4.** *Symbol* **coth** The *hyperbolic cotangent,* defined by the equation $\coth z = \cosh z/\sinh z$. **5.** *Symbol* **sech** The *hyperbolic secant,* defined by the equation $\operatorname{sech} z = 1/\cosh z$. **6.** *Symbol* **cosech** and **csch.** The *hyperbolic cosecant,* defined by the equation $\operatorname{cosech} z = 1/\sinh z$.

hyperbolic paraboloid *n.* See **paraboloid.**

hy·per·bo·lise, hy·per·bo·lize (hī-pérbə-līz) *v.* **-lised, -lising, -lises.** **—intr.** To use hyperbole; exaggerate. **—tr.** To express with hyperbole; exaggerate.

hy·per·bo·lism (hī-pérbə-liz'm) *n.* **1.** The use of hyperbole. **2.** A hyperbole.

hy·per·bo·loid (hī-pérbə-loyd) *n. Geometry.* Either of two quadric surfaces having a finite centre with certain plane sections that are hyperbolas and others that are ellipses or circles.

hy·per·bo·re·an (hípər-baw-rée-ən, -bo-, -báwri-ən || -bóri-) *adj.* **1.** Of or pertaining to the far north; arctic. **2.** Very cold; frigid. [Latin *Hyperborei,* HYPERBOREAN.]

Hy·per·bo·re·an *n. Greek Mythology.* A member of a people known to the ancient Greeks from the earliest times, living in an unidentified country in the far north, and renowned as pious and divinely favoured adherents of the cult of Apollo.
~*adj.* Of or pertaining to the Hyperboreans. [Latin *Hyperborei,* from Greek *Huperboreoi* (plural) : *huper-,* beyond, extreme + *boreios,* northern, from *Boreas,* "north wind", north.]

hy·per·cap·ni·a (hípər-kápni-ə) *n.* The presence of an abnormally high carbon dioxide concentration in the blood. Also called "hypercarbia". [HYPER- + *-capnia,* from Greek *kapnos,* smoke.]

hy·per·cat·a·lex·is (hípər-káttə-lék-siss) *n.* The addition of one or more syllables in excess of the normal number in the last foot of a line of verse. [New Latin : HYPER- + *catalexis,* omission in the last foot of a line, from Greek *katalēxis,* from *katalēgein,* to leave off (see **catalectic**).] **—hy·per·cat·a·lec·tic** (-tik) *adj.*

hy·per·charge (hípər-chaarj) *n. Symbol* **Y** *Physics.* A quantum number numerically equal to twice the average electric charge of a particle multiplet or, equivalently, to the sum of the strangeness and the baryon number.

hy·per·cor·rec·tion (hípər-kə-réksh'n) *n.* A mistake in grammar, pronunciation, or the like, made as a result of trying especially hard to be correct; for example, saying *badmington* for *badminton.* **—hy·per·cor·rect** (-rékt) *adj.* **—hy·per·cor·rect·ly** *adv.*

hy·per·crit·ic (hípər-kríttik) *n.* A person who is excessively critical.

hy·per·crit·i·cal (hípər-kríttik'l) *adj.* Overcritical; especially, excessively critical about trivial matters. **—hy·per·crit·i·cal·ly** *adv.* **—hy·per·crit·i·cism** (-krítti-siz'm) *n.*

hy·per·du·li·a (hípər-dew-lée-ə || -doo-) *n.* In the Roman Catholic and Eastern Orthodox churches, the special reverence given to the Virgin Mary. Compare **dulia, latria.** [Medieval Latin : HYPER- + DULIA.] **—hy·per·du·lic** (-déwlik || -dóolik) **hy·per·du·li·cal** *adj.*

hyperemia *U.S.* Variant of **hyperaemia.**

hyperesthesia *U.S.* Variant of **hyperaesthesia.**

hy·per·eu·tec·tic (hípər-yōo-téktik) *adj. Chemistry.* Having the minor component present in a larger amount than in the eutectic composition of the same components. Said of mixtures.

hy·per·ex·ten·sion (hípər-iks-ténsh'n, -eks-) *n.* Extension of a limb beyond normal limits, usually as part of an orthopaedic exercise.

hy·per·fine structure (hípər-fīn) *n. Abbr.* **hfs** *Physics.* The splitting of a spectral line into two or more components as a result of the spin or magnetic moment of the atomic nucleus.

hy·per·ga·my (hī-pérgəmi) *n.* The practice or state of being married to a person of equal or superior rank, caste, or class. [HYPER- + -GAMY.] **—hy·per·ga·mous** *adj.*

hy·per·gly·cae·mi·a (hípər-glī-séemi-ə) *n.* The presence of an abnormally high concentration of glucose in the blood, as occurs in diabetes. **—hy·per·gly·cae·mic** (-séemik) *adj.*

hy·per·gol·ic (hípə-góllik) *adj.* Igniting spontaneously on contact with an oxidiser. Said of a rocket fuel. [German *Hypergol* : HYP(ER)- + Greek *ergon,* work + -OL(E).]

hy·per·i·cum (hī-pérrikəm) *n.* Any plant of the genus *Hypericum,* which includes **St. John's wort** and **rose of Sharon** *(both of which see).* [New Latin *Hypericum* (genus), from Greek *hupereikon* : HYPER- + *ereikē,* heath.]

hy·per·in·fla·tion *n. Economics.* Extraordinarily high inflation.

hy·per·in·sew·lin·ism (hípər-ín·sew-lin-iz'm || -sə-) *n.* The presence of abnormally large quantities of insulin in the blood, resulting in hypoglycaemia.

Hy·pe·ri·on¹ (hī-péer-i-ən, -pérri-) *n. Greek Mythology.* A Titan, the son of Gaea and Uranus, and father of Helios, the sun god.

Hyperion² *n.* One of the smallest satellites of the planet Saturn.

hy·per·ker·a·to·sis (hípər-kérrə-tō-siss) *n.* Hypertrophy of the horny, outer layer of the skin. [New Latin : HYPER- + Greek *keras* (stem *kerat-*), horn + -OSIS.] **—hy·per·ker·a·tot·ic** (-tóttik) *adj.*

hy·per·ki·ne·sis (hípər-kī-néezi-ə, -ki-, -néezhə) *n.* Also **hy·per·ki·ne·sis** (-née-siss). Pathologically excessive restlessness, occurring particularly in children as a symptom of certain types of disorder. [New Latin : HYPER- + Greek *kinēsis,* movement, from *kinein,* to move.] **—hy·per·ki·net·ic** (-néttik) *adj.*

hy·per·mar·ket (hípər-maarkit) *n.* A very large self-service store, similar to a supermarket but usually selling a wider variety of goods. [From French *hypermarché.* See **hyper-, market.**]

hy·per·me·ter (hī-pérmitər) *n.* **1.** A verse or metrical line having one or more syllables in excess of the normal number. **2.** An extra or redundant syllable. **—hy·per·met·ric** (hípər-méttrik), **hy·per·met·ri·cal** *adj.*

hy·per·me·tro·pi·a (hípər-me-trōpi-ə, -mi-) *n.* The condition in which light entering the eye is focused behind the retina, resulting in inability to see near objects clearly. Also called "long-sightedness", "far-sightedness", *chiefly U.S.* "hyperopia". Compare **myopia.** [New Latin, from Greek *hupermetros,* beyond measure, excessive : *huper-,* beyond, excessive + *metron,* measure.] **—hy·per·me·trop·ic** (-trópik), **hy·per·me·trop·i·cal** *adj.* **—hy·per·met·ro·py** (-méttrəpi) *n.*

hy·perm·ne·si·a (hípərm-néezi-ə, -néezhə) *n.* Unusually exact or vivid memory. [New Latin : HYPER- + (A)MNESIA.]

hy·per·mo·til·i·ty (hípər-mō-tílləti) *n.* Abnormally increased movement, especially of the stomach or intestines.

hy·per·on (hípər-on) *n. Physics.* A subatomic particle with mass greater than the nucleon, decaying into a nucleon or another hyperon and lighter particles, and having $2I + 1$ charge states, where I is the isospin of the particle multiplet. [HYPER- + -ON.]

hy·per·o·pi·a (hípər-ṓpi-ə) *n. Chiefly U.S.* Hypermetropia. **—hy·per·ope** (-ṓp) *n.* **—hy·per·op·ic** (-óppik) *adj.*

hy·per·os·to·sis (hípər-oss-tō-siss) *n.* Excessive or abnormal thickening or growth of bone tissue. [New Latin : HYPER- + OST(EO)- + -OSIS.] **—hy·per·os·tot·ic** (-tóttik) *adj.*

hy·per·par·a·site (hípər-párrə-sīt) *n.* An organism that is parasitic on or in another parasite. **—hy·per·par·a·sit·ic** (-síttik) *adj.*

hy·per·par·a·thy·roid·ism (hípər-párrə-thír-oydiz'm) *n.* An abnormal increase in the activity of the parathyroid glands.

hy·per·phys·i·cal (hípər-fízzik'l) *adj.* Beyond the physical or material; supernatural.

hy·per·pi·tu·i·ta·rism (hípər-pi-téw-i-tə-riz'm ‖ -tóō-) *n.* Pathologically excessive production of anterior pituitary hormone, especially growth hormones, resulting in acromegaly or gigantism. —**hy·per·pi·tu·i·tar·y** (-təri ‖ -terri) *adj.*

hy·per·plane (hípər-playn) *n. Mathematics.* A plane, or an analogue of a plane, with more than three dimensions.

hy·per·pla·si·a (hípər-pláyzi-ə, -plázzi-ə, -pláyzhə) *n.* An abnormal increase in the number of cells in an organ or tissue with consequent enlargement of the affected part. [New Latin : HYPER- + -PLASIA.] —**hy·per·plas·tic** (-plástik, -pláastik) *adj.*

hy·per·ploid (hípər-ployd) *adj. Genetics.* Having a chromosome number in excess of an exact multiple of the normal haploid number. [HYPER- + -PLOID.] —**hy·per·ploid·y** *n.*

hy·per·pnoe·a (hípərp-née-ə, hípər-) *n.* Abnormally deep and rapid breathing, as after exercise. [New Latin : HYPER- + Greek *pnoia,* breath, from *pnein,* to breathe.]

hy·per·py·rex·i·a (hípər-pīr-éksi-ə) *n.* Abnormally high fever, with a body temperature of 41.1°c (106°F) or above; hyperthermia. —**hy·per·py·rex·i·al, hy·per·py·ret·ic** (-éttik) *adj.*

hy·per·sen·si·tive (hípər-sén-sətiv) *adj.* **1.** Abnormally sensitive; especially, oversensitive. **2.** Liable to respond abnormally to the presence of an antigen or drug. —**hy·per·sen·si·tive·ness, hy·per·sen·si·tiv·i·ty** (-sə-tívvəti) *n.*

hy·per·son·ic (hípər-sónnik) *adj.* Of, pertaining to, or relating to speed equal to or exceeding five times the speed of sound. —**hy·per·son·ics** *n.*

hy·per·space (hípər-spayss) *n. Mathematics.* Space with more than three dimensions, especially a four-dimensional space.

hy·per·sthene (hípərss-theen) *n.* A green, brown, or black, splintery, cleavable, pyroxene mineral, essentially (Fe,Mg)₂Si₂O₆. [French *hypersthène* : HYPER- + Greek *sthenos,* strength.] —**hy·per·sthen·ic** (-thénnik) *adj.*

hy·per·ten·sion (hípər-ténsh'n) *n.* **1.** Abnormally high arterial blood pressure. **2.** *Informal.* A state of high emotional tension. —**hy·per·ten·sive** (-tén-siv) *adj.* & *n.*

hy·per·text (hípər-tekst) *n.* Computerized text that allows multiple modes of access to its information and makes cross-referring easy.

hy·per·ther·mi·a (hípər-thérmi-ə) *n.* Unusually high fever; hyperpyrexia. [New Latin : HYPER- + THERM(O)- + -IA.] —**hy·per·therm·al** (-thérm'l) *adj.*

hy·per·thy·roid·ism (hípər-thír-oyd-iz'm) *n.* Overactivity of the thyroid gland, resulting in excessive production of thyroid hormones. See thyrotoxicosis. —**hy·per·thy·roid** *adj.* & *n.*

hy·per·ton·ic (hípər-tónnik) *adj.* **1.** *Pathology.* Having extreme muscular or arterial tension. **2.** *Chemistry.* Having the higher osmotic pressure of two solutions. —**hy·per·to·ni·a** (-tóni-ə), **hy·per·to·ni·ci·ty** (-tō-níssəti, -tə-) *n.*

hy·per·tro·phy (hī-pértrəfi) *n.* Also **hy·per·tro·phi·a** (hípər-trōfi-ə, -trō-fée-ə). *Pathology.* Abnormal enlargement of an organ or part as a result of the enlargement, without increase in number, of its constituent cells.

~*v.* **hypertrophied, -phying, -phies.** —*tr.* To cause to grow abnormally large. —*intr.* To grow abnormally large. [HYPER- + -TROPHY.] —**hy·per·troph·ic** (-tróffik) *adj.*

hy·per·ven·ti·la·tion (hípər-vénti-láysh'n) *n.* Abnormally fast or deep respiration in which excessive quantities of air are taken in, causing buzzing in the ears, tingling of extremities, and sometimes fainting. —**hy·per·ven·ti·late** (-layt) *v.*

hy·per·vi·ta·min·o·sis (hípər-víttə-min-ō-siss, -vítə-) *n.* Any of various abnormal conditions due to excessive intake of a vitamin.

hy·pha (hī-fə) *n., pl.* **-phae** (-fee) Any of the threadlike filaments forming the mycelium of a fungus. [New Latin, from Greek *huphē,* web.] —**hy·phal** *adj.*

hy·phen (híf'n) *n.* A punctuation mark (-) used to connect the words of phrases to make a compound, to separate parts of a compound word or name, or between syllables, especially of a word that is split over two consecutive lines.

~*tr.v.* **hyphened, -phening, -phens.** To hyphenate. [Late Latin, from Late Greek *huphen,* a sign written below two consecutive letters to show that they belong to the same word, from Greek, in the same word : *hupo-,* under + *hen,* neuter of *heis,* one.]

hy·phen·ate (hífə-nayt) *tr.v.* **-ated, -ating, -ates.** To divide or connect (syllables, words, names, or word elements) with a hyphen. —**hy·phen·a·tion** (-náysh'n) *n.*

hy·phen·at·ed (hífə-naytid) *adj. U.S. Informal.* Of foreign birth or mixed national origin: *German-Americans and other hyphenated Americans.*

hy·phen·ise, hy·phen·ize (hífə-nīz) *tr.v.* **-ised, -ising, -ises.** To hyphenate. —**hy·phen·i·sa·tion** (-nī-záysh'n ‖ *U.S.* -ni-) *n.*

hyp·na·gog·ic, hyp·no·gog·ic (hípnə-gójik, -gŏjik) *adj.* **1.** Inducing sleep. **2.** Of or pertaining to the state of drowsiness preceding sleep. [French *hypnagogique* : HYPN(O)- + Greek *agōgos,* leading, from *agein,* to lead.]

hypno–, hypn– *comb. form.* Indicates: **1.** Sleep; for example, **hypnopompic. 2.** Hypnosis; for example, **hypnoanalysis, hypnotherapy.** [Greek *hupnos,* sleep.]

hyp·no·a·nal·y·sis (hípnō-ə-nál-ə-siss) *n.* A psychoanalytic technique in which hypnosis is used to elicit unconscious material from a patient.

hyp·no·gen·e·sis (hípnō-jénnə-siss) *n.* The process of inducing or

entering a hypnotic state or sleep. —**hyp·no·ge·net·ic** (-jə-néttik) *adj.* —**hyp·no·ge·net·i·cal·ly** *adv.*

hyp·noid (hípnoyd) *adj.* Also **hyp·noid·al** (hip-nóyd'l). Of or resembling hypnosis or sleep. [HYPN(O)- + -OID.]

hyp·nol·o·gy (hip-nólləji) *n.* The scientific study of sleep. [HYPNO- + -LOGY.] —**hyp·no·log·ic** (hípnə-lójik), **hyp·no·log·i·cal** *adj.* —**hyp·nol·o·gist** *n.*

hyp·no·pae·di·a (híp-nō-péedi-ə, -nə-) *n.* A method of teaching in which information is heard while asleep and is supposed to be retained when awake. [HYPNO- + Greek *paideia,* education, from *pais* (stem *paid-*), boy.] —**hyp·no·pae·dic** *adj.*

hyp·no·pho·bi·a (hípnə-fŏbi-ə, hípnō-, -fŏb-yə) *n.* Abnormal fear of sleep. [New Latin : HYPNO- + -PHOBIA.] —**hyp·no·pho·bic** (-fŏbik) *adj.*

hyp·no·pom·pic (hípnə-pómpik, hípnō-) *adj.* Of or pertaining to the partially conscious state preceding complete awakening. [HYPNO- + Greek *pompē,* a sending off, procession, POMP + -IC.]

Hyp·nos (híp-noss) Also **Hyp·nus** (-nəss). *Greek Mythology.* The god of sleep. [Greek.]

hyp·no·sis (hip-nō-siss) *n., pl.* **-ses** (-seez). **1.** An artificially induced sleeplike condition in which an individual is extremely responsive to suggestions made by the hypnotist. **2.** Hypnotism. **3.** Any sleeplike condition. [New Latin : Greek *hupnos,* sleep.]

hyp·no·ther·a·py (hípnō-thérrəpi) *n.* Treatment for mental or physical illness based on or using hypnosis.

hyp·not·ic (hip-nóttik) *adj.* **1. a.** Of, involving, or inducing hypnosis. **b.** Resembling hypnosis, or inducing a state that resembles hypnosis; fascinating; mesmerising: *hypnotic music.* **c.** Of, pertaining to, or practising hypnotism. **2.** Inducing sleep; soporific.

~*n.* **1. a.** A person who is hypnotised. **b.** A person who can be hypnotised. **2. a.** An agent that causes sleep; a soporific. **b.** An agent used to produce a hypnotic state. [French *hypnotique,* from Late Latin *hypnōticus,* from Greek *hupnōtikos,* sleepy, from *hupnoun,* to put to sleep, from *hupnos,* sleep.] —**hyp·not·i·cal·ly** *adv.*

hyp·no·tise, hyp·no·tize (hípnə-tīz) *tr.v.* **-tised, -tising, -tises. 1.** To put in a state of hypnosis. **2.** To fascinate; entrance. —**hyp·no·tis·a·ble** *adj.* —**hyp·no·ti·sa·tion** (-tī-záysh'n ‖ *U.S.* -ti-) *n.* —**hyp·no·tis·er** *n.*

hyp·no·tism (hípnə-tiz'm) *n.* **1.** The theory or practice of inducing hypnosis. **2.** An act of inducing hypnosis.

hyp·no·tist (hípnə-tist) *n.* A person who induces hypnosis.

hy·po¹ (hípō) *n.* In photography, **sodium thiosulphate** *(see).* [Short for HYPOSULPHITE.]

hypo² *n., pl.* **-pos.** *Slang.* A hypodermic syringe or injection.

hypo–, hyp– *comb. form.* Indicates: **1.** Below or beneath; for example, **hypodermic. 2.** At a lower point; for example, **hypogenous. 3.** Abnormally low; for example, **hypoglycaemia. 4.** Deficient; for example, **hypoxia. 5.** Partial or incomplete; for example, **hypoaesthesia. 6.** *Chemistry.* Designating an acid containing a low amount of oxygen; for example, **hypophosphorous acid.** [Greek *hupo-,* from *hupo,* under, from under, beneath.]

hy·po·a·cid·i·ty (hípō-ə-síddəti, -a-) *n.* **1.** *Chemistry.* Slight acidity. **2.** *Medicine.* Below normal acidity.

hy·po·aes·the·si·a (hípō-eess-théezi-ə, -théezhə ‖ *U.S.* -ess-) *n.* Also **hy·paes·the·si·a** (híp-ess-théezi-ə, -théezhə). *Pathology.* Partial loss of sensation; diminished sensibility. [New Latin : HYPO- + (AN)-AESTHESIA.]

hy·po·bar·ic (hípə-bárrik) *adj.* Below normal pressure. [HYPO- + BAR(O)- + -IC.] —**hy·po·bar·ism** *n.*

hy·po·blast (hípə-blast) *n. Embryology.* **Endoblast** *(see).* [HYPO- + -BLAST.] —**hy·po·blas·tic** (-blástik) *adj.*

hy·po·caust (hī-pə-kawst, -pō-) *n.* In ancient Rome, a space under the floor where heat from a furnace was accumulated to heat a room or a bath. [Latin *hypocaustum,* from Greek *hupokauston,* from *hupokaiein,* to burn underneath : *hupo-,* under + *kaiein,* to burn.]

hy·po·cen·tre (hípō-sentər) *n.* **Ground zero** *(see).*

hy·po·chlo·rite (hī-pə-kláw-rīt, -pō- ‖ -klŏ-) *n.* A salt or ester of hypochlorous acid.

hy·po·chlo·rous acid (hī-pə-kláw-rəss) *n.* A weak, unstable acid, HOCl, occurring only in solution and used as a bleach, oxidiser, deodorant, and disinfectant. Also called "chloric (I) acid".

hy·po·chon·dri·a (hípə-kóndri-ə) *n.* The persistent neurotic conviction that one is or is likely to become ill, sometimes involving experiences of real pain, when illness is neither actually present nor likely. Also called "hypochondriasis". [Originally a region of the abdomen (formerly held to be the seat of melancholy), from Late Latin, from Greek *hupokhondria,* plural of *hupokhondrion,* belly, abdomen, from *hupokhondrios,* under the cartilage of the breastbone : *hupo-,* under + *khondros,* cartilage.]

hy·po·chon·dri·ac (hípə-kóndri-ak, híppə-) *n.* A person afflicted with hypochondria.

~*adj.* **1.** Pertaining to or afflicted with hypochondria. **2.** *Anatomy.* Pertaining to or located in the hypochondrium. —**hy·po·chon·dri·a·cal** (-kon-drí-ak'l, -kon-) *adj.* —**hy·po·chon·dri·a·cal·ly** *adv.*

hy·po·chon·dri·um (hípə-kón-dri-əm, híppə-) *n., pl.* **-dria** (-dri-ə). The upper lateral region of the abdomen, below the ribs. [New Latin, from Greek *hupokhondrion,* abdomen. See hypochondria.]

hy·poc·o·rism (hī-pókə-riz'm) *n.* **1.** A name of endearment or pet name. **2.** The use of such names. **3.** A euphemism. [Late Latin *hypocorisma,* from Greek *hupokorisma,* from *hupokorizesthai,* to call by endearing names : *hupo-,* below, beneath + *korizesthai,* to caress, from *koros,* boy, and *korē,* girl.] —**hy·po·co·ris·tic** (hí-pokə-rístik), **hy·po·co·ris·ti·cal** *adj.* —**hy·po·co·ris·ti·cal·ly** *adv.*

hy·po·cot·yl (hī́pə-kóttil) *n. Botany.* The part of the axis of a plant embryo or seedling plant that is below the cotyledons. [HYPO- + COTYL(EDON).] —**hy·po·cot·yl·ous** *adj.*

hy·poc·ri·sy (hi-póckrə-si) *n., pl.* **-sies.** **1.** The feigning of beliefs, feelings, or virtues that one does not hold or possess; gross insincerity. **2.** An instance of such falseness. [Middle English *ipocrisie, ypocrisy,* from Old French *ypocrisie,* from Late Latin *hypocrisis,* from Greek *hupokrisis,* playing of a part on the stage, from *hupokrinein,* to separate gradually, answer, answer one's fellow actor, play a part : *hupo-,* under + *krinein,* to separate.]

hyp·o·crite (híppə-krit) *n.* A person given to hypocrisy. [Middle English *ipocrite, ypocrite,* from Old French *ypocrite,* from Late Latin *hypocrita,* from Greek *hupocritēs,* actor, hypocrite, from *hupokrinein,* to play a part. See **hypocrisy.**] —**hyp·o·crit·i·cal** (-kríttik'l) *adj.* —**hyp·o·crit·i·cal·ly** *adv.*

hy·po·cy·cloid (hī́pō-síkloyd) *n. Geometry.* The plane locus of a point fixed on a circle that rolls on the inside circumference of a fixed circle.

hy·po·der·mal (hī́pə-dérm'l) *adj.* **1.** Of or pertaining to the hypodermis. **2.** Lying below the epidermis.

hy·po·der·mic (hī́pə-dérmik) *adj.* **1.** Of or pertaining to the layer just beneath the epidermis. **2.** Pertaining to the hypodermis. **3.** Injected beneath the skin.
—*n.* **1.** A hypodermic needle or syringe. **2.** A hypodermic injection. [HYPO- + DERM(ATO)- + -IC.] —**hy·po·der·mi·cal·ly** *adv.*

hypodermic injection *n.* A subcutaneous, intramuscular or intravenous injection by means of a hypodermic syringe and needle.

hypodermic needle *n.* **1.** A hollow needle used with a hypodermic syringe. **2.** A hypodermic syringe complete with needle.

hypodermic syringe *n.* A tubular, piston-operated syringe fitted with a hypodermic needle for hypodermic injections, withdrawing blood, and the like.

hy·po·der·mis (hī́pə-dérmiss) *n.* Also **hy·po·derm** (-derm). **1.** *Zoology.* An epidermal layer of cells that secretes an overlying chitinous cuticle, as in arthropods. **2.** *Botany.* A layer of cells lying immediately below the epidermis, in certain plants, that acts as water-storing or strengthening tissue. [New Latin : HYPO- + *dermis,* DERMA (skin).]

hy·po·eu·tec·tic (hī́pō-yŏŏ-téktik) *adj. Chemistry.* Having the minor component present in a smaller amount than in the eutectic composition of the same components. Said of mixtures, especially alloys.

hy·po·gas·tri·um (hī́-pō-gástri-əm, -pə-) *n.* The lowest of the three median regions of the abdomen. [New Latin, from Greek *hupogastrion* : HYPO- + GASTR(O)- + -IUM.] —**hy·po·gas·tric** *adj.*

hy·po·ge·al (hī́-pə-jée-əl, -pō-) *adj.* Also **hy·po·ge·an** (-ən), **hy·po·ge·ous** (-əss). **1.** Located under the earth's surface; underground. **2.** *Botany.* Designating germination in which the cotyledons remain below the surface of the ground. [Late Latin *hupogēus,* from Greek *hupogaios* : HYPO- + *gē, gaia,* earth.]

hy·po·gene (hī́-pə-jeen, -pō-) *adj.* Formed or situated below the earth's surface. Said of rocks. [HYPO- + (EPI)GENE.]

hy·pog·e·nous (hī-pójənəss) *adj. Botany.* Developing or growing on a lower surface, as fungi on leaves. [HYPO- + -GENOUS.]

hyp·o·ge·um (hī́-pə-jée-əm, -pō-) *n., pl.* **-gea** (-jée-ə). **1.** A subterranean chamber of an ancient building. **2.** An ancient subterranean burial chamber, such as a catacomb. [Latin *hypogēum,* from Greek *hupogaion,* from *hupogaios,* HYPOGEAL.]

hy·po·glos·sal (hī́-pə-glóss'l, -pō-) *adj.* **1.** Located under the tongue. **2.** *Anatomy.* Of or pertaining to the hypoglossal nerve.
—*n.* The hypoglossal nerve. [New Latin *hypoglossus,* hypoglossal nerve : HYPO- + Greek *glōssa,* tongue.]

hypoglossal nerve *n.* The twelfth cranial nerve, which supplies motor fibres to the muscles of the tongue.

hy·po·gly·cae·mi·a (hī́pō-glī-séemi-ə) *n.* An abnormally low level of sugar in the blood. —**hy·po·gly·cae·mic** *adj.*

hy·pog·y·nous (hī-pójinəss) *adj. Botany.* Having or characterising floral parts or organs that are below and not in contact with the ovary. [HYPO- + -GYNOUS.] —**hy·pog·y·ny** *n.*

hy·poid gear (hípoyd) *n.* A gear in which the shapes of the teeth are hypocycloids, used for applications in which a high surface load is desirable. [*Hypoid,* shortened from HYPOCYCLOID.]

hy·po·lim·ni·on (hī́-pō-lím-ni-ən, -pə- ‖ *U.S.* -on) *n., pl.* **-nia** (-ni-ə). The lower, colder layer of a lake or other body of water that is divided into two layers at different average temperatures. [*hypo-* + Greek *limnion,* diminutive of *limnē,* lake.]

hy·po·ma·ni·a (hī́-pō-máyni-ə, -pə-, -máyn-yə) *n.* A mild state of mania involving slightly abnormal elation and overactivity. —**hy·po·ma·nic** (-mánnik, -máynik) *adj.*

hy·po·nas·ty (hī́-pō-nasti, -pə-) *n.* An upward bending of leaves or other plant parts, resulting from growth of the lower side. [German *Hyponastie* : HYPO- + -NASTY.] —**hy·po·nas·tic** *adj.*

hy·po·ni·trite (hī́-pə-nítrīt, -pō-) *n.* A salt or ester of hyponitrous acid.

hy·po·ni·trous acid (hī́-pə-nítrəss, -pō-) *n.* An unstable white crystalline acid, $H_2N_2O_2$.

hy·po·nym (hī́-pə-nim, po-) *n.* A word which includes the meaning of another, more general word, such that the two can never be entirely interchangeable; for example, *cabbage* is a hyponym of *vegetable.* [HYP(O)- + -ONYM.] —**hy·pon·y·mous** (hī-pónniməss) *adj.* —**hy·pon·y·my** (hī-pónnimi) *n.*

hy·po·phos·phate (hī́-pə-fóss-fayt, -pō-) *n.* A salt or ester of hypophosphorous acid.

hy·po·phos·phite (hī́-pə-fóss-fīt, -pō-) *n.* A salt of hypophosphorous acid.

hy·po·phos·pho·rous acid (hī́-pə-fóss-fərəss, -pō-) *n.* A clear, colourless or slightly yellow, oily liquid, H_3PO_2, used in the preparation of hypophosphites.

hy·poph·y·sis (hī-póffə-siss) *n., pl.* **-ses** (-seez). *Anatomy.* The **pituitary gland** (*see*). [New Latin, outgrowth, from Greek *hupophusis,* attachment underneath, growth, from *hupophuein,* to grow up under : *hupo-,* under + *phuein,* to bring forth, grow.] —**hy·po·phys·e·al** (hī́pə-fízzi-əl, hī-póffə-sée-əl) *adj.*

hy·po·pi·tu·i·ta·rism (hī́pō-pi-téw-i-tə-riz'm ‖ -tŏŏ-) *n.* Deficient or diminished production of pituitary hormones. —**hy·po·pi·tu·i·tar·y** (-təri ‖ -terr-i) *adj.*

hy·po·pla·si·a (hī́-pə-pláyzi-ə, -pō-, -plázzi-ə, -pláyzhə) *n. Pathology.* Incomplete or arrested development of an organ or part. [New Latin : HYPO- + -PLASIA.] —**hy·po·plas·tic** (-plástik, -plaastik) *adj.*

hy·po·ploid (hī́-pə-ployd, -pō-) *adj. Genetics.* Having a chromosome number less by only a few chromosomes than a multiple of the normal haploid number. [HYPO- + -PLOID.] —**hy·po·ploid·y** *n.*

hy·po·pnoe·a (hī́-pəp-née-ə, -pōp-, -pə-, -pō-) *n.* Abnormally slow and shallow breathing. [New Latin : HYPO- + Greek *pnoē,* breathing, from *pnein,* to breathe.]

hy·po·sen·si·tiv·i·ty (hī́pō-sén-sə-tívvəti) *n.* Also **hy·po·sen·si·tive·ness** (-tiv-nəss, -niss). Less than normal sensitivity. —**hy·po·sen·si·tive** *adj.*

hy·po·sen·si·tise, hy·po·sen·si·tize (hī́pō-sén-sə-tīz, -si-) *tr.v.* **-tised, -tising, -tises.** To make less sensitive; desensitise. —**hy·po·sen·si·ti·sa·tion** (-tī-záysh'n ‖ *U.S.* -ti-) *n.*

hy·pos·ta·sis (hī́-póstə-siss) *n., pl.* **-ses** (-seez). **1.** *Philosophy.* **a.** That which underlies something else; substance or essence, as distinguished from attributes or qualities. **2.** *Theology.* **a.** Any of the persons of the Trinity as distinguished from the single nature of the godhead. **b.** The essential person of Christ in which his human and divine natures are united. **3.** *Medicine.* The accumulation of blood or fluid in a part of the body, such as the lungs, that is caused by poor circulation. **4.** *Genetics.* A condition in which the action of one gene conceals or suppresses the action of another gene that is not its allele. [Late Latin, substance, from Greek *hupostasis,* "a standing under", origin, substance, existence : *hupo-,* under + *stasis,* a standing.] —**hy·po·stat·ic** (hī́pə-státtik) *adj.* —**hy·po·stat·i·cal** *adj.* —**hy·po·stat·i·cal·ly** *adv.*

hypostatic union *n. Theology.* The union of Christ's human and divine natures in one hypostasis or person. [Greek *hupostatikos,* of substance, from *hupostatos,* standing under, from *huphistasthai,* to stand under : *hupo-,* under + *histasthai,* middle voice of *histanai,* to cause to stand.]

hy·pos·ta·tise, hy·pos·ta·tize (hī-póstə-tīz) *tr.v.* **-tised, -tising, -tises.** **1.** To symbolise (a concept) in a concrete form. **2.** To ascribe material existence to. [Greek *hupostatos,* standing under. See **hypostatic union.**] —**hy·pos·ta·ti·sa·tion** (-tī-záysh'n ‖ *U.S.* -ti-) *n.*

hy·po·sthe·ni·a (hī́-pəss-théeni-ə, -pōss-, -poss-) *n.* Abnormal lack of strength; extreme weakness. [New Latin : HYPO- + Greek *sthenos,* strength.] —**hy·po·sthe·nic** (-thénnik) *adj.*

hyp·o·style (hī́-pə-stīl, -pō-) *n.* A building having a roof or ceiling supported by rows of columns, as in ancient Egyptian architecture. [Greek *hupostulos,* resting upon pillars set underneath : *hupo-,* under + *stulos,* pillar.] —**hyp·o·style** *adj.*

hy·po·sul·phite (hī́-pə-súlfīt, -pō-) *n.* **Sodium thiosulphate** (*see*).

hy·po·sul·phu·rous acid (hī́-pə-súlfərəss, -pō-, -sul-féwr-əss) *n.* An unstable acid, $H_2S_2O_4$, known only in aqueous solution, and used as a bleaching and reducing agent. Also called "hydrosulphurous acid".

hy·po·tax·is (hī́-pō-táksiss, -pə-, -taksiss) *n.* The subordination of one clause to another using a connective; for example, *I shall despair if you don't come.* Compare **parataxis.** [Greek *hupotaxis,* subjection, submission, from *hupotassein,* to arrange under : *hupo-,* under + *tattein,* to arrange.] —**hy·po·tac·tic** (-táktik) *adj.*

hy·po·tension (hī́-pə-ténsh'n) *n.* Abnormally low arterial blood pressure. —**hy·po·ten·sive** (-tén-siv) *adj.*

hy·pot·e·nuse (hī-póttə-newz, -newss ‖ -nŏŏz, -nŏŏss) *n. Abbr.* **hyp.** The side of a right-angled triangle opposite the right angle. [Latin *hypotēnūsa,* from Greek *hupoteinousa,* line subtending the right angle, hypotenuse, from *hupoteinein,* to stretch under : *hupo-,* under + *teinein,* to stretch.]

hypoth. hypothesis.

hy·po·thal·a·mus (hī́-pō-thál-əməss, -pə-) *n.* The part of the brain that lies below the thalamus, and regulates bodily temperature, hunger, thirst, and other autonomic activities. —**hy·po·tha·lam·ic** (-thə-lámmik) *adj.*

hy·poth·ec (hī-póthik) *n.* In Roman and Scots law, a security granted a creditor on the property of a debtor without transfer of possession or title. [French *hypothèque,* from Late Latin *hypothēca,* pledge, mortgage, from Greek *hupothēkē,* from *hupotithenai,* "to place under", put down as a deposit : *hupo-,* under + *tithenai,* to place.] —**hy·poth·ec·ar·y** (-əri ‖ -erri) *adj.*

hy·poth·e·cate (hī-póthi-kayt) *tr.v.* **-cated, -cating, -cates.** *Law.* To pledge (property) as security to a creditor without transfer of title or possession; mortgage. [Medieval Latin *hypothēcāre,* from Late Latin *hypothēca,* HYPOTHEC.] —**hy·poth·e·ca·tion** (-káysh'n) *n.* —**hy·poth·e·ca·tor** (-ər) *n.*

hy·po·ther·mal (hī́-pə-thérm'l, -pə-) *adj.* **1.** *Geology.* Of, pertaining to, or designating high-temperature deposits derived from magmatic emanations forced under pressure into pre-existing rock openings. **2.** Of, pertaining to, or characterised by hypothermia.

hy·po·ther·mi·a (hī-pə-thérmi-ə, -pō-) *n.* **1.** Abnormally low body temperature caused by exposure to cold. **2.** The deliberate lowering of body temperature to reduce metabolic rate during surgery. [HYPO + Greek *thermē*, heat + -IA.]

hy·poth·e·sis (hī-póthə-siss) *n., pl.* **-ses** (-seez). *Abbr.* **hyp., hypoth.** **1.** An assertion subject to verification or proof, as: **a.** A proposition stated as a basis for argument or reasoning. **b.** A premise from which a conclusion is drawn. **c.** A conjecture that accounts, within a theory or set of coherent beliefs for a set of facts and that can be used as a basis for further investigation. **d.** A theory supported by no objective evidence; a groundless assumption. **2.** An assumption used as the basis for action. [Late Latin, from Greek *hupothesis*, proposal, suggestion, supposition, from *hupotithenai*, "to place under", propose, suppose : *hupo-*, under + *tithenai*, to place.]

hy·poth·e·sise, hy·poth·e·size (hī-póthə-sīz) *v.* **-sised, -sising, -sises.** —*tr.* To assert as a hypothesis. —*intr.* To form a hypothesis or hypotheses.

hy·po·thet·i·cal (hīp-ə-théttik'l) *adj.* Also **hy·po·thet·ic** (-théttik). **1.** Of or based on a hypothesis. **2. a.** Suppositional; conjectural; uncertain. **b.** Conditional; contingent. **3.** Existing as an idea or possibility, but not actual: *That's only a hypothetical case.* [Late Latin *hypotheticus*, from Greek *hupothetikos*, from *hupothesis*, HYPOTHESIS.] —**hy·po·thet·i·cal·ly** *adv.*

hypothetical imperative *n.* In the philosophy of Immanuel Kant, a principle of conduct arising from expediency or necessity rather than from moral law. Compare **categorical imperative.**

hy·po·thy·roid (hī-pō-thír-oyd, -pə-) *adj.* Affected by or manifesting hypothyroidism.
~*n.* A person affected by hypothyroidism.

hy·po·thy·roid·ism (hī-pō-thír-oydiz'm, -pə-) *n.* **1.** Insufficient production of thyroid hormones. **2.** A pathological condition resulting from severe thyroid insufficiency; especially, **myxoedema** or **cretinism** (*both of which see*). Also called "hypothyrea", "hypothyroidea". [HYPO- + THYROID + -ISM.]

hy·po·ton·ic (hī-pō-tónnik, -pə-) *adj.* **1.** *Pathology.* Having less than normal muscular or arterial tone or tension. **2.** *Chemistry.* Having the lower osmotic pressure of two fluids. —**hy·po·to·nic·i·ty** (-tə-níssəti, -to-, -tō-) *n.*

hy·po·troch·oid (hī-pə-trókoyd, -pō-) *n. Geometry.* The locus of a point anywhere on the radius, or radius extended, of a circle that rolls inside a fixed circle. A hypotrochoid for which the moving point is on the circumference of the rolling circle is a hypocycloid.

hy·po·xan·thine (hī-pō-zán-theen, -pə-, -thin) *n.* A white powder, $C_5H_4N_4O$, that is an intermediate in the metabolism of purines.

hy·pox·i·a (hī-póksi-ə) *n.* Deficiency in the amount of oxygen reaching bodily tissues. [New Latin : HYP(O)- + OX(Y)- + -IA.] —**hy·pox·ic** *adj.*

hypso– *comb. form.* Indicates height; for example, **hypsometry.** [Greek *hupsos*, height, summit.]

hyp·sog·ra·phy (hip-sóggrəfi) *n.* **1.** The scientific study of the earth's topological configuration above sea level, especially the measurement and mapping of land elevations. **2.** A representation or description of such features, as on a map or in an atlas. **3.** Hypsometry. [HYPSO- + -GRAPHY.] —**hyp·so·graph·ic** (hípsə-gráffik), **hyp·so·graph·i·cal** *adj.*

hyp·som·e·ter (hip-sómmitər) *n.* An instrument using the altitude-pressure dependence of boiling points to determine land elevations. [HYPSO- + -METER.]

hyp·som·e·try (hip-sómmətri) *n.* The measurement of elevation relative to sea level. [HYPSO- + -METRY.] —**hyp·so·met·ric** (híp-sə-méttrik, -sō-) **hyp·so·met·ri·cal** *adj.* —**hyp·so·met·ri·cal·ly** *adv.* —**hyp·som·e·trist** (hip-sómmətrist) *n.*

hy·rax (hír-aks) *n., pl.* **-raxes** or **-races** (-ə-seez). Any of several herbivorous mammals of the family Procaviidae of Africa and adjacent Asia, resembling hamsters but more closely related to elephants. Also called "dassie", and, especially in the Old Testament, "cony". [New Latin, from Greek *hurax†*, shrew mouse.]

Hyr·ca·ni·a (hur-káyni-ə). A province of the ancient Persian empire, on the southeastern shore of the Caspian Sea.

hy·son (hī-s'n) *n.* A type of Chinese green tea, the leaves of which are twisted or curled. [Cantonese *hei chon,* corresponding to Mandarin Chinese *xī chūn,* "bright spring", after the name of a famous tea grower, *Li Xi-chun.*]

hys·sop (híssəp) *n.* **1.** A woody plant, *Hyssopus officinalis,* native to Asia, having spikes of small blue flowers and aromatic leaves used in perfumery and as a condiment. **2.** Any of several similar or related plants. **3.** An unidentified plant mentioned in the Bible as the source of twigs used for sprinkling in certain Hebraic purificatory rites. Exodus 12:22. [Middle English *ysop,* from Old English *hysope* and Old French *ysope,* both from Latin *hyssōpus,* from Greek *hussōpos,* from Semitic, akin to Hebrew *'ezōbh.*]

hys·ter·ec·tom·ise, hys·ter·ec·tom·ize (hístər-éktə-mīz) *tr.v.* **-ised, -ising, -ises.** To perform a hysterectomy on.

hys·ter·ec·to·my (hístər-éktəmi) *n., pl.* **-mies.** The removal of either the whole of the uterus, or the body of the uterus but not the cervix. [HYSTER(O)- + -ECTOMY.]

hys·ter·e·sis (hístə-rée-siss) *n., pl.* **-ses** (-seez). *Physics.* The failure of a property that has been changed by an external agent to return to its original value when the cause of the change is removed. See **magnetic hysteresis.** [New Latin, from Greek *husterēsis,* a shortcoming, from *husterein,* to be behind, come later, from *husteros,* later, behind.] —**hys·ter·et·ic** (-réttik) *adj.*

hysteresis loop *n. Physics.* A closed curve obtained by plotting a graph of the magnetic induction of a ferromagnetic substance (as ordinate) against the external magnetic field. The shape of the curve is characteristic of the magnetic properties of the material and shows the ease with which it is magnetised and the ability to retain magnetisation.

hys·ter·i·a (hi-stéer-i-ə) *n.* **1.** A neurosis characterised by susceptibility to suggestion, emotional instability, amnesia, and other mental aberrations. **2.** Excessive or uncontrollable fear or other strong emotion. [New Latin, from Latin *hystericus,* HYSTERIC.]

hys·ter·ic (hi-stérrik) *n.* A person suffering from hysteria.
~*adj.* Hysterical. [Latin *hystericus,* from Greek *husterikos,* suffering in the womb (hysteria was once thought to be caused by uterine disturbances), from *hustera,* womb.]

hys·ter·i·cal (hi-stérrik'l) *adj.* **1.** Of, characterised by, or arising from hysteria. **2.** Having or prone to having hysterics: *hysterical paralysis.* **3.** *Informal.* Extremely funny. —**hys·ter·i·cal·ly** *adv.*

hys·ter·ics (hi-stérriks) *n.* Used with a singular or plural verb. **1.** An attack of hysteria. **2.** *Informal.* **a.** A fit of uncontrollable laughing. **b.** A fit of wild anger: *He'll have hysterics if he finds out.*

hystero–, hyster– *comb. form.* Indicates: **1.** Womb or uterus; for example, **hysterectomy. 2.** Hysteria; for example, **hysterogenic.** [Greek *hustera,* womb.]

hys·ter·o·gen·ic (hístərō-jénnik) *adj.* Causing hysteria. [HYSTERO- + -GENIC.]

hys·ter·oid (hístə-royd) *adj.* Also **hys·ter·oid·al** (-róyd'l). Resembling hysteria. [HYSTER(O)- + -OID.]

hys·ter·on prot·er·on (hístə-ron próttə-ron, -prótə-) *n.* **1.** A figure of speech in which the natural or rational order of its terms is reversed; for example, *bred and born* instead of *born and bred.* **2.** *Logic.* The fallacy of assuming as a premise a proposition following something yet to be proved. [Late Latin, from Greek *husteron proteron,* "latter first" : *husteron,* neuter of *husteros,* latter + *proteron,* neuter of *proteros,* first, former.]

hys·ter·ot·o·my (hístə-róttəmi) *n., pl.* **-mies.** Surgical incision into the uterus. [New Latin *hysterotomia* : HYSTERO- + -TOMY.]

hys·tric·o·morph (hi-stríckə-mawrf, -stríkə-) *n.* Any rodent belonging to the suborder *Hystricomorpha,* which includes the porcupines, chinchillas, guinea pigs, and agoutis. [Greek *hustrix* (stem *hustrik-*), porcupine + -MORPH.] —**hys·tric·o·morph, hys·tric·o·morph·ic** (-mórfik) *adj.*

Hyw·el the Good (hów-əl, hó-, -el), also known as Howel Dda (thaa) (died 950). Welsh prince. He formalised Welsh law and was the only Welsh ruler to issue his own coins.

Hz hertz (unit of frequency).

I

i, I (ī) *n., pl.* **i's, I's,** or **Is. 1.** The ninth letter of the modern English alphabet. **2.** Any of the speech sounds represented by this letter. **3.** Something shaped like an I. —**dot (one's) i's and cross (one's) t's.** To pay rigorous attention to detail; be exhaustively comprehensive.

i, I, i., I. *Note:* As an abbreviation or symbol, *i* may be a small or a capital letter, with or without a full stop. Established forms or those generally preferred precede the definition. When no form is given, all four forms are in general use in that sense. **1. i,** *Electricity.* current. **2. i** *Mathematics.* imaginary unit; especially the symbol for √-1 **3. i.** incisor. **4. I.** independence; independent. **5. I.** institute. **6. i.** interest. **7. I.** international. **8. i.** intransitive. **9. I** The symbol for the element iodine. **10. i., I.** island; isle. **11. I** isospin. **12. i, I,** The Roman numeral for one. **13.** The ninth in a series.

I (ī) *pron.* The first person singular pronoun in the nominative case. **1.** Used to represent the speaker or writer. **2.** Sometimes used in a conditional construction depending on the elliptically understood clause *if I were you,* to express advice or indirect injunction: *I wouldn't go out without a coat today.* See Usage note at **me.** ∼*n., pl.* **I's.** The self; the ego. [Middle English *i, ich,* Old English *ic,* from Germanic *eka* (unattested).]

i-[1]. Variant of **y-.**

i-[2]. Variant of **in-** (not).

-i *n. & adj. suffix.* Indicates a specified region, nation, origin, or people; for example, **Kashmiri, Pakistani, Tandoori.** [Adjective suffix in Semitic and Indo-Iranian languages.]

-i- *infix.* Used to connect the elements of a compound word, especially when they are of Latin origin; for example, **patrilineal, homicide.** [From or by analogy with French *-i-,* from Latin.]

i.a. in absentia.

-ia[1] *n. suffix.* Indicates: **1.** Diseases and disorders; for example, **alexia, diphtheria. 2.** Plants or genera of plants; for example, **poinsettia, begonia. 3.** Zoological classes; for example, **Amphibia. 4.** Areas and countries; for example, **Manchuria.** [New Latin, from Latin and Greek, suffix of feminine abstract nouns.]

-ia[2] *n. suffix.* Indicates: **1.** Collective nouns; for example, **trivia, genitalia. 2.** Things relating or belonging to; for example, **pedodontia.** [New Latin, from Latin, neuter plural of *-ius,* and from Greek, neuter plural of *-ios.*]

IAEA International Atomic Energy Agency.

-ial *adj. suffix.* Indicates of, pertaining to, or characterised by; for example, **managerial, residential.** [Middle English, from Old French *-ial, -iel,* from Latin *-iālis : -i-,* stem + *-ālis,* -AL.]

i·amb (ī-amb, -am) *n.* **1.** A metrical foot consisting of a short syllable followed by a long (in quantitative verse), or an unstressed syllable followed by a stressed (in accentual verse). Also called "iambic", "iambus". There are four iambs in the following line: *"I-am'bics march' from short' to long'"* (S.T. Coleridge). **2.** A line of verse consisting of such feet. Compare **trochee.** [French *iambe,* from Latin *iambus,* IAMBUS.]

i·am·bic (ī-ámbik) *adj.* **1.** Consisting of iambs or characterised by their predominance: *iambic pentameter.* **2.** Employing this rhythm: *the iambic poets of antiquity.* ∼*n.* **1.** An iamb. **2.** *Usually plural.* A verse, stanza, or poem written in iambs. [Latin *iambicus,* from Greek *iambikos,* from *iambos,* IAMBUS.]

i·am·bus (ī-ámbəss) *n., pl.* **-buses** or **-bi** (-bī). An iamb. [Latin, from Greek *iambos†.*]

-ian. Variant of **-an.** [Old French *-ien,* from Latin *-iānus : -i-,* stem + *-ānus,* -AN.]

-iana. Variant of **-ana** (a collection).

IAS *Aeronautics.* indicated air speed.

-iasis *comb. form.* Indicates a pathological condition; for example, **teniasis.** [New Latin, from Greek, suffix of action.]

I.A.T.A., IATA International Air Transport Association.

i·at·ric (ī-áttrik) *adj.* Also **i·at·ri·cal** (-'l). *Rare.* Pertaining to medicine or physicians; medical. [Greek *iatrikos,* from *iatros,* physician, healer, from *iasthai†,* to heal, cure.]

-iatric *n. & adj. comb. form.* Indicates a specified kind of patient or medical treatment; for example, **geriatric.** [From IATRIC.]

-iatrics *n. comb. form.* Indicates medical treatment; for example, **paediatrics.** [From IATRIC.]

i·at·ro·gen·ic (ī-áttrō-jénnik, ī-átrō-) *adj.* Induced in a patient by a doctor's actions or treatment: *an iatrogenic disease.* [Greek *iatros,* physician (see **iatric**) + -GENIC.]

-iatry *n. comb. form.* Indicates medical treatment; for example, **psychiatry.** [French *-iatrie,* from New Latin *-iatria,* from Greek *iatreia,* the art of healing, from *iatros,* physician. See **iatric.**]

ib. ibidem.

I.B.A. Independent Broadcasting Authority (in Britain).

I·ba·dan (i-bádd'n). A city in southwestern Nigeria, lying about 130 kilometres (80 miles) north of Lagos. It is the second largest city in the country and one of the oldest settlements in Africa.

Ib·ár·ru·ri Gómez (i-bárroor-i gő-mez), **Dolores** (1895–1989). Spanish Communist leader. Her oratory in the Spanish Civil War won her the nickname of La Pasionaria (the passionflower). She sought refuge in the U.S.S.R. (1939), but returned to Spain in 1977.

I-beam (ī-beem) *n.* A steel beam or girder with a cross-section formed like the capital letter I.

I·be·ri·a (ī-béer-i-ə). **1.** The ancient name for the region roughly corresponding to the eastern part of modern Georgia. **2.** An ancient name for the **Iberian Peninsula.**

I·be·ri·an (ī-béer-i-ən) *adj.* **1. a.** Of or pertaining to the ancient ethnological group or groups that inhabited the Iberian Peninsula. **b.** Of or pertaining to the language or culture of these groups. **2. a.** Of or pertaining to the Iberian Peninsula. **b.** Broadly, Spanish, or Spanish and Portuguese. **3.** Of or pertaining to ancient Iberia in the Caucasus, to its inhabitants, their language, or their culture. ∼*n.* **1. a.** A member of the ancient Caucasoid people that inhabited the Iberian Peninsula. **b.** The language of this people. **2.** An inhabitant of the Iberian Peninsula. **3.** An inhabitant of ancient Iberia in the Caucasus.

Iberian Peninsula. Land mass of extreme southwestern Europe, comprising Spain and Portugal, separated from the rest of Europe by the Pyrenees and from Africa by the Strait of Gibraltar.

Ibero- *comb. form.* Indicates the Iberian Peninsula or Iberian; for example, **Ibero-Celtic.**

i·bex (íbeks) *n., pl.* **ibexes, ibices** (íbi-seez, íbbi-), or collectively **ibex.** Any of several wild goats of the genus *Capra,* of mountainous regions of the Old World; especially, *C. ibex,* having long, ridged, backward-curving horns. Also called "steinbok". [Latin, perhaps of Alpine origin.]

I·bib·i·o (i-bíbbi-ō) *n., pl.* **-os** or collectively **Ibibio. 1.** A member of a people of southeastern Nigeria. **2.** The Niger-Congo language of this people. —**I·bib·i·o** *adj.*

ibid. ibidem.

i·bi·dem (ibbi-dem, i-bī- ‖ -dəm) *adv.* Latin. *Abbr.* **ib., ibid.** In the same place. Used in footnotes and bibliographies to refer to the book, chapter, article, or page cited just before.

-ibility. Variant of **-ability.**

i·bis (íbiss) *n., pl.* **ibises** or collectively **ibis.** Any of various long-billed, mainly tropical, wading birds of the family Threskiornithidae such as the sacred ibis, *Threskiornis aethiopica.* See **wood ibis.** [Latin *ībis,* from Greek *ibis,* from Egyptian *hīb.*]

I·bi·za (i-béetha; *Spanish* i-béetha). The third largest of the Balearic Islands, in the Mediterranean Sea, and the one nearest the east coast of Spain. Ibiza is also the name of the largest town. The island is a popular tourist resort.

-ible. Variant of **-able.**

Ibn Gabirol (íbbən ga-béer-ol), **Solomon ben Yehuda,** also known as Avicebrón (*c.*1021–58). Jewish philosopher and poet. He was a leading contributor to the growth of Jewish culture in Moorish Spain; his Neoplatonist philosophy, particularly in *Fons Vitae,* had great influence on Jews and Christians.

Ibn Rushd. See **Averroes.**

Ibn Saud (sowd) (*c.*1880–1953). Founder and first king of modern Saudi Arabia, which he ruled from 1932 until his death. His long struggle to gain control of central Arabia began in 1902. It continued against the Turks, with British support during World War I, and against rival Arab factions in the 1920s. The discovery of oil in 1936, which later brought great wealth, occurred in his reign.

Ibn Sina. See **Avicenna.**

I·bo (ée-bō) *n., pl.* **Ibos** or collectively **Ibo. 1.** A member of a Negroid people of Nigeria. **2.** The Kwa language of this people.

Ib·sen (ib-s'n), **Henrik Johan** (1828–1906). Norwegian dramatist and poet, whose plays created a major scandal in his lifetime because of their realism, but are now acclaimed as classics. His chief works include *A Doll's House* (1879), *Ghosts* (1881), and *An Enemy of the People* (1882). Other major plays are *Hedda Gabler* (1890) and *The Master Builder* (1892).

-ic, -ical *adj. suffix.* Indicates: **1.** Of, pertaining to, or characteristic of; for example, **seismic, Gaelic, geological, metrical. 2.** *Chemistry.* Having or taking a valency higher than in corresponding *-ous* compounds; for example, **ferric.** Compare **-ous.** [Middle English *-ic, -ik,* from Latin *-icus.*]

Usage: Sometimes the endings *-ic* and *-ical* can be used interchangeably without affecting the sense, as in *astronomic* and *astronomical.* In many pairs, however, such as *comic, comical,* or *economic, economical,* the *-ic* form suggests an actual example of something, and the *-ical* form a general tendency towards something, in these cases *comedy* and *economy.* American usage sometimes keeps *-ic* forms, for example *geologic,* which have been superseded by *-ical* forms in British English.

IC integrated circuit.

ICA 1. Institute of Contemporary Arts. **2.** International Cooperation Administration.

ICAO International Civil Aviation Organisation.

Ic·a·rus[1] (íckərəss). *Greek Mythology.* The son of Daedalus, who, in escaping from Crete on artificial wings made for him by his father, flew so close to the sun that the wax with which his wings were fastened melted, so that he fell into the Aegean Sea and drowned.

Icarus[2] *n. Astronomy.* A small asteroid, the one that passes closest to the sun. [After ICARUS.]

ICBM intercontinental ballistic missile.

ice (īss) *n.* **1.** Water frozen solid. **2.** A surface, layer, or mass of frozen water. **3. a.** Pieces of ice, as those put in a drink, for example, to chill it. **b.** Anything resembling frozen water, such as **dry ice** *(see).* **4.** An **ice cream** or **water ice** *(both of which see).* **5.** *Slang.* Diamonds. **6. a.** The skating surface in an ice rink. **b.** The playing field in ice hockey. **7.** *Astronomy.* A mixture of solid water, carbon dioxide, other gases, and dust, forming the nucleus of a comet. **8.** An addictive, smokable methamphetamine drug. —**break the ice.** To dispel the initial mood of reserve or formality of a social situation. —**cut no ice.** *Informal.* To have no influence or effect; make no impression. —**on ice. 1.** In a refrigerator or freezer. **2.** *Informal.* **a.** In reserve or readiness. **b.** Put aside; shelved; postponed. **c.** Held incommunicado. **d.** Certain to be won. Said of games. —**on thin ice.** In a risky situation; on uncertain ground.
~*v.* **iced, icing, ices.** —*tr.* **1.** To coat with ice. **2.** To cause to become ice; freeze. **3. a.** To chill by setting in or as if in ice. **b.** To put ice in (a drink, for example). **4.** To cover or decorate (a cake) with icing. —*intr.* To turn into, or become coated with, ice; freeze. Often used with *over* or *up.* [Middle English *is,* Old English *īs,* from Germanic.]

I.C.E. Institution of Civil Engineers.

Ice. Iceland; Icelandic.

ice age *n.* **1.** A **glaciation period** *(see).* **2.** *Capital* **I,** *capital* **A.** The Pleistocene or glacial epoch.

ice axe *n.* An axe used by mountaineers for cutting steps in ice.

ice bag *n.* A small waterproof bag used as an **ice pack** *(see).*

ice barrier *n.* That part of the ice sheet covering Antarctica that extends beyond the coastline. Also called "barrier".

ice·berg (íss-berg) *n.* **1.** A massive floating body of ice broken away from a glacier or ice sheet. Also called "berg". **2.** *Informal.* One who appears to be cold or aloof. [Probably partial translation of Danish and Norwegian *isberg* : *is,* ice + *berg,* mountain.]

iceberg lettuce *n.* A type of lettuce characterised by its light green colouring, crisp leaves, and compact head.

ice·blink (íss-blingk) *n.* A yellowish glare in the sky over an ice field. Also called "blink".

ice block *n. Australian & N.Z.* An ice lolly.

ice-blue (íss-blōō ‖ -bléw) *n.* A pale greenish blue. —**ice-blue** *adj.*

ice·boat (íss-bōt) *n.* **1.** A boatlike vehicle set on runners that sails on ice. **2.** An icebreaker.

ice·bound (íss-bownd) *adj.* **1.** Locked in by ice: *an icebound ship.* **2.** Jammed or covered over by ice: *an icebound harbour.*

ice·box (íss-boks) *n.* **1.** A freezing compartment in a refrigerator. **2.** An insulated chest or box in which ice is put to cool and preserve food. Also called "cool box". **3.** *U.S.* A refrigerator.

ice·break·er (íss-braykər) *n.* A sturdy ship built for breaking a passage through icebound waters. Also called "iceboat".

ice bucket *n.* **1.** A small insulated bucket with a lid, containing ice for adding to drinks. **2.** A somewhat larger bucket of this sort, used without a lid to cool bottles placed inside it.

ice cap *n.* An extensive perennial cover of ice and snow, smaller than an ice sheet.

ice-cold (íss-kṓld) *adj.* Very cold; freezing cold.

ice cream *n.* **1.** A smooth, sweet, cold food prepared from a frozen mixture of milk products and sometimes egg yolks and flavoured in a variety of ways. **2.** Such a food, but with animal fat or seaweed products used as substitues for milk products.

ice-cream cone (íss-kréem ‖ *U.S. also* -kreem) *n.* **1.** A conical wafer used to hold a scoop of ice cream. **2.** This wafer with the ice cream in it.

iced (īst) *adj.* **1.** Covered over with ice. **2.** Chilled with ice. **3.** Decorated or coated with icing.

ice-fall (íss-fawl) *n.* **1.** A broken, tumbled mass of ice where a glacier becomes steeper. **2.** An avalanche of ice.

ice field *n.* **1.** A large, level expanse of floating ice. Also called "floe". **2.** A large expanse of ice on land.

ice floe *n.* A floe *(see).*

ice hockey *n.* A game played on ice in which two opposing teams of skaters, using curved sticks, try to drive a flat disc, or puck, into the opponents' goal. Also called "hockey".

ice house *n.* A building, often underground, formerly used for storing ice and preserving it by natural means.

Ice·land (íssland ‖ -land) *n.* An independent island republic lying in the north Atlantic Ocean, just south of the Arctic Circle. Much of the island is of volcanic origin and there are about 200 volcanoes, several of which are still active, as well as a number of geysers and lakes of boiling mud. Less than two per cent of the land is cultivated, and the economy is heavily dependent on the cod-fishing industry. Area, 103 000 square kilometres (39,769 square miles). Population, 270,000. Capital, Reykjavík. See map at **Western Europe.**

Ice·land·er (íss-ləndər, -landər) *n.* A native of Iceland.

Ice·land·ic (íss-lándik) *adj. Abbr.* **Ice., Icel.** Of or pertaining to Iceland, its inhabitants, their language, or their culture.
~*n.* The North Germanic language spoken in Iceland, specifically: **1.** This language as spoken since the 16th century. **2. Old Icelandic** *(see).*

Iceland moss *n.* A brittle, greyish-brown, edible lichen, *Cetraria islandica,* of artic regions and northern Europe.

Iceland poppy *n.* **1.** An arctic poppy, *Papaver nudicaule,* widely cultivated for its white or yellow flowers. **2.** Any of several similar arctic poppies.

Iceland spar *n.* A doubly refracting, transparent, crystalline form of calcite used in experiments on optical polarisation.

ice lolly *n. British.* A water ice or other frozen sweet held on a small stick. Also *U.S.* "Popsicle" (a trademark).

ice machine *n.* A machine that freezes water into ice cubes.

ice needle *n.* Any of the thin ice crystals that float high in the atmosphere in certain conditions of clear, cold weather.

ice pack *n.* **1.** A bag or folded cloth filled with crushed ice and applied to sore or swollen parts of the body. Also called "pack". **2.** A container filled with a liquid of high thermal capacity that can be frozen, used to keep food or other materials cool.

ice pick *n.* A pointed awl for chipping or breaking ice.

ice plant *n.* A plant, *Mesembryanthemum* (or *Cryophytum*) *crystallinum,* native to southern Africa, having fleshy leaves and stems covered with glistening encrustations, and white or pink flowers.

ice point *n.* The temperature at which pure water and ice are in equilibrium in a mixture at one atmosphere of pressure; the melting point of ice, or freezing point of water, under normal atmospheric pressure.

ice rink *n.* **1.** A building housing a level ice surface for skating. **2.** The ice surface itself. Also called "skating rink".

ice-scouring *n. Geology.* The erosion of rock by glacial ice. —**ice-scoured** *adj.*

ice sheet *n.* A vast, continuous expanse of land ice, such as that covering the Antarctic continent. See **glacier.**

ice shelf *n.* A thick, floating ice sheet attached to a coastline.

ice show *n.* An entertainment performed by skaters on ice.

ice skate *n.* **1.** A metal runner or blade that is fitted to the sole of a shoe for skating on ice. **2.** A shoe or light boot with such a runner permanently fixed to it.

ice-skate (íss-skayt) *intr.v.* **-skated, -skating, -skates.** To skate on ice. —**ice-skat·er** *n.*

ice-tray (íss-tray) *n.* A shallow oblong tray of metal or plastic in which water is frozen into cubes of ice in a freezer or icebox.

ice wall *n.* A cliff of ice forming the seaward margin of an ice sheet.

ice water *n.* **1. a.** Very cold drinking water. **b.** Such water containing ice. **2.** Melted ice.

ICFTU International Confederation of Free Trade Unions.

Ich dien (ikh déen). *German.* I serve. The motto of the Prince of Wales.

I Ching (í ching, ée jíng) *n.* A classical book of ancient China whose philosophy seeks to explain nature and human nature in terms of changing balances. As a form of fortune-telling, the book is used to explain each of 64 hexagrams, one of which is chosen at random by the person consulting it. [Chinese, "book of changes".]

ich·neu·mon (ik-néw-mən ‖ -nōō-) *n.* A mongoose of the genus *Herpestes;* especially, *H. ichneumon,* of Africa. [Latin, from Greek *ikhneumōn,* "tracker", a weasel that hunts out crocodile eggs, from *ikhneuein,* to track, from *ikhnos†,* track.]

ichneumon fly *n.* Any of numerous wasplike insects of the family Ichneumonidae, having larvae that are parasitic on the larvae of other insects. Also called "ichneumon wasp".

ich·nite (ík-nīt) *n.* A fossilised footprint. Also called "ichnolite". [Greek *ikhnos,* footstep, track (see **ichneumon**) + -ITE.]

ich·nog·ra·phy (ik-nóggrəfi) *n., pl.* **-phies. 1.** The art or process of drawing up ground plans. **2.** A ground plan of a building. [French *ichnographie,* from Latin, from Greek *ikhnographia* : *ikhnos,* track + -*graphia,* -GRAPHY.]

i·chor (í-kawr) *n.* **1.** *Greek Mythology.* The rarefied fluid said to run in the veins of the gods. **2.** A fluid likened to blood. **3.** *Pathology.* A watery, acrid discharge from a wound or ulcer. [Greek *ikhōr†.*] —**i·chor·ous** (íkərəss) *adj.*

ich·thy·ic (íkthi-ik) *adj.* Of, pertaining to, or characteristic of fishes. [Greek *ikhthus,* fish. See **ichthyo-.**]

ichthyo-, ichthy- *comb. form.* Indicates fish; for example, **ichthyology, ichthyornis.** [Latin, from Greek *ikhthuo-,* from *ikhthus,* fish.]

ich·thy·oid (íkthi-oyd) *adj.* Also **ich·thy·oid·al** (-óyd'l). Characteristic of or resembling a fish.
~*n.* A fish or fishlike vertebrate. [Greek *ikhthuoeidēs* : ICHTHY(O)- + -OID.]

ich·thy·ol·o·gy (íkthi-ólləji) *n. Abbr.* **ichthyol., ichth.** A branch of zoology specialising in the study of fishes. [ICHTHYO- + -LOGY.] —**ich·thy·o·log·ic** (-ə-lójik), **ich·thy·o·log·i·cal** *adj.* —**ich·thy·ol·o·gist** *n.*

ich·thy·oph·a·gous (íkthi-óffə-gəss) *adj.* Feeding on fish; fish-eating. [Greek *ikhthuophagos* : ICHTHYO- + -PHAGOUS.] —**ich·thy·oph·a·gy** (-ji) *n.*

ich·thy·or·nis (íkthi-órniss) *n.* Any of various extinct, fish-eating birds of the genus *Ichthyornis,* that existed during the Cretaceous period. [New Latin "fish bird" : ICHTHY(O)- + Greek *ornis,* bird.]

ich·thy·o·saur (íkthi-ə-sawr) *n.* Also **ich·thy·o·saur·us** (-sáw-rəss) *pl.* **-sauri** (-rī), **-sauruses.** Any of various extinct fishlike marine reptiles of the order Ichthyosauria, of the Triassic to the Cretaceous periods. [New Latin *Ichthyosaurus* : ICHTHYO- + -SAUR.]

ich·thy·o·sis (íkthi-ṓ-siss) *n.* A congenital skin disease, characterised by dry, thickened, scaly skin. Also called "fishskin disease", "xeroderma". [New Latin : ICHTHY(O)- + -OSIS.]

-ician *n. suffix.* Indicates a person who practises or is a specialist in a specified field; for example, **beautician, phonetician.**

i·ci·cle (ī-sik'l) *n.* A tapering spike of ice formed by the freezing of dripping or falling water. [Middle English *isikel* : *is,* ICE + *ikel,* icicle, Old English *gicel.*]

i·ci·ly (ī-sili) *adv.* In an icy or chilling manner.

i·ci·ness (ī-si-nəss, -niss) *n.* The condition or quality of being icy.

ic·ing (ī-sing) *n.* **1. a.** A covering for cakes and other confectionery, made from icing sugar and water or butter and sometimes flavoured. **b.** Frosting for cakes. **2.** The formation of ice; especially, the formation of ice from moisture in the atmosphere, as on an aircraft or ship.

icing sugar *n. British.* Finely powdered sugar used to make cake icing. Also U.S. "confectioners' sugar".

ickle (ick'l) *adj. British Informal.* Little. Used by or to children. [Baby talk variant of LITTLE.]

ick·y (icki) *adj. Chiefly U.S. Slang.* **1.** Sticky; cloying. **2.** Sentimental; mawkish. **3.** Nasty; unpleasant. [20th century : origin obscure.]

ICJ International Court of Justice.

Ick·nield Way (ík-neeld). Prehistoric road in England. It ran southwest from the Wash, along the line of the Chiltern Hills and the Berkshire Downs, to Salisbury Plain.

i·con, i·kon (ī-kon, -kən) *n.* Also **ei·kon** (for sense 2). **1. a.** An image; a representation. **b.** One that is both a symbol and a representative of something specified; exemplar: *that icon of revolution, Che Guevara.* **2.** A representation or picture of a sacred Christian personage, itself regarded as sacred, especially in the tradition of the Eastern Churches. **3.** A term which in some way resembles that which it designates. [Latin *īcōn,* from Greek *eikōn,* likeness, image.]

i·con·ic (ī-kónnik) *adj.* **1.** Pertaining to or having the character of an icon. **2.** Having a conventional style. Said of certain memorial statues and busts, such as the ancient statues of victorious athletes.

Iconium. See **Konya.**

icono– *comb. form.* Indicates likeness, image; for example, **iconolatry.** [Greek *eikono-,* from *eikōn,* image, ICON.]

i·con·o·clasm (ī-kónnə-klaz'm) *n.* The action or doctrine of an iconoclast.

i·con·o·clast (ī-kónnə-klast) *n.* **1.** A destroyer of sacred images, specifically: **a.** Any of the opponents of the use and veneration of icons in the Eastern Churches during the eighth and ninth centuries A.D. **b.** A Protestant in the 16th and 17th centuries who opposed the veneration of sacred images and traditions. **2.** One who attacks and seeks to overthrow traditional or popular ideas or institutions. [Medieval Latin *īconoclāstēs,* from Medieval Greek *eikonoklastēs,* "image breaker" : ICONO- + -CLAST.] —**i·con·o·clas·tic** (-klástik) *adj.* —**i·con·o·clas·ti·cal·ly** *adv.*

i·co·nog·ra·phy (ī'kə-nóggrəfi) *n., pl.* **-phies. 1. a.** Pictorial illustration of a given subject. **b.** The collected representations illustrating a subject. **2. a.** A given set of symbolic forms bearing the meaning of a stylised work of art. **b.** The conventions defining them and governing their interrelationship. [Greek *eikonographia,* description, sketch, "drawing of images" : ICONO- + -GRAPHY.] —**i·con·o·graph·ic** (ī-kónnə-gráffik), **i·con·o·graph·i·cal** *adj.*

i·co·nol·a·try (ī'kə-nóllətri) *n.* The worship of images or icons. [ICONO- + -LATRY.] —**i·co·nol·a·ter** *n.*

i·co·nol·o·gy (ī'kə-nólləji) *n., pl.* **-gies. 1.** The branch of art history dealing with the description, analysis, and interpretations of icons or iconic representations. **2.** Symbolic representation. [French *iconologie* : ICONO- + -LOGY.] —**i·con·o·log·i·cal** (ī-kónnə-lójik'l) *adj.* —**i·co·nol·o·gist** *n.*

i·con·o·scope (ī-kónnə-skōp) *n.* A television-camera tube equipped for rapid scanning of an information-storing, photoactive mosaic by a beam of electrons. [Originally a trademark : ICONO- + -SCOPE.]

i·co·nos·ta·sis (ī'kō-nóstə-siss) *n., pl.* **-ses** (-seez). The screen dividing the sanctuary from the main body of an Eastern Church. [Late Greek *eikonostasion,* shrine, "place where images stand" : ICONO- + Greek *stasis,* a standing.]

i·co·sa·he·dron (ī-kossə-hée-drən, -kəssə-, -hé- ‖ ī-kóssə-, -kōssə-) *n., pl.* **-dra** (-drə) or **-drons.** A polyhedron having 20 faces. A regular icosahedron has faces that are equilateral triangles. [Greek *eikosaedron* : *eikosi,* twenty.] —**i·co·sa·he·dral** *adj.*

-ics *n. suffix.* Indicates: **1.** *Used with a singular verb.* The science or art of; for example, **graphics, poetics. 2.** *Used with a plural verb.* The act, practices, or activities of; for example, **acrobatics, athletics. 3.** *Used with a plural verb.* Characteristic properties or operations of; for example, **mechanics, dynamics.** [From -IC, originally used to render the Greek plural noun ending *-ika,* as in *mathēmatika,* MATHEMATICS.]

ICSH interstitial-cell stimulating hormone.

ic·ter·ic (ik-térrik) *adj.* **1.** Pertaining to or having jaundice. **2.** Used to treat jaundice.

~*n.* A remedy for jaundice.

ic·ter·us (íktərəss) *n. Pathology.* Jaundice (see). [New Latin, from Greek *ikterost,* jaundice.]

ic·tus (íktəss) *n., pl.* **-tuses** or **ictus. 1.** A metrical or rhythmical stress in verse. **2.** *Pathology.* A sudden attack; a fit; a stroke. [Latin, blow, stroke, from the past participle of *īceret,* to strike.]

i·cy (ī-si) *adj.* **icier, iciest. 1.** Containing or covered with ice; frozen; slippery: *an icy road.* **2.** Resembling ice; cold or slippery. **3.** Bitterly cold; freezing. **4.** Chilling in manner; frigid: *an icy smile.*

id (id) *n. Psychoanalysis.* That division of the psyche associated with instinctive impulses and demands for immediate satisfaction of primitive needs. See **ego, superego.** [New Latin (translation of German *es,* it), from Latin, it, neuter of *is,* he.]

I'd (īd). **1.** Contraction of *I had.* **2.** Contraction of *I would.* **3.** Contraction of *I should.*

-id *n. suffix.* Indicates: **1.** *Zoology.* A member of a family; for example, **hominid. 2.** *Chemistry.* Variant of **-ide.** [Partly from New Latin -IDAE and partly from French *-ide,* from Latin *-is* (stem *-id-*), feminine patronymic suffix.]

id. idem.

i.d. inside diameter.

I.D. 1. identification. **2.** intelligence department.

IDA International Development Association.

I·da, Mount (ī-də). Mountain in central Crete associated with the worship of Zeus. It rises to 2 456 metres (8,058 feet) and is the highest mountain on the island.

-idae *pl.n. suffix.* Indicates taxonomic names of families in zoology; for example, **Hominidae.** [New Latin. See **-id.**]

I·da·ho (ī-də-hō). State (since 1890) in the northwestern United States, one of the group of Rocky Mountain states. The capital and largest city is Boise. It is noted for its unspoilt natural beauty, two fifths of the state being covered by natural forest. Hell's Canyon, also known as "Grand Canyon of the Snake", is at one point 2 401 metres (7,900 feet) below the mountain peaks, and is the deepest gorge in North America. —**I·da·ho·an** *adj. & n.*

I.D.B. *South African.* illicit diamond buying.

-ide, -id *n. suffix.* Used to form the names of chemical compounds, especially salts derived from acids that contain no oxygen; for example, **chloride.** [German *-id,* from French *-ide* (first used in *oxide,* OXIDE), from *acide,* ACID.]

i·de·a (ī-déer, ī-, -dée-ə ‖ ī-dee) *n.* **1.** That which comes into existence in the mind as a product of mental activity, such as thought or knowledge; a thought; a conception: *many good ideas.* **2.** An opinion, conviction, or principle produced after thought or observation: *Upon what do you base your political ideas?* **3.** A plan, scheme, or method. **4.** The gist or significance of a specific action or situation. **5.** A notion; a fancy. **6.** *Obsolete.* A mental image of something remembered. **7.** *Music.* A theme or motif. **8.** *Philosophy.* **a.** In the philosophy of Plato, an archetype of which a corresponding being in phenomenal reality is an imperfect replica. **b.** In the philosophy of Kant, a concept of reason that is transcendent but nonempirical. **c.** In the philosophy of Hegel, absolute truth, the complete and ultimate product of reason. [Latin, from Greek, form, model, class, notion.]

Synonyms: idea, thought, notion, conception, concept.

i·de·al (ī-déerl, ī-, -dée-əl, -déel) *n.* **1.** A conception of something in its absolute perfection. **2.** One regarded as a standard or model of perfection. **3.** An ultimate object of endeavour; a goal. **4.** A worthy principle or aim. **5.** That which exists only in the mind.

~*adj.* **1.** Conforming to an ultimate form of perfection or excellence. **2.** Considered the best of its kind. **3.** Completely or highly satisfactory. **4.** Existing only in the mind; visionary; imaginary. **5.** Of, pertaining to, or consisting of ideas or mental images. **6.** *Philosophy.* **a.** Existing as an archetype or pattern, especially as a Platonic idea. **b.** Of or pertaining to idealism. [French *idéal,* from Late Latin *ideālis,* from Latin *idea,* model, IDEA.]

Synonyms: ideal, model, exemplar, standard, archetype.

ideal gas *n. Physics.* A hypothetical gas that obeys the gas laws. In kinetic theory, a model of such a gas is a large number of particles of negligible size, moving randomly and making elastic collisions with the walls of the container.

ideal gas law *n. Physics.* Gas equation (see).

i·de·al·ise, i·de·al·ize (ī-déer-līz, -dée-ə) *v.* **-ised, -ising, -ises.** —*tr.* **1. a.** To regard as ideal. **b.** To treat (a person or thing) as if ideal. **2.** To depict or imagine as ideal. —*intr.* **1.** To render something as an ideal. **2.** To conceive an ideal or ideals. —**i·de·al·i·sa·tion** (-ī-záysh'n ‖ U.S. -i-) *n.* —**i·de·al·is·er** *n.*

i·de·al·ism (ī-déer-liz'm, -dée-ə-, ídi-ə-) *n.* **1.** The envisaging of things in an ideal form. **2.** Pursuit of one's ideals. **3.** An idealising treatment of a subject in literature or art. **4.** The theory that the object of external perception, in itself or as perceived, consists of ideas. In this sense, compare **materialism, realism.**

i·de·al·ist (ī-déer-list, -dée-ə-, ídi-ə-) *n.* **1.** One whose conduct is influenced by idealism. **2.** One who is unrealistic and impractical; a visionary. **3.** An artist or writer whose work is imbued with idealism. **4.** An adherent of any system of philosophical idealism.

i·de·al·is·tic (ī-déer-lístik, -dée-ə-, ídi-ə-) *adj.* Pertaining to or having the nature of an idealist or idealism. —**i·de·al·is·ti·cal·ly** *adv.*

i·de·al·i·ty (ī-di-ál-əti) *n., pl.* **-ties. 1.** The state or quality of being ideal. **2.** Existence in idea only.

i·de·al·ly (ī-déer-li, ídi-ə-) *adv.* **1.** In conformity with an ideal; perfectly. **2.** In ideal conditions; theoretically.

i·de·ate (ī-dée-ayt, ídi-) *v.* **-ated, -ating, -ates.** —*tr.* To form an idea of; imagine; conceive. —*intr.* To conceive mental images; think. [IDEA.] —**i·de·a·tion** (ídi-áysh'n) *n.* —**i·de·a·tion·al** *adj.*

i·dée fixe (ee-day feeks) *n., pl.* **idées fixes** (*pronounced as singular*). A fixed idea; an obsession. [French.]

i·dée re·çue (ee-day rə-séw, -sü) *n., pl.* **idées reçues** (*pronounced as singular*). A received idea; an opinion that is held out of respect for convention rather than from conviction. [French.]

i·dem (ī-dem, íddem). *Abbr.* **id.** The same. Used to indicate a reference previously mentioned. [Latin *īdem* (masculine), *idem* (neuter), the same, from *id*, it, neuter of *is*, he.]

i·dem·po·tent (ídem-pōtənt, i-démpətənt) *adj. Mathematics.* Unchanged by multiplication by itself. Said of matrices, functions, operators, and the like. [Latin *idem*, same + POTENT.]

i·den·tic note (ī-déntik) *n.* A diplomatic communication with wording that has been agreed by two or more governments, copies of which are dispatched simultaneously on behalf of these governments. [Medieval Latin *identicus*, IDENTICAL.]

i·den·ti·cal (ī-déntik'l, i-) *adj.* **1.** Being the same. **2.** Being exactly alike or equal. —See Synonyms at **same.** [Medieval Latin *identicus*, from Late Latin *identitās*, IDENTITY.] **—i·den·ti·cal·ly** *adv.* **—i·den·ti·cal·ness** *n.*

Usage: Standard English recommends that the preposition following *identical* should be *with (That picture is identical with the one in my office)*, but *to* is becoming increasingly common.

identical twin *n.* Either of a pair of twins of the same sex developed from a single fertilised ovum that split in half. Identical twins have identical genetic constitutions and show pronounced mutual resemblance. Also called "monozygotic twin".

i·den·ti·fi·ca·tion (ī-déntifi-káysh'n, i-) *n.* **1.** The act of identifying. **2.** The state of being identified. **3.** *Abbr.* **I.D.** Proof of one's identity, such as a document, for example. **4.** *Psychology.* **a.** An individual's recognition of a personal or group identity. **b.** The transferral of response to an object considered identical to another. **5.** Loosely, the recognition of oneself in another character, such as one in fiction or public life.

identification parade *n.* A police procedure in which a witness to or victim of a crime is invited to identify the criminal from a group of persons which includes the person under suspicion.

i·den·ti·fy (ī-dénti-fī, i-) *v.* **-fied, -fying, -fies.** *—tr.* **1. a.** To establish the identity of. **b.** To ascertain the origin, nature, or definitive characteristics of: *His accent was difficult to identify.* **c.** To determine and select: *identify the best method.* **2.** To determine the taxonomic classification of. **3.** To consider as identical; equate. **4.** To associate with. **5.** *Psychology.* **a.** To associate or affiliate (oneself) closely with a person or group. **b.** Loosely, to imagine (oneself) as another person, such as a literary character or a prominent figure. *—intr.* To establish an identification with another or others. [Medieval Latin *identificāre* : Late Latin *identitās*, IDENTI(TY) + -FY.] **—i·den·ti·fi·a·ble** (-fī-əb'l, -fī-) *adj.* **—i·den·ti·fi·er** *n.*

Usage: This verb is widely used with a reflexive pronoun: *He identified himself with the hero of the novel.* To omit the pronoun *(He identified with the hero of the novel)* is widespread in American English, and is increasingly common in British English, but formal styles still prefer the use of the pronoun. Used technically, in the field of psychology, *identify* expresses close association with a person or group, and also lacks the reflexive pronoun *(He identifies with his father).*

I·den·ti·kit (ī-dénti-kit) *n.* A trademark for a method of combining drawings of facial features from which an image of a police suspect, missing person, or the like can be made up according to descriptions given to the police. Compare **Photofit.**
~adj. **1.** Made up from such drawings. **2.** *Often small* **i.** Typical; conforming to a conventional type: *an identikit executive.*

i·den·ti·ty (ī-déntəti, i-) *n., pl.* **-ties. 1.** The collective aspect of the set of characteristics by which a thing is definitively recognisable or known. **2.** The set of behavioural or personal characteristics by which an individual is recognisable as a member of a group. **3.** The name or nature of a person or thing: *reveal one's identity.* **4.** The quality or condition of being exactly the same as something else. **5.** The quality or condition of being or remaining the same. **6.** The personality of an individual regarded as a persisting entity. **7.** *Mathematics.* **a.** An equality satisfied by all values of the variables for which the expressions involved in the equality are defined. **b.** A member of a set that combines with other members and leaves them unchanged for a particular operation; for example, the integer 1 is the identity for real numbers under multiplication. Also called "identity element". [Late Latin *identitās*, from Latin *idem*, the same, IDEM.]

identity crisis *n. Psychology.* A period of disorientation and anxiety resulting from difficulties experienced in resolving personal conflicts, adjusting to social demands and pressures, or the like.

ideo– *comb. form.* Indicates idea; for example, **ideogram.** [French *idéo-*, from Greek *idea*, form, notion.]

id·e·o·gram (íddi-ō-gram, ídi-, -ə-) *n.* Also **id·e·o·graph** (-graf, -graaf). **1.** A character or symbol representing an idea or thing without indicating pronunciation, as the characters in Chinese. **2.** A graphic symbol; for example, &, %, @. [IDEO- + -GRAM.]

id·e·og·ra·phy (íddi-óggrəfi, ídi-) *n.* **1.** The representation of ideas by graphic symbols. **2.** The use of ideograms to express ideas. [IDEO- + -GRAPHY.] **—id·e·o·graph·ic** (-ə-gráffik) *adj.*

i·de·o·log·i·cal (īdi-ə-lójik'l, íddi-) *adj.* **1.** Of or relating to ideology. **2.** Of or concerned with ideas. **—i·de·o·log·i·cal·ly** *adv.*

i·de·ol·o·gist (īdi-óllәjist, íddi-) *n.* **1.** An advocate or adherent of a given ideology. **2.** A student of ideologies. **3.** *Archaic.* A visionary; a theorist.

i·de·o·logue (īdi-ə-log, íddi-) *n.* An advocate of a given ideology, especially one of its official exponents. [French *idéologue*, back-formation from *idéologie*, IDEOLOGY.]

i·de·ol·o·gy (īdi-óllәji, íddi-) *n., pl.* **-gies. 1.** The body of ideas reflecting the needs and aspirations of an individual, group, or culture. **2.** A set of doctrines or beliefs that form the basis of a political, economic, or other system. [French *idéologie* : IDEO- + -LOGY.]

i·de·o·mo·tor (īdi-ə-mōtər, íddi-, -ō-) *adj.* Of or being a motor response to an ideational rather than a sensory stimulus.

ides (īdz) *n. Used with a singular or plural verb.* In the ancient Roman calendar, the 15th day of March, May, July, or October or the 13th day of the other months. [Middle English *idus, ides*, from Old French *ides*, from Latin *īdūs*†.]

id est (id ést). *Abbr.* **i.e.** *Latin.* That is.

idio– *comb. form.* Indicates individuality, peculiarity, isolation, or distinctness; for example, **idiolect.** [Greek, from *idios*†, personal, peculiar, separate.]

id·i·o·blast (íddi-ō-blast) *n.* A specialised plant cell that differs from the cells around it. [IDIO- + -BLAST.] **—id·i·o·blast·ic** (-blástik) *adj.*

id·i·o·cy (íddi-ə-si) *n., pl.* **-cies. 1.** *Psychiatry.* Formerly, a condition of subnormal intellectual development or ability, characterised by an intelligence quotient in the range 20–50. No longer in technical usage. Compare **imbecility. 2.** Extreme folly or stupidity. **3.** A foolish or stupid utterance or deed.

id·i·o·gram (íddiō-gram) *n.* A **karyotype** *(see).* [IDIO- + -GRAM.]

id·i·o·lect (íddi-ə-lekt) *n.* The speech of an individual, considered as a linguistic pattern unique among speakers of his language or dialect. [IDIO- + (DIA)LECT.] **—id·i·o·lect·al** (-lékt'l), **id·i·o·lect·ic** (-léktik) *adj.*

id·i·om (íddi-əm) *n.* **1.** An expression or phrase, often informal, that has a meaning of its own that is not apparent from the meanings of its individual words; for example, *round the bend* meaning "mad" is an idiom. **2.** The specific grammatical, syntactical, and structural character of a given language. **3.** A regional speech or dialect. **4.** A specialised vocabulary used by a particular group of people; jargon: *legal idiom.* **5.** A style of artistic expression characteristic of a given individual, school, period, or medium. [Old French *idiome*, from Late Latin *idiōma*, from Greek, peculiarity, idiom, from *idiousthai*, to make one's own, from *idios*†, own, personal.]

id·i·o·mat·ic (íddi-ə-máttik) *adj.* **1.** Peculiar to or characteristic of a given language. **2.** Resembling or having the nature of an idiom. **3.** Using many idioms; fluent and natural: *spoke idiomatic French.* **—id·i·o·mat·i·cal·ly** *adv.*

id·i·o·mor·phic (íddi-ō-mórfik) *adj.* Occurring as crystals. Said of minerals. [Greek *idiomorphos*, having one's own form : IDIO- + -MORPHOUS.] **—id·i·o·mor·phic·al·ly** *adv.* **—id·i·o·mor·phism** *n.*

id·i·op·a·thy (íddi-óppəthi) *n. Medicine.* A disease of unknown origin or cause. [Greek *idiopathia*, disease having its own origin : IDIO- + -PATHY.] **—id·i·o·path·ic** (-ō-páthik) *adj.*

id·i·o·syn·cra·sy (íddi-ō-síngkrə-si, -ə-) *n., pl.* **-sies. 1.** Structural or behavioural characteristics peculiar to an individual or group. **2.** A physiological or temperamental peculiarity. **3.** Unusual hypersensitivity to a drug or food. —See Synonyms at **eccentricity.** [Greek *idiosunkrasia* : IDIO- + *sunkrasis*, a mingling, mixture, temperament : *syn-*, together + *krasis*, mixture, CRASIS.] **—id·i·o·syn·crat·ic** (-sing-kráttik) *adj.* **—id·i·o·syn·crat·i·cal·ly** *adv.*

id·i·ot (íddi-ət) *n.* **1.** A mentally deficient person, having an intelligence quotient in the 20 to 50 range, and classified as severely subnormal. No longer in technical usage. **2.** A very stupid person. [Middle English, from Old French *idiote*, from Latin *idiōta*, ignorant person, from Greek *idiōtēs*, private person, plebeian, layman, ignorant person, from *idios*†, peculiar, private.]

id·i·ot·ic (íddi-óttik) *adj.* Very stupid. **—id·i·ot·i·cal·ly** *adv.*

–idium *n. suffix.* Indicates a small structure or form; for example, **nephridium.** [New Latin, from Greek *-idion*.]

i·dle (íd'l) *adj.* **idler, idlest. 1.** Not employed; inactive: *an idle man.* **2.** Avoiding employment; lazy; shiftless. **3.** Not in operation or working order. **4.** Empty; pointless: *idle talk.* **5.** Unfounded; baseless: *idle rumours.* —See Synonyms at **inactive.**
~v. **idled, idling, idles.** *—intr.* **1.** To pass time without working or in avoiding work. **2.** To move lazily and without purpose. **3.** To run at a slow speed or out of gear. Used of a motor or a machine. *—tr.* **1.** To pass (time) without working or in avoiding work; waste. Often used with *away*: *idle the afternoon away.* **2.** *U.S.* To cause to be unemployed or inactive. **3.** To cause (a motor or machine) to idle. [Middle English *idel*, idle, void, empty, Old English *īdel*, from West Germanic *īdal* (unattested).] **—i·dle·ness** *n.* **—i·dly** *adv.*

idle pulley *n.* A pulley on a shaft that rests on or presses against a drive belt to guide it or take up slack. Also called "idler", "idler pulley", "idle wheel".

i·dler (ídlər) *n.* **1.** One that idles. **2.** An idle wheel or idle pulley. **3.** A sailor exempt from night watch.

idle wheel *n.* **1.** A gear, wheel, or roller interposed between two similar parts to convey motion from one to the other without change in speed or direction of motion. Also called "idler". **2.** An idle pulley.

I·do (éedō) *n.* An artificial language based on Esperanto. [Ido, offspring, from Greek *-id*, "daughter of".]

id·o·crase (ídə-krayss, íddə-, -krayz) *n.* A green, brown, yellow, or blue mineral, essentially $Ca_{10}Al_4(Mg,Fe)_2(Si_2O_4)_2(SiO_4)_5(OH)_4$. Also called "vesuvianite". [French : Greek *eidos*, form, shape + *krasis*, mixture.]

i·dol (íd'l) *n.* **1. a.** An image used as an object of worship. **b.** A false god. **2.** One that is the object of deep love or devotion. **3.** *Archaic.* Something visible but without substance. [Middle English *idol, idel*, from Old French *idole, idele*, from Late Latin *īdōlum*, from Greek *eidōlon*, image, form, apparition, from *eidos*, form.]

i·dol·a·ter (ī-dóllətər) *n.* **1.** One who worships idols. **2.** One who blindly admires or adores another. [Middle English *idolatrer*, from Old French *idolatre*, from Late Latin *īdōlolatrēs*, from Greek *eidōlolatreia* : *eidōlon*, IDOL + *-latrēs*, worshipper.]

i·dol·a·trise, i·dol·a·trize (ĭ-dŏllə-trīz) *tr.v.* **-trised, -trising, -trises.** To make an idol of. See Synonyms at **revere**.

i·dol·a·trous (ĭ-dŏllətrəss) *adj.* **1.** Given to idolatry. **2.** Constituting idolatry. **—i·dol·a·trous·ly** *adv.* **—i·dol·a·trous·ness** *n.*

i·dol·a·try (ī-dŏllətri) *n., pl.* **-tries. 1.** The worship of idols. **2.** Blind admiration of or devotion to something or someone. [Middle English, from Old French, from Medieval Latin *īdōlatrīa*, from Greek *eidōlolatreia* : *eidōlon*, IDOL + *-latreia*, -LATRY.]

i·dol·ise, i·dol·ize (ĭd'l-īz) *tr.v.* **-ised, -ising, -ises. 1.** To regard with blind admiration or devotion. **2.** To worship as an idol. **—**See Synonyms at **revere**. **—i·dol·i·sa·tion** (-ī-záysh'n ‖ *U.S.* -i-) *n.* **—i·dol·is·er** *n.*

i·do·lum (ī-dṓ-lōōm, -ləm) *n., pl.* **-la** (-lə). **1.** An image in the mind. **2.** A fallacy. [Latin, IDOL.]

Idun. Variant of **Ithunn**.

i·dyll, *U.S.* **i·dyl** (ĭddil, ĭ-dil) *n.* **1.** A short poem describing a picturesque episode or scene of rustic life. **2.** A scene or event of rural simplicity. **3.** A delightful and simple episode in life or literature. **4.** A piece of calm pastoral music. [Latin *īdyllium*, from Greek *eidullion*, diminutive of *eidos*, form, picture.]

i·dyl·lic (i-dĭllik, ī-) *adj.* **1.** Of, pertaining to, or having the nature of an idyll. **2.** Having a natural charm and picturesqueness. **—i·dyl·li·cal·ly** *adv.*

i·dyl·list (iddil-ist, ĭd'l-) *n.* A writer of idylls.

-ie. Variant of **-y**.

i.e. id est.

> *Usage:* The abbreviations *i.e.* and *e.g.* are not interchangeable, though they are sometimes confused. The distinction can easily be made by reference to their meanings: *i.e.* stands for the Latin *id est*, meaning "that is"; *e.g.* stands for the Latin *exempli gratia*, meaning "for example". Thus, *i.e.* always gives a fuller explanation of what precedes it: *the manager, i.e. the one in charge*, whereas *e.g.* introduces an example, or set of examples: *the people in charge, e.g. supervisors, stewards.* It is unacceptable to use such expressions as: *schoolchildren, i.e. five-year-olds and six-year-olds,* when what follows the abbreviation is an example rather than an explanation.

if (if ‖ iv) *conj.* **1.** Used to introduce a conditional clause, meaning: **a.** In the event that: *If I were to go, I would be late.* **b.** Granting that: *Even if that's true, what should we do?* **c.** On condition that: *She will sing only if she is paid.* **d.** Whenever: *I always go if she asks me.* **e.** Although: *they are gifted, if inexperienced.* **2.** Used to introduce an indirect question, meaning whether: *Ask if he will come.* **3.** Used to introduce an exclamatory clause, indicating: **a.** A wish: *If she had only come earlier!* **b.** Surprise, anger, or a similar emotion: *If she ever does that again!* **—as if. 1.** As might be the case if: *I felt as if I was dying.* **2.** It is ridiculous to claim that: *As if you couldn't have telephoned.* **—if not. 1.** Though perhaps not: *certainly comfortable, if not rich.* **2.** And possibly even: *a millionaire, if not a billionaire.*
~*n.* A possibility, condition, or stipulation. [Middle English *(y)if*, Old English *gif*.]

> *Usage:* Both *if* and *whether* may be used to introduce an indirect question, but *whether* is slightly more formal. It is also more likely whenever more than one condition is being expressed and linked by *or: He asked whether John would arrive on time or whether he would be late.* Sometimes it is necessary to use *whether* in order to avoid ambiguity: *Tell me if you want an answer,* for example, could mean either "Tell me whether you want an answer", or "If you expect an answer, there is something you should tell me".

IF, i.f. intermediate frequency.

IFC International Finance Corporation.

I·fe (ée-fi, -fay). City in southwestern Nigeria, a leading centre for the marketing and exporting of cocoa. It is believed to be the most ancient settlement of the Yoruba tribe, dating from *c.*1300. The terracotta and bronze sculptures made there in that period are considered some of the finest treasures of West African art.

if·fy (iffi) *adj.* Informal. Doubtful; uncertain. [From IF.] **—if·fi·ly** *adv.* **—if·fi·ness** *n.*

—i·form *adj. comb. form.* **—form** *(see).*

IGFET *n.* Insulated-gate *f*ield-*e*ffect *t*ransistor: a type of field-effect transistor.

I-girder *n.* A girder with an I-shaped cross-section.

ig·loo (íglōō) *n., pl.* **-loos.** An Eskimo house, traditionally dome-shaped and built of blocks of ice or hard snow. [Eskimo *iglu, igdlu,* house.]

Ign. ignition.

Ig·na·ti·us Loy·o·la, Saint (ig-náyshəss loy-ṓlə, lóy-ələ) (1491-1556). Spanish priest who founded the Society of Jesus (the Jesuits). He was canonised in 1622. His feast day is July 31.

ig·ne·ous (igni-əss) *adj.* **1.** Of, pertaining to, or characteristic of fire. **2.** *Geology.* **a.** Formed by solidification from a molten or partially molten state. Said of rocks. **b.** Of or pertaining to rock so formed; pyrogenic. [Latin *igneus*, from *ignis*, fire.]

ig·nis fat·u·us (ig'niss fáttew-əss) *n., pl.* **ignes fatui** (ig-neez fát-tew-ī). **1.** A phosphorescent light that hovers or flits over swampy ground at night, caused by spontaneous combustion of methane and other gases emitted by rotting organic matter. Also called "will-o'-the-wisp". **2.** Something that misleads or deludes; a deception. [Medieval Latin, "foolish fire".]

ig·nite (ig-nīt) *v.* **-nited, -niting, -nites. —***tr.* **1. a.** To cause to burn.

b. To set fire to. **2.** To arouse or kindle. **—***intr.* To begin to burn; catch fire. [Latin *ignīre*, to set on fire, from *ignis*, fire.] **—ig·nit·a·ble, ig·nit·i·ble** *adj.* **—ig·nit·er, ig·ni·tor** *n.*

ig·ni·tion (ig-nísh'n) *n.* **1.** The act of igniting or the point at which this occurs. **2.** *Abbr.* **Ign. a.** An electrical system, typically powered by a battery or magneto, that provides the spark to ignite the fuel mixture in an internal-combustion engine. **b.** A switch or other device that activates this system.

ignition point *n.* The minimum temperature at which a substance will continue to burn without additional external heat.

ig·ni·tron (ig-nĭ-tron, ígni-) *n.* A single-anode, mercury-vapour rectifier in which current passes as an arc between the anode and a mercury-pool cathode, used in power rectification. [Latin *ignis*, fire + -TRON.]

ig·no·ble (ig-nṓb'l) *adj.* **1.** Not having an honourable character or purpose; contemptible. **2.** Not of the nobility; common. **—**See Synonyms at **mean** (base). [Latin *ignōbilis* : *in-*, not + *nōbilis*, NOBLE.] **—ig·no·bil·i·ty** (ig-nō-bílləti), **ig·no·ble·ness** *n.* **—ig·no·bly** *adv.*

ig·no·min·i·ous (ig-nə-mínni-əss) *adj.* **1.** Characterised by shame or disgrace. **2.** Deserving disgrace or shame; despicable. **3.** Degrading; debasing. **—ig·no·min·i·ous·ly** *adv.* **—ig·no·min·i·ous·ness** *n.*

ig·no·min·y (ig-nə-mini ‖ *U.S. also* ig-nómmini) *n., pl.* **-ies. 1.** Dishonour; infamy. **2.** That which causes dishonour; a disgraceful act or disgraceful conduct. **—**See Synonyms at **disgrace**. [Latin *ignōminia* : *in-*, not + *nōmen* (stem *nōmin-*), name, reputation.]

ig·no·ra·mus (ig-nə-ráyməss) *n., pl.* **-muses.** An ignorant person. [New Latin, from Latin, "we do not know", from *īgnōrāre*, to be ignorant, IGNORE.]

ig·no·rance (íg-nərənss) *n.* The condition of being ignorant; lack of knowledge.

ig·no·rant (íg-nərənt) *adj.* **1.** Without education or knowledge. **2.** Exhibiting lack of education or knowledge. **3.** Unaware or uninformed. **4.** *Nonstandard.* Ill-mannered. [Middle English *ignoraunt*, from Old French *ignorant*, from Latin *īgnōrāns* (stem *īgnorant-*), present participle of *īgnōrāre*, to be ignorant, IGNORE.] **—ig·no·rant·ly** *adv.*

> *Synonyms:* ignorant, uneducated, untaught, unlearned, untutored, unlettered.

ig·no·ra·ti·o e·len·chi (íg-nə-ráyshi-ō i-léng-kī, -ráati-, -ki) *n. Latin.* The procedure of disproving an extraneous proposition rather than one actually advanced. ["Ignoring of proof", translation of Greek *elenkhou agnoia*.]

ig·nore (ig-nór ‖ -nŏr) *tr.v.* **-nored, -noring, -nores.** To refuse to pay attention to; disregard. See Synonyms at **refuse**. [French *ignorer*, from Latin *īgnōrāre*, not to know, disregard.] **—ig·nor·a·ble** *adj.* **—ig·nor·er** *n.*

ig·no·tum per ig·no·ti·us (ig-nṓ-tōōm pər ig-nóti-ōōss, -təm, -əss) *n. Latin.* An explanation which is more confusing than that which it purports to explain. ["The unknown by means of the more unknown."]

I·go·rot (íggə-rŏt, éegə-) *n., pl.* **-rots** or collectively **Igorot.** Also **I·gor·ro·te** (-rṓti). **1.** A member of any of several related peoples of mountainous northern Luzon in the Philippines. **2.** The Malayo-Polynesian language of these people.

i·gua·na (i-gwáanə; *also* íggew-áanə) *n.* Any of various large tropical American lizards of the family Iguanidae, often having spiny projections along the back. [Spanish, from Arawak *iwana*.]

i·guan·o·don (i-gwáanə-don, íggew-áanə-, -dən) *n.* Any of various large dinosaurs of the genus *Iguanodontidae*, of the Jurassic and Cretaceous periods. [New Latin *Iguanodon*: IGUAN(A) + -ODON.]

IGY International Geophysical Year.

ih·ram (i-ráam) *n.* **1.** The sacred dress of Muslim pilgrims, consisting of two lengths of white cotton. **2.** The sacred state in which the pilgrim exists while wearing this dress. [Arabic *iḥrām*, "prohibition", from *ḥarama*, he prohibited. See **haram**.]

IHS A graphic symbol for Jesus. [From ΙΗΣΟΤΣ or IHSOUS, Jesus (in Greek capitals).]

IJs·sel·meer or **Ys·sel·meer** (*Dutch* áy-səl-mair). Lake of the north Netherlands. It was formed in 1932 from the Zuider Zee by the Wieringen-Friesland Barrage. Four polders are now farmland. Work on a fifth polder, Markermeer, was planned, but because of ecological objections these plans were abandoned.

i·ke·ba·na (ícke-báanə) *n.* The Japanese art of formal flower arrangement. [Japanese, "living flowers".]

Ikhnaton. See **Akhenaton**.

ikon. Variant of **icon**.

ilang-ilang. Variant of **ylang-ylang**.

-ile *adj. suffix.* Indicates relationship with, similarity to, or capability of; for example, **prehensile, virile**. [Middle English, from Old French, from Latin *-ilis*.]

ILEA Inner London Education Authority.

il·e·ac (illi-ak) *adj.* **1.** Of or pertaining to ileus. **2.** Of or pertaining to the ileum; ileal.

Ile-de-France (éel-də-frónss). A region and former province in north central France, occupying the Paris basin in the Seine lowland, with Paris as its centre.

Ile du Diable. See **Devil's Island**.

il·e·i·tis (illi-ítiss) *n.* Inflammation of the ileum. [New Latin : IL-E(UM) + -ITIS.]

il·e·os·to·my (illi-ósstəmi) *n., pl.* **-mies.** The surgical formation of an artificial opening through the abdominal wall into the ileum so that the intestinal contents can be discharged without passing through the colon. [ILEO- + -STOMY.]

il·e·um (ílli-əm) n., pl. **-ea** (-ə). The lower portion of the small intestine extending from the jejunum to the caecum. [New Latin, from Latin *īlium, īleum†,* groin, flank.] **—il·e·al** adj.

il·e·us (ílli-əss) n. Intestinal obstruction due to loss of peristalsis or to mechanical obstruction, causing colic, vomiting, and toxaemia. [Latin *īleus,* from Greek *(e)ileos,* "a twisting", from *eilein, illein,* to roll, wind.]

i·lex (ílleks) n. **1.** Any of various trees or shrubs of the genus *Ilex;* a holly. **2.** The **holm oak** (see). [Latin *īlex,* holm oak, of Mediterranean origin.]

Il·i·ad (ílli-əd, -ad) n. A Greek epic poem attributed to Homer, recounting the siege of Troy.

il·i·um (ílli-əm) n., pl. **-ia** (-ə). The uppermost and widest of three bones comprising one of the lateral halves of the pelvis. [New Latin, from Latin *īlium, īleum†,* groin, flank.] **—il·i·ac** (-ak) adj.

ilk¹ (ilk) n. **1.** Type or kind: *people of that ilk.* Sometimes used humorously. **2.** *Scottish.* Used following a name in the phrase *of that ilk* to indicate that the one named resides on an estate bearing the same name: *Duncan of that ilk.* —See Synonyms at **type.** [Middle English *ilke, ilk,* Old English *ilca,* same.]

ilk². Variant of **ilka.**

il·ka (ílkə) adj. Also **ilk** (ilk). *Scottish.* Each; every. [Middle English *ilka(n),* each one : *ilk, ech,* EACH + a, A.]

ill (il) adj. **worse, worst. 1.** Not healthy; sick. **2.** Not normal; unsound: *ill health.* **3.** Resulting in suffering; distressing. **4.** Characterised by animosity or an unpleasant disposition: *ill humour.* **5.** Boding evil; unpropitious. **6.** Disreputable; wicked: *a house of ill repute.* **7.** *Archaic & Regional.* Difficult; hard: *he's ill to please.* —See Synonyms at **sick.**
~adv. worse, worst. 1. In an ill manner; badly. **2.** Scarcely or with difficulty. **Note:** The adverb *ill* combines with many adjectives, usually derived from the participles of verbs, to form attributive modifiers before nouns: *an ill-regulated life; an ill-deserving man.* In such use, the elements are joined with a hyphen. However, when *ill* modifies an adjective coming after the noun or pronoun, the two words are written separately: *His life was ill regulated. The man is ill deserving.*
~n. 1. Evil; wrongdoing. **2.** Disaster or harm. **3.** A physical or moral trouble. [Middle English *ill(e),* from Old Norse *illr†,* bad.]

I'll (īl). **1.** Contraction of *I will.* **2.** Contraction of *I shall.*

ill. illustrated; illustration; illustrator.

ill-ad·vised (íl-əd-vízd ‖ -ad-) adj. Unwise; foolish. **—ill-ad·vis·ed·ly** (-ídli) adv.

ill-as·sort·ed (íl-ə-sórtid) adj. Poorly matched: *an ill-assorted couple.*

ill-at-ease (íl-ət-éez) adj. Nervous; uncomfortable.

il·la·tion (i-láysh'n) n. **1.** The act of inferring or drawing conclusions. **2.** A conclusion drawn; a deduction. [Late Latin *illātiō* (stem *illātiōn-*) from Latin, "a carrying in", deduction, from *illātus* (past participle of *inferre,* to bring in) : *in-,* in + *-lātus,* "carried".]

il·la·tive (íl-láytiv, íllətiv) adj. *Grammar.* **1.** Expressing or preceding an inference: *"therefore" is an illative word.* **2.** Designating a case in Finnish and Hungarian that expresses movement or direction towards. **—il·la·tive** n.

ill-behaved (íl-bi-háyvd) adj. Ill-mannered.

ill-bred (íl-bréd) adj. **1.** Badly brought up; ill-mannered; impolite. **2.** Not thoroughbred.

ill-considered (íl-kən-síddərd ‖ -kon-) adj. Unwise; foolish.

ill-defined (íl-di-fínd) adj. Not defined clearly.

ill-disposed (íl-di-spózd) adj. **1.** Having an unfriendly or hostile attitude. **2.** Unwilling.

il·le·gal (i-léeg'l, í) adj. **1.** Prohibited by law. **2.** Prohibited by official rules. **—il·le·gal·ly** adv.

il·le·ga·lise, il·le·ga·lize (i-léeg'l-īz) tr.v. **-ised, -ising, -ises.** To make illegal. **—il·le·gal·i·sa·tion** (-ī-zaysh'n ‖ U.S. -i-) n.

il·le·gal·i·ty (ílli-gál-əti, illee-) n., pl. **-ties. 1.** The state or quality of being illegal. **2.** An illegal act.

il·leg·i·ble (i-léj-ib'l) adj. Not legible or decipherable. **—il·leg·i·bil·i·ty** (-bíllə̆ti), **il·leg·i·ble·ness** n. **—il·leg·i·bly** adv.

il·le·git·i·ma·cy (illi-jíttimə-si) n. The condition or state of being illegitimate; specifically, bastardy.

il·le·git·i·mate (ílli-jítti-mət, -mit) adj. **1.** Against the law; illegal. **2.** Born to unmarried parents. **3.** Improper; unfair. **4.** Incorrectly deduced. **—il·le·git·i·mate·ly** adv.

ill-fat·ed (il-fáytid) adj. **1.** Destined for misfortune; doomed. **2.** Marked by causing misfortune; unlucky.

ill-fa·voured (il-fáyvərd) adj. **1.** Having an ugly or unattractive face. **2.** Objectionable; offensive. **—ill-fa·voured·ly** adv. **—ill-fa·voured·ness** n.

ill feeling n. Feelings of animosity or rancour.

ill-founded (il-fówndid) adj. Having no factual basis.

ill-got·ten (il-gótt'n) adj. Obtained in an evil manner or by dishonest means. Used chiefly in the phrase *ill-gotten gains.*

ill humour n. An irritable state of mind; surliness.

ill-hu·moured (íl-héwmərd) adj. Irritable and surly. **—ill-hu·moured·ly** adv. **—ill-hu·moured·ness** n.

ill-judged (il-júj'd) adj. Unwise; foolish.

il·lib·er·al (i-líbbərəl, í-, -líbbrəl) adj. **1.** Narrow-minded; bigoted. **2.** Ungenerous, mean, or stingy. **3.** *Archaic.* **a.** Lacking liberal culture. **b.** Ill-bred; ungentlemanly; vulgar. [Latin *illīberālis : in-,* not + *līberālis,* LIBERAL.] **—il·lib·er·al·i·ty** (i-líbbə-rál-əti, íllibə-), **il·lib·er·al·ness** n. **—il·lib·er·al·ly** adv.

il·lic·it (i-líssit) adj. Not sanctioned by custom, morality, or law; illegal; unlawful. [Latin *illicitus,* not allowed : *in-,* not + *licitus,* LICIT.] **—il·lic·it·ly** adv. **—il·lic·it·ness** n.

il·lim·it·a·ble (i-límmitə-b'l) adj. Incapable of being limited or circumscribed; limitless. See Synonyms at **infinite.** **—il·lim·it·a·bil·i·ty** (-ə-bíllə̆ti), **il·lim·it·a·ble·ness** n. **—il·lim·it·a·bly** adv.

Il·li·nois¹ (íllə-nóy, -nóyz). State in the north central United States, one of the group of Midwest states. The capital is Springfield; the largest city is Chicago. Its fertile prairies make it a leading agricultural state. It also has rich mineral reserves and is a leading producer of coal and fluorspar. Illinois joined the Union in 1818. **—Il·li·nois·an** (usually -nóy-ən) n. & adj.

Il·li·nois² n., pl. **Illinois. 1.** A member of a confederacy of Algonquian-speaking Indian peoples that inhabited Illinois and parts of Iowa, Wisconsin, and Missouri. **2.** The Algonquian language of the Illinois and Miami peoples.

il·liq·uid (i-líkwid) adj. **1.** Incapable of being readily converted into cash: *illiquid assets.* **2.** Lacking in cash or liquid assets: *not bankrupt but just illiquid.* [IN-, not + LIQUID.] **—il·li·quid·i·ty** (ílli-kwíd-əti) n.

il·lit·er·ate (i-líttə-rət, -rit) adj. **1.** Unable to read or write. **2. a.** Marked by inferiority to an expected standard of familiarity with language and literature. **b.** Violating prescribed standards of speech or writing. **3.** Ignorant of the fundamentals of a specified art or branch of knowledge: *musically illiterate.*
~n. One who is illiterate. [Latin *illiterātus : in-,* not + *literātus,* LITERATE.] **—il·lit·er·a·cy** (-rə-si) n. **—il·lit·er·ate·ly** adv. **—il·lit·er·ate·ness** n.

ill-man·nered (il-mánnərd) adj. Lacking or indicating a lack of good manners; impolite; rude. **—ill-man·nered·ly** adv.

ill nature n. A disagreeable, irritable, or malevolent disposition.

ill-na·tured (il-náychərd) adj. Disagreeable; surly. **—ill-na·tured·ly** adv. **—ill-na·tured·ness** n.

ill·ness (íl-nəss, -niss) n. **1. a.** Sickness of body or mind. **b.** A sickness; a disease. **2.** *Obsolete.* Evil; wickedness.

il·log·ic (i-lójik) n. The lack of logic.

il·log·i·cal (i-lójik'l) adj. **1.** Contradicting or disregarding the principles of logic. **2.** Without logic; senseless. **—il·log·i·cal·i·ty** (-kál-əti), **il·log·i·cal·ness** n. **—il·log·i·cal·ly** adv.

ill-o·mened (íl-ô-mend, -mənd) adj. Marked by bad omens.

ill-sort·ed (il-sórtid) adj. Badly matched; ill-assorted.

ill-starred (il-stárd) adj. Ill-fated; unlucky.

ill-tem·pered (il-témpərd) adj. **1.** Having a bad temper; irritable. **2.** *Archaic.* Out of sorts; unwell. **—ill-tem·pered·ly** adv.

ill-timed (il-tímd) adj. Done or occurring at an inappropriate time; untimely.

ill-treat (il-tréet) tr.v. **-treated, -treating, -treats.** To maltreat. See Synonyms at **abuse. —ill-treat·ment** n.

il·lude (i-lóod, -lêwd) tr.v. **-luded, -luding, -ludes.** *Literary.* To deceive; trick. [Latin *illūdere,* to trick, sport with, from *lūdus,* game.]

il·lume (i-lóom, -lêwm) tr.v. **-lumed, -luming, -lumes.** *Poetic.* To illuminate. [Shortened from ILLUMINE.]

il·lu·min·ance (i-lóomi-nənss, -lêwmi-) n. *Physics.* Symbol **E** The luminous flux per unit area falling on a surface, usually measured in lux. Also called "illumination".

il·lu·mi·nant (i-lóomi-nənt, -lêwmi-) n. Something that gives off or provides light.

il·lu·mi·nate (i-lóomi-nayt, -lêwmi-) v. **-nated, -nating, -nates.** —tr. **1.** To provide with light; turn or focus light upon. **2.** To decorate or hang with lights. **3.** To make understandable; clarify. **4.** To enable to understand; enlighten. **5.** *Literary.* To endow with fame or splendour. **6.** To adorn (a text, page, or initial letter) with ornamental designs, miniatures, or lettering in brilliant colours or precious metals. —intr. To become lighted; glow.
~n. (-nit, -nayt). One who has or professes to have an unusual degree of enlightenment. [Latin *illūmināre : in-,* in + *lūmināre,* to light up, from *lūmen,* light.]

il·lu·mi·na·ti (i-lóomi-naáti, -lêwmi-) pl.n. **1.** Persons claiming to be unusually enlightened with regard to some subject. **2.** *Capital* **I. a.** The members of a secret society of freethinkers and republicans that flourished in Germany during the late 18th century. Also called "Illuminaten". **b.** Persons regarded as atheists, libertines, or radical republicans during the 18th century (such as the French Encyclopedists, the Freemasons, or the freethinkers). **3.** *Capital* **I.** The members of a heretical sect of 16th-century Spain, who claimed special religious enlightenment. [Latin *illūmināti,* "enlightened ones", plural of *illūminātus,* past participle of *illūmināre,* ILLUMINATE.]

il·lu·mi·na·tion (i-lóomi-náysh'n, -lêwmi-) n. **1.** The act of illuminating. **2.** The state of being illuminated. **3.** A light source. **4.** *Often plural.* Lights used as decoration. **5.** Spiritual or intellectual enlightenment. **6.** Clarification; elucidation. **7. a.** The art or act of decorating a text, page, or initial letter with ornamental designs, miniatures, or lettering. **b.** An example of this art. **8.** *Physics.* Illuminance.

il·lu·mi·na·tive (i-lóomi-nətiv, -lêwmi-, -náytiv) adj. Causing or able to cause illumination.

il·lu·mi·na·tor (i-lóomi-naytər, -lêwmi-) n. **1.** One that illuminates. **2.** A device for producing, concentrating, or reflecting light. **3.** A person who illuminates manuscripts, texts, or the like.

il·lu·mine (i-lóo-min, -lêw-) v. **-mined, -mining, -mines.** *Literary.* —tr. To illuminate; give light to. —intr. To be or become illuminated. [Middle English *illuminen*, from Latin *illūmināre*, to ILLUMI-NATE.] —**il·lu·mi·na·ble** *adj.*

il·lu·mi·nism (i-lōōmi-niz'm, -lēwmi-) *n.* **1.** Belief in or proclamation of a special personal enlightenment. **2.** *Capital* I. The ideas and principles of various groups of illuminati. [ILLUMIN(ATI) + -ISM.] —**il·lu·mi·nist** *n.*

illus. illustrated; illustration; illustrator.

ill-use (il-yōōz) *tr.v.* **-used, -using, -uses.** To maltreat. ~*n.* (-yōōss). Also **ill-us·age** (-yōō-sij, -zij). Bad or unjust treatment.

il·lu·sion (i-lōō-zh'n, -lēw-) *n.* **1. a.** An erroneous perception of reality. **b.** An erroneous concept or belief. **c.** Loosely, a delusion. **2.** The state or condition of being deceived by erroneous perceptions or beliefs. **3.** Something that causes an erroneous belief or perception. **4.** *Art.* Illusionism. **5.** A fine transparent silk or lace, used for dresses or trimmings. **6.** A conjuring trick. [Middle English *illusioun*, from Old French *illusion*, from Late Latin *illūsiō* (stem *illūsiōn*-), from Latin, a mocking, jeering, from *illūdere* (past participle *illūsus*), to mock, jeer at : *in-*, against + *lūdere*, to play, from *lūdus*, game.] —**il·lu·sion·al, il·lu·sion·ar·y** (-zh'n-əri, -ri ‖ *U.S.* -erri) *adj.*

il·lu·sion·ism (i-lōō-zh'n-iz'm, -lēw-) *n.* **1.** The doctrine that the material world is an immaterial product of the senses. **2.** The use of illusionary techniques and devices in art or decoration. —**il·lu·sion·is·tic** (-istik) *adj.*

il·lu·sion·ist (i-lōō-zh'nist, -lēw-) *n.* **1.** An adherent of the doctrine of illusionism. **2.** A conjuror or ventriloquist. **3.** An artist whose work is marked by illusionism.

il·lu·sive (i-lōō-siv, -lēw- ‖ -ziv) *adj.* Of, pertaining to, or of the nature of an illusion; lacking reality; illusory. [From ILLUSION.] —**il·lu·sive·ly** *adv.* —**il·lu·sive·ness** *n.*

il·lu·so·ry (i-lōō-səri, -lēw-, -zəri) *adj.* Tending to deceive; of the nature of an illusion; illusive.

il·lus·trate (i-lləs-trayt ‖ *U.S. also* i-lúss-) *v.* **-trated, -trating, -trates.** —*tr.* **1. a.** To clarify by use of examples, comparisons, or the like. **b.** To clarify by serving as an example, comparison, or the like. **2.** To provide (a publication) with explanatory or decorative pictures, photographs, diagrams, or the like. **3.** *Obsolete.* To illuminate. —*intr.* To present a clarification, example, or explanation. [Latin *illūstrāre* : *in-*, in + *lūstrāre*, to make bright, enlighten.] —**il·lus·tra·tor** *n.*

il·lus·tra·tion (illə-stráysh'n) *n. Abbr.* **ill., illus. 1. a.** The action of clarifying or explaining. **b.** The state of being clarified or explained. **2.** Material used to clarify or explain. **3.** A picture, photograph, or the like; visual matter collectively, used to clarify or to decorate a text. **4.** *Obsolete.* Illumination. —See Synonyms at **example.**

il·lus·tra·tive (illə-strətiv, -straytiv; *rarely* i-lústrətiv) *adj.* Acting as an illustration. —**il·lus·tra·tive·ly** *adv.*

il·lus·tri·ous (i-lústri-əss) *adj.* Renowned; famous; celebrated. [Latin *illūstris*, shining, clear, probably back-formation from *illūstrāre*, ILLUSTRATE.] —**il·lus·tri·ous·ly** *adv.* —**il·lus·tri·ous·ness** *n.*

il·lu·vi·a·tion (i-lōō-vi-áysh'n, -lēw-) *n.* The deposition in an underlying soil layer of colloids, soluble salts, and mineral particles leached out of an overlying soil layer. [IN- (in) + (AL)LUVI(UM) + -ATION.] —**il·lu·vi·al** *adj.*

ill will *n.* Unfriendly feeling; hostility; enmity.

il·ly (illi, il-li) *adv. Rare.* Badly; ill.

Il·lyr·i·a (i-lírri-ə). *Latin* **Il·lyr·i·cum** (-kōōm). Ancient region of the Balkan peninsula, of vague extent. The name is most commonly used for the region extending from the Adriatic coast of northern Albania to the Dinaric Alps.

Il·lyr·i·an (i-lírri-ən) *n.* **1.** A member of a people inhabiting Illyria. **2.** The Indo-European language of the Illyrians. ~*adj.* Of, pertaining to, or characteristic of the Illyrians or their language.

il·men·ite (ilme-nīt) *n.* A lustrous black-to-brownish titanium ore, essentially a mixed ferrous and titanium oxide, FeO.TiO$_2$. [German *Ilmenit*; first found in *Ilmen*, range in the Ural Mountains.]

ILO International Labour Organisation.

I·lo·ca·no (illō-ka'anō) *n., pl.* **-nos** or collectively **Ilocano.** Also **I·lo·ka·no. 1.** A member of a people inhabiting northwestern Luzon in the Philippines. **2.** The Austronesian language of these people. ~*adj.* Of, pertaining to, or characteristic of the Ilocano or their language. [Spanish, from *iloko*, native name in the Philippines.]

I.L.P. Independent Labour Party (in Britain).

ILS *Aeronautics.* instrument landing system.

ILTF, I.L.T.F. International Lawn Tennis Federation.

im–. Variant of **in–.**

I.M. 1. intramuscular. **2.** International Master (in chess).

I'm (īm). Contraction of *I am.*

im·age (immij) *n.* **1.** A reproduction of the appearance of someone or something; especially, a sculptured likeness. **2.** A duplicate, counterpart, or other representative reproduction of an object, such as: **a.** An optical reproduction formed by a lens or mirror. **b.** A photographic reproduction, either visible or undeveloped (*latent image*). **c.** A reproduction of a picture on a television screen. **3.** One that closely resembles another; a double: *He is the image of his uncle.* **4. a.** The opinion or concept of someone or something that is held by the public. **b.** The character projected by someone or something to the public. **5.** A personification of something specified: *He is the image of health.* **6.** A mental picture of something not real or present. **7. a.** A comparison or metaphor: *Plato's image of the cave.* **b.** A figure, usually recurrent, in art or literature that has

a symbolic value: *the image of the Fool in Shakespeare.* **8.** *Mathematics.* The function of a specific variable or the value of the function for a specific value of the variable. **9.** *Obsolete.* An apparition. ~*tr.v.* **imaged, -aging, -ages. 1.** To make or produce a likeness of; copy or portray. **2.** To mirror or reflect. **3.** To symbolise or typify. **4.** To picture mentally; imagine or recall; especially, to call up pleasant images or thoughts. **5.** To describe; especially, to describe so as to call up a mental picture of. [Middle English, from Old French, from Latin *imāgō*; akin to *imitārī*, IMITATE.]

image converter *n.* A device for converting invisible electromagnetic radiation, such as infrared or ultraviolet radiation, into a visible optical image. Also called "image tube".

image intensifier *n.* A device for increasing the intensity of a faint optical image, generally using photoemission of electrons from a cathode and acceleration of these electrons onto a screen.

im·age-ma·ker (immij-maykər) *n. Informal.* One who employs skilful publicity and advertising to create a favourable public image of a person or organisation. —**im·age-ma·king** *n.*

image orthicon *n.* An orthicon (*see*).

im·age·ry (immij-ri, -əri) *n., pl.* **-ries. 1.** The production of mental pictures or images. **2. a.** The employment of comparisons or vivid descriptions in writing or speaking to produce mental images. **b.** Any metaphorical representation, as in literature or art. **3. a.** Representative images, particularly statues or icons. **b.** The art of making such images. [Middle English *imagerie*, from Old French, from *image*, IMAGE.]

im·ag·i·na·ble (i-máji-nəb'l, -nəb'l) *adj.* Capable of being conceived of by the imagination: *chose the worst time imaginable for a holiday.* —**im·ag·i·na·bly** *adv.*

im·ag·i·nal (i-májin'l) *adj.* Of or relating to an imago. [New Latin *imago* (stem *imagin*-), IMAGO.]

im·ag·i·nar·y (i-máji-nəri, -nri ‖ -nerri) *adj.* **1.** Having existence only in the imagination; unreal. **2.** *Mathematics.* **a.** Of, pertaining to, or being the coefficient of the imaginary unit in a complex number. **b.** Of, pertaining to, involving, or being an imaginary number. **c.** Involving only a complex number of which the real part is zero. ~*n., pl.* **imaginaries.** *Mathematics.* An imaginary number. —**im·ag·i·nar·i·ly** *adv.* —**im·ag·i·nar·i·ness** *n.*

imaginary number *n.* A complex number (*see*) in which the real part is zero and the coefficient of the imaginary unit is not zero. Also called "imaginary".

imaginary unit *n. Symbol* i The square root of –1.

im·ag·i·na·tion (i-máji-náysh'n) *n.* **1. a.** The formation of a mental image or concept of that which is not real or present. **b.** A mental image or idea. **2.** The ability or tendency to form such mental images or concepts. **3. a.** The mental faculty permitting visionary and creative thought. **b.** Visionary and creative thought. **4.** *Archaic.* **a.** An unrealistic idea or notion; a fancy. **b.** A plan or scheme. —**im·ag·i·na·tion·al** *adj.*

im·ag·i·na·tive (i-máj-inətiv, -nətiv ‖ -inaytiv) *adj.* **1.** Having a strong imagination, especially a creative imagination. **2.** Tending to indulge in the fanciful or in make-believe. **3.** Created by, indicative of, or characterised by imagination or creativity. —**im·ag·i·na·tive·ly** *adv.* —**im·ag·i·na·tive·ness** *n.*

im·ag·ine (i-májin) *v.* **-ined, -ining, -ines.** —*tr.* **1.** To form a mental picture or image of; create in the mind. **2.** To suppose; conjecture. **3.** To believe (something that has no basis in reality). —*intr.* **1.** To employ the imagination. **2.** To make a guess; conjecture. [Middle English *imaginen*, from Old French *imaginer*, from Latin *imāginārī*, to picture to oneself, from *imāgō*, IMAGE.] —**im·ag·in·er** *n.*

im·a·gism (immi-jiz'm) *n.* A literary movement among British and U.S. poets, launched about 1912, to promote free verse and precise imagery. —**im·a·gist** *n.* —**im·a·gis·tic** (-jístik) *adj.*

i·ma·go (i-máygō, -má'agō) *n., pl.* **-goes** or **imagines** (i-máji-neez, -maagi-). **1.** An insect in its sexually mature adult stage after metamorphosis. **2.** *Psychoanalysis.* An often idealised image of a person, usually a parent, formed in childhood and persisting into adulthood. [New Latin, from Latin *imāgō*, IMAGE.]

i·mam (i-ma'am) *n.* Also **i·maum** (i-ma'am, -máwm). **1.** A prayer leader of Islam. **2.** A Muslim scholar; especially, an authority on Islamic law. **3.** *Capital* I. **a.** A title accorded to Muhammad and his four immediate successors. **b.** Any of the leaders regarded by the Shiites as successors of Muhammad. **c.** Any of various religious and temporal leaders claiming descent from Muhammad. [Arabic *imām*, leader, from *amma*, he led.]

i·mam·ate (i-ma'a-mayt) *n.* **1.** The office of an imam. **2.** A country governed by an imam.

I. Mar. E. Institute of Marine Engineers (in Britain).

i·ma·ret (i-máret) *n.* An inn or hostel for pilgrims in Turkey. [Turkish, from Arabic *imārah*, hospice, "cultivated land", from *amara*, he built.]

im·bal·ance (im-bálənss) *n.* A lack of balance or proportion.

im·be·cile (imbə-seel, -sīl ‖ *U.S. also* -s'l) *n.* **1.** A feeble-minded person. **2.** A dolt. **3.** A person affected by imbecility. No longer in technical usage. ~*adj.* Also **im·be·cil·ic** (-síllik). **1.** Deficient in mental ability. **2.** Stupid. [Old French *imbecille*, from Latin *imbēcillus*, "without support", feeble : *in-*, not + *bacillum*, diminutive of *baculum*, staff, rod.] —**im·be·cile·ly** *adv.*

im·be·cil·i·ty (imbə-sílləti) *n.* A condition of moderate to severe subnormal intellectual development, characterised by an intelligence quotient in the upper range of idiocy. Not recommended in technical usage. Compare **idiocy.**

imbed. Variant of **embed.**

im·bibe (im-bíb) v. **-bibed, -bibing, -bibes.** —tr. **1.** To drink (especially alcoholic drink). **2.** To absorb or take in as if by drinking. **3.** To receive and absorb into the mind. **4.** Obsolete. To permeate; saturate. —intr. To drink. [Middle English enbiben, to absorb, from Old French embiber, from Latin imbibere, to drink in : in-, in + bibere, to drink.] —**im·bib·er** n.

im·bi·bi·tion (ímbi-bísh'n) n. **1.** Chemistry. The absorption or adsorption of a liquid by a solid or a gel. **2.** In photography, the absorption of a dye by gelatine. **3.** Rare. The act of imbibing. [IMBIBE + -TION.]

im·bri·cate (ímbri-kət, -kit, -kayt) adj. **1.** Having the edges overlapping in a regular pattern, as tiles on a roof, the scales of a fish, or bracts or sepals of a plant. **2.** Covered or ornamented with a pattern or design of overlapping parts or edges.
~v. (-kayt) **imbricated, -cating, -cates.** —tr. To overlap in a regular pattern. —intr. To be arranged with regular overlapping edges. [Latin imbricātus, past participle of imbricāre, to cover with roof tiles, from imbrex (stem imbric-), roof tile, from imber (stem imbr-), rain.]

im·bri·ca·tion (ímbri-káysh'n) n. **1.** A regular overlapping of edges. **2.** A pattern or design having such overlapping.

im·bro·gli·o (im-brŏl-yō) n., pl. **-glios. 1.** A confused or difficult situation; a predicament; an entanglement. **2.** Rare. A confused heap; a tangle. [Italian imbroglio : probably in-, in + broglio, grove, bush, from Old French breuil, from Late Latin brogilus, from Gaulish brogilos (unattested), from brogos, broga†, field.]

im·brue (im-brōō || -brēw) tr.v. **-brued, -bruing, -brues.** Also **embrue** (em-). Rare. **1.** To stain or dye. Used of blood. **2.** To soak or saturate. [Middle English enbrewen, enbrowen, from Old French embruer, embrouer, to soak : en-, in + breu, broth, from Germanic.]

im·brute (im-brōōt || -brēwt) v. **-bruted, -bruting, -brutes.** Rare. —tr. To cause to become brutal. —intr. To become brutal.

im·bue (im-bēw) tr.v. **-bued, -buing, -bues. 1.** To inspire, permeate, or pervade. **2.** Rare. To make thoroughly wet; saturate, as with stain or dye. [Latin imbuere, to moisten, stain.]

I. Mech. E. Institution of Mechanical Engineers (in Britain).

IMF, I.M.F. International Monetary Fund.

Im·ho·tep (ímhō-tep) (c. 2650 B.C.). Egyptian architect, astrologer, physician, and chief minister to Pharoah Djoser (c. 2686–2613 B.C.). He is thought to have designed the first pyramid at Saqqara.

im·id·az·ole (ímmi-dázzōl, -də-zōl) n. Any of a group of heterocyclic nitrogen compounds, especially the white crystalline base, $C_3H_4N_2$; 1,3-diazole. Also called "glyoxaline". [IMID(E) + AZOLE.]

im·ide (ímmíd) n. A compound derived from ammonia containing the divalent group —CO.NH.CO— combined with two other radicals. [Alteration of AMIDE.]

im·ine (ímmeen, i-méen) n. A compound derived from ammonia containing the divalent NH group combined with alkyl or other radicals. [Alteration of AMINE.]

I. Min. E. Institution of Mining Engineers.

im·i·no acid (i-méenō) n. An organic compound, such as proline or hydroxyproline, similar to an amino acid and also a constituent of proteins, but containing an imino group (–NH) rather than an amino group (C–NH₂).

im·i·tate (ímmi-tayt) tr.v. **-tated, -tating, -tates. 1.** To model oneself on the behaviour or actions of. **2. a.** To copy the appearance, mannerisms, or speech of; mimic. **b.** To copy the literary, artistic, or musical style of. **3.** To copy; reproduce. **4.** To resemble. [Latin imitārī† (past participle imitātus).] —**im·i·ta·tor** n.
Synonyms: imitate, copy, mimic, ape, parody, simulate.

im·i·ta·tion (ímmi-táysh'n) n. **1.** An act of imitating. **2.** Something derived or copied from an original. **3.** Music. The repetition of a phrase or sequence often with variations in key, rhythm, and voice. —**im·i·ta·tion·al** adj.

im·i·ta·tive (ímmi-tətiv, -taytiv) adj. **1.** Of or involving imitation. **2.** Not original; derivative; copied. **3.** Tending to imitate. **4.** Onomatopoeic. —**im·i·ta·tive·ly** adv. —**im·i·ta·tive·ness** n.

I.M.M. Institution of Mining and Metallurgy (in Britain).

im·mac·u·la·cy (i-máckewlə-si) n. The quality or condition of being immaculate; immaculateness.

im·mac·u·late (i-máckew-lət, -lit) adj. **1.** Free from stain or blemish; spotless; pure. **2.** Free from fault or error. **3.** Impeccably clean. **4.** Having no markings or spots. Said of plants and animals. [Middle English immaculat, from Latin immaculātus : in-, not + maculātus, past participle of maculāre, to stain, blemish, from macula, spot.] —**im·mac·u·late·ly** adv. —**im·mac·u·late·ness** n.

Immaculate Conception n. **1.** The Roman Catholic doctrine that the Virgin Mary was conceived in her mother's womb free from all stain of original sin. Compare **virgin birth. 2.** The day, December 8, on which this is celebrated.

im·ma·nent (ímmənənt) adj. **1.** Existing or remaining within; inherent. **2.** Restricted entirely to the mind; subjective. Compare **transeunt. 3.** Present throughout the universe. Said of God. Compare **transcendent.** [Late Latin immanēns (stem immanent-), present participle of immanēre, to remain in : Latin in-, in + manēre, to remain.] —**im·ma·nent·ly** adv.

Im·man·u·el, Em·man·u·el (i-mánnew-əl) n. **1.** The child whose birth was prophesied by Isaiah, as a sign that Judah would not be destroyed. Isaiah 7:14. **2.** A name applied to Jesus. Matthew 1:23. [Hebrew, "God with us".]

im·ma·te·ri·al (ímmə-téer-i-əl) adj. **1.** Having no material body or form. **2.** Of no importance or relevance; inconsequential. —**im·ma·te·ri·al·ly** adv. —**im·ma·te·ri·al·ness** n.

im·ma·te·ri·al·ise, im·ma·te·ri·al·ize (ímmə-téeri-ə-līz) tr.v. **-ised, -ising, -ises.** To render immaterial.

im·ma·te·ri·al·ism (ímmə-téer-i-ə-liz'm) n. A metaphysical doctrine asserting that things only have an existence through perception by the mind. —**im·ma·te·ri·al·ist** n.

im·ma·te·ri·al·i·ty (ímmə-téer-i-álati) n., pl. **-ties. 1.** The state or quality of being immaterial. **2.** Something immaterial.

im·ma·ture (ímmə-téwr, -choor || -toor) adj. **1.** Not fully grown or developed. **2.** Behaving with less than normal maturity. **3.** Not having a chance to achieve a mature state due to constant erosion. Said of soils. **4.** Informal. Childish; silly. [Latin immātūrus : in-, not + mātūrus, MATURE.] —**im·ma·ture·ly** adv. —**im·ma·tur·i·ty, im·ma·ture·ness** n.

im·meas·ur·a·ble (i-mézhərə-b'l) adj. **1.** Incapable of being measured. **2.** Vast; limitless. —**im·meas·ur·a·bil·i·ty** (-bílləti), **im·meas·ur·a·ble·ness** n. —**im·meas·ur·a·bly** adv.

im·me·di·a·cy (i-méedi-ə-si) n., pl. **-cies. 1.** The condition or quality of being immediate; directness. **2.** Something immediate. **3.** Immediate or direct perception; intuitiveness. **4.** Philosophy. Direct consciousness as opposed to that involving an intermediary such as memory.

im·me·di·ate (i-méedi-ət, -méej-, -it) adj. **1.** Acting or occurring without mediation or interposition; direct: immediate consequence. **2.** Directly apprehended or perceived; intuitive: immediate awareness. **3.** Next in line or relation: the immediate successor. **4.** Occurring without delay: an immediate response. **5.** Of or near the present time: the immediate future. **6.** Close at hand; near: the immediate vicinity. **7.** Of direct concern or importance. [Late Latin immediātus : Latin in-, not + mediātus, past participle of mediāre, to be in the middle, MEDIATE.] —**im·me·di·ate·ness** n.

immediate constituent n. Linguistics. Abbr. **I.C.** Any of the main divisions into which a word, phrase, or sentence can be most immediately divided; for example, the immediate constituents of the watch has stopped are the watch and has stopped.

im·me·di·ate·ly (i-méedi-ət-li, -méej-, -it-) adv. **1.** Without intermediary; directly. **2.** Without delay. **3.** Nearby.
~conj. As soon as; directly.
Synonyms: immediately, instantly, forthwith, directly, promptly.

im·med·i·ca·ble (i-méddikəb'l) adj. Incurable.

Im·mel·mann turn (ímm'l-man, -mən) n. A manoeuvre in which an aircraft first completes half a loop then half a roll in order to gain altitude and change direction in flight simultaneously. [After Max Immelmann (1890–1916), German pilot.]

im·me·mo·ri·al (immi-máwri-əl || -móri-) adj. Reaching beyond the limits of memory, tradition, or recorded history. Used chiefly in the phrase from time immemorial. [Medieval Latin immemoriālis : Latin in-, not + memoriālis, memorial, from memoria, MEMORY.] —**im·me·mo·ri·al·ly** adv.

im·mense (i-ménss) adj. **1.** Extremely large; huge. **2.** Boundless. **3.** Informal. Very great: immense pleasure. —See Synonyms at **enormous.** [Old French, from Latin immēnsus, immeasurable : in-, not + mēnsus, past participle of mētīrī, to measure.] —**im·mense·ly** adv. —**im·mense·ness** n.

im·men·si·ty (i-mén-səti) n., pl. **-ties. 1.** The quality or state of being immense. **2.** Something immense. **3.** Informal. A very large amount.

im·men·sur·a·ble (i-ménshərəb'l) adj. Rare. Immeasurable.

im·merge (i-mérj) v. **-merged, -merging, -merges.** Archaic. —tr. To immerse. —intr. To submerge or disappear in or as if in a liquid. [Latin immergere, IMMERSE.] —**im·mer·gence** n.

im·merse (i-mérss) tr.v. **-mersed, -mersing, -merses. 1.** To cover completely in a liquid; submerge. Used with in. **2.** To baptise by submerging in water. **3.** To involve profoundly; absorb. Used with in, especially reflexively or passively. [Latin immergere (past participle immersus), to dip in : in-, in + mergere, to dip.]

im·mer·sion (i-mér-sh'n || -zh'n) n. **1.** An act of immersing. **2.** The condition of being immersed. **3.** Baptism performed by totally submerging a person in water. **4.** Absorption: her total immersion in politics. **5.** Astronomy. The obscuring of a celestial body by another or by the shadow of another, as in an eclipse or occultation. Also called "ingress".

immesh. Variant of **enmesh.**

immersion heater n. An electric element immersed in a liquid and used to heat it; especially, such an element used in a domestic hot-water tank.

im·mi·grant (ímmigrənt) n. **1.** One who enters a country to settle permanently. Compare **emigrant. 2.** An organism living or growing in a place to which it has recently migrated. —**im·mi·grant** adj.

im·mi·grate (ímmi-grayt) v. **-grated, -grating, -grates.** —intr. To enter and settle in a country or region of which one is not a native. —tr. To bring in or introduce as immigrants. —See Usage note at **migrate.** [Latin immigrāre, to remove into, go in : in-, in + migrāre, to remove, MIGRATE.]

im·mi·gra·tion (immi-gráysh'n) n. **1.** The act, process, or an instance of immigrating. **2. a.** The area in a port or airport, where passengers arriving from abroad have their passports and visas checked. **b.** The government officials in charge of this process.

im·mi·nence (ímmi-nənss) n. Also **im·mi·nen·cy** (-nən-si) pl. **-cies. 1.** The condition of being imminent. **2.** Something imminent.

im·mi·nent (ímminənt) adj. **1.** About to occur; impending. **2.** Archaic. Jutting out; overhanging. See Usage note at **eminent.** [Latin

imminēns (stem imminent-), present participle of imminēre, to project over or towards, threaten : in-, towards + -minēre, to project.]
—im·mi·nent·ly adv.

Im·ming·ham (imming-əm). Seaport of northern England. Lying to the south of the Humber estuary, on the North Sea, it has petrochemical and iron ore processing facilities, and it exports steel.

im·min·gle (i-míng-g'l) v. -gled, -gling, -gles. Archaic. —intr. To intermingle; blend. —tr. To blend.

im·mis·ci·ble (i-míssi-b'l) adj. Incapable of mixing or blending. Said of two or more liquids. —im·mis·ci·bil·i·ty (-bílləti) n. —im·mis·ci·bly adv.

im·mit·i·ga·ble (i-míttigəb'l) adj. Rare. Incapable of being mitigated. —im·mit·i·ga·bly adv.

im·mix (i-míks) tr.v. -mixed, -mixing, -mixes. Rare. To commingle; blend. [Back-formation from Middle English immixte, mixed in, from Latin immixtus, past participle of immiscēre, to mix in : in-, in + miscēre, to mix.] —im·mix·ture n.

im·mo·bile (i-mṓ-bīl || U.S. also -b'l, -beel) adj. 1. a. Unable to move. b. Incapable of being moved. 2. Not moving; motionless. 3. Not fluid; viscous. Said of liquids. [Middle English inmobile, from Latin immōbilis : in-, not + mōbilis, MOBILE.] —im·mo·bil·i·ty (immō-bílləti) n.

im·mo·bi·lise (i-mṓbi-līz, -b'l-īz) tr.v. -lised, -lising, -lises. 1. To render immobile. 2. To impede movement or use of: immobilise troops. 3. Medicine. To fix (a broken limb, for example) so that no movement is possible. 4. a. Finance. To withdraw (specie) from circulation and reserve as security for other money. b. To convert (floating capital) into fixed capital. —im·mo·bi·li·sa·tion (-lī-záysh'n || U.S. -li-) n. —im·mo·bi·lis·er n.

im·mo·bil·ism (i-mṓbi-liz'm) n. A highly reactionary political stance. —im·mo·bi·list n. & adj.

im·mod·er·ate (i-móddər-ət, -it) adj. Not moderate; extreme. See Synonyms at excessive. [Middle English immoderat, from Latin immoderātus : in-, not + moderātus, MODERATE.] —im·mod·er·ate·ly adv. —im·mod·er·ate·ness, im·mod·er·a·tion (-ráysh'n) n.

im·mod·est (i-móddist) adj. 1. Lacking modesty. 2. a. Contrary to conventional standards of sexual propriety. b. Morally offensive. 3. Arrogant. [Latin immodestus : in-, not + modestus, MODEST.] —im·mod·est·ly adv. —im·mod·es·ty n.

im·mo·late (ímmō-layt, immə-) tr.v. -lated, -lating, -lates. 1. To kill as a sacrifice. 2. To destroy or renounce for the sake of something else. [Latin immolāre, to sacrifice, originally "to sprinkle with sacrificial meal" : in-, on + mola, meal.] —im·mo·la·tion (-láysh'n) n. —im·mo·la·tor n.

im·mor·al (i-mórrəl || -máwrəl) adj. 1. Contrary to established morality, especially in sexual matters. 2. Morally dissolute. 3. Unethical or unfair. 4. Tending to corrupt. —im·mor·al·ly adv.

Usage: Immoral and amoral are sometimes confused. Immoral applies to situations or behaviour that are contrary to established morality; it is therefore opposed to moral, and always carries a pejorative implication. Amoral (sense 1), however, has no such implication. It applies to situations where moral judgments cannot or should not be made, and is neutral on the question of right or wrong. Amoral (sense 2), a more modern sense, is used only of a person who lacks moral judgment or is not interested in the distinction between right and wrong.

im·mo·ral·i·ty (immə-ráliti) n., pl. -ties. 1. The state or condition of being immoral. 2. An immoral act. 3. Immoral behaviour; especially, sexual promiscuity. 4. South African. Formerly, unlawful sexual intercourse between a man and a woman of different race groups.

im·mor·tal (i-mórt'l) adj. 1. Not subject to death. 2. Having eternal fame; imperishable. 3. Of or pertaining to immortality.
~n. 1. One not subject to death. 2. One whose fame is enduring. 3. Plural. Often capital I. The gods of ancient Greece and Rome. 4. Capital I. A member of the French Academy. [Latin immortālis: in-, not + mortālis, MORTAL.] —im·mor·tal·ly adv.

im·mor·tal·ise, im·mor·tal·ize (i-mórt'l-īz) tr.v. -ised, -ising, -ises. 1. To make immortal. 2. To give permanent fame to.

im·mor·tal·i·ty (immawr-táləti) n. 1. The quality or condition of being immortal. 2. Endless life. 3. Enduring fame.

im·mor·telle (ímmawr-tél) n. Any plant with flowers that retain their colour when dried. Also called "everlasting". [French, from the feminine of immortel, from Latin immortālis, IMMORTAL.]

im·mo·tile (i-mṓ-tīl || U.S. also -t'l) adj. Not motile. Said of living organisms. —im·mo·til·i·ty (-tílləti) n.

im·mov·a·ble, im·move·a·ble (i-mṓvəb'l) adj. 1. a. Incapable of being moved. b. Incapable of movement. 2. Not capable of alteration. 3. Unyielding in principle, purpose, or adherence; steadfast. 4. Showing no sign of emotional stress; unimpressionable. 5. Law. Not liable to be physically removed: immovable property. 6. Occurring on the same date each year. Said of feast days and holidays.
~n. 1. One that is incapable of movement. 2. Immovable property. Compare movable. —im·mov·a·ble·ness, im·mov·a·bil·i·ty (-bílləti) n. —im·mov·a·bly adv.

im·mune (i-méwn) adj. 1. Biology. a. Having immunity to infection. b. Relating to or conferring immunity: the body's immune system; an immune reaction. 2. a. Exempt, as from an obligation or a duty. b. Not affected or responsive. 3. Protected from danger. [Latin immūnis.] —im·mune n.

Usage: In the senses of "exempt" and "protected from", immune is followed by from (immune from tax, immune from commercial pressures). In the senses of "resistant to a disease" and "not

affected by or responsive to", immune is followed by to (immune to diphtheria, immune to their entreaties).

im·mu·nise, im·mu·nize (ímmew-nīz) tr.v. -nised, -nising, -nises. To render immune by artificial methods. —im·mu·ni·sa·tion (-nī-záysh'n || U.S. -ni-) n.

Usage: Immunise is followed by against (to immunise someone against a particular disease). See also immune.

im·mu·ni·ty (i-méwnəti) n., pl. -ties. 1. The quality or condition of being immune. 2. An inherited, acquired, or induced resistance to a specific pathogen, especially by the production of antibodies or by inoculation.

immuno– comb. form. Indicates immune response or immunity; for example, immunogenetics, immunogenic. [From IMMUNE.]

im·mu·no·as·say (ímmew-nō-ássay) n. A method of identifying substances, particularly proteins, by studying the antibodies they induce when injected into an animal.

im·mu·no·chem·is·try (immew-nō-kémmi-stri) n. The chemistry of immunological phenomena, as of antigen stimulation of tissue or of antigen-antibody reactions.

im·mu·no·ge·net·ics (immew-nō-ji-néttiks) n. Used with a singular verb. The study of the interrelation between immunity to disease and genetic make-up.

im·mu·no·gen·ic (immew-nō-jénnik) adj. Producing immunity.

im·mu·no·glob·u·lin (immew-nō-glóbbewlin) n. Any one of a group of structurally similar proteins that show antibody activity.

im·mu·nol·o·gy (ímmew-nólləji) n. The study of immunity to disease. [IMMUNO- + -LOGY.] —im·mu·no·log·ic (nə-lójik), im·mu·no·log·i·cal adj. —im·mu·no·log·i·cal·ly adv.

im·mu·no·sup·pres·sive (ímmew-nō-sə-préssiv) adj. Tending to suppress a natural immune response of an organism to an antigen. ~n. An immunosuppressive drug.

im·mure (i-méwr) tr.v. -mured, -muring, -mures. 1. To confine within walls; imprison. 2. To build into a wall; entomb in a wall. 3. To shut (oneself) away in seclusion. [Medieval Latin immūrāre : Latin in-, in + mūrus, wall.] —im·mure·ment n.

im·mu·ta·ble (i-méwtə-b'l) adj. Not mutable; not susceptible to change; ageless. [Middle English, from Latin immūtābilis : in-, not + mūtābilis, MUTABLE.] —im·mu·ta·bil·i·ty (-bílləti), im·mu·ta·ble·ness n. —im·mu·ta·bly adv.

imp (imp) n. 1. A mischievous child. 2. A mischievous elf. 3. A small or young demon. 4. Archaic. A descendant.
~tr.v. imped, imping, imps. 1. To graft (new feathers) onto the wing of a falcon to repair damage or to increase flying capacity. 2. Archaic. To furnish with wings. 3. Archaic. To eke out. [Middle English impe, scion, offspring, child, Old English impa, young shoot, sapling, from impian, to graft on, from Common Romance impotare (unattested), from Medieval Latin impotus, graft, from Greek emphutos, implanted, from emphuein, to implant : en-, in + phuein, plant.]

imp. 1. imperative. 2. imperfect. 3. imperial. 4. import; imported; importer. 5. important. 6. imprimatur.

Imp. 1. imperator. 2. imperatrix.

im·pact (im-pakt) n. 1. The striking of one body against another; a collision. 2. The effect of one thing upon another. 3. The influence or force of a person, thing, or idea.
~ v. (im-pákt) impacted, -pacting, -pacts. —tr.v. To pack firmly together. —intr.v. To have an impact: policies that impact on inflation. [Latin impactus, past participle of impingere, to dash or strike against, IMPINGE.] —im·pac·tion (im-páksh'n) n.

im·pact·ed (im-páktid) adj. 1. Wedged together at the broken ends. Said of a fractured bone. 2. a. Placed in the alveolus in a manner prohibiting eruption into a normal position. Said of a tooth. b. Driven upwards into the alveolar process or surrounding tissue. Said of a tooth.

im·pair (im-páir) tr.v. -paired, -pairing, -pairs. To diminish in strength, value, quantity, or quality. See Synonyms at injure. [Middle English empairen, from Old French empeirer, from Vulgar Latin impējōrāre (unattested), to make worse : in- (intensive) + Late Latin pējōrāre, to make or become worse, from Latin pējor, worse.] —im·pair·ment n. —impaired adj. comb. form. Indicates handicapped or, euphemistically, challenged; for example, hearing-impaired.

im·pa·la (im-paálə) n. An African antelope, Aepyceros melampus, having a reddish coat, and ridged, curved horns in the male. [Zulu.]

im·pale, em·pale (im-páyl) tr.v. -paled, -paling, -pales. 1. a. To pierce with a sharp stake or point. b. To torture or kill by impaling. 2. To render helpless as if by impaling. 3. Heraldry. To display (arms) on either side of a vertical line on a shield. [Medieval Latin impālāre : Latin in-, in + pālus, stake, pole.] —im·pale·ment n. —im·pal·er n.

im·pal·pa·ble (im-pálpə-b'l) adj. 1. a. Not perceptible to the touch; intangible. b. So fine that individual grains cannot be felt. Said of powder. 2. Not easily perceived or grasped by the mind. —im·pal·pa·bil·i·ty (-bílləti) n. —im·pal·pa·bly adv.

impanel. Chiefly U.S. Variant of empanel.

im·par·i·syl·la·bic (im-párri-si-lábbik) adj. Not having the same number of syllables in all its forms. Said of nouns or verbs in inflected languages.

im·par·i·ty (im-párrəti) n., pl. -ties. Rare. Inequality; disparity; dissimilarity. [Late Latin impāritās (stem impāritāt-), from Latin impār, not equal : in-, not + pār, equal.]

im·park (im-párk) tr.v. -parked, -parking, -parks. 1. To confine (deer, for example) in a park. 2. To enclose (land) for a park. —im·par·ka·tion (ímpaar-káysh'n) n.

im·part (im-párt) *tr.v.* **-parted, -parting, -parts. 1.** To grant a share of; bestow. **2.** To make known; disclose. —See Synonyms at **reveal.** [Latin *impartīre,* to cause to share in, share with : *in-,* in + *partīre,* to share, divide, from *pars* (stem *part-*), part, share.] **—im·part·a·ble** *adj.* **—im·part·er** *n.* **—im·part·ment** *n.*

im·par·tial (im-pársh'l) *adj.* Not partial; unprejudiced; fair. See Synonyms at **fair. —im·par·ti·al·i·ty** (-shi-áliti), **im·par·tial·ness** *n.* **—im·par·tial·ly** *adv.*

im·part·i·ble (im-párti-b'l) *adj. Law.* Not partible; indivisible. Said of land. [Late Latin *impartibilis* : Latin *in-,* not + *partībilis,* PARTIBLE.] **—im·part·i·bil·i·ty** (-bílləti) *n.* **—im·part·i·bly** *adv.*

im·pass·a·ble (im-paáss-əb'l || -páss-) *adj.* Unable to be traversed. **—im·pass·a·bil·i·ty** (-ə-bílləti), **im·pass·a·ble·ness** *n.* **—im·pass·a·bly** *adv.*

im·passe (am-paáss, ám-paass, ím- || ím-pass, im-páss) *n.* **1.** A situation where no progress can be made; a deadlock. **2.** A road or passage having no exit; a dead end; a cul-de-sac. [French : Old French *in-,* not, in- + *passer,* to PASS.]

im·pas·si·ble (im-paáss-əb'l || -páss-) *adj.* **1. a.** Not subject to suffering or pain. **b.** Incapable of being injured: *"The Godhead is impassible."* (Aldous Huxley). **2.** Impassive. [Middle English, from Old French, from Late Latin *impassibilis* : *in-,* not + *passibilis,* PASSIBLE.] **—im·pas·si·bil·i·ty** (-ə-bílləti), **im·pas·si·ble·ness** *n.* **—im·pas·si·bly** *adv.*

im·pas·sion (im-pásh'n) *tr.v.* **-sioned, -sioning, -sions.** To arouse the passions of. [Italian *impassionare* : *in-,* in, from Latin + *passione,* passion, from Late Latin *passiō,* PASSION.]

im·pas·sioned (im-pásh'nd) *adj.* Filled with passion; ardent.

im·pas·sive (im-pássiv) *adj.* **1.** Devoid of or not subject to emotion; apathetic. **2.** Revealing no emotion; expressionless. **3.** Incapable of physical sensation. [IN- (not) + Latin *passīvus,* capable of feeling, PASSIVE.] **—im·pas·sive·ly** *adv.* **—im·pas·sive·ness, im·pas·siv·i·ty** (ímpa-sívvəti) *n.*

im·paste (im-páyst) *tr.v.* **-pasted, -pasting, -pastes.** *Rare.* **1.** To make into a paste. **2.** To apply pigment thickly to. [Italian *impastare* : *in-,* in, + *pasta,* PASTE.]

im·pas·to (im-páss-tō, -paáss-) *n.* **1.** The application of thick layers of pigment. **2.** The layers of pigment thus applied. [Italian, from *impastare,* IMPASTE.]

im·pa·tience (im-páysh'nss) *n.* **1.** The inability to wait patiently. **2.** The inability to endure irritation. **3.** Restive eagerness, desire, or anticipation. [Middle English *impacience,* from Old French *impatience,* from Latin *impatientia,* from *impatiēns* (stem *impatient-*), not patient : *in-,* not + *patiēns,* PATIENT.]

im·pa·ti·ens (im-páyshi-enz || *U.S. also* -enss) *n.* Any plant of the genus *Impatiens,* which includes the busy lizzie. [New Latin *Impatiens,* from Latin *impatiēns,* IMPATIENT (so called because the ripe pods burst open when touched).]

im·pa·tient (im-páysh'nt) *adj.* **1.** Lacking patience, as in enduring delay or imperfection. **2.** Restively eager. **—im·pa·tient·ly** *adv.*

im·peach (im-peéch) *tr.v.* **-peached, -peaching, -peaches. 1. a.** To accuse of a crime, especially a crime against the state such as treason. **b.** *Chiefly U.S.* To charge with improper conduct in office before a proper tribunal. **2.** To challenge or discredit; attack. [Middle English *empeachen,* to impede, accuse, from Old French *empe(s)cher,* impede, from Late Latin *impedicāre,* to entangle, put in fetters : Latin *in-,* in + *pedica,* fetter.] **—im·peach·a·ble** *adj.* **—im·peach·er** *n.* **—im·peach·ment** *n.*

im·pearl (im-pérl) *tr.v.* **-pearled, -pearling, -pearls.** *Archaic.* **1.** To form into pearls. **2.** To adorn with or as if with pearls.

im·pec·ca·ble (im-péckə-b'l) *adj.* **1.** Without flaw; faultless. **2.** Not to be doubted: *impeccable sources.* **3.** *Rare.* Not capable of sin or wrongdoing. [Latin *impeccābilis,* not liable to sin : *in-,* not + *peccāre,* to sin.] **—im·pec·ca·bil·i·ty** (-bílləti) *n.* **—im·pec·ca·bly** *adv.*

im·pe·cu·ni·ous (impi-kéwni-əss) *adj.* Lacking money; penniless. [IN- (not) + obsolete *pecunious,* rich, Middle English *pecunyous,* from Latin *pecūniōsus,* from *pecūnia,* money.] **—im·pe·cu·ni·ous·ly** *adv.* **—im·pe·cu·ni·ous·ness, im·pe·cu·ni·os·i·ty** (-óssəti) *n.*

im·pe·dance (im-peéd'nss) *n.* **1.** *Symbol* **Z** A measure of the total opposition to current flow in an alternating-current circuit, equal to the ratio of the rms electromotive force in the circuit to the rms current produced by it, and usually represented in complex notation as $Z = R + iX$, where R is the ohmic resistance and X is the reactance. **2.** An analogous measure of resistance to an alternating effect, such as the resistance to vibration of the medium in sound transmission *(acoustic impedance)* or to vibration by an applied force *(mechanical impedance).* [From IMPEDE.]

impedance matching *n.* The use of electric circuits, transmission lines, and other devices to make the impedance of a load equal to the internal impedance of the source of power, thereby making possible the most efficient transfer of power.

im·pede (im-peéd) *tr.v.* **-peded, -peding, -pedes.** To obstruct the way of; hinder the progress of; block. See Synonyms at **hinder.** [Latin *impedīre,* to entangle, fetter.] **—im·ped·er** *n.*

im·ped·i·ment (im-péddimənt) *n.* **1.** A hindrance; an obstruction. **2.** Something that impedes, as: **a.** An organic defect, especially one preventing clear articulation: *a speech impediment.* **b.** *Law.* Something that obstructs the making of a legal contract. —See Synonyms at **obstacle.** [Latin *impedīmentum,* from *impedīre,* IMPEDE.] **—im·ped·i·men·tal** (-mént'l), **im·ped·i·men·tar·y** (-méntəri) *adj.*

im·ped·i·men·ta (im-péddi-méntə) *pl.n.* Objects, such as provisions, baggage, or military equipment that impede or encumber. [Latin *impedīmenta,* plural of *impedīmentum,* IMPEDIMENT.]

im·pel (im-pél) *tr.v.* **-pelled, -pelling, -pels. 1.** To urge to action, as through moral pressure or necessity; compel; constrain. **2.** To drive forward; propel. [Latin *impellere,* to drive on or against : *in-,* against + *pellere,* to drive.] **—im·pel·lent** *adj. & n.*

im·pel·ler (im-péllər) *n.* **1.** One that impels. **2.** *Mechanics.* **a.** A rotating device used to force a gas in a given direction under pressure. **b.** A rotor or rotor blade in such a device.

im·pend (im-pénd) *intr.v.* **-pended, -pending, -pends. 1.** To hang or hover menacingly. **2.** To be about to take place. **3.** *Archaic.* To overhang. [Latin *impendēre* : *in-,* against + *pendēre,* to hang.]

im·pen·dent (im-pénd'nt) *adj. Rare.* Impending.

im·pend·ing (im-pénding) *adj.* Due to happen soon; imminent.

im·pen·e·tra·ble (im-pénnitrəb'l) *adj.* **1.** Not capable of being penetrated or entered. **2.** Incomprehensible; inscrutable; unfathomable. **3.** Impervious to argument or sentiment. **4.** *Physics.* Incapable of occupying space already occupied by matter. Said of bodies or particles. [Middle English *impenetrabel,* from Old French *impenetrable,* from Latin *impenetrābilis* : *in-,* not + *penetrābilis,* PENETRABLE.] **—im·pen·e·tra·bil·i·ty** (-bílləti), **im·pen·e·tra·ble·ness** *n.* **—im·pen·e·tra·bly** *adv.*

im·pen·i·tent (im-pénnit'nt) *adj.* **1.** Not penitent; unrepentant. **2.** Hardened; resolute: *an impenitent philistine.* [Late Latin *impaenitēns* (stem *impaenitent-*) : Latin *in-,* not + *paenitēns,* PENITENT.] **—im·pen·i·tence** *n.* **—im·pen·i·tent** *n.* **—im·pen·i·tent·ly** *adv.*

imper. imperative.

im·per·a·tive (im-pérrətiv) *adj. Abbr.* **imp., imper. 1.** Expressing a command or plea; peremptory. **2.** Assuming the power or authority to command or control. **3.** *Grammar.* Of, pertaining to, or designating the mood that expresses a command or request. **4.** Extremely important; essential. **5.** Obligatory; mandatory. —See Synonyms at **urgent.**
~*n. Abbr.* **imp., imper. 1.** *Grammar.* **a.** The imperative mood. **b.** A verb form of the imperative mood. **2. a.** A command; an order. **b.** Something that is important or essential. **c.** An obligation. [Late Latin *imperātīvus,* from Latin *imperāre,* "to prepare against (an occasion)", hence to command : *in-,* against + *parāre,* to prepare.] **—im·per·a·tive·ly** *adv.* **—im·per·a·tive·ness** *n.*

im·pe·ra·tor (impə-raá-tawr, -tər) *n.* **1.** A title given to a victorious commander in ancient Rome. **2.** *Abbr.* **Imp.** An emperor, especially of the Roman Empire. [Latin *imperātor,* EMPEROR.]

im·pe·ra·trix (impe-raátrikss) *n. Abbr.* **Imp.** An empress. [Latin.]

im·per·cep·ti·ble (impər-séptə-b'l) *adj.* **1.** Not perceptible. **2.** Barely perceptible. **3.** Extremely slight or subtle. **—im·per·cep·ti·bil·i·ty** (-bílləti), **im·per·cep·ti·ble·ness** *n.* **—im·per·cep·ti·bly** *adv.*

im·per·cep·tive (impər-séptiv) *adj.* Not perceptive; lacking perception. **—im·per·cep·tiv·i·ty** (-sep-tívvəti), **im·per·cep·tive·ness** *n.*

im·per·cip·i·ent (impər-síppi-ənt) *adj.* Imperceptive. **—im·per·cip·i·ence** *n.*

im·per·fect (im-pérfikt, ím-) *adj. Abbr.* **imp., imperf. 1. a.** Not perfect; having some flaw or defect. **b.** Incomplete. **2.** Of or designating the tense of a verb that shows, usually in the past, an action or condition as incomplete, continuous, or coincident with another action. **3.** *Botany.* **a.** Having either stamens or a pistil only: *imperfect flowers.* **b.** Designating fungi in which the sexual reproductive stage has not been discovered or has been lost during evolution. **4.** *Law.* Not legally enforceable because of a technical defect. **5.** *Music.* **a.** Designating a cadence ending on the dominant rather than the direct chord of the tonic. **b.** Of or designating intervals other than the fourth, fifth, and octave.
~*n. Abbr.* **imp., imperf. 1.** The imperfect tense. **2.** A verb in this tense. [Middle English *imperfit,* from Old French *imparfait,* from Latin *imperfectus* : *in-,* not + *perfectus,* PERFECT.] **—im·per·fect·ly** *adv.* **—im·per·fect·ness** *n.*

imperfect competition *n.* **Monopolistic competition** *(see).*

im·per·fec·tion (impər-féksh'n) *n.* **1.** The quality or condition of being imperfect. **2.** Something imperfect; a defect; a flaw. —See Synonyms at **blemish.**

im·per·fec·tive (impər-féktiv) *adj. Grammar.* Of or designating a verb in the imperfective aspect.
~*n. Grammar.* **1.** The imperfective aspect. **2.** A verb in the imperfective aspect.

imperfective aspect *n.* An aspect of verbs that expresses action without regard to its beginning or completion. Compare **perfective aspect.** See **aspect.**

im·per·fo·rate (im-pérfərit, -rət) *adj.* **1.** Not perforated. **2.** Not perforated into detachable rows. Said of stamps and sheets of stamps. **3.** *Anatomy.* Lacking a normal opening. Said of a bodily part.
~*n.* An imperforate stamp.

im·pe·ri·al[1] (im-peér-i-əl) *adj. Abbr.* **imp 1. a.** Of or pertaining to an empire or a sovereign, especially an emperor or empress. **b.** Of or pertaining to the British Empire. **2.** Designating a nation or government having sovereign rights over colonies or dependencies. **3. a.** *Obsolete.* Having supreme authority; sovereign. **b.** Regal; majestic. **4.** Outstanding in size or quality. **5.** Of or pertaining to the Imperial system of weights and measures.
~*n.* **1.** *Capital* **I.** A supporter or a soldier of the Holy Roman Empire. **2.** An emperor or empress. **3.** A dome with a pointed top. **4.** Something outstanding in size or quality. **5. a.** A 22 by 30 inches size of paper. **b.** A size of book; especially, *imperial octavo* (7½ by 11 inches) or *imperial quarto* (11 by 15 inches). **6.** Formerly, a Russian gold coin. [Middle English *emperial, imperial,* from Old French, from Late Latin *imperiālis,* from Latin *imperium,* command, EMPIRE.] **—im·pe·ri·al·ly** *adv.*

imperial² *n.* A pointed beard grown from the lower lip and chin. [French *impériale,* IMPERIAL (after Napoleon III).]
im·pe·ri·al·ism (im-peér-i-ə-liz'm) *n.* **1.** The policy of extending a nation's authority by territorial acquisition or by the establishment of economic and political hegemony over other nations. Often used derogatorily. **2.** The system, policies, or practices of an imperial government. **3.** The imposing of its will on others by a country or powerful organisation, as in social, cultural, or other matters. Used derogatorily. **—im·pe·ri·al·ist** *n.* & *adj.* **—im·pe·ri·al·is·tic** (-lístik) *adj.* **—im·pe·ri·al·is·ti·cal·ly** *adv.*
imperial system *n.* The system of weights and measures used in Britain and various other countries, using units of weights such as the ounce, pound, and stone; units of length such as the inch, foot, yard, and mile; and units of volume such as the pint, quart, and gallon.
im·per·il (im-pérril) *tr.v.* **-illed** or *U.S.* **-iled, -illing** or *U.S.* **-iling, -ils.** To put in peril; endanger. **—im·per·il·ment** *n.*
im·pe·ri·ous (im-peér-i-əss) *adj.* **1.** Domineering; overbearing. **2.** *Obsolete.* Regal; imperial. **3.** *Rare.* Urgent; pressing. —See Synonyms at **dictatorial.** [Latin *imperiōsus,* from *imperium,* IMPERIUM.] **—im·pe·ri·ous·ly** *adv.* **—im·pe·ri·ous·ness** *n.*
im·per·ish·a·ble (im-pérrish-əb'l) *adj.* Not perishable. **—im·per·ish·a·bil·i·ty** (-ə-bílləti), **im·per·ish·a·ble·ness** *n.* **—im·per·ish·a·bly** *adv.*
im·pe·ri·um (im-peér-i-əm) *n., pl.* **-ria** (-i-ə). **1.** Absolute rule; supreme power. **2.** A sphere of power or dominion; an empire. [Latin, EMPIRE.]
im·per·ma·nent (im-pérmənənt) *adj.* Not permanent; not lasting or durable. **—im·per·ma·nence, im·per·ma·nen·cy** *n.*
im·per·me·a·ble (im-pérmi-əb'l) *adj.* **1.** Not permeable. **2.** *Physics.* Not allowing the passage of fluids. **3.** *Geology.* Not allowing water or other fluid to pass through it easily. Said of rock. [Late Latin *impermeābilis* : *in-,* not + *permeābilis,* PERMEABLE.] **—im·per·me·a·ble·ness** *n.* **—im·per·me·a·bly** *adv.*
im·per·mis·si·ble (impər-míss-əb'l) *adj.* Not permissible. **—im·per·mis·si·bil·i·ty** (-ə-bílləti) *n.* **—im·per·mis·si·bly** *adv.*
im·per·script·i·ble (impər-skríptib'l) *adj.* Not supported by written authority; unrecorded.
im·per·son·al (im-pérss'n-'l) *adj.* **1.** *Grammar.* **a.** Pertaining to or designating a verb or construction that expresses the action of an unspecified agent and is used in the third person singular without a separate subject (as *methinks*) or with a non-personal, non-specific subject (as in *it snowed*). **b.** Indefinite. Said of pronouns. **2.** Not personal; not related or connected to a person or persons: *impersonal possessions.* **3.** Exhibiting little or no individuality or personality. **4.** Lacking sympathy or human warmth. **—im·per·son·al·i·ty** (-ál-əti) *n.* **—im·per·son·al·ly** *adv.*
im·per·son·al·ise, im·per·son·al·ize (im-pérss'n'l-īz) *tr.v.* **-ised, -ising, -ises.** To make impersonal.
im·per·son·ate (im-pérss'n-ayt) *tr.v.* **-ated, -ating, -ates. 1.** To act the character or part of, especially in order to entertain. **2.** To assume the identity of for unlawful purposes. **3.** *Archaic.* To embody; personify. [IN- (in) + PERSON + -ATE.] **—im·per·son·ate** (-ət) *adj.* **—im·per·son·a·tion** (-áysh'n) *n.* **—im·per·son·a·tor** *n.*
im·per·ti·nence (im-pérti-nənss) *n.* Also **im·per·ti·nen·cy** (-nən-si) *pl.* **-cies. 1.** The quality or condition of being impertinent; insolence. **2.** *Rare.* Irrelevance. **3.** An impertinent act, person, statement, or the like.
im·per·ti·nent (im-pértinənt) *adj.* **1.** Impudent; presumptuous; rude. **2.** Not pertinent; irrelevant. [Middle English, irrelevant, from Old French, from Late Latin *impertinēns* (stem *impertinent-*) : Latin *in-,* not + *pertinēns,* PERTINENT.] **—im·per·ti·nent·ly** *adv.*
im·per·turb·a·ble (impər-túrb-əb'l) *adj.* Not capable of being perturbed; calm. See Synonyms at **cool. —im·per·turb·a·bil·i·ty** (-ə-bílləti), **im·per·turb·a·ble·ness** *n.* **—im·per·turb·a·bly** *adv.*
im·per·vi·ous (im-pérvi-əss) *adj.* **1.** Incapable of being penetrated, as by water or light. **2.** Not affected; unable to be influenced: *impervious to her charm.* [Latin *impervius* : *in-,* not + *pervius,* PERVIOUS.] **—im·per·vi·ous·ly** *adv.* **—im·per·vi·ous·ness** *n.*
im·pe·ti·go (impi-tī́-gō || *U.S. also* -teé-) *n.* A contagious skin disease characterised by pustules that burst and form characteristic thick yellow crusts. [Latin *impetīgō,* "an attack", from *impetere,* to assail, attack. See **impetus.**]
im·pe·trate (ímpi-trayt) *tr.v.* **-trated, -trating, -trates.** *Theology.* **1.** To obtain by entreaty or petition. **2.** To beseech. [Latin *impetrāre,* to accomplish : *in-* (intensive) + *patrāre,* to father, achieve, accomplish, from *pater,* father.] **—im·pe·tra·tion** (-tráysh'n) *n.* **—im·pe·tra·tor** *n.*
im·pet·u·ous (im-péttew-əss) *adj.* **1.** Characterised or prompted by sudden energy, emotion, or the like; impulsive; rash. **2.** Having great impetus; rushing with violence: *impetuous, heaving waves.* [Middle English, from Old French *impetueux,* from Latin *impetuōsus,* from *impetus,* IMPETUS.] **—im·pet·u·os·i·ty** (-óssiti), **im·pet·u·ous·ness** *n.* **—im·pet·u·ous·ly** *adv.*
Synonyms: impetuous, heedless, hasty, headlong.
im·pe·tus (ímpitəss) *n., pl.* **-tuses. 1. a.** An impelling force; an impulse. **b.** Something that incites; a stimulus. **2.** Loosely, the force associated with a moving body. [Latin, attack, from *impetere,* to assail, attack : *in-,* against + *petere,* to go towards, seek, attack.]
im·pi (ímpi) *n., pl.* **-pis** or collectively **impi. 1.** Formerly, a regiment or army of a black South African people. **2.** In South Africa, an armed band of black men. [Nguni, "military unit".]
im·pi·e·ty (im-pī́-əti) *n., pl.* **-ties. 1.** The quality or state of being impious. **2.** An impious act. **3.** Undutifulness.
im·pinge (im-pínj) *intr.v.* **-pinged, -pinging, -pinges. 1.** To encroach; trespass. Used with *on* or *upon.* **2.** To collide; strike; dash. Used with *on, upon,* or *against.* [Latin *impingere,* to push against : *in-,* against + *pangere,* to fasten, drive in.] **—im·pinge·ment** *n.* **—im·ping·er** *n.*
impingement attack *n. Metallurgy.* Erosion of a metal surface that is in contact with a turbulent fluid containing small gas bubbles or solid particles.
im·pi·ous (ímpi-əss || im-pī́-) *adj.* **1.** Not pious; lacking reverence; profane. **2.** Lacking due respect. [Latin *impius* : *in-,* not + *pius,* PIOUS.] **—im·pi·ous·ly** *adv.* **—im·pi·ous·ness** *n.*
imp·ish (ímpish) *adj.* Of or like an imp; mischievous. See Synonyms at **playful. —imp·ish·ly** *adv.* **—imp·ish·ness** *n.*
im·pla·ca·ble (im-pláck-əb'l || *U.S. also* -pláyk-) *adj.* **1.** Not placable; incapable of appeasement; inexorable. **2.** Unalterable; inflexible. [Latin *implācābilis* : *in-,* not + *plācābilis,* PLACABLE.] **—im·pla·ca·bil·i·ty** (-ə-bílləti), **im·pla·ca·ble·ness** *n.* **—im·pla·ca·bly** *adv.*
im·plant (im-plaánt || -plánt) *tr.v.* **-planted, -planting, -plants. 1.** To entrench or set in firmly, as in the ground; infix. **2.** To establish decisively, as in the mind or consciousness; instil; ingrain. **3.** *Medicine.* To insert or embed surgically, as in grafting.
~*n.* (im-plaant || -plant). Something implanted; especially, a drug or surgically implanted tissue.
im·plan·ta·tion (implaan-táysh'n, -plan-) *n.* **1.** An act or instance of implanting. **2.** The condition of being implanted. **3.** An implanted object. **4.** The attachment and embedding of the fertilised ovum in the uterine wall.
im·plau·si·ble (im-pláwzə-b'l) *adj.* Not plausible. **—im·plau·si·bil·i·ty** (-bílləti), **im·plau·si·ble·ness** *n.* **—im·plau·si·bly** *adv.*
im·plead (im-pleéd) *tr.v.* **-pleaded, -pleading, -pleads.** To sue or prosecute in a court of law. [Middle English *impleden,* from Old French *empleid(i)er* : *en-* (intensive) + *pleid(i)er,* PLEAD.]
im·ple·ment (ímpli-mənt) *n.* **1.** A tool, utensil, or instrument. **2.** An article used to outfit or equip. **3.** A means employed to achieve a given end; an agent. **4.** In Scots law, performance of a contract or an obligation. —See Synonyms at **tool.**
~*tr.v.* (-ment) **implemented, -menting, -ments. 1.** To fulfil (an order, for example); comply with. **2.** To carry out (a plan, for example); execute. **3.** *Rare.* To supply with implements. [Middle English, from Late Latin *implēmentum,* a filling up, supplement, from Latin *implēre,* to fill up, fulfil : *in-* (intensive) + *plēre,* to fill.] **—im·ple·men·ta·tion** (-men-táysh'n) *n.*
im·pli·cate (ímpli-kayt) *tr.v.* **-cated, -cating, -cates. 1.** To involve intimately or incriminatingly. **2.** To imply. **3.** *Archaic.* To interweave or entangle; entwine.
~*n. Rare.* That which is implied. [Latin *implicāre* : *in-,* in + *plicāre,* to fold.]
im·pli·ca·tion (ímpli-káysh'n) *n.* **1.** The act of implicating or the condition of being implicated. **2.** The act of implying or the condition of being implied. **3.** That which is implied, especially: **a.** An indirect suggestion. **b.** An inference.
im·pli·ca·tive (im-plíckə-tiv, ímpli-kaytiv) *adj.* Also **im·pli·ca·to·ry** (-təri, -tri) **1.** Having a tendency to implicate. **2.** Of or pertaining to implication. **—im·pli·ca·tive·ly** *adv.*
im·plic·it (im-plíssit) *adj.* **1.** Implied or understood although not directly expressed: *His anger was implicit.* **2.** Inherent or contained in the nature of something although not directly expressed. Used with *in*: *Suspicion is implicit in such a tone of voice.* **3.** Having no doubts or reservations; unquestioning: *Her trust in him was implicit.* **4.** *Mathematics.* Pertaining to or designating a function of two or more variables of the form $f(x, y) = 0$. For example, in $2xy + 1 = 0$, x is an implicit function of y. [Latin *implicitus,* earlier *implicātus,* involved, entangled, from the past participle of *implicāre,* to involve, IMPLICATE.] **—im·plic·it·ly** *adv.* **—im·plic·it·ness** *n.*
im·plied (im-plī́d) *adj.* Suggested, involved, or understood although not clearly or openly expressed.
im·plode (im-plṓd) *v.* **-ploded, -ploding, -plodes.** —*intr.* To undergo implosion. —*tr.* **1.** To cause implosion in. **2.** *Phonetics.* To pronounce by implosion. [IN- (in) + (EX)PLODE.]
im·plore (im-plór || -plṓr) *v.* **-plored, -ploring, -plores.** —*tr.* **1.** To appeal to in supplication; entreat; beseech: *I implore you to have mercy on the defendant.* **2.** To plead or beg for urgently: *I implore your mercy.* —*intr.* To make an earnest appeal. —See Synonyms at **beg.** [Latin *implōrāre,* to invoke with tears : *in-,* in + *plōrāre,* to weep, bewail, lament (perhaps imitative).] **—im·plo·ra·tion** (im-plaw-ráysh'n) *n.* **—im·plor·er** *n.* **—im·plor·ing·ly** *adv.*
im·plo·sion (im-plṓzh'n) *n.* **1.** A more or less violent collapse inwards, as of a highly evacuated glass vessel. **2.** *Phonetics.* The stopping of the breath while breathing in to form a stop consonant. Compare **plosion.** [IN- + (EX)PLOSION.]
im·plo·sive (im-plṓ-siv || -ziv) *adj. Phonetics.* Pronounced by implosion.
~*n. Phonetics.* A consonant pronounced by implosion.
im·ply (im-plī́) *tr.v.* **-plied, -plying, -plies. 1.** To say or express indirectly; hint; suggest. **2.** To involve or suggest by logical necessity; entail: *His aims imply a good deal of energy.* —See Synonyms at **suggest.** [Middle English *implien, emplien,* from Old French *emplier,* from Latin *implicāre,* infold, involve, IMPLICATE.]
Usage: It is a common mistake to confuse *imply* (to hint, or state something indirectly) with *infer* (to deduce, or draw a conclusion from what is stated). The speaker or writer *implies*: *Your report*

implies that the mechanism was faulty. The listener or reader *infers*: *I infer from your report that the mechanism was faulty.*

im·pol·i·cy (im-pólli-si) *n., pl.* **-cies. 1.** The state of or an instance of being impolitic. **2.** A bad policy.

im·po·lite (ímpə-līt) *adj.* Not polite; discourteous; rude. [Latin *impolītus,* unpolished : *in-,* not + *polītus,* polished, POLITE.] **—im·po·lite·ly** *adv.* **—im·po·lite·ness** *n.*

im·pol·i·tic (im-póllitik) *adj.* Not wise or expedient; not politic. **—im·pol·i·tic·ly** *adv.* **—im·pol·i·tic·ness** *n.*

im·pon·der·a·ble (im-póndərəb'l) *adj.* Incapable of being weighed, measured, or evaluated with precision.
~n. Sometimes plural. Something which is imponderable; an indeterminable factor: *Public support is a great imponderable.* **—im·pon·der·a·ble·ness** *n.* **—im·pon·der·a·bly** *adv.*

im·po·nent (im-pōnənt) *n.* One who imposes a duty. [From IMPOSE, by analogy with *opponent.*] **—im·po·nent** *adj.*

im·port (im-pórt ‖ -pōrt) *v.* **-ported, -porting, -ports.** *—tr.* **1.** To bring or carry in from an outside source; especially, to bring in (goods) from a foreign country for trade or sale. Compare **export. 2.** To mean; signify. **3.** To imply. **4.** *Archaic.* To have importance for. *—intr.* To be significant. —See Synonyms at **mean** (convey sense).
~n. (ím-pawrt ‖ -pōrt). **1.** *Abbr.* **imp.** Something imported. **2. a.** The business of importing. **b.** Importation. **3.** Meaning; signification. **4.** Importance; significance. —See Synonyms at **importance, meaning.** [Middle English *importen,* from Latin *importāre,* to carry in : *in-,* in + *portāre,* to carry.] **—im·port·a·bil·i·ty** (im-pórtə-bílləti ‖ -pōrtə) *n.* **—im·port·a·ble** *adj.* **—im·port·er** *n.*

im·por·tance (im-pórt'nss ‖ -pōrt'nss) *n.* **1.** The condition or quality of being important; significance; consequence. **2.** Personal status; standing. **3.** *Obsolete.* An important matter.
Synonyms: *importance, consequence, moment, significance, import, weight.*

im·por·tant (im-pórt'nt ‖ -pōrt'nt) *adj. Abbr.* **imp. 1.** Having a great effect on or being of great concern; significant: *an important decision to many people.* **2.** Holding or considered as holding a high position in people's estimation. **3.** Self-important. [Old French, from Old Italian *importante,* from Medieval Latin *importāns* (stem *important-*), present participle of *importāre,* to mean, be significant, from Latin, to carry in, IMPORT.] **—im·por·tant·ly** *adv.*
Usage: When used as part of a connecting phrase, such as *More important, he failed his exam,* there is a tendency, especially in formal American English, to add an *-ly* ending. This usage is criticised by traditional grammarians, who argue that the phrase is short for *What is more important,* but the use of *importantly* is now very common.

im·por·ta·tion (ímpawr-táysh'n ‖ -pōr-) *n.* **1.** The act, occupation, or business of importing. **2.** Something imported; an import.

im·por·tu·nate (im-pórtew-nət, -nit) *adj.* **1.** Stubbornly or unreasonably persistent in request or demand. **2.** Urgent; pressing. **—im·por·tu·nate·ly** *adv.* **—im·por·tu·nate·ness** *n.*

im·por·tune (im-pór-tewn, ím-pawr-téwn ‖ -pər-, -tōōn, -tóōn) *tr.v.* **-tuned, -tuning, -tunes. 1.** To beset with repeated and insistent requests. **2.** To solicit, especially for immoral purposes. **3.** *Obsolete.* To ask for insistently and repeatedly. **4.** *Obsolete.* To annoy; vex. —See Synonyms at **beg.**
~adj. Importunate. [Medieval Latin *importūnārī,* to be troublesome, from Latin *importūnus,* "without a port", difficult of access, unfit, unsuitable : *in-,* not + *portus,* port, harbour.] **—im·por·tune·ly** *adv.* **—im·por·tun·er** *n.*

im·por·tu·ni·ty (im-pawr-téw-nəti ‖ -pər-, -tōō-) *n., pl.* **-ties. 1. a.** The act of importuning. **b.** The state or quality of being importunate. **2.** *Plural.* Insistent demands or requests.

im·pose (im-pōz) *v.* **-posed, -posing, -poses.** *—tr.* **1.** To establish or apply as compulsory; levy: *The amount of duties imposed now constitutes a protective tariff.* **2.** To lay (something burdensome) upon another or others: *impose extra duties.* **3.** To obtrude or force (oneself, for example) upon another or others. **4.** *Printing.* To arrange (type or plates) in the correct order and lock them into a chase. **5.** To pass off (something) on others: *He imposed a fraud on his company.* **6.** To lay (hands) on the head of a person receiving certain sacraments. Used of a bishop or priest. *—intr.* **1.** To take unfair advantage of something or someone. Used with *on* or *upon.* **2.** To make an impression, often fraudulently. Used with *on* or *upon.* [Old French *imposer,* from Latin *impōnere* (past participle *impositus*), to put on : *in-,* on + *pōnere,* to put, place.] **—im·pos·er** *n.*

im·pos·ing (im-pōzing) *adj.* Impressive, as in size or appearance. See Synonyms at **grand.**

imposing stone *n. Printing.* A stone or metal slab on which material to be printed is arranged. Also called "imposing table".

im·po·si·tion (ímpə-zísh'n) *n.* **1.** The act of imposing. **2. a.** Something imposed, as a tax, undue burden, or fraud. **b.** *British.* Extra work given to school children as a punishment. **3.** *Printing.* The arrangement of printed matter to form a sequence of pages.

im·pos·si·bil·i·ty (im-póssi-bílləti) *n., pl.* **-ties. 1.** The condition or quality of being impossible. **2.** Something impossible.

im·pos·si·ble (im-póss-əb'l, -ib'l) *adj.* **1.** Not capable of existing or happening. **2.** Having little likelihood of happening or being accomplished. **3.** Unacceptable. **4.** Untrue or ridiculously exaggerated: *an impossible claim.* **5.** Not capable of being dealt with or tolerated: *an impossible request.* **6.** Troublesome; behaving in an annoying way: *her boss is impossible.* [Middle English, from Old French, from Latin *impossibilis* : *in-,* not + *possibilis,* POSSIBLE.] **—im·pos·si·bly** *adv.*

im·post¹ (ímpōst) *n.* **1.** Something imposed or levied, as a tax or duty. **2.** The weight a horse must carry in a handicap race. [Old French, from Medieval Latin *impositum,* from Latin *impositus,* past participle of *impōnere,* IMPOSE.]

impost² *n. Architecture.* The uppermost part of a column or pillar supporting an arch, usually projecting from a wall like a bracket. [French *imposte,* from Italian *imposta,* from Latin, feminine past participle of *impōnere,* IMPOSE.]

im·pos·tor (im-póstər) *n.* A person who deceives, especially by assuming a false identity. [Old French *imposteur,* from Late Latin *impos(i)tor,* from Latin *impōnere* (past participle *impositus*), IMPOSE.]

im·pos·ture (im-pósschər) *n.* Deception or fraud; especially, assumption of a false identity. [Late Latin *impostura,* from Latin *impos(i)tus,* past participle of *impōnere,* IMPOSE.]

im·po·tent (ímpətənt) *adj.* **1.** Lacking physical strength or vigour; weak. **2.** Powerless; ineffectual. **3.** Incapable of sustaining an erection. Said of males. Compare **frigid. 4.** *Obsolete.* Lacking self-restraint. —See Synonyms at **sterile.** [Middle English, from Old French, from Latin *impotēns* : *in-,* not + *potēns,* POTENT.] **—im·po·tence, im·po·ten·cy** *n.* **—im·po·tent·ly** *adv.*

im·pound (im-pównd) *tr.v.* **-pounded, -pounding, -pounds. 1.** To confine in or as if in a pound. **2.** To seize and retain, especially in legal custody. **3.** To accumulate (water) in a reservoir. **—im·pound·age, im·pound·ment** *n.* **—im·pound·er** *n.*

im·pov·er·ish (im-póvvərish) *tr.v.* **-ished, -ishing, -ishes. 1.** To diminish or exhaust the wealth of; reduce to poverty. **2.** To deprive of natural richness or strength. —See Synonyms at **deplete.** [Middle English *enpoverisen,* from Old French *empovrir* (present stem *empovriss-*), to make poor : *en-* (causative) + *povre,* POOR.] **—im·pov·er·ish·ment** *n.*

im·prac·ti·ca·ble (im-práktikəb'l) *adj.* **1.** Not capable of being done or carried out. **2.** Unfit for use or passage, as a road may be. **3.** *Archaic.* Unmanageable; intractable. —See Usage note at **impractical. —im·prac·ti·ca·bil·i·ty** (-bílləti), **im·prac·ti·ca·ble·ness** *n.* **—im·prac·ti·ca·bly** *adv.*

im·prac·ti·cal (im-prákti-k'l) *adj.* **1.** Difficult to implement or maintain in practice. **2.** Incapable of dealing efficiently with practical matters, especially financial or mechanical matters. **3.** *Chiefly U.S.* Impracticable. **—im·prac·ti·cal·i·ty** (-kál-əti), **im·prac·ti·cal·ness** *n.*
Usage: There is a certain overlap of usage between *impracticable* and *impractical,* but generally the senses are distinct. *Impracticable* has the more absolute sense, applying to something that is not capable of being carried out *(It is impracticable to make the journey on foot). Impractical* means that something could be carried out, but it would be unwise or inefficient to do so *(That's a very impractical suggestion).*

im·pre·cate (ímpri-kayt) *tr.v.* **-cated, -cating, -cates.** To invoke (evil or a curse) upon. [Latin *imprecārī* : *in-,* on + *precārī,* to pray, entreat.] **—im·pre·ca·tor** *n.* **—im·pre·ca·to·ry** (-káytəri, im-prékətri, -təri) *adj.*

im·pre·ca·tion (ímpri-káysh'n) *n.* **1.** The act of imprecating. **2.** A curse.

im·pre·cise (ímpri-síss) *adj.* Not precise; inexact. **—im·pre·cise·ly** *adv.* **—im·pre·ci·sion** (-sízh'n) *n.*

im·preg·na·ble¹ (im-prégnəb'l) *adj.* **1.** Able to resist capture or entry by force: *an impregnable castle.* **2.** Unable to be shaken, refuted, or criticised: *impregnable convictions.* [Middle English *imprenable,* from Old French : *in-,* not + *prenable,* PREGNABLE.]

impregnable² *adj.* Able to be impregnated. [From IMPREGNATE.]

im·preg·nate (ímpreg-nayt, im-prég-) *tr.v.* **-nated, -nating, -nates. 1.** To make pregnant; inseminate. **2.** To fertilise (an ovum, for example). **3.** To fill throughout or saturate. **4.** To permeate or imbue.
~adj. Impregnated; made pregnant. [Late Latin *impregnāre* : Latin *in-,* in + *praegnās,* PREGNANT.] **—im·preg·na·tion** (impreg-náysh'n) *n.* **—im·preg·na·tor** *n.*

im·pre·sa (im-práyzə) *n.* Also **im·prese** (im-préez). An emblem or device with a motto. [French *impresse,* from Italian *impresa,* undertaking, emblem. See **impresario.**]

im·pre·sa·ri·o (imprə-saári-ō, -zaári- ‖ *U.S. also* -sárri-) *n., pl.* **-sarios** or **-sari** (-saári, -zaári). **1.** One who sponsors or produces entertainments, especially theatrical and musical ones. **2.** A manager; a producer. [Italian, undertaker, manager, from *impresa,* undertaking, chivalric deed, emblem, from the feminine of *impreso,* past participle of *imprendere,* to undertake, from Vulgar Latin *imprendere* (unattested). See **emprise.**]

im·pre·scrip·ti·ble (ímpri-skríptib'l) *adj. Law.* Immune from prescription; inalienable. **—im·pre·scrip·ti·bly** *adv.*

im·press¹ (im-préss) *tr.v.* **-pressed, -pressing, -presses. 1.** To produce or apply with pressure. **2.** To mark or stamp with or as if with pressure. **3.** To produce a vivid perception or image of. **4.** To affect or influence deeply or forcibly. **5.** To emphasise; stress. **b.** To transmit a force or motion to. —See Synonyms at **affect.**
~n. (ím-press). **1.** The act of impressing. **2.** A mark or pattern produced by impressing. **3.** A stamp or seal meant to be impressed. **4.** A characteristic quality. [Middle English *impressen,* from Latin *imprimere* (past participle *impressus*) : *in-,* in + *premere,* to press.]

im·press² (im-préss) *tr.v.* **-pressed, -pressing, -presses. 1.** Formerly, to compel (a person) to serve in a military force. **2.** To confiscate (property).
~n. Impressment. [IN- (intensive) + PRESS (to force into service).]

im·press·i·ble (im-préssib'l) *adj.* Susceptible to being impressed. **—im·press·i·bly** *adv.*

im·pres·sion (im-présh'n) *n.* **1.** The act or process of impressing. **2.** The effect, mark, or imprint made on a surface by pressure. **3. a.** An effect, image, or feeling retained as a consequence of experience. **b.** An effect produced by an event or action. **4.** A vague notion, remembrance, or belief. **5.** An imitation or mimicking of another person or thing. **6.** *Printing.* **a.** All the copies of a publication printed at one time from the same set of type. **b.** A single copy of this printing. **c.** A print taken from an engraving or from type. **7.** In dentistry, an imprint of the teeth and surrounding tissue in material such as wax or plaster, used as a mould in making dentures or inlays. —See Synonyms at **opinion.**

im·pres·sion·a·ble (im-présh'n-əb'l) *adj.* Readily influenced; suggestible. **—im·pres·sion·a·bil·i·ty** (-ə-bílləti), **im·pres·sion·a·ble·ness** *n.*

im·pres·sion·ism (im-présh'n-iz'm) *n.* *Sometimes capital* **I. 1.** A theory or style of painting originating and developed in France during the 1870s, characterised chiefly by concentration on the general impression produced by a scene or object and by the use of unmixed primary colours and small strokes to simulate actual reflected light. **2.** A literary style characterised generally by the use of details and mental associations to evoke subjective and sensory impressions rather than the re-creation of objective reality. **3.** A musical style of the late 19th and early 20th centuries, using unusual harmonies to evoke suggestions of mood, place, and natural phenomena. **—im·pres·sion·ist** *n.* & *adj.*

im·press·ion·ist·ic (im-présh'n-ístik) *adj.* **1.** Of or pertaining to impressionism. **2.** Of or pertaining to a subjective, sketchy approach or attitude: *an impressionistic survey of recent history.*

im·pres·sive (im-préssiv) *adj.* Making a strong, favourable impression; awesome or stirring. **—im·pres·sive·ly** *adv.* **—im·press·ive·ness** *n.*

im·press·ment (im-préssmənt) *n.* The act or policy of impressing men or property for public service or use: *army ranks swelled by impressment.*

im·pres·sure (im-préshər) *n. Archaic.* An impression.

im·prest (im-prést, ím-prest) *n.* An advance or loan of government or public funds towards the performance of some service for the government. [Probably from Italian *imprestare,* to make a loan to : *in-,* towards, from Latin + *prestare,* to lend, from Latin *praestāre,* to pay, give, from *praestō,* at hand (see **presto**).]

im·pri·ma·tur (ímpri-máytər, -maátər) *n.* **1.** *Abbr.* **imp.** Official approval or licence to print or publish, especially under conditions of censorship. **2.** Broadly, any official sanction. [Latin, let it be printed, from Latin *imprimere,* to print, IMPRESS.]

im·pri·mis (im-prī́-miss || -prée-) *adv. Archaic.* In the first place. [Middle English, from Latin *in prīmīs,* among the first (things) : *in,* in + *prīmīs,* ablative plural of *prīmus,* first.]

im·print (im-prínt) *v.* **-printed, -printing, -prints.** —*tr.* **1.** To produce or impress (a mark or pattern) on a surface. **2.** To stamp or produce a mark on. **3.** To establish firmly or impress, as on the mind or memory. **4.** To subject (a young animal) to imprinting. —*intr.* To become imprinted. Used of young animals.
~*n.* (imprint). **1.** A mark or pattern produced by imprinting. **2.** A distinguishing manifestation: *the imprint of defeat.* **3. a.** The publisher's name, often with the date, address, and edition of a publication, printed at the bottom of a title page. **b.** The printer's name, usually placed on the copyright page. [Middle English *imprenten,* from Old French *empreinter,* from *empreinte,* impression, from *empreindre,* to print, from Latin *imprimere,* to IMPRESS.]

im·print·ing (im-prínting) *n.* A learning process occurring early in the life of certain animals, whereby the young recognise and associate with members of their own species or with a surrogate parent.

im·pris·on (im-prízz'n) *tr.v.* To put in or as if in prison. [Middle English *inprisonen, emprisonen,* from Old French *emprisoner* : *en-* (causative) + *prison,* PRISON.] **—im·pris·on·ment** *n.*

im·prob·a·bil·i·ty (im-próbbə-bílləti, ím-) *n., pl.* **-ties. 1.** The condition of being improbable. **2.** Something improbable.

im·prob·a·ble (im-próbbəb'l, ím-) *adj.* Not probable; doubtful or unlikely. [Latin *improbābilis* : *in-,* not + *probābilis,* PROBABLE.] **—im·prob·a·ble·ness** *n.* **—im·prob·a·bly** *adv.*

im·pro·bi·ty (im-prṓbəti) *n.* Lack of probity; dishonesty. [Latin *improbitās,* from *improbus,* dishonest : *in-,* not + *probus,* honest, good.]

im·promp·tu (im-prómp-tew || -tōō) *adj.* Not rehearsed; improvised. See Synonyms at **extemporaneous.**
~*adv.* Spontaneously; in the manner of improvisation.
~*n.* Something made or done impromptu; specifically, a musical composition that is improvisatory in style. [French, from Latin *in promptū,* at hand : *in,* in + *promptū,* ablative of *promptus,* ready, PROMPT.]

im·prop·er (im-próppər, ím-) *adj.* **1.** Not suited to the circumstances or intention. **2.** Not in keeping with propriety; indecorous: *improper conduct.* **3.** Not consistent with fact or rule; incorrect: *improper reasoning.* **4.** Irregular or abnormal. [Old French *impropre,* from Latin *improprius* : *in-,* not + *proprius,* one's own, PROPER.] **—im·prop·er·ly** *adv.* **—im·prop·er·ness** *n.*
Synonyms: *improper, unbecoming, unseemly, indelicate, indecent, indecorous.*

improper fraction *n.* A fraction that is greater than or equal to one, such as $^9/_5$, $^{21}7/_4$, $^{12}/_{12}$. Compare **proper fraction.**

improper integral *n.* An integral having at least one nonfinite limit or having an integrand that becomes infinite between the limits of integration.

im·pro·pri·ate (im-prṓpri-ayt) *tr.v.* **-ated, -ating, -ates.** To transfer (church property, tithes, or the like) into lay hands. [Anglo-Latin *impropriāre,* from *proprius,* own.] **—im·pro·pri·a·tion** *n.* **—im·pro·pri·a·tor** *n.*

im·pro·pri·e·ty (imprə-prī́-əti) *n., pl.* **-ties. 1.** The quality or condition of being improper. **2.** An improper act. **3.** An improper or unacceptable usage in speech or writing.

im·prove (im-prōōv) *v.* **-proved, -proving, -proves.** —*tr.* **1.** To advance to a better state or quality; make better. **2.** To increase the productivity or value of (property or land, for example). —*intr.* **1.** To become or get better. **2.** To make beneficial additions or changes: *improve on the translation.* [Earlier *improwe,* from Anglo-French *emprouer,* to turn to profit : Old French *en-* (causative) + *prou,* profit, from Late Latin *prōde,* advantageous (see **proud**).] **—im·prov·a·ble** (-əb'l) *adj.* **—im·prov·a·bil·i·ty** (-ə-bílləti) *n.*
Synonyms: *improve, better, help, ameliorate, enhance.*

im·prove·ment (im-prōōvmənt) *n.* **1.** The act of improving. **2.** The state of being improved. **3. a.** A change or addition that improves. **b.** A person or thing that incurs a change for the better.
Usage: *Improvement* may be followed by *in* or *on,* depending on the context. To say that there is an *improvement in* something is simply to say that "something has improved". *Improvement on* is used only in the context of comparison: *That is a great improvement on yesterday's performance.*

im·prov·er (im-prōōvər) *n.* **1.** One that improves. **2.** *British.* One who works for no wages in return for instruction in his particular job or trade.

im·prov·i·dent (im-próvvid'nt) *adj.* **1.** Not providing for the future; thriftless. **2.** Rash; incautious. **—im·prov·i·dence** *n.* **—im·prov·i·dent·ly** *adv.*

im·pro·vi·sa·tion (ím-prə-vī-záysh'n, -pró-, -vi-) *n.* **1.** The act of improvising. **2.** Something improvised. **—im·pro·vi·sa·tion·al** *adj.*

im·prov·i·sa·tor (im-prə-vī-zaytər, -pró-, -vi-) *n.* One who improvises; especially, one who improvises music or verse, for example. **—im·pro·vi·sa·to·ri·al** (-zə-táwr-i-əl || -tṓr-) *adj.* **—im·pro·vi·sa·to·ry** (-záytəri, -zaytəri) *adj.*

im·pro·vise (ímprə-vīz) *v.* **-vised, -vising, -vises.** —*tr.* **1.** To invent, compose, or recite without preparation. **2.** To make or provide from available materials. —*intr.* To invent, compose, recite, or execute something spontaneously or without preparation. [French *improviser,* from Italian *improvvisare,* from *improvviso,* unforeseen, impromptu, from Latin *imprōvīsus,* : *in-,* not + *prōvīsus,* past participle of *prōvīdere,* to foresee, PROVIDE.] **—im·pro·vis·er** *n.*

im·pro·vised (ímprə-vīz'd) *adj.* **1.** Invented, composed, or recited spontaneously or without preparation. **2.** Made with whatever was available at the time. —See Synonyms at **extemporaneous.**

im·pru·dent (im-prōō-d'nt || -préw-) *adj.* Not prudent; unwise or injudicious; rash. [Middle English, from Latin *imprūdēns* : *in-,* not + *prūdēns,* PRUDENT.] **—im·pru·dence** *n.* **—im·pru·dent·ly** *adv.*

im·pu·dent (impewdənt) *adj.* **1.** Impertinent; rude; disrespectful. **2.** *Archaic.* Immodest. —See Synonyms at **shameless.** [Middle English, from Latin *impudēns* : *in-,* not + *pudēns* (stem *pudent-*), present participle of *pudēre,* to be ashamed.] **—im·pu·dence, im·pu·den·cy** *n.* **—im·pu·dent·ly** *adv.*

im·pu·dic·i·ty (ímpew-díssəti) *n. Archaic.* Immodesty; shamelessness. [Old French *impudicite,* from Latin *impudicus,* immodest : *in-,* not + *pudicus,* modest, from *pudēre,* to be ashamed.]

im·pugn (im-péwn) *tr.v.* **-pugned, -pugning, -pugns.** To oppose or attack as false; criticise; challenge. [Middle English *impugnen,* from Old French *impugner,* from Latin *impugnāre,* to fight against : *in-,* against + *pugnāre,* to fight.] **—im·pugn·a·ble** *adj.* **—im·pugn·er** *n.* **—im·pugn·ment** *n.*

im·pu·is·sance (im-pweéss'nss, -péw-iss'nss) *n.* Lack of power or effectiveness; weakness; impotence. **—im·pu·is·sant** *adj.*

im·pulse (ím-pulss) *n.* **1.** An impelling force or the motion it produces; a thrust; a push; momentum; impetus. **2.** A sudden inclination or urge; a desire; a whim: *an impulse to speak up.* **3.** A motivating propensity; a drive; an instinct. **4.** *Physics.* The product of the average value of a force and the time during which it acts, equal in general to the change in momentum produced by the force in this time interval. **5.** *Physiology.* A **nerve impulse** *(see).* [Latin *impulsus,* from the past participle of *impellere,* IMPEL.]

impulse buying *n.* The purchasing of goods as a result of a sudden urge rather than deliberate planning.

impulse turbine *n.* A type of turbine that is driven by jets of fluid directed onto the blades, used especially in the generation of hydroelectricity.

im·pul·sion (im-púlsh'n) *n.* **1.** The act of impelling or the condition of being impelled. **2.** An impelling force; a thrust. **3.** Motion produced by an impelling force. **4.** An urging; a compulsion.

im·pul·sive (im-púl-siv) *adj.* **1.** Inclined to act on impulse rather than thought. **2.** Produced as a result of impulse; precipitate; uncalculated: *an impulsive act.* **3.** Having force or power to impel or incite; forceful. **4.** *Physics.* Acting within brief time intervals. Said especially of a force. —See Synonyms at **spontaneous. —im·pul·sive·ly** *adv.* **—im·pul·sive·ness** *n.*

im·pu·ni·ty (im-péwnəti) *n., pl.* **-ties. 1.** Exemption from punishment or penalty. **2.** Immunity or preservation from recrimination, retribution, regret, or the like. [Latin *impūnitās* (stem *impūnitāt-*), from *impūnis,* not punished : *in-,* not + *poena,* penalty, pain, from Greek *poina, poinē,* expiation, punishment.]

im·pure (im-péwr, ím-) *adj.* **1.** Not pure or clean; contaminated. **2.** Not purified by religious rite; defiled. **3.** Immoral or obscene; unchaste. **4.** Mixed with another substance; alloyed; adulterated. **5.** Being a composite of more than one colour, or mixed with black or white. Said of colour. **6.** Deriving from more than one source, style, or convention; bastardised. Said of the arts. **7.** Containing improper usages or foreign elements. Said of language. **—im·pure·ly** *adv.* **—im·pure·ness** *n.*

im·pu·ri·ty (im-péwr-əti, ím-) *n., pl.* **-ties. 1.** The quality or condition of being impure: *moral impurity.* **2. a.** Something that is impure. **b.** Something that renders something else impure; a contaminant. **3.** *Electronics.* An element added in small controlled amounts to a pure crystal of another element in order to produce or modify semiconductor properties.

im·put·a·ble (im-péwt-əb'l) *adj.* Capable of being ascribed or imputed; attributable. **—im·put·a·bil·i·ty** (-ə-bílləti) *n.* **—im·put·a·bly** *adv.*

im·pu·ta·tion (ímpew-táysh'n) *n.* **1.** The act of imputing. **2.** Something imputed or ascribed.

im·pu·ta·tive (im-péwtətiv) *adj.* Characterised by or arising from imputation. **—im·pu·ta·tive·ly** *adv.*

im·pute (im-péwt) *tr.v.* **-puted, -puting, -putes. 1.** To ascribe (a crime or fault) to another. **2.** To attribute to a cause or source. **3.** *Theology.* To attribute (wickedness or merit) to a person. —See Synonyms at **attribute.** [Middle English *inputen,* from Old French *imputer,* from Latin *imputāre,* to bring into the reckoning : *in-*, in, into, + *putāre,* to reckon, compute, consider.]

in (in) *prep.* **1. a.** Within the confines of; inside: *in the safe.* **b.** Within the area covered by: *playing in the mud; We live in Spain.* **c.** *Informal.* Into: *came in my office.* **2.** On or affecting some part of: *He was hit in the head.* **3. a.** As a part, aspect, or property of: *a delay in delivery.* **b.** Within the scope or context of: *in the story; in physics.* **c.** Included as part of: *in the first batch.* **d.** Resulting from the operations of: *in his imagination.* **4. a.** During the course of or before the expiration of: *ready in a few minutes.* **b.** At the time of: *in winter.* **5. a.** At the position of: *put in command.* **b.** Closely associated with, especially in a professional way or as an occupation: *in banking.* **6.** After the pattern or form of: *going round in circles.* **7.** To or at the condition or situation of; into: *in trouble.* **8.** As an expression of; out of; by way of: *said in anger; in answer to the question.* **9. a.** During or as part of the act or process of: *in hot pursuit.* **b.** While affected by: *in his delirium.* **10.** With the attribute of: *in silence.* **11. a.** By means of: *paid in cash.* **b.** Made with or through the medium of; using: *a text written in French.* **12.** Within the category or class of: *the latest thing in fashion.* **13.** With reference to; as regards: *in my opinion; equal in speed.* **14.** Wearing: *in pyjamas.* **15.** Used to indicate ratio, rate, or number: *a one in five hill; killed in their hundreds.* **—in all.** Taking the whole sum into account: *two pounds in all.* **—in on.** Involved or associated with: *in on the latest project.* **—in that.** Inasmuch as; since.
~*adv.* **1.** To or towards the inside or a centre; inwards: *He stepped in; the group closed in.* **2. a.** Towards a particular or appropriate destination or location: *sailed in; news is coming in.* **b.** At a particular or appropriate place: *slotted in.* **3.** Into a given place or position: *Let her in.* **4. a.** Present or as being present: *tell me when he's in; count me in.* **b.** Indoors: *time to go in.* **5.** Into a given activity together: *joined in and sang.* **6.** Inwards: *caved in.* **7.** So as to blend with or be part of something: *mix in.* **8.** So as to achieve a state of popularity or power: *skirts are coming back in; the Tories got in.* **9.** *Sports.* **a.** In cricket and certain other games, so as to be the team or player that is batting. **b.** Within the designated limits of a playing area, such as a tennis or squash court. **10.** *British.* Burning; alight: *keep the fire in.* **—in at.** Present or involved: *in at the start.* **—in for.** About to experience something, usually something unpleasant: *He's in for a big surprise.* **—in with.** On familiar or friendly terms with: *get in with the boss.*
~*adj.* **1.** Fashionable; popular; prestigious: *the in film to see.* **2.** Exclusive or private; appealing to a clique: *a member of the in crowd; telling in jokes.* **3.** Having power; incumbent: *the in party.*
~*n. Chiefly U.S.* **1.** *Often plural.* Those in power or having the advantage. **2.** *Informal.* A means of access or favour. **—ins and outs. 1.** The twists and turns, as of a road. **2.** The intricacies of an activity, situation, or process. [Middle English *in,* Old English *in, inn.*]

In The symbol for the element indium.

in-¹ *prefix.* Also **i-** (before *g*), **il-** (before *l*), **im-** (before *b,m,p*), **ir-** (before *r*). Indicates not, lacking, or without; for example, **inaction.** See Usage note at **un-**. [Middle English, from Old French, from Latin.]

in-² *prefix.* Also **il-** (before *l*), **im-** (before *b,m,p*), **ir-** (before *r*). Indicates: **1.** In, into, within, or inward; for example, **incretion, intubation. 2.** Intensive action; for example, **impress, implant, inosculate. 3.** Causative function (with basic meaning "to cause to become," "to put in"); for example, **integrate, impound, imperil.** Compare **en-¹**. [Middle English, from Old French, from Latin, from *in,* in, within. In borrowed Latin compounds, *in-* indicates (in addition to the above senses): 1. On, upon, as in **inunction.** 2. Towards, to, as in **irradiate, imminent.** 3. Against, as in **impugn, infest.**]

in-³ *comb. form.* Indicates found or taking place within a specified context: for example, **in-flight, in-service.**

in. inch or inches.

-in¹ *n. comb. form.* Also **-ein** (for sense 1). Indicates: **1.** A neutral chemical compound, such as glyceride or protein, as distinguished from an alkaloid or basic substance; for example, **globulin, phthalein. 2.** Enzyme; for example, **pancreatin. 3.** Names of drugs and other pharmaceutical products; for example, **penicillin, aspirin. 4.** Variant of **-ine** (chemical suffix). [French *-ine,* from Latin *-īna,* feminine of *-īnus,* belonging to. See **-ine.**]

-in² *n. comb. form.* Indicates organised participatory activity: **phone-in; love-in.**

-ina *n. suffix.* Indicates feminine names or titles: for example, **Georgina, Tsarina.**

in·a·bil·i·ty (innə-bílləti) *n.* Lack of ability or means.

in ab·sen·ti·a (in ab-sén-ti-ə, -shi-, -aa, -shə) *adv.* In absence; while or although not present: *she was sentenced in absentia by the judge.*

in·ac·ces·si·ble (ínak-séss-əb'l) *adj.* **1.** Not accessible; difficult to approach or reach. **2.** Difficult to obtain. **—in·ac·ces·si·bil·i·ty** (-ə-bílləti) *n.* **—in·ac·ces·si·bly** *adv.*

in·ac·cu·ra·cy (in-áckewr-ə-si) *n., pl.* **-cies. 1.** The quality or condition of being inaccurate. **2.** An error or mistake.

in·ac·cu·rate (in-áckewr-ət, -it) *adj.* **1.** Not accurate. **2.** Mistaken or incorrect. **—in·ac·cu·rate·ly** *adv.* **—in·ac·cu·rate·ness** *n.*

in·ac·tion (in-áksh'n, ín-) *n.* Lack or absence of action or activity; idleness.

in·ac·ti·vate (in-ákti-vayt) *tr.v.* **-vated, -vating, -vates.** To render inactive. **—in·ac·ti·va·tion** (-váysh'n) *n.*

in·ac·tive (in-áktiv) *adj.* **1.** Not active or not tending to be active. **2. a.** Not functioning; being out of use. **b.** Retired from or not engaged in military duty or service. **3. a.** *Chemistry.* Not readily participating in chemical reactions. **b.** *Biology.* Having no significant effect on or interaction with living organisms. **c.** *Medicine.* Quiescent. Said especially of a disease. **d.** *Physics.* Displaying little or no radioactivity. **—in·ac·tive·ly** *adv.* **—in·ac·tive·ness, in·ac·tiv·i·ty** (-tívvəti) *n.*
Synonyms: *inactive, idle, inert, passive, dormant, torpid, supine.*

in·ad·e·qua·cy (in-áddikwə-si) *n., pl.* **-cies. 1.** The quality or condition of being inadequate. **2.** A failing or lack; a defect.

in·ad·e·quate (in-áddi-kwət, -kwit) *adj.* **1.** Not adequate; insufficient. **2.** Not able; incapable. **3.** Socially awkward or ill-at-ease; gauche. **—in·ad·e·quate·ly** *adv.*

in·ad·mis·si·ble (ínnəd-míssə-b'l) *adj.* Not admissible or allowed: *inadmissible evidence.* **—in·ad·mis·si·bil·i·ty** (-bílləti) *n.* **—in·ad·mis·si·bly** *adv.*

in·ad·ver·tence (ínnəd-vért'nss) *n.* Also **in·ad·ver·ten·cy** (-i) *pl.* **-cies. 1.** The quality of being inadvertent. **2.** An instance of being inadvertent; a mistake; an oversight. [Medieval Latin *inadvertentia* : Latin *in-*, not + *advertēns,* present participle of *advertēre,* to ADVERT.]

in·ad·ver·tent (ínnəd-vért'nt) *adj.* **1.** Not duly attentive; negligent. **2.** Accidental; unintentional. [Back-formation from INADVERTENCE.] **—in·ad·ver·tent·ly** *adv.*

in·ad·vis·a·ble (ínnəd-vízəb'l) *adj.* Unwise; not recommended. **—in·ad·vis·a·bil·i·ty** (-bílləti) *n.*

-inae *n. suffix.* Indicates the names of zoological subfamilies.

in ae·ter·num (in ee-térnəm, i-) *adv. Latin.* Forever; to eternity.

in·al·ien·a·ble (in-áyli-ənəb'l) *adj.* Not to be removed or transferred to another; not alienable: *inalienable rights.* **—in·al·ien·a·bil·i·ty** (-ənə-bílləti) *n.* **—in·al·ien·a·bly** *adv.*

in·al·ter·a·ble (in-áwl-tərəb'l ‖ -ól-) *adj.* Not alterable; unchangeable. **—in·al·ter·a·bil·i·ty** (-tərə-bílləti) *n.* **—in·al·ter·a·bly** *adv.*

in·am·o·ra·ta (in-ámmə-raátə, ínnamə-) *n., pl.* **-tas.** A woman with whom one is in love. [Italian, from feminine of *inamorato,* past participle of *inam(m)orare,* to inspire love in, enamour : *in-*, in, into + *amore,* love, from Latin *amor,* love, from *amāre,* to love.]

in·am·o·ra·to (in-ámmə-raátō, ínnamə-) *n., pl.* **-tos.** A man with whom one is in love. [Italian, from the past participle of *inam(m)orare,* enamour. See **inamorata.**]

in-and-in (ín-ənd-ín) *adv.* Repeatedly within the same or closely related stocks: *to breed pigs in-and-in.* **—in-and-in** *adj.*

in·ane (i-náyn) *adj.* Lacking intelligence, sense, or substance; empty; silly: *an inane comment.* See Synonyms at **foolish.**
~*n. Rare.* Something that is empty; specifically, the empty void of infinite space. [Latin *inānis*†, empty, vain.] **—in·ane·ly** *adv.*

in·an·i·mate (in-ánni-mət, -mit) *adj.* **1.** Not animate; not having the qualities associated with active, living organisms. **2.** Not exhibiting life; appearing lifeless or dead. **3.** Not animated or energetic; listless; spiritless. —See Synonyms at **dead. —in·an·i·mate·ly** *adv.* **—in·an·i·mate·ness** *n.* **—in·an·i·ma·tion** (-máysh'n) *n.*

in·a·ni·tion (ínnə-nísh'n) *n.* **1.** Exhaustion, as from lack of nourishment. **2.** The condition or quality of being spiritually or mentally empty. [Middle English, from Late Latin *inānītiō* (stem *inānītiōn-*), from *inānīre,* to make empty, from *inānis,* empty, INANE.]

in·an·i·ty (i-nánnəti) *n., pl.* **-ties. 1.** The condition or quality of being inane. **2.** An inane or absurd act or remark.

in·ap·peas·a·ble (ínnə-peézəb'l) *adj.* Incapable of being appeased.

in·ap·pel·la·ble (ínnə-pélləb'l) *adj. Law.* Incapable of being appealed against: *an inappellable decision.* [Obsolete French *inappelable,* from *appeler,* to APPEAL.]

in·ap·pe·tence (in-áppitənss) *n.* Also **in·ap·pe·ten·cy** (-i). Lack of appetite or desire. **—in·ap·pe·tent** *adj.*

in·ap·pli·ca·ble (in-áplik-əb'l, ínnə-plíck-) *adj.* Not applicable. **—in·ap·pli·ca·bil·i·ty** (-ə-bílləti) *n.* **—in·ap·pli·ca·bly** *adv.*

in·ap·po·site (in-áppəzit) *adj.* Not pertinent; unsuitable. **—in·ap·po·site·ly** *adv.* **—in·ap·po·site·ness** *n.*

in·ap·pre·ci·a·ble (ínnə-preésh-əb'l, -i-əb'l) *adj.* Not appreciable;

insignificant; negligible. **—in·ap·pre·ci·a·bly** *adv.*

in·ap·pre·ci·a·tive (ínnə-préesh-ətiv, -i-ətiv, -i-aytiv) *adj.* Feeling or showing no appreciation; unappreciative. **—in·ap·pre·ci·a·tive·ly** *adv.* **—in·ap·pre·ci·a·tive·ness** *n.*

in·ap·proach·a·ble (ínnə-prŏchə-b'l) *adj.* Not approachable; inaccessible. **—in·ap·proach·a·bil·i·ty** (-bíllətí) *n.* **—in·ap·proach·a·bly** *adv.*

in·ap·pro·pri·ate (ínnə-prŏpri-ət, -ít) *adj.* Not appropriate; unsuitable. **—in·ap·pro·pri·ate·ly** *adv.* **—in·ap·pro·pri·ate·ness** *n.*

in·apt (in-ápt, ín-) *adj.* **1.** Not appropriate; unsuitable. **2.** Unskilful; inept.

> **Usage:** *Inapt* and *inept* are frequently interchangeable, but there is a tendency in modern English to differentiate their contexts of use. *Inept* generally applies to clumsiness of language or behaviour: *an inept remark, inept handling of the situation. Inapt* tends to be used more with abstract ideas and has the sense of something inappropriate: an *inapt comparison* would be one which did not make its intended point. *Unapt* is also used in this way.

in·ap·ti·tude (in-ápti-tewd ‖ -tōod) *n.* **1.** Inappropriateness. **2.** Lack of skill; ineptitude.

in·arch (in-árch) *tr.v.* **-arched, -arching, -arches.** To graft by joining independently growing scions that have not been removed from the parent stock. [IN + ARCH.]

in·arm (in-árm) *tr.v.* **-armed, -arming, -arms.** *Rare.* To embrace.

in·ar·tic·u·late (innaar-tíckew-lət, -lit) *adj.* **1.** Uttered without the use of normal words or syllables; incomprehensible. **2. a.** Unable to speak; speechless. **b.** Unable to speak with clarity or eloquence. **3.** Unable to be expressed in words: *inarticulate sorrow.* **4.** *Biology.* Not having joints or segments. **—in·ar·tic·u·late·ly** *adv.* **—in·ar·tic·u·la·cy** (-lə-si), **in·ar·tic·u·late·ness** *n.*

in·ar·tis·tic (innaar-tístik) *adj.* Not artistic; not appreciating or possessing skill in art. **—in·ar·tis·ti·cal·ly** *adv.*

in·as·much as (innəz-múch) *conj.* **1.** Because of the fact that; since. **2.** To the extent that; insofar as. —See Usage note at **insofar.**

in·at·ten·tion (innə-ténsh'n) *n.* Lack of attention, notice, or regard; heedlessness; neglect.

in·at·ten·tive (innə-téntiv) *adj.* Showing a lack of attention; negligent. **—in·at·ten·tive·ly** *adv.* **—in·at·ten·tive·ness** *n.*

in·au·di·ble (in-áwdə-b'l, ín-) *adj.* Incapable of being heard; not audible. **—in·au·di·bil·i·ty** (-bíllətí) *n.* **—in·au·di·bly** *adv.*

in·au·gu·ral (in-áwgewr-əl) *adj.* Of, pertaining to, or characteristic of an inauguration.
~*n.* A speech or address made at an inauguration.

in·au·gu·rate (in-áwgewr-ayt ‖ -áwgər-) *tr.v.* **-rated, -rating, -rates.** **1.** To admit (a president, prime minister, or the like) into office by a formal ceremony. **2.** To begin or start officially. **3.** To open or begin use of formally with a ceremony; dedicate. —See Synonyms at **begin.** [Latin *inaugurāre,* to take omens from the flight of birds, to consecrate, install : *in,* in + *augurāre,* to augur, from AUGUR, soothsayer.] **—in·au·gu·ra·tor** *n.*

in·au·gu·ra·tion (in-áugewr-áysh'n ‖ -áwgər-) *n.* **1.** A formal beginning or introduction. **2.** Formal introduction to an office or position of power.

Inauguration Day *n.* The day, January 20, on which the newly elected president of the United States is installed in office.

in·aus·pi·cious (ínnaw-spíshəss) *adj.* Not auspicious; ill-omened. **—in·aus·pi·cious·ly** *adv.* **—in·aus·pi·cious·ness** *n.*

in between *prep.* Between two things, limits, or the like. **—in between** *adv.*

in·be·tween (ín-bi-twéen, -bə-) *adj.* Intermediate.
~*n.* An intermediate or intermediary: *conservatives, radicals, and in-betweens.*

in·board (ín-bawrd ‖ -bōrd) *adj.* **1.** *Nautical.* Within the hull or towards the centre of a ship: *an inboard engine.* **2.** *Aeronautics.* Designating either of the two engines that are closest to the fuselage in an aircraft with four or more wing-mounted engines. **3.** Towards the centre of a machine.
~*n.* A motor attached to the inside of the hull of a boat. Compare **outboard motor.** [IN + BOARD.] **—in·board** *adv.*

in·born (ín-bórn) *adj.* **1.** Possessed by an organism at birth. **2.** Inherited or hereditary. —See Synonyms at **innate.**

in·bound (ín-bownd) *adj.* Homeward bound or incoming.

in·breathe (in-breéth) *tr.v.* **-breathed, -breathing, -breathes.** **1.** To breathe in; inhale. **2.** *Rare.* To inspire.

in·bred (ín-bréd) *adj.* **1.** Produced by inbreeding. **2.** Innate; deep-seated. —See Synonyms at **innate.**

in·breed (in-breéd) *tr.v.* **-bred** (-bréd), **-breeding, -breeds.** **1.** To produce by the continued breeding of closely related individuals. **2.** To breed or develop within; engender. **—in·breed·ing** *adj. & n.*

in·built *adj.* Built-in.

inc. **1.** income. **2.** incorporated. **3.** increase. **4.** including. **5.** inclusive.

Inc. incorporated.

In·ca (íngkə) *n., pl.* **-cas** or collectively **Inca.** **1.** A member of the group of Quechuan Indian peoples who ruled Peru before the Spanish conquest. **2.** A king or other member of the royal family of this group of peoples. [Spanish, from Quechua *inka,* king, prince.]

in·cal·cu·la·ble (in-kálkew-ləb'l) *adj.* **1.** Not calculable; indeterminate. **2.** Incapable of being foreseen; unpredictable; uncertain: *the incalculable consequences of her actions.* **—in·cal·cu·la·bil·i·ty** (-lə-bíllətí), **in·cal·cu·la·ble·ness** *n.* **—in·cal·cu·la·bly** *adv.*

in·ca·les·cent (ín-kə-léss'nt, -ka-) *adj. Chemistry.* Growing warm; increasing in temperature. [Latin *incalescēns* (stem *incalescent-*),

present participle of *incalescere* : IN- + *calescere,* grow warm, from *calēre,* be warm.] **—in·ca·les·cence** *n.*

in camera *adv.* **1.** In secret, private, or closed session. **2.** *Law.* In private with a judge rather than in open court; in the chambers of a judge. [Latin, "in the chamber".]

in·can·desce (in-kan-déss, -kən-) *v.* **desced, -descing, -desces.** —*intr.* To become incandescent. —*tr.* To cause to become incandescent. [Latin *incandēscere,* to become white with heat, glow : *in-* (intensive) + *candēscere,* to become white, glow, from *candēre,* to be white, shine.]

in·can·des·cence (in-kan-déss'nss, -kən-) *n.* **1.** The emission of visible light by a hot object. **2.** The light emitted by an incandescent object. **3.** A high degree of emotion, intensity, brilliance, or the like: *his rhetoric reached incandescence.* —See Synonyms at **blaze.**

in·can·des·cent (in-kan-déss'nt, -kən-) *adj.* **1.** Emitting a visible white glow as a result of being heated. **2.** Very intense, brilliant or bright: *incandescent eyes; incandescent anger.* —See Synonyms at **bright.** **—in·can·des·cent·ly** *adv.*

incandescent lamp *n.* An electric lamp in which a filament is heated to incandescence by an electric current.

in·can·ta·tion (ín-kan-táysh'n) *n.* **1. a.** Ritual recitation or chanting of charms or spells to produce a magical effect. **b.** The casting of these spells. **2.** The formulaic words, phrases, or sounds used in this manner. [Middle English *incantacioun,* from Old French *incantation,* from Late Latin *incantātiō* (stem *incantātiōn-*), enchantment, spell, from Latin *incantāre,* ENCHANT.] **—in·can·ta·tion·al** *adj.*

in·can·ta·to·ry (íng-kan-táytəri, in-kántə-təri, -tri) *adj.* **1.** Of or pertaining to incantation. **2.** Of or producing a monotonously regular sound: *incantatory verse.*

in·ca·pa·ble (in-káypə-b'l, ín-) *adj.* **1.** Not capable; lacking the requisite ability or power. **2.** Not admitting of or susceptible to: *incapable of improvement.* **3.** *Law.* Lacking legal qualifications or requirements; ineligible: *incapable of holding office.* **—in·ca·pa·bil·i·ty** (-bílləti), **in·ca·pa·ble·ness** *n.* **—in·ca·pa·bly** *adv.*

in·ca·pac·i·tate (ín-kə-pássi-tayt) *tr.v.* **-tated, -tating, -tates.** **1.** To deprive of strength or ability. **2.** To make legally ineligible; disqualify. **—in·ca·pac·i·tant** *n.* **—in·ca·pac·i·ta·tion** (-táysh'n) *n.*

in·ca·pac·i·ty (in-kə-pássəti) *n., pl.* **-ties.** **1.** Lack of strength or ability; disability; helplessness. **2.** *Law.* That which renders legally ineligible; a disqualification.

incapsulate. Variant of **encapsulate.**

in·car·cer·ate (in-kár-sə-rayt) *tr.v.* **-ated, -ating, -ates.** **1.** To put in jail. **2.** To shut in; confine. [Latin *incarcerāre* : *in-,* in + *carcer,* prison, enclosed place.] **—in·car·cer·a·tion** (-ráysh'n) *n.* **—in·car·cer·a·tor** *n.*

in·car·na·dine (in-kárnə-dīn ‖ -deen, -d'n) *adj.* **1.** Flesh-coloured; incarnate. **2.** Blood-red.
~*n.* A colour resembling flesh or blood.
~*tr.v.* **incarnadined, -dining, -dines.** To make the colour of blood or flesh. [Old French *incarnadin,* from Old Italian *incarnadino, incarnatino,* from *incarnato,* flesh-coloured, from Late Latin *incarnāre,* INCARNATE.]

in·car·nate (in-kár-nayt, -nit) *adj.* **1. a.** Invested with bodily nature and form: *a god incarnate.* **b.** Embodied or personified: *wisdom incarnate.* **2.** Incarnadine.
~*tr.v.* (in-kaar-nayt, in-kár-) **incarnated, -nating, -nates.** **1.** To give bodily, especially human, form to. **2.** To embody or personify. **3.** To actualise; realise. [Late Latin *incarnāre,* to make flesh : Latin *in-* (causative) + *carō* (stem *carn-*), flesh.]

in·car·na·tion (in-kaar-náysh'n) *n.* **1.** A manifestation or the act of making a divinity, spirit, or the like manifest in bodily form. **2.** *Capital* l. *Theology.* The embodiment of God in the human form of Jesus. **3.** Any bodily manifestation of a supernatural being. **4.** One held to personify a given abstract quality or idea.

incase. Variant of **encase.**

in·cen·di·ar·y (in-séndi-əri ‖ -erri) *adj.* **1. a.** Causing or capable of causing fire. **b.** Producing intense fire. Said of a military weapon. **c.** Of or involving arson. **2.** Tending to inflame or produce anger or violence; inflammatory.
~*n., pl.* **incendiaries.** **1.** One who sets fire to property; an arsonist. **2.** One who stirs up violent feelings or quarrels. **3.** An incendiary bomb. [Latin *incendiārius,* from *incendium,* burning, fire, from *incendere,* to set on fire.] **—in·cen·di·a·rism** *n.*

incendiary bomb *n.* A bomb used to start a fire. Also called "fire bomb", "incendiary".

in·cense¹ (in-sénss) *tr.v.* **-censed, -censing, -censes.** To cause to be angry or indignant; outrage. [Middle English *encensen,* from Old French *incenser,* from Latin *incendere* (past participle *incensus*), to set on fire, enrage.] **—in·cense·ment** *n.*

in·cense² (in-senss) *n.* **1.** An aromatic substance, as a gum or wood, that burns with a pleasant odour. **2.** The smoke or odour produced by the burning of such a substance. **3.** Broadly, any pleasant smell. **4.** Adulation; praise; admiration.
~*tr.v.* **incensed, -censing, -censes.** **1.** To perfume with incense. **2.** To burn incense in front of, especially as a ritual act. [Middle English *insens, encens,* from Old French *encens,* from Late Latin *incensum,* neuter past participle of Latin *incendere,* to set on fire.]

in·cen·so·ry (in-sénsəri) *n.* An incense burner, a censer *(see).*

in·cen·tive (in-séntiv) *n.* Something inciting to action or effort, such as the fear of punishment or the expectation of reward.
~*adj.* Inciting; motivating. [Middle English, from Latin *incentīvum,* from the neuter of *incentīvus,* that sets the tune, inciting, from

incinere (past participle *incentus*), to sing, sound : *in-* (intensive) + *canere,* to sing.]

in·cept (in-sépt) *tr.v.* **-cepted, -cepting, -cepts.** **1.** *Biology.* To take in (food); ingest. **2.** Formerly, to take the degree of master or doctor at a university. [Latin *inceptus,* begun, attempted, past participle of *incipere,* to begin : IN- + *capere,* to take.]

in·cep·tion (in-sépsh'n) *n.* The beginning of something. See Synonyms at **origin.** [Latin *inceptiō* (stem *inceptiōn-*), from *incipere,* to take in hand, begin : *in-,* in + *capere,* to take.]

in·cep·tive (in-séptiv) *adj.* **1.** Incipient; beginning. **2.** *Grammar.* Expressing an action, state, or occurrence in its initial phase. Used of certain verbs, for example, *start* or *wake.*
∼*n.* An inceptive verb.

in·cer·ti·tude (in-sérti-tewd || -tōōd) *n.* **1.** Uncertainty; doubt. **2.** Insecurity or instability. [Old French, from Late Latin *incertitūdō* : *in-,* not + *certitūdō,* CERTITUDE.]

in·ces·sant (in-séss'nt) *adj.* Continuing without respite or interruption; unceasing. See Synonyms at **continual.** [Late Latin *incessāns* : *in-,* not + *cessāns* (stem *cessant-*), present participle of *cessāre,* CEASE.] **—in·cess·an·cy, in·cess·ant·ness** *n.* **—in·ces·sant·ly** *adv.*

in·cest (ín-sest) *n.* **1.** Sexual union between persons who are so closely related that their marriage is illegal or contrary to custom. **2.** The crime committed by such closely related persons who marry, cohabit, or copulate illegally. [Middle English, from Latin *incestus,* "unchaste", "impure" : *in-,* not + *castus,* CHASTE.]

in·ces·tu·ous (in-séstew-əss) *adj.* **1.** Of or involving incest. **2.** Having committed incest. **3.** Resulting from incest. **4.** Excessively introspective or mutually involved: *an incestuous group of friends.* **—in·ces·tu·ous·ly** *adv.* **—in·ces·tu·ous·ness** *n.*

inch¹ (inch) *n. Abbr.* **in.** **1.** A unit of length in the Imperial system, equal to $^1/_{12}$ of a foot or 25.4 millimetres. **2.** A unit of pressure equal to the pressure required to balance a column of mercury one inch high in a barometer. **3.** A depth of water or snow that would cover a surface with a layer one inch deep: *two inches of rain.* **4.** A very small amount or distance: *wouldn't budge an inch.* **—by inches.** Gradually; by small degrees. **—every inch.** In every respect: *every inch a gentleman.* **—inch by inch.** Very gradually. **—within an inch of.** Almost to the point of. **—within an inch of (one's) life.** **1.** Close to death. **2.** Thoroughly; soundly: *beat him within an inch of his life.*
∼*v.* **inched, inching, inches.** *—intr.* To move slowly or by small degrees. *—tr.* To cause to move in such a manner. [Middle English *inch(e),* Old English *ince, ynce,* from Latin *uncia,* twelfth part, inch, ounce, from *ūnus,* one.]

inch² *n. Scottish.* A small island, especially one near the seacoast. Used in place names. [Middle English *inch, ynche,* from Scottish Gaelic *innis,* akin to Old Irish *inis*†.]

Inchcape Rock. See **Bell Rock.**

inch·meal (ínch-meel) *adv.* Gradually; little by little. [*inch* + piece-*meal.*]

in·cho·ate (in-kṓ-ayt, ín-kō-, -ət, -it) *adj.* **1.** In an initial or early stage; just beginning; incipient. **2.** Immature; imperfect.
∼*tr.v.* (-ayt) **inchoated, -ating, -ates.** To begin. [Latin *inchoātus,* past participle of *inchoāre, incohāre,* to begin, originally "to harness" : *in-,* in + *cohum,* strap fastening the plough beam to the yoke.] **—in·cho·ate·ly** *adv.*

in·cho·a·tion (ín-kō-áysh'n) *n.* A beginning; a start; an origin.

in·cho·a·tive (in-kṓ-ətiv) *adj. Grammar.* Inceptive. Used of certain verbs. **—in·cho·a·tive** *n.*

inch·worm (ínch-wurm) *n.* A **measuring worm** *(see).*

in·ci·dence (ín-sidənss) *n.* **1.** An act, instance, or manner of occurring or affecting; an occurrence. **2.** The extent or frequency of the occurrence of something. **3.** *Physics.* The arrival of incident radiation or of an incident projectile at a surface.

in·ci·dent (ín-sidənt) *n.* **1.** A definite, distinct occurrence; an event. **2.** An event that is subordinate to another. **3.** Something contingent upon or related to something else. **4. a.** A relatively minor occurrence or event that precipitates a public crisis. **b.** An event involving violence or hostilities: *an incident on the football terraces.* —See Synonyms at **occurrence.**
∼*adj.* **1.** Tending to arise or occur as a minor concomitant. Used with *to*: *"There is a professional melancholy . . . incident to the occupation of a tailor"* (Charles Lamb). **2.** Related to or dependent on another thing. **3.** *Law.* Contingent upon or related to something else. **4.** *Physics.* Falling upon; striking. [Middle English, from Old French, from Latin *incidēns* (stem *incident-*), present participle of *incidere,* to fall upon, happen to : *in-,* on + *cadere,* to fall.]

in·ci·den·tal (ín-si-dént'l) *adj.* **1.** Occurring as a fortuitous or minor concomitant: *incidental expenses.* **2.** Attending or related. Often used with *to*: *action incidental to the main plot.* **3.** Following upon incidentally. Often used with *upon.* —See Synonyms at **accidental.**
∼*n. Usually plural.* A minor concomitant circumstance, event, expense, or the like.

in·ci·den·tal·ly (ín-sidént'l-i) *adv.* **1.** Casually; by chance. **2.** Parenthetically; by the way.

incidental music *n.* Music that accompanies the action of a play, film, or the like.

in·cin·er·ate (in-sínnə-rayt) *v.* **-ated, -ating, -ates.** *—tr.* To consume by burning to ashes. *—intr.* To burn or burn up. [Medieval Latin *incinerāre* : Latin *in-,* in, into + *cinis* (stem *ciner-*), ashes.] **—in·cin·er·a·tion** (-ráysh'n) *n.*

in·cin·er·a·tor (in-sínnə-raytər) *n.* One that incinerates; especially, a furnace or other apparatus for burning waste.

in·cip·i·ent (in-síppi-ənt) *adj.* In an initial or early stage; just beginning to exist or appear. [Latin *incipiēns* (stem *incipient-*), beginning, present participle of *incipere,* to take in hand, begin : *in-,* in + *capere,* to take.] **—in·cip·i·en·cy, in·cip·i·ence** *n.* **—in·cip·i·ent·ly** *adv.*

in·ci·pit (ín-sipit, -kipit) *n.* A beginning; specifically, an introductory word of a medieval manuscript.

in·cise (in-sīz) *tr.v.* **-cised, -cising, -cises.** **1.** To cut into or mark with a sharp instrument. **2.** To cut (designs or writing, for example) into a surface; engrave; carve. [Old French *inciser,* from Latin *incīdere* (past participle *incīsus*) : *in-,* into, in + *caedere,* to cut.]

in·cised (in-sīzd) *adj.* **1.** Cut into; engraved; carved. **2.** Made with or as if with a sharp instrument. **3.** Deeply notched.

in·ci·sion (in-sízh'n) *n.* **1.** The act of incising. **2.** A surgical cut into soft tissue. **3.** A notch, as in the edge of a leaf. **4.** Incisiveness.

in·ci·sive (in-sī-siv || -ziv) *adj.* **1.** Cutting; penetrating. **2.** Trenchant; marked by directness, clarity, and decisiveness: *incisive comments.* [Medieval Latin *incīsīvus,* from Latin *incisus,* past participle of *incīdere,* INCISE.] **—in·ci·sive·ly** *adv.* **—in·ci·sive·ness** *n.*
Synonyms: *incisive, trenchant, biting, cutting, crisp, mordant.*

in·ci·sor (in-sīzər) *n.* A tooth adapted for cutting, located at the front of the mouth. In man there are four incisors in each jaw.

in·cite (in-sīt) *tr.v.* **-cited, -citing, -cites.** To provoke to action, stir up, or urge on. See Synonyms at **provoke.** [Old French *inciter,* from Latin *incitāre,* to urge, set in violent motion : *in-* (intensive) + *citāre,* frequentative of *ciēre, cīre,* to set in violent motion, rouse, provoke.] **—in·ci·ta·tion** (ín-sī-táysh'n || *U.S. also* -si-) *n.* **—in·cite·ment** *n.* **—in·cit·er** *n.*

in·ci·vil·i·ty (ín-si-vílləti) *n., pl.* **-ties.** **1.** Coarse or ill-mannered behaviour; rudeness. **2.** An act of incivility.

incl. including; inclusive.

in·clem·ent (in-klémmənt) *adj.* **1.** Wild; stormy. Said of weather. **2.** *Rare.* Severe or unmerciful. [Latin *inclēmēns* : *in-,* not + *clēmens,* CLEMENT.] **—in·clem·en·cy** *n.* **—in·clem·ent·ly** *adv.*

in·clin·a·ble (in-klīnəb'l) *adj.* **1.** Disposed; inclined. Often used with *to.* **2.** Favourably disposed; amenable. Often used with *to.*

in·cli·na·tion (ín-kli-náysh'n) *n.* **1.** An attitude or disposition towards something. **2.** A trend or general tendency towards a particular aspect, condition, or character: *an inclination to be serious.* **3.** Something for which one has a preference or leaning: *an inclination to watch films.* **4.** The act of inclining. **5.** The state of being inclined. **6.** A deviation from a definite direction, especially from a horizontal or vertical. **7.** The degree of deviation from a horizontal or vertical. **8.** *Mathematics.* The angle between a line on a graph and the positive limb of the *x*-axis. **9.** *Astronomy.* The angle between the plane of a planet's orbit and that of the ecliptic. **10. Magnetic dip** *(see).* —See Synonyms at **tendency.**

in·cline (in-klīn) *v.* **-clined, -clining, -clines.** *—intr.* **1.** To deviate from a horizontal or vertical; lean; slant; slope. **2.** To have or express a mental tendency; be disposed: *inclines to an opposite view.* **3.** To tend towards a particular state or condition. **4.** To lower or bend the head or body, as in a nod or bow. *—tr.* **1.** To cause to lean, slant, or slope; place at an inclination. **2.** To influence (someone or something) to have a certain preference, leaning, or disposition; dispose. **3.** To bend or lower in a nod or bow.
∼*n.* (ín-klīn). An inclined surface; a slope or gradient. [Middle English *inclinen, enclinen,* from Old French *encliner,* from Latin *inclīnāre* : *in-,* towards + *-clīnāre,* to bend, lean.] **—in·clin·er** *n.*

in·clined (in-klīnd) *adj.* **1.** Having a preference, or tendency; disposed. Often used with *to.* **2.** Sloping, slanting, or leaning.

inclined plane *n.* **1.** A plane surface inclined to the horizontal. **2.** A simple machine, such as an inclined track or plank, allowing a load to be raised or lowered by rolling or sliding.

in·cli·nom·e·ter (in-kli-nómmitər) *n.* **1.** An instrument used to determine **magnetic dip** *(see);* a dip circle. **2.** An instrument for showing the attitude of an aircraft or ship relative to the horizontal. Also called "dip needle". **3.** *Machinery.* A **clinometer** *(see).*

inclose. *Rare.* Variant of **enclose.** **—inclosure** *n.*

in·clude (in-klóod || -kléwd) *tr.v.* **-cluded, -cluding, -cludes.** **1.** To have as a part or member; be made up of, at least in part; contain. **2.** To contain as a minor or secondary element. **3.** To cause to be a part of something; consider with or put into a group, class, or total. [Middle English *includen,* from Latin *inclūdere,* to shut in : *in-,* in + *claudere,* to close.] **—in·clud·a·ble, in·clud·i·ble** *adj.*
Synonyms: *include, comprise, comprehend, embrace, involve.*

in·clud·ed (in-klóō-did || -kléw-) *adj.* **1.** *Botany.* Not protruding beyond a surrounding part. Said of stamens that do not project from a corolla. **2.** *Geometry.* Formed by and between two intersecting straight lines: *an included angle.*

in·clu·sion (in-klóō-zh'n || -kléw-) *n.* **1.** The act of including or the state of being included. **2.** Something included. **3.** *Mineralogy.* Any solid, liquid, or gaseous foreign body enclosed in a mineral or rock. **4.** *Biology.* Any nonliving mass in cytoplasm. **5.** *Mathematics.* A relationship between two sets valid only when the member of one set are all members of the other. [Latin *inclūsiō* (stem *inclūsiōn-*), from *inclūdere* (past participle *inclūsus*), to INCLUDE.]

inclusion body *n.* Any of various abnormal structures in a cell nucleus or cytoplasm having characteristic staining properties and associated especially with the presence of viruses.

in·clu·sive (in-klóō-siv || -kléw-, -ziv) *adj. Abbr.* **incl.** **1.** Taking everything into account; including everything; comprehensive. **2.** Including the specified extremes or limits as well as the area between them. Often used after the noun: *23–84 inclusive.* **3.** Including; taking in. Used with *of*: *the whole family, inclusive of grandparents.* **4.** *Logic.* Designating a disjunction that needs only one of its elements to be true for it to be valid. [Medieval Latin *inclūsīvus,* from Latin *inclūdere* (past participial stem *inclūs-*), to INCLUDE.] **—in·clu·sive·ly** *adv.* **—in·clu·sive·ness** *n.*

in·co·er·ci·ble (ìng-kō-ér-sib'l) *adj.* Not subject to coercion.

incog. incognito.

in·cog·i·tant (in-kójitənt) *adj. Rare.* Thoughtless; unthinking; inconsiderate. [Latin *incōgitāns* : *in-,* not + *cōgitāns* (stem *cōgitant-*), present participle of *cōgitāre,* to think about, COGITATE.]

in·cog·ni·sant, in·cog·ni·zant (in-kógnizənt) *adj.* Lacking knowledge or awareness of something; unaware. Often used with *of.* **—in·cog·ni·sance** *n.*

in·cog·ni·ta (ín-kog-née̍tə, in-kóg-nitə) *adv.* Incognito. Used of a woman.
~*n.* A woman who is incognito. **—in·cog·ni·ta** *adj.*

in·cog·ni·to (ín-kog-née̍tō, in-kóg-nitō) *adv. Abbr.* **incog.** In a nonofficial capacity or under a name or title intended to elude public notice: *travel incognito.*
~*n. Abbr.* **incog.** **1.** One who is incognito. **2.** The anonymity or disguised appearance assumed by one who is incognito. [Italian, from Latin *incognitus,* unknown : *in-,* not + *cognitus,* past participle of *cognōscere,* to know (see **cognition**).] **—in·cog·ni·to** *adj.*

in·co·her·ent (ín-kō-hée̍r-ənt) *adj.* **1.** Not coherent; disordered; unconnected; inharmonious. **2.** Characterised by an inability to think or express thoughts in a clear or orderly manner: *incoherent with grief.* **—in·co·her·ence, in·co·her·en·cy** *n.* **—in·co·her·ent·ly** *adv.* **—in·co·her·ent·ness** *n.*

in·com·bus·ti·ble (ín-kəm-bústə-b'l) *adj.* Incapable of burning.
~*n.* An incombustible object or material. [Middle English, from Medieval Latin *incombustibilis* : Latin *in-,* not + *combūrere* (past participle *combustus*), to burn up (see **combust**).] **—in·com·bus·ti·bil·i·ty** (-bílləti) *n.* **—in·com·bus·ti·bly** *adv.*

in·come (íng-kum, ín-, -kəm) *n. Abbr.* **inc.** **1.** The amount of money or its equivalent received during a period of time, such as a year, in exchange for labour or services, from the sale of goods or property, or as profit from financial investments. **2.** *Archaic.* An influx. [Middle English, a coming in, entry : IN + *comen,* COME.]

income group *n.* A section of a population having roughly the same income.

incomes policy *n.* An economic policy aimed at controlling wage increases.

in·com·er (ín-kummər) *n.* One that comes in; especially, a person who is not considered to be integrated with his new environment.

income tax *n.* A graduated tax levied on annual income.

in·com·ing (ín-kumming) *adj.* **1. a.** Coming in; entering or arriving: *incoming telephone calls.* **b.** Coming in as profits. **2.** About to come in; next in succession: *the incoming president.*
~*n.* **1.** The act of coming in; an entrance; an arrival. **2.** *Usually plural.* Income; revenue.

in·com·men·su·ra·ble (ín-kə-ménshə-rəb'l || -ménsə-) *adj.* **1.** Having no common quality upon which to make a comparison; incapable of being measured or judged comparatively; incommensurate. **2.** *Mathematics.* **a.** Having no common measure; not having the same units. **b.** Not having a common factor other than one.
~*n.* Something that is incommensurable. **—in·com·men·su·ra·bil·i·ty** (-rə-bílləti) *n.* **—in·com·men·su·ra·bly** *adv.*

in·com·men·su·rate (ín-kə-ménshə-rət, -rit || -mensə-) *adj.* **1. a.** Not commensurate; unequal; disproportionate: *a reward incommensurate with his efforts.* **b.** Inadequate. **2.** Incommensurable. **—in·com·men·su·rate·ly** *adv.* **—in·com·men·su·rate·ness** *n.*

in·com·mode (ín-kə-mṓd) *tr.v.* **-moded, -moding, -modes.** To cause to be inconvenienced; disturb. [French *incommoder,* from Old French, from Latin *incommodāre,* from *incommodus,* inconvenient : *in-,* not + *commodus,* convenient.]

in·com·mo·di·ous (ín-kə-mṓdi-əss) *adj.* Inconvenient or uncomfortable, as by affording insufficient room. **—in·com·mo·di·ous·ly** *adv.* **—in·com·mo·di·ous·ness** *n.*

in·com·mod·i·ty (ín-kə-móddìti) *n., pl.* **-ties.** *Rare.* **1.** Inconvenience; discomfort. **2.** Something that is inconvenient.

in·com·mu·ni·ca·ble (ín-kə-méwnikə-b'l) *adj.* **1.** Not communicable; that cannot be told or shared. **2.** *Rare.* Incommunicative. **—in·com·mu·ni·ca·bil·i·ty** (-bílləti) *n.* **—in·com·mu·ni·ca·bly** *adv.*

in·com·mu·ni·ca·do (ín-kə-méwni-káadō) *adj.* Without the means or right of communicating with others, as one held in solitary confinement. [Spanish, past participle of *incomunicar,* to deny communication : *in-,* not, from Latin + *comunicar,* to communicate, from Latin *commūnicāre,* COMMUNICATE.] **—in·com·mu·ni·ca·do** *adv.*

in·com·mu·ni·ca·tive (ín-kə-méwni-kətiv, -kaytiv) *adj.* Not communicative; reticent. **—in·com·mu·ni·ca·tive·ly** *adv.* **—in·com·mu·ni·ca·tive·ness** *n.*

in·com·mut·a·ble (ín-kə-méwtə-b'l) *adj.* **1.** Incapable of being exchanged. **2.** Not changeable; unalterable. **—in·com·mut·a·bil·i·ty** (-bílləti), **in·com·mut·a·ble·ness** *n.* **—in·com·mut·a·bly** *adv.*

in·com·pa·ra·ble (in-kóm-pərə-b'l, -prə- || íng-kəm-páir-ə-, -kom-) *adj.* **1.** Incapable of being compared; incommensurable. **2.** Above all comparisons; unsurpassed; matchless. **—in·com·pa·ra·bil·i·ty** (-bílləti), **in·com·pa·ra·ble·ness** *n.* **—in·com·pa·ra·bly** *adv.*

in·com·pat·i·bil·i·ty (ín-kəm-pátti-bílləti) *n., pl.* **-ties.** **1.** The state or quality of being incompatible; lack of harmony or consistency; disagreement; incongruity. **2.** *Plural.* Mutually exclusive or antagonistic qualities or things.

in·com·pat·i·ble (ín-kəm-páttib'l) *adj.* **1.** Not compatible, as in being: **a.** Unable to live or work together. **b.** Not consistent with something else. **2.** Incapable of being held simultaneously by one person, as offices, ranks, or the like. **3.** *Logic.* Incapable of being simultaneously true; mutually exclusive. **4.** *Medicine.* **a.** Designating blood transfusions or tissue grafts that evoke adverse reactions in the recipient due to antibody formation. **b.** Designating drugs that in combination do not produce their desired therapeutic effects. **5.** *Botany.* **a.** Not capable of self-fertilisation. **b.** Not capable of forming a viable graft union. —See Synonyms at **inconsistent.**
~*n. Usually plural.* An incompatible element, person, object, or the like. [Medieval Latin *incompatibilis* : *in-,* not + *compatibilis,* COMPATIBLE.] **—in·com·pat·i·ble·ness** *n.* **—in·com·pat·i·bly** *adv.*

in·com·pe·tent (in-kómpitənt) *adj.* **1.** Not competent; not able or not in a position to act. **2.** Lacking competence; clumsy or very inefficient. **3.** *Law.* Not qualified to act in law.
~*n.* An incompetent person. **—in·com·pe·tence, in·com·pe·ten·cy** *n.* **—in·com·pe·tent·ly** *adv.*

in·com·plete (ín-kəm-pléet || -kom-) *adj.* **1.** Not complete. **2.** Not fully formed. **—in·com·plete·ly** *adv.* **—in·com·plete·ness, in·com·ple·tion** *n.*

in·com·pli·ant (ín-kəm-plī́-ənt || -kom-) *adj.* Not compliant; unyielding. **—in·com·pli·ance, in·com·pli·an·cy** *n.* **—in·com·pli·ant·ly** *adv.*

in·com·pre·hen·si·ble (ín-kom-pri-hén-sə-b'l, in-kóm-) *adj.* **1.** Incapable of being understood or comprehended, as: **a.** Unintelligible. **b.** Unknowable; unfathomable. **2.** *Archaic.* Without limits; boundless. **—in·com·pre·hen·si·bil·i·ty** (-bílləti), **in·com·pre·hen·si·ble·ness** *n.* **—in·com·pre·hen·si·bly** *adv.*

in·com·pre·hen·sion (ín-kom-pri-hénsh'n, in-kóm-) *n.* Lack of comprehension or understanding.

in·com·pre·hen·sive (ín-kom-pri-hénsiv, in-kóm-) *adj.* Not comprehensive or all-inclusive; limited in range or scope. **—in·com·pre·hen·sive·ly** *adv.* **—in·com·pre·hen·sive·ness** *n.*

in·com·press·i·ble (ín-kəm-préssə-b'l || -kom-) *adj.* Incapable of being compressed. **—in·com·press·i·bil·i·ty** (-bílləti) *n.*

in·com·put·a·ble (ín-kəm-péwtə-b'l || -kom-) *adj.* Incapable of being computed or calculated. **—in·com·put·a·bil·i·ty** (-bílləti) *n.*

in·con·ceiv·a·ble (ín-kən-sée̍və-b'l || -kon-) *adj.* Incapable of being conceived or thought of; unbelievable. **—in·con·ceiv·a·bil·i·ty** (-bílləti), **in·con·ceiv·a·ble·ness** *n.* **—in·con·ceiv·a·bly** *adv.*

in·con·clu·sive (ín-kən-klóo-siv || -kon-, -kléw-) *adj.* Not conclusive; not allowing a proper conclusion to be drawn. **—in·con·clu·sive·ly** *adv.* **—in·con·clu·sive·ness** *n.*

in·con·den·sa·ble, in·con·den·si·ble (ín-kən-dén-sə-b'l || -kon-) *adj.* Incapable of being condensed; especially, that cannot be reduced to a solid or liquid. **—in·con·den·sa·bil·i·ty** (-bílləti) *n.*

in·con·dite (in-kón-dit, -dīt) *adj. Rare.* Badly constructed; crude. Said of literary or artistic compositions. [Latin *inconditus* : *in-,* not + *conditus,* past participle of *condere,* to put together.] **—in·con·dite·ly** *adv.*

in·con·form·i·ty (ín-kən-fórməti || -kon-) *n. Archaic.* Resistance to or lack of conformity; nonconformity.

in·con·gru·ent (in-kóng-groo-ənt) *adj.* **1.** Not congruent. **2.** Incongruous. **—in·con·gru·ence** *n.* **—in·con·gru·ent·ly** *adv.*

in·con·gru·i·ty (ín-kong-gróo-əti || -kən-) *n., pl.* **-ties.** **1.** The state or quality of being incongruous. **2.** That which is incongruous.

in·con·gru·ous (in-kóng-groo-əss) *adj.* **1.** Inharmonious or incompatible with the surroundings; incongruent: *a plan incongruous with good sense.* **2.** Made up of disparate, inconsistent, or discordant parts or qualities. **3.** Not consistent with what is correct, appropriate, or logical; out-of-place: *an incongruous remark.* —See Synonyms at **inconsistent.** [Latin *incongruus* : *in-,* not + *congruus,* CONGRUOUS.] **—in·con·gru·ous·ly** *adv.* **—in·con·gru·ous·ness** *n.*

in·con·sec·u·tive (ín-kən-séckewtiv) *adj.* Not consecutive; not in a logical sequence.

in·con·se·quent (in-kón-sikwənt) *adj.* **1.** Not obtained as a result. **2.** Not derived from the premises or obtained by logic or reason; irrelevant. **3.** Proceeding without logical sequence; haphazard. **4.** Out of character with the nature or style of something. **5.** Unimportant; insignificant. [Late Latin *inconsequēns* : Latin *in-,* not + *consequēns,* CONSEQUENT.] **—in·con·se·quence** *n.* **—in·con·se·quent·ly** *adv.*

in·con·se·quen·tial (ín-kon-si-kwén-sh'l, in-kón-) *adj.* **1.** Without consequence; lacking importance; petty. **2.** Inconsequent. **3.** Designating the behaviour of a person who disregards the consequences of his or her behaviour. **—in·con·se·quen·ti·al·i·ty** (-shi-ál-əti), **in·con·se·quen·tial·ness** *n.* **—in·con·se·quen·tial·ly** *adv.*

in·con·sid·er·a·ble (ín-kən-síddərəb'l || -kon-) *adj.* Too small or unimportant to merit attention or consideration; trivial. **—in·con·sid·er·a·ble·ness** *n.* **—in·con·sid·er·a·bly** *adv.*

in·con·sid·er·ate (ín-kən-síddə-rət, -síd-, -rit || -kon-) *adj.* Not considerate; thoughtless. [Latin *inconsīderātus* : *in-,* not + *consīderātus,* CONSIDERATE.] **—in·con·sid·er·ate·ly** *adv.* **—in·con·sid·er·ate·ness, in·con·sid·er·a·tion** (-ráysh'n) *n.*

in·con·sis·ten·cy (ín-kən-sístən-si || -kon-) *n., pl.* **-cies.** Also **in·con·sis·tence** (-tənss) (for sense 1). **1.** The state or quality of being inconsistent; lack of consistency or uniformity; incongruity. **2.** Something that is inconsistent.

in·con·sis·tent (ín-kən-sístənt || -kon-) *adj.* **1.** Not consistent, especially: **a.** Erratic. **b.** Incongruous. **c.** Contradictory. **d.** Illogical. **2.** *Mathematics.* Designating two or more equations that do not have one set of values of the variable in common. **—in·con·sis·tent·ly** *adv.*

Synonyms: inconsistent, incongruous, incompatible, discordant.

in·con·sol·a·ble (ín-kən-sốlə-b'l ‖ -kon-) *adj.* Incapable of being consoled or solaced; deeply despondent. —**in·con·sol·a·bil·i·ty** (-bíllǝti), **in·con·sol·a·ble·ness** *n.* —**in·con·sol·a·bly** *adv.*

in·con·so·nant (in-kón-sǝnǝnt) *adj.* Lacking harmony, agreement, or compatibility; discordant. —**in·con·so·nance** *n.* —**in·con·so·nant·ly** *adv.*

in·con·spic·u·ous (ín-kǝn-spíckew-ǝss ‖ -kon-) *adj.* Not readily noticeable. —**in·con·spic·u·ous·ly** *adv.* —**in·con·spic·u·ous·ness** *n.*

in·con·stan·cy (in-kón-stǝn-si) *n., pl.* **-cies.** **1.** Fickleness; faithlessness. **2.** Unreliability; instability. **3.** An act or instance of being inconstant.

in·con·stant (in-kón-stǝnt) *adj.* **1.** Not constant. **2.** Fickle. —See Synonyms at **faithless.** —**in·con·stant·ly** *adv.*

in·con·sum·a·ble (ín-kǝn-séwm-ǝb'l, -sõom- ‖ -kon-, -shõom-) *adj.* **1.** Incapable of being consumed. **2.** Satisfying an economic requirement without being consumed, as currency. —**in·con·sum·a·bly** *adv.*

in·con·test·a·ble (ín-kǝn-tésta-b'l ‖ -kon-) *adj.* Incapable of being contested; unquestionable. —**in·con·test·a·bil·i·ty** (-bíllǝti), **in·con·test·a·ble·ness** *n.* —**in·con·test·a·bly** *adv.*

in·con·ti·nent (in-kóntinǝnt) *adj.* **1.** Not continent; unrestrained; uncontrolled. Often said of sexual behaviour. **2.** Incapable of holding back, containing, or retaining. Usually used with *of: incontinent of anger.* **3.** Incapable of controlling the passage of urine or faeces. [Middle English, from Old French, from Latin *incontinēns,* unrestrained : *in-,* not + *continēns,* restrained, CONTINENT.] —**in·con·ti·nence** *n.*

in·con·ti·nent·ly (in-kóntinǝntli) *adv.* **1.** In an incontinent manner. **2.** *Archaic.* Immediately; straightaway.

in·con·trol·la·ble (ín-kǝn-trốlǝb'l ‖ -kon-) *adj. Rare.* Not controllable; difficult to restrain.

in·con·tro·vert·i·ble (in-kon-trǝ-vérta-b'l, in-kón-) *adj.* Not able to be contradicted; indisputable; unquestionable. —**in·con·tro·vert·i·bil·i·ty** (-bíllǝti), **in·con·tro·vert·i·ble·ness** *n.* —**in·con·tro·vert·i·bly** *adv.*

in·con·ven·i·ence (ín-kǝn-véen-i-ǝnss, -yǝnss ‖ -kon-) *n.* **1.** The state or quality of being inconvenient; lack of ease or comfort; trouble; difficulty. **2.** Something that causes difficulty, trouble, or discomfort; an inconvenient thing or situation.
~*tr.v.* **inconvenienced, -iencing, -iences.** To cause inconvenience to; trouble; bother.

in·con·ven·i·ent (ín-kǝn-véen-i-ǝnt, -yǝnt ‖ -kon-) *adj.* Not convenient, especially: **1.** Not accessible or handy. **2.** Difficult, awkward, or troublesome. [Middle English, from Old French, from Latin *inconveniēns* : *in-,* not + *conveniēns,* CONVENIENT.] —**in·con·ven·i·ent·ly** *adv.*

in·con·vert·i·ble (ín-kǝn-vérta-b'l ‖ -kon-) *adj.* Incapable of being converted, changed, or exchanged; especially, designating currency not redeemable for another currency or for gold or silver. —**in·con·vert·i·bil·i·ty** (-bíllǝti), **in·con·vert·i·ble·ness** *n.* —**in·con·vert·i·bly** *adv.*

in·con·vin·ci·ble (ín-kǝn-vín-sib'l ‖ -kon-) *adj.* Incapable of being convinced.

in·co·or·di·nate (ín-kō-órdi-nǝt, -nit, -nayt) *adj.* **1.** Not of the same order. **2.** Uncoordinated. —**in·co·or·di·nate·ly** *adv.*

in·co·or·di·na·tion (ín-kō-órdi-náysh'n) *n.* **1.** Lack of coordination. **2.** The inability to exercise normal voluntary control of relatively complex muscular movement.

in·cor·po·rate¹ (in-kórpǝ-rayt) *v.* **-rated, -rating, -rates.** —*tr.* **1.** To unite with or blend indistinguishably into something already in existence. **2.** To cause to merge or combine together into a united whole. **3.** To admit as a member to a corporation or similar organisation. **4.** To cause to form into a legal corporation. **5.** *Rare.* To give substance or material form to; embody; substantiate. —*intr.* **1.** To become united or combined into an organised body. **2.** To form a legal corporation.
~*adj.* (-rǝt, -rit). **1.** Combined into one united body; merged. **2.** Formed into a legal corporation. [Middle English *incorporaten,* from Late Latin *incorporāre,* to form into a body : Latin *in-* (intensive) + *corporāre,* to form into a body (see **corporate**).] —**in·cor·po·ra·tion** (-ráysh'n) *n.* —**in·cor·po·ra·tive** (-rǝtiv, -raytiv) *adj.* —**in·cor·po·ra·tor** *n.*

in·cor·po·rate² (in-kórpǝ-rǝt, -rit) *adj. Rare.* Incorporeal. [Late Latin *incorporātus,* not in the body, spiritual : Latin *in-,* not + *corporātus,* embodied, CORPORATE.]

in·cor·po·rat·ed (in-kórpǝ-raytid) *adj.* **1.** United into one body; combined. **2.** *Abbr.* **Inc., inc.** *Chiefly U.S.* Organised and maintained as a legal business corporation.

in·cor·po·rat·ing (in-kórpǝ-rayting) *adj. Linguistics.* Polysynthetic.

in·cor·po·re·al (ín-kawr-páwr-i-ǝl ‖ -pôr-) *adj.* **1.** Lacking material form or substance. **2.** Spiritual. **3.** *Law.* Lacking material substance but existing in the eyes of the law; intangible, such as a right or patent might be. [Latin *incorporeus* : *in-,* not + *corporeus,* CORPOREAL.] —**in·cor·po·re·al·ly** *adv.*

in·cor·po·re·i·ty (in-kórp-ǝ-rée-ǝti, ín-, -ráy-) *n.* Immateriality. [Latin *incorporeus,* INCORPOREAL.]

in·cor·rect (ín-kǝ-rékt) *adj.* Not correct, especially: **1.** Erroneous. **2.** Improper; inappropriate. —**in·cor·rect·ly** *adv.* —**in·cor·rect·ness** *n.*

in·cor·ri·gi·ble (in-kórri-jǝb'l ‖ -káwri-) *adj.* **1.** Incapable of being corrected or reformed: *an incorrigible drunkard.* **2.** Firmly rooted; impossible to eliminate; ineradicable: *incorrigible innocence.*
~*n.* A person or animal that will not be tamed or corrected. [Middle English, from Late Latin *incorrigibilis* : Latin *in-,* not + *corrigere,* to CORRECT.] —**in·cor·ri·gi·bil·i·ty** (-jǝ-bíllǝti), **in·cor·ri·gi·ble·ness** *n.* —**in·cor·ri·gi·bly** *adv.*

in·cor·rupt (ín-kǝ-rúpt) *adj. Rare.* **1.** Not corrupt or immoral. **2.** Not decayed; unspoilt. **3.** Free from error or deterioration. Said of a text or manuscript. [Middle English, from Latin *incorruptus* : *in-,* not + *corruptus,* CORRUPT.] —**in·cor·rupt·ly** *adv.* —**in·cor·rupt·ness** *n.*

in·cor·rupt·i·ble (ín-kǝ-rúpta-b'l) *adj.* **1.** Incapable of being morally corrupted, as by bribery; honest. **2.** Not subject to decay or decomposition. —**in·cor·rupt·i·bil·i·ty** (-bíllǝti) *n.* —**in·cor·rupt·i·bly** *adv.*

in·cras·sate (in-kráss-ǝt, -it, -ayt) *adj.* Also **in·cras·sat·ed** (-aytid). *Biology.* Thickened; enlarged. Said especially of cell walls. [Late Latin *incrassāre* (past participle *incrassātus*), become thick, from *crassus,* thick.]

in·crease (in-kréess, ín-) *v.* **-creased, -creasing, -creases.** —*intr.* **1.** To become greater or larger. **2.** To multiply; reproduce. **3.** *Literary.* To advance, as in power or attainment; thrive; prosper. —*tr.* To make greater or larger.
~*n.* (ín-kreess; *also* in-kréess) *Abbr.* **inc., incr. 1.** The act of increasing; enlargement; multiplication. **2.** The amount of such increase; an increment: *a tax increase of ten per cent.* **3.** *Archaic.* Crops and other produce. —**on the increase.** Increasing. [Middle English *encresen,* from Old French *encreistre* (present stem *encreiss-*), from Latin *incrēscere,* to grow in or on : *in-,* in + *crēscere,* to grow.] —**in·creas·a·ble** *adj.* —**in·creas·er** *n.* —**in·creas·ing·ly** *adv.*

Synonyms: increase, magnify, enlarge, expand, extend, augment, grow.

in·cre·ate (in-krée-ayt, ín-kri-) *adj. Archaic.* Existing without having been created. Said especially of divine beings. —**in·cre·ate·ly** *adv.*

in·cred·i·bil·i·ty (in-kréddi-bíllǝti) *n., pl.* **-ties. 1.** The condition or quality of being incredible. **2.** Something incredible.

in·cred·i·ble (in-kréddib'l) *adj.* **1.** Unbelievable. **2.** *Informal.* Marvellous; wonderful. [Middle English, from Latin *incrēdibilis* : *in-,* not + *crēdibilis,* CREDIBLE.] —**in·cred·i·ble·ness** *n.* —**in·cred·i·bly** *adv.*

Usage: Incredible and *incredulous* are sometimes confused, but there is a clear distinction between them. *Incredible* means simply "unbelievable"; *incredulous* means "disbelieving" or "sceptical." A story may be *incredible;* the sceptical person to whom it is told is *incredulous.*

in·cre·du·li·ty (íng-kri-déw-lǝti ‖ -dǒo-) *n.* Also **in·cred·u·lous·ness** (in-kréjõõlǝss-nǝss, -niss). Disbelief.

in·cred·u·lous (in-kréjõõlǝss) *adj.* **1.** Disbelieving; sceptical. **2.** Expressing disbelief: *an incredulous stare.* [Latin *incrēdulus* : *in-,* not + *crēdulus,* CREDULOUS.] —**in·cred·u·lous·ly** *adv.*

in·cre·ment (íng-kri-mǝnt) *n.* **1.** An increase in number, size, or extent; growth; enlargement. **2.** Something added or gained; especially, an increase in salary awarded to an employee according to his progress, along a salary scale. **3.** A small increase in quantity. **4.** *Mathematics.* A small positive or negative change in a variable.
~*tr.v.* (-ment) **incremented, -menting, -ments.** To add a small amount to, often at regular intervals. [Middle English, from Latin *incrēmentum,* from *incrēscere,* to INCREASE.] —**in·cre·men·tal** (-mént'l) *adj.*

incremental plotter *n.* A device for plotting graphs from the output of a computer.

in·cres·cent (in-kréss'nt) *adj.* Waxing. Said of the moon. Compare **decrescent.** [Latin *incrēscēns,* present participle of *incrēscere,* to INCREASE.]

in·cre·tion (in-kréesh'n) *n.* **1.** Secretion directly into the bloodstream, characteristic of endocrine glands. **2.** The product of such secretion; a hormone. [IN- (in) + (SE)CRETION.]

in·crim·i·nate (in-krímmi-nayt) *tr.v.* **-nated, -nating, -nates. 1.** To charge with or involve in a crime or other wrongful act. **2.** To indicate the guilt of. [Late Latin *incrīmināre* : Latin *in-,* in + *crīmen* (stem *crīmin-*), CRIME.] —**in·crim·i·na·tion** (-náysh'n) *n.* —**in·crim·i·na·to·ry** (-nǝ-tǝri, -tri) *adj.*

in·cross (ín-kross ‖ -krawss) *n.* An organism produced as a result of continuous inbreeding.
~*v.* **incrossed, -crossing, -crosses.** —*tr.* To produce by continuous inbreeding. —*intr.* To produce an incross.

incrust. Variant of **encrust.**

in·crus·ta·tion (ín-kruss-táysh'n) *n.* **1.** An encrusting; a hard coating; especially, a deposit of a fine material. **2.** A facing of marble or mosaic on a building. **3.** A scab or other concretion on a surface. [French or from Late Latin *incrustātiō,* from Latin *incrustāre,* to ENCRUST.]

in·cu·bate (íng-kew-bayt) *v.* **-bated, -bating, -bates.** —*tr.* **1.** To warm (eggs), as by bodily heat, so as to promote embryonic development and the hatching of young; brood. **2.** To maintain (a bacterial culture or an embryo, for example) at optimum environmental conditions for development, especially in an incubator. **3.** To cause to develop; foment. —*intr.* **1.** To brood eggs. **2.** To develop in favourable conditions. Used of eggs, embryos, bacteria, and the like. **3.** To undergo incubation. [Latin *incubāre,* to hatch, lie down upon : *in-,* on + *cubāre,* to lie down.] —**in·cu·ba·tive** *adj.*

in·cu·ba·tion (íng-kew-báysh'n) *n.* **1.** The act of incubating or the state of being incubated. **2.** *Medicine.* **a.** The development of an infection from the time an organism is first exposed to it up to the time of the first appearance of signs or symptoms. **b.** The time

between exposure to an infection and the first appearance of signs or symptoms. In this sense, also called "incubation period". **—in·cu·ba·tion·al** *adj.*
in·cu·ba·tor (íng-kew-baytər) *n.* One that incubates, especially: **1.** A cabinet in which a uniform temperature can be maintained, used in growing bacterial cultures or hatching eggs. **2.** An apparatus for maintaining an infant, especially a premature infant, in an environment of controlled temperature, humidity, and oxygen.
in·cu·bus (íng-kew-bəss) *n., pl.* **-buses** or **-bi** (-bī). **1.** An evil spirit believed to descend upon and have sexual intercourse with sleeping women. Compare **succubus. 2.** A nightmare. **3.** Something oppressively or nightmarishly burdensome. [Middle English, from Late Latin, from Latin *incubāre,* to lie down upon, INCUBATE.]
incudes. Plural of **incus.**
in·cul·cate (íng-kul-kayt, in-kúl-) *tr.v.* **-cated, -cating, -cates.** To teach or impress by forceful urging or frequent repetition; instil: *inculcate a code of ethics.* [Latin *inculcāre,* to trample in, impress upon : *in-,* in + *calcāre,* to trample, from *calx* (stem *calc-*), heel.] **—in·cul·ca·tion** (íng-kul-káysh'n) *n.* **—in·cul·ca·tor** *n.*
in·cul·pa·ble (in-kúlpəb'l) *adj.* Not culpable; free from guilt; blameless.
in·cul·pate (íng-kul-payt, in-kúl-) *tr.v.* **-pated, -pating, -pates.** To incriminate; cause blame to be attached to. [Late Latin *inculpāre* : *in-,* on + *culpāre,* to blame, from Latin *culpa,* fault, CULPA.] **—in·cul·pa·tion** (íng-kul-páysh'n) *n.* **—in·cul·pa·to·ry** (in-kúlpə-təri, íng-kul-pay-, -páy-, -tri) *adj.*
in·cult (in-kúlt) *adj. Archaic.* **1.** Not cultured; uncultivated. **2.** Not tilled or cultivated. [Latin *incultus,* uncultivated : *in-,* not + *cultus,* past participle of *colere,* to till.]
in·cum·ben·cy (in-kúmbən-si) *n., pl.* **-cies. 1.** The condition or quality of being incumbent. **2.** Something that is incumbent. **3.** The holding and administering of an office or ecclesiastical benefice. **4.** The term of such a benefice or office.
in·cum·bent (in-kúmbənt) *adj.* **1.** Lying, leaning, or resting upon something else. **2.** Imposed as an obligation or duty; required; obligatory. **3.** Holding a specific office or ecclesiastical benefice.
~n. A person who holds an office or ecclesiastical benefice. [Middle English, from Latin *incumbēns* (stem *incumbent-*), present participle of *incumbere,* to lean upon : *in-,* on + *cumbere,* to lean, recline.] **—in·cum·bent·ly** *adv.*
in·cu·nab·u·lum (íng-kew-nábbew-ləm) *n., pl.* **-la** (-lə). **1.** A book printed from movable type before 1501. Also called "incunable". **2.** An artefact of an early period. **3.** *Plural.* The earliest stages in the development of something. [Latin *incūnābula* (plural), swaddling clothes, cradle, infancy : *in-,* in + *cūnābula,* infancy, origin, cradle, from *cūnae,* cradle.] **—in·cu·nab·u·lar** *adj.*
in·cur (in-kúr) *tr.v.* **-curred, -curring, -curs. 1.** To meet with; run into. **2.** To become liable or subject to as a result of one's own actions; bring upon oneself. [Latin *incurrere,* to run into, come upon : *in-,* in + *currere,* to run.]
in·cur·a·ble (in-kéwr-əb'l, ín-) *adj.* **1.** Not curable. Said of a disease. **2.** Broadly, not susceptible to modification.
~n. A person suffering from an incurable disease. **—in·cur·a·bil·i·ty** (-ə-bílləti), **in·cur·a·ble·ness** *n.* **—in·cur·a·bly** *adv.*
in·cu·ri·ous (in-kéwr-i-əss, ín-) *adj.* **1.** Not curious; uninterested. **2.** Not arousing interest; lacking novelty. **3.** Heedless; negligent. —See Synonyms at **indifferent.** [Latin *incūriōsus,* indifferent : *in-,* not + *cūriōsus,* CURIOUS.] **—in·cu·ri·os·i·ty** (-óssəti), **in·cu·ri·ous·ness** *n.* **—in·cu·ri·ous·ly** *adv.*
in·cur·rent (in-kúrrənt) *adj.* Affording passage to an inflowing current. Said of anatomical ducts and vessels. [Latin *incurrēns* (stem *incurrent-*), present participle of *incurrere,* to run into, INCUR.]
in·cur·sion (in-kúr-sh'n || -zh'n) *n.* **1.** A sudden attack on or invasion of hostile territory; a raid. **2.** An entering into. [Middle English, from Old French, from Latin *incursiō* (stem *incursiōn-*), from *incurrere* (past participle *incursus*), to run into, attack, INCUR.]
in·cur·vate (ín-kur-vayt || -kúr-) *tr.v.* **-vated, -vating, -vates.** To bend (something) into an inward curve.
~adj. (-vayt, -vət, -vit). Curved, especially inwards. [Latin *incurvāre* (past participle *incurvātus*) : *in-,* in + *curvāre,* to bend, from *curvus,* CURVE.] **—in·cur·va·tion** (ín-kur-váysh'n) *n.* **—in·cur·va·ture** (-kúrvə-chər) *n.*
in·curve (in-kúrv, íng-) *v.* **-curved, -curving, -curves.** *—intr.* To bend into an inward curve. *—tr.* To incurvate.
~n. (íng-kurv). An inward curve. [Latin *incurvāre,* INCURVATE.]
in·cus (íng-kəss) *n., pl.* **incudes** (in-kéwdeez). An anvil-shaped bone in the mammalian middle ear. Also called "anvil". Compare **malleus, stapes.** [Latin *incūs,* anvil, from *incūdere* (past participle *incūsus*), to forge with a hammer : *in-,* in + *cūdere,* to strike, stamp.].
in·cuse (in-kéwz || -kéwss) *adj.* Hammered, stamped, or pressed in. Said of a design or feature of a design on a coin or medal.
~n. A design impressed in such a manner.
~tr.v. **incused, -cusing, -cuses. 1.** To impress (a design) on a coin. **2.** To impress (a coin or medal) with a design. [Latin *incūsus,* past participle of *incūdere,* to beat or stamp in. See **incus.**]
Ind (ind) *n.* India.
ind. 1. independence; independent. **2.** index. **3.** indicative. **4.** indigo. **5.** indirect. **6.** industrial; industry.
Ind. 1. Independent. **2.** India. **3.** Indian. **4.** Indiana. **5.** Indies.
in·da·ba (in-daábə) *n.* **1.** A conference or meeting of indigenous peoples in southern Africa to discuss a serious issue. **2.** *South African Informal.* **a.** A discussion. **b.** A personal concern. [Zulu, "business, affair".]

in·da·mine (ində-meen, -min) *n.* Any of a group of organic bases that form unstable bluish or greenish salts used as dyes, especially the base, $NH_2C_6H_4N{:}C_6H_4{:}NH$, used to produce the dye safranine. Also called "phenylene blue". [*indigo* + *amine.*]
in·debt·ed (in-déttid) *adj.* **1.** Owing gratitude or recognition for something: *indebted to her for her help.* **2.** Owing money. [Middle English *endetted,* from Old French *endette,* from the past participle of *endetter,* to involve in debt, oblige : *en-,* in + *dette,* DEBT.]
in·debt·ed·ness (in-déttid-nəss, -niss) *n.* **1.** The state of being indebted. **2.** That which is owed to another.
in·de·cen·cy (in-deé-s'n-si) *n., pl.* **-cies. 1.** The state or quality of being indecent. **2.** Something that is indecent.
in·de·cent (in-deé-s'nt) *adj.* **1.** Offensive to good taste; unseemly. **2.** Offensive to public moral values; immodest. —See Synonyms at **improper. —in·de·cent·ly** *adv.*
indecent assault *n.* The act or offence of making a sexual attack other than rape on a person who has not consented.
indecent exposure *n.* The act or offence of indecently exposing one's body, especially the genitals, to public view. Also called "exposure".
in·de·ci·pher·a·ble (índi-sífərə-b'l, -sífrə-) *adj.* Incapable of being deciphered, especially by being illegible. **—in·de·ci·pher·a·bil·i·ty** (-bílləti), **in·de·ci·pher·a·ble·ness** *n.*
in·de·ci·sion (índi-sízh'n) *n.* Irresolution; indecisiveness.
in·de·ci·sive (índi-sī́-siv) *adj.* **1.** Not decisive; inconclusive. **2.** Prone to or characterised by indecision; vacillating; hesitant. **3.** Not clearly defined; indefinite. **—in·de·ci·sive·ly** *adv.* **—in·de·ci·sive·ness** *n.*
in·de·clin·a·ble (índi-klī́nəb'l) *adj.* Having no set of grammatical inflections; not declinable.
in·de·com·pos·a·ble (ín-dee-kəm-pṓzəb'l || -kom-) *adj.* Not capable of being split into component parts.
in·dec·o·rous (in-déckərəss, ín-) *adj.* Lacking propriety or good taste; unseemly. See Synonyms at **improper. —in·dec·o·rous·ly** *adv.* **—in·dec·o·rous·ness** *n.*
in·de·cor·um (índi-káwr-əm || -kṓr-) *n.* **1.** Lack of decorum; lack of propriety or good taste. **2.** An instance of indecorous behaviour.
in·deed (in-deéd) *adv.* **1.** Without a doubt; certainly; truly. **2.** In fact; in reality. **3.** Admittedly; unquestionably. **4.** What is more.
~interj. Used to express surprise, scepticism, or irony. [Middle English *in dede,* in reality : *in,* IN + *dede,* DEED.]
indef. indefinite.
in·de·fat·i·ga·ble (índi-fáttigə-b'l) *adj.* **1.** Untiring; tireless. **2.** Unremitting. [Latin *indēfatīgābilis* : *in-,* not + *dēfatīgāre,* to tire out : *de-* (intensive) + *fatīgāre,* to FATIGUE.] **—in·de·fat·i·ga·bil·i·ty** (-bílləti), **in·de·fat·i·ga·ble·ness** *n.* **—in·de·fat·i·ga·bly** *adv.*
in·de·fea·si·ble (índi-feézə-b'l) *adj.* Not capable of being annulled or made void. **—in·de·fea·si·bil·i·ty** (-bílləti) *n.* **—in·de·fea·si·bly** *adv.*
in·de·fec·ti·ble (índi-féktə-b'l) *adj.* **1.** Having the ability to resist defect or failure; permanent; lasting. **2.** Without flaw or defect; perfect. **—in·de·fec·ti·bil·i·ty** (-bílləti) *n.* **—in·de·fec·ti·bly** *adv.*
in·de·fen·si·ble (índi-fén-sə-b'l) *adj.* Not capable of being defended, especially: **1.** Inexcusable. **2.** Invalid; untenable. **3.** Vulnerable to attack. **—in·de·fen·si·bil·i·ty** (-bílləti), **in·de·fen·si·ble·ness** *n.* **—in·de·fen·si·bly** *adv.*
in·de·fin·a·ble (índi-fī́nəb'l) *adj.* Not capable of being defined, described, or analysed.
~n. A word, concept, or quality that cannot be defined. **—in·de·fin·a·ble·ness** *n.* **—in·de·fin·a·bly** *adv.*
in·def·i·nite (in-déffi-nət, ín-, -déf-, -nit) *adj. Abbr.* **indef. 1.** Not definite, especially: **a.** Unclear; vague. **b.** Lacking precise limits. **c.** Uncertain; undecided. **2.** *Grammar.* Not specifying whether an action is complete or continuous. Said of verb tenses. **3.** *Botany.* Indeterminate. [Latin *indēfīnītus* : *in-,* not + *dēfīnītus,* DEFINITE.] **—in·def·i·nite·ly** *adv.* **—in·def·i·nite·ness** *n.*
indefinite article *n. Grammar.* An article, as English *a* or *an,* that does not fix or immediately fix the identity of the noun modified. Compare **definite article.**
indefinite integral *n. Mathematics.* The set of all functions of which a given function is the derivative, usually represented by $\int f(x)dx + C$, where $\int f(x)dx$ is any member of the set and C is an arbitrary constant.
indefinite pronoun *n. Grammar.* A pronoun, for example *any* or *some,* that does not specify the identity of its object.
in·de·his·cent (índi-híss'nt) *adj.* Not splitting open at maturity: *indehiscent fruit.* Compare **dehiscent. —in·de·his·cence** *n.*
in·del·i·ble (in-déllə-b'l) *adj.* **1.** Incapable of being removed, erased, or washed away. **2.** Making a mark not easily erased or washed away: *an indelible laundry pencil.* **3.** Permanent; enduring: *indelible memories.* [Latin *indēlēbilis* : *in-,* not + *dēlēbilis,* that can be obliterated, from *dēlēre,* to obliterate, DELETE.] **—in·del·i·bil·i·ty** (-bílləti), **in·del·i·ble·ness** *n.* **—in·del·i·bly** *adv.*
in·del·i·ca·cy (in-déllikə-si) *n., pl.* **-cies. 1.** The quality or condition of being indelicate. **2.** An instance of indelicate speech or behaviour; a crudity.
in·del·i·cate in-délli-kət, -kit) *adj.* **1. a.** Offensive to propriety. **b.** Coarse; tasteless. **2.** Tactless. —See Synonyms at **coarse, improper. —in·del·i·cate·ly** *adv.* **—in·del·i·cate·ness** *n.*
in·dem·ni·fi·ca·tion (in-dém-ni-fi-káysh'n) *n.* **1.** The act of indemnifying or the condition of being indemnified. **2.** Something that indemnifies, such as a sum paid in compensation.
in·dem·ni·fy (in-dém-ni-fī) *tr.v.* **-fied, -fying, -fies. 1.** To protect

against possible damage, legal suit, or bodily injury; insure. **2.** To compensate for incurred damage or hurt. [Latin *indemnis,* uninjured (see **indemnity**) + -FY.] **—in·dem·ni·fi·er** *n.*

in·dem·ni·ty (in-dém-nəti) *n., pl.* **-ties. 1.** Insurance or other security against possible damage, loss, or hurt. **2.** A legal exemption from prosecution or liability for damages resulting from one's actions. **3.** Compensation for damage, loss, or hurt incurred, as sought by a victor in a war, for example; indemnification. —See Synonyms at **reparation.** [Middle English *indempnyte,* from Old French *indemnite,* from Late Latin *indemnitās* (stem *indemnitāt-*), from Latin *indemnis,* unhurt, uninjured : *in-,* not + *damnum,* hurt, harm.]

in·de·mon·stra·ble (in-démmən-strə-b'l, índi-món-) *adj.* Incapable of being proved or demonstrated. Said especially of axiomatic truths. **—in·de·mon·stra·bil·i·ty** (-bílləti) *n.* **—in·de·mon·stra·bly** *adv.*

in·dene (in-deen) *n.* A colourless organic liquid, C_9H_8, obtained from coal tar and used in preparing synthetic resins.

in·dent[1] (in-dént) *v.* **-dented, -denting, -dents.** *—tr.* **1.** To cut or tear (a document with two or more copies) along an irregular line so that the parts can later be matched for establishing authenticity. **2.** To draw up (a deed or other document) in duplicate or triplicate. **3. a.** To notch or serrate the edge of; make jagged. **b.** To form indentations in: *a deeply indented coastline.* **4. a.** To make notches, grooves, or holes in (wood, for example) for the purpose of mortising. **b.** To fit or join together by or as if by mortising. **5.** To set in from the margin (the first line of a paragraph, for example). **6.** *Chiefly British.* To order (goods) by an indent. **7.** To bind (an apprentice) by indenture. *—intr.* **1.** To form an indentation. **2.** *Chiefly British.* To draw up or order an indent for something. *~n.* (indent). **1.** An indenture. **2.** *Chiefly British.* An official requisition or purchase order for goods. **3.** An indention. [Middle English *indenten, endenten,* to make a toothlike incision into, from Old French *endenter* : *en-,* in + *dent,* tooth, from Latin *dēns* (stem *dent-*).] **—in·dent·er, in·den·tor** *n.*

in·dent[2] *tr.v.* **-dented, -denting, -dents. 1.** To push in or press down upon so as to form a dent or impression. **2.** To make a dent in. *~n.* An indentation.

in·den·ta·tion (inden-táysh'n) *n.* **1.** The act of indenting or the condition of being indented. **2. a.** A notch or jagged cut in an edge. **b.** A series of notches or jagged cuts. **3.** A deep recess in a border, coastline, or other boundary. **4.** *Printing.* An indention.

in·den·tion (in-dénsh'n) *n.* **1.** *Printing.* The blank space between a margin and the beginning of an indented line. **2.** Indentation. **3.** *Archaic.* A dint or dent.

in·den·ture (in-dénchər) *n.* **1.** *Law.* A deed or contract executed between two or more parties. **2.** *Usually plural.* A contract binding one party into the service of another for a stipulated term. **3.** *Archaic.* A document having indented edges. **4.** An official or authenticated inventory, list, or voucher. **5.** *Archaic.* Indentation. *~tr.v.* **indentured, -turing, -tures. 1.** To bind by indenture. **2.** *Archaic.* To form an indentation in. [Middle English *indenture, endenture,* from Old French *endenture,* from *endenter,* INDENT.]

in·de·pend·ence (índi-péndənss) *n. Abbr.* **ind. 1.** The state or quality of being independent. **2.** The point in time at which a state attains national independence: *has made great strides since independence.* **3.** *Archaic.* Sufficient income for self-support; a sufficiency.

In·de·pend·ence (índi-péndənss). City in western Missouri, central United States. In the mid-19th century it was the departure point for expeditions along the Santa Fe, Oregon, and California trails.

Independence Day *n.* **1.** In the United States, a public holiday (July 4) celebrating the anniversary of the adoption of the Declaration of Independence in 1776. **2.** A similar holiday in other countries, celebrating the attainment of national independence.

in·de·pend·en·cy (índi-péndən-si) *n., pl.* **-cies. 1.** Independence. **2.** An independent territory or state. **3.** *Capital* **I.** The Independent movement in England; Congregationalism.

in·de·pend·ent (índi-péndənt) *adj. Abbr.* **ind. 1.** Politically autonomous; self-governing. **2. a.** Free from the influence, guidance, or control of another or others. **b.** Self-reliant; not seeking or relying on help or guidance from others. **3.** Not contingent upon another person or thing. **4.** Affiliated with or loyal to no one political party or organisation: *the independent vote.* **5.** Not dependent on or affiliated with a larger or controlling group, system, or the like; separate: *an independent brewery.* **6.** Financially self-sufficient; self-supporting. **7.** Not having to work for a living; wealthy in one's own right. **8.** Providing a sufficient income upon which to live: *independent means.* **9.** *Mathematics.* **a.** Not dependent on other variables: *independent variable.* **b.** Of or pertaining to a system of equations, no one of which is necessarily satisfied by a set of values of the independent variables that satisfy all the others. **c.** Of, pertaining to, or designating an outcome of a trial of a chance experiment the probability of which does not depend on the outcome of any other trial of the chance experiment. *~n. Abbr.* **ind.** One that is independent; especially, a voter or politician who does not pledge allegiance to any one political party. **—in·de·pend·ent·ly** *adv.*

In·de·pend·ent (índi-péndənt) *n.* **1.** A member of a movement in England in the 17th century advocating the political and religious independence of individual congregations. **2.** *British.* A Congregationalist. **—In·de·pend·ent** *adj.*

independent clause *n.* A **main clause** *(see).*

independent school *n.* A school which is not maintained or controlled by central government or a local authority, and which usually charges fees.

in-depth (ín-dépth) *adj.* Detailed; thorough: *an in-depth study.*

in·de·scrib·a·ble (índi-skríbə-b'l) *adj.* **1.** Incapable of description; undefinable. **2.** Beyond description. **—in·de·scrib·a·bil·i·ty** (-bílləti), **in·de·scrib·a·ble·ness** *n.* **—in·de·scrib·a·bly** *adv.*

in·de·struc·ti·ble (índi-strúktə-b'l) *adj.* Not capable of being destroyed. **—in·de·struc·ti·bil·i·ty** (-bílləti), **in·de·struc·ti·ble·ness** *n.* **—in·de·struc·ti·bly** *adv.*

in·de·ter·mi·na·ble (índi-términəb'l) *adj.* **1.** Not capable of being fixed or measured; not ascertainable. **2.** Incapable of being finally settled or decided. **—in·de·ter·mi·na·bly** *adv.*

in·de·ter·mi·na·cy (índi-términə-si) *n.* The state or quality of being indeterminate. [From INDETERMINATE.]

in·de·ter·mi·nate (índi-térmi-nət, -nit) *adj.* **1. a.** Not precisely or quantitatively determined. **b.** Incapable of being so determined. **c.** Lacking clarity or precision. **d.** Not capable of clear interpretation; inconclusive; ambiguous. **e.** Not known in advance. **2.** *Botany.* **a.** Not terminating in a flower and continuing to grow at the apex: *an indeterminate inflorescence.* **b.** Not fixed in number, being too numerous to count: *indeterminate stamens.* **3.** *Mathematics.* **a.** Designating an equation containing more than one variable that has an unlimited number of solutions. **b.** Having no numerical meaning: *0 ÷ 0 is indeterminate.* **c.** Designating a structure or framework consisting of forces that cannot be analysed into a set of vectors. **4.** *Physics.* Designating an effect that appears to have no cause or does not obey a causal law. [Middle English *indeterminat,* from Late Latin *indēterminātus* : Latin *in-,* not + *dēterminātus,* DETERMINATE.] **—in·de·ter·mi·nate·ly** *adv.* **—in·de·ter·mi·nate·ness, in·de·ter·mi·na·tion** (-náysh'n) *n.*

indeterminate sentence *n.* A sentence whose length is determined by the prisoner's conduct while in prison.

indeterminate vowel *n. Phonetics.* **Schwa** *(see).*

in·de·ter·min·ism (índi-términi-niz'm) *n.* The philosophical doctrine that human actions are not necessarily predetermined by physiological and psychological factors. **—in·de·ter·min·ist** *n. & adj.* **—in·de·ter·min·is·tic** (-nístik) *adj.*

in·dex (índeks) *n., pl.* **-dexes** or **indices** (índi-seez) (for senses 5 and 6). **1.** Anything that serves to guide, point out, or otherwise facilitate reference, as: **a.** *Abbr.* **ind.** An alphabetised listing of names, places, and subjects included in a printed work that gives for each item the page on which it may be found. **b.** A series of notches cut into the edge of a book for easy access to chapters or other divisions; a thumb index. **c.** Any table, file, or catalogue which enables a reference to be located. **2.** Anything that reveals or indicates; a sign; a token: *"Her face . . . was a fair index to her disposition."* (Samuel Butler). **3.** A character (☞) used in printing to call attention to a particular paragraph or section. Also called "fist", "hand". **4.** Something that serves as an indicator or pointer, as in a scientific instrument. **5.** *Mathematics.* **a.** A number or symbol, often written as a subscript or superscript to a mathematical expression, that indicates an operation to be performed on, an ordering relation involving, or a use of the associated expression. **b.** A number indicating a specific property of a particular material: *refractive index.* **6.** A formula indicating the current level of something, such as prices, by reference to a standard, usually taken to be 100: *cost-of-living index.* **7.** An index finger. *~tr.v.* **indexed, -dexing, -dexes. 1.** To compile an index for. **2.** To enter (an item) in an index. **3.** To indicate or signal. **4.** To make index-linked. [Latin *index* (plural *indicēs*), forefinger, indicator.]

Usage: The plural of index is *indexes* if you are referring to books or papers: it is *indices* only if you are referring to symbols in mathematics, economics, and the like.

in·dex·a·tion (índek-sáysh'n) *n.* **1.** An act of indexing. **2.** The act of relating salaries, pensions, and the like to the cost-of-living index. Also called "index-linking".

index finger *n.* The finger next to the thumb; the forefinger.

In·dex Li·bro·rum Pro·hib·i·to·rum (índeks lī-bráwr-əm prō-híbbi-táwr-əm || -brṓr-, -tṓr-) *n.* A list formerly published by Church authority for Roman Catholics, restricting or forbidding the reading of certain books. Also shortened to "Index". [New Latin, "index of prohibited books".]

in·dex-linked (índeks-língkt) *adj.* Directly related to the cost-of-living index. Said of salaries, pensions, and the like. **—in·dex-link·ing** *n.*

index number *n.* A number indicating change in magnitude, as of price, wage, employment, or production shifts, relative to the magnitude at some given point usually taken as 100.

index of refraction *n.* **Refractive index** *(see).*

In·di·a, Republic of (índi-ə). *Sanskrit* **Bha·rat** (baáraat). Independent republic of southern Asia, within the Commonwealth. Much of India came under British domination in the mid-18th century. Its government, initially in the hands of the East India Company, was transferred to the Crown (1858) following the **Indian Mutiny.** India became independent in 1947, when the country was partitioned and the Muslim areas of the east and northwest made into the new nation of Pakistan. India has three main natural divisions: the triangular Deccan plateau of the south, the great northern plains, and the Himalayan mountains. The whole peninsula south of the Himalayas is often referred to as the "Indian subcontinent". The northern plains, which are crossed by the Indus, Ganges, and Brahmaputra rivers, form the world's largest alluvial lowland and the most densely populated part of the country. India's population

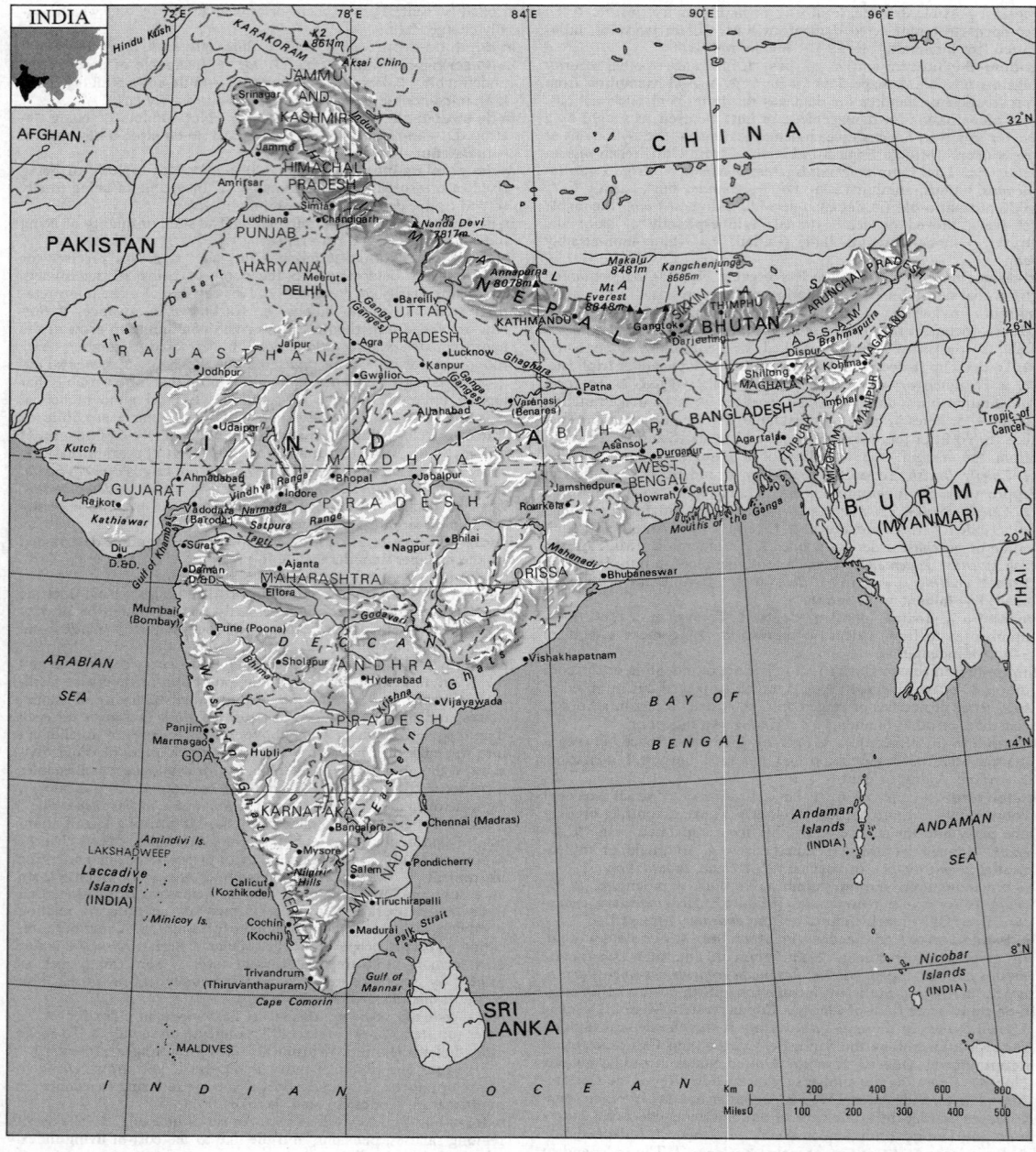

INDIA

is exceeded only by that of China. Although 40 per cent of the national income is derived from agriculture, especially rice and wheat, India is also rich in mineral reserves. Its iron ore is the basis of its rapidly expanding steel, machinery, and transport equipment industries. India is one of the leading producers of mica, coal, manganese, and aluminium, but still relies on imported oil. Area, 3 288 000 square kilometres (1,269,496 square miles). Population, 939,420,000. Capital, New Delhi.

In·di·a·man (índi-ə-mən) *n., pl.* **-men** (-mən, -men). A large merchant ship formerly used on trade routes to India.

In·di·an (índi-ən) *n. Abbr.* **Ind. 1.** A native or inhabitant of India or of the East Indies. **2.** A member of any of the aboriginal peoples of North America, South America, or the West Indies. **3.** Loosely, any of the languages spoken by the American Indians.
~*adj.* **1.** Of or pertaining to India or the East Indies, their culture, their languages, or their people. **2.** Of or pertaining to the aboriginal people of North America, South America, or the West Indies. **3.** Of or pertaining to the former British administration in India: *the Indian Civil Service.*

In·di·an·a (índi-ánnə, -a′ənə). State in the north central United States, one of the group of Midwest states. The capital and largest city is Indianapolis. Arable farming and cattle-rearing remain important, but Indiana is now a major manufacturing state and producer of petroleum. It was admitted to the Union in 1816.

Indian almond *n.* A tree, *Terminalia catappa,* of tropical Asia, having fruit with edible seeds. Also called "myrobalan".

In·di·an·ap·o·lis (índi-ə-náppəliss). Largest city and capital of the

state of Indiana, lying on the White River in the centre of the state. Situated in the centre of a rich agricultural region, it is a major grain and livestock market and food-processing centre. The formula one motor race, the Indianapolis "500", is held there each summer.

Indian bean *n.* A tree, the **catalpa** *(see).*

Indian club *n.* A bottle-shaped wooden club used in juggling or other gymnastic exercises.

Indian corn *n.* **Maize** *(see).*

Indian file *n.* Single file *(see).*

Indian giver *n. Chiefly U.S. Informal.* One who gives something as a gift to another and then takes or demands it back.

Indian hemp *n.* **1.** A plant, **hemp** *(see).* **2.** A North American plant, *Apocynum cannabinum,* whose stem fibres were formerly used by Indians for making matting and ropes.

Indian ink *n.* **1.** A black pigment made from lampblack mixed with a binding agent and moulded into cakes or sticks. **2.** A liquid ink made from this.

Indian liquorice *n.* A woody tropical Asian plant, *Abrus precatorius,* whose roots have been used as a substitute for liquorice and whose red and black seeds are used as beads.

Indian millet *n.* **Durra** *(see).*

Indian mulberry *n.* A small tree, *Morinda citrifolia,* of Indonesia and Australia from which red and yellow dyes are obtained.

Indian Mutiny *n.* A revolt by native Indian troops in 1857–58 leading to the end of the rule of the East India Company and the subsequent administration of India by the British Crown.

Indian National Congress *n.* One of the main political parties in

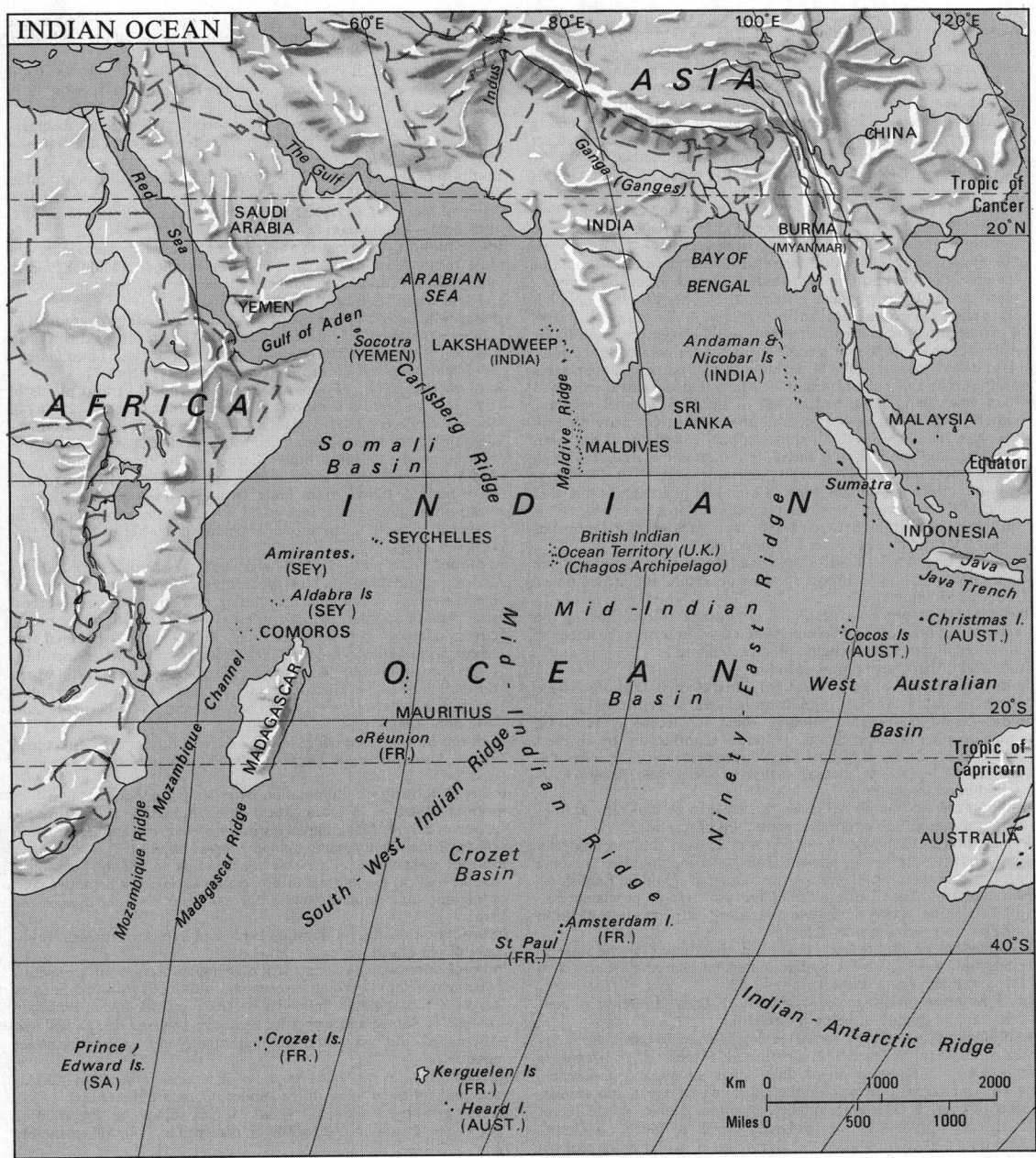

INDIAN OCEAN

India, founded in 1885, which has frequently been the governing party since India's independence.

Indian Ocean. World's third largest ocean, occupying an area of about 73 427 000 square kilometres (28,350,000 square miles) and having a width of about 6 400 kilometres (4,000 miles) at the equator. It extends from southern Asia to the Antarctic and from east Africa to southeastern Australia. It is divided into eastern and western halves by the Mid-Oceanic ridge, a few peaks of which emerge as islands. The average depth of the ocean is about 3 400 metres (11,000 feet).

Indian pipe *n.* A waxy white or sometimes pinkish saprophytic woodland plant, *Monotropa uniflora,* having scalelike leaves and a solitary, nodding flower.

Indian red *n.* An iron oxide used as a paint and cosmetic pigment.

Indian rope trick *n.* The feat of climbing an unsupported rope, which some Indians are supposed to be able to perform.

Indian summer *n.* **1.** A period of mild weather, occurring in late autumn or early winter. **2.** A pleasant, tranquil, or flourishing period occurring during the end of a condition or period, such as the late stage of one's life.

Indian Territory. An area of the United States, occupying part of the modern state of Oklahoma. It was set aside in 1834 by the U.S. government as a homeland for five Indian tribes expelled from the east. From 1889, the land was forcibly repurchased and the surviving Indians placed on reservations.

Indian wrestling *n.* A contest of strength between two people who clasp each other's hand with the elbow resting on a table, the winner being the one who forces his opponent's hand down to the table.

India paper *n.* **1.** A thin, uncoated, delicate paper made of vegetable fibre, used especially for taking impressions of engravings. **2. Bible paper** *(see).*

India rubber *n.* **Rubber** *(see).* —**in·di·a-rub·ber** *adj.*

In·dic (indik) *adj.* **1.** Of, pertaining to, or constituting the Indic languages. **2.** Of or pertaining to India, its people, or their culture. —*n.* A branch of the Indo-European languages that comprises Sanskrit and its modern descendants (including Hindi and Urdu), and Pali, Prakrits, and Dard.

in·di·can (indikən) *n.* **1.** A compound, $C_8H_6NOSO_2OH$, excreted, usually in the form of its potassium salt, in the urine. **2.** A glycoside, $C_{14}H_{17}NO_6$, occurring in the indigo plant. [Latin *indicum,* IN-DIGO + -AN.]

in·di·cant (indikənt) *n.* Something that serves to indicate. [Latin *indicāns* (stem *indicant-*), present participle of *indicāre,* to INDI-CATE.]

in·di·cate (indi-kayt) *tr.v.* **-cated, -cating, -cates. 1. a.** To demonstrate or point out with precision: *indicate a route.* **b.** To state or exhibit in complete detail. **c.** To show a reading of. Used of instruments. **2.** To serve as a sign, symptom, or token of; signify. **3.** To suggest or demonstrate the necessity, expedience, or advisability of: *The symptoms indicate immediate surgery.* **4.** To state, disclose, or express briefly. [Latin *indicāre,* to show, from *index,* forefinger, indicator, INDEX.] —**in·di·ca·to·ry** (in-dícka-təri, -tri) adj.

in·di·ca·tion (índi-káysh'n) n. **1.** The action of indicating. **2. a.** Something that indicates; a sign, token, or symptom. **b.** Something indicated as necessary or expedient. **3.** The reading shown on a measuring instrument. —See Synonyms at **sign**.

in·dic·a·tive (in-díckətiv) adj. **1.** Serving to point out or indicate: *indicative of their cynical attitude.* **2.** *Abbr.* **ind.** *Grammar.* Pertaining to or designating a verb mood used to indicate that the denoted act or condition is an objective fact. Compare **subjunctive**. ~n. *Abbr.* **ind.** *Grammar.* **1.** The indicative mood. **2.** A verb in this mood. —**in·dic·a·tive·ly** adv.

in·di·ca·tor (índi-kaytər) n. **1. a.** A device that indicates, such as a pointer or index. **b.** A circumstance or characteristic that serves to indicate: *all the usual indicators of a weak economy.* **2.** Any of various meters, gauges, or other instruments that are used to monitor the operation or condition of an engine, furnace, electrical network, reservoir, or other physical system. **3.** The needle, dial, or other registering device on such an instrument. **4.** An indicator board. **5.** An accurate measuring instrument used to measure small linear distances or to check that a component has the correct dimensions. Also called "dial gauge". **6. a.** Either of two pairs of amber lights on the front and back of a motor vehicle that the driver causes to flash when he is about to turn left or right. **b.** A small, sticklike switch inside a car, used to operate these lights. Compare **trafficator**. **7.** A plant species that requires special conditions of soil, temperature, and the like, and therefore indicates these conditions in places where it grows. Also called "indicator species". **8.** *Chemistry.* Any of various substances, such as litmus or phenolphthalein, that indicate the presence, absence, or concentration of a substance, or the degree of reaction between two or more substances, by means of a characteristic change, especially in colour.

indicator board n. A board displaying information; especially, one in a railway station or airport showing departure and arrival times. Also called "indicator".

indicator diagram n. A graph or oscilloscope record showing the variation of pressure and volume within the combustion chamber of an internal-combustion engine or steam engine.

in·di·ces. Alternative plural of **index**.

in·di·ci·a (in-díshi-ə) pl.n. Identifying marks or indications; signs. [Latin, plural of *indicium*, sign, from *indicāre*, to INDICATE.]

in·dict (in-dít) tr.v. **-dicted, -dicting, -dicts.** To accuse formally of a crime or other offence; charge. [Alteration (influenced by obsolete *indict*, to proclaim) of Middle English *enditen*, to accuse, from Anglo-French *enditer*, to dictate, INDITE.] —**in·dict·ee** (ín-di-tée) n. —**in·dict·er, in·dic·tor** n.

in·dict·a·ble (in-dítəb'l) adj. *Law.* **1.** Liable to be indicted. **2.** Rendering a person liable to indictment. Said of a crime.

in·dic·tion (in-díksh'n) n. **1.** A 15-year cycle used as a chronological unit for tax purposes in ancient Rome and incorporated in some medieval systems. **2.** *Archaic.* A proclamation. [Middle English *indiccioun*, from Late Latin *indictiō* (stem *indictiōn-*), "proclamation" (of Diocletian, fixing a 15-year assessment of property tax), from *indīcere*, to proclaim, INDITE.]

in·dict·ment (in-dítmənt) n. **1.** The act of indicting or the state of being indicted. **2.** *Law.* A written statement charging a party with the commission of a crime.

in·dif·fer·ence (in-diff-rənss, -ərənss) n. **1.** Lack of interest or concern. **2.** The quality of being indifferent.

in·dif·fer·ent (in-diff-rənt, -ərənt) adj. **1.** Having no particular interest or concern; apathetic. **2.** Unaffected; insensible: *indifferent to their pleas.* **3.** Showing no partiality, bias, or marked preference. **4.** Not mattering one way or the other; of no great importance; insignificant. **5.** Of average quality, extent, or degree. **6.** Mediocre; fairly bad. **7.** Not active or involved; neutral. **8.** *Biology.* **a.** Undifferentiated, as cells or tissue. **b.** Occurring in two or more ecological communities. Said of a species. —See Synonyms at **average**. [Middle English, from Old French, from Latin *indifferēns* : *in-*, not + *differēns*, DIFFERENT.] —**in·dif·fer·ent·ly** adv.

Synonyms: indifferent, unconcerned, apathetic, incurious, detached.

Usage: The usual preposition following this word is *to* (He was *indifferent to her advances*) but *as to* is sometimes used, especially in the context of abstract ideas (He was *indifferent as to the consequences of his action*), and *about* is often heard in less formal usage (I'm *indifferent about money*).

in·dif·fer·ent·ism (in-diff-rən-tiz'm, -ərən-) n. The belief that religions are all of like validity. —**in·dif·fer·ent·ist** n.

in·di·gen (índi-jən, -jen) n. Also **in·di·gene** (-jeen). One that is native or indigenous to an area. [Latin *indigena*, native.]

in·di·gence (índijənss) n. Want or neediness.

in·dig·e·nous (in-díjinəss) adj. **1.** Occurring or living naturally in an area; not introduced; native. **2.** Intrinsic; innate. [Latin *indigena*, native.] —**in·dig·e·nous·ly** adv. —**in·dig·e·nous·ness** n.

in·di·gent (índijənt) adj. **1.** Lacking the means of subsistence; impoverished; needy. **2.** *Archaic.* Lacking or deficient in something specified. Usually used with *of.* —See Synonyms at **poor**. ~n. A destitute or needy person. [Middle English, from Old French, from Latin *indigēns* (stem *indigent-*), present participle of *indigēre*, to lack : *indi-*, strengthened form of *in-*, in + *egēre*, to lack, want.] —**in·di·gent·ly** adv.

in·di·gest·ed (índi-jéstid ‖ -dī-) adj. **1.** Not carefully thought over or considered. **2.** Shapeless or chaotic.

in·di·gest·i·ble (in-di-jésta-b'l ‖ -dī-) adj. **1.** Difficult or impossible to digest. **2.** Difficult for the mind to assimilate, especially because of poor expression or presentation. —**in·di·gest·i·bil·i·ty** (-billəti) n. —**in·di·gest·i·bly** adv.

in·di·ges·tion (ín-di-jéss-chən ‖ -dī-) n. **1.** The inability to digest food. **2.** Discomfort or illness resulting from this; dyspepsia. **3.** A mental reaction against information that is hard to assimilate.

in·dign (in-dín) adj. *Obsolete.* **1.** Unworthy. **2.** Shameful; disgraceful. [Middle English *indigne*, from Old French, from Latin *indignus* : *in-*, not + *dignus*, worthy.]

in·dig·nant (in-dígnənt) adj. Characterised by or filled with indignation; outraged. [Latin *indignāns* (stem *indignant-*), present participle of *indignārī*, to regard as unworthy, from *indignus*, unworthy, INDIGN.] —**in·dig·nant·ly** adv.

in·dig·na·tion (índig-náysh'n) n. Anger aroused by something unjust, mean, or unworthy. See Synonyms at **anger**. [Middle English *indignacioun*, from Latin *indignātiō* (stem *indignātiōn-*), from *indignārī*, to regard as unworthy. See **indignant**.]

in·dig·ni·ty (in-dig-nəti) n., pl. **-ties. 1. a.** Humiliating, degrading, or abusive treatment of an individual. **b.** An offence to dignity; an affront. **2.** *Obsolete.* The want of dignity or honour. [Latin *indignitās* (stem *indignitāt-*), from *indignus*, unworthy, INDIGN.]

in·di·go (índigō) n., pl. **-gos** or **-goes. 1.** Any of various plants of the genus *Indigofera*, some of which yield a blue dyestuff. **2.** Any of several similar or related plants. **3.** A blue dye obtained from indigo or other plants or produced synthetically. **4.** *Abbr.* **ind.** Dark blue to greyish purplish blue. [Earlier *indico*, from Spanish, from Latin *indicum*, from Greek *indikon (pharmakon)*, "Indian (dye)", from *Indikos*, Indian, from *India*, INDIA.] —**in·di·go** adj.

in·di·go·tin (in-díga-tin, índi-gō-) n. A dark blue, crystalline compound, $C_{16}H_{10}N_2O_2$, the principal colouring matter of indigo. [INDIGO + -IN.]

in·di·rect (in-di-rékt, -dī-) adj. *Abbr.* **ind. 1. a.** Not taking a direct course; roundabout. **b.** Not proceeding or operating directly: *an indirect connection.* **2.** Not descending in a straight line of succession. Said of an inheritance or title. **3. a.** Not straight to the point; circumlocutory. **b.** Evasive; devious. **4.** Not directly planned for; secondary: *indirect benefits.* **5.** Pertaining to or characteristic of indirect speech; oblique. **6.** In soccer, designating a free kick in which the ball cannot be kicked directly at goal but must have been touched previously by at least two players. —**in·di·rect·ly** adv. —**in·di·rect·ness** n.

in·di·rec·tion (in-di-réksh'n, -dī-) n. Lack of direction or directness, as: **1.** Aimlessness. **2.** Lack of straightforwardness. **3.** Deviousness.

indirect lighting n. Illumination by reflected or diffused light.

indirect object n. A grammatical object indirectly affected by the action of a verb; for example, *me* in *Sing me a song* and *the rabbit* in *He feeds the rabbit lettuce.* Compare **direct object**.

indirect passive n. A passive construction in which the subject corresponds to the indirect or prepositional object in an active construction; for example, *they* in the sentence *They were given the papers.*

indirect question n. A question expressed in indirect speech. Compare **direct question**.

indirect speech n. A construction giving an account of a previous statement without quoting it verbatim, introduced by a verb such as *say* or *tell*, sometimes followed by *that*, and having appropriate changes in person and tense; for example, *She said that he had left.* Also called "indirect discourse", "reported speech". Compare **direct speech**.

indirect tax n. A tax levied on goods or services rather than individuals and collected through the vendor. Compare **direct tax**.

in·dis·cern·i·ble (índi-sérnib'l) adj. **1.** Not able to be discerned or perceived. **2.** Barely discernible or perceptible. —**in·dis·cern·i·bly** adv.

in·dis·ci·pline (in-díssiplin) n. Lack of discipline; unruly behaviour.

in·dis·creet (índi-skréet) adj. **1.** Lacking discretion; injudicious. **2.** Too frank; inclined to reveal more than is wise. —**in·dis·creet·ly** adv. —**in·dis·creet·ness** n.

in·dis·crete (índi-skréet) adj. Not divided or divisible into separate parts; unified.

in·dis·cre·tion (índi-skrésh'n) n. **1.** Lack of discretion. **2.** An indiscreet act or remark.

in·dis·crim·i·nate (índi-skrími-nət, -nit) adj. **1.** Wanting in discrimination or discernment: *indiscriminate admiration of power.* **2.** Random; haphazard. **3.** Confused; motley. **4.** Not restricted or restrained; promiscuous. —**in·dis·crim·i·nate·ly** adv. —**in·dis·crim·i·nate·ness** n.

in·dis·crim·i·na·tion (índi-skrímmi-náysh'n) n. The condition or quality of being indiscriminate. —**in·dis·crim·i·na·tive** (-nətiv, -naytiv) adj.

in·dis·pen·sa·ble (índi-spén-sə-b'l) adj. **1.** Incapable of being dispensed with; essential; required. **2.** Incapable of being set aside or escaped; inevitable. —See Synonyms at **necessary**. ~n. An indispensable person or thing. —**in·dis·pen·sa·bil·i·ty** (-bílləti), **in·dis·pen·sa·ble·ness** n. —**in·dis·pen·sa·bly** adv.

in·dis·pose (índi-spóz) tr.v. **-posed, -posing, -poses. 1.** To make averse; disincline. **2.** To render unfit; disqualify. **3.** To cause to be or feel ill; sicken.

in·dis·posed (índi-spózd) adj. **1.** Mildly ill. **2.** Disinclined; unwilling. —See Synonyms at **sick**.

in·dis·po·si·tion (índi-spə-zísh'n) n. **1.** Disinclination; unwillingness. **2.** A minor ailment.

in·dis·put·a·ble (índi-spéwtəb'l) *adj.* Beyond doubt; undeniable. —**in·dis·put·a·ble·ness** *n.* —**in·dis·put·a·bly** *adv.*

in·dis·sol·u·ble (índi-sóllew-b'l) *adj.* **1.** Impossible to break or undo; binding: *an indissoluble contract.* **2.** Incapable of being dissolved, disintegrated, or decomposed. —**in·dis·sol·u·bil·i·ty** (-bílləti), **in·dis·sol·u·ble·ness** *n.* —**in·dis·sol·u·bly** *adv.*

in·dis·tinct (índi-stíngkt) *adj.* **1.** Not clearly delineated; blurred. **2.** Faint; dim. **3.** Difficult to understand or make out: *indistinct speech.* —**in·dis·tinct·ly** *adv.* —**in·dis·tinct·ness** *n.*

in·dis·tinc·tive (índi-stíngktiv) *adj.* Lacking distinctive qualities; not distinctive. —**in·dis·tinc·tive·ly** *adv.* —**in·dis·tinc·tive·ness** *n.*

in·dis·tin·guish·a·ble (índi-stíng-gwishə-b'l) *adj.* Not distinguishable, especially: **1.** Difficult or impossible to perceive or make out. **2.** So similar as to be incapable of being distinguished from another or each other. —**in·dis·tin·guish·a·ble·ness, in·dis·tin·guish·a·bil·i·ty** (-bílləti) *n.* —**in·dis·tin·guish·a·bly** *adv.*

in·dite (in-dít) *tr.v.* **-dited, -diting, -dites. 1.** To write; compose. **2.** To set down in writing. **3.** *Obsolete.* To dictate. [Middle English *enditen,* to compose, write down, from Anglo-French *enditer,* from Vulgar Latin *indictāre* (unattested), frequentative of Latin *indīcere* (past participle *indictus*), to proclaim : *in-,* towards + *dīcere,* to pronounce.] —**in·dite·ment** *n.* —**in·dit·er** *n.*

in·di·um (índi-əm) *n. Symbol* **In** A soft, malleable, silvery-white metallic element found primarily in ores of zinc and tin, used as a plating over silver in making mirrors, in plating aircraft bearings, and in compounds for transistors. Atomic number 49, atomic weight 114.82, melting point 156.61°C, boiling point 2,000°C, relative density 7.31, valencies 1, 2, 3. [New Latin, from Latin *indicum,* INDIGO (from the indigo-blue colour of its spectrum).]

in·di·ver·ti·ble (ín-di-vértib'l, -dī-) *adj.* Incapable of being diverted or turned aside. —**in·di·ver·ti·bly** *adv.*

in·di·vid·u·al (índi-víddew-əl) *adj.* **1. a.** Of or pertaining to a single human being. **b.** By or for one person: *an individual portion.* **2.** Existing as a distinct entity; single; separate. **3.** Distinguished by particular characteristics; peculiar to one person; distinctive. **4.** *Obsolete.* Indivisible; inseparable. —See Synonyms at **characteristic, single.**
~*n.* **1. a.** A single human being considered separately from his group or from society. **b.** A single organism as distinguished from a group or colony. **2.** An independent, strong-willed person. **3.** A person. [Middle English *indyvyduall,* separate, indivisible, from Medieval Latin *indīviduālis,* from Latin *indīviduus,* indivisible : *in-,* not + *dīviduus,* divisible, from *dīvidere,* to DIVIDE.] —**in·di·vid·u·al·ly** *adv.*

Usage: Individual, in the sense of "a person", is used without nuance when a single human being is being distinguished from a group: *the individual's right to dissent.* When this contrast is absent, there is usually a humorous or pejorative implication: *Look at that bearded individual.* If a special sense is not intended, it is best to use a neutral word, such as *people.*

in·di·vid·u·al·ise, in·di·vid·u·al·ize (índi-víddew-ə-līz) *tr.v.* **-ised, -ising, -ises. 1.** To give individuality to. **2.** To consider individually; specify; particularise. **3.** To modify to suit a particular individual. —**in·di·vid·u·al·i·sa·tion** (-lī-záysh'n ‖ *U.S.* -i-) *n.*

in·di·vid·u·al·ism (índi-víddew-ə-liz'm) *n.* **1.** Individuality. **2.** The assertion of one's uniqueness; egoism. **3.** An individual peculiarity or foible. **4.** *Economics.* **a.** The theory that a citizen should have freedom in his economic pursuits and should succeed by his own initiative. **b.** The practice of this: *rugged individualism.* **5.** The doctrine that the interests of the individual should take precedence over the interests of the state or social group. **6.** *Philosophy.* The doctrine that reality is composed of individual entities.

in·di·vid·u·al·ist (índi-víddew-ə-list) *n.* **1.** One who asserts his individuality by his independence of thought and action. **2.** One who advocates individualism. —**in·di·vid·u·al·ist, in·di·vid·u·al·is·tic** (-lístik) *adj.* —**in·di·vid·u·al·is·ti·cal·ly** *adv.*

in·di·vid·u·al·i·ty (índi-víddew-ál-əti) *n., pl.* **-ties. 1.** The quality of being individual; distinctness. **2.** The aggregate of distinguishing attributes of a person or thing. **3.** A single, distinct entity. **4.** *Archaic.* Indivisibility.

in·di·vid·u·ate (índi-víddew-ayt) *tr.v.* **-ated, -ating, -ates. 1.** To individualise. **2.** To form into a separate and distinct entity.

in·di·vid·u·a·tion (índi-víddew-áysh'n) *n.* **1.** The act or process of individuating; specifically, the process by which social individuals become differentiated one from the other. **2.** The condition of being individuated; individuality.

in·di·vis·i·ble (índi-vizzə-b'l) *adj.* **1.** Incapable of being divided. **2.** *Mathematics.* Incapable of being divided exactly. —**in·di·vis·i·ble·ness, in·di·vis·i·bil·i·ty** (-bílləti) *n.* —**in·di·vis·i·bly** *adv.*

Indo- *comb. form.* Indicates India or East Indian; for example, *Indochina.*

In·do-Ar·y·an (índo-áir-i-ən) *adj.* **1.** Belonging to or characteristic of any of the Indo-European-speaking peoples of the Indian subcontinent. **2.** Indo-Iranian.
~*n.* **1.** A member of an Indo-Aryan people. **2.** Indo-Iranian.

In·do·chi·na (índo-chínə). Region of Southeast Asia. It includes Burma (Myanmar), Thailand, Laos, Cambodia, Vietnam and the Malay Peninsula. See **French Indochina.** —**In·do·chi·nese** *n. & adj.*

in·doc·ile (in-dó-sīl ‖ *U.S.* -dóss'l) *adj.* Difficult to control or instruct; not docile. —**in·do·cil·i·ty** (-dō-síllɐti ‖ *U.S.* -i-) *n.*

in·doc·tri·nate (in-dóktri-nayt) *tr.v.* **-nated, -nating, -nates. 1.** To instruct in a body of doctrine. **2.** To teach to accept a system of thought uncritically. —**in·doc·tri·na·tion** (-náysh'n) *n.*

In·do-Eu·ro·pe·an (índo-yóor-ə-pée-ən) *adj.* **1.** Belonging to or constituting a family of languages that includes the Germanic, Celtic, Italic, Baltic, Slavic, Greek, Armenian, Hittite, Tocharian, Iranian, and Indic groups. **2.** Belonging to or constituting Proto-Indo-European. **3.** Of, pertaining to, or characteristic of cultural traits appearing to be common to or widely distributed among peoples who speak Indo-European languages, and presumed to be inherited from the original speakers of Proto-Indo-European.
~*n.* **1.** The Indo-European family of languages. **2. Proto-Indo-European** *(see).* **3.** A member of any of the peoples who speak Indo-European languages. **4.** A member of the presumed prehistoric people who spoke Proto-Indo-European. [Named after the geographical extremities of the distribution of the languages : INDO- + EUROPEAN.]

In·do-Eu·ro·pe·an·ist (índo-yóor-ə-pée-ənist) *n.* A historical linguist specialising in the study of Indo-European.

In·do-Ger·man·ic (índo-jər-mánnik, -jer-) *adj.* Indo-European.
~*n.* Indo-European. [Translation of German *indogermanisch.*]

In·do-Hit·tite (índo-híttīt) *n.* Indo-European together with Hittite. Used by those who do not consider Hittite to be itself within the Indo-European family proper.

In·do-I·ra·ni·an (índo-I-ráyni-ən, -ī-) *adj.* Belonging to or constituting the branch of Indo-European made up of the Indic and the Iranian language groups.
~*n.* The Indo-Iranian branch of Indo-European.

in·dole (ín-dōl) *n.* Also **in·dol** (-dōl, -dol). A white crystalline compound, C_8H_7N, obtained from coal tar and used in perfumery, medicine, and as a flavouring; I-benzopyrrole. —**in·dol·ic** *adj.* [IND(IGO) + -OLE.]

in·dole·a·ce·tic acid (índōlə-sée-tik, -sé) *n. Abbr.* **IAA.** An organic compound, $C_{10}H_9NO_2$, which is the most common of the group of substances that regulate plant growth (auxins).

in·dole·a·ce·to·ni·trile (índōlə-séetō-nītrīl) *n. Abbr.* **IAN.** A common auxin, $C_{10}H_8N_2$.

in·do·lent (índələnt) *adj.* **1.** Averse to work or activity; habitually lazy. **2.** *Pathology.* **a.** Causing little or no pain: *an indolent tumour.* **b.** Slow to heal; persistent: *an indolent ulcer.* [Late Latin *indolēns,* painless : Latin *in-,* not + *dolēns* (stem *dolent-*), present participle of *dolēre,* to give pain, feel pain.] —**in·do·lence** *n.*

In·dol·o·gy (in-dólləji) *n.* The study of Indian history, languages, and culture. [INDO- + -LOGY.] —**In·dol·o·gist** *n.*

in·do·meth·a·cin (índō-méthə-sin) *n.* A drug, $C_{19}H_{16}ClNO_4$, that relieves pain and inflammation, used particularly in the treatment of rheumatoid arthritis. [INDO(LE) + METH- + AC(ETIC ACID) + -IN.]

in·dom·i·ta·ble (in-dómmitəb'l) *adj.* Incapable of being overcome, subdued, or vanquished; unconquerable. [Late Latin *indomitābilis,* untamable : Latin *in-,* not + *domitāre,* frequentative of *domāre* (past participle *domitus*), to tame.] —**in·dom·i·ta·bly** *adv.*

In·do·ne·si·a, Republic of (índə-néez-yə, -néeshə, -néezhə). Independent republic in southeastern Asia, the fifth-largest nation in the world and the world's largest Muslim nation. It consists of more than 13,000 islands lying between the Indian and Pacific oceans. Despite fertile land, prolific sea fisheries, and abundant minerals, Indonesia is still one of the world's poorest countries because of lack of development. The chief agricultural product is rice and cash crops include tea, rubber, copra, coffee, and sugar. Indonesia also exports petroleum, petroleum products, and tin. It gained its independence from the Netherlands in 1949 under Achmed Sukarno. He was removed by a bloody military coup (1965), and since then General Suharto has reversed his Communist policies. Area 1 919 317 square kilometres (741,653 square miles). Population 196,810,000. Capital, Jakarta, on the island of Java. See map, next page.

In·do·ne·sian (índə-néez-yən, -néesh'n, -néezh'n) *n.* **1.** A native or inhabitant of the Republic of Indonesia. **2.** A member of a hypothetical non-Malay race of Indonesia, Malaysia, and the Philippines, having both Mongoloid and Polynesian characteristics. **3.** The official language of Indonesia, **Bahasa Indonesia** *(see).*
~*adj.* Of or pertaining to Indonesia, its people, or their language.

Indonesian Borneo. See **Kalimantan.**

in·door (in-dór ‖ -dór) *adj.* **1.** Of, pertaining to, or situated in the interior of a house or other building: *an indoor pool.* **2.** Carried on or used indoors: *indoor games; indoor fireworks.* **3.** Of or belonging to the workhouse or poorhouse. [Short for earlier *within-door* : WITHIN + DOOR.]

in·doors (in-dórz ‖ -dórz) *adv.* In or into a house or other building. [Short for earlier *withindoors* : WITHIN + DOORS.]

in·do·phe·nol (índo-féenol) *n.* A green or blue organic dye, OH $C_6H_4NC_6H_4O$, or its derivatives.

indorse. Variant of **endorse.**

In·dra (índrə). *Hinduism.* A principal Vedic deity associated with rain and thunder. [Sanskrit *Indraḥ†.*]

in·draught (in-draaft ‖ -draft) *n.* **1.** A pulling or drawing inwards. **2.** An inward flow or current: *an indraught of cold air.*

in·drawn (in-dráwn) *adj.* **1.** Drawn in. **2.** Introspective; aloof.

in·dri (índri) *n., pl.* **-dris.** Also **in·dris** (índriss). A large lemur, *Indri indri,* of Madagascar, having silky fur and a short tail. [Malagasay *indry!* look! (mistakenly assumed to be the animal's name).]

in·du·bi·ta·ble (in-déw-bitə-b'l ‖ -dóo-) *adj.* Too obvious to be doubted; unquestionable. —**in·du·bi·ta·bil·i·ty** (-bílləti) *n.* —**in·du·bi·ta·bly** *adv.*

in·duce (in-déwss ‖ -dóoss) *tr.v.* **-duced, -ducing, -duces. 1.** To lead

INDONESIA

or move by influence or persuasion; prevail upon: *finally induced him to give up smoking.* **2.** To stimulate the occurrence of; especially, to hasten (childbirth) artificially, as by the use of drugs. **3.** To infer by inductive reasoning. **4.** *Physics.* To produce (an electric current or magnetic effect) by induction. —See Synonyms at **persuade.** [Middle English *inducen,* from Latin *indūcere* : *in-,* in + *dūcere,* to lead.] —**in·duc·er** *n.* —**in·duc·i·ble** *adj.*

in·duce·ment (in-déwss-mənt ‖ -dōōss-) *n.* **1.** The act or process of inducing: *the inducement of sleep.* **2.** That which induces; an incentive; a motive. **3.** An introductory or background statement explaining the main allegations in a legal proceeding.

in·duct (in-dúkt) *tr.v.* **-ducted, -ducting, -ducts.** **1. a.** To place ceremoniously or formally in an office or benefice; install. **b.** To introduce, as to facts or knowledge; initiate. **2.** *Physics.* To induce. [Middle English *inducten,* from Medieval Latin *indūcere* (past participle *inductus*), from Latin, to lead in, INDUCE.]

in·duc·tance (in-dúktənss) *n.* **1.** The property of an electric circuit that enables an electromagnetic force to be generated as a result of a change of current in the same circuit *(self-inductance)* or in a nearby circuit with which it is magnetically linked *(mutual inductance).* **2.** A measure of this property in henries. **3.** A circuit element that introduces this property.

in·duc·tile (in-dúk-tīl ‖ *U.S. also* -t'l) *adj.* Unyielding; not pliant or ductile.

in·duc·tion (in-dúksh'n) *n.* **1.** The act of inducting or of being inducted. **2.** *Electricity.* **a.** The generation of electromotive force in a closed circuit by a varying magnetic flux through the circuit. Also called "electromagnetic induction". **b.** The charging of an isolated conducting object by momentarily earthing it while a charged body is nearby. Also called "electrostatic induction". **3. a.** *Logic.* A principle of reasoning to a conclusion about all the members of a class from examination of only a few members of the class; broadly, reasoning from the particular to the general. Compare **deduction.** **b.** A conclusion reached by this method. **4.** *Mathematics.* A deductive method of proof in which verification of a proposition consists of proving the first case and the case immediately following an arbitrary case for which the proposition is assumed to be correct. **5.** The act of inducing. **6.** *Archaic.* A preface or preamble.

induction coil *n.* A transformer, often used in the ignition systems of petrol engines, in which an interrupted, low-voltage direct current in the primary is converted into an intermittent, high-voltage current in the secondary.

induction hardening *n.* A method of hardening the surface of a metal component by inducing eddy currents in it to heat it rapidly, then rapidly cooling it.

induction heating *n.* A method of heating a conducting material by inducing electric currents within it as a result of applying an alternating magnetic field to it.

induction motor *n.* A brushless electric motor in which an alternating current fed to the stator induces a current in the windings of the rotor. Rotation occurs as a result of the interaction of the magnetic field of the stator with that of the rotor.

in·duc·tive (in-dúktiv) *adj.* **1.** Of or utilising induction: *inductive method.* **2.** *Electricity.* Of or arising from inductance: *inductive reactance.* **3.** Causing or influencing; inducing. —**in·duc·tive·ly** *adv.* —**in·duc·tive·ness** *n.*

in·duc·tor (in-dúktər) *n.* **1.** A person who inducts, as into office. **2.** *Electricity.* Symbol L. A device that functions by or introduces inductance into a circuit.

indue. Variant of **endue.**

in·dulge (in-dúlj) *v.* **-dulged, -dulging, -dulges.** —*tr.* **1.** To yield to the desires and whims of (oneself or another), especially to an excessive degree; humour; pamper. **2.** To gratify or yield to: *indulge a craving for chocolate.* **3.** To grant an ecclesiastical indulgence or

dispensation to. —*intr.* **1.** To allow oneself some special pleasure; indulge oneself. Used with *in: indulge in an afternoon nap.* **2.** *Informal.* To consume an excessive amount of alcohol. —See Synonyms at **pamper.** [Latin *indulgēre†,* to be forbearing, grant as a favour.] —**in·dulg·er** *n.*

in·dul·gence (in-dúljənss) *n.* **1.** The act of indulging or the fact of being indulgent; tolerance, forbearance, or absence of restraint. **2. a.** The act of indulging in something. **b.** Something indulged in: *Sports cars are an expensive indulgence.* **3. a.** Something granted as a favour or privilege. **b.** Permission to extend the time of payment or performance, as in business. **4.** *Roman Catholic Church.* The remission of temporal punishment due for a sin after the guilt has been forgiven. **5.** A royal dispensation during the reigns of Charles II and James II of England granting special religious freedom to the Nonconformists and the Roman Catholics.
~*tr.v.* **indulgenced, -gencing, -gences.** *Roman Catholic Church.* To grant an indulgence to.

in·dul·gent (in-dúljənt) *adj.* Showing, characterised by, or given to indulgence; lenient: *an indulgent employer.* See Synonyms at **thoughtful.** —**in·dul·gent·ly** *adv.*

in·du·line (indew-līn, -leen, -lin) *n.* Also **in·du·lin** (-lin). Any of a group of blue or black synthetic azine dyestuffs used for colouring varnishes and dyeing wool.

in·dult (in-dúlt) *n.* A temporary exemption from the common law of the Roman Catholic Church granted by the pope. [Middle English, from Medieval Latin *indultum,* from Latin *indultus,* past participle of *indulgēre†,* INDULGE.]

in·du·na (in-dōōnə) *n.* In South Africa: **1.** A leading adviser or official appointed by a tribal chief. **2.** A black overseer, as on a farm or mine. [Zulu *induna,* an official.]

in·du·pli·cate (in-déw-pli-kət, -kit, -kayt ‖ -dōō-) *adj. Botany.* Having the edges folded or turned inwards but not overlapping. Said of the parts of a bud. [IN- (in, inward) + Latin *duplicātus,* doubled up, DUPLICATE.]

in·du·rate (índewr-ayt ‖ -door-) *v.* **-rated, -rating, -rates.** —*tr.* **1.** To make hard; harden. **2.** To make callous. —*intr.* **1.** To harden. **2.** To become obdurate.
~*adj.* (-ət, -it). Hardened; obstinate; unfeeling. [Latin *indūrāre,* to harden : *in-* (intensive) + *dūrāre,* to harden, from *dūrus,* hard.] —**in·du·ra·tion** (-ráysh'n) *n.* —**in·du·ra·tive** (-raytiv) *adj.*

In·dus¹ (índəss). Chief river of Pakistan, rising in the Kailas mountains in Tibet and flowing to the Arabian Sea southeast of Karachi. It is about 3 060 kilometres (1,900 miles) long. The Indus valley is the most populous part of Pakistan. Its alluvial plains were the site of the early Indus Valley civilisation which flourished from *c.* 2500 B.C. to *c.* 1500 B.C.

In·dus² *n.* A constellation in the Southern Hemisphere near Tucana and Pavo.

in·du·si·um (in-déw-zi-əm ‖ -dōō-, -zhi-) *n., pl.* **-sia** (-zē-ə). An enclosing membrane, such as that covering and protecting the sorus of a fern. [Latin, tunic, from Greek *endusis,* from *enduein,* to sink or slip into, put on : *en-,* in + *duein,* to sink.]

in·dus·tri·al (in-dústri-əl) *adj. Abbr.* **ind. 1.** Of, pertaining to, or derived from industry: *an industrial exhibition.* **2.** Having highly developed industries: *an industrial nation.* **3.** Employed, required, or used in industry: *industrial diamonds.* **4.** Involving or concerning workers in industry: *industrial relations.*
~*n. Plural.* Shares in industrial companies. —**in·dus·tri·al·ly** *adv.*

industrial action *n. Chiefly British.* Any action, such as striking, working to rule, or boycotting, taken by workers to protest against working conditions, managerial policy, or the like.

industrial archaeology *n.* The study of machines, methods, and sites characteristic of the early history of the Industrial Revolution.

industrial design *n.* The study or practice of designing manufacturable products.

industrial disease *n.* An occupational disease characteristic of workers in a particular industry, for example **asbestosis** *(see)*.

industrial estate *n. British.* A district planned in relatively recent times to be the site of many factories and businesses. Also *U.S.* "industrial park".

industrial injury benefit *n. British.* A weekly payment formerly made under the National Insurance scheme to a person who has incurred injury while at work. Also called "injury benefit".

in·dus·tri·al·ise, in·dus·tri·al·ize (in-dústri-ə-līz) *v.* **-ised, -ising, -ises.** —*tr.* **1.** To develop industry, in especially on an extensive scale. **2.** To organise as an industry. —*intr.* To become industrial. —**in·dus·tri·al·i·sa·tion** (-lī-záysh'n ‖ *U.S.* -li-) *n.*

in·dus·tri·al·ism (in-dústri-ə-liz'm) *n.* An economic system in which industries are dominant.

in·dus·tri·al·ist (in-dústri-əlist) *n.* A person, such as the owner, the managing director, or a large shareholder of an industrial enterprise, who has a substantial interest in the running and profits of that enterprise.

industrial melanism *n.* Melanism *(see)*.

industrial relations *n.* **1.** *Used with a plural verb.* The relations that exist between the management and workers in an enterprise. **2.** *Used with a singular verb.* The art or study of managing these relations, especially from the point of view of improving them.

industrial revolution *n.* **1.** Social and economic changes brought about when extensive mechanisation of production systems results in a shift from home manufacturing to large-scale factory production. **2.** *Capital* **I,** *capital* **R.** A period of such change beginning in the middle of the 18th century in England. Preceded by *the*.

industrial union *n.* A union to which all the workers of a particular industry can belong regardless of their trade. Also *U.S.* "vertical union". Compare **craft union**.

in·dus·tri·ous (in-dústri-əss) *adj.* **1.** Diligently active; assiduous in work or study. **2.** *Obsolete.* Skilful; clever. —See Synonyms at **busy**. [Latin *industriōsus*, from *industria*, skill, INDUSTRY.] —**in·dus·tri·ous·ly** *adv.* —**in·dus·tri·ous·ness** *n.*

in·dus·try (in-dəss-tri ‖ -duss-) *n., pl.* **-tries.** *Abbr.* **ind. 1.** The commercial production and sale of goods, including the extraction and processing of raw materials and construction. **2.** A particular branch of manufacture and trade: *the textile industry.* **3. a.** Industrial management as distinguished from the work force. **b.** Manufacturing enterprises as distinguished from agriculture. **4.** Diligence; assiduity. **5.** Study or interest in a specified subject, cause, or the like, especially when considered exploitative: *the Shakespeare industry; the race relations industry.* —See Synonyms at **business**. [Middle English *industrie*, skill, diligence, from Old French, from Latin *industria*.]

in·dwell (ín-dwél) *v.* **-dwelt** (-dwélt), **-dwelling, -dwells.** —*intr.* **1.** To abide as a divine inner spirit, force, or principle. Usually used with *in*. **2.** To exist within permanently. Used with *in*. —*tr.* To abide within as a divine spirit, force, or principle. —**in·dwell·er** *n.*

-ine¹ *adj. suffix.* Indicates of, pertaining to, or belonging to; for example, **Ursuline, elephantine.** [Middle English *-ine, -in,* from Old French *-in,* from Latin *-īnus, -inus,* from Greek *-inos.*]

-ine² *n. comb. form.* Also **-in** (for sense 3). *Chemistry.* **1.** Indicates a halogen element; for example, **chlorine, astatine. 2.** Indicates any of various nitrogen-containing compounds, such as: **a.** An amine; for example, **cadaverine. b.** An amino acid; for example, **glycine. c.** An alkaloid; for example, **strychnine. d.** An azine; for example, **induline. 3.** Indicates certain other individual chemical compounds; for example, **glycerine.** [Middle English *-ine,* -INE (pertaining to).]

-ine³ *adj. suffix.* Indicates made of or resembling; for example, **opaline, petaline.** [Middle English *-ine,* -INE (pertaining to).]

in·e·bri·ant (in-éebri-ənt) *adj.* Intoxicating.
~*n.* An intoxicant.

in·e·bri·ate (in-éebri-ayt) *tr.v.* **-ated, -ating, -ates. 1.** To make drunk; intoxicate. **2.** To exhilarate or stupefy with or as if with alcohol.
~*adj.* (in-éebri-ət, -it). Intoxicated.
~*n.* (in-éebri-ət, -it). An intoxicated person; especially, a drunkard. [Latin *inēbriāre* : *in-* (intensive) + *ēbriāre* (past participle *ēbriātus*), to intoxicate, from *ēbrius*.] —**in·e·bri·a·tion** (-áysh'n) *n.*

in·e·bri·at·ed (in-éebri-aytid) *adj.* Exhilarated or confused by or as if by alcohol; intoxicated; drunk.

in·e·bri·e·ty (ínni-brí-əti) *n.* Drunkenness; intoxication.

in·ed·i·ble (in-éddi-b'l, ín-) *adj.* Not suitable for consumption; not edible. —**in·ed·i·bil·i·ty** (-bílləti) *n.*

in·ed·it·ed (in-édditid) *adj.* **1.** Not edited. **2.** Not published.

in·ed·u·ca·ble (in-éddəkwəb'l) *adj.* Not able to be educated; unable to learn.

in·ef·fa·ble (in-éffəb'l) *adj.* **1.** Beyond expression; indescribable or unspeakable: *ineffable delight.* **2.** Not to be uttered; taboo: *the ineffable name of the Deity.* [Middle English, from Old French, from Latin *ineffābilis* : *in-,* not + *effābilis,* EFFABLE.] —**in·ef·fa·bil·i·ty** (-bílləti), **in·ef·fa·ble·ness** *n.* —**in·ef·fa·bly** *adv.*

in·ef·face·a·ble (ínni-fáysə-b'l) *adj.* Not effaceable; indelible. —**in·ef·face·a·bil·i·ty** (-bílloti) *n.* —**in·ef·face·a·bly** *adv.*

in·ef·fec·tive (ínni-féktiv) *adj.* **1.** Not effective; having no effect. **2.** Incompetent; not performing to the required standard. —**in·ef·fec·tive·ly** *adv.* —**in·ef·fec·tive·ness** *n.*

in·ef·fec·tu·al (ínni-fék-choo-əl, -tew-) *adj.* **1.** Not effectual; inad-

equate. **2.** Powerless; lacking in force or competence: *an ineffectual king.* —**in·ef·fec·tu·al·i·ty** (-ál-əti), **in·ef·fec·tu·al·ness** *n.* —**in·ef·fec·tu·al·ly** *adv.*

in·ef·fi·ca·cious (ínnefi-káyshəss) *adj.* Not producing a desired effect or result. —**in·ef·fi·ca·cious·ly** *adv.* —**in·ef·fi·ca·cious·ness** *n.*

in·ef·fi·ca·cy (in-éffika-si) *n.* The state or quality of being inefficacious.

in·ef·fi·cient (inni-fish'nt) *adj.* **1.** Wanting in ability; incompetent. **2.** Wasteful of time, energy, or materials. **3.** Not producing the intended result. —**in·ef·fi·cien·cy** *n.* —**in·ef·fi·cient·ly** *adv.*

in·e·las·tic (inni-lástik, -laástik) *adj.* Not elastic; unyielding; unadaptable. See Synonyms at **stiff**. —**in·e·las·tic·i·ty** (-la-stíssəti) *n.*

in·el·e·gant (in-élligənt) *adj.* **1.** Lacking elegance or polish. **2.** Coarse; vulgar. [Old French, from Latin *inēlegāns* : *in-,* not + *ēlegāns,* ELEGANT.] —**in·el·e·gant·ly** *adv.* —**in·el·e·gance** *n.*

in·el·i·gi·ble (in-éllija-b'l) *adj.* **1.** Not qualified; not fulfilling the necessary conditions: *ineligible to enter the competition.* **2.** Not worthy of being chosen.
~*n.* A person who is not eligible. —**in·el·i·gi·bil·i·ty** (-billəti) *n.* —**in·el·i·gi·bly** *adv.*

in·el·o·quent (in-éllakwənt) *adj.* Not eloquent; not fluent or vivid in expression. —**in·el·o·quence** *n.* —**in·el·o·quent·ly** *adv.*

in·e·luc·ta·ble (inni-lúktə-b'l) *adj.* Not to be avoided or overcome; inevitable. [Latin *inēluctābilis* : *in-,* not + *ēluctārī,* to struggle out : *ex-,* out + *luctārī,* to struggle.] —**in·e·luc·ta·bil·i·ty** (-bílləti) *n.* —**in·e·luc·ta·bly** *adv.*

in·ept (in-épt) *adj.* **1.** Not apt or fitting; unsuitable; inappropriate: *an inept comparison.* See Usage note at **inapt**. **2.** Not sensible; foolish: *an inept remark.* **3.** Awkward; clumsy; incompetent. —See Synonyms at **awkward**. [Latin *ineptus* : *in-,* not + *aptus,* APT.] —**in·ept·ly** *adv.* —**in·ept·ness** *n.*

in·ep·ti·tude (in-épti-tewd ‖ -tōōd) *n.* **1.** The quality of being inept. **2.** An inept act or remark.

in·e·qua·ble (in-ékwəb'l) *adj.* Not uniform; unevenly distributed.

in·e·qual·i·ty (ínni-kwóllati) *n., pl.* **-ties. 1.** The condition of being unequal. **2.** Lack of equality, as of opportunity, distribution of wealth, or the like. **3.** Unevenness; lack of smoothness or regularity. **4.** Variability; changeability. **5.** An instance of being unequal. **6.** *Mathematics.* An algebraic statement that a quantity is greater than another quantity or that it is less than another quantity.

in·eq·ui·ta·ble (in-ékwitəb'l) *adj.* Not equitable; unfair; unjust. —**in·eq·ui·ta·ble·ness** *n.* —**in·eq·ui·ta·bly** *adv.*

in·eq·ui·ty (in-ékwəti) *n., pl.* **-ties. 1.** Lack of equity; injustice; unfairness. **2.** An instance of injustice or unfairness.

in·e·rad·i·ca·ble (ínni-ráddikəb'l) *adj.* That cannot be uprooted, eradicated, or erased. —**in·e·rad·i·ca·ble·ness** *n.* —**in·e·rad·i·ca·bly** *adv.*

in·er·ra·ble (in-érra-b'l, -ér-ə-) *adj.* Inerrant. —**in·er·ra·bil·i·ty** (-billəti), **in·er·ra·ble·ness** *n.* —**in·er·ra·bly** *adv.*

in·er·rant (in-érrənt ‖ -ér-ənt) *adj.* Making no errors; unerring. —**in·er·ran·cy** *n.*

in·ert (in-ért) *adj.* **1.** Inherently unable to move or act. **2.** Resisting motion or action; sluggish. **3.** *Chemistry.* **a.** Exhibiting no chemical activity; totally unreactive. **b.** Exhibiting chemical activity under special or extreme conditions only. —See Synonyms at **inactive**. [Latin *iners* (stem *inert-*), inactive, unskilled : *in-,* not + *ars,* skill, ART.] —**in·ert·ly** *adv.* —**in·ert·ness** *n.*

inert gas *n.* Any of the elements helium, neon, argon, krypton, xenon, and radon that were formerly thought to be completely inert but which are now known to form some compounds. Also called "rare gas".

in·er·tia (in-érsh-ə, -i-ə) *n.* **1.** *Physics.* **a.** The tendency of a body to resist acceleration. **b.** The tendency of a body at rest to remain at rest or of a body in motion to stay in motion in a straight line unless disturbed by an external force. **2.** Resistance or disinclination to motion, action, or change. **3.** *Medicine.* Reduction or absence of activity in certain smooth muscles: *uterine inertia.* [New Latin, from Latin, lack of skill, idleness, from *iners,* INERT.]

in·er·tial (in-érsh'l) *adj.* **1.** Of or pertaining to inertia. **2.** Arising from or depending upon the effects of inertia. **3.** Referred to an inertial frame of reference.

inertial frame *n.* Any frame of reference relative to which the Newtonian law of motion, that a mass m subjected to a force F moves in accordance with the equation $F = ma$, where a is the acceleration, is valid. Also called "inertial system", "Newtonian frame".

inertial guidance *n.* Guidance of a missile in which data from a gyroscope and an accelerometer are used by a computer to maintain a predetermined course.

inertial mass *n.* The mass of a body as determined by its momentum. Compare **gravitational mass**.

in·er·tia-reel seat belt (in-érsha-reel) *n.* A type of seat belt used in cars, in which the belt is only restrained from unwinding from a metal drum when the car is decelerating. The occupant of the seat therefore has freedom of movement except during a collision or very sharp braking.

inertia selling *n. British.* The illegal sending of unrequested goods to people in the hope that they will not be returned and payment can be demanded.

inertia welding *n.* The welding together of two metal parts caused by the heat of friction when a spinning part is pressed against a stationary part.

in·es·cap·a·ble (ínni-skáypə-b'l) *adj.* That cannot be escaped; un-

avoidable; inevitable. —**in·es·cap·a·bil·i·ty** (-bílləti) *n.* —**in·es·cap·a·bly** *adv.*
in·es·cutch·eon (ínni-skúchən) *n. Heraldry.* A small escutcheon placed at the centre of a larger escutcheon.
in es·se (in éssi) *adj. Latin.* In actual existence. Compare **in posse.**
in·es·sen·tial (ínni-sénsh'l) *adj.* **1.** Not essential; unnecessary. **2.** Without essence.
~*n.* Something inessential. —**in·es·sen·ti·al·i·ty** (-sénshi-ál-əti) *n.*
in·es·ti·ma·ble (in-éstimab'l) *adj.* **1.** Incapable of being estimated or computed; indeterminable: *inestimable damage.* **2.** Of incalculable value. —**in·es·ti·ma·bly** *adv.*
in·ev·i·ta·ble (in-évvitə-b'l) *adj.* **1.** Incapable of being avoided or evaded. **2.** That cannot be prevented; certain to take place. **3.** Invariably appearing or occurring; predictable: *made the inevitable jokes about the bridegroom.*
~*n.* Something that is inevitable. Preceded by *the.* —**in·ev·i·ta·bil·i·ty** (-bílləti), **in·ev·i·ta·ble·ness** *n.* —**in·ev·i·ta·bly** *adv.*
in·ex·act (ín-ig-zákt || -eg-, -ik-) *adj.* Not exact; not quite accurate or precise. —**in·ex·act·ly** *adv.* —**in·ex·act·ness** *n.*
in·ex·act·i·tude (ín-ig-zákti-tewd || -eg-, -ik-, -tōōd) *n.* **1.** Lack of exactness. **2.** An example thereof: *a terminological inexactitude.*
in·ex·cus·a·ble (ínnik-skéwzəb'l) *adj.* Not excusable; unpardonable. —**in·ex·cus·a·bil·i·ty** (-bílləti), **in·ex·cus·a·ble·ness** *n.* —**in·ex·cus·a·bly** *adv.*
in·ex·haust·i·ble (ín-ig-záwstə-b'l || -eg-, -ik-) *adj.* **1.** Incapable of being exhausted or used up. **2.** Unfailing; tireless; indefatigable. —**in·ex·haust·i·bil·i·ty** (-bílləti), **in·ex·haust·i·ble·ness** *n.* —**in·ex·haust·i·bly** *adv.*
in·ex·o·ra·ble (in-éksərə-b'l) *adj.* **1.** Not capable of being persuaded by entreaty; unyielding: *"and more inexorable far / Than empty tigers or the roaring sea."* (Shakespeare). **2.** Relentless; unremitting. [Latin *inexōrābilis* : *in-*, not + *exōrābilis,* from *exōrāre,* to move by entreaty, from *ex-*, completely + *ōrāre,* to plead.] —**in·ex·ora·bil·i·ty** (-bílləti), **in·ex·o·ra·ble·ness** *n.* —**in·ex·o·ra·bly** *adv.*
in·ex·pe·di·ent (ín-ik-spéedi-ənt, -ek-) *adj.* Not expedient; inadvisable. —**in·ex·pe·di·ence, in·ex·pe·di·en·cy** *n.* —**in·ex·pe·di·ent·ly** *adv.*
in·ex·pen·sive (ín-ik-spén-siv || -ek-) *adj.* Not expensive; fairly cheap. —**in·ex·pen·sive·ly** *adv.* —**in·ex·pen·sive·ness** *n.*
in·ex·pe·ri·ence (ín-ik-spéer-i-ənss || -ek-) *n.* Lack of experience.
in·ex·pe·ri·enced (ín-ik-spéer-i-ənst || -ek-) *adj.* Lacking experience and the knowledge gained from experience.
in·ex·pert (in-ék-spert, ín-ek-spért) *adj.* Not expert; not skilful or adept. —**in·ex·pert·ly** *adv.* —**in·ex·pert·ness** *n.*
in·ex·pi·a·ble (in-ék-spi-əb'l) *adj.* **1.** Not capable of being expiated or atoned for: *inexpiable crimes.* **2.** *Archaic.* Implacable; unrelenting. —**in·ex·pi·a·ble·ness** *n.* —**in·ex·pi·a·bly** *adv.*
in·ex·pli·ca·ble (ín-ik-splíckə-b'l, -ek-, in-ék-splikə-) *adj.* Not explicable; not capable of being explained or accounted for. —**in·ex·pli·ca·bil·i·ty** (-bílləti), **in·ex·pli·ca·ble·ness** *n.* —**in·ex·pli·ca·bly** *adv.*
in·ex·plic·it (ín-ik-splíssit, -ek-) *adj.* Not explicit; indefinite; vague.
in·ex·press·i·ble (ín-ik-spréssə-b'l, -ek-) *adj.* Not capable of being expressed; indescribable: *inexpressible joy.* —**in·ex·press·i·bil·i·ty** (-bílləti), **in·ex·press·i·ble·ness** *n.* —**in·ex·press·i·bly** *adv.*
in·ex·pres·sive (ín-ik-spréssiv, -ek-) *adj.* **1.** Expressing nothing or little. **2.** *Archaic.* Inexpressible. —**in·ex·pres·sive·ness** *n.* —**in·ex·pres·sive·ly** *adv.*
in·ex·pug·na·ble (ín-ik-spúgnəb'l, -ek- || -spéwn-) *adj.* Not expugnable; impregnable. —**in·ex·pug·na·bly** *adv.*
in·ex·pung·i·ble (ín-ik-spúnjib'l, -ek-) *adj.* Incapable of being expunged or obliterated.
in·ex·ten·si·ble (ín-ik-stén-sib'l, -ek-) *adj.* Not extensible; unable to be extended.
in ex·ten·so (in ik-stén-sō) *adv. Latin.* At full length; in full: *His article was published in extenso.*
in·ex·tin·guish·a·ble (ín-ik-stíng-gwishəb'l, -ek-) *adj.* Not capable of being extinguished or quenched. —**in·ex·tin·guish·a·ble·ness** *n.* —**in·ex·tin·guish·a·bly** *adv.*
in ex·tre·mis (in ek-strée-meess, ik-, -miss) *adv.* **1.** At the point of death. **2.** In grave difficulties. [Latin, "in the last (straits)".]
in·ex·tri·ca·ble (in-ék-strikə-b'l, ínnik-stríckə-) *adj.* **1. a.** Incapable of being disentangled or untied. **b.** Too intricate or complicated to solve. **2. a.** Firmly resisting one's attempts at escape or resolution: *an inextricable quandary.* **b.** Incapable of being freed: *The screws were rusted in and quite inextricable.* —**in·ex·tri·ca·bil·i·ty** (-billəti), **in·ex·tri·ca·ble·ness** *n.* —**in·ex·tri·ca·bly** *adv.*
inf. **1.** infantry. **2.** inferior. **3.** infinitive. **4.** influence. **5.** information.
Inf. infantry.
in·fal·li·bil·ism (in-fál-əb'l-izm) *n. Roman Catholic Church.* The principle of the pope's infallibility. —**in·fal·li·bil·ist** *n.*
in·fal·li·ble (in-fál-əb'l) *adj.* **1.** Incapable of erring; entirely dependable: *an infallible source of information.* **2.** Incapable of failing; certain: *an infallible antidote.* **3.** Incapable of error in expounding doctrine on faith or morals. Said especially of the pope speaking ex cathedra. [French, from Medieval Latin *infallibilis* : *in-*, not + *fallibilis,* FALLIBLE.] —**in·fal·li·bil·i·ty** (-ə-bílləti), **in·fal·li·ble·ness** *n.* —**in·fal·li·bly** *adv.*
in·fa·mous (ínfəməss) *adj.* **1.** Having an exceedingly bad reputation; notorious. **2.** Causing or deserving infamy; loathsome; grossly shocking: *an infamous deed.* **3.** *Law.* **a.** Formerly, deprived of all or some civil rights as a result of being convicted of certain serious crimes. **b.** Designating a crime, such as treason or perjury that entailed this deprivation. —See Synonyms at **outrageous, mean** (base). [Middle English, from Medieval Latin *infamōsus,* from Latin *infāmis* : *in-*, not + *fāma,* FAME.] —**in·fa·mous·ly** *adv.* —**in·fa·mous·ness** *n.*
in·fa·my (ínfəmi) *n., pl.* **-mies.** **1.** Evil fame or reputation. **2.** The condition of being infamous. **3.** An infamous act. —See Synonyms at **disgrace.** [Middle English *infamye,* from Old French *infamie, infame,* from Latin *infāmia,* from *infāmis,* INFAMOUS.]
in·fan·cy (ínfən-si) *n., pl.* **-cies.** **1.** The state or period of being an infant. **2.** The earliest years or stage of something: *television in its infancy.* **3.** *Law.* The state or period of being a minor.
in·fant (ínfənt) *n.* **1.** A child in the earliest period of its life; a baby. **2.** *Law.* One under the legal age of majority; a minor. **3.** *British.* A schoolchild under a certain age, usually under eight.
~*adj.* **1.** Of or being in infancy. **2.** Intended for infants or very young children. **3.** Young and growing: *an infant enterprise.* [Middle English *enfaunt,* from Old French *enfant,* from Latin *infāns,* "(one) unable to speak" : *in-*, not + *fāns* (stem *fant-*), present participle of *fārī,* to speak.]
in·fan·ta (in-fántə || *U.S. also* -fáantə) *n.* **1.** A daughter of a Spanish or Portuguese king. **2.** The wife of an infante. [Spanish, feminine of *infante,* INFANTE.]
in·fan·te (in-fán-tay || *U.S. also* -faan-) *n.* Any son of a Spanish or Portuguese king other than the heir to the throne. [Spanish and Portuguese, "infant", from Latin *infāns,* INFANT.]
in·fan·ti·cide (in-fánti-sīd) *n.* **1. a.** The killing of an infant. **b.** *Law.* The killing by its mother of a child under one year old. **2.** A person who kills an infant. **3.** The practice of killing infants. [Late Latin *infanticidium* (killing) and *infanticida* (killer) : Latin *infāns,* INFANT + *-cidium, -cida,* -CIDE.] —**in·fan·ti·cid·al** (-sīd'l).
in·fan·tile (ínfən-tīl || *U.S. also* -t'l, -teel) *adj.* **1.** Of or pertaining to infants or infancy. **2.** Lacking maturity, sophistication, or reasonableness. **3.** *Pathology.* Designating diseases occurring in adults that are recognisable in childhood: *infantile paralysis.* [French, from *infantilis,* from *infāns,* INFANT.]
infantile autism *n. Psychology.* **Autism** *(see).*
infantile paralysis *n. Pathology.* **Poliomyelitis** *(see).*
in·fan·til·ise, in·fan·til·ize (in-fánti-līz) *tr.v.* **-ised, -ising, -ises.** To treat (a person, especially an adolescent) as if still at an early stage of development.
in·fan·til·ism (in-fántil-iz'm || ínfəntīl-) *n.* **1.** A state of arrested development in an adult, characterised by a retention of infantile mentality accompanied by stunted growth and sexual immaturity. **2.** Childish behaviour or speech.
infant mortality rate *n.* The number of deaths of infants aged under one year for every 1000 live births, occurring in any one year.
in·fan·try (ínfəntri) *n., pl.* **-tries.** *Abbr.* **Inf., inf.** The branch of an army made up of units trained to fight on foot. [French *infanterie,* from Italian *infanteria,* from *infante,* youth, foot soldier, from Latin *infāns,* INFANT.]
in·fan·try·man (ínfəntri-mən, -man) *n., pl.* **-men** (-mən, -men). A soldier serving in the infantry.
infant school *n. British.* A school for children aged between approximately five and seven years. Compare **junior school.**
in·farct (in-fárkt, ín-faarkt) *n.* Also **in·farc·tion** (in-fárksh'n). A dead area of tissue resulting from failure of local blood supply. [New Latin *infarctus,* from Latin *infarctus, infartus,* past participle of *infarcīre,* to stuff in, cram : *in-*, in + *farcīre,* to stuff.]
in·farc·tion (in-fárksh'n) *n.* **1.** Death of an organ or part of an organ that occurs when its blood supply is obstructed by a blood clot or embolus. **2.** An infarct.
in·fat·u·ate (in-fáttew-ayt) *tr.v.* **-ated, -ating, -ates.** **1.** To cause to behave foolishly. **2.** To inspire with powerful but foolish and unreasoning passion or attraction.
~*adj.* (-ət, -ayt). *Archaic.* Infatuated. [Latin *infatuāre* : *in-* (causative) + *fatuus,* FATUOUS.]
in·fat·u·at·ed (in-fáttew-aytid) *adj.* Possessed by a powerful, unreasoning, often short-lived, passion or attraction. —**in·fat·u·at·ed·ly** *adv.*
in·fat·u·a·tion (in-fáttew-áysh'n) *n.* **1.** The state or an instance of being infatuated. **2.** An object of extravagant, short-lived passion. —See Synonyms at **love.**
in·fau·na (ín-faw-nə) *n., pl.* **-nas** or **-nae** (-nee). The mass of aquatic animals that live just beneath the bed of a sea, lake, or river. [Danish *ifauna* : IN- + FAUNA.]
in·fea·si·ble (in-féezəb'l) *adj.* Not feasible; impracticable.
in·fect (in-fékt) *tr.v.* **-fected, -fecting, -fects.** **1.** To contaminate with pathogenic microorganisms. **2.** To communicate a disease to (another person). **3.** To invade and produce infection in. **4.** To corrupt; contaminate. **5.** To affect as if by contagion. [Middle English *infecten,* from Latin *inficere* (past participle *infectus*), to work in, dye, taint : *in-*, in + *facere,* to do.]
in·fec·tion (in-féksh'n) *n.* **1.** Invasion of the body by pathogenic microorganisms. **2.** An instance of such invasion. **3.** The pathological state resulting from such invasion, characterised by inflammation and tissue damage due to the action of toxins produced by the microorganisms. **4.** An agent or contaminated substance responsible for such invasion. **5.** An infectious disease. **6. a.** Moral contamination or corruption, as by the communication of harmful influences. **b.** The communication or spreading from one to another of ideas, emotions, or the like, as if by contagion.
in·fec·tious (in-fékshəss) *adj.* **1.** Capable of causing infection. **2.** Capable of being transmitted by infection without actual con-

tact; communicable. Said of a disease. Compare **contagious.** **3.** Caused by a microorganism. Said of a disease. **4.** Tending to spread or affect others easily: *an infectious chuckle.* **—in·fec·tious·ly** *adv.* **—in·fec·tious·ness** *n.*

infectious enterohepatitis *n.* In veterinary medicine, the disease **blackhead.**

infectious hepatitis *n.* See **hepatitis.**

infectious mononucleosis *n.* **Glandular fever** *(see).*

in·fec·tive (in-féktiv) *adj.* Capable of producing infection; infectious. **—in·fec·tive·ness, in·fec·tiv·i·ty** (ínfek-tívvəti) *n.*

in·fe·lic·i·tous (ínfi-lissitəss) *adj.* **1.** Not happy; unfortunate; sad. **2.** Inappropriate; inapt, as in style or manner of expression. **—in·fe·lic·i·tous·ly** *adv.*

in·fe·lic·i·ty (ínfi-lissəti) *n., pl.* **-ties. 1.** The quality or condition of being infelicitous. **2.** Something inappropriate or inapt. [Middle English *infelicite,* from Latin *infēlīcitās,* from *infēlix,* unhappy : *in-,* not + *fēlix,* happy.]

in·fer (in-fér) *v.* **-ferred, -ferring, -fers.** *—tr.* **1.** To conclude from evidence; deduce. **2.** *Nonstandard.* To suggest; imply. See Usage note at **imply.** *—intr.* To draw inferences. [Old French *inferer,* from Latin *inferre,* to bring in, introduce, deduce : *in-,* in- + *ferre,* to bear.] **—in·fer·a·ble** *adj.* **—in·fer·a·bly** *adv.*

in·fer·ence (ín-fərənss, -frənss) *n.* **1.** The act or process of inferring. **2.** Something inferred; a conclusion based on a premise. **3.** *Logic.* A process of reasoning consisting of forming conclusions from premises.

in·fer·en·tial (ínfə-rénsh'l) *adj.* Derived or capable of being derived from inference. **—in·fer·en·tial·ly** *adv.*

in·fe·ri·or (in-féer-i-ər) *adj. Abbr.* **inf. 1. a.** Low or lower in quality, status, or estimation. **b.** Mediocre; second-rate. **2.** Low or lower in order, degree, or rank. **3.** Situated under or beneath. **4.** *Botany.* Located below the perianth and other floral parts. Said of an ovary. **5.** *Printing.* Set below the normal line. Said of type. **6.** *Astronomy.* **a.** Orbiting between the Sun and the Earth: *an inferior planet.* **b.** Lying below the horizon.
~n. **1.** A person of lesser rank or status than another. **2.** *Printing.* An inferior character. [Middle English, from Latin *īnferior,* comparative of *īnferus,* low.] **—in·fe·ri·or·i·ty** (-órrəti) *n.*

inferior court *n.* A court of law of lower rank than another, usually with a limited jurisdiction, the decisions of which are subject to appeal to a superior court, as for example the county and magistrates' courts in England and the sheriff and district courts in Scotland.

inferiority complex *n.* A neurotic condition resulting from a persistent, unrealistic sense of inadequacy, characterised by withdrawal or by compensatory and often aggressive attempts to attract attention.

in·fer·nal (in-férn'l) *adj.* **1.** Of or pertaining to the world of the dead in classical mythology. **2.** Of, pertaining to, or characteristic of hell or those in it. **3.** Abominable; damnable: *Stop that infernal racket!* [Middle English, from Old French, from Late Latin *īnfernālis,* from *īnfernus,* hell, from Latin, lower.] **—in·fer·nal·ly** *adv.*

infernal machine *n. Archaic.* An explosive device maliciously designed to harm or destroy.

in·fer·no (in-férnō) *n., pl.* **-nos. 1.** *Often capital* **I.** Hell. **2.** Any place or situation likened to hell; especially, a conflagration. [Italian, hell, from Late Latin *īnfernus.* See **infernal.**]

in·fer·tile (in-fér-tīl || *U.S.* -t'l) *adj.* **1.** Not fertile; unproductive; barren. **2.** Incapable of producing offspring. —See Synonyms at **sterile. —in·fer·til·i·ty** (ínfər-tílləti) *n.*

in·fest (in-fést) *tr.v.* **-fested, -festing, -fests. 1.** To inhabit or overrun in large numbers so as to be harmful or unpleasant. **2.** To invade and live on or within a living organism. Said of animal parasites, such as ticks and tapeworms. [Middle English *infesten,* to attack, molest, trouble, from Old French *infester,* from Latin *infestāre,* from *infestus,* hostile. **—in·fes·ta·tion** (ínfess-táysh'n) *n.*

in·feu·da·tion (infew-dáysh'n) *n.* In feudal society: **1.** The process of granting legal possession of an estate. **2.** The deed used for this.

in·fib·u·late (in-fíbbew-layt) *tr.v.* **-lated, -lating, -lates.** To enclose or fasten (especially, the female genitals) with a clasp or stitches to prevent sexual intercourse. [Latin *infībulāre* : IN- + *fībula,* clasp.] **—in·fib·u·la·tion** (-láysh'n) *n.*

in·fi·del (ínfi-d'l, -del) *n.* **1.** One who has no religious beliefs. **2.** One who is an unbeliever with respect to a particular religion, especially Christianity or Islam. [Middle English *infydel,* from Old French *infidel,* from Latin *infidēlis,* unfaithful : *in-,* not + *fidēs,* faith.] **—in·fi·del** *adj.*

in·fi·del·i·ty (ínfi-délləti) *n., pl.* **-ties. 1.** Lack of fidelity or loyalty. **2.** Unfaithfulness to a sexual partner, especially a spouse. **3.** An act of disloyalty or sexual unfaithfulness. **4.** Lack of religious faith, especially in Christianity or Islam.

in·field (ín-feeld) *n.* **1.** A field located near a farmhouse. **2.** In cricket, the area of the field close to and around the wicket. **3.** In baseball: **a.** The area of the field enclosed by the bases. **b.** The defensive positions of first base, second base, third base, and shortstop. Compare **outfield.**

in·field·er (ín-feeldər) *n.* A player who plays in the infield. Also called "infieldsman".

in·fight·ing (ín-fīting) *n.* **1.** Rivalry or competition, often bitter, between members of the same group or organisation: *political infighting.* **2.** In boxing, hitting at close range, especially in order to tire out one's opponent. **—in·fight·er** *n.*

in·fil·trate (ínfil-trayt, in-fíl) *v.* **-trated, -trating, -trates.** *—tr.* **1.** To pass (a liquid or gas) into something through its interstices. **2.** To permeate with a liquid or gas passed through interstices. **3.** To send (troops, for example) surreptitiously into enemy-held territory. **4.** To gain entry or cause to gain entry to (an organisation or political party, for example) surreptitiously, and with subversive intent. *—intr.* To gain entrance gradually or surreptitiously.
~n. Any substance that accumulates gradually in bodily tissues.

in·fil·tra·tion (ínfil-tráysh'n) *n.* **1.** The act or process of infiltrating. **2.** The state of being infiltrated. **3.** Something that infiltrates. **—in·fil·tra·tive** (-trətiv, in-fíl-) *adj.* **—in·fil·tra·tor** *n.*

infin. infinitive.

in·fi·nite (ínfi-nət, -nit; *also, chiefly for sense 5,* -nīt) *adj.* **1.** Having no boundaries or limits. **2.** Immeasurably or uncountably large. **3.** *Mathematics.* **a.** Existing beyond or being greater than any arbitrarily large value. **b.** Unlimited in spatial extent. **c.** Of or designating a set capable of being put into one-to-one correspondence with a proper subset of itself. **4.** Continuing endlessly in time, space, extent, or magnitude. **5.** All-encompassing; total: *God's infinite love.*
~n. Something infinite; infinity. Preceded by *the.* **—the Infinite (Being).** God. [Middle English *infinit,* from Old French, from Latin *infīnītus* : *in-,* not + *fīnītus,* FINITE.] **—in·fi·nite·ly** *adv.* **—in·fi·nite·ness** *n.*

Synonyms: *infinite, limitless, illimitable, boundless, measureless, eternal, innumerable, numberless, countless.*

in·fin·i·tes·i·mal (ínfini-téssi-m'l || *U.S. also* -téezi-) *adj.* **1.** Immeasurably or incalculably minute. **2.** Loosely, very small; minute. **3.** *Mathematics.* Capable of having values arbitrarily close to zero. —See Synonyms at **small.**
~n. **1.** An infinitesimal amount or quantity. **2.** *Mathematics.* A function having values arbitrarily close to zero. [New Latin *infinitesimus* : Latin *infīnītus,* INFINITE + *-esimus,* ordinal suffix.] **—in·fi·i·tes·i·mal·ly** *adv.*

infinitesimal calculus *n.* Differential and integral calculus.

in·fin·i·tive (in-fínnətiv) *n. Abbr.* **inf., infin.** *Grammar.* **1.** A verb form that is not inflected to indicate person, number, or tense. **2.** Such a verb form used in English: **a.** To serve as a substantive while retaining some verbal aspects, such as modification by adverbs and connection with an object, preceded by *to;* for example, *To go willingly is to show strength.* **b.** To form verb phrases, preceded by *to;* for example, *He wished to go.* In this usage, the *to* may be dropped with certain verbs; for example, *He may go.*
~adj. Of, pertaining to, or using the infinitive. [Late Latin *infīnītīvus,* "unlimited" (because it has no definite numbers or persons), from Latin *infīnītus,* INFINITE.] **—in·fin·i·ti·val** (ínfini-tīv'l, in-fínni-)

in·fin·i·tude (in-fínni-tewd || -tōōd) *n.* **1.** The state or quality of being infinite. **2.** An infinite quantity, number, or extent.

in·fin·i·ty (in-fínnəti) *n., pl.* **-ties. 1.** The quality or condition of being infinite. **2.** Unbounded space, time, or quantity. **3.** An indefinitely large number or amount. **4.** *Mathematics.* The limit that a function f is said to approach at $x = a$ when for x close to a, $f(x)$ is larger than any preassigned number. **5.** A point that is sufficiently far away from a lens or mirror for it to be assumed that light emitted by it will fall in parallel rays on the lens or mirror.

in·firm (in-fúrm, ín-) *adj.* **1.** Weak in body, especially from old age; feeble. **2.** Lacking moral firmness; irresolute. —See Synonyms at **weak.** [Middle English *infirme,* from Latin *infirmus* : *in-,* not + *firmus,* FIRM.] **—in·firm·ly** *adv.* **—in·firm·ness** *n.*

in·fir·ma·ry (in-fúrməri) *n., pl.* **-ries.** A place for the care of the sick or injured; especially, a hospital or dispensary. [Medieval Latin *infirmāria,* from Latin *infirmus,* INFIRM.]

in·fir·mi·ty (in-fúrməti) *n., pl.* **-ties. 1.** A disability, especially one caused by an illness or old age. **2.** Bodily weakness; frailty. **3.** Moral weakness.

in·fix (in-fíks, ín-fikss) *tr.v.* **-fixed, -fixing, -fixes. 1.** To fix into another. **2.** To fix in the mind; inculcate; instil. **3.** *Grammar.* To insert (a morphological element) as an infix.
~n. (ín-fiks). *Grammar.* **1.** An inflectional or derivational element inserted into the body of a word; for example, an infix *-n-* is added to the Old Latin verb root *frag-,* "break", to form the imperfective *frang-,* "is breaking". **2.** An intermediate letter or sound, in English usually a vowel, that connects the elements of a compound word; for example, the *-o-* in *meritocracy* is an infix. [Latin *infigere* (past participle *infixus*) : *in-,* in + *fīgere,* to FIX.]

infl. influence; influenced.

in fla·gran·te de·lic·to (in flə-gránti di-líktō) *adv. Law.* Also *Informal.* **in fla·gran·te.** In the actual act of committing an offence; red-handed. [Latin, with the crime still blazing.]

in·flame (in-fláym) *v.* **-flamed, -flaming, -flames.** *—tr.* **1.** To set on fire; kindle. **2. a.** To arouse or excite into a state of strong emotion or passion. **b.** To arouse (strong emotion or passion) in. **3.** To intensify intolerably: *"inflamed to madness an already savage nature"* (Robert Graves). **4.** To produce inflammation in. *—intr.* **1.** To catch fire. **2.** To become excited or aroused. **3.** To be affected by inflammation. [Middle English *inflamen,* from Old French *enflammer,* from Latin *inflammāre* : *in-* (intensive) + *flammāre,* to set on fire, from *flamma,* FLAME.]

in·flam·ma·ble (in-flámmə-b'l) *adj.* **1.** Tending to ignite easily and burn rapidly; flammable. **2.** Quickly or easily aroused to strong emotion; passionate. See Usage note at **flammable.**
~n. Something flammable. [French, from Medieval Latin *inflammābilis,* from Latin *inflammāre,* to INFLAME.] **—in·flam·ma·bil·i·ty** (-bílləti), **in·flam·ma·ble·ness** *n.* **—in·flam·ma·bly** *adv.*

in·flam·ma·tion (ínflə-máysh'n) *n.* **1.** The act of inflaming or the state of being inflamed. **2.** Localised heat, redness, swelling, and pain as a result of irritation, injury, or infection.

in·flam·ma·to·ry (in-flámmə-təri, -tri) *adj.* **1.** Arousing strong emotion, especially anger or aggression. **2.** Characterised or caused by inflammation.

in·fla·ta·ble (in-fláytəb'l) *adj.* Having to be inflated for use: *an inflatable rubber dinghy.*
~*n.* Any object that can be inflated; especially, a large inflatable object made of sturdy material and used for children to play on.

in·flate (in-fláyt) *v.* **-flated, -flating, -flates.** —*tr.* **1.** To fill and swell with a gas. **2.** To cause to increase unduly: *Success inflated his ego.* **3.** *Economics.* To raise or expand abnormally, as prices, wages, or circulating currency. —*intr.* To become inflated. [Latin *inflāre,* to blow into : *in-,* in, + *flāre,* to blow.] —**in·flat·er, in·flat·or** *n.*

in·flat·ed (in-fláytid) *adj.* **1.** Distended or expanded by or as if by gas or air. **2.** Unduly increased or puffed up: *inflated ideas.* **3.** Increased or raised to abnormal economic levels: *inflated wages.* **4.** Resulting from inflation. **5.** *Botany.* Hollow and enlarged: *an inflated calyx.* —**in·flat·ed·ness** *n.*

in·fla·tion (in-fláysh'n) *n.* **1.** The act of inflating or the state of being inflated. **2.** *Economics.* A continuing increase in available currency and credit beyond the proportion of available goods, or an increase in the costs of production, resulting in a sharp and continuing rise in price levels and a fall in the purchasing power of money. Compare **deflation.** See **cost-push, demand-pull.**

in·fla·tion·ar·y (in-fláy-sh'n-əri, -ri ‖ -erri) *adj. Economics.* Pertaining to or tending to cause inflation.

inflationary spiral *n. Economics.* Continually increasing inflation attributed to the mutually reinforcing effects of rising costs, wages, or the like interacting with rising prices.

in·fla·tion·ist (in-fláysh'n-ist) *n.* One who advocates inflation by increasing the supply of available currency and credit. —**in·fla·tion·ism** *n.*

in·fla·tion-proof (in-fláysh'n-prōōf ‖ -prōof) *adj.* Increasing in value at the same rate as inflation: *an inflation-proof investment.*
~*tr.v.* **inflation-proofed, -proofing, -proofs.** To make the value of (pensions, wages, or the like) rise at the same rate as inflation.

in·flect (in-flékt) *v.* **-flected, -flecting, -flects.** —*tr.* **1.** To turn from a course or alignment; bend. **2.** To alter (the voice) in tone or pitch; modulate. **3.** *Grammar.* To alter (a word) as by conjugating or declining. —*intr. Grammar.* To be modified by inflection. [Middle English *inflecten,* from Latin *inflectere,* to bend, warp, change : *in-* (intensive) + *flectere,* to bend.] —**in·flec·tive** *adj.* —**in·flec·tor** *n.*

in·flec·tion (in-fléksh'n) *n.* Also chiefly British **in·flex·ion.** **1.** The act of inflecting or a state of being inflected. **2.** An alteration in pitch or tone of the voice. **3.** *Grammar.* **a.** An alteration of the form of a word, usually by means of affixes, to indicate different grammatical and syntactical relations, such as the declension of nouns, adjectives, and pronouns or the conjugation of verbs. **b.** An element added to a word to denote a grammatical function, such as the *s* in *apples* indicating the plural form or the *'s* in *girl's* indicating the possessive case. **c.** An inflected form of a word. **4.** *Mathematics.* A change in direction of a geometric curve, occurring at a point (the *point of inflection*) at which the curvature of the curve changes sign. —**in·flec·tion·al** *adj.* —**in·flec·tion·al·ly** *adv.*

in·flexed (in-flékst) *adj.* Bent or curved inwards or downwards, as petals or sepals. [Latin *inflexus,* past participle of *inflectere,* to bend, INFLECT.]

in·flex·i·ble (in-flék-səb'l) *adj.* **1.** Not flexible; stiff; rigid. **2.** Incapable of being changed; unalterable: *inflexible rules.* **3.** Rigidly adhering to a purpose or stance; unyielding. —See Synonyms at **stiff.** —**in·flex·i·bil·i·ty** (-sə-bíllə́ti), **in·flex·i·ble·ness** *n.* —**in·flex·i·bly** *adv.*

Synonyms: inflexible, unyielding, inexorable, adamant, obdurate.

in·flict (in-flíkt) *tr.v.* **-flicted, -flicting, -flicts.** **1.** To deal or give (a blow, wound, or the like). Used with *on* or *upon.* **2.** To impose (someone or something considered unpleasant): *"malignant Nature, who reserves the right to inflict upon her children the most terrifying jests"* (Thornton Wilder). [Latin *inflīgere* (past participle *inflictus*) : *in-,* on + *flīgere,* to strike.] —**in·flict·er, in·flic·tor** (-flíktər) *n.* —**in·flic·tive** *adj.*

Usage: Inflict is sometimes confused with *afflict,* but their meanings are different. Something (such as a heavy burden) is *inflicted on* a person; but a person is *afflicted with* something (such as some form of suffering).

in·flic·tion (in-flíksh'n) *n.* **1.** The act or process of inflicting. **2.** Something inflicted, such as blows or punishment.

in-flight (ín-flīt, -flĭt) *adj.* **1.** Carried out or made while in flight: *in-flight refuelling.* **2.** Provided for use or enjoyment while in flight: *in-flight entertainment.*

in·flo·res·cence (ín-flaw-réssənss, -flə-) *n.* **1.** *Botany.* **a.** A characteristic arrangement of flowers on a single main stalk. **b.** The part of a plant consisting of the flower-bearing stalk. **2.** A flowering. [New Latin *inflorescentia,* from Late Latin *inflōrēscere,* to begin to flower : Latin *in-* (intensive) + *flōrēscere,* to begin to flower (see **florescence**).]

in·flow (ín-flō) *n.* **1.** The act or process of flowing in or into. **2.** Something that flows in; an influx.

in·flu·ence (ín-floo-ənss) *n. Abbr.* **inf., infl. 1.** A power indirectly or intangibly affecting a person or a course of events. **2.** Power to sway or affect, based on prestige, wealth, ability, character, or position. **3.** A person or thing exercising such power. **4.** An effect or

change produced by such power. **5.** *Astrology.* **a.** An occult ethereal fluid believed to flow from the stars to affect the fate of humankind. **b.** The occult power emanating from the stars. —**under the influence.** *Informal.* Intoxicated, especially with alcohol.
~*tr.v.* **influenced, -encing, -ences. 1.** To have power over; affect. **2.** To cause a change in the nature or development of; have a modifying effect upon. —See Synonyms at **affect.** [Middle English, from Old French, from Medieval Latin *influentia,* "a flowing in", from Latin *influēns* (stem *influent-*), present participle of *influere,* to flow in : *in-,* in + *fluere,* to flow.] —**in·flu·enc·er** *n.*

in·flu·ent (ínfloo-ənt) *adj.* Flowing in.
~*n.* Something that flows in; especially, a tributary. [Middle English, from Latin *influēns,* flowing in. See **influence.**]

in·flu·en·tial (ínfloo-énsh'l) *adj.* Having or exercising influence. —**in·flu·en·tial·ly** *adv.*

in·flu·en·za (ínfloo-énzə) *n.* An acute infectious viral disease characterised by inflammation of the respiratory tract, fever, muscular pain, and irritation in the intestinal tract. Also called "flu", "grippe". [Italian, influence, hence "intangible visitation", specifically the European epidemic of influenza of 1743), from Medieval Latin *influentia,* INFLUENCE.]

in·flux (ín-fluks) *n.* **1.** A flowing in of substance. **2.** A sudden invasion or arrival of many people or things: *an influx of visitors.* **3.** The mouth of a river or stream. [Late Latin *influxus,* from Latin, past participle of *influere,* to flow in. See **influence.**]

influx control *n.* In South Africa formerly, the legal control exercised on the movement by black people into urban areas.

in·fo (ínfō) *n. Informal.* Information. Also used in combinations; for example, *infotainment,* combining information and entertainment.

in·fold (in-fṓld) *tr.v.* **-folded, -folding, -folds. 1.** To fold inwards. **2.** Variant of **enfold.** —**in·fold·er** *n.* —**in·fold·ment** *n.*

in·form (in-fórm) *v.* **-formed, -forming, -forms.** —*tr.* **1. a.** To impart information to. **b.** To acquaint (oneself) with knowledge of a subject. **2.** To give form or character to; be the formative principle of. **3.** To animate or inspire with a particular quality or character; imbue. **4.** *Archaic.* To form or shape (the mind or character) by teaching or training. —*intr.* To disclose or provide information, usually of an incriminating nature. Used with *on* or *against.* [Middle English *enfourmen,* from Old French *enfourmer,* from Latin *informāre,* to give form to, form an idea of : *in-* (intensive) + *formāre,* to form, from *forma,* FORM.]

in·for·mal (in-fórm'l, ín-) *adj.* **1.** Not performed or made according to prescribed regulations or forms; unofficial; irregular: *an informal truce.* **2.** Completed or performed without ceremony or formality: *an informal gathering.* **3.** Of, for, or pertaining to ordinary everyday use; casual; relaxed: *informal clothes.* **4.** Belonging to the usage of spoken or written language as used in face-to-face communication by familiar equals and considered inappropriate in certain cultural contexts, as in the standard written prose of ceremonial and official communications. **5.** *Australian & N.Z.* Invalid. Said of a vote or ballot-paper. —**in·for·mal·ly** *adv.*

in·for·mal·i·ty (in-fawr-mál-əti ‖ -fər-) *n., pl.* **-ties. 1.** The state or quality of being informal. **2.** An informal act or usage.

in·for·mant (in-fórmənt) *n.* **1.** One who discloses information; an informer. **2.** A person who gives information about a subject of study; especially, a speaker of a particular language or dialect used as a source of linguistic evidence in research. **3.** *Law.* A person who makes a statement of alleged criminal conduct to a justice of the peace in the initiation of criminal proceedings.

in·for·mat·ics (ínfər-máttiks) *n. Used with a singular verb.* **Information science** *(see).*

in·for·ma·tion (in-fər-máysh'n, *rarely* -fawr-) *n. Abbr.* **inf. 1.** The act of informing or the condition of being informed; communication of knowledge. **2.** Knowledge derived from study, experience, or instruction. **3.** Knowledge of a specific event or situation; news; word. **4.** A service or agency supplying facts or news. **5.** *Law.* **a.** The initiation of criminal proceedings in a magistrate's court before a justice of the peace, in the form of a statement of the alleged criminal conduct made by the informant or prosecutor. **b.** Formerly, a complaint filed on behalf of the Crown by the Attorney General. **6.** A nonaccidental signal used as an input to a computer or communications system. —See Synonyms at **knowledge.** —**in·for·ma·tion·al** *adj.*

information officer *n.* A person employed by an organisation to answer enquiries from the media and the public, and often to edit its own publications.

information retrieval *n.* The branch of computer science concerned with the classification, storage, and retrieval of information by computers and associated electronic devices.

information science *n.* The science concerned with gathering, classifying, storing, retrieving, manipulating, and evaluating information, especially by means of computers. Also called "informatics".

information technology *n.* The technology used in information science.

information theory *n.* The theory of the probability of transmission of messages with a given degree of accuracy when the items of information forming the messages are subject, with certain probabilities, to transmission failure, distortion, and accidental additions.

in·form·a·tive (in-fórmə-tiv) *adj.* Also **in·form·a·to·ry** (-təri, -tri). Providing or conveying information; instructive.

in·formed (in-fórmd) *adj.* **1.** Knowledgeable; educated. **2.** Reflecting or resulting from thorough knowledge of a subject: *an informed opinion.*

in·form·er (in-fórmər) *n.* **1.** One who informs against others, often for payment. **2.** An informant.

in·fra (ínfrə) *adv. Latin.* Below; specifically, in a subsequent part of the text. Compare **supra.**

infra– *prefix.* Indicates: **1.** Below, beneath, inferior to; for example, **infrared. 2.** After, later; for example, **infralapsarianism.** [Latin *infrā*, below, beneath.]

in·fract (in-frákt) *tr.v.* **-fracted, -fracting, -fracts.** To break (a rule, law, or agreement); infringe; violate. [Latin *infringere* (past participle *infractus*), to destroy, INFRINGE.] **—in·frac·tor** (-fráktər) *n.*

in·frac·tion (in-fráksh'n) *n.* The act or an instance of breaching or violating; a violation. See Synonyms at **breach.**

in·fra dig (ínfrə díg) *adj. Informal.* Beneath one's dignity. [Latin *infrā dignitātem.*]

in·fra·lap·sar·i·an·ism (ínfrə-lap-saír-i-ə-niz'm) *n.* The chiefly Calvinist predestinarian doctrine that it was only after the Fall that God elected some from the fallen to be saved by a redeemer. Also called "sublapsarianism". [From INFRA- + Latin *lapsus*, to fall, LAPSE.] **—in·fra·lap·sar·i·an** *n.* & *adj.*

in·fran·gi·ble (in-fránjəb'l) *adj.* **1.** Unbreakable. **2.** Inviolable. [Old French, from Late Latin *infrangibilis* : Latin *in-*, not + *frangere*, to break.] **—in·fran·gi·bil·i·ty** (-fránjə-bílləti) *n.* **—in·fran·gi·bly** *adv.*

in·fra·red (ínfrə-réd) *adj.* **1.** Of, pertaining to, or designating electromagnetic radiation having wavelengths greater than those of visible light and shorter than those of microwaves; radiation with wavelengths between 0.8 micrometre and 1 millimetre. **2.** Generating, using, or sensitive to such radiation. **—in·fra·red** *n.*

in·fra·son·ic (ínfrə-sónnik) *adj.* Generating or using waves or vibrations with frequencies below that of audible sound.

in·fra·sound (ínfrə-sownd) *n.* A wave phenomenon having the general characteristics of sound waves except that its frequency range is below that of sound.

in·fra·struc·ture (ínfrə-strukchər) *n.* **1.** An underlying base or supporting structure. **2.** The basic facilities, equipment, services, and installations needed for the growth and functioning of a country, community, operation, or organisation.

in·fre·quent (in-fréekwənt) *adj.* **1.** Not frequent; rare. **2.** Not steady; irregular; occasional: *an infrequent guest.* **—in·fre·quence, in·fre·quen·cy** *n.* **—in·fre·quent·ly** *adv.*

in·fringe (in-frínj) *v.* **-fringed, -fringing, -fringes.** *—tr.* To break or ignore the terms or obligations of (an oath, agreement, law, or the like); disregard; violate. *—intr.* To go beyond the limits of something; trespass; encroach. Used with *on* or *upon.* [Latin *infringere* : *in-* (intensive) + *frangere*, to break.] **—in·fring·er** *n.*

in·fringe·ment (in-frínjmənt) *n.* **1.** A violation, as of a law, regulation, or agreement; a breach. **2.** An encroachment, as of a right or privilege. **—See** Synonyms at **breach.**

in·fu·la (ínfew-lə) *n., pl.* **-lae** (-lee). Either of the two ribbons attached to a bishop's mitre. [Latin, woollen fillet (worn on the forehead by ancient Romans at religious rites).]

in·fun·dib·u·li·form (infun-díbbewli-fawrm) *adj. Botany.* Funnel-shaped.

in·fun·dib·u·lum (infun-díbbew-ləm) *n., pl.* **-la** (-lə). Any of various funnel-shaped bodily passages or parts; especially, the conical stalk connecting the pituitary gland to the hypothalamus at the base of the brain. [Latin, funnel, from *infundere*, to pour in, INFUSE.] **—in·fun·dib·u·lar, in·fun·dib·u·late** (-lit, -lāt, -lāyt) *adj.*

in·fu·ri·ate (in-féwr-i-ayt) *tr.v.* **-ated, -ating, -ates. 1.** To make furious; enrage. **2.** To annoy or irritate intensely: *an infuriating delay.* *~adj.* (in-féwr-i-ət, -it). *Archaic.* Furious. [Medieval Latin *infuriāre*, to enrage : Latin *in-* (intensive) + *furiāre*, to enrage, from *furia*, FURY.] **—in·fu·ri·at·ing·ly** *adv.*

in·fuse (in-féwz) *v.* **-fused, -fusing, -fuses.** *—tr.* **1.** To put in or introduce into by or as if by pouring. Used with *into.* **2.** To pervade or imbue, as with a quality or emotion. Used with *with.* **3.** To instil or inculcate (a quality). Used with *into.* **4.** To steep or soak without boiling, in order to extract soluble elements or active principles. *—intr.* To undergo infusion. [Middle English *infusen*, from Old French *infuser*, from Latin *infundere* (past participle *infūsus*), to pour in : *in-* + *fundere*, to pour.] **—in·fus·er** *n.*

in·fus·i·ble¹ (in-féwzə-b'l) *adj.* Incapable of being fused or melted; resistant to heat. **—in·fus·i·bil·i·ty** (-bílləti), **in·fus·i·ble·ness** *n.*

infusible² *adj.* Capable of being infused. **—in·fus·i·bil·i·ty, in·fus·i·ble·ness** *n.*

in·fu·sion (in-féwzh'n) *n.* **1.** The act or process of infusing. **2.** A liquid product obtained by infusing. **3.** An admixture. **4.** The introduction of a solution into a vein by slow injection.

in·fu·sion·ism (in-féwzh'n-iz'm) *n. Theology.* The Christian doctrine that a pre-existing soul of divine origin is infused into the body at conception or birth. Compare **creationism. —in·fu·sion·ist** *n.* & *adj.*

in·fu·so·ri·al (ínfew-záwri-əl, -sáwri- ‖ -zóri-, -sóri-) *adj.* **1.** Of or pertaining to infusorians. **2.** Containing or consisting of infusorians.

in·fu·so·ri·an (ínfew-záwri-ən, -sáwri- ‖ -zóri-, -sóri-) *n.* Any of numerous microscopic organisms, especially of the phylum Protozoa or the order Rotifera, occurring in stagnant water or in infusions containing organic material. No longer in technical usage. [New Latin *Infusoria*, "found in infusions".] **—in·fu·so·ri·an** *adj.*

–ing¹ *v.* & *adj. suffix.* Indicates: **1.** The present participle of verbs; for example, **going, seeing, hoping. 2.** Participial adjectives; for example, **striking, gripping. 3.** Adjectives resembling participial adjectives but not derived from verbs; for example, **swashbuckling.**

4. Adjectives used adverbially as intensives, in the sense "to the point of"; for example, **dripping** wet. [Middle English *-inge, -ing*, variants of *-end, -ind*, Old English *-ende*, related to Latin *-āns*, -ANT.] **—ingly** *adv. suffix.*

–ing² *n. suffix.* Indicates: **1.** The act, process, or art of performing a specified action; for example, **dancing, thinking. 2.** The thing or substance used in accomplishing such an action; for example, **coating, wadding. 3.** Something that is to undergo such an action; for example, **washing, mending. 4.** The result of such an action; for example, **peeling, opening, drawing. 5.** Something that belongs to, is connected with, used in making, or has the character of; for example, **lagging, boarding. 6.** An action upon or involving; for example, **sounding, berrying.** [Middle English *-ing*, Old English *-ung, -ing.*]

–ing³ *n. suffix.* Indicates the possession of a certain quality or nature; for example, **sweeting, wilding.** [Middle English *-ing*, Old English *-ing, -ung*, of, belonging to, descended from.]

in·gath·er (in-gáthər, in-gathər) *tr.v.* **-ered, -ering, -ers. 1.** To reap or gather in (especially, a harvest). **2.** To collect, gather together, or gather back (dispersed people or objects). Used especially in the phrase *the ingathering of the exiles*, with reference to the founding of the state of Israel. **—in·gath·er·er** *n.*

Inge (ing), **William Ralph** (1860–1954). English religious leader, Dean of St. Paul's (1911–34). His brilliant but pessimistic sermons and articles got him nicknamed "the Gloomy Dean". His books include *Outspoken Essays* (1919, 1922) and *Lay Thoughts of a Dean* (1926, 1931).

in·gem·i·nate (in-jémmi-nayt) *tr.v.* **-nated, -nating, -nates.** To urge or reiterate constantly.

Ing·en·housz (íngən-hōoss), **Jan** (1730–99). Dutch scientist who discovered the principle of photosynthesis (1779). He demonstrated that plants absorb carbon dioxide in daylight and release oxygen at night.

in·gen·i·ous (in-jéeni-əss) *adj.* **1.** Having or arising from an inventive or cunning mind; characterised by ingenuity; clever: *an ingenious idea; an ingenious gadget.* **2.** *Obsolete.* Having genius; brilliant. **—See** Synonyms at **clever.** [French *ingénieux*, from Latin *ingeniōsus*, from *ingenium*, inborn talent, skill.] **—in·gen·i·ous·ly** *adv.* **—in·gen·i·ous·ness** *n.*

Usage: Ingenious and *ingenuous* are often confused in everyday use because of the similarity of their spelling. *Ingenious* means "clever", "original" (*an ingenious plot, an ingenious solution to a problem*); *ingenuous* means "innocent", "naive" (*an ingenuous manner; his behaviour was ingenuous*). The noun *ingenuity* has come to mean "ingeniousness" and not, as might have been expected, "ingenuousness".

in·gé·nue (án-zhay-new ‖ -nōo; *French* -nǘ) *n.* **1.** An artless, innocent girl or young woman. **2.** An actress playing an ingénue. [French, feminine of *ingénu*, guileless, artless, from Latin *ingenuus*, INGENUOUS.]

in·ge·nu·i·ty (inji-néw-əti ‖ -nóo-) *n., pl.* **-ties. 1.** Inventive skill or imagination; cleverness. **2.** The state of being ingeniously contrived. **3.** *Usually plural.* An ingenious or imaginative device: *"sophistication in the ingenuities of language"* (T.S. Eliot). **4.** *Archaic.* Ingenuousness. [Latin *ingenuitās*, frankness, innocence (but influenced in meaning by INGENIOUS), from *ingenuus*, INGENUOUS.]

in·gen·u·ous (in-jénnew-əss) *adj.* **1.** Without sophistication or worldliness; artless; innocent. **2.** Open or honest; frank; candid. **—See** Synonyms at **frank, naive. —See** Usage note at **ingenious.** [Latin *ingenuus*, native, free-born, noble, honest, frank.] **—in·gen·u·ous·ly** *adv.* **—in·gen·u·ous·ness** *n.*

in·gest (in-jést) *tr.v.* **-gested, -gesting, -gests. 1.** To take (food, for example) in by or as if by swallowing. **2.** To take in (air). Used of a jet engine. [Latin *ingerere* (past participle *ingestus*), to carry in : *in-*, in + *gerere*, to bear, carry.] **—in·ges·tion** *n.* **—in·ges·tive** *adj.*

in·ges·ta (in-jéstə) *pl.n.* Ingested matter, especially food. [New Latin, from Latin, neuter plural of *ingestus*, past participle of *ingerere*, to INGEST.]

in·gle·nook (ing-g'l-nōōk ‖ -nōōk) *n.* A space by or beside a large fireplace, often with seats inside it facing each other. [*Ingle*, Scottish, probably from Scots Gaelic *aingeal*, fire + NOOK.]

in·glo·ri·ous (in-gláwri-əss ‖ -glóri-) *adj.* **1.** Ignominious; dishonourable. **2.** Obscure; unknown. [Latin *inglōrius* : *in-*, not + *glōria*, GLORY.] **—in·glo·ri·ous·ly** *adv.* **—in·glo·ri·ous·ness** *n.*

in·go·ing (in-gó-ing) *adj.* Entering; coming in. *~n.* The sum paid by a new tenant or purchaser for fixtures left in a property.

in·got (ing-gət, -got) *n.* **1.** A mass of metal shaped for convenient storage or transportation. **2.** A casting mould for metal. [Middle English *ingot*, mass of metal, "something poured into (the mould)": *in*, IN + Old English *goten*, past participle of *geotan*, to pour.]

ingot iron *n.* A form of low-carbon steel containing small quantities of other elements.

ingraft. Variant of **engraft.**

in·grain, en·grain (in-gráyn, ín-) *tr.v.* **-grained, -graining, -grains. 1.** To impress indelibly on the mind or nature; fix; infuse. Used with *in, into,* and *on.* **2.** *Archaic.* To cause (a dye or stain) to 'sink indelibly into the fibre of something. *~adj.* (in-grayn). **1.** Deeply rooted; instilled. **2.** Dyed in the yarn before weaving or knitting. **3.** Made of fibre or yarn dyed before weaving. Said especially of rugs. *~n.* (in-grayn). **1.** Yarn or fibre dyed before manufacture. **2.** Any article made of ingrained yarns, such as a carpet. [IN- (in) + GRAIN (dye).]

in·grained (in-gráynd, ín-graynd) *adj.* **1.** Deeply infused; imbued; deep-seated: *ingrained faults.* **2.** Deeply worked into the grain, pores, or the like: *ingrained mud.* **3.** Complete; utter: *an ingrained cad.*

in·grate (ín-grayt, in-gráyt) *n.* An ungrateful person. ~*adj. Archaic.* Ungrateful. [Middle English *ingrat,* from Latin *ingrātus,* ungrateful : *in-,* not + *grātus,* pleasing, thankful.]

in·gra·ti·ate (in-gráyshi-ayt) *tr.v.* **-ated, -ating, -ates.** To bring (oneself) deliberately into the good graces or favour of another. [IN- (in) + Latin *grātia,* GRACE.] **—in·gra·ti·at·ing·ly** *adv.* **—in·gra·ti·a·tion** (-áysh'n) *n.* **—in·gra·ti·a·to·ry** (-ə-təri, -tri) *adj.*

in·grat·i·tude (in-grátti-tewd ‖ -tōod) *n.* Lack of gratitude; ungratefulness. [Middle English, from Old French, from Medieval Latin *ingrātitūdō : in-,* not + *grātitūdō,* GRATITUDE.]

in·gra·ves·cent (ín-grə-véss'nt, -gra-) *adj.* Gradually increasing in severity. Said of a disease. [Latin *ingravescēns* (stem *ingravescent-*), present participle of *ingravescere,* to become heavier, from *gravis,* heavy, GRAVE.] **—in·gra·ves·cence** *n.*

in·gre·di·ent (in-gréedi-ənt) *n.* **1.** Something added or required to form a mixture or compound: *ingredients for onion soup.* **2.** A component or constituent: *Hard work is an ingredient of success.* [Middle English, "something that enters into a mixture", from Latin *ingrediēns* (stem *ingredient-*), present participle of *ingredī,* to enter into. See **ingress.**

Ingres (angr), **Jean Auguste Dominique** (1780–1867). French artist, who led the French Classical school of painting after the death of David. He is noted for his historical paintings, drawings, and mythological works, and for his superb draughtsmanship.

in·gress (ín-gress) *n.* Also **in·gres·sion** (in-grésh'n) (for sense 1). **1.** A going in or entering. **2.** The right or permission to enter. **3.** A means or place of entering. **4.** *Astronomy.* **Immersion** *(see).* [Middle English *ingresse,* from Latin *ingressus,* from the past participle of *ingredī,* to enter into : *in-,* in, into + *gradī,* to step.]

in·gres·sive (in-gréssiv) *adj.* **1.** Of or pertaining to entering. **2.** Of or designating a speech sound pronounced with an inhalation of breath. ~*n.* An ingressive speech sound. **—in·gres·sive·ness** *n.*

in·group (ín-grōop) *n.* A group united by common beliefs, attitudes, and interests, characteristically excluding outsiders.

in·grow·ing (ín-grō-ing) *adj.* Growing inwards; especially, designating a toenail that grows into the surrounding flesh.

in·grown (ín-grōn, in-grón) *adj.* **1.** Grown abnormally into the flesh: *an ingrown toenail.* **2.** Grown within; innate: *an ingrown habit.*

in·growth (ín-grōth) *n.* **1.** The act of growing inwards. **2.** Something that grows inwards or within.

-ings *pl.n. suffix.* Indicates the bits, scraps, dregs, or leftovers resulting from or caused by a specified activity; for example, **shavings, grindings, cuttings.**

in·gui·nal (ín-gwin'l) *adj.* Of, pertaining to, or located in the groin. [Latin *inguinālis,* from *inguen* (stem *inguin-*), groin.]

ingulf. Variant of **engulf.**

in·gur·gi·tate (in-gúrji-tayt) *tr.v.* **-tated, -tating, -tates.** To swallow greedily or in excessive amounts; gorge. [Latin *ingurgitāre : in-,* in + *gurges* (stem *gurgit-*), whirlpool, abyss.] **—in·gur·gi·ta·tion** (-táysh'n) *n.*

INH isoniazid.

in·hab·it (in-hábbit) *v.* **-ited, -iting, -its.** —*tr.* To live or reside in. —*intr. Archaic.* To dwell. [Middle English *enhabiten,* from Old French *enhabiter,* from Latin *inhabitāre : in-,* in + *habitāre,* to dwell, frequentative of *habēre* (past participle *habitus*), to have, possess.] **—in·hab·it·a·bil·i·ty** (-ə-bílləti) *n.* **—in·hab·ita·ble** *adj.* **—in·hab·i·ta·tion** (-hábbi-táysh'n) *n.* **—in·hab·it·er** *n.*

in·hab·i·tan·cy (in-hábbitən-si) *n., pl.* **-cies.** Occupancy.

in·hab·i·tant (in-hábbitənt) *n.* A person or animal that inhabits a place; a permanent resident.

in·hab·it·ed (in-hábbitid) *adj.* Having inhabitants; populated.

in·ha·lant (in-háylənt) *adj.* Used in or for inhaling. ~*n.* Something that is inhaled, such as a medicine.

in·ha·la·tion (ínhə-láysh'n, ínnə-) *n.* **1.** The act or an instance of inhaling. **2.** A medicinal preparation that is inhaled.

in·ha·la·tor (ínhə-laytər, ínnə-) *n.* A device that produces a vapour to ease breathing or to medicate the respiratory system. Also called "inhaler."

in·hale (in-háyl) *v.* **-haled, -haling, -hales.** —*tr.* To draw in by breathing. —*intr.* **1.** To breathe in. **2.** To draw cigarette smoke into the lungs. [Latin *inhālāre : in-,* in + *hālāre,* to breathe (see **halitosis**).]

in·hal·er (in-háylər) *n.* **1.** One that inhales. **2.** An inhalator.

in·har·mon·ic (ínhaar-mónnik) *adj.* Not harmonic.

in·har·mo·ni·ous (ín-haar-mṓni-əss) *adj.* **1.** Not in harmony; discordant. Said of sounds. **2.** Not in accord or agreement. **—in·har·mo·ni·ous·ly** *adv.* **—in·har·mo·ni·ous·ness** *n.*

in·haul (ín-hawl) *n.* Also **in·haul·er** (in-háwlər). *Nautical.* A rope used to draw in a ship's sail.

in·here (in-héer) *intr.v.* **-hered, -hering, -heres.** To be inherent or innate. Used with *in.* [Latin *inhaerēre : in-,* in + *haerēre,* to stick, remain fixed.] **—in·her·ence** (-héer-ənss, -hérrənss), **in·her·en·cy** *n.*

in·her·ent (in-héer-ənt, -hérrənt) *adj.* Existing as an essential or characteristic constituent or attribute; intrinsic. [Latin *inhaerēns*

(stem *inhaerent-*), present participle of *inhaerēre,* INHERE.] **—in·her·ent·ly** *adv.*

in·her·it (in-hérrit) *v.* **-ited, -iting, -its.** —*tr.* **1.** To receive (property, a title, or the like) from a parent, ancestor, or another person by legal succession or will. **2.** To receive or take over from a predecessor. **3.** *Biology.* To receive (a character or characteristic) genetically from a parent or ancestor. **4.** To come into possession of; possess. —*intr.* To succeed as an heir; take possession of an inheritance. [Middle English *enheriten,* from Old French *enheriter,* from Late Latin *inhērēditāre : in-* (intensive) + *hērēditāre,* to inherit, from *hērēs* (stem *hērēd-*), heir.] **—in·her·i·tor** (-hérritər) *n.* **—in·her·i·trix** (-hérri-trikss) *n.*

in·her·it·a·ble (in-hérri-təb'l) *adj.* **1.** Capable of being inherited. **2.** Capable of inheriting; having the right to inherit. **3.** *Law.* Capable of being transferred by a will from one generation to a later generation. **—in·heri·ta·bil·i·ty** *n.* **—in·her·i·ta·bly** *adv.*

in·her·i·tance (in-hérri-tənss) *n.* **1.** The act or right of inheriting. **2.** That which is inherited or to be inherited; a legacy; a bequest. **3.** Anything regarded as a heritage: *the cultural inheritance of Rome.* **4.** *Biology.* **a.** The process of genetic transmission of characters or characteristics. **b.** The configuration of characters or characteristics so inherited.

in·hib·it (in-híbbit) *tr.v.* **-ited, -iting, -its.** **1.** To restrain or hold back (an impulse, natural reaction, or the like). **2.** To prohibit or forbid, especially in ecclesiastical law. **3.** *Psychology.* To cause inhibition in. **4.** To act as an inhibitor. —See Synonyms at **restrain.** [Middle English *inhibiten,* from Latin *inhibēre* (past participle *inhibitus*), to restrain, hold in : *in-,* in + *habēre,* to have, hold.] **—in·hib·it·a·ble** *adj.* **—in·hib·it·ed** *adj.* **—in·hib·i·tive, in·hib·i·to·ry** (-híbbi-təri, -tri) *adj.*

in·hi·bi·tion (ínhi-bísh'n, ínni-) *n.* **1.** The act of inhibiting or the state of being inhibited. **2. a.** *Psychology.* Restraint of an instinctive impulse or the condition inducing such restraint. **b.** Any emotion, idea, habit, or the like, which holds back one's impulses or desires. **3.** The prevention or reduction of the functioning of an organ or part by affecting its nerve supply.

in·hib·i·tor, in·hib·it·er (in-híbbitər) *n.* One that inhibits, as: **1.** A substance used to retard or halt a chemical reaction, such as rusting. Also called "anti-catalyst". **2.** An inert substance added to another substance to inhibit some reaction. **3.** An impurity in a solid that inhibits luminescence. **4.** A substance, such as a drug, that prevents or reduces a physiological action.

in·ho·mo·ge·ne·ous (ín-hómmə-jéeni-əss, -hṓmə-) *adj.* Not homogeneous; lacking in uniformity: *an inhomogeneous magnetic field.* **—in·ho·mo·gen·e·i·ty** (-ji-née-əti, -náy-) *n.*

in·hos·pi·ta·ble (in-hóspi-təb'l, ín-ho-spíttəb'l) *adj.* **1.** Displaying no hospitality; unfriendly. **2.** Not affording shelter or sustenance; barren. **—in·hos·pi·ta·ble·ness** *n.* **—in·hos·pi·ta·bly** *adv.* **—in·hos·pi·tal·i·ty** (ínho-spi-tál-əti, in-hóspi-) *n.*

in·house (ín-hówss) *adj.* Working, originating, or produced within an organisation or group: *an in-house editor, not a freelance.* **—in·house** *adv.*

in·hu·man (in-héwmən ‖ -yṓomən) *adj.* **1.** Not possessing desirable human qualities; lacking kindness or pity; barbarous; brutal. **2.** Not of ordinary human form or type. —See Synonyms at **cruel.** [Latin *inhūmānus : in-,* not + *hūmānus,* HUMAN.] **—in·hu·man·ly** *adv.* **—in·hu·man·ness** *n.*

in·hu·mane (ínhew-máyn) *adj.* Not humane; lacking in pity or compassion. **—in·hu·mane·ly** *adv.*

in·hu·man·i·ty (ínhew-mánnəti) *n., pl.* **-ties.** **1.** Lack of pity or compassion. **2.** An inhumane or cruel act.

in·hume (in-héwm) *tr.v.* **-humed, -huming, -humes.** To place in a grave; bury; inter. [Latin *inhumāre : in-,* in + *humus,* earth, ground.] **—in·hum·er** *n.* **—in·hu·ma·tion** (ínhew-máysh'n) *n.*

in·im·i·cal (i-nímmik'l) *adj.* **1.** Not conducive; harmful; adverse: *habits inimical to good health.* **2.** Unfriendly; hostile; antagonistic: *"a voice apparently cold and inimical"* (Arnold Bennett). [Late Latin *inimīcālis,* from Latin *inimīcus,* enemy : *in-,* not + *amīcus,* friend.]

in·im·i·ta·ble (i-nímmitə-b'l) *adj.* Defying imitation; matchless; unique. **—in·im·i·ta·bil·i·ty** (-bílləti) *n.* **—in·im·i·ta·bly** *adv.*

in·i·on (ínni-ən) *n.* The projecting point of the occipital bone at the base of the skull, used as a measuring point in craniometry. [Greek, back of the head.]

in·iq·ui·tous (i-níkwitəss) *adj.* **1.** Of the nature of iniquity; wicked; sinful. **2.** *Informal.* Disgraceful; scandalous: *an iniquitous waste of money.* **—in·iq·ui·tous·ly** *adv.* **—in·iq·ui·tous·ness** *n.*

in·iq·ui·ty (i-níkwəti) *n., pl.* **-ties.** **1.** Moral turpitude or sin; wickedness: *"the human mind, since the Fall, was nothing but a sink of iniquity"* (Henry Fielding). **2.** A grossly immoral act; a sin. [Middle English *iniquite,* from Old French, from Latin *iniquitās* (stem *iniquitāt-*), from *inīquus,* unjust : *in-,* not + *aequus,* just, EQUAL.]

init. initial.

in·i·tial (i-nísh'l) *adj. Abbr.* **init. 1.** Occurring or existing at the beginning or outset; first. **2.** Occurring first in a word, syllable, or the like. ~*n. Abbr.* **init. 1. a.** The first letter of a person's name, used as a shortened signature or for identification. **b.** *Plural.* The first letters of each part of a person's full name, used as a shortened signature or for identification. **2.** The first letter of a word. **3.** A large, often highly decorated letter set at the beginning of a chapter, verse, paragraph, or the like. ~*tr.v.* **initialled** or *U.S* **initialed, -tialling** or *U.S.* **-tialing, -tials.** To mark or sign with one's own initial or initials, especially in order to indicate approval or authorisation. [Latin *initiālis*, from *initium*, beginning.] —**in·i·tial·ly** *adv.*

i·ni·tial·ism (i-nísh'l-iz'm) *n.* An abbreviation of a phrase consisting of the initial letter of each word in the phrase; distinguishable from an acronym in that it is not pronounced as a single word; for example **B.B.C., C.I.A.**

in·i·ti·ate (i-níshi-ayt) *tr.v.* **-ated, -ating, -ates.** **1.** To begin or originate. **2.** To introduce (a person) to a new field, interest, skill, or the like. **3.** To admit into membership, as with ceremonies or ritual. —See Synonyms at **begin.** —*adj.* (i-níshi-ət, -it, -ayt). Initiated. —*n.* (i-níshi-ət, -it, -ayt). **1.** One who has been initiated. **2.** A novice; a beginner. [Latin *initiāre*, from *initium*, beginning. See **initial.**] —**in·i·ti·a·tor** (-aytər) *n.*

in·i·ti·a·tion (i-nishi-áysh'n) *n.* **1.** The act of initiating or the fact of being initiated. **2.** A ceremony, ritual, test, or period of instruction by which a new member is admitted to an organisation, office, or status or to knowledge.

in·i·ti·a·tive (i-níshi-ətiv, -nísh-) *n.* **1.** **a.** The ability or instinct to initiate and follow through a plan or task; enterprise and determination. **b.** The right or power to initiate: *has the initiative.* **2.** The first step or action; the opening move: *take the initiative; new peace initiatives.* **3.** **a.** The power or right to introduce a new legislative measure. **b.** The right and procedure by which citizens can propose a law by petition and ensure its submission to the electorate, as in many U.S. states and in Switzerland. —**on (one's) own initiative.** Without instruction or coercion; unprompted. —*adj.* **1.** Of, pertaining to, or requiring initiative: *an initiative test.* **2.** Used to initiate. —**in·i·ti·a·tive·ly** *adv.*

in·i·ti·a·to·ry (i-níshi-ə-təri, -ay-, -tri) *adj.* **1.** Introductory; initial. **2.** Used to initiate; initiative.

inj. injection.

in·ject (in-jékt) *tr.v.* **-jected, -jecting, -jects.** **1.** To force or drive (a fluid) into something. **2.** *Medicine.* **a.** To introduce (a fluid) into the skin, subcutaneous tissue, muscle, blood vessels, or a bodily cavity by means of a syringe. **b.** To introduce a fluid into (an individual or a part of the body) in this way. **3.** To introduce (a new element) into consideration: *inject a note of humour into the negotiations.* **4.** To place (a satellite, rocket, or the like) in an orbit, trajectory, or stream. [Latin *inicere, injicere* (past participle *injectus*), to throw or put in : *in-,* in + *jacere,* to throw.]

in·ject·a·ble (in-jékt-əb'l) *adj.* Able to be injected. Said of a drug. —*n.* A drug or medicine that can be injected directly into the bloodstream.

in·jec·tion (in-jéksh'n) *n. Abbr.* **inj.** **1.** The act or an instance of injecting. **2.** A fluid that is injected. **3.** Broadly, anything injected.

injection moulding *n.* **1.** A process for making moulded articles by forcing a liquid under pressure into a mould. **2.** An article made by such a process.

in·jec·tor (in-jéktər) *n.* **1.** A device used to force water into a steam boiler. **2.** A device for spraying atomised fuel into the combustion chamber of an internal-combustion engine.

in·ju·di·cious (injōō-díshəss) *adj.* Lacking judgment or discretion. —**in·ju·di·cious·ly** *adv.* —**in·ju·di·cious·ness** *n.*

In·jun (ínjən) *n. U.S. Informal & Regional.* A North American Indian. [Facetious respelling of INDIAN.]

in·junc·tion (in-júngkshən) *n.* **1.** The act of enjoining. **2.** That which is enjoined; a command, directive, or order. **3.** *Law.* A court order enjoining or prohibiting a party from a specific course of action. [Late Latin *injunctiō*, from Latin *injungere* (past participle *injunctus*), to enjoin : *in-,* in + *jungere,* to join.] —**in·junc·tive** *adj.*

in·jure (ínjər) *tr.v.* **-jured, -juring, -jures.** **1.** To cause harm or damage to; hurt. **2.** To commit an injustice or offence against; wrong. [Back-formation from INJURY.] —**in·jur·er** *n.*

Synonyms: injure, harm, hurt, damage, impair, mar, wound.

in·ju·ri·ous (in-jóor-i-əss) *adj.* **1.** Harmful or damaging. **2.** Slanderous; libellous. —**in·ju·ri·ous·ly** *adv.* —**in·ju·ri·ous·ness** *n.*

in·ju·ry (ínjəri) *n., pl.* **-ries.** **1.** Damage of or to a person, property, reputation, or thing. **2.** A specific damage or wound: *a leg injury.* **3.** Injustice. **4.** *Law.* Any wrong or damage done to persons, property, reputation, or rights that gives grounds for legal action. —See Synonyms at **injustice.** [Middle English *injurie*, from Anglo-French, from Latin *injūria*, injustice, wrong, from *injūrius,* unjust, wrongful : *in-,* not + *jūs* (stem *jūr-*), right, law.]

injury benefit *n. British.* **Industrial injury benefit** *(see).*

injury time *n. Sports.* Extra playing time allowed at the end of a match to compensate for the time lost in treating injured players.

in·jus·tice (in-jústiss) *n.* **1.** The fact, practice, or quality of being unjust; lack of justice. **2.** An unjust act; a wrong. [Middle English, from Old French, from Latin *injūstitia,* from *injūstus,* unjust : *in-,* not + *jūstus,* JUST.]

Synonyms: injustice, injury, wrong, grievance.

ink (ingk) *n.* **1.** A pigmented liquid or paste used especially for writing or printing. **2.** A dark liquid secreted by cuttlefish and other cephalopods for protective concealment. —*tr.v.* **inked, inking, inks.** To mark or stain with ink. —**ink in.** To retrace the pencil lines of (a drawing) in ink. —**ink up.** To put ink onto (a printing machine) to prepare for printing. [Middle English *enke,* from Old French *enke, enque,* from Late Latin *encaustum,* from Greek *enkauston,* purple ink, from *enkaiein,* to paint in encaustic.] —**ink·er** *n.*

In·ka·tha (in-káətə) *n.* A Zulu national liberation movement founded in 1928 with the aim of a single multiracial South Africa.

ink·blot (íngk-blot) *n.* **1.** A blotted pattern of spilled ink. **2.** Such a pattern used in the Rorschach test.

ink cap *n.* Any of various mushrooms of the genus *Coprinus,* having gills that dissolve into a dark liquid on maturing.

ink·horn (íngk-hawrn) *n.* A small container made of horn or similar material, formerly used to hold writing ink. —*adj.* Pedantic; recondite: *an inkhorn term.*

ink·ling (íngkling) *n.* **1.** A hint or intimation. **2.** A vague idea or notion. [Middle English *inkle†*, to mutter.]

ink pad *n.* An ink-soaked cushion used to ink a rubber stamp. Also called "pad".

ink sac *n.* A gland near the anus in an octopus or other cephalopod mollusc, that secretes ink.

ink·stand (íngk-stand) *n.* **1.** A tray or rack for bottles of ink, pens, and other writing implements. **2.** An inkwell.

ink·well (íngk-wel) *n.* A small ink reservoir into which a pen is dipped for filling.

ink·y (íngki) *adj.* **-ier, -iest. 1.** Of or containing ink. **2.** Dark or murky. **3.** Stained or smeared with ink. —**ink·i·ness** *n.*

inlace. Variant of **enlace.**

in·laid (ín-layd, in-láyd) *adj.* **1.** Set into a surface in a decorative pattern. **2.** Decorated with a pattern set into a surface.

in·land (ín-lənd, -land) *adj.* **1.** Of, pertaining to, or located in the interior part of a land mass. **2.** Operating or applying within the borders of a country, region, or state; domestic: *inland trade.* —*adv.* (in-lánd, ín-land, -lənd). In, towards, or into the interior of a land mass. —*n.* The interior of a country, region, or state.

inland drainage *n.* **Internal drainage** *(see).*

in·land·er (ín-lənd-ər, -land-) *n.* A person who lives in or near the centre of a land mass, especially in a large continent such as Australia.

Inland Revenue *n. Abbr.* **I.R.** *British.* **1.** The government department responsible for the assessment and collection of taxes, especially direct taxes such as income tax or capital gains tax. **2.** *Small* i, *small* r. Government income from such taxation.

inland sea *n.* An isolated, landlocked expanse of water, with no outlet to the world's main seas.

Inland Sea. *Japanese* **Se·to—nai·kai** (sétō-nákkī). An arm of the Pacific Ocean, enclosed by the Japanese islands of Honshu, Shikoku, and Kyushu, except for a narrow channel connecting it to the Sea of Japan. Within it are about 950 small islands, about two-thirds of which form the Inland Sea (or Seto-naikai) National Park.

in-law (ín-law) *n.* Any relative by marriage. [From -IN-LAW.]

-in-law *n. comb. form.* Indicates relation through marriage; for example, **sister-in-law.**

in·lay (in-láy, ín-lay) *tr.v.* **-laid, -laying, -lays. 1.** To set (pieces of wood, ivory, or the like) into a surface, usually at the same level, to form a design. **2.** To decorate (a surface) with wood, ivory, or the like. —*n.* (ín-lay). **1.** An article, material, or substance that has been inlaid. **2.** A design, pattern, or decoration made by inlaying. **3.** *Dentistry.* A solid filling of gold, porcelain, or the like, fitted to a cavity in a tooth and cemented in place. **4.** A piece of tissue, such as bone, surgically inserted into an organ or part to repair a defect. —**in·lay·er** *n.*

in·let (ín-let, -lət) *n.* **1.** A relatively narrow channel or pocket of water. **2.** A stream or bay leading inland, as from the ocean; an estuary. **3.** A narrow passage of water between two islands. **4.** An entry or drainage passage, as to a culvert. **5.** Something that is inserted, let in, or inlaid. **6.** A way or means of entering; especially, a valve or part through which a fluid enters a machine, engine, or the like. Also used adjectivally: *inlet manifold; inlet valve.* —*tr.v.* **inletted, -letting, -lets.** To insert; let in.

in·li·er (ín-lī-ər) *n.* An older rock formation completely surrounded by newer strata.

in loc. cit. Variant of **loc. cit.**

in lo·co pa·ren·tis (in lōkō pə-réntiss, lóckō) *adv. Latin.* In the position or place of a parent.

in·ly (ínli) *adv. Poetic.* Inwardly.

in·ly·ing (ín-lī-ing) *adj.* Positioned within or inside.

in·mate (ín-mayt) *n.* **1.** A resident in a building or dwelling. **2.** A person confined to an institution such as a prison or mental hospital. [Perhaps INN (influenced by IN) + MATE.]

in me·di·as res (in méedi-ass ráyss, méddi-, -aass, ráyz) *adv. Latin.* Into the middle of things. Used chiefly of the classical literary or dramatic device whereby an author starts a narrative by plunging the audience into the middle of an objective sequence of events. [Taken from the passage *"in medias res . . . auditorem rapit"*, "(the poet) plunges his hearer . . . into the middle of things" (Horace, *Ars Poetica*).]

in me·mo·ri·am (in mi-máwri-am, -əm ‖ -móri-) *prep. Latin. Abbr.* **in mem.** In memory of; as a memorial to. Used in epitaphs.

inmesh. Variant of **enmesh.**

in·mi·grant (ín-mīgrənt) *n. Chiefly U.S.* A person who moves to another area within the same country.

in·mi·gra·tion (ín-mī-gráysh'n) *n. Chiefly U.S.* The movement of people to another area within the same country.

in·most (ín-mōst) *adj.* Innermost.

inn (in) *n.* **1.** A public house or small hotel providing food, drink, and lodging for travellers. **2.** A tavern or restaurant. **3.** *British.* Formerly, a hall of residence for students. [Middle English *inn,* Old English *inn.*]

in·nards (ínnərdz) *pl.n. Informal.* **1.** Internal bodily organs; viscera. **2.** Broadly, any inner parts. [Variant of INWARDS.]

in·nate (i-náyt, ínnayt) *adj.* **1.** Possessed at birth; inborn. **2.** Possessed as an essential feature; inherent. **3.** Of or produced by thought as distinguished from experience: *innate ideas.* [Middle English *innat,* from Latin *innātus,* past participle of *innāscī,* to be born in : *in-,* in + *nāscī,* to be born.] **—in·nate·ly** *adv.* **—in·nate·ness** *n.*

Synonyms: *innate, inborn, inbred, congenital, hereditary.*

in·ner (ínnər) *adj.* **1.** Located further inside: *an inner room.* **2. a.** Occurring within. **b.** Closer to the centre; more secret or exclusive: *inner circles of government.* **3.** Less apparent; underlying: *the inner meaning of a poem.* **4.** Pertaining to the soul or mind: *an inner struggle.* **5.** *Chemistry.* Designating a cyclic compound formed by the reaction of one functional group in a molecule with another in the same molecule. [Middle English *inner,* Old English *inn(e)ra.*]

inner bar *n. British.* Queen's Counsel or King's Counsel considered as a body.

inner child *n.* The childlike part of the personality, easily damaged or suppressed by psychological trauma, stress, or social pressure. [Perhaps coined as a non-derogatory counterpart of Freud's *id* and the *child* of transactional analysis.]

inner city *n.* The older, central part of a city, as when characterised by crowded, run-down, low-income districts. **—in·ner-cit·y** *adj.*

in·ner-di·rect·ed (ínnər-di-réktid, -dī-) *adj.* Guided by personal principles rather than those shared by society at large: *an inner-directed personality.* Compare **other-directed. —in·ner-di·rec·tion** *n.*

inner ear *n.* The **internal ear** *(see).*

Inner Hebrides. See **Hebrides.**

inner man *n.* **1.** The mind, soul, or spirit. **2.** The hungry stomach. Used humorously: *feeding the inner man.*

Inner Mongolian Autonomous Region. Autonomous region in northeast China. Since the coming of Communist rule in China in 1949 it has had limited powers of self-government within the Chinese state. Most of the Mongols in China live here, although they form less than ten per cent of the region's population. The region comprises largely steppe lands and arid near-desert; stock-raising is the chief economic activity.

in·ner·most (ínnər-mōst) *adj.* **1.** Situated or occurring farthest within. **2.** Most intimate: *innermost feelings.*

inner planet *n.* Any of the planets Mercury, Venus, Earth, or Mars, with orbits inside the asteroid belt. Compare **outer planet.**

inner product *n. Mathematics.* **Scalar product** *(see).*

Inner Temple *n.* In England, one of the four legal societies forming the **Inns of Court** *(see).*

inner tube *n.* The inflatable rubber tube that fits inside the outer casing of a pneumatic tyre.

in·ner·vate (ínner-vayt, i-nér-) *tr.v.* **-vated, -vating, -vates. 1.** To supply (a bodily part) with nerves. **2.** To stimulate (a nerve or bodily part). [IN- + NERV(E) + -ATE.] **—in·ner·va·tion** *n.*

in·nerve (i-nérv) *tr.v.* **-nerved, -nerving, -nerves.** To give nervous energy to; stimulate.

in·ning (ínning) *n.* **1.** In baseball, one of nine divisions or periods of a regulation game, in which each team has a turn at bat as limited by three outs. **2.** *Archaic.* **a.** The reclamation of flooded or marshy land. **b.** *Often plural.* Land that has been reclaimed. [From IN.]

in·nings (ínningz) *n., pl.* **innings. 1.** The period or division of a game of cricket during which one team bats. **2.** The play or the number of runs of a batsman during his turn at batting: *He had a magnificent innings.* **3.** Any period of opportunity and action: *She had a good innings at the top.* [From *in* (verb), to go in.]

inn·keep·er (ín-keepər) *n.* One who owns or manages an inn.

in·no·cence (ínnə-sənss, ínnō-) *n.* **1.** The state, quality, or virtue of being innocent. **2.** A plant, **bluets** *(see).*

in·no·cent (ínnə-sənt, ínnō-) *adj.* **1.** Uncorrupted by evil, malice, or wrongdoing; sinless; untainted; pure: *as innocent of evil as a babe.* **2. a.** Not guilty of a specific crime; legally blameless: *found innocent on all charges.* **b.** Not responsible for or guilty of something wrong or unethical: *innocent of negligence.* **3.** Not dangerous or harmful; not serious: *an innocent prank.* **4.** Not experienced or worldly; credulous; naive: *innocent tourists.* **5.** Not exposed to or familiar with something; devoid. Used with *of*: *innocent of learning.* **6.** Betraying or suggesting no deception or guile; simple; artless: *an innocent smile.* **7.** Not malignant; benign. Said of a tumour. —See Synonyms at **naive.**

~n. **1.** A person who is free of evil or sin; one who is pure or uncorrupted. **2.** A simple, guileless, inexperienced, or unsophisticated person; one who is vulnerable or credulous: *an innocent abroad.* **3.** A very young child. [Middle English, from Old French, from Latin *innocēns* : *in-,* not + *nocēns* (stem *nocent-*), present participle of *nocēre,* to harm, hurt.] **—in·no·cent·ly** *adv.*

in·noc·u·ous (i-nóckew-əss) *adj.* **1.** Having no adverse effect; harmless: *an innocuous snakebite.* **2.** Inoffensive; unobjectionable: *an innocuous speech.* [Latin *innocuus* : *in-,* not + *nocuus,* harmful, from *nocēre,* to harm.] **—in·noc·u·ous·ly** *adv.* **—in·noc·u·ous·ness** *n.*

in·nom·i·nate (i-nómmi-nət, -nit, -nayt) *adj.* **1.** Having no specific name. **2.** Anonymous. [Late Latin *innōminātus* : Latin *in-,* not + *nōminātus,* past participle of *nōmināre,* to name, NOMINATE.]

innominate artery *n.* A short artery that arises from the aortic arch and divides in the neck to form the right common carotid and right subcarian arteries.

innominate bone *n. Anatomy.* A large flat bone forming the lateral half of the pelvis, consisting of the fused ilium, ischium, and pubis. Also called "hip bone".

innominate vein *n.* Either of a pair of veins in the neck formed by the union of the internal jugular and subclavian veins. The innominate veins join to form the superior vena cava.

in·no·vate (ínnə-vayt, ínnō-) *v.* **-vated, -vating, -vates.** *—tr.* To begin or introduce (something new). *—intr.* To begin or introduce something new; be inventive. [Latin *innovāre,* to renew : *in-* (intensive) + *novāre,* to make new, renew, from *novus,* new.] **—in·no·va·tive, in·no·va·to·ry** *adj.* **—in·no·va·tor** (-vaytər) *n.*

in·no·va·tion (ínnə-váysh'n, ínnō-) *n.* **1.** The act of innovating. **2.** That which is newly introduced; a change. **—in·no·va·tion·al** *adj.*

Inns·bruck (ínz-brōōk, *German* ínss-). City in western Austria, the capital of Tirol province. It is a popular summer and winter resort and was the site of the 1964 and 1976 Winter Olympics.

Inns of Court *pl.n.* **1.** The four legal societies in England founded at the beginning of the 14th century, consisting of Gray's Inn, Lincoln's Inn, the Inner Temple, and the Middle Temple, which have the exclusive right to grant law students admission to the bar as barristers. **2.** The buildings housing these societies.

in·nu·en·do (innew-én-dō) *n., pl.* **-does. 1.** An indirect, oblique, or subtle implication, often derogatory in nature. **2.** *Law.* **a.** An interpretation, as in a libel suit, of allegedly libellous or slanderous material. **b.** Any explanation of a word or charge. [Latin *innuendō,* by hinting, from *innuendum,* gerund of *innuere,* to nod to, signal to : *in,* towards + *-nuere,* to nod.]

Innuit. Variant of **Inuit.**

in·nu·mer·a·ble (i-néw-mər-əb'l || -nōō-) *adj.* Also **in·nu·mer·ous** (-mər-əss). Too many to be counted or numbered. See Synonyms at **infinite. —in·nu·mer·a·bil·i·ty** (-ə-bílləti), **in·nu·mer·a·ble·ness** *n.* **—in·nu·mer·a·bly** *adv.*

in·nu·tri·tion (í-new-trísh'n, ín-new- || -nōō-) *n.* Lack of nutrition; poor nourishment. **—in·nu·tri·tious** *adj.*

in·ob·serv·ance (in-əb-zérv'nss || -ob-) *n.* **1.** Lack of heed or attention; disregard. **2.** Nonobservance, as of a law or custom. **—in·ob·serv·ant** *adj.*

in·oc·u·la·ble (i-nóckew-ləb'l) *adj.* **1.** Transmissible by inoculation. **2.** Susceptible to a disease transmitted by inoculation. [From INOCULATE.] **—in·oc·u·la·bil·i·ty** (-lə-bílləti) *n.*

in·oc·u·late (i-nóckew-layt) *tr.v.* **-lated, -lating, -lates. 1.** To introduce the virus of a disease or other antigenic material into the body of (a person or animal) in order to immunise, cure, or experiment: *inoculated against polio.* **2.** To communicate a disease to by transferring its virus or other causative agent. **3.** To implant (microorganisms or infectious material) into a medium suitable for their growth. **4.** To introduce nitrogen-fixing bacteria or mycorrhizal fungi into (the soil) to enhance plant growth. **5.** To influence or penetrate (someone) with ideas, opinions, or the like. [Middle English, from Latin *inoculāre,* to engraft : *in-,* in + *oculus,* eye, bud.] **—in·oc·u·la·tive** (-lətiv, -laytiv) *adj.* **—in·oc·u·la·tor** *n.*

in·oc·u·la·tion (i-nóckew-láysh'n) *n.* **1.** The act, process, or an instance of inoculating. **2.** Inoculum.

in·oc·u·lum (i-nóckew-ləm) *n.* **1.** The material used in an inoculation. Also called "inoculant", "inoculation". **2.** Fungal spores, bacteria, or other pathogens that initiate an outbreak of plant disease.

in·o·dor·ous (in-ōdərəss) *adj.* Having no odour.

in·of·fen·sive (ínnə-fén-siv) *adj.* Giving no offence; harmless; unobjectionable. **—in·of·fen·sive·ly** *adv.* **—in·of·fen·sive·ness** *n.*

in·of·fi·cious (ínnə-físhəss) *adj. Law.* Contrary to natural affection or moral duty. Said of a will in which the testator unreasonably disinherits the rightful heirs. [Latin *inofficiōsus* : *in-,* not + *officiōsus,* dutiful, OFFICIOUS.] **—in·of·fi·cious·ly** *adv.*

in·op·er·a·ble (in-óppərə-b'l, -óppr-) *adj.* **1.** Not operable. **2.** Not susceptible to surgery. Said especially of malignant tumours. **—in·op·er·a·bly** *adv.*

in·op·er·a·tive (in-óppərə-tiv, -óppr-) *adj.* Not working or functioning; not taking effect: *inoperative measures.*

in·op·por·tune (in-óppər-tewn, ín-, -téwn || -tōōn) *adj.* Not opportune; ill-timed; inappropriate. **—in·op·por·tune·ly** *adv.* **—in·op·por·tune·ness** *n.*

in·or·di·nate (i-nórd'n-ət, -nórdin-, -it) *adj.* **1.** Exceeding reasonable limits; immoderate; unrestrained: *inordinate desires.* **2.** Not regulated; disorderly. —See Synonyms at **excessive.** [Middle English *inordinat,* from Latin *inordinātus* : *in-,* not + *ōrdinātus,* past participle of *ōrdināre,* to set in order, from *ōrdō* (stem *ōrdin-*), order.] **—in·or·di·na·cy** (-ə-si), **in·or·di·nate·ness** *n.* **—in·or·di·nate·ly** *adv.*

in·or·gan·ic (ínnawr-gánnik) *adj. Abbr.* **inorg. 1. a.** Involving neither organic life nor the products of organic life. **b.** Not composed of organic matter; especially, mineral. **2.** Of or pertaining to the chemistry of noncarbon compounds not usually classified as **organic** *(see).* **3.** Not arising in normal growth; artificial. **4.** Lacking system or structure. **—in·or·gan·i·cal·ly** *adv.*

inorganic chemistry *n.* The branch of chemistry that deals with the formation, structure, and properties of compounds of elements other than carbon, usually considered to include some simple carbon compounds such as carbon dioxide and carbonate salts. Compare **organic chemistry.**

in·os·cu·late (i-nóss-kew-layt) *v.* **-lated, -lating, -lates.** *—tr.* **1.** To unite (blood vessels, nerve fibres, or ducts) by small openings. **2.** To make continuous; blend (as fibres, for example). *—intr.* **1.** To open into one another. **2.** To unite so as to be continuous; blend. **3.** To communicate by means of small channels or openings. Used of blood vessels, nerve fibres, and the like. [IN- + Latin *ōsculāre,* to provide with an opening, from *ōsculum,* little mouth, opening, diminutive of *ōs,* mouth.] **—in·os·cu·la·tion** (-láysh'n) *n.*

in·o·si·tol (i-nṓ-si-tol || ī-, -tōl) *n.* One of nine isomeric alcohols, $C_6H_6(OH)_6$; especially, one found in plant and animal tissue and classified as a member of the vitamin B complex. [Greek *īs* (genitive *īnos*), tendon, sinew, muscle + -IT(E) + -OL.]

in·o·trop·ic (ínnə-tróppik, ínə- || *U.S. also* éenə-, -trṓpik) *adj.* Affecting the contraction of muscles, especially heart muscle: *Digitalis is an inotropic drug.* [Greek *īs* (stem *īn-*), tendon + -TROPIC.]

in·pa·tient (ín-paysh'nt) *n.* A patient living or staying in a hospital. Compare **outpatient.**

in per·so·nam (in per-sṓ-nam, pər-, -nəm, -naam) *adv. Law.* Against a person. Said of a proceeding. Compare **in rem.** [Latin.] —**in per·so·nam** *adj.*

in pet·to (in péttō) *adv.* Secretly; privately. Said of appointments of cardinals by the pope undisclosed in consistory. [Italian, "in the breast".] —**in pet·to** *adj.*

in-phase (ín-fáyz) *adj. Physics.* Designating or pertaining to two or more waves, alternating signals, or other periodically varying quantities for which the maximum (and minimum) values of each quantity occur at the same time.

in pos·se (in póssi) *adj. Latin.* Possible but not actual; potential. Compare **in esse.** [Literally, in possibility.]

in pro·pri·a per·so·na (in prṓpri-ə per-sṓnə, próppri-ə) *adv. Latin.* In one's own person; in one's self.

in·put (ín-pŏŏt) *n.* **1.** Anything put into a system or expended in its operation to achieve a result or output, especially: **a.** Energy, work, or power used to drive a machine. **b.** Current, electromotive force, or power supplied to an electric circuit, network, or device. **c.** Information put into a communications system for transmission or into a data-processing system for processing. **d.** The entirety of basic resources, including materials, equipment, and funds, required to complete a project. **2.** A position, terminal, or station at which any such input enters a system.
~*tr.v.* **input** or **inputted, -putting, -puts.** To insert (data) into a data-processing system.

in·put-out·put (ínpŏŏt-ówtpŏŏt) *adj.* **1.** Designating the equipment forming part of a computer system that controls the passage of information into or out of the system. **2.** Concerned with or pertaining to the passage of information into or out of a computer. **2.** Designating an analysis of the input into a system in relation to output, especially in terms of economics.

in·quest (ín-kwest) *n.* **1.** A judicial enquiry concerning some matter, usually before a jury; especially, an investigation into the cause of someone's death held before a jury and a coroner. **2.** A jury making such an enquiry. **3.** An investigation. [Middle English *enquest,* from Old French *enqueste,* from Vulgar Latin *inquesta* (unattested), from the feminine past participle of *inquaerere* (unattested), to ENQUIRE.]

in·qui·e·tude (in-kwī́-ə-tewd || -tŏŏd) *n.* **1.** Restlessness. **2.** Uneasiness; disquietude. [Middle English, from Late Latin *inquiētūdō,* from Latin *inquiētus,* restless : *in-,* not + *quiētus,* QUIET.]

in·qui·line (ínkwi-līn, -lin) *n.* An animal that characteristically lives commensally in the burrow or dwelling place of an animal of another kind. [Latin *inquilīnus,* tenant, dweller.] —**in·qui·line** *adj.* —**in·qui·lin·ism** (-li-niz'm), **in·qui·lin·i·ty** (-línnəti) *n.* —**in·qui·lin·ous** (-līnəss) *adj.*

inquire. Variant of **enquire.**

inquiring. Variant of **enquiring.**

inquiry. Variant of **enquiry.** —See Usage note at **enquiry.**

in·qui·si·tion (ínkwi-zísh'n) *n.* **1.** The act of enquiring into a matter; investigation. **2. a.** A judicial enquiry. **b.** The verdict of a judicial enquiry. **3.** *Capital* **I.** A former tribunal in the Roman Catholic Church directed at the suppression and punishment of heresy. See **Spanish Inquisition. 4.** Any inquisitorial investigation or scrutiny. [Middle English *inquisicioun,* from Old French *inquisition,* from Latin *inquīsītiō* (stem *inquīsitiōn-*), from *inquīrere* (past participle *inquīsītus*), to ENQUIRE.] —**in·qui·si·tion·al** *adj.*

in·quis·i·tive (in-kwízzətiv) *adj.* **1.** Unduly curious and enquiring; prying. **2.** Eager to learn. —See Synonyms at **curious.** —**in·quis·i·tive·ly** *adv.* —**in·quis·i·tive·ness** *n.*

in·quis·i·tor (in-kwízzitər) *n.* **1.** One who enquires; a questioner. **2.** One who investigates officially. **3.** *Capital* **I.** A member of the Inquisition.

In·quis·i·tor-Gen·er·al (in-kwízzitər-jénnərəl, -jénnrəl) *n.* The head of the court of Inquisition in Spain.

in·quis·i·to·ri·al (in-kwìzzi-táwri-əl, ín-kwizzi- || -tṓri-) *adj.* **1.** Pertaining to, resembling, or having the function of an inquisitor. **2.** *Law.* Designating a form of criminal procedure, often conducted in secrecy, in which one party acts as both prosecutor and judge. Compare **accusatorial. 3.** Involving or imposing browbeating interrogation. —**in·quis·i·to·ri·al·ly** *adv.*

in re (in ráy, rée) *prep. Law.* In the matter or case of; with regard to. [Latin.]

in rem (in rém) *adv. Law.* Against a thing, as a property, status, or right. Compare **in personam.** [Latin.] —**in rem** *adj.*

I.N.R.I. Jesus of Nazareth, King of the Jews. Used as an inscription on a crucifix. [Latin *Iesus Nazarenus Rex Iudaeorum.*]

in·road (ín-rōd) *n.* **1.** A hostile invasion; a raid; an incursion. **2.** *Often plural.* An encroachment; an intrusion: *Her work made inroads on her free time.* [IN + ROAD (obsolete sense "raid").]

in·rush (ín-rush) *n.* A sudden rushing in; an irruption; an influx.

ins. 1. inches. **2.** inspector. **3.** insulated. **4.** insurance.

in·sa·lu·bri·ous (in-sə-lŏŏ-bri-əss, -léw) *adj.* Not salubrious; unhealthy: *an insalubrious climate.* —**in·sa·lu·bri·ty** *n.*

in·sane (in-sáyn) *adj.* **1.** Of, exhibiting, or suffering from insanity. **2.** Characteristic of, used by, or for the insane. **3.** Very foolish; rash; wild. [Latin *insānus* : *in-,* not + *sānus,* SANE.] —**in·sane·ly** *adv.* —**in·sane·ness** *n.*

in·san·i·tar·y (in-sánni-təri, -tri || *U.S.* -terri) *adj.* Not sanitary; unhealthy: *insanitary conditions.*

in·san·i·ty (in-sánnəti) *n., pl.* **-ties. 1.** Persistent mental disorder or derangement. **2.** Unsoundness of mind sufficient to exempt a person from legal responsibility for his actions. **3. a.** Extreme foolishness; total folly. **b.** Something foolish.
Synonyms: *insanity, lunacy, madness, mania, dementia.*

in·sa·tia·ble (in-sáyshə-b'l, -sáyshi-ə-) *adj.* Incapable of being satiated or satisfied: *an insatiable lust for power.* [Middle English *insaciable,* from Old French, from Latin *insatiābilis* : *in-,* not + *satiāre,* to SATIATE.] —**in·sa·tia·bil·i·ty** (-bílləti), **in·sa·tia·ble·ness** *n.* —**in·sa·tia·bly** *adv.*

in·sa·ti·ate (in-sáyshi-ət, -it) *adj.* Not satisfied; never satisfied; insatiable. —**in·sa·ti·ate·ly** *adv.* —**in·sa·ti·ate·ness** *n.*

in·scribe (in-skrī́b) *tr.v.* **-scribed, -scribing, -scribes. 1.** To write, print, carve, or engrave (words or letters) on or in a paper, stone, wood, or other surface. **2.** To mark or engrave (a surface) with words or letters. **3.** To enter (a name) on a list or in a register. **4.** To write an inscription, such as a message or autograph, on (a book or photograph, for example) as an informal dedication to another. **5.** *Geometry.* To enclose (a polygon or polyhedron) within a closed configuration of lines, curves, or surfaces so that every vertex of the enclosed figure is incident on the enclosing configuration. **6.** *British.* To issue (loan stocks) in the form of shares whose holders' names are registered: *inscribed securities.* [Latin *inscrībere* : *in-,* in + *scrībere,* to write.] —**in·scrib·a·ble** *adj.* —**in·scrib·er** *n.*

in·scrip·tion (in-skrípsh'n) *n.* **1.** The act or an instance of inscribing. **2.** That which is inscribed, such as the wording on a coin or monument, or a dedication of a book or work of art. [Middle English *inscripcioun,* from Latin *inscriptiō* (stem *inscriptiōn-*), a writing in or upon, from *inscrībere* (past participle *inscriptus*), to INSCRIBE.] —**in·scrip·tion·al, in·scrip·tive** *adj.* —**in·scrip·tive·ly** *adv.*

in·scru·ta·ble (in-skrŏŏtə-b'l) *adj.* Not able to be fathomed or understood; impenetrable; enigmatic: *an inscrutable look.* —**in·scru·ta·bil·i·ty** (-bílləti), **in·scru·ta·ble·ness** *n.* —**in·scru·ta·bly** *adv.*

in·sect (ín-sekt) *n.* **1.** Any of numerous usually small invertebrate animals of the class Insecta (or Hexapoda), having an adult stage characterised by three pairs of legs, a segmented body with three major divisions, and usually two pairs of wings. **2.** Loosely, any of various similar invertebrate animals such as the spider, centipede, or tick. **3.** One who is small or contemptible. [Latin *insectum (animale),* "segmented (animal)" (translation of Greek *entomon*; see **entomo-**), from *insectus,* past participle of *insecāre,* to cut into : *in-,* in + *secāre,* to cut.]

in·sec·tar·i·um (ín-sek-taír-i-əm) *n., pl.* **-ums** or **-ia** (-i-ə). Also **in·sec·tar·y** (in-sék-təri, ín-sek-) *pl.* **-ies.** A place in which living insects are kept or bred.

in·sec·ti·cide (in-sékti-sīd) *n.* A substance used to kill insects. —**in·sec·ti·ci·dal** (-sī́d'l) *adj.*

in·sec·ti·vore (in-sékti-vawr || -vōr) *n.* **1.** Any of various mammals of the order Insectivora, characteristically feeding on insects, and including the shrews, moles, and hedgehogs. **2.** An organism that feeds on insects. [New Latin *Insectivora* (order) : Latin *insectum,* INSECT + *-vorus,* -VOROUS.]

in·sec·tiv·o·rous (in-sek-tívvərəss) *adj.* **1.** Feeding on insects. **2.** *Botany.* Capable of trapping and absorbing insects, as the pitcher plant or Venus's flytrap. [INSECT + -VOROUS.]

insectivorous bat *n.* Any of various bats of the suborder Microchiroptera, characteristically having large ears and feeding on insects.

in·se·cure (ín-si-kéwr) *adj.* **1.** Not secure or safe; inadequately guarded or protected. **2.** Not firm or firmly fixed; unstable; shaky. **3.** Apprehensive or lacking self-confidence: *felt insecure in company.* —**in·se·cure·ly** *adv.* —**in·se·cu·ri·ty, in·se·cure·ness** *n.*

in·sel·berg (ínz'l-berg) *n.* A domed hill or hard rock rising steeply from the surrounding region. [German : *Insel,* island + *Berg,* mountain.]

in·sem·i·nate (in-sémmi-nayt) *tr.v.* **-nated, -nating, -nates. 1.** To sow seed in. **2.** To introduce semen into the uterus of. **3.** To introduce (ideas) into the mind of another. [Latin *insēmināre* : *in-,* in + *sēmināre,* to plant, from *sēmen* (stem *sēmin-*), seed, SEMEN.] —**in·sem·i·na·tion** (-náysh'n) *n.* —**in·sem·i·na·tor** (-naytər) *n.*

in·sen·sate (in-sén-sayt, -sət, -sit) *adj.* **1. a.** Lacking sensation; inanimate. **b.** Unconscious. **2.** Lacking sensibility; inhuman; unfeeling. **3.** Lacking sense; foolish. —**in·sen·sate·ly** *adv.*

in·sen·si·ble (in-sénsəb'l) *adj.* **1.** Deprived of the power of feeling; unconscious. **2.** Imperceptible; inappreciable: *an insensible change.* **3. a.** Insusceptible; unaffected: *insensible to the cold.* **b.** Unaware; unmindful: *I am not insensible of your concern.* **c.** Not emotionally affected; unfeeling; indifferent: *insensible to their cries of pain.* **4.** *Archaic.* Lacking intelligence; irrational. —**in·sen·si·bil·i·ty** (-sə-bílləti) *n.* —**in·sen·si·bly** *adv.*

in·sen·si·tive (in-sén-sə-tiv) *adj.* **1.** Lacking sensation; not physically sensitive. **2.** Lacking sensitivity; unfeeling, unresponsive, or tactless. —**in·sen·si·tiv·i·ty** (-tívvəti), **in·sen·si·tive·ness** *n.* —**in·sen·si·tive·ly** *adv.*

in·sen·ti·ent (in-sén-shi-ənt, -shənt) *adj.* Without sensation or consciousness; inanimate. —**in·sen·ti·ence** *n.*

in·sep·a·ra·ble (in-séppərə-b'l, -sépprə-) *adj.* **1.** Incapable of being separated. **2.** Always together; intimate. —**in·sep·a·ra·bil·i·ty** (-bíl-

lǝti), **in·sep·a·ra·ble·ness** *n.* **—in·sep·a·ra·bly** *adv.*
in·sert (in-sért) *tr.v.* **-serted, -serting, -serts.** **1.** To put or set into, between, or among another or other things. **2.** To introduce into the body or text of something; interpolate.
~n. (ín-sert). Something inserted; especially, printed material, such as a map or advertising feature, inserted in a book or magazine. [Latin *inserere* (past participle *insertus*) : *in-*, in + *serere,* to sow, plant.] **—in·sert·er** (in-sértǝr) *n.*
in·sert·ed (in-sértid) *adj.* **1.** Joined to another part, as stamens to a corolla. **2.** *Anatomy.* Attached to the bone or other part that it moves. Said of a muscle.
in·ser·tion (in-sérsh'n) *n.* **1.** The act of inserting. **2.** Something inserted, such as an advertisement in a newspaper. **3.** *Anatomy.* A point or mode of attachment of a muscle to a bone. **4.** A strip of lace, embroidery, or other trimming to be inserted in a garment, tablecloth, or the like. **5.** *Botany.* The point at which one part is attached to another. **—in·ser·tion·al** *adj.*
in·ser·vice (in-sérviss) *adj.* Occurring while one is employed or in the context of one's work: *in-service training.*
in·ses·so·ri·al (in-se-sáwri-ǝl || -sṓri-) *adj.* *Rare.* Perching or adapted for perching: *insessorial claws.* [Late Latin *insessor,* "one that perches", from Latin *insidēre* (past participle *insessus*), to sit upon : *in-*, on + *sedēre,* to sit.]
in·set (in-sét) *tr.v.* **-set, -setting, -sets.** To insert; set in.
~n. (ín-set). **1.** Something set in, as: **a.** A small map or illustration set within a larger one. **b.** A leaf or group of pages inserted in a publication. **c.** A piece of material set into a dress as trimming. **2.** An inflow, as of water.
in·shore (ín-shór || -shṓr) *adj.* **1.** Situated or taking place close to the shore. **2.** Coming towards the shore. **—in·shore** *adv.*
in·side (ín-sī́d) *n.* **1.** The inner or interior part. **2.** An inner side or surface. **3.** The middle part; the part away from the edge: *the inside of the path.* **4.** *Plural. Informal.* **a.** The inner organs; the entrails. **b.** The inner parts or workings. **5.** A position affording access to exclusive or confidential information. **—inside out. 1.** With the inner surface turned out; reversed. **2.** Completely; thoroughly: *knows her inside out.*
~adj. **1.** Situated within; interior. **2.** Involving or coming from those having access to exclusive knowledge: *inside information.*
~adv. (in-sī́d). **1.** Into or in the interior; within. **2.** *British Slang.* In or into prison. **3.** In one's inner feelings or nature: *made me feel good inside.*
~prep. (in-sī́d). **1. a.** Within: *inside an hour.* **b.** Less than: *Her running time is well inside the record.* **2.** Into: *to go inside the house.* **—inside of.** Within the boundaries or limits of.
inside centre *n.* **1.** In Rugby football, a player taking a position outside the scrum, just beyond the stand-off half. **2.** The position of any of such players.
inside forward *n.* An inside left or inside right.
inside job *n.* *Chiefly British.* A crime committed by, or with the complicity of, someone who works or lives where the crime is committed.
inside left *n.* In ball games such as soccer or hockey: **1.** An attacking player on the left-hand side of the team. **2.** The position of such a player.
in·sid·er (in-sī́dǝr) *n.* **1.** An accepted member of a clique. **2.** One who has access to exclusive or confidential information.
inside right *n.* In ball games such as soccer or hockey: **1.** An attacking player on the right-hand side of the team. **2.** The position of such a player.
insider trading *n.* *Stock Market.* In share dealing, the use of confidential information for personal profit.
in·sid·i·ous (in-síddi-ǝss) *adj.* **1.** Working or spreading harmfully in a subtle or stealthy manner: *insidious disease.* **2.** Intended or seeking to entrap with guile: *insidious argument.* **3.** Wily; treacherous. [Latin *insidiōsus,* "lying in wait for", from *insidiae,* ambush, from *insidēre,* to sit in or on, lie in wait for. See **insessorial.**] **—in·sid·i·ous·ly** *adv.* **—in·sid·i·ous·ness** *n.*
in·sight (ín-sīt) *n.* **1.** The capacity to discern the true nature of a situation; penetration. **2.** An elucidating glimpse. **3.** *Psychology.* **a.** In behavioural studies, the sudden perception by an animal of a solution to a problem or difficulty. **b.** In psychoanalysis, a patient's perception of his own mental condition. **—in·sight·ful** *adj.* **—in·sight·ful·ly** *adv.*
in·sig·ni·a (in-síg-ni-ǝ) *n., pl.* **insignia** or **-as.** Also **in·sig·ne** (-nee). **1.** A badge of office, rank, membership, or nationality; an emblem. **2.** A distinguishing sign: *the insignia of success.* [Latin, plural of *insigne,* sign, mark, from *insignis,* distinguished, marked : *in-*, in + *signum,* SIGN.]
Usage: This word is now generally used as a singular, with plural forms being either *insignia* or *insignias.* The original singular, *insigne,* is rare, and is restricted to technical contexts.
in·sig·nif·i·cant (ín-sig-níffikǝnt, *also* -nívvikǝnt) *adj.* **1. a.** Trivial; unimportant. **b.** Lacking significant features or character: *an insignificant little man.* **c.** Contemptible. **2.** Small; trifling. **—in·sig·nif·i·cance, in·sig·nif·i·can·cy** *n.* **—in·sig·nif·i·cant·ly** *adv.*
in·sin·cere (ín-sin-séer) *adj.* Not sincere; hypocritical. **—in·sin·cere·ly** *adv.* **—in·sin·cer·i·ty** (-sérrǝti) *n.*
in·sin·u·ate (in-sínnew-ayt) *v.* **-ated, -ating, -ates.** *—tr.* **1.** To introduce gradually, subtly, artfully, or insidiously. **2.** To convey or imply with oblique hints and allusions; hint covertly: *insinuated that I wasn't telling the truth.* *—intr.* To make insinuations. —See Synonyms at **suggest.** [Latin *insinuāre,* to wind one's way into : *in-*, in + *sinuāre,* to curve, from *sinus,* curve, SINUS.] **—in·sin·u·at·ing·ly** *adv.* **—in·sin·u·a·tive** (-ǝtiv, -aytiv) *adj.* **—in·sin·u·a·tor** (-aytǝr) *n.*
in·sin·u·a·tion (in-sínnew-áysh'n) *n.* **1.** The act or practice of insinuating. **2.** An artfully indirect suggestion.
in·sip·id (in-síppid) *adj.* **1.** Lacking flavour or zest; unpalatable: *insipid food.* **2.** Lacking excitement or the ability to excite; spiritless; dull; unstimulating: *an insipid character.* [Late Latin *insipidus* : Latin *in-*, not + *sapidus,* SAPID.] **—in·si·pid·i·ty** (ín-si-píddǝti), **in·sip·id·ness** *n.* **—in·sip·id·ly** *adv.*
in·sist (in-síst) *v.* **-sisted, -sisting, -sists.** *—intr.* To emphasise or keep resolutely to an assertion, demand, or course of action. Usually used with *on* or *upon*: *insisted on his rights*; *insisted on paying the bill.* *—tr.* To assert or demand positively and persistently: *He insisted that he was right.* [Latin *insistere,* to stand on, persist : *in-*, on + *sistere,* to stand, stand firm.] **—in·sis·tence, in·sis·ten·cy** *n.*
in·sis·tent (in-sístǝnt) *adj.* **1.** Persistent; pertinacious. **2.** Demanding notice: *insistent hunger.* **—in·sis·tent·ly** *adv.*
in si·tu (in síttew, sī́-tew) *adv.* *Latin.* In (its original) place.
in·so·bri·e·ty (ín-sǝ-brī́-ǝti, -sō-) *n.* Lack of sobriety; intemperance.
in so far, in·so·far (ín-sō-fár, -sǝ-) *adv.* To such an extent. Used with *as.*
Usage: The writing of this form as a single word, followed by *as,* is now widespread, though it is still criticised by traditionalist writers on usage, who recommend separate words: *in so far as.*
in·so·late (ín-sō-layt) *tr.v.* **-lated, -lating, -lates.** To expose to sunlight, as for bleaching. [Latin *insōlāre* : *in-*, in + *sōl,* sun.]
in·so·la·tion (ín-sō-láysh'n) *n.* **1.** Exposure to sunlight, as for therapeutic purposes. **2. Sunstroke** *(see).* **3. a.** The solar radiation falling on the earth or another planet. **b.** The rate of delivery of such radiation per unit surface area.
in·sole (ín-sōl) *n.* **1.** The inner sole of a shoe or boot. **2.** An extra strip of material put inside a shoe for comfort or protection.
in·so·lent (ín-sǝlǝnt) *adj.* **1.** Presumptuous and insulting in manner or speech; arrogant. **2.** Audaciously impudent; impertinent. [Middle English, from Latin *insolēns,* perhaps originally "unusual", "quaint" : *in-*, not + *solēns* (stem *solent-*), present participle of *solēre,* to use (see **obsolete**).] **—in·so·lence** *n.* **—in·so·lent·ly** *adv.*
in·sol·u·ble (in-sóllew-b'l) *adj.* **1. a.** Incapable of being dissolved in water. **b.** Incapable of being dissolved in the specified solvent. **2.** Not able to be solved or explained. [Middle English *insolible,* from Latin *insolūbilis* : *in-*, not + *solvere,* to SOLVE.] **—in·sol·u·bil·i·ty** (-bíllǝti), **in·sol·u·ble·ness** *n.* **—in·sol·u·bly** *adv.*
in·solv·a·ble (in-sól-vǝb'l || *South of England also* -sṓl-) *adj.* Incapable of being solved. **—in·solv·a·bil·i·ty** *n.* **—in·solv·a·bly** *adv.*
in·sol·vent (in-sól-vǝnt || *South of England also* -sṓl-) *adj.* **1.** Unable to meet debts or discharge liabilities; bankrupt. **2.** Pertaining to bankruptcy or bankrupt persons.
~n. One who is insolvent. **—in·sol·ven·cy** *n.*
in·som·ni·a (in-sóm-ni-ǝ) *n.* Chronic inability to sleep. [Latin, from *insomnis,* sleepless : *in-*, not + *somnus,* sleep.] **—in·som·ni·ous** *adj.*
in·som·ni·ac (in-sóm-ni-ak) *n.* A person suffering from insomnia.
~adj. Causing or exhibiting insomnia.
in·so·much (ín-sō-múch, -sǝ-) *adv.* **1.** To such extent or degree. Used with *as* or *that.* **2.** Since; inasmuch. Used with *as.* [Middle English *in so muche,* translation of Old French *en tant (que).*]
in·sou·ci·ance (in-sóo-si-ǝnss; *French* aɴ-sooss-yóɴss) *n.* Lack of concern; lighthearted indifference.
in·sou·ci·ant (in-sóo-si-ǝnt; *French* aɴ-sooss-yóɴ) *adj.* Blithely indifferent; carefree. [French : *in-*, not + *souciant,* present participle of *soucier,* to trouble, upset (reflexively, "to care"), from Latin *sollicitāre,* to agitate, vex (see **solicit**).] **—in·sou·ci·ant·ly** *adv.*
in·span (in-span) *v.* **-spanned, -spanning, -spans.** *Chiefly South African.* *—tr.* **1.** To harness (a draught animal) as to a wagon. **2.** To prepare (a wagon, for example) for a journey. *—intr.* **1.** To inspan a draught animal. **2.** To prepare for a journey, as by making a wagon ready. [Afrikaans, from Middle Dutch *inspannen,* from *spannen,* to yoke.]
in·spect (in-spékt) *tr.v.* **-spected, -specting, -spects.** **1.** To examine carefully and critically, especially for flaws. **2.** To review or examine officially: *inspecting the troops.* [Latin *inspectāre,* frequentative of *inspicere* (past participle *inspectus*), to look into : *in-*, in + *specere,* to look.] **—in·spect·ive** *adj.*
in·spec·tion (in-spékshǝn) *n.* **1.** The act of inspecting. **2.** An examination, scrutiny, or review, especially one of a formal or official character: *an inspection of the troops.* **—in·spec·tion·al** *adj.*
inspection chamber *n.* A **manhole** *(see).*
in·spec·tor (in-spéktǝr) *n.* *Abbr.* **ins., insp. 1.** One who inspects; especially, an official whose job it is to examine and supervise the running of a particular operation, institution, organisation, and to ensure that the appropriate rules and standards are maintained. **2.** A police officer of the rank next below superintendent and above sergeant. **—in·spec·to·ral, in·spec·to·ri·al** (-spek-táwri-ǝl || -tṓri-) *adj.* **—in·spec·tor·ship** *n.*
in·spec·tor·ate (in-spéktǝr-ǝt, -it) *n.* **1.** The office or duties of an inspector. **2.** A staff of inspectors. **3.** An inspector's district.
inspector general *n., pl.* **inspectors general. 1.** A person in charge of a staff of inspectors or a system of inspection. **2.** *U.S.* An officer having investigative powers in the armed forces.
insphere. Variant of **ensphere.**
in·spi·ra·tion (ín-spǝ-ráysh'n, -spi-) *n.* **1.** Stimulation of the mental or emotional faculties to a high level of feeling, animation, or creative activity. **2.** The condition of being so stimulated. **3.** Someone or something perceived as the source of such stimulation: *His ex-*

ample was an inspiration to us all. **4.** Something that is inspired, such as an idea or action. **5.** *Theology.* Divine guidance or influence exerted directly upon the mind and soul of humankind. **6.** The act of breathing in; inhalation.

in·spi·ra·tion·al (in-spə-ráysh'n-'l, -spi-) *adj.* **1.** Of or pertaining to inspiration. **2.** Providing or intended to convey inspiration. **3.** Resulting from inspiration. **—in·spi·ra·tion·al·ly** *adv.*

in·spi·ra·tor (ín-spə-raytər, -spi-) *n.* A device for drawing in vapour or liquid.

in·spir·a·to·ry (in-spír-ə-təri, -spírrə-, -tri) *adj.* Pertaining to or used for the drawing in of air.

in·spire (in-spír) *v.* **-spired, -spiring, -spires.** *—tr.* **1.** To animate the mind or emotions of; serve as a source of inspiration to: *inspired by his rousing speech.* **2.** To stimulate or impel to a particular feeling or action: *inspired her to be brave.* **3. a.** To elicit; bring forth: *a woman capable of inspiring love.* **b.** To suggest or bring about; serve as a source of inspiration for: *a whole poem inspired by that fleeting smile.* **4. a.** To affect, guide, or arouse by divine influence. **b.** To communicate by divine influence: *oratory inspired by God.* **5.** To inhale (air). **6.** *Archaic.* **a.** To breathe upon. **b.** To breathe life into. *—intr.* **1.** To rouse latent energies, ideals, or reverence. **2.** To inhale. [Middle English *inspiren,* from Old French *inspirer,* from Latin *inspīrāre,* to breathe into : *in-,* into + *spīrāre,* to breathe.] **—in·spir·er** *n.* **—in·spir·ing·ly** *adv.*

in·spired (in-spírd, -spiərd) *adj.* Resulting from or as if from inspiration: *an inspired guess, an inspired performance.*

in·spir·it (in-spírrit) *tr.v.* **-ited, -iting, -its.** To instil courage or life into; animate; enliven.

in·spis·sate (in-spíssayt, ín-spi-sayt) *v.* **-sated, -sating, -sates.** *—tr.* To cause to thicken, as by boiling or evaporation; condense. *—intr.* To thicken. [Late Latin *inspissāre* : Latin *in-* (intensive) + *spissāre,* to thicken, from *spissus*†, thick.] **—in·spis·sa·tion** (in-spi-sáysh'n) *n.* **—in·spis·sa·tor** (ín-spiss-aytər, in-spíss-) *n.*

inst. 1. instant. **2.** instance. **3.** institute; institution. **4.** instrument.

in·sta·bil·i·ty (in-stə-bílləti) *n., pl.* **-ties.** Lack of stability, firmness, or steadiness: *emotional instability.*

in·stall, in·stal (in-stáwl) *tr.v.* **-stalled, -stalling, -stalls** or **-stals. 1.** To set (a machine, for example) in position and connect or adjust for use. **2.** To put in an office, rank, or position, especially with ceremonies. **3.** To settle in the place or condition specified; establish. Often used reflexively: *He installed himself by the window.* [Old French *installer,* from Medieval Latin *installāre* : *in-* (causative) + *stallum,* place, stall.] **—in·stall·er** *n.*

in·stal·la·tion (in-stə-láysh'n, -staw-) *n.* **1.** The act of installing or the state of being installed. **2. a.** A system of machinery or other apparatus set up for use. **b.** A work of art that is an arrangement of still or moving objects, perhaps complemented by films, lights, and the like. **3.** A military base or camp.

in·stal·ment[1], *U.S.* **in·stall·ment** (in-stáwlmənt) *n.* **1.** One of several successive payments in settlement of a debt. **2.** A portion of anything issued at intervals. **3.** A chapter, episode, or part of a work presented serially. [Variant of earlier *estallment,* from Anglo-French *estalement,* from *estaler,* to fix (as payments), from *estal,* place, fixed position, from Old High German *stal,* place, stall.]

in·stal·ment[2] *U.S.* **in·stall·ment** *n.* The act of installing (sense 2) or state of being installed.

instalment plan *n. U.S.* **Hire-purchase** *(see).* Used with *the.*

in·stance (ín-stənss) *n. Abbr.* **inst. 1.** A case or example. **2.** A legal proceeding or process; a suit: *a court of first instance.* **3.** A specified step in a procedure or list of considerations: *Apply in the first instance to the personnel manager.* **4. a.** Prompting; request: *He called at the instance of his wife.* **b.** *Archaic.* Urgent solicitation. —See Synonyms at **example. —for instance.** For example.
~tr.v. **instanced, -stancing, -stances. 1.** To offer as an example; cite. **2.** To demonstrate or show by being an example of; exemplify. [Middle English *instaunce,* from Old French *instance,* from Latin *instantia,* presence, perseverance, urgency, from *instāns,* INSTANT.]

in·stan·cy (ín-stən-si) *n.* **1.** Urgency. **2.** *Rare.* Immediateness.

in·stant (ín-stənt) *n. Abbr.* **inst 1.** A very brief time; a moment: *He came in an instant.* **2.** A particular point in time: *the instant she arrives.* —See Synonyms at **moment.**
~adj. Abbr. **inst. 1.** Immediate: *instant attention.* **2.** Imperative; urgent: *an instant need.* **3.** Of the current month: *my letter of the fifth instant.* Compare **proximo, ultimo. 4.** Prepared or devised so as to be made usable or accessible rapidly and with minimal effort: *instant soup; instant history.*
~adv. Poetic. Instantly. [Middle English, urgent, immediate, from Old French, from Latin *instāns* (stem *instant-*), present participle of *instāre,* to be present, persist : *in-,* upon + *stāre,* to stand.]

in·stan·ta·ne·ous (ín-stən-táyni-əss) *adj.* **1.** Occurring or completed without perceptible delay. **2.** Occurring or applying at a specific instance of time. Said of changing physical quantities that are considered at a given instance: *instantaneous pressure.* [Medieval Latin *instantāneus,* from Latin *instāns,* urgent, INSTANT.] **—in·stan·ta·ne·ous·ly** *adv.* **—in·stan·ta·ne·ous·ness** *n.*

in·stan·ter (in-stántər) *adv.* Instantly. [Medieval Latin, from Latin, urgently, from *instāns,* urgent, INSTANT.]

in·stan·ti·ate (instan-shi-ayt) *tr.v.* **-ated, -ating, -ates.** To be an instance of. **—in·stan·ti·a·tion** (-áysh'n) *n.*

in·stant·ly (ín-stənt-li) *adv.* **1.** At once. **2.** *Archaic.* Urgently. —See Synonyms at **immediately.**
~conj. As soon as: *tell me instantly she comes.*

instant replay *n. Chiefly U.S.* An **action replay** *(see).*

in·star (ín-staar) *n.* **1.** An insect or other arthropod between moults, as during metamorphosis. **2.** This stage of development. [New Latin, from Latin *instar*†, form, likeness (referring to the successive forms of the arthropod after each moult, as *first instar, second instar,* and so on).]

in·state (in-stáyt) *tr.v.* **-stated, -stating, -states.** To put in office; install. [IN- (causative) + STATE (rank).] **—in·state·ment** *n.*

in sta·tu quo (in státtōō kwō, stáytōō) *adv. Latin.* In the same state or condition as before.

in·stau·ra·tion (ín-staw-ráysh'n, -stə-) *n. Archaic.* Renovation; restoration. [Latin *instaurātiō* (stem *instaurātiōn-*), from *instaurāre,* to restore.] **—in·stau·ra·tor** (-raytər) *n.*

in·stead (in-stéd) *adv.* In the place of that previously mentioned or implied; as an alternative or substitute: *Planning to drive, he walked instead.* **—instead of.** In lieu of; rather than: *"Instead of eating monkeys/They are eating Christians"* (T.S. Eliot). [Middle English *in sted (of)* : IN + STEAD.]

in·step (ín-step) *n.* **1.** The arched, middle section of the human foot. **2.** The part of a shoe, stocking, or the like, covering the instep. [Probably IN + STEP.]

in·sti·gate (ín-sti-gayt) *tr.v.* **-gated, -gating, -gates. 1.** To urge on; goad; incite, especially to wrongdoing. **2.** To foment; stir up. [Latin *instīgāre* : *in-* (intensive) + *stīgāre,* to spur on.] **—in·sti·ga·tion** (-gáysh'n) *n.* **—in·sti·ga·tive** *adj.* **—in·sti·ga·tor** (-gaytər) *n.*

in·stil, *U.S.* **in·still** (in-stíl) *tr.v.* **-stilled, -stilling, -stils** or *U.S.* **-stills. 1.** To introduce or impart by gradual, persistent efforts; implant. **2.** To pour in drop by drop. [Latin *instillāre,* to drip in : *in-,* in + *stillāre,* to drip, from *stilla*†, drop.] **—in·stil·la·tion** (ín-sti-láysh'n) *n.* **—in·still·er** *n.* **—in·stil·ment** *n.*

in·stinct (ín-stingkt) *n.* **1. a.** The aspect of behaviour that is innate, complex, and normally adaptive. **b.** A powerful intuition or impulse. **2.** An innate aptitude: *an instinct for picking a winner.*
~adj. (in-stíngkt). *Archaic.* Imbued or charged with something, such as energy. [Middle English, from Latin *instinctus,* instigation, from the past participle of *instinguere,* to instigate, urge on : *in-,* on + *stinguere,* to prick, incite.] **—in·stinc·tu·al** *adj.*

in·stinc·tive (in-stíngktiv) *adj.* **1.** Of or pertaining to instinct. **2.** Arising from instinct. —See Synonyms at **spontaneous. —in·stinc·tive·ly** *adv.*

in·sti·tute (ín-sti-tewt || -tōōt) *tr.v.* **-tuted, -tuting, -tutes. 1. a.** To establish, organise, and set in operation. **b.** To initiate; begin. **2.** To establish or invest in a position; especially, to install (a clergyman) in a position of spiritual authority.
~n. **1.** Something instituted, especially: **a.** An authoritative rule or precedent. **b.** *Plural.* A digest of the principles or rudiments of some subject, especially law. **2.** *Abbr.* **inst. a.** An organisation or association set up to promote some cause. **b.** An educational institution. **c.** The building or buildings of such an organisation or institution. **3.** *Chiefly U.S.* A short, intensive workshop or seminar on one specific subject. [Middle English *instituten,* from Latin *instituere,* to establish, ordain : *in-,* in + *statuere,* to set up, from *stāre* (past participle *status*), to stand.] **—in·sti·tu·tor** *n.*

in·sti·tu·tion (ín-sti-téwsh'n || -tōōsh'n) *n. Abbr.* **inst. 1.** The act of instituting. **2. a.** A relationship or behavioural pattern of importance in the life of a community or society: *the institution of marriage.* **b.** *Informal.* An ever-present feature; a fixture: *His corny jokes were a family institution.* **3.** An organisation or establishment set up to perform a specific charitable, religious, educational, or other public service: *the Royal National Lifeboat Institution.* **4.** The building or buildings housing such an organisation. **5.** A place of confinement, such as a mental hospital.

in·sti·tu·tion·al (ín-sti-téwsh'n-'l || -tōōsh'n-) *adj.* **1.** Of or pertaining to institutions. **2.** Organised through institutions or as an institution: *institutional religion.* **3.** Characteristic or suggestive of an institution, especially in being uniform, dull, or unimaginative: *institutional furniture.* **4.** Of or pertaining to the principles or institutes of a subject such as law. **—in·sti·tu·tion·al·ly** *adv.*

in·sti·tu·tion·al·ise, in·sti·tu·tion·al·ize (ín-sti-téwsh'n-ə-līz || -tōōsh'n-) *tr.v.* **-ised, -ising, -ises. 1.** To make into an institution; give legal or institutional status to; *a society that has institutionalised injustice.* **2.** To confine (a person) in an institution. **3.** To expose to the harmful effects of long-term confinement in an institution, producing apathy, dependence, and boredom. **—in·sti·tu·tion·al·i·sa·tion** (-lī-záysh'n || *U.S.* -li-) *n.*

in·sti·tu·tion·al·ism (ín-sti-téwsh'n-ə-liz'm || tōōsh'n-) *n.* **1.** Belief in established forms, such as those of a religion, sometimes to the virtual exclusion of other considerations. **2.** The provision of institutional care or maintenance for those in need. **—in·sti·tu·tion·al·ist** *n. & adj.*

in·struct (in-strúkt) *tr.v.* **-structed, -structing, -structs. 1.** To furnish with knowledge; teach; educate. **2.** To provide with authoritative directions; give orders to. **3.** *Law.* **a.** To provide (a solicitor) with information relevant to a case. Used of a client. **b.** To provide (a barrister) with such information. Used of a solicitor. **c.** To authorise (a solicitor or barrister) to appear on one's behalf. **d.** To provide (a jury) with a full elucidation of the points of law in a particular case. —See Synonyms at **command, teach.** [Middle English *instructen,* from Latin *instruere* (past participle *instructus*), to build, prepare, instruct : *in-,* in + *struere,* to build.]

in·struc·tion (in-strúkshən) *n. Abbr.* **instr. 1.** The act, practice, or profession of instructing; education. **2. a.** Imparted knowledge. **b.** An imparted or acquired item of knowledge; a lesson. **3.** *Plural.* **a.** Directions; orders. **b.** *Law.* Information or directions given by a client to a solicitor or by a solicitor to a barrister. **4.** *Computing.* A part of a program that causes the computer to perform a specific operation. **—in·struc·tion·al** *adj.*

in·struc·tive (in-strúktiv) *adj.* Conveying knowledge or information. **—in·struc·tive·ly** *adv.* **—in·struc·tive·ness** *n.*

in·struc·tor (in-strúktər) *n. Abbr.* **instr. 1.** One who instructs; a teacher. **2.** *U.S.* **a.** An academic rank below that of assistant professor. **b.** One who holds such a rank. **—in·struc·tor·ship** *n.*

in·struc·tress (in-strúktriss) *n.* A female instructor.

in·stru·ment (ín-strə-mənt, -strōō-) *n. Abbr.* **inst., instr. 1.** A means by which something is done; an agency. **2.** One used to accomplish some purpose. **3.** A mechanical implement; a tool. **4.** A device for recording or measuring; especially, such a device functioning as part of a control system, as in an aircraft, for example. **5.** A device for producing or playing music: *a stringed instrument.* **6.** A legal document. **—See Synonyms at tool.**

~ *tr.v.* **instrumented, -menting, -ments. 1.** To provide or equip with instruments. **2.** To arrange (music) for instruments. [Middle English, from Latin *instrūmentum,* implement, equipment, tool, from *instruere,* to prepare, equip, INSTRUCT.]

in·stru·men·tal (ín-strə-mént'l, -strōō-) *adj.* **1.** Serving as a means or instrument; contributing decisively to some outcome. **2.** Of, pertaining to, or accomplished with an instrument or tool. **3.** Performed on or written for a musical instrument or instruments rather than the voice. **4.** *Grammar.* Of or designating a case in Russian, Sanskrit, and certain other inflected languages, used typically to express means, agency, or accompaniment.

~ *n.* **1.** The instrumental case. **2.** A form or construction in this case. **—in·stru·men·tal·ly** *adv.*

in·stru·men·tal·ism (ín-strə-mént'l-iz'm, -strōō-) *n.* A pragmatic theory that ideas are instruments that function as guides of action, their validity being measured by the success of the action.

in·stru·men·tal·ist (ín-strə-mént'l-ist, -strōō-) *n.* **1.** One who plays a musical instrument. **2.** A student or advocate of instrumentalism.

in·stru·men·tal·i·ty (ín-strə-men-tál-í-tē, -strōō-, -mən-) *n., pl.* **-ties. 1.** The quality or circumstance of being instrumental. **2.** Agency; means.

in·stru·men·ta·tion (ín-strə-men-táysh'n, -strōō-, -mən-) *n.* **1. a.** The application or use of instruments in the performance of some work. **b.** Instruments collectively. **2.** The study and practice of arranging music for instruments. **3.** The study, development, and manufacture of instruments, as for scientific use. **4.** Instrumentality.

instrument flying *n.* The flying of an aircraft using only the recording instruments and radio instructions from the ground, without visual observation.

instrument panel *n.* A mounted array of instruments used to monitor performance. Also called "instrument board".

in·sub·or·di·nate (in-sə-bórd'n-ət, -bórdin-, -it) *adj.* Not submissive to authority; rebellious.

~ *n.* An insubordinate person. **—in·sub·or·di·nate·ly** *adv.* **—in·sub·or·di·na·tion** (-áysh'n) *n.*

Synonyms: insubordinate, rebellious, mutinous, factious, seditious.

in·sub·stan·tial (ín-səb-stánsh'l) *adj.* **1.** Lacking substance; imaginary. **2.** Not firm; unsubstantial. **—in·sub·stan·ti·al·i·ty** (-stán-shi-ál-ə-ti) *n.*

in·suf·fer·a·ble (in-súffərə-b'l, -súffrə-) *adj.* Not endurable; intolerable. **—in·suf·fer·a·ble·ness** *n.* **—in·suf·fer·a·bly** *adv.*

in·suf·fi·cien·cy (in-sə-físh'n-si) *n., pl.* **-cies. 1.** The quality or state of being insufficient. **2.** A lack or deficiency, as of some requisite thing or quality. **3.** *Medicine.* Inability of an organ to function properly.

in·suf·fi·cient (ín-sə-físh'nt) *adj.* Not sufficient; inadequate: *insufficient evidence.* **—in·suf·fi·cient·ly** *adv.*

in·suf·flate (ín-sufflayt ‖ in-súfflayt) *tr.v.* **-flated, -flating, -flates. 1.** To blow or breathe into or upon. **2.** To treat medically by blowing a powder, gas, or vapour into a bodily cavity. [Late Latin *insufflāre* : Latin *in-,* into + *sufflāre,* to blow.] **—in·suf·fla·tor** (-ər) *n.*

in·suf·fla·tion (in-su-fláysh'n) *n.* **1.** The act or an instance of insufflating. **2.** *Ecclesiastical.* A ritual breathing upon a person or thing as a symbol of the influence of the Holy Spirit.

in·su·lar (ín-sew-lər ‖ -sə-, -shə-) *adj.* **1.** Of, pertaining to, or constituting an island. **2.** Characteristic or suggestive of the isolated life of an island, especially: **a.** Circumscribed and detached in outlook and experience. **b.** Narrow; prejudiced. **3.** *Anatomy.* Designating isolated tissue or an island of tissue. [Late Latin *īnsulāris,* from Latin *īnsula,* island, ISLE.] **—in·su·lar·ism, in·su·lar·i·ty** (-lárrəti) *n.* **—in·su·lar·ly** *adv.*

in·su·late (ín-sew-layt ‖ -sə-) *tr.v.* **-lated, -lating, -lates. 1. a.** To detach; isolate. **b.** To shield (a person), as from unpleasant realities. **2.** To prevent the passage of heat, electricity, or sound into or out of (a body or region), especially by interposition of an appropriate material. [Originally "to convert into an island", from Latin *īnsula,* island, ISLE.]

in·su·lat·ing tape (in-sew-layting ‖ -sə-) *n.* Adhesive tape, as of plastic or waterproofed fabric, to insulate electrical conductors.

in·su·la·tion (in-sew-láysh'n ‖ -sə-) *n.* **1.** The act of insulating or state of being insulated. **2.** Material used in insulating.

in·su·la·tor (in-sew-laytər ‖ -sə-) *n.* **1.** A material that insulates; especially, a substance that is a poor conductor of heat, electricity, or sound. **2.** A device that insulates.

in·su·lin (ín-sew-lin ‖ -sə-) *n.* **1.** A polypeptide hormone secreted by the islets of Langerhans in the pancreas and functioning to regulate carbohydrate metabolism by controlling blood glucose levels. **2.** A preparation produced by genetic engineering or derived from the pancreas of the pig or the ox for use in the medical treatment of diabetes. [Latin *īnsula,* island.]

insulin shock *n.* **1.** Acute hypoglycaemia that typically results from an overdose of insulin given to a diabetic and may lead to coma. Also called "insulin reaction". **2.** Such a condition formerly induced artificially for therapeutic purposes in schizophrenics.

in·sult (in-súlt) *v.* **-sulted, -sulting, -sults. —tr. 1. a.** To speak to or treat in a callous or contemptuous way. **b.** To reveal a disdainful estimate of: *The paper's political analysis insults its readers' intelligence.* **2.** *Archaic.* To make an attack upon; assault. **—intr.** *Obsolete.* To behave arrogantly. **—See Synonyms at offend.**

~ *n.* (in-sult). **1.** An offensive action or remark; an affront. **2.** A slur; an aspersion: *Your refusal to confide is an insult to my discretion.* **3.** *Medicine.* An injury, irritation, or trauma. [French *insulter,* to triumph over, behave arrogantly, from Latin *insultāre,* to leap on, jump over : *in-,* on, upon + *saltāre,* frequentative of *salīre,* to jump.]

in·su·per·a·ble (in-sōō-pərə-b'l, -séw-, -prə-) *adj.* Incapable of being overcome; insurmountable: *an insuperable barrier.* **—in·su·per·a·bil·i·ty** (-bíllə-ti) *n.* **—in·su·per·a·bly** *adv.*

in·sup·port·a·ble (ín-sə-pórt-əb'l ‖ -pórt-) *adj.* **1.** Unbearable; intolerable. **2.** Lacking grounds or defence; unjustifiable: *an insupportable claim.* **—in·sup·port·a·ble·ness** *n.* **—in·sup·port·a·bly** *adv.*

in·sup·press·i·ble (in-sə-préssəb'l) *adj.* That cannot be suppressed; irrepressible.

in·sur·ance (in-shōōr-ənss ‖ -shéwr-) *n. Abbr.* **ins. 1. a.** The act, business, or process of insuring persons or property. **b.** The state of being insured. **2.** A contract binding a company to indemnify an insured party against stipulated loss, damage, or injury in return for premiums paid. Also called "insurance policy". **3.** The sum or coverage so insured. **4.** The periodical premium paid for this indemnification. **5.** A protective measure or device: *took an umbrella as an insurance against rain.*

in·sur·ant (in-shōōr-ənt ‖ -shéwr-) *n.* One who is insured.

in·sure (in-shōōr ‖ -shéwr) *v.* **-sured, -suring, -sures. —tr. 1.** To cover with insurance: *Am I insured if I drive your car?* **2.** To make sure or certain; ensure. **3.** To make safe or secure. Used with *from* or *against: Nowadays a degree doesn't insure you against unemployment.* **—intr.** To buy or sell insurance. [Middle English *insuren, ensuren,* to guarantee, from Anglo-French *enseurer,* perhaps variant of Old French *ass(e)urer,* to ASSURE.] **—in·sur·a·bil·i·ty** (-ə-bílləti) *n.* **—in·sur·a·ble** *adj.*

in·sured (in-shōórd ‖ -shéwrd) *n., pl.* **insured.** One covered by insurance.

in·sur·er (in-shōór-ər ‖ -shéwr-) *n.* One who insures; an underwriter.

in·sur·gence (in-súrjənss) *n.* **1.** Uprising. **2.** An act of revolt.

in·sur·gen·cy (in-súrjən-si) *n.* **1.** The quality or state of being insurgent. **2.** Insurgence.

in·sur·gent (in-súrjənt) *adj.* Rising in revolt against civil authority or a government in power.

~ *n.* **1.** One who revolts against authority. **2.** *U.S.* A member of a political party who rebels against its leadership. [Latin *insurgēns* (stem *insurgent-*), present participle of *insurgere,* to rise up : *in-* (intensive) + *surgere,* to rise, SURGE.]

in·sur·mount·a·ble (ín-sər-mówntəb'l) *adj.* Incapable of being surmounted; insuperable: *struggling against insurmountable difficulties.* **—in·sur·mount·a·bly** *adv.*

in·sur·rec·tion (ín-sə-réksh'n) *n.* An act or instance of open revolt against civil authority or a constituted government. See Synonyms at **rebellion.** [Middle English *insurrecioun,* from Old French *insurrection,* from Latin *insurrectiō* (stem *insurrection-*), from *insurgere* (past participle *insurrectus*), to rise up. See **insurgent.**] **—in·sur·rec·tion·al** *adj.* **—in·sur·rec·tion·ar·y** *adj. & n.* **—in·sur·rec·tion·ist** *n.*

in·sus·cep·ti·ble (in-sə-séptəb'l) *adj.* Not susceptible; unaffected.

in·swing·er (ín-swing-ər) *n.* A ball bowled in cricket that swerves through the air from off to leg.

in·tact (in-tákt) *adj.* **1.** Not impaired in any way. **2.** Having all parts; whole. [Middle English *intacte,* untouched, from Latin *intactus* : *in-,* not + *tactus,* past participle of *tangere,* to touch.] **—in·tact·ness** *n.*

in·ta·glio (in-táali-ō, -tál-i-; *Italian* in-táa-lyō) *n., pl.* **-glios** or **-tagli** (-táal-yee, -tál-; *Italian* -táa-lyee). **1. a.** A figure or design incised into the surface of hard metal or stone. **b.** The art or process of making intaglios. **2.** Something, such as a gemstone, carved in intaglio. Compare **cameo. 3.** Printing done with a plate bearing an image in intaglio. **4.** A die incised to produce a design in relief. [Italian, from *intagliare,* to engrave : *in-,* in + *tagliare,* to cut, from (unattested) Vulgar Latin *tālliāre* (see **tailor**).] **—in·ta·glia·ted** *adj.*

in·take (ín-tayk) *n.* **1.** An opening by which a fluid is admitted into a container or conduit. **2.** An airway into a mine. **3. a.** The act of taking in. **b.** A person, thing, or quantity that is taken in or received: *an intake of energy; a fresh intake of members.*

in·tan·gi·ble (in-tánjə-b'l) *adj.* **1.** Incapable of being perceived by touch; impalpable. **2.** Imprecisely defined or identified; elusive: *intangible ideas.* **—in·tan·gi·ble** *n.* **—in·tan·gi·bil·i·ty** (-bílləti), **in·tan·gi·ble·ness** *n.* **—in·tan·gi·bly** *adv.*

in·tar·si·a (in-tár-si-ə) *n.* **1.** A mosaic worked in wood. **2.** The art or process of making such mosaics. **3. a.** A knitting technique by which large patches of different colour are juxtaposed in stocking stitch to form an asymmetrical design, keeping several yarns on the needle at once and joining them by overlapping behind the work. **b.** Work produced or decorated by this method. [Perhaps IN(LAY) + *tarsia,* an inlaid mosaic, from Arabic *tarsī.*]

in·te·ger (íntijər) *n.* **1.** Any member of the set of positive whole numbers (1, 2, 3, . . .), negative whole numbers (–1, –2, –3, . . .), and zero (0). **2.** Any intact unit or entity. [Latin, whole, complete, perfect, virtuous.]

in·te·gra·ble (ínti-grəb'l) *adj. Mathematics.* Capable of being integrated. Said of a function.

in·te·gral (íntigrəl || in-téggrəl, -teégrəl) *adj.* **1. a.** Essential for completion; necessary to the whole. **b.** Forming a constituent or intrinsic part; not separate: *a house with an integral garage.* **2.** Whole; entire; intact. **3.** *Mathematics.* **a.** Expressed or expressible as or in terms of integers. **b.** Expressed as or involving integrals.

~n. **1.** A complete unit; a whole. **2.** *Mathematics.* The limit of a sum of terms as the number of terms tends to infinity and the terms tend to zero. There are two types: the **definite integral** and the **indefinite integral** *(both of which see).* [Middle English, from Late Latin *integrālis,* making up a whole, from Latin *integer,* whole.] **—in·te·gral·i·ty** (ínti-grál-əti) *n.* **—in·te·gral·ly** *adv.*

integral calculus *n.* The mathematical study of integration, the properties of integrals, and their applications.

integral domain *n. Mathematics.* A commutative ring with unity having no proper divisors of zero, that is, having no nonzero elements *a, b* such that $a \cdot b = 0$, where 0 is the additive identity.

in·te·grand (ínti-grand) *n.* A mathematical function or equation to be integrated. [Latin *integrandus,* from *integrāre,* to INTEGRATE.]

in·te·grant (íntigrənt) *adj.* Integral; constituent. [Latin *integrāns* (stem *integrant-*), present participle of *integrāre,* to INTEGRATE.]

in·te·grate (ínti-grayt) *v.* **-grated, -grating, -grates.** *—tr.* **1.** To make into a whole by bringing all parts together; unify. **2.** To unite with or incorporate into a larger body or unit; especially, to cause (members of an ethnically or culturally distinct group) to be assimilated into a society. **3.** To desegregate. **4.** *Mathematics.* To calculate the integral of (a function). **5.** To bring about the harmonious integration of (personality traits): *an integrated personality.* *—intr.* To become integrated or undergo integration. [Latin *integrāre,* to make complete, from *integer,* whole.] **—in·te·gra·tive** *adj.*

in·te·grat·ed circuit (ínti-graytid) *n. Abbr.* **IC.** An electronic circuit made of a number of components connected in a single small package, either by fixing small separate components on a ceramic wafer or by building them into the surface of a silicon chip.

in·te·gra·tion (ínti-gráysh'n) *n.* **1. a.** An act or the process of integrating. **b.** The state of becoming integrated. **c.** Desegregation. **2.** The organisation of the psychological or social traits and tendencies of a personality into a harmonious whole. **3.** *Physiology.* The processing of information received by the nervous system in such a way that a flexible and coordinated response is made. **4.** *Mathematics.* The process of finding the equation or function of which a given quantity or function is the derivative.

in·te·gra·tor (ínti-graytər) *n.* **1.** One that integrates. **2.** An instrument for mechanically calculating definite integrals.

in·teg·ri·ty (in-téggrəti) *n.* **1.** Strict adherence to a code of moral values, artistic principles, or other standards; complete sincerity or honesty. **2.** The state of being unimpaired; soundness. **3.** Completeness; unity. —See Synonyms at **honesty.** [Middle English *integrite,* from Old French, from Latin *integritās* (stem *integritāt-*), completeness, purity, from *integer,* whole. See **integer.**]

in·teg·u·ment (in-téggew-mənt) *n.* An outer covering or coat, such as the skin of an animal, the coat of a seed, or the membrane enclosing an organ. [Latin *integumentum,* from *integere,* to cover : *in-,* on + *tegere,* to cover.] **—in·teg·u·ment·al** (-ménť'l), **in·teg·u·men·ta·ry** (-mén-təri, -tri) *adj.*

in·tel·lect (íntə-lekt) *n.* **1. a.** The ability to learn and reason as distinguished from the ability to feel or will; the capacity for knowledge and understanding. **b.** The ability to think abstractly or profoundly. **2. a.** A person of great intellectual ability. **b.** The intellectual members of a group. —See Synonyms at **mind.** [Middle English, from Old French, from Latin *intellectus,* perception, comprehension, from the past participle of *intellegere,* to perceive, choose between. See **intelligent.**]

in·tel·lec·tion (íntə-léksh'n) *n.* **1.** The act or process of exercising the intellect; mental activity. **2.** A thought or idea. [Middle English *intelleccioun,* understanding, from Latin *intellectiō* (stem *intellectiōn-*), from *intellectus,* INTELLECT.]

in·tel·lec·tive (íntə-léktiv) *adj.* Of, pertaining to, or generated by the intellect. **—in·tel·lec·tive·ly** *adv.*

in·tel·lec·tu·al (íntə-léktew-əl) *adj.* **1. a.** Of or pertaining to the intellect. **b.** Rational rather than emotional: *an intellectual debate.* **2.** Appealing to or requiring the exercise of the intellect. **3. a.** Having superior intelligence. **b.** Involved in activity requiring the use of the intellect. **c.** Given to or marked by the creative use of the intellect, as expressed in abstract thought, study, and developed artistic and literary tastes. —See Synonyms at **intelligent.**

~n. **1.** An intellectual person. **2.** One belonging to an intellectual group or class, and involved in mental rather than manual labour. **—in·tel·lec·tu·al·i·ty** (-ál-əti) *n.* **—in·tel·lec·tu·al·ly** *adv.*

in·tel·lec·tu·al·ise, in·tel·lec·tu·al·ize (íntə-léktew-ə-līz) *tr.v.* **-ised, -ising, -ises.** **1.** To make rational. **2.** To treat in an intellectual way, especially at the expense of an emotional response or interpretation. **—in·tel·lec·tu·al·i·sa·tion** (-lī-záysh'n || *U.S.* -li-) *n.*

in·tel·lec·tu·al·ism (íntə-léktew-ə-liz'm) *n.* **1.** Devotion to the exercise or development of the intellect, especially to the extent of disregarding emotional or spiritual factors. **2.** The doctrine that knowledge is the product of pure reason; rationalism. **—in·tel·lec·tu·al·ist** *n.* **—in·tel·lec·tu·al·is·tic** (-lístik) *adj.*

in·tel·li·gence (in-téllijənss) *n.* **1. a.** The capacity to acquire and apply knowledge. **b.** The faculty of thought and reason. **c.** Superior powers of mind. **2. a.** *Often capital* **I.** An intelligent being, especially one that is incorporeal, such as an angel. **3.** Received information; news. **4. a.** Secret information, especially about an enemy. **b.** The work of gathering such information. **c.** An agency, staff, or office employed in such work.

intelligence quotient *n. Abbr.* **IQ, I.Q.** An index of an individual's tested mental ability as compared to the rest of the population, usually arrived at by dividing an individual's mental age by his chronological age and multiplying by 100.

in·tel·li·genc·er (in-téllijən-sər) *n. Archaic.* **1.** One who conveys news; an informant. **2.** A secret agent, informer, or spy.

intelligence test *n.* A standardised test used to establish an intelligence level rating by measuring an individual's ability to form concepts, solve problems, and perform other intellectual operations.

in·tel·li·gent (in-téllijənt) *adj.* **1.** Having intelligence. **2.** Having a high degree of intelligence; mentally acute. **3.** Showing intelligence; perceptive and sound. **4.** Guided or motivated by the intellect; rational. **5.** Designating or pertaining to a computer terminal that can be used or programmed to perform logical operations as well as the input and output of data. [Latin *intelligēns* (stem *intelligent-*), present participle of *intellegere, intelligere,* to perceive, choose between : *inter-,* between + *legere,* to gather, choose.] **—in·tel·li·gen·tial** (in-télli-jénsh'l) *adj.* **—in·tel·li·gent·ly** *adv.*

Synonyms: *intelligent, bright, brilliant, knowing, quick-witted, clever, smart, intellectual.*

in·tel·li·gent·si·a (in-télli-jént-si-ə, -gént-) *n. Used with a singular or plural verb.* The class within a society consisting of those who are cultured, well-educated, or intellectual. [Russian *intelligyentsia,* from Polish *inteligiencja,* from Latin *intelligentia,* intelligence, from *intelligēns,* INTELLIGENT.]

in·tel·li·gi·ble (in-téllijə-b'l) *adj.* **1.** Comprehensible. **2.** Capable of being apprehended by the intellect alone. [Middle English, from Latin *intelligibilis,* from *intelligere,* to perceive. See **intelligent.**] **—in·tel·li·gi·bil·i·ty** (-bílləti) *n.* **—in·tel·li·gi·bly** *adv.*

In·tel·sat (in-tel-sat) *n.* *I*nternational *Tel*ecommunications *Sat*ellite Consortium: an international organisation formed in 1964, whose member countries cooperate in establishing and promoting non-military satellite communications.

in·tem·per·ance (in-tém-pərənss, -prənss) *n.* Lack of temperance or restraint, as in the indulgence of an appetite or passion.

in·tem·per·ate (in-tém-pə-rət, -rit, -prət, -prit) *adj.* Not temperate or moderate: *an intemperate drinker.* **—in·tem·per·ate·ly** *adv.* **—in·tem·per·ate·ness** *n.*

in·tend (in-ténd) *tr.v.* **-tended, -tending, -tends.** **1.** To have in mind; plan: *She intended to leave.* **2.** To design for a specific purpose or destine for a particular use. **3.** To signify; mean. [Middle English *entenden,* from Old French *entendre,* from Latin *intendere,* to stretch or direct towards : *in,* towards + *tendere,* to stretch, tend.]

in·ten·dance (in-téndənss) *n.* **1.** The function of an intendant; management; superintendence. **2.** An intendancy.

in·ten·dan·cy (in-téndən-si) *n., pl.* **-cies.** **1.** The position or function of an intendant. **2.** Intendants collectively. **3.** The district supervised by an intendant in Latin America.

in·ten·dant (in-téndənt) *n.* **1.** Formerly, a provincial or colonial administrative official of France, Spain, or Portugal. **2.** A district administrator in some countries of Latin America. **3.** *Archaic.* A manager of superintendent. [French, from Old French, "director", administrator, from Latin *intendēns* (stem *intendent-*), present participle of *intendere,* to direct one's mind to, INTEND.]

in·tend·ed (in-téndid) *adj.* **1.** Planned; intentional. **2.** Prospective; future.

~n. Informal. A person's prospective husband or wife.

in·tend·ment (in-téndmənt) *n.* The true meaning or intention of something as fixed by law.

in·ten·er·ate (in-ténnə-rayt) *tr.v.* **-ated, -ating, -ates.** To make tender; soften. [IN- (causative) + Latin *tener,* TENDER + -ATE.] **—in·ten·er·a·tion** (-ráysh'n) *n.*

in·tense (in-ténss) *adj.* **1.** Of great intensity; extreme in degree, concentration, or extent. **2.** Involving or showing strain: *intense effort.* **3. a.** Deeply felt; profound. **b.** Tending to feel deeply: *an intense writer.* [Middle English, from Old French, from Latin *intensus,* stretched tight, from the past participle of *intendere,* to stretch towards, INTEND.] **—in·tense·ly** *adv.* **—in·tense·ness** *n.*

in·ten·si·fi·er (in-tén-si-fī-ər) *n.* **1.** One that intensifies. **2.** An intensive. **3.** *Photography.* A substance added to an emulsion to increase its sensitivity.

in·ten·si·fy (in-tén-si-fī) *v.* **-fied, -fying, -fies.** *—tr.* **1.** To make intense or more intense. **2.** To increase the contrast of (a photographic image). *—intr.* To become intense or more intense. [INTENSE + -FY.] **—in·ten·si·fi·ca·tion** (-fi-káysh'n) *n.*

in·ten·sion (in-ténsh'n) *n.* **1.** *Logic.* The sum of the properties or attributes connoted by a term. Compare **extension.** **2.** Intensity. [Latin *intensiō* (stem *intensiōn-*), from *intensus,* INTENSE.]

in·ten·si·ty (in-tén-səti) *n., pl.* **-ties.** **1.** Exceptionally great concentration, power, or force. **2.** *Physics.* **a.** The measure of effectiveness of a force field given by the force per unit test element. **b.** The energy transferred by a wave per unit time across a unit area perpendicular to the direction of propagation.

in·ten·sive (in-tén-siv) *adj.* **1.** Of, pertaining to, or characterised by intensity. **2.** Pertaining to or being a linguistic intensive. **3.** Concentrated and exhaustive: *intensive study.* **4.** Designating or pertaining to a method of land cultivation calling for large-scale employment of capital and labour and designed to increase productivity. **5.** *Physics.* Having the same value for any subdivision of a thermodynamic system. Said of pressure, for example. **6.** Having a greater than average requirement of the specified resource. Used in combination: *labour-intensive; an energy-intensive system.*
~*n.* A linguistic element that intensifies the effect of a word or phrase but has itself little or no semantic content; for example, in the sentence *She is terribly pretty, terribly* is an intensive.

intensive care *n.* Continuous and carefully monitored medical treatment given to patients who are seriously ill, especially in a specialised section (*intensive-care unit*) of a hospital.

in·tent (in-tént) *n.* **1.** That which is intended; an aim; a purpose. **2.** The state of mind prevailing at the time of an action: *acted with malicious intent.* **3.** Meaning; purport. —See Synonyms at **intention.** **—to all intents and purposes.** Practically; virtually.
~*adj.* **1.** Firmly fixed; concentrated. **2.** Having the attention applied; engrossed. **3.** Having the mind fastened upon some purpose. [Middle English *entent,* from Old French, from Latin *intentus,* a stretching out, from the alternative past participle of *intendere,* to stretch towards, INTEND.] **—in·tent·ly** *adv.* **—in·tent·ness** *n.*

in·ten·tion (in-ténsh'n) *n.* **1.** A plan of action; a design. **2. a.** An aim that guides action; an object. **b.** *Plural.* Purpose in regard to marriage: *honourable intentions.* **3.** *Logic.* **a.** A concept derived from an object of thought. **b.** The general connotation or concept of something. **4.** *Medicine.* The course or manner of healing of a surgical wound. **5.** *Archaic.* Import; meaning. **6.** *Archaic.* Intentness. [Middle English *entencioun,* from Old French *entention,* from Latin *intentiō* (stem *intentiōn-*), "a stretching out", from *intendere,* to stretch towards, INTEND.]
Synonyms: *intention, intent, purpose, object, goal, end, aim, objective.*

in·ten·tion·al (in-ténshən'l) *adj.* **1.** Done deliberately; intended: *an intentional slight.* **2.** Having to do with logical intention or connotation. —See Synonyms at **voluntary.** **—in·ten·tion·al·i·ty** (in-ténshə-nál-əti) *n.* **—in·ten·tion·al·ly** *adv.*

in·ter (in-tér) *tr.v.* **-terred, -terring, -ters.** To place (a dead body) in a grave; bury. [Middle English *enteren,* from Old French *enterrer,* from Vulgar Latin *interrāre* (unattested) : Latin *in,* in + *terra,* earth, ground.]

inter- *prefix.* Indicates: **1.** Between or among; for example, **intercollegiate, international. 2.** Mutually or together; for example, **interact, intermingle.** ***Note:*** Many compounds other than those entered here may be formed with *inter-*. In forming compounds, *inter-* is normally joined with the following element without space or hyphen: *intercontinental.* However, if the second element begins with a capital letter, it is separated with a hyphen: *inter-American.* In Latin phrases used in English, the Latin preposition remains a separate word: *inter alia.* [Middle English *inter-, entre-,* from Old French, from Latin *inter-,* from *inter,* between, among. In borrowed Latin compounds, *inter-* indicates: 1. Between, among, as in **interregnum.** 2. Mutually, each other, as in **intersect.** 3. At intervals, as in **intermit.** 4. Preventively, destructively, as in **internecine.**]

inter. intermediate.

in·ter·act (íntər-ákt) *intr.v.* **-acted, -acting, -acts.** To act on each other.

in·ter·ac·tion (íntər-ákshən) *n.* **1.** The action, state, or result of interacting. **2.** *Physics.* Any of four fundamental ways in which elementary particles and bodies can influence each other, characterised by the strength and range of such interaction and classified as strong, weak, electromagnetic, and gravitational.

in·ter·ac·tive (íntər-áktiv) *adj.* **1.** Acting on each other. **2.** *Computing.* Designating or pertaining to a system in which information and instructions can be continuously transferred between computer and operator.

in·ter a·li·a (íntər áyli-ə, ál-i-, áali-) *adv. Latin.* Among other things.

in·ter a·li·os (íntər áyli-ōss, ál-i-, áali-) *adv. Latin.* Among other persons.

in·ter·a·tom·ic (íntərə-tómmik) *adj.* Occurring or operating between atoms.

in·ter·brain (íntər-brayn) *n.* A part of the brain, the **diencephalon.**

in·ter·breed (íntər-bréed) *v.* **-bred** (-bréd), **-breeding, -breeds.** —*intr.* **1.** To breed with another kind or species; crossbreed; hybridise. **2.** To breed within a narrow range or with closely related types or individuals; inbreed. —*tr.* To cause to interbreed.

in·ter·ca·lar·y (in-térkə-ləri, íntər-kál-əri || *U.S.* in-térkə-lerri) *adj.* **1.** Added to the calendar to make the calendar year correspond to the solar year. Said of a day or a month. **2.** Having such a day or month added. Said of a year. **3.** Interpolated; constituting an insertion. **4.** Designating non-localised plant growth occurring in regions other than the apical meristems, as at internodes and leaf bases. [Latin *intercalārius,* from *intercalāre,* to INTERCALATE.]

in·ter·ca·late (in-térkə-layt) *tr.v.* **-lated, -lating, -lates. 1.** To add (a day or month) to a calendar. **2.** To insert, interpose, or interpolate. [Latin *intercalāre,* to proclaim the insertion of a day : *inter-,* among, between + *calāre,* to call.] **—in·ter·ca·la·tion** (-láysh'n) *n.* **—in·ter·ca·la·tive** *adj.*

in·ter·cede (íntər-séed) *intr.v.* **-ceded, -ceding, -cedes. 1.** To plead on another's behalf: *interceded with the father for the child.* **2.** To act as mediator in a dispute. [Latin *intercēdere,* to come between : *inter-,* between + *cēdere,* to go.] **—in·ter·ced·er** *n.*

in·ter·cel·lu·lar (íntər-séllewlər) *adj. Biology.* Among or between cells.

in·ter·cept (íntər-sépt) *tr.v.* **-cepted, -cepting, -cepts. 1. a.** To stop, deflect, or interrupt the progress or intended course of: *intercepted a message; intercepted her at the port.* **b.** In ball games such as football, hockey or the like, to cut off, or take possession of (a ball) by anticipating an opponent's pass. **2.** *Archaic.* **a.** To cut off from access or communication. **b.** To prevent. **3.** *Mathematics.* To cut off or bound a part of (a line, plane, surface, or solid).
~*n.* (íntər-sept). *Mathematics.* **1.** A point of interception. **2.** A line segment formed by an intercept; for example, the distance from the origin of coordinates along a coordinate axis to the point at which a line, curve, or surface intersects the axis. [Latin *intercipere* (past participle *interceptus*), to intercept, seize in transit : *inter,* preventively + *capere,* to take, seize.] **—in·ter·cep·tion** (-sépsh'n) *n.* **—in·ter·cep·tive** (-séptiv) *adj.*

in·ter·cep·tor, in·ter·cep·ter (íntər-séptər) *n.* One that intercepts; especially, a fast-climbing, highly manoeuvrable fighter plane designed to intercept enemy aircraft.

in·ter·ces·sion (íntər-sésh'n) *n.* **1.** Entreaty in favour of another; especially, a prayer or petition to God on behalf of another. **2.** Mediation in a dispute. [Old French, from Latin *intercessiō* (stem *intercessiōn-*), from *intercēdere* (past participle *intercessus*), INTERCEDE.] **—in·ter·ces·sion·al** *adj.* **—in·ter·ces·sor** (-séssər) *n.* **—in·ter·ces·so·ry** (-séssəri) *adj.*

in·ter·change (íntər-cháynj) *v.* **-changed, -changing, -changes.** —*tr.* **1.** To switch each of (two things) into the place of the other. **2.** To give and receive mutually; exchange. **3.** To cause to succeed each other; alternate: *interchanging wit with wisdom in the course of conversation.* —*intr.* **1.** To change places with each other. **2.** To succeed each other; alternate.
~*n.* (íntər-chaynj). **1.** The act or process or an instance of interchanging, especially: **a.** A switch of places. **b.** An exchange. **2.** Alternation. **3.** A road junction, especially on a motorway, designed to permit traffic to move freely from one road to another. [Middle English *entrechaungen,* from Old French *entrechangier* : INTER- + *changier,* to CHANGE.] **—in·ter·chang·er** (-cháynjər) *n.*

in·ter·change·a·ble (íntər-cháynjə-b'l) *adj.* Capable of being interchanged; admitting transposition. **—in·ter·change·a·bil·i·ty** (-bílləti), **in·ter·change·a·ble·ness** *n.* **—in·ter·change·a·bly** *adv.*

in·ter·col·le·giate (íntər-kə-lée-ji-ət, -ko-, -it, -jət, -jit) *adj.* Involving or representing two or more colleges.

in·ter·co·lum·ni·a·tion (íntər-kə-lúm-ni-áysh'n) *n. Architecture.* **1.** The open spaces between the columns in a colonnade. **2.** The system whereby they are spaced.

in·ter·com (íntər-kom) *n. Informal.* An internal communication system, as between two rooms. [Short for INTERCOMMUNICATION.]

in·ter·com·mu·ni·cate (íntər-kə-méwni-kayt) *intr.v.* **-cated, -cating, -cates. 1.** To communicate with each other. **2.** To be connected or adjoined, as rooms. **—in·ter·com·mu·ni·ca·tion** (-káysh'n) *n.* **—in·ter·com·mu·ni·ca·tive** *adj.*

in·ter·com·mun·ion (íntərkə-méwn-yən) *n.* The practice by members of different Christian denominations of receiving communion at each other's eucharistic services or at a common service.

in·ter·con·nect (íntərkə-nékt) *v.* **-nected, -necting, -nects.** —*intr.* To be connected one to the other. —*tr.* To connect (one thing with another). **—in·ter·con·nec·tion** *n.*

in·ter·con·ti·nen·tal (íntər-kónti-nént'l) *adj.* **1.** Extending from one continent to another: *intercontinental flight.* **2.** Carried on between continents: *intercontinental warfare.* **3.** Capable of flight from one continent to another: *intercontinental ballistic missile.*

in·ter·cos·tal (íntər-kóst'l) *adj.* Located or occurring between the ribs. [New Latin *intercostalis* : Latin *inter-,* between + *costa,* rib.]

in·ter·course (íntər-kawrss || -kōrss) *n.* **1.** Interchange between persons or groups; communication. **2. Sexual intercourse** *(see).* [Middle English *intercurse,* from Old French *entrecours,* from Latin *intercursus,* past participle of *intercurrere,* to run between : *inter-,* between + *currere,* to run.]

in·ter·crop (íntər-króp, -krop) *v.* **-cropped, -cropping, -crops.** —*intr.* To grow a secondary crop between the rows of a principal crop. —*tr.* To plant such a crop between (another crop).
~*n.* (íntər-krop). A secondary crop grown between the rows of a principal crop.

in·ter·cross (íntər-kross) *n.* A **crossbreed** *(see).* **—in·ter·cross** *v.*

in·ter·cur·rent (íntər-kúrrənt) *adj.* **1.** Occurring as an interruption in a process. **2.** *Pathology.* Occurring during the course of an existing disease. [Latin *intercurrēns* (stem *intercurrent-*), present participle of *intercurrere,* to run between. See **intercourse.**]

in·ter·cut (íntər-kút) *tr.v.* **-cut, -cutting, -cuts.** To insert (a scene or camera shot) into a film sequence, so as to achieve dramatic contrast or to make it appear that two or more actions are taking place simultaneously.

in·ter·de·nom·i·na·tion·al (íntərdi-nómmi-náysh'n-əl) *adj.* Of or involving different religious denominations.

in·ter·den·tal (íntər-dént'l) *adj.* **1.** Located between the teeth. **2.** *Phonetics.* Pronounced with the tip of the tongue protruding between the teeth, as (th) in *that* or (th) in *thumb.*
~*n. Phonetics.* A consonant pronounced in this manner.

in·ter·de·pen·dent (íntərdi-péndənt) *adj.* Dependent on each other. **—in·ter·de·pen·dence** *n.* **—in·ter·de·pen·dent·ly** *adv.*

in·ter·dict (íntər-dikt, -dīt) *tr.v.* **-dicted, -dicting, -dicts. 1.** To prohibit or place under an ecclesiastical or legal sanction. **2.** To cut or

destroy (an enemy line of communication) by firepower so as to halt an enemy's advance.
~*n.* (íntər-dikt, -dīt). **1.** An authoritative prohibition or legal injunction. **2.** A Roman Catholic ecclesiastical censure whereby an offending person or district is excluded from participation in most sacraments and from Christian burial. [Learned respelling of Middle English *entrediten,* to announce ecclesiastical censure, from Old French *entredire* (past participle *entredit*), from Latin *interdīcere,* to forbid : *inter-,* preventively + *dīcere,* to say.] **—in·ter·dic·tion** *n.* **—in·ter·dic·tive, in·ter·dic·to·ry** *adj.* **—in·ter·dic·tive·ly** *adv.* **—in·ter·dic·tor** (-díktər) *n.*

in·ter·dis·ci·pli·nar·y (íntər-díssi-plín-əri, -plin- || -erri) *adj.* Concerned with two or more academic disciplines usually considered distinct: *an interdisciplinary degree.*

in·ter·est (ín-trist, -tə-rest, -trəst) *n.* **1. a.** A feeling of curiosity, fascination, or absorption. **b.** The cause of any such feeling. **c.** The quality or aspect of something that enables it to cause any such feeling. **2.** *Often plural.* Advantage; self-interest. **3. a.** A right, claim, or legal share in something. **b.** *Usually plural.* Something in which such a legal right, claim, or share is held. **4. a.** Involvement with or participation in something. **b.** A leisure activity or pursuit: *What are your interests?* **5. a.** *Abbr.* **i., int.** A charge for a financial loan, usually a percentage of the amount lent. **b.** An excess or bonus beyond what is expected or due: *She returned his ardour with interest.* **6.** *Usually plural.* A group of persons sharing an interest in an enterprise, industry, or segment of society. **—in the interest** or **interests of.** For the sake of; on behalf of.
~*tr.v.* **interested, -esting, -ests. 1.** To arouse the curiosity or hold the attention of. **2.** To cause to become involved or concerned. **3.** *Archaic.* To concern or affect. [Middle English, variant (influenced by Old French *interest,* damage) of *interesse,* concern, share, from Anglo-French, substantive use of Latin *interesse,* "to be in between", to matter, be of concern : *inter-,* between + *esse,* to be.]

in·ter·est·ed (ín-tri-stid, -trə-, -tre-, -tə-restid) *adj.* **1.** Having or showing curiosity, fascination, or concern. **2.** Possessing a right, claim, or share; personally concerned: *the interested parties.* **3.** Influenced by considerations of personal gain; self-seeking. **—in·ter·est·ed·ly** *adv.* **—in·ter·est·ed·ness** *n.*

in·ter·est·ing (ín-tri-sting, -trə-, -tre-, -tə-resting) *adj.* Arousing or holding attention; absorbing. **—in·ter·est·ing·ly** *adv.*

in·ter·face (íntər-fayss) *n.* **1.** A surface forming a common boundary between adjacent bodies, liquids, or regions. **2.** A link between two circuits or parts, especially in a computer. **3.** The meeting-point or boundary at which two theories, systems, groups of people or the like meet and affect each other.
~*v.* **interfaced, -facing, faces.** —*tr.* To connect (material) with or through an interface. —*intr.* To become interfaced. **—in·ter·fa·cial** (-fáysh'l) *adj.*

in·ter·fac·ing (íntər-fay-sing) *n.* A strip of firm fabric sewn between the layers of a garment to thicken or stiffen it.

in·ter·fas·cic·u·lar (íntər-fə-síckewlər, -fa-) *adj. Botany.* Occurring between fascicles: *interfascicular cambium.*

in·ter·fere (íntər-féer) *intr.v.* **-fered, -fering, -feres. 1.** To be a hindrance or obstacle. Often used with *with.* **2.** To intervene or intrude in the affairs of others; meddle. **3.** In various sports, to impede an opponent contrary to the rules of the game. **4.** To strike one hoof against the opposite hoof or leg while moving. Used of a horse. **5.** *Chiefly British.* To molest or assault sexually. Used with *with.* **6.** *Physics.* To produce interference with another wave. **7.** *Electronics.* To inhibit or prevent clear reception of broadcast signals. [Old French *(s')entreferir,* to strike each other : INTER- + *ferir,* to strike, from Latin *ferīre.*] **—in·ter·fer·er** *n.* **—in·ter·fer·ing·ly** *adv.*
Synonyms: *interfere, meddle, tamper, tinker.*

in·ter·fer·ence (íntər-féer-ənss) *n.* **1.** The act, process, or an instance of interfering. **2.** *Physics.* The phenomenon of two or more waves of the same frequency combining to form a wave in which the disturbance at any point is the algebraic or vector sum of the disturbances due to the interfering waves at that point. **3.** *Electronics.* **a.** The inhibition or prevention of clear reception of broadcast signals. **b.** The distorted portion of a received signal. **—in·ter·fer·en·tial** (-fə-rénsh'l) *adj.*

in·ter·fe·rom·e·ter (íntər-fə-rómmitər) *n.* **1.** Any of several optical, acoustic, or radio-frequency instruments that use interference phenomena between a reference wave and an experimental wave, or between two parts of an experimental wave, to determine wavelengths, wave velocities, distances, and directions. **2.** A type of radio telescope in which the received waves are collected by two separate antennae, connected so as to combine the signals. See **aperture synthesis.** [INTERFER(E) + -METER.]

in·ter·fer·on (íntər-féer-on) *n.* A protein produced in response to, and acting to prevent replication of, an infectious viral form within a cell. [INTERFER(E) + -ON.]

in·ter·fer·tile (íntər-fér-tīl || -t'l) *adj.* Able to interbreed.

in·ter·fluve (íntər-flōōv) *n.* The region of higher land between two rivers that are in the same drainage system. [Back-formation from *interfluvial* : INTER- + Latin *fluvius,* river.] **—in·ter·flu·vi·al** *adj.*

in·ter·fuse (íntər-féwz) *v.* **-fused, -fusing, -fuses.** —*tr.* **1.** To fuse or blend. **2.** To spread throughout; diffuse. —*intr.* **1.** To become fused or blended. **2.** To become diffused.

in·ter·ga·lac·tic (íntər-gə-láktik) *adj.* Between galaxies.

in·ter·gla·ci·al (íntər-gláy-si-əl, -shi-, -sh'l) *n.* A comparatively short period of warmth during an overall period of glaciation. **—in·ter·gla·ci·al** *adj.*

in·ter·grade (íntər-gráyd) *intr.v.* **-graded, -grading, -grades.** To merge or grow into each other in a series of stages, forms, or types, Used especially of biological species.
~*n.* (íntər-grayd). A transitional step, grade, or form. **—in·ter·gra·da·tion** (-grə-dáysh'n) *n.* **—in·ter·gra·di·ent** (íntər-gráydi-ənt) *adj.*

in·ter·im (íntərim) *n.* An interval of time between one event, process, or period and another.
~*adj.* Belonging to, made, or taking place during an interim; temporary, provisional, or partial: *interim measures; an interim payment.* [Latin, in the meantime, from *inter,* among, at intervals.]

in·te·ri·or (in-téer-i-ər) *adj. Abbr.* **int. 1.** Of, pertaining to, or located on the inside; inner. **2.** Of or pertaining to one's mental or spiritual being. **3.** Situated away from a coast or border; inland.
~*n. Abbr.* **int. 1.** The internal portion or area of something, especially of a building; the inside. **2.** One's mental or spiritual being. **3. a.** A representation of the inside of a building or room, as in a painting. **b.** A film scene that is shot indoors. **4.** The inland part of a given political or geographical entity. **5.** *Capital* **I.** The internal or domestic affairs of a country: *Minister of the Interior.* [Latin, comparative of *inter,* in, within.] **—in·te·ri·or·i·ty** (-órrəti) *n.* **—in·te·ri·or·ly** *adv.*

interior angle *n.* **1.** Any of four angles formed between two straight lines cut by a transversal. **2.** The angle formed inside a polygon by two adjacent sides.

interior decorator *n.* One who plans and executes the layout and decoration of an architectural interior. Also called "interior designer". **—interior decoration** *n.*

interior monologue *n.* In literature, the direct representation of a character's thoughts and feelings, as opposed to a narrative description of them.

interj. interjection.

in·ter·ject (íntər-jékt) *tr.v.* **-jected, -jecting, -jects.** To interpose parenthetically or by way of an interruption. [Latin *interjicere* (past participle *interjectus*), to throw between : *inter-,* between + *jacere,* to throw.] **—in·ter·jec·tor** (-jéktər) *n.* **—in·ter·jec·to·ry** (-jék-təri) *adj.*

in·ter·jec·tion (íntər-jéksh'n) *n.* **1.** An exclamation; an ejaculation. **2.** *Abbr.* **interj. a.** A part of speech consisting of an exclamatory word capable of standing alone; for example, *oh!* or *ahem!* **b.** A word, phrase, or other sound used exclamatorily and capable of standing alone; for example, *Heavens!* or *Shut up!* **—in·ter·jec·tion·al** *adj.* **—in·ter·jec·tion·al·ly** *adv.*

in·ter·lace (íntər-láyss) *v.* **-laced, -lacing, -laces.** —*tr.* **1.** To connect together by or as if by weaving; interweave. **2.** To intersperse. **3.** *Electronics.* To scan (a television picture, for example) in two stages, each composed of alternate lines. —*intr.* To intertwine. Used with *with.* **—in·ter·lace·ment** *n.*

In·ter·la·ken (íntər-laakən). Town in Switzerland on the river Aar, between lakes Thun and Brienz. It is the tourist centre of the Bernese Alps.

in·ter·lam·i·nate (intər-lámmi-nayt) *tr.v.* **-nated, -nating, -nates. 1.** To insert (a layer) between other layers. **2.** To arrange in alternating layers. **—in·ter·lam·i·nar** (-nər) *adj.* **—in·ter·lam·i·na·tion** (-náysh'n) *n.*

in·ter·lard (intər-lárd) *tr.v.* **-larded, -larding, -lards. 1.** To modify or diversify by interspersing with something different or foreign. **2.** To be interspersed through; occur in repeatedly. [Old French *entrelarder,* to alternate layers of fat and lean : INTER- + *larder,* to insert fat, cover with lard, from LARD.]

in·ter·leaf (íntər-leef) *n., pl.* **-leaves** (-leevz). A blank leaf inserted between the regular pages of a book.

in·ter·leave (íntər-léev) *tr.v.* **-leaved, -leaving, -leaves. 1.** To provide (a book) with an interleaf or interleaves. **2.** To insert (an interleaf) into a book. **3.** To arrange in alternating layers.

in·ter·line[1] (íntər-līn) *tr.v.* **-lined, -lining, -lines. 1.** To insert (writing) between printed or written lines. **2.** To insert words between the lines of (a text). **—in·ter·lin·e·a·tion** (-línni-áysh'n) *n.*

in·ter·line[2] *tr.v.* **-lined, -lining, -lines.** To fit with an interlining.

in·ter·lin·e·ar (íntər-línni-ər) *adj.* **1.** Inserted between the lines of a text. **2.** Written or printed with different languages or versions in alternating lines.

In·ter·lin·gua (íntər-líng-gwə) *n.* An artificially devised international language comprising elements of both English and the Romance languages. [Italian : INTER- + *lingua,* language.]

in·ter·lin·ing (íntər-līning) *n.* An extra lining between the outer fabric and the ordinary lining of a garment.

in·ter·lock (íntər-lók) *v.* **-locked, -locking, -locks.** —*tr.* **1.** To unite firmly or join closely, as by hooking or dovetailing. **2.** To arrange or connect (separate parts of a system) so that they cannot be operated independently. —*intr.* To engage or be joined firmly.
~*n.* (íntər-lok). **1.** A mechanism that ensures that a particular activity cannot take place until a prescribed sequence of operations has been carried out. **2.** A fabric knitted with interlocking stitches.

in·ter·lo·cu·tion (íntər-lə-kéwsh'n) *n. Formal.* Conversation. [Latin *interlocūtiō* (stem *interlocūtiōn-*) from *interloquī* (past participle *interlocūtus*), to speak between : *inter-,* between + *loquī,* to speak.]

in·ter·loc·u·tor (íntər-lóckewtər) *n.* **1.** Someone who takes part in a conversation. **2.** A partner in such a dialogue.

in·ter·loc·u·to·ry (íntər-lóckew-təri, -tri) *adj.* **1.** Made during the course of a suit, divorce trial, or the like: *an interlocutory decree.* **2.** Interspersed, as into a text or talk. **3.** Of, pertaining to, or resembling a conversation.

in·ter·lope (íntər-lōp, -lōp) *intr.v.* **-loped, -loping, -lopes. 1.** To violate the legally established trading rights of others. **2.** To interfere in the affairs of others; intrude. —See Synonyms at **intrude.** [Back-formation from *interloper* : INTER- + Dutch *loper,* running, from Middle Dutch, from *loopen,* to run.] **—in·ter·lo·per** *n.*

in·ter·lude (íntər-lo͞od, -lewd) *n.* **1.** An intervening episode, feature, or period of time. **2. a.** A short farcical entertainment performed between the acts of a medieval mystery or morality play. **b.** A 16th-century genre of comedy derived from this. **c.** An entertainment between the acts of a play. **3.** A short musical piece inserted between the parts of a longer composition. [Middle English *enterlude,* from Medieval Latin *interlūdium,* performance between acts : Latin *inter-,* between + *lūdus,* play.]

in·ter·lun·a·tion (íntər-lo͞o-náysh'n, -lo͞o-, -lew-) *n.* The period during which the moon is invisible, occurring between the old and new moon. **—in·ter·lu·nar** (-lo͞onər, -léwnər) *adj.*

in·ter·mar·ry (íntər-márri) *intr.v.* **-ried, -rying, -ries. 1.** To marry a member of another group. **2.** To be bound together by the marriages of members. **3.** To marry within one's own family, tribe, or clan. **—in·ter·mar·riage** *n.*

in·ter·me·di·a·cy (íntər-méedi-ə-si) *n.* **1.** The state of being intermediate. **2.** The act of intermediating.

in·ter·me·di·ar·y (íntər-méedi-əri || -erri) *n., pl.* **-ies. 1.** One who acts as a mediator. **2.** One that acts as an agent between persons or things; a means. **3.** An intermediate state or stage.
~*adj.* **1.** Acting as a mediator. **2.** In between; intermediate.

in·ter·me·di·ate (íntər-méedi-ət, -it, -méed-yət) *adj. Abbr.* **inter. 1.** Lying or occurring at a point, degree, or level between two extremes; in between; in the middle. **2.** *Geology.* Designating a class of igneous rocks containing less than ten per cent free quartz, some feldspar, and about 52 to 66 per cent silica.
~*n. Abbr.* **inter. 1.** One that is intermediate. **2.** An intermediary. **3.** *Chemistry.* A substance formed as a necessary stage in the change from reactants to products during a chemical reaction.
~*intr.v.* (-ayt) **intermediated, -ating, -ates.** To act as an intermediary; mediate. [Medieval Latin *intermediātus,* from Latin *intermedius* : *inter-,* between + *medius,* middle.] **—in·ter·me·di·ate·ly** *adv.* **—in·ter·me·di·ate·ness** *n.* **—in·ter·me·di·a·tion** (-áysh'n) *n.* **—in·ter·me·di·a·tor** (-aytər) *n.*

in·ter·ment (in-térmənt) *n.* The act or ritual of interring.

in·ter·mez·zo (íntər-mét-sō, -méd-zō) *n., pl.* **-zos** or **-zi** (-see, -zee). **1.** A brief musical, theatrical, or dance performance during an interval; an entr'acte. **2. a.** A short movement separating the major sections of a symphonic work. **b.** An independent instrumental composition having the character of such a movement. [Italian, from Latin *intermedius,* INTERMEDIATE.]

in·ter·mi·na·ble (in-términəb'l) *adj.* Tiresomely protracted; endless. See Synonyms at **continual. —in·ter·mi·na·bly** *adv.*

in·ter·min·gle (íntər-míng-g'l) *v.* **-gled, -gling, -gles.** —*tr.* To mix or mingle. —*intr.* To mix or mingle with one another.

in·ter·mis·sion (íntər-mísh'n) *n.* **1. a.** The act of intermitting. **b.** The state of being intermitted. **2.** A respite; a temporary cessation. **3.** The period between the separate acts or parts of a play, film, or other entertainment; an interval. [Latin *intermissiō* (stem *intermissiōn-*), from *intermittere,* to INTERMIT.]

in·ter·mit (íntər-mít) *v.* **-mitted, -mitting, -mits.** —*intr.* To cease activity temporarily or repeatedly. —*tr.* To suspend (activity) temporarily or repeatedly; interrupt. [Latin *intermittere,* to interrupt at intervals : *inter-,* at intervals + *mittere,* to send, let go.] **—in·ter·mit·tence** *n.*

in·ter·mit·tent (íntər-mítt'nt) *adj.* Stopping and starting at intervals. See Synonyms at **periodic. —in·ter·mit·tent·ly** *adv.*

intermittent current *n.* A periodically interrupted unidirectional electric current.

intermittent fever *n.* A fever, such as malaria, in which periods of improvement alternate with periods of deterioration.

in·ter·mix (íntər-míks) *v.* **-mixed, -mixing, -mixes.** —*tr.* To mix together. —*intr.* To be or become mixed together. [Back-formation from earlier *intermixt,* from Latin *intermixtus,* past participle of *intermiscēre,* to mix together : *inter-,* mutually + *miscēre,* to mix.]

in·ter·mix·ture (íntər-míks-chər) *n.* **1.** The process of intermixing of the state of being intermixed. **2.** Something composed of various ingredients; a mixture. **3.** Something added to a mixture; an admixture.

in·ter·mo·lec·u·lar (íntər-mə-léckewlər) *adj.* Occurring or operating between molecules.

in·tern (ín-tern) *n. U.S.* An advanced student or recent graduate undergoing supervised practical training, especially medical training in a hospital. Compare **houseman, house officer.**
~*v.* **interned, -terning, -terns.** —*intr.* (ín-tern). *U.S.* To train or serve as an intern. —*tr.* (in-térn). To detain or confine, especially in wartime. [French *interner,* to confine, from *interne,* inmate, resident assistant physician, from Old French, from Latin *internus,* INTERNAL.] **—in·tern·ship** *n.*

in·ter·nal (in-térn'l, ín-) *adj.* **1.** Of, relating to, or located within the limits or surface of something; inner; interior. **2.** Emanating from, belonging to, or dependent on the nature of something; intrinsic; inherent: *the internal contradictons of his theory.* **3.** Located, acting, or effective within the body. **4.** Pertaining to mental or spiritual life, as opposed to material things; subjective. **5.** Of or relating to the domestic affairs of a country. **6.** Of or involving those who belong to a group or organisation, as opposed to those outside it: *the party's internal squabbles; an internal appointment.* **7. a.** Designating an examination set and marked by the teaching institution itself, rather than by a public examinations board. **b.** Designating an examiner from one's own educational institution, as opposed to one brought in from outside. **8.** Designating a medical examination of the vagina or uterus.
~*n. Informal.* An internal medical examination. [New Latin *internalis,* from Latin *internus,* from *inter,* in, within.] **—in·ter·nal·i·ty** (in-ter-nál-əti) *n.* **—in·ter·nal·ly** *adv.*

in·ter·nal-com·bus·tion engine (in-térn'l-kəm-búss-chən, ín- || -kom-). *n.* An engine, such as a piston engine or a gas turbine, in which fuel is burned within the engine proper rather than in an external furnace as in a steam engine.

internal drainage *n.* A system of drainage with no outlet to the sea. Also called "inland drainage".

internal ear *n.* The portion of the ear that includes the semicircular canals, the vestibule, and the cochlea. Also called "inner ear", "labyrinth".

internal energy *n. Symbol* **U** A thermodynamic property of a system equal to the total kinetic and potential energies of all the molecules present. It is the quantity that changes when the system alters or suffers external work without energy transfer from or to its surroundings.

in·ter·nal·ise, in·ter·nal·ize (in-térn'l-īz) *tr.v.* **-ised, -ising, -ises. 1.** To take (external conditions, values, or the like) into one's consciousness as part of one's own thinking; assimilate. **2.** To keep within oneself; repress: *internalise feelings of aggression.* **—in·ter·nal·i·sa·tion** (-ī-záysh'n || *U.S.* -i-) *n.*

internal medicine *n. Chiefly U.S.* The medical study and treatment of nonsurgical constitutional diseases in adults.

Internal Revenue Service *n. Abbr.* **I.R.S.** The U.S. government department responsible for the collection of Federal taxes.

internal rhyme *n.* Rhyme within a single line of verse, or between lines of verse, in which at least one of the rhyming syllables is not at the end of a line.

internal secretion *n. Physiology.* A secretion of an endocrine gland discharged directly into the blood.

in·ter·na·tion·al (íntər-násh'n'l) *adj. Abbr.* **int., intl., internat. 1.** Of, pertaining to, or involving two or more nations or nationalities: *an international incident.* **2.** Ordered, demanded, or controlled by a group of nations: *an international commission.* **3.** Equally accessible to all nations: *international waters.* **4.** In South Africa formerly, of, pertaining to, or designating the status of certain hotels and restaurants licensed to cater for both black and white patrons.
~*n. Sports.* **1.** A contest or match between representative teams of two or more nations. **2.** A member of any such team. **—in·ter·na·tion·al·ly** *adv.*

In·ter·na·tion·al *n.* **1.** Any of several socialist organisations of international scope formed during the late 19th and early 20th centuries; especially: **a.** The *First International* (International Workingmen's Association), organised (1864) by Marx and Engels to associate the trade unions of all nations. **b.** The *Second International* (Socialist International), an association formed (1889) to promote the unity of socialist parties in various countries. **c.** The *Third International* (Communist International), organised (1919) by the Bolsheviks to coordinate the activities of communist movements throughout the world. In this sense, also called "Comintern". **d.** The *Fourth International* formed (1937) by followers of Trotsky in opposition to Stalin and the Third International. **2.** The Internationale.

International Bank for Reconstruction and Development *n.* The official name for the **World Bank** *(see).*

international candle *n. Physics.* A **candle** *(see).*

International Court of Justice *n. Abbr.* **ICJ** The main judicial body of the United Nations founded in 1945, and based in The Hague. Also called "World Court".

International Criminal Police Organisation *n.* See **Interpol.**

International Date Line *n.* The **date line** *(see).*

In·ter·na·tio·nale (íntər-nash'n-aál, -ál; *French* aN-tair-na-syo-nál) *n.* A revolutionary song adopted at different times by various syndicalist and Communist movements as an international socialist anthem. Preceded by *the.* [French, "the International".]

International Grandmaster *n.* In chess, a player of the highest ranking, as certified by the F.I.D.E. Also called "grandmaster".

in·ter·na·tion·al·ise, in·ter·na·tion·al·ize (íntər-násh'n-ə-līz) *tr.v.* **-ised, -ising, -ises. 1.** To make international. **2.** To put under international control. **—in·ter·na·tion·al·i·sa·tion** (-lī-záysh'n) *n.*

in·ter·na·tion·al·ism (íntər-násh'n-ə-liz'm) *n.* **1.** The state or quality of being international in character, principles, concern, or attitude. **2.** The policy or principle of cooperation among nations, especially in politics and economics. **—in·ter·na·tion·al·ist** *n.*

International Labour Organisation *n. Abbr.* **ILO** A specialised agency of the United Nations originally established in 1919 to standardise and improve international labour conditions.

international law *n.* A set of rules generally regarded as binding in relations between states and nations. Also called "law of nations".

International Master *n.* In chess, a player of the highest ranking but one, as certified by the F.I.D.E. Also called "master".

International Monetary Fund *n. Abbr.* **IMF** An international financial organisation set up (1945) by the United Nations to regulate the exchange values of currencies, and thereby promote international trade. Loans are made to member nations in difficulties with their balance of payments, often with strict conditions attached.

International Phonetic Alphabet *n. Abbr.* **IPA, I.P.A.** A phonetic alphabet sponsored by the International Phonetic Association to provide a uniform, universally comprehensible system of letters and

symbols for writing the speech sounds of all languages.
international pitch *n. Music.* **Concert pitch** *(see).*
International Practical Temperature Scale *n. Abbr.* **IPTS** A temperature scale based on 11 fixed points with agreed methods of determining temperatures between these points. It ranges from 13.81 K (triple point of hydrogen) to 1337.58 K (melting point of gold).
international time zone. See **time zone.**
in·ter·ne·cine (íntər-née-sīn || *U.S. also* -néss-een, in-térnə-seen, -sən) *adj.* **1.** Mutually destructive; ruinous or fatal to both sides. **2.** Characterised by bloodshed or carnage. **3.** Carried on within a nation or organisation: *internecine struggles.* [Latin *internecīnus,* from *interneciō,* massacre, from *internecāre,* to slaughter, massacre : *inter* (intensive) + *necāre,* to kill.]
in·tern·ee (ín-ter-née) *n.* One who is interned, especially during a war.
Inter·net (íntər-net) *n.* An international computer network that facilitates greatly the worldwide exchange of information and may be accessed via the World Wide Web. Preceded by *the.*
in·ter·neu·rone (íntər-néwr-ōn) *n.* Also **in·ter·neu·ron** (-on). *Physiology.* A neurone that acts as a link between motor neurones and sensory neurones in a reflex arc.
in·ter·nist (ín-ter-nist, in-tér-) *n. Chiefly U.S.* A doctor who specialises in internal medicine. [INTERN(AL MEDICINE) + -IST.]
in·tern·ment (in-térn-mənt) *n.* The act of interning or the state of being interned.
in·ter·node (íntər-nōd) *n.* A section or part between two nodes, as of a nerve or stem. **—in·ter·no·dal** (-nṓd'l) *adj.*
in·ter·nun·ci·o (íntər-nún-shi-ō, -si- || -nóon-) *n., pl.* **-os.** A Vatican diplomatic envoy or representative ranking just beneath a nuncio. [Italian *internunzio,* from Latin *internuntius,* go-between : *inter-,* between + *nūntius,* messenger, NUNCIO.] **—in·ter·nun·cial** *adj.*
in·ter·o·cep·tor (íntərō-séptər) *n. Physiology.* A specialised sensory nerve receptor responding to stimuli originating in internal organs. [From INTER(IOR) + (RE)CEPTOR.] **—in·ter·o·cep·tive** *adj.*
in·ter·par·ti·cle (íntər-pártik'l) *adj.* Occurring or existing between particles.
in·ter·par·ti·cle (íntər-pártik'l) *adj.* Occurring or existing between particles.
in·ter·pel·late (in-tér-pe-layt, -pə- || *U.S. also* íntər-péll-ayt, -pə-láyt) *tr.v.* **-lated, -lating, -lates.** In some legislative bodies, to question (a minister) formally about government policy or action. [Latin *interpellāre,* to interrupt by speaking.] **—in·ter·pel·lant** (íntər-péllənt) *n. & adj.* **—in·ter·pel·la·tion** (-láysh'n) *n.* **—in·ter·pel·la·tor** (-laytər) *n.*
in·ter·pen·e·trate (íntər-pénni-trayt) *v.* **-trated, -trating, -trates.** *—tr.* **1.** To penetrate thoroughly; permeate. **2.** To penetrate (each other). *—intr.* To penetrate mutually. **—in·ter·pen·e·tra·tion** (-tráysh'n) *n.* **—in·ter·pen·e·tra·tive** (-trətiv, -traytiv) *adj.*
in·ter·per·son·al (íntər-pérss'n'l) *adj.* Occurring between or involving two or more people: *interpersonal relations.*
in·ter·phase (íntər-fayz) *n. Biology.* A period or stage between two successive mitotic divisions of a cell nucleus.
in·ter·plan·e·tar·y (íntər-plánni-təri, -tri || -terri) *adj.* Between planets.
in·ter·play (íntər-play, -pláy) *n.* Reciprocal action and reaction; interaction.
~intr.v. **interplayed, -playing, -plays.** To act or react on each other; interact.
in·ter·plead (íntər-pleéd) *intr.v.* **-pleaded, -pleading, -pleads.** *Law.* To go to court together in order to settle a point in which a third party is involved. [Anglo-French *entrepleder* : INTER- + *pleder,* to plead, from Old French *plaidier, pleidier,* to PLEAD.]
in·ter·plead·er (íntər-pleédər) *n. Law.* **1.** A legal procedure to determine which of two persons bringing the same suit against a third person is the rightful claimant. **2.** One who interpleads.
In·ter·pol (íntər-pol) *n.* An international police organisation comprising the police forces of over 100 countries and concentrating on international crimes. The General Secretariat is in Paris. Also officially called "International Criminal Police Organisation".
in·ter·po·late (in-tér-pə-layt, -pō-) *v.* **-lated, -lating, -lates.** *—tr.* **1.** To insert or introduce between other things or parts; interpose; interject. **2.** To insert (additional or false material) in a text. **3.** To change or falsify (a text) by introducing new or false material. **4.** *Mathematics.* To determine a value of (a function) between known values by a procedure different from that specified by the function itself. *—intr.* To make insertions, additions, or interjections. [Latin *interpolāre* : *inter-,* between + *polīre,* to adorn, furbish, POLISH.] **—in·ter·po·la·tion** (-láysh'n) *n.* **—in·ter·po·la·tive** (-lətiv, -laytiv) *adj.* **—in·ter·po·lat·or** (-laytər) *n.*
in·ter·pose (íntər-pṓz) *v.* **-posed, -posing, -poses.** *—tr.* **1.** To place in an intervening position; insert or introduce between parts. **2.** To introduce or interject (a remark, question, or digression) during a conversation or speech. **3.** To exert (influence or authority) in order to interfere, obstruct, or intervene: *interpose one's veto. —intr.* **1.** To come between; intervene. **2.** To introduce a remark, question, or argument; interrupt. [Old French *interposer,* from Latin *interpōnere* (past participle *interpositus*), to place between : *inter-,* between + *pōnere,* to place.] **—in·ter·pos·er** *n.* **—in·ter·po·si·tion** *n.*
in·ter·pret (in-tér-prit) *v.* **-preted, -preting, -prets.** *—tr.* **1.** To clarify the meaning of; elucidate. **2.** To explain or perceive the significance of; construe: *interpreted his grunt as a refusal.* **3.** To represent the meaning or character of (a piece of music or a dramatic role, for example). **4.** To translate. *—intr.* **1.** To offer an explanation. **2.** To act as an interpreter. —See Synonyms at **explain.** [Middle English *interpreten,* from Old French *interpreter,* from Latin *interpretārī,* from *interpres,* interpreter, negotiator.] **—in·ter·pret·a·ble** *adj.* **—in·ter·pret·a·bil·i·ty** (-ə-bílləti), **in·ter·pret·a·ble·ness** *n.*
in·ter·pre·ta·tion (in-tér-pri-táysh'n) *n.* **1.** The act or process of interpreting; elucidation. **2.** The result of interpreting; an explanation or inference. **3.** A concept of a work of art as expressed by the character and style of its representation or performance. **—in·ter·pre·ta·tion·al** *adj.*
in·ter·pre·ta·tive (in-tér-pri-tə-tiv, -tay-) *adj.* Also **in·ter·pre·tive** (-pri-tiv). Expository; explanatory. **—in·ter·pre·ta·tive·ly** *adv.*
Usage: *Interpretative* is now often replaced by *interpretive* in formal English, presumably on account of easier pronunciation and spelling. See also **orientate.**
in·ter·pret·er (in-tér-pri-tər) *n.* **1.** One who translates orally the words of parties communicating with each other in different languages. **2.** One who makes and expounds an interpretation: *medieval interpreters of Aristotle.* **3.** *Computing.* A program or circuit for changing from the language in which instructions are written into machine code for use by the computers.
in·ter·ra·cial (íntər-ráysh'l) *adj.* Involving or existing between members of different racial groups: *interracial tension.*
in·ter·reg·num (íntər-rég-nəm) *n., pl.* **-nums** or **-na** (-nə). **1.** The interval of time between the end of a sovereign's reign and the accession of a successor. **2.** A period of temporary suspension of the usual functions of government or control. **3.** Any gap in continuity. [Latin *interrēgnum* : *inter-,* between + *rēgnum,* REIGN.] **—in·ter·reg·nal** *adj.*
in·ter·re·late (íntər-ri-láyt) *v.* **-lated, -lating, -lates.** *—tr.* To place in mutual relationship. *—intr.* To come into mutual relationship. **—in·ter·re·la·tion** *n.* **—in·ter·re·la·tion·ship** *n.*
in·ter·rex (íntər-réks) *n., pl.* **interreges** (íntər-reé-jeez). One who holds supreme state power during an interregnum. [Latin *interrex* : *inter-,* between + *rēx,* king.]
in·ter·ro·gate (in-térrə-gayt) *tr.v.* **-gated, -gating, -gates.** **1.** To question closely and formally; especially, to subject to prolonged and systematic questioning, sometimes with the use of threats or force. **2.** To obtain specific information from (a computer or data store) by program. —See Synonyms at **ask.** [Latin *interrogāre,* to consult, question : *inter-,* between + *rogāre,* to ask.] **—in·ter·ro·gat·ing·ly** *adv.* **—in·ter·ro·ga·tor** (-gaytər) *n.* **—in·ter·ro·ga·tion** (-gáysh'n) *n.* **—in·ter·ro·ga·tion·al** *adj.*
interrogation point *n.* **A question mark** *(see).* Also called "interrogation mark".
in·ter·rog·a·tive (íntə-róggətiv) *adj. Abbr.* **interrog. 1.** Having the form or character of a question; asking or serving to ask a question: *an interrogative raising of the eyebrows.* **2.** Designating a word or form used in asking a question: *an interrogative pronoun.* Compare **demonstrative, relative.**
~n. **1.** A word or form used in asking a question. **2.** An interrogative sentence or expression. **3.** A question mark. **—in·ter·rog·a·tive·ly** *adv.*
in·ter·rog·a·to·ry (íntə-róggə-təri, -tri) *adj.* Interrogative.
~n., pl. **interrogatories.** *Usually plural. Law.* A formal statement of questions that one party to a civil action may require the rival party to answer under oath. **—in·ter·rog·a·tor·i·ly** *adv.*
in·ter·rupt (íntə-rúpt) *v.* **-rupted, -rupting, -rupts.** *—tr.* **1. a.** To break the continuity or uniformity of. **b.** To be in the way of; obstruct (a view, for example). **2.** To hinder or stop the action or discourse of (someone) by breaking in. *—intr.* To break in upon an action or discourse. —See Synonyms at **intrude.**
~n. Computing. A signal or code for temporarily interrupting the processing of one computer program in order to process a different program. [Middle English *interrupten,* from Latin *interrumpere* (past participle *interruptus*), to break in : *inter,* between + *rumpere,* to break.] **—in·ter·rup·tion** *n.* **—in·ter·rup·tive** *adj.*
in·ter·rupt·ed (íntə-rúptid) *adj.* **1.** Broken in continuity; discontinuous. **2.** *Botany.* Having an uneven arrangement, as of leaflets along a stem. **—in·ter·rup·ted·ly** *adv.*
in·ter·rupt·er, in·ter·rup·tor (íntə-rúptər) *n.* **1.** One that interrupts. **2.** A device for periodically and automatically opening or closing an electric circuit.
in·ter se (íntər sáy, seé) *adv. Latin.* Between or among themselves.
in·ter·sect (íntər-sékt) *v.* **-sected, -secting, -sects.** *—tr.* To divide or penetrate (a line or space, for example) by cutting across or through. *—intr.* **1.** To cut across or overlap each other. **2.** To form an intersection. [Latin *intersecāre* (past participle *intersectus*) : *inter-,* mutually + *secāre,* to cut.]
in·ter·sec·tion (íntər-séksh'n) *n.* **1. a.** The act or process of intersecting. **b.** A place where things intersect; especially, a place where two or more roads cross. **2.** *Mathematics.* **a.** The point or locus of points common to two or more geometric figures. **b.** A set every member of which is an element of each of two or more given sets.
in·ter·sex (íntər-seks) *n.* An intersexual individual.
in·ter·sex·u·al (íntər-sék-sew-əl, -shoo-) *adj.* **1.** Existing or occurring between the sexes. **2.** Having sexual characteristics intermediate between those of a typical male and a typical female. **—in·ter·sex·u·al·i·ty** (-ál-əti) *n.* **—in·ter·sex·u·al·ly** *adv.*
in·ter·space (íntər-spáyss) *tr.v.* **-spaced, -spacing, -spaces.** To make or occupy a space between.
~n. (íntər-spayss). A space between two things; an interval. **—in·ter·spa·tial** (-spáysh'l) *adj.*
in·ter·sperse (íntər-spérss) *tr.v.* **-spersed, -spersing, -sperses.**

1. To scatter or distribute among other things at irregular intervals. 2. To supply or diversify with things distributed at irregular intervals. [Latin *interspergere* (past participle *interspersus*), to scatter among : *inter-*, among + *spargere*, to scatter.] **—in·ter·spers·ed·ly** (-spér-sidli) *adv.* **—in·ter·sper·sion** (-spérsh'n || -spérzh'n) *n.*

in·ter·state (íntər-stáyt) *adj.* Involving, existing between, or connecting two or more states, especially in the United States.
~*n. U.S.* A major road running between states.

in·ter·stel·lar (íntər-stéllər) *adj.* Between the stars.

in·ter·stice (in-tér-stiss) *n., pl.* **-stices** (-sti-siz, -seez). A narrow or small space between things or parts; a hole; a crevice. [French, from Late Latin *interstitium*, from Latin *intersistere* (past participle *interstitus*), to stand in the middle of : *inter-*, in the middle of, between + *sistere*, to stand.]

in·ter·sti·tial (íntər-stísh'l) *adj.* **1.** Of or occurring in interstices. **2.** Affecting or based on interstices.
~*n.* **1.** Any of various cells occurring in the spaces between tissues or organs, especially those interspersed between the seminiferous tubules of the testis. **2.** An atom or ion in a crystal, in a position between two normal lattice positions. **—in·ter·sti·tial·ly** *adv.*

interstitial compound *n. Chemistry.* A solid compound in which atoms of a nonmetal such as carbon or boron occupy interstitial positions in a metal lattice.

in·ter·strat·i·fy (íntər-strátti-fī) *tr.v.* **-fied, -fying, -fies.** To alternate or vary with other strata. Used in the passive. **—in·ter·strat·i·fi·ca·tion** (-fi-káysh'n) *n.*

in·ter·tex·ture (íntər-téks-chər) *n.* **1.** The act of interweaving or the state of being interwoven. **2.** Something interwoven.

in·ter·tid·al (íntər-tī́d'l) *adj.* Of, pertaining to, or designating the region between the extremes of high and low tide.

in·ter·tri·bal (íntər-trī́b'l) *adj.* Existing or carried on between tribes.

in·ter·tri·go (íntər-trī́gō) *n.* Inflammation of two moist skin surfaces that are in contact and between which there is friction, as may occur on the inside of the thighs.

in·ter·trop·i·cal (íntər-tróppik'l) *adj. Geography.* **1.** Between or within the tropics. **2.** Of or pertaining to the tropics.

in·ter·twine (íntər-twī́n) *v.* **-twined, -twining, -twines.** *—tr.* To twist or braid together. *—intr.* To interweave with one another; become entwined. **—in·ter·twine·ment** *n.*

in·ter·val (íntərv'l) *n. Abbr.* **int. 1.** A space between two objects, points, or units. **2.** The temporal duration between two instants, events, or states. **3.** *Mathematics.* **a.** A set consisting of all the numbers between a pair of given numbers, either including the end points *(closed interval)* or excluding the end points *(open interval).* **b.** A line segment representing such a set. **c.** A set of numbers greater than or less than a given number and including or excluding the given number. **4.** *Chiefly British.* A short pause between the acts of a play, parts of a concert, and the like; an intermission. **5.** *Music.* The difference in pitch between two notes on a given scale. **—at intervals. 1.** Intermittently; now and then. **2.** Separated by spaces. [Middle English *intervalle*, from Latin *intervallum*, space between ramparts : *inter-*, between + *vallum*, rampart.]

in·ter·vene (íntər-véen) *intr.v.* **-vened, -vening, -venes. 1.** To enter, appear, or have an effect as an extraneous element: *At this point fate intervened.* **2.** To come, appear, or lie between two things. **3.** To occur or come between two periods or points of time. **4.** To come in or between so as to mediate, prevent, or otherwise affect an outcome. Often used with *between* or *in.* **5.** To interfere, usually through force or threat of force, in the affairs of another nation. **6.** *Law.* To enter into a suit as a third party for the protection of an alleged interest. [Latin *inter-*, between + *venīre*, to come.] **—in·ter·ven·er** *n.*

in·ter·ven·tion (íntər-vénshən) *n.* **1.** The act or result of intervening. **2.** Active medical treatment to deal with a serious condition; specifically, surgical intervention.

in·ter·ven·tion·ism (íntər-vénsh'n-iz'm) *n.* **1.** The policy of intervening in the affairs of another sovereign state. **2.** Government action designed to control or influence domestic economic activity, as through nationalisation of industries. **—in·ter·ven·tion·ist** *adj. & n.*

in·ter·ver·te·bral disc (íntər-vérti-brəl) *n. Anatomy.* Any of the flexible plates of fibrocartilage connecting adjacent vertebrae in the spinal column.

in·ter·view (íntər-vew) *n.* **1. a.** A face-to-face meeting. **b.** Such a meeting arranged for a particular purpose, especially the assessment of a candidate for a job or award. **2. a.** A conversation between a reporter and a person from whom he seeks facts or statements. **b.** An account or reproduction of such a conversation.
~*v.* **interviewed, -viewing, -views.** *—tr.* To have an interview with. *—intr.* To undergo an interview: *She didn't interview well.* [Earlier *entervewe*, from Old French *entrevue*, from *entrevu*, past participle of *(s')entrevoir*, to see each other : *entre-*, INTER- + *voir*, to see, from Latin *vidēre.*] **—in·ter·view·ee** (-vew-ée) *n.* **—in·ter·view·er** *n.*

in·ter·war (íntər-wáwr) *adj.* Occurring between wars; especially, occurring between World War I and World War II.

in·ter·weave (íntər-wéev) *tr.v.* **-wove** (-wṓv) or *rare* **-weaved, -woven** (-wṓv'n) or *rare* **-wove, -weaving, -weaves. 1.** To weave together. **2.** To intermix.

in·tes·tate (in-téss-tayt, -tət, -tit) *adj.* **1.** Having made no legal will: *died intestate.* **2.** Not disposed of by a legal will. Said of property.
~*n.* One who dies without a legal will. [Middle English, from Latin *intestātus* : *in-*, not + *testātus*, TESTATE.] **—in·tes·ta·cy** (-tə-si) *n.*

intestinal flora *n.* All the harmless and beneficial bacteria that live in the intestinal tract.

in·tes·tine[1] (in-téstin) *n.* The portion of the **alimentary canal** *(see)* extending from the stomach to the anus. See **small intestine, large intestine.** [Latin *intestīnum*, from *intestīnus*, internal, from *intus*, within.] **—in·tes·ti·nal** (in-téstin'l, ínte-stī́n'l) *adj.* **—in·tes·ti·nal·ly** *adv.*

in·tes·tine[2] *adj.* Involving or restricted to the people of a country; internal; internecine: *intestine conflicts.*

in·ti·fa·da (ínti-faádə) *n.* A campaign begun in 1987 by Palestinian Arabs, especially in the West Bank and the Gaza Strip, to assert their national identity and resist the Israeli occupation of their territories. [From Arabic *intifada*, uprising; literally tremor, shaking (as in shaking or dusting off).]

in·ti·ma (ínti-mə) *n., pl.* **-mae** (-mee) or **-mas.** *Anatomy.* The innermost layer of an organ or part, especially the wall of a lymphatic vessel, artery, or vein. [New Latin, from Latin, feminine of *intimus*, innermost.]

in·ti·ma·cy (íntimə-si) *n., pl.* **-cies. 1.** The condition of being intimate. **2.** An instance of being intimate. **3.** *Sometimes plural.* Sexual intercourse. Used formally or euphemistically. [From INTIMATE.]

in·ti·mate[1] (ínti-mət, -mit) *adj.* **1.** Marked by close acquaintance, association, or familiarity: *an intimate friend.* **2. a.** Pertaining to or indicative of one's deepest nature. **b.** Very personal; private; secret. **3.** Essential; innermost. **4.** Characterised by informality and privacy: *an intimate nightclub.* **5.** Involved in a sexual relationship.
~*n.* A close friend or confidant. [Late Latin *intimātus*, past participle of *intimāre*, to put in, announce, INTIMATE (to hint).] **—in·ti·mate·ly** *adv.* **—in·ti·mate·ness** *n.*

in·ti·mate[2] (ínti-mayt) *tr.v.* **-mated, -mating, -mates. 1.** To communicate with a hint or other indirect sign; imply subtly. **2.** To announce; proclaim. —See Synonyms at **suggest.** [Late Latin *intimāre*, to make known or announce (one's inmost thoughts), from Latin *intimus*, inmost, deepest.] **—in·ti·mat·er** *n.* **—in·ti·ma·tion** (-máysh'n) *n.*

in·tim·i·date (in-tímmi-dayt) *tr.v.* **-dated, -dating, -dates. 1.** To make timid; frighten. **2.** To discourage, silence, or inhibit by or as if by threats. —See Synonyms at **threaten.** [Medieval Latin *intimidāre* : Latin *in-* (causative) + *timidus*, TIMID.] **—in·tim·i·da·tion** (-dáysh'n) *n.* **—in·tim·i·da·tor** (-daytər) *n.* **—in·tim·i·da·to·ry** (-daytəri, -dáytəri) *adj.*

in·tinc·tion (in-tíngksh'n) *n. Ecclesiastical.* The administration of the Eucharist by dipping the host into the wine before offering it to the communicant. [Late Latin *intinctiō* (stem *intinctiōn-*), from Latin *intingere* (past participle *intinctus*), to dip in : *in-*, in + *tingere*, to moisten, dye.]

in·tine (ín-tin, -teen, -tīn) *n.* The inner layer of the cell wall surrounding a grain of pollen. Also called "endosporium". [Latin *inti(-mus)*, innermost + -INE.]

in·tit·ule (in-títtewl) *tr.v.* **-uled, -uling, -ules.** *British.* To give a title to (an Act of Parliament). [Old French *intituler*, from Late Latin *intitulāre* : Latin *in-*, in + *titulus*, TITLE.]

intl. international.

in·to (íntoo, -too; *weak form, chiefly before a consonant sound,* intə) *prep.* **1.** To the inside or middle part of; to a point within. **2.** To the action or occupation of: *go into banking.* **3.** To the condition, state, or form of: *break into pieces; get into debt.* **4.** So as to be in or within: *enter into an agreement.* **5.** To a time or place in the course of: *well into the week.* **6.** Against: *ram into a tree.* **7.** Towards; in the direction of: *look into the distance.* **8.** As a divisor of: *Two into eight is four.* **9.** *Informal.* Interested in or involved with: *They are into vegetarianism.* [Middle English *into*, Old English *intō* : IN + TO.]

in·tol·er·a·ble (in-tóllərə-b'l) *adj.* **1.** Insupportable; unbearable. **2.** *Informal.* Extremely annoying; maddening. **—in·tol·er·a·bil·i·ty** (-billəti), **in·tol·er·a·ble·ness** *n.* **—in·tol·er·a·bly** *adv.*

in·tol·er·ance (in-tóllərənss) *n.* **1.** The quality or condition of being intolerant. **2.** Inability to withstand or consume: *an intolerance to certain drugs.*

in·tol·er·ant (in-tóllərənt) *adj.* **1.** Not tolerant of different characteristics or habits in others; bigoted. **2.** Irritable; short-tempered. **3.** Unable or indisposed to endure. **—in·tol·er·ant·ly** *adv.*

in·to·na·tion (ín-tə-náysh'n, -tō-) *n.* **1. a.** The act of intoning or chanting. **b.** An intoned utterance. **2.** A manner of producing musical notes, especially with regard to accuracy of pitch. **3. a.** The use of pitch as an element of meaning in language: *a questioning intonation.* **b.** A characteristic pattern of rising and falling pitch in speaking: *a lilting intonation in his voice.* **4.** *Music.* The opening phase of a plainsong composition, sung as a solo part.

in·tone (in-tṓn) *v.* **-toned, -toning, -tones.** *—tr.* **1.** To recite in a singing voice. **2.** To utter in a monotone. *—intr.* **1.** To speak with a given intonation. **2.** To sing a plainsong intonation. [Middle English *entonen*, from Old French *entoner*, from Medieval Latin *intonāre*, to utter in a musical tone : Latin *in-*, in + *tonus*, TONE.] **—in·ton·er** *n.*

in to·to (in tṓ-tō) *adv. Latin.* Totally; altogether.

in·tox·i·cant (in-tók-si-kənt) *n.* An agent that intoxicates; especially, an alcoholic drink. **—in·tox·i·cant** *adj.*

in·tox·i·cate (in-tók-si-kayt) *tr.v.* **-cated, -cating, -cates. 1.** To affect, especially by ingested alcohol, with any of a series of progressively deteriorating states from exhilaration to stupefaction; make drunk. **2.** To stimulate or excite: *"a man whom life intoxicates, who has no need of wine"* (Anaïs Nin). **3.** To administer poison. [Medieval Latin *intoxicāre*, to put poison in, poison : Latin *in-*, in +

toxicum, poison.] **—in·tox·i·ca·tion** (-káysh'n) *n.* **—in·tox·i·ca·tive** *adj.* **—in·tox·i·ca·tor** (-kaytər) *n.*

intr. intransitive.

intra– *prefix.* Indicates in, within, or inside of; for example, **intracranial, intramuscular.** ***Note:*** Many compounds other than those entered here may be formed with *intra-.* In forming compounds, *intra-* is normally joined with the following element without space or hyphen: *intraorbital.* However, if the second element begins with a capital letter or with the letter *a,* it is separated with a hyphen: *intra-European, intra-atomic.* [Late Latin, from Latin *intrā,* within.]

in·tra·a·tom·ic (íntrə-ə-tómmik) *adj.* Within an atom.

in·tra·car·di·ac (íntrə-kárdi-ak) *adj.* Within the heart.

in·tra·car·ti·lag·i·nous (íntrə-kárti-lájinəss) *adj.* Within cartilage.

in·tra·cel·lu·lar (íntrə-séllewlər) *adj.* Occurring or situated within a cell or cells.

in·tra·cra·ni·al (íntrə-kráyni-əl) *adj.* Within the skull.

in·trac·ta·ble (in-tráktə-b'l) *adj.* **1.** Difficult to manage or govern; stubborn. **2.** Difficult to mould or manipulate. **3.** Difficult to deal with or solve. **4.** Difficult to alleviate, remedy, or cure. —See Synonyms at **unruly.** **—in·trac·ta·bil·i·ty** (-bílləti), **in·trac·ta·ble·ness** *n.* **—in·trac·ta·bly** *adv.*

in·tra·cu·ta·ne·ous (íntrə-kew-táyni-əss) *adj.* Within the skin: *an intracutaneous injection.*

in·tra·dermal (íntrə-dérm'l) *adj.* Within the skin; intracutaneous.

in·tra·dos (in-tráy-doss || *U.S. also* -dōss, íntrə-doss, -dō) *n., pl.* **in·trados** (-dōz, -doss) or **-doses.** *Architecture.* The inner curve of an arch. [French, "inside back" : INTRA- + *dos,* back, from Old French, from Latin *dorsum.*]

in·tra·ga·lac·tic (íntrə-gə-láktik) *adj.* Occurring or situated within one galaxy.

in·tra·mo·lec·u·lar (íntrə-mə-léckewlər) *adj.* Within a molecule.

in·tra·mu·ral (íntrə-méwr-əl) *adj.* **1.** Existing or carried on within the bounds of an institution, especially a university. **2.** *Anatomy.* Within the wall of a cavity or organ. **—in·tra·mu·ral·ly** *adv.*

in·tra·mus·cu·lar (íntrə-múss-kewlər) *adj.* Within muscle.

in·tran·si·gent (in-trán-si-jənt, -traán-, -zi-) *adj.* Refusing to moderate a position; uncompromising. [French *intransigeant,* from Spanish *los intransigentes,* "the uncompromising" (name of a party of extreme republicans) : *in-,* not, from Latin + *transigente,* present participle of *transigir,* to compromise, from Latin *trānsigere,* to drive through, come to an understanding : *trāns-,* through + *agere,* to drive.] **—in·tran·si·gence, in·tran·si·gen·cy** *n.* **—in·tran·si·gent** *n.* **—in·tran·si·gent·ly** *adv.*

in·tran·si·tive (in-trán-si-tiv, -traán-) *adj. Abbr.* **intr., i.** **1.** *Grammar.* Designating a verb or verb construction that does not require a direct object to complete its meaning; for example; the verb *triumph* is always intransitive, and the verb *win* is sometimes intransitive. **2.** *Logic.* Designating a relationship such that if A and B have the relationship, and B and C have the relationship then it is not true that A and C have the relationship; for example, if A is the uncle of B, and B is the uncle of C, it is not true to say that A is the uncle of C, and therefore "is the uncle of" is an intransitive relationship. Compare **transitive.**

~n. An intransitive verb. [Late Latin *intransitīvus* : *in-,* not + *transitīvus,* TRANSITIVE.] **—in·tran·si·tive·ly** *adv.* **—in·tran·si·tive·ness** *n.*

in·tra·nu·cle·ar (íntrə-néw-kli-ər || -nōō-) *adj.* Within a nucleus.

in·tra·spe·cif·ic (íntrə-spə-síffik) *adj.* Occurring within a species: *intraspecific selection.*

in·tra·state (íntrə-stáyt) *adj.* Within the boundaries of a state.

in·tra·tel·lu·ric (íntrə-tə-léwr-ik) *n. Geology.* Formed or found below the earth's surface. Said of rocks.

in·tra·u·ter·ine (íntrə-yōōtə-rīn, -rin) *adj.* Within the uterus.

intrauterine device *n. Abbr.* **IUD, I.U.D.** A piece of metal or plastic, often in the shape of a loop, ring, or spiral, inserted into the uterus as a contraceptive.

in·tra·va·sa·tion (in-trávvə-sáysh'n) *n.* The entry of foreign matter into a blood vessel. [INTRA- + VAS + -ATION.]

in·tra·vas·cu·lar (íntrə-váss-kewlər) *adj.* Within the blood vessels or lymphatics.

in·tra·ve·na·tion (íntrə-vee-náysh'n) *n.* The entry of foreign matter into a vein.

in·tra·ve·nous (íntrə-veénəss) *adj. Abbr.* **IV** Within or into a vein or veins.

~n., pl. **intravenouses.** An intravenous injection, drip, or transfusion. **—in·tra·ve·nous·ly** *adv.*

in-tray (ín-tray) *n.* A tray, usually on an office desk, for incoming mail, documents needing attention, and the like. Compare **out-tray.**

intreat. Variant of **entreat.**

intrench. Variant of **entrench.**

intrenchment. Variant of **entrenchment.**

in·trep·id (in-tréppid) *adj.* Resolutely courageous; fearless; bold. See Synonyms at **brave.** [French, *intrépide,* from Latin *intrepidus* : *in-,* not + *trepidus,* agitated, alarmed.] **—in·tre·pid·i·ty** (ín-trə-píddəti, -tre-), **in·trep·id·ness** *n.* **—in·trep·id·ly** *adv.*

in·tri·ca·cy (íntri-kə-si) *n., pl.* **-cies.** **1.** The condition or quality of being intricate. **2.** Something intricate.

in·tri·cate (íntri-kət, -kit) *adj.* **1.** Having many elements in a complex arrangement; convoluted. **2.** Soluble or comprehensible only with painstaking effort; complicated. —See Synonyms at **complex, hard.** [Middle English, from Latin *intrīcātus,* past participle of *intrīcāre,* to entangle : *in-,* in + *trīcae,* trifles, troubles, perplexities.] **—in·tri·cate·ly** *adv.* **—in·tri·cate·ness** *n.*

in·tri·gant, in·tri·guant (íntri-gənt; *French* aN-tri-góN) *n. Feminine* **in·tri·gante** (íntri-gónt, -gánt; *French* aN-tri-góNT). *Archaic.* One who intrigues; a plotter. [French, "intriguing", from Italian *intrigante,* present participle of *intrigare,* to INTRIGUE.]

in·trigue (ín-treeg, in-treég) *n.* **1.** A covert manoeuvre to achieve an unavowed purpose; a secret or underhand scheme. **2.** The use of or involvement in such schemes. **3.** *Archaic.* A clandestine love affair. **4. a.** The quality of exciting interest or curiosity; allurement. **b.** Mystery; suspense. —See Synonyms at **conspiracy.**

~v. (in-treég) **intrigued, -triguing, -trigues.** *—intr.* **1.** To engage in covert schemes; plot. **2.** *Archaic.* To engage in a secret love affair. Often used with *with.* *—tr.* **1.** To insinuate (one's way, for example) by scheming. **2.** To arouse the interest or curiosity of. [French, from Italian *intrigo,* from *intrigare,* to perplex, from Latin *intrīcāre,* to entangle. See **intricate.**] **—in·tri·guer** *n.* **—in·trigu·ing·ly** *adv.*

in·trin·sic (in-trín-sik, -zik) *adj.* Also *archaic* **in·trin·si·cal** (-sik'l, -zik'l). **1.** Belonging to the essential nature of a thing; inherent: *"the exploitive and oppressive relationships intrinsic to capitalism."* (E.P. Thompson). **2.** *Anatomy.* Situated within or belonging solely to a body part, as certain nerves and muscles are. [Old French *intrinseque,* inner, from Late Latin *intrinsecus,* inward, from Latin, inwardly, on the inside : *intrim* (unattested), inward, from *intrā,* within + *secus,* alongside.] **—in·trin·si·cal·ly** *adv.*

intrinsic factor *n. Biochemistry.* A protein secreted in the stomach that is essential for the uptake of vitamin B_{12}.

intrinsic semiconductor *n.* A semiconductor that has no dopant added, having equal numbers of current-carrying holes and electrons.

in·tro (ín-trō) *n. Informal.* An introduction.

intro– *prefix.* Indicates: **1.** In or into; for example, **introjection.** **2.** Inward; for example, **introvert.** [Latin, from *intrō,* to the inside, inwardly.]

intro., introd. introduction; introductory.

in·tro·duce (íntrə-déwss || -dōōss) *tr.v.* **-duced, -ducing, -duces.** **1.** To identify and present; especially: **a.** To present to an audience. **b.** To make (a stranger) known to another person. Often used with *to.* **c.** To make (strangers) acquainted. **2.** To present and recommend (a plan, for example) for consideration. **3.** To bring into currency, use, or practice; institute. **4.** To bring in and establish: *introduce exotic birds.* **5.** To insert or inject. **6.** To make (a person) acquainted with something new: *introduced them to sailing.* **7.** To preface; open. [Latin *intrōdūcere,* to lead in : *intrō-,* in + *dūcere,* to lead.] **—in·tro·duc·er** *n.* **—in·tro·duc·i·ble** *adj.*

in·tro·duc·tion (íntrə-dúksh'n) *n. Abbr.* **intro., introd.** **1.** An act of introducing. **2.** The state of being introduced. **3.** A means of presenting one person to another, such as a personal presentation or formal letter. **4.** Something recently introduced; an innovation. **5.** Anything spoken, written, or otherwise presented in introducing, especially: **a.** A preface, as in a book. **b.** A short preliminary movement in a musical work. **6.** A basic instructive text or course of study. [Middle English *introduccion,* from Old French *introduction,* from Latin *intrōductiō* (stem *intrōductiōn-*), from *intrōdūcere,* to INTRODUCE.]

in·tro·duc·to·ry (íntrə-dúk-təri, -tri) *adj.* Also **in·tro·duc·tive** (-tiv). *Abbr.* **intro., introd.** Serving to introduce. **—in·tro·duc·to·ri·ly** *adv.*

in·tro·gres·sion (íntrə-grésh'n) *n. Genetics.* The introduction of genetic material to one gene pool from another by hybridisation. Also called "introgressive hybridisation". [INTRO- + *-gression* (as in *digression*).]

in·troit, In·tro·it (ín-troyt, -trō-it, in-trō-it) *n. Ecclesiastical.* **1.** A hymn or psalm sung at the opening of a service, especially in the Anglican Church. **2.** *Roman Catholic Church.* The beginning of the proper of the Tridentine Mass usually consisting of a psalm verse, antiphon, and the Gloria Patri followed by the repeated verse. [Middle English, "entrance", beginning, from Old French *introït,* from Latin *introitus,* from the past participle of *introīre,* to go in, enter : *intrō-,* into + *īre,* to go.]

in·tro·jec·tion (íntrə-jékshən) *n.* **1.** The unconscious incorporation into one's personality of the characteristics of another person or of an inanimate object. **2.** The incorporation or adoption of any attitude or belief. [INTRO- + (PRO)JECTION.] **—in·tro·ject** *tr.v.*

in·tro·mis·sion (íntrə-mísh'n) *n.* **1.** Introduction; admission. **2.** *Biology.* The introduction of one organ or part into another, such as the penis into the vagina. [Medieval Latin *intrōmissiō* (stem *intrōmissiōn-*), from Latin *intrōmittere,* to INTROMIT.] **—in·tro·mis·sive** *adj.*

in·tro·mit (íntrə-mít) *tr.v.* **-mitted, -mitting, -mits.** To cause or permit to enter; introduce or admit. [Middle English *intromitten,* from Latin *intrōmittere,* to send or put in, introduce : *intrō-,* in + *mittere,* to send.] **—in·tro·mit·tent** *adj.* **—in·tro·mit·ter** *n.*

in·trorse (in-trórss) *adj. Botany.* Facing inwards; turned towards the axis. Said especially of anthers that shed their pollen towards the flower. [Latin *introrsus,* contracted from *intrōversus,* turned inwards : *intrō-,* inwards + *versus,* past participle of *vertere,* to turn.]

in·tro·spect (íntrə-spékt) *intr.v.* **-spected, -specting, -spects.** To turn one's thoughts inwards; examine one's own feelings. [Latin *intrōspicere* (past participle *intrōspectus*), to look into : *intrō-,* into + *specere,* to look.]

in·tro·spec·tion (íntrə-spéksh'n) *n.* Contemplation of one's own thoughts and sensations; self-examination.

in·tro·spec·tive (íntrə-spéktiv) *adj.* **1.** Of, pertaining, or given to introspection. **2.** Given to private thought; contemplative. **—in·tro·spec·tive·ly** *adv.* **—in·tro·spec·tive·ness** *n.*

in·tro·ver·sion (íntrə-vérsh'n || -vérzh'n) *n.* **1. a.** *Psychology.* The directing of one's thoughts and interests inwards, especially to an excessive degree, accompanied by absence of interest in or aptitude for dealing with the external world and other people. **b.** Loosely, shy, reserved, or unsociable behaviour. Compare **extroversion. 2.** *Medicine.* The turning inwards of a hollow organ. **—in·tro·ver·sive** *adj.*

in·tro·vert (íntrə-vért) *v.* **-verted, -verting, -verts.** *—tr.* **1.** To turn or direct inwards. **2.** *Psychology.* To concentrate (one's thoughts or feelings) inwards upon themselves. **3.** To turn (a tubular organ or part) inwards upon itself. *—intr.* To exhibit introversion.

~n. (íntrə-vert). **1.** A person whose manner and behaviour are characterised by introversion. Compare **extrovert. 2.** An anatomical structure, such as the intestine, that is turned inwards upon itself.

~adj. Characterised by introversion; introverted. [New Latin *introvertere* : INTRO- + Latin *vertere*, to turn.]

in·trude (in-trōōd || -tréwd) *v.* **-truded, -truding, -trudes.** *—tr.* **1.** To interpose (oneself or something) without invitation or permission, or quite inappropriately. **2.** *Geology.* To force (molten rock) into existing rocks. *—intr.* To come in rudely or inappropriately; enter as an improper or unwanted element: *intruding on a private conversation.* [Latin *intrūdere,* to thrust in : *in-*, in + *trūdere,* to thrust.] **—in·trud·er** *n.*

Synonyms: *intrude, obtrude, interrupt, interlope.*

in·tru·sion (in-trōōzh'n || -tréwzh'n) *n.* **1.** The act or an instance of intruding, or the state of being intruded upon. **2.** An inappropriate or unwelcome addition: *"The fields were a timid intrusion on a landscape hardly marked by man"* (Doris Lessing). **3.** *Law.* Illegal entry upon or appropriation of the property of another. **4.** *Geology.* **a.** The forcing of molten rock into existing rocks. **b.** The intrusive mass so produced.

in·tru·sive (in-trōō-siv || -tréw-, -ziv) *adj.* **1.** Intruding or tending to intrude. **2.** *Geology.* Designating igneous rock forced into existing rocks while in molten state; irruptive. **3.** *Linguistics.* Constituting an **epenthesis** *(see).* —See Synonyms at **curious. —in·tru·sive·ly** *adv.* **—in·tru·sive·ness** *n.*

intrust. Variant of **entrust.**

in·tu·bate (ín-tew-bayt || -tə-) *tr.v.* **-bated, -bating, -bates.** *Medicine.* To insert a tube into (an organ or passage); cannulate. **—in·tu·ba·tion** (-báysh'n) *n.*

in·tu·it (in-téw-it || -tōō-) *v.* **-ited, -iting, -its.** *—tr.* To know or sense by intuition. *—intr.* To acquire knowledge by intuition. [Back-formation from INTUITION.]

in·tu·i·tion (ín-tew-ísh'n || -tōō-) *n.* **1. a.** The act or faculty of knowing without the use of rational processes; immediate cognition. **b.** Knowledge so gained; a perceptive insight. **2.** A capacity for guessing accurately; sharp insight. **3.** A sense of something not evident or deducible; an impression; a notion. —See Synonyms at **reason.** [Middle English *intuycion,* contemplation, from Old French *intuition,* from Late Latin, view, contemplation, from Latin *intuērī,* to look at or towards, contemplate : *in-*, on, towards + *tuērī,* to look at, watch.]

in·tu·i·tion·al (ín-tew-ísh'n'l || -tōō-) *adj.* Of, pertaining to, or based on intuition. **—in·tu·i·tion·al·ly** *adv.*

in·tu·i·tion·al·ism (ín-tew-ísh'n-ə-liz'm || -tōō-) *n. Philosophy.* Intuitionism. **—in·tu·i·tion·al·ist** *n.*

in·tu·i·tion·ism (ín-tew-ísh'n-iz'm || -tōō-) *n.* **1.** The theory that basic truths are known by intuition rather than reason. **2.** The theory that objects of perception are known to be real by intuition. **3.** The theory that ethical principles are known to be valid and universal through intuition. **4.** The theory that mathematical statements are true or false only if they can be proved to be so. **—in·tu·i·tion·ist** *n. & adj.*

in·tu·i·tive (in-téw-i-tiv || -tōō-) *adj.* **1.** Of or pertaining to intuition; intuitional. **2.** Known or arising from intuition. **3.** Possessing or demonstrating intuition. **—in·tu·i·tive·ly** *adv.* **—in·tu·i·tive·ness** *n.*

in·tu·i·tiv·ism (in-téw-i-ti-viz'm || -tōō-) *n. Philosophy.* The theory of intuitionism in ethics. **—in·tu·i·tiv·ist** *n.*

in·tu·mesce (ín-tew-méss || -tōō-) *intr.v.* **-mesced, -mescing, -mesces.** To swell or expand; enlarge. [Latin *intumēscere,* to swell up : *in-* (intensive) + *tumēscere,* to begin to swell, from *tūmere,* to swell.]

in·tu·mes·cence (ín-tew-méss'nss || -tōō-) *n.* **1.** Intumescing; swelling. **2.** A swollen organ or part. **—in·tu·mes·cent** *adj.*

in·turn (ín-turn) *n.* A curving inwards. **—in·turned** *adj.*

in·tus·sus·cept (íntə-sə-sépt, íntəss-) *tr.v.* **-cepted, -cepting, -cepts.** *Pathology.* To fold or turn inwards; invaginate. [Probably back-formation from INTUSSUSCEPTION.] **—in·tus·sus·cep·tive** *adj.*

in·tus·sus·cep·tion (íntə-sə-sépsh'n, íntəss-) *n.* **1.** *Pathology.* Invagination; especially, an infolding of one part of the intestine into another. **2.** *Botany.* The deposition of molecules into a cell wall, thereby increasing the surface area. [New Latin *intussusceptio* : Latin *intus,* within + *susceptiō* (stem *susceptiōn-*), taking up, from *suscipere,* to take up : *sub-*, up from under + *capere,* to take, seize.]

intwine. Variant of **entwine.**

intwist. Variant of **entwist.**

In·u·it, In·nu·it (innew-it) *n., pl.* **-its** or collectively **Inuit. 1.** An Eskimo of North America and Greenland as distinguished from one of Asia and the Aleutian Islands. **2.** The language of these Eskimos.

in·u·lin (innew-lin) *n.* A fructose polysaccharide, $(C_6H_{10}O_5)_3$ or $(C_6H_{10}O_5)_4$, stored as a food reserve in the roots of many plants.

in·unc·tion (in-úngkshən) *n.* The process of applying and rubbing in an ointment. [Middle English, from Latin *inunctiō* (stem *inunctiōn-*), from *inunguere,* to smear oil on, anoint : *in-*, on + *unguere,* to smear, anoint.]

in·un·date (ínnun-dayt) *tr.v.* **-dated, -dating, -dates. 1.** To cover with water, especially flood water; overflow. **2.** To overwhelm as if with a flood; swamp: *inundated with requests.* [Latin *inundāre,* "to flow in" : *in-*, in + *undāre,* to flow, from *unda,* wave.] **—in·un·da·tion** (-dáysh'n) *n.* **—in·un·da·tor** (-daytər) *n.* **—in·un·da·to·ry** (in-úndə-təri, -tri, ínnun-dáytəri) *adj.*

in·ure, en·ure (i-néwr || -nóor) *v.* **-ured, -uring, -ures.** *—tr.* To make used to something unpleasant by prolonged subjection. Usually used in the passive, and with *to*: *He became inured to the flies.* *—intr.* To come into operation; take effect, especially in law. [Middle English *enewren* : *en-* (causative) + *ure,* use, custom, from Old French *uevre, euvre,* custom, work, from Latin *opera,* work.] **—in·ure·ment** *n.*

in·urn (in-úrn) *tr.v.* **-urned, -urning, -urns.** *Archaic.* **1.** To put or seal (ashes of the dead, for example) in an urn. **2.** To bury or entomb.

in u·ter·o (in yōōtə-rō, ōōtə-) *adj. Latin.* In the womb. **—in u·ter·o** *adv.*

in·u·tile (i-néw-tīl || *U.S.* -néwt'l) *adj.* Useless. [Middle English, from Old French, from Latin *inūtilis* : *in-*, not + *ūtilis,* useful, from *ūtī*†, to use.] **—in·u·tile·ly** *adv.* **—in·u·til·i·ty** (innew-tillәti) *n.*

inv. 1. invented; invention; inventor. **2.** invoice.

in va·cu·o (in váckew-ō) *adj. Latin.* **1.** In a vacuum. **2.** In isolation; considered without reference to related evidence. **—in va·cu·o** *adv.*

in·vade (in-váyd) *v.* **-vaded, -vading, -vades.** *—tr.* **1.** To enter (a territory, for example) by force in order to conquer or overrun. **2.** To encroach or intrude upon; violate: *to invade someone's privacy.* **3.** To overrun or infest: *The kitchen was invaded by ants.* **4.** To enter and spread harm through: *Infection has invaded the membranes.* *—intr.* To make an invasion. [Middle English *invaden,* from Latin *invādere,* "to go in" : *in-*, in + *vādere,* to go.] **—in·vad·er** *n.*

in·vag·i·nate (in-váji-nayt) *v.* **-nated, -nating, -nates.** *—tr.* **1.** To enclose in or as in a sheath. **2.** To turn within; introvert. *—intr.* To become enclosed or turned within itself. [Medieval Latin *invāgīnāre*: Latin *in-*, in + *vāgīna,* sheath.] **—in·vag·i·na·ble** (-nəb'l) *adj.*

in·vag·i·na·tion (in-váji-náysh'n) *n.* **1.** The act or process of invaginating or the condition of being invaginated. **2.** Something invaginated, as an organ or part. **3.** The infolding of an outer layer of cells to form a cavity, especially as in the embryonic development of the gastrula from the blastula.

in·va·lid[1] (ínvə-lid, -leed) *n.* A chronically ill or disabled person.

~adj. **1.** Disabled by illness or injury; sickly or infirm. **2.** Of, pertaining to, or for invalids.

~v. (*usually* -leed) **invalided, -liding, -lids.** *—tr.* **1.** To make an invalid of; disable physically. **2.** To release or exempt from duty because of ill health. *—intr.* To become invalided. [Latin *invalidus,* not strong, ineffective : *in-*, not + *validus,* strong, VALID.]

in·val·id[2] (in-válid) *adj.* **1.** Null; legally ineffective. **2.** Falsely based or reasoned; unjustified: *an invalid conclusion.* [Latin *invalidus,* ineffective, INVALID (infirm).] **—in·val·id·ly** *adv.*

in·val·i·date (in-vál-i-dayt) *tr.v.* **-dated, -dating, -dates. 1.** To make legally ineffective or void. **2.** To undermine or destroy the force or effectiveness of (an argument, for example). —See Synonyms at **nullify. —in·val·i·da·tion** (-dáysh'n) *n.* **—in·val·i·da·tor** (-daytər) *n.*

in·va·lid·ism (ínvə-lid-iz'm, -leed-) *n.* The condition of being chronically ill or disabled.

in·val·i·di·ty[1] (ínvə-líddəti) *n.* The condition or quality of being void or unjustifiable; lack of validity.

invalidity[2] *n.* The condition of being ill or disabled, usually for a long period of time. Also used adjectivally: *invalidity benefit.*

in·val·u·a·ble (in-vál-yoo-əb'l, -yə-b'l) *adj.* **1.** Of inestimable use or help; indispensable; much appreciated: *an invaluable service.* **2.** Having extremely high value; priceless: *invaluable paintings.* —See Synonyms at **costly. —in·val·u·a·bly** *adv.*

In·var (in-vár) *n.* A trademark for an iron alloy containing 36 per cent nickel, with an extremely low coefficient of expansion, and used chiefly in measuring rods and tapes, pendulums, balance wheels, tuning forks, and in temperature-regulating devices.

in·var·i·a·ble (in-váir-i-əb'l) *adj.* Not changing or subject to change; constant.

~n. Something that does not change; especially, a mathematical expression or a physical quantity. **—in·var·i·a·bil·i·ty** (-ə-billəti), **in·var·i·a·ble·ness** *n.* **—in·var·i·a·bly** *adv.*

in·var·i·ant (in-váir-i-ənt) *adj.* **1.** Not varying; constant. **2.** Unaffected by a given mathematical operation, such as a transformation of coordinates.

~n. An invariant quantity, function, configuration, or system. **—in·var·i·ance** *n.*

in·va·sion (in-váyzh'n) *n.* **1.** The act or an instance of invading; especially, entrance by force. **2.** The onset of something injurious or harmful, as of a disease. **3.** Any intrusion or encroachment. [Middle English *invasioune,* from Old French *invasion,* from Late Latin *invāsiō* (stem *invāsiōn-*), from Latin *invādere,* to INVADE.]

in·va·sive (in-váy-siv || -ziv) *adj.* **1. a.** Tending to spread; especially tending to invade healthy tissue. **b.** Relating to or designating a medical procedure that "invades" (i.e. enters) the body, as by puncture or incision. **2.** *Archaic.* Of, relating to, or given to armed aggression.

in·vec·tive (in-véktiv) *n.* Vehement accusation or abuse; denunciation; vituperation. [Middle English *invectiff,* abusive, vituperative, from Old French *invectif,* from Late Latin *invectīva (ōrātiō),* "abusive (speech)", from Latin *invehere,* to attack, INVEIGH.] **—in·vec·tive** *adj.* **—in·vec·tive·ly** *adv.* **—in·vec·tive·ness** *n.*

in·veigh (in-váy) *intr.v.* **-veighed, -veighing, -veighs.** To give vent to angry censure; protest vehemently; rail. Used with *against.* [Latin *invehī,* passive infinitive of *invehere,* to carry in, sail into, assail, attack : *in-,* in + *vehere,* to carry.] **—in·veigh·er** *n.*

in·vei·gle (in-váyg'l, -véeg'l) *tr.v.* **-gled, -gling, -gles.** **1.** To lead astray or win over by deceitful flattery or persuasion: *She inveigled me into joining her plot.* **2.** To obtain by cajolery. —See Synonyms at **lure.** [Earlier *invegle,* from Anglo-French *envegler,* alteration of Old French *aveugler,* to blind, from *aveugle,* blind, from Medieval Latin *ab oculīs,* without eyes : Latin *ab,* out of + *oculus,* eye.] **—in·vei·gle·ment** *n.* **—in·vei·gler** *n.*

in·vent (in-vént) *tr.v.* **-vented, -venting, -vents.** **1.** To conceive of or devise (something entirely new); produce (an invention). **2.** To fabricate; make up. [Middle English *inventen,* to come upon, find, from Latin *invenīre* (past participle *inventus*) : *in-,* on + *venīre,* to come.] **—in·vent·i·ble** *adj.*

in·ven·tion (in-vénsh'n) *n. Abbr.* **inv. 1.** The act or process of inventing. **2.** A new device or process developed from study and experimentation. **3.** A mental fabrication; a falsehood or fictitious story. **4.** Skill in inventing; inventiveness. **5.** A short musical piece developing a single theme contrapuntally. **6.** *Archaic.* A discovery; a finding. **—in·ven·tion·al** *adj.*

in·ven·tive (in-véntiv) *adj.* **1.** Of or characterised by invention or imagination: *an inventive spy-story.* **2.** Adept or skilful at inventing; creative; ingenious. **—in·ven·tive·ly** *adv.* **—in·ven·tive·ness** *n.*

in·ven·tor (in-véntər) *n.* Also *Chiefly U.S.* **in·ven·ter.** *Abbr.* **inv.** One who invents a previously unknown device, method, or process.

in·ven·to·ry (ínvən-təri, -tri. *Note: not* in-véntəri.) *n., pl.* **-ries. 1.** A detailed list of things, such as articles or goods in one's possession. **2.** The process of making such a list. **3.** The items so listed. **4.** The total quantity of goods and materials held by an organisation or company. **5.** Broadly, an evaluation or survey.

~tr.v. **inventoried, -rying, -ries. 1.** To make an inventory of. **2.** To include in an inventory. [Medieval Latin *inventōrium,* list, altered from Late Latin *inventārium,* "a finding out", "enumeration", from Latin *invenīre,* to come upon, find, INVENT.] **—in·ven·to·ri·al** (-táwri-əl || -tōri-) *adj.* **—in·ven·to·ri·al·ly** *adv.*

in·ve·rac·i·ty (ín-və-rássəti) *n., pl.* **-ties. 1.** Lack of veracity; untruthfulness. **2.** An untruth; a falsehood.

In·ver·car·gill (ínvər-kárgil). A city in New Zealand on the southeast coast of South Island. It is the capital of Southland and the centre of a dairy and agricultural district.

In·ver·ness[1] (ínvər-néss). Royal burgh in northeast Scotland. The administrative centre of the Highland Unitary Authority area, it supports distilling, tweed-manufacturing, saw-milling, tourism, and some coal-shipping from its port at the head of the Moray Firth.

Inverness[2]. Formerly the largest county in Scotland (10 269 square kilometres; 4,211 square miles). Between the western Cairngorms and the Outer Hebrides, it is now in the Highland Unitary Authority area.

Inverness[3] *n. Often small* **i. 1.** A loose overcoat with a detachable cape. **2.** The cape of such a coat. Also called "Inverness cape". [First popularised in INVERNESS.]

in·verse (in-vérss, ín-verss) *n.* **1.** That which is opposite, as in sequence or character; the reverse. **2.** *Mathematics.* An element in a set that yields the identity element of the set when combined with another element in a binary operation; especially: **a.** The reciprocal of a designated quantity. Also called "multiplicative inverse". **b.** The negative of a designated quantity. Also called "additive inverse".

~adj. **1.** Reversed in order, nature, or effect. **2.** Turned upside down; inverted. **3.** *Mathematics.* Pertaining to an inverse. Said of relationships, proportions, or functions. [Latin *inversus,* past participle of *invertere,* to INVERT.] **—in·verse·ly** *adv.*

in·ver·sion (in-vérsh'n || -vérzh'n) *n.* **1.** The act of inverting or the state of being inverted. **2.** An interchange of position, especially of adjacent objects in a sequence. **3.** A change in normal word order, such as the placing of a verb before its subject. **4.** *Music.* **a.** A rearrangement of notes in which upper and lower voices are transposed, as in counterpoint, or in which each interval in a single melody is applied in the opposite direction. **b.** An interval, chord, or melody resulting from such rearrangement. **5.** Homosexuality. **6.** *Medicine.* The turning inwards or inside out of an organ or part. **7.** *Genetics.* A type of chromosome mutation in which a chromosome segment is inserted in reverse order. **8.** *Chemistry.* Conversion from the dextrorotatory to the laevorotatory or from the laevorotatory to the dextrorotatory form. **9.** *Meteorology.* A state in which the air temperature increases with increasing altitude, holding surface air down. [Latin *inversiō* (stem *inversiōn-*), from *invertere,* to INVERT.] **—in·ver·sive** (in-vér-siv || -ziv) *adj.*

in·vert (in-vért) *v.* **-verted, -verting, -verts.** *—tr.* **1.** To turn inside out or upside down. **2.** To reverse the position, order, or condition of. **3.** To subject to inversion. *—intr.* To be subjected to inversion.

~n. (ín-vert). **1.** Something inverted. **2.** A homosexual. [Latin *invertere,* to turn inside out or upside down : *in-,* in, inwards + *vertere,* to turn.] **—in·vert·i·ble** *adj.*

in·ver·tase (in-vér-tayz, -tayss) *n.* A plant and animal enzyme that catalyses the conversion of sucrose to glucose and fructose. Also called "sucrase", "saccharase".

in·ver·te·brate (in-vérti-brət, -brit, -brayt) *adj.* **1.** Having no backbone or spinal column; not vertebrate. **2.** Lacking strength of character; spineless.

~n. An invertebrate animal. [New Latin *Invertebrata,* neuter plural of *invertebratus,* having no backbone : IN- (no) + VERTEBRATE.]

in·vert·ed comma (in-vértid) *n. Chiefly British.* A **quotation mark** *(see).*

inverted mordent *n. Music.* A **pralltriller** *(see).*

inverted snobbery *n.* **1.** The conscious affirmation of values, tastes, or habits characteristic of one's lower-class background, or the affectation of values, tastes, or habits supposedly characteristic of a class lower than one's own. **2.** A sense of social exclusiveness resulting from such an image of oneself.

in·vert·er (in-vértər) *n.* **1.** One that inverts. **2.** *Electronics.* A device used to convert direct current into alternating current. **3.** *Computing.* A logic component, a **NOT gate** *(see).*

invert sugar *n.* A hygroscopic mixture of equal parts of glucose and fructose resulting from the hydrolysis of sucrose and used chiefly in brewing and in medicine. [Commercially produced by inversion of sucrose.]

in·vest (in-vést) *v.* **-vested, -vesting, -vests.** *—tr.* **1.** To commit (money or capital) in order to gain profit or interest, as by purchasing property or shares. **2.** To spend or utilise (time, money, or effort) for future advantage or benefit. Often used with *in.* **3.** To endow with rank, authority, or power. **4.** To inaugurate with ceremony; install in office. **5.** To provide with some enveloping or pervasive quality. **6.** *Rare.* To clothe; adorn. **7.** To cover completely; envelop; shroud. **8.** *Military. Rare.* To surround with hostile troops or ships; besiege. *—intr.* **1.** To invest money; make an investment. Often used with *in.* **2.** *Informal.* To buy. Used with *in.* [Old French *investir,* from Medieval Latin *investīre,* from Latin, to clothe in, surround : *in-,* in + *vestīre,* to clothe, from *vestis,* clothes.] **—in·ves·tor** (-véstər) *n.*

in·ves·ti·gate (in-vésti-gayt) *v.* **-gated, -gating, -gates.** *—tr.* To observe or inquire into in detail; examine systematically. *—intr.* To make an investigation. [Latin *investīgāre,* to trace out, search into : *in-,* in + *vestīgāre,* to trace, track, from *vestīgium,* trace, footprint, VESTIGE.] **—in·ves·ti·ga·ble** (-gəb'l), **in·ves·ti·ga·tive, in·ves·ti·ga·to·ry** (-gay-təri, -gə-, -tri) *adj.* **—in·ves·ti·ga·tor** (-gaytər) *n.*

in·ves·ti·ga·tion (in-vésti-gáysh'n) *n.* The act, process, or an instance of investigating; an inquiry.

investigative journalism *n.* The gathering of news, especially news of crime, corruption, official mismanagement, or controversial plans, by means of investigation. **—investigative journalist** *n.*

in·ves·ti·tive (in-vésti-tiv) *adj.* Of or pertaining to investiture.

in·ves·ti·ture (in-vésti-chər, -tewr) *n.* **1.** The act or formal ceremony of conferring upon a person the authority and symbols of a high office. **2.** *Chiefly British.* An act or formal ceremony of conferring honours or awards, especially one performed by a sovereign. **3.** *Archaic.* A thing that covers or adorns, as a garment. [Middle English, from Medieval Latin *investītūra,* from *investīre,* INVEST.]

in·vest·ment (in-véstmənt) *n.* **1.** The act of investing or the state of being invested. **2.** An amount invested. **3.** Property or another possession acquired or invested in for future income or benefit. **4.** Investiture. **5.** *Archaic.* A garment; a vestment. **6.** An outer covering or layer. **7.** *Rare.* A siege.

investment trust *n. Finance.* A company that invests its capital, acquired by the issue of shares, solely in other companies.

in·vet·er·ate (in-véttə-rət, -vét-, -rit) *adj.* **1.** Firmly established by long standing; deep-rooted. **2.** Persisting in an ingrained habit; habitual: *an inveterate liar.* [Latin *inveterātus,* past participle of *inveterāre,* to render old : *in-* (causative) + *vetus* (stem *veter-*), old.] **—in·vet·er·a·cy** (-rə-si), **in·vet·er·ate·ness** *n.* **—in·vet·er·ate·ly** *adv.*

in·vi·a·ble (in-vī́-əb'l) *adj.* Nonviable; especially, biologically incapable of growth or reproduction: *an inviable seed.*

in·vid·i·ous (in-víddi-əss) *adj.* **1.** Tending to rouse ill will or animosity; offensive: *an invidious clause in the contract.* **2.** Containing or implying a slight; unfairly discriminatory. [Latin *invidiōsus,* envious, hostile, from *invidia,* ENVY.] **—in·vid·i·ous·ly** *adv.* **—in·vid·i·ous·ness** *n.*

in·vig·i·late (in-víji-layt) *v.* **-lated, -lating, -lates.** *—intr. British.* **1.** To keep watch over students during a written examination. **2.** *Archaic.* To keep guard; keep watch. *—tr.* To watch over students during (an examination). [Latin *invigilāre,* watch over : IN- + *vigilāre,* to keep watch; see **vigil.**] **—in·vig·i·la·tor** (-laytər) *n.*

in·vig·or·ate (in-víggə-rayt) *tr.v.* **-ated, -ating, -ates.** To impart vigour, strength, or vitality to: *"A few whiffs of the raw, strong scent of phlox invigorated her."* (D.H. Lawrence). [IN- (causative) + VIGOUR + -ATE.] **—in·vig·or·at·ing·ly, in·vig·or·a·tive·ly** *adv.* **—in·vig·or·a·tion** (-ráysh'n) *n.* **—in·vig·or·a·tive** (-rətiv, -raytiv) *adj.* **—in·vig·or·a·tor** (-raytər) *n.*

in·vin·ci·ble (in-vín-sə-b'l) *adj.* **1.** Unconquerable; unbeatable. **2.** Incapable of being surmounted; insuperable. [Middle English, from Latin *invincibilis* : *in-,* not + *vincibilis,* VINCIBLE.] **—in·vin·ci·bil·i·ty** (-bílləti), **in·vin·ci·ble·ness** *n.* **—in·vin·ci·bly** *adv.*

in vi·no ve·ri·tas (in véenō vérri-tass, -taass). *Latin.* When drunk, one speaks the truth. [Latin, "in wine (there is) truth".]

in·vi·o·la·ble (in-vī́-ələ-b'l) *adj.* **1.** Safe from or secured against violation or profanation; kept sacred. **2.** Impregnable to assault, trespass, or disturbance. **—in·vi·o·la·bil·i·ty** (-bílləti), **in·vi·o·la·ble·ness** *n.* **—in·vi·o·la·bly** *adv.*

in·vi·o·late (in-vī́-ə-lət, -lit, -layt) *adj.* Not violated; intact: *an inviolate shrine.* [Middle English *invyolat,* from Latin *inviolātus* : *in-,* not + *violātus,* past participle of *violāre,* VIOLATE.] **—in·vi·o·la·c**

(-lə-si), **in·vi·o·late·ness** n. **—in·vi·o·late·ly** adv.

in·vis·i·ble (in-vízzə-b'l) adj. **1.** Incapable of being seen; not visible. **2.** Not accessible to view; hidden. **3. a.** Not easily noticed or detected; inconspicuous; especially, of or designating mending of clothes that is intended to be undetectable. **b.** Hidden from public view. **4.** Economics. **a.** Not published in financial statements: an invisible asset. **b.** Designating items of international trade consisting of services rather than goods: invisible exports. **~n. 1.** One that is invisible. **2.** Plural. Economics. Imports and exports of services such as tourism, banking, or insurance, as opposed to goods. **—in·vis·i·bil·i·ty** (-bílləti), **in·vis·i·ble·ness** n. **—in·vis·i·bly** adv.

invisible ink n. Ink that is colourless and invisible until treated by a chemical, heat, or special light. Also called "sympathetic ink".

in·vi·ta·tion (invi-táysh'n) n. **1.** The act of inviting. **2.** A spoken or written request for one's presence or participation. Also used adjectivally: an invitation dance. **3.** An allurement, enticement, or attraction.

in·vi·ta·tion·al (invi-táysh'n'l) adj. Chiefly U.S. Restricted to invited participants: an invitational golf tournament.

in·vi·ta·to·ry (in-vítə-təri, -tri) n., pl. **-ries.** A psalm or other piece sung as an invitation to prayer in church services. [Middle English invytatory, from Medieval Latin invītātōrium, from the neuter of Late Latin invītātōrius, inviting, antiphonal, from Latin invītāre, INVITE.]

in·vite (in-vít) v. **-vited, -viting, -vites.** **—tr. 1.** To request the presence or participation of. **2.** To request politely or formally. **3.** To tend to bring on; provoke. **4.** To lure; entice; tempt. **—intr.** To give an invitation. **~n.** (ín-vīt). Informal. An invitation. [Old French inviter, from Latin invītāre.]

in·vit·ing (in-víting) adj. Attractive; tempting: an inviting dessert. **—in·vit·ing·ly** adv. **—in·vit·ing·ness** n.

in vi·tro (in véetrō, víttrō) adj. Designating biological processes made to occur in an artificial environment outside the living organism: in vitro fertilisation. [New Latin, "in glass".] **—in vi·tro** adv.

in vi·vo (in véevō) adj. Designating biological processes or experiments conducted or occurring within the living organism. [New Latin, "in a living body".] **—in vi·vo** adv.

in·vo·cate (ín-və-kayt, -vō-) tr.v. **-cated, -cating, -cates.** Archaic. To invoke. [Latin invocāre, INVOKE.] **—in·voc·a·tive** (in-vóckətiv) adj. **—in·vo·ca·tor** (-kaytər) n.

in·vo·ca·tion (ín-və-káysh'n, -vō-) n. **1.** The act of invoking; especially, an appeal to a higher power for assistance. **2.** A prayer or other formula used in invoking, as at the opening of a religious service. **3. a.** A conjuring or calling up of a spirit by incantation. **b.** The incantation used in conjuring. [Middle English, from Old French, from Latin invocātiō (stem invocātiōn-), from invocāre, INVOKE.] **—in·voc·a·to·ry** (in-vóckə-təri, -tri) adj.

in·voice (in-voyss) n. Abbr. **inv.** A detailed list of goods supplied or sent or services rendered, with an account of all costs; a bill. **~tr.v. invoiced, -voicing, -voices.** **1.** To list on an invoice. **2.** To present an invoice to. [Originally invoyes, plural of invoy, invoice, from Old French envoy, a sending, shipment of goods. See envoi.]

in·voke (in-vōk) tr.v. **-voked, -voking, -vokes.** **1.** To call upon (a higher power) for assistance. **2.** To appeal to; petition. **3.** To call for (help, for example) earnestly; solicit. **4.** To summon (a spirit, for example) with incantations; conjure up. **5.** To cite in support or justification of one's cause. [Old French invoquer, from Latin invocāre, "to call upon" : in-, in, on + vocāre, to call.] **—in·vo·ca·ble** adj. **—in·vok·er** n.

in·vol·u·cel (in-vóllew-sel) n. Botany. A secondary involucre, as at the base of an umbellule in a compound umbel. [New Latin involucellum, diminutive of involucrum, INVOLUCRE.]

in·vo·lu·crate (ínvə-lóō-krət, -krit, -krayt) adj. Botany. Having an involucre.

in·vo·lu·cre (ínvə-lóōkər, -lewkər) n. Also **in·vo·lu·crum** (-lóō-krəm, -léw-) pl. **-cra** (-krə). Botany. A whorl or series of leaflike scales or bracts beneath or around a flower or flower cluster. [New Latin involucrum, from Latin, wrapper, case, envelope, from involvere, to enwrap, INVOLVE.] **—in·vo·lu·cral** adj.

in·vo·lu·crum (invə-lóō-krəm, -léw-) n., pl. **-cra** (-krə). **1.** An enveloping sheath or envelope. **2.** Botany. Variant of **involucre.** [New Latin, INVOLUCRE.]

in·vol·un·tar·y (in-vóllən-təri, -tri ‖ -terri) adj. **1.** Not desired; enforced: involuntary exile. **2.** Performed without conscious willing; unintentional. **3.** Physiology. Not subject to conscious control: an involuntary muscle. **—See Synonyms at spontaneous.** **—in·vol·un·tar·i·ly** adv. **—in·vol·un·tar·i·ness** n.

in·vo·lute (ínvə-lōōt, -lewt) adj. Also **in·vo·lut·ed** (-lōōtid, -lewtid). **1.** Intricate; complex. **2.** Botany. Having the margins rolled inwards. **3.** Having whorls that obscure the axis or other volutions, as the shell of a cowry. **~n.** Mathematics. **1.** The locus of a fixed point on a tangent line as it rolls but does not slide around a fixed curve. **~intr.v.** (-lōōt, -léwt) **involuted, -luting, -lutes.** To become involute. [Latin involutus, past participle of involvere, to enwrap, INVOLVE.]

in·vo·lu·tion (invə-lóōsh'n, -léwsh'n) n. **1.** The act of involving or the state of being involved. **2.** Anything that is internally complex or convoluted. **3.** Grammar. A complicated construction. **4.** Mathematics. The multiplying of a quantity by itself a specified number of times; raising to a power. In this sense, compare **evolution.** **5.** Physiology. The shrinking of an organ, as of the womb after

childbirth, or as a result of old age. [Latin involūtiō (stem involūtiōn-) from involvere, INVOLVE.] **—in·vo·lu·tion·al** adj.

in·volve (in-vólv ‖ Southern English also -vólv) tr.v. **-volved, -volving, -volves.** **1.** To contain or include as a part. **2.** To have as a necessary feature or consequence; imply. **3.** To draw in as an associate or participant; embroil; implicate. **4.** To occupy or engross completely; absorb. **5.** To make complex or intricate; complicate. **6.** Poetic. To wrap; envelop: a castle involved in mist. **7.** Archaic. To wind or coil about. **8.** Mathematics. To raise (a number) to a specified degree. Not in technical usage. **—See Synonyms at include.** [Middle English involven, from Latin involvere, to enwrap, "roll in" : in-, in + volvere, to roll, turn.] **—in·volve·ment** n. **—in·volv·er** n.

in·volved (in-vólvd ‖ Southern English also -vólvd) adj. **1.** Complicated; intricate. **2.** Involute; twisted. **3.** Confused; tangled. **4.** Associated; implicated; concerned. Used with in: involved in a conspiracy. **5.** Having a romantic or sexual relationship. Used with with. **—See Synonyms at complex.**

in·vul·ner·a·ble (in-vúln-ərə-b'l, -rəbl; also -vún-) adj. **1.** Immune to attack; impregnable: an invulnerable position. **2.** Incapable of being damaged, injured, or wounded. [Latin invulnerābilis : in-, not + vulnerāre, to wound (see vulnerable).] **—in·vul·ner·a·bil·i·ty** (-bílləti), **in·vul·ner·a·ble·ness** n. **—in·vul·ner·a·bly** adv.

in·ward (ínwərd) adj. **1.** Located inside; inner. **2.** Directed or moving towards the interior. **3.** Existing in thought or mind. **4.** Intimate; familiar. Used with with. **~adv.** Variant of **inwards.** **~n. 1.** An inner or central part. **2.** An inner essence or spirit. **3.** Plural. Entrails; innards. [Middle English inward, Old English inweard.]

in·ward·ly (ínwərdli) adv. **1.** On or in the inside; within. **2.** Within one's own mind or thoughts: inwardly alarmed. **3.** Privately; to oneself: inwardly laughing. **4.** Archaic. Intimately; closely.

in·ward·ness (ínwərd-nəss, -niss) n. **1.** Intimacy; familiarity. **2. a.** Self-preoccupation; introspection. **b.** Concern with the spiritual aspect of life. **3.** Essential or fundamental nature. **4.** Internal quality or essence.

in·wards (ínwərdz) adv. Also **in·ward** (ínwərd). **1.** Towards the inside or centre. **2.** In, into, or towards the mind or the self. **—in·ward** adj.

in·weave (ín-wéev) tr.v. **-wove** (-wṓv) or **-weaved, -woven** (-wṓv'n) or rare **-wove, -weaving, -weaves.** To weave into a fabric or design.

in·wrought (ín-ráwt) adj. **1.** Worked or woven in, as thread might be. **2.** Having a pattern worked or woven in, as a fabric might.

in·ya·la (in-yaála) n. An antelope, the **nyala** (see).

in-your-face (in-yor-fáys, -yoor-) adj. Slang. Assertively up-front; confrontationist and provocative: the in-your-face attitude of those pop stars.

I·o¹ (ī-ō). Greek Mythology. A maiden who was loved by Zeus and transformed by him or by Hera into a heifer.

Io² n. The largest of Jupiter's four large satellites, and the second nearest to the surface of the planet.

IOC International Olympic Committee.

i·o·date (ī-ə-dayt, -ō-) tr.v. **-dated, -dating, -dates.** To iodise. **~n.** A salt of iodic acid. [IOD(O)- + -ATE.]

i·od·ic acid (ī-óddik) n. A colourless or white crystalline powder, HIO_3, used as an antiseptic and deodorant. [French iodique, from iode, IODINE.]

i·o·dide (ī-ə-dīd, -ō-) n. A binary compound of iodine with a more electropositive atom or group. [IOD(O)- + -IDE.]

i·o·dine (ī-ə-deen, -ō-, -dīn, -din) n. Symbol **I 1.** A lustrous, greyish-black, corrosive, poisonous halogen element having radioactive isotopes, especially I-131, used as tracers and in thyroid disease diagnosis and therapy. Its compounds are used as germicides, antiseptics, and dyes. Atomic number 53, atomic weight 126.9044, melting point 113.5°C, boiling point 184.35°C, relative density (solid, 20°C) 4.93, valencies 1, 3, 5, 7. **2.** A **tincture** (see) of iodine and sodium iodide, NaI, or potassium iodide, KI, used as an antiseptic for wounds. [French iode, from Greek iōdēs, ioeidēs, violet-coloured : ion, violet, of Mediterranean origin + -INE.]

i·o·dise, i·o·dize (ī-ə-dīz, -ō-) tr.v. **-dised, -dising, -dises.** To treat or combine with iodine or an iodide. [IOD(O)- + -ISE.]

i·o·dism (ī-ə-diz'm, -ō-) n. Poisoning by iodine or iodine compounds. [IOD(O)- + -ISM.]

iodo-, iod- comb. form. Indicates iodine; for example, **iodoform, iodide.** [French iode, IODINE.]

i·o·do·form (ī-óddə-fawrm, -ṓdə-) n. A yellowish iodine compound, CHI_3, used as an antiseptic. Also called "tri-iodomethane". [IODO- + FORM(YL).]

i·o·lite (ī-ə-līt, -ō-) n. A blue silicate mineral, $Al_3(Mg,Fe)_2AlSi_5O_{18}$, occurring chiefly in metamorphic rocks. Also called "cordierite".

I.O.M. Isle of Man.

i·on (ī-ən, -on) n. An atom or group of atoms that has acquired a net electric charge by gaining electrons in or losing electrons from an initially electrically neutral configuration. [Greek ion, "going particle" (referring to the passage of ions to either of the electrodes in electrolysis), neuter present participle of ienai, to go.]

–ion n. suffix. Indicates: **1.** An act or process or the outcome of an act or process; for example, **indention. 2.** A state of being; for example, **cohesion.** [Middle English -io(u)n, from Old French -ion, from Latin -iō (stem -iōn-).]

I·o·na (ī-ṓnə). Small island of the Inner Hebrides. Of religious importance since St. Columba founded his monastery here (563), it is also the burial place of many of the monarchs of Scotland, Ireland,

Norway, and Denmark. It is also rich in Celtic remains.

ion engine *n.* A rocket engine that develops thrust by expelling ions rather than gaseous combustion products. Also called "ion rocket". See **ionic propulsion**.

i·o·nes·co (ee-ə-ness-kō; *French* yo-ness-kô), **Eugene** (1912–94). Romanian-born French playwright, whose play, *The Bald Prima Donna* (1956), marked a new era in the Theatre of the Absurd. He continued to stress his rejection of realism in plays such as *Rhinoceros* (1960) and *Exit the King* (1963).

ion exchange *n.* A reversible chemical reaction between a solid and a solution by means of which ions may be interchanged, used in water softening and separation of radioactive isotopes.

I·o·ni·a (ī-ōni-ə). A region on the west coast of Asia Minor. An ancient Greek settlement, it was probably colonised (c.1100 B.C.) by refugees from Achaea. The Ionians became the cultural leaders of the Greek world between the eighth and sixth centuries B.C. Conquered by the Lydians (550 B.C.) and by the Persians (546 B.C.), they were eclipsed following their unsuccessful revolt (499–494 B.C.).

I·o·ni·an (ī-ōni-ən) *adj.* **1.** Of or pertaining to Ionia or the Ionians. **2.** *Music.* Of or designating an authentic mode represented by the scale of C on a keyboard instrument.
~*n.* A member of a Hellenic people who settled in Attica and on the northern coast of the Peloponnese in about 1100 B.C. and founded colonies in Asia Minor.

Ionian Islands. Chain of Greek Islands in the Ionian Sea. They extend from Corfu (Kérkira), off the west coast of Greece and Albania, southwards to Zákynthos (Zante), off the southwest Greek coast, and include Paxoi, Lefkáda (Levkás), Kefallonica (Cephalonia), and Ithaca (Itháki), the legendary home of Odysseus.

Ionian Sea. Area of the central Mediterranean. Bounded by Sicily and southern Italy in the west, the Strait of Otranto in the north, and Greece in the east, it includes the Ionian Islands.

i·on·ic (ī-ónnik) *adj.* Of, containing, or involving ions.

Ionic *adj.* **1.** Ionian. **2.** *Architecture.* Pertaining to the Ionic order. **3.** In Greek verse: **a.** Designating a metrical foot consisting of two long syllables followed by two short ones, or two short syllables followed by two long ones. **b.** Designating a verse or metre having such feet.
~*n.* **1.** The ancient Greek dialect of Ionia, belonging to Attic-Ionic, early developed as a medium for scientific and historical prose. **2.** In Greek verse, an Ionic foot, verse, or metre.

ionic bond *n.* A chemical bond characteristic of salts and formed by the complete transfer of one or more electrons from one kind of atom to another. Also called "electrovalent bond".

ionic crystal *n.* A crystal formed of an array of positive and negative ions held together by electrostatic forces.

Ionic order *n. Architecture.* An order of classical Greek architecture characterised by fluted columns and two opposed volutes in the capital. Compare **Corinthian order, Doric order.**

ionic propulsion *n.* Propulsion by the reactive thrust of a high-speed beam of similarly charged ions ejected by an ion engine. Also called "ion propulsion".

ion implantation *n.* A technique for introducing controlled amounts of impurity into a material, usually into a semiconductor, by bombarding it with ions of the impurity.

i·on·i·sa·tion (ī-ə-nī-záysh'n || *U.S.* -ni-) *n.* **1.** The formation of one or more ions by the addition of electrons to or the removal of electrons from an electrically neutral atomic or molecular configuration, by heat, electrical discharge, radiation, or chemical reaction. **2.** The state or condition of being ionised.

ionisation chamber *n.* A gas-filled enclosure fitted with electrodes between which electric current flows upon ionisation of the gas by incident radiation, the electrodes being maintained at a potential difference just sufficient to collect ions thus produced without causing further ionisation.

ionisation potential *n.* The energy required to remove completely the weakest bound electron from its ground state in an atom or molecule so that the resulting ion is also in its ground state.

i·on·ise, i·on·ize (ī-ə-nīz) *v.* **-ised, -ising, -ises.** —*tr.* To convert totally or partially into ions. —*intr.* To become converted totally or partially into ions.

ionising radiation *n.* Radiation capable of producing ionisation, including energetic charged particles such as alpha and beta rays, and electromagnetic radiation such as X-rays, and neutrons.

i·o·none (ī-ə-nōn) *n.* Either of two yellowish to colourless liquid isomers, $C_{13}H_{20}O$, having a strong odour of violets and used in perfumes. [Greek *ion,* violet (see **iodine**) + -ONE.]

i·on·o·sphere (ī-ónnə-sfeer) *n.* An electrically conducting set of layers of the Earth's atmosphere, extending from altitudes of approximately 60 to 400 kilometres (35 to 250 miles) and more, caused by ionisation of rarefied atmospheric gases by incident solar radiation; the D, E, and F layers. [ION + -SPHERE.]

i·on·o·spher·ic wave (ī-ónnə-sférrik) *n. Electronics.* A **sky wave** (*see*).

ion rocket *n.* **1.** A rocket using ionic propulsion. **2.** An **ion engine** (*see*).

i·o·ta (ī-ōtə) *n.* **1.** The ninth letter in the Greek alphabet, written I, *i.* Transliterated in English as *I, i.* **2.** A very small amount. Often used in the phrase *not one iota.* [Greek *iōta,* of Semitic origin; akin to Hebrew *yōdh,* YOD.]

IOU (ī-ō-yōō) *n., pl.* **IOU's, IOUs.** A promise to pay a debt. [Short for *I owe you.*]

-ious *adj. suffix.* Indicates characterised by or full of; for example, **sagacious, edacious.** [Middle English, partly from Latin *-ius,* and partly from Old French *-ieus, -ieux,* from Latin *-iōsus* : *-i-,* stem + *-ōsus,* -OUS.]

I.O.W. Isle of Wight.

I·o·wa¹ (ī-ō-ə, ī-ə-wə). State in the north central United States, lying between the Mississippi and Missouri rivers. It was part of the Louisiana Purchase and was admitted to the Union in 1846. Almost 95 per cent of its gently undulating land is given over to agriculture. The capital, Des Moines, is a meat-processing centre.

Iowa² *n., pl.* **-was** or collectively **Iowa. 1.** A member of a Siouan-speaking North American Indian people formerly inhabiting the region of Minnesota, Iowa, and Missouri. **2.** The Siouan language of this people. —**I·o·wa** *adj.*

IPA, I.P.A. 1. India Pale Ale. **2.** International Phonetic Alphabet. **3.** International Phonetic Association.

ip·e·cac (íppi-kak) *n.* Also **ip·e·cac·u·an·ha** (íppi-káckew-ánnə, -aänə) **1.** A low-growing South American shrub, *Cephaelis ipecacuanha.* **2.** A medicinal extract from the dried roots of this shrub used as an expectorant and to induce vomiting. [Shortened from Portuguese *ipecacuanha,* from Tupi *ipekaaguéne.*]

Iph·i·ge·ni·a (i-fiji-nī-ə, íffiji-). *Greek Mythology.* The daughter of Clytemnestra and Agamemnon, offered as a sacrifice to Artemis to enable the Greek fleet to sail for Troy.

ip·o·moe·a (ippə-mée-ə, ípə-) *n.* Any tropical or subtropical climbing plant of the genus *Ipomoea,* such as the sweet potato and morning glory, having trumpet-shaped flowers. [New Latin, from Greek *ips* (stem *ipo-*), worm + *homoios,* like.]

ip·pon (íppon) *n.* In judo, a full scoring point, resulting directly in victory. [Japanese, "point".]

ip·se dix·it (ip-si díksit, -say) *n., pl.* **ipse dixits. 1.** An unsupported assertion, usually by a person of authority or standing. **2.** An arbitrary statement; a dictum. [Latin, he himself said (it), translation of Doric Greek *autos epha,* expression used by the Pythagoreans of sayings of Pythagoras.]

ip·si·lat·er·al (ip-si-láttərəl, -láttrəl) *adj.* On or affecting the same side of the body. [Irregularly from Latin *ipse,* self + LATERAL.]

ip·sis·si·ma ver·ba (ip-síssimə vérbə) *pl. n. Latin.* The very words.

ip·so fac·to (íp-sō fáktō) *adv. Latin.* By the fact itself; by that very fact: *An alien, ipso facto, has no right to a British passport.*

ip·so ju·re (íp-sō jóor-i, yóor-i) *adv. Latin.* By the law itself.

Ips·wich (ip-swich). Town and port in Suffolk, east England, at the head of the Orwell estuary. It is the administrative centre for the county and supports engineering and chemical industries.

IQ, I.Q. intelligence quotient.

Iq·bal (ík-bal), **Sir Muhammed** (c. 1876 – 1938). Indian poet, philosopher, and Muslim leader, noted for his opposition to the British. He advocated a separate Muslim state which later came with the formation of modern Pakistan (1947).

Ir The symbol for the element iridium.

ir-¹. Variant of **in-¹.**

ir-². Variant of **in-².**

I.R.A., IRA *n.* Irish Republican Army: a secret Irish Nationalist organisation formed to oppose the partition of Ireland, active in anti-British terrorist acts in the 1930s and 1940s, and again in the 1970s and 1980s. In 1969 it split into the **Official** and **Provisional** wings (*both of which see*). See **Sinn Fein.**

i·ra·de (i-raádi) *n.* A decree by a Muslim ruler. [Turkish, from Arabic *'irāda,* will.]

I·rá·kli·o (i-rákli-ō) (Modern Greek) or **I·ra·kli·on** (i-rákli-ən), **He·ra·kli·on, He·ra·klei·on;** *Italian* **Can·di·a** (kándi-ə). Port on the north coast of the island of Crete, Greece. It is the island's chief port, and exports wine, olive oil, and fruit. It is noted for its Venetian fortifications, the relics of 15th- and 16th-century Venetian rule.

I·ran, Islamic Republic of (i-raán || -rán) (*see*). Formerly **Per·sia** (pér-shə || -zhə) (*see*). Country of western Asia. Mountainous and sparsely populated, its geographical position has made it a crossroads for trade and culture, and a target for conquest. Overrun by many, including Alexander the Great (c. 325 B.C.) and the Arabs (7th century A.D.), who introduced Islam, Persia was always able eventually to overthrow or absorb each occupation and re-establish its own power. By the late 18th century, however, it had declined into a buffer state between Russia, Turkey, and British India. In World War II, the country (known since 1935 as Iran) was occupied jointly by Russia and Britain, who installed Muhammad Reza Pahlavi as Shah (1941). Despite massive U.S. aid, the Shah was overthrown (1979) by a revolution led by the Muslim fundamentalist leader, Ayatollah Khomeini. War with Iraq, which began in 1980, ended in 1990 when the two sides agreed to a United Nations peace plan. Ninety per cent uncultivated, the country is economically dependent on its vast oil reserves, up to ten per cent of the world's total. Area, 1 648 000 square kilometres (636,290 square miles). Population, 61,130,000. Capital, Tehran. See map, next page.

I·ra·ni·an (i-ráyni-ən, ī-) *adj.* Of or pertaining to Iran, its inhabitants, or their language.
~*n.* **1.** A native or inhabitant of Iran. **2. a.** A group of languages including Persian, Kurdish, and Pashto, spoken principally in Iran, Afghanistan, and west Pakistan, and forming a subbranch of the Indo-Iranian branch of the Indo-European language family. **b.** The modern Persian language as spoken in Iran; Farsi.

I·raq (i-raák || -rák). Republic of western Asia. Its area includes the geographical location of ancient Mesopotamia, on the fertile plain between the rivers Tigris and Euphrates. Wrested from the Turkish

IRAN AND IRAQ

empire and established as an independent kingdom (1921), it joined the Arab League (1945), and following the assassination of the king (1958) became a socialist republic. In 1980 it began an inconclusive war with Iran, which ended in 1990. In the same year Iraq occupied Kuwait, from which it was ejected in 1991 by a coalition of United Nations forces. Since then tension has erupted from time to time through Iraqi intransigence concerning United Nations resolutions. Iraq's economy rests heavily on oil, which accounts for over 90 per cent of its exports. Area, 438 317 square kilometres (169,235 square miles). Population, 20,610,000. Capital, Baghdad. See map at **Iran and Iraq.**

I·ra·qi (i-raáki ‖ -rácki) *adj.* Of or pertaining to Iraq, its inhabitants, or their language.
~n., pl. **-qis. 1.** A native or inhabitant of Iraq. **2.** The Arabic dialect spoken in Iraq.

i·ras·ci·ble (i-rásse-b'l, ĭ-) *adj.* **1.** Prone to outbursts of temper; easily angered. **2.** Characterised by or resulting from anger. [Old French, from Late Latin *īrāscibilis,* from Latin *īrāscī,* to get angry, from *īra,* anger, IRE.] **—i·ras·ci·bil·i·ty** (-bílləti), **i·ras·ci·ble·ness** *n.* **—i·ras·ci·bly** *adv.*

i·rate (ī-ráyt, ír-) *adj.* **1.** Angry; enraged. **2.** Characterised or occasioned by anger: *an irate phone call.* [Latin *īrātus,* from *īra,* anger, IRE.] **—i·rate·ly** *adv.*

IRBM Intermediate Range Ballistic Missile.

ire (īr) *n. Literary.* Wrath; anger. See Synonyms at **anger.** [Middle English, from Old French, from Latin *īra,* anger.]

ire·ful (īr-fˈl) *adj. Literary.* Full of ire; angry; wrathful. **—ire·ful·ly** *adv.* **—ire·ful·ness** *n.*

Ire·land (īr-lənd). *Irish* **Éi·re** (aír-ə). Second largest of the British Isles. Its fertile central lowlands contain many peat bogs, and are surrounded by several low mountain ranges, including the mountains of Mourne, Wicklow, Kerry, and Ox. Once occupied by a number of Celtic kingdoms, from the 12th century it fell increasingly under English domination. Following violence and unrest during and after World War I, the predominantly Roman Catholic southern 26 counties became an autonomous state, the 6 northern counties remaining within the United Kingdom as the province of Northern Ireland.

Ireland, Republic of. Country of northwest Europe. After much bitter fighting and civil unrest, the Anglo-Irish Treaty (1921) paved the way for the 26 southern counties of Ireland to become the Irish Free State (1922). In 1937 a new constitution with full sovereignty was adopted by plebiscite, and the people called their country Eire. It left the Commonwealth in 1949, and since then has been known officially as the Republic of Ireland. Mainly agricultural, its economy rests chiefly on beef and dairy cattle, sheep, pig, and poultry farming, two-thirds of the land being used for crop or pasture. Distilling, brewing, food-processing, and electronics, chemicals, and textile manufacture are also important. The republic has been a member of the European Economic Community (now the European Union) since 1973. Area, 70 283 square kilometres (27,136 square miles). Population, 3,520,000. Capital, Dublin.

I·re·ne (ī-réeni). *Greek Mythology.* The goddess of peace. [From Greek *eirēnē,* peace.]

i·ren·ic, ei·ren·ic (ī-réenik, -rénnik) *adj.* Also **i·ren·i·cal, ei·ren·i·cal** (ī-réenik'l, -rénnik'l). Promoting peace; conciliatory; pacific. [Greek *eirēnikos,* from *eirēnē,* peace.] **—i·ren·i·cal·ly** *adv.*

i·ren·ics (ī-réeniks, -rénniks) *n. Used with a singular verb.* The branch of theology dealing with the promotion of peace and unity among Christian churches.

Ire·ton (īr-t'n), **Henry** (1611–51). English Parliamentary general during the English Civil War (1642–51). Ireton married Cromwell's daughter Bridget and later helped to bring Charles I to trial.

Irian Jaya. See **West Irian.**

ir·i·dec·to·my (irri-déktəmi, ír-i-) *n., pl.* **-mies.** Surgical removal of part of the eye's iris. [Latin *īris* (stem *īrid-*), IRIS + -ECTOMY.]

ir·i·des·cent (irri-déss'nt) *adj.* Producing a display of lustrous, rainbow-like colours. [Latin *īris* (stem *īrid-*), rainbow, IRIS + -ESCENT.] **—ir·i·des·cence** *n.*

i·rid·ic (i-ríddik, ī-) *adj.* Pertaining to the iris of the eye.

i·rid·i·um (ī-ríddi-əm, i-) *n. Symbol* **Ir** A very hard and brittle, exceptionally corrosion-resistant, whitish-yellow metallic element occurring in platinum ores and used principally to harden platinum and in high-temperature materials, electrical contacts, and wear-resistant bearings. Atomic number 77, atomic weight 192.2, melting point 2,410°C, boiling point 4,527°C, relative density 22.42 (17°C), valencies 3, 4. [New Latin, from Latin *īris* (stem *īrid-*), rainbow, IRIS (from the variety of colours it gives in solutions).]

ir·i·dol·o·gy (irri-dólləji) *n.* Detailed examination of the iris of the eye as a diagnostic technique, based on the claim that different parts of the iris represent different organs of the body, with changes in the state of health of the latter discernible from changes in the former. [Latin *īrid-* (stem of *iris,* IRIS) + -O- + -LOGY.] **—ir·i·dol·o·gist** *n.*

ir·i·dos·mine (irri-dóss-mīn, ír-i-, -dóz-, -min, -meen) *n.* An alloy, **osmiridium** (see). [German *Iridosmin* : IRID(IUM) + OSM(IUM) + -INE.]

i·ris (īr-iss) *n., pl.* **irises** or **irides** (ír-i-deez, írri-). **1.** The pigmented, round, contractile membrane of the eye, situated between the cornea and lens, and perforated by the pupil. **2.** Any of numerous plants of the genus *Iris,* having sword-shaped leaves and variously coloured flowers. **3.** *Rare.* A rainbow or rainbow-like display of colours. [Middle English *iris, yris,* rainbow, kind of prismatic crystal, from Latin *īris,* from Greek *iris,* rainbow, iris of the eye.]

Iris. *Greek Mythology.* The goddess of the rainbow and messenger of the gods.

iris diaphragm *n.* A diaphragm that can be adjusted to vary the diameter of a central aperture, commonly used on cameras to regulate the amount of light admitted to a lens.

I·rish (īr-ish) *adj. Abbr.* **Ir.** Of or pertaining to Ireland, its people, or their language.
~n. Abbr. **Ir. 1.** *Used with a plural verb.* **a.** The inhabitants of Ireland. **b.** People of immediate Irish descent. **2.** The Celtic language spoken in Ireland; Irish Gaelic. **3.** The English spoken in Ireland. **4.** *Informal.* Fieriness of temper or passion; high spirit. [Middle

IRELAND

10°W · 8°W · 6°W

SCOTLAND

Lifford

Slieve League ▲ · Donegal · DONEGAL · NORTHERN IRELAND · U L S T E R

ATLANTIC OCEAN

Donegal Bay · Ballyshannon

North Channel

Sligo Bay · Sligo · Monaghan

Lough Conn

Dundalk · 54°N

Achill I. · Carrick-on Shannon · Cavan · Dundalk Bay

Westport · C O N N A U G H T · Longford · Kells · Drogheda

IRISH SEA

Lough Mask · Dunmore · Roscommon · Lough Ree · Navan · Mullingar

Lough Corrib · Athlone · Boyne

Galway · DUBLIN · Dún Laoghaire

Galway Bay · I R E L A N D · Tullamore · Naas

Aran Is · Port Laoise · 926m▲ · Wicklow

Lough Derg · Roscrea · L E I N S T E R · Wicklow Mts

CLARE · Ennis · Nenagh · Carlow

Ardnacrusha · Limerick · Kilkenny · Slaney

Tipperary · Cashel

M U N S T E R · Clonmel · Wexford

Tralee · Waterford

K E R R Y · Blackwater · ST. GEORGE'S CHANNEL · WALES · 52°N

Dingle Bay · Killarney · Lee

▲ Carrauntoohil 1041m · Blarney · Cobh

Cork

Bandon

Bantry Bay

Km 0 · 40 · 80
Miles 0 · 20 · 40 · 60

English *Irisc(h),* from Old English *Íras,* the Irish.]

Irish coffee *n.* A drink of sweetened hot coffee and Irish whiskey, topped with thick cream.

Irish elk *n.* A large extinct European deer of the genus *Megaloceros,* of the Pliocene and Pleistocene epochs, having palmate antlers.

Irish Free State. A former name (1922–37) for the Republic of Ireland.

Irish Gaelic *n.* The Goidelic language of Ireland, an official language of the Republic of Ireland. Also called "Erse", "Irish".

I·rish·ism (ī-rish-iz'm) *n.* An Irish idiom or custom.

I·rish·man (ī-rish-mən) *n., pl.* **-men** (-mən, -men). A man of Irish birth, citizenship, or descent.

Irish moss *n.* A seaweed, **carrageen** *(see).*

Irish Republic. **1.** The free state proclaimed by Irish rebels against British rule during the abortive Easter Rising in Dublin (1916). **2.** The Republic of Ireland. Used erroneously.

Irish Republican Army *n.* The I.R.A. *(see).*

Irish Sea. An arm of the Atlantic Ocean. It separates Britain from Ireland and is connected to the Atlantic by the North Channel in the north, and by St. George's Channel in the south.

Irish setter *n.* A breed of dog, having a silky reddish-brown coat. Also called "red setter".

Irish stew *n.* A stew of meat and vegetables.

Irish terrier *n.* A breed of dog having a wiry brown coat.

Irish water spaniel *n.* A dog of a breed having a dark curly coat and a characteristic topknot.

Irish whiskey *n.* A whisky made in Ireland by the distillation of barley.

Irish wolfhound *n.* A large dog of an ancient breed, having a rough, shaggy coat.

I·rish·wom·an (ī-rish-wŏŏmən) *n., pl.* **-women** (-wimmin). A woman of Irish birth, citizenship, or descent.

i·ri·tis (ī-rītiss) *n.* Inflammation of the iris of the eye. [New Latin : IR(IS) + -ITIS.]

irk (urk) *tr.v.* **irked, irking, irks.** To vex; weary; irritate. See Synonyms at **annoy.** [Middle English *irken, yrken,* perhaps from Old Norse *yrkja,* to work.]

irk·some (úrks'm) *adj.* Causing annoyance or bother; wearisome; tedious: *irksome restrictions.* See Synonyms at **boring.** —**irk·some·ly** *adv.* —**irk·some·ness** *n.*

IRO 1. Inland Revenue Office (in Britain). **2.** International Refugee Organisation.

i·ro·ko (i-rōkō) *n.* **1.** A tropical tree, *Chlorophora excelsa.* **2.** The wood of this tree, often used as a substitute for teak. [Yoruba.]

i·ron (īrn, í-ərn) *n. Symbol* **Fe** A silvery-white, lustrous, malleable, ductile, magnetic or magnetisable, metallic element occurring abundantly in combined forms, notably in haematite, limonite, magnetite, and taconite, and used alloyed in a wide range of important structural materials. Atomic number 26, atomic weight 55.847, melting point 1,535°C, boiling point 3,000°C, relative density 7.874 (20°C), valencies 2, 3, 4, 6. **2.** Great hardness or strength; firmness: *a will of iron.* **3. a.** An implement made of iron alloy or similar metal; especially, a bar heated for use in branding, cauterising, or soldering. **b.** A **calliper** (sense 3). **4.** Any of various golf clubs with a metal head, numbered from one or two to nine or ten according to the degree of slant of the face of the club. **5.** A metal appliance with a handle and a weighted flat bottom, used when heated to press wrinkles from fabric. **6.** *Informal.* A harpoon. **7.** *Plural.* **a.** Fetters; shackles. **b.** Stirrups. **8.** Iron taken as a dietary supplement in the form of a tonic, pill, or other medication. —**have many irons in the fire.** To be engaged in many undertakings simultaneously. —**in**

irons. **1.** Fettered. **2.** *Nautical.* Lying head to the wind and unable to turn either way. **—pump iron.** *Informal.* In bodybuilding, to exercise with weights. **—strike while the iron is hot.** To seize an opportunity to act.
~adj. **1.** Made of or containing iron. **2.** Extremely hard and strong: *an iron fist.* **3.** Hardy; robust: *an iron constitution.* **4.** Inflexible; unyielding: *an iron will.* **5.** Base; degraded.
~v. **ironed, ironing, irons.** *—tr.* **1. a.** To press and smooth (clothing, for example) with a heated iron. **b.** To remove (creases) by pressing. Sometimes used with *out.* **2.** *Rare.* To put in irons; fetter. **3.** To fit or clad with iron. *—intr.* **1.** To iron clothes. **2.** To be capable of being ironed: *this fabric irons well.* **—iron out.** To settle through discussion or compromise; work out: *iron out our problems.* [Middle English *yren, yron, iren,* Old English *īren,* earlier *īsern, īsen.*]
iron age *n. Classical Mythology.* The last of the ages of the history of the world, a very degenerate age, and supposedly the one we are in now. Compare **golden age, silver age.**
Iron Age *n.* The generally prehistoric period succeeding the Bronze Age, characterised by the introduction and spread of iron tools and weapons, beginning in the Middle East around the 12th century B.C., and in Europe around the 8th century B.C.
i·ron·bark (ī́rn-baark, ī́-ərn-) *n.* Any of several Australian trees of the genus *Eucalyptus,* often having hard, rough bark.
i·ron·bound (ī́rn-bownd, ī́-ərn-) *adj.* **1.** Bound with iron. **2.** Rigid and unyielding. **3.** Bound with rocks and cliffs, as a coast.
Iron Chancellor *n.* An epithet or nickname for **Bismarck** *(see).*
i·ron·clad (ī́rn-klad, ī́-ərn-) *adj.* **1.** Sheathed with iron plates for protection. **2.** Rigid: *an ironclad rule.* **3.** Fully protected from attack; unshakeable: *an ironclad argument.*
~n. A 19th-century warship having sides armoured with metal plates.
Iron Cross *n.* A medal formerly awarded to German soldiers for the highest degree of bravery.
Iron Curtain *n.* A barrier that prevents free exchange or communication; specifically, the political and ideological barrier between the Soviet bloc and western Europe after World War II. [Popularised (1946) by Winston Churchill.]
Iron Duke *n.* A nickname for the Duke of **Wellington** *(see).*
iron glance *n.* A mineral, **haematite** *(see).*
iron hand *n.* Rigorous or despotic control: *ruling with an iron hand.* **—i·ron·hand·ed** (ī́rn-hándid, ī́-ərn-) *adj.*
iron horse *n. Informal. Archaic.* **1.** A railway engine. **2.** A bicycle or tricycle.
i·ron·ic (ī-rónnik, īr-) *adj.* Also **i·ron·ic·al** (-'l). **1.** Characterised by or constituting irony. **2.** Given to the use of irony. —See Usage note at **sarcastic.** **—i·ron·i·cal·ly** *adv.* **—i·ron·i·cal·ness** *n.*
i·ron·ing (ī́r-ning, ī́-ər-) *n.* **1.** The pressing of clothes with a heated iron. **2.** The clothing to be pressed or that has been pressed.
ironing board *n.* A long narrow padded board on a collapsible support, used as a working surface for ironing.
i·ron·ist (ī́r-ə-nist) *n.* A notable user of irony. **—i·ron·ise** *v.*
iron lung *n.* An airtight tank in which the entire body except the head is enclosed and by means of which pressure is regularly increased and decreased to provide artificial respiration. Also called "respirator".
iron maiden *n.* A medieval torture device, consisting of a coffin-like case lined with iron spikes, in which the victim was enclosed.
i·ron·mas·ter (ī́rn-maastər, ī́-ərn- || -mastər) *n. British.* A manufacturer of iron.
i·ron·mon·ger (ī́rn-mung-gər, ī́-ərn- || -mong-gər) *n. Chiefly British.* A hardware merchant, selling metal tools and utensils.
i·ron·mon·ger·y (ī́rn-mung-gəri, ī́-ərn- || -mong-gəri) *n., pl.* **-ies.** *Chiefly British.* **1.** Ironware. **2.** The shop or business of an ironmonger. **3.** *Slang.* Firearms.
iron pyrites *n.* A mineral, **pyrite** *(see).*
iron rations *pl.n.* Emergency rations, especially those carried by a soldier.
I·ron·side (ī́rn-sīd, ī́-ərn-), **William Edmund, 1st Baron** (1880–1959). British soldier. He was Chief of the Imperial General Staff at the outbreak of World War II, but was replaced after the fall of France. He was the model for John Buchan's hero, Richard Hannay.
i·ron·sides (ī́rn-sīdz, ī́-ərn-) *n., pl.* **i·ron·sides. 1.** A person with great stamina or powers of endurance. **2.** An ironclad ship. **3.** *Plural. Often capital* **I.** In the English Civil War: **a.** Cromwell's soldiers. **b.** Cromwell's personal cavalry regiment. **c.** The Parliamentary Army.
i·ron·smith (ī́rn-smith, ī́-ərn-) *n.* One who works in iron; a blacksmith.
i·ron·stone (ī́rn-stōn, ī́-ərn-) *n.* **1.** Any of several kinds of iron ore with admixtures of silica and clay. **2.** A hard white pottery.
i·ron·ware (ī́rn-wair, ī́-ərn-) *n.* Iron utensils and other products made of iron.
i·ron·wood (ī́rn-wŏŏd, ī́-ərn-) *n.* **1.** Any of various trees having very hard wood, such as the **hornbeam** and the **hop hornbeam** *(both of which see).* **2.** The wood of such a tree.
i·ron·work (ī́rn-wurk, ī́-ərn-) *n.* **1.** Iron objects, such as gratings or gates, especially when made by hand. **2.** The craft or profession of making such objects.
i·ron·work·er (ī́rn-wurkər, ī́-ərn-) *n.* **1.** A person who makes ironwork. **2.** A person who works in an ironworks.
i·ron·works (ī́rn-wurks, ī́-ərn-) *n., pl.* **ironworks.** A building or establishment where iron is smelted or where heavy iron products are made.
i·ro·ny¹ (ī́r-əni) *n., pl.* **-nies. 1.** The use of words to convey the opposite of their literal meaning. **2.** An expression or utterance marked by such a deliberate contrast between apparent and intended meaning. **3.** A literary style employing such contrasts for humorous or rhetorical effect. **4.** Incongruity between what might be expected and what actually occurs: *the irony of being run over by an ambulance.* **5.** An occurrence, result, or circumstance notable for such incongruity. **6. Dramatic irony** *(see).* **7. Socratic irony** *(see).* —See Synonyms at **wit.** [Latin *īrōnia,* from Greek *eirōneia,* dissembling, feigned ignorance, from *eirōn,* dissembler, "one who says less than he thinks", from *eirein,* to say.]
i·ron·y² (ī́-ərni) *adj.* Of, like, or containing iron.
Ir·o·quoi·an (írrə-kwóy-ən) *n.* **1.** A family of North American Indian languages spoken in Canada and the eastern United States by such peoples as the Iroquois, Cherokee, Conestoga, Erie, and Wyandot. **2.** A member of a people using a language of this family.
~adj. **1.** Of or designating this language family. **2.** Of or pertaining to the Iroquois or their culture.
Ir·o·quois (írrə-kwoy, -kwoyz) *n., pl.* **Iroquois. 1.** A member of any of several Iroquoian-speaking North American Indian peoples formerly inhabiting New York State, and forming the confederacy known as the *Five Nations,* including the Cayuga, Mohawk, Oneida, Onondaga, and Seneca peoples. After 1722 the confederacy was joined by the Tuscaroras to form the *Six Nations.* **2.** Any of the languages spoken among these peoples. **—Ir·o·quois** *adj.*
ir·ra·di·ant (i-ráydi-ənt) *adj.* Sending forth radiant light. [Latin *irradiāns* (stem *irradiant-*), present participle of *irradiāre,* IRRADIATE.]
ir·ra·di·ance (i-ráydi-ənss) *n. Symbol* **E** *Physics.* The radiant flux or radiation reaching a surface per unit area. Compare **radiance.**
ir·ra·di·ate (i-ráydi-ayt) *v.* **-ated, -ating, -ates.** *—tr.* **1. a.** To expose to radiation. **b.** To treat with radiation. **2.** To emit in a manner analogous to the emission of light. **3.** To make intellectually interesting or spiritually radiant; clarify; illumine. *—intr. Archaic.* **1.** To send forth rays; radiate. **2.** To become radiant. [Latin *irradiāre,* to shine forth : *in-,* towards + *radiāre,* to shine, RADIATE.] **—ir·ra·di·a·tive** (-ətiv, -aytiv) *adj.* **—ir·ra·di·a·tor** (-aytər) *n.*
ir·ra·di·a·tion (i-ráydi-áysh'n, í-) *n.* **1.** The act of irradiating or the condition of being irradiated. **2.** *Medicine.* Therapy or treatment by exposure to radiation.
ir·ra·tion·al (i-rásh'n'l) *adj.* **1. a.** Not endowed with reason. **b.** Affected by loss of usual or normal mental clarity; incoherent, as, for example, from shock. **c.** Contrary to reason; illogical: *an irrational dislike.* **2.** In Greek and Latin verse: **a.** Designating a syllable whose length does not fit the metrical pattern. **b.** Designating a metrical foot containing such a syllable. **3.** *Mathematics.* Incapable of being expressed as an integer or a ratio or quotient of integers. **—ir·ra·tion·al·ly** *adv.* **—ir·ra·tion·al·ness** *n.*
ir·ra·tion·al·i·ty (i-rásh'n-ál-əti) *n., pl.* **-ties.** Also **ir·ra·tion·al·ism** (-'l-iz'm). **1.** The state or quality of being irrational. **2.** An irrational idea or action.
irrational number *n. Mathematics.* A member of the set of real numbers that is not a member of the set of rational numbers; a number that cannot be expressed as an integer or an exact ratio of two integers; for example, the number π (pi).
Ir·ra·wad·dy (írrə-wóddi). Also **Ayeyarwady.** The chief river of Burma (Myanmar). Rising in the Patkai hills in the northeast of the country, it flows 2 010 kilometres (1,250 miles) south to the Bay of Bengal. Its delta, west of the Gulf of Martaban, is a major rice-growing area.
ir·re·claim·a·ble (írri-kláymə-b'l) *adj.* Incapable of being reclaimed: *irreclaimable wasteland.* **—ir·re·claim·a·bil·i·ty** (-bílləti), **ir·re·claim·a·ble·ness** *n.* **—ir·re·claim·a·bly** *adv.*
ir·rec·on·cil·a·ble (i-réck'n-sīlə-b'l, -sīlə-) *adj.* **1.** Not capable of being reconciled; implacably hostile. **2.** Incompatible; incongruous.
~n. **1.** A person who will not compromise or adjust. **2.** *Plural.* Conflicting ideas or beliefs that cannot be brought into harmony. **—ir·rec·on·cil·a·bil·i·ty** (-bílləti) *n.* **—ir·rec·on·cil·a·bly** *adv.*
ir·re·cov·er·a·ble (írri-kúvvərə-b'l, -kúvvrə-) *adj.* Incapable of being recovered; irreparable: *irrecoverable losses.* **—ir·re·cov·er·a·ble·ness** *n.* **—ir·re·cov·er·a·bly** *adv.*
ir·re·cu·sa·ble (írri-kéwzəb'l) *adj.* Not subject to challenge or objection; unexceptionable; undeniable. [French *irrécusable,* from Late Latin *irrecūsābilis* : *in-,* not + *recūsābilis,* that should be rejected, from Latin *recūsāre,* to reject.] **—ir·re·cu·sa·bly** *adv.*
ir·re·deem·a·ble (írri-déemə-b'l) *adj.* **1.** Incapable of being bought back or paid off: *an irredeemable annuity.* **2.** Not convertible into coin: *irredeemable banknotes.* **3.** Incapable of being remedied. **4.** Incapable of being saved or reformed.
~n. A bond, annuity, or similar investment that cannot be redeemed before it matures. **—ir·re·deem·a·bil·i·ty** (-bílləti) *n.* **—ir·re·deem·a·bly** *adv.*
ir·re·den·tist (írri-déntist) *n.* One who advocates the recovery of lands of which his nation has been deprived, or of territory culturally or historically related to his nation but now subject to a foreign government. [Italian *irredentista,* from *(Italia) irredenta,* "unredeemed (Italy)" (Italian-speaking areas subject to other countries), from *irredento,* not redeemed : *in-,* not, from Latin + *redento,* redeemed, from Latin *redemptus,* past participle of *redimere,* REDEEM.] **—ir·re·den·tist** *adj.* **—ir·re·den·tism** *n.*
ir·re·duc·i·ble (írri-déw-sə-b'l || -dŏŏ-) *adj.* **1.** Incapable of being reduced to a desired, simpler, or smaller form or amount. **2.** *Medicine.* Incapable of being replaced in a normal position. Said especially of a hernia. **—ir·re·duc·i·bil·i·ty** (-bílləti), **ir·re·duc·i·ble·ness** *n.* **—ir·re·duc·i·bly** *adv.*

ir·ref·ra·ga·ble (i-réffrəgə-b'l ‖ írri-frággə-) adj. Incapable of being refuted or controverted; indisputable. [Late Latin *irrefrāgābilis* : Latin *in-*, not + *refrāgārī*, to oppose, akin to *frangere*, to break.] —**ir·ref·ra·ga·bil·i·ty** (-bílləti) n. —**ir·ref·ra·ga·bly** adv.

ir·re·fran·gi·ble (irri-fránjə-b'l) adj. **1.** Incapable of being violated or broken; indestructible. **2.** *Physics.* Incapable of being refracted. —**ir·re·fran·gi·bil·i·ty** (-bílləti) n. —**ir·re·fran·gi·bly** adv.

ir·ref·u·ta·ble (i-réffew-tə-b'l, írri-féwtə-b'l) adj. Incapable of being refuted or disproved; incontrovertible: *irrefutable arguments.* —**ir·ref·u·ta·bil·i·ty** (-bílləti) n. —**ir·ref·u·ta·bly** adv.

irreg. irregular; irregularly.

ir·re·gard·less (irri-gárd-ləss, -liss) adv. *Nonstandard.* Regardless.

ir·reg·u·lar (i-réggew-lər) adj. *Abbr.* **irreg. 1.** Not according to rule, accepted order, or general practice. **2.** Not conforming to legality, moral law, or social convention: *an irregular marriage.* **3.** Not straight, uniform, or symmetrical: *a path of irregular width; irregular facial features.* **4.** Of uneven rate, occurrence, or duration: *an irregular heartbeat; irregular attendance.* **5.** Deviating from type; asymmetrically arranged or atypical. **6.** *Botany.* Having differing floral parts, especially petals. **7.** *Chiefly U.S.* Falling below the manufacturer's standard or usual specifications; flawed; imperfect. **8.** *Grammar.* Departing from the usual set of inflectional forms; for example, the verb *be* is an irregular verb. **9.** Not belonging to a permanent, organised military force: *irregular troops.* ~n. **1.** A person or thing that is irregular. **2.** A soldier, such as a guerrilla, who is not a member of a regular military force. —**ir·reg·u·lar·ly** adv.

ir·reg·u·lar·i·ty (i-réggew-lárrəti) n., pl. **-ties. 1.** The quality or state of being irregular. **2.** That which is irregular.

ir·rel·a·tive (i-réllətiv) adj. **1.** Having no correlative relationship; unconnected. **2.** Irrelevant. —**ir·rel·a·tive·ly** adv.

ir·rel·e·vance (i-rélla-vənss, -rélli-) n. Also **ir·rel·e·van·cy** (-vən-si) pl. **-cies. 1.** The quality or state of being irrelevant. **2.** That which is irrelevant.

ir·rel·e·vant (i-réllə-vənt, -rélli-) adj. **1.** Having no applications or effects in a specified circumstance; unrelated to the subject under discussion or the matter to be dealt with. **2.** Lacking in contemporaneity; failing to deal with current concerns. —**ir·rel·e·vant·ly** adv.

ir·re·lig·ion (irri-líjən) n. Hostility or indifference to religion.

ir·re·lig·ious (írri-líjəss) adj. Indifferent or hostile to religion; ungodly. —**ir·re·lig·ious·ly** adv. —**ir·re·lig·ious·ness** n.

ir·rem·e·a·ble (i-rémmi-əb'l, -réemi-) adj. *Archaic.* Affording no possibility of return. [Latin *irremeābilis* : *in-*, not + *remeāre*, to return : *re-*, back + *meāre*, to go.]

ir·re·me·di·a·ble (irri-méedi-əb'l) adj. Impossible to remedy, correct, or repair; incurable. —**ir·re·me·di·a·bly** adv.

ir·re·mis·si·ble (irri-míssə-b'l) adj. **1.** Not remissible; unpardonable. **2.** In need of doing; unavoidable; obligatory. —**ir·re·mis·si·bil·i·ty** (-bílləti) n. —**ir·re·mis·si·bly** adv.

ir·re·mov·a·ble (írri-móovə-b'l) adj. **1.** Not physically removable. **2.** Not liable to removal from office. —**ir·re·mov·a·bil·i·ty** (-bílləti) n. —**ir·re·mov·a·bly** adv.

ir·rep·a·ra·ble (i-réppərə-b'l, -répprə- ‖ írri-páir-əb'l) adj. Incapable of being repaired, rectified, or amended; beyond repair: *irreparable harm.* —**ir·rep·a·ra·bil·i·ty** (-bílləti) n., **ir·rep·a·ra·ble·ness** n. —**ir·rep·a·ra·bly** adv.

ir·re·peal·a·ble (irri-péeləb'l) adj. Not capable of being repealed.

ir·re·place·a·ble (írri-pláy-səb'l) adj. Incapable of being replaced because too valuable.

ir·re·pres·si·ble (irri-préssə-b'l) adj. Not capable of being repressed; impossible to control or restrain. —**ir·re·pres·si·bil·i·ty** (-bílləti) n., **ir·re·pres·si·ble·ness** n. —**ir·re·pres·si·bly** adv.

ir·re·proach·a·ble (írri-prōchə-b'l) adj. Not meriting any reproach; beyond reproach; perfect. —**ir·re·proach·a·bil·i·ty** (-bílləti), **ir·re·proach·a·ble·ness** n. —**ir·re·proach·a·bly** adv.

ir·re·sis·ti·ble (írri-zístə-b'l) adj. **1.** Impossible to resist. **2.** Having an overpowering appeal: *an irresistible urge to kick him.* **3.** Very attractive; alluring: *an irresistible woman.* —**ir·re·sis·ti·bil·i·ty** (-bílləti), **ir·re·sis·ti·ble·ness** n. —**ir·re·sis·ti·bly** adv.

ir·res·o·lu·ble (i-rézzə-lewb'l ‖ írri-zóllewb'l) adj. Not capable of being solved.

ir·res·o·lute (i-rézzə-lōōt, -lewt) adj. **1.** Unresolved as to action or procedure. **2.** Lacking in resolution; vacillating; wavering; indecisive. —**ir·res·o·lute·ly** adv. —**ir·res·o·lute·ness**, **ir·res·o·lu·tion** (-lōōsh'n, -léwsh'n) n.

ir·re·solv·a·ble (írri-zólvəb'l) adj. **1.** Incapable of being solved or resolved. **2.** Not capable of being separated into component parts; irreducible.

ir·re·spec·tive (írri-spéktiv) adj. *Archaic.* Characterised by disregard; heedless. —**irrespective of.** Regardless of; without consideration of. ~adv. *Informal.* Regardless; without considering: *We advised him against that he carried on irrespective.* —**ir·re·spec·tive·ly** adv.

ir·re·spir·a·ble (i-réspirəb'l, írri-spír-ə-b'l) adj. Not fit for breathing; not respirable.

ir·re·spon·si·ble (írri-spón-sə-b'l) adj. **1.** Not mentally or financially fit to assume responsibility. **2.** Showing no sense of responsibility or due care; reckless; untrustworthy. **3.** *Archaic.* Not liable to be called to account by a higher authority. ~n. An irresponsible person. —**ir·re·spon·si·bil·i·ty** (-bílləti), **ir·re·spon·si·ble·ness** n. —**ir·re·spon·si·bly** adv.

ir·re·spon·sive (írri-spón-siv) adj. **1.** Not responsive, as to treat-

ment or stimuli. **2.** Not responding or answering readily. —**ir·re·spon·sive·ly** adv. —**ir·re·spon·sive·ness** n.

ir·re·triev·a·ble (írri-tréevə-b'l) adj. **1.** Not capable of being retrieved or recovered. **2.** Beyond help or repair. —**ir·re·triev·a·bil·i·ty** (-bílləti), **ir·re·triev·a·ble·ness** n. —**ir·re·triev·a·bly** adv.

ir·rev·er·ence (i-révvərənss, -révvrənss) n. **1.** Absence of reverence or due respect. **2.** A disrespectful act or remark.

ir·rev·er·ent (i-révvərənt, -révvrənt) adj. **1.** Lacking in reverence; disrespectful: *an irreverent person.* **2.** Proceeding from irreverence: *an irreverent act.* —**ir·rev·er·ent·ly** adv.

ir·re·vers·i·ble (írri-vér-sə-b'l) adj. **1.** Incapable of being reversed. **2.** *Chemistry.* **a.** Designating or pertaining to a chemical reaction that takes place almost completely in one direction. **b.** Designating or pertaining to a change in which intermediate stages do not attain thermodynamic equilibrium. —**ir·re·vers·i·bil·i·ty** (-bílləti), **ir·re·vers·i·ble·ness** n. —**ir·re·vers·i·bly** adv.

ir·rev·o·ca·ble (i-révvəkə-b'l) adj. Incapable of being retracted or revoked; irreversible. —**ir·rev·o·ca·bil·i·ty** (-bílləti), **ir·rev·o·ca·ble·ness** n. —**ir·rev·o·ca·bly** adv.

ir·ri·ga·ble (írrigəb'l) adj. Capable of irrigation; able to be irrigated.

ir·ri·gate (írri-gayt) tr.v. **-gated, -gating, -gates. 1. a.** To supply (dry land) with water by means of ditches, pipes, or streams. **b.** To water or provide (land) with water. Used of a river, stream, or the like. **2.** To wash out (a cavity or wound) with water or a medicated fluid. **3.** To make fertile or vital by or as if by watering. [Latin *irrigāre*, to lead water : *in-*, in + *rigāre*, to wet, water.] —**ir·ri·ga·tion** (-gáysh'n) n. —**ir·ri·ga·tion·al** (-gáysh'n'l) adj. —**ir·ri·ga·tor** (-gaytər) n.

ir·ri·ta·bil·i·ty (írrita-bílləti) n. **1.** The quality or state of being irritable; testiness; petulance. **2.** *Medicine.* Excessive sensitivity. **3.** *Biology.* The capacity to respond to stimuli.

ir·ri·ta·ble (írritəb'l) adj. **1.** Easily annoyed; ill-tempered. **2.** *Medicine.* Abnormally sensitive. **3.** *Biology.* Responsive to stimuli. [Latin *irritābilis*, from *irritāre*, IRRITATE.] —**ir·ri·ta·ble·ness** n. —**ir·ri·ta·bly** adv.

ir·ri·tant (írritənt) adj. Causing physical or mental irritation. ~n. Something that causes irritation. [Latin *irritāns* (stem *irritant-*), present participle of *irritāre*, IRRITATE.]

ir·ri·tate (írri-tayt) tr.v. **-tated, -tating, -tates. 1. a.** To annoy; vex. **b.** To provoke. **2.** To chafe or inflame. —See Synonyms at **annoy.** [Latin *irritāre†.*] —**ir·ri·tat·ing·ly** adv. —**ir·ri·ta·tive** (-taytiv, -tətiv) adj. —**ir·ri·ta·tor** (-taytər) n.

ir·ri·ta·tion (irri-táysh'n) n. **1.** The act of irritating. **2.** A source of irritation. **3.** The condition of being irritated; vexation. **4.** *Medicine.* Incipient inflammation, soreness, roughness, or irritability of a bodily part.

ir·rupt (i-rúpt) intr.v. **-rupted, -rupting, -rupts. 1.** To break or burst in; make an incursion or invasion. **2.** *Ecology.* To increase irregularly in number. Used of a human or animal population. [Latin *irrumpere* (past participle *irruptus*) : *in-*, in + *rumpere*, to break, burst.] —**ir·rup·tion** n.

ir·rup·tive (i-rúptiv) adj. **1.** Irrupting or tending to irrupt. **2.** *Geology.* Intrusive. **3.** Characterised by irruption.

IRS *U.S.* Internal Revenue Service.

Ir·tysh. River in western Siberia in the U.S.S.R. It rises in Xinjiang Uygur A.R. in China, and flows some 4 260 kilometres (2,650 miles) to join the Ob.

Ir·vine (úrvin). Port on the west coast of Scotland. Situated on the mouth of the river Irvine, in East Ayrshire, it has been developed as a New Town since 1967.

Ir·ving (úrving), **Sir Henry,** born John Henry Brodribb (1838–1905). Great Shakespearian actor. His productions, particularly those at London's Lyceum theatre, won him the first theatrical knighthood to be awarded to an Englishman (1895).

Irving, Washington (1783–1859). U.S. diplomat and writer. His best-known work is *The Sketch Book* (1819–20), containing the classic stories "Rip van Winkle" and "The Legend of Sleepy Hollow".

is (iz). The third person singular present indicative of the verb **be.**

is. island(s); isle(s).

Is. 1. Isaiah (Old Testament). **2.** island; isle.

is–. Variant of **iso–.**

Isa. Isaiah (Old Testament).

I·saac (ízək). A Hebrew patriarch, the son of Abraham and Sarah and the father of Jacob and Esau. Genesis 21:1–4. [Late Latin *Isaacus*, from Greek *Isaak*, from Hebrew *Yiṣḥāq*, "he laughs".]

I·sa·bel·la I of Castile (izzə-béllə), also called "Isabella the Catholic" (1451–1504). Queen of Castile. Her marriage to Ferdinand of Aragon (1469) led to the eventual unification of Spain. She was the patron of Christopher Columbus.

i·sa·go·gic (ī-sə-gójik) adj. Pertaining to or designating studies, especially Bible studies, of an introductory kind. [Latin, from Greek *eisagōgikos*, introductory, from *eisagōgē*, introduction : *eis*, into + *agōgē*, leading, from *agein*, to lead.]

i·sa·gog·ics (ī-sə-gójiks) pl.n. Introductory studies, especially of the Bible.

I·sa·iah¹ (ī-zí-ə ‖ ī-záy-ə). Also in Douay Bible **I·sa·ias** (ī-zí-əss ‖ ī-záy-əss). A Hebrew prophet of the eighth century B.C. in Judah. [Hebrew *Yasha‘yāh(u)*, "salvation of the Lord" : *yēsha‘*, *yəshū‘āh*, salvation + *yāh(u)*, the Lord.]

Isaiah² n. *Abbr.* **Isa.**, **Isa.** A book in the Old Testament attributed to Isaiah, though now considered to be the work of three hands.

i·sal·lo·bar (ī-sál-ə-baar) n. *Meteorology.* A line on a weather map connecting places exhibiting equal changes in barometric pressure within a given period of time. [IS(O)- + ALLO- + Greek *baros*, weight.]

ISBN *n.* International Standard Book Number; a number assigned under an international system to each newly published book, to facilitate ordering and identification.

Iscariot. See **Judas**[1].

is·chae·mi·a (i-skéemi-ə) *n. Pathology.* A local anaemia caused by mechanical obstruction of the blood supply. [New Latin *ischaemia*, from Greek *iskhaimos*, stanching, stopping blood : *iskhein*, to keep back, hold, restrain + *haima*, blood.]

is·chi·um (iss-ki-əm) *n., pl.* **-chia** (-ki-ə). *Anatomy.* The lowest of three major bones comprising each half of the pelvis. [Latin, hip joint, from Greek *iskhion*†.]

ISD *n.* International Subscriber Dialling: a system of direct dialling between countries.

-ise, -ize *v. suffix.* Indicates: **1. a.** To cause to be or to become; make into; for example, **dramatise. b.** To make conform with; make like: for example, **Hellenise, Anglicise. c.** To treat or regard as; for example, **idolise. 2.** To cause to acquire a specified quality; for example, **legalise, modernise, sterilise. 3.** To become or become similar to; for example, **crystallise, oxidise, materialise. 4. a.** To subject to; for example, **jeopardise, anaesthetise. b.** To affect with; for example, **magnetise, galvanise. 5.** To do or follow some practice; for example, **pasteurise, bowdlerise.** [Old French *-iser*, Latin *-izāre*, Greek *-izein*.] **—isation** *n. suffix.*

Usage: Several verbs in English must be spelt with *-ise*: for example, *advise, comprise, exercise, surprise.* For most verbs, however, there is an alternative spelling, *-ize.* British English prefers the *-ise* spelling, American English the *-ize* spelling, but there is considerable variablility in both. New verbs created by adding *-ise/-ize* to a noun or adjective are often the butt of criticism by conservative language users, who feel that excessive use of this ending results in imprecise thinking. However, alternatives can sound long-winded or awkward and the popularity of this affix in modern English continues unabated. British English is perhaps a little slower to accept the trend than American English. Words such as *hospitalise/-ize* and *finalise/-ize* still sound slightly unacceptable to many British speakers.

is·en·trop·ic (í-sen-tróppik ‖ -trópik) *adj.* Without change in entropy; at constant entropy. [IS(O)- + ENTROP(Y) + -IC.]

I·seult, Y·seult (ee-zǒolt, i-, -sǒolt). Also **I·sol·de** (i-zóldə, -zóldə). **1.** A legendary Irish princess who married Mark, the king of Cornwall, and had a doomed love for his nephew, Tristan. **2.** A legendary princess of Brittany, whom Tristan in some accounts married.

Is·fa·han (iss-fə-háan). Formerly **As·pa·da·na** (áspə-daána). City in central Iran and the capital of the Isfahan province. It is noted for its carpet-manufacturing and metalwork. It was the capital of Persia under Shah Abbas the Great (c.A.D. 1600).

-ish *adj. suffix.* Indicates: **1. a.** Having the nationality of; for example, **Swedish, Finnish. b.** Having the qualities or character of; for example, **childish, sheepish. c.** Tending to or preoccupied with; for example, **bookish, selfish. d.** Somewhere near or approximately. Used informally in naming hours or years: *She's fortyish.* **2.** Somewhat or rather; for example, **greenish.** [Middle English *-is(c)h*, Old English *-isc*, from Common Germanic *-iskaz* (unattested), corresponding to Greek *-iskos*, diminutive noun suffix.]

Ish·er·wood (íshər-wǒod), **Christopher** (1904–86). English novelist, best known for his portrayals of Berlin in the early 1930s in works such as *Mr. Norris Changes Trains* (1935) and *Good-bye to Berlin* (1939), on which the musical *Cabaret* is based.

Ish·ma·el[1] (ish-may-əl, -mayl, -mee-əl). The son of Abraham by Sarah's handmaid, Hagar. Genesis 16:1–16. [Late Latin *Ismaël*, from Hebrew *Yishmā'ēl*, "God hears" : *yishmā*, he hears, from *shāma'*, he heard + *'Ēl*, God.]

Ishmael[2] *n.* An outcast. [From ISHMAEL, referring to Abraham's expulsion of Ishmael and Hagar after the birth of Isaac (Genesis 21:14).]

Ish·ma·el·ite (ish-mi-ə-līt, -may-ə-, -may- -mə-) *n.* **1.** A member of a group of desert-dwelling people believed by the ancient Hebrews to be descended from Ishmael. **2.** An outcast. **—Ish·ma·el·it·ism** *n.*

Ish·tar (ish-taar). *Assyrian & Babylonian Mythology.* The goddess of love, fertility, and war; identified with the Phoenician Astarte. [Akkadian *Ishtar*, akin to Hebrew *'Ashtōreth*, ASHTORETH.]

Is·i·dore of Seville, Saint (ízzi-dawr) (c.560–636). Spanish priest and theologian. His chief work, *Etymologiae*, is an encyclopedic glossary in 20 sections. He was Bishop of Seville.

i·sin·glass (ízing-glaass ‖ īz'n-, -glass) *n.* **1.** A transparent, almost pure gelatine prepared from the air bladder of certain fishes, such as the sturgeon. **2.** A mineral, **muscovite** *(see).* [Alteration (influenced by GLASS) of obsolete Dutch *huizenblas*, from Middle Dutch *huusblase* : *huus*, sturgeon, from Germanic *hūson-* (unattested) + *blase*, bladder.]

I·sis[1] (í-siss). *Egyptian Mythology.* A goddess of fertility, and sister and wife of Osiris.

Isis[2]. See **Thames**.

isl. island; isle.

Is·lam (íz-laam, is-, -lam, -ləm, iz-laám, is-, -lám) *n.* **1.** A religion based upon the teachings of the prophet Muhammad, believing in one God (Allah) and in Paradise and Hell, and having a body of law set forth in the Koran and the Sunna; the Muslim religion. **2. a.** All those nations of the world, especially in Asia and Africa, whose populations are Muslim; the Muslim world. **b.** Islamic civilisation. **3.** Muslims collectively. [Arabic *islām*, "submission (to

God)", from *aslama*, he surrendered, he resigned himself, from *salama*, he was safe.] **—Is·lam·ic** (-lámmik; *rarely* -laámik) *adj.*

Is·la·ma·bad (iz-laámə-baad, is-, -lámmə-, -bad). A new city in north Pakistan, the national capital since 1967.

Is·lam·ise, Is·lam·ize (ízzlə-mīz) *tr.v.* **-ised, -ising, -ises. 1.** To convert to Islam. **2.** To impose the laws and practices of Islam on. **—Is·lam·i·sa·tion** (ízzlə-mī-záysh'n ‖ *U.S.* -mi-) *n.*

is·land (ílənd) *n.* **1.** *Abbr.* **i., I., is., Is., isl.** A land mass, especially one smaller than a continent, entirely surrounded by water. **2.** Anything completely isolated or regarded as resembling such an isolated land mass. **3.** A **traffic island** *(see).* **4.** *Anatomy.* A tissue or cluster of cells separated from surrounding tissue by a groove or differing from surrounding tissue in structure. **5.** A free-standing kitchen unit or set of units, having a work surface and often a hob, placed in the centre of the kitchen.
~*tr.v.* **islanded, -landing, -lands. 1. a.** To make into or as if into an island; insulate. **b.** To place on an island. **2.** To dot or intersperse with or as if with islands. [Middle English *eland, ilond, ylond* (influenced by ISLE), Old English *ī(e)gland, īland*.]

is·land·er (íləndər) *n.* An inhabitant of an island.

is·land-hop·ping (ílənd-hopping) *n.* The making of short boat trips or short-haul flights to a number of islands in the same area.

Islands of the Blessed *pl.n. Greek Mythology.* See **Hesperides**.

Islas Malvinas. See **Falkland Islands**.

Is·lay (í-lay; *locally* í-lə). Island lying off the west coast of Scotland, the most southerly of the Inner Hebrides. Its comparative prosperity is due chiefly to an established whisky-distilling industry.

isle (īl) *n. Abbr.* **i., I., is., Is., isl.** An island, especially a small one. Used poetically and in place names. [Middle English *i(s)le*, from Old French, from Latin *insula*†.]

Isle of Ely. See **Ely**.

Isle of Man. See **Man, Isle of**.

Isle of Wight. See **Wight, Isle of**.

Isles of the Blest. The **Hesperides** *(see).*

is·let (ílit) *n.* A little island.

is·lets of Lang·er·hans (lángər-hanss ‖ *U.S.* laángər-haanz, -haanss) *pl.n.* Also **islands of Lang·er·hans.** Irregular masses of small endocrine cells that lie in the interstitial tissue of the pancreas and secrete insulin and glucagon. [After Paul *Langerhans* (1847–88), German doctor.]

Is·ling·ton (ízzling-tən). Borough in the north of Greater London, incorporating the former boroughs of Islington and Finsbury.

ism (iz'm) *n. Informal.* A distinctive doctrine, system, or theory. Usually used derogatorily. [From -ISM.]

–ism *n. suffix.* Indicates: **1.** An action, practice, or process; for example, **terrorism, favouritism. 2.** A state or condition of being; for example, **pauperism, parallelism. 3.** A characteristic behaviour or quality; for example, **heroism, individualism. 4.** A distinctive usage or feature, especially of language; for example, **malapropism, Latinism. 5.** A doctrine, theory, system, or principle; for example, **Platonism, expressionism, capitalism, pacifism.** [Middle English *-isme*, from Old French, from Latin *-ismus*, from Greek *-ismos*, suffix used to form nouns of action from verbs in *-izein*, -ISE.]

Is·ma·il·i, Is·ma'il·i (iz-maa-éeli, is-,) *n.* Also **Is·ma·il·i·an** (-ən, -il-li-ən). A Muslim of a Shiite sect. [Arabic *Isma'īlīy*, after *Isma'īl* (died A.D. 760), son of the sixth Imam Jafar.]

is·n't (iz'nt). Contraction of *is not.*

ISO International Standards Organisation.

iso–, is– *comb. form.* Indicates: **1.** Equal, identical, or similar; for example, **isallobar, isogon. 2.** *Chemistry.* Isomeric; for example, **isopropyl alcohol.** [Greek, from *isos*†, equal.]

i·so·ag·glu·ti·na·tion (í-sō-ə-glǒoti-náysh'n) *n.* The agglutination of red blood cells by the serum of another individual of the same species.

i·so·ag·glu·tin·in (í-sō-ə-glǒoti-nin) *n.* An isoantibody that causes agglutination of red blood cells.

i·so·ag·glu·tin·o·gen (í-sō-ágglǒo-tínnə-jən, -jen) *n.* An isoantigen that on exposure to its isoantibody induces agglutination of the red blood cells to which it is attached. [ISOAGGLUTIN(IN) + -GEN.]

i·so·am·yl acetate (í-sō-ámmil) *n.* A colourless compound, $(CH_3)_2CHCH_2CH_2OOCCH_3$, used as a solvent and a flavouring.

i·so·an·ti·bod·y (í-sō-ánti-boddi) *n., pl.* **-ies.** An antibody that occurs in only some individuals of a species and reacts specifically with the corresponding isoantigen from a different individual of the same species.

i·so·an·ti·gen (í-sō-ánti-jən, -jen) *n.* An antigen that occurs in only some individuals of a species and never in those having cells that contain the corresponding isoantibody.

i·so·bar (í-sō-baar, -sə-) *n.* **1.** A line on a map connecting points of equal atmospheric pressure. **2.** *Physics.* Any of two or more nuclides having the same mass number but different atomic numbers. [ISO- + Greek *baros*, weight.] **—i·so·bar·ic** (-bárrik) *adj.*

i·so·bath (í-sō-baath) *n.* A line on a chart connecting points of equal water depth. [Greek *isobathēs*, of equal depth : ISO- + *bathēs*, depth.]

i·so·bu·tane (í-sō-béw-tayn) *n.* An isomer of **butane** *(see).*

i·so·chor, i·so·chore (í-sō-kawr ‖ -kōr) *n.* A line on a graph showing how the temperature of fluid kept at constant volume varies with pressure. [ISO- + Greek *khōros*, space, place.]

i·so·chro·mat·ic (í-sō-krō-máttik, -sə-, -krə-) *adj.* **1.** Having the same colour. **b.** Of uniform colour. **2.** *Photography.* Orthochromatic.

i·soch·ro·nal (ī-sóckrə-n'l ‖ *U.S. also* í-sə-krŏn'l) *adj.* Also **i·soch·**

ro·nous (-nəss), **i·so·chron·ic** (ī-sō-krónnik, -sə-). **1.** Equal in duration. **2.** Characterised by or occurring at equal intervals of time. [Greek *isokhronos,* ISOCHRONOUS.] —**i·soch·ro·nal·ly** *adv.* —**i·soch·ro·nism** (ī-sóckrəniz'm) *n.*

i·soch·ro·nise, i·soch·ro·nize (ī-sóckrə-nīz) *tr.v.* **-nised, -nising, -nises.** To make isochronal.

i·soch·ro·ous (ī-sóckrō-əss) *adj.* Having the same colour throughout. [ISO- + -CHROOUS.]

i·so·cli·nal (ī-sō-klīn'l, -əss-) *adj.* Also **i·so·clin·ic** (ī-sō-klínnik, -sə-). **1.** Having the same inclination or angle of dip. **2.** *Geology.* Designating folds having limbs parallel to each other.
~*n.* Also **i·so·clin·ic.** An isoclinal line.

i·so·cline (ī-sō-klīn, -sə-) *n.* An anticline or syncline with its limbs so tightly folded as to have the same dip. [ISO- + -CLINE.]

isoclinic line *n.* Also **isoclinal line.** A line on a map connecting points of equal magnetic dip.

i·soc·ra·cy (ī-sóckrə-si) *n.* A form of government in which all have equal power. [ISO- + -CRACY.] —**i·soc·ra·tic** (ī-sō-kráttik, -sə-) *adj.*

i·so·cy·an·ide (ī-sō-sī-ə-nīd) *n. Chemistry.* **1.** An organic compound containing the group –NCO. Also called "carbylamine". **2.** A salt containing the ion NCO$^-$.

i·so·di·a·met·ric (ī-sō-dī-ə-méttrik) *adj.* **1.** Having equal diameters. **2.** Designating a crystal that has three equal axes.

i·so·di·a·phere (ī-sō-dī-ə-feer) *n.* Any of two or more nuclides that have the same difference between their total number of constituent neutrons and constituent protons. [ISO- + *-diaphere,* from Greek *diapherein,* to differ, "carry across" : DIA- + *pherein,* to carry.]

i·so·di·mor·phism (ī-sō-dī-mór-fiz'm) *n.* Isomorphism between crystalline forms of two dimorphic substances.

i·so·dy·nam·ic (ī-sō-dī-námmik) *adj.* **1.** Having equal force or strength. **2.** Designating an imaginary line drawn on the earth's surface that connects points of equal horizontal magnetic intensity.

i·so·e·lec·tric (ī-sō-i-léktrik) *adj.* Having equal electric potential.

isoelectric point *n. Chemistry.* The pH value of a solution in which a given substance, especially an amino acid or protein, forms neutral zwitterions or neutral colloidal particles.

i·so·e·lec·tron·ic (ī-sō-i-lek-trónnik) *adj.* Having equal numbers of electrons or the same electronic configuration.

iso·en·zyme (ī-sō-én-zīm) *n.* Also **i·so·zyme** (ī-sō-zīm). Any one of the variant forms of a given enzyme. Isoenzymes catalyse the same type of reaction but differ slightly in physical and immunological properties. —**i·so·en·zy·mic** (-zímik) *adj.*

i·so·gam·ete (ī-sō-ga-méet, -gə-, -gámmeet) *n.* A gamete that is morphologically indistinguishable from one with which it unites. —**i·so·ga·met·ic** (-méttik) *adj.*

i·sog·a·my (ī-sóggəmi) *n.* Sexual union of isogametes, such as occurs in certain algae, fungi, and protozoans. [ISO- + -GAMY.] —**i·sog·a·mous** *adj.*

i·sog·e·nous (ī-sójinəss) *adj.* Also **i·so·ge·nic** (ī-sə-jénnik, -sō-) (for sense 2). *Biology.* **1.** Having a similar origin. Said, for example, of organs derived from the same embryonic tissue. **2.** Genetically identical. [ISO- + -GENOUS.] —**i·sog·e·ny** *n.*

i·so·ge·o·therm (ī-sō-jée-ō-therm) *n. Geology.* An imaginary line below the earth's surface connecting points of equal temperature. [ISO- + GEO- + Greek *thermē,* heat.]

i·so·gloss (ī-sō-gloss, -sə-) *n.* A geographical boundary line delimiting the area in which a given linguistic feature occurs. [ISO- + Greek *glōssa,* language, tongue.] —**i·so·gloss·al** (-glóss'l) *adj.*

i·so·gon (ī-sō-gon, -sə-) *n.* An equiangular polygon. [ISO- + -GON.]

i·so·gon·ic (ī-sō-gónnik, -sə-) *adj.* Also **i·sog·o·nal** (ī-sóggən'l) Having equal angles.
~*n.* Also **i·sog·o·nal.** An isogonic line.

isogonic line *n.* A line on a map connecting points of equal magnetic declination.

i·so·graft (ī-sō-graaft ‖ -graft) *n.* A tissue graft in which the donor and recipient are genetically identical, as, for example, by being identical twins. Also called "syngraft".

i·so·gram (ī-sō-gram, -sə-) *n.* An **isopleth** *(see).*

i·so·hel (ī-sō-hel, -sə-) *n.* A line drawn on a map connecting points receiving equal sunlight. [ISO- + Greek *hēlios,* sun.]

i·so·hy·et (ī-sō-hī-it, -sə-) *n.* A line drawn on a map connecting points receiving equal rainfall. [ISO- + Greek *huetos,* rain.]

i·so·la·ble (ī-sə-ləb'l ‖ *U.S. also* íssə-) *adj.* Capable of being isolated.

i·so·late (ī-sə-layt ‖ *U.S. also* íssə-) *tr.v.* **-lated, -lating, -lates. 1. a.** To separate from a group or whole and set apart. **b.** To identify; pick out. **2.** To place in quarantine. **3.** *Chemistry.* To obtain (a substance) in an uncombined form. **4.** To obtain (a species or strain of bacterium or fungus, especially a pathogen) in a pure form. **5.** To render free of external influence; insulate. [Back-formation from *isolated,* from French *isolé,* from Italian *isolato,* from Late Latin *īnsulātus,* converted into an island, from Latin *īnsula,* island.] —**i·so·la·tor** (-laytər) *n.*

i·so·lat·ed (ī-sə-laytid ‖ *U.S. also* íssə-) *adj.* **1.** Having undergone isolation. **2.** Infrequent; sporadic: *an isolated incident.* **3.** Lacking in or having failed to maintain human contact; psychologically cut off from others. —See Synonyms at **alone.**

isolated point *n.* An **acnode** *(see).*

i·so·lat·ing (ī-sə-layting ‖ *U.S. also* íssə-) *adj.* Pertaining to or designating languages that have no inflections but convey each unit of meaning through a separate word.

isolating mechanism *n. Biology.* Any factor that prevents the breeding of one population with another. Isolating mechanisms en-courage the evolution of the separated populations into new varieties and species.

i·so·la·tion (ī-sə-láysh'n ‖ *U.S. also* íssə-) *n.* **1.** The act of isolating. **2.** The condition of being isolated, especially psychologically isolated from others. **3.** Separation or quarantine imposed on a person having or suspected of having a highly infectious or contagious disease. Also used adjectivally: *isolation ward; isolation hospital.* —**in isolation.** Considered apart from context, surrounding factors, relationships, or the like. —See Synonyms at **solitude.**

i·so·la·tion·ism (ī-sə-láysh'n-iz'm ‖ *U.S. also* íssə-) *n.* A national policy of remaining aloof from political or economic relations with other countries. —**i·so·la·tion·ist** *n. & adj.*

Isolde. Variant of **Iseult.**

i·so·lec·i·thal (ī-sō-léssithəl) *adj. Biology.* Having the yolk evenly distributed throughout the egg. Said of the eggs of mammals and some other vertebrates. Compare **heterolecithal.**

i·so·leu·cine (ī-sō-lṓō-seen, -sə-, -léw-, -sin) *n.* An essential amino acid, $C_6H_{13}NO_2$, isomeric with leucine.

i·so·line (ī-sō-līn) *n.* An **isopleth** *(see).*

i·sol·o·gous (ī-sóllagəss) *adj.* Designating two or more organic compounds that have a similar structure but contain some different atoms of the same valency. [ISO- + (HOMO)LOGOUS.]

i·so·mag·net·ic (ī-sō-mag-néttik) *adj.* **1.** Designating or pertaining to points of equal magnetic induction. **2.** Designating an imaginary line on the earth's surface connecting points of equal magnetic intensity.

i·so·mer (ī-səmər) *n.* **1.** *Chemistry.* **a.** A compound having the same percentage composition and molecular weight as another compound but differing in chemical or physical properties. **b.** Such a compound so differing because of the manner of linkage of its constituent atoms. Also called "structural isomer". **c.** Such a compound so differing because of the manner of arrangement of its constituent atoms in space. Also called "stereoisomer". **d.** A stereoisomer manifesting one of two structures that rotate the plane of polarisation of polarised light either to the left or to the right. Also called "optical isomer". **e.** A stereoisomer having no effect on polarised light but exhibiting isomerism because of a structural asymmetry about a double bond in the molecule. Also called "geometric isomer". **2.** *Physics.* An atom whose nucleus can exist in any of several bound excited states for a measurable period of time. In this sense, also called "nuclear isomer". [Greek *isomerēs,* equally divided, equal : ISO- + *meros,* part.] —**i·so·mer·ic** (ī-sə-mérrik) *adj.*

i·som·er·ase (ī-sómmə-rayz, -rayss) *n.* Any of a group of enzymes that catalyse the conversion of one isomer into another.

i·som·er·ise, i·som·er·ize (ī-sómmə-rīz) *v.* **-ised, -ising, -ises.** —*tr.* To cause to change into an isomeric form. —*intr.* To become an isomeric form. —**i·som·er·i·sa·tion** (-rī-záysh'n ‖ *U.S.* -ri-) *n.*

i·som·er·ism (ī-sómmə-riz'm) *n.* **1.** The phenomenon of the existence of isomers. **2.** The complex of chemical and physical phenomena characteristic of or attributable to isomers. **3.** The state or condition of being an isomer.

i·som·er·ous (ī-sómmərəss) *adj.* **1.** Having an equal number of parts or markings. **2.** Having or designating floral whorls with equal numbers of parts. [ISO- + -MEROUS.]

i·so·met·ric (ī-sō-méttrik, -sə-) *adj.* Also **i·so·met·ri·cal** (-méttrik'l). **1.** Of or exhibiting equality in dimensions or measurements. **2.** *Crystallography.* Of or being a crystal system of three equal and mutually orthogonal axes. **3.** *Physiology.* Of or involving muscular contraction occurring when the ends of the muscle are fixed in place so that increase in tension occurs without appreciable decrease in length.
~*n.* A line connecting isometric points. [Greek *isometros,* of equal measure : ISO- + *metron,* measure.]

i·so·met·rics (ī-sō-méttriks, -sə-) *n. Used with a singular verb.* Exercise involving isometric contraction, used to build up muscles and improve fitness. Also called "isometric exercise".

i·so·me·tro·pi·a (ī-sō-mi-trópi-ə, -mee-) *n.* Equality of refraction in both eyes. [New Latin : Greek *isometros,* of equal measure, ISOMETRIC + -OPIA.]

i·som·e·try (ī-sómmətri) *n.* Equality of measure. [ISO- + -METRY.]

i·so·morph (ī-sō-mawrf, -sə-) *n.* An object, organism, or group exhibiting isomorphism. [ISO- + -MORPH.]

i·so·mor·phism (ī-sō-mór-fiz'm, -sə-) *n.* **1.** *Biology.* Similarity in form, as in different kinds of organisms or cells. **2.** *Mathematics.* A one-to-one correspondence between the elements of two sets such that the result of an operation on elements of one set corresponds to the result of the analogous operation on their images in the other set. **3.** *Crystallography.* The existence or an instance of the existence of two or more different substances having closely similar crystalline structure, crystalline dimensions, and chemical composition. **4.** Structural similarity, due to resemblance of corresponding parts. —**i·so·mor·phic, i·so·mor·phous** *adj.*

i·so·oc·tane (ī-sō-ók-tayn) *n.* A highly flammable liquid, $(CH_3)_3CCH_2CH(CH_3)_2$, used to determine the octane numbers of fuels.

i·so·ni·a·zid (ī-sō-ní-ə-zid) *n. Abbr.* **INH** A soluble, colourless, crystalline compound, $C_6H_7N_3O$, usually administered orally for the treatment of tuberculosis. [From *isoni*cotinic acid hydr*azide.*]

i·so·pi·es·tic (ī-sō-pī-éstik) *adj.* Marked by or indicating equal pressure; isobaric.
~*n.* An isobar. [ISO- + Greek *piestos,* capable of being compressed, from *piezein,* to press tight, compress.]

i·so·pleth (ī-sō-pleth) *n.* A line on a map connecting places at which some geographical or meteorological feature is the same. Also called "isogram", "isoline". [Greek *isoplēthēs*, of equal number : ISO- + *plēthos*, great number.]

i·so·pod (ī-sō-pod, -sə-) *n.* Any of numerous crustaceans of the order Isopoda, which includes the woodlice and gribbles. [New Latin *Isopoda*, "those having pairs of legs" : ISO- + *-poda*, plural of -POD.]

i·so·pren·a·line (ī-sō-prénnə-lin, -sə-, -leen) *n.* A drug used in the treatment of asthma and similar conditions to dilate the air passages.

i·so·pro·pyl alcohol (ī-sō-própil, -sə-) *n.* A clear, colourless, mobile flammable liquid, $(CH_3)_2CHOH$, used in antifreeze compounds, lotions and cosmetics, and as a solvent for gums, shellac, and essential oils. [ISO- + PROPYL.]

i·sos·ce·les (ī-sóssi-leez) *adj. Geometry.* Having two equal sides: *isosceles triangle; isosceles trapezoid.* [Late Latin *isoscelēs*, from Greek *isoskelēs*, "having equal legs" : ISO- + *skelos*, leg.]

i·so·seis·mic (ī-sō-síz-mik) *adj.* Also **i·so·seis·mal** (-m'l). *Geology.* Of, pertaining to, or exhibiting equal seismic intensities.

i·sos·mot·ic (ī-soz-móttik, -soss-) *adj. Chemistry.* Of or exhibiting equal osmotic pressure; isotonic. [IS(O)- + OSMOTIC.]

i·so·spin (ī-sō-spin, -sə-) *n.* Symbol **I** A quantum number related to the number of charge states of a subatomic particle by the equation $2I + 1 = M$, where M is the number of such states. Also called "isotopic spin". [Short for *isotopic spin*.]

i·sos·ta·sy (ī-sóstə-si) *n. Geology.* A theoretical state of equilibrium of the earth's crust in which the crust rests on a denser underlying medium and has equal pressure at all points. [ISO- + Greek *stasis*, a standing, standstill.]

i·so·ster·ic (ī-sō-stérrik) *adj.* Designating two molecules, such as CO_2 and N_2O, that have the same number of atoms and the same configuration of valency electrons.

i·so·tac·tic (ī-sō-táktik) *adj. Chemistry.* Designating a polymer in which the groups attached to the main chain are not arranged regularly, although the same irregularity is repeated along the chain. Compare **syndiotactic**. [ISO- + -TACTIC.]

i·so·therm (ī-sō-therm, -sə-) *n.* **1.** A line drawn on a weather map or chart linking all points of equal atmospheric temperature. **2.** A line on a graph connecting points of equal temperature. [French *isotherme*, having the same temperature : ISO- + -THERM.]

i·so·ther·mal (ī-sō-thérm'l) *adj.* **1.** Of, pertaining to, or indicating equal temperatures. **2.** Of or designating changes of pressure and volume at constant temperature. **3.** Of or pertaining to an isotherm. ~*n.* An isotherm.

i·so·tone (ī-sō-tōn, -sə-) *n.* One of two or more atoms, the nuclei of which have the same number of neutrons but different numbers of protons. [ISO- + Greek *tonos*, stretching, TONE.]

i·so·ton·ic (ī-sō-tónnik, -sə-) *adj.* **1.** Of equal tension. Said of two or more muscles. **2.** Isosmotic. **3.** *Music.* Of equal tone; of equal intervals of the well-tempered scale. [ISO- + Greek *tonos*, tension, stretching, TONE.]

i·so·tope (ī-sō-tōp) *n.* Any of two or more atoms, the nuclei of which have the same number of protons but different numbers of neutrons. Compare **nuclide**. [ISO- + Greek *topos*, place, "position in the periodic table" (see **topic**).] —**i·so·top·ic** (-tóppik) *adj.* —**i·so·top·i·cal·ly** *adv.*

i·so·tron (ī-sə-tron) *n.* An instrument for separating small quantities of isotropes by ionising them and applying an electric field to the ions. [ISO- + -TRON.]

i·so·trop·ic (ī-sō-tróppik, -sə-) *adj.* Also **i·so·tro·pous** (ī-sóttrəpəss). **1.** Identical in all directions; invariant with respect to direction. **2.** *Biology.* Lacking predetermined axes. Said of certain ova. [ISO- + -TROPIC.] —**i·sot·ro·py** (ī-sóttrə-pi), **i·sot·ro·pism** (-piz'm) *n.*

Is·ra·el¹, State of (izz-ray-əl, -ri-, -el). Republic of west Asia. The country was created as a United Nations mandate (1947) from the former British League of Nations mandate of Palestine, as a homeland for Jews. It declared its independence in 1948. Largely regarded as invaders by the native Palestinians, many of whom now live as refugees in neighbouring countries, the Israelis have four times (1948, 1956, 1967, 1973) defeated surrounding Arab states. In 1982, the Israelis invaded southern Lebanon to secure their northern border against guerrillas of the Palestine Liberation Organisation. From December 1987 Israel was troubled by the *intifada*, a Palestinian uprising in the Gaza Strip and West Bank, which, along with the Golan Heights, Israel occupied in 1967. However, in 1993 Israel and the PLO issued a declaration of principles by which the PLO was to recognise Israel, and Israel was to allow Palestinians autonomy in Jericho and the Gaza Strip, as first steps to a general settlement; but mutual distrust has impeded progress. Israel has few natural resources, but large areas of desert have been reclaimed and an industrial economy built up. The chief exports are cut diamonds, textiles, fruit, and vegetables. Area, 21 946 square kilometres (8,473 square miles). Population, 5,700,000. Capital, Jerusalem.

Israel² *n.* **1.** The descendants of Jacob. **2.** The whole Hebrew people, past, present, and future, regarded as the chosen people of Jehovah by virtue of the covenant of Jacob. **3.** Any group considered or considering itself to be God's chosen people or the inheritors of God's covenant with Jacob, especially the Christian Church or any of various Christian sects. [Latin *Israēl*, from Greek, from Hebrew *Yisrā'ēl*, the name given to Jacob by the angel with whom he wrestled (Genesis 32:28), "he who struggles with God".]

Israel³. A name of the patriarch **Jacob** (see).

Is·rae·li (iz-ráyli) *adj.* Of or relating to the state of Israel or its

Is·rae·li (iz-ráyli) *adj.* Of or relating to the state of Israel or its people.

~*n., pl.* **-lis.** Natives or inhabitants of the state of Israel.

Is·ra·el·ite (ízz-ri-ə-līt, -ray-, -ri-līt) *n.* **1.** A Hebrew. **2.** A member of any of various Christian groups regarded as heirs of the covenant of Jacob.
~*adj.* Also **Is·ra·el·it·ic** (-líttik). Of or relating to Israel or the Israelites.

Is·sa·char¹ (íssə-kaar). One of the patriarchs of Israel, son of Jacob and Leah. Genesis 30:18.

Issachar² *n.* The tribe descended from Issachar.

is·su·a·ble (íshoō-ə-b'l, ishew-, íssew-) *adj.* **1.** Capable of issuing or being issued. **2.** Capable of being established as an issue; open to debate or litigation. **3.** Authorised for issue.

is·su·ance (ishoo-ənss, íssew-, íshew-) *n.* An act of issuing; issue.

is·su·ant (ishoo-ənt, íssew-, íshew-) *adj. Archaic & Heraldry.* Emerging; issuing or proceeding from.

is·sue (íshoō, íssew, íshew) *n.* **1. a.** An act or instance of flowing, passing, or giving out. **b.** An act of circulating, distributing, or publishing by an office or official group: *government issue of new bonds.* **2.** Something produced, published, or offered, as: **a.** An item or set of items, such as stamps or coins, made available at one time by a government department or other organisation. **b.** A new set of bonds, shares, or the like made available for purchase at the same time. **c.** All the copies of a periodical printed for publication at the same time. **d.** The contents of these copies: *in the June issue of Reader's Digest.* **3.** An allocation; that which is given out: *an issue of ammunition.* **4.** The result of an action or series of events. **5.** Something proceeding from a specified source: *suspicions that were the issue of a deranged mind.* **6. a.** A point of discussion, debate, or dispute. **b.** A matter of wide public concern. **c.** The essential point; the crux: *the real issue.* **d.** A point of dispute in a legal action: *an issue of fact; an issue of law.* **e.** A culminating point leading to a decision; a result. Used chiefly in legal contexts: *bring a case to an issue.* **7.** A place of egress; an outlet: *a lake with no issue to the sea.* **8.** Children; offspring or descendants. Used chiefly in legal contexts. **9.** *Pathology.* **a.** A discharge, as of blood. **b.** A suppurating sore. **10.** *Archaic.* Termination; close. **—at issue. 1.** In question; in dispute. **2.** At variance; in disagreement. **—force the issue.** To make decisive action unavoidable. **—join issue.** To enter into controversy. **—take issue with.** To take an opposing point of view to; disagree with.
~*v.* **issued, -suing, -sues.** —*intr.* **1.** To go or come forth; emerge. **2.** To accrue as proceeds or profit: *Little money issued from the stocks.* **3.** To be circulated or published. **4.** To originate or be derived. Used with *from.* **5.** To terminate or result. Used with *in.* —*tr.* **1.** To cause to flow out; emit. **2.** To circulate, allocate, or distribute, especially in an official capacity: *The school issued uniforms to the players.* **3.** To make public; announce: *issue a stern warning.* [Middle English, from Old French *(e)issue*, from Vulgar Latin *exūta* (unattested), "exit", altered from Latin *exita*, feminine of *exitus*, past participle of *exīre*, to go out : *ex-*, out + *īre*, to go.] —**is·su·er** *n.*

–ist *n. suffix.* Indicates: **1.** A person who does, makes, produces, operates, plays, or sells a specified thing; for example, **dramatist, lobbyist, motorist, organist, tobacconist.** **2.** A person who is skilled, trained, or employed in a specified field; for example, **machinist, radiologist, industrialist.** **3.** An adherent or proponent of a

doctrine, system, or school of thought; for example, **anarchist, federalist, Platonist. 4.** A person characterised by a certain trait or predilection; for example, **romanticist, sadist. 5.** A person having a disparaging or hostile attitude towards a particular social group on the basis of a specified characteristic; for example **sexist, ageist, racist.**
~*adj. suffix.* Indicates: **1.** Pertaining to or designating a doctrine, system, or school of thought; for example, **anarchist, federalist, Platonist. 2.** Pertaining to or designating a disparaging or hostile attitude towards a particular social group on the basis of a specified characteristic; for example, **sexist, ageist, racist.** [Middle English -*iste,* from Old French, from Latin -*ista,* -*istēs,* from Greek -*istēs,* agential suffix for verbs in -*izein,* -ISE.] — -**istic,** -**istical** *adj. suffix.*

Is·tan·bul (iss-tan-bóol, -taan-, -bóol). Largest city and chief port of Turkey, called **Constantinople** before 1930. It is a major manufacturing, cultural, and tourist centre, with many museums, including Hagia Sophia and the Seraglio (royal palace).

isth·mi·an (ísth-mi-ən, íst-, íss-) *adj.* **1.** Of, pertaining to, or forming an isthmus. **2.** *Capital* **I.** Of or pertaining to the Isthmus of Corinth, especially with regard to the biennial pan-Hellenic games held there in antiquity. **3.** *Capital* **I.** Of or pertaining to the Isthmus of Panama.

isth·mus (íss-məss, ísth-, íst-) *n., pl.* -**muses** or -**mi** (-mī). **1.** A narrow strip of land connecting two larger masses of land. **2.** *Anatomy.* **a.** A narrow strip of tissue joining two larger organs or parts of an organ. **b.** A narrow passage connecting two larger cavities. [Latin, from Greek *isthmos†*.]

–**istics** *n. suffix.* Indicates study of a specified subject; for example, **statistics, cladistics.**

is·tle, ix·tle (ístli) *n.* A plant, **pita** *(see).* [Mexican Spanish *ixtle,* from Nahuatl *ichtli.*]

is·tri·a (istri-ə). Peninsula of the northwest Croatian coast. It separates the Gulf of Venice from the Bay of Kvarner in the Adriatic Sea.

it¹ (it) *pron.* The third person singular pronoun, neuter gender in the nominative or objective case. **1.** Used to represent the thing, non-human being, or person whose sex is unknown or disregarded, last mentioned or implied. **2.** Used without a previously understood antecedent or consequent as **a.** The formal subject of an impersonal verb: *It is raining.* **b.** The object, having little meaning, of various verbs: *Live it up; leg it.* **3.** Used to represent a word, phrase, or clause that follows: *It is he. It's certain that he'll win.* **4.** Used to represent a situation, topic for consideration, or any other item of discourse that the speaker assumes the hearer will comprehend without antecedent: *Always try to do it right the first time.* **5.** Used to represent all the experience that can be endured or desired. *He'd had it; he resigned.* **6.** Used to represent the crucial moment upon which an outcome depends: *This is it! he thought, as the plane's engine sputtered.* **7.** Used to represent a human life: *The old man's eyes closed; it was all over.*
~*n.* **1. a.** A game, **tag** *(see).* **b.** The child who chases the others in a game of tag. **2.** *Informal.* An important person. Usually used derogatorily, especially in such phrases as *he thinks he's it.* **3.** *Informal.* **a.** Sexual intercourse. **b.** *Rare.* Sexual attractiveness. [Middle English *(h)it, (h)yt,* Old English *hit, hyt.*]

it² *n. Informal.* Italian vermouth.

It. Italian; Italy.

ITA. See **IBA.**

i.t.a., I.T.A. *n.* Initial *teaching* alphabet: a 44-letter phonetic alphabet used in teaching young children to read.

it·a·col·u·mite (itta-kóllew-mīt) *n.* A variety of sandstone that is slightly flexible when cut into thin slabs. Also called "flexible sandstone". [Found in *Itacolumi,* a mountain in Brazil.]

it·a·con·ic ac·id (itta-kónnik) *n.* A white crystalline substance, $CH_2:C(COOH) CH_2COOH$, obtained by the fermentation of carbohydrates and used in the manufacture of synthetic resins. [Anagram of *aconitic.*]

ital. italic.

Ital. Italian; Italy.

Italia See **Italy.**

I·tal·ian (i-tál-yən) *adj. Abbr.* **It., Ital.** Pertaining to Italy, its people, their culture, or their language.
~*n. Abbr.* **It., Ital. 1.** A native or citizen of Italy, or a person of Italian descent. **2.** The Romance language of Italy and one of the three official languages of Switzerland. **3.** Italian vermouth. [Middle English, from Italian *Italiano,* from *Italia,* ITALY.]

I·tal·ian·ate (i-tál-yə-nayt, -nət, -nit) *adj.* Italian in character. [Italian *Italianato,* from *Italiano,* ITALIAN.]

Italian East Africa. Former Italian colony in East Africa. It comprised Italian Somaliland Eritrea (another Italian colony, now part of Ethiopia); and Abyssinia (the rest of Ethiopia, conquered by the Italians in 1935–6). The territory was captured by Allied and Ethiopian forces in 1941 and broken up.

Italian greyhound *n.* A dog of a breed of small greyhound having a long, narrow skull, a deep, narrow chest, and sloping hindquarters.

Italian hand *n.* A forward-slanting script employed by 15th-century Italian calligraphers and used as a model for modern, especially English penmanship. Also called "Italian handwriting".

I·tal·ian·ise, I·tal·ian·ize (i-tál-yə-nīz) *v.* -**ised,** -**ising,** -**ises.** —*tr.* To give an Italian aspect to. —*intr.* To become Italian; adopt Italian speech, manners, or customs. —**I·tal·ian·i·sa·tion** (-nī-záysh'n ‖ *U.S.* -ni-) *n.*

I·tal·ian·ism (i-tál-yə-niz'm) *n.* **1.** An Italian custom, trait, or expression. **2.** A quality characteristic of Italy or its people.

Italian Somaliland. See **Somalia.**

Italian sonnet *n.* A Petrarchan sonnet *(see).*

Italian vermouth *n.* A sweet, aromatic wine distilled and flavoured with herbs. Also called "Italian", "it".

i·tal·ic (i-tál-ik ‖ ī-) *adj. Abbr.* **ital. 1.** Of, pertaining to, or being a style of printing type patterned upon a Renaissance script with the letters slanting to the right, now chiefly used to set off a word or passage within a text printed in roman type, indicating that the word or passage is emphatic, in a foreign language, or has a structurally independent function within the main text: *This sentence is printed in italic type.* Compare **roman. 2.** Pertaining to or designating a modern style of handwriting similar to Italian hand.
~*n.* **1.** Italic handwriting. **2. a.** *Often plural.* Italic type or print. **b.** An italic character. [Introduced in the Aldine Virgil printed in Venice in 1501, which was dedicated to Italy.]

I·tal·ic (i-tál-ik) *adj.* **1.** Of or pertaining to ancient Italy or its peoples. **2.** Of or pertaining to a branch of Indo-European languages that includes the Latino-Faliscan and Osco-Umbrian groups.
~*n.* The Italic branch of the Indo-European family of languages. [Latin *Italicus,* from Greek *Italikos,* from *Italia,* Italy, from Latin.]

i·tal·i·cise, i·tal·i·cize (i-tál-i-sīz) *v.* -**cised,** -**cising,** -**cises.** —*tr.* **1.** To print in italic type. **2.** To underscore (written matter) with a single line to indicate italics. —*intr.* To print or put words in italics; use italics. —**i·tal·i·ci·sa·tion** (-sī-záysh'n ‖ *U.S.* -si-).

I·tal·i·cism (i-tál-i-siz'm) *n.* Italianism; especially, a word or idiom borrowed from or suggestive of the Italian language.

Italo- *comb. form.* Indicates Italian or Italy; for example, **Italophile.**

It·a·ly (íttəli, ítt'li). *Italian* **I·ta·lia** (ee-taʾal-ya). Republic of southern Europe. It includes Sardinia to the west. The mainland peninsula's spine is formed by the Apennine mountains, the only lowlands of any size being the fertile Po valley in the northeast. After the fall of the Western Roman Empire (A.D. 476), Italy was dominated by successive foreign powers until its unification (1870) under the Piedmontese royal family. The Republic was declared (1946) following the country's defeat in World War II. Industries, especially textiles and motor vehicles, are concentrated in the north, with much of the south being economically depressed. Rich in cultural heritage, and with many holiday resorts, much of the country is heavily dependent on tourism. Italy was a founder member of the European Economic Community (now the European Union). Area, 301 225 square kilometres (116,303 square miles). Population, 57,300,000. Capital, Rome. See map, next page.

itch (ich) *n.* **1.** An irritating or tickling skin sensation, causing a desire to scratch. **2.** Any of various contagious skin diseases, such as scabies, marked by intense irritation, eruptions, and itching. **3.** A restless desire or craving: *an itch for foreign travel.*
~*v.* **itched, itching, itches.** —*intr.* **1.** To feel, have, or produce an itch; have a desire to scratch. **2.** To have a persistent, restless craving. —*tr.* To cause to itch. [Middle English *(y)icchen,* Old English *giccan,* from Germanic *juk-* (unattested).]

itch mite *n.* **1.** A parasitic mite, *Sarcoptes scabiei,* that causes scabies. **2.** Any of various related mites that infest the skin.

itch·y (ichi) *adj.* -**ier,** -**iest.** Having or causing an itching sensation: *an itchy jumper.* —**itch·i·ness** *n.*

–**ite¹** *n. suffix.* Indicates: **1.** A person who is: **a.** A native or resident of a specified place; for example, **Surreyite, Guernseyite. b.** A member of a tribe or family; for example, **Ammonite. c.** An adherent of a doctrine, idea, way of life, or the like; for example, **toryite, socialite. d.** A supporter of someone specified, or their views; for example, **Luddite, Bennite. 2.** *Biology.* A part of an organ or body; for example, **somite. 3.** A fossil; for example, **trilobite, ammonite. 4.** A mineral or rock; for example, **graphite. 5. a.** An explosive; for example, **gelignite, ammonite. b.** A commercial product; for example, **Araldite.** [Middle English, from Old French, from Latin -*ita,* -*itēs,* from Greek -*itēs.*] —-**ite** *adj. suffix.*

–**ite²** *n. suffix.* Indicates a salt or ester of an acid whose adjectival denomination ends in -*ous;* for example, **sulphite.** [French, arbitrarily altered from -ATE.]

i·tem (í-təm; *rarely* -tem, -tim) *n.* **1.** A single article listed on a bill or unit included in a collection, enumeration, or series and specified separately. **2.** A separate matter for consideration, such as a topic or proposal listed on an agenda. **3.** An entry in an account. **4. a.** A bit of information; a detail. **b.** A short piece in a newspaper or magazine. **c.** *Informal.* An unmarried couple in a relationship obvious enough to be noticed. **5.** A member of a set of minimal units: *a lexical item.*
~ *tr.v.* **itemed, iteming, items.** *Archaic.* To itemise.
~*adv.* Also; likewise. Used to introduce each article in an enumeration or list. [Middle English, from Latin, from *ita,* so.]

i·tem·ise, i·tem·ize (ítə-mīz) *tr.v.* -**ised,** -**ising,** -**ises.** To set down item by item; list. —**i·tem·i·sa·tion** (-mī-záysh'n ‖ *U.S.* -mi-) *n.* —**i·tem·is·er** *n.*

it·er·ate (íttə-rayt) *tr.v.* -**ated,** -**ating,** -**ates.** To say or perform again; repeat. [Latin *iterāre,* from *iterum,* again.] —**it·er·a·tion** (-ráysh'n), **it·er·ance** *n.* —**it·er·ant** *adj.*

it·er·a·tive (íttə-rə-tiv, -ray-) *adj.* **1.** Repetitious. **2.** *Grammar.* Frequentative.

Ith·a·ca (ithəkə). See **Ionian Islands.**

I·thunn, I·thun (ée-thóon). Also **I·dun** (-dóon). *Norse Mythology.*

ITALY

SWITZERLAND
AUSTRIA
HUNGARY
FRANCE
SLOVENIA
CROATIA
BOSNIA
AND
HERZEGOVINA
MONACO
SAN MARINO
VATICAN CITY
ROMA
(ROME)
ALGERIA
TUNISIA
MALTA
VALLETTA

The wife of Bragi, goddess of youth and spring. [Old Norse *Idhunn*, probably from *idh*, again, anew.]

ith·y·phal·lic (íthi-fál-ik, íthi-) *adj.* **1.** Of or pertaining to the phallus carried in the ancient festival of Bacchus. **2.** Relating to or composed in the trochaic meter of the hymns to Bacchus. **3.** Having the penis erect. Said of graphic and sculptural representations. **4.** Lascivious; salacious; obscene.

~*n.* **1.** A poem in ithyphallic meter. **2.** An indecent or obscene verse. [Late Latin *īthyphallicus*, from Greek *ithuphallikos*, from *ithuphallos*, erect phallus : *ithus†*, straight + *phallos*, phallus.]

i·tin·er·an·cy (i-tínnə-rən-si, ī-) *n.* Also **i·tin·er·a·cy** (-rə-si). A state or system of itinerating, especially in the role or office of public speaker, minister, or judge.

i·tin·er·ant (i-tínnərənt, ī-) *adj.* Travelling from place to place, especially to perform some duty or work: *an itinerant preacher.*

~*n.* One who so travels. [Late Latin *itinerāns* (stem *itinerant*-), present participle of *itinerārī*, ITINERATE.]

i·tin·er·ar·y (ī-tínnə-rəri, i- ‖ -ri, -rair-i) *n., pl.* **-ies. 1.** A route or proposed route of a journey. **2.** An account or record of a journey. **3.** A travellers' guidebook.

~*adj.* **1.** Of or pertaining to a journey or to a route. **2.** Travelling from place to place; itinerant. [Middle English *itinerarie*, from Late Latin *itinerārium*, course of travel, from *itinerārius*, of travelling, from Latin *iter* (stem *itiner*-), journey.]

i·tin·er·ate (i-tínnə-rayt, ī-) *intr.v.* **-ated, -ating, -ates.** *Rare.* To travel from place to place. [Late Latin *itinerārī*, from Latin *iter* (stem *itiner*-), journey.] —**i·tin·er·a·tion** (-ráysh'n) *n.*

–itis *n. comb. form.* Indicates: **1.** An inflammatory medical condition or disease; for example, **laryngitis, bronchitis. 2.** *Informal.* An excessive preoccupation with or influence by a person or thing; for example, **footballitis.** [New Latin, from Greek *-itis*, feminine of *-itēs*, -ITE (pertaining to, native).]

it'll (itt'l). **1.** Contraction of *it will.* **2.** Contraction of *it shall.*

iTO International Trade Organisation.

–itol *n. suffix. Chemistry.* Indicates an alcohol containing more than one hydroxyl group; for example, **mannitol.** [-ITE + -OL.]

its (its). The possessive form of the pronoun *it.* Used to indicate possession, agency, or reception of an action by the thing, nonhuman being, or person whose sex is not known or disregarded, spoken of: *its forepaw.* [Originally *it's* : IT + -'s, possessive ending.]

it's (its). **1.** Contraction of *it is.* **2.** Contraction of *it has.*

it·self (it-sélf) *pron.* A specialised form of the third person singular neuter pronoun. It is used: **1.** As a reflexive pronoun, forming the direct or indirect object of a verb or the object of a preposition: *This record player turns itself off.* **2.** For emphasis, after a noun or it: *The trouble is in the machine itself.* **3.** As an emphasising substitute: *Itself in difficulties, the bank could not help us.* Sometimes nonstandard: *Despite the damage, itself was unhurt.* **4.** As an indication of its real identity or normal, healthy condition: *The computer is acting itself again since the program was corrected.* —**in itself.** Considered in isolation: *in itself, quite a good idea.* [Middle English *itself,* Old English *hit self* : IT + SELF.]

it·sy-bit·sy (ĭt-si-bĭt-si) *adj.* Also **it·ty-bit·ty** (ĭti-bíti). *Informal.* Very small; tiny. Usually used humorously. [Baby-talk reduplication of LITTLE (influenced by BIT).]

–ity *n. suffix.* Indicates a state or quality; for example, **authenticity, jollity.** [Middle English *-it(i)e,* from Old French *-ite,* from Latin *-itās* : thematic vowel *-i-* + *-tās* (stem *-tāt-*), -TY.]

IUD *n.* An **intrauterine device** *(see).*

–ium *n. comb. form.* Indicates: **1.** *Chemistry.* **a.** A metallic chemical element; for example, **aluminium, unnilquadium. b.** A positive ion formed from a group or molecule; for example, **ammonium, hydroxonium. 2.** A biological or anatomical structure; for example, **pericardium.** [New Latin, from Latin, from Greek *-ion,* diminutive suffix.]

IV, i.v. intravenous; intravenously.

I·van (III) the Great, of Russia (ĭv'n), born Ivan Vasilyevich (1440–1505). Grand Prince of Muscovy (1462–1505), whose successful campaigns against the Tatars laid the foundations for eventual Russian unity. He also set up a strong central government.

Ivan (IV) the Terrible, of Russia, born Ivan Vasilyevich (1530–84). First ruler of Russia to be proclaimed tsar (1547). He greatly expanded the Russian state by war and conquest, but his later pathological fear of treachery led him to the violent suppression of suspected opposition, earning him his nickname "the Terrible".

I've (īv). Contraction of *I have.*

–ive *adj. suffix.* Indicates having a tendency towards or inclination to perform some action; for example, **degenerative, disruptive.** [Middle English *-if, -ive,* from Old French *-if* (feminine *-ive*), from Latin *-īvus* (feminine *-īva,* neuter *-īvum*).]

Ives (īvz), **Charles (Edward)** (1874–1954). U.S. composer. Many of his works anticipated those of later 20th-century musicians in their abandonment of conventional tonality. His *Third Symphony* (1904–11) won the 1947 Pulitzer Prize.

IVF. in vitro fertilisation.

i·vied (ī-vid) *adj.* Overgrown or covered with ivy.

i·vo·ry (ī-vəri, -vri) *n., pl.* **-ries. 1. a.** The hard, smooth, yellowish-white dentine forming the main part of the tusks of the elephant, and used as an ornamental material. **b.** A similar substance forming the tusks or teeth of certain other animals, such as the walrus. **2.** A tusk, especially an elephant's tusk. **3.** A substance, such as a plant product, resembling ivory. **4.** Pale or greyish yellow to yellowish white. **5.** *Often plural.* An article made of ivory. **6.** *Usually plural. Slang.* **a.** Piano keys. **b.** Dice. **c.** The teeth. *~adj.* **1.** Made of or resembling ivory. **2.** Of the colour ivory. [Middle English *ivor(ie), yvory,* from Old French *ivurie, ivoire,* from Vulgar Latin *eboreus* (unattested), from neuter of Latin *eboreus,* of ivory, from *ebur* (stem *ebor-*), ivory.]

ivory black *n.* A black pigment prepared from charred ivory.

Ivory Coast. French **Côte d'Ivoire** (kōt-dee-vwár). Republic in West Africa, on the Gulf of Guinea. Ceded to France (1842), it became an independent republic in 1960. It was once the centre of the slave and ivory trade, and is now Africa's largest exporter of timber and coffee. Area 322 500 square kilometres (124,518 square miles). Population, 14,780,000. Capital, Yamoussoukro. See map at West African States.

ivory gull *n.* An Arctic gull, *Pagophila eburnea.*

ivory nut *n.* The hard seed of the American ivory palm, *Phytelephas macrocarpa,* yielding an ivory-like substance.

ivory tower *n.* A place or attitude of retreat; especially, a preoccupation with lofty, remote, or intellectual considerations rather than with practical everyday life. [Translation of French *tour d'ivoire,* first used by C.A. Sainte-Beuve with reference to Alfred de Vigny, who was anxious to preserve the purity of his inspiration unmixed with practical matters.]

i·vy (ī́vi) *n., pl.* **ivies. 1.** Any of several woody, climbing or trailing plants of the genus *Hedera,* native to the Old World, especially *H. helix,* having lobed, evergreen leaves and berry-like black fruit. **2.** Any of various other climbing or creeping plants, such as ground ivy or poison ivy. [Middle English *ivi, ivye,* Old English *īfig,* from Germanic *ibahs* (unattested), obscurely related to Latin *ibex,* "climber", IBEX.]

Ivy League *n.* An association of eight traditional and prestigious universities in the northeastern United States, comprising Brown, Columbia, Cornell, Dartmouth, Harvard, Princeton, the University of Pennsylvania, and Yale. *~adj.* Of or resembling the traditions of the Ivy League, especially in being conservative and restrained in style. [Referring to the ivy-covered university buildings.] **—Ivy Leaguer** *n.*

i·wis, y·wis (i-wíss) *adv. Archaic.* Certainly; assuredly. [Middle English *iwis(se), gewis,* Old English *gewis,* certain.]

I·wo Ji·ma (ée-wō jéemə). The largest of the Volcano Islands. Lying in the Pacific Ocean, 1 200 kilometres (750 miles) south of Tokyo, it has been part of Japan since 1887, and was the scene of fierce fighting during World War II.

IWW, I.W.W. Industrial Workers of the World.

ix·i·a (ĭk-si-ə) *n.* Any plant of the genus *Ixia,* of southern Africa, having ornamental funnel-shaped flowers. [New Latin, from Greek *ixos,* a type of thistle.]

Ix·i·on (ĭk-sī́-ən). *Greek Mythology.* A Thessalian king whom Zeus punished for his temerity in seeking Hera's love by having him bound to a perpetually revolving wheel in Hades.

ix·o·di·a·sis (ĭk-sō-dī́-ə-siss) *n.* Any disease caused by infestation with ticks. [New Latin, from Greek *ixōdēs,* resembling birdlime, sticking, from *ixos,* birdlime + -IASIS.]

ixtle. Variant of **istle.** See **pita.**

I·yar, Iy·yar (ee-yár, ée-yaar) *n.* The eighth month of the year on the Hebrew calendar. [Hebrew *iyyār.*]

iz·ar (i-zár) *n.* A long cotton outer garment, usually white, worn by women in many Muslim countries. [Arabic *'izār, 'izr,* veil, covering.]

iz·ard (ĭzzərd) *n.* A variety of the chamois occurring in the Pyrenees. [French *isard†.*]

–ize. Variant of **-ise.**

Iz·mir (iz-meer). Formerly **Smyr·na** (smúrnə). City and port in west Turkey. At the head of the Gulf of Izmir, on the Aegean Sea, it is the commercial centre of the Levant, with strong Greek connections.

iz·zard (ĭzzərd) *n. Archaic.* The letter *z.* [Earlier *ezed,* probably from Old French *et zède,* "and zed".]

J

j, J (jay) *n., pl.* **j's** or rare **js, Js** or **J's. 1.** The tenth letter of the modern English alphabet. **2.** Any of the speech sounds represented by this letter. **3.** Anything shaped like the letter J.

j, J, j., J. Note: As an abbreviation or symbol, *j* may be a small or capital letter, with or without a full stop. Established forms or those generally preferred precede the definition. When no form is given, all four forms are in general use in that sense. **1.** J jack (playing card). **2.** current density. **3.** J joule. **4.** J. journal. **5.** J. judge; justice. **6.** The Roman numeral for 1, used as a substitute for i or I in the final position. **7.** The tenth in a series.

ja (yaa) *interj. South African Informal.* Yes. [Afrikaans.]

J.A. 1. joint account. **2.** judge advocate.

jaap (yaap) *n. South African.* Also **ja·pie** (ya'api). A simple-minded, innocent person; a country bumpkin. [Afrikaans, from *Jaap,* pet form of *Jakob, Jacob.*]

jab (jab) *v.* **jabbed, jabbing, jabs.** *—tr.* **1.** To poke abruptly, especially with something sharp. **2.** To stab or pierce. **3.** To thrust into or against something with a rough, abrupt movement. **4.** To punch with short blows. *—intr.* **1.** To make an abrupt jabbing motion. **2.** To deliver a quick punch. *~n.* **1.** A quick stab or blow. **2.** *Informal.* An injection. [Variant of JOB.]

jab·ber (jábbər) *v.* **-bered, -bering, -bers.** *—intr.* To talk rapidly, unintelligibly, or idly. *—tr.* To utter rapidly or unintelligibly.

~n. Rapid or babbling talk. [Middle English *jaberen* (imitative).] **—jab·ber·er** *n.*

jab·ber·wock·y (jábbər-wocki) *n.* **1.** Nonsense verse. **2.** Unintelligible speech or writing; nonsense; gibberish. [Title of a poem in Lewis Carroll's *Through the Looking Glass* (1871).]

jab·i·ru (jábbi-roō) *n.* **1.** A large tropical American wading bird, *Jabiru mycteria,* having white plumage and a dark, naked head and neck. **2.** A similar Australian bird, *Xenorhyncus asiaticus.* Also called "black-necked stork". **3.** Any of various other similar birds, such as the **saddlebill** *(see).* [Portuguese *jabiru,* from Tupi-Guarani.]

jab·o·ran·di (jábbə-rándi, -ran-dée) *n., pl.* **-dis. 1.** Either of two tropical American shrubs, *Pilocarpus jaborandi* or *P. microphyllus.* **2.** The dried leaves of these shrubs, which yield **pilocarpine** *(see).* [Portuguese, from Tupi-Guarani *jaburandi.*]

jab·ot (zhábbō ‖ U.S. also zha-bō) *n.* A cascade of frills down the front of a shirt, blouse, or bodice. [French, from Auvergne or Limousin dialect, akin to Old French dialectal *gave,* throat, from a Romance root *gab-* (unattested), crop, gullet, perhaps from Gaulish.]

jac·a·mar (jácke-maar) *n.* Any of various tropical American birds of the family Galbulidae, related to the woodpeckers. [French, from Tupi-Guarani *jacamaciri.*]

ja·ça·na (jássə-naa, zha'a-sə-) *n.* Any of several tropical marsh birds of the family Jacanidae, having long toes adapted for walking on floating vegetation. Also called "lily-trotter". [From Portuguese *jaçaná,* from Tupi-Guarani *jasaná.*]

jac·a·ran·da (jáckə-rándə) *n.* **1.** Any of several trees of the genus *Jacaranda,* native to tropical America, having clusters of pale purple flowers. **2.** The wood of such a tree. **3.** Any similar wood, or the tree yielding it. [Portuguese *jacarandá,* from Tupi-Guarani.]

ja·cinth (jássinth, jáy-sinth) *n.* **1.** A reddish-orange variety of zircon, **hyacinth** (*see*). **2.** *Obsolete.* A hyacinth plant or flower. [Middle English *iacynth, iacin(c)t,* from Old French *iacinte* or Medieval Latin *jacinthus,* from Latin *hyacinthus,* HYACINTH.]

jack (jak) *n.* **1.** *Usually capital* **J.** A man; a fellow; a chap. Often used in direct address. **2. a.** *Archaic.* One who does odd jobs. **b.** One who works in the specified manual trade. Used in combination: *lumberjack; steeplejack.* **3.** A sailor; a tar. **4.** A playing card showing the figure of a young man or prince and ranking below a queen; a knave. **5. a.** Any of several devices or contrivances replacing human labour. Often used in combination: *bootjack.* **b.** A usually portable device for raising heavy objects, especially one for raising a motor vehicle when changing a tyre, by means of force applied with a lever, screw, or hydraulic press. **c.** A wooden wedge for cleaving rock. **d.** A support or brace; especially, the iron crosstree on a topgallant masthead. **e.** A device that turns a spit for roasting meat. **6.** The male of certain animals, especially the ass. **7.** Any of several food and game fishes chiefly of the genus *Caranx,* of Atlantic and Pacific waters. **8.** A piece of wood holding the leather or quill pluck in a harpsichord or the hammer in other keyboard instruments, such as the piano. **9.** A small bowl, usually white, that players aim at in the game of bowls. **10.** Any of the metal pieces used in the game of **jacks** (*see*). Also called "jackstone". **11.** A socket that accepts a plug at one end and attaches to an electric circuit at the other. **12.** A small flag flown at the bow of a ship, usually to indicate nationality. **—every man jack.** Every single person of a group.

~v. jacked, jacking, jacks. —jack in. *Informal.* To give up; leave or abandon. **—jack up. 1.** To raise with or as if with a jack. **2.** *Informal.* To increase (prices, for example). **3.** *U.S.* To bolster confidence in; support. **4.** *N.Z.* To arrange; set up; put in order. **5.** *Australian.* To refuse to cooperate; resist or rebel.

~adj. *Australian Informal.* Tired or dissatisfied. Used with *of:* jack of it all. [Transferred use of the name *Jack,* familiar form of *John,* used to represent "any man".]

jack·al (jáckawl, jáck'l) *n.* **1.** Any of several doglike carnivorous mammals of the genus *Canis,* of Africa and Asia, which feed on carrion or prey on other animals. **2.** An accomplice or lackey characterised by the greed and baseness attributed to the jackal. [Turkish *chakāl,* from Persian *shagāl, shaghāl†.*]

jack·a·napes (jáckə-nayps) *n.* **1.** A conceited, cheeky young man. **2.** A mischievous child. **3.** *Archaic.* A monkey or ape. [Earlier, "an ape", originally (about 1450) *Jack Napes,* perhaps referring to the nickname of William de la Pole, first Duke of Suffolk (1396–1450), whose badge was a figure of the ball and chain of a tame ape.]

jack·ass (jáck-ass, *in sense 2 also* -aass) *n.* **1.** A male ass or donkey. **2.** A foolish or stupid person; a blockhead. **3.** An Australian bird, the **kookaburra** (*see*). [JACK (male) + ASS.]

jackass penguin *n.* The northernmost of penguins, *Spheniscus demersus,* found especially on the islets off the west coast of Africa, so called because of its donkey-like braying.

jackass rig *n.* *Nautical.* Any nonstandard combination of square rig and fore-and-aft rig on a sailing ship having two or more masts. Also called "hermaphrodite rig".

jack·boot (jáck-bōot) *n.* **1.** A stout military boot extending to or above the knee. **2.** Oppressive, bullying behaviour. Also used adjectivally: *jackboot tactics.*

jack·daw (jáck-daw) *n.* A Eurasian bird, *Corvus monedula,* related to and resembling the crow, having a black and grey plumage. Also called "daw".

jack·e·roo, jack·a·roo (jáckə-rōo) *n., pl.* **-roos.** *Australian Informal.* An apprentice hand on a sheep or cattle station.

~intr.v. jackerooed, -rooing, -roos. To work as a jackeroo. [Blend of JACK (man) and KANGAROO.]

jack·et (jáckit) *n.* **1.** A short coat, usually waist- or hip-length, worn by men or women. **2.** Any of various coverings worn on the upper part of the body. Used in combination: *a straitjacket.* **3.** The coat of certain animals. **4.** An outer covering or casing, especially: **a.** The skin of a baked potato. **b.** A dust jacket (*see*). **c.** Insulation covering a steam pipe, wire, boiler, or the like. **d.** *U.S.* A record sleeve.

~tr.v. jacketed, -eting, -ets. To supply or cover with a jacket. [Middle English *jaket,* from Old French *jacquet, jaquet,* diminutive of *jaque,* short jacket, perhaps from the name *Jacques.*]

jacket potato *n.* A potato baked in its skin; a baked potato.

Jack Frost *n.* Frost or cold weather personified.

jack·fruit (jáck-frōot) *n.* **1.** A tree, *Artocarpus heterophyllus,* of tropical Asia, bearing large, edible fruit. **2.** The fruit of this tree, resembling breadfruit. [Portuguese *jaca,* from Malayalam *chakka* + FRUIT.]

jack·ham·mer (jáck-hammər) *n.* **1.** A hand-held pneumatic machine for drilling rock. **2.** *Chiefly U.S.* A pneumatic drill (*see*).

jack-in-of·fice (jáck-in-offiss ‖ -awfiss) *n., pl.* **jacks-in-office.** A pompous, obnoxious minor official.

jack-in-the-box (jáck-in-thə-boks) *n., pl.* **jack-in-the-boxes** or **jacks-in-the-box.** A toy consisting of a grotesque puppet that springs out of a box when the lid is opened.

jack-in-the-pul·pit (jáck-in-thə-pŏol-pit ‖ -púl-) *n.* A plant, the **cuckoopint** (*see*).

Jack Ketch *n.* *Archaic. British.* A hangman. [After John KETCH.]

jack-knife (jáck-nīf) *n., pl.* **-knifes** (for senses 2,3) or **-knives** (-nīvz). **1.** A large pocketknife. **2.** A dive executed by jumping headfirst and then bending the body at the waist and, with the legs straight, touching the feet with the hands before straightening out to enter the water, hands first. **3.** An uncontrollable manoeuvre of an articulated lorry, in which the trailer swings round at an angle, usually of less than 90°, to the tractor or cab.

~v. jackknifed, -knifing, -knifes. —tr. To fold or double like a jackknife. **—intr. 1.** To bend or fold up like a jackknife. **2.** To make a jackknife dive. **3.** To go out of control by performing a jackknife. Used of an articulated vehicle. [Probably JACK + KNIFE.]

jack-of-all-trades (jáck-əv-áwl-traydz, -tráydz) *n., pl.* **jacks-of-all-trades.** A person who can do many different kinds of work. Sometimes used derogatorily.

jack-o'-lan·tern (jáck-ə-lantərn, -lántərn) *n.* **1. a.** A lantern made from a hollowed pumpkin with a carved face. **b.** A commercial imitation of this. **2.** A phosphorescent light over marshy ground or similar phenomenon; a will-o'-the-wisp.

jack·plane (jáck-playn) *n.* A bench plane for rough surfacing. [JACK + PLANE.]

jack plug *n.* A usually single-pronged electrical plug for use with a jack.

jack·pot (jáck-pot) *n.* **1. a.** The accumulated stakes in a kind of poker that requires one to hold a pair of jacks or better in order to open the betting. **b.** Any cumulative pool or kitty in various games and competitions. **2.** A top prize or reward. **—hit the jackpot.** *Informal.* To experience great success or sudden good fortune. [JACK (playing card) + POT.]

jack rabbit *n.* Any of several large long-eared, long-legged hares of the genus *Lepus,* of western North America. [JACK(ASS) (from its long ears) + RABBIT.]

Jack Russell terrier *n.* A dog of a breed developed from the fox terrier, having a smooth, white coat with black and tan markings, short legs, and a stocky body. Also called "Jack Russell". [After John *Russell* (1795–1883), English clergyman known as the "sporting parson".]

jacks (jaks) *n.* *Used with a singular verb.* A game played with a set of six-pointed metal pieces and a small ball, the object being to pick up the pieces in various combinations while bouncing and catching the ball. Also called "jackstones". [Shortened from *jackstones* : JACK (man) + STONE.]

jack-shaft (jáck-shaaft ‖ -shaft) *n.* An auxiliary or intermediate shaft that transmits motion from a motor to a machine.

jack-snipe (jáck-snīp) *n., pl.* **-snipes** or collectively **jacksnipe. 1.** A Eurasian wading bird, *Limnocryptes minima,* having brownish plumage and a long bill. **2.** Any of several similar birds. [JACK + SNIPE.]

Jack·son (jáks'n). State capital of Mississippi since 1821, situated on the Pearl River in the United States. The city was the scene of bitter fighting during the American Civil War, and of civil rights agitation after World War II.

Jackson, Andrew (1767–1845). Seventh U.S. president. He became a national hero after his defence of New Orleans against the British in 1815, and was elected president in 1828 and 1832.

Jackson, Michael (Joseph) (1958–). American pop singer. His album *Thriller* (1982) had by 1986 achieved worldwide sales of more than 50 million, making it the most successful LP to that date.

Jackson, Thomas (Jonathan) (1824–63). Confederate general in the U.S. Civil War. He won his nickname—"Stonewall"—for his resistance to Union forces at Bull Run (1861). He was accidentally shot dead by his own troops at Chancellorsville (1863).

jack-stay (jáck-stay) *n.* **1.** A stay for racing or cruising vessels used to steady the mast against the strain of the gaff. **2.** A rope, rod, or batten along the upper side of a yard, gaff, or boom to which a sail is fastened. **3.** A rope or rod running vertically on the forward side of the mast on which the yard moves.

jack-stones (jáck-stōnz) *n.* **1.** *Used with a singular verb.* The game of jacks (*see*). **2.** *Singular.* A **jack** (*see*).

jack-straws (jáck-strawz) *n.* **1.** *Used with a singular verb.* The game of spillikins (*see*). **2.** *Singular.* A spillikin (*see*). [JACK + STRAW.]

jack-sy (jáksi) *n., pl.* **-sies.** *Slang.* The buttocks. [JACK (fellow) + -*sy,* hypocoristic diminutive suffix.]

Jack Tar, Jack tar *n.* A sailor. [*Jack* (name) + TAR.]

Jack the lad *n.* A clever and important person. Often used humorously or derogatorily: *He thinks he's Jack the lad.*

Jack the Ripper. An unknown murderer who killed and mutilated a number of prostitutes in the East End of London in 1888.

Ja·cob (jáykəb). Hebrew patriarch; son of Isaac and grandson of Abraham; father of 12 sons, ancestors of the 12 tribes of Israel. See Israel[2,3].

Jac·o·be·an (jáckə-bée-ən) *adj.* **1.** Of or pertaining to the reign of James I of England or his times. **2.** Pertaining to or designating an architectural style of 17th-century England, blending late Gothic and Palladian elements.

~n. Any prominent figure of this period. [New Latin *Jacobaeus,* from *Jacobus,* JAMES.]

Jac·o·be·than (jáckə-béeth'n) *adj.* Pertaining to, suggestive of, or designating a style, especially in architecture, characteristic of the reigns of Elizabeth I and James I. Often used humorously. [Blend of JACOBEAN + ELIZABETHAN, coined (1933) by Sir John Betjeman.]

Jac·o·bin (jáckə-bin) *n.* **1.** A member of the most radical republican group during the French Revolution, led by Robespierre, which overthrew the Girondins in 1793 and instituted the Reign of Terror. **2.** A leftist or extreme left-wing revolutionary. Often used derogatorily. **3.** A French Dominican friar. [French, from Late Latin *Jacobus,* after the church of *Saint-Jacques,* Paris, near which the Jacobin friars built their first convent. The French political group was founded (1789) in this convent.] —**Jac·o·bin·ic** (-bínnik), Jac·o·bin·i·cal *adj.* —**Jac·o·bin·ism** *n.*

Jac·o·bin·ise, Jac·o·bin·ize (jáckəbin-īz) *tr.v.* **-ised, -ising, -ises.** To imbue with or convert to revolutionary ideas characteristic of the Jacobins.

Jac·o·bite (jáckə-bīt) *n.* A supporter of James II of England or of the Stuart pretenders after 1688. [From New Latin *Jacobus,* JAMES.] —**Jac·o·bit·i·cal** (-bíttik'l) *adj.* —**Jac·o·bit·ism** (-bīt-iz'm) *n.*

Jacobite Rebellion *n.* **1.** The failed Jacobite uprising (1715–16) led by the Earl of Mar in support of James Edward Stuart, the Old Pretender. Also called the "Fifteen". **2.** The later Jacobite uprising (1745–46) led by Charles Edward Stuart, the young Pretender, in which all hopes of restoring the Stuarts to the throne were finally crushed. Also called the "Forty-Five".

Jac·ob·sen (yáckəb-s'n), **Arne** (1902–71). Danish designer. His severely functional style, such as his three-legged stacking stool, influenced much modern design. He summed up his work in the motto "economy plus function equals style".

Jacob's ladder *n.* **1.** *Nautical.* A rope or chain ladder with rigid rungs. **2.** A widely cultivated garden plant, *Polemonium caeruleum,* having blue flowers and numerous paired leaflets. [From the ladder seen by the patriarch JACOB in a dream. Genesis 28:12.]

ja·co·bus (jə-kṓbəss) *n., pl.* **-buses.** A gold coin issued during the reign of James I. [New Latin *Jacobus,* JAMES.]

jac·o·net (jáckə-net, -nit) *n.* A light, cotton cloth with a soft finish used especially for bandages and poulticing. [Urdu *jagannāthī,* first made in *Jagannath* (now Puri), India.]

Jac·quard (jákaard ‖ *chiefly U.S.* jə-kárd) *adj.* Made on or pertaining to a Jacquard loom.
~*n.* A fabric with an intricately woven pattern made on a Jacquard loom. Also called "Jacquard weave". [After Joseph-Marie JACQUARD.]

Jac·quard (jákaard ‖ jə-kárd; *French* zha-ka'ar), **Joseph-Marie** (1752–1834). French silk-weaver. His invention of the Jacquard loom (1801) made it possible to weave complex patterns automatically. The silk-workers of his native Lyons smashed his machines, but by 1812 11,000 looms were in use and they were adopted worldwide.

Jacquard loom *n.* A loom fitted with perforated cards to facilitate the weaving of a figured fabric. [After Joseph-Marie JACQUARD.]

Jac·que·rie (zháckə-ri, -rée ‖ *U.S.* zha'ak-) *n.* **1.** The uprising of the French peasants against the nobility in 1358. **2.** *Often small* j. A violent peasant revolt. [French, from Old French, from *jacques,* "peasant", from *Jacques,* James.]

jac·ta·tion (jak-táysh'n) *n.* **1.** *Rare.* Bragging; boasting. **2.** *Pathology.* Jactitation. [Latin *jactātiō* (stem *jactātiōn-*), from *jactāre,* "to toss about", discuss, boast, frequentative of *jacere* (past participle *jactus*), to throw.]

jac·ti·ta·tion (jákti-táysh'n) *n.* **1.** *Law.* A false boast or claim, especially of marriage, detrimental to the interests of another. **2.** *Pathology.* Extreme restlessness or tossing in bed, often associated with a high fever. Also called "jactation". [Medieval Latin *jactitātiō* (stem *jactitātiōn-*), a false assertion made to the injury of another, from *jactitāre,* frequentative of Latin *jactāre,* to boast, declare publicly. See **jactation**.]

Ja·cuz·zi (jə-kṓozi, ja-) *n.* A trademark for a deep bath with a device that makes the water swirl around.

jade¹ (jayd) *n.* **1.** Either of two distinct minerals, **nephrite** and **jade·ite** *(both of which see),* that are generally pale green or white and are used mainly as gemstones or in carved ornaments. **2.** A dull yellowish-green. [French *jade, ejade,* from Spanish *(piedra de) ijada,* "(stone of the) flank" (from the belief that it was a cure for renal colic), from Vulgar Latin *iliata* (unattested), flanks, from Latin *īlia,* plural of *īlium,* flank, ILEUM.] —**jade** *adj.*

jade² *n.* **1.** A broken-down or useless horse; a nag. **2.** A worthless or disreputable woman.
~*v.* **jaded, jading, jades.** —*tr.* To exhaust or wear out. —*intr.* To become weary or spiritless. [Middle English *jade†,* a broken-down horse.]

jad·ed (jáydid) *adj.* **1.** Wearied; spiritless as through fatigue: *jaded after his efforts.* **2.** Dulled as by surfeit; sated. —See Synonyms at **tired.** [From JADE (verb).] —**jad·ed·ly** *adv.* —**jad·ed·ness** *n.*

jade·ite (jáyd-īt) *n.* A rare, emerald to light green, white, red-brown, yellow-brown, or violet jade, $NaAlSi_2O_6$, used as a gem and for ornamental carvings. [French : JADE + -ITE.]

j'a·doube (zha-dṓob) *interj. French.* Used in chess to express the intention not to move a piece that one is about to touch. [Literally "I adjust".]

jae·ger (yáygər; *also* jáygər *for sense* 2) *n.* **1.** A marksman or sniper in some units of the German and Austrian armed forces. **2.** *Chiefly U.S.* Any of several sea birds of the genus *Stercorarius.* See **skua.** **3.** *Rare.* A huntsman or hunting attendant. [German *Jäger,* "hunter".]

Jaf·fa (jáffə). *Hebrew* **Jafo;** *Arabic* **Yafa.** Ancient city of west central

Israel. Founded by the Phoenicians, it was taken by the Israelites in the sixth century B.C. The city fell to the Arabs (A.D. 636), to the Crusaders (1126 and 1191), and to the Ottoman Turks (16th century). It became part of Tel Aviv–Yafo in 1950.

Jaffa orange *n.* A variety of orange having a large, thick-skinned fruit. Also called "jaffa". [After JAFFA, near which it was originally grown.

jag¹, jagg (jag) *n.* **1.** A sharp projection; a barb. **2. a.** A hanging flap along the edge of a garment. **b.** A slash or slit in a garment. **3.** *Regional.* An injection.
~*tr.v.* **jagged, jagging, jags.** Also **jagg. 1.** To cut jags in; notch. **2.** To cut unevenly; make (an edge) ragged. **3.** *Regional.* To prick; jab sharply. [Middle English *jagge†.*]

jag² *n.* **1.** *Slang.* **a.** A bout of drinking, drug-taking, or the like. **b.** Any period of indulgence in an activity: *a crying jag.* **2.** *Regional.* A small load or portion. [16th century : origin obscure.]

J.A.G. Judge Advocate General.

jag·ad·gu·ru (júggəd-gṓo-rōo, -gṓor-ōo) *n.* A title for a revered Hindu guru. [Hindi, from Sanskrit : *jagat-,* world + GURU.]

Jag·an (jággən), **Cheddi Bharat** (1918–97). Guyanese politician. During his country's drive for independence, Jagan's Communist-inspired People's Progressive Party was banned and he was imprisoned, but he became Guyana's first prime minister (1961–64). He was elected president in 1992.

Jagannath, Jagannatha. Variants of **Juggernaut.**

jag·ged (jággid) *adj.* **1.** Toothed or serrated; having jags. **2.** Roughly torn; having a ragged edge. See Synonyms at **rough.** —**jag·ged·ly** *adv.* —**jag·ged·ness** *n.*

Jag·ger (jággər), **Michael Philip,** known as Mick (1943–). English rock singer and songwriter, lead singer of the Rolling Stones. He has also appeared as a film actor, as in the film *Ned Kelly* (1970).

jag·ger·y (jággəri) *n.* Unrefined sugar made from palm sap. [From Indo-Portuguese *jagara,* from Kanarese *sharkare,* from Sanskrit *śarkarā†,* "gravel", sugar.]

jag·gy (jággi) *adj.* **-gier, -giest.** Having jags; jagged.

jag·u·ar (jággew-ər ‖ -aar, *U.S. also* jág-waar) *n.* A large feline mammal, *Panthera onca,* of tropical America, having a tawny coat spotted with black rosette-like markings. [Spanish *jaguar, yaguar* and Portuguese *jaguar,* from Tupi-Guarani *jaguara, yaguara.*]

ja·gua·ron·di, ja·gua·run·di (jágwə-róndi, jággew-ə-, -rúndi) *n., pl.* **-dis.** A long-tailed greyish-brown wild cat, *Felis yagouaroundi,* of tropical America. [American Spanish and Portuguese, from Tupi-Guarani.]

Jah (jaa) *n.* Yahweh; God. Used especially by Rastafarians. [Shortened from Hebrew, YAHWEH.]

Jahveh, Jahweh. Variants of **Yahweh.**

Jahvist, Jahwist. Variants of **Yahwist.**

jai a·lai (hī-lī, -ə-lī, -ə-lī) *n.* A ball game, a version of **pelota** *(see).*

Jai Hind (jī hínd, jä) *interj.* Victory to India. Used in India as a greeting or as an affirmation of friendship, solidarity, or the like, as at the end of a public function. [Hindi.]

jail (jayl) *n.* Also *chiefly British* **gaol.** A place for the confinement of persons in lawful detention; a prison. See Usage note at **gaol.**
~*tr.v.* **jailed** or *chiefly British* **gaoled, jailing** or *chiefly British* **gaoling, jails** or *chiefly British* **gaols.** To detain in custody; imprison. [*Jail* and *gaol,* respectively from Middle English *jaiole* and *gayole,* from Old French *jaiole* and Old Northern French *gaiole,* both from Vulgar Latin *gaviola* (unattested), variant of *caveola* (unattested), diminutive of Latin *cavea,* a hollow, den, coop.]

jail·bird (jáyl-burd) *n. Informal.* A prisoner or ex-convict; especially, one who has a long record of imprisonment.

jail·break (jáyl-brayk) *n.* An escape from prison. —**jail·break·er** *n.*

jail·er, jail·or (jáylər) *n.* A keeper of or warder in a jail.

jail fever *n.* A virulent type of typhus fever, formerly endemic in crowded and dirty prisons.

jail·house (jáyl-howss) *n. U.S.* A jail.

Jain (jīn) *n.* Also **Jai·na** (jīnə). A believer in or follower of Jainism. [Hindi *jaina,* from Sanskrit *jainas,* saintly, from *jinas,* saint, "overcomer", from *jayati,* to conquer.] —**Jain, Jai·na** *adj.*

Jain·ism (jīn-iz'm) *n.* An ascetic religion of India, founded in the 6th century B.C. It teaches that the soul is immortal and will be reincarnated until it reaches perfection and is liberated. The deity of Jainism consists not of a single supreme being but of the collection of these perfect liberated souls.

Jai·pur (jī-poor, -pór). The capital of Rajasthan state, northwestern India. Founded in 1728, it was the capital of the Rajput state of Jaipur and came under British protection in 1818.

Ja·kar·ta or **Dja·kar·ta** (jə-kártə). Formerly **Ba·ta·vi·a** (bə-táyvi-ə). The capital of Indonesia, situated on the river Chiliwong on the northwestern coast of Java. Founded by the Dutch (*c.* 1619), it became an important centre of the Dutch East India Company. It was renamed Jakarta on independence and in 1949. From its port, Tandjung Priok, oil, rubber, timber, and tea are exported.

jake (jayk) *adj. Chiefly Australian & N.Z. Informal.* Fine; suitable; all right: *She'll be jake mate, as long as the beer lasts.* [Origin unknown.]

jakes (jayks) *n., pl.* **jakes.** *Regional & Archaic.* A lavatory. [Perhaps from the French name *Jacques.*]

Ja·kob·son (yaäkəb-s'n), **Roman** (1896–1982). Russian-born U.S. linguist. He was a principal founder (1926) of the Prague School, and a major influence on contemporary linguistics. His works include *Fundamentals of Language* (with M. Halle, 1956).

jal·ap (jál-əp) *n*. **1.** A Mexican plant, *Exogonium purga,* having a tuberous rootstock that is dried, powdered, and used medicinally as a cathartic. **2.** Any of several similar or related plants. **3.** The dried rootstock of such a plant. [French *jalap,* from Mexican Spanish *jalapa,* short for *(purga de) Jalapa,* "(purgative of) Jalapa", capital of Veracruz State, Mexico.]

ja·lop·y (jə-lóppi) *n., pl.* **-ies.** *Informal.* An old, dilapidated car. [20th century : origin obscure.]

ja·lou·sie (zháloo-zee, -zée || *U.S. and West Indies* jál-ŏŏ-si, jéllə-) *n.* A blind or shutter having adjustable horizontal slats for regulating the passage of air and light. [French, "jealousy" (probably because one sees through it without being seen).]

jam[1] (jam) *v.* **jammed, jamming, jams.** —*tr.* **1.** To drive or wedge forcibly; squeeze into a tight position. **2. a.** To force or push suddenly: *jam the lid down.* **b.** To apply (brakes) suddenly. Used with *on.* **3. a.** To cause to be stuck in a position, so that movement or extrication is difficult or impossible: *Her skirt was jammed in the bicycle wheel.* **b.** To cause to lock in an unworkable position: *jam the typewriter keys.* **4.** To fill or pack to excess; cram: *He jammed the drawer with old socks.* **5.** To block, congest, or clog: *The drain was jammed by debris.* **6.** To crush or bruise between two bodies or surfaces: *jammed her finger in the door.* **7.** *Electronics.* To interfere with or prevent the clear reception of (broadcast signals) by electronic means. —*intr.* **1.** To become wedged; stick. **2.** To become inoperable because of jammed parts. **3.** *Slang.* To play in a jam session.

~*n.* **1.** The act of jamming or the condition of being jammed. **2.** A crush or congestion of people or things in a limited space: *a traffic jam.* **3.** *Slang.* A **jam session** *(see).* **4.** *Informal.* A predicament: *in a jam with the police.* [18th century : imitative.]

jam[2] *n.* **1.** A preserve made from whole fruit boiled to a pulp with sugar. **2.** *British.* Something pleasant or coming as a bonus: *always promised jam tomorrow.* [Probably from JAM (act of jamming).]

Jam. James (New Testament).

Ja·mai·ca (jə-máykə). An island in the Caribbean Sea. Its central uplands rise to 2 256 metres (7,402 feet) in the Blue Mountains to the east. The island was discovered by Columbus (1494), settled by the Spanish, but taken by the British in 1655. Jamaica became a major centre of the slave trade with extensive sugar plantations. In 1962 the island became an independent Commonwealth state. In the election of 1980, with high unemployment and street violence, the left-wing Michael Manley was replaced as prime minister by the pro-Western Edward Seaga, and much-needed foreign investment became available. Since then, through a number of changes of government, the island has moved hesitantly towards a greater prosperity. The island once depended on exports of bananas, but bauxite is now the main export. Tourism is the second-largest earner of foreign exchange, and sugar is also important. Area, 10 991 square kilometres (4,243 square miles). Population, 2,490,000. Capital, Kingston. —**Ja·mai·can** *n. & adj.*

jamb, jambe (jam) *n.* **1.** A vertical post or piece forming the side of a door or window frame. **2.** A jambeau. [Middle English *jambe,* from Old French, "leg", jamb, from Late Latin *gamba,* hoof, from Greek *kampē,* joint.]

jam·ba·lay·a (júmbə-lí̄-ə) *n.* A southern U.S. dish consisting of rice with shrimps, chicken, turkey, or similar ingredients. [Louisiana French, from Provençal *jambalaia* (a stew of chicken and rice).]

jam·beau (jámbō) *n., pl.* **-beaux** (-z). A piece of armour for the leg below the knee. Also called "jambe". [Middle English, from Anglo-French *jambeau* (unattested), from Old French *jambe,* leg.]

jam·bo·ree (jámbə-rée) *n.* **1.** A lively celebration. **2.** A large assembly, often international, especially of Scouts or Guides. [19th century : origin obscure.]

James (jaymz) *n. Abbr.* **Jam., Jas.** The 20th book of the New Testament, attributed to St. James the Less.

James IV of Scotland (1473–1513). King of Scotland from 1488. He led Scotland to its greatest military defeat—at Flodden (1513), against the English, in which he died with many of his nobles.

James V of Scotland (1512–42). King of Scotland from 1513. He allied himself with Church and people to curb the nobility, but in 1542, dissent between king and nobles allowed the English to over-

whelm the Scottish army at Solway Moss.

James VI of Scotland and I of England (1566–1625). King of Scotland from 1567 and first Stuart King of England from 1603, when he succeeded the childless Elizabeth I. James believed in the Divine Right of Kings, and quarrelled with Parliament, sowing the seeds of civil war.

James VII of Scotland and II of England (1633–1701). Last Stuart king to rule both countries (1685–88). His fervent Roman Catholicism almost denied him accession. A rebellion against him by the Duke of Monmouth (1685) was unsuccessful, but in 1688 seven leading political figures invited William of Orange to invade the country. James was deserted by his own troops and fled to France.

James, Henry (1843–1916). U.S. novelist and critic. He settled in England in 1876, and his early novels, *The Americans* (1877), *Portrait of a Lady* (1881), and *The Bostonians* (1886) deal with the impact of European civilisation on Americans. His other works include *The Turn of the Screw* (1898), *The Ambassadors* (1903), and *The Golden Bowl* (1904). —**James·i·an** *n. & adj.*

James, Saint[1], called "the Less". Described by Saint Paul (Galatians 1:19) as the brother of Jesus, considered to be the author of the Epistle of James and first bishop of Jerusalem.

James, Saint[2], called "the Greater". One of the Twelve Apostles; son of Zebedee and brother of John; traditionally supposed to have been martyred by Herod Agrippa (*c.* A.D. 44).

James, Saint[3]. One of the Twelve Apostles; often identified with Saint James the Less.

James, William (1842–1910). U.S. psychologist and philosopher, brother of Henry James. He developed the theory of pragmatism, and is noted for his pioneering study, *The Varieties of Religious Experience* (1902).

Jam·e·son (jémmi-s'n, jáym-), **Sir Leander Starr** (1853–1917). South African politician. His disastrous raid into the Boer Transvaal Republic (1895) led to the fall of Cecil Rhodes. Jameson later became prime minister of Cape Colony (1904–08).

James·town (jáymz-town). Ruined village on the James River in Virginia, eastern United States. It was the first permanent English settlement in the New World (founded 1607).

jam·mer (jámmər) *n.* A device for jamming broadcast signals.

Jam·mu and Kash·mir (jámmōō, júmmōō; kásh-méer). A state in northern India, in the Indian part of Kashmir. The Himalayan and Karakoram ranges lie in the north and east of the state. There are two capitals: Jammu (winter) and Srinagar (summer).

jam·my (jámmi) *adj.* **-mier, -miest. 1.** Covered with jam. **2.** *British Informal.* Lucky. **b.** Easy or pleasant: *a jammy job.*

jam·packed (jám-pakt, -pákt) *adj. Informal.* Full, crowded, or crammed: *an article jam-packed with new ideas.*

jam·pan (jám-pan) *n.* A type of sedan chair, used in parts of India, that is carried by four people. [Bengali *jhāmpān.*]

jam session *n.* An informal gathering at which musicians, especially jazz musicians, play improvised music together, usually for their own enjoyment.

Jam·shid, Jam·shyd (jám-shid, -sheed, -sheéd) *n.* In Persian mythology, a fairy king who drank a cup of the elixir of life. He was punished for boasting that he was immortal by being made human, after which he became a great ruler for 700 years.

Jan. January.

Ja·ná·ček (yán-ə-chek, -aa-), **Leoš** (1854–1928). Czech composer, influenced by folk music. His works include the operas *Jenůfa* (1904), *Kátya Kabanová* (1921), and the *Glagolitic Mass* (1926).

Ja·na·ta (júnnə-taa) *n.* A political coalition that held power in India between 1977 and 1979. [Hindi, "group of the people".]

jan·gle (jáng-g'l) *n.* A harsh, discordant, metallic sound.

~*v.* **jangled, -gling, -gles.** —*intr.* **1.** To make a jangle. **2.** *Archaic.* To wrangle; dispute. —*tr.* **1.** To cause (something metallic) to jangle: *jangled the bells.* **2.** To grate on or jar (the nerves). [Middle English *janglen,* from Old French *jangler,* probably from Germanic, akin to Middle Dutch *jangelen†.*] —**jan·gler** *n.*

jan·is·sar·y (jánni-səri || -serri) *n., pl.* **-ies.** Also **jan·i·zar·y** (-zəri || -zerri). A soldier in an elite guard of Turkish troops organised in the 14th century and abolished in 1826. [French *janissaire,* from Turkish *yeniçeri : yeni,* new + *çeri,* militia.]

jan·i·tor (jánni-tər) *n.* **1.** *Chiefly U.S. & Scottish.* A caretaker. **2.** *Archaic.* A doorman. [Latin *jānitor,* from *jānua,* door, from *jānus,* arched passage.] —**jan·i·to·ri·al** (-táwri-əl || -tóri-) *adj.*

Jan·sen (ján-s'n; *Dutch* yán-), **Cornelis Otto** (1585–1638). Dutch theologian. He founded a reform movement in the Roman Catholic Church, known as Jansenism. In the posthumous *Augustinus* (1640) he argued against the concept of a state of grace, and his movement was condemned as heretical by Pope Innocent X.

Jan·sen·ism (ján-s'n-iz'm) *n.* The heretical theological principles of Cornelis Jansen, which emphasise predestination, deny free will, and maintain that human nature is incapable of good. —**Jan·sen·ist** *n. & adj.* —**Jan·sen·is·tic** (-ístik) *adj.*

Jan·sky (jánski), **Karl Guthe** (1905–50). U.S. engineer. He discovered in 1931 that the stars transmit radio waves, and laid the foundations of the science of radio astronomy.

Jan·u·ar·y (jánnew-əri, -ri || -erri) *n., pl.* **-ies.** *Abbr.* **Jan.** The first month of the year in the Gregorian calendar. January has 31 days. [Middle English *Januarie,* from Latin *Jānuārius (mensis),* "(month) of Janus", from JANUS.]

Ja·nus (jáynəss). *Mythology.* An ancient Roman god of gates and doorways, depicted with two faces looking in opposite directions, whose festival month was January.

JAMAICA

CUBA   75°W   20°N

JAMAICA   HAITI

Montego Bay

Spanish Town   ▲2256m   KINGSTON

CARIBBEAN SEA

Km 0   100
Miles 0   100

Ja·nus-faced (jáynəss-fayst) *adj*. Hypocritical; two-faced.

Jap. Japan; Japanese.

ja·pan (jə-pán) *n*. **1.** A black enamel or lacquer of a type originating in the Orient, used to produce a durable glossy finish. **2.** Any object decorated and varnished in the Japanese manner. ~*adj*. Relating to or varnished with japan. ~*tr.v*. **japanned, -panning, -pans. 1.** To enamel with japan. **2.** To coat with a glossy finish. [From JAPAN, from Malay *Japang*, from Chinese *Jih-pun* : *jih*, sun + *pun*, origin.]

Ja·pan (jə-pán). *Japanese* **Nip·pon** (níppon) or **Ni·hon** (née-hón). Nation consisting of a group of islands in the North Pacific Ocean, lying off the mainland of east Asia. The four main islands, Honshū, Shikoku, Kyūshū, and Hokkaidō, are mountainous. The highest peak is Fujiyama (3 776 metres; 12,388 feet). Japan has been ruled from the 5th century A.D. by emperors of the Yamato dynasty, though legends trace their origins back to the 7th century B.C. The native Shinto religion was challenged by Buddhism from the 6th century A.D. From the 12th to 19th centuries, real power lay in the hands of the shoguns, feudal warlords whose dominance ended with the accession of the emperor Mutsuhito (Meiji Tenno). During his reign (1868-1912), Japan opened its doors to Western trade and technology. Victory in the Russo-Japanese war (1904-05) encouraged expansion into Asia, and Japan occupied Korea and parts of China during the first half of the 20th century. One of the Axis powers in World War II, Japan surrendered in 1945 after atomic bombs were dropped on Hiroshima and Nagasaki. In 1946, the Emperor Hirohito renounced the imperial claim to divinity, remaining head of state in a constitutional monarchy. A highly industrialised country with few natural resources, Japan depends on imported oil, and nuclear power generation is very important. It is the world's leading fishing nation, and relies on imports of food, and exports, particularly of motor vehicles, electric and electronic products, ships, synthetic fibres, and steel. Area, 377 750 square kilometres (145,850 square miles). Population, 125,760,000. Capital, Tokyo.

Japan clover *n*. A leguminous plant, *Lespedeza striata*, native to Asia, cultivated as a forage plant and for soil improvement.

Japan Current *n*. *Japanese* **Ku·ro·shi·o** (kóor-ō-shée-ō). A warm ocean current flowing northeast from the Philippine Sea past southeastern Japan to the North Pacific.

Jap·a·nese (jáppə-néez ‖ -néess) *adj*. *Abbr*. **Jap.** Of or pertaining to Japan, or to the people, language, or culture of Japan. ~*n., pl.* **Japanese. 1.** A native or inhabitant of Japan, or a descendant of one. **2.** *Abbr*. **Jap.** The language of Japan, having no proven affinities to any other language.

Japanese andromeda *n*. An ornamental shrub, *Pieris japonica*, native to Japan, having small, early-blooming white flowers.

Japanese beetle *n*. A metallic-green and brownish beetle, *Popillia japonica*, native to eastern Asia, the larvae and adults of which are serious plant pests in North America.

Japanese cedar *n*. A tree, the **cryptomeria** *(see)*, or its wood.

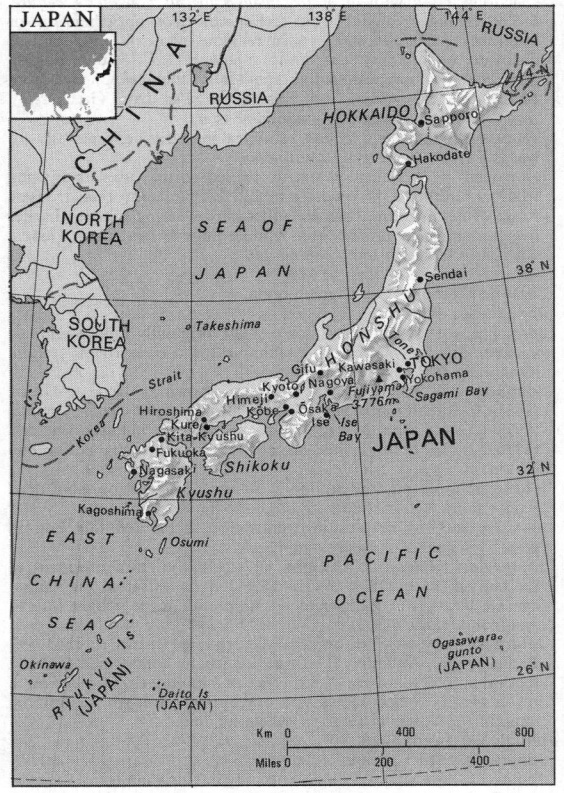

Japanese iris *n*. A plant, *Iris kaempferi*, native to Asia, and cultivated in many horticultural varieties for its large, flat, showy flowers.

Japanese ivy *n*. **Virginia creeper** *(see)*.

Japanese lantern *n*. A paper lantern; a Chinese lantern.

Japanese maple *n*. A shrub or small tree, *Acer palmatum*, native to eastern Asia and widely cultivated for its decorative foliage.

Japanese river fever *n*. *Pathology*. **Scrub typhus** *(see)*.

Japan paper *n*. A strong fibrous paper made in Japan, and often used for printing etchings.

Japan wax *n*. A pale yellow, solid wax obtained from the berries of certain plants of the genus *Rhus* and used in wax matches, soaps, food packaging, and as a substitute for beeswax.

jape (jayp) *v*. **japed, japing, japes.** *Archaic & Literary.* —*intr*. To joke or quip. —*tr*. To joke about; make sport of. ~*n*. **1.** A trick or prank. **2.** *Literary*. A joke or quip. [Middle English *japen*, to trick, joke, from Old French *japper*, to yap (imitative).] —**jap·er** *n*. —**jap·er·y** *n*.

Ja·pheth (jáy-feth, -fith). Also **Ja·phet** (-fet, -fit). The third son of Noah, in some traditions considered the ancestor of the Indo-European race. Genesis 5:32.

Ja·phet·ic (jə-féttik) *adj*. **1.** Of or pertaining to Japheth or his descendants. **2.** Designating a discredited linguistic grouping that attempted to associate Basque, Etruscan, and sometimes Sumerian and Elamite with the Caucasian languages.

japie. Variant of **jaap**.

ja·pon·i·ca (jə-pónnikə) *n*. **1.** A shrub, *Chaenomeles speciosa*, native to Japan, that has quincelike fruit and is cultivated for its red flowers. Also called "flowering quince", "Japanese quince". **2.** A shrub, the **camellia** *(see)*. [New Latin, "Japanese", from *Japonia*, JAPAN.]

Jaques-Dal·croze (zhaák-dal-krōz), **Emile** (1865-1950). Swiss composer. He developed eurhythmics, an expression of the rhythm of music through physical movement, which influenced dance through Dame Marie Rambert.

jar¹ (jar) *n*. **1.** A cylindrical glass or earthenware vessel with a wide mouth and usually without handles. **2.** The contents of such a vessel; a jarful. **3.** *British Informal*. A glass of beer. [French *jarre*, from Provençal *jarra*, from Arabic *jarrah*, large earthen vase.]

jar² *v*. **jarred, jarring, jars.** —*intr*. **1.** To make or utter a harsh, discordant sound. **2.** To have an unpleasant or disturbing effect; grate: *His voice jarred on her nerves.* **3.** To shake or shiver from impact. **4.** To clash or conflict. —*tr*. **1.** To cause to make a harsh, discordant sound. **2.** To bump or cause to move or shake from impact. **3.** To startle or unsettle; shock. ~*n*. **1.** A jolt; a shock. **2.** A harsh or grating sound. [16th century : probably imitative.]

jar·di·nière (zhárdin-yaír ‖ *U.S.* járd'n-éer) *n*. **1.** A large, decorative stand or pot for plants. **2.** Diced, cooked vegetables served as a garnish with meat. [French, feminine of *jardinier*, gardener, from *jardin*, garden, from Old French, from Vulgar Latin *gardīnus* (unattested), GARDEN.]

jar·ful (jár-fool) *n., pl.* **-fuls. 1.** The amount a jar will hold. **2.** The contents of a jar.

jar·gon¹ (járgən) *n*. **1.** The specialised or technical language of a trade, profession, class, or fellowship; cant: *"She could not follow the ugly academic jargon"* (Virginia Woolf). Compare **argot, slang. 2.** A hybrid language or dialect; pidgin. **3.** Nonsensical, incoherent, or meaningless utterance; gibberish: *"Wholly a blessed time: when jargon might abate, and . . . genuine speech begin"* (Thomas Carlyle). —*intr.v*. **jargoned, -goning, -gons.** To speak in or use jargon. [Middle English *iargoun, gargoun*, meaningless chatter, from Old French *jargoun, gargon*, "twittering" (probably imitative).] —**jar·gon·ise** *v*. —**jar·gon·is·tic** (-ístik) *adj*.

jar·gon² *n*. Also **jar·goon** (-gōon). A smoky, yellow, or colourless variety of zircon. [French, ZIRCON.]

jarl (yarl). *n*. A great chieftain or nobleman of the medieval Scandinavians. [Old Norse, from Germanic *erilaz* (unattested), EARL.]

Jarls·berg (yárlz-berg, -bair) *n*. A mild, pale yellow Norwegian cheese. [After *Jarlsberg*, Norway, an estate west of Oslo.]

jar·o·site (járrə-sīt) *n*. A yellow to brown mineral, $KFe_3(SO_4)_2(OH)_6$, occurring in masses or hexagonal crystals. [After *Barranco Jaroso*, Almeria, Spain, where it was first found.]

jar·rah (járrə) *n*. An Australian eucalyptus tree, *Eucalyptus marginata*, widely grown for its hard, red-brown timber. [From a native Australian language.]

Jar·row (járrō). An industrial town in northeast England, situated on the river Tyne. The early historian, the Venerable Bede, lived at Jarrow in a 7th-century monastery, whose ruins survive. In the 20th century, Jarrow developed important shipyards and steelworks, whose collapse during the 1930s Depression led to 80 per cent local unemployment. The Jarrow March (1936) of the unemployed to London is famous in trade union history.

Jar·ry (zha-rée), **Alfred** (1873-1907). French writer. His play *Ubu Roi* (1896), which denounced bourgeois lust for power, is regarded as perhaps the earliest example of the Theatre of the Absurd.

Ja·ru·zel·ski (jarrōō-zélski), **Wojciech Witold** (1923-). Polish general and politician. From 1981-85 he was Chairman of Poland's Council of Ministers, and was President and Head of State 1985-92.

Jas. 1. James. **2.** James (New Testament).

jas·mine (jáz-min, jass-) *n*. **1.** Any of several shrubs of the genus *Jasminum*; especially, *J. officinalis*, native to Asia, having fragrant white flowers used in making perfume. Also called "jessamine". See **winter jasmine. 2.** Any of several other plants or shrubs having

823

fragrant flowers, such as the frangipani *(red jasmine).* **3.** Light to brilliant yellow. [French *jasmin,* from Arabic *yās(a)mīn,* from Persian *yasmīn, yāsman†.*]

Ja·son (jáyss'n). *Greek Mythology.* The leader of the Argonauts in quest of the Golden Fleece; husband of Medea.

jas·pé (jáspay) *adj.* Being randomly coloured like jasper. [French.]

jas·per (jáspər) *n.* An opaque variety of quartz, red or reddish brown in colour. [Middle English *jaspre,* from Old French *jasp(r)e,* from Latin *jaspis,* from Greek *iaspis,* from Semitic, akin to Assyrian *ashpū,* Aramaic *yashb,* and Hebrew *yashpāh.*]

Jasper National Park. Second largest national park in Canada, established in 1907 in the Rocky Mountains of Alberta. It has glaciers, hot springs, and game reserves.

Jas·pers (yáss-pərz, German -pərss), **Karl (Theodor)** (1883–1969). German philosopher and psychologist, advocate of existentialism. His works include *Philosophie* (1932).

jasper ware *n.* A fine stoneware invented by Josiah Wedgwood, often coloured by metallic oxides with raised designs in white.

Jat (jaat ‖ jaat) *n.* A member of an Indo-Aryan people of the Punjab and Uttar Pradesh. [Hindi *jāt†.*]

ja·to (jáytō) *n.* **1.** A takeoff aided by an auxiliary jet or rocket. **2.** An auxiliary unit providing thrust for such a takeoff. [From JATO.]

JATO jet assisted takeoff.

jaun·dice (jáwn-diss ‖ jaán-) *n.* **1.** Yellowish discoloration of the skin and white of the eyes due to excess bile pigment in the blood. It is caused by any of several pathological conditions such as hepatitis, in which normal processing of bile is interrupted. Also called "icterus". **2.** A state of jealousy or bitterness. [Middle English *jaun(d)is,* from Old French *jaunice,* from *jaune,* yellow, from Latin *galbinus,* greenish yellow, pale green, from *galbus†.*]

jaun·diced (jáwn-dist ‖ jaán-) *adj.* **1.** Affected with jaundice. **2.** Affected by envy, cynicism, prejudice, or hostility; embittered. **3.** Yellow or yellowish.

jaunt (jawnt ‖ jaant) *n.* A short trip or excursion, usually taken for pleasure; an outing.
~*intr.v.* **jaunted, jaunting, jaunts.** To make a short journey, especially for pleasure. [16th century : origin obscure.]

jaunt·ing car (jáwnting ‖ jaánting) *n.* A light, open cart with seats hung back to back over its two wheels, once commonly used in Ireland. Also called "jaunty car".

jaun·ty (jáwnti ‖ jaánti) *adj.* **-tier, -tiest. 1.** Having or expressing a buoyant or self-confident air; carefree. **2.** Crisp and dapper in appearance; smart. [Earlier *jentee, jantee,* elegant, "genteel", from French *gentil.*] —**jaun·ti·ly** *adv.* —**jaun·ti·ness** *n.*

Jav. Javanese.

ja·va (jáavə ‖ jávvə) *n. U.S. Informal.* Coffee. [From JAVA.]

Ja·va (jáavə ‖ *U.S. also* jávvə). The most populous island of Indonesia, situated between the Indian Ocean and the Java Sea. From the 1st century A.D. a distinctive Hindu-Javanese civilisation flourished for 16 centuries. Java was later converted to Islam, and was colonised by the Dutch from the 17th century. The island became part of the Republic of Indonesia in 1950. The island has well-irrigated soil producing rice, sugar, tea, and kapok. Java also has reserves of oil and is an important producer of textiles. The most industrialised of the Indonesian islands, Java includes the nation's three largest cities: Jakarta (the capital), Surabaya, and Bandung.

Java man *n.* A type of primitive man, **Pithecanthropus** *(see).*

Jav·a·nese (jaávə-née̯z ‖ -néess, *U.S.* jávvə-) *adj. Abbr.* **Jav.** Of or pertaining to Java, or to the people, language, or culture of Java.
~*n., pl.* **Javanese.** *Abbr.* **Jav. 1.** A native or inhabitant of Java. **2.** The Indonesian language spoken in Java.

Java sparrow *n.* A small, greyish weaver bird, *Padda oryzivora,* native to tropical Asia and often kept as a cage bird.

jave·lin (jáv-lin, jávvə-) *n.* **1.** A light spear thrown with the hand and used as a weapon. **2.** A metal or metal-tipped spear, weighing 800 grams (1 pound 12 ounces) for men, 600 grams (1 pound 5 ounces) for women, used in contests of distance throwing. **3.** The athletic field event in which such a spear is thrown. [French *javeline,* from Old French, variant of *javelot,* from Celtic.]

Ja·velle water, Ja·vel water (jávv'l, jə-vél, zhə-) *n.* An aqueous solution of potassium or sodium hypochlorite, used as a disinfectant and bleaching agent. [From *Javel,* former French town, now part of Paris.]

jaw (jaw) *n.* **1.** Either of two bony or cartilaginous structures in most vertebrates forming the framework of the mouth and holding the teeth. See **mandible, maxilla. 2. a.** The anatomical part forming the wall of the mouth and serving to open and close it. **b.** The corresponding parts in insects and other invertebrate animals. **3.** *Plural.* A mechanical device resembling the jaws, such as the hinged parts in a mechanical grab or the gripping parts of a vice. **4.** *Plural.* The walls or narrow mouth of a pass, canyon, or cavern. **5.** *Plural.* The engulfing power of some undesirable force: *the jaws of death.* **6.** *Informal.* **a.** Impudent argument or expression of opposition: *Don't give me any jaw.* **b.** Idle chatter. **c.** A moralising lecture.
~*intr.v.* **jawed, jawing, jaws.** *Informal.* To talk or chat, especially at tedious length. [Middle English *iawe, iowe,* from Old French *joe†.*]

ja·wan (jə-waán) *n.* A soldier in the Indian Army, especially a private. [Urdu, "young man".]

Ja·wa·ra (jaá-wərə), **Sir Dawda (Kairaba)** (1924–). Prime minister (1962) and president (1970) of The Gambia, until the union with

Senegal (1982), when he became vice-president of Senegambia. He was deposed in 1994.

jaw·bone (jáw-bōn) *n.* Any bone of the jaw; especially, the bone of the lower jaw. See **mandible.**

jaw·break·er (jáw-braykər) *n.* **1.** *Informal.* A word which is difficult to pronounce. **2.** A machine that crushes rock or ore.

jay (jay) *n.* **1.** Any of various often crested birds of the family Corvidae, often having a loud, harsh call. The Eurasian jay, *Garrulus glandarius,* is brownish-pink with blue and white wings and a black and white crest. **2.** A noisy or talkative person; a chatterbox. **3.** *Chiefly U.S.* A gullible or inexperienced person. [Middle English, from Old French, from Late Latin *gāius* and *gāia†.*]

Ja·ya Peak (jī-ə). Also **Mount Sukarno.** Highest mountain in Indonesia (5 039 metres; 16,532 feet), situated in the Maoke range of West Irian.

Ja·ya·war·den·e (jī-ə-waár-dinə, jáy-), **Junius Richard** (1906–96). Sri Lankan politician. He became president in 1978 (stepped down 1989), and was Prime Minister 1977–88.

jay·walk (jáy-wawk) *intr.v.* **-walked, -walking, -walks.** To cross a street or recklessly or at an unauthorised place. [From JAY (inexperienced person).] —**jay·walk·er** *n.*

jazz (jaz) *n.* **1.** A kind of native American music first played extemporaneously by black bands in Southern U.S. towns at the turn of the century. In most styles it has syncopated rhythms with solo and ensemble improvisations on basic tunes and chord patterns, and, in more recent styles, a highly sophisticated harmonic idiom. **2.** Bigband dance music, popular especially in the 1920s and 1930s. **3.** *Chiefly U.S. Informal.* Animation; enthusiasm. **4.** *Informal.* Extreme exaggeration; nonsense: *all that jazz about his big deals.* —**and all that jazz.** *Informal.* And so on; and all that sort of thing. ~*v.* **jazzed, jazzing, jazzes.** —*tr.* To play in a jazz style. —*intr. Informal.* To play or dance to jazz. —**jazz up.** *Informal.* **1.** To play or arrange (music) in a more lively or improvised way, as by a jazz arrangement. **2.** To make more interesting; enliven. [20th century : origin obscure.] —**jazz·er** *n.*

jazz ballet *n.* **1.** A choreographed dance work performed to jazz music. **2.** This style of dancing.

jazz-rock (jáz-rók) *n.* Music that blends jazz elements and the heavy repetitive rhythms of rock.

jazz·y (jázzi) *adj.* **-ier, -iest. 1.** Resembling jazz; rhythmical. **2.** *Slang.* Showy; vivid; flashy. —**jazz·i·ly** *adv.* —**jazz·i·ness** *n.*

J.C. **1.** Jesus Christ. **2.** Julius Caesar.

J.C.D. **1.** Doctor of Canon Law [Latin *Juris Canonici Doctor*]. **2.** Doctor of Civil Law [Latin *Juris Civilis Doctor*].

J.C.R. Junior Common Room.

J.C.S. Joint Chiefs of Staff.

jct. junction.

J.D. **1.** Doctor of Laws [Latin *Jurum Doctor*]. **2.** juvenile delinquent.

jeal·ous (jélləss) *adj.* **1.** Fearful or wary of being supplanted; apprehensive of loss of position or affection. **2.** Resentful or bitter in rivalry; envious. Often used with *of.* **3.** Possessively watchful; vigilant: *He kept a jealous guard on what he had hoarded.* **4.** Protective; solicitous. Used with *of* or *for: jealous for his daughter's welfare.* **5.** Concerning or arising from feelings of envy, apprehension, or bitterness: *jealous thoughts.* **6.** In religious contexts, intolerant of disloyalty or infidelity; autocratic: *a jealous God.* [Middle English *gelus, ielus,* jealous, zealous for, from Old French *gelos, jelous,* from Medieval Latin *zēlōsus,* from Late Latin *zēlus,* from Greek *zēlos,* zeal.] —**jeal·ous·ly** *adv.* —**jeal·ous·ness** *n.*

jeal·ous·y (jéllə-si) *n., pl.* **-ies. 1.** A jealous attitude, especially towards a rival. **2.** Close watchfulness.

jean (jeen) *n.* **1.** A heavy, strong, twilled cotton, used in making trousers, uniforms, and work clothes. **2.** *Plural.* Informal trousers made of denim, jean, or some other hard-wearing fabric. [Earlier *iene fustian, geane fustian,* from Middle English *Jene, Gene,* Genoa, where it was first made.] —**jean** *adj.*

Jeanne d'Arc. See **Joan of Arc.**

Jean de Bologne. See **Giambologna.**

Jedda. See **Jiddah.**

Jeep (jeep) *n.* A trademark for a small, originally military, motor vehicle with four-wheel drive, suitable for use on rough terrain. [Originally *G.P.,* "general purpose".]

Jeeps (jeeps), **Richard Eric Gautrey,** known as Dick or Dickie (1931–). British rugby player and chairman of the Sports Council (1978–85). He won 24 rugby caps as a scrum half for England (1956–62). In 1976–77, he was president of the Rugby Football Union.

jeer (jeer) *v.* **jeered, jeering, jeers.** —*intr.* To speak or shout derisively; mock. Often used with *at.* —*tr.* To deride; taunt.
~*n.* A scoffing or taunting remark or shout. [Middle English *geere†.*] —**jeer·er** *n.* —**jeer·ing·ly** *adv.*

Jef·fer·son (jéffər-s'n), **Thomas** (1743–1826). Third president of the United States (1801–09). In 1776 Jefferson drafted the American Declaration of Independence. As president, he bought Louisiana from France (1803).

Jef·freys of Wem (jéffriz əv wém), **George, 1st Baron** (*c.* 1648–89). English judge. As James II's Chief Justice, he condemned to death more than 150 followers of the Duke of Monmouth, who had led a revolt (1685). When James was overthrown, Jeffreys was imprisoned in the Tower of London, where he died.

jehad. Variant of **jihad.**

Jehan. See **Shah Jahan.**

Je·ho·vah (ji-hṓvə, jə-). God, especially in Christian translations of the Old Testament. See **Tetragrammaton**. [From the Hebrew Tetragrammaton YHWH with the addition of the vowel points of ADO-NAI.]

Jehovah's Witness *n.* A member of a religious sect founded in the United States during the late 19th century, the followers of which practise active evangelism, preach the imminent approach of the millennium, and are strongly opposed to war and to the authority of organised government in matters of conscience.

Je·ho·vist (ji-hṓvist, jə-) *n.* The author of portions of the Hexateuch, **Yahwist** (*see*).

je·june (ji-jōōn ‖ jə-) *adj.* **1.** Childish; immature; unsophisticated. **2.** Lacking in substance; insipid; dull: *"and there pour forth jejune words and useless empty phrases"* (Anthony Trollope). **3.** Not nourishing; insubstantial. [From Latin *jējūnus*, hungry, fasting.] —**je·june·ly** *adv.* —**je·june·ness** *n.*

je·ju·num (ji-jōō-nəm ‖ jə-) *n., pl.* **-na** (-nə). The section of the small intestine between the duodenum and the ileum. [Medieval Latin *jējūnum* (*intestīnum*), "the fasting (intestine)", translation of Greek *nēstis*, the jejunum, from *nēstis*, fasting, so named because it was always found (in dissection) empty.] —**je·ju·nal** *adj.*

Jekaterinburg. See **Yekaterinburg.**

Je·kyll and Hyde (jéck'l, jéckil, *rarely* jéekil; hīd) *n. Informal.* A person who has two distinct alternating personalities. [After *The Strange Case of Dr. Jekyll and Mr. Hyde* (1886), novel by R.L. Stevenson.] —**Je·kyll-and-Hyde** *adj.*

jell (jel) *v.* **jelled, jelling, jells.** —*intr.* **1.** To become firm or gelatinous; congeal. **2.** *Informal.* To take shape or fall into place; become clear and definite; crystallise: *My ideas on the subject haven't jelled yet.* —*tr.* To cause to jell. [Back-formation from JELLY.]

jel·la·ba, jel·la·bah, djel·la·ba (jéllabə) *n.* A long, loose garment with a hood worn by men, especially in North Africa. [Arabic.]

Jel·li·coe (jélliko͞, **John Rushworth Jellicoe, 1st Earl,** (1859-1935). British naval officer, and governor of New Zealand (1920-24). He was Commander in Chief of the Grand Fleet that fought at Jutland (1916). He was created an earl (1925).

jel·lied (jéllid ‖ jélleed) *adj.* Prepared or cooked within jelly.

jel·li·fy (jélli-fī) *v.* **-fied, -fying, -fies.** —*intr.* To become jelly. —*tr.* To make into jelly. —**jel·li·fi·ca·tion** (-fi-káysh'n) *n.*

jel·ly¹ (jélli) *n., pl.* **-lies. 1.** A soft, semisolid food substance with a resilient consistency, made by the setting of a liquid containing pectin or gelatine, or by the addition of gelatine or a similar substance to a liquid, especially: **a.** A fruit-flavoured dessert set with gelatine. **b.** A preserve made from fruit juice and sugar set with pectin and used as a jam. **c.** A savoury food such as aspic or calf's-foot jelly. **2.** Any substance with the consistency of jelly, such as a petroleum ointment. **3.** Anything similar or likened to jelly. ~*v.* **jellied, -lying, -lies.** —*tr.* **1.** To make into or cause to become jelly. **2.** To set or prepare with jelly. —*intr.* To become jelly; set. [Middle English *geli, gely*, from Old French *gelee*, frost, jelly, from Vulgar Latin *gelāta* (unattested), from Latin, feminine past participle of *gelāre*, to freeze.]

jelly² *n. British Slang.* Gelignite.

jelly baby *n.* A small soft gelatinous sweet in the shape of a baby.

jel·ly·bean (jélli-been) *n.* A small bean-shaped sweet with a hardened sugar coating over a chewy centre.

jel·ly·fish (jélli-fish) *n., pl.* **-fishes** or collectively **jellyfish. 1.** Any of numerous usually free-swimming marine coelenterates of the class Scyphozoa, characteristically having a gelatinous, tentacled, often bell-shaped medusoid stage as the dominant or only phase of its life cycle. **2.** Any of various similar or related coelenterates or other organisms. **3.** *Informal.* A person who lacks force of character, resilience, or self-control.

jem·a·dar (jémmə-daar) *n.* A native officer of the former British army in India with a rank corresponding to lieutenant. [Urdu *jama'dār* : Persian *jama'at*, body of men, from Arabic *jam'*, collection + *dār*, holder, from Old Persian.]

jem·be (jém-bi ‖ *locally* -be) *n. East African.* A short-handled hoe with the blade set at right angles, used with a swinging, overarm motion to break up the soil. [Swahili.]

jem·my (jémmi) *n., pl.* **-mies.** Also *U.S.* **jim·my** (jímmi). A short crowbar with curved ends, especially when regarded as a burglar's tool. ~*tr.v.* **jemmied, -mying, -mies.** Also *U.S.* **jimmy.** To prise open with or as if with a jemmy. [From the pet name for *James*.]

Je·na (yáynə). A town in eastern Germany, situated on the river Saale. Fichte, Hegel, and others taught at its university (founded 1557-58). The town is also the headquarters of the Zeiss optical firm, founded in 1846. Napoleon defeated the Prussians at Jena (1806).

je ne sais quoi (zhə-nə-say-kwáa, zhən-say-) *n. French.* An indefinable or unspecifiable distinctive quality. ["I don't know what".]

Jenghiz Khan. See **Genghis Khan.**

Jen·kins (jéng-kinz, jén-). **Roy (Harris), Baron Jenkins of Hillhead** (1920-). British politician. He was Home Secretary (1965), Chancellor of the Exchequer (1967-70), and President of the European Commission (1977-81). Jenkins was a founder member of the Social Democratic Party (launched 1981) and its first elected leader (1982-83). Chancellor of Oxford University (1987); biographer of W.E. Gladstone (1995).

Jen·ner (jénnər), **Edward** (1749-1823). British physician and pioneer of vaccination. In 1796 he found that smallpox could be prevented by inoculation with the substance from cowpox lesions.

jen·net, gen·et (jénnit) *n.* **1.** A small Spanish saddle horse. **2.** A

female donkey or ass; a jenny. [Middle English *jennett, genett*, from Old French *genet*, from Spanish *jinete*, light horseman, from Arabic *Zenetī*, Berber tribe famed for horsemanship.]

jen·ny (jénni) *n., pl.* **-nies. 1.** A female donkey or ass. **2.** A female wren. **3.** A spinning jenny. **4.** A hand-operated machine for bending sheet metal at an angle. [From *Jenny*, pet form of *Jane*.]

jeop·ard·ise, jeop·ard·ize (jéppər-dīz) *tr.v.* **-ised, -ising, -ises.** To expose to danger of loss or injury; make vulnerable or precarious; imperil.

jeop·ard·y (jéppərdi) *n., pl.* **-ies. 1.** Danger or risk of loss or injury; peril; vulnerability. **2.** *Law.* The defendant's risk or danger of conviction when put on trial. —See Synonyms at **danger**. [Middle English *jeopartie*, even chance, from Old French *jeu parti*, "divided play, even chance" : *jeu*, game, from Latin *jocus*, jest, game + *parti*, past participle of *partir*, to divide, from Latin *partīre*, from *pars* (stem *part-*), PART.]

Jeph·thah (jéf-thə ‖ jép-). A judge of Israel who sacrificed his daughter to fulfil a rash vow. Judges 11-12.

je·quir·i·ty bean (ji-kwírrəti) *n.* The **Indian liquorice** (*see*) or any of its seeds. [From Tupi-Guarani *jekirití*.]

jer·bo·a (jər-bṓ-ə, jér-) *n.* Any of various small, leaping rodents of the family Dipodidae, of desert regions of Asia and northern Africa, having long hind legs and a long, tufted tail. Also called "desert rat". [New Latin, from Medieval Latin *jerbōa*, from Arabic *yerbō', yarbu'*, flesh of the loins (from the animal's highly developed thighs).]

jer·e·mi·ad (jérri-mí-əd, -ad) *n.* An elaborate and prolonged lamentation or a tale of woe. [French *jérémiade*, after *Jérémie*, JEREMIAH (the prophet who lamented the decline of morals).]

Jer·e·mi·ah¹ (jérri-mí-ə). Also in Douay Bible **Jer·e·mi·as** (-əss, -ass). A Major Prophet of the seventh and sixth centuries B.C. See **Lamentations**. [Late Latin *Jeremias*, from Hebrew *Yirmayāh(ū)*, "the Lord is exalted".]

Jeremiah² *n.* Also in Douay Bible **Jer·e·mi·as** (-əss, -ass). *Abbr.* **Jer.** A book in the Old Testament with the prophecies of Jeremiah.

Jeremiah³ *n. Sometimes small j.* A person given to bewailing the evils of his day or prophesying disasters to come. [After the Old Testament prophet.]

jer·e·pi·go (jérri-pée-gō) *n.* In South Africa, a sweet fortified red or white wine. [Portuguese *cheripiga*.]

Je·rez (de la Fron·te·ra) (he-réth, khe-; de la fron-taír-ə). A city in southwest Spain, situated on the river Guadalete in Andalusia. It is famous for the making of sherry, whose name derives from that of the city.

Jer·i·cho (jérri-kō). Ancient city near the modern village of Al Ariha, just north of the Dead Sea, in the part of Jordan occupied by Israel in 1967. The earliest remains date back to before 7000 B.C. and probably represent the world's oldest known settlement. By the time the Israelites under Joshua captured Jericho (c.1300 B.C.) it was a thriving Canaanite town. Herod the Great destroyed it (c.30 B.C.) and later rebuilt it with a great fortress and palace in Hellenistic style.

jerk¹ (jerk) *v.* **jerked, jerking, jerks.** —*tr.* **1.** To move (something) with a sharp, sudden, abrupt motion; give an abrupt thrust, push, pull, or twist to: *He jerked his head as a signal.* **2.** To throw or toss with a quick, abrupt motion. **3.** In weightlifting, to raise (the weight) from shoulder-height to above the head. **4.** To utter abruptly or sharply. Used with *out.* —*intr.* **1.** To move in sudden abrupt motions; jolt: *The train jerked ahead.* **2.** To make spasmodic motions: *His legs jerked from fatigue.* ~*n.* **1.** A sudden, abrupt motion, such as a yank, tug, or twist. **2.** A jolting or lurching motion. **3.** *Physiology.* A sudden spasmodic, muscular movement, especially a reflex movement. **4.** *Plural.* Violent convulsive twitching and shaking, often resulting from excitement. **5.** *Plural. U.S. Informal.* **Chorea** (*see*). **6.** *Plural.* **Physical jerks** (*see*). **7.** *Slang.* A stupid, objectionable, or fatuous person. [16th century : perhaps imitative.] —**jerk·er** *n.*

jerk² *tr.v.* **jerked, jerking, jerks.** To cut (meat) into long strips and dry in the sun or cure by exposing to smoke. [Back-formation from JERKY (cured meat).]

jer·kin (jérkin) *n.* **1.** A man's or woman's sleeveless and collarless jacket. **2.** A short, close-fitting coat or jacket, usually of leather, worn in former times. [16th century : origin obscure.]

jerk·y¹ (jérki) *adj.* **-ier, -iest.** Characterised by jerks or jerking. —**jerk·i·ly** *adv.* —**jerk·i·ness** *n.*

jerky² *n.* Cured meat, **charqui** (*see*). [Earlier *jerkin beef*, from CHARQUI.]

jer·o·bo·am (jérrə-bṓ-əm) *n.* An outsize wine bottle of varying capacity, usually holding, in Britain, the equivalent of six normal-sized bottles. [Humorously after *Jeroboam I*, king of northern Israel, who was a "mighty man of valour" (I Kings 11:28).]

Je·rome (jə-rṓm, ji-, je-, jérrəm), **Saint,** born Sophronius Eusebius Hieronymus (c. 347-420). Dalmatian priest, scholar, and Doctor of the Church. His *Vulgate* was the first authentic Latin translation of the Bible from Hebrew.

jer·ry (jérri) *n., pl.* **-ries. British Informal.** A chamber pot. [Perhaps short for JEROBOAM.]

Jer·ry (jérri) *n., pl.* **-ries. Chiefly British Slang.** A German; especially, a German soldier. [Alteration of GERMAN.]

jer·ry·build (jérri-bild) *tr.v.* **-built** (-bilt), **-building, -builds.** To build shoddily, flimsily, and cheaply. [19th century : origin obscure.] —**jer·ry·build·er** *n.*

jerry can *n.* Also **jer·ri·can.** A flat-sided can for storing or transporting liquids, used especially for motor fuels and having a capacity of between 20 and 23 litres (4.4 and 5 gallons). [*Jerry* (German) + CAN, probably from its German origin.]

jer·sey (jérzi) *n., pl.* **-seys.** **1.** A soft, plain-knitted fabric used for clothing. **2.** A knitted shirt worn, especially by men, as a uniform in certain sports. **3.** A close-fitting knitted garment for the upper part of the body, usually made of wool. [Originally worn by the fishermen of JERSEY.]

Jer·sey¹ (jérzi). The largest of the Channel Islands, situated in the English Channel to the west of Normandy. The island was annexed by the Normans in A.D. 933, and French influence has persisted since autonomy was granted in 1204. Dairy goods, early potatoes, and tomatoes are important products. The capital is St. Helier.

Jersey² *n.* Any of a breed of fawn-coloured dairy cattle developed on the island of Jersey.

Jersey City. Coastal city in New Jersey, United States, situated by the mouth of the Hudson River. It is connected to Manhattan Island by the Hudson River tunnels. Its industries include oil refining, chemicals, and paper.

Je·ru·sa·lem (jə-róō-sə-ləm, -lem, -sləm). *Arabic* **Al Quds.** The capital of Israel, situated in the east of the country. Of immense historical and religious importance, it was the royal city of King David in the 10th century B.C., and destroyed by Nebuchadnezzar in the 6th. Subsequently rebuilt, it was occupied by Alexander the Great (332 B.C.). Jerusalem was taken by Pompey (65 B.C.) and Jesus Christ was crucified there under the Roman procurator Pontius Pilate. The city was in Islamic hands (7th–11th centuries A.D.), and made capital of a Crusader kingdom (1099) by Godfrey of Bouillon. Reconquered by Saladin (1187), Jerusalem remained in Islamic hands, apart from brief intervals (1229–39, 1243–44), until World War I. In 1917, the city was captured from the Turks by the British. In 1948 it was divided between Israel and Jordan. Israel occupied the Jordanian sector in the Six Day War (1967), and its status remains disputed today. Jerusalem has innumerable mosques, churches, and synagogues, as well as holy places of great historical importance, such as the Western or Wailing Wall, sacred to the Jews as the major surviving part of the second Hebrew Temple. The Mount of Olives and the 4th-century Church of the Holy Sepulchre are among many Christian sites, while the 7th-century Dome of the Rock is sacred to Islam.

Jerusalem artichoke *n.* **1.** A North American sunflower, *Helianthus tuberosus*, having yellow, rayed flowers and widely cultivated for its edible tubers. **2.** The tuber of this plant, eaten as a vegetable. Also called "artichoke". [*Jerusalem,* alteration (by folk etymology) of Italian *girasole,* sunflower, GIRASOL.]

Jerusalem Bible *n.* A translation of the Bible into various modern European languages, initiated by the Biblical School of Jerusalem and used especially in the Roman Catholic Church.

Jerusalem cherry *n.* A small shrub, *Solanum pseudo-capsicum,* native to the Old World, bearing inedible reddish fruit and used as a house plant.

Jerusalem cross *n.* A cross with four arms, each terminating in a crossbar.

jess (jess) *n.* A short strap fastened around the leg of a hawk or other bird used in falconry, and to which a leash may be fastened. —*tr.v.* **jessed, jessing, jesses.** To put jesses on (a hawk). [Middle English *ges(se),* from Old French *ges,* "a throwing", "something thrown around", from Vulgar Latin *jectus* (unattested), variant of Latin *jactus,* from *jacere,* to throw.]

jessamine. Variant of **jasmine.**

Jes·se (jéssi). Father of King David. I Samuel 16.

Jesse tree *n.* A pictorial representation of the genealogy of Christ, proceeding from the stem of Jesse, found in church carvings and paintings, stained-glass windows, and manuscript illuminations. [After JESSE, father of David and ancestor of Christ, whose birth, in Christian belief, is prophesied by Isaiah: "And there shall come forth a rod out of the stem of Jesse, and a branch shall grow out of his roots" (Isaiah 11:1).]

jest (jest) *n.* **1.** Something said or done to provoke amusement and laughter. **2.** A humorous or frivolous tone or mood: *spoken in jest.* **3.** A jeering remark; a taunt. **4.** An object of ridicule; a laughing stock. **5.** *Obsolete.* A notable exploit. —See Synonyms at **joke.** —*v.* **jested, jesting, jests.** —*intr.* **1.** To act or speak playfully; make sport; joke. **2.** To make witty or amusing remarks. **3.** To utter scoffs or jeers; gibe. —*tr.* To say in jest. [Middle English *geste,* deed, tale, from Old French *geste, jeste,* from Latin *gesta,* exploits, from *gerere,* to do.]

jest·er (jéstər) *n.* One given to jesting; especially, a clown or buffoon employed by a king or nobleman at medieval courts.

Je·su (jée-zew ‖ -zōō; *Latin* yáy-sōō). *Poetic.* A form of the name *Jesus* used in addressing Him in hymns and prayers. [Late Latin.]

Jes·u·it (jézzew-it, jézhoo-) *n.* **1.** A member of the Society of Jesus, a Roman Catholic order founded by St. Ignatius Loyola in 1534, active in missionary and other work. **2.** *Often small* **j.** One given to excessively subtle debating or legalistic arguments. Used derogatorily. [French *Jésuite,* from New Latin *Jesuita,* from JESUS.] —**Jes·u·it·i·cal** (-ittik'l) *adj.* —**Jes·u·it·i·cal·ly** *adv.*

Je·sus (jéezəss) (c. 4 B.C.–c. A.D.29). Son of Mary; founder of Christianity; regarded by Christians as the son of God and the Messiah. Also, in various contexts, "Jesus Christ", "Christ", "Christ Jesus", or "Jesus of Nazareth". —*interj.* Also **Jesus Christ.** Used as an oath or to express outrage

or surprise. [Late Latin *Jēsūs,* from Greek *Iēsous,* from Hebrew *yēshūa‘,* from *Yəhōshūa‘,* JOSHUA.]

Jesus freak *n.* A member of a movement among young Christians adapting traditional evangelicalism to a pop culture.

jet¹ (jet) *n.* **1.** A dense, black lignite that takes a high polish and is used for jewellery. **2.** A deep, dark black. [Middle English *ge(e)t, jeet,* from Anglo-French *geet,* Old French *jaiet,* from Latin *gagātēs,* from Greek *gagatēs,* "stone of *Gagai*" (town in Lycia).] —**jet** *adj.*

jet² *n.* **1.** A high-velocity fluid stream forced under pressure out of a small-diameter opening or nozzle. **2.** Something emitted in or as if in such a stream: *a jet of sparks.* **3.** An outlet, such as a spout or nozzle, for emitting such a stream. **4. a.** A jet-propelled vehicle; especially, a jet-propelled aircraft. **b.** A jet engine. —*v.* **jetted, jetting, jets.** —*intr.* **1.** To spurt or squirt out in a jet or jets. **2.** To travel by jet aircraft. —*tr.* To propel outwards or squirt, as under pressure. [Old French, from *jeter,* to spout forth, "to throw", from Vulgar Latin *jectāre* (unattested), from Latin *jactāre,* frequentative of Latin *jacere* (past participle *jactus*), to throw.]

jet black *n.* The colour of jet; a deep dark black.

je·té (zhə-táy) *n.* A ballet step executed by springing from one leg to the other, with a backward kick of the first leg. [French, from past participle of *jeter,* to throw.]

jet engine *n.* **1.** Any engine that develops thrust by ejecting a jet, especially by ejecting a jet of gaseous combustion products. **2.** Such an engine, using a gas turbine, equipped to consume atmospheric oxygen and used mainly to propel aircraft.

jet·foil (jét-foyl) *n.* A hydrofoil propelled by a jet engine.

jet lag *n.* The psychological dislocation and disruption of bodily rhythms due to high-speed air travel across several time zones.

jet·lin·er (jét-līnər) *n.* A large passenger-carrying jet aircraft.

jet pipe *n.* A pipe or duct fitted to the rear end of a jet engine, through which the exhaust gases are discharged.

jet-plane (jét-playn) *n.* A jet-propelled aircraft.

jet-pro·pelled (jét-prə-péld) *adj.* Propelled or powered by one or more jet engines.

jet propulsion *n.* Propulsion derived from the high-velocity expulsion of fluid or gas in a jet; especially, propulsion by jet engines.

jet·sam (jét-səm, -sam) *n.* **1.** Cargo or equipment thrown overboard to lighten a ship in distress. **2.** Discarded cargo or equipment found washed ashore. Used in the phrase *flotsam and jetsam.* Compare **flotsam.** **3.** Discarded odds and ends. [Earlier *jetson,* from JETTISON.]

jet set *n.* A social set made up of people who are rich, sophisticated, and fashionable, and who spend much of their time travelling from one fashionable place to another. —**jet-set·ter** *n.*

jet stream *n.* **1.** A high-altitude, narrow airstream in the troposphere, generally moving from a westerly direction. It may reach speeds of more than 320 kilometres (c. 200 miles) an hour. **2.** A high-speed stream of emitted fluid; a jet.

jet·ti·son (jétti-s'n, -z'n) *tr.v.* **-soned, -soning, -sons.** **1.** To cast off or overboard. **2.** To discard or abandon (something unwanted or burdensome) —*n.* **1.** The act of jettisoning. **2.** Jetsam. [From Middle English *jetteson,* a throwing overboard, from Anglo-French *getteson,* from Latin *jactātiō* (stem *jactātiōn-*), from *jactāre,* to throw. See **jet** (to propel).]

jet·ton (jétt'n) *n.* A stamped and engraved counter used especially as a chip in casinos. [French *jeton,* from *jeter,* to throw, add up (accounts).]

jet·ty¹ (jétti) *n., pl.* **-ties.** **1.** A pier, groyne, mole, or other structure projecting into a body of water to influence the current or tide or to protect a harbour or shoreline. **2.** A wharf. [Middle English *jette,* from Old French *jetee,* a jutting, projection, from the feminine past participle of *jeter,* to throw, project. See **jet** (to propel).]

jetty² *adj.* Resembling jet, especially in colour. —**jet·ti·ness** *n.*

jeu d'es·prit (zhér dess-prée, zhō) *n., pl.* **jeux d'esprit** (*pronounced as singular*). *French.* A display or stroke of wit, especially in literature. ["Play of wits".]

jeu·nesse do·rée (zhér-ness do-ráy, zher-néss, zhō-, daw-) *n.* *French. Used with a singular or plural verb.* Fashionable and wealthy young people. ["Gilded youth".]

Jew (jōō ‖ jew) *n.* **1.** An adherent of Judaism in its religious or cultural aspects. **2.** A descendant of the Hebrew people. [Middle English *Giw, Ju,* from Old French *giu, juiu,* from Latin *Jūdaeus,* from Greek *Ioudaios,* from Aramaic *Yəhūdāy* and Hebrew *Yəhūdī,* after the tribe of *Yəhūdāh,* JUDAH.]

Jew-bait·ing (jōō-bayting ‖ jéw-) *n.* Systematic persecution of Jews. —**Jew-bait·ing** *adj.* —**Jew-bait·er** *n.*

jew·el (jōō-əl, joorl, jōōl ‖ jéw-) *n.* **1.** A costly ornament of precious metal or gems used as an adornment. **2.** A precious stone; a gemstone. **3.** A small gem or gem substitute used as a bearing in a watch. **4.** A person or thing that is treasured or esteemed. **5.** A decorative glass boss in a stained glass window. —*tr.v.* **jewelled** or *U.S.* **jeweled, -elling** or *U.S.* **-eling, -els.** **1.** To adorn with jewels. **2.** To fit (a watch, for example) with jewels. [Middle English *iuel, gewel,* from Anglo-French *juel,* perhaps from *jeu,* game, jest, from Latin *jocus.*]

jew·el·fish (jōō-əl-fish) *n., pl.* **-fishes** or collectively **jewelfish.** A small, brilliantly coloured freshwater cichlid fish, *Hemichromis bimaculatus,* of tropical Africa, popular in home aquariums.

jew·el·ler, *U.S.* **jew·el·er** (jōō-əl-ər, joorl- ‖ jōōl-, jéw-) *n.* **1.** A person who makes, repairs, or deals in jewellery. **2.** A person who is skilled in the art of cutting, polishing, and setting gemstones.

jeweller's rouge *n.* Finely powdered ferric oxide, used as a metal polish.

jew·el·ler·y, *U.S.* **jew·el·ry** (jōō-əl-ri, -il-, jōorl- ‖ jōol-, jéw-, jōoləri) *n.* **1.** Jewels collectively. **2.** Any objects, such as bracelets, rings, necklaces, or the like, worn or used for adornment.

Jew·ess (jōō-iss, -ess ‖ jéw-) *n.* A Jewish woman or girl. See Usage note at **-ess.**

jew·fish (jōō-fish ‖ jéw-) *n. pl.* **-fishes** or collectively **jewfish.** Any of several large, dark marine fishes of the family Serranidae, such as *Epinephelus itajara,* of tropical Atlantic waters, and the Australian **mulloway** *(see).*

Jew·ish (jōō-ish ‖ jéw-) *adj.* Of, concerning, or characteristic of the Jews, their customs, or their religion. ~*n.* Yiddish. Not in technical usage. **—Jew·ish·ly** *adv.* **—Jew·ish·ness** *n.*

Jewish Autonomous Region. Also **Bi·ro·bi·dzhan** (bírrəbi-jáan). Former autonomous region of the R.S.F.S.R. (Russia), created in 1934 as a Siberian area of settlement for Soviet Jews. The area's remoteness and severe climate discouraged colonisation, and Jews remain in the minority.

Jewish calendar *n.* The lunisolar calendar used by the ancient Hebrews and for religious purposes today, calculating the date from the supposed year of creation, 3761 B.C. and based on a meteoric cycle of 19 years, with the 3rd, 6th, 8th, 11th, 14th, 17th, and 19th years of each cycle designated leap years. Also "Hebrew calendar".

Jew·ry (jōor-i ‖ jōō-ri, jéw-) *n.* **1.** Jews collectively; the Jewish people. **2.** The district of a medieval city inhabited by Jews.

jew's-ear (jōōz-éer ‖ jéwz-) *n.* An edible fungus, *Auricularia auricula,* having a brown or flesh-coloured saucer-shaped fruiting body and growing on wood.

jew's-harp, jews'-harp (jōōz-hárp ‖ jéwz-, *U.S. also* jōoss-, -haarp) *n.* A small musical instrument with a lyre-shaped metal frame that is held between the teeth when played, and a projecting steel tongue that is plucked to produce a soft, twanging sound. [Earlier *jew's trump,* perhaps alteration (influenced by JEW) of Dutch *jeugdtromp,* children's trumpet.]

jez·e·bel (jézzə-b'l, -bel) *n. Sometimes capital* **J.** A shamelessly immoral or scheming woman. [After JEZEBEL.]

Jez·e·bel (jézzə-b'l, -bel). Also in Douay Bible **Jez·a·bel.** Phoenician princess of the ninth century B.C. who as Ahab's wife and queen of Israel encouraged idolatry and the killing of the prophets of Israel. I Kings 16:31, 18:3.

JHVH, JHWH. Variants of YHWH.

–ji *suffix. Indian.* Used with a person's name as a sign of respect; for example, *Gandhiji.* [Hindi.]

Jiang Jie-shi (jyáng jáyshə), also known as Chiang Kai-shek (1887–1975). Chinese general and statesman. He joined the army and was active in the 1911 revolution. In 1918 he joined the Guomindang (Nationalist People's Party), and became its leader after the death of Sun Yat-sen in 1925. In 1926 he allied his forces with the Communists against the Chinese warlords, but a year later purged left-wingers from his own forces, and the alliance broke up (1928). Later he waged war on the Communists. After World War II civil war broke out again (1946–49) and when the Guomindang was defeated Jiang withdrew to Taiwan. He was president of Taiwan until his death.

Jiang Qing (jáng ching), also known as Chiang Ch'ing (1914–91). Wife of Mao Ze-dong (Tse-tung). She was an actress before she married him in 1939. After his death (1976) she was arrested, expelled from the Chinese Communist Party, and given a suspended death sentence for plotting rebellion. The government notice announcing her death said she had killed herself.

Jiang·su or **Chiang·su** or **Kiang·su** (ji-áng-sōō). Province of eastern China. It largely comprises the deltas of the Huang He and Chang Jiang, and is one of the country's smallest and most densely populated provinces. Nanjing is the capital.

Jiang·xi or **Chiang·hsi** or **Kiang·si** (jyáng-shée). Province of central southern China. It is a major rice-growing area, with resources of coal, uranium, tin, and lead. The capital is Nanchang. The southern part of the province was held by Mao Ze-dong's Communists (1930–34) during the war against the Guomindang, and it was from here that the Long March was begun.

jib¹ (jib) *n.* **1.** A triangular sail stretching from the foretopmast head to the jib boom and in small craft to the bowsprit or the bow. **2. a.** The arm of a mechanical crane. **b.** The boom of a derrick. **—the cut of (someone's) jib.** *Informal.* Someone's appearance, style, or manner. [17th century : origin obscure.]

jib² *intr.v.* **jibbed, jibbing, jibs. 1.** To draw back, baulk, or show reluctance. Often used with *at.* **2.** To stop short and turn restively from side to side; shy. **3.** Used of an animal. ~*n.* Also **jib·ber** (jíbbərr). An animal that jibs. [19th century : origin obscure.]

jib³. Variant of **gybe** (to shift a sail).

jibbah. Variant of **jubbah.**

jib boom *n.* A spar forming a continuation of the bowsprit.

jibe¹. Variant of **gybe** (to shift a sail).

jibe² (jīb) *intr.v.* **jibed, jibing, jibes.** *Chiefly U.S. Informal.* To be in accord; harmonise; agree. [19th century : origin obscure.]

jibe³. Variant of **gibe** (taunt).

Jibuti. See **Djibouti.**

Jid·dah (jíddə). Also **Jed·da** (jéddə) or **Jud·dah** (jéddə, júddə). A Red Sea port in western Saudi Arabia. It serves Mecca, which lies about 74 kilometres (46 miles) inland.

jif·fy (jíffi) *n., pl.* **-fies.** Also **jiff** (jif). *Informal.* A moment; no time at all: *I'll be there in a jiffy.* See Synonyms at **moment.** [18th century : origin obscure.]

jig (jig) *n.* **1. a.** Any of various lively kicking or leaping dances, usually in 6/8 time. **b.** A piece of music for such a dance. Also called "gigue". **2.** A joke or trick. **3.** A fishing lure, usually made of metal, and having one or more hooks, that darts or bobs about when pulled through the water. **4.** An apparatus for cleaning or separating ore by agitation in water. **5.** A device for guiding a tool or for holding machine work in place. ~*v.* **jigged, jigging, jigs.** —*intr.* **1.** To dance or play a jig. **2.** To move or bob up and down jerkily and rapidly. **3.** To operate a jig, as in fishing, machine work, or refining ore. —*tr.* **1.** To shake or jerk up and down or to and fro. **2.** To machine with the aid of a jig. **3.** To separate or clean (ore) by shaking a jig. [16th century : origin obscure.]

jig·ger¹ (jíggər) *n.* **1.** A person who jigs or operates a jig. **2. a.** A small measure for alcoholic drinks especially spirits. **b.** A small quantity of alcoholic drink. **3.** A short golf club with an iron head. **4.** In fishing, mining, or mechanics, a jig. **5.** Any device that operates with a jerking or jolting motion, such as a drill. **6.** *Nautical.* **a.** A light tackle. **b.** A small sail, set in the stern of a yawl, for example. **c.** A boat having such a sail. **d.** A jigger mast. **7.** *U.S. Informal.* Any trivial article or device whose name eludes one. **8.** A rest for a billiard cue.

jigger² *n.* A flea, the **chigoe** *(see).*

jig·gered (jíggərd) *adj. British Slang.* **1.** Very surprised. Used as a mild oath: *I'll be jiggered.* **2.** Exhausted; tired out.

jigger mast *n. Nautical.* **1.** The short after mast from which the jigger sail is set on a ketch or yawl. Also called "mizzenmast". **2.** The fourth mast aft on a four-masted ship. Also called "jigger".

jig·ge·ry-po·ke·ry (jíggəri-pókəri) *n. Chiefly British Informal.* Underhand scheming or behaviour; trickery. [From Scottish dialect *joukery-pawkery,* based on dialect *jouk*†, to duck, dodge.]

jig·gle (jígg'l) *v.* **-gled, -gling, -gles.** —*intr.* To move or rock lightly up and down or to and fro in an unsteady, jerky manner. —*tr.* To cause to move in this manner. ~*n.* A jiggling motion. [Frequentative of JIG (verb).]

jig·saw (jig-saw) *n.* **1.** A saw, often power-driven, with a narrow, vertical reciprocating blade, used to cut sharp curves. **2.** A jigsaw puzzle.

jigsaw puzzle *n.* A puzzle consisting of a picture pasted on cardboard or wood and cut into numerous interlocking pieces, the object being to reassemble the picture by fitting the pieces together. Also called "jigsaw".

ji·had, je·had (ji-hád ‖ -ha'ad) *n.* **1.** A Muslim holy war against infidels. **2.** A crusade. [Arabic *jihād.*]

Ji·lin or **Ki·rin** (jee-lín). Province of northeast China. It lies on the fertile Manchurian Plain, and is a major cereal producer. It also has extensive coal and iron deposits, the basis of a large industrial region centred on the cities of Changchun (the capital) and Jilin.

jil·la·roo (jíllə-rōo) *n., pl.* **-roos.** *Australian Informal.* A female jackeroo. [Alteration of JACKEROO, with allusion to *Jack and Jill.*]

jilt (jilt) *tr.v.* **jilted, jilting, jilts.** To reject or cast aside (a lover), especially after an engagement. ~*n.* A woman who discards a lover. [17th century : origin obscure.]

jim-crow (jim-krō) *adj. U.S. Slang.* Also **Jim-Crow. 1.** Favouring or promoting the segregation of blacks: *jim-crow policies.* **2.** For blacks only: *a jim-crow waiting room.* Usually considered offensive in both senses. [From JIM CROW.]

Jim Crow *n. U.S. Slang.* **1. a.** The systematic practice of segregating and suppressing black people. **b.** A black person. Used derogatorily in both senses. **2.** A device for straightening iron bars or rails. [After *Jim Crow,* a character in an act by Thomas D. Rice (1808–60), U.S. entertainer who based it on an anonymous 19th-century song called *Jim Crow.*] **—Jim-Crow·ism** *n.*

jim-jams (jim-jamz) *pl. n. Slang.* **1.** A state of extreme nervousness; the jitters. **2.** Delirium tremens. **3.** *British.* Pyjamas. [Whimsical reduplication.]

jimmy. *U.S.* Variant of **jemmy.**

Jim·my (jímmi) *n. Scottish Informal.* Used as a humorous form of address to a man whose name is not known by the speaker. [Pet form of *James,* considered as a very common Scottish name.]

Jimmy Woods·er (wŏodzər) *n. Australian Informal.* **1.** A person who drinks alone in a bar. **2.** A drink consumed when alone. [19th century (also *Jimmy Wood(s)*) : origin obscure.]

Ji·nan or **Chi·nan** or **Tsi·nan** (jee-nán). Capital of Shandong province, northeast China, situated in the Huang He valley. A rail and marketing centre of a rich farming area, its products include iron and steel, flour, textiles, chemicals, and agricultural machinery.

Jinghiz. See **Ghengis Khan.**

jin·gle (jíng-g'l) *v.* **-gled, -gling, -gles.** —*intr.* **1.** To make a repeated tinkling or ringing metallic sound. **2.** To have the sound of a verse jingle. —*tr.* To cause to jingle. ~*n.* **1. a.** The tinkling sound produced by light bits of metal striking together: *the jingle of sleigh bells.* **b.** Something resembling or suggesting this. **2.** A simple, repetitious, catchy rhyme or song, especially one used in an advertisement. [Middle English *ginglen* (probably imitative).]

jin·go (jíng-gō) *n., pl.* **-goes.** One who vociferously supports his country, especially one who supports a belligerent foreign policy;

an uncritical patriot; a chauvinist. Also used adjectivally: *jingo policies.* **—by jingo.** Used to express surprise or for emphasis. [From the refrain of a music-hall song sung by supporters of Disraeli's policy against Russia in 1878: *"We don't want to fight, yet by Jingo! if we do,/We've got the ships, we've got the men, and got the money too."* Originally used in conjuring, perhaps euphemistic for *by Jesus.*] **—jin·go·ish, jin·go·is·tic** (-istik) *adj.* **—jin·go·ism** *n.* **—jin·go·ist** *n. & adj.*

Jin·ja (jínjə). A city in eastern Uganda, situated on Lake Victoria. Its industries include copper and steel processing.

jink (jingk) *intr.v.* **jinked, jinking, jinks.** To make a quick, evasive turn, especially when flying or playing Rugby football.
~*n.* **1.** A sudden evasive turn. **2.** *Plural.* Boisterous play; frolic. Used chiefly in the phrase *high jinks.* [18th century (originally Scottish): perhaps imitative of quick movement.]

Jin·men or **Chin·men** (jín·mén, chín·) Also **Que·moy** (ke·móy). Island group, a possession of Taiwan, lying in the Taiwan Strait close to the mainland of China. It remained in Nationalist hands after 1949 and is still a military base. Its bombardment from the mainland (1949–1958) served only to strengthen defence ties between Taiwan and the United States.

Jin·nah (jínnə), **Mohammed Ali** (1876–1948). First governor-general of Pakistan. When India was about to achieve independence from Britain, Jinnah feared the Muslim minority would be kept from power by the Hindus, and he insisted on a Muslim homeland.

jin·ni, jin·ee (jínni, ji·née) *n., pl.* **jinn** (jin). Also **djin·ni, djin·ny** *pl.* **djinn.** In Muslim legend, a spirit capable of assuming human or animal form and exercising supernatural influence over men. [Arabic *jinnīy.*]

jin·rick·sha (jin·rík-shaw, -shə) *n.* Also **jin·rik·i·sha** (-ríck-). a **rickshaw** *(see).* [Japanese : *jin,* man + *riki,* power + *sha,* vehicle.]

jinx (jingks) *n. Informal.* Something or someone believed to bring bad luck or misfortune.
~*tr.v.* **jinxed, jinxing, jinxes.** *Informal.* To bring bad luck or misfortune to. [Perhaps from *Jynx,* genus name of the wryneck, from Greek *iunx,* wryneck (a bird used in magic), from *iuzein,* to call.]

ji·pi·ja·pa (heèpi-haá-pə, -paa) *n.* A plant, *Carludovica palmata,* of Central and South America, having long-stalked, fanlike leaves used to make Panama hats. [Spanish, after *Jipijapa,* Ecuador.]

jit·ter (jíttər) *intr.v.* **-tered, -tering, -ters.** *Informal.* To be nervous or uneasy; fidget. [20th century : origin obscure.] **—jit·ter·y** *adj.*

jit·ter·bug (jíttər-bug) *n. Slang.* **1.** A fast dance performed to quick-tempo jazz or swing music and consisting of various two-step patterns embellished with twirls and throws, especially popular in the United States in the 1940s. **2.** A person who does such a dance. **3.** A highly nervous person.
~*intr.v.* **jitterbugged, -bugging, -bugs.** To dance the jitterbug. [JITTER + BUG.]

jit·ters (jíttərz) *pl.n. Informal.* A fit of nervousness; anxiety.

jiujitsu, jiujutsu. Variants of **jujitsu.**

Jiu·long or **Chiu·lung** (jyŏ-lóng). Also **Kow·loon** (ków-lŏon). A port and peninsula on mainland China, forming part of the former British Crown Colony of Hong Kong. It was ceded to Britain in 1860 and returned to China in 1997.

jive (jīv) *n.* **1. a.** A style of lively, fast jazz music. **b.** A fast, jerky dance, similar in style to rock'n'roll, originally performed to jive music and later to rock'n'roll music. **2. a.** *Informal.* Glib or deceptive talk: *don't give me that jive.* **b.** A slang or jargon used by black Americans and by jazz musicians and enthusiasts. [20th century : origin obscure.] **—jive** *intr.v.*

jnr., Jnr. junior.

jo, joe (jō) *n., pl.* **joes.** *Scottish.* A sweetheart. [16th century : variant of JOY.]

Joan of Arc (jōn, ärk), **Saint,** *French* **Jeanne d'Arc** (zhan dárk). (1412–31). French heroine, known as the Maid of Orléans. She led the French resistance that forced the English to raise the siege of Orléans (1429). The same year, aged 17, she led an army of 12,000 to Rheims and had the Dauphin crowned Charles VII. She was captured and sold to the English (1430) by the Burgundians, and tried for heresy and sorcery. Joan was burned at the stake in Rouen (1431). She was beatified (1909) and canonised (1920).

job¹ (job) *n.* **1.** An action requiring some exertion; a task; an undertaking. **2.** An activity performed in exchange for payment; especially, one performed regularly as one's trade, occupation, or profession. **3. a.** A specific piece of work to be done for a set fee. **b.** The object to be worked on. **c.** Anything resulting from or produced by work. **4.** A position in which one is employed. **5. a.** An assigned or assumed duty or responsibility: *It was her job to get her younger brother ready for school.* **b.** Anything which must be done: *Stitching up her cuts was a very messy job.* **6.** *Informal.* A difficult or strenuous task: *We had a job getting the piano up the stairs.* **7.** *Informal.* A thing which is notable of its kind: *driving a nice little red job.* **8.** *Chiefly British Informal.* A state of affairs: *It's a good job you called the fire brigade.* **9.** *Informal.* A criminal act, especially a robbery: *pull a bank job.* **10.** Something done ostensibly in the public interest, but actually for private gain or advantage. **—See Synonyms at task. —just the job.** Precisely what is or was required. **—lie down on the job.** *Informal.* To neglect the responsibilities of one's job. **—on the job.** *Informal.* **1.** Working at one's occupation or task; at work. **2.** *Vulgar Slang.* In the act of having sexual intercourse.
~*v.* **jobbed, jobbing, jobs.** *—intr.* **1.** To do odd jobs or piecework: *a jobbing builder.* **2.** To act as a middleman or jobber. **3.** To exploit a position of trust for private advantage. **—***tr.* **1. a.** To purchase (merchandise) from manufacturers and sell it to retailers. **b.** *British.* To buy and sell (stocks and shares) as a jobber. **2.** To arrange for (contracted work) to be done in portions by others; subcontract. **3.** To transact (official business) dishonestly for private profit. **4.** *British.* **a.** To hire out (a horse, for example). **b.** To hire. [Originally a piece of work, perhaps from obsolete *job†,* "piece".]

job² *v.* **jobbed, jobbing, jobs.** *Archaic.* **—***tr.* To jab. **—***intr.* To make a jab.
~*n. Archaic.* A jab. [Middle English *jobben†.*]

Job¹ (jōb). In the Old Testament, an upright man whose faith in God survived the test of repeated calamities, and who is taken as a model of patient endurance: *the patience of Job.* [Hebrew *Iyyŏbh,* "hated, persecuted", from *ayabh,* to be hostile.]

Job² *n.* A book of the Old Testament, recounting the story of Job.

job·ber (jóbbər) *n.* **1.** One who buys merchandise from manufacturers and sells it to retailers. **2.** A person who does piecework or odd jobs. **3.** A public official who exploits his position for personal gain. **4.** *Chiefly British.* Formerly, a middleman in the exchange of stocks and securities among brokers; a stockjobber.

job·ber·y (jóbbəri) *n.* Corruption among public officials. [From JOB (to seek graft).]

Job·cen·tre (jób-sentər) *n.* In Britain, an office run by the Department of Employment that lists and advertises current employment vacancies in a locality.

job·hold·er (jób-hōldər) *n.* One who has a regular job.

job-hop (jób-hop) *intr.v.* **-hopped, -hopping, -hops.** To change jobs frequently. **—job-hop·per** *n.*

job·less (jób-ləss, -liss) *adj.* Unemployed. **—job·less·ness** *n.*

job lot *n.* **1.** Miscellaneous goods sold in one lot. **2.** Any collection of unsorted items.

job reservation *n.* In South Africa formerly, the practice of limiting various categories of employment to particular race groups, thereby effectively excluding black people from many trades and professions.

Job's comforter *n.* One who discourages or saddens while seemingly offering sympathy or comfort. [From JOB, who was treated in such a way by his friends.]

job-shar·ing (jób-shàiring) *n.* A practice whereby the responsibility for a post is shared between two alternating part-time workers.

Job's-tears (jōbz-teérz) *n. Used with a singular or plural verb.* **1.** A grass, *Coix lacryma-jobi,* of tropical Asia, having edible seeds enclosed in beadlike modified leaves. **2.** The seeds of this plant. **3.** The beadlike, seed-containing structures of this plant, used for ornamentation.

jobs·worth (jóbz-wurth) *n. British Informal.* A person unwilling to do anything, however trivial or decent, that might conceivably compromise the security of his own position. [From the catchphrase "It's more than my *job's worth* to do it".]

Jo·cas·ta (jō-kástə). In Greek legend, a Theban queen who unknowingly married her own son Oedipus.

Joch·um (yókhəm), **Eugen** (1902–87). German conductor. He conducted the Berlin and Vienna Philharmonic Orchestras, and was the conductor laureate of the London Symphony Orchestra.

jock¹ (jok) *n. Informal.* A jockey. [Short for JOCKEY.]

jock² *n.* **1.** *Informal.* A jockstrap. **2.** *U.S. Slang.* **a.** A male athlete, especially in college or university. **b.** A virile and promiscuous man; a playboy.

Jock (jok) *n. Informal.* A Scotsman. Often used as a familiar, humorous, or derogatory form of address. [Scottish form of *Jack.*]

jock·ey (jócki) *n., pl.* **-eys.** A person who rides horses in races, especially as a profession.
~*v.* **jockeyed, -eying, -eys.** *—tr.* **1.** To ride (a horse) as jockey. **2.** To direct or manoeuvre by cleverness or skill. **3.** To trick; outwit. *—intr.* **1.** To ride a horse in a race. **2.** To manoeuvre for a certain position or advantage. Used chiefly in the phrase *jockey for position.* **3.** To employ trickery; cheat; swindle. [Originally "lad", diminutive of Scottish *Jock,* JACK (a man).]

jock·strap (jók-strap) *n.* An elasticated support for the male genitals, worn when playing strenuous sports. Also called "athletic support", "jock". [Slang *jock,* "penis", earlier *jockum†* + STRAP.]

jo·cose (jō-kŏss, jə-) *adj.* **1.** Given to good-humoured joking; merry. **2.** Characterised by joking; humorous. [Latin *jocōsus,* from *jocus,* jest, joke.] **—jo·cose·ly** *adv.* **—jo·cos·i·ty** (jō-kóssəti, jə-) *n.*

joc·u·lar (jóckew-lər) *adj.* **1.** Given to or characterised by joking. **2.** Meant in jest; facetious. **—See Synonyms at jolly.** [Latin *joculāris,* from *joculus,* diminutive of *jocus,* jest, joke.] **—joc·u·lar·i·ty** *n.* **—joc·u·lar·ly** *adv.*

joc·und (jóckənd, jŏk-ənd, -und) *adj.* Having a cheerful disposition or quality; merry; gay. [Middle English, from Old French, from Late Latin *jōcundus,* from Latin *jūcundus,* agreeable, pleasant, from *juvāre,* to entertain, delight, AID.] **—joc·und·ly** *adv.* **—jo·cund·i·ty** (jō-kúndəti, jə-, jo-) *n.*

Jodh·pur (jód-pər, -pur, -poor). A city in northwestern India, in Rajasthan state. Founded in 1459, it became the capital of a large princely state, and now has a university (founded 1962).

jodh·purs (jód-pərz) *pl.n.* Wide-hipped riding breeches of heavy cloth, fitting tightly at the knees and ankles. [After JODHPUR.]

Jo·do (jō-dō) *n.* Pure Land Buddhism *(see).* [Japanese.]

Jod·rell Bank (jóddrəl). A site near Macclesfield in Cheshire in northwest England. The Jodrell Bank Experimental Station (also called the Nuffield Radio Astronomy Laboratory) was established here in 1945 as part of the University of Manchester. One of the world's largest steerable radio telescopes, with a diameter of 76.2

metres (250 feet), was installed between 1952–57.

Joe Bloggs (jō blógz) *n. British Informal.* The average man; the man in the street. Also *U.S. & Australian.* "Joe Blow", *U.S.* "Joe Sixpack", *British* "Joe Public".

Jo·el[1] (jṓ-əl, -el ‖ jōl). A Hebrew Minor Prophet.

Joel[2] *n.* A book of the Old Testament containing Joel's prophecies of the judgment of Judah.

jo·ey (jṓ-i) *n., pl.* **-eys. 1.** *Australian.* **a.** A young kangaroo or other young animal. **b.** A young child. **2.** *N.Z.* An opossum. [Native Australian name.]

jog[1] (jog) *v.* **jogged, jogging, jogs.** *—tr.* **1.** To jar or move by shoving, bumping, or jerking. **2.** To give a slight push or shake to; nudge. **3.** To stimulate; stir (one's memory, for example). *—intr.* **1.** To ride at a steady, slow trot. **2.** To run at a moderate pace, especially for exercise. **3.** To proceed in a leisurely, monotonous, or uneventful way.
~*n.* **1.** A slight jolt or shake. **2.** A nudge. **3.** A slow steady pace; a trot. [Middle English (probably imitative).] **—jog·ger** *n.*

jog[2] *n. U.S.* **1.** A protruding or receding part in a surface or line. **2.** An abrupt change in direction. [Perhaps variant of JAG.]

jog·gle[1] (jógg'l) *v.* **-gled, -gling, -gles.** *—tr.* To shake or jar repeatedly. *—intr.* To move with a shaking or jolting motion.
~*n.* A shaking or jolting motion. [Frequentative of JOG.]

joggle[2] *n.* **1.** A joint between two pieces of building material formed by a notch and a fitted projection. **2.** The notch or the projecting piece used in such a joint.
~*tr.v.* **joggled, -gling, -gles.** To join or attach by means of a joggle. [From JOG (protruding part).]

Jog·ja·kar·ta or **Djog·ja·kar·ta** (jóg-yə-kártə ‖ -jə-, *U.S.* jǒg-). A city in Indonesia, situated in southern central Java. Palaces and temples have been sited in the surrounding area since the 8th century B.C., and include the magnificent Buddhist monument of Borobudur. Founded in 1755, Jogjakarta was the capital of the Indonesian republic (1946–49). It has a university (founded 1949) and markets tea, tobacco, and handicrafts.

jog trot *n.* **1.** A moderate, steady, jolting pace; a jog. **2.** A regular, humdrum way of living or of doing something.

Jo·han·nes·burg (jə-hánniss-burg, jō-, -hánniz- ‖ *locally also* -hónniss-). The largest city in South Africa, informally known as Jo'burg, situated in Gauteng province in the northeast of the country. It lies on the Witwatersrand and was founded in 1886 when gold was discovered. Now the centre of the world's largest gold field, Johannesburg is at the heart of South Africa's most highly industrialised region.

Jo·han·nine (jō-hánnīn) *adj.* Pertaining to or designating those parts of the New Testament attributed to Saint John. [From Latin *johannīnus,* from *Johannes,* JOHN.]

john (jon) *n. U.S., Australian, & N.Z. Slang.* A lavatory. [From *John* (masculine name).]

John[1] (jon) *n.* **1.** A book of the New Testament, the fourth Gospel, attributed to St. John. **2.** Any of three New Testament Epistles attributed to St. John.

John[2], also known as John Lackland (1167–1216). King of England from 1199. He was the youngest son of Henry II, and intrigued against his father and then his brother, Richard I. Under him, the English lost most of their possessions in France. The barons rose against John and forced him to set his seal on the Magna Carta (1215), a cornerstone of English liberty.

John, Augustus (Edwin) (1878–1961). British painter. He often stayed with and painted gypsies, as in *Encampment on Dartmoor* (1906). He painted portraits of his wife *Dorelia,* of *George Bernard Shaw Esq.* (1914), *Thomas Hardy O.M.* (1923), and *Dylan Thomas* (c. 1936). He was elected to the Royal Academy (1928).

John, Barry (1945–). Welsh Rugby Union player. He played for Wales 25 times. On the British Lions tour of New Zealand (1971), scored a record 180 points.

John, Saint, also called "the Evangelist", "the Divine". One of the Twelve Apostles; reputed author of the fourth Gospel, three epistles, and the Book of Revelation.

John XXIII, Pope, born Angelo Giuseppe Roncalli (1881–1963). He became pope in 1958. He called a general council of the Church, the first for almost a century, and worked for world peace and Christian unity. See **Vatican Council.**

John Bar·ley·corn (bárli-kawrn) *n.* A personification of malt spirits or of alcoholic drinks in general.

John Birch Society (búrch) *n.* An ultraconservative anticommunist organisation founded in the United States by Robert Welch in 1958. [Named after *John Birch* (died 1945), U.S. intelligence officer.]

John Bull *n.* **1.** A personification of England or the English. **2.** A typical Englishman. [After *The History of John Bull* (1712), a satire by John ARBUTHNOT.]

John Doe *n.* **1.** A name formerly used in U.S. legal proceedings to designate a fictitious or unidentified person. **2.** *U.S.* An average citizen; the man in the street.

John Do·ry (dáwri ‖ dóri). Any fish of the family Zeidae; especially, *Zeus faber,* of the eastern Atlantic and Mediterranean, having spiny fins and a laterally compressed body.

John Han·cock (hán-kok, háng-) *n. U.S. Informal.* A person's signature. [After *John Hancock* (1737–93), whose signature appears prominently on the American Declaration of Independence.]

john·ny (jónni) *n., pl.* **-nies. 1.** *Informal.* A bloke; a fellow. **2.** *Slang.* A condom. [From *Johnny,* diminutive of JOHN.]

john·ny·cake (jónni-kayk) *n. Australian.* A thin cake made with wheatmeal or flour, often cooked on the embers of a campfire.

john·ny-come-late·ly (jónni-kum-láytli) *n., pl.* **-lies.** *Informal.* A newcomer or latecomer, especially one who is regarded as an upstart.

John·ny Reb (reb) *n. U.S. Informal.* A Confederate soldier during the American Civil War.

John of Gaunt (1340–99). Duke of Lancaster, fourth son of Edward III. He effectively ruled England during his father's last years and in the first years of Richard II's reign.

John of the Cross, Saint, born Juan de Yepes y Alvarez (1542–91). Spanish monk, mystic, and poet. He tried to restore austerity to Carmelite life. Friction among the Carmelites led to his imprisonment (1577) and finally retreat to a life of solitude. He was canonised in 1726.

John O'Groats (jón-ə-gróts). Location in the extreme northeast of Scotland, named after John de Groat, a Dutchman, who built an octagonal house there in the 16th century. The northern extremity of Britain is popularly marked by John O'Groats.

John Paul II, Pope, born Karol Jozef Wojtyla (1920–). The first Polish-born pope. He was Archbishop of Kraków before his election in 1978 as the first non-Italian pope since the Dutch-born Adrian VI (1522–23).

Johns (jonz), **Jasper** (1930–). U.S. artist. He aims to remove the boundary between art and real life, and has made bronze casts of light bulbs, toothbrushes, and beer cans.

John·son (jon-s'n), **Amy** (1903–41). Pioneer British aviator. She was the first woman to fly solo from London to Australia (1930). She drowned after baling out over the Thames estuary while on war service.

Johnson, Andrew (1808–75). Seventeenth U.S. president (1865–69). A Southerner who remained loyal to the Union during the Civil War, Johnson was elected vice-president in 1864 and succeeded the assassinated Abraham Lincoln. He pursued a policy of conciliation towards the defeated Confederate states to the point of readmitting them to the Union without requiring political reforms or ensuring civil rights for freed slaves.

Johnson, Lyndon (Baines) (1908–73). 36th U.S. president. Johnson succeeded after John F. Kennedy's assassination (1963). He launched a welfare programme, termed the "Great Society", and overwhelmingly won the presidential election in 1964. He faced increasing criticism over the mounting U.S. involvement in Vietnam, and did not stand for re-election in 1968.

Johnson, Samuel (1709–84). British writer and lexicographer. His works include *Dictionary of the English Language* (1755) and *Lives of the Poets* (1779–81). **—John·so·ni·an** (jon-sṓniən) *n. & adj.*

Johnson grass *n.* A coarse grass, *Sorghum halepense,* native to the Mediterranean area, cultivated for forage but often a troublesome weed. [Developed by William *Johnson,* 19th-century U.S. agriculturalist.]

John the Baptist, Saint. Son of Elizabeth and Zacharias; cousin of Jesus, whom he baptised; executed by Herod Antipas.

John Thomas *n. Slang.* A penis. [Humorous use of male Christian names.]

Jo·hore or **Jo·hor** (jō-hór, jə- ‖ -hór). A state in Malaysia, situated in the south of the Malay peninsula. Its extensive forests produce rubber, copra, and palm oil, and there are important reserves of tin and bauxite. The capital, Johore Baharu, is connected to Singapore by a causeway.

joie de vi·vre (zhwáa də véev, zhwáad véevr) *n.* Hearty or carefree enjoyment of life. [French, "joy of living".]

join (joyn) *v.* **joined, joining, joins.** *—tr.* **1.** To put or bring together; unite or make continuous: *The children joined hands in a circle.* **2.** To put or bring into close association or relationship: *joined in marriage.* **3.** *Geometry.* To connect (points), as with a straight line. **4.** To form a junction with. **5.** To become a part or member of (a club, society, or the like). **6.** To take a place among, in, or with; enter into the company of: *I shall join you later.* **7.** *Informal.* To adjoin. *—intr.* **1.** To come or act together; form a connection, junction, or alliance. Often used with *with.* **2.** To become a member of a group. **3.** To take part; participate. Used with *in: He joined in the singing.* **—join up.** To enlist, especially in the armed forces.
~*n.* A joint; a junction. [Middle English *joinen,* from Old French *joindre* (stem *joign-*), from Latin *jungere.*]

Synonyms: join, combine, unite, consolidate, link, connect, relate, associate.

Usage: The use of *together* following this verb is often felt to be redundant: *He joined (together) the two wires.* . . . The longer form does have a certain value in adding emphasis, however, and it is well-established in a few fixed phrases, for example: *whom God hath joined together.* . . .

join·der (jóyndər) *n.* **1.** The act of joining. **2.** *Law.* **a.** A joining of causes of action or defence in a suit. **b.** A joining of parties in a suit. **c.** The formal acceptance of an issue offered. [From French *joindre* (mistaken as a substantive), to JOIN.]

join·er (jóynər) *n.* **1.** One that joins. **2.** A person who makes furniture, house fittings, door frames, or the like. Compare **carpenter. 3.** *Informal.* A person given to joining groups, organisations, or causes.

join·e·ry (jóynəri) *n.* **1.** The skill or craft of a joiner. **2.** Work done by a joiner, such as the fittings in a house.

joint (joynt) *n. Abbr.* **jt. 1. a.** A point or position at which two or more things are joined. **b.** A configuration in or by which two or more things are joined. **2.** The manner of joining. **3. a.** *Anatomy.* A point of connection or articulation between two or more bones, consisting of cartilage and connective tissue. **b.** A similar connection between segments in the body or leg of an arthropod. **4.** *Botany.* A point on a stem from which a leaf or branch may grow; a node. **5.** *Geology.* A fracture or crack in a rock mass along which no movement has occurred. **6.** A large cut of meat, such as the shoulder or leg, used for roasting. **7.** *Slang.* A cheap or disreputable gathering place, such as a nightclub or bar. **8.** *Slang.* Any dwelling or public establishment. Often used humorously. **9.** *Slang.* A rolled cigarette containing cannabis. **—out of joint. 1.** Dislocated, as a bone. **2.** Not harmonious; inconsistent. **3.** Out of order; unsatisfactory.

~adj. **1.** Shared by or common to two or more: *a joint belief; the divorced couple received joint custody of the children.* **2.** Sharing with another or others: *joint heirs.* **3.** Formed, created, involving, or characterised by cooperation or united action: *a joint effort.* **4.** *Law.* Regarded as one legal body; united in identity of interest, ownership, or liability.

~tr.v. **jointed, jointing, joints. 1.** To combine or attach at a joint or joints. **2.** To provide or construct with joints. **3.** To cut (meat) into joints. [Middle English, from Old French, from the past participle of *joindre,* to JOIN.] **—joint·ly** *adv.*

joint account *n.* A bank account in the name of two or more people, any of whom may use it for deposits and withdrawals.

joint·ed (jóyntid) *adj.* Having a joint or joints, often of a specified type. Often used in combination: *double-jointed.*

joint·er (jóyntər) *n.* **1.** One that joints; especially, a machine or tool used in making joints. **2.** A long plane for smoothing the edges of planks to enable them to be fitted together. Also called "jointing plane".

joint resolution *n. U.S.* A resolution passed by both houses of a bicameral legislature and eligible to become a law if signed by the chief executive or passed over his veto.

joint stock *n.* Stock or capital funds of a company held jointly or in common by the owners.

joint-stock company (jóynt-stók) *n.* A business with a separate legal identity whose capital is held in shares by joint owners, each of whom enjoys limited liability.

join·ture (jóynchər) *n. Law.* An estate settled on a woman by her husband, by an arrangement that takes effect in the event of her widowhood.

~tr.v. **jointured, -turing, -tures.** *Law.* To arrange a jointure for. [Middle English, from Old French, from Latin *junctūra,* JUNCTURE.]

joist (joyst) *n.* Any of the parallel horizontal beams set from wall to wall to support the boards of a floor or ceiling.

~tr.v. **joisted, joisting, joists.** To construct with joists. [Middle English *gyste, giste,* from Old French *giste,* beam supporting a bridge, from Latin *jacitum,* from the past participle of *jacēre,* to lie down.]

jo·jo·ba (hō-hṓbə ‖ jə-jṓbə) *n.* A flowering shrub, *Simmondsia chinensis,* of northern and central America, whose seeds contain a high proportion of liquid wax. Used in lubrication, polishes, pharmaceuticals, and cosmetics.

joke (jṓk) *n.* **1.** An amusing story, especially one with a punch line. **2.** An amusing or jesting remark; a witticism, quip, or pun. **3.** A mischievous trick; a prank. **4. a.** An amusing or ludicrous incident or situation. **b.** The amusing aspect of something: *couldn't see the joke.* **5.** Something not to be taken seriously; a triviality: *His accident was no joke.* **6.** A laughing-stock.

~v. **joked, joking, jokes.** *—intr.* **1.** To tell or play jokes; jest. **2.** To speak in fun; be facetious. *—tr.* To make fun of; tease. [Latin *jocus,* jest, joke.] **—jok·ey, jok·y** *adj.* **—jok·i·ly** *adv.* **—jok·i·ness** *n.* **—jok·ing·ly** *adv.*

Synonyms: *joke, jest, witticism, quip, sally, crack, wisecrack, gag.*

jok·er (jṓkər) *n.* **1. a.** A person who tells or plays jokes; a clown; a prankster. **b.** An insolent person who seeks to make a show of cleverness. **2.** A playing card, usually printed with a picture of a jester, used in certain games as the highest ranking card or as a wild card. **3.** An unpredictable person or factor that may prove troublesome. Used chiefly in the phrase *joker in the pack.* **4.** *Slang.* A fellow; a man. **5.** *U.S.* A minor clause in a document, such as a legislative bill, that voids or changes its original purpose.

jo·lie laide (zhóllee láyd, zho-lée léd) *n., pl.* **jolies laides.** *French.* A woman or girl whose features are not conventionally pretty but are nonetheless attractive. [Literally, "pretty-ugly".]

Jo·liot-Cu·rie (zhólli-ō kéwr-i, zhol-yṓ kewr-ée, kü-rée), **(Jean) Frédéric** (1900-58), born Jean Frédéric Joliot, and **Irène** (1897-56). French physicists. Irène Joliot-Curie was the daughter of Pierre and Marie Curie. She married Frédéric Joliot, her mother's assistant, who added Curie to his name. Together they discovered artificial radioactivity, for which they won the 1935 Nobel prize for chemistry. Both died of cancer, after life-long exposure to radioactivity.

jol·li·fi·ca·tion (jóllifi-káysh'n) *n.* Festivity; revelry; merry-making. [From JOLLY.]

jol·li·fy (jólli-fī) *v.* **-fied, -fying, -fies.** *—tr.* To cause to become jolly; cheer up. *—intr.* To make merry; celebrate.

jol·li·ty (jólləti) *n.* Gaiety; merriment.

jol·ly (jólli) *adj.* **-lier, -liest. 1.** Full of merriment and good spirits; fun-loving; gay. **2.** Exhibiting or occasioning happiness or mirth; cheerful; festive. **3.** Greatly pleasing; enjoyable.

~adv. British Informal. Very; extremely: *a jolly good cook.*

~tr.v. **jollied, -lying, -lies. 1.** To keep amused or diverted for one's

own purposes; humour. Often used with *up* or *along.* **2.** To poke fun at good-naturedly; tease. [Middle English *jolif, joli,* from Old French, gay, pleasant, probably from Old Norse *jōl,* name of the midwinter festival, yule, from Common Germanic *jegol* (unattested), YULE.] **—jol·li·ly** *adv.* **—jol·li·ness** *n.*

Synonyms: *jolly, jovial, merry, blithe, jocular, convivial.*

jol·ly-boat (jólli-bōt) *n.* A small boat kept by the stern of a larger ship. [Probably an alteration of earlier *jolywart†.*]

Jolly Rog·er (rójər) *n.* A black flag bearing the emblematic white skull and crossbones of a pirate ship.

Jol·son (jṓl-s'n), **Al,** born Asa Yoelson (1888-1950). U.S. singer, born in Russia. He imitated black singers. His hits include *Mammy* and *Sonny Boy.* He starred in *The Jazz Singer,* the first major film with synchronised sound (1927), and later in *Swanee River* (1939).

jolt (jṓlt) *v.* **jolted, jolting, jolts.** *—tr.* **1.** To shake or cause to move with a sudden jerk or blow. **2.** To bump into; jostle. **3.** To put into a specified condition by or as if by a jolt: *He was jolted out of his reverie by a police siren.* *—intr.* To move in an irregular, bumpy, or jerky fashion.

~n. **1.** A sudden jarring or jerking, as from a blow. **2.** An abrupt or unexpected shock or reversal: *a jolt to his complacency.* [16th century : origin obscure.] **—jolt·er** *n.* **—jolt·i·ly** *adv.* **—jolt·y** *adj.*

Jomada. Variant of **Jumada.**

Jo·nah¹ (jṓnə). An Old Testament prophet who was thrown overboard during a storm at sea caused by his disobedience to God. He was swallowed by a great fish and disgorged unharmed three days later. [Hebrew *Yōnāh,* "the moaning one", dove, pigeon, akin to *ānāh,* "moan".]

Jonah² *n.* A book of the Old Testament containing the story of Jonah.

Jonah³ *n.* One thought to bring bad luck. [After JONAH.]

Jon·a·than¹ (jónnəthən). Eldest son of King Saul of Israel and friend of David. I Samuel 20.

Jonathan² *n.* A variety of red, late-ripening apple. [After *Jonathan* Hasbrouck (died 1846), American jurist.]

Jonathan³ *n.* **Brother Jonathan** (see).

Jones, (Alfred) Ernest (1879-1958). British psychoanalyst, a follower of Sigmund Freud. Jones was instrumental in developing the use of psychoanalysis in Britain and North America. He wrote a a biography of Freud (1953-56).

Jones, (Everett) LeRoi, also called Baraka, Imamu Amiri (1934-). U.S. playwright and poet. Founder of the Black Community Development and Defense Organization (1968), his works include *Blues People* (1963), about the social significance of African-American music.

Jones, Inigo (1573-1652). English architect. Jones studied in Italy and brought the Palladian classical style to England. Among the buildings he designed are The Queen's House, Greenwich, and the Banqueting Hall, Whitehall, London. He also introduced movable scenery and the proscenium arch into the English theatre.

Jones, James Larkin, known as Jack (1913-). English trade union leader. He was general secretary of the Transport and General Workers' Union (1969-78). He was awarded the M.B.E. (1950) and made a Companion of Honour (1978).

Jones, John Paul, born John Paul (1747-92). U.S. naval hero, born in Scotland. He settled in Virginia and on the outbreak of the War of American Independence gained a commission from Congress. In command of a French force he raided the British coast in 1779, destroying two British warships. Jones later became an admiral in the Russian navy. He died in Paris.

Jones, Robert Tyre, known as Bobby (1902-71). U.S. golfer. He was the only golfer ever to win the "Grand Slam", the British and U.S. amateur and open golf championships in the same year (1930).

jong (yong) *n. South African Informal.* Used as a familiar term of address to a man, woman, or child. [From Cape Dutch *jonger,* boy.]

Jong·lei Canal (jóng-gli). Internationally financed canal project in southern Sudan, begun in 1979. The canal, from Bor on the Bahr al Jebel to Malakal on the White Nile, will be 320 kilometres (c. 200 miles) long, and will divert water from the Sudd swamp and so reduce its massive evaporation.

jon·gleur (zhoN-glúr, -glṓr ‖ jóng-glər) *n.* A wandering minstrel and storyteller in medieval England and France. [French, from Old French, variant of *joglere,* JUGGLER.]

jon·quil (jóng-kwil ‖ *U.S. also* jón-) *n.* A widely cultivated plant, *Narcissus jonquilla,* having long, narrow leaves and short-tubed, fragrant yellow flowers. [New Latin *jonquilla,* from Spanish *junquillo,* diminutive of *junco,* rush, reed, from Latin *juncus†.*]

Jon·son (jón-s'n), **Ben(jamin)** (1572-1637). English playwright and poet. He developed the comedy of humours in England. His plays include *Volpone* (1606), *The Alchemist* (1610), and *Bartholomew Fair* (1614).

jook. Variant of **juk.**

Jor·dan (jórd'n). River flowing south from Syria and Lebanon, partially marking the border between Israel and Jordan, and issuing into the Dead Sea. John the Baptist baptised his followers in the river, which is 320 kilometres (199 miles) long.

Jordan, Hashemite Kingdom of (jórd'n). A largely agricultural desert Arab state in southwest Asia. Most of its fertile land lies in the Jordan valley. However, with foreign aid, the cultivated area is expanding. Jordan, then part of the Nabatacan empire, fell to the Romans (c. A.D. 110), and later to the Arabs, Crusaders, and Turks (1516). After the Arab Revolt against the Turks in World War I, Transjordan, a British mandate east of the Jordan, led by the

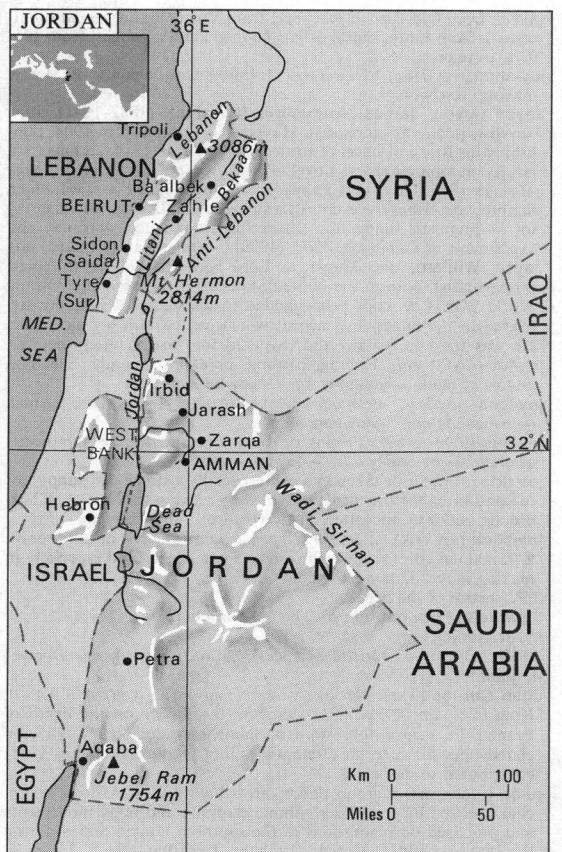

JORDAN 36 E
Tripoli
LEBANON ▲3086m
Ba'albek SYRIA
BEIRUT Zahle
Sidon (Saida)
Tyre (Sur) Mt. Hermon 2814m
MED. SEA
Irbid
Jarash
WEST BANK Zarqa 32°N
AMMAN
Hebron Dead Sea
ISRAEL JORDAN
SAUDI ARABIA
Petra
EGYPT
Aqaba
Jebel Ram 1754m
Km 0 100
Miles 0 50

Hashemite family, was established (1923). Its independence became effective in 1948. The same year, Transjordan occupied the West Bank, adopting its present name in 1949. Resident units of the Palestine Liberation Organisation provoked a civil war in 1970–71. Jordan assisted Syria in the Yom Kippur War (1973) and supported Iraq against Iran in 1980. King Hussein, ruler since 1952, while pressing for a Palestinian-Arab homeland, has been a mediating influence between the militant Arab states and the West. Area, 97 740 square kilometres (37,738 square miles) including the West Bank. Population, 5,580,000. Capital, Amman. —**Jor·da·ni·an** (jor-dáy-nian) *n. & adj.*

Jordan almond *n.* A large variety of almond from Málaga, Spain, used widely in confectionery. [By folk etymology from Middle English *jardin,* probably from Old French *jardin,* from Vulgar Latin *gardīnus* (unattested), GARDEN + ALMOND.]

jo·rum (jáwrəm ‖ jórəm) *n.* **1.** A large drinking bowl. **2.** The amount such a bowl contains. [Perhaps after *Joram* (II Samuel 8:10), who brought vessels of silver, gold, and brass to King David.]

jo·seph (jṓ-zif ‖ -sif) *n.* A long riding coat with a small cape, worn by women in the 18th century. [Probably after Joseph's (son of Jacob) "coat of many colours" (Genesis 37:3).]

Jo·seph[1] (jṓ-zif ‖ -sif). Son of Jacob and Rachel, sold into slavery in Egypt. Genesis 3; 37; 41; 45.

Joseph[2]. Husband of Mary the mother of Jesus. Matthew 1:16.

Joseph, Keith (Sinjohn), Baron (1918–94). British Conservative politician. In the government of Mrs. Thatcher he was Secretary of State for Industry (1979–81) and for Education and Science (1981–86).

Jo·seph (zhō-zéf). **Père,** born François le Clerc du Tremblay (1577–1638). French Franciscan friar and diplomat. He was a close friend and adviser of Cardinal Richelieu, and the original "éminence grise".

Jo·sé·phine (jṓ-zi-feen, zhō-ze-féen), born Marie Josèphe Rose Tascher de la Pagerie (1763–1814). Wife of Napoleon I, Empress of France (1804–09). Born in Martinique, she married Napoleon in 1796 after the execution of her first husband, Viscount Beauharnais. Her failure to bear a child led Napoleon to repudiate their marriage in 1809, although she continued to advise him.

Joseph of Ar·i·ma·the·a (árri-mə-thée-ə). An Israelite who provided a tomb for Jesus; the subject of many legends.

Joseph's coat *n.* A tropical plant, *Amaranthus tricolor,* cultivated for its variously coloured foliage. [From JOSEPH. See joseph.]

Jo·seph·son (jṓ-zif-s'n ‖ -sif-), **Brian David** (1940–). British physicist. He predicted theoretically the **Josephson effect** and **Josephson junction.** He shared the 1973 Nobel prize for physics with Leo Esaki and Ivar Giaever for this work.

Josephson effect *n. Physics.* Any of certain electrical phenomena

observed at very low temperatures at a junction between two superconducting materials separated by a thin insulating layer. Under such conditions a direct current can flow with no applied voltage up to a critical value. A small direct voltage across the junction can cause an alternating current to flow. [Predicted theoretically by B.D. JOSEPHSON in 1962.]

Josephson junction *n. Physics.* A junction in which two superconductors at very low temperature are separated by a thin insulating layer such that Josephson effects can be observed. Josephson junctions are used in physics for accurate measurement of magnetic fields and definition of physical quantities and, in particular, for high-speed switches in advanced computers.

Josephson memory *n.* A computer memory consisting of a number of interconnected Josephson junctions, which are switched between conducting and superconducting states by variations in magnetic field.

josh (josh) *v.* **joshed, joshing, joshes.** *U.S. Informal.* —*tr.* To tease (someone) good-humoredly. —*intr.* To banter; joke. ~*n.* A teasing or joking remark. [19th century : origin obscure.]

Josh. Joshua (Old Testament).

Josh·u·a[1] (jósh-wə, jóshew-ə, jóshoo-ə). Also in Douay Bible **Jos·u·e** (jóssew-ee, jóshew-). Successor of Moses in the Exodus.

Joshua[2] *n.* Also in Douay Bible **Josue.** *Abbr.* **Josh.** An Old Testament book with the narrative of Joshua.

Joshua tree *n.* A treelike plant, *Yucca brevifolia,* of the southwestern United States, having sword-shaped leaves and greenish-white flowers. [From the greatly extended branches, recalling the outstretched arm of the prophet Joshua as he pointed with his spear to the city of Ai. Joshua 8:18.]

Jo·si·ah (jō-sí-ə). Also in Douay Bible **Jo·si·as** (-əss). King of Judah (*c.* 638– *c.* 608 B.C.).

Jos·quin des Prez or **des Prés** (zhoss-kán day práy) (*c.* 1450–1521). Flemish composer. His musical style bridged the early and later Renaissance periods and he helped to introduce the northern polyphonic manner to Italy.

joss (joss) *n.* An image of a Chinese god. [Pidgin English, from Portuguese *deos,* god, from Latin *deus.*]

joss house *n.* A Chinese temple or shrine.

joss stick *n.* A stick of fragrant tinder mixed with clay and burned as incense.

jos·tle (jóss'l) *v.* **-tled, -tling, -tles.** —*intr.* **1.** To come in contact or collide repeatedly, as in a crowd; knock or push together. Often used with *with.* **2.** To make one's way by pushing or elbowing. **3.** To vie for an advantage or favourable position. **4.** To be in close proximity. Often used with *with.* —*tr.* **1. a.** To force (one's way) by pushing, shoving, and elbowing. **b.** To push or shove roughly or unceremoniously. **2.** To come into close contact or collision with. **3.** To vie with for an advantage or favourable position. **4.** To be in close proximity with. ~*n.* A rough shove or push. [Earlier *justle,* from Middle English *justlen,* to come against in combat, frequentative of *justen,* from Old French *juster,* to JOUST.]

jot (jot) *n.* The smallest bit or particle; an iota. ~*tr.v.* **jotted, jotting, jots.** To write down briefly and hastily: *jot down an address.* [Earlier *iote,* from Latin *iōta,* from Greek, IOTA.]

jot·ting (jótting) *n.* A brief note or memorandum.

jot·ter (jóttər) *n.* A small pad or notebook for notes or messages.

Jo·tun·heim (yŏt'n-haym, yóttōōn-) Also **Jö·tunn·heim** (jö-tōōn-), **Jo·tunn·heim·r** (-haymər). *Norse Mythology.* **Utgard** (*see*).

jou·al (zhōō-ál, zhwaal) *n. Canadian.* Uneducated, nonstandard, or dialectal Canadian French. [Respelling of French *cheval,* horse, as it would sound in nonstandard or dialectal Canadian French.]

Jou·bert (yō-báir, yōō-), **Piet,** born Petrus Jacobus Joubert (1831–1900). Afrikaner statesman and commandant general of the Boer forces. Favouring political equality for British immigrants, he three times failed against Paul Kruger in bids for the presidency of the Transvaal (1883, 1893, 1898).

jougs (jōōgz, jugz) *pl.n.* A former Scottish instrument of punishment consisting of a hinged iron collar chained to a wall or post. [Perhaps from Middle French *joug,* yoke, from Latin *jugum.*]

joule (jōōl, *rarely* jowl) *n. Abbr.* **J** The SI unit of energy, equal to the work done when a current of 1 ampere is passed through a resistance of 1 ohm for 1 second. This is equivalent to the work done when the point of application of a force of 1 newton is displaced 1 metre in the direction of the force. Compare **calorie.** [After James P. JOULE.]

Joule (jōōl), **James Prescott** (1818–89). British physicist who was the first to measure the mechanical equivalent of heat. He performed a number of experiments to prove that a given amount of electrical energy will always produce the same amount of heat. He provided the evidence for the law of conservation of energy.

Joule's law *n.* **1.** The principle that the heat generated by an electric current passing through a wire is equal to the product of the potential difference between the ends of the wire, the current flowing through it, and the time for which it flows. **2.** The principle that the internal energy of a gas at a constant temperature is independent of the volume of the gas. This law applies only to ideal gases; in real gases the internal energy varies with volume as a result of intermolecular forces.

Joule-Thom·son effect (jōōl-tóm-s'n) *n.* The fall in temperature of a gas when it expands through a small hole, caused by work being done against the intermolecular forces within the gas. Also called "Joule-Kelvin effect".

jounce (jownss) *v.* **jounced, jouncing, jounces.** —*intr.* To move with bumps and jolts. —*tr.* To cause to jounce. [Middle English *jouncen†*.]

jour. **1.** journal; journalist. **2.** journeyman.

jour·nal (júrn'l) *n. Abbr.* J., jour. **1.** A daily record of occurrences or transactions, especially: **a.** A personal record of experiences and reflections; a diary. **b.** An official record of daily proceedings, as of a legislative body. **c.** A ship's log. **2.** *Bookkeeping.* **a.** A daybook. **b.** A book of original entry in a double-entry system, listing all transactions and indicating the accounts to which they belong. **3. a.** A newspaper. **b.** A periodical presenting news or containing scholarly articles on a particular subject: *a medical journal.* **c.** Used as part of the title of certain newspapers or periodicals: *The Wessex Journal.* **4.** The part of a shaft or axle supported by a bearing. [Middle English, from Old French *jurnal, jornal,* from *journal, jornel,* "daily", from Late Latin *diurnālis,* diurnal, from *diurnus,* daily, from *diēs,* day.]

journal box *n.* A housing enclosing a journal and its bearings.

jour·nal·ese (júrn'l-éez ‖ -éess) *n.* The slick, superficial style of writing often held to be characteristic of newspapers and magazines. [JOURNAL + -ESE.]

jour·nal·ise, jour·nal·ize (júrn'l-īz) *v.* **-ised, -ising, -ises.** —*tr.* To record in a journal. —*intr.* To keep a journal. —**jour·nal·is·er** *n.*

jour·nal·ism (júrn'l-iz'm) *n.* **1. a.** The collecting, reporting, writing, photographing, editing, and publishing of news or articles for any of the media, especially for newspapers and magazines. **b.** The business or occupation of working in the news media. **2.** Material written for publication in a newspaper or magazine. **3.** A style of writing associated with newspapers and magazines, characterised by direct presentation of facts or occurrences with little attempt at analysis or interpretation. **4.** Newspapers and magazines collectively. **5.** Written material of current interest or wide popular appeal.

jour·nal·ist (júrn'l-ist) *n.* **1.** *Abbr.* jour. A person whose occupation is journalism. **2.** A person who keeps a journal.

jour·nal·is·tic (júrn'l-ístik) *adj.* Pertaining to or characteristic of journalism or journalists. —**jour·nal·is·ti·cal·ly** *adv.*

jour·ney (júrni) *n., pl.* **-neys.** **1. a.** An act of travelling from one place to another; a trip. **b.** A long overland trip as distinguished from a voyage or a flight. **2. a.** The distance travelled on a journey. **b.** The time required for such a trip. **3.** A process of transition or progress: *our journey through life.*

—*intr.v.* **journeyed, -neying, -neys.** To travel; make a trip. [Middle English *journey, jorne,* period of travel, a day's travelling, from Old French *jornee,* from Vulgar Latin *diurnāta* (unattested), from Latin *diurnum,* daily portion, neuter of *diurnus,* daily, from *diēs,* day.] —**jour·ney·er** *n.*

jour·ney·man (júrni-mən) *n., pl.* **-men** (-mən, -men). **1.** *Abbr.* jour. One who has fully served his apprenticeship in a trade or craft and is a qualified worker in another's employ. **2.** Any competent workman. [Middle English : JOURNEY (in the dialectal sense of "a day's work") + MAN.]

jour·ney·work (júrni-wurk) *n.* **1.** The work of a journeyman. **2.** Menial or routine work.

journ·o (júrnō) *n. Australian Informal.* A journalist.

joust (jowst, *sometimes* jōost, just) *n.* **1.** A combat with lances between two mounted knights or men-at-arms; a tilting match. **2.** *Usually plural.* A series of these matches; a tournament. **3.** Any combat or exchange suggestive of a joust.

—*intr.v.* **jousted, jousting, jousts.** To engage in such combat or exchange; tilt. [Middle English, from Old French *juste, jouste,* from *juster,* to join battle, joust, from Vulgar Latin *juxtāre* (unattested), to come together, from Latin *juxtā,* close together.]

j'ou·vert (zhoo-váir) *n. West Indian.* The eve of Mardi Gras. [Shortened from French *jour ouvert,* "the day having been opened".]

Jove (jōv) *n.* **1.** The god **Jupiter** *(see).* **2.** *Poetic.* The planet Jupiter. —**by Jove.** A mild oath used to express surprise or to give emphasis. [Middle English, from Latin *Jov-,* stem of the oblique cases of Old Latin *Jovis.*]

jo·vi·al (jōv-yəl, -i-əl) *adj.* Marked by hearty conviviality. See Synonyms at **jolly.** [Originally "born under the influence of Jupiter" (the planet, regarded as the source of happiness), from French *jovial,* from Italian *gioviale,* from Jove, from Latin *Jov-.*] —**jo·vi·al·i·ty** (-i-ál-əti) *n.* —**jo·vi·al·ly** *adv.*

Jo·vi·an (jōv-yən, -i-ən) *adj.* **1.** Of, pertaining to, or resembling the God Jove. **2.** Of, relating to, or occurring on the planet Jupiter.

Jow·ett (jów-it, jō-), **Benjamin** (1817–93). British classical scholar and Master of Balliol College, Oxford (1870–93). His essay *The Interpretation of Scripture* (1860), provoked charges of heresy from orthodox Anglicans. He also published classical translations, the most notable being of Plato's *Dialogues.*

jowl¹ (jowl) *n.* **1.** The jaw, especially the lower jaw. **2.** The cheek. [Middle English *chawle, chauel,* Old English *ceafl.*]

jowl² *n.* **1.** The flesh under the lower jaw, especially when plump or flaccid. **2.** A similar fleshy part, such as a dewlap or a wattle. [Middle English *cholle,* probably Old English *ceole, ceolu,* throat.]

joy (joy) *n.* **1.** A condition or deep feeling of pleasure or delight; happiness; gladness. **2.** The expression or manifestation of such a feeling. **3.** A source or object of pleasure or satisfaction. **4.** *Informal.* Satisfaction or assistance. Used chiefly in *any* or *no joy.* —See Synonyms at **pleasure.**

—*v.* **joyed, joying, joys.** —*intr. Literary.* To take pleasure; rejoice. —*tr. Archaic.* **1.** To fill with joy. **2.** To enjoy. [Middle English

joy(e), from Old French *joie, joye,* from Vulgar Latin *gaudia* (unattested), from Latin, plural of *gaudium,* gladness, delight, from *gaudēre,* to rejoice.]

joy·ance (jóy-ənss) *n. Literary.* **1.** Enjoyment; delight. **2.** Merrymaking; festivity.

Joyce (joyss), **James (Augustine Aloysius)** (1882–1941). Irish novelist, poet, and dramatist. He lived in Europe from 1904, publishing his first collection of stories, *Dubliners,* in 1914, and his first, largely autobiographical novel, *Portrait of the Artist as a Young Man,* in 1916. He is best known for *Ulysses* (1922), a novel which minutely describes the events of a single day in Dublin, and is noted for its linguistic innovation. Joyce further pursued wordplay and experiment in *Finnegans Wake* (1939). —**Joy·ce·an** (jóyssiən) *adj.*

Joyce, William, also known as Lord Haw-Haw (1906–46). Nazi propagandist, born in the United States of Irish parentage. During World War II he made propaganda broadcasts from Germany, delivered in the upper-class accent which earned him his nickname. He was tried in Britain and executed for treason after the war.

joy·ful (jóyf'l) *adj.* Feeling, causing, or expressing joy. See Synonyms at **glad.** —**joy·ful·ly** *adv.* —**joy·ful·ness** *n.*

joy·less (jóy-ləss, -liss) *adj.* Destitute of joy; cheerless; dismal. —**joy·less·ly** *adv.* —**joy·less·ness** *n.*

joy·ous (jóy-əss) *adj.* Feeling or causing joy; joyful. See Synonyms at **glad.** —**joy·ous·ly** *adv.* —**joy·ous·ness** *n.*

joy ride *n.* **1.** A ride taken in a car, especially a stolen car, simply for fun and often for the thrills provided by reckless driving. **2.** A hazardous, reckless, and often costly venture. —**joy-ride** *intr.v.*

joy·stick (jóy-stik). *n. Informal.* **1.** The control stick of an aircraft. **2.** A manual control device linked to a computer, used especially in making moves in a video game.

J.P. justice of the peace.

J particle, j psi particle *n.* The **psi particle** *(see).*

jr., Jr. junior.

J.S.D. Doctor of Juristic Science. [Latin *Juris Scientiae Doctor.*]

jt. joint.

Juan Car·los (waán kár-loss, wán, hwáan, hwán ‖ -lōss) (1938–). King of Spain (1975–). Acceding to the throne on the death of Franco, he helped to restore parliamentary democracy. His declared opposition to an attempted military coup (February 1981) contributed to its failure.

ju·ba (joobə) *n.* A group dance, probably of West African origin, characterised by complex rhythmic clapping and body movements and practised on plantations in the southern United States during the 18th and 19th centuries. [Probably from Bantu.]

Ju·bal (joo-b'l, -bal). A descendant of Cain and the reputed inventor of musical instruments. Genesis 4:21.

jub·bah (joobə) *n.* Also **jib·bah** (jíbə). A long, loose, open, outer garment with sleeves, worn by Muslims and Parsees. [Arabic.]

ju·be¹ (joo-bi ‖ jéw-) *n.* A loft or rood screen and gallery that separate the choir from the nave in a church. [French *jubé,* from Medieval Latin, opening word of the prayer *Jube, Domine, benedicere,* bid, Lord, a blessing : perhaps applied to the structure because the prayer was recited there by the deacon.]

jube² (joob) *n. Australian & N.Z.* A soft, chewy sweet coated with sugar. [Shortened from JUJUBE.]

ju·bi·lant (joobi-lənt ‖ jéwbi-) *adj.* Filled with or expressing great joy, especially through success or triumph. [Latin *jūbilāns* (stem *jūbilant-*), present participle of *jūbilāre,* to JUBILATE.] —**ju·bi·lance, ju·bi·lan·cy** *n.* —**ju·bi·lant·ly** *adv.*

ju·bi·late (joobi-layt ‖ jéwbi-) *intr.v.* **-lated, -lating, -lates.** To rejoice; exult. [Latin *jūbilāre,* to raise a shout of joy.]

Ju·bi·la·te (joobi-laáti, yoobi- *old-fashioned* -láyti ‖ jéwbi-) *n.* **1.** The 100th Psalm in the King James Bible, or the 99th in the Vulgate and the Douay Bible. **2.** A musical setting of the Jubilate. **3.** *Roman Catholic Church.* The third Sunday after Easter. **4.** A song or outburst of joy and triumph. [Latin *jūbilāte!,* rejoice! (the first word in the Jubilate), imperative of *jūbilāre,* to JUBILATE.]

ju·bi·la·tion (joobi-láysh'n ‖ jéwbi-) *n.* **1.** The state of being jubilant; exultation. **2.** A celebration or other expression of joy.

ju·bi·lee (joobi-lee, -lée ‖ jéwbi-) *n.* **1. a.** A special anniversary, as of a monarch's accession; especially, a 25th, 50th, 60th, or 75th anniversary. **b.** The celebration of such an anniversary. **2.** A season or occasion of joyful celebration. **3.** Jubilation; rejoicing. **4.** In the Old Testament, a year of rest to be observed by the Israelites every 50th year, during which slaves were to be set free, alienated property restored to its former owners, and the land left untilled. Leviticus 25:8–17. **5.** *Roman Catholic Church.* A year during which plenary indulgence may be obtained by the performance of certain pious acts. It is usually granted at intervals of 25 years. [Middle English, from Old French *jubilé,* from Late Latin *jūbilaeus (annus),* "(year) of jubilee", alteration (influenced by Latin *jūbilāre,* to JUBILATE) of Late Greek *iōbēlaios,* from *iōbēlos,* jubilee, from Hebrew *yōbhēl,* "ram's horn" (used to proclaim the jubilee), originally, "leading animal", akin to *hōbhīl,* to lead, conduct.]

Jud. **1.** Judges (Old Testament). **2.** Judith (Apocrypha).

J.U.D. Doctor of Canon and Civil Law. [Latin *Juris Utriusque Doctor,* "Doctor of either law".]

Ju·dae·a or **Ju·de·a** (joo-déer, joo-, -dée-ə ‖ jew-). The southern part of ancient Palestine. The Kingdom of Judah, sited here, lay south of Israel. Under David, the two kingdoms were united, the Judaean city of Jerusalem becoming his capital. Judah became independent in *c.* 922 B.C., later falling to the Assyrians, Babylonians,

Greeks, and Persians. In A.D. 135 it was absorbed into the Roman province of Syria. —**Ju·dae·an** *n. & adj.*

Judaeo-, *U.S.* **Judeo-**. *comb. form.* Indicates Judaism; for example, *Judaeo-Christian*. [From Latin *judaeus*, Jewish.]

Ju·dae·o·Ger·man (jōō-dáyō-jérmən, -déeō-) *n.* **Yiddish** *(see).*

Ju·dae·o·Span·ish (jōō-dáyō-spánnish, -déeō-) *n.* **Ladino** *(see).*

Ju·dah[1] (jōōdə ‖ jéwdə). Son of Jacob and Leah; ancestor of one of the twelve tribes of Israel. [Hebrew *Yəhūdāh*, "praised".]

Judah[2] *n.* The tribe of Israel descended from Judah.

Judah[3]. An ancient kingdom in southern Palestine, occupied by the tribes of Judah and Benjamin and governed by the descendants of Solomon. I Kings 11:31, 12:17–21. See **Judaea**.

Ju·da·ic (jōō-dáy-ik ‖ jew-) *adj.* Also **Ju·da·i·cal** (-ik'l). Of or pertaining to Jews or Judaism. [Latin *Jūdaicus*, from Greek *Ioudaikos*, from *Ioudaios*, JEW.] —**Ju·da·i·cal·ly** *adv.*

Ju·da·i·ca (jōō-dáy-ikə, jōō-) *n.* Books, documents, and artefacts representing the literature, history, and culture of the Jewish people. [Latin, "Jewish matters".]

Ju·da·ise, Ju·da·ize (jōō-day-īz ‖ jéw-, -di-) *v.* **-ised, -ising, -ises.** —*tr.* To bring into conformity with or convert to Judaism. —*intr.* To adopt Jewish customs and beliefs. —**Ju·da·i·sa·tion** (-ī-záysh'n ‖ U.S. -i-) *n.* —**Ju·da·is·er** *n.*

Ju·da·ism (jōō-day-iz'm ‖ jéw-, -di-) *n.* **1.** The monotheistic religion of the Jewish people, tracing its origins to Abraham, having its spiritual and ethical principles embodied chiefly in the Old Testament and the Talmud. **2.** Conformity to the traditional ceremonies and rites of the Jewish religion. **3.** The cultural, spiritual, and social way of life of the Jewish people. **4.** The Jewish people. [Late Latin *Jūdaismus*, from Greek *Ioudaismos*, from *Ioudaios*, JEW.] —**Ju·da·ist** *n.* —**Ju·da·is·tic** (-ístik) *adj.*

Ju·das[1] (jōō-dəss ‖ jéw-). Called "Judas Iscariot". One of the Twelve Apostles, who betrayed Jesus for 30 pieces of silver. [Late Latin *Jūdas*, from Greek *Ioudas*, from Hebrew *Yəhūdāh*, JUDAH.]

Judas[2]. Known as Saint Jude to distinguish him from Judas Iscariot. One of the Twelve Apostles.

Judas[3] *n.* **1.** One who betrays under the appearance of friendship. **2.** *Usually small* **j.** A one-way peephole in a door. [From JUDAS (Iscariot).]

Judas Maccabaeus. See **Maccabaeus**.

Judas tree *n.* Any of various trees of the genus *Cercis;* especially, the ornamental Eurasian species *C. siliquastrum*, having clusters of pinkish-red flowers that appear before the leaves. Also called "red-bud". [From a belief that Judas Iscariot hanged himself on it.]

Juddah. See **Jiddah**.

jud·der (júddər) *intr.v.* **-dered, -dering, -ders.** To shake, shudder, or vibrate violently. —*n.* A juddering movement, especially in a mechanical system. [Probably from JAR + SHUDDER.]

Jude (jōōd ‖ jewd) *n.* The Epistle of Jude, a book of the New Testament often attributed to Saint Jude. See **Judas**[2].

Judg. Judges (Old Testament).

judge (juj) *v.* **judged, judging, judges.** —*tr.* **1. a.** To pass judgment upon in a court of law. **b.** To sit in judgment upon; try; hear. **2.** To determine authoritatively after deliberation, especially: **a.** To decide or settle (a controversy, for example). **b.** To appraise discriminatingly as an expert. **c.** To declare after deliberation: *They judged her a witch.* **d.** To choose the winners of (a competition). **3.** To form an appraisal or estimate of: *judge character; judge distances.* **4.** To criticise; censure. **5.** To consider, especially as a result of careful thought; conclude: *judged that the moment was right.* —*intr.* **1.** To act or decide as a judge; pass judgment. **2.** To form an opinion or estimation; make a critical determination or appraisal. —*n.* **1.** *Abbr.* **J.** A public official who hears and decides cases brought before a court of law for the purpose of administering justice. See **justice, justice of the peace, magistrate. 2.** An appointed arbiter in a contest or competition. **3.** One who makes critical judgments: *He's a poor judge of character.* **4.** A leader of the Israelites during a period of about 400 years between the death of Joshua and the accession of Saul. [Middle English *jugen*, from Old French *jugier*, from Latin *jūdicāre*, from *jūdex* (stem *jūdic-*), judge.]

Synonyms: *judge, arbitrator, arbiter, referee, umpire.*

judge advocate *n., pl.* **judge advocates.** *Abbr.* **J.A.** An officer who superintends proceedings at a court-martial.

Judge Advocate General *n., pl.* **Judge Advocates General** or **Judge Advocate Generals.** *Abbr.* **J.A.G.** In England and Wales, a military legal officer who exercises judicial functions in relation to courts-martial and who advises the government on military law.

Judg·es (jújiz) *n.* Used with a singular verb. *Abbr.* **Jud., Judg.** A book of the Old Testament containing the history of the Israelites during the rule of the judges.

judge·ship (júj-ship) *n.* The office, duties, or jurisdiction of a judge.

judg·es' rules (jújiz) *pl.n.* *Law.* In England and Wales, a set of rules that are not legally binding, laid down by judges for the guidance of the police when dealing with suspected offenders.

judg·mat·ic (juj-máttik) *adj.* Also **judg·mat·i·cal** (-'l). *Informal.* Judicious. [From JUDGMENT.] —**judg·mat·i·cal·ly** *adv.*

judg·ment, judge·ment (újjmənt) *n.* **1. a.** The capacity to appraise, discriminate, and compare, and so arrive at a sound evaluation; discernment. **b.** The capacity to make reasonable decisions, especially in regard to the practical affairs of life; good sense; wisdom. **c.** The exercise of such a capacity. **2.** A formal decision, as of an arbiter in a contest. **3.** A discriminating appraisal; an authoritative opinion. **4.** Estimation: *make a judgment of the distance.* **5.** An as-

sertion of something believed; an idea; an opinion: *It's my judgment that we ought to leave soon.* **6.** Criticism; censure. **7.** *Law.* **a.** A verdict by a court of law; a judicial decision. **b.** A court act creating or affirming an obligation, such as a debt. **c.** A writ in witness of such an act. —See Synonyms at **opinion, reason.** [Middle English *juge-ment*, from Old French, from *juger*, to JUDGE.]

judg·ment·al (juj-mént'l) *adj.* **1.** Of, pertaining to, or involving a judgment. **2.** Given to making judgments, especially moral judgments.

Judgment Day *n.* **1.** In Judaism, Christianity, and Islam, the day of God's final judgment upon mankind. **2.** Any day of reckoning or final judgment. Also called "Day of Judgment".

ju·di·ca·ble (jōōdi-kəb'l ‖ jéwdi-) *adj.* **1.** Capable of being judged. **2.** Liable to be judged. [Late Latin *jūdicābilis*, from Latin *jūdicāre*, to JUDGE.]

ju·di·ca·tive (jōōdi-kətiv, -kaytiv ‖ jéwdi-) *adj.* Having the capacity to judge; judicial. [Medieval Latin *jūdicātivus*, from Latin *jūdicāre*, to JUDGE.]

ju·di·ca·tor (jōōdi-kaytər ‖ jéwdi-) *n.* One who acts as judge. [Late Latin *jūdicātor*, from Latin *jūdicāre*, to JUDGE.]

ju·di·ca·to·ry (jōōdi-kətri, -kətəri, -kaytəri ‖ jéwdi-, -káytəri, *U.S.* -kə-tawri, -tōri) *n., pl.* **-ries. 1.** A court of justice; a tribunal. **2.** A system of courts of law for the administration of justice; a judiciary. —*adj.* Of or pertaining to the administration of justice. [Medieval Latin *jūdicātōrium*, from Latin *jūdicāre*, to JUDGE.]

ju·di·ca·ture (jōōdikə-chər, jōō-dickə-, -tewr ‖ jéwdikə-, -choor) *n.* **1.** The administering of justice. **2.** The position, function, or authority of a judge. **3.** A court of law. **4.** A system of law courts and their judges. [Old French, from Medieval Latin *jūdicātūra*, from Latin *jūdicāre*, to JUDGE.]

ju·di·cial (jōō-dísh'l ‖ jew-) *adj.* **1.** Of, pertaining to, or proper to courts of law or to the administration of justice: *the judicial branch of the government.* Compare **executive, legislative. 2.** Decreed by or proceeding from a court of justice. **3.** Pertaining or appropriate to the office of a judge. **4.** Characterised by or expressing judgment. **5.** *Theology.* Proceeding from a divine judgment. [Middle English, from Old French, from Latin *jūdiciālis*, from *jūdicium*, judgment, from *jūdex* (stem *jūdic-*), JUDGE.] —**ju·di·cial·ly** *adv.*

Judicial Committee of the Privy Council *n.* The final appeal court for citizens of certain Commonwealth countries and for appellants against decisions of certain ecclesiastical and prize courts and various professional bodies.

judicial separation *n.* A court order recognising that husband and wife are living apart and regulating their mutual rights and liabilities. Also called "legal separation".

ju·di·ci·ar·y (jōō-dísh-əri, -i-əri, -yəri ‖ jew-, *U.S.* -i-erri) *adj.* Of or pertaining to courts, judges, or judicial decisions. —*n., pl.* **judiciaries. 1.** The judicial branch of government. Compare **executive, legislature. 2.** A system of courts of justice. **3.** Judges collectively. [Latin *jūdiciārius*, from *jūdicium*, judgment. See **judicial**.]

ju·di·cious (jōō-díshəss ‖ jew-) *adj.* Having or exhibiting sound judgment. [Old French *judicieux*, from Latin *jūdicium*. See **judicial**.] —**ju·di·cious·ly** *adv.* —**ju·di·cious·ness** *n.*

Ju·dith[1] (jōō-dith ‖ jew-). In the Apocrypha, a Jewish woman who rescued her people by slaying the Assyrian general Holofernes.

Judith[2] *n.* A book of the Apocrypha and the Douay Bible relating the story of Judith.

ju·do (jōō-dō ‖ jéw-) *n.* A modern form of jujitsu applying principles of balance and leverage, often used as physical training. [Japanese *jūdō : jū*, soft (see **jujitsu**) + *dō*, way.] —**ju·do·ist** *n.*

ju·do·gi (jōō-dōgi) *n.* A white costume worn by contestants in judo, consisting of loose trousers and a loose-sleeved jacket fastened by a belt. [Japanese.]

ju·do·ka (jōōdō-kaa) *n.* One who takes part in a judo contest. [Japanese.]

Ju·dy (jōōdi ‖ jéwdi) *n., pl.* **-ies. 1.** A character in the puppet show *Punch and Judy.* See **Punch. 2.** *Often small* **j.** *British Slang.* A woman or girl.

jug (jug) *n.* **1. a.** A vessel of earthenware, glass, or metal with a lip or spout, a handle, and sometimes a stopper or cap, made for holding and pouring liquids. **b.** The contents of a jug. **c.** The amount of liquid a jug will hold. **2.** *British Informal.* A glass for beer or some other alcoholic drink, especially one with a handle. **3.** *Slang.* Jail. —*tr.v.* **jugged, jugging, jugs. 1.** To stew (a hare, for example) in an earthenware vessel. **2.** *Slang.* To put in jail. [From *Jug*, pet form of *Joan* or *Judith*.]

ju·gal (jōōg'l ‖ jéwg'l) *adj.* Of or pertaining to the zygomatic bone. —*n.* The zygomatic bone. Also called "jugal bone". [Latin *jugālis*, of a yoke, from *jugum*, a yoke.]

ju·gate (jōō-gayt, -gət, -git ‖ jéw-) *adj.* Joined in or forming a pair or pairs. Said especially of compound leaves. [From New Latin *jugum*, yoke, from Latin.]

jug band *n. Music.* A country-and-western group playing improvised instruments, such as empty jugs and washboards.

JUG·FET (júg-fet) *n. Electronics.* *J*unction-*G*ate *F*ield-*E*ffect Transistor: a type of field-effect transistor in which the gate is a p-n junction with the conducting channel.

jug·ger·naut (júggər-nawt) *n.* **1.** *British.* A very large, heavy motor vehicle, especially a long-distance lorry. **2.** Anything that draws blind and destructive devotion, or to which people are ruthlessly sacrificed, such as a belief or institution. [From JUGGERNAUT.]

Jug·ger·naut *n.* **1.** *Hinduism.* Also **Jag·an·nath, Jag·an·na·tha.**

1. A title of the deity Krishna. **2.** A huge car or wagon on which an idol of the god Krishna is drawn in procession; specifically, such a vehicle used in an annual procession in Puri, in the Indian state of Orissa. [From Hindi *Jagannath,* from Sanskrit *Jagannātha* : *jagat-,* world + *nāthás,* lord.]

jug·gle (júgg'l) *v.* **-gled, -gling, -gles.** —*tr.* **1.** To keep (two or more balls, plates, or other objects) in the air at one time by alternately tossing and catching. **2.** To keep (more than one activity) in motion or progress at one time. **3.** To attempt to balance or otherwise cope with: *juggle a handbag and glass at a cocktail party.* **4.** To manipulate, especially in order to deceive: *juggle figures in a ledger.* —*intr.* **1.** To perform the tricks of a juggler. **2.** To use trickery to deceive. —*n.* **1.** An act of juggling. **2.** A piece of trickery for some dishonest purpose. [Middle English *jogelen,* from Old French *jogler,* from Latin *joculārī,* to jest. See **juggler.**]

jug·gler (júgglər) *n.* **1.** An entertainer who performs tricks of dexterity; especially, one who juggles balls or other objects. **2.** One who uses tricks, deception, or fraud. [Middle English *iugelere, iugelour,* jester, magician, from Old French *joglere, juglere,* from Latin *joculātor,* from *joculārī,* to jest, from *joculus,* diminutive of *jocus,* jest, joke.]

jug·gler·y (júggləri) *n., pl.* **-ies. 1.** The art or performance of a juggler. **2.** Trickery; deception.

Jugoslavia. See **Yugoslavia.**

jug·u·lar (júggewlər) *adj.* **1.** Of, pertaining to, or located in the region of the neck or throat. **2.** Of, designating, or having pelvic fins in front of the pectoral fins. —*n.* A jugular vein. [Late Latin *jugulāris,* from Latin *jugulum,* collarbone, diminutive of *jugum,* yoke.]

jugular vein *n.* Any of several veins in the neck. The *internal jugular* is a large paired vein conveying blood from the brain, face, and neck to the subclavian vein. The *external jugular* is a smaller paired vein taking blood from the face, scalp, and neck to the subclavian vein.

ju·gum (jōō-gəm ‖ jéw-) *n., pl.* **-ga** (-gə) or **-gums.** A paired or yokelike structure, such as a pair of opposite leaflets, a ridge or furrow connecting two parts of a bone, or a lobe joining the bases of the forewings and hind wings of certain insects. [New Latin, from Latin *jugum,* yoke.]

juice (jōōss ‖ jewss) *n.* **1. a.** Any fluid naturally contained in plant or animal tissue. **b.** Any bodily secretion. **c.** Any extracted fluid, especially that of a fruit. **2. a.** The essence or animating spirit of something. **b.** Vigorous life and vitality. **3.** *Slang.* **a.** Electric current. **b.** Fuel for an engine. **4.** *Chiefly U.S. Slang.* Alcoholic drink. —**stew in (one's) own juice.** To suffer from problems of one's own making. —*tr.v.* **juiced, juicing, juices. 1.** To extract the juice from. **2.** *U.S. Slang.* To make lively. Used with *up.* [Middle English *iuys, jus,* from Old French *jus,* from Latin *jūs,* broth, sauce, juice.]

juic·er (jōō-sər) *n.* A kitchen appliance for extracting juice from fruits and vegetables.

juic·y (jōō-si ‖ jéw-) *adj.* **-ier, -iest. 1.** Full of juice; succulent. **2.** Richly interesting; suggestive; racy: *a juicy bit of gossip.* —**juic·i·ly** *adv.* —**juic·i·ness** *n.*

ju·jit·su, ju·jut·su, jiu·jut·su, jiu·jit·su (jōō-jitsōō ‖ jew-) *n.* A Japanese art of self-defence or hand-to-hand combat based on manoeuvres that seek to turn an opponent's weight and strength against himself. [Japanese *jūjitsu* : *jū,* soft, yielding, + *jitsu,* art.]

ju·ju (jōōjōō) *n., pl.* **-jus. 1.** An object used as a fetish, charm, or amulet in West Africa. **2.** The supernatural power ascribed to such an object. [Probably of West African origin.] —**ju·ju·ism** *n.*

ju·jube (jōōjōōb) *n.* **1. a.** Any of several spiny trees of the genus *Ziziphus;* especially, *Z. jujuba,* native to the Old World, having small yellowish flowers and dark red fruit. **b.** The fleshy, edible fruit of this tree. Also called "Chinese date". **2.** A fruit-flavoured, usually chewy sweet or lozenge. [Middle English *iuiube,* from Old French *jujube* or Medieval Latin *jujuba,* both from Latin *zizyphum,* from Greek *zizuphon†.*]

juk, jook (jōōk) *tr.v.* **juked** or **jooked, juking** or **jooking, jukes** or **jooks.** *West Indian Informal.* To prick; jab. —*n.* A prick or jab. [West African, probably Fulani *jukka,* to poke.]

juke·box (jōōk-boks) *n.* A coin-operated machine, typically encased in an illuminated and decorated cabinet, and equipped with push buttons for the selection and playing of records. [From earlier *jukehouse,* a brothel, from Gullah *juke,* disorderly.]

ju·lep (jōō-lep, -lip) *n.* **1.** A sweet syrupy drink, especially one to which medicine may be added. **2.** *U.S.* A **mint julep** (see). [Middle English *iulep,* from Old French *julep,* from Arabic *julāb,* from Persian *gulāb,* "rose water" : *gul,* rose + *āb,* water.]

Ju·li·an (jōōl-yən, -i-ən ‖ jéwl-), known as Julian the Apostate, born Flavius Claudius Julianus (A.D. 331–363). Roman emperor (361–363). Brought up as a Christian, he began to take measures to restore the old Roman religion. He died in battle.

Ju·li·an·a (jōōli-aánə), born Louise Emma Marie Wilhelmina (1909–). Queen of the Netherlands (1948–80). She married Prince Bernhard (1911–) in 1937, and came to the throne after the abdication of her mother, Wilhelmina (1880–1962). In 1980, Juliana abdicated in favour of her daughter, Beatrix (1938–).

Julian calendar *n.* The calendar introduced by Julius Caesar in Rome in 46 B.C., that fixed the length of the year at 365 days, with an extra day every fourth, or leap, year. It was eventually replaced by the Gregorian calendar.

ju·li·enne (jōō-li-én, zhōō-, zhül-yén) *adj.* Cut into thin strips about

the size of a matchstick: *julienne potatoes.* —*n.* Consommé or broth garnished with strips of julienne vegetables. [From French *à la julienne,* probably from the given name *Julien* or *Jules.*]

Jul·i·us II (jōōl-yəss, -i-əss ‖ jéwl-), born Giuliano della Rovere (1443–1513). Pope (1503–13). A soldier and statesman more than a spiritual leader, he restored papal authority in central Italy through campaigns against Venice, and formed the Holy League to expel the French from Italy. He ordered the reconstruction of St. Peter's in Rome, and commissioned Michelangelo to decorate the Sistine chapel and Raphael to decorate his papal apartments.

Julius Caesar. See **Caesar.**

Ju·ly (jōō-lí, jōō-, jə-, jōō-) *n., pl.* **-lys.** *Abbr.* **Jul.** The seventh month of the year according to the Gregorian calendar. July has 31 days. [Middle English *Julie,* from Anglo-French, from Latin *Jūlius (mēnsis),* (month of) Julius Caesar.]

Ju·ma (jōō-mə, -maa) *n.* The Islamic Sabbath, falling on Friday.

Ju·ma·da, Jo·ma·da (jōō-maádə) *n.* **1.** The fifth month of the year in the Muslim calendar, having 30 days. **2.** The sixth month of the year in the Muslim calendar, having 29 days. [Arabic *Jumādā.*]

jum·ble¹ (júmb'l) *v.* **-bled, -bling, -bles.** —*intr.* To move, mix, or mingle in a confused, disordered manner. —*tr.* **1.** To stir or mix in a disordered mass. **2.** To muddle; confuse. —*n.* **1.** A confused or disordered mass: *a jumble of disconnected ideas.* **2.** A disordered state; a muddle. **3.** *Chiefly British.* Goods to be sold at a jumble sale. [16th century : perhaps imitative.]

jumble² *n.* A light, thin, crisp biscuit, variously flavoured with fruit or almonds and usually tightly rolled. [17th century (originally, a cake made in rings) : perhaps from earlier *gimmal,* variant of GIMBALS.]

jumble sale *n.* A sale of miscellaneous secondhand articles, chiefly clothes, donated in order to raise money for a charity, club, or the like. Also *chiefly U.S.* "rummage sale".

jum·bo (júmbō) *n., pl.* **-bos. 1.** An unusually large person, animal, or thing. **2.** *Informal.* A jumbo jet. —*adj.* Larger than average: *jumbo pack of detergent.*

Jum·bo (júmbō). A name for an elephant, as used by children and in folktales. [Probably from the second element of MUMBO JUMBO.]

jumbo jet *n.* A large jet airliner.

jum·buck (júm-buk) *n. Australian Informal.* A sheep. [From a native Australian name.]

Jum·na (júm-nə). Also **Yam·u·na** (yámmōōnə). A river in northern India. It rises in the Himalayas of Uttar Pradesh and flows roughly south through Delhi to its confluence with the Ganges. The juncture of the two rivers is known as the Prayag, a place of pilgrimage in Hindu religion. The Jumna is 1 385 kilometres (860 miles) long.

jump (jump) *v.* **jumped, jumping, jumps.** —*intr.* **1. a.** To spring off the ground or other base by a muscular effort of the legs and feet: *jumped three feet into the air.* **b.** To perform this movement repeatedly or rhythmically, as for exercise. **2. a.** To move or propel oneself, legs downwards, down, off, out, or into something. **b.** To involve or commit oneself enthusiastically: *He jumped into the political fray.* **c.** To parachute from an aircraft. **3.** To spring or pounce with the intent to upbraid or censure. Used with *on* or *at: He jumped on me for saying such a thing.* **4.** To form judgments hastily or haphazardly. Used with *to: jump to conclusions.* **5.** To grab at eagerly; respond with alacrity. Used with *at: jump at the chance.* **6.** To start involuntarily: *You made me jump.* **7.** To rise suddenly and pronouncedly: *Prices jumped.* **8. a.** To skip over space or material, leaving a break in continuity. **b.** To be displaced vertically or laterally because of improper alignment: *The film jumped during projection.* **9.** In board games, to move over an opponent's playing piece. **10.** In bridge, to make a jump bid. **11.** To be in agreement; coincide. **12.** *Slang.* To have a lively, pulsating quality: *a nightclub that jumps.* **13.** *Physics.* To change from one quantum state to another. —*tr.* **1.** To leap over or across: *jump a gate.* **2.** *Chiefly U.S.* To leap aboard or jump on (a vehicle) illegally: *jump a train.* **3.** *Slang.* To spring upon in sudden attack: *The muggers jumped him.* **4.** To cause to leap: *jump a horse over a hurdle.* **5.** To cause to increase suddenly and markedly. **6.** To miss out; skip: *The typewriter jumped a space.* **7.** To drive through or move away from (traffic lights), before they change to green. **8.** In bridge, to raise (a partner's bid) by more than is necessary. **9.** In board games, to take (an opponent's piece) by moving over it with one's own. **10.** To leave (a course or track) through mishap: *The train jumped the rails.* **11.** To leave or abandon without authorisation: *jump ship; jump bail.* —**jump to it.** *Informal.* To get going promptly and eagerly. —*n.* **1.** The act of jumping; a leap. **2. a.** The space or distance covered by a leap: *a jump of seven feet.* **b.** A descent by parachute from an aircraft. **3.** A hurdle, fence, barrier, or span to be jumped. **4.** An athletic event featuring skill in jumping: *the high jump.* **5.** A sudden, pronounced rise, as in price or salary. **6.** A step or level: *a jump ahead of the others.* **7.** A major transition, as from one career to another. **8.** A short trip: *just a hop, skip, and a jump to the shore.* **9.** A break in continuity, as in a film. **10.** In board games, a move made by jumping. **11. a.** An involuntary nervous movement, as when startled. **b.** *Plural. Informal.* The fidgets. **12.** *Physics.* A change between two quantum states. **13.** *West African.* A dance with live music. [16th century : probably imitative.]

jump bid *n.* In bridge, a bid at a higher level than that required to exceed the preceding bid.

jumped-up (júmpt-úp, -up) *adj. Informal.* Showing arrogance or conceit as a result of having risen from a humble to a significant position; upstart.

jump·er¹ (júmpər) *n.* **1.** One that jumps. **2.** *Electricity.* A short length of wire used temporarily to complete or by-pass a circuit. **3.** A bit or other boring device in a hammer drill.

jumper² *n.* **1.** *Chiefly British.* **a.** A jersey or sweater. **b.** Loosely, any knitted top. **2.** *U.S.* A sleeveless dress worn over a blouse or sweater; a pinafore dress. [Probably from British dialectal *jump, jup,* man's loose jacket, woman's underbodice, from French *juppe,* variant of *jupe,* skirt, from Arabic *jubbah,* JUBBAH.]

jump·ing bean (júmping) *n.* A seed, as of certain Mexican shrubs or plants of the genera *Sebastiania* and *Sapium,* containing the larva of a moth, *Carpocapsa* (or *Enarmonia*) *saltitans,* the movements of which cause the seed to jerk or roll.

jumping jack *n.* **1.** A toy figure with jointed limbs that can be moved using an attached string or frame. **2.** A firework that jumps along the ground when lit.

jumping mouse *n.* Any of various small rodents of the family Zapodidae, having a long tail and long hind legs.

jump·ing-off place (júmping-óff, -áwf) *n.* **1.** A starting point for an enterprise. Also called "jumping-off point". **2.** *U.S.* A very remote place.

jump jet *n.* A fixed-wing jet aircraft in which the engine ducts can be rotated downwards so that the aircraft can take off and land vertically.

jump leads *pl.n.* A pair of heavily insulated cables with clips on each end, used to start a motor vehicle by connecting its battery to the battery of another vehicle. Also *chiefly U.S.* "jumper cables".

jump-off (júmp-off, -awf) *n.* In show-jumping, a round that decides which of two or more horses previously tying for first place is the winner.

jump seat *n.* A portable or folding seat in an aircraft or in a car between the front and rear seats.

jump-start (júmp-staart, -stárt) *tr.v.* **-started, -starting, -starts. 1.** To start (a car engine) by pushing or rolling and suddenly releasing the clutch; bump-start. **2.** To start (a car engine) using jump leads. **3.** To cause to start or restart with or as if with a whoosh: *jump-start a flagging economy.*
~ *n.* The process or an instance of jump-starting.

jump·suit (júmp-sōot, -sewt) *n.* A one-piece woman's outfit with legs, reaching from neck to ankles, and usually made of a close-fitting, stretch fabric.

jump-up (júmp-up) *n.* A West Indian festival dance.

jump·y (júmpi) *adj.* **-ier, -iest. 1.** Characterised by fitful, jerky movements. **2.** Easily unsettled or alarmed; nervous or on edge, as with apprehension. —**jump·i·ness** *n.*

jun (jun, jōon) *n., pl.* **jun.** A coin equal to ¹/₁₀₀ of the won of North Korea. [Korean.]

jun·co (júng-kō) *n., pl.* **-cos.** Any of various North American sparrows of the genus *Junco,* having predominantly grey plumage. [Spanish, "rush", junco. See **jonquil**.]

junc·tion (júngk-sh'n, júng-) *n.* **1.** The act or process of joining or the condition of being joined. **2.** *Abbr.* **jct.** The place where two things join or meet; specifically, the place where two roads or railway routes join or cross paths. **3.** A transition layer or boundary between two different materials or between physically different regions in a single material, especially: **a.** A connection between conductors or sections of a transmission line. **b.** The interface between a region of predominantly positive charge carriers and another of predominantly negative charge carriers in a semiconductor. **c.** A mechanical or alloyed contact between different metals or other materials, as in a thermocouple. [Latin *junctiō* (stem *junctiōn-*), from *junctus,* past participle of *jungere,* to join.] —**junc·tion·al** *adj.*

junction box *n.* An enclosed panel used to connect or branch electric circuits without making permanent splices.

junction transistor *n.* A common type of transistor in which contact is made between regions of different conductivity type.

junc·ture (júngk-chər, júng-) *n.* **1.** The act of joining, or the condition of being joined. **2.** A line or point where two things are joined; a junction; a joint; a hinge. **3.** A point or interval in time; especially, a crisis or similar turning point. **4.** The transition or mode of transition from one sound to another in speech. [Middle English, from Latin *junctūra,* from *junctus,* past participle of *jungere,* to join.]

June (jōon ‖ jewn) *n. Abbr.* **Jun.** The sixth month of the year according to the Gregorian calendar. June has 30 days. [Middle English, from Old French *juin,* from Latin *Jūnius (mēnsis),* (month consecrated to) the goddess JUNO.]

Ju·neau (jōo-nō). The capital of Alaska in the northwestern United States, situated on the Gastineau channel.

June·ber·ry (jōon-bəri, -berri ‖ jewn-) *n., pl.* **-ries.** The **serviceberry** *(see),* or its fruit.

Jung (yoong), **Carl Gustav** (1875–1961). Swiss psychiatrist, a pioneer of psychoanalysis. He worked with Freud but developed his own approach to psychoanalysis, based in part on his study of schizophrenia. Jung coined the terms introvert and extrovert to define psychological types. His best-known work is *Psychology of the Unconscious* (1912). —**Jung·i·an** *n. & adj.*

Jung·frau (yoong-frow). One of the highest peaks (4 158 metres; 13,642 feet) in the Swiss Alps, situated in the Bernese Oberland, overlooking Interlaken. Its summit was first scaled in 1811.

jun·gle (júng-g'l) *n.* **1.** Land densely overgrown with tropical vegetation and trees. **2.** Any dense thicket or growth. **3.** A milieu characterised by intense, often ruthless competition. **4.** Any maze, entanglement, or confusion, especially one that is fruitless or leads

nowhere. [Originally, "wasteland", from Hindi and Marathi *jangal,* from Sanskrit *jāṅgala†,* "dry", desert.] —**jun·gly** *adj.*

jungle fever *n.* A pernicious malaria occurring in the East Indies.

jungle fowl *n.* Any of several birds of the genus *Gallus,* of southeastern Asia; especially, *G. gallus,* considered to be the ancestor of the common domestic fowl.

jungle gym *n.* A **climbing frame** *(see).* [From a trademark.]

jungle juice *n. Slang.* Alcoholic drink, especially when homemade.

ju·ni·or (jōon-yər, -i-ər ‖ jewn-) *adj. Abbr.* **Jnr., jnr., Jr., Jun., jun. 1.** Designed for or including youthful persons: *a junior tennis match; junior dress sizes.* **2.** Lower in rank or shorter in length of tenure: *the junior minister.* **3.** *British.* Of or pertaining to schoolchildren between the ages of 7 and 11. **4.** Younger. Used especially after a name to denote the younger of two persons who share the same name, such as a father and son: *William Jones, Jnr.* **5.** *U.S.* Designating the third or penultimate year of a high school or college.
~ *n.* **1.** A younger person or individual. **2.** A person lesser in rank or length of service; a subordinate. **3.** *Law.* In England, a barrister who is not a Queen's or King's Counsel. **4.** *British.* A schoolchild between the ages of 7 and 11. **5.** *U.S.* An undergraduate in his third or penultimate year of a high school or college. [Latin *jūnior,* from pre-classical *juvenior* (unattested), comparative of *juvenis,* young.]
Usage: British English prefers the abbreviation of *Jr.* to contain the *n* — either *jnr.* or *Jnr.* American English prefers *Jr.,* and also sometimes uses *Jun.* Note also that in American English, but not in British English, *junior* is occasionally attached to the name of a woman.

junior college *n.* An educational institution in the U.S. system offering a two-year course that is generally the equivalent of the first two years of a four-year undergraduate course.

Junior Common Room *n. Abbr.* **J.C.R. 1.** In certain universities, colleges, and schools, a common room for the use of students. **2.** The student body collectively.

junior high school *n.* A school in the U.S. system intermediate between grammar school and high school, and generally including the seventh, eighth, and sometimes ninth grades. Also called "junior high".

junior lightweight *n.* A professional boxer who weighs between 126 and 130 pounds (57 and 59 kilograms).

junior middleweight *n.* A professional boxer who weighs between 147 and 154 pounds (66.5 and 70 kilograms).

junior school *n.* In Britain, a school for children aged between 7 and 11. Compare **infant school**.

junior welterweight *n.* A professional boxer who weighs between 135 and 140 pounds (61 and 63.5 kilograms).

ju·ni·per (jōoni-pər ‖ jewni-) *n.* Any of various evergreen coniferous trees or shrubs of the genus *Juniperus* in the cypress family (cupressaceae), having spine-tipped needles and aromatic, bluish-grey, berry-like cones. An oil from the berries of *J. communis* is used to flavour gin. [Middle English *junipere,* from Latin *jūniperus†.*]

junk¹ (jungk) *n.* **1.** Discarded articles or waste materials of little or no value. **2.** *Informal.* **a.** Anything worn-out or fit to be discarded. **b.** Something of inferior quality; something cheap or shoddy. **c.** Anything meaningless, fatuous, or unbelievable; nonsense. **3.** *Slang.* A narcotic drug; especially, heroin. **4.** *Nautical.* **a.** Hard salt beef. **b.** Old cordage, reused for gaskets, oakum, and mats.
~ *adj.* Worthless; junky.
~ *tr.v.* **junked, junking, junks.** *Chiefly U.S.* To throw away or discard as useless; scrap. [Originally (until the 20th century) a nautical term meaning old, worn-out pieces of rope or cable, from Middle English *jonke†.*] —**junk·y** *adj.*

junk² *n.* A flat-bottomed ship used in China and Southeast Asia with a high poop and battened sails. [Chiefly from Portuguese *junco* and Dutch *jonk,* from Malay *jong,* sea-going ship.]

junk bond *n.* A high-yield, high-risk bond issued typically to finance a corporate takeover bid.

Jun·ker (yŏongkər) *n.* A member of the Prussian landed aristocracy, especially of its ultrareactionary section. [German, from Old High German *junchērro : jung,* young + *hērro,* comparative of *hēr,* worthy, exalted.] —**Jun·ker·dom** *n.*

jun·ket (júngkit) *n.* **1.** A sweet pudding made from flavoured milk set with rennet. **2.** A party, banquet, or outing. **3.** *Chiefly U.S.* A trip or excursion, especially one taken by an official and underwritten with public funds.
~ *intr.v.* **junketed, -keting, -kets. 1.** To hold a party or banquet. **2.** *Chiefly U.S.* To make an excursion using public funds. [Middle English *jonket,* a kind of egg custard served on rushes or made in a rush mat, from *junket,* rush basket, from Old Northern French *jonquette,* from *jonc,* rush, from Latin *juncus.* See **jonquil**.] —**jun·ket·er** *n.* —**jun·ket·ing** *n.*

junk food *n. Informal.* Food that has been processed so as to be easily prepared and that is often of low nutritional value.

junk·ie, junk·y (júngki) *n., pl.* **-ies.** *Slang.* A drug addict, especially one using heroin.

junk mail *n.* Unsolicited post that typically advertises something.

Ju·no (jōo-nō ‖ jew-). *Roman Mythology.* The principal Roman goddess, wife and sister of Jupiter, patroness primarily of marriage and the well-being of women, identified with the Greek goddess Hera. [Latin *Jūno†.*]

Ju·no·esque (jōo-nō-ésk ‖ jew-) *adj.* Having the stately bearing and imposing beauty of the goddess Juno.

jun·ta (júnta, jŏontə, hŏontə, khŏontə) *n.* **1.** A group of military officers holding state power in a country after a coup d'état. **2.** A council or small legislative body in a government, especially in Central and South American countries. **3.** Variant of **junto.** [Spanish and Portuguese, from Vulgar Latin *juncta* (unattested), "joined", from Latin, feminine past participle of *jungere,* to join.]

jun·to (júntō) *n., pl.* **-tos.** Also **jun·ta.** A small, usually secret group or committee that gathers for some common interest or aim; a cabal; a clique; a faction. [Variant of JUNTA.]

Ju·pi·ter¹ (jóopi-tər || jéwpi-). *Roman Mythology.* The supreme god, patron of the Roman state, brother and husband of Juno, identified with the Greek god Zeus. Also called "Jove". [Middle English, from Latin *Jūpiter, Jūppiter,* Old Latin *Jovis Pater,* "Jove Father".]

Jupiter² *n. Astronomy.* The fifth planet from the Sun, the largest and most massive in the solar system, having a diameter of approximately 142 800 kilometres (88,700 miles), a mass approximately 318 times that of Earth, and a sidereal period of revolution about the Sun of 11.86 years at a mean distance of 773 million kilometres (483 million miles). [After JUPITER.]

ju·ra. Plural of **jus.**

Ju·ra (jóor-ə). A sparsely populated island in the Inner Hebrides, western Scotland. Cattle and sheep are raised and there is some fishing.

Ju·ra Mountains (jóor-ə, *French* zhü-raá). A mountain range in eastern France and western Switzerland. It forms a natural boundary between the two countries. Crêt de la Neige (1 723 metres; 5,653 feet) is the highest point.

ju·ral (jóor-əl || jéwr-) *adj.* **1.** Of or pertaining to law. **2.** Of, pertaining to, or arising from rights and obligations. [From Latin *jūs* (stem *jūr-*), right, law.] **—ju·ral·ly** *adv.*

Ju·ras·sic (joor-ássik, jər- || jewr-) *adj. Geology.* Of, belonging to, or designating the time and deposits of the second period of the Mesozoic era, characterised by the existence of dinosaurs and primitive mammals and birds.
~*n. Geology.* The Jurassic period. Preceded by *the.* [French *jurassique,* after the JURA MOUNTAINS.]

ju·rat (jóor-at) *n.* **1.** A certification on an affidavit declaring when, where, and before whom it was sworn. **2.** In the Channel Islands, any of a body of magistrates occupying the position of assistant to a bailiff. **3.** Formerly, a municipal officer of the Cinque Ports holding a position similar to that of an alderman. [Latin *jūrātum (est),* "(it has been) sworn", from *jūrāre,* to swear. See **jury.**]

Jur. D. Doctor of Law. [Latin *Juris Doctor.*]

ju·rid·i·cal (joor-íddik'l || jewr-) *adj.* Also **ju·rid·ic** (-íddik). Of or pertaining to the law and its administration. [From Latin *jūridicus* : *jūs* (stem *jūr-*), law + *dīcere,* to say.] **—ju·rid·i·cal·ly** *adv.*

juridical days *pl.n.* The days on which courts are in session. Compare **dies non.**

ju·ris·con·sult (jóor-iss-kən-sult, -kón- || jéwr-) *n.* A person learned in law; a jurist. [Latin *jūrisconsultus* : *jūris,* genitive of *jūs,* law + *consultus,* past participle of *consulere,* to CONSULT.]

ju·ris·dic·tion (jóor-iss-díksh'n || jéwr-) *n.* **1.** The right and power to interpret and apply the law. **2.** Authority or control. **3.** The extent of authority or control. **4.** The territorial range of authority or control. [Middle English *jurisdiccioun,* from Old French *juridiction,* from Latin *jūrisdictiō* (stem *jūrisdictiōn-*) : *jūris,* genitive of *jūs,* law + *dictiō,* declaration (see **diction**).] **—ju·ris·dic·tion·al** *adj.* **—ju·ris·dic·tion·al·ly** *adv.*

ju·ris·pru·dence (jóor-iss-próod'nss || jéwr-, -préwd'nss) *n.* **1.** The philosophy of law or the formal science of law. **2.** A division or department of law. **3.** A system or body of laws. [Originally "skill in law", from Late Latin *jūrisprūdentia* : *jūris,* genitive of *jūs,* law + *prūdentia,* foresight, knowledge, from *prūdēns,* knowing, PRUDENT.] **—ju·ris·pru·den·tial** (-proo-dénsh'l || -prew-) *adj.* **—ju·ris·pru·den·tial·ly** *adv.*

ju·ris·pru·dent (jóor-iss-próod'nt || jéwr-, -préwdn't) *n* One who is versed in jurisprudence. **—ju·ris·pru·dent** *adj.*

ju·rist (jóor-ist || jéwr-) *n.* **1.** A person who is skilled in the law; especially, one who studies or writes about legal matters. **2.** *U.S.* **a.** A judge. **b.** A lawyer. [Old French, from Medieval Latin *jūrista,* from Latin *jūs* (stem *jūr-*), law.]

ju·ris·tic (joor-ístik || jewr-) *adj.* Also **ju·ris·ti·cal** (-'l). **1.** Of or pertaining to a jurist or to jurisprudence. **2.** Of or pertaining to law or legality. **—ju·ris·ti·cal·ly** *adv.*

ju·ror (jóor-ər || jéwr-, -awr) *n.* **1. a.** A person serving as a member of a body sworn to hear and deliver a verdict on a case. **b.** A person called or designated for jury duty. **2.** A person who serves on any body acting in a capacity analogous to that of a jury, as when judging the entries in a competition. [Middle English *juroure,* from Anglo-French *jurour,* from Latin *jūrātor,* "swearer", from *jūrātus,* past participle of *jūrāre,* to swear. See **jury.**]

ju·ry¹ (jóor-i || jéwr-i) *n., pl.* **-ries. 1.** A group of persons forming a body sworn to give a verdict on some matter; specifically, a body of 12 persons summoned by law and sworn to hear and deliver a verdict upon a case presented in court. See **grand jury, petit jury. 2.** A group of persons forming a committee to judge, for example, a competition and award prizes. [Middle English *jurie,* from Anglo-French *juree,* from Old French *juree,* oath, inquest, from Latin *jūrāta,* "thing sworn", from the feminine past participle of *jūrāre,* to swear, from *jūs* (stem *jūr-*), law.]

jury² *adj. Nautical.* Intended or designed for emergency or temporary use; makeshift: *a jury rig.* [Perhaps ultimately from Old French *ajurie,* aid.]

jury box *n.* The enclosed area in a court where the jury sits.

ju·ry·man (jóor-i-mən || jéwr-) *n., pl.* **-men** (-mən, -men). A man serving on a jury; a male juror.

ju·ry-rigged (jóor-i-rigd || jéwr-) *adj. Nautical.* Rigged for emergency or temporary use.

ju·ry·wom·an (jóor-i-wŏomən) *n., pl.* **-women** (-wimmin). A woman serving on a jury; a female juror.

jus (juss, yŏoss, yóoss) *n., pl.* **jura** (jóor-ə, yóor-). *Latin.* **1.** Right; justice; law. **2.** A given right; a legal power.

jus gen·ti·um (jénshəm, jénti-əm, génti-). *n. Latin.* The law of nations; international law.

Jus·sieu (zhőss-yő). A family of eminent French botanists. **Antoine de Jussieu** (1686–1758) was a director of the Jardin des Plantes in Paris, and his younger brother **Bernard de Jussieu** (1699–1777) worked at the Jardins du Roi. **Joseph de Jussieu** (1704–79), the youngest of the three brothers, lived for many years in South America and introduced the common garden heliotrope into Europe. **Antoine-Laurent de Jussieu** (1748–1836), the nephew of Joseph, was professor of botany at the Paris Museum of Natural History, and his *Genera Plantarum* (1789) was a major work of plant classification which remains fundamental to modern botany.

jus·sive (júsiv) *adj. Grammar.* Expressing or used to express a command.
~*n. Grammar.* A word, mood, or construction used to express command. [From Latin *jussus,* past participle of *jubēre,* to command.]

just (just) *adj.* **1.** Honourable and fair in one's dealings and actions. **2.** Consistent with moral right; fair; equitable. **3.** Properly due or merited: *just deserts.* **4.** Legally valid or correct; lawful: *just title.* **5.** Suitable; fitting. **6.** Well-founded; justified; legitimate: *just resentment.* **7.** Exact; accurate: *a just measure.* **8.** Upright before God; righteous. —See Synonyms at **fair.**
~*adv.* (just; *weak form* jəst, *sometimes used as strong form; the pronunciation* jest *is non-standard*). **1.** Precisely; exactly: *That's just what I was going to say.* **2.** At the exact moment of: *Just as I was leaving, he turned up.* **3.** Only a moment ago: *He has just come.* **4.** By a narrow margin; barely: *You have just missed Tom.* **5.** But a little distance: *You'll find it just down the road.* **6.** Merely; only: *I just meant that I agree.* **7.** Conceivably; possibly: *There's just a chance she won't notice.* **8.** Simply; certainly. Used as an intensive: *It's just beautiful!* **—just about.** Almost; very nearly: *I've just about had enough.* **—just now. 1.** At this very moment. **2.** Only a moment ago. **3.** *South African.* In the near future; shortly; very soon. **—just so. 1.** Carried out, arranged, or presented with due regard for neatness, accuracy, tidiness, or the like. **2.** Used to express agreement. [Middle English *just(e),* from Old French *juste,* from Latin *jūstus.*] **—just·ly** *adv.* **—just·ness** *n.*

Usage: *Just* is normally used with the present perfect tense form in standard English, as in *He's just left the house.* Informal American English allows the use of the past tense *(He just went out),* which is occasionally heard in informal British English too, although the usage attracts criticism.

jus·tice (jústiss) *n.* **1.** Moral rightness; equity. **2.** The quality of being just, fair, or in conformity with what is right or legal: *recognised the justice of our cause.* **3.** Good reason: *He's very angry, and with justice.* **4.** Fair handling; due reward or treatment. **5.** The administration and procedure of law. **6.** *Abbr.* **J.** A judge; especially, a judge of the Supreme Court of Judicature. **7.** A justice of the peace. **—bring to justice.** To effect the arrest and trial of (a lawbreaker). **—do justice to. 1.** To approach with proper appreciation; enjoy fully. **2.** To show to full advantage: *The picture doesn't do justice to her eyes.* [Middle English, from Old French, from Latin *jūstitia,* from *jūstus,* JUST.] **—jus·tice·ship** *n.*

justice of the peace *n. Abbr.* **J.P.** In England and Wales, a local unpaid lay magistrate appointed by the Lord Chancellor, to try minor cases and commit more serious cases to a higher court.

jus·tic·es' court (jústi-siz) *n.* A court presided over by a justice of the peace.

jus·ti·ci·a·ble (juss-tíshi-əb'l, -tísh-) *adj.* Appropriate for or subject to court trial; liable to be brought before a court of law. [French, from Old French, from *justicier,* to try, from *justice,* JUSTICE.]

jus·ti·ci·ar (juss-tíshi-aar, -tíssi-) *n.* Also **jus·ti·ci·a·ry.** Formerly, an English legal officer who acted for the king in his absence.

jus·ti·ci·ar·y (juss-tíshi-əri, -tísh-, -tíssi- || -erri) *adj.* Pertaining to the administration of the law.
~*n., pl.* **justiciaries. 1.** One who administers the law. **2.** Variant of **justiciar.** [Medieval Latin *jūstitiārius,* from Latin *jūstitia,* JUSTICE.]

jus·ti·fi·a·ble (jústi-fī-əb'l, -fī́-) *adj.* Capable of being justified. **—jus·ti·fi·a·bil·i·ty** (-ə-bílləti), **jus·ti·fi·a·ble·ness** *n.* **—jus·ti·fi·a·bly** *adv.*

jus·ti·fi·ca·tion (jústifi-káysh'n) *n.* **1.** The act of justifying. **2.** The condition or fact of being justified. **3.** A fact, circumstance, or evidence that justifies; a ground for defence.

jus·ti·fi·ca·to·ry (jústi-fi-kaytəri, -káytəri, -fíckətri) *adj.* Also **jus·ti·fi·ca·tive** (-kaytiv, -káytiv, -fíckətiv). Serving as justification.

jus·ti·fi·er (jústi-fī-ər || -fī́-) *n.* **1.** One that justifies. **2.** *Printing.* A space that varies as necessary to justify a line.

jus·ti·fy (jústi-fī) *v.* **-fied, -fying, -fies.** —*tr.* **1.** To demonstrate or prove to be just, right, or valid. **2.** To show to be well-founded; warrant. **3.** To declare free of blame; absolve. **4.** *Theology.* To free (man) of the guilt and penalty attached to grievous sin. Used only of God. **5.** *Law.* **a.** To demonstrate good reason for (an action taken). **b.** To prove to be qualified to act as a surety. **6.** *Printing.* To adjust or space (a line of type) to the proper length. —*intr.*

Printing. To be or become properly spaced and of the correct length. Said of a line of type. [Middle English *justifien*, originally, to judge, punish, from Old French *justifier*, from Late Latin *jūstificāre*, to do justice towards, to forgive, pardon : *jūstus*, JUST + *facere*, to do.]

Jus·tin·i·an I (juss-tínni-ən) (A.D. 483–565). Byzantine emperor (527–565). He held the eastern frontier of his empire against the Persians and with the brilliant generalship of Belisarius, reconquered former Roman territories in Africa, Italy, and Spain. A devout if autocratic Christian, he also achieved the temporary unity of the Eastern and Western churches and built the great cathedral of St. Sophia in Constantinople. As an administrator, he revised Roman law according to a system known as the **Justinian Code.**

Justinian Code *n.* The codification of Roman law made by order of Justinian I and published in A.D. 529.

jut (jut) *intr.v.* **jutted, jutting, juts.** To project, usually sharply, beyond the limits of the main body; protrude. Often used with *out:* *"He had a sharp crooked nose jutting out of a lean dancer's face"* (Graham Greene).
~*n.* Something that protrudes; a projection. [Variant of JET (to project).] —**jut·ting·ly** *adv.*

jute (jōōt) *n.* **1.** Either of two Asian plants, *Corchorus capsularis* or *C. olitorius,* yielding a fibre used for sacking and cordage. **2.** The fibre obtained from such a plant. **3.** The coarse fabric made from the fibre of this plant. [Bengali *jhōṭo, jhuṭo,* from Sanskrit *jūṭaṭ.*]

Jute (jōōt) *n.* A member of any of several Germanic tribes, some of whom invaded Britain and settled in Kent in the fifth century A.D. —**Jut·ish** (jōōtish) *adj.*

Jut·land (jút-lənd). *Danish* **Jyl·land** (yülan). A peninsula of northern Europe, almost entirely flat, situated between the North and Baltic seas. Mainland Denmark occupies the northern part, the southern region lying in Germany. The Battle of Jutland (1916), fought in the North Sea off the Danish coast between the British and German fleets, was the largest naval engagement of World War I. Though the Germans inflicted the greater losses, they failed to break British control of the seas and afterwards remained in harbour until the end of the war.

juv. juvenile.

Ju·ve·nal (jōōvən'l), born Decimus Junius Juvenalis (*c.*A.D. 60–*c.*140). Roman satirical poet. He is remembered for his 16 *Satires* (probably written after A.D. 100), which denounce the extravagance, snobbery, and corruption of the privileged classes in Rome.

ju·ve·nes·cent (jōōvə-néss'nt ‖ jéwvə-) *adj.* Becoming young or youthful. [JUVEN(AL) + -ESCENT.] —**ju·ve·nes·cence** *n.*

ju·ve·nile (jōōvə-nīl ‖ jéwvə-, *U.S. also* -n'l) *adj.* Also *chiefly U.S.* **ju·ve·nal** (-n'l) (for sense 3). *Abbr.* **juv. 1.** Young; youthful. **2.** Not fully developed; not yet adult. Said of animals and plants or their parts. **3.** Of or pertaining to a young bird having its first plumage of true feathers though often lacking the adult characteristics of its species: *juvenile plumage.* **4.** Characteristic of youth or children; immature: *juvenile behaviour.* **5.** Intended for or appropriate to children or young persons: *juvenile fashions.*
~*n. Abbr.* **juv. 1. a.** A young person; a child. **b.** A young animal that has not reached sexual maturity. **c.** A plant bearing the juvenile form of foliage. **2.** An actor who plays children or young persons. **3.** A children's book. —See Synonyms at **young.** [Latin *juvenīlis,* from *juvenis,* young, a youth.] —**ju·ve·nile·ly** *adv.* —**ju·ve·nile·ness** *n.*

juvenile court *n.* A court dealing with children and young offenders.

juvenile delinquency *n.* Antisocial or criminal behaviour exhibited by a child or adolescent.

juvenile delinquent *n. Abbr.* **J.D.** A child or adolescent who exhibits antisocial or criminal behaviour. —**juvenile delinquency** *n.*

juvenile hormone *n.* An insect hormone that prevents metamorphosis into the adult form and maintains larval characteristics.

ju·ve·nil·i·a (jōōvə-nílli-ə ‖ jéwvə-) *pl.n.* Works, particularly written or artistic works, produced in childhood or youth. [Latin *juvenīlia,* neuter plural of *juvenīlis,* JUVENILE.]

ju·ve·nil·i·ty (jōōvə-nílloti ‖ jéwvə-) *n., pl.* **-ties. 1.** The quality or condition of being foolishly juvenile; immaturity. **2.** The quality or condition of being young or youthful. **3.** *Plural.* Juvenile or immature acts or characteristics. **4.** Young persons collectively.

jux·ta·pose (júkstə-pōz) *tr.v.* **-posed, -posing, -poses.** To place or situate side by side or close together, especially so as to produce or exhibit a contrasting effect. [French *juxtaposer,* probably from JUXTAPOSITION.]

jux·ta·po·si·tion (júkstə-pə-zish'n) *n.* The act of juxtaposing or the state of being juxtaposed. [French : Latin *juxtā,* close together + POSITION.] —**jux·ta·po·si·tion·al** *adj.*

J.W.V. Jewish War Veterans.

Jylland. See **Jutland.**

k, K (kay) *n., pl.* **k's, Ks** or **K's. 1.** The 11th letter of the modern English alphabet. **2.** Any of the speech sounds represented by this letter. **3.** *Slang. Capital* **K.** A thousand pounds. **4.** *Capital* **K.** *Computing.* A unit of storage capacity equal to 1024 words, bytes, or bits.

k, K, k., K. *Note:* As an abbreviation or symbol, *k* may be a small or a capital letter, with or without a full stop. Established forms or those generally preferred precede the definition. When no form is given, all four forms are in general use in that sense. **1. K** kaon. **2. k** karat. **3. K** a. kelvin (temperature unit). **b.** Kelvin (temperature scale). **4. k** kilo-. **5. k., K** king. **6. K** *Chess.* king. **7. Card Games. K.** king. **8. k., K** kip. **9. k., K** knight. **10. K** Köchel number. **11. k., K.** kopeck. **12. k., K** koruna. **13. k., K** krona. **14. k., K** krone. **15. k** The symbol for the Boltzmann constant. **16. K** The symbol for the element potassium. **17.** The 11th in a series; 10th when *J* is omitted.

K2. See **Godwin-Austen, Mount.**

ka (kaa) *n.* A spirit believed by the ancient Egyptians to dwell in a man or statue.

Kaa·ba, Caa·ba (ka'a-bə, -əbə) *n.* A Muslim shrine in Mecca which houses a sacred black stone said to have been given to Abraham by the archangel Gabriel, and towards which followers of Muhammad face when praying. [Arabic *ka'bah,* "square building", from *ka'b, ka'ba,* cube.]

Kalaallit Nunaat. See **Greenland.**

ka·ba·ka (kə-báakə) *n.* Any of the former dynastic rulers of the Baganda people native to southern Uganda. [Luganda.] —**ka·ba·ka·ship** *n.*

kabala, kabbala. Variants of **cabala.**

kab·el·jou (kább'l-yō, -jō) *n., pl.* **kabeljou.** *South African.* **1.** An edible codlike fish *Argyrosmus hololepidotus,* of the family Sciaenidae. **2.** A fish, the **cod** *(see).* [Afrikaans, from Dutch *kabeljauw,* from Germanic.]

Ka·bu·ki (kə-bōōki) *n.* A type of popular Japanese drama, evolved from the older Noh theatre, in which elaborately costumed performers, usually male, enact both tragedies and comedies using stylised movements, dances, and songs. [Japanese, "art of singing and dancing" : *kabu,* singing and dancing, + *ki,* art.]

Ka·bul (ka'a-bōōl, káw-, -b'l). Capital of Afghanistan. It commands the northeast trade route into Pakistan, and has frequently been occupied by foreign invaders during its 3,000-year history, most recently by Soviet forces. From 1504 to 1526, it was the capital of the Mogul Empire. It became Afghanistan's capital in 1773.

Kab·we (ka'ab-way, -wi). Formerly **Broken Hill.** Town in central Zambia. It is a railway junction and heart of a mining district, producing lead, zinc, and vanadium.

Ka·byle (kə-bîl, ka-) *n., pl.* **-byles** or collectively **Kabyle. 1.** A member of one of the Berber tribes inhabiting Tunisia or Algeria. **2.** The Hamitic Berber dialect spoken by these people.

Ká·dár (ka'a-daar), **János** (1912–89). First secretary of the Hungarian Communist Party (1956–88). He joined the invading Soviet forces during the 1956 revolution and was prime minister (1956–58, 1961–65).

Kad·dish (kádish, ka'a-dish) *n., pl.* **Kaddishim** (ka-dishim). *Judaism.* A prayer in praise of God said in daily synagogue services and by mourners after the death of a close relative. [Aramaic *qaddīsh.*]

kaf·fer·boet·ie (káffər-bōōti) *n., pl.* **-boeties.** *South African Slang.* A white person regarded as being excessively friendly towards black people or unduly concerned with their welfare. Used derogatorily, often as a term of address. [Afrikaans *kaffer,* KAFFIR + *boet,* brother + *-ie,* diminutive suffix.]

Kaf·fir, Ka·fir (káffər) *n., pl.* **-firs** or collectively **Kaffir.** *Often small* **k. 1.** Any black African, especially one living in southern Africa. Used derogatorily. **2. a.** A member of any of the Bantu-speaking tribes inhabiting South Africa. **b.** The language spoken by these people. Not in current usage. **3.** A non-Muslim. Used derogatorily by Muslims. **4.** Variant of **Kafir. 5.** *Capital* **K.** *Plural.* On the London Stock Exchange, South African mining shares. [Arabic *kafir,* "infidel", present participle of *kafara,* to deny, be sceptical.]

kaffir beer *n.* In South Africa, a kind of beer brewed from kaffircorn or millet.

kaf·fir·boom (káffər-bōō-əm) *n.* A deciduous tree, *Erythrina caffra,* native to southern Africa, having large, showy clusters of bright orange or red flowers. [Afrikaans: KAFFIR + *boom,* tree.]

kaf·fir·corn (káffər-kawrn) *n.* A variety of sorghum, *Sorghum caffrorum,* of Africa, cultivated in dry regions for its grain and as fodder. [From KAFFIR.]

kaffir lily *n.* A bulbous plant, *Schizostylis coccinea,* native to South

Africa but widely cultivated as a garden ornamental for its autumn-blooming, pink or red flowers.

kaf·fi·yeh (kə-fée-yə, -ye) *n.* Also **kef·fi·yeh** (ke-). An Arab head-dress consisting of a folded triangle of material held in place with a cord. [Arabic, perhaps from Late Latin *cofea*, COIF.]

Ka·fir, Kaf·fir (káffər) *n.*, *pl.* **-firs** or collectively **Kafir**. 1. A member of a people of ancient Iranian stock living in northeastern Afghanistan. 2. Variant of **Kaffir**.

Ka·fi·ri (ka-féer-i) *n.* The Indic language of the Iranian Kafirs.

Kaf·ka (káfkə) **Franz** (1883–1924). Czech novelist, writing in German. He wrote enigmatic stories in which individuals were constantly threatened by a nightmarishly impersonal world. Most of his work, including the novels *The Trial* (1925) and *The Castle* (1926), was published posthumously.

Kafka·esque (káf-kər-ésk, -kə-) *adj.* Of, pertaining to, or suggestive of the works of Franz Kafka, especially their surrealistic evocation of some sinister impersonal force controlling human affairs.

kaftan. Variant of **caftan.**

Ka·fu·e (ka-fóo-i, kaa-, -ay). River of central Zambia. It flows 960 kilometres (600 miles) from the Congo border to join the Zambezi. The Kafue Dam provides much of Zambia's hydroelectric power.

Kagoshima (kago-shéemə). Port and naval base on Kagoshima Bay, southern Kyushu, Japan. The first European missionary to Japan, St. Francis Xavier, landed here in 1549.

kagoule. Variant of **cagoule.**

kai (ki) *n. N.Z.* Food, foodstuffs. Maori.

kaiak. Variant of **kayak.**

Kai·kou·ra Ranges (kī-kóor-ə). Two mountain ranges in the South Island of New Zealand. They run parallel to the Pacific coast, with the Clarence river valley between them. Tapuaenuku (2 885 metres; 9,465 feet) is the highest peak.

kail. Variant of **kale.**

kail·yard (káyl-yaard) *n.* Also **kale·yard.** *Scottish.* A vegetable garden. [*Kail, kale,* COLE.]

kain. Variant of **cain.**

kai·nite (kī-nīt, káy-) *n.* A mineral, essentially $KCl·MgSO_4·3H_2O$, found in potash deposits, and used mainly as fertiliser and as a source of potassium compounds. [German *Kainit* : Greek *kainos*, new, recently formed + -ITE.]

Ka·in·ji Dam (ka-ínji) Series of hydroelectric dams on the river Niger in Nigeria. It is one of Africa's largest hydroelectric and irrigation projects.

kai·ser (kízər) *n. Sometimes capital* **K.** Any of the emperors of the Holy Roman Empire (A.D. 800–1806), Austria (1804–1918), and Germany (1871–1918). [German *Kaiser,* from Old High German *Keisar,* from Latin *Caesar,* CAESAR.]

kai·ser·in (kízər-in) *n. Sometimes capital* **K.** The wife of a kaiser; an empress. [German.]

kak (kak) *n. South African Vulgar.* Faeces.
~*interj. South African Vulgar Slang.* Rubbish; nonsense. [Afrikaans, from Dutch, from Latin *cacāre,* to defecate; akin to CAK.]

ka·ka (káa-kaa) *n.* A brownish or greenish parrot, *Nestor meridionalis,* of New Zealand. [Maori, imitative of its cry.]

ka·ka·po (káako-pō) *n.*, *pl.* **-pos.** A ground-dwelling owl-like nocturnal parrot, *Strigops habroptilus,* of New Zealand, having greenish plumage. [Maori KAKA (parrot) + *po,* night.]

ka·ke·mo·no (kácki-mǒnǒ || *U.S.* káaki-nó-) *n.*, *pl.* **-nos.** A Japanese scroll painting on silk or paper and hung vertically. [Japanese, "hanging thing," scroll : *kake,* hanging + *mono,* thing.]

ka·la·a·zar (kál-ə-ə-zár, káal-) *n.* A chronic disease, **leishmaniasis** (*see*). [Hindi *kālā-āzār,* "black disease" : *kālā,* black, from Sanskrit *kālah,* blue-black, black, from Dravidian + *āzār,* disease, from Persian *āzār†.*]

Ka·la·ha·ri Desert (kál-ə-haári || *U.S.* káal-). Arid, sand-covered plateau between the Zambezi and Orange rivers in southern Africa. It occupies most of Botswana and parts of South Africa and Namibia, and is inhabited by Bushmen.

kal·an·cho·e (kál-ən-kó-i, -əng-) *n.* Any of various small shrubs of the tropical genus *Kalanchoe,* having clusters of variously coloured, often red, flowers on tall stems, and cultivated as a house plant. [French, ultimately from Cantonese name *goh leung choi* (Mandarin *gāo liáng cái*), tall cool plant.]

Ka·lash·ni·kov (kə-láshni-koff, ka-) *n.* A trademark for an automatic rifle designed in the former U.S.S.R. that is operated by gas, has a calibre of 7.62 millimetres, and has a high degree of accuracy over ranges of up to 300 metres. Also called "AK 47".

kale, kail (kayl) *n.* 1. A variety of cabbage, *Brassica oleracea* var. *acephala,* eaten as a vegetable or used for livestock feed, having ruffled or crinkled leaves that do not form a tight head. Also called "borecole". 2. *Scottish.* **a.** A cabbage. **b.** Broth containing cabbage. 3. *U.S. Slang.* Money. [Middle English (northern dialect) *cal(e),* variant of COLE.]

ka·lei·do·scope (kə-lídə-skōp) *n.* 1. A small tube in which patterns of colours are optically produced and viewed for amusement; especially, one in which a pair of angled mirrors reflect light transmitted through bits of loose coloured glass contained at one end, causing them to appear as symmetrical designs when viewed at the other. 2. A constantly changing set of colours. 3. A series of changing phases or events. [Greek *kalos,* beautiful + *eidos,* form + -SCOPE.] —**ka·lei·do·scop·ic** (-skóppik), **ka·lei·do·scop·i·cal** *adj.* —**ka·lei·do·scop·i·cal·ly** *adv.*

kalends. Variant of **calends.**

Ka·le·va·la (káa-lev-aa-lə, kə-lévv'l-ə, káalə-vaálə) *n.* The Finnish

national epic poem, recounting the legendary adventures of the hero Kaleva. The work, compiled during the 19th century from ancient folk tales and oral poetry, inspired creative artists such as Sibelius. [After the name of the legendary land in the epic, from Finnish *Kaleva,* and the hero Kaleva + —*la,* home area, dwelling place.]

kale yard Variant of **kailyard.**

Kale·yard School (káyl-yaard). A loose-knit group of Scottish writers between about 1880 and 1914 who depicted, in rather sentimental fiction and with the use of much Scots dialect, the lives of the common people in the Scottish Lowlands. [Adapted from the old Jacobite song, "There grows a bonny brier bush in our kailyard", part of which formed the title of an early book of short stories typical of the school's style. See **kailyard.**]

Kal·goor·lie-Boul·der (kal-góorli-bóldər). A town in south Western Australia. It grew from 1892 after gold-mining began at Coolgardie nearby. It is now a nickel-mining centre.

ka·li (káyli, kálli) *n.* A plant, the **saltwort** (*see*).

Ka·li (káali). In Hindu mythology, Devi, considered as the goddess of death and destruction.

Kal·i·man·tan (kál-i-mán-tən || -maán-). Also **Indonesian Borneo.** The Indonesian section of the island of Borneo, occupying two-thirds of the island. It is densely forested and produces timber.

Ka·li·nin (kə-léenin, ka-), **Mikhail Ivanovich** (1875–1946). President of the supreme council of the U.S.S.R. (1937–46). He was born a peasant, took part in the 1917 revolution, and joined the Politburo in 1926. He was a founder of *Pravda* (1912).

Ka·lin·in·grad (kə-léen-in-grad, -ing- || -graad; *Russian* -gráat). Also (until 1946) **Kö·nigs·berg** (kérn-igz-bairg, -burg || kǒn-; *German* kön-ikhs-bairk). A Baltic port in northwest Russia. It was founded (1255) by the Teutonic Knights, and eventually became the capital of East Prussia.

Ka·li·yu·ga (káali-yōogə) *n.* In Hindu mythology, the fourth and present age of the world, characterised by moral degeneration.

kal·li·din (kál-i-din) *n.* A type of **kinin** (*see*).

kal·li·krein (kál-i-krīn) *n.* Any of several enzymes that act on globulins in the blood to synthesise the kinins bradykinin and kallidin.

kal·mi·a (kál-mi-ə) *n.* Any evergreen shrub of the genus *Kalmia,* which includes the **mountain laurel** (*see*).

Kal·muck (kál-muk, kal-múk) *n.*, *pl.* **-mucks** or collectively **Kalmuck.** Also **Kal·myk** (-mik, -mík). 1. A member of one of the Buddhist Mongol peoples originally inhabiting northwestern China, and later migrating westwards to the lower Volga. 2. The Mongolian language spoken by the Kalmucks.

ka·long (káa-long) *n.* An East Indian fruit bat, *Pteropus vampyrus,* having a wingspan of over 1.5 metres (4 feet). [Javanese.]

kalpak. Variant of **calpac.**

Ka·ma (káamə). In Hindu mythology, the god of erotic love, son of Brahma and husband of Rati.

kam·a·cite (kámmə-sīt) *n.* A nickel-iron alloy found in certain meteorites. [Obsolete German *Kamacit,* from Greek *kamax* (stem *kamak-*), shaft.]

ka·ma·la (kámmələ, kə-maálə) *n.* 1. An Asian tree, *Mallotus philippinensis,* having hairy, capsular fruit. 2. A powder obtained from the capsules of this tree, used as a dye and formerly to treat tapeworm and ringworm infestations. [Sanskrit *kamala,* probably from Dravidian, akin to Kanarese *kōmale.*]

Ka·ma·su·tra (káamə-sóotrə) *n.* A treatise in Sanskrit (4th–7th century A.D.), setting forth rules for erotic love and marriage in accordance with Hindu law. [Sanskrit, "book on love" : *kāma,* love, desire + *sūtra,* warp.]

Kam·chat·ka (kam-chát-kə). A large, volcanically active peninsula in Siberia, lying in the far northeast of Russia, in the Pacific Ocean between the Sea of Okhotsk and the Bering Sea. —**Kam·chat·kan** *n. & adj.*

kame (kaym) *n.* A mound or long, low ridge of sand and gravel deposited during the melting of glacial ice. [Scottish, from Middle English *camb,* northern variant of COMB.]

ka·mi (káami) *n.*, *pl.* **kami.** A divinity or god in the Shinto religion. [Japanese, "god".]

ka·mi·ka·ze (kámmi-kaázi || *U.S.* káami-) *n.* 1. During World War II, a Japanese pilot trained to make a suicidal crash attack at a target, such as a naval vessel. 2. An aeroplane loaded with explosives to be exploded in such an attack.
~*adj.* 1. Of or being a kamikaze. 2. *Informal.* Courting disaster; reckless: *a kamikaze driver.* Often used humorously. [Japanese, "divine wind" : *kami,* god + *kaze,* wind.]

Kam·pa·la (kam-paálə). The capital of Uganda, situated on Lake Victoria. It was founded by the British near Mengo, the seat of the Kabaka (King) of Buganda. It became the country's capital in 1962.

kam·pong (kám-pong, kam-póng) *n.* A compound or village in Malaysia. [Malay.]

Kam·pu·che·a, People's Republic of (kámpoo-cheér, -chée-ə). See **Cambodia.** —**Kam·pu·ch·e·an** *n. & adj.*

karnsin. Variant of **khamsin.**

ka·na (káanə) *n.* Either of two Japanese syllabaries, **hiragana** or **katakana** (*both of which see*). Compare **kanji.** [Japanese, "pseudo-characters" (as distinguished from **kanji,** which are regarded as originally Chinese characters) : *ka,* false + *na,* name, character.]

Ka·nak·a (kə-náckə || -naákə, kánnəkə) *n.* 1. A native of the South Sea Islands, especially one who in former times was abducted to work in Australia. 2. A native of Hawaii. [Hawaiian, "person".]

kan·a·my·cin (kánnə-mí-sin) *n.* An antibiotic, $C_{18}H_{36}O_{11}N_4$, obtained from the soil actinomycete bacterium *Streptomyces kanamyceticus*, used to treat a wide range of bacterial infections. [New Latin *Streptomycetes kanamyceticus* (specific epithet of the bacterium).]

Ka·na·ra (kə-náarə). District of Karnataka state (formerly Mysore state), southwest India. It is largely hilly and produces rice, coffee, and copra.

Ka·na·rese (kánnə-réez || -réess) *adj.* Of or relating to Kanara, its people, or their language.
~ *n., pl.* **Kanarese.** **1.** A member of any of the Kannada-speaking peoples of Kanara. **2.** A Dravidian language, **Kannada** *(see).*

Kanchenjunga, Mount. See **Kangchenjunga, Mount.**

Kan·da·har or **Qan·da·har** (kándə-hár). A city in southern Afghanistan. It is the centre of a fertile region and lies on the trade route between Pakistan and the former U.S.S.R.

Kan·din·sky (kan-dínski), **Wassily** (1866–1944). Russian abstract painter, who also worked in Germany and France. He considered form and colour capable of spiritual expression, and is often considered to be the first painter to use an entirely abstract style in a watercolour he produced in 1910.

Kan·dy (kándi). Formerly **Can·dy.** A city in the central tea-growing district of Sri Lanka. It was the seat of the Sinhalese kings until the British occupation in 1815. **—Kand·y·an** *n. & adj.*

kane. Variant of **cain.**

kan·ga, khan·ga (kángə) *n.* A piece of brightly coloured cloth worn as a garment by women in East Africa.

kan·ga·roo (kángə-rōō) *n., pl.* **-roos.** Any of various herbivorous marsupials of the family Macropodidae, of Australia and adjacent areas, characteristically having short forelimbs, large hind limbs adapted for leaping, and a long, tapered tail. [Probably from a native name in Queensland, Australia.]

kangaroo closure. A form of closure in a parliamentary debate where the speaker limits discussion to selected amendments. Compare **guillotine.**

kangaroo court *n.* **1.** An unofficial court set up in violation of established legal procedure. **2.** Any court characterised by dishonesty or incompetence. [By allusion to its irregular procedures suggesting the leaps of a kangaroo.]

kangaroo dog. A large, rough-haired dog of a breed developed in Australia for hunting kangaroos.

kangaroo paw. Any of various plants of the Australian genus *Anigozanthus*, having swordlike leaves and clusters of tubular flowers, which when unopened resemble kangaroos' paws.

kangaroo rat *n.* Any of various long-tailed rodents of the genera *Dipodomys* and *Microdipodops*, of arid areas of western North America, having long hind legs adapted for jumping.

kangaroo vine *n.* An evergreen climbing plant, *Cissus antarctica*, widely grown as a house plant for its glossy green foliage.

Kang·chen·jun·ga or **Kan·chen·jun·ga, Mount** (káng-chən-jŏóng-gə, kán-, -chen-). Also **Kin·chin·jun·ga** (kín-chin-). After Everest and K2, the world's third highest peak (8585 metres; 28,166 feet), on the India-Nepal border. It was first climbed in 1955.

kan·ji (kán-ji, káan-) *n., pl.* **kanji** or **-jis.** **1.** A Japanese system of writing based upon borrowed or modified Chinese characters. **2.** A character used in the kanji system of writing. Compare **kana.** [Japanese, from Chinese (Mandarin) *hànzi* : *hàn*, Chinese (originally a dynastic name) + *zi*, word.]

Kan·na·da (kánnədə || káanədə). A Dravidian language spoken chiefly in the state of Karnataka, in southern India. Also called "Canarese", "Kanarese". **—Kan·na·da** *adj.*

Ka·no (káanō). A city in northern Nigeria, capital of Kano state. It was once the terminus of a major Sahara caravan route, and is still a trade centre.

Kan·pur (káan-póor). *English* **Cawn·pore** (káwn-pór || -pór). The largest city in Uttar Pradesh in northern India, on the river Ganges. It is a communications junction and manufacturing centre. Its British garrison was massacred (1857) during the Indian Mutiny.

Kan·sas (kán-zəss, -səss; *locally always* -zəss). State of the United States, lying on the Great Plains. Its main products are agricultural. It joined the Union in 1861. Topeka is the capital.

Kansas City. Either of a pair of twin cities in the United States. Kansas City, Kansas, lies west of the Kansas river; the much larger Kansas City, Missouri, lies to its east.

Kansu. See **Gansu.**

Kant (kant || kaant), **Immanuel** (1724–1804). German idealist philosopher, born in Königsberg, where he stayed all his life. In the *Critique of Pure Reason* (1781), Kant argued that reason was the means by which the phenomena of experience are translated into understanding. He put forward his system of ethics based on the **categorical imperative** in the *Critique of Practical Reason* (1788). **—Kant·i·an** *n. & adj.* **—Kant·i·an·ism** *n.*

kan·tar (kan-tár) *n.* Any of various units of weight used in some eastern Mediterranean countries, usually corresponding to about 45 kilograms (100 pounds). [Arabic *qinṭār*, ultimately from Latin *centēnārius*, of a hundred, from *centum*, hundred.]

KANU (káa-nōō). Kenya African National Union.

kan·zu (kán-zoo) *n.* A long, usually white garment, worn by men in East Africa. [Swahili.]

ka·o·lin (káyə-lin) *n.* A fine white to yellowish or greyish clay, mostly kaolinite, used as an absorbent in medicine and in ceramics and refractories, and as a filler or coating for paper and textiles. Also called "china clay", "porcelain clay", "terra alba". [French,

from Mandarin Chinese *gaō lǐng*, name of a hill in Jiangxi Province where it was first obtained, "high mountain" : *gaō*, high + *lǐng*, mountain, peak.]

ka·o·lin·ite (káy-əli-nīt) *n.* A mineral, essentially $Al_2O_3 \cdot 2SiO_2 \cdot 2H_2O$, the principal constituent of kaolin.

ka·on (káy-on) *n. Symbol* **K** *Physics.* **1.** Either of two elementary particles in the meson family, a neutral particle, κ zero, or a positively charged particle, κ plus, having strangeness quantum number –1. **2.** Either of two corresponding antiparticles, κ zero bar or κ minus. [*ka,* the letter *k* + (MES)ON.]

Ka·pell·meis·ter (kə-pél-mīstər, ka- || kaa-) *n., pl.* **Kapellmeister.** The leader of a choir or orchestra, especially at the court of an 18th-century German prince. [German, "choir master".]

kaph, caph (kawf, kaaf) *n.* The 11th letter in the Hebrew alphabet. Transliterated in English as *K, k,* or *kh.* [Hebrew *kāph,* "palm of the hand" (from the ancient form of this letter).]

Ka·pit·za (kə-pítsə, ka-), **Peter Leonidovich** (1894–1984). Soviet physicist. He liquefied helium and oxygen, and was awarded the Nobel prize in 1978.

ka·pok (káypok) *n.* A silky fibre from the fruit of the **silk-cotton tree** *(see),* used for insulation and as padding in pillows, mattresses, and life belts. Also called "silk cotton". [Malay.]

Ka·po·si's sarcoma (ka-pōzis) *n.* A disease mainly afflicting people with a defective immune system, now especially associated with AIDS patients, involving malignant tumours of the lymph nodes or skin. [After M. K. *Kaposi* (1837–1902), Hungarian dermatologist, who first described the condition in detail.]

kap·pa (káppə) *n.* The tenth letter in the Greek alphabet, written K, κ. Transliterated in English as *K, k,* or, for words of Greek origin, *C, c.* [Greek, from Semitic, akin to Hebrew *kāph,* KAPH.]

ka·put (kə-pŏot, ka- || *U.S. also* kaa-) *adj. Informal.* **1.** Destroyed; wrecked. **2.** Incapacitated or out of order. [German *kaputt,* from French *capot,* as in the expression *être capot,* to have lost all tricks at cards, "be hoodwinked", from *capot,* cloak with hood, from *cape,* CAPE (garment).]

kar·a·bi·ner (kárrə-béenər) *n.* An oblong steel ring that is snapped to the eye of a piton and through which a rope is run, used in mountaineering. [German *Karabiner(haken),* "carbine hook" (originally used to fasten carbines to a belt) : *Karabiner,* carbine, from French *carabine,* CARBINE + *Haken,* hook.]

Ka·ra·chi (kə-ráachi). Largest city and chief port and naval base of Pakistan, lying on the Arabian Sea. It was the national capital from 1947–59.

ka·ra·hi (kə-ráahi) *n.* **1.** A wok from the Indian subcontinent, typically smaller than its Chinese counterpart, in which food is cooked and typically served. **2.** The food cooked in a karahi. Compare **balti.** [Indic, from Sanskrit *katāha,* cauldron, wok.]

Ka·ra·jan (kárr-yaan || kaárə-), **Herbert von** (1908–89). Austrian conductor. He was musical director of the Berlin Philharmonic orchestra (1955–89), and artistic director of the Vienna State Opera (1957–64). He founded the Salzburg Easter Festival in 1967. Among his vast output of recordings, his various interpretations of the Beethoven symphonies are particularly renowned.

Ka·ra·Kal·pak[1] (kəráa-kəl-pák) *n.* Former autonomous republic of the Soviet Union, now integrated within Uzbekistan. It comprises parts of the Kyzul Kum desert and the Amu Darya delta on the Aral Sea.

Kara-Kalpak[2] *n.* **1.** A native or inhabitant of Kara-Kalpak. **2.** The language spoken by the Kara-Kalpaks. **—Ka·ra·Kal·pak** *adj.*

Kar·a·ko·ram Range (kárrə-káw-rəm || -kō-). Range of mountains in central Asia, stretching through Jammu and Kashmir to Tibet. It includes Mount Godwin-Austen, K2, which at 8 611 metres (28,250 feet), is the world's second highest mountain.

kar·a·kul, car·a·cul (kárrak'l) *n.* **1.** Any of a breed of sheep native to central Asia, having wool that is curled and glossy in the young and wiry and coarse in the adult. Also called "broadtail". **2.** Fur made from the pelt of a karakul lamb. Compare **broadtail, Persian lamb.** [Originally bred near *Kara Kul,* "black lake", lake in Tajikistan.]

Ka·ra·man·lis (kárrə-man-léess || kaárə-), **Constantine** (1907–). Greek prime minister (1955–63, 1974–80). In 1963 he resigned and went to Paris, returning after the fall of the Greek military government (1974). He was president (1980–85; 1990–95).

ka·ra·o·ke (kárrə-ōki) *n.* A form of entertainment of Japanese origin, in which guests sing popular songs solo to a prerecorded accompaniment, as in bars and restaurants. Also used adjectivally: *a karaoke bar.* [Japanese, "empty orchestra" : *kara,* empty + *ōke (sutora),* ORCHESTRA.]

karat. *Chiefly U.S.* Variant of **carat** (sense 2).

ka·ra·te (kə-ráati, ka-) *n.* A Japanese system of unarmed self-defence that uses sharp blows struck with the hands or feet. [Japanese, "empty-handed" : *kara,* empty + *te,* hand.]

Ka·re·li·an (kə-réel-i-ən, -rávl-) *n.* **1.** A native or inhabitant of the former Karelian A.S.S.R. **2.** The Finnish dialect spoken by the Karelians. **—Ka·re·li·an** *adj.*

Karelian Isthmus. An isthmus in northwest Russia, lying between the Gulf of Finland and Lake Ladoga. From 1917 the greater part was Finnish, but this was surrendered to the U.S.S.R. in 1944.

Ka·re·li·ya (kə-réel-i-ə, -rávl-). Former autonomous administrative region of the U.S.S.R., now part of Russia. The area lies between the White Sea and Finland and is rich in timber and mineral deposits.

Karen (kə-rén) *n., pl.* **-ens** or collectively **Karen.** **1.** A member of a

Thai people living in south Burma. **2.** Any of the Karen languages.
Ka·ri·ba, Lake (kə-reébə). A reservoir on the Zambia-Zimbabwe border. It was formed on the Zambezi River after the building of the Kariba Dam (1955–59), which provides hydroelectricity for Copper Belt in Zambia and also parts of Zimbabwe.
Kar·loff (kár-lof), **Boris,** born William Henry Pratt (1887–1969). British film actor. He played the monster in *Frankenstein* (1931), and starred in many horror films.
Kar·lo·vy Va·ry (kárləvi vaári). *German* **Karls·bad** (kárlz-bad; *German* kárlss-baat). Famous spa in Bohemia in the Czech Republic. Its hot medicinal springs were popular with European royalty and aristocrats before World War I.
Karls·ruh·e or **Carls·ruh·e** (kárlz-rōō-ə; *German* kárlss-rōō-ə). Canal-port and industrial city in western Germany, and capital of the former state of Baden.
kar·ma (kár-mə, kúr-) *n.* **1.** *Hinduism & Buddhism.* The sum of a person's actions during the successive phases of his existence, regarded as determining his destiny in future incarnations. **2.** Fate; destiny. [Sanskrit *karman* (nominative *karma*), act, deed, work, from *karoti,* he makes, he does.] **—kar·mic** (-mik) *adj.*
Kar·nak (kár-nak). Village in central Egypt on the river Nile. It is the site of ancient **Thebes,** with its Great Temple of Amen.
Kar·na·ta·ka (kárnə-taákə). Formerly **My·sore** (mī-sór || -sŏr). State of India, on the Arabian Sea coast. It produces most of the world's sandalwood. Bangalore is the capital.
Kärn·ten (kayrntən). *English* **Ca·rin·thi·a** (kə-rínthi-ə, ka-). State of southern Austria. It produces cereals and livestock, and has deposits of magnesite, iron ore, zinc, and lead. Klagenfurt is the capital.
ka·ross (kə-róss) *n.* A simple cloak made from animal skins, worn by southern African tribesmen. [Afrikaans *karos,* perhaps from Dutch *kuras,* from French *cuirasse,* CUIRASS.]
Kar·pov (kár-pov; *Russian* kár-pəf), **Anatoly Yevgeniyevich** (1951–). Russian chess grandmaster. He became world champion (1975) and beat Victor Korchnoi in 1978 and 1981 to keep the title. He drew with Garry Kasparov in 1984, but Kasparov defeated him in 1985 and again in 1988. F.I.D.E. champion (1994).
kar·ri (kárri) *n.* **1.** A eucalyptus tree of Western Australia, *Eucalyptus diversicolor.* **2.** The hard red timber of this tree. [Native Australian name.]
Kar·roo or **Ka·roo** (kə-rōō). Plateau of southern South Africa. It is divided by the Groot-Swartberge range into the lower, southern Little Karroo and the higher Great Karroo. It is a grazing and fruit-growing area.
Karroo System. Vast system of rocks found in Africa south of the equator. Dating from the Permo-Carboniferous to late Triassic periods, it comprises nonmarine sediments, with coal and oil deposits, and volcanic rocks. The system is noted for its reptilian fossils.
karst (karst) *n.* A barren limestone or dolomite region in which erosion has produced fissure, sinkholes, underground streams, and caverns. Usually used adjectivally: *karst scenery.* [German *Karst,* name of limestone region near Trieste.]
kart (kart) *n.* A **go-kart** *(see).* **—kart·ing** *n.*
karyo-, caryo- *comb. form.* Indicates the nucleus of a living cell; for example, **karyogamy, karyotype.** [New Latin, from Greek *karuon,* kernel, nut.]
kar·y·og·a·my (kárri-óggəmi) *n.* The coming together and fusing of two gamete nuclei. [KARYO- + -GAMY.]
kar·y·o·ki·ne·sis (kárri-ō-kī-neé-siss) *n.* A form of cell division, **mitosis** *(see).* **—kar·y·o·ki·ne·tic** *adj.*
kar·y·o·lymph (kárri-ō-limf, -ə-) *n.* The clear homogeneous liquid portion of nuclear protoplasm.
kar·y·o·plasm (kárri-ō-plaz'm, -ə-) *n.* Nuclear protoplasm, **nucleoplasm** *(see).* [KARYO- + -PLASM.] **—kar·y·o·plas·mic** (-plázmik) *adj.*
kar·y·o·some (kárri-ō-sōm, -ə-) *n.* **1.** An aggregation of chromatin in a resting nucleus during mitosis. **2.** A cell nucleus. [KARYO- + -SOME (body).]
kar·y·o·type (kárri-ə-tīp, -ō-) *n.* A photomicrograph of metaphase chromosomes of a given species in a standard array showing their number, size, and shape. Also called "idiogram". **—kar·y·o·typ·ic** (-tippik), **kar·y·o·typ·ic·al** *adj.*
Kas·a·vu·bu (kássə-vōōbōō), **Joseph** (1917–69). First president of Congo (now Congo, Dem. Rep.) (1960–65). He was ousted by Colonel Joseph Mobutu (1965).
kas·bah, cas·bah (káz-baa) *n. Often capital* **K.** The old quarter of certain North African towns, surrounding a castle or citadel. [French *casbah,* from Arabic *kas(a)ba,* citadel.]
ka·sha (káshə || *U.S.* kaáshə) *n.* An eastern European dish traditionally consisting of coarse buckwheat, boiled or baked. [Russian *kasha,* from Old Slavonic *kāsyā* (unattested).]
Kash·mir (kásh-meér). Former princely state on the northwestern border of India. Then a Hindu-ruled region with a largely Muslim people, it became a source of conflict between India and Pakistan after Indian independence (1947), and was partitioned in 1949, becoming Jammu and Kashmir, an Indian state, and Azad Kashmir under Pakistani control. Sporadic fighting continued until 1972; in 1989, border tensions were renewed.
Kashmir goat *n.* Also **Cashmere goat.** A goat native to the Himalayan regions of India and Tibet, prized for its wool.
Kash·mi·ri (kash-meér-i) *n., pl.* **-miris** or collectively **Kashmiri. 1.** A native or inhabitant of Kashmir. **2.** An Indic language spoken in Jammu and Kashmir. **—Kash·mi·ri** *adj.*
kash·ruth, kash·rut (kash-rōōt || *U.S.* kaash-). *n.* **1.** The body of Jewish dietary laws. **2.** The state of being kosher. [Hebrew, "appropriateness".]
Kas·par·ov (kəs-paárəf), **Garry (Kimovich)** (1963–), born Gary Weinstein. Azerbaijani chess grandmaster. In 1985 he became the youngest-ever world champion, by defeating Anatoly Karpov for the title; he retained supremacy in 1988 and again in 1993, but lost to IBM's computer "Deep Blue" in 1997.
Kas·sel or **Cas·sel** (káss'l). City in Hessen in Germany.
Käst·ner (késtnər), **Erich** (1899–1974). German writer. He wrote children's books, including *Emil and the Detectives* (1929).
kat, khat (kat, kaat) *n.* An evergreen shrub, *Catha edulis,* native to Africa and Arabia, whose leaves have narcotic properties and are used to make a beverage (Arabian tea) and to flavour wine.
ka·ta·ba·tic (káttə-báttik) *adj.* Of, pertaining to, or designating cold wind currents travelling downhill. Compare **anabatic.** [Late Greek *katabatikos,* from Greek, falling, from *katabainein,* to go down.]
ka·ta·ka·na (káttə-kaánə || *U.S.* kaátə-) *n.* A phonetic Japanese syllabary used for writing foreign words or documents, such as telegrams. Also called "kana". See **hiragana.** [Japanese : *kata,* one, one-sided + KANA.]
Katanga. See **Shaba.**
kath·ak (kúttək) *n.* A classical dance of northern India that uses complex, rhythmic patterns and contains elements of mimed narrative. [Bengali, "story-teller", from Sanskrit *kathayati,* he tells.]
kath·a·ka·li (kúttə-kaáli) *n.* A vigorous classical dance of Kerala in southern India, performed by men wearing elaborate costumes and make-up and based on episodes from Hindu literary texts. [Malayalam, drama : *katha,* story, from Sanskrit *kathā,* talk + *kali,* play.]
Ka·tha·re·vu·sa, Ka·tha·re·vou·sa (káthə-révvōō-sə, -révvə- || *U.S. also* kaáthə-, -saa) *n.* The literary and official form of Modern Greek, showing many morphological and lexical features restored from Classical Greek. Also called "Puristic". Compare **Dhimotiki.** [Modern Greek *kathareuousa,* from Greek, feminine present participle of *kathareuein,* to be pure, from *katharos,* pure.]
Kath·man·du or **Kat·man·du** (kát-man-dōō, kaát-maan-). Capital of Nepal. It was founded in the 8th century on the Baghmati river, and became the capital when taken by the Gurkhas in 1768.
Ka·to·wi·ce (káttō-veét-say, káttə-). *German* **Kat·to·witz** (-vits). City in southern Poland, producing coal, and iron and steel. It was part of Germany until the partition of Silesia (1921).
Kat·te·gat or **Cat·te·gat** (kátigat). Strait between Sweden and Jutland, Denmark, connecting with the North Sea via the Skagerrak, and with the Baltic Sea via the Øresund, Store Baelt, and Little Baelt.
ka·ty·did (káyti-did) *n.* Any of various green, long-horned grasshoppers of the predominantly tropical family Tettigoniidae, having specialised organs in the wings of the male that when rubbed together produce a distinctive sound. [Imitative.]
Ka·tyn (katín). Village near Smolensk in Russia. It was occupied by German forces in World War II. Mass graves of more than 4,000 Polish officers were found in the forest nearby, and they were widely thought to have been massacred by the Russians.
Kauff·man (kówf-man, -mən), **(Maria Anna Catharina) Angelica** (1741–1807). Swiss painter. She worked chiefly in England, and was a founder member of the Royal Academy.
Ka·un·da (kaa-ōōndə), **Kenneth (David)** (1924–). Zambian President (1964–91). He led his country (formerly Northern Rhodesia) to full independence under the name of Zambia (1964). He has been influential in the Organisation of African Unity.
kau·ri, kau·ry (kówr-i) *n.* **1.** Any of several coniferous trees of the genus *Agathis*; especially, *A. australis,* of New Zealand, having close-grained, durable wood. **2.** The wood of such a tree. In both senses, also called "kauri pine". **3.** A resin obtained from the kauri or from deposits of fossilised exudations of such trees, used in varnishes and enamels. In this sense, also called "kauri gum", "kauri resin". [Maori *kawri.*]
ka·va (kaávə) *n.* **1.** A shrub, *Piper methysticum,* of tropical Pacific islands, the dried roots of which are used to make an intoxicating drink. **2.** The drink made from this plant. Also called "kava-kava". [Tongan *kava,* "bitter".]
Ka·wa·sa·ki (ków-ə-saáki, kaá-wə-). City in Japan, part of the Tokyo Bay industrial complex. Its industries include shipbuilding, engineering, and oil-refining.
Kay (kay), **Sir.** In Arthurian Legend, the rude, boastful foster brother and steward of King Arthur.
kay·ak, kai·ak (kī-ak) *n.* **1.** A watertight Eskimo canoe made of skins stretched over a light wooden frame and having a deck covering that closes around the waist of the paddler. Compare **umiak. 2.** A lightweight and highly manoeuvrable, usually canvas-covered canoe popular for sports. [Eskimo *qajaq.*]
Ka·zakh (kázzak, kə-zák || *U.S.* -zaák) *n., pl.* **-zakhs** or collectively **Kazakh.** Also **Ka·zak. 1.** A member of a Turkic people dwelling in Kazakhstan and in northwestern China. **2.** The Turkic language of this people. **—Ka·zakh** *adj.*
Kaz·akh·stan (kázzak-staán), **Republic of.** Country in northwestern Asia, formerly a constituent republic of the U.S.S.R. The world's first fast-breeder nuclear reactor was opened there on the Mangyshlak peninsula. Area, 2 717 300 square kilometres (1,049,151 square miles). Population, 16,530,000. Capital, Astana (Akmola). See map at **Commonwealth of Independent States.**
Ka·zan or **Ka·san** (kə-zán, -záan). City in Russia, on the Volga river. It was capital of a Tatar khanate until captured by Russia in 1552. Tolstoy and Lenin studied at its university.

Ka·zan (kə-zaán), **Elia,** born Elia Kazanjoglou (1909–). U.S. stage and film director, born in Turkey of Greek parents. He directed Tennessee Williams's *A Streetcar Named Desire* (1947), and the films *On the Waterfront* (1954) and *East of Eden* (1955).

Ka·zan·tza·kis (kázzan-dzaákeess), **Nikos** (1885–1957). Greek writer and translator. Among his novels are *Zorba the Greek* (1946) and *Christ Recrucified* (1954).

ka·zoo (kə-zōō) *n., pl.* **-zoos.** A toy musical instrument in which a paper membrane at the end of a tube is vibrated by the player's voice, to make a buzzing sound. [Probably imitative of its sound.]

kb kilobar.

KB *Chess.* king's bishop.

K.B. 1. King's Bench. 2. Knight Bachelor.

K.B.E. Knight (Commander of the Order) of the British Empire.

KBP *Chess.* king's bishop's pawn.

kc kilocycle.

K.C. 1. King's Counsel. 2. King's College.

kcal kilocalorie.

K.C.B. Knight Commander (of the Order) of the Bath (in Britain).

K.C.M.G. Knight Commander (of the Order) of St. Michael and St. George (in Britain).

kcs, kc/s kilocycles per second.

K.C.V.O. Knight Commander of the Royal Victorian Order (in Britain).

ke·a (káy-ə, kée-ə) *n.* A brownish-green parrot, *Nestor notabilis,* of mountainous areas of New Zealand, reputed to kill sheep by pecking at their flesh. [Maori, imitative of its cry.]

Kean (keen), **Edmund** (*c.* 1787–1833). British actor. He was hailed as a great tragic actor for his roles as Shylock at the Drury Lane theatre (1814), as Richard III, and as Iago.

Kea·ting (keeting), **Paul John** (1944–). Australian politician, leader of the Labor Party and Prime Minister of Australia (1991–96).

Kea·ton (kéet'n), **Buster,** born Joseph Francis Keaton (1895–1966). U.S. film actor. His skill as a mime made him a great comedian of the silent screen. His films include *The Navigator* (1924).

Keats (keets), **John** (1795–1821). British Romantic poet. His collection *Lamia and Other Poems* (1820) includes "The Eve of St. Agnes" and the famous odes "To a Nightingale", "To Autumn", "To Psyche", and "On a Grecian Urn". He died of tuberculosis at the age of 26. **—Keats·i·an** (kéetsi-ən) *adj. & n.*

ke·bab (ki-báb ‖ *U.S.* -baáb) *n.* 1. Pieces of meat, seafood, or vegetables threaded onto skewers and grilled; especially, **shish kebab** *(see).* **b.** See **doner kebab.**

Ke·ble (kéeb'l), **John** (1792–1866). British clergyman. He delivered a sermon in Oxford (1833) defending Catholic principles in the Church of England, so initiating the Oxford Movement.

Kechua. Variant of **Quechua.**

keck¹ (kek) *intr.v.* **kecked, kecking, kecks.** To retch. **—keck at.** To refuse or shrink from with an expression of disgust. [Imitative.]

keck² *n.* Also **kex** (keks). A tall, white-flowered umbelliferous plant; especially, cow parsley or hogweed. [*Keck,* from *kext†* (mistaken as a plural, as if *kecks*).]

ked (ked) *n.* Any of various wingless parasitic flies; especially, the sheep ked, *Melophagus orinus,* and the deer ked, *Liptoptena cervi.* [16th century : origin obscure.]

kedge (kej) *n.* A light anchor used for kedging. **~v.** **kedged, kedging, kedges.** **—tr.** To move (a ship) by pulling on a rope attached to an anchor lowered some distance away. **—intr.** To move in this way. Used of a ship. [From *kedge,* earlier *cadge,* to warp a ship, perhaps from Middle English *cagge†,* to tie, bind.]

ked·ger·ee (kéjə-rée, -ree) *n.* 1. An Indian dish of rice, lentils, onions, eggs, and spices. 2. An English dish of flaked fish, boiled rice, and eggs, usually served hot. [Hindi *khichṛī,* from Sanskrit *khiccā†.*]

keef. Variant of **kif.**

Kee·gan (keégən), **Kevin (Joseph)** (1951–). English footballer. He has played for Liverpool, Hamburg, Southampton, and Newcastle. He captained the England team and was European Footballer of the Year (1978, 1979).

keek (keek) *intr.v.* **keeked, keeking, keeks.** *Scottish.* To peek; peep. **~n.** *Scottish.* A quick or furtive look; a peek. [Middle English *kike,* probably from Middle Dutch *kiken,* to peep.]

keel¹ (keel) *n.* 1. The main structural member of a ship, running fore and aft on the centre line, extending from bow to stern, forming the backbone of the vessel to which the frames are attached. 2. *Poetic.* A ship. 3. A structure that resembles a ship's keel in function or shape, such as the member extending lengthways at the bottom of an aircraft fuselage. 4. *Biology.* A structure having a longitudinal ridge suggestive of a ship's keel, as: **a.** The anterior part of the breastbone of a flying bird. **b.** A pair of united petals in certain flowers. **—on an even keel.** Balanced; steady. **~v.** **keeled, keeling, keels.** **—tr.** To cause to capsize or turn over. Usually used with *over.* **—intr.** 1. To roll on her keel; capsize. Used of a ship, usually with *over.* 2. To collapse or fall over in or as if in a faint. Used with *over.* [Middle English *ke(o)le,* from Old Norse *kjölr.*] **—keeled** *adj.*

keel² *n.* 1. **a.** A barge, especially one for carrying coal on the Tyne. **b.** The amount carried by such a barge. 2. A British unit of weight formerly used for coal, equal to 21.2 tons. [Middle English *kele,* from Middle Dutch *kiel,* ship.]

keel³ *tr.v.* **keeled, keeling, keels.** *Archaic & Regional.* To cool (a hot liquid), as by stirring in order to prevent boiling over. Used chiefly in the phrase *keel the pot.* [Middle English *kelen,* Old English *cēlan.*]

keel·boat (kéel-bōt) *n.* A large, covered, flat-bottomed boat with a keel but without sails, used for river transport.

keel·haul (kéel-hawl) *tr.v.* **-hauled, -hauling, -hauls.** 1. To punish by dragging under the keel of a ship from one side to the other or from stem to stern. 2. To castigate; scold severely. [Dutch *kielhalen* : Middle Dutch *kiel,* keel of a ship + *halen,* to pull, haul.]

Keeling Islands. See **Cocos Islands.**

keel·son (kél-s'n, kéel-) *n.* Also **kel·son** (kél-). *Nautical.* A timber or girder placed parallel with and bolted to the keel of a ship for additional strength. [Probably from Low German *kielswīn* : Middle Low German *kiel,* keel of a ship + *swīn,* swine, "timber".]

keen¹ (keen) *adj.* **keener, keenest.** 1. Having a fine, sharp cutting edge or point. 2. Intellectually acute; penetrating; trenchant. 3. Acutely sensitive. Said of the senses. 4. Sharp; vivid; strong. 5. Bitter; piercing: *a keen wind.* 6. Offering strong competition: *keen prices.* 7. **a.** Ardent; enthusiastic and willing. Used with *on.* **b.** Eager: *keen on going.* 8. *Informal.* Strongly attracted to or fond of. Used with *on: he's been keen on her for ages.* **—See Synonyms at eager, sharp.** [Middle English *kene,* Old English *cēne,* wise, bold, powerful, from Common Germanic *kōnjaz* (unattested).] **—keen·ly** *adv.* **—keen·ness** *n.*

keen² *n.* A loud wailing lamentation for the dead. **~intr.v.** **keened, keening, keens.** To wail over the dead. [Irish Gaelic *caoine,* lamentation, from *caoninim,* I wail, from Old Irish *coínim,* from Common Celtic *koinyo-* (unattested), to wail.]

keen·er (kéenər) *n.* One who keens; especially, a professional mourner at an Irish funeral.

keep (keep) *v.* **kept** (kept), **keeping, keeps.** **—tr.** 1. To retain possession of: *keep the change; kept his nerve.* 2. To store; put customarily: *Where do you keep your saw?* 3. To take in one's charge temporarily: *Keep this for me until I return.* 4. **a.** To provide with the necessities of life; support: *"There's little to earn and many to keep."* (Charles Kingsley). **b.** To support (a mistress or lover) financially. Used chiefly in the past participle: *a kept woman.* 5. **a.** To supply with room and board for a charge: *keep boarders.* **b.** To raise and feed: *keep chickens.* 6. To have the resources to retain for pleasure or use: *"It is not too much for me now, in degree or cost, to keep a coach."* (Samuel Pepys). 7. To have in ready supply. 8. To manage: *keeps a tobacconist's shop.* 9. To maintain by making regular entries: *keep records.* 10. To cause to remain in some specified condition or position: *kept us all guessing; keep her away.* 11. **a.** To preserve and protect; save. **b.** To withhold for the time being; reserve: *keep some for tomorrow.* 12. To detain: *What kept you? kept us in after school.* 13. To confine: *keep in quarantine.* 14. To prevent or deter. Used with *from: keep ice from melting.* 15. **a.** To observe habitually: *keep late hours.* **b.** To observe in the appropriate or prescribed manner: *keep the Sabbath.* 16. To adhere to; fulfil: *keep a schedule; keep one's word.* 17. To refrain from divulging: *keep a secret; keep counsel.* 18. To associate with habitually: *She kept bad company.* **—intr.** 1. To remain in a specified position, place, or condition; stay: *keep in line; keep quiet.* 2. To persevere in some action or on some course; continue: *keep guessing; keep left.* 3. To be in the specified state of health: *How are you keeping?* 4. **a.** To remain fresh or unspoiled: *The dessert won't keep.* **b.** To admit of being withheld: *I've got some interesting gossip, but it'll keep till tomorrow.* **—See Synonyms at observe. —keep at it.** To persevere in an action or work. **—keep back.** To refuse to tell or give; withhold. **—keep down.** 1. To repress or control. 2. To retain (food or drink) in the stomach. **—keep from.** To prevent oneself from. Used with the present participle: *I can't keep from worrying.* **—keep in with.** To remain on friendly terms with. **—keep off.** To refrain from approaching, discussing, or the like. **—keep on.** 1. To continue in an action. Used with the present participle: *keep on smiling.* 2. To continue to employ: *keep on five men.* 3. **a.** To talk incessantly: *keeps on about his bad leg.* **b.** To nag persistently. Used with *at.* **—keep out.** To prevent from entering and taking control or possession: *keep out the unions.* **—keep to.** To adhere to: *keep to the original purpose.* **—keep to (oneself).** 1. To shun company. 2. To refrain from sharing or divulging: *He's keeping the news to himself.* **—keep under.** To cause to remain in subjection. **—keep up.** 1. To maintain in good condition. 2. To persevere in; carry on: *keep up traditions; can't keep this up forever.* 3. To remain at the same level or pace: *keep up with the leaders.* 4. To remain informed or in touch: *keep up with current research.* 5. To cause to stay up late at night. **—keep up with the Joneses.** To strive competitively with one's neighbours or associates. **~n.** 1. Care; charge: *The child is in my keep for the day.* 2. The means by which one is supported; the necessities of life: *earn one's keep.* 3. The main tower or donjon of a medieval castle; a stronghold. **—See Synonyms at livelihood. —for keeps.** 1. To keep forever: *He gave it to me for keeps.* 2. Seriously and permanently: *We're separating for keeps.* [Middle English *kepen,* Old English *cēpan†,* to seize, hold, guard.]

Synonyms: keep, retain, withhold, reserve, maintain.

keep·er (kéepər) *n.* 1. One who keeps; especially: **a.** An attendant, guard, or warden, as in a museum, art gallery, or the like. **b.** One who has the charge or care of animals in a zoo or circus. **c.** A person who preserves or protects someone or something. **d.** *Chiefly British.* A gamekeeper, goalkeeper, or wicketkeeper *(all of which see).* 2. A device for keeping something in place, such as a pin or clip. 3. A guard ring *(see).* 4. A small piece of iron placed across the poles of a permanent magnet when it is not in use, in order to complete the magnetisation.

Keeper of the Privy Purse *n.* An official of the royal household, the **Privy Purse** (see).

keep·ing (kéeping) *n.* 1. Custody; care; guardianship. 2. Harmony; conformity. Used chiefly in the phrases *in* or *out of keeping.*

keep·net (kéep-net) *n.* A cylindrical net, open at one end and suspended in the water, into which anglers put fish to keep them alive.

keep·sake (kéep-sayk) *n.* Something given or kept as a reminder of the giver; a memento.

kees·hond (káyss-hond, kéess-) *n., pl.* **-honden** (-ən) or **-honds.** A dog of a small breed originating in the Netherlands, having a thick greyish-black coat. [Dutch : probably *Kees,* pet form of name *Cornelis,* from Latin *Cornēlius†,* name of a Roman gens + *hond,* dog.]

kef. Variant of **kif.**

keffiyeh. Variant of **kaffiyeh.**

Kef·la·vík (kéflə-vik, képlə-, -veek). A fishing port in southwest Iceland. Its international airport, built by the United States in World War II as Meeks Field, has also been a NATO base since 1951.

keg (keg) *n.* 1. A small cask or barrel, usually with a capacity of five to ten gallons. 2. *British.* An aluminium container for transporting and storing beer. [Earlier *cag,* Middle English *kag,* from Old Norse *kaggi†.*]

keg beer *n.* Beer that has been pasteurised and artificially recarbonated and is able to be stored for long periods in aluminium kegs. Compare **real ale.**

keg·ler (kéglər) *n. U.S. Informal.* A tenpin bowler. [German *Kegler,* from *kegeln,* to bowl, from *Kegel,* bowling pin, from Old High German *kegit†,* stick, peg.]

ke·ku·lé formula (kékkew-lay) *n. Chemistry.* A structural formula for benzene in which the six carbon atoms are positioned at the corners of a regular hexagon and linked by alternate double and single bonds. [After KEKULE VON STRADONITZ.]

Ke·ku·lé von Stradonitz (kékkew-lay, *German* káy-kōō-), **(Friedrich) August** (1829-96). German chemist. He carried out important research concerning the structure and combining power of atoms, and in 1865 formulated the structure of benzene.

kelim. Variant of **kilim.**

Kel·ler (kéllər), **Helen (Adams)** (1880-1968). U.S. writer and lecturer. She was deaf and blind from early childhood, but learnt to read, write, and speak. She became noted for her work for the blind and other causes.

Kells (kelz). Market town in County Meath, Republic of Ireland. *The Book of the Kells,* an eighth-century illuminated Gospel, is said to have been written at a monastery founded there by St. Columba in the sixth century.

Kel·ly (kélli), **Grace (Patricia)** (1929-82). U.S. film actress. She starred in *High Noon* (1952) and *To Catch a Thief* (1955). In 1956 she gave up her career to marry Prince Rainier III of Monaco.

Kelly, Ned, born Edward Kelly (1855-80). Australian bushranger. He headed a four-man gang robbing banks in the Victoria/New South Wales borderlands (1878-80), but was eventually captured and hanged.

ke·loid, che·loid (kée-loyd) *n.* A mass of fibrous connective tissue, usually at the site of a scar. [French *kéloïde* : Greek *khēlē,* claw, CHELA + -OID.]

kelp (kelp) *n.* 1. Any of various brown, often very large seaweeds of the order Laminariales. Also called "oarweed". 2. The ash of such seaweeds, used as a source of potash and iodine. Also called "varec". [Middle English *cülpe†.*]

kelp·er (kélpər) *n. Informal.* A native of the Falkland Islands. [KELP + -ER (from the importance of kelp in the Falklands).]

kel·pie¹ (kélpi) *n.* A water spirit in Scottish legend, usually having the shape of a horse and causing or rejoicing in drownings. [18th century : origin obscure.]

kelpie² *n.* A dog of an Australian breed of sheepdog developed from the Scottish collie. Also called "barb".

kelson. Variant of **keelson.**

kelt (kelt) *n.* A salmon after spawning, usually in an exhausted condition. [Middle English : origin obscure.]

Kelt. Variant of **Celt.** —**Keltic** *adj.*

kelter. *Chiefly British.* Variant of **kilter.**

kel·vin (kélvin) *n. Symbol* **K** The unit of thermodynamic temperature, equal to ¹⁄273.16 of the thermodynamic temperature of the triple point of water. [After Baron KELVIN.]

Kel·vin (kélvin) *adj. Abbr.* **K** Of, pertaining to, or designating an **absolute scale** (see) of temperature, the zero point of which is approximately −273.15°C.

Kel·vin (kélvin), **William Thomson, 1st Baron** (1824-1907). British physicist and inventor. He established the Kelvin scale of temperature and supervised the laying of a cable across the Atlantic (1866). He also did important work in thermodynamics.

Kemal Ataturk. See **Ataturk.**

Kem·ble (kémb'l). British theatrical family, founded by Roger Kemble (1721-1802). His sons, John Philip Kemble (1757-1823) and Charles Kemble (1775-1854) were both distinguished actors, and his eldest daughter was Sarah Siddons. Frances Ann Kemble, known as Fanny (1809-93), was the daughter of Charles Kemble.

kempt (kempt) *adj.* Combed; tidy. [Back-formation from UN-KEMPT; originally, past participle of *kemb,* dialect variant of COMB.]

ken (ken) *v.* **kenned** or **kent** (kent), **kenning, kens.** —*tr.* 1. *Chiefly Scottish.* To know (a person, fact, or thing). 2. *Chiefly Scottish.* To recognise. 3. *Archaic.* To descry; make out. —*intr. Chiefly Scottish.* To have an understanding of something.

~*n.* 1. Range of knowledge or understanding: *beyond my ken.* 2. *Rare.* Range of vision; view. [Middle English *kennen,* Old English *cennan,* to make known (probably influenced in sense by Old Norse cognate *kenna,* to know).]

Ken·dal green (kéndal) *n.* 1. A coarse, green, woollen fabric. Also called "Kendal". 2. The colour of this fabric. [Originally manufactured at *Kendal,* England.]

ken·do (kéndō) *n.* A traditional Japanese martial art, in which two contestants wearing protective armour fight with bamboo swords. [Japanese *kendō* "the art of fencing", from Chinese *jiàn,* sword + *daò,* way.]

Kennedy, Cape. See **Canaveral, Cape.**

Kennedy, John F(itzgerald) (1917-63). 35th President of the United States (1961-63). A Democrat and the youngest president ever to be elected and also the first Roman Catholic president. He studied at Harvard where he wrote *Why England Slept,* a study of the British failure to judge adequately the Nazi threat, which became a best seller. After a distinguished war career in the navy he entered the House of Representatives (1947) and the U.S. Senate (1952). He executed (although did not plan) the disastrous invasion attempt on Cuba (1961) by Cuban exiles, but caused Khrushchev to back down over his attempts to establish Soviet nuclear missiles there in 1962. A liberal on domestic policy, he established the Peace Corps, fought for slum clearance and cheap public housing, and raised the minimum wage. He agreed a partial Test Ban Treaty with the U.S.S.R. (1963) and insisted on continued U.S. access to West Berlin. He was assassinated in Dallas, Texas, allegedly by Lee Harvey Oswald.

Kennedy, Joseph Patrick (1888-1969). U.S. multimillionaire and father of the Kennedy brothers. He made a fortune from banking and the stock market, and became U.S. ambassador to Britain (1937-40). He resigned because he opposed aid to the Allies.

Kennedy, Robert Francis (1925-68). U.S. Democratic politician. He was Attorney General (1961-64) during the presidency of his brother, John F. Kennedy. He was elected to the Senate (1964), and was campaigning for the Democratic nomination for the presidency when he was assassinated.

ken·nel¹ (kénn'l) *n.* 1. A shelter for a dog or dogs. 2. A pack of dogs, especially hounds. 3. *Usually plural.* An establishment where dogs are bred, trained, or boarded. 4. A wretched house; a hovel. ~*v.* **kennelled** or *U.S.* **kenneled, -nelling** or *U.S.* **-neling, -nels.** —*tr.* To keep or place in or as if in a kennel. —*intr.* To stay or take cover in or as if in a kennel. [Middle English *kenel,* from Old Northern French *kenil* (unattested), variant of Old French *chenil,* from Vulgar Latin *canile* (unattested), from Latin *canis,* dog.]

kennel² *n. Archaic.* A gutter along a street. [Variant of *cannel,* Middle English *canel, canal,* CANAL.]

Ken·nel·ly (kénn'l-i), **Arthur Edwin** (1861-1939). U.S. electrical engineer. At the same time as Oliver Heaviside, he correctly predicted the existence of an ionised layer in the upper atmosphere, the **Kennelly-Heaviside layer.**

Ken·nel·ly-Heav·i·side layer (kénn'l-i-hévvi-sīd) *n.* The **E** layer *(see)* of the ionosphere.

Ken·neth I Mac·Al·pine or **Mac·Al·pin** (kénnith məcálpin) (died 860). First King of Alba (846), a united kingdom of Picts and Scots.

ken·ning (kénning) *n.* A metaphorical, usually compound expression substituted for the name of something, especially in Old English and Old Norse poetry; for example, *storm of swords* is a kenning for "battle". [Old Norse *kenning,* "naming", symbol, from *kenna,* to know, name (with a kenning).]

Ken·ny (kénni), **Elizabeth** (1886-1952). Australian pioneer of polio treatment. She applied hot towels to affected limbs, instead of wrapping them in plaster casts, the traditional treatment.

ke·no (kéenō) *n. U.S.* A game of chance similar to bingo, but using balls rather than counters. [Probably from French *quine,* set of five (winning numbers), back-formation from Old French *quines,* five each, from Latin *quīnī* (accusative *quīnas*).]

ke·no·sis (ke-nṓ-siss, ki-) *n. Theology.* Christ's relinquishment of the form of God in becoming man and suffering death. Philippians 2:5-8. [Late Greek *kenōsis,* from Greek, an emptying, from *kenoun,* to empty, from *kenos,* empty.] —**ke·not·ic** (-nóttik, -nótik) *adj. & n.*

Ken·sing·ton and Chel·sea (kénzing-tən; chél-si). Since 1965, a royal borough of Greater London.

ken·speck·le (kén-speck'l) *adj. Scottish.* Easily recognised; conspicuous. [From dialect *kenspeck,* from Scandinavian; akin to Old Norse *kennispeki,* power of recognition. See **ken.**]

kent. Alternative past tense and past participle of **ken.**

Kent (kent). A county of southeast England, called the Garden of England for its fruit and hop crops. The Saxon kingdom of Kent was the first to be converted to Christianity (597), by St. Augustine. The administrative centre is Maidstone.

Kent, Bruce (1929-). Former British Roman Catholic priest. He was active in the Campaign for Nuclear Disarmament (CND) from the mid-1960s. He was CND's General Secretary (1980-85), its Vice-Chairman (1985), and its Chairman (1987-90).

Kent, William (1684-1748). English architect and painter. He designed Holkham Hall in Norfolk, Horse Guards Parade in Whitehall, and Esher Place.

ken·te (kén-ti, -tay) *n.* 1. A brightly coloured cloth of Ghana, woven in strips. 2. A large cloth made up of such strips, worn as dress in the style of a toga by Ghanaian men. [Probably from Akan.]

ken·ti·a palm (kénti-ə) *n.* A palm, *Howea belmoreana* (or *Kentia belmoreana*), often grown as a house plant. Also called "sentry palm".

Kent·ish (kéntish) *adj.* Of, relating to, or inhabiting Kent.
~*n.* The dialect originally spoken in Kent.

Kentish glory *n.* A handsome, large, European moth, *Endromis versicolora*, no longer found in Kent but plentiful elsewhere.

kent·ledge (kéntlij) *n. Nautical.* Pig iron used as permanent ballast. [Old French *quintelage*, ballast, from *quintal*, hundredweight, from Medieval Latin *quintale*, from Arabic *qinṭār*, KANTAR.]

Ken·tuck·y (ken-túcki ‖ *U.S.* kən-). A state of central United States. Known as the "Bluegrass State" because of the rich pastures of bluegrass in its central area, it also has coal deposits, and heavy industry has been developed at Louisville. Kentucky joined the Union in 1792. Frankfort is its capital.

Kentucky bluegrass *n.* See **bluegrass.**

Kentucky Derby *n.* An annual horse race for three-year-olds run since 1875 at Churchill Downs in Louisville, Kentucky.

Ken·ya, Mount (kén-yə, kéen-). Extinct volcano in Kenya. It is Africa's second highest mountain at 5 199 metres (17,057 feet).

Kenya, Republic of. East African republic lying across the equator. The fertile southwest highlands are Africa's major source of coffee and tea, the country's main exports, along with pyrethrum and sisal. Tourists to Amboseli, Tavo and other national parks and game reserves is a major industry. Kenya was proclaimed a British colony in 1920. The savage Mau Mau rebellion of the Kikuyu (1952–60) hastened independence (1963) under Jomo Kenyatta, and stability and prosperity ensued. Despite multi-party elections (1992), Kenya remains a one-party state in practice. Daniel arap Moi, in power for 20 years, won the 1998 election. Area, 580 367 square kilometres (224,081 square miles). Population, 31,800,000. Capital, Nairobi. —**Ken·yan** *n. & adj.*

Ken·yat·ta (ken-yáttə), **Jomo (Kamau)**, born Kamau Ngengi (1894–1978). First president of independent Kenya (1964–78). In 1947, he became leader of the Kenya African Union. He was a suspected organiser of the Mau Mau rebellion (1952) and was imprisoned by the British (1952–61). Kenyatta negotiated independence, and was elected prime minister (1963).

Ken·yon (kén-yən), **Dame Kathleen** (1906–78). British archaeologist. She excavated the ruins of Jerusalem and Jericho in Jordan.

kep (kep) *tr.v.* **kepped, kepping, keps.** *Northern British.* To catch. [Variant of KEEP (in obsolete sense, seize, hold).]

ke·pi (káypee, képpi) *n., pl.* **-is.** A French military cap with a flat, circular top and a peak. [French *képi*, from Swiss German *käppi*, diminutive of German *Kappe*, cap.]

Kep·ler (képplər), **Johannes** (1571–1630). German astronomer, founder of modern astronomy. His three laws, based on the observations made by his teacher Tycho Brahe, made sense of the theory that the planets revolve around the sun. —**Kep·ler·i·an** (kep-léer-i-ən) *adj.*

Kep·ler's laws (képplərz) *pl.n.* Three laws describing planetary motion, published by Kepler between 1609 and 1619: the path of a planet is an ellipse with the sun at one focus; a line from the sun to a planet sweeps out equal areas in equal time periods; the square of the orbital period of a planet is proportional to the cube of its average distance from the sun.

kept. Past tense and past participle of **keep.**

Ker·a·la (kérrələ). The most densely populated state in India. It lies in the southwest part of the country, between the Western Ghats and the coast. Though poor and undeveloped, Kerala has the highest literacy rate in India.

ker·a·tin (kérrə-tin) *n.* A tough, fibrous protein containing sulphur and forming the outer layer of epidermal structures such as hair, nails, horns, and hoofs. [Greek *keras* (stem *kerat-*), horn + -IN.]

—ke·rat·i·nous (ki-ráttinəss, ke-) *adj.*

ker·a·tin·ise, ker·a·tin·ize (kérrətin-īz) *v.* **-ised, -ising, -ises.** —*tr.* To form keratin in or on. —*intr.* To form a keratinous layer. —**ker·a·tin·i·sa·tion** (-ī-záysh'n ‖ *U.S.* -i-) *n.*

ker·a·ti·tis (kérrə-tī-tiss) *n.* Inflammation of the cornea.

kerato-, kerat– *comb. form.* Indicates: **1.** Horny tissue, especially of the skin; for example, **keratin. 2.** The cornea of the eye; for example, **keratitis.**

ker·a·to·sis (kérrə-tṓ-siss) *n.* Any horny growth or condition of the skin, such as a wart.

kerb, *U.S.* **curb** (kerb, kurb) *n., pl.* **kerbs.** A concrete border or row of joined stones forming the edge of a pavement.
~*tr.v.* **kerbed, kerbing, kerbs.** To provide with a kerb.

kerb crawler *n. Chiefly British.* A person who is in a vehicle moving slowly along beside a kerb and who sexually harasses or propositions passers-by. —**kerb crawling** *n.*

kerb drill *n.* A basic safety procedure to be followed by pedestrians before crossing a road.

kerb market *n.* **1.** An unofficial after-hours market for buying and selling securities. **2.** A market dealing in securities that are not quoted on the stock exchange.

kerb weight *n.* The weight of a car without its passengers and their belongings.

ker·chief (kér-cheef, -chif) *n.* **1.** A square scarf, often worn around the neck or as a head covering. **2.** *Archaic.* A handkerchief. [Middle English *c(o)urchef, kercheffe*, from Old French *couvrechef, cuerchief*, "head covering" : *co(u)vrir*, from COVER + *ch(i)ef*, head, from Latin *caput*.]

Ke·ren·sky (kə-rénski; *Russian* kérrinski), **Aleksandr Feodorovich** (1881–1970). Russian politician. He was head of government between the two Russian revolutions in 1917, being expelled by the Bolsheviks because of his moderate policies. He went to Australia (1940) and lived in the United States (1946–70).

kerf (kerf) *n.* **1.** A groove or notch made by a saw, axe, or the like. **2.** The cut end of a tree that has been felled. [Middle English *kyrf, kerf*, Old English *cyrf*, act of cutting.]

ker·fuf·fle (kər-fúff'l) *n. Chiefly British Informal.* A fuss or commotion. [20th century : origin obscure.]

Ker·gue·len Islands (kérgilin). See **French Southern and Antarctic Territories.**

Kerkira or **Kerkyra.** See **Corfu.**

ker·ma (kérmə) *n. Physics.* The sum of all the initial kinetic energies of particles produced in a given sample by ionising radiation divided by the mass of the sample. [*kinetic energy released in matter.*]

Kermanshahr (kér-man-shaá) Formerly Qahremanshahr and Bakhtaran, capital of Kermanshahan province, western Iran, founded by the Sassanids in the fourth century A.D. It is a market centre for a rich agricultural region.

ker·mes (kér-meez, -miz) *n.* **1.** A red dyestuff prepared from the dried bodies of female scale insects of the genus *Kermes*, especially the Eurasian species *K. ilices*. **2.** A small evergreen Eurasian oak, *Quercus coccifera*, on which *Kermes* scale insects live. [French *kermès*, short form for *alkermès*, from Spanish *alkermez*, from Arabic *al-qirmiz*, from Sanskrit *the kermes*, from Sanskrit *kṛmi-ja-*, (red dye) produced by a worm : *kṛmi-*, worm + *ja-*, born, produced.]

ker·mis, ker·mess, kir·mess (kér-miss) *n.* **1.** Especially formerly in Belgium and the Netherlands, an annual outdoor fair. **2.** *Chiefly U.S.* A fund-raising fair or carnival. [Dutch *kermis(se)*, from Middle Dutch *kercmisse* : *kerke, kerc*, church, from West Germanic *kirika* (unattested), from Late Greek *kurikon*, CHURCH + *misse*, Mass.]

kern, kerne[1] (kern) *n.* **1.** A medieval Scottish or Irish foot soldier. **2.** *Archaic.* A country bumpkin; a rustic. [Middle English *kerne*, from Middle Irish *ceithern*, from Old Irish, band of foot soldiers, possibly from *cath*, battle, troop.]

kern[2] *n. Printing.* The portion of a character or typeface that projects beyond the body or shank.
~*tr.v.* **kerned, kerning, kerns.** *Printing.* To provide (a character or typeface) with a kern. [French *carne*, corner, salient angle, from Latin *cardō* (stem *cardin-*), hinge.]

kern[3] *n. Engineering.* The middle part of a wall, column, or other supporting structure regarded as the part subject to compressive forces. [Perhaps from German *Kern*, nucleus.]

Kern (kern), **Jerome (David)** (1885–1945). U.S. songwriter. He wrote more than 50 stage and film musicals and more than a thousand songs. His most successful musical was *Showboat* (1927), and his songs include *Ol' Man River* and *Smoke Gets in Your Eyes*.

ker·nel (kérn'l) *n.* **1.** A grain or seed, as of a cereal grass, enclosed in a hard husk. **2.** The inner, usually edible part of a nut or fruit stone. **3.** A nucleus; an essence; a core: *"that hard kernel of gaiety that never breaks"* (Evelyn Waugh). [Middle English *kirnel, kernell*, Old English *cyrnel*, seed, kernel, diminutive of *corn*, corn, berry, seed.]

kern·ite (kérn-īt) *n.* A colourless to white crystalline mineral, $Na_2B_4O_7 \cdot 4H_2O$, that is a major source of boron. [Found in *Kern* County, California.]

ker·o·gen (kérrə-jən, -jen) *n.* Solid organic remains found in rocks, which produce hydrocarbons similar to petroleum when heated. Oil shale is rich in kerogen. [Greek *kēros*, wax + -GEN.]

ker·o·sene, ker·o·sine (kérrə-seen, -séen) *n. Chiefly U.S.* Paraffin oil, especially when used as fuel for jet aircraft. [Greek *kēros*, wax (see **ceruse**) + -ENE (from the use of paraffin in its distillation).]

Ke·rou·ac (kérroo-ak), **Jack** (1922–69). U.S. writer and leading figure of the beat generation. His mainly autobiographical books in-

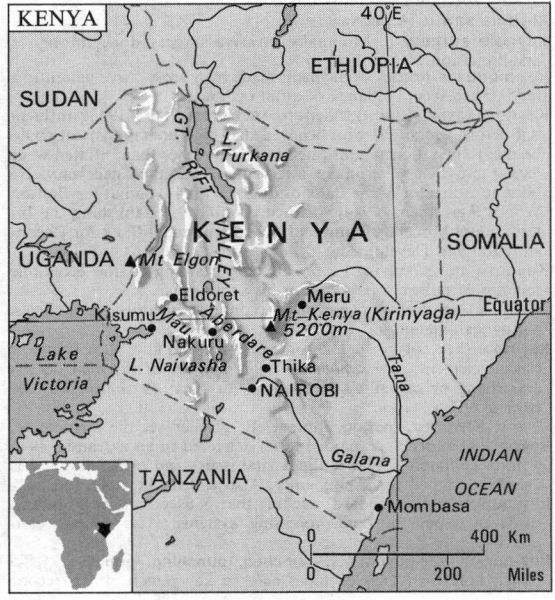

KENYA

SUDAN

ETHIOPIA

L. Turkana

KENYA

UGANDA · Mt Elgon

SOMALIA

Eldoret · Meru

Kisumu · Mt Kenya (Kirinyaga) 5200m · Equator

Nakuru

Lake Victoria

L. Naivasha · Thika

NAIROBI

Galana

TANZANIA

INDIAN OCEAN

· Mombasa

0 — 400 Km

200 Miles

clude *On the Road* (1957), *Dharma Bums* (1958), and *Desolation Angels* (1965).

Kerr cell (ker) *n.* A cell consisting of a transparent liquid to which a strong electric field can be applied to stop the passage of light through the cell. The device, which depends for its action on the electrical Kerr effect, is used for producing short pulses of light for laser experiments, high speed photography, and the like. [After John *Kerr* (1824–1907), British physicist.]

Kerr effect (ker) *n. Physics.* **1.** The production of double refraction in certain transparent solids or liquids by application of a strong electric field. **2.** The slight elliptical polarisation of light that is reflected from the surface of strongly magnetised material. [After John *Kerr* (1824–1907), British physicist.]

Ker·ry[1] (kérri). A county on the southwest coast of the Republic of Ireland. Its mountains and lakes are a tourist attraction.

Kerry[2] *n., pl.* **-ries.** Any of a breed of small, black dairy cattle originally raised in the county of Kerry, Ireland.

Kerry blue terrier *n.* Any of a breed of terriers of Irish origin, having a dense, wavy, bluish-grey coat.

Kerry Hill *n.* A large, broad-bodied sheep of a breed originally from the Kerry Hills of Montgomeryshire (Powys).

ker·sey (kérzi) *n., pl.* **-seys. 1.** A woollen fabric, often ribbed, formerly used for hose and trousers. **2.** A twilled woollen fabric, sometimes with a cotton warp, used for coats. [Middle English, probably after *Kersey*, village in Suffolk.]

ker·sey·mere (kérzi-meer) *n.* A type of fine woollen cloth with a twill weave. Also called "cassimere". [Altered from CASSIMERE (by association with KERSEY).]

ke·ryg·ma (ki-rígmə, ke-) *n., pl.* **ke·ryg·ma·ta** (-tə). *Theology.* The proclamation of religious truths, especially as taught in the Gospels. [Greek, proclamation, from *kērussein*, to proclaim.]

Ke·sey (kéezi), **Ken (Elton)** (1935–). U.S. novelist. He wrote *One Flew Over the Cuckoo's Nest* (1962, filmed 1975), set in a mental ward, and *Sometimes A Great Notion* (1964, filmed 1971).

Kes·sel·ring (késs'l-ring), **Albert** (1885–1960). German military commander. In World War II, he led blitzkrieg operations against Poland, France, the U.S.S.R., and Britain. He was convicted of war crimes and sentenced to death, but was reprieved and freed (1952).

Kes·te·ven, Parts of (késtivən). Formerly, a division of **Lincolnshire.**

kes·trel (késtrəl) *n.* **1.** A small Old World falcon, *Falco tinnunculus*, noted for its habit of hovering while searching for prey. Also called "windhover". **2.** Any of several similar birds. [Middle English *castrell*, alteration of Old French *cresserelle, crecelle*, "rattle", kestrel (from its cry), from Vulgar Latin *crepicella* (unattested), diminutive formation from Latin *crepitāre*, to rattle, creak, crackle, frequentative of *crepāre*, to crack.]

ketch (kech) *n.* A two-masted fore-and-aft-rigged sailing vessel with a mizzen or jigger mast situated aft of a taller mainmast but forward of the rudder. Compare **yawl.** [Earlier *catch*, Middle English *cache*, probably from *cachen, cacchen*, to hunt, CATCH.]

Ketch (kech), **John,** known as Jack (died 1686). English executioner, famous for his cruelty and incompetence. He bungled the execution of, among others, the Duke of Monmouth (1685). The name has passed into English folklore, and is still given to the hangman in Punch and Judy puppet shows.

ketch·up (kéch-əp, -up ‖ *Chiefly U.S.* kách-) *n.* Also **cat·sup** (káts-) A thick, smooth, spicy sauce usually made with tomatoes. [Malay *kichap*, from Chinese (Amoy) *kôechiap* "brine of fish" : *kôe* (Mandarin *qui*), a kind of fish + *chiap* (Mandarin *zhī*), juice.]

ke·tene (kéeteen, kétteen) *n.* A pungent, toxic, colourless gas, H_2CCO, used chiefly as an acetylation agent. Also called "ethonone". [KET(O)- + -ENE.]

keto–, ket– *comb. form. Chemistry.* Indicates a ketone or ketonic properties; for example, ketosis. [From KETONE.]

ke·to·e·nol tautomerism (kéetō-ée-nol ‖ -nōl) *n. Chemistry.* A type of tautomerism involving an equilibrium between the keto and enol forms of a molecule, occurring because of migration of a hydrogen atom.

ke·to form (kéetō) *n. Chemistry.* A structural form of an organic compound in which its molecules contain a ketone group (CO) linked to an adjacent carbon atom.

ke·tone (kéetōn) *n.* Any of a class of organic compounds having a carbonyl group linked to a carbon atom in each of two hydrocarbon radicals and having the general formula $R_1(CO)R_2$, where R_1 may be the same as R_2. [German *Keton*, from *Aketon, Azeton*, ACETONE.] **—ke·ton·ic** (ke-tónnik) *adj.*

ketone body *n.* Any of several substances, such as acetoacetic acid, increasing in the blood during starvation and in certain diabetic and other pathological conditions. Also called "acetone body".

ketone group *n. Chemistry.* A carbonyl group (CO) linked to two carbon atoms, as in a ketone.

ke·to·nu·ri·a (kée-tō-néwr-i-ə) *n.* The presence of ketone bodies in the urine.

ke·tose (kée-tōz, -tōss) *n.* Any of various carbohydrates containing a ketone group in each molecule. Compare **aldose.** [KET(O)- + -OSE.]

ke·to·sis (ki-tṓ-siss, kee-) *n.* A pathological accumulation of ketone bodies in the body. [New Latin : KET(O)- + -OSIS.]

ket·tle (kétt'l) *n.* **1.** A metal pot, usually with a lid and spout and often having an electric heating element, used for boiling water. **2.** See **fish kettle. 3.** A kettledrum. **4.** A depression left in a mass of glacial drift, apparently formed by the melting of an isolated block

of glacial ice. Also called "kettle hole". **5.** Any of various large vessels used for refining metals, distilling, or other industrial processes. **—a (pretty** or **fine) kettle of fish.** A troublesome, awkward, or embarrassing situation. [Middle English *ketel*, from Old Norse *ketill*, from Common Germanic *katilaz* (unattested), from Latin *catillus*, small bowl or dish, from *catīnus†*, bowl, dish, pot.]

ket·tle·drum (kétt'l-drum) *n.* A large copper or brass hemispherical drum with a head that may be tuned by adjusting the tension.

keV kiloelectron volt.

kev·el (kévv'l) *n.* A sturdy cleat or pin for securing the heavier cables of a ship. [Middle English *kevile*, peg, from Old North French *keville*, from Late Latin *clāvicula*, bolt, bar, from Latin, small key, from *clāvis*, key.]

Kew Gardens (kew). The Royal Botanic Gardens at Kew in the London borough of Richmond. Founded in 1759, they were presented to the nation in 1841.

kex. *Botany.* Variant of **keck.**

key[1] (kee) *n., pl.* **keys. 1.** An implement designed to open a lock; especially, a metallic, notched and grooved piece inserted into and turned to open or close a lock. **2. a.** Any means of control or possession. **b.** An essential ingredient or requisite: *A good diet is the key to a long life.* **3. a.** A small instrument for winding a spring. **b.** A slotted metal strip used to open tins. **4. a.** An explanation of a set of symbols or abbreviations. **b.** A set of answers to a test or puzzle. **c.** A table, gloss, or cipher for decoding or interpreting. **d.** Anything that serves to explain or interpret. **5.** A pin or wedge inserted to lock together mechanical or structural parts. **6.** The keystone in the crown of an arch. **7. a.** A control button or lever on a machine, such as a typewriter, that is operated with the fingers. **b.** A button or lever on a musical instrument, such as a clarinet or piano, that is pressed with the fingers to produce or modulate a sound. **8.** *Music.* **a.** A tonal system consisting of seven notes in fixed relationship to a tonic, having a characteristic key signature, and being, since the Renaissance, the structural foundation of the bulk of Western music; tonality. **b.** The principal tonality of a musical work: *an étude in the key of E.* **9.** The pitch of a voice or other sound: *She spoke in a high key.* **10. a.** A general tone, or level of intensity, as of a speech, theatrical performance, or sales campaign. **b.** The general tone or intensity of colour in a picture. **11.** *Botany.* A samara *(see).* **12.** *Biology.* A list of taxonomic characters used on a presence or absence system to identify plants and animals. **13.** A roughness on a surface that provides a bond for the application of another finish, such as paint. **14.** *Slang.* A kilogram of a drug, especially heroin or marijuana. **—in** (or **out of) key.** In (or out of) tune with other factors.
~tr.v. **keyed, keying, keys. 1.** To lock together with pins, bolts, wedges, or the like. **2.** To furnish (an arch) with a keystone. **3.** To supply with a key or keys. **4. a.** To adjust the pitch of (a musical instrument). **b.** To bring into tune or harmony; coordinate. **5.** To identify by means of a key, such as a set of symbols. **6.** To roughen (a surface) so as to provide a bond for a subsequent finish. **—key up.** To raise to a high pitch; make tense or excited.
~adj. Of crucial importance: *Mining is a key industry in South Wales.* [Middle English *key(e), kay*, Old English *cǣg(e)†*.]

key[2]. Variant of **cay.**

key·board (kée-bawrd ‖ -bōrd) *n.* A set of keys, as on a piano, an organ, or a typewriter. Also used adjectivally: *keyboard instruments.*
~tr.v. **keyboarded, -boarding, -boards.** To set or record (copy or data) by means of a keyed typesetting machine, key punch, or the like. **—key·board·er** *n.*

key fruit *n.* A samara *(see).* [From its shape.]

key·hole (kée-hōl) *n.* **1.** The hole in a lock into which a key fits. **2.** Any aperture resembling this hole.

keyhole saw *n.* A padsaw *(see).*

keyhole surgery *n.* Minimally invasive surgery done through a small incision.

key money *n. British.* A payment made by a prospective tenant to a landlord to secure tenancy of a flat or house.

Keynes (kaynz), **(John) Maynard,1st Baron** (1883–1946). Influential British economist who believed that high unemployment could be due to insufficient consumer spending rather than inflated wage levels, and that government intervention was then necessary. He became a director of the Bank of England (1941) and at the Bretton Woods Agreement (1944) was instrumental in establishing the International Monetary Fund and the International Bank for Reconstruction and Development.

Keynes·i·an (káynz-i-ən) *adj.* Of or pertaining to the economic theories or policies of Keynes or his supporters.
~n. A supporter of Keynes's economic theories or policies. **—Keynes·i·an·ism** *n.*

key·note (kée-nōt) *n.* **1.** The tonic of a musical key. **2.** A prime or crucial element: *saw simplicity as the keynote of the plan.* **3.** An underlying or prevailing tone, spirit, or idea: *Pessimism was the keynote of her speech.*
~tr.v. **keynoted, -noting, -notes.** To give or set the keynote of.

keynote speech *n.* A major speech delivered to an assembly, as at a party conference, that outlines vital issues and principles, and is usually designed to inspire unity. Also called "keynote address".

key punch *n.* A keyboard machine that is used to punch holes in cards or tapes for data-processing systems. Also called "card punch".

key-punch (kée-punch) *tr.v.* **-punched, -punching, -punches. 1.** To punch holes in (cards or tape) using a key punch. **2.** To record (data) by using a key punch. —**key-punch-er** n.

key signature n. The group of sharps or flats placed to the right of the clef on a musical stave to identify the key. Also called "signature".

key-stone (kée-stōn) n. **1.** *Architecture.* The central wedge-shaped stone of an arch that locks the others together. **2.** An essential part on which other parts depend.

key-stroke (kée-strōk) n. A single depression of a key of a typewriter, typesetting machine, key punch, or other keyboard device.

key-way (kée-way) n., pl. -**ways. 1.** A slot in a wheel hub or shaft for a key. **2.** The keyhole of a cylinder lock.

Key West. Seaport at the western tip of the Florida Keys in the United States, a site of U.S. naval and air bases.

key word n. Also **key-word** (kée-wurd). **1.** A word serving as a key to a cipher or code. **2.** A significant word or quality. **3.** A word used as an index to other words or information.

kg, kg. 1. kilogram. **2.** keg.

K.G. Knight of the (Order of the) Garter (in Britain).

KGB, K.G.B. n. The Commission of State Security (Russian *Komityet Gosudarstvyennoi Byezopasnosti*): an intelligence agency of the former U.S.S.R. See **Cheka.**

Khach-a-tu-ri-an (kácho-tewr-i-án, -toor-, -téwr-i-ən, -toor-, áan), **Aram Ilyich** (1903–78). Soviet composer. He composed concertos for piano (1936) and violin (1940), three symphonies (1934, 1943, 1947), and wrote the ballets *Gayaneh* (1942) and *Spartacus* (1954).

kha-di (káadi) n. Also **khad-dar** (káʹadər). A plain, hand-woven fabric, usually made from hand-spun cotton. [Hindi.]

khak-i (kárki, káaki ‖ *chiefly U.S.* kácki) n., pl. **khakis. 1.** Light olive brown to moderate or light yellowish brown. **2.** A sturdy wool or cotton cloth of this colour, used especially for military uniforms. [Urdu *khākī*, dusty, dust-coloured, from *khāk*, dust, from Persian *khāk*†.] —**khak-i** adj.

Kha-lid (kaʹa-lid, khaʹa-), **Ibn Abdul Aziz** (1913–82). Fourth king of Saudi Arabia. He succeeded on the assassination of his half-brother, King Faisal (1975).

khalif. Variant of **caliph.**

Kha-ma (káamə), **Sir Seretse** (1921–80). First President of independent Botswana (1966–80). He was exiled by Britain from Bechuanaland (1950) after his marriage to a white woman, Ruth Williams (1948). He was elected prime minister (1965), became president on independence, and was knighted in 1966.

kham-sin, kham-seen, kam-sin (kam-séen, kám-sin) n. A generally southerly hot wind from the Sahara that blows across Egypt and the southeast Mediterranean from March to early May. [Arabic *(rīḥ al-)khamsīn,* (wind of the 50 (days), from *khamsūn,* 50.]

khan[1] (kaan ‖ *U.S. also* kan) n. **1.** A title of respect for rulers, officials, or important persons in Pakistan and other parts of central Asia. **2.** Formerly, a title given to the rulers of Mongol, Tatar, or Turkish tribes who succeeded Genghis Khan, as well as to the emperors of China. [Middle English *caan, c(h)an,* from Old French, from Medieval Latin *caanus,* from Turkish *khān,* contraction of *khāqān,* sovereign, ruler.]

khan[2] n. A caravanserai or inn in the East. [Middle English from Arabic and Persian *khān,* inn.]

khan-ate (kaʹan-ayt ‖ kán-) n. The realm or position of a khan.

khanga. Variant of **kanga.**

Khan-i-a (kaá-ni-ə) or **Chan-ia** (*Modern Greek*). Capital of the Greek island of Crete and of the Khania nome (province) in the northwest of the island. Under the Venetians (13th–17th centuries), it was taken by the Turks (1645). The Venetian fortifications and town walls can still be seen.

kha-rif (kə-réef) n. A crop harvested at the end of autumn in India and neighbouring countries. Compare **rabi.** [Urdu, from Arabic *kharafa,* to gather.]

Kharkiv. See **Kharkov.**

Khar-kov (kár-kov, -kof; *Russian* khárkəf). *Ukrainian* **Khar-kiv** (khárkif). A city in western Ukraine, formerly capital of the Ukraine (1919–34).

Khar-toum (kár-tōom). *Arabic* **al-Kartum** or **Al Khartum.** Capital of Sudan. Founded as an army camp by Muhammad Ali (1821), it was destroyed by Mahdists in 1885, when General Gordon was killed defending it. General Kitchener recaptured the city in 1898.

khazi. Variant of **carzey.**

khe-dive (ki-déev, ke-) n. *Often capital* **K.** The title of the Turkish viceroys of Egypt from 1867 to 1914.

Khirbar Qumran. See **Qumran.**

Khmer (kmair) n., pl. **Khmrs** or collectively **Khmr. 1.** A member of a people of Cambodia whose culture flourished during the Middle Ages. **2.** The Mon-Khmer language of this people. —**Khmer-i-an** adj.

Khmer Republic. See **Cambodia.**

Khmer Rouge n. A Communist movement in Cambodia. Khmer Rouge guerrillas fought against the U.S.-backed government of General Lon Nol (1970s). See **Cambodia.** [French, Red Khmer.]

Khoi-san (kóy-sán ‖ -saʹan, -san, -saan) n. A family of languages of southwestern Africa including those of the Bushmen and Hottentots and characterised by the use of clicks.

Kho-mei-ni (ko-máyni), **Ayatollah Ruholla** (c. 1902–89). Iranian leader and head of the Shiite Muslims. He was arrested in 1964 and exiled for his opposition to Shah Muhammad Reza Pahlavi. When the Shah fled to Egypt (1979), Khomeini returned to Tehran (1979) amid wild celebrations. He established a new constitution giving himself supreme power. Under his rule, there was steady economic decline in Iran.

Khor-ram-shahr (ko-ram-shár). Town in Khuzestan, western Iran. It lies at the confluence of the river Karun and the Shatt-al-Arab, and is a major port and oil refining centre.

Khrush-chev (krōosh-chof, krōoss-; *Russian* khroo-shchóf), **Nikita Sergeyevich** (1894–1971). Soviet leader (1955–64). He was political head of the Ukraine (1938–49) under Stalin. He succeeded Georgi Malenkov as First Secretary of the All Union Party (1953). He later denounced Stalin (1956). He was deposed (1964) after the Cuban missile crisis (1962) and the failure of economic reforms.

Khu-fu (kóofōo), also known as Cheops (c. 2590–2568 B.C.). Second Egyptian king of the fourth dynasty. He built the Great Pyramid named after him, which took 20 years to complete.

khur-ta, kur-ta (koórtə) n. A long, loose-fitting, collarless shirt worn by Indians. [Hindi.]

khus-khus (kóoss-kóoss) n. **1.** An aromatic perennial Indian grass, *Vetiveria zizanioides* (or *Andropogon squarrosus*). **2.** The root of this plant, used to make fans, mats, and the like. [Hindi.]

Khu-ze-stan (kōozəstán). Province in southwest Iran. A fertile region producing dates, citrus fruits, melons, cotton, and rice, it is also rich in petroleum, and has many refineries. More than half the population is Arab.

Khy-ber Pass (kíbər). Main mountain pass between Afghanistan and Pakistan, frequently fought over. Its gorge runs 53 kilometres (33 miles) through the Safid Koh range, and for 8 kilometres (5 miles) is no more than 180 metres (c. 600 feet) wide.

kHz kilohertz.

ki-ang (ki-áng, kee-) n. A Tibetan variety of the wild ass, *Equus hemionus.* [Tibetan *rkyaṅ.*]

Kiangsi. See **Jiangxi.**

Kiangsu. See **Jiangsu.**

kia-ora (kéa-óra) interj. Good health or good luck. Used as a greeting. [Maori.]

kib-ble[1] (kíbb'l) n. An iron bucket used in wells, mines, and the like for hoisting water, ore, or rubbish to the surface. [German *Kübel*; akin to Old English *cyfel,* from Medieval Latin *cupellus,* a measure for corn, diminutive of *cuppa,* CUP.]

kibble[2] tr.v. -**bled, -bling, -bles.** To crush or grind (grain, for example) coarsely. [18th century : origin obscure.]

kib-butz (ki-bóots) n., pl. **kibbutzim** (kíbbōot-séem). A collective farm or settlement in modern Israel. [Hebrew *qibbūtz,* "gathering", from *qibbētz,* he gathered.]

kibe (kīb) n. An ulcerated chilblain, especially one on the heel. [Middle English *kybe,* perhaps from Welsh *cibi, cibwst*†.]

kib-itz-er (kíbbitsər) n. *U.S. Informal.* **1.** An onlooker at a card game who gives unwanted advice to the players. **2.** Any person who offers unwanted advice; a meddler. [Yiddish, from German *Kiebitz,* plover, busybody.] —**kib-itz** intr.v.

kib-lah (kíbblaa) n. **1.** The direction towards which Moslems face when they pray. **2.** A niche in the wall of a mosque indicating this direction. [Arabic *qiblah,* from *qábilah,* he lay opposite.]

kibosh. Variant of **kybosh.**

kick (kik) v. **kicked, kicking, kicks.** —intr. **1.** To strike out with the foot or feet. **2.** To recoil, as a gun does when fired. **3.** *Informal.* To object vigorously; protest or rebel. **4.** To rise almost vertically from the ground on pitching. Used of a ball. —tr. **1.** To strike with the foot. **2.** To drive or move by striking with the foot. **3. a.** In Rugby football, to make (a conversion or drop goal) by means of a kick. **b.** In soccer, to score (a goal) by kicking the ball. **4.** *Slang.* To give up (a bad habit, for example). —**kick about** or **around.** *Informal.* **1.** To treat roughly. **2.** To give consideration or thought to (an idea). **3.** To travel or wander aimlessly. **4.** To lie neglected or unobserved: *There's a pen kicking about somewhere here.* —**kick (oneself).** To reproach (oneself). —**kick out.** *Informal.* To eject; dismiss. —**kick up.** *Informal.* To make or stir up (trouble, fuss, or the like).

~n. **1. a.** A vigorous thrust or blow with the foot. **b.** The motion of the legs used in swimming. **2.** The jolting recoil of a gun. **3.** *Informal.* Power, force, or resilience: *still a lot of kick in that engine.* **4.** *Slang.* Stimulating or intoxicating impact: *quite a kick in that martini.* **5.** *Slang.* **a.** A feeling of excitement or pleasure. **b.** *Plural.* Fun; thrills: *just for kicks.* **6.** *Informal.* A temporary interest or enthusiasm: *on a health food kick.* **7. a.** The action of kicking a ball, as in Rugby football. **b.** A kicked ball. **c.** The distance travelled by a kicked ball: *a 47-yard kick.* **8.** A sudden momentary increase in pressure forcing drilled mud back up the bore of an oil or gas well. In this sense, also called "kick-back". [Middle English *kiken, kyken*†.]

kick back intr.v. **1.** To recoil unexpectedly and violently. **2.** To suffer a momentary increase in pressure. Used of an oil or gas well. **3.** *U.S. Slang.* To pay a kickback.

kick-back (kík-bak) n. **1.** A sharp response or reaction; a repercussion. **2.** *Chiefly U.S. Slang.* **a.** A percentage payment to a person able to influence or control a source of income, as by confidential arrangement or coercion. **b.** The money paid. **3.** A kick (sense 8).

kick-er (kíckər) n. **1.** A person, animal, or thing that kicks. **2.** In Rugby football, a **place-kicker** (see).

kick off intr.v. **1.** In Rugby football and soccer, to start either half of a game by kicking the ball from the centre of the field. **2.** To start a discussion, debate, programme of events, or the like.

kick-off (kík-off, -awf) n. **1.** In Rugby football or soccer: **a.** A place kick that starts play in either half of a game. **b.** The time a game is due to begin. **2.** A beginning.

kick pleat *n.* A short pleat at the hem in the back of a straight skirt that enables the wearer to walk more easily.

kick·shaw (kík-shaw) *n.* Also **kick·shaws** (-shawz). **1.** A trinket or trifle; a gewgaw. **2.** *Archaic.* A fancy food; a delicacy. Usually used derogatorily. [Earlier *kickshose, quelkchose,* from French *quelque-chose,* something.]

kick sorter *n. Physics.* A device for sorting a train of pulses according to their height, used to investigate the pulses from a radiation counter to determine the energy spectrum of the incident radiation.

kick·stand (kík-stand) *n.* A retractable metal bar at the base of a motorcycle or bicycle that keeps it upright when not in use.

kick·start (kík-staart, -stárt) *tr.v.* **-started, -starting, -starts. 1.** To start (an engine, especially of a motorcycle) by kicking downwards on a special pedal. **2. Jump-start** (*sense* 3). **—kick·start** *n.*

kick turn *n.* In skiing, a turn made while stationary by lifting each ski separately and turning it to face the opposite direction.

kid¹ (kid) *n.* **1. a.** A young goat. **b.** The young of a similar animal, such as an antelope. **2.** The flesh of a young goat. **3.** Leather made from the skin of a young goat. **4.** An article made from this leather. **5.** *Informal.* **a.** A child. **b.** A young person.
~*adj.* **1.** Made of kid. **2.** *Informal.* Younger: *my kid brother.*
~*v.* **kidded, kidding, kids.** —*tr. Informal.* **1.** To mock playfully; tease. **2.** To deceive in fun; fool. —*intr.* **1.** *Informal.* To engage in teasing or good-humoured deception. **2.** To bear young. Used of a goat or an antelope. [Middle English *kide, kyde,* from Old Norse *kidh,* young goat, from Germanic *kidhja-* (unattested).] **—kid·der** *n.*

kid² *n.* **1.** A small wooden tub. **2.** Formerly, a dish used as a sailor's mess container. [Probably variant of KIT (tub).]

Kidd (kid), **William,** known as Captain Kidd (1645–1701). British pirate. He sailed from Deptford in 1696 with a commission to defend ships of the East India Company. He was to be paid according to ships taken, so he turned pirate, attacking friendly ships. Kidd was brought from America to London, found guilty, and hanged.

Kid·der·min·ster¹ (kiddər-minstər). Market town in Worcestershire, famous for its carpets.

Kidderminster² *n.* An ingrain carpet. [Originally manufactured at KIDDERMINSTER.]

Kid·dush (kiddəsh, ki-dōōsh) *n. Judaism.* A traditional blessing and prayer recited over a cup of wine or bread on the Sabbath or a festival. [Hebrew *qiddūsh,* sanctification, from *qiddesh,* he sanctified.]

kid·dy, kid·die (kíddi) *n., pl.* **-dies.** *Informal.* A small child. Used affectionately.

kid glove *n.* A glove made of fine, soft leather, especially kidskin. **—handle with kid gloves.** To treat tactfully and cautiously. **—kid-glove** (kíd-glúv) *adj.*

kid·nap (kídnap) *tr.v.* **-napped** or *U.S.* **-naped, -napping** or *U.S.* **-naping, -naps.** To abduct and detain (a person or animal), often for ransom. [Back-formation from *kidnapper* : KID (child) + *napper,* (slang) thief, from *nap,* to seize, probably from Scandinavian; akin to Swedish *nappa†,* to snatch.] **—kid·nap·per** *n.*

kid·ney (kídni) *n., pl.* **-neys. 1.** *Anatomy.* Either of a pair of organs in the dorsal region of the vertebrate abdominal cavity, functioning to maintain proper water balance, regulate acid-base concentration, and excrete metabolic wastes as urine. **2.** The kidney of certain animals, eaten as food. **3.** An excretory organ of certain invertebrates. **4. a.** Disposition; temperament. **b.** A kind or class. [Middle English *kidenei, kydney* : possibly *kiden-* (an obscure element) + *ei,* egg, Old English *ǣg.*]

kidney bean *n.* Any of various green beans with kidney-shaped beans; especially, the **French bean** *(see).*

kidney machine *n.* An apparatus for filtering waste products and water from the blood of a patient whose kidneys have ceased to function. Also called "artificial kidney", "dialyser".

kidney stone *n. Pathology.* A renal **calculus** *(see).*

kidney vetch *n.* A plant, *Anthyllis vulneraria,* native to Europe, having greyish-green leaves and small yellow flowers. [Formerly used to treat kidney disorders.]

kid·skin (kíd-skin) *n.* Soft leather made from the skin of a young goat. Also called "kid".

kids' stuff (kidz) *n. Slang.* **1.** Something very easy or simple to perform. **2.** Something suitable only for children.

kief. Variant of **kif.**

Kiel (keel). Capital of Schleswig-Holstein, northern Germany. It is a Baltic seaport and was an important naval base (1871–1945).

Kiel Canal. German **Nord-Ostsee Kanal** or **Kaiser Wilhelm Kanal.** Canal in Germany. It runs 98 kilometres (61 miles) from Kiel to the Elbe estuary, connecting the Baltic with the North Sea.

kier (keer) *n.* A vat for boiling, dyeing, or bleaching cloth or yarn. [Earlier *keare,* from Old Norse *ker,* tub, akin to Old High German *char,* Gothic *kas†,* vessel.]

Kier·ke·gaard (keerkə-gaard, *Danish* -gawr), **Søren (Aabye)** (1813–55). Danish philosopher. He opposed Hegel's idea that truth was absolute and attacked the reliance on ritual and dogma in Christianity. His books include *Either-Or* (1843) and *Stages on Life's Way* (1845). **—Kier·ke·gaard·i·an** (-gárd-i-ən) *adj. & n.*

kie·sel·guhr (keez'l-goor) *n. Mineralogy.* Diatomite *(see).*

kie·ser·ite (keezər-īt) *n.* A whitish to yellowish hydrous magnesium sulphate mineral, used as a source of Epsom salts. [German *Kieserit,* after Dietrich G. Kieser (died 1862), German physicist.]

Ki·ev (kee-ev, -ef; *Russian* -if). *Ukrainian* **Ki·yev.** Capital and largest city of Ukraine, situated at the confluence of the rivers Dnepr, Pripet,

and Dvina. It was the third largest city in the U.S.S.R., and is the traditional centre of Russian Christianity.

kif, keef, kief (keef) *n.* Also **kef** (kayf). **1.** A pleasurable state of idleness or dreamy intoxication. **2.** Cannabis or any similar drug that produces such a state when smoked. [Arabic *kayf,* euphoria, enjoyment.]

kike (kīk) *n. U.S. Slang.* A Jew. Used derogatorily. [Perhaps from *kiki,* reduplication of *-(s)ki, -(s)ky,* ending in names common among Jews from Slavonic countries.]

Ki·ku·yu (ki-kōō-yōō) *n., pl.* **-yus** or collectively **Kikuyu. 1.** A member of a Bantu people of Kenya. **2.** The Bantu language of this people. **3.** *Small* **k.** A hardy grass, *Pennisetum clandestinum,* used for lawns and pasture in southern Africa and central America.

Ki·lau·e·a (keelow-áy-ə). Volcanic crater of Hawaii. On the southeast slopes of Mauna Loa, it is one of the largest craters in the world (about 3 kilometres; 2 miles across) still volcanically active.

Kil·dare (kil-dáir). *Irish* **Contae Cill Dara.** County of the Republic of Ireland. The Bog of Allen lies in the north. Kildare, a market town, was founded by St. Bride in A.D. 490. Naas, in the northeast, is the county town.

kil·der·kin (kíldərkin) *n.* **1.** A cask equal in capacity to half a barrel. **2.** The amount held by such a cask, used formerly as a measure of capacity and equal to approximately 18 gallons. [Middle English *kilderkyn,* earlier *kyn(d)erkyn,* from Middle Dutch *kinderkin, kinnekijn,* diminutive of *kintal,* hundredweight, from Medieval Latin *quintāle,* from Arabic *qinṭār,* KANTAR.]

ki·lim, ke·lim (ki-léem, kee-) *n.* An oriental tapestry-woven rug or other textile piece. [Turkish, from Persian *kilīm†.*]

Ki·li·man·ja·ro (killi-mən-jaárō, -man-). Extinct volcano in northern Tanzania. It has two peaks, Mount Kibo (5 895 metres; 19,340 feet), Africa's highest peak, and Mount Mawenzi (5 354 metres; 17,564 feet). The surrounding plain is a wildlife reserve.

Kil·ken·ny¹ (kil-kénni). *Irish* **Contae Cill Choinnigh.** County of the Republic of Ireland. In the southeast of the country, in the province of Leinster, it is ringed by hills and drains towards Waterford harbour in the southeast.

Kilkenny². County town of Kilkenny, it was once the capital of the ancient kingdom of Ossory, and is one of Ireland's oldest settlements.

kill (kil) *v.* **killed, killing, kills.** —*tr.* **1. a.** To put to death; slay. **b.** To deprive of life: *Famine killed thousands.* **2.** To put an end to; extinguish. **3.** To harm greatly; ruin: *killed the taste.* **4.** *Informal.* To pass (time) idly or unproductively. **5.** *Informal.* To consume entirely; finish off: *kill a bottle of whisky.* **6.** *Informal.* To cause extreme pain or discomfort to: *My shoes are killing me.* **7.** *Informal.* To mark for deletion; rule out. **8.** *Informal.* To thwart; veto: *kill a bill.* **9.** *Informal.* To cause to stop; turn off. **10.** *Informal.* To exhaust by overexertion. **11.** *Informal.* To destroy the effect of or neutralise (a colour, for example) by contrast. **12.** In tennis and similar sports, to hit (a ball) with such force as to make a return impossible. —*intr.* **1.** To be fatal; cause death or extinction: *speed kills.* **2.** To commit murder.
~*n.* **1.** The act or moment of killing. **2.** The animal or animals killed, especially in hunting. **3.** *Informal.* Something hilariously funny or amusing. **—in at the kill.** Present at the moment of triumph. [Middle English *kullen, killen, kellen,* Old English *cyllan* (unattested).]

Kil·lar·ney (ki-lárni). *Irish* **Cill Airne.** Market town and tourist centre in County Kerry, in the Republic of Ireland.

kill·deer (kíl-deer) *n., pl.* **-deers** or collectively **killdeer.** A New World bird, *Charadrius vociferus,* of inland ponds, streams, and fields, having a distinctive cry. [Imitative of its cry.]

killed spirits (kild) *n.* A solution of zinc chloride used as a flux for soldering, made by adding zinc to hydrochloric acid. [Referring to the action of zinc as killing or neutralising hydrochloric acid.]

kill·er (kíllər) *n.* One that kills, especially: **1.** A murderer. **2.** An animal or disease that kills habitually.

killer whale *n.* A black and white predatory whale, *Orcinus orca,* of cold seas. Also called "grampus", "orc".

kil·lick (kíl-ik) *n.* Also **kil·lock** (-ək). A small anchor, especially one made of a stone in a wooden frame. [Origin unknown.]

Kil·lie·cran·kie, Pass of (killi-kránki). Pass in the Grampian Mountains in central Scotland. At the Battle of Killiecrankie (1689), a Jacobite force defeated troops of William III.

kil·li·fish (kílli-fish) *n., pl.* **-fishes** or collectively **killifish.** Any of numerous small fishes of the family Cyprinodontidae, chiefly of fresh and brackish waters of warm regions. [KILL (creek) + FISH.]

kill·ing (kílling) *n.* **1.** A murder. **2.** Quarry; kill. **3.** *Informal.* A sudden large profit: *made a killing on the stock market.*
~*adj.* **1.** Designed or apt to kill; fatal. **2.** Exhausting: *a killing ordeal.* **3.** *Informal.* Hilarious. **—kill·ing·ly** *adv.*

kill·joy (kíl-joy) *n.* A person who spoils the enjoyment or fun of others.

kiln (kiln, kil) *n.* Any of various types of oven for hardening, burning, or drying substances, such as grain, meal, or clay; especially, a brick-lined oven used to bake or fire ceramics.
~*tr.v. Rare.* **kilned, kilning, kilns.** To process in a kiln. [Middle English *kylne,* Old English *cyline, cylen,* from Latin *culīna,* kitchen, irregular variant of *coquīna,* cookery, from *coquīnus,* of cooking, from *coquere,* to cook.]

Kil·ner jar (kílnər) *n.* A trademark for a glass jar having a tightly fitting lid and used in preserving and bottling.

ki·lo (keelō || kíllō) *n., pl.* **-los. 1.** A kilogram. **2.** A kilometre.

kilo– *prefix. Symbol* **k** Indicates 1,000 (10³); for example, **kilowatt,** **kilocalorie.** [French, arbitrarily from Greek *khilioi,* thousand.]

kil·o·cal·o·rie (kíl-ō-kal-əri, -ə-) *n. Abbr.* **kcal** A large calorie; 1,000 calories.

ki·lo·cy·cle (kíl-ə-sīk'l, -ō-) *n. Abbr.* **kc** 1. A unit equal to 1,000 cycles. 2. Loosely, 1,000 cycles per second.

kil·o·gram, kil·o·gram·me (kíl-ə-gram, -ō-) *n. Abbr.* **kg** 1. The fundamental SI unit of mass equal to the mass of a prototype block of platinum–iridium kept at the International Bureau of Weights and Measures at Sèvres. It is equal to about 2.20462 pounds. 2. A force equal to a kilogram weight, that is, the product of a kilogram mass with the acceleration of free fall.

kil·o·gram-me·tre (kíl-ə-gram-méetər, -ō-) *n.* A metre-kilogram-second unit of work, equal to the work performed by a one-kilogram force acting through a distance of one metre.

ki·lo·hertz (kíl-ə-herts, -ō-, -hairts) *n. Abbr.* **Khz** One thousand hertz.

kil·o·joule (kíl-ə-jōōl, -ō-, *rarely* -jowl) *n.* One thousand joules.

kil·o·me·tre (kíl-ə-meetər, -ō-, ki-lómmitər) *n. Abbr.* **km** One thousand metres, approximately 0.62137 mile. —**kil·o·met·ric** (-méttrik) *adj.*

kil·o·ton (kíl-ə-tun, -ō-) *n.* 1. One thousand tons. 2. An explosive force equivalent to that of 1,000 tons of TNT.

ki·lo·volt (kíl-ə-vōlt, -ō- ‖ -volt) *n. Abbr.* **kV** One thousand volts.

kil·o·watt (kíl-ə-wot, -ō-) *n. Abbr.* **kW** One thousand watts.

kil·o·watt-hour (kíl-ə-wot-ówr, -ō-) *n. Abbr.* **kWh** The total energy developed by a power of one kilowatt acting for one hour, a common unit of electric power consumption.

kilt (kilt) *n.* A knee-length skirt with deep pleats, usually of a tartan wool, worn especially as part of formal dress for men in Scotland. ~*tr.v.* **kilted, kilting, kilts.** To tuck up around the body. [From dialectal verb *kilt,* to fasten up, tuck up, Middle English (northern dialect) *kilten,* from Scandinavian, akin to Danish *kilte,* to tuck up, Old Norse *kjalta†,* shirt.] —**kilt·ed** *adj.*

kil·ter (kíltər) *n.* Also *chiefly British* **kel·ter** (kéltər). Good condition or proper form. Used chiefly in the phrase *out of kilter.* [17th century : origin obscure.]

Kim·ber·ley (kímbərli). City in central South Africa. In Northern Cape province, south of the river Vaal, it was founded (1870) as a diamond-mining camp and is still a major mining centre.

kim·ber·lite (kímbər-līt) *n.* A type of rock (a variety of periodtite) found especially in South Africa and often containing diamonds. —**kim·ber·li·tic** (-líttik) *adj.*

Kim Il Sung (kím il sōong), born Kim Song Ju (1912–94). North Korean political and military leader. He led the Korean People's army against Japan (1932–45) and became leader of Soviet-dominated North Korea in 1945. He was supreme commander during the Korean War (1950–53). He proclaimed the Democratic People's Republic of Korea in 1948 (premier 1948–72; president 1972–94). His son, Kim Jong Il (1942–) succeeded him.

ki·mo·no (ki-mō-nō ‖ -nə) *n., pl.* **-nos.** 1. A long, loose, wide-sleeved Japanese robe, worn with a broad sash. 2. A dressing gown modelled after this. [Japanese, "thing for wearing" : *ki,* to wear + *mono,* person, thing.]

kin (kin) *n.* One's relatives collectively; family; kindred; kinsfolk. See **next of kin.** ~*adj.* Related; akin. [Middle English *kin(n), kyn,* Old English *cyn(n).*]

–kin *n. suffix.* Indicates small or diminutive; for example, **bodkin,** **lambkin.** [Middle English, from Middle Dutch *-kin, -kijn,* from West Germanic *-kin* (unattested).]

ki·na (kéenə) *n., pl.* **kina.** The basic monetary unit of Papua New Guinea, equal to 100 toea. [Native name.]

kin·aes·the·sia, *U.S.* **kin·es·the·sia** (kín-ees-théezi-ə, kín-, -théezhə ‖ *U.S.* -ess-) *n.* Also **kin·aes·the·sis** (-thée-siss). The sensation of bodily position, presence, or movement resulting chiefly from stimulation of sensory nerve endings in muscles, tendons, and joints. Also called "muscle sense". [New Latin, from Greek *kinein,* to move + AESTHESIA.] —**kin·aes·the·tic** (-théttik) *adj.*

ki·nase (kín-ayz, -ayss) *n.* An enzyme or metal ion that activates the inactive precursor of another enzyme. [KIN(ETIC) + -ASE.]

Kin·car·dine (kin-kár-din, king-, -d'n). Also **Kin·car·dine·shire** (-shər, -sheer ‖ -shīr). Former county of east Scotland, in Grampian Region (1975–96), then Aberdeenshire (1996–).

Kinchinjunga. See **Kangchenjunga, Mount.**

kind¹ (kīnd) *adj.* **kinder, kindest.** 1. Of a friendly, generous, and hospitable nature; warmhearted; good. 2. Showing sympathy, generosity, or thoughtfulness: *a kind act; his kind remarks about your work.* 3. Humane; considerate: *kind to animals.* 4. Forbearing; tolerant; charitable: *very kind about the broken window.* 5. Favourable; well-disposed: *Fate has been kind to her.* 6. *Informal.* Not harmful; beneficial: *a soap kind to the skin.* [Middle English *kynde, kind,* Old English *gecynde,* natural, innate.]
Synonyms: kindly, benign, benevolent, caring, compassionate.

kind² (kīnd) *n.* 1. Variety; sort; type: *the kind of people who are cheerful in the morning.* —See Usage note at **sort.** 2. A class or category of similar or related individuals: *What kind of dog is that?* 3. A rough, often not very good, approximation to the thing specified: *a kind of shelter; gave us soup of a kind.* 4. Nature; essential character. Used chiefly in such phrases as *a difference in kind; to differ in kind.* —See Synonyms at **type.** —**in kind.** 1. With produce or commodities rather than with money: *pay in kind.* 2. In the same manner or with something equivalent; accordingly: *returned the slight in kind.*

—**kind of.** *Informal.* Somewhat: *I'm kind of hungry.* [Middle English *kynd(e), kind(e),* Old English *cynd, gecynd(e),* birth, nature, race.]

kin·der·gar·ten (kíndər-gaart'n) *n.* 1. A **nursery school** (*see*). 2. The lowest form in a primary school. [German *Kindergarten,* "children's garden".]

kind·heart·ed (kīnd-hártid) *adj.* Having or proceeding from a kind nature; sympathetic; generous and helpful. See Synonyms at **kind.** —**kind·heart·ed·ly** *adv.* —**kind·heart·ed·ness** *n.*

kin·dle (kínd'l) *v.* **-dled, -dling, -dles.** —*tr.* 1. To set fire to; cause to start burning; ignite. 2. To cause to glow; light up: *The sunset kindled the skies.* 3. **a.** To inflame; excite. **b.** To arouse; inspire: *"no spark had yet kindled in him an intellectual passion"* (George Eliot). —*intr.* 1. To catch fire; burst into flame. 2. To become bright; glow. 3. To become inflamed; be aroused or stirred up. [Middle English *kind(e)len,* from Old Norse *kynda,* to kindle, catch fire (but influenced in form by Old Norse *kyndill,* torch), akin to Middle High German *künden†,* to set on fire.] —**kin·dler** *n.*

kind·less (kīnd-ləss, -liss) *adj. Archaic.* 1. Heartless. 2. Inhuman.

kind·li·ness (kíndli-nəss, -niss) *n.* 1. The quality of being kindly. 2. A kindly deed; a good turn; a kindness.

kin·dling (kíndling) *n.* Easily ignited material, such as dry sticks of wood, used to start a fire.

kind·ly (kíndli) *adj.* **-lier, -liest.** 1. Having a sympathetic, helpful, or benevolent nature; customarily showing kindness: *a kindly old soul.* 2. Expressive of a sympathetic, helpful, or benevolent nature or impulse: *a kindly interest.* 3. Agreeable; pleasant. 4. *Archaic.* **a.** Lawful; legitimate. **b.** Native-born. —See Synonyms at **kind.** ~*adv.* 1. Out of kindness: *He kindly overlooked their mistake.* 2. In a kind manner; graciously; cordially: *She spoke kindly to him.* 3. Pleasantly; agreeably: *The sun shone kindly.* 4. Please; as a matter of courtesy. Used in a request to express formality or impatience: *Would you kindly refrain from doing that?* 5. *Archaic.* In a way or course that is natural; fittingly. —**take kindly to.** 1. To be receptive or favourably disposed to: *doesn't take kindly to people who criticise him.* 2. To be naturally attracted or fitted to; thrive on.

kind·ness (kīnd-nəss, -niss) *n.* 1. The quality or state of being kind: *We relied upon their kindness.* 2. An instance of kind behaviour.

kin·dred (kíndrid) *n.* 1. Relationship; kinship. 2. **a.** A group of related persons; a family, clan, tribe, or the like. **b.** A person's own relatives; one's family. ~*adj.* 1. Of the same ancestry or family: *kindred clans.* 2. Having a similar or related origin, nature, or character. 3. Having the same interests or outlook as oneself. Used chiefly in the phrase *a kindred spirit.* [Middle English *kin(d)red(e), kinraden* : KIN + *-rede,* from Old English *ræden,* condition, rule, from *rædan,* to advise, rule, read.] —**kin·dred·ness** *n.*

kine. *Archaic.* Plural of **cow.**

kin·e·mat·ics (kínni-máttiks, kíni-) *n. Used with a singular verb. Physics.* A branch of mechanics concerned with the study of motion exclusive of the influences of mass and force. Compare **dynamics, statics.** [Greek *kinēma* (stem *kinēmat-*), motion, from *kinein,* to move.]

kin·e·mat·ic viscosity (kínni-máttik, kíni-) *n. Symbol* **ν** *Physics.* The viscosity of a fluid divided by its density.

kin·e·scope (kínni-skōp, kíni-) *n.* 1. A cathode-ray tube in a television receiver that translates received electrical signals into a visible picture on a luminescent screen. 2. A film of a transmitted television programme. [KINE(TIC) + -SCOPE.]

ki·ne·sics (kī-néez-iks, ki-, -néess-) *n. Used with a singular verb.* The study of bodily movements, facial expressions, gestures, and the like as a systematic mode of communication. [Greek *kinēsis,* motion + -ICS.]

ki·ne·si·ol·o·gy (kī-née-zi-óllji, -si-) *n.* The study of locomotion in relation to the structure and working of human muscles.

–kinesis *n. comb. form.* Indicates: 1. Division; for example, **cytokinesis.** 2. Movement or motion; for example, **photokinesis.** [New Latin, from Greek *kinēsis,* movement, from *kinein,* to move.]

kinesthesia. *U.S.* Variant of **kinaesthesia.**

ki·net·ic (kī-néttik, ki-) *adj.* Of, relating to, or produced by motion or change. [Greek *kinētikos,* from *kinētos,* moving, from *kinein,* to move.]

kinetic art *n.* Art or art objects that move, have moving parts, or depend on a moving observer for their effect.

kinetic energy *n.* Energy associated with motion, equal for a body in pure translational motion at nonrelativistic speeds to half the product of its mass and the square of its speed. Compare **potential energy.**

ki·net·ics (kī-néttiks, ki-) *n.* 1. *Used with a singular verb. Physics.* The study of all aspects of motion, comprising both kinematics and dynamics. 2. *Used with a singular verb. Physics.* The study of the relationship between motion and the forces affecting motion. 3. *Used with a singular verb. Chemistry.* The study of the rates of chemical reactions. 4. *Used with a plural verb. Physics.* The general motion of a particle or system. 5. *Used with a plural verb. Chemistry.* The rate of a given chemical reaction, especially as affected by changes in temperature, concentration, or the like.

kinetic theory *n.* A theory of the behaviour of matter, especially of pressure-volume-temperature relationships in gases, based in its simplest form on the identification of heat with the kinetic energy of a substance's rapid, randomly moving molecules and on statistical analysis of this motion for large numbers of molecules.

ki·ne·tin (kī-néetin, ki-) *n.* An artificial cytokinin. [Greek *kinētos,* moving + -IN.]

kinfolk, kinfolks. *U.S.* Variants of **kinsfolk.**

king (king) *n.* **1.** *Abbr.* **k, K.** A male monarch. **2.** One that is supreme or pre-eminent in its own class or sphere: *the king of the jungle.* **3.** *Capital* **K.** God or Christ. **4.** *Abbr.* **K.** A playing card bearing a picture of a king. **5.** *Chess. Abbr.* **K** The principal piece, which can move one square in any direction and must be protected against checkmate. **6.** In draughts, a piece that has reached the opponent's side of the board and been crowned, and can then move both backwards and forwards. [Middle English *king,* Old English *cyning.*]

King (king), **Billie Jean,** born Billie Jean Moffitt (1943–). U.S. tennis player. She won 20 Wimbledon titles and four U.S. Championships.

King, Jr., Martin Luther (1929–68). American clergyman and civil rights leader. He organised the Southern Christian Leadership Council to press for black rights (1957), and led a civil rights march on Washington (1963). He preached nonviolence, but his assassination by James Earl Ray in Memphis, Tennesse led to widespread rioting. His books include *Why We Can't Wait* (1964) and *Where Do We Go From Here: Chaos or Community?* (1967). He won the Nobel peace prize in 1964.

King, William Lyon Mackenzie (1874–1950). Liberal politician and Canada's longest-serving prime minister (1921–26, 1926–30, and 1935–48).

king·bolt (king-bōlt ‖ -bolt) *n.* A vertical bolt used for such purposes as joining the body of a wagon to the front axle, and usually serving as a pivot. Also called "kingpin".

King Charles spaniel *n.* A dog of a breed of toy (small) spaniel having a curly black and tan coat and long ears. [After King CHARLES II of England.]

king cobra *n.* A large venomous snake, *Ophiophagus hannah,* of tropical Asia. Also called "hamadryad".

king crab *n.* **1.** A large crab, *Paralithodes camtschatica,* of coastal waters of Alaska, Japan, and Siberia, valued commercially for its edible flesh. **2.** A marine arthropod, the **horseshoe crab** (*see*).

king·craft (king-kraaft ‖ -kraft) *n. Archaic.* The art or method used by a king to rule; especially, the use of cunning in the exercise of royal power.

king-cup (king-kup) *n. Chiefly British.* Any of several plants having cup-shaped yellow flowers; the name is used in particular of the **marsh marigold** (*see*).

king·dom (king-dəm) *n.* **1.** A government, territory, state, or population that is nominally or actually ruled by a king or queen. **2. a.** The eternal spiritual sovereignty of God. **b.** The realm over which this sovereignty extends. **3.** An area, province, or realm in which one thing is dominant: *the kingdom of the imagination.* **4. a.** The broadest, most inclusive taxonomic category of organisms having certain basic characteristics: *the plant kingdom.* **b.** Any such large general category of natural forms: *the mineral kingdom.* [Middle English *kingdom,* Old English *cyningdōm* : KING + -DOM.]

kingdom come *n. Informal.* **1.** The next world; life after death: *gone to kingdom come.* **2.** The Day of Judgment; the end of the world: *You can scream till kingdom come but he won't take any notice.* [From the phrase *Thy kingdom come* in The Lord's Prayer.]

king·fish (king-fish) *n., pl.* **-fishes** or collecitvely **kingfish.** Any of various large fish; especially, the **opah** (*see*).

king·fish·er (king-fishər) *n.* Any of various birds of the family Alcedinidae, especially *Alcedo atthis,* which has blue-green and orange plumage. [Originally *king's fisher,* Middle English *kyngys fischare.*]

king hit *n. Australian Informal.* A sudden knockout blow, especially one delivered without warning. **—king-hit** (king-hit) *tr.v.*

King James Bible *n.* The **Authorised Version** (*see*) of the Bible. Also called "King James Version".

king·klip (kingklip) *n., pl.* **kingklip.** *Chiefly South African.* Either of two edible marine fish of the Ophidiidae family, *Xiphiuris capensis* and *Hoplobrotula gnathopus.* [Afrikaans, from Dutch *koning,* KING + *klip,* stone.]

king·let (king-lit, -lət) *n.* A petty or insignificant king.

king·ly (king-li) *adj.* **-lier, -liest. 1.** Having the status or rank of king. **2.** Of or pertaining to a king; regal: *kingly power.* **3.** Like a king or suitable for a king; majestic.
~*adv. Rare.* As a king; regally; royally. **—king·li·ness** *n.*

king·mak·er (king-maykər) *n.* **1.** One who can make a person of his choice king; one who has control over who is king. **2.** One able to ensure that persons of his choice are placed in positions of power.

King of Arms *n., pl.* **Kings of Arms.** The title of the highest-ranking heraldic officer in the United Kingdom.

king·pin (king-pin) *n.* **1.** In tenpin bowling, the foremost or central pin of the arrangement of pins to be knocked down. **2.** The most important or essential person or thing in an enterprise or system. **3. a.** A hardened steel pin in the steering system of a motor vehicle that does not have independent front suspension. Also called "swivel pin". Compare **ball-joint. b.** A kingbolt (*see*).

king post, king·post (king-pōst) *n.* A supporting post extending vertically from a bearer beam to the apex of a triangular truss. Compare **queen post.**

king prawn *n.* Any of various large edible prawns of the genus *Enaeus.*

Kings (kingz) *n. Used with a singular verb.* **1.** Either of the two Old Testament books, I Kings or II Kings, which tell the history of the kings of Israel and Judah. **2.** Any of a group of four books, I, II,

III, and IV Kings, in the Douay version of the Old Testament corresponding to I Samuel, II Samuel, I Kings, and II Kings in the King James Bible.

King's Bench *n.* See **Queen's Bench.**

King's Counsel *n. Abbr.* K.C. See **Queen's Counsel.**

King's English *n.* See **Queen's English.**

king's evidence *n.* See **queen's evidence.**

King's evil *n.* A disease, **scrofula** (*see*). [From the belief that scrofula could be healed by the king's touch.]

king's highway *n.* See **queen's highway.**

king·ship (king-ship) *n.* **1.** The position, power, province, or prerogative of a king. **2.** The period or tenure of a king; reign. **3.** A monarchy.

king-size (king-sīz) *adj.* Also **king-sized** (-sīzd). Larger or longer than a standard or usual size: *king-size cigarettes; a king-size duvet.*

Kings·ley (kingzli), **Charles** (1819–75). British author. He was professor of modern history at Cambridge (1860), Canon of Chester (1869) and of Westminster (1873), and Chaplain to the Queen (1873). He wrote the adventure novels *Westward Ho!* (1855) and *Hereward the Wake* (1865), and *The Water Babies* (1863).

king snake *n.* Any of various nonvenomous New World snakes of the genus *Lampropeltis,* having yellow or reddish markings.

King's Regulations *pl.n.* See **Queen's Regulations.**

King's shilling *n.* A shilling given to recruits to the British Army until 1879. Also called "queen's shilling" during the reign of a queen. **—take the king's shilling.** *Archaic.* To enlist in the army.

King's speech *n.* See **speech from the throne.**

King·ston[1] (king-stən). The capital and chief port of Jamaica. Founded in 1693 following the destruction of Port Royal by earthquake, it became the capital in 1872.

Kingston[2]. A city on Lake Ontario, Canada, connected to Ottawa by the Rideau Canal. It stands on the site of Fort Frontenac, and was the capital of Canada from 1841 to 1844.

Kingston upon Hull. See **Hull.**

Kingston upon Thames. Royal borough in southwest Greater London. The Coronation Stone near the Guildhall is a relic of the days (A.D. 901–978) when Saxon kings were crowned here.

king·wood (king-wood) *n.* **1.** A South American tree, *Dalbergia cearensis,* having hard, fine-textured, purplish-brown wood used in cabinetmaking. **2.** The wood of this tree.

ki·nin (kínin) *n.* **1.** Any of a class of polypeptides found in the blood that act in the contraction of smooth muscle and the dilation of blood vessels. **2.** Cytokinin (*see*). In this sense, not in technical usage. [Greek *kinein,* to move + -IN.]

kink (kingk) *n.* **1.** A tight curl, as in a hair, or a sharp twist in a line or wire, typically caused by the tensing of a looped section. **2.** A painful muscle spasm, as in the neck or back; a crick. **3.** A quirk of personality. **4.** *Chiefly British.* A sexual peculiarity or deviation. **5.** *Chiefly U.S.* A clever or eccentric idea or notion.
~*v.* **kinked, kinking, kinks. —tr.** To cause to have a kink or kinks. **—intr.** To form kinks. [Low German *kinke,* a twist in a rope, from Middle Low German *kinkel.*]

kink·a·jou (king-kə-jōō) *n.* An arboreal mammal, *Potos flavus,* of tropical America, having brownish fur and a long, prehensile tail. Also called "honey bear", "potto". [French *quincajou,* from Algonquian; akin to Ojibwa *gwingwâage,* wolverine.]

kink·y (kingki) *adj.* **-ier, -iest. 1.** Tightly curled; frizzy: *kinky hair.* **2.** *Chiefly British.* Bizarre or perverse; especially, sexually deviant.

kin·ni·kin·nick, kin·ni·kin·nic (kínniki-ník, -nik) *n.* **1.** A tobacco-like preparation made from the dried leaves or bark of various plants and used for smoking, especially by American Indians. **2.** A plant having leaves or bark used in such a preparation, such as the **bearberry** (*see*). [Algonquian; akin to Natick *kinukkinuk,* mixture.]

Kinnock (kínnək), **Neil (Gordon)** (1942–). British politician. Leader of the Labour Party (1983–92); EU commissioner (1995–).

ki·no (kéenō) *n., pl.* **-nos.** A reddish resin obtained from several Old World tropical trees of the genera *Pterocarpus* and *Butea* and used to treat dysentery and diarrhoea. [A West African word, akin to Mandingo *keno.*]

Kin·ross (kin-róss). Also **Kin·ross·shire.** (-shər, -sheer ‖ -shīr). Former county of east central Scotland. From Tayside Region it passed (1996) into Perthshire and Kinross.

kin selection *n.* The theory that natural selection in animal populations may operate through the mechanism of cooperation among a group of related individuals, which ensures that the average fitness for survival of the group is increased, although one member's individual fitness may be decreased through apparently altruistic behaviour.

Kin·sey (kínzi), **Alfred Charles** (1894–1956). U.S. zoologist. He founded the Institute of Sex Research, Indiana, and published *Sexual Behaviour in the Human Male* (1948) and *Sexual Behaviour in the Human Female* (1953), pioneer studies of their kind.

kins·folk (kínz-fōk) *pl.n.* Also *U.S. informal* **kin·folk** (kin-), **kin·folks** (-fōks). Members of a family; kindred.

Kin·sha·sa (kin-shaá-sə; *rarely* -zə). Formerly **Léopoldville.** Capital of Congo (Dem. Rep.). An ancient settlement on the river Congo, it was discovered by Stanley (1881). It is one of Africa's major cities.

kin·ship (kin-ship) *n.* **1.** The state of being related by blood. **2.** The state of being related in character, origin, or the like; similarity.

kins·man (kínz-mən) *n., pl.* **-men** (-mən, -men). A male blood relation or, loosely, a relation by marriage. **—kins·wo·man** *n.*

ki·osk (kee-osk; *rarely* ki-ósk) *n.* **1.** A small, sometimes ornamental, structure used for selling newspapers, cigarettes, refreshments, or the like. **2.** *Chiefly British.* A booth for a public telephone; a telephone box. **3.** An open gazebo or pavilion, especially in Turkey or Iran. [French *kiosque,* from Turkish *köshk,* pavilion, from Persian *kūshk†,* palace.]

kip¹ (kip) *n., pl.* **kip.** The basic monetary unit of Laos, equal to 100 at. [Thai.]

kip² *n.* The untanned hide of a small or young animal, such as a calf. [Obsolete Dutch *kip,* bundle (of hides), from Middle Dutch; akin to Old Norse *kippi†,* bundle.]

kip³ *n. British Slang.* **1. a.** Sleep. **b.** A period of sleep. **2.** A place to sleep, such as a room or bed. **3.** A lodging house.
~*intr.v.* **kipped, kipping, kips.** *British Slang.* **1.** To sleep. **2.** To go to bed or prepare to sleep. Usually used with *down: can we kip down here?* [Danish *kippe†,* cheap inn.]

kip⁴ *n. Engineering.* A 1,000-pound unit of weight, used to express loads. [KI(LO)- + P(OUND).]

kip⁵ *n. Australian.* A small flat piece of wood on which coins are spun in the game of two-up. [Variant of KEP.]

Kip·ling (kíppling), **(Joseph) Rudyard** (1865–1936). Indian-born British poet and novelist. His first volume of poetry, *Departmental Ditties* (1886), was followed by *Plain Tales from the Hills* (1888). His later works include the two *Jungle Books* (1894–95), *Kim* (1901), and the *Just So Stories* (1902). He received the Nobel prize for literature (1907).

kip·per (kíppər) *n.* **1.** A male salmon or sea trout in the spawning season. **2.** A herring that has been split, salted, and smoked.
~*tr.v.* **kippered, -pering, -pers.** To cure (fish) in this manner. [Middle English *kypre,* Old English *cypera,* perhaps from *coper,* COPPER (from the colour of the fish).]

Kipp's apparatus (kips) *n. Chemistry.* A laboratory apparatus for the controlled production of a gas by the action of a liquid on a solid, used especially to prepare hydrogen sulphide by the action of sulphuric acid on iron sulphide. [After P.J. *Kipp* (1808–64), Dutch chemist.]

kir (keer) *n.* A drink consisting of white wine flavoured with cassis. [After Canon *Kir,* former mayor of Dijon, who is said to have invented the drink.]

kir·by grip (kúrbi-grip) *n.* A small thin metal hair clip with the ends pressed tightly together. Also *U.S.* "bobby pin". [Originally *Kirbigrip,* trademark (Kirby, Beard, and Co. Ltd., Birmingham).]

Kir·giz (kúr-giz, kéer-‖ *U.S.* keer-géez) *n., pl.* **Kirgiz** or **-gizes.** Also **Kir·ghiz, Kyr·gyz. 1.** A member of a Turkic people living principally in Kirgizia or Kyrgyzstan. **2.** The Turkic language of this people. See Kyrgyzstan.

Ki·ri·ba·ti (kírri-báati). Formerly the **Gilbert Islands.** Republic in the west Pacific. It includes the Phoenix Islands, the southern Line Islands, and Ocean Island (Banaba). Formerly part of the Gilbert and Ellice Islands Colony, Kiribati gained independence from the United Kingdom in 1979. The same year the phosphate deposits of Banaba became exhausted, and the country now depends on copra exports and British aid. Fishing and tourism are expanding. Area, 810 square kilometres (312 square miles). Population, 80,000. Capital, Tarawa. See map at **Pacific Ocean.**

ki·ri·ga·mi (kírri-gáami) *n.* The Japanese art of making ornamental designs by cutting and folding paper. Compare **origami.** [Japanese : *kiri,* to cut + *-gami,* from *kami,* paper.]

Ki·ri·ti·ma·ti (kírri-ti-máati). Formerly Christmas Island, coral atoll just north of the Equator in the central-north Pacific Ocean, part of Kiribati.

kirk (kurk) *n.* **1.** *Chiefly Scottish.* A church. **2.** *Capital* **K.** The Presbyterian Church of Scotland. Preceded by *the.* [Middle English *kirk(e),* from Old Norse *kirkja,* from Old English *cir(i)ce,* CHURCH.]

Kirk·cal·dy (kər-kóddi, kur-, -káwdi). Royal burgh of east central Scotland. In Fife, it is a port and coal-mining centre on the Firth of Forth.

Kirk·cud·bright (kər-kóobri, kur-). Former county of southwest Scotland, that is now part of Dumfries and Galloway.

Kir·kuk or **Ker·kuk** (keer-kóok). City in northeast Iraq. It is the centre of the country's oil industry, connected to the Mediterranean by pipeline.

Kirk·wall (kúrk-wawl). Royal burgh of north Scotland. On Mainland or Pomona Island in Orkney, it is the islands' largest town and chief port, and the administrative centre.

Kir·li·an (kúr-li-n, keér-) *adj.* Pertaining to or designating a photographic process used for recording the radiation discharges of the human body, electrically stimulated objects, or the like. [After V. K. and S. D. *Kirlian,* the 20th-century Russian inventors of the process.]

Kir·man, Ker·man (keer-máan, kur-) *n.* A Persian rug with an elaborate border pattern and muted colours. [After *Kirman,* province of Iran.]

Kirmanshah. See Kermanshah.

kirmess. Variant of **kermis.**

kirsch (keersh) *n.* A colourless brandy made from the fermented juice of cherries. Also called "kirschwasser". [German *Kirsch(wasser),* "cherry (water)", from Old High German *kirsa,* cherry, from Vulgar Latin *cerasia* (unattested).]

kir·tle (kúrt'l) *n. Archaic.* **1.** A knee-length tunic or coat for a man. **2.** A woman's long dress or skirt. [Middle English *ki(e)rtel, curtle,* Old English *cyrtel,* from Germanic *kurtilaz* (unattested), "short coat", diminutive of *kurt-* (unattested), short, from Latin *curtus,* cut short.]

kish (kish) *n. Metallurgy.* Graphite formed on the surface of molten iron when the iron contains large amounts of carbon. [Perhaps alteration of German *Kies,* gravel.]

Kish (kish). A city of ancient Mesopotamia. Excavated in the 1920s, it revealed its pre-Sumerian origins, when the earliest existing example of writing was discovered there: a pre-cuneiform tablet dating from 3500 B.C.

kish·ke (kíshkə) *n.* A food, **derma** (*see*). [Yiddish, probably from Russian *kishka,* gut.]

Kis·lev (kíss-ləf, kiss-lév) *n.* The third month of the Hebrew year. [Hebrew *kislēw.*]

kis·met (kíz-met, kíss-, -mət) *n.* Fate; fortune. [Turkish *kismet,* from Arabic *qismah,* lot, from *qasama,* he divided, he allotted.]

kiss (kiss) *v.* **kissed, kissing, kisses.** —*tr.* **1.** To touch or caress with the lips as a sign of sexual passion, affection, greeting, or respect. **2.** To touch lightly; brush against. **3.** In billiards and snooker, to touch or hit lightly against (another ball). Used of a ball. —*intr.* **1.** To touch or caress someone, something, or each other with the lips. **2.** To brush against each other. **3.** In billiards and snooker, to touch another ball lightly. Used of a ball. **—kiss hands.** To kiss the sovereign's hand ceremonially, on taking high office.
~*n.* **1.** A caress or touching with the lips. **2.** A slight or gentle touching. **3.** In billiards and snooker, a gentle impact between balls. **4.** A small piece of confectionery. [Middle English *kissen, cussen,* Old English *cyssan.*]

kiss-curl (kiss-kurl) *n.* A small, almost circular, curl of hair lying flat against the cheek, forehead, or nape of the neck.

kiss·er (kíssər) *n.* **1.** A person who kisses. **2.** *Slang.* The mouth or face.

kis·sing bug (kíssing) *n.* An assassin bug, *Melanolestes picipes,* that inflicts a painful bite, often on the lips of a sleeping person.

Kis·sin·ger (kíssinjər), **Henry (Alfred)** (1923–). U.S. foreign policy adviser. He was born in Germany and fled the Nazis (1938) to live in the United States. Under presidents Nixon and Ford he was executive secretary of the National Security Council (1969) and Secretary of State (1973–77). He helped to negotiate the Vietnam ceasefire (1973), for which he shared the Nobel peace prize (1973) with the North Vietnamese negotiator, Le Duc Tho.

kissing gate *n.* A gate that is partially enclosed on the side opposite to the hinge, in a U- or V-shaped structure so as to allow only one person to pass through at a time.

kiss of death *n.* That which is ruinous, disastrous, or fatal. [From Judas's kiss that betrayed Jesus.]

kiss of life *n.* Mouth-to-mouth resuscitation, used when breathing has stopped. Air is blown into the victim's mouth by the rescuer to inflate the lungs, and allowed to escape before the next blow.

kiss of peace *n.* A ceremonial kiss or, more usually, a handshake, made as a sign of unity between all those at the Eucharist.

kist¹ (kist ‖ *South African also* kiss) *n. Chiefly Scottish & South African.* A large, lidded chest. [Middle English, from Old Norse *kista,* CHEST.]

kist². Variant of **cist** (coffin).

kit¹ (kit) *n.* **1. a.** A set of instruments or equipment used for a specific job or purpose: *a survival kit.* **b.** A collection of clothing and other personal effects, as for travel, a sporting activity, or the like. **c.** A container for any such set or collection, such as a box, bag, or rucksack. **2.** A set of parts or materials to be assembled: *a model aeroplane kit.* **3.** *British Regional.* A wooden tub or barrel for holding water or foodstuffs. **—the whole kit and caboodle.** *Chiefly U.S. Informal.* The entire collection or lot.
~*tr.v.* **kitted, kitting, kits.** *Chiefly British.* To equip; provide with a kit or outfit. Usually used with *out* or *up.* [Middle English *kytt, kitt,* wooden tub, from Middle Dutch *kitte†,* jug, tankard.]

kit² *n.* A kitten or other young fur-bearing animal. [Short for KITTEN.]

kit³ *n. N.Z.* A basket, especially one woven from flax. [Maori *kete,* bag.]

kit·bag (kít-bag) *n.* A bag, such as a rucksack, for carrying kit; especially, a long narrow canvas bag used by servicemen.

kitch·en (kích-in, -'n) *n.* A room or area in which food is cooked or prepared. [Middle English *kichene, kuchene,* Old English *cycene,* from West Germanic *kocina* (unattested), from Late Latin *coquīna,* from Latin, feminine of *coquīnus,* of cooking, from *coquere,* to cook.]

kitchen cabinet *n.* An unofficial but influential group of advisers to a prime minister, president, or the like.

Kitch·e·ner of Khartoum and of Broome (kíchinər), **Horatio Herbert, 1st Earl** (1850–1916). British soldier and statesman. As Sirdar (commander in chief) of the Egyptian army, he won back the Sudan for Egypt at the Battle of Omdurman (1898). He brought the second Boer War (1899–1902) to a conclusion. As Secretary for War in World War I he recruited 3,000,000 volunteers ("Kitchener armies") for the armed forces. He went down with H.M.S. *Hampshire* when it was mined in the North Sea.

kitch·en·ette (kíchin-ét) *n.* A small kitchen.

kitchen garden *n.* A garden in which vegetables and fruits are grown for household consumption.

kitchen midden *n.* A refuse heap or mound of the Mesolithic or later prehistoric periods, containing numerous artefacts, shells, and often animal bones. [*Midden,* Middle English *myddyng,* from Scandinavian; akin to Danish *mødding.*]

kitchen police *pl.n. U.S. Military.* Enlisted men assigned to work in the kitchen.

kitch·en·sink (kíchin-síngk) *adj.* Portraying working-class domestic life realistically and unromantically: *kitchen-sink drama.*

kitch·en·ware (kíchin-wair) *n.* Utensils for use in the kitchen, such as pots and pans.

kite (kīt) *n.* **1.** A flying device made up of one or more cloth or paper surfaces stretched over a light framework, designed to climb and hover in the breeze at the end of a long string. **2.** Any of the highest sails of a ship, used only in a light wind. **3.** Any of various predatory birds of the subfamilies Milvinae and Elaninae, having a long, often forked tail. **4.** *Finance. Informal.* An **accommodation bill** *(see).* **5.** *Geometry.* A quadrilateral that has two pairs of equal adjacent sides. **—fly a kite. 1.** To test opinion, especially by making a preliminary experiment. **2.** *Informal.* To raise money using accommodation bills.
~*v.* **kited, kiting, kites.** —*intr.* To fly like a kite; soar or glide. —*tr. Finance. Informal.* To use up as a kite. [Middle English *kyte, kete,* kite (bird), Old English *cȳta,* from Common German *kūtja-* (unattested), probably imitative of its cry.]

Kite·mark (kīt-maark) *n.* A kite-shaped emblem that is the official mark of approval of the British Standards Institution, placed on manufactured goods that meet the Institution's required standards.

kith (kith) *n.* Friends and neighbours. Now used only in the phrase *kith and kin.* [Middle English *kith, kyth,* Old English *cȳth(the), cȳthu,* "knowledge", "acquaintance", friend.]

kitsch (kich) *n.* **1.** Vulgarity, sentimentality, and pretentious bad taste, especially in the arts, sometimes achieved deliberately for effect or fun. **2.** Examples or an example of kitsch. [German, from *kitschen†,* to put together (a work of art) sloppily.] **—kitsch, kitsch·y** *adj.*

kit·ten (kítt'n) *n.* A young cat. **—have kittens.** To be very angry, nervous, or upset.
~*intr.v.* **kittened, -tening, -tens.** To bear kittens. [Middle English *kitoun,* from Old North French *caton* (unattested), diminutive of *cat,* cat, from Late Latin *cattus,* CAT.]

kit·ten·ish (kítt'n-ish) *adj.* Playful; coy. **—kit·ten·ish·ly** *adv.*

kit·ti·wake (kítti-wayk) *n.* Either of two gulls, *Rissa tridactyla* or *R. brevirostris,* of northern regions. [Imitative of its cry.]

kit·tle (kítt'l) *adj. Scottish.* Requiring careful handling; tricky; delicate. [Scottish *kittle,* to tickle, Middle English (Scottish) *kytyllen,* probably from Old Norse *kitla.*]

kit·ty¹ (kítti) *n., pl.* **-ties. 1.** In some card games, a sum of money contributed by each player at the start of a hand, all of which is won by the winner of that hand. **2.** Any shared sum of money, especially one contributed to equally by a group of people and used to buy something that they all share. **3.** In bowls, the **jack** *(see).* [Originally "small bowl", diminutive of KIT (tub).]

kit·ty² *n., pl.* **-ties.** *Informal.* A kitten or cat. [From *kit,* short for KITTEN.]

ki·va (kéevə) *n.* An underground or partly underground room in a Pueblo Indian village, used by the men especially for ceremonies or councils. [Hopi.]

Kivu, Lake (kéevoo). Africa's highest lake. It lies at 1 459 metres (4,788 feet) on the Congo (Dem. Rep.)-Rwanda border, in the western arm of the Great Rift Valley.

ki·wi (kée-wee) *n.* **1.** Any of several nocturnal flightless birds of the genus *Apteryx,* of New Zealand, having vestigial wings and a long, slender bill. **2. a.** A vine, *Actinidia chinensis,* native to Asia, bearing hairy, edible fruit. **b.** The fruit of this vine. In this sense, also called "Chinese gooseberry", "kiwi fruit". **3.** *Capital* **K.** *Informal.* A New Zealander. [Maori, imitative of its cry.]

Ki·wi·land (kée-wee-land) *n. Informal.* New Zealand.

K.K.K. Ku Klux Klan.

Klai·pe·da (klī-peddə). *German* **Me·mel** (máym'l). Ice-free Baltic port and industrial city in Lithuania. A strategic fortress, it was held by the Prussians from 1635 until 1919. The city was the capital of Memelland, a Lithuanian autonomous territory from 1924. Memelland was ceded to Germany (March 1939), and fell to the Russians in 1945.

Klan (klan) *n.* The **Ku Klux Klan** *(see).*

Klans·man (klánz-mən) *n., pl.* **-men** (-mən). A member of the Ku Klux Klan.

klax·on (kláks'n) *n.* A loud warning hooter or horn, formerly used on cars. [Greek *klazein,* to roar.]

Klee (klay), **Paul** (1879-1940). Swiss painter. His works, mainly small abstracts, are reminiscent of doodles or children's art, as in *Twittering Machine, The Zoo,* and *Fish Magic.*

Kleen·ex (kléeneks) *n.* A trademark for a soft paper tissue.

Klein (klīn), **Melanie** (1882-1960). Austrian psychoanalyst. She moved to England in 1926 and studied the behaviour of children in terms of their desires and anxieties through play. **—Klein·i·an** *adj. & n.*

Klein bottle (klīn) *n.* A one-sided topological surface having no inside or outside, formed by inserting the small open end of a tapered tube through the side of the tube and making it contiguous with the larger open end. Compare **Möbius strip.** [After Felix *Klein* (1849-1925), German mathematician.]

Klem·pe·rer (klémpərər), **Otto** (1885-1973). German conductor. He conducted several orchestras in Germany, but left in 1933 and went on to conduct many major orchestras all over the world.

klep·to·ma·ni·a (klépt-ə-máyni-ə, -ō-) *n.* An obsessive impulse to steal, especially in the absence of economic necessity or personal desire. [New Latin : Greek *kleptein,* to steal + -O- + -MANIA.] **—klep·to·ma·ni·ac** (-ak) *n.*

klieg light (kleeg) *n.* A powerful carbon-arc lamp producing an intense light, used especially in cinematography. [Invented by the brothers John H. *Kliegl* (1869-1959) and Anton T. *Kliegl* (1872-1927), U.S. lighting experts.]

Klimt (klimmt), **Gustav** (1862 - 1918). Austrian Art Nouveau artist. He founded the Vienna Secession group and achieved fame as a portrait and landscape painter of great exotic and erotic sensibility. His mosaics and paintings are characterised by large predominant patterns of gold as in *The Kiss* (Vienna).

klip·spring·er (klíp-spring-ər). *n.* A small-hoofed African antelope, *Oreotragus oreotragus,* having large ears. [Afrikaans, "cliff springer" : Dutch *klip,* cliff, from Middle Dutch *klippe,* from Germanic *klibam* (unattested), CLIFF + *springer,* from *springen,* to leap, from Middle Dutch.]

Klon·dike (klón-dīk). A region of the Yukon Territory, Canada. It was the scene of a famous gold rush (1897-98); the gold yield, however, has steadily declined since 1910. It takes its name from the Klondike river, a tributary of the Yukon.

klon·kie (klóngki) *n., pl.* **-kies.** Also **klong** (klong). *South African.* A young coloured boy. [Afrikaans, perhaps a blend of *klein,* small + *jong,* boy + *-kie,* diminutive suffix.]

kloof (kloōf) *n.* In South Africa, a deep ravine. [Afrikaans, from Dutch, from Middle Dutch *clove,* cleft.]

klutz (kluts) *n. U.S. Slang.* A clumsy or dull-witted person. [German *Klotz,* clod, "block", from Middle High German *kloz,* block, lump.]

klys·tron (klíss-tron, klíss-, -trən) *n.* An electron tube used to amplify or generate radio waves of microwave range frequencies by means of velocity modulation. [Greek *klustēr,* syringe, clyster pipe, from *kluzein,* to wash out + (ELECTR)ON.]

km kilometre.

K-me·son (káy-mee-zon) *n. Physics.* A type of meson, a **kaon** *(see).*

km/h kilometres per hour.

kn. *Nautical.* knot(s).

knack (nak) *n.* **1.** A clever, expedient way of doing something. **2.** A specific skill or talent for something, especially one difficult to explain or teach. [Middle English *knak(ke),* probably identified with *knak,* sharp blow, from Dutch and Low German *knak.*]

knack·er (náckər) *n. British.* **1.** A person who buys useless or worn-out horses and slaughters them for their hides or to make pet foods, for example. **2.** A person who buys up discarded structures and dismantles them to sell the materials. **3.** *Slang.* A testicle.
~*tr.v.* **knackered, -ering, -ers.** *British Slang.* To wear out; exhaust. [Originally "harness maker", saddler, probably from Scandinavian, akin to Old Norse *hnakkur,* saddle.] **—knack·er·y** *n.*

knack·wurst, knock·wurst (nák-wurst, -woorst; *German* -voorst ‖ *U.S.* nók-) *n.* A short, thick sausage resembling a frankfurter. [German *Knackwurst,* "sausage whose skin cracks open when bitten" : *knacken,* to crack, from Middle High German + *Wurst,* sausage, WURST.]

knap¹ (nap) *v.* **knapped, knapping, knaps.** *Archaic & British Regional.* —*tr.* **1.** To strike sharply; rap. **2.** To break or chip (flints, for example) with a sharp blow. **3.** To utter; chat about. —*intr.* To deliver a sharp blow. [Middle English *knappen,* probably from Low German, akin to Middle Dutch *cnappen,* Low German *knappen.*]

knap² *n. Regional.* The crest of a hill; a summit. [Middle English *knap,* Old English *cnæpp.*]

knap·sack (náp-sak) *n.* A case or bag, usually of canvas or leather, worn on the back to carry supplies and equipment, especially on a hike or march. [Low German *knappsack* : probably *knappen,* to snap, bite, eat + *sack,* bag, from Middle Low German, from Germanic, from Latin *saccus,* SACK (bag).]

knap·weed (náp-weed) *n.* Any of various plants of the genus *Centaurea,* having purplish, thistle-like flowers. [Middle English *knopwed* : KNOP (from the knobby head of its flower) + WEED.]

knar (nar) *n.* A knot or protuberance on a tree or in wood. [Middle English *knarre,* probably from Scandinavian; akin to Norwegian *knart.*]

knave (nayv) *n.* **1.** An unprincipled, crafty man. **2.** In card games, the jack. [Middle English *knave,* Old English *cnafa,* boy, lad, from Common Germanic *knabōn-* (unattested).]

knav·er·y (náyvəri) *n., pl.* **-ies. 1.** Dishonest or crafty dealing. **2.** A piece of mischief or trickery.

knav·ish (náyvish) *adj.* Like or characteristic of a knave; dishonest; unprincipled. **—knav·ish·ly** *adv.* **—knav·ish·ness** *n.*

knaw·el (náw-əl, nawl) *n.* A low-growing, weedy plant, *Scleranthus annuus,* native to Eurasia, having narrow leaves and inconspicuous green flowers. [German *Knäuel,* knot, knob, ball of yarn, from Middle High German *kniuwel, kliuwel(in),* from Old High German *kliuwilin,* from *kliuwa,* ball.]

knead (need) *tr.v.* **kneaded, kneading, kneads. 1.** To mix and work (a substance) into a uniform mass; especially, to fold, press, and stretch (dough) with the hands. **2.** To make (bread or pottery, for example) by kneading. **3.** To squeeze, press, or roll with the hands, as in massaging. **4.** To blend together or manipulate as if by kneading. [Middle English *kneden,* Old English *cnedan.*] **—knead·er** *n.*

knee (nee) *n.* **1.** *Anatomy.* The joint of the human leg that is the articulation for the tibia and fibula with the femur, which is covered in front by the patella. **2.** A corresponding joint of a leg of other animals, as in the forelimb of a hoofed animal. **3.** The region of the leg around this joint, especially at the front. **4.** The part of a garment, for example trousers or tights, that covers the knee. **5.** Anything resembling the knee in action, such as a pivoted device, or in shape, such as a bent pipe or piece of wood. **6.** The lap: *sit on my*

knee. —**to (one's) knees** To a state of submission or defeat.
~*tr.v.* **kneed, kneeing, knees.** *Informal.* To strike with the knee. [Middle English *kne(e), kn(e)ow,* Old English *cnēo.*]
knee breeches *pl.n.* Breeches extending to or just below the knee.
knee·cap (née-kap) *n.* **1.** A bone, the **patella** *(see).* Also called "kneepan". **2.** A kneepad.
~*tr.v.* **kneecapped, -capping, -caps.** To shoot or injure in the knee as a form of punishment.
knee-deep (née-deep) *adj.* **1.** As high as the knees; reaching to the knees; knee-high. **2.** Submerged to the knees. **3.** Deeply occupied or engaged.
knee-high (née-hí) *adj.* As tall or high as the knee.
knee·hole (née-hōl) *n.* A space or opening for the knees, as under a desk or counter. Also used adjectivally: *a kneehole desk.*
knee jerk *n.* A sudden, involuntary, reflex kick forward produced by a smart tap to the tendon below the patella as the leg hangs relaxed forming a right angle with the thigh. Also called "patellar reflex".
knee-jerk (née-jerk) *adj. Informal.* **1.** As unthinking, automatic, and predictable as a knee jerk: *His anger was a knee-jerk reaction.* **2.** Characterised by knee-jerk reactions: *a knee-jerk liberal.*
kneel (neel) *intr.v.* **knelt** (nelt) or *chiefly U.S. & Literary* **kneeled, kneeling, kneels.** To fall or rest on bent knees. [Middle English *kne(w)len,* Old English *cnēowlian.* Knelt (past tense and past participle) is an analogous formation after FEEL, FELT.]
knee-length (née-length ‖ -lenth) *adj.* Reaching the knee or just below the knee: *knee-length socks.*
kneel·er (néelər) *n.* **1.** One who kneels. **2.** Something to kneel on, as in a church, such as a stool, cushion, or board.
knee·pad (née-pad) *n.* A protective covering for the knee. Also called "kneecap".
knees-up (néez-up) *n. Informal.* A lively celebration; a party.
knee·trem·bler (née-tremblər) *n. Slang.* An act of sexual intercourse performed while standing up.
knell (nel) *v.* **knelled, knelling, knells.** —*intr.* **1.** To ring or sound, especially for a funeral; toll. Used of a bell. **2.** To produce a mournful or ominous sound. —*tr.* To signal, summon, or proclaim by tolling.
~*n.* **1.** The slow, solemn sounding of a bell, as at a funeral; a tolling. **2.** An omen or signal of disaster, failure, or extinction. [Middle English *knillen, knellen,* Old English *cnyllan.*]
Knes·set (k-néss-et) *n.* The Israeli parliament. [Hebrew (Mishnaic) *Kəneseth,* "assembly", from *kānas,* he gathered.]
knew. Past tense of **know.**
Knick·er·bock·er (nícker-bockər) *n. U.S.* **1.** A descendant of the Dutch settlers of New York. **2.** A New Yorker. [From Diedrich *Knickerbocker,* fictitious Dutch settler and pretended author of Washington Irving's *History of New York* (1809).]
knickerbocker glory *n.* An ice cream and fruit dessert served in a tall glass.
knick·er·bock·ers (nícker-bockərz) *pl.n.* Full breeches gathered and banded just below the knee. Also *U.S.* "knickers". [Supposed to have been worn by Dutch settlers.]
knick·ers (níckərz) *pl.n.* **1.** Underpants worn by women and girls. **2.** *U.S.* Knickerbockers.
knick-knack, nick-nack (ník-nak) *n.* A small, ornamental article; a trinket. [Reduplication of KNACK (device).]
knick·point, *U.S.* **nick·point** (ník-poynt) *n.* A place in the long or longitudinal profile of a river valley where the slope changes. [German *Knickpunkt.*]
knife (nîf) *n., pl.* **knives** (nîvz). **1.** A cutting instrument or weapon consisting of a sharp blade with a handle. **2.** Any cutting edge or blade. **3.** *Informal.* Malicious harm. Used chiefly in such phrases as *put the knife in* or *get one's knife into.* —**under the knife.** *Informal.* Undergoing surgery.
~*v.* **knifed, knifing, knifes.** —*tr.* **1.** To use a knife on, especially to cut, stab, or wound. **2.** *Chiefly U.S. Informal.* To hurt, defeat, or betray by underhand means. —*intr.* To cut or slash a way through, with or as if with a knife. [Middle English *knyf, knif,* Old English *cníf.*]
knife-edge (nîf-ej) *n.* **1.** The cutting edge of a blade. **2.** A sharp mountain ridge. **3.** Any sharp, knifelike edge, such as a sharp pleat or fold. **4.** A wedge of metal used as a low-friction fulcrum for a balancing beam or lever. **5.** A position of extreme precariousness.
knife pleat *n.* A narrow, flat pleat lying in one direction and often overlapping another.
knife-point (nîf-poynt) *n.* The tip of a knife. —**at knife-point.** Threatened with injury by a person using a knife.
knife switch *n.* A type of electrical switch in which flat, hinged, metal blades are pushed between fixed contact clips.
knight (nît) *n. Abbr.* **k., K., Knt, Kt 1.** The holder of a nonhereditary rank conferred by a sovereign in recognition of personal merit or services rendered to the country, and in Britain bearing the title *Sir* before the Christian name. **2.** A member of any of several orders or brotherhoods that call their members *knights.* **3.** A medieval tenant giving military service as a mounted man-at-arms to a feudal landholder. **4.** A medieval gentleman-soldier, usually of high birth, raised by a sovereign to privileged military status after training as a page and squire. **5. a.** A defender, champion, or zealous upholder of a cause or principle. **b.** The devoted champion of a lady. **6.** A chess piece usually having the shape of a horse's head and able to be moved two squares horizontally and one vertically, or two vertically and one horizontally.

~*tr.v.* **knighted, knighting, knights.** To give (a person) a knighthood; make a knight. [Middle English *cniht, knyght,* Old English *cniht,* originally "boy", "lad", "servant", from West Germanic *knih-tas* (unattested).]
knight bachelor *n., pl.* **knights bachelor.** One who holds a knighthood but does not belong to any special order, such as the Bath or Garter.
knight banneret *n.* A banneret *(see).*
knight errant *n., pl.* **knights errant. 1.** A knight of medieval romance who wandered in search of adventure. **2.** One given to adventurous or quixotic conduct. —**knight-er·rant·ry** (nît-érrəntri) *n.*
knight·head (nît-hed) *n.* Either of two timbers rising from the keel of a sailing ship to support the inner end of the bowsprit. [They were sometimes adorned with a carved knight's head.]
knight·hood (nît-hŏod) *n.* **1.** The rank or dignity of a knight. **2.** The behaviour of or qualities befitting a knight; chivalry. **3.** Knights as a body or class.
knight·ly (nît-li) *adj.* Of, pertaining to, or befitting a knight. —**knight·li·ness** *n.*
knight marshal *n., pl.* **knights marshal.** A royal court official, a marshal *(see).*
Knight Templar *n., pl.* **Knights Templars** or **Knights Templar.** *Abbr.* **K.T.** A member of an order of knights founded in 1119 to protect pilgrims in the Holy Land during the second Crusade and suppressed (1311–14). Also called "Templar".
knish (k'nish) *n.* A piece of dough stuffed with potato or other filling and baked or fried. [Yiddish, from Russian, akin to Ukrainian *knyš,* Polish *knysz†.*]
knit (nit) *v.* **knit** or **knitted, knitting, knits.** —*tr.* **1.** To make (a fabric or garment) by intertwining yarn or thread in a series of connected loops either on a machine or by hand with knitting needles. **2.** To make (yarn or thread) into a fabric or garment in this manner. **3. a.** To knit by using a **plain stitch** *(see).* **b.** To make (a plain stitch): *knit one, purl one.* **4.** To join closely; unite securely. Often used in the passive: *a tightly knit community.* **5.** To draw (the brows) together in wrinkles; furrow. —*intr.* **1. a.** To make a fabric or garment by intertwining yarn or thread in connected loops. **b.** To make a plain stitch; knit using a plain stitch. **2.** To come or grow together securely. Used especially of fractured bones. **3.** To come together in wrinkles or furrows. —**knit up. 1.** To repair by or as if by knitting. **2.** To conclude or complete by or as if by knitting.
~*n.* **1.** A fabric or garment made by knitting. **2.** The method, style, or way in which a garment has been knitted: *a loose knit.* [Middle English *knitten,* Old English *cnyttan,* to tie in a knot.] —**knit·ter** *n.*
knit·ting (nítting) *n.* **1.** The process of producing something knitted. **2.** Knitted work.
knitting needle *n.* A long, thin, pointed rod used in knitting.
knit·wear (nít-wair) *n.* Knitted clothing, especially sweaters.
knives. Plural of **knife.**
knob (nob) *n.* **1. a.** A rounded protuberance on a surface or extremity. **b.** A rounded handle, as on a drawer or door. **c.** A small rounded control switch or dial. **2.** A small rounded piece, as of butter. **3.** *British Vulgar Slang.* The penis. —**with (brass) knobs on.** That and even more so. Used as a retort to an insult or an ironic expression of disbelief. [Middle English *knobbe,* from Middle Low German, tree knot, knob.] —**knobbed** *adj.* —**knob·by** *adj.*
knob·bly (nóbbli) *adj.* Having small knoblike protrusions; lumpy; knobby: *knobbly knees.*
knob·ker·rie (nób-kerri) *n.* Also **knob·kie·rie** (-kirri) *n.* A short club with one knobbed end, used as a weapon by South African tribesmen. [Afrikaans *knopkierie* : *knop,* knob, from Middle Dutch *cnoppe* + *kieri,* club, from Hottentot *kïrri,* a stick.]
knock (nok) *v.* **knocked, knocking, knocks.** —*tr.* **1.** To strike with a hard blow; hit. **2.** To put into a specified place or condition with a blow: *knocked senseless.* **3.** To send into collision; cause to collide. **4.** To produce by hitting or striking: *She knocked a hole in the wall.* **5.** To instil with or as if with blows: *Try to knock some sense into his head.* **6.** *Slang.* To criticise adversely; disparage. **7.** *British Slang.* To astonish. —*intr.* **1.** To strike a sharp, audible blow or series of blows, as at a door when requesting admittance; rap. **2.** To collide; bump. **3. a.** To make the pounding or clanking noise of a labouring or defective engine. **b.** To emit a characteristic metallic sound as a result of faulty combustion. Used of a petrol engine. —**knock off. 1.** *Informal.* **a.** To take a break or rest from. **b.** To cease; stop. **c.** To cease work. **2.** *Informal.* To make, accomplish, or consume hastily or easily. **3.** *Informal.* To eliminate; deduct: *The grocer knocked off a little from the bill.* **4.** *Slang.* To kill. **5.** *Slang.* To steal; rob. —**knock sideways** or **for six.** *Informal.* **1.** To astonish; dumbfound. **2.** To disconcert; discomfit. **3.** To put an end to; ruin: *a decision that knocked the whole project for six.* —**knock together.** To make or assemble quickly or carelessly.
~*n.* **1.** An instance of knocking; a blow. **2.** The sound of a sharp tap on a hard surface; a rap. **3. a.** A pounding, clanking noise made by an engine, especially one in poor operating condition. **b.** A characteristic metallic sound emitted by an engine as a result of faulty combustion. **4.** *Slang.* A criticism or insult; a cutting remark. **5.** *Informal.* A misfortune, setback, or trouble: *has taken a few knocks over the years.* **6.** *Informal.* A player's innings in a game of cricket. —**take the knock.** To suffer financial hardship. [Middle English *knokken,* Old English *cnocian.*]
knock about Also **knock around.** *Informal. tr.v.* **1.** To be rough or brutal with; maltreat. **2.** To discuss or consider. —*intr.v.* **1.** To travel about, often aimlessly. **2.** To be present or active in a place

constantly or regularly but often inconspicuously. **3.** To go out with or spend time with someone, especially a girlfriend or boy-friend.

knock·a·bout (nóckə-bowt) *n. U.S.* A small sloop with a mainsail, a jib, and a keel, but no bowsprit.
~*adj.* **1.** Rough; boisterous; rowdy. **2.** Appropriate for rough wear or use.

knock back *tr.v. Informal.* **1.** To drink (alcohol, for example) quickly or in large quantities. **2.** To cost; especially, to cost (a person) a large amount of money. **3.** To surprise and disconcert. **4.** To reject; refuse; rebuff.

knock·back (nók-bak) *n.* A rejection, refusal, or rebuff.

knock down *tr.v.* **1.** To disassemble into parts, as for storage or shipping. **2.** To declare as sold at an auction, as by striking a blow with a gavel. **3.** To demolish. **4.** *Informal.* **a.** To reduce (a purchase price). **b.** To cause (a seller) to reduce a price: *knocked him down to £10.*

knock·down (nók-down ‖ *West Indies also* -dung) *adj.* **1.** Strong enough to knock down or overwhelm; powerful. **2.** Designed to be assembled or disassembled quickly and easily: *knockdown furniture.* **3.** *Informal.* Cheap: *knockdown prices.*
~*n.* **1.** The act of knocking down; a toppling or overwhelming. **2.** An overwhelming blow or shock. **3.** *Australian & U.S. Informal.* An introduction (to a person).

knock·er (nóckər) *n.* **1.** One that knocks, especially: **a.** An often decorative fixture used for knocking on a door. **b.** *Slang.* One who constantly criticises. **—on the knocker. 1.** *British Informal.* From door to door; especially, as a door-to-door salesman: *working on the knocker.* **2.** *Australian Informal.* Punctually; promptly.

knock·ers (nóckərz) *pl.n. British Slang.* A woman's breasts.

knock·er-up (nóckər-úp) *n., pl.* **knockers-up.** Also **knocker-upper** (úppər), *pl.* **knocker-uppers.** *British.* **1.** One who goes from door to door, for example as a salesman or as a political canvasser. **2.** Formerly, one whose job was to wake people up, as for work, by going from house to house knocking on windows.

knock·ing-shop (nócking-shop) *n. British Slang.* A brothel.

knock-knee (nók-née ‖ -nee) *n.* An abnormal condition in which one knee is turned towards the other, or in which each is turned towards the other. **—knock-kneed** *adj.*

knock on *intr.v.* In Rugby football, to hit, drop, or otherwise play the ball with hand or arm so that it moves in the direction of the opponent's goal-line. **—***tr.v.* To knock on (a ball).

knock-on (nók-ón) *n.* In Rugby football, the action of hitting, dropping, or otherwise playing the ball with hand or arm so that it moves in the direction of the opponent's goal-line.
~*adj.* Of or designating a process whereby an initial event leads to a series of related effects: *The closure of a large factory inevitably has a knock-on effect on its major suppliers.*

knock out *tr.v.* **1.** To render unconscious. **2.** In boxing, to defeat (an opponent) by knocking him to the canvas for a count of ten. **3.** To defeat or overcome; especially, to eliminate from a knockout competition. **4.** *Informal.* To exert or exhaust (oneself or another) to the utmost. **5.** *Informal.* To delight or amaze: *We've been really knocked out by the book's success.*

knock·out (nók-owt) *n.* **1.** A blow that induces unconsciousness. **2.** In boxing, the knocking out of an opponent. **3.** *Slang.* Something or someone very impressive or attractive. **4.** A competition with a series of matches, in each of which a competitor is eliminated.
~*adj.* Effecting a knockout.

knockout drops *pl.n. Slang.* A solution, as of chloral hydrate, put into a drink to render the drinker unconscious.

knock up *intr.v.* In tennis, squash, and similar games, to hit the ball in practice for a period before starting to play a game. **—***tr.v.* **1.** To make or assemble quickly or carelessly. **2.** *British Informal.* To exhaust; wear out. **3.** *British.* To wake up, as by knocking at a door. **4.** In cricket, to score (runs) quickly. **5.** *Slang.* To make pregnant.

knock-up (nók-up) *n.* In tennis, squash, and similar games, a practice session or warming-up period before a game starts.

knockwurst. Variant of **knackwurst.**

knoll (nōl) *n.* A small rounded hill or mound; a hillock. [Middle English *knol(le),* Old English *cnoll.*]

knop (nop) *n.* A decorative knob or boss, as on the end of the handle of a spoon. [Middle English *knoppe,* probably from Middle Low German or Middle Dutch.]

Knos·sos or **Cnos·sos** (knóss-oss, knóss-, -əss). City of ancient Crete. Just south of modern Iráklio, it was occupied from *c.* 3000 B.C., and by the time of its destruction, probably by earthquake (*c.* 1400 B.C.), it was, as the centre of Minoan culture, one of the leading cities of the ancient world. The legends of the Labyrinth, the Minotaur, and Atlantis probably originated here. It was excavated and extensively restored between 1899 and 1935. Now named Knosós.

knot¹ (not) *n.* **1.** A more or less complex, compact intersection of interlaced cord, ribbon, rope, or the like. **2.** A fastening made by tying together lengths, as of rope, in a prescribed way. **3.** A decorative bow of ribbon, fabric, or braid. **4.** Any tie or bond, especially a marriage bond. **5.** A tight cluster of persons or things. **6.** A difficulty; a problem. **7. a.** A hard place or node on a plant, especially on a tree, at a point from which a stem or branch grows. **b.** The circular, contrastingly dark-coloured cross section of such a node as it appears cross-grained on a piece of cut timber. **8.** A growth on or enlargement of a gland, muscle, or the like. **9.** *Nautical.* **a.** A division on a log line used to measure the speed of a ship. **b.** *Abbr.* **kn.**,

kt. A unit of speed of ships or aircraft, one nautical mile per hour, 1.85 kilometres (1.15 statute miles) per hour. **c.** *Informal.* A distance of one nautical mile. **—at a rate of knots.** At great speed. **—tie in knots.** To make (a person) confused. **—tie the knot.** *Slang.* To get married.
~*v.* **knotted, knotting, knots.** **—***tr.* **1.** To tie in or fasten with a knot or knots. **2.** To entangle. **3.** To cause to form knots. **—***intr.* To form a knot or knots. [Middle English *knot(te),* Old English *cnotta.*]

knot² *n.* A shore bird, *Calidris canutus,* related to the sandpipers, having a greyish, mottled plumage in winter and brick-red in summer, and a short, black bill. [Middle English, origin obscure.]

knot garden *n.* A formal garden having the flower beds arranged in an intricate, knot-like pattern.

knot·grass (nót-graas ‖ -grass) *n.* **1.** A low-growing, weedy plant *Polygonum aviculare,* having very small greenish flowers. Also called "allseed". **2.** Any of several similar plants.

knot·hole (nót-hōl) *n.* A hole in a piece of timber where a knot has dropped out or been removed.

knot·ted (nóttid) *adj.* **1.** Tied or fastened in or with a knot or knots. **2.** Intricate; knotty. **3.** Characterised by knots and knobs; gnarled: *a knotted branch.* **—get knotted.** *British Slang.* Used interjectionally to express disagreement, disapproval, or rejection.

knot·ty (nótti) *adj.* **-tier, -tiest. 1.** Tied or tangled in knots: *a knotty cord.* **2.** Covered with knots or knobs; gnarled: *a knotty plank.* **3.** Difficult to understand or solve; intricate; puzzling. **—**See Synonyms at **complex. —knot·ti·ness** *n.*

knot·weed (nót-weed) *n.* Any of several plants of the genus *Polygonum,* having jointed stems and inconspicuous flowers.

knout (nowt) *n.* A leather scourge formerly used for flogging criminals in Russia.
~*tr.v.* **knouted, knouting, knouts.** To flog with a knout. [French, from Russian *knut,* from Old Norse *knūtr,* knot.]

know (nō) *v.* **knew** (new ‖ nōō), **known** (nōn ‖ nó-ən), **knowing, knows.** **—***tr.* **1.** To perceive directly with the senses or mind; apprehend with clarity or certainty: *didn't know the answer.* **2.** To be certain of; regard or accept as true beyond doubt. **3.** To be capable of; have the skill to. Used with *how: know how to swim.* **4.** To have a thorough or practical understanding of, as through experience or study: *knows the rules of bridge.* **5. a.** To have personal experience of: *has never known real hunger.* **b.** To be subjected to or limited by: *grief that knows no bounds.* **6.** To have firmly secured in the mind or memory. **7.** To be able to distinguish; recognise: *Do you know him from his twin brother?* **8.** To be acquainted or familiar with. **9.** To see, hear, or experience. Used only in perfect tenses: *I've never known her lose her temper; He's never been known to be late.* **10.** *Archaic.* To have sexual intercourse with: *"And Adam knew Eve his wife; and she conceived"* (Genesis 4:1). **—***intr.* **1.** To possess knowledge. **2.** To be cognisant or aware. **—in the know.** Possessing correct or exclusive information. [Know, knew, known; Middle English *knowen, knew, knowe(n),* Old English *(ge)cnāwan, (ge)cnēow, (ge)cnāwen.*] **—know·a·ble** *adj.* **—know·er** *n.*
Usage: In negative constructions, *know* may be followed by clauses introduced by *that, whether,* or *if: I don't know that/ whether/if he can come.* There is, however, a difference of meaning between *I don't know whether/if he can come* and *I don't know that he can come.* The latter is a milder version of *I doubt that he can come,* whereas the former pair are neutral with respect to whether he can come or not.

know-all (nó-awl) *n. Informal.* A person who believes himself to be exceptionally well-informed and displays his knowledge in an arrogant or outspoken fashion.

know-how (nó-how) *n. Informal.* Knowledge, skill, or ingenuity.

know·ing (nó-ing) *adj.* **1.** Possessing knowledge or understanding. **2.** Suggestive of secret or private information: *a knowing glance.* **3.** Clever; shrewd. **4.** Planned; deliberate. **—**See Synonyms at **intelligent. —know·ing·ly** *adv.* **—know·ing·ness** *n.*

know-it-all (nó-it-awl) *n. Chiefly U.S. Informal.* A know-all.

knowl·edge (nóllij) *n.* **1.** The state or fact of knowing. **2.** Familiarity, awareness, or understanding gained through experience or study. **3.** That which is known, as: **a.** The sum or range of what has been perceived, discovered, or inferred. **b.** Specific information about something. **4.** Learning; erudition: *men of knowledge.* **5.** *Archaic.* Sexual intercourse; copulation. Now used only in the legal phrase *carnal knowledge.* **—to (one's) knowledge. a.** So far as one knows. **b.** Known to one as a certain fact. [Middle English *knowlege, know(e)lech,* from *cnawlechen, know(e)lechen,* to confess, recognise, Old English *cnāwlǣcan* (unattested), from *cnāwan,* to KNOW.]
Synonyms: knowledge, information, learning, erudition, lore, scholarship, wisdom, enlightenment.

knowl·edge·a·ble, knowl·edg·a·ble (nóllijəb'l) *adj.* Well-informed.

known (nōn ‖ nó-ən). Past participle of **know.**
~*adj.* Proved or generally recognised: *a known crook; the only known case of recovery from the disease.*
~*n.* Something that is known: *proceed from the known to the unknown.*

know-noth·ing (nó-nuthing ‖ -nothing) *n.* A complete ignoramus.

Knox (noks), **John** (*c.* 1505–72). Leader of the Scottish Reformation. He became chaplain to Edward VI (1551) but after the accession of the Roman Catholic Mary Tudor (1553) he fled to Geneva, where he was influenced by Calvin. After Mary's death (1558), Knox returned to Scotland (1559) and by 1560 the Confession of

Faith was drawn up, and Protestantism became the established religion in Scotland despite the subsequent efforts of Mary, Queen of Scots.

Knox·ville (nóks-vil). Industrial port in Tennessee, in the United States. On the Tennessee river, it was settled in 1786, and was twice state capital (1796-1812, 1817-19). It is the seat of the Tennessee Valley Authority.

knuck·le (núck'l) n. **1.** Anatomy. **a.** Any joint or region around a joint of a finger, especially one of the joints connecting the fingers to the hand. **b.** Any of the rounded protuberances formed by the bones in such a joint. **2.** A cut of meat centring on the carpal joint, such as that of a pig. **3.** The part of a hinge through which the pin passes. **4.** A joint between two members of a structure or mechanism in which the two components are at an angle to each other. **—near** or **close to the knuckle.** Approaching what is conventionally regarded as indecent.
~tr.v. **knuckled, -ling, -les. 1.** To press, rub, or hit with the knuckles of the fist. **2.** To shoot (a marble) with the thumb over the bent forefinger. **—knuckle down.** Informal. To apply oneself earnestly: knuckled down to his work. **—knuckle under.** To yield to pressure; give in. [Middle English knokel, from Middle Low German knökel.]

knuck·le·bone (núck'l-bōn) n. A knobbed bone, as of a knuckle or joint.

knuck·le·bones n. Used with a singular verb. The game of **jacks** (see).

knuck·le·dust·er (núck'l-dustərz) n. A weapon consisting of a piece of metal that fits snugly over the knuckles.

knuckle joint n. **1.** A joint forming a knuckle. **2.** A hinged, flexible joint formed by the juncture of two rods or projections, one inside the other and the two locked by a pin that functions as an axle.

knuck·le·head (núck'l-hed) n. Informal. A fool or idiot.

knuckle sandwich n. Slang. A punch in the mouth.

knur, knurr (nur) n. A bump or knot, as on a tree trunk. [Middle English knorre, swelling, from Germanic, akin to Middle Low German and Middle High German knorre, knot, knob.]

knurl (nurl) n. **1.** A knob, knot, or similar protuberance. **2.** Any of a series of small ridges or beads placed along the edge of a metal object to aid in gripping. [Probably from KNUR (influenced by GNARL).] **—knurled, knurl·y** adj.

Knut. See **Canute.**

KO (káy-ṓ) tr.v. **KO'd, KO'ing, KO's.** Also **K.O., k.o., ka·yo.** Slang. To knock out.
~n., pl. **KOs, KO's.** Slang. In boxing, a **knockout** (see).

ko·a (kṓ-ə) n. **1.** A Hawaian tree, Acacia koa. **2.** The hard, reddish wood of this tree, used especially for making furniture. [Hawaiian.]

ko·a·la (kō-áälə) n. An arboreal marsupial, Phascolarctos cinereus, of Australia, having greyish fur and feeding chiefly on the leaves and bark of eucalyptus trees. Also called "koala bear", Australian "native bear". [Earlier koola, from native Australian name külla.]

ko·an (kṓ-an) n. In Zen Buddhism, a problem or riddle that aims to break down logical reasoning. [Japanese.]

Ko·be (kṓ-bi, -bay). City in south Honshu in Japan. On Osaka Bay at the eastern end of the Inland Sea, it is the chief port of the industrial Osaka and Kinki plain districts. It has major shipbuilding facilities, and produces sugar, rubber, and ferrous metals.

København. See **Copenhagen.**

Ko·blenz or **Coblenz** (kō-blénts, kə-; German kṓ-blents) A city in Germany, founded by the Romans (first century A.D.) at the confluence of the Rhine and Mosel rivers. The centre of the Moselle wine trade, it also produces pianos, furniture, clothing, and paper.

ko·bo (kṓbō) n., pl. **kobo.** A Nigerian coin equal to ¹/₁₀₀ of a naira. [Alteration of English copper (penny).]

ko·bold (kṓ-bōd, kó-; German -bolt) n. In German folklore: **1.** A mischievous household elf. **2.** A gnome that haunts underground places such as mines and caves. [German Kobold, from Middle High German kobolt.]

Koch (kokh), **Robert** (1843-1910). German bacteriologist. He discovered the cholera bacillus and the bacterial origin of anthrax. He was awarded the Nobel prize (1905) for his work on tuberculosis.

Köch·el number (kérk'l, kókh'l) n. Abbr. **K.** A number assigned to each of the compositions of Mozart as listed in the catalogue of Ludwig Köchel (1800-77).

Kochi (kṓ-chī). See **Cochin.**

Ko·dály (kṓ-dī), **Zoltán** (1882-1967). Hungarian composer. His works include an opera Háry János (1926), Te Deum (1936), and Missa Brevis (1945).

Ko·di·ak (kṓdi-ak). An island of the United States. Lying in the Shelikof Strait off the south coast of Alaska, it was settled by Russians (1784) as a whale- and seal-hunting centre.

Kodiak bear n. A form of the brown bear, Ursus arctos, of islands and coastal areas of Alaska, sometimes considered a separate species, U. middendorffi.

koek·sis·ter (kṓok-sistər) n. In South Africa, a sweet cake consisting of a plait or twisted roll of dough deep-fried and coated with thin syrup. [Afrikaans, from Dutch koek, cake + sister, sizzler, from sissen, to hiss, sizzle.]

ko·el (kṓ-əl) n. A cuckoo, Eudynamys scolopacea, found in India, southeast Asia, and Australia, that lays its eggs in the nests of crows. [Hindi, from Sanskrit kokila.]

Koest·ler (kérst-lər, kóst- || kést-), **Arthur** (1905-83). Hungarian-born British author and journalist. Educated in Vienna, he became a Communist, but his novel Darkness at Noon (1940) shows his disillusionment with communism as practised in the U.S.S.R. While reporting the Spanish Civil War he narrowly escaped execu-

tion by Franco. In his later works, such as The Sleepwalkers (1959) and The Ghost in the Machine (1968), he explores various philosophical aspects of science and psychology.

Koff·ka (kóf-kə || U.S. káwf-), **Kurt** (1886-1941). German-U.S. psychologist. With Wolfgang Köhler and Max Wertheimer (1880-1943), he helped to formulate the principles of **Gestalt psychology.**

kof·ta (kóftə) n. An Indian dish in which the ingredients, usually chopped meat or vegetables together with spices, are formed into balls and served in a sauce. [Urdu.]

kohl (kōl) n. A preparation used chiefly in Muslim and Asian countries as a cosmetic around the eyes, on the eyebrows, or the like. [Arabic kuḥl, koḥl, powder of antimony. See also **alcohol.**]

Kohl (kōl), **Helmut** (1930-). German politician. He became Chancellor of West Germany in 1982, and in 1990 formed the first government after German reunification. He was re-elected in 1994.

Köhl·er (kérl-ər, kṓl-), **Wolfgang** (1887-1967). German-U.S. psychologist, cofounder with Kurt Koffka and Max Wertheimer (1880-1943) of **Gestalt psychology.**

kohl·ra·bi (kōl-ra'abi || U.S. also -rábbi) n., pl. **-bies.** A plant, Brassica caulorapa, with a thickened stem that is eaten as a vegetable. Also called "turnip cabbage". [German Kohlrabi (influenced by Kohl, cabbage), from Italian cavoli rape, plural of cavolo rapa : cavolo, cole, cabbage, from Latin caulis + rapa, turnip, from Latin rāpa, rāpum.]

koi·ne (kóy-nee, -nay) n. **1.** Usually capital **K.** A dialect of Ancient Greek during the Hellenistic age, developed primarily from Attic and eventually replacing the local dialects, forming a common language used throughout the Hellenistic world from which the later stages of Greek are descended. **2.** A language common to people speaking different languages; a lingua franca. [Greek koinē (dialektos), "common (language)", from koinos, common.]

Koko Nor. See **Qinghai.**

Ko·kosch·ka (ko-kóshkə, kō-), **Oskar** (1886-1980). Austrian-born expressionist painter, skilled at portraits and landscapes. He left Nazi Germany and settled in England and later in Switzerland.

kok·sa·ghyz (kók-sə-géez, -gízz || U.S. also kók-) n. A dandelion, Taraxacum kok-saghyz, of central Asia, having fleshy roots that yield a form of rubber. [Russian kok-sagyz, from Turkish kok-sagiz : kok, root + sagiz, rubber.]

kola. Variant of **cola** (nut-bearing tree).

kola nut. Variant of **cola nut.**

Kol·chak (kól-chək, -chak), **Alexandr Vasilyevich** (1874-1920). Russian admiral. He was commander of the Black Sea fleet during World War I and after the 1917 October Revolution, led the White Russians against the Bolsheviks. He was recognised by the Allies as head of the provisional Russian government (1918-20), but he was captured and shot by the Bolsheviks.

ko·lin·sky (kə-línski) n., pl. **-skies. 1.** Any of several minks of northern Eurasia, especially Mustela siberica. **2.** The tawny fur of such an animal. [Russian kolinský, "(mink) of Kola", from Kola, district in northwestern Russia.]

kol·khoz, kol·koz (kol-kóz, -káwz; Russian kəl-kháwss) n. pl. **-khozes** or **-khozy.** A collective farm in the former U.S.S.R. [Russian, contraction of kollektivnoe khozyaistvo : kollektivnoe, neuter of kollektivny, collective + khozyaistvo, household, farm.]

Köln (köln). English **Co·logne** (kə-lōn). City and port on the west bank of the Rhine in North Rhine-Westphalia, Germany. It is a major industrial city, producing iron and steel, machinery, chemicals, textiles, and eau de Cologne.

Kol Ni·dre (káwl níddray, nee-dráy || U.S. kōl) n. Judaism. The opening prayer recited on the eve of Yom Kippur, containing a declaration of the annulment of all personal vows of the preceding year. [Aramaic kol nidhrē, "all vows", from its opening words.]

Komenský, Jan. See **Comenius, John Amos.**

Ko·mo·do dragon (kə-mṓdō) n. A large monitor lizard, Varanus komodoensis, of the Indonesian islands of Komodo and Flores. It is the largest living lizard, growing up to 3 metres (10 feet) long.

Kom·so·mol (kóm-sə-mol, -mól; Russian kəm-) n. In the former U.S.S.R., a communist youth organisation. [Russian, acronym of Kommunistichesky Soyuz Molodyozhi, Communist Union of Youth.]

kon·fyt (kón-fayt) n. South African. Crystallised or preserved fruit, often in syrup. [Afrikaans, from Dutch konfijt, preserves.]

Kon·go¹ (kóng-gō). **1.** Variant of Congo. **2.** A powerful African state founded in the 14th century. It covered the area now occupied by the republic of Angola and both Congo republics.

Kongo² n., pl. **Kongos** or collectively **Kongo. 1.** A member of a Bantu people of the region of the lower Congo River. **2.** The language of this people.

kon·go·ni (kong-gṓni, kəng-) n. A large antelope, Alcelaphus buselaphus, of East Africa that is a species of hartebeest. [Swahili.]

Königsberg. See **Kaliningrad.**

ko·ni·ol·o·gy (kṓni-óllaji) n. The scientific study of atmospheric dust and its effects. [Greek konia, dust + -LOGY.]

Kon·ka·ni (kóngkəni) n. An Indic language related to Marathi and spoken on the west coast of India south of Maharashtra and north of Kerala.

Kon·stanz or **Con·stanz** (kon-shtánts). English **Con·stance** (kónstənss). Port in Baden-Württemberg in southwestern Germany, lying on the Bodensee (Lake Constance). Its industries include chemicals, electrical equipment, textiles, and tourism.

Kon·ya (kon-yáä). Latin **I·co·ni·um** (ī-kṓni-əm). Capital of Konya province in central Turkey. It markets grains, sugar, flax, fruit, and livestock, and produces carpets, silk goods, and cotton. In the 13th century, the order of the dancing dervishes was founded in the city.

koodoo. Variant of **kudu.**

kook (kook) *n. Chiefly U.S. Informal.* An amusingly eccentric or zany person. [Perhaps from CUCKOO.] —**kook·y** *adj.* —**kook·i·ness** *n.*

kook·a·bur·ra (kookə-burrə) *n.* A large kingfisher, *Dacelo novaeguineae* (or *D. gigas*), of Australia and adjacent areas, having a call resembling raucous laughter. Also called "laughing jackass". [Native Australian name.]

kop (kop) *n. South African.* An isolated hill or peak. [Afrikaans, "head, hill".]

ko·peck, co·peck, ko·pek (kṓ-pek, kó-) *n. Abbr.* **k., K.** A coin equal to $\frac{1}{100}$ of the Russian rouble. [Russian *kopyeika*, from *kopye*, lance (from the figure of the tsar with a lance in his hand originally stamped on the coin), from *kopat'*, to hack.]

koppie, kopje (kóppi) *n. South African.* A small, isolated hill. [Afrikaans, diminutive of KOP.]

Ko·ran, Qur'an (ko-raán, kaw-, kə- || -rán) *n.* The sacred text of Islam, believed to contain the revelations made by Allah to Muhammad. Also called "Alcoran". [Arabic *qur'ān*, reading, recitation, from *qara'a*, to read, recite.] —**Ko·ran·ic** (-ránnik) *adj.*

Kor·but (kór-boot), **Olga (Valentinovna)** (1955–). Belarussian gymnast. She won three gold medals and one silver at the 1972 Olympic Games, and one gold and one silver medal at the 1976 Olympics.

Kor·da (kórdə), **Sir Alexander,** born Sándor Laszlo (1893–1956). Hungarian-born British film producer. His productions include *The Scarlet Pimpernel* (1934) and *The Third Man* (1949). Knighted 1942.

Kor·do·fan (kórdə-fán, -faán). Province in southern Sudan. —**Kor·do·fan·i·an** (-fánni-ən) *adj.*

Ko·re·a (kə-réer, ko-, kaw-, -rée-ə). *Korean* **Cho·son** (chṓ-són); *Japanese* **Cho·sen** (chṓ-sén). Peninsula in northeast Asia. Extending southwards between the Yellow Sea and the Sea of Japan, it is mainly mountainous. Civilised from *c.* 1200 B.C., it was united under the kingdom of Silla (A.D. 668), and despite a Mongol invasion (13th century) it survived until a Japanese occupation (1910–45). Following World War II, the Soviet and U.S. occupied zones became separate republics; the northern, Soviet-sponsored republic invaded the south (1950), which resisted with the aid of U.N. forces. The border was established by treaty (1953), dividing the peninsula into South Korea and North Korea.

Korea, North. Official name the **People's Democratic Republic of Korea.** Asian republic. Lying north of the 1953 ceasefire line, it has the bulk of the peninsula's mineral resources. With Soviet aid, it built up its industries and intensified the cultivation of its limited fertile land, but has had economic problems recently. Its chief exports are metals. Area, 120 538 square kilometres (46,528 square miles). Population, 22,470,000. Capital, Pyongyang.

Korea, South. Official name the **Republic of Korea.** Asian republic. It has few natural resources apart from coal, iron ore, and graphite. Though more than a third of the population is still engaged in agriculture, the republic has developed its industries

with U.S. aid and its growth rates were among the world's highest from the 1980s until its problems of the later 1990s. Area, 99 392 square kilometres (38,375 square miles). Population, 45,540,000. Capital, Seoul.

Ko·re·an (kə-réern, ko-, kaw-, -rée-ən) *adj.* Of or pertaining to Korea, its inhabitants, or their language.

~*n.* **1.** A native or inhabitant of Korea. **2.** The language of Korea, containing many words of Chinese origin.

Korean War *n.* A war between North Korea, helped by China, and South Korea, helped by United Nations forces consisting of mainly U.S. troops (1950–53).

korf·ball (kórf-bawl) *n.* A game of Dutch origin that resembles basketball and is played by teams of both sexes. [Dutch *korfbal,* basketball.]

Korinthos. See **Corinth.**

Kort·rijk (kórt-rīk). *French* **Cour·trai** (koortray). City of West Flanders province in Belgium, lying on the river Leie (Lys). It was a major centre of the medieval cloth industry of Flanders.

ko·ru·na (ko-roōn-ə, kō̄-, -aa) *n., pl.* **-ny** (-ee) or **-nas.** *Abbr.* **k., K.** **1.** The basic monetary unit of Czechoslovakia, equal to 100 halers. Also called "crown". **2.** A coin worth one koruna. [Czech, "crown", from Latin *corōna,* CROWN.]

Kos. See **Cos.**

Kos·ci·us·ko[1] (kossi-úskō). Australia's highest mountain (2 228 metres; 7,310 feet). Part of the Snowy Mountains of southeast New South Wales, it is a winter sports centre. It is named after the Polish patriot, Tadeusz Kościuszko (1746–1817).

Kosciusko[2] *adj.* Of or designating an epoch of the Cenozoic era in Australia, or the rocks laid down during it. The epoch corresponds with the Pliocene and Pleistocene epochs of other parts of the world. [From KOSCIUSKO[1].]

ko·sher (kṓshər) *adj.* **1.** Conforming to or prepared in accordance with Jewish dietary laws, as: **a.** Slaughtered or prepared for eating according to rabbinic law; ritually pure: *kosher meat.* **b.** Restricting one's diet to such food. **c.** Specialising in the preparation or sale of such food: *a kosher delicatessen.* Compare **tref.** **2.** *Informal.* **a.** Proper; correct; permissible. **b.** Genuine; legitimate. —**keep kosher.** To obey the Jewish dietary laws.

~*n.* Kosher food.

~*tr.v.* **koshered, -shering, -shers.** To make kosher. [Yiddish, from Hebrew *kāshēr,* proper.]

Ko·so·vo (kósso-vō), **Republic of.** Former province of Serbia. Its population is mainly ethnic Albanian, with a Serb minority. In 1992, during the disintegration of Yugoslavia, elections in the province were won by the Democratic Alliance of Kosovo, which proclaimed an independent republic. The elections were declared illegal by the Serbian authorities, whose repression of the ethnic Albanians has brought international condemnation. Capital, Pristina.

Kos·suth (kóshoot), **Lajos** (1802–94). Hungarian revolutionary leader. He aimed for Hungarian independence from Austria. He was appointed provisional governor of the 1849 Hungarian Republic, but after Russian intervention, he fled to Turkey.

Ko·sy·gin (ko-séegin, kə-), **Alexei Nikolayevich** (1904–80). Soviet premier (chairman of Council of Ministers) (1964–80). He was deputy chairman of the Council of Ministers (1940–53) but he lost his position after Stalin's death (1953). He became a full member of the Politburo (1966) and premier on the fall of Khrushchev.

ko·to (kṓtō) *n.* A Japanese musical instrument that has 13 strings stretched over an oblong box. [Japanese.]

koumis, koumiss. Variants of **kumiss.**

Kous·se·vits·ky (koo-sə-vítski), **Sergei** (1874–1951). Russian-U.S. conductor. He left Russia in 1920 and eventually settled in the United States. He set up the Koussevitsky Music Foundation (1942) to encourage new composers.

ko·whai (kṓ-wī, -fī, -hwī) *n.* A New Zealand tree, *Sophora tetraptera,* with golden, sweet-smelling flowers.

Kowloon. See **Jiulong.**

kow·tow (ków-tów, kō̄- || *U.S.* -tow) *n.* Also **ko·tow** (kō̄́). **1.** A Chinese salutation in which one touches the forehead to the ground as an expression of respect or submission. **2.** An obsequious act.

~*intr.v.* **kowtowed, -towing, -tows.** **1.** To perform a kowtow. **2.** To show servile deference; fawn: *kowtowed to the directors.* [Mandarin Chinese *ké tóu* : *ké,* to knock, bump + *tóu,* head.]

KP *Chess.* king's pawn.

Kr The symbol for the element krypton.

KR *Chess.* king's rook.

kr. **1.** krona. **2.** krone.

kraal, craal (kraal || krawl) *n.* **1.** A village of rural black people in southern Africa, typically consisting of huts surrounded by a stockade. **2.** An enclosure for livestock in southern Africa.

~*tr.v.* **kraaled, kraaling, kraals.** To put or keep (livestock) in a kraal. [Afrikaans, "enclosure for cattle", from Portuguese *curral,* of Latin origin. See also **corral.**]

kraft (kraaft || kraft) *n.* A tough wrapping paper made from sulphate wood pulp. [German *Kraft,* force, strength, from Old High German, from Germanic *kraftaz* (unattested). See **craft.**]

Krafft-E·bing (kraáft-ébbing, kráft-; *German* -áybing), **Baron Richard von** (1840–1902). German neurologist and psychiatrist. He studied paranoia, epilepsy, and sexual deviance. He is best known today for his work, *Psychopathia Sexualis* (1886).

krait (krīt) *n.* Any of several brightly coloured, venomous snakes of the genus *Bungarus,* of southeastern Asia. [Hindi *karait†.*]

Kra·ka·to·a (krácka-tṓ-ə, kraáka-). Also **Kra·ka·tau** (-tow). Small volcanic island. Lying in the Strait of Sunda, west of Java and east of Sumatra, it was blown apart (1883) by one of the largest volcanic eruptions ever recorded, causing a tsunami that killed over 36,000 people. The explosion was heard in Australia, 5 000 kilometres (3,000 miles) away.

kra·ken (kraáken) *n.* A legendary sea monster said to dwell in Norwegian waters. [Dialectal Norwegian : *krake†,* kraken + *-n,* suffix used as the definite article.]

Kra·ków, Cra·cow (krák-ow, kraák-, -ō; *Polish* krákōōf). City and river port in southern Poland. Founded in the 8th century, on the river Vistula, it was the national capital from 1305 to 1595, and remains an important cultural centre. The Jagiellonian University (1364) is one of the oldest in Europe. Kraków produces metals, machinery, chemicals, clothing, and rolling stock.

kra·me·ri·a (krə-méer-i-ə) *n.* A dried root, the **rhatany** *(see).* [New Latin (Linnaeus), after J.G.H. *Kramer,* 18th-century Austrian botanist.]

krans (kraans) *n. South African.* An overhanging, sheer wall of rock; a precipice. [Afrikaans.]

K ration *n.* A U.S. Army emergency field ration used in World War II, consisting of a single compact meal. [After A. B. *Keys* (1904–), U.S. physiologist and nutritional consultant.]

kraton. Variant of **craton.**

kraut (krowt) *n. Slang.* A German. Used derogatorily.

Krebs (krebz), **Sir Hans (Adolf)** (1900–81). British biochemist, born in Germany. He discovered the **Krebs cycle.** He shared the Nobel prize for medicine (1953) with Fritz Lipmann.

Krebs cycle *n.* A series of enzymatic reactions that constitute the second stage of respiration in aerobic organisms, involving the breakdown of acetyl units, especially during respiration, to provide the main source of energy for cells in the form of ATP. Also called "citric acid cycle", "tricarboxylic acid cycle". [After Hans KREBS.]

Kreis·ler (kríss-lər), **Fritz** (1875–1962). Austrian virtuoso violinist and composer.

krem·lin (krém-lin) *n.* **1.** The citadel of a Russian town or city. **2.** *Capital* **K. a.** The citadel of Moscow, housing the offices of the Russian government. **2.** The former Soviet government. [French, from Russuan *kreml',* citadel, of Tatar origin.]

krem·lin·ol·o·gy (krémlin-óllǝji) *n.* The study and analysis of the politics of the former Soviet government. —**krem·lin·ol·o·gist** *n.*

kreut·zer (króytsǝr) *n.* Any of several small coins of low value, formerly used in Austria and Germany. [German *Kreuzer,* from Middle High German *kriuzer,* from *kriuze,* a cross (originally stamped with a cross), from Old High German *krūzi,* from Latin *crux,* CROSS.]

Kriem·hild (kréem-hild; *German* -hilt). Also **Kriem·hil·de** (-hildǝ). In the Nibelungenlied, the wife of Siegfried and avenger of his murder.

krill (kril) *pl.n.* Small marine crustaceans of the order Euphausiacea, constituting the principal food of whalebone whales. [Norwegian *kril†,* young of fish.]

krim·mer (krímmǝr) *n.* Grey, curly fur made from the pelts of lambs of the Crimean region. [German *Krimmer,* from *Krim,* the Crimean peninsula.]

Kri·o (krée-ō) *n., pl.* **-os.** **1.** A creolised language based on English and spoken in Sierra Leone. **2.** A native speaker of Krio. [Alteration of CREOLE.]

kris, crease, creese (kreess; *sometimes* kriss) *n.* A sword of Malayan origin having a wavy double-edged blade. [Malay *kěris.*]

Krish·na (kríshnǝ). *Hinduism.* The eighth and principal avatar of the deity Vishnu, often depicted as a handsome young man playing a flute. See **Bhagavad-Gita.** [Hindi, "the black one", from Sanskrit *kṛṣṇáh,* black.] —**Krish·na·ism** *n.*

Kris·tian·sand, Chris·tian·sand (kríss-chǝn-sand, -ti-ǝn-; *Norwegian* -san). Seaport of southern Norway. In Vest-Agder county, on the Skagerrak, it has shipbuilding, fishery, and timber industries.

kro·na (krṓ-nǝ) *n., pl.* **-nor** (-nawr). *Abbr.* **k., K., kr. 1.** The basic monetary unit of Sweden, equal to 100 öre. **2.** A coin worth one krona. [Swedish, "crown", from Old Swedish *krūna, krōna,* from Latin *corōna,* wreath, CROWN.]

kró·na (krṓ-nǝ) *n., pl.* **-nur** (-nǝr). *Abbr.* **k., K., kr. 1.** The basic monetary unit of Iceland, equal to 100 aurar. **2.** A coin worth one króna. [Icelandic *krōna,* from Old Norse *krūna,* crown, from Middle Low German, from Latin *corōna,* CROWN.]

kro·ne (krṓ-nǝ) *n., pl.* **-ner** (-nǝr). *Abbr.* **k., K., kr. 1.** The basic monetary unit of Denmark and Norway, equal to 100 öre. **2.** A coin worth one krone. [Danish *krone* and Norwegian *krune,* "crown", from Old Norse *krūna,* from Latin *corōna,* CROWN.]

Kronos. Variant of **Cronos.**

Kron·shtadt (krón-shtat; *Russian* krun-shtát). *German* **Kron·stadt** (krṓn-shtat). Russian seaport and naval base on the island of Kotlin in the Gulf of Finland. Its importance declined in the 19th century after the construction of a deep-water canal to St. Petersburg. The Kronshtadt Mutiny (1921) of disaffected sailors precipitated Lenin's New Economic Policy.

Kro·pot·kin (krǝ-pót-kin, kro-), **Prince Pyotr Alexeyevich** (1842–1921). Russian anarchist revolutionary. He joined the anarchist movement in 1872 and was imprisoned in Russia (1874–76), but escaped, and again in France (1883–86). He settled in England in 1886 and wrote *Memoirs of a Revolutionist* (1899). In 1917 he returned to Russia, but disliked the extremism of the Bolsheviks.

KRP *Chess.* king's rook's pawn.

Kru (krṓ) *n., pl.* **Krus** or collectively **Kru.** Also **Kroo. 1.** A member

of a Negro people living mainly on the coast of Liberia. **2.** The language of these people.

Kru·ger (krṓōgǝr), **(Stephanus Johannes) Paul(us)** (1825-1904). Afrikaner leader of South Africa. His nationalist policies as president of the Transvaal Republic from 1883 led to the second Boer War (1899-1902). He fled the advancing British in 1900 and died in exile in Switzerland.

Kruger National Park. A wildlife reserve in northeast South Africa. Extending along the Mozambique border of Mpumalanga province, it occupies an area of 21 000 square kilometres (8,106 square miles). It originated as the Sabi Game Reserve established by President Kruger in 1898, and opened to the public in 1928.

kru·ger·rand (krṓōgǝr-rand, -ront) *n.* A coin containing one troy ounce of pure gold, minted in South Africa but widely used by investors or speculators in gold. [Afrikaans, after S.J.P. KRUGER, whose portrait appears on the obverse.]

krummhorn. Variant of **crumhorn.**

Krung Thep (krōong tepp). *English* **Bang·kok** (báng-kok, bang-kók). Capital and chief port of Thailand, situated on the Chao Phraya near the Gulf of Thailand. It is the country's main cultural, commercial, and industrial centre, and one of the leading cities of Southeast Asia, with an international jewellery market. Within the city are the royal palace, and more than 400 Buddhist temples.

Krupp (krṓōp). German family of arms manufacturers, whose factories in Essen were founded in the early 19th century, and are still in production.

kryp·ton (krípton) *n. Symbol* **Kr** A whitish, inert, gaseous element used chiefly in gas-discharge lamps, fluorescent lamps, and electronic flash tubes. Atomic number 36, atomic weight 83.80, melting point –156.6°C, boiling point –152.30°C, density 3.73 kg per m³ (0°C). [New Latin, "hidden (element)", from Greek *krupton,* neuter of *kruptos,* hidden, from *kruptein,* to hide.]

Ksha·tri·ya (kshát-ri-ǝ, shát-) *n.* **1.** One of the four Hindu castes, including the professional, governing, and military occupations. **2.** A member of this caste. See **caste.** [Sanskrit *kṣatriya,* "ruling, ruler", from *kṣatra,* rule, dominion, from *kṣayati,* he possesses, he rules.]

K.St.J. Knight (of the Order) of St. John.

Kt knight.

kt. 1. karat. **2.** *Nautical.* knot.

K.T. 1. Knight (of the Order) of the Thistle. **2.** Knight Templar.

Kua·la Lum·pur (kwaála lṓom-poor, -lúm-). The capital of Malaysia. On the river Kelang, in Peninsular Malaysia, it is the commercial centre of a tin-mining and rubber-growing area.

Kuang-tung. See **Guangdong.**

Ku·be·lík (kṓōbǝ-lik; *Czech* kṓobeleek), **Jan** (1880–1940). Czech violinist. He was a child prodigy, but in later life, though technically brilliant, had a small repertoire. He wrote three violin concertos. His son, Rafael (1914–96) left Prague in 1948. He was music director of the Royal Opera, Covent Garden (1955–58) and of the New York Metropolitan Opera (1972–74).

Ku·blai Khan (kṓōb-lī kảan, kṓōb-) (1215–94). Fifth of the Mongol Great Khans and first Mongol emperor of China. He was a grandson of Genghis Khan, and became Khan in 1259. He founded the Yuan dynasty (1279) and made Buddhism the state religion. Marco Polo, the traveller, spent 17 years at Kublai Khan's court.

Ku·brick (kéwbrik), **Stanley** (1928–). U.S. film director. His films include *Lolita* (1962), *Dr. Strangelove* (1963), *2001: A Space Odyssey* (1969), *A Clockwork Orange* (1971), and *Eyes Wide Shut* (1997).

ku·chen (kṓō-kh'n, -kǝn) *n. Chiefly U.S.* A yeast-raised cake originally from Germany that contains fruits and nuts and is usually crusted with sugar and spices. [German *Kuchen,* from Middle High German *kuoche,* cake, from Old High German *kuocho.*]

ku·dos (kéw-doss ‖ *U.S. also* -dōss) *n.* Acclaim or prestige as a result of achievement or position: *The prize gave him little material benefit but much kudos.* [Originally British university slang, from Greek *kudos,* glory, fame.]

ku·du, koo·doo (kṓō-dṓo; *South African* kṓo-) *n.* Either of two African antelopes, *Tragelaphus strepsiceros* or *T. imberbis,* having a brownish coat with narrow white vertical stripes and long, spirally curved horns in the male. [Afrikaans *koedoe,* from Xhosa *iqudu.*]

kud·zu (kṓōdzṓo) *n.* A vine, *Pueraria lobata,* native to Japan, having compound leaves and clusters of reddish-purple flowers and grown for fodder and forage. [Japanese *kuzu.*]

Ku·fic, Cu·fic (kṓō-fik, kéw-) *adj.* Designating or pertaining to an early form of the Arabic alphabet used for making fine copies of the Koran. [Arabic *Al Kufah,* town in south-central Iraq, where such copies of the Koran were made.] —**Ku·fic** *n.*

Ku Klux Klan (kṓō klúks klán, kéw) *n. Abbr.* **K.K.K. 1.** A secret society organised in the southern United States after the Civil War to reassert white supremacy by terroristic methods. **2.** A secret organisation founded in Georgia in 1915, chiefly composed of white protestants, and modelled upon the earlier society in aims and practice. [Said to be Greek *kuklos,* circle, CYCLE + *klan,* from CLAN.] —**Ku Kluxer, Ku Klux Klan·ner** *n.* —**Ku Klux·ism** *n.*

kuk·ri (kṓōkri) *n.* A large knife with a blade broadening to the point, used especially by the Gurkhas. [Hindi.]

ku·lak (kṓō-lak ‖ kéw-, -laak) *n.* **1.** In Tsarist Russia and during the October Revolution, a rich peasant or village usurer notorious as an exploiter. **2.** One of a class of Russian peasants after the revolution who opposed the collectivisation of farms and later had their property confiscated or were themselves liquidated. [Russian, "fist", "tight-fisted person", from Turkic, akin to Turkish *kol,* arm.]

Kul·tur (kŏŏl-tŏŏr) *n.* Culture; especially, the authoritarian and chauvinistic aspects of German culture and civilisation as idealised by the exponents of German imperialism during the period 1900–45. [German, from Latin *cultūra,* CULTURE.]

Kul·tur·kampf (kŏŏl-tŏŏr-kampf ‖ -kaampf) *n.* **1.** The struggle (1872–87) between the Roman Catholic Church and the German government for control over civil marriage and school and church appointments. **2.** Any conflict between secular and religious authorities. [German, "culture struggle".]

Ku·mas·i (kŏŏ-mássi, kŏŏ-). Formerly **Coo·mas·sie.** The second city of Ghana. Capital of the Ashanti region west of Lake Volta, it is the country's major centre for cocoa production and an important transport junction.

ku·miss, kou·mis, kou·miss (kŏŏ-miss) *n.* The fermented milk of a mare or ass, drunk by certain peoples of western and central Asia. [Russian *kumys,* from Kazan Tatar *kumyz.*]

küm·mel (kŏŏmm'l, kímm'l; *German* kümm'l) *n.* A colourless liqueur flavoured with caraway seeds or cumin. [German *Kümmel,* "cumin seed", from Old High German *kumil, kumīn,* from Latin *cumīnum,* CUMIN.]

kum·quat, cumquat (kúm-kwot) *n.* **1.** Any of several trees of the genus *Fortunella,* native to China, having small, edible, orange-like fruit. **2.** The fruit of such a tree, having acid pulp and a thin, edible rind, used in preserves. [Cantonese *kam kwat, gam gwat,* corresponding to Mandarin Chinese *jīn jú,* "golden orange".]

Kun (kŏŏn), **Béla** (1885 – *c.* 1939). Hungarian Communist leader. He formed the Hungarian Communist Party and became president of a coalition (1919), promising his allies Soviet support for war against Romania, but no support came. Kun fled to Vienna and then to the U.S.S.R., where he was executed in one of Stalin's purges.

Kunene, River. See **Cunene, River.**

kung fu (kúng-fŏŏ, kŏŏng-) *n.* A martial art originating in China and resembling karate. [From Chinese *gōng fu,* skill.]

Kun·ming, K'un-ming (kŏŏn-míng). Ancient walled city of southwest China. It is the capital of Yunnan province and the seat of Yunnan University.

kunz·ite (kŏŏn-sīt, kŏŏnt-) *n.* A transparent lilac-coloured variety of spodumene, used as a gemstone. [After George F. *Kunz* (1856–1932), U.S. gem expert.]

Kuomintang See **Guomindang.**

Kuo·yü, guo·yu (gwáw-yŏŏ) *n.* **Mandarin Chinese** *(see).* [Mandarin Chinese *gúoyü* : *gúo,* nation, nation + *yüh,* language.]

Kur·cha·to·vi·um (kúrcha-tŏvi-əm) *n.* The former name, in the U.S.S.R., for the chemical element **unnilquadium** *(see).* [New Latin, after I.V. *Kurchatov* (1903–1960), Soviet physicist.]

Kurd (kurd ‖ kŏŏrd) *n.* A member of a formerly nomadic Muslim people living chiefly in Kurdistan.

Kurd·ish (kúrd-ish ‖ kŏŏrd-) *adj.* Of or pertaining to the Kurds, their culture, or their language.
~*n.* The northwestern Iranian language of the Kurds.

Kurd·i·stan (kúrd-i-staán, kŏŏrd-, -stán). Area of western Asia. Lying west and southwest of the Caspian Sea, it was split between southeast Turkey, north Syria, north Iraq, northwest Iran, and south U.S.S.R. with the dissolution of the Ottoman Empire (1918). Its inhabitants, the Kurds, have been fighting in all these countries for the establishment of an independent state.

Ku·ro·sa·wa (kŏŏr-ō-saá-wa), **Akira** (1910–). Japanese film director. His *Rashomon* won the 1951 Venice Film Festival Grand Prize, and gave Japanese films international status. His films include *The Seven Samurai* (1954), *Dersu Uzala* (1975, Oscar), *Kagemusha* (1980), *Ran* (1985), and *Rhapsody in August* (1990).

Ku·ro·shi·o (kŏŏr-ō-shée-ō) *n.* The **Japan Current** *(see).*

kur·ra·jong (kúrrə-jong) *n.* **1.** An Australian tree, *Brachychiton populneus,* having evergreen leaves and yellowish or reddish flowers. **2.** Any of several other Australian trees, such as the green kurrajong, *Hibiscus heterophyllus,* which has edible leaves and shoots. [Native Australian name.]

Kursk (koorsk). Industrial city in western Russia. In 1943 Soviet forces routed a German army here in the world's largest tank battle.

kurta. Variant of **khurta.**

kur·to·sis (kur-tŏ-siss) *n. Statistics.* A deviation from the normal distribution curve in which the curve remains symmetrical but is either too sharp at the peak values *(positive kurtosis)* or too flat at the peak values *(negative kurtosis).* [Greek *kurtōsis,* convexity, curvature, from *kurtos,* convex.]

ku·ru (kŏŏr-ōō) *n.* A fatal neurological disease that is a spongiform encephalopathy caused by a virus, occurring in New Guinea and characterised by tremors affecting the whole body. Also called "trembling disease". [New Guinea native name.]

ku·ruş (kŏŏ-rŏŏsh) *n., pl.* **kuruş.** A Turkish coin, the **piaster** *(see).* [Turkish.]

Kush. See **Cush.**

Kushitic. Variant of **Cushitic.**

Kut-al-Amara. See **Al Kut.**

Kuwait, State of Sheikhdom of western Asia. On the east coast of the Arabian Peninsula, it was settled in 1756, and was a British protectorate from 1899 to 1961. Oil was discovered in 1938 and Kuwait became one of the world's major oil-producing countries, with oil accounting for 80 per cent of its exports. However, its abundant overseas investments have freed the economy from dependence on oil exports. In 1990 Kuwait was occupied by Iraq, whose forces were subsequently ejected by a United Nations coalition in the Gulf War, which caused massive damage to oil installations. Area,

17 818 square kilometres (6,878 squares miles). Population 1,690,000. Capital, Kuwait. See map at **Gulf States.** —**Ku·wai·ti** *n. & adj.*

Kuybyshov. See **Samara.**

Kuz·bas (kŏŏz-báss). Also **Kuz·netsk Basin** (kooz-nyétsk). Major industrial area of Russia, situated in western Siberia. Novokuznetsk and Novosibirsk are the main centres.

kV kilovolt.

kvass, kvas (kvass, kvaass) *n.* A fermented Russian beverage similar to beer, made from rye or barley. [Russian *kvas.*]

kvetch (kvech) *intr.v.* **kvetched, kvetching, kvetches.** *U.S. Slang.* To complain or find fault in a persistent, querulous manner.
~*n. U.S. Slang.* A chronic and annoying complainer. [Yiddish, from German *quetschen,* to crush, squeeze, from Middle High German *quetzen.*]

kW kilowatt.

Kwa (kwaa) *n.* A branch of the Niger-Congo language family, including Ibo, Yoruba, and other languages. —**Kwa** *adj.*

kwa·cha (kwácha, kwaáchaa) *n.* **1.** The basic monetary unit of Zambia, equal to 100 ngwee. **2.** The basic monetary unit of Malawi, equal to 100 tambala. [Native word in Zambia.]

KwaN·de·be·le (kwaán-de-béllay, -báylay). In South Africa, the tribal homeland for the South Ndebele people.

Kwangchow. See **Guangzhou.**

Kwangtung. See **Guangdong.**

kwan·za (kwánzə, kwaán-) *n.* The standard monetary unit of Angola, equal to 100 lwei. [From a Bantu language.]

kwash·i·or·kor (kwáshi-ór-kər, kwóshi-, -kawr) *n.* Severe malnutrition due to protein deficiency, occurring especially in African children, characterised by anaemia, oedema, potbelly, depigmentation of the skin, and loss of hair or change in hair colour. [Native word in Ghana.]

Kwa·Zu·lu-Na·tal (kwaá-zŏŏlōō-nətáal). Province in South Africa corresponding to the former province of Natal. Inland, uplands rise to the Drakensberg Mountains. Industries, dominated by sugar refining, are concentrated around Durban and the capital Pietermaritzburg.

kWh kilowatt-hour.

kwic (kwik) *adj.* Designating an index, usually generated by computer, in which key words are extracted together with the context in which the words appear in the text. [*k*ey*w*ord *i*n *c*ontext.]

ky·an·ise, ky·an·ize (kī-ə-nīz) *tr.v.* **-ised, -ising, -ises.** To treat (wood) with mercuric chloride in order to preserve it. —**ky·an·i·sa·tion** (-nī-záysh'n ‖ *U.S.* -ni-) *n.*

ky·a·nite (kī-ə-nīt) *n.* Also **cy·a·nite** (sī-). A bluish, greenish, or colourless mineral, essentially Al_2SiO_5, used as a refractory. [German *Zyanit* : *zyan(o)-,* CYANO- + -ITE.]

kyat (ki-aát) *n.* **1.** The basic monetary unit of Burma, equal to 100 pyas. **2.** A coin worth one kyat. [Burmese.]

ky·bosh, ki·bosh (kī-bosh) *n. Informal.* A check or restraint. Used chiefly in the phrase *put the kybosh on.* [Origin unknown.]

kyle (kīl) *n.* In Scotland, a narrow strait, as between two islands. [Gaelic *caol,* narrow.]

ky·lin (kée-lín, kī-lin) *n.* Also **qi·lin** (chée-lín). A mythical, composite creature found on Chinese and Japanese pottery. [Mandarin Chinese *qílín* : *qí* male + *lín* female.]

ky·lix (kī-lix, kíl-) *n., pl.* **kylikes** (-i-keez). Also **cy·lix** (sī-, síl-). A shallow, typically tall-stemmed drinking cup with two handles, used in ancient Greece. [Greek *kulix,* cup.]

ky·loe (kī-lō) *n.* Any of a breed of long-horned, long-haired beef cattle from northwest Scotland. [19th century : origin obscure.]

ky·mo·graph (kīmə-graaf, -graf) *n.* An instrument for recording pressure variations, especially in blood pressure. [*Kymo-,* variant of *cymo-,* from CYME + -GRAPH.]

Kymric. Variant of **Cymric.**

Kymry. Variant of **Cymry.**

Kyo·to (ki-ō-tō, kyō-). City in south central Honshu, Japan. On the river Kamo, it is the capital of Kyoto prefecture, and was Japan's capital from A.D. 794 until 1868. It is still the centre of Buddhism in Japan. Noted for its craft industries, it also manufactures chemicals, textiles, and machinery.

ky·pho·sco·li·o·sis (kīfō-skōli-ō-siss) *n.* Abnormal curvature of the spine both forwards and sideways.

ky·pho·sis (kī-fō-siss) *n.* Abnormal outward curvature of the spine, due to bone disease, bad posture, or congenital deformity. Also called "humpback", "hunchback". [Greek *kuphōsis,* from *kuphos,* bent, hunchbacked.] —**ky·phot·ic** (-fóttik) *adj.*

Kyrgyz. Variant of **Kirgiz.**

Kyr·gyz·stan (kúr-giz-staán, -stán) or **Kyr·gyz Republic** (keér-giz, kúr-, -geéz). Former constituent republic of the U.S.S.R. Bounded on the southeast by China, it is almost entirely mountainous, the Tian Shan being on the Chinese border. It is rich in mineral deposits, especially coal, lead, mercury, antimony, and uranium, of which it was one of the U.S.S.R.'s major producers. Area, 198 500 square kilometres (76,600 square miles). Population, 4,570,000. Capital, Bishkek. See map at **Commonwealth of Independent States.**

Kyr·i·e e·le·i·son (kírri-ay i-láy-i-son, keér-i-, -i) *n.* **1.** A liturgical prayer in some Christian churches beginning with or composed of the words "Lord, have mercy". **2.** A musical setting for such a prayer, as in a choral mass. Also called "Kyrie". [Late Latin, from Greek *Kurie eleēson,* "Lord, have mercy" : *Kurie,* vocative of *kurios,* lord, master, "powerful (one)", from *kuros,* power, supreme authority + *eleēson,* aorist imperative of *elein,* to show mercy, from *eleos,* pity, mercy (see **alms**).]

Kyu·shu (kéw-shoo). One of the four major islands of Japan. The most southerly, the third largest, and most densely populated of Japan's islands, it lies to the east of the Korea Strait, and is joined to Honshu, across the Shimonoseki Strait, by a road and rail bridge. Much of the island is mountainous, forcing a concentration of agri-culture around the Chikugo river in the northwest. Its industries have developed around important coalfields in the north.

Ky·zyl Kum (kə-zíl koom). Desert in Central Asia, lying across the Kazakhstan-Uzbekistan border. It was the major atomic testing ground of the U.S.S.R.

L

l, L (el) *n., pl.* **l's** or *rare* **ls, L's** or **Ls. 1.** The 12th letter of the modern English alphabet. **2.** Any of the speech sounds represented by this letter. **3.** Anything shaped like the letter **L**.

l, L, I., L. *Note:* As an abbreviation or symbol, *l* may be a small or a capital letter, with or without a full stop. Established forms or those generally preferred precede the definition. When no form is given, all four forms are in general use in that sense. **1. l., L.** lake. **2. L** lambert. **3. L** large. **4. L.** Latin. **5. L** *British.* learner driver. **6. l.** length. **7. L.** Liberal. **8. L.** licentiate (in titles). **9. l.** line. **10. L.** Linnaean. **11. l.** lira. **12. l** litre. **13. L** The Roman numeral for 50. **14. L** *Electricity.* inductor. **15. L** *Physics.* latent heat.

l- *n. comb. form. Chemistry.* Indicates a laevorotatory compound. Usually written in italics: for example, **l- glucose.** Compare **d-.**

L- *n. comb. form. Chemistry.* Indicating an optically active compound with a molecular structure derived from or related to the structure of laevorotatory glyceraldehyde: for example **L- alanine.** Compare **D-.** An isomer designated **L-** may itself be laevorotatory (**l-**) but is not necessarily so.

la¹ Variant of **lah.**

la² (law, laa) *interj. Archaic.* Used to express emphasis or to indicate surprise. [Perhaps variant of LO.]

La¹ The symbol for the element lanthanum.

La² (laa) **1.** A respectful title prefixed to the surname of an eminent female artiste: *La Sutherland.* **2.** A title facetiously prefixed to the surname of a woman who is regarded as formidable, temperamental, or troublesome. [Feminine definite article of Romance languages.]

La. Louisiana.

L.A. 1. Legislative Assembly. **2.** Library Association. **3.** local agent. **4.** Los Angeles.

laa·ger, la·ger (láagər) *n. Chiefly South African.* **1.** A defensive encampment encircled by wagons or armoured vehicles. **2.** A narrow and protective social or intellectual environment.

~*v.* **laagered, -gering, -gers.** —*tr.* To form into a laager. —*intr.* To camp in a laager. [Afrikaans *lager,* from Dutch *leger,* camp, LAIR.]

laager mentality *n.* An attitude or policy of isolationism and inflexible opposition to change, especially as thought by its opponents to characterise the ruling Afrikaners of South Africa.

lab (lab) *n. Informal.* A **laboratory** *(see).*

lab. laboratory.

Lab. 1. Labour. **2.** Labrador.

lab·a·rum (láb-ərəm) *n., pl.* **-ara** (-ərə). **1.** The banner adopted by Constantine the Great after his conversion to Christianity, combining the Roman military standard and Christian symbols. **2.** Any banner, especially an ecclesiastical one. [Late Latin *labarum†.*]

lab·da·num (lábdənəm) *n.* Also **lad·a·num** (láddˈn-əm). A resinous exudation of certain Old World plants of the genus *Cistus,* yielding a fragrant essential oil used in flavourings and perfumes. [Medieval Latin, from Latin *lādanum,* from Greek *ladanon, lēdanon,* from *lēdon,* shrub from which labdanum exudes, from Semitic.]

la·bel (láyb'l) *n.* **1.** Anything functioning as a means of identification; especially: **a.** A piece of paper, card, or the like attached to an article such as a parcel or suitcase to designate its origin, owner, and destination. **b.** A piece of paper or similar material attached to a container such as a bottle or packet, providing printed or written information, about the contents. **2.** A term serving to describe or categorise; an epithet. **3.** The brand or trademark of a particular company, especially of a record company. **4.** A moulding over a door or window; a dripstone. **5.** The heraldic device distinguishing an eldest son, consisting of a horizontal band across the upper part of the shield with a set of usually three downward projections. **6.** *Chemistry.* A radioactive element in a compound, used to trace the pathway of the compound through a system.

~*tr.v.* **labelled** or *U.S.* **labeled, -belling** or *U.S.* **-beling, -bels. 1.** To attach a label to. **2.** To describe, classify, or designate. **3.** To make an atom in (a molecule or compound) radioactive so that the pathway of the molecule or compound can be traced through a system. [Middle English, label, narrow strip, from Old French, ribbon, strip, from Germanic.] —**la·bel·ler** *n.*

la·bel·lum (lə-béllum) *n., pl.* **-bella** (-béllə). **1.** The often enlarged lip of an orchid. **2.** The lobe at the top of a fly's proboscis. [New Latin, from Latin, "small lip", diminutive of *labrum,* lip.]

la·bi·al (láybi-əl) *adj.* **1.** Of or pertaining to the lips or labia. **2.** Resembling or serving as a lip. **3.** *Music.* Producing tones by the impact of a stream of air upon the edge of a lip, as in a flute or the flue pipes of an organ. **4.** *Phonetics.* Formed mainly by closing or partly closing the lips.

~*n.* A labial sound, such as (b), (m), (v), (w), or a rounded vowel. [Medieval Latin *labiālis,* from Latin *labium,* lip.] —**la·bi·al·ly** *adv.*

la·bi·al·ise, la·bi·al·ize (láybi-ə-līz) *tr.v.* **-ised, -ising, -ises.** *Phonetics.* To round (a vowel); make labial. —**la·bi·al·ism, la·bi·al·i·sa·tion** (-lī-záysh'n ‖ *U.S.* -li-) *n.*

la·bi·a ma·jo·ra (láybi-ə mə-jáwrə ‖ -jóˈrə) *pl.n.* Two rounded folds of tissue that form the external lateral boundaries of the vulva. [New Latin, "greater lips".]

labia mi·no·ra (mi-náwrə ‖ -nóˈrə) *pl.n.* Two narrow folds of tissue enclosed within the cleft of the labia majora. Also called "nymphae". [New Latin, "lesser lips".]

la·bi·ate (láybi-ət, -it, -ayt) *adj.* **1.** Having lips or liplike parts. **2.** *Botany.* **a.** Having or designating flowers with the corolla divided into two liplike parts. **b.** Of or belonging to the family Labiatae, which includes the mints.

~*n.* A labiate plant. [New Latin *labiatus,* from Latin *labium,* lip.]

la·bile (láy-bīl ‖ *U.S. also* -b'l) *adj.* Constantly liable to undergo change or fluctuation; unstable. [Late Latin *lābilis,* from Latin *lābī,* to slide.] —**la·bil·i·ty** (lə-bílləti) *n.*

labio– *comb. form.* Indicates formed with the lips (and another organ); for example, **labiodental.** [Latin *labium,* lip.]

la·bi·o·den·tal (láybi-ō-dént'l) *adj. Phonetics.* Articulated with the lip or lips and teeth.

~*n. Phonetics.* A labiodental sound, such as (f) or (v).

la·bi·o·ve·lar (láybi-ō-véelər) *adj.* Also **la·bi·al·ve·lar** (-əl-). *Phonetics.* Simultaneously labial and velar.

~*n. Phonetics.* A labiovelar sound, such as (w).

la·bi·um (láybi-əm) *n., pl.* **-bia** (-bi-ə). **1.** *Anatomy.* Any of four folds of tissue of the female external genitalia. See **labia majora, labia minora. 2.** *Zoology.* A liplike structure, such as the appendage forming the lower lip in insects. **3.** *Botany.* Any of the liplike divisions of a labiate corolla. [New Latin, from Latin, lip.]

lab·lab (láb-lab) *n.* **1.** A tropical African twining plant, *Dolichos lablab.* **2.** The edible pod or seed of this plant. [Arabic.]

lab·o·ra·to·ry (lə-bórrə-təri, -tri ‖ *U.S.* lábbrə-tawri, lábbərə-, -tōri) *n., pl.* **-ries.** *Abbr.* **lab. 1.** A room or building equipped for scientific experimentation, research, or testing. Also used adjectively: *laboratory conditions; a laboratory assistant.* **2.** A place where drugs and chemicals are manufactured. **3.** Any place equipped for study, practice, or testing, such as a **language laboratory** *(see).* Also informally called "lab". [Medieval Latin *labōrātōrium,* workshop, from Latin *labōrātus,* past participle of *labōrāre,* TO LABOUR.]

la·bo·ri·ous (lə-báwri-əss ‖ -bóri-) *adj.* **1.** Requiring long, hard work. **2.** Hard-working; industrious. **3.** Not fluent or spontaneous; laboured: *a laborious explanation.* [Middle English, from Old French *laborieus,* from Latin *labōriōsus,* from *labor,* LABOUR.] —**la·bo·ri·ous·ly** *adv.* —**la·bo·ri·ous·ness** *n.*

la·bour, *U.S.* **la·bor** (láybər) *n.* **1.** Physical or mental exertion of a

la·bour, *U.S. & Australian* **la·bor** (láybər) *n.* **1.** Physical or mental exertion of a practical nature, rather than exertion for the sake of pleasure or recreation; work. **2.** A specific task, especially one requiring physical effort. **3.** The contribution of workers to the production of goods and provision of services in a community; work done for wages rather than for profit. **4.** The class of people who make such a contribution; workers collectively, rather than management and employers. **5.** *Capital* **L.** A political party claiming to represent the interests of this class, such as the Labour Party of Great Britain. **6. a.** The physical effort involved in giving birth; parturition. **b.** An instance or period of this: *a long labour; a difficult labour.* —See Synonyms at **work.**

~*v.* **laboured** or *U.S. & Australian.* **labored, -bouring** or *U.S. & Australian* **-boring, -bours** or *U.S. & Australian* **-bors.** —*intr.* **1.** To expend great physical or mental effort; work; toil. **2.** To strive painstakingly or strenuously for a particular end. **3. a.** To proceed slowly; plod. **b.** To pitch and roll. Used of a ship. **4.** To be hampered. Used with *under: labouring under a misconception.* **5.** To undergo the pains of childbirth. —*tr.* **1.** To deal with in exhaustive detail; treat laboriously: *labour a point.* **2.** To cultivate; till. [Middle English, from Old French, from Latin *labor.*]

labour camp *n.* **1.** A penal settlement where the prisoners undertake forced labour. **2.** A camp for migrant workers.

Labour Day *n.* **1.** A public holiday celebrated in many countries in honour of the working class, usually on May 1. **2.** A similar holiday (Labor Day) observed in the United States and Canada on the first Monday in September.

la·boured (láybərd) *adj.* **1.** Done or produced with labour or difficulty: *laboured breathing*. **2.** Showing evidence of labour; lacking natural ease; overworked.

la·bour·er (láy-bərər, -brər) *n.* A person who performs physical work, especially of an unskilled nature.

la·bour·in·ten·sive (láybər-in-ten-siv, -tén-) *adj.* Requiring a high degree of human as opposed to mechanical work.

la·bour·ite (láybə-rīt) *n. Sometimes capital* L. A member or supporter of a Labour Party.

labour of love *n.* A task performed for the enjoyment it brings to oneself or another.

Labour Party *n.* **1.** A British political party, formed in 1900 from the Independent Labour Party and various trade unions, cooperative societies, and other socialist bodies, and claiming to represent the interests of workers. **2.** Any of several similar parties in other countries, especially in the Commonwealth.

la·bour·sav·ing (láybər-sayving) *adj.* Designed to reduce or eliminate the labour required to carry out a task.

labour union *n. U.S.* A trade union.

lab·ra·dor (lábbrə-dawr) *n.* A dog of a breed originating in Newfoundland, having a short, dense, black or yellow-brown coat and a tapering tail. Also called "labrador retriever".

Lab·ra·dor¹ (lábbrə-dawr). Also **Lab·ra·dor-Un·ga·va** (lábbrə-dáwr-ən-gaávə). Peninsula of east Canada, divided between Quebec and Newfoundland provinces. A high plateau, with barren tundra in the north and coniferous forest in the south, it has large mineral, forest, and hydroelectric resources. —**Lab·ra·dor·i·an** (-dáw-ri-ən ‖ -dô-) *n. & adj.*

Labrador². The mainland part of Newfoundland province, Canada.

Labrador Current *n.* A cold ocean current flowing southwards from Baffin Bay along the coast of Labrador to unite with the Gulf Stream over the Grand Banks off southeast Newfoundland. Also called "Arctic Current".

lab·ra·dor·ite (lábbrə-dawr-īt, -dáwr-) *n.* A plagioclase feldspar, found in igneous rocks, and characterised by brilliant colours in some specimens. [After LABRADOR.]

la·bret (láy-bret, -brət) *n.* An ornament inserted in a perforation in the lip. [Latin *labrum*, lip + -ET.]

la·brum (láy-brəm) *n., pl.* **-bra** (-brə). A lip or liplike structure, such as the upper lip in insects. [New Latin, from Latin, lip.]

La Bru·yère (laábrōō-yáir; *French* la brü-yáir), **Jean de** (1645–96). French writer. His *Caractères de Théophraste traduits du grec, avec les caractères ou les moeurs de ce siècle* (1688–96), satirises society under Louis XIV.

la·bur·num (lə-búrnəm) *n.* Any of several poisonous trees or shrubs of the genus *Laburnum;* especially, *L. anagyroides,* cultivated for its drooping clusters of yellow flowers. Also called "golden chain". [Latin *laburnum*, perhaps from Etruscan.]

lab·y·rinth (lábbə-rinth) *n.* **1. a.** An intricate structure of interconnecting passages; a maze. **b.** *Capital* L. *Greek Mythology.* The maze in which the Minotaur was confined. **2.** Something highly intricate or tortuous in character, composition, or construction. **3.** *Anatomy.* **a.** A group of communicating anatomical cavities. **b.** The internal ear, comprising the semicircular canals, vestibule, and cochlea. **4.** *Electronics.* A loudspeaker housing containing a number of air chambers, used to reduce the production of standing waves and improve the quality of sound reproduction. [Learned respelling of Middle English *laborintus*, from Latin *labyrinthus*, from Greek *laburinthos*, probably akin to *labrus*, LABYRIS.]

labyrinth fish *n.* Any small freshwater fish of the family Anabantidae, of tropical Africa and Asia, having a lunglike breathing organ.

lab·y·rin·thi·an (lábbə-rínthi-ən) *adj.* Labyrinthine.

lab·y·rin·thine (lábbə-rín-thīn, -theen ‖ -thin) *adj.* **1.** Of, pertaining to, or constituting a labyrinth. **2.** Intricate; complicated.

lab·y·rinth·o·dont (lábbi-rínthə-dont) *n.* Any primitive extinct amphibian of the subclass Labyrinthodontia, having hollow teeth convoluted in cross-section.
~*adj.* Of or pertaining to the Labyrinthodontia. [New Latin *Labyrinthodontia* : LABYRINTH + -ODONT.]

lab·y·ris (lábbi-riss) *n.* Also **lab·rys** (láb-). **1.** In ancient Minoan civilisation, a sacred double-headed axe. **2.** A similarly-shaped modern feminist symbol of strength, especially of lesbian solidarity. [Greek *labrus*, double-headed axe.]

lac¹ (lak) *n.* A resinous secretion of the lac insect *(see),* used in making shellac. [Dutch *lak* or French *laque*, from Hindi *lākh*, from Prakrit *lakkha*, from Sanskrit *lākshā*.]

lac². Variant of **lakh**.

L.A.C. leading aircraftman (in Britain).

Laccadive, Minicoy, and Amindivi Islands. See **Lakshadweep**.

lac·co·lith (láckə-lith) *n.* A mushroom-shaped body of igneous rock intruded between layers of sedimentary rock. [Greek *lakkos*, cistern (referring to the shape) + -LITH.]

lace (layss) *n.* **1.** A delicate fabric woven of silk, cotton, nylon, or other thread in an open weblike pattern. **2.** A cord or ribbon threaded through eyelets or around hooks on two opposite edges, as of a shoe or garment, for drawing and tying them together. **3.** Gold or silver braid ornamenting an officer's uniform.
~*v.* **laced, lacing, laces.** —*tr.* **1.** To thread a cord through the eyelets or around the hooks of: *laced her shoes.* **2. a.** To draw together and tie the laces of. Used with *up.* **b.** To pinch in the waist of by tightening corset laces. **3.** To intertwine: *lace shoots of a plant through a trellis.* **4.** To apply lace to. **5.** To add spirits to (a drink). **6.** To streak with colour. **7.** *Informal.* To give a beating to; thrash. —*intr.* To be fastened with a lace. —**lace into.** To attack; assail.

[Middle English *lace, laas, las,* braid, cord, from Old French *laz, las,* from Vulgar Latin *lacium* (unattested), from Latin *laqueus*, noose, trap, probably related to *lacere*, to allure.] —**lac·er** *n.*

Lacedaemon. See **Laconia**, **Sparta**.

lac·er·ate (lássə-rayt) *tr.v.* **-ated, -ating, -ates. 1.** To tear (especially flesh) roughly or jaggedly. **2.** To distress deeply.
~*adj.* (-rayt, -rət, -rit). Also **lac·er·at·ed** (-raytid). **1.** Torn; mangled. **2.** Deeply wounded; distracted. **3.** Having jagged, deeply cut edges: *lacerate leaves.* [Latin *lacerāre*, from *lacer*, torn, rent, mangled.] —**lac·er·a·tion** (-ráysh'n) *n.* —**lac·er·a·tive** (-rətiv) *adj.*

La·cer·ta (lə-súrtə) *n.* A constellation in the Northern Hemisphere situated near Cygnus and Andromeda. [New Latin, from Latin, LIZARD.]

lace·wing (láyss-wing) *n.* Any of various greenish or brownish insects of the families Chrysopidae and Hemerobiidae, having four gauzy wings, threadlike antennae, and larvae that feed on insect pests such as aphids. [From the texture of the wings.]

lach·es (láychiz, láchiz) *n., pl.* **laches.** *Law.* Culpable negligence; especially, delay in asserting a right or a claim. [Middle English *lachesse,* from Anglo-French, Old French, from *lasche*, lax, from Vulgar Latin *lascus* (unattested), from Latin *laxus*, LAX.]

Lach·e·sis (lácki-siss). *Greek Mythology.* One of the three **Fates** *(see).* [Greek *Lakhesis*, "disposer of lots", from *lakhein*, aorist infinitive of *lankhanein†*, to obtain by lot.]

Lach·ry·ma Chris·ti (láckrimə krísti) *n.* A dryish white or occasionally red wine produced from grapes grown on the southern slopes of Vesuvius. [Latin, "tear of Christ".]

lach·ry·mal, lac·ri·mal (láckrim'l) *adj.* **1.** Of or pertaining to tears. **2.** Of or pertaining to the lachrymal glands.
~*n.* **1.** A lachrymatory. **2.** *Plural.* The lachrymal glands. [Medieval Latin *lachrymālis, lacrimālis,* from Latin *lacrima, lacruma,* tear.]

lachrymal duct *n.* The short duct in the inner corner of the eyelid through which tears are drained into the nasal cavity. Also called "tear duct".

lachrymal gland *n.* A gland that lies beneath the upper eyelid in humans and many vertebrates and secretes tears.

lach·ry·ma·tor, lac·ri·ma·tor (láckri-maytər) *n.* Any substance that induces an excessive flow of tears; especially, **tear gas** *(see).* [Latin *lacrima*, tear + -OR.]

lach·ry·ma·to·ry (láckri-mə-təri, -may-, -máy-, -tri) *n., pl.* **-ries.** Formerly, a vase or phial for holding the tears of mourners.
~*adj.* Of, pertaining to, or causing tears. [Medieval Latin *lachrymatórium,* from Late Latin *lacrimatórius,* of tears, from Latin *lacrimāre*, to cry, from *lacrima,* tear.]

lach·ry·mose (láckri-mōss, -mōz) *adj.* **1.** Weeping or inclined to weep; tearful. **2.** Causing tears; sorrowful. **3.** Lugubrious; morose. [Latin *lacrimōsus,* from *lacrima*, tear.] —**lach·ry·mose·ly** *adv.*

lac·ing (láy-sing) *n.* **1.** *British.* A course of stone or brick built into a stone or rubble wall so as to bind the facing to the core. **2.** *Informal.* A thrashing.

la·cin·i·ate (lə-sínni-ayt, -ət, -it) *adj.* Also **la·cin·i·a·ted** (-aytid). *Biology.* **1.** Fringed. **2.** Having edges cut into narrow, fringelike segments or lobes: *laciniate petals.* [Latin *lacīnia*, fringe, tuft.] —**la·cin·i·a·tion** (-áysh'n) *n.*

lac insect *n.* Any of various insects of the subfamily Lacciferinae; especially, *Laccifer lacca,* of southern Asia, the female of which secretes the resinous substance lac.

lack (lak) *n.* **1.** A deficiency or want: *a lack of money.* **2.** A need.
~*v.* **lacked, lacking, lacks.** —*tr.* To be entirely without or have too little of (a thing or quality). —*intr.* **1.** To be wanting or deficient. Used with *in* or *for.* **2.** *Archaic.* To be missing. [Middle English *lac, lacke,* perhaps from Middle Dutch, deficiency, fault.]

Usage: Intransitive *lack*, followed by *for*, has attracted criticism: *They lack for nothing; You will not be lacking for support.* In both examples, the transitive use of *lack* provides an alternative: *They lack nothing; You will not lack support.*

lack·a·dai·si·cal (lackə-dáyzik'l) *adj.* Lacking spirit or enthusiasm; languid. [From earlier *lackadaisy*, extended form of LACKADAY.] —**lack·a·dai·si·cal·ly** *adv.* —**lack·a·dai·si·cal·ness** *n.*

lack·a·day (láckə-day, -dáy) *interj. Archaic.* Used to express regret or disapproval. [From the phrase *alack the day.*]

lack·ey (lácki) *n., pl.* **-eys.** Also **lac·quey** *pl.* **-queys. 1.** A liveried male servant; a footman. **2.** A servile follower; a toady.
~*tr.v.* **lackeyed, -eying, -eys.** Also **lac·quey, -queyed, -queying, -queys.** To attend as a lackey. [French *laquais*, from Old French, from Catalan *alacay*, akin to Spanish ALCALDE.]

lack·ing (lácking) *adj. British Informal.* Mentally deficient. —**lacking in.** Deficient in; in need of.

lack·lus·tre, *U.S.* **lack·lus·ter** (láck-lustər) *adj.* Lacking lustre, brightness, or vitality; dull.

La·clos (la-klō), **Pierre Choderlos de** (1741–1803). French writer and general. His novel *Les Liaisons dangereuses* (1782), is a study of moral and sexual corruption. He died fighting in Italy.

La·co·ni·a (lə-kōni-ə). Also **Lac·e·dae·mon** (lássi-déemən). Ancient region of the southern Peloponnese, Greece. Sparta, its capital, stood on the river Evrotás, and dominated the area before the rise of the Achaean League in the third century B.C.

la·con·ic (lə-kónnik) *adj.* Expressed in or using few words; terse; succinct. See Synonyms at **concise.** [Latin *laconicus,* from Greek *Lakōnikos,* of or resembling the Laconians or Spartans (known for their brevity of speech): a famous anecdote concerns Philip of Macedon's warning, "If I enter Laconia, I shall raze Sparta to the ground", to which the Spartans returned the laconic message "If"), from *Lakōn*†, native of Laconia, Spartan.] —**la·con·i·cal·ly** *adv.*

lac·o·nism (láckə-niz'm) *n.* Also **la·con·i·cism** (lə-kónni-siz'm). **1.** Succinctness of expression. **2.** A laconic expression.

La Co·ru·ña (lá kō-rōon-yə). *English* **Co·run·na** (kə-rúnnə). City in northwest Spain, capital of the province of La Coruña. It is an Atlantic port and a summer resort. The English commander, John Moore, was killed here in 1809 during the Peninsular campaign against Napoleon.

lac·quer (láckər) *n.* **1.** Any of various clear or coloured synthetic coatings, made by dissolving cellulose derivatives together with plasticisers and pigments in a mixture of volatile solvents, and used to give wood and metal surfaces a high gloss. **2.** Any glossy, often resinous material used as a surface coating, such as the exudation of the lacquer tree. **3.** A baked-on finish on the inside of food and drink tins. **4.** A substance sprayed on hair to keep a style in place. ~*tr.v.* **lacquered, -quering, -quers. 1.** To coat with lacquer. **2.** To give a sleek, glossy finish to. [Earlier *lacker,* from obsolete French *lacre,* sealing wax, variant of Portuguese *laca,* LAC (resin).] —**lac·quer·er** *n.*

lacquer tree *n.* A tree, *Rhus verniciflua,* of eastern Asia, having a toxic exudation from which a black lacquer is obtained. Also called "varnish tree".

lacrimal. Variant of **lachrymal.**

lac·ri·ma·tion (láckri-máysh'n) *n.* The secretion of tears, especially in excess.

lacrimator. Variant of **lachrymator.**

la·crosse (lə-króss, la- ‖ -kráwss) *n.* A team game of American Indian origin played with long-handled sticks fitted with nets for catching, carrying, and throwing the ball. [Canadian French, from French *(le jeu de) la crosse,* (the game of) the hooked stick, from Old French *crosse, croce,* staff, crosier, from Germanic.]

lac·tal·bu·min (lak-tál-bew-min, lák-tal-béw-) *n.* The albumin contained in milk. [LACT(O)- + ALBUMIN.]

lac·tam (lák-tam) *n.* Any of various amides containing the group -CONH-. [LACT(ONE) + AM(IDE).]

lac·tase (lák-tayz, -tayss) *n.* An enzyme occurring in certain yeasts and in the intestinal juices of mammals that catalyses the conversion of lactose into glucose and galactose. [LACT(O)- + -ASE.]

lac·tate (lák-tayt, lak-táyt) *intr.v.* **-tated, -tating, -tates.** To secrete or produce milk. ~*n.* A salt or ester of lactic acid. [Latin *lactāre,* to suckle, from *lac* (stem *lact-*), milk.] —**lac·ta·tion** (-táysh'n) *n.*

lac·te·al (lákti-əl) *adj.* **1.** Of, pertaining to, or like milk; milky. **2.** *Anatomy.* Of or pertaining to the lacteals. ~*n. Anatomy.* Any of numerous minute lymph-carrying vessels that convey chyle from the intestine to the thoracic duct. [Latin *lacteus,* of milk, from *lac* (stem *lact-*), milk.] —**lac·te·al·ly** *adv.*

lac·tes·cent (lak-téss'nt) *adj.* **1.** Becoming milky. **2.** Milky. **3.** *Biology.* Secreting or yielding a milky juice. Said of certain plants and insects. [Latin *lactescēns* (stem *lactescent-*), present participle of *lactescēre,* to become milky, from *lactēre,* to be milky, from *lac* (stem *lact-*), milk.] —**lac·tes·cence** *n.*

lac·tic (láktik) *adj.* Pertaining to or derived from milk. [French *lactique,* from Latin *lac* (stem *lact-*), milk.]

lactic acid *n.* A hygroscopic syrupy liquid, $CH_3CH(OH) \cdot CO_2H$, present in sour milk, molasses, various fruits, and wines, and used in foods and beverages as an acidulant, flavouring, and preservative, and in adhesives, plasticisers, and pharmaceuticals.

lac·tif·er·ous (lak-tíffərəss) *adj.* **1.** Producing, secreting, or conveying milk. **2.** *Botany.* Yielding latex or a similar milky juice; laticiferous. [Late English *lactifer* : LACT + -I- + -FEROUS.]

lac·ti·fuge (lákti-fewj) *n.* Any drug or other agent used to suppress the secretion of milk in mothers not breast-feeding their babies. [LACT + -I- + -FUGE.]

lacto–, lact– *comb. form.* Indicates milk; for example, **lactoprotein.** [French, from Late Latin, from Latin *lac* (stem *lact-*), milk.]

lac·to·ba·cil·lus (láktō-bə-síllass) *n., pl.* **-cilli** (-síllī). Any of various bacilli of the genus *Lactobacillus,* that ferment carbohydrates to produce lactic acid.

lac·to·fla·vin (lák-tō-fláyvin, -tə-) *n. Chemistry.* **Riboflavin** (see).

lac·to·gen·ic (láktə-jénnik) *adj.* Inducing lactation: *lactogenic hormone.* [LACTO- + -GENIC.]

lac·tone (lák-tōn) *n.* A cyclic ester of a hydroxyl acid, formed by removing the constituents of water from a molecule of the acid. [LACT(O)- + -ONE.] —**lac·ton·ic** (lak-tónnik) *adj.*

lac·to·pro·tein (láktō-prṓ-teen ‖ -tee-in) *n.* Any protein normally present in milk.

lac·tose (lák-tōss, -tōz) *n.* A white crystalline disaccharide, $C_{12}H_{22}O_{11}$, occurring in milk and used in pharmaceuticals, infant foods, bakery products, and confections. Also called "milk sugar", "sugar of milk". [French : LACT(O)- + -OSE.]

la·cu·na (lə-kéw-nə, la-, -kṓ-) *n., pl.* **-nae** (-nee) or **-nas. 1.** An empty space or missing part, especially in an ancient manuscript; a gap. **2.** *Biology.* A cavity or depression. [Latin *lacūna,* pool. See **lagoon.**] —**la·cu·nal, la·cu·nar·y** *adj.*

la·cu·nar (lə-kéw-nər, -kṓ-) *n., pl.* **-nars** or **lacunaria** (láckew-naír-i-ə). *Architecture.* **1.** A ceiling or soffit decorated with a pattern of recessed panels. **2.** A panel in such a pattern. ~*adj. Biology.* Of, pertaining to, or containing lacunae. [Latin *lacūnar,* from *lacūna,* cavity, cleft, pool. See **lagoon.**]

la·cus·trine (lə-kúss-trīn, la-, -trin) *adj.* **1.** Of or pertaining to a lake. **2.** Living or growing in or along the edges of lakes. [French *lacus-tre,* of a lake, from Latin *lacus,* LAKE (influenced in form by Latin *palūster,* marshy, from *palus,* swamp).]

L.A.C.W. leading aircraftwoman (in Britain).

lac·y (láy-si) *adj.* **-ier, -iest.** Of, pertaining to, or resembling lace. —**lac·i·ness** *n.*

lad (lad) *n.* **1.** A boy or young man. **2.** *Informal.* A man of any age. Used familiarly. **3.** *British.* A person of any age who looks after horses: *a stable lad.* [Middle English *ladde*†.]

ladanum. Variant of **labdanum.**

lad·der (láddər) *n.* **1.** A device consisting of two long structural members crossed by parallel, equally spaced rungs, used for climbing up or down. **2.** A length of unravelled stitches, as in a stocking. Also called "run". **3. a.** A means of ascent and descent: *ascending the social ladder.* **b.** A series of ranked stages or levels: *high on the executive ladder.* See **fish ladder. 4.** *Sports.* A competition in a game, such as squash or tennis, in which each competitor tries to beat the competitor above him and so take his place. ~*v.* **laddered, -dering, -ders.** —*intr.* To develop a ladder. Used especially of stockings. —*tr.* To cause (a stocking, for example) to ladder. [Middle English *ladder,* Old English *hlǣd(d)er.*]

lad·der-back (láddər-bak) *n.* **1.** A chair back consisting of two upright posts connected by horizontal slats. **2.** A chair with this type of back. —**lad·der-back** *adj.*

lad·die (láddi) *n.* A young lad.

lade (layd) *v.* **laded, laded** (láyd'n) or **laded, lading, lades.** —*tr.* **1. a.** To load with or as if with cargo. **b.** To ship (cargo). **2.** To take up or remove water with a ladle or the like; bale. —*intr.* To take on cargo. [Lade (infinitive), laden (past participle); Middle English *laden, laden,* Old English *hladan, gehladen.*]

lad·en (láyd'n) *adj.* **1.** Weighed down with a load; heavy. **2.** Oppressed; burdened: *laden with grief.* **3.** Saturated or suffused. Also used in combination: *a guilt-laden atmosphere.*

la-di-da (láa-di-dáa) *adj. Informal.* Affectedly genteel; pretentious. ~*n. Informal.* A person showing such affectation. [Imitative of affected speech.]

la·dies, la·dies' (láydiz) *n. Used with a singular verb. Informal.* A public lavatory for women. Also called "ladies' room".

ladies' fingers *n. Used with a singular or plural verb.* A plant, the kidney vetch (see). Compare **lady's finger.**

ladies' man *n.* A man who enjoys and attracts the company of women.

la·dies'-tress·es, la·dy's-tress·es (láydiz-tressiz) *n. Used with a singular or plural verb.* Any of various orchids of the genus *Spiranthes,* having a spike of small white flowers usually in a spiral.

La·din (la-déen) *n.* **1.** The Rhaeto-Romanic dialect of southeast Switzerland, contiguous parts of northern Italy, and the Tirol; Romansch. It is a distinct Romance language. **2.** Someone from this region who speaks Ladin. [Italian *Ladino,* from Latin *Latīnus,* LATIN.]

La·di·no (lə-déenō) *n.* A Romance language, derived from Spanish with Hebrew elements and modifications, spoken by Sephardic Jews, especially in the Balkans. Also called "Judaeo-Spanish". [Spanish, "Latin", from Latin *Latīnus,* LATIN.]

la·dle (láyd'l) *n.* **1.** A long-handled spoon with a deep bowl for serving liquids. **2.** A large container used to transfer molten metals. ~*tr.v.* **ladled, -dling, -dles. 1.** To lift out or convey with a ladle. **2.** To distribute (money or food, for example) liberally. Used with *out.* [Middle English *ladel,* Old English *hlædel,* from *hladan,* to draw out, LADE.]

Lad·o·ga (lád-ə-gə, laád-, -ō-). *Russian* **Ladozhskoye Ozero;** *Finnish* **Laatokka.** Largest freshwater lake in Europe, in northwest Russia. It covers 18 130 square kilometres (7,000 square miles).

la·dy (láydi) *n., pl.* **-dies. 1.** A woman having the refined habits, gentle manners, and other characteristics typically associated with breeding, culture, and high station; the female equivalent of a gentleman. **2. a.** An adult female. Used as a polite term, especially in her presence: *Would you ask the lady to wait?* Also used adjectively: *a lady doctor.* **b.** *U.S. & South African. Informal.* Madam. Used in direct address: *Can I help you, lady?* **3.** A woman considered especially from the point of view of some specified ability or quality: *She's a very dynamic lady.* **4. a.** A woman to whom a man is romantically attached; a ladylove. **b.** *Informal.* A wife or mistress. **5.** *Capital L.* A term prefixed to the title of certain positions of office when such a position is held by a woman: *the Lady Mayor.* **6.** *Capital L. British.* The general feminine title of nobility and of other rank, used in the following specific ways: **a.** For the wife or widow of a knight or baronet: *Lady Smith* (wife of Sir Harry Smith). **b.** Semiformally for a marchioness, countess, viscountess, or baroness: *Lady Salisbury* (the Marchioness of Salisbury). **c.** As the usual style for the wife or widow of a baron: *Lady Snow* (wife of Lord Snow); **d.** As a courtesy title for the daughter of a duke, marquis, or earl: *Lady Hester Stanhope* (daughter of Earl Stanhope); **e.** As a courtesy title for the wife or widow of a younger son of a duke or marquis: *Lady John Russell* (wife of Lord John Russell, third son of the Duke of Bedford). **Note:** In direct address, *my lady* and *your ladyship* are deferential substitutes for any of the above. With all except **a,** the formal usage (as in addressing a letter), is *The Lady Snow, The Lady Ruthven,* and the like. [Middle English *la(ve)di, lafdi,* Old English *hlǣfdige,* "kneader of bread", lady : *hlǣf,* LOAF + *dig-* (unattested), knead.]

Usage: Apart from its special uses with reference to the British aristocracy, *lady* is the normal form to use when referring to a female person in her presence: *Show the lady to her seat; Has one of you ladies dropped a handkerchief?* Woman would be blunt or rude, or imply some kind of nuance, in such contexts. In fixed phrases or special contexts, however, *woman* is a permissible variant for *lady:* one may refer to either the *ladies' finals* or the *women's finals* in a sport, or to a *young lady* or *young woman.* In such cases, *lady* is the form which implies an extra degree of courtesy or formality. On the other hand, in the context of jobs, *woman* is often used adjectivally without any special implication: *a woman teacher, women students.*

la·dy·bird (láydi-burd) *n.* Any of numerous small beetles of the family Coccinellidae, often reddish with black spots. Also *U.S.* "ladybug". [After OUR LADY.]

Lady Chapel *n. Sometimes small* **l**, *small* **c**. A chapel in a church or cathedral dedicated to the Virgin Mary.

Lady Day *n.* The Feast of the Annunciation, celebrated on March 25, one of the four quarter days in England and Wales.

lady in waiting *n., pl.* **ladies in waiting.** A lady of a court appointed to serve or attend a queen or princess. Also called "lady of the bedchamber".

la·dy-kill·er (láydi-killər) *n. Slang.* A man reputed to be exceptionally successful and often ruthless with women.

la·dy·like (láydi-lik) *adj.* **1.** Characteristic of or befitting a lady; refined; well-bred. **2.** Unduly sensitive to matters of propriety or decorum. **3.** Effeminate. Said of a man.

la·dy·love (láydi-luv) *n.* A beloved woman; a sweetheart.

lady of the house *n.* The female head of a household.

lady's finger *n.* A vegetable, **okra** *(see).* Compare **ladies' fingers.**

la·dy·ship (láydi-ship) *n. Sometimes capital* **L**. Used in addressing or referring to a woman holding the title of Lady, or ironically of any woman. Used with *Your* or *Her.* See Note at **lady.**

lady's mantle *n.* Any of various plants of the genus *Alchemilla,* having clusters of small greenish flowers.

La·dy·smith (láydi-smith). Market town in eastern South Africa. During the second Anglo-Boer War, a British garrison there was besieged from November, 1899, until relieved in February, 1900.

la·dy's-slip·per (láydiz-slíppər ‖ -slippər) *n.* Any of various orchids of the genus *Cypripedium,* having variously coloured flowers with an inflated, pouchlike lip.

la·dy's-smock (láydiz-smok) *n.* A plant, the **cuckooflower** *(see).*

lady's-tresses. Variant of **ladies'-tresses.**

La·ën·nec (la-e-nék), **René Théophile Hyacinthe** (1781–1826). French physician who invented the stethoscope.

La·er·tes (lay-ér-teez). *Greek Mythology.* The father of Odysseus.

La·e·trile (láy-ə-tril) *n.* A trademark for a cyanide-containing compound extracted from the seeds of peaches and related plants and used experimentally in the treatment of cancer.

laevo–, *U.S.* **levo–** *comb. form.* Indicates: **1.** Towards the left-hand side; for example, **laevorotatory. 2.** A laevorotatory chemical compound; for example, **laevulose.** [Latin *laevus,* left.]

laevodopa. Variant of **levodopa.**

lae·vo·ro·ta·tion (léevō-rō-táysh'n) *n.* An anticlockwise rotation; a rotation to the left, especially of the plane of polarised light.

lae·vo·ra·to·ry (léevō-rōtə-tri, -rō-táy-, -təri) *adj.* Also **lae·vo·ro·ta·ry** (-rōtəri). **1.** In optics, turning or rotating the plane of polarisation of light to the left or anticlockwise. **2.** *Chemistry.* Of or pertaining to a solution that rotates the plane of polarised light in this way. Compare **dextrorotatory.**

laev·u·lin (lévvew-lin, léevew-) *n.* A polysaccharide that occurs in the tubers of certain plants of the genus *Helianthus,* such as the Jerusalem artichoke. [LAEVULOSE + -IN.]

laev·u·lose (lévvew-lōss, léevew-, -lōz) *n.* A sugar, **fructose** *(see).* [LAEVO- + -ULE + -OSE.]

La Fa·yette (laa-fī-ét, lá-, -fay-; *French* la-fa-yét), **Marie Joseph Paul Yves Roch Gilbert du Motier, Marquis de** (1757–1834). French soldier and politician. He served on Washington's staff in the War of American Independence. In France he took part in the 1789 and 1830 revolutions. He designed the modern French flag.

La Fayette, Marie-Madeleine Pioche de la Vergne, Comtesse de (1634–93). French writer. Her novel *La Princesse de Clèves* (1678) examines the conflicts between passion and duty in marriage.

La·fon·taine (lá-fon-táyn, laa-, lə-fón-; *French* la-foN-tén), **Henri-Marie** (1854–1943). Belgian jurist and statesman. He was President of the International Peace Bureau (1907–43), and was awarded the Nobel peace prize in 1913.

La Fon·taine (lá-fon-táyn, laa-, lə-fón; *French* la-foN-tén), **Jean de** (1621–95). French poet, who collected the fables of Aesop and others in his *Fables* (1668–94).

lag¹ (lag) *intr.v.* **lagged, lagging, lags. 1.** To fail to keep up a pace; fall behind; straggle; loiter. Often used with *behind.* **2.** To fail, weaken, or slacken gradually; flag.
~*n.* **1.** The act, process, or condition of lagging. **2.** An extent or duration of lagging; a time lag. [Probably from *lag* (noun), last person; compare dialect *fog, seg, lag,* fanciful distortions of *first, second,* last in children's games.] —**lag·ger** *n.*

lag² *n.* Any covering for a cylindrical object, especially the insulating covering of a hot-water cylinder, steam pipes, or the like.
~*tr.v.* **lagged, lagging, lags.** To furnish or cover with lagging. [Perhaps from Scandinavian, akin to Swedish *lagg,* barrel stave.] —**lag·ger** *n.*

lag³ *tr.v.* **lagged, lagging, lags.** *Slang.* **1.** To arrest. **2.** To send to prison.
~*n. Slang.* **1.** A convict. Used especially in the phrase *an old lag.* **2.** A term of imprisonment. [19th century : origin obscure.]

lag·an (lággən) *n.* Also **li·gan** (lígən), **lag·end** (lággənd). *Law.* Cargo

or equipment thrown into the sea from a ship in distress, often attached to a float or buoy to enable it to be recovered. [Old French, perhaps from Old Norse *lögn* (stem *lagn-*), dragnet.]

Lag b'O·mer (lág bŏmər, laág, bə-ŏmər) *n.* A Jewish holiday, originally an agricultural festival, celebrated on the 33rd day after the second day of Passover, on the 18th day of Iyar. [Hebrew, "33rd (day) of the Omer".]

la·ge·na (lə-jéenə) *n.* The structure in the inner ear of fishes and amphibians that is homologous to the cochlea of higher vertebrates. [Latin, from Greek *lagēnos,* flask (referring to the shape).]

la·ger¹ (laágər) *n.* A light, usually effervescent beer of a type originally brewed in Germany, that contains a relatively small amount of hops. [Short for German *Lager(bier),* (beer) for storing, from *lager,* store, lair, from Old High German *legar,* lair.]

lager². Variant of **laager.**

La·ger·löf (laágər-löv), **Selma (Ottiliaa Louisa)** (1858–1940). Swedish novelist. She wrote *Gösta Berlings Saga* (1891), and in 1909 became the first woman to win the Nobel prize for literature.

lag·gard (lággərd) *adj.* Lagging behind or tending to lag behind; dawdling; straggling. [LAG (fall behind) + -ARD.] —**lag·gard** *n.* —**lag·gard·ly** *adv.* —**lag·gard·ness** *n.*

lag·ging (lágging) *n.* **1.** Insulation used to prevent heat diffusion from steam pipes, boilers, and the like. **2.** A wooden frame built to support the sides of an arch until the keystone is positioned. [From LAG (insulating covering).]

lag·o·morph (lággō-mawrf, lággə-) *n.* Any of various gnawing mammals of the order Lagomorpha, which includes the rabbits and hares. [New Latin *Lagomorpha* : Greek *lagōs,* hare + -MORPH.] —**lag·o·mor·phic** (-mórfik) *adj.*

la·goon (lə-gōōn) *n.* **1.** A body of salt water separated from the sea by sand or shingle bars or coral reefs. **2.** *Australian & N.Z.* A small body of fresh water. [French *lagune* and Italian or Spanish *laguna,* from Latin *lacūna,* pool, cavity, from *lacus,* LAKE.]

La·gos (láy-goss). Largest city of Nigeria, lying on the Gulf of Guinea. Abuja has replaced it as capital. Lagos consists of four islands and four mainland sections, joined to one another by bridges and causeways. It is Nigeria's chief port and industrial centre.

lag screw *n.* A heavy screw having a square bolt head. [Originally used in securing barrel staves. See **lag** (insulate).]

Lag·ting, Lag·thing (laág-ting) *n.* The upper house in the Storthing, or parliament, of Norway. Compare **Odelsting.** [Norwegian : *lag,* society, from Old Norse, due place (influenced in meaning by plural *lög,* law) + *ting,* parliament, from Old Norse *thing,* parliament, assembly.]

La Guar·di·a (lə gwárdi-ə), **Fiorello (Henry)** (1882–1947). U.S. politician. He was a congressman (1917–21, 1923–33), and mayor of New York (1934–45). One of the city's airports is named after him.

lah, la (laa) *n. Music.* In tonic sol-fa, a syllable representing the sixth note of a diatonic scale.

La·hore (lə-hór ‖ -hór). A city in east central Pakistan, the capital of Punjab province and Pakistan's second largest city. It is notable for its architecture, especially the palace and mausoleum of the emperor Jahangir.

la·ic (láy-ik) *adj.* Also **la·i·cal** (-ik'l). Of or pertaining to the laity; secular.
~*n.* A layman. [Late Latin *lāicus,* LAY.] —**la·i·cal·ly** *adv.*

la·i·cise, la·i·cize (láy-i-sīz) *tr.v.* **-cised, -cising, -cises. 1.** To free from ecclesiastical control; give over to laymen. **2.** To secularise. —**la·i·ci·sa·tion** (-sī-záysh'n ‖ *U.S.* -si-) *n.*

laid. Past tense and past participle of **lay** (verb).

laid-back (láyd-bák) *adj. Informal.* Relaxed; easy-going.

laid paper *n.* **1.** A paper made on wire moulds that give it a characteristic watermark of fine lines. Compare **wove paper. 2.** A machine-made paper imitating this.

laik (layk) *v.* **laiked, laiking, laiks.** *British Regional.* —*intr.* **1.** To have a day off work; be on holiday. **2.** To be out of work. **3.** To play about. —*tr.* To play (a game). [Middle English *leiken,* to frolic, play, from Old Norse *leika;* akin to LARK.]

lain. Past participle of **lie** (to recline).

Laing (lang, layng), **R(onald) D(avid)** (1927–89). British psychiatrist. His controversial theories about sanity were outlined in *The Politics of Experience* (1967). His other books include *The Divided Self* (1960) and a book of poetry, *Knots* (1970). —**Laing·i·an** *adj. & n.*

lair (lair) *n.* **1.** The den or dwelling of a wild animal. **2.** *British.* An enclosure for cattle to stay in on their way to market. **3.** *Archaic.* A resting place; a couch. **4.** *Informal.* A place of hiding or seclusion.
~*v.* **laired, lairing, lairs.** —*tr.* To put in a lair. —*intr.* To retreat to or lie in a lair. [Middle English *lair, leir,* Old English *leger.*]

laird (laird) *n.* In Scotland, the owner of a landed estate. [Scottish, variant of LORD.]

Laird (laird), **Macgregor** (1808–61). British explorer, who helped to open up the Niger river.

lair·y (láir-i) *adj.* **-ier, -iest.** *Australian Informal.* Flashily dressed; exhibitionistic. [Variant of LEERY.]

lais·sez-al·ler, lais·ser-al·ler (léssay-ál-ay, láy-say-) *n.* Also **laisser-aller.** An absence of constraint; uncontrolled freedom. [French, "let go".]

lais·sez-faire, lais·ser-faire (léssay-faír, láy-say-) *n.* **1.** The doctrine that government should not interfere with commerce. **2.** *Informal.* Noninterference in the affairs of others. [French, "allow (them) to do".] —**lais·sez-faire** *adj.* —**lais·sez-faire·ism** *n.*

lais·sez-pas·ser, lais·ser-pas·ser (léssay-pássay, láy-say-, -páa-say) *n.* A pass; especially, a permit allowing one to enter a restricted area. [French, "allow (them) to pass".]

la·i·ty (láy-əti) *n., pl.* **-ties. 1.** Laymen collectively, as distinguished from the clergy. **2.** All those persons outside a given profession, art, or other specialised field; nonprofessionals. [From LAY (non-clergy).]

La·ius (lí-əss, láy-əss). *Greek Mythology.* The king of Thebes who was killed by his own unwitting son, Oedipus.

lake¹ (layk) *n. Abbr.* **L., l. 1.** A large inland body of fresh or salt water. **2.** A scenic pond as in a park. **3.** A large pool of any liquid. [Middle English *lac,* from Old French *lac,* from Latin *lacus,* basin for water.]

lake² *n.* A pigment consisting of organic colouring matter with an inorganic base or carrier. [Variant of LAC (resin).]

lake³ *tr.v.* **laked, laking, lakes.** To cause (blood) to become a homogeneous solution by releasing haemoglobin from erythrocytes, as by suspending the erythrocytes in water. [From LAKE (pigment).]

Lake Dis·trict (láyk-distrikt). Scenic district and tourist area of northwest England, lying between Morecambe Bay and the Solway Firth. It includes the Cumbrian mountains and 15 lakes, among them Windermere, Ullswater, and Derwent Water. The Lake District National Park, covering about 32 375 hectares (80,000 acres), was established in 1951.

lake dwelling *n.* A dwelling built on piles in a shallow lake, especially in prehistoric times. **—lake dweller** *n.*

lake herring *n.* **1.** A fish, the powan *(see).* **2.** A North American food fish, *Coregonus artedii* (or *Leucichthys artedii*), of the Great Lakes region, related to the whitefishes.

Lake·land terrier (láyk-lənd) *n.* A terrier of a breed developed in the Lake District for flushing foxes from cover.

Lake Poets *pl.n.* Coleridge, Wordsworth, and Southey, grouped as a school because they lived for a time in the Lake District.

lakh, lac (laak, lak) *n.* In India: **1.** The number 100,000: *12 lakhs of rupees.* **2.** A very large number. Compare **crore.** [Hindi *lākh,* from Sanskrit *laksha.*]

Lak·shad·weep (lak-shád-weep). Formerly **Laccadive, Minicoy, and Amindivi Islands.** Indian territory off the coast of Kerala, comprising 27 coral islands, 10 of which are inhabited. The total area is only 32 square kilometres (12 square miles). Administered as separate island groups by Britain (1877–1947), it became a single territory, the Laccadive, Minicoy, and Amindivi Islands, in 1956. The name was changed to Lakshadweep in 1973.

lak·y (láyki) *adj.* **-ier, -iest.** Of the colour of lake or of blood.

–lalia *n. comb. form.* Indicates a speech defect; for example, *echolalia.* [New Latin, from Greek *lalia,* chatter, Greek *lalein,* to babble.]

La·lique (la-léek, lə-), **René** (1860–1945). French jeweller and glassmaker, who applied Art Nouveau designs to crystal ware.

Lal·lans (lál-ənz) *n. Used with a singular verb.* The dialect of Scottish English spoken in the Lowlands. **—Lal·lan, Lal·lans** *adj.*

lal·la·tion (la-láysh'n) *n.* The pronunciation of the sound (r) as (l). [Latin *lallāre,* to make lulling sounds.]

lam (lam) *v.* **lammed, lamming, lams.** *Slang.* **—tr.** To thrash; wallop. **—intr.** To strike. Used with *into* or *out.* [Of Scandinavian origin, akin to Old Norse *lemja,* to flog, make lame by beating.]

Lam. Lamentations (Old Testament).

la·ma (laámə) *n.* A Buddhist monk of Tibet or Mongolia. [Tibetan *bla-ma,* superior one.]

La·ma·ism (laámə-iz'm) *n.* The religion of Tibet and Mongolia and neighbouring areas, a form of Mahayana Buddhism with an admixture of animism, characterised by elaborate rituals. [From LAMA (priest).] **—La·ma·ist** *n. & adj.* **—La·ma·is·tic** (-ístik) *adj.*

La·marck (la-márk, la-), **Jean Baptiste Pierre Antoine de Monet, Chevalier de** (1744–1829). French naturalist. His idea of human evolution influenced Darwin's theory, but Lamarck believed that acquired characteristics could be inherited, a belief since discredited. **—La·marck·i·an** *n. & adj.*

La·marck·ism (lə-már-kiz'm) *n.* The theory that adaptive responses to environment cause structural changes capable of being inherited. Compare **Darwinism.** See **acquired characteristic.** [Developed by Chevalier de LAMARCK.]

La·mar·tine (la-maar-téen), **Alphonse Marie Louis de** (1790–1869). French romantic poet who was briefly minister of foreign affairs in 1848.

la·ma·ser·y (laámə-səri ‖ -serri) *n., pl.* **-ies.** A Lamaist monastery.

lamb (lam) *n.* **1.** A young sheep, especially one not yet weaned. **2.** The flesh of a young sheep used as meat. **3.** Lambskin. **4. a.** A sweet, mild-mannered person; a dear. **b.** One who is easily cheated; a dupe. **5.** A member of a Christian flock. **—the Lamb.** Christ. Also called "Lamb of God".

~intr.v. **lambed, lambing, lambs.** To give birth to a lamb. **—lamb down.** *Australian Informal.* **1.** To spend one's money wastefully or recklessly. **2.** To persuade (a person) to do this. [Middle English, Old English, from Germanic *lambiz-* (unattested).]

Lamb (lam), **Charles** (1775–1834). English essayist. He and his sister, Mary Lamb (1764–1847), wrote *Tales from Shakespeare* (1807) for children.

lam·ba·da (lam-baádə) *n.* **1.** A Brazilian dance in which couples hold each other, typically with bellies touching, and gyrate sexily. **2.** The rhythmic music of the lambada [Portuguese, "slap; rebuff".]

lam·baste, lam·bast (lam-báyst, -bást) *tr.v.* **-basted, -basting, -bastes** or **-basts.** *Slang.* **1.** To give a thrashing to; whip; beat. **2.** To attack verbally; berate or criticise. [Perhaps LAM (beat) + BASTE (beat).]

lamb·da (lámdə) *n.* The 11th letter in the Greek alphabet, written Λ, λ. Transliterated in English as *L, l.* [Greek *lambda,* of Semitic origin, akin to Hebrew *lāmedh,* LAMED.]

lambda particle *n. Symbol* Λ *Physics.* An electrically neutral subatomic particle in the baryon family, having a mass 2,183 times that of the electron and a mean lifetime of approximately 2.5×10^{-10} second. [From LAMBDA.]

lambda point *n.* **1.** The temperature at which the transition from helium I to superfluid helium II occurs, approximately 2.19° K. **2.** The temperature of any phase transition in which the specific heat capacity regarded as a function of temperature has a logarithmic singularity.

lamb·doid (lám-doyd) *adj.* Also **lamb·doi·dal** (lam-dóyd'l). Designating the deeply serrated suture in the skull between the two parietal bones and the occipital bone. [French *lambdoïde,* from Greek *lambdoeidēs,* "lambda-shaped" : LAMBDA + -OID.]

lam·bent (lámbənt) *adj.* **1.** Flickering lightly and gently over a surface: *lambent flames.* **2.** Flitting over subjects with effortless brilliance: *a lambent wit.* **3.** Having a gentle glow; luminous. **—See** Synonyms at **bright.** [Latin *lambens* (stem *lambent-*), present of *lambere,* to lick, tap.] **—lam·ben·cy** *n.* **—lam·bent·ly** *adv.*

lam·bert (lámbərt) *n. Symbol* **L** A unit of illumination equal to one lumen per square centimetre. [After J.H. *Lambert* (1728–77), German physicist.]

Lam·bert (lámbərt), **Constant** (1905–51). British composer and conductor. Much of his work, notably *The Rio Grande* (1929), a choral piece, experimented with the jazz idiom. His *Music Ho!* (1934) is a noted critical study of the music of the 1920s.

Lam·beth (lámbəth). Borough of central Greater London, lying south of the river Thames. In it are situated the South Bank arts complex and Lambeth Palace, the London residence of the archbishop of Canterbury.

Lambeth Conference *n.* An assembly of all the diocesan bishops of the Anglican Communion throughout the world, held every 10 years at Lambeth Palace to discuss matters of interest.

Lambeth Walk *n. British.* A dance popular in the 1930s and 1940s.

lamb·kin (lám-kin) *n.* **1.** A small lamb. **2.** A small endearing child.

lam·bre·quin (lám-brə-kin, -bər-) *n.* **1. a.** A piece of material worn over a helmet in medieval times. **b.** A heraldic representation of this, **mantling** *(see).* **2.** A scalloped band of colour ornamenting the top of a piece of porcelain. [French, from Dutch *lamperkin* (unattested), diminutive of *lamper,* veil, from Middle Dutch *lampert†.*]

lamb·skin (lám-skin) *n.* **1.** The skin of a lamb, especially when dressed without removing the fleece, as for a garment. **2.** Leather made from the dressed hide of a lamb.

lamb's-let·tuce (lámz-lettiss) *n.* A plant, **corn salad** *(see).*

lambs' tails *pl.n. British.* Hazel catkins.

lame¹ (laym) *adj.* **lamer, lamest. 1.** Disabled or crippled in one or more limbs, especially in a leg or foot so that walking is impaired. **2.** Weak and ineffectual; unsatisfactory: *a lame excuse.*

~tr.v. **lamed, laming, lames. 1.** To cause to become lame. **2.** To make ineffective; disable. [Middle English *lame,* Old English *lama.*] **—lame·ly** *adv.* **—lame·ness** *n.*

lame² *n.* A thin metal plate such as an overlapping plate in medieval armour. [Old French, from Latin *lāmina,* thin plate.]

la·mé (laá-may ‖ *U.S.* laa-máy) *n.* A fabric in which are woven metallic threads, often of gold or silver. [French, from adjective, "worked with silver and gold thread", from Old French *lame,* thin metal plate, LAME.]

la·med, la·medh (laá-mid, -med) *n.* The 12th letter in the Hebrew alphabet. [Hebrew *lāmedh,* "ox goad" (from the shape of the letter).]

lame duck *n. Informal.* **1.** An ineffectual, helpless, or disabled person. **2.** A company that is chronically unable to achieve profitability. **3.** A speculator on a stock market who is unable to meet all his obligations. **4.** *U.S.* An official or body during the period between an election defeat and the inauguration of a successor; broadly, one whose term is nearly over.

la·mel·la (lə-méllə) *n., pl.* **-mellae** (-mellee) or **-las. 1.** A thin scale, plate, or layer; especially: **a.** Any of the gills of a mushroom. **b.** Any of the concentric layers of calcified material of which bone is formed. **c.** Any of the layers of membranes in a plant chloroplast. **2.** A thin layer of a fluid. **3.** A wooden, metal, or concrete member forming the frame of a vaulted roof. [New Latin, from Latin *lāmella,* diminutive of *lāmina,* thin plate.] **—la·mel·lar** (-méllər) *adj.* **—la·mel·lar·ly** *adv.*

la·mel·late (lámmi-layt, lət, -lit, lə-mé-) *adj.* Also **lam·el·la·ted** (-laytid). **1.** Having, composed of, or arranged in thin layers or lamellae. **2.** Resembling a lamella. **—lam·el·la·tion** (lámmi-láysh'n) *n.*

lamelli– *comb. form.* Indicates a lamella or lamellae; for example, *lamellibranch.* [From LAMELLA.]

la·mel·li·branch (lə-mélli-brangk) *n.* Any of the molluscs of the class Lamellibranchia (or Bivalvia). See **bivalve.** **~adj.** Of or pertaining to lamellibranchs. [New Latin *Lamellibranchia,* "plate gilled" : LAMELLI- + BRANCHIA.]

la·mel·li·corn (lə-mélli-kawrn) *n.* A beetle of the superfamily Lamellicornia (or Scarabaeoidea), which includes the scarabs and other beetles having antennae tipped with movable leaflike plates. [New Latin *Lamellicornia,* "plate horned" : LAMELLI- + Latin *cornū,* horn.] **—la·mel·li·corn** *adj.*

la·mel·li·form (lə-mélli-fawrm) *adj.* Having the form of a thin plate or lamella. [LAMELLI- + -FORM.]

la·ment (lə-mént) *v.* **-mented, -menting, -ments.** **—tr. 1.** To express

grief for or about; mourn over: *lament a death.* **2.** To regret deeply; deplore. —*intr.* **1.** To grieve. **2.** To wail; complain.
~*n.* **1.** An expression of sorrow or grief; a lamentation. **2.** A song or poem expressing grief; an elegy; a dirge. [French *lamenter,* from Old French, from Latin *lāmentārī,* from *lāmentum,* expression of sorrow.] —**la·ment·er** *n.*

lam·en·ta·ble (lámmən-təb'l, lə-mén-) *adj.* **1.** To be lamented; deplorable; highly regrettable. **2.** *Archaic.* Exhibiting sorrow or grief; mournful. —See Synonyms at **pathetic.** —**lam·en·ta·bly** *adv.*

lam·en·ta·tion (lámmen-táysh'n, lámmən-) *n.* **1.** The act of lamenting. **2.** An instance of such expression of grief; a lament.

Lam·en·ta·tions (lámmen-táysh'nz, lámmən-) *n. Used with a singular verb. Abbr.* **Lam.** A book of the Old Testament, attributed to Jeremiah.

la·ment·ed (lə-méntid) *adj.* Mourned for. Used chiefly in the phrase *the late lamented.* —**la·ment·ed·ly** *adv.*

la·mi·a (láymi-ə) *n., pl.* **-mias** or **-miae** (-ee). **1.** *Greek Mythology.* A monster, represented as a serpent with the head and breasts of a woman, reputed to prey upon humans and suck their blood. **2.** A sorceress; a vampire. [Middle English, from Latin, from Greek.]

lam·i·na (lámmi-nə) *n., pl.* **-nae** (-nee) or **-nas.** **1.** A thin plate, sheet, or layer, as of bone or mineral. **2.** *Botany.* The expanded area, or blade, of a leaf or thallus. **3.** *Zoology.* A scalelike or platelike structure, such as any of the thin layers of sensitive tissue in the hoof of a horse. **4.** *Geology.* A narrow bed of rock. [New Latin, from Latin *lāmina,* thin plate.] —**lam·i·nar** (-nər), **lam·i·nal** *adj.*

laminar flow *n.* Nonturbulent flow of a viscous fluid in layers near a boundary, as of lubricating oil in bearings. Compare **streamline flow, turbulent flow.**

lam·i·nar·i·a (lámmi-naír-i-ə) *n.* Any seaweed of the genus *Laminaria,* having large, brown, leathery fronds. Also called "oarweed". See **kelp.** [New Latin, from Latin *lāmina,* tissue, plate. See **lamina.**]

lam·i·nate (lámmi-nayt) *v.* **-nated, -nating, -nates.** —*tr.* **1.** To beat or compress into a thin plate or sheet. **2.** To divide into thin layers. **3.** To make by uniting several layers. **4.** To cover with thin sheets. —*intr.* To split into thin layers or sheets.
~*adj.* (lámmi-nayt, -nət, -nit). Also **lam·i·nose** (-nōss), **lam·i·nous** (-nəss). Consisting of, arranged in, or covered with a lamina or laminae.
~*n.* A laminated product, such as plywood. [LAMIN(A) + -ATE.] —**lam·i·na·tor** (-naytər) *n.*

lam·i·nat·ed (lámmi-naytid) *adj.* **1.** Composed of layers bonded together. **2.** Arranged in laminae; laminate.

laminated glass *n.* See **safety glass.**

laminated iron *n.* Thin sheets of iron or a steel-silicon alloy shaped to form the core of a transformer to reduce the eddy current losses that occur with a solid iron core.

lam·i·na·tion (lámmi-náysh'n) *n.* **1.** The process or state of being laminated. **2.** Something laminated. **3.** A lamina.

lam·i·ni·tis (lámmi-nítiss) *n.* Inflammation of the sensitive laminae in the hoof of a horse. Also called "founder". [New Latin : LAMIN(A) + -ITIS.]

Lam·mas (lámməss) *n.* August 1, one of the four Scottish quarter days. [Middle English *Lammasse,* Old English *hlāfmæsse* : *hlāf,* LOAF + *mæsse,* MASS.] —**Lam·mas·tide** *n.*

lam·mer·gei·er, lam·mer·gey·er (lámmər-gī-ər) *n.* A large predatory bird, *Gypaetus barbatus,* of mountainous regions of the Old World, having black bristles around the bill. Also called "bearded vulture" and sometimes "ossifrage". [German *Lämmergeier* : *Lämmer,* genitive plural of *Lamm,* lamb, from Old High German *lamb,* from Germanic *lambiz-* (unattested), LAMB + *Geier,* vulture, from Old High German *gīr.*]

Lam·mer·muir Hills (lámmər-mewr). Range of low-lying mountains in southeast Scotland, southeast of Edinburgh. The highest peak, Meikle Says Law, rises to 535 metres (1,755 feet).

lamp (lamp) *n.* **1. a.** Any of various devices that generate light, heat, or therapeutic radiation. **b.** A vessel containing oil, paraffin, or alcohol burned through a wick for illumination. **2.** *Poetic.* A star, planet, meteor, or other celestial body regarded as lighting the heavens. **3.** *Literary.* That which illumines the mind or the soul. [Middle English *lampe,* from Old French, from Latin *lampas,* from Greek, torch, from *lampein,* to shine.]

lamp·black (lámp-blak) *n.* A grey or black pigment made from the soot of incompletely burned carbonaceous materials, used as a pigment, and in matches, explosives, lubricants, and fertilisers.

Lam·pe·du·sa (lámpi-dōozə), **Giuseppe (Tomasi) di** (1896–1957). Italian novelist. His best-known work, *The Leopard* (1958), published posthumously, deals with his own experience of the Sicilian aristocracy in decline at the beginning of the century.

lam·per eel (lámpər) *n.* The lamprey. [Variant of LAMPREY.]

lam·pern (lámpərn) *n.* A European lamprey, *Lampetra fluviatilis,* that migrates up rivers from the sea to spawn. [Middle English *laumprun,* from Old French, from *lampreie,* LAMPREY.]

lam·pi·on (lámpi-ən) *n.* An oil-burning lamp, often of coloured glass, for outdoor use. [French, from Italian *lampione,* augmentative of *lampa,* lamp, from Old French *lampe,* LAMP.]

lamp·light (lámp-līt) *n.* The light shed by a lamp.

lamp·light·er (lámp-lītər) *n.* **1.** Formerly, a person employed to light and extinguish street lamps. **2.** *U.S.* Something, such as a torch or taper, used to light lamps.

lam·poon (lam-pōon) *n.* **1.** A bitingly satirical piece of writing that is strongly personal in its flavour and ridicule. **2.** A light, good-humoured satire. —See Synonyms at **caricature.**

~*tr.v.* **lampooned, -pooning, -poons.** To assail in a satirical composition; write a lampoon concerning. [French, perhaps from *lampons,* let us drink (used as a refrain in 17th-century poetry), first person plural imperative of *lamper,* to gulp down, guzzle, from Germanic.] —**lam·poon·er, lam·poon·ist** *n.* —**lam·poon·er·y** *n.*

lamp·post (lámp-pōst) *n.* A post supporting a street lamp.

lam·prey (lámpri) *n., pl.* **-preys.** Any of various primitive elongated freshwater or anadromous fishlike vertebrates of the family Petromyzontidae, characteristically having a jawless sucking mouth with a rasping tongue. Also called "lamper eel". [Middle English *lamprei,* from Old French *lampreie,* from Medieval Latin *lamprēda*†. See also **limpet.**]

lam·pro·phyre (lámprə-fīr) *n.* Any of several intermediate igneous rocks comprising feldspar and ferromagnesian minerals that occur as dykes and minor intrusions. [Greek *lampros,* bright + *-phyre,* from PORPHYRY.]

lamp·shade (lámp-shayd) *n.* Any of various protective or ornamental coverings used for screening a light bulb.

lamp shell *n.* A marine invertebrate, a **brachiopod** *(see).* [From the shape of one of the valves in certain species.]

LAN Local area network.

Lan·ark (lánnərk) *n.* Town in south central Scotland, lying on the river Clyde. At New Lanark, nearby, Robert Owen built his model industrial village for his mill hands in the early 19th century.

la·nate (láy-nayt) *adj. Biology.* Covered with or consisting of woolly hairs. [Latin *lānātus,* from *lāna,* wool.]

Lancang Jiang. See **Mekong.**

Lan·ca·shire[1] (láng-kə-shər, -sheer). County in northwest England. In the late 18th and early 19th centuries it was the greatest cotton-manufacturing region in the world. Preston is the administrative centre, and Lancaster is the county town. Since 1974 the Liverpool and Manchester areas, Lancashire's old industrial heartland, are no longer part of the county.

Lancashire[2] *n.* A white, crumbly, English cheese made from cow's milk. [Originally made in Lancashire.]

Lan·cas·ter[1] (láng-kə-stər || -kaa-, -ka-). The family name of the English royal family (1399–1461).

Lancaster[2]. County town of Lancashire, northwest England, lying on the river Lune. It stands on the site of a Roman military station.

Lancaster, Duchy of. Collection of estates scattered throughout England and Wales, with its own administration. Created as an earldom in 1267, it was attached to the Crown when Henry IV became king in 1399, and it still provides revenue for the Crown.

Lan·cas·tri·an (lang-káss-tri-ən) *adj.* **1.** Of or pertaining to the English royal house of Lancaster. **2.** Of or pertaining to Lancashire or its inhabitants.
~*n.* **1.** A member of the Lancastrian faction in the Wars of the Roses (1455–85). **2.** An inhabitant of Lancashire.

lance (laanss || lanss) *n.* **1.** A thrusting weapon with a long wooden shaft and a sharp metal head, used by horsemen. **2.** A similar implement for spearing fish or killing whales. **3.** A lancer. **4.** A lancet.
~*tr.v.* **lanced, lancing, lances.** **1.** To pierce with a lance. **2.** *Archaic.* To fling; hurl. **3.** To make an incision in with a lancet; cut into: *lance a boil.* [Middle English *la(u)nce,* from Old French *lance,* from Latin *lancea*†.]

lance corporal *n. Abbr.* **L/Cpl.** **1.** In the British Army, a noncommissioned officer of the lowest rank. **2.** In the U.S. Marine Corps, an enlisted man ranking above a private first class and below a corporal. [From obsolete *lancepesade,* from Old French *lancepesade,* from Old Italian *lancia spezzata,* old soldier, "broken lance" : *lancia,* LANCE + *spezzata,* feminine past participle of *spezzare,* to break in pieces.]

lance-jack (laanss-ják || lánss-) *n. British Slang.* A lance corporal.

lance·let (laanss-lit || lánss-) *n.* Any of various small, flattened marine organisms of the genus *Amphioxus* and subphylum Cephalochordata, allied to the vertebrates but having a notochord rather than a true vertebral column. Also called "amphioxus".

Lan·ce·lot, Laun·ce·lot (laan-slət, -slot, -sə-lət, -lot || lán-). In Arthurian legend, a knight of the Round Table whose love affair with Queen Guinevere resulted in a war with King Arthur.

lan·ce·o·late (laan-si-ə-layt, -lət, -lit || lán-) *adj.* Narrow and tapering at each end: *lanceolate leaves.* [Late Latin *lanceolātus,* from Latin *lanceola,* diminutive of *lancea,* LANCE.]

lanc·er (laan-sər || lán-) *n.* **1.** Formerly, a cavalryman armed with a lance. **2.** A soldier belonging to a regiment that was originally armed with lances. [French *lancier,* from Old French, from LANCE.]

lanc·ers (laan-sərz || lán-) *n.* Also **lan·ciers** (lán-seerz, laan-). *Used with a singular verb.* **1.** A form of quadrille for 8 or 16 couples. **2.** The music for this dance.

lance sergeant *n.* In certain regiments of the British Army, a corporal.

lan·cet (laan-sit || lán-) *n.* **1.** A surgical knife with a short, wide, pointed, double-edged blade. **2.** *Architecture.* **a.** A lancet arch. **b.** A lancet window. [Middle English *lancette,* from Old French, diminutive of *lance,* LANCE.]

lancet arch *n. Architecture.* An arch that is narrow and pointed like the head of a spear. Also called "lancet".

lancet fish *n.* Either of two large marine fishes, *Alepisaurus ferox,* of the Atlantic, or *A. richardsoni,* of the Pacific, having long, sharp teeth and a large dorsal fin.

lancet window *n. Architecture.* A tall narrow window set in a lancet arch. Also called "lancet".

lance·wood (laanss-wŏod || lánss-) *n.* **1.** Any of several tropical trees, such as *Oxandra lanceolata* of tropical America or *Acacia doratoxylon* of Australia, having hard, durable, uniformly grained wood. **2.** The wood of such a tree.

lan·cin·at·ing (láan-si-nayting ‖ lán-) *adj.* Acute; stabbing. Said of a pain.

land (land) *n.* **1.** The solid ground of the Earth, especially as distinguished from the sea. **2. a.** The soil; the earth: *till the land.* **b.** Any tract of ground considered in terms of its potential or nature: *desert land; prime building land.* **c.** *Plural. South African.* An area of land used for the cultivation of crops. **d.** The rural as opposed to the urban life: *back to the land.* **3. a.** A nation. **b.** A district or region inhabited by a particular people. **c.** *Plural.* Territorial possessions. **d.** A sphere or domain: *no longer in the land of the living.* **4.** Public or private landed property; real estate. **5.** *Law.* **a.** Any tract of land that may be owned, together with everything growing or constructed upon it. **b.** A landed estate. **6. a.** Any of the raised strips in a field that is divided by furrows. **b.** The raised portion of a grooved surface. **—how the land lies.** The nature of the prevailing state of affairs.
~*v.* **landed, landing, lands.** —*tr.* **1. a.** To bring to and unload on land: *land cargo.* **b.** To set or bring down on land or other surface: *land an aircraft.* **2.** To cause to arrive; bring to a specified place or condition: *landed me in trouble.* **3. a.** To catch and pull in (a fish). **b.** *Informal.* To win; secure: *land a big contract.* **4.** To deliver: *land a blow on the head.* —*intr.* **1. a.** To come to shore. **b.** To disembark. **2. a.** To descend towards and settle on the ground or other surface. **b.** To meet or come to rest on a surface in a specified way: *landed on her back.* —**land up.** **1.** To reach a specified place or condition in the end; finish up: *You'll land up in court if you carry on this way.* **2.** To cause to reach a specified place or condition in the end. —**land with.** To present with something that is not wanted or appreciated: *Don't land me with your problems.* [Middle English, Old English.] —**land·less** *adj.*

-land *n. comb. form.* Indicates: **1.** A region of a specified quality or kind; for example, **grassland.** **2.** A realm of a specified nature; for example, **dreamland.**

land agent *n.* **1.** *Chiefly Australian & N.Z.* An estate agent. **2.** A person who manages a landed estate.

lan·dau (lán-daw ‖ -dow) *n.* **1.** A four-wheeled closed carriage with passenger seats facing front and back and a roof made in two sections for lowering or detaching. **2.** An early type of car with a roof similar to this. [First manufactured in *Landau,* Bavaria.]

lan·dau·let, lan·dau·lette (lándaw-lét) *n.* **1.** A small landau. **2.** An early type of car having a collapsible roof over the back seat and an open driver's seat.

land bank *n.* A bank that issues long-term loans on real estate in return for mortgages.

land breeze *n.* Wind blowing from the land towards the sea or a lake centre in the early part of the day, most commonly in the tropics.

land bridge *n.* **1.** A tract of land once thought to have connected one continent to another, providing a passage for migrating animals and thereby influencing their distribution. **2.** A tract of land, such as the Panama isthmus, joining two continents.

land crab *n.* Any terrestrial crab of the tropical family Gecarcinidae, having a large, square body.

land·drost (lánd-drost ‖ *South African* lúnt-) *n. South African.* Formerly, a government official serving as magistrate or sheriff of a particular district. [Afrikaans, from Dutch : *land,* country + *drost,* sheriff.]

land·ed (lándid) *adj.* **1.** Owning land: *landed gentry.* **2.** Consisting of land or real estate: *a landed estate.*

land·fall (lánd-fawl) *n.* **1.** The sighting or reaching of land on a voyage or flight. **2.** The land sighted or reached.

land·form (lánd-fawrm) *n.* Any physical feature of the earth's surface, such as a mountain or river valley.

land·grab·ber (lánd-grabbər) *n.* One who seizes land illegally or unscrupulously; specifically, one who took over a farm in Ireland following the eviction of its tenant.

land·grave (lánd-grayv) *n.* **1.** In medieval Germany, a count having jurisdiction over a particular territory. **2.** The title of certain German princes. [German *Landgraf,* from Middle High German *lantgrāve* : *lant,* land, + *grāve,* count.]

land·gra·vi·ate (land-gráyvi-ət, -it, -ayt) *n.* The office, jurisdiction, or territory of a landgrave.

land·gra·vine (lánd-grə-veen) *n.* **1.** The wife or widow of a landgrave. **2.** The female ruler of a landgraviate. [German *Landgräfin,* from Middle High German *lantgrævinne,* from *lantgrāve,* LANDGRAVE.]

land·hold·er (lánd-hōldər) *n.* A person who owns or holds land. —**land·hold·ing** *n.*

land·ing (lánding) *n. Abbr.* **ldg.** **1. a.** The act or process of coming to land or rest, especially after a sea voyage or flight. **b.** A termination, especially of a sea voyage or flight. **2.** A site for landing. **3. a.** An intermediate platform on a flight of stairs. **b.** The area at the top or bottom of a staircase.

landing beam *n.* A radio beam transmitted from an airfield to enable incoming aircraft to make a landing using instruments only.

landing craft *n. Abbr.* **L.C.** A flat-bottomed naval craft specifically designed to convey troops and equipment from ship to shore.

landing field *n.* A tract of land providing a runway for aircraft.

landing gear *n.* The undercarriage of an aircraft, designed to support the weight of the craft and its load on the ground.

landing strip *n.* An aircraft runway without airport facilities.

land·la·dy (lánd-laydi) *n., pl.* **-dies.** **1.** *Rare.* A woman who owns and rents or leases land, commercial property, or residential units. **2.** A woman who runs a boarding house or inn. **3.** A female publican or the wife of a publican.

länd·ler (léntlər) *n.* **1.** An Austrian country dance for couples in triple time. **2.** The music for this dance. [German, from dialectal *Landl,* Upper Austria, where the dance originated.]

land line *n.* **1.** A telephone or telegraph link consisting of a cable laid over land rather than under the sea. **2.** A radio link.

land·locked (lánd-lokt) *adj.* **1.** Surrounded or nearly surrounded by land. **2.** Confined to inland waters, as certain salmon are.

land·lop·er (lánd-lōpər) *n. Chiefly Scottish.* A tramp or vagabond. [Dutch : LAND + *loper,* from *loopen,* to walk, LEAP.]

land·lord (lánd-lawrd) *n.* **1.** A person who owns and leases land or buildings. **2.** A man who runs a boarding house or inn. **3.** A man who runs a public house; a publican.

land·lord·ism (lánd-lawr-diz'm) *n.* **1.** A system of land management in which ownership of land is vested in a private individual or group that leases it at a fixed rate to tenants. **2.** The advocacy of such a system.

land·lub·ber (lánd-lubbər) *n.* A person with little or no experience of the sea or seamanship.

land·mark (lánd-maark) *n.* **1.** A fixed marker, such as a concrete block, indicating a boundary line. **2.** A prominent and identifying natural or man-made feature of a landscape. **3.** An event marking an important stage of development or a turning point in history.

land·mass (lánd-mass) *n.* Any large area of land, such as a continent.

land mine *n.* An explosive mine laid usually just below the surface of the ground.

land of milk and honey *n.* A region or country offering the promise of a high standard of living and material comforts. [Referring to the Promised Land and God's promise to Moses to lead the Israelites "unto a land flowing with milk and honey" (Exodus 3:8).]

Land of Nod *n. Informal.* Sleep. [Punning phrase from NOD (to fall asleep) and the biblical Land of Nod: "And Cain . . . dwelt in the land of Nod, on the East of Eden" (Genesis 4:16).]

Land of the Long White Cloud *n.* New Zealand.

Land of the Midnight Sun *n.* **1.** Land lying north of the Arctic circle. It has at least one day in summer when the sun does not set. **2.** Any region or country whose borders lie within this area, especially Lappland.

Land of the Rising Sun *n.* Japan.

Lan·dor (lán-dawr), **Walter Savage** (1775–1864). British poet and prose-writer. A romantic republican, he is best known for his *Imaginary Conversations of Literary Men and Statesmen* (1824–29), written in Florence.

land·own·er (lánd-ōnər) *n.* One who owns land. —**land·own·er·ship** *n.* —**land·own·ing** *n. & adj.*

land·poor (lánd-poor) *adj.* Owning much unprofitable land but lacking the capital to improve or maintain it.

land·race (lánd-rayss) *n.* **1.** A pig of a white, lop-eared breed, yielding good-quality bacon and pork. **2.** Any primitive variety of a cultivated crop. [Danish: *land,* LAND + *race,* breed, RACE.]

land rail *n.* A bird, the corncrake *(see).*

Land Registry *n. Law.* In Britain, an office where the title, registrable leases, mortgages, restrictive covenants, or the like, of or affecting a piece of land are registered, and where a purchaser may go to inspect these before buying a piece of land.

Land-Ro·ver (lánd-rōvər) *n.* A trademark for a powerful four-wheel drive motor car that is especially suited for rough terrain.

land·scape (lánd-skayp, *old-fashioned* -skip) *n.* **1.** A wide view or vista of natural scenery: *a desert landscape.* **2.** A painting, photograph, or other pictorial representation depicting such scenery. **3.** The branch of art dealing with the representation of natural scenery. **4. a.** A locality as seen with regard to its natural and man-made features: *an industrial landscape.* **b.** The scenery or appearance, natural or as modified by man, characteristic of a particular locality: *the Highland landscape.* **5.** An extensive mental view; a prospect; a vista: *whole landscapes of thought.*
~*v.* **landscaped, -scaping, -scapes.** —*tr.* To adorn or improve (grounds) by contouring the land and planting flowers, shrubs, or trees. —*intr.* To arrange grounds artistically as a profession. [Dutch *landschap,* from Middle Dutch *landscap, lantscap,* landscape, region : *land,* land + *-schap, -scap,* suffix indicating condition.]

landscape architecture *n.* The decorative and functional alteration, planning, and planting of a piece of land, especially with reference to the siting of buildings. —**landscape architect.** *n.*

landscape gardening *n.* The planning and planting of gardens or grounds in order to obtain a picturesque or harmonious result. —**landscape gardener** *n.*

land·scap·ist (lánd-skaypist) *n.* A painter of landscapes.

Land·seer (lán-seer), **Sir Edwin Henry** (1802–73). British painter. His paintings, often depicting animals, were popular with both Queen Victoria and the public, combining sentimentality with photographic realism; *The Monarch of the Glen* (1851) is probably one of the best known of all animal paintings. He also designed the lions in Trafalgar Square.

Land's End. Rugged, westernmost peninsula of Cornwall and of England. It is the furthest point on the mainland of Great Britain from John O' Groats, which is traditionally considered to be its northernmost point.

land·side (lánd-sīd) *n.* The flat side of a plough opposite the furrow.

lands·knecht (lántsk-nekht, laántsk-) *n.* A European mercenary soldier in the 16th or 17th century; especially, a German foot soldier armed with a pike or lance. [German *Landsknecht* : *land* + *knecht,* soldier, KNIGHT.]

land·slide (lánd-slīd) *n.* **1. a.** The dislodging and fall of a mass of earth or rock or both. **b.** The dislodged mass. Also *chiefly British* "landslip". **2. a.** An overwhelming majority of votes for a political party or candidate. **b.** An election that sweeps a party or person into office. **c.** Any great victory.

land·slip (lánd-slip) *n. Chiefly British.* A landslide.

lands·man[1] (lándz-mən) *n., pl.* **-men** (-mən). One who lives and works on land as distinguished from a seaman.

lands·man[2] (lándz-mən, laánts-) *n., pl.* **landsleit** (-līt). A fellow Jew coming from one's own district or town in Eastern Europe. [Yiddish, compatriot, from Middle High German *lantsman* : Old High German *lant,* land + *man,* man.]

Land·stei·ner (lánd-stī-nər, laánt-, -shtī-), **Karl** (1868–1943). Austrian physician. Noted for his discovery of blood groups (1900), and for devising the ABO classification which enabled blood transfusions to be made, he also discovered the Rh factor, and was the first to isolate the poliomyelitis virus. He was awarded the Nobel prize in 1930.

Land·tag (laánt-taak) *n.* **1.** A legislative assembly of a German state. **2.** In some German states in the 19th century, a diet or assembly. [German, "land-day".]

land tax *n.* Formerly in Britain, a tax paid by the owner of land.

land·ward (lándwərd) *adj.* Being towards the land.

land·wards (lándwərdz) *adv.* Towards the land or the shore.

Land·wehr (laánt-vair) *n.* In German-speaking countries, a trained military reserve. [German, "land defence".]

land yacht *n.* A wind-powered vehicle having wheels and sails and used on flat ground, such as beaches. **—land yachting** *n.*

lane[1] (layn) *n.* **1. a.** A narrow way or passage between walls, hedges, or fences. **b.** A narrow road, as in the country. **2.** Any narrow passage, course, or track, such as: **a.** A prescribed course for ships or aircraft. **b.** Any of two or more strips delineated on a road or motorway to accommodate a single line of traffic. **c.** Any of a set of parallel courses marking the bounds for contestants in a race, especially a swimming or running race. **d.** A bowling alley. [Middle English, Old English, akin to Middle Dutch *lāne*†.]

lane[2] *adj. Scottish.* Lone.

Lane (layn), **Sir Allen** (1902–70). British publisher. In 1936 he founded Penguin books, the first paperback publishing house in the United Kingdom.

Lan·franc (lán-frangk) (c.1010–89). Italian churchman. He was appointed Archbishop of Canterbury (1070) by William I, in which post he reorganised the English church as a mainstay of the Norman administration.

lang (lang) *adj. Scottish.* Long.

lang. language.

Lang (lang), **Fritz** (1890–1976). German film director. After pioneering the German film industry with such films as *Metropolis* (1926) and *M* (1931), he moved to Hollywood where he made many Westerns and thrillers, noted for their sombreness of tone.

Lange (lóngi), **David Russell** (1942–). New Zealand politician. He became an M.P. in 1977; two years later, in 1979, he was made deputy leader of the Labour Party and in 1983, its leader. He was Prime Minister 1984–9, and an M.P. until 1996.

Langerhans, islets of *pl.n.* **Islets of Langerhans** (*see*).

Lang·land (láng-lənd), **William** (c.1332–c.1400). English poet. Probably a minor cleric, he is attributed with the authorship of *The Vision of William concerning Piers the Plowman* (earliest complete known edition: 1392). Its religious allegory is combined with social comment on inequality and clerical abuse.

lang·lauf (laáng-lowf) *n.* A cross-country ski run. [German *Langlauf,* "long race" : *lang,* long, from Old High German + *Lauf,* a running, from Old High German *hlouf,* a leap, from *hlouffan,* to leap.] **—lang·lauf** *intr.v.* **—läng·lauf·er** (-loyfər) *n.*

lang·ley (lángli) *n.* A unit of illumination used to measure temperature, as of a star, equal to one gram calorie per square centimetre of irradiated surface. [After S.P. *Langley* (1834–1906), U.S. astronomer.]

Lan·go·bard (láng-gə-baard, -gō-) *n., pl.* **-bardi** (-bárdi). A **Lombard** (*see*). **—Lan·go·bar·dic** (-bárdik) *adj.*

lan·gouste (lóng-gōost, long-gōost) *n.* The **spiny lobster** (*see*). [French, from Old French, from Old Provençal *langosta,* from Vulgar Latin *lacusta* (unattested), perhaps variant of Latin *lócusta,* lobster, LOCUST.]

lan·gous·tine (lón-gōoss-téen) *n.* A **Dublin Bay prawn** (*see*). [French, diminutive of LANGOUSTE.]

lan·grage (láng-grij) *n.* Also **lan·grel** (-grəl), **lan·gridge** (-grij). A type of shot consisting of scrap iron loaded into a case, formerly used in naval warfare to damage sails and rigging.

lang·syne, lang syne (láng-sīn, -zīn) *adv. Scottish.* Long ago. **~***n. Scottish.* Time long past; times past. [Middle English *lang sine* : *lang,* long + *syne,* contraction of *sithen,* SINCE.]

Lang·try (láng-tri), **Lillie,** born Emilie Charlotte le Breton (1853–1929). British actress. Known as the "Jersey Lily", she was already a society figure before making her stage debut (1881). She

---

was for a time the mistress of Edward, Prince of Wales.

lan·guage (láng-gwij) *n. Abbr.* **lang. 1. a.** The aspect of human behaviour that involves the use of vocal sounds in meaningful patterns and, when they exist, corresponding written symbols to form, express, and communicate thoughts and feelings. **b.** The faculty in human beings which enables them to communicate in this way. **2.** A pattern of such behaviour, historically established among a social or cultural group, involving a grammar and vocabulary that offers substantial communication only among its users: *the English language.* **3.** Any method of communicating ideas, as by a system of signs, symbols, gestures, or the like: *the language of algebra; body language.* **4.** The transmission of meaning, feeling, or intent by significance of act or manner: *"There's language in her eye"* (Shakespeare). **5.** The special vocabulary and usages of a scientific, professional, or other group. **6.** A characteristic style of speech or writing: *Miltonic language.* **7. a.** Speech or writing which uses vulgar or abusive terms: *Less of the language!* **b.** A particular manner of utterance or choice of words: *gentle language.* **8.** The manner or means of communication between living creatures other than man: *the language of dolphins.* **9. a.** *Often plural.* A language, especially a foreign language, as a subject of study: *He did languages at university.* **b.** Linguistics. **10.** *Law.* The wording of a document or statute as distinct from its spirit. **11.** A computer programming code enabling human language to be translated into a form intelligible to computers. **—speak the same language.** To have the same background, experience, or understanding as another person. [Middle English *langage,* from Old French, from Gallo-Roman *linguāticum* (unattested), from Latin *lingua,* tongue, language.]

language laboratory *n.* A room designed for learning foreign languages, using audiovisual equipment such as tape recorders and a monitoring device that enables the teacher to listen and speak to students individually or all together.

langue (laangg, lONG) *n. Linguistics.* Language considered as an abstract pattern or system shared by a speech community, as opposed to **parole** (*see*), the actual instances of its use in speech or writing. Compare **competence.** [French (specialised sense introduced by Saussure), tongue, language.]

langue de chat (də shaa) *n.* A thin, flat, finger-shaped, sweet biscuit or piece of chocolate. [French, "cat's tongue".]

langue d'oc (dok) *n.* The Romance language spoken in and around Provence and the Roussillon surviving in Provençal and Occitan. [French, from Old French, "language of *oc*". *Oc* is the word for "yes" in Provençal.]

Langue·doc (lóng-dók). Wine-producing region of southern France, formerly a province, lying on the Mediterranean Sea to the west of the Rhône. Its largest city is Toulouse.

langue d'o·ïl (do-éel) *n.* The Romance language of Gaul north of the Loire on which modern French is based. [French, "language of *oïl*". *Oïl* is the word for "yes" in northern medieval French.]

lan·guet (láng-gwet, -gwit) *n. Rare.* A tonguelike thing or part. [Middle English, from Old French *languette,* diminutive of *langue,* tongue, language, from Latin *lingua.*]

lan·guid (láng-gwid) *adj.* **1.** Lacking energy or vitality; faint; weak. **2.** Showing little or no spirit or animation; listless. **3.** Slow of movement; sluggish. [Old French *languide,* from Latin *languidus,* from *languēre,* to LANGUISH.] **—lan·guid·ly** *adv.* **—lan·guid·ness** *n.*

lan·guish (láng-gwish) *intr.v.* **-guished, -guishing, -guishes. 1. a.** To become weak or feeble; sag with loss of strength or vigour; flag. **b.** To continue in a state of apathy, debility, or suffering; exist under miserable or disheartening conditions. **c.** To be left ignored or neglected. **2.** To fall off; fade. **3.** To become listless as with longing; pine. Often used with *for.* **4.** To affect a mawkish air of nostalgia, tenderness, or wistfulness. [Middle English *languishen,* from Old French *languir* (stem *languiss-*), from Vulgar Latin *languīre* (unattested), from Latin *languēre,* to be faint or weak.] **—lan·guish·er** *n.* **—lan·guish·ment** *n.*

lan·guish·ing (láng-gwishing) *adj.* **1.** Becoming weak; fading. **2.** Slow; lingering. **3.** Expressing languor; full of sentimentality. **—lan·guish·ing·ly** *adv.*

lan·guor (láng-gər || láng-ər) *n.* **1.** Physical or mental lassitude; sluggishness. **2.** Oppressive quiet or stillness. **3.** An atmosphere or feeling of soft or wistful tenderness. **4.** *Archaic.* Debility; sickness. —See Synonyms at **lethargy.** [Middle English, from Old French, from Latin, from *languēre,* to LANGUISH.] **—lan·guor·ous** *adj.* **—lan·guor·ous·ly** *adv.* **—lan·gour·ous·ness** *n.*

lan·gur (lung-góor, laang-) *n.* Any of various slender, long-tailed, leaf-eating, Asian monkeys of the genus *Presbytis* and related genera. Also called "leaf monkey". [Hindi *langūr,* perhaps from Sanskrit *lāngūla*†, "tailed".]

laniard. Variant of **lanyard.**

la·ni·ar·y (lánni-əri || -erri) *adj.* Adapted for tearing. Said of teeth, especially canines. **~***n., pl.* **laniaries.** A laniary tooth; a canine. [Latin *laniāre,* to tear.]

la·nif·er·ous (lə-nífferəss) *adj. Biology.* Having wool or wool-like hair. [Latin *lānifer,* "wool-bearing" : *lāna,* wool + -FEROUS.]

lank (langk) *adj.* **1.** Long and lean; gaunt. **2.** Long, straight, and limp: *lank hair.* —See Synonyms at **lean.** [Old English *hlanc,* loose, hollow, from Germanic.] **—lank·ly** *adv.* **—lank·ness** *n.*

lank·y (lángki) *adj.* **-ier, -iest.** Tall, thin, and ungainly. See Synonyms at **lean.** **—lank·i·ly** *adv.* **—lank·i·ness** *n.*

lan·ner (lánnər) *n.* **1.** A falcon, *Falco biarmicus,* of Africa and the Mediterranean region. **2.** *Archaic.* The female of this species, used in falconry. [Middle English *laner,* from Old French *lanier (faucon),* cowardly (falcon), scornful application of *lanier,* weaver, from Latin *lānārius,* wool worker, from *lāna,* wool.]

lan·ner·et (lánnə-ret) *n. Archaic.* A male lanner, smaller than the female, used in falconry. [Middle English *lanerette,* from Old French *laneret,* diminutive of *lanier,* LANNER.]

lan·o·lin, lan·o·line (lánnə-lin, -leen) *n.* A yellowish-white fatty substance obtained from wool and used in soaps, cosmetics, and ointments. Also called "wool fat". [German *Lanolin* : Latin *lāna,* wool + -OL (hydrocarbon) + -IN.]

la·nose (láy-nōss, -nōz) *adj.* Having woolly hair. [Latin *lānōsus,* from *lāna,* wool.] **—la·nos·i·ty** (lay-nóssəti) *n.*

Lans·bu·ry (lánz-bəri, -bri), **George** (1859–1940). British politician. As an M.P. (1910–12, 1922–40), he espoused women's suffrage and pacifism. He was leader of the Labour Party (1931–35).

lans·que·net (lán-skə-net) *n.* 1. A card game involving betting. 2. A landsknecht. [French.]

lan·ta·na (lan-táynə, -táanə) *n.* Any of various aromatic, chiefly tropical shrubs of the genus *Lantana,* having dense clusters of small, variously coloured flowers. [New Latin *Lantana*†.]

lan·tern (lántərn) *n.* Also *obsolete* **lant·horn** (lánt-hawrn, lántərn). 1. A case that has transparent or translucent sides for holding and protecting a light, and is either fixed or portable. 2. The room at the top of a lighthouse where the light is located. 3. *Architecture.* A structure built on top of a roof with open or windowed walls to let in light and air. 4. A magic lantern *(see).* [Middle English *lanterne,* from Old French, from Latin *lanterna,* from Greek *lamptēr,* lantern, torch, from *lampein,* to shine.]

lantern fish *n.* Any of numerous small deep-sea fishes of the family Myctophidae, having phosphorescent light organs on the body.

lantern fly *n.* Any of various chiefly tropical insects of the subfamily Fulgorinae, having an enlarged, elongated head. [They were once erroneously thought to be luminous.]

lantern jaw *n.* 1. A protruding, usually square-shaped, lower jaw. 2. *Plural.* Long thin jaws with sunken cheeks. **—lan·tern-jawed** *adj.*

lantern slide *n.* A photographic slide for projection, used in a magic lantern.

lantern wheel *n.* A small pinion consisting of circular discs connected by cylindrical bars that serve as teeth, used now chiefly in inexpensive clocks. Also called "lantern pinion".

lan·tha·nide (lánthə-nīd) *n.* Also **lan·tha·non** (-non). A rare-earth element *(see).* [LANTHAN(UM) + -IDE.]

lanthanide series *n.* The set of chemically related elements with atomic numbers from 57 to 71; the rare-earth elements.

lan·tha·num (lánthənəm) *n. Symbol* La A soft, silvery-white, malleable, ductile, metallic, rare-earth element, obtained chiefly from monazite and bastnaesite, used in glass manufacture and with other rare earths in carbon lights for film and television studio lighting. Atomic number 57, atomic weight 138.91, melting point 920°C, boiling point 3,469°C, relative density 5.98 to 6.186, valency 3. [New Latin, from Greek *lanthanein,* to hide (from the finding of lanthanum concealed in cerium oxide).]

la·nu·gi·nous (lə-néw-ji-nəss ‖ -nŏŏ-) *adj.* Also **la·nu·gi·nose** (-nōss, -nōz). Covered with soft, short hair; downy. [Latin *lānūginōsus,* from *lānūgō,* down, LANUGO.] **—la·nu·gi·nous·ness** *n.*

la·nu·go (lə-néw-gō ‖ -nŏŏ-) *n., pl.* **-gos.** Fine, soft hair, such as that covering a foetus. [Latin *lānūgō,* down, from *lāna,* wool.]

lan·yard, lan·iard (lán-yərd, -yaard) *n.* 1. *Nautical.* A short rope or gasket for seizing a ladder, for example, or to secure rigging. 2. A cord worn around the neck for carrying a knife, keys, or a whistle. 3. A cord with a hook at one end used to fire a cannon. [Middle English *lanyer, lasniere,* from *lasne,* thong, strap : perhaps *laz,* LACE + *nasle,* string, from Germanic.]

Lao (low) *n., pl.* **Laos** or collectively **Lao.** Also **La·o·tian** (lów-shi-ən, -shən, lay-ṓ-shən). 1. A member of a Buddhist people of Thai stock living in the area of the Mekong River in Laos and Thailand. 2. The Thai language of this people, the official language of Laos. *~adj.* Of the Lao or their language.

La·oc·o·on (lay-óckō-on, -ən). *Greek Mythology.* A Trojan priest of Apollo who was killed with his two sons by two sea serpents for having warned his people against the Trojan horse.

La·o·di·ce·a (láy-ōdi-sée-ə). Name given to several cities built in Asia and Asia Minor by the Greek Seleucid dynasty in the third century B.C. The chief one, Laodicea ad Lycum, near present-day Denizli in western Turkey, was a prosperous market town on the Roman trading route from the Orient and an early centre of Christianity. **—La·od·i·ce·an** *n. & adj.*

la·od·i·ce·an (láy-ōdi-sée-ən) *adj.* Indifferent or lukewarm. [After *Laodicea ad Lycum,* whose early church is reproved in Revelation 3:14–16 as being "lukewarm, and neither hot nor cold".] **—la·od·i·ce·an** *n.*

Laois. See Leix.

Laos (laa-oss, lowss, lowz). Officially **The Lao People's Democratic Republic.** Country in southeast Asia. It is largely mountainous and forested, most of the population living in the Mekong valley. Rice dominates the economy; teak and tin are exports. Laos was part of French Indochina, becoming fully independent in 1953. Pathet Lao Communists fought two civil wars (1953-54; 1960–73), and finally swept away the 600-year monarchy in 1975. The country aided the Vietnamese invasion of Cambodia (1979), and by 1980 there was a massive Vietnamese presence in Laos, still racked by guerrilla activity. Area, 236 800 square kilometres (91,428 square miles).

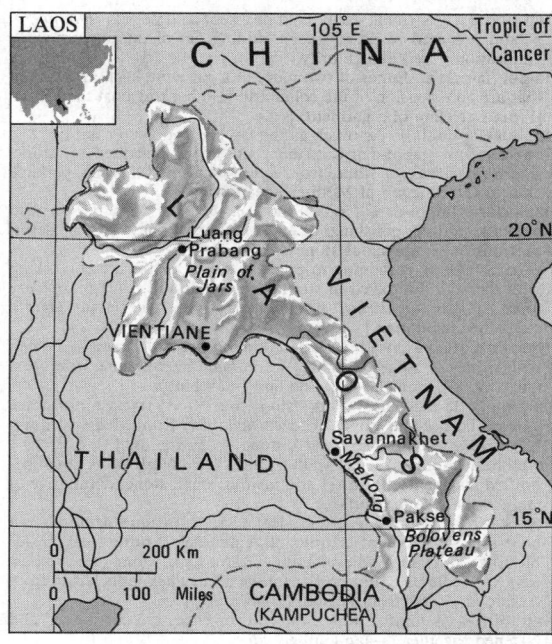

Population, 5,040,000. Capital, Vientiane (Viangchan). **—Lao·ti·an** (lówshən) *n. & adj.*

Lao Zi (lów dzə́), also known as **Lao Tzu** or **Lao Tze** (c. 6th century B.C.). Chinese philosopher. In legend he is a hermit from the Imperial Court who became deified as the founder of Taoism and author of Tao-te-Ching (Way of Life). [Chinese, "old master".]

lap¹ (lap) *n.* 1. The front region or area of a seated person extending from the lower trunk to the knees. 2. a. The portion of a garment that covers this area. b. The front part of a skirt or dress used to hold or carry something. c. A hanging or flapping part of a garment. 3. A hollow or depressed area as in the land. 4. A secure place or environment: *in the lap of luxury.* **—in (someone's) lap.** Under someone's responsibility. **—in the lap of the gods.** To be decided by fate or some impersonal power. [Middle English *lappe,* Old English *læppa,* flap of a garment, from Germanic.]

lap² *v.* **lapped, lapping, laps.** *—tr.* 1. To fold, wrap, or wind over or around something: *lap pie crust over a filling.* 2. To envelop in something; enwrap; swathe: *lapped in sables.* 3. a. To place (a thing) so as to overlap another. b. To lie partly over (something underneath); project onto or over the edge of. 4. In cabinetmaking, to join as by scarfing. 5. To get ahead of (an opponent) in a race by one or more complete circuits of the course. 6. To polish until smooth, especially to hone (two mating parts against each other) with or without an abrasive. 7. To convert (cotton or other fibres) into a sheet or layer. *—intr.* 1. To fold or wind around something. 2. To extend beyond an edge; overlap.
~n. 1. A part that overlaps. 2. a. One complete turn or circuit, especially of a racecourse or racetrack. b. A segment or stage of a race, journey, or comparable undertaking. 3. A length, as of rope, required to encircle a drum or wheel, for example. 4. A continuous band, layer, or sheet of cotton, flax, or other fibres ready for further processing. 5. A wheel, disc, or slab of leather or metal, either stationary or rotating, for polishing stone, glass, or the like. [Middle English *lappen,* probably from *lappe,* LAP (as of a garment).]

lap³ *v.* **lapped, lapping, laps.** *—tr.* 1. To take in (a liquid or food) with the tongue. Often used with *up.* Usually used of animals, especially dogs and cats. 2. To wash against with a gentle intermittent slapping sound. Used of waves or a body of water. *—intr.* 1. To drink by lifting a liquid with the tongue. 2. To dash or slap softly against a shore or other surface. **—lap up.** *Informal.* To receive eagerly and uncritically: *lap up praise.*
~n. 1. The act or process of lapping. 2. A watery food for animals. 3. An amount ingested by a lap. 4. The sound of lapping water. [Middle English *lappen,* Old English *lapian.*] **—lap·per** *n.*

lap·a·ro·scope (láppərə-skōp) *n.* A surgical instrument that is inserted through the abdominal wall to inspect the abdominal organs. [Greek *lapara,* flank, from *laparos,* soft + -SCOPE.] **—lap·a·ros·co·py** (láppə-róskəpi) *n.*

lap·a·rot·o·my (láppə-róttəmi) *n., pl.* **-mies.** Surgical incision into the abdominal wall, either as a prelude to further surgery or to aid diagnosis. [Greek *lapara,* flank, from *laparos,* soft + -TOMY.]

La Paz (laa páz, la, *Spanish* páss). Also **La Paz de Ayacucho** (ī-ə-kŏŏchō). Capital of Bolivia, founded in 1548. Independence from Spain was declared there in 1809 and it became the capital in 1898. It is the world's highest capital at 3 577 metres (11,735 feet).

lap·board (láp-bawrd ‖ -bōrd) *n.* A flat board to hold on the lap as a substitute for a table or desk.

lap dissolve *n.* A cinematic technique of overlapping a fade-out and a fade-in so that one scene dissolves into the next.

lap dog *n.* **1.** A small, easily held dog kept as a pet. **2.** *Informal.* A person prepared to do another's bidding out of uncritical love or admiration. Used derogatorily.
la·pel (lə-pél) *n.* Either of two parts of a garment, such as a jacket, that are an extension of the collar and fold back against the breast. [From LAP (flap of a garment).]
lap·ful (láp-fōol) *n.* As much as the lap can support or hold.
lap·i·dar·i·an (láppi-dáir-i-ən) *adj.* Cut in or inscribed on stone. [Latin *lapidārius,* of stone, from *lapis* (stem *lapid-*), stone, perhaps akin to Greek *lepas,* of Mediterranean origin.]
lap·i·dar·y (láppi-dəri ‖ *U.S.* -derri) *n., pl.* **-ies. 1.** A person who works at cutting, polishing, or engraving gemstones. **2.** A dealer in precious or semiprecious stones.
~*adj.* **1.** Of or pertaining to precious stones or the art of working with them. **2.** Engraved in stone. **3.** Elegant and concise: *lapidary prose.* [Latin *lapidārius,* stoneworker, from *lapis* (stem *lapid-*), stone. See **lapidarian.**]
lap·i·date (láppi-dayt) *tr.v.* **-dated, -dating, -dates.** *Literary.* To pelt with stones or stone to death. [Latin *lapidāre,* to stone, from *lapis* (stem *lapid-*), stone.] **—lap·i·da·tion** (-dáysh'n) *n.*
la·pid·i·fy (lə-píddi-fī) *v.* **-fied, -fying, -fies.** —*tr.* To turn into stone. —*intr.* To become stone. [French *lapidifier,* from Medieval Latin *lapidificāre* : *lapis* (stem *lapid-*), stone + *-ficāre,* -FY.]
la·pil·lus (lə-pílləss) *n., pl.* **-pilli** (-píllī). *Usually plural.* A small solidified fragment of lava. [Latin *lapillus,* small stone, diminutive of *lapis,* stone. See **lapidarian.**]
lap·is laz·u·li (láppiss lázzew-lī, -lee) *n.* **1.** An opaque, azure-blue to deep-blue gemstone of lazurite. **2.** A mineral, **lazurite** *(see).* [Middle English, from Medieval Latin : Latin *lapis,* stone (see **lapidarian**) + Medieval Latin *lazuli,* genitive of *lazulum,* lapis lazuli, from Arabic *lāzaward,* from Persian *lāzhuward*†.]
lap joint *n.* A joint in which the ends or edges are overlapped and fastened together. **—lap-joint·ed** *adj.*
La·place (laa-pláss, la-, lə-), **Pierre Simon, Marquis de** (1749–1827). French mathematician and astronomer. His speculation, in *Mécanique céleste* (1798–1825), that the solar system evolved from a rotating nebula, is thought to be broadly correct.
Laplace operator *n. Mathematics.* *Symbol* ∇^2 The differential operator $\partial^2/\partial x^2 + \partial^2/\partial y^2 + \partial^2/\partial z^2$. Also called "Laplacian". [After P.S. de LAPLACE.]
La Pla·ta (laa plaáatə, la, pláttə). City in eastern Argentina, the capital of Buenos Aires province, lying 8 kilometres (5 miles) inland from Ensenada, its port on the Río de la Plata. It is Argentina's leading oil-refining centre.
lap of honour *n.* A celebratory circuit made of a racetrack, or other sports ground by the winner or winners of a sports event.
Lapp (lap) *n.* Also **Lap·pish** (láppish) (for sense 2). **1.** A member of a people of nomadic tradition who inhabit Lappland. Also called "Lapplander". **2.** The Finno-Ugric language of this people.
~*adj.* Also **Lappish.** Of the Lapps or their language.
lap·pet (láppit) *n.* **1.** A decorative flap, streamer, or loose fold on a garment or headdress. **2.** A flaplike structure, such as the wattle of a bird. [From LAP (fold or flap).]
lap·pie (lúppi) *n., pl.* **-pies** (-pis, -piz). *South African Informal.* A cloth or rag, as for cleaning. [Afrikaans, diminutive of *lap,* rag, cloth.]
Lapp·land (lápp-land). *Norwegian* **Lapland**; *Finnish* **Lappi.** Vast Arctic region of Europe, extending over the north of Norway, Sweden, Finland, and the Kola peninsula of Russia. It consists of tundra, swamps, forests, and mountains, and is inhabited by the reindeer-herding Lapps or Lapplanders, about two-thirds of whom live in Norway. There are large forest and mineral resources. **—Lapp·land·er** *n.*
lapse (laps) *intr.v.* **lapsed, lapsing, lapses. 1. a.** To fall away by degrees; decline; vanish: *My enthusiasm soon lapsed.* **b.** To subside gradually; drift: *lapse into dreaminess.* **c.** To drop in standard or quality, usually temporarily. **d.** To cease practising or adhering to a belief, custom, or the like: *a lapsed Catholic.* **2.** To elapse: *Years had lapsed since we last met.* **3. a.** *Law.* To pass to another through neglect or omission. Said of a right or privilege, a benefice, or an estate. **b.** To become void or ineffective.
~*n.* **1.** The act of lapsing; a gradual or imperceptible falling or sliding away. **2. a.** A minor slip or failure: *a lapse of the memory.* **b.** A fall from rectitude; moral error. **3.** A slipping into a lower state or degree; a decline: *his lapse into premature senility.* **4. a.** The passage of time. **b.** An interval. **5.** *Law.* The termination of a right, interest, or privilege through disuse, a death, or other failure. **6.** An abandonment of a practice, especially of religious faith. **7.** A failure to renew membership of an organisation. [Latin *lapsus,* error, a sliding, from *lābī* (past participle *lapsus*), to slide.] **—laps·er** *n.*
lapse rate *n.* The rate of change of a meteorological parameter with increasing height, such as the rate of change of atmospheric temperature for every 100 metres increase in altitude.
lap·strake (láp-strayk) *adj.* Also **lap·streak** (-streek). *Nautical.* Built with each strake overlapping the one below; clinker-built.
~*n.* Also **lap·streak.** A clinker-built boat. [LAP (to overlap) + STRAKE.]
lap·sus (láp-səss) *n., pl.* **-sus.** *Formal.* A lapse; a slip.
lap-top (láp-top) *adj.* Portable and compact enough to be used without a supporting table or desk, as when propped on someone's lap: *a lap-top computer.* **—lap-top** *n.*
La·pu·tan (lə-péwt'n) *adj.* Impractical and visionary; absurd. [After *Laputa,* a country in Swift's *Gulliver's Travels* (1726) devoted to absurdly visionary schemes.]
lap·wing (láp-wing) *n.* Any of several Eurasian birds of the genus *Vanellus,* related to the plovers; especially, *V. vanellus,* having a narrow crest. Also called "peewit", "pewit", "green plover". [Middle English *lapwinge,* variant (influenced by *winge,* wing, and *lappen,* to overlap) of *lappewinke,* Old English *hlēapewince* : *hlēapan,* to LEAP + *-wince* (unattested), WINK (referring to its way of flying).]
lar (lar) *n., pl.* **lares** (láir-eez, laáar-, -ayz) or **lars.** *Sometimes capital* **L.** A tutelary deity or spirit of an ancient Roman household. [Latin *Lār*†.]
lar·board (lárbərd) *n. Nautical.* The port side.
~*adj. Nautical.* On the port side. [Middle English *lathebord, lad(d)borde,* probably "the loading side" (but influenced by STARBOARD) : *laden,* to load, LADE + *bord,* ship's side, BOARD.]
lar·ce·ny (lár-səni) *n., pl.* **-nies.** *Law.* The felonious taking and removing of another's personal property; theft. In Britain the offence was abolished in 1968 and is now covered by the laws on theft. See **grand larceny, petit larceny.** [Middle English, from Old French *larcin,* from Latin *latrōcinium,* military service for pay, freebooting, from *latrō,* mercenary soldier, from Greek *latron,* pay.] **—lar·ce·nist, lar·ce·ner** *n.* **—lar·ce·nous** *adj.* **—lar·ce·nous·ly** *adv.*
larch (larch) *n.* **1.** Any of several coniferous trees of the genus *Larix,* such as *L. decidua,* the European larch, having deciduous needles and heavy, durable wood. **2.** The wood of a larch. [German *Lärche,* from Middle High German *larche, lerche,* from Old High German *larihha* (unattested), from Latin *larix*† (stem *laric-*).]
lard (lard) *n.* The white solid or semisolid rendered fat of a pig.
~*tr.v.* **larded, larding, lards. 1.** To cover or coat with fat. **2.** To insert strips of bacon or the like in (lean meat or poultry) before cooking. **3.** To enrich (speech or writing) with witticisms, quotations, or similar additions. Often used derogatorily. [Middle English, from Old French, from Latin *lārdum, lāridum*†.] **—lard·y** *adj.*
lar·der (lárdər) *n.* A small room, cupboard, or the like where meat and other foods are kept. [Middle English, from Old French *lardier,* from *lard,* LARD.]
larder beetle *n.* A small black beetle, *Dermestes lardarius,* found in houses, where it feeds on bacon and other fatty foods.
lar·don (lárd'n) *n.* Also **lar·doon** (laar-dōōn). A strip of fat for larding meat. [French, from Old French, from *lard,* LARD.]
lardy cake *n.* A breadlike cake containing currants. [From LARD.]
lar·es and pe·na·tes *pl.n.* Esteemed household possessions. [From two kinds of Roman household gods. See **lar, penates.**]
large (larj) *adj.* **larger, largest.** *Abbr.* **L, lg., lge. 1.** Of considerable size, extent, quantity, capacity, or amount; big; not small: *a large house.* **2.** Important; on a considerable scale: *a large steel producer.* **3. a.** Of wide scope or capacity: *a large mind.* **b.** Having breadth or sweep; comprehensive. **4. a.** Liberal; generous: *a large heart.* **b.** Prodigal. **5.** *Rare.* **a.** Pretentious; big. Said of speech or manners. **b.** Unrestrained; loose; gross. Said of speech or language. **6.** *Nautical.* Designating a favourable wind. **—at large. 1.** At liberty; free. **2.** At length; copiously: *He spoke at large on the housing problem.* **3.** As an entity or whole; in general. **—in the large.** On a broad scale. [Middle English, from Old French, from Latin *largus*†, generous, bountiful.] **—large·ness** *n.*
large calorie *n.* A unit of heat, a **calorie** *(see).*
large-heart·ed (lárj-hártid) *adj.* Having a generous disposition; sympathetic. **—large-heart·ed·ness** *n.*
large intestine *n.* The portion of the intestine that extends from the ileum to the anus, forming an arch around the convolutions of the small intestine, and including the caecum, colon, and rectum.
large·ly (lárjli) *adv.* **1.** In a large manner; on a large scale. **2.** To a large extent; mainly.
large-mind·ed (lárj-mīndid) *adj.* Having a breadth of ideas; of liberal views; open-minded. **—large-mind·ed·ness** *n.*
larg·er-than-life, larger than life (lárjər-thən-līf) *adj.* Seeming to belong to the world of fiction rather than to real life; possessing extraordinary qualities.
large-scale (lárj-skáyl, -skayl) *adj.* **1.** Of large scope; conducted as or operating a major undertaking. **2.** Drawn or made large to show detail. Said of maps and models.
lar·gesse, lar·gess (laar-jéss, lár-jess, -zhéss) *n.* **1. a.** Generosity, especially as displayed by an important person on a great occasion. **b.** The money, favours, or gifts bestowed. **2.** Generosity of attitude. [Middle English, from Old French, from *large,* generous, LARGE.]
lar·ghet·to (laar-géttō) *adv. Music.* Moderately slow in tempo. Used as a direction.
~*n., pl.* **larghettos.** *Music.* A larghetto movement or passage.
~*adj. Music.* Moderately slow. [Italian, diminutive of LARGO.]
larg·ish (lárjish) *adj.* Fairly large.
lar·go (lárgō) *adv. Music.* In a slow, solemn manner. Used as a direction.
~*adj. Music.* Slow and solemn.
~*n., pl.* **largos.** *Music.* A largo movement or passage. [Italian, slow, "broad", from Latin *largus,* LARGE.]
lar·i·at (lárri-ət) *n. U.S.* **1.** A long rope with a running noose for catching wild livestock; a lasso. **2.** A rope for picketing grazing horses or mules. [Spanish *la reata,* lasso, rope for tying mules : *la,* the + *reatar,* to tie again : *re-,* again, from Latin + *atar,* to tie, from Latin *aptāre,* to fit, from *aptus,* APT.]
Lá·ri·sa or **La·ris·sa** (lə-ríssə; *Greek* lárree-sa). Capital of ancient Thessaly in Greece. It now produces silk and tobacco.
lark¹ (lark) *n.* **1.** Any of various chiefly Old World birds of the

family Alaudidae, having a sustained, melodious song. See **skylark.** **2.** Any of several similar birds, such as the meadowlark. **—up with the lark.** Out of bed early. [Middle English *larke,* Old English *lāwerce, lǣwerce,* from West Germanic *larw(a)rikōn* (unattested).]

lark² *n. Informal.* **1.** A carefree adventure. **2.** A harmless prank. **3.** An amusing situation or event: *What a lark!*
~intr.v. **larked, larking, larks.** *Informal.* **1.** To play or have fun. Often used with *about* or *around.* **2.** To play tricks. [Probably variant of dialectal *lake,* to play, from Middle English *leiken,* from Old Norse *leika.*]

Lar·kin (lár-kin), **Philip (Arthur)** (1922–85). British poet, novelist, and editor of *The Oxford Book of Twentieth Century English Verse* (1973). His books of poetry include *The Whitsun Weddings* (1964) and *High Windows* (1974). His novels include *A Girl in Winter* (1947).

lark·spur (lárk-spur) *n.* Any of various plants of the genus *Delphinium,* having spurred, variously coloured flowers.

Lar·mor precession (lár-mər, -mawr) *n.* The precession of the orbit of an electron in an atom subjected to a magnetic field. The frequency of the precession (the *Larmor frequency*) is $eH/4\pi mv$, where H is the field strength and $m,e,$ and v are the mass, charge, and velocity of the electron respectively. [After Sir Joseph *Larmor* (1857–1942), British physicist.]

larn (larn) *v.* **larned, larning, larns.** *Nonstandard.* *—intr.* To learn. Often used humorously. *—tr.* To teach; especially, to teach (a person) a lesson: *That'll larn you!*

Larne (larn). Seaport and resort in Northern Ireland. It is the ferry terminal to Stranraer (Scotland), the shortest sea route between Ireland and Britain.

La Roche·fou·cauld (laa rósh-fōō-kō || rōsh-; *French* la-rosh-fōō-kō), **François, Duc de** (1613–80). French moralist. He wrote *Maximes* (1664), a collection of cynical epigrams suggesting that people are ruled by self-interest.

La Ro·chelle (laa ro-shél; *French* la-ro-shél). City in western France, lying on the Bay of Biscay. It is the chief French Atlantic fishing port. During the 16th-century Wars of Religion it was the most important stronghold of the Protestant Huguenots.

La·rousse (lə-rōōss, la-), **Pierre** (1817–75). French lexicographer, who compiled the *Grand Dictionnaire universel du XIXe Siècle* (1866–76). His company still publishes reference books.

lar·ri·gan (lárrigən) *n. Sometimes capital* **L.** A moccasin with knee-high leggings made of oiled leather. [17th century : origin obscure.]

lar·ri·kin (lárri-kin) *n. Australian & N. Z. Informal.* A rowdy youth; a hooligan. [From English dialect, probably from *Larry* (pet form of *Lawrence*) + -KIN.]

lar·rup (lárrəp) *tr.v.* **-ruped, -ruping, -rups.** *Regional.* To beat; flog. *~n. Regional.* A blow. [19th century : origin obscure.]

Lars Por·se·na (lárz pór-sinə) (*c.* 6th century B.C.). Etruscan king who, in Roman legend, attacked Rome after the proclamation of the Republic (509 B.C.) but was foiled by Horatius (Cocles).

lar·um (lárrəm) *n. Archaic.* An alarm. [Short for ALARUM.]

lar·va (lár-və) *n., pl.* **-vae** (-vee). **1.** The wingless, often wormlike form of a newly hatched insect before metamorphosis. **2.** The newly hatched stage of any of various animals that undergo metamorphosis, differing markedly in appearance from the adult. [Latin *lārva*†, disembodied spirit, mask.] **—lar·val** *adj.*

lar·vi·cide (lárvi-sīd) *n.* An insecticide designed to kill larval pests. [LARV(A) + -I- + -CIDE.] **—lar·vi·ci·dal** (-sīd'l) *adj.*

la·ryn·ge·al (lárrin-jée-əl, -jéel, lə-rínji-əl, -rínjəl) *adj.* Also **la·ryn·gal** (lə-ríng-g'l). **1.** Of, pertaining to, affecting, or near the larynx. **2.** *Phonetics.* Produced in or with the larynx; glottal.
~n. **1.** A part of the larynx. **2.** *Phonetics.* A laryngeal sound. **3.** Any of a set of sounds reconstructed for Proto-Indo-European, of uncertain character (but originally thought to be laryngeal in nature), manifested in various environments, typically involving loss of the original sound in most languages of the family. [New Latin *laryngeus,* from *larynx* (stem *laryng-*), LARYNX.]

lar·yn·gec·to·my (lárrin-jéktəmi) *n., pl.* **-mies.** Surgical removal of part or all of the larynx, as for the treatment of laryngeal cancer. [LARYNG(O)- + -ECTOMY.]

lar·yn·gi·tis (lárrin-jītiss) *n.* Inflammation of the larynx, causing hoarseness and sometimes temporary loss of speech. [New Latin : LARYNG(O)- + -ITIS.] **—lar·yn·git·ic** (-jíttik) *adj.*

laryngo-, laryng- *comb. form.* Indicates the larynx or pertaining to the larynx; for example, **laryngoscope, laryngitis.** [New Latin, from Greek *larungo-,* from *larunx* (stem *larung-*), LARYNX.]

la·ryn·go·graph (lə-ríng-gə-graaf, -graf) *n.* An instrument used to observe the functioning of the vocal cords by means of electrodes placed on the surface of the neck. [LARYNGO- + -GRAPH.] **—la·ryn·go·graph·ic** (-gráffik) *adj.* **—la·ryn·gog·ra·phy** (lárring-góggrəfi) *n.*

lar·yn·gol·o·gy (lárring-gólləji) *n.* The medical study or treatment of the larynx and its diseases. [LARYNGO- + -LOGY.] **—lar·yn·go·log·i·cal** (lə-ríng-gə-lójik'l) *adj.* **—lar·yn·gol·o·gist** *n.*

la·ryn·go·scope (lə-ríng-gə-skōp) *n.* A tubular instrument used to observe the interior of the larynx. [LARYNGO- + -SCOPE.] **—la·ryn·go·scop·ic** (-skóppik), **la·ryn·go·scop·i·cal** *adj.* **—la·ryn·go·scop·i·cal·ly** *adv.* **—lar·yn·gos·co·py** (lárring-góskəpi) *n.*

lar·yn·got·o·my (lárring-góttəmi) *n., pl.* **-mies.** Surgical incision into the larynx. [LARYNGO- + -TOMY.]

lar·ynx (lárringks) *n., pl.* **larynges** (lə-rín-jeez) or **-ynxes.** The upper part of the respiratory tract between the pharynx and the trachea, having cartilaginous walls and containing the vocal cords. [New Latin, from Greek *larunx*†.]

la·sa·gne, la·sa·gna (lə-zán-yə, -sán-, -zaán-, -saán-) *n.* **1.** Flat wide noodles. **2.** A dish made by baking such noodles in layers with minced meat, tomatoes, and cheese. [Italian, from Latin *lasanum,* cooking pot, originally "chamber pot", from Greek *lasanon*†.]

La Salle (lə sál, laa, la), **Robert Cavelier, Sieur de** (1643–87). French explorer. He led expeditions to North America and claimed Louisiana for France (1682). He was murdered by mutineers on his final expedition.

las·car (láskər) *n.* A sailor from the East Indies. [Hindi *lashkarī,* soldier, from *lashkar,* army, from Persian, from Arabic *al-'askar,* the army.]

Las Ca·sas (lass kaá-səss), **Bartolomé de** (1474–1566). Spanish planter in the West Indies, who joined the Dominican order and campaigned for the abolition of Indian slavery.

Las·caux (láss-kō; *French* la-skō). Cave near Montignac in southwest France, lying above the Vézère valley in the Dordogne. Discovered in 1940, it is one of the most important sites of prehistoric cave art in Europe. The paintings are mostly of animals.

las·civ·i·ous (lə-sívvi-əss) *adj.* **1.** Of or characterised by lust; lewd; lecherous. **2.** Exciting sexual desires. [Late Latin *lascīviōsus,* from Latin *lascīvia,* licentiousness, wantonness, from *lascīvus,* wanton, lustful.] **—las·civ·i·ous·ly** *adv.* **—las·civ·i·ous·ness** *n.*

Las·dun (láz-dən), **Sir Denys (Louis)** (1914–). British architect, who designed the University of East Anglia, Norwich (1961), the National Theatre, London (1968–76), and the Institute of Education, London (1970–78).

lase (layz) *intr.v.* **lased, lasing, lases.** To function as a laser; emit coherent radiation by laser. [Back-formation from LASER.]

la·ser (láyzər) *n.* **1.** Any of several devices that convert incident electromagnetic radiation of mixed frequencies to one or more discrete frequencies of highly amplified and coherent visible radiation. Also called "optical maser". **2.** Any such device, including the **maser** *(see),* the output of which is in an invisible region of the electromagnetic spectrum. [*L*ight *a*mplification by *s*timulated *e*mission of *r*adiation.]

laser disc *n.* A disc on which pictures or sound are recorded for playing through a television set or specially adapted record player. A laser beam senses variations in height on the surface of the disc and converts them into electronic pulses for playback.

lash¹ (lash) *n.* **1.** A stroke or blow with or as if with a whip, rope, or the like. **2.** The thin stinging part or parts of a whip; the thongs. **3.** A remark that insults, reprimands, or ridicules. **4.** A powerful or violent impact: *the lash of rain on the windows.* **5.** An eyelash. **—have a lash.** *Australian Informal.* To attempt; have a go.
~v. **lashed, lashing, lashes.** *—tr.* **1.** To strike with or as if with a whip. **2.** To strike against with force or violence: *waves lashing the sides of the ship.* **3.** To move or wave rapidly to and fro: *a lion lashing his tail.* **4.** To make a vehement verbal or written attack on. **5.** To incite or urge as with lashes. *—intr.* **1.** To move a limb, tail, or the like rapidly or suddenly. **2.** To make a sudden or violent attack. Used with *at* or *against.* **—lash out. 1.** To make a sudden or violent attack. **2.** To express vehement criticism. **3.** To kick out violently. Used of a horse. **4.** *Informal.* To spend money in an apparently extravagant way. [Middle English *lashe*†.] **—lash·er** *n.*

lash² *tr.v.* **lashed, lashing, lashes.** To secure or bind, as with a rope, cord, or chain. [Middle English *lasshen,* from Old French *lac(h)ier,* from Latin *laqueāre,* to ensnare, from *laqueus,* snare.] **—lash·er** *n.*

lash·ing (láshing) *n.* **1.** Something used for securing or binding, such as a rope or cord. **2.** A beating or flogging.

lash·ings (láshingz) *pl.n. Chiefly British.* Lavish quantities. [From LASH (whip) in an obsolete sense "lavish".]

Las·ki (láski), **Harold (Joseph)** (1893–1950). British socialist and political theorist. He was a professor at the London School of Economics.

Las Pal·mas (lass pál-məss, paál-). Also **Las Palmas de Gran Canaria.** Capital of Spain's Las Palmas province in the Canary Islands, lying on the Isla de Gran Canaria. It was founded in 1478 and named after the palm trees growing there. It was an important station for Spanish trade ships on the African-South American route. Today it is a major tourist resort.

La Spe·zia (laa spét-siə, la, spétss-yə). Seaport in northwest Italy, lying on the Gulf of La Spezia. It has been an important fortified town since the Middle Ages and is today the largest naval station and arsenal in Italy.

lass (lass) *n.* **1.** A girl or young woman. **2.** A sweetheart. [Middle English *lasce, lasse*†.]

Las·sa fever (laá-sə, lássə) *n.* A severe viral disease of Central West Africa, typically causing fever, headache, and muscular pain and often leading to death from heart or kidney failure.

las·si (lassi, lussi) *n.* A sweet or salty cold drink, originating in India, made from yoghurt or buttermilk and spices. [Hindi.]

las·sie (lássi) *n.* A lass. [Diminutive of LASS.]

las·si·tude (lássi-tewd || -tōōd) *n.* A state of exhaustion or torpor. See Synonyms at **lethargy.** [Latin *lassitūdō,* from *lassus,* tired, weary.]

las·so (la-sōō, lə- || *Chiefly U.S.* lássō) *n., pl.* **-sos** or **-soes.** A long rope or leather thong with a running noose at one end used especially to catch horses and cattle.
~tr.v. **lassoed, -soing, -sos** or **-soes.** To catch with or as if with a lasso; rope. [Spanish *lazo,* from Latin *laqueus,* snare.]

last¹ (laast || last). Alternative superlative of **late.**
~adj. **1.** Being or coming after all others: *last on the list.* **2.** Being the only remaining part of a collection or sequence: *my last stamp.* **3.** Most recent; latest: *last year.* **4.** Highest; greatest; utmost: *the*

last degree. **5.** Most valid, authoritative, or conclusive: *The boss always has the last say.* **6** Least appropriate; most unexpected: *the last man we suspected.* **7.** The lowest in rank, size, or importance: *the last prize.* **8.** Final or ultimate, as just before death: *famous last words.* —See Usage note at **first.** —**every last.** *Informal.* All; omitting none: *He took every last cigarette.* —**last but not least.** Important or significant although coming at the end.

~*adv.* **1.** After all others, as in chronology or sequence: *They left last.* **2.** Most recently: *last heard of in May.* Often used in combination: *the last-mentioned item.*

~*n.* **1.** One that is last: *the last of the Plantagenets.* **2.** The end: *He held out until the last.* **3.** The final mention or appearance of something: *I fear we haven't seen the last of her.* **4.** The person or thing most recently mentioned: *You need glue, string, and paper, the last being the most important.* **5.** The last instance or occasion of something: *This day will be your last.* —**at (long) last.** After a considerable length of time; finally. —**breathe one's last.** To die. [Middle English *last*, Old English *latost*, superlative of *laet, late*, LATE.]

Synonyms: last, final, terminal, eventual, ultimate.

last² *v.* **lasted, lasting, lasts.** —*intr.* **1.** To continue in existence; go on: *The war lasted for four years.* **2.** To remain in good condition; endure: *Clay lasts longer than paper.* **3.** To endure or get through. Often used with *out*: *His strength won't last out.* **4.** To remain in adequate supply. Often used with *out*: *Will our water last out?* —*tr.* **1.** To be adequate or sufficient for: *Five pounds will last me till tomorrow.* **2.** To continue throughout: *He didn't last the course.* **3.** To take or go on for (a specified time): *It lasts half an hour.* [Middle English *lasten*, Old English *lǣstan*.] —**last·er** *n.*

last³ *n.* A block or form shaped like a human foot, used by shoemakers in making or repairing shoes.

~*tr.v.* **lasted, lasting, lasts.** To mould or shape on a last. —**stick to (one's) last.** To do the work to which one is accustomed. [Middle English *laste*, Old English *lǣste*, from *lāst*, sole, footprint.]

last⁴ *n. Chiefly British.* A unit of weight or volume varying for different commodities and in different districts, and approximating to 80 bushels, 640 gallons, or 2 tons. [Middle English *last*, "load", "burden", Old English *hlæst*.]

last-ditch (laást-dích ‖ lást-) *adj.* Of or designating a final desperate effort: *a last-ditch attempt to save the company.*

last honours *pl.n.* Observances or signs of respect at a funeral. Also called "funeral honours".

last·ing¹ (laást-ing ‖ lást-) *adj.* Continuing for a long time; durable. —**last·ing·ly** *adv.* —**last·ing·ness** *n.*

lasting² *n.* A durable twilled fabric.

Last Judgment *n.* According to the Bible, the final judgment by God of all mankind. Preceded by *the.*

last·ly (laást-li ‖ lást-) *adv.* In the end; in conclusion; finally.

last minute *n.* The moment or time immediately before an event or deadline: *She always does everything at the last minute.* Also called "last moment". —**last-minute** (laást-mínnit) *adj.*

last name *n.* A surname.

last post *n. Sometimes capital* L, *capital* P. *Military.* **1.** A bugle call blown as a signal for the hour for retiring to bed. **2.** A bugle call blown at funerals.

last resort *n.* A final measure or course of action open to one.

last straw *n.* An additional difficulty, irritation, or trouble that stretches one's tolerance or endurance beyond the limit. Preceded by *the.* [Based on the proverbial phrase, *It's the last straw that breaks the camel's back.*]

Last Supper *n.* Christ's supper with his disciples on the night before his Crucifixion, at which he instituted the Eucharist. Preceded by *the.* Also called the "Lord's Supper".

last thing *adv. Informal.* As the last or final action: *She'll do that last thing before she leaves.*

last word *n.* **1.** The final statement in a verbal argument. **2. a.** A conclusive or authoritative statement or treatment: *the last word in car safety.* **b.** The power or authority of ultimate decision. **3.** *Informal.* The newest in fashion; the latest thing. Preceded by *the.*

Las Ve·gas (lass váygəss ‖ *U.S.* laass). City in southern Nevada, in the southwest United States. Set in a remote ranching and mining region, it is nevertheless the leading gambling city in the country and the site of many famous nightclubs.

lat. latitude.

Lat. Latin.

lat·a·ki·a (láttə-kée-ə) *n.* A grade of Turkish tobacco. [After *Latakia*, Syrian port in a tobacco-growing region.]

latch (lach) *n.* **1.** A fastening or lock, typically a bar that falls into a groove or cavity and is lifted by a lever. **2.** A small spring-lock for an outside door that can be opened from the outside by a key.

~*v.* **latched, latching, latches.** —*tr.* To close or lock with a latch. —*intr.* To have a latch for closing or locking. —**latch on.** *Informal.* **1.** To attach oneself; cling. Used with *to.* **2.** To understand; perceive: *The fool still hasn't latched on.* Often used with *to.* **3.** To single out (an idea, for example). Used with *to: latched on to idealism as the key to his work.* [Middle English *lache*, from *lachen*, to latch, seize, Old English *lǣccan*, to grasp.]

latch·et (láchit) *n. Archaic.* A thong used to fasten a shoe or sandal. [Middle English, from Old French *lachet, lacet*, shoestring, from *las*, noose, snare.]

latch·key (lách-kee) *n.* **1.** A key for opening a latch, especially one on an outside door or gate. **2.** A symbol of freedom from parental authority.

latchkey child *n.* A child who has a key to his home because both

parents are out working when he returns from school.

latch·string (lách-string) *n.* A cord attached to a latch and often passed through a hole in the door to allow lifting of the latch from the outside.

late (layt) *adj.* **later** or *rare* **latter** (láttər), **latest** or **last** (laast ‖ last). **1.** Coming or occurring after the correct, usual, or expected time; delayed. **2. a.** Beginning at, occurring at, or lasting until a relatively advanced hour or time: *a late breakfast.* **b.** Occurring, being, or continuing towards the end: *the late 19th century.* **c.** Coming from near the end of a period or life: *a late Rembrandt.* **d.** At an advanced hour at night: *It was very late by then.* **3.** Taking longer than usual to reach a given stage: *a late developer.* **4.** Having recently begun or occurred; just previous to the present: *the latest developments.* **5.** Being the immediate past occupant of a position or place; former. **6.** Dead, especially recently deceased: *the late Mr. Foster.* —See Synonyms at **tardy.**

~*adv.* **later, latest. 1.** After the correct, usual, or expected time; tardily. **2. a.** At a relatively advanced time: *undertaken late in his life.* **b.** At an advanced hour of the night: *called very late.* **c.** Far into a period of time. **3.** In the recent past: *As late as last week, he was still alive.* —**of late.** In the near past; lately. [Middle English, Old English *lǣt.*] —**late·ness** *n.*

lat·ed (láytid) *adj. Poetic.* Belated. [From LATE.]

la·teen (lə-téen) *adj. Nautical.* **1.** Designating a triangular sail hung on a long yard attached to a short mast. **2.** Rigged with such a sail.

~*n.* A lateen-rigged boat. [French *(voile) latine*, "Latin (sail)" (from its use in the Mediterranean), from Old French, feminine of *Latin*, LATIN.]

Late Greek *n.* Greek during the early Byzantine Empire, from about the fourth to about the seventh century A.D.

Late Latin *n.* Latin from the third to the seventh century A.D.

late·ly (láytli) *adv.* Not long ago; recently.

La Tène (laa tén, la) *adj.* Pertaining to or designating an Iron Age European civilisation dating from the fifth to the first century B.C. [After *La Tène*, on Lake Neuchâtel, Switzerland, where the remains were first discovered.]

la·tent (láyt'nt) *adj.* Present or potential, but not manifest: *latent talent.* [Latin *latēns* (stem *latent-*), present participle of *latēre*, to lie hidden, be concealed.] —**la·ten·cy** *n.* —**la·tent·ly** *adv.*

Synonyms: latent, dormant, potential, quiescent.

latent heat *n. Symbol* L The quantity of heat absorbed or released by a substance undergoing a change of state, as by ice changing to water or water to steam.

latent image *n.* In photography, an invisible image produced in an emulsion after exposure but before development.

latent period *n.* **1.** The incubation period of an infectious disease. **2.** The interval between stimulus and response.

lat·er (láytər) Comparative of **late.**

~*adj.* Subsequent.

lat·er·al (láttərəl, láttrəl) *adj.* **1.** Of, pertaining to, or situated at or on the side or sides. **2.** *Phonetics.* Designating a sound produced by breath passing along one or both sides of the tongue.

~*n.* **1.** A lateral part, projection, passage, or appendage. **2.** *Phonetics.* A lateral sound, such as (l). [Latin *laterālis*, from *latus†* (stem *later-*), side.] —**lat·er·al·ly** *adv.*

lateral inversion *n.* Inversion between right and left, such as that which occurs in the formation of an image in a plane mirror.

lateral line *n.* A linear series of sensory pores and tubes for sensing sound and vibration, as along the side of a fish.

lateral thinking *n.* A method of solving problems by using an associational, sometimes apparently illogical, approach, especially one that uses the imagination as opposed to step-by-step reasoning. [Coined by Edward de Bono (1933–), British psychologist and author of *The Use of Lateral Thinking* (1967).]

Lat·er·an (láttərən) *n.* **1.** The church of Saint John Lateran, cathedral church of the pope as bishop of Rome. **2.** The palace, now a museum, adjoining this church. Preceded by *the.* [Latin *Laterana*, district of ancient Rome, residence of the family Plautii *Laterani.*]

la·te·ra rec·ta. Plural of **latus rectum.**

lat·er·ite (láttə-rīt) *n.* A reddish-brown earthy substance, the residue produced by leaching of the soil in tropical regions, consisting of a preponderance of hydrated iron oxide with some hydrated aluminium oxide. Compare **bauxite.** [Latin *later†*, brick, tile + -ITE.]

lat·est (láytist) Alternative superlative of **late.**

~*adj.* Most recent, modern, or up-to-date.

~*n. Informal.* The most recent or up-to-date news, fashion, or the like. Preceded by *the.*

la·tex (láy-teks) *n., pl.* **latices** (láyti-seez) or **-texes. 1.** The usually milky, viscous sap of certain trees and plants, such as the rubber tree, that coagulates on exposure to air. **2.** An emulsion of rubber or plastic globules in water, used in paints, adhesives, and other products. [New Latin, from Latin *latex*, fluid.] —**la·tex** *adj.*

latex paint *n.* A paint having a binder that is a latex. Also called "rubber-base paint".

lath (laath ‖ lath) *n., pl.* **laths** (laaths, laathz ‖ laths, lathz). **1.** A narrow, thin strip of wood or metal, used especially in making a supporting structure for plaster, shingles, slates, or tiles. **2.** Any other building material, such as a sheet of metal mesh, used for similar purposes. **3.** A slat. **4.** Lathing.

~*tr.v.* **lathed, lathing, laths.** To build, cover, or line with laths. [Middle English *lat, lathe*, Old English *lætt.*]

lathe (layth) *n.* **1.** A machine on which a piece of wood or metal, for example, is spun on a horizontal axis and shaped by a fixed cutting or abrading tool. **2.** A potter's wheel.

~*tr.v.* **lathed, lathing, lathes.** To cut or shape on a lathe. [Perhaps Middle English *lath,* Old Danish *lad,* supporting stand, perhaps a special use of *lad,* pile, from Old Norse *hladh.*]

lath·er (laáth-ǝr, láth-) *n.* **1.** A light foam formed by soap or detergent agitated in water. **2.** Froth formed by profuse sweating, as on a horse. —**in a lather.** *Informal.* Highly excited or upset; agitated. ~*v.* **lathered, -ering, -ers.** —*tr.* **1.** To put lather on; coat with lather. **2.** *Informal.* To give a beating to; whip. —*intr.* **1.** To produce lather; foam. **2.** To become coated with lather. Used especially of horses. [Revival of Old English *léathor,* washing soda.] —**lath·er·er** *n.* —**lath·er·y** *adj.*

lath·ing (laáth-ing ‖ laáth-, láth-) *n.* **1.** The act or process of building with laths. **2.** A structure made of laths. Also called "lath".

la·ti·ci·fer (la-tíssifǝr, lay-) *n.* A cell or vessel containing latex, found in such plants as rubber, poppy, and euphorbia. [New Latin, from *latex* (stem *latic-*), LATEX + -i- + -FER.]

lat·i·cif·er·ous (látti-siffǝrǝss, láyti-) *adj.* Secreting or exuding latex. [New Latin *latex* (stem *latic-*), LATEX + -i- + FEROUS.]

lat·i·fun·di·um (látti-fúndi-ǝm) *n., pl.* **-dia** (-ǝ). A landed estate, especially one in the ancient Roman world or in Latin America. [Latin *latifundium : latus,* broad + *fundus,* estate, bottom.]

Lat·i·mer (láttimǝr), **Hugh** (*c.* 1485–1555). English churchman during the Reformation, who became Bishop of Worcester (1535). He was martyred at Oxford by Queen Mary I.

Lat·in (láttin ‖ látt'n) *adj.* **1.** *Abbr.* **L., Lat.** Of or pertaining to Latium, its people, or its culture. **2.** Of or pertaining to ancient Rome, its people, or its culture. **3.** Of, pertaining to, or composed in the language of ancient Rome and Latium. **4.** Of or pertaining to those countries or peoples using Romance languages, especially the countries of Latin America. **5.** Of or pertaining to the Roman Catholic Church, as distinguished from the Eastern Orthodox Church. ~*n. Abbr.* **L., Lat. 1.** The ancient Italic dialect of Latium or the language into which it evolved, which through the political and cultural expansion of Rome became the dominant language of the Western Roman Empire, and survived into the Middle Ages as a language of learning and state documents, and until modern times as the official language of the Roman Catholic Church. See **Late Latin, Medieval Latin, New Latin, Old Latin, Vulgar Latin. 2.** A native or resident of ancient Latium. **3.** A member of a Latin people, especially of Latin America. **4.** A Roman Catholic.

Latin alphabet *n.* The **Roman alphabet** (*see*).

Latin America. A division of the Americas, consisting broadly of the countries of Central and South America (specifically those speaking Romance languages), together with Mexico. The region constitutes the fourth largest of the world's major divisions, with 14 per cent of its land, and 8 per cent of its people.

Latin America's backbone of young fold mountains, the Sierra Madre of Mexico and the Andes, is earthquake-prone, and forms part of the Pacific's "Ring of Fire", with active volcanoes. To the east lie highland blocks, and vast lowlands drained by great rivers such as the Amazon and Paraná.

The region has some of the driest places on earth—some 20 per cent is thorn forest, savannah, steppe, or desert. Its tropical rain forest (selvas) covers 30 per cent of the area, and supplies more than 15 per cent of the world's hardwoods.

Less than 25 per cent of Latin America is cultivated; 34 per cent of its workers are in agriculture. It produces much of the world's coffee, sugar cane, and bananas, and also beef and wool.

The area has vast reserves of silver, copper, high-grade iron ore, bauxite, chrome, and nickel. It has little coal but considerable oil and gas, soon to supply most of the energy for its increasing industrialisation, especially in Mexico and Brazil.

The region's basic problems persist, however: a shortage of cultivable land, overpopulation and the drift of people to the cities, social disparities, and political instability. See map, next page.

Lat·in·ate (látti-nayt) *adj.* Imitative of the style of Latin or using many Latinisms: *Latinate English prose.*

Latin Church *n.* The Roman Catholic Church.

Latin cross *n.* A cross with the lower limb longest.

Lat·in·ise, Lat·in·ize (látti-nīz) *v.* **-ised, -ising, -ises.** —*tr.* **1.** To translate into Latin. **2.** To transliterate into the Latin alphabet; Romanise. **3.** To cause to adopt or acquire Latin characteristics or customs. **4.** To cause to follow or resemble the Roman Catholic Church in dogma or practices. —*intr.* To use Latinisms. —**Lat·in·i·sa·tion** (-nī-záysh'n ‖ *U.S.* -ni-) *n.* —**Lat·in·i·ser** *n.*

Lat·in·ism (látti-niz'm) *n.* An idiom, structure, or word derived from or in imitation of Latin.

Lat·in·ist (láttinist) *n.* A Latin scholar.

La·tin·i·ty (lǝ-tínnǝti, la-) *n.* **1.** The use of Latin. **2.** The manner in which Latin is used in speaking or writing; Latin style.

Latin lover *n.* A vain, ostentatiously seductive man, apparently of Italian or Spanish parentage. Used humorously.

Latin Quarter *n.* A section of Paris on the left bank of the Seine, a centre for university students for many centuries.

Latin square *n. Mathematics.* A set of *n* numbers or symbols arranged in a square array of *n* rows and *n* columns such that each number or symbol occurs only once in each row and column. Such squares are used for the statistical analysis of variability.

lat·ish (láytish) *adj. Informal.* Fairly late. —**lat·ish** *adv.*

lat·i·tude (látti-tewd ‖ -tŏōd) *n. Abbr.* **l., L., lat. 1.** Extent; breadth; range. **2.** Freedom from normal restraints, limitations, or regula-

tions. **3.** *Geography.* The angular distance north or south of the equator, measured in degrees along a meridian, as on a map, globe, or the celestial sphere. **4.** A region of the Earth considered in relation to its distance from the equator: *temperate latitudes.* **5.** The range of values or conditions over which something operates or is effective; for example, the range of exposures over which a photographic film yields usable images. [Middle English, from Latin *lātitūdō,* from *lātus,* wide, broad.] —**lat·i·tu·din·al** (-tēwdin'l) *adj.*

lat·i·tu·di·nar·i·an (látti-tēwdi-naíri-ǝn ‖ -tŏŏdi-) *adj.* Favouring freedom of thought and behaviour, especially in religion. ~*n.* A latitudinarian person. [Latin *lātitūdō* (stem *lātitūdin-*), LATITUDE + -ARIAN.] —**lat·i·tu·di·nar·i·an·ism** *n.*

La·ti·um (láy-shi-ǝm, -sh'm). **1.** An ancient country in west-central Italy. **2.** See **Lazio.**

La Tour (la tŏor), **Georges de** (1593–1652). French painter. He specialised in genre painting and religious subjects, and is famous for the dramatic lighting of his night scenes, as in *La Madeleine à la veilleuse.*

la·tri·a (lǝ-trī-ǝ) *n.* In the Roman Catholic and Eastern Orthodox churches, the special reverence due to God alone. Compare **dulia, hyperdulia.** [Latin, from Greek *latreia,* worship.]

la·trine (lǝ-tréen) *n.* A lavatory, as in a barracks or camp. [French, from Latin *latrīna,* contraction of *lavātrīna,* bath.]

-latry *n. comb. form.* Indicates the worship of; for example, **idolatry.** [Greek *latreia,* service, worship.]

lat·ten (látt'n) *n.* **1.** An alloy formerly made of or made to resemble brass, hammered thin, and used in the manufacture of church vessels. **2.** Any thin sheet of metal, especially of tin. [Middle English *laton,* from Old French *leiton, laton,* from Arabic *lāṭūn,* copper, from Turkish dialectal *altan,* gold.]

lat·ter (láttǝr). *Rare.* Alternative comparative of **late.** ~*adj.* **1.** Designating the second of two persons or things mentioned. **2.** Further advanced in time or sequence; later. **3.** Closer to the end: *the latter part of the book.* ~*n.* The second of two persons or things mentioned. [Middle English, Old English *lætra,* comparative of *læt,* LATE.]

Usage: *Latter* is appropriate only in referring to the second of two previously mentioned entities: *We could travel by car or train—the latter would be quicker. Latter* is sometimes loosely used to refer to the last-mentioned item in a sequence of three or more (*We could travel by car, train or boat. . .*), but formal usage prefers an alternative form, such as *the last-named, the last of these,* or simply *the last.* Similarly, *latter* is not acceptable when only one item is referred to: *We could travel by car—the latter is very convenient.*

lat·ter-day (láttǝr-dáy) *adj.* Belonging to present or recent time; modern.

Latter-day Saint *n.* A **Mormon** (*see*).

lat·ter·ly (láttǝr-li) *adv.* Recently; lately.

lat·tice (láttiss) *n.* **1.** An open framework made of strips of metal, wood, or other material interwoven to form regular, patterned spaces. **2.** A screen, window, gate, or the like made of such a framework. **3.** Something, such as a heraldic bearing, that resembles such a framework. **4.** *Chemistry.* A regular, periodic configuration of points, particles, or objects throughout an area or space; especially, the arrangement of ions or molecules in a crystalline solid. ~*tr.v.* **latticed, -ticing, -tices.** To construct or furnish with a lattice or latticework. [Middle English *latis,* from Old French *lattis,* from *latte,* lath, from Germanic, akin to Old English *lætt,* LATH.] —**latticed** *adj.*

lat·tice·work (láttiss-wurk) *n.* **1.** A lattice or something resembling a lattice; trelliswork. **2.** A structure made of lattices.

la·tus rec·tum (láttǝss réktǝm, laátǝss) *n., pl.* **latera recta** (láttǝrǝ réktǝ). In geometry, a chord through the focus of a parabola, hyperbola, or ellipse parallel to a transverse axis. [New Latin, "straight side".]

Lat·vi·a, Republic of (látvi-ǝ). Formerly a constituent republic of the U.S.S.R., lying on the Baltic Sea. It consists largely of a fertile lowland, although there are numerous lakes and hills to the east. Latvia came under Russian control in the 18th century. From 1918 to 1940 it was an independent republic, but during World War II it was annexed by the U.S.S.R. In 1991 moves towards independence were at first frustrated by Soviet military intervention, but the break-up of the U.S.S.R. confirmed independent statehood. Area, 64 589 square kilometres (24,937 square miles). Population, 2,490,000. Capital, Riga. See map at **Baltic States.**

Lat·vi·an (látvi-ǝn) *adj.* Of or pertaining to Latvia, its people, or its language. ~*n.* **1.** A native or inhabitant of Latvia. **2.** The Baltic language of these people. In this sense, also called "Lettish".

lau·an (low-aán, lŏō-) *n.* Timber obtained from any of various trees native to the Philippines, such as *Shorea,* having light yellow to brown, close-grained wood. [Tagalog *lawaan.*]

laud (lawd) *tr.v.* **lauded, lauding, lauds.** To give praise or express devotion to; glorify. See Synonyms at **praise.** ~*n.* **1.** Praise; glorification. **2.** A hymn or song of praise. **3.** *Plural.* Usually capital **L.** *Ecclesiastical.* **a.** An early-morning church service at which psalms of praise are sung. **b.** The service of prayers following the matins and constituting with them the first of the seven canonical hours. [Latin *laudāre,* to praise, from *laus* (stem *laud-*), praise.] —**laud·er** *n.*

Laud (lawd), **William** (1573–1645). Archbishop of Canterbury (1633–45). His attempts to introduce the Book of Common Prayer

LATIN AMERICA

into Scotland led to the Bishops' Wars, and his eventual imprisonment and execution by Parliament.

Lau·da (lówdə), **(Andreas Nikolaus) "Niki"** (1949–). Austrian motor-racing driver. He was Formula 1 world champion (1975, 1977). He recovered from severe facial burns sustained in a crash (1976) to continue racing until his retirement in 1985.

laud·a·ble (láwdə-b'l) *adj.* Deserving approbation; commendable; praiseworthy. **—laud·a·bil·i·ty** (-bílləti), **laud·a·ble·ness** *n.* **—laud·a·bly** *adv.*

lau·da·num (lód-nəm, láwd'n-əm) *n.* A tincture of opium. [New Latin *laudanum* (coined by Paracelsus), possibly from Latin *lādanum*, *labdanum*, resin, LABDANUM.]

laud·a·tion (law-dáysh'n) *n.* The act of lauding; praise.

laud·a·tive (láwdətiv) *adj.* Laudatory.

laud·a·to·ry (láwdə-təri, -tri) *adj.* Including, expressing, or bestowing praise; eulogistic. [Late Latin *laudātōrius*, from Latin *laudāre* (past participle *laudātus*), to praise, LAUD.]

Lau·der (láwdər), **Sir Harry,** born Hugh MacLennan (1870–1950). Scottish music-hall star who created the comic figure of a wry but sentimental Highlander.

laugh (laaf ‖ laf) *v.* **laughed, laughing, laughs.** *—intr.* **1.** To express emotion, typically mirth, by a series of inarticulate sounds, characteristically with the mouth open in a wide smile. **2.** To produce sounds or cries resembling laughter. **3.** To manifest or appear

to manifest joy in any way. —*tr.* **1.** To drive, induce, or effect with or by laughter: *They laughed him off the stage.* **2.** To utter or express by or as if by laughing: *laughing their appreciation.* **—be laughing.** *Informal.* To be in a position of good fortune, satisfaction, or easy success. **—laugh at. 1.** To exhibit amusement at. **2.** To poke fun at; ridicule; deride. **3.** To refuse to consider seriously. **—laugh down.** To silence with laughter. **—laugh off** or **away.** To dismiss lightly (especially, something unpleasant or painful), by or as if by laughing.
~*n.* **1.** A burst or sound of laughter. **2.** *Informal.* Something amusing, improbable, or ridiculous; a joke or absurdity: *That's a laugh.* **—have the last laugh.** To enjoy vindication. [Middle English *laughen,* Old English *hliehhan, hlœhhan.*] **—laugh·er** *n.* **—laugh·ing·ly** *adv.*

laugh·a·ble (laáf-əb'l || láff-) *adj.* Causing or deserving of laughter or derision. **—laugh·a·ble·ness** *n.* **—laugh·a·bly** *adv.*

laugh·ing gas (laáfing || láffing) *n.* An anaesthetic, **nitrous oxide** *(see).*

laughing hyena *n.* The **spotted hyena** *(see).*

laughing jackass *n.* A bird, the **kookaburra** *(see).*

laughing stock *n.* An object of jokes or ridicule; a butt; a fool.

laugh·ter (laáf-tər || láf-) *n.* **1.** The act of laughing. **2.** The sound produced by laughing. **3.** The experience or appearance of joy, merriment, amusement, or the like. **4.** *Archaic.* A cause or subject for laughter. [Middle English, Old English *hleahtor.*]

laughter line *n.* A line that forms as a wrinkle on the face as a result of laughing or smiling.

Laugh·ton (láwt'n), **Charles** (1899–1962). British actor. Among many starring Hollywood roles was his screen triumph as Captain Bligh in *Mutiny on the Bounty* (1935).

launce (laanss || lawnss) *n.* A fish, the **sand eel** *(see).* [Perhaps variant of LANCE.]

Launcelot. Variant of **Lancelot.**

Laun·ces·ton (láwn-sə-stən, lón-). City in Tasmania, southeast Australia. It is Tasmania's second largest city and the main port for trade between the island and the Australian mainland.

launch[1] (lawnch, *rarely* laanch) *v.* **launched, launching, launches.** —*tr.* **1.** To move or set in motion with force; propel: *launch a missile; launched a volley of snowballs.* **2.** To slide or lower (a boat) into the water, especially for the first time. **3.** To put into action; inaugurate; initiate. **4.** To set or start (a person or group) on a particular course of action. **5.** To engage (oneself) vigorously and enthusiastically in a new activity. **6.** To introduce (a new book, film, product, or the like) to the public through a publicity campaign. —*intr.* **1.** To begin a new project or venture; especially, to widen or extend one's current activities or enterprises. Usually used with *out: The company is launching out into plastics this year.* **2.** To make a rousing or enthusiastic beginning. Used with *into* or *forth into: The whole crowd launched into song.* **3.** To start talking or writing, especially eagerly and at length. Used with *on* or *forth* or *into: launched forth into a tirade.*
~*n.* An act of launching. Also used adjectivally: *a launch complex.* [Middle English *launchen,* to hurl, pierce, from Old North French *lancher,* variant of Old French *lancier,* from *lance,* LANCE.]

launch[2] *n.* **1.** A large ship's boat formerly sloop-rigged but now powered. **2.** Any large, open motorboat. [Portuguese *lancha,* from Malay, akin to Malay *lancharan,* boat.]

launch·er (láwn-chər, laán-) *n.* One that launches, such as: **1.** A device for firing grenades. **2.** A device for firing rockets.

launching pad (láwnching) *n.* Also **launch pad.** The base or platform from which a rocket or space vehicle is launched.

launch vehicle *n. Aerospace.* A **booster** *(see).*

laun·der (láwn-dər, *rarely* laán-) *v.* **-dered, -dering, -ders.** —*tr.* **1.** To wash, or wash and iron (clothes, linen, or the like). **2.** To pass (money from a dubious source) through a bank or other intermediary, in order to obscure its origin. —*intr.* **1.** To withstand washing in a specified way: *This material launders well.* **2.** To wash, or wash and iron, clothes or linens.
~*n.* In mining, a wooden trough for water, used for washing ore. [From obsolete *launder,* launderer, from Middle English *launder,* variant of *lavender,* from Old French *lavandier,* from Vulgar Latin *lavandārius* (unattested), from Latin *lavanda,* things that need washing, from the gerundive of *lavāre,* to wash, LAVE.] **—laun·der·er** *n.*

laun·derette (láwn-də-rét, -drét) *n.* Also **laun·drette** (-drét). A commercial establishment equipped with washing machines and dryers, usually coin-operated and self-service. [LAUNDER + -ETTE.]

laun·dress (láwn-driss, *rarely* laán-, -dress) *n.* A woman who launders clothes, linen, or the like, as an occupation.

laun·dry (láwn-dri, *rarely* laán-) *n., pl.* **-dries. 1.** Soiled or laundered clothes and linens; washing. **2.** A place where laundering is done. [From obsolete *launder,* launderer. See **launder.**]

laun·dry·man (láwn-dri-mən, laán-) *n., pl.* **-men** (-mən). **1.** A man who makes collections and deliveries for a commercial laundry. **2.** A man who works in a laundry.

laun·dry·wom·an (láwn-dri-wŏŏmən, laán-) *n., pl.* **-women** (wimmin). A female laundryman.

Laur·as·i·a (law-ráy-shə, -zhə). Ancient supercontinent which formed the northern land mass of the world when the single continent of Pangaea split into two sections at the end of the Palaeozoic era. It comprised North America, Greenland, Europe, and Asia (excluding the Indian subcontinent), and itself split during the Mesozoic era, into North America and Eurasia.

lau·re·ate (láwri-ət, lórri-) *adj.* **1.** Worthy of laurels for one's achievements; pre-eminent. **2.** Crowned or decked with laurel as a mark of honour. **3.** Honoured for achievement in a field. **4.** *Archaic.* Made of laurel sprigs, as a wreath or crown.
~*n.* **1.** A poet laureate. **2.** One honoured with a crown of laurel. **3.** One who has received an honour or award: *a Nobel laureate.* [Latin *laureātus,* crowned with laurel, from *laurea,* laurel tree or crown, from *laureus,* of laurel, from *laurus,* LAUREL.] **—lau·re·ate·ship** *n.*

lau·rel (lórrəl || láwrəl) *n.* **1.** A shrub or tree, the **bay** *(see).* **2.** Any of several similar or related shrubs or trees, such as **California laurel, cherry laurel, mountain laurel, spotted laurel,** and **spurge laurel** *(all of which see).* **3.** *Usually plural.* Leaves or twigs of a laurel, especially *L. nobilis,* formed into a wreath and conferred as a mark of honour in ancient times upon poets, heroes, and victors in athletic contests. **4.** *Plural.* Honour and glory won for achievement. **—look to (one's) laurels.** To protect one's position of eminence against rivals. **—rest on (one's) laurels.** To be content with past achievements and to cease striving.
~*tr.v.* **laurelled** or *U.S.* **-reled, -relling** or *U.S.* **-reling, -rels.** To crown with laurel. [Middle English *lorel, laurer,* laurel tree, from Old French *lorier,* from *lor,* laurel, from Latin *laurus,* perhaps of Mediterranean origin.]

Lau·rel and Har·dy (lórrəl ənd hárdi). Film comedy team, the first great innovative comedians of talking films. Stan Laurel, born Arthur Stanley Jefferson (1890–1965), was British, Oliver Hardy (1892–1957), American. They made many short films between 1926 and 1945. *The Music Box* (1932) won an Academy Award.

lau·ric acid (láwr-ik, lórr-) *n.* A fatty acid, $C_{12}H_{24}O_2$, obtained chiefly from coconut oil, and used in making soaps, cosmetics, insecticides, and alkyd resins. Also called "dodecanoic acid". [Latin *laurus,* LAUREL (from its occurrence in some laurel).]

Lau·ri·er (lórri-ər), **Sir Wilfrid** (1841–1919). The first French-Canadian prime minister of Canada (1896–1911). His Liberal administration fought to improve Canada's status within the Commonwealth.

lau·rus·ti·nus (lórrə-stīnəss || láwrə-) *n.* A Mediterranean shrub, *Viburnum tinus,* often grown for ornament, having glossy, dark green foliage and flattish clusters of small pink or white flowers. [New Latin : Latin *laurus,* laurel + *tinus,* name of a plant (probably laurustinus), probably from Germanic.]

lau·ryl alcohol (láwr-il, lórr-) *n.* A white crystalline solid, $C_{12}H_{25}OH$, used in the manufacture of detergents. [LAURIC ACID + -YL.]

Lau·sanne (lō-zán). A city in western Switzerland, lying on Lake Geneva. It is the trading and marketing centre of a fertile agricultural region and also a popular resort and conference centre.

lav (lav) *n. Chiefly British Informal.* A lavatory.

lav. lavatory.

la·va (laávə || lávvə) *n.* **1.** Molten rock that issues from a volcano or a fissure in the earth's surface. **2.** The same rock when cooled and solidified. [Italian, lava stream from Vesuvius, stream caused by rain, from *lavare,* to wash, from Latin *lavāre,* to wash, LAVE.]

la·va·bo (lə-váy-bō, -vaá-, lávvə-) *n., pl.* **-boes. 1.** *Often capital* **L. a.** In the Roman Catholic and Anglican churches, the ceremonial washing of the celebrant's hands after the offertory of the Mass. **b.** The psalm passage formerly recited at this point. **2.** The basin or small towel used in this ritual. **3.** A washbowl and water tank with a spout used in medieval monasteries. [Latin *lavābo,* "I shall wash" (first word in Psalm 26:6), from *lavāre,* to wash, LAVE.]

lav·age (lávvij, la-vaázh) *n. Medicine.* A washing, especially of a hollow organ, such as the stomach or lower bowel, with repeated injections of water. [French, a washing, from Old French, from *laver,* to wash, from Latin *lavāre,* to wash, LAVE.]

La·val (la-vál), **Pierre** (1883–1945). French politician. He twice served as prime minister (1931–32, 1935–36). After the surrender of France he became premier of the Vichy government (1942–44). He was executed for treason for collaborating with the Germans.

la·va-la·va (laávə-laávə) *n.* A rectangular strip of printed cotton cloth tied around the waist and worn as a skirt by Polynesians, especially Samoans. [Samoan *lavalava.*]

lav·a·liere (lávvə-léer) *n.* Also **la·val·lière** (lávval-yáir). *U.S.* **1.** A pendant worn on a chain around the neck. **2.** A **neck microphone** *(see).* [French *lavallière,* after Louise de *La Vallière,* a mistress of Louis XIV.]

la·va·tion (la-váysh'n, lay-) *n. Formal.* The process of washing; a cleansing. [Latin *lavātiō* (stem *lavātiōn-*), from *lavāre,* LAVE.]

lav·a·to·ry (lávvə-təri, -tri) *n., pl.* **-ries.** *Abbr.* **lav. 1.** A disposal apparatus consisting of a bowl fitted with a flushing device, used for urination and defecation. **2.** A room equipped with one or more lavatories and usually with washing facilities. [Middle English *lavatorie,* from Late Latin *lavātorium,* washing place, washing vessel, from Latin *lavāre,* to wash, LAVE.] **—la·va·to·ri·al** (-táwri-əl || -tōri-) *adj.*

lavatory paper *n. Chiefly British.* Toilet paper.

lave (layv) *v.* **laved, laving, laves.** —*tr. Archaic & Literary.* **1.** To wash; bathe. **2.** To lap or wash against: *The stream laved the rocks.* —*intr. Archaic & Literary.* To bathe oneself. [Middle English *laven,* from Old French *laver,* from Latin *lavāre.*]

lav·en·der (lávv'ndər) *n.* **1.** Any of various aromatic Old World plants of the genus *Lavandula;* especially, *L. officinalis* (or *L. spica* or *L. vera*), having clusters of small purplish flowers and yielding an oil used in perfumery. **2.** The fragrant dried leaves, stems, and flowers of such a plant. **3.** Any of various similar or related plants, such as **sea lavender** and **spike lavender** (both of which see). **4.** Pale to light bluish purple, to very light or pale violet. [Middle English *lavendre*, from Anglo-French, from Medieval Latin *lavendula, livendula*†.] —**lav·en·der** adj.

la·ver¹ (láyvər) n. **1.** A large basin used in ancient Judaism by the priest for ablutions before making a sacrificial offering. **2.** Archaic. A stone basin or trough used for washing. **3.** Archaic. The baptismal font or the water in it. [Middle English *laver, lavor*, from Old French *laveoir*, perhaps from Late Latin *lavātorium*, LAVATORY.]

la·ver² (láavər) n. Any of several edible seaweeds of the genus *Porphyra*. [New Latin, from Latin *laver*†.]

La·ver (láyvər), **Rod(ney George)** (1938–). Australian tennis player. He was Wimbledon champion in 1961, 1962, 1968, and 1969. He won the world's four major singles titles in 1962 as an amateur, and in 1969 as a professional.

La·ve·ran (lávvə-róN), **(Charles Louis) Alphonse** (1845–1922). French physician. He isolated the parasitic protozoa responsible for malaria (1880), for which he was awarded the Nobel prize in physiology or medicine (1907).

laver bread (láavər) n. The fronds of laver seaweed dipped in oatmeal, fried and eaten, especially in Wales.

lav·ish (lávvish) adj. **1.** Extravagant; prodigal. **2.** Characterised by or produced with extravagance and profusion. **3.** Showing unrestrained generosity: *a lavish present.* —See Synonyms at ornate. ~tr.v. **lavished, -ishing, -ishes.** To give or pour forth unstintingly: *the loving care they lavished on the work.* [Middle English *lavas*, from noun, "an outpouring", profusion, from Old French *lavasse*, torrent of rain, from *laver*, to wash, LAVE.] —**lav·ish·er** n. —**lav·ish·ly** adv. —**lav·ish·ness** n.

La·voi·sier (laa-vwaázi-ay, French, -vwaz-yáy), **Antoine Laurent** (1743–94). French chemist, and father of modern chemistry. He isolated the major constituents of air, disproved the phlogiston theory by explaining the role of oxygen in combustion, and organised the classification of compounds. He was guillotined during the Revolution for having held various government posts.

law¹ (law) n. Abbr. **L, L. 1.** A rule established by authority, society, or custom. **2. a.** The body of rules governing the affairs of people within a community or among states; a legal system: *the law of nations.* **b.** The condition of social order or justice resulting from the existence of a legal system in a society. **c.** A declaration or position which is not to be questioned or disputed: *His word is law.* **3.** A set of rules or customs dealing with a specified area of a legal system: *the law of contracts; criminal law.* **4.** In Britain: **a.** The body of rules and principles originally followed by the common law courts, as opposed to those which were administered by the courts of equity. **b.** That part of the law which arises out of legislation; statute law as opposed to common law. **5. a.** The system of courts, judicial processes, and legal officers giving effect to the laws of a society: *resort to the law in defence of one's interests.* **b.** An impromptu system of justice, usually illegal, substituted for established juridical procedure: *gang law.* **6.** The science and study of law; jurisprudence. **7.** Knowledge of law: *His law is good.* **8.** The profession of a lawyer. **9.** Capital L. **a.** Often plural. A code of behaviour of divine origin: *Mosaic Law.* **b.** In the Old Testament, the Pentateuch and the precepts laid down in it. **10. a.** Often plural. Principles of conduct conceived to be of natural origin: *the laws of decency.* **b.** A way of life: *law of the jungle.* **11.** Often plural. A code of principles and regulations observed by a profession or association or by sportsmen: *the law of the turf.* **12. a.** Often plural. A formulation of the observed recurrence, order, relationship, or interaction of natural phenomena: *laws of motion.* **b.** A generalisation based on the observation of repeated events: *Parkinson's law.* **13.** Mathematics. A general principle or rule that is obeyed in all cases to which it is applicable. **14.** Often plural. The rules of an art; principles or elements: *the laws of harmony; the laws of grammar.* **15.** Slang. The police or a policeman. Preceded by the. —**be a law unto (oneself).** To disregard established laws and conventions; make one's own rules. —**go to law.** To take a complaint to court for settlement. —**lay down the law.** To speak in a firm, authoritarian way. —**take the law into (one's) own hands.** To redress a wrong or proceed by one's own methods rather than proper authority. [Middle English *law(e)*, binding custom or practice, Old English *lagu*, code of rules.]

law² n. In Scotland and Northern England, a hill, especially a rounded one. Used in place names: *Berwick Law.* [Middle English (northern dialect), from Old English *hlāw*.]

Law (law), **Andrew Bonar** (1858–1923). Canadian-born leader of the British Conservative Party. He succeeded Lloyd George as prime minister (1922).

law·a·bid·ing (láw-ə-bīding) adj. Abiding by the law.

law agent n. Formerly in Scotland, a solicitor.

law and order n. Used with a singular or plural verb. **1.** A state of peace in a law-abiding society. **2.** The use or advocacy of stringent measures to reduce crime and eliminate violence in a society.

law·break·er (láw-braykər) n. A person who breaks the law. —**law·break·ing** n. & adj.

law centre n. In Britain, an office, often financed by a local authority, that provides free legal advice and information to the public.

law·ful (láwf'l) adj. **1.** Within the law; allowed by law: *lawful methods.* **2.** Established or recognised by the law; legally acknowledged: *the lawful heir.* **3.** Legally sanctioned; legitimate: *a lawful marriage.* —**law·ful·ly** adv. —**law·ful·ness** n.

law·giv·er (láw-givvər) n. **1.** One who gives a code of laws to a

people. **2.** A lawmaker; a legislator. —**law·giv·ing** n. & adj.

lawks (lawks) interj. British. Used to express astonishment, dismay, or the like. [Variant of *Lord!* (perhaps influenced by ALACK).]

law·less (láw-ləss, -liss) adj. **1. a.** Unrestrained by law; disobedient: *a lawless person.* **b.** Unbridled: *lawless passion.* **2.** Heedless of or contrary to the law: *a lawless act.* **3.** Not governed by law: *the lawless border.* —**law·less·ly** adv. —**law·less·ness** n.

Law Lord n. In Britain, a member of the House of Lords who sits in the highest court of appeal; a Lord of Appeal in Ordinary.

law·mak·er (láw-maykər) n. One who draughts or helps to enact laws; a legislator. —**law·mak·ing** n. & adj.

law·man (láw-mən, -mən) n., pl. **-men** -men, -mən. Chiefly U.S. A law enforcement officer, such as a sheriff.

law merchant n. The rules of trade and commerce, drawn from the customs of merchants in the past; commercial law.

lawn¹ (lawn) n. A usually closely mown plot or area planted with grass or similar plants. [Variant of obsolete *laund*, from Middle English *launde, lawnde*, from Old French *launde*, heath, from Germanic.] —**lawn·y** adj.

lawn² n. A very fine fabric of cotton or linen. [Middle English, probably from *Laon*, France, linen-making town.] —**lawn·y** adj.

lawn mower n. A machine with a revolving blade or blades for cutting grass.

lawn tennis n. **1.** Tennis played on a grass court. **2.** Formal. Tennis.

law of averages n. The assertion that what happens at one extreme will be counteracted by what happens at the other, thus maintaining an average.

law officer n. In Britain, any of various officials who advise the Crown and Parliament on legal matters, and who are sometimes concerned with prosecutions on behalf of the Crown. For England, Wales, and Northern Ireland, they are the Attorney-General and the Solicitor-General, and in Scotland, the Lord Advocate and the Solicitor-General.

Law of large numbers n. Mathematics. **Bernouilli's principle** (see).

Law of Moses n. **Mosaic Law** (see).

law of nations n. **International law** (see).

Law·rence (lórrənss), **D(avid) H(erbert)** (1885–1930). British novelist, short-story writer, essayist, and poet. Among his novels are *Sons and Lovers* (1913), *The Rainbow* (1915), and *Women in Love* (1920). The sex scenes in his work aroused controversy: publication of *Lady Chatterley's Lover* (1928) was not allowed in Britain until 1961. —**Law·ren·ti·an** (law-rénsh'n) adj.

Lawrence, Ernest Orlando (1901–58). U.S. physicist. He designed the cyclotron, a particle accelerator, and was awarded the Nobel prize in physics (1939).

Lawrence, Gertrude, born Gertrud Alexandra Dagmar Lawrence Klasen (1898–1952). British actress. She partnered her childhood friend, Noël Coward, notably in his play *Private Lives* (1931), and was in *The King and I* (1951).

Lawrence, Sir Thomas (1769–1830). British portrait painter, artist to George III (1792), and President of the Royal Academy (1820).

Lawrence, T(homas) E(dward), also known as T.E. Shaw, J.H. Ross, Lawrence of Arabia (1888–1935). British soldier and writer. He was sent in 1916 to organise Arab insurgency in the Turkish empire, and led a legendary guerrilla action. He wrote a philosophical record of the desert campaign, *The Seven Pillars of Wisdom* (1926). He was killed in a motorcycling accident.

law·ren·ci·um (lo-rén-si-əm, law-) n. Symbol **Lw** A synthetic transuranic element. The most stable isotope has a mass number 256 and a half-life of 35 seconds. Also called "unniltrium". [After Ernest O. LAWRENCE.]

Law Society n. An organisation representing, conducting examinations for, and regulating the admission of solicitors in various countries, such as England, Scotland, and Australia.

law stationer n. **1.** A person who sells stationery required by lawyers. **2.** A person who engrosses legal documents.

law·suit (láw-sŏot, -sewt) n. A case brought before a court, usually a civil case.

law term n. **1.** A word or expression used in legal contexts. **2.** A period of time appointed for the sitting of a lawcourt or lawcourts.

law·yer (láw-yər, lóy-ər) n. **1.** One whose profession is to give legal advice and assistance to clients and represent them in court. **2.** British. Loosely, a solicitor. **3.** A student or teacher of law. **4.** Regional. A burbot. [Middle English *lawyere*, from *lawe*, LAW.]

Usage: lawyer, solicitor, barrister, advocate, counsel, attorney, counsellor. These nouns denote members of the legal profession. *Lawyer* is the general and most comprehensive term for one authorised to manage the legal affairs of a client, give legal advice, and represent clients in court. *Solicitor*, especially in Britain and some other Commonwealth countries, refers to a lawyer who gives legal advice, acts as a legal agent, represents clients in lower courts, and prepares cases for trial in higher courts. *Barrister*, in England and some other Commonwealth countries, refers to a lawyer who represents and argues cases for clients in higher courts. *Advocate* refers generally to a person who pleads a case on behalf of another. In Scotland and South Africa, it is the usual term for a *barrister. Counsel* refers to a barrister or group of barristers engaged in pleading a case in court: *counsel for the prosecution. Attorney* refers generally to a person, usually a lawyer, who is appointed or empowered to act for another. In the United States, *attorney* is the usual term for a *lawyer* and in South Africa, for a *solicitor. Counsellor*, in the United States, is used as another term for an *attorney*, especially one who represents clients in court.

lax (laks) *adj.* **1. a.** Showing little concern; remiss; negligent: *lax about paying bills.* **b.** Not strict; unenforced. **2.** Not taut, firm, or compact; slack. **3.** Loose and not easily retained or controlled. Said of bowel movements. **4.** *Phonetics.* Pronounced with the muscles of the tongue and jaw partially relaxed; wide. Said of certain vowel sounds, such as *e* in *let* or *i* in *hid.* Compare **tense.** —See Synonyms at **careless.** [Middle English, from Latin *laxus,* slack, loose.] —**lax·a·tion** (-sáysh'n) *n.* —**lax·ly** *adv.* —**lax·i·ty, lax·ness** *n.*

lax·a·tive (láksətiv) *n. Medicine.* A drug that stimulates evacuation of the bowels. Also called "cathartic", "purgative".
~*adj.* **1.** Stimulating evacuation of the bowels. **2.** Unrestrained. [Middle English *laxatif,* from adjective, "producing looseness", from Old French, from Latin *laxātīvus,* from *laxāre,* to relax, from *laxus,* loose, LAX.]

Lax·ness (laăks-ness), **Halldór (Kiljan),** pseudonym of Halldór Guðjónsson (1902–98). Icelandic novelist, writing in the epic tradition of his country. He was awarded the Nobel prize (1955).

lay[1] (lay) *v.* **laid** (layd), **laying, lays.** —*tr.* **1.** To cause to lie; put in a recumbent position: *lay a child in its cot.* **2.** To place or rest in a particular state or position: *lay the books on the table.* **3.** To put or set down, especially for a particular purpose or as a basis: *lay a trail; lay foundations.* **4.** To produce and deposit: *lay eggs.* **5. a.** To cause to settle or subside: *The fog laid the wind.* **b.** To scotch (a rumour, for example). **c.** To exorcise (a ghost). **6.** To put or apply: *lay an ear to the door.* **7.** To assign or attribute: *laid the blame on him.* **8.** To put in a setting; locate: *laid the story in Italy.* **9.** To bury; sink in the ground: *lay a cable.* **10.** To place in the proper position or spot: *lay a carpet; lay bricks.* **11. a.** To arrange in a required order for use; make ready: *lay a trap; lay a fire.* **b.** To arrange knives, forks, mats, and the like on (a table) ready for eating. **12.** To devise; make: *lay plans.* **13.** To apply in a thick layer or coat: *lay paint on a canvas.* **14.** To place or give (importance): *lay stress on clarity.* **15.** To impose as a burden or punishment. Usually used with *upon*: *lay a penalty upon him.* **16.** To put forth for examination; present; submit. Often used with *before: lay a case before a committee.* **17.** To place (a bet); stake; wager: *lay ten pounds on a horse.* **18.** To bring or deliver forcefully: *laid a blow on his jaw.* **19.** *Archaic.* To take possession of; annex. **20.** *Military.* To aim (a gun or cannon). **21. a.** To place together (strands) to be twisted into rope. **b.** To make in this manner. Used with *up: lay up cable.* **22.** To inlay: *The floor was laid in semiprecious stones.* **23.** To bring (a ship) to a specified position: *lay the vessel alongside the wharf.* **24.** In hunting, to put (hounds) on a scent. **25.** *Vulgar Slang.* To have sexual intercourse with. Used especially of men. —*intr.* **1.** To produce and deposit eggs. **2. a.** *Nonstandard.* To lie; recline. **b.** *Nautical.* To lie in a specified position: *The ship laid aft.* —**lay about (one).** To hit out in all directions; fight vigorously. —**lay aloft.** *Nautical.* To go up into the rigging of a ship. —**lay aside. 1.** To put off to one side; abandon: *lay aside all hope.* **2.** To put aside for the future; save. **3.** To disregard for the moment. —**lay away. 1.** To reserve for the future; save. **2.** To hold (merchandise) for future delivery. —**lay bare.** To expose to view; reveal. —**lay down. 1.** To store (wine or provisions), especially in a cellar. **2.** To place (a bet); wager. **3.** To relinquish or sacrifice (one's hopes or life, for example). **4.** To begin the construction of (a ship, railway, or the like). **5.** To make or formulate (a rule, principle, or the like). **6.** To convert (land) into pasture: *lay down a field with grass.* **7.** To put down (a chart, diagram, or the like) on paper. —**lay hold of.** To seize; grasp. —**lay in.** To obtain and store (provisions or supplies). —**lay into.** *Informal.* To attack, either physically or verbally. —**lay it on.** *Informal.* **1.** To be effusive with praise, flattery, excuses, or the like. **2.** To inflict blows on; strike. —**lay on. 1.** To provide (refreshments or entertainment, for example). **2.** To install the necessary pipes and fittings for supplying (gas, electricity, or water). —**lay (oneself) open.** To make oneself vulnerable; expose oneself, as to criticism, blame, or the like. —**lay open. 1.** To cut open. **2.** To expose; reveal. —**lay to. 1.** To apply oneself vigorously. **2.** *Nautical.* **a.** To bring (a sailing ship) to a stop in open water, steadying her with a jib or other small sail. **b.** To remain stationary, facing into the wind. —**lay to rest.** To bury. —**lay up. 1.** To store for future needs. **2.** *Informal.* To confine to bed through illness. Used in the passive. —**lay waste.** To ravage (land, for example).
~*n.* **1.** A share of the profits of a whaling or fishing expedition allotted in place of wages. **2. a.** The direction the strands of a rope or cable are twisted in: *a left lay.* **b.** The amount of such twist. **3.** The position, way, or direction in which something, such as land, lies. **4.** *Chiefly British Slang.* A line of activity, especially one of a questionable nature. **5.** *Vulgar Slang.* **a.** An act of sexual intercourse. **b.** A partner in sexual intercourse. —**in lay.** In a period of ovulation. Said of laying hens. [Lay, laid, laid; Middle English *leggen, leide, leid,* Old English *lecgan, lēde, gelēd.*]

Usage: The overlap in the forms of the verbs *lay* and *lie* often leads to uncertain usage. *Lay* has the senses "put, place, prepare", a past tense *laid,* and a past participle *laid. Lie* has the senses "recline, be situated", a past tense *lay,* and a past participle *lain.* The crucial difference in grammar is that *lay* takes a direct object, whereas *lie* does not. Thus one says: *I laid the table* (not *lay*); *The hen has laid an egg* (not *lain*); *I lay down to sleep* (not *laid*). The forms in brackets are sometimes heard in informal speech, and are common in some regional dialects, but only occasionally does the confusion surface in the written language (usually in idiomatic constructions, such as *to lie/lay low; the lie/lay of the land*).

lay[2] *adj.* **1.** Pertaining to, coming from, or serving the laity; secular: *a lay preacher.* **2.** Nonprofessional; not formally qualified or trained. **3.** Of or typical of the average or common man: *a lay opinion.* [Middle English *laie,* from Old French *lai,* from Late Latin *lāicus,* from Greek *laikos,* from *laos*†, the people.]

lay[3] *n.* A ballad. [Middle English, from Old French *lai,* akin to Provençal *lais*†.]

lay[4]. Past tense of **lie** (recline).

lay·a·bout (láy-ə-bowt) *n. British Informal.* One who avoids work; an idler.

lay brother *n.* A man who has taken religious vows but who is not ordained and is usually employed in manual duties.

lay by *tr.v.* **1.** To keep on hand for future needs; save. **2.** To lay (a sailing vessel) to. —*intr.v.* To lay to. Used of a sailing vessel.

lay-by (láy-bī) *n., pl.* **-bys. 1.** *Chiefly British.* An area beside a main road where vehicles can stop without obstructing other traffic. **2.** A similar area on a canal or beside a railway for boats or railway coaches. **3.** *Australian & N.Z.* A method of reserving an article in a shop by paying a deposit: *put a dress on lay-by.*

lay clerk *n.* A lay male member of a cathedral or church choir.

lay-day (láy-day) *n. Finance.* A day in port allowed to the lessee of a ship without charge; a free day. [From LAY (verb).]

lay·er (láy-ər) *n.* **1. a.** A single thickness, coating, or stratum spread out or covering a surface. **b.** A superimposed level: *layers of meaning.* **2.** One that lays; specifically, a hen. **3.** In horticulture, a stem covered with soil for rooting while still part of a living plant.
~*v.* **layered, -ering, -ers.** —*tr.* **1.** To cut (hair) into layers. **2.** In horticulture, to propagate (a plant) by layering. —*intr.* **1.** To separate or split into layers. **2.** In horticulture, to take root as a result of layering. [Middle English *leyer,* from *leyen, leggen,* to LAY.]

layer cake *n.* A usually iced cake of two or more layers separated by a filling, such as jam or cream.

lay·ered (láy-ərd) *adj.* **1.** Having or arranged in layers. **2.** Consisting of one garment or layer of fabric worn over another: *the layered look; a layered skirt.*

lay·er·ing (láy-ər-ing) *n.* Also **lay·er·age** (-ij). The process of rooting branches, twigs, or stems that are still attached to a parent plant, as by placing a specially treated part in moist soil.

lay·ette (lay-ét) *n.* Clothing and other accessories for a newborn baby. [French, from Old French, diminutive of *laie,* box, from Middle Dutch *laege*†.]

lay figure *n* **1.** A jointed model of the human body used by artists, especially to demonstrate the arrangement of drapery. Also called "mannequin". **2.** A subservient person.

lay·man (láy-mən) *n., pl.* **-men** (-mən). **1.** A member of a congregation as distinguished from the clergy. **2.** One who does not have special or advanced training or skill.

lay off *tr.v.* **1.** To suspend (workers) from employment, especially during a slack period. **2.** To mark off; chart the boundaries of. **3.** *Informal.* **a.** To desist from (an activity): *lay off shouting.* **b.** To leave (a person or thing) alone. —*intr.v. Informal.* To desist.

lay·off (láy-off, -awf) *n.* **1.** The suspension or dismissal of employees. **2.** The interval for which employment has been suspended.

lay out *tr.v..* **1.** To put or spread out in readiness, as for wear, packing, display, or inspection. **2. a.** To arrange according to plan: *laid out the grounds of the castle.* **b.** To set out (an argument, for example). **3.** *Informal.* To spend or invest (money), especially on a large scale. **4.** To clothe and prepare (a corpse) for burial. **5.** *Informal.* To knock down; especially, to knock unconscious. **6.** *Informal.* to put (oneself) to a lot of trouble.

lay·out (láy-out) *n.* **1.** The laying out of something. **2.** The arrangement, plan, or structuring of something laid out; the overall picture or form: *the layout of a factory.* **3. a.** The arrangement and juxtaposition of printed matter, photographs, or the like, as for a newspaper or magazine page. **b.** A dummy, sketch, or paste-up for matter to be printed. **4.** A diagram showing how something, such as a machine, is constructed.

lay reader *n.* A layman in the Anglican and Episcopal churches authorised by a bishop to preach and conduct certain services. Also called "reader".

lay·shaft (láy-shaaft || -shaft) *n.* A secondary shaft to which motion is transmitted from the main shaft in a gear box.

lay sister *n.* A female lay brother.

lay·wo·man (láy-wŏŏmən) *n., pl.* **-women** (-wimmin). A female layman.

la·zar (lázzər || láyzər) *n. Archaic.* A beggar afflicted with some loathsome disease, especially leprosy; a leper. [Middle English, from Medieval Latin *Lazarus,* LAZARUS.]

laz·a·ret·to (lázzə-réttō) *n., pl.* **-tos.** Also **laz·a·ret, laz·a·rette** (-rét). **1.** Formerly, a hospital treating contagious diseases. Also called "lazar house", "pest house". **2.** A building or ship used as a quarantine station. **3.** A storage space between the decks of a ship. [Italian *lazaretto,* from *lazzaro,* leper, beggar, from Medieval Latin *Lazarus,* LAZARUS.]

Laz·a·rus (lázzərəss). **1.** The brother of Mary and Martha whom Jesus raised from the dead. John 11:1–44. **2.** The diseased beggar in the parable of the rich man and the beggar. Luke 16:19–31.

laze (layz) *v.* **lazed, lazing, lazes.** —*intr.* To be lazy; loaf. —*tr.* To spend (time) in loafing. Often used with *away.*
~*n.* Time spent in idleness. [Back-formation from LAZY.]

La·zio (látsi-ō, laăts-yō). Region of west central Italy, bordering on the Tyrrhenian Sea, embracing ranges of the central Apennines in the east and the lowlands of the Campagna di Roma and Pontine marshes in the west. In ancient times the region was called Latium. The largest city and capital is Rome.

lazuli *n.* **Lapis lazuli** *(see).*

laz·u·lite (lázzew-līt) *n.* A relatively rare, deep sky-blue or azure mineral, essentially $Mg,Al_2(PO_4)_2(OH)_2$, in which iron usually replaces some of the magnesium. [Medieval Latin *lazulum,* LAPIS LAZULI + -ITE.]

laz·u·rite (lázzewr-īt) *n.* A relatively rare, azure, violet-blue, or Prussian blue mineral, $3(NaAlSiO_4)\cdot Na_2S$. Also called "lapis lazuli". [German *Lasurit,* from Medieval Latin *lazur,* from Arabic *lāzaward,* LAPIS LAZULI.]

la·zy (láyzi) *adj.* **-zier, -ziest. 1.** Resistant to work or exertion; given to idleness; slothful. **2.** Slow-moving; sluggish: *a lazy river.* **3.** Conducive to languor or indolence: *a lazy day.* [Perhaps from Low German and akin to *lasich,* idle.] **—la·zi·ly** *adv.* **—la·zi·ness** *n.*

la·zy·bones (láyzi-bōnz) *n., pl.* **-bones.** *Informal.* A lazy person.

lazy tongs *pl.n.* Tongs having a jointed extensible framework operated by scissor-like handles for grasping an object at a distance.

lb pound [Latin *libra*].

l.b. leg bye (in cricket).

l.b.w. leg before wicket (in cricket).

l.c. 1. letter of credit. **2.** In the place cited [Latin *loco citato*]. **3.** *Printing.* lower-case.

L.C.C. London County Council (formerly in Britain).

L/C letter of credit.

LCD *n.* A *l*iquid-*c*rystal *d*isplay: a digital display, as in electronic calculators, containing liquid crystal between sheets of glass, and becoming readable when a voltage is applied.

l.c.d., L.C.D. lowest common denominator.

L.C.J. Lord Chief Justice (in England and Wales).

l.c.m., L.C.M. lowest common multiple.

L/Cpl. lance-corporal.

ld. 1. *Printing.* lead. **2.** load.

Ld. Lord (title).

LD lethal dose. LD_{50} is an index of toxicity indicating the amount of poison that causes the death of 50 per cent of a batch of experimental organisms.

L-D converter *n. Metallurgy.* A converter for producing steel by blowing oxygen through a water-cooled pipe into molten pig iron, thus burning off some of the carbon. [From *Linz-Donawitz,* after two towns in Austria where the method was first used.]

L-do·pa (él-dṓpə) *n.* An amino acid, $C_9H_{11}NO_4$, that occurs naturally in the body and is used to treat Parkinson's disease. Also called "levodopa". [From *L-dihydroxyphenylalanine.*]

L-driver (él-drīvər) *n. British.* A **learner-driver** *(see).*

lea[1] (lee || *U.S. also* lay) *n.* Also **ley** (lay || lee). *Poetic.* **1.** Grassland; meadow. **2.** Land sown temporarily with grass. [Middle English *ley(e),* Old English *lēah, lēa.*]

lea[2] (lee) *n.* A measure of yarn that is 300, 200, 120, or 80 yards (275, 183, 110, or 73 metres) depending on the type. [Middle English *lee,* perhaps from French *lier,* from Latin *ligāre,* to bind.]

lea. 1. league (unit of distance). **2.** leather.

L.E.A. local education authority (in Britain).

leach (leech) *v.* **leached, leaching, leaches.** *—tr.* **1.** To remove soluble constituents from (a substance) by the action of a percolating liquid. **2.** To remove (soluble constituents) from a substance in this way. *—intr.* **1.** To be dissolved and washed out by a percolating liquid. **2.** To lose or yield soluble matter to a percolating liquid. *~n.* **1.** The process of leaching. **2.** A porous, perforated, or sieve-like vessel that holds material to be leached. **3.** The substance through which a liquid is leached. **4.** The solution thus leached. [Variant of obsolete *letch,* to wet, probably ultimately from Old English *leccan,* to moisten.] **—leach·er** *n.*

Leach (leech), **Bernard (Howell)** (1887–1979). British potter. He set up a pottery at St. Ives, Cornwall (1920), and described his innovative ideas in *A Potter's Book* (1940).

leach·ing (léeching) *n. Geology.* Separation and removal of soluble components from soil by percolating water. Also called "chemical weathering".

Lea·cock (léekok), **Stephen (Butler)** (1869–1944). British-born Canadian humorist. He was a professor of economics at McGill University, Montreal, while writing humorous essays and books.

lead[1] (leed) *v.* **led** (led), **leading, leads.** *—tr.* **1. a.** To show the way to by going in advance; conduct, escort, or direct. **b.** To show (the way) by going in advance or by setting an example. **2.** To guide physically, as by taking by the hand or by holding by a rope: *lead a horse.* **3.** To serve as a route for; conduct on a particular course: *The path led him to a cemetery.* **4. a.** To cause to follow some course of action or line of thought; induce: *led him to believe otherwise.* **b.** To influence the answer of a (witness) by phrasing a question in a certain way. **5. a.** To direct the performance or activities of: *lead a battalion.* **b.** To inspire the conduct of: *led the nation.* **6.** To assume leadership in; steer; guide: *lead a discussion.* **7.** To be at the head of: *His name led the list.* **8.** To have an advance over: *led the field in aerodynamics.* **9.** To pursue; live: *leading a hectic life.* **10.** In card games, to begin a round of play by putting down (a card): *led an ace.* **11.** To aim in front of (a moving target). **12.** *Chiefly British.* To be the principal first violinist in (an orchestra). **13.** To guide (a partner) when dancing. **14.** To be a channel for (water, electricity, or the like). *—intr.* **1.** To be first; be ahead: *leading by a length.* **2.** To go first as a guide. **3.** To act as commander, director, or conductor. **4.** To guide a partner in dance steps. **5.** To be guided: *The horse leads easily.* **6.** To afford a passage, course, or route: *a door leading into the kitchen.* **7.** To tend towards a certain goal or result. Used with *to: led to complications.* **8.** To make the initial play, as in a card game. **9.** *British.* To be the principal first violinist in an orchestra. **10.** In boxing, to deliver attacking punches with a specified fist: *leading with his left.* **11.** To begin a presentation in a given way: *led with the election news.* **12.** In dancing, to start off on a specified foot: *leading with your right foot.* **13.** *Music.* To have a lead in a piece of music. **—lead astray.** To lead into error or wrongdoing. **—lead on.** To draw along; lure; entice, especially by deception. **—lead up to. 1.** To result in by a series of steps. **2.** To proceed towards (one's true purpose or subject) with preliminary remarks.
~n. **1.** The first place; the foremost position. **2.** The margin by which one is ahead: *he was losing his lead.* **3. a.** A piece of information of possible use in a search: *several good leads for a job.* **b.** A clue; a hint. **4.** Command; leadership: *take the lead.* **5.** An example; a precedent. **6. a.** The principal role in a dramatic production. **b.** The person playing such a part. **7.** In journalism: **a.** The opening line or paragraph of a news story. **b.** A prominently displayed news story. **8.** In card games: **a.** The first play. **b.** The prerogative of making or turn to make the first play. **c.** The card played. **9.** In boxing: **a.** The arm with which a boxer usually leads. **b.** A punch using this arm. **10.** A leash, rope, or strap for leading an animal. **11.** *Nautical.* The direction in which a rope runs. **12.** *Mining.* **a.** A deposit of gold ore in an old riverbed. **b.** A lode. **13.** A wire or cable for making an electrical connection. **14.** The act of aiming ahead of and firing at a moving target. **15.** *Music.* A major part at the beginning of a piece of music for an instrument or voice. **16.** A stream or other channel leading up to a mill. [Middle English *leden,* Old English *lǣdan, lǣdde, lǣded.*]

lead[2] (led) *n.* **1.** *Symbol* **Pb** A soft, malleable, ductile, bluish-white, dense metallic element, extracted chiefly from galena and used in containers and pipes for corrosives, in solder and type metal, bullets, radiation shielding, paints, and antiknock compounds. Atomic number 82, atomic weight 207.19, melting point 327.5°C, boiling point 1,744°C, relative density 11.35, valencies 2, 4. **2.** A lump of lead suspended by a line, used to make soundings to determine the depth of water. **3.** *Plural. British.* **a.** A flat or slightly pitched roof covered with sheets of lead. **b.** The sheets of lead used for such a roof. **4.** Bullets from or for firearms; shot. **5.** *Plural.* Strips of lead used in fitting windows with small panes or stained glass pieces. **6.** *Printing. Abbr.* **ld.** A thin strip of type metal used to separate lines of type. **7. a.** Any of various, often graphitic, compositions used as the writing substance in pencils. **b.** A thin stick of such material. **—swing the lead.** To shirk one's duties, especially by malingering.
~adj. Containing or made of lead.
~v. **leaded, leading, leads.** *—tr.* **1.** To cover, line, weight, fill, or treat with lead. **2.** *Printing.* To provide space between (lines of type) with leads. **3.** To secure (window glass) with leads. *—intr.* To become filled, covered, or clogged with lead. [Middle English *lead, lęd,* Old English *lēad,* from West Germanic *lauda* (unattested), akin to Gaelic *luaidh*†.]

lead acetate (led) *n.* A poisonous white crystalline compound, $Pb(C_2H_3O_2)_2\cdot 3H_2O$, used in dyes, waterproofing compounds, and varnishes. Also called "sugar of lead".

lead arsenate (led) *n.* A poisonous white crystalline compound, $Pb_3(AsO_4)_2$, used in insecticides and herbicides.

Lead·bel·ly (léd-belli), **Lead Belly,** born Huddie William Ledbetter (1888–1949). U.S. songwriter and blues singer. Among his compositions is *Good Night Irene.*

lead carbonate (led) *n.* A poisonous white amorphous powder, $PbCO_3$, used as a paint pigment.

lead chromate (led) *n.* A poisonous yellow crystalline compound, $PbCrO_4$, used as a paint pigment.

lead·en (lédd'n) *adj.* **1.** Made of or containing lead. **2.** Heavy and inert like lead. **3.** Dull and listless; sluggish. **4.** Burdened; weighted down; depressed: *a leaden heart.* **5.** Dull, dark grey: *a leaden sky.* **—lead·en·ly** *adv.* **—lead·en·ness** *n.*

lead·er (léedər) *n.* **1.** A person who leads others along a way; a guide. **2.** One in charge or in command of others. **3.** The head of a political party or organisation. **4.** *British. Capital* **L. a.** A member of the House of Commons who is responsible for organising the programme of parliamentary business. Also called "Leader of the House of Commons". **b.** A peer who has a similar function in the House of Lords. Also called "Leader of the House of Lords". In both senses, also called "Leader of the House". **5. a.** The principal performer in an orchestra, quartet, choir, or the like; especially, a principal first violinist who represents the orchestra to the conductor and often plays solos. **b.** *U.S.* The conductor of an orchestra, band, or choral group. **6.** The foremost horse, dog, or other animal in a harnessed team. **7.** *British.* The senior counsel, usually a Queen's Counsel, who conducts a case in court. **8.** *Chiefly British.* The main editorial article in a newspaper or periodical. Also called "leading article". **9.** *Plural. Printing.* Dots or dashes in a row leading the eye across a page, as in an index entry. **10.** A pipe for conveying rainwater from the roof to the ground. **11.** A short length of gut, wire, or the like by which the hook is attached to a fishing line. **12.** *Botany.* The growing apex or main shoot of a shrub or tree. **13.** A tab on the end of a film or tape, used to thread it. **—lead·er·ship** *n.*

lead glance (led) *n.* A mineral, **galena** *(see).*

lead glass (led) *n.* **Flint glass** *(see).*

lead-in (léed-in) *n.* **1.** An introduction, as to a subject or programme. **2.** The part of an antenna or aerial that leads to an electronic transmitter or receiver.

lead·ing¹ (léeding) *adj.* **1.** Major; principal: *a leading factor.* **2.** At the head; in the lead; foremost: *the leading candidate.* **3.** Playing a lead or principal role in a theatrical production: *a leading lady.* **4.** Phrased to elicit a desired response: *a leading question.* —See Synonyms at **chief.** —**lead·ing·ly** *adv.*

lead·ing² (lédding) *n.* **1.** A border or rim of lead, as around a window-pane. **2.** *Printing.* The spacing between lines.

leading aircraftman (léeding) *n., pl.* **-men.** *Abbr.* **L.A.C..** A serviceman in the Royal Air Force ranking between a senior aircraftman and an aircraftman.

leading aircraftwoman (léeding) *n., pl.* **-women.** *Abbr.* **L.A.C.W.** A member of the British Women's Royal Air Force holding a rank equivalent to that of a leading aircraftman.

leading edge (léeding) *n.* **1.** The edge of a sail that faces the wind. **2.** The front edge of an aircraft propeller blade or wing.

leading light (léeding) *n. Informal.* A person of great importance or value, especially to a group or undertaking.

leading note (léeding) *n. Music.* The seventh note, or degree, of a scale, a half tone below the tonic; a subtonic.

leading-rein (léeding-rayn) *n.* A rope or rein attached to a horse's bridle or halter by which to lead it.

leading reins (léeding) *pl.n.* A harness with straps attached to it, that is used to support a baby learning to walk. Also called "leading strings".

leading seaman (léeding) *n., pl.* **-men.** A serviceman in the Royal Navy ranking between a petty officer and an able seaman.

leading strings (léeding) *pl.n.* **1.** Excessive control or guidance. Used especially in the phrase *keep someone in leading strings.* **2.** Leading reins.

lead lights (led) *pl.n.* Also **lead·ed lights** (léddid). Windows made up of small pieces of glass held together by lead strips.

lead line (led) *n. Nautical.* A sounding line with a lump of lead on it used to determine the depth of water.

lead monoxide (led) *n. Chemistry.* **Litharge** *(see).*

lead off (led) *intr.v.* To make the initial play or move; start.

lead-off (léed-off, -awf) *n.* **1.** An opening play or move; a start; a beginning. **2.** A person or thing that starts something.

lead pencil (led) *n.* A pencil that contains a thin stick of graphite as its marking substance.

lead poisoning (led) *n.* Acute or chronic poisoning by lead or any of its salts, the acute form causing severe gastroenteritis, and the chronic form anaemia, abdominal pain, constipation, partial paralysis, and convulsions. Also called "plumbism", "saturnism".

lead screw (led) *n.* A threaded screw along the bed of a lathe, used to drive the tool carriage along at a controlled rate, as in cutting threads.

leads·man (lédz-mən) *n., pl.* **-men** (-mən). *Nautical.* The man who uses the lead line in taking soundings.

lead tetraethyl (led) *n.* **Tetraethyl lead** *(see).*

lead time (léed) *n.* The time needed or available between the decision to start a project and the completion of the work.

lead·wort (léd-wurt) *n.* **1.** Any of various plants of the genera *Plumbago* or *Ceratostigma*, having clusters of variously coloured flowers. **2.** Any of several similar plants. Also called "plumbago". [Some species were thought to cure lead poisoning.]

leaf (leef) *n., pl.* **leaves** (leevz). *Abbr.* **l., L.** **1.** A usually green, flattened structure of vascular plants, characteristically consisting of a bladelike expansion attached to a stem, and functioning as a principal organ of photosynthesis and transpiration. **2.** A leaflike organ or structure. **3.** Leaves collectively; foliage. **4.** The leaves of a plant used or processed for a specific purpose: *tobacco leaf.* **5.** Any of the sheets of paper bound in a book, each side of which constitutes a page. **6.** Metal in the form of a very thin sheet: *gold leaf.* **7.** A hinged or removable section for a table top. **8.** A hinged or otherwise movable section of a folding door, shutter, or gate. **9.** Any of the metal strips forming a leaf spring. —**in leaf.** Having sprouted or produced leaves; green with foliage. —**turn over a new leaf.** To make a significant change in one's life by mending one's ways. —*intr.v.* **leafed, leafing, leafs.** **1.** To produce leaves; put forth foliage. **2.** To turn pages rapidly; glance: *leafed through the catalogue.* [Middle English *le(e)f*, Old English *lēaf.*]

leaf·age (léefij) *n.* Leaves; foliage.

leaf beet *n.* A vegetable, **chard** *(see).*

leaf-cutter ant (léef-kuttər) *n.* Any of various ants of the genus *Atta*, native to South America, that cut away leaf pieces to use them as fertiliser for their fungus gardens.

leaf-cutter bee *n.* Any of various carpenter bees of the genus *Megachile* that use pieces of leaf to construct the walls of their egg cells. *M. centuncularis* is a pest of garden roses.

leaf fat *n.* A dense fat that collects around the kidneys of certain animals, notably pigs.

leaf·hop·per (léef-hoppər) *n.* Any of numerous insects of the family Cicadellidae, that suck juices from plants.

leaf insect *n.* Any of various chiefly Asiatic insects of the genus *Phyllium* and related genera, that resemble leaves.

leaf-lard (léef-laard) *n.* High-grade lard made from the leaf fat of a pig.

leaf·less (léef-ləss, -liss) *adj.* Having or putting forth no leaves.

leaf·let (léef-lət, -lit) *n.* **1.** Any of the segments of a compound leaf. **2.** A small leaf or leaflike part. **3.** A printed, usually folded sheet of paper for distribution, such as an advertising circular. —*v.* **leafleted** or **leafletted, -leting** or **-letting, -lets.** —*intr.* To distribute leaflets. —*tr.* **1.** To distribute leaflets in (an area). **2.** To distribute leaflets to (people).

leaf miner *n.* Any of numerous small flies and moths that in the larval state dig into and feed on leaf tissue.

leaf monkey *n.* The **langur** *(see).*

leaf mould *n.* Humus or compost consisting of decomposed leaves and other organic material.

leaf spot *n.* Any of various plant diseases resulting in well-defined darkened areas on the leaves.

leaf spring *n.* A composite spring consisting of several layers of flexible metallic strips joined to act as a single unit.

leaf-stalk (léef-stawk) *n.* The stalk by which a leaf is attached to a stem; a petiole.

leaf·y (léefi) *adj.* **-ier, -iest.** **1.** Having or covered with leaves. **2.** Consisting of leaves. **3.** Leaflike. —**leaf·i·ness** *n.*

league¹ (leeg) *n. Abbr.* **l., L.** **1.** An association of states, organisations, or individuals formed to promote common interests; an alliance. **2.** An association of sports teams or clubs that play one another. **3.** *Informal.* A class of competition; a level: *out of his league.* —**in league.** Allied; in close cooperation. —*v.* **leagued, leaguing, leagues.** —*intr.* To come together for a common purpose; unite. —*tr.* To bring together under a common agreement; join. [Middle English *ligg*, from Old French *ligue*, from Italian *liga, lega*, from *legare*, to bind, from Latin *ligāre.*]

league² *n. Abbr.* **lea.** **1.** Formerly, a unit of distance, usually equal to three statute miles. **2.** A square league. [Middle English *leg(h)e*, from Late Latin *leuca, leuga*, perhaps from Gaulish.]

League of Nations *n.* An international organisation of nations established in 1920 to promote world peace and dissolved in 1946.

lea·guer¹ (léegər) *n. Archaic.* **1.** A siege; beleaguerment. **2.** A besieging army or its camp. —*tr.v.* **leaguered, -guering, -guers.** To besiege; beleaguer. [Dutch *leger*, camp, siege, from Middle Dutch, camp, lair.]

leaguer² *n.* A person who belongs to a league.

league table, league tables *n.* A comparative rating or ranking of those in the same line of activity: *Where is our school in the league tables?*

Le·ah (leer, lée-ə). The elder daughter of Laban and first wife of Jacob. Genesis 29:16–23. [Hebrew, "wild cow".]

leak (leek) *n.* **1.** An escape from normal or proper confinement; especially, an accidental escape from a container or conduit. **2.** Something escaping normal or proper confines, such as: **a.** A liquid or gas abnormally flowing out of a pipe or reservoir. **b.** An electric current diverted through faulty insulation. **c.** Light or other radiation passing through an accidental opening. **3.** A flaw, crack, hole, or passage through which an escape occurs. **4.** The path followed by the escaping material. **5. a.** A disclosure of confidential information, either intentional or deliberate. **b.** The information disclosed. **c.** The source of such information. **6.** *Vulgar Slang.* An act of urinating. —**spring a leak.** To contract or develop an opening or other flaw that allows the escape or entrance of a substance. —*v.* **leaked, leaking, leaks.** —*intr.* **1.** To permit the escape or passage of something through a hole, crack, or similar opening. **2.** To escape or pass through such an opening. **3.** To become publicly known through a breach of secrecy. Often used with *out: The news leaked out.* **4.** *Vulgar Slang.* To urinate. —*tr.* **1.** To permit (a substance) to escape or pass through a hole, crack, or similar opening. **2.** To disclose (information) without authorisation or official sanction. [Middle English *leke*, perhaps from Old Norse *leki.*]

leak·age (léekij) *n.* **1.** The process or an instance of leaking. **2.** That which escapes by leaking. **3.** An allowance made for loss of stock by leaking, as in commerce.

Lea·key (léeki), **Louis (Seymour Bazett)** (1903–72). British palaeontologist. He influenced evolutionary thinking with his account and analysis of the discovery, but his wife Mary Leakey (1913–96), of the 1.75 million-year-old *Zinjanthropus* skull at Olduvai Gorge, in Tanzania. Their son Richard Leakey (1944–) continues his research.

leak·y (léeki) *adj.* **-ier, -iest.** Having leaks or tending to leak.

Leam·ing·ton (lémmingtən). Town in Warwickshire, central England, on the river Leam. Its full name is Royal Leamington Spa, and its saline waters made it a popular spa and health resort in the late 18th and 19th centuries.

lean¹ (leen) *v.* **leaned** (lent, leend) or **leant** (lent), **leaning, leans.** —*intr.* **1.** To bend or slant away from the vertical. **2.** To incline the weight of the body so as to be supported: *leaning against the railing.* **3.** To rely for assistance or support: *Lean on me for help.* **4.** To have a tendency or preference. Used with *to* or *towards: She leans towards the group approach.* **5.** *Informal.* To exert pressure. Used with *on: Their boss is leaning on them.* —*tr.* **1.** To set or place so as to be resting or supported. **2.** To cause to incline: *Lean your head back.* —**lean over backwards.** To put oneself to great inconvenience to achieve something.

—*n.* A tilt or inclination away from the vertical. [Middle English *lenen*, Old English *hleonian, hlinian.*]

Usage: *Leant* is the usual past tense and participle form in British English, *leaned* in American English; the latter is more widespread in the English-speaking world, especially in written English. Many users of British English write *leaned*, but say (lent).

lean² *adj.* **leaner, leanest.** **1.** Not fleshy or fat; thin. **2.** Containing little or no fat. Said of meat. **3.** Not productive or abundant: *lean years.* **4. a.** Lacking mineral value: *lean ore.* **b.** Lacking a high proportion of combustible material; containing much air: *lean fuel.* **5.** Downsized and competitive: *leaner, meaner, and fitter companies.* ~*n.* Meat with little or no fat. [Middle English *lene,* Old English *hlæne,* from Germanic *hlainjaz* (unattested).] **—lean·ly** *adv.* **—lean·ness** *n.*

Synonyms: *lean, spare, skinny, scrawny, lank, lanky, gaunt.*

Lean (leen), **Sir David** (1908–91). British film director. His work includes *The Bridge On the River Kwai* (1957) and *Lawrence of Arabia* (1962), both of which won Academy Awards.

Le·an·der (li-ándər). *Greek Mythology.* Youth who loved Hero and drowned while swimming the Hellespont one night to be with her.

lean·ing (léening) *n.* A tendency; a proclivity; an inclination.

lean-to (léen-tōō, -tŏŏ) *n., pl.* **-tos. 1.** A shed with a single-pitch roof attached to the side of a building. **2.** A shelter made from planks or branches raised in the front on poles.

leap (leep) *v.* **leapt** (lept) or **leaped** (lept, leept), **leaping, leaps.** —*intr.* **1.** To jump off the ground with a spring of the legs. **2.** To jump forwards; vault; bound. **3.** To move quickly, abruptly, or impulsively: *leaps from one loyalty to another.* —*tr.* **1.** To jump over; hurdle: *leap the brook.* **2.** To cause to jump: *leap a horse.* ~*n.* **1.** The act of springing up or forwards; a vault; a bound. **2.** The distance cleared in a forward spring. **3.** An abrupt or precipitous passage, shift or transition. **4.** Something, such as a fence, that is or is to be leapt. **—a leap in the dark.** A course of action or a risk taken without knowing what the consequences will be. **—by leaps and bounds.** Very quickly and by large degrees. [Middle English *le(a)pen,* Old English *hlēapan.*] **—leap·er** *n.*

Usage: *Leapt* is the usual past tense and participle form in British English, *leaped* in American English; the latter is more widespread in the English-speaking world, especially in written English.

leap·frog (léep-frog || -frawg) *n.* A game in which one player kneels or bends over while the next in line jumps over him straddle-legged. ~*v.* **leapfrogged, -frogging, -frogs.** —*tr.* **1.** To jump over or as if in leapfrog. **2.** *Military.* To advance (two military units) by engaging one with the enemy while moving the other to a forward position. —*intr.* To move forwards or progress by or as if by alternating leaps.

leap year *n.* **1.** A year in the Gregorian calendar having 366 days, with the extra day, February 29, intercalated to compensate for the quarter-day difference between an ordinary year and the astronomical year. Every year whose number is divisible by 4 is a leap year, except centennial numbers, which are leap years only when divisible by 400. **2.** An intercalary year in any calendar.

Lear (leer), **Edward** (1812–88). British artist and writer. He was a skilled painter of birds, but is famous for the whimsical humour of his limericks and works such as his first *Book of Nonsense* (1846).

Lear (leer) *n.* A foolish, self-deceiving father, especially one whose behaviour has tragic consequences. [After *King Lear,* hero of Shakespeare's tragedy (1605).]

learn (lern) *v.* **learned** (lernt, lernd) or *chiefly British* **learnt** (lernt), **learning, learns.** —*tr.* **1.** To gain knowledge, comprehension, or mastery of through experience or study. **2.** To fix in the mind or memory; memorise: *learnt the poem by heart.* **3.** To acquire through experience: *learnt humility in the hands of his captors.* **4.** To become informed of; find out. **5.** *Obsolete.* To give information of. **6.** *Nonstandard.* To teach. —*intr.* **1.** To gain knowledge, comprehension, or skill. **2.** To become informed. Used with *of* or *about.* [Middle English *lernen,* Old English *leornian.*] **—learn·er** *n.*

Usage: *Learnt* is the usual past tense and participle form in British English, *learned* in American English; the latter is more widespread in the English-speaking world, especially in written English. *Learned* pronounced as one syllable (lernt *or* lernd) should not be confused with the adjective *learned* (as in *a learned historian),* which is pronounced as two syllables (lérnid). *Learn* in the sense of "teach, impart knowledge" has no status in standard English.

learn·ed (lérnid) *adj.* **1.** Having or demonstrating profound knowledge or scholarship; erudite; scholarly. **2.** Scholarly or directed towards scholars: *a learned journal.* **3.** Designating a member of the legal profession, especially a barrister: *my learned friend.*

learner-driver (lérnər-drīvər) *n.* A driver with a provisional licence who is learning to drive and in Britain has L-plates on his or her car. Also *British* "L-driver".

learn·ing (lérning) *n.* **1.** Instruction; education. **2.** Acquired wisdom, knowledge, or skill. **3.** *Psychology.* The process of development through experience which leads to relatively permanent changes in behaviour. —See Synonyms at **knowledge.**

learning curve *n.* **1.** A graph representing progress in learning, usually showing a fairly steady increase, especially at the beginning, and then levelling off towards the end. **2.** *Informal.* The rate of progress in learning: *have a steep learning curve in a new job.*

lease (leess) *n.* **1. a.** A contract granting use or possession of property for a specified period in exchange for rent. **b.** The legal document granting such use or possession. **2.** The term or duration of use or possession granted by such a contract. **3.** Property used or possessed by contract in exchange for rent. **—a new lease of life.** Renewed strength, enthusiasm, or usefulness. ~*tr.v.* **leased, leasing, leases. 1.** To grant use or possession of by lease. **2.** To use or possess by lease. [Middle English *les,* from Anglo-French, from *lesser,* to lease, from Old French *laissier,* to let go, leave, from Latin *laxāre,* to let go, loosen, from *laxus,* LAX.] **—leas·a·ble** *adj.*

lease-back (léess-bak) *n.* The leasing of property by a new owner back to the previous owner: *sale and lease-back.*

lease·hold (léess-hōld) *n.* **1.** Use or possession by lease. **2.** Property held under a lease for a term of years. Compare **freehold.** ~*adj.* Designating property held under a lease for a term of years.

lease·hold·er (léess-hōldər) *n.* A person who uses or possesses property through a lease.

leash (leesh) *n.* **1.** A chain, rope, or strap attached to the collar or harness of an animal and used to hold it in check or lead it. **2.** A control or check kept on something, as if by a leash. **3.** In hunting, a group of three animals, such as hounds, foxes, or hares. **—straining at the leash.** Eager and impatient to start. ~*tr.v.* **leashed, leashing, leashes.** To restrain with or as if with a leash. [Middle English *lees, leshe,* from Old French *laisse,* from *laissier,* to loosen, let (a dog run slack). See **lease.**]

leas·ing (lée-sing) *n. Archaic.* A lie, or the act of lying; falsehood. [Middle English *le(e)sing,* Old English *lēasung,* from *lēasian,* to lie, from *lēas,* untrue, false.]

least (leest). Alternative superlative of **little.** ~*adj.* **1.** Lowest in importance or rank. **2.** Smallest in magnitude, amount, or degree. **3.** Slightest; remotest: *He hasn't the least notion.* ~*adv.* To or in the smallest degree or amount. **—at least. 1.** According to the lowest possible assessment; no less than. **2.** In any event; anyway: *You might at least answer.* ~*n.* The smallest or slightest degree, amount, or the like. **—at the (very) least.** At the lowest calculation; as a minimum. **—in the least.** At all: *I don't mind in the least.* [Middle English *leest, least,* Old English *læst,* from Germanic *loisiz* (unattested), little. See **less.**]

least common denominator *n. Mathematics.* The **lowest common denominator** *(see).*

least common multiple *n. Mathematics.* The **lowest common multiple** *(see).*

least squares *n. Used with a singular verb.* A method of determining the line or curve that best fits an experimental set of data, using the criterion that the sums of the squares of deviations of experimental points from curve ordinates be a minimum.

least·ways (léest-wayz) *adv.* Also *chiefly U.S.* **least·wise** (-wīz). *Informal.* Anyway; at least.

leat (leet) *n.* An open ditch or trench that conducts water to a mill, mining works, or the like. [Old English *-gelæt* (as in *wætergelæt,* water-channel), from the root of LET.]

leath·er (léthər) *n. Abbr.* **lea. 1.** The dressed or tanned hide of an animal, usually with the hair removed. **2.** Any of various articles made of leather, such as a strap or boot. **3.** The flap of a dog's ear. ~*adj.* Of or made of leather. ~*tr.v.* **leathered, -ering, -ers. 1. a.** To cover with leather. **b.** To add leather parts to. **2.** *Informal.* To beat with or as if with a leather strap. [Middle English *lether, leder,* Old English *lether.*]

leath·er·back (léthər-bak) *n.* A large, chiefly tropical marine turtle, *Dermochelys coriacea,* having a leathery, ridged carapace.

Leath·er·ette (léthə-rét) *n.* A trademark for a paper or cloth imitation leather.

leath·er·head (léthər-hed) *n.* The **friarbird** *(see).*

leath·er·jack·et (léthər-jackit) *n.* **1.** The tough-skinned larva of certain crane flies, which feeds on the roots of grasses. **2.** Any of various fish of the genera *Scomberoides* and *Oligoplites,* having a leathery skin. **3.** Any of various triggerfish of the genus *Monacanthus* and related genera.

leath·ern (léthərn) *adj. Archaic.* **1.** Made of or covered with leather. **2.** Resembling leather.

leath·er·neck (léthər-nek) *n. U.S. Slang.* A marine. [Referring to the U.S. marine uniform which formerly had a leather neckband.]

leath·er·y (léthəri) *adj.* Having the texture or appearance of leather; tough or weathered: *leathery hands.*

leave[1] (leev) *v.* **left** (left), **leaving, leaves.** —*tr.* **1.** To go out of or away from. **2.** To go without taking or removing. Often used with *behind: left his book behind on the train.* **3. a.** To cause to remain as a consequence or aftereffect: *left a trail of smoke.* **b.** To bring to a specified state or condition: *left her in a rage.* **4. a.** To forgo moving, changing, proceeding with, or interfering with; let remain: *Leave the dishes in the sink.* **b.** To allow (a person or thing) or do something without intervening: *left the house to burn down.* **c.** To postpone: *leave packing till the morning.* **5.** To have remaining alive after one's death: *He leaves a son.* **6.** To give as or as if as a bequest. **7.** To submit to another to be done, acted upon, or accomplished: *Leave the hard work for Jones to do.* **8.** To abandon; forsake: *She's leaving home.* **9.** To give (information) to be acted upon at a later stage: *I left my number with his wife.* **10.** To have as remainder: *6 from 12 leaves 6.* —*intr.* To depart; set out; go. **—leave alone.** To refrain from disturbing, upsetting, or dealing with. **—leave be.** To refrain from interfering with, changing, or disturbing. **—leave go or hold of.** *Informal.* To let go of; stop holding. **—leave it at that.** To stop at the point indicated and do or say no more. **—leave much to be desired.** To fall far short of the appropriate standard or quality. **—leave off. 1.** To stop; cease. **2.** To stop doing or using: *leave off alcohol.* **—leave out. 1.** To omit. **2.** To disregard or ignore, especially in social matters. [Leave, left, left; Middle English *leven, left, lefte,* Old English *læfan, læfde, læfed.*]

Usage: In the sense of "refrain from interfering", *leave* and *let* are often interchangeable *(leave him alone/let him alone)* but some users try to maintain a distinction between the verbs: *leave alone* is felt to imply "leave someone in solitude", *let alone* simply "stop interfering with". In the sense of "allow", *let* is the usual form *(let him be, let it go),* though *leave* is often heard in less formal speech.

leave[2] *n.* **1.** Permission: *With your leave, I must go.* **2.** Official permission, as for military personnel, to be absent from work or duty for a considerable length of time: *leave of absence.* **3.** The duration of absence granted by such permission. **4.** Formal or verbal farewell: *took leave of her with a heavy heart.* **—on leave.** Absent with official permission. [Middle English *leve,* Old English *lēaf.*]

leave³ *intr.v.* **leaved, leaving, leaves.** To put forth foliage; leaf. [Middle English *leven,* from *le(e)f,* LEAF.]

leaved (leevd) *adj.* **1.** Having or bearing a leaf or leaves. **2.** Having a specified number or kind of leaves. Usually used in combination: *three-leaved; wide-leaved.*

leav·en (lévv'n) *n.* **1. a.** A substance, such as yeast, added to batters and doughs to produce fermentation. **b.** A portion of fermented dough used to produce fermentation in a new batch of dough. **2.** Any element or influence which works to enliven the whole.
~*tr.v.* **leavened, -ening, -ens. 1.** To add yeast or some other fermenting agent to. **2.** To produce fermentation in. **3.** To pervade with a lightening or enlivening influence: *leavened with a gentle humour.* [Middle English *levain,* from Old French, probably from Latin *levāmen,* alleviation, hence (in Vulgar Latin) "that which raises", from *levāre,* to raise.]

leaves. Plural of **leaf.**

leave-tak·ing (leév-tayking) *n.* **1.** A departure or farewell. **2.** An act of saying farewell.

leav·ings (leévingz) *pl.n.* Scraps or remains; leftovers; residue. See Synonyms at **remainder.**

Lea·vis (leéviss), **F(rank) R(aymond)** (1895–1978). British literary critic. He was editor of *Scrutiny* (1932–53), and his books include *The Great Tradition* (1948) and studies of D.H. Lawrence (1955) and Dickens (1971), this last work in collaboration with his wife, the critic Q.D. Leavis (1900–81). **—Lea·vis·ite** *n. & adj.*

Leb·a·non, Republic of (lébbənən). Small country in the Middle East. It has few resources, but developed as the regional centre of international finance, trade, and tourism. Unlike other Arab countries, it has a large Christian population, mainly Maronite (about 40 per cent of the total). It also has more than 200,000 Palestinian refugees. Lebanon was created as a French League of Nations mandate in 1920, and proclaimed its independence in 1941. It played a minor role in the 1948 and 1956 Arab-Israeli wars, but did not participate in those of 1967 and 1973. Civil war between rival groups occurred in 1958, 1969, 1973, 1975-76, when a Syrian peace-keeping force entered the country, in 1977, and again in 1983. To counter Palestine Liberation Organisation (PLO) attacks on northern Israel, the Israelis occupied south Lebanon in 1978, after which a U.N. peace-keeping force took over, and again in 1982, when more than 10,000 PLO guerrillas were evacuated, mainly from Beirut, under U.S., French, and Italian supervision. The Taif Accord of October 1989 has brought fragile peace between the opposing factions so far. Area, 10 452 square kilometres (4,036 square miles). Population, 3,080,000. Capital, Beirut. See map at **Jordan.** —**Leb·a·nese** (lébbə-neéz || -neéss) *n. & adj.*

Le·bens·raum (láybənz-rowm) *n.* **1.** Additional territory deemed, especially by the Nazis, to be necessary to a nation for its economic well-being. **2.** Broadly, any extra space needed to facilitate working or living. [German, "living space".]

Le Brun (lə brōN), **Charles** (1619–90). Artist to Louis XIV. He decorated Versailles, directed the Gobelins works (1663), responsible for royal furnishings, and was a founder of the Académie de France (1666), set up to enable French artists to study abroad.

Le Car·ré (lə kárray), **John,** pen name of David John Moore Cornwell (1931–). British writer of espionage novels. These include *The Spy Who Came in from the Cold* (1963), *Tinker, Tailor, Soldier, Spy* (1974), and *Smiley's People* (1980).

lech, letch (lech) *n. Informal.* **1.** A strong desire or craving, especially of a sexual nature. **2.** A lecherous act.
~*intr.v.* **leched** or **letched, leching** or **letching, leches** or **letches.** *Informal.* To behave in a lecherous manner. Often used with *after.* [Back-formation from LECHER.]

Le Cha·te·lier's principle (lə sha-télli-ayz) *n. Chemistry.* The principle that if a chemical reaction is at equilibrium and the conditions (such as pressure, temperature, or concentration) are changed, then there will be a compensating change in the position of equilibrium tending to restore the original conditions. [After H.L. *Le Châtelier* (1850–1936), French chemist.]

lech·er (léchər) *n.* A man given to excessive sexual cravings or indulgence. [Middle English *lech(o)ur,* from Old French *lecheor, lecheur,* from *lechier,* to live in debauchery, lick, from Frankish *likkōn* (unattested).] **—lech·er·ous** *adj.* **—lech·er·ous·ly** *adv.* **—lech·er·ous·ness** *n.*

lech·er·y (léchəri) *n.* **1.** Excessive indulgence in sexual activity. **2.** Prurience; lasciviousness.

lec·i·thin (léssithin) *n.* Any of a group of phospholipids found in all plant and animal tissues, produced commercially from egg yolks, soyabeans, and maize, and used in the processing of foods, pharmaceuticals, cosmetics, paints and inks, and rubber and plastics. [Greek *lekithos*†, egg yolk + -IN.]

le·cith·i·nase (lə-síthi-nayz, léssithi-, -nayss) *n.* Any of several enzymes that break down lecithin.

Le·clan·ché cell (lə-klóNshay) *n.* A voltaic cell of a type having a carbon anode, a zinc cathode, and ammonium chloride electrolyte. Manganese dioxide is used as a depolariser. The dry form is widely used in small batteries.

Le Cor·bu·sier (lə kawr-béwzi-ay, *French* -büz-yáy), pseudonym of Charles-Edouard Jeanneret (1887–1965). Swiss-born French architect. His design and use of modular housing units has greatly influenced modern town planning.

lec·tern (léktərn) *n.* **1.** A reading desk with a slanted top holding the books from which Scriptural passages are read during a church service. **2.** Broadly, any stand that serves as a support for notes or books, especially those of a speaker. [Middle English *lectorn, lettron,* from Old French *lettrun,* from Medieval Latin *lectrīnum,* from *lectrum,* from Latin *lectus,* past participle of *legere,* to read.]

lec·tion (léksh'n) *n.* **1.** A variant reading or transcription of a text as given in a particular edition or copy. **2.** A reading from Scripture that forms a part of a church service. [Latin *lectiō* (stem *lectiōn-*), "a reading", from *legere,* to read. See **lectern.**]

lec·tion·ar·y (léksh'n-əri || *U.S.* -erri) *n., pl.* **-ies.** A book containing lessons or a list of lessons from Scripture to be read at services. [Late Latin *lectiōnārium,* from Latin *lectiō,* LECTION.]

lec·tor (lék-tawr || -tər) *n.* **1. a.** A cleric of the second lowest of the four minor orders in the early Christian church and formerly in the Roman Catholic Church, having the office of reading the sacred books in church. **b.** In the Roman Catholic Church, an ordinand who has been admitted to one of the first stages of the priestly ministry. **2.** A person who reads aloud certain of the Scriptural passages used in a church service; a reader. **3.** A lecturer or reader in certain universities. [Late Latin, from Latin, "reader", from *legere,* to read. See **lecture.**] **—lec·tor·ship** *n.*

lec·ture (lékchər) *n.* **1.** An exposition of a given subject delivered before an audience or class for the purpose of instruction; a discourse. **2.** A method of teaching by discourse, as is used in universities. **3.** A sober admonition or correction; a solemn scolding.
~*v.* **lectured, -turing, -tures.** —*intr.* To deliver a lecture. —*tr.* **1.** To give a lecture to. **2.** To scold soberly and at length. [Middle English, "a reading", from Old French, from Medieval Latin *lectūra,* from *lectus,* past participle of *legere,* to read.]

lec·tur·er (lékchərər) *n.* **1.** A person who gives a lecture. **2. a.** A teacher in a college or university ranking below a reader or professor. **b.** The rank or position of such a teacher. **—lec·ture·ship** *n.*

lec·ture·ship (lékchər-ship) *n.* **1.** The status or position of a lecturer. **2.** An endowment or foundation supporting a series or course of lectures.

led. Past tense and past participle of **lead.**

LED *n. Electronics.* A *l*ight-*e*mitting *d*iode: a semiconductor device that emits light when a voltage is applied, used extensively in visual displays on calculators, digital measuring instruments, and the like.

Le·da (leédə). *Greek Mythology.* A queen of Sparta and the mother, by Zeus, who had taken the form of a swan, of Helen and Pollux, and by her husband Tyndareus of Castor and Clytemnestra.

le·der·ho·sen (láydər-hōz'n) *pl.n.* Men's leather shorts worn as part of traditional Tirolean or Bavarian costume. [German, "leather trousers".]

ledge (lej) *n.* **1.** A horizontal projection forming a narrow shelf on a wall. **2.** A cut or projection forming a shelf on a cliff or rock wall. **3.** A ridge or rock shelf under water. **4.** A level of rock bearing ore; a vein. [Middle English *legge,* a raised strip or bar, perhaps from *leggen,* to lay, Old English *lecgan.*] **—ledged, ledg·y** *adj.*

ledg·er (léjər) *n.* **1. a.** A book in which the monetary transactions of a business are recorded as debits and credits. **b.** A book to which the record of accounts is transferred as final entry from original listings. **2.** A slab of stone laid flat over a grave. **3.** A horizontal timber in scaffolding, attached to the uprights and supporting the putlogs. **4.** In fishing, ledger bait, line, or tackle. [Middle English *legger,* book fixed in one place, probably from Middle Dutch *legger, ligger,* respectively from *leggen,* to lay, and *liggen,* to lie.]

ledger bait *n.* Fishing bait that is designed to rest on the bottom.

ledger board *n.* The top railing of a fence or balustrade.

ledger line, leg·er line (léjər) *n.* **1.** *Music.* A short line placed above or below a staff to accommodate notes higher or lower than the staff's range. **2.** A fishing line used with ledger bait.

ledger tackle *n.* Fishing tackle used with ledger bait.

Le Duc Tho (láy dŏŏk tő) (1911–). Vietnamese politician, who negotiated the North Vietnamese-U.S. ceasefire (1973) with Henry Kissinger. Both were awarded the Nobel peace prize (1973), but Le Duc Tho refused it. He retired from the Vietnam politburo (1986).

lee (lee) *n.* **1. a.** *Nautical.* The side or quarter away from the direction from which the wind blows; the side sheltered from the wind. **b.** Any place sheltered from the wind. **2.** Cover; shelter: *under the lee of a large tree.*
~*adj.* Located on or moving in the direction of the side towards which the wind blows: *the lee side of a ship.* Compare **weather.** [Middle English *le(e),* from Old English *hlēo,* covering, shelter.]

Lee (lee), **Robert E(dward)** (1807–70). Commander of the Confederate armies in the U.S. Civil War. He led the U.S. marines when they captured John Brown at Harpers Ferry in 1859. Loyalty to his native Virginia led him to resign from the Federal army in April, 1861, and become a Confederate general. He won victories at Bull Run (1862), Fredericksburg (1862), and Chancellorsville (1863). Lee was appointed Confederate general-in-chief in February 1865, two months before surrendering to Grant at Appomattox.

lee·board (leé-bawrd || -bōrd) *n.* Either of a pair of movable boards or plates attached to the sides of certain flat-bottomed sailing vessels, that is lowered into the water on the lee side when the vessel is sailing to windward to prevent its drifting leeward.

leech¹ (leech) *n.* **1.** Any of various chiefly aquatic bloodsucking or carnivorous annelid worms of the class Hirudinea, having suckers

at each end of the body. One species, *Hirudo medicinalis,* was formerly used by physicians to bleed patients. **2.** One who preys on or clings to another; a parasite. **3.** *Archaic.* A physician.
~*tr.v.* **leeched, leeching, leeches.** *Medicine.* **1.** To bleed (someone) with leeches. **2.** To drain in a parasitic way: *leeched them penniless.* **3.** *Archaic.* To heal. [Middle English *leche,* from Old English *lǣce,* leech; akin to Middle Dutch *leke*† and *lǣce,* physician.]
leech² *n. Nautical.* **1.** Either vertical edge of a square sail. **2.** The after edge of a fore-and-aft sail. [Middle English *leche,* earlier *liche,* probably from Middle Low German *līk,* leech line.]
Leech (leech), **John** (1817–64). English illustrator. From 1841 he contributed over 3,000 illustrations to *Punch.* He illustrated the novels of Surtees, and Dickens' *A Christmas Carol.*
Leeds (leedz). City in west Yorkshire, north England, lying on the river Aire. Since the 14th century it has been a centre of the wool industry. Its neoclassical town hall (1858) is an example of grandiose Victorian civic architecture.
leek (leek) *n.* **1.** A plant, *Allium porrum,* related to the onion and having a cylindrical bulb that is the base of the flat, overlapping leaves. It is a national emblem of Wales. **2.** The blanched leaves of this plant, used as food. **3.** Any of various similar wild plants of the genus *Allium.* [Middle English *le(e)k,* Old English *lēac.*]
Lee Kuan Yew (lée kwán yōō) (1923–). Singapore politician. In 1954 he helped to found the Socialist People's Action Party, which campaigned for a self-governing constitution. Singapore's first prime minister (1959–90); succeeded by Goh Chok Tong (1941–).
leer (leer) *intr.v.* **leered, leering, leers.** To look or glance slyly, lasciviously, or with hostile intent: *leered at her with a dirty grin.*
~*n.* A sly or lascivious look. [Probably from obsolete *leer,* cheek, Middle English *ler(e),* Old English *hlēor.*]
leer·y (léer-i) *adj.* **-ier, -iest.** *Informal.* Suspicious or distrustful; wary. [From LEER, sly look.]
lees (leez) *pl.n.* The sediment or dregs of an alcoholic drink, such as wine. [Plural of obsolete *lee,* sediment, from Middle English *lie,* from Old French, from Medieval Latin *lia,* from Celtic.]
lee shore *n.* A shore towards which the wind is blowing and towards which a ship is likely to be driven.
leet (leet) *n.* **1.** A former manorial court in England. Also called "court-leet". **2.** The jurisdiction of this court. [Middle English *lete,* from Anglo-French *lete* and Medieval Latin *leta*†.]
Leeu·wen·hoek (láy-v'n-hōōk, -wən-), **Anton van** (1632–1723). Dutch naturalist. He was a pioneer in microscopy.
lee·ward (lée-wərd; *Nautical* loord) *adj.* Located on or moving in the direction of the side towards which the wind is blowing.
~*n.* **1.** The lee direction. **2.** The lee side or quarter.
~*adv.* Towards the lee side. Compare **windward.**
Lee·ward Islands¹ (léewərd). Northern group of the Lesser Antilles in the West Indies, extending from Puerto Rico to the Windward Islands. The chief islands or groups are the Virgin Islands, Guadeloupe, Anguilla, Antigua, Saint Kitts-Nevis, and Montserrat.
Leeward Islands² *French* **Îles sous le Vent** (éel sōō lə vóN). The western group of the Society Islands, part of French Polynesia.
Leeward Islands³. Chain of islets to the northwest of Hawaii, United States. Only Midway Island is inhabited.
lee·way (lée-way) *n.* **1.** The drift of a ship or aircraft to leeward of true course. **2.** A margin of freedom or variation, as of activity, time, or expenditure; latitude.
Le Fa·nu (léffə-new, lə-faánōō), **(Joseph) Sheridan** (1814–73). Irish writer. His novels of suspense include *The House by the Churchyard* (1863), *Uncle Silas* (1864). Short stories: *In a Glass Darkly* (1872).
left¹ (left) *adj.* **1. a.** Designating, belonging to, or located on the side of the body in which most of the heart is located and which has the hand that is weaker in most people: *left arm.* **b.** Designating or located on the corresponding side of anything that can be said to have a front: *the bird's left wing.* **c.** Designating or located on that side of anything which an observer facing it perceives to be on or towards his left side. **2.** *Often capital* **L.** Of, belonging to, or towards the political or intellectual Left.
~*n.* **1. a.** The left side or direction: *My house is on the left.* **b.** That which is on or towards the left-hand side. **2.** A turn in the direction of the left hand or side: *took a left at the traffic lights.* **3.** *Often capital* **L. a.** The individuals and groups pursuing generally egalitarian political goals by reformist or revolutionary means, as opposed to broadly conservative, established, or reactionary interests. **b.** A stance of favouring such goals, considered as part of a roughly measurable political continuum: *moving further to the left.* **4.** In boxing, the left hand or a blow struck by the left hand.
~*adv.* On or towards the left side or direction. [Middle English *luft, lift, left,* Old English *left, lyft* (attested only in *lyftādl,* paralysis, "left-disease"), akin to Middle Dutch *luft, lucht*†, weak, useless.]
left². Past tense and past participle of **leave.**
Left Bank *n.* In Paris, a district situated on the left or southern bank of the River Seine, noted for its artistic and bohemian atmosphere. [Translation of French *rive gauche.*]
left-hand (léft-hánd) *adj.* **1.** Of, pertaining to, or located on the left: *a left-hand drive car.* **2.** Moving or turning to the left: *a left-hand turn.* **3.** Intended for the left hand or a left-handed person.
left-hand·ed (léft-hándid) *adj.* **1.** Having more power or skill in the left hand, or using the left hand more easily than the right: *a left-handed batsman.* **2.** Executed with the left hand. **3.** Designed for wear on or use by the left hand. **4.** Awkward; clumsy; maladroit. **5.** Obliquely derisive; dubious; insincere: *a left-handed compliment.* **6.** Of, pertaining to, or born of a morganatic marriage. **7.** Turning or spiralling from right to left; anticlockwise.
~*adv.* With the left hand. **—left-hand·ed·ly** *adv.* **—left-hand·ed·ness** *n.*
left-hand·er (léft-hándər) *n.* **1.** One who is left-handed or uses the left hand. **2.** A blow with the left hand.
left·ism (léft-iz'm) *n. Often capital* **L.** The ideology of the Left. **—left·ist** *n. & adj.*
left-lug·gage office (léft-lúggij) *n.* A room at a railway station, airport, or the like, where luggage can be stored temporarily for a fee. Also *U.S.* "checkroom".
left·o·ver (léft-ōvər) *adj.* Of or designating something that has been left as an unused remnant or portion.
left·o·vers (léft-ōvərz) *pl.n.* An unused portion or remnant of something, especially of food.
left wing *n.* **1.** The troops on the left-hand side of an army. **2.** In ball games such as soccer or hockey: **a.** An attacking player on the far left-hand side of his team. **b.** The position of such a player. **3.** *Often capital* **L,** *capital* **W.** The radical or leftist faction of a group or party. **—left-wing** (léft-wing) *adj.* **—left-wing·er** (-wing-ər) *n.*
left·y (léfti) *n., pl.* **-ies.** *Informal.* **1.** A person on the political Left. **2.** *Chiefly U.S.* A left-handed person.
leg (leg) *n.* **1.** A limb or appendage of an animal, used for locomotion or support. **2.** The lower or hind limb in man and primates. **3.** The edible back part of the hindquarter of an animal such as a chicken or sheep. **4.** Any supporting part resembling a leg in shape or function: *a table leg.* **5.** Either or any of the branches of a forked or jointed object, such as a pair of compasses. **6.** Any part of a garment, especially of a pair of trousers, that covers all or part of the leg. **7.** In geometry, either side of a right-angled triangle that is not the hypotenuse. **8. a.** A stage of a journey, course, or race: *ran the first leg quickly.* **b.** A stage of a sporting contest that counts towards the final result: *won the first leg but lost the second.* **9.** *Nautical.* The distance travelled by a sailing vessel on a single tack. **10.** In cricket, the side of the field that is on the left of or behind the left shoulder of a right-handed batsman who is facing the bowling, or on the right of or behind the right shoulder of a left-handed batsman. Also used adjectivally: *the leg stump.* **—give a leg up.** To assist by boosting or providing support. **—not have a leg to stand on.** To have no justifiable or logical basis for a defence or proposition. **—on (one's) last legs.** On the verge of failure, exhaustion, collapse, or death. **—pull (someone's) leg.** *Informal.* To tease, make fun of, or fool someone. **—shake a leg.** *Slang.* To hasten; hurry. Often used in the imperative. **—show a leg.** *Informal.* To rise from bed in the morning. **—stretch (one's) legs.** To stand or walk, especially after sitting for a long time.
~*intr.v.* **legged, legging, legs.** *Informal.* To walk or run, especially so as to escape. Usually used with *it:* *We legged it to the station.* [Middle English *leg, legge,* from Old Norse *leggr*†.]
leg. 1. legal. **2.** legate. **3.** *Music.* legato. **4.** legislation; legislative; legislature.
leg·a·cy (léggə-si) *n., pl.* **-cies. 1.** Money or property bequeathed to someone by will. **2.** Something handed down from an ancestor or predecessor, or from the past: *a legacy of madness.* [Middle English *legacie,* from Old French, from Medieval Latin *lēgantia,* from Latin *lēgāre,* to depute, commission, bequeath.]
le·gal (lée g'l) *adj. Abbr.* **leg. 1.** Of, pertaining to, or concerned with law: *legal papers.* **2. a.** Authorised by or based on law: *a legal act.* **b.** Established by law; statutory. **3.** In conformity with or permitted by law. **4.** Recognised or enforced by law rather than by equity. **5.** In terms of or created by the law: *a legal offence.* **6.** Applicable to or characteristic of lawyers or their profession: *legal advice.* **7.** *Theology.* **a.** Of or pertaining to Mosaic law. **b.** Of or pertaining to salvation through works rather than through faith. [Old French, from Latin *lēgālis,* from *lēx* (stem *lēg-*), law.] **—le·gal·ly** *adv.*
legal age *n.* The age of legal responsibility. See **age.**
legal aid *n.* In Britain, financial assistance towards court costs and legal fees given to people whose disposable income and capital assets fall below a certain limit.
legal holiday *n. U.S.* A **bank holiday** *(see).*
le·gal·ise, le·gal·ize (lée g'l-īz) *tr.v.* **-ised, -ising, -ises.** To make legal or lawful. **—le·gal·i·sa·tion** (-ī-záysh'n ‖ *U.S.* -i-) *n.*
le·gal·ism (lée g'l-iz'm) *n.* **1.** Strict, literal adherence to law. **2.** *Theology.* Adherence to the doctrine of salvation by works rather than by faith. **—le·gal·ist** *n.* **—le·gal·is·tic** (-istik) *adj.* **—le·gal·is·ti·cal·ly** *adv.*
le·gal·i·ty (lee-gál-əti) *n., pl.* **-ties. 1.** The state or quality of being legal; lawfulness. **2.** Adherence to or observance of the law. **3.** A requirement of law: *Legalities prevented the merger.*
legal memory *n. Law.* The period of time required for certain customs to attain legal significance, approximately 20 years in British common law.
legal separation *n.* **Judicial separation** *(see).* Not in technical usage.
legal tender *n.* Currency that may legally be offered in payment of a debt and that a creditor must accept.
leg·ate (lég-ət, -it) *n. Abbr.* **leg. 1.** An official emissary; especially, an official representative of the pope. **2.** In Roman history: **a.** The deputy of a general. **b.** The deputy of a provincial governor. **c.** During the empire, a provincial governor. [Middle English, from Old French, from Latin *lēgātus,* from the past participle of *lēgāre,* to depute, commission, send on an embassy.] **—leg·ate·ship** *n.* **—leg·a·tine** (léggə-tīn ‖ -teen, -tin) *adj.*
leg·a·tee (léggə-tée) *n.* The inheritor of a legacy.

le·ga·tion (li-gáysh'n) *n.* **1.** The sending of a legate. **2.** The mission on which a legate is sent. **3. a.** A diplomatic mission in a foreign country, ranking below an embassy. **b.** The legate and staff of such a mission. **4.** The position or office of a legate. **5.** The premises occupied by a legation. [Middle English *legacioun,* from Old French *legation,* from Latin *lēgātiō* (stem *lēgātiōn-*), from *lēgātus,* LEGATE.]

le·ga·to (li-gaátō) *adv. Abbr.* **leg.** *Music.* In an even, smooth style. Used as a direction.
~*n., pl.* **legatos.** A smooth, even style, performance, or passage. [Italian, connected, continuous, bound, from *legare,* to bind, from Latin *ligāre.*] —**le·ga·to** *adj.*

leg·a·tor (légga-tór ‖ *U.S.* la-gáytar) *n.* A person who makes a will; a testator. [Latin *lēgātōr,* from *lēgāre,* to bequeath. See legacy.] —**leg·a·tor·i·al** (léggə-táwri-əl ‖ -tóri-) *adj.*

leg before wicket *n. Abbr.* **l.b.w.** In cricket, a dismissal occurring when a correctly bowled ball, which would otherwise have hit the wicket, strikes the batsman's leg.

leg break *n.* In cricket, a ball bowled with a spin that makes it move from leg to off upon landing.

leg bye *n. Abbr.* **l.b.** In cricket, a run scored when a bowled ball is deflected off the batsman's legs or any other part of his body except his hands.

leg·end (léjənd) *n.* **1. a.** An unverified popular story handed down from earlier times. **b.** A story of the life of a saint. **2.** A body or collection of such stories. **3.** A romanticised or popularised myth of modern times. **4.** A person who achieves legendary fame: *He was a legend in his own lifetime.* **5.** An inscription or title on an object, such as a coat of arms or coin. **6.** An explanatory caption accompanying a map, chart, or illustration. [Middle English *legende,* originally, story of a saint's life, from Old French, from Medieval Latin *legenda,* "things for reading", from Latin *legendus,* gerundive of *legere,* to collect, gather, read.]

leg·en·dar·y (léjən-dəri, -dri ‖ -derri) *adj.* **1.** Of, constituting, based on, or of the nature of a legend. **2.** Famous or described in legend. **3.** Celebrated or notorious to such an extent as to form the basis of a legend.

Lé·ger (lay-zháy), **Fernand** (1881–1955). French painter. One of the early Cubists, he exhibited with the Orphist group (1910–14). His obsession with machinery led to his being called "the primitive of the machine age".

leg·er·de·main (léjərdə-máyn) *n.* **1.** Sleight of hand *(see).* **2.** Any deception or trickery; hocus-pocus. [Middle English *legerdemayn,* from Old French *leger de main,* "light of hand" : *leger,* light, from Vulgar Latin *leviārius* (unattested), from Latin *levis* + *main,* hand, from Latin *manus.*]

leger line. Variant of **ledger line.**

le·ges. Plural of **lex.**

leg·ged (léggid, legd) *adj.* **1.** Having a leg or legs. **2.** Having a specified number or kind of legs. Used in combination: *bowlegged; six-legged.*

leg·gings (léggingz) *pl.n.* Coverings for the legs, as of canvas or leather, usually extending from the knee to the foot.

leg·gy (léggi) *adj.* **-gier, -giest.** **1.** Having disproportionately long legs: *a leggy colt.* **2.** *Informal.* Having attractively long and slender legs. **3.** Having long, spindly, often leafless stems.

leg·horn (le-górn, li-; *for senses 1,2,3 also* lég-hawrn ‖ ərn) *n.* **1.** The dried and bleached straw of an Italian variety of wheat. **2.** A plaited fabric made from this straw. **3.** A hat made from this fabric. **4.** *Often capital* L. A domestic fowl of a breed of Mediterranean origin, noted for prolific production of eggs. [After LEGHORN.]

Leghorn. See **Livorno.**

leg·i·ble (léji-b'l) *adj.* Capable of being read or deciphered. [Middle English *legibille,* from Late Latin *legibilis,* from Latin *legere,* to read.] —**leg·i·bil·i·ty** (-bílləti), **leg·i·ble·ness** *n.* —**leg·i·bly** *adv.*

le·gion (leéjən) *n.* **1.** The major unit of the ancient Roman army consisting of 3,000 to 6,000 infantry troops and 100 to 200 cavalrymen. **2.** *Sometimes plural.* Any large number; a multitude: *He surveyed the massed, singing legions.* **3.** *Usually capital* L. Any of several honorary or military organisations: *the Foreign Legion; the British Legion.* —See Synonyms at **multitude.**
~*adj.* Very numerous; abundant: *Examples are legion.* [Middle English *legioun,* from Old French *legion,* from Latin *legiō,* from *legere,* "to gather", levy troops.]

le·gion·ar·y (leéjən-əri, -ri ‖ *U.S.* -erri) *adj.* Of, pertaining to, or constituting a legion.
~*n., pl.* **legionaries.** A soldier of a legion.

legionary ant *n.* An army ant *(see).*

le·gion·naire (leéjə-naír) *n.* A member of a legion. [French *légionnaire,* from Old French *legion,* LEGION.]

le·gion·naires' disease (leéjə-naírz) *n.* A serious, often fatal, bacterial infection of the lungs, characterised by fever, chest pain, dry cough, and breathlessness. [First identified when it struck members attending an American Legion convention in Philadelphia (1976).]

Legion of Honour. A high French civilian and military decoration, instituted in 1802.

legis. Legislation; legislative; legislature.

leg·is·late (léji-slayt) *v.* **-lated, -lating, -lates.** —*intr.* **1.** To pass a law or laws. **2.** *Informal.* To make provision by taking prior measures. Used with *for: You can't legislate for a rainy day.* —*tr.* To create or bring about by legislation; enact into law. [Back-formation from LEGISLATOR.]

leg·is·la·tion (leji-sláysh'n) *n. Abbr.* **leg., legis.** **1.** The act or procedure of legislating; lawmaking. **2.** A law or laws made by such a procedure.

leg·is·la·tive (léji-slətiv, -slaytiv) *adj. Abbr.* **leg., legis.** **1.** Of or pertaining to legislation. **2.** Resulting from or decided by legislation. **3.** Having the power to create laws; designed to legislate: *a legislative body.* **4.** Of or pertaining to a legislature. Compare **executive, judicial.**
~*n.* The legislative body of a government. —**leg·is·la·tive·ly** *adv.*

legislative assembly *n. Sometimes capital* L, *capital* A. **1.** A bicameral legislature, as in some U.S. states. **2.** A unicameral legislature, as in a Canadian Province. **3.** The lower house of a bicameral legislature, as in Australia.

legislative council *n. Sometimes capital* L, *capital* C. **1.** The upper house of a bicameral legislature, as in Australia. **2.** A unicameral legislature, as in certain dependent states or territories.

leg·is·la·tor (léji-slaytər) *n.* **1.** A person who creates or enacts laws. **2.** A member of a legislative body. [Latin *lēgis lātor,* "proposer of law" : *lēgis,* genitive of *lēx,* law + *lātor,* bearer, proposer, from *lātus,* "carried", past participle of *ferre,* to bear, carry.] —**leg·is·la·to·ri·al** (-slay-táwri-əl ‖ -tóri-) *adj.*

leg·is·la·ture (léji-slaychər) *n. Abbr.* **leg., legis.** An official body of persons having the responsibility and power to legislate for a political unit, such as a nation or state. Compare **executive, judiciary.**

le·gist (leéjist) *n.* A specialist in law. [Medieval Latin *lēgista,* from Latin *lēx,* law.]

le·git (lə-jít) *n. Slang.* Legitimate drama; stage plays collectively as opposed to films and musicals.
~*adj. Slang.* Legitimate.

le·git·i·mate (li-jítti-mət, -mit) *adj.* **1.** In compliance with the law; lawful. **2.** In accordance with traditional or established patterns and standards. **3.** Based on logical reasoning; reasonable: *a legitimate solution.* **4.** *Archaic.* Authentic; genuine. **5.** Born in wedlock. **6.** Of, pertaining to, or ruling by hereditary right. **7.** Of, pertaining to, or designating stage plays as opposed to films, musicals, music-hall, and the like.
~*tr.v.* (-mayt) **legitimated, -mating, -mates.** **1.** To justify as legitimate; authorise. **2.** To make, establish, or declare legitimate. [Middle English, born in wedlock, from Medieval Latin *lēgitimātus,* past participle of *lēgitimāre,* to make lawful, from Latin *lēgitimus,* lawful, legal, from *lēx* (stem *lēg-*), law.] —**le·git·i·ma·cy** (-mə-si) *n.* —**le·git·i·mate·ly** *adv.*

le·git·i·mise, le·git·i·mize (li-jítti-mīz) *tr.v.* Also **le·git·i·ma·tise** (-mə-tīz). To make or claim to be legitimate or acceptable.

le·git·i·mist (li-jíttimist) *n.* A person who believes in or supports legitimate authority; especially, a supporter of rule by hereditary right. —**le·git·i·mism** *n.* —**le·git·i·mist, le·git·i·mis·tic** *adj.*

leg·less (lég-ləss, -liss) *adj.* **1.** Without legs. **2.** *Slang.* So drunk as to be unable to walk.

leg·man (lég-man) *n., pl.* **-men** (-men). *Chiefly U.S.* **1.** A news reporter who gathers news in person away from the office, interviewing people and visiting the scenes of incidents. **2.** A person employed to deliver messages, run errands, and perform other tasks requiring legwork.

Leg·o (léggō) *n.* **1.** A trademark for any of various construction sets consisting of small, plastic interlocking toy bricks. **2.** Such bricks collectively.
~*adj. Often small* l. Resembling Lego in being made up of uniform blocks: *a lego housing scheme.*

leg-of-mut·ton (lég-əv-mútt'n) *adj.* Resembling a leg of mutton in shape; tapering sharply from one large end to a point or smaller end, as in a sleeve or sail.

leg-pull (lég-pŏol) *n. Informal.* A humorous deception or hoax; a practical joke.

leg-room (lég-rŏom, -rŏom) *n.* Space that enables one to stretch one's legs, as in a car or cinema.

leg·ume (léggewm, li-géwm) *n.* **1.** A pod, such as that of a pea or bean, that splits into two halves with the seeds attached to the lower edge of one of the halves. **2.** Such a pod or seed, used as food. **3.** Any plant of the family Leguminosae, characteristically bearing such pods. [French *légume,* from Latin *legūmen†,* pulse, bean.]

le·gu·mi·nous (li-géwminəss) *adj.* **1.** Of, belonging to, or characteristic of the family Leguminosae, which includes peas, beans, clover, alfalfa, and other plants. **2.** Resembling or of the nature of a legume. [New Latin *leguminosus,* from Latin *legūmen,* bean, LEGUME.]

leg·work (lég-wurk) *n. Informal.* Work, such as collecting information, that involves walking or travelling about.

Le·hár (láy-haar, li-hár), **Franz** (1870–1948). Hungarian composer of light operas. His first success was *Viennese Ladies* (1902). His most popular work remains *The Merry Widow* (1905).

Le Ha·vre (lə aávrə). Commercial port on the north coast of France, lying on the Seine estuary. One of France's leading ports, it handles much transatlantic trade, and is the main port for transatlantic passage liners. The city is built around one of the largest central squares in Europe, the Place de l'Hôtel de Ville.

Leh·mann (láymən), **Lotte** (1888–1976). German soprano. She sang chiefly with the Vienna State Opera (1914–38), then settled in the United States, singing at the Metropolitan Opera, New York. She created the role of Ariadne in Richard Strauss's *Ariadne auf Naxos,* and Strauss wrote *Arabella* especially for her.

lehr (leer) *n.* A long oven for annealing glass. [17th century : origin obscure.]

lei¹ (lay, láy-ee) *n., pl.* **leis.** A garland, usually of flowers. [Hawaiian.]

lei². Plural of **leu.**

Leib·niz or **Leib·nitz** (lībnīts), **Baron Gottfried Wilhelm von** (1646–1716). German philosopher and mathematician. He devised the infinitesimal calculus independently of Newton. His philosophy includes the theories that the universe is made of indivisible units called **monads** (*see*), and—since God disposes these in the best possible combination—that we live in the best possible world. —**Leib·niz·i·an** *adj.*

Leices·ter¹ (léstər). City and Unitary Authority area in central England. It has been an industrial centre, chiefly associated with hosiery and shoe manufacturing, since the 14th century.

Leicester² *n.* **1.** A sheep of a breed developed in Leicestershire, having long, fine wool. **2.** A hard, flaky, orange-coloured cheese. In this sense, also called "red Leicester".

Leicester, Robert Dudley, 1st Earl of (*c.* 1532–88). English courtier and favourite of Elizabeth I. In 1553 he helped to place his sister-in-law, Lady Jane Grey, on the throne. He was condemned to death, but pardoned. He was a confidant of Elizabeth, who shortly after her accession made him a privy councillor (1559) and later captain general of her armies (1587).

Leices·ter·shire (léstər-shər, -sheer). Unitary Authority area in central England. Although Leicester and other towns in the western part of the county are industrial centres, Leicestershire remains primarily an agricultural county, the home of Stilton cheese.

Lei·den or **Ley·den** (līd'n). City in south Holland, Netherlands. The **Leyden jar** was invented at its famous university, founded (1575) by William of Orange.

Leif Er·ic·sson (léef érrik-sən) (*fl.* 1000). Norse discoverer of America. He was the son of Eric the Red, and probably born in Iceland. According to Norse sagas, on his return from Greenland in 1000 he was blown off course to an unknown land, called Vinland after the vines supposedly growing there. It is thought to lie somewhere between Newfoundland and Virginia.

Leigh, (lee), **Vivien,** born Vivian Mary Hartley (1913–67). English actress. She won an Academy Award as best actress for her roles in *Gone with the Wind* (1939) as Scarlett O'Hara and in *A Streetcar Named Desire* (1951) as Blanche Dubois.

Leigh·ton (láyt'n), **Frederic, 1st Baron** (1830–96). English painter. With Alma-Tadema and Poynter, he revived a fashion for scenes of ancient Greek and Roman life. His first exhibited painting, *Cimabue's Madonna Carried in Procession,* was bought by Queen Victoria in 1855. He was president of the Royal Academy (1878–96), and became a peer in 1896.

Lein·ster (lén-stər). Province in the east of the Republic of Ireland, consisting of the counties of Carlow, Dublin, Kildare, Kilkenny, Leix, Longford, Louth, Meath, Offaly, Westmeath, Wexford, and Wicklow. The major city is Dublin.

Leip·zig (līp-sig ‖ German līp-tsikh). City in eastern Germany, one of the great historic industrial and cultural centres of Europe. Originally a Slav settlement called Lipsk, it developed by the early Middle Ages into a major trading and commercial town, famous from the 15th to the mid-20th centuries for its book and music publishing. Its university was founded in 1409. At the battle of Leipzig (the Battle of the Nations) in 1813, the armies of Russia, Prussia, and Austria inflicted a decisive defeat on the army of Napoleon.

leish·man·i·a·sis (léeshmə-nī-ə-siss) *n.* **1.** Infection with flagellate protozoans of the genus *Leishmania.* **2.** A disease, such as kala-azar or various ulcerative skin diseases, caused by such infection. [New Latin, from *Leishmania,* genus of protozoans, identified by Sir William B. *Leishman* (1865–1926), British medical officer.]

leis·ter (léestər) *n.* A three-pronged spear used for catching fish, such as salmon.
~*tr.v.* **leistered, -tering, -ters.** To spear (a fish) with a leister. [Old Norse *ljóstr,* from *ljósta†,* to strike.]

lei·sure (lézhər ‖ U.S. also léezhər) *n.* Freedom from time-consuming duties, responsibilities, or activities. See Synonyms at **rest.** —**at leisure. 1.** Having free time. **2.** Not employed, occupied, or engaged. **3.** Unhurried. —**at (one's) leisure.** When one has free time; at one's convenience.
~*adj.* **1.** Not spent in work or compulsory activity; free: *leisure time.* **2.** Having much leisure; leisured. [Middle English *leisour, leiser,* freedom, opportunity, from Anglo-French *leisour,* variant of Old French *leisir,* to be permitted, from Latin *licēre†,* to be lawful, be permitted.]

lei·sured (lézhərd ‖ U.S. also léezhərd) *adj.* **1.** Having much leisure: *the leisured classes.* **2.** Unhurried; leisurely.

lei·sure·ly (lézhərli ‖ U.S. also léezhərli) *adj.* Without haste; unhurried: *a leisurely meal.*
~*adv.* In a steady, relaxed manner; slowly. —**lei·sure·li·ness** *n.*

Leith (leeth). The second largest port in Scotland, absorbed by Edinburgh in 1920.

leit·mo·tif, leit·mo·tiv (līt-mōteef) *n.* **1.** *Music.* A thematic passage, as in Wagnerian opera, associated with a specific character, thing, or element. **2.** A dominant theme or recurring image or use of words, as in a novel. [German *Leitmotiv,* "leading motif".]

Lei·trim (léetrim). County in the north of the Republic of Ireland, having a short border with Northern Ireland. The county town is Carrick on Shannon. The county is divided by Lough Allen into a lowland southern half and a mountainous northern half.

Leix or **Laois** or **Laoighis** (leesh). County in the central part of the Republic of Ireland, occupying the valleys of the upper Nore and upper Barrow rivers. From 1556 to 1922 it was known as the Queen's County. The county town is Port Laoise (Maryborough).

lek¹ (lek) *n.* **1.** The basic monetary unit of Albania, equal to 100 quintars. **2.** A coin worth one lek. [Albanian.]

lek² *n.* An area used for courtship display and mock fighting by certain male birds, especially the black grouse. [Probably from Scandinavian; akin to Swedish *lek,* sport, play, Old Norse *leikr,* play; compare LAIK.]

lek·ker (léckər) *adj. South African Informal.* **1.** Very good-tasting; delicious. **2.** Very pleasing, attractive, or enjoyable. **3.** Slightly drunk; tipsy. [Afrikaans, from Dutch.]

Le·ly (léeli), **Sir Peter** (1618–80). Dutch painter. He worked in England from about 1643 and in 1660 was appointed principal painter to Charles II recording in portraits the Restoration court.

LEM (lem) *n. Aerospace.* A lunar excursion module.

lem·an (lémmən, léemən) *n. Archaic.* **1.** A lover. **2.** A mistress. [Middle English *leofman, lemman : lef, leof,* dear, from Old English *lēof* + MAN.]

Léman, Lac. See Geneva, Lake.

Le Mans (lə món). City in northwest France, capital of the Sarthe département, lying on the river Sarthe. It was settled from pre-Roman times and was for a time the Merovingian capital. Its Romanesque cathedral is renowned for its flamboyant flying buttresses. Since 1923 Le Mans has been the site of the annual 24-hour motor race.

Lemberg. See L'viv.

lem·ma¹ (lémmə) *n., pl.* **-mas** or **lemmata** (lémmətə). **1.** *Logic.* A subsidiary proposition assumed to be valid and used to demonstrate a principal proposition. **2.** A theme, argument, or subject indicated in a title. **3.** A glossed word in a glossary or other listing. [Latin, from Greek *lēmma,* anything received, argument, proof, from *lambanein* (past perfect *eilēmmai*), to grasp, take.]

lem·ma² *n., pl.* **-mas** or **lemmata.** *Botany.* The outer, lower bract enclosing the flower in a grass spikelet. [Greek *lemma,* rind, husk, from *lepein,* to peel.]

lem·ma·tise, lem·ma·tize (lémmə-tīz) *tr.v.* **-tised, -tising, -tises.** To arrange (words in a text) in such a way that all words which are inflected or variant forms of the same word are grouped together. [Latin *lemma* (stem *lemmat-*), proposition (see LEMMA) + -ISE.]

lem·ming (lémming) *n.* **1.** Any of various volelike rodents of the genus *Lemmus* and related genera, of northern regions, such as the European species *L. lemmus,* noted for its mass migrations as a result of periodic population increases. **2.** A person who wilfully follows a disastrous course of action; a self-destructive person. [Norwegian *lemming, lemende,* akin to Swedish *lemmel†.*]

lem·nis·cate (lem-nis-kət, -kit) *n.* In geometry: **1.** A plane curve that is the locus of the foot of a perpendicular from the origin to a tangent moving on a rectangular hyperbola. The curve, which has two symmetrical lobes, has the equation $(x^2 + y^2) = a^2 (x^2 - y^2)$, where *a* is the greatest distance from the node to the curve. Also called "lemniscate of Bernoulli". **2.** A plane curve that is the locus of the vertex of a triangle with the side opposite the vertex of fixed length and the other two sides having a constant product (*k*) equal to one quarter of the square of the fixed side. Its equation is $[(x + a)^2 + y^2][(x - a)^2 + y^2] = k^4$, where *a* is one half of the length of the fixed side. Also called "lemniscate of Cassini". [Greek *lēmniskos,* fillet, ribbon.]

lem·nis·cus (lem-niskəss) *n., pl.* **-nisci** (-nissī, -nískī). A bundle of sensory nerve fibres located in the brain. [New Latin, from Latin *lēmniscus,* ribbon, from Greek *lēmniskos†.*]

lem·on (lémmən) *n.* **1.** A spiny evergreen tree, *Citrus limon,* native to Asia, widely cultivated for its yellow, egg-shaped fruit. **2.** The fruit of this tree, having an aromatic rind and acid, juicy pulp. **3. Lemon yellow** (*see*). **4.** *Informal.* Something or someone that is or proves to be defective, inadequate, or unsuitable. [Middle English *lymon,* from Old French *limon,* from Arabic *laymūn,* variant of *līmūn,* from Persian *līmūn†.*] —**lem·on** *adj.*

lem·on·ade (lémmə-náyd) *n.* A cold, often carbonated, drink made of lemon juice or flavouring, water, and sugar. [French *limonade :* obsolete *limon,* LEMON + -ADE.]

lemon balm *n.* A plant, **balm** (*see*).

lemon curd *n.* A sweet, viscous, yellow paste used in tarts or on sandwiches, prepared from lemons, sugar, and eggs. Also called "lemon cheese".

lemon drop *n.* A small, hard, lemon-flavoured sweet.

lemon geranium *n.* A widely cultivated plant, *Pelargonium limoneum* (or *P. mellisimum*), having lemon-scented leaves and small, pale purple flowers.

lem·on·grass (lémmən-graass ‖ -grass) *n.* Any of several tropical grasses of the genus *Cymbopogon;* especially, *C. citratus,* yielding an aromatic oil used in perfumery and as flavouring.

lemon sole *n.* An edible marine flatfish, *Microstomus kitt* (or *Limanda limanda*), having a variegated brown body. Also called "lemon dab". [French *limande,* from Old French, irregularly from *lime,* file, lemon sole (from its shape), from Latin *lima,* file.]

lemon verbena *n.* An aromatic plant, *Lippia citriodora,* native to South America, cultivated for its fragrant foliage and flowers.

lem·on·y (lémməni) *adj.* **1.** Having the characteristic odour or flavour of lemons. **2.** *Australian Slang.* Irritable; peevish.

lemon yellow *n.* Brilliant, vivid yellow to greenish yellow. —**lem·on-yel·low** *adj.*

lem·pi·ra (lem-péer-ə) *n.* **1.** The basic monetary unit of Honduras, equal to 100 centavos. **2.** A coin or note worth one lempira. [After *Lempira,* indigenous Indian leader who resisted the Spanish.]

le·mur (léemər) *n.* Any of several arboreal primates chiefly of the family Lemuridae, of Madagascar and adjacent islands, having large eyes, soft fur, and a long tail. [New Latin, coined by Linnaeus after Latin *lemurēs*, LEMURES, from the ghostly appearance of its face and its nocturnal habits.] **—le·mur·ine** (-īn, lémmewr-, -in), **le·mur·oid** *adj.*

lem·u·res (lémmewr-eez) *pl.n.* In ancient Rome, the spirits of the dead considered as frightening spectres. Compare **manes**. [Latin *lemurēs*.]

Le·na (léenə ‖ *Russian* lyáynə). Easternmost of the great rivers of Siberia, rising near Lake Baikal and flowing northeast for 4 300 kilometres (2,670 miles) into the Arctic Ocean. It broadens into a vast delta about 400 kilometres (250 miles) wide.

Le Nain (lə nán), **Antoine** (*c.* 1588 – 1648), **Louis** (*c.* 1593 – 1648), and **Mathieu** (*c.* 1607 – 77). French painters. The brothers worked in Paris after about 1630, painting mostly peasant scenes. They signed their paintings without initials, so it is difficult to separate their work. Mathieu was made painter to the city of Paris in 1633.

lend (lend) *v.* **lent** (lent), **lending, lends.** *—tr.* **1.** To give out or allow the use of (something) temporarily on the condition that it or its equivalent in kind will be returned. **2.** To provide (money) temporarily on the condition that the amount borrowed will be returned, often with an interest fee. **3.** To contribute or impart, especially a desirable attribute or quality; add: *She lent elegance to the proceedings.* **4.** To put at another's service or needs; give. **5.** To accommodate or offer (itself) to something; be suited to. Used reflexively: *This medium lends itself to many styles.* *—intr.* To make a loan or loans. —See Usage note at **loan**. [Middle English *len(d)en*, Old English *lǣnan*, to lend, give.] **—lend·er** *n.*

lending library *n.* A library from which books may be borrowed or rented for a fee. Also *U.S.* "circulating library".

Len·dl (lénd'l), **Ivan** (1960–). Czech-born U.S. tennis player. He was U.S. champion in 1985, 1986, and 1987. Retired 1994.

lend-lease (lénd-léess) *n.* The U.S. aid programme during World War II providing food, munitions, and other goods to strategic countries threatened by Germany and Italy.

~tr.v. **lend-leased, -leasing, -leases.** To provide (aid) to a country, as under the provisions of the U.S. Lend-Lease Act (1941).

Leng·len (lon-glón), **Suzanne** (1899–1938). French tennis player. She won the Wimbledon women's singles championship six times from 1919 to 1925, the French championship six times, and singles and doubles gold medals (1920 Olympics).

length (length, lengkth ‖ lenth) *n. Abbr.* **l. 1.** The state, quality, or fact of being long. **2. a.** The measurement of the extent of something along its greatest dimension. **b.** The measurement of the extent of something from back to front as distinguished from its width or height. **3.** A piece of something, often of a standard size, normally measured along the greatest dimension: *a length of cloth.* **4.** A unit of measurement based on the approximate extent from front to back of an animal or vehicle in a race: *The boat won by two lengths.* **5.** The extent of a thing from start to finish as measured by space, pages, or words: *the length of a story.* **6.** The amount of time between particular moments; a duration; a period. **7.** The distance between particular points or locations: *the length of their journey.* **8.** The state or quality of extending greatly in time or space. **9.** *Phonetics.* **a.** The quantity or duration of a vowel. **b.** Loosely, the quality of a vowel. **10.** In verse, the quantity or duration of a syllable. **11.** In cricket, the distance in front of the batsman at which the ball strikes the pitch: *bowled a good length.* **12.** The longer side or dimension of a swimming pool, or the distance from end to end: *swam ten lengths.* **—at length. 1.** After some time; eventually. **2.** For a considerable time; fully. **—go to any or great length or lengths.** To take great trouble. **—keep at arm's length.** To refuse to become closely associated with. **—measure (one's) length.** To fall flat.

~adj. **1.** Extending up to or down to a specified part or point. Used in combination: *shoulder-length hair.* **2. a.** Having a specified length. Used in combination: *a full-length opera.* **b.** Being as long as something specified. Used in combination: *a book-length manuscript.* [Middle English *lengthe*, Old English *lengthu.*]

length·en (léng-th'n, léngk- ‖ lénth-) *v.* **-ened, -ening, -ens.** *—tr.* To make longer. *—intr.* To become longer. **—length·en·er** *n.*

length·man (léngth-mən, léngkth- ‖ lénth-) *n., pl.* **-men** (-mən). *British.* A person employed to maintain a stretch of railway line or road.

length·ways (léngth-wayz, léngkth- ‖ lénth-) *adv.* Also *chiefly U.S.* **length·wise** (-wīz). In or along the direction of a length: *He cut the cloth lengthways.*

length·y (léng-thi, léngk- ‖ lén-) *adj.* **-ier, -iest.** Of considerable length, especially in time; drawn-out. **—length·i·ly** *adv.* **—length·i·ness** *n.*

le·ni·en·cy (léeni-ən-si, léen-yən-) *n., pl.* **-cies.** Also **le·ni·ence** (léeni-ənss, léen-yən-nss). **1.** The condition or quality of being lenient. **2.** A lenient action. —See Synonyms at **mercy.**

le·ni·ent (léeni-ənt, léen-yənt) *adj.* **1.** Merciful, restrained, or forgiving; gentle or understanding. **2.** Not austere or strict; liberal; generous: *lenient rules.* **3.** *Archaic.* Soothing or relaxing. [Latin *léniēns* (stem *léníent-*), present participle of *lénīre*, to soothe, make soft, from *lénis*, soft.] **—le·ni·ent·ly** *adv.*

Le·nin (lénnin; *Russian* lyáy-neen), **Vladimir Ilich**, born Vladimir Ilich Ulyanov; also known as Nikolai Lenin (1870–1924). Russian revolutionary leader. He was exiled to Siberia for subversive activities in 1895. In 1900 he went abroad to study Marx's theories, returning briefly to Russia during the abortive 1905 revolution.

Lenin was in Switzerland in 1917 when the revolution broke out in Russia, and the German government secretly helped him to travel to Petrograd. On November 7 (October 25 by the Russian calendar) he led the Bolshevik overthrow of Kerensky's government and was head of the Soviet government until his death following a stroke.

Leningrad. See **St Petersburg.**

Len·in·ism (lénni-niz'm) *n.* The theory and practice of proletarian revolution as developed by Lenin. See **Marxism-Leninism.** **—Len·in·ist** *n. & adj.*

Lenin Peak. Highest peak in the Trans-Alai range of mountains, on the border between Tajikistan and Kyrgyzstan. It rises to 7 134 metres (23,405 feet).

le·nis (lée-niss, láy-) *adj. Phonetics.* Articulated with little or no aspiration; weak; soft. The consonants *b* and *d* are lenis compared with *p* and *t.* Compare **fortis.**

~n., pl. **lenes** (lée-neez, láy-). *Phonetics.* A speech sound pronounced with little or no aspiration; a lenis consonant. [Latin *lēnis*, soft, mild, smooth.]

len·i·tive (lénnitiv) *adj.* Capable of easing pain or discomfort.

~n. A lenitive medicine. [Old French *lenitif*, from Medieval Latin *lēnītīvus*, from Latin *lēnīre*, to soothe, soften, from *lēnis*, soft.]

len·i·ty (lén-ŏti, léen-) *n., pl.* **-ties. 1.** The state, condition, or quality of being lenient; leniency. **2.** A lenient action. [Latin *lēnitas* (stem *lēnitāt-*), gentleness, mildness, from *lēnis*, soft, mild.]

Len·non (lénnən), **John (Winston)** (1940–80). English pop musician, one of the Beatles. He and Paul McCartney wrote most of the group's songs of the 1960s. Lennon married the singer Yoko Ono in 1969. He was shot dead in New York by Mark Chapman.

le·no (léenō) *n., pl.* **-nos. 1.** A weaving of a type in which the warp yarns are paired and twisted. **2.** A fabric having such a weave. [Probably from French *linon*, fine linen, from *lin*, flax, linen, from Latin *lĭnum.*]

lens (lenz) *n.* **1.** A carefully ground or moulded piece of glass, plastic, or other transparent material, in which either or both opposite surfaces are curved such that light rays are refracted to converge or diverge and form an image. **2.** A combination of two or more such lenses, sometimes with other optical devices such as prisms, used to form an image for viewing or photographing. Also called "compound lens". **3.** Any device that causes radiation other than light to converge or diverge by an action analogous to that of an optical lens. **4.** A transparent, biconvex body of the eye between the iris and the vitreous humour, that focuses light rays entering through the pupil to form an image on the retina. In this sense, also called "crystalline lens". **5.** A combination of electrodes or magnets used to cause a beam of electrons or other charged particles to converge or diverge. Also called "electron lens". [New Latin, from Latin *lēns*, LENTIL (from the resemblance of an optical lens to a lentil seed).]

lens hood *n.* A protective extension or attachment to a camera lens, especially to shield it from glare.

lent. Past tense and past participle of **lend.**

Lent (lent) *n.* **1.** The 40 weekdays before Easter (beginning on Ash Wednesday), observed as a season of penitence. **2.** *Plural.* At Cambridge University, boat races occurring during the Lent term. [Middle English *lente, lenten*, originally "spring", Old English *lencten*, probably from Germanic *lang-* (unattested), LONG (referring to the lengthening days of spring).]

Lent·en (léntən) *adj.* **1.** Of or pertaining to Lent. **2.** *Sometimes small* **l.** *Archaic.* Characteristic of or appropriate to Lent; meagre; sombre: *Lenten fare; a Lenten face.*

len·tic (léntik) *adj.* Of, pertaining to, or designating ecological communities living in still water. Compare **lotic.** [Latin *lentus*, slow, still.]

len·ti·cel (lénti-sel) *n. Botany.* Any of the small pores on the surface of the stems of woody plants, allowing the passage of gases to and from the interior tissue. [New Latin *lenticella*, diminutive of Latin *lēns* (genitive *lentis*), LENTIL.] **—len·ti·cel·late** (-séll-it, -ət) *adj.*

len·tic·u·lar (len-tíckewlər) *adj.* **1. a.** Shaped like a biconvex lens. **b.** Shaped like a lentil seed. **2.** Of or pertaining to a lens, especially that of the eye. [Latin *lenticulāris*, like a lentil, from *lenticula*, LENTIL (compare **lens**).]

len·ti·form (lénti-fawrm) *adj.* Lens-shaped, having the form of a lens or lentil seed. [Latin *lens* (stem *lent-*), LENTIL + -FORM.]

len·ti·go (len-tīgō) *n., pl.* **-tigines** (-tiji-neez) **1.** A freckle. **2.** A naevus. [Latin *lentīgo*, freckles, from *lēns*, LENTIL.] **—len·tig·i·nous** (-tíji-nəss), **len·tig·i·nose** (-nŏss, -nŏz) *adj.*

len·til (léntil, lént'l) *n.* **1.** A leguminous plant, *Lens esculenta* (or *L. culinaris*), native to the Old World, having pods containing edible seeds. **2.** The round, brown or orange, flattened seed of this plant. [Middle English, from Old French *lentille*, from Vulgar Latin *lentīcula* (unattested), variant of Latin *lenticula*, diminutive of *lēns†*, lentil.]

len·tisk (lén-tisk) *n.* The **mastic tree** (see). [Middle English, from Latin *lentīscus†*.]

len·tis·si·mo (len-tíssi-mō) *adv.* Very slowly. Used as a direction. *adj. Music.* Very slow. *n. Music.* A lentissimo passage. [Italian, from Latin *lentissimus*, from *lentus*, slow.]

len·to (léntō) *adv. Music.* Slowly. Used as a direction. *~adj. Music.* Slow. *~n. Music.* A lento passage. [Italian, from Latin *lentus*, slow.]

len·toid (lén-toyd) *adj.* Lenticular.

Lent term *n.* In some universities, the term during which most of the period of Lent falls.

Len·ya (lén-yə), **Lotte**, born Karoline Wilhelmine Blamauer (1900–81). Austrian singer and actress. In 1926 she married Kurt Weill, who composed *The Seven Deadly Sins* for her.

Lenz's law (léntsiz) *n. Physics.* The principle that if the magnetic flux linked with a circuit changes, the current induced in the circuit flows in such a way as to produce a field opposing the change. [After H.F.E. *Lenz* (1804–65), German physicist.]

Le·o¹ (lée-ō) *n.* **1.** A constellation in the Northern Hemisphere near Cancer and Virgo, containing the bright stars Regulus and Denebola. **2. a.** The fifth sign of the **zodiac** (*see*). Also called the "Lion". **b.** One born under this sign. [New Latin, from Latin *leō,* LION.]

Leo². A name for a lion, as used by children and in folk tales. [Latin, lion.]

Leo I, Saint, known as Leo the Great (*c.* 400–461). Italian pope from 440–61. His negotiations with Attila in 452 and Gaiseric the Vandal in 455 saved Rome from barbarian invasions. *The Leonian Sacramentary,* the oldest existing form of the Roman missal, is named after him though probably not his work. His feast day is April 11.

Leo Minor *n.* A constellation in the Northern Hemisphere near Leo and Ursa Major.

Le·ón (lay-ón). Capital of León province in northwest Spain. It was the capital of the medieval kingdom of León, and is today a major tourist centre.

Le·o·nar·do da Vin·ci (lée-ə-nárdō də vínchi, láy-, -ō-, daa), also known as Leonardo (1452–1519). Italian artistic and scientific genius of the Renaissance. He trained in Florence under Verrocchio, and became engineer and adviser to Duke Ludovico Sforza in Milan, Cesare Borgia in Florence, and finally Francis I in Amboise in France. Few of his paintings survive, but among these are *The Virgin of the Rocks* (1485) and *Mona Lisa* (or *La Giaconda*) (1503).

Le·on·ca·val·lo (láy-ongka-vál-ō), **Ruggiero** (1858–1919). Italian composer. He wrote several operas, including *I Pagliacci* (1892), in the style of Italian *verismo,* or realism.

le·one (lee-ōni) *n.* **1.** The basic monetary unit of Sierra Leone, equal to 100 cents. **2.** A note worth one leone. [From SIERRA LEONE.]

Le·o·nid (lée-ənid) *n., pl.* **-nids** or **Leonides** (li-ónni-deez). Any of the meteors constituting the shower that recurs annually in mid-November. [New Latin *Leōnidēs,* from Latin *Leō,* lion (the meteors seem to radiate from the constellation Leo).]

Le·on·i·das I (li-ónni-dass) (died 480 B.C.). King of Sparta. He led a handful of Spartans and Thespians in the heroic defence of the pass at Thermopylae in 480 B.C. during the Persian Wars. He was killed in the battle.

le·o·nine (lée-ə-nīn) *adj.* Of, pertaining to, or characteristic of a lion: *a leonine sigh.* [Middle English, from Old French *leonin(e),* from Latin *leōnīnus,* from *leō* (stem *leōn-*), LION.]

Le·o·nine (lée-ə-nīn) *adj.* Of or pertaining to any of the popes called Leo. [Latin *leōnīnus,* from Leo.]

Leonine verse *n.* **1.** A Latin verse of a type written in the Middle Ages, usually consisting of alternating hexameters and pentameters, each line having internal rhyme. **2.** A similar verse in English poetry. [After *Leo* or *Leonius,* medieval poet who used this verse.]

leop·ard (léppərd) *n.* **1.** A large feline mammal, *Panthera pardus,* of Africa and Asia, having a tawny coat with dark rosette-like markings. There is also a black colour variant. See **panther. 2.** Any of several similar felines, such as the cheetah or the snow leopard. **3.** The pelt or fur of a leopard. **4.** *Heraldry.* A lion in side view, having one forepaw raised and the head facing the observer. [Middle English *leopard, leupard,* from Old French, from Late Latin *leopardus,* from Late Greek *leopardos, leontopardos,* "lion pard" (it was thought to be a hybrid) : *leōn* (genitive *leontos*), LION + *pardos,* PARD.]

leop·ard·ess (léppərd-iss, -ess) *n.* A female leopard.

Le·o·par·di (láy-ō-párdee), **Giacomo, Count** (1798–1837). Italian poet. His *Canti* ("Songs") (1816–36) combine patriotic appeals against Austrian rule with lyrical nature poetry.

leopard lily *n.* A tall plant, *Lilium pardalinum,* of the western United States, having orange-red, dark-spotted flowers and long stamens.

leopard moth *n.* A moth, *Zeuzera pyrina,* having black-spotted white wings and larvae that damage trees by boring into the wood.

leop·ard's-bane (léppərdz-bayn) *n.* **1.** Any of several plants of the genus *Doronicum,* especially *D. plantagineum,* having rayed yellow flowers. **2.** Any of several similar or related plants.

Le·o·pold II (1835–1909). King of the Belgians (1865–1909). In 1885 he was given personal rule of the Congo Free State, established in that year at an international congress at Berlin. He imposed slavery on the natives in rubber plantations, and was forced by public opinion to hand over control to the Belgian government in 1908.

Léopoldville. See **Kinshasa**.

le·o·tard (lée-ətaard) *n.* A sleeveless, skin-tight garment worn by dancers, gymnasts, or the like. [After Jules *Léotard,* 19th-century French acrobat who popularised it.]

Le·pan·to, Battle of (li-pántō). A naval battle (1571) in a strait between the Gulf of Corinth and the Ionian Sea, in which Ottoman sea power was temporarily destroyed by a Christian armada.

Lep·cha (lépchə) *n., pl.* **-chas** or collectively **Lepcha. 1.** A member of a Mongoloid people living in Sikkim, India. **2.** The Tibeto-Burman language of this people.

lep·er (léppər) *n.* **1.** A person afflicted with leprosy. **2.** One who is spurned on moral or social grounds. [Middle English, from *leper,* leprosy, from Old French *lepre,* from Late Latin *lepra,* from Greek *lepra,* from *lepros,* scaly, from *lepos, lepis,* a scale.]

lepido-, lepid- *comb. form.* Indicates a scale or flake; for example, **lepidopteran**. [Greek *lepis* (stem *lepid-*), scale.]

le·pid·o·lite (li-piddə-līt, léppidə-) *n.* A lilac or pink to grey mica, $K_2Li_3Al_4Si_7O_2(OH,F)_3$, used as a lithium ore and in glass and ceramic production. [German *Lepidolith* : LEPIDO- + -LITH.]

lep·i·dop·ter·an (léppi-dóp-tərən) *n., pl.* **-terans** or **-tera** (-tərə). Also **lep·i·dop·ter·on** (-tərən, -təron) *pl.* **-tera** (-tərə). A lepidopterous insect. [New Latin *Lepidoptera,* "scale-winged ones" : LEPIDO- + -PTER.] **—lep·i·dop·ter·an** *adj.*

lep·i·dop·ter·ist (léppi-dóptərist) *n.* An entomologist specialising in the study of butterflies and moths.

lep·i·dop·ter·ous (léppi-dóptərəss) *adj.* Of or belonging to the order Lepidoptera, which includes the butterflies and moths, having four wings covered with small scales, and with caterpillars forming the larval stage.

lep·i·dote (léppi-dōt) *adj.* Covered with small scales. [Greek *lepidōtos,* from *lepis,* scale.]

lep·o·rine (léppə-rīn ‖ -rin, -rən) *adj.* Of or characteristic of hares. [Latin *leporīnus,* from *lepus* (stem *lepor-*), hare.]

lep·re·chaun (lépprə-kawn) *n.* In Irish folklore, any of a race of elves who are cobblers and have hidden treasure. [Earlier *lubrican,* from Irish *lupracán, leipracán,* from Middle Irish *luchrupán,* from Old Irish *luchorpán* : *lū,* small + *corp,* body, from Latin *corpus.*]

lep·ro·sar·i·um (lépprə-saír-i-əm) *n., pl.* **-ums** or **-saria** (-i-ə). A hospital for the treatment of lepers. [Medieval Latin, from Late Latin *leprōsus,* LEPROUS.]

lep·rose (lép-rōss, -rōz) *adj.* Scurfy or scaly; leprous. [Late Latin *leprōsus,* LEPROUS.]

lep·ro·sy (léprə-si) *n.* A chronic, infectious, granulomatous disease occurring chiefly in tropical and subtropical regions, caused by a bacillus, *Mycobacterium leprae,* and ranging in severity from noncontagious and spontaneously remitting forms to contagious, malignant forms with progressive anaesthesia, paralysis, ulceration, nutritive disturbances, gangrene, and mutilation. Also called "Hansen's disease". [From LEPROUS.] **—lep·rot·ic** (le-próttik) *adj.*

lep·rous (léprəss) *adj.* **1.** Having leprosy. **2.** Of, pertaining to, or resembling leprosy. **3.** *Biology.* Having or consisting of loose, scurfy scales. [Middle English *lepro(u)s,* from Late Latin *leprōsus,* from *lepra,* leprosy. See **leper.**] **—lep·rous·ly** *adv.* **—lep·rous·ness** *n.*

-lepsy *n. comb. form.* Indicates a fit or seizure; for example, **narcolepsy**. [Greek *-lēpsia,* from *lēpsis,* taking, seizure, from *lambanein* (future stem *lēps-*), to take, seize.] **—leptic** *adj. comb. form.*

lepto-, lept- *comb. form.* Indicates slender, thin, fine; for example, **leptocephalus, lepton**. [Greek *leptos,* peeled, fine, small, thin, from *lepein,* to peel.]

lep·to·ceph·a·lus (léptō-séff'l-əss) *n., pl.* **-li** (-lī). Any of the slender, transparent larvae of eels and certain other fishes. [New Latin, "slender-headed" : LEPTO- + -CEPHALOUS.]

lep·ton¹ (lép-ton) *n., pl.* **-ta** (-tə). **1.** A monetary unit equal to ¹/₁₀₀ of the drachma of Greece. **2.** An ancient Greek coin. [Modern Greek, from Greek, small coin, from *leptos,* fine, small, from *lepein,* to peel.]

lep·ton² *n., pl.* **-tons.** Any of a family of elementary particles including the electron, the muon, the tau particle, and their associated neutrinos, all having spin equal to ¹/₂ and masses less than those of the mesons. [LEPT(O)- + -ON.]

lepton number *n. Symbol* L *Physics.* A quantum number equal to the number of leptons in an interaction minus the number of antileptons. Each type of lepton has its own quantum number that is separately conserved.

lep·to·some (léptə-sōm) *n. Physiology.* A person with a slender, thin, or frail body. [German *Leptosom* : LEPTO- + -SOME (body).] **—lep·to·so·mat·ic** (-sōmáttik) *adj.*

lep·to·spi·ro·sis (léptō-spīr-ō-siss) *n.* An infectious disease caused by bacteria of the genus *Leptospira,* that may be transmitted to humans by contact with rodents, dogs, and other mammals, and is characterised by fever and either jaundice or meningitis. [New Latin *Leptospira* (LEPTO- + Greek *speira,* coil) + -OSIS.]

lep·to·spo·ran·gi·ate (léptō-spə-ránji-ət, -spaw-, -it, -ayt) *adj.* Of or pertaining to ferns in which the sporangium develops from a single cell. Compare **eusporangiate.**

lep·to·tene (lép-tə-teen, -tō-) *n. Biology.* The first stage of prophase in mitosis and meiosis when the nuclear material becomes visible as slender single-stranded threads. [LEPTO- + *-tene,* from Greek *taina,* band, thread.]

Lep·us (léppəss, léepəss) *n.* A constellation in the Southern Hemisphere near Orion and Columba. [New Latin, from Latin, hare.]

Le Puy (lə pwée). *French* Le Puy en Ve·lay (ON və-láy). The administrative centre of the Haute-Loire département, south central France, built around towering rock pinnacles. It is a liqueur and lace-making centre.

Lé·ri·da (láyreeda). Capital of Lérida province, Catalonia, northeast Spain. An ancient fortified city on the river Segre, it was taken by Julius Caesar (49 B.C.). The city commanded the approaches to Barcelona during the Spanish Civil War, and fell to the Nationalists in 1938 after a nine-month battle.

Ler·mon·tov (laír-montof ‖ *Russian* -məntəf), **Mikhail Yuryevich** (1814–41). Russian writer. He wrote the novel *A Hero of Our Times* (1840), and many poems. He was killed in a duel.

Ler·ner (lérnər), **Alan Jay** (1918–86). U.S. lyricist. He wrote musicals with the composer, Frederick Loewe, including *Brigadoon* (1947) and *My Fair Lady* (1956).

Ler·wick (lér-wik). Most northerly town in the British Isles, in Shetland, Scotland. It has a sheltered harbour with a fishing industry, and serves the North Sea oil industry.

Le Sage (lə saázh), **Alain René** (1668–1747). French writer. His novel *Gil Blas de Santillane* (1715–35) was one of the earliest examples of modern realistic fiction.

les·bi·an (lézbi-ən) *n. Sometimes capital* **L.** A female homosexual. ~*adj. Sometimes capital* **L.** Of or pertaining to female homosexuals. [After LESBOS, alluding to the supposed homosexuality of Sappho who lived there.] **—les·bi·an·ism** *n.*

Les·bi·an (lézbi-ən) *n.* **1.** A native or resident of Lesbos. **2.** The Ancient Greek dialect of Lesbos, belonging to Aeolic, used in the lyric poetry of Sappho and Alcaeus.
~*adj.* **1.** Of or pertaining to Lesbos or its people. **2.** Of or pertaining to the Ancient Greek dialect of Lesbos. **3.** Of, pertaining to, or characteristic of Sappho, or her poetry.

Les·bos (lézboss). *Greek* **Lés·vos** (lézvoss). Mountainous Greek island off western Turkey, the home of Sappho and Aristotle.

lese majesty (leez) *n.* Also *French* **lèse ma·jes·té** (láyz mázhess-tay, léz, -táy). **1.** An offence or crime committed against the ruler or supreme power of a state; treason. **2.** The act or an instance of affronting another's dignity or overstepping authority. [Old French *lese-majeste,* from Latin *laesa mājestās,* "violated majesty" : *laesa,* past participle of *laedere,* to injure, damage, offend + MAJESTY.]

le·sion (leézh'n) *n.* **1.** A wound or injury. **2.** A circumscribed pathological alteration of tissue or an organ. **3.** A point or patch of a skin disease. [Middle English *lesioun,* from Old French *lesion,* from Latin *laesiō* (stem *laesiōn-*), from *laedere*†, to injure, damage.]

Le·so·tho, Kingdom of (li-sóotóo, lə-, -sōtō). Independent Commonwealth country, formerly Basutoland, surrounded by the Republic of South Africa. It became a British protectorate in 1868 and an independent kingdom in 1966. It is mountainous, but produces wheat and maize. Area, 30 355 square kilometres (11,720 square miles). Population, 2,080,000. Capital, Maseru. See map at **South Africa.**

less (less). Alternative comparative of **little.**
~*adj.* **1.** Not as great in extent, quantity, magnitude, or degree: *takes less sugar; needs less attention.* **2.** Lower in importance, esteem, or rank: *No less a person than a marquis is considered.* **—no less. 1.** Used, sometimes ironically, as a comment on a preceding statement, when surprised or impressed: *She's going to Oxford, no less.* **2.** None other: *The surprise guest turned out to be no less than the chairman himself.* —See Usage note at **fewer.**
~*adv.* To a smaller extent, degree, or frequency.
~*n.* A smaller amount. **—less of.** To stop or desist from. Used in the imperative: *Less of your cheek!*
~*prep.* Minus; subtracting: *Five less one is four.* [Middle English *less(e),* Old English *lǣssa* (adjective) and *lǣs* (adverb and noun), from Germanic *loisiz* (unattested), little.]

-less *adj. comb. form.* Indicates: **1.** Lack of, free of, not having, or without; for example, **toothless, sleepless, blameless. 2.** Not acting or able to be acted upon in a specified way; for example, **tireless, ceaseless, countless.** [Middle English *-les(se),* Old English *-lēas,* from *lēas,* lacking, free from.]

les·see (le-seé) *n.* One holding a lease. [Middle English, from Anglo-French *lessee,* variant of Old French *lesse,* past participle of *lesser,* to LEASE.] **—les·see·ship** *n.*

less·en (léss'n) *v.* **-ened, -ening, -ens.** *—tr.* **1.** To cause to decrease; make less. **2.** To make little of; minimise; belittle. *—intr.* To become less; decrease. —See Synonyms at **decrease.** [Middle English *lessenen,* from *lesse,* LESS.]

Les·seps (léssəps || *French* le-séps), **Ferdinand Marie, Vicomte de** (1805–94). French engineer and diplomat. He planned and supervised construction of the Suez Canal, opened in 1869. His company began building the Panama Canal in 1881, but went bankrupt in 1888. The canal was completed by the U.S. government.

less·er (léssər) *adj.* Smaller or less in size, amount, value, or importance, especially in a comparison of two elements. [Middle English double comparative, from LESS.]

Lesser Antilles. A chain of islands in the West Indies, forming a barrier between the Atlantic Ocean and the Caribbean Sea. They are made up of the Leeward and Windward Islands. See map at **Latin America.**

lesser brethren *pl.n.* Those members of a group regarded as less important than the other members.

lesser celandine *n.* A plant, *Ranunculus ficaria,* having heart-shaped leaves and yellow flowers. Also called "pilewort".

lesser doxology *n.* The **Gloria Patri** *(see).*

lesser panda *n.* See **panda.**

Les·sing (léssing), **Doris (May)** (1919–). British novelist, born in Iran, reared in Rhodesia. Her works include *The Grass is Singing* (1950), the 5-volume semiautobiographical *Children of Violence* (1952–69), science fiction such as *The Sirian Experiments* (1981), the autobiographical *Under my Skin* (1994), and *Love, Again* (1995).

Lessing, Gotthold Ephraim (1729–81). German dramatist and critic. He wrote the plays *Minna von Barnhelm* (1763) and *Nathan der Weise* (1779) which advocated tolerance.

les·son (léss'n) *n.* **1.** Something to be learned. **2. a.** A period of instruction; a class: *a tennis lesson.* **b.** The material taught in one such period. **3. a.** An experience or observation that imparts beneficial new knowledge or wisdom. **b.** The knowledge or wisdom learned in such a manner. **4.** A reprimand or punishment. **5.** A reading from the Bible or other sacred writing as part of a religious service.
~*tr.v.* **lessoned, -soning, -sons.** *Rare.* **1.** To teach a lesson or lessons to; instruct. **2.** To reprimand or punish. [Middle English *lesso(u)n,* a reading, lesson, from Old French *lecon,* from Latin *lectiō,* LECTION.]

les·sor (léssawr, le-sáwr) *n.* One who lets property under a lease; a landlord. [Middle English *lessour,* from Anglo-French, from *lesser,* to LEASE.]

lest (lest) *conj. Literary.* **1.** So as to prevent the possibility that; for fear that: *Tiptoe lest the guard should hear you.* **2.** That. Used after phrases denoting fear, worry, or the like: *anxious lest he should become ill.* [Middle English *leste,* short for *les the,* whereby less, Old English *thȳ lǣs the,* from *lǣs,* LESS.]

let[1] (let) *tr.v.* **let, letting, lets. 1.** Used as an auxiliary followed by an infinitive omitting *to:* **a.** To grant permission to; allow: *She let him continue.* **b.** To cause to. Used with *know* or *hear: He let me know the results.* **2.** Used as an auxiliary in the imperative: **a.** In order to convey a command, request, or proposal: *Let's finish the job!* **b.** In order to convey a warning or threat: *Just let her try!* **c.** In order to convey an assumption or hypothesis: *Let x equal y.* **d.** In order to convey acceptance of or resignation to the inevitable: *Let death come!* **3.** To permit to move or change in a specified manner: *let the dog through.* **4.** To rent or lease: *let a room to a bachelor.* **5.** To assign (a contract for work, for example): *let the construction job to a new firm.* **—let alone.** Not to speak of; much less: *Don't whisper, let alone speak.* **—let in.** To permit to enter: *They let in three goals.* **—let in for.** To involve in: *let them in for a lot of trouble.* **—let in on. 1.** To take into one's confidence; inform: *Were they let in on the secret?* **2.** To allow to participate: *Let him in on the robbery.* **—let into. 1.** To permit to enter or be inserted into. **2.** To take into one's confidence; inform. **—let on. 1.** To allow it to be known: *Don't let on that you helped me.* **2.** To pretend. [Middle English *leten,* Old English *lǣtan,* to leave behind, leave undone.]

Usage: In negative constructions, the form *let's not* has widespread currency in both British and American English speech. *Don't let's* is largely British; *let's don't* is to be found in American English, but is considered nonstandard. *Let* is followed by pronouns in their objective form: *Let Jane and me/him/us decide.* See also **leave.**

let[2] *n.* **1.** An obstacle. Used chiefly in the phrase *without let or hindrance.* **2.** *Sports.* **a.** In certain games such as tennis or squash, a small irregularity in the play that causes the point to be replayed. **b.** A point replayed for this reason.
~*tr.v.* **letted** or **let, letting, lets.** *Archaic.* To obstruct or hinder. [Middle English *let(te),* a hindrance, from *letten,* to hinder, prevent, Old English *lettan.*]

-let *n. suffix.* Indicates: **1.** Diminutive size or minor status; for example, **brooklet, starlet. 2.** An article worn on some part of the body; for example, **bracelet, anklet.** [Middle English *-lette,* from Old French *-elet* : noun ending *-el* + *-et(te),* -ETTE.]

letch. Variant of **lech.**

Letch·worth (léch-wərth, -wurth). Britain's first garden city. It lies in Hertfordshire and was planned in 1903 as an industrial and residential town surrounded by a rural belt.

let down *tr.v..* **1.** To take down; lower: *let down the sails.* **2.** To fail to satisfy; disappoint: *The mayor let down the electorate.* **3.** To undo so as to add length: *let down a dress; let down her hair.* **4.** To release air from: *let down tyres.*

let·down (lét-down) *n.* **1.** A slowing down, relaxing, or decrease, as of effort or energy. **2.** *Informal.* A disappointment. **3.** The descent made by an aircraft in order to land.

le·thal (leéth'l) *adj.* **1.** Sufficient to cause or capable of causing death. **2.** Of, pertaining to, or causing death. —See Synonyms at **fatal.** [Latin *lethālis,* from *lēthum,* death, variant of *lētum.*] **—le·thal·i·ty** (lee-thál-əti) *n.* **—le·thal·ly** *adv.*

lethal dose *n.* See **LD.**

lethal gene *n.* A gene that, under certain conditions, brings about the death of the organism carrying it, usually when its effect is not masked by a normal dominant gene.

lethargic encephalitis *n. Pathology.* **Encephalitis lethargica** *(see).*

leth·ar·gy (léthərji) *n.* **1.** Sluggish indifference or slowness; a feeling of laziness or lack of arousal. **2.** A state of unconsciousness resembling deep sleep, from which an individual can be roused but into which he at once relapses. [Middle English *litargie, letargie,* from Old French *litargie,* from Latin *lēthargia,* drowsiness, from Greek, from *lēthargos,* forgetful, from *lēthē,* forgetfulness.] **—leth·ar·gic** (le-thárjik, li-, lə-) *adj.* **—leth·ar·gic·al·ly** *adv.*

Synonyms: *lethargy, lassitude, sluggishness, torpor, languor.*

Le·the (leéthi) *n. Greek Mythology* **1.** The river of forgetfulness in Hades. **2.** Oblivion; loss of memory. [Greek *lēthē,* forgetfulness (later personified).] **—Le·the·an** (li-theé-ən, leéthi-) *adj.*

Le·to (leétō). *Greek Mythology.* A consort of Zeus and the mother of Apollo and Artemis.

let off *tr.v.* **1.** To emit or release: *let off steam.* **2.** To excuse or dismiss: *let the workmen off early.* **3.** To give little or no punishment to for an offence: *He was let off with a year on probation.* **4.** To detonate or fire: *let off a bomb.*

let-off (lét-off, -awff) *n.* An escape or reprieve: *a lucky let-off.*

let out *tr.v.* **1.** To release from confinement. **2.** To give forth, emit: *The dog let out a yelp.* **3.** To make known, (a secret, for example); reveal: *Who let that story out?* **4.** To increase the size of (a garment, for example). **5.** To rent or lease (buildings, land, or the like).

let-out (lét-owt) *n.* A way of escape; a loophole.

let's (lets). Contraction of *let us.*

Lett (let) *n.* A Latvian.

let·ter (lettər) *n.* **1.** A written symbol or character representing a speech sound; a component of an alphabet. **2.** A written or printed communication directed to an individual or organisation. **3.** *Often plural.* A formal or legal document giving information or granting rights to its bearer or recipient. **4.** The literal meaning of something: *the letter of the law.* **5.** *Printing.* **a.** A piece of type that prints a single character. **b.** A specific style of type. **c.** The characters in one style of type. **6.** *Plural.* Honour, distinction, or the like, displayed in a written, abbreviated form: *letters after his name.* —**to the letter.** Precisely as directed, as when following orders. ~*tr.v.* **lettered, -tering, -ters. 1.** To write letters on. **2.** To write in letters. [Middle English *letter, lettre,* from Old French *lettre,* from Latin *littera,* letter (of the alphabet), document (in plural only).] —**let·ter·er** *n.*

letter bomb *n.* An explosive device that is thin enough to fit into a large envelope and is designed to explode when the envelope is opened.

let·ter·box, letter box (léttər-boks) *n.* **1.** A postbox *(see).* **2.** A slot in a front door, usually covered with a flap, through which post is delivered. **3.** A private box for receiving incoming letters. Also *chiefly U.S.* "mailbox".

letter card *n.* A card, often with a printed stamp, that has gummed edges and can be folded and sent as a letter.

let·tered (léttərd) *adj.* **1. a.** Educated to read and write; literate. **b.** Erudite; learned. **2.** Of or pertaining to literacy or learning. **3.** Inscribed or marked with letters.

let·ter·head (léttər-hed) *n.* **1.** The printed heading at the top of a sheet of writing paper, usually a person's address or the name and address of an organisation. **2.** Paper with such a printed heading.

let·ter·ing (léttəring) *n.* **1.** The act, process, or art of forming or inscribing with letters. **2.** The letters themselves.

letter of advice *n.* A letter containing specific information about a commercial transaction, as from a consignor to a consignee.

letter of credit *n. Abbr.* **l.c., L/C** A letter issued by a bank authorising the bearer or person named to draw a stated amount of money from it or its branches, or from associated banks or agencies.

let·ter-per·fect (léttər-pér-fikt, -fekt) *adj. Chiefly U.S.* Correct in every detail; word-perfect.

let·ter·press (léttər-press) *n.* **1. a.** The process of printing from a raised inked surface. **b.** Anything printed in this fashion. **2.** The text itself as distinct from illustrations or other ornamentation.

let·ters (léttərz) *n. Used with a singular verb.* Literary culture or learning; literature as a discipline or profession: *a man of letters.*

letters of administration *pl.n.* A legal document entrusting an individual with the administration of a deceased person's estate.

letters of credence *pl.n.* Also **letter of credence.** An official document conveying the credentials of a diplomatic envoy to a foreign government. Also called "letters credential".

letters of marque *pl.n.* Also **letter of marque. 1.** A document issued by a nation allowing a private citizen to seize citizens or goods of another nation. **2.** A document issued by a nation allowing a private citizen to equip a ship with arms in order to attack enemy ships. Also called "letters of marque and reprisal". [Middle English, from Old French *marque,* reprisal, from Old Provençal *marca,* from *marcar,* to seize as a pledge, from Germanic.]

letters patent *pl.n. Law.* A document issued by a government granting a patent to an inventor.

Let·tish (léttish) *adj.* Of or pertaining to the Latvians or their language. ~*n.* A language, **Latvian** *(see).*

let·tre de cac·het (léttrə də ka-sháy) *n., pl.* **lettres de cachet** *(pronounced as singular).* French. Formerly, a document issued or sanctioned by the French sovereign, granting powers of arrest or banishment without trial.

let·tuce (léttiss) *n.* **1.** Any of various plants of the genus *Lactuca;* especially, *L. sativa,* cultivated for its edible leaves. **2.** The leaves of *L. sativa,* eaten as salad. **3.** Any of various plants resembling lettuce, such as the sea lettuce. [Middle English *letus(e),* from Old French *laituës,* plural of *laituë,* from Latin *lactūca,* from *lac* (stem *lact-*), milk (from its milky juice).]

let up *intr.v.* **1.** To diminish; slacken; lessen. **2.** To stop.

let·up (lét-up) *n.* **1.** A slackening of pace, force, intensity, or effort; a slowdown. **2.** A temporary stop; a pause.

le·u (láy-ōō) *n., pl.* **lei** (lay). **1.** The basic monetary unit of Romania, equal to 100 bani. **2.** A coin worth one leu. [Romanian, "lion", from Latin *leō* (stem *leōn-*), LION.]

leu·cine (lōō-seen, léw-) *n.* An essential amino acid, $C_6H_{13}NO_2$, derived from the hydrolysis of protein by pancreatic enzymes. [LEUC(O)- + -INE.]

leu·cite (lōō-sīt, léw-) *n.* A white or grey mineral, consisting essentially of $KAl(SiO_3)_2$. [German *Leucit* : LEUC(O)- + -ITE.]

leuco-, leuc-, leuko- *comb. form.* Indicates: **1.** White or colourless; for example, **leucoderma, leucoplast. 2.** Leucocyte; for example, **leucopenia, leukaemia.** [New Latin, from Greek *leukos,* clear, white.]

leu·co base (lōōkō, léwkō) *n. Chemistry.* A colourless dyestuff produced by reducing a dye. It can be oxidised back to the original dye in the fabric. [Greek *leukos,* lacking colour, white.]

leu·co·cyte (lōōkə-sīt, léwkə-) *n.* Any of the white or colourless nucleated cells occurring in blood. Also called "white blood cell",

"white corpuscle". [LEUCO- + -CYTE.] —**leu·co·cyt·ic** (-síttik) *adj.*

leu·co·cy·topoi·e·sis (lōōkō-sítō-pay-ée-siss, léwks) *n.* Leucopoiesis. [LEUCOCYT(E) + -POIESIS.] —**leu·co·cy·to·poi·et·ic** (-ettik) *adj.*

leu·co·cy·to·sis (lōōkō-sī-tō-siss, léwkō-) *n., pl.* **-ses** (-seez). A large increase in the number of leucocytes in the blood, generally in response to infection. [New Latin : LEUCOCYT(E) + -OSIS.] —**leu·co·cy·tot·ic** (-tóttik) *adj.*

leu·co·der·ma (lōōkō-dérmə, léwkō-) *n.* Partial or total lack of skin pigmentation. Also called "vitiligo". [New Latin : LEUCO- + -DERMA.] —**leu·co·der·mal, leu·co·der·mic** *adj.*

leu·co·ma (lōō-kōmə, lew-) *n.* A dense, white opacity of the cornea of the eye. [New Latin, from Greek *leukōma* : LEUC(O)- + -OMA.]

leu·co·pe·ni·a (lōōkō-pééni-ə, léwkō-) *n.* An abnormally low number of leucocytes in the blood. [New Latin : LEUCO- + -PENIA.]

leu·co·plast (lōōkō-plast, léwkə-) *n.* Also **leu·co·plas·tid** (-plásstid). A colourless plastid in the cytoplasm of plant cells, around which starch collects. [LEUCO- + PLAST(ID).]

leu·co·poi·e·sis (lōōkō-poy-ée-siss, léwkō-) *n.* The formation and development of leucocytes. Also called "leucocytopoiesis". [New Latin : LEUCO- + -POIESIS.] —**leu·co·poi·et·ic** (-éttik) *adj.*

leu·cor·rhoe·a (lōōkə-réer, léwkə-, -rée-ə) *n.* A whitish or yellowish vaginal discharge containing mucus, which in excessive amounts may indicate infection of the lower reproductive tract. [New Latin: LEUCO- + -RRHOEA.]

leu·cot·o·my (lōō-kóttəmi, lew-) *n., pl.* **-omies.** The surgical interruption of certain of the nerve fibres in the brain to relieve severe emotional tension and other mental disorders, especially when all other treatment has failed. The original form of this operation was called "prefrontal lobotomy". [LEUCO- (referring to the white tissue of the frontal lobe) + -TOMY.]

leu·kae·mi·a (lōō-kéemi-ə, lew-) *n.* Any of a group of usually fatal diseases of the reticuloendothelial system, involving uncontrolled proliferation of leucocytes, which suppress the production of normal blood cells. [New Latin : LEUC(O)- + -AEMIA.]

leuko-. Variant of **leuco-.**

Leuven. See **Louvain.**

lev (lef) *n., pl.* **leva** (lévvə). *Abbr.* **L. 1.** The basic monetary unit of Bulgaria, equal to 100 stotinki. **2.** A coin worth one lev. [Bulgarian, "lion", from Old Bulgarian *livu,* probably from Old High German *lewo,* from Latin *leō,* LION.]

Lev. Leviticus (Old Testament).

Lev·al·loi·si·an (lévvə-lóyzi-ən) *adj.* Of or pertaining to a western European stage in lower Palaeolithic culture distinguished by the method of striking off flake tools from pieces of flint. [After *Levallois*-Perret, district near Paris.]

lev·al·lor·phan (li-vál-ər-fan) *n.* A drug used to counteract the slowing in breathing caused by narcotic pain relievers without reducing their analgesic effects. [*Levorotatory* + *all*yl + *morph*ine + *-an* (unsaturated carbon compound).]

le·vant¹ (li-vánt) *n.* A type of heavy, coarse-grained morocco leather often used in bookbinding. Also called "Levant morocco". [Originally imported from the LEVANT.]

le·vant² *intr.v.* **-vanted, -vanting, -vants.** To run away or abscond, usually leaving unpaid debts behind. [Slang use of LEVANT.]

Le·vant (li-vánt). A term for the countries bordering on the eastern Mediterranean. Preceded by *the.* [Middle English *levaunt,* "the Orient", from Old French *levant,* "rising" (said of the sun), present participle of *lever,* to rise, raise.]

le·vant·er (li-vántər) *n.* **1.** One who levants; an absconder. **2.** A strong easterly wind in the extreme west Mediterranean area. In this sense, also called "levante". **3.** *Capital* **L.** A Levantine.

le·van·tine (lévv'n-tīn, -teen ‖ lə-vánt-) *n.* A strong, closely woven silk fabric. [Originally made in the LEVANT.]

Le·van·tine (lévv'n-tīn ‖ -teen, lə-vánt-) *adj.* Of or pertaining to the Levant. ~*n.* **1.** A native or resident of the Levant. **2.** A ship from the Levant.

le·va·tor (li-váytər) *n., pl.* **levatores** (lévvə-táwr-eez ‖ -tōr-). **1.** *Anatomy.* Any muscle that raises a part of the body. **2.** In surgery, an instrument for lifting the depressed part of a fractured skull. [New Latin, from Latin *levāre,* to raise.]

lev·ee¹ (lévvi, lə-vée) *n.* **1.** A natural embankment built up by a river. **2.** An embankment raised to prevent a river from overflowing. **3.** A small ridge or raised area bordering an irrigated field. **4.** *U.S.* A landing place on a river; a pier. [French *levée,* from Old French *levee,* "raising", from the past participle of *lever,* to raise.]

lev·ee² (lévvi, lévvay) *n.* **1.** A reception held by a monarch or other high-ranking person on rising from bed. **2.** A formal reception, as at a royal court. [French *levé,* from *lever,* to rise.]

lev·el (lévv'l) *n.* **1. a.** Relative position or rank on a scale, as in a hierarchy, society, or other grouping. Also used in combination and adjectivally: *high-level talks between diplomats.* **b.** Loosely, any grade or step in a series or position on a range: *a deeper level of meaning; at the spiritual level.* **c.** A natural or proper position, place, or stage: *finally found her own level.* **2.** An amount, degree, standard, or value achieved: *a level of output; sound levels.* **3.** Position along a vertical axis; elevation; height: *the level of the windows.* **4. a.** A horizontal line or plane at right angles to the plumb or vertical. **b.** The position or height of such a line or plane: *eye level.* **5. a.** A flat, horizontal surface. **b.** A layer, as of land or rock. **6.** A tract of land of uniform elevation. **7. a.** A spirit level *(see).* **b.** A spirit level combined with a telescope, used in surveying. **c.** A computation of the difference in elevation between two points, using a spirit level. **—on a level with.** Equal to. **—on the level.** *Informal.* Without deception.

~*adj.* **1.** Having a flat, smooth surface. **2.** On a horizontal plane. **3.** Being at the same height as another; even. **4.** Poured or measured into a container so as to be even with its rim: *a level teaspoonful.* **5.** Being of the same degree or rank as another; equal. **6.** Without abrupt variations; uniform; consistent. **—(one's) level best.** The best one is capable of doing.

~*v.* **levelled** or *U.S.* **-leveled, -elling** or *U.S.* **-eling, -els.** *—tr.* **1.** To make horizontal, flat, or even. Often used with *off.* **2.** To tear down; raze. **3.** To knock down with or as if with a blow. **4.** To put (two persons or things) in the same rank, degree, or plane. **5.** To aim along a horizontal plane: *levelled a gun at my head.* **6.** To direct (a gaze or remark, for example) emphatically or forcefully towards someone. **7.** To measure the different elevations of (a tract of land) with a level. *—intr.* **1.** To render persons or things equal, as in rank, importance, or size. **2.** To achieve or come to a level. **3.** To aim a weapon horizontally. **4.** *Chiefly U.S. Informal.* To be frank. Used with *with: Level with me on what happened.* **—level off** or **out. 1.** To move towards stability or consistency. **2.** To manoeuvre an aircraft into horizontal flight after gaining or losing altitude.

~*adv.* Along a flat or even line or plane. [Middle English *level, livel,* from Old French *livel,* from Vulgar Latin *libellum* (unattested), variant of Latin *libella,* level, water level, plummet line, diminutive of *libra,* "a pound", balance, level.] **—lev·el·ly** *adv.* **—lev·el·ness** *n.*

Synonyms: *level, flat, plane, even, smooth, flush.*

level crossing *n.* A place where a railway line crosses a road on the same level, usually having a protective barrier that closes the road when a train is coming. Also *U.S.* "grade crossing".

lev·el·head·ed (lévv'l-héddid) *adj.* Characteristically self-composed; sensible; calm. **—lev·el·head·ed·ly** *adv.* **—lev·el·head·ed·ness** *n.*

lev·el·ler, *U.S.* **lev·el·er** (lévv'l-ər) *n.* **1.** One that levels. **2.** One who advocates the abolition of social inequalities.

Lev·el·ler (lévv'l-ər) *n.* A member of an English radical political movement active in the 1640s that advocated universal male suffrage, parliamentary democracy, and religious tolerance.

lev·el·ling rod (lévv'l-ing) *n.* A graduated pole or stick with a movable marker, used with a surveyor's level to measure differences in elevation. Also called "levelling pole", "levelling staff".

level-pegging (lévv'l-pégging) *n.* A state of equality, especially between contestants.

~*adj.* Running equal in output, performance, or the like.

level playing field *n.* A set of conditions fair to everyone. [From the principle that a level playing field gives neither side an unfair advantage.]

Le·ven, Loch (leev'n). Lake in Perthshire and Kinross, Scotland. Mary, Queen of Scots was imprisoned on one of its seven islands, Castle Island, in the 16th century.

le·ver (leevər ‖ *U.S. also* lévvər) *n.* **1.** A simple **machine** (*see*) consisting of a rigid body, typically a metal bar, pivoted on a fixed fulcrum. **2.** A projecting handle used to adjust or operate a mechanism. **3.** A means of advancement or accomplishment.

~*v.* **levered, -vering, -vers.** *—tr.* To move or lift with a lever. *—intr.* To use a lever. [Middle English *lever, levour,* from Old French *levier, leveor,* from *lever,* to raise, from Latin *levāre,* from *levis,* light.]

le·ver·age (leevərij ‖ *U.S. also* lévvərij) *n.* **1.** The action of a lever. **2.** The mechanical advantage of a lever. **3.** Positional advantage; power to act effectively; influence.

lev·er·et (lévvərit) *n.* A young hare, especially one less than a year old. [Middle English, from Anglo-French, diminutive of *levre,* variant of Old French *lievre,* hare, from Latin *lepus* (stem *lepor-*).]

Le·ver·hulme (leevər-hewm), **William Hesketh Lever, 1st Viscount** (1851–1925). British philanthropic soap magnate. He founded Lever Brothers (1884), developing "Sunlight", a soap made from vegetable oils rather than tallow. Lever became an M.P. in 1906, and was made baron in 1917 and viscount in 1922.

Le·ver·rier (lə-vérri-ay), **Urbain Jean Joseph** (1811–77). French astronomer. His calculations led to the discovery of the planet Neptune in 1846, independently of its prediction by the English astronomer J.C. Adams.

Le·vesque (lə-véck), **René** (1922–87). Canadian politician. In 1967 he co-founded the Parti Québecois, a French-Canadian separatist party. He was premier of Quebec 1976–85.

Le·vi[1] (leevī). A son of Jacob and Leah. Genesis 29:34.

Levi[2] *n.* A tribe of Israel descended from Levi.

lev·i·a·ble (lévvi-əb'l) *adj.* **1.** Liable to be levied, as a tax is. **2.** Liable to be taxed or to have a levy imposed, as imports might be.

le·vi·a·than (li-vī-əthən) *n.* **1.** A monstrous sea creature mentioned in the Old Testament. Job 41:1. **2.** Any very large animal. **3.** Anything unusually large for its kind. [Middle English, from Late Latin, from Hebrew *libhyāthōn.*]

lev·i·gate (lévvi-gayt) *tr.v.* **-gated, -gating, -gates. 1.** To make into a smooth, fine powder, as by grinding when moist. **2.** To suspend in a liquid. **3.** To make smooth; polish.

~*adj. Botany.* Smooth; glabrous. [Latin *lēvigāre : lēvis,* smooth + *agere,* to do, make.] **—lev·i·ga·tion** (-gáysh'n) *n.*

lev·in (lévvin) *n. Archaic.* Lightning. [Middle English *leven(e),* probably from Scandinavian; akin to Old Swedish *liughn(elder),* lightning (flash).]

lev·i·rate (lévvi-rət, -rit) *n.* The practice of marrying the widow of one's brother, as required by ancient Hebrew law. Compare **soro-**rate. [Latin *lēvir,* husband's brother.] **—lev·i·rat·ic** (-ráttik), **lev·i·rat·i·cal** *adj.*

Le·vis (leevīz) *pl.n.* A trademark for snugly fitting trousers of heavy denim with rivets reinforcing points of strain.

Lé·vi-Strauss (lévvi-strówss; *French* -stráwss), **Claude** (1908–). French social anthropologist, born in Belgium. He is a leading exponent of the theory of structuralism, and believes that there are similar underlying patterns of social life in all cultures, resulting from the unconscious structure of the human mind.

lev·i·tate (lévvi-tayt) *v.* **-tated, -tating, -tates.** *—intr.* To rise into the air and float, in apparent defiance of gravity. *—tr.* **1.** To cause to rise into the air and float. **2.** To support (a patient with severe burns) on an **air bed** (*see*). [From LEVITY.] **—lev·i·ta·tion** (-táysh'n) *n.* **—lev·i·ta·tor** (-taytər) *n.*

Le·vite (leevīt) *n.* A member of the tribe of Levi, the men of which were assistants to the Temple priests.

Le·vit·i·cal (li-víttik'l) *adj.* Also **Le·vit·ic** (-víttik). **1.** Of or pertaining to the Levites. **2.** Of or pertaining to Leviticus.

Le·vit·i·cus (li-víttikəss) *n. Abbr.* **Lev.** The third book of the Old Testament, containing the Hebrew ceremonial laws.

lev·i·ty (lévvəti) *n., pl.* **-ties. 1.** Lightness of speech or manner, especially when inappropriate; frivolity. **2.** Changeableness; inconstancy. **3.** *Archaic.* Lack of weight; lightness; buoyancy. [Latin *levitās* (stem *levitat-*), from *levis,* light.]

le·vo·do·pa (leevə-dōpə) *n.* Also *rare* **lae·vo·do·pa. L-dopa** (*see*).

lev·y (lévvi) *v.* **-ied, -ying, -ies.** *—tr.* **1.** To impose or collect (a tax, for example). **2.** To conscript into military service. **3.** To declare, begin, or wage (a war). *—intr.* To confiscate property, especially in accordance with a legal judgment.

~*n., pl.* **levies. 1.** The act or process of levying. **2. a.** The money, property, or number of soldiers levied. **b.** *Usually plural.* The men or troops levied. [Middle English *leve(e), levie,* from Old French *levee,* a raising, from *lever,* to raise.] **—lev·i·er** *n.*

lewd (lood, lewd) *adj.* **lewder, lewdest. 1.** Licentious; lustful. **2.** Obscene; indecent. **3.** *Obsolete.* Wicked. [Middle English *lew(e)d,* originally, ignorant, vulgar, Old English *lǣwede†,* lay (nonclergy).] **—lewd·ly** *adv.* **—lewd·ness** *n.*

Lew·es (loo-iss, lew-). County town of East Sussex, England. The old market town grew around a Norman castle, still standing.

Lewes, G(eorge) H(enry) (1817–78). English writer. His works include *Life of Goethe* (1855) and a five-volume philosophical work. *Problems of Life and Mind* (1874–79). He met George Eliot (Mary Ann Evans) in 1851 and lived with her from 1854.

lew·is (loo-iss, lew-) *n.* A dovetailed iron tenon made of several parts and designed to fit into a dovetail mortise in a large stone so that it can be lifted by a hoisting apparatus. Also called "lewisson".

Lewis, Cecil Day. See Day Lewis, Cecil.

Lewis, (loo-iss), C(live) S(taples) (1898–1963). British author and critic. His works include the medieval study, *The Allegory of Love* (1936), and the autobiographical *Surprised by Joy* (1954). He also wrote poems, theological works, space fantasies, and the famous children's fantasy series of Narnia tales.

Lewis, Frederick Carlton "Carl" (1961–). U.S. athlete. He won four Olympic gold medals in 1984, two each in 1988 and 1992, and a ninth in 1996, including the long jump four times. By 1992 he had set two world records at 100 metres.

Lewis, (Harry) Sinclair (1855–1951). U.S. novelist. He satirised middle-class America in his 22 novels, including *Main Street* (1920), *Babbit* (1922), and *Elmer Gantry* (1927). In 1930 he became the first American to win a Nobel prize for literature.

Lewis, (Percy) Wyndham (1884–1957). English painter and author, born in the United States. In 1914–15 he edited with Ezra Pound the organ of the Vorticist movement, *Blast.* His writings include *The Apes of God* (1930) and *Self-Condemned* (1954).

Lewis acid *n. Chemistry.* A compound capable of accepting a pair of electrons from a donor to form a coordinate bond. [After G.N. *Lewis* (1875-1946), U.S. chemist.]

Lewis base *n. Chemistry.* A compound capable of donating a pair of electrons to an acceptor to form a coordinate bond. [After G.N. *Lewis* (see **Lewis acid**).]

Lewis with Harris. Largest and most northerly island in the Outer Hebrides off northwest Scotland, now part of Western Isles Region. Lewis is low-lying, Harris mountainous. The largest town is Stornoway. Harris tweed is spun and woven by the island crofters.

lex·eme (lék-seem) *n.* An abstract linguistic unit, posited as the smallest vocabulary unit in the semantic system of a language, consisting typically of: **1.** A word root abstracted from its inflections, such as *run-* in the group *runs, running, runner.* **2.** A set consisting of a word together with all its inflections and derivations. **3.** An idiomatic phrase that makes no sense when broken down into its components, such as *to kick the bucket* ("to die").

lex·i·cal (lék-sik'l) *adj.* **1.** Of or pertaining to the vocabulary, words, or morphemes of a language. **2.** Of, pertaining to, or appropriate to lexicography or a lexicon. [From LEXICON.]

lex·i·cog·ra·pher (léksi-kóggrəfər) *n.* One who writes, compiles, or edits a dictionary.

lex·i·cog·ra·phy (léksi-kóggrəfi) *n.* The writing or compilation of a dictionary or dictionaries. [LEXICO(N) + -GRAPHY.] **—lex·i·co·graph·ic** (-kə-gráffik), **lex·i·co·graph·i·cal** *adj.* **—lex·i·co·graph·i·cal·ly** *adv.*

lex·i·col·o·gy (léksi-kólləji) *n.* The study of the lexical component of language. [LEXICO(N) + -LOGY.] **—lex·i·co·log·i·cal** (-kə-lójik'l) *adj.* **—lex·i·co·log·i·cal·ly** *adv.* **—lex·i·col·o·gist** *n.*

lex·i·con (lék-si-kən || -kon) *n. Abbr.* **lex.** **1.** A dictionary, especially of an ancient language such as Latin or Hebrew. **2.** A vocabulary of terms used in or of a particular profession, subject, or style; a specialised list of terms: *the lexicon of the sports page.* **3.** *Linguistics.* The morphemes of a language. [New Latin, from Greek *lexikon (biblion),* (book) pertaining to words, from *lexis,* speech, word, phrase, from *legein,* to speak.]

lex·i·gra·phy (lek-siggrəfi) *n.* A system of writing, such as that of Chinese, in which each word is represented by a single character or symbol. [Greek *lexis,* word (see **lexis**) + -GRAPHY.] **—lex·i·graph·ic** (-gráffik) *adj.* **—lex·i·graph·ic·al·ly** *adv.*

lex·is (léksiss) *n.* Vocabulary; the total set of words in a language. [Greek, word, from *legein,* to speak.]

lex ta·li·o·nis (tál-i-ṓ-niss) *n.* The principle of retribution according to which the punishment matches the offence in nature and severity, as encapsulated in such phrases as "an eye for an eye". [New Latin, "law of retaliation".]

ley. Variant of **lea** (meadow).

Leyden. See **Leiden.**

Ley·den jar (líd'n) *n.* An early form of capacitor, consisting of a glass jar lined inside and out with tinfoil and having a conducting rod connected to the inner foil lining and passing out of the jar through an insulated stopper. [After LEYDEN (Leiden), where it was invented (1745).]

ley farming *n.* The rotation, or alternate growing, of crops and grass on arable land.

Ley·land cypress (láy-lənd, -land) *n.* A fast-growing hybrid conifer tree, *Cupressocyparis leylandii.* [After C. J. *Leyland* (1849–1926), British botanist.]

ley lines (lay || lee) *pl.n.* Straight lines linking hilltops, tumuli, church sites, and other traditional places of sanctity in the British isles. They sometimes appear to correspond with prehistoric tracks. [From LEY, variant of LEA (grassland) : the lines are supposed to have demarcated ancient meadows.]

lf, l.f. 1. *Printing.* lightface. **2.** low frequency.

LG, L.G. Low German.

lg., lge. large.

LH luteinising hormone.

Lha·sa or **Las·sa** (laá-sə, lá-). Capital of the Tibet Autonomous Region, southwest China. Formerly the national capital of Tibet and centre of Tibetan Buddhism, it had numerous monasteries, temples, and convents, many of which were closed or razed following the Tibetan revolt against the Chinese in 1959. Until 1904 Lhasa was closed to foreign visitors.

Lhasa ap·so (ápsō) *n.* A small dog of a Tibetan breed, having a long, straight coat. [LHASA + Tibetan *apso,* Lhasa apso.]

li (lee) *n., pl.* **li.** A traditional Chinese measure of distance, today standardised at 500 metres (547 yards). [Chinese *lǐ.*]

Li The symbol for the element lithium.

li·a·bil·i·ty (lī-ə-bílləti) *n., pl.* **-ties. 1.** Something for which one is liable; an obligation or debt. **2.** *Plural.* The financial obligations entered in the balance sheet of a business enterprise. Compare **assets. 3.** A hindrance; a handicap. **4.** Likelihood.

li·a·ble (lī́-əb'l) *adj.* **1.** Legally obliged; responsible. Used with *for: liable for military service.* **2.** Susceptible; subject. Used with *to: liable to fainting fits.* **3.** Likely; apt. Used with an infinitive: *You're liable to get hurt if you fall for her.* —See Synonyms at **responsible.** [Middle English, perhaps from Anglo-French *liable* (unattested), from Old French *lier,* to bind, from Latin *ligāre.*]

li·aise (li-áyz) *intr.v.* **-aised, -aising, -aises.** To contact and communicate, often on a regular or official basis; effect a liaison. Often used with *with* or *between.* [Back-formation from LIAISON.]

li·ai·son (li-áy-z'n, -zon, -ZON) *n., pl.* **-sons. 1.** An instance or means of communication between bodies, groups, or units. **2. a.** A close relationship. **b.** A sexual relationship. **3.** The pronunciation of the usually silent final consonant of a word when followed by a word beginning with a vowel. **4.** In cookery, a thickening agent, such as egg yolks or cream, for sauces, soups, or the like. [French *liaison,* "binding", from Old French, from *lier,* to bind.]

li·an·a (li-aánə || -ánnə) *n.* Also **li·ane** (-aán || -án). Any of various high-climbing, usually woody vines common in the tropics. [French *liane,* perhaps from *lier,* to bind.]

li·ar (lī́-ər) *n.* One who tells lies.

li·as (lī́-əss) *n.* **1.** A pale grey, clayey limestone, usually found with clays and shales, particularly in southwest England. Also used adjectivally: *lias limestone.* **2.** *Capital* **L.** The earliest series of rocks formed in the Jurassic period, consisting of beds of sandstone, clay, lias limestone, and shale, and often containing ammonite fossils. [Middle English, from Old French *liais,* a kind of limestone, probably from Germanic.] **—li·as, li·as·sic** (lī-ássik) *adj.*

lib (lib) *n. Informal.* Liberation. Often used as an abbreviation in titles such as *animal lib* or *gay lib,* and sometimes considered to be offensive, as in *women's lib.*

lib. 1. a. liberal. **b.** *Capital* **L.** Liberal. **2.** librarian; library.

li·ba·tion (lī-báysh'n) *n.* **1. a.** The pouring of a liquid offering as a religious ritual. **b.** The liquid poured. **2.** *Informal.* An intoxicating drink. [Middle English *libacioun,* from Latin *lībātiō* (stem *lībātiōn-*), from *lībāre,* to taste, pour out as an offering.]

lib·ber (líbbər) *n. Informal.* **1.** A feminist. Used derogatorily. **2.** A member of or a believer in any of various liberation movements. Usually used in combination: *a gay libber.* [From LIB.]

Lib·by (líbbi), **Willard Frank** (1908–80). U.S. chemist. He developed the method of radiocarbon dating. He won the Albert Einstein award (1959) and the Nobel prize in chemistry (1960).

Lib Dem (líb-dém) *n. Informal.* A Liberal Democat. **—Lib Dem** *adj.*

li·bel (lī́b'l) *n.* **1.** *Law.* **a.** Any written, printed, or pictorial statement that damages a person by defaming his character or reputation. **b.** The act of presenting such a statement to the public. Compare **slander. 2.** Any slighting statement. **3.** The written claims presented by a plaintiff to an ecclesiastical court.

~tr.v. **libelled** or *U.S.* **-libeled, -belling** or *U.S.* **-beling, -bels. 1.** To make or publish a defamatory statement about. **2.** To speak slightingly of. **3.** To make a claim or bring an action against in an ecclesiastical court. —See Synonyms at **malign.** [Middle English, formal written claim of a plaintiff, from Old French *libel,* from Latin *libellus,* a little book, diminutive of *liber,* book.] **—li·bel·ist, li·bel·ler** *n.*

li·bel·lant, *U.S.* **li·bel·ant** (lī́b'l-ənt) *n.* The plaintiff in a case of ecclesiastical libel.

li·bel·lous, *U.S.* **li·bel·ous** (lī́b'l-əss) *adj.* Containing or constituting a libel; defamatory. **—li·bel·lous·ly** *adv.*

lib·er·al (líbbrəl, líbbərəl) *adj. Abbr.* **lib. 1.** Having, expressing, or following social or political views or policies that favour nonrevolutionary progress and reform. **2. a.** Having, expressing, or following views or policies that favour the freedom of individuals to act or express themselves in a manner of their own choosing. **b.** Having, expressing, or following a belief in laissez-faire economic policies. **3.** *Capital* **L.** *Abbr.* **Lib.** Of, designating, or belonging to a Liberal political party. **4.** Of, pertaining to, or designating a wide cultural education, as opposed to a technical or specialised one. **5.** Tolerant of the ideas or behaviour of others. **6. a.** Tending to give freely; generous: *a liberal benefactor.* **b.** Generously given; bountiful: *a liberal helping.* **7.** Not strict or literal: *a liberal translation.*

~n. **1.** A person with liberal ideas or opinions. **2.** *Capital* **L.** *Abbr.* **Lib.** A member of a Liberal political party. [Middle English, from Old French, from Latin *līberālis,* of freedom, from *līber,* free.] **—lib·er·al·ly** *adv.* **—lib·er·al·ness** *n.*

liberal arts *pl.n.* Academic disciplines, such as languages, history, philosophy, and pure science, that provide information of general cultural concern, as distinguished from narrow practical training.

Liberal Democrat Party. A political party formed in British in 1988 from the merger of the Liberal Party with the majority of SDP members. **—Liberal Democrat** *n. & adj.*

lib·er·al·ise, lib·er·al·ize (líbbrə-līz, líbbərə-) *v.* **-ised, -ising, -ises.** *—tr.* To make liberal or more liberal. *—intr.* To become liberal or more liberal. **—lib·er·al·i·sa·tion** (-ī-záysh'n || *U.S.* -i-) *n.*

lib·er·al·ism (líbbrə-líz'm, líbbərə-) *n.* Liberal views and policies, especially with regard to social or political questions.

lib·er·al·i·ty (líbbə-rál-əti) *n., pl.* **-ties. 1.** The quality or state of being liberal. **2.** A generous gift.

Liberal Party *n.* A political party advocating liberalism; especially, a party formed in Great Britain in the 19th century.

liberal studies *n. Usually used with a singular verb.* An arts course consisting of literature, social studies, and the like, taken by students undergoing further education whose main courses are usually technical, professional, or scientific.

lib·er·ate (líbbə-rayt) *tr.v.* **-ated, -ating, -ates. 1.** To free, as from oppression, repression, bondage, or foreign control. **2.** *Chemistry.* To release from combination. Used especially of gases. **3.** *Slang.* To obtain by looting; steal. In this sense, used ironically. [Latin *līberāre,* from *līber,* free.] **—lib·er·a·tion** (-ráysh'n) *n.* **—lib·er·a·tion·ist** *n.* **—lib·er·a·tor** (-raytər) *n.*

liberation theology *n.* A school of theology, especially prevalent in the Catholic Church in Latin America, seeing in the Gospel a call to liberate people from political and material oppression.

Li·be·ri·a, Republic of (lī-beér-i-ə). Africa's oldest independent republic, founded as a home for freed U.S. slaves early in the 19th century, lately in civil war. It has a large flag-of-convenience merchant navy. Most Liberians are subsistence farmers, although the country exports iron ore, rubber, rice, coffee, and sugar. Area, 97 754 square kilometres (37,743 square miles). Population 2,810,000. Capital, Monrovia. **—Li·be·ri·an** *n. & adj.*

lib·er·tar·i·an (líbbər-taír-i-ən) *n.* **1.** One who believes in freedom, especially individual freedom, of action and thought. **2.** One who believes in free will as opposed to determinism. [From LIBERTY.] **—lib·er·tar·i·an** *adj.* **—lib·er·tar·i·an·ism** *n.*

lib·er·tine (líbbər-teen, -tin, -tīn) *n.* **1.** One who acts without moral or sexual restraint; a dissolute person. **2.** One standing in defiance of established moral precepts.

~adj. Morally or sexually unrestrained. [Middle English *libertyn* (only in the sense "freed slave"), from Latin *lībertīnus,* from *lībertus,* set free, from *līber,* free.]

lib·er·tin·ism (líbbərti-niz'm) *n.* Also **lib·er·tin·age** (-nij). **1.** Sexual promiscuity. **2.** *Rare.* Freedom of thought.

lib·er·ty (líbbərti) *n., pl.* **-ties. 1. a.** The condition of being not subject to restriction or control. **b.** The right to act in a manner of one's own choosing. **2.** The state of not being in confinement or servitude. **3.** Permission or right to do a specific thing; a privilege. **4.** *Often plural.* **a.** A social action regarded as more familiar than polite convention permits: *Is it a liberty to address you by your first name?* **b.** A statement, attitude, or action not warranted by conditions or actualities: *a historical novel that takes liberties with chronology.* **5.** Authorised leave from naval duty. **—at liberty. 1.** Not in confinement or under constraint; free. **2.** Not occupied or in use. [Middle English *liberte,* from Old French, from Latin *lībertās* (stem *lībertāt-*), from *līber,* free.]

liberty bodice *n. Sometimes capital* **L**. A trademark for an item of underwear for women and children, similar to a sleeveless vest, and usually made of thick cotton with buttons down the front.

liberty cap *n.* **1.** A brimless cap that fits snugly around the head and has a soft conical crown. Compare **Phrygian cap**. **2.** A magic mushroom *(see)*. [Adopted as a symbol of liberty during the French Revolution. In ancient Rome such caps were presented to slaves when they were freed.]

liberty hall *n. Informal.* **1.** A place in which one can behave as one likes. **2.** A state of absolute freedom.

liberty ship *n.* A large U.S. cargo ship of a type produced in large numbers during World War II.

li·bid·i·nous (li-bíddinəss) *adj.* Characterised by or having lustful desires; licentious; lascivious. [Middle English *lybydynous,* from Latin *libīdinōsus,* from *libīdō,* desire, LIBIDO.]

li·bi·do (li-bée-dō, -bí-, líbbi-dō) *n., pl.* **-dos. 1.** The psychic and emotional energy associated with instinctual biological drives. **2. a.** Sexual desire. **b.** Manifestation of the sexual drive. [Latin *libīdō,* desire, lust.] —**li·bid·i·nal** (li-biddin'l) *adj.*

li·bra (lí-brə *for sense 1;* lee-brə *for sense 2*) *n., pl.* **-brae** (-bree) (for sense 1) or **-bras** (-brəz) (for sense 2). **1.** A unit of weight in ancient Rome like a pound and equivalent to approximately 12 ounces. **2.** A former gold coin of Peru. [Latin *libra,* "pound", balance.]

Li·bra (lée-brə, lí-, líbbrə) *n.* **1.** A constellation in the Southern Hemisphere near Scorpius and Virgo. **2. a.** The seventh sign of the **zodiac** *(see)*. Also called the "Balance", the "Scales". **b.** One born under this sign. [New Latin, from Latin *libra,* balance. See **libra**.] —**Lib·ran** *n. & adj.*

li·brar·i·an (li-braír-i-ən) *n. Abbr.* **lib. 1.** A person in charge of a library. **2.** One trained or employed in library administration.

li·brar·i·an·ship (lí-braír-i-ən-ship ‖ *U.S.* -brérri-) *n. Chiefly British.* The principles or practice of library administration.

li·brar·y (lí-brəri, -bri ‖ *U.S.* -brerri) *n., pl.* **-ies.** *Abbr.* **lib. 1.** A repository for literary and artistic materials, such as books, periodicals, newspapers, pamphlets, and prints, kept for reading or reference. **2.** A collection of such material, especially when systematically arranged for reference or borrowing. **3. a.** An institution or foundation maintaining such a collection. **b.** A room in a private home set aside to house such a collection. **4.** A series or set of books issued by a publisher. **5.** A collection of standard computer programs. [Middle English *librarie,* from Old French *librairie,* from Vulgar Latin *librāriā* (unattested), alteration of Latin *librāria (taberna),* book (shop), from *liber†,* book.]

library edition *n.* A special edition of a book, usually large, strongly bound, and of superior quality.

Library of Congress classification *n.* A system of classification of books and other publications using a notation of letters of the alphabet and numbers. Compare **Dewey Decimal System**. [After the *Library of Congress,* the national library of the United States in Washington, D.C. founded in 1800.]

library science *n.* Librarianship.

li·brate (lí-bráyt ‖ lí-brayt) *intr.v.* **-brated, -brating, -brates. 1.** To oscillate; undergo libration. **2.** To balance; hover. [Latin *librāre* (past participle *librātus*), from *libra,* balance.] —**li·bra·to·ry** (-əri, líbrə-tri, -təri) *adj.*

li·bra·tion (li-bráysh'n) *n.* A real or apparent very slow oscillation of a satellite as viewed from its parent celestial body.

li·bret·tist (li-bréttist) *n.* The author of a libretto.

li·bret·to (li-bréttō) *n., pl.* **-tos** or **-bretti** (-bréttee). The text of an opera or other dramatic musical work. [Italian, diminutive of *libro,* book, from Latin *liber†.*]

Li·bre·ville (lée·brə-vil). Capital and chief port of Gabon, lying on the Gabon river estuary. It was founded as a French trading post, and renamed Libreville (1848) after freed slaves were settled there.

Lib·y·a (líbbi-ə, líb-yə). Also **Socialist People's Libyan Arab Jamahiriya**. Republic in North Africa, the first independent state created by the United Nations (1951). Oil discoveries brought great

prosperity in the 1970s, and the nationalised oil industry remains the basis of the economy. In 1969 King Idris was deposed by Colonel Gaddafi, and the country has since been run as an Islamic state. Area, 1 775 540 square kilometres (685,524 square miles). Population, 5,590,000. Capital, Tripoli.

Lib·y·an (líbbi-ən, líb-yən) *adj.* Of or pertaining to Libya, its people, or their language.
~*n.* **1.** A native or resident of Libya. **2.** The extinct Hamitic language used in ancient Libya.

lice. Plural of **louse**.

li·cence, *U.S.* **li·cense** (lí-s'nss) *n.* **1.** Official or legal permission to do or own a specified thing. **2.** Proof of permission granted, usually in the form of a document, card, or plate: *a television licence.* Compare **certificate**. **3.** Deviation from normal rules, practices, or methods in order to achieve a certain end or effect: *artistic licence.* **4.** An instance of such deviation. **5.** Freedom from strict rules, especially concerning behaviour or speech. **6.** Excessive or undisciplined freedom constituting an abuse of a privilege. **7.** Lust; licentiousness. [See **license**.]

Usage: The spelling of *licence* and *license* is often confused in British English (not so in American English, where *license* is the normal form in all uses). *Licence* is the noun; *license* is the correct form for the verb and derivative uses (as in *licensed premises*).

li·cense (lí-s'nss) *tr.v.* **-censed, -censing, -censes. 1.** To give or yield permission to or for. **2.** To grant a licence to or for; authorise. **3.** To obtain a licence for: *Have you licensed the car yet?* [Middle English *licence,* from Old French *licence,* from Latin *licentia,* freedom, from *licēre,* to be lawful, be permitted. See **leisure**.] —**li·cens·a·ble** *adj.* —**li·cen·ser, li·cen·sor** *n.*

licensed premises *pl.n.* A place, such as a public house or hotel, licensed to sell alcohol to be consumed there. Compare **off-licence**.

li·cen·see (lí-s'n-sée) *n.* One to whom a licence is granted; especially, one licensed to sell beer and spirits.

li·cen·ti·ate (li-sénshi-ət, -it ‖ li-) *n.* **1. a.** A person who is granted a licence by an authorised body to practise a specific profession. **b.** A person licensed to preach, especially in the Presbyterian Church. **2.** *Abbr.* **L. a.** A degree from certain European universities ranking below that of a doctorate. **b.** One holding such a degree. [Medieval Latin *licentiātus,* from *licentiāre,* to allow, from Latin *licentia,* freedom, LICENCE.]

li·cen·tious (li-sénshəss) *adj.* **1.** Lacking moral discipline or sexual restraint. **2.** Having no regard for accepted rules or standards. [Latin *licentiōsus,* from *licentia,* freedom, dissoluteness, LICENCE.] —**li·cen·tious·ly** *adv.* —**li·cen·tious·ness** *n.*

lichee. Variant of **lychee**.

li·chen (líkən, lichən) *n.* **1.** Any of numerous plants consisting of a fungus, usually of the class Ascomycetes, in close combination with certain algae, characteristically forming a crustlike, scaly, or branching growth on rocks or tree trunks. **2.** *Pathology.* Any of various skin eruptions occurring primarily in lichen-like patches. ~*tr.v.* **lichened, -chening, -chens.** To cover with lichen or lichens. [Latin *līchēn,* from Greek *leikhēn,* "licker", from *leikhein,* to lick.] —**li·chen·ose** (-ōss, -ōz), **li·chen·ous** *adj.*

li·chen·ol·o·gy (líkə-nólləji) *n.* The botanical study of lichens. —**li·chen·ol·o·gist** *n.*

lich gate, lych gate (lich) *n.* A roofed gateway to a churchyard used originally to rest biers before burial. [Middle English *lycheyate: lich,* body, corpse, Old English *līc* + *gate, yate,* GATE.]

Lich·ten·stein (líktən-stīn, -steen), **Roy** (1923–97). U.S. painter and sculptor. He was a leading exponent of Pop art.

lic·it (líssit) *adj.* Within the law; legal. [Middle English, from Latin *licitus,* from the past participle of *licēre,* to be permitted. See **leisure**.] —**lic·it·ly** *adv.* —**lic·it·ness** *n.*

lick (lik) *v.* **licked, licking, licks.** —*tr.* **1.** To pass the tongue over or along. **2.** To lap up. **3.** To move or flicker over like a tongue: *The waves licked the rocks lining the shore.* **4.** *Informal.* To thrash; whip. **5.** *Informal.* To get the better of; defeat. —*intr.* **1.** To pass over something with or as if with the tongue: *The flames licked at our feet.* **2.** To move rapidly.
~*n.* **1.** The act or process of licking. **2.** A small quantity; a bit: *a lick of paint.* **3.** A place frequented by animals that lick the exposed natural salt deposits. **4.** *Informal.* A blow. **5.** *Informal.* Speed; pace: *at a good lick.* —**lick and a promise.** A quick and not very thorough wash. [Middle English *licken,* Old English *liccian.*] —**lick·er** *n.*

lick·er·ish, li·quor·ish (líckərish) *adj. Archaic.* **1.** Lascivious; lecherous. **2.** Relishing pleasurable sensations. **3.** Greedy. **4.** Arousing hunger; appetising. [Alteration of Middle English *lickerous,* from Anglo-French *likerous* (unattested), variant of Old French *lechereus,* from *lecheor,* LECHER.]

lick·e·ty-split (líckəti-split) *adv. Chiefly U.S. Informal.* With great speed. [From LICK and SPLIT.]

lick·ing (lícking) *n. Informal.* **1.** A beating or spanking. **2.** A resounding defeat.

lick·spit·tle (lík-spitt'l) *n.* A fawning underling; a toady. —**lick·spit·tle** *adj.*

licorice. *U.S.* Variant of **liquorice**.

lic·tor (lík-tər, -tawr) *n.* A Roman functionary who carried fasces in attendance on a magistrate. [Middle English *littour,* from Latin *lictor.*]

lid (lid) *n.* **1.** A removable or sometimes hinged cover for any hollow receptacle. **2.** An eyelid. **3.** *Biology.* A flaplike covering, such as an operculum. **4.** A curb or restraint. **5.** *Slang.* A hat. —**flip (one's)**

lid. *Informal.* **1.** To have a sudden and violent feeling, as of rage or infatuation. **2.** To lose one's sanity; go mad. **—put the (tin) lid on.** *British Slang.* **1.** To be the climax of a series of misfortunes. **2.** To put an end to. **—take the lid off.** To expose the scandalous truth about. [Middle English, Old English *hlid,* covering, gate, opening.] **—lid·ded** *adj.*

li·dar (lī-daar) *n.* A type of radar using a directional laser or maser beam. [*Li*ght + ra*dar.*]

Li·di·ce (líddit-se). Mining village west of Prague, Czechoslovakia, destroyed in 1942 by the German army in retaliation for the assassination of the Nazi chief Reinhard Heydrich. The men were killed and the women and children deported. After the war, a new village was built, the old site being maintained as a memorial.

lid·less (lid-ləss, -liss) *adj.* **1.** Having no lid. **2.** Having no eyelids. Said of animals. **3.** *Archaic.* Sleepless; watchful.

li·do (léedō || līdō) *n., pl.* **-dos.** **1.** An open-air swimming pool for public use, often providing other recreational facilities. **2.** A bathing beach. [Italian, beach of sand or silt separated from the mainland by a lagoon, such as the *Lido,* name of fashionable bathing beach near Venice, from Latin *litus,* shore.]

li·do·caine (līdə-kayn) *n. U.S.* An anaesthetic, **lignocaine** *(see).* [From acetani*lide* + (CO)CAINE.]

lie[1] (lī) *intr.v.* **lay** (lay), **lain** (layn), **lying, lies.** **1.** To be in or place oneself in a prostrate or recumbent position; rest; recline. Often used with *down.* **2. a.** To be placed on or supported by a surface that is usually horizontal. **b.** To float at anchor. Used of a ship. **3.** To be or remain in a specified condition: *The conflict lies dormant.* **4.** To exist; be inherent: *Her good nature lies within her.* **5.** To be located: *The spring lies several miles beyond this village.* **6.** To be buried or entombed. **7.** To extend: *Our land lies between these trees and the river.* **8.** *Archaic.* To stay for a night or short while: *The regiment is lying not far from here.* **9.** To remain on the ground. Used of game birds. **10.** *Law.* To be admissible or maintainable. —See Usage note at **lay.** **—lie down.** To remain impassive in the face of provocation: *She won't take those insults lying down.* **—lie low.** To keep oneself or one's plans hidden. **—lie off.** *Nautical.* To anchor away from the shore or from another ship. **—lie over.** To remain and wait until a future time. **—lie to.** *Nautical.* To remain stationary while facing the wind. **—lie up.** **1.** To remain in one's room, usually when ill. **2.** To be out of use or in need of repair. **—lie with.** **1.** To be decided by, dependent upon, or up to: *The choice lies with you.* **2.** *Archaic.* To have sexual intercourse with.

~n. **1.** The manner or position in which something is situated. **2.** A lair or hiding place of an animal. **3.** In golf, the position of a ball that has come to a stop. **—the lie of the land.** **1.** The physical characteristics of a piece of land. **2.** A social or political state of affairs, usually in the process of changing. [Lie, lay, lain; Middle English *lien* or *lig(g)en, lay, ley(e)n,* Old English *licgan, læg, legen.*]

lie[2] *n.* **1.** A false statement or piece of information deliberately presented as being true; a falsehood. **2.** Anything meant to deceive or give a wrong impression. **—give the lie to.** **1.** To prove to be untrue; belie. **2.** To accuse of lying; contradict.

~v. **lied, lying, lies.** *—intr.* **1.** To present false information with the intention of deceiving. **2.** To convey a false image or impression: *Appearances often lie.* *—tr.* To put in a specific condition through deceit: *lied herself into trouble.* [Middle English *ligen, lien,* Old English *lēogan.*]

Lie (lee), **Trygve (Halvdan)** (1896–1968). Norwegian politician and first Secretary-General of the United Nations (1946–53).

Lieb·frau·milch (léeb-frow-milk || *German* léep-, -milkh) *n.* A white wine from the Rhine region. [German : *Liebfrau,* the Virgin Mary (to whom the convent where the wine was first produced was dedicated) + *Milch,* milk.]

Lie·big (lée-big, *German* -bikh), **Justus, Baron von** (1803–73). German chemist. He discovered chloral, and later revealed the importance in plant growth of atmospheric nitrogen and carbon dioxide and of soil minerals.

Liebig condenser *n. Chemistry.* A simple laboratory condenser, usually of glass, having a straight central tube surrounded by a jacket through which cold water is passed. [After Justus von LIEBIG.]

Lieb·knecht (*German* léep-knekht), **Karl** (1871–1919). German politician, son of Wilhelm. Expelled from the Social Democratic Party in 1916, he engaged in illegal antiwar activity with Rosa Luxemburg in the Spartacusbund, which was to become the German Communist Party. In 1919 he led an unsuccessful uprising and was arrested and murdered by army officers.

Liebknecht, Wilhelm (1826–1900). German pacifist politician. With August Bebel (1840–1913), he founded the German Social Democratic Labour party in 1869.

Liech·ten·stein (liktən-stīn). *German* **Für·sten·tum Liech·ten·stein** (fűrstəntōōm léekht'n-shtīn). Small, landlocked Alpine principality in central Europe. It has a customs and currency union with neighbouring Switzerland, which looks after its defence and foreign affairs. Area 160 square kilometres (64 square miles). Population 30,000. Capital, Vaduz.

lied (leed; *German* leet) *n., pl.* **lieder** (léedər). A German song in the style of a ballad for solo voice and piano. [German *Lied,* song, from Old High German *liod.*]

lie detector *n.* A **polygraph** *(see)* used to detect lying in a person undergoing interrogation.

lief (leef) *adv. Archaic.* Readily; willingly: *as lief go now as later.*

~adj. Archaic. **1.** Beloved; dear. **2.** Ready or willing. [Middle English *le(e)f, lif,* from *le(e)f,* "beloved", Old English *lēof.*]

liege (leej, *also* leezh) *n.* **1.** A lord or sovereign in feudal law. **2.** A vassal or subject owing allegiance and services to a lord or sovereign under feudal law.

~adj. **1.** Of, pertaining to, or designating the relationship between a vassal or subject and his lord. **2.** Entitled to the loyalty and services of his vassals or subjects. Said of a feudal lord. **3.** Bound to give such allegiance and services to a lord or monarch. Said of a feudal vassal or subject. **4.** Loyal. [Middle English *li(e)ge, lege,* from Old French *li(e)ge,* from Medieval Latin *lēticus, laeticus,* from *lētus, lītus,* serf, from Germanic.]

Li·ège (li-áyzh, *French* -ézh). *Flemish* **Luik** (loyk); *German* **Lüt·tich** (lűttikh). City on the river Meuse, Belgium. It is a centre of the country's steel, engineering, and arms industries.

liege·man (léej-man, -mən) *n., pl.* **-men** (-men, -mən). **1.** A feudal vassal or subject. **2.** A loyal supporter or follower.

lie in *intr.v.* **1.** *Archaic.* To be in confinement for childbirth. **2.** To stay in bed late into the morning.

lie-in (lī-ín) *n.* A long sleep or stay in bed late into the morning.

lien (léern, lée-ən || leen) *n. Law.* The right to take and hold or sell the property of a debtor as security or payment for a debt. [Old French *l(o)ien,* bond, tie, from Latin *ligāmen,* from *ligāre,* to bind.]

li·e·nal (lī-ən'l, lī-éen'l) *adj.* Of or pertaining to the spleen. [Latin *liēn,* spleen.]

li·en·ter·y (lī-ən-tri, -təri || -terri) *n.* Diarrhoea in which the faeces contains undigested food. [French, *lientérie,* from Greek *leienteria* : *leios,* smooth + *entera,* intestine.]

li·erne (li-érn) *n. Architecture.* A reinforcing rib used in Gothic vaulting to connect the intersections and bosses of the primary ribs. [French, from Old French, from *lier,* to bind, from Latin *ligāre,* to bind.]

lieu (lew, lōō) *n.* Place; stead. Used chiefly in the phrase *in lieu of.* [Middle English *liue,* from Old French *lieu,* from Latin *locus,* place, LOCUS.]

lieu·ten·ant (lef-ténnənt, ləf-; *but for sense 2* lə-ténnənt, le-, lōō-, *and for sense 3* lōō-ténnənt) *n. Abbr.* **Lieut., Lt.** *Military.* **1.** Either of two officers in the British and other armies and various other military, police, and civilian organisations: **a.** A commissioned officer of the lowest rank, a **second lieutenant** *(see).* **b.** An officer ranking between a captain and a second lieutenant. In this sense, also *U.S.* "first lieutenant". **2.** An officer of the British and other navies, ranking between a lieutenant-commander and a sublieutenant, equivalent in rank to a captain in the army. **3.** Either of two officers in the U.S. navy: **a.** A *lieutenant junior grade,* ranking between a lieutenant senior grade and an ensign. **b.** A *lieutenant senior grade,* ranking between a lieutenant-commander and a lieutenant junior grade. **4.** One who is second in command to and sometimes acts in place of a superior; a deputy. [Originally, "officer who acts for a superior", from Middle English *lieutenaunt,* vice regent, from Old French *lieutenant* : *lieu,* LIEU + *tenant,* present participle of *tenir,* to hold, from Vulgar Latin *tenīre* (unattested), from Latin *tenēre.*] **—lieu·ten·an·cy** *n.*

lieu·ten·ant-colo·nel, *U.S.* **lieutenant colonel** (lef-ténnənt-kérn'l, ləf- || *U.S.* lōō-) *n. Abbr.* **Lt. Col.** *Military.* An officer of the British army and various other armies, air forces, and marine corps, ranking between a colonel and a major.

lieu·ten·ant-com·mand·er, *U.S.* **lieutenant commander** (lə-ténnənt-kə-maándər, le-, lōō- || -mándər) *n. Abbr.* **Lt. Comdr.** An officer of the British and other navies ranking between a commander and a lieutenant.

lieu·ten·ant-gen·e·ral, *U.S.* **lieutenant general** (lef-ténnənt-jénrəl, ləf-, -ərəl || *U.S.* lōō-) *n. Abbr.* **Lt. Gen.** An officer of the British army and various other armies, air forces, and marine corps, ranking between a general and a major general.

lieutenant governor *n. Abbr.* **Lt. Gov.** **1.** Also **lieu·ten·ant-gov·er·nor** (lef-ténnənt-gúv-nər, ləf-, -ərnər || *U.S.* lōō-). A deputy governor. **2.** An elected state official ranking just below the governor of a U.S. state. **3.** The appointed head of government of a Canadian province.

life (līf) *n., pl.* **lives** (līvz). **1.** The property or quality manifested in functions such as metabolism, growth, response to stimulation, and reproduction, by which living organisms are distinguished from dead organisms or from inanimate matter. **2.** The characteristic state or condition of a living organism. **3.** Living organisms collectively: *plant life.* **4.** A living being, especially a person, contrasted with one no longer alive: *lives lost in battle.* **5.** The interval between the birth or inception of an organism and its death. **6. a.** The remainder of one's life: *paralysed for life.* Also used adjectivally: *a life sentence.* **b.** *Slang.* A sentence of life imprisonment: *For such a vicious murder, he should have got life.* **7.** The period of one's life that has already passed: *She has suffered from rheumatism all her life.* **8.** The interval or amount of time during which anything exists or functions: *the operating life of a machine.* **9. a.** A spiritual state regarded as a transcending of death. **b.** Salvation. **10.** An account of a person's life; a biography: *lives of the saints.* **11. a.** Human activities, relationships, and interests collectively: *everyday life.* **b.** A career; prospects: *made a new life for herself in Australia.* **c.** A mode of activity or existence: *country life.* **12.** A pleasant, easy, or luxurious manner of existence: *That's the life.* **13.** An animating force; a source of vitality. **14.** Animation, spirit, or liveliness: *full of life.* **15.** Strength or freshness of flavour. **16.** In fine arts: **a.** A living person or model regarded as an artistic subject: *painted from* *life.* Also used adjectivally: *life drawing.* **b.** Actual environment or reality; nature. **17. a.** A chance to live again; specifically, an immunity to fatal accident or an exemption from death at the last moment: *That cat has nine lives.* **b.** In games, any of an allotted number of chances to take part prior to exclusion. **—as big or large as life. 1.** Life-size. **2.** *Informal.* Physically real; living; vital. **—bring to life. 1.** To cause to regain consciousness. **2.** To put spirit into; animate. **3.** To make lifelike. **—come to life. 1.** To regain consciousness. **2.** To become or seem to become animated; grow lively or lifelike. **—for dear life.** Desperately or urgently. **—for life. 1.** Until the end of one's life. **2.** So as to save one's life. **—for the life of (one).** *Informal.* Though trying hard. Used with negative expressions: *For the life of me I couldn't remember her name.* **—get a life.** *Informal.* To get a life worth living and stop being a misery. **—lay down (one's) life.** To sacrifice one's life. **—not on your life.** *Informal.* Not for any reason; definitely not. **—take (someone's) life.** To kill. **—the good life.** An affluent, luxurious lifestyle. **—the life and soul of the party.** An animated or amusing person who is the centre of attention at a social gathering. **—the life of Riley.** *Informal.* An easy or good lifestyle. **—to save (one's) life.** No matter how hard one tries: *I can't dance to save my life.* **—to the life.** Exactly or closely resembling a model or original. **—true to life.** Not deviating from reality; faithfully representing real life. [Middle English *lif(e)*, Old English *līf*.]

Life. See **Liffey.**

life assurance *n.* Assurance that guarantees a specific sum of money to a beneficiary when the insured dies or to the insured if he lives beyond a certain age. Also called "life insurance".

life belt *n.* A large ring of buoyant material designed to keep a person afloat.

life·blood (līf-blud, -blúd) *n.* **1.** Blood regarded as essential for life. **2.** The indispensable vital part of a thing.

life·boat (līf-bōt) *n.* **1.** A boat carried on a ship to sustain persons abandoning the ship. **2.** A boat used for rescuing people at sea.

life buoy *n.* Any of various devices for keeping people afloat.

life cycle *n.* **1.** The course of developmental changes through which an organism passes from its inception as a fertilised zygote to the mature state in which another zygote may be produced. **2.** A progression through a series of differing stages of development, as in insect metamorphosis.

life estate *n.* Property which a person can hold during his lifetime, but may not sell or bequeath to anyone else.

life expectancy *n.* The statistically determined number of years that an individual is expected to live.

life·guard (līf-gaard) *n.* An expert swimmer trained and employed to safeguard swimmers or bathers. Also called "lifesaver".

Life Guards *pl.n.* A British regiment, formerly of cavalry and now (in combat) of armour, making up with the Blues and Royals the mounted section of the Household Division. **—Life Guardsman** *n.*

life history *n.* **1.** The history of changes undergone by an organism from inception or conception to death. **2.** The developmental history of an individual or group in society.

life instinct *n. Psychology.* An instinct that includes the impulses for self-preservation and reproduction.

life insurance *n.* **Life assurance** *(see).*

life interest *n.* Interest payable to a person during his lifetime, which lapses when he dies.

life jacket *n.* An inflatable sleeveless jacket designed to keep the wearer afloat in water.

life·less (līf-ləss, -liss) *adj.* **1.** Having no life; inanimate. **2.** Having lost life; dead. **3.** Incapable of sustaining life; not inhabited by living beings. **4.** Lacking vitality or animation; dull; listless. —See Synonyms at **dead. —life·less·ly** *adv.* **—life·less·ness** *n.*

life·like (līf-līk) *adj.* **1.** Resembling a living thing. **2.** Accurately representing real life. **—life·like·ness** *n.*

life·line (līf-līn) *n.* **1.** An anchored line thrown as a support to someone falling or drowning. **2.** A line shot to a ship in distress either to connect it with the shore or for hauling aboard other lifesaving devices such as heavier lines or breeches buoys. **3.** A line used to raise and lower deep-sea divers. **4. a.** Any means or route by which necessary supplies are transported. **b.** Any person or thing that provides continuous or sustained support in times of difficulty or distress. **5.** A diagonal line crossing the palm of the hand and alleged to indicate the length and major events of one's life.

life·long (līf-long, -lóng || -lawng) *adj.* Continuing for a lifetime.

life peer *n. British.* A peer whose title is bestowed for a lifetime only and lapses at death. **—life peerage** *n.*

life preserver *n.* **1.** *British.* A weapon, such as a club or bludgeon. **2.** *U.S.* A buoyant device, usually in the shape of a ring, belt, or jacket, designed to keep a person afloat in the water.

lif·er (līfər) *n. Slang.* A prisoner serving a life sentence.

life raft *n.* A raft usually made of wood or inflatable material and used in an emergency at sea.

life·sav·er (līf-sayvər) *n.* **1.** One that saves a life. **2.** A **lifeguard** *(see).* **3.** One that provides help in a minor crisis or emergency.

life·sav·ing, life-sav·ing (līf-sayving) *n.* A set of skills or techniques for rescuing and resuscitating the victims of accidents, especially victims of drowning.

~*adj.* **1.** Of or pertaining to the techniques studied in lifesaving: *a lifesaving medal.* **2. a.** Saving life. **b.** Providing help in a minor crisis or emergency.

life science *n.* Any of the fields of science dealing with the structure and function of organisms, such as botany, zoology, biochemistry, genetics, or immunology. Compare **physical science.**

life-size (līf-sīz) *adj.* Also **life-sized** (-sīzd). Being of the same size as the person, animal, or thing represented.

life span *n.* The period of time during which an organism or machine remains alive or functional under normal conditions.

life·style, life-style (līf-stīl) *n.* An internally consistent way of life or style of living that reflects the attitudes and values of an individual or a culture.

life-sup·port system (līf-sə-pawrt || -pōrt) *n.* **1.** The equipment that provides a viable environment where this would not normally be possible, as in a spacecraft or below the sea. **2.** Hospital equipment that artificially sustains life.

life·time (līf-tīm) *n.* **1.** The period of time during which an individual is alive. **2.** The interval or amount of time during which an object, property, process, or phenomenon exists or functions. **3.** *Physics.* The average time of existence of an unstable particle or nucleus. Also called "mean life".

~*adj.* Continuing or lasting a lifetime: *a lifetime guarantee.*

life·work (līf-wúrk) *n.* Also **life's work.** The chief work or creation of one's lifetime.

Lif·fey (líffi). *Irish* **Li·fe.** River in the Republic of Ireland, flowing from the Wicklow Mountains into the Irish Sea at Dublin.

lift (lift) *v.* **lifted, lifting, lifts.** —*tr.* **1.** To direct or carry from a lower to a higher position; raise; elevate: *lift the suitcase; lift one's eyes.* **2.** To pick up for the purpose of moving or removing: *lift the child from the sandpit; lift a suitcase down.* **3. a.** To take back or remove; revoke; rescind: *lift a ban.* **b.** To bring an end to (a blockade or siege) by removing forces. **c.** To cease (artillery fire) on an area. **4.** To raise in condition, rank, esteem, or value; exalt: *Her courage lifted her in their eyes.* **5.** To remove (plants) from the ground for transplanting. **6.** To project or sound in loud, clear tones: *lifted their voices in song.* **7.** *Informal.* To steal; pilfer. **8.** *Informal.* To plagiarise. **9.** *U.S.* To pay off or clear (a debt or mortgage, for example). **10.** To perform cosmetic surgery on (the face or breasts), especially to remove wrinkles or sag. **11. a.** In golf and cricket, to hit (the ball) very high into the air. **b.** In golf, to pick up (the ball) in the hand to put in a better position. **12.** To carry (a passenger or goods) in a vehicle. —*intr.* **1.** To rise; ascend. **2.** To disappear or disperse by or as if by rising: *The clouds had lifted.* **3.** To use force or energy in or as if in lifting something. **4.** To yield to upward force: *The window won't lift.* **5.** To stop temporarily.

~*n.* **1.** The act or process of raising or rising to a higher position. **2.** Power or force available for raising: *the lift of a pump.* **3.** An amount or weight raised or capable of being raised at one time; a load. **4.** The extent or height to which something is raised; the amount of elevation. **5.** The distance or space through which something is raised. **6.** A rising of the level of the ground. **7.** A rising of spirits; a mood of exhilaration or happiness. **8.** A raised, high, or erect position: *the lift of her chin.* **9.** A machine or device designed to pick up, raise, or carry something. **10.** Any of the layers of leather, rubber, or other material making up the heel of a shoe. **11. a.** *Chiefly British.* A platform or enclosure raised and lowered in a vertical shaft to transport goods or people. Also *chiefly U.S.* "elevator". **b.** An apparatus for transporting people up and down a mountain; a **chair lift** *(see).* **12.** A ride given in a vehicle to help someone reach a destination. **13.** Any kind of assistance or help. **14.** A set of pumps used in a mine. **15.** *Aeronautics.* **a.** The component of the total aerodynamic force acting on an aerofoil, or on an entire aircraft or winged missile, perpendicular to the relative wind and normally exerted in an upward direction, opposing the pull of gravity. **b.** The upward force on a balloon, airship, or the like. [Middle English *liften,* from Old Norse *lypta.*] **—lift·er** *n.*

Synonyms: *lift, raise, elevate, hoist, heave, boost.*

lifting body *n.* An aircraft or spacecraft that has no wings and gains lift by the action of aerodynamic forces on its body.

lift off *intr.v.* To commence flight. Used of a rocket or other craft.

lift·off (lift-off, -awff) *n.* **1.** The initial movement by which a rocket or other craft commences flight. **2.** The instant at which this occurs.

lift pump *n.* A simple pump for lifting a liquid to a higher level, typically having a piston with a valve in the base moving vertically in a cylinder.

lig·a·ment (líggə-mənt) *n.* **1.** *Anatomy.* A sheet or band of tough, fibrous tissue connecting two or more bones or cartilages, or supporting an organ, fascia, or muscle. **2.** Any unifying or connecting tie or bond. [Middle English, from Latin *ligāmentum,* bond, bandage, from *ligāre,* to bind.] **—lig·a·men·tal** (-mént'l), **lig·a·men·ta·ry** (-méntəri), **lig·a·men·tous** (-méntəss) *adj.*

ligan. Variant of **lagan.**

lig·and (líggənd, līgənd) *n. Chemistry.* An atom, ion, group, or molecule that is linked to a central atom in an inorganic coordination compound. [Latin *ligandum,* gerund of *ligāre,* to bind.]

li·gase (lī-gayz, -gayss) *n.* An enzyme that catalyses the linkage of molecules, using ATP as an energy source. [Latin *ligāre,* to bind + -ASE.]

li·gate (lī-gáyt || lī-gayt) *tr.v.* **-gated, -gating, -gates.** To tie up, bind, or constrict with a ligature. [Latin *ligāre,* to bind.]

li·ga·tion (lī-gáysh'n) *n.* **1.** The act of binding or applying a ligature. **2.** The state of being bound. **3.** Something that binds; a ligature.

lig·a·ture (líggə-chər, -tewr) *n.* **1.** The act of tying together, binding, or constricting. **2.** A cord, wire, or bandage used for tying, binding, or constricting. **3.** Something that unites; a bond. **4.** In surgery, a thread, wire, cord, or the like, applied in a tight loop, as to close vessels, tie off ducts, or constrict a growth. **5.** A character or type

combining two or more letters, such as *fi.* **6.** *Music.* **a.** A group of notes intended to be played or sung as one phrase. **b.** A curved line indicating such a phrase; a slur.
~tr.v. **ligatured, -turing, -tures.** To ligate. [Middle English, from Latin *ligātūra,* from *ligāre,* to bind.]

li·ger (līgər) *n.* A hybrid produced by the mating of a female tiger and a male lion. [Blend of *lion* + *tiger.*]

Li·ge·ti (líggeti), **György (Sándor)** (1923–). Hungarian avant-garde composer. In Vienna after 1956. Works include: *Apparitions* (1958–59), a double concerto (1972), *The San Francisco Polyphony* (1996).

light[1] (līt) *n.* **1.** *Physics.* **a.** Electromagnetic radiation that has a wavelength in about the range 380–780 nanometres and that may be perceived by the normal, unaided human eye. **b.** Loosely, other electromagnetic radiation that is close to light in wavelength, but not visible: *ultraviolet light.* **2.** The sensation of the perception of such radiation; brightness. **3.** A source of illumination, such as the sun or an electric lamp. **4. a.** The illumination derived from such a source: *by the light of the moon.* **b.** The particular quality or amount of such illumination: *Play was abandoned because of bad light.* **c.** The path by which light reaches a person: *You're standing in my light.* **5.** Daylight. **6.** Dawn; daybreak. **7. a.** Something that admits light, such as a window. **b.** *Often plural.* Daylight falling on a window. See **ancient lights. 8.** A means or agent, such as a match or cigarette lighter, for igniting something. **9. a.** Something that provides clarification or elucidation: *shed some light on the problem.* **b.** A state of understanding or awareness, especially as derived from a particular source: *saw the light; in the light of experience.* **10.** The state of being visible, publicly available, or generally known; public attention or awareness: *bring new facts to light.* **11.** A way of regarding something; an angle; an aspect: *saw the situation in a new light.* **12.** *Archaic & Poetic.* Eyesight. **13.** *Plural.* One's individual opinions, choices, or life philosophy: *acted according to their own lights.* **14.** A person who inspires or is adored by another: *Her son is the light of her life.* **15.** A prominent or distinguished person, especially one serving as an example for others; a notable or luminary: *the brighter lights of Irish art.* **16.** An expression of the eyes, usually indicative of animation or liveliness. **17. a.** Spiritual illumination. **b.** *Capital* **L.** In Quaker doctrine, the guiding spirit or divine presence in each person. **18. a.** The representation of light in art. **b.** An area of pronounced illumination in a painting or photograph. **19. a.** A traffic light. **b.** A lighthouse beacon.
~v. **lighted** or **lit** (lit), **lighting, lights.** *—tr.* **1.** To set on fire; ignite; kindle. **2.** To cause to give out light; make luminous. **3.** To provide, cover, or fill with light; illuminate. **4.** To guide or direct with or as if with lights. **5.** To enliven or animate: *a smile lighting her face.* *—intr.* To start to burn; be ignited or kindled: *Green wood will not light easily.* —See Usage note at **light[2]**. **—light up. 1.** To become or cause to become light, radiant, or bright. **2.** To become or cause to become animated or cheerful. **3.** *Informal.* To start smoking a cigarette, cigar, or pipe.
~adj. **lighter, lightest.** *Abbr.* **lt. 1.** Having a greater rather than lesser degree of **lightness** *(see).* Said of a colour. **2.** Characterised by or filled with light; radiant; bright. **3.** Pale, as if mixed with white; fair: *a light complexion.* [Middle English *liht, light,* Old English *lēoht, līht.*]

light[2] *adj.* **lighter, lightest. 1.** Of relatively low weight; not heavy. **2.** Of low weight in proportion to bulk; of relatively low density. **3.** Of less than the correct, standard, or lawful weight; underweight: *a light pound.* **4.** Exerting little pressure; having relatively little force or impact: *a light kick.* **5. a.** Having relatively little volume, quantity, or intensity: *a light rain; light traffic.* **b.** Moderate; abstemious: *a light eater; a light smoker.* **6. a.** Having little importance or value; insignificant: *light chatter.* **b.** Characterised by frivolity; silly; trivial. **7.** Intended as entertainment; not serious or profound: *a light comedy.* **8.** Free from worries or troubles; blithe. **9.** Having little moral discipline; wanton. **10.** Suffering from mild delirium or faintness; dizzy. **11.** Moving quickly and easily; graceful; nimble. **12. a.** Designed for ease and quickness of movement; having a slim structure and little weight: *light aircraft.* **b.** Designed to carry relatively small loads: *a light lorry.* **13.** Concerned with the production of relatively small consumer goods: *light industry.* **14.** Performed or endured without significant difficulty or effort: *Many hands make light work.* **15.** Easily disturbed or woken: *a light sleeper.* **16.** *Military.* Carrying little equipment or arms: *a light brigade.* **17.** Characterised by lightness and elegance in design or construction; not ponderous or massive. **18.** Easily digested. **19.** Having a spongy or flaky texture; well-leavened: *light pastries.* **20.** Having a loose, porous consistency; not packed together or solid: *light earth.* **21.** Containing a relatively small amount of alcohol: *a light wine.* **22.** Faint; not bold. Said of type. **23.** In phonetics and prosody, designating a vowel or syllable pronounced with little or no stress. **24.** *Informal.* Lacking an adequate supply of something. Used with *on.* **—make light of.** To regard or treat as insignificant or petty.
~adv. **1.** Lightly. **2.** Without additional weight or burdens; in an unencumbered manner: *travelling light.*
~intr.v. **lighted** or **lit** (lit), **lighting, lights. 1.** To get down, as from a mount or vehicle; dismount; alight. **2.** To descend to the ground after flight; perch; land. **3.** To come upon one unexpectedly; strike suddenly, as a blow or stroke of luck may. Often used with *on* or *upon: Misfortune lighted upon her.* **4.** To come upon an object or idea by chance or accident. Used with *on* or *upon.* **—light into.** *Informal.* To attack verbally or physically; assail. **—light out.** *Informal.* To leave hastily; run off. [Middle English *liht, light,* Old English *lēoht, līht.*]
Usage: The past tense and participle of **light[1]** and **light[2]** is generally *lit. Lighted* is used only in a few special senses; for example, when **light[1]** means "provide with light" (*I was lighted along the corridor by candles*). When **light[2]** is used in the phrases *light on* or *light upon,* meaning "discover", *lighted* and *lit* are both possible: *We lighted/lit upon an old map.* In adjectival use, *lighted* is the usual form, although *lit* is sometimes found, especially if there is a preceding adverb: *a lighted cigarette,* but *a well-lit arcade.*

light air *n.* A wind whose speed is 0.3 to 1.5 metres per second, force 1 on the Beaufort scale.

light breeze *n.* A wind whose speed in 1.6 to 3.3 metres per second, force 2 on the Beaufort scale.

light bulb, light·bulb (līt-bulb) *n.* An electric lamp in which a filament is heated to incandescence by an electric current.

light-emitting diode *n.* See **LED.**

light·en[1] (līt'n) *v.* **-ened, -ening, -ens.** *—tr.* **1. a.** To make light or lighter; illuminate; brighten. **b.** To make (a colour) lighter. **2.** *Archaic.* To enlighten mentally or spiritually, as by imparting knowledge or wisdom to. *—intr.* **1.** To become light or lighter; brighten. **2.** To be luminous; glow; shine. **3.** To produce or give off flashes of lightning. —See Usage note at **lightning.**

lighten[2] *v.* **-ened, -ening, -ens.** *—tr.* **1.** To make less heavy, as by a reduction in weight or load. **2.** To lessen the oppressiveness, trouble, or severity of. **3.** To relieve of cares or worries; gladden. *—intr.* **1.** To become lighter. **2.** To become less oppressive, severe, or troublesome. **3.** To become cheerful. —See Synonyms at **relieve.**

light·er[1] (lītər) *n.* **1.** One that lights or ignites something. **2.** A mechanical device for lighting a cigarette, cigar, or pipe.

lighter[2] *n. Nautical.* A large barge used to transport goods over short distances or to deliver to or unload from a larger cargo ship unable to navigate in shallow water.
~v. **lightered, -ering, -ers.** *—tr.* To convey (cargo) in a lighter. *—intr.* To use a lighter to transport cargo. [Middle English, from Middle Dutch *lichter* (unattested), from *lichten,* to lighten, unload.]

light·er·age (lītərij) *n.* **1.** The transport of goods on a lighter. **2.** The fee charged for such service.

light·er-than-air (lītər-thən-áir) *adj.* Having a weight less than that of the air displaced. Said of certain aircraft.

light·face (līt-fayss) *n. Printing. Abbr.* **lf** A typeface or font of characters having relatively thin, light lines. Compare **boldface. —light·face, light·faced** *adj.*

light-fin·gered (līt-fing-gərd) *adj.* **1.** Having quick and nimble fingers. **2.** Skilled at or given to petty thievery. **—light-fin·gered·ness** *n.*

light flyweight *n.* A wrestler or amateur boxer weighing not more than 48 kilograms (106 pounds).

light-foot·ed (līt-fŏŏtid) *adj.* Also *poetic* **light·foot** (-fŏŏt). Treading with light and nimble ease. **—light-foot·ed·ly** *adv.* **—light-foot·ed·ness** *n.*

light-head·ed (līt-héddid) *adj.* **1.** Delirious, giddy, or faint: *light-headed with wine.* **2.** Frivolous; silly. **—light-head·ed·ly** *adv.* **—light-head·ed·ness** *n.*

light-heart·ed (līt-hártid) *adj.* **1.** Blithe; carefree; gay. **2.** Not serious: *a light-hearted look at the week's news.* —See Synonyms at **glad. —light-heart·ed·ly** *adv.* **—light-heart·ed·ness** *n.*

light heavyweight *n.* **1. a.** An amateur boxer weighing between 75 and 81 kilograms (165 and 178.5 pounds). **b.** A professional boxer weighing between 160 and 175 pounds (72.5 and 79.5 kilograms). **2.** A wrestler weighing between 82 and 90 kilograms (181 and 198.5 pounds).

light·house (līt-howss) *n.* A tall structure topped by a powerful light used as a beacon or signal to aid marine navigation.

light·ing (līting) *n.* **1.** The state of being lighted; illumination. **2. a.** The method or equipment used to provide artificial illumination. **b.** The illumination so provided.

lighting-up time (līting-úp) *n.* The time by which vehicles must have their lights on along public highways.

light·ly (lītli) *adv.* **1.** With little weight or force; gently. **2.** To a slight extent or amount; sparingly; little: *use lightly.* **3.** With buoyancy or ease; quickly and gracefully. **4.** In a carefree manner; cheerfully; blithely: *take the bad news lightly.* **5.** Without enough care or serious consideration; thoughtlessly; indifferently. **6.** Depreciatingly; slightingly.

light meter *n.* In photography, an **exposure meter** *(see).*

light middleweight *n.* An amateur boxer weighing between 67 and 71 kilograms (148 and 157 pounds).

light-mind·ed (līt-mīndid) *adj.* Frivolous, silly, or inane; giddy. **—light-mind·ed·ly** *adv.* **—light-mind·ed·ness** *n.*

light·ness[1] (līt-nəss, -niss) *n.* **1.** The dimension of the colour of an object by which the object appears to reflect or transmit more or less of the incident light, varying from black to white for surface colours, and from black to colourless for transparent volume colours. **2.** The relative paleness of an object or the brightness of a place.

lightness[2] *n.* **1.** The state or quality of having little weight or force. **2.** Ease or quickness of style or movement; agility; nimbleness. **3.** Freedom from worry or trouble; blitheness; gaiety. **4.** Lack of appropriate seriousness; levity.

light·ning (līt-ning) *n.* A large-scale natural electric discharge in the atmosphere in the form of a visible flash of light.
~intr.v. **lightninged** (-ningd), **-ning, -nings.** To discharge a flash or flashes of lightning. Sometimes used impersonally.

~*adj.* Moving with extreme alacrity; very fast or sudden, like a flash of lightning [Middle English *light(e)ning,* from *lightenen,* to illuminate, from LIGHT (illumination).]

Usage: *Lightning* and *lightening* are sometimes confused in spelling, on account of their similar pronunciations. *Lightning* is the noun (as in *thunder and lightning*); *lightening* is a participle form of the verbs **lighten¹** and **lighten²**. Note that it is possible, though rare, to use **lighten¹** to refer to the process that produces lightning: *It was thundering and lightening by the time I returned.*

lightning bug *n. U.S.* A firefly.

lightning conductor *n.* An earthed metal rod placed high on a structure to prevent damage by conducting lightning to the ground. Also *chiefly U.S.* "lightning rod".

lightning strike *n.* **1.** A strike of a work force called at very short notice. **2.** A sudden and intensive military attack.

light opera *n.* An **operetta** *(see).*

light pen *n. Computing.* A photoelectric device shaped like a pen, used to sense and amend data or lines on a visual-display unit.

light ratio *n. Astronomy.* The ratio of the brightness of a star to that of any other star one magnitude fainter, approximately 2.512.

lights (līts) *pl.n.* The lungs, especially of sheep, pigs, or bullocks, used chiefly as pet food. [Middle English *lihte,* from *liht,* LIGHT (not heavy).]

light·ship (līt-ship) *n.* A ship with a powerful light or warning signals anchored in dangerous waters to alert other vessels.

light show *n.* A display of moving coloured lights or slides projected onto a screen or wall, especially in a discotheque.

light·some (līt-səm) *adj.* **1.** Light, nimble, or graceful in movement; buoyant. **2.** Carefree; blithe; cheerful. **3.** Frivolous; silly. —**light·some·ly** *adv.* —**light·some·ness** *n.*

lights out *n. Used with a singular verb.* The time when all lights must be extinguished for the night, as in a military camp, boarding school, or the like.

light water *n.* Ordinary water as distinguished from heavy water.

light·weight (līt-wayt) *n.* **1.** A person, animal, or thing that weighs relatively little. **2.** A person of little ability, intelligence, influence, or importance. **3. a.** An amateur boxer weighing between 57 and 60 kilograms (126 and 132 pounds). **b.** A professional boxer weighing between 130 and 135 pounds (59 and 61 kilograms). **4.** A wrestler weighing between 62 and 68 kilograms (137 and 150 pounds).
~*adj.* **1.** Weighing relatively little; not heavy: *lightweight wool.* **2.** Lacking substance: *lightweight novels.*

light·well (līt-wel) *n.* A vertical shaft running the full depth of a building to admit light into it. Compare **stairwell.** [LIGHT + WELL (sense 3).]

light welterweight *n.* An amateur boxer weighting between 60 and 63.5 kilograms (132 and 140 pounds).

light-year, light year (līt-yeer, -yer) *n.* The distance that light covers travelling in a vacuum for a period of one year, approximately 9.4607×10^{12} kilometres (5.878×10^{12} miles).

lig·ne·ous (líg-ni-əss) *adj.* Consisting of or having the texture or appearance of wood; woody. Said of a plant. [Latin *ligneus,* from *lignum,* wood.]

ligni-, ligno-, lign- *comb. form.* Indicates wood; for example, **lignocellulose, lignin.** [Latin *lignum,* wood.]

lig·ni·fy (líg-ni-fī) *v.* **-fied, -fying, -fies.** —*intr.* To form or turn into wood through the formation and deposit of lignin in cell walls. —*tr.* To make woody or woodlike by the deposit of lignin. [French *lignifier* : LIGNI- + -FY.] —**lig·ni·fi·ca·tion** (-fi-káysh'n) *n.*

lig·nin (líg-nin) *n.* The chief noncarbohydrate constituent of wood, a polymer that functions as a natural binder and support for the cellulose fibres of woody plants. [LIGN- + -IN.]

lig·nite (líg-nīt) *n.* A low-grade, brownish-black coal. Also called "brown coal". [French : LIGN- + -ITE.] —**lig·nit·ic** (-níttik) *adj.*

lig·no·caine (líg-nə-kayn, -nō-) *n.* A local anaesthetic administered by injection or direct application for dental and minor surgical operations. Also *U.S.* "lidocaine". [LIGNO- + (CO)CAINE.]

lig·no·cel·lu·lose (líg-nō-séllew-lōss, -lōz) *n.* Any combination of lignin and cellulose that strengthens plant cells.

lig·num vi·tae (líg-nəm vīti, vée-tī) *n., pl.* **lignum vitaes. 1.** Either of two tropical American trees, *Guaiacum officinale* or *G. sanctum,* having evergreen leaves and heavy, durable, resinous wood. **2.** The wood of either of these trees, used for machine bearings. **3.** Any of several similar or related trees. [New Latin, from Late Latin, "tree or wood of life" : *lignum,* wood + *vītae,* genitive of *vīta,* life.]

lig·ro·in (líggrō-in) *n.* A volatile, flammable fraction of petroleum boiling in the range 70–130°C and used chiefly as a solvent. [20th century : origin obscure.]

lig·u·late (líggew-lət, -lit, -layt) *adj.* **1.** Strap-shaped. **2.** Having a ligule or ligula. [New Latin *ligula,* LIGULE + -ATE.]

lig·ule (líggewl) *n.* A straplike structure, such as a ray flower of a daisy or a sheathlike organ at the base of a grass leaf. [New Latin *ligula,* from Latin, tongue of a shoe, shoe-strap, variant of *lingula,* from *lingua,* tongue.]

lig·ure (líggewr) *n.* A precious stone of ancient Israel. Exodus 28:19. [Middle English *lugre, ligurie,* from Late Latin *ligūrius,* from Greek *ligurion*†, a precious stone.]

Li·gu·ria (li-géwr-i-ə). Autonomous region of northwest Italy. The industrial port of Genoa is the capital.

lik·a·ble, like·a·ble (līk-əb'l) *adj.* Pleasing; attractive. —**lik·a·bil·i·ty** (-ə-bílliti), **lik·a·ble·ness** *n.*

like¹ (līk) *v.* **liked, liking, likes.** —*tr.* **1.** To find pleasant; enjoy. **2.** To feel an attraction, tenderness, or affection for; be fond of. **3.** To want, wish, or prefer. **4.** To feel towards or respond to; view; regard: *How do you like that!* **5.** *Archaic & Poetic.* To agree with; suit or please: *This likes me not.* —*intr.* To have an inclination or preference; desire; choose; wish: *If you like, we can go fishing.*
~*n. Plural.* Preferences or predilections. Used in the phrase *likes and dislikes.* [Middle English *lik(i)en,* Old English *līcian,* to please, be sufficient.] —**lik·er** *n.*

Synonyms: *like, love, enjoy, relish, fancy, dote.*

Usage: *Like* is often followed by an infinitive form of the verb, which may be preceded by a noun or pronoun: *I would like you to travel by bus.* The insertion of *for* (*I would like for you to travel by bus*) is often heard in informal American English, and occasionally in some other English dialects, but it is not considered standard. The forms *would have/should have liked* are usually followed by a simple infinitive form (*They would have liked to go*), rather than by a perfect infinitive as in *They would have liked to have gone*: the double use of *have* is considered unnecessary.

like² *prep.* **1.** Possessing the characteristics of; resembling closely; similar to. **2. a.** In the same way as: *to live like pigs.* **b.** In the typical manner of: *It's not like you to take offence.* **3.** Desirous of; disposed to: *He felt like swimming.* **4.** As if the probability exists for; indicative of: *It looks like a bad season for the English team.* **5.** Such as; for example: *The better wines, like claret, cost more.*
~*adj.* **1.** Possessing the same or almost the same characteristics; similar: *on this and like occasions.* **2.** Having equivalent value or quality. Usually used in negative phrases: *There's nothing like an open fire.* **3.** Alike: *They are as like as two brothers.* **4.** *Archaic & Regional.* Likely: *He's like to cause trouble.*
~*adv.* **1.** *Informal.* Probably; likely: *Like as not she'll change her mind.* **2.** *Nonstandard.* As it were. Used to provide an emphasis or pause: *I thought I would just teach him a lesson, like.*
~*n.* **1.** Similar or related persons or things. Used with *the: He was subject to fevers, coughs, asthma, and the like.* **2.** *Often plural. Informal.* An equivalent or similar person or thing; an equal or match: *I've never seen the likes of this before.*
~*conj. Nonstandard.* **1.** In the same way that; as: *She talks just like you do.* **2.** As if: *He acts like he owns the place.* [Middle English *lic, lik,* Old English *līc* (unattested), short for *gelīc.*]

Usage: The use of *like* as a conjunction is hardly ever acceptable in formal English, where *as* (or *as if, as though*) is preferred. Such sentences as *He acts like he owns the place* and *It looks like we'll win* would have the *like* replaced by *as if* in formal English. *Sort out the books like I told you* would become *as I told you.* There is, however, one case where *like* is a more acceptable variant of *as,* namely, when it introduces a clause in which the verb is not expressed: *The dress looks like new* (compare *The dress looks as if it is new*). Of course, *like* is quite acceptable in its other uses, and there is no need to use *as* in preference. For example, the prepositional use of *like* expresses comparison—*works like a charm, sings like an angel*—whereas the use of *as* here would instead imply a contrast (of manner or role): compare *He asked a question as a beginner* (i.e. he is a beginner) and *He asked a question like a beginner* (i.e. he is behaving as if he were a beginner).

-like *adj. comb. form.* Indicates: **1.** A resemblance or similarity to something specified; for example, **lifelike. 2.** A characteristic of or appropriateness to something specified; for example, **childlike, ladylike.** [From LIKE (preposition).]

like·li·hood (līkli-hŏŏd) *n.* The state of being likely; probability.

like·ly (līkli) *adj.* **-lier, -liest. 1.** Having, expressing, or exhibiting an inclination or probability; apt. Used with an infinitive: *They are likely to become angry with him.* **2.** That can with reasonable confidence be expected to occur; probable: *the likely outcome; More rain is likely.* **3.** Within the realm of credibility; seeming to be true; plausible: *a likely excuse.* **4.** Apparently appropriate or suitable for a purpose: *phoned round all the likely shops.* **5.** Apparently capable of doing well or becoming successful; promising: *a likely lad.* **6.** *Chiefly U.S.* Attractive; pleasant; enjoyable.
~*adv.* Probably. —**not likely.** Definitely not. [Middle English *likely,* from Old Norse *līkligr,* from *līkr,* like.]

Usage: As an adverb, *likely* normally requires a qualifying word, in British English, such as *quite, very,* or *most: I will very likely arrive by six.* If you do not wish to use a qualifying word, it is preferable to use an alternative word, such as *probably.*

like-mind·ed (līk-mīndid) *adj.* Of the same turn of mind.

lik·en (līkən) *tr.v.* **-ened, -ening, -ens.** To see, mention, or show as being like or similar; compare. [Middle English *lik(n)en,* from *lik,* LIKE (adjective).]

like·ness (līk-nəss, -niss) *n.* **1.** The state or quality of resembling or being like something. **2.** An imitative appearance; a semblance or guise. **3.** A pictorial, graphic, or sculptured representation of someone or something; an image.

Synonyms: *likeness, similarity, similitude, resemblance, analogy, affinity.*

like·wise (līk-wīz) *adv.* **1.** In the same way; similarly. **2.** As well; also; too. —See Synonyms at **also.**

Usage: *Likewise* is considered to be an adverb (*She did likewise*) in standard English, and its occasional informal use as a conjunction attracts criticism: *Her speech, likewise her manner, upset me.*

lik·ing (līking) *n.* **1.** The state or act of someone who likes. **2.** A feeling of attraction, tenderness, or love; fondness; affection. **3.** Preference; inclination; taste: *Was the meal to your liking?*

li·ku·ta (li-kŏŏtaa) *n., pl.* **makuta** (maa-). A coin equal to 1/100 of the zaire of Zaire. [Native word in Zaire.]

li·lac (lī́-lək || -lak, -lok) *n.* **1.** Any of various shrubs of the genus *Syringa;* especially, *S. vulgaris,* widely cultivated for its clusters of fragrant purplish or white flowers. **2.** Pale purple; mauve. [Obsolete French, from Spanish, from Arabic *līlak,* from Persian, variant of *nīlak,* from *nīl,* indigo, blue.] **—li·lac** *adj.*

li·la·ngeni (lée-lang-gáyni) *n., pl.* **emalangeni** (émma-). The standard monetary unit of Swaziland equal to 100 cents. [SiSwati : *li-,* singular prefix + *-langeni,* money.]

lil·i·a·ceous (lílli-áyshəss) *adj.* Of, pertaining to, or belonging to the Liliaceae, a family of flowering plants including lilies, tulips, and onions. [Late Latin *līliāceus,* from *līlium,* lily.]

Lil·ith (líllith). **1.** In ancient Semitic legend, an evil female spirit or demon alleged to haunt lonely, deserted places and attack children. **2.** In Hebrew folklore, the first wife of Adam, believed to have been in existence before the creation of Eve. **3.** A witch in medieval legend. [Hebrew *līlīth.*]

Lille (leel). Administrative centre of the Nord département, north France. It was the birthplace of Charles de Gaulle.

Lil·lie (lílli), **Beatrice (Gladys)** (1898–1989). British actress and singer, born in Canada. She made her London stage debut in 1914 and her first film, *Exit Smiling,* in 1926.

Lil·li·pu·tian (lílli-péwsh'n) *n.* **1.** A very small person or being. **2.** A person of little intelligence, worth, or significance.
~adj. **1.** Very small; diminutive. **2.** Trivial; petty. [After *Lilliput,* the land of tiny people, in Swift's *Gulliver's Travels* (1726).]

Li·lō, li·lo (lī́lō) *n., pl.* **-lōs.** A trademark for a type of air bed, popular as a floating mattress in swimming pools.

Li·lon·gwe (li-lóng-gway). Capital of Malawi, lying in its western highlands. It replaced Zomba as the capital in 1975.

lilt (lilt) *n.* **1.** A light, happy tune or song. **2.** A cheerful or lively manner of speaking marked by a pleasantly varied cadence. **3.** A light, springing manner of moving or walking.
~v. **lilted, lilting, lilts.** *—tr.* To say, sing, or play in a cheerful, rhythmic manner. *—intr.* To speak, sing, or play with liveliness or rhythm. [Middle English *lulten*†, to sound, sing.]

lil·y (lílli) *n., pl.* **-ies.** **1.** Any of numerous plants of the genus *Lilium,* having showy, variously coloured, often trumpet-shaped flowers. **2.** Any of various similar or related plants, such as the tiger lily or the water lily. **3.** The flower of such a plant. **—gild the lily.** To try to improve what is already excellent or beautiful. [Middle English *lilie,* Old English, from Latin *līlium,* akin to Greek *leirion,* probably of Mediterranean origin.]

lily iron *n.* A harpoon with a barbed head that may be detached. [From its shape.]

lil·y-liv·ered (lílli-lívvərd) *adj.* Cowardly; timid.

lily of the valley *n., pl.* **lilies of the valley.** A plant, *Convallaria majalis,* having a spike of fragrant, bell-shaped white flowers.

lily pad *n.* Any of the broad, floating leaves of a water lily.

lil·y-trot·ter (lílli-trottər) *n.* A bird, the **jacana** *(see).*

lil·y-white (lílli-wīt, -hwīt) *adj.* **1.** White as a lily. **2.** Beyond reproach; blameless; pure.

Li·ma (léema). Capital of Peru, founded in 1535 by Francisco Pizarro. It is now an industrial centre, joined to its port of Callao.

li·ma bean (lī́mə) *n.* **1.** Any of several varieties of a tropical American plant, *Phaseolus lunatus* (or *P. limensis*), having flat pods containing large, light-green, edible seeds. **2.** The seed of such a plant. See **butter bean.** [After *Lima,* Peru.]

lim·a·cine (límmə-sīn, lī́mə-, -sin) *adj.* Of, pertaining to, or resembling a slug. [New Latin *limacinus* : Latin *līmax* (stem *līmac-*), slug, snail, from *līmus,* slime + -INE.]

li·ma·çon (límmə-son) *n.* In geometry, a type of curve: the locus of a point on a straight line such that the point is always a fixed distance from the intersection of the line with a fixed circle as the line rotates about a point on the circle. [French, snail (named by Pascal with reference to the shape).]

Li·mas·sol (límmə-sol). Seaport on the south coast of Cyprus, centre of the island's wine industry.

limb[1] (lim) *n.* **1.** Any of the jointed appendages of a person or an animal, used for locomotion or grasping, such as an arm, leg, wing, or flipper. **2.** Any of the larger branches of a tree. **3.** Any extension or projecting part, as of a building or a mountain range. **4.** One that is considered to be an extension, member, or representative of a larger body, group, or the like. **5.** *Geology.* Either of the sides of a fold in rock strata, away from the central axis. **6.** *Rare.* An impish or naughty child. **—out on a limb.** *Informal.* **1.** In a difficult, awkward, or vulnerable position. **2.** *British.* Isolated, especially in holding unpopular or controversial opinions. **—tear limb from limb.** To dismember.
~tr.v. **limbed, limbing, limbs.** *Rare.* To dismember. [Middle English *lim, lymm,* Old English *lim;* akin to Old Norse *limr*†.] **—limb·less** *adj.*

limb[2] *n.* **1.** *Astronomy.* The circumferential edge of the apparent disc of a celestial body. **2.** The edge of a graduated arc or circle used in an instrument to measure angles. **3.** *Botany.* The expanded tip of a petal or the expanded upper part of a united corolla. [French *limbe,* from Latin *limbus*†, border, hem, seam.]

lim·bate (límbayt) *adj. Botany.* Having an edge of a different colour. [Late Latin *limbātus,* bordered, from *limbus*†, border.]

limbed (limd) *adj.* **1.** Having a limb or limbs. **2.** Having a specified number or kind of limbs: *strong-limbed athletes.*

lim·ber[1] (límbər) *adj.* **1.** Bending or flexing readily; pliable. **2.** Capable of moving, bending, or contorting easily; agile; supple.
~v. **limbered, -bering, -bers.** *—tr.* To make limber. Often used with *up.* *—intr.* To make oneself limber. Used with *up*: *The football players limbered up before the game.* [16th century : perhaps from LIMBER (vehicle).] **—lim·ber·ly** *adv.* **—lim·ber·ness** *n.*

limber[2] *n.* A two-wheeled horse-drawn vehicle that carries ammunition and behind which a field gun may be towed.
~v. **limbered, -bering, -bers.** *—tr.* To fasten a limber to (a gun). Often used with *up.* *—intr.* To fasten a limber and a gun together. Often used with *up.* [Middle English *lymo(u)r,* shaft of a carriage, perhaps from Medieval Latin *limōnārius,* of a shaft, from *limō,* shaft, perhaps from Celtic.]

limber[3] *n. Nautical.* A channel on either side of the keelson into which water drains and can then be pumped away. [French *lumière,* hole, limber (literally, light).]

lim·bic system (límbik) *n.* The part of the brain governing basic activities, such as self-preservation, reproduction, and the expression of fear and rage. [French *limbique,* from *limbe,* LIMBUS.]

lim·bo (límbō) *n., pl.* **-bos.** **1.** *Often capital* **L.** *Theology.* The abode of just souls kept from Heaven through circumstance, such as lack of baptism. **2.** A region or condition of oblivion or neglect. **3.** A state or place of confinement. **4.** An intermediate state, usually of an unpleasant or unsatisfactory nature. [Middle English, from Medieval Latin *in limbō,* "(region) on the border (of hell)" : *in,* on + *limbus*†, border.]

limbo[2] *n., pl.* **-bos.** A West Indian dance in which the performer has to pass under a low bar, bending his knees and leaning backwards. [20th century : origin obscure.]

Lim·burg·er, Lim·bourg·er (lím-burgər) *n.* A soft, often pungent, white cheese made with herbs, originally produced in Limburg province, Belgium.

lim·bus (lím-bəss) *n., pl.* **-bi** (-bī). *Biology.* A distinctive border or edge. [Latin *limbus*†, border, hem, seam.]

lime[1] (līm) *n.* **1.** A spiny, evergreen tree, *Citrus aurantifolia,* native to Asia, having fragrant white flowers, and egg-shaped fruit with a green rind and acid juice used as flavouring. **2.** The fruit of this tree. [French, from Provençal *limo,* from Arabic *līmah.*]

lime[2] *n.* Any of several Old World trees of the genus *Tilia,* having sweet-scented flowers; especially the common lime, *T.* × *europaea,* which is a hybrid of the small-leaved lime, *T. cordata,* and the large-leaved lime, *T. platyphyllos.* Also called *U.S.* "linden". [Variant of *line,* dialectal variant of obsolete *lind,* LINDEN.]

lime[3] *n.* **1. a. Calcium oxide** *(see).* **b. Calcium hydroxide** *(see).* **2.** A sticky substance smeared on twigs to catch birds; birdlime.
~tr.v. **limed, liming, limes.** **1.** To treat with lime. **2.** To smear with birdlime. **3.** To catch or snare with or as with birdlime. [Middle English *lim,* Old English *līm.*]

lime green *n.* A bright yellowish green. **—lime-green** *adj.*

lime·kiln (lī́m-kiln, -kil) *n.* A furnace used to reduce naturally occurring forms of calcium carbonate to lime.

lime·light (lī́m-līt) *n.* **1.** An early type of stage light in which lime was heated to incandescence producing brilliant illumination. **2.** The brilliant light so produced. Also called "calcium light". **3.** The state of being at the centre of public attention. Used especially in the phrase *in the limelight.*

li·men (lī́-men) *n., pl.* **-mens** or **limina** (límminə) The threshold of a physiological or psychological response. [Latin *līmen,* threshold, akin to *līmes,* boundary, LIMIT.] **—lim·i·nal** (límmin'l) *adj.*

lime pit *n.* A pit containing lime and water in which hides are soaked to remove the hair before they are tanned.

lim·er (lī́mər) *n. West Indian Informal.* A person who hangs about the streets; a loafer. **—lim·ing** *n.*

lim·er·ick (límmərik, límrik) *n.* A light humorous or nonsensical verse of five anapaestic lines usually with the rhyme scheme *aabba.* [From the line "Will you come up to Limerick?" (the refrain of a convivial verse in a similar form).]

Lim·e·rick[1] (límmərik). County in Munster province, Republic of Ireland. Its fertile pastures support dairy and beef cattle.

Limerick[2]. Port on the river Shannon, the county town of County Limerick, Republic of Ireland. It was founded by the Vikings on an island on the river. It has long been noted for its lace.

lime·stone (lī́m-stōn) *n.* A sedimentary rock, chiefly $CaCO_3$. The chief mineral is calcite, but dolomite may also be present. It is used as building stone, and in the manufacture of lime, carbon dioxide, and cement.

lime-twig (lī́m-twig) *n.* **1.** A twig covered with birdlime to catch birds. **2.** A snare.

lime·wa·ter (lī́m-wawtər || *U.S. also* -wottər) *n.* A clear, colourless, alkaline, aqueous solution of calcium hydroxide, used in calamine lotion and other skin preparations and as an antacid. It is used in a laboratory test for carbon dioxide, which causes it to go milky.

lim·ey (lī́mi) *n., pl.* **-eys.** *U.S. Slang.* **1.** A British person. **2.** A British sailor. [From earlier *lime-juicer,* American term for a British sailor or ship (the drinking of lime-juice as an antiscorbutic was compulsory in the Royal Navy).] **—lim·ey** *adj.*

li·mic·o·line (lī-míckə-līn, -lin) *adj.* Of, pertaining to, or designating shore birds, such as sandpipers, of the suborder Charadrii. [New Latin *Limicolae* (former order name), "mud dwellers" : Latin *līmus,* slime, mud + *-colae,* from *-colus,* -COLOUS.]

lim·it (límmit) *n.* **1.** The point, edge, or line beyond which something is no longer possible or allowable; the final or furthest confines or extent of something. **2.** *Usually plural.* The boundary surrounding a specific area; bounds: *within the city limits.* **3.** The maximum or minimum amount or number allowed: *an overdraft limit of £250; no minimum age limit.* **4.** *Informal.* Someone or something that goes

beyond the limits of forbearance or acceptability. Preceded by *the.* **5.** *Archaic.* A region or section enclosed within or as if within boundaries. **6.** *Mathematics.* **a.** A number that is approached by a function as the variable approaches zero, infinity, or some other number. **b.** A value that a sequence or series approaches as the number of terms approaches infinity. **7.** Either of the two values between which a definite integral is defined. —See Synonyms at **boundary.** **—off limits.** *Chiefly U.S.* Out of bounds.
~tr.v. **limited, -iting, -its. 1.** To confine or restrict within a limit or limits. **2.** To specify; fix definitely. [Middle English *limite,* from Latin *līmes*† (stem *līmit-*), border between fields, boundary.] **—lim·it·a·ble** *adj.* **—lim·i·ta·tive** (límmi-tətiv, -taytiv) *adj.* **—lim·it·er** *n.*
Synonyms: *limit, restrict, confine, circumscribe, bound.*

lim·i·tar·y (límmi-təri, -tri || *U.S.* -terri) *adj.* **1. a.** Of or pertaining to a limit or boundary. **b.** Limiting; restrictive. **2.** Limited.

lim·i·ta·tion (límmi-táysh'n) *n.* **1.** The act of limiting or the state of being limited. **2.** A restriction. **3.** A shortcoming. **4.** *Law.* A limited period during which, by statute, an action may be brought.

lim·it·ed (límmitid) *adj. Abbr.* **Ltd., ltd. 1. a.** Having a limit or limits. **b.** Confined or restricted. **2. a.** Not attaining the highest goals or achievement: *a limited success.* **b.** Having only moderate talent or range of ability: *a rather limited writer.* **3.** Having governmental or ruling powers restricted by enforceable limitations, as a constitution or legislative body might. **4.** *U.S.* Designating transport facilities, such as trains or buses, that make few stops and carry relatively few passengers. **—lim·i·ted·ly** *adv.* **—lim·i·ted·ness** *n.*

limited edition *n.* An edition, as of a book or print, limited to a stated number of copies.

limited liability company *n. British. Abbr.* **Limited, Ltd.** A public or private company in which the liability of a shareholder for the company's debts is limited to his actual investment, such that his other assets are not affected if the company fails.

lim·i·ter (límmitər) *n. Electronics.* A circuit that cuts off an alternating signal and restricts it to a predetermined maximum or minimum value. Also called "clipper".

lim·it·less (límmit-ləss, -liss) *adj.* **1.** Having no limit or limits. **2.** Unconfined or unrestricted. —See Synonyms at **infinite.**

limit point *n. Mathematics.* A limit.

lim·i·trophe (límmi-trōf) *adj.* Near or on a frontier. Said of a country or region. [French, from Late Latin *limitrophus,* from Latin *līmes* (stem *limit-*), boundary + Greek *-trophos,* supporting, feeding (referring to frontier land devoted to supporting troops guarding the border).]

limn (lim) *tr.v.* **limned, limning** (límming, lím-ning), **limns.** *Archaic.* **1.** To describe. **2.** To depict by painting or drawing. [Middle English *limnen,* to illuminate (manuscripts), shortened from *luminen,* from Old French *luminer,* from Latin *lūmināre,* from *lūmen,* light.] **—lim·ner** (lím-nər) *n.*

lim·net·ic (lim-néttik) *adj.* Of or occurring in the water of lakes or ponds to the level of light penetration. [Greek *limnē*†, pool, lake.]

lim·nol·o·gy (lím-nólləji) *n.* The scientific study of the life and phenomena of lakes, ponds, and streams. [Greek *limnē,* pool, lake + -LOGY.] **—lim·no·log·i·cal** (-nə-lójik'l) *adj.* **—lim·no·log·i·cal·ly** *adv.* **—lim·nol·o·gist** (-nólləjist) *n.*

lim·o (límmō) *n., pl.* **-mos.** *Informal.* A limousine.

Li·moges[1] (li-mōzh). Capital of the Haute-Vienne département, central France.

Limoges[2] *n.* A variety of fine porcelain made at Limoges. Also called "Limoges ware".

lim·o·nene (límmə-neen) *n.* A liquid, $C_{10}H_{16}$, with a characteristic lemon-like fragrance, used as a solvent, wetting agent, and dispersing agent, and in the manufacture of resins. [French *limon,* lime, from Old French, LEMON + -ENE.]

li·mo·nite (līmə-nīt) *n.* A widely occurring yellowish-brown to black natural iron oxide, essentially $FeO(OH){\cdot}nH_2O$, used as an ore of iron. [German *Limonit,* "meadow ore", bog iron ore : Greek *leimōn*†, meadow + -ITE.] **—li·mo·nit·ic** (-níttik) *adj.*

lim·ou·sine (límmə-zeen, -zéen) *n.* **1.** Formerly, a large car with an enclosed passenger compartment and an open but roofed driver's seat. **2.** Any large and luxurious car. [Originally a cloak popular in *Limousin,* former province of France, which the projecting roof was thought to resemble.]

limp (limp) *intr.v.* **limped, limping, limps. 1.** To walk lamely, especially with irregularity, when or as if one leg is weaker or shorter than the other. **2.** To move or proceed haltingly or unsteadily.
~n. An irregular, jerky, or awkward way of walking.
~adj. **limper, limpest. 1.** Lacking or having lost rigidity; flaccid; flabby. **2.** Lacking vitality, vigour, or strength of character; weak. **3.** Not stiffened; paperbacked. Said of a bookbinding. [Probably shortened from obsolete *limphalt,* lame, ultimately from Old English *lempheal t, læmpihalt.*] **—limp·ly** *adv.* **—limp·ness** *n.*

lim·pet (límpit) *n.* **1.** Any of numerous, generally marine gastropod molluscs, as of the families Acmaeidae and Patellidae, characteristically having a tent-shaped shell and adhering to rocks of tidal areas. **2.** One who clings persistently. **3.** A type of explosive designed to cling to the hull of a ship and detonate on contact or signal. [Middle English *lempet,* Old English *lempedu,* from Medieval Latin *lamprēda,* LAMPREY.]

lim·pid (límpid) *adj.* **1.** Characterised by transparent clearness; pellucid. **2.** Easily intelligible; clear. Said especially of literary style. **3.** Calm and untroubled; serene. [French *limpide,* from Latin *limpidus*†.] **—lim·pid·i·ty** (lim-píddəti), **lim·pid·ness** *n.* **—lim·pid·ly** *adv.*

limp·kin (límpkin) *n.* A brownish wading bird, *Aramus guarauna,* of warm, swampy regions of the New World, having a distinctive, wailing call. Also called "courlan". [LIMP (referring to its movements) + -KIN.]

Lim·po·po (lim-pṓpō). River in southern Africa. It flows 1 600 kilometres (1,000 miles) from near Pretoria, South Africa, to the Indian Ocean north of Maputo, Mozambique.

lim·u·lus (límmew-ləss) *n., pl.* **-li** (-lī). A horseshoe crab; especially, *Limulus polyphemus.* [New Latin, from Latin, diminutive of *limus,* sidelong.]

lim·y (līmi) *adj.* **-ier, -iest.** Of, resembling, or containing lime.

lin. 1. lineal. **2.** linear.

lin·ac (línnak) *n. Physics.* A **linear accelerator** *(see).* [From *lin*ear *ac*celerator.]

lin·age, line·age (līnij) *n.* **1.** The number of lines of printed or written material. **2.** Payment for written work according to the number of such lines.

lin·al·o·ol (li-nál-ō-ol || -ōl) *n.* Also **lin·al·ol** (línnə-lol || -lōl). A colourless, fragrant liquid, $C_{10}H_{18}O$, distilled from the oils of rosewood, bergamot, and other plants and trees, and used in perfume manufacture. [Earlier *linaloe,* fragrant wood of a Mexican tree, from Mexican Spanish *lináloe,* from Spanish, from Late Latin *lignum aloēs,* "wood of the aloe" : Latin *lignum,* wood + *aloē,* ALOE.]

Lin Biao or **Lin Piao** (lín byów) (1907–71). Chinese Communist politician. He fought with Mao Ze-dong in the communist campaign to gain power in China. Defence minister after 1959, heir-apparent to Mao after 1969, killed in a plane crash.

linch·pin, lynch·pin (línch-pin) *n.* **1.** A locking pin inserted in the end of a shaft, as in an axle to prevent a wheel from slipping off. **2.** A central or cohesive element: *the linchpin of the family.* [Middle English *lynspin* : *lins,* linchpin, Old English *lynis,* akin to Old Saxon *lunisa*† + PIN.]

Lin·coln (língkən). County town and market centre of Lincolnshire, England. In the tower of its (11th–15th century) cathedral is the famous bell, Great Tom of Lincoln.

Lincoln, Abraham (1809–65). 16th President of the United States (1861–65). From 1836 he practised law in Illinois, until becoming a Whig congressman (1847–49). Lincoln opposed slavery, and in 1856 joined the new Republican party, winning the 1860 presidential election. He vigorously led the North in the Civil War, and in 1863 issued the Emancipation Proclamation, freeing the slaves in the areas still under Confederate control. He was re-elected president in 1864, and during its session of 1864–65 Congress approved the 13th Amendment to the Constitution, abolishing slavery in the United States. Lincoln was assassinated in April, days after the end of the war, at Ford's Theatre in Washington, by John Wilkes Booth, a southern actor.

Lincoln green *n.* **1.** A yellowish- or brownish-green colour. **2.** Cloth of this colour, which Robin Hood and his men are supposed to have worn. [After LINCOLN, where the cloth was originally made.] **—Lincoln green** *adj.*

Lincoln Red *n.* Any of a breed of short-horned, red-coated beef cattle developed in eastern England.

Lin·coln·shire (língkən-shər, -sheer). Largely flat county in eastern England, intersected by canals and dykes. Much of its fenland has been drained for agricultural use.

Lincoln's Inn *n.* One of the four legal societies forming the **Inns of Court** *(see)* in England.

linc·tus (língktəss) *n.* A liquid, syrupy medicine taken to relieve coughs. [Latin, from the past participle of *lingere,* to lick.]

Lind (lind), **Jenny,** also known as The Swedish Nightingale (1820–87). Swedish soprano. After 1852, she lived mainly in London, and taught at the Royal College of Music (1883–86).

lin·dane (líndayn) *n.* A white poisonous powder used as a weed killer and insecticide. It is an isomer of hexachlorocyclohexane. [After T. van den *Linden,* 20th-century Dutch chemist.]

Lind·bergh (líndberg), **Charles (Augustus)** (1902–74). U.S. pilot. In May, 1927, he made the first solo nonstop transatlantic flight (New York–Paris) in his plane *The Spirit of Saint Louis.* His baby son was notoriously kidnapped and murdered in 1932.

lin·den (líndən) *n. U.S.* A lime tree. Not in current British usage.

Lindisfarne. See **Holy Island.**

Lind·sey (líndzi), **Parts of.** See **Lincolnshire.**

Lind·wall (línd-wawl), **Ray(mond Russell)** (1921–96). Australian cricketer. By the time of his retirement in 1960, he had taken 228 Test wickets, then the Australian record for a bowler.

line[1] (līn) *n. Abbr.* **l., L. 1.** In geometry: **a.** The locus of a point having one degree of freedom; a curve. **b.** A set of points (x, y) that satisfy the linear equation $ax + by + c = 0$, where a and b are not both zero. **2.** A thin, continuous mark, such as that made by a pen, pencil, or brush applied to a surface. **3.** A similar mark cut or scratched into a surface. **4.** An indentation or crease in the skin, especially on the face or palm; a wrinkle. **5.** *Sports.* **a.** A mark on a playing court or field indicating a boundary of play. **b.** A mark or imaginary point at which a race starts or ends. **6.** *Chiefly U.S.* A border or boundary: *the county line.* **7.** Any demarcation: *a picket line.* **8.** A contour or outline. **9.** In art: **a.** A mark used to define a shape or represent a contour. **b.** Any of the marks that make up the formal design of a picture. **10.** A cable, rope, string, cord, or wire, such as: **a.** One used on a ship. **b.** One used for catching fish. **c.** A clothes line. **d.** A string or cord used, as by builders or surveyors, for taking measurements, levelling, or straightening. **e.** A cable transmitting electric power of telecommunications signals: *telephone lines.* **11.** An open or functioning telephone connection.

12. **a.** A system of public transport, as by ship, aircraft, or bus, usually over a definite route. **b.** A company owning or managing such a system. Sometimes used in combination: *an airline.* **13. a.** A railway track. **b.** A particular section of a railway network: *the London to Glasgow line.* **14.** A course of progress or movement: *the line of flight.* **15. a.** A general method, manner, or course of procedure: *different lines of thought.* **b.** A manner or course of procedure determined by a specified factor: *development along communist lines; a society divided along tribal lines.* **16.** An official or prescribed policy: *the party line.* **17.** A state of alignment, conformity, or agreement: *brought the front wheels into line; a wages agreement in line with recent settlements.* **18. a.** One's trade or occupation. **b.** The range of one's competence or preferred activity: *not really in my line.* **19.** Merchandise of a similar or related nature: *This store carries a line of small tools.* **20.** A group of persons or things arranged in a row or series. **21.** A series of persons, especially belonging to the same family, who succeed each other chronologically: *comes of a long line of bankers.* **22. a.** A row of words printed or written across a page or a column. **b.** A unit of verse made up of such a row, or formed of a certain number of metrical feet characteristic of the verse. **c.** *Plural. British.* A usually specified number of lines of prose or verse to be written out by a pupil as a punishment. **23.** A brief letter; a note. **24.** *Often plural.* The dialogue of a play or other theatrical presentation: *learning his lines.* **25.** A calculated or glib way of speaking, usually to obtain some undeclared end. **26.** A hint or snippet of information: *tried to get a line on their secret plans.* **27.** A horizontal demarcation in bridge dividing categories of points scored: *Points above the line do not count towards game.* **28.** *Music.* Any of the five parallel marks composing a staff. **29.** *Military.* **a.** A formation in which elements, such as troops, tanks, or ships, are arranged abreast of each other. **b.** The battle area closest to the enemy. **c.** The troops in this area. **d.** A bulwark or trench. **e.** An extended system of such fortifications or defences. **f.** *Capital* **L.** In the British army, the regular numbered regiments, as distinguished from the Guards and auxiliary units. Preceded by *the.* **30.** The equator. Preceded by *the*: *crossed the line.* **31.** Any of the horizontal bands that make up a television picture. **32.** The course followed when hunting a fox. **33.** In cricket, the degree of a bowler's control over the direction of the ball: *good line and length.* **34.** A unit of magnetic flux, one **maxwell** *(see).* **35.** The proportion of an insurance risk assumed by a particular underwriter or company. **—all along the line. 1.** In every place. **2.** At every stage or moment. **—draw the line (at).** To refuse to go as far as or beyond; consider as unacceptable. **—hold the line. 1.** To keep open a telephone connection. **2.** To maintain a firm position. **—in line for.** Likely or due to receive: *in line for promotion.* **—in the line of duty.** As a part of one's responsibilities in a given job. **—keep in line.** To keep in order; restrain. **—lay** or **put on the line.** *Informal.* **1.** To make payment. **2.** To jeopardise; put at risk: *put his reputation on the line.* **3.** To be candid or explicit: *He sure laid it on the line.* **—read between the lines.** To deduce the implicit rather than explicit meaning of a statement. **—shoot a line.** To try to deceive by lying or exaggerating. **—toe the line.** To obey the rules; conform.
~*v.* **lined, lining, lines.** —*tr.* **1.** To mark or incise with a line or lines. **2.** To represent or depict with a line or lines. **3.** To place in a series or row. Often used with *up.* **4.** To form a bordering line along: *Small stalls lined the alleys.* —*intr.* To form a line. Usually used with *up.* See **line up.** [Middle English *ligne, line,* cord, stroke, mark, line, partly from Old French *ligne,* from Vulgar Latin *linja* (unattested), from Latin *līnea,* thread, line, from *līnum,* flax, and partly from Old English *līne,* cord, rope, series, representing a Common Germanic borrowing of Latin *līnea.*]

line² *tr.v.* **lined, lining, lines. 1.** To sew or fit a covering to the inside surface of: *a coat lined with fur.* **2.** To cover the inner surface of: *Moisture lined the cave's walls.* **3.** To fill plentifully, as with money or food. [Middle English *linen,* from *line,* flax, Old English *līn,* from Germanic *līnam* (unattested), from Latin *līnum,* flax.]

lin·e·age¹ (línni-ij) *n.* **1.** Direct descent from a particular ancestor; ancestry. **2.** Derivation. **3.** The descendants of a certain ancestor considered as the founder of the line. [Middle English *linage,* from Old French *li(g)nage,* from *ligne,* LINE.]

line·age². Variant of **linage.**

lin·e·al (línni-əl) *adj. Abbr.* **lin. 1.** Belonging to or being in the direct line of descent from an ancestor. Compare **collateral. 2.** Derived from or pertaining to a particular line of descent: *the lineal rights of royalty.* **3.** Linear. [Middle English, from Old French, from Late Latin *līneālis,* from Latin *līnea,* LINE.] **—lin·e·al·ly** *adv.*

lin·e·a·ment (línni-əmənt) *n.* **1.** A distinctive shape, contour, or line, especially of the face. **2.** A definitive or characteristic mark or feature. [Middle English *liniament,* from Latin *līneāmentum,* from *līneāre,* to make straight, from *līnea,* LINE.]

lin·e·ar (línni-ər) *adj. Abbr.* **lin. 1.** Of, pertaining to, or resembling a line or lines; straight. **2.** In geometry: **a.** In, of, describing, described by, or related to a straight line. **b.** Having only one dimension. **3.** In art, characterised chiefly by forms and shapes that are precisely defined by line. Compare **painterly. 4.** Narrow and elongated: *a linear leaf.* **5.** Designating a form of script made up of lines rather than pictorial symbols. See **Linear A, Linear B.** [Latin *līneāris,* from *līnea,* LINE.] **—lin·e·ar·ly** *adv.*

Linear A *n.* A partly linear, partly pictographic script used in Crete from about 1900 to 1500 B.C., and as yet undeciphered.

linear accelerator *n.* An electron, proton, or heavy-ion **accelerator** *(see)* in which the paths of the particles accelerated are essentially straight lines rather than circles or spirals. Also called "linac".

linear algebra *n.* **1.** A branch of mathematics dealing with the theory of systems of linear equations, matrices, vector spaces, determinants, and linear transformations. **2.** A mathematical ring and vector space with scalars from an associated field, the multiplication of which is of the form $(aA)(bB)=(ab)(AB)$ where a and b are scalars and A and B are vectors.

Linear B *n.* A syllabic script, probably a modification of Linear A, used in Mycenaean Greek documents from the 14th to the 12th century B.C. and deciphered by Michael Ventris in 1952.

linear equation *n.* An algebraic equation, such as $x + y + 5 = 0$, in which the highest degree term in the variable or variables is of the first degree.

linear measure *n.* **1.** Measurement of length. **2.** A unit or system of units for measuring length. Also called "long measure".

linear momentum *n. Physics.* **Momentum** *(see).*

linear motor *n.* A type of electric motor in which the moving and stationary parts are linear and parallel so that a current causes motion along a line. Commonly, the moving part, which may be a vehicle, such as a locomotive, contains horizontal coils which induce a voltage in a long metal rail.

linear perspective *n.* See **perspective.**

linear programming *n. Mathematics.* A technique using successive approximations to find the optimum value of a function that is subject to linear constraints, used extensively in planning industrial processes, economic models, and the like.

lin·e·a·tion (línni-áysh'n) *n.* **1.** A marking or outlining with lines. **2.** An outline. **3.** An arrangement of lines.

line breeding *n.* Selective inbreeding to perpetuate certain qualities or characteristics in a strain of stock.

line cut *n.* A letterpress printing plate made from a line drawing by a photoengraving process. Also called "line engraving".

line drawing *n.* A drawing made with lines only, especially one used as copy for a line engraving.

line engraving *n. Printing.* **1.** A metal plate, used in intaglio printing, on the surface of which design lines have been hand engraved. **2.** The process of making such an engraving. **3.** A print made from such an engraving. **4.** A line cut.

Line Islands (līn). Group of small islands in the central Pacific Ocean. Eight of them are part of Kiribati. The other three are uninhabited, and are dependencies of the United States.

lin·en (línnin) *n.* **1.** Thread made from fibres of the flax plant. **2.** Cloth woven from this thread. **3.** Garments or other articles, such as sheets and tablecloths, made from this or similar cloth. ~*adj.* **1.** Made of flax or linen. **2.** Resembling linen. [Middle English, Old English *līnen, linnen,* "made of flax" (not used of linen cloth), from Germanic *līnin* (unattested), from *līnam* (unattested), flax, from Latin *līnum.*]

line of credit *n.* **A credit line** *(see).*

line of fire *n.* The flight path of a bullet or other missile discharged from a firearm.

line of force *n. Physics.* An imaginary line in a field of force, any tangent to which gives the direction of the field at the point of tangency.

line of scrimmage *n.* In American football, an imaginary line across the field on which the ball rests and at which the teams line up for a new play.

line of sight *n.* An imaginary line from the eye to the object being looked at. Also called "line of vision".

lin·e·o·late (línni-ə-layt) *adj. Biology.* Marked with fine lines. [New Latin *lineolatus,* from Latin *līneola,* diminutive of *līnea,* LINE.]

line-out (līn-owt) *n.* In Rugby football, the grouping of the opposing forwards into two parallel lines between which the ball is thrown from the touchline after it has gone out of play.

line printer *n.* A fast printer that prints characters a whole line at a time, used especially for printing the output from computers.

lin·er¹ (līnər) *n.* **1.** One that draws or makes a line or lines. **2.** A commercial ship or aircraft, especially one carrying passengers on a regular route. **3. Eyeliner** *(see).*

liner² *n.* **1.** One who makes or puts in linings. **2.** Something used as a lining: *a dustbin liner.*

lines·man (līnz-mən) *n., pl.* **-men** (-mən, -men). *Sports.* An official assisting the referee or umpire, as in soccer or tennis, whose main duty is to indicate when the ball has gone out of play.

line spectrum *n.* A spectrum consisting of a set of discrete, fairly narrow lines.

line squall *n.* A band of extremely stormy weather with gusting winds, hail, and thunderstorms, associated with a cold front.

line up *intr.v.* To form or take a place in a line. —*tr.v.* **1.** To put into line or into alignment. **2.** To assemble, organise, or prepare: *lined up a lot of evidence against him.*

line-up, line·up (līn-up) *n.* **1.** A line of persons formed for inspection or identification. **2.** A group or arrangement of people or things brought together for a particular purpose: *an interesting line-up of acts for the show; in the Leeds line-up for tonight's game.*

ling¹ (ling) *n., pl.* **lings** or collectively **ling.** Any of various marine food fishes related to or resembling the cod, such as *Molva molva,* of northwest European waters. [Middle English *leng(e),* probably of Low German origin; akin to Dutch *lenghe, linghe.*]

ling² *n.* A plant, **heather** *(see).* [Middle English *lyng,* from Old Norse.]

-ling¹ *n. suffix.* Indicates: **1.** The young of a specified animal; for example, **duckling, gosling. 2.** A smaller, lesser, or inferior version; for example, **princeling, underling. 3.** One produced by or under the care or control of; for example, **earthling, nursling, hireling.** Often used derogatorily. [Middle English, Old English, from Common Germanic *-linga-* (unattested) : noun ending *-ilaz* (unattested) + patronymic ending *-inga-*.]

–ling² *adj. & adv. suffix.* Indicates: **1.** Direction or position; for example, **sideling, flatling. 2.** Condition; for example, **darkling.** [Middle English, from Old English, from West Germanic *-ling-, -lang-* (unattested).]

ling. linguistics.

lin·gam (líng-gəm) *n.* Also **lin·ga** (-gə). A stylised phallus worshipped as a symbol of the Hindu god Siva. [Sanskrit *linga†,* "distinctive mark", penis.]

ling·cod (líng-kod) *n., pl.* **-cods** or collectively **lingcod.** A food fish, *Ophiodon elongatus,* of northern Pacific waters.

lin·ger (líng-gər) *v.* **-gered, -gering, -gers.** —*intr.* **1.** To delay departure; be slow and reluctant to leave; tarry. **2.** To hover between life and death for some time before dying. **3.** To remain, in dilute form; be slow in disappearing: *The smell of frying lingered on; The memory still lingers.* **4.** To delay; procrastinate. **5.** To proceed slowly; saunter. —*tr. Archaic.* To prolong; protract. Used with *on* or *out.* —See Synonyms at **stay.** [Middle English (northern dialect) *lengeren,* frequentative of *lengen,* to tarry, from Old Norse *lengja.*] —**lin·ger·er** *n.* —**lin·ger·ing·ly** *adv.*

lin·ge·rie (láɴzhə-ri, lónzhə-, -ray) *n.* **1.** Women's underwear and night wear. **2.** *Archaic.* Linen articles, especially garments. [French, "linen garments", from *linge,* linen, from Latin *līneus,* made of linen, from *līnum,* flax.]

lin·go (líng-gō) *n., pl.* **-goes.** *Informal.* Language that is distinctive, unintelligible, or unfamiliar through being foreign or a jargon. [Portuguese *lingoa,* "tongue", language, from Latin *lingua.*]

lin·gua (líng-gwə) *n., pl.* **-guae** (-gwee). A tongue or tonguelike organ. [Latin.]

lingua fran·ca (fráng-kə) *n., pl.* **linguae francae** (-kee) or **lingua francas. 1.** Any hybrid language used as a medium of communication between peoples of different languages. **2.** Any mutually intelligible medium of communication. **3.** *Capital* L. A mixture of Italian with French, Spanish, Arabic, Greek, and Turkish, formerly spoken in eastern Mediterranean ports. [Italian, "the Frankish tongue".]

lin·gual (líng-gwəl ‖ -gew-əl) *adj.* **1.** Of, pertaining to, or resembling the tongue or a tonguelike organ. **2.** *Phonetics.* Formed with the tongue in conjunction with other organs of speech. **3.** *Rare.* Linguistic.
~*n. Phonetics.* A sound that is pronounced with the tongue in conjunction with other organs of speech, such as the sounds (t), (l), or (n). —**lin·gual·ly** *adv.*

lin·gui·form (líng-gwi-fawrm) *adj.* Having the form of a tongue.

lin·gui·ni (ling-gwéeni) *n.* **1.** *Used with a singular or plural verb.* Pasta in the form of long, thin, flat strands. **2.** A dish consisting of or containing such pasta. [Italian, plural of *linguino,* "small tongue", from *lingua,* tongue, from Latin.]

lin·guist (líng-gwist) *n.* **1.** A person who speaks several languages fluently. **2.** A student of a language or languages. **3.** A specialist in linguistics. **4.** *West African.* The spokesman of a chief, especially in Ghana. [Latin *lingua,* tongue, language.]

lin·guis·tic (ling-gwístik) *adj.* Of or pertaining to language or linguistics. —**lin·guis·ti·cal·ly** *adv.*

linguistic form *n.* Any meaningful unit of speech, such as an affix, word, phrase, or sentence. Also called "form".

lin·guis·tic·ian (líng-gwiss-tísh'n) *n.* A specialist in linguistics. Usually used derogatorily.

lin·guis·tics (ling-gwístiks) *n. Used with a singular verb. Abbr.* **ling.** The science of language; the study of the nature and structure of human speech.

lin·gu·late (líng-gew-layt) *adj.* Tongue-shaped. [Latin *lingulātus,* from *lingula,* diminutive of *lingua,* tongue.]

lin·i·ment (línnimənt) *n.* A medicinal fluid applied to the skin by rubbing as an anodyne or to relieve stiffness. [Middle English *lynyment,* from Late Latin *linīmentum,* from Latin *linere,* to anoint.]

li·nin (línin) *n.* The filamentous, achromatic material in the nucleus of a cell that interconnects the chromatin granules. [Latin *līnum,* flax + -IN.]

lin·ing (líning) *n.* **1. a.** An interior covering or coating. **b.** Material that may be used for such covering or coating. **2.** The act or process of applying a lining to something.

link¹ (lingk) *n.* **1.** Any of the rings or loops forming a chain. **2.** Anything resembling a chain link in its physical arrangement or its connecting function, such as a cuff link or a loop in crochet. **3.** Anything that connects or provides a connection, such as: **a.** Something constituting a causal relation: *the link between stress and heart disease.* **b.** A system of transport or communications, as between two or more points: *a satellite link; the Heathrow to Gatwick helicopter link.* **c.** A single unit or element in such a system: *the islanders' only link with the outside world.* **d.** A passage, continuity, or progression, as in music, prose, or a broadcast. **4.** A unit of length used in surveying, equal to 0.01 chain or 20.1 centimetres (7.92 inches). **5.** A rod or lever transmitting motion in a machine.
~*v.* **linked, linking, links.** —*tr.* **1.** To connect or couple with or as if with links. **2.** To intertwine: *link arms.* —*intr.* To become connected with or as with links. —See Synonyms at **join.** [Middle

English, from Old Norse *hlenkr* (unattested), variant of *hlekkr,* link, ring.]

link² *n.* A torch formerly used at night for lighting one's way in the streets. [Perhaps from Medieval Latin *linchinus,* variant of *lichinus,* from Latin *lychnus,* from Greek *lukhnos,* lamp.]

link·age (língkij) *n.* **1.** The act or process of linking. **2.** The state or condition of being linked. **3.** A system of interconnected machine elements, such as rods, springs, and pivots, used to transmit power or motion. **4.** *Electricity.* A measure of the induced voltage in a circuit caused by a magnetic flux, and equal to the flux multiplied by the number of turns in the coil that surrounds it. **5.** *Genetics.* The occurrence of genes together on the same chromosome such that they are likely, in proportion to their proximity, to be inherited together rather than independently. **6.** In international relations, a bargaining tactic whereby apparently diverse issues are combined so that agreement on one is dependent on agreement on another or others.

linked (lingkt) *adj.* **1.** Connected, especially by or as if by links. **2.** Intertwined: *linked arms.* **3.** *Genetics.* Exhibiting linkage.

linking verb *n.* A verb, such as *appear, be, feel, grow,* or *seem,* that connects a subject and a predicate adjective or predicate nominative; a copula.

Link·lat·er (língk-laytər), **Eric** (1899–1974). British writer. He wrote many novels, including *Private Angelo* (1946).

link·man (língk-man) *n., pl.* **-men** (-men). **1.** A person responsible for providing continuity between different items in a radio or television broadcast. **2.** In games such as football and hockey, a player who acts as a link between the forwards and the backs.

Lin·kö·ping (*Swedish* línt-khöping). Ancient city in southern Sweden, capital of Östergötland county.

links (lingks) *pl.n.* **1.** A golf course, especially one along a seashore. **2.** *Chiefly Scottish.* Relatively flat or undulating ground, sandy and turf-covered, along a seashore. [Middle English, from Old English *hlincas,* plural of *hlinc,* ridge.]

Link trainer *n. Aeronautics.* A trademark for a flight simulation device used to train aircrew.

Lin·lith·gow (lin-líthgō). Ancient burgh in West Lothian, Scotland. James V and his daughter Mary, Queen of Scots, were born at the now ruined Linlithgow Palace.

linn (lin) *n. Chiefly Scottish.* **1.** A waterfall. **2.** A steep ravine. [Scottish Gaelic *linne.*]

Lin·nae·us (li-née-əss, -náy-), **Carolus,** also known as Karl Linné (after 1761 von Linné) (1707–78). Swedish biologist. He created the system of classification of plants and animals used today. In his *Systema Naturae* (1735) and *Species Plantarum* (1753), animals and plants were described by genus and species. —**Lin·ne·an, Lin·nae·an** (-née-ən, -náy-) *adj.*

lin·net (línnit) *n.* **1.** A small Old World songbird, *Acanthis cannabina,* having brownish plumage. **2.** A similar bird, *Carpodacus mexicanus,* of western North America. [Old French dialectal *linette,* from *lin,* flax (the bird feeds on linseed), from Latin *līnum.*]

li·no (línō) *n., pl.* **-nos.** Linoleum.

li·no·cut (línō-kut) *n.* **1.** A print taken from a block of linoleum on which a design has been carved with a gouging tool. **2.** The technique of producing such prints.

lin·o·le·ic acid (lín-ō-lée-ik, -ə-, -láy-) *n.* A clear to straw-coloured liquid, $C_{18}H_{32}O_2$, an important component of drying oils and an essential fatty acid in the human diet, being obtained from vegetable seed oils and some animal fats. [Greek *linon,* flax + OLEIC ACID (so called because found in linseed oil).]

lin·o·len·ic acid (lín-ō-lénnik, -ə-) *n.* A colourless liquid, $C_{18}H_{30}O_2$, an important component of natural drying oils and an essential fatty acid in the human diet, being obtained from vegetable oils. [Arbitrarily from LINOLEIC ACID.]

li·no·le·um (li-nóli-əm) *n.* A durable, washable material made in sheets by pressing a mixture of heated linseed oil, rosin, powdered cork, and pigments onto a burlap or canvas backing, used chiefly as a floor covering. Also called "lino". [Latin *līnum,* flax + *oleum,* OIL.]

Li·no·type (línə-tīp) *n.* A trademark for a machine that can set an entire line of type on a single metal slug and that is operated by a keyboard similar to that of a typewriter. —**Li·no·type** *v.* —**Li·no·typ·er, Li·no·typ·ist** *n.*

Lin Piao. See **Lin Biao.**

lin·sang (lín-sang) *n.* Any of several Asian or African catlike carnivorous mammals of the genera *Poiana* and *Prionodon,* having a spotted coat and a long striped tail. [Malay.]

lin·seed (lín-seed) *n.* The seed of flax, especially when used as the source of linseed oil. [Middle English, Old English *līnæd* : Old English *līn,* flax, from Latin *līnum* + SEED.]

linseed oil *n.* A golden-yellow, amber, or brown oil that thickens and hardens on exposure to air, extracted from the seeds of flax, and used as a drying oil in paints and varnishes, and in linoleum, printing inks, and synthetic resins.

lin·sey-wool·sey (línzi-wŏŏlzi) *n., pl.* **-seys.** A coarse fabric of cotton or linen woven with wool. [Middle English *lynsy-wolsye* : probably after *Lindsey,* village in Suffolk (where it was originally manufactured) + WOOL.]

lin·stock (lín-stok) *n.* A long forked stick for holding a match, formerly used to fire cannon. [Dutch *lontstok* : *lont,* match, wick, akin to Middle Low German *lunte†* + *stok,* stick.]

lint (lint) *n.* **1.** Downy material obtained by scraping linen cloth and used for dressing wounds. **2.** The mass of soft fibres surrounding the seeds of unginned cotton. **3.** Clinging bits of fibre and fluff; fuzz. [Middle English *lynet,* from Latin *linteum,* linen cloth, from *linteus,* made of linen, from *linum,* flax.]

lin·tel (líntʹl) *n.* The horizontal beam that forms the upper member of a window or door frame and supports part of the structure above it. [Middle English, from Old French *lintel, lintier,* from Vulgar Latin *līmitāris* (unattested), alteration (influenced by Latin *līmes,* stem *līmit-,* boundary, LIMIT) of Latin *līmināris,* of a threshold, from *līmen,* threshold, LIMEN.]

lint·er (líntər) *n. U.S.* **1.** A machine that removes the short fibres that cling to cotton seeds after the first ginning. **2.** *Plural.* The fibres thus removed.

lint-white (línt-wīt, -hwīt) *n. Poetic & Regional.* A linnet. [Middle English *lynkwhyte,* Old English *līnetwige,* "linseed eater" : *līn,* flax + *-twige,* "plucker", "eater", from West Germanic *twig-* (unattested), to pluck.]

Linz (lints). Capital of Upper Austria, situated on the river Danube. It is an iron and steel centre.

li·on (līʹən) *n., pl.* **lions** or collectively (senses 1, 2) **lion. 1.** A large, carnivorous feline mammal, *Panthera leo,* of Africa and India, having a short tawny coat and a long, heavy mane around the neck and shoulders in the male. **2.** Any of several related animals considered to resemble a lion in some way. **3.** A person resembling a lion, as in bravery or ferocity. **4.** One whose eminence, as in arts and letters, has led to social prestige; a sought-after celebrity. **5.** A heraldic representation of a lion, the national emblem of Great Britain. **6.** *Capital* L. A member of the British international Rugby Union team. **7.** *Capital* L. *Astronomy.* The constellation and sign of the zodiac, Leo (*see*). Preceded by *the.* —**beard the lion in his den.** To face or defy the opposition in its own territory or home. —**twist the lion's tail.** To irritate or insult the nation or government of Great Britain. [Middle English *li(o)un, leoun,* from Anglo-French *liun* and Old French *lion,* both from Latin *leō* (stem *leōn-*), from Greek *leōn,* perhaps from Semitic.]

li·on·ess (līʹən-ess, -iss, -éss) *n.* A female lion. [Middle English *leonesse,* from Old French *lionnesse,* from *lion,* LION.]

li·on-heart·ed (līʹən-haartid, -hártid) *adj.* Extraordinarily courageous.

lionise, li·on·ize (līʹən-īz) *tr.v.* **-ised, -ising, -ises.** To look upon or treat (a person) as a celebrity. —**li·on·i·sa·tion** (-ī-záysh'n ‖ *U.S.* -i-) *n.* —**li·on·is·er** *n.*

lion's share *n.* The largest or best part of a whole.

lip (lip) *n.* **1.** *Anatomy.* Either of two fleshy, muscular folds that together surround the opening of the mouth. **2.** Any structure or part that similarly encircles or bounds an orifice, as: **a.** *Anatomy.* A labium. **b.** The margin of flesh around a wound. **c.** Either of the margins of the aperture of a gastropod shell. **d.** The rim of a vessel, bell, crater, or the like. **3.** *Botany.* Any of the protruding divisions of an irregular corolla or calyx, either paired, as in the snapdragon, or single, as in an orchid. **4.** The tip of a pouring spout. **5.** *Slang.* Insolent talk. **6.** *Music.* The ability to shape the lips properly in playing a brass instrument; embouchure. —**bite (one's) lip. 1.** To hold back one's anger or other feeling. **2.** To show vexation. ~*tr.v.* **lipped, lipping, lips. 1. a.** To touch the lips to. **b.** *Poetic.* To kiss. **2.** To utter; especially, to whisper or murmur. **3.** *Literary.* To lap. Used of water. **4.** To serve as a lip or rim to. **5.** *Golf.* To hit the ball so that it stops just at the edge of (the hole). [Middle English *lip(pe),* Old English *lippa.*]

Li·pa·ri Islands (líppəri; *Italian* lée-paa-ree). Formerly **Aeolian Islands.** Italian islands lying north of Sicily. They are volcanic, and include Lipari, Vulcano, Stromboli, and Salina.

lip·ase (lípʹayz, líp-, -ayss) *n.* An enzyme that hydrolyses fats to form glycerol and fatty acids. [LIP(O)- + -ASE.]

lip gloss *n.* A clear or coloured cosmetic grease used to add shine to the lips.

lip·id (líppid) *n.* Also **lip·ide** (lí-pīd). Any of numerous fats and fatlike materials that are generally insoluble in water but soluble in common organic solvents, that are related to the fatty-acid esters, and that together with carbohydrates and proteins constitute the principal structural material of living cells. [French *lipide* : LIP(O)- + -ID.]

Lip·iz·za·ner, Lip·pi·zan·er (líppit-saánər) *n.* Any of a breed of nearly white horses, used by the Spanish Riding School in Vienna and trained in feats of dressage. [German, after *Lippiza,* near Trieste, where the breed was developed.]

Lip·mann (lípmən), **Fritz Albert** (1899–1986). U.S. biochemist, born in Germany. He discovered coenzyme A, which is necessary for the oxidation of carbohydrate during metabolism, and shared the 1953 Nobel prize in physiology or medicine with H.A. Krebs.

lipo-, lip- *comb. form.* Indicates fat or fatty; for example, **lipolysis, lipoma.** [New Latin, from Greek *lipos,* fat.]

li·po·gen·e·sis (lipō-jénnə-siss) *n.* The synthesis of fatty acids in living cells. [LIPO- + -GENESIS.]

lip·oid (lípʹoyd, líp-) *adj.* Also **lip·oi·dal** (li-póydʹl). Resembling fat; fatty. [LIP(O)- + -OID.] —**lip·oid** *n.*

li·pol·y·sis (li-póllə-siss, lī-) *n.* The hydrolysis of fats or lipids. [LIPO- + -LYSIS.]

li·po·ma (li-pṓmə) *n., pl.* **-mata** (-tə) or **-mas.** A benign tumour of fatty cells. [LIP(O)- + -OMA.] —**li·pom·a·tous** (-pómmətəss) *adj.*

lip·o·pro·tein (lippō-prṓ-teen, lípō-, -tee-in) *n.* A conjugated protein consisting of a simple protein combined with a lipid group.

lip·o·some (lip-ō-sṓm, líp-, -ə-) *n.* A small sac consisting of a synthetic membrane made of phospholipid, used to convey relatively toxic drugs to target organs or cancerous tumours. [LIPO- + -SOME.]

lip·o·trop·ic (líppō-tróppik, lípō-) *adj.* Preventing abnormal or excessive accumulation of fat in the liver. [LIPO- + -TROPIC.] —**li·pot·ro·pism, li·pot·ro·py** (li-póttrəpi, lī-) *n.*

Lip·pe (lipp-e). Former independent state of Germany, now part of North Rhine-Westphalia, western Germany.

lipped (lipt) *adj.* **1.** Having a lip or lips. **2.** Having a specified number or kind of lips: *thick-lipped.*

Lip·per·shey (líppər-shay), **Hans,** also called Jan or Hans Lippersheim (líppərss-hīm) (*c.*1570–*c.*1619). German-born Dutch inventor of the telescope.

Lip·pi (líppi), **Filippino** (*c.*1457–1504). Florentine painter, son of Fra Filippo. He completed (*c.*1480) Masaccio's frescoes in the Brancacci chapel, Florence. He also painted the *Vision of St. Bernard* (*c.*1486), and the *Madonna Enthroned.*

Lippi, Fra Filippo, also known as Fra Lippo (*c.*1406–69). Florentine painter, father of Filippino. He left the Carmelite order to become a pupil of Masaccio. His paintings, such as the *Annunciation* (*c.*1438) and the *Coronation of the Virgin* (*c.*1441), display a bold three-dimensional style.

Lippizaner. Variant of *Lipizzaner.*

lip-read (lip-reed) *v.* **-read** (-red), **-reading, -reads.** —*tr.* To interpret (another's utterance) by lip-reading. —*intr.* To use lip-reading. —**lip-read·er** *n.*

lip-read·ing (lip-reeding) *n.* A technique used, especially by the deaf, to understand inaudible speech by interpreting lip and facial movements.

lip service *n.* Superficial respect or agreement.

lip·stick (líp-stik) *n.* A stick of waxy or creamy lip colouring enclosed in a small cylindrical case.

liq. 1. liquid. **2.** liquor.

li·quate (lí-kwáyt ‖ lí-kwayt) *tr.v.* **-quated, -quating, -quates.** To separate (the metals in an alloy) by melting some constituents while leaving others solid. [Latin *liquāre,* to melt, dissolve.] —**li·qua·tion** (-kwáysh'n) *n.*

liq·ue·fac·tion (líkwi-fáksh'n) *n.* **1.** The process of liquefying. **2.** The state of being liquefied.

liq·ue·fi·er (líkwi-fī-ər) *n.* A device that liquefies; especially, an apparatus for liquefying gases.

liq·ue·fy (líkwi-fī) *v.* **-fied, -fying, -fies.** —*tr.* To cause to become liquid, especially: **1.** To melt (a solid) by heating. **2.** To condense (a gas) by cooling. —*intr.* To become liquid. —See Synonyms at **melt.** [Old French *liquefier,* from Latin *liquefacere* : *liquēre,* to be liquid + *facere,* to make.] —**liq·ue·fa·cient** (-fáysh'nt) *n.*

li·ques·cent (li-kwéss'nt) *adj.* Becoming or tending to become liquid; melting. [Latin *liquescēns* (stem *liquescent-*), present participle of *liquescere,* to become liquid, from *liquēre,* to be liquid.] —**li·ques·cence, li·ques·cen·cy** *n.*

li·queur (li-kéwr, -kér, -kör) *n.* **1.** A sweet syrupy alcoholic beverage, often with a brandy base, usually drunk in small quantities at the end of a meal. **2.** A mixture of sugar and wine used for inducing the second fermentation in the making of champagne. [French, from Old French *licour,* liquid, LIQUOR.]

liq·uid (líkwid) *n. Abbr.* **liq. 1.** The state of matter in which a substance exhibits a characteristic readiness to flow, little or no tendency to disperse, and relatively high incompressibility. **2.** Matter or a specific body of matter in this state. **3.** *Phonetics.* A liquid consonant.

~*adj.* **1.** Of or being a liquid. **2.** Liquefied, especially: **a.** Melted by heating: *liquid wax.* **b.** Condensed by cooling: *liquid oxygen.* **3.** Clear; shining: *liquid eyes.* **4.** Flowing and clear; musical: *a liquid voice.* **5.** *Phonetics.* Designating a consonant, especially (l) or (r), that is produced without friction and can be prolonged like a vowel. **6.** Flowing gracefully in motion. **7.** Readily converted into cash: *liquid assets.* [Middle English *liquide* (adjective), from Old French, from Latin *liquidus,* from *liquēre,* to be liquid.] —**liq·uid·ly** *adv.*

liquid air *n.* Air in the liquid state, condensed from the gas by cooling and sometimes pressure, and used as a refrigerant.

liq·uid·am·bar (líkwid-ámbər) *n.* A tree of the genus *Liquidambar,* such as the sweet gum. [New Latin *Liquidambar,* "liquid amber" (from its aromatic resin) : LIQUID + Medieval Latin *ambar,* ambergris, AMBER.]

liq·ui·date (líkwi-dayt) *v.* **-dated, -dating, -dates.** —*tr.* **1.** To pay off or settle (a debt, claim, or obligation). **2.** To wind up the affairs of (a business, a bankrupt estate, or the like) by determining the liabilities and applying the assets to their discharge. **3.** To convert (assets) into cash. **4.** To abolish. **5.** To dispose of; kill, especially by impersonal means: *The double agent was liquidated.* —*intr.* To go into liquidation. [Late Latin *liquidāre,* to make clear, melt, from Latin *liquidus,* LIQUID.] —**liq·ui·dat·or** *n.*

liq·ui·da·tion (líkwi-dáysh'n) *n.* **1.** The action or process of liquidating. **2.** The state of being liquidated.

liquid crystal *n.* Any of various liquids in which the atoms or molecules have partial order and are regularly arrayed in either one dimension or two dimensions, the order giving rise to optical properties, such as anisotropic scattering, associated with the crystals.

liquid-crystal display (líkwid-krístʹl) *n.* See **LCD.**

liquid glass *n.* Sodium silicate (*see*).

liq·uid·ise, liq·uid·ize (líkwi-dīz) *v.* **-ised, -ising, -ises.** —*tr.* **1.** To make liquid. **2.** To process (food) in a blender so as to reduce it to a liquid. —*intr.* To become liquid.

liq·uid·ise·r (líkwi-dīzər) *n. Chiefly British.* A **blender** *(see).*
li·quid·i·ty (li-kwíddəti) *n., pl.* **-ties.** **1.** The condition or quality of being liquid. **2.** The condition of having sufficient cash or liquid assets to pay debts or assume obligations.
liquidity preference *n. Economics.* A preference, influenced by factors such as income level and interest rates, for keeping one's assets in the form of money rather than investing them.
liquid measure *n.* **1.** A unit or system of units of liquid capacity. **2.** A measure for liquids.
liquid oxygen *n.* A pale blue liquid produced by distilling liquid air and used as a rocket fuel. Boiling point −182.9°C. Also called "lox".
liquid paraffin *n.* A clear oily liquid obtained by distillation of petroleum and used as a laxative. Also *chiefly U.S.* "mineral oil".
liq·uor (líckər) *n. Abbr.* **liq.** **1. a.** Alcoholic drink made by distillation or fermentation. **b.** *U.S.* Alcoholic spirits. **2.** A liquid substance, such as broth or juice, which has been used in cooking. **3.** *Pharmacy.* An aqueous solution of a nonvolatile substance. **4.** A solution, emulsion, or suspension for industrial use. **5.** Warm water used in brewing.
~*tr.v.* **liquored, -uoring, -uors.** **1. a.** To treat (leather) with grease. **b.** To steep (malt, for example) in warm water. **2.** *Chiefly U.S. Slang.* To cause to become drunk with alcoholic spirits. Used with *up.* [Middle English *lic(o)ur,* liquid, beverage, from Old French, from Latin *liquor,* from *liquēre,* to be liquid.]
li·quo·rice, *U.S.* **li·co·rice** (líckə-riss, -rish) *n.* Also **li·quo·rish** (-rish). **1.** A plant, *Glycyrrhiza glabra,* of the Mediterranean region, having blue flowers and a sweet, distinctively flavoured root. **2.** The root of this plant, used as a flavouring in sweets, drinks, tobacco, and medicines. **3.** A sweet made from or flavoured with this root. **4.** Any of various plants resembling or tasting like liquorice, especially the wild liquorice, *Astragalus glycyphyllos.* [Middle English *licoris, licorice,* from Anglo-French *lycorys* and Old French *licoresse, licorece,* from Late Latin *liquirītia,* alteration (influenced by Latin LIQUOR) of Greek *glukurrhiza,* "sweetroot": *glukus,* sweet + *rhiza,* root.]
liquorice all·sort (áwl-sort) *n.* Any of a number of variously coloured and shaped sweets, typically made from liquorice and sugar icing.
liquorish. **1.** Variant of **lickerish.** **2.** Variant of **liquorice.**
li·ra (léer-ə) *n., pl.* **lire** (-ay) or **-ras.** *Abbr.* **l.** **1.** The standard monetary unit of Italy. **2.** The standard monetary unit of Turkey, equal to 100 kurus. **3.** A coin or note worth one lira. [Italian, from Latin *lībra,* balance, measure.]
lir·i·o·den·dron (lírri-ə-déndrən) *n., pl.* **-drons** or **-dra.** Any of various trees of the genus *Liriodendron* in the family Magnoliaceae, especially the tulip tree, *L. tulipifera,* from North America, or *L. chinense* from China. [New Latin, from greek *leirion,* lily + *dendron,* tree.]
Lis·bon (lízbən). *Portuguese* **Lis·bo·a** (lizh-bṓ-ə). Capital and chief port of Portugal lying on the Tagus estuary. It exports wine, cork, and tinned fish, and produces textiles, chemicals, and paper. Voyages of discovery in the 15th and 16th centuries made it one of Europe's wealthiest cities. The city was rebuilt after an earthquake destroyed it in 1755.
-lish *n. comb. form. Informal.* Indicates English language. Used to suggest that another language (such as Japanese or Tagalog) has been heavily influenced by English; for example, **Japlish, Taglish.** [Abstracted from *English.*]
lisle (līl) *n.* **1.** A fine, smooth, tightly twisted cotton thread used especially for hosiery and underwear. Also called "lisle thread". **2.** Fabric knitted of lisle. [From *Lisle,* earlier form of LILLE, where it was originally made.]
lisp (lisp) *n.* **1.** A speech defect or mannerism characterised by the failure to produce normal sibilants, especially by the substitution of the sounds (th) and (th) for the sibilants (s) and (z). **2.** A sound suggestive of a lisp, such as the rustling of leaves.
~*v.* **lisped, lisping, lisps.** —*intr.* **1.** To speak with a lisp. **2.** To speak imperfectly, as a child does. —*tr.* To pronounce or express with a lisp. [Middle English *(w)lispen,* Old English *wlispian* (attested only in compound *awlispian*), from *wlisp,* a lisping, akin to Old High German *lisp* (imitative).] **—lisp·er** *n.*
Lis·sa·jous figure (lée-sə-zhōō, -zhōō) *n.* A type of curve: the locus of a point that moves with two simple harmonic motions in mutually perpendicular directions, the shape depending on the frequencies and relative phase of the motions. Lissajous figures can be formed from two electrical signals on an oscilloscope and used to measure frequency and phase. [After Jules *Lissajous* (1822-80), French physicist.]
lis·som, lis·some (líss'm) *adj.* **1.** Lithe; supple. **2.** Capable of moving with ease; limber; nimble. [Variant of LITHESOME.] **—lis·som·ly** *adv.* **—lis·som·ness** *n.*
list¹ (list) *n.* An item-by-item printed or written entry of persons or things, often arranged in a particular order, and usually of a specified nature or category: *a guest list; a shopping list.*
~*v.* **listed, listing, lists.** —*tr.* **1.** To make a list of; itemise. **2.** To enter in a list or register, especially: **a.** To register (a security) as officially approved for trading on the stock exchange. **b.** *British.* To classify as a listed building. **3.** *Archaic.* To enlist. —*intr. Archaic.* To enlist in the armed forces. [Old French *liste,* band, border, strip of paper, list, from Old Italian *lista,* from Germanic.]
list² *n.* **1.** A border or selvage of cloth, usually of a different material from the cloth it is bordering. **2.** A stripe or band of colour. **3.** *Obsolete.* A boundary; a border. **4.** *Plural.* **a.** An arena for tournaments or other contests. **b.** Any scene of combat. **5.** *U.S.* A ridge thrown up between two furrows in ploughing. [Middle English *liste,* border, edge, strip, Old English *līste.*]
list³ *n.* An inclination to one side, as of a ship; a tilt.
~*v.* **listed, listing, lists.** *Nautical.* —*intr.* To lean or tilt to the side. —*tr.* To cause (a ship) to list. [Origin unknown.]
list⁴ *v.* **listed, listing, lists.** *Poetic.* —*tr.* To listen to. —*intr.* To listen. [Middle English *listen, lusten,* Old English *hlystan.*]
list⁵ *v.* **listed, listing, lists.** *Archaic.* —*tr.* To be pleasing to; satisfy; please. —*intr.* To be disposed; choose.
~*n. Archaic.* A desire or inclination. [Middle English *listen,* Old English *lystan.*]
list·ed building (lístid) *n. British.* A building designated as being of particular historical or architectural interest and therefore subject to restrictions regarding to its alteration or demolition.
lis·tel (líst'l) *n. Architecture.* A narrow border, moulding, or fillet. [Old French, from Old Italian *listello,* diminutive of *lista,* band, border, LIST.]
lis·ten (líss'n) *intr.v.* **-tened, -tening, -tens.** **1.** To apply oneself to hearing something. **2.** To take notice; heed: *begged her to reconsider, but she wouldn't listen.* **3.** To be alert so as to hear. Used with *for.* **—listen in.** **1.** To tune in and listen to a broadcast. **2.** To listen to a conversation, sometimes surreptitiously. [Middle English *listnen,* Old English *hlysnan.*] **—lis·ten·er** *n.*
Lis·ter (lístər), **Joseph, 1st Baron** (1827–1912). British surgeon. He demonstrated in 1865 that carbolic acid was an effective antiseptic agent, showing that hygiene could save lives during surgery.
lis·ter·ia (li-stéer-i-ə) *n.* The bacterium *Listeria monocytogenes,* which can cause meningitis, septicaemia, and listeriosis (a form of food poisoning). [After Joseph LISTER.]
list·ing (listing) *n.* **1.** An entry in a list. **2.** A list. **3.** *Computing.* A series of records on a file. **4.** *Plural.* Information, such as details of forthcoming events, presented in the form of lists. Also used adjectivally: *listings magazines.*
list·less (líst-ləss, -liss) *adj.* Marked by a lack of energy or enthusiasm; disinclined towards any effort; indifferent; languid. [Middle English *listles* : *list,* desire, from *listen,* to be pleasing, to LIST + -LESS.] **—list·less·ly** *adv.* **—list·less·ness** *n.*
list price *n.* A basic published or advertised price, often subject to discount.
Liszt (list), **Franz** (1811–86). Hungarian composer. In his lifetime he was more famous for his virtuoso piano playing than his compositions. His popular works include 20 *Hungarian Rhapsodies,* 6 Paganini *Études,* and 2 piano concertos.
lit¹. **1.** Alternative past tense and past participle of **light** (to illuminate). **2.** Alternative past tense and past participle of **light** (to descend).
lit². **1.** literal; literally. **2.** literary; literature.
lit·a·ny (líttəni, lítt'n-i) *n., pl.* **-nies.** **1.** A liturgical prayer consisting of phrases recited by a leader alternating with responses by the congregation. **2.** *Capital* **L.** The set of prayers in this form in the Book of Common Prayer. **3.** Any repetitive or incantatory recital. [Middle English *letanie,* from Old French, from Late Latin *litanīa,* from Greek *litaneia,* entreaty, from *litanuein,* to entreat, from *litanos,* entreating, from *litē*†, supplication.]
litchi. Variant of **lychee.**
lit. crit. (lít krít) *n. Informal.* Literary criticism.
-lite *n. comb. form.* Indicates stone. Used in names of minerals; for example, **cryolite, actinolite.** [French *-lite* and German *-lit,* variants of *-lithe* and *-lith,* from Greek *lithos,* stone.]
liter. *U.S.* Variant of **litre.**
lit·er·a·cy (líttrə-si, líttərə-) *n.* **1.** The condition or quality of being literate; especially, the ability to read, write, and use language. **2.** A basic understanding of or ability in a specified discipline.
lit·e·rae hu·man·i·o·res (líttər-ee hew-mánni-áwr-eez; *also* -ī -ayz) *n. Used with a singular verb.* The faculty of classics, philosophy, and ancient history at Oxford University. [Latin, "the more humane studies".]
lit·er·al (líttrəl, líttərəl) *adj. Abbr.* **lit.** **1.** In accordance with, conforming to, or upholding the explicit or primary meaning of a word or the words of a text. **2.** Word for word; verbatim: *a literal translation.* **3.** Matter-of-fact; prosaic: *a literal mind.* **4.** Avoiding exaggeration, metaphor, or embellishment; plain: *a literal statement.* **5.** Consisting of, using, or expressed by letters: *literal notation.*
~*n.* A misspelling or misprint. Also called "literal error". [Middle English *lit(t)eral,* of letters, written, from Old French *literal,* from Late Latin *litterālis,* from Latin *littera,* letter.] **—lit·er·al·ness** *n.*
lit·er·al·ise, lit·er·al·ize (líttrəl-īz, líttərəl-) *tr.v.* **-ised, -ising, -ises.** To make literal.
lit·er·al·ism (líttrəl-iz'm, líttərəl-) *n.* **1.** Adherence to the explicit sense of a given text or doctrine. **2.** Literal portrayal; realism. **—lit·er·al·ist** *n.* **—lit·er·al·is·tic** (-ístik) *adj.*
lit·er·al·ly (líttrəli, líttərəli) *adv. Abbr.* **lit.** **1.** In a literal or strict sense. **2.** Really; actually: *She literally works 12 hours a day.* **3.** *Nonstandard.* Used as an intensive: *The company is literally bleeding to death.*
lit·er·ar·y (líttrəri, líttə-rəri || -rerri. *Note: the pronunciation* littri *is nonstandard*) *adj. Abbr.* **lit.** **1.** Of, pertaining to, or dealing with literature. **2. a.** Found in or appropriate to literature: *a literary style.* **b.** Employed chiefly in writing rather than speaking: *a literary language.* **3.** Versed in or fond of literature or learning: *a literary woman.* **4.** Of or pertaining to writers or the profession of literature: *literary circles.* [French *littéraire,* from Latin *litterārius,* of

writing, from *litterae,* epistle, writing, plural of *littera,* letter.] —**lit·er·ar·i·ly** *adv.* —**lit·er·ar·i·ness** *n.*

literary agent *n.* A person who handles an author's business affairs, especially in dealing with publishers. —**literary agency** *n.*

lit·er·ate (líttrət, líttər-ət, -it) *adj.* **1. a.** Able to read and write. **b.** Able to write well. **2.** Knowledgeable; educated. **3.** Familiar with literature; literary.
~*n.* **1.** A literate person. **2.** One admitted to holy orders in the Church of England without having a university degree. [Middle English *litterate,* from Latin *lit(t)erātus,* acquainted with writings, learned, from *litterae,* epistle, writing, plural of *littera,* letter.]

lit·e·ra·ti (líttə-raáti, *old-fashioned* -ráytī) *pl.n.* The literary intelligentsia. [Italian, from Latin *litterātī,* plural of *litterātus,* LITERATE.]

lit·e·ra·tim (líttə-raátim, -ráytim) *adv.* Literally; letter for letter. [Medieval Latin, from *lit(t)era,* letter.]

lit·er·a·ture (líttri-chər, líttrə-, líttəri-, -tewr) *n. Abbr.* **lit. 1.** A body of writings in prose or verse. **2.** Writings of particular excellence or artistic value. **3.** The art or occupation of a writer of artistic or critical works. **4.** The body of written work produced by scholars or researchers in a given field: *medical literature.* **5.** Printed material of any kind, as for a political or publicity campaign. **6.** *Archaic.* Literary culture; learning. [Middle English *litterature,* from Old French, from Latin *litterātūra,* writing, learning, from *litterātus,* learned, LITERATE.]

-lith *n. comb. form.* Indicates stone or rock; for example, **monolith, palaeolith.** [Greek *lithos,* stone.]

lith. lithograph; lithographic; lithography.

lith·arge (líthaarj || *U.S. also* li-thárj) *n.* A yellow lead oxide, PbO, used in storage batteries, glass, and as a pigment. Also called "lead monoxide". Compare **massicot.** [Middle English *lit(h)arge,* from Old French, from Latin *lithargyrus,* from Greek *litharguros,* "silver stone" : LITH(O)- + *arguros,* silver.]

lithe (lī̲th) *adj.* **1.** Supple; limber. **2.** Marked by effortless grace. [Middle English *lith(e), lythe,* meek, mild, flexible, Old English *līthe.*] —**lithe·ly** *adv.* —**lithe·ness** *n.*

lithe·some (lī̲th-s'm) *adj.* Lithe; lissom.

li·thi·a·sis (li-thī-ə-siss) *n. Pathology.* The formation of stones in the body. [New Latin, from Greek : LITH(O)- + -IASIS.]

lithia water *n.* Mineral water containing some lithium salts.

lith·ic (líthik) *adj.* **1.** Pertaining to stone. **2.** Pertaining to lithium. [Greek *lithikos,* from *lithos,* stone.] —**lith·ic·al·ly** *adv.*

-lithic *adj. comb. form.* Indicates the use of stone; for example, **Neolithic.**

lith·i·um (líthi-əm) *n.* **1.** *Symbol* **Li** A soft, silvery, highly reactive metallic element that is used as a heat-transfer medium, in thermonuclear weapons, and in various alloys, ceramics, and optical forms of glass. Atomic number 3, atomic weight 6.939, melting point 179°C, boiling point 1317°C, relative density 0.534, valency 1. **2.** *Informal.* Lithium carbonate as a drug. [New Latin : LITH (from its mineral origin) + -IUM.]

lithium carbonate *n.* A white crystalline solid, Li_2CO_3, used in the ceramic and glass industries and as a drug in the treatment and prevention of manic-depression and some depressive conditions.

lithium oxide *n.* A strongly alkaline white powder, Li_2O, used in ceramics and glass. Also called "lithia".

litho–, lith– *comb. form.* Indicates stone; for example, **lithosphere, lithia.** [Latin, from Greek, from *lithos*†, stone.]

litho., lithog. lithograph; lithographic; lithography.

lith·o·graph (líth-ə-graaf, -ō-, -graf; *in technical usage often* līth-) *n. Abbr.* **lith., litho., lithog.** A print produced by lithography.
~*tr.v.* **lithographed, -graphing, -graphs.** To produce by lithography. [Back-formation from LITHOGRAPHY.] —**li·thog·raph·er** (li-thógrəfər, lī-) *n.* —**lith·o·graph·ic** (-gráffik), **lith·o·graph·i·cal** *adj.* —**lith·o·graph·i·cal·ly** *adv.*

li·thog·ra·phy (li-thógrəfi, lī-) *n. Abbr.* **lith., litho., lithog.** A printing process in which the image to be printed is rendered on a flat surface, as on stone or now chiefly on sheet zinc or aluminium, and treated so that it will retain ink while the nonimage areas are treated to repel ink. [German *Lithographie* : LITHO- + -GRAPHY.]

li·thol·o·gy (li-thólləji) *n.* **1.** The physical character of a rock or rock formation. **2.** The study, description, and classification of rock, generally in handheld specimens and outcrops. [New Latin *lithologia* : LITHO- + -LOGY.] —**lith·o·log·ic** (líthə-lójik), **lith·o·log·i·cal** *adj.* —**lith·o·log·i·cal·ly** *adv.* —**li·thol·o·gist** (li-thólləjist) *n.*

lith·o·phyte (líthə-fīt) *n.* **1.** *Botany.* A plant that grows on a rocky surface. **2.** An organism, such as coral, having a stony structure. [French : LITHO- + -PHYTE.] —**lith·o·phyt·ic** (-fíttik) *adj.*

lith·o·pone (líth-ə-pōn, -ō-) *n.* A white pigment consisting of a mixture of zinc sulphide, zinc oxide, and barium sulphate. [LITHO- + Greek *ponos,* artefact, product.]

lith·o·sphere (líth-ə-sfeer, -ō-) *n.* The solid outer layer of the Earth. It lies above the asthenosphere, and includes the crust and solid upper part of the mantle down to about 75 kilometres (47 miles).

lith·o·stra·tig·ra·phy (líth-ə-stra-tíggrəfi, -ō-, -strə-) *n.* **1.** Stratigraphy based on the physical and petrographic properties of rocks. **2.** The interpretation of the physical characters of sedimentary rocks. —**lith·o·strat·i·graph·ic** (-strátti-gráffik) *adj.*

li·thot·o·my (li-thóttəmi) *n., pl.* **-mies.** A surgical operation to remove stones from the urinary tract. [Late Latin *lithotomia,* from Greek : LITHO- + -TOMY.]

li·thot·ri·ty (li-thóttrəti) *n., pl.* **-ties.** A surgical operation to pulverise stones in the bladder or urethra. [Irregularly from Greek *lithōn thrutika,* "stone-crushing (drug)" : *lithōn,* genitive plural of *lithos,* stone + *thrutikos,* crushing, from *thruptein,* to crush.]

Lith·u·a·ni·a, Republic of (líthew-áyni-ə, líthoo-). *Lithuanian* **Lie·tu·va** (lye-tōō-vaá). Formerly a constituent republic of the U.S.S.R., bordering on the Baltic Sea. Once a flourishing state, Lithuania was a province of the Russian empire from 1795, but became an independent republic in 1918. It was incorporated into the U.S.S.R. in 1940. From 1988 a nationalist movement gained majority support, leading to a unilateral declaration of independence. In 1991 Soviet forces seized key buildings to restore control, but independence was achieved after the break-up of the U.S.S.R. Area 65 200 square kilometres (25,174 square miles). Population, 3,710,000. Capital, Vilnius. See map at **Baltic States.**

Lith·u·a·ni·an (líthew-áyni-ən, lithōō-) *adj.* Of or pertaining to Lithuania, its people, or their language.
~*n.* **1.** An inhabitant or native of Lithuania. **2.** The Baltic language of Lithuania.

lit·i·gant (líttigənt) *n.* One who is engaged in a lawsuit.
~*adj.* Engaged in a lawsuit. [Latin *lītigāns* (stem *lītigant-*), present participle of *lītigāre,* LITIGATE.]

lit·i·gate (lítti-gayt) *v.* **-gated, -gating, -gates.** —*tr.* To subject (something) to legal proceedings; contest. —*intr.* To engage in legal proceedings. [Latin *lītigāre,* to dispute, quarrel, sue : *līs*† (stem *līt-*), lawsuit + *agere,* to drive, lead, act.] —**lit·i·ga·tor** (-gaytər) *n.*

lit·i·ga·tion (lítti-gáysh'n) *n.* Legal action or process.

li·ti·gious (li-tíjəss) *adj.* **1.** Given to or fond of litigation. **2.** Disputable at law; litigable. —**li·ti·gious·ly** *adv.* —**li·ti·gious·ness** *n.*

lit·mus (lít-məss) *n.* A blue, amorphous powder derived from certain lichens, that takes on a red colour in acid solutions and a blue in alkaline solutions. [Perhaps from Old Norse *litmosi,* "dye moss" : *litr,* a dye, colour + *mosi,* moss.]

litmus paper *n.* An unsized white paper impregnated with litmus and used as an acid-base indicator.

litmus test *n.* **1.** A test to determine alkalinity or acidity using litmus paper. **2.** Any decisive test: *The strike will be a litmus test of the government's industrial relations policy.*

li·to·tes (lī-tō-teez, lī-tō-, -tə- || *U.S. also* líttə-) *n.* A figure of speech consisting of an understatement in which an affirmative is expressed by the negation of its opposite, as in *This is no small problem.* [Greek *litotēs,* from *lītos,* simple, plain, unadorned.]

li·tre, *U.S.* **li·ter** (leétər) *n. Abbr.* **l. 1.** A unit of volume equal to one cubic decimetre (0.22 gallon). **2.** Formerly, a unit of volume equal to the volume of one kilogram of pure water at its temperature of maximum density (4° C) and at standard pressure (760mmHg); it is equivalent to 1.000 028 cubic decimetres. ***Note:*** The first definition is a special name for the cubic decimetre in SI units. The second definition, based on a volume of water, is still applicable for purposes of the British 1963 Weights and Measures Act. Because of the small difference between the two defined volumes, use of the term *litre* is not recommended for expressing precise measurements. [French, from *litron,* (an obsolete measure of capacity), from Medieval Latin, from Greek, a monetary unit of Sicily.]

Litt. B., Lit. B. Bachelor of Letters [Latin *Litterarum Baccalaureus.*]

Litt.D., Lit.D. Doctor of Letters [Latin *Litterarum Doctor.*]

lit·ter (líttər) *n.* **1.** A disorderly accumulation of objects; especially, carelessly discarded rubbish, paper, and the like. **2.** The young produced at one birth by a multiparous mammal. **3. a.** Straw or other material used as bedding for livestock. **b.** Granules of a porous material based on fuller's earth or sawdust, kept in a tray so that pets may excrete indoors. Also called "cat litter". **4.** A conveyance carried by people or animals, typically an enclosed couch mounted on shafts. **5.** A stretcher for the sick or wounded. **6.** The uppermost layer of a forest floor, consisting chiefly of decaying leaves.
~*v.* **littered, -tering, -ters.** —*tr.* **1.** To give birth to (young). **2. a.** To make untidy by discarding rubbish carelessly. **b.** To lie scattered untidily about (a place): *discarded cans and bottles littering the streets.* **3.** To scatter about. **4.** To supply (animals) with litter for bedding. —*intr.* **1.** To give birth to a litter. **2.** To scatter litter. [Middle English *litere,* bed, offspring at birth, from Anglo-French, variant of Old French *litiere,* from Medieval Latin *lectāria,* from Latin *lectus,* bed.]

lit·tér·a·teur, lit·ter·a·teur (líttə-rə-tér, -ra-, -tóor, -tŏr) *n.* A literary person, especially a writer. [French, from Latin *litterātor,* elementary teacher, grammarian, from *littera,* LETTER.]

lit·ter·lout (líttər-lowt) *n. Informal.* One who litters public areas with discarded rubbish. Also *U.S.* "litterbug".

lit·tle (lítt'l) *adj.* **littler** or **less** (less) (especially for senses 2, 3, 4), **littlest** or **least** (leest) (especially for senses 2, 3, 4). **1.** Small, or smaller by comparison. **2.** Short in extent or duration; brief: *in a little while.* **3. a.** Small in quantity or degree; not as much as needed or desired: *little hope of a recovery; speaks little English.* **b.** Small, but not too small, in quantity or degree. Preceded by *a*: *speaks a little English; Would you like a little sugar?* **4.** Unimportant; trivial; insignificant: *life's little troubles.* **5.** Without much force; weak. **6.** Narrow; petty. **7.** Without much power or influence; of minor status. **8. a.** Being at an early stage of growth. Said of children and animals. **b.** Younger: *my little sister.* **c.** Smaller or smallest of a set: *little toe.* **9.** Operating on a relatively small scale: *the little man who mends radios.* **10.** Resembling the specified person, place, or thing, but on a smaller scale: *Little Venice.* **11.** Appealing; endearing: *the little rascal; a pretty little cottage.* —See Synonyms at **small.**
~*adv.* **less, least. 1.** Not much; scarcely: *He sleeps little.* Often used in combination: *little-known; little-loved.* **2.** Rarely: *I see her very little.* **3.** Not at all; not in the least. Used before a verb: *I little*

thought I'd see you here; little did she know . .
~*n.* **1.** A small quantity: *Give me a little.* **2.** An insignificant amount. **3.** A short distance or time: *a little down the road; a little past four o'clock.* —**in little.** On a small scale. —**little by little.** By small degrees or increments; gradually. —**make little of.** To regard or treat as not very important; dismiss. —**think little of.** **1.** To have no hesitation about (some course of action). **2.** To think of as relatively unimportant or valueless. [Middle English *litel, lutel,* Old English *lȳtel.*] —**lit·tle·ness** *n.*

little auk *n.* A small, short-billed, stout-bodied diving bird, *Plautus alle,* with a black and white plumage. It is found in northern oceans. Also called "dovekie".

Little Bear *n.* **Ursa Minor** *(see).* Also *U.S.* "Little Dipper".

little bird *n.* An informant whose name is supposedly not known. Used humorously or ironically. [From the traditional phrase refusing to name one's informant, "A little bird told me".]

little end *n. Mechanics.* **1.** The smaller end of a connecting rod. **2.** The bearing between this and the gudgeon pin.

little Eng·land·er (ing-glǝndǝr) *n.* One who advocates a self-sufficient British foreign policy, as: **1.** In the 19th century, an opponent of imperialist expansion. **2.** An opponent of involvement in the European Economic Community.

little finger *n.* The smallest finger on the hand, the fifth and last as counted from the thumb.

little grebe *n.* A small Old World grebe, *Podiceps ruficollis,* having a chestnut throat.

little hours *pl.n. Roman Catholic Church.* The canonical hours of prime, terce, sext, and nones, and sometimes including vespers and compline.

little magazine *n.* A literary magazine specialising in experimental writings and appealing to a limited readership.

little owl *n.* A small Old World owl, *Athene noctua,* having speckled brownish plumage.

little people *pl.n. Chiefly Irish.* Fairies, pixies, and the like; especially, leprechauns.

little slam. See **slam.**

Lit·tle·wood (litt'l-woŏd), **Joan (Maud)** (1914–). British theatre director. In 1945 she founded the Theatre Workshop in Manchester and in 1953 moved it to the Theatre Royal, Stratford, in London's East End. It specialised in plays about contemporary social issues. Her productions include *Oh, What a Lovely War!* (1963).

lit·to·ral (littǝrǝl) *adj.* Of or existing on a shore.
~*n.* A shore or coastal region, especially the zone between the high- and low-tide marks of spring tides. [Latin *littorālis, lītorālis,* from *lītus (lītor-),* shore.]

li·tur·gics (li-túrjiks) *n. Used with a singular verb.* The study of liturgies. Also called "liturgiology".

lit·ur·gist (littǝrjist) *n.* **1.** One who uses or advocates the use of liturgical forms. **2.** A scholar in liturgics.

lit·ur·gy (littǝrji) *n., pl.* **-gies.** **1.** The rite of the Eucharist. **2. a.** A system of public worship in the Christian church. **b.** The Book of Common Prayer. [Late Latin *lītūrgia,* from Greek *leitourgia,* public service, service of a priest, from *leitourgos,* public servant, minister, priest : *leōs* (stem *leit-*), variant of *laos,* people, multitude + *ergon,* work.] —**li·tur·gi·cal** (li-túrjik'l) *adj.* —**li·tur·gi·cal·ly** *adv.*

Lit·vi·nov (lit-vée-noff; *Russian* -nǝf), **Maxim Maximovich,** born Maxim Maximovich Wallach (1876–1951). Soviet politician. He was Soviet Foreign Minister (1930–39) and ambassador to the United States (1941–43).

Liu Shao-qi or **Liu Shao-ch'i** (lyō shów-chée) (*c.* 1898–1973). Chinese Communist leader. He was Chairman of the People's Republic of China from 1959 until he was purged in 1966 during the Cultural Revolution. He was officially rehabilitated in 1980.

liv·a·ble, live·a·ble (lívvǝb'l) *adj.* **1.** Fit to live in; habitable. **2.** Worth living.

live¹ (liv) *v.* **lived, living, lives.** —*intr.* **1.** To exhibit the characteristic signs of life. **2.** To continue to remain alive: *lived to a great age.* **3.** To subsist; be maintained: *living on rice and fish; lived on inherited income.* **4. a.** To have one's usual dwelling in a particular place; reside. **b.** *Informal.* To be usually kept: *Where do these knives live?* **5.** To conduct one's existence in a particular manner: *lived by the old code of personal honour; lives for her work.* **6.** To enjoy life and experience it to the full: *They really know how to live.* **7. a.** To remain in human memory: *She lives in the minds of us all.* Often used with *on.* **b.** To remain in existence; escape destruction. Often used with *on: Despite persecution, the faith lived on.* —*tr.* **1.** To go through (a particular form of existence or experience): *lived a nightmare.* **2.** To embody in one's manner of existence: *We lived our beliefs.* —**live and let live.** To be tolerant. —**live down.** *Informal.* To live sufficiently long, or sufficiently blamelessly, to overcome the effects of (a scandal, for example). —**live it up.** *Informal.* To have fun, especially in an extravagant way. —**live out.** **1.** To reside away from the place where one works or studies. **2.** To live through (a period); live beyond (a time limit): *The injured butterfly lived out the day.* —**live together.** To reside together, especially in sexual intimacy. —**live up to.** **1.** To succeed in guiding one's life by: *live up to religious ideals.* **2.** To show oneself to be as good as: *live up to a great reputation.* —**live with.** **1.** To reside with, especially in sexual intimacy. **2.** To put up with (a continuing adverse factor). [Middle English *liven,* Old English *libban, lifian.*]

live² (līv) *adj.* **1.** Having life. **2.** Characteristic of life. **3.** Of current interest: *a live topic.* **4.** Actual, as opposed to pretended or imitation: *a real live princess.* **5.** Glowing; burning: *a live coal.* **6.** Brilliant; vivid. **7. a.** Explosible: *a live bomb.* **b.** Charged with a bullet or shell; not blank: *live ammunition.* **8.** *Electricity.* Carrying current or electric potential. **9.** Native; not mined or quarried. Said of rocks and ores. **10. a.** Designating or participating in a programme broadcast at the time of filming rather than recorded in advance. **b.** Involving actual performers rather than recorded material: *a party with live music.* **11.** *Printing.* **a.** Not yet set into type: *live copy.* **b.** Set and still in use. Said of type. **12.** *Sports.* Being or capable of being in play: *a live ball.*
~*adv.* As, participating in, or during a live broadcast, performance, or the like: *a rock band playing live.* [Shortened from ALIVE.]

live-bear·er (līv-báir-ǝr, -bair-) *n.* An ovoviviparous fish, such as a guppy. —**live-bear·ing** *adj.*

live in *intr.v.* To reside in the place where one works or studies.

live-in (lív-in) *adj.* **1.** Living in the place where one works: *a live-in barmaid.* **2.** Living with another person without being married: *her live-in companion.*

live·li·hood (lívli-hoŏd) *n.* Means of support; subsistence. [Variant (influenced by LIVELY and -HOOD) of Middle English *liv(e)lode,* course of life, sustenance, Old English *līflād* : *līf,* LIFE + *lād,* course.]

Synonyms: *livelihood, living, subsistence, maintenance, keep.*

live load (līv) *n.* A moving, variable weight added to the dead load or intrinsic weight of a structure or vehicle. Compare **dead load.**

live·long (liv-long ‖ līv-, *U.S. also* -lawng) *adj.* **1.** Long or seemingly long in passing. **2.** Complete; whole. Used chiefly in the phrase *the livelong day.* **3.** *British.* A plant, the **orpine** *(see).* [Middle English *lefe longe,* "dear long" : *lef,* "dear" (here used as an intensive), Old English *lēof* + LONG.]

live·ly (lívli) *adj.* **-lier, -liest.** **1.** Full of life; vigorous; energetic. **2.** Full of activity, interest, or excitement. **3.** Exhibiting or characterised by intense intellectual or emotional activity; keen: *a lively debate.* **4.** Exhibiting or inspiring liveliness; gay; cheerful. **5.** Effervescent; sparkling. **6.** Invigorating; brisk. **7.** Bouncing readily upon impact; resilient, as a ball is. **8.** *Nautical.* Buoyant; rising lightly with the sea swell. **9.** Lifelike. —See Synonyms at **active.**
~*adv.* In a vigorous, energetic, or spirited manner. —**look lively.** To hurry up; make haste. Usually used in the imperative. [Middle English *lifliche,* Old English *līflic,* living, vital, from *līf,* life.] —**live·li·ly** *adv.* —**live·li·ness** *n.*

li·ven (līv'n) *v.* **-vened, -vening, -vens.** —*tr.* To cause to become lively. Often used with *up.* —*intr.* To become lively. Often used with *up.*

live oak (līv) *n.* Any of several evergreen North American oaks, such as *Quercus virginiana,* of the southeastern United States.

liv·er¹ (lívvǝr) *n.* **1.** *Anatomy.* A large, reddish-brown, multilobed, vertebrate gland situated in the top right hand part of the abdominal cavity. It secretes bile and acts in the formation of blood and in the metabolism of carbohydrates, fats, proteins, minerals, and vitamins. **2.** A similar invertebrate organ. **3.** The liver of an animal, used as food. [Middle English *liver,* Old English *lifer.*]

liver² *n.* One who lives in a specified manner: *a loose liver.*

liver extract *n.* A dry, brownish powder containing vitamin B_{12}, which is prepared from mammalian livers and is capable of increasing the number of healthy red blood corpuscles in persons suffering from pernicious anaemia.

liver fluke *n.* **1.** Any of several parasitic trematode worms, such as *Fasciola hepatica* or *Opisthorchis sinensis* (or *Clonorchis sinensis*), that infest the liver of various animals, including human beings. **2.** Infestation with such parasites. Also called "liver rot".

liv·er·ied (lívvǝ-rid ‖ -reed) *adj.* Wearing livery, especially as a servant.

liv·er·ish (lívvǝrish) *adj.* **1.** Resembling liver, particularly in colour. **2.** Having a liver disorder; bilious. **3.** Having a disagreeable disposition; irritable.

Liv·er·pool (lívvǝr-poŏl). City, port and Unitary Authority area in northeast England, Britain's second largest port after London. The city's Anglican cathedral, begun in 1904 and completed in 1978, is the largest Anglican cathedral in the world. The modernist Roman Catholic cathedral, designed by Frederick Gibberd, was opened in 1968. Liverpool's industries include chemicals and engineering.

Liverpool, Robert Banks Jenkinson, 2nd Earl of (1770–1828). English Tory politician. He was prime minister (1812–27) longer than anyone except Walpole and the younger Pitt.

Liv·er·pud·li·an (lívvǝr-púddli-ǝn) *n.* A native or inhabitant of Liverpool.
~*adj.* Of or pertaining to Liverpool, its inhabitants, or its characteristic speech. [From *Liverpool,* with humorous substitution of *puddle* for *pool.*]

liver salts *pl.n.* A mixture of mineral salts taken to relieve indigestion or biliousness.

liver sausage *n.* A type of sausage made of or containing liver. Also *chiefly U.S.* "liverwurst".

liver spot *n.* A localised brown discoloration of the skin occurring especially in old age; a lentigo.

liver starch *n.* A carbohydrate, **glycogen** *(see).*

liv·er·wort (lívvǝr-wurt ‖ -wawrt) *n.* Any of numerous green non-flowering plants of the class Hepaticae within the division Bryophyta, found in moist habitats and lacking true roots. Also called "hepatic". [Referring to its liver-shaped leaves.]

liv·er·y (lívvǝri) *n., pl.* **-ies.** **1.** The distinctive uniform or insignia worn by a person's servants or retainers. **2.** The distinctive dress or garb worn by the members of a particular organisation or group.

899

3. Any distinctive dress or outward marking. **4.** Persons collectively who wear such costumes or uniforms, such as the members of a livery company. **5.** *Archaic.* **a.** The provision of food or clothing to servants. **b.** The boarding and care of horses for a fee. **6.** *U.S.* A livery stable. **7.** *Archaic. Law.* The official transfer of property, especially land, to a new owner. [Middle English *livere, liverye,* from Anglo-French *livere,* variant of Old French *livree,* "something delivered or given", allowance (later clothes) granted to servants, from the feminine past participle of *livrer,* to deliver, relieve, from Latin *līberāre,* to set free, from *līber,* free.]

livery company *n.* Any of various associations in the City of London that originated from the early trade guilds. Their members are no longer necessarily connected with the trades after which the companies are named, but they retain considerable influence over the election of the Lord Mayor and other City officers.

liv·er·y·man (lívvəri-mən) *n., pl.* **-men** (-mən, -men). **1.** A keeper or employee of a livery stable. **2.** A member of a livery company.

livery stable *n.* A stable that boards horses and keeps horses and carriages for hire.

lives. Plural of **life**.

live steam (līv) *n.* Steam coming from a boiler at full pressure.

live·stock (līv-stok) *n. Used with a singular or plural verb.* Domestic animals, such as cattle, sheep, or goats, raised for home use or for profit, especially on a farm.

live·ware (līv-wair) *n.* Programmers and other operating personnel working in a computer installation. [By analogy with **hardware, software**.]

live wire (līv) *n.* **1.** A wire carrying electric current. **2.** *Slang.* An extremely vivacious, alert, or energetic person.

liv·id (lívvid) *adj.* **1.** Having a bluish discoloration of the skin, as from a bruise. **2.** Ashen or pallid, as with illness or rage. **3.** Extremely angry; furious. [French *livide,* from Latin *līvidus,* from *līvēre,* to be bluish.] **—li·vid·i·ty** (li-víddəti), **liv·id·ness** *n.* **—liv·id·ly** *adv.*

liv·ing (lívving) *adj.* **1.** Possessing life; alive. **2. a.** Still alive; not yet dead. **b.** In active function or use. **c.** Still in existence as a species; extant. **3.** Of or pertaining to persons who are alive. **4. a.** Of, pertaining to, or characteristic of daily life: *living standards.* **b.** Of or pertaining to the maintenance of existence: *living costs.* **5.** True to life; real: *the living image of her mother.* **6.** Experienced while still alive: *a living hell.*
~*n.* **1.** The state or condition of being alive. **2.** A manner or style of life: *plain living.* **3.** A manner or means of maintaining life; a livelihood. **4.** *British.* A church benefice, including the revenue attached to it. **—See Synonyms at livelihood.**
Synonyms: living, alive, extant.

living fossil *n.* An extant organism, such as a coelacanth, that belongs to a taxonomic group whose other members have become extinct.

living memory *n.* The collective experience or memory of all those currently alive: *the worst winter in living memory.*

living room, living-room (lívving-room, -room) *n.* A room in a private residence intended for the general use of the members of the household and for the reception and entertainment of guests.

Liv·ing·stone (lívving-stən || -stōn). City of southern Zambia, on the Zambezi river. Named after David Livingstone (1905), it was the capital of Northern Rhodesia from 1911 to 1935, when Lusaka replaced it.

Livingstone, David (1813–73). British missionary and explorer. He discovered the Zambezi river in 1851 and Victoria Falls in 1855. While searching for the source of the Nile (from 1866), he discovered Lake Mweru and Lake Bangweulu. Sickness forced him to return to Ujiji, on Lake Tanganyika, where Stanley found him in 1871.

living wage *n.* A wage sufficient to provide minimally satisfactory living conditions.

living will *n.* A person's directive that if terminally ill or fatally injured he or she is not officiously to be kept alive in demeaning conditions.

Li·vor·no (li-vórnō). *English* **Leg·horn** (lég-hawrn, -hórn). Seaport and capital of Livorno province, Tuscany, Italy.

li·vre (léevrə; *French* leevr) *n. Abbr.* **lv.** A former French unit of account originally worth a pound of silver. [French, from Latin *lībra,* a pound.]

Liv·y (lívvi). Latin name Titus Livius (*c.*59 B.C.–A.D. 17). Roman historian, born in Padua. His history of Rome originally consisted of 142 books, of which only 35 survive.

lix·iv·i·ate (lik-sívvi-ayt) *tr.v.* **-ated, -ating, -ates.** To wash or percolate the soluble matter from. [Late Latin *lixīvium,* lye, from the neuter of *lixīvius,* of lye, from *lixa,* lye.] **—lix·iv·i·al** *adj.* **—lix·iv·i·a·tion** (-áysh'n) *n.*

lix·iv·i·um (lik-sívvi-əm) *n., pl.* **-ums** or **-ivia** (-ivvi-ə). A solution obtained by lixiviation; especially, the lye obtained by leaching wood ash. [Late Latin, from *lixivius,* of lye, from *lix,* lye.]

liz·ard (lízzərd) *n.* **1.** Any of numerous reptiles of the suborder Sauria (or Lacertilia), characteristically having an elongated, scaly body, four legs, and a tapering tail. **2.** Broadly, any reptile or amphibian resembling a lizard. **3.** Leather made from the skin of a lizard. [Middle English *liserd, lesard(e),* from Old French *lesard, laisarde,* from Latin *lacertus, lacerta†.*]

lizard fish *n.* Any of various bottom-dwelling fishes of the family Synodontidae, of warm seas, having a lizard-like head.

Liz·ard Point (lízzərd). The most southerly point of England, at the end of the Lizard peninsula in Cornwall.

Ljub·lja·na (léwbli-aánə, loóbli-, loóbli-). Capital of Slovenia, lying on the Sava river. It is an industrial and tourist centre.

II. lines.

lla·ma (laámə; *Spanish* yaámə) *n.* **1.** A South American ruminant mammal, *Lama peruana* (or *L. glana*), domesticated as a beast of burden and for its soft, fleecy wool. **2.** Any other animal of the genus *Lama,* such as the guanaco and the alpaca. [Spanish, from Quechua.]

Llan·daff (hlan-dəf, hlán-, -dáf). *Welsh* **Llan·daf** (hlan-daáv). City that since 1922 has formed part of the city of Cardiff, Wales.

Llan·dud·no (hlan-díd-nō, lan-, -dúd-). Holiday resort on the north coast of Wales.

Llan·ell·i (hla-néhli, lə-néthli, la-). Town on the Burry estuary, Carmarthenshire, Wales. Its port was closed in 1951, and tin-plate manufacturing and petrochemicals are now the main industry.

Llan·fair PG (lán-fair peé jeé; *Welsh* hlán-vīr). Also **Llan·fair·pwll** (-poóhl) or **Llan·fair·pwll·gwyn·gyll** (-poóhl-gwín-gihl). Village in Anglesey, north Wales, with the longest possibly authentic place name in Britain: Llanfairpwllgwyngyllgogerychwyrndrobwllllantysiliogogogoch, formed from the names of two neighbouring hamlets.

Llan·goll·en (hlan-góhlen, lan-góthlən). Market town in central Denbighshire, north Wales, where the International Eisteddfod, an annual festival of traditional music, poetry, and dance, has been held since 1947.

lla·no (laánō || *U.S. also* lánnō) *n., pl.* **-nos.** A large, grassy, almost treeless plain, as in Latin America; savannah. [Spanish, from Latin *plānum,* a plain, from the neuter of *plānus,* level.]

LL.B. Bachelor of Laws [Latin *Legum Baccalaureus*].

LL.D. Doctor of Laws [Latin *Legum Doctor*].

Lle·well·yn (hlə-wéllin, lə-, loo-éllin), **Sir Harry,** also known as Lieutenant-Colonel Sir Henry Morton Llewellyn (1911–). British show-jumper. He won many prizes with his horse Foxhunter.

Llewellyn, Richard, pen name of Richard Dafydd Vivian Llewellyn Lloyd (1907–83). British novelist, born in Wales. He wrote *How Green Was My Valley* (1939), a portrait of life in a South Wales mining village.

LL.M. Master of Laws [Latin *Legum Magister*].

Lloyd, Harold (Clayton) (1893–1971). U.S. comedian of the silent screen. His stunts included hanging from a clockface high above a street in *Safety Last* (1923).

Lloyd, Marie, stage name of Matilda Wood (1870–1922). British music-hall artiste, famous for such songs as *Oh, I Do Like to be Beside the Seaside.* Her Cockney humour won her great popularity.

Lloyd George, David, 1st Earl of Dwyfor (1863–1945). British prime minister (1916–22). He was elected a Liberal M.P. in 1890, and as Chancellor of the Exchequer (1908–15) initiated the welfare state, introducing old-age pensions, unemployment benefit, and national health insurance. In 1916 he succeeded Asquith as prime minister. His postwar coalition government set up the Irish Free State, but resigned in 1922. Lloyd George remained Liberal party leader until 1931, but never held office again.

Lloyd's (loydz) *n.* An association of underwriters founded in London in 1688, originally specialising in marine insurance and shipping information and now noted for the variety of insurance dealt with. [After *Lloyd's* Coffee House in London, a gathering place of marine underwriters.]

Lloyd's List *n.* A daily newssheet concerned with shipping matters, published by Lloyd's of London.

Lloyd's Register *n.* A compilation of data about oceangoing vessels, published annually by Lloyd's Register of Shipping.

Lloyd-Web·ber (wébbər), **Andrew, Baron** (1948–). British composer. He was responsible for several popular musicals, such as *Joseph and the Amazing Technicolor Dreamcoat, Jesus Christ Superstar, Evita, Cats,* and *The Phantom of the Opera.*

Lly·wel·yn ap Gru·ffudd (hlə-wéllin ap gríffith), also called Llywelyn II (died 1282). Native-born Prince of Wales (1258–82), known as Llywelyn the Last. His death in a war with the English king Edward I marked the end of Welsh independence.

Llywelyn ap Ior·werth (ap yór-wairth), also called Llywelyn I (1173–1240). Welsh Prince of Gwynedd (1194–1238), known as Llywelyn the Great. He paid homage to King John of England, but commanded the allegiance of lesser princes in Wales. In 1238 he became a monk, handing over the succession to his son.

lm lumen.

LM lunar module.

LMT local mean time.

lo (lō) *interj.* Used to attract attention or to show surprise. Now archaic except in the phrase *lo and behold.* [Middle English *lo, la,* Old English *lā.*]

loach (lōch) *n.* Any of various Eurasian and African freshwater fishes of the family Cobitidae, having barbels around the mouth. [Middle English *loch(e),* from Old French *lochet†.*]

load (lōd) *n. Abbr.* **ld.** **1. a.** A supported weight or mass. **b.** The overall force to which a structure is subjected in supporting a weight or mass, or in resisting externally applied forces. **2. a.** Anything that is transported by a motor vehicle, ship, or aircraft, or carried by a person or pack animal. **b.** The quantity so transported or capable of being so transported: *a full load.* Often used in combination: *a busload of football supporters.* **3. a.** The share of work allocated to or required of an individual, machine, group, or organisation: *has a fairly light teaching load.* **b.** The demand for services

or performance made on a machine or system. **4.** The amount that can be loaded into a machine or device at one time. **5.** A single charge of ammunition for a firearm. **6.** A source of stress or anxiety, regarded as a depressing weight on the mind; a burden. **7.** The external mechanical resistance against which a machine acts. **8. a.** The power output of a generator or power plant. **b.** A device, or the resistance of a device, to which power is delivered. **9.** *Geology.* Material carried by a river, stream, sea, glacier, or wind during the process of denudation. **10.** *Usually plural. Informal.* Any large amount or quantity. —**get a load of.** *Chiefly U.S. Slang.* To look at or pay attention to: *Get a load of that!* —**shed** or **shoot (one's) load.** *Vulgar Slang.* To ejaculate semen.
~*v.* **loaded, loading, loads.** —*tr.* **1.** To put or place (a load) in or on a structure, device, or conveyance. **2.** To put or place in or on (a structure, device, or conveyance). **3.** To provide with an abundant or excessive supply. **4.** To weigh down; burden; oppress. **5.** To charge (a firearm) with ammunition. **6. a.** To insert (film or tape, for example) into a holder or magazine. **b.** To insert film or tape, for example, into (a magazine, camera, or similar device). **7.** To tamper with; especially, to make (dice) heavier on one side by adding weight. **8. a.** To twist or bias (evidence). **b.** To charge (a question) with broader implications that may not be immediately obvious, especially so as to trap the person being questioned. **9.** To dilute, adulterate, or doctor. **10.** To increase (an insurance premium) by adding a loading. **11.** *Electricity.* **a.** To raise the power demand in (a circuit), as by adding resistance. **b.** To draw power from (a generator). **12.** To raise the power output of (an engine). **13.** *Physics.* To add a material such as barium to (concrete, for example) in order to increase radiation-shielding efficiency. —*intr.* **1.** To receive a load; take on cargo. **2.** To be charged with ammunition. **3.** To insert ammunition, film, or tape, for example. [Middle English *lode* (influenced in sense by Middle English *laden,* to load, LADE), Old English *lād,* way, course, conveyance.]
Usage: The past tense and past participle of this verb are both *loaded: We loaded the goods; The goods were loaded. Laden* is an adjective, generally used after the verb unless premodified itself: *The table was laden with good things to eat; a heavily laden table.* In contexts where either word could be used, there is usually a difference in meaning: *The ship was loaded with ammunition* (i.e. ammunition was put on board by someone or something), but *The ship was laden with ammunition* (it was weighed down with ammunition).
load displacement *n. Nautical.* The displacement of a fully loaded ship.
load·ed (lṓdid) *adj. Slang.* **1.** Extremely wealthy. **2.** Drunk. **3.** *Chiefly U.S.* Drugged.
load·er (lṓdər) *n.* **1.** One that loads. **2.** *Computing.* A program that transfers data from an off-line memory to an on-line memory by means of an input or storage device. **3.** An apparatus, such as a washing machine or firearm, that is loaded in the specified way. Used in combination: *top-loader; breechloader.*
load·ing (lṓding) *n. Abbr.* **ldg. 1.** A weight, stress, or burden. **2.** The act of supplying a load. **3.** A substance added to something; a filler. **4.** An addition to an insurance premium taking account of special circumstances: *an extra loading for those with hazardous occupations.* **5.** *Electricity.* The addition of inductance to a transmission line to improve its transmission characteristics. **6.** *Aeronautics.* The ratio of the weight of an aircraft to its power (the *power loading*), to its wing span (the *span loading*), or to its wing area (the *wing loading*). **7.** *Psychology.* The correlation or degree of correlation between a specific factor or variable, such as a test score, and a broad condition or constant, such as a personality trait. **8.** A contractually agreed bonus or extra payment added to basic wages or salary in certain conditions; a weighting.
loading program *n. Computing.* A sequence of computer instructions that starts the processing of a program entered by means of an automatic input device.
load line *n. Nautical.* A Plimsoll line *(see).*
load shedding *n.* Temporary reduction of the electric power supply in an area to avoid overloading the generators.
loadstar. Variant of **lodestar.**
loadstone. Variant of **lodestone.**
loaf[1] (lōf) *n., pl.* **loaves** (lōvz). **1.** A shaped mass of bread baked in one piece. **2.** Any shaped, typically oblong mass of food: *nut loaf.* **3.** *British Slang.* The head; the brains: *Use your loaf.* [Middle English *lo(o)f, laf,* Old English *hlāf,* loaf, bread, from Germanic *hlaibaz* (unattested). See also **lord, lady.** Sense 3, rhyming slang, *loaf of bread, head.*]
loaf[2] *v.* **loafed, loafing, loafs.** —*intr.* **1.** To spend time lazily or aimlessly. Used with *around* or *about.* **2.** To waste time on a job; dawdle. —*tr.* To spend (time) lazily or idly. Usually used with *away.* [Probably back-formation from LOAFER.]
loaf·er (lṓfər) *n.* **1.** One who loafs. **2.** *Chiefly U.S.* A casual or informal moccasin-like shoe. [Perhaps from German *Landläufer,* wanderer, vagabond.]
loam (lōm) *n.* **1.** Fertile soil consisting of sand, clay, silt, and organic matter. **2.** A mixture of moist clay and sand, together with straw, used principally in making bricks and foundry moulds. [Middle English *lome, lame,* Old English *lām.*] —**loam·y** *adj.*
loan[1] (lōn) *n.* **1.** A sum of money lent at interest. **2.** Anything lent for temporary use. **3.** An act of lending or permission to borrow: *gave me the loan of her bike.* **4.** A loanword. —**on loan. 1.** Borrowed: *She has my coat on loan.* **2.** Transferred temporarily to some duty or place away from a regular position or location.

~*tr.v.* **loaned, loaning, loans.** To lend; grant a loan of. [Middle English *lone, lane,* from Old Norse *lān.*]
Usage: The use of *loan* as a verb is increasingly common, especially in American English, where it is encountered in formal as well as informal contexts: *Can you loan me 50 dollars?* Many people prefer to restrict *loan* to its use as a noun, especially in British English, using *lend* as the analogous verb. But *loan* is now often used in the sense of "making a formal act of lending, especially to an institution" in British English: *She has loaned her collection to a museum.*
loan[2] *n.* Also **loan·ing** (lōning). *Chiefly Scottish.* **1.** A lane. **2.** An open space where cows are milked. [Middle English, variant of LANE.]
loan translation *n.* The process or an instance of verbal borrowing from one language to another, whereby the semantic components or morphemes of a given term are literally translated into their equivalents in the borrowing language; for example, *superman* is a loan translation of the German word *Übermensch* (*über,* over = *super-; Mensch,* man = *man*). Also called "calque".
loan word *n.* A word adopted from another language that has become at least partly naturalised; for example, *angst, hors d'oeuvre.*
loath, loth (lōth ‖ lōth) *adj.* Unwilling; reluctant. Usually used with an infinitive: *loath to go.* —**nothing loath.** Willing; willingly. [Middle English *loth(e), lath,* Old English *lāth,* hateful, loathsome.]
loathe (lōth) *tr.v.* **loathed, loathing, loathes.** To detest greatly; abhor. [Middle English *lothen,* Old English *lāthian.*] —**loath·er** *n.* —**loath·ing·ly** *adv.*
loath·ing (lṓthing) *n.* Abhorrence.
loath·some (lṓth-səm, lōth-) *adj.* Also *archaic* **loath·ly** (-li). Repulsive; disgusting. [Middle English *lothsum : loth,* hatred, Old English *lāth,* from adjective (see **loath**) + -SOME.] —**loath·some·ly** *adv.*
loaves. Plural of **loaf.**
lob (lob) *v.* **lobbed, lobbing, lobs.** —*tr.* **1.** To hit, toss, or propel slowly in or as if in a high arc. **2.** *Informal.* To throw casually; toss. —*intr.* To hit a ball in a high arc.
~*n.* **1.** A ball hit, bowled, or thrown in a high arc. **2.** An act of lobbing a ball. [Probably of Low German origin, akin to Low German *lubbe,* awkward person. [Middle Low German *lobbe†,* hanging lip, thus extended to anything clumsy, pendulous, or slow.]
Lo·ba·chev·ski (lóbbə-chéfski; *Russian* ləbə-), **Nikolai Ivanovich** (1793–1856). Russian mathematician. His revolutionary system of geometry, published in 1829, challenged the accepted Euclidean theory.
lo·bar (lṓb-ər ‖ -aar) *adj.* Of or pertaining to a lobe, such as one of those in the lungs: *lobar pneumonia.*
lo·bate (lṓbayt) *adj.* Also **lo·bat·ed** (lō-báytid ‖ *chiefly U.S.* lṓ-bay-tid) **1.** Having lobes. **2.** Resembling a lobe. **3.** Having separate toes, each bordered with a weblike lobe. Said of certain birds. —**lo·bate·ly** *adv.*
lo·ba·tion (lō-báysh'n) *n.* **1.** The state of being lobed. **2.** A lobe or part resembling a lobe.
lob·by (lóbbi) *n., pl.* **-bies. 1. a.** An entrance hall or corridor. **b.** A foyer, waiting room, or reception area in a hotel, theatre, or other public building. **2. a.** A public room next to the assembly chamber of a legislative body, where legislators and members of the public can meet. **b.** Any of three anterooms in the British Houses of Parliament, the *members' lobby* for members of the House of Commons, the *peers' lobby* for members of the House of Lords, and the *central lobby* for all members of Parliament and members of the public. **3.** *Chiefly British.* Either of the two corridors attached to a legislative chamber to which the members go to register their votes. In this sense, also called "division lobby". **4.** A group of people, usually representing a particular interest, who seek to influence legislation: *the environmental lobby.* **5.** *Often capital* L. A group of British political journalists having access to cabinet ministers and senior civil servants, from whom they acquire confidential information on *lobby terms,* allowing the information to be reported without the source being identified.
~*v.* **lobbied, -bying, -bies.** —*intr.* To seek to influence legislators in favour of some special interest. —*tr.* **1.** To seek to influence or gain the support of (legislators or public opinion, for example). **2.** To seek to influence legislators to pass (legislation). [Medieval Latin *lobium, lobia, laubia,* a monastic cloister, from Germanic.] —**lob·bi·er, lob·by·er** *n.*
lob·by·ist (lóbbi-ist) *n.* One employed to influence legislators to introduce or vote for measures favourable to the interest he represents. —**lob·by·ism** *n.*
lobe (lōb) *n.* **1.** A rounded projection; especially, a rounded, projecting anatomical part such as the ear lobe *(see).* **2.** A subdivision of an organ or part bounded by fissures, connective tissue, or other structural boundaries. **3.** A loop forming part of a curve or graph. [Late Latin *lobus,* from Greek *lobos,* lobe (of the ear or liver).]
lo·bec·to·my (lōb-ĕktəmi) *n., pl.* **-mies.** A surgical operation for the excision of a lobe. [LOB(E) + -ECTOMY.]
lobed (lōbd) *adj.* Having lobes: *lobed leaves.*
lobe·fin (lṓb-fin) *n.* Any of various mostly extinct bony fishes of the subclass Sarcopterygii, of which the coelacanth is a living representative.
lo·be·li·a (lō-béel-i-ə, lə-, -yə) *n.* Any of numerous plants of the genus *Lobelia,* having terminal clusters of variously coloured, often blue, flowers. It is widely grown as an ornamental border plant. [New Latin, after Matthias de Lobel (1538–1616), Flemish botanist.]

Lo·ben·gu·la (lṓ-ben-gŏͦ-lə, -géw-) (c.1836–94). King of the Nde-bele (1870–94), ruling in Bulawayo. In 1888 he granted mineral concessions to Cecil Rhodes's British South Africa Company, which later subjugated his kingdom (1893), forcing him into exile.

lo·bo (lṓ-bō) n., pl. **-bos**. U.S. The grey or timber wolf, Canis lupus. [Spanish, from Latin lupus, wolf.]

lo·bo·la (lō-bŏ́-lə, law-báw-) n. Also **lo·bo·lo** (-lō). South African. 1. A wedding gift, comparable to a dowry, among black African peoples, consisting of a payment in cash or cattle made by the bridegroom or his family to the family of his prospective wife. 2. The amount involved in such a transaction; the bride price. [Zulu.]

lo·bot·o·mise, lo·bot·o·mize (lō-bottəmīz) tr.v. **-mised, -mising, -mises**. 1. To perform a labotomy on. 2. Informal. To make dull, zombie-like, or conformist: lobotomised couch potatoes.

lo·bot·o·my (lō-bóttəmi, lə-) n., pl. **-mies** 1. A surgical division of one or more cerebral nerve tracts in the frontal lobe of the brain. See **leucotomy**. 2. Surgical incision into a lobe. [LOB(E) + -TOMY.] **—lo·bot·o·mise** (-mīz) tr.v.

lob·scouse (lób-skowss) n. A seaman's stew made of meat, vegeta-bles, and hardtack. [Perhaps dialectal lob, to bubble, boil + scouse†, broth.]

lob·ster (lób-stər) n., pl. **-sters** or collectively **lobster**. 1. Any of several relatively large marine crustaceans of the genus Homarus, having five pairs of legs, the first pair modified into large claws. 2. Any of several related crustaceans, such as the **spiny lobster** (see). 3. The flesh of any of these crustaceans, used as food. 4. A bright orange-red, the colour of cooked lobster. [Middle English lobster, lopster, Old English loppestre, lopystre, from Latin locusta, locust, lobster (influenced by Old English loppe, spider).] **—lob·ster** adj.

lobster pot n. A slatted cage with an opening covered by a funnel-shaped net, used for trapping lobsters underwater. Also called "lob-ster trap".

lob·u·late (lóbbew-lət, -lit, -layt) adj. Also **lob·u·lat·ed** (-laytid) Having or consisting of lobules. **—lob·u·la·tion** (-láysh'n) n.

lob·ule (lóbbewl) n. 1. A small lobe. 2. A section or subdivision of a lobe. [French, from New Latin lobulus, diminutive of Late Latin lobus, LOBE.] **—lob·u·lar** (-ər), **lob·u·lose** (-ōz, -ōss) adj. **—lob·u·lar·ly** adv.

lob·worm (lób-wurm) n. A lugworm (see). [LOB (obsolete sense "lump") + WORM.]

lo·cal (lṓk'l) adj. 1. Of or pertaining to a place. 2. Pertaining to, existing in, of interest to, peculiar to, or serving a certain locality: local government. 3. Not broad or general; confined: a little local difficulty. 4. Medicine. Of or affecting a limited part of the body; not systemic: a local disease. 5. Making many stops; not express: a local train.
~n. 1. A local person; a native inhabitant. 2. A public conveyance that makes all possible or scheduled stops. 3. British Informal. A pub close to one's work or home. 4. Informal. A local anaesthetic. 5. U.S. A local branch of an organisation, especially of a trade union. [Middle English, from Old French, from Late Latin locālis, from Latin locus, place, LOCUS.]

local anaesthetic n. Medicine. An injected or topically applied anaesthetic that induces loss of sensation in a particular region of the body. Compare **general anaesthetic**.

local area network n. Abbr. **LAN** A network of word processors or computers connected together, for example in an office building, so that information can be transferred from one to another or accessed from a main store.

local authority n. British. A local council and its officials, respon-sible for administering the services of an area; the organ of local government.

local colour n. The atmosphere or flavour of a locality imparted by the presentation, as in a novel, of the customs and sights peculiar to that locality.

lo·cale (lō-ka·al ‖ chiefly U.S. -kál) n. 1. A locality, with reference to some event. 2. The scene or setting, as of a novel. [French local, locality, from Old French, LOCAL.]

lo·cal·ise, lo·cal·ize (lṓkə-līz) v. **-ised, -ising, -ises**. 1. To make local. 2. To confine or restrict to a particular area or part. 3. To assign to a locality or determine more precisely the origin or source of: localise a dialect. **—lo·cal·is·a·tion** (-lī-záysh'n ‖ U.S. -li-) n.

lo·cal·ism (lṓk'l-iz'm) n. 1. An idiom, mannerism, custom, or the like peculiar to a locality. 2. Provincialism.

lo·cal·i·ty (lə-kál-əti, lō-) n., pl. **-ties**. 1. A neighbourhood, place, or district. 2. A site, as of an event. 3. The fact or quality of having position in space. **—See Synonyms at area**. [French localité, from Late Latin locālitās (stem locālitāt-), from locālis, LOCAL.]

lo·cal·ly (lṓkəli) adv. At or near a particular location: lives locally.

local option n. An option granted usually by a central or regional government to a community or a local government, allowing it dis-cretion, sometimes subject to a referendum, in such issues as whether to keep shops open or to sell spirits on Sundays.

local solar time n. Local time.

local time n. The time of day at any point on Earth indicated by the apparent movement of the sun, as shown on a sundial. Also called "apparent time", "local solar time". Compare **mean solar time**.

Lo·car·no (lə-kárnō, lō-, lo-). Resort on Lake Maggiore in the south of canton Ticino, Switzerland. It was here in 1925 that representa-tives of Belgium, Czechoslovakia, France, Germany, Great Britain, Italy, and Poland drew up the Locarno Pact. Among other things this resolved the status of the Rhineland and guaranteed the French-German and Belgian-German borders.

lo·cate (lō-káyt, lə- ‖ chiefly U.S. lṓ-kayt) v. **-cated, -cating, -cates**. —tr. 1. To determine or specify the position and boundaries of: locate Timbuktu on the map. 2. To find by searching, examining, or experimenting: locate the source of error. 3. To station, situate, or place: locate an agent in Nice. —intr. U.S. To become established in a spot; settle. [Latin locāre, to place, from locus, place, LOCUS.]

lo·ca·tion (lə-káysh'n, lō-) n. 1. The act or process of locating. 2. The fact of being located or settled. 3. A place or position where something is or might be located. 4. In television or film produc-tion, a site away from the studio grounds, where a scene is shot: That safari film was made on location. 5. South African. A small township for black or Coloured residents. [Latin locātio (stem locā-tiōn-), a placing, from locāre, to place, LOCATE.]

loc·a·tive (lóckətiv) n. Grammar. 1. The noun case in certain Indo-European languages, such as Sanskrit or Old Church Slavonic, that denotes the place where. 2. A form or construction in this case. ~adj. Designating, pertaining to, or inflected in the locative. [French locatif, from Old French, from Latin locāre, to LOCATE.]

loc. cit. adv. In the place cited. [Latin locō citātō.]

loch (lokh, lok) n. In Scotland: 1. A lake. 2. A sea loch. [Middle English (Scottish) louch, from Scottish Gaelic loch, probably from Old Irish.]

loch·an n. In Scotland, a small lake. [LOCH and Gaelic diminutive suffix -an.]

lo·chi·a (lócki-ə ‖ lṓki-ə) pl.n. The normal discharge of blood, tis-sue, and mucus from the vagina after childbirth. [New Latin, from Greek lokhia, from neuter plural of lokhios, of childbirth, from lok-hos, childbirth.] **—lo·chi·al** adj.

lo·ci. Plural of locus.

lock[1] (lok) n. 1. A device used to provide restraint; especially, a key- or combination-operated mechanism used to fasten shut a door, lid, or the like. 2. Such a device used to prevent unauthorised operation of a machine: a telephone lock. 3. A section of a canal closed off by gates, within which a vessel may be raised or lowered by the raising or lowering of the section's water level. 4. A mechanism in a fire-arm for exploding its charge of ammunition. Usually used in combi-nation: a flintlock. 5. A jamming or locking together of elements or parts. 6. Any of several holds in wrestling. 7. In Rugby football: a. Either of the two forwards who form the second row of the scrum. b. The position of such a player. In both senses, also called "lock forward". 8. British. The degree of turn of which a motor vehicle is capable; the turning base. 9. A gas bubble or pocket preventing the flow of liquid through a pipe. **—lock, stock, and barrel**. Completely; totally. **—under lock and key**. In complete security or safety.
~v. **locked, locking, locks**. —tr. 1. To fasten with a lock, as: a. To secure against passage or entry: lock a door. b. To secure against loss or theft: lock a bicycle. 2. a. To confine or safeguard by putting behind a lock. Used with in or up: lock the dog in for the night. 3. To engage and fix together securely; intertwine. 4. To clasp or embrace tightly. 5. To entangle in struggle or battle. 6. To jam or force together so as to make unmovable. 7. To pass (a ves-sel) through a lock. 8. To provide or section off (a waterway) with locks. —intr. 1. a. To become fastened by or as if by a lock. b. To admit of being locked: Does this drawer lock? 2. To become entan-gled; interlock. 3. To become rigid or unmovable. 4. To pass or flow through a lock. 5. To find, fasten onto, and automatically follow a target, especially with radar. Used with on or onto. [Middle English lo(c)k, Old English loc.] **—lock·a·ble** adj.

lock[2] n. 1. A strand or curl of hair; a tress. 2. Plural. The hair of the head. 3. A small wisp or tuft, as of wool or cotton. [Middle English lock, lok(k), Old English locc.]

lock·age (lóckij) n. Nautical. 1. The passage of a vessel through a lock by operation of the lock. 2. The toll for the use of a lock. 3. a. A system of locks. b. The works of a lock. 4. The amount of the rise and fall effected by a lock or system of locks.

Locke (lok), **John** (1632–1704). English empiricist philosopher, au-thor of An Essay Concerning Human Understanding (1690). His Two Treatises of Government (1690) justified the English Revolution of 1688, opposing the notion of the divine right of kings.

lock·er (lóckər) n. 1. One that locks. 2. A small metal cupboard or enclosure that may be locked; especially, one of many provided at a sporting centre or school for the safekeeping of clothing and valu-ables. 3. A flat storage trunk.

locker room n. 1. A room in a gymnasium, school, clubhouse, or the like, furnished with rows of lockers. 2. A room for changing one's clothes, as at public swimming baths.

lock·et (lóckit) n. A small ornamental metal case for a picture or keepsake, such as a lock of hair, usually worn as a pendant. [Old French locquet, latch, small lock, diminutive of loc, lock, probably from Old English loc, lock.]

lock·jaw (lók-jaw) n. Pathology. 1. Tetanus (see). 2. A symptom of tetanus, in which the jaws are clamped shut because of a tonic spasm of the muscles of mastication. Also called "trismus".

lock·nut (lók-nut) n. 1. A usually thin nut screwed down on a pri-mary nut to keep the latter from loosening. 2. A self-locking nut.

lock out tr.v. 1. To bar or shut out by locking a door. 2. To refuse work to (employees) during a dispute.

lock·out (lók-owt) n. The closing down of a place of employment by an employer to coerce the workers into meeting his terms or modi-fying theirs. Also called "shutout".

lock·smith (lók-smith) n. One who makes or repairs locks.

lock step *n.* A marching technique in which the marchers follow each other as closely as possible.
lock stitch *n.* A stitch made on a sewing machine by the interlocking of the upper thread and the bobbin thread.
lock up *tr.v.* **1.** To shut and make secure by fastening all locks: *lock up a house.* **2.** To put in jail or some other place of confinement. **3.** *Printing.* **a.** To secure (letterpress type) in a chase or press bed by tightening the quoins. **b.** To fasten (a curved plate) to the cylinder of a rotary press. **4.** To invest (funds) in such a way that they cannot easily be converted back into cash.
~*intr.v.* To shut and make secure a house or other premises, as when going out in the evening.
lock·up (lók-up) *n.* **1.** An act of locking up or the state of being locked up. **2.** *Informal.* A jail, especially a local one in which offenders are held while awaiting a court hearing. **3.** *British.* A small shop or other business premises where the manager or proprietor does not live. Also used adjectivally: *a lockup shop.* **4.** *British.* A garage or row of garages, often at some distance from the owner's home or place of work.
lo·co[1] (lṓkō) *adj. Chiefly U.S. Slang.* Mad; insane. [Spanish *loco*†, crazy, insane.]
lo·co·mo·tion (lṓkə-mṓsh'n) *n.* **1.** The act of moving or ability to move from place to place. **2.** Movement from place to place; travel. [Latin *locō,* ablative of *locus,* place, LOCUS + MOTION.]
lo·co·mo·tive (lṓkə-mōtiv, -mṓtiv) *n.* Also *Informal* **loco**[2]. A self-propelled engine, now usually electric or diesel-powered, that pulls or pushes trains along railway tracks.
~*adj.* **1.** Of or involved in locomotion. **2.** Able to move independently from place to place. **3.** Of or pertaining to travel. [Latin *locō* (see **locomotion**) + MOTIVE.]
lo·co·mo·tor (lṓkə-mṓtər, -mōtər) *adj.* Locomotive. [Latin *locō* (see **locomotion**) + *mōtor,* mover, MOTOR.]
locomotor ataxia *n. Pathology.* **Tabes dorsalis** *(see).*
lo·co·weed (lṓkō-weed) *n.* Any of several plants of the genera *Oxytropis* and *Astragalus,* of the western and central United States, causing severe poisoning when eaten by livestock. [Mexican Spanish *loco,* locoweed, from Spanish, LOCO (referring to the effects of the poison, which seems to drive livestock mad).]
loc·u·lar (lóckew-lər) *adj.* Also **loc·u·late** (-layt, -lat, -lit), **loc·u·lat·ed** (-laytid). *Biology.* Having, formed of, or divided into small cells or cavities. **—loc·u·la·tion** (-láysh'n) *n.*
loc·ule (lóckewl) *n.* Also **loc·u·lus** (-əss) *pl.* **-li** (-ī). A small cavity or compartment within an organ or part, such as any of the cavities within a plant ovary. [Latin, diminutive of *locus,* place, LOCUS.]
lo·cum (lṓkəm) *n. Chiefly British.* A clergyman, chemist, or, especially, a doctor, temporarily replacing another. Also called "locum tenens". [Medieval Latin *locum tenēns,* "(one) holding the place".]
lo·cus (lṓkəss, lóckəss) *n., pl.* **-ci** (lṓ-sī, lóckee). **1.** A place, especially when considered as the site of a particular activity. **2.** *Mathematics.* The set or configuration of all points satisfying given conditions. **3.** *Genetics.* The position that a gene occupies on a chromosome. [Latin *locus*†, place.]
locus clas·si·cus (klássi-kəss) *n., pl.* **loci classici** (-sī, -kee). A passage from a classic or standard work that is often cited as an authoritative illustration or instance. [Latin, "classical place".]
locus stan·di (stán-dī, -dee) *n.* **1.** *Law.* The right of a party to be heard in court. **2.** Any recognised right or official status, such as the right to participate in meetings. [Latin, "place of standing".]
lo·cust[1] (lṓkəst) *n.* **1.** Any of numerous grasshoppers of the family Locustidae, often travelling in swarms and devouring vegetation in huge quantities. **2.** A cicada such as the **seventeen-year locust** *(see).* [Middle English, from Old French *locuste,* from Latin *lōcusta,* locust, lobster.]
locust[2] *n.* **1.** *British.* A tree, the **carob** *(see).* **2.** *U.S.* A tree, the **false acacia** *(see).* [From the locust-shaped pods of some species.]
locust bird *n.* Any of the African pratincoles, such as *Glareola pratincola,* that feed on swarms of locusts.
lo·cu·tion (lə-kéwsh'n, lo-, lō-) *n.* **1.** A particular word, phrase, or expression considered from the point of view of style. **2.** Style of speaking; phraseology. [Middle English *locucion,* from Latin *locūtiō* (stem *locūtiōn-*), speech, utterance, from *loquī* (past participle *locūtus*), to speak.]
Lod (lod). Also **Lyd·da** (líddə). Ancient Hebrew city, southeast of Tel Aviv, Israel, the site of Israel's main international airport.
lode (lōd) *n.* **1.** A mineral deposit contained in hard rock, usually in the form of a group of veins. **2.** A rich source or supply. **3.** In East Anglia, an artificial watercourse. [Middle English *lode, lade,* course, way, Old English *lād.*]
lo·den (lṓd'n) *n.* **1.** A thick, waterproof, woollen fabric, used in making coats. **2.** A dark green colour. [German, from Old High German *lodo,* heavy cloth.]
lode·star, load·star (lṓd-staar) *n.* **1.** A star that is used as a point of reference; especially, the North Star. **2.** A guiding principle, interest, or ambition: *Nuclear disarmament was her constant lodestar.* [Middle English *lo(o)de sterre,* "guiding star" : *lode, lade,* course, guidance (see **lode**) + STAR.]
lode·stone, load·stone (lṓd-stōn) *n.* **1.** A magnetised piece of magnetite. **2.** One that attracts or magnetises. [From its former use by sailors as a compass to guide their course.]
lodge (loj) *n.* **1.** A small house on the grounds of an estate or park for a caretaker, gatekeeper, or the like. **2.** A cottage or hut, often located in an isolated place, used as temporary accomodation or shelter by huntsmen, climbers, or the like: *a skiing lodge.* **3.** The room or rooms near the entrance of a university, college, or similar building which house the porter's office, the notice boards, and the students' pigeon holes. **4.** At Cambridge university, the residence of the head of a college. **5. a.** A local chapter of certain fraternal organisations. **b.** The members of such a chapter considered collectively. **c.** The meeting hall of such a society. **6.** The den of certain animals, such as otters. **7.** *Chiefly U.S.* The central building in a camping ground or nature park. **8. a.** A North American Indian living unit such as a hogan, wigwam, or long house. **b.** The group living in such a unit.
~*v.* **lodged, lodging, lodges.** —*tr.* **1.** To provide with temporary quarters. **2.** To rent a room or rooms to; take in as a paying guest. **3.** To place or establish in quarters: *lodge children with relatives.* **4.** To serve as a depository for; harbour. **5.** To place, leave, or deposit for safety. **6.** To fix, embed, or implant. **7.** To register (a charge) in court or with an appropriate authority or official: *lodge a complaint.* **8.** To vest (authority or power, for example). Used with *in* or *with.* **9.** To beat down (crops). Used of wind or rain: *"If rye or wheat be lodged, cut it though it be not ripe."* (Robert Browning). —*intr.* **1.** To reside temporarily. **2.** To rent living accommodation; be a lodger. **3.** To be or become embedded. [Middle English *log(g)e,* from Old French *loge,* shed, small house, from Frankish *laubja* (unattested).]
lodg·er (lójər) *n.* A person who rents and lives in a furnished room or rooms in the landlord's home.
lodg·ings (lójing) *pl.n.* **1.** Rented rooms. **2.** *Sometimes singular.* Sleeping accommodation. **3.** *Sometimes singular.* At Oxford university, the residence of the head of a college.
lodg·ment, lodge·ment (lójmənt) *n.* **1. a.** The act of lodging. **b.** The state of being lodged. **2.** A place for lodging. **3.** An accumulation or deposit. **4.** *Military.* A foothold, beach-head, or salient gained in enemy or neutral territory.
lod·i·cule (lóddi-kewl || lṓdi-) *n. Botany.* Any of the small scales at the base of the ovary in grasses. [Late Latin *lōdīcula,* diminutive of *lōdīx* (stem *lōdīc-*), covering, perhaps from Celtic.]
Łódź (loj; *Polish* wŏŏch). Second largest city in Poland, renowned for its textiles.
lo·ess, löss (lṓ-iss, lerss, löss || *U.S. also* less) *n.* A fine-grained, friable, porous, yellowish to grey silt or dust, generally thought to have been initially worn away and then deposited by the wind. [German *Löss,* from Swiss German *Lösch,* from *lösch,* loose.]
loft (loft || lawft) *n.* **1.** An open space under a roof; an attic. **2.** A gallery or balcony, as in a church: *a choir loft.* **3.** *U.S.* The top floor, usually unpartitioned, as of a factory or warehouse. **4.** A **hayloft** *(see).* **5. a.** A coop in which pigeons are kept. **b.** A flock of pigeons kept in such a coop. **6.** In golf: **a.** The backward slant of the face of a club head, designed to drive the ball in a high arc. **b.** A golf stroke that lofts the ball. **c.** The upward course of a lofted ball.
~*v.* **lofted, lofting, lofts.** —*tr.* **1.** To put, store, or keep in a loft. **2.** To send (a ball) in a high arc. **3.** To give a loft to (a golf club). —*intr.* To loft a golf ball. [Middle English *lofte,* upper room, sky, Old English *loft,* sky, air, from Old Norse *lopt,* air, attic.]
loft·er (lóftər || láwftər) *n.* A golf club designed to loft the ball. Also called "lofting iron".
loft·y (lófti || láwfti) *adj.* **-ier, -iest. 1.** Of imposing height; towering. **2.** Elevated in character; exalted; noble. **3.** High-flown; affecting grandness; pompous. **4.** Arrogant; haughty. **—See Synonyms at high.** [Middle English, from *lofte,* raised, elevated, from *lofte,* sky, LOFT.] **—loft·i·ly** *adv.* **—loft·i·ness** *n.*
log[1] (log || *chiefly U.S.* lawg) *n.* **1. a.** The trunk of a large fallen or felled tree. **b.** A thick section of trimmed but unhewn timber. **2.** *Nautical.* A device trailed from a ship to determine its speed through the water. **3. a.** A record of a ship's speed, progress, and shipboard events of navigational importance. **b.** The book in which this record is kept. Also called "logbook". **c.** Any record of performance, such as the flight record of an aircraft. **d.** Any record of events or experiences, such as the journal of an expedition. **4.** A record of radio transmissions, frequencies, and the like. **—sleep like a log.** To sleep soundly.
~*v.* **logged, logging, logs.** —*tr.* **1. a.** To cut down the timber of (a section of land). **b.** To cut (trees) into logs. **2.** To achieve and record (a specified time, distance, or speed, for example) in a ship's or other log. **3.** *Informal.* To achieve: *She's logged 25 years with her company.* —*intr.* To cut down, trim, and haul timber. **—log on.** To register, especially with a computer as an authorised user. [Middle English *logge*†.]
log[2] *n. Informal.* **1.** A logarithm. **2.** *Plural.* Logarithmic tables.
Lo·gan, Mount (lṓgən). Canada's highest peak at 6 050 metres (19,850 feet). It lies in the St. Elias Mountains in southwest Yukon Territory and was first climbed in 1925.
lo·gan·ber·ry (lṓgən-bri, -bəri || -berri) *n., pl.* **-ries. 1.** A trailing, prickly plant, *Rubus loganobaccus,* cultivated for its raspberry-like edible fruit. **2.** The dark red fruit of this plant. [First grown 1881 by James H. *Logan* (1841–1928), U.S. judge and horticulturist.]
log·a·oe·dic (lóggə-éedik) *adj.* Of, pertaining to, or designating a form of verse in which different metrical units occur within a single line.
~*n.* A line of such verse. [Late Latin, from Greek *logaoidikos,* (of verse) like natural (prose) speech : *logos,* speech + *aoidē,* poetry.]
log·a·rithm (lóggə-rith'm, *rarely* -rith'm || *U.S. also* láwgə-) *n.* The exponent indicating the power to which a fixed number, the base, must be raised to produce a given number. For example, if $n^x = a$, the logarithm of a, with n as the base, is x; symbolically, $\log_n a = x$.

See **common logarithm, natural logarithm.** [New Latin *logarithmus* : Greek *logos,* reckoning, reason, ratio + *arithmos,* number.]
log·a·rith·mic (lóggə-ríthmik, -ríthmik) *adj.* **1.** Of or pertaining to logarithms. **2.** Involving a logarithmic function. Said of a scale in which successive distances are proportional to logarithms, as in certain measuring instruments, slide rules, and graph paper, for example. **—log·a·rith·mi·cal** *adj.* **—log·a·rith·mi·cal·ly** *adv.*
logarithmic function *n. Mathematics.* A function containing an expression of the form log *x.*
log·book (lóg-bŏŏk || láwg-, -bŏŏk) *n.* **1.** The official record book of a ship, aircraft, or expedition, for example. **2.** *British.* Formerly, the identifying document of a motor vehicle, listing its specifications, registration number, and owner. Also called "log".
loge (lōzh) *n.* **1.** A small compartment; especially, a box in a theatre. **2.** The front rows of the upper block of seating in a theatre, especially in continental Europe or the United States. [French, from Old French, shed, small house. See **lodge.**]
log·ger (lóggər || láwgər) *n.* **1.** A lumberjack. **2.** A tractor, crane, or other machine used for hauling or loading logs.
log·ger·head (lóggər-hed || láwgər-) *n.* **1.** A marine turtle, *Caretta caretta,* having a large, beaked head. **2.** An iron tool consisting of a long handle with a bulbous end, used when heated to melt tar or to warm liquids. **3.** *Nautical.* A post on a whaleboat used to help secure a rope holding a harpooned whale. **4.** *Archaic & Regional.* **a.** A blockhead; a dolt. **b.** A disproportionately large head. **5.** A loggerhead shrike. **—at loggerheads.** Engaged in a dispute. [Dialectal *logger,* wooden block, from LOG + HEAD.]
loggerhead shrike *n.* A North American bird, *Lanius ludovicianus,* having grey and white plumage and a hooked beak. Also called "loggerhead".
log·gi·a (lōj-ə, lój-, -i-ə) *n., pl.* **-gias** or **-gie** (-ay). **1.** A roofed but open gallery or arcade along the front or side of a building, often at an upper level. **2.** An open balcony in a theatre. [Italian, from French *loge,* LOGE.]
log·ging (lógging || láwging) *n.* The work or business of felling and trimming trees and transporting the logs to a mill.
log·ic (lójik) *n.* **1.** *Philosophy.* The study of the principles of reasoning, especially of the structure of propositions as distinguished from their content and of method and validity in deductive reasoning. **2. a.** A system of reasoning. **b.** A mode of reasoning. **c.** The formal, guiding principles of a discipline, school, or science. **3.** Valid reasoning as distinguished from invalid or irrational argument. **4.** The relationship of elements to one another and to the whole in a set of objects, individuals, principles, or events. **5.** *Computing.* The way in which signals are combined in a circuit to perform logical operations. **6.** The apparently irresistible force which brings about or holds together a sequence of events: *the logic of circumstances.* **7.** *Informal.* Reasonableness; good sense: *What's the logic of trying to do it before you're ready?* [Middle English *logik,* from Old French *logique,* from Late Latin *logica,* from Greek *logikē (tekhnē),* "(art) of reasoning", from the feminine of *logikos,* of speech, of reasoning, from *logos,* speech, reason.]
log·i·cal (lójik'l) *adj.* **1.** Pertaining to, in accordance with, or of the nature of logic. **2.** Showing consistency of reasoning. **3.** Reasonable on the basis of earlier statements or events: *a logical development; a logical choice.* **4.** Able to reason clearly: *a logical thinker.* **—log·i·cal·i·ty** (lóji-kál-əti), **log·i·cal·ness** *n.* **—log·i·cal·ly** *adv.*
logical positivism *n. Philosophy.* A doctrine, developed in the 20th century, asserting the primacy of observation in assessing the truth of statements of fact and holding that metaphysical and subjective arguments not based on observable data are meaningless, meaningful statements being either a priori and analytic or a posteriori and synthetic.
logic gate *n. Computing.* An electronic gate that gives an output signal for certain combinations of two or more input signals, used for performing logical operations. Also called "logic circuit".
lo·gi·cian (lə-jísh'n, lo-, lō-) *n.* A person who is trained in or expert at logic.
lo·gi·on (lóggi-on || *chiefly U.S.* lōgi-) *n., pl.* **-gia** (-ə || -aa). Any of the sayings of Jesus not recorded in the Gospels but supposed to have belonged to the source material from which they were compiled. [Greek, "saying".]
lo·gis·tic (lə-jístik, lo-, lō-) *adj.* Also **lo·gis·tic·al** (for sense 1). **1.** Of or pertaining to logistics. In this sense, also "logistical". **2.** *Rare.* Of or skilled in arithmetical calculation. [French *logistique,* from Late Latin *logisticus,* of reason, from Greek *logistikos,* skilled in calculation, from *logistēs,* calculator, from *logizein,* to calculate, from *logos,* reckoning.] **—lo·gis·tic·al·ly** *adv.* **—lo·gis·ti·cian** (-jís-s-tísh'n, lójiss-) *n.*
lo·gis·tics (lə-jístiks, lo-, lō-) *n.* **1.** *Used with a singular verb. Military.* The science or study of the procurement, distribution, maintenance, and replacement of equipment and personnel. **2.** *Used with a plural verb.* The planning and control of any complex operation, as for example in finance or transport.
log jam *n. Chiefly U.S.* **1.** A mass of floating logs crowded immovably together. **2.** *Informal.* A deadlock in the progress of negotiations, debates, or the like.
log·log (lóg-lóg || *U.S. also* láwg-láwg) *n.* The logarithm of a logarithm. Also used adjectivally: *a loglog scale.*
lo·go (lōgō, lóggō || *U.S. also* láwgō) *n., pl.* **-gos.** A logotype.
logo– *comb. form.* Indicates word or speech; for example, **logogram.** [Greek, from *logos,* speech, word, reason, account.]
log·o·gram (lóggə-gram, lóggō- || *U.S. also* láwgə-) *n.* Also **log·o·graph** (-graaf, -graf). A symbol or letter representing an entire word, such as £ for pounds or *e* for energy (in physics). [LOGO- + -GRAM.] **—log·o·gram·mat·ic** (-grə-máttik) *adj.* **—log·o·gram·mat·i·cal·ly** *adv.*
log·o·graph·ic (loggə-gráffik) *adj.* Of or pertaining to logography or logograms. **—log·o·graph·i·cal·ly** *adv.*
lo·gog·ra·phy (lə-góggrəfi, lo-, lō-) *n.* The use of logotypes in design and printing. Also called "logotypy". [LOGO- + -GRAPHY.]
log·o·griph (lóggə-grif || *U.S. also* láwgə-) *n.* A word puzzle, such as an anagram or one in which clues are given in a set of verses. [French *logogriphe* : LOGO- + Greek *griphos*†, fishing basket.]
lo·gom·a·chy (lə-gómməki, lo-, lō-) *n.* **1.** An argument about words or their meanings. **2.** An argument apparently about something substantial but in fact turning merely on different definitions of the terms involved. [Greek *logomakhia* : LOGO- + -MACHY.]
log·o·pae·dics (lóg-ə-peédiks, -ō- || *U.S. also* láwg-) *n. Usually used with a singular verb.* **Speech therapy** *(see).* [LOGO- + Greek *paideia,* education (see **paedo-**) + -ICS.]
log·or·rhoe·a (lóg-ə-reé-ə, -ō-, -reér || *U.S. also* láwg-) *n.* A compulsive tendency to talk, often incoherently, as in mental illness; excessive talkativeness. [LOGO- + -RRHOEA.]
Log·os (lóggoss || lōgōss) *n.* **1.** *Often small* **l. a.** Cosmic reason, regarded in ancient Greek philosophy as the source of world order and intelligibility. **b.** Reason or an expression of reason in words or things. **2.** The self-revealing thought and will of God, as set forth in the Gospel of St. John, often associated with the second person of the Trinity. In this sense, also called the "Word". [Greek *logos,* speech, word, reason.]
lo·go·type (lóg-ō-tīp, -ə- || *U.S. also* láwg-) *n. Printing.* **1.** A single piece of type bearing two or more usually separate elements. **2. a.** The name, trademark, or, especially, the identifying symbol of an organisation or publication. In this sense, also called "logo". **b.** A piece of type bearing this. [LOGO- + TYPE.]
log·roll (lóg-rōl || láwg-, -rol) *v.* **-rolled, -rolling, -rolls.** *Chiefly U.S.* *—tr.* To work towards the passage of (legislation) by logrolling. *—intr.* To engage in political logrolling.
log·roll·ing (lóg-rōlling || láwg-, -rolling) *n.* **1. Birling** *(see).* **2.** The transportation of logs by water. **3.** *Chiefly U.S.* The exchanging of political favours; especially, the swapping of influence or votes between legislators to their mutual advantage. **—log·roll·er** *n.*
-logue, *U.S.* **-log** *n. comb. form.* Indicates speech, discourse, recitation, or description; for example, **monologue, travelogue.** [Greek *-logos,* from *legein,* to speak.]
log·wood (lóg-wŏŏd || láwg-) *n.* **1.** A tropical American tree, *Haematoxylon campechianum,* having dark heartwood from which a dyestuff is obtained. **2.** The wood of this tree. **3.** The blackish or brownish dye, haematoxylin, obtained from this wood.
-logy *n. comb. form.* Indicates: **1.** Discourse or expression; for example, **phraseology. 2.** The science, theory, or study of; for example, **palaeontology.** [Middle English *-logie,* from Old French, from Latin *-logia,* from Greek, from *logos,* word, speech.] **—-logist** *n. comb. form.* **—-logistic, -logistical** *adj. comb. form.*
Lo·hen·grin (lō-ən-grin, -in-; *German* -green). In Germanic legend, a son of Parsifal and knight of the Holy Grail.
loin (loyn) *n.* **1.** *Usually plural. Anatomy.* The part of the side and back between the ribs and the pelvis. **2.** A cut of meat taken from this part of an animal. **3.** *Plural.* **a.** The pelvic region, including the thighs and groin. **b.** *Literary.* The reproductive organs. **—gird up (one's) loins.** To prepare oneself for strenuous effort. [Middle English *loyne,* from Old French *loigne,* dialectal form for *longe,* from Vulgar Latin *lumbia* (unattested), from feminine of *lumbeus* (unattested), of the loin, from Latin *lumbus,* loin.]
loin·cloth (lóyn-kloth || -klawth) *n., pl.* **-cloths** (-kloths || -klawths, -klawthz). A strip of cloth worn around the loins.
Loire (lwaar). France's longest river. It flows some 1 015 kilometres (630 miles) from the Cévennes Mountains in the southeast roughly northwards to Orléans, and then westwards through Tours and Nantes to the Bay of Biscay at St. Nazaire. The middle and lower Loire valley is noted for its fine chateaux.
loi·ter (lóytər) *intr. v.* **-tered, -tering, -ters. 1. a.** To stand idly about; linger aimlessly. **b.** To linger or wait somewhere with the intention of committing a crime. **2.** To proceed slowly or with many stops. **3.** To dawdle: *loiter over a job.* [Middle English *loyteren,* perhaps from Middle Dutch *loteren,* to shake, totter.] **—loi·ter·er** *n.*
Lo·ki (lōki). *Norse Mythology.* The god who creates discord, especially among his fellow gods. [Old Norse, probably related to *logi,* flame, fire.]
Lo·li·ta (lə-leétə, lo-, lō-) *n.* A pubescent girl considered sexually precocious and attractive to adult men. [After Vladimir Nabokov's novel *Lolita* (1955).]
loll (lol) *v.* **lolled, lolling, lolls.** *—intr.* **1.** To move, stand, or recline in an indolent or relaxed manner. **2.** To hang or droop loosely. *—tr.* To allow to hang or droop loosely.
~n. Archaic. An act or attitude of lolling. [Middle English *lollen,* probably of Low German origin, akin to Middle Dutch *lollen,* to lull to sleep.] **—loll·er** *n.* **—loll·ing·ly** *adv.*
Lol·lard (lól-əd, -aard) *n.* A member of a sect of reformers who were followers of John Wycliffe in the 14th, 15th, and 16th centuries. [Middle English, from Middle Dutch *lollaerd,* "mumbler (of prayers)", from *lollen,* to mutter.] **—Lol·lard·ism, Lol·lard·ry** *n.*
lol·li·pop, lol·ly·pop (lólli-pop) *n.* **1.** A piece of hard sweet attached to a narrow stick. **2.** The sign held by a lollipop man. **3.** *Informal.* A short piece of light orchestral music, suitable for playing as an

encore. [Perhaps northern English dialect *lolly,* the tongue, from LOLL, to hang out (the tongue) + POP.]

lollipop lady *n.* See **lollipop man.**

lollipop man *n. British.* A man employed to assist schoolchildren in crossing roads by stopping traffic with a large portable traffic sign consisting of a pole and brightly coloured disc.

lol·lop (lólləp) *intr.v.* **-loped, -loping, -lops.** *British Informal.* **1.** To walk or run in an ungainly way. **2.** To loll. [From LOLL + *-op,* perhaps from GALLOP.]

lol·ly (lólli) *n., pl.* **-lies. 1.** *Informal.* A lollipop. **2.** *British.* An **ice lolly** (see). **3.** *British Slang.* Money. **4.** *Australian Informal.* A boiled sweet.

Lo·lo (lṓlō) *n.* **1.** A member of a Tibeto-Burman people living in the mountains between Sichuan and Yunnan provinces, southwest China. **2.** The language of this people. —**Lo·lo** *adj.*

Lom·bard (lóm-bərd, lúm-, -baard) *n.* **1.** A member of a Germanic people that invaded northern Italy in A.D. 568 and established a kingdom in the Po Valley. Also called "Langobard", "Longobard". **2.** A native of Lombardy. **3.** *Archaic.* A banker or pawnbroker. *~adj.* Also **Lom·bar·dic** (lom-bárdik, lum-). Of or pertaining to the Lombards or to Lombardy.

Lombard Street *n.* The British banking and financial world. [After the moneychangers and bankers from LOMBARDY who once occupied this street in the City of London.]

Lom·bar·dy (lóm-bərdi, lúm-). *Italian* **Lom·bar·di·a** (lom-bárdi-ə). Region in north Italy bounded by the Alps and the river Po. It is the most densely populated region in Italy. The Po valley is a rich agricultural area, while Milan, the capital, lies at the centre of an industrial region.

Lombardy poplar *n.* A tree, *Populus nigra italica,* having upward-pointing branches that form a slender, columnar outline.

Lo·mé (lṓ-may || lṓ-máy). Capital city of the republic of Togo, West Africa. Its deepwater port exports phosphates, cocoa, and coffee.

Lomé Convention *n.* Either of two trade and economic cooperation agreements signed in Lomé by members of the European Economic Community and certain ACP states (less developed countries in Africa, the Caribbean, and Pacific). *Lomé I* signed in 1975 to run from April 1976 to February 1980, involved 46 ACP states. *Lomé II,* signed in 1979 to run from March 1980 to February 1985, involved 57 ACP states.

lo·ment (lṓ-ment) *n.* A pod, as of the tick trefoil or similar leguminous plants, having constrictions separating the individual seeds, such that it divides into one-seeded portions when ripe. [New Latin *lomentum,* from Latin *lōmentum, lōvimentum,* a bean meal used by Roman women as a wash or cosmetic, from *lavāre,* to wash.]

Lo·mond, Loch (lṓmənd). Largest natural freshwater lake in Britain, 39 kilometres (24 miles) long and 8 kilometres (5 miles) wide at its broadest, northeast of Glasgow, Scotland.

Lon·don (lúndən). Capital city of the United Kingdom and one of the largest cities in the world, covering 1 580 square kilometres (610 square miles) north and south of the river Thames. The City (of London), about one square mile in area and occupying the site of a Roman settlement, is surrounded by Greater London, which consists of 32 boroughs. One of these, the City of Westminster, contains the Houses of Parliament, Westminster Abbey, and the governmental ministries, and Buckingham Palace. Much of the City was destroyed by the Great Fire of 1666, after which Sir Christopher Wren rebuilt St. Paul's Cathedral and many other buildings. London is one of the world's most important banking and insurance centres, and Britain's largest port. It is also a major industrial area, its products ranging from machinery, chemicals, and motor vehicles to films, clothing, and luxury goods. London is also one of the world's major cultural and tourist centres.

London, Jack, pen name of John Griffith London (1876–1916). U.S. writer. He was a tramp and a prospector in the Klondike Gold Rush (1897). His tales include *The Call of the Wild* (1903) and *The People of the Abyss* (1903).

London Bridge. First recorded bridge to span the river Thames in London, England. The first London Bridge of stone, which replaced a wooden one, was completed in 1209 and was lined with houses and a chapel. It was demolished after a new bridge, designed by John Rennie, was built to its west in 1824–31. In 1973, a 32-metre (105-foot) wide bridge replaced the Rennie bridge, which was re-erected at the resort of Lake Havasu City, in Arizona, United States.

Lon·don·der·ry[1] (lúndən-dérri, -derri, -dəri). Also **Der·ry** (dérri). Hilly county in Northern Ireland. It is mostly agricultural, with coastal and inland fishing and some light industries. In the 17th century much of the land was confiscated from its Irish owners (the O'Neill family) and granted to City Companies of London.

Londonderry[2]. Also **Derry.** Second largest city of Northern Ireland, on the river Foyle, Co. Londonderry. Derry dates from 546 when St. Columba founded a monastery there. In 1613 the city was granted to the Corporation of the City of London (hence the name Londonderry).

Lon·don·er (lúndənər) *n.* A native or inhabitant of London.

London plane *n.* A hybrid plane tree, *Platanus hybrida,* often planted in cities, having a bark which flakes off, making it resistant to smoke and fumes.

London pride *n.* An alpine garden plant that is a hybrid between *Saxifraga spathularis* and *S. umbrosa.* It has a basal rosette of leaves and a cluster of small pink flowers borne on a long stem.

lone (lōn) *adj.* **1.** Single; solitary: *a lone spectator.* **2.** Isolated; set apart: *a lone cottage.* **3.** *Poetic.* Lonely. **4.** *Rare.* Unmarried or widowed. [Shortened from ALONE (*a-* being taken for the indefinite article).]

lone hand *n.* **1.** In some card games, a hand played without help from a partner's hand. **2.** A cardplayer without a partner.

lone·ly (lṓnli) *adj.* **-lier, -liest. 1. a.** Without companions; lone. **b.** Characterised by aloneness; solitary: *a lonely existence.* **2.** Unfrequented; empty of people; desolate: *a lonely crossroads.* **3. a.** Dejected by the awareness of being alone. **b.** Producing such dejection: *the loneliest night of the week.* [From LONE.] —**lone·li·ly** *adv.* —**lone·li·ness** *n.*

lonely hearts *pl.n.* People who are distressed by lack of emotional companionship, especially those who seek it through advertisements in newspapers or periodicals. Also used adjectivally: *a lonely hearts club.*

lon·er (lṓnər) *n. Informal.* One who prefers to be or work alone.

lone·some (lṓn-səm) *adj. Chiefly U.S.* Lonely. —**by** or **on (one's) lonesome.** *Chiefly U.S. Informal.* Alone; by oneself.

lone wolf *n.* A person who likes to live or work alone.

long[1] (long || *U.S. also* lawng) *adj.* **longer** (-gər), **longest** (-gist). **1. a.** Having great length. **b.** *Rare.* Tall. **2.** Of relatively great duration: *a long time.* **3. a.** Of a specified linear extent or duration; in length: *a mile long; an hour long.* **b.** Lengthways: *two inches long, and one inch wide.* **4.** Extending beyond an average or a standard: *a long game; a long memory.* **5.** Tediously protracted; lengthy: *a long speech.* **6.** Concerned with distant issues; far-reaching: *the long view.* **7.** Risky; chancy: *long odds.* **8.** Having an abundance or an excess of. Used with *on: long on hope.* **9.** *Finance.* Having an unsold holding of a security or commodity in expectation of a rise in price: *long in steel.* **10.** *Phonetics.* Having a comparatively protracted sound: *a long vowel.* **11.** In verse: **a.** Designating a vowel sound of relatively great duration, as *feed* compared with *feet.* **b.** Bearing stress: *a long syllable.* **12.** In cricket, designating a fielding position near to the boundary: *long leg.*
~adv. **1.** During or for an extended period of time: *The promotion was long due.* Often used in combination: *long-lasting; long-lost.* **2.** Far: *He read long into the night.* **3.** For or throughout a specified period: *They talked all night long.* **4.** At a point of time distant from that referred to: *long before we were born.* —**as** or **so long as. 1.** Since; inasmuch as. **2.** During or only during the time that. **3.** Provided that; on condition that. —**no longer.** Not now as formerly; no more: *He no longer smokes.*
~n. **1.** A long time. **2.** A relatively long sound, such as a vowel or a signal in Morse code. **3.** *Finance.* **a.** One who acquires large holdings of a security expecting a rise in price or commodity. **b.** *Plural.* Long-dated gilt-edged securities. **4.** A clothing size for a tall person. —**before long.** Soon. —**the long and the short of.** The essential details; the substance: *The long and short of it is they won.* [Middle English *long, lang,* Old English *long, lang.*] —**long·ish** *adj.*

long[2] (long || lawng) *intr.v.* **longed, longing** (-ing), **longs.** To yearn; wish earnestly; desire greatly: *He longed to go home.* See Synonyms at **yearn.** [Middle English *longen,* Old English *langian,* "to seem long (to some)", to yearn for.]

long. longitude.

lon·gan (lóng-gən || láwng-) *n.* **1.** A Chinese tree, *Euphoria longana.* **2.** The edible fruit of this tree, which is similar to but smaller than a lychee. [Chinese *lóng yăn,* dragon's eye.]

long-and-short work (lóng-ən-shórt || láwng-) *n. Architecture.* The alternation of vertical and horizontal stone slabs at the corner of an Anglo-Saxon or Early English building.

Long Beach. Coastal resort south of Los Angeles, California, United States. It has a large harbour, naval shipyard, dry dock, and refineries for oil, discovered nearby in the 1920s.

long·boat (lóng-bōt || láwng-) *n.* **1.** The longest boat carried by a sailing ship. **2.** A **longship** (see).

long·bow (lóng-bō || láwng-) *n.* **1.** A wooden bow roughly 1.5 to 1.8 metres (five to six feet) long. **2.** A powerful hand-drawn bow, sometimes as much as two metres (over six feet) in length, much used in medieval England.

long-case clock (lóng-kayss || láwng-) *n.* A **grandfather clock** (see).

long-chain *adj.* Designating a molecule whose constituent atoms are arranged in an extended chainlike structure.

long-dat·ed (lóng-dáytid || láwng-) *adj. Finance.* Designating gilt-edged securities redeemable after a time more than 15 years away. Compare **medium-dated, short-dated.**

long-day (lóng-dáy) *adj.* Of or designating plants that will flower only when exposed to periods of daylight in excess of ten hours. Compare **short-day.**

long-dis·tance (lóng-distənss || láwng-) *adj.* **1.** Located or from far away. **2.** Covering a long distance. **3.** Of or designating telephone communications to a distant place. —**long-distance** *adv.*

long division *n.* A process of division in arithmetic, usually used when the divisor has more than one digit, in which the remainders leading to succeeding steps of the procedure are recorded in a determinate pattern.

long dozen *n.* Thirteen; a baker's dozen.

long-drawn-out (lóng-dráwn-owt || láwng-) *adj.* Unduly prolonged.

long drink *n.* A thirst-quenching drink, usually served chilled in a tall glass, having little or no alcohol and often diluted with water, soda water, or a soft drink.

lon·ge·ron (lónjə-rən || *U.S. also* -ron) *n.* A structural member that runs from front to rear of an aircraft's fuselage. [French, from *longer,* to pass along, extend along, from Late Latin *longāre,* to lengthen, from Latin *longus,* long.]

lon·gev·i·ty (lon-jévvəti, *also* long-) *n.* **1.** A long duration of life. **2.** Long duration, as in an occupation or political office. [Late Latin *longevitās* (stem *longevitāt-,* from Latin *longaevus,* living to a great age : *longus,* long + *aevum,* age.] **—lon·ge·vous** (-jéevəss) *adj.*

long face *n.* A discontented or sullen facial expression.

Long·fel·low (lóng-fellō || láwng-), **Henry Wadsworth** (1807–82). U.S. poet. He wrote *The Wreck of the Hesperus* (1841), *Paul Revere's Ride* (1863), and *The Song of Hiawatha* (1855), an epic of Native American life.

Long·ford (lóng-fərd || láwng-). Inland county in Leinster province, Republic of Ireland. The rearing of beef cattle and butter-making are its main industries.

long·hair (lóng-hair || láwng-) *n.* **1.** A man with long hair who is considered to be a social misfit. **2.** *Chiefly U.S.* **a.** One dedicated to the arts and especially to classical music. **b.** One whose taste in the arts is held to be overrefined. In all senses, usually used derogatorily. **—long·hair, long·haired** *adj.*

long·hand (lóng-hand || láwng-) *n.* Handwriting as distinct from shorthand, typing, or printing.
~*adj.* Handwritten. **—long·hand** *adv.*

long haul *n.* **1.** A journey covering a great distance or taking a long time. **2.** Any task or project that takes a long time to carry out.

long-haul (lóng-hawl || láwng-) *adj.* Designating flights or other journeys over a long distance.

long·head·ed (lóng-héddid || láwng-) *adj.* **1.** Dolichocephalic. **2.** Possessing foresight; shrewd; astute; cunning.

long·horn (lóng-hawrn || láwng-) *n.* A member of any of several breeds of beef cattle having long horns.

long-horned beetle (lóng-hawrnd || láwng-) *n.* Any of numerous beetles of the family Cerambycidae, having long legs and long antennae. Also called "longicorn", "longicorn beetle".

long house *n.* A long, often communal, wooden dwelling used by various peoples, as in North America, Borneo, and New Guinea.

longi– *n. comb. form.* Indicates long; for example, **longicorn**. [Latin, from *longus,* long.]

lon·gi·corn (lónji-kawrn) ~*adj.* Having long antennae.
~*n.* A long-horned beetle. Also called "longicorn beetle". [New Latin *Longicornia* (former classification) : LONGI- + Latin *cornū,* horn.]

long·ing (lóng-ing || láwng-) *n.* A persistent, unfulfilled yearning or desire.
~*adj.* Affected by or expressing such a yearning: *look with longing eyes.* **—long·ing·ly** *adv.*

Long Island. Island in New York state, United States, including part of New York City.

lon·gi·tude (lónji-tewd, lóng-gi- || -tōōd) *n. Abbr.* **long. 1.** The angular distance east or west of the prime meridian at Greenwich, England, to the point on the earth's surface for which the longitude is being ascertained, expressed either in degrees or in hours, minutes, and seconds. **2.** *Astronomy.* The angular distance, measured in degrees eastward along the ecliptic from the vernal equinox to the great circle passing through the pole of the ecliptic and the celestial point being measured. Also called "celestial longitude". [Middle English, from Latin *longitūdō,* from *longus,* LONG.]

lon·gi·tu·di·nal (lónji-téwd-in'l, lóng-gi- || -tōōd-) *adj.* **1.** Of or pertaining to length. **2.** Placed or running lengthways. **3.** Pertaining to longitude. **—lon·gi·tu·di·nal·ly** *adv.*

longitudinal wave *n.* A wave propagated in the same direction as the displacement of the transmitting medium. Compare **transverse wave.**

long johns (jonz) *pl.n. Informal.* Long, warm underpants reaching to the ankle.

long jump *n.* In athletics, an event in which the participants compete to cover the greatest distance by jumping, after a sprinting run, from a fixed mark into a flat pit of sand. Also U.S. "broad jump".

long-leaf pine (lóng-leef || láwng-) *n.* An evergreen coniferous tree, *Pinus australis* (or *P. palustris*), of the southeastern United States, having long needles and heavy, tough, resinous wood valued as timber and as a source of turpentine.

long lease *n. Chiefly British.* A lease that can be bought and sold, by contrast with one that is held in exchange only for rent. [Because such a lease is typically for a longer period than one granted to someone who rents.] **—long-lease-holder** *n.*

Long·leat (lóng-leet). Historic house, near Warminster, Wiltshire, in England. It was begun in 1568 and is owned by the Marquess of Bath. It has a safari park.

long-lived (lóng-lívd || láwng-, -lívd) *adj.* **1.** Having a long life. **2.** Persistent: *a long-lived rumour.* **—long-lived-ness** *n.*

Long March. The hazardous journey to safety undertaken (1934–35) by an army of about 100,000 Communist Chinese soldiers and officials, of whom a third at most survived. Their route led northwest across China from Jiangxi to Shaanxi, a distance of about 10 000 kilometres (6,000 miles).

long measure *n.* **Linear measure** *(see).*

long multiplication *n.* A method for obtaining the product of two numbers, especially when both numbers consist of several digits. The multiplicand is multiplied by each digit of the multiplier in turn, the partial products so obtained being set out in an array that takes account of the position of their decimal points; the final product is the sum of the partial products.

Lon·go·bard (lóng-gō-baard || láwng-) *n., pl.* **-bards** or **-bardi** (-bár-

dee). An early **Lombard** *(see).* **—Lon·go·bar·di·an** (-bárdi-ən), **Lon·go·bar·dic** (-bárdik) *adj.*

Long Parliament *n.* The English Parliament that was convened by Charles I in 1640, dismissed by Oliver Cromwell in 1653, and reconvened in 1659–1660. See **Rump Parliament.**

long pig *n.* A human being used for meat by cannibals. [Translation of a Polynesian term.]

long-play·ing (lóng-pláy-ing || láwng-) *adj. Abbr.* **LP** Pertaining to or designating a microgroove gramophone record, especially one turning at 33¹⁄₃ revolutions per minute.

long-range (lóng-ráynj || láwng-) *adj.* **1.** Requiring or involving a span of years; not immediate: *long-range planning.* **2.** Of, suitable for, or equipped to travel long distances: *long-range aircraft.*

long-ship (lóng-ship || láwng-) *n.* A narrow uncovered vessel powered by oars and sail, used by the Vikings and other peoples in Europe during the early Middle Ages. Also called "longboat".

long-shore (lóng-shawr || láwng-, -sháwr, -shōr, -shór) *adj.* Occurring, living, or working along a seacoast. [Short for ALONGSHORE.]

long-shore·man (lóng-shawr-mən || láwng-, -sháwr-, -shōr-, -shór), *n., pl.* **-men** (-mən, -men). *U.S.* A **docker** *(see).*

long shot *n.* **1. a.** An entry, as in a horse race, with only a slight chance of winning. **b.** A bet made at and against great odds. **2. a.** A risky venture that will pay off handsomely if successful. **b.** An attempt or guess that has only a slight chance of proving successful. **3.** A film scene shot at some distance from the subject. **—not by a long shot.** Not by any means; nor nearly.

long-sight·ed (lóng-sítid || láwng-) *adj.* **1.** Suffering from **hypermetropia** *(see);* able to see only distant objects clearly. **2.** Possessing foresight; planning for the future. **—long-sight·ed·ness** *n.*

long-stand·ing (lóng-stánding || láwng-) *adj.* Having been in existence or force for a long time.

long-stop (lóng-stop || láwng-) *n.* **1. a.** In cricket, the fielding position behind the wicketkeeper and near the boundary. **b.** The fielder in this position, whose function is to stop balls that the wicketkeeper has missed. **2.** *British.* A secondary or supplementary safeguard: *The second check is a longstop to catch minor errors.*

long-suf·fer·ing (lóng-súffər-ing, -súffring || láwng-) *adj.* Patiently enduring wrongs or difficulties.
~*n.* Also **long-suf·fer·ance** (-ənss). Patient endurance. **—long-suf·fer·ing·ly** *adv.*

long suit *n.* **1.** In card games, a suit containing more cards than any of the other suits in a hand. **2.** *Informal.* The personal quality or talent that is one's strongest asset.

long-tailed tit (lóng-tayld || láwng-) *n.* A small Eurasian songbird, *Aegisthalos caudatus,* with a black, pink, and white plumage and a long, black and white tail.

long-term (lóng-térm || láwng-) *adj.* In effect for, involving, or maturing after a number of years: *a long-term investment.*

long-time (lóng-tím || láwng-) *adj.* Having existed or persisted for a long time: *a long-time acquaintance.*

long tom *n. Sometimes capital* L, *capital* T. **1.** A long pivoted cannon formerly used on warships. **2.** A similar long-range gun used on land. **3.** A trough in which gold-bearing sand is washed.

long ton *n.* A ton *(see).*

lon·gueur, lon·geur (long-gér, LON-, -gór) *n. Often plural.* **1.** A boring or tedious period of time. **2.** A tedious, overlong passage, as in a book or film. [French, "length".]

long vacation, *Informal.* **long vac.** *n.* The summer vacation at the end of an academic year.

long-waisted (lóng-waystid) *adj.* Having or being of more than average length between shoulders and waist.

long wave *n.* A radio waveband in which the wavelength exceeds 1 000 metres (frequency less than 300 kilohertz).

long·ways (lóng-wayz || láwng-) *adj.* Also *chiefly U.S.* **long·wise** (-wīz). Lengthways.

long-wind·ed (lóng-wíndid || láwng-) *adj.* **1.** Wearisomely verbose: *a long-winded bore.* **2.** Not subject to quick loss of breath. **—long·wind·ed·ly** *adv.* **—long·wind·ed·ness** *n.*

Lons·dale (lonz-dayl), **Dame Kathleen,** born Kathleen Yardley (1903–71). British physicist. She worked on the structure and growth of crystals and in 1945 she became one of the first two women to be elected to the Royal Society.

loo¹ (lōō) *n., pl.* **loos.** *British Informal.* A lavatory. [Perhaps from French *lieux (d'aisances),* privy.]

Usage: Words for lavatory constitute one of the most changeable areas of vocabulary, as people search for the most polite or neutral expressions. *Loo* is a recent development in British English, used widely but only informally. *Lavatory* and *toilet* are both acceptable in middle-class usage, but the latter is more frequently used. There are several euphemisms (*powder room, men's room, rest room,* and the like) available for formal use, and several colloquial and semijocular expressions (*gents, ladies,* and so on) available for informal use. The use of *bathroom* in the sense of "toilet" has a different range of usage in British and American English. In British English, a bathroom has to contain a bath, and it may contain a toilet; in American English, the reference would be to a room which contains a toilet, and which may not contain a bath.

loo² *n., pl.* **loos.** A card game in which each player contributes stakes to a pool. [Shortened from *lanterloo,* from French *lanturlu,* originally the refrain of a popular song.]

loo·by (lōōbi) *n., pl.* **-bies.** *Chiefly U.S. Informal.* A stupid or clumsy person. [Middle English *loby,* probably of Low German origin, akin to Middle Low German *lobbe,* loose lip, bumpkin. See **lob.**]

loo·fah (lŏŏfə) *n.* Also *chiefly U.S.* **loo·fa, luf·fa** (lúffə). **1.** The dried, fibrous, spongelike interior of the fruit of the dishcloth gourd, used as a washing sponge or as a filter. **2.** The **dishcloth gourd** *(see).* [New Latin *luffa,* from Arabic *lūf, lūfah.*]

look (lŏŏk || lŏŏk) *v.* **looked, looking, looks.** *—intr.* **1.** To employ one's eyes in seeing. **2. a.** To turn one's glance. **b.** To turn one's attention. Often used with *at.* **3.** To seem or appear to be: *look morose.* **4.** To face in a specified direction. Often used with *onto* or *out onto*: *The cottage looks onto the river.* **5.** *Informal.* To hope or expect. Used with an infinitive: *He looked to hear from her.* *—tr.* **1.** To turn one's eyes on. **2.** To express by one's appearance: *She looked her joy.* **3.** To have an appearance in conformity with: *look one's age.* **—look after.** To take care of. **—look as if.** To seem likely that. **—look back.** To reflect on the past; remember. **—look down on** or **upon.** To regard with contempt or condescension. **—look for. 1.** To search for. **2.** To expect. **—look forward to.** To anticipate eagerly. **—look into.** To investigate. **—look like.** To indicate as a likely possibility: *It looks like war.* **—look on. 1.** To be a spectator. **2.** To consider; regard: *look on the accident as a stroke of luck.* **—look over.** To inspect; especially, to inspect casually. **—look sharp** or **lively.** To hurry up, or respond quickly. Usually used as an imperative. **—look through. 1.** To inspect briefly: *look through a report.* **2.** To pretend to be unacquainted with (a person); ignore; snub. **—look to. 1.** To expect. **2.** To attend to. **3.** To rely upon. **4.** To resort to: *If you won't agree, I must look to force.* **—look towards.** To be a pointer to; herald; prefigure: *His poetry looks towards the modernist revolution.* **—look up. 1.** To search for and find, as in a reference book. **2.** To locate and call upon; visit. **3.** *Informal.* To improve: *Things are looking up.* **—look up and down. 1.** To inspect critically, coldly, or disdainfully. **2.** To search everywhere. **—look up to.** To admire. **—never look back.** To make uninterrupted progress. **—not look at.** To refuse to have anything to do with: *He won't look at Spanish wines.*
~n. **1.** The action or an instance of looking; a gaze or glance. **2.** An appearance or aspect. **3.** *Plural.* Physical appearance, especially when pleasing. **—by the look of.** Taking appearances as a guide or indication: *by the look of her, she's ill.*
~interj. Used to request attention, preface an objection, or express impatience or insistence. [Middle English *loken,* to look, have the appearance, Old English *lōcian,* to look, from West Germanic *lokōn* (unattested).]

-look *adj. comb. form.* Indicates resemblance to or imitation of something specified; for example, *a leather-look handbag.*

look·a·like (lŏŏk-ə-līk || lŏŏk-) *n.* One that closely resembles another; especially, one resembling a celebrity. **—look·a·like** *adj.*

look·er (lŏŏkər || lŏŏkər) *n.* **1.** One that looks. **2.** *Chiefly U.S. Informal.* A very pretty woman or a very handsome man.

look·er-on (lŏŏkər-ón || lŏŏkər-, -áwn) *n., pl.* **lookers-on.** A spectator.

look in *intr.v.* To drop in; make a brief visit. Often used with *on.*

look-in (lŏŏk-in || lŏŏk-) *n.* **1.** A short visit. **2.** *Informal.* An opportunity to take part, prove oneself, or achieve something: *His opponent never gave him a look-in.*

looking glass *n.* A mirror.

look·ing-glass (lŏŏk-ing-glaass || lŏŏk-, -glass) *adj.* Topsy-turvy; disconcertingly unfamiliar: *Travelling in the East, she felt herself to be in a looking-glass world.* [After the fantastic logic of Lewis Carroll's *Through the Looking-Glass.*]

look out *intr.v.* **1.** To be careful or protective: *looking out for one's interests.* **2.** To be careful to notice some hazard: *Look out for the step!* **3.** To watch in the hope of finding something: *looking out for bargains.*
~tr. To make some effort to find: *I'll look out that book for you.*

look·out (lŏŏk-owt || lŏŏk-) *n.* **1.** The act of observing or keeping watch. **2.** A high place or structure commanding a wide view for observation. **3.** One who keeps watch. **4.** An outlook; prospects. **5.** *Informal.* An unfortunate prospect: *If they don't work, that's their lookout!* **—on the lookout.** Watching out, as for a hazard or something needed.

look-see (lŏŏk-see || lŏŏk-) *n. Informal.* A quick survey or glance.

loom¹ (lōōm) *intr.v.* **loomed, looming, looms. 1.** To come into view as a massive, distorted, or indistinct image. **2.** To appear to the mind in a magnified and threatening form. **3.** To seem imminent; impend. **4.** To tower above; overhang. Used with *over*: *The crag looms over the house.* **—loom large. 1.** To be a preoccupation. **2.** To be a significant element: *Beethoven's influence looms large in his earlier works.*
~n. A distorted, threatening appearance of something, as through fog or darkness. [Probably of Low German origin; akin to East Frisian *lōmen,* to move slowly, *lōm,* lame, crippled.]

loom² *n.* **1.** A machine or device from which a textile is produced by interweaving thread or yarn at right angles. **2.** *Nautical.* The shaft of an oar. [Middle English *lome,* Old English *gelōma,* utensil, tool : *ge-* (collective prefix) + *-lōma,* akin to Middle Dutch *allame*†, tool.]

loon¹ (lōōn) *n. Chiefly U.S.* Any of several northern diving birds of the genus *Gavia,* a **diver** *(see).* [Probably from Old Norse *lomr.*]

loon² *n. Informal.* A simple-minded or mad person. [Middle English *loun, lown*†.]

loon·y, loon·ey (lōōni) *adj.* **-ier, -iest.** *Informal.* **1.** So odd as to appear demented; mad; crazy. **2.** Foolish; senseless.
~n., pl. **loonies.** *Informal.* A loony person.

loony bin *n. Slang.* A mental hospital. Often considered offensive.

loop¹ (lōōp) *n.* **1.** A length of line, as of wire, thread, rope, or ribbon, that is folded over and joined at the ends. **2.** The opening formed by such a doubled line. **3.** Any roughly oval, closed, or nearly closed turn or figure. **4.** Something having such a turn or figure. **5.** *Electricity.* A closed circuit. **6.** A flight manoeuvre in which an aircraft flies a circular path in a vertical plane with the lateral axis of the aircraft remaining horizontal. **7.** The commonest of the basic patterns of ridges making up the human fingerprint. Compare **arch, whorl. 8.** *Anatomy.* A bend in a tubular organ, such as *Henle's loop* in a kidney tubule. **9.** An intrauterine contraceptive consisting of a small device in the shape of a loop. **10.** *Mathematics.* A closed curve on a graph. **11.** *Computing.* A series of program instructions that are performed repeatedly until one specific condition is fulfilled. **12.** A loop aerial. **13.** A loopline. **14.** A **tape-loop** *(see).* **15.** A figure executed by an ice-skater by describing a figure of eight on one edge and doubling back into and out of the eight at the top and bottom.
~v. **looped, looping, loops.** *—tr.* **1.** To form (thread, for example) into a loop or loops. **2.** To fasten, join, or encircle with a loop or loops. **3.** To fly (an aircraft) in a loop. **4.** *Electricity.* To join (conductors) so as to complete a circuit. *—intr.* **1.** To form a loop or loops. **2.** In aviation, to make a loop or loops. **3.** To progress by looping the body. Used of measuring worms. **—loop the loop.** To make a vertical loop or loops in the air. Used of an aircraft. [Middle English *loupe*†.]

loop² *n. Archaic.* A small opening in a wall; a loophole. [Middle English *loupe*†.]

loop aerial *n.* A radio aerial consisting of one or more coils of wire wound on a frame. Also called "frame aerial", "loop".

loop·er (lōōpər) *n.* **1.** One that makes loops. **2.** The caterpillar of a geometrid moth; a **measuring worm** *(see).*

loop·hole (lōōp-hōl) *n.* **1.** A small hole or slit in a wall, especially one through which small arms may be fired. **2.** A way of escaping a difficulty; especially, an omission or an ambiguity, as in the wording of a contract or law, that provides a means of evasion. [LOOP (opening) + HOLE.]

loop·line (lōōp-līn) *n.* A railway line that leaves and later rejoins a main line.

loop·y (lōōpi) *adj.* **1.** Containing, resembling, or pertaining to loops: curly. **2.** *Informal.* Eccentric; crazy.

loose (lōōss) *adj.* **looser, loosest. 1. a.** Not fastened or restrained; unbound. **b.** Not tightly anchored or secured: *a loose tooth.* **2.** Not taut or drawn up tightly; slack. **3.** Free from confinement or imprisonment; unfettered. **4.** Not tight-fitting or tightly fitted. **5.** Allowing some latitude; not rigidly arranged: *a loose association.* **6.** Not bound, bundled, packed, stapled, or gathered together. **7.** Not compact or dense. **8.** Not fast: *a loose dye.* **9.** Lacking a sense of restraint or responsibility; idle: *loose talk.* **10.** Licentious; unchaste; immoral: *a loose woman; a loose way of life.* **11.** Not precise or exact: *a loose translation.* **12.** Not strict or totally correct: *a loose use of the term.* **13.** Readily available; not committed: *loose cash.* **14.** *Chiefly U.S. Informal.* Calm; unruffled. **15.** Designating bowels that empty easily or overactively. **16.** Designating a cough that produces or results from an excess of phlegm in the throat.
~n. In Rugby football, the period of play when possession of the ball is being disputed in a ruck. **—on the loose.** *Informal.* **1.** At large; free from confinement. **2.** Acting in an uninhibited or licentious fashion.
~adv. In a loose manner.
~v. **loosed, loosing, looses.** *—tr.* **1.** To let loose; set free; release. **2.** To undo, untie, or unwrap. **3.** To release pressure on; make less tight, firm, or compact. **4.** To relax (rules or regulations); make less strict. **5.** To let fly (a projectile). *—intr.* **1.** To become loose. **2.** To discharge a projectile; fire. [Middle English *lous(e), lo(o)s,* from Old Norse *lauss, louss.*] **—loose·ly** *adv.* **—loose·ness** *n.*

loose box *n.* A covered stall in which a horse is kept without having to be tied up.

loose cannon *n.* **1.** A reckless person, whose behaviour endangers others' safety. **2.** An unpredictable politician, teammate, or the like, whose actions threaten the success of the group; a maverick [After the mobile carriage-mounted cannons on old fighting ships, which could roll about dangerously when not securely fastened.]

loose cover *n.* A fitted, removable cover of cloth or other material for a piece of upholstered furniture.

loose-joint·ed (lōōss-jóyntid) *adj.* **1.** Having freely articulated joints. **2.** Supple in movement. **—loose-joint·ed·ness** *n.*

loose-leaf (lōōss-léef) *adj.* Designating a binder or folder that allows the insertion and removal of pages.

loose-limbed (lōōss-límd) *adj.* Having supple limbs.

loos·en (lōōss'n) *v.* **-ened, -ening, -ens.** *—tr.* **1.** To make looser. **2.** To untie. **3.** To free from restraint, pressure, or strictness. **4.** To free (the bowels) from constipation. *—intr.* To become loose or looser. [Middle English *lo(o)snen,* from *lo(o)s,* LOOSE.]

loose·strife (lōōss-strīf) *n.* **1.** Any of various plants of the genus *Lysimachia,* having typically yellow flowers. **2.** Any of various plants of the genus *Lythrum.* See **purple loosestrife. 3.** Any of various related or similar plants. [LOOSE + STRIFE (literal translation of Latin *lysimachia,* from Greek *lusimakheion.*]

loot (lōōt) *n.* **1.** Stolen valuables; spoils. **2.** *Informal.* Goods illicitly obtained, as by theft or bribery. **3.** *Informal.* Money. *~v.* **looted, looting, loots.** *—tr.* **1.** To steal from during war or civil disturbance. **2.** To take as spoils. *—intr.* To loot property. —See Synonyms at **rob.** [Hindi *lūt,* from Sanskrit *lō(p)tra,* booty.]

lop¹ (lop) *tr.v.* **lopped, lopping, lops. 1.** To cut off branches or twigs

from; trim. **2.** To cut off (branches) from a tree or shrub. **3.** To cut off (a part), especially with a single swift blow. Usually used with *off.* **4.** To eliminate or excise as superfluous. Used with *off.*
~*n.* **1.** The trimmings of a felled tree; twigs and branches. **2.** Anything lopped off. [Middle English, Old English *loppian* (unattested), to prune.] —**lop·per** *n.*

lop² *v.* **lopped, lopping, lops.** —*intr.* **1.** To hang loosely; droop. **2.** To slouch; dawdle; loiter. **3.** To lope. —*tr.* To allow or cause to hang loosely. [Akin to LOB.]

lope (lōp) *intr.v.* **loped, loping, lopes.** To run or ride with a steady, easy gait.
~*n.* A steady, easy stride or movement. [Middle English *lo(u)pen,* from Old Norse *hlaupa,* to leap.] —**lop·er** *n.*

lop-eared (lŏp-êerd) *adj.* Having bent or drooping ears. Said of certain animals: *lop-eared beagles.*

Lope de Vega. See **Vega (Carpio), Lope Félix de.**

lopho- *comb. form.* Indicates a crested or tufted part; for example, **lophobranch.** [From Greek *lophos,* crest.]

lo·pho·branch (lōfə-brangk, lŏffə-) *n.* Any fish of the suborder Lophobranchii, having gills arranged in tufts, and including the sea horses. [LOPHO- + -BRANCH.] —**lo·pho·branch** *adj.*

lo·pho·phore (lōfə-fawr, lŏffə- ‖ -fōr) *n.* The filter-feeding organ of certain small, aquatic, invertebrate animals, such as brachiopods, consisting of a circular or horseshoe-shaped ring of tentacles around the mouth. [LOPHO- + -PHORE.] —**lo·pho·phor·ate** (-fáwr-ayt, -ət, -it ‖ -fōr-) *adj.*

Lop Nur or **Lop Nor** (lŏp nŏor). Also **Lo-pu p'o, Luo Bu Po.** Largely dried-up salt lake in the Tarim basin, Xinjiang Uygur Autonomous Region, Western China. Since 1964 it has been the country's nuclear research and testing site.

lop·o·lith (lŏppo-lith) *n.* A saucer-shaped body of intrusive igneous rock. [Greek *lopos,* shell + -LITH.]

lop·py (lŏppi) *adj.* **-pier, -piest.** Hanging limp; pendulous.

lop·sid·ed (lŏp-sĩdid) *adj.* **1.** Heavier, larger, or higher on one side than on the other; not symmetrical. **2.** Sagging or leaning to one side. **3.** Not showing proper balance. —**lop·sid·ed·ly** *adv.* —**lop·sid·ed·ness** *n.*

loq. loquitur.

lo·qua·cious (lə-kwáyshəss, lo-, lō-) *adj.* Very talkative. See Synonyms at **talkative.** [Latin *loquāx* (stem *loquāc-*), from *loquī,* to speak.] —**lo·qua·cious·ly** *adv.* —**lo·qua·cious·ness, lo·quac·i·ty** (-kwássəti) *n.*

lo·quat (lō-kwot, -kwŏt) *n.* **1.** A small tree, *Eriobotrya japonica,* native to eastern Asia, having white flowers and yellow, pear-shaped fruit. **2.** The edible fruit of this tree. [Cantonese *lō kwat, lō kat.*]

lo·qui·tur (lōkwi-tər, -toor ‖ lōkwi-). *Abbr.* **loq.** He or she speaks or begins to speak. Used as a stage direction. [Latin.]

lo·ran (láwr-ən, -an ‖ lōr-) *n.* A long-range navigational system based on pulsed radio signals from two or more pairs of ground stations of known position, with which a navigator can establish his own position by an analysis involving the time intervals between pulses. [*Lo*ng-*ra*nge *n*avigation.]

Lor·ca (lórkə), **Federico García** (*c.* 1899–1936). Spanish poet and playwright. His work, notably *Gipsy Ballads* (1928), draws on Andalusian culture. He was shot by Falangists in the Civil war.

lord (lord) *n.* **1.** A man of high rank in a feudal society or in one that retains feudal forms and institutions, as: **a.** A king. **b.** A territorial magnate. **c.** The proprietor of a manor. **2.** *Capital* L. *British. Abbr.* **Ld.** The general masculine title of nobility and other ranks, used: **a.** Semiformally for any peer other than a duke: *Lord Cardigan* (the Earl of Cardigan). **b.** As the usual style for a baron: *Lord Morrison* (titularly, Baron Morrison of Lambeth). **c.** As a courtesy title for a younger son of a duke or marquis: *Lord Randolph Churchill* (third son of the Duke of Marlborough). **d.** As part of the titles of certain high officials and dignitaries, as *the Lord Mayor of London, the Lord Chancellor, the Lords of the Admiralty.* **e.** As a nominal title for a bishop. *Note:* In direct address, *my lord* and *your lordship* are deferential appellations for any of the above. *My lord,* usually pronounced (mə-lúd), is also used in addressing a British judge in court. In direct address and in informal reference, **c** may be shortened to *Lord Randolph,* but it may never be given as *Lord Churchill,* while **a** and **b** may never be used with first names. With **b** and **c,** the formal usage (as in addressing a letter) is *The Lord Morrison.* **3. a.** *Capital* L. God or Jesus. **b.** *Archaic.* The head of a household. **c.** A husband. **d.** A man of renowned power. **e.** A man who has mastery in some field or activity. —**the Lords.** The House of Lords.
~*interj.* Used to express surprise, distress, and the like. Often used in phrases such as *Lord knows!* and *Good Lord!*
~*intr.v.* **lorded, lording, lords.** To play the lord; domineer. Used with *it: lording it over the newcomers.* [Middle English *lord, loverd,* Old English *hlāford, hlāfweard,* "keeper of the bread" : *hlāf,* LOAF + *weard,* WARD.]

Lord Advocate *n.* In Scotland, the senior **law officer** (*see*).

Lord Chamberlain *n.* The senior member of the British royal household, responsible especially for the ceremonial aspects of royal activities.

Lord Chancellor *n., pl.* **Lords Chancellor.** The presiding officer and speaker of the House of Lords, Keeper of the Great Seal, Head of the judiciary in England and Wales, and usually a senior cabinet minister. Also called "Lord High Chancellor".

Lord Chief Justice *n. Abbr.* **L.C.J.** A senior English judge, the highest judicial officer after the Lord Chancellor, head of the

Queen's Bench Division of the High Court of Justice, and President of the Criminal Division of the Court of Appeal.

lord·ing (lórding) *n. Archaic & Poetic.* Lord; sir. Used chiefly as a form of address.

Lord Lieutenant *n., pl.* **Lords Lieutenant. 1.** In Britain, a representative officer of the Crown in a county or in some Scottish burghs, performing largely ceremonial duties and nominally responsible for the proper administration of justice. **2.** Formerly, the British viceroy in Ireland.

lord·ling (lórdling) *n.* A young or unimportant lord.

lord·ly (lórdli) *adj.* **-lier, -liest. 1.** Of or pertaining to a lord. **2.** Dignified; noble. **3.** Arrogant; overbearing; haughty.
~*adv. Archaic.* In a lordly fashion. —**lord·li·ness** *n.*

Lord Mayor *n.* The mayor in certain cities such as London.

Lord of Appeal *n.* Any of several judges appointed to hear appeal cases in the House of Lords. Also called "Lord of Appeal in Ordinary".

Lord of Hosts *n.* Jehovah; God.

Lord of Misrule *n.* The master of traditional Christmas revelry in England during the 15th and 16th centuries.

lor·do·sis (lawr-dō-siss) *n. Pathology.* An abnormal forward curvature of the spine in the lumbar region. [New Latin, from Greek *lordōsis : lordos,* bent backwards + -OSIS.] —**lor·dot·ic** (-dóttik) *adj.*

Lord Privy Seal *n.* The official who is Keeper of the Privy Seal, usually a senior cabinet member with some other ministerial responsibility.

Lord Provost *n.* The provost in any of the six major Scottish burghs.

Lord's (lordz). A cricket ground in northwest London, the headquarters of the M.C.C. and Test and County Cricket Board.

lords-and-la·dies (lórdz'n-láydiz) *n. Used with a singular verb.* A plant, the **cuckoopint** (*see*). [From its dark (for lords) and light (for ladies) spadices.]

Lord's Day, Lord's day *n.* The Christian Sabbath; Sunday.

lord·ship (lórd-ship) *n.* **1.** *Usually capital* L. A title of or form of address for a British nobleman, judge, or bishop. Used with *Your, His,* or *Their.* See Note at **lord. 2.** The position or authority of a lord. **3.** The territorial fief of a feudal lord.

Lord's Prayer *n.* The prayer taught by Jesus to his disciples. Matthew 6:9-13. Also called "Our Father", "paternoster".

Lords Spiritual *pl.n.* Those members of the House of Lords who are Anglican bishops.

Lord's Supper *n.* **1.** The **Last Supper** (*see*). **2.** The Eucharist.

Lord's Table *n.* The Communion table.

Lords Temporal *pl.n.* Those members of the House of Lords who are not Anglican bishops.

Lord Steward *n.* An officer of the British royal household ranking between the Lord Chamberlain and the Master of the House, whose main duties are to supervise the servants.

lore¹ (lor ‖ lōr) *n.* **1.** Accumulated fact, tradition, or belief about a particular subject: *country lore.* **2.** Knowledge acquired through education or experience. —See Synonyms at **knowledge.** [Middle English *lore,* Old English *lār.*]

lore² *n.* The area between a bird's eye and the base of the bill. [New Latin *lorum,* from Latin *lōrum*†, thong.]

Lo·re·lei (láwrə-lī, lórrə- ‖ lōrə-) *n. Germanic Mythology.* A siren of the Rhine whose singing lures sailors to shipwreck.

Lo·ren (láwr-ən, -en, lə-rén), **Sophia,** born Sophia Scicoloni (1934–). Italian film actress. Her films include *Two Women* (1961), for which she won an Academy Award, *Yesterday, Today, and Tomorrow* (1963), and *Man of La Mancha* (1972). She married (1957–62, 1966–) the film producer Carlo Ponti (1913–).

Lo·rentz (láw-rənts, lō- ‖ lō-), **Hendrik Antoon** (1853–1928). Dutch physicist. His studies of the influence of magnetism on radiation won him and his pupil, Zeeman, the 1902 Nobel prize in physics.

Lo·renz (láw-rents, lō, -rənts ‖ lō), **Konrad (Zacharias)** (1903–89). Austrian zoologist. He was the first to describe imprinting, the learning process which occurs during the first hours of life. His book *On Aggression* (1963) describes the ritualisation of aggressive impulses in animals. He was awarded a Nobel prize in physiology or medicine (1973) jointly with Frisch and Tinbergen.

Lorentz contraction *n.* The contraction in length of a moving body, as measured by an observer at rest with respect to the body, by the factor $(1-v^2/c^2)^{1/2}$, where v is the relative speed of the moving body and c the speed of light. Also called "Lorentz-Fitzgerald contraction". [After Hendrik LORENTZ.]

Lo·re·to (lə-réttō, lo-, -ráytō). Town in Ancona, Italy. The Virgin Mary's house was reputed to have been miraculously transported there in 1295 from Nazareth.

lor·gnette (lawrn-yét) *n.* A pair of spectacles or opera glasses with a short handle. Also called "lorgnon". [French, from *lorgner,* to leer at, from Old French, from *lorgne*†, squinting.]

lo·ri·ca (lo-rī-kə, lə-, law- ‖ lō-) *n., pl.* **-cae** (-see, -kee). **1.** *Zoology.* A protective external shell or case, as of a rotifer. **2.** A cuirass or body armour, usually of leather and metal, worn by soldiers in ancient Rome. [Latin *lōrīca,* leather cuirass, from *lōrum,* thong.] —**lor·i·cate** (lórri-kayt, -kət, -kit ‖ láwri-), **lor·i·ca·ted** (-kaytid) *adj.*

lor·i·keet (lórri-keet, -keet' ‖ láwri-) *n.* Any of several small Australasian parrots of the subfamily Loriinae; a small lory. [LOR(Y) + (PARA)KEET.]

lor·i·mer (lórrimər) *n.* One who made spurs, bits, and similar metal accessories for horse riders in former times. [Middle English, from Old French *loremier, lorenier,* from *lorain,* harness strap, from Vulgar Latin *loranum* (unattested), from Latin *lōrum*, thong, strap.]

lo·ris (láw-riss ‖ lố-) *n., pl.* **lorises.** Any of several slow-moving, nocturnal, arboreal, prosimian primates of the genera *Loris* and *Nycticebus,* of tropical Asia, having dense, woolly fur, large eyes, and a vestigial tail. [French, probably from obsolete Dutch *loeris†,* simpleton, clown.]

lorn (lorn) *adj. Poetic.* Forlorn; desolate. [Middle English *lorn, loren,* lost, Old English *-loren,* past participle of *-lēosan,* to lose.]

Lor·rain (lo-ráyn, lə), **Claude,** born Claude Gellée (1600–82). French landscape painter, who settled in Rome. He produced luminous landscapes and coastal scenes suffused with golden light.

Lor·raine (lo-ráyn, lə-). *German* **Loth·ring·en** (lốtring-ən). Former province in northeast France, now comprising the départements of Vosges, Moselle, Meurthe-et-Moselle, and Meuse. It was originally part of the kingdom of Lotharingia, belonging to Charlemagne's grandson Lothair I. Lorraine, with its neighbour Alsace, disputed between France and Germany for many years, was returned to France after World War I. The area contains deposits of iron ore. The main industrial towns are Metz and Nancy.

lor·ry (lórri ‖ lúrri, láwri) *n., pl.* **-ries.** 1. A large road vehicle designed to carry goods. Also *chiefly U.S.* "truck". 2. Any of various flat carts or vehicles that run on rails and are used for carrying goods. [19th century (northern dialect) : perhaps akin to dialect *lurry,* to tug, pull.]

lo·ry (láwri ‖ lốri) *n., pl.* **-ries.** Any of various brightly coloured Australasian parrots of the subfamily Loriinae, having a tongue with a brushlike tip for feeding on pollen and nectar. [Malay *luri, nuri.*]

Los An·ge·les (loss ánji-leez, áng-gi-, -liss ‖ *U.S. also* lawss, lōss). Commercial, industrial, and tourist city in southern California, United States. It is the second largest city in the United States, and its greater metropolitan area, including independent cities such as Long Beach, Santa Monica, and Beverly Hills, stretches 80 kilometres (50 miles). Los Angeles harbour handles oil and petrol, and the city's main industries include the manufacture of cars, planes, textiles, and electrical equipment. It also produces films for cinema and television in Hollywood, now a suburb of the city.

lose (lōōz) *v.* **lost** (lost ‖ lawst) **losing, loses.** —*tr.* 1. To experience the disappearance of (a possession, for example); be unable to find; mislay. 2. a. To be unable to maintain, sustain, or keep: *lose one's balance.* b. To cease to feel: *lose hope.* 3. a. To be deprived of: *lose a friend.* b. To be deprived of through death. 4. To fail to win: *lose the game.* 5. To fail to use or take advantage of: *lose a chance.* 6. To fail to hear, see, or understand: *lose the thread of an argument.* 7. To remove (oneself), as from everyday reality into a fantasy world; engross. Often used in the passive: *lost in thought.* 8. To rid oneself of: *lose ten pounds.* 9. To stray or wander from: *lose one's way.* 10. To allow to disappear or fade from view: *We lost him in the crowd.* 11. To elude or outdistance: *lose one's pursuers.* 12. To cause or result in the loss of: *Failure to reply lost her a job.* 13. To cause to die or be destroyed. Used in the passive: *Both planes were lost in the crash.* 14. To fail to keep alive or resuscitate: *The surgeon lost his patient on the operating table.* 15. To fail to give birth to (a living baby), as through miscarriage. —*intr.* 1. To suffer loss. 2. To be defeated. 3. To run slow. Used of a timepiece. 4. To suffer a reduction in impact or value: *The play lost slightly in translation.* —**lose out.** To be defeated. —**lose out on.** To fail to benefit from: *lose out on the sponsorship scheme.* [*Lose, lost, lost;* Middle English *losen, lost, loste,* Old English *lōsian, lōsode, gelōsod,* from *los,* loss, perdition, destruction.]

lo·sel (lốz'l, lốōz'l) *n. Archaic.* One that is worthless. [Middle English, profligate, "lost one", from *losen,* alternative past participle of *losen,* to lose, Old English *-lēosan.*]

los·er (lốōzər) *n.* 1. One that loses or seems fated to lose. 2. One who accepts defeat in a specified way: *a good loser.* 3. One who fails repeatedly, or is always being taken advantage of: *a born loser.*

Lo·sey (lố-si, -zi), **Joseph** (1909–84). U.S. film director. In 1952, he was blacklisted in Hollywood because of alleged Communist sympathies. He made several films in Britain, including *The Servant* (1963), and *The Go-Between* (1970).

los·ing (lốōzing) *adj.* 1. Unprofitable: *sell off the losing parts of the company.* 2. Being defeated: *the losing team.*

loss (loss ‖ lawss) *n.* 1. The act or an instance of losing. 2. Something or someone that is lost. 3. The harm or suffering caused by losing or by being lost. 4. *Plural.* The number of people killed in war or an accident. 5. *Electricity.* The power decrease in a circuit, circuit element, or device caused by resistance. 6. a. A failure to make a profit on a commercial transaction. b. The amount of money lost on an unprofitable transaction. c. *Often plural.* The amount by which a business enterprise's spending exceeds its income. 7. *Insurance.* a. An instance of theft, damage by fire, or the like, as a result of which a policyholder may make a claim. b. The amount of such a claim by an insured. —**at a loss.** Reduced to a state of helplessness or perplexity: *at a loss for words.* —**cut (one's) losses.** To withdraw from a situation so that losses or damage are kept to a minimum. [Middle English *los,* probably back-formation from *loste,* past participle of *losen,* to lose, Old English *lōsian,* to perish, be destroyed or ruined, from *los,* destruction, loss.]

löss. Variant of **loess.**

loss leader *n.* An item of merchandise offered by a retailer at cost price or less to attract customers. Also called "leader".

loss ratio *n.* The ratio between the premiums paid to an insurance company and the claims settled by the company.

los·sy (lốssi ‖ láwssi) *adj.* Designating a transmission line, dielectric material, or the like that has a high attenuation. [From LOSS.]

lost (lost ‖ lawst) *adj.* 1. Strayed; unable to find one's way. 2. Misplaced; missing. 3. Gone in time; passed away: *lost youth.* 4. Gone morally astray; fallen: *a lost woman.* 5. Bewildered or bemused. 6. No longer possessed or practised: *a lost art.* 7. Not appreciated or made use of. Used with *on: His hints were lost on her.* 8. Dead or destroyed: *his lost comrades.* 9. Unavailable; forfeited: *That opportunity is now lost to you.* 10. Unconscious; not susceptible. Used with *to: lost to reason.* 11. Absorbed; engrossed: *lost in her book.* 12. Damned: *lost souls.* —**get lost.** *Informal.* To go away. Usually used in the imperative. [From the past participle of LOSE.]

lost cause *n.* A case that seems hopeless or bound for failure.

Lost Generation *n.* The generation of promising young men who died as soldiers in World War I.

lost wax process *n.* A technique of casting bronze, in which a wax model is used to form a mould and is then melted and drained off. Also called "cire perdue". [Translation of French *cire perdue.*]

lot (lot) *n.* 1. Any of a group of nearly identical objects used in making a determination or choice by chance. 2. The use of such objects for selection. 3. The selections made. 4. That which befalls an individual as a result of such a selection. 5. a. A share; an allotted portion. b. One's fortune in life; one's fate. 6. A number or group of people or things: *Let's get rid of that lot.* 7. Kind, type, or sort: *him and his lot.* 8. a. A job lot *(see).* b. An item or group of items sold at an auction. 9. *Sometimes plural.* A large amount or number. 10. a. *Chiefly U.S.* A piece of land: *a parking lot.* b. A piece of land having fixed boundaries. c. A film studio. —**a lot.** A great deal: *I like him a lot.* —**draw** or **cast lots.** To arrive at a decision or selection by means of lots. —**the lot.** All of a specific collection, quantity, or group. —**throw** or **cast in (one's) lot with.** To join with voluntarily. ~*v.* **lotted, lotting, lots.** —*tr.* 1. To apportion by lots; allot. 2. To draw lots for. 3. To divide (land) into lots. —*intr.* To draw lots. [Middle English *lot(te),* Old English *hlot.*]

Usage: Lot is frequently criticised as inelegant in expressions such as *a lot of money* and *lots of people.* The alternative would be to use such phrases as *a variety of, a great deal of, a great many,* and these are often preferred in formal speech and writing.

Lot (lot). Abraham's nephew, whose wife was turned into a pillar of salt when she looked back as they fled from Sodom. Genesis 19:1–26. [Hebrew *lōṭ,* "covering".]

loth. Variant of **loath.**

Lo·thar·i·o (lə-thaár-i-ō, lō-, -thaír-) *n., pl.* **-os.** A seducer; a sexually promiscuous man. [Name of a seducer in *The Fair Penitent* (1703) by Nicholas Rowe.]

Lo·thi·an (lốthi-ən). Former region in southeast Scotland along the south shore of the Firth of Forth now administratively subdivided. It comprised the former counties of East Lothian, Midlothian, and West Lothian. Edinburgh was the administrative centre.

Lothringen. See **Lorraine.**

loti (lốti) *n., pl.* **maloti** (mə-lốti). The basic monetary unit of Lesotho, equal to 100 lisente.

lo·tic (lốtik) *adj.* Of, pertaining to, or designating ecological communities living in fast-flowing rivers or streams. Compare **lentic.** [Latin *lotus,* past participle of *lavāre,* to wash.]

lo·tion (lốsh'n) *n.* 1. A medicated liquid for external application, especially one containing a substance in suspension, having a soothing or antiseptic effect. 2. Any of various externally applied cosmetic liquids. [Middle English *loscion,* from Old French *lotion,* from Latin *lōtiō* (stem *lōtiōn-*), washing, from *lavere* (past participle *lautus, lōtus*), to wash.]

lots (lots) *adv. Informal.* A great deal; very much: *She's lots prettier than she used to be.*

lot·ter·y (lốttəri) *n., pl.* **-ies.** 1. A game of chance offering money or prizes in which tickets are distributed or sold, the winning ticket or tickets being secretly predetermined or ultimately selected in a chance drawing. 2. An activity or event regarded as having an outcome depending on fate. [Old French *loterie,* from Middle Dutch *loterije,* from *lot,* lot.]

lot·to (lốttō) *n.* A game of chance resembling bingo, played mainly by children. [French *loto,* from Italian *lotto,* from Old French *lot,* lot, from Frankish *lot* (unattested).]

lo·tus, lo·tos (lốtəss) *n.* 1. a. An aquatic plant, *Nelumbo nucifera,* native to southern Asia and widely regarded as sacred there, having large leaves, fragrant, pinkish flowers, and a broad, rounded, perforated seed pod. b. Any of several similar or related plants, such as certain water lilies of the genus *Nymphaea;* especially, *N. lotus,* a white-flowered species regarded as sacred in ancient Egypt. 2. A representation of such a plant in sculpture, architecture, and art. 3. Any of several leguminous plants of the genus *Lotus.* 4. a. A plant in Greek legend whose fruit was eaten by the lotus-eaters. b. The fruit of this tree. [Latin *lōtus,* from Greek *lōtos,* fruit eaten by the lotus-eaters, of Semitic origin; akin to Hebrew *lōṭ,* myrrh.]

lo·tus-eat·er (lốtəss-eetər) *n.* 1. A member of a North African people described in the *Odyssey* who lived on the lotus, in a drugged, indolent state. 2. One who defers the tasks of life in favour of self-indulgent pleasure; an indolent sybarite.

lotus position *n.* A sitting position in which the legs are crossed with the feet resting on opposite thighs and the hands resting on the knees, used in yoga and meditation.

louche (loosh) *adj.* Dubious; appearing unsavoury or shady. [French, "squinting".]

loud (lowd) *adj.* **louder, loudest.** **1.** Characterised by high volume and intensity of sound: *a loud crash.* **2.** Producing or capable of producing a sound of high volume and intensity. **3.** Clamorous and insistent: *loud denials.* **4. a.** Having offensively bright colours: *a loud tie.* **b.** Brash and vulgar in manner. ~*adv.* **louder, loudest.** In a loud manner. —**out loud.** Audibly. [Middle English *l(o)ud, lowde,* Old English *hlūd.*] —**loud·ly** *adv.* —**loud·ness** *n.*

Usage: *Loud* and *loudly* are often interchangeable: *Don't shout so loud(ly)!* Loudly is, however, somewhat more formal, and is the usual form found in writing, and when the meaning is not simply "intensity of the sound", but "clamorous and insistent": *They aired their grievances loudly.*

loud·en (lówd'n) *v.* **-ened, -ening, -ens.** —*tr.* To make louder. —*intr.* To become louder.

loud·hail·er (lówd-háylər ‖ -haylər) *n.* A portable megaphone with a built-in microphone, amplifier, and loudspeaker.

loud·mouth (lówd-mowth) *n.* One whose speech is loud and irritating or indiscreet. —**loud·mouthed** (-mowthd, -mowtht) *adj.*

loud pedal *n. Music.* A sustaining pedal (*see*).

loudspeak·er (lówd-speékər ‖ *chiefly U.S.* -speekər) *n.* A device that converts electric signals to audible sound. Also called "speaker".

lough (lokh, lok) *n.* In Ireland: **1.** A lake. **2.** A bay or inlet of the sea. [Middle English *lough, lowe,* perhaps from Old English *luh,* from Old Irish *loch.*]

Lough·bor·ough (lúf-brə, -bərə ‖ -burrə). Industrial and market town in Leicestershire, England. It has a bell foundry and engineering works and produces knitwear and hosiery.

Lou·is XIV (loo-i), also known as the Sun King (1638–1715). King of France (1643–1715), the greatest of the Bourbon monarchs. After the death of Cardinal Mazarin in 1661, Louis asserted his authority, insisting on the divine right of kings. He waged three major wars: the Dutch War (1672–78), the War of the Grand Alliance (1688–97), and the War of the Spanish Succession (1701–13). Louis presided over a brilliant court at Versailles, but the unity of France which he sought was foiled by his own persecution of the Huguenots, after his revocation of the Edict of Nantes (1685).

Louis XV (1710–74). King of France (1715–74). Louis was a weak ruler much influenced by his mistresses, Madame de Pompadour and Madame du Barry. He led France into the War of the Austrian Succession (1740–48), and the Seven Years' War (1756–63), which led to the loss of the French territories in India, Canada, and the West Indies.

Louis XVI (1754–93). King of France (1774–93), whose reign ended in the turmoil of the French Revolution. In the French economic crisis following the American War of Independence, Louis summoned the States General (1789), but was reluctant to grant the wide-ranging reforms demanded. Revolution followed. Louis and his queen Marie Antoinette fled but were arrested at Varennes (1791) and brought back to Paris. In 1792, the monarchy was abolished. Louis was guillotined the following year.

Lou·is (loo-iss), **Joe,** born Joseph Louis Barrow (1914–81). U.S. boxer, known as the Brown Bomber. He held the world heavyweight title for nearly 12 years (1937–49), successfully defending it for a record 25 times.

lou·is d'or (loo-i-dór) *n., pl.* **louis d'or** (*pronounced as singular*). **1.** A gold coin of France from 1640 until the Revolution. **2.** A 20-franc gold coin of post-Revolutionary France. Also called "louis". [French, "gold Louis", first minted in the reign of Louis XIII.]

Lou·i·si·an·a (loo-eézi-ánnə, loo-izi-, -áanə ‖ loozi-). State in the southern United States, on the Gulf of Mexico. It is dominated by the marshy valley of the river Mississippi. Louisiana is the United States' main source of salt and sulphur, and a major producer of oil and natural gas, cotton, sugar cane, and rice. It was part of a French province, named after Louis XIV, and was sold to the United States (1803). It became a state in 1812. Baton Rouge is the state capital and New Orleans the largest city.

Louisiana French *n.* French as spoken by descendants of the original French settlers of Louisiana.

Louisiana Purchase. The purchase in 1803 by the United States from France of a vast area of land between the Mississippi and the Rocky Mountains. This area, extending over some 2 144 500 square kilometres (about 828,000 square miles), doubled the national territory of the United States at a cost of $15 million.

Louis Napoleon. See Napoleon III.

Louis Phi·lippe (loo-i fi-leép) (1773–1850). King of France (1830–48), son of the Duke of Orléans. When the Bourbons were overthrown in the July Revolution (1830), Louis succeeded to the throne. He was known as the Citizen King. He abdicated during the revolution of 1848, and retired to England.

Louis Qua·torze (ka-tórz) *adj.* Pertaining to the baroque style of architecture, furniture, and decoration of the reign of Louis XIV. [French, "Louis XIV".]

Louis Quinze (kánz) *adj.* Pertaining to the rococo style in architecture, furniture, and decoration of the reign of Louis XV. [French, "Louis XV".]

Louis Seize (séz, sáyz) *adj.* Pertaining to the neoclassical style in architecture, furniture, and decoration of the reign of Louis XVI. [French, "Louis XVI".]

Louis Treize (tráyz, tréz) *adj.* Pertaining to the heavy late-Renaissance style in architecture, furniture, and decoration of the reign of Louis XIII. [French, "Louis XIII".]

Lou·is·ville (loo-i-vil). Industrial city and port on the Ohio river in Kentucky, United States. It makes cars, electrical equipment, and whiskey.

lounge (lownj) *v.* **lounged, lounging, lounges.** —*intr.* **1.** To stand, lean, sit, or lie in a lazy, relaxed way; loll. **2.** To walk in a leisurely way. **3.** To pass time idly. —*tr.* To pass (time) in lounging. ~*n.* **1.** The act of lounging. **2.** A period of lounging. **3.** A lounging walk or gait. **4. a.** A public waiting room with seats, as in a theatre, or air terminal. **b.** A lounge bar. **5. a.** A living room in a house. **b.** A sitting room in a hotel: *a TV lounge.* **6.** *Chiefly U.S.* A long couch, especially one having no back and a headrest at one end. [16th century : origin obscure.] —**loung·er** *n.*

lounge bar *n.* A bar in a hotel, or a **saloon bar** (*see*).

lounge chair *n.* A deep, comfortable chair.

lounge lizard *n. Informal.* A man who does nothing but frequent social gatherings; a hanger-on in fashionable society.

lounge suit *n.* A man's ordinary two-piece suit.

loupe (loop) *n.* A small magnifying glass usually set in an eyepiece and used chiefly by watchmakers and jewellers. [French, from Old French *loupe†,* imperfect gem.]

loup-ga·rou (loo-ga-roo) *n., pl.* **loups-garous** (-roo, -roo). A werewolf. [French, from Old French *leu garoul* : *leu,* wolf, from Latin *lupus* + *garoul, garulf,* werewolf, from Frankish *werwulf* (unattested), "man wolf".]

loup·ing ill (lówp-ing, loop-) *n.* A disease of sheep caused by a virus and transmitted by ticks, characterised by partial paralysis and twitching. Also called "trembles". [From earlier *loup,* to leap, Middle English *loupen,* to LOPE.]

lour. Variant of **lower** (scowl).

Lourdes (loord, *often* loordz). Town at the foot of the Pyrenees in the département of Hautes-Pyrénées, France. The Virgin Mary is said to have appeared in a grotto there to a peasant girl, Marie Bernarde Soubirous (St. Bernadette), several times in 1858. Since that time, pilgrims have flocked there, many seeking cures.

Lourenço Marques. See **Maputo.**

louse (lowss) *n., pl.* **lice** (līss) or **louses** (for sense 4). **1.** Any of numerous small, flat-bodied, wingless, bloodsucking insects of the order Anoplura, many of which are external parasites on various animals, including man. Common species are the head louse, *Pediculus capitis,* and the body louse, *Pediculus corporis.* **2.** Any of numerous small, wingless, biting insects of the order Mallophaga, which are external parasites on birds. In this sense, also called "biting louse", "bird louse". **3.** Any of various similar insects, such as the book louse. **4.** *Slang.* A mean or despicable person. ~*tr.v.* **loused, lousing, louses.** **1.** *Slang.* To bungle. Often used with *up: louse up a deal.* **2.** To remove lice from; delouse. [Louse, lice; Middle English *lous, lys,* Old English *lūs, lȳs.*]

louse·wort (lówss-wurt ‖ -wawrt) *n.* Any of numerous plants of the genus *Pedicularis,* having clusters of irregular, variously coloured flowers. [Sheep feeding on it were believed to be subject to vermin.]

lous·y (lówzi) *adj.* **-ier, -iest.** **1.** Infested with lice. **2.** *Slang.* Mean; nasty; contemptible: *a lousy trick.* **3.** *Slang.* **a.** Painful; unpleasant: *a lousy headache.* **b.** Unwell; sick: *feel lousy.* **c.** Paltry; mere: *a lousy £5.* **4.** *Slang.* Inferior; worthless. **5.** *Slang.* Abundantly supplied; having a surfeit of. Used with *with: lousy with money.* —**lous·i·ly** *adv.* —**lous·i·ness** *n.*

lout[1] (lowt) *n.* An awkward or ill-mannered man or youth; a boor. [Perhaps ultimately from Old Norse *lūtr,* bent low, from *lūta,* to bend down, bow.] —**lout·ish** *adj.*

lout[2] *intr.v.* **louted, louting, louts.** *Archaic.* **1.** To bow or curtsy. **2.** To bend or stoop. [Middle English *l(o)uten,* Old English *lūtan,* to bend down, bow.]

Louth (lowth; *also* lowth). Smallest county in the Republic of Ireland, on the northeast coast. Cattle rearing, fishing, crop raising, brewing, food processing, and textile manufacturing are its main industries. Dundalk is the county town.

Lou·vain (loo-ván). *Flemish* **Leu·ven** (lóvən). Market town in north Brabant, Belgium, with a 15th-century university.

lou·var (loo-vaar) *n.* A widely distributed, silvery whalelike fish, *Louvaris imperialis,* that feeds on plankton. [Italian (Calabrian and Sicilian dialect) *luvaru,* perhaps akin to Latin *ruber,* red.]

L'Ouverture, Toussaint. See **Toussaint L'Ouverture.**

lou·vre, lou·ver (loovər) *n.* **1. a.** A framed opening, as in a wall, fitted with fixed or movable slanted slats. **b.** Such a slatted frame. Also called "louvre boards". **c.** A structure, such as a door or window, incorporating a slatted frame. **2.** Any of the slats used in a louvre. Also called "louvre board". **3.** *Architecture.* A lantern-shaped cupola on the roof of many medieval buildings to admit air and provide for the escape of smoke. **4.** Any slatted ventilating opening. [Middle English *luver, lover,* from Old French *lov(i)er†.*] —**lou·vered** *adj.*

lov·a·ble, love·a·ble (lúvvəb'l) *adj.* Having characteristics that attract love or affection; endearing. —**lov·a·bil·i·ty** (lúvvə-bílləti), **lov·a·ble·ness** *n.* —**lov·a·bly** *adv.*

lov·age (lúvvij) *n.* **1.** A European plant, *Levisticum officinale,* having small, aromatic seeds used as seasoning. **2.** A similar and related plant, *L. scoticum.* [Middle English *lov(e)ache,* from Old French *luvesche, levesche,* from Late Latin *levisticum (apium),* "Ligurian (parsley)", variant of *ligusticum,* neuter of *ligusticus,* of LIGURIA.]

love (luv) *n.* **1.** An intense affectionate concern for another person. **2.** An intense sexual desire and overwhelming affection for another person. **3.** A beloved person. Often used as a term of endearment. **4.** A strong fondness or enthusiasm for something: *a love of the woods.* **5. a.** *Capital* **L.** Eros or Cupid, the god of sexual love in classical mythology. **b.** Sexual love as a force, as a literary subject or personified. **6.** *Theology.* **a.** God's benevolence and mercy towards man. **b.** Man's devotion to or adoration of God. **c.** The benevolence, kindness, or brotherhood that human beings should rightfully feel towards others. **7.** An expression of one's warm feelings: *give them my love.* **8.** One that is liked or thought of as sweet and endearing: *He's a love.* **9.** *British Informal.* Used as a term of address, especially in northern England. **10.** A zero score in tennis. **—fall in love.** To become enamoured of or feel strong affection and sexual desire for someone. **—for love.** As a favour; out of fondness; without payment. **—for love or money.** Under any circumstances. Usually used in the negative: *He would not do that for love or money.* **—for the love of.** **1.** For the sake of. **2.** Used in expressions of impatience or surprise: *for the love of Mike!* **—in love.** Feeling love for someone or something; enamoured. **—make love.** **1.** To have sexual intercourse. **2.** To embrace and caress. **3.** *Archaic.* To court; pay amorous attention to a person.

~v. **loved, loving, loves.** *—tr.* **1.** To feel love for. **2.** To make love to. **3.** To like or desire enthusiastically; delight in. **4.** To thrive on: *The cactus loves hot, dry air.* *—intr.* **1.** To experience loving tenderness for another. **2.** To be in love. **—**See Synonyms at **like.** [Middle English *love,* Old English *lufu.*]

Synonyms: *love, affection, devotion, fondness, infatuation.*

love affair *n.* **1.** An intimate sexual episode between lovers. **2.** An episode characterised by an enthusiastic liking or desire.

love apple *n. Archaic.* A tomato.

love·bird (lúv-burd) *n.* **1.** Any of various small African parrots, chiefly of the genus *Agapornis,* often kept as a cage bird. **2.** *Plural. Informal.* Sweethearts; lovers.

love-bomb·ing (lúv-bomming) *n.* A technique of demonstrating strong concern and affection for a person in order to convert him to the views or beliefs of an organisation.

love child *n.* An illegitimate child. Used euphemistically.

love feast *n.* **1.** Among early Christians, a meal eaten with others as a symbol of love. **2.** A similar symbolic meal among certain modern Christians.

love game *n.* In tennis, a game in which the winner loses no points.

love-hate (lúv-háyt) *adj.* Characterised by alternating feelings of love and hatred or approval and disapproval: *a love-hate relationship.*

love-in-a-mist (lúv-in-ə-mist) *n.* A plant, *Nigella damascena,* native to Europe, having blue or whitish flowers surrounded by numerous threadlike bracts.

love-in-i·dle·ness (lúv-in-ī́d'l-nəss, -niss) *n. Archaic.* A plant, **heartsease** *(see).*

love knot *n.* A stylised knot, generally in the form of a bow, regarded as a symbol of the constancy of two lovers or as an emblem of love. Also called "true lover's knot".

Love·lace (lúv-layss, -ləss, -liss), **Richard** (1618–57). English poet. He supported the Royalists during the English Civil War and was twice imprisoned. He wrote "To Althea, from Prison" (1642).

love·less (lúv-ləss, -liss) *adj.* **1.** Characterised by an absence of love. **2.** Feeling no love; unloving. **3.** Receiving no love; unloved.

love-lies-bleed·ing (lúv-līz-bléeding) *n.* A tropical plant, *Amaranthus caudatus,* having clusters of small red flowers.

Lov·ell (lúvv'l), **Sir (Alfred Charles) Bernard** (1913–). British astronomer, director of Jodrell Bank Experimental Station (now Nuffield Radio Astronomy Laboratories) (1951–81). His written works include *The Exploration of Outer Space* (1961).

love·lock (lúv-lok) *n.* **1.** A lock of hair, often curled and tied with ribbon, worn over the shoulder by men of fashion during the 17th and 18th centuries. **2.** A lock of hair curled over the forehead.

love·lorn (lúv-lawrn) *adj.* Suffering because of love; feeling unrequited love or bereft of love or one's lover.

love·ly (lúvli) *adj.* **-lier, -liest.** **1. a.** Having pleasing or attractive qualities: *a lovely landscape.* **b.** Beautiful; graceful: *a lovely girl.* **2.** Enjoyable; delightful: *a lovely party.* **3.** Inspiring love or affection. **4.** *Rare.* Full of love; loving. **—lovely and.** *Informal.* Pleasingly: *lovely and hot.* **—**See Synonyms at **beautiful.**

~n., pl. **lovelies.** *Informal.* **1.** A beautiful woman, especially an entertainer or model. **2.** Used as a term of endearment or address. **—love·li·ness** *n.* **—love·ly** *adv.*

love·mak·ing (lúv-mayking) *n.* **1.** Sexual activity between lovers; especially, sexual intercourse. **2.** *Archaic.* Courtship.

love match *n.* A marriage based on love, rather than on financial, dynastic, or other considerations.

love nest *n.* A place, such as a house or flat, used by lovers, especially in an illicit love affair. Often used euphemistically.

lov·er (lúvvər) *n.* **1.** Someone who loves another; especially, a man in love with a woman. **2.** *Plural.* A couple having a love affair. **3. a.** Someone engaged in an extramarital love affair. **b.** A sexual partner. **4.** One who is fond of or devoted to something. Usually used in combination: *a dog-lover.* **—lov·er·ly** *adj. & adv.*

love seat *n.* A small sofa or double chair that seats two people.

love set *n. Tennis.* A set in which the winner loses no games.

love·sick (lúv-sik) *adj.* **1.** Stricken, as if with illness, by love. **2.** Exhibiting unhappiness because of love. **—love·sick·ness** *n.*

lov·ey (lúvvi) *n. British Informal.* Used as an affectionate form of address.

lov·ey-dov·ey (lúvvi-dúvvi) *adj. Informal.* Exhibiting excessive sentimentality and affection towards a loved one.

lov·ing (lúvving) *adj.* **1.** Feeling love; affectionate; tenderly devoted. **2.** Indicative of or exhibiting love.

loving cup *n.* **1.** A large, ornamental wine vessel, usually made of silver and having two or more handles, from which each person drinks in turn, as at a ceremonial banquet. **2.** A similar cup given as an award in modern sporting events and similar contests.

lov·ing-kind·ness (lúvving-kīnd-nəss, -niss) *n.* Affection or tenderness stemming from sincere love for someone.

low[1] (lō) *adj.* **lower, lowest.** **1. a.** Having little relative height; not tall. **b.** Rising only slightly above surrounding surfaces: *a low hill.* **c.** Situated or placed below normal height: *a low lighting fixture.* **d.** Situated below the surrounding surfaces, especially below sea level: *water standing in low spots.* **e.** Dead or prostrate. **f.** Cut to show the wearer's chest, back, and neck; décolleté. **2.** Near or at the horizon: *The sun is low in the sky.* **3.** *Phonetics.* Sounded with all or part of the tongue depressed. Said of a vowel, for example (aa) in *large.* **4.** Of less than usual or average depth; shallow: *The river is low.* **5. a.** Of inferior quality or character: *low intelligence.* **b.** Of relatively simple structure in the scale of living organisms. **c.** Inferior in rank or scale: *a low priority.* **6. a.** Morally base. **b.** Having inferior social, moral, or cultural status. **c.** Vulgar; coarse: *low jokes.* **7. a.** Wanting vigour; weak. **b.** Emotionally or mentally depressed. **c.** Giving little nourishment. **8. a.** Below average in quantity, degree, or intensity: *a low temperature.* **b.** Below an average or standard figure: *low wages.* **c.** Pertaining to or designating latitudes nearest to the equator. **d.** Of relatively small price: *The cost is low.* **e.** Involving or having a small amount: *low in fat.* **9. a.** *Music.* Being a sound produced by a relatively small frequency of vibrations: *a low note.* **b.** Hushed; not loud: *a low voice.* **10.** Being almost without money: *low in funds.* **11.** Not well supplied with; not adequately provided with or equipped for. **12.** Of small value or quality; depreciatory; disparaging: *a low opinion of his qualities.* **13.** Brought down or reduced in health or wealth. **14.** Overthrown; defeated. **15.** Designating a gear designed to produce power and slow speed. **16.** *Often capital* **L.** Low-Church. **—**See Synonyms at **mean** (ignoble).

~adv. **1. a.** In a low position, level, or space. **b.** In a low condition or rank; humbly: *You value yourself too low.* **2.** In or to a reduced, humbled, or degraded condition: *"A woman too brought Parnell low."* (James Joyce). **3.** Softly; quietly: *speak low.* **4.** With a deep pitch. **5.** At a small price: *bought low, sold high.* **6.** In hiding; biding one's time: *keep low; lie low.*

~n. **1.** A low level, position, or degree: *The stock market fell to a new low.* **2.** *Meteorology.* A **depression** *(see).* **3.** The gear configuration or setting that produces the lowest range of output speeds, as in the transmission of a motor vehicle. **4.** In some card games, the lowest trump. **5.** In some other games, the lowest score. [Middle English *low(e), lah,* from Old Norse *lāgr.*] **—low·ness** *n.*

low[2] *n.* The characteristic sound uttered by cattle; a moo.

~v. **lowed, lowing, lows.** *—intr.* To emit a low. *—tr.* To utter by means of a low. [Middle English *loowen,* Old English *hlōwan.*]

Low, Sir David (Alexander Cecil) (1891–1963). British cartoonist, born in New Zealand. He created a character called Colonel Blimp, a pompous and diehard reactionary.

low·born (lṓ-bórn) *adj. Rare.* Of humble birth.

low·bred (lṓ-bréd) *adj.* **1.** Lowborn. **2.** Coarse; vulgar.

low·brow (lṓ-brow) *n. Informal.* One having uncultivated tastes. Compare **highbrow, middlebrow.** **—low·brow, low·browed** *adj.*

Low Church *n.* A movement or faction in the Anglican Church that is opposed to excessive ritualism and favours a more evangelical doctrine. Compare **Broad Church, High Church.** **—Low-Church** (lṓ-chúrch) *adj.* **—Low-Church·man** (-mən) *n.*

low comedy *n.* Comedy characterised by slapstick, visual, and physical humour.

Low Countries. Region in northwest Europe comprising Belgium, the Netherlands, and Luxembourg.

low-down (lṓ-dówn || *West Indies also* -dúng) *adj.* Mean; unfair; despicable.

low·down *n. Informal.* All the facts; the relevant information from an informed source. Preceded by *the.*

Low Dutch *n.* The language of the Netherlands, **Dutch** *(see).*

Low·ell (lṓ-əl), **Amy** (1874–1925). U.S. poet. She was a leading imagist writer. Her works include *Men, Women, and Ghosts* (1916).

Lowell, Robert (Traill Spence) (1917–77). U.S. poet. He was imprisoned as a conscientious objector in World War II. His works include *Lord Weary's Castle* (1946), and *For the Union Dead* (1964).

low·er[1] (low-ər, lowr) *intr.v.* **-ered, -ering, -ers.** Also **lour, loured, louring, lours.** **1.** To look angry, sullen, or threatening; scowl. **2.** To appear dark or threatening. Said especially of the sky or weather.

~n. Also **lour.** **1.** A threatening, sullen, or angry look. **2.** A dark and ominous look. [Middle English *l(o)uren*†.] **—low·er·ing·ly** *adv.*

low·er[2] (lṓ-ər). Comparative of **low.**

~adj. **1.** Below someone or something in rank, position, or authority. **2.** Below a similar or comparable thing: *a lower shelf.* **3.** *Capital* **L.** *Geology & Archaeology.* Being an earlier division of.

~n. One that is beneath another; especially, a lower berth.

~v. **lowered, -ering, -ers.** *—tr.* **1.** To let, bring, or move something down to a lower level. **2.** To reduce in value, degree, intensity, or quality. **3.** To weaken; undermine: *lower one's energy.* **4.** To reduce in standing or respect. *—intr.* To diminish; become less.

Lower Austria. *German* **Nie·der·öster·reich** (needər-ōstərīkh). Formerly (1938–1945) **Lower Danube.** *German* **Nie·der·do·nau** (nee-dər-dónnow). State in northeast Austria. It is a largely agricultural region, crossed by the Danube. Vienna is the capital.

lower bound *n. Mathematics.* A number that is not greater than any number in a set.

Lower California. *Spanish* **Ba·ja California** (báakhə). Mountainous peninsula in western Mexico separated from the mainland by the Gulf of California. It is mainly desert with limited agriculture. However, it has pearl and deep-sea fisheries, and considerable mineral resources, including gold, silver, copper and iron.

lower case *n. Abbr.* **l.c.** 1. Small letters, as opposed to capitals. 2. The case of printing type containing the small letters.

low·er-case (lṓ-ər-káyss, -kayss) *adj. Abbr.* **l.c.** *Printing.* Pertaining to or designating small letters as distinguished from capitals: *a, b, and c are lower-case letters.*
~*tr.v.* **lower-cased, -casing, -cases.** To print in lower-case letters.

lower class *n. Often plural.* The class of lower than middle rank in a society; the working class. —**low·er-class** *adj.*

lower criticism *n.* Textual criticism and verbal examination of Biblical texts. Compare **higher criticism.**

lower deck *n.* 1. The deck of a ship immediately above the hold. 2. *Informal.* The petty officers and seamen of a navy, or of a ship, collectively.

Lower House *n.* The branch of a bicameral legislative body that is larger and more representative of the population, such as the House of Commons in the British Parliament. Also called "Lower Chamber". Compare **Upper House.**

low·er·most (lṓ-ər-mōst) *adj.* Lowest.

Lower Saxony. *German* **Nied·er·sach·sen** (néedər-zaks'n). State in northwestern Germany comprising the former province of Hanover and the states of Brunswick, Oldenburg, and Schaumburg-Lippe. It is mainly agricultural, but has several manufacturing centres, including Brunswick and Hanover (the state capital).

lower world *n.* 1. The realm of the dead, considered in ancient times to be beneath the surface of the earth; hell. Also called "lower regions". 2. The earth.

low·er·y (lów-əri, lówr-i) *adj.* Overcast; threatening: *a lowery sky.*

lowest common denominator *n. Abbr.* **l.c.d., L.C.D.** 1. The least common multiple of the denominators of a set of fractions. Also called "least common denominator". 2. **a.** The most basic, least sophisticated level of taste, sensibility, or opinion among a group of people. **b.** A group reacting at such a level.

lowest common multiple *n. Abbr.* **l.c.m., L.C.M.** The least quantity that is exactly divisible by each of two or more specified quantities; for example, 12 is the lowest common multiple of 2, 3, 4, and 6. Also called "least common multiple".

Lowes·toft (lṓ-stoft, lṓ-i-, -stəft; *locally* lṓ-stəf). Fishing port and resort in Suffolk, England, the most easterly town in England.

low explosive *n.* An explosive, as used in firearms, that has relatively low power.

low frequency *n. Abbr.* **lf** A **radio frequency** *(see)* in the range from 30 to 300 kilohertz.

Low German *n. Abbr.* **LG, L.G.** 1. Any of several German dialects spoken in northern Germany. 2. All of the West Germanic languages except High German. See **High German.**

low-key (lṓ-kée) *adj.* 1. Having low intensity; restrained, as in style or quality. 2. In photography, having or producing uniformly dark tones with little contrast.

low-keyed (lṓ-kéed) *adj.* Restrained; low-key.

low·land (lṓ-lənd) *n.* 1. Low-lying ground. **b.** *Plural.* A flat lowlying region of a country.
~*adj.* Pertaining to or characteristic of low, usually level, land.

Low·land (lṓ-lənd) *n.* The English dialect of the Scottish Lowlands; Lallans.
~*adj.* Of or from the Scottish Lowlands.

low·land·er (lṓ-ləndər) *n.* 1. A native or inhabitant of a lowland. 2. *Capital* **L.** A native of the Scottish Lowlands.

Low·lands, The (lṓ-ləndz). Scotland south of the Highlands.

Low Latin *n.* Loosely, late or medieval latin.

low-level language (lṓ-levv'l) *n.* A computer language that bears more resemblance to a machine language than to human language. Compare **high-level language.**

low life *n.* Life among the less respectable sections of society. —**low-life** *adj.*

low·ly (lṓ-li) *adj.* **-lier, -liest.** 1. Having or suited for a low rank or position. 2. Humble; meek. 3. Plain; simple; undistinguished.
~*adv.* 1. In a low manner, condition, or position. 2. Humbly; meekly. —**low·li·ness** *n.*

Low Mass *n.* A Mass without singing or ceremonial.

low-mind·ed (lṓ-míndid) *adj.* Exhibiting a coarse, vulgar character. —**low-mind·ed·ly** *adv.* —**low-mind·ed·ness** *n.*

low-necked (lṓ-nékt) *adj.* Also **low-neck** (-nék). Having a low-cut neckline; décolleté.

low-pass filter (lṓ-paass ‖ -pass) *n.* An electronic filter that allows frequencies below a specific value to pass but substantially attenuates frequencies above this value.

low-pitched (lṓ-pícht) *adj.* 1. Low in tone or tonal range. 2. Having a moderate slope: *a low-pitched roof.*

low-pres·sure (lṓ-préshər) *adj.* 1. Having, working under, or exerting little pressure. 2. Relaxed; calm; easy-going.

low profile *n.* An unobtrusive, restrained behaviour or stance; especially, an avoidance of militancy, publicity, or intervention.

low relief *n.* **Bas-relief** *(see).* [Translation of French *bas-relief.*]

low-rise (lṓ-ríz) *adj.* Of or designating a building or buildings having few storeys: *a low-rise development.* Compare **high-rise.**

Low·ry (lówr-i), **(Clarence) Malcolm** (1909–57). British novelist. His best-known work is *Under the Volcano* (1947), a partly autobiographical novel about an alcoholic ex-consul in Mexico.

Lowry, L(awrence) S(tephen) (1887–1976). British painter. He mirrored working-class life as a clerk in Lancashire, filling his canvasses with matchstick figures in dark industrial towns.

low season *n.* The time of year, for example winter at seaside resorts, when there is least demand for a service or product.

low-spir·it·ed (lṓ-spírritid) *adj.* In low spirits; depressed.

Low Sunday *n.* The Sunday following Easter.

low-ten·sion (lṓ-ténsh'n) *adj. Abbr.* **LT** Having, carrying, or operating at a low voltage.

low-test (lṓ-tést) *adj.* Having low volatility and a high boiling point. Said of petrol.

low tide *n.* 1. The tide at its lowest ebb. 2. The time of this ebb.

Low·veld (lṓ-felt). In South Africa, the savannah of the African plateau below 900 metres (about 3,000 feet).

low water *n. Abbr.* **L.W.** 1. Low tide. 2. The lowest level of water in a body of water, such as a river, lake, or reservoir.

low-wa·ter mark (lṓ-wáwtər ‖ *U.S. also* -wóttər) *n.* 1. A mark that indicates the lowest level reached by a river or sea water at low tide or on some other regular occasion. 2. The lowest point in something, when there seems the least prospect of success: *the low-water mark in her career.*

lox¹ (loks) *n. U.S.* Smoked salmon. [Yiddish *laks,* from Middle High German *lahs,* salmon, from Old High German.]

lox² *n.* **Liquid oxygen** *(see).*

lox·o·drome *n.* A **rhumb line** *(see).* Also called "loxodromic curve".

lox·o·drom·ic (lóksə-drómmik) *adj.* Also **lox·o·drom·i·cal** (-'l). *Nautical.* Pertaining to sailing on a rhumb line. [Greek *loxos*†, slanting + *dromos,* a running, course.] —**lox·o·drom·i·cal·ly** *adv.*

loy·al (lóy-əl) *adj.* 1. Steadfast in support of and devotion to and never betraying the interests of one's homeland, government, or sovereign. 2. Faithful to a person, ideal, or custom; constantly supporting or following. 3. Of or professing loyalty. —See Synonyms at **faithful.** [French, from Old French *loyal, loial, leial,* faithful to obligations, legal, from Latin *lēgālis,* legal, from *lēx* (stem *lēg-*), law.] —**loy·al·ism** *n.* —**loy·al·ly** *adv.*

loy·al·ist (lóy-əl-ist) *n.* 1. One who maintains loyalty to a lawful government, political party, or sovereign, especially during war or revolutionary change. 2. *Capital* **L.** A Northern Irish Protestant wishing to keep Northern Ireland as part of the United Kingdom and strongly opposed to the unification of Ireland. 3. *Capital* **L.** One who supported the lawful government of Spain during the Spanish Civil War; a Republican.

loyal toast *n. British.* A toast to the monarch drunk during a formal dinner.

loy·al·ty (lóy-əlti) *n., pl.* **-ties.** 1. The state or quality of being loyal. 2. *Plural.* Feelings of devoted attachment, affection, or duty: *divided loyalties.* —See Synonyms at **fidelity.**

Loyalty Islands. *French* **îles Loy·au·té** (eel lwa-yō-táy). Group of coral islands in the southwest Pacific Ocean, forming part of the French Overseas Territory of New Caledonia. It comprises Maré, Lifou, Uvéa, and numerous islets, and exports copra and rubber.

Lo-yang. See **Luoyang.**

Loyola, Saint Ignatius. See Saint **Ignatius Loyola.**

loz·enge (lózzinj) *n.* 1. **a.** A four-sided planar figure with a diamond-like shape; a rhombus that is not a square. **b.** Something with this shape, especially a heraldic device. 2. **a.** A medicated drop that dissolves slowly in the mouth for local medication of the mouth or throat. **b.** A sugary tablet like this, eaten as a sweet. [Middle English *losenge,* from Old French, originally a diamond-shaped figure in heraldic design, from Gaulish *lausa* (unattested), flat stone.]

LP *adj.* Long-playing.
~*n., pl.* **LP's** or **LPs.** A long-playing gramophone record.

LPG liquefied petroleum gas.

L-plate (él-playt) *n.* In Britain, a white plate bearing a capital L in red that must be displayed on a vehicle driven by a learner-driver.

Lr The symbol for the element lawrencium.

L.S. the place of the seal [Latin *locus sigilli.*]

LSD *Lysergic acid diethylamide:* a crystalline compound, $C_{20}H_{25}N_3O$, prepared from lysergic acid, used illegally as a hallucinogenic drug. Also called "acid".

L.S.D., £.s.d. pounds, shillings, and pence [Latin *Librae, solidi, denarii.*]
~*n. British Informal.* Money.

L.S.E. London School of Economics.

lt. light.

Lt. lieutenant.

l.t. *Chiefly U.S.* local time.

LT low tension.

Lt. Col. lieutenant-colonel.

Lt. Comdr. lieutenant-commander.

ltd, ltd., Ltd. limited.

Lt. Gen. lieutenant-general.

Lt. Gov. lieutenant governor.

Lu The symbol for the element lutetium.

Lu·an·da (loo-án-də). Capital and port of Angola, on the Atlantic coast of Africa. It was founded as São Paulo de Loanda by the Portuguese in 1575. The city has a fine natural harbour, an oil refinery, and chemical, cement, and textile industries.

lu·au (lōo-ow) *n.* An elaborate Hawaiian feast. [Hawaiian *lu'au.*]

lub. lubricant; lubrication.

Lu·ba (lōobə) *n., pl.* **Luba. 1.** A member of a Negroid people of the southeastern Congo. **2.** The language of this people. —**Lu·ba** *adj.*

lub·ber (lúbbər) *n.* **1.** A clumsy fellow. **2.** An inexperienced sailor; a landlubber. [Middle English *lobur, lobre†.*] —**lub·ber·ly** *adj. & adv.*

lubber line *n.* Also **lubber's line.** A line or mark on a compass or cathode-ray indicator that represents the heading of a ship or aircraft.

lubber's hole *n.* A hole through the platform surrounding the upper part of a ship's mast, through which one may climb to go aloft.

Lub·bock (lúbbək). City in northwest Texas, United States. It is the major distribution centre for the southern Great Plains.

Lü·beck (lōo-bek, lếw-; *German* lǘ-). Commercial city and river port in Schleswig-Holstein, northern Germany. A major Baltic port and industrial centre, it has foundries and shipyards, and is connected to the river Elbe by canal. The present city, dating from 1143, was the leading town of the Hanseatic League. It remained a free city until 1937, when it was included in Schleswig-Holstein, a province of the Prussian state.

Lu·bitsch (lōo-bich), **Ernst** (1892–1947). U.S. film director, born in Germany. His Hollywood productions include *Design For Living* (1933), *Ninotchka* (1939), and *Heaven Can Wait* (1943).

Lub·lin (lōobleen). *Russian* **Lyu·blin** (lew-blín). Industrial and agricultural marketing city of central Poland. It is also a regional capital and cultural centre. A council of workers and peasants proclaimed Poland's independence from Russia there in 1918. There also, a Soviet-sponsored liberation group proclaimed itself the provisional government of Poland in December 1944, and this was recognised by the Allies at the Potsdam Conference (August 1945).

lu·bri·cant (lōo-bri-kənt, lếw-) *n.* Abbr. **lub. 1.** Any of various usually oily liquids or solids, such as grease, machine oil, or graphite, that reduce friction, heat, and wear when applied as a surface coating to moving parts. **2.** *Informal.* Something or someone that helps to reduce difficulty or conflict. [Latin *lubricāns* (stem *lubricant-*), present participle of *lubricāre*, to LUBRICATE.] —**lu·bri·cant** *adj.*

lu·bri·cate (lōo-bri-kayt, lếw-) *v.* **-cated, -cating, -cates.** —*tr.* **1.** To apply a lubricant to. **2.** To make slippery. **3.** *Informal.* To reduce friction or difficulty in. —*intr.* To act as a lubricant. [Latin *lubricāre*, from *lubricus*, slippery.] —**lu·bri·ca·tion** (-káysh'n) *n.* —**lu·bri·ca·tive** (-kaytiv, -kətiv) *adj.* —**lu·bri·ca·tor** *n.*

lu·bric·i·ty (lōo-bríssəti, lew-) *n.* **1.** Lewdness; salaciousness. **2.** Shiftiness; trickiness. **3.** Slipperiness. [Late Latin *lubricitās* (stem *lubricitāt-*), slipperiness, from Latin *lubricus*, slippery.]

lu·bri·cous (lōo-bri-kəss, lếw-) *adj.* Also **lu·bri·cious** (lōo-bríshəss, lew-) **1.** Characterised by lewdness. **2.** Elusive. **3.** Slippery. [Latin *lubricus*, slippery.]

Lu·bum·bash·i (loo-bŏom-báshi). Formerly **E·liz·a·beth·ville** (ilízzə-bəth-vil). Capital of Shaba province, Congo (Dem. Rep.). It is a copper mining and smelting centre, and also a marketing point. The city was the capital of the secessionist state of Katanga (the former name of Shaba province) in the civil war (1960–63).

Lu·can (lōo-kən, lếw-) *adj.* Pertaining to those parts of the New Testament attributed to St. Luke. [Ecclesiastical Latin *Lucas*, from Greek *Loukas*, Luke.]

lu·carne (lōo-kárn, lew-) *n.* A dormer window. [Variant (influenced by French *lucarne*) of earlier *lucane*, Old French *lucanne*, from Frankish *lukinna* (unattested), from *lūk* (unattested), something that closes.]

luce (lōoss) *n.* A pike, especially when full-grown. [Middle English, from Old French *lu(i)s*, from Latin *lūcius.*]

lu·cent (lōoss'nt, lếwss'nt) *adj. Literary.* **1.** Giving off light; luminous. **2.** Translucent. [Latin *lūcēns* (stem *lūcent-*), present participle of *lūcēre*, to shine.] —**lu·cen·cy** *n.* —**lu·cent·ly** *adv.*

lu·cerne (lōo-sérn, lew-, lōo-, lōo-sern) *n. Chiefly British.* A plant, **alfalfa** (see). [French *luzerne*, from Provençal *luzerno*, special use of *luzerno*, glowworm (from its shiny seeds), perhaps from Latin *lucerna*, lamp.]

Lu·cerne (lōo-sérn, lew-; *French* lü-sáirn). *German* **Lu·zern** (lōo-tsáirn). Canton in central Switzerland, noted for dairy and forest products. The city of Lucerne, on Lake Lucerne, is the capital and one of Switzerland's leading resorts.

Lucerne, Lake. *German* **Vier·wald·stät·ter·see** (feer-váalt-shtettər-zay). Resort lake in central Switzerland, its German name meaning "Lake of the Four Forest Cantons" (Lucerne, Schwyz, Unterwalden, and Uri).

lu·cid (lōo-sid, lếw-) *adj.* **1.** Easily understood; clear: *a lucid speech.* **2.** Sane; rational: *a lucid moment.* **3.** *Poetic.* Shining. [French *lucide* and Italian *lucido*, from Latin *lūcidus*, from *lūcēre*, to shine.] —**lu·cid·i·ty** (lōo-síddəti, lew-), **lu·cid·ness** *n.* —**lu·cid·ly** *adv.*

lu·ci·fer (lōo-si-fər, lếw-) *n.* A friction match. Not in current usage. [After LUCIFER.]

Lu·ci·fer¹ (lōo-si-fər, lếw). The archangel cast from Heaven for leading a revolt of the angels; Satan. [Middle English *Lucifer*, Old English *Lucifer*, from Latin *Lūcifer*, "light-bearer" : *lūx* (stem *lūc-*), light + *-FER.*]

Lucifer² *n.* The planet Venus in its appearance as the morning star.

lu·cif·er·ase (lōo-síffər-ayz, lew-, -ayss) *n.* An enzyme that catalyses the oxidation of luciferin. [LUCIFER(IN) + -ASE.]

lu·cif·er·in (lōo-síffərin, lew-) *n.* A pigment in bioluminescent animals, such as fireflies or certain marine crustaceans, that produces

an almost heatless, bluish-green light when oxidised. [Latin *lūcifer*, "light-bearer". See Lucifer.]

luck (luk) *n.* **1.** The fortuitous happening of fortunate or adverse events; fortune. **2.** One's (often specified) fate or lot. **3.** Good fortune; prosperity or success that comes by chance: *I wish you luck.* —**down on (one's) luck.** Afflicted by misfortune. —**in luck.** Fortunate; enjoying success. —**out of luck.** Unsuccessful; not having good fortune. —**push (one's) luck.** To take a risk, often by acting overconfidently and relying on luck. —**try (one's) luck.** To attempt something without knowing if one will be successful. [Middle English *lucke*, perhaps from Low German *luk* or Middle Dutch *luc*, akin to Middle High German *gelücke†.*]

luck·i·ly (lúckili) *adv.* With or by favourable chance.

luck·less (lúck-ləss, -liss) *adj.* Unlucky; having poor luck.

Luck·now (lúk-now; *also* lōok-). Capital city and rail centre in Uttar Pradesh, north India, once the capital of the kings of Oudh (1775–1856). The city was besieged for five months during the Indian Mutiny (1857).

luck·y (lúcki) *adj.* **-ier, -iest. 1.** Having or resulting in good luck. **2.** Occurring by fortunate chance. **3.** Believed to bring good luck: *a lucky number.* —See Usage note at **fortuitous.** —**luck·i·ness** *n.*

lucky dip *n. British.* **1.** A large barrel or box containing concealed prizes which are selected at random. **2.** *Informal.* Any undertaking whose outcome is uncertain.

lu·cra·tive (lōo-krətiv, lếw-) *adj.* Producing wealth; profitable. [Middle English *lucratif*, from Old French, from Latin *lucrātīvus*, from *lucrārī*, to profit, from *lucrum*, gain, LUCRE.]

lu·cre (lōo-kər, lếw-) *n.* Money; profits. Often used humorously in the phrase *filthy lucre.* [Middle English, from Latin *lucrum*, gain, profit.]

Lu·cre·ti·us (lōo-kréesh-əss, lew-, -yəss). Latin name Titus Lucretius Carus (*c.* 95–*c.* 55 B.C.). Roman poet. He wrote *De rerum natura*, a philosophical poem on the teachings of Democritus and Epicurus, which tried to explain the universe without a divinity.

lu·cu·brate (lōo-kew-brayt, lếw-) *intr.v.* **-brated, -brating, -brates.** To write in a scholarly fashion. [Latin *lūcubrāre*, to work at night by lamplight.]

lu·cu·bra·tion (lōo-kew-bráysh'n, lew-) *n.* **1. a.** Laborious study or writing. **b.** A product of such study, such as a treatise. **2.** Pedantry in speech or writing.

lu·cu·lent (lōo-kew-lənt, lếw-) *adj. Archaic.* Easily understood; clear; lucid. [Middle English, full of light, clear, from Latin *lūculentus*, from *lūx* (stem *lūc-*), light.]

Lu·cul·lan (lōo-kúllən, lew-) *adj.* Lavish; luxurious. [After Lucius Lucullus, first-century B.C. Roman general noted for his luxurious banquets.]

lud (lud) *n.* Lord. Used when addressing a judge, in the phrase *m'lud* (my lord).

Lü·da or **Lü·ta** (lú-daá). Also **Dai·ren** (dí-ren), **Da·lian**, or **Ta·lien** (daa-lyen). Industrial conurbation and rail terminus in southern Liaoning province, northeast China. It now includes the city of Lüshun (Lü-shun or Port Arthur), northeast China's chief port and also a major naval station.

Lud·dite (lúddīt) *n.* **1.** Any of a group of British workmen who, between 1811 and 1816, rioted and destroyed textile machinery in the belief that mechanisation would diminish employment. **2.** One who aggressively opposes technical or technological progress. [Probably after Ned *Lud(d)*, an insane person who destroyed some stocking frames about 1779.]

Lu·den·dorff (lōo'dn-dawrff), **Erich** (1865–1937). German general and politician. He was Hindenburg's chief of staff in the east during World War I, and won the battle of Tannenberg (1916). He was defeated as a Nazi candidate for the presidency in 1925.

lu·dic (lōo-dik, lếw-) *adj.* Pertaining to play. [Latin *lūdus*, game, and *lūdere*, to play.]

lu·di·crous (lōo-di-krəss, lếw-) *adj.* Laughable or hilarious through obvious absurdity or incongruity. See Synonyms at **foolish.** [Latin *lūdicrus*, done playfully, from *lūdus*, game.] —**lu·di·crous·ly** *adv.* —**lu·di·crous·ness** *n.*

Lud·low (lúd-lō). Market town in Shropshire, England, dominated by ruins of its massive 11th–16th century castle.

lu·do (lōo-dō || lếw-) *n.* A board game played with counters that are moved according to the throw of a dice. [Latin, "I play".]

lu·es (lōo-eez, lếw-) *n., pl.* **lues.** *Pathology.* **1.** Syphilis. **2.** A plague; a pestilence. [New Latin, from Latin *luēs*, plague.] —**lu·et·ic** (lōo-éttik, lew-) *adj.* —**lu·et·i·cal·ly** *adv.*

luff (luf) *n.* **1.** The forward side of a fore-and-aft sail. **2.** The fullest part of the bow of a ship.

~*v.* **luffed, luffing, luffs.** —*intr.* **1.** To steer a sailing vessel nearer into the wind, especially with the sails flapping. **2.** To flap while losing wind. Used of a sail. **3.** To sail closer to the wind than, or to come between the jib and, an opponent's yacht during a race. **4.** To move the jib of a crane or the boom of a derrick. —*tr.* To cause (a ship, for example) to sail closer to the wind. [Earlier *loufe*, Middle English *luff, lof*, from Old French *lof*, perhaps from Middle Dutch *loef* (unattested).]

luffa. *Chiefly U.S.* Variant of **loofah.**

Luft·waf·fe (lōoft-vaaffə) *n.* The German air force. [German, "air weapon".]

lug¹ (lug) *n.* **1.** An earlike handle or projection on a vessel or machine, used as a hold or support. **2.** In machinery, a nut, especially one that is closed at one end to serve as a cap. **3.** A loop, usually of leather, at the side of the saddle of a harness rig through which one of the shafts of a cart or other conveyance passes. **4.** A projection from a battery plate to which an electrical connection can be made. **5.** *Chiefly Scottish.* An ear. **6.** A lugsail. [Middle English (Scottish) *lugge,* flap, ear, perhaps from *luggen,* to LUG (to pull, as the ear).]

lug² *v.* **lugged, lugging, lugs.** —*tr.* **1.** To drag or haul (something) laboriously. **2.** To introduce or include (something irrelevant) in a forced manner. —*intr.* To pull with difficulty; tug.
~*n.* **1.** The act or an instance of lugging. **2.** Something that is lugged. [Middle English *luggen,* to pull, perhaps from Scandinavian, akin to Swedish *lugga†,* to pull one's hair.]

lug³ *n.* The lugworm.

Lu·gan·da (lōō-gándǝ, -gaǎndǝ) *n.* The Bantu language of the Ganda, a people of Uganda. —**Lu·gan·da** *adj.*

luge (lōōzh) *n.* A light, short toboggan for one person.
~*intr.v.* **luged, luging, luges.** To ride or travel on a luge. [French.]

Lu·ger (lōōgǝr) *n.* A trademark for a German automatic pistol.

lug·gage (lúggij) *n.* The suitcases, trunks, bags, and the like of a traveller; baggage. [Probably LUG (to drag) + (BAG)GAGE.]

luggage van *n.* A **railway van** *(see).*

lug·ger (lúggǝr) *n.* A small boat used for fishing, sailing, or coasting and having two or three masts, each with a lugsail, and two or three jibs set on the bowsprit. [From LUG(SAIL).]

lug·hole (lúg-hōl) *n. British Slang.* An ear.

lug·sail (lúg-sayl, *nautical* -s'l) *n.* A quadrilateral sail lacking a boom and having the foot larger than the head, bent to a yard hanging obliquely on the mast. Also called "lug". [Perhaps from LUG "ear".]

lu·gu·bri·ous (lōō-gōōbri-ǝss, lǝ-, lōō-, lew-) *adj.* Mournful or doleful, especially to an excessive degree. [Latin *lūgubris,* mournful, from *lūgēre,* to mourn.] —**lu·gu·bri·ous·ly** *adv.* —**lu·gu·bri·ous·ness** *n.*

lug·worm (lúg-wurm) *n.* Any of various segmented, burrowing marine worms of the genus *Arenicola;* especially, *A. marina,* often used as fishing bait. Also called "lug", "lobworm". [17th century : origin obscure.]

Luik. See **Liège.**

Luke (lōōk, lewk) *n.* A book of the New Testament, the third Gospel, attributed to St. Luke.

Luke, Saint. A companion of the Apostle Paul, traditionally regarded as author of the third Gospel and The Acts of the Apostles.

luke·warm (lōōk-wáwrm, léwk-, -wawrm) *adj.* **1.** Mildly warm; tepid. **2.** Lacking in enthusiasm; indifferent. [Middle English : *luke,* perhaps from *lew,* tepid, Old English *hlēow,* warm + WARM.] —**luke·warm·ly** *adv.* —**luke·warm·ness** *n.*

lull (lul) *v.* **lulled, lulling, lulls.** —*tr.* **1.** To cause to sleep or rest; soothe; calm. **2.** To dispel or quieten (fears or suspicions). **3.** To deceive into trustfulness. —*intr.* To become calm.
~*n.* **1.** A relatively calm interval in a storm or other turbulence. **2.** An interval of lessened activity: *a lull in sales.* [Middle English *lullen,* perhaps of German origin; akin to Middle Low German *lollen.*]

lull·a·by (lúllǝ-bī) *n., pl.* **-bies.** A soothing song with which to lull a child to sleep.
~*tr.v.* **lullabied, -bying, -bies.** To quieten with or as if with a lullaby. [Perhaps LULL + good*bye.*]

Lul·ly (lōō-lée; *French* lü-), **Jean Baptiste,** born Giovanni Battista Lulli (1632–87). Italian-born French composer. He was court composer to Louis XIV of France, founding French opera and producing court ballets for Molière's plays.

lu·lu (lōō-lōō) *n. Chiefly U.S. Slang.* An object, action, or idea that is remarkable. [Perhaps from *Lulu,* pet form of the name *Louise.*]

lum·ba·go (lum-báygō) *n.* Pain in the region of the lower back, resulting from various causes. [Latin *lumbāgo,* from *lumbus,* loin.]

lum·bar (lúm-bǝr || -baar) *adj.* Of, near, or situated in the part of the back and sides between the lowest ribs and the pelvis. [New Latin *lumbaris,* from Latin *lumbus,* loin.]

lumbar puncture *n.* The insertion of a hollow needle into the lumbar region of the spinal cord in order to withdraw cerebrospinal fluid for diagnostic examination or inject drugs.

lum·ber¹ (lúmbǝr) *n.* **1.** *Chiefly British.* Miscellaneous stored articles. **2.** Anything useless or cumbersome. **3.** *U.S. & Canadian.* Timber.
~*v.* **lumbered, -bering, -bers.** —*tr.* **1.** *Chiefly British.* To clutter with or as if with unused articles. **2.** To jumble or heap together. **3.** *Informal.* To burden or encumber, as with difficulties or responsibilities. **4.** *Chiefly U.S.* To cut or saw into timber. —*intr. Chiefly U.S.* To cut and prepare timber for the market. [Perhaps from LUMBER (to move clumsily, hence something clumsy).] —**lum·ber** *adj.* —**lum·ber·er, lum·ber·man** (-mǝn) *n.*

lum·ber² *intr.v.* **-bered, -bering, -bers.** To walk or move with heavy clumsiness. [Middle English *lomeren,* perhaps from Scandinavian; akin to Swedish dialectal *loma,* to move heavily.]

lum·ber·jack (lúmbǝr-jak) *n.* One who fells trees and transports the timber to a mill; a logger. [LUMBER (wood) + JACK (man).]

lum·ber·jack·et (lúmbǝr-jackit) *n.* A heavy, waist-length jacket worn especially by outdoor workers.

lum·bri·coid (lúmbri-koyd) *adj.* Resembling or pertaining to an earthworm.
~*n.* A parasitic roundworm, *Ascaris lumbricoides,* that infests the human intestine. [New Latin *lumbricoides* : Latin *lumbrīcus,* earthworm + -OID.]

lu·men (lōō-min, léw-, -men, -mǝn) *n., pl.* **-mens** or **-mina** (-mi-nǝ). **1.** *Anatomy.* The inner open space of a tubular organ, as of a blood

vessel or an intestine. **2.** *Botany.* The space enclosed by the cell walls of a plant cell that has lost its living contents. **3.** *Abbr.* **lm** *Physics.* The SI unit of luminous flux, equal to the luminous flux emitted in a solid angle of one steradian by a uniform point source having an intensity of one candela. [New Latin, from Latin *lūmen,* light, eye, opening.] —**lu·men·al, lu·min·al** *adj.*

Lu·mière (lōōmi-aír; *French* lüm-yaír), **Auguste** (1862–1954). French photographer. Auguste and his brother Louis Jean Lumière (1864–1948) gave the first public showing of a projected cinematic film in Paris (1895).

lu·mi·nance (lōō-mi-nǝnss, léw-) *n.* **1.** The condition or quality of being luminous. **2.** *Physics.* The luminous intensity in a given direction of a small element of surface area divided by the orthogonal projection of this area onto a plane at right angles to the direction. Formerly called "brightness". [Latin *lūmen* (stem *lūmin-*), light + -ANCE.]

lu·mi·nar·y (lōō-mi-nǝri, léw- || -nerri) *n., pl.* **-ies. 1.** An object, as a celestial body, that gives light. **2.** A source of intellectual or spiritual enlightenment. **3.** A notable person in a given field. [Middle English *luminarye,* from Old French *luminarie,* from Late Latin *lūmināre,* lamp, heavenly body, from Latin *lūmen* (stem *lūmin-*), light.] —**lu·mi·nar·i·al** *adj.*

lu·mi·nesce (lōō-mi-néss, léw-) *intr.v.* **-nesced, -nescing, -nesces.** To be or become luminescent. [Back-formation from LUMINESCENT.]

lu·mi·nes·cence (lōō-mi-néss'nss, léw-) *n.* **1.** The emission of light, as in phosphorescence, fluorescence, and bioluminescence, by processes that derive energy from essentially nonthermal sources such as chemical, biochemical, or crystallographic changes, the motion of subatomic particles, or the excitation of an atomic system by radiation; especially, such emission distinguished from incandescence. **2.** The light so emitted.

lu·mi·nes·cent (lōō-mi-néss'nt, léw-) *adj.* Capable of, exhibiting, or suitable for the emission of luminescence. [Latin *lūmen* (stem *lūmin-*), light + -ESCENT.]

lu·mi·nif·er·ous (lōō-mi-níffǝrǝss, léw-) *adj.* Generating, yielding, or transmitting light. [Latin *lūmen* (stem *lūmin-*), light (see **luminous**) + -FEROUS.]

lu·mi·nos·i·ty (lōō-mi-nóssǝti, léw-) *n.* **1.** The condition or quality of being luminous. **2.** Something luminous. **3.** The attribute of an object or colour that enables the observation of the extent to which an object emits light. **4.** *Astronomy.* A measure of the absolute brightness of a star, equal to the total power radiated.

lu·mi·nous (lōō-mi-nǝss, léw-) *adj.* **1.** Emitting light; especially, emitting self-generated light. **2.** Full of light; illuminated. **3.** Designating a photometric physical quantity that is evaluated on the basis of the visual sensation it produces in the observer. Compare **radiant. 4.** Intelligible; clear. —See Synonyms at **bright.** [Middle English, from Old French *lumineux,* from Latin *lūminōsus,* full of light, from *lūmen* (stem *lūmin-*), light.] —**lu·min·ous·ly** *adv.* —**lu·min·ous·ness** *n.*

luminous efficacy *n.* **1.** The ratio of the total luminous flux to the total radiant flux of an emitting source. **2.** The ratio of the luminous flux emitted by a source of radiation to the power it consumes, usually expressed in lumens per watt.

luminous efficiency *n.* The efficiency of polychromatic radiation in producing a visual sensation measured as the ratio of the radiant flux, weighed according to the spectral luminous efficiencies of its constituent wavelengths, to the corresponding radiant flux.

luminous energy *n.* Energy in the form of light, expressed as luminous flux multiplied by its duration and measured in lumen seconds.

luminous exitance *n.* The ability of a surface to emit light, equal to the luminous flux per unit area at a specific position on the surface.

luminous flux *n.* The rate of flow of luminous energy evaluated on the basis of its ability to produce a visual sensation. For monochromatic light it is the radiant flux multiplied by the spectral luminous efficiency and is measured in lumens.

luminous intensity *n.* The amount of light radiated by a point source in a given direction expressed as the luminous flux in that direction per unit of solid angle. It is measured in candelas.

luminous paint *n.* A paint containing a phosphorescent or fluorescent substance that makes it glow in the dark.

lum·me, lum·my (lúmmi) *interj. Informal.* Used to express surprise or mild dismay. [Pronunciation of *(Lord) love me.*]

lump¹ (lump) *n.* **1.** An irregularly shaped mass or piece. **2.** A small cube or cuboid of sugar. Also used adjectivally: *lump sugar.* **3.** *Pathology.* A swelling or small, palpable tumour. **4.** An aggregate; a collection; a totality. **5.** An ungainly, heavy or lazy person. **6.** A piece of coal or coke suitable for use in a stove or fireplace. —**a lump in the throat.** A feeling of constriction in the throat caused by emotion. —**the lump.** *British.* Casual workers in the building trade operating as self-employed, often to avoid paying tax or national insurance contributions.
~*v.* **lumped, lumping, lumps.** —*tr.* **1.** To put together or amass in a single group or pile. **2.** To treat as a single group; fail to differentiate. Often used with *together.* **3.** To make lumpy. —*intr.* **1.** To become lumpy. **2.** To move heavily. [Middle English, perhaps of Low German origin; Low German *lump,* coarse.]

lump² *tr.v.* **lumped, lumping, lumps.** *Informal.* To tolerate (what must be endured): *like it or lump it.* [16th century : origin obscure.]

lump·ec·tomy (lúmp-éktǝmi) *n., pl.* **-mies.** A surgical operation for the removal of a tumour from the breast. [LUMP + -ECTOMY.]

lump·en (lúmpən) *adj.* Ignorant or stupid. Used derogatorily or humorously. [German *Lumpen*, rag, vagabond.]

lum·pen·pro·le·tar·i·at (lúmpən-prōli-taÍr-i-ət, -at) *n.* **1.** According to Marxist analysis, a social grouping consisting of outcasts such as tramps and thieves, considered to be below the proletariat. **2.** The unthinking, ignorant lower classes, uninterested in advancement or social change. Used derogatorily. Compare **underclass**. [German, "ragged proletariat".]

lump·fish (lúmp-fish) *n., pl.* **-fishes** or collectively **lumpfish.** Any of various fishes of the family Cyclopteridae; especially, *Cyclopterus lumpus,* of Atlantic waters, having a body covered with tuberous excrescences, a ventral sucker formed from fused pelvic fins, and an edible roe resembling caviar. Also called "lumpsucker". [Obsolete *lump,* lumpfish, from Middle Dutch *lumpe* + FISH.]

lump·ish (lúmpish) *adj.* **1.** Stupid; dull. **2.** Clumsy; heavy; cumbersome. **—lump·ish·ly** *adv.* **—lump·ish·ness** *n.*

lump sum *n.* A sum of money as an inclusive payment.

lump·y (lúmpi) *adj.* **-ier, -iest. 1.** Covered with lumps. **2.** Full of lumps. **3.** Thickset or cumbersome in appearance. **4.** Characterised by short, choppy waves. Said of a windblown sea.

lumpy jaw *n. Pathology.* **Actinomycosis** *(see).*

Lu·mum·ba (lŏo-mŏombə), **Patrice** (1925–61). First prime minister (1960–61) of the Congo (now Congo Dem. Rep.). He fought to form a united Congo, but was ousted in 1961, and murdered by Katanga secessionists.

lu·na (lŏo-nə, léw-) *n.* In alchemy, silver. [Middle English, from Medieval Latin *lūna,* from Latin, moon (from its colour).]

Lu·na (lŏo-nə, léw-). The Roman goddess of the moon. [Latin.]

lu·na·cy (lŏo-nə-si, léw-) *n., pl.* **-cies. 1.** Insanity. Not in technical usage. **2.** Foolish and irresponsible conduct. **3.** *Archaic.* Mental derangement associated with certain phases of the moon. **—See** Synonyms at **insanity.** [From LUNATIC.]

luna moth *n.* A large, pale green North American moth, *Actias luna,* having a long projection on each hind wing. [Latin *lūna,* moon (from the yellow rings on its wings).]

lu·nar (lŏo-nər, léw-) *adj.* **1.** Of, involving, caused by, or affecting the moon. **2.** Measured by or based on the revolution of the moon: *a lunar month; a lunar calendar.* **3.** Of or pertaining to silver. [Latin *lūnāris,* from *lūna,* moon.]

lunar caustic *n.* Silver nitrate in the form of sticks, formerly used in cauterisation.

lunar excursion module *n. Abbr.* **LEM** A spacecraft designed to transport astronauts from a command module orbiting the Moon to the lunar surface and back. Also called "lunar module".

lunar month *n.* A **month** *(see).*

lunar year *n.* An interval of 12 lunar months.

lu·nate (lŏo-nayt, léw-, -nət, -nit) *adj.* Also **lu·nat·ed** (lŏo-náytid, lew-) Crescent-shaped. [Latin *lūnātus,* from *lūnāre,* to form into a crescent, from *lūna,* moon.]

lunate bone *n.* The second of three bones forming the upper row of bones in the wrist. Also called "semilunar bone".

lu·na·tic (lŏo-nətik, léw-) *adj.* **1.** Suffering from lunacy; insane. Not in technical usage. **2.** Of or for the insane: *a lunatic asylum.* Not in technical usage. **3.** Wildly or absurdly foolish: *a lunatic decision.* [Middle English *lunatik,* from Old French *lunatique,* from Latin *lūnāticus,* "moonstruck", crazy, insane, from *lūna,* moon.] **—lu·na·tic** *n.*

lunatic fringe *n.* The fanatical, extreme, or irrational members of a society or group.

lu·na·tion (lŏo-náysh'n, lew-) *n.* A lunar **month** *(see).* [Middle English *lunacioun,* from Medieval Latin *lūnātiō* (stem *lūnātiōn-*), from Latin *lūna,* moon.]

lunch (lunch) *n.* **1.** A meal eaten at midday. **2.** The food provided for this meal. **—out to lunch** *Slang.* Crazy; mad. **~v. lunched, lunching, lunches.** To take (a prospective client, for example) to lunch, especially to discuss business. **~intr. 1.** To have one's lunch. **2.** To lunch clients or others. [Shortened from LUNCHEON.] **—lunch·er** *n.*

lunch·eon (lúnchən) *n.* **1.** A lunch, especially a formal one. **2.** An early afternoon party at which a light meal is served. [17th century : origin obscure.]

luncheon meat *n.* Meat, often pork, processed and pressed into a small loaf shape and usually tinned.

luncheon voucher *n. Abbr.* **L.V.** A trademark for a voucher, given by an employer to an employee, that can be exchanged for food in certain shops and restaurants.

Lund (lŏond). A market and industrial city north of Malmö, Sweden. It was the largest town in Scandinavia during the Middle Ages, and is now an educational centre with a university.

Lun·dy (lúndi). Island in the Bristol Channel off Hartland Point, Devon, England, preserved by the National Trust as a sanctuary for wild flowers, seals, and birds, particularly puffins.

lune (lŏon, lewn) *n.* A portion of a sphere enclosed between two semicircles having their common end points at opposite poles. [Latin *lūna,* moon.]

Lü·ne·burg (lŏonə-burg; *German* lünə-bŏork). City and river port in Lower Saxony, Germany. It is also a spa. On Lüneburg Heath (Lüneburger Heide) to the south, the Nazi forces in the West surrendered to the Allies in May 1945.

lu·nette (lŏo-nét, lew-) *n.* **1.** *Architecture.* **a.** A small, circular or crescent-shaped opening in a vaulted roof. **b.** A crescent-shaped or semicircular space, usually over a door or window, that may contain another window, a sculpture, or a mural. **2.** *Military.* A type of

fieldwork fortification that has two projecting faces and two parallel flanks. **3.** A flattened, glass covering for a watch. **4.** *Roman Catholic Church.* A flat, round case with a hinged glass lid used for holding the consecrated host in a monstrance. [French, diminutive of *lune,* from Latin *lūna,* moon.]

lung (lung) *n.* **1.** Either of two spongy, saclike respiratory organs in air-breathing vertebrates, occupying the chest cavity together with the heart, and functioning to remove carbon dioxide from the blood and provide it with oxygen. **2.** A comparable invertebrate structure. [Middle English *lunge,* from Old English *lungen.*]

lunge¹ (lunj) *n.* **1.** A sudden thrust or pass, as with a sword or rapier. **2.** Any sudden forward movement or plunge. **~v. lunged, lunging, lunges. —intr. 1.** To make a thrust or pass. **2.** To move with a lunge. **—tr.** To thrust forward suddenly. [Earlier *allonge, elonge,* from French *allonger, alongier,* to lengthen, extend, from Vulgar Latin *allongāre* (unattested) : Latin *ad-* (towards) + *longus,* long.] **—lung·er** *n.*

lunge² *n.* A long rope or leather rein used for schooling or exercising a horse by someone on foot. Also called "lunging rein". **~tr.v. lunged, lunging, lunges.** To school or exercise (a horse) by means of a lunge. [French *longe,* "long (rein)", from Latin *longus,* long.]

lung·fish (lúng-fish) *n., pl.* **-fishes** or collectively **lungfish.** Any of several elongated tropical freshwater fishes of the order Dipnoi (or Dipneusti), having lungs as well as gills, and in certain species constructing a mucus-lined mud covering in which to withstand an extended drought.

lun·gi, lun·gee (lŏong-gee) *n.* **1.** A loincloth, turban, or scarf, as worn by Indian men. **2.** The long piece of fabric used to form this. [Hindi, from Persian *lungī.*]

lung·worm (lúng-wurm) *n.* Any of various parasitic nematode worms that are parasites of the lungs of mammals, such as any of the family Metastrongylidae.

lung·wort (lúng-wurt ‖ -wawrt) *n.* **1.** Any of several plants of the genus *Pulmonaria,* native to Europe, with long-stalked leaves and coiled clusters of blue or purple flowers. **2.** Any of various plants of the genus *Mertensia,* having drooping clusters of tubular, usually blue flowers. [Formerly used to treat lung diseases.]

lu·ni·so·lar (lŏo-ni-sōlər, léw-) *adj.* Of, caused or measured by both the Sun and the Moon. [Latin *lūna,* moon + -I- + SOLAR.]

lu·ni·ti·dal (lŏo-ni-tíd'l, léw-) *adj.* Of or pertaining to tidal phenomena caused by the Moon. [Latin *lūna,* moon + -I- + TIDAL.]

lunitidal interval *n.* The time elapsing between the Moon's transit at a place and the next high tide there.

lu·nu·la (lŏo-new-lə, léw-) *n., pl.* **-lae** (-lee). Also **lu·nule** (-newl). A small crescent-shaped structure or marking; especially, the white crescent-shaped area at the base of a fingernail. [Latin *lūnula,* crescent-shaped ornament, "little moon", from *lūna,* moon.]

lu·nu·lar (lŏo-new-lər, léw-) *adj.* Crescent-shaped.

lu·nu·late (lŏo-new-lət, léw-, -lit, -layt) *adj.* Also **lu·nu·lat·ed** (-laytid). **1.** Small and lunular. **2.** Having lunular markings.

Luo·yang or **Lo·yang** (lwŏ-yáng). Formerly **Ho·nan** (ńnán). Industrial city in Henan province, north central China. It is the market centre of an agricultural and coalmining region. An ancient city, it was a Chinese capital under the Han, Tang, and Song dynasties.

Lu·per·ca·li·a (lŏo-pər-káyli-ə, léw-) *n.* A fertility festival in ancient Rome, celebrated on February 15 in honour of the pastoral god Lupercus. **—Lu·per·ca·li·an** *adj.*

lu·pin, *U.S.* **lu·pine** (lŏo-pin, léw-) *n.* Any of various plants of the genus *Lupinus,* having tall spikes of brightly coloured flowers. [Middle English, from Latin *lupīnum,* from *lupīnus,* LUPINE (wolflike), from the ancient belief that it destroyed the soil.]

lu·pine (lŏo-pīn, léw-) *adj.* **1.** Wolflike. **2.** Rapacious; ravenous. [Latin *lupīnus,* from *lupus,* wolf.]

lu·pu·lin (lŏo-pew-lin, léw-) *n.* Minute yellowish-brown hairs from the female flowers of the hop plant, formerly used as a sedative. [New Latin *lupulus,* hop plant, diminutive of Latin *lupus,* wolf, hop plant + -IN.]

lu·pus (lŏo-pəss, léw-) *n.* Any of several diseases of the skin and mucous membranes, many causing disfiguring lesions, especially: **1.** *Lupus vulgaris,* tuberculosis of the skin characterised by ulcerating, nodular facial lesions, especially around the nose and ears. **2.** *Lupus erythematosus,* a chronic inflammatory disease affecting the skin and internal organs characterised by a scaly red rash on the face. [New Latin, from Latin, wolf.]

Lupus *n.* A constellation in the Southern Hemisphere near Centaurus and Scorpius. [Latin *lupus,* wolf. See **lupine.**]

lurch¹ (lurch) *intr.v.* **lurched, lurching, lurches. 1.** To stagger. **2.** To roll or pitch suddenly or erratically, as a ship during a storm. **~n. 1.** A staggering or tottering movement or gait. **2.** An abrupt rolling or pitching. [From *lee-lurch,* variant of *lee-latch,* drifting to leeward.]

lurch² *n.* **1.** A position of difficulty or discomfort. Now used only in the phrase *to leave (someone) in the lurch.* **2.** In the game of cribbage, the losing position of a player who scores 30 points or less to the winner's 61. [French *lourche,* a game resembling backgammon, also a defeat or bad score in this game, probably from Middle High German *lurz,* left, wrong, "defeat".]

lurch·er (lúrchər) *n.* **1.** *Chiefly British.* A crossbred hunting dog, especially one formerly used by poachers. **2.** *Archaic.* A lurker; a sneak thief. [From obsolete *lurch,* to lurk, Middle English *lorchen,* variant of *lurken,* to LURK.]

lure (lewr, loor) *n.* **1. a.** Anything that entices, tempts, or attracts

with the promise of gaining a pleasure or reward. **b.** An attraction or appeal. **2.** Any decoy used in catching animals; especially, an artificial bait used in catching fish. **3.** A bunch of feathers attached to a long cord, used in falconry to recall the hawk.
~tr.v. **lured, luring, lures. 1.** To attract by wiles or temptation; entice. **2.** To recall (a falcon) with a lure. [Middle English, from Old French *loirre,* bait, from Germanic *lōthr* (unattested).]
Synonyms: *lure, entice, inveigle, decoy, tempt, seduce, beguile.*
Lu·rex (léwr-eks, lóor-) *n.* A trademark for a shiny plastic-coated thread, or for a fabric made from this thread.
lur·gy, lurg·i (lúrgi) *n. Informal.* A disease or illness. Used humorously, often in the phrase *the dreaded lurgy.* [Phrase invented and popularised by the Goons (radio show).]
lu·rid (léwr-id, lóor-) *adj.* **1.** Causing shock or horror. **2.** Vivid; glaring; unnaturally bright. **3.** Glowing or glaring through a haze. **4.** *Rare.* Sallow in colour; pallid. —See Synonyms at **ghastly.** [Latin *lūridus,* pallid, ghastly, from *lūror*†, pale yellow, ghastliness.] **—lu·rid·ly** *adv.* **—lu·rid·ness** *n.*
lurk (lurk) *intr.v.* **lurked, lurking, lurks. 1.** To lie in wait, as in ambush or for some other evil purpose. **2.** To move furtively; sneak; slink. **3.** To exist unobserved or unsuspected. [Middle English *lurken,* probably frequentative of *luren,* LOWER (to frown).]
lurk·ing (lúrking) *adj.* Concealed; hitherto unacknowledged or unsuspected: *a lurking suspicion; lurking sympathy.*
Lu·sa·ka (lōō-saákə). Capital city and industrial centre of Zambia, central Africa. It replaced Livingstone as the capital of the then British colony of Northern Rhodesia in 1935.
Lu·sa·tia (loo-sáyshə, lew-). *German* **Lau·sitz** (lów-zits). Home of the Sorbs, an ancient Slav people. The area successively part of Brandenburg, Bohemia, Saxony, and Prussia, is now confined between the rivers Elbe and Oder in eastern Germany.
Lu·sa·tian (lōō-sáysh'n, -sáysh-yən || lew-) *n.* **1.** A native of Lusatia. **2.** A language, **Wendish** *(see).* **—Lu·sa·tian** *adj.*
lus·cious (lúshəss) *adj.* **1.** Sweet and pleasant to taste or smell; delicious: *a luscious melon.* **2.** Having strong sensual appeal; voluptuous. **3.** *Archaic.* Excessively rich or sweet; cloying. [Perhaps from Middle English *lucius, licius,* possibly shortened from DELICIOUS.]
lush[1] (lush) *adj.* **lusher, lushest. 1.** Having or characterised by luxuriant growth or vegetation. **2.** Luxurious; opulent: *lush carpets.* **3.** Succulent; juicy. [Middle English *lusch,* lax, soft, perhaps variant of *lasche,* soft, watery, from Old French, lax, slack, from Latin *laxus,* spacious, loose.]
lush[2] *n. Chiefly U.S. Slang.* **1.** A drunkard. **2.** Intoxicating drink. [18th century : perhaps humorous use of LUSH, opulent, delicious.]
Lushün. See **Lüda.**
Lusitania. See **Portugal.**
lust (lust) *n.* **1.** Sexual desire, especially excessive or unrestrained. **2.** Any overwhelming desire or craving: *a lust for power.*
~intr.v. **lusted, lusting, lusts.** To have or feel lust. Usually used with *after* or *for.* [Middle English *lust,* Old English *lust.*]
lust·ful (lúst-f'l) *adj.* **1.** Excited by lust. **2.** *Archaic.* Vigorous.
lus·tral (lústrəl) *adj.* **1.** Of, pertaining to, or used in a rite of purification. **2.** Pertaining to a lustrum. [Latin *lustrālis,* from LUSTRUM.]
lus·trate (luss-tráyt || *U.S.* lúss-trayt) *tr.v.* **-trated, -trating, -trates.** To purify ceremonially. [Latin *lustrāre,* to purify, from LUSTRUM.] **—lus·tra·tion** (luss-tráysh'n) *n.* **—lus·tra·tive** (lústrə-tiv) *adj.*
lus·tre, *U.S.* **lus·ter** (lústər) *n.* **1.** Soft reflected light; sheen; gloss. **2.** Brilliance or radiance of light; brightness. **3. a.** Brilliant or radiant quality. **b.** Glory; distinction. **4.** A glass pendant, especially on a chandelier. **5.** A decorative object, such as a chandelier having glass pendants. **6.** Any of various substances, such as wax, used to give an object a gloss or polish. **7.** An opalescent, shiny glaze on pottery and porcelain. Also used adjectivally: *lustre ware.* **8.** *Mineralogy.* The appearance of a mineral surface judged by its brilliance and ability to reflect light in comparison with metals, glasses, diamonds, and other materials regarded as standards.
~v. **lustred** or *U.S.* **-tered, -tring** or *U.S.* **-tering, -tres** or *U.S.* **-ters.** *—tr.* To give a gloss or sheen to. *—intr.* To become or be lustrous. [French *lustre,* from Italian *lustro,* from *lustrare,* to brighten, from Latin *lūstrāre,* to purify, make bright, from *lūstrum,* purification.]
lus·trous (lústrəss) *adj.* **1.** Having a sheen. **2.** Radiant; bright: *a lustrous gaze.* —See Synonyms at **bright. —lus·trous·ly** *adv.* **—lus·trous·ness** *n.*
lus·trum (lústrəm) *n., pl.* **-trums** or **-tra. 1.** A ceremonial purification of the entire ancient Roman population after the census every five years. **2.** A period of five years. [Latin *lustrum.*]
lust·y (lústi) *adj.* **-ier, -iest. 1.** Full of vigour; robust. **2.** Powerful; strong: *a lusty drink.* **3.** Lustful. **4.** *Archaic.* Merry; joyous. **—lust·i·ly** *adv.* **—lust·i·ness** *n.*
lu·sus na·tu·rae (lōō-səss nə-téwr-ee, léw-, na-, -ī) *n.* A freak of nature. [Latin *lūsus nātūrae,* "a joke of nature".]
Luta. See **Lüda.**
lu·ta·nist, lu·te·nist (lōō-tən-ist, léw-, -t'n-) *n.* A lute player. [Medieval Latin *lūtānista,* from *lūtāna,* from Old French *lut,* LUTE.]
lute[1] (lōōt, lewt) *n.* A musical stringed instrument having a body shaped like a pear halved lengthways and usually a bent neck with a fretted fingerboard with pegs for tuning it. [Middle English, from Old French *lut,* earlier *leut,* from Arabic *al-'ud,* "the wood".]
lute[2] *n.* A substance, such as dried clay or cement, used to pack and seal joints and other connections or seal a porous surface.
~tr.v. **luted, luting, lutes. 1.** To apply lute to. **2.** To seal with lute. [Middle English, from Old French *lut,* from Latin *lutum,* mud, clay.]
lute-, luteo- *comb. form.* Indicates corpus luteum; for example, **luteal.** [New Latin (corpus) *luteum,* from Latin, neuter of *luteus,* yellow.]
lu·te·al (lōō-ti-əl, léw-) *adj.* Of or pertaining to the **corpus luteum** *(see)* or to the phase of the oestrous cycle during which it develops.
lu·te·in (lōō-ti-in, léw-, -teen) *n.* **1.** A yellow pigment isolated from the corpus luteum and found in body fats and egg yolk. **2.** A photosynthetic pigment found in green leaves and certain algae. [LUTE- + -IN.]
lu·te·in·is·ing hormone (lōō-ti-in-īzing, léw-, -teen-) *n. Abbr.* **LH** A hormone, secreted by the anterior lobe of the pituitary gland, that stimulates ovulation and corpus luteum formation in female mammals and androgen synthesis by the interstitial cells of the testis in male mammals. Also called "interstitial-cell-stimulating hormone".
lu·te·o·tro·phic hormone (lōō-ti-ə-tróffik, léw-, -ō-, -trōfik) *n.* **Prolactin** *(see).* [LUTEO- + -TROPHIC.]
lu·te·ous (lōō-ti-əss, léw-) *adj.* Of a light or moderate greenish yellow. [Latin *lūteus,* yellow, from *lūtum*†, yellow weed.]
lu·te·ti·um, lu·te·ci·um (lōō-tée-shi-əm, lew-, -shəm) *n. Symbol* **Lu** A silvery-white rare-earth element that is exceptionally difficult to separate from the other rare-earth elements, used in nuclear technology. Atomic number 71, atomic weight 174.97, melting point 1 652°C, boiling point 3 327°C, relative density 9.872, valency 3. [New Latin, from *Lūtēia,* Latin name for Paris, native city of its discoverer, Georges Urbain (1872–1938), French chemist.]
Lu·ther (lōō-thər, léw-; *German* lóotər), **Martin** (1483–1546). German leader of the Reformation. Luther, an Augustinian monk, visited Rome in 1510–11 and was shocked by the wealth and corruption of the papacy. In 1517 he nailed to the chapel door at Wittenberg castle 95 theses attacking the sale of papal indulgences. In 1520, Luther launched the Protestant Reformation, publicly burning a papal bull of condemnation against him, and was excommunicated in 1521. He refused to recant at the Diet of Worms (1521), and was sheltered by the Elector of Saxony. He translated the New Testament into German and married in 1525, breaking the rule of celibacy. Luther confirmed the Augsburg Confession (1530), which effectively established the Lutheran churches.
Lu·ther·an (lōō-thərən, léw-) *adj.* **1.** Of or pertaining to Martin Luther or his religious teachings and especially to the doctrine of justification by faith alone. **2.** Of, pertaining to, or designating the branch of the Protestant Church adhering to the views of Martin Luther.
~n. A member of the Lutheran Church. **—Lu·ther·an·ism** *n.*
Lutheran Church *n.* The Protestant denomination founded in Germany in the 16th century by Martin Luther.
Lu·thu·li (lōō-tōōli), **Albert (John Mvumbi)** (*c.* 1898–1967). Black South African political leader. As president of the African National Congress, he came into conflict with the government of white-ruled South Africa. He advocated universal suffrage, but rejected the use of violence as a means of attaining it. He was awarded the Nobel Peace prize in 1960.
Lu·tine bell (lōō-téen) *n.* A bell kept at Lloyd's and rung to announce news of a missing ship insured at Lloyd's, once for bad news and twice for good. [Bell salvaged from the *Lutine,* ship wrecked in 1799.]
Lu·ton (lōōt'n). Manufacturing town in central England, which expanded rapidly in the 19th century with the straw hat industry. It now manufactures vehicles and aircraft components.
Lut·yens (lúchənz, lút-yənz), **Sir Edwin (Landseer)** (1869–1944). British architect. He combined traditional and modern influences in his work, which includes the Whitehall Cenotaph. He was chief architect of New Delhi (1912–30).
Lutyens, (Agnes) Elizabeth (1906–83). British composer, daughter of Sir Edwin. She wrote many chamber and orchestral works, often using a 12-tone technique, as well as music for films.
lutz (lōōts) *n., pl.* **lutzes.** A jump by an ice-skater, performed by taking off from the back off one blade, making a complete spin in the air, and landing on the rear of the other blade. [Probably after Gustave *Lussi* (born 1898), Swiss figure skater.]
luv·vie, luv·vy (lúvvi) *n. British Informal.* **1. Lovey** *(see).* **2.** A bohemian whose displays of affection and social concern are more showy than sincere. [Sense 2 from the supposedly widespread use of *lovey* as a form of address by such people.]
lux (luks) *n., pl.* **lux.** *Abbr.* **lx** The SI unit of illumination, equal to one lumen per square metre. [Latin *lūx,* light.]
lux·ate (luk-sáyt, lúksayt) *tr.v.* **-ated, -ating, -ates.** To put out of joint; dislocate. [Latin *luxāre,* from *luxus,* dislocated.] **—lux·a·tion** (luk-sáysh'n) *n.*
luxe *n.* See **de luxe.**
Lux·em·bourg (Ville) (lúksəm-burg; *French* lüksoN-bóor (veel). *German* **Lux·em·burg** (lóoks'm-boork). Capital of the Grand Duchy of Luxembourg, on the river Alzette. The city has several offices of the European Economic Community, the European Court of Justice, and the European Parliament, and a commercial radio station transmitting in six languages.
Luxembourg, Grand Duchy of. *French* **Grand-Duché de Luxembourg.** Small independent state in northwest Europe. The north is part of the Ardennes, the south being a continuation of Lorraine. From 1443 to 1839 it was ruled in turn by Burgundians, Spaniards, Austrians, French, and Dutch. Its neutrality was guaranteed in 1867. Luxembourg joined with Belgium and the Netherlands in the Benelux Customs Union in 1948. Area, 2 586 square kilometres (998 square miles). Population, 420,000. Capital, Luxembourg (Ville). See map at **Belgium.**

Lux·em·burg (lúksəm-burg; *German* lŏoks'm-boork), **Rosa** (*c.* 1870–1919). German socialist leader, born in Poland. She took part in the revolution of 1905 while in Russian Poland. With Karl Liebknecht she led the antiwar Spartacus party (1916), which became the German Communist Party after the war. She was arrested and killed by soldiers during the Spartacist revolt in Berlin.

Lux·or (lúk-sawr ‖ lŏok-). *Arabic* **Al Uqsor**. Town on the east bank of the river Nile in central Egypt. It covers part of the site of the ancient city of Thebes, with the great Temple of Luxor.

lux·u·ri·ant (lug-zéwr-i-ənt, ləg-, -zhŏor-) *adj.* **1.** Growing abundantly, vigorously, or lushly. **2.** Exuberantly elaborate; ornate; florid. **3.** Abundantly fertile or productive. [Latin *luxuriāns (stem luxuriant-),* present participle of *luxuriāre,* to grow profusely, LUXURIATE.] —**lux·u·ri·ance** *n.* —**lux·u·ri·ant·ly** *adv.*

Usage: There is a slight tendency in modern English to use *luxuriant* where one would expect *luxurious (a luxuriant meal),* but this should be avoided. *Luxury* is being increasingly used as an adjective in place of *luxurious (luxury hotel, luxury goods)* to refer to something of exceptional quality or comfort.

lux·u·ri·ate (lug-zéwr-i-ayt, ləg-, -zhŏor-) *intr.v.* **-ated, -ating, -ates.** **1.** To take luxurious pleasure; indulge oneself. Used with *in.* **2.** To proliferate. **3.** To grow profusely. [Latin *luxuriāre,* to grow profusely, from *luxuria,* excess, LUXURY.]

lux·u·ri·ous (lug-zéwr-i-əss, ləg-, -zhŏor-). **1.** Sensuously comfortable: *a luxurious hot bath.* **2.** Characterised by or contributing to luxury. **3.** Fond of or given to luxury. —See Synonyms at **sensuous.** —**lux·u·ri·ous·ly** *adv.* —**lux·u·ri·ous·ness** *n.*

lux·u·ry (lúksħəri ‖ lúgzhəri) *n., pl.* **-ries.** **1.** Rich or sumptuous comfort. **2.** An item or activity that is expensive, pleasurable, and unnecessary: *I can't afford luxuries.* **3.** Anything conducive to physical comfort. **4.** The enjoyment of sumptuous living.
~ *adj.* **1.** Providing sumptuous comfort: *a luxury hotel.* **2.** Of high quality, and usually expensive: *luxury goods.* See Usage note at **luxuriant.** [Middle English *luxurie,* from Old French, from Latin *luxuria,* excess, rankness, from *luxus,* excess, extravagance.]

Luzern. See **Lucerne.**

Lu·zon (lŏo-zón). Main island of the Philippines. It has fertile volcanic soils and many fine natural harbours, including Manila Bay, on which the country's capital, Manila, is situated.

L.V. luncheon voucher.

L'viv (lviv), **Russian Lvov** (lə-vóv; *Russian* lvawf). *Polish* **Lwów** (lvŏof); *German* **Lem·berg** (lém-bairk). Capital of the L'viv Region of Ukraine. It is a centre of communications, learning, trade, and industry. The city was founded by Ukrainians in the 13th century and captured by the Poles a century later. From 1772 it was the capital of Galicia, an Austrian province. The Poles regained the city in 1919, but formally ceded it to the U.S.S.R. in 1945. When the U.S.S.R. broke up, L'viv became Ukrainian again.

Lvov, Georgi Yevgenyevich, Prince (1861–1925). Russian prime minister (1917). He headed the first provisional government after the February Revolution of 1917.

lwei (lway) *n.* A unit of currency equal to ¹⁄₁₀₀ of the kwanza of Angola.

–ly¹ *adj. suffix.* Indicates: **1.** Having the characteristics of or resembling; for example, **sisterly.** **2.** Appearing or occurring at specified intervals; for example, **weekly, monthly.** [Middle English *-li, -lich,* Old English *-lic,* "having the form of".]

–ly² *adv. suffix.* Indicates: **1.** In a specified manner or degree; for example, **gradually, partly.** **2.** From a specified point of view; for example, **politically.** **3.** At every specified interval; for example, **hourly, daily.** **4.** The event or statement in question is viewed as specified; for example, **regrettably, ironically.** **5.** Speaking in a specified way; for example, **frankly, honestly.** [Middle English *-li, -liche,* Old English *-lice,* from *-lic,* LY (adjectival suffix).]

ly·ase (lí-ayz, -ayss) *n.* Any of a group of enzymes that catalyse the formation of double bonds or the addition of groups to double bonds. [LYO- + -ASE.]

ly·can·thrope (líkən-thrōp, lī-kán-) *n.* **1.** A werewolf. **2.** A person suffering from the delusion that he is a wolf. [New Latin *lycanthropus,* from Greek *lukanthrōpos,* werewolf : *lukos,* wolf + *anthrōpos,* man.]

ly·can·thro·py (lī-kánthrəpi) *n.* **1.** The mythical, supernatural ability to assume the form and characteristics of a wolf. **2.** A psychological illness in which someone believes himself to be a wolf.

ly·cée (lée-say) *n. pl.* **lycées.** A state secondary school in France or a French-speaking country; or one run on similar lines elsewhere. [French, "lyceum".]

ly·ce·um (lī-sée-əm) *n.* A large public building or hall. Now used chiefly in place names. [Latin *Lyceum,* garden near temple of Apollo where Aristotle taught, from Greek *Lukeion,* neuter of *Lukeios* (epithet of Apollo).]

ly·chee, li·chee, li·chi, li·tchi (lí-chée, -chée ‖ lée-, lichi) *n.* **1.** A Chinese tree, *Nephelium chinensis,* bearing edible fruit. **2.** The small, round fruit of this tree, consisting of a thin, brown, scaly shell enclosing a white fleshy interior with a seed at the centre. [Cantonese *lai ji.*]

lych gate. Variant of **lich gate.**

lych·nis (lik-niss) *n.* Any of various plants of the genus *Lychnis,* which includes the campions and ragged robin. [New Latin *Lychnis,* from Latin, a kind of rose of fiery colour, from Greek *lukhnis,* from *lukhnos,* lamp.]

Lyc·i·a (líssi-ə, líshi-ə ‖ líshə). Ancient country and later a Roman province on the southwestern coast of Asia Minor.

Lyc·i·an (líssi-ən, líshi-ən ‖ líshən) *n.* **1.** An inhabitant of ancient Lycia in Asia Minor. **2.** The Anatolian language of the Lycians. —**Lyc·i·an** *adj.*

ly·co·pod (lík-ə-pod, -ō-) *n.* Any pteridophyte plant of the order Lycopodiales; especially, any of the genus *Lycopodium.*

ly·co·po·di·um (līkə-pŏdi-əm) *n.* **1.** Any plant of the genus *Lycopodium;* a **club moss** *(see).* **2.** The yellowish powdery spores of certain club mosses, especially *Lycopodium clavatum,* used in fireworks and explosives, and as a covering for pills. [New Latin *Lycopodium,* "wolf foot" (from its claw-shaped roots) : Greek *lukos,* wolf + *pous* (stem *pod-),* foot.]

Lydda. See **Lod.**

lyd·dite (líddīt) *n.* An explosive consisting chiefly of picric acid. [From *Lydd,* town in Kent where it was first tested.]

Lyd·i·a (líddi-ə, lid-yə). Ancient country which in 546 B.C. covered all Asia Minor west of the river Halys, excluding Lycia. The Lydians probably coined the first money.

Lyd·i·an (líddi-ən, líd-yən) *n.* **1.** A member of a people of ancient Lydia. **2.** The Anatolian language of this people. —**Lyd·i·an** *adj.*

Lydian mode *n. Music.* A church mode with F as final and C as dominant. [After an ancient Greek mode associated with Lydia.]

lye (lī) *n.* **1.** The alkaline liquid containing potassium hydroxide obtained by leaching wood ashes. **2. Potassium hydroxide** *(see).* **3. Sodium hydroxide** *(see).* [Middle English *lye, ley(e),* Old English *lēag.*]

Ly·ell (lí-əl), **Sir Charles** (1797–1875). British geologist. He established the theory of uniformitarianism. His *Principles of Geology* (1830–33) made him the most influential 19th-century geologist.

ly·ing (lí-ing) *adj.* Untruthful; false; mendacious. See Synonyms at **dishonest.**

ly·ing-in (lí-ing-in) *n., pl.* **lyings-in** or **lying-ins.** The confinement of a woman during childbirth.

Lyle (lil), **Alexander Walter Barr,** known as Sandy (1958–). British golfer. He won the British Open tournament in 1985, and in 1988 became the first ever British winner of the U.S. Masters tournament.

Lyme disease (lim) *n.* An inflammatory disease involving more than one of the body's systems, transmitted by ticks and caused by a spirochaete *(Borrelia burgdorferi).* [After the village of *Lyme* in Connecticut, U.S.A., where the disease was first noticed.]

lyme grass *n.* A perennial grass, *Elymus arenarius,* with bluish-green leaves, that grows on sand dunes in north temperate regions. [Perhaps from LIME (respelling influenced by genus name, *Elymus*), alluding to its binding effect (as lime in mortar).]

lymph (limf) *n.* **1.** A clear, transparent, watery, sometimes faintly yellowish liquid, derived from body tissues, that contains mainly white blood cells and travels through the lymphatic system to return to the venous blood stream through the thoracic duct. It acts to remove bacteria and certain proteins from the tissues, to transport fat from the intestines, and to supply lymphocytes to the blood. **2.** *Archaic.* A spring or stream of pure, clear water. [Latin *lympha,* earlier *lumpa, limpa,* water.]

lym·phad·e·ni·tis (límf-addi-nī-tiss, lim-fáddi-) *n.* Inflammation of the lymph nodes. [New Latin : *lympha,* LYMPH + Greek *adēn,* gland + -ITIS.]

lym·phan·gi·tis (limfan-jī-tiss) *n.* Inflammation of the lymphatic vessels, most commonly occurring during a streptococcal infection. [LYMPH + ANGIO- + -ITIS.]

lym·phat·ic (lim-fáttik) *adj.* **1.** Of or pertaining to lymph, a lymph vessel, or a lymph node. **2.** Sluggish; indifferent; phleḡnatic.
~ *n.* A vessel that conveys lymph. [New Latin *lympnaticus,* from *lympha,* LYMPH.]

lymphatic system *n.* The interconnected system of spaces and vessels between tissues and organs by which lymph is circulated throughout the body and returned to the venous system.

lym·pha·ti·tis (límfə-tîtiss) *n.* Inflammation of lymph nodes or vessels. [LYMPHAT(IC) + -ITIS.]

lymph node *n.* Any of numerous oval or round bodies, located along the lymphatic vessels, that supply lymphocytes to the circulatory system and remove bacteria and foreign particles from the lymph. Also called "lymph gland".

lympho–, lymph– *comb. form.* Indicates lymph or lymphatic system; for example, **lymphocyte, lymphoma.** [From LYMPH.]

lym·pho·blast (límf-ō-blaast, -ə-, -blast) *n.* An abnormal cell found in the blood in a type of leukaemia. [LYMPHO- + -BLAST.] —**lym·pho·blas·tic** (-blástik) *adj.*

lym·pho·cyte (límf-ō-sīt, -ə-) *n.* A white blood cell formed in lymphoid tissue, as in the lymph nodes, spleen, thymus, and tonsils, and constituting between 22 to 28 per cent of all leucocytes in the normal adult human's blood. Also called "lymph cell". [LYMPHO- + -CYTE.] —**lym·pho·cyt·ic** (-sittik) *adj.*

lym·pho·cy·to·sis (límf-ō-sī-tō-siss, -ə-) *n. Pathology.* A form of leucocytosis in which lymphocytes are greatly increased in number. —**lym·pho·cy·tot·ic** (-tóttik) *adj.*

lym·phoid (límfoyd) *adj.* Of or pertaining to lymph or the lymphatic system. [LYMPH(O)- + -OID.]

lymphoid tissue *n.* Tissue responsible for the production of lymphocytes, which includes the lymph nodes, tonsils, thymus, and spleen.

lym·pho·ma (lim-fṓmə) *n., pl.* **-mata** (-tə) or **-mas.** Any of various malignant tumours of lymph nodes or lymphoid tissue. —**lym·pho·ma·toid, lym·phom·a·tous** (-fṓmətoss, -fṓmmətəss) *adj.*

lyn·ce·an (lin-sée-ən) *adj.* **1.** Of or resembling a lynx. **2.** *Rare.* Sharp-sighted. [Latin *lyncēus,* from Greek *Lunkeios,* pertaining to

Lynceus (an Argonaut noted for his keenness of sight), from *Lunkeos,* Lynceus.]

lynch (linch) *tr.v.* **lynched, lynching, lynches.** To kill (a person suspected of a crime), especially by hanging, without due process of law. [Probably after William *Lynch,* Virginia planter and justice of the peace.]

Lynch (linch), **Jack,** born John Lynch (1917–). Prime minister of the Republic of Ireland (1966–73, 1977–79). He was a Fianna Fáil M.P. from 1948, and tried to moderate his party's demands for a united Ireland. Retired from politics 1981.

lynch·et (línchit) *n.* A man-made terrace on a hillside resulting from culturation, probably in the Iron Age. [From dialect *linch,* from Old English *hlinc,* ridge.]

lynch law *n.* The punishment of persons suspected of crime without due process of law.

lynch mob *n.* A group or crowd of people wishing to kill or succeeding in killing a person they suspect of a crime.

lynchpin. Variant of **linchpin.**

lynx (lingks) *n.* Any of several wild cats of the genus *Lynx;* especially, *L. lynx* (or *canadensis*), of Eurasia and northern North America, having thick, soft fur, a short tail, and tufted ears. [Latin, from Greek *lunx.*]

Lynx *n.* A constellation in the Northern Hemisphere near Ursa Major and Auriga.

lynx-eyed (língks-īd) *adj.* Keen of vision; sharp-sighted.

lyo– *comb. form.* Indicates dispersion or dissolution; for example, **lyophilic.** [Green *luein,* to loosen, dissolve.]

Lyon (lée-ON; *French* lyón). *English* **Ly·ons** (lí–ənz). Administrative centre of the Rhône *département* in east central France, and the country's second metropolis after Paris. A communications, cultural, and financial centre, the city grew after Italians introduced silk manufacturing in the 15th century. It now specialises in artificial fibres, and also makes cars, clothing, chemicals, and machinery.

ly·on·naise (lée-ə-náyz, lí–, *French* -néz) *adj.* Cooked, usually fried, with onions: *potatoes lyonnaise.* [French *à la Lyonnaise,* in the manner of LYON.]

ly·o·phil·ic (lí-ō-fíllik, -ə-) *adj. Chemistry.* Of, pertaining to, or exhibiting a strong affinity between the dispersed phase and the dispersing medium of a colloid. [LYO- + -PHILIC.]

ly·o·pho·bic (lí-ō-fṓbik, -ə-) *adj. Chemistry.* Of, pertaining to, or exhibiting a lack of strong affinity between the dispersed phase and the dispersing medium of a colloid. [LYO- + PHOBIC.]

Ly·ra (lír-ə) *n.* A constellation in the Northern Hemisphere near Cygnus and Hercules containing the star Vega. [Latin *lyra,* LYRE.]

ly·rate (lír-ət, -it, -ayt) *adj.* **1.** Having a form or curvature suggestive of a lyre. **2.** Designating leaves having a large terminal lobe and smaller lateral lobes. [New Latin *lyratus,* from Latin *lyra,* LYRE.]

lyre (līr) *n.* A stringed instrument of the harp family used to accompany a singer or reader of poetry, especially in ancient Greece. [Middle English *lire,* Old French, from Latin *lyra,* from Greek *lura†.*]

lyre·bird (lír-burd) *n.* Either of two Australian birds, *Menura superba* (or *M. novaehollandae*) or *M. alberti,* the male of which has a long tail spread during courtship in a lyre-shaped display.

lyr·ic (lírrik) *adj.* **1. a.** Of or pertaining to a category of poetry or verse that is distinguished from the narrative and dramatic, is typically lucid and simple or direct, with smooth, regular rhythms, and is often considered representational of music in its sound patterns. **b.** Writing this type of verse. **2. a.** Of or pertaining to the lyre or harp. **b.** Appropriate for accompaniment by the lyre. **3.** *Music.* **a.** Having a singing voice of a light, rather than dramatic quality. **b.** Pertaining to or designating opera or musical drama, especially of the lighter kind.

~*n.* **1.** A lyric poem. **2.** *Often plural.* The words of a song, especially a popular song. [Old French *lyrique,* of a lyre, from Latin *lyricus,* from Greek *lurikos,* from *lura,* LYRE.]

lyr·i·cal (lírrik'l) *adj.* **1.** Highly enthusiastic or emotional; exuberant. **2.** Romantic and poetic. **3.** Lyric.

lyr·i·cism (lírri-siz'm) *n.* **1.** The character or quality of subjectivism and sensuality of expression, especially in the arts. **2.** An intense outpouring of exuberant emotion.

lyr·i·cist (lírri-sist) *n.* A writer of lyrics for a popular song or musical.

lyr·ism (lírriz'm) *n.* Lyricism. [French *lyrisme,* from Greek *lurismos,* played on the lyre, from *lura,* LYRE.]

lyr·ist (lírrist *for sense 1;* lír-ist *for sense 2*) *n.* **1.** *Rare.* A lyricist. **2.** One who plays a lyre. [Latin *lyristēs,* one who plays a lyre, from Greek *luristēs,* from *lura,* LYRE.]

lyse (līz, līss) *v.* **lysed, lysing, lyses.** —*tr.* To cause (something) to undergo lysis. —*intr.* To undergo lysis. [From LYSIS.]

–lyse, *U.S.* **–lyze** *v. comb. form.* Indicates the causing of chemical decomposition; for example, **pyrolyse.** [From -LYSIS.]

Ly·sen·ko (li-sáng-kō; *Russian* -kə), **Trofim Denisovich** (1898–1976). Soviet biologist. Stalin backed his belief that acquired characteristics could be inherited. This seriously hampered Soviet research into chromosomes and the mechanics of inheritance. —**Ly·sen·ko·ism** *n.*

ly·ser·gic acid (lī-sérjik, li-) *n.* A crystalline alkaloid, $C_{16}H_{16}N_2O_2$, derived from ergot and used in medical research. [From LYS(O)- + ERG(OT) + -IC.]

lysergic acid di·eth·yl·am·ide (dī-ethil-ámmīd) *n.* See **LSD.**

ly·sin (lí-sin) *n.* A specific antibody that acts to destroy blood cells, tissues, or microorganisms. [LYS(O)- + -IN.]

ly·sine (lí-seen, -sin) *n.* An essential, crystalline amino acid, $C_6H_{14}N_2O_2$, used in nutrition studies, in culture media, and to fortify foods and feeds. [LYS(O)- + -INE.]

ly·sis (lí-siss) *n.* **1.** *Biochemistry.* The dissolution or destruction of red blood cells, bacteria, or other antigens by a specific lysin. **2.** *Medicine.* The gradual subsiding of the symptoms of an acute disease. [New Latin, from Greek *lusis,* a loosing, deliverance, from *luein,* to loosen, unbind.]

–lysis *n. comb. form.* Indicates dissolving or decomposition; for example, **hydrolysis.** [New Latin, from Greek *lusis.* See **lysis.**]

lyso–, lys– *comb. form.* Indicates loosening, dissolving, or freeing; for example, **lysin, lysogenesis.** [Greek *lusis,* a loosening. See **lysis.**]

ly·so·gen·e·sis (lí-sō-jénnə-siss) *n.* The production of lysins. [New Latin : LYSO- + -GENESIS.]

Ly·sol (lí-sol ‖ -sōl) *n.* A trademark for a liquid antiseptic and disinfectant. [LYS(O)- + -OL (phenol).]

ly·so·some (lí-sō-sōm, -sə-) *n.* Any of a number of particles in the cytoplasm of cells that contain enzymes capable of breaking down substances in the cell. [LYSO- + -SOME (body).]

ly·so·zyme (lí-sō-zīm, -sə-) *n.* An enzyme occurring naturally in tears, capable of destroying the cell walls of certain bacteria, thereby acting as a mild antiseptic. [LYSO- + -ZYME.]

–lyte *n. comb. form.* Indicates a substance that can be decomposed by a specified process; for example, **electrolyte.** [Greek *lutos,* soluble, from *luein,* to loosen.]

lyt·ic (líttik) *adj.* **1.** Of, pertaining to, or causing lysis. **2.** Of or pertaining to a lysin. [Greek *lutikos,* able to loosen, laxative, from *lutos,* capable of being untied, from *luein,* to untie, loosen. See **lysis.**]

–lytic *adj. comb. form.* Indicates a loosening or dissolving; for example, **hydrolytic.** [Greek *lutikos,* able to loose. See **lytic.**]

lyt·ta (líttə) *n., pl.* **lyttae** (littee). A thin cartilaginous strip on the underside of the tongue of certain carnivorous mammals, such as dogs. [Latin, "worm under a dog's tongue" (believed to cause madness), from Greek *lutta, lussa,* madness, frenzy.]

Lyt·tel·ton (lítt'l-tən), **Humphrey** (1921–). British jazz trumpeter and broadcaster. His *Bad Penny Blues* (1955) was the first jazz record to get into the Top Twenty in Britain.

Lyt·ton (lítt'n), **Edward George Earle Bulwer-Lytton, 1st Baron.** British novelist. He wrote *Pelham* (1828) and *The Last Days of Pompeii* (1834), a historical romance. He sat as a Liberal, then a Tory, M.P., and was Secretary for the colonies (1858–59).

Lytton (Edward) Robert Bulwer-Lytton, 1st Earl of Lytton, also known as Owen Meredith. (1831–91). British colonial administrator and poet, the son of the novelist, Bulwer-Lytton. He was viceroy of India (1876–80) and instigated the second Afghan War (1878–80) in which the British occupied Kabul. He was ambassador to France (1887–91).

Lyublin. See **Lublin.**

M

m, M (em) *n., pl.* **m's** or *rare* **ms, Ms** or **M's**. **1.** The 13th letter of the modern English alphabet. **2.** Any of the speech sounds represented by the letter **M**.

m, M, m., M. *Note:* As an abbreviation or symbol, *m* may be a small or a capital letter, with or without a full stop. Established forms or those generally preferred precede the definition. When no form is given, all four forms are in general use in that sense. **1. m, M** *Printing.* **a.** em. **b.** pica em. **2. M** *Physics.* Mach number. **3. M.** majesty (in titles). **4.** male; masculine. **5. M.** mark (currency). **6. m, M** *Physics.* mass. **7. M.** master (in titles). **8. M.** medieval. **9.** medium. **10. M** mega-. **11. M.** member (in titles). **12. m., M.** meridian. **13. M** *Chemistry.* metal. **14. m** metre (measure). **15. M** *Logic.* middle term of a syllogism. **16. m.** mile. **17. m** milli-. **18. m, M.** million. **19. M** minim (liquid measure). **20. m, M** *Physics.* modulus. **21. M** *Chemistry.* molar. **22. M** *Physics.* moment. **23. M.** Monday. **24. M.** *French.* Monsieur. **25.** month. **26. M** motorway. **27. M** *Physics.* mutual inductance. **28. m., M.** noon [Latin *meridies.*] **29. M** Roman numeral for 1,000 [Latin *mille.*] **30.** The 13th in a series; 12th when *J* is omitted.

M1 *n. Economics.* See **money supply.**

M2 *n. Economics.* See **money supply.**

M3 *n. Economics.* See **money supply.**

ma (maa ‖ *U.S. also* maw) *n. Informal.* Mother. [Shortened form of MAMMA.]

mA milliampere.

M.A. **1.** Master of Arts [Latin *Magister Artium.*] **2.** mental age.

Ma'am (mam, maam, məm). Contraction of *Madam.*

maar (mar) *n.* A flat-bottomed, roughly circular volcanic crater of explosive origin, often filled with water. [Dialectal North German *maar,* from Middle Low German *mare,* lake.]

Maas. See **Meuse.**

Maas·tricht or **Maes·tricht** (maʹa-strikht, *Dutch* maa-strıʹkht). Industrial city in southeast Netherlands, capital of Limburg province. Its cathedral of St. Servatius, founded in the sixth century, is the country's oldest church. The Treaty of European Union was signed here in 1992.

Mab·i·nog·ion (mábbi-nóggi-on) *n.* A collection of medieval Welsh folk tales translated by Lady Charlotte Guest in 1838–49. [Welsh, plural of *mabinogi,* "tales of youth", from *mab,* youth, son, from Old Welsh *map,* from Common Celtic *makwos* (unattested), son.]

mac, mack (mak) *n. Chiefly British Informal.* A mackintosh.

Mac (mak) *n. U.S. Slang.* Used as a familiar term of address. [Abstracted from (especially Scottish) surnames (*Macdonald, Macleod,* and so on).]

Mac-, M'-, Mc- *prefix.* Indicates son of. Used in surnames [Gaelic *Mac-,* from Celtic *makkos* (unattested), son.]

Mac. Maccabees (books of the Apocrypha).

ma·ca·bre (mə-kaʹa-brə, ma-, -bər) *adj.* **1.** Suggesting the horror of death and decay; gruesome; ghastly. **2.** Associated with or suggestive of the *danse macabre,* in which an allegorical figure of death summons those about him to dance with him to their deaths. —See Synonyms at **ghastly.** [French, ghastly, from Old French *Danse Macabre,* the Dance of Death, probably originally *Danse Macabé,* "the Maccabean Dance", translation of Medieval Latin *Chorea Maccabaeorum,* probably referring to a representation of the slaughter of the Maccabees in a miracle play.] —**ma·ca·bre·ly** *adv.*

ma·ca·co (mə-kaʹa-kō, -káy-) *n. pl.* **-cos.** Any of various lemurs; especially, the species *Lemur macaco.* [French *mococo*[!].]

mac·ad·am (mə-káddəm) *n.* **1.** A surface, especially of a road, made of layers of compacted small stones, now usually bound with tar or asphalt. **2.** The material used to make this surface. [After John L. McADAM.]

mac·a·da·mi·a (mácka-dáymi-ə) *n.* Any of five trees of the genus *Macadamia,* native to eastern Australia; especially, *M. tetraphylla* which has edible, nutlike seeds called *macadamia nuts.* [New Latin, after John *Macadam* (1827–1865), Australian chemist.]

mac·ad·am·ise, mac·ad·am·ize (mə-káddə-mīz) *tr.v.* **-ised, -ising, -ises.** To construct or pave (a road) with macadam. —**mac·ad·am·i·sa·tion** (-mī-záysh'n ‖ *U.S.* -mi-) *n.* —**mac·ad·am·is·er** *n.*

Macao. See **Macau.**

ma·caque (mə-kaʹak, -kák) *n.* Any of several short-tailed monkeys of the genus *Macaca,* of southeast Asia, Japan, Gibraltar, and north Africa. See **Barbary ape, rhesus monkey.** [French, from Portuguese *macaco,* from Fiot *makaku,* "some monkeys" : *ma,* numerical sign + *kaku,* monkey.]

mac·a·ro·ni, mac·ca·ro·ni (mácka-rŏni) *n., pl.* **-roni** (for senses 1 and 2), **-nis** or **-nies** (for all senses). **1.** A pasta of wheat flour in the form of hollow tubes or other shapes, dried, and prepared for eating by boiling. **2.** A dish containing macaroni. **3.** A fashionable fop of the 18th century. [Italian (Neapolitan dialect), plural of *maccarone,* from Late Greek *makaria,* food made from barley.]

mac·a·ron·ic (mácka-rónnik) *adj.* **1.** Of or pertaining to a literary composition containing a mixture of vernacular words with Latin or with mock-Latin words: *macaronic verse.* **2.** Of or involving a mixture of two or more languages.

~ *n. Usually plural.* A macaronic composition. [New Latin *macaronicus,* "like macaroni" (i.e., a crude rustic mixture), from Italian *maccaroni,* MACARONI.]

macaroni cheese *n.* A dish consisting of macaroni coated in a cheese sauce and baked.

mac·a·roon (mácka-rōʹon) *n.* A chewy biscuit made with sugar, egg whites, and ground almonds or coconut. [French *macaron,* from Italian *maccarone,* MACARONI.]

Mac·Ar·thur (mə-kárthər), **Douglas** (1880–1964). U.S. general. Much-decorated in World War I, he rose to become U.S. Chief of Staff (1935–37). Recalled from retirement by the Army in 1941, he was driven from the Philippines by the Japanese, but regained the islands (1944–45), and with the war's end became Supreme Commander of the Allied Forces in Japan (1945–50). He was Commander (1950–51) of the United Nations Forces in the Korean War.

Ma·cas·sar oil (mə-kássər) *n.* A perfumed oil used, especially in the 19th century, for the hair. [After *Macassar* (Makassar), port and region in Celebes (Sulawesi), Indonesia, which was claimed to be the source of the ingredients.]

Ma·cau or **Ma·cao** (mə-ków). Portuguese overseas province in southeast China. The Portuguese founded a trading post between the Xi Jiang and Zhujiang (Pearl river) estuaries in 1557, and paid China tribute for it until 1849, when it became a free port. In 1887 China formally leased Macau to Portugal until 1997. It reverts to China in December 1999. It is now a gambling, tourist, and transit trade centre. Area, 16 square kilometres (6 square miles). Population, 492,000. Capital, Macau Town. —**Mac·a·nese** (mácka-neʹez ‖ -neʹess) *n.*

Macaulay, Thomas Babington, 1st Baron (1800–59). English historian, politician, and poet. He was elected an M.P. (1830), then after a period in India, became Secretary for War (1839–41). He was made a peer in 1857. Besides his essays for the *Edinburgh Review,* he wrote the uncompleted *History of England* (1849–61) and *Lays of Ancient Rome* (1842).

ma·caw (mə-káw) *n.* Any of various tropical and subtropical American parrots of the genera *Ara* and *Anodorhynchus,* including the largest parrots, characterised by long sabre-shaped tails, curved powerful bills, and usually brilliant plumage. [Portuguese *macaú,* perhaps from *macaúba,* a kind of palm (on whose fruit the parrot feeds), from Tupi *macahuba, macahiba* : probably *maca-,* thorn (of African origin) + *-yba,* tree.]

Mac·beth (mək-béth, mak-) (died 1057). King of Scotland (1040–57). In pursuit of a tenuous claim to the throne, he killed Duncan in battle (1040) to become king. He was later killed by Malcolm, son of Duncan. Shakespeare based *Macbeth* on the account of him in Holinshed's *Chronicles.*

Mac·ca·be·an (mácka-béeʹən) *adj.* Of or pertaining to Judas Maccabeus or to the Maccabees.

Mac·ca·bees (mácka-beez) *pl.n.* **1.** A Jewish dynasty of patriots, high priests, and kings of the second and first centuries B.C. See Judas **Maccabeus.** **2.** *Abbr.* **Mac., Macc.** Four books in the Old Testament Apocrypha, the first two of which tell about the feats of this family. In the Roman Catholic and Eastern Orthodox churches, the first two books are canonical. Also called in the Douay Bible "Machabees".

Mac·ca·be·us (mácka-béeʹəss), **Judas** (died 160 B.C.). Jewish patriot, most famous of the Maccabees; leader of a Jewish revolt against Syria in 166 B.C. His rededication of the Temple at Jerusalem (164 B.C.) is commemorated by the Feast of Chanukkah.

mac·ca·boy (mácka-boy) *n.* A perfumed snuff made in Martinique. [French *macouba,* after *Macouba,* district of Martinique.]

maccaroni. Variant of **macaroni.**

Mac·cles·field (máck'lz-feeld). Market town in Cheshire, northwest England. It is the silk-milling centre of England.

Mac·Diar·mid (mək-dúr-mid ‖ mak-), **Hugh,** born Christopher Murray Grieve (1892–1978). Scottish poet, Marxist, and founder member of the Scottish Nationalist Party (1928). He wrote in Scots. *A Drunk Man Looks at the Thistle* (1926), giving his view on Scottish independence, was a landmark in modern Scots poetry.

Mac·Don·ald (mək-dónn'ld ‖ mak-), **Flora** (1722–90). Scottish Jacobite heroine. On the Isle of Benbecula, she met Prince Charles Edward Stuart, the Young Pretender, who was in hiding after Culloden (1746). She took him, disguised as a maid, to Skye, and he escaped to France. She was imprisoned briefly in the Tower.

MacDonald, (James) Ramsay (1866–1937). Britain's first Labour prime minister, born in Scotland. He became an M.P. (1906) and prime minister and Secretary of State for foreign affairs (1924). He was out of parliament (1924–29), but returned as prime minister of a minority government until he lost the support of his own party (1931). He then formed a coalition government made up mainly of

Conservatives and resigned in 1935.

Macdonald, Sir John Alexander (1815–91). Scottish-born Canadian politician, the first prime minister (1867–73, 1878–91) of the Dominion of Canada. He was a powerful advocate of the movement which led to Canadian confederation in 1867.

mace[1] (mayss) *n.* **1.** A heavy medieval war club, usually with a spiked or flanged metal head, used to crush armour. **2.** A ceremonial staff borne or displayed as the symbol of authority of a legislative body. **3.** A macebearer. [Middle English, from Old French *mace, masse,* from Vulgar Latin *mattea†* (unattested), club.]

mace[2] *n.* An aromatic spice made from the dried, waxy, scarlet or yellowish covering that partly encloses the kernel of the nutmeg. [Middle English, formed as singular of *macis* (wrongly taken to be plural), from Medieval Latin, misreading of Latin *macir,* from Greek *makir,* an Indian spice.]

Mace (mayss) *n.* Chemical Mace (*see*).

~*tr.v.* **Maced, Macing, Maced.** *Often small* **m.** To spray with Chemical Mace.

mace·bear·er (máyss-bair-ər) *n.* An official who carries a mace of office. Also called "mace", "macer".

Maced. Macedonia; Macedonian.

mac·é·doine (mássi-dwáan, -dwaan) *n.* **1.** A mixture of finely cut or diced vegetables or fruits, sometimes jellied, served as a salad, dessert, or appetiser. **2.** Any mixture; a medley; a hotchpotch. [French *macédoine,* "Macedonian" (the population of Macedonia is a mixture of various peoples).]

Mac·e·do·ni·a (massi-dṓni-ə). *Abbr.* **Maced.** Region in the Balkans, in southeast Europe. Largely mountainous, it was peopled by Slavs in the sixth century A.D. and is now divided between Bulgaria, Greece, and FYROM. A powerful empire under Philip II and his son Alexander the Great (fourth century B.C.), Macedonia was later ruled by the Romans, Byzantine Greeks, Bulgars, Serbs, and Turks. The present division resulted largely from the Second Balkan War (1913).

Macedonia, Former Yugoslav Republic of. *Abbr.* **FYROM.** Country in south central Europe, formerly the southernmost republic of Yugoslavia, bordering Greece. It lies chiefly in plateau regions; its economy is primarily agricultural. Area, 25 713 square kilometres (9,928 square miles). Population, 4,200,000. Capital, Skopje.

Mac·e·do·ni·an (mássi-dṓni-ən) *adj. Abbr.* **Maced.** Of or pertaining to ancient or modern Macedonia, or the people or languages of these regions.

~*n. Abbr.* **Maced. 1.** A native or inhabitant of ancient or modern Macedonia. **2.** The language of ancient Macedonia, having characteristics regarded as Indo-European. **3.** The Slavonic language of modern Macedonia.

mac·er (máy-sər) *n.* **1.** A macebearer. **2.** A Scottish usher in a law court.

mac·er·ate (mássə-rayt) *v.* **-ated, -ating, -ates.** —*tr.* **1.** To soften (a solid substance) by soaking or steeping in a liquid, sometimes using heat. **2.** To separate (a solid substance) into constituents by soaking. **3.** To cause to become lean; emaciate, usually by starvation. —*intr.* To become macerated; undergo macerating. [Latin *mācerāre,* to soften.] —**mac·er·a·tion** (-ráysh'n) *n.* —**mac·er·a·tor,** **mac·er·a·ter** *n.*

Mac·gil·li·cud·dy's Reeks (mə-gílli-kuddiz reeks). Mountain range in County Kerry, Republic of Ireland. This range borders the Lakes of Killarney and Lough Caragh, and rises to 1 041 metres (3,414 feet) at Carrantuohill, the highest mountain in Ireland.

Mach, machine (mak, maak). *n.* **Mach number** (*see*).

Mach (maakh, maak; *German* makh), **Ernst** (1838–1916). Austrian physicist and philosopher. He gave his name to the **Mach number,** and contributed to the philosophy of scientific positivism.

mach. machine; machinery; machinist.

Mach·a·bees (máckə-beez). In the Douay Bible, **Maccabees** (*see*).

mach·air (mákhər) *n.* **1.** A whitish, almost entirely calcareous sand forming undulating lowlands along the coasts of western Scotland and the Hebrides, and providing light, arable soils. **2.** A coastal lowland formed from such sand. [Gaelic *machair(e).*]

Ma·chel (ma-shél, mə-), **Samora** (Moïsés) (1933–86). Mozambique politician. As leader of the Mozambique Liberation Front (FRELIMO), he led the movement against Portuguese rule (1966–74). He became the first president of independent Mozambique (1975–86).

ma·chet·e (mə-chétti, -shétti, -cháyti) *n.* Also **ma·tchet** (máchit). A large, heavy knife with a broad blade, used for cutting vegetation and as a weapon. [American Spanish, from Spanish, diminutive of *macho,* axe, club, hammer, from Late Latin *marcus†,* hammer.]

Mach·i·a·vel·li (mácki-ə-vélli), **Niccolò** (1469–1527). Italian statesman and writer. As diplomat and statesman, he served the Florentine Republic (1498–1512). His book, *The Prince* (published 1532), describes the achievement and maintenance of power by a determined ruler indifferent to moral considerations.

Mach·i·a·vel·li·an (mácki-ə-vélli-ən) *adj.* **1.** Of or pertaining to Niccolò Machiavelli. **2.** Of or pertaining to Machiavellianism. **3.** *Often small* **m.** Devious; cunning.

~*n.* One who believes in or practises Machiavellianism.

Mach·i·a·vel·li·an·ism (mácki-ə-vélli-ə-niz'm) *n.* Also **Mach·i·a·vel·lism** (-vélliz'm). The political doctrine of Machiavelli, which denies the relevance of morality in political affairs and holds that craft and deceit are justified in pursuing and maintaining political power; political opportunism.

ma·chic·o·late (mə-chíckō-layt, ma-, -chíckə-) *tr.v.* **-lated, -lating, -lates.** To build or furnish with machicolations. [Old French *ma-*

chicoler, from Anglo-Latin *machicollāre,* from Provençal *machacol* : *macar,* crush + *col,* neck.] —**ma·chic·o·la·ted** *adj.*

ma·chic·o·la·tion (mə-chíckō-láysh'n, ma-, -chíckə-) *n.* **1. a.** A projecting gallery at the top of a castle wall or above an entrance, supported by a row of corbelled arches, having openings in the floor through which stones and boiling liquids could be dropped on attackers. **b.** Any of these openings. **c.** Any of these corbelled arches. **2.** *Usually plural.* A row of small corbelled arches used as an ornamental architectural feature.

mach·i·nate (mácki-nayt, -máshi-) *v.* **-nated, -nating, -nates.** —*tr.* To devise (a plot). —*intr.* To plot. [Latin *māchinārī,* from *māchina,* contrivance, MACHINE.] —**mach·i·na·tor** *n.*

mach·i·na·tion (mácki-náysh'n, máshi-) *n.* **1.** The act of plotting. **2.** *Usually plural.* A hostile intrigue. —See Synonyms at **conspiracy.**

ma·chine (mə-shéen) *n. Abbr.* **mach. 1. a.** Any system or device formed and connected to alter, transmit, and direct applied forces in a predetermined manner to accomplish a specific objective, such as the performance of useful work. **b.** Any of a number of simple devices, such as the lever, the pulley, the wedge, the screw, or the inclined plane, that alters the magnitude or direction, or both, of an applied force. In this sense, also called "simple machine". **2.** Any such system or device together with its power source and auxiliary equipment, for example, a car, aircraft, or jackhammer. **3. a.** Any system or device, such as an electronic computer, that performs or assists in the performance of a human task. **b.** Any automated device, such as a slot machine. **4.** *Archaic.* **a.** An intricate natural system or organism, such as the human body. **b.** A functional unit of such a system, for example, an organ such as the heart or kidney. **5.** A person who acts in a rigid, mechanical, or unfeeling manner. **6. a.** Any complex system, organisation, or agency of people that functions in what appears to be an inexorable manner: *the military machine; a propaganda machine.* **b.** Any established group of people controlling a political or other organisation. Often used derogatorily: *the party machine.* **7.** A **deus ex machina** (*see*).

~*v.* **machined, -chining, -chines.** —*tr.* To make, cut, shape, or finish using a machine, for example a sewing machine. —*intr.* To undergo machining: *This metal machines easily.* [French, from Old French, from Latin *māchina,* engine, contrivance, from Doric Greek *makhana,* from *makhos,* contrivance, means.] —**ma·chin·a·ble** *adj.*

machine bolt *n.* A bolt with a square or hexagonal head.

machine finish *n.* A finish on paper surfaces, **mill finish** (*see*).

machine gun *n.* An automatic gun, usually mounted, that fires rapidly and repeatedly. Compare **submachine gun.**

ma·chine-gun (mə-shéen-gun) *tr.v.* **-gunned, -gunning, -guns.** To fire at or kill with a machine gun.

~*adj.* Fast and staccato.

machine language *n.* Any of various systems of symbols used to code information that is to be fed into a computer. Also called "machine code".

ma·chine-read·a·ble (mə-shéen-réedəb'l) *adj.* Able to be fed directly into a computer. Said of data stored magnetically or on punched cards or punched tape.

ma·chin·er·y (mə-shéenəri) *n., pl.* **-ies.** *Abbr.* **mach. 1.** Machines or machine parts collectively. **2.** The working parts of a particular machine. **3. a.** An organised, highly interdependent system, often exerting power: *bureaucratic machinery; the machinery of government.* **b.** Any system of related elements that operates in a definable manner: *the machinery of grammar.* **4.** A generally unsubtle device in literature, for example the introduction of a new character or an unlikely event, for bringing about a calculated effect such as a happy ending. See **deus ex machina.**

machine screw *n.* A screw with a thread along the whole length of its shank.

machine shop *n.* A workshop where power-driven tools are used for making, finishing, or repairing machines or machine parts.

machine tool *n.* A power-driven tool for machining, such as a lathe or milling machine.

ma·chine-wash (mə-shéen-wósh) *v.* **-washed, -washing, -washes.** —*tr.* To wash (clothing, material, or the like) in a washing machine. —*intr.* To undergo washing in a washing machine without damage: *Wool doesn't machine-wash easily.* —**ma·chine-wash·able** *adj.*

ma·chin·ist (mə-shéenist) *n. Abbr.* **mach. 1.** One who operates and makes objects with a machine, for example a sewing machine, for a

living. **2.** One skilled in operating machine tools. **3.** One who makes, operates, or repairs machines.

ma·chis·mo (ma-chíz-mō, mə-, -kíz- ‖ *U.S. also* maa-, -chéez-) *n.* An exaggerated sense of masculinity stressing such attributes as physical courage, virility, domination of women, and aggressiveness or violence. [Spanish : MACHO + -*ismo*, -ISM.]

Mach·me·ter (mák-meetər, maák-) *n. Sometimes small* **m.** An aircraft instrument that indicates speed in Mach numbers.

Mach number, mach number *n. Abbr.* **M** The ratio of the speed of an object to the speed of sound in the surrounding medium. For example, an aircraft moving twice as fast as sound is said to be travelling at Mach 2. [After Ernst MACH.]

ma·cho (máchō, maá-chō) *adj.* Characterised by machismo.
~*n., pl.* **machos.** *Chiefly U.S.* **1.** Machismo. **2.** A macho man. [Spanish, male, virile, from Latin *masculus*, MALE.]

ma·chree (mə-krée) *n. Irish.* A dear; a darling. Used as a term of endearment. [Irish *mo chroidhe*, "my heart".]

Mach's principle *n. Physics.* The principle that inertia is not an intrinsic property of a body but results from the presence of other matter in the universe. [After Ernst MACH.]

Ma·chu Pic·chu (maáchōō péek-chōō). Inca city northwest of Cusco, Peru. Built on a mountain overlooking the Urubamba valley, it lay forgotten after the Spanish conquest in the 16th century until discovered almost intact in 1911.

–machy *n. comb. form.* Indicates struggle or fight; for example, **logomachy.** [Greek *makhē*, battle.]

mach·zor, mah·zor (maak-zór, maakh-) *n., pl.* **machzorim** or **-zors.** A Jewish prayer book containing rituals prescribed for holidays and festivals. Compare **siddur.** [Hebrew, "cycle".]

macintosh. Variant of **mackintosh.**

Mac·in·tosh (máckin-tosh), **Charles** (1766–1843). British chemist and inventor. He produced a waterproof material (patented 1823) by dissolving rubber in naphtha, a by-product of tar, and sandwiching it between layers of cloth.

mack (mak) *n. Slang.* A pimp. [Shortening of obsolete *mackerel*, from Old French *maquerel*, from Middle Dutch *makelaer*, broker.]

Mac·kay (mə-kí). Seaport of eastern Queensland, Australia. Built on the Pioneer river, it processes and exports sugar.

Mac·ken·zie¹ (mə-kénzi). District in Canada's Northwest Territories, rich in gold, oil, zinc, natural gas, and uranium. It is peopled mainly by Eskimos and North American Indians. Yellowknife is the capital.

Mackenzie². River in Northwest Territories, Canada. It flows from Great Slave Lake to the Arctic Ocean and is navigable from June to October. The Finlay-Peace-Mackenzie system is Canada's longest river (4 212 kilometres; 2,635 miles).

Mackenzie, Alexander¹ (1822–92). First Liberal prime minister (1873–78) of the Dominion of Canada. He left Scotland to settle in Canada in 1842 and was elected to the Canada assembly in 1861.

Mackenzie, Sir Alexander² (c. 1755–1820). Canadian fur-trader and explorer, born in Scotland. He charted the Mackenzie river (1789) and was the first European to cross the North American continent north of Mexico.

Mackenzie, Sir (Edward Montague) Compton (1883–1972). British novelist. His books include *Sinister Street* (1914), *Whisky Galore* (1947, filmed 1949), two volumes of autobiography.

mack·er·el (máckrəl, máckərəl) *n., pl.* **-els** or collectively **mackerel. 1.** Any of several marine fishes of the family Scombridae, found worldwide. Some species are important food fishes, especially the Atlantic mackerel, *Scomber scombrus*, which has dark, wavy bars on the back and a silvery belly. **2.** Any of the smaller fishes of the suborder Scombroidea, such as the **Spanish mackerel** (*see*). **3.** Any of various fishes resembling mackerel. [Middle English *makerel*, from Anglo-French, from Old French *maquerel*†.]

mackerel shark *n.* The porbeagle (*see*).

mackerel sky *n.* A striped formation of high, white cirrocumulus or altocumulus clouds suggesting the bars on a mackerel's back.

Mac·ker·ras (mə-kérrəss), **Sir (Alan) Charles** (1925–). U.S.-born Australian conductor and oboist. A noted Janáček interpreter, he directed the Hamburg State Opera (1966–69), the English National Opera (1970–77), and the Welsh National Opera (1987–92).

mack·i·naw (mácki-naw) *n. U.S.* **1.** A short, double-breasted coat of heavy woollen material, usually plaid. **2.** The cloth from which such a coat is made, usually of wool, often with a heavy nap. [After *Mackinac*, island in Lake Huron, Michigan, a 19th-century entrepôt where the cloth and the coat were traded.]

mack·in·tosh, mac·in·tosh (máckin-tosh) *n. Chiefly British.* **1. a.** A raincoat of patented rubberised cloth. **b.** This cloth. **2.** Any raincoat. Also informally called "mac", "mack". [After Charles MAC·INTOSH.]

Mack·in·tosh (máckin-tosh), **Charles Rennie** (1868–1928). Scottish architect and artist in the Art Nouveau style. He redesigned Glasgow School of Art (completed 1909).

mack·le (máck'l) *n. Also* **mac·ule** (máckewl). *Printing.* A spot, especially a blurred or double impression caused by a slipping of the type or a wrinkle in the paper.
~*v.* **mackled, -ling, -les.** *Also* **mac·ule, -uled, -uling, -ules.** —*tr.* To blur or double (a printed impression). —*intr.* To become blurred. [French *macule*, from Latin *macula*, spot.]

Mac·lau·rin series (mə-kláwrin, -klórrin) *n. Mathematics.* An infinite series by which a function can be expressed in terms of the values of its derivatives when the independent variable is zero. It

has the form $f(x) = f(0) + f'(0)/1! + f''(0)/2! + f'''(0)/3! + \ldots$ [After Colin *Maclaurin* (1698–1746), Scottish mathematician.]

mac·le (máck'l) *n.* **1.** A mineral, chiastolite (*see*). **2.** A crystalline form, twin (*see*). **3.** A spot or discoloration in a mineral. [French, double crystal, from Old French *macle*, heraldic term for a "voided lozenge" (one diamond shape within another), originally a stylised mesh of a net, from Latin *macula*, mesh, hole in a net, spot.]

Mac·leish (mə-kléesh), **Archibald** (1892–1982). U.S. poet and playwright. He was Librarian of Congress (1939–44). His works include *Streets in the Moon* (1926), and he won Pulitzer prizes for *Conquistador* (1932), *Collected Poems 1917–52* (1952), and *J.B.* (1958).

Mac·lise (mə-kléess), **Daniel** (1806–70). Irish painter and illustrator. He decorated the Royal Gallery of the House of Lords, and painted *Wellington and Blücher at Waterloo* (1859–61) and *The Death of Nelson* (1863–64).

Mac·Mil·lan (mək-millən ‖ mak-), **Sir Kenneth** (1929–92). British choreographer. Beginning as a ballet dancer, he turned to choreography in 1953, directing the Royal Ballet, Covent Garden (1970–77) and becoming its principal choreographer (1977). His many creations included *Romeo and Juliet*, *Song of the Earth*, *Manon*, and *Isadora*.

Macmillan, (Maurice) Harold, Earl of Stockton (1894–1986). British prime minister (1957–63). He became an M.P. in 1924, and during the 1930s he backed Churchill in condemning British appeasement of Hitler. After the re-election of the Conservatives (1951), he was in turn minister of housing (1951–54), of defence (1954–55), and of foreign affairs (1955), and then Chancellor of the Exchequer (1955–57). Ill health made him resign.

Mac·Neice (mək-néess ‖ mak-), **(Frederick) Louis** (1907–63). British poet and playwright, born in Northern Ireland. He wrote satirical poetry in colloquial style in a literary group with Christopher Isherwood, Cecil Day Lewis, and W.H. Auden. His works include *Blind Fireworks* (1929), *Autumn Journal* (1939), *Holes in the Sky* (1948), and *The Strings are False* (published 1965).

Mâ·con¹ (má-koɴ, maá-, -kon, -kən). French town, capital of the Saône-et-Loire département. Built on the river Saône, it is noted for its fine Burgundy wines.

Mâcon² *n.* A red or white Burgundy wine produced in the area around Mâcon.

Mac·on·chy (mə-kóngki), **Dame Elizabeth Violet** (1907–94). British composer, who studied with Vaughan Williams. She composed chamber music and twelve string quartets as well as choral and ballet music and one-act operas.

Mac·quar·ie (mə-kwórri). River of New South Wales, Australia, flowing 950 kilometres (590 miles) from the Blue Mountains to the Darling river.

Macquarie, Lachlan (1761–1824). Scottish colonial administrator. He was governor of New South Wales (1809–21), where he encouraged the convicts to learn trades, and extended the road system.

mac·ra·mé (mə-kraámi, máckrə-may, -máy) *n.* **1.** Ornamental lacework made by weaving and knotting cords, especially string, into a pattern. **2.** The art of making this kind of lacework. [French, from Italian *macramè*, from Turkish *makrama*, napkin, towel, from Arabic *miqramah*, striped cloth.]

mac·ren·ceph·a·ly (mák-rən-séffəli, -ren–) *n. Also* **mac·ren·ceph·a·li·a** (-sə-fáyli-ə). *Pathology.* Abnormal enlargement of the brain. [MACR(O)- + ENCEPHAL(O)- + -Y.]

macro–, macr– *comb. form.* Indicates: **1.** Largeness in extent, duration, or size; for example, **macrocosm. 2.** Abnormal largeness or overdevelopment, especially in some part; for example, **macrencephaly.** Compare **micro-.** [Greek *makros*, large, long.]

mac·ro·bi·o·sis (máckrō-bī-ō-siss) *n.* Longevity. [Late Greek *makrobiōsis* : MACRO- + -BIOSIS.]

mac·ro·bi·o·ta (máckrō-bī-ótə) *n.* The macroscopic plant and animal life of a region. [New Latin : MACRO- + Greek *biotos*, life.]

mac·ro·bi·ot·ics (máckrō-bī-óttiks) *n. Used with a singular verb.* The theory or practice of promoting longevity, especially by means of a diet consisting of completely unprocessed cereals and vegetables grown without chemical additives. [Greek *makrobiotos*, long-lived : MACRO- + *biotos*, life + -ICS.] —**mac·ro·bi·ot·ic** *adj.*

mac·ro·ceph·a·ly (máckrō-séffəli) *n. Also* **mac·ro·ce·pha·li·a** (-sə-fáyli-ə). *Pathology.* Abnormally large cranial capacity, often observed in the mentally handicapped. Also called "megacephaly", "megalocephaly". [French *macrocéphalie*, from *macrocéphale*, having a long head, from Greek *makrokephalos* : MACRO- + -CEPHA-LOUS.] —**mac·ro·ce·phal·ic** (-sə-fál-ik), **mac·ro·ceph·a·lous** (-séffələss) *adj.*

mac·ro·chem·is·try (máckrō-kémmiss-tri, -kemmiss-) *n.* Chemistry requiring neither microscopy nor microanalysis. Compare **microchemistry.** —**mac·ro·chem·i·cal** (-kémmik'l) *adj.*

mac·ro·cli·mate (máckrō-klī-mət, -mit) *n. Meteorology.* The climate of a large geographical area. Compare **microclimate.** —**mac·ro·cli·mat·ic** (-klī-máttik) *adj.*

mac·ro·code (máckrō-kōd) *n.* **1.** A coding system that assembles sets of computer instructions. **2.** A single code representing a set of computer instructions. Also informally called "macro".

ma·cro·con·sum·er (máckrō-kən-sewmər) *n.* An organism in an ecological community that feeds on other organic matter.

mac·ro·cosm (máckrō-koz'm, máckrə-) *n.* **1.** The universe itself, or the concept of universe. **2.** A system regarded as an entity containing subsystems. Compare **microcosm.** [French *macrocosme*, from Medieval Latin *macrocosmus*, from Late Greek *makros kosmos*, the great world : MACRO- + *kosmos,* world.] —**mac·ro·cos·mic** (-kózmik) *adj.*

mac·ro·cyte (máckrō-sīt) *n. Pathology.* An abnormally large red blood cell associated with some forms of anaemia. [MACRO- + (ERYTHRO)CYTE.] —**mac·ro·cyt·ic** (-síttik) *adj.*

mac·ro·cy·to·sis (máckrō-sī-tō-siss) *n. Pathology.* A condition of macrocytes in the blood. —**mac·ro·cy·tot·ic** (-tóttik) *adj.*

mac·ro·e·co·nom·ics (máckrō-éekə-nómmiks, -éckə-) *n. Used with a singular verb.* The study of the economics of large-scale systems or aggregates, such as the economy of a country. Compare **microeconomics.** —**mac·ro·e·co·nom·ic** *adj.*

mac·ro·ev·o·lu·tion (máckrō-éevə-lōōsh'n, -évvə-, -léwsh'n) *n.* Evolution involving whole genera, or larger groups, of organisms. —**mac·ro·ev·o·lu·tion·ar·y** *adj.*

mac·ro·ga·mete (máckrō-ga-méet, -gə-, -gámmeet) *n.* Also **meg·a·ga·mete** (mégga-). *Biology.* The larger of two conjugating cells, usually female, in protozoans. Compare **microgamete.**

mac·ro·glob·u·lin (máckrō-glóbbew-lin) *n.* A plasma globulin that has an unusually large molecular weight.

mac·ro·glob·u·lin·ae·mi·a (máckrō-glóbbew-li-néemi-ə) *n.* The presence in the blood of an abnormal form of macroglobulin.

mac·ro·graph (máckrō-graaf, -graf) *n.* A representation of an object which is at least as large as the object. [MACRO- + -GRAPH.]

ma·crog·ra·phy (mə-króggrəfi, ma-) *n.* 1. Examination of objects with the unaided eye. Compare **micrography.** 2. Abnormally large handwriting, sometimes indicating a nervous disorder. [MACRO- + -GRAPHY.] —**mac·ro·graph·ic** (máckrō-gráffik) *adj.*

mac·ro·mol·e·cule (máckrō-mólli-kewl) *n.* 1. A very large molecule, especially in a natural or synthetic polymer, such as a protein or synthetic resin. 2. A covalent or ionic crystal, such as diamond or salt, in which individual atoms or molecules cannot be distinguished. —**mac·ro·mo·lec·u·lar** (-mə-léckewlər, -mo-, -mō-) *adj.*

ma·cron (máckron ‖ *U.S. also* máy-kron, -krən) *n.* A diacritical mark placed above a vowel to indicate a long sound or phonetic value in pronunciation, such as the mark in (ō). Compare **breve.** [Greek *makron,* neuter of *makros,* long.]

mac·ro·nu·cle·us (máckrō-néw-kli-əss ‖ -nōō-) *n., pl.* **-clei** (-ī) or *rare* **-cleuses.** The larger of the two nuclei in ciliate protozoans, which is involved in the nonreproductive functions of the cell. Compare **micronucleus.**

mac·ro·nu·tri·ent (máckrō-néw-tri-ənt ‖ -nōō-) *n.* An element, such as carbon, hydrogen, oxygen, or nitrogen, required in relatively large proportion for growth and development.

mac·ro·phage (máckrō-fayj, máckrə-) *n.* A large phagocytic cell present in connective tissue, bone marrow, lymph nodes, and the like. [MACRO- + -PHAGE.] —**mac·ro·phag·ic** (-fájik) *adj.*

mac·ro·phys·ics (máckrō-fízziks) *n. Used with a singular verb.* The physics of macroscopic phenomena.

ma·crop·ter·ous (ma-króptərəss, mə-) *adj. Zoology.* Having unusually large wings. [Greek *makropteros* : MACRO- + -PTEROUS.]

mac·ro·scop·ic (máckrō-skóppik, máckrə-) *adj.* Also **mac·ro·scop·i·cal** (-'l). 1. Large enough to be perceived or examined without instruments, especially as by the naked eye. 2. Pertaining to observations made without magnifying instruments, especially by the naked eye; megascopic. 3. *Physics.* Of or pertaining to systems or properties that depend on large numbers of atoms rather than individual atoms or molecules. 4. Of, pertaining to, or concerned with large units or whole issues; large-scale. [MACRO- + -SCOP(Y) + -IC.] —**mac·ro·scop·i·cal·ly** *adv.*

mac·ro·spo·ran·gi·um (máckrō-spawr-ánji-əm, -spər-) *n., pl.* **-gia** (-ji-ə). *Botany.* A **megasporangium** *(see).*

mac·ro·spore (máckrō-spawr, máckrə- ‖ -spōr) *n. Botany.* A **megaspore** *(see).*

mac·u·la (máckew-lə) *n., pl.* **-lae** (-lee). Also **macule** (for sense 2). 1. A spot, stain, blemish, or pit; especially, a discoloration of the skin caused by excess or lack of pigment. 2. *Anatomy.* A small area distinguishable from surrounding tissue, such as the macula lutea. 3. A sunspot. [Latin *macula,* spot, blemish.] —**mac·u·lar** (-lər) *adj.*

macula lu·te·a (lōō-ti-ə, léw-) *n., pl.* **maculae luteae** (-ee). *Anatomy.* An area in the eye near the centre of the retina at which visual perception is most acute. [New Latin, "yellow spot".]

mac·u·late (máckew-layt) *tr.v.* **-lated, -lating, -lates.** To spot, blemish, or pollute.

~*adj.* (-lət, -lit). 1. Spotted or blotched. 2. Stained; impure. [Middle English *maculaten,* to stain, from Latin *maculāre,* from *macula,* spot, blemish.]

mac·u·la·tion (máckew-láysh'n) *n.* 1. The act of spotting or staining. 2. A spotted or stained condition. 3. The spotted markings collectively of a plant or animal, such as the spots of the leopard.

mac·ule (máckewl) *v.* **-uled, -uling, -ules.** —*tr.* To blur; mackle. —*intr.* To become blurred or mackled.

~*n.* 1. *Printing.* Variant of **mackle.** 2. *Anatomy.* Variant of **macula.** [Middle English, from Latin *macula,* spot, blemish.]

mad (mad) *adj.* **madder, maddest.** 1. Suffering from a disorder of the mind; insane. 2. As if insane; temporarily or apparently deranged by violent sensations, emotions, or ideas: *mad with pain; mad with love.* 3. *Informal.* Feeling or showing strong liking or enthusiasm. Used with *about, on,* or *over: mad about golf.* Sometimes used in combination: *golf-mad.* 4. *Informal.* Angry; resentful. 5. Lacking restraint or reason; wildly foolish; senseless. 6. Marked by extreme excitement, confusion, or agitation; frantic. 7. Boisterously gay; hilarious: *to have a mad time.* 8. Affected by rabies; rabid. —**like mad.** *Slang.* Wildly; impetuously: *He drove like mad.*

—**mad keen.** Wildly enthusiastic.

~*v.* **madded, madding, mads.** *Archaic.* —*tr.* To madden or make mad. —*intr.* To act, be, or become mad. [Middle English *madd,* Old English *gemǣdd,* past participle of *gemǣdan,* to madden, from *gemād,* mad.]

MAD mutual(ly) assured destruction.

Madagascan periwinkle *n.* A plant, *Catharanthus roseus* (or *Vinca rosea*), native to Madagascar, having pink or white flowers. It is a source of various alkaloids used in treating leukaemia.

Mad·a·gas·car (máddə-gáskər), **Republic of.** Island state off southeast Africa. Its coastal plains in the east and west rise to a central plateau. Rice-growing and livestock-rearing are the main occupations, and exports include chrome ore, coffee, vanilla, cloves, and meat. Made a French colony in 1896, it was granted self-rule as the Malagasy Republic in 1958 and full independence in 1960. It became a democratic republic in 1975. The island separated from Africa 150 million years ago and is noted for its unique wildlife. Area, 587 041 square kilometres (226,658 square miles). Population, 15,350,000. Capital, Antananarivo (Tananarive) —**Mad·a·gas·can** (-gáskən) *n. & adj.*

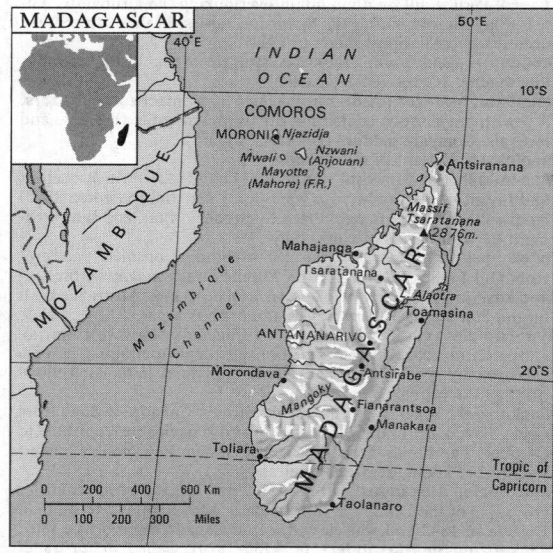

MADAGASCAR

mad·am (máddəm) *n., pl.* **mesdames** (may-dám, -daʹam, máy-dam) (for sense 1) or **madams** (for senses 3 and 4). 1. *Capital* **M. a.** A title of courtesy used as a form of address, originally to a woman of rank, now to any woman. **b.** A conventional form of address used instead of a woman's name at the opening of a letter. 2. A respectful form of address used before a woman's surname or the title of her office: *Madam Chairwoman.* 3. *Informal.* A bossy or impudent girl. Used chiefly in the phrase *a little madam.* 4. A woman who manages a brothel. [Middle English, from MADAME.]

mad·ame (máddəm, mə-dám) *n., pl.* **mesdames** (may-dám, máy-dam). *Abbr.* **Mme., Mme** 1. The French title of courtesy for a married woman, equivalent to the English *Mrs.*; sometimes used of older unmarried women. 2. A title of courtesy prefixed to the surname of certain foreign women, especially heads of state or the wives of heads of state and artists in the opera or ballet. [Middle English, from Old French *ma dame,* my lady.]

mad·cap (mád-kap) *n.* A rash or impulsive person.

~*adj.* Rash; impulsive; wild. [MAD + CAP (head).]

mad cow disease *n.* **bovine spongiform encephalopathy** *(see).*

mad·den (mádd'n) *v.* **-dened, -dening, -dens.** —*tr.* 1. To make mad; drive insane. 2. *Informal.* To make angry; excite or irritate. —*intr.* To become infuriated.

mad·den·ing (mádd'n-ing) *adj.* 1. Causing madness or serving to drive mad. 2. *Informal.* Extremely irritating; infuriating. —**mad·den·ing·ly** *adv.*

mad·der¹ (máddər) *n.* 1. Any of various plants of the genus *Rubia*; especially, a Eurasian species, *R. tinctoria,* having small, yellow flowers and a red, fleshy root. 2. The root of this plant, formerly an important source of dye. 3. A red dye obtained from the madder root. 4. Medium to strong red or reddish orange. [Middle English *mader,* Old English *mædere.*]

madder² Comparative of **mad.**

mad·ding (mádding). *adj. Archaic.* 1. Acting as if mad; frenzied. 2. Maddening.

made (mayd). The past tense and past participle of **make.**

~*adj.* 1. Produced or manufactured by constructing, shaping, forming, or the like. Used in combination: *handmade.* 2. Produced or created artificially; not found naturally. 3. Having a packed, smooth surface; sealed. Said of a road. 4. Invented; designed; contrived. 5. Assured of success or fortune: *a made man.* —**have (got) it made.** *Informal.* To be assured in advance of success. —**made for.** Perfectly suited for: *made for each other.*

Ma·dei·ra¹ (mə-déer-ə) *n.* A fortified white dessert wine from the island of Madeira.

Madeira². River in Brazil, the most important tributary of the Amazon. It forms on the Bolivian border and flows 3 315 kilometres (2,060 miles) to the Amazon below Manáus.

Madeira³. Island of the Madeira Islands.

Madeira cake *n.* A rich, pale yellow, densely textured sponge cake. [Eaten with Madeira wine.]

Madeira Islands. Also **Fun·chal Islands** (fōōn-shaál). Archipelago off northwest Africa, forming the Funchal overseas district of Portugal. Only two of the volcanic islands are inhabited, Madeira being the larger. The main industries are tourism, fishing, agriculture, and the production of Madeira wine. See map at **Atlantic Ocean.** —**Ma·dei·ran** *adj. & n.*

mad·e·leine (mádd'l-in, -ayn, -én) *n.* A small, rich cake, usually coated with jam or coconut. [French, perhaps after *Madeleine* Paulmier, 19th-century French pastry cook.]

mad·e·moi·selle (máddəm-wə-zél, -ə-, mam-zél; *French* mad-mwa-zél ‖ mam-zél) *n., pl.* **mesdemoiselles** (máyd-mwə-zél). *Abbr.* **Mlle., Mlle 1.** The French title of courtesy for a young girl or unmarried woman, equivalent to the English *Miss.* It may be used separately or prefixed to either a first or last name. **2.** A French governess or teacher. [French, from Old French *ma demoiselle : ma,* my, from Latin *mea,* + *demoiselle,* young lady, from Gallo-Roman *dom(i)nicella* (unattested), diminutive of Latin *domina,* lady, feminine of *dominus,* lord.]

made-to-meas·ure (máyd-tə-mézhər) *adj.* **1.** Made to fit certain measurements, as of a person. **2.** Made-to-order.

made-to-or·der (máyd-too-órdər ‖ -tə-) *adj.* **1.** Made in accordance with particular instructions to fill the requirements of a customer. Compare **ready-made. 2.** Highly appropriate; just right.

made-up (máyd-úp) *adj.* **1.** Fabricated; fictitious; imaginary; invented: *a made-up story.* **2.** Wearing cosmetics or make-up: *a made-up actress.* **3. a.** Complete; finished: *a made-up package.* **b.** Put together; assembled; arranged: *a made-up page of type.*

mad·house (mád-howss) *n. Informal.* **1.** A mental hospital. Not in technical usage. **2.** A place of uproar or great disorder.

Madison, James (1751–1836). Fourth president of the United States (1809–17). As a member of the Philadelphia Convention (1787) he helped to frame the U.S. constitution and the Bill of Rights. As president he instigated a war with Britain (1812–15) known as "Mr. Madison's War".

Madison Avenue *n.* **1.** A street in Manhattan, New York City, the centre of the American advertising business. **2.** The principles, attitudes, ideas, and methods of advertising and mass communications. Often used derogatorily.

mad·ly (mádli) *adv.* **1.** Insanely. **2.** Wildly; furiously; frantically. **3.** Foolishly; rashly. **4.** *Informal.* To an extreme or excessive degree; very much: *madly in love.*

mad·man (mád-mən) *n., pl.* **-men** (-mən, -men). An insane man; especially, a maniac or lunatic, or a person who behaves like one. Not in technical usage.

mad·ness (mád-nəss, -niss) *n.* **1.** Insanity. **2.** Great folly. **3.** Fury; rage. **4.** Wild enthusiasm; excitement. —See Synonyms at **insanity.**

ma·don·na (mə-dónnə) *n.* **1.** *Capital* **M. a.** The Virgin Mary. Usually preceded by *the.* **b.** An artistic representation of the Virgin Mary. **2.** A woman having qualities of purity, serenity, gentleness, or steadfast love that suggest the Madonna. **3.** Formerly, an Italian title for a married woman, equivalent to *madam.* It has been replaced in current usage by *signora.* [Italian : *ma,* my, from Latin *mea* + *donna,* lady, from Latin *domina,* feminine of *dominus,* lord.]

Madonna lily *n.* A plant, *Lilium candidum,* native to Eurasia and widely cultivated for its white, trumpet-shaped flowers. Also called "Annunciation lily".

ma·dras (mə-dráss, -draáss, máddrəss) *n.* **1.** A fine cotton cloth, usually with a plaid, striped, or checked pattern. **2.** A light cloth, usually of cotton, used for curtains. **3.** A large kerchief of brightly coloured silk or cotton. [Originally produced in MADRAS, India.]

Ma·dras¹ (mə-draáss, -dráss). Also **Chennai.** Indian seaport and capital of Tamil Nadu State, regarded as the traditional burial place of St. Thomas. It was founded as Fort St. George on the Cooum estuary by the British East India Company in 1639. Its chief manufacturing products are bicycles, cars, cement, textiles, and leather products.

Madras². *adj.* With a very hot, spicy curry sauce: *chicken Madras.*

Madras hemp *n.* A plant, **sunn** (see), or its fibre.

mad·re·pore (máddri-pór, -pawr ‖ -pŏr, -pōr) *n.* Any of various corals of the genus *Madrepora,* including the reef builders of tropical seas. [French, from Italian *madrepora,* "mother-stone", referring to the manner in which polyps produce coral : *madre,* mother, from Latin *māter* + Latin *pŏrus,* tufa, from Greek *pōros†.*] —**mad·re·por·ic** (-pórrik) *adj.*

mad·re·por·ite (máddri-pawr-īt ‖ -pōr-) *n.* A sievelike structure that forms the inlet of the water vascular system in echinoderms. [MA-DREPOR(E) + -ITE.]

Ma·drid (mə-dríd; *Spanish* ma-thréeth). Capital city of Spain and of Madrid province. Built on the Castile plateau overlooking the river Manzanares, it is a cultural, commercial, and industrial centre, producing leather, textiles, and chemicals. Begun on the site of a Moorish fortress in the tenth century, it became capital under Philip II in 1561, and was a Republican stronghold during the Spanish Civil War (1936–39). Its fine buildings include the Prado art gallery.

mad·ri·gal (máddri'l) *n.* **1.** An unaccompanied vocal composition for two or three voices in simple harmony, following a strict poetic form, developed in Italy in the early 14th century. **2.** A contrapuntal part song, typically unaccompanied and with parts for five or six voices, using a secular text. This form was developed in Italy in the 16th century, and was popular in England in the 16th and early 17th centuries. **3.** A lyric poem with a pastoral, idyllic, or amatory subject, developed from the lyrics of the 14th-century Italian madrigal. **4.** Any part song. [Italian *madrigale,* earlier *madriale,* "(piece) without accompaniment", probably from Medieval Latin *mātrīcālis,* "of the womb", newly sprung from the womb, simple, from *mātrix,* womb, from *māter,* mother.] —**mad·ri·gal·ist** *n.*

ma·dri·lène, ma·dri·lene (máddri-len, -layn) *n.* A consommé flavoured with tomato, generally chilled. [Abbreviation of French *consommé madrilène,* from Spanish *madrileño,* of MADRID.]

Ma·du·rai (mád-yŏōrī). Formerly **Ma·thu·rai** (mát-yŏōrī). City on the river Vaigai in Tamil Nadu State, south India. Known as the "city of festivals and temples", it is a centre of Hindu pilgrimage, with the great temple complex of Sundareswara and Meenakshi, which has 1,000 exquisitely carved columns. The city is a cultural, craft, and market centre. It was the capital of the Pandya kingdom (5th century B.C. to 11th century A.D.) and part of the Hindu Vijayanagar kingdom (1378 to *c.* 1550).

Mad·u·rese (máddewr-éez ‖ -éess) *n., pl.* **Madurese. 1.** A member of a Malayan people inhabiting the Indonesian island of Madura. **2.** The Austronesian language of the Malayans of Madura and eastern Java. —**Mad·u·rese** *adj.*

ma·du·ro (mə-dŏór-ō) *n., pl.* **-ros.** A strong-flavoured cigar with a dark wrapper. [Spanish, MATURE.] —**ma·du·ro** *adj.*

mad·wo·man (mád-wŏōmən) *n., pl.* **-women** (-wimmin). An insane woman; especially, a maniac or lunatic or a woman who behaves like one. Not in technical usage.

mad·wort (mád-wurt ‖ -wawrt) *n.* **1.** A low-growing plant, *Asperugo procumbens,* native to Eurasia, having rough stems and small blue flowers. **2.** Any of several plants of the genus *Alyssum.* [Formerly believed to cure madness.]

Mae·an·der (mee-ándər). Now known as **Büyük Menderes.** Turkish river, flowing about 400 kilometres (250 miles) from the west of Afyonkarahisar into the Aegean Sea.

Mae·ce·nas (mī-sée-nass, mi-, mee-, -nəss) *n.* A patron, especially one generous to artists. [Gaius *Maecenas* (died 8 B.C.), Roman statesman, patron of Horace and Virgil.]

mael·strom (máyl-strom, -strŏm) *n.* **1.** A whirlpool. **2.** A strong eddy in a tidal current in a restricted, irregular channel. **3.** A state of great confusion or turbulence that resembles such a whirlpool in violence or power to engulf. [Early Modern Dutch *maelstrom,* "whirlstream" : *malen,* to whirl, grind + *stroom,* stream.]

Mael·strom (máyl-strŏm) *n.* A notoriously dangerous tidewater whirlpool, between the Lofoten Islands off the northwest coast of Norway. Preceded by *the.*

mae·nad, me·nad (mée-nad) *n., pl.* **-nads** or **-nades** (ménnə-deez). **1.** *Greek Mythology.* A woman member of the orgiastic cult of Dionysus. **2.** A frenzied woman. [Latin *maenas* (stem *maenad-*), from Greek *mainas,* "she who is mad", from *mainesthai,* to be mad.] —**mae·nad·ic** (mee-náddik) *adj.*

maes·to·so (mī-stō-sō, maá-e-, -zō) *adv. Music.* In a majestic and stately manner. Used as a direction. [Italian, majestic, from *maestà,* majesty, from Latin *mājestās.*] —**maes·to·so** *n. & adj.*

Maestricht. See **Maastricht.**

maes·tro (míss-trō; *Italian* ma-éss-trō) *n., pl.* **-tros** or **-tri** (-tree). A master in any art, especially a composer, conductor, or teacher of music. Often used as a term of address. [Italian, from Latin *magister,* master.]

Mae·ter·linck (máytər-lingk; *French* méttair-láNk, *Dutch* maátər-lingk), **Count Maurice (Polydore Marie Bernard)** (1862–1949). Belgian poet and playwright, and a leading member of the Symbolist movement. Among his plays were *Pelléas et Mélisande* (1892), on which Debussy based his opera (1902), and *The Blue Bird* (1909). He received the Nobel prize for literature (1911).

Mae West (máy wést) *n.* An inflatable life jacket. [After *Mae* WEST, whose generous figure it was thought to be reminiscent of.]

Mafeking. See **Mafikeng.**

maf·fick (máffik) *intr.v.* **-ficked, -ficking, -ficks.** *British.* To rejoice or celebrate with boisterous public demonstrations. No longer in current usage. [Back-formation from *Mafeking,* MAFIKENG, referring to the celebration of the raising of the siege there (1900).]

Ma·fi·a, Maf·fi·a (máffi-ə ‖ maáfi-) *n.* **1.** An international criminal organisation active, especially in Italy and the United States, since the late 19th century. Preceded by *the.* Compare **Black Hand, Camorra, Cosa Nostra. 2.** A secret terrorist organisation in Sicily, operating since the early 19th century in opposition to legal authority. Preceded by *the.* **3.** Any organisation using terrorist methods to control an activity. **4.** *Often small* **m.** Any exclusive group or clique, especially an influential one. [Italian (Sicilian dialect) *mafia,* boldness, "boasting", from Arabic *mahyah,* boasting.]

Ma·fi·keng (máffi-keng, -king). Formerly **Ma·fe·king** (-king). A town in the North West province of South Africa. The 217-day siege and relief of Mafeking (October 1899–May 1990) was one of the celebrated events of the Boer War.

Ma·fi·o·so (máffi-ố-sō ‖ maáfi-) *n., pl.* **-si** (-see). A member of the Mafia. [Italian.]

mag (mag) *n. British Informal.* A magazine or periodical.

mag. 1. magnetism. **2.** magnitude.

mag·a·zine (mággə-zéen, -zeen) *n. Abbr.* **mag. 1. a.** A place where goods are stored; especially, a building (as in a fort) or storeroom (as on a warship) where ammunition is stored. **b.** The contents of a storehouse; a stock of ammunition. **2.** A publication appearing at regular intervals, containing articles, stories, photographs, or other features. **3. a.** A compartment in some types of firearms, often a small, detachable box, in which cartridges are held to be fed into the firing chamber. **b.** A compartment in a camera in which rolls or cartridges of film are held for feeding through the exposure mechanism. **c.** Any of various other compartments attached to machines, for storing or supplying necessary material. [Old French *magazin*, storehouse, from Italian *magazzino*, from Arabic *makhāzin*, plural of *makhzan*, storehouse, from *khazana*, to store up.]

mag·da·len (mágdə-lin) *n.* Also **mag·da·lene** (-leen). *Rare.* **1.** A reformed prostitute. **2.** A reformatory for prostitutes. [From MARY MAGDALENE.]

Mag·da·le·ni·an (mágdə-léeni-ən) *adj. Archaeology.* Of, belonging to, or designating the last upper Palaeolithic culture of Europe, and characterised by cave art and decorative work in bone and ivory. [French *magdalénien*, from *La Madeleine*, village in Dordogne, France, near which artefacts were found.]

Mag·de·burg (mágdə-burg; *German* mákdə-boork). City in eastern Germany, built on the river Elbe. It became self-governing (13th century) and was a leader of the Hanseatic League.

mage (mayj) *n. Archaic.* **1.** A magician. **2.** One of the Magi. [Middle English, from Latin *magus*, sorcerer. See **Magi**.]

Ma·gel·lan (mə-géllən, -jéllən), **Ferdinand** (*c.* 1480–1521). Portuguese navigator. He was financed by Charles V of Spain (1519) to find a westward route to the Moluccas. Magellan crossed the Atlantic without charts and was blown by storms into the strait that carries his name (1520). He crossed the ocean, which he named the Pacific, reaching the Marianas and the Philippines, where he was killed fighting for the King of Cebu. One of his ships arrived back in Sanlúcar (1522), thereby completing the world's first circumnavigation.

Magellan, Strait of A passage between the Atlantic and Pacific Oceans, between mainland South America and Tierra del Fuego. It is some 530 kilometres (330 miles) long and a maximum of only 24 kilometres (15 miles) wide. Magellan discovered it in 1520.

Mag·el·lan·ic cloud (mággi-lánnik, máji-) *n.* Either of two small companion galaxies of the Milky Way, faintly visible near the south celestial pole. They are the *Large Magellanic Cloud* (Nubecula Major) and the *Small Magellanic Cloud* (Nubecula Minor). [After Ferdinand MAGELLAN.]

Ma·gen Da·vid, Mo·gen Da·vid (máwgən dáyvid, má'agən, dá'avid, dáwvid) *n.* The **Star of David** (*see*). [Hebrew *māgen Dāwid*, shield of (King) David.]

ma·gen·ta (mə-jéntə) *n.* **1.** A coal-tar dye, **fuchsine** (*see*). **2.** Moderate to vivid purplish red, or strong reddish purple; one of the subtractive primaries. See **primary colour**. [After the bloodshed of the battle of MAGENTA : the dye was discovered that same year (1859).]

Magenta. North Italian town, to the west of Milan, in Lombardy. The nearby river Ticino was the scene of the decisive French-Sardinian victory over the Austrians in 1859.

mag·gie (mággi) *n. Australian Informal.* A magpie.

Mag·gi·o·re, Lake (máji-áwri, maj-). *Italian* **Lago Maggiore** or **Ver·ba·no** (vair-bá'anō). Italy's second largest lake, on the Swiss border. Lying in the Alpine foothills, it is a tourist area with resorts such as Locarno and Stresa.

mag·got (mággət) *n.* **1.** The legless, soft-bodied larva of any of various insects of the order Diptera, especially of the housefly and the bluebottle, usually found in decaying matter or as a parasite. **2.** *Rare.* An extravagant notion; a whim. [Middle English *magot, maked*, earlier *maddock, madhek*, from Old Norse *mathkr*.]

mag·got·y (mággəti) *adj.* **1.** Infested with maggots. **2.** *Rare.* Full of strange whims. **3.** *Australian Informal.* Angry.

Ma·ghreb or **Ma·ghrib** (mág-reb, -rib, múggrəb). *Arabic* **Djezira el Maghreb.** Region of northwest Africa comprising the coastlands and Atlas ranges of Algeria, Morocco, and Tunisia. Its Arabic name means "the western island", the island of land between the Sahara and the Mediterranean. —**Ma·ghre·bi, Ma·ghri·bi** (-ee) *adj. & n.*

Ma·gi (máy-jī) *pl.n. Singular* **Ma·gus** (máygəss). **1.** *Sometimes small* **m.** The Zoroastrian priestly caste of the Medes and Persians. **2.** The "wise men from the East", traditionally three in number, who travelled to Bethlehem to pay homage to the infant Jesus. Matthew 2:1–12. According to St. Augustine their names were Balthasar, Caspar, and Melchior. [Middle English, from Latin, plural of *magus*, sorcerer, from Greek *magos*, from Old Persian *maguš*.] —**Ma·gi·an** (máyji-ən) *adj. & n.*

mag·ic (májik) *n.* **1.** The art that purports to control or forecast natural events, effects, or forces by invoking the supernatural. **2.** The practice of using charms, spells, or rituals to attempt to produce supernatural effects or to control events in nature. **3.** The exercise of sleight of hand for entertainment; the use of deception to produce baffling effects. **4.** Any mysterious and overpowering quality that lends singular distinction and enchantment. ~*adj.* **1.** Pertaining to the supernatural; having to do with magic and its practice. **2.** Possessing distinctive qualities that produce unaccountable or baffling effects: *a magic wand.* **3.** *British Slang.* Wonderful; marvellous: *His new car is really magic.* ~*tr.v.* **magicked, -gicking, -gics.** To produce or make by or as if by magic. [Middle English, from Old French *magique*, from Late Latin *magica*, from Greek *magikē (tekhnē)*, the sorcerer's art, from *magikos*, pertaining to sorcery, from *magos*, sorcerer, from Old Persian *maguš.*]

Synonyms: magic, black magic, sorcery, voodoo, witchcraft, necromancy, alchemy.

mag·i·cal (májik'l) *adj.* **1.** Of or produced by or as if by magic. **2.** Having a mysteriously captivating quality. —**mag·i·cal·ly** *adv.*

magic bullet *n.* A drug or other medical treatment that will destroy a pathogen without side effects, as a magic bullet hits only what it is aimed at.

magic carpet *n.* A mythical carpet possessing magical powers that enable it to transport a person through the air.

magic eye *n.* A **photoelectric cell** (*see*).

ma·gi·cian (mə-jísh'n) *n.* **1.** A sorcerer; a wizard. **2.** A person who performs magic for entertainment or diversion. **3.** One whose skill or art seems to be magical: *a magician with words.*

magic lantern *n.* An early type of slide projector used to project the enlarged image of a picture. Also called "lantern".

magic mushroom *n.* A hallucinogenic mushroom, *Psilocybe semilanceata*, having a conical pileus with a sharply pointed umbo. Also called "liberty cap".

magic number *n. Physics.* Any of the numbers 2, 8, 20, 28, 50, 82, 126, that represent the number of neutrons, protons, or both, in strongly bound, exceptionally stable, and abundant atomic nuclei.

magic realism *n.* The realistic depiction of the magically surreal, as in the paintings of Magritte or the novels of García Márquez —**magic realist** *n.*

magic square *n.* A square arrangement of numbers such that the numbers in any row, column, or diagonal all add up to the same sum.

magilp. Variant of **megilp.**

Ma·gi·not Line (mázhi-nō) *n.* A 320-kilometre (200-mile) line of fortifications built by France along its border with Germany before World War II. It was thought to be impregnable but fell to the Germans in 1940 after they had bypassed it through Belgium. [After André *Maginot* (1877–1932), French minister of war.]

mag·is·te·ri·al (máji-stéer-i-əl) *adj.* **1.** Pertaining to a master, teacher, or person in a similar position of authority. **2. a.** Characteristic of a master; authoritative; commanding. **b.** Dictatorial; dogmatic; overbearing: *offended by his magisterial manner of giving advice.* **3.** Of or pertaining to a magistrate or his official functions. [Latin *magisterius*, from *magister*, master.] —**mag·is·te·ri·al·ly** *adv.*

mag·is·te·ri·um (máji-stéer-i-əm) *n.* The teaching authority of the Roman Catholic Church. [Late Latin, from Latin *magister*, teacher, MASTER.]

mag·is·ter·y (máji-stəri, -stri ‖ *U.S.* -sterri) *n., pl.* **-ies.** Also **ma·gis·ter** (mə-jístər). A substance or power in nature supposed by alchemists to be capable of effecting transmutation, such as the philosopher's stone. [Medieval Latin *magisterium*, from Latin, position of a master, from *magister*, MASTER.]

mag·is·tra·cy (máji-strə-si) *n., pl.* **-cies.** **1.** The position, function, or term of office of a magistrate. **2.** A body of magistrates. **3.** The district under the jurisdiction of a magistrate.

mag·is·tral (mə-jístrəl, máji-strəl) *adj.* **1.** Magisterial. **2.** In pharmacology, prepared or prescribed for a specific occasion. Compare **officinal. 3.** Principal; main: *the magistral line of fortifications.* [Latin *magistrālis*, masterful, from *magister*, MASTER.]

mag·is·trate (máji-strayt, -strət, -strit) *n.* **1.** A civil officer with power to administer and enforce law. **2.** A person conducting a magistrate's court, such as a justice of the peace. [Latin *magistrātus*, magistracy, magistrate, from *magister*, MASTER.]

magistrate's court *n.* In England, a minor court with summary jurisdiction presided over by a minimum of two justices of the peace or a stipendiary magistrate, that deals with minor crimes and local civil matters, and holds preliminary criminal hearings.

mag·is·tra·ture (máji-strə-tewr, -chər) *n.* A magistracy.

Ma·gle·mo·si·an (mágglə-mōzi-ən) *adj. Archaeology.* Of, designating, or pertaining to an early Mesolithic forest culture of northern Europe, characterised by wood-working tools and dugout canoes. [After *Maglemose*, Denmark, where evidence was found.]

mag·ma (mág-mə) *n., pl.* **magmata** (-mətə, -má'atə) or **-mas.** **1.** A mixture of finely divided solids with enough liquid to produce a pasty mass. **2.** *Geology.* Molten matter formed within the earth's crust or upper mantle, which may consolidate on cooling to form igneous rock. **3.** In pharmacology, a suspension of particles in a liquid. [Middle English, dregs of a liquid, from Latin, sediment, from Greek *magma*, unguent.] —**mag·mat·ic** (-máttik) *adj.*

Mag·na Car·ta, Mag·na Char·ta (mág-nə kártə) *n.* **1.** The great charter of English political and civil liberties granted by King John at Runnymede on June 15, 1215. **2.** Any document or piece of legislation that serves as a guarantee of basic rights. [Medieval Latin, "Great Charter".]

mag·na cum lau·de (mág-nə kōōm lów-day ‖ má'ag-, láw-, -də) *adv. Chiefly U.S.* With great praise. Used on university and college diplomas to designate the second-highest degree of academic distinction. Compare **cum laude, summa cum laude.** [Latin.]

Mag·na Grae·ci·a (mág-nə grée-shi-ə, -shə). The colonies of ancient Greece in southern Italy and Sicily in the eighth to fourth centuries B.C. [Latin, "Great Greece".]

mag·nan·i·mous (mag-nánniməss) *adj.* Noble of mind and heart; generous in forgiving; above revenge or resentment. [Latin *magnanimus*, "great-souled" : *magnus*, great + *animus*, soul.] —**mag·nan·i·mous·ly** *adv.* —**mag·na·nim·i·ty** (mág-nə-nímmiti), **mag·nan·i·mous·ness** *n.*

mag·na op·er·a. Plural of **magnum opus.**

mag·nate (mág-nayt, -nit) *n.* A powerful or influential man, especially in business or industry: *a steel magnate.* [Middle English *magnates* (plural only), from Late Latin *magnātēs*, plural of *magnās*, "great man", from Latin *magnus*, great.]

mag·ne·sia (mag-née-shə, mag-, -zi-ə, -zhə) *n.* **Magnesium oxide** *(see)*, especially when processed for purity. [Middle English, from Medieval Latin, from Late Greek *magnēsia*, name of various minerals, from *Magnēsia*, name of a metalliferous region of Thessaly.] —**mag·ne·sian** (-shən, -zi-ən, -zhən) *adj.*

magnesian limestone *n. Geology.* **Dolomite** *(see).*

mag·ne·site (mág-ni-sīt) *n.* **1.** A white, yellowish, or brown, mineral composed of magnesium carbonate, $MgCO_3$. It is used in the manufacture of refractory bricks. **2.** Any of several grades of magnesium oxide obtained from this material. [MAGNES(IUM) + -ITE.]

mag·ne·si·um (mag-née-zi-əm, mag-, -si-əm, -shi-əm, -zhəm) *n.* *Symbol* **Mg** A light, silvery, moderately hard, metallic element that in ribbon or powder form burns with a brilliant white flame. It is used in structural alloys, pyrotechnics, flash photography, and incendiary bombs. Atomic number 12, atomic weight 24.312, melting point 651°C, boiling point 1,107°C, relative density 1.74, valency 2. [New Latin, from MAGNESIA.]

magnesium carbonate *n.* A very light, odourless, white powdery compound, $MgCO_3$, used in a wide variety of manufactured products including inks, glass, dentifrices, and cosmetics.

magnesium hydroxide *n.* A white powder, $Mg(OH)_2$, used as an antacid and laxative, especially in milk of magnesia.

magnesium oxide *n.* A white, powdery compound, MgO, having a high melting point (2,800°C), and used in high-temperature refractories, electric insulation, semiconductor devices and in medicine as a mild antacid and laxative. Also called "magnesia".

magnesium sulphate *n.* A colourless, crystalline compound, $MgSO_4$, used in fireproofing, ceramics, matches, explosives, and fertilisers. The hydrate, $MgSO_4 \cdot 7H_2O$, is **Epsom salts** *(see).*

mag·net (mág-nit) *n.* **1.** A body that attracts iron and certain other materials by virtue of a surrounding field of force produced by the motion of its atomic electrons and the alignment of its atoms. **2.** An **electromagnet** *(see).* **3.** A person, place, object, or situation that exerts attraction, especially irresistible attraction. [Middle English *magnete*, from Old French, from Latin *magnēs* (stem *magnēt-*), from Greek *magnēs*, short for *Magnēs lithos*, "the Magnesian stone", from *Magnēs*, pertaining to *Magnēsia.* See **magnesia**.]

mag·net·ic (mag-néttik, məg-) *adj.* **1.** Of or relating to magnetism or magnets. **2.** Having the properties of a magnet; exhibiting magnetism. **3.** Relating to the magnetic poles of the earth: *a magnetic compass bearing.* **4.** Capable of being magnetised or of being attracted by a magnet. **5.** Operating by means of magnetism: *a magnetic recorder.* **6.** Exerting great powers of attraction: *a magnetic personality.* —**mag·net·i·cal·ly** *adv.*

magnetic bearing *n.* The angular direction from magnetic north.

magnetic bottle *n.* An arrangement of magnetic fields used to confine the plasma in a controlled thermonuclear reaction.

magnetic bubble *n.* A small, nonvolatile, cylindrical region of magnetisation in a thin film of material that can be manipulated by an external magnetic field and used to represent data in the memory of a computer.

magnetic character recognition *n.* A method of introducing printed or written information into a computer. The information is printed using magnetic ink and the resulting text is scanned with a *magnetic character reader*, which recognises each character by its magnetic outline.

magnetic circuit *n.* A closed path through which a magnetic flux can pass, analogous to a circuit through which a current flows.

magnetic compass *n.* An instrument using a **magnetic needle** *(see)* to show direction relative to the earth's magnetic field.

magnetic constant *n.* The permeability of free space. It has the value $4\pi \times 10^{-7}$ henry per metre. Also called "absolute permeability".

magnetic core *n. Computing.* A **core** *(see).*

magnetic declination *n.* The angle between the geographical meridian and the local magnetic meridian, in navigation indicated as degrees plus (+) to the east, or degrees minus (–) to the west, of the geographical meridian. Also called "declination", "magnetic variation".

magnetic dip *n.* The angle that the earth's magnetic field makes with the horizontal plane at any specific location. Also called "dip", "magnetic inclination".

magnetic dipole moment *n.* A measure of the strength of a magnet or coil expressed as the torque produced when the magnet or coil is set with its axis perpendicular to unit magnetic field. Also called "magnetic moment".

magnetic disk *n.* **1.** A computer storage device consisting of a stack of plates coated with a magnetic layer arranged so that they can be rotated at high speed as one unit. A read-write head can move radially on concentric tracks to enter or remove data from the store. **2.** A **floppy disk** *(see).*

magnetic domain *n. Physics.* A **domain** *(see).*

magnetic equator *n.* A line connecting all points on the earth's surface at which there is no magnetic dip. Also called "aclinic line". Compare **geomagnetic equator**.

magnetic field *n.* A condition in a region of space, established by the presence of a magnet, or of an electric current, and characterised by the existence of a detectable magnetic force at every point in the region.

magnetic field strength *n.* **1.** Magnetic intensity. **2.** Magnetic induction.

magnetic flux *n.* The total number of magnetic lines of force passing through a bounded area in a magnetic field.

magnetic flux density *n.* Magnetic induction.

magnetic force *n.* **1.** The force on a **magnetic pole** *(see)* in a magnetic field. **2.** The force on an electrically charged particle, or on an electric current, in a magnetic field.

magnetic head *n.* A device, as in a tape recorder, that converts electric impulses into variations in the magnetism of a surface for storage and subsequent retrieval. See **magnetic recording**.

magnetic hysteresis *n.* The failure of the **magnetisation** *(see)* in a body to return to its original value when the external field is reduced.

magnetic inclination *n.* **Magnetic dip** *(see).*

magnetic induction *n.* **1.** A vector quantity that specifies the direction and magnitude of magnetic force at every point in a magnetic field. Also called "magnetic field strength", "magnetic flux density". **2.** The temporary conversion of a piece of iron or of certain other materials into a magnet by a magnetic field.

magnetic ink *n.* Ink that contains particles of a magnetic material to enable it to be used in **magnetic character recognition** *(see).*

magnetic intensity *n.* That part of a magnetic field related solely to external currents as a cause, without reference to the presence of matter.

magnetic lens *n.* An arrangement of magnets, usually electromagnets, used to focus a beam of particles in such devices as an electron microscope or particle accelerator.

magnetic meridian *n.* A meridian passing through the earth's magnetic poles.

magnetic mine *n.* A marine mine detonated by a mechanism that responds to magnetic material, such as the steel hull of a ship.

magnetic mirror *n.* An arrangement of magnetic fields that can reflect charged particles, used to contain the plasma in thermonuclear reactors.

magnetic moment *n.* **Magnetic dipole moment** *(see).*

magnetic monopole *n.* A hypothetical elementary particle that has a single north or south magnetic pole, predicted theoretically.

magnetic needle *n.* A needle-shaped bar magnet usually suspended on a low-friction mounting and used in various instruments, especially in the magnetic compass, to indicate the alignment of a local magnetic field.

magnetic north *n.* The direction of the earth's magnetic pole, to which the north-seeking pole of a magnetic needle points when free from local magnetic influence. See **magnetic declination**.

magnetic permeability *n.* A characteristic of a medium in a magnetic field, that is equal to the ratio of magnetic induction to magnetic intensity. Also called "permeability".

magnetic pick-up *n.* A type of gramophone pick-up that utilises a coil in a magnetic field to receive vibrations from the stylus and convert them into electric impulses. Compare **crystal pick-up**.

magnetic pole *n.* **1.** Either of two limited regions in a magnet at which the magnet's field is most intense, each of which is designated by the approximate geographical direction to which it is attracted: *a north, or north-seeking pole; a south, or south-seeking pole.* **2.** Either of two variable points on the earth, close to but not coinciding with the North and South Poles, corresponding to the poles of the earth's magnetic field.

magnetic pole strength *n.* A measure of the effectiveness of a magnet, equal to the magnetic moment divided by the magnetic induction.

magnetic pyrites *n.* A mineral, **pyrrhotite** *(see).*

magnetic recording *n.* **1.** A recording of a signal, such as sound or computer instructions, in the form of a magnetic pattern on a magnetisable surface for storage and subsequent retrieval. **2.** A surface containing such a magnetic pattern. —**magnetic recorder** *n.*

magnetic resonance imaging *n. Abbr.* **MRI.** Imaging of parts of the body produced via NMR and used in medical diagnosis like CAT scanning or X-raying.

magnetic storm *n.* A severe but short-lived disturbance in the earth's magnetosphere field believed to be produced by currents of charged particles and gamma rays, resulting from abnormal solar activity and fluctuations in the earth's magnetic field.

magnetic susceptibility *n.* The ratio of the magnetic permeability of a medium to that of a vacuum, minus one. It is positive for a paramagnetic or ferromagnetic medium, negative for a diamagnetic medium. Also called "susceptibility".

magnetic tape *n.* A plastic tape coated with a magnetisable material such as iron oxide for use in magnetic recording.

magnetic variation *n.* **Magnetic declination** *(see).*

mag·net·i·sa·tion (mág-ni-tī-záysh'n ‖ U.S. -ti-) *n.* **1.** The process of making a substance temporarily or permanently magnetic, as by insertion in a magnetic field. **2.** The magnetic moment per unit volume induced in a body by an external field. **3.** The property of being magnetic.

mag·net·ise, mag·net·ize (mág-ni-tīz) *tr.v.* **-ised, -ising, -ises. 1.** To make magnetic. **2. a.** To exert a strong influence on. **b.** To attract strongly. —**mag·net·is·able** *adj.* —**mag·net·is·er** *n.*

mag·net·ism (mág-ni-tiz'm) *n. Abbr.* **mag.** **1.** The class of phenomena exhibited by the field of force produced by a magnet or by an electric current. **2.** The study of magnets and their effects. **3.** The force exerted by a magnetic field. **4.** Unusual power to attract, fascinate, or influence: *the magnetism of money*. **5. Animal magnetism** *(see)*.

mag·net·ite (mág-ni-tīt) *n.* A black mineral of iron oxide, Fe_3O_4, often occurring with titanium or magnesium, and an important ore of iron. A magnetically polarised piece of this mineral is called a **lodestone** *(see)*.

mag·ne·to (mag-néetō, məg-) *n., pl.* **-tos.** A small generator of alternating current using permanent magnets, used in the ignition systems of some internal-combustion engines. [Short for *magnetoelectric machine.*]

magneto– *comb. form.* Indicates magnetic properties; for example, **magnetometer, magnetohydrodynamics.**

mag·ne·to·chem·is·try (mag-néetō-kémmistri) *n.* The study of the interrelation of magnetic and chemical phenomena. **—mag·ne·to·chem·i·cal** *adj.*

mag·ne·to·elec·tric (mag-néetō-i-léktrik) *adj.* Pertaining to both magnetism and electricity, especially to electricity produced using magnetic fields. **—mag·ne·to·elec·tric·i·ty** *n.*

mag·ne·to·graph (mag-néetō-graaf, -graf) *n.* A magnetometer with three variometers that are equipped for recording three perpendicular components of a magnetic field. [MAGNETO- + -GRAPH.]

mag·ne·to·hy·dro·dy·nam·ics (mag-néetō-hīdrō-dī-námmiks, -néttō-, -di-) *n. Abbr.* **MHD.** *Used with a singular verb.* **1.** The study of electrically conducting fluids, such as molten metal or plasma, in electric and magnetic fields. **2.** A method of generating electricity by subjecting a plasma to a magnetic field so that the flow of free electrons constitutes a current. Also called "hydromagnetics", "magnetoplasmadynamics". **—mag·ne·to·hy·dro·dy·nam·ic** *adj.*

mag·ne·tom·e·ter (mag-ni-tómmitər) *n.* An instrument for comparing the magnitude and direction of magnetic fields. [MAGNETO- + -METER.]

mag·ne·to·mo·tive force (mag-néetō-mŏtiv, -néttō-) *n. Abbr.* **mmf, m.m.f. 1.** The agency that produces **magnetic flux** *(see)* in a magnetic circuit. **2.** The strength of such an agency, equal to the work required to carry a hypothetical isolated magnetic pole of unit strength completely round the circuit.

mag·ne·ton (mág-ni-ton, mag-néeton) *n.* A unit of magnetic moment applied to atoms, molecules, and subatomic particles, equal to $eh/4\pi mc$, where e is the particle's electric charge, m its mass, h Planck's constant, and c the speed of light; especially: **1.** The *Bohr magneton,* calculated using the mass and charge of the electron. **2.** The *nuclear magneton,* calculated using the mass of the nucleon. [French *magnéton* : MAGNET + -ON.]

mag·ne·to·plas·ma·dy·nam·ics (mag-néetō-plázmə-dī-námmiks, -néttō- -di-) *n. Used with a singular verb.* Magnetohydrodynamics. **—mag·ne·to·plas·ma·dy·na·mic** *adj.*

mag·ne·to·sphere (mag-néetō-sfeer, -néttō-) *n.* An asymmetric region surrounding the earth, extending from about 400 to several thousand miles above the surface, in which charged particles are trapped and their behaviour dominated by the earth's magnetic field. [MAGNETO- + -SPHERE.] **—mag·ne·to·spher·ic** (-sférrik) *adj.*

mag·ne·to·stric·tion (mag-néetō-stríksh'n, -néttō-) *n.* The deformation of a ferromagnetic material subjected to a magnetic field. **—mag·ne·to·stric·tive** *adj.*

mag·ne·tron (mág-ni-tron) *n.* A thermionic valve in which the electron beam is controlled by electromagnetic fields and generates high-power microwaves. [MAGNE(T) + -TRON.]

mag·nif·ic (mag-níffik) *adj.* Also **mag·nif·ic·al** (-'l). *Archaic.* Magnificent; grand. [Middle English *magnifyque,* from Old French *magnifique,* from Latin *magnificus,* "great in deeds" : *magnus,* great + -FIC.] **—mag·nif·i·cal·ly** *adv.*

Mag·nif·i·cat (mag-níffi-kat, mag- ‖ -kaat) *n.* **1.** The canticle beginning *Magnificat anima mea Dominum* ("My soul doth magnify the Lord"). The text is Luke 1:46-55. **2.** A musical setting of this text. **3.** *Small* **m.** Any hymn or song of praise.

mag·ni·fi·ca·tion (mág-ni-fi-káysh'n) *n.* **1. a.** The act of magnifying or the state of being magnified. **b.** The process of enlarging the size of something, such as an optical image. **c.** Something that has been magnified; an enlarged representation, image, or model. **d.** The degree to which something is magnified. **2.** In optics, the ratio of image size to object size.

mag·nif·i·cence (mag-níffi-sənss, məg-) *n.* **1.** Greatness or lavishness of surroundings or ornament; splendour; sumptuousness. **2.** Grand or imposing beauty: *the magnificence of the scenery.*

mag·nif·i·cent (mag-níffi-sənt, məg-) *adj.* **1. a.** Splendid; stately; grand. **b.** Lavishly decorated; sumptuous. **2.** Grand or imposing to the mind; marked by nobility of thought or deed; exalted. **3.** Outstanding of its kind; superlative: *a magnificent sunset.* See Synonyms at **grand.** [Latin *magnificent-,* variant stem of *magnificus,* MAGNIFIC.] **—mag·nif·i·cent·ly** *adv.*

mag·nif·i·co (mag-níffi-kō) *n., pl.* **-coes. 1.** A person of distinguished rank, importance, or appearance. Often used humorously. **2.** A nobleman of the Venetian Republic. [Italian, from *magnifico,* magnificent, from Latin *magnificus,* MAGNIFIC.]

mag·ni·fi·er (mág-ni-fī-ər) *n.* **1. a.** A magnifying glass. **b.** Broadly, any system of optical components that magnifies. **2.** A person who magnifies.

mag·ni·fy (mág-ni-fī) *v.* **-fied, -fying, -fies.** **—tr. 1.** To make greater in size; enlarge, amplify, or intensify: *Our problems are magnified by lack of time.* **2.** To cause to appear greater or seem more important; exaggerate. **3.** To increase the apparent size of, especially by means of a lens. **4.** *Archaic.* To glorify. **—intr.** To increase or have the power to increase the size or volume of an image or sound. **—See**

Synonyms at **increase.** [Middle English *magnifien,* from Old French *magnifier,* from Latin *magnificāre,* to make great, from *magnificus,* MAGNIFIC.]

magnifying glass *n.* A converging lens that enlarges the image of an object. Also called "magnifier".

mag·nil·o·quent (mag-níllə-kwənt) *adj.* Lofty and extravagant in speech; grandiloquent. [Latin *magniloquus : magnus,* great + *loquī,* to speak.] **—mag·nil·o·quence** *n.* **—mag·nil·o·quent·ly** *adv.*

mag·ni·tude (mág-ni-tewd ‖ -tōōd) *n. Abbr.* **mag. 1. a.** Greatness of rank or position. **b.** Greatness in size or extent. **c.** Greatness in significance or influence: *the magnitude of the achievement.* **2.** *Astronomy.* The relative brightness of a celestial body designated on a numerical scale, originally integers from 1 (brightest) to 6 (faintest visible), now extended to include negative integers, integers above 6, and decimals, with the scale rule that a decrease of 1 unit represents an increase in apparent brightness by a factor of 2.512. Also called "apparent magnitude". **3.** *Mathematics.* A property that can be quantitatively described, such as the volume of a sphere or the length of a vector. **4.** The force of an earthquake as measured on the **Richter scale.** [Middle English, from Latin *magnitūdō,* greatness, from *magnus,* great.]

mag·no·lia (mag-nŏli-ə, məg-) *n.* **1.** Any of various evergreen or deciduous trees and shrubs of the genus *Magnolia,* of the Western Hemisphere and Asia, many of which are cultivated for their showy white, pink, purple, or yellow flowers. **2.** The flower of any of these trees or shrubs. **3.** A creamy white tinged with pink. [New Latin, after Pierre *Magnol* (1638–1715), French botanist.]

mag·num (mág-nəm) *n.* **1.** A bottle holding the equivalent of two normal-sized wine bottles. **2.** The amount of liquid contained in such a bottle. **3.** An extremely powerful .44 calibre handgun. [Latin, "a big one", neuter of *magnus,* great.]

magnum opus *n., pl.* **magna opera, magnum opuses. 1.** A great work; especially, a literary or artistic masterpiece. **2.** The greatest single work of an artist, writer, or composer. [Latin, "great work".]

mag·nus hitch (mág-nəss) *n.* A knot, a clove hitch with one extra turn. [Probably from Latin *magnus,* "large".]

Magog. See Gog and Magog.

ma·got (maa-gŏ, mággət) *n.* A Chinese or Japanese figurine, usually grotesque and rendered in a crouching position. [French *magot, magog,* a monstrous figure, after the Biblical giant Magog.]

mag·pie (mág-pī) *n.* **1.** Any of various birds of the genus *Pica,* found throughout the Northern Hemisphere and noted for their chattering call. *P. pica,* the black-billed magpie, has black plumage with prominent white markings. **2.** Any of various birds resembling the magpie. **3.** Any of several piping crows and bell magpies of the genus *Gymnorhina,* of Australia. **4.** A person who chatters. **5.** *British.* A person who compulsively collects miscellaneous small objects. **6. a.** The outermost ring but one of a target. **b.** A shot that hits this ring. [*Mag,* a dialectal name for a chatterbox (probably from *Mag,* pet form of *Margaret*) + PIE (magpie).]

magpie lark *n.* A distinctively marked black and white bird, *Grallina cyanoleuca,* found throughout Australia and parts of New Zealand. Also called "mudlark".

Ma·gritte (ma-gréet, mə-), **René (François Ghislain)** (1898–1967). Belgian surrealist painter. From 1922, he produced dreamlike paintings showing ordinary objects in impossible situations.

ma·guey (mág-way, mə-gáy) *n.* **1.** Any of various plants of the genus *Agave,* native to tropical America; especially, any yielding a fibre or beverage. Also called "mescal". **2.** Any plant of the related genus *Furcraea.* **3.** The fibre obtained from any of these plants. [Spanish, from Taino.]

Ma·gus (máy-gəss) *n., pl.* **-gi** (-jī). **1.** A member of the Zoroastrian caste, the **Magi** *(see).* **2.** A wizard or sorcerer, especially in ancient times. **3.** Any of the **Magi** *(see).*

Mag·yar (mág-yaar, maág-; *Hungarian* mód-yaar) *n.* **1.** A member of the principal ethnic group of Hungary. **2.** The Finno-Ugric language of the Magyars, the official language of Hungary; Hungarian. **~***adj.* **1.** Of or pertaining to the Magyars or their language. **2.** Designating a loose-fitting sleeve or a blouse with sleeves that is cut as one whole with the bodice. [Hungarian *Magyar†.*]

Magyarország. See Hungary.

Ma·ha·bha·ra·ta (mə-háa-báarə-tə) *n.* Also **Ma·ha·bha·ra·tam** (-təm). A great epic poem of ancient India, written in Sanskrit and containing the Bhagavad-Gita. Compare **Ramayana.** [Sanskrit *Mahābhārata,* "the great story" : *mahā,* great + *bhārata,* story.]

ma·ha·ra·jah, ma·ha·ra·ja (máa-hə-ráa-jə, máa-ə-, -zhə) *n.* A king or prince in India, especially the sovereign of any of the former States. [Hindi *mahārājā,* from Sanskrit : *mahā,* great + *rājā,* king.]

ma·ha·ra·ni, ma·ha·ra·nee (máa-hə-ráa-nee) *n.* **1.** The wife of a maharajah. **2.** A queen or princess in India, especially the sovereign ruler of any of the former States. [Hindi *mahārānī,* from Sanskrit *mahārājñī : mahā,* great + *rājñī,* queen.]

Ma·ha·rash·tra (máa-haa-rásh-trə, -hə-, -ráash-). Western state of India bordering the Arabian Sea. Its rice-producing coastlands rise to the Western Ghats, beyond which lies the Deccan plateau, where cotton is grown. Mostly peopled by Marathas, the state was created when the former Bombay state was divided between its Marathi and Gujarati inhabitants. Bombay is the capital.

ma·ha·ri·shi (máa-hə-ríshi, -réeshi, mə-háar-i-shi) *n. Hinduism.* **1.** A great sage or spiritual leader. **2.** *Capital* **M.** A title or form of address for a guru or spiritual leader, preceding the person's name. [Sanskrit *māha,* great + *rishi,* sage.]

ma·hat·ma (mə-háat-mə, -hát-) *n.* **1.** In India and Tibet, any of a class of persons venerated for great knowledge and love of humanity. 2. *Capital* **M.** A Hindu title of respect for a man renowned for spirituality and thought to possess extraordinary powers. [Sanskrit *mahātman* : *mahā,* great + *ātman,* soul.]

Ma·ha·ya·na (maá-hə-yaánə) *n.* One of the major schools of Buddhism, active in Japan, Korea, Nepal, Tibet, Mongolia, and China. Compare **Hinayana.** [Sanskrit *mahāyāna,* "the great vehicle" : *mahā,* great + *yāna,* vehicle.]

Mah·di (maádi) *n.* 1. The Islamic messiah who it is believed will appear at the end of the world and establish a reign of peace and righteousness. 2. A title assumed by various Islamic religious leaders; especially, Mohammed Ahmed (1844–85), Sudanese leader of a religious war against the British and Egyptians. [Arabic *mahdīy,* "rightly guided (one)", past participle of *madā,* to lead rightly.] —**Mah·dism** *n.* —**Mah·dist** *adj. & n.*

Ma·hi·can (mə-héekən) *n., pl.* **-cans** or collectively **Mahican.** Also **Mo·hi·can** (mó-i-kən, mō-héekən, mə-). A member of a group or confederacy of Algonquian-speaking North American Indians that formerly lived between the upper Hudson River Valley and Lake Champlain.

mah·jong, mah·jongg (maá-jóng, -zhóng) *n.* A game of Chinese origin usually played by four persons. Tiles bearing various designs, are drawn and discarded until one player wins with a hand of four combinations of three tiles each and a pair of matching tiles. [Chinese *má jiàng,* possibly from *máquè,* sparrow (from the figure of a sparrow on a leading piece of one of the suits).]

Mah·ler (maálər), **Gustav** (1860–1911). Austrian composer and conductor. He was conductor at the Vienna State Opera House (1897–1907). He completed nine symphonies, some with voices, and the song cycles *Das Lied von der Erde* (1908) and *Kindertotenlieder* (1902). —**Mah·ler·i·an** (maa-léer-i-ən) *adj. & n.*

mahlstick. Variant of **maulstick.**

ma·ho·e (maá-hō-i) *n.* A New Zealand tree, *Melicytus ramiflorus,* yielding a useful fibre and a wood from which charcoal is produced. [Maori.]

ma·hog·a·ny (mə-hóggəni) *n., pl.* **-nies.** 1. a. Any of various tropical American trees of the genus *Swietenia,* valued for their hard, reddish-brown wood. b. The wood of any of these trees; especially, that of *S. mahogani,* much used for making furniture. 2. a. Any of several trees having wood resembling true mahogany. b. The wood of any of these trees. See **African mahogany, Philippine mahogany.** 3. Moderate reddish brown. [17th century : origin obscure.]

Mahomet. Variant of **Muhammad.**

Mahometan. Variant of **Muhammadan.**

Mahometanism. Variant of **Muhammadanism.**

ma·ho·ni·a (mə-hŏni-ə) *n.* An evergreen plant of the genus *Mahonia,* certain of which are cultivated as ornamental shrubs. [New Latin, after Bernard *McMahon* (1775–1816), U.S. botanist.]

Ma·hore (mə-hór, ma-ór). See **Mayotte.**

Ma·hound (mə-hównd, -hōónd). *Archaic.* Muhammad. Typically used derogatorily.

ma·hout (mə-hówt) *n.* In India and the East Indies, the keeper and driver of an elephant. [Hindi *mahāut, mahāwat,* from Sanskrit *mahāmātra,* "great measure", originally an honorific title : *mahā,* great + *mātra,* measure.]

Mahrati, Mahratti. Variants of **Marathi.**

Mahratta. Variant of **Maratha.**

Mähren. See **Moravia.**

mah·seer (maá-seer) *n.* Any of several large Indian freshwater fishes of the carp family, such as *Barbus tor.* [Hindi, probably from Sanskrit *mahāciras,* "big-head".]

mahzor. Variant of **machzor.**

Mai·a¹ (mí-ə, máy-ə). *Greek Mythology.* A goddess, the eldest of the **Pleiades** *(see).* [Greek, from *maia,* mother, nurse.]

Maia² *n.* The brightest star in the **Pleiades** *(see).*

maid (mayd) *n.* 1. A female servant. 2. A spinster. Used chiefly in the phrase *old maid.* 3. *Archaic & Literary.* a. A girl or young woman. b. A virgin. [Middle English *maide,* shortening of MAIDEN.]

mai·dan (mī-daán, ma-) *n.* In India and Southeast Asia, an open space in or near a town, used for parades, sports, or the like. [Urdu, from Arabic.]

maid·en (máyd'n) *n.* 1. *Archaic & Literary.* a. An unmarried girl or woman. b. A virgin. 2. A machine resembling the guillotine, used for executions in the 16th and 17th centuries in Scotland. 3. A racehorse that has never won a race. 4. In cricket, a maiden over. ~*adj.* 1. Of, pertaining to, or befitting a maiden: *a maiden blush.* 2. Unmarried. Said only of women: *a maiden aunt.* 3. Inexperienced; untried. Said especially of a soldier or weapons. 4. Designating a racehorse that has never won a race. 5. First or earliest: *a maiden voyage.* 6. Designating territory that has never been explored or captured. [Middle English *maiden,* Old English *mægden,* diminutive of *mægeth,* maid, from Germanic.]

maid·en·hair (máyd'n-hair) *n.* Any of various ferns of the genus *Adiantum,* having dark stems and light green, feathery fronds with fan-shaped leaflets. Also called "maidenhair fern". [From the fineness of the stems.]

maidenhair tree *n.* The **ginkgo** *(see).*

maid·en·head (máyd'n-hed) *n.* 1. The hymen. Not in technical usage. 2. *Poetic.* Virginity.

maid·en·hood (máyd'n-hōōd) *n.* The condition or time of being a maiden or virgin.

maid·en·ly (máyd'n-li) *adj.* Pertaining to or suitable for a maiden.

—**maid·en·li·ness** *n.*

maiden name *n.* A woman's family name before marriage.

maiden over *n.* In cricket, an over during which no runs are scored. Also called "maiden".

maid in waiting *n., pl.* **maids in waiting.** An unmarried woman attending a queen or princess.

Maid Mar·i·an (márri-ən) *n.* The Queen of the May in morris dances and May Day games.

maid of honour *n., pl.* **maids of honour.** 1. An unmarried noblewoman attending upon a queen or princess. 2. *U.S.* The chief unmarried female attendant of a bride. Compare **bridesmaid, matron of honour.** 3. *British.* An almond-flavoured custard tart.

Maid of Orléans. See **Joan of Arc.**

maid·ser·vant (máyd-servənt) *n.* A female servant.

Maid·stone (máyd-stən, -stōn). County town of Kent, southeast England, on the river Medway. Its main industries are paper-making and brewing, and it is a major market for hops and grain.

mai·eu·tic (may-óotik, mī-) *adj.* Also **mai·eu·ti·cal** (-'l). Pertaining to the Socratic method of bringing forth latent ideas through a logical sequence of questions and answers. [Greek *maieutikos,* obstetric, "bringing ideas to birth", from *maieuesthai,* to act as midwife, from *maia,* midwife, nurse.]

mai·gre (máygər) *adj.* 1. Not containing meat or its juices: *a maigre diet.* 2. *Roman Catholic Church.* Formerly, of or designating a day of abstinence on which only maigre food was permitted. [French, thin, from Old French, from Latin *macer,* thin.]

mail¹ (mayl) *n.* 1. a. Letters, packages, and other material handled in a postal system; post. b. *Chiefly U.S.* Postal material for a specific person or organisation: *I received my mail today.* c. *Chiefly U.S.* Material collected or processed for distribution from a post office at a specified time: *the morning mail.* 2. The postal system; the post. 3. A train, ship, or aircraft by which mail is transported: *The ship is a fast mail.* 4. *Capital* **M.** Used as part of the title of certain newspapers: *Daily Mail.* ~*adj.* Of, pertaining to, carrying, or used in the handling of mail: *mail delivery.* ~*tr.v.* **mailed, mailing, mails.** *Chiefly U.S.* To send by mail; post. [Middle English *male,* mailbag, from Old French *male,* pouch, bag, from Old High German *malha.*] —**mail·a·ble** *adj.*

mail² *n.* 1. Flexible body armour composed of small overlapping metal rings, interlocking loops of chain, or scales. See **chain mail, coat of mail.** 2. The protective shell or covering of certain animals, such as the turtle. ~*tr.v.* **mailed, mailing, mails.** To cover with mail. [Middle English *maille,* from Old French, from Latin *macula,* spot, mesh.]

mail·bag (máyl-bag) *n.* 1. A large canvas sack used for transporting mail. 2. A leather or canvas bag suspended from the shoulder, used by postmen. Also called "postbag".

mail·box (máyl-boks) *n. Chiefly U.S.* A **letter box** (see).

mail carrier *n. Chiefly U.S.* A postman.

mail coach *n.* A railway wagon designed to carry mail.

mail drop *n. U.S.* 1. Any receptacle for holding mail at the address of delivery. 2. A slot for the insertion of mail. 3. An address at which a person receives mail but does not reside.

mailed (mayld) *adj.* 1. Covered with or made of plates of mail. 2. Having a hard covering of scales, spines, or horny plate. Said, for example, of an armadillo or lobster.

mailed fist *n.* The threat of the use of force, as between nations.

mail·er (máylər) *n.* A person or device that addresses, stamps, or otherwise prepares mail.

Mail·er (máylər), **Norman (Kingsley)** (1923–). U.S. author. Concerned with political, moral, and social questions, he rose to prominence with a World War II novel, *The Naked and the Dead* (1948). His other books include *Why Are We In Vietnam?* (1967) and *The Armies of the Night* (1968), which won a Pulitzer prize, as did *The Executioner's Song* (1979). He has also written screenplays and biographies.

mail·ing list (máyling) *n.* A list of persons to whom advertising leaflets, brochures, or the like are to be posted.

Mail·lol (mī-ó, maa-yó), **Aristide** (1861–1944). French sculptor. He was noted for his large, classically influenced statues of female nudes.

mail·lot (mī-ó, maa-yó) *n.* 1. A coarsely knitted, stretchable jersey fabric. 2. a. A pair of tights or a leotard made of this material and worn for ballet or gymnastics. b. A bathing suit of this material, usually of one piece. [French, tight garment, originally a child's swaddling bands, from Old French, from *maille,* band of cloth, mail, from Latin *macula,* spot, mesh.]

mail·man (máyl-man) *n., pl.* **-men** (-men) *Chiefly U.S.* A postman.

mail order *n. Abbr.* **m.o., M.O.** 1. A request for goods or services that is received, and usually dealt with, through the post. 2. The system of ordering and receiving goods through the post.

mail-or·der firm (máyl-awrdər, -órdər) *n.* A business establishment that is primarily organised to promote, receive, and deal with requests for goods or services through the post.

mail·ship (máyl-ship) *n.* A ship carrying mail, and often passengers, regularly between two ports or countries; especially, that between South Africa and Britain.

mail shot *n.* A dispatch of promotional mail in bulk. [MAIL + SHOT¹ 7 (attempt).]

maim (maym) *tr.v.* **maimed, maiming, maims.** 1. To deprive (a person) of, or of the use of, a limb or bodily part; mutilate; disable; cripple. 2. To make imperfect or defective; impair. [Middle English *maymen,* to wound, from Old French *mahaigner*†.]

Mai·mon·i·des (mī-mónni-deez), **Moses ben Maimon,** also known as Rambam (1135–1204). Jewish doctor, rabbi, and philosopher. He codified Jewish laws and philosophy in such works as *The Mishneh Torah* and *The Guide to the Perplexed.*

main[1] (mayn) *adj.* **1. a.** Most important; principal; major. **b.** Being the largest or greatest in size, extent, or degree: *the main road.* **2.** Exerted to the utmost; sheer; utter. **3.** Of or pertaining to a continuous area or stretch, as of land or water: *the main ocean.* **4.** *Archaic.* **a.** Very great or considerable of its kind; remarkable: *"I am a main bungler at a long story."* (R.B. Sheridan). **b.** Highly important; momentous. **5.** *Grammar.* Designating the principal clause, verb, or phrase referring to the subject in a complex sentence. **6.** *Nautical.* Connected to or located near the mainmast: *a main skysail.*
~*n.* **1.** The principal, most important, or largest part or point: *"The main of life is composed of small incidents."* (Samuel Johnson). **2. a.** The principal pipe or conduit in a system for conveying switches, gas, oil, or other utility. **b.** *Plural.* The place from which switches, valves, or the like can be operated to control the supply of electricity, water, or gas to an entire building or area. **3.** Physical strength. Used chiefly in the phrase *might and main.* **4.** *Rare.* The mainland, as distinguished from islands. See **Spanish Main. 5.** *Poetic.* The open ocean. **6.** *Nautical.* **a.** The **mainsail** *(see).* **b.** The **mainmast** *(see).* —**in the main.** Mostly; on the whole; chiefly. —See Synonyms at **chief.** [Middle English, from Old English *mægen,* strength, and *mægn-* (used in compounds), strong, great.]

main[2] *n.* **1.** In dice playing, a throw of the dice. **2.** A series of cockfights consisting of an odd number of matches. [16th century : perhaps from the phrase MAIN CHANCE.]

main-brace (máyn-brayss) *n.* A rope that controls the movement of the main yard on a sailing ship.

main chance *n.* One's most advantageous opportunity.

main clause *n. Grammar.* A clause in a complex sentence, containing a subject, verb and sometimes an object and modifiers, capable of standing alone syntactically as a complete sentence.

main course *n.* The largest and usually most substantial course of a meal that consists of more than one course.

main deck *n.* The principal deck of a ship or other large vessel.

main drag *n. Chiefly U.S. Slang.* The principal street of a city or town.

Maine[1] (mayn; *French* men). Former province of northwest France, largely corresponding with the départements of Mayenne and Sarthe. Le Mans was its capital. The region is noted for its cattle.

Maine[2] (mayn). Largest state in New England, United States. The north and west are mountainous, the east hilly with a fragmented coast. There are more than 2,200 lakes. Maine is four-fifths forested. Tourism, timber, dairying, market gardening, fishing, and the making of paper and wood products are its chief industries. It has considerable mineral wealth. Augusta is the capital.

main·frame (máyn-fraym) *n.* **1.** A high-speed computer with a large memory store. Also called "mainframe computer". Compare **mini-computer. 2.** The central processing unit of a computer exclusive of peripheral and remote devices.

main·land (máyn-lənd, -land) *n.* The principal land mass of a country, area, or continent, as distinguished from an island or peninsula.

Main·land[1] (máyn-land). Also **Po·mo·na** (pə-mōnə). Largest of the 65 Orkney Islands. It has Stone Age and other prehistoric remains. The main town is Kirkwall.

Mainland[2]. Largest of the Shetland Islands. The main town is Lerwick.

main line *n.* **1.** A principal section of a railway line. Compare **branch line. 2.** *Slang.* A principal and easily accessible vein, usually in the arm or leg, into which narcotics can be injected.

main·line (máyn-līn) *v.* **-lined, -lining, -lines.** *Slang.* —*tr.* To inject (narcotics) directly into a major vein. —*intr.* To take drugs in this way. —**main·lin·er** *n.*

main·ly (máynli) *adv.* Most importantly; for the most part.

main·mast (máyn-maast, *nautical* -məst ‖ -mast) *n.* **1.** The principal mast of a vessel. **2.** The taller mast, whether forward or aft, of any two-masted sailing vessel. **3.** The second mast aft of any sailing ship with three or more masts.

main·plane (máyn-playn) *n.* **1.** Either of the wings of an aircraft. **2.** The principal supporting surfaces of an aircraft, including both wings.

main·sail (máyn-sayl, *nautical* -s'l) *n.* **1.** The principal sail of a vessel. **2.** A quadrilateral or triangular sail set from the after part of the mainmast on a fore-and-aft rigged vessel. **3.** A square sail set from the main yard on a square-rigged vessel.

main sequence *n.* A major grouping of stars, containing the Sun and 90 per cent of the known stars, characterised by an approximately uniform average increase of luminosity with surface temperature as represented by a single band on the **Hertzsprung-Russell diagram** *(see).*

main·sheet (máyn-sheet) *n.* The rope that controls the angle at which the mainsail is adjusted to take advantage of the wind.

main·spring (máyn-spring) *n.* **1.** The principal spring in a mechanical device, especially in a watch or clock, that drives the mechanism by uncoiling. **2.** A motivating force; an impelling cause: *He was the mainspring of the reform movement.*

main·stay (máyn-stay) *n.* **1.** A strong rope that serves to steady and support the mainmast of a sailing vessel. **2.** A principal support: *Agriculture is a mainstay of the economy.*

main·stream (máyn-streem) *n.* The prevailing current or direction of a movement, activity, or influence: *writers in the mainstream of 18th-century thought.*
~*adj.* Avoiding extremes; neither traditional nor avant-garde: *mainstream jazz.*

main street *n.* **1.** The principal street of an American town or city. **2.** *U.S. Capital* **M,** *capital* **S.** The culture of smug, materialistic, and provincial small towns. [Sense 2 influenced by *Main Street* (1920), novel by Sinclair LEWIS.]

main·tain (mayn-táyn, mən-, men-) *tr.v.* **-tained, -taining, -tains. 1.** To continue; carry on; keep up: *maintain good relations; maintain a custom.* **2.** To preserve or retain: *tried to maintain her composure.* **3.** To keep in a condition of good repair or efficiency: *maintain public roads.* **4. a.** To provide for; bear the expenses of: *maintain a family.* **b.** To keep in existence; sustain: *food to maintain life.* **5.** To defend or sustain; hold against attack. **6. a.** To declare to be true; defend against dispute: *The defendant maintains his innocence.* **b.** To assert in or as if in an argument; state; declare: *He maintained that he was innocent.* —See Synonyms at **keep, support.** [Middle English *mainteine,* from Old French *maintenir,* from Medieval Latin *manūtenēre,* from Latin *manū tenēre,* "to hold in the hand", support, know : *manū,* ablative of *manus,* hand + *tenēre,* to hold.] —**main·tain·a·ble** *adj.* —**main·tain·er** *n.*

maintained school *n.* In Britain, a school maintained by funds from the local authority, rather than by private money.

main·te·nance (máyntə-nənss, máynt- ‖ mayn-táynənss) *n.* **1.** The action of maintaining or the state of being maintained: *the maintenance of tribal custom.* **2.** *Law.* An interference in a lawsuit by someone who is a disinterested party. **3.** The act or work of keeping something in proper condition. Also used adjectivally: *a maintenance man.* **4. a.** The provision or means of support or livelihood: *maintenance of serfs by a lord.* **b.** *Law.* Financial support ordered by a court to be given by one person to another, as in the case of a divorced couple. In this sense, also *U.S.* "alimony". —See Synonyms at **livelihood.** [Middle English *maintenaunce,* from Old French *maintenance,* from *maintenir,* to MAINTAIN.]

Main·te·non (mán-tə-noN; *French* maNt-nón), **Marquise de,** born Françoise d'Aubigné (1635–1719). Second wife of Louis XIV. Her first husband, Paul Scarron, died in 1660. She married Louis in secret in 1684 after the death of the Queen.

main·top (máyn-top) *n.* A platform at the head of the mainmast on a square-rigged vessel.

main topgallant *n.* A sail or yard set from the topgallant section of a mainmast.

main topgallantmast *n.* The section of the mainmast immediately above the main topmast on a square-rigged vessel.

main topmast *n.* The section of the mainmast on a square-rigged sailing vessel between the lower mast and the main topgallantmast.

main topsail *n.* The sail that is set above the mainsail.

main yard *n.* The lower yard on a mainmast.

Mainz (mīnts). *French* **Ma·yence** (ma-yoNs). River port and capital of Rhineland-Palatinate, western Germany. At the confluence of the rivers Rhine and Main, it grew on an early Roman camp site (c. 13 B.C.), was the seat of the first German archbishopric (8th century), and was made Europe's first printing centre by Johann Gutenberg (15th century). An industrial and communications centre, it is also important in the wine trade.

mai·ol·i·ca (mī-óllikə, mə-yóllikə) *n.* A type of richly coloured and decorated pottery that is enamelled and glazed, especially as produced in Italy in the 16th century. [From *Majolica,* medieval form of MALLORCA where the ceramic style originated.]

mai·son·ette, mai·son·nette (máyzə-nét, máysə-) *n.* A self-contained unit of living accommodation, especially that occupying two or more floors of a larger building and having its own outside front door. [Diminutive of French *maison,* house.]

maî·tre d'hô·tel (méttrə-dō-tél, máytrə-) *n., pl.* **maîtres d'hôtel** (*pronounced as singular*). **1.** A head steward or butler, a **major-domo** *(see).* **2.** A **head waiter** *(see).* **3.** A sauce of melted butter, chopped parsley, lemon juice, salt, and pepper. [French, "master of hotel".]

maize (mayz) *n.* **1.** A New World grass, *Zea mays,* widely cultivated for animal feed and for its yellow cob, which may be cooked and eaten as a vegetable. Also called "Indian corn", "corn". **2.** Light yellow to moderate orange yellow. [Spanish *maíz,* or French *maïs,* probably from Taino *mahiz.*] —**maize** *adj.*

ma·jes·tic (mə-jéstik) *adj.* Also **ma·jes·ti·cal** (-'l). Having or exhibiting stateliness or great dignity; royal; dignified: *a majestic gesture.* See Synonyms at **grand.** —**ma·jes·ti·cal·ly** *adv.*

maj·es·ty (májə-sti) *n., pl.* **-ties. 1. a.** The greatness and dignity of a sovereign. **b.** The sovereignty and power of God. **2. a.** A royal personage. **b.** *Capital* **M.** *Abbr.* **M.** A title of or form of address for a sovereign monarch. Used with *His, Her,* or *Your: His Majesty's wish; Your Majesty.* **3. a.** Royal dignity of bearing or aspect; grandeur. **b.** Stateliness, splendour, or magnificence, as of appearance, style, or character; imposing quality. [Middle English *maieste, majeste,* from Old French *majeste,* from Latin *mājestās* (stem *mājestāt-*), authority, grandeur.]

ma·jol·i·ca (mə-yólli-kə, -jólli-) *n.* **1.** A type of pottery made, chiefly in the 19th century, in imitation of maiolica. **2.** Loosely, maiolica. [Alteration of MAIOLICA.]

ma·jor (máyjər) *adj.* **1.** Great in importance, rank, or stature: *a major writer; a major scientific discovery.* **2.** Serious or dangerous; requiring great attention or concern: *major difficulties; a major illness.* **3.** *Law.* Having attained full legal age. **4.** Designating the senior or older of two pupils with the same surname. Used especially in some British schools. **5.** *Chiefly U.S.* Designating or pertaining to the principal field of academic specialisation chosen by students in a college or university. **6.** *Logic.* More inclusive in scope; broader, as are the **major premise** and **major term** *(both of which see).* **7.** *Music.* **a.** Designating a scale or mode having semitones between the third and fourth and the seventh and eighth degrees. **b.** Equivalent to the distance between the tonic note and the second or third or sixth or seventh degrees of a major scale or mode: *a major interval.* **c.** Based on a major scale: *major key.* Compare **minor.**

~n. **1.** *Abbr.* **Maj.** *Military.* **a.** An officer of the British Army or Royal Marines ranking between a lieutenant colonel and a captain, equivalent in rank to lieutenant-commander in the Royal Navy and squadron leader in the Royal Air Force. **b.** An officer of corresponding rank in the U.S. and certain other armies. **2.** *Law.* One who has reached full legal age. **3.** *Chiefly U.S.* **a.** The principal field of academic specialisation of a student in a college or university: *His major is chemistry.* **b.** A student specialising in such a field: *a history major.* **4.** A **major premise** or **major term** *(both of which see).* **5.** *Music.* A major scale, key, interval, or mode.

~intr.v. **majored, -joring, -jors.** *Chiefly U.S.* To pursue academic studies in a major field. Used with *in.* [As adjective, Middle English, from Latin *mājor,* greater. As noun (in military sense), from French, shortened from SERGEANT MAJOR.]

major axis *n.* In geometry: **1.** The line intersecting an ellipse and passing through both its focuses. **2.** The longest axis of an ellipsoid.

Ma·jor (máyjər), **John** (1943–). British Conservative prime minister and party leader (1990–97). He was Chancellor of the Exchequer (1989–90) until replacing Margaret Thatcher as premier.

Ma·jor·ca (mə-jáwr-kə, -yáwr). Spanish **Ma·llor·ca** (ma-yáwr-kə, mə-). Largest of the Balearic Islands, Baleares province, Spain. Its northern mountains give it a mild climate and tourism is the economy's mainstay, together with agriculture, fishing, and mining. Palma is the capital and chief port. **—Ma·jor·can** *adj. & n.*

ma·jor-do·mo (máyjər-dṓmō) *n., pl.* **-mos. 1.** The head steward or butler in the household of a sovereign or great nobleman. Also called "maître d'hôtel". **2.** Broadly, any steward or butler. [Italian *maggiordomo* and Spanish *mayordomo,* from Medieval Latin *mājor domūs,* "head of the house", "mayor of the palace" : *mājor,* noun use of Latin *mājor,* greater + *domūs,* genitive of *domus,* house.]

ma·jor·ette (máyjə-rét) *n.* A **drum majorette** *(see).*

major general *n. Abbr.* **Maj. Gen.** *Military.* **1.** An officer of the British Army or Royal Marines ranking between a lieutenant-general and a brigadier, and equivalent in rank to a rear admiral in the Royal Navy and an air vice marshal in the Royal Air Force. **2.** An officer of corresponding rank in the U.S. and certain other armies. [French *major-général* : MAJOR (officer) + *général* (adjective), "of general rank".] **—major generalcy, major generalship** *n.*

ma·jor·i·ty (mə-jórrəti) *n., pl.* **-ties. 1.** The greater number or part: *the majority of the consumers.* **2.** The number of votes cast in any election above the total number obtained by the runner-up or all other votes cast. See **absolute majority, relative majority. 3.** The political party, group, or faction having the most power by virtue of its larger representation or electoral strength. **4.** The status of legal age when full civil and personal rights may be exercised legally, in Britain at 18, in various other countries at 21. **5.** The military rank, commission, or office of a major. [French *majorité,* from Medieval Latin *mājōritās* (stem *mājōritāt-*), the state of being greater, greater number, from Latin *mājor,* greater.]

Usage: *Majority* is used only with reference to estimates of number, and not for general statements of quantity: thus one may say *The majority of the strikers have decided to go back to work,* but not *The majority of the strike action has been unsuccessful.* In precise contexts, *majority* can apply to anything over 50 per cent, but it is more commonly used to mean "most", and often "almost all", where it is frequently preceded by an intensive, such as *vast* or *great.* The construction *greater majority* is used only with reference to a comparison of two specific numbers (i.e. two majorities) in careful English, but loosely it can be heard as an equivalent of *great majority* (i.e. "most of").

When *majority* signifies a specific number, it takes a singular verb: *His majority was five votes.* When it signifies the larger of two groups it (like such other collective nouns as *committee* or *jury*) may be singular or plural, depending on the sense: *The majority is determined* stresses the unity of the group in question, whereas *The majority are of different minds* stresses the individuality of the group's members. When discussing politics, speakers of British English can use *majority* to mean either the difference between the number of votes for the winner and the number of votes for the runner-up, or the difference between the number of votes for the winner and the number of votes for all other candidates combined. Speakers of American English tend to use *majority* for the latter sense and *plurality* for the former.

majority carrier *n.* The electrons in n-type semiconductors and the holes in p-type semiconductors that carry the majority of the current. Compare **minority carrier.**

majority leader *n. U.S.* The leader of the majority party in a legislative body. Compare **minority leader.**

majority rule *n.* A political doctrine and practice by which a numerical majority of the voters holds the power to make decisions binding on all the voters.

major league *n.* **1.** In the United States, either of the two principal groups of professional baseball teams: the **American League** or the **National League** *(both of which see).* **2.** Any league of principal importance in other professional sports, such as basketball or football. **—major-league** *adj.*

major orders *pl.n.* See **holy orders.**

major planet *n.* Any of the four planets, Jupiter, Saturn, Uranus, or Neptune, that are larger than Earth. Compare **terrestrial planet.**

major premise *n. Logic.* In a **syllogism** *(see),* the premise containing the major term.

Major Prophets *pl.n.* **1.** The Hebrew prophets Isaiah, Jeremiah, and Ezekiel. **2.** In the Old Testament, the books of these prophets.

major scale *n. Music.* A diatonic scale having semitones between the third and fourth and the seventh and eighth notes. Compare **minor scale.**

major suit *n.* In the game of bridge, a suit, either spades or hearts, of superior scoring value.

major term *n. Logic.* A term of a **syllogism** *(see)* that forms the predicate of the conclusion and the subject or predicate of the major premise.

Ma·ju·ba Hill (mə-jo͞obə). Also **A·ma·ju·ba** (ámmə-). A mountain in the Drakensberg range, South Africa. It was the scene in 1881 of the rout of 554 British soldiers by 150 Boers.

ma·jus·cule (májə-skewl || *U.S. also* mə-júss-kewl) *n.* A large letter, either capital or uncial, used in writing or printing. Compare **minuscule.**

~adj. **1.** Of or pertaining to such a letter. **2.** Written in such letters. [French *majuscule,* from Medieval Latin *(littera) mājuscula,* largish (script), from *mājusculus,* somewhat larger, diminutive of *mājor,* larger.] **—ma·jus·cu·lar** (mə-júss-kewlər) *adj.*

Ma·ka·lu (máckə-lo͞o). Also **Chomo Lonzo.** The world's fifth highest mountain, lying in the Himalayas of Nepal. Its higher peak, rising to 8 481 metres (27,825 feet), was first climbed in 1955.

Ma·kar·i·os III (mə-kaári-oss), **Archbishop,** born Mikhail Christodoulou Mouskos (1913–77). Primate of the Orthodox Church of Cyprus. He was deported by the British (1956) for alleged support of the EOKA terrorists. He returned in 1959 to become president.

make (mayk. *Note: the pronunciation* (mek) *is not considered standard.*) *v.* **made** (mayd), **making, makes.** *—tr.* **1.** To create; construct; form; shape: *make a statue.* **2.** To give a new form or use to: *make a stone into a weapon.* **3.** To cause to become: *That'll make him sorry.* **4.** To cause to acquire a specified characteristic or property: *make a stone sharp.* **5. a.** To cause to behave in a specified manner: *Heat makes a gas expand.* **b.** To compel: *make him obey.* **6.** To use or adopt for a specified purpose: *make Perth one's home.* **7.** To bring about; cause: *make trouble; make a noise.* **8.** To engage in: *make war.* **9.** To perform: *make a phone call.* **10.** To arrive at; come round to: *make a decision.* **11.** To form as one's own; acquire: *make a friend.* **12. a.** To score; achieve: *make a run in cricket; make two tricks in bridge.* **b.** To earn: *make money.* **c.** To manage to come within reach of; attain: *make the grade.* **13.** To confer rank upon: *made him president.* **14. a.** To put into proper condition; prepare: *make the bed.* **b.** *South African.* To cook or prepare: *making chicken for dinner.* **15.** To prepare and start: *make a fire.* **16.** To regard as the nature or meaning of something. Used with *of*: *What do you make of his behaviour?* **17.** To allow provision for; provide: *make room.* **18.** To be suitable for; serve as: *Oak makes good building material.* **19. a.** To constitute: *Twenty members make a quorum.* **b.** To add up to: *One and one makes two.* **c.** To amount to: *It makes no difference.* **20.** To be the completion or satisfaction of: *That makes my day.* **21.** To succeed in becoming a member of: *He didn't make the cricket team.* **22.** To calculate as being; estimate: *We make the distance 20 miles.* **23.** To reach or arrive at: *made Salisbury by sunset; made the train in time.* **24.** To develop into: *She will make a fine doctor.* **25.** To cause to be or seem: *The beard makes him quite distinguished.* **26.** To close an electrical circuit. **27.** *Slang.* To have sexual intercourse with. **28.** In some card games: **a.** To name (the trump). **b.** To win a trick with (a card). **c.** To shuffle (the cards). *—intr.* **1. a.** To give an appearance of doing something: *She made as if to shake my hand.* **b.** To behave or act in a specified manner: *make merry.* **2.** To head in a specified direction; set out: *a ship making for shore.* **—make after.** To chase or pursue. **—make away with.** To carry off; especially, to steal. **—make for. 1.** To move towards with haste. **2.** To attack or assail: *made for his throat.* **3.** To lead to; be conducive to: *Champagne makes for a good time.* **—make it. 1.** To arrange or come to a meeting: *Let's make it tomorrow; I can't make it on Friday.* **2.** *Informal.* To become successful: *Made it as a dancer.* **3.** *Slang.* To have sexual intercourse. Often used with *with*: *made it with a girl.* **—make it up.** To satisfy a grievance or debt. **—make like.** *U.S. Slang.* To imitate: *make like a bird.* **—make off.** To leave or run away in a hurry. **—make off with.** *Informal.* To take away; steal. **—make out. 1. a.** To discern or see, especially with difficulty. **b.** To decipher: *I can't make out her handwriting.* **2.** To understand or comprehend: *I can't make out what he is saying.* **3. a.** To write out or draw up: *She made out the invoices.* **b.** To fill in by writing: *make out an application.* **4.** To attempt to prove, show, or imply: *He makes me out to be a liar.* **5.** To get along; manage: *How is he making out in his new job?* **—make with.** *U.S. Slang.* To perform; produce. Usually followed by *the*: *Start making with the hard work.*

~n. **1.** The act or process of making. **2.** The style or manner in which a thing is made: *I dislike the make of this coat.* **3. a.** A manufacturing style. **b.** A specific line of manufactured goods, identified by the maker's name or the registered trademark: *a famous make of*

shirt. **4.** The physical or moral nature of a person: *Let's see what make of man you are.* **5.** *Rare.* The amount produced; the yield or output, especially of a factory. **6.** In cards: **a.** The act of naming trumps. **b.** The act of shuffling the cards. **—on the make. 1.** Applying oneself brashly to social or financial advancement. **2.** *Slang.* Seeking out a sexual partner. [Make (infinitive), made (past tense), made (past participle); Middle English *maken, mad, mad,* Old English *macian, macode, macod,* from Germanic.]

make believe *tr.v.* To feign; pretend.

make-be·lieve (máyk-bi-leev, -bə-) *n.* Playful pretence or fanciful belief, as in the conscious suspension of reality in a child's game. **—make-be·lieve** *adj.* **—make-be·liev·er** *n.*

make-or-break (máyk-awr-bráyk) *adj.* Liable to end in either complete success or complete failure: *a make-or-break policy.*

make over *tr.v.* **1.** To change or remake; renovate: *We made over the cellar into a playroom.* **2.** To change or transfer the ownership of, typically by means of a legal document: *He made the property over to his son.*

make-o·ver (máyk-ōvər) *n. Informal.* A transformation, as of someone's appearance.

mak·er (máykər) *n.* **1.** One that makes. **2.** *Law.* An individual who signs a promissory note. **3.** *Archaic.* A poet.

Mak·er (máykər) *n. Capital* **M.** God. Usually used with a possessive pronoun: *our Maker.* **—go to meet (one's) Maker.** To die.

make-read·y (máyk-reddi) *n. Printing.* The operation of preparing a forme for printing by adjusting and levelling the plates to ensure a clear impression.

make·shift (máyk-shift) *adj.* Used or assembled as a temporary or expedient substitute. **—make·shift** *n.*

make up *tr.v.* **1.** To create or put together by assembling parts or ingredients: *make up a prescription.* **2.** To prepare or organise for use: *make up the beds.* **3.** To apply cosmetics to (the face). **4.** To devise a fiction or falsehood; invent: *make up an excuse.* **5.** *Printing.* To arrange (type in columns or pages) ready for printing. **6. a.** To add up to or constitute. **b.** To make complete: *make up a foursome at golf.* **7. a.** To make good (a deficit or lack): *make up the difference.* **b.** To resolve (a personal difference or quarrel). **—intr.v. 1. a.** To apply cosmetics to the face. **b.** To apply theatrical make-up. **2.** To be reconciled after a personal difference: *Let's kiss and make up.* **—make up for.** To compensate for: *make up for lost time.* **—make up to. 1.** To act in a friendly or ingratiating manner towards. **2.** To make amorous overtures to.

make-up (máyk-up) *n.* **1.** The way in which something is composed or arranged; construction: *the complex make-up of UNESCO.* **2.** *Printing.* The arrangement or composition, as of type or illustrations, on a page or in a book. **3.** The qualities or temperament that constitute a personality; disposition: *Lying is not in her make-up.* **4.** Cosmetics applied especially to the face. **5.** The cosmetics, costumes, wigs, and the like, that an actor uses in playing a role.

make-weight (máyk-wayt) *n.* **1.** Something added to a scale in order to meet a required weight. **2.** A person or thing added to make good a deficiency or lack.

mak·ing (máyking) *n.* **1.** The act of one that makes or the process of being made. Often used in combination: *matchmaking.* **2.** A means of gaining success or realising potential: *The job will be the making of him.* **3. a.** Something made. **b.** The amount or quantity of something made at one time: *the largest making of pastry for the week.* **4.** *Often plural.* The materials or substances necessary for making or achieving something: *We have the makings of a fine team.* **5.** *Often plural.* Earnings or profits. **6.** *Plural. Chiefly U.S. Slang.* The paper and tobacco for rolling a cigarette. **—in the making.** In the process of being realised; potential: *a politician in the making.*

-making *adj. comb. form. Chiefly British Informal.* Indicates causing or producing a specified emotional reaction or condition; for example, **anxious-making, sick-making.**

ma·ko (máakō) *n., pl.* **-kos.** Any shark of the genus *Isurus,* such as *I. oxyrinchus.* [Maori.]

ma·ko-ma·ko (máakō-máakō) *n., pl.* **-kos.** A small evergreen tree *Arisfotelia serrata,* native to New Zealand, having large racemes of reddish flowers. [Maori.]

ma·ku·ta. Plural of **likuta.**

mal– *comb. form.* Indicates: bad, badly, not, or wrongly; for example, **maladminister, malodorous.** [Middle English, from Old French *mal-* (prefix) and *mal* (adverb and adjective), from Latin *mal-, male-* (prefix), *male* (adverb), ill, and *malus* (adjective), bad.]

Mal. 1. Malachi (Old Testament). **2.** Malay; Malayan.

Mal·a·bar Coast (mál-ə-bár). The southwest coast of India. It stretches from Goa in the north to Cape Comorin, and produces coconuts, rice, spices, and hardwoods.

Mal·a·bo (ma-láa-bō). Formerly **Santa Isabel.** Capital of Equatorial Guinea, and the chief town of the island of Bioko.

Ma·lac·ca¹ or **Me·la·ka** (mə-láckə). Seaport of Peninsular Malaysia and capital of Malacca state. Founded on the Strait of Malacca in about 1400, the city became one of the chief trading centres of the Far East. It was later colonised in turn by the Portuguese, Dutch, and British (1824), and its commercial importance declined with the expansion of Singapore.

Malacca² or **Melaka.** State of Peninsular Malaysia. Formerly one of the Straits Settlements, it consists mainly of swampy plains on the southwest coast of the Malay Peninsula, rising to low hills inland. Its main products are rubber, tin, rice, and copra.

Malacca, Strait of. Sea channel in Southeast Asia, between Suma-

tra and the Malay Peninsula. It is a major world shipping route and has been claimed by both Indonesia and Malaysia.

Malacca cane *n.* The stem of the rattan palm of Asia, used for walking sticks. Also called "Malacca". [After MALACCA.]

Mal·a·chi¹ (mál-ə-kī). A Hebrew prophet of the fifth century B.C., the last of the **Minor Prophets** *(see).*

Malachi² *n. Abbr.* **Mal.** A prophetic book of the Old Testament attributed to Malachi.

mal·a·chite (mál-ə-kīt) *n.* A green mineral, copper carbonate, $CuCO_3 \cdot Cu(OH)_2$, used as a source of copper and for ornamental stoneware. [French, from Old French *melochite,* from Latin *molochitēs,* from Greek *molokhitis,* malachite, "the mallow-green stone", from *molokhē,* variant of *malakhē,* mallow.]

Mal·a·chy (mál-əki), **Saint,** born Mael Maedoc ua Morgair (1095–1148). Irish churchman. He became Bishop of Connor (1124) and Archbishop of Armagh (1134–37), and founded the first Cistercian abbey in Ireland (1142). The "Prophesies of St. Malachy" are incorrectly attributed to him. His feast day is November 3.

mal·a·col·o·gy (mál-ə-kólləji) *n.* The scientific study of molluscs. [French *malacologie,* abbreviation of *malacozoologie;* New Latin *Malacozoa,* molluscs : Greek *malakos,* soft + -ZOA + -LOGY.] **—mal·a·col·o·gist** *n.*

mal·a·cop·te·ryg·i·an (mál-ə-kóptə-ríji-ən) *adj.* Of or pertaining to the Malacopterygii, a group of soft-finned fishes including the herring and salmon.
~*n.* A malacopterygian fish. Compare **acanthopterygian.** [Greek *malakos,* soft + *pterux* (stem *pterug-*), wing, fin + -IAN.]

mal·ad·just·ment (mál-ə-jústmənt) *n.* **1.** Faulty adjustment, as in a machine. **2.** *Psychology.* Inability to adjust one's personality to the demands of one's social environment. **—mal·ad·just·ed** *adj.*

mal·ad·min·is·ter (mál-əd-mínni-stər ‖ -ad-) *tr.v.* **-tered, -tering, -ters.** To administer inefficiently or dishonestly. **—mal·ad·min·is·tra·tion** (-stráysh'n) *n.* **—mal·ad·min·is·tra·tor** (-straytər) *n.*

mal·a·droit (mál-ə-dróyt) *adj.* Lacking dexterity; clumsy; awkward. **—**See Synonyms at **awkward.** [French, from Old French : MAL- + ADROIT.] **—mal·a·droit·ly** *adv.* **—mal·a·droit·ness** *n.*

mal·a·dy (mál-ədi) *n., pl.* **-dies. 1.** A disease, disorder, or ailment. **2.** Broadly, any unwholesome condition. [Middle English *maladie,* from Old French, from *malade,* sick, from Latin *male habitus,* "ill-kept", "in poor condition" : *male,* ill, from *malus,* bad + *habitus,* past participle of *habēre,* to have, keep.]

ma·la fi·de (mál-ə fídi, máalə) *adv. Latin.* In bad faith. Compare **bona fide. —ma·la fi·de** *adj.*

Mal·a·ga (mál-əgə) *n.* A sweet white wine originally from Málaga.

Mál·ag·a (mál-əgə). Seaport and capital of Málaga province, Spain. Founded in the 12th century B.C. by the Phoenicians on the coast of Andalusia, it became a Moorish city (711–1487) and is now a major resort of the Costa del Sol. It exports wine, almonds, dried fruits, and olives. Pablo Picasso was born here.

Mal·a·gas·y (mál-ə-gássi, -gáazi) *n., pl.* **-gasies** or collectively **Malagasy. 1.** A native of Madagascar. **2.** The Austronesian language spoken in Madagascar. **—Mal·a·gas·y** *adj.*

Malagasy Republic. See **Madagascar, Democratic Republic of.**

ma·la·gue·ña (mál-ə-gáyn-yə) *n.* **1.** A dance native to Málaga, a variety of the fandango. **2.** The music for such a dance. [Spanish, feminine of *malagueño,* of MÁLAGA.]

mal·aise (ma-láyz, mə-) *n.* **1.** A feeling of illness or depression. **2.** A vague feeling of unease. **3.** An unwholesome or undesirable condition or state of affairs: *Violence is a symptom of a malaise in society.* [French, from Old French : MAL- + *aise,* EASE.]

ma·la·mute, ma·le·mute (mál-ə-mōōt, -mewt) *n.* A powerful dog of a breed developed in Alaska as a sledge dog, having a thick grey, black, or white coat. Also called "Alaskan malamute". [Inuit Eskimo *Mahlemut,* name of the Alaskan tribe that bred the dog.]

Ma·lan (mə-lán, -láan), **Daniel (François)** (1874–1959). South African politician. Formerly a preacher in the Dutch Reformed Church (1905–15), he became an M.P. (1918), Nationalist Party leader (1934–54), and prime minister (1948–54). He introduced the country's first apartheid laws.

mal·a·pert (mál-ə-pert, -pért) *adj. Archaic.* Impudent in speech or manner; saucy; bold.
~*n. Archaic.* An impudent, saucy person. [Middle English, from Old French : MAL- + *apert,* clever, from Latin *apertus,* open, from past participle of *aperīre,* to open.] **—mal·a·pert·ly** *adv.* **—mal·a·pert·ness** *n.*

mal·a·prop·ism (mál-ə-prop-iz'm) *n.* **1.** A humorous misuse of a word by confusing it with one of similar sound; for example, "a shrewd awakening" instead of "a rude awakening". **2.** A word so misused. [After *Mrs. Malaprop* in Sheridan's play *The Rivals* (1775), from MALAPROPOS.] **—mal·a·prop·i·an** (-própi-ən) *adj.*

mal·a·pro·pos (mál-ápprə-pṓ) *adj.* Inappropriate; out of place.
~*adv.* In an inappropriate or inopportune manner. [French *mal à propos,* "not to the purpose".]

ma·lar (máy-lər ‖ -laar) *adj. Anatomy.* Of or pertaining to the cheekbone or the cheek.
~*n. Anatomy.* The cheekbone, the **zygomatic bone** *(see).* [Latin *mālāris,* from *māla†,* cheekbone, upper jaw. See **maxilla.**]

ma·lar·i·a (mə-láir-i-ə) *n.* **1.** An infectious disease characterised by cycles of chills, fever, and sweating, transmitted by the bite of a female anopheles mosquito infected with a protozoan parasite of the genus *Plasmodium.* Also called "paludism", "marsh fever". **2.** *Rare.* Bad or foul air. [Italian *mal'aria,* foul air (hence, also the

fever once erroneously associated with it) : *mal(a)*, bad + *aria*, air.]
—**ma·lar·i·al, ma·lar·i·an, ma·lar·i·ous** *adj.*

ma·lar·key, ma·lar·ky (mə-lárki) *n. Slang.* Exaggerated or meaningless talk; nonsense. [20th century : origin obscure.]

mal·ate (mál-ayt, máyl-) *n.* A salt or an ester of malic acid. [MAL(IC ACID) + -ATE.]

Mal·a·thi·on (mál-ə-thĭ-on) *n.* A trademark for an organic compound, $C_{10}H_{19}O_6PS_2$, similar to but less toxic than parathion and used as a garden insecticide.

Ma·la·wi (mə-láa-wi). Formerly **Nyasaland** (nī-ássə-land). Small, landlocked country in east central Africa. Mostly highland, it depends on agriculture, exporting sugar, tobacco, tea, and groundnuts. However, it has untapped deposits of bauxite and coal and considerable hydroelectric potential. A British protectorate from 1891, the country joined Northern and Southern Rhodesia (now Zambia and Zimbabwe) in a federation (1953–63). Led by Dr. Hastings Banda, it became independent as Malawi in 1964 and a republic in 1966. Area, 118 484 square kilometres (45,747 square miles). Population, 10,140,000. Capital, Lilongwe.

Malawi, Lake. Also **Lake Nyasa** (nī-ássə). Lake of east central Africa, at the southern end of the Great Rift Valley. With an area of some 30 040 square kilometres (11,600 square miles), it is the third largest of Africa's lakes, and drains southwards via the river Shiré to the Zambezi. David Livingstone reached the lake in 1859.

Ma·lay (mə-láy ‖ máy-lay) *n. Abbr.* **Mal.** 1. A member of a people inhabiting much of Malaysia and Indonesia, and some adjacent areas. 2. The Austronesian language of this people. 3. In South Africa, a Muslim of Malay or Indonesian descent.
~*adj.* 1. Of or pertaining to the Malays or their language. 2. Of or pertaining to Malaya or Malaysia. —**Ma·lay·an** *adj. & n.*

Ma·lay·a, Federation of (mə-láy-ə). Former state in Southeast Asia. The British established trading centres on Penang (now Pinang) Island (1786) and Singapore (1819). In 1824 they formally acquired Malacca from the Dutch. The three territories were joined as the Straits Settlements (1926). By 1930 the British controlled the entire Malay Peninsula, and the independent Federation of Malaya was formed in 1957. See **Malaysia, Federation of.**

Mal·a·ya·lam (mál-i-áaləm, -ay-) *n.* A Dravidian language spoken on the Malabar coast in Kerala, in southwestern India.

Ma·lay Archipelago. Chain of islands off Southeast Asia separating the Indian and Pacific Oceans. Extending some 6 100 kilometres (about 3,800 miles) from Sumatra to Timor, it includes the Indonesian, Malaysian, and Philippine islands. The island of New Guinea (without the Bismarck Archipelago) is sometimes included.

Ma·lay·o·Pol·y·ne·sian (mə-láy-ō-pólli-néezh'n, -néesh'n) *n.* **Austronesian** *(see).* —**Ma·lay·o·Pol·y·ne·sian** *adj.*

Ma·lay Peninsula. Also **Kra Peninsula** (kraa) or **Malaya.** Peninsula of Southeast Asia. Extending south between the Andaman Sea and the South China Sea, it includes part of Thailand in the north, Peninsular Malaysia in the south, and the island of Singapore.

Ma·lay·si·a (mə-láy-zi-ə, zhi-, zhə). State in Southeast Asia. Formed in 1963, it comprised West Malaysia (the former **Federation of Malaya** and now called Peninsular Malaysia) and East Malaysia, the former British colonies of Sabah (North Borneo) and Sarawak on the northwest coast of Borneo, now called by their original names. Singapore seceded in 1965. Generally mountainous, with much tropical rain forest, Malaysia is the world's leading producer of tin and natural rubber, and Sabah and Sarawak have valuable oilfields. Tension between the Malay (44 per cent) and Chinese (36 per cent) populations has contributed to a history of political unrest. Area, 329 749 square kilometres (127,317 square miles). Population, 20,570,000. Capital, Kuala Lumpur.

Mal·colm III (mál-kəm), also known as Malcolm Canmore (1031–93). King of Scotland (1057–93). He was the son of Duncan, and became king on the death of Macbeth (1057). He was killed at Alnwick while raiding England.

Malcolm X, born Malcolm Little; also known as El Hajj Malik El-Shabass (1925–65). U.S. black militant leader. Joining the Black Muslims (1952), he preached that Western society was inherently

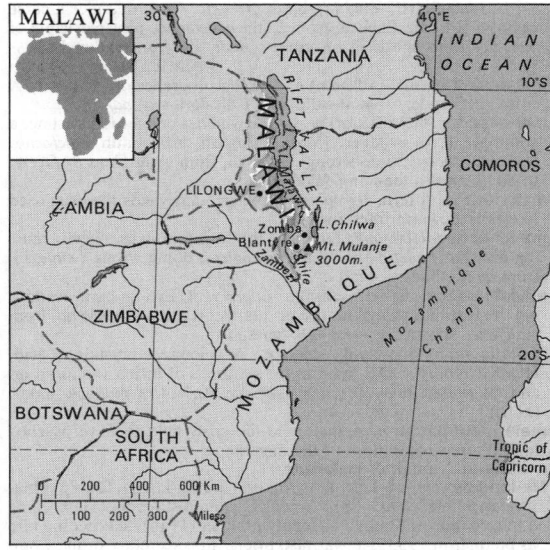

racist and that black people must create a separate society, by violence if necessary. Suspended from the Black Muslims (1963), he founded the Organisation of Afro-American Unity (1964) and was assassinated in Harlem while addressing a rally.

mal·con·tent (mál-kən-tent ‖ -tént) *adj.* Discontented with or in rebellion against established conditions.
~*n.* A discontented or rebellious person. [French : MAL- + CONTENT.]

mal de mer (mál də maír) *n.* Seasickness. [French.]

Mal·dives (máwl-divz ‖ mól-, -dīvz), **Republic of.** Formerly **Maldive Islands.** South Asian state comprising a group of some 2,000 coral islands in the Indian Ocean, 220 of which are inhabited. It was a sultanate (1100–1965), and from 1887 was under British protection. The sultanate gained full independence in 1965 and became a republic in 1968. Fishing, coconuts and tourism are the mainstay of the economy. Area, 298 square kilometres (115 square miles). Population, 260,000. Capital, Malé. See map at **Indian Ocean.** —**Mal·div·i·an** *adj. & n.*

male (mayl) *adj. Abbr.* **m, M, m., M.** 1. **a.** Of, pertaining to, or designating the sex that has organs to produce spermatozoa for fertilising ova. **b.** Capable of fertilising ova. Said of gametes. 2. Of or characteristic of the male sex; masculine: *male aggression.* 3. Virile; manly. 4. Composed of men or boys, or both: *a male choir.* 5. *Botany.* Bearing stamens but not pistils; staminate: *male flowers.* 6. Designating the projecting part of a machine, plug, or the like designed for insertion into a corresponding hollow part or socket.
~*n. Abbr.* **m, M, m., M.** 1. A male human or animal. 2. A plant having only staminate flowers. [Middle English, from Old French *male, masle,* from Latin *masculus,* diminutive of *mas,* male.]
—**male·ness** *n.*

ma·le·ate (máli-ayt) *n.* A salt or an ester of maleic acid. [MALEIC + -ATE.]

Male·branche (mal-brónsh), **Nicolas** (1638–1715). French philosopher. He tried to reconcile Cartesianism with religion.

male chauvinist *n.* A man who regards women as being innately inferior to men. —**male chauvinism** *n.*

male chauvinist pig *n. Abbr.* **M.C.P.** A male chauvinist. Used derogatorily.

mal·e·dict (mál-i-dikt, -díkt) *adj. Archaic.* Accursed.

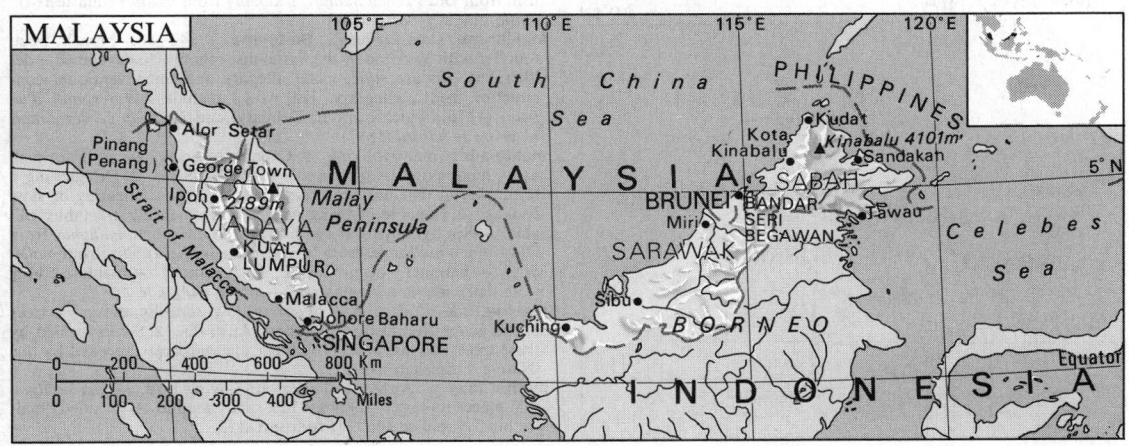

~*tr.v.* **maledicted, -dicting, -dicts.** *Archaic.* To pronounce a curse against. [Middle English, from Latin *maledictus,* past participle of *maledīcere,* to speak ill of, curse : *male,* ill, from *malus,* bad + *dīcere,* to say.]

mal·e·dic·tion (mál-i-díksh'n) *n.* **1. a.** The utterance of a curse. **b.** A curse. **2.** Slander. —**mal·e·dic·to·ry** (-dík-təri, -tri) *adj.*

mal·e·fac·tor (mál-i-faktər) *n.* **1.** One who has committed a crime; a criminal. **2.** An evildoer. [Middle English, from Latin *malefactor,* from *malefacere,* to do wrong : *male,* ill, from *malus,* bad + *facere,* to do.] —**mal·e·fac·tion** (-fáksh'n) *n.*

male fern *n.* A fern, *Dryopteris filix-mas,* that yields the drug used to treat tapeworm infestation.

ma·lef·ic (mə-léffik) *adj. Literary.* Producing or causing evil; causing disaster: *malefic arts.* [Latin *maleficus,* doing wrong : *male,* ill, from *malus,* bad + -FIC.]

ma·lef·i·cence (mə-léffi-sənss) *n. Literary.* **1.** Evil or harm; evildoing. **2.** Harmful or evil nature or quality. [Latin *maleficentia,* from *maleficus,* MALEFIC.] —**ma·lef·i·cent** *adj.*

ma·le·ic ac·id (mə-láy-ik, -lee´-) *n.* A colourless crystalline acid, HOOCCH:CHCOOH, used in the synthesis of resins and as an oil and fat preservative. [French *maléique,* variant of *malique,* MALIC (ACID).]

male menopause *n.* A male mid-life crisis held to have psychological effects like those of the menopause.

malemute. Variant of **malamute.**

Ma·len·kov (mál-ən-kof, -kov; *Russian* mullin-káwf), **Georgi Maximilianovich** (1901–88). Soviet Communist leader. He became a trusted aide of Stalin and deputy premier (1946), succeeding him as premier in 1953. He was also briefly first secretary of the Communist Party. He resigned in 1955 because of the failure of the government's agricultural policy. See also **Molotov.**

ma·lev·o·lent (mə-lévvələnt) *adj.* **1.** Having or exhibiting ill will; wishing harm to others; malicious. **2.** *Obsolete.* Having an evil influence: *malevolent stars.* [Latin *malevolēns* (stem *malevolent-*) : *male,* ill, from *malus,* bad + *volēns,* present participle of *velle,* to will, wish.] —**ma·lev·o·lence** *n.* —**ma·lev·o·lent·ly** *adv.*

mal·fea·sance (mal-féez'nss) *n. Law.* Misconduct or wrongdoing; especially, wrongdoing that is committed by one who has official obligations. Compare **misfeasance, nonfeasance.** [MAL- + Old French *faisance,* doing, from Medieval Latin *faciēntia,* from Latin *facere,* to do.] —**mal·fea·sant** *adj.* & *n.*

mal·for·ma·tion (mál-fawr-máysh'n) *n.* **1.** The condition of being malformed. **2.** An abnormal structure or form, especially a deformity present at birth.

mal·formed (mál-fórmd) *adj.* Abnormally or faultily formed.

mal·func·tion (mál-fúngksh'n) *intr.v.* **-tioned, -tioning, -tions. 1.** To fail to function. **2.** To function abnormally; perform imperfectly. —*n.* The act or an instance of malfunctioning.

Mal·herbe (ma-laírb), **François de** (1555–1628). French poet. He helped to formulate the norms of the French classical style.

Ma·li (maáli), **Republic of.** A landlocked West African state. The Sahara covers the north and savannah the south. The country's agricultural economy has been ravaged by drought, and its exports of cotton and groundnuts have to be supplemented by foreign aid, especially from France. The seat of several ancient empires, Mali was conquered by the French (1893) and as French Sudan became part of French West Africa. In 1959 it joined Senegal in the Mali Federation, but broke away to full independence the next year. Area, 1 240 192 square kilometres (478,841 square miles). Population, 11,130,000. Capital, Bamako.

mal·ic acid (mál-ik, máyl-) *n.* A colourless, crystalline compound, COOHCH₂CH(OH)COOH, that occurs naturally in a wide variety of unripe fruit, including apples, cherries, and tomatoes, and is used as a flavouring and an aid in ageing wine. [French *acide malique;* *malique* from Latin *mālum,* apple, from Doric Greek *malon,* variant of Attic *mēlon.*]

mal·ice (mál-iss) *n.* **1.** The desire to harm others, or to see others suffer; ill will; spite: *Her eyes glittered with malice.* **2.** *Law.* The intent, without just cause or reason, to commit an unlawful act that will result in harm to another or others. Often used in the phrases *malice aforethought* and *malice prepense.* [Middle English, from Old French, from Latin *malitia,* from *malus,* bad.]

ma·li·cious (mə-líshəss) *adj.* **1.** Resulting from or having the nature of malice: *malicious rumours.* **2.** *Law.* Motivated by or experiencing malice. —**ma·li·cious·ly** *adv.* —**ma·li·cious·ness** *n.*

ma·lign (mə-lín) *tr.v.* **-ligned, -ligning, -ligns.** To speak evil of; slander; defame.
~*adj.* **1.** Evil in nature or intent. **2.** Evil in influence; injurious; baleful. [Middle English *maligne,* evil, from Old French, from Latin *malignus,* from *malus,* bad.] —**ma·lign·er** *n.* —**ma·lign·ly** *adv.*
Synonyms: *malign, defame, traduce, vilify, revile, vituperate, slander, calumniate, libel.*

ma·lig·nan·cy (mə-lígnən-si) *n., pl.* **-cies.** Also **ma·lig·nance** (-lígnənss). **1.** The state or quality of being malignant. **2.** A malignant tumour.

ma·lig·nant (mə-líg-nənt) *adj.* **1.** Showing great malevolence; actively evil in nature. **2.** Highly injurious; pernicious. **3.** *Pathology.* **a.** Designating an abnormal growth that tends to metastasise. Compare **benign. b.** Threatening to life or health; virulent: *a malignant disease.*
~*n.* A Cavalier in the English Civil War. Used derogatorily. —**ma·lig·nant·ly** *adv.*

ma·lig·ni·ty (mə-líg-nəti) *n., pl.* **-ties. 1. a.** Intense ill will or hatred; great malice. **b.** An act or feeling of great malice. **2.** The condition or quality of being highly dangerous or injurious; deadliness.

ma·li·hi·ni (maáli-héeni) *n.* A newcomer, foreigner, or stranger among the natives of Hawaii. [Hawaiian.]

ma·lines, ma·line (mə-léen) *n., pl.* **malines. 1.** A thin, stiff, gauzy material woven in a hexagonal pattern. **2.** A fine lace, **Mechlin** (*see*). [French, from *Malines* (MECHELEN), Belgium, where the lace was made.]

Malines. See **Mechelen.**

ma·lin·ger (mə-líng-gər) *intr.v.* **-gered, -gering, -gers.** To pretend to be ill or injured in order to avoid duty or work. [French *malingre,* sickly, from Old French *malingre†* : perhaps MAL- + *haingre,* weak.] —**ma·lin·ger·er** *n.*

ma·lin·ke (mə-língki) *n., pl.* **-kes** or collectively **Malinke. 1.** A member of a people of west Africa related to the Mandingos. **2.** The language of the Malinke.

Ma·li·now·ski (mál-i-nófski), **Bronislaw (Kasper)** (1884–1942). Polish-born anthropologist. He believed that customs and beliefs have specific social functions. His works, based on his research in New Guinea and the Trobriand Islands, include *Crime and Custom in Savage Society* (1926) and *The Sexual Life of Savages in Northwestern Melanesia* (1929).

mal·i·son (mál-i-sən, -zən) *n. Archaic.* A curse. [Middle English *malisoun,* from Old French *maleison,* from Latin *maledictiō* (stem *maledictiōn-*), from *maledīcere,* MALEDICT.]

mal·kin (máw-kin, máwl- ‖ mál-) *n. British Regional.* **1.** A slovenly woman. **2.** A cat. **3.** A hare. [Middle English, diminutive of *Maalde,* Matilda.]

mall (mawl; *in sense 3, and in the names of certain thoroughfares,* mal) *n.* **1.** A shady public walk or promenade. **2.** *Chiefly U.S.* A street lined with shops and closed to vehicles. **3.** A game, **pall-mall** (*see*). [After The *Mall* in London, originally a pall-mall lane, shortened from PALL-MALL.]

mal·lard (mál-aard, -ərd) *n., pl.* **-lards** or collectively **mallard.** A wild duck, *Anas platyrhynchos,* the male of which has a green head and neck. It is the ancestor of most domestic ducks. [Middle English, from Old French *mallart,* probably from *maslart* (unattested) : *masle,* MALE + *-art,* -ARD.]

Mal·lar·mé (mál-aar-máy), **Stéphane** (1842–98). French poet, founder with Verlaine of the Symbolist school. He developed a deliberately obscure style, using allegory and unconventional construction and vocabulary. His works include *L'Après-midi d'un faune* (1876) (which inspired Debussy) and *Un coup de dés jamais n'abolira le hasard* (1897).

mal·le·a·ble (mál-i-əb'l) *adj.* **1.** Capable of being shaped or formed, as by hammering or pressure: *a malleable metal.* **2.** Designating a form of iron that has been toughened by gradual heating or slow cooling. **3.** Capable of being altered or influenced; tractable; pliable. —See Synonyms at **flexible.** [Middle English *malliable,* from Old French *malleable,* from Medieval Latin *malleābilis,* from *malleāre,* to hammer, from *malleus,* a hammer.] —**mal·le·a·bil·i·ty** (-ə-bílləti), **mal·le·a·ble·ness** *n.* —**mal·le·a·bly** *adv.*

mal·lee (mál-ee) *n.* **1.** Any of several low, scrubby, evergreen trees of the genus *Eucalyptus,* of western Australia. **2.** Scrub formed by these trees. **3.** *Australian.* The bush; the outback. Preceded by *the.* [Native Australian name.]

mallee fowl *n.* An Australian ground-living bird, *Leipoa ocellata,* that places its eggs to incubate in a sandy mound. Also called "mallee bird", "mallee hen". [From MALLEE.]

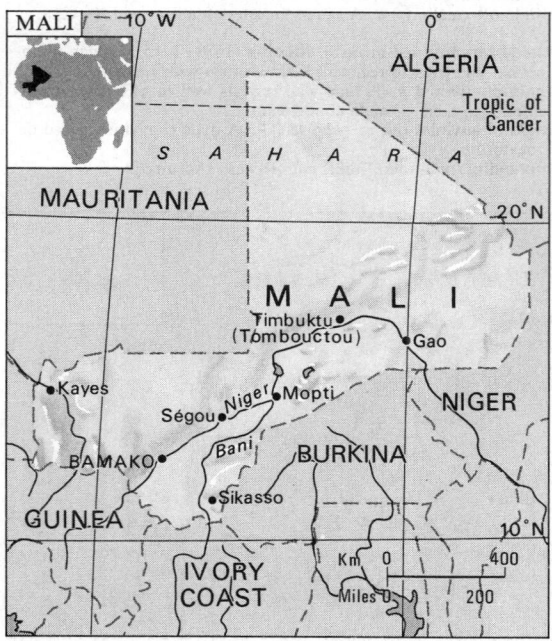

mal·le·muck (mál-i-muk) *n.* Any of several sea birds, such as the fulmar, the petrel, or the shearwater. [Dutch *mallemok*, fulmar : Middle Dutch *mal*, silly + *mocke*, thing.]

mal·le·o·lus (mə-lée-ə-ləss) *n., pl.* **-li** (-lī). *Anatomy.* Either of the two rounded protuberances on each side of the ankle, formed by a projection of the tibia or fibula. [New Latin, diminutive of Latin *malleus*, hammer (from the resemblance to a hammerhead).]

mal·let (mál-it) *n.* **1. a.** A short-handled hammer, usually with a wooden head, used chiefly to drive a chisel or wedge. **b.** Any of various specialised forms of this tool. **2.** *Sports.* A longer handled, similar implement used to strike the ball, as in croquet and polo. **3.** A light hammer with a spherical, often padded head, used to play instruments such as the vibraphone or xylophone. [Middle English *maillet*, from Old French, from *mailler*, to hammer, from *mail*, a hammer, from Latin *malleus*, hammer.]

mal·le·us (mál-i-əss) *n., pl.* **mallei** (-i-ī). The largest of three small bones in the middle ear. Also called "hammer". Compare **incus**, **stapes**. See **ear**. [Latin, hammer.]

Ma·llor·ca (ma-yáwr-kə, mə-). See **Majorca**. —**Ma·llor·can** *adj. & n.*

mal·low (mál-ō) *n.* **1.** Any plant of the widely distributed genus *Malva*, typically having pink flowers. **2.** Any of various related plants, such as the marsh mallow or musk mallow. [Middle English *malwe*, Old English *mealuwe*, *mealwe*, from Latin *malva*.]

malm (maam) *n.* **1. a.** A soft, easily crumbled limestone. **b.** Loam formed by the disintegration of such limestone. **2.** A mixture of clay and chalk used in making bricks. [Middle English *malme*, Old English *mealm*- (only in compounds).]

Mal·mö (mál-mö; *Swedish* -mö). Seaport in Sweden, situated on the Øresund opposite Copenhagen. It is a naval port and a shipbuilding and textile centre.

malm·sey (maámzi) *n., pl.* **-seys.** A sweet fortified white wine originally made in Greece, but now also produced in Madeira, the Canary Islands, the Azores, and Spain. [Middle English, from Medieval Latin *Malmasia*, alteration of Greek *Monembasia*, Greek seaport from which it was shipped.]

mal·nour·ished (mál-núrrisht) *adj.* Suffering from improper nutrition or insufficient food.

mal·nu·tri·tion (mál-new-trísh'n ‖ -nōō-) *n.* A lack of, or condition resulting from a lack of, adequate nutrition. It is caused by an insufficient or ill-balanced diet or by defective digestion or utilisation of food.

mal·oc·clu·sion (mál-ə-klōō-zh'n ‖ -klēw-) *n.* Failure of the upper and lower teeth to meet when the mouth is closed.

mal·o·dor·ous (mal-ṓdərəss) *adj.* Having a bad odour; ill-smelling. —**mal·o·dor·ous·ly** *adv.* —**mal·o·dor·ous·ness** *n.*

ma·lo·nic acid (mə-lṓnik, -lónnik) *n.* **Propanedioic acid** *(see).*

Mal·o·ry (mál-əri), **Sir Thomas** (died 1471). English writer. He was the author of *Le Morte d'Arthur* (published by Caxton, 1485), a collection of Arthurian romances adapted from French sources.

Mal·pi·ghi (mal-péegi), **Marcello** (1628–94). Italian physiologist. He was the first to use a microscope in the study of anatomy. He became physician to Pope Innocent XII (1691).

Mal·pigh·i·an body (mal-píggi-ən, -péegi-) *n. Anatomy.* A mass of arterial capillaries enveloped in a capsule and attached to a tubule in the kidney. Also called "Malpighian corpuscle". [Discovered by Marcello MALPIGHI.]

Malpighian layer *n. Anatomy.* The deepest layer of the epidermis, from which the outer layers develop.

Malpighian tubule *n.* Any of the excretory tubes leading into the rear part of the gut of arthropods. Also called "Malpighian tube".

mal·po·si·tion (mál-pə-zísh'n) *n.* An abnormal position, especially of a foetus or of a bodily part.

mal·prac·tice (mal-práktiss) *n.* **1.** Improper or negligent treatment of a patient by a doctor or surgeon, for example, resulting in damage or injury. **2.** Improper or unethical conduct by the holder of an official or professional position. **3.** An improper practice. —**mal·prac·ti·tion·er** (mál-prak-tísh'n-ər) *n.*

Mal·raux (mal-rṓ), **André** (1901–76). French writer and political figure. Under de Gaulle's Fifth Republic he served as Minister of Information (1945–46) and Minister for Culture (1959–69). His books include *La Condition humaine* (1933), *Le Temps du mépris* (1935), and an autobiography, *Antimémoires* (1967).

malt (mawlt ‖ molt) *n.* **1.** Grain, usually barley, that has been allowed to sprout, used chiefly in brewing and distilling. **2. Malt liquor** *(see).* **3.** A whisky that is made from malt and not blended with grain spirit. **4.** *Informal.* Malted milk. —*v.* **malted, malting, malts.** —*tr.* **1.** To process (grain) into malt. **2.** To treat or to mix with malt or a malt extract. —*intr.* To become malt. [Middle English, Old English *mealt*.] —**malt·y** *adj.*

Mal·ta (máwltə ‖ móltə), **Republic of.** Mediterranean state comprising the islands of Malta, Gozo, and Comino, and two uninhabited islets. Its strategic value led to a series of foreign invasions, starting with that of the Phoenicians before 1000 B.C., and it became a British colony (1814). A naval base was built on Grand Harbour, and during World War II the Maltese people were awarded the George Cross for gallantry under bombardment. Malta became an independent Commonwealth republic in 1974 and in 1979 the naval base closed. The economy now depends on shipping, tourism, and light industries. Area, 316 square kilometres (122 square miles). Population, 370,000. Capital, Valletta.

Malta fever *n.* **Brucellosis** *(see).*

mal·tase (máwl-tayz, -tayss ‖ mól-) *n.* An enzyme that hydrolyses maltose to glucose.

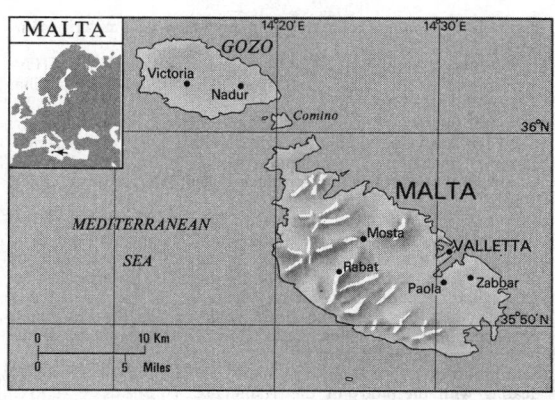

mal·ted milk (máwltid ‖ móltid) *n.* **1.** A soluble powder made of dried milk, malted barley, and wheat flour. **2.** A beverage made by mixing milk with this powder. In this sense, also called "malt", "malted".

Mal·tese (máwl-téez ‖ mól-, -téess) *adj.* Of or pertaining to Malta, its inhabitants, or the language spoken in Malta. —*n., pl.* **Maltese.** **1.** A native or inhabitant of Malta. **2.** The language spoken in Malta, a dialect of North Arabic with elements of Italian. **3.** A Maltese dog. **4.** A Maltese cat.

Maltese cat *n.* A North American domestic cat with short, silky, bluish-grey fur.

Maltese cross *n.* A cross having the form of four triangles, often with the outer edges indented, placed with their points towards the centre of a circle.

Maltese dog *n.* A dog of a toy breed, probably originating in Malta, having a long, silky, white coat, short legs, and a tail arched over the back. Also called "Maltese", "Maltese poodle", "Maltese terrier".

mal·tha (mál-thə) *n.* **1.** A black, viscous natural bitumen. **2.** Any of certain mineral waxes composed of mixtures of hydrocarbons. [Latin, from Greek *maltha*, a mixture of wax and pitch.]

malt house *n.* A building where malt is made or stored. Also called "malting".

Mal·thus (mál-thəss), **Thomas Robert** (1766–1834). British economist. He wrote *Essay on the Principle of Population* (1798), arguing that a population without planning increased faster than food production. His ideas were used to justify birth control. —**Mal·thu·si·an** (mal-théw-zi-ən, -thōō-) *n. & adj.* —**Mal·thu·si·an·ism** *n.*

malt liquor *n.* Any alcoholic drink, such as beer, brewed from malt.

mal·tose (máwl-tōz ‖ mól-, -tōss) *n.* A sugar, $C_{12}H_{22}O_{11}$, formed during the digestion of starch and also occurring in germinating cereal grains. Also called "malt sugar".

mal·treat (mál-tréet) *tr.v.* **-treated, -treating, -treats.** To treat cruelly; handle roughly. See Synonyms at **abuse**. [French *maltraiter* : MAL- + *traiter*, to TREAT.] —**mal·treat·ment** *n.*

malt·ster (máwlt-stər ‖ mólt-) *n.* One employed to make malt. [Middle English : MALT + -STER.]

mal·va·ceous (mal-váyshəss) *adj.* Of or pertaining to the Malvaceae, a family of flowering plants that includes the mallow, cotton, and hollyhock. [Latin *malvaceus*, from *malva*, MALLOW.]

mal·va·si·a (mál-və-sée-ə) *n.* **1.** A grape from which malmsey wine is made. **2.** Malmsey wine. Also called "malvoisie". [Italian, from Medieval Greek *Monemvasia*, MALMSEY.] —**mal·va·si·an** *adj.*

Mal·vern (máwl-vərn ‖ mól-, *locally also* máw-). Spa in west central England, in the Malvern Hills, in Worcestershire. It is the site of an important annual drama and music festival.

mal·ver·sa·tion (mál-vor-sáysh'n) *n.* Misconduct committed while in public office. [Old French, from *malverser*, to misbehave, from Latin *male versāri* : *male*, ill, from *malus*, bad + *versāri*, to behave.]

Malvinas, Islas. See **Falkland Islands**.

mal·voi·sie (mál-voy-zi, -və-) *n.* Malmsey wine, or a type of grape from which it is made; malvasia. [Middle English *malvesie*, from Old French, from Medieval Greek *Monemvasia*, MALVASIA.]

mam (mam) *n. British Regional.* Mother. Used familiarly, especially by children.

mama. *Chiefly U.S.* Variant of **mamma**.

mam·ba (mámbə) *n.* Any of several venomous arboreal snakes of the genus *Dendroaspis*, found in equatorial and southern Africa; especially, *D. angusticeps*, a green tree snake. [Zulu *im-amba*.]

mam·bo (mámbō) *n., pl.* **-bos.** **1.** A dance of Latin American origin, resembling the rumba. **2.** The music for this dance, in 4/4 time. —*intr.v.* **mamboed, -boing, -boes.** To dance the mambo. [American Spanish, from Haitian Creole *mambo*, a voodoo priestess.]

mam·e·lon (mámm'l-ən) *n.* A small, rounded hill. [French, "nipple", from *mamelle*, breast. See **mamilla**.]

Mam·e·luke (mámmi-lōōk ‖ -lewk) *n.* A member of a former military caste, originally composed of slaves from Turkey, that held the Egyptian throne from about 1250 until 1517 and remained powerful until 1811. [Arabic *mamlūk*, slave.]

mamey. Variant of **mammee**.

mam·il·la (ma-míl'ə) *n., pl.* **-illae** (-ee). Also *chiefly U.S.* **mam·mil·la.** **1.** A nipple or teat. **2.** Any nipple-shaped protuberance. [Latin, diminutive of *mamma,* breast.] —**mam·il·lar·y** (mə-míllərı, mám-mi-lərı ‖ *U.S.* -lerri) *adj.*

mam·il·late (mámmi-layt) *adj.* Also **mam·il·lat·ed** (-laytid). 1. Having nipples or mamillae. 2. Shaped like a nipple or mamilla. —**mam·il·la·tion** (-láysh'n) *n.*

mam·ma¹ (mə-maá ‖ mámmə) *n.* Also chiefly *U.S.* **ma·ma.** Mother. Used familiarly, as by children. [Reduplication of baby-talk *ma.*]

mam·ma² (mámmə) *n., pl.* **mammae** (mámmee). An organ of female mammals that contains milk-producing glands; a breast or udder. [Latin.]

mam·mal (mámm'l) *n.* A member of the class Mammalia. [New Latin MAMMALIA.] —**mam·mal·i·an** (ma-máyli-ən, mə-) *adj. & n.*

Mam·ma·li·a (ma-máyli-ə, mə-) *pl.n.* A class of vertebrate animals of more than 15,000 species, including humans, distinguished by self-regulating body temperature, separation of oxygenated and deoxygenated blood in the heart, and, in the females, milk-producing mammae. [New Latin, from Latin *mammalis,* of the breast, from *mamma,* breast.]

mam·mal·o·gy (ma-mál-əji, mə-, -mól-) *n.* The branch of zoology dealing with the study of the Mammalia. [MAMMAL + -LOGY.] —**mam·ma·log·i·cal** (mámmə-lójik'l) *adj.* —**mam·mal·o·gist** (ma-mál-əjist, mə-, -mól-) *n.*

mam·ma·ry (mámməri) *adj.* Of or pertaining to a mamma.

mammary gland *n.* 1. A milk-producing organ in female mammals, consisting of clusters of alveoli or small cavities with ducts terminating in a nipple or teat. 2. A woman's breast. Used humorously.

mam·mee (ma-mée) *n.* Also **ma·mey** *pl.* **-meys.** 1. A tropical American tree, *Mammea americana,* bearing edible fruits. 2. The large, red-rinded fruit of this tree, having a yellow, pulpy centre. In this sense, also called "mammee apple". [Spanish *mamey, mamei,* from Haitian.]

mam·mif·er·ous (ma-míffərəss) *adj.* Having mammary glands. [French *mammifère* : MAMMA (breast) + -FEROUS.]

mammilla. Chiefly *U.S.* Variant of mamilla. —**mammillate** *adj.*

mam·mo·gram (mámmə-gram) *n.* An X-ray photograph or radiograph of the breast. [MAMMA (breast) + -GRAM.]

mam·mog·ra·phy (ma-móggrəfi, mə-) *n.* Examination of the breast by X-rays, used for the early detection of abnormal growths. [MAMMA (breast) + -GRAPHY.]

Mam·mon (mámmən) *n.* 1. In the New Testament, riches, avarice, and worldly gain personified as a false god. Matthew 6:24; Luke 16:9,11,13. 2. *Often small* **m.** Riches regarded as a worldly goal or an evil influence. [Middle English *Mammona,* from Medieval Latin *mammōna,* from Greek *mamōnas,* from Aramaic *māmōnā,* riches.] —**mam·mon·ism** *n.* —**mam·mon·ist** *n.*

mam·mo·plas·ty (mámmō-plasti) *n., pl.* **-ties.** The altering of the shape or size of the breast by plastic surgery. [MAMMA (breast) + -PLASTY.]

mam·moth (mámməth) *n.* 1. An extinct elephant of the genus *Mammuthus,* once found throughout the Northern Hemisphere. The best-known species is the woolly mammoth, *M. primigenius,* of northern Eurasia and North America. 2. Something of great size. ~*adj.* Of enormous size, scale, or importance; gigantic. See Synonyms at **enormous.** [Obsolete Russian *mammot,* from Tartar *mamont,* "earth" (because the first mammoth remains were dug out of the earth in Siberia).]

mam·my, mam·mie (mámmı̄) *n., pl.* **-mies.** 1. Mother. Used familiarly, especially by children. 2. *Chiefly southern U.S.* A black nurse for white children. Often considered offensive. [Baby talk, variant of MAMMA.]

mam·poer (mam-poór) *n.* In South Africa, a brandy, usually homemade, distilled from the juice of peaches or other soft fruits. [Afrikaans, possibly after *Mampura,* a Sotho chieftain.]

man (man) *n., pl.* **men** (men). 1. An adult male human being, as distinguished from a female. Sometimes used in combination: *milkman; he-man.* 2. Loosely, any human being, as distinguished from an animal or deity; a member of the human race; a person. Sometimes used in combination: *draughtsman; workmanlike; man-day.* See Usage note at **-person.** 3. *Often capital* M. The human race; mankind. Used without an article: *the family of man.* 4. *Zoology.* A member of the genus *Homo,* family Hominidae, order Primates, class Mammalia, characterised by erect posture and an opposable thumb; especially, a member of the only extant species, *Homo sapiens,* distinguished by the ability to communicate by means of organised speech and to record information in a variety of symbolic systems. 5. A male human being endowed with such qualities as courage, strength, and fortitude, considered characteristic of manhood: *Stop snivelling and be a man!* 6. A husband, lover, or boyfriend. Now used chiefly informally, except in the phrase *man and wife.* 7. A member of the armed forces, especially one who is not an officer: *officers and men.* 8. Any workman, servant, or subordinate, as opposed to an employer or master. 9. A valet; a male servant. 10. *Informal.* Fellow: *Look here, my good man!* 11. One who swore allegiance to a lord in the Middle Ages; a liegeman; a vassal. 12. Any of the pieces used in chess, draughts, backgammon, and other board games. 13. *Nautical.* A ship. Used in combination: *merchantman; man-of-war.* 14. A representative of a government, large company, or the like in a specified town or country: *our man in Paris.* —**as one man.** Unanimously: *They answered him as one man.* —**be (one's) own man.** To be independent in judgment and action. —**man and boy.** From boyhood on: *Man and boy, I've lived here 40 years.* —**the Man.** *U.S. Slang.* 1. The police. 2. A white man. Used derogatorily, especially by blacks. —**the man on the**

Clapham omnibus. The ordinary citizen regarded as the embodiment of common sense. —**to a man.** Including everyone; without exceptions. See Usage note at **gentleman.**
~*tr.v.* **manned, manning, mans.** 1. To supply or furnish with men for defence, support, or service: *manning a ship.* 2. To be stationed at in order to defend, care for, or operate: *man the guns.*
~*interj. Chiefly U.S. Slang.* Used as an expletive to indicate strong feeling or to draw attention: *Man! it's hot in here.* [Middle English *man* (plural *men*), Old English *mann* (plural *menn*), from Germanic *mann-* (unattested).]

Man (man), **Isle of.** Island in the Irish Sea, an autonomous possession of the British Crown. Its parliament, the Court of Tynwald, is one of the oldest legislative assemblies in the world. The island depends on tourism, and is famous for the annual T.T. motorcycle racing. Douglas is the capital. See map at **United Kingdom.**

ma·na (maánə) *n.* 1. In the native religions of Oceania, an impersonal supernatural force inherent in gods and sacred objects. 2. Broadly, any power, prestige, or influence. [Maori.]

man-about-town (mán-əbówt-tówn) *n., pl.* **men-about-town** (mén-). A worldly and sophisticated man, especially one who frequents fashionable places.

man·a·cle (mánnək'l) *n.* 1. A device for confining the hands, usually consisting of two metal rings that are fastened about the wrists and joined by a metal chain. 2. Anything that confines or restrains. ~*tr.v.* **manacled, -cling, -cles.** 1. To restrain with manacles. 2. To confine or restrain as if with manacles; shackle; fetter. [Middle English *manicle,* from Old French, from Latin *manicula,* little hand, handle, diminutive of *manus,* hand.]

man·age (mánnij) *v.* **-aged, -aging, -ages.** —*tr.* 1. To direct or control the use of; handle, wield, or use (a tool, machine, or weapon, for example). 2. To exert control over; make submissive to one's authority, discipline, or persuasion: *Her mother can't manage her.* 3. To direct or administer the affairs of (an organisation, estate, or the like): *He manages a football team.* 4. **a.** To contrive or arrange; succeed in doing or accomplishing, especially with difficulty: *I'll manage to come on Friday.* **b.** To deal or cope with: *She couldn't manage any more food.* —*intr.* 1. To direct, supervise, or carry on business affairs; perform the duties of a manager. 2. To carry on or get along, especially in financial matters: *They can't manage without her.* —See Synonyms at **conduct.** [Italian *maneggiare,* to handle (a horse), probably from Vulgar Latin *manidiāre* (unattested), to handle, from Latin *manus,* hand.] —**man·age·a·bil·i·ty** (-bíllətı), **man·age·a·ble·ness** *n.* —**man·age·a·ble** *adj.* —**man·age·a·bly** *adv.*

managed currency *n.* A monetary system in which the money supply and its buying power are controlled by government, rather than automatically regulated by the gold standard.

man·age·ment (mánnijmənt) *n.* 1. The act, manner, or practice of managing, handling, or controlling something. 2. The person or persons who manage a business establishment, organisation, or institution. 3. Skill in managing; executive ability.

man·ag·er (mánnijər) *n. Abbr.* **mgr., Mgr.** 1. A person who manages a business or other enterprise. 2. A person who is in charge of the business affairs of an entertainer or group of entertainers. 3. *Sports.* A person in charge of the training and performance of an athlete or team. 4. In Britain, any of a number of members of either of the Houses of Parliament appointed to arrange business matters in which both Houses are involved. 5. *Law.* One who is appointed by a court to run a business while it is in the hands of the receiver. —**man·ag·er·ship** *n.*

man·ag·er·ess (mánnijə-réss ‖ -ress, -rəss) *n.* A female manager; especially, a woman in charge of a restaurant, shop, or the like.

man·a·ger·i·al (mánnə-jéer-i-əl) *adj.* Of, pertaining to, or characteristic of a manager or management. —**man·a·ge·ri·al·ly** *adv.*

man·ag·ing (mánnijing) *adj.* Having administrative power or control: *managing director; managing editor.*

Ma·na·gua (mə-nág-wə, -naág-). Capital of Nicaragua since 1855. It lies on the south shore of Lake Managua, and is a centre for industry, trade, and administration. It was badly damaged by earthquakes (1931 and 1972) and in the civil war (1979).

man·a·kin (mánnəkin) *n.* 1. Any of various small, colourful birds of the family Pipridae, found in forests of Central and South America. 2. Variant of **manikin.**

Ma·na·ma (mə-naámə). *Arabic* **Al Ma·na·mah.** Capital of Bahrain since 1971. Formerly a pearl fishing centre, its newer activities include oil-refining, fishing, petrochemicals, and (at Mina Sulman) marine industries. It is also the free transit port for the southern (Persian) Gulf.

ma·ña·na (man-yaánə) *adv.* 1. Tomorrow. 2. At some unspecified future time. ~*n.* Some indefinite time in the future. [Spanish, tomorrow, from Vulgar Latin (*cras*) *māneāna* (unattested), "early tomorrow" : *crās,* tomorrow (see **procrastinate**) + *māneāna,* early, from Latin *māne,* in the morning.]

Ma·nas·seh¹ (mə-nássi, -nássə). The elder son of Joseph. Genesis 41:51.

Manasseh². A king of Judah in the seventh century B.C. II Kings 21:1–18.

Manasseh³ *n.* A tribe of Israel descended from Manasseh, son of Joseph.

man-at-arms (mán-ət-ármz) *n., pl.* **men-at-arms** (mén-). A soldier; especially, a medieval cavalryman supplied with heavy arms.

man·a·tee (mánnə-tée) *n.* Any whalelike mammal of the genus *Trichechus,* found in Atlantic coastal waters of the tropical Americas and Africa. Each has paddle-like forelimbs and a horizontally flattened tail. [Spanish *manati,* from Carib *manattouï.*]

Ma·náus or **Ma·náos** (mə-nówss). Capital of Amazonas state, Brazil. Situated on the Rio Negro, near the Amazon, it is a free port, accessible to ocean-going ships, and the commercial centre for the upper Amazon basin. Around 1900 it was the centre of a rubber boom. With the opening up of Amazonas and the discovery of oil nearby, it is booming again.

Man·cha, La (mánchə). Region and former province of central Spain. A bleak plateau notable for its windmills, it was the setting for Cervantes' novel, *Don Quixote de la Mancha.* **—Man·che·go** (man-cháygō) *adj. & n.*

Man·ches·ter (mán-chistər, -chestər, -chəstər). City and Unitary Authority area in northwest England. It began as a Roman camp, Mancunium, and its people are still known as Mancunians. A medieval wool town, it became the country's main cotton centre in the Industrial Revolution. England's first passenger railway linked it with Liverpool in 1830, and with the completion of the Manchester Ship Canal (1894) the city became a major port and financial centre.

Manchester terrier *n.* A short-haired, black-and-tan dog of a breed that originated in Manchester. Formerly called "black-and-tan terrier".

man·chi·neel (mánchi-néel) *n.* A tropical American tree, *Hippomane mancinella,* having poisonous sap and fruit. [French *mancenille,* from Spanish *manzanilla,* "small apple", MANZANILLA.]

Man·chu (mán-chōō) *n., pl.* **-chus** or collectively **Manchu. 1.** A member of a nomadic Mongoloid people, native to Manchuria, who conquered China in 1644 and established the **Ch'ing** *(see)* dynasty that was overthrown by revolution in 1911. **2.** The Tungusic language of the Manchu.
~*adj.* **1.** Of or pertaining to the Manchu, their dynasty, language, or culture. **2.** Of or pertaining to Manchuria. [Manchu, "pure".]

Man·chu·guo, Man·chu·kuo (mán-chōō-gwáw). Also **Man·zhou·guo** (-jō-gwáw). See **Manchuria.**

Man·chu·ri·a (man-chóor-i-ə). Region of northeast China, composed of the modern provinces of Heilongjiang, Jilin, and Liaoning. It was the home of the Manchu conquerors of China in the 17th century. Of great strategic value, it was subsequently seized by the Russians, then the Japanese, who in 1932 set up their protégé state of Manchuguo (Manchuria plus the former province of Jehol, now mostly in the Inner Mongolian Autonomous Region). China regained this territory in 1946. **—Man·chu·ri·an** *adj. & n.*

man·ci·ple (mán-sip'l) *n.* In Britain, a steward responsible for purchasing the provisions of a college, an Inn of Court, or similar institution. [Middle English, from Anglo-French, from Latin *mancipium,* purchase : *manus,* hand + *cip-,* from *capere,* to take.]

Man·cu·ni·an (man-kéwni-ən) *n.* A native or inhabitant of Manchester. [Medieval Latin *Mancunium,* MANCHESTER.] **—Man·cu·ni·an** *adj.*

-mancy *n. comb. form.* Indicates divination by a specified means or in a specified manner; for example, **chiromancy, necromancy.** [Middle English, from Old French *-mancie,* from Late Latin *-mantīa,* from Greek *manteia,* divination, from *manteuesthai,* to prophesy, from *mantis,* a prophet.]

Man·dae·an, Man·de·an (man-dée-ən). *n.* **1.** A member of an ancient Gnostic sect still surviving in Iraq. **2.** A form of the Aramaic language used by the Mandaeans. [Aramaic *mandaiia,* Gnostics, from *manda,* knowledge.]
~*adj.* Of or pertaining to the Mandaeans or their language.

man·da·la (mándələ, man-dáalə) *n.* In Oriental art and religion, any of various usually circular designs symbolic of the universe. [Sanskrit *maṇḍala,* circle, probably from Tamil *muṭalai.*]

Man·da·lay (mándə-láy, -lay). Last capital of the Burman kingdom, annexed by the British in 1885. Situated on the Ayeyarwady river it is a major port and commercial centre of Upper Burma (Myanmar).

man·da·mus (man-dáyməss) *n., pl.* **-muses.** *Law.* An order issued by a higher court ordering a public official or body or a lower court to perform a specific duty.
~*tr.v. Law.* **mandamused, -musing, -muses.** To serve with a mandamus. [Latin *mandāmus,* "we order", from *mandāre,* to order.]

man·da·rin[1] (mándə-rin ‖ -rin) *n.* **1.** In imperial China, a member of any of the nine ranks of high public officials. **2. a.** A high civil servant thought to exercise wide undefined powers outside political control. **b.** A member of any influential intellectual or highbrow circle, especially when conservative or elderly. **3.** *Capital* **M.** Mandarin Chinese. **4.** *Capital* **M.** In imperial China, the dialect used by mandarins and other officials of the empire.
~*adj.* **1.** Of or resembling a mandarin. **2.** Marked by elaborate and intricate language or literary style. [Portuguese, from Malay *mĕntĕri,* from Hindi *mantrī,* from Sanskrit *mantrin,* counsellor, from *mantra,* counsel.]

man·da·rin[2] (mándə-rin) *n.* Also **man·da·rine** (-réen). **1.** A small citrus tree, *Citrus nobilis* or *C. deliciosa,* cultivated for its edible, orange-like fruit. **2.** The small, loose-skinned fruit of this tree. Also called "mandarin orange". [French *mandarine,* perhaps from MANDARIN (Chinese public official), comparing the colour of· the fruit to the yellow robes worn by mandarins.]

Mandarin Chinese *n. Chinese* **guo yu** (gwó yǔ) or **pu·tong·hua** (pṓo-tǒong-hwá). The national language of the People's Republic of China and of Taiwan, based on the principal dialect spoken in the area around Beijing (Peking).

mandarin collar *n.* A narrow, stiff collar that stands up around the neck and does not quite meet at the front.

mandarin duck *n.* A perching duck, *Aix galericulata,* of Asia, having brightly coloured plumage and a crested head in the male.

man·da·tar·y, man·da·to·ry (mándə-təri, -tri ‖ *U.S.* -terri) *n., pl.* **-ies.** A person or nation that receives a mandate. [Late Latin *mandātārius* : MANDATE + -ARY.]

man·date (mándayt) *n.* **1.** An authoritative command or instruction. **2.** An instruction or authorisation to a government to follow a particular policy, supposedly expressed in election results. **3. a.** Formerly, a commission from the League of Nations authorising a nation to administer a territory. **b.** Formerly, a region under such administration. Compare **trusteeship, trust territory. 4.** In Roman and Scots law, a contract by which an individual agrees to perform services for another without payment.
~*tr.v.* *(also* man-dáyt) **mandated, -dating, -dates. 1.** To assign (a colony or territory) to a particular nation under a mandate. **2.** To give authority to by means of a mandate. [Latin *mandātum,* a command, from *mandāre,* to command.]

man·da·tor (mán-daytər, man-dáytər) *n.* One who gives a mandate.

man·da·to·ry (mándə-tri, -təri, man-dáytəri) *adj.* **1.** Of, pertaining to, having the nature of, or containing a mandate. **2.** Required as if by mandate; obligatory. **3.** Holding a mandate over some region. Said of a nation.
~*n., pl.* **mandatories.** Variant of **mandatary.**

man·day (mán-dáy) *n., pl.* **man-days.** The work performed by one person during one day.

Man·de (mán-day, maán-) *n., pl.* **-des** or collectively **Mande. 1.** A Mandingo. **2.** A branch of the Niger-Congo language family, spoken chiefly in Mali, Liberia, and Sierra Leone. [Mandingo : *ma-,* "mother" + *-nde,* diminutive suffix. See **Mandingo.**]

Mandean. Variant of **Mandaean.**

Man·de·la (man-déllə, -dáylə), **Nelson (Rolihlahla)** (1918–). South African black political leader and first black president (1994–). While a practising lawyer in Johannesburg, he became the national organiser of the banned African National Congress. He was tried for treason and acquitted (1956–61), retried (1963–64), and sentenced to life imprisonment. His publications include *No Easy Walk to Freedom* (1965). He was released in 1990. He shared the Nobel peace prize in 1993 with President de Klerk for his efforts on behalf of peace and democracy in South Africa.

man·di·ble (mándib'l) *n.* A jaw, especially : **1.** The lower jaw in vertebrates. **2.** Either the upper or lower part of the beak in birds. **3.** Any of various mouth-parts in insects. [Middle English, from Old French, from Latin *mandibula,* from *mandere,* to chew.] **—man·dib·u·lar** (man-díbbewlər) *adj.*

man·dib·u·late (mən-díbbew-lət, -lit, -layt) *n.* An animal having mandibles. **—man·dib·u·late** *adj.*

Man·din·go (man-díng-gō) *n., pl.* **-gos, -goes,** or collectively **Mandingo. 1.** A member of any of various Negroid peoples inhabiting the region of the upper Niger river valley of west Africa. **2.** Any language or dialect of the Mandingo. [Mandingo : *ma-,* "mother" + *-ndi, -nde,* diminutive suffix + *-ngo,* variant of *-ko,* suffix of nationality or tribe.] **—Man·din·go** *adj.*

man·do·la (mán-dələ) *n.* Also **man·dor·a** (-dawrə). An early, larger form of mandolin. [Italian.]

man·do·lin, man·do·line (mándə-lín, -léen, -lin, -leen) *n.* **1.** A musical instrument with a usually pear-shaped wooden body and a fretted neck over which several pairs of metal strings are stretched. **2.** A utensil for slicing vegetables finely, consisting of a wooden board fitted with an adjustable metal blade. [French *mandoline,* from Italian *mandolino,* diminutive of *mandola, mandora,* lute, from Greek *pandoura.*] **—man·do·lin·ist** *n.*

man·dor·la (man-dórlə) *n.* An oval aureole used especially in medieval painting and sculpture. [Italian, almond.]

man·drag·o·ra (man-drággərə) *n. Chiefly Poetic.* The mandrake, or a narcotic drug prepared from it. [Old English. See **mandrake.**]

man·drake (mándrayk) *n.* **1.** A Eurasian plant, *Mandragora officinarum,* having purplish flowers and a branched root thought to resemble the human body, from which a narcotic drug was formerly prepared. This plant was once widely believed to have magical powers and to shriek when pulled up by the roots. **2.** A North American plant, the **May apple** *(see).* [Middle English *mandragge, mandrake* (probably influenced by DRAKE, dragon), from Middle Dutch *mandragre* and Old English *mandragora,* both from Latin *mandragoras,* from Greek *mandragoras†.*]

man·drel, man·dril (mándrəl) *n.* **1.** A spindle or axle used to secure or support material being machined or milled. **2.** A metal core around which wood and other materials may be shaped. **3.** A shaft on which a working tool is mounted, as in a dental drill. **4.** A miner's pick with a large flattish blade on one side of the head. [16th century : perhaps akin to French *madrin,* lathe.]

man·drill (mándril) *n.* A large, fierce baboon, *Mandrillus sphinx,* of west Africa, having a beard, a crest, and a mane, with brilliant blue, purple, and scarlet markings on the face, and scarlet markings on the hindquarters in the adult male. [MAN + DRILL (baboon).]

mane (mayn) *n.* **1. a.** The long hair along the top and sides of the neck of such mammals as the horse and the male lion. **b.** The feathers on the back of the neck and head of some pigeons. **2.** A long, thick growth of hair on a person's head. [Middle English, Old English *manu.*] **—maned** *adj.*

man-eat·er (mán-eetər) *n.* **1.** An animal or fish that eats or is reputed to eat human flesh. **2.** A cannibal. **3.** *Informal.* A type of woman seen as habitually dominating and discarding male lovers. **—man-eat·ing** *adj.*

ma·nège, ma·nege (ma-náyzh, -nézh) n. **1.** The art and practice of training a horse in the more difficult exercises of riding. **2.** A riding academy. [French *manège*, from Italian *maneggio*, from *maneggiare*, to MANAGE.]

ma·nes (máanayz, máyneez) *pl.n. Sometimes capital* **M.** In ancient Rome: **1.** The spirits of the dead, especially ancestors, deified as minor gods. **2.** *Used with a singular verb.* Any revered spirit of one who has died. Compare **lemures.** [Latin *mānēs*, probably "the good ones", from *mānis*, good.]

Ma·net (mánnay, ma-náy), **Edouard** (1832–83). French painter. His *Déjeuner sur l'herbe* (1863), showing a nude woman at a picnic, was rejected by the Paris Salon and caused a scandal. He had a considerable influence on the impressionists.

maneuver. *U.S.* Variant of **manoeuvre.**

man Friday n. Any devoted male servant, aide, or employee, especially one having a high degree of responsibility. [After *Friday*, the devoted native servant in Defoe's novel *Robinson Crusoe* (1719).]

man·ful (mánf'l) *adj.* Having or displaying qualities considered as befitting a man; brave and resolute. **—man·ful·ly** *adv.* **—man·ful·ness** n.

man·ga (máng-gə) n., *pl.* **manga** or **mangas.** A Japanese comic strip or animated film in comic-strip style; specifically: one intended for adults that is violent and/or sexy. [Japanese.]

man·ga·bey (máng-gə-bay) n., *pl.* **-beys.** Any monkey of the genus *Cercocebus*, of equatorial Africa, having a long tail and a relatively long muzzle. [After *Mangaby*, a region of Madagascar.]

man·ga·nate (máng-gə-nayt) n. Any salt containing manganese in its anion, especially a salt containing the $MnO_4{}^{2-}$ ion. [MANGA-N(ESE) + -ATE (salt).]

man·ga·nese (máng-gə-néez, -neez ‖ -néess, -neess) n. *Symbol* **Mn** A grey-white or silvery, brittle metallic element, occurring in several allotropic forms, found worldwide, especially in the ore pyrolusite. Manganese is alloyed with steel to increase hardness, resistance, and other properties, and with other metals to form highly ferromagnetic materials. Atomic number 25, atomic weight 54.9380, melting point 1,244°C, boiling point 2,097°C, relative density 7.21 to 7.44, valencies 2,3,4,6,7. [French *manganèse*, from Italian *manganese*, probably alteration of Medieval Latin *magnēsia*, manganese, magnesia, from Late Greek *magnēsia*. See **magnesia**.]

manganese dioxide n. A black crystalline compound, MnO_2, used as a depolariser for electric cells and in textile dyeing.

manganese nodule n. An irregular fragment of rock found on the deep ocean floor, and containing on average 20 per cent manganese, 6 per cent iron, and also nickel and copper. The nodules will probably prove an important commercial resource in future.

manganese spar n. A mineral, **rhodonite** *(see).*

man·gan·ic (mang-gánnik) *adj.* Pertaining to or containing manganese. Used especially to designate compounds of manganese with a valency of 3 or 6. [MANGAN(ESE) + -IC.]

Man·gan·in (máng-gə-nin) n. A trademark for an alloy of copper, manganese, and nickel used for making electrical resistors that do not vary much with changes in temperature.

man·ga·nite (máng-gə-nīt) n. A steel-grey to black mineral form of manganese oxide, MnO(OH), found in North America and Europe. It is an important ore of manganese. [MANGAN(ESE) + -ITE.]

man·ga·nous (máng-gə-nəss, mang-gánnəss) *adj.* Pertaining to or containing manganese. Used especially to designate compounds of manganese with a valency of 2. [MANGAN(ESE) + -OUS.]

mange (maynj) n. A contagious skin disease of many mammals, occasionally affecting humans. It is caused by parasitic mites and characterised by itching and loss of hair. [Middle English *maniewe*, from Old French *manjue*, "eating", itch, from *mangier*, to eat, from Latin *mandūcāre*, to eat, chew, from *mandūcō*, glutton, from *mandere*, to chew.]

man·gel·wur·zel (máng-g'l-wurz'l) n. A variety of the common beet having a large yellowish root, used chiefly as cattle fodder. Also called "mangel", "mangold". [German, (properly) *Mangold-wurzel*, "beet-root" : *Mangold*, beet, from Old High German *mānegolt†* + *Wurzel*, root, from Old High German *wurzala*.]

man·ger (máynjər) n. **1.** A trough or open box in which feed for horses or cattle is placed. **2.** *Nautical.* A small basin-like device in the bows of a ship for catching any water entering through the hawseholes. [Middle English *maniure, ma(w)nger*, from Old French *mangeoire, manjeure*, from Vulgar Latin *mandūcātōria* (unattested), feeding place, from *mandūcāre*, to chew. See **mange**.]

mange·tout (mónzh-tōō, -tóō) n., *pl.* **mange·tout. 1.** A variety of pea, *Pisum sativum* or *P. saccharatum*, the pods of which are picked when fairly young and eaten entire. **2.** The pod of this plant. Also called "sugar pea". [French, "eat all".]

man·gle¹ (máng-g'l) *tr.v.* **-gled, -gling, -gles. 1.** To mutilate or disfigure by battering, hacking, cutting, or tearing. **2.** To ruin or spoil through ineptitude or ignorance: *mangle a speech.* [Middle English *manglen*, from Anglo-French *mangler, mahangler*, probably frequentative of Old French *mahaignier*, to MAIM.] **—man·gler** n.

mangle² n. **1.** A laundry machine for wringing out or pressing fabrics. **2.** *Chiefly British.* A clothes wringer.
~*tr.v.* **mangled, -gling, -gles.** To wring out or press with a mangle. [Dutch *mangel*, from German, diminutive of Middle High German *mange*, mangle, from Late Latin *manganum*, MANGONEL.]

man·go (máng-gō) n., *pl.* **-goes** or **-gos. 1.** A tropical evergreen tree, *Mangifera indica*, native to Asia, cultivated for its edible fruit. **2.** The ovoid fruit of this tree, having a smooth rind and sweet, juicy, yellow-orange flesh. **3.** Any of various types of pickle; especially, mango chutney. [Portuguese *manga*, from Malay *mangā*, from Tamil *mānkāy* : *mān*, mango tree + *kāy*, fruit.]

man·go·nel (máng-gə-nel) n. A military machine used during the Middle Ages for hurling stones and other missiles. [Middle English, from Old French, from Medieval Latin *mangonellus, manganellus*, diminutive of Late Latin *manganum*, mangonel, from Greek *manganon*, enchantment, contrivance, war machine.]

man·go·steen (máng-gō-steen, -gə-) n. **1.** A tropical tree, *Garcinia mangostana*, having thick, leathery leaves and edible fruit. **2.** The fruit of this tree, having a hard rind and segmented, sweet, juicy pulp. [From obsolete Malay *manggustan*.]

man·grove (máng-grōv) n. **1.** Any of various tropical evergreen trees or shrubs of the genus *Rhizophora*, having stiltlike, aerial roots and forming dense thickets along tidal shores. **2.** Any of various similar shrubs or trees, especially any of the genus *Avicennia*. [Portuguese *mangue* (influenced by GROVE), from Taino *mangle*.]

man·gy, man·gey (máynji) *adj.* **-gier, -giest. 1.** Having, resembling, or caused by mange. **2.** Having many bare spots; shabby: *a mangy old mink coat.* **3.** Having a squalid appearance; wretched: *mangy tenements.* **—man·gi·ly** *adv.* **—man·gi·ness** n.

man·han·dle (mán-hánd'l, -hand'l) *tr.v.* **-dled, -dling, -dles. 1.** To handle roughly. **2.** To move by manpower, without machinery.

Man·hat·tan¹ (man-hátt'n, mən-) n., *pl.* **-tans** or collectively **Manhattan.** A member of an Algonquian-speaking North American Indian people, formerly inhabiting the area that is now roughly New York City. **—Man·hat·tan** *adj.*

Manhattan². Borough of New York City, New York state, United States. Most of it lies on Manhattan Island, the original nucleus of the city, bounded by the Hudson, East, and Harlem rivers and New York Bay. The financial, business, and cultural heart of the city, it includes Broadway, Wall Street, and Greenwich Village.

Manhattan³ n. *Sometimes small* **m.** A cocktail made from vermouth, rye whiskey or bourbon, and angostura bitters. [After MANHATTAN, New York.]

Manhattan District n. In World War II, the name given to a unit of the U.S. Army Corps of Engineers established in 1942 to administer the nuclear energy project that produced the atomic bomb. Also unofficially called "Manhattan Project".

man·hole (mán-hōl) n. A hole through which a person may enter a boiler, pipe, conduit, or drain. Also called "inspection chamber".

man·hood (mánhŏod) n. **1.** The state or condition of being an adult male as distinguished from being a boy or a woman: *Green youths grow to manhood.* **2.** The composite of qualities, such as courage, determination, and vigour, considered desirable in an adult male. **3.** Men collectively. **4.** Loosely, the state or condition of being part of or endowed with humanity.

man·hour (mán-owr) n., *pl.* **man·hours.** An industrial unit of production equal to the work a person can produce in one hour.

man·hunt (mán-hunt) n., *pl.* **manhunts.** An organised and extensive search for a man, usually a fugitive criminal.

ma·ni·a (máyni-ə) n. **1.** *Psychology.* A state of mind characterised by profuse and rapidly changing ideas, exaggerated gaiety that may quickly change to irritability or violence, and physical overactivity. **2.** *Informal.* An inordinately intense desire or enthusiasm for something; a craze. **3.** Any violent abnormal behaviour. [Middle English, madness, from Late Latin, from Greek.]

–mania n. *comb. form.* Indicates an exaggerated desire for or pleasure in, or a pathological excitement induced by something; for example, **monomania, pyromania.** **— -maniac** n. & adj. *comb. form.*

ma·ni·ac (máyni-ak) n. **1.** An insane person; a lunatic. **2.** *Informal.* A person who has excessive enthusiasm or desire for something: *a bridge maniac.* **3.** A person who behaves in a wild, irresponsible way: *Look out for maniacs on the motorway.*
~*adj.* Maniacal. [Greek *maniakos*, from *mania*, madness.]

ma·ni·a·cal (mə-nī-ək'l) *adj.* Also **maniac. 1.** Insane: *a maniacal killer.* **2.** *Informal.* Characterised by excessive enthusiasm: *a maniacal fondness for gambling.* **—ma·ni·a·cal·ly** *adv.*

man·ic (mánnik) *adj.* **1.** Of, pertaining to, or afflicted with mania; hyperactive. **2.** Loosely, crazy; apparently insane, especially in a frenetic way: *manic humour.*
~n. A person afflicted with mania. [MANIA + -IC.]

man·ic-de·pres·sive (mánnik-di-préssiv) *adj. Psychology.* Designating, displaying, or suffering from a mood disorder in which periods of manic excitation alternate with melancholic depressions.
~n. *Psychology.* A manic-depressive person. **—man·ic-de·pres·sion** n.

Man·i·chae·an, Man·i·che·an (mánni-kée-ən) n. Also **Man·i·chee** (-kee). A believer in Manichaeism.
~*adj.* Of or pertaining to Manichaeism. [Middle English, from Medieval Latin *Manichaeus*, from Late Greek *Manikhaios*, a follower of *Manikhaios* or *Manes*, the Persian founder of the sect.]

Man·i·chae·ism, Man·i·che·ism (mánni-kee-iz'm) n. Also **Man·i·chae·an·ism, Man·i·che·an·ism** (-kée-ən-iz'm). **1.** The syncretic, dualistic religious philosophy taught by the Persian prophet Manes about the third century A.D., according to which God and Satan reigned as equals. It combined elements of Zoroastrian, Christian, and Gnostic thought. **2.** Any similar dualistic philosophy holding that there is an evil deity who exists in opposition to God, especially any considered a heresy by the Roman Catholic Church.

man·i·cot·ti (mánni-kótti) n. An Italian dish consisting of pasta with a filling of chopped ham and ricotta cheese, usually served hot with a tomato sauce. [Italian, "sleeves", plural of *manicotto*, augmentative of *manica*, sleeve, from Latin *manica*, from *manus*, hand.]

man·i·cure (mánni-kewr) *n.* A cosmetic treatment of the hands and fingernails, including shaping, cleaning, and polishing of the nails. Also used adjectively: *a manicure set.*
~*tr.v.* **manicured, -curing, -cures. 1.** To care for (the hands and fingernails) by shaping, cleaning, and polishing, or other treatment. **2.** To clip or trim evenly and closely: *manicured lawns.* [French *manicure,* "hand-care" : Latin *manus,* hand + *cūra,* care.] —**man·i·cur·ist** *n.*

man·i·fest (mánni-fest) *adj.* **1.** Clearly apparent to the sight or understanding; obvious. **2.** *Psychology.* Of or pertaining to impulses which appear to be conscious but which may hide unconscious ones. —See Synonyms at **evident.**
~*v.* **manifested, -festing, -fests.** —*tr.* **1.** To show or demonstrate plainly; reveal. **2.** To be evidence of; prove. **3. a.** To record or list in a ship's manifest. **b.** To display or present a manifest of (cargo). —*intr.* To manifest itself: *frustration manifesting as aggression.*
~*n.* **1. a.** A list of cargo or passengers; especially one for use by customs. **b.** *U.S.* A list of railway trucks, according to owner and location. **2.** *U.S.* A fast freight train, usually one that carries perishable goods. [Middle English, from Latin *manifestus, manufestus,* palpable, "grasped by hand" : *manus,* hand + *-festus,* "gripped".] —**man·i·fest·a·ble** *adj.* —**man·i·fest·ly** *adv.*

man·i·fes·ta·tion (mánnifess-táysh'n) *n.* **1. a.** The act of manifesting or the state of being manifested. **b.** The demonstration of the existence, reality, or presence of a person, object, or quality: *a manifestation of ill will.* **c.** Any of the forms in which someone or something, such as an individual, a divine being, or an idea, is revealed. **2.** A public demonstration, usually of a political nature.

Manifest Destiny *n.* The 19th-century doctrine that the United States had the right and duty to expand throughout the North American continent.

man·i·fes·to (mánni-féstō) *n., pl.* **-toes** or **-tos.** A public declaration of principles, policies, or intentions, especially of a political party.
~*intr.v. Rare.* **manifestoed, -toing, -toes.** To issue a manifesto. [Italian, "manifestation", from adjective, manifest, from Latin *manifestus,* MANIFEST.]

man·i·fold (mánnifōld) *adj.* **1.** Of many kinds; varied; multiple: *our manifold failings.* **2.** Having many features or forms: *manifold intelligence.* **3.** Consisting of or operating several of one kind.
~*n.* **1.** A whole composed of diverse elements. **2.** Any one of many copies; a copy made by manifolding. **3.** A pipe so fitted that it has several apertures for making multiple connections. **4.** *Mathematics.* A topological space consisting of matched, overlapping open sets in which each point is homeomorphic to an open subset of Euclidean space.
~*tr.v.* **manifolded, -folding, -folds. 1.** To make several copies of. **2.** To make manifold; multiply. [Middle English, Old English *manig-feald* : MANY + -FOLD.] —**man·i·fold·ly** *adv.* —**man·i·fold·ness** *n.*

man·i·fold·er (mánni-fōldər) *n.* A machine for making manifold copies of documents or other writings.

man·i·kin, man·ni·kin (mánni-kin) *n.* Also **man·a·kin** (mánnə-) (for sense 1). **1. a.** A dwarf or pixie. **b.** A little boy. **2.** An anatomical model of the human body, used primarily for study in art and medical schools. **3.** Variants of **mannequin.** [Middle Dutch *mannekīn,* diminutive of *man,* MAN.]

ma·nil·a, ma·nil·la (mə-níllə) *n. Often capital* **M. 1.** A cigar or cheroot of a type made in Manila. **2.** A fibre, Manila hemp. **3.** Manila paper. **4.** Light yellowish brown.

Ma·nil·a (mə-níllə). Capital and main seaport of the Philippines. It was founded (1571) by the Spanish on Manila Bay, Luzon Island, and is the country's industrial centre.

Manila hemp *n.* The fibre of a tropical plant, the **abaca** (*see*), used for making rope, cordage, and paper. Also called "Manila".

Manila paper *n.* Strong paper or thin cardboard with a smooth finish, usually buff in colour, made from Manila hemp or wood fibres similar to it. Also called "manila": *a manila envelope.*

ma·nil·la (mə-níllə) *n.* A metal bracelet worn by certain West African peoples, formerly used as currency. [Spanish, bracelet, probably diminutive of *mano,* hand.]

ma·nille (ma-níl) *n.* The second-best trump in the card games quadrille and ombre. [French, from Spanish *malilla,* diminutive of *mala,* bad.]

man in the moon *n.* The face or shape of a man in the light and dark areas of the Moon's surface, as apparently visible from the earth. Preceded by *the.*

man in the street *n.* The ordinary citizen; the common man. Preceded by *the.*

man·i·oc (mánni-ok) *n.* Also **man·i·o·ca** (-ōkə). A tropical plant, the **cassava** (*see*). [French, from Tupi *mandioca.*]

man·i·ple (mánnip'l) *n.* **1.** A former ecclesiastical vestment, a coloured band on the left arm near the wrist. **2.** A subdivision of an ancient Roman legion, containing 60 or 120 men. [Sense 1, Middle English, from Old French *handkerchief,* from Latin *manipulus,* handful. Sense 2, direct from Latin *manipulus,* handful, hence, a bundle of hay on a pole used as a standard, hence a detachment of troops : *manus,* hand + -*pulus*†.]

ma·nip·u·late (mə-níppew-layt) *tr.v.* **-lated, -lating, -lates. 1.** To operate or control by skilled use of the hands; handle. **2. a.** To influence or manage shrewdly or deviously: *She manipulated public opinion in her favour.* **b.** To control the will or emotions of (another person) by exploiting guilt or affection, for example, to one's own ends: *His parents quite openly manipulate him.* **3.** To tamper with or

falsify (financial records) for personal gain. **4.** *Medicine.* To handle and move (a limb, for example), either in an examination or for therapeutic purposes. —See Synonyms at **handle.** [Back-formation from MANIPULATION.] —**ma·nip·u·la·bil·i·ty** (-lə-bílləti) *n.* —**ma·nip·u·la·ble** *adj.* —**ma·nip·u·lat·ive** (-lətiv ‖ -laytiv), **ma·nip·u·la·to·ry** (-lə-təri, -tri) *adj.* —**ma·nip·u·la·tor** *n.*

ma·nip·u·la·tion (mə-níppew-láysh'n) *n.* **1.** The act of manipulating. **2.** The state of being manipulated. **3.** Shrewd or devious effort to manage or influence for one's own purposes: *manipulation of popular feeling.* **4.** The therapeutic movement of bones or other tissue, as by an osteopath or physiotherapist, to restore normal action. [Latin *manipulus,* handful. See **maniple.**]

ma·ni·pu·ri (mánni-poóri, múnni-) *n., pl.* **-ris.** One of the four classical Hindu dance forms, presenting episodes from the life of the god Krishna. [After *Manipur,* region of India, where the dance originated.]

Man·i·to·ba (mánni-tōbə). Province of central Canada, the most easterly of the Prairie Provinces. The southwest produces vast amounts of wheat, and the northern tundra, furs. There are large reserves of timber, oil, and metal ores. Winnipeg is the capital.

man·i·tou, man·i·tu (mánni-tōō) *n., pl.* **-tous, -tus** or **-tou, -tu.** Also **man·i·to** (-tō) *pl.* **-tos** or **-to. 1.** A spirit or force of nature, either good or bad, deified in the religion of the Algonquian Indians. **2.** A representation or image of such a spirit. [French, from Ojibwa *manitu,* "he has surpassed".]

man jack *n. Informal.* A single individual. See **every man jack** at **jack** *n.* [MAN + JACK (fellow, chap).]

man·kind (man-kínd *for sense 1;* mán-kínd *for sense 2) n.* **1.** The human race. **2.** *Rare.* Men as distinguished from women.

mank·y (mángki) *adj.* **-ier, -iest. 1.** *Scottish.* Decaying; dirty. **2.** *Northwest English.* Spoilt; naughty. [From obsolete (Scottish) *mank,* maimed, defective, from Old French *manc,* from Latin *mancus,* maimed; current sense perhaps influenced by French *manqué,* failed, missed, miscarried.]

Man·ley (mánli), **Michael (Norman)** (1923 – 97). Jamaican politician. He worked as a journalist before entering politics, leading the People's National Party in opposition (1969 – 72) and as prime minister (1972-80, 1989-92). As a socialist in his first term, he strengthened his country's links with Cuba, spoke out for Third World interests, and gave the state a majority holding in the bauxite industry.

man·like (mán-līk) *adj.* **1.** Resembling a man. **2.** Pertaining to or befitting a man.

man·ly (mánli) *adj.* **-lier, -liest. 1.** Having qualities generally considered desirable in a man: *manly courage.* **2.** Suited to or befitting a man; masculine: *manly clothes.*
~*adv. Rare.* In a manly manner. —**man·li·ness** *n.*

man-made (mán-máyd) *adj.* Made by people; manufactured; not of natural origin.

Mann (man), **Thomas** (1875-1955). German novelist. Concerned with the artist's role in society, his works include *Death in Venice* (1912), *The Magic Mountain* (1924), and *Dr. Faustus* (1947). He was awarded the Nobel prize in 1929.

man·na (mánnə) *n.* **1.** The food miraculously provided for the Israelites in the wilderness during their flight from Egypt. Exodus 16:14–36. **2.** Any spiritual nourishment of divine origin, especially the Eucharist. **3.** Something of value that a person receives unexpectedly when in need. **4.** The dried exudate of certain plants; especially, that of a Eurasian ash tree, *Fraxinus ornus,* formerly used as a laxative. [Aramaic *mannā,* from Hebrew *mān.*]

manned (mand) *adj.* **1.** Having the personnel required for operation. **2.** Involving a human crew or having humans on board as well as or instead of machinery: *a manned space capsule.*

man·ne·quin (mánnikin) *n.* Also **manikin, mannikin** (for sense 1). **1.** A life-size, full or partial representation of the human body, used for the fitting or displaying of clothes; a dummy. **2.** A **lay figure** (*see*). **3.** A woman who models clothes; a model. [French, from Middle Dutch *mannekīn,* MANIKIN.]

man·ner (mánnər) *n.* **1.** A way of doing something, or the way in which a thing is done or happens: *boasting in their usual manner.* **2.** A way of acting; a person's bearing or behaviour: *a very flirtatious manner.* **3.** *Plural.* **a.** The socially correct way of acting; polite bearing or behaviour; etiquette. **b.** The prevailing systems or modes of social conduct of a specific society, period, or group. **4.** Practice, style, execution, or method in the arts: *This fresco is typical of the painter's early manner.* **5.** Exaggerated style; a mannerism. **6.** *Archaic.* Kind or sort: *What manner of man is that?* —See Synonyms at **bearing, method.** —**by all manner of means.** Of course; surely. —**in a manner of speaking.** In a way; so to speak. —**not by any manner of means.** In no way whatever. —**to the manner born. 1.** Born to follow or obey usual practices or customs. **2. a.** Fitted by birth, education, or experience to occupy a specific position, usually one of leadership. **b.** As if naturally equipped for an activity. [Middle English *manere,* from Anglo-French, from Old French *maniere,* from Vulgar Latin *manuāria* (unattested), "way of handling", manner, from Latin *manuārius,* of the hand, from *manus,* hand.]

man·nered (mánnərd) *adj.* **1.** Having a manner or manners of a specified kind. Often used in combination: *ill-mannered.* **2.** Artificial or affected: *His mannered speech irks me.* **3.** Of, pertaining to, or exhibiting mannerisms. Said of art or literature.

man·ner·ism (mánnə-riz'm) *n.* **1.** A distinctive behavioural trait; an idiosyncrasy. **2.** An exaggerated or affected style or habit, as in dress, speech, or art. **3.** *Capital* M. An artistic style of the late 16th century characterised by distortion of such elements as scale and perspective. —**man·ner·ist** n.

man·ner·ly (mánnərli) adj. Having good manners; polite. ~adv. With good manners; politely. —**man·ner·li·ness** n.

mannikin. Variant of **manikin.**

Man·ning (mánning), **Henry Edward, Cardinal** (1808–92). British cardinal. Educated at Oxford and an adherent of the Oxford Movement, he entered the Anglican ministry and became archdeacon of Chichester (1841) before his conversion to Roman Catholicism (1851). He was archbishop of Westminster (1865) and became a cardinal (1875). He was a staunch defender of papal infallibility.

man·nish (mánnish) adj. 1. Of or befitting a man. 2. Resembling a man in appearance or bearing. Said of a woman. —**man·nish·ly** adv. —**man·nish·ness** n.

man·ni·tol (mánni-tol || -tōl) n. Also **man·nite** (mánnīt). An alcohol, $C_6H_8(OH)_6$, used as a nutrient, a dietary supplement, and as the basis of dietetic sweets. [MANN(A) + -IT(E) + -OL.]

man·nose (mán-ōz, -ōss) n. A sugar, $C_6H_{12}O_6$, occurring in various polysaccharides. [MANN(A) + -OSE.]

ma·noeu·vre, U.S. **ma·neu·ver** (mə-nóō-vər || -néw-) n. **1. a.** A strategic or tactical military movement. **b.** Often plural. A large-scale military training exercise simulating combat. **2.** A movement or way of doing something generally requiring skill and dexterity; especially: **a.** An act of changing direction in a car, boat, or other transport. **b.** A controlled change in the flight path of an aircraft, rocket, or space vehicle. **3.** A calculated procedure intended to further personal or partisan interests: devious political manoeuvres. See Synonyms at **artifice.** ~v. **manoeuvred** or U.S. **maneuvered, -vring** or U.S. **-vering, -vres** or U.S. **-vers.** —intr. **1.** To perform or carry out a military manoeuvre. **2.** To make a change, or a series of changes, in position or direction for some desired end. **3.** To make tactical changes, as in debate or negotiation: The opposition had no room in which to manoeuvre. **4.** To attempt to bring about something by planning or scheming. —tr. **1.** To alter the tactical placement of (troops or warships, for example). **2.** To move into a desired position. **3.** To manipulate (people, for example) for one's own ends: manoeuvred her into signing the contract. [French, from Medieval Latin man(u)operāri, from Latin manus, hand + operāri, to work.] —**man·oeuv·ra·bil·i·ty** (-vrə-bílləti, -vərə-) n. —**man·oeuv·rable** adj.

man of God n. **1.** A man who is notably holy. **2.** A clergyman.

man of straw n. **1.** A person without financial substance. **2.** A person who is nominally, but not actually responsible, especially one involved in a dubious enterprise. Also U.S. "straw man". **3.** A spurious argument, put forward only to be refuted immediately. Also U.S. "straw man".

man of the world n. A sophisticated or worldly-wise man.

man-of-war (mán-ə-wáwr, -əv-) n., pl. **men-of-war** (mén-). **1.** A warship. **2.** A jellyfish, the **Portuguese man-of-war** (see).

ma·nom·e·ter (mə-nómmitər) n. **1.** Any of various instruments for measuring the pressure of liquids and gases. **2.** An instrument for measuring blood pressure, a **sphygmomanometer** (see). [French manomètre : Greek manos, sparse (here used of gaseous conditions) + -METER.] —**man·o·met·ric** (mánnə-méttrik), **man·o·met·ri·cal** adj. —**man·o·met·ri·cal·ly** adv. —**ma·nom·e·try** (mə-nómmətri) n.

man·or (mánnər) n. **1. a.** The district over which a lord had domain in medieval western Europe. **b.** The lord's residence in such a district. **2.** Any landed estate. **3.** The main house on any estate; a mansion. In this sense, also "manor house". **4.** In certain North American colonies, a tract of land with hereditary rights granted by royal charter. **5.** British Slang. **a.** A police district. **b.** The area of operations or pitch of a criminal or gang. **c.** An area that one lives in and knows well: South London's my manor. [Middle English maner, from Anglo-French manere, Old French maneir, "dwelling place", from maneir, to dwell, from Latin manēre, to dwell, remain.] —**ma·no·ri·al** (mə-náwr-i-əl || -nōr-) adj.

man-o'-war bird n. the **frigate bird** (see).

man·pow·er (mán-powr) n. **1.** The power of human physical strength. **2.** Power in terms of the people available to a particular group, or required for a particular task.

man·qué (móng-kay, MON-káy) adj. Unsuccessful or frustrated; unfulfilled. Used after the noun: an artist manqué. [French, from manquer, to fail, lack, from Italian mancare, from manco, lacking, defective, from Latin mancus, maimed.]

man·sard (mán-saard, -sərd) n. **1.** A roof having two slopes on all four sides, the lower slope almost vertical, and the upper almost horizontal. Also called "mansard roof". **2.** The upper storey formed by the lower slope of such a roof. [French (toit en) mansarde, "mansard (roof)"; originally designed by François MANSART.]

Man·sart (mon-sáar), **François** (1598–1666). French classical architect. He adapted the Baroque style and developed the mansard roof for the château of Blois (1635–38). His works include the Hôtel de la Vrillière (1635–38), the Church of Val-de-Grâce (1645), and the château of Maisons-Laffitte (1642–51).

manse (manss) n. **1. a.** Chiefly Scottish. A Church of Scotland clergyman's house and land. **b.** A Methodist or Nonconformist clergyman's house. **2.** Rare. A mansion. [Medieval Latin mansa, mansus, mansum, dwelling place, from Latin manēre, to dwell, remain.]

Man·sell (mánss'l), **Nigel (Ernest James)** (1953–). British motor racing driver. After being runner-up on three occasions (1986, 1987, 1991) in the World Drivers' Championship, he won it in 1992 when he won a record nine Grands Prix in a season. He won the IndyCar Championship in his first year in the U.S. in 1993.

man·ser·vant (mán-serv'nt) n., pl. **menservants** (mén-serv'nts). A male servant, especially a valet.

Mans·field (mánss-feeld, mánz-), **Katherine,** born Kathleen Mansfield Beauchamp (1888–1923). New Zealand short-story writer. Educated in London, she settled in Europe (1908) and wrote chiefly short stories in a style reminiscent of Chekhov's. Her works include Bliss (1920) and The Garden Party (1922).

-manship n. comb. form. Indicates: **1.** Skill in a specified field; for example, **horsemanship. 2.** Manoeuvring to gain advantage; for example, **gamesmanship.** [Abstracted from terms such as workmanship (workman + -ship) and used to create new terms such as one-upmanship (one up + -manship).]

man·sion (mánsh'n) n. **1.** A large, stately house. **2.** A manor house. **3.** Archaic. A dwelling; an abode. **4.** Plural. British. Used as part of the name of certain blocks of flats: Gresham Mansions. **5.** Astrology. **a.** A house (see). **b.** Any one of the 28 divisions of the moon's monthly path. [Middle English, house, from Old French, from Latin mānsiō (stem mānsiōn-), dwelling, from manēre, to dwell, remain.]

Mansion House n. The official residence of the Lord Mayor of London. Preceded by the.

man-sized (mán-sīzd) adj. Informal. Large enough for a man; hefty: a man-sized piece of cheese.

man·slaugh·ter (mán-slawtər) n. **1.** The taking of human life without premeditation. **2.** Law. The unlawful killing of one human being by another without express or implied intent to take life. Compare **murder.**

man·sue·tude (mán-swi-tewd || -tōōd) n. Archaic. Gentleness of manner; mildness. [Middle English, from Latin mānsuētūdō, from mānsuēscere, to tame, "to accustom to the hand" : manus, hand + suēscere, to accustom.]

man·ta (mántə) n. **1.** A rough-textured cotton fabric or blanket made and used in Latin America and the southwestern United States. **2.** Any of several fishes of the family Mobulidae, having large, flattened bodies with winglike pectoral fins. Also called "devilfish", "manta ray". [Spanish, cape, blanket, hence (in American Spanish) fish trap shaped like a blanket, manta ray (caught with such a trap), from Vulgar Latin manta (unattested), cloak, variant of Latin mantus, shortened from mantellum†, MANTLE.]

man·teau (mán-tō; French MON-tō) n., pl. **-teaus** (-tōz) or **-teaux** (-tō). A loose cloak or mantle. [French, from Old French mantel, from Latin mantellum†, MANTLE.]

Man·teg·na (man-tén-yə), **Andrea** (c. 1431–1506). Italian painter and engraver. Influenced by Donatello, his works reflect an interest in the classical period, and include a Pietà and the nine paintings of the Triumph of Caesar. (c. 1486).

man·tel, man·tle (mánt'l) n. **1.** An ornamental facing around a fireplace. **2.** The protruding shelf over a fireplace. Also called "mantelpiece". [Middle English mantel, cloak, covering, from Old French, from Latin mantellum†, MANTLE.]

man·tel·et (mánt'l-et, mántlit) n. Also **mant·let** (mántlit) (for sense 2). **1.** A short cape worn by women in the mid-19th century. **2.** A mobile screen or shield formerly used to protect soldiers. [Middle English, from Old French, diminutive of mantel, mantle, from Latin mantellum†, MANTLE.]

man·tel·piece (mánt'l-peess) n. The shelf over a fireplace, a mantel.

man·tel·tree (mánt'l-tree) n. A beam, stone, or arch that functions as a lintel over a fireplace, supporting the masonry above. [Middle English : MANTEL + TREE (beam).]

man·tic (mántik) adj. Of, pertaining to, or having the power of divination; prophetic. [Greek mantikos, from mantis, prophet.]

man·ti·core (mánti-kor || -kōr) n. A fabulous monster having the head of a man, the body of a lion, and the tail of a dragon or scorpion. [Middle English, from Latin mantichōra, from Greek mantikhōras, a misreading of martikhoras, a fabulous Oriental beast, from an unattested Old Iranian word meaning "man-eater" : represented by Old Persian martīya-, man + Avestan khvar-, to eat.]

man·til·la (man-tíllə) n. **1.** A scarf, usually of lace, worn over the head and shoulders, often over a high comb, by women in Spain and Latin America. **2.** A shawl or a short veil, as worn by Roman Catholic women in church. [Spanish, diminutive of manta, cape, MANTA.]

man·tis (mán-tiss) n., pl. **-tises** or **-tes** (-teez). Any of various carnivorous insects of the family Mantidae, primarily tropical but including a few Temperate Zone species. They are usually pale green and have two pairs of walking legs and powerful forelimbs that are often folded in a praying position. See **praying mantis.** [New Latin, from Greek mantis, prophet, diviner, hence (from its praying appearance) mantis.]

man·tis·sa (man-tissə) n. Mathematics. The decimal part of a common logarithm when the logarithm is written as the sum of an integer and a decimal. In 1.7041 the mantissa is .7041. [Latin, makeweight, probably from Etruscan.]

mantis shrimp n. A burrowing crustacean, the **squilla** (see).

man·tle (mánt'l) n. **1.** A loose, sleeveless cloak worn over outer garments. **2.** Anything that covers, envelops, or conceals: a mantle of ivy. **3.** Variant of **mantel. 4.** A zone of hot gases around a flame. **5.** A device in lamps consisting of a conical or cylindrical gauze, impregnated with certain salts, that gives off brilliant illumination when heated by the flame. **6.** Anatomy. The outer part of the brain, the **cerebral cortex** (see). **7.** Geology. The layer of the earth between the crust and the core. See **Mohorovičić discontinuity. 8.** Zoology.

The wings, shoulder feathers, and back of a bird, when differently coloured from the rest of the body. **9.** *Zoology.* In molluscs and brachiopods, a membrane that covers most of the body and secretes the substance forming the shell. **10.** A clay mould placed around a wax model and used for making a cast.
~v. **mantled, -tling, -tles.** *—tr.* To cover with or as if with a mantle; cloak; conceal: *mountains mantled in snow.* *—intr.* **1.** To spread or become extended over a surface. **2.** To become covered with a coating, such as scum or froth on the surface of a liquid. **3.** To be or become covered or overspread by blushes or colours: *Her face mantled.* **4.** To spread the wings over food. Used of hawks. [Middle English, from Old French, from Latin *mantellum†,* cloak.]

mantle rock *n. Geology.* **Regolith** *(see).*

mantlet. Variant of **mantelet.**

mant·ling (mántling) *n. Heraldry.* The ornamental drapery or scrollwork around an achievement. [MANTLE + -ING.]

man-to-man (mán-tə-mán) *adj.* **1.** Characterised by forthrightness and candour between two participants, usually male: *man-to-man talks.* **2.** *Sports.* Involving or designating a strategy in which each defending player deals with one particular player on the attacking team: *man-to-man marking.* **—man to man** *adv.*

Man·toux test (man-tōō; *French* MON-) *n.* A test to determine whether a person has developed any immunity to tuberculosis. Some tuberculin is injected below the skin and the appearance of inflammation during the next 24 hours indicates a certain degree of immunity. Also called "tuberculin test". [After C. *Mantoux* (1877–1947), French doctor.]

man·tra (mántrə, múntrə) *n.* **1.** *Hinduism.* A sacred formula believed to embody the divinity invoked and to possess magical power. It is used in prayer and incantation. **2.** A similar formula or word repeated, often in one's head, to induce a contemplative state in some techniques of meditation, or to increase one's powers of concentration. **3.** A Vedic psalm of praise. [Sanskrit, "prayer", "hymn".]

man·tu·a (mántew-ə) *n.* A loose gown, caught open in front to reveal an underskirt, worn in the 17th and 18th centuries. [French *manteau,* mantle (influenced by MANTUA, formerly famous for silks), from Old French *mantel,* from Latin *mantellum,* MANTLE.]

Man·tu·a (mántew-ə). *Italian* **Man·to·va** (mántŏva). City on the river Mincio, Lombardy, Italy. It is the capital of Mantova province, and is a tourist, manufacturing, and agricultural centre. **—Man·tu·an** *adj. &. adj.*

man·u·al (mánnew-əl) *adj.* **1. a.** Of, pertaining to, or done by the hands. **b.** Used by or operated with the hands, as a weapon, tool, or simple machine may be: *manual controls.* **c.** Employing human rather than mechanical energy: *manual labour.* **d.** Pertaining to unskilled work done with the hands, as opposed to clerical or administrative work, for example: *manual workers.* **2.** Of, pertaining to, or resembling a manual or guidebook.
~n. **1.** Any small reference book, especially one giving instructions; a guidebook; a handbook. **2.** The keyboard of an organ. **3.** *Military.* A set of prescribed movements in the handling of a weapon, especially a rifle. **4.** Manual control: *on manual.* [Middle English *manuel,* from Old French, from Latin *manuālis,* of the hand, from *manus,* hand.] **—man·u·al·ly** *adv.*

manual alphabet *n.* An alphabet of hand signals used for communication with or between deaf people.

ma·nu·bri·um (mə-néw-bri-əm ‖ -nōō-) *n., pl.* **-bria** (-bri-ə). *Anatomy.* **1.** The upper part of the breastbone. **2.** The handle-shaped projection of the malleus in the ear. [New Latin, from Latin *manubrium,* handle : *manus,* hand + an obscure second element.]

Manucci. See **Manutius.**

Ma·nu·el I (mánnew-el, -əl; *Portuguese* man-wél), also called Emmanuel; also known as **Manuel the Great** or **the Fortunate** (1469–1521). King of Portugal (1495–1521). He presided over the golden age of Portugal's overseas exploration, including the discovery of the sea route to India by Vasco da Gama.

man·u·fac·to·ry (mánnew-fák-təri, -tri) *n., pl.* **-ries.** *Archaic.* A factory. [MANUFACT(URE) + (FACT)ORY.]

man·u·fac·ture (mánnew-fákchər ‖ mánnə-) *v.* **-tured, -turing, -tures.** *—tr.* **1. a.** To make or process (a raw material) into a finished product, especially by means of a large-scale industrial operation. **b.** To make or process (a product), especially by industrial machines. **2.** To create, produce, or turn out in a mechanical manner: *A street artist manufacturing portraits to order.* **3.** To concoct or invent; fabricate. *—intr.* To make or process goods, especially in large quantities and by means of industrial machines.
~n. Abbr. **manuf., manufac., mfg., mfr. 1.** The act, craft, or process of manufacturing. **2.** A product that is manufactured. [French, a making by hand, handiwork, from Late Latin *manūfactus,* handmade : Latin *manus,* hand + *factus,* from *facere,* to make.] **—man·u·fac·tur·a·ble** *adj.*

man·u·fac·tured gas (mánnew-fákchərd ‖ mánnə-) *n.* A gaseous fuel made from various petroleum products or from soft coal.

man·u·fac·tur·er (mánnew-fákchərər ‖ mánnə-) *n. Abbr.* **mfr.** A person or enterprise that manufactures; especially, the owner or operator of a factory.

ma·nu·ka (máanəkə, mə-nōōkə) *n.* An ornamental tree or shrub, *Leptospermum scoparium,* native to New Zealand, with aromatic leaves and hard timber. [Maori.]

man·u·mit (mánnew-mít) *tr.v.* **-mitted, -mitting, -mits.** To free from slavery or bondage; emancipate. [Middle English *manumitten,* from Old French *manumitter,* from Latin *manumittere,* from *manū ēmit-*

tere, to liberate, release from one's hand : *manū,* ablative of *manus,* hand + *ēmittere,* to EMIT.] **—man·u·mis·sion** (-mísh'n) *n.* **—man·u·mit·ter** *n.*

ma·nure (mə-néwr ‖ -nōōr) *n.* Animal dung, compost, or other material used to fertilise soil.
~tr.v. **manured, -nuring, -nures.** To apply manure to. [Middle English *manour,* cultivation of soil, from *manouren,* to till, from Anglo-French *mainoverer,* from Old French *manoeuvrer,* to till, "work by hand", from Medieval Latin *manuoperārī* : Latin *manus,* hand + *operārī,* to work.] **—ma·nur·er** *n.*

ma·nus (máynəss) *n., pl.* **manus. 1.** *Zoology.* The end of the forelimb in vertebrates, such as the hand, claw, or hoof. **2.** In Roman law, the authority of a husband over his wife. [Latin, hand.]

man·u·script (mánnew-skript) *n. Abbr.* **ms, MS, ms., MS. 1.** A book, document, or other composition written by hand. **2.** A typewritten or handwritten version of a book, article, document, or other work, prepared and submitted for publication in print. **3.** Handwriting, as opposed to printing.
~adj. Handwritten or typewritten. [Medieval Latin *manūscrīptus,* handwritten : Latin *manus,* hand + *scrīptus,* from *scrībere,* to write.]

Ma·nu·ti·us (mə-néw-shi-əss, -shəss ‖ -nōō-), also called Manucci. Family of Italian printers. Aldus Manutius (1450–1518) established the Aldine Press in Venice (*c.* 1498) to publish Greek and Latin classics. Paulus Manutius (1512–74) and Aldus Manutius the Younger (1547–97) directed the papal press.

Manx (mangks) *adj.* Of or pertaining to the Isle of Man or Manx (the language).
~n., pl. **Manx. 1.** A native or resident of the Isle of Man. **2.** The nearly extinct Goidelic Celtic language spoken on the Isle of Man. **3.** A Manx cat.

Manx cat *n. Sometimes small* **m.** A domestic cat of a breed having short hair and an internal vestigial tail. Also called "Manx". [Originally bred on the Isle of MAN.]

Manx shearwater *n.* A small European oceanic bird, *Puffinus puffinus,* that shows remarkably accurate homing ability.

man·y (ménni ‖ *Irish also* mánni) *adj.* **more, most. 1.** Amounting to or consisting of a large or indefinite number: *many friends; as many eggs as you can eat.* **2.** Designating each of a large number of persons or things. Used with *a, an,* or *another: many a woman; many another day.*
~pl.n. **1.** A large, indefinite number of persons or things. Often used with *of: Many of the children were ill.* **2.** The great body of the people; the masses. Usually preceded by *the:* "*The many fail; the one succeeds.*" (Alfred, Lord Tennyson).
~pl. pron. A large number of persons or things: "*Many are called, but few are chosen.*" (Matthew 22:14). **—as many.** The same number of: *had six cars in as many years.* **—many's the.** Often. **—one too many.** One more than is necessary or desirable: *drank one too many.* [Middle English, Old English *manig, mœnig.*]

man·y·plies (ménni-plīz) *n.* The third stomach of a cud-chewing mammal, the **omasum** *(see).* [MANY + *plies,* plural of PLY (modelled by analogy on *manifolds*).]

man·y·sid·ed (ménni-sídid) *adj.* Having a variety of aspects or qualities: *a many-sided book.* **—man·y·sid·ed·ness** *n.*

man·za·ni·lla (mánzə-nílla) *n.* A pale dry sherry from Spain. [Spanish, small apple, hence (from its aromatic bouquet) manzanilla sherry, diminutive of *manzana,* apple, from Old Spanish, from Latin *(māla) Matiāna,* "(apples) of *Matius*", a particular kind of apple, probably named after Caius *Matius* Calvena, Roman author of a cookery book (first century B.C.).]

Man·zo·ni (man-dzóni), **Alessandro** (1785–1873). Italian novelist and poet. He was the leader of the Italian romantic school and is best known for his romantic-historical novel *I Promessi Sposi (The Betrothed,* 1825–27). The refined Florentine dialect which he used as a literary language set the standard for modern Italian prose.

Mao (mow) *adj.* Being of a plain, uniform-like style characteristic of clothing worn in China under Mao Ze-dong: *a Mao jacket.*

Mao·ism (mów-iz'm) *n.* The Communist political philosophy and practice developed in China chiefly by Mao Ze-dong, emphasising the peasantry's role in a revolution. **—Mao·ist** *n. & adj.*

Ma·o·ri (mówr-i, mów-ri) *n., pl.* **-ris** or collectively **Maori. 1.** A member of the aboriginal people of New Zealand, of Polynesian-Melanesian descent. **2.** The Austronesian language of this people. **—Ma·o·ri** *adj.*

mao-tai, mao tai (mów-tí) *n.* A potent, colourless Chinese alcoholic drink distilled from a mixture of Chinese sorghum and millet. [Chinese, after *Maotai,* town in southwest China where it is produced.]

Mao Ze-dong or **Mao Tse-t'ung** (mów-dzə-dŏong), also known as Chairman Mao (1893–1976). Chinese Communist leader. In 1921 he helped to form the Chinese Communist Party, and with its split from the Guomindang Nationalist Party (1927) became a leader of the Chinese Soviet Republic in southeast China (1931). He led the Long March (1934–35) to Yan'an where, after the collapse of the Japanese, he defeated the Nationalists and proclaimed the People's Republic of China (1949). As Chairman of the People's Republic (1949–59), he instituted the Great Leap Forward (1958–60) and the founding of the communes. He continued as party chairman after 1959 and instituted the Cultural Revolution (1966–69) to reestablish the revolutionary spirit. His writings have had great influence on revolutionary thinking throughout the world.

map (map) *n.* **1. a.** A representation, usually on a plane surface, of a region of the earth showing geographical, political, or other features. **b.** A similar representation of stars, planets, and other

heavenly bodies. **2.** Something suggesting a map, as in comprehensiveness or clarity of representation. **3.** *Mathematics*. A **mapping.** **4.** *Slang*. The face. **5.** The arrangement of genes on a chromosome. **—put on the map.** To make famous or known. **—wipe off the map.** To destroy completely; annihilate.
~*tr.v.* **mapped, mapping, maps. 1.** To make a map of. **2.** To explore or make a survey of (a region) for the purpose of making a map. **3.** To plan or delineate, especially in detail; arrange. Often used with *out: mapping out holiday plans.* **4.** *Mathematics*. To establish a mapping of (a set or aggregate). **5.** To locate (a gene) on a chromosome. [Medieval Latin *mappa (mundī),* map (of the world), from *mappa,* napkin, sheet, cloth.] **—map·per** *n.*

ma·ple (mayp'l) *n.* **1.** Any tree or shrub of the genus *Acer,* found in the North Temperate Zone. Most are deciduous trees, having lobed leaves and winged seeds borne in pairs. **2.** The wood of a maple, especially the hard, close-grained wood of the **sugar maple** *(see).* **3.** The flavour of the concentrated sap of the sugar maple. [Middle English, Old English *mapel(treow),* maple (tree).]

maple sugar *n.* A sugar made by boiling down maple syrup.

maple syrup *n.* **1.** A sweet syrup made from the sap of maple trees, especially the **sugar maple** *(see).* **2.** Syrup made from other sugars and flavoured with maple syrup or artificial maple flavouring.

map·ping (mápping) *n. Mathematics*. A rule of correspondence between two sets that associates each member of the first set with one or more members of the second; a function. Also called "map."

map projection *n.* A representation of the earth's parallels of latitude and meridians of longitude as a network, or graticule, on a plane surface.

Ma·pu·to (mə-pōótō). Formerly **Lou·ren·ço Mar·ques** (lə-rén-sō márks; *Portuguese* lō-rán-su márkish). Capital of Mozambique, situated on Maputo Bay. It is a resort and a major seaport, exporting metal ores and coal from southern Africa.

maq·uette (ma-két) *n.* A preliminary model or sketch made by a sculptor. [French, from Italian *machietta,* diminutive of *macchia,* spot, ultimately from Latin *macula,* spot.]

ma·quill·age (máckee-aàzh) *n.* **1.** Cosmetics; make-up. **2.** The application of cosmetics. [French, from *maquiller,* to make up, from Old French *masquiller,* to stain.]

ma·quis (máckee, maàkee, ma-kée) *n., pl.* **maquis.** In the Mediterranean area, a shrubby vegetation made up of mainly evergreen small trees and bushes. [French (via Corsica), from Italian *macchia,* thicket, "spot", from Latin *macula,* spot.]

Ma·quis (ma-kée) *n., pl.* **Maquis. 1.** The French underground organisation that fought against German occupation forces during World War II; the resistance. **2.** A member of this organisation. [French, from *maquis,* MAQUIS, "bush" (referring to undergrowth as a hiding place).]

mar (mar) *tr.v.* **marred, marring, mars. 1.** To damage or deface. **2.** To spoil the quality of: *"Mend your speech lest it mar your fortunes."* (Shakespeare). **—See Synonyms at injure.**
~*n.* A mark that disfigures; a blemish. [Middle English *marren, merran,* Old English *merran, mierran.*]

Mar. March.

mar·a·bou, mar·a·bout (márrə-bōō) *n.* **1.** A large Old World stork, *Leptoptilus crumeniferus.* Also called "adjutant", "adjutant stork". **2.** A neckpiece, hat, dress, or coat trimmed with the down of the marabou. **3. a.** A raw silk that can be dyed without being separated from the gum. **b.** A fabric or an article of clothing made from such silk. [French *marabout,* from Portuguese *marabuto,* from Arabic *murābit,* holy man, hermit, hence stork (the stork is a sacred bird in Islam). See **marabout.**]

mar·a·bout[1] (márrə-bōō, -bōōt) *n.* **1.** A Muslim hermit or saint, especially in north Africa. **2.** The tomb of a marabout or a shrine to his memory. [French, from Portuguese *marabuto,* from Arabic *murābit,* hermit, holy man, "(one) stationed (at a frontier post)", from *ribāt,* frontier post (those stationed there fought against infidels and were thus considered holy).]

marabout[2]. Variant of **marabou.**

ma·ra·bun·ta (márrə-buntə) *n. West Indian.* **1.** Any of several social wasps. **2.** *Slang.* A bad-tempered, nagging woman. [Probably of West African origin.]

ma·rac·a (mə-rácka ‖ -raàkə) *n.* A percussion instrument consisting of a hollow gourd rattle containing pebbles or beans. Maracas are often played in pairs. [Brazilian Portuguese *maracá,* from Tupi.]

Ma·ra·do·na (márə-dōnə), **Diego Armando** (1960–). Argentinian soccer player. He captained Argentina to win the World Cup in 1986.

ma·rae (mə-rí) *n.* A Maori meeting place.

mar·ag·ing (maàr-ayjing) *n. Metallurgy.* The process of heating a martensite steel at around 500°C followed by cooling in air without quenching. It is used to modify the martensite structure and produce strong low-carbon steels. [MAR(TENSITE) + AG(E)ING.]

Ma·ram·ba (mə-rámbə). See **Liv·ing·stone** (lívving-stən ‖ -stōn).

ma·ran·ta (mə-rántə) *n.* **1.** Any plant of the tropical American genus *Maranta,* one species of which, *M. arundinacea,* yields arrowroot. Several species are cultivated for their ornamental foliage. **2.** A starch made from arrowroot. [New Latin, after Bartolomeo *Maranta* (died 1600), Italian herbalist.]

ma·ran·ta (mə-rántə) *n.* **1.** Any plant of the tropical American genus *Maranta,* one species of which, *M. arundinacea,* yields arrowroot. Several species are cultivated for their ornamental foliage. **2.** A starch made from arrowroot. [New Latin, after Bartolomeo *Maranta* (died 1600), Italian herbalist.]

ma·ras·ca (mə-ráskə) *n.* A European cherry tree, *Prunus cerasus marasca,* bearing bitter red fruit from which maraschino is made. [Italian, shortened from *amarasca (ciliegia),* bitter (cherry), from *amaro,* bitter, from Latin *amārus,* bitter.]

mar·a·schi·no (márrə-skéenō, *also* -shéenō) *n.* A liqueur made from the fermented juice and crushed kernels of the marasca cherry. [Italian, from MARASCA.]

maraschino cherry *n.* A maraschino-flavoured preserved cherry.

ma·ras·mus (mə-rázməss) *n. Pathology.* A wasting away of the body, especially of infants, associated with inadequate or inadequately assimilated food. [Late Latin, from Greek *marasmos,* from *marainein,* to waste away.] **—ma·ras·mic** *adj.*

Ma·rat (márraa; *French* ma-rá), **Jean Paul** (1743–93). French journalist, and Revolutionary politician. He was trained as a doctor and wrote scientific works before founding (1789) and editing *l'Ami du Peuple* which supported the French Revolution. Hero of the working classes, he was elected to the National Convention (1792) and struggled against the Girondins, one of whose supporters, Charlotte Corday, murdered him in his bath.

Ma·ra·tha (mə-raàtə) *n., pl.* **-thas** or collectively **Maratha.** Also **Mah·rat·ta** (-ráttə). A member of a Scythian-Dravidian people of southwest India.

Ma·ra·thi (mə-raàti) *adj.* Also **Mah·rat·i, Mah·rat·ti** (-rátti). Of or pertaining to the state of Maharashtra, India.
~*n.* Also **Mahrati, Mahratti.** The major Indic language in Maharashtra.

mar·a·thon (márrə-th'n ‖ -thon) *n.* **1.** A race on foot of 42.195 kilometres (26 miles 385 yards). It is an event in the Olympic games. **2.** Any long-distance race: *a swimming marathon.* **3.** A contest of endurance: *a dance marathon.* **4.** A task or action that requires endurance: *a letter-writing marathon.* [Named in commemoration of the feat of the messenger Pheidippides, who ran to Athens to report the news of the Greek victory over the Persians at *Marathon* (490 B.C.).] **—mar·a·thon** *adj.*

ma·raud (mə-ráwd) *v.* **-rauded, -rauding, -rauds.** —*intr.* To rove in search of booty; raid for plunder. —*tr.* To invade for loot; raid or pillage.
~*n. Archaic.* A raid. [French *marauder,* from *maraud,* vagabond, rogue, perhaps from dialectal *maraud,* tomcat (imitative of purring).] **—ma·raud·er** *n.*

mar·ble (márb'l) *n.* **1.** A metamorphic rock, chiefly calcium carbonate, $CaCO_3$, often irregularly coloured by impurities. It is used for architectural and ornamental purposes. **2.** A piece of marble. **3.** A sculpture of marble: *the Elgin marbles.* **4.** A small hard ball made of stone or glass, used in children's games. See **marbles. —lose (one's) marbles.** *Slang.* **1.** To take leave of one's senses; go mad. **2.** To become senile. **—make (one's) marble good with.** *Australian Slang.* To make oneself popular with; win the approval of.
~*tr.v.* **marbled, -bling, -bles.** To mottle and streak with colours and veins in imitation of marble: *marbled paper.*
~*adj.* **1.** Consisting of or constructed with marble: *marble halls.* **2.** Resembling marble in consistency, texture, venation, colour, or coldness: *a marble heart.* [Middle English *marbel,* from Old French *marbre,* from Latin *marmor,* from Greek *marmaros*†, marble, originally any hard stone.] **—mar·bly** *adj.*

marble cake *n.* A sponge cake with a marbled appearance, made with a light and a dark mixture of ingredients, swirled together slightly just before cooking.

mar·bled white (márb'ld) *n.* A widely distributed butterfly, *Melariargia galathea,* with distinctive black and cream marking.

mar·ble·ise, mar·ble·ize (márb'l-īz) *tr.v.* **-ised, -ising, -ises.** To give a veined or mottled appearance to.

mar·bles (márb'lz) *n. Used with a singular verb.* Any of various children's games played with marbles, the object usually being to strike a marble or group of marbles belonging to one's opponent by throwing at it a marble of one's own.

mar·bling (márbling) *n.* **1.** A mottling or streaking that resembles marble. **2.** The process or operation of giving something the surface appearance of marble. **3.** The decorative imitation of marble patterns printed on page edges and endpapers of books. **4.** The streaks of fat found in beef of good quality.

Mar·burg[1] (már-burg; *German* -bóork). City in Hesse, central Germany. It is the site of Germany's first Protestant university (1527) and the 13th- to 14th-century castle where Luther and Zwingli held their famous religious debate (1529). It produces precision machinery, pharmaceuticals, and pottery.

Marburg[2]. See **Maribor.**

Marburg disease *n.* A fatal virus disease that is transmitted to humans from the vervet or green monkey by contact with infected tissue in a laboratory. Also called "green monkey disease". [After MARBURG, Germany, where laboratory technicians contracted the disease in 1967.]

marc (mark, mar) *n.* **1.** The pulpy residue left after the juice has been pressed from grapes, apples, or other fruit. **2.** Brandy distilled from grape residue. [French, from Old French *marcher,* to trample (grapes), MARCH.]

Marc·an (márkən) *adj.* Pertaining to or designating St. Mark's Gospel. [Latin *Marcus,* Mark + -AN.]

mar·ca·site (márkə-sīt ‖ -zīt) *n.* **1.** A mineral form of iron disulphide, FeS_2, having the same composition as pyrite but differing in crystalline structure. Also called "white iron pyrites". **2.** An ornament of pyrite, polished steel, or white metal. [Middle English *mar-*

chasite, from Medieval Latin *marcasīta,* from Arabic *marqashīṭā,* probably from Persian.]

Mar·ceau (maar-sṓ), **Marcel** (1923–). French mime, trained as a conventional actor. His most famous character is the clown-harlequin Bip. His films include *Un Jardin public* (1955).

mar·cel (már-sél) *n.* A once fashionable hairstyle characterised by regular waves. Also called "marcel wave".

~*tr.v.* **marcelled, -celling, -cels.** To style (the hair) in a marcel. [After *Marcel* Grateau (1852–1936), French hairdresser.]

mar·ces·cent (maar-séss'nt) *adj. Botany.* Withering but not falling off. Said especially of a blossom that persists on a twig after flowering. [Latin *marcēscēns* (stem *marcēscent-*), present participle of *marcēscere,* inceptive of *marcēre,* to wither.]

march¹ (march) *v.* **marched, marching, marches.** —*intr.* **1. a.** To walk in a formal military manner with measured steps at a steady rate. **b.** To begin to move in such a manner: *The troops will march at dawn.* **2.** To advance or proceed assertively or belligerently: *marched up to the shop assistant to make a complaint.* —*tr.* **1.** To cause to march: *soldiers being marched into battle.* **2.** To traverse by marching: *They marched the route in a day.*

~*n.* **1. a.** The act of marching. **b.** The steady forward movement of a body of troops. **2.** A long tiring journey on foot. **3.** Forward movement; advancement; progression: *the march of time.* **4.** A regulated pace: *quick march.* **5.** The distance covered by marching: *a week's march away.* **6.** A procession held as a form of public demonstration. **7.** *Music.* A musical composition in regularly accented, usually duple, time with a rhythm suitable for accompanying marching. —**on the march.** Advancing; progressing: *Science is on the march.* —**steal a march on.** To get ahead of, especially by quiet enterprise. [French *marcher,* to walk, tramp, trample, from Frankish *markôn* (unattested), to mark out with footprints.] —**march·er** *n.*

march² *n.* **1.** The border or boundary of a country or area of land. **2.** A tract of land bordering on two countries: *the Welsh Marches.* ~*intr.v.* **marched, marching, marches.** To border upon a country or have a common boundary. Used with *with: England marches with Scotland.* [Middle English *marche,* from Old French, *marche, marc,* borderland, from Germanic.]

March (march) *n. Abbr.* **Mar.** The third month of the Gregorian calendar. March has 31 days. [Middle English, from Old French *Marche, Marz,* from Latin *Mārtius (mēnsis),* (month) of Mars, from *Mārs* (stem *Mārt-*), MARS (god).] **March.** marchioness.

Mar·che (márkay). Also **the Marches.** Coastal region of central Italy, covered largely by Apennine ranges and foothills. It produces cereals, fruit, wine, tobacco, cattle, and fish. It is so called because it lay on the southern border (or march) of the Holy Roman Empire. Ancona is the capital.

Mär·chen (maírkhən) *n., pl.* **Märchen.** *German.* A folk tale or fairy story.

March·es, the (márchiz). The areas along the English-Welsh and English-Scottish borders. In medieval times, the lords of these areas were given wide-ranging powers to defend the borders.

mar·che·sa (mar-káy-za, -sa, -zə, -sə) *n., pl.* **-se** (-ze, -se). A wife or widow of a marchese. [Italian, feminine of MARCHESE.]

mar·che·se (mar-kay-zə) *n., pl.* **-si** (-zee). An Italian nobleman ranking between a prince and a count. [Italian, from Late Latin *marcēnsis,* "ruler of a march", from *marca,* borderland, MARCH.]

Marcheshvan. Variant of **Cheshvan.**

marching orders *pl.n.* **1. a.** Orders to move on or depart. **b.** Official instructions to proceed. **2.** *Informal.* A warning that one is no longer wanted: *was given her marching orders by her lover.*

mar·chion·ess (mársh'n-iss, -éss) *n., pl.* **-esses.** *Abbr.* **March. 1.** The wife or widow of a marquis. **2.** A peeress of the rank of marquis in her own right. In certain countries, also called "marquise". [Medieval Latin *marchionissa,* feminine of *marchiō,* marquis, "ruler of the march", from *marca,* borderland, MARCH.]

march·land (márch-land, -lənd) *n.* A borderland; a march.

march·pane (márch-payn) *n. Archaic.* A confection, **marzipan** *(see).*

march past *n.* The ceremonial marching of troops or other uniformed personnel past a saluting base during a review.

Mar·cio·nism (mársh'n-izm) *n.* A Gnostic movement of the second and third centuries A.D. that rejected the Old Testament and emphasised the teachings of St. Paul. [After *Marcion* of Sinope (*c.* 100–160), who founded the sect (144).]

Mar·co·ni (maar-kṓni), **Guglielmo, Marchese** (1874–1937). Italian physicist and electrical engineer. He developed the equipment for converting radio waves into electrical signals: in 1895 he successfully transmitted long-wave radio signals, and in 1901 sent signals across the Atlantic. He shared the Nobel prize for physics (1909).

Marconi rig *n.* A Bermuda rig *(see).* [After Guglielmo MARCONI, since the rig resembles an early radio transmitting aerial.]

Mar·cos (már-koss), **Ferdinand (Edralin)** (1917–89). President of the Philippines (1965–86). He declared martial law (1972), and suppressed political opposition. In 1986 he was replaced as president by Cory Aquino.

Mar·cus (Ae·li·us) Au·re·li·us (An·to·ni·nus) (márkəss eeli-əss aw-rééli-əss ántə-nínəss), born Marcus Annius Verus (121–180). Roman emperor (161–180) and Stoic philosopher. An active emperor, he ruled with Lucius Verus until A.D. 169, afterwards ruling alone. Sometimes called the Philosopher Emperor, he wrote the *Meditations,* 12 volumes of aphorisms, illustrating his Stoic ideals.

Mar·cus·e (maar-kṓozə), **Herbert** (1898–1979). U.S. Marxist phi-

losopher. A Jewish refugee from Nazi Germany, he criticised both orthodox Marxism and western positivism, and advocated using the tolerance of contemporary society to overthrow that very society. His works include *Eros and Civilisation* (1954), *One Dimensional Man* (1965), and *Counter-Revolution and Revolt* (1972).

Mar·di gras (márdi gráa) *n.* Shrove Tuesday, the last day before Lent. It is celebrated in some places, such as New Orleans, United States, by carnivals, masquerade balls, and parades of costumed merrymakers. [French, "fat Tuesday".]

Mar·duk (márdōōk). The chief god of ancient Babylon.

mar·dy (márdi) *adj. British Regional.* **1.** Spoilt. **2.** Naughty; sulky. Said of a child. [From *marred,* past participle of MAR.]

mare¹ (mair) *n.* A female horse or the female of other equine species. [Middle English *mare, mere,* Old English *mēre* (unattested).]

ma·re² (máa-ray, -ri, márray, márri) *n., pl.* **-ria** (máari-ə, márri-ə). *Astronomy.* Any of the large dark areas on the moon or Mars, originally thought to be seas. [New Latin, from Latin, sea.]

mare clau·sum (klów-səm, -sōōm) *n. Law.* A sea under the jurisdiction of one nation and closed to all others. [Latin, "closed sea".]

mare li·be·rum (léebə-rəm, -rōōm) *n. Law.* A sea open to navigation by all nations. [Latin, "free sea".]

ma·rem·ma (mə-rémmə) *n.* Low, unhealthy coastal marshland, especially in Italy. [Italian, from Latin *maritima.* See **maritime.**]

Ma·ren·go (mə-réng-gō) *adj.* Browned in oil and sautéed in a sauce of tomatoes, mushrooms, garlic or onion, and white wine. Used after the noun: *veal Marengo.* [Said to be from the chicken dish served to Napoleon after the battle of *Marengo* (1800).]

mare's nest (mairz) *n.* **1.** A hoax or fraud. **2.** An extraordinarily complicated situation. [From the proverbial expression "to find a mare's nest" (that is, an impossible fantasy).]

mare's-tail (maírz-tayl) *n.* **1.** An aquatic plant, *Hippuris vulgaris,* of the North Temperate Zone, having minute flowers and whorls of tapering leaves. **2.** *Usually plural.* A drawn out, wispy cirrus cloud.

marg. Variant of **marge.**

Mar·ga·ret (márg-rit, márgə-, -rət), **Maid of Norway** (1283–90). Queen of Scotland (1286–90). Daughter of Eric II, King of Norway, and Princess Margaret of Scotland, she became queen on the death of her grandfather Alexander III. Betrothed to the future Edward II of England, she died in the Orkneys on her way to Scotland, thereby causing a war of succession.

Margaret (Rose), H.R.H. Princess, Countess of Snowdon (1930–). A princess of the United Kingdom, the younger daughter of George VI and sister of Queen Elizabeth II. She was married (1960–78) to Anthony Armstrong-Jones, later Earl of Snowdon.

Margaret of Anjou (1430–82). Queen of England. Daughter of René of Anjou, she was married to Henry VI of England (1445) in an attempt to establish peace between France and England. The incompetent rule of Henry led to the Wars of the Roses (1455–85) during which Margaret led the Lancastrian faction, hoping to secure the succession of her son Edward (1453–71). Defeated and captured at the Battle of Tewkesbury (1471), she was ransomed to France (1476), where she died in poverty.

Margaret of Scotland, Saint (*c.* 1045–93). Queen of Scotland. The grand-daughter of the English king Edmund Ironside, she married Malcolm III of Scotland (1067). She reformed the Scottish Church, and was canonised (1250).

Margaret of Valois (1553–1615). Queen of Navarre and France. She was the daughter of Henry II of France and Catherine de' Medici. Her marriage to Henry of Navarre (later Henry IV of France) in 1572 was annulled in 1599. Remembered for her *Mémoires,* she formed a literary circle during her stay at Usson (1587–1605).

Margaret Tudor (1489–1541). Regent of Scotland (1513–14). Daughter of Henry VII of England, she married James IV of Scotland (1503), after whose death she was regent for her son James V. Her marriage to Archibald Douglas, Earl of Angus (1514), lost her the regency.

mar·gar·ic (maar-gárrik). *adj.* Also **mar·ga·rit·ic** (márgə-ríttik). Resembling pearl; pearly. [French *margarique,* from Greek *margaron,* pearl.]

margaric acid *n.* A synthetic crystalline fatty acid, $C_{16}H_{33}COOH$. Also called "heptadecanoic acid". [French *margarique,* "pearly" (referring to its colour), from Greek *margaron,* pearl.]

mar·ga·rine (márjə-réen, *occasionally* márgə- ‖ -reen) *n.* Also **mar·ga·rin** (-rin). A fatty solid consisting of a blend of hydrogenated vegetable or animal oils mixed with emulsifiers, vitamins, colouring matter, and other ingredients. It is used as a butter substitute. Also called "marge", "oleomargarine". [French, from *margarique,* MARGARIC (ACID).]

mar·ga·ri·ta (márgə-réetə) *n.* A cocktail made with tequila, orange liqueur, and lemon or lime juice, usually served in a salt-rimmed glass. [Mexican Spanish, probably from *Margarita,* a feminine name.]

mar·ga·rite (márgə-rīt) *n.* **1.** A mineral, $CaAl_2(Si_2Al_2)O_{10}(OH)_2$, with a pearly, translucent lustre, formed in sheets of monoclinic crystals and related to mica. **2.** *Archaic.* A pearl. **3.** A rock formation that resembles beads. [Sense 1, from German *Margarit,* from Greek *margaritēs,* pearl. Sense 2, Middle English, from Old French, from Latin *margarīta,* from Greek *margaritēs,* pearl. Sense 3, from sense 2.]

Mar·gate (márgayt, márgit). Popular seaside resort of Kent, southeast England. It includes Westgate-on-Sea and Cliftonville.

marge (marj) *n.* Also **marg** (marg). *Informal.* Margarine.

mar·gin (márjin) *n.* **1.** An edge and the area adjacent to it; a border; a rim; a verge. **2. a.** The blank space bordering the written or printed area on a page. **b.** A vertical line drawn usually on the left-hand side of a page marking off such blank space. **3.** A limit of a state or process: *the margins of reality.* **4.** An amount allowed beyond what is strictly necessary; a surplus measure or amount: *a margin of safety.* **5.** A measure, quantity, or degree of difference: *a margin of 500 votes.* **6.** *Economics.* **a.** The minimum return that an enterprise may earn and still pay for itself. **b.** The difference between the cost and the selling price of securities or commodities. **7.** *Finance.* An amount in money, or represented by securities, deposited by a customer with a broker as a provision against loss on transactions made on account. **8.** *Australian.* An additional or bonus payment made to an employee, especially for extra responsibilities. **9.** *Botany.* The border of a leaf. **10.** *Zoology.* The boundary area of an insect's wing. —See Synonyms at **border.**
~*tr.v.* **margined, -gining, -gins. 1.** To provide with a margin. **2.** *Finance.* To deposit a margin upon. [Middle English, from Latin *margō* (stem *margin-*).]

mar·gin·al (márjin'l) *adj.* **1.** Of, pertaining to, or constituting a margin: *the marginal strip of beach.* **2.** Geographically adjacent: *counties marginal to Wales.* **3.** Written or printed in the margin of a book: *marginal notes.* **4. a.** Barely within a lower standard or limit of quality: *marginal writing ability.* **b.** Amounting to mere subsistence: *a marginal existence.* **c.** Barely noticeable; very small: *a marginal difference.* **5.** *Economics.* **a.** Designating enterprises that produce goods or are capable of producing goods at a rate that barely covers production costs. **b.** Pertaining to commodities thus manufactured and sold. **6.** *Psychology.* Pertaining to the fringe of consciousness. **7.** Lying next to more fertile agricultural land and yielding only a small crop. **8.** Only loosely associated with a main body; fringe: *marginal social groups.* **9.** *British.* Designating an electoral district where the majority of the elected councillor or Member of Parliament is so small that it may easily be won by an opposing candidate at a subsequent election. [Medieval Latin *marginālis,* from Latin *margō* (stem *margin-*), margin.] —**mar·gin·al·i·ty** (márji-nál'-ǝti) *n.* —**mar·gin·al·ly** *adv.*

mar·gi·na·li·a (márji-náyli-ǝ) *pl.n.* Notes in the margin of a book or other printed matter. [New Latin, neuter plural of Medieval Latin *marginālis,* MARGINAL.]

mar·gin·al·ise, mar·gin·al·ize (márjin'līz) *tr. v.* **-ised, -ising, -ises.** To relegate to the margin, away from the centre of attention, interest, concern, or significance: *"They fear that Britain will be marginalised by its more dynamic neighbours."* (*The Spectator.*) —**mar·gin·al·i·sa·tion** (-ī-záysh'n || *U.S.* -i-) *n.*

mar·gin·ate (márji-nayt) *tr.v.* **-ated, -ating, -ates.** To provide with margins or a margin.
~*adj.* Also **mar·gin·at·ed** (-naytid). *Biology.* Having a border or edge of distinctive colour or pattern. —**mar·gin·a·tion** (-náysh'n) *n.*

mar·grave (már-grayv) *n.* **1.** The lord or military governor of a medieval German border province. **2.** A hereditary title of certain princes in the Holy Roman Empire. [Middle Dutch *markgrave,* "count of the march" : *mark,* border, MARCH + *grave,* count.]

mar·gra·vi·ate (maar-gráyvi-ǝt, -ayt) *n.* Also **mar·gra·vate** (márgrǝv-ǝt, -ayt). The territory governed by a margrave.

mar·gra·vine (márgrǝ-veen) *n.* The wife or widow of a margrave. [Middle Dutch *markgravin,* feminine of *markgrave,* MARGRAVE.]

Mar·gre·the II (maar-gráy-tǝ, -dǝ) (1940–). Queen of Denmark. She inherited the throne from her father Frederick IX (1972) after alterations in the constitution to permit the accession of women.

mar·gue·rite (márgǝ-réet) *n.* **1.** A garden plant, *Chrysanthemum frutescens,* native to the Canary Islands, having white or pale yellow flowers. **2.** Any of several similar or related plants having daisy-like flowers. [French, from Old French *margarite,* daisy, from Latin *margarīta,* pearl, from Greek *margaritēs,* pearl.]

Ma·ri (maári). Ancient Amorite city of Mesopotamia (now Tel Hariri, Syria), on the Euphrates river. Excavations began in 1933 and the royal palace yielded over 20,000 cuneiform tablets, mostly letters and historical accounts.

ma·ri·a. *Astronomy.* Plural of **mare.**

Ma·ri·am (márri-ǝm), **Mengistu Haile** (1937–). Ethiopian soldier and politician. He played a leading part in the overthrow of Emperor Haile Selassie in 1974, and in 1977 became Head of State. In 1991, facing defeat by rebels, he fled the country.

Mar·i·an (maír-i-ǝn) *n.* **1.** A devotee of the Virgin Mary. **2. a.** A supporter of Queen Mary I of England. **b.** An adherent of Mary, Queen of Scots.
~*adj.* Of or pertaining to the Virgin Mary, Queen Mary I of England, or Mary, Queen of Scots.

Mar·i·a·nas, Northern (márri-áanǝz). Also **Mariana Islands, Marianas.** A commonwealth of the United States in the northwest Pacific. The Mariana Islands, from 1947 part of the United Nations Trust Territory of the Pacific Islands administered by the United States, voted for their present status (like that of Puerto Rico) in 1978, with the exception of **Guam.** They rely heavily on tourism and exports of copra. Saipan is the largest island, with most inhabitants. Their area is 471 square kilometres (182 square miles), and their capital is Saipan. See map at **Pacific Ocean.**

Marianas Trench. Ocean trench just east of the Mariana Islands in the northwest Pacific. It includes Challenger Deep, the deepest point of any ocean in the world (11 033 metres; 36,197 feet).

Ma·ri·án·ské Láz·ně (márri-aanske laázn-ye). *German* **Ma·ri·en·bad** (mǝ-reé-ǝn-bad, *German* -baat). A spa in Bohemia, Czech Republic. Popular since the late 18th century, it was visited by such notables as King Edward VII and Richard Wagner.

Ma·ri·bor (márribawr). *German* **Mar·burg** (már-boork). City in Slovenia, lying on the river Drava. It is one of the principal industrial centres of the country, producing aeroplanes, cars, armaments, and machinery.

Ma·rie An·toi·nette (márri ón-twǝ-nét, mǝ-reé, maá-ri, -twa-) (1755–1793). Austrian princess and wife of Louis XVI of France. Her origins, extravagances, and political intrigue made her highly unpopular. She attempted to influence French policy in favour of Austria and resisted the post-revolutionary settlement for the monarchy proposed by Mirabeau. She was tried for treason by the Revolutionary Tribunal and guillotined.

Ma·rie de Mé·di·cis (márri dǝ may-di-séess, mǝ-reé, maá-ri, méddichi) (1573–1642). Queen of France. Married to Henry IV of France from 1600 to 1610, she was regent, after his murder, for her son Louis XIII (1610–1617). She was banished by Louis (1617), but they were reconciled in 1622. She encouraged the rise of Richelieu to chief minister, but then lost all influence. She fled to the Netherlands (1631) and died in poverty.

Mari-El (maari-él). Formerly the Mari Autonomous Soviet Socialist Republic of the Soviet Union. Now a constituent republic of the Russian Federation, lying on the east bank of the Volga between Nizhniy Novgorod and Kazan.

Marienbad. See **Mariánské Lázně.**

mar·i·gold (márri-gōld) *n.* **1.** Any plant of the genus *Tagetes,* native to tropical America. Several species are widely cultivated for their showy yellow or orange flowers. **2.** Any of several plants having similar flowers, such as the **corn marigold** and the **marsh marigold** (*both of which see*). [Middle English *marygould* : *Mary* (with some reference to the Virgin Mary) + dialect *gold,* a marigold, Old English *gold,* probably from GOLD.]

mar·i·jua·na, mar·i·hua·na (márri-hwáanǝ, -waánǝ, -yoo-áanǝ) *n.* The dried flower clusters and leaves of the hemp plant, especially when taken as a drug to induce euphoria. Slang equivalents include "pot", "grass", "weed", and as a cigarette, "joint", "reefer". See **hashish.** [Mexican Spanish *mariguana, marihuana†.*]

ma·rim·ba (mǝ-rímbǝ) *n.* Any of various xylophones with resonators. [Bantu : *ma-,* plural prefix + *rimba, limba,* musical note.]

ma·ri·na (mǝ-réenǝ) *n.* A boat basin that has docks, moorings, supplies, and other facilities for small boats. [Italian, feminine of *marino,* MARINE.]

mar·i·nade (márri-náyd) *n.* A pickling liquid of vinegar or wine and oil, with various spices and herbs, in which meat and fish are soaked before cooking.
~*tr.v.* **marinaded, -nading, -nades.** To marinate. [French, from Spanish *marinada,* from *marinar,* to marinate, from *marino,* "briny", MARINE.]

mar·i·nate (márri-nayt) *tr.v.* **-nated, -nating, -nates.** To soak in a marinade. [French *mariner* or Italian *marinare* + -ATE.]

ma·rine (mǝ-réen) *adj.* **1. a.** Of or pertaining to the sea: *marine exploration.* **b.** Native to or formed by the sea: *marine plant life.* **2.** Of or pertaining to shipping or maritime affairs: *marine insurance.* **3.** Of or pertaining to sea navigation; nautical: *a marine chart.* **4.** Designating of or troops that serve at sea as well as on land.
~*n.* **1.** Shipping in general; maritime interests as represented by ships. Now rare except in the phrase *merchant marine.* **2. a.** A soldier serving on a ship or at a naval installation. **b.** *Capital* **M.** A member of the Marine Corps or similar military grouping. **3.** In some nations, the government department in charge of naval affairs. **4.** A painting or photograph of the sea. —**tell it to the marines.** *U.S. Informal.* Used to express scepticism. [Middle English, from Old French *marin,* from Latin *marīnus,* from *mare,* sea.]

Marine Corps *n. Abbr.* **MC, USMC, U.S.M.C.** A branch of the U.S. Armed Forces composed chiefly of amphibious troops under the authority of the Secretary of the Navy. Also officially called "United States Marine Corps".

mar·i·ner (márrinǝr) *n.* A person who navigates or serves on a ship; a sailor or seaman. [Middle English, from Old French *marinier,* from *marin,* MARINE.]

Mar·i·ol·a·try (maíri-óllǝtri, márri-) *n.* Excessive veneration of the Virgin Mary. Used derogatorily. [Latin *Maria,* Mary + -LATRY (by analogy with *idolatry*).]

Mar·i·ol·o·gy (maíri-óllǝji, márri-) *n.* Also **Mar·y·ol·o·gy.** The body of belief pertaining to the Virgin Mary. [MARY + -LOGY.]

mar·i·o·nette (márri-ǝ-nét) *n.* A jointed puppet manipulated by strings or wires attached to its limbs. [French, diminutive of the feminine name *Marion.*]

mar·i·po·sa lily (márri-pṓ-zǝ, -sǝ) *n.* Any of several bulbous plants of the genus *Calochortus,* of the southwestern United States and Mexico, having variously coloured, tulip-like flowers. Sometimes called "mariposa tulip". [Spanish *mariposa,* butterfly : probably *Maria,* Mary + *posar,* to perch, alight.]

Mar·ist (maír-ist) *n.* **1.** A member of the Society of Mary, a congregation of Roman Catholic missionary priests founded in 1824. **2.** A member of the Little Brothers of Mary, a Roman Catholic teaching order founded in 1817. —**Mar·ist** *adj.*

Ma·ri·tain (marri-táN), **Jacques** (1882–1973). French Catholic philosopher. He abandoned the philosophy of Bergson to become a neo-Thomist, applying the medieval techniques of St. Thomas Aquinas to modern social problems. His works include *Les Degrés du savoir* (1932) and *La Philosophie morale* (1960).

mar·i·tal (márrit'l, *rarely* mə-rī́t'l) *adj.* **1.** Of, pertaining to, or required by marriage. **2.** *Rare.* Of or pertaining to a husband. [Latin *marītālis,* from *marītus,* married, husband.] **—mar·i·tal·ly** *adv.*

marital status *n.* Whether a person is married, single, divorced, separated, or widowed.

mar·i·time (márri-tīm) *adj. Abbr.* **mar. 1.** Located on or near the sea. **2.** Of or concerned with shipping or navigation. **3.** Designating a climate characteristic of coastal areas, with relatively small seasonal and daily temperature changes. [French, from Latin *maritimus,* from *mare,* sea.]

Mar·i·time Alps (márri-tīm). *French* **Alpes Mar·i·times** (álp marri-tée͞m). A branch of the western Alps along the French-Italian border, extending to the Mediterranean. They give their name to the French département of Alpes Maritimes, whose resorts include Cannes, Nice, and Grasse. Punta Argentera (3 297 metres; 10,817 feet) is the highest peak.

maritime pine *n.* A tree, the **pinaster** *(see).*

Maritime Provinces. Atlantic region of Canada, comprising the provinces of New Brunswick, Nova Scotia, and Prince Edward Island. It covers most of the area of the former Acadia (Acadie), French Canada (1605–1713).

Ma·ri·vaux (marri-vṓ), **Pierre Carlet de Chamblain de** (1688–1763). French dramatist, a writer of sophisticated romantic comedies. His works include *Le Jeu de l'amour et du hasard* (1730) and the unfinished *La Vie de Marianne* (1731–41).

mar·jo·ram (márjərəm) *n.* **1.** An aromatic plant, *Origanum marjorana,* having small purplish or white flowers and leaves used as seasoning. Also called "sweet marjoram". **2.** A similar plant, *Origanum vulgare,* having spikes of pinkish flowers, and leaves used in cooking. Also called "oregano", "wild marjoram". **3.** A similar plant, *Origanum onites,* having white or pinkish flowers, of the Mediterranean region. Also called "pot marjoram". [Middle English *majorane,* from Old French, from Medieval Latin *majorāna*†.]

mark[1] (mark) *n. Abbr.* **mk. 1.** A visible trace or impression on something, such as a spot, dent, or line. **2.** A cross or other sign made in lieu of a signature by an illiterate person. **3. a.** A written or printed symbol used for punctuation; a punctuation mark. **b.** A written or printed symbol used to give information or instructions: *proofreaders' marks.* **4. a.** A number, letter, or point awarded to indicate the quality of academic work: *high marks in History.* **b.** *Plural.* An indication of how strongly one approves of a person's actions: *I give her full marks for initiative.* **5. a.** A name, stamp, label, seal, or inscription placed on an article to signify ownership, quality, manufacture, or origin. See **trademark, hallmark. b.** A notch in an animal's ear or hide indicating ownership. **6.** *Nautical.* A knot or piece of material placed at various measured lengths on a lead line to indicate the depth of the water. **7.** Something that indicates a position; a marker. **8. a.** A sign or indication of some quality, property, or feature: *bore all the marks of dejection; as a mark of my respect.* **b.** A visible sign or symbol, such as a badge or brand adopted by or imposed on a person: *Trouble had set its mark on her.* **c.** *Capital* **M.** A particular type or version, especially of machines or vehicles under development. Usually followed by a designation such as a numeral, and also used adjectivally: *the Mark 3 model.* **9.** Quality; note; importance. Usually preceded by *of: "A fellow of no mark nor likelihood."* (Shakespeare). **10.** Notice; attention; heed. Usually preceded by *of*: *Little worthy of mark happened.* **11.** A target: *The arrow hit the mark.* **12.** That which one wishes to achieve; a goal. **13.** An object or point that serves as a guide. **14.** *Slang.* A person who is an easy target for a swindler; a dupe. **15.** *Usually plural.* The place from which competitors in a race begin and sometimes end their contest: *on your marks.* **16.** A stationary ball in bowls; the jack. **17.** In Rugby and Australian Rules football, a mark deliberately made in the ground with the heel by a player who has caught the ball. **18.** The middle of a boxer's stomach, just above the waistband of his shorts. **19.** A boundary between countries. **20.** In medieval England and Germany, a tract of land held in common by a community. **21.** *Statistics.* A **class mark** *(see).* **—**See Synonyms at **sign. —beside the mark.** Beside the point; irrelevant. **—God** or **Heaven save** or **bless the mark!** *Archaic.* Used to express ironic deprecation. **—make (one's) mark.** To achieve recognition; be successful.

~interj. Used by a Rugby football player on catching the ball, whereupon he is entitled to a free kick.

~v. **marked, marking, marks.** *—tr.* **1.** To make a visible impression on, as with a spot, line, or dent. **2.** To form, make, or depict by making a visible impression on, as with a spot, line, or dent: *She marked a square on the board.* **3. a.** To distinguish or indicate by making a visible impression: *She marked the spot where the treasure is buried.* **b.** To distinguish, indicate, or characterise: *This year marks the tenth anniversary.* **c.** To show (an emotion, for example): *marked her anger by leaving the room.* **4. a.** To set off by or separate as if by a mark. **b.** To limit or demarcate (a boundary, for example). **5. a.** To attach price tags, maker's labels, or other identification to (articles for sale). **b.** To write or print (a price, for example), as on a label. **6.** To correct and assess (scholastic work) by evaluating it according to a scale of letters or numbers. **7. a.** To give attention to; notice: "*Mark what radiant state she spreads.*" (John Milton). **b.** To take note of in writing; write down. **8.** To consider; study; observe: *Mark my word.* **9.** To keep (score) in various games. **10.** *Sports.* **a.** *British.* To keep close to (an opponent) so as to hamper him. **b.** In Australian Rules football, to catch (the ball). *—intr.* **1.** To make a visible impression: *This pen will still mark under water.* **2.** To receive a visible impression: *The floor marks easily.* **3.** *Archaic & Poetic.* To notice; pay attention: *"Pray you, mark."* (Shakespeare). **4.** To keep score. Used of various games. **5.** To determine scholastic grades: *Our teacher marks strictly.* [Middle English, Old English *mearc,* boundary, hence landmark, sign, trace, from Germanic *markō* (unattested), boundary.]

mark[2] *n. Abbr.* **M. 1.** A former English and Scottish monetary unit equal to 13 shillings and 4 pence. **2.** *Capital* **M. a.** A former German monetary unit, the **Reichsmark** *(see).* **b.** The **Deutschmark** *(see).* **c.** The basic monetary unit of the former East Germany, divided into 100 pfennigs. Formerly called "Ostmark". **3.** Any of several former European units of weight equal to about 225 grams (eight ounces), used especially for weighing gold and silver. **4.** A Finnish monetary unit, a **markka** *(see).* [Sense 1, Middle English *mark,* Old English *marc.* Sense 2, German *Mark,* from Middle High German *marke.* The word exists in all Germanic and Romance languages; the source is probably identical with that of MARK (sign), in a sense such as "a mark on a bar of metal".]

Mark[1] (mark). In Arthurian legend, the king of Cornwall who was the husband of Iseult and the uncle of Tristan.

Mark[2] *n.* A book of the New Testament, the second Gospel, attributed to St. Mark.

Mark, Saint. A disciple of St. Peter, reputedly the author of the second Gospel of the New Testament.

Mark An·to·ny (ántəni), Latin name Marcus Antonius (*c.* 83–30 B.C.). Roman soldier and statesman. Dissolute in his youth, he fought under Julius Caesar in Gaul (54–50 B.C.) and after Caesar's assassination (44 B.C.) formed a triumvirate with Octavius and Lepidus, which defeated Cassius and Brutus at Philippi (42 B.C.). He met and fell in love with Cleopatra (41 B.C.) while in Egypt, gaining her territory in his division of the empire. When the senate declared war on Egypt, Antony was defeated at the naval battle of Actium (31 B.C.) and committed suicide, as did Cleopatra.

mark down *tr.v.* **1.** To reduce (goods) in price. **2.** To single out, usually for an undesirable end. **3.** To note down; record.

mark-down (márk-down) *n.* A reduction in price.

marked (markt) *adj.* **1.** Having a mark or marks. **2.** Having a noticeable character or trait; distinctive; clearly defined: *"certain strongly marked variations, which no one would rank as mere individual differences"* (Charles Darwin). **3.** Singled out, especially for an exceptional fate: *a marked man.* **4.** *Linguistics.* Of or pertaining to that one of a closely connected pair of words or other linguistic units which has some feature held to distinguish it from the other more neutral or general form; for example, in the pairs *dog/dogs* and *dog/bitch, dogs* and *bitch* are the marked forms. **—mark·ed·ly** (márkidli) *adv.* **—mark·ed·ness** (márkid-nəss, -niss) *n.*

marked cheque *n. British.* A cheque guaranteed by a bank as being covered by sufficient funds on deposit. Also *U.S.* "certified cheque".

mark·er (márkər) *n.* **1.** Something that marks or distinguishes, such as a bookmark, tombstone, milestone, or buoy. **2.** A person who marks objects, especially for industrial purposes. **3.** A person who corrects examination papers. **4.** *Sports.* **a.** A line, stake, flag, or other device on a playing field that shows the playing or scoring position. **b.** One who marks another player. **5. a.** A person or device that keeps score in various games. **b.** A score in a game. **6.** A pen or other writing instrument used for making marks on objects, as for identification or pricing. **7.** *Chiefly U.S. Slang.* A written, signed promissory note; an IOU.

mar·ket (márkit) *n. Abbr.* **mkt. 1.** A public gathering held at regular intervals for buying and selling merchandise. **2.** An open place or building where goods are offered for sale. Also called "marketplace". **3.** A store or shop that sells a particular type of merchandise: *a meat market.* **4. a.** The business of buying and selling a specified commodity. **b.** Market price. **c.** Commercial activity; trading: *a brisk market; a free market.* **5. a.** The opportunity to buy or sell; demand for or availability of merchandise. **b.** An area in which sales may be made: *one of our biggest export markets.* **6. a.** An exchange for buying and selling stocks or commodities: *securities sold on the London market.* **b.** The entire enterprise of buying and selling commodities and securities. Usually preceded by *the.* **—at the market.** At the price prevailing when a customer's order to buy or sell is placed. **—be in the market for.** To desire to acquire or buy. **—play the market.** To speculate on the stock exchange. **—price out of the market.** To price so highly as to remove demand. **—put on the market.** To put up for sale.

~v. **marketed, -keting, -kets.** *—tr.* **1.** To offer for sale. **2.** To sell. **3.** To promote the sale of (a product) by means of marketing techniques. *—intr.* **1.** To deal in a market. **2.** To buy household supplies: *He marketed for Sunday dinner.* [Middle English, Old English, from Vulgar Latin *marcātus* (unattested), variant of Latin *mercātus,* from the past participle of *mercārī,* to trade, from *merx,* merchandise.] **—mar·ket·er** *n.*

mar·ket·a·ble (márkitə-b'l) *adj.* **1.** Fit to be offered for sale. **2.** Salable. **3.** Of selling or buying. **—mar·ket·a·bil·i·ty** (-bílləti) *n.*

market economy *n.* An economy regulated mainly or exclusively by market forces.

Mark·e·teer (márki-tée͞r) *n.* In Britain, one who has a specified attitude to Britain's membership of the European Economic Community. Used in the combinations *anti-Marketeer* and *pro-Marketeer.*

market forces *pl.n. Economics.* The effects on an economy of supply and demand, unmodified by government intervention.

market garden *n. Chiefly British.* An establishment, larger than a smallholding but smaller than a farm, where fruit and vegetables are cultivated on a commercial scale. Also *U.S.* "truck farm". —**market gardener** *n.* —**market gardening** *n.*

mark·et·ing (márkiting) *n.* The act or business of promoting sales of a product, as by market research, advertising, and packaging.

market maker *n.* Any of the people (such as brokers) or organisations always willing to buy or sell in a securities market on their own account, if the price is appropriate.

market order *n.* An order to buy or sell stocks or commodities at the prevailing market price.

mar·ket·place, market place (márkit-playss) *n.* **1.** A public square or other place in which a market is set up. In this sense, also called "market". **2.** The processes of buying and selling goods or services: *prices determined by the marketplace.* **3.** A forum, such as a journal or a conference, where views or information can be exchanged.

market price *n.* The prevailing price at which merchandise, securities, or commodities are sold. Also called "market".

market research *n.* The study of how a product or service is likely to sell or is already selling, usually carried out by asking questions of a cross-section of the population in order to determine consumers' reactions.

market value *n.* The amount that a seller may expect to obtain for merchandise, services, or securities in the open market.

mar·khor (márkawr) *n.* A Himalayan goat, *Capra falconeri*, having a red-brown coat and large, spirally curved horns. [Persian, "snake-eater" : *mār*, snake + *khōr*, -eating.]

Mar·kie·wicz (márk-yevich), **Constance (Georgine), Countess,** born Constance Gore-Booth (1868–1927). Irish nationalist, married to a Polish count. She was imprisoned and sentenced to death for fighting in the Easter Rebellion of 1916. Her sentence commuted, she was released in 1917, and as a Sinn Fein candidate became the first woman M.P. elected to the British parliament (1918), although she did not take her seat.

mark·ing (márking) *n.* **1.** The act of making a mark or marks. **2.** A mark or marks. **3.** The arrangement or pattern of characteristic coloration of a plant or animal.

marking ink *n.* An indelible ink used for marking clothes, linen, and the like.

mark·ka (már-kə) *n., pl.* **-kaa** (-kaa). *Abbr.* **mk.** The basic monetary unit of Finland, equal to 100 penniä. Also called "mark". [Finnish, from Swedish *mark*. See **mark** (money).]

mark of mouth *n.* A depression in the incisor tooth of a horse that indicates the animal's age.

Mar·ko·va (maar-kṓva), **Dame Alicia,** born Lilian Alicia Marks (1910–). British ballet dancer. She studied with Pavlova and Astafieva and worked with Diaghilev's company. With Anton Dolin (1904–83) she formed the Markova-Dolin company (1935). She was noted for her delicacy and graceful lightness, as in *Swan Lake* and *Giselle.*

Mar·kov chain (márkof) *n. Statistics.* A sequence of events in which the probability of each event's taking place depends on the event immediately preceding it. [After Andrei *Markov* (1856–1922), Russian mathematician.]

marks·man (márks-mən) *n., pl.* **-men** (-mən, -men). A person skilled at shooting a gun or other weapon, especially one who has reached a certain standard of proficiency. [*Mark's man*, from MARK (target).] —**marks·man·ship** *n.*

mark up *tr.v.* To raise the price of.

mark·up, mark-up (márk-up) *n.* **1.** An increase in price. **2.** The amount added to the cost of an item when calculating the selling price.

marl[1] (marl) *n.* **1.** A fine-grained mixture of clay, calcium carbonate (including shell fragments), and magnesium carbonate, forming a loam used as a fertiliser. **2.** Any friable clay soil.
~*tr.v.* **marling, marled, marls.** To fertilise with marl. [Middle English, Old English *marle*, from Late Latin *margila*, diminutive of *marga*†.]

marl[2] *tr.v.* To bind with a marline. [Back-formation from MARLINE.]

Marlborough, John Churchill, 1st Duke of (1650–1722). English soldier and statesman. He served under James II at the defeat of Monmouth and was made a baron (1685), but supported William of Orange against James in the revolution of 1688, receiving an earldom. He served in the War of the Spanish Succession with victories at Blenheim (1704), Ramillies (1706), Oudenaarde (1708), and Malplaquet (1709). Dismissed for alleged corruption in 1711, he fled to Holland, returning to England in 1714.

mar·lin (márlin) *n.* Any of several large game fish of the family Istiophoridae, of the Atlantic and Pacific oceans, having a long upper jaw. Also called "spearfish". [Short for MARLINESPIKE (from the pointed shape of the snout).]

mar·line, mar·lin (már-lin) *n.* Also **mar·ling** (-ling). *Nautical.* A light rope made of two loosely twisted strands. [Middle English, from Middle Dutch *marlijn*, "tie-line" : *marren*, to tie + *lijn*, LINE.]

mar·line·spike, mar·lin·spike (már-lin-spīk) *n.* Also **mar·ling·spike** (-ling-). *Nautical.* A pointed metal spike, used to separate strands of rope in splicing and for similar purposes.

mar·lite (márlīt) *n.* A marl containing 25 to 75 per cent clay, the remainder being calcium carbonate, that is resistant to decomposition in air. Also called "marlstone". [MARL (loam) + -ITE.] —**mar·lit·ic** (maar-líttik) *adj.*

Mar·lowe (márlō), **Christopher** (1564–93). English playwright and poet. His development of blank verse influenced Shakespeare. Among his plays are *Tamburlaine the Great* (c. 1587), *Dr. Faustus* (c.

1588), and *Edward II* (1592). While awaiting trial for atheism, he was killed in a tavern brawl in Deptford.

mar·ma·lade (mármə-layd) *n.* A preserve made from the pulp and rind of citrus fruits, especially oranges. [French *marmelade*, from Portuguese *marmelada*, "quince jam", from *marmelo*, quince, from Latin *melimēlum*, from Greek *melimēlon*, "honey-apple", the fruit of an apple tree grafted on a quince : *meli*, honey + *mēlon*, apple, fruit.]

marmalade box *n.* A tree, the **genipap** (see).

marmalade cat *n.* A domestic cat with orange-coloured stripes.

Mar·ma·ra, Sea of (mármərə). Small sea in northwest Turkey between Asia and Europe. It is connected to the Aegean Sea by the Dardanelles, and to the Black Sea by the Bosporus.

mar·mite (már-mīt; *in senses 1 and 2, also* -meet) *n.* **1. a.** A large covered pot, usually made of earthenware or metal. **b.** A small, covered earthenware casserole designed to hold an individual serving. **2.** The broth made in such a pot or served in such a casserole. **3.** *Capital* **M.** A trademark for a savoury spread made from yeast extract. [French, kettle, pot.]

mar·mo·re·al (maar-máwr-i-əl ‖ -mṓr-) *adj.* Also **mar·mo·re·an** (-ən). **1.** Of or pertaining to marble. **2.** Resembling marble, as in being cold, smooth, white, or hard: *a complexion of marmoreal lustre.* [Latin *marmoreus*, from *marmor*, MARBLE.]

mar·mo·set (mármə-zet ‖ -set) *n.* Any of various small monkeys of the genera *Callithrix, Cebuella, Saguinus,* and *Leontideus,* found in tropical forests of the Americas. They have soft, dense fur, tufted ears, and long tails. [Middle English, from Old French *marmoset*†, grotesque figure.]

mar·mot (mármət) *n.* Any of various stocky, coarse-furred rodents of the genus *Marmota,* having short legs and bushy tails, found throughout the Northern Hemisphere. [French *marmotte,* from earlier *marmottaine,* from Medieval Latin *mormotāna,* "mountain mouse" : Latin *mūs* (stem *mūr-*), mouse + *montānus,* mountain.]

Marne (marn). River of northern France. Flowing 525 kilometres (326 miles) from the Plateau de Langres to the Seine at Paris, it forms, with the Marne-Rhine and the Marne-Saône canals, a major inland waterway network. The two Battles of the Marne (1914, 1918) ended in decisive victories for the Allies.

mar·o·cain (márrə-kayn) *n.* **1.** A crepe dress fabric, especially one made of silk. **2.** A garment made of this fabric. [French, "Moroccan", from *Maroc,* Morocco.]

Mar·o·nite (márrə-nīt) *n.* A member of a Christian sect established in Syria in the fifth century, and now found mainly in Lebanon. [Medieval Latin *Marōnīta,* from *Maro,* 5th-century Syrian monk and founder of the sect.] —**Mar·o·nite** *adj.*

ma·roon[1] (mə-rṓon) *v.* **-rooned, -rooning, -roons.** —*tr.* **1.** To put (a person) ashore on a deserted island or coast. **2.** To abandon or isolate (a person) with little hope of rescue or escape. —*intr.* To wander or wait around in an idle manner.
~*n.* **1. a.** A fugitive slave in the West Indies in the 17th and 18th centuries. **b.** A descendant of such a slave. **2.** A person who is marooned. [French *marron,* alteration of American Spanish *cimarrón,* fugitive slave, originally, "living on the mountain tops", possibly from *cima,* summit, from Latin *cȳma,* sprout, from Greek *kuma.*]

maroon[2] *n.* **1.** Dark reddish brown to dark purplish red. **2.** An explosive device; especially, one used as a warning signal. [Originally "chestnut", from French *marron*†.] —**ma·roon** *adj.*

mar·plot (már-plot) *n. Literary.* A stupid and officious meddler whose interference compromises the success of any undertaking. [After *Marplot* ("to spoil plots"), character in *The Busybody* (1709), a comic play by Susanna Centlivre (c. 1667–1723), English author.]

marque (mark) *n.* **1.** A make of car or other product. **2.** An emblem or nameplate used to identify such a make. [French, mark.]

marque, letters of *pl.n.* See **letters of marque.**

mar·quee (maar-kée) *n.* **1.** A large tent, sometimes with open sides, used chiefly for outdoor entertainment or for serving refreshments. **2.** *U.S.* A rooflike structure, often made of canvas and bearing a signboard, projecting over an entrance to a building. In this sense, also called "marquise". [French *marquise* (taken as a plural), a linen tent pitched above an officer's tent to distinguish it from others, from *marquis,* MARQUIS (disparagingly).]

Mar·que·san (maar-káy-z'n, -s'n) *n.* **1.** An inhabitant of the Marquesas Islands. **2.** The Austronesian language of the Marquesans. ~*adj.* Of or pertaining to the Marquesas Islands, their inhabitants, or their language.

Mar·que·sas Islands (maar-káy-səss, -sass, -zass). *French* Îles Marquises (eel maar-kéez). Group of 11 volcanic islands in the east Pacific, part of French Polynesia. They were annexed by France in 1842, and now export copra, vanilla, cotton, and tobacco. Gauguin is buried on Hiva Oa, near the capital, Atuona. See map at **Pacific Ocean.**

mar·que·try, mar·que·terie (márkətri) *n.* Inlaid work in wood, ivory, or the like, used chiefly in decorating furniture. [French *marqueterie,* from *marqueter,* to checker, from MARQUE.]

Már·quez (már-kess), **Gabriel García** (1928–). Colombian novelist and short-story writer. His most famous work is the novel *One Hundred Years of Solitude* (1967). He was awarded the Nobel prize (1982). Recent work includes *Love in the Time of Cholera* (1985), *News of a Kidnapping* (1997).

mar·quis (márkwiss; *French* maar-kée) *n., pl.* **marquis** or **-quises.** Also *chiefly British* **mar·quess** (márkwiss). A nobleman ranking below a duke and above an earl or count. [Middle English *marchis,* *markis,* from Old French *marquis, marchis,* "count of the march (frontier)", from *marche,* MARCH.]

mar·quis·ate (márkwi-zət, -zayt, -zit ‖ -sət, -sit) *n.* The rank or territory of a marquis.

mar·quise (már-kéez) *n.* **1.** A **marchioness** *(see).* **2.** *U.S.* A **marquee** *(see).* **3. a.** A finger ring set with a pointed oval stone or cluster of pointed oval stones. **b.** A pointed oval shape in diamonds or other gems. [French, feminine of *marquis,* MARQUIS.]

mar·qui·sette (már-ki-zét, -kwi-) *n.* A sheer fabric of cotton, rayon, silk, or nylon, used for clothing, curtains, and mosquito nets. [From MARQUISE (marquee).]

Marquis of Queensberry Rules *pl.n.* See **Queensberry Rules.**

Mar·ra·kesh (márrə-késh, *rarely* mə-ráckesh). *French* **Mar·ra·kech** (márrə-késh). Former capital of Morocco. A major Islamic, commercial, and tourist centre, it is best known for its leatherwork.

mar·ram (márrəm) *n.* **1.** A beach grass, *Ammophila arenaria,* widely planted to stabilise shifting dunes. **2.** Any of several other grasses of the genus *Ammophila.* Also called "marram grass". [East Anglian dialect, from Old Norse *maralmr : marr,* sea + *halmr,* grass.]

mar·riage (márrij) *n.* **1. a.** The state of being wife and husband; wedlock. **b.** The legal union of a woman and man as wife and husband. **2.** The act of marrying or the ceremony of being married; a wedding. **3.** Any close union: *a true marriage of minds.* **4.** In some card games, such as pinochle, the combination of the king and queen of the same suit. [Middle English *mariage,* from Old French, from *marier,* to MARRY.]

Synonyms: marriage, matrimony, wedlock, wedding, nuptials.

mar·riage·a·ble (márrijə-b'l) *adj.* Suitable or ready for marriage. **—mar·riage·a·bil·i·ty** (-billəti), **mar·riage·a·ble·ness** *n.*

marriage guidance *n.* Counsel given to help couples with their marital problems.

marriage of convenience *n.* A marriage contracted for financial, social, or similar reasons, rather than out of love.

mar·ried (márrid) **1. a.** Having a spouse: *a married man.* **b.** United in matrimony: *a married couple.* **2.** Of or pertaining to the state of marriage: *married bliss.*

~ *n.* *Often plural.* A married person: *young marrieds.*

mar·rons gla·cés (*French* ma-rón gla-sáy) *pl.n. French.* Sweet chestnuts preserved in or coated with sugar.

mar·row (márrō) *n.* **1.** The soft material that fills bone cavities, consisting, in varying proportions, of fat cells and maturing blood cells, together with supporting connective tissue and numerous blood vessels. **2.** Spinal marrow; the spinal cord. **3.** A cucurbitaceous plant, *Cucurbita peop,* cultivated for its large, white-fleshed, green-skinned gourd which is eaten as a vegetable. Also called "vegetable marrow". **4. a.** The inmost, choicest, or essential part; the pith: *chilled to the marrow.* **b.** Strength or vigour; vitality. [Middle English *marowe, margh,* Old English *mærg, mærh.*]

mar·row·bone (márrō-bōn) *n.* A bone containing marrow, used for example for flavouring soup.

mar·row·fat (márrō-fat) *n.* **1.** Any of several varieties of pea that produce large seeds. **2.** The seed of such a plant. Also called "marrow pea".

mar·ry[1] (márri) *v.* **-ried, -rying, -ries.** **—***tr.* **1. a.** To become united with in matrimony: *They married each other in June.* **b.** To take as a husband or wife: *She married her sweetheart.* **c.** To give in marriage. **2.** To obtain by marriage: *marry wealth.* **3.** To join together (a couple) in marriage. **4.** To join together or unite closely: *a woman in whom wisdom and love were married.* **5.** To manoeuvre into a matching or locking position. Used with *up: marry up the two edges before gluing.* **6.** *Nautical.* To join (two ropes) end to end by interweaving their strands. **—***intr.* **1.** To take a wife or husband; wed. **2. a.** To match; join easily. **b.** To enter into a close relationship; unite. **—marry into. 1.** To become a member of (a family) by marriage. **2.** To obtain or become involved in through marriage: *married into money.* **—marry off.** To find an appropriate spouse for. Often used derogatorily. [Middle English *marien,* from Old French *marier,* from Latin *marītāre,* from *marītus,* husband.]

marry[2] *interj. Archaic.* Used to express surprise, indignation, or emphasis. [Middle English *Marie,* "Mary!" (the Virgin).]

Mar·ry·at (márri-ət), **Captain Frederick** (1792–1848). British naval officer and author. He used the experiences of his naval career (1806–30) as a source for novels such as *Mr. Midshipman Easy* (1834–36). His children's books include *The Children of the New Forest* (1847) and *Masterman Ready* (1841).

Mars[1] (marz). *Roman Mythology.* The god of war; identified with the Greek god Ares.

Mars[2] *n.* The fourth planet from the Sun, having a sidereal period of revolution around the sun of 687 days at a mean distance of 227.9 million kilometres (141.6 million miles), a mean radius of approximately 3 363 kilometres (2,108 miles), and a mass approximately 0.11 that of Earth.

Mar·sa·la[1] (maar-sáalə). Ancient name **Lil·y·bae·um** (lílli-bée-əm). Seaport and major fishing centre in west Sicily, Italy. Founded by the Carthaginians (397 B.C.), it exports Marsala wine, salt, and grain. Garibaldi landed here in 1860 for his campaign against the Kingdom of the Two Sicilies.

Marsala[2] *n.* A pale brown, sweet dessert wine, originally exported from Marsala, Sicily.

Mar·seil·laise (már-say-áyz, -éz, -sə-láyz) *n.* The French national anthem, written in 1792 by Claude Joseph Rouget de Lisle. [French *(chanson) Marseillaise,* (song) of Marseilles.]

mar·seille (maar-sáyl) *n.* Also **mar·seilles** (-sáylz). A heavy cotton fabric with a raised pattern of stripes or figures, used for bedspreads, curtains, or the like. [Shortened from *Marseille quilting,* originally made in MARSEILLE.]

Mar·seille (maar-sáy). *English* **Mar·seilles** (-sáylz). Principal seaport of France and capital of Bouches-du-Rhône département, founded on the Mediterranean by the Greeks (*c.* 600 B.C.). It is linked to the Rhône by canal, and its industries include oil-refining, ore-smelting, chemicals, shipbuilding, and food processing.

marsh (marsh) *n.* **1.** An area of temporarily flooded land beside a river or lake, characterised by water-loving plants such as reeds, and often silty. **2.** Loosely, any area of low-lying, wet land; a fen, swamp, or bog. **3.** A **salt marsh** *(see).* [Middle English *mersh,* Old English *mersc, merisc.*] **—marsh·i·ness** *n.* **—marsh·y** *adj.*

Marsh (marsh), **Dame Ngaio (Edith)** (1899–1982). New Zealand author. She wrote many detective novels which include *A Man Lay Dead* (1934), *Death in a White Tie* (1938), and *Last Ditch* (1977).

mar·shal (mársh'l) *n.* **1.** In some countries, a military officer of the highest rank. See **field marshal. 2.** In the United States: **a.** A Federal officer who carries out court orders. **b.** A city officer who carries out court orders. **c.** The head of a police or fire department. **3.** A person in charge of a ceremony, parade, or the like. **4.** Formerly in England, a high official in the royal court, especially one aiding the sovereign in judicial matters. Also called "knight marshal". **5.** In England, a clerical assistant accompanying a judge on circuit.

~ *v.* **marshalled** or *U.S.* **marshaled, -shalling** or *U.S.* **-shaling, -shals.** **—***tr.* **1.** To arrange or place (soldiers) in line for a parade, manoeuvre, or review. **2.** To arrange, place, or set in methodical order: *marshalled facts; marshalled her thoughts.* **3.** To enlist and organise. **4.** To guide (a person) ceremoniously; conduct or usher. **5.** *Heraldry.* To join together (two or more coats of arms) on one shield. **—***intr.* To take form or order; especially, to take up positions in or as if in a military formation. **—See Synonyms at gather.** [Middle English *mareschal,* from Old French, from Late Latin *mariscalcus,* from Germanic *marhas kalkaz* (unattested), "keeper of the horses" : *marhaz,* horse + *skalkaz,* servant.] **—mar·shal·cy, mar·shal·ship** *n.*

Mar·shall (márshəl), **George C(atlett)** (1880–1959). U.S. soldier and statesman. While secretary of state (1947–49) he initiated the European Recovery Programme, known as the Marshall Plan, which gave economic aid to Europe. He served briefly as secretary of defence (1950–51) and received the Nobel prize for peace (1953).

mar·shal·ling yard (mársh'l-ing) *n.* An area in which railway rolling stock is kept and in which locomotives, carriages, goods wagons, and the like, are made up into trains.

Marshall Islands, Republic of the. State in the central Pacific Ocean, comprising some 1,259 islets and atolls. The economy depends on exports of copra, and U.S. payments for a military base. Fishing is also important. Germany bought the islands from Spain (1899), and they became a Japanese mandate (1920). From 1947 they were part of the U.N. Trust Territory of the Pacific Islands, but became self-governing in 1979. Area, 181 square kilometres (70 square miles). Population, 60,000. Capital, Majuro. See map at **Pacific Ocean.**

Marshall Plan *n.* See **European Recovery Program.**

marsh andromeda *n.* A plant, **bog rosemary** *(see).*

marsh crocodile *n.* A crocodile, the **mugger** *(see).*

marsh fever *n.* Malaria *(see).*

marsh gas *n.* Methane produced by rotting vegetation in marshes.

marsh harrier *n.* A Eurasian hawk, *Circus aeruginosus,* that frequents reedbeds and marshes. It has a dark brown plumage with paler markings.

marsh hawk *n.* *U.S.* The **hen harrier** *(see).*

marsh hen *n.* Any of various marsh birds of the family Rallidae, which includes the gallinules, coots, and rails.

marsh·land (mársh-land, -lənd) *n.* Land consisting of marshes.

marsh mallow *n.* A plant, *Althaea officinalis,* native to Europe, having showy pink flowers and a mucilaginous root used as a demulcent and in confectionery.

marsh·mal·low (mársh-mál-ō) *n.* **1.** A confection of sweetened paste, formerly made from the root of the marsh mallow. **2.** A soft confection made of gelatine, sugar, and starch, and dusted with powdered sugar. [From MARSH MALLOW.] **—marsh·mal·low** *adj.*

marsh marigold *n.* Any plant of the genus *Caltha;* especially, *C. palustris,* growing in swampy places and having bright yellow flowers. Also called "king-cup".

marsh samphire *n.* A plant, the **glasswort** *(see).*

marsh tit *n.* A small European songbird, *Parus palustris,* having a greyish body and a black head.

Mars·ton (már-stən), **John** (1576–1634). English dramatist. His literary career began with satirical and frequently licentious poetry, such as *The Scourge of Villainy* (1598), and declined after he took holy orders (1609). His plays include *The Malcontent* (1604) and *What You Will* (1607).

Marston Moor. The site in North Yorkshire of the first decisive battle of the English Civil War (July 2, 1644), won by the Parliamentarians.

mar·su·pi·al (maar-séw-pi-əl, -sōō-) *n.* Any mammal of the order Marsupialia, including kangaroos, opossums, bandicoots, and wombats, found principally in the Australian region and South and Central America. The female of most species lacks a placenta and possesses a marsupium.

~ *adj.* **1.** Of or pertaining to the Marsupialia. **2.** Of or pertaining to a marsupium. [New Latin *marsupialis,* from MARSUPIUM.]

marsupial mole *n.* **1.** An Australian marsupial, *Notoryctes typhlops,* that resembles the mole. **2.** Any of several related animals.

mar·su·pi·um (maar-séw-pi-əm, -sŏŏ-) *n., pl.* **-pia** (-pi-ə). **1.** An external abdominal pouch in female marsupials that contains mammary glands and that shelters the young. **2.** A temporary egg pouch in various animals. [Latin *marsupium,* pouch, from Greek *marsupion, marsipion,* diminutive of *marsipos,* purse, probably from Avestan *maršu†,* belly.]

mart (mart) *n.* **1.** A market; a trading or auction centre. **2.** *Archaic.* A fair. [Middle English, shortened from MARKET.]

mar·ta·gon (mártəgən) *n.* A Eurasian lily, *Lilium martagon,* having pinkish-purple, spotted flowers. Also called "martagon lily". See **Turk's-cap lily.** [Middle English, from Old French, from Spanish *martagón,* from Turkish *martagān,* a kind of turban.]

Mar·tel·lo tower (maar-téllō) *n.* A small circular fort, formerly used in Europe for coastal defence. Also called "martello". [Alteration from Cape *Mortella,* Corsica, where a tower of this type had proved effective in a battle in 1794.]

mar·ten (mártin) *n., pl.* **-tens** or collectively **marten. 1.** Any carnivore of the genus *Martes,* similar to the weasel, and found in northern wooded areas. See **pine marten. 2.** The fur of the marten. See **sable.** [Middle English *martren,* marten, marten's fur, from Old French *martrine,* marten's fur, from *martre,* marten, from Germanic *marthuz* (unattested).]

mar·ten·site (mártin-zīt) *n.* A solid solution of iron and up to one per cent of carbon, the chief constituent of hardened carbon tool steels. [After Adolf *Marten* (1914–), German metallurgist.] **—mar·ten·sit·ic** (-zíttik) *adj.*

Mar·tha (mártha). A sister of Lazarus and Mary, and friend of Jesus, who busied herself with household chores while her sister listened to Jesus. Luke 10:38–41.

mar·tial (mársh'l) *adj.* **1.** Of, pertaining to, or suggesting war. **2.** Pertaining to or connected with the armed forces or the military profession: *court martial.* **3.** Resembling, characteristic of, or befitting a warrior: *a martial roar of indignation.* [Middle English, from Latin *mārtiālis,* from *Mārs* (stem *Mārt-*), MARS.] **—mar·tial·ism** *n.* **—mar·tial·ist** *n.* **—mar·tial·ly** *adv.*

Mar·tial (márshəl), Latin name Marcus Valerius Martialis (A.D. 40 – 104). Latin poet. Spanish-born, he came to Rome (A.D. 64), gaining patronage through the Senecas. His 12 books of epigrams are keen, witty observations of contemporary Roman life.

martial art *n.* Any of several methods of fighting or self-defence, such as judo or karate, originating in the East.

martial law *n.* Rule by military authorities imposed upon a civilian population in time of war or when civil authority is considered to be functioning inadequately. Compare **military law.**

Mar·tian (mársh'n) *adj.* Of or pertaining to the planet Mars. **—~n.** An inhabitant of the planet Mars, especially as a stock fictional character. [Middle English, from Latin *mārtius,* from *Mārs* (stem *Mārt-*), MARS.]

mar·tin (már-tin ‖ -t'n) *n.* Any of several birds resembling and closely related to the swallows, such as the **house martin** *(see).* [Middle English, after St. *Martin* (the birds migrate from England near the time of Martinmas).]

Mar·ti·neau (márti-nō), **Harriet** (1802–76). British writer. Her work dealt with economic and religious themes based on the ideas of Ricardo and Mill. Her works include *Illustrations of Political Economy* (1832–34) and the children's story *The Play Fellow* (1841).

mar·ti·net (márti-nét) *n.* **1.** A rigid military disciplinarian. **2.** A person who demands absolute adherence to standards or rules. [After Jean *Martinet,* 17th-century French general.]

mar·tin·gale (mártin-gayl) *n.* Also **mar·tin·gal** (-gal). **1.** A part of a harness designed to prevent a horse from throwing back its head. **2.** *Nautical.* Any of several parts of standing rigging strengthening the bowsprit and jib boom against the force of the head stays. **3.** A method of gambling in which one doubles the stakes after each loss. [16th century : from French *martingale†.*]

mar·ti·ni (maar-téeni) *n., pl.* **-nis.** A cocktail usually made of three or more parts of gin to one part of dry vermouth, sometimes with a dash of angostura bitters. [Supposedly after a New York barman, *Martinez,* who invented the drink; the name was quickly confused with that of the Italian vermouth firm.]

Mar·ti·ni (maar-téeni) *n.* A trademark for an Italian vermouth.

Mar·ti·nique (márti-néek). Overseas département of France in the Caribbean, settled by the French in 1635. The small volcanic island is dominated by Mont Pelée, which erupted in 1902, killing more than 30,000 people and destroying the town of Saint Pierre. The economy depends on bananas, sugar, pineapple canning, and rum. Fort-de-France is the capital. See map at **Latin America. —Mar·ti·ni·can** *adj. & n.*

Mar·tin·mas (már-tin-məss, -mass ‖ -t'n-) *n.* A Christian festival celebrated annually on St. Martin's Day, November 11. It is one of the Scottish quarter days.

Mar·ti·nů (márti-nŏŏ), **Bohuslav** (1890–1959). Czech composer. He studied in Prague and Paris, and fled to the United States in 1941. His works include the ballet *Ishtar* (1920), the opera *Julietta* (1938), symphonies, and chamber music.

mart·let (márt-lət, -lit) *n.* **1.** *Archaic.* A martin. **2.** *Heraldry.* A representation of a bird without feet, used as a crest or bearing to indicate a fourth son. [French *martelet,* probably an alteration of *martinet,* diminutive of MARTIN.]

mar·tyr (mártər) *n.* **1.** One who suffers death through refusing to renounce religious or political principles. **2.** One who sacrifices

something very important to him in order to further a belief, cause, or principle. **3.** A person who endures great suffering: *a martyr to migraine.* **4.** A person who makes a great show of suffering in order to arouse sympathy. **—~tr.v.** **martyred, -tyring, -tyrs. 1.** To make a martyr of (a person). **2.** To inflict great pain upon; torment: *martyred by toothache.* [Middle English *martir,* Old English *martyr,* from Late Latin *martyr,* from Greek *martus†* (stem *martur-*), witness (of Christ).]

mar·tyr·dom (mártər-dəm) *n.* **1.** The state of being a martyr; the suffering of death by a martyr. **2.** Extreme suffering.

mar·tyr·ise, mar·tyr·ize (mártər-īz) *tr.v.* **-ised, -ising, -ises.** To martyr.

mar·tyr·ol·o·gy (mártə-róllǝji) *n.* **1.** An official catalogue of saints and martyrs. **2.** A list of those who have suffered or died for their beliefs: *Islamic martyrology.*

mar·tyr·y (mártəri) *n.* A monument, such as a shrine or chapel, erected in honour of a martyr. [Middle English, from Medieval Latin *martyrium,* from Greek *marturion,* martyrdom.]

mar·vel (márv'l) *n.* **1.** Something that evokes surprise, admiration, or wonder. **2.** *Archaic.* A sense of wonder or astonishment. **—~v.** **marvelled** or *U.S.* **marveled, -velling** or *U.S.* **-veling, -vels.** **—intr.** To be or become filled with wonder or astonishment. **—tr.** *Archaic.* To wonder at or about. [Middle English *marveile,* from Old French *merveile,* from Vulgar Latin *mīrābilia* (unattested), marvel, originally "wonderful things", Latin neuter plural of *mīrābilis,* wonderful, from *mīrārī,* to wonder, from *mīrus,* wonderful.]

Mar·vell (márvəl), **Andrew** (1621 – 78). English Metaphysical poet. His frequently satirical work includes the poems *To His Coy Mistress* and *The Definition of Love,* and pamphlets attacking the monarchy and political corruption.

mar·vel·lous, *U.S.* **mar·vel·ous** (márv-ləss, -'l-əss) *adj.* **1.** Causing wonder or astonishment: *a marvellous cure.* **2.** Of the highest or best kind or quality: *a marvellous recipe.* **3.** *Archaic.* Miraculous; supernatural. **—mar·vel·lous·ly** *adv.* **—mar·vel·lous·ness** *n.*

mar·vel-of-Pe·ru (márv'l-əv-pə-rŏŏ) *n.* A plant, the **four-o'clock** *(see).* [Originally found in Peru.]

Marx (marks), **Karl (Heinrich)** (1818–83). German journalist and philosopher. He edited the *Rheinische Zeitung* (1842–43) before working with Friedrich Engels, producing the *Communist Manifesto* in 1848. Expelled from Prussia (1849), he settled in London. He adapted Hegel's ideas to produce a theory of social change, dialectical materialism, and believed that violent revolution by the proletariat is necessary to create a classless society. *Das Kapital* (1867) greatly influenced subsequent socialism and communism.

Marx Brothers. U.S. family of comedians. Touring from early childhood in vaudeville, they later starred in films full of irreverent and anarchic humour, both verbal and visual, including *Duck Soup* (1933), *A Night at the Opera* (1935), and *A Day At the Races* (1937). Julius (Groucho) (1895–1977), with his comic moustache, cigar, and biting sarcasm, Arthur (Harpo) (1893–1964), the dumb clown and harpist, and Leonard (Chico) (1891–1961), the piano-playing confidence trickster, contrasted with Herbert (Zeppo) (1901–79), who played the straight man before retiring from films. Milton (Gummo) (1894–1977) followed his own career.

Marx·i·an (márks-i-on, -yən) *n.* One who studies or makes use of Karl Marx's philosophical or other concepts as a method of analysis and interpretation, as in political economy or in historical or literary criticism. **—Marx·i·an** *adj.* **—Marx·i·an·ism** *n.*

Marx·ism (márks-iz'm) *n.* The political and economic ideas of Karl Marx and Friedrich Engels; specifically, a system of thought in which the concept of class struggle plays a primary role both in analysing Western society in general, and in understanding its allegedly inevitable development from bourgeois oppression under capitalism to a socialist society and thence to communism.

Marx·ism-Len·in·ism (márks-iz'm-lénnin-iz'm) *n.* Marxism as developed to include Lenin's concept of imperialism as the final form of capitalism, and a shift in the focus of struggle from the developed to the underdeveloped countries. **—Marx·ist-Lenin·ist** *n. & adj.*

Marx·ist (márks-ist) *n.* **1.** One who believes in or follows the ideas of Marx and Engels. **2.** Loosely, any militant Communist. **—~adj.** Of or pertaining to Marxism.

Mar·y (maír-i). The mother of Jesus. Matthew 1:18–25. Also called the "Virgin Mary", "Our Lady".

Mary I, also known as Mary Tudor (1516–58). Queen of England (1553–58). Daughter of Henry VIII and Catherine of Aragon, she came to the throne on the death of her half-brother, Edward VI. She married Philip II of Spain (1554) and restored papal supremacy in England: the persecution of the Protestants followed, including the burning of bishops Cranmer, Latimer, and Ridley, thus earning her the nickname of "Bloody Mary".

Mary II, (1662–94). Queen of England, Scotland, and Ireland (1689–94). Daughter of James II, she married her cousin William of Orange (1677), ruling jointly with him after the "Glorious Revolution" (1688) which forced her father's abdication.

Mary, Queen of Scots, also known as Mary Stuart (1542–87). Queen of Scotland (1542–67). The daughter of James V and Mary of Guise, she was brought up as a Catholic in France, where she married the dauphin (later Francis II). She returned to Scotland after the death of her husband (1561). She married her cousin, Lord Darnley (1565), by whom she had a son, later to be James VI of Scotland and James I of England. Darnley was murdered by the Earl of Bothwell (1567), whom Mary married three months later. Forced to abdicate by the nobles in favour of her son, she fled to

England (1568) and was imprisoned by Elizabeth I. Catholic supporters plotted to place her on the throne of England, and this resulted in her trial and execution.

Mar·y·land (máir-i-lənd, -land, *also* mérri-, márri- *in imitation of U.S. pronunciation*). Atlantic state of the United States. One of the original 13 states, it had been founded (1634) by Lord Baltimore as a refuge for English Roman Catholics. Its Atlantic plain, divided by Chesapeake Bay, rises in the northwest to the Blue Ridge Mountains (Appalachians). Although livestock, cereal, and tobacco farming are important, the economy rests mainly on manufacturing, particularly of steel, metal products, and machinery. Annapolis is the capital.

Mary Mag·da·len·e (mágdə-léeni, -leen, -lin). Also **Mary Mag·da·len** (-lin). A woman in the New Testament (Luke 8:2) whom Jesus cured of evil spirits. She is usually considered identical with the repentant prostitute in Luke 7:36–50. Also called the "Magdalene".

Maryology. Variant of **Mariology.**

mar·zi·pan (márzi-pan, -pán ‖ *U.S. also* mártsə-, -paan) *n.* A confection in the form of a paste, made from ground almonds and sugar, often moulded into decorative forms or used in icing cakes. [German *Marzipan,* from Italian *marzapane,* fine box for confections, originally a box containing a tenth of a load, from Venetian *matapan,* coin bearing a seated Christ figure, originally a ten per cent tax, from Arabic *mawthabān,* "seated king", name given to similar coins in circulation since the Crusades.]

–mas *n. comb. form.* Indicates a Christian festival; for example, **Christmas.** [Middle English *-masse,* MASS.]

Ma·sac·cio (ma-zácho), born Tommaso di Giovanni di Simone Guidi (1401–28). Early Italian Renaissance painter. His revolutionary use of linear perspective and mastery of light and shade are illustrated in his fresco series in the Brancacci Chapel at Santa Maria del Carmine, Florence.

Ma·sa·da (ma-saádə, mə-). Mountain fortress in the Judaean Desert, Israel, overlooking the Dead Sea. In A.D. 73, after a two-year siege, the Zealots, a Jewish sect who were defending the fortress, committed mass suicide rather than surrender to the Romans.

Ma·sai (maá-sī, maa-sī) *n., pl.* **-sais** or collectively **Masai.** 1. A member of a nomadic people of Kenya and parts of Tanzania. 2. The Nilotic language of this people. —**Ma·sai** *adj.*

Ma·sa·ryk (mázzə-rik, mássə-), **Tomáš (Garrigue)** (1850–1937). Czech statesman. He became first president of the independent Czech Republic (1918), retiring in 1935. His son, Jan Masaryk (1886–1948), entered the Czech diplomatic service (1918), was minister to Britain (1925–38), and foreign minister in the exiled Czech government in London (1940–45) and in Czechoslovakia itself (1945–48). After the Communist takeover, he is alleged to have committed suicide.

masc. masculine.

Mas·ca·gni (ma-skaán-yee), **Pietro** (1863–1945). Italian composer. He wrote several operas, none of which equalled the success of his one-act work *Cavalleria Rusticana* (1890).

mascanonge. Variant of **muskellunge.**

mas·car·a (mass-kaárə ‖ *U.S.* -kárrə) *n.* A cosmetic applied to darken or thicken the eyelashes. [Italian *mascara, maschera,* MASK, probably from Arabic *maskharah,* "buffoon".]

mas·cle (mássk'l, maásk'l) *n. Heraldry.* A charge consisting of a lozenge with the inner area also shaped like a lozenge. [Middle English, from Anglo-French, from Anglo-Latin *mascula,* from Latin *macula,* spot.]

mas·con (máss-kon) *n.* Any of several areas of high-density mass below the surface of the Moon causing an exceptionally high gravitational attraction in that vicinity. [From *mass con*centration.]

mas·cot (máss-kət, -kot) *n.* A person, animal, or object believed to bring good luck: *She took a toy bear into her exam as a mascot.* [French *mascotte,* from Provençal *mascotto,* diminutive of *masco,* sorcerer, from Late Latin *masca,* witch, from Langobard.]

mas·cu·line (máss-kew-lin, maáss-) *adj. Abbr.* **masc.** 1. **a.** Of or , pertaining to men or boys; male. **b.** Manly or virile. 2. Mannish; unwomanly: *She had a masculine face.* 3. *Grammar.* Belonging or pertaining to a category of words or forms which in some languages, such as French or German, are assigned a grammatical gender associated with maleness, and in others, such as English, actually refer to males. —*n. Abbr.* **masc.** 1. The masculine gender. 2. A word or word form of the masculine gender. [Middle English *masculin,* from Old French, from Latin *masculīnus,* from *masculus,* male, diminutive of *mas,* male.] —**mas·cu·line·ly** *adv.* —**mas·cu·line·ness, mas·cu·lin·i·ty** (-línnəti), *n.*

masculine ending *n.* The ending of a line of verse with a stress on the last syllable. Compare **feminine ending.**

masculine rhyme *n.* A rhyme of only a single syllable, terminal and stressed, as in *cat, hat* and *annoy, enjoy.* Compare **feminine rhyme.**

mas·cu·lin·ise, mas·cu·lin·ize (máss-kew-lin-īz, maáss-) *v.* **-nised, -nising, -nises.** —*tr.* To make masculine. —*intr.* To become masculine. Used especially of a woman who has developed masculine characteristics owing to hormonal imbalance or male hormone therapy. —**mas·cu·lin·i·sa·tion** (-ī-záysh'n ‖ *U.S.* -i-) *n.*

Mase·field (máyss-feeld, máyz-), **John (Edward)** (1878–1967). British poet and novelist. His poetry includes the colloquial *Everlasting Mercy* (1911), *Dauber* (1913), and the Chaucerian *Reynard the Fox* (1919), while his novels include *Sard Harker* (1924) and *Basilissa* (1940). He became Poet Laureate (1930).

ma·ser (máyzər) *n. Physics.* Any of several devices that convert incident electromagnetic radiation from a wide range of frequencies to one or more discrete frequencies of highly amplified and coherent microwave radiation. Compare **laser.** [*M*icrowave *a*mplification by *s*timulated *e*mission of *r*adiation.]

Ma·se·ru (ma-saír-ōo, mə-). Capital of Lesotho.

mash (mash) *n.* 1. Any fermentable, starchy mixture from which alcohol or spirits can be distilled. 2. A mixture of ground grain and nutrients fed to livestock and poultry. 3. **a.** Any soft, pulpy mixture or mass. **b.** *British Informal.* Mashed potatoes. —*v.* **mashed, mashing, mashes.** —*tr.* 1. To convert (malt or grain) into mash. 2. To convert (something) into a soft, pulpy mixture resembling mash: *to mash potatoes.* 3. To crush or grind. 4. *Northern English.* To brew (tea). 5. *Archaic Slang.* To flirt with. —*intr. Northern English.* To brew: *Leave the tea to mash.* [Middle English, Old English *māsc.*]

mash·er (máshər) *n.* 1. A kitchen utensil for mashing vegetables or fruit. 2. *U.S. Slang.* A man who attempts to force his sexual attentions upon a woman. [Sense 2 originally "a flirt", from *mash* (verb), to flirt, make advances, from obsolete *mash* (noun), a "crush".]

Mash·had or **Me·shed.** Ancient city of northeast Iran at the junction of major caravan routes. It is a provincial capital, and centre of a rich agricultural region.

mash·ie, mash·y (máshi) *n., pl.* **-ies.** A golf club of medium loft. [Perhaps from French *massue,* club.]

Mashona. Variant of **Shona.**

Ma·sho·na·land (mə-shónnə-land, -shónə-). Region of northeast Zimbabwe, now divided into the provinces of Northern Mashonaland and Southern Mashonaland. Inhabited by the Shona people (or Mashona), it includes the country's capital, Harare (Salisbury).

mas·jid (múss-jid) *n.* A **mosque** (see).

mask (maask ‖ mask) *n.* 1. A covering worn on the face to conceal one's identity; especially: **a.** A cloth, plastic, or paper covering that has openings for the eyes, entirely or partly conceals the face, and is worn especially at a masquerade ball, fancy-dress dance, or the like. **b.** A representation of a grotesque face: *a horror mask.* **c.** A facial covering worn for a parade, carnival, ritual, or the like. **d.** A complete facial covering and headdress, usually made of plaster or wood, worn by actors in Greek and Roman drama to emphasise a single character trait. 2. **a.** A protective covering for the face or head, as worn in fencing and some other sports. **b.** A facial covering worn to prevent infection, especially during surgery. 3. **a.** A **gas mask** (see). **b.** A device fitting over the mouth and nose through which oxygen or an anaesthetic gas may be supplied. 4. A representation of a face or head: **a.** A **death mask** (see). **b.** An often grotesque representation of a head and face, used for ornamentation. 5. The face or facial markings of certain animals, such as a fox or dog. 6. A face having a blank, fixed, or enigmatic expression: *She displayed an impenetrable mask to the world.* 7. Something, often a trait, that disguises or conceals: *hid his shyness under a mask of confidence.* 8. A natural or artificial feature of terrain that conceals and protects military forces or installations. 9. **a.** An opaque border or pattern placed between a source of light and a photosensitive surface to prevent exposure of specific portions of the surface. **b.** The translucent border framing a television picture tube and screen. 10. See **face mask.** 11. A **masque** (see). 12. *Archaic.* A person wearing a mask. 13. *Electronics.* A thin sheet of material with a pattern cut into it to enable a semiconducting chip to be made into an integrated circuit. —*tr.v.* **masked, masking, masks.** 1. To cover (the face, for example) with a decorative or protective mask. 2. To disguise; especially, to make indistinct or blurred to the senses: *The spice masks the strong flavour of the meat.* 3. To cover up for concealment or protection: *They masked their guns with branches.* 4. To block the view of: *Undergrowth masked the entrance.* 5. To cover (a part of a photographic film) by the application of an opaque border. 6. To apply masking paper or masking tape to (an area not to be painted). 7. *Chemistry.* To inhibit (a compound or radical) with a reagent more active in a specific reaction. [French *masque,* from Italian *maschera,* perhaps from Arabic *maskharah,* "buffoon".]

maskalonge. Variant of **muskellunge.**

masked (maaskt ‖ maskt) *adj.* 1. Wearing a mask. 2. Disguised; concealed: *masked intentions.* 3. Latent or hidden, as a symptom or disease may be. 4. *Botany.* Resembling a mask; personate. 5. *Zoology.* Having masklike markings on the head or face.

maskeg. Variant of **muskeg.**

mask·er, mas·quer (maáskər, máskər) *n.* A participant in a masquerade or masque.

mas·o·chism (mássə-kiz'm ‖ mázzə-) *n.* 1. The deriving of pleasure, especially sexual arousal, from having physical or emotional pain inflicted on one. 2. Loosely, the practice of deliberately undergoing unpleasant experiences, usually in the pursuit of some higher satisfaction: *the sheer masochism of entering a marathon.* [After Leopold von Sacher-*Masoch* (1836–95), Austrian novelist who wrote on the theme of sexual masochism.] —**mas·o·chist** *n.* —**mas·o·chis·tic** (-kístik) *adj.* —**mas·o·chis·ti·cal·ly** *adv.*

ma·son (máyss'n) *n.* 1. **a.** A person who builds with stone. **b.** A person who dresses stone. **c.** *South African.* A bricklayer. 2. *Capital* **M.** A **Freemason** (see). —*tr.v.* **masoned, -soning, -sons.** To build or strengthen with masonry. [Middle English *masoun, machoun,* from Anglo-French *machun,* from Old French *masson,* from Frankish *makjo* (unattested), from *makōn,* to make (unattested).]

mason bee *n.* Any of various solitary bees of the family Megachilidae which build nests of sand or clay under stones or in cavities.

Ma·son-Dix·on Line (máyss'n-díks'n). Former political boundary between Pennsylvania and Maryland, United States. Drawn up (1763–67) by the astronomers Charles Mason (1730–87) and Jeremiah Dixon (died 1777), it was extended (1779) as the boundary between Pennsylvania and Virginia (now West Virginia). The line became a cultural boundary between the Northern and Southern States.

Ma·son·ic (mə-sónnik) *adj.* Of Freemasons or Freemasonry.

ma·son·ry (máyss'n-ri) *n., pl.* **-ries.** 1. The trade of a mason. 2. Stonework or brickwork. 3. *Capital* **M. Freemasonry** (*see*).

masonry cement *n.* A kind of cement especially prepared to be used in the mortar of block and brick masonry.

Ma·so·ra, Ma·so·rah (mə-sáwrə ‖ -sórə) *n.* 1. The body of tradition pertaining to correct textual reading of the Old Testament. The critical notes in which this tradition is embodied, popular in the tenth century A.D. [Middle Hebrew *māsōrāh,* "tradition", from Hebrew *māsar,* root of *limsor,* to hand over, transmit.] —**Mas·o·ret·ic** (mássə-réttik) *adj.*

masque, mask (maask, mask) *n.* 1. A dramatic entertainment, usually based on a mythological or allegorical theme, popular in England in the 16th and early 17th centuries. 2. A dramatic verse composition written for a masque production. 3. A masquerade. [Variant of MASK.]

masquer. Variant of **masker.**

mas·quer·ade (máss-kə-ráyd, maáss-) *n.* 1. A costume ball or party at which masks are worn; a masked ball. Also called "masque". 2. The costume for such a party or ball. 3. Any disguise or false outward show; a pretence: *a masquerade of humility.*
~*intr.v.* **masqueraded, -ading, -ades.** 1. To wear a mask or disguise, as at a masquerade: *She masqueraded as a shepherdess.* 2. To pretend to be something one is not: *He masqueraded as the ship's surgeon.* [French *mascarade,* from Italian *mascherata* or Spanish *mascarada,* from Italian *maschera,* MASK.] —**mas·quer·ad·er** *n.*

mass (mas) *n.* 1. A unified body of matter with no specific shape. 2. A grouping of individual parts or elements that compose a unified body of unspecified size or quantity: *A mass of people poured into the streets.* 3. Any large but nonspecific amount or number: *a mass of bruises.* 4. The major part of something; the majority. 5. The bulk of a solid body. 6. *Physics. Abbr.* **m, M** The measure of a body's resistance to acceleration. The mass of a body is different from but proportional to its **weight** (*see*), is independent of the body's position but dependent on its velocity relative to other bodies, and may be expressed in mass units, such as kilograms or slugs, or corresponding energy units, by means of the mass-energy relationship of the special theory of relativity. 7. In painting, an area of unified light, shade, or colour. 8. In pharmacology, a thick, pasty mixture of drugs used to form pills. 9. In mining, a mineral deposit with no specific shape. Compare **bed, vein.** —**in the mass.** Considered as a whole. —**the masses.** The body of common people; the many; the proletariat.
~*v.* **massed, massing, masses.** —*tr.* To gather or form into a mass. —*intr.* To assemble in a mass.
~*adj.* 1. Of, pertaining to, characteristic of, or involving a large number of people: *mass education; mass destruction.* 2. Done on a large scale; involving great numbers or large amounts: *mass production.* [Middle English, from Old French *masse,* from Latin *massa,* from Greek *maza,* barley cake, lump, mass.]

Mass (mass, maass) *n. Sometimes small* **m.** 1. In the Roman Catholic and some Protestant churches, such as the Lutheran, the celebration of the Eucharist. See **High Mass, Low Mass.** 2. A musical setting of certain parts of the Mass, especially the Kyrie, Gloria, Credo, Sanctus, Benedictus, and Agnus Dei. [Middle English *masse,* Old English *mæsse, messe,* from Late Latin *missa,* eucharist, perhaps deriving from the final words, *Ite, missa est,* "Go, it is the dismissal", from *mittere* (past participial stem *miss-*), to send away.]

Mass. Massachusetts.

Mas·sa·chu·set (mássə-chōō-sit, -zit) *n., pl.* **-sets** or collectively **Massachuset.** Also **Mas·sa·chu·sett.** 1. A member of an Algonquian-speaking Indian people who lived on or near Massachusetts Bay. 2. The Algonquian language of these Indians.

Mas·sa·chu·setts (mássə-chōō-sits, -zits). State in New England, United States. It was the destination of the *Mayflower* (1620), and became one of the 13 original states. Massachusetts is largely a manufacturing state with shipping, machinery, paper, printing, textile, and leather industries. Boston is the capital.

mas·sa·cre (mássə-kər) *n.* 1. An act of savage and indiscriminate killing, especially of large numbers of people. 2. *Informal.* A severe defeat, as in a sports event. 3. *Informal.* An act of wanton destruction: *the massacre of our hopes.*
~*tr.v.* **massacred** (-kərd), **-cring** (-kring, -kər-ing), **-cres.** 1. To kill indiscriminately and wantonly; slaughter. 2. *Informal.* To defeat decisively, as in a sports event. [French, from Old French *maçacre†,* slaughterhouse.] —**mas·sa·crer** (-kər-ər, -krər) *n.*

mas·sage (máss-aazh, -aaj ‖ *chiefly U.S.* mə-saázh, -saáj) *n.* The rubbing or kneading of parts of the body, so as to aid circulation or relax the muscles.
~*tr.v.* **massaged, -saging, -sages.** 1. To give a massage to. 2. To treat by or as if by means of a massage: *massaged her ego.* 3. *Informal.* To mould or adjust to suit a preconceived interpretation: *massage statistics.* [French, from *masser,* to massage, probably from Portuguese *amassar,* to knead, from *massa,* dough, MASS.]

Mas·sa·wa or **Ma·sau·a** (mə-saáwə). Ancient Red Sea port in Eritrea. It is also the main port serving Ethiopia, as well as being a fishing and industrial centre.

mass defect *n. Physics.* The amount by which the mass of an atomic nucleus is less than the sum of the masses of its constituent particles. It is equivalent to the **binding energy** (*see*) of the nucleus. Also called "mass deficiency".

mas·sé (mássi) *n.* In billiards, a stroke made by hitting the cue ball on its side with the cue held nearly perpendicular to the table, such that the cue ball will curve around a ball that is immediately obstructing it. [French, from *masser,* to cue, from *masse,* cue, MACE.]

mass-energy equivalence *n. Physics.* The principle that a measured quantity of energy is equivalent to a measured quantity of mass. The equivalence is expressed by Einstein's equation, $E = mc^2$, where E represents energy, m the equivalent mass, and c the speed of light.

Mas·se·net (mássə-nay; *French* mass-náy), **Jules (Émile Frédéric)** (1842–1912). French composer. Both a student and professor at the Paris Conservatoire, he composed over 20 operas, including *Manon Lescaut* (1884) and *Thaïs* (1894).

mas·se·ter (ma-séetər, mə-) *n.* A large muscle in the cheek that acts to close the jaws and is therefore important in chewing. [Greek *masētēr,* one who chews, from *masasthai,* to chew.] —**mas·se·ter·ic** (mássi-térrik) *adj.*

mas·seur (ma-súr ‖ -séwr, -sóor) *n. Feminine* **mas·seuse** (-súrz ‖ -séwz, -sóoz, -sóz).* A person who gives massages professionally. [French, from *masser,* to MASSAGE.]

mas·si·cot (mássi-kot, -kō) *n.* 1. A rare mineral, the yellow crystalline mineral form of lead monoxide, PbO. Compare **litharge.** 2. A yellow pigment, lead monoxide. [Middle English *masticot,* from Old French, akin to Italian *marzacotto,* ointment.]

mas·sif (ma-séef, másseef) *n.* 1. A large plateau-like region with marked edges, often formed by faults. 2. A compact group of connected mountains forming a distinct portion of a mountain range. [French, from *massif,* MASSIVE.]

Mas·sif Cen·tral (ma-séef son-traál). The "central upland" of France, covering nearly a sixth of the country. It is a mountainous plateau: its highest point is the Puy de Sancy (1 886 metres; 6,186 feet). Stock rearing and dairying are the chief occupations, but peripheral coal and kaolin deposits support industrial centres such as Limoges and Clermont-Ferrand.

Mas·sine (ma-séen), **Léonide,** born Leonid Fyodorovitch Myassin (1896–1979). Russian ballet dancer and choreographer. He worked with Diaghilev's Ballets Russes. He created *Parade* (1917), *La Boutique Fantasque* (1919), and *Les Présages* (1933).

mas·sive (mássiv) *adj.* 1. Consisting of or making up a large mass; bulky; heavy; solid: *a massive piece of furniture.* 2. Unusually large or imposing: *a massive head.* 3. Large or impressive in quantity, scope, or scale: *a massive work of the finest scholarship; massive profits.* 4. *Medicine.* Large in comparison with the usual amount. Said of dosage. 5. *Pathology.* Affecting a large area of bodily tissue; widespread and severe: *massive gangrene.* 6. *Physics.* Having mass: *a massive particle.* 7. *Geology.* Lacking obvious layering, banding, or foliation, or having very thick layers. Said of rock or rocks. 8. *Mineralogy.* Lacking externally observable crystalline form. —See Synonyms at **heavy.** [Middle English, from Old French *massif,* from Vulgar Latin *massīceus* (unattested), from Latin *massa,* MASS (amount).] —**mas·sive·ly** *adv.* —**mas·sive·ness** *n.*

mass·less (máss-ləss, -liss) *adj.* Having no mass: *a massless particle.* —**mass·less·ness** *n.*

mass media *pl.n. Singular* **mass medium.** The means of communication, such as television, radio, or sometimes newspapers, that can reach large numbers of people over a widespread area, in a relatively short time.

mass noun *n.* A **noncountable** (*see*) noun. Compare **count noun.**

mass number *n.* The total number of neutrons and protons in an atomic nucleus. Also called "nucleon number". See **atomic number, atomic mass.**

mass production *n.* The manufacture of goods in large quantities, using assembly-line techniques. —**mass-pro·duce** (máss-prə-déwss ‖ -dōoss) *tr.v.* —**mass-pro·duced** *adj.*

mass ratio *n.* The mass of a rocket loaded with fuel at liftoff divided by the mass of the rocket without fuel.

mass spectrograph *n. Physics.* An instrument used to separate charged particles in a prepared beam by means of an electromagnetic field and to photograph the resulting distribution or spectrum of masses.

mass spectrometer *n.* An instrument used to separate charged particles in a prepared beam by means of an electromagnetic field according to their charge to mass ratio. An electrical detector moves across the beam, recording the relative amounts of the various types of ion present.

mass spectrum *n.* The record produced by a mass spectrometer or mass spectrograph, characteristic of the compound analysed.

mass·y (mássi) *adj.* **-ier, -iest.** *Archaic.* Massive; solid; having great mass or bulk. [Middle English, perhaps from Old French *massiz,* variant of *massif,* MASSIVE.] —**mass·i·ness** *n.*

mast¹ (maast ‖ mast) *n.* 1. A tall vertical spar, sometimes sectioned, that rises from the keel of a sailing vessel to support the sails and running rigging. 2. Any tall, narrow pole or structure: *a radio mast.* —**before the mast.** Serving as an ordinary seaman.
~*tr.v.* **masted, masting, masts.** To fit out (a ship) with masts. [Middle English *maste,* Old English *mæst.*]

mast² *n.* The nuts of forest trees, such as beech and oak, accumulated on the ground, used especially as food for pigs. [Middle English *maste,* Old English *mæst.*]

mas·ta·ba, mas·ta·bah (mástəbə) *n.* An ancient Egyptian tomb with a rectangular base and sloping sides. [Arabic *maṣṭabah,* stone bench.]

mast cell *n.* A cell present in connective tissue that releases histamine and other chemicals during inflammatory conditions. [Partial translation of German *Mastzelle* : *Mast,* food MAST (referring to the cell's appearance) + *Zelle,* CELL.]

mas·tec·to·my (mast-éktəmi) *n., pl.* **-mies.** Surgical removal of a breast, usually as a treatment for cancer. [MAST(O)- + -ECTOMY.]

mas·ter (maástər || mástər) *n.* **1.** A man having control over the action of another or others. **2.** The captain of a merchant ship. Also called "master mariner". **3.** An employer. **4.** The owner of a slave or an animal. **5.** The male head of a household: *Who is the master of the house?* **6. a.** One who has complete mastery over something requiring skill, such as the playing of a game or a musical instrument: *a master of the backhand pass.* **b.** One who has the ability to control or deal with something: *master of his emotions; master of the situation.* **7.** One who defeats another; a victor. **8.** A male teacher; a schoolmaster. **9. a.** A person whose teachings or doctrines are accepted by followers. **b.** *Capital* **M.** Jesus. Preceded by *our* or *the.* **10.** A person holding a master's degree such as a Master of Arts or Master of Science. **11.** A skilled craftsman, especially one qualified to teach apprentices. Also used adjectivally: *a master engraver.* **12.** An **old master** *(see).* **13.** A former title for a naval officer just below a lieutenant and in charge of navigation on a warship. **14.** The title of the head or presiding officer of certain societies, clubs, orders, university colleges, or other institutions. **15.** *Chiefly British.* The title of any of various law court officers, such as the chief clerks in Chancery. **16.** A master of foxhounds. **17.** *Capital* **M.** A title prefixed to the name of a boy or youth not considered old enough to be addressed as Mr. **18.** An **International Master** *(see).* **19. a.** An original from which copies can be made. Also called "master copy". **b.** The machine playing a video-tape master from which **slave** *(see)* machines can copy.
~*adj.* **1.** Of, pertaining to, or characteristic of a master. **2.** Chief; principal: *the master bedroom.* **3.** Highly skilled, masterful: *a master thief.* **4.** Being a part of a mechanism that controls all other parts: *a master switch.* **5.** Being an original from which copies are made.
~*tr.v.* **mastered, -tering, -ters. 1.** To make oneself a master of (an art, craft, or science). **2.** To overcome or defeat: *mastered the tyranny of gambling.* **3.** To reduce to subjugation; break or tame (a person or animal). [Middle English, from Old English *mægister, magister* and Old French *maistre,* both from Latin *magister.*] **—mas·ter·dom** *n.* **—mas·ter·hood** *n.* **—mas·ter·ship** *n.*

mas·ter-at-arms (maástər-ət-ármz || mástər-) *n., pl.* **masters-at-arms.** A naval petty officer assigned to maintain discipline.

master cylinder *n.* A large cylinder in a hydraulic system, in which a fluid is compressed by a piston so that the compressed fluid will operate the pistons in smaller slave cylinders.

mas·ter·ful (maástər-f'l || mástər-) *adj.* **1.** Revealing an inclination to play the master; imperious; domineering. **2.** Revealing mastery; expert; skilful: *a masterful rendition of Othello.* See Usage note below. **—mas·ter·ful·ly** *adv.* **—mas·ter·ful·ness** *n.*

Usage: *Masterful* generally means "domineering or powerful"; *masterly* means "showing the knowledge or skill of a master". Thus one would expect *a masterful woman* but *a masterly argument.* Occasionally, *masterful* is used in contexts where *masterly* would normally be expected *(masterful Spanish, a masterful speech),* but this use has been criticised and is best avoided.

master key *n.* A key that opens several locks which each usually have different keys. Also called "passkey".

mas·ter·ly (maástər-li || mástər-) *adj.* Like a master; indicating the knowledge or skill of a master. See Usage note at **masterful.**
~*adv.* With the skill of a master. **—mas·ter·li·ness** *n.*

master mason *n.* **1.** An expert mason. **2.** *Capital* **M,** *capital* **M.** One who has achieved the third degree of Freemasonry.

mas·ter·mind (maástər-mīnd || mástər-) *n.* **1.** A highly intelligent person. **2.** Such a person who plans and directs a project.
~*tr.v.* **masterminded, -minding, -minds.** To direct, plan, or supervise (a project, often one of a criminal nature).

Master of Arts *n. Abbr.* **M.A. 1.** A degree granted by a university or other institution of higher education, normally to a person who has completed at least one year of postgraduate study, or at Scottish universities to a person completing an undergraduate course, especially in nonscientific subjects. **2.** A person holding such a degree. Compare **Bachelor of Arts, Doctor of Philosophy.**

master of ceremonies *n. Abbr.* **M.C. 1.** A person who acts as host at a formal event, making the welcoming speech and introducing other speakers. **2.** A performer who acts as the host of a variety show; a compere. Also called "emcee".

master of foxhounds *n. Abbr.* **M.F.H.** The chief officer of a hunt, who is responsible for the hounds and for organising the hunting programme. Also called "master".

Master of Science *n. Abbr.* **M.Sc. 1.** A degree granted by a university or other institution of higher education to a person who has completed at least one year of postgraduate study in the sciences. **2.** A person holding such a degree. Compare **Bachelor of Science, Doctor of Philosophy.**

Master of the Horse *n.* An officer of the British royal household, ranking below the Lord Chamberlain and the Lord Steward, whose main duty is to attend the sovereign on State occasions.

Master of the Rolls *n.* One who keeps the roll of solicitors in England and Wales and is one of the judges of the Court of Appeal, Keeper of the Records at the Public Records Office, and President of the Civil Division of the Court of Appeal.

mas·ter·piece (maástər-peess || mástər-) *n.* **1. a.** An outstanding work of art or craft. **b.** An artist's greatest work: *"Paradise Lost" was Milton's masterpiece.* **2.** Any superlative achievement: *a masterpiece of public speaking.* [Probably translation of Dutch *meesterstuk* or German *Meisterstück,* the piece of work presented to a guild by a craftsman for admission to the rank of master.]

master race *n. Sometimes capital* **M,** *capital* **R.** A people who consider themselves endowed with the right to dominate and exploit other supposedly inferior peoples; specifically, the German nation viewed as such a master race in the ideology of German imperialism (about 1890–1945). Also called "Herrenvolk".

master sergeant *n. Abbr.* **MSgt, M. Sgt.** A noncommissioned officer of the next to highest rating in the U.S. Army, Air Force, and Marine Corps.

mas·ter·sing·er (maástər-sing-ər || mástər-) *n.* A **Meistersinger** *(see).*

mas·ter·stroke (maástər-strōk || mástər-) *n.* A masterly achievement or manoeuvre: *a masterstroke of statesmanship.*

mas·ter·work (maástər-wurk || mástər-) *n.* A masterpiece.

mas·ter·y (maástəri || mástəri) *n., pl.* **-ies. 1.** Possession of consummate skill: *displayed mastery in handling the situation.* **2.** The state or condition of having power or control: *mastery of the seas.* **3.** Full command of some subject of study: *a poet's mastery of the language.*

mast·head (maást-hed || mást-) *n.* **1.** The top of a ship's mast. **2.** The listing in a newspaper, magazine, or other publication of information about its staff and operation.

mas·tic (mástik) *n.* **1.** The aromatic resin of the mastic tree, used in varnishes and lacquers and as an astringent. **2.** A pastelike cement, especially one made with powdered lime or brick and tar. [Middle English *mastyk,* from Old French *mastic,* from Late Latin *mastichum,* variant of *masticē,* from Greek *mastikhē,* mastic, "chewing gum", from *mastikhān,* to grind the teeth.]

mas·ti·cate (másti-kayt) *tr.v.* **-cated, -cating, -cates. 1.** To chew. **2.** To grind and knead. [Late Latin *masticāre,* from Greek *mastikhān,* to grind the teeth.] **—mas·ti·ca·tion** (-káysh'n) *n.* **—mas·ti·ca·tor** (-kaytər) *n.*

mas·ti·ca·to·ry (másti-kə-tri, -təri, -káytəri) *adj.* **1.** Of, pertaining to, or used in mastication. **2.** Being adapted for chewing.
~*n., pl.* **masticatories.** A substance chewed to increase salivation.

mastic tree *n.* A small evergreen tree, *Pistacia lentiscus,* of the Mediterranean region, that yields mastic. Also called "lentisk".

mas·tiff (mástif, maástif) *n.* A large dog of an ancient breed, probably originating in Asia, having a short fawn-coloured coat. [Middle English *mastif,* from Old French *mastin,* from Vulgar Latin *mānsuētīnus* (unattested), "tame", from Latin *mānsuētus,* tamed, "accustomed to the hand" : *manus,* hand + *suēscere,* to accustom.]

mastiff bat *n.* Any of various bats of the family Molossidae, found in the tropics, having narrow wings and brown, grey, or black fur. [So called because of its apparently doglike ears.]

mas·ti·goph·o·ran (másti-góffərən) *n.* Any member of the class Mastigophora, which includes protozoans with one or more flagella. [New Latin *Mastigophora,* "whip bearers" : Greek *mastix*† (stem *mastig-*), whip, lash + *-phora,* -PHORE.] **—mas·ti·goph·o·ran** *adj.*

mas·ti·tis (mass-tī́-tiss) *n.* Inflammation of the breast or udder. [MAST(O)- + -ITIS.]

masto–, mast– *comb. form.* Indicates the breast or protuberances resembling a breast or nipple; for example, **mastitis, mastodon.** [New Latin, from Greek *mastos*†, breast.]

mas·to·don (mástə-don, -dən) *n.* Any of several extinct mammals of the genus *Mammut* (sometimes called *Mastodon*), resembling the elephant. [New Latin, "breast-tooth" : MAST(O)- + -ODON; from the nipple-shaped protuberances on the teeth.] **—mas·to·don·tic** (-dóntik) *adj.*

mas·toid (mástoyd) *n.* The mastoid process.
~*adj.* Pertaining to the mastoid process. [New Latin *mastoides,* "breast-shaped" : MAST(O)- + -OID.]

mas·toid·ec·to·my (mástoyd-éktəmi) *n., pl.* **-mies.** *Surgery.* Removal of part or all of the mastoid process.

mas·toid·i·tis (mástoyd-ī́-tiss) *n. Pathology.* Inflammation of part or all of the mastoid process.

mastoid process *n. Anatomy.* The nipple-shaped rear portion of the temporal bone on each side of the head behind the ear in humans and many other vertebrates. Also called "mastoid", "mastoid bone".

mas·tur·bate (mástər-bayt, maástər-) *v.* **-bated, -bating, -bates.** *—intr.* To perform an act of masturbation. *—tr.* To perform an act of masturbation on. [Latin *masturbārī*†.]

mas·tur·ba·tion (mástər-báysh'n, maástər-) *n.* **1.** Excitation of the genital organs, especially one's own, and usually to orgasm, by means other than sexual intercourse. **2.** Loosely, any act of blatant self-indulgence. Used derogatorily: *He regards his fantasising as poetry, but it's just mental masturbation.* **—mas·tur·ba·tion·al, mas·tur·ba·to·ry** (-baytəri, -báytəri) *adj.* **—mas·tur·ba·tor** (-baytər) *n.*

ma·su·ri·um (mə-séwr-i-əm, -zéwr-, -soór-, -zoór-) *n.* A chemical element, **technetium** *(see).* Not in current technical usage. [New Latin, after *Masuria,* region of north-east Poland (formerly East Prussia), where it was discovered.]

mat¹ (mat) *n.* **1.** A flat piece of fabric or other material used for

wiping one's shoes or feet, or as a floor covering. **2.** A small, flat piece of decorated material, such as cloth or cork, placed under a lamp, dish of food, or other object, to protect a surface or for ornament. **3.** A thick floor pad to protect athletes, as in wrestling or gymnastics. **4.** Any densely woven or thickly tangled mass: *a mat of hair.* **5.** A heavy, woven net of rope or wire cable placed over a blasting site to keep debris from scattering.
~*v.* **matted, matting, mats.** —*tr.* **1.** To cover, protect, or decorate with a mat or mats. **2.** To interweave into or cover with a thick mass: *A heavy growth of vines matted the tree.* —*intr.* To be interwoven into a thick mass; become entangled. [Middle English, Old English *matt(e)*, from Late Latin *matta†*, mat.]

mat² *n.* **1.** A decorative border of cardboard or similar material placed around a picture to serve as a frame or act as a contrast between the picture and the frame. **2.** Variant of **matt.**
~*tr.v.* **matted, matting, mats. 1.** To put a mat around (a picture). **2.** Variant of **matt.**
~*adj.* Variant of **matt.** [French, Old French, "dead". See **checkmate.**]

mat³ *n. Printing.* A **matrix** (see).

Mat·a·be·le (mátta-béeli, -bélli) *n., pl.* **-les** or collectively **Matabele. 1.** An Ndebele (see). **2.** A language, Ndebele (see). [Sotho, from *letebele*, "the disappearing ones"; so called because the warriors of this people would sink down (*teba*) behind their huge shields during battle.]

Mat·a·be·le·land (mátta-béeli-land, -bélli-). Region of southwest Zimbabwe. Inhabited by the Ndebele people (or Matabele), it has important gold deposits. Bulawayo is the chief town.

mat·a·dor (mátta-dawr) *n.* **1.** A bullfighter who kills the bull. **2.** One of the highest trumps in certain card games, such as ombre. [Spanish, "killer", from *matar*, to kill, from Latin *mactāre*, to sacrifice, from *mactus*, sacred.]

Ma·ta Ha·ri (maáta haári), born Margaretha Geertruida Zelle; also known as Lady MacLeod (1876-1917). Dutch spy. Married to a Dutch army officer, she became a professional "oriental" dancer in Paris (1905) and adopted her stage name. During World War I she is said to have worked for both the French and the Germans and was finally shot by the French for espionage.

Mat·a·pan, Cape (mátta-pan, -pán). *Greek* **Ak·ra Taí·na·ron** (áckra ténna-ron). The southernmost tip of the Greek mainland. It gave its name to a sea battle (1941), in which an Italian fleet was heavily defeated by the British.

match¹ (mach) *n.* **1. a.** A person or thing that is exactly like another; a counterpart. **b.** A person or thing that is similar to another in some specified quality: *He is John's match for bravery.* **2. a.** A person or thing that closely resembles or harmonises with another. **b.** A pair made up of two things or persons that resemble or harmonise with each other: *The colours were a close match.* **3.** A person or thing equal in qualities or able to compete with another of the same class or type: *The boxer had met his match.* **4. a.** An organised athletic contest or game in which individuals or teams oppose and compete with each other: *a boxing match; a football match.* **b.** A tennis contest decided on the basis of victory in a certain number of sets, usually two out of three or three out of five. **5. a.** A marriage or an arrangement of marriage: *Her parents tried to arrange a match for her.* **b.** A person viewed as a prospective marriage partner.
~*v.* **matched, matching, matches.** —*tr.* **1.** To be exactly like; correspond exactly to. **b.** To be equal or comparable to (another) with respect to some specified quality: *The new model doesn't match the old one for speed.* **c.** To equal; rival: *beauty that could never be matched.* **2.** To resemble or harmonise with: *The coat matches the dress.* **3.** To adapt or suit so that a balanced or harmonious result is achieved; cause to correspond: *matching skill with speed.* **4.** To fit together or cause to fit together. **5.** To join or give in marriage; find a suitable match for. **6.** To place in opposition or competition with; pit: *The only way to ensure peace is to match strength with strength.* **7.** To provide with an adversary or competitor, especially one of equivalent worth: *well-matched contestants.* **8.** To couple (electric circuits) by means of a transformer. —*intr.* To be a close counterpart; correspond. [Middle English *macche*, match, mate, Old English *gemæcca*, mate.] —**match·a·ble** *adj.* —**match·er** *n.*

match² *n.* **1.** A narrow strip of wood, cardboard, or wax coated on one end with a compound that ignites easily by friction. See **safety match. 2.** An easily ignited cord or wick, formerly used for detonating powder charges or firing cannons and muzzle-loading firearms. [Middle English *macche, mecche*, lamp wick, candle, from Old French *meiche*, from Medieval Latin *myxa*, lamp wick, from Latin, nozzle of a lamp.]

match·board (mách-bawrd ‖ -bōrd) *n.* A board cut with a tongue on one side and a matching groove on the other to fit with other boards of identical cut.

match·book (mách-bŏŏk ‖ -bŏŏk) *n.* A small folded piece of card containing rows of detachable matches, and a rough strip for striking them against.

match·box (mách-boks) *n.* A box for holding matches, edged on one or two sides with a strip of rough card or treated paper for striking the matches against.

matchet. Variant of **machete.**

match·less (mách-ləss, -liss) *adj.* Having no match or equal; peerless; unsurpassed: *matchless beauty.* —**match·less·ly** *adv.* —**match·less·ness** *n.*

match·lock (mách-lok) *n.* **1.** A gunlock in which powder is ignited by a match. **2.** A musket having such a gunlock.

match·mak·er (mách-maykər) *n.* One who attempts to arrange marriages by bringing unmarried people together, either for personal satisfaction or, in some societies, as a profession. —**match·mak·ing** *n.* & *adj.*

match·mark (mách-maark) *n.* Any of several marks made on the mating components of a machine or engine to ensure that the components are assembled in the correct relative positions.
~*tr.v.* **-marked, -marking, -marks.** To stamp such marks on (components).

match play *n.* The form of competition in golf in which the basis of the score is the number of holes won by each side rather than the number of strokes taken. Compare **medal play.**

match point *n.* The final point needed to win certain sports games, such as tennis or squash.

match·wood (mách-wŏŏd) *n.* **1.** Wood in small pieces or splinters, suitable especially for making matches. **2.** Splinters.

mate¹ (mayt) *n.* **1. a.** Either of a conjugal pair of animals or birds. **b.** Either of a pair of animals brought together for breeding. **2.** A spouse. **3.** A person with whom one is in close association. Often used in combination: *flatmate; teammate.* **4.** Either of a matched pair: *the mate to this glove.* **5.** *Chiefly British.* **a.** *Slang.* A friend. **b.** An informal form of address used to men. **6.** A deck officer on a merchant ship ranking below the master. **7.** In some professions, an assistant: *a plumber's mate.*
~*v.* **mated, mating, mates.** —*tr.* **1.** To pair (animals) for breeding. **2.** To unite in marriage. **3.** To join closely; pair; couple. **4.** To connect (gear wheels, machine parts, or the like) together so that parts interlock. —*intr.* **1.** To pair for reproduction; breed. **2.** To become mated; join together. **3.** To become joined in marriage. **4.** To fit or interlock exactly. Used of gears, machine parts, and the like. [Middle English, from Middle Low German *mate, gemate*, companion.]

mate² *n.* In chess, a **checkmate** (see).
~*v.* **mated, mating, mates.** —*tr.* To checkmate. —*intr.* To achieve a checkmate: *White mated in 20 moves.* [Middle English *mat*, from Old French, short for *eschec mat*, CHECKMATE.]

ma·té (máttay, maá-tay) *n.* **1.** An evergreen tree, *Ilex paraguayensis*, of South America, where it is widely cultivated. **2.** A mildly stimulant beverage, popular in South America, made from the dried leaves of this tree. Also called "Paraguay tea", "yerba maté". [American Spanish *maté*, alteration (influenced by *té*, tea) of *mate* (with initial stress), from Quechua.]

mate·lot (mát-lō) *n. Chiefly British Slang.* A sailor. [French.]

mate·e·lote (mátta-lōt ‖ *U.S. also* -lŏt) *n.* **1.** A wine sauce for fish. **2.** Fish stewed in such a sauce. [French (sauce) *matelote*, "sailor (sauce)".]

ma·ter (máytər) *n. British Slang.* Mother. Now used only humorously. [Latin *māter.*]

ma·ter·fa·mil·i·as (máytər-fə-mílli-ass, -əss) *n., pl.* **matresfamilias** (máytreez-). The mother of a family. [Latin : *māter*, mother + *familias*, archaic genitive of *familia*, FAMILY.]

ma·te·ri·al (mə-téer-i-əl) *n.* **1.** The substance or substances out of which a thing is or may be constructed: *raw material; building material.* **2.** The basic elements, such as factual data, plans, and ideas, to be refined and made or incorporated into a finished effort: *material for a novel.* **3.** *Plural.* Tools or apparatus for the performance of a given task: *writing materials.* **4.** Fabric or cloth. **5.** A person having sufficient qualities for a specified job or level of achievement: *a competent athlete, but not world record material.*
~*adj.* **1.** Composed of or pertaining to physical substances; relating to matter; corporeal. **2.** Of, pertaining to, or affecting the enjoyment of physical well-being: *material comfort.* **3.** Of or concerned with the physical as distinct from the intellectual or spiritual. **4.** Of substantial or crucial importance: *a material part of the plan.* **5.** *Law.* Relevant to or having significant bearing upon the case: *a material witness.* **6.** *Philosophy.* Of or pertaining to the matter of reasoning, rather than the form. —See Synonyms at **relevant.** [Middle English, from Old French *materiel*, from Late Latin *māteriālis*, from *māteria*, matter.] —**ma·te·ri·al·ness** *n.*

ma·te·ri·al·ise, ma·te·ri·al·ize (mə-téer-i-ə-līz) *v.* **-ised, -ising, -ises.** —*tr.* **1.** To invest with material or physical characteristics; cause to become real or actual: *By building the house, he materialised his dream.* **2.** To cause to adopt materialistic values. —*intr.* **1.** To assume material or effective form: *The promised reinforcements did not materialise.* **2.** To take form or shape. **3.** To take bodily form or shape. Used of a ghost, spirit, or the like. —**ma·te·ri·al·i·sa·tion** (-ī-záysh'n ‖ *U.S.* -i-) *n.* —**ma·te·ri·al·is·er** *n.*
Usage: The intransitive use of this verb to mean "happen" or "occur" (as in *Nothing has yet materialised*) still attracts criticism as being unnecessarily complicated. However, it is frequently used in all styles of spoken and written English. See **transpire.**

ma·te·ri·al·ism (mə-téer-i-ə-liz'm) *n.* **1.** *Philosophy.* **a.** The theory or doctrine that physical matter in its movements and modifications is the only reality and that everything in the universe, including thought, feeling, mind, and will, can be explained in terms of physical laws. Compare **idealism. b.** The theory or doctrine that physical well-being constitutes the greatest good and highest value in life. **2.** An excessive devotion to worldly rather than spiritual concerns, and especially to the acquisition of material possessions. —**ma·te·ri·al·ist** *adj.* & *n.* —**ma·te·ri·al·is·tic** (-ístik) *adj.* —**ma·te·ri·al·is·ti·cal·ly** *adv.*

ma·te·ri·al·i·ty (mə-téer-i-ál-əti) *n., pl.* **-ties. 1.** The state or quality of being material. **2.** Matter; physical substance.

ma·te·ri·al·ly (mə-téer-i-əli) *adv.* **1.** *Philosophy.* With regard to matter as distinguished from form. **2.** To a significant extent or degree; importantly. **3.** With regard to the physical world.

ma·te·ri·a med·i·ca (mə-téer-i-ə méddika) *n. Medicine.* **1.** The study of medicinal drugs and their sources, preparation, and use. **2.** A substance used in preparing medicinal drugs or as a medicine. [Latin, "medical material".]

ma·te·ri·el, ma·té·ri·el (mə-téer-i-él, ma-) *n.* **1.** The equipment, apparatus, and supplies, such as guns and ammunition, of a military force. **2.** The equipment, apparatus, and supplies of any organisation. [French, from *matériel,* MATERIAL (adjective).]

ma·ter·nal (mə-térn'l) *adj.* **1.** Pertaining to or characteristic of a mother or motherhood; motherly: *maternal instinct.* **2.** Received or inherited from one's mother: *a maternal trait.* **3.** Related through one's mother: *my maternal uncle.* [Middle English, from Old French *maternel,* from Latin *māternus,* from *māter,* mother.] —**ma·ter·nal·ly** *adv.*

ma·ter·ni·ty (mə-térnəti) *n.* **1.** The state of being a mother; motherhood. **2.** The feelings or characteristics associated with being a mother; motherliness.

~*adj.* Associated with or adapted for pregnancy and childbirth: *a maternity dress.* [French *maternité,* from Medieval Latin *māternitās* (stem *māternitāt-*), from *māternus,* MATERNAL.]

ma·tey (máyti) *adj. Chiefly British Informal.* Sociable; friendly. —See Synonyms at **familiar.**

~ *n. Chiefly British Informal.* **Mate**[1] (sense 5b). Sometimes used threateningly. —**ma·tey·ness, ma·ti·ness** *n.* —**ma·ti·ly** *adv.*

math (math) *n. U.S.* Mathematics.

math·e·mat·i·cal (máthə-máttik'l, máth-, máthi-, math-) *adj.* Also **math·e·mat·ic** (-máttik). **1.** Of or pertaining to mathematics. **2.** Precise; rigorous; exact. [Old French *mathematique,* from Latin *mathēmaticus,* from Greek *mathēmatikos,* from *mathēma,* science, from *manthanein* (stem *math-*), to learn.] —**math·e·mat·i·cal·ly** *adv.*

mathematical induction *n.* A principle and method of proof in mathematics. See **induction.**

mathematical logic *n.* **Symbolic logic** *(see).*

math·e·ma·ti·cian (máthə-mə-tísh'n, máth-, máthi-) *n.* A person skilled or learned in mathematics.

math·e·mat·ics (máthə-máttiks, máth-, máthi-, math-) *n.* **1.** *Used with a singular verb.* The study of number, form, arrangement, and associated relationships, using rigorously defined literal, numerical, and operational symbols. **2.** *Used with a plural verb.* The application of mathematics to a calculation or problem. [Probably from French *(les) mathématiques,* from Latin *mathēmatica* (neuter plural), from Greek *(ta) mathēmatika.* See **mathematical.**]

Usage: In the sense of the academic subject, *mathematics* takes a singular verb: *Mathematics is an enormous field.* In the sense of "performing calculations", it takes a plural verb: *Your mathematics are wrong.* In U.S. English, the contraction is *math,* not *maths.*

maths (maths) *n.* Mathematics.

Ma·thu·ra (múttoor-ə, mu-thóor-ə). Also **Mut·tra** (múttra). City in Uttar Pradesh, northern India. Lying on the river Jumna, it is the region's commercial centre, and, as the traditional birthplace of Krishna, a place of pilgrimage for Hindus. It was the centre of the Mathura school of Indian art (second to fifth century A.D.).

Mathurai. See **Madurai.**

ma·til·da (mə-tíldə) *n. Australian Informal.* A bushman's pack or bundle. [From *Matilda,* woman's name.]

Ma·til·da (mə-tíldə), also known as the Empress Maud (1102–67). Lady of England (1141–53). The daughter of Henry I, she married Emperor Henry V (1114) and, after his death, Geoffrey of Anjou (1128), by whom she bore Henry II. When her cousin Stephen was elected king, she waged civil war against him and was acknowledged as "Lady of England" (1141) though never crowned. She established her son's succession after Stephen by the Treaty of Wallingford (1153).

mat·in (máttin ‖ mátt'n) *adj.* Also **mat·in·al** (-'l). **1.** Of or pertaining to matins. **2.** *Literary.* Of or pertaining to the early morning.

mat·i·née, matinee (máttin-ay, -áy ‖ mátt'n-) *n. Abbr.* **mat.** A concert, theatrical performance, or showing of a film given in the daytime, usually in the afternoon. [French *matinée,* "morning", early performance, from Old French *matinee,* from *matin,* morning, from Latin *(tempus) mātūtīnum,* morning (time), from *mātūtīnus,* of the morning, from *Mātūta,* goddess of dawn.]

matinée jacket *n.* A baby's short coat, usually knitted. Also called "matinée coat".

mat·ins (máttinz ‖ mátt'nz) *n. Used with a singular or plural verb.* Also *chiefly British* **mat·tins.** **1.** In the Roman Catholic Church, the office that, together with lauds, constitutes the first of the seven **canonical hours** *(see).* **2.** In the Anglican Church, **Morning Prayer** *(see).* **3.** *Poetic.* The morning song of a bird. [Middle English *matines,* from Old French, from Medieval Latin *(vigiliae) mātūtīnae,* morning (watches, vigils). See **matinée.**]

Ma·tisse (ma-téess), **Henri** (1869–1954). French painter and sculptor. Having studied under Gustave Moreau, he led the artistic group Les Fauves from 1905, with colourful, strongly patterned, and often distorted portraits, still lifes, and nudes. He was also influenced by impressionist, cubist, and Islamic art. His works include *The Pink Nude* and *Woman With the Hat.*

Ma·to Gros·so (máttō gróssō; *Portuguese* máatoo grössōō). A state in west central Brazil, comprising the plateau of Mato Grosso. Its name means "thick forest", but this is largely confined to its great river valleys, with extensive wooded savannas between. The state is being opened up, with new roads, development of a beef industry

and exploitation of its rich mineral deposits. Cuiabá is the capital.

mat·rass, mat·trass (máttrəss) *n.* A glass vessel with a long neck, formerly used in chemistry for distilling. [French *matras†.*]

mat·res·fa·mil·i·as. Plural of **materfamilias.**

matri– *comb. form.* Indicates mother; for example, **matriclinous.** [Latin *māter,* mother.]

ma·tri·arch (máytri-aark) *n.* **1.** A woman who rules a family, clan, or tribe. **2.** A woman who dominates any group or activity. [MATRI- + -ARCH.] —**ma·tri·ar·chal** (-árk'l), **ma·tri·ar·chic** (-árkik) *adj.* —**ma·tri·ar·chal·ism** *n.*

ma·tri·ar·chate (máytri-aar-kət, -kit, -kayt) *n.* **1.** A matriarchy. **2.** A hypothetical stage in the evolution of primitive society in which authority is held by matriarchs.

ma·tri·ar·chy (máytri-aarki) *n., pl.* **-chies.** A social system in which women are dominant and descent is traced through the mother of the family.

ma·tric (mə-trík) *n.* Matriculation.

mat·ri·cide (máytri-sīd ‖ máttri-) *n.* **1.** The act of killing one's mother. **2.** One who kills his mother. [Latin *mātricīda* (person), and *mātricīdium* (act) : MATRI- + -CIDE.] —**mat·ri·ci·dal** (-sīd'l) *adj.*

mat·ri·cli·nous (máttri-klínəss, máytri-) *adj.* Having predominantly maternal hereditary traits. Said of plants and animals. Compare **patriclinous.** [MATRI- + *-clinous,* from Greek *-klinēs,* "leaning", from *klinein,* to lean.]

ma·tric·u·lant (mə-tríckew-lənt) *n.* A person who matriculates or is a candidate for matriculation.

ma·tric·u·late (mə-tríckew-layt) *v.* **-lated, -lating, -lates.** —*tr.* To admit formally to membership of a college, university, or the like. —*intr.* To be so admitted.

~*n.* One who has matriculated. [Medieval Latin *mātriculāre,* to enrol, from *mātricula,* list, roll, from *mātrīx,* list, originally, womb, source. See **matrix.**]

ma·tric·u·la·tion (mə-tríckew-láysh'n) *n.* **1.** The act or process of matriculating. **2.** The qualification acquired by matriculating. **3.** In South Africa, the final set of high-school examinations, the successful completion of which entitles the candidate to undertake university studies. Also called "matric".

mat·ri·lin·e·al (máttri-línni-əl, máytri-) *adj.* Pertaining to, based upon, or tracing ancestral descent through the maternal line rather than through the paternal. Compare **patrilineal.**

mat·ri·lo·cal (máttri-lōk'l, máytri-) *adj.* Designating or following a system of marriage in primitive societies, whereby the couple go to live in the home territory of the wife's kin group or clan. Compare **patrilocal.** —**mat·ri·lo·cal·ly** *adv.*

mat·ri·mo·ny (máttri-məni ‖ U.S. -mōni) *n., pl.* **-nies.** **1.** The state of being married. **2.** The sacrament or rite of marriage. **3. a.** A card game in which the combination of a king and queen is needed to win. **b.** Such a winning combination. —See Synonyms at **marriage.** [Middle English, from Anglo-French *matrimonie,* from Latin *mātrimōnium,* marriage, "motherhood" : MATRI- + -*mōnium,* abstract noun suffix.] —**mat·ri·mo·ni·al** (-mōni-əl, -mōn-yəl) *adj.* —**mat·ri·mo·ni·al·ly** *adv.*

ma·trix (máytriks; *for sense 10 also* máttriks) *n., pl.* **matrices** (máytri-seez, máttri-) or **-trixes.** **1.** The environment or surrounding substance within which something originates, develops, or is contained: *contented children nurtured in the matrix of parental love.* **2.** The womb. No longer in technical usage. **3.** *Anatomy.* **a.** The formative cells of a tooth, fingernail, or toenail. **b.** The substance between the cells of animal or plant tissue. **4.** *Geology.* The fine-grained rock material in which a fossil or crystal is embedded. **5.** A mould or die. **6.** The principal metal in an alloy, such as the iron in steel. **7.** A binding substance, such as cement in concrete. **8.** *Mathematics.* A rectangular array of numerical or algebraic quantities treated as an algebraic entity. **9.** The network of intersections between input and output leads in a computer, functioning as an encoder or decoder. **10.** *Printing.* **a.** A metal plate used for casting type faces. **b.** A mould used in stereotyping and designed to receive positive impressions of type or illustrations from which metal plates can be cast. In this sense, also called "mat". [Latin *mātrix,* womb, originally, pregnant animal, from *māter,* mother.]

matrix mechanics *n. Used with a singular verb. Physics.* A formulation of quantum mechanics developed by Heisenberg using matrix algebra to determine the behaviour of physical systems, mathematically equivalent to **wave mechanics** *(see).* Physical quantities are represented by operators in matrix element form.

ma·tron (máytrən) *n.* **1.** A married woman; especially, a mother of mature age with established dignity and social position. **2.** A woman who supervises the medical and domestic arrangements of a boarding school or other institution. **3.** A woman in charge of the nursing staff of a hospital. In this sense, now called "senior nursing officer". [Middle English, from Old French *matrone,* from Latin *mātrōna,* matron, wife, from *māter,* mother.] —**ma·tron·al** (-'l, mə-trōn'l) *adj.* —**ma·tron·li·ness** *n.* —**ma·tron·ly** *adj. & adv.*

matron of honour *n., pl.* **matrons of honour.** A married woman serving as chief attendant of the bride at a wedding. Compare **bridesmaid, maid of honour.**

matronymic. Variant of **metronymic.**

matt, mat, matte (mat) *n.* A dull, often rough finish, as on glass, metal, or paper.

~*tr.v.* **matted, matting, matts.** To produce a dull finish on.

~*adj.* Having a dull surface; not shiny. [French *mat,* "dead". See **checkmate.**]

Matt. Matthew (New Testament).

matte¹ (mat) *n. Metallurgy.* A mixture of a metal with its oxides and sulphides, produced by smelting certain sulphide ores. Also called "regulus". [French, from dialectal *mate*†, a lump.]

matte². Variant of **matt.**

mat·ted (máttid) *adj.* **1.** Covered with or made from mats. **2.** Tangled in a dense mass: *matted hair.* **—mat·ted·ly** *adv.*

mat·ter (máttər) *n.* **1. a.** That which occupies space, can be perceived by one or more senses, and constitutes any physical body or the universe as a whole; that which is corporeal as distinguished from that which is spiritual or intellectual. **b.** *Physics.* Any entity displaying gravitation and inertia when at rest as well as when in motion. **2.** A specified type of substance: *inorganic matter.* **3.** Discharge or waste from a living organism, such as pus or faeces. **4.** The actual substance of thought or expression; the theme of what is expressed as distinguished from the manner in which it is stated or conveyed. **5.** *Philosophy.* In Aristotelian and scholastic use, that which is in itself undifferentiated and formless and which, as the subject of change and development, receives form and becomes substance and experience. **6.** *Law.* **a.** That which must be proved or is the subject of litigation. **b.** Statements, allegations, or the like brought before the court. **7.** Something that is the subject of consideration or attention; a concern or affair, especially of a specified kind: *a personal matter; In matters of finance, his advice is usually reliable.* **8. a.** A circumstance tending to evoke a specified response: *a matter for regret.* **b.** Something largely dependent on or likely to be determined by a specified factor: *a matter of luck.* **c.** A situation presenting a choice that depends on the application of a specified faculty: *a matter of conscience; a matter of opinion.* **9.** A particular factor adversely affecting a person or thing; a trouble or difficulty. Preceded by *the: What's the matter with the car?* **10.** An indefinite or approximate quantity, amount, or extent: *a matter of a few hours.* **11.** Something that is printed or otherwise set down in writing: *reading matter.* **12.** *Printing.* **a.** Composed, or set, type. **b.** Material to be set in type. **—for that matter.** With regard to that: *For that matter, we didn't know when to come.* **—no matter.** Irrespective or regardless of: *No matter what the time is, come!*
~*intr.v.* **mattered, -tering, -ters. 1.** To be of importance: *It matters very much.* **2.** To suppurate. [Middle English *matere,* from Anglo-French, from Latin *māteria,* matter.]

Mat·ter·horn (máttər-hawrn). *French* **Mont Cer·vin** (sair-váN), *Italian* **Monte Cer·vino** (chair-véenō). Mountain (4 477 metres; 14,688 feet) in the Pennine Alps, on the Swiss-Italian border near Zermatt. Its distinctive pyramidal crest was first climbed (1865) by the Englishman Edward Whymper.

matter of course *n.* An expected, natural, or logical outcome. **—mat·ter-of-course** (máttər-əv-kórss || -kŏrss) *adj.*

matter of fact *n.* That which pertains to fact as opposed to opinion; especially, the establishing of the truth of certain alleged facts in the course of a judicial inquiry.

mat·ter-of-fact (máttər-əv-fákt) *adj.* Adhering to or solely concerned with facts; prosaic, unemotional, or unimaginative: *discussed her divorce in a very matter-of-fact way.* **—mat·ter-of-fact·ly** *adv.* **—mat·ter-of-fact·ness** *n.*

Mat·the·an (mə-theé-ən, ma-) *adj.* Of, pertaining to, or designating the Gospel of Saint Matthew. [MATTHE(W) + -AN.]

Mat·thew (máthew) *n. Abbr.* **Matt.** A book of the New Testament, the first Gospel, attributed to Saint Matthew.

Matthew, Saint. One of the Apostles of Christ and traditionally the author of the first Gospel.

Matthew Paris (*c.* 1200–59). English chronicler. He was a monk in the Benedictine monastery at St. Albans. His major work was the *Chronica Majora,* a history of the world from the Creation to 1259.

Mat·thews (máthewz), **Sir Stanley** (1915–). English soccer-player. He played for Stoke City (1931–47, 1961–65) and Blackpool (1947–61) and 56 times for England. He was knighted in 1965.

Mat·thi·as (mə-thī́-əss), **Saint.** One of the Apostles of Jesus, chosen by lot to take the place of Judas Iscariot. Acts 1:23–26.

mat·ting¹ (mátting) *n.* **1.** A coarsely woven fabric used for covering floors and similar purposes. **2.** Mat-making.

matting² *n.* **1.** A dull surface or finish. **2.** A border or mat used for framing a picture.

mattins. *Chiefly British.* Variant of **matins.**

mat·tock (máttək) *n.* A digging tool with a blade set at right angles to the handle and used with a downward motion. [Middle English *mattok,* Old English *mattuc*†.]

mat·tress (máttrəss, máttriss) *n.* **1.** A rectangular pad of heavy cloth enclosing soft material, such as foam rubber, and sometimes coiled springs, used as or on a bed. **2.** A closely woven mat of brush and poles used to protect an embankment, dyke, or dam from erosion. **3.** A raft or slab, made of concrete or metal, used as a foundation. **4.** A network of reinforcing rods or expanded metal forming the basis of reinforced concrete. [Middle English *materas,* from Old French, from Italian *materasso,* from Arabic *maṭraḥ,* place where something is thrown, from *ṭaraḥa,* to throw, fling.]

mat·u·rate (máttewr-ayt, máchər-) *v.* **-rated, -rating, -rates.** *—intr.* **1.** *Archaic.* To mature, ripen, or develop. **2.** To suppurate. *—tr.* To cause to suppurate. [Latin *mātūrāre,* to mature, from *mātūrus,* MATURE.] **—mat·u·ra·tive** (-ətiv, -aytiv) *adj.*

mat·u·ra·tion (máttewr-áysh'n) *n.* **1.** The process of becoming mature; development or ripening: *the maturation of the personality.* **2.** *Biology.* **a.** Formation of a sex cell, **gametogenesis** *(see).* **b.** The final differentiation processes in biological systems, such as the final ripening of a seed. **3.** Discharge of pus, **suppuration** *(see).*

ma·ture (mə-téwr, -chóor || -tóor) *adj.* **-turer, -turest. 1. a.** Complete and finished in natural growth or development: *a mature cell.* **b.** Fully developed; ripe: *a mature cheese.* **c.** Fully established: *a mature garden.* **2. a.** Having reached a stage of intellectual and emotional development usually associated with adulthood: *mature for her age.* **b.** Characteristic of one who has reached such a stage. **3.** Worked out fully by the mind; carefully considered: *a mature piece of criticism.* **4.** *Finance.* At the limit of its time; payable; due: *a mature bond.* **5.** *Geology.* Designating a landscape in which hills and valleys predominate over flat areas as a result of erosion.
~*v.* **matured, -turing, -tures.** *—tr.* **1.** To bring to full development; ripen. **2.** To work out fully in the mind: *to mature one's views.* *—intr.* **1.** To evolve towards or attain full development: *Judgement matures with age.* **2.** *Finance.* To become due. Used of notes, bonds, or the like. [Middle English, from Latin *mātūrus,* timely.] **—ma·ture·ly** *adv.* **—ma·ture·ness** *n.*

mature student *n.* **1.** A college or university student who is above a specific age, usually 25, and is or has been financially self-supporting. **2.** Any student who is older than average.

ma·tur·i·ty (mə-téwr-əti, -chóor- || -tóor-) *n., pl.* **-ties. 1.** The state or quality of being fully grown or fully developed. **2. a.** The time at which a note, bill, or bond is due. **b.** The state of being due, as of a note, bill, or bond. **3.** *Geology.* The state of being mature. [Middle English *maturite,* from Latin *mātūritās* (stem *mātūritāt-),* from *mātūrus,* MATURE.]

ma·tu·ti·nal (máttew-tīn'l, mə-téwtin'l || -tóotin'l) *adj.* Of, pertaining to, or occurring in the morning; early. [Late Latin *mātūtīnālis,* from Latin *mātūtīnus,* from *Mātūta,* goddess of dawn.] **—ma·tu·ti·nal·ly** *adv.*

mat·zo (mát-sō, mót-, -sə) *n., pl.* **-zoth** (-sōt, -sŏt) or **-zos** (-sōz, -səz) or **-zot** (-sōt). A brittle, flat piece of unleavened bread, eaten especially during the Passover. [Yiddish *matse,* from Hebrew *maṣṣah.*]

maud (mawd) *n.* In Scotland, a grey woollen plaid, used as a shawl, rug, or the like. [18th century : origin obscure.]

maud·lin (máwdlin) *adj.* **1.** Effusively sentimental. **2.** Tearfully emotional, especially because of drunkenness. [From *Maudlin,* MARY MAGDALENE (who was depicted as a weeping penitent).] **—maud·lin·ly** *adv.*

Maugham (mawm), **(William) Somerset** (1874–1965). British novelist and dramatist. Born in Paris and trained as a doctor, he wrote such realistic novels as *Liza of Lambeth* (1897), *Of Human Bondage* (1915), and *Cakes and Ale* (1930). He was a popular dramatist too and is most famous of all perhaps for his short stories.

mau·gre (máwgər) *prep. Archaic.* In spite of; notwithstanding. [Middle English, in spite of, "to the displeasure of", from noun, "ill will", from Old French *maugré* (whence French *malgré) : mal,* bad, from Latin *malus* + *gré,* pleasure, from Latin *gratus,* pleasing.]

maul (mawl) *n.* **1.** A heavy, long-handled hammer used to drive stakes, piles, or wedges. **2.** In Rugby football, a loose scrum.
~*tr.v.* **mauled, mauling, mauls. 1.** To handle roughly; bruise or mangle: *a hunter mauled by a bear.* **2.** To injure by or as if by beating: *badly mauled by his critics.* [Middle English *meall, mal,* from Old French *mail,* from Latin *malleus,* hammer.] **—maul·er** *n.*

maul·stick (máwl-stik) *n.* Also **mahl·stick** (máwl-, maál-). A long wooden stick used by painters to support the hand that holds the brush. [Partial translation and alteration of Dutch *maalstok : maalen,* to paint, from Middle Dutch *malen* + *stok,* STICK.]

Mau Mau (mów-mow, -mów) *n., pl.* **Mau Maus** or collectively **Mau Mau. 1.** A secret organisation of Kikuyu tribesmen in Kenya that used terrorism during the 1950s with the aim of driving out white settlers and ending colonial rule. **2.** A member of this organisation. [Origin obscure.]

Mau·na Lo·a (máwnə lṓ-ə). Volcano lying in Hawaii Volcanoes National Park, United States. It is the world's largest volcano, rising to 4 170 metres (13,681 feet).

maund (mawnd) *n.* Any of several Asian units of weight of varying amounts; especially, the official maund in India, equivalent to about 37 kilograms (82 pounds). [Hindi *mān,* from Persian, from Akkadian *manū,* designating a unit of weight. See **mina.**]

maun·der (máwndər) *intr.v.* **-dered, -dering, -ders. 1.** To talk incoherently or aimlessly. **2.** To move or act aimlessly or vaguely; wander. [Perhaps from obsolete *maunder*†, to beg.] **—maun·der·er** *n.*

Maun·dy (máwndi) *n. Sometimes small* **m. 1. a.** The distribution of specially minted coins by the British sovereign to a selected group of poor people on Maundy Thursday. **b.** The coins so distributed. Also called "Maundy money". **2.** In the Roman Catholic Church, the ceremony of washing the feet of twelve people on Maundy Thursday, in commemoration of Jesus' washing of his apostles' feet at the Last Supper. [Middle English, from Old French *mandé,* a thing commanded, from Medieval Latin *mandātum,* the ceremony, "command", from the words of Christ in the first antiphon of Maundy Thursday, *Mandātum novum dō vōbis,* "A new commandment give I unto you" (John 13).]

Maundy Thursday *n.*. The Thursday before Easter, commemorating Jesus' Last Supper. In the Roman Catholic Church, also called "Holy Thursday".

Mau·pas·sant, (mṓ-pa-soN, -paa-), **(Henri René Albert) Guy de** (1850–93). French novelist and short-story writer. While a civil servant, he was encouraged to write by Flaubert, and produced his first success with *Boule de Suif* (1880). His works, mainly realistic short stories, examine the themes of hypocrisy, madness, the social world of Paris, and peasant life in Normandy.

Mau·re·ta·ni·a (mórri-táyni-ə, máwri-). North African district of the Roman Empire, comprising the Atlas Mountains of Morocco and western Algeria and land to the north. Settled before 2000 B.C. by Maures (Moors), a Berber people, it fell to Rome in about 100 B.C. Arabs overran the area in the seventh century A.D., and by 1000 the Moors, fanatical Muslims, had spread into Spain and south-westwards in Africa. Their Arab-Berber descendants now form the majority in Algeria, Mauritania, and Morocco.

Mau·riac (mórri-ak ‖ máwri-, mõ̃ri-, -ák; *French* mō-ryák), **François** (1885–1970). French novelist. His works include *Le Baiser au lépreux* (1922), *le Noeud de vipères* (1932), and his play *Asmodée* (1938). He was awarded the Nobel prize for literature (1952).

Mau·ri·ta·ni·a, Islamic Republic of (mórri-táyni-ə, máwri-). *Arabic* **Muritaniyah,** *French* **Republique Islamique de Mauritanie.** A large, sparsely populated, mostly desert country of northwest Africa. Its only major fertile area is along the Senegal river, and most people live by stock rearing. The country, badly hit by recurring Sahel droughts, depends on exports of iron ore. Fish is also exported. The area was settled by Berbers from the north in about A.D. 1000, and their Arab-Berber descendants, the Maures (Moors), make up 75 per cent of the population. The rest, mostly in the south, are black Africans. European traders plied the coast from the 15th century. The French took over the country (1860–1903) and governed it until it became fully independent in 1960. In 1964 it became a one-party state, and was under military rule from 1979, the year it renounced its claim to southern Western Sahara (Tiris al Gharbia), until multi-party elections in 1992. Area, 1 030 700 square kilometres (397,956 square miles). Population, 2,350,000. Capital, Nouakchott. —**Mau·ri·ta·ni·an** *adj. & n.*

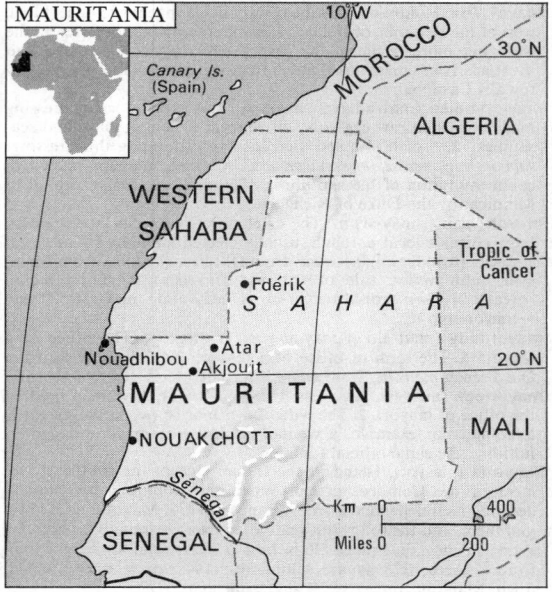

Mau·ri·tius (mə-rishəss, mo-, maw-), **Republic of.** Formerly **Île de France.** State in the Indian Ocean, comprising the mountainous island of Mauritius and several tiny dependencies. The economy once rested on the growing and processing of sugar cane, but now tourism and clothing manufacture are equally important. The first European settlers were Dutch (1598–1710). During French occupation (1715–1810), black African slaves were imported to work the sugar plantations. Creoles (of French-African descent) now make up about one third of the population. The British captured the islands (1810), abolished slavery, and brought in Indian contract labourers, whose descendants now account for some two thirds of Mauritians. Tension between the two groups has been a major problem for the country, independent since 1968. Area, 2040 square kilometres (788 square miles). Population, 1,130,000. Capital, Port Louis. —**Mau·ri·tian** (-rishən) *n. & adj.*

Mau·rois (máw-rwaa ‖ mõ̃-, -rwaá), **André,** born Émile Herzog (1885–1967). French biographer and novelist. Having served with the British army during World War I, he produced two perceptive portrayals of the British character with *Les Silences du Colonel Bramble* (1918) and *Les Discours du Docteur O'Grady* (1921), plus biographies of Shelley, Disraeli, and others.

Mau·ser (mów-zər) *n.* A trademark for a repeating rifle or pistol. [After Paul *Mauser* (1838–1914), German arms manufacturer, who invented it.]

mau·so·le·um (máw-sə-lée-əm ‖ -zə-) *n., pl.* **-leums** or **-lea** (-ə). A large and stately tomb, or a building housing such a tomb or tombs. [Latin *mausōleum,* from Greek *mausōleion,* originally, the tomb of *Mausōlos,* satrap of Caria (377–353 B.C.), at Halicarnassus.] —**mau·so·le·an** *adj.*

mau·vais quart d'heure (mõ̃-vay kaar dér, -váy, dõ̃r) *n.* A short-lived but unpleasant experience. [French, bad quarter of an hour.]

mauve (mõv) *n.* **1.** Brilliant violet to strong or brilliant purple to moderate reddish purple. **2. a.** A mauve dye. **b.** Mauveine. [French *mauve,* "mallow(-coloured)", from Latin *malva,* mallow.] —**mauve** *adj.*

mau·veine (mõ̃-veen, -vin) *n.* A purple dye made from aniline; the first synthetic dye. Also called "mauve", "Perkin's mauve". [MAUVE + -INE.]

mav·er·ick (mávvərik, mávvrik) *n.* **1.** *U.S.* An unbranded calf or colt that has strayed from the herd, traditionally considered the property of the first person who brands it. **2. a.** One who refuses to abide by the dictates of his group; a dissenter. **b.** One who resists adherence to or affiliation with any single organised group or faction; an independent. Often used adjectively: *maverick politicians.* [After Samuel A. *Maverick* (1803–1870), Texas cattleman who did not brand his calves.]

ma·vis (máyviss) *n.* A bird, the **song thrush** *(see).* [Middle English *mavys,* from Old French *mauvis†.*]

ma·vour·neen, ma·vour·nin (mə-võor-neen) *n. Irish.* My darling. [Irish *mo mhuirnín : mo,* my + *muirnín,* darling, diminutive of *muirn,* delight, from Old Irish, revels, banquet, tumult.]

maw (maw) *n.* **1.** The stomach, mouth, jaws, or gullet of a voracious carnivore. **2.** Something suggestive of a gaping opening or the appetite of a voracious animal. [Middle English *mawe,* Old English *maga.*]

mawk·ish (máwkish) *adj.* **1.** Excessively and objectionably sentimental. **2.** *Archaic.* Sickly; nauseating. [Earlier senses "nauseating", "nauseous", from obsolete *mawk,* maggot, whim, fastidious person, from Middle English *mathek,* MAGGOT.] —**mawk·ish·ly** *adv.* —**mawk·ish·ness** *n.*

max. maximum: *We're talking £8,000 max!*

max·i (máksi) *n.* **1.** An ankle- or floor-length skirt or coat. **2.** Something larger or longer than other members of its class. Often used adjectively and in combination: *a maxicoat.* Compare **mini, mini-.** [Short for MAXIMUM.]

max·il·la (mak-síl-ə) *n., pl.* **-lae** (-ee) or **-las. 1.** *Anatomy.* Either of a pair of bones forming part of the upper jaw. See **skull. 2.** *Zoology.* Either of two laterally moving appendages behind the mandibles in insects and most other arthropods, used in feeding. [Latin, "lower jaw", akin to *mālā†,* upper jaw. See also **malar.**] —**max·il·lar, max·il·lar·y** (-əri ‖ *U.S.* máksə-lerri) *adj.*

max·il·li·ped (mak-sílli-ped) *n.* The first pair or first three pairs of appendages in crustaceans, situated behind the maxillae and used for feeding. [MAXILL(A) + -PED.]

max·im (máksim) *n.* A succinct formulation of some fundamental principle or rule of conduct. —See Synonyms at **saying.** [Middle English, from Old French *maxime,* from Medieval Latin (*prōpositiō*) *maxima,* "greatest proposition", philosophical term for a fundamental axiom, from *maximus,* greatest.]

max·i·mal (máksim'l) *adj.* **1.** Of, pertaining to, or consisting of a maximum. **2.** The greatest or highest possible. **3.** *Mathematics.* Designating an element, in an ordered set, that is followed by no other.

~*n. Mathematics.* A maximal element. —**max·i·mal·ly** *adv.*

max·i·mal·ist (máksim'l-ist) *n.* **1.** *Sometimes capital* **M.** One who advocates direct revolutionary action to secure social and political gains. **2.** One who rejects all compromise and insists on all his demands being met. [French *maximaliste* (probably from English MAXIMAL).]

Max·im gun (máksim) *n.* The first automatic repeating gun. [After Sir Hiram *Maxim* (1840–1916), U.S.-born British engineer, who invented it.]

Max·i·mil·i·an (máksi-míl-yən, -i-ən), **(Ferdinand Joseph)** (1832–67). Emperor of Mexico (1864–67). The younger brother of Francis Joseph I of Austria, he accepted the title of Emperor of Mexico from the French, who had recently captured the country. Lacking popular support, he was captured and shot by the republicans when the French withdrew under American pressure.

max·i·min (máksi-min) *n.* **1.** *Mathematics.* The highest of a set of minimum values. **2.** In games theory, the selection of a strategy for a member of the group that gives the maximum value for the member's minimum gains. Compare **minimax.** [*Maximum* + *minimum.*]

max·i·mise, max·i·mize (máksi-mīz) *tr.v.* **-mised, -mising, -mises. 1.** To make as great as possible; increase to a maximum. **2.** To represent as having the greatest degree of importance or value. **3.** *Mathematics.* To find a maximum value of (a function). —**max·i·mi·sa·tion** (-mī-záysh'n ‖ *U.S.* -mi-) *n.* —**max·i·mis·er** *n.*

max·i·mum (máksi-məm) *n., pl.* **-mums** or **-ma** (-mə). *Abbr.* **max. 1. a.** The greatest possible quantity, degree, or number. **b.** The time or period during which the highest point or degree is attained. **2.** An upper limit stipulated by law or otherwise fixed or agreed: *a price maximum; a wage increase maximum.* **3.** *Astronomy.* **a.** The moment when a variable star is most brilliant. **b.** The magnitude of the star at such a moment. **4.** *Mathematics.* **a.** The value of a function that is not exceeded by neighbouring values. **b.** The greatest value assumed by a function within some subset of its domain of definition. **c.** The largest number in a set.

~*adj. Abbr.* **max. 1.** Having, being, or showing the greatest quantity or the highest degree that has been or can be attained: *maximum temperature.* **2.** Of, pertaining to, or making up a maximum or maximums: *a maximum number in a series.* [Latin *maximum,* "greatest (quantity)", neuter of *maximus,* greatest.]

maximum permissible dose. *Physics.* A **dose** *(see).*

max·i·sin·gle (máksi-sing-g'l) *n.* **1.** A record the size of an LP but designed to be played at 45 r.p.m. **2.** An EP.

ma·xi·xe (mə-shée-shay, -shə, -shéesh) *n.* A Brazilian dance similar to the two-step. [Brazilian Portuguese *maxixe†*.]

max·well (máks-wəl, -wel) *n. Abbr.* **Mx** A unit of magnetic flux in the centimetre-gram-second electromagnetic system, equal to the flux perpendicularly intersecting an area of one square centimetre in a region where the magnetic induction is one gauss. [After James Clerk MAXWELL.]

Max·well (máks-wəl, *also* -wel), **James Clerk** (1831–79). British physicist. Educated at Edinburgh and Cambridge, he published in 1873 the *Treatise on Electricity and Magnetism,* expounding a set of four equations which were applicable to electricity, magnetism, and light. He predicted the existence of radio waves and worked on the kinetic theory of gases and the study of colour perception.

Maxwell, (Ian) Robert, born Jan Ludvik Hoch (1923–   ). Czech-born British publisher and newspaper proprietor. Chairman of the British Printing and Communication Corporation (1981), in 1985 he acquired control of the Mirror Group of newspapers.

may¹ (may) *v.* Past **might** (mīt), present **may** or *archaic* **mayest** (mayst, máy-ist) or **mayst** (mayst) (for second person singular). Used as an auxiliary, followed by an infinitive without *to,* or with the infinitive understood, to indicate: **1.** A requesting or granting of permission: *May I take a swim? You may.* See Usage note at **can. 2.** Possibility: *It may rain this afternoon.* **3.** Ability or capacity, with the force of *can: If I may be of service.* **4.** Obligation or function, with the force of *must* or *shall,* in statutes, deeds, and other legal documents. **5.** Desire or fervent wish. Used chiefly in exclamatory phrases: *Long may he live!* **6.** Purpose or result, in clauses introduced by *that* or *so that: expressing ideas so that the average person may understand.* **7.** Contingent or conditional: *Whatever you may think, I still believe he's innocent.* **8.** Less abrupt or pointed questioning: *How old may this little boy be?* —**be that as it may.** Nevertheless; despite that. —**come what may.** Whatever happens. —**may as well.** To have no compelling reason not to. —**may well.** To be very likely. [Middle English *may,* past *mighte, moghte,* Old English *maeg* (first and third person singular), past *mighte, moghte,* infinitive *magan,* to be strong, be able, have permission.]
   Usage: Might and may: might functions in context as a past form and subjunctive *(She said she might leave early; so that the average person might understand).* It is often interchangeable with *may,* however, though it tends to emphasise the hypothesis more strongly: *Might I take a swim?; It might rain this afternoon.*

may² *n. British.* The **hawthorn** *(see).* Also called "may tree". [From MAY (month).]

May (may) *n.* **1.** The fifth month of the year according to the Gregorian calendar. May has 31 days. **2.** *Poetic.* The springtime of life; youth. **3.** The festivities of May Day. [Middle English, from Old French *Mai,* from Latin *Maius (mēnsis),* (the month) of *Maia,* Italic goddess.]

ma·ya (mī-ə, maá-yə) *n. Hinduism.* Illusion; especially, the visible material world conceived of as being purely illusory. [Sanskrit *māyā†*.]

Ma·ya (mī-ə, maá-yə) *n., pl.* **Mayas** or collectively **Maya. 1.** A member of an Indian people of southern Mexico and Central America whose civilization reached its height in about A.D. 300–900. **2.** The language spoken by the Maya; Mayan. —**Ma·ya** *adj.*

Ma·ya·kov·sky (mī-ə-kóf-ski; *Russian* mə-yi-káwf-), **Vladimir** (1893–1930). Soviet poet and playwright. He combined experimental poetic techniques with Bolshevik propaganda, and was a leading member of the futurist movement. His works include the poems *150 Million* (1920) and *Mystery-Bouffe* (1918), and the plays *The Bedbug* (1928) and *The Bath-House* (1929). He committed suicide.

Ma·yan (mī-ən, maá-yən) *adj.* Of or pertaining to the Maya, their culture, their language or the language group to which it belongs. —*n.* **1.** A Maya. **2.** A family of Central American languages, including the language of the Maya.

May apple *n.* **1.** A North American plant, *Podophyllum peltatum,* having a single, nodding white flower and oval edible fruit. **2.** The fruit of this plant.

may·be (máy-bee, -bi; *occasionally* -bée) *adv.* Perhaps; possibly.
   Usage: Written as a single word, it has the meaning "perhaps" and tends, especially in British English, to be restricted to informal usage *(Maybe they'll attack tomorrow),* except in certain cases where it occurs in rather formal British English in final position and has stress on the second syllable *(They will attack tomorrow maybe, but we shall be ready to repel them).* Written as two words, it functions as a verb phrase *(It may be that they will attack).*

May bug *n.* The **cockchafer** *(see).*

May Day *n.* **1.** The first day of May, traditionally marked by the celebration of spring. **2.** May 1, or the first working day of May, widely observed as a public holiday in honour of workers.

may·day (máy-day) *n.* An international radio-telephone signal word used by aircraft and ships in distress. [Phonetic rendering of French *m'aider,* help me.]

Mayence. See **Mainz.**

May·er (máy-ər), **Sir Robert** (1879–1985). British music patron, born in Germany. In 1923 he organised the Robert Mayer Children's Concert, which has continued every year since. In 1954 he founded the Youth and Music scheme. He was knighted in 1939.

May·fair (máy-fair) *n.* A district of the City of Westminster, Greater London. A wealthy residential, recreational, and commercial area of London's West End, it takes its name from the annual fair held

there until the end of the 18th century.

may·flow·er (máy-flowr, -flow-ər) *n.* Any of a wide variety of plants that bloom in May, such as the hawthorn and cowslip.

May·flow·er (máy-flowr, -flow-ər). The name of the ship on which the Pilgrims sailed to America in 1620.

may·fly (máy-flī) *n., pl.* **-flies.** Any of various fragile, winged insects of the order Ephemeroptera that develop from aquatic nymphs and live in the adult stage for a few days at most. Also called "dayfly". [So named because it swarms in May.]

may·hap (máy-hap, -háp) *adv. Archaic.* Perhaps; perchance. [From the phrase *it may hap.*]

may·hem (máy-hem ‖ -əm) *n.* **1.** The infliction of violent injury upon a person or thing; wanton destruction: *children committing mayhem in the flower beds.* **2.** A state of violent disorder or riotous confusion; havoc. **3.** *Law.* Formerly, the offence of wilfully maiming or crippling a person. [Middle English, from Anglo-French *maihem, mahaym,* injury, from Old French *mahaignier,* MAIM.]

May·hew (máy-hew), **Henry** (1812–87). English journalist and sociologist. He pioneered a study of London's poor for the *Morning Chronicle,* which were published in three volumes (1851). A fourth, *London Labour and the London Poor,* appeared in 1862.

may·ing (máy-ing) *n. Poetic.* The celebration of or participation in traditional May Day festivities. [From MAY (month).]

may·n't (maynt, máy-ənt). Contraction of *may not.*

May·o¹ (máy-ō ‖ *Irish also* may-ő). Family of U.S. physicians and surgeons. William Worrall (1819–1911), born in England, went to the United States in 1845 and concentrated on gynaecological surgery. A clinic he started in Rochester, Minnesota, grew into the renowned Mayo Clinic under the supervision of his sons, William James (1861–1939) and Charles Horace (1865–1939).

Mayo². *Irish* **Muigheo.** Atlantic county in Connacht province, in the west of the Republic of Ireland. It is mountainous and barren in the west, but more fertile in the east, producing oats, potatoes, and livestock. It has many lakes and a fragmented coastline. The county town is Castlebar.

may·on·naise (máy-ə-náyz, -nayz) *n.* **1.** A creamy salad dressing made of beaten raw egg yolk, oil, vinegar or lemon juice, and seasonings. **2.** A dish of a specified food incorporating this dressing: *salmon mayonnaise; egg mayonnaise.* [French, perhaps named in commemoration of the capture in 1756 of Port *Mahon,* capital of Minorca, by the Duke of Richelieu.]

mayor (mair ‖ máy-ər) *n.* The chief officer of a city, town, or (in large cities) a local borough, usually elected annually by the local council. [Middle English *mair,* from Old French *maire,* from Medieval Latin *major,* title of various officials, from Latin *mājor,* "greater".] —**mayor·al** (maír-əl ‖ máy-ərəl, may-áwrəl) *adj.* —**mayor·ship** *n.*

mayor·al·ty (maír-əlti ‖ máy-ər-) *n., pl.* **-ties. 1.** The office of a mayor. **2.** The term of office of a mayor. [Middle English, from Old French *mairalté,* from *maire,* MAYOR.]

mayor·ess (maír-iss, -ess, -éss ‖ máy-ər-) *n.* **1.** A woman holding the office of mayor. **2.** The wife of a mayor or (when the mayor is a woman, for example) a woman, such as the mayor's daughter, fulfilling the same official function.

Ma·yotte (ma-yót). Island in the Indian Ocean, the southeasternmost of the Comoros group. When the Comoros government declared its independence from France in 1975, Mayotte refused to join them, and the following year voted overwhelmingly to become a dependency of France. It is now a Territorial Collectivity of France. Area, 373 square kilometres (144 square miles). Chief town, Mamoudzou. —See **Madagascar** map p922.

May·pole (máy-pōl) *n. Sometimes small* **m.** A pole decorated with streamers that May Day celebrants hold while dancing round it.

May queen *n.* A young woman or girl who is crowned with a ring of flowers and presides over the traditional May Day celebrations. Also called "Queen of the May".

may tree *n. British.* The **hawthorn** *(see).*

may·weed (máy-weed) *n.* A widespread weed, *Anthemis cotula,* having unpleasant-smelling leaves and white flowers. Also called "dog fennel", "stinking mayweed".

Ma·za·rin (mázzərin; *French* ma-za-rán), **Jules,** born Giulio Mazarini (1602–61). French statesman, born in Italy. He became adviser to Louis XIII's chief minister, Richelieu. After the death of Louis (1643), he was the chief minister of the regent, Anne of Austria, and after 1653 was all-powerful in the French government. He was never ordained a priest, but was made a cardinal on the recommendation of Louis XIII in 1641.

Maz·da·ism (máz-dər-iz'm, -də-) *n.* A religion, **Zoroastrianism** *(see).* Avestan *mazda,* the good principle in Zoroastrianism + -ISM.]

maze (mayz) *n.* **1. a.** An intricate, usually confusing, network of walled or hedged pathways; a labyrinth. **b.** Any physical situation resembling such a network, in which it is easy to get lost. **c.** Any elaborate, confusing, or impenetrable network: *a maze of regulations.* **2.** A puzzle consisting of a graphic representation of a maze. **3.** *Archaic.* A state of confusion or perplexity.
   —*tr.v.* **mazed, mazing, mazes.** *Archaic.* To daze, bewilder, or perplex. [Middle English, a maze, earlier, "delusion", from *mazen,* to bewilder, amaze. See **amaze.**] —**ma·zy** *adj.*

ma·zer (máyzər) *n.* A large, often elaborately ornamented, drinking bowl made of hard wood or metal. [Middle English *mazer,* originally, "an outgrowth of maple wood" (from which a mazer was made), from Germanic.]

ma·zu·ma (mə-zōomə) *n. U.S. Slang.* Money; cash. [Yiddish *mezumen,* "ready" (i.e., ready cash), from Hebrew *məzumān.*]

ma·zur·ka, ma·zour·ka (mə-zúr-kə, -zóor-) *n.* **1.** A lively Polish dance resembling the polka. **2.** A piece of music for such a dance. [French, from Polish *Mazurka,* oblique form of *mazurek,* diminutive of *mazur,* one from *Mazovia* province.]

maz·zard (máz-ərd, -aard) *n.* A wild sweet cherry, *Prunus avium,* often used as grafting stock. [Perhaps akin to MAZER.]

Maz·zi·ni (mat-séeni), **Giuseppe** (1805–72). Italian revolutionary nationalist. He was exiled in 1830 for joining a secret society, the Carbonari, and lived mainly in London after 1837. In 1849 he was a leader of the Roman republic, and after its fall he organised an unsuccessful uprising in Milan (1853). In 1858, in London, he began the revolutionary paper *Thought and Action,* stirring Italian nationalist opinion.

M.B. Bachelor of Medicine [Latin *Medicinae Baccalaureus.*]

M.B.A. Master of Business Administration.

Mba·ba·ne (m-baa-báani). Capital of Swaziland, situated in the Mdimba Mountains. It is also a commercial centre.

M.B.E. Member of the Order of the British Empire.

M·bo·ya (m-bóy-ə), **Thomas Joseph,** known as Tom (1930–69). Kenyan politician. In 1957 he was one of the first eight Africans elected to the legislative council. A year later he was elected president of the All-African People's Conference at Accra. After independence in 1963 he served in Jomo Kenyatta's government as minister of justice (1963–64) and minister of economic planning (1964–69). He was assassinated in 1969.

M.C. **1.** Master of Ceremonies. **2.** *U.S.* Member of Congress. **3.** *British.* Military Cross.

M.C.C. Marylebone Cricket Club.

Mc·Ad·am (mə-káddəm), **John Loudon** (1756–1836). British engineer. He developed the technique of improving roads by raising their level and covering them with graded stones. He became surveyor general of Britain's roads (1827).

Mc·Car·thy (mə-kárthi), **Joseph R(aymond),** known as Joe (1908–57). U.S. politician. He was elected to the U.S. Senate (1947). As chairman of the permanent subcommittee on investigations, he began public hearings, accusing army officials, media employees, and public personalities of communism. His charges were never proved and he was censured by the Senate (1954).

McCarthy, Mary (Therese) (1912–89). U.S. writer. She satirised urban American life in novels such as *The Company She Keeps* (1942), *The Group* (1963), and *Birds of America* (1971).

Mc·Car·thy·ism (mə-kárthi-iz'm) *n.* **1.** A political stance, especially prevalent in the United States in the 1950s, of intense anticommunism, characterised by the practice of driving suspected communists from government office by means of well-publicised but often unsubstantiated allegations. **2.** The use of underhand methods or unsupported allegations in order to suppress opposition. [Coined by opponents of Joseph R. MCCARTHY.] —**Mc·Car·thy·ist, Mc·Car·thy·ite** *n.* & *adj.*

Mc·Cart·ney (mə-kártni), **Sir (James) Paul** (1942–). British rock musician and composer. As a Beatle (1960–71), he wrote with John Lennon many memorable songs, including *She Loves You* and *Yesterday.* Since the Beatles, he has worked as a solo artist and (1971–81) with the group Wings. Knighted 1997.

Mc·Coy (mə-kóy) *n. Slang.* The authentic thing or quality; something that is not an imitation or substitute. Used in the phrase *the real McCoy.* [After Kid McCoy, professional name of Norman Selby (1873–1940), American boxer.]

Mc·Cul·lers (mə-kúllərz), **Carson (Smith)** (1917–67). U.S. novelist. Her books, set in the South, are compassionate studies of the macabre and grotesque. They include *The Heart is a Lonely Hunter* (1940) and *The Member of the Wedding* (1946).

Mc·En·roe (mácken-rō), **John (Patrick)** (1959–). U.S. tennis player. He was U.S. singles champion (1979–81, 1984) and Wimbledon champion (men's doubles 1979, 1981, 1983–84, 1992; singles 1981, 1983, 1984).

Mc·Gon·a·gall (mə-gónnəg'l) **William** (1830–1902). British writer. He is often called "the world's worst poet": his poems, such as *The Tay Bridge Disaster* and *Attempted Assassination of the Queen,* frequently fail to rhyme or scan and are full of unintentional bathos.

Mc·Kel·len (mə-kéllən), **Sir Ian (Murray)** (1939–). British actor. He played Marlowe's Doctor Faustus, Shakespeare's Macbeth, Romeo, and many other major roles, and made a number of television and film appearances. In 1984–86 he was Associate Director of the National Theatre in London.

Mc·Kin·ley, Mount (mə-kinli). The highest mountain in North America. It lies in Mount McKinley National Park, in the Alaska Range, Alaska, United States, and rises to 6 194 metres (20,322 feet). It is named after William **McKinley.**

McKinley, William (1843–1901). 25th President of the United States (1897–1901). He was elected to Congress as a Republican in 1876, where he introduced the protectionist McKinley Tariff Act (1890). His presidency was imperialist, with the destruction of the Spanish fleet in the Spanish-American war (1898) to gain Cuba, and the annexation of the Philippines. He was shot by an anarchist.

Mc·Lu·han (mə-klóo-ən), **(Herbert) Marshall** (1911–80). Canadian literary critic and communications sociologist. He argued that the media, such as print or television, affect or overshadow the message they convey. His books include *Understanding Media* (1964) and *The Medium is the Message* (1967).

Mc·Mil·lan (mək-millən), **Edwin Mattison** (1907–91). U.S. physicist. He discovered the first transuranic element, neptunium, in 1940 by bombarding uranium with neutrons. Together with Glenn Seaborg (1912–), he was awarded the Nobel Prize for chemistry (1951).

M.C.P. male chauvinist pig.

Md The symbol for the element mendelevium.

M.D. **1.** Doctor of Medicine [Latin *Medicinae Doctor.*] **2.** Managing Director.

M.D.S. Master of Dental Surgery.

mdse. merchandise.

me¹ (mee, *weak form* mi) *pron.* The objective case of the first person pronoun *I.* It is used: **1.** As the direct object of a verb: *He assisted me.* **2.** As the indirect object of a verb: *They offered me a lift.* **3.** As the object of a preposition: *This letter is addressed to me.* **4.** After *than* or *as* in comparisons in which the first term is in the objective case: *The judges praised you more than me.* **5.** *U.S. Informal.* In place of the reflexive pronoun *myself,* as the indirect object of a verb: *I'm going to get me a gun.* **6.** In various elliptical, absolute, or interjectional phrases in which it is neither subject nor object: *Goodness me! Unlucky me. Who, me?*

~*n.* The speaker's image or personality: *This dress isn't really me; the real me.* [Middle English, Old English *mē, mē.*]

Usage: Until about thirty years ago, grammarians taught that the correct answer to the question *"Who is there?"* is *"It is I",* not *"It's me".* They pointed out that the verb "to be" has no object, so that any pronoun following it should be in the subjective form. Today, however, *It is I* sounds overcareful to the point of being pedantic, and objective forms of the pronouns *(me, him, her, us, them)* are acceptable even in formal contexts, unless there is a following construction (as in *It was he who told the vicar).* In such cases, formal speech requires the subjective form, informal speech the objective. Similarly, following *than* or *as,* subjective forms of the pronoun are used in formal writing *(John is bigger than I),* objective forms in other styles. If the construction continues, the subjective form must be used in standard English whether written or spoken, formal or informal *(John is bigger than I am).* The choice of an objective as opposed to a possessive form of these pronouns is an issue when an *-ing* form of a verb follows. Purists insist on the possessive form, in such sentences as *I remember your doing that.* But the objective form has become normal in informal usage, and is often heard in all but the most formal contexts. Sometimes a subtle distinction of meaning is involved: *I remember you acting in Macbeth* means "I remember the fact that you acted in that play"; whereas *I remember your acting in Macbeth* may additionally mean "I remember the quality of your acting".

me², **mi** (mee) *n. Music.* In tonic sol-fa, a syllable representing the third note of a diatonic scale. [Originally *mi,* Medieval Latin, from Latin *mīra,* "wonders", a word sung to this note in a hymn to St. John the Baptist (see **gamut**), from Latin *mīrārī,* to be amazed at, from *mīrus,* wonderful.]

Me methyl group (CH₃-).

ME **1.** Middle English. **2.** Myalgic encephalomyelitis.

M.E. **1.** mechanical engineer; mechanical engineering. **2.** Middle English. **3.** mining engineer.

me·a cul·pa (máy-ə kóol-pə, mée-, kúl-) *n. Latin.* An admission of fault or error. Often used interjectionally. [Literally, my fault.]

mead¹ (meed) *n.* An alcoholic drink made from fermented honey and water. [Middle English *mede,* Old English *medu, meodu.*]

mead² *n. Archaic.* A meadow. [Middle English *mede,* Old English *mǣd.*]

Mead (meed), **Margaret** (1901–78). U.S. anthropologist. She was a curator of ethnology at the American Museum of Natural History in New York (1926–69). She wrote *Coming of Age in Samoa* (1928) and *Growing Up in New Guinea* (1930).

mead·ow (méddō) *n.* **1.** A tract of grassland mown for hay, as opposed to pasture, which is grazed by animals. **2.** A **water meadow** *(see).* [Middle English *medwe,* Old English *mǣdwe,* oblique case of *mǣd,* MEAD.] —**mead·ow·y** *adj.*

meadow fescue *n.* A grass, *Festuca pratensis* (or *eliator),* native to Eurasia and introduced in North America.

meadow grass *n.* A perennial grass, *Poa pratensis,* widely distributed in meadows and fields in northern temperate regions.

mead·ow·lark (méddō-laark) *n.* **1.** Either of two North American songbirds, *Sturnella magna* or *S. neglecta,* related to the Baltimore oriole. **2.** Any of various other birds of the genus *Sturnella,* of North, Central, and South America.

meadow mushroom *n.* A field mushroom *(see).*

meadow pipit *n.* A European songbird, *Anthus pratensis,* with a brown and white speckled plumage.

meadow rue *n.* Any of various plants of the genus *Thalictrum,* having clusters of small white, yellowish, or purplish flowers.

meadow saffron *n.* A plant, the **autumn crocus** *(see).*

mead·ow·sweet (méddō-sweet) *n.* Any of several plants of the genera *Filipendula* or *Spiraea;* especially, *F. ulmaria,* of Eurasia, having clusters of small, creamy white, fragrant flowers.

Meads (meedz), **Colin (Earl)** (1935–). New Zealand Rugby football player. He played lock forward for the All Blacks a record 100 times, and appeared in 55 test matches.

mea·gre, *U.S.* **mea·ger** (mée̱gər) *adj.* **1.** Having little flesh; thin; lean. **2.** Markedly deficient in quantity, fullness, or extent; scanty. **3.** Markedly deficient in richness, fertility, or vigour; barren or feeble. [Middle English *megre,* from Anglo-French *megre* and Old French *maigre,* from Latin *macer* (stem *macr*-), thin.] —**mea·gre·ly** *adv.* —**mea·gre·ness** *n.*

Synonyms: meagre, spare, sparse, skimpy, scanty, scant.

meal¹ (meel) *n.* **1.** The edible seed or other edible part of a pulse or grain, usually excluding wheat, coarsely ground. **2.** *Scottish.* Oatmeal. **3.** Any granular substance produced by grinding. [Middle English *mele*, Old English *melu*, flour.]

meal² *n.* **1.** An amount of food served and eaten, often as several courses, in one sitting. **2.** A customary time or occasion of eating food. **—make a meal of.** To devote unnecessary effort or attention to (a task, for example). [Middle English *meel*, Old English *mæl*, "mark", "measure", fixed time, mealtime.]

meal·ie *n. South African.* **1.** An ear of maize. **2.** *Plural.* Maize. [Afrikaans *mielie*, from Portuguese *milho*, millet, from Latin *milium*.]

meals on wheels *n. Used with a singular verb.* A service, usually funded by a local authority, providing hot meals to elderly or disabled people in their own homes.

meal ticket *n.* **1.** *Chiefly U.S.* A card or ticket entitling the holder to a meal or meals. **2.** *Slang.* A person or thing depended on as a source of financial support.

meal·time (meel-tīm) *n.* The usual time for eating a meal.

meal·worm (meel-wurm) *n.* The larva of any of several beetles of the genus *Tenebrio*. Mealworms infest flour and other grain products and are raised for bird feed.

meal·y (meeli) *adj.* **-i·er, -i·est.** **1.** Resembling meal in texture or consistency; granular: *mealy potatoes.* **2. a.** Made of or containing meal. **b.** Sprinkled or covered with meal or a similar granular substance. **3.** Flecked with spots; mottled. **4.** Unhealthily pale. Said of the complexion. **5.** Mealy-mouthed. **—meal·i·ness** *n.*

meal·y·bug (meeli-bug) *n.* Any insect of the genus *Pseudococcus* and related genera. Some species, such as *P. citri*, are destructive to plants, especially citrus trees. [So named because they are covered with a white powdery substance.]

meal·y-mouthed (meeli-mówthd, -mowthd ‖ -mowtht) *adj.* Unwilling to state facts or opinions simply and directly.

mean¹ (meen) *v.* **meant** (ment), **meaning, means.** **—tr.** **1. a.** To be defined or described as; refer to; denote: *The word "dog" means a certain species of mammal.* **b.** To convey the same sense as; refer to the same thing as: *The French word "chien" means "dog".* **c.** To act as a symbol of; represent. **d.** To signify; serve as a sign. Used with a clause: *The flashing light means that you can cross.* **2. a.** To intend to convey or indicate: *What do you mean by that look?* **b.** To have in mind as one's true meaning or intention: *said £12 but meant 12 pence; said she would resign, and meant it.* **3.** To have as a purpose, aim, or intention; want: *I mean to get to the bottom of this.* **4.** To design or intend for a certain purpose, person, or end: *a building meant for storage; Was this letter meant for me?* **5.** To have as a consequence; entail; imply: *This decision means another 20% on the rates.* **6.** To have as its full implications and true character: *He doesn't know what hard work means.* **7.** To require or oblige. Used in the passive: *You're meant to knock before you go into his office.* **—intr.** **1.** To be of a specified importance or significance; matter: *The opinions of critics meant little to him.* **2.** To have intentions of a specified kind; be disposed. Followed by *well* or *ill*: *She means well, despite her blunders.* [Middle English *menen*, Old English *mǣnan*, to intend, tell, signify.]

Synonyms: mean, signify, import, denote, represent, purport.

Usage: In clauses conveying the idea of intention or purpose, the following construction is introduced by *that* in standard English: *I did not mean that you should leave.* British English can also use the infinitive: *I didn't mean you to leave.* A construction using *for* is sometimes encountered in American English: *I didn't mean for you to leave.*

mean² *adj.* **meaner, meanest.** **1.** Ignoble; small-minded; petty: *a mean motive.* **2.** Lacking elevating human qualities, such as kindness, generosity, and goodwill: **a.** Reluctant to help or oblige; selfish. **b.** Cruel; malicious; spiteful. **c.** Reluctant to give; stingy. See Synonyms at **stingy.** **3.** Low in quality or grade; inferior. **4.** Low in social status; of humble origin or rank. **5.** Common or poor in appearance; shabby. **6.** *U.S. Informal.* Ill-tempered. Said of animals. **7.** *Chiefly U.S. Informal.* In poor health; out of sorts; ill. **8.** *Slang.* Skilful; hard to beat: *She plays a mean game of bridge.* **—no mean.** Very good: *He's no mean cook.* [Middle English *mene*, *imene*, Old English *gemǣne*, "common".] **—mean·ly** *adv.* **—mean·ness** *n.*

Synonyms: mean, low, base, abject, infamous, ignoble.

mean³ *n.* **1.** That which lies between two extremes; a middle point, condition, quality, or course of action. See **golden mean.** **2.** *Mathematics.* **a.** A number that represents a set of numbers in any of several ways determined by a rule involving all members of the set; an average. **b.** The **arithmetic mean** *(see).* Compare **geometric mean.** **3.** *Logic.* The middle term in a syllogism. **—See means.** **~adj.** **1.** Occupying a middle or intermediate position between two extremes. **2.** Intermediate in size, extent, quality, time, or degree; medium. **3.** Constituting a mean; average. [Middle English *mene*, from Anglo-French *meen* and Old French *meien*, from Latin *mediānus*, median, from *medius*, middle.]

me·an·der (mee-ándər, mi-) *intr.v.* **-dered, -dering, -ders.** **1.** To follow a winding and turning course: *Streams tend to meander through level land.* **2.** To wander aimlessly and idly without fixed direction: *vagabonds meandering through life.* **—See Synonyms at wander.** **~n.** **1.** *Plural.* Circuitous, sinuous windings, as of a stream or path. **2.** A circuitous journey or excursion; a ramble. **3.** An ornamental pattern of intertwining lines, used in art and architecture; a fret. [Originally as a noun, from Latin *maeander*, from Greek *maiandros*,

from *Maiandros*, the river MAEANDER, noted for its windings.] **—me·an·der·er** *n.* **—me·an·der·ing·ly** *adv.* **—me·an·drous** (-ándrəs) *adj.*

mean deviation *n. Statistics.* The arithmetic mean of the absolute values of deviations from the arithmetic mean, or from the median, in a statistical distribution.

mean distance *n.* The average distance between two bodies; especially, the average of the greatest and the least distances between an orbiting body and the body about which it is orbiting.

mean free path *n.* The average distance covered by a particle, molecule, ion, or the like, between collisions.

mean free time *n.* The average time that elapses between collisions of a particle, molecule, ion, or the like.

meanie. Variant of **meany.**

mean·ing (meening) *n.* **1.** That which is signified or denoted by a linguistic expression such as a word or phrase; sense; semantic content: *a word with several different meanings.* **2.** That which one wishes to convey by words or actions; import: *I listened carefully to grasp his meaning.* **3.** The full implications or true character of something: *doesn't know the meaning of pain.* **4.** That which is felt to be the inner significance of something: *the meaning of dreams.* **5.** Functional value; efficacy; significance. **~adj.** **1.** Full of meaning; expressive: *a meaning look.* **2.** Intentioned or disposed in a specified manner. Used in the combinations *ill-meaning* and *well-meaning.*

Synonyms: meaning, sense, significance, signification, import, purport.

mean·ing·ful (meening-f'l) *adj.* Having meaning, function, value, or purpose; significant. **—mean·ing·ful·ly** *adv.*

mean·ing·less (meening-lass, -liss) *adj.* Having no meaning or significance; senseless. **—mean·ing·less·ly** *adv.*

mean life *n.* The average time for which an unstable or reactive particle, ion, or the like, can exist; a lifetime.

means (meenz) *pl.n.* **1.** *Sometimes used with a singular verb.* A method, instrument, or course of action by which some act or end can be accomplished: *The fastest means of communication is the telephone.* **2.** Material resources; income, wealth, or property: *a man of means.* **—by all means.** Without fail; certainly. **—by means of.** With the use of; owing to: *They succeeded by means of patience and sacrifice.* **—by no means** or **not by any means.** In no sense; certainly not: *by no means an easy opponent.*

Usage: Means, in the sense of "resources" (of money or property, for example), takes a plural verb: *His means are sufficient to keep him alive. Means,* in the sense of "way to an end", takes either a singular or a plural verb, depending on the type of construction in which it occurs. Used with *a, any, each* and so on, it takes a singular verb *(A means of transport is essential);* used with *all, several, such,* and the like, it takes a plural verb *(Several means of transport are available).* Used with *the,* it takes a verb that may be singular or plural, depending on whether or not a collective sense of the noun is intended: *The means of transport is for you to decide* (collective), but *The means of transport are many and various* (individualised).

mean sea level *n.* The average level of the sea, used in geography as a basis from which to measure height.

mean solar day *n.* The average period between successive transits of the Sun, equal to 24 hours, and now measured from midnight to midnight. It is used because the apparent solar day, the actual period between successive transits of the Sun, varies. Also called "civil day".

mean solar time *n.* Time based on the mean solar day. Also called "civil time", loosely "mean time".

mean square *n. Mathematics.* The arithmetic mean of the squares of a set of numbers.

means test *n.* An official examination of a person's material resources to establish eligibility for social security or other benefits. **—means-test** (meenz-test) *tr.v.*

mean sun *n.* A hypothetical sun defined as moving at a uniform rate along the celestial equator so that it completes its orbit in the same period as the apparent sun. It is used in computing the mean solar day.

meant. Past tense and past participle of **mean.**

mean time *n.* Loosely, mean solar time.

mean·time (meen-tīm, -tīm) *n.* The time between one occurrence and another; an interval. **~adv.** During a period of intervening time; meanwhile.

Usage: Meantime is used principally as a noun, usually in the phrase *in the meantime. Meanwhile* is used principally as an adverb: *Meanwhile, we were waiting in the shop.* But some speakers, in Scotland for example, do use *meantime* as an adverb, and *meanwhile* as a noun, without any change of meaning.

mean·tone system (meen-tōn) *n. Music.* A former system for tuning keyboard instruments. It has now been replaced by **equal temperament** *(see).*

mean·while (meen-wīl, -wīl, -hwīl, -hwīl) *adv.* **1.** During or in the intervening time: *Meanwhile, life goes on.* **2.** At the same time: *The court is deliberating; meanwhile, we must be patient.* **~n.** The intervening time. See Usage note at **meantime.**

mean·y, mean·ie (meeni) *n., pl.* **-nies.** *Informal.* **1.** A miserly, ungenerous person. **2.** A malicious, spiteful person.

meas. measurable; measure.

mea·sles (meez'lz) *n. Used with a singular verb.* **1.** An acute, contagious virus disease, usually occurring in childhood. Its symptoms include those of the common cold and the eruption of red spots.

Also called "rubeola". See **German measles.** **2.** A disease of cattle and pigs, caused by tapeworm larvae. **3.** A plant disease, usually caused by fungi, and producing minute spots on leaves and stems. [Middle English *maseles,* plural of *masel,* from Middle Dutch *măsel,* blemish.]

mea·sly (méez-li, -'l-i) *adj.* **-slier, -sliest.** **1.** Infected or spotted with measles; measled. **2.** Infected with larval tapeworms. Said of meat. **3.** *Slang.* Contemptibly small; meagre: *a measly tip.*

meas·ur·a·ble (mézh-rəb'l, mézhə-) *adj. Abbr.* **meas.** **1.** Capable of being measured. **2.** Important; significant: *a measurable feat.*

meas·ure (mézhər) *n. Abbr.* **meas.** **1.** The dimensions, quantity, or capacity of anything as ascertained by measuring: *Length, area, volume, and mass are basic measures of material properties.* **2.** A reference standard or sample used for the quantitative comparison of properties: *The standard kilogram is maintained as a measure of mass.* **3.** A unit specified by a scale, such as an inch, or by variable conditions, such as a day's march. **4.** A system of measurement, such as the metric system. **5.** A device, such as a marked tape or a graduated container, used for measuring. **6.** An act of measurement. **7.** A basis for evaluation or comparison: *the measure of an achievement.* **8.** An amount taken or prescribed as a standard: *a good measure of oats; short measure.* **9.** A specified extent, degree, or amount: *achieved some measure of success; hasn't yet grasped the full measure of the calamity.* **10.** An implied extent, degree or amount, such as: **a.** A fitting amount: *a measure of recognition.* **b.** A limited amount: *a measure of happiness.* **11.** Limit; bounds: *a generosity knowing no measure.* **12.** Appropriate restraint; moderation: *criticism in measure.* **13.** An action taken as a means to an end; an expedient: *desperate measures.* **14.** A legislative bill or enactment: *"I have opposed measures, not men."* (Lord Chesterfield). **15. a.** Poetic metre. **b.** Poetic rhythm or cadence. **16. a.** *Archaic.* A dance. **b.** *Poetic.* A tune. **17.** *Music.* **a.** The time of a piece of music. **b.** *Chiefly U.S.* The metrical unit between two bars on the staff; a **bar** *(see).* **18.** *Printing.* The width of a page or column of type. **—for good measure.** In addition to the required amount.

~v. **measured, -uring, -ures.** *—tr.* **1.** To ascertain the dimensions, quantity, or capacity of. **2.** To mark, lay out, or establish dimensions for by measuring. Often followed by *off: measure off an area.* **3.** To evaluate, especially by comparison with something else: *an encouraging result when measured against last year's figures.* **4.** To bring into opposition: *She measured her power with that of a dangerous adversary.* **5.** To serve as a measure of: *The inch measures length.* **6.** To mark off or separate, usually with reference to some unit of measurement. Often followed by *out: measure out a pint of milk.* **7.** To have a measurement of: *The room measures 10 by 12 metres.* **8.** To allot or distribute as if by measuring; mete. Often followed by *out: The revolutionary tribunal measured out harsh justice.* **9.** To consider or choose with care; weigh: *She measures her words with pedantic caution.* **10.** *Archaic.* To travel over or through. *—intr.* To take measurements; work out the dimensions of something. **—measure up.** To have the right qualifications. **—measure up to.** To match (expectations, standards, or the like). [Middle English *mesure,* from Old French *mesure,* from Latin *mēnsūra,* a measure, from *mētīrī* (past participial stem *mēns-*), to measure.] **—meas·ur·er** *n.*

meas·ured (mézhərd) *adj.* **1.** Regular in rhythm. **2.** Carefully weighed; calculated; deliberate: *with measured irony.* **3.** Written in metre. **—meas·ured·ly** *adv.* **—meas·ured·ness** *n.*

meas·ure·less (mézhər-ləss, -liss) *adj.* Limitless; immeasurable; infinite: *"Through caverns measureless to man"* (S.T. Coleridge). See Synonyms at **infinite.** **—meas·ure·less·ly** *adv.*

meas·ure·ment (mézhərmənt) *n.* **1.** The act of measuring or the process of being measured. **2.** A system of measuring: *measurement in miles.* **3.** The dimensions, quantity, or capacity determined by measuring: *room measurements.*

meas·ur·ing jug (mézhəring) *n.* A transparent or semitransparent jug marked with a graduated scale and used in cookery to measure dry or liquid ingredients.

measuring worm *n.* The caterpillar of a geometrid moth, which moves in alternate contractions and expansions suggestive of measuring. Also called "inchworm", "looper".

meat (meet) *n.* **1.** The edible flesh of mammals, as distinguished from that of fish or poultry. **2.** Edible flesh including poultry and some fish and shellfish: *crab meat.* **3.** The edible portions of eggs, fruits, or nuts. **4. a.** The essence or principal part of something: *the meat of the editorial.* **b.** Valuable or significant content; substance: *a witty book, but without much meat in it.* **5.** *Archaic & Regional.* Food in general, especially solid food. [Middle English *mete,* "food", meat, Old English *mete,* food.]

meat and drink *n.* Something from which one derives great satisfaction or enjoyment.

meat·ball (méet-bawl) *n.* **1.** A small ball of minced meat variously prepared and cooked. **2.** *U.S. Slang.* A stupid person; especially, a stupid boy or man.

Meath (meeth; *locally always* meeth). *Irish* **Mhidhe.** County in Leinster province, Republic of Ireland, on the Irish Sea. It is mainly fertile, producing grain, potatoes, cattle, and horses. Its many historical sites include Newgrange, Tara, Kells, and the Boyne valley. Trim is the county town.

meat·less (méet-ləss, -liss) *adj.* **1.** Lacking meat or food. **2.** When meat is not to be eaten: *meatless days.*

meat loaf *n.* A dish of meat and other ingredients shaped into a loaf and usually baked.

meat-safe (méet-sayf) *n.* A cupboard for storing meat, usually consisting of a boxlike frame covered with wire netting or gauze.

me·a·tus (mi-áytəss, mee-) *n., pl.* **-tuses** or **meatus.** A body canal or opening, such as the opening of the ear or the urethral canal. [Latin *meātus,* passage, from *meāre* (past participial stem *meāt-*), to pass.]

meat·y (méeti) *adj.* **-ier, -iest.** **1.** Of, resembling, or full of meat. **2.** Supplying ample food for thought; substantial: *a meaty theme for study and debate.* **—meat·i·ness** *n.*

mec·a·myl·a·mine (méckə-míllə-meen) *n.* A drug, $C_{11}H_{21}N.HCL$, taken orally to treat high blood pressure.

mec·ca (méckə) *n. Sometimes capital* **M.** **1.** A place that is the centre of an activity or the goal to which adherents of a faith or practice aspire. **2.** Any place visited by many people. [After MECCA, as a goal of pilgrims.]

Mec·ca (méckə). *Arabic* **Mak·kah** (máck-kə). Holiest city of Islam. Capital of Hejaz province, western Saudi Arabia, it is circled by hills. The birthplace of Muhammad (*c.* A.D. 570) and site of the **Kaaba,** Mecca is a pilgrimage centre which all Muslims hope to visit at least once in their lives.

Mec·ca·no (mi-kaánō, me-, mə-) *n.* A trademark for any of various miniature construction sets consisting of metal or plastic parts that may be bolted together to make mechanical models.

mech. **1.** mechanical; mechanics. **2.** mechanism.

me·chan·ic (mi-kánnik, mə-) *n.* **1.** A worker skilled in making, using, or repairing machines and tools. **2.** *Archaic.* A craftsman; an artisan. [Earlier form of MECHANICAL.] **—me·chan·ic** *adj.*

me·chan·i·cal (mi-kánnik'l, mə-) *adj. Abbr.* **mech.** **1.** Of or pertaining to machines or tools. **2.** Operated or produced by a machine. **3.** Of or pertaining to mechanics. **4.** Acting like a machine or performed as if by a machine; automatic: *The speaker's delivery was mechanical.* **5.** Pertaining to, produced by, or dominated by physical forces. **6.** Interpreting and explaining the phenomena of the universe by reference to causally determined material forces; mechanistic. **7.** *Archaic.* Of or pertaining to manual labour, its tools, and its skills.

~n. U.S. Printing. A **paste-up** *(see).* [Middle English, pertaining to manual labour, earlier *mechanic,* from Latin *mēchanicus,* from Greek *mēkhanikos,* from *mēkhanē,* MACHINE.] **—me·chan·i·cal·ly** *adv.* **—me·chan·i·cal·ness** *n.*

mechanical advantage *n.* The ratio of the output force of a machine to the input force.

mechanical drawing *n.* **1.** Any drawing to scale of a machine, engine, building, or the like, from which measurements can be taken. **2.** The art or skill of producing such drawings; draughtsmanship.

mechanical engineering *n. Abbr.* **M.E.** The branch of engineering that encompasses the generation and application of heat and mechanical power and the design, production, and use of machines and tools. **—mechanical engineer** *n.*

me·chan·ics (mi-kánniks, mə-) *n. Abbr.* **mech.** **1.** *Used with a singular verb.* The analysis of the action of forces on matter or material systems. See **dynamics, statics, quantum mechanics, statistical mechanics.** **2.** *Used with a singular verb.* The design, construction, operation, and application of machinery or mechanical structures. **3.** *Used with a plural verb.* The process by or way in which something operates, is constructed, or is carried out; the technical or procedural aspects of something: *grasps the mechanics of music but has no feel for it; the mechanics of getting a bill through Parliament.*

mech·a·nise, mech·a·nize (méckə-nīz) *tr.v.* **-nised, -nising, -nises.** **1.** To equip with or perform by means of machinery: *mechanise a factory; mechanised farming.* **2.** To equip (a military unit) with motor vehicles, such as tanks and trucks. **3.** To make (something) mechanical, automatic, or unspontaneous. [MECHAN(ICAL) + -ISE.] **—mech·a·ni·sa·tion** (-nī-záysh'n || *U.S.* -ni-) *n.*

mech·a·nism (méckə-niz'm) *n.* **1.** *Abbr.* **mech.** **a.** A machine or mechanical appliance. **b.** The arrangement of connected parts in a machine. **2.** Any system of parts that operate or interact like those of a machine: *the mechanism of the Solar System.* **3.** An instrument or process, physical or mental, by which something is done or comes into being: *The mechanism of learning includes studying.* **4.** *Psychology.* **a.** The automatic and consistent response of an organism to various stimuli. **b.** A usually unconscious mental and emotional pattern that influences behaviour: *a defence mechanism.* **5.** *Philosophy.* The doctrine that all natural phenomena are explicable by material causes and mechanical principles. [Late Latin *mēchanisma,* from Greek *mēkhanē,* machine.]

mech·a·nist (méckə-nist) *n.* One who subscribes to the philosophical doctrine of mechanism.

mech·a·nis·tic (méckə-nístik) *adj.* **1.** Of or pertaining to mechanics as a branch of physics. **2.** Of or pertaining to the philosophy of mechanism; specifically, tending to explain phenomena only by reference to physical or biological causes. **—mech·a·nis·ti·cal·ly** *adv.*

mech·a·no·chem·i·cal coupling (méckənō-kémmik'l) *n. Biochemistry.* The reversible conversion of chemical energy into mechanical work, as in the control of muscle contraction and relaxation by ATP.

mech·a·no·ther·a·py (méckənō-thérrəpi) *n.* Physiotherapy using mechanical methods to improve the functioning of joints and muscles by producing repeated movements.

Me·chel·en (mékhə-lən). *French* **Ma·lines** (ma-léen). City on the Dijle river, Antwerp province, north central Belgium. Once a famous lace-making centre, it is now an important commercial and industrial city and a transport centre.

Mech·lin (mécklin) *n.* A delicate lace in which the pattern details are defined by a flat thread. Also called "malines". [After MECHE-LEN, where it was made.]

Meck·len·burg (mécklən-burg; *German* -boork). Former north German state. A much forested lowland along the Baltic with many lakes, it produces potatoes, rye, and sugar beet.

Mecklenburg-Pomerania. State of Germany, created from former East German counties.

me·co·ni·um (mi-kŏni-əm) *n.* Excrement in the foetal intestinal tract that is discharged after birth. [New Latin, from Latin, from Greek *mēkŏnion*, "poppy juice", from *mēkŏn*, poppy; from a fancied resemblance.]

Med (med) *n. Informal.* The Mediterranean Sea and its coastal regions. Preceded by *the.*

med. 1. medical; medicine. 2. medieval. 3. medium.

M. Ed. Master of Education.

med·al (médd'l) *n.* A piece of metal, stamped with a design or inscription commemorating an event or person, often given as an award.

~*tr.v.* **medalled** or *U.S.* **medaled, -alling** or *U.S.* **-aling, -als.** To honour or decorate with a medal. [French *médaille*, from Italian *medaglia*, from Common Romance *medallia* (unattested), from Vulgar Latin *metallea* (unattested), from Latin *metallum*, METAL.]

me·dal·lion (mi-dál-yən, me-, mə-) *n.* 1. A large medal. 2. Something resembling a large medal, such as an oval or circular panel or tablet bearing a design or portrait. 3. A medallion-shaped portion of meat. [French *médaillon*, from Italian *medaglione*, augmentative of *medaglia*, MEDAL.]

med·al·list, *U.S.* **med·al·ist** (médd'l-ist) *n.* 1. One who designs, makes, or collects medals. 2. One who receives a medal.

Medal of Honour *n. Abbr.* **MH** The highest U.S. military decoration, awarded for bravery beyond the call of duty in action against the enemy. Also called "Congressional Medal of Honour".

medal play *n.* A form of competition in golf in which the total number of strokes taken is the basis of the score. Also called "stroke play". Compare **match play.**

Med·a·war (méddə-wər), **Sir Peter (Brian)** (1915–87). British zoologist and anatomist. He was awarded, with Sir Macfarlane Burnet, the Nobel prize for physiology or medicine (1960) for work on tissue transplants.

med·dle (médd'l) *intr.v.* **-dled, -dling, -dles.** 1. To intrude in other people's affairs or business; interfere. Used with *in* or *with.* 2. To handle something idly or ignorantly; tamper. Used with *with.* —See Synonyms at **interfere.** [Middle English *medlen*, "to mix", meddle, from Old French *medler*, variant of *mesler*, from Vulgar Latin *misculāre* (unattested), frequentative of Latin *miscēre*, to mix.] —**med·dler** (médd'l-ər, méddlər) *n.*

med·dle·some (médd'l-səm) *adj.* Inclined to meddle or interfere. —**med·dle·some·ly** *adv.* —**med·dle·some·ness** *n.*

Mede (meed) *n.* A native or inhabitant of ancient Media.

Me·de·a (mi-déer, -dée-ə). *Greek Mythology.* A princess and sorceress of Colchis who helped Jason to obtain the Golden Fleece, lived as his consort, and killed their children as revenge for his infidelity.

Me·de·llín (medde-lín, -yín). Major industrial city of Colombia, and capital of Antioquia department in the northwest of the country. It has an important coffee market, a mint, and four universities.

me·di·a¹ (méedi-ə) *n., pl.* **-diae** (-ee). 1. The middle layer of the wall of an artery or vein. 2. The middle layer of various other parts or organs. 3. Any of the main veins in an insect's wing. [Latin, feminine of *medius*, middle.]

media². Alternative plural of **medium.**

~*pl.n. Informal.* The mass media as a whole. Preceded by *the.* Also used adjectivally: *a media personality.*

Usage: In the sense "means of mass communication", *media* is a plural noun, derived from **medium.** The incorrect use of *media* as a singular is sometimes heard (*Television is an unpredictable media*). A new plural form is sometimes used *(medias)*, but it is still considered unacceptable. The phrase *the mass media* is more commonly encountered as a singular, and attracts less criticism.

Me·di·a (méedi-ə). Ancient country of western Asia, in what is now northern Iran. —**Me·di·an** *adj. & n.*

me·di·a·cy (méedi-ə-si) *n.* The state or quality of being mediate.

mediaeval. Variant of **medieval.**

me·di·al (méedi-əl) *adj.* 1. Pertaining to, situated in, or extending towards the middle; median. 2. *Phonetics.* Designating a sound, syllable, or letter occurring between the initial and final positions in a word or morpheme. 3. Designating or pertaining to a mathematical average or mean. 4. Of average or ordinary size. [Late Latin *mediālis*, from Latin *medius*, middle.] —**me·di·al·ly** *adv.*

me·di·an (méedi-ən) *adj.* 1. Pertaining to, located in, or directed towards the middle; medial. 2. *Anatomy & Zoology.* Of, pertaining to, or lying in the plane that divides a bilaterally symmetrical animal into right and left halves; mesial. 3. *Statistics.* Pertaining to or constituting the middle value in a distribution.

~*n.* 1. A median point, plane, line, or part. 2. *Statistics.* The middle value in a distribution, above and below which lie an equal number of values. 3. In geometry: **a.** The line that joins a vertex of a triangle to the midpoint of the opposite side. **b.** The line that joins the midpoints of the nonparallel sides of a trapezoid. [Latin *mediānus*, from *medius*, middle.] —**me·di·an·ly** *adv.*

median plane *n.* A plane dividing a bilaterally symmetrical animal into right and left halves.

median point *n.* The intersection of the medians of a triangle.

me·di·ant (méedi-ənt) *n.* The third note in a diatonic musical scale between the tonic and the dominant, traditionally related harmonically to them.

me·di·as·ti·num (méedi-ə-stī-nəm, -a-) *n., pl.* **-na** (-nə). 1. The space between the pleural sacs in mammals, containing all the thoracic viscera except the lungs. 2. A membrane between two parts of a cavity or organ. [New Latin, from neuter of Latin *mediastīnus*, median, from *medius*, middle.] —**me·di·as·ti·nal** *adj.*

me·di·ate (méedi-ayt) *v.* **-ated, -ating, -ates.** —*tr.* 1. To resolve or settle (differences) by acting as an intermediary agent between two or more conflicting parties. 2. To bring about (a settlement, agreement, or compromise) by action as an intermediary. 3. To serve as a vehicle for bringing about (a result) or for transmitting (information, for example) to others. —*intr.* 1. To occupy an intermediate or middle position. 2. To intervene between parties in a dispute in order to effect an agreement, settlement, or compromise.

~*adj.* (-ət, -it). Acting through, involving, or dependent upon some intervening agency. [Latin *mediāre*, to be in the middle, from *medius*, middle.] —**me·di·ate·ly** *adv.* —**me·di·a·tive** (-ətiv, -aytiv) *adj.*

me·di·a·tion (méedi-áysh'n) *n.* 1. The act of mediating; intervention. 2. The intervention of a neutral power in an attempt to bring about a peaceful settlement between disputing nations.

Synonyms: mediation, conciliation, arbitration.

me·di·a·tise, me·di·a·tize (méedi-ə-tīz) *tr.v.* **-tised, -tising, -tises.** To annex (a small state) to a large one, leaving the ruler of the smaller power with his title and some authority. [German *mediatisieren*, from *mediat*, mediate, from Latin *mediāre*, to be in the middle, MEDIATE.] —**me·di·a·ti·sa·tion** (tī-záysh'n ‖ *U.S.* -ti-) *n.*

me·di·a·tor (méedi-aytər) *n.* One that mediates; especially, a person who serves as an intermediary to reconcile differences. —**me·di·a·tor·y** (-ətri, -ətəri, -áytəri) *adj.*

medic¹. *U.S.* Variant of **medick.**

med·ic² (méddik) *n. Informal.* A doctor, medical orderly, or medical student. [Latin *medicus*, doctor.]

medic-. Variant of **medico-.**

med·i·ca·ble (méddikəb'l) *adj.* Potentially responsive to treatment with medicine; curable.

Med·i·caid (méddi-kayd) *n.* In the United States, a publicly-funded scheme providing medical aid for people who fall below a certain income level. [MEDIC(AL) + AID.]

med·i·cal (méddik'l) *adj. Abbr.* **med.** 1. Of or pertaining to the study or practice of medicine. 2. Requiring or concerned with treatment by medicine as distinct from surgery. 3. Medicinal; curative. ~*n. Informal.* A thorough physical examination. [French *médical*, from Medieval Latin *medicālis*, from Latin *medicus*, doctor, from *medērī*, to heal.]

medical card *n.* In the United Kingdom, a card issued by the National Health Service and bearing the name of the card holder's doctor and general information about medical services.

medical certificate *n.* A certificate given by a medical practitioner after a medical examination, stating a person's fitness or unfitness, as for work, military service, or the like.

medical examiner *n.* In the United States, a public official responsible for determining the cause of death in cases of death by crime or violence. Compare **coroner.**

medical jurisprudence *n.* **Forensic medicine** *(see).*

medical social worker *n.* In Britain, a social worker attached to a hospital and responsible for the general welfare of patients. Formerly called "almoner".

me·dic·a·ment (mi-díkkə-mənt, mi-, mə-, méddikə-) *n.* An agent that promotes recovery from injury or ailment; a medicine. [Latin *medicāmentum*, from *medicārī*, TO MEDICATE.]

Med·i·care (méddi-kair) *n.* 1. In the United States, a government health scheme providing medical care for the elderly. 2. In Canada, a government health insurance scheme. [MEDI(CAL) + CARE.]

med·i·cate (méddi-kayt) *tr.v.* **-cated, -cating, -cates.** 1. To treat medicinally. 2. To tincture or permeate with a medicinal substance. [Latin *medicārī*, from *medicus*, a doctor, from *medērī*, to heal.] —**med·i·ca·tive** (-kətiv, -kaytiv) *adj.*

med·i·ca·tion (méddi-káysh'n) *n.* 1. A medicine. 2. The act or process of being medicated. 3. The administration of medicine.

Me·di·ci (méddi-chee, -chi, me-dée-; *Italian* méddee-chee). Italian noble and banking family, which produced three popes (Leo X, Clement VII, and Leo XI) and two queens of France (Catherine de Médicis and Marie de Médicis). The family's lavish patronage of the arts helped to make Florence one of the richest storehouses of European culture. The first of the family to rule Florence was Cosimo the Elder (1389–1464). The most outstanding patron of learning and the arts was Lorenzo the Magnificent (1449–92), whose artists included Michelangelo and Botticelli. Cosimo the Great (1519–74) became Grand Duke of Tuscany in 1569. The line ended with Gian Gastone's death in 1737. —**Me·di·ce·an** (méddi-cheeən) *adj.*

me·dic·i·nal (me-díssin'l, mi-, mə-) *adj.* Pertaining to or having the properties of medicine; healing; curative.

~*n.* A medicinal substance. —**me·dic·i·nal·ly** *adv.*

med·i·cine (méd-s'n, méddi-, -sin) *n.* 1. *Abbr.* **med.** The science of diagnosing, treating, alleviating, or preventing disease and other damage to the body or mind. 2. The branch of this science encompassing treatment by drugs, diet, exercise, and other nonsurgical means. 3. The practice of medicine. 4. Any drug or other agent used to treat disease or injury. 5. Among various tribal peoples, something believed to control natural or supernatural powers and to serve as a preventive or remedy. —**(someone's) own medicine.**

Treatment, especially unkind or unfriendly treatment, given to a person who usually gives it to others. Used chiefly in the phrases *give someone a taste* or *dose of his own medicine.* —**take (one's) medicine.** To endure deserved punishment. [Middle English, from Old French, from Latin *medicīna,* the art of a physician, from *medicus,* doctor, from *medērī,* to heal.]

medicine ball *n.* A large, heavy ball used for exercise.

medicine chest *n.* A cabinet, chest, or cupboard containing medicines, bandages, and the like.

medicine lodge *n.* A large wooden structure used by some North American Indian peoples for various ritualistic ceremonies.

medicine man *n.* A person believed, especially among North American Indians, to possess supernatural powers for healing, invoking spirits, and other purposes; a sorcerer; a shaman.

medicine show *n.* A travelling show, popular especially in 19th-century America, that offered various entertainments and acts, between which medicines were peddled.

med·ick, *U.S.* **med·ic** (méddik) *n.* Any of several plants of the genus *Medicago,* native to the Old World and having clusters of small, usually yellow or purple flowers and compound leaves with three leaflets. [Middle English, from Latin *mēdica,* from Greek *Medikē (poa),* Median (grass).]

med·i·co (méddikō) *n., pl.* **-cos.** *Informal.* A doctor or medical student. [Italian and Spanish, from Latin *medicus,* doctor, from *medērī,* to heal.]

medico-, medic- *comb. form.* Indicates medical; for example, **medicodental.** [Latin *medicus,* doctor.]

me·di·e·val, me·di·ae·val (méddi-éev'l, med-, méedi- ‖ meed-) *adj. Abbr.* **M., med.** **1.** Of, pertaining to, or characteristic of the Middle Ages. **2.** *Informal.* Old-fashioned or out-of-date. [New Latin *Medium Aevum,* the Middle Age : Latin *medium,* neuter of *medius,* middle + *aevum,* age.] —**me·di·e·val·ly** *adv.*

Medieval Greek *n. Abbr.* **Med. Gr.** Greek as used from about A.D. 700 to 1500. Also called "Middle Greek".

me·di·e·val·ism, me·di·ae·val·ism (méddi-éev'l-iz'm, med-, méedi- ‖ meed-) *n.* **1.** The spirit, beliefs, or practices of the Middle Ages. **2.** Devotion to or acceptance of the ideas of the Middle Ages. **3.** Scholarly study of the Middle Ages. —**me·di·e·val·ist** *n.*

Medieval Latin *n. Abbr.* **ML, M.L.** Latin as used throughout Europe in the Middle Ages, from about A.D. 700 to 1500.

me·di·na (me-déenə, mi-) *n.* The ancient native quarter of various North African towns. [Native name in North Africa.]

Me·di·na (me-déenə, mi-). *Arabic* **Al Madinah.** Second most holy city of Islam, in western Saudi Arabia. It lies in a fertile date-producing oasis, some 355 kilometres (220 miles) north of Mecca. Muhammad lived in the city after fleeing from Mecca (A.D. 622) and died there. The Mosque of the Prophet contains his tomb.

me·di·o·cre (méedi-ōkər, méddi-, -ōkər) *adj.* Neither good nor very bad; lacking in commendable qualities; very ordinary. See Synonyms at **average.** [Latin *mediocris,* "halfway up the mountain", in a middle state : *medius,* middle + *ocris,* mountain, peak.]

me·di·oc·ri·ty (méedi-óckrəti, méddi-) *n., pl.* **-ties.** **1.** The state or quality of being mediocre. **2.** Mediocre ability, achievement, or performance. **3.** A person who displays mediocre qualities.

Medit. Mediterranean Sea.

med·i·tate (méddi-tayt) *v.* **-tated, -tating, -tates.** —*tr.* **1.** To plan or intend in the mind: *He meditated revenge.* **2.** *Archaic.* To reflect upon; ponder; contemplate. —*intr.* **1.** To direct one's thoughts; reflect. Used with *on* or *upon: He meditated upon his loss.* **2.** To engage in deep, contemplative thought, or to concentrate on one thing or nothing, having emptied the mind of all thoughts, especially as a religious exercise or a means of achieving spiritual enlightenment. [Latin *meditārī.*] —**med·i·ta·tor** (-taytər) *n.*

med·i·ta·tion (méddi-táysh'n) *n.* **1. a.** The act of meditating. **b.** A devotional exercise of contemplation. **2.** A contemplative discourse, usually on a religious or philosophical subject. —See **transcendental meditation.**

med·i·ta·tive (méddi-tətiv, -taytiv) *adj.* Devoted to, characterised by, or expressing meditation. See Synonyms at **pensive.** —**med·i·ta·tive·ly** *adv.* —**med·i·ta·tive·ness** *n.*

Med·i·ter·ra·ne·an (médditə-ráyni-ən) *adj.* **1.** Designating a subgroup of the Caucasian race, characterised by dark hair and complexion, and relatively short stature. **2.** Of, pertaining to, or characteristic of the Mediterranean Sea or the countries bordering it and their inhabitants: *a lazy, Mediterranean life-style.* **3.** *Meteorology.* Having or pertaining to a type of climate with hot dry summers and warm, wet winters. **4.** *Small* **m.** Surrounded or almost surrounded by land. Said of large bodies of water. —*n.* **1.** The Mediterranean Sea. **2.** A member of the Mediterranean racial subgroup. **3.** A native or inhabitant of the Mediterranean region. [Latin *mediterrāneus : medius,* middle + *terra,* land.]

Mediterranean fever *n.* A disease, **brucellosis** *(see).*

Mediterranean Sea. *Abbr.* **Medit.** Almost landlocked body of water lying between Europe, North Africa, and Asia. It connects with the Atlantic through the Strait of Gibraltar, with the Black Sea through the Dardanelles, the Sea of Marmara, and the Bosporus, and with the Red Sea through the Suez Canal. Its larger islands include Crete, Cyprus, Sardinia, Corsica, and Sicily, and its shores have cradled many civilisations. Commercial developments have caused severe pollution which is aggravated by the Sea's nearly tideless nature; nevertheless, tourism remains a major industry.

me·di·um (méedi-əm, méed-yəm) *n., pl.* **-dia** (méedi-ə, méed-yə) or **-ums** (the only form for sense 5). *Abbr.* **m, M, m., M., med.** **1.** Some-

thing occupying a position or having a condition midway between extremes; a mean; a compromise. **2.** *Physics.* An intervening substance through which something is transmitted or carried, such as an agency for transmitting energy. **3.** An agency, such as a person, object, or quality, by means of which something is accomplished, conveyed, or transferred: *Money is used as a medium of exchange.* **4.** A means of mass communication, such as newspapers, magazines, or television. See Usage note at **media.** **5.** A person thought to have powers of communicating with the spirits of the dead. **6.** A surrounding environment in which something functions and thrives; especially: **a.** The substance in which a specific organism lives and thrives. **b.** A substance in which microorganisms are cultivated for scientific purposes; a culture medium. **7. a.** A specific type of artistic technique or means of expression as determined by the materials used or the creative methods involved. **b.** The materials used. **8.** Any solvent with which paint is thinned to the proper consistency. **9.** *Chemistry.* A filtering substance, such as filter paper. **10.** A size of paper, usually 46 × 58 centimetres (18 × 23 inches). —See Synonyms at **average.** —*adj. Abbr.* **m, M, m., M., med.** **1.** Occurring or being between two degrees, positions, or quantities; intermediate: *a medium steak.* **2.** Average; mean: *a medium-grade ore.* [Latin *medium,* the middle, from *medius,* middle.]

me·di·um-dat·ed (méedi-əm-dáytid, méed-yəm-) *adj. Finance.* Designating gilt-edged securities that are redeemable at any time between 5 and 15 years after the date of purchase. Compare **long-dated, short-dated.**

medium frequency *n. Abbr.* **MF, M.F.** A radio frequency or radio-frequency band in the range 3,000 to 300 kilohertz.

medium of exchange *n.* Anything that is commonly used in a specific area or among a certain group of people as money. See **circulating medium, money.**

medium wave *n. Abbr.* **MW, M.W.** A radio wave or band of radio waves with wavelengths between 100 and 1 000 metres.

med·lar (méddlər) *n.* **1.** A tree, *Mespilus germanica,* cultivated for its fruit. **2.** The fruit of this tree, similar in appearance to a crab apple but eaten when soft. [Middle English, from Old French *medler,* from *medle* (unattested), variant of *mesle,* a medlar fruit, from Latin *mespila,* from Greek *mespilē†.*]

med·ley (méddli) *n., pl.* **-leys.** **1.** A jumbled assortment; a mixture: *a medley of grating noises.* **2.** A musical arrangement made up of a series of melodies from various sources. **3.** A swimming race in which each participant swims lengths using various different, prescribed strokes (in individual races) or in which each member of a team swims using a different stroke (in relay races). —*adj.* **1.** Made up of a jumbled mixture of elements. **2.** Of or pertaining to a swimming medley: *a medley relay.* [Middle English *medlee,* from Old French, variant of *meslee,* from Vulgar Latin *misculāta* (unattested), from Late Latin *musculāre,* to mix up, frequentative of *miscēre,* to mix.]

Mé·doc¹ (máy-dok, méddok, may-dók). A region of southwest France, north of Bordeaux, between the Gironde estuary and the Bay of Biscay. It is particularly famous for its red wines, its vineyards including those of Château Lafite and Château Latour.

Médoc² *n.* A red Bordeaux wine made in Médoc.

me·dul·la (me-dúllə, mi-) *n., pl.* **-las** or **-lae** (-dúllee). **1.** *Anatomy.* The inner core of certain animal body structures where this differs in form or function from the outer zone; for example, the marrow of bone. **2.** The medulla oblongata. **3.** *Botany.* The **pith** *(see)* or central tissue in stems of certain plants. [Latin *medulla,* marrow.] —**me·dul·lar** (-dúllər), **med·ul·lar·y** (-dúlləri ‖ *U.S.* also méddə-lerri) *adj.*

medulla ob·lon·ga·ta (ób-long-gaá-tə, -gáy-) *n., pl.* **medulla oblongatas** or **medullae oblongatae** (-tee). The nervous tissue at the bottom of the brain that controls respiration, circulation, and certain other bodily functions. [New Latin, "elongated marrow".]

medullary ray *n. Botany.* The undifferentiated tissue between the vascular bundles in young plants and in plants not undergoing secondary thickening.

medullary sheath *n.* **1.** *Anatomy.* **Myelin** *(see).* **2.** *Botany.* A layer of thick-walled cells surrounding the pith in the stems of various plants.

med·ul·lat·ed (me-dúl-aytid, mi-, méddəl- ‖ *U.S.* also méjəl-) *adj.* **1.** *Anatomy.* Myelinated. **2.** Having a medulla. [Late Latin *medullātus,* having a marrow, from Latin *medulla,* MEDULLA.] —**med·ul·la·tion** (-áysh'n) *n.*

med·ul·li·sa·tion (me-dúl-ī-záysh'n, mi-, méddəl- ‖ *U.S.* -i-, *also* méjəl-) *n.* Replacement of bone tissue by marrow, as in inflammatory bone disease.

me·du·sa (mi-déw-zə, me-, -sə ‖ -dō͞o-) *n., pl.* **-sas** or **-sae** (-zee, -see). The tentacled, free-swimming sexual stage in the life cycle of a coelenterate of the class Scyphozoa or Hydrozoa; a jellyfish. Compare **polyp.** [New Latin.] —**me·du·san** *adj.*

Me·du·sa (mi-déw-zə, me-, -sə ‖ -dō͞o-) *Greek Mythology.* One of the three Gorgons, slain by Perseus.

me·du·soid (mi-déw-zoyd, -soyd, me- ‖ -dō͞o-) *n.* A jellyfish or a shape resembling a jellyfish. —**me·du·soid** *adj.*

Med·way (méd-way). River of southeast England, rising in Sussex to flow some 113 kilometres (70 miles) through Kent to join the Thames estuary at Sheerness. It divides the "Kentish Men", born west of the river, from the "Men of Kent", born to the east.

meed (meed) *n. Archaic.* A merited gift or reward. [Middle English *mede,* Old English *mēd.*]

meek (meek) *adj.* **meeker, meekest. 1. a.** Showing patience and humility; long-suffering. **b.** Easily imposed upon; submissive. **2.** *Archaic.* Kind; merciful: *"that I am meek and gentle with these butchers."* (Shakespeare). —See Synonyms at **humble.** [Middle English *mēk, mēoc,* from Old Norse *mjūkr,* gentle, soft.] —**meek·ly** *adv.*

meer·kat (méer-kat) *n.* Any of several small South African mammals similar to the mongoose; especially, *Suricata suricatta.* [Afrikaans, from Dutch, "sea-cat", originally a type of monkey, so called because imported from overseas.]

meer·schaum (méer-shəm, -showm ‖ -shawm) *n.* **1.** A compact, usually white mineral of hydrous magnesium silicate, $Mg_4[Si_6O_{15}](OH)_2 \cdot 6H_2O$, found chiefly in the Mediterranean area and used in fashioning tobacco pipes and as a building stone. Also called "sepiolite". **2.** A tobacco pipe with a bowl of meerschaum. [German, "sea-foam", translation of Persian *kef-i-daryā,* referring to its frothy appearance.]

Mee·rut (méer-ət). City of Uttar Pradesh, north central India, where the Indian Mutiny began (1857).

meet¹ (meet) *v.* **met** (met), **meeting, meets.** —*tr.* **1.** To come into the presence or company of, by chance or by arrangement: *met her on the stairs.* **2.** To come into the presence or company of, for the purpose of conferring: *meeting the directors at 11.* **3.** To be present at the arrival of: *I plan to meet the train.* **4.** To be introduced to; make the acquaintance of: *We'd like to meet your sister.* **5.** To come into association or conjunction with; join: *where the sea meets the sky.* **6.** To come to the notice of (the senses): *more than meets the eye.* **7.** To experience; undergo; suffer: *to meet one's fate.* **8.** To encounter in conflict or competition; oppose: *Spurs will meet Leeds in the final.* **9.** To cope or contend effectively with: *met every accusation with a satisfactory explanation.* **10.** To come into conformity with the views, wishes, or opinions of: *The firm must meet us on that point.* **11.** To satisfy (a demand, obligation, or the like); fulfil: *meet a need.* **12.** To pay; settle: *enough money to meet the expenses.* —*intr.* **1.** To come together by chance or by arrangement. Often used with *up* or *up with*: *met up with an old friend; Let's meet for a drink.* **2.** To come into conjunction or contact; be joined: *"East is East, and West is West, and never the twain shall meet"* (Rudyard Kipling). **3.** To come together as opponents; contend. **4.** To be introduced or become acquainted. **5.** To assemble, as for a meeting or other common purpose. —**meet with. 1.** To experience or encounter: *The housing bill met with approval.* **2.** To suffer or undergo: *meet with an accident.* **3.** To have a meeting with: *Blair met with Clinton.* —*n.* **1.** A meeting or contest, especially an athletic competition. **2.** The gathering of hounds and riders for a hunt. [Middle English *meten,* Old English *mētan.*]

meet² *adj. Archaic.* Fitting; proper; suitable. [Middle English *mete, y-mete,* Old English *gemǣte.*] —**meet·ly** *adv.*

meet·ing (méeting) *n. Abbr.* **mtg. 1. a.** A coming together of people for a common purpose; an assembly. **b.** The persons so assembled. **2.** A place or point where things meet; a conjunction. **3.** A hostile or competitive encounter. **4.** A programme of horse-racing or dog-racing at a particular racecourse.

meeting house *n.* **1.** A place of worship, especially one used by Quakers. **2.** In New Zealand, the central large building on a Maori marae where gatherings of the community take place.

meet·ing-point (méeting-poynt) *n.* **1.** A place of assembly. **2.** An area where different cultures, ideas, or the like converge: *a meeting-point between East and West.*

mega– *comb. form.* Indicates: **1.** *Abbr.* **M** One million (10^6); for example, megahertz. **2. a.** Large; for example, megalith. **b.** Large in comparison with others of its kind; for example, megatanker. **3.** *Informal.* Great or exaggeratedly large; for example **megastar, megahype.** Can be used independently: *That star is mega!* [Greek, from *megas,* great.]

meg·a·ceph·a·ly (méggə-kéffəli, -séffəli) *n.* Enlargement of the head, **macrocephaly** *(see).* [MEGA- + -CEPHALY.] —**meg·a·ce·phal·ic** (-kə-fál-ik, -si-), **meg·a·ceph·a·lous** (-kéffə-ləss, -séffə-) *adj.*

meg·a·cy·cle (méggə-sīk'l) *n. Physics.* One million cycles per second; a megahertz. Not in current technical usage.

meg·a·death (méggə-deth) *n.* **1.** The death of one million people, especially as the result of a war. **2.** Loosely, the death of a very large number of people.

Me·gae·ra (mi-jéer-ə). *Greek Mythology.* One of the **Furies** *(see).*

megagamete. Variant of **macrogamete.**

meg·a·hertz (méggə-herts, -hairts) *n., pl.* **megahertz.** *Abbr.* **MHz** *Physics.* One million cycles per second, used especially as a radio-frequency unit.

meg·a·lith (méggə-lith) *n.* A very large stone used in various prehistoric architectures or monumental styles, notably in western Europe during the second millennium B.C. See **dolmen, menhir.** [MEGA- + -LITH.] —**meg·a·lith·ic** (-líthik) *adj.*

megalo–, megal– *comb. form.* Indicates largeness, greatness, or exaggerated size; for example, **megalocephaly, megalomania.** [Greek, from *megas* (extended stem *megal-*), great.]

meg·a·lo·blast (méggəlō-blast, -blaast) *n.* A large blood cell that is an abnormal form of a red-blood-cell precursor. It occurs in certain types of anaemia *(megaloblastic anaemias).* [MEGALO- + -BLAST.] —**meg·a·lo·blas·tic** (-blástik) *adj.*

meg·a·lo·car·di·a (méggəlō-kárdi-ə) *n. Pathology.* Enlargement of the heart. Also called "cardiomegaly". [MEGALO- + Greek *kardia,* heart.]

meg·a·lo·ceph·a·ly (méggəlō-séffəli) *n.* Enlargement of the head, **macrocephaly** *(see).* [MEGALO- + -CEPHALY.] —**meg·a·lo·ce·phal·ic** (-si-fál-ik), **meg·a·lo·ceph·a·lous** (-séffələss) *adj.*

meg·a·lo·ma·ni·a (méggəlō-máyni-ə) *n.* A psychopathological condition involving fantasies of wealth or power. —**meg·a·lo·ma·ni·ac** *adj.* & *n.* —**meg·a·lo·ma·ni·a·cal** (-mə-nī-ək'l) *adj.*

meg·a·lop·o·lis (méggə-lóppə-liss) *n.* A region made up of several large cities and their surrounding areas in sufficiently close proximity to be considered a single urban complex. [MEGALO- + Greek *polis,* city.] —**meg·a·lo·pol·i·tan** (-lə-póllit'n, -lō-) *adj.*

meg·a·lo·saur (méggə-lō-sawr, -lə-) *n.* Also **meg·a·lo·sau·rus** (-sáwrəss). An extinct gigantic carnivorous dinosaur, genus *Megalosaurus,* of the Jurassic period. [New Latin *Megalosaurus :* MEGALO- + -SAURUS.] —**meg·a·lo·sau·ri·an** (-sáwri-ən) *n.* & *adj.*

meg·a·phone (méggə-fōn) *n.* A funnel-shaped device used to direct and amplify the voice. Compare **loud-hailer.** —**meg·a·phon·ic** (-fónnik) *adj.* —**meg·a·phon·i·cal·ly** *adv.*

meg·a·pode (méggə-pōd) *n.* Any bird of the family Megapodiidae, found in Australia and many South Pacific islands, that incubates its eggs by natural heat from mounds of rotting vegetation, sand, and the like. Also called "scrub fowl", "scrub turkey". [New Latin *Megapodius :* MEGA- + -PODE.]

Még·a·ra (méggə-rə). The capital of Megaris, a small Dorian state. It was a wealthy centre of sea trade (eighth to fifth century B.C.), and its people founded many colonies, including Byzantium.

meg·a·ron (méggə-ron) *n., pl.* **-ra** (-rə). The main hall or central room of an ancient Greek house, having a hearth. [Greek, from *megas,* large.]

meg·a·scop·ic (méggə-skóppik) *adj.* Visible to the naked eye; macroscopic. —**meg·a·scop·i·cal·ly** *adv.*

meg·a·spo·ran·gi·um (méggə-spaw-ránji-əm, -spə-) *n., pl.* **-gia** (-ránji-ə). *Botany.* A structure that encloses a megaspore. Sometimes called "macrosporangium".

meg·a·spore (méggə-spawr ‖ -spōr) *n. Botany.* **1.** The larger of two types of spores formed by heterosporous plants, such as certain ferns, giving rise to the female gametophyte. Compare **microspore. 2.** A spore that forms the embryo sac in seed plants. Sometimes called "macrospore". —**meg·a·spor·ic** *adj.*

meg·a·spo·ro·phyll (méggə-spáwr-ə-fil ‖ -spŏr-) *n. Botany.* A leaf-like structure that bears megasporangia.

meg·a·there (méggə-theer) *n.* A member of the extinct family Megatheriidae, composed of large ground sloths of the Miocene and Pleistocene epochs. [New Latin *Megatherium :* MEGA- + -THERE.] —**meg·a·ther·i·an** (-théer-i-ən) *adj.*

meg·a·ton (méggə-tun) *n.* A unit of explosive force equal to one million tons of TNT. —**meg·a·ton·nage** *n.*

meg·a·watt (méggə-wot) *n. Abbr.* **MW, M.W.** One million watts.

me generation *n.* People collectively, especially in the United States, who lived or live by the self-preoccupied and self-advancing values of the *me decade,* the 1970s. [Coined by Tom WOLFE, probably influenced by earlier phrase, *now generation* (1960s).]

Me·gid·do (mə-gíddō). Ancient fortress town of north Israel. Strategically situated in the valley of Esdraelon, on the route between Mesopotamia and Egypt, it was the site of many battles, and it may be the Armageddon of the Bible (Revelation 16:16), where the last battle on earth will be fought.

Me·gil·lah (mə-gíllə) *n.* **1.** The Judaic scroll containing the Biblical narrative of the Book of Esther, traditionally read in synagogues to celebrate the festival of Purim. **2.** *Small m. Informal.* A prolix, tediously detailed narrative or explanation. [Hebrew *məgillāh,* "scroll", from *gālal,* to roll.]

me·gilp, ma·gilp (mə-gílp) *n.* A base used for oil colours, usually linseed oil and mastic varnish. [18th century : origin obscure.]

meg·ohm (méggōm) *n. Symbol* **M** Ω. One million ohms. [MEGA- + OHM.]

me·grim (mée-grim) *n.* **1.** A severe headache, a **migraine** *(see).* **2.** *Often plural.* A caprice or fancy: *"Can't one work for sober truth as well as for megrims?"* (George Eliot). **3.** *Plural.* Depression or unhappiness: *"If these megrims are the effect of Love, thank Heaven, I never knew what it was."* (Samuel Richardson). **4.** *Plural.* A disease of cattle and horses. In this sense, also called "blind staggers". [Middle English *mygreyn,* from Old French, MIGRAINE.]

Me·hem·et A·li (mi-hémmit áali), also called Mohammed Ali (*c.* 1769–1849). Turkish soldier, pasha of Egypt (1805–49). He rose from common soldier to command the Turkish army in Egypt and became pasha of Egypt, then an Ottoman province. In the late 1830s he attacked Turkey. The European powers forced a peace which made Mehemet's line hereditary in Egypt.

Mei·ji (máy-jée), also known as Mutsuhito (1852–1912). Emperor of Japan (1867–1912). After the Meiji Restoration of 1867, he presided over the transformation of Japan from a feudal state into a modern constitutional one. His name means "enlightened government".

mei·o·sis (mī-ṓ-siss) *n., pl.* **-ses** (-seez). **1.** *Biology.* The cell division in sexually reproducing organisms that reduces the number of chromosomes in reproductive cells to half that found in the somatic cells, leading to the production of gametes in animals and spores in plants. Also called "reduction division". Compare **mitosis. 2.** Rhetorical understatement; litotes. [New Latin, from Greek *meiōsis,* diminution, from *meioun,* to diminish, from *meiōn,* less.] —**mei·ot·ic** (-óttik) *adj.* —**mei·ot·i·cal·ly** *adv.*

Me·ir (may-éer), **Golda,** born Golda Mabovitch (1898–1978). Russian-born Israeli stateswoman, prime minister of Israel (1969–74). She lived in the United States from 1906 and settled in Palestine in

1921. After Israel was created (1948) she became minister of labour (1949–56) and foreign minister (1956–66). In 1966 she became leader of the Mapai (later Labour) Party and succeeded Levi Eshkol as prime minister in 1969. She resigned in April, 1974.

Meis·sen (míss'n). City near Dresden, eastern Germany, on the river Elbe. It is famous for its porcelain, known as Meissen ware or Dresden china, made from local kaolin. Production moved here from Dresden in 1710.

Meissen ware *n.* A delicate porcelain ware made in Meissen, eastern Germany. Also called "Dresden china".

Meis·ter·sing·er (mī-stər-sing-ər; German -zing-) *n., pl.* **-ers** or **Meistersinger.** *German.* A member of any of the guilds organised in the principal cities of Germany in the 14th, 15th, and 16th centuries for the purpose of establishing competitive standards for the composition and performance of music and poetry. Also called "mastersinger". [German, mastersinger.]

Meit·ner (mītnər), **Lise** (1878–1968). Austrian-born physicist. She worked in Berlin with Otto Hahn, and in 1918 they discovered the element protactinium. Her analysis of Hahn's experiments on uranium nuclei marks the discovery of nuclear fission (1939). Meitner became a Swedish citizen in 1949, and worked on subatomic physics at the Nobel Institute at Stockholm.

Méjico. See **Mexico.**

Me·kong (mée-kóng, máy-). *Chinese* **Lancang Jiang** or **Lan-ts'ang Chiang.** Major river of southeast Asia, 4 184 kilometres (2,600 miles) long. Rising in Tibet, China, it flows mainly south through China, Laos, Cambodia, and Vietnam to join the South China Sea. Its delta is a major rice-growing area, and its last 550 kilometres (340 miles) can take moderate-sized ships.

mel (mel) *n.* A constituent of certain pharmaceutical preparations, consisting of a pure form of honey. [Latin, honey.]

mel·a·mine resin (méllə-meen) *n.* A thermosetting resin produced from melamine, $C_3H_6N_6$, used for moulded products, adhesives, and surface coatings. [German *Melamin* : *Melam* (arbitrary term for distillate of ammonium thiocyanate) + AMINE.]

mel·an·cho·li·a (méllən-kóli-ə) *n.* A mental disorder characterised by feelings of dejection and usually by withdrawal. It is often a phase of manic-depression. [New Latin, MELANCHOLY.] —**mel·an·cho·li·ac** *adj.* & *n.*

mel·an·chol·ic (méllən-kóllik) *adj.* **1.** Suffering from or subject to melancholy; depressed. **2.** Pertaining to, subject to, or suffering from melancholia. —**mel·an·chol·ic** *n.* —**mel·an·chol·i·cal·ly** *adv.*

mel·an·chol·y (méllən-kəli, -kolli) *n.* **1.** Sadness or depression of the spirits; gloom. **2.** Pensive reflection or contemplation. **3.** *Archaic.* **a.** Black bile, one of the four humours of ancient or medieval physiology. **b.** An emotional state characterised by sullenness and outbreaks of violent anger, believed to arise from the bile. ~*adj.* **1.** Sad; depressed; gloomy. **2. a.** Tending to cause sadness or gloom. **b.** Expressive of gloom or sadness: *a melancholy sigh.* **3.** Pensive; thoughtful: *"He had a pleasing face and a melancholy air."* (Jane Austen). —See Synonyms at **sad.** [Middle English *malencolie*, *melancholye*, from Old French *melancolie*, from Late Latin *melancholia*, from Greek *melankholia*, sadness, "(an excess of) black bile" : *melas* (stem *melan-*), black + *kholē*, bile.] —**mel·an·chol·i·ly** *adv.* —**mel·an·chol·i·ness** *n.*

Me·lanch·thon (mə-lángk-thən, me-, -thon, me-lánkh-ton), **Philip,** born Philip Schwarzerd (1497–1560). German theologian and a leader of the German Reformation. He was a friend of Luther, and wrote *Loci Communes* (1521), outlining Lutheran doctrine.

Mel·a·ne·si·a (méllə-née-zi-ə, -zhi-ə, -zhə, -si-ə, -shi-ə, -shə). A division of the Pacific islands, including Papua New Guinea, the Solomons, Vanuatu, New Caledonia, the Bismarck Archipelago, Fiji, and other islands in the southwest. The name comes from the Greek word *melas* (black), referring to the dark skin of the dominant race of inhabitants. See **Micronesia, Polynesia.**

Mel·a·ne·sian (méllə-née-zi-ən, -zhi-ən, -zhən, -si-ən, -shi-ən, -shən) *adj.* Of or pertaining to Melanesia, its people, or their languages. ~*n.* **1.** An indigenous inhabitant of Melanesia. **2.** A subfamily of Austronesian languages spoken in Melanesia.

mé·lange, me·lange (may-lónzh) *n.* **1.** A mixture. **2.** *Geology.* A mixture of different rock types, of diverse origin and age. [French, from Old French, from *mesler*, to mix, from Vulgar Latin *misculāre* (unattested), from Latin *miscēre*, to mix.]

me·lan·ic (me-lánnik) *adj.* **1.** Of, pertaining to, or exhibiting melanism. **2.** Suffering from melanosis.

mel·a·nin (méllənin) *n.* A dark pigment found in the skin, retina, and hair. [MELAN(O)- + -IN.]

mel·a·nism (méllə-niz'm) *n.* **1.** Dark coloration of skin, hair, fur, feathers, or the like, due to excessive production of melanin. It occurs, for example, among populations of moths in regions blackened by pollution *(industrial melanism),* where dark coloration provides camouflage. **2.** *Pathology.* Melanosis. [MELAN(O)- + -ISM.] —**mel·a·nist** *n.* —**mel·a·nis·tic** (-nístik) *adj.*

mel·a·nite (méllə-nīt) *n.* A black variety of garnet. [German *Melanit* : MELAN(O)- + -ITE.] —**mel·a·nit·ic** (-níttik) *adj.*

melano-, melan- *comb. form.* Indicates blackness or darkness; for example, **melanocyte, melanoma.** [New Latin, from Greek, from *melas* (stem *melan-*), black.]

Mel·a·noch·ro·i (méllə-nóckrō-ī, -nóck-roy) *pl.n.* The members of a subdivision of Caucasians, having dark hair and light skin. [New Latin, "the dark-pale (people)" : MELAN(O)- + Greek *ōkhroi,* plural of *ōkhros,* pale.] —**Mel·a·noch·roid** (-nóck-royd) *adj.*

mel·a·no·cyte (méllənō-sīt) *n. Biology.* An epidermal cell capable of

synthesising the black pigment melanin, and responsible for colour variations in the skin of many animals including humans. [MELANO- + -CYTE.]

mel·a·noid (méllə-noyd) *adj.* **1.** Black-pigmented; dark in colour. **2.** Suffering from or resembling melanosis. [Greek *melanoeidēs,* black-looking : MELAN(O)- + -OID.] —**mel·a·noid** *n.*

mel·a·no·ma (méllə-nō-mə) *n., pl.* **-mas** or **-mata** (-mətə). A dark-pigmented malignant tumour. [New Latin : MELAN(O)- + -OMA.]

mel·a·no·sis (méllə-nō-siss) *n. Pathology.* Abnormally dark pigmentation of the skin or other tissues, resulting from sunburn and various dermatoses. [New Latin : MELAN(O)- + -OSIS.] —**mel·a·not·ic** (-nóttik) *adj.*

mel·a·nous (méllə-nəss) *adj.* Having a swarthy or black complexion and black hair. Compare **xanthous.** [MELAN(O)- + -OUS.] —**mel·a·nos·i·ty** (-nóssəti) *n.*

mel·a·to·nin (méllə-tōnin) *n.* A hormone secreted by the pineal gland that causes lightening of the skin in certain animals. [*Mel*anocyte + serotonin (referring to its ability to lighten melanocytes).]

Mel·ba (mélbə), **Dame Nellie,** stage name of Helen Porter Mitchell (1859–1931). Australian soprano. She made her debut in Brussels (1887), and sang regularly at Covent Garden (1888–1926) and the Metropolitan Opera (1893–1910).

Melba toast *n.* Very thin crisp toast. [After Dame Nellie MELBA.]

Mel·bourne (mél-bərn, -bawrn; *locally* -bərn). Capital of Victoria, southeast Australia, and the country's second largest city. It was founded (1835) at the mouth of the Yarra river on Port Phillip Bay, and after the gold rush of 1851 developed into a financial and market centre. Its industries include engineering, vehicle and textile production, and food processing. Melbourne was the national capital (1901–27) and the venue for the 1956 Olympic Games.

Mel·bourne (mél-bərn, -bawrn), **William Lamb, 2nd Viscount** (1779–1848). British prime minister (1834 and 1835–41). He was home secretary in Lord Grey's government (1830–34) and succeeded Grey as prime minister. As home secretary he was responsible for the deportation of the Tolpuddle martyrs (1834).

Mel·chi·or (mélki-awr). One of the three **Magi** *(see)* who travelled to see the infant Jesus.

Mel·chite (mélkīt) *n.* A member of the Uniat Greek Catholic Church, concentrated in the Middle East. [Medieval Latin *Melchita,* from Greek *Melkhitēs,* "royalist", from Syriac *malkā,* king.] —**Mel·chite** *adj.*

Mel·chiz·e·dek, Mel·chis·e·dec (mel-kízzə-dek). The king of Salem and high priest who blessed Abraham. Genesis 14:18.

meld[1] (meld) *v.* **melded, melding, melds.** —*tr.* To declare or display (a card or combination of cards) for inclusion in one's score in a game such as canasta or rummy. —*intr.* To present a meld. ~*n.* **1.** An act of melding. **2.** A combination of cards to be declared for a score. [German *melden,* to declare, from Old High German *meldōn.*]

meld[2] *v.* **melded, melding, melds.** —*tr.* To cause to unite, blend, or combine. —*intr.* To become blended or combined. [Perhaps MELT + WELD.]

me·lee, mê·lée (méllay, máy-lay, me-láy) *n.* **1. a.** A confused, hand-to-hand fight. **b.** Any riotous skirmish or brawl. **2.** Any confused and tumultuous mingling, as of a crowd: *the rush-hour melee.* **3.** An argumentative or noisy debate between several people. —See Synonyms at **conflict.** [French *mêlée,* a mixture, from Old French *meslee,* MEDLEY.]

mel·ic (méllik) *adj.* Designating poetry intended to be sung, especially ancient Greek lyric poems. [Latin *melicus,* from Greek *melikos,* from *melos,* song.]

mel·i·lot (mélli-lot) *n.* Any of several plants of the genus *Melilotus,* native to the Old World, having compound leaves and narrow clusters of small, fragrant, white or yellow flowers. Also called "sweet clover". [Middle English *melilot,* from French *meliloti,* from Latin *melilōtus,* from Greek *melilōtos,* sweet clover, "honey-lotus" : *meli,* honey + *lōtos,* LOTUS.]

mel·i·nite (mélli-nīt) *n.* A high explosive made with picric acid. [French *mélinite,* from Greek *mēlinos,* quince-yellow, pertaining to quinces or apples, from *mēlon,* fruit, apple.]

me·li·o·rate (méeli-ə-rayt) *v.* **-rated, -rating, -rates.** —*tr.* To make better; improve. —*intr.* To grow better; evolve towards higher forms. [Latin *meliorāre,* from *melior,* better.] —**me·li·o·ra·ble** (-rəb'l) *adj.* —**me·li·o·ra·tive** (-rətiv, -raytiv) *adj.* & *n.* —**me·li·o·ra·tor** (-raytər) *n.*

me·li·o·ra·tion (méeli-ə-ráysh'n) *n.* **1. a.** The act or process of improving something or the state of being improved. **b.** A specific instance of this; an improvement. **2.** *Linguistics.* **Amelioration** *(see).*

me·li·o·rism (méeli-ə-riz'm) *n.* The belief that society has an innate tendency towards improvement and that this tendency may be furthered through deliberate human effort. [Latin *melior,* better.] —**me·li·o·rist** *adj.* & *n.* —**me·li·o·ris·tic** (-rístik) *adj.*

me·lis·ma (me-líz-mə) *n., pl.* **-mas** or **-mata** (-mətə). *Music.* **1.** A passage of several notes sung to one syllable of text, as in Gregorian chant. **2.** Any elaborate vocal passage. [Greek, from *melizein,* to sing, from *melos,* song.] —**mel·is·mat·ic** (mélliz-máttik) *adj.*

mel·lif·er·ous (mə-líffərəss, me-) *adj.* Also **mel·lif·ic** (-líffik). Forming or bearing honey. [Latin *mellifer* : *mel,* honey + -FER.]

mel·lif·lu·ous (mə-líffloo-əss, me-) *adj.* Also **mel·lif·lu·ent** (-ənt). **1.** Flowing with honey or sweetness. **2.** Smooth and sweet; rich and harmonious. Said especially of sounds and utterances. [Latin *melli-*

fluus : *mel,* honey + *-fluus,* flowing.] —**mel·lif·lu·ous·ly** *adv.* —**mel· lif·lu·ous·ness** *n.*

mel·lo·phone (méllǝ-fōn, méllō-) *n.* A brass musical wind instrument, sometimes used as a substitute for the French horn, which it resembles in tone. [MELLO(W) + -PHONE.]

mel·lo·tron (méllǝ-tron) *n.* An electronic keyboard instrument that uses prerecorded tape loops to imitate the individual sounds of an orchestra. [*Mellow* + electro*nic.*]

mel·low (méllō) *adj.* **-lower, -lowest. 1. a.** Soft, sweet, juicy, and full-flavoured because of ripeness. Said of fruit. **b.** Suggesting any of these qualities. **2.** Rich and soft in quality; not harsh: *a mellow sound.* **3.** Having the gentleness, wisdom, or dignity often characteristic of maturity. **4.** *Informal.* Relaxed and at ease; genial. **5.** *Informal.* Slightly and pleasantly intoxicated. **6.** Moist, rich, soft, and loamy. Said of soil. **7.** Fully matured and free from acidity. Said of wine.
~*v.* **mellowed, -lowing, -lows.** —*tr.* To bring to maturity; ripen. —*intr.* **1.** To become ripe; mature. **2.** To become gentle and sympathetic: *He mellowed as he aged.* [Middle English *mel(o)we,* probably from an attributive use of Old English *melu,* meal, "soft and rich, like meal".] —**mel·low·ly** *adv.* —**mel·low·ness** *n.*

me·lo·de·on (mi-lōdi-ǝn, me-) *n.* A small reed organ, similar to the harmonium. [Alteration of earlier *melodium,* from MELODY (by analogy with HARMONIUM).]

me·lod·ic (mi-lóddik, me-) *adj.* Pertaining to or containing melody. —**me·lod·i·cal·ly** *adv.*

me·lod·i·ca (mi-lóddikǝ) *n.* A small instrument like a harmonica but with a small keyboard on top that is played with the fingers. [*Melode*on + harmon*ica.*]

melodic minor scale *n. Music.* A minor scale that has the sixth and seventh notes sharpened in its ascending form. Compare **harmonic minor scale.**

me·lo·di·ous (mi-lōdi-ǝss, me-) *adj.* **1.** Containing or pertaining to a pleasing succession of sounds; tuneful. **2.** Agreeable or pleasant to the ear. —**me·lo·di·ous·ly** *adv.* —**me·lo·di·ous·ness** *n.*

mel·o·dise, mel·o·dize (méllǝ-dīz) *v.* **-dised, -dising, -dises.** —*tr.* **1.** To write a melody for (a song lyric). **2.** To make melodious. —*intr.* **1.** To make melody; play on a musical instrument. Often used humorously. **2.** *Poetic.* To mingle or blend melodiously: *"To murmur through the . . . groves, and melodise with man's blest nature there."* (P.B. Shelley). —**mel·o·dis·er, mel·o·dist** *n.*

mel·o·dra·ma (méllǝ-draamǝ, méllō- ‖ -drammǝ) *n.* **1.** A dramatic presentation characterised by use of suspense, sensational episodes, romantic sentiment, and usually a happy ending. **2.** The dramatic genre characterised by this treatment. **3.** Behaviour or occurrences, in fiction or real life, having melodramatic characteristics. **4.** *Music.* Spoken words with a musical accompaniment, especially as part of an opera. [French *mélodrame,* originally "musical drama" : Greek *melos,* song + French *drame,* DRAMA.]

mel·o·dra·mat·ic (méllǝ-drǝ-máttik, méllō-) *adj.* **1.** Having the excitement and emotional appeal of melodrama: *a melodramatic account of her arrest by the police.* **2.** Exaggeratedly sensational, emotional, or sentimental; histrionic.
~*n. Plural.* Melodramatic behaviour. —**mel·o·dra·mat·i·cal·ly** *adv.*

mel·o·dra·ma·tise, mel·o·dram·a·tize (méllō-drámmǝ-tīz, méllō-, -draamǝ-) *tr.v.* **-tised, -tising, -tises.** To create a melodrama out of; make melodramatic. —**mel·o·dram·a·ti·sa·tion** (-tī-záysh'n ‖ *U.S.* -ti-) *n.*

mel·o·dy (méllǝdi) *n., pl.* **-dies. 1.** A pleasing succession or arrangement of sounds. **2.** Musical quality: *the melody of verse.* **3.** *Music.* **a.** A rhythmically organised sequence of single notes so related to one another as to make up a particular musical phrase or idea; a tune. **b.** The structure of music with respect to the arrangement of single notes in succession. Together with harmony and rhythm, melody is one of the three basic elements of traditional Western music. **c.** The leading part or the air in a harmonic composition. [Middle English *melodie,* from Old French, from Late Latin *melōdia,* from Greek *melōidia,* choral song : *melos,* tune + *-ōidia,* "singing", from *aoidein,* to sing.]

mel·oid (mélloyd) *n.* Any beetle of the family Meloidae, which includes the oil beetles and blister beetles.
~*adj.* Of or pertaining to such beetles. [New Latin *meloidae* (family), from *Meloe†* (genus name).]

mel·on (méllǝn) *n.* **1.** Any of several varieties of two related vines, *Cucumis melo* or *Citrullus vulgaris,* widely cultivated for their edible fruit. **2.** The fruit of any of these vines, characteristically having a hard rind and juicy flesh. See **cantaloupe, honeydew melon, muskmelon, watermelon.** [Middle English, from Old French, from Late Latin *mēlo* (stem *mēlōn-*), shortening of *mēlopepōn,* from Greek, melon, "apple-gourd", from *mēlon,* apple.]

Me·los (mée-loss). *Greek* **Mílos.** Greek island in the Cyclades group in the Aegean Sea. It was a thriving centre of early Aegean civilisation, but later declined and was conquered by the Athenians (416 B.C.). Excavations on the island have unearthed many treasures, including (1820) the Venus de Milo, a marble statue of the second or first century B.C., now in the Louvre, Paris.

Mel·pom·e·ne (mel-pómmini). *Greek Mythology.* The Muse of tragedy. [Latin *Melpomenē,* from Greek, "the singing one", from the feminine present participle of *melpesthai,* to sing, sing of, from *melpein†,* to sing.]

melt (melt) *v.* **melted, melted** or *archaic* **molten** (mōltǝn), **melting, melts.** —*intr.* **1.** To be changed from a solid to a liquid state, as by the application of heat. **2.** To become liquid; dissolve: *Icing melts in the mouth.* **3.** To disappear or vanish gradually as if by melting. Often used with *away: The crowd melted away.* **4.** To pass or merge imperceptibly into something else; blend gradually. Used with *into: Sea melted into sky.* **5.** To become softened in feeling, as by compassion; be made gentle: *Her heart melted at the child's tears.* **6.** *Informal.* To be extremely hot; perspire from heat. —*tr.* **1. a.** To reduce from a solid to a liquid state, as by the application of heat. **b.** To reduce (manufactured metal articles) to the state of raw material, usually for making other metal articles. Used with *down: They melted everything down, from statues to spoons, for shell casings.* **2.** To dissolve: *She melted some honey in hot milk.* **3.** To cause to disappear gradually; disperse: *The sun melted the fog.* **4.** To cause to pass or merge imperceptibly; blend (colours or outlines, for example): *"This effect is produced by melting . . . the shadows in a ground still darker."* (Sir Joshua Reynolds). **5.** To soften (someone's feelings); make gentle or tender: *"O ye critics! will nothing melt you?"* (Laurence Sterne).
~*n.* **1. a.** A melted solid. **b.** A blended or fused mass. **2.** The state of being melted. **3. a.** The act or operation of melting. **b.** The quantity melted in one period or operation. [Melt (infinitive), molten (past participle); Middle English *melten, molten,* Old English *meltan, gemolten,* from Germanic *maltjan* (unattested), dissolve.] —**melt·a·bil·i·ty** (méltǝ-bílləti) *n.* —**melt·a·ble** *adj.* —**melt·er** *n.*
Synonyms: melt, liquefy, thaw, dissolve, deliquesce.
Usage: The standard past tense form is *melted (The sun melted the ice),* but *melt* is often heard in casual use, and is a common alternative in regional speech. *Molten* can be used only as an adjective; it differs from the adjectival use of *melted* in that it refers only to substances that melt at a very high temperature. Thus one may refer to *molten rock,* but to *melted ice cream.*

melt·age (méltij) *n.* **1.** The quantity or substance produced by a melting process. **2.** The process or act of melting.

melt·down (mélt-down) *n.* Severe overheating of the core of a nuclear reactor causing melting of the core and supporting base, so that molten radioactive material flows into the space below the reactor.

melting point *n. Abbr.* **mp, m.p. 1.** The temperature at which a solid becomes a liquid at standard atmospheric pressure. **2.** The temperature at which a solid and its liquid are in equilibrium, at any fixed pressure.

melting pot *n.* A place where much change or mixing occurs, as of people, ideas, or cultures. —**in the melting pot.** Under consideration and therefore uncertain and likely to change.

mel·ton (méltǝn) *n.* A heavy, woollen cloth used chiefly for making overcoats and hunting jackets. [After *Melton* Mowbray, town in Leicestershire.]

melt·wa·ter (mélt-wawtǝr ‖ *U.S. also* -wottǝr) *n.* Water produced by the melting of snow or ice.

Mel·ville (mélvil), **Herman** (1819–91). U.S. novelist. Many of his works, such as his allegorical masterpiece *Moby Dick* (1851), draw on his experiences as a crewman on a whaler. He also wrote *Redburn* (1849) and the story *Billy Budd* (published 1924).

mem (mem) *n.* The thirteenth letter of the Hebrew alphabet. [Hebrew, perhaps from *mayim,* water.]

mem. 1. member. **2.** memoir. **3.** memorandum. **4.** memorial.

mem·ber (mémbǝr) *n.* **1.** *Abbr.* **M., mem.** An individual belonging to a group or organisation. **2.** *Abbr.* **M., mem.** *Often capital* **M.** One who serves on or is elected to a political body such as Parliament. **3.** A distinct part of a whole, such as an architectural support in a building or a proposition of a syllogism. **4.** A part or organ of a human or animal body; especially: **a.** A limb, such as an arm or leg. **b.** The penis. **5.** A part of a plant. **6.** *Biology.* Any individual organism belonging to a taxonomic group. **7.** *Mathematics.* **a.** The expression on either side of an equality sign. **b.** An element of a set. [Middle English, from Old French *membre,* from Latin *membrum.*]

Member of Parliament *n. Abbr.* **M.P.** A person who has been elected to the House of Commons or a similar legislative body, as in many Commonwealth countries.

mem·ber·ship (mémbǝr-ship) *n.* **1.** The state of being a member. **2.** The total number of members of a group or organisation.

mem·brane (mém-brayn) *n.* **1.** *Biology.* A thin, pliable layer of tissue covering surfaces or separating or connecting regions, structures, or organs of an animal or plant. **2.** A piece of parchment. **3.** *Chemistry.* A thin sheet of natural or synthetic material that is permeable to substances in solution. **4.** A thin piece of skin or plastic stretched over a drumhead. [Latin *membrāna,* membrane, "skin covering an organ or member of the body", from *membrum,* member.]

membrane bone *n.* A bone formed directly in the connective tissue, as some cranial bones are. Compare **cartilage bone.**

mem·bra·nous (mémbrǝ-nǝss, mem-bráy-) *adj.* Also **mem·bra·na·ceous** (mémbrǝ-náyshǝss). Made of or similar to a membrane.

Memel. See **Klaipeda.**

me·men·to (mi-méntō, me-) *n., pl.* **-tos** or **-toes.** Any reminder of the past; a keepsake, souvenir, or relic. [Middle English, from Latin *mementō,* "remember", imperative of *meminisse,* to remember.]

memento mo·ri (mórree, máwree) *n.pl.* **memente mori.** Any reminder of death or mortality, such as a skull or an ornament bearing symbols of death. [Latin, "remember that you must die".]

Mem·ling (mémling), **Hans** (c. 1430–94). Flemish painter of religious works and portraits, born in Germany. Among his paintings are *Tomaso Portinari and his Wife* (c. 1468) and the *Diptych of Martin van Nieuwenhoven* (1487).

Mem·non¹ (mém-non). *Greek Mythology.* An Ethiopian king killed by Achilles in the Trojan War and made immortal by Zeus.

Memnon² *n.* A huge statue of the Egyptian Pharaoh Amenhotep III at Thebes.

mem·o (mémmō) *n., pl.* **-os.** A memorandum.

mem·oir (mém-waar, -wawr) *n. Abbr.* **mem.** **1. a.** A narrative of one's experiences or a historical account based on personal experience. **b.** *Usually plural.* An autobiography. **c.** A biography or biographical sketch. **2.** A monograph: *a memoir on anthills.* **3.** *Plural.* The report or a collection of reports of the proceedings of a learned society. [French *mémoire*, MEMORY.]

mem·o·ra·bil·i·a (mémmərə-bílli-ə) *pl.n.* Things worthy of remembrance. [Latin *memorābilia,* from *memorābilis,* MEMORABLE.]

mem·o·ra·ble (mémmə-ra-b'l, mémmrə-) *adj.* Worth being remembered; notable. [Middle English, from Latin *memorābilis,* from *memorāre,* to remember, from *memor,* mindful.] **—mem·o·ra·bil·i·ty** (-bílləti), **mem·o·ra·ble·ness** *n.* **—mem·o·ra·bly** *adv.*

mem·o·ran·dum (mémmə-rán-dəm) *n., pl.* **-dums** or **-da** (-də). *Abbr.* **mem.** **1.** A short note written as a reminder. **2.** A written record or communication, as in a business office. **3.** *Law.* A short, written statement outlining the terms of an agreement, transaction, or contract. **4.** A brief, unsigned diplomatic communication. [Middle English, from Latin, "let it be remembered", neuter singular gerundive of *memorāre,* to remember, from *memor,* mindful.]

me·mo·ri·al (mi-máwri-əl ‖ -mŏri-) *n. Abbr.* **mem.** **1.** Something, such as a monument or a public holiday, designed or established to serve as a remembrance of a person or an event. **2.** *Plural.* A historical record. **3.** A written statement of facts or a petition presented to a legislative body or an executive.

~adj. **1.** Serving as a remembrance of a person or event; commemorative. **2.** Of, pertaining to, or in memory. [Middle English, from Latin *memoriālis,* belonging to memory, from *memoria,* MEMORY.] **—me·mo·ri·al·ly** *adv.*

me·mo·ri·a·lise, me·mo·ri·a·lize (mi-máwri-ə-līz) *tr.v.* **-ised, -ising, -ises.** **1.** To commemorate. **2.** To present a memorial to; petition. **—me·mo·ri·a·li·sa·tion** (-lī-záysh'n ‖ *U.S.* -li-) *n.* **—me·mo·ri·a·li·ser** *n.*

me·mo·ri·al·ist (mi-máwri-ə-list ‖ -mŏri-) *n.* **1.** A person who writes memoirs. **2.** A person who writes or signs a memorial.

me·mo·ri·a tech·ni·ca (mi-máwri-ə téknikə) *n.* A device or system that is used to aid the memory, such as a mnemonic. [New Latin, artificial memory.]

mem·o·rise, mem·o·rize (mémmə-rīz) *tr.v.* **-rised, -rising, -rises.** To commit to memory; learn by heart. **—mem·o·ris·a·ble** *adj.* **—mem·o·ri·sa·tion** (-rī-záysh'n ‖ *U.S.* -ri-) *n.* **—mem·o·ris·er** *n.*

mem·o·ry (mémməri, mémmri) *n., pl.* **-ries.** **1.** The mental faculty of retaining and recalling past experience; the ability to remember. **2.** An act or instance of remembrance; a recollection: *pleasant memories of his childhood.* **3.** All that a person can remember, or all that is retained in the mind. **4.** Something remembered of a person, thing, or event: *He has no memory of that occasion.* **5. a.** The fact of being remembered, as after death. **b.** Remembrance; recollection: *in memory of our loved ones.* **6.** The period of time covered by the remembrance or recollection of a person or group of persons: *within the memory of man.* **7.** *Physics.* The property of a substance or system that depends on past treatment or states of the substance or system. **8. a.** A unit, such as one in or attachable to a computer, calculator, or word processor, that preserves data for retrieval. Also called "memory store", "store". **b.** The capacity of such a unit. **9.** *Statistics.* The set of past events affecting a given event in a stochastic process. [Middle English *memorie,* from Old French, from Latin *memoria,* from *memor,* mindful.]

Synonyms: memory, remembrance, recollection, reminiscence.

memory span *n.* The length of time that a person is able to retain something in his short-term memory.

memory trace *n.* A hypothetical change to a brain cell or to structures of brain cells as a result of learning.

Mem·phis¹ (mémfiss). Ruined city on the river Nile 18 kilometres (12 miles) south of Cairo, Egypt. Reputedly founded by the pharaoh Menes, it was the capital of the Old Kingdom (*c.* 3100 – *c.* 2258 B.C.), the first united Egyptian state, and was the centre for the worship of Ptah. The city declined with the rise of Thebes, but temporarily revived under the Persians, Ptolemies, and Romans. Its remains include the temple of Ptah.

Memphis². City of southwest Tennessee, United States, at the confluence of the Mississippi and Wolf rivers.

mem·sa·hib (mém-saa-ib, -hib, -saab) *n.* Formerly, a title of respect or form of address for a European woman in India. [MA'AM + SAHIB.]

men. Plural of **man.**

men·ace (ménnəss, ménniss) *n.* **1.** *Literary.* **a.** A threat: *menace of the gun.* **b.** The act of threatening. **2.** A dangerous or potentially dangerous person or thing. **3.** *Informal.* A troublesome or annoying person: *She has become a menace by her gossip.*

~v. menaced, -acing, -aces. **—tr.** To threaten in a hostile or nasty manner. **—intr.** To make threats; indicate danger or coming harm. **—See Synonyms at threaten.** [Middle English *manace,* from Old French, from Latin *minācia,* menace, originally "threatening things", neuter plural of *mināx* (stem *mināc-),* threatening, from *minārī,* to threaten, from *minae,* threats.] **—men·ac·er** *n.* **—men·ac·ing·ly** *adv.*

men·a·di·one (ménnə-dí-ōn, -dī-ŏn) *n.* A yellow crystalline powder, $C_{11}H_8O_2$, having physiological effects similar to vitamin K. It is used as a medicine and as a fungicide. [*methyl* + *naphtha* + DI- + -ONE.]

mé·nage, me·nage (may-naázh, me-) *n.* **1.** A group of people living together as a unit; a household. **2.** The management of a household. [French, from Old French *menage,* from Vulgar Latin *mansiōnāticum* (unattested), household, from *mansiō* (stem *mansiōn-*), house, dwelling, from *manēre,* to dwell.]

ménage à trois (aa trwaá) *n., pl.* **ménages à trois** (*pronounced as singular*). A sexual relationship involving three people who live together, such as a married couple and the lover of one of them. [French, household of three.]

me·nag·er·ie (mi-nájəri, me-, -naázhəri) *n.* **1.** A collection of live wild animals on exhibition. **2.** The enclosure in which such animals are kept. [French *ménagerie,* originally "the management of domestic animals", from *ménage,* MÉNAGE.]

Men·ai Strait (ménnī). Channel of the Irish Sea separating the island of Anglesey from the mainland, in Gwynedd, Wales. It is 23 kilometres (14 miles) long and is crossed by the famous road suspension bridge of Thomas Telford (built 1819–26) and the tubular rail bridge of Robert Stevenson (1850).

Me·nan·der (me-nándər, mi-) (*c.* 342 B.C.–*c.* 290 B.C.). Greek dramatist, who wrote tangled love plays. Only one, *The Curmudgeon,* discovered at Cairo in 1957, survives complete.

men·a·qui·none (ménnə-kwi-nōn) *n.* A form of **vitamin K** (*see*). [*methylnaphthoquinone.*]

me·nar·che (me-nárki, mə-, ménnaarki) *n.* The first occurrence of menstruation in young women. [New Latin : Greek *mēn,* month + *arkhē,* beginning.] **—me·nar·che·al** *adj.*

Menck·en (méngkən), **H(enry) L(ouis)** (1880–1956). U.S. journalist and literary critic. He founded the magazine *American Mercury* with George Nathan in 1924. His essays are collected in six volumes, *Prejudices* (1919–27). He also wrote a four-volume work on philology, *The American Language* (1919).

mend (mend) *v.* **mended, mending, mends.** **—tr.** **1.** To make right or correct; repair. **2.** To reform or improve. Used chiefly in the phrases *mend one's ways* or *manners.* **—intr.** **1.** To undergo a moral improvement; reform. **2. a.** To improve in health: *He is mending well.* **b.** To heal: *The bone mended in a month.*

~n. **1.** The act of mending. **2.** A part or place mended or repaired after breaking or coming apart. **3.** A place on a piece of material that has been mended, as by a patch or darning. **—on the mend.** Improving, especially in health; recuperating. [Middle English *menden,* shortening of *amenden,* to AMEND.] **—mend·a·ble** *adj.* **—mend·er** *n.*

men·da·cious (men-dáyshəss) *adj. Formal.* **1.** Lying; untruthful: *a mendacious child.* **2.** False; untrue: *a mendacious statement.* **—See Synonyms at dishonest.** [Latin *mendāx* (stem *mendāc-*).] **—men·da·cious·ly** *adv.* **—men·dac·i·ty** (-dássəti) *n.*

Men·del (ménd'l), **Gregor (Johann)** (1822–84). Moravian (Austrian) monk and founder of the science of genetics. He entered the Augustinian monastery at Brno in 1843 and for 25 years experimented with plants, chiefly garden peas. He discovered the principle of the inheritance of characteristics through the combination of genes from parent cells. His conclusions, published in 1866 and ignored during his lifetime, form the basis of scientific genetics.

men·de·le·vi·um (méndi-léevi-əm, *also* -láyvi-) *n. Symbol* **Md** A radioactive transuranic element of the actinide series. Atomic number 101, half-life of the most stable isotope (Md²⁵⁸) 60 days. Also called "unnilunium". [New Latin, after Dmitri MENDELEYEV.]

Men·de·le·yev (méndə-láy-ef, -ev; *Russian* mindi-láy-əf), **Dmitri Ivanovich** (1834–1907). Russian chemist. He formulated the periodic table of the elements noting the regular recurrence of their chemical and physical properties when they are arranged by their atomic numbers. Other scientists, notably Lothar Meyer, independently reached the same conclusions, but Mendeleyev was the first to draw attention to gaps in the periodic arrangement and to postulate the existence of undiscovered elements to fill them.

Men·de·li·an (men-déeli-ən) *adj.* Of or pertaining to Gregor Mendel or his theories of genetics.

Men·del·ism (méndə-liz'm) *n.* Also **Men·de·li·an·ism** (men-déeli-ə-niz'm) *n.* The theoretical principles of heredity formulated by Gregor Mendel. See **Mendel's laws.**

Mendel's laws *pl.n.* The principles of heredity of sexually reproducing organisms formulated by Gregor Mendel, now usually summarised in two laws: **1.** *Law of Segregation:* Certain paired characteristics, one from each parent, do not blend with or alter each other in the offspring, thus accounting for contrasting traits in successive generations. **2.** *Law of Independent Assortment:* The genes determining such pairs of traits combine in the offspring according to the laws of chance.

Men·dels·sohn (ménd'l-s'n; *German* ménd'l-zōn), **Felix,** born Jacob Ludwig Felix Mendelssohn-Bartholdy (1809–47). German composer. Mendelssohn was a child prodigy; his overture to *A Midsummer Night's Dream* and his *Octet* for strings were both written by the time he was 17. He wrote five symphonies, the oratorios *St. Paul* (1836) and *Elijah* (1846), the violin concerto in E Minor (1844), and six string quartets.

Men·de·res (méndə-réss), **Adnan** (1889–1961). Turkish prime minister (1950–60). During his period of office, Turkey joined NATO (1952) and the Baghdad Pact (1955). He was ousted in a military coup led by General Cemal Gürsel and executed.

Men·dès-France (mén-dess fraánss; *French* maN-dess-frónss), **Pierre** (1907–82). French prime minister (1954–55). He was economic minister in de Gaulle's government (1944–45). As prime minister he negotiated France's withdrawal from Indochina, but he resigned when his liberal policies on the North African colonies were rejected. He led the Radical Socialist Party until 1957.

men·di·cant (méndi-kənt) *adj.* **1.** Depending upon alms for a living; practising begging. **2.** Characteristic of a beggar or begging.
~ *n.* **1.** *Rare.* A beggar. **2.** A member of a mendicant order of friars. [Latin *mendīcāns* (stem *mendīcānt*-), present participle of *mendīcāre*, to beg, from *mendīcus*, beggar, poor man, originally "injured", from *mendum*, physical defect.] —**men·di·can·cy, men·dic·i·ty** (men-díssəti) *n.*

mend·ing (ménding) *n.* Articles, especially clothes, that are to be or have been mended.

Men·dip Hills (méndip). Limestone range in Somerset, southwest England. The range runs northwest from the Frome valley, reaching 325 metres (1,068 feet) at Blackdown.

Men·e·la·us (ménni-láy-əss). *Greek Mythology.* The king of Sparta, brother of Agamemnon, and husband of Helen whose abduction gave rise to the Trojan War.

me·ne, me·ne, tek·el, u·phar·sin (méeni méeni téck'l yōō-fár-sin). *Aramaic.* Numbered, numbered, weighed, divided. The phrase appeared on the wall at Belshazzar's feast, and was interpreted by Daniel to mean that God had doomed Belshazzar's kingdom. Daniel 5:25–28.

men·folk (mén-fōk) *pl.n.* **1.** Men collectively. **2.** A particular group of men, as in a family: *They lost their menfolk.*

Mengistu Haile Mariam. See **Mariam, Mengistu Haile.**

men·ha·den (men-háyd'n, mən-) *n., pl.* **-dens** or collectively **menhaden.** An abundant inedible fish, *Brevoortia tyrannus,* of American Atlantic and Gulf waters, used as a source of fish oil, fish meal, fertiliser, and bait. Also *U.S.* "mossbunker", "oldwife". [Algonquian; akin to Natick *munnohquohteau,* "the fertilises" (menhaden were used by the Algonquins as fertiliser for maize).]

men·hir (mén-heer) *n.* A prehistoric monument consisting of a single tall, upright megalith. Compare **dolmen.** [French, from Breton *men hir,* "long stone" : *men,* stone + *hir,* long.]

me·ni·al (méeni-əl) *adj.* **1.** Of, pertaining to, or appropriate for a servant. **2.** Of or pertaining to work or a job regarded as servile or degrading. **3.** Of, pertaining to, or involving work, such as cleaning, that is routine, boring, and requires little skill.
~ *n.* **1.** A servant, especially a domestic servant. **2.** A person who has a servile or low nature. [Middle English *meynial,* from Anglo-French *menial,* Old French *meinie, mesne,* servant, from Vulgar Latin *mānsiōnatā* (unattested), household, from *mānsiō,* house dwelling. See **mansion.**] —**me·ni·al·ly** *adv.*

Mé·nière's disease (ménni-airz, mayn-yaírz) *n.* A disorder of the inner ear involving progressive deafness, loss of balance, ringing in the ear, and nausea. Also called "Ménière's syndrome". [After Prosper *Ménière* (1799–1862), French physician.]

me·nin·ge·al (mə-nínji-əl, ménnin-jée-əl) *adj.* Of, pertaining to, or concerned with a meninx or meninges.

men·in·gi·tis (ménnin-jítiss) *n. Pathology.* Inflammation of any meninx or all of the meninges of the brain and the spinal cord, usually caused by either a bacterium or a virus. [New Latin : *meninges* + -ITIS.] —**men·in·git·ic** (-jíttik) *adj.*

me·ninx (mée-ningks, ménningks) *n., pl.* **meninges** (mə-nín-jeez, me-). Any of the three membranes enclosing the brain and spinal cord in vertebrates. [New Latin, from Greek *mēninx* (stem *mēning*-), membrane.]

me·nis·cus (mi-níss-kəss, me-) *n., pl.* **-cuses** or **menisci** (-níssī). **1.** A crescent-shaped body. **2.** A concavo-convex lens. **3.** The curved upper surface of a stationary liquid in a container. It is concave if the liquid wets the container walls and convex if it does not. **4.** *Anatomy.* A cartilage disc that cushions the ends of bones in a joint. [New Latin, from Greek *mēniskos,* crescent, diminutive of *mēnē,* moon.] —**me·nis·cal** (-k'l), **me·nis·cate** (-kayt), **me·nis·coid** (-koyd), **men·is·coi·dal** (ménniss-kóyd'l) *adj.*

Men·non·ite (ménnə-nīt) *n.* A member of a Protestant Christian sect opposed to infant baptism, taking oaths, holding public office, or performing military service. [German *Mennonit,* after *Menno* Simons (1492–1559), religious reformer.]

me·nol·o·gy (mi-nólləji) *n., pl.* **-gies. 1.** An ecclesiastical calendar of the months with important religious events recorded. **2.** In the Eastern Orthodox Church, a collection of short biographies of the lives of the saints arranged in the form of a calendar. [Medieval Greek *mēnologion,* "list of months" : Greek *mēn,* month + -LOGY.]

me·no mos·so (ménnō móssō, máynō, móss-sō) *adv. Music.* With less speed. Used as a direction. [Italian, "less rapid".]

Men·on (ménnən), **(Vengalil Krishnan) Krishna** (1897–1974). Indian politician. After independence (1947) he became High Commissioner to the United Kingdom. In 1952 he headed the Indian delegation to the United Nations, and in 1957 became defence minister. He resigned in 1962, after China's border attacks.

men·o·pause (ménnə-pawz, ménnō-) *n.* The period of cessation of menstruation in a woman, occurring typically between the ages of 45 and 50. Also called "change of life", "climacteric". [New Latin *menopausis : meno-,* from Greek *mēn,* month + *pausis,* PAUSE.] —**men·o·paus·al** (-páwz'l) *adj.*

me·no·rah (mi-náwrə ‖ -nōrə) *n.* **1.** A ceremonial seven-branched candelabrum of the Jewish Temple symbolising the seven days of Creation. Exodus 37:17–24. **2.** A nine-branched candelabrum used in celebrating Chanukkah. [Hebrew *monōrāh,* candlestick.]

Me·nor·ca (me-nórkə). See **Minorca.** —**Me·nor·can** *adj. & n.*

men·or·rha·gi·a (ménnə-ráy-ji-ə, ménnaw-, -jə ‖ -ráa-, -zhə) *n. Pathology.* Abnormally heavy menstrual flow. [New Latin : Greek *mēn,* month + -RRHAGIA.]

Me·not·ti (mə-nótti, me-), **Gian Carlo** (1911–). Italian composer, who has lived chiefly in the United States since 1927. He has written his own English libretti for most of his operas, which include *The Medium* (1946), *The Consul* (1950), and *Amahl and the Night Visitors* (1951). He established (1958) a festival at Spoleto in Italy.

Men·sa[1] (mén-sə) *n.* A southern constellation between Hydrus and Carina. [Latin *mēnsa*†, table.]

Mensa[2] *n.* An international society established in 1946 for the stimulation of and exchange of ideas among its members. Membership is restricted to those with an I.Q. in the top two per cent in each member country.

men·sal[1] (mén-s'l) *adj. Rare.* Belonging to or used at the table. [Late Latin *mēnsālis,* from *mēnsa*†, table.]

mensal[2] *adj. Rare.* Monthly. [Latin *mēnsis,* month.]

mensch (mensh) *n. U.S. Informal.* A person having admirable characteristics, such as fortitude and decency. [Yiddish *mens(c)h,* from Middle High German *mensch,* man, from Old High German *mennisco.*]

men·ses (mén-seez) *pl.n.* **1.** *Physiology.* Blood and dead cell debris that is discharged from the uterus through the vagina by nonpregnant adolescent girls and women at approximately monthly intervals between puberty and menopause. **2.** Menstruation. [Latin *mēnsēs,* months, hence also "monthly periods", plural of *mēnsis,* month.]

Men·she·vik (ménshə-vik) *n., pl.* **-viks** or **-viki** (-véekee). **1. a.** A member of the liberal minority faction of the Russian Social Democratic Party, which struggled against the more radical majority element, the Bolsheviks, from 1903 until the Russian Revolution in 1917. Also called "Minimalist". **b.** A member of a liberal socialist group established after the Russian Revolution to oppose the Bolshevik Party. **2.** A person having views in accord with the Menshevik faction. Compare **Bolshevik.** [Russian *men'shevik,* a member of the smaller (faction), from *men'she,* less, from Old Church Slavonic *mĭnĭshĭ,* less.] —**Men·she·vism** *n.* —**Men·she·vist** *adj. & n.*

mens re·a (ménz ráy-ə, rée-) *n. Law.* Criminal intent, the essential mental element that in theory has to be proved for all crimes, although in practice some statutory offences are crimes of absolute liability, regardless of criminal intent. [Latin, guilty mind.]

men·stru·al (mén-stroo-əl) *adj.* Also **men·stru·ous** (-əss). Pertaining to menstruation. [Middle English *menstruall,* from Latin *mēnstruālis,* from *mēnstruus,* menstrual, monthly, from *mēnsis,* month.]

men·stru·ate (mén-stroo-ayt) *intr.v.* **-ated, -ating, -ates.** To undergo menstruation. [Latin *mēnstruāre,* from *mēnstruus,* MENSTRUAL.]

men·stru·a·tion (mén-stroo-áysh'n) *n.* **1.** *Physiology.* The process or an instance of discharging the menses. **2.** The period of time during which this occurs. Also called "menses".

men·stru·um (mén-stroo-əm) *n., pl.* **-ums** or **-strua** (-stroo-ə). A solvent, especially one used in extracting and preparing drugs. [Middle English, from Medieval Latin *mēnstruum,* solvent, originally "menstrual blood" (alchemists regarded the gold-transmuting solvent as similar to menstrual blood, which they believed transformed sperm in the womb into an embryo), from Latin *mēnstruus,* MENSTRUAL.]

men·su·ra·ble (mén-shər-əb'l, -sewr-) *adj.* **1.** Capable of being measured. **2.** Having fixed rhythm and measure, as in music; mensural. —**men·su·ra·bil·i·ty** (-ə-bílləti) *n.*

men·su·ral (mén-shər-əl, -sewr-) *adj.* **1.** Of or pertaining to measure. **2.** *Music.* Of, pertaining to, or designating music having notes of fixed rhythmic value. [Latin *mēnsūrālis,* from *mēnsūra,* MEASURE.]

men·su·ra·tion (mén-shə-ráysh'n, -sewr-) *n.* **1.** The process, act, or art of measuring. **2.** The measurement of geometric quantities. —**men·su·ra·tive** (-rətiv, -raytiv) *adj.*

mens·wear (ménz-wair) *n.* Clothing and accessories for men.

–ment *n. suffix.* Indicates: **1.** Product or result; for example, **pavement, statement. 2.** Means, action, or process; for example, **appeasement, measurement. 3.** State or condition; for example, **amazement, merriment.** [Middle English, from Old French, from Latin *-mentum,* abstract noun suffix originally added only to verbs.]

men·tal[1] (mént'l) *adj.* **1.** Of or pertaining to the mind. **2.** Done or performed by the mind; existing in the mind: *a mental image; mental arithmetic.* **3.** Concerning, involving, or dealing with disorders of the mind: *mental illness; mental institutions.* **4.** Suffering from a disorder or illness of the mind: *a mental patient.* **5.** *Informal.* Very stupid or crazy. [Middle English, from Old French, from Latin *mentālis,* from *mēns* (stem *ment*-), mind.] —**men·tal·ly** *adv.*

mental[2] *adj. Rare.* Of or pertaining to the chin. [French, from Latin *mentum,* chin.]

mental age *n. Abbr.* **MA, M.A.** A measure of mental development, as determined by intelligence tests, generally restricted to children and expressed as the age at which the level achieved is considered to be average.

mental block *n.* A temporary inability to think, remember, or concentrate.

mental cruelty *n.* Cruel behaviour towards or ill-treatment of another person that causes emotional and psychological distress but does not involve physical violence. It is sometimes cited as grounds for divorce in the United States.

mental deficiency *n.* Subnormal intellectual development, either congenital or induced by brain injury or disease, characterised broadly by deficiencies ranging in severity from impaired learning ability through social and vocational inadequacy to inability to learn connected speech or guard against common dangers. Also called "amentia", "mental handicap", "mental retardation", "subnormality".

mental hospital n. A hospital or institution that provides care and treatment for the mentally ill. Also called "mental institution".

men·tal·ism (mént'l-iz'm) n. **1.** *Philosophy.* The doctrine that the mind is the only true reality and that the material world exists only on a subjective level as aspects of the individual's mind. **2.** *Philosophy & Linguistics.* The doctrine that mental processes exist independently of, and can account for, their manifestations in observable behaviour. —**men·tal·ist** n. & adj. —**men·tal·is·tic** (-ístik) adj.

men·tal·i·ty (men-tál-əti) n., pl. **-ties. 1.** The sum of a person's intellectual capabilities or endowments; mental capacity; intelligence. **2.** Cast or turn of mind; mental make-up or inclination: *She has a very conservative mentality.* —See Synonyms at **mind.**

mental retardation n. Mental deficiency.

mental telepathy n. **Telepathy** (see).

men·thol (mén-thol ‖ -thöl) n. A white, crystalline, organic compound, $C_{10}H_{20}O$, obtained from peppermint oil or synthesised. It is used in perfumes, as a mild anaesthetic, and as a flavouring. [German *Menthol* : Latin *mentha,* MINT + -OL.] —**men·tho·lat·ed** (-thə-laytid) adj.

men·tion (ménsh'n) tr.v. **-tioned, -tioning, -tions. 1.** To cite or refer to incidentally. **2.** To refer to by name, especially as an acknowledgement or to show appreciation. —**don't mention it.** A formula of courtesy used as a self-deprecating reply to proffered thanks or apologies. —**not to mention.** Used to draw attention to or emphasise the importance of: *Our thanks to all those who helped with the cooking, not to mention the chef herself, who planned the entire meal.* ~n. **1. a.** The act of briefly or casually referring to something. **b.** An incidental reference or allusion. **2.** A reference to a person by name, especially in order to acknowledge or honour him. [Middle English *mencioun,* from Old French *mention,* from Latin *mentiō* (stem *mention-*), remembrance, mention.] —**men·tion·a·ble** adj. —**men·tion·er** n.

men·tor (mén-tawr ‖ -tər) n. A wise and trusted counsellor or teacher. ~ tr.v. **-tored, -toring, -tors.** To be a mentor to. [French, after *Mentor,* a character in Fénelon's *Télémaque* (1699), based on Homer's MENTOR.]

Men·tor (mén-tawr ‖ -tər). *Greek Mythology.* Odysseus' trusted counsellor who became the guardian and teacher of Telemachus. [Greek *Mentōr,* name probably meaning "adviser", "wise man", from *men-* (unattested), to think.]

men·u (ménnew ‖ méenew, *U.S. also* máynew) n. **1.** A list of the dishes that are served or that can be ordered, as in a restaurant. **2.** The dishes served or available. **3.** *Computing.* A list of available options, usually displayed on a VDU, from which a user can select and access a particular program, function, or file. [French, menu, list, from *menu,* detailed, small, from Latin *minūtus,* minute, diminished, past participle of *minuere,* to diminish.]

Me·nu·hin (ménnew-in), **Yehudi, Baron Menuhin of Stoke d'Abernon** (1916-). American-born British violinist. He made his professional debut in San Francisco in 1924. Bartók's sonata for solo violin (1945) was written for him. Resident in England since 1959, he was director of the Bath music festival (1959-68), and in 1963 founded a school for musically gifted children.

Men·zies (ménziz), **Sir Robert (Gordon)** (1894-1978). Australian prime minister (1939-41; 1949-66). He was attorney-general in Joseph Lyons's government (1935-39), and succeeded Lyons as prime minister. His second period as prime minister was as the head of a Liberal/Country Party coalition.

me·ow, mi·aou, mi·aow (mee-ów) n. **1.** The characteristic high-pitched crying sound of a cat. **2.** Any similar sound. ~v. **meowed, -owing, -ows.** —intr. To emit a meow. —tr. To express by means of a meow. [Imitative.]

mep, m.e.p. mean effective pressure.

M.E.P. Member of the European Parliament.

mep·a·crine (méppəkrin) n. A drug, $C_{23}H_{30}ClN_3O$, formerly used in the treatment of malaria.

me·per·i·dine hydrochloride (me-pérri-deen, mə-, -din) n. An organic compound, $C_{15}H_{21}NO_2 \cdot HCl$, used as an analgesic and sedative. Also called "meperidine".

meph·i·stoph·e·les (méffi-stóffə-leez) n. **1.** The part of a beard directly below the lower lip. **2.** A beard consisting solely of the hairs between the lower lip and the chin, often waxed and shaped in an upward curve. [19th century : after MEPHISTOPHELES, represented in medieval and Renaissance painting as having a pronounced beard or part of a beard of this type.]

Meph·i·stoph·e·les (méffi-stóffə-leez). The devil in the Faust legend to whom Faust sold his soul. —**Me·phis·to·phe·le·an, Me·phis·to·phe·li·an** (méffi-stə-féeli-ən, mə-fístə-) adj.

me·phi·tis (me-fítiss, mi-) n. **1.** An offensive smell; a stench. **2.** A poisonous or foul-smelling gas emitted from the earth. [Latin *mefitis†,* stench.] —**me·phit·ic** (me-fíttik, mi-), **me·phit·i·cal** adj. —**me·phit·i·cal·ly** adv.

me·pro·ba·mate (mə-próbə-mayt, me-, mépprō-bámmayt) n. A bitter white powder, $CH_3(C_3H_7)C(CH_2OOCNH_2)_2$, used as a tranquilliser.

mer. meridian.

-mer. Variant of **-mere.**

mer·bro·min (mər-brómin) n. A green, crystalline, organic compound, $C_{20}H_8Br_2HgNa_2O_6$, that forms a red aqueous solution. It is used as a germicide and antiseptic under the trademark Mercurochrome.

mer·can·tile (mérkən-tíl ‖ *U.S. also* -teel, -til) adj. **1.** Of or pertaining to merchants, trade, or commerce. **2.** Of or pertaining to mercantilism. [French, from Italian, from *mercante,* MERCHANT.]

mer·can·til·ism (mérkən-ti-liz'm, -tī- ‖ -tee-, mər-kánti-) n. The theory and system of political economy prevailing in Europe after the decline of feudalism, based on national policies of accumulating bullion, establishing colonies and a merchant navy, and developing industry and mining to attain a favourable balance of trade. Also called "mercantile system". [French *mercantilisme,* from MERCANTILE.] —**mer·can·til·ist** n. & adj.

mer·cap·tan (mer-káp-tan, mər-) n. Any sulphur-containing organic compound with the general formula RSH, R being any radical; for example, ethyl mercaptan, C_2H_5SH. Also called "thiol". [German, from Danish, from Medieval Latin *(corpus) mercurium captans,* "(substance) seizing mercury" : *mercurium,* MERCURY + *captāns,* present participle of *captāre,* frequentative of *capere,* to take.]

mer·cap·tide (mer-káp-tīd, mər-) n. A salt of a mercaptan containing the ion RS-, where R is an alkyl or aryl group.

mercapto- comb. form. Indicates an HS- group in a chemical compound; for example, **mercaptopurine.** [From MERCAPTAN.]

Mer·ca·tor (mer-káy-tawr, mər-, -tər), **Gerardus,** born Gerhard Kremer (1512-94). Flemish inventor of the map projection (1569) which bears his name. He produced his first world map in 1538 and his first globe in 1541. His great atlas, started in 1585, was completed by his son (1594).

Mercator projection n. Also **Mercator's projection.** A map projection in which the globe is projected onto a cylinder, the meridians and parallels appearing as straight lines crossing at right angles. Lines of constant direction are straight lines, so it is used widely for navigation, despite increasing expansion and distortion of areas the further they are from the equator.

mer·ce·nar·y (mér-sinnəri, -sinri ‖ *U.S.* -si-nerri) adj. **1. a.** Motivated solely by a desire for monetary or material gain. **b.** Greedy; venal. **2.** Hired for service in a foreign army. ~n., pl. **mercenaries. 1.** A professional soldier who is hired by a foreign country or organisation. **2.** A person who serves or works merely for monetary gain; a hireling. [Middle English *mercenarie,* from Latin *mercēnārius,* from *mercēs,* pay.] —**mer·ce·nar·i·ly** (*also* -si-nérrili) adv. —**mer·ce·nar·i·ness** n.

mer·cer (mér-sər) n. British. A dealer in textiles, especially in expensive fabrics such as silks. [Middle English, from Old French *mercier,* trader, from Vulgar Latin *merciārius* (unattested), from Latin *merx* (stem *merc-*), merchandise.]

mer·cer·ise, mer·cer·ize (mér-sə-rīz) tr.v. **-ised, -ising, -ises.** To treat (cotton thread) with sodium hydroxide in order to shrink the fibre and increase its colour absorption and lustre. [After John Mercer (1791-1866), English textile maker.] —**mer·cer·i·sa·tion** (-rī-záysh'n ‖ *U.S.* -ri-) n.

mer·chan·dise (mérchən-dīz, -dīss) n. Abbr. **mdse.** Commodities of commerce; goods that may be bought or sold. ~v. (-dīz) **merchandised, -dising, -dises.** —tr. **1.** To buy and sell (commodities). **2.** To promote the sale of, as by advertising or display. —intr. To trade commercially. [Middle English, from Old French, from *marcheant,* MERCHANT.] —**mer·chan·dis·er** n.

mer·chant (mérchənt) n. **1.** A person whose occupation is the wholesale purchase and retail sale of goods for profit; a trader. **2.** *Chiefly U.S.* A person who runs a retail business; a shopkeeper. **3.** Someone fond of or involved with something specified that is generally thought undesirable: *a speed merchant.* ~adj. **1.** Of or pertaining to a merchant, merchandise, or commercial trade; dealing in commerce: *a merchant guild.* **2.** Of or pertaining to the merchant navy. [Middle English, from Old French *marcheant,* trader, from Vulgar Latin *mercātāns* (unattested), present participle of *mercātāre* (unattested), to trade, from Latin *mercārī,* to trade, from *merx* (stem *merc-*), merchandise.]

mer·chant·a·ble (mérchənt-əb'l) adj. Suitable for buying and selling; marketable.

merchant bank n. British. An institution engaged in a number of financial activities, such as accepting foreign bills of exchange, dealing in loans and securities, and supervising the issue of new securities. —**merchant banker** n. —**merchant banking** n.

mer·chant·man (mérchənt-mən) n., pl. **-men** (-mən, -men). **1.** A ship used in commerce. **2.** *Archaic.* A merchant.

merchant navy n. **1.** A nation's ships that are engaged in commerce. **2.** The personnel of such ships. Also called "mercantile marine", *U.S.* "merchant marine".

Mer·ci·a (mér-si-ə, -shi-ə, -shə). Anglo-Saxon kingdom of England, roughly corresponding with the Midlands. It became a major power under Penda (c. 632-54), overlord of all England south of the Humber: East Anglia, Kent, Mercia, Sussex, and Wessex. Offa (757-96) extended this power, controlling Northumberland too. Mercia came under Wessex overlordship (825), and the east was incorporated into the Danelaw (877).

Mer·ci·an (mér-si-ən, -shi-, -shən) n. **1.** A native or inhabitant of Mercia. **2.** The dialect of Old English used in Mercia. —**Mer·ci·an** adj.

mer·ci·ful (mér-sif'l) *adj.* Full of mercy; compassionate; lenient. —**mer·ci·ful·ness** *n.*

mer·ci·ful·ly (mér-sif'l-i, -si-fli) *adv.* **1.** In a merciful manner. **2.** It is a mercy that: *The climber fell, but mercifully landed in a tree.*

mer·ci·less (mér-si-ləss, -liss) *adj.* Having no mercy; pitiless; cruel. —**mer·ci·less·ly** *adv.* —**mer·ci·less·ness** *n.*

Merckx (mairks), **Eddy** (1945–). Belgian racing cyclist. He was world amateur champion (1964) and equalled the record of Jacques Anquetil by winning the Tour de France five times (1969–74). Also Tour of Italy, five times, and over 400 other races. He retired in 1978.

Mer·cou·ri (mer-koòr-i, mər-), **Melina**, born Anna Amalia Mercouri (1925–94). Greek film actress. She starred in *Never on Sunday* (1959). In 1981 she was elected to the Greek parliament and appointed Minister of Culture and Sciences (1981–85), and of Culture, Youth, and Sports (1985–90).

mer·cur·ate (mér-kewr-ayt) *tr.v.* **-curated, -curating, -curates.** To treat or mix with mercury. —**mer·cu·ra·tion** (-áysh'n) *n.*

mer·cu·ri·al (mər-kéwr-i-əl) *n.* A medical or chemical preparation containing mercury.
~*adj.* **1.** *Usually capital* **M.** Of or pertaining to the Roman god Mercury or the planet Mercury. **2.** Having the characteristics of eloquence, shrewdness, swiftness, and thievishness attributed to the god Mercury in Roman mythology. **3.** Containing or caused by the action of the element mercury. **4.** Being quick and changeable in character: *a mercurial temperament.* [Latin *mercuriālis,* from *Mercurius,* the god MERCURY.] —**mer·cu·ri·al·ly** *adv.*

mer·cu·ri·al·ism (mər-kéwr-i-ə-liz'm) *n.* Poisoning caused by mercury or its compounds. Also called "hydrargyria", "hydrargyrism".

mer·cu·ric (mər-kéwr-ik) *adj. Chemistry.* Pertaining to or containing bivalent mercury.

mercuric chloride *n.* A poisonous white crystalline compound, HgCl₂, used as an antiseptic and disinfectant and in insecticides, preservatives, and batteries, and in metallurgy and photography. Also called "corrosive sublimate".

mercuric oxide *n.* A poisonous compound, HgO, existing as red and yellow crystals and used as a pigment.

mercuric sulphide *n.* A poisonous compound, HgS, having two forms: **1.** *Black mercuric sulphide,* a black powder obtained from mercury salts or by the reaction of mercury with sulphur, used as a pigment. Also called "metacinnabarite". **2.** *Red mercuric sulphide,* a bright scarlet powder derived from heating mercury with sulphur, used as a pigment. Also called "artificial cinnabar", "vermilion".

Mer·cu·ro·chrome (mər-kéwr-ə-krōm) *n.* A trademark for a solution of **merbromin** *(see),* used as an antiseptic.

mer·cu·rous (mér-kewr-əss ‖ mər-kéwr-əss) *adj. Chemistry.* Pertaining to or containing monovalent mercury.

mercurous chloride *n.* A white powder, Hg₂Cl₂, used as a fungicide and formerly used in medicine as a cathartic.

mer·cu·ry (mérkewr-i) *n., pl.* **-ries. 1.** Symbol **Hg** A silvery-white poisonous metallic element, liquid at room temperature. It is used in thermometers, barometers, vapour lamps, and batteries, and in the preparation of chemical pesticides. Atomic number 80, atomic weight 200.59, melting point –38.87°C, boiling point 356.58°C, relative density 13.546, valencies 1, 2. Also called "quicksilver". **2.** Temperature. **3.** Any of several weedy plants of the genera *Mercurialis* or *Acalypha.* See **dog's mercury. 4.** *Archaic.* A messenger or guide. Now used only in the titles of some newspapers. [Middle English *Mercurie,* god, planet, metal, and plant (after Greek *Hermou poa,* "herb of Hermes"), from Latin *Mercurius,* MERCURY.]

Mer·cu·ry¹ (mérkewr-i) *Roman Mythology.* A god, often identified with the Greek god **Hermes** *(see),* serving as messenger to the other gods and being the god of commerce, travel, and thievery.

Mercury² *n.* The second smallest of the planets (after Pluto) and the one nearest the Sun. It has a sidereal period of revolution around the Sun of 88 days at a mean distance of 58 million kilometres (36 million miles), a mean radius of approximately 2 440 kilometres (1,516 miles), and a mass 0.05 that of the Earth. [Latin *Mercurius,* the god, the planet.]

mercury arc *n.* A bluish discharge containing some ultraviolet radiation produced by passing a high current through ionised mercury vapour.

mercury barometer *n.* A type of **barometer** *(see)* in which pressure is measured by the height of a column of mercury.

mer·cu·ry-va·pour lamp (mérkewr-i-váypər) *n.* A lamp in which ultraviolet and yellowish-green to blue visible light is produced by an electric discharge through mercury vapour. It is used as a source of ultraviolet light and for outdoor lighting.

mer·cy (mér-si) *n., pl.* **-cies. 1.** Kind and compassionate treatment of an offender, enemy, prisoner, or other person under one's power who might deserve harsh treatment; clemency. Also used ironically in the phrase *tender mercies: He was left to the tender mercies of the Inquisition.* **2.** A possible disposition to be kind and forgiving: *I threw myself on her mercy.* **3.** Something for which to be thankful; a fortunate occurrence. **4.** Alleviation of distress; relief: *Her death was a mercy.* —**at the mercy of.** Totally in the power of.
~*adj.* Of or involving an emergency or the alleviation of critical distress: *a mercy dash; a mercy flight.* [Middle English *merci,* from Old French *merci,* compassion, forbearance (to someone in one's power), from Late Latin *mercēs,* reward, God's gratuitous compassion, from Latin, pay, reward.]
Synonyms: mercy, leniency, clemency, forbearance.

mercy killing *n.* **Euthanasia** *(see).*

mercy seat *n.* **1.** The golden covering of the ark of the covenant

regarded as the resting place of God. Exodus 25:12–22. Also called "propitiatory". **2.** The throne of God.

mere¹ (meer) *adj.* Superlative **merest. 1.** Being nothing more than what is specified: *Her fee was a mere ten pounds.* **2.** *Archaic.* Pure; unadulterated. [Latin *merus,* clear, pure, unmixed.]

mere² (meer) *n.* A small, usually circular lake or pond. [Middle English, Old English, sea, lake.]

mere³ (meer) *n. Archaic.* A boundary. [Middle English, Old English *mǣre, gemǣre,* boundary.]

–mere, –mer *n. comb. form. Zoology.* Indicates a part or segment; for example, **blastomere, elastomer.** [French, from Greek *meros,* a part.]

Mer·e·dith (mérrədith), **George** (1828–1909). British novelist and poet. His novels include *The Ordeal of Richard Feverel* (1859), *The Adventures of Harry Richmond* (1871), *The Egoist* (1879), and *Diana of the Crossways* (1885), his poems, *Modern Love* (1862).

Meredith, Owen. See Lytton, (Edward) Robert Bulwer-Lytton, 1st Earl Lytton.

mere·ly (méerli) *adv.* **1.** Nothing more than what is specified; only: *"Although he seems so firm to us / He is merely flesh and blood."* (T.S. Eliot). **2.** *Archaic.* Purely. **3.** *Obsolete.* Absolutely; completely.

mer·e·tri·cious (mérri-tríshəss) *adj.* **1. a.** Superficially attractive. **b.** Attracting attention in a vulgar manner: *meretricious ornamentation.* **2.** Lacking sincerity: *a meretricious argument.* **3.** *Archaic.* Pertaining to or resembling a prostitute. [Latin *meritricius,* from *meretrix,* a prostitute, from *merere,* to earn pay.] —**mer·e·tri·cious·ly** *adv.* —**mer·e·tri·cious·ness** *n.*

mer·gan·ser (mer-gán-sər, -zər) *n., pl.* **-sers** or collectively **merganser.** Any marine fish-eating duck of the genus *Mergus,* having a slim, hooked, serrated bill. Also called "sawbill". [New Latin, "diver-goose" : Latin *mergus,* diver (bird) + *anser,* goose.]

merge (merj) *v.* **merged, merging, merges.** —*tr.* To cause to blend, fuse, or be absorbed so as to lose identity. —*intr.* To blend together so as to lose identity. —See Synonyms at **mix.** [Latin *mergere,* to dive, plunge.] —**mer·gence** *n.*

merg·er (mérjər) *n.* **1.** The union of two or more commercial interests or companies. **2.** *Law.* The absorption of a lesser estate, liability, right, action, or offence into a greater one.

me·rid·i·an (mə-ríddi-ən) *n. Abbr.* **m., M., mer. 1.** *Geography.* **a.** Half of any of the imaginary great circles on the Earth's surface passing through both geographical poles. **b.** A representation of such a half-circle; a line of longitude on a map. **2.** *Astronomy.* A great circle passing through the two poles of the celestial sphere and the observer's zenith; the celestial meridian. **3.** *Mathematics.* **a.** A curve on a surface of revolution, formed by the intersection of a plane containing the axis of revolution with the surface. **b.** A plane section of a surface of revolution containing the axis of revolution. **4.** The highest point or stage of development of anything; a zenith: *"Men come to their meridian at various periods of their lives."* (J.H. Newman). **5.** *Obsolete.* Noon. [Middle English *meridien,* noon, meridian circle, from Old French, from Latin *merīdiānus,* from *merīdiēs,* midday, dissimulated variant of *medidiēs : medius,* middle + *diēs,* day.] —**me·rid·i·an** *adj.*

meridian circle *n.* **1.** *Geography.* Any of the imaginary great circles on the Earth's surface passing through both geographical poles, and consisting of a meridian and its complementary meridian, such as 0° and 180°. **2.** An astronomical instrument consisting of a telescope mounted on a graduated circle, used to determine the declination and right ascension of stars.

me·rid·i·o·nal (mə-ríddi-ən'l) *adj.* **1.** Of or pertaining to a meridian. **2.** Characteristic of southern areas or people. **3.** Located in the south; southerly.
~*n.* An inhabitant of a southern region, especially of France. [Middle English, from Old French *meridionel,* from Late Latin *merīdionālis,* variant extension of Latin *merīdiānus,* MERIDIAN.]

Mé·ri·mée (mérri-may; *French* may-ree-máy), **Prosper** (1803–70). French writer. His work includes *The Chronicle of the Reign of Charles IX* (1829), a historical novel, and *Carmen* (1845), on which Bizet's opera is based.

me·ringue (mə-ráng) *n.* **1.** Beaten egg whites mixed with sugar and baked, used as a topping for puddings or pies. **2.** A small, crisp shell or cake made of meringue, often eaten with whipped cream. [French *méringue†.*] —**me·ringue** *adj.*

me·ri·no (mə-réenō) *n., pl.* **-nos. 1. a.** A sheep of a breed originally from Spain. **b.** The fine wool of this sheep. **2.** A soft, lightweight fabric made originally of merino wool but now of any fine wool. **3. a.** A type of fine wool and cotton yarn used for knitting underwear, hosiery, and other articles of clothing. **b.** A knitted fabric made from merino yarn.
~*adj.* Made of merino wool, yarn, or cloth. [Spanish, perhaps from Berber *Benī Merīn,* a people that developed the breed.]

Mer·i·on·eth·shire (mérri-ónnith-sheer, -shər). Former county of Wales, now in Gwynedd. It borders Cardigan Bay and its mountain scenery, with Cader Idris (892 metres; 2,927 feet), attracts many tourists. Dolgellau was the county town.

mer·i·stem (mérri-stem) *n. Botany.* The growing point or area of rapidly dividing cells in the cambium or at the tip of a stem, root, or branch. [Greek *meristos,* divided, divisible, from *merizein,* to divide, from *meris,* a division, part + *-em,* by analogy with *xylem.*] —**mer·i·ste·mat·ic** (-sti-máttik) *adj.*

me·ris·tic (mə-rístik) *adj. Biology.* **1.** Made up of segments, as some worms are. **2.** Modified by changes in the number or placement of entire body parts, as contrasted with modification by gradual change of the entire organism. [Greek *meristos*, divided, divisible. See **meristem**.]

mer·it (mérrit) *n.* **1.** Value, excellence, or superior quality: *a play of some merit.* **2.** An aspect of a person's character or behaviour deserving approval or disapproval: *to each according to his merits.* **3.** *Theology.* Spiritual credit granted for good works. **4.** *Plural. Law.* **a.** A party's strict legal rights, excluding jurisdictional or technical aspects. **b.** The factual substance of a case as distinguished from its form and procedural aspects. **5.** *Plural.* **a.** The intrinsic right or wrong of any matter. **b.** The actual facts of a matter. ~*tr.v.* **merited, -iting, -its.** To earn; deserve; warrant: *"How can the unknown merit reverence?"* (Harold Pinter). [Middle English, from Old French *merite,* that which is deserved, from Latin *meritum,* recompense, desert, from *merēre* (past participle *meritus*), to earn, deserve.] —**mer·it·ed·ly** *adv.*

mer·i·toc·ra·cy (mérri-tóckrə-si) *n., pl.* **-cies. 1.** A system in which advancement is based on ability or achievement. **2. a.** An elite composed of talented people who have achieved success through their own efforts. **b.** Leadership by such an elite. [MERIT + -CRACY.] —**mer·it·o·crat** (-tə-krat) *n.* —**mer·it·o·crat·ic** (-tə-kráttik) *adj.*

mer·i·to·ri·ous (mérri-táwri-əss ‖ -tóri-) *adj.* Deserving reward or praise; having merit. [Latin *meritōrius,* earning money, from *merēre* (past participle *meritus*), to earn, MERIT.] —**mer·i·to·ri·ous·ly** *adv.*

merle, merl (merl) *n.* The European blackbird, *Turdus merula.* See **blackbird.** [Middle English, from Old French, from Latin *merulus, merula,* blackbird.]

mer·lin (mérlin) *n.* A small falcon, *Falco columbarius,* which has dark plumage and a black-striped tail. [Middle English *meriloun,* from Anglo-French *merilun,* from Old French *esmerillon, esmeril,* merlin, from Frankish *smeril†* (unattested).]

Mer·lin (mérlin) *n.* In Arthurian legend, a wizard and prophet serving as mentor and counsellor to King Arthur.

mer·lon (mérlən) *n.* The solid portion of a crenellated wall between two open spaces. [French, from Italian *merlone,* from *merlo,* blackbird, battlement (probably from ranks of blackbirds perched on castle walls), from Latin *merulus, merula,* blackbird.]

mer·maid (mér-mayd) *n.* A fabled creature of the sea with the head and upper body of a woman and the tail of a fish. [Middle English : MERE (sea) + MAID.]

mermaid's purse *n.* A flat, rectangular envelope containing fertilised eggs, produced by certain sharks and skates such as the dogfish. Also called "sea purse".

mer·man (mér-man, -mən) *n., pl.* **-men** (-men, -mən). A male mermaid. [By analogy with MERMAID.]

mero– *comb. form.* Indicates parts or segments; for example, **meroblastic, merocrine.** [New Latin, from Greek *meros,* part, division.]

mer·o·blas·tic (mérrō-blástik, mérrə-) *adj. Biology.* Undergoing partial cleavage. Said of an egg with a large yolk. Compare **holoblastic.** [MERO- + -BLAST + -IC.] —**mer·o·blas·ti·cal·ly** *adv.*

mer·o·crine (mérrə-krīn, -krin, -kreen) *adj.* Of or pertaining to a gland the cells of which remain intact during secretion; eccrine. Compare **holocrine.** [Literally, "partly separating" (referring to the cells) : MERO- + Greek *krinein,* to separate.]

Meroë. See **Merowe.**

Mer·o·pe[1] (mérrəpi, mer-ópi). *Greek Mythology.* One of the **Pleiades** (*see*), who, after marrying a mortal, hid her face in shame.

Merope[2] *n.* The seventh star in the Pleiades cluster and the only one not visible to the naked eye.

me·ro·pi·a (mə-rópi-ə) *n.* Partial blindness. [New Latin : MER(O)- + -OPIA.] —**me·ro·pic** (mə-róppik, -rópik) *adj.*

-merous *adj. comb. form. Biology.* Having a specified number or kind of parts; for example, **pentamerous.** [New Latin *-merus,* from Greek *-meres,* from *meros,* a part.]

Mer·o·vin·gi·an (mérrō-vín-ji-ən, mérrə-, -jən) *adj.* Of or pertaining to the first dynasty of Frankish kings that ruled over Gaul from about A.D. 500 until 751. ~*n.* A member of this dynasty. [French *mérovingien,* from Medieval Latin *Merovingī,* "the descendants of Merovaeus", from Frankish *Merowig,* the eponymous ancestor.]

Mer·o·we or **Me·ro·ë** (mérrō-wi) *n.* Ruined capital of Cush (ancient Ethiopia) on the Nile north of Khartoum, Sudan.

mer·o·zo·ite (mérrō-zṓ-īt, mérrə-) *n.* A cell produced by fission of a sporozoan. [MERO- + ZO(O)- + -ITE.]

mer·ri·ment (mérrimənt) *n.* Gay conviviality; hilarity. See Synonyms at **mirth.**

mer·ry (mérri) *adj.* **-rier, -riest. 1.** Full of spirited gaiety; jolly. **2.** Marked by or offering humour and fun; festive. **3.** *Informal.* Slightly drunk. —See Synonyms at **jolly.** [Middle English *merie,* Old English *mirige,* pleasant.] —**mer·ri·ly** *adv.* —**mer·ri·ness** *n.*

mer·ry-an·drew (mérri-án-drōō) *n.* A prankster, jester, or clown. [17th century : reference to the name *Andrew* unexplained.]

mer·ry-go-round (mérri-gō-rownd) *n.* **1. a.** A circular platform fitted with seats, often in the form of wooden animals, revolved mechanically, usually to music, and ridden for amusement. **b.** A piece of playground equipment consisting of a small circular platform that revolves when pushed or pedalled. In both senses, also called "roundabout". **2.** Any whirl or swift round: *a merry-go-round of parties.*

merry hell *n. Informal.* Great disruption or disturbance. Often used in the phrase *to play merry hell.*

mer·ry·mak·ing (mérri-mayking) *n.* **1.** Participation in a party or revel. **2.** A festivity; revelry. —**mer·ry·mak·er** *n.*

mer·ry·thought (mérri-thawt) *n. Rare.* A wishbone.

Mer·sey (mérzi). River of northwest England. Formed by the confluence of the rivers Tame and Goyt, it flows 113 kilometres (70 miles) from Stockport to the Irish Sea where its estuary, 26 kilometres (16 miles) long, can be used by ocean-going ships. The river connects with the Manchester Ship Canal.

Mer·sey·side (mérzi-sīd). From 1974 to 1997 a metropolitan county centred on Liverpool, which had been created from northeast Cheshire and southwest Lancashire. It is now divided into Unitary Authority areas.

Mer·thyr Tyd·fil (mérthər tidvil). Town in South Wales. Situated on the river Taff in the South Wales Coalfield, it was once an iron and steel town of great importance. It now relies on light industries, including engineering, textiles, and clothing.

Mer·ton (múrt'n). Borough of southwest Greater London, incorporating the former boroughs of Mitcham and Wimbledon.

mes–. Variant of **meso-.**

me·sa (máy-sə) *n.* A flat-topped elevation with one or more clifflike sides, common in the southwestern United States. [Spanish, from Old Spanish, from Latin *mēnsa†,* table.]

mé·sal·li·ance (me-zál-i-ɔnss, may-; *French* may-zal-yónss) *n.* A marriage with a person of inferior social position. [French : *més-,* MIS- + *alliance,* ALLIANCE.]

mes·cal (me-skál) *n.* **1.** A spineless, globe-shaped cactus, *Lophophora williamsii,* of Mexico and the southwestern United States, having button-like tubercles (*mescal buttons*) that are dried and chewed as a drug. Also called "peyote". See **mescaline. 2.** A Mexican alcoholic drink distilled from the fermented juice of certain species of **agave** (*see*). **3.** A plant, the **maguey** (*see*). [Spanish *mescal, mezcal, mexcal,* from Nahuatl *mexcalli.*]

mes·ca·line, mes·ca·lin (méskə-leen, -lin) *n.* An alkaloid drug, $(CH_3O)_3C_6H_2(CH_2CH_2NH_2)$, that produces hallucinations and other psychedelic effects.

Mes·dames. *Abbr.* **Mmes.** Plural of **Madame** or **Madam.**

Mes·de·moi·selles. *Abbr.* **Mlles.** Plural of **Mademoiselle.**

mes·em·bry·an·the·mum (mi-zémbri-ánthə-məm) *n.* Any of various succulent plants of the chiefly South African genus *Mesembryanthemum,* having showy, daisy-like flowers. They are widely grown as ornamentals. See **ice plant.** [New Latin : Greek *mesēmbria,* noon + *anthemon,* flower.]

mes·en·ceph·a·lon (méss-en-séffə-lon, mézz-, mée-sen-, -zen-, -lən) *n.* Also **mes·o·ceph·a·lon** (méssō-). The region of the brain that develops from the middle section of the embryonic brain. Also called "midbrain". See **brain.** [New Latin : MES(O)- + ENCEPHALON.] —**mes·en·ce·phal·ic** (-si-fál-ik) *adj.*

mes·en·chyme (méss-eng-kīm, mézz-, mée-seng-, -zeng-) *n.* Also **mes·en·chy·ma** (me-séng-kimə, -zéng-). The part of the embryonic mesoderm from which develop connective tissue, cartilage, and the circulatory and lymphatic systems. [German *Mesenchym* : MESO- + ENCHYMA.] —**mes·en·chy·mal** (me-séng-kim'l, -zéng-), **mes·en·chym·a·tous** (mésseng-kímmətəss, mézzeng-, mée-seng-, -zeng-) *adj.*

mes·en·ter·i·tis (me-séntə-rítiss, mee-, -zéntə-) *n.* Inflammation of the mesentery. [New Latin : *mesenterium,* MESENTERY + -ITIS.]

mes·en·ter·on (me-séntə-ron, mee-, -zéntə-) *n. Biology.* **1.** The middle part of the intestinal cavity, the **midgut** (*see*). **2.** The middle part of the gastrovascular cavity in sea anemones and corals. [New Latin : MES(O)- + ENTERON.] —**mes·en·ter·on·ic** (-rónnik) *adj.*

mes·en·ter·y (méssən-təri, mézzən- ‖ -terri) *n., pl.* **-ies.** Also **mes·en·ter·i·um** (méssən-téer-i-əm, mézzən-) *pl.* **-ia** (-i-ə). Any of several peritoneal folds that connect the intestines to the dorsal abdominal wall. [New Latin *mesenterium* : MES(O) + ENTERON.] —**mes·en·ter·ic** (-térrik) *adj.*

mesh (mesh) *n.* **1.** Any of the open spaces in a cord, thread, or wire network. **2.** *Often plural.* The cords, threads, or wires surrounding these spaces. **3.** A net or network. **4.** Either of two measures of the fineness of a net, according to the frequency of strands or the distance between strands. **5.** Something that snares or entraps: *entangled in the meshes of politics.* **6.** The engagement of gear teeth. —**in mesh.** In gear. ~*v.* **meshing, meshes.** —*tr.* **1.** To entangle or ensnare. **2.** To cause (gear teeth) to become engaged. **3.** To cause to work closely together or harmoniously. —*intr.* **1.** To be or become entangled. **2.** To be or become engaged or interlocked, as gear teeth might. **3. a.** To coordinate or fit harmoniously and effectively: *mesh with the boss's idiosyncratic methods.* **b.** To accord with another; harmonise. [Earlier *meash, mash,* from Middle Dutch *masche, maesche.*] —**mesh·ing** *n.* —**mesh·y** *adj.*

Me·shach (mée-shak). A Hebrew captive who, with Shadrach and Abednego, miraculously escaped death in Nebuchadnezzar's fiery furnace. Daniel 3.

Meshed. See **Mashhad.**

me·shu·ga, me·shug·ga (mi-shṓogə, mə-) *adj. Informal.* Mad; crazy. [Yiddish, from Hebrew.]

mesh·work (mésh-wurk) *n.* Meshes; network.

me·si·al (mée-zi-əl, -si-) *adj.* Of, in, near, or towards the middle; medial. [MES(O)- + -IAL.] —**me·si·al·ly** *adv.*

me·si·tes (mə-sīteez) *n.* A flightless, rail-like bird, *Monias benschi,* found in the forests and brushlands of Madagascar.

me·sit·y·lene (mə-sítti-leen, méssi-ti-) *n.* A hydrocarbon, $(CH_3)_3C_6H_3$, occurring in petroleum and coal tar and synthesised from acetone; 1,3,5-trimethylbenzene.

mes·i·tyl oxide (méssi-til) *n.* An oily liquid, $(CH_3)_2C:CHCOCH_3$, obtained from acetones and used as a solvent and insect repellent.

[Greek *mesitēs*, mediator, from *mesos*, middle + -YL.]

Mes·mer (méz-mər; German méss-), **Franz Anton**, also known as Friedrich Anton Mesmer (1734–1815). German medical practitioner who pioneered hypnotism and psychoanalysis in medicine. He first used magnets in treatment, then treated patients by psychological suggestion. He settled in Paris in 1778, and although denounced by the French Academy of Medicine, his methods, known as "mesmerism", led to the development of therapeutic hypnotism.

mes·mer·ise, mes·mer·ize (méz-mə-rīz, méss-) *tr.v.* **-ised, -ising, -ises.** 1. To hypnotise. 2. To enthral: *She mesmerised the audience.* —**mes·mer·ic** (mez-mérrik, mess-) *adj.* —**mes·mer·is·er** *n.*

mes·mer·ism (méz-mə-riz'm, méss-) *n.* Hypnotism or a theory concerning it. Not in technical usage. See **animal magnetism**. [After Franz Anton MESMER.] —**mes·mer·ist** *n.*

mesne (meen) *adj. Law.* Intermediate; intervening. [Middle English, from Anglo-French *mesne, meen,* from Old French *meien,* from Latin *mediānus,* median, from *medius,* middle.]

mesne lord *n.* A feudal lord intermediate between a superior lord and his own vassals or tenants.

meso-, mes- *comb. form.* Indicates centre or intermediate; for example, **mesoblast, mesoderm.** [Greek, from *mesos,* middle.]

mes·o·blast (méss-ō-blast, mézz-, méess-, méez-, -ə-, -blaast) *n.* The middle germinal layer of the embryo; the mesoderm in its early stage of development. [MESO- + -BLAST.] —**mes·o·blas·tic** (-blástik) *adj.*

mes·o·carp (méss-ō-kaarp, mézz-, méess-, méez-, -ə-) *n. Botany.* The middle, usually fleshy layer of a **pericarp** *(see).* [MESO- + -CARP.]

mes·o·ceph·al·ic (méss-ō-séff'l-ik, mézz-, méess-, méez-, -ə-) *n.* 1. Having a head form intermediate between **brachycephalic** and **dolichocephalic** *(both of which see).* 2. A medium cranial capacity. [MESO- + -CEPHALIC.]

mesocephalon. Variant of **mesencephalon.**

mes·o·derm (méss-ō-derm, mézz-, méess-, méez-, -ə-) *n.* The embryonic germ layer, lying between the ectoderm and the endoderm, from which develop connective tissue, muscles, and the urogenital and vascular systems. [MESO- + -DERM.] —**mes·o·der·mal** (-dérm'l), **mes·o·der·mic** (-dérmik) *adj.*

mes·o·gle·a, mes·o·gloe·a (méss-ō-glée-ə, mézz-, méess-, méez-, -ə-) *n.* The layer of jelly-like material that separates the inner and outer cell layers in coelenterates. [New Latin : MESO- + Greek *gloia,* glue.]

Mes·o·lith·ic (méss-ō-líthik, mézz-, méess-, méez-, -ə-) *adj. Archaeology.* Designating the cultural period between the Palaeolithic and Neolithic Ages, marked by the appearance of microlithic cutting tools, and the introduction of boats and fishing.

~*n. Archaeology.* The Mesolithic Age. Preceded by *the.* Also called "Middle Stone Age". [MESO- + -LITHIC.]

mes·o·morph (méss-ō-mawrf, mézz-, méess-, méez-, -ə-) *n.* A human build characterised by powerful musculature and a predominantly bony framework. Compare **ectomorph, endomorph.** [MESO- + -MORPH.]

mes·o·mor·phic (méss-ō-mór-fik, mézz-, méess-, méez-, -ə-) *adj.* Also **mes·o·mor·phous** (-fəss) (for sense 1). 1. *Chemistry.* Of, pertaining to, or existing in a state of matter intermediate between liquid and crystal. 2. *Anatomy.* Of or pertaining to a mesomorph. —**mes·o·mor·phy** (-mawrfi) *n.*

mes·on (mée-zon, -son, mésson, mézzon) *n. Physics.* Any of several elementary particles, having integral spins and masses generally intermediate between those of leptons and baryons. Formerly called "mesotron". [MES(O)- + -ON.] —**me·son·ic** (mi-zónnik, mee-, -sónnik) *adj.*

mes·o·neph·ros (méss-ō-néff-ross, mézz-, méess-, méez-, -ə-, -rəss) *n.* The middle part of the embryonic excretory system in vertebrates that becomes the functioning kidney in fish and amphibians and the epididymis in reptiles, birds, and mammals. Also called "Wolffian body". [New Latin : MESO- + Greek *nephros,* kidney.] —**mes·o·neph·ric** *adj.*

mes·o·pause (méss-ō-pawz, mézz-, méess-, méez-, -ə-) *n.* The atmospheric zone, about 80 kilometres (50 miles) above the Earth, forming the upper limit of the mesosphere.

mes·o·phil·ic (méss-ō-fíllik, mézz-, méess-, méez-, -ə-) *adj.* Pertaining to or designating an organism, usually a bacterium, thriving at moderate temperatures, between 20°C and 40°C. Compare **psychrophilic, thermophilic.** [MESO- + -PHIL(E) + -IC.]

mes·o·phyll (méss-ō-fil, mézz-, méess-, méez-, -ə-) *n.* The soft tissue of a leaf, between the upper and lower epidermis, that contains the chloroplasts and is involved in photosynthesis. [New Latin *mesophyllum* : MESO- + -PHYLL.] —**mes·o·phyl·lic** (-fíllik), **mes·o·phyl·lous** (-fílləss) *adj.*

mes·o·phyte (méss-ō-fīt, mézz-, méess-, méez-, -ə-) *n.* A land plant that grows in a temperate environment having a moderate amount of moisture. Compare **xerophyte, hydrophyte.** [MESO- + -PHYTE.] —**mes·o·phyt·ic** (-fíttik) *adj.*

Mes·o·po·ta·mi·a (méssəpə-táymi-ə). Ancient region of southwest Asia, between the Euphrates and Tigris rivers. Its name is derived from the Greek for "between rivers". Most of it lies in modern Iraq. The site of some of the earliest human settlements, such as Jarmo (*c.* 7000 B.C.), it saw the rise of early civilisations: Sumer (*c.* 3100 B.C.), Akkad (*c.* 2370 B.C.), and Babylon (*c.* 1800 B.C.).

mes·o·sphere (méss-ō-sfeer, mézz-, méess-, méez-, -ə-) *n.* 1. The portion of the atmosphere from about 50 to 80 kilometres (30 to 50 miles) above the Earth, characterised by a temperature range that decreases from 10°C to –90°C with increasing altitude. See **atmosphere.** 2. The solid part of the Earth's mantle, lying between the semi-fluid asthenosphere and the fluid outer core. [MESO- + -SPHERE.] —**mes·o·spher·ic** (-sférrik, -sféer-ik) *adj.*

mes·o·spor·i·um (méss-ō-spáwri-əm, mézz-, méess-, méez-, -ə-) *n. Botany.* The **exo-intine** *(see).*

mes·o·the·li·um (méss-ō-thée-li-əm, mézz-, méess-, méez-, -ə-) *n., pl.* **-lia** (-li-ə). A layer of squamous cells of the epithelium lining the peritoneum, pericardium, and pleura, derived from the mesoderm. [New Latin : MESO- + (EPI)THELIUM.] —**mes·o·the·li·al** *adj.*

mes·o·tho·rax (méss-ō-tháwr-aks, mézz-, méess-, méez-, -ə- || -thór-) *n., pl.* **-raxes** or **-races** (-ə-seez). The middle section of an insect's thoracic region, bearing the middle legs and the front wings.

mes·o·tho·ri·um (méssō-tháwr-i-əm, mézz-, méess-, méez-, -ə- || -thór-) *n. Abbr.* **Ms-Th.** Either of two decay products of thorium: 1. Mesothorium I, now called radium-228. 2. Mesothorium II, now called actinium-228. Not in technical usage.

mes·o·tron (méss-ə-tron, mézz-, méess-, méez-) *n. Physics.* A **meson** *(see).* No longer in technical usage. [MESO- + (ELEC)TRON.]

Mes·o·zo·ic (méss-ō-zṓ-ik, mézz-, méess-, méez-, -ə-) *adj.* Of, belonging to, or designating the third era of geological time, which includes the Cretaceous, Jurassic, and Triassic periods, and is characterised by the predominance of reptilian life forms.

~*n.* The Mesozoic era. Preceded by *the.* [MESO- + -ZOIC.]

mes·quite, mes·quit (me-skéet, mess-, méss-keet) *n.* Any of several shrubs or small trees of the genus *Prosopis*; especially, *P. juliflora,* of the southwestern United States and Mexico. Its pods are used as forage. Also called "algarroba", "honey locust". [Spanish *mezquite,* from Nahuatl *mizquitl.*]

mess (mess) *n.* 1. A disorderly accumulation of items. 2. **a.** A cluttered, untidy, usually dirty state or condition. **b.** *Informal.* An untidy or dirty person or thing. 3. **a.** A disturbing, confusing, and troublesome state of affairs; a muddle. **b.** *Informal.* A confused, muddled, or disturbed person or thing. 4. *Archaic.* An amount of food for a meal, course, or dish: *"at their savoury dinner set / Of herbs, and other country messes"* (John Milton). 5. *Archaic.* A serving of soft, semiliquid food: *a mess of gruel.* 6. A distasteful and unappetising concoction. 7. An animal's faeces, especially those of a pet: *The cat's made a mess on the carpet again.* 8. **a.** A group of persons, usually in the military, who regularly eat meals together. **b.** A meal eaten in such a group. **c.** The place where such meals are served, and, in the armed forces, where there are facilities for recreation, entertainment, and accommodation: *the officers' mess.* —**make a mess of.** To bungle or ruin.

~*v.* **messed, messing, messes.** —*tr.* 1. To make disorderly and soiled; clutter. Often used with *up: messed up the kitchen with pots and pans.* 2. To bungle, mismanage, or botch. Usually used with *up: She messed up the test.* 3. *Slang.* To be rough with; manhandle. Usually used with *up: a mugger messing up his victim.* —*intr.* 1. To take a meal in a military mess. 2. To cause or make a mess. 3. To interfere; meddle. Usually used with *with* or *about* with. —**mess about** or **around.** *Informal.* 1. To occupy time by pottering or tinkering; work aimlessly: *"there is nothing . . . half so much worth doing as simply messing about in boats"* (Kenneth Grahame). 2. To waste time; procrastinate. 3. To treat (someone) inconsiderately or badly. [Middle English *mes,* course of a meal, dish of food, group of messmates, from Old French, from Latin *missus,* "placement", course of a meal, from *mittere* (past participle *missus*), to send, place, put.]

mes·sage (méssij) *n. Abbr.* **msg.** 1. A communication transmitted by spoken or written words, by signals, or by other means from one person or group to another. 2. A formal diplomatic communication. 3. A statement made or read before a gathering: *a farewell message.* 4. An apparent communication from God, delivered by a prophet. 5. A moral or religious point or theme. 6. The basic theme, inspiration, or significance of something: *"the life of Britain, her message, and her glory"* (Winston Churchill). 7. *Regional.* An errand: *run a message.* —**get the message.** *Informal.* To understand; learn the truth. —**off message.** Not on message. —**on message.** Displaying support for agreed or official policy. [Middle English, from Old French, from Vulgar Latin *missāticum* (unattested), "something sent", communication, from Latin *mittere* (past participle *missus*), to send.]

mes·sa·line (méssə-léen, -leen) *n.* A lightweight, soft, shiny silk cloth with a twilled or satin weave. [French *messaline†.*]

Mes·sei·gneurs. Plural of **Monseigneur.**

mes·sen·ger (méssinjər) *n.* 1. One charged with transmitting messages or performing errands; especially: **a.** One employed to carry telegrams, letters, or parcels. **b.** A military or official dispatch bearer; a courier. 2. A bearer of news. Also used in the titles of some newspapers. 3. *Archaic.* A forerunner or prophet; a harbinger. 4. *Nautical.* A chain or rope used for hauling in a cable. [Middle English *messager, messanger,* from Old French *messagier,* from MESSAGE.]

messenger RNA *n.* A ribonucleic acid *(see)* that carries the genetic information required for protein synthesis in cells from DNA to the ribosomes. Also called "messenger ribonucleic acid", "mRNA".

Mes·ser·schmitt (méssər-shmit), **Wilhelm**, known as Willy (1898–1978). German aircraft designer. He designed the Messerschmitt 109 (1937), which set a world speed record; the Messerschmitt 163 Komet, the first aircraft to be powered by a liquid-fuel rocket; and the Messerschmitt 262, the first jet aeroplane used in combat (1944).

Mes·si·aen (méss-yon, mess-yón), **Olivier (Eugène-Prosper-Charles)** (1908–92). French organist and composer. His organ works include *La Nativité du Seigneur* (1935) and *Les Corps glorieux* (1939), and a mammoth symphony in ten movements, *Turangalîla* (1946–48). He used bird songs in *Réveil des oiseaux* (1953), *Oiseaux exotiques* (1955), and *Catalogue d'oiseaux* (1956–58).

Mes·si·ah (mi-sí-ə, me-) *n.* Also **Mes·si·as** (-əss, me-). **1.** *Judaism.* The anticipated deliverer and king of the Jews. **2.** Jesus Christ. **3.** *Small* **m.** Any expected or supposed deliverer or liberator. [Middle English, from Old French *Messie*, from Late Latin, from Greek *Messias*, from Aramaic *məshîḥā*, Hebrew *māshiaḥ*, "the anointed", the Messiah.]

mes·si·an·ic (méssi-ánnik) *adj.* Also capital **M.** Of or pertaining to a messiah or the salvation and ideal state he is expected to produce.

Mes·sieurs. *Abbr.* **Messrs., M.M.** Plural of **Monsieur.**

Mes·si·na (me-séenə, mə-). Port of northeast Sicily, Italy, on the Strait of Messina. It exports wine, fruit, and olive oil and manufactures chemicals and pasta. It was founded by the Greeks (late eighth century B.C.). Its many occupiers included the Carthaginians, Romans, and Spaniards. Garibaldi took the city in 1860–61. It was destroyed by earthquakes in 1783 and 1908.

Messina, Strait of. Channel of the Mediterranean Sea between Sicily and mainland Italy. Linking the Ionian and Tyrrhenian seas, it is 32 kilometres (20 miles) long and at its narrowest 3 kilometres (2 miles) wide. Its rocks, currents, and whirlpools may have given rise to the legend of Scylla and Charybdis.

mess jacket *n.* An officer's fitted, waist-length jacket, often worn in the mess on formal occasions. Also called "monkey jacket".

mess kit *n.* **1.** *British.* A military officer's formal evening wear. **2.** Special cooking and eating utensils for soldiers in the field.

mess·mate (méss-mayt) *n.* A person with whom one eats regularly, as in a military or naval mess.

Messrs. **1.** Messieurs. **2.** Plural of **Mr.**

mes·suage (méss-wij, méssew-ij) *n. Law.* A dwelling house with its outbuildings and adjoining lands. [Middle English, from Anglo-French, household, probably based on a misreading of Old French *me(s)nage*, MÉNAGE.]

mess·y (méssi) *adj.* **-ier, -iest.** Resembling, being in, or causing a mess; untidy; dirty; disordered. **—mess·i·ly** *adv.* **—mess·i·ness** *n.*

mestee. Variant of **mustee.**

mes·ti·zo (me-stée-zō, mə-) *n., pl.* **-zos** or **-zoes.** Feminine **mes·ti·za** (-zə). In Latin America, a person of mixed European and American Indian ancestry. [Spanish, from *mestizo*, mixed, from Old Spanish, from Vulgar Latin *mixtīcius* (unattested), of mixed race, from Latin *mixtus*, from the past participle of *miscēre*, to mix.]

mes·tra·nol (méss-trə-nol ‖ -nōl) *n.* A synthetic oestrogen, $C_{21}H_{26}O_2$, used as an oral contraceptive in combination with progestogens. [*Methyl oestrogen pregnane* + -OL.]

met. Past tense and past participle of **meet.**

met. **1.** metaphor. **2.** metaphysics. **3.** meteorological; meteorology. **4.** metropolitan.

me·ta (méttə) *adj. Chemistry.* **1.** Of, pertaining to, or designating positions in a benzene ring separated by one carbon atom. Used in combination: *metadichlorobenzene.* Compare **ortho, para, pyro.** **2.** Of, pertaining to, or designating the least hydrated form of an acid. Used in combination: *metaphosphoric acid.* **3.** Of, pertaining to, or designating a polymer of an organic compound. Used in combination: *metaldehyde.* [Independent use of META-.]

meta–, met– *prefix.* Indicates: **1.** *Anatomy.* Situated behind; for example, **metacarpus. 2.** Occurring later; for example, **metazoan. 3. a.** Going beyond or transcending; for example, **metalanguage. b.** A discipline concerned with the analysis of a specified and related discipline; for example, **metalinguistics. 4.** Changed or involving change; for example, **metachromatism. 5.** Alternating; for example, **metagenesis. 6.** *Geology.* Having undergone metamorphic change. [In borrowed Greek compounds, *meta-* indicates: 1. Between, as in **metope.** 2. After, following, as in **method.** 3. Behind, backward, hence reversed, changed, as in **metathesis, metamorphosis.** 4. Intensified action, as in **meteor.** *Meta-* is the preverbal form of the preposition *meta*, between, with, beside, after.]

met·a·bol·ic (méttə-bóllik) *adj. Biology.* Of, pertaining to, or exhibiting metabolism. [Greek *metabolikos*, changeable, from *metabolē*, change. See **metabolism.**] **—met·a·bol·i·cal·ly** *adv.*

metabolic pathway *n.* Any of the chains or cycles of reactions occurring in living cells, during which materials are broken down or built up with accompanying release or expenditure of energy.

me·tab·o·lise, me·tab·o·lize (mi-tábbə-līz, me-) *v.* **-lised, -lising, -lises. —tr.** To subject (a substance) to metabolism or produce (a substance) by metabolism. **—intr.** To undergo change or be produced by metabolism.

me·tab·o·lism (mi-tábbə-liz'm, me-) *n. Biology.* **1. a.** The complex of physical and chemical processes involved in the maintenance of life. See **anabolism, catabolism. b.** The rate at which such processes function: *a slow metabolism.* **2.** The functioning of any specified substance within the living body: *water metabolism; iodine metabolism.* [Greek *metabolē*, change, from *metaballein*, to change : *meta* (denoting change) + *ballein*, to throw.]

me·tab·o·lite (mi-tábbə-līt, me-) *n.* Any of various organic compounds produced by or taking part in metabolism. [METABOL(ISM) + -ITE.]

met·a·car·pal (méttə-kárp'l) *adj. Anatomy.* Pertaining to the metacarpus.

~*n. Anatomy.* Any of the bones of the metacarpus.

met·a·car·pus (méttə-kárpəss) *n. Anatomy.* The part of the hand or forefoot in mammals that includes the five bones between the fingers and the wrist. [New Latin : META- (behind) + CARPUS.]

met·a·cen·tre (méttə-sentər) *n.* The intersection of the verticals through the centre of buoyancy of a floating body when in equilibrium and when tilted. This point must be above the centre of gravity for stability. **—met·a·cen·tric** (-séntrik) *adj.*

met·a·chro·mat·ic (méttə-krō-máttik) *adj.* **1.** Changing to a different colour from that of the dye used for staining. Said of cells and tissues stained for microscopic examination. **2.** Designating a dye that is able to stain cells or tissues a different colour from its own. **3.** Characteristic of or pertaining to metachromatism.

met·a·chro·ma·tism (méttə-krōmə-tiz'm) *n.* A change in colour caused by variation of the physical conditions to which a body is subjected, as in heating. [META- (denoting change) + CHROMAT(O)- + -ISM.]

met·a·cin·na·bar (méttə-sínnə-bar) *n.* The black form of **mercuric sulphide** *(see).*

met·a·gal·ax·y (méttə-gál-ək-si, -gal-) *n., pl.* **-ies.** The entire collection of all galaxies, considered as the total physical universe.

met·age (méetij) *n.* **1.** The official measurement of weight or contents. **2.** The fee charged for metage. [From METE (to measure).]

met·a·gen·e·sis (méttə-jénni-siss) *n. Biology.* **Alternation of generations (see). —met·a·ge·net·ic** (-ji-néttik) *adj.* **—met·a·ge·net·i·cal·ly** *adv.*

me·tag·na·thous (mi-tág-nə-thəss) *adj.* Having a beak in which the tips of the mandibles cross, as the crossbill does. [META- + -GNATHOUS.] **—me·tag·na·thism** *n.*

met·al (métt'l) *n.* **1.** *Symbol* **M** Any of a category of electropositive elements that are usually silvery-white, lustrous, good conductors of electricity and heat, and, in the transition metals, typically ductile and malleable with high tensile strength. Typical metals form salts with nonmetals, basic oxides with oxygen, and alloys with one another. **2.** An alloy of two or more metallic elements. **3.** An object made of metal. **4.** Basic character; mettle. **5.** Broken stones used to form the surface of a macadamised road. In this sense, also called "road metal". **6.** Molten glass, especially when used in glassmaking. **7.** Molten cast iron. **8.** *Printing.* Type made of metal. **9.** *Plural.* Railway-line rails. **10.** The total weight, number, or power of a warship's guns. **11.** *Heraldry.* Either of the tinctures *or* (gold) and *argent* (silver), as distinguished from the colours and the furs.

~*tr.v.* **metalled** or *U.S.* **metaled, -alled** or *U.S.* **-aling, -als. 1.** To cover or equip with metal. **2.** To make (a road) with broken stones. [Middle English, from Old French, from Latin *metallum*, from Greek *metallon*†, a mine, mineral, metal.]

met·a·lan·guage (méttə-lang-gwij) *n.* The natural language, formal language, or logical system used to discuss or analyse another language, the **object language** *(see).*

met·a·lin·guis·tics (méttə-ling-gwístiks) *n. Used with a singular verb.* The study of the interrelationship between language and other cultural or behavioural phenomena.

me·tal·lic (mi-tál-ik) *adj.* **1.** Of, pertaining to, or having the characteristics of a metal. **2.** Containing a metal: *a metallic compound.* **3.** Having a quality characteristic of metal: *a metallic tinkle.* [French *métallique*, from Latin, from Greek *metallikos*. See **metal.**] **—me·tal·li·cal·ly** *adv.*

metallic bond *n.* The chemical bond characteristic of metals, produced by the sharing of valency electrons between atoms in a usually stable crystalline structure.

metallic soap *n.* A soft, waxlike organic compound composed of a metal and a fatty acid, used as a drier or lubricant.

met·al·lif·er·ous (métt'l-íffərəss) *adj.* Containing metal. [Latin *metallifer* : *metallum*, METAL + -FEROUS.]

met·al·line (métt'l-īn) *adj.* **1.** Of, resembling, or having the properties of a metal. **2.** Containing metal ions. [METAL + -INE.]

met·al·lise, met·al·lize, *U.S.* **met·al·ize** (métt'l-īz) *tr.v.* **-ised, -ising, -ises.** To make metallic; coat with metal. **—met·al·li·sa·tion** (-ī-záysh'n ‖ *U.S.* -i-) *n.*

met·al·list, *U.S.* **met·al·ist** (métt'l-ist) *n.* **1.** One who works with metals; especially, a craftsman producing fine metal objects. **2.** One who has an expert knowledge of metals. **3.** One who advocates metal money instead of paper currency.

met·al·log·ra·phy (métt'l-óggrəfi) *n.* **1.** The study of the structure of metals and their compounds, especially with a microscope. **2.** A printing process, **lithography** *(see),* in which metal plates are used. [METAL + -GRAPHY.] **—met·al·log·ra·pher** *n.* **—me·tal·lo·graph·ic** (mi-tál-ə-gráffik) *adj.* **—me·tal·lo·graph·i·cal·ly** *adv.*

met·al·loid (métt'l-oyd) *n.* A nonmetallic element, such as arsenic, that has some of the chemical properties of a metal, or one, such as carbon, that can form an alloy with metals.

~*adj.* Also **met·al·loi·dal** (-óyd'l). **1.** Pertaining to or having the properties of a metalloid. **2.** Having the appearance of a metal. [METAL + -OID.]

met·al·lo·phone (me-tál-ə-fōn) *n.* **1.** Any of various musical instruments resembling the xylophone but having metal bars. **2.** A musical instrument resembling a piano but having metal bars rather than strings. [METAL + -PHONE.]

met·al·lur·gy (mi-tál-ər-ji, me-, métt'l-urji) *n. Abbr.* **metal., metall. 1.** The science or procedures of extracting metals from their ores, of purifying metals, and of creating useful objects from metals. **2.** The knowledge and study of metals and their properties in bulk and at the atomic level. [New Latin *metallurgia*, from Greek *metallourgos*, a miner : *metallon*†, a mine + -*ourgos*, agent suffix of *ergon*, work.]

—**met·al·lur·gic** (mett'l-úrjik), **met·al·lur·gi·cal** adj. —**met·al·lur·gi·cal·ly** adv. —**met·al·lur·gist** (mett'l-urjist, mi-tál-ər-jist) n.

met·al·work (mett'l-wurk) n. **1.** The craft of working in or making objects from metal. **2.** Articles of or work done in metal.

met·al·work·ing (mett'l-wurking) n. **1.** The craft or process of shaping things out of metal. **2.** The processing of metal to prepare it for industrial use, as by rolling or flattening it. —**met·al·work·er** n.

met·a·math·e·mat·ics (mettə-máthi-máttiks) n. The study of the principles, conceptual elements, consistency, and other aspects of logical systems, especially of mathematical systems. —**met·a·math·e·mat·i·cal** adj. —**met·a·math·e·ma·ti·cian** (-mə-tísh'n) n.

met·a·mer (méttə-mər) n. Any pair or larger group of isomeric compounds that exhibit metamerism. [META- + -MER.]

met·a·mere (méttə-meer) n. Any of a series of similar body segments, as in worms and lobsters. Also called "somite". [META- + -MERE.]

met·a·mer·ic (mettə-mérrik, -meer-ik) adj. **1.** Zoology. Of, pertaining to, or having metameres. **2.** Chemistry. Of, pertaining to, or exhibiting metamerism. —**met·a·mer·i·cal·ly** adv.

metameric segmentation n. The repetition of similar body segments along the length of an animal, as seen in the earthworm. In most animals such segmentation is confined to embryonic stages. Also called "metamerism", "segmentation".

me·tam·er·ism (mi-támmə-riz'm, me-) n. **1.** Chemistry. A form of isomerism in which different organic radicals form compounds (metamers) by attachment to the same central atom or group. **2.** Zoology. Metameric segmentation.

met·a·mor·phic (mettə-mórfik) adj. Also **met·a·mor·phous** (méttə-mórfəss). **1.** Of or pertaining to metamorphosis. **2.** Geology. Characteristic of, pertaining to, or changed by metamorphism. [From METAMORPHOSIS.]

met·a·mor·phism (méttə-mór-fiz'm) n. **1.** Geology. Any alteration in composition, texture, or structure of rock masses, caused by great heat or pressure or both. **2.** Metamorphosis (of an insect). [METAMORPH(OSIS) + -ISM.]

met·a·mor·phose (méttə-mór-fōz, -fōss) v. **-phosed, -phosing, -phoses.** —tr. **1.** To transform, as by sorcery: *"His eyes turned bloodshot, and he was metamorphosed into a raging fiend."* (Jack London). **2.** To cause to change in form, structure, or character; subject to metamorphosis or metamorphism. —intr. To be changed or transformed by or as if by metamorphosis or metamorphism. [French *metamorphoser,* from *metamorphose,* transformation, from METAMORPHOSIS.]

met·a·mor·pho·sis (méttə-mórfə-siss, -mawr-fō-siss) n., pl. **-ses** (-seez). **1.** A transformation, as by magic or sorcery. **2.** A marked change in appearance, character, condition, or function. **3.** One that has been transformed or changed in this way. **4.** Biology. Change in the structure and habits of an animal during normal growth, usually in the postembryonic stage. Metamorphosis includes, in insects, the emerging of an adult fly from a maggot or of a butterfly from a caterpillar, and, in amphibians, the changing of a tadpole into a frog. **5.** Physiology. Transformation of one kind of tissue into another; especially, degeneration; metaplasia. [Latin *metamorphōsis,* from Greek : *meta-* (involving change) + MORPHOSIS.]

met·a·neph·ros (mettə-néff-ross, -rəss) n. The section of the embryonic kidney that is the third and last stage to be formed in reptiles, birds, and mammals. It develops into the adult kidney. [New Latin : META- + Greek *nephros,* kidney.]

metaph. 1. metaphor; metaphorical. **2.** metaphysics.

met·a·phase (méttə-fayz) n. Biology. The stage of mitosis or meiosis during which the chromosomes are aligned along the equator of the nuclear spindle.

met·a·phor (méttə-fər, -fawr) n. **1.** Abbr. **met., metaph.** A figure of speech in which a term is transferred from the object it ordinarily designates to an object it may designate only by implicit comparison or analogy, as in the phrase *evening of life.* Compare **simile.** **2.** Figurative language: *the effective use of metaphor in her poetry.* [Old French *metaphore,* from Latin *metaphora,* from Greek, transference, from *metapherein,* to transfer : *meta-* (involving change) + *pherein,* to bear.] —**met·a·phor·ic** (-fórrik ‖ -fáwrik), **met·a·phor·i·cal** adj. —**met·a·phor·i·cal·ly** adv.

met·a·phos·phate (méttə-fóss-fayt) n. The inorganic anion PO_3^-, or a compound containing it.

met·a·phos·phor·ic acid (méttə-foss-fórrik ‖ -fáwrik, -fóss-fər-ik) n. A polymeric inorganic compound, $(HPO_3)_n$, used as a dehydrating agent and in dental cements.

met·a·phrase (méttə-frayz) n. A word-for-word translation. —tr.v. **metaphrased, -phrasing, -phrases. 1.** To manipulate the wording of (a text), especially as a means of subtly altering the sense. **2.** To make a word-for-word translation of. [New Latin *metaphrasis,* from Greek, from *metaphrazein,* to translate : *meta-* (involving change) + *phrazein,* to relate, tell.] —**met·a·phras·tic** (-frástik) adj.

met·a·phrast (méttə-frast) n. One who changes a text into a different form, as by recasting prose into verse. [Middle Greek *metaphrastēs,* from Greek *metaphrazein,* to METAPHRASE.]

met·a·phys·i·cal (méttə-fízzik'l) adj. Also rare **met·a·phys·ic** (-fízzik). **1.** Of or pertaining to metaphysics. **2.** Based on speculative or abstract reasoning. **3.** Too abstract; excessively subtle: *metaphysical speculations.* **4. a.** Immaterial; incorporeal. **b.** Supernatural. **5.** Usually capital **M.** Of or designating a group of 17th-century English poets, such as John Donne, whose verse is characterised by scholarly imagery and elaborate metaphors. —n. Usually capital **M.** Any of the Metaphysical poets or their imitators. [Middle English, from Medieval Latin *metaphysicālis,* from *metaphysica,* METAPHYSICS.] —**met·a·phys·i·cal·ly** adv.

met·a·phy·si·cian (méttə-fi-zísh'n) n. One who specialises or is skilled in metaphysics.

met·a·phys·ics (méttə-fízziks) n. Used with a singular verb. Also rare **met·a·phys·ic** (-fízzik). **1.** Abbr. **met., metaph.** The branch of philosophy that systematically investigates the nature of first principles and problems of ultimate reality. Metaphysics includes the study of being (ontology) and, often, the study of the structure of the universe (cosmology). See **epistemology. 2.** Speculative or critical philosophy in general. **3.** Excessively subtle, abstract, or speculative reasoning. Used derogatorily. [Medieval Latin *metaphysica,* metaphysics, from Greek *Ta meta ta phusika,* "the (works) after the *Physics*", Aristotle's treatise on transcendental philosophy, so called because it followed his work on physics.]

met·a·pla·sia (mettə-pláyzi-ə ‖ U.S. -pláyzhi-, -pláyzhə) n. The change of cells from a normal to an abnormal state. [New Latin : META- + -PLASIA.]

met·a·plasm (méttə-plaz'm) n. **1.** Biology. Inert material in the protoplasm of a cell, such as the yolk of an egg. **2.** Grammar. The changing of a word by adding, subtracting, or transposing letters or syllables, or the changing of the word order of a sentence. [Sense 1, META- + PLASM; sense 2, Latin *metaplasmus,* transformation, from Greek *metaplasmos,* from *metaplassein,* to remould : *meta-* (change) + *plassein,* to mould.] —**met·a·plas·mic** (-plázmik) adj.

met·a·pro·tein (mettə-prō-teen, -tee-in) n. Any of various organic compounds resulting from a reaction between an acid or alkali and a protein. Metaproteins are soluble in weak acids or alkalis, and insoluble in neutral solutions.

met·a·psy·chol·o·gy (méttə-sī-kóllə·ji) n. **1.** Philosophical speculation on the origin, structure, and function of the mind, and on the relationship between the mind and objective reality. **2.** The philosophical analysis of the foundations or laws of psychology. —**met·a·psy·cho·log·i·cal** (sīk'l-ójik'l) adj.

met·a·so·ma·tism (méttə-sōmə-tiz'm) n. Also **met·a·so·ma·to·sis** (-tō-siss). Geology. Metamorphism in which chemical as well as physical changes occur as a result of reaction with external material. [META- + SOMAT(O)- + -ISM.]

met·a·sta·ble (méttə-stáyb'l) adj. Designating a relatively unstable, transient, but significant state or condition of a chemical or physical system, as of a supersaturated solution or an energetically excited atom. —**met·a·sta·bil·i·ty** (-stə-billəti) n.

me·tas·ta·sis (mi-táss-tə-siss, me-) n., pl. **-ses** (-seez). **1.** Pathology. Transmission of disease from an original site to one or more sites elsewhere in the body, as in tuberculosis or cancer. **2.** Rhetoric. A sudden transition from one point to another. **3.** A geological process, **paramorphism** (see). [New Latin, from Late Latin, transition, from Greek, from *methistanai,* to change : *meta-* (involving change) + *histanai,* to cause to stand.] —**met·a·stat·ic** (-státtik) adj.

me·tas·ta·sise, me·tas·ta·size (mi-táss-tə-sīz, me-) intr.v. **-sised, -sising, -sises.** To be transmitted, transferred, or transformed by metastasis.

met·a·tar·sal (méttə-tár-s'l) adj. Of or pertaining to the metatarsus. —n. Any of the bones of the metatarsus.

met·a·tar·sus (méttə-tár-səss) n., pl. **-si** (-sī). **1.** The middle part of the foot in humans, composed of the five bones between the toes and the tarsus, that forms the instep. **2.** A corresponding part of the hind foot in four-legged animals, or of the foot in birds.

met·a·the·ri·an (méttə-theer-i-ən) adj. Of or pertaining to the Metatheria, a group of mammals consisting of the marsupials. —n. A metatherian mammal; a marsupial.

me·tath·e·sis (mi-táthə-siss, me-) n., pl. **-ses** (-seez). **1.** Transposition within a word of letters, sounds, or syllables, as in the change from Old English *brid* to modern English *bird,* or in the confused use of *revelant* for *relevant.* **2.** Chemistry. **Double decomposition** (see). [Late Latin, from Greek, from *metatithenai,* to transpose : *meta-* (involving change) + *tithenai,* to place.] —**met·a·thet·ic** (méttə-théttik), **met·a·thet·i·cal** adj.

me·tath·e·sise, me·tath·e·size (mi-táthə-sīz) v. **-sised, -sising, -sises.** —tr. To subject to metathesis. —intr. To undergo metathesis.

met·a·tho·rax (méttə-tháwr-aks ‖ -thór-) n., pl. **-raxes** or **-thoraces** (-tháwr-ə-seez ‖ -thór-). The hindmost of the three thoracic segments of an insect, which bears the third pair of legs and the hind wings.

met·a·xy·lem (méttə-zí-lem, -ləm) n. Botany. Xylem that is differentiated after the protoxylem is distinguished by wider vessels and thickening of supporting cells. Compare **protoxylem.**

met·a·zo·an (méttə-zō-ən) n. A member of a division of the animal kingdom, the Metazoa, which includes all animals more complex than protozoans and sponges. [New Latin *Metazoa :* META- + -ZOA.] —**met·a·zo·al, met·a·zo·an, met·a·zo·ic** adj.

mete[1] (meet) tr.v. **meted, meting, metes. 1.** To distribute by or as if by measure; deal out; allot. Often used with *out: a judge meting out justice.* **2.** Archaic. To measure. —n. Archaic. A measure. [Middle English *meten,* Old English *metan.*]

mete[2] n. Rare. A boundary line or limit. Used chiefly in the phrase *metes and bounds.* [Middle English, from Old French, from Latin *meta,* boundary.]

me·tem·psy·cho·sis (méttem-sī-kō-siss, méttemp-, -si- ‖ mətém-si-)

n., pl. **-ses** (-seez). The passing of a soul into another body or form of existence, after bodily death; the transmigration of souls. [Greek *metempsukhōsis*, from *metempsukhousthai*, (of the soul) to transmigrate : *meta-* (involving transfer) + *empsukhos*, animate : *en-*, in + *psukhē*, soul.]

met·en·ceph·a·lon (métten-séffə-lon, -lən) *n., pl.* **-la** (-lə). The part of the embryonic hindbrain from which the cerebellum and the pons develop. [New Latin : MET(A)- + ENCEPHALON.] —**met·en·ce·phal·ic** (-si-fál-ik) *adj.*

me·te·or (méeti-ər, -awr) *n.* **1.** The luminous trail or streak that appears in the sky when a meteoroid, usually no larger than a grain of sand, is made incandescent by friction with the earth's atmosphere. Also called "shooting star". **2.** A meteoroid. **3.** *Obsolete.* Any atmospheric phenomenon, such as a rainbow or lightning. [Middle English, from Old French *meteore*, from Medieval Latin *meteōrum*, from Greek *meteōron*, astronomical phenomenon, from *meteōros*, high in the air : *meta-* (intensifier) + *aeirein*, to raise.] **meteor.** meteorological; meteorology.

me·te·or·ic (méeti-órrik ‖ -áwrik) *adj.* **1.** Of, pertaining to, or formed by a meteor or meteors. **2.** Resembling a meteor in speed and brilliance: *a meteoric rise to fame.* **3.** Of or pertaining to the earth's atmosphere. —**me·te·or·i·cal·ly** *adv.*

me·te·or·ite (méeti-ə-rīt) *n.* The stony or metallic object consisting of the material of a meteoroid that is large enough to survive the passage through the atmosphere and reach the Earth's surface. —**me·te·or·it·ic** (-ríttik) *adj.*

me·te·or·o·graph (méeti-ərə-graaf, -graf ‖ *U.S.* -áwrə-, -órrə-) *n.* An instrument that records simultaneously several meteorological conditions, such as temperature, barometric pressure, and moisture. [French *météorographe* : METEOR + -GRAPH.]

me·te·or·oid (méeti-ə-royd) *n.* Any of numerous celestial bodies, ranging in size from specks of dust to asteroids weighing many tons, which appear as meteors when entering the Earth's atmosphere.

me·te·or·ol·o·gy (méeti-ə-rólləji) *n. Abbr.* **met., meteor., meteorol.** The science dealing with the phenomena of the atmosphere, especially weather and weather conditions. [Greek *meteōrologia*, discussion of astronomical phenomena : *meteōron*, METEOR + -LOGY.] —**me·te·or·o·log·i·cal** (-ərə-lójik'l), **me·te·or·o·log·ic** *adj.* —**me·te·or·o·log·i·cal·ly** *adv.* —**me·te·or·ol·o·gist** (-rólləjist) *n.*

meteor shower *n.* Any group of meteors that appear together and have an apparent common origin.

me·ter¹ (méetər) *n.* Any of various devices designed to measure time, distance, speed, or intensity, or to indicate and record or regulate the amount or volume of something, such as a flow of fluid or an electric current, or the passage of time, as in a coin-operated parking meter.
~*tr.v.* **metered, -tering, -ters. 1.** To measure or regulate with a metering device. **2.** To imprint with postage or other revenue stamps by means of a postage meter or similar device: *metered mail.* [From -METER.]

meter² *U.S.* Variant of **metre**.

-meter *n. comb. form.* Indicates: **1.** A measuring device; for example, **barometer, speedometer. 2.** A line of verse having a specified number of feet; for example, **hexameter**. [New Latin *-metrum*, or French *-mètre*, both from Greek *metron*, meter, measure.]

meter maid *n. Informal.* A female traffic warden.

meth- *comb. form.* Indicates chemical compounds containing methyl; for example, **methacrylate**. [From METHYL.]

meth·ac·ry·late (meth-áckri-layt) *n.* **1.** An ester of methacrylic acid, CH_2:$C(CH_3)COOR$, R being an organic radical. It is used in the manufacture of plastics. **2.** A resin derived from methacrylic acid.

meth·a·cryl·ic acid (méthə-kríllik) *n.* A colourless liquid, CH_2:$C(CH_3)COOH$, used in the manufacture of resins and plastics.

meth·a·done hydrochloride (méthə-dōn) *n.* Also *informal* **methadone**. A synthetic organic compound, $C_{21}H_{27}NO$·HCl, used as an analgesic and in treating heroin addiction.

met·hae·mo·glo·bin (met-héemə-glóbin, me-théemə- ‖ -glóbin) *n.* A brownish-red, crystalline, organic compound formed by oxidation of haemoglobin and found in the blood after poisoning by chlorates, nitrates, ferricyanides, or after ingestion of oxidising drugs. [MET(A)- + HAEMOGLOBIN.]

meth·am·phet·a·mine (métham-féttə-min, -meen) *n.* An amine derivative, $C_{10}H_{15}N$, of amphetamine in the form of its crystalline hydrochloride as a stimulant. [METH- + AMPHETAMINE.]

me·thane (mée-thayn ‖ *chiefly U.S.* méth-ayn) *n.* An odourless, colourless, flammable gas, CH_4, that is the major constituent of natural gas. It is used as a fuel and is an important source of hydrogen and a wide variety of organic compounds. See **marsh gas**. [METH- + -ANE.]

methane series *n.* A group of hydrocarbons of similar structure, the **alkanes** *(see).*

meth·a·nol (méthə-nol ‖ -nōl) *n.* A colourless, flammable, poisonous liquid, CH_3OH, used as an antifreeze, general solvent, fuel, and denaturant for ethanol. Also called "methyl alcohol", "wood alcohol", "wood spirit". [METHAN(E) + -OL.]

me·theg·lin (me-thégglin) *n.* A kind of spiced mead. [Welsh *meddyglyn* : *meddyg*, medicinal, from Latin *medicus*, MEDICAL + *llyn*, alcoholic liquor.]

me·the·na·mine (me-théenə-meen, -mīn, -min) *n. Chemistry.* **Hexamine** *(see).*

me·thinks (mi-thíngks) *v.* Past tense **me·thought** (mi-tháwt). *Archaic.* It seems to me. [Middle English *me thinketh*, Old English *mē*

thyncth (impersonal) : *mē*, ME + *thyncth*, third person singular present of *thyncan*, to seem.]

me·thi·o·nine (me-thí-ə-neen, mə-, -nīn) *n.* An essential amino acid, $C_5H_{11}NO_2S$, used as a dietary supplement and in pharmaceuticals.

meth·od (méthəd) *n.* **1.** A means or manner of procedure; especially, a regular and systematic way of accomplishing anything. **2.** Orderly and systematic arrangement; orderliness. **3.** *Often plural.* The procedures and techniques characteristic of a particular discipline or field of knowledge. —**the Method.** A system of acting formulated by Stanislavsky, in which the actor recalls emotion and reactions from his past experience and utilises them in the role he is playing. Also used adjectivally: *a Method actor.* [French *méthode*, from Latin *methodus*, from Greek *methodos*, "a going after", pursuit (as of knowledge) : *met(a)-*, after + *hodos*, road, journey.]
Synonyms: method, system, routine, manner, mode, way.

me·thod·i·cal (mi-thóddik'l, me-, mə-) *adj.* Also **me·thod·ic** (-thóddik). **1.** Arranged or proceeding in regular, systematic order. **2.** Characterised by ordered and systematic habits or behaviour. —See Synonyms at **orderly.** —**me·thod·i·cal·ly** *adv.* —**me·thod·i·cal·ness** *n.*

meth·od·ise, meth·od·ize (méthə-dīz) *tr.v.* **-ised, -ising, -ises.** To reduce to or organise according to a method; systematise. —**meth·od·i·sa·tion** (-dī-záysh'n ‖ *U.S.* -di-) *n.* —**meth·od·is·er** *n.*

Meth·od·ism (méthə-diz'm) *n.* The beliefs, worship, and system of organisation of the Methodists.

Meth·od·ist (méthə-dist) *n. Abbr.* **Meth.** A member of any of various Nonconformist Protestant Christian denominations having an evangelistic theology based on the teachings of John and Charles Wesley and others in the early 18th century, and characterised by an emphasis on Arminian doctrines of free grace and on individual responsibility. [From METHOD; Wesley's early followers at Oxford were apparently contemptuously described as methodical in their devotions.] —**Meth·od·ist, Meth·od·is·tic** (-dístik), **Meth·od·is·ti·cal** *adj.*

meth·od·ol·o·gy (méthə-dólləji) *n., pl.* **-gies. 1.** The system of principles, practices, and procedures applied to any specific branch of knowledge. **2.** The philosophical study of scientific method; the branch of logic dealing with the general principles of the formation of knowledge. —**meth·od·o·log·i·cal** (-də-lójik'l) *adj.* —**meth·od·o·log·i·cal·ly** *adv.*

methought. Past tense of **methinks**.

meth·ox·ide (meth-óksīd) *n.* A methylate.

meths (meths) *n. Informal.* Methylated spirits.

me·thu·se·lah (mə-théw-zə-lə, mi-, -thóo-) *n.* **1.** A champagne bottle holding the equivalent of eight standard bottles. **2.** An extremely old man. [After METHUSELAH.]

Methuselah. A Biblical patriarch said to have lived for 969 years, Genesis 5:27.

meth·yl (méthil, mée-thīl) *n.* The univalent organic radical CH_3, derived from methane, and occurring in many important organic compounds. [French *méthyle*, back-formation from *méthylène*, METHYLENE.] —**me·thyl·ic** (mə-thíllik) *adj.*

methyl acetate *n.* An organic compound, CH_3COOCH_3, used as a paint remover, general solvent, and in the manufacture of perfumes.

meth·yl·al (méthi-lal) *n.* A colourless flammable liquid, $CH_2(OCH_3)_2$, used in the manufacture of perfumes, adhesives, and protective coatings.

methyl alcohol *n.* **Methanol** *(see).*

meth·yl·a·mine (mee-thí-lə-meen, mə-thíllə-, méthi-lə-méen) *n.* A flammable gas, CH_3NH_2, produced by the decomposition of organic matter, and synthesised for use as a solvent and in the manufacture of many products, such as dyes and insecticides.

meth·yl·ate (méthi-layt) *n.* An organic compound in which the hydrogen of the hydroxyl group (OH) of methanol is replaced by a metal. Also called "methoxide".
~*tr.v.* **methylated, -lating, -lates. 1.** To mix or combine with methanol. **2.** To combine with the methyl radical. —**meth·yl·a·tion** (-láysh'n) *n.*

meth·yl·at·ed spirits (méthi-laytid) *pl.n. Sometimes singular.* A denatured form of ethanol containing methanol, pyridine, and a violet dye. Also informally called "meths".

methyl chloride *n.* An explosive gas, CH_3Cl, used in organic synthesis and polymerisation, as a refrigerant, and as an anaesthetic.

meth·yl·ene (méthi-leen) *n.* A bivalent organic radical, CH_2, a component of unsaturated hydrocarbons. [French *méthylène* : Greek *methu*, wine, mead + *hulē*, wood + -ENE.]

methylene blue *n.* An organic compound, $C_{16}H_{18}ClN_3S$·$23H_2O$, the dark green crystals or powder of which forms a deep-blue solution when dissolved in water. It is used to treat the accumulation of methaemoglobin induced by drugs and as a bacteriological stain.

methyl ethyl ketone *n. Chemistry.* **Butanone** *(see).*

methyl methacrylate *n.* A colourless liquid, CH_2:$C(CH_3)COOCH_3$, that is used as a monomer in plastics.

meth·yl·naph·tha·lene (mée-thil-náp-thə-leen, méthil-, -náf-) *n.* An organic compound, $C_{10}H_7CH_3$, obtained from coal tar in two isomeric forms, one a liquid, the other a solid. The liquid is used to standardise diesel fuels, the solid for insecticides, and both are used in organic synthesis.

me·thyl·prop·ane (mée-thil-prô-payn, méthil-) *n.* A gaseous hydrocarbon, $CH_3C_3H_7$; an isomer of **butane** *(see).*

met·ic (méttik) *n.* In ancient Greece, an alien enjoying certain rights of citizenship in the city where he resided. [Greek *metoikos* : META- + *oikos*, house.]

me·tic·u·lous (mi-tíckew-ləss, me-) *adj.* **1.** Extremely careful and precise. **2.** Excessively concerned with details; overscrupulous. [Latin *meticulōsus*, over concerned, fearful : *metus†*, fear + *(per)īculōsus*, perilous, from *perīculum*, PERIL.] —**me·tic·u·los·i·ty** (-lóssəti), **me·tic·u·lous·ness** *n.*

    Synonyms: meticulous, conscientious, scrupulous, fastidious, punctilious.

mé·ti·er (máyti-ay, métti-; *French* mayt-yáy) *n.* **1.** An occupation, trade, or profession; especially, the work for which one is especially suited. **2.** One's special interest, talent, or strong point; a speciality. [French, from Old French *mestier*, from Vulgar Latin *misterium* (unattested), from Latin *ministerium*, trade, service.]

mé·tis (may-téess, me-) *n., pl.* **métis** (*pronounced as singular*). *Feminine* **mé·tisse** (-téess). *Sometimes capital* **M. 1.** A person of mixed American Indian and French-Canadian ancestry. **2.** Any person of mixed descent. [Canadian French, from Old French *metis*, mongrel, from Vulgar Latin *mixtīcius* (unattested). See **mestizo**.]

met·oes·trus (met-éess-trəss ‖ *U.S.* -éss-) *n.* The period of sexual inactivity that follows oestrus in the female of most mammals apart from higher primates and mankind. [META- (after) + OESTRUS.]

Met Office (met) *n.* The Meteorological Office: a government department that records and studies the weather and issues weather forecasts and reports.

me·tol (mée-tol ‖ -tōl) *n.* A colourless substance, $CH_3(NH_2)C_6H_3OH$, used in photographic developers.

Me·ton·ic cycle (mi-tónnik) *n.* A period of 235 lunar months or about 19 Julian years, at the end of which the phases of the moon recur in the same order and on the same days as in the preceding cycle. [Discovered by *Meton*, Athenian astronomer of the fifth century B.C.]

met·o·nym (méttə-nim) *n.* A word or phrase used in metonymy. [Back-formation from METONYMY, after *synonym*.]

me·ton·y·my (mi-tónnim, me-) *n., pl.* **-mies.** A figure of speech in which an idea is evoked or named by means of a term designating some associated notion, for example the use of *the Law* for *the Police.* [Late Latin *metōnymia*, from Greek *metōnumia*, "substitute naming" : *meta-* (involving transfer) + *onoma*, name.] —**met·o·nym·i·cal** (méttə-nímmik'l) *adj.*

met·o·pe (méttōp, méttəpi) *n. Architecture.* The space between any two triglyphs on a Doric frieze. [Latin *metopa*, from Greek *metopē*, area between two beam-ends : *meta*, between + *opē*, opening.]

me·top·ic (mi-tóppik) *adj. Anatomy.* Of or pertaining to the forehead. [Greek *metōpikos*, from *metōpon*, forehead.]

me·tre¹, *U.S.* **me·ter** (méetər) *n. Abbr.* **m.** The fundamental unit of length (equivalent to 39.37 inches) in the metric system. It is defined (1960) as the length equal to 1,650,763.73 wavelengths in a vacuum of the orange-red light emitted by krypton-86 in a discharge tube. [French *mètre*, from Greek *metron*, measure.]

metre², *U.S.* **meter** *n.* **1. a.** The measured rhythm characteristic of verse. **b.** A specified rhythmic pattern of verse, usually determined by the number and kinds of metric units in a typical line. See **foot** (prosody). **2.** *Music. Chiefly U.S.* Time. See Synonyms at **rhythm.** [Middle English *meter*, *metre*, from Old English *meter* and Old French *metre*, from Latin *metrum*, measure, from Greek *metron*.]

    Usage: British English uses the spelling *metre* for the senses "rhythm" and "unit of length", but *meter* for any of the instruments which measure (*gas meter, speedometer,* and so on) and for the types of poetic line (*pentameter,* for example). American English uses the spelling *meter* in all senses.

me·tre-kil·o·gram-sec·ond-am·pere system (méetər-kíllə-gram-séckənd-ám-pair) *n. Abbr.* **MKSA.** A coherent system of units for mechanics, electricity, and magnetism, using the metre, the kilogram, the second, and the ampere as basic units for length, mass, time, and current intensity. See **SI units.**

me·tre-kil·o·gram-sec·ond system (méetər-kíllə-gram-séckənd) *n. Abbr.* **mks.** A coherent system of units for mechanics, using the metre, the kilogram, and the second as basic units of length, mass, and time. See **centimetre-gram-second system.**

met·ric¹ (méttrik) *adj.* Designating, pertaining to, or using the metric system. [French *métrique,* from *mètre,* METRE (unit of length).]

met·ric² *n.* **1.** A standard of measurement. **2.** In geometry, a function defined for a coordinate system such that the distance between any two points in that system may be determined from their coordinates.

met·ri·cal (méttrik'l) *adj.* **1.** Of, pertaining to, or composed in rhythmic metre. **2.** Of, or pertaining to measurement. [From Latin *metricus,* from Greek *metrikos,* from *metron,* measure, meter.] —**met·ri·cal·ly** *adv.*

met·ri·cate (méttri-kayt) *v.* **-cated, -cating, -cates.** —*tr.* To convert to the metric system. —*intr.* To adopt the metric system.

met·ri·ca·tion (méttri-káysh'n) *n.* Conversion to the metric system of weights and measures; metrification.

metric centner *n.* A unit of mass equal to 100 kilograms.

metric grain *n.* A unit of weight, a **grain** (*see*).

metric hundredweight *n.* A unit of mass equal to 50 kilograms.

met·rics (méttriks) *n. Used with a singular verb.* The branch of prosody dealing with measure and metrical structures; the use of poetic metre: *Greek metrics.*

metric system *n.* A decimal system of weights and measures based on the metre as a unit length and the kilogram as a unit mass. Derived units include the litre for liquid volume, the stere for solid volume, and the are for area. See **SI units.**

metric ton *n. Abbr.* **m.t., M.T.** A unit of mass equal to 1 000 kilograms.

met·ri·fi·ca·tion (méttri-fi-káysh'n) *n.* Metrication.

me·tri·tis (mi-trítiss) *n.* Inflammation of the uterus. [New Latin : METR(O)- + -ITIS.]

met·ro, Mét·ro (méttrō; *French* may-trŏ) *n.* The underground railway system in various cities, especially that of Paris. [French, short for *(chemin de fer) métropolitain,* "metropolitan (railway)".]

metro-, metr- *comb. form.* Indicates the uterus or things pertaining to the uterus; for example, **metritis.** [New Latin, from Greek *mētro-, mētr-,* from *mētra,* womb, uterus, from *mētēr,* mother.]

me·trol·o·gy (me-tróllǝji, mi-) *n., pl.* **-gies. 1.** The science that deals with measurement. **2.** A system of measurement. [French *métrologie,* from Greek *metrologia,* theory of measurements : *metron,* measure + -LOGY.]

met·ro·nome (méttrǝ-nōm) *n.* A device to mark time at a steady beat in adjustable intervals, used especially as an aid to keeping time when practising music. [Greek *metron,* measure + *nomos,* rule, law.] —**met·ro·nom·ic** (-nómmik) *adj.*

met·ro·nym·ic (mét-rō-nímmik, méet-, rǝ-) *n.* Also **mat·ro·nym·ic.** (mát-) A name derived from the name of one's mother or a female ancestor. [Medieval Greek *mētronumikos* : Greek *mētēr,* mother + *onoma,* name.] —**me·tro·nym·ic, ma·tro·nym·ic** *adj.*

me·trop·o·lis (mi-tróppǝliss, me-) *n., pl.* **-lises. 1.** A major city; especially, the capital, largest, or most important city of a particular country, state, or region. **2.** A large urban centre of culture, trade, or other activity. **3.** The chief see of a metropolitan bishop; especially, the main diocese of a specific ecclesiastical province. **4.** The mother city of a state or colony in ancient Greece. —**the Metropolis.** *British Informal.* London. [Late Latin *mētropolis,* from Greek : *mētēr,* mother + *polis,* city.]

met·ro·pol·i·tan (méttrǝ-póllitǝn) *adj. Abbr.* **met. 1. a.** Of, pertaining to, or characteristic of a metropolis. **b.** Making up a metropolis. **2.** Pertaining to or constituting the home territory of a sovereign state, as distinguished from its dependencies, protectorates, or overseas territories and provinces: *metropolitan France.* **3.** Of or pertaining to a metropolitan. **4.** *Often capital* **M.** Of or pertaining to London: *the Metropolitan Police.*
    ~*n.* **1.** In the Roman Catholic and other episcopal churches, an archbishop who has authority over bishops. **2.** In the Eastern Orthodox Church, a bishop ranking just below the patriarch, who serves as the head of an ecclesiastical province. [Middle English, from Late Latin *mētropolītānus,* from Greek *mētropolītēs,* a citizen of a METROPOLIS.]

metropolitan county *n.* Any of the six urban areas established in England (1974–97) as units of local government on a par with counties. They were: Greater Manchester, Merseyside, South Yorkshire, Tyne and Wear, West Midlands, and West Yorkshire.

me·tror·rha·gi·a (méet-raw-ráyji-ǝ, mét-, -rǝ-) *n.* An abnormal haemorrhage of the uterus, especially between menstrual flows. [New Latin : METRO- + -RRHAGIA.]

-metry *n. comb. form.* Indicates the science or process of measuring; for example, **calorimetry, photometry.** [Middle English *-metrie,* from Old French *-metrie,* from Latin *-metria,* from Greek, from *metron,* meter, measure.]

Met·ter·nich (méttǝr-nikh), **Klemens Wenzel Nepomuk Lothar, Fürst von** (1773–1859). Austrian statesman. In 1809 he became the Austrian foreign minister and helped form the Quadruple Alliance which ultimately defeated Napoleon. For the next 30 years he upheld Austrian rule in Italy.

met·tle (métt'l) *n.* **1.** Inherent quality of character and temperament. **2.** Courage and fortitude; spirit: *show one's mettle in combat.* —See Synonyms at **courage.** —**on (one's) mettle.** Ready to put one's spirit, courage, or energy to the test. [Middle English *metel,* fortitude, metal, variant of *metal,* METAL.]

met·tled (métt'ld) *adj.* Mettlesome; full of mettle.

met·tle·some (métt'l-sǝm) *adj.* Full of mettle; high-spirited; plucky. See Synonyms at **brave.**

Metz (mets; *French* mess). Capital of Moselle département, northeast France. Situated on the river Moselle, it is a cultural and market centre in a fertile agricultural and wine-producing area and at the heart of the Lorraine iron and steel region.

meu·nière (mǝn-yáir, mŏn-) *adj.* Designating a fish dish, or a style of cooking fish, in which the fish is lightly coated with flour and fried in butter, and served with melted butter, lemon juice, and parsley. [French (*à la*) *meunière,* (in the manner of) miller's wife.]

Meuse (merz ‖ mewz; *French* mŏz). *Dutch* **Maas** (maass). River of western Europe. Rising in the Plateau de Langres, northeast France, it flows through Belgium and The Netherlands, entering the North Sea by the Rhine delta.

MeV mega electronvolts.

mew¹ (mew) *n.* **1.** A cage for hawks, especially when moulting. **2.** A secret place; a hideaway.
    ~*v.* **mewed, mewing, mews.** —*tr.* To confine in a cage or as if in a cage. Often followed by *up.* —*intr. Archaic.* To moult. Used of a hawk. [Middle English *mewe,* hawk cage, from Old French *mue,* a moulting, from *muer,* to moult, from Latin *mūtāre,* to change.]

mew² *n.* **1.** The crying sound of a cat; a meow. **2.** Any similar sound.
    ~*v.* **mewed, mewing, mews.** —*intr.* To emit a mew. —*tr.* To express by means of a mew. [Middle English *mewen* (imitative).]

mew³ *n.* A sea bird, *Larus canus,* one of the gulls. It is found in northern Eurasia and western North America. [Middle English *mew*, Old English *mǣw*, from Germanic *mai(g)wiz* (unattested).]

mewl (mewl) *n.* A whimper or weak cry.
~*v.* **mewled, mewling, mewls.** —*intr.* To cry weakly; emit a mewl. —*tr.* To express by means of a mewl. [Imitative.]

mews (mewz) *n., pl.* **mews. 1.** A small street behind a residential street, formerly containing private stables for town houses, now mostly converted into small houses and flats. **2.** Such a house or flat, or a row of such houses or flats. [After the *Mews* at Charing Cross, London, medieval royal stables built on a site previously used for hawk cages, plural of MEW (cage).]

Mex·i·can (méksikən) *n.* A native or inhabitant of Mexico.
~*adj. Abbr.* **Mex.** Of or pertaining to Mexico or to its inhabitants, their language, or their culture.

Mexican hairless *n.* A small dog of a breed of unknown origin, found in Mexico, having a smooth almost hairless body.

Mexican War *n.* A war between the United States and Mexico (1846–48) settled by the Treaty of Guadalupe Hidalgo.

Mexican wave *n.* A show of enthusiasm among spectators at a sporting event, consisting of the concerted rising and sitting of successive sections of the crowd, giving a ripple effect around the stadium. Used by spectators at the football World Cup in Mexico in 1986.

Mex·i·co, United States of (méksi-kō). *Spanish* **Estados Unidos Mexicanos** or **Méjico** (mekhi-kō). Central American republic. Three-quarters of it lies above 500 metres (1,640 feet), the Sierra Madre ranges flanking a central plateau. Half the land is too dry for crops, but farming is the chief occupation, with maize the main crop. Tourism and fishing are also important. Large mineral deposits, including iron ore, oil, natural gas, and some coal, give Mexico great industrial potential, and it has established iron and steel, vehicle, engineering, textile, and fertiliser plants. Mexico's Indian civilisations included the Maya, Toltec, and finally the Aztec, conquered by Hernán Cortés (1521). Mexico, the nucleus of New Spain (Nueva España), achieved independence only after a struggle (1810–20). It lost its territory north of the Rio Grande to the United States after the war of 1846–48. Internal strife finally erupted in revolution (1910–17), and the present constitution was adopted. Since 1930 the republic has been one of Latin America's most stable countries. Area, 1 958 201 square kilometres (756,066 square miles). Population, 96,580,000. Capital, Mexico City.

Mexico City *Spanish* **Ciudad de México.** The capital and largest city of Mexico. It lies on the southern edge of the earthquake-prone central plateau at about 2 380 metres (7,800 feet), on the site of the Aztec city of Tenochtitlán, destroyed by Cortés (1521). An earthquake in 1985 ruined much of the city and killed more than 7,000 people. The city is a centre of industry, commerce, finance and culture, with much Spanish colonial and modern architecture, and it is a major tourist attraction.

Mey·er·beer (mí̄-ər-beer, -bair), **Giacomo,** born Jakob Liebmann Beer (1791–1864). German composer. He worked mainly in France, and wrote operas such as *Les Huguenots* (1836).

Mey·er·hof (mí̄-ər-hōf), **Otto** (1884–1951). German physiologist. He studied oxygen consumption in muscle tissues, and was awarded the Nobel prize in physiology or medicine, with A.V. Hill, in 1922.

Mey·nell (ménn'l, máyn'l), **Alice (Christiana Gertrude),** born Alice Thompson (1847–1922). English poet, whose work includes *Preludes* (1875) and the essays *The Second Person Singular* (1921).

me·ze (mé-ze ‖ -záy, máy-zay), **me·zes** (-s, -z), **me·ze·des** (mézze-des, -dez) *pl. n.* A Greek, Turkish, or Near Eastern meal consisting of a variety of cold and hot savoury regional dishes. [Modern Greek *mezes*, from Turkish *meze*, snack, appetiser, perhaps from regional Arabic.]

me·ze·re·on (mə-zéer-i-ən) *n.* **1.** A shrub, *Daphne mezereum*, native to Eurasia, having fragrant lilac-purple flowers and small scarlet fruit. **2.** A bark, mezereum. [Middle English *mizerion*, from Medieval Latin *mezereon*, from Arabic *māzaryūn*.]

me·ze·re·um (mə-zéer-i-əm) *n.* **1.** A shrub, the mezereon. **2.** The dried bark of certain shrubs of the genus *Daphne*, once used externally as a vesicant (blistering agent) and internally for arthritis. [New Latin, variant of Medieval Latin *mezereon*, MEZEREON.]

me·zu·zah, me·zu·za (mə-zŌ͡O-zə, -zŌ͡O-) *n., pl.* **mezuzoth** (-zot, -zəss) or **-zahs.** *Judaism.* A small piece of parchment inscribed with the Biblical passages Deuteronomy 6:4–9 and 11:13–21 and marked with the word "Shaddai", a name for God. The parchment is rolled up in a container and affixed to a door frame as a sign that a Jewish family lives within. [Hebrew *məzūzāh*, "doorpost".]

mez·za·nine (mét-sə-neen, mézzə-, -néen) *n.* **1.** A partial storey situated between two main storeys of a building, especially one between the ground and first floors. **2.** *British.* A floor beneath a theatre stage. **3.** *U.S.* The lowest balcony in a theatre or its first few rows. [French, from Italian *mezzanino,* from *mezzano,* middle, from Latin *mediānus,* MEDIAN.]

mez·zo (mét-sō, méd-zō) *n., pl.* **-zos.** A mezzo-soprano.

mez·zo-re·lie·vo (mét-sō-ri-léevō, méd-zō-) *n., pl.* **-vos.** Also *Italian* **mez·zo-ri·lie·vo** (mét-sō-ril-yáyvō, méd-zō-) *pl.* **-vi** (-vee). Sculptural relief in which the modelled forms project about halfway from the background. Also called "demirelief", "half relief". [Italian *mezzorilievo* : *mezzo,* half + *rilievo,* relief, from *rilevare,* to raise.]

mez·zo-so·pran·o (mét-sō-sə-práanō, méd-zō- ‖ -pránnō) *n., pl.* **-os** or **-prani** (-práanee ‖ -pránnee). **1.** A voice or voice part having a range between soprano and contralto. **2.** A woman having such a voice. [Italian : *mezzo,* half + SOPRANO.]

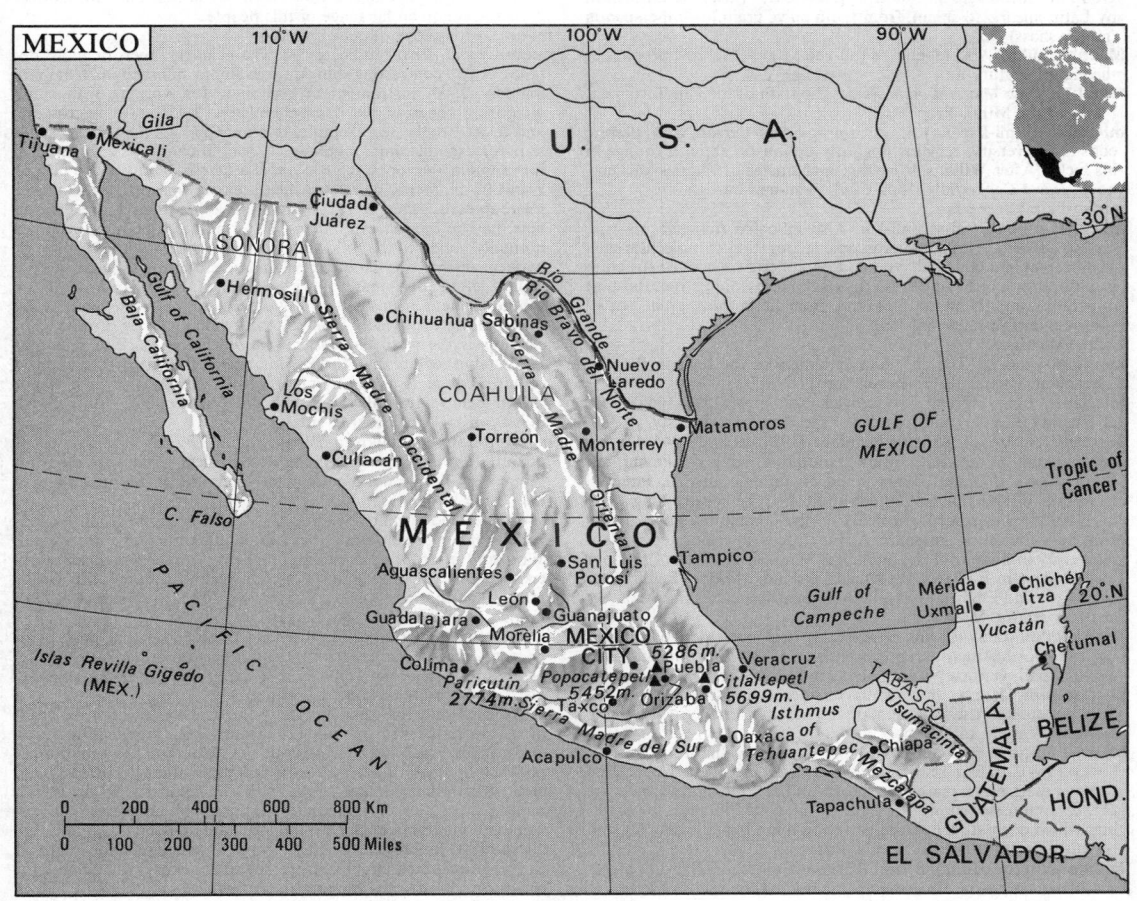

mez·zo·tint (mét-sō-tint, méd-zō-) *n.* **1.** A method of engraving a copper plate by scraping and burnishing areas to produce effects of light and shadow. **2.** A print made from a plate so treated. *~tr.v.* **mezzotinted, -tinting, -tints.** To engrave (a metal plate) using the method of mezzotint. [Italian *mezzotinto* : *mezzo,* half + *tinto,* tint, from Latin *tingere* (past participle stem *tinctus*), to TINT.]

mF millifarad.

MF, M.F. medium frequency.

m.f. *Music.* mezzo-forte.

mfg. manufacture; manufactured; manufacturing.

MFH Master of Foxhounds.

mfr. manufacture; manufacturer.

mg milligram.

Mg The symbol for the element magnesium.

mgr. manager.

Mgr. **1.** manager. **2.** Monseigneur; Monsignor.

mH millihenry.

MHA Member of the House of Assembly (in Australia).

MHD magnetohydrodynamics.

MHG Middle High German.

mho (mō) *n., pl.* **mhos.** *Electricity.* A unit of conductance; a **siemens** *(see).* [Backward spelling of OHM.]

MHR Member of the House of Representatives (in Australia).

MHz megahertz.

mi. *Music.* Variant of **me.**

MI Military Intelligence.

mi. **1.** mile. **2.** mill (monetary unit).

Mi·am·i[1] (mī-ámmi || *U.S. also* -ámmə) *n., pl.* **-is** or collectively **Miami.** A member of an Algonquian North American Indian people who lived in what is now Ohio, Indiana, Illinois, and Wisconsin. **—Mi·am·i** *adj.*

Miami[2] A city and port in southeast Florida, United States. It grew in the 1920s land boom and is now a famous holiday resort and cruise centre for the Caribbean.

miaou, miaow. Variants of **meow.**

mi·as·ma (mi-áz-mə, mī-) *n., pl.* **-mas** or **-mata** (-mətə). **1. a.** A poisonous atmosphere formerly thought to rise from swamps and putrid matter and cause disease. **b.** A thick, vaporous atmosphere: *a miasma around the factory.* **2.** Any noxious atmosphere or influence: *a miasma of evil.* [New Latin, from Greek, from *miainein,* to pollute.] **—mi·as·mal** (-məl), **mi·as·mat·ic** (mée-əz-máttik, mī-), **mi·as·mic** *adj.*

Mic. Micah (Old Testament).

mi·ca (mīkə) *n.* Any of a group of chemically and physically related complex mineral silicates, common in igneous and metamorphic rocks, occurring as thin flaky sheets. The two main members of the group are muscovite and biotite. [New Latin (meaning influenced by Latin *micāre,* to shine), from Latin *mīca,* grain.] **—mi·ca·ceous** (mī-káyshəss) *adj.*

Mi·cah[1] (mīkə). Also **Mi·che·as** (mī-kée-əss). A Hebrew prophet of the eighth century B.C.

Micah[2] *n.* Also **Micheas** *Abbr.* **Mic.** The sixth of the Old Testament books of the Minor Prophets.

mi·caw·ber (mi-káwbər) *n.* An improvident person who, despite constant adversity, remains doggedly optimistic about a change in his luck. [After Wilkins *Micawber,* a character in Charles Dickens' novel *David Copperfield* (1849–50).] **—mi·caw·ber·ish** *adj.*

mice. Plural of **mouse.**

mi·celle, mi·cell (mi-sél, mī-) *n.* Also **mi·cel·la** (mi-séllə, mī-) *pl.* **-cellae** (-séllee). **1.** A submicroscopic aggregation of molecules such as a droplet in a colloidal system. **2.** A coherent strand or structure in natural or synthetic fibres. **3.** A submicroscopic structural unit of protoplasm. [New Latin *micella,* from Latin *mīca,* grain, MICA.] **—mi·cel·lar** (mi-séllər, mī-) *adj.*

Mich. Michigan.

Mi·chael[1] (mīk'l). The guardian archangel of the Jews in the Old Testament. Daniel 10:13; Revelation 12:7–9.

Michael[2], born Mikhail Fyodorovich Romanov (1596–1645). Tsar of Russia (1613–45) and founder of the Romanov dynasty.

Michael I (1921–). King of Romania (1927–30 and 1940–47). He became king on the death of his grandfather, King Ferdinand, but was reduced to Crown Prince when his father, Carol II, returned from exile in 1930. On his father's abdication, he became king again in 1940. He was forced into exile by the communist government.

Mich·ael·mas (mick'l-məss) *n.* A church festival celebrated on September 29 in honour of the archangel Michael. It is one of the four quarter days in England, Wales, and Ireland. [Middle English *mychelmesse,* Old English *Michaeles mæsse* : *Michaeles,* genitive of *Michael* + *mæsse,* MASS.]

Michaelmas daisy *n.* Any of several hybrid asters derived primarily from North American species such as *A. novi-belgii,* having clusters of small, variously coloured, daisy-like flowers.

Michaelmas term *n.* In some universities, schools, or the like, the term beginning near Michaelmas; the autumn term.

Micheas. Variant of **Micah.**

Mi·chel·an·ge·lo Buo·nar·ro·ti (mīk'l-ánjə-lō bwónnə-rótti, mick'l-) (1475–1564). Italian sculptor, painter, and architect. He created some of the greatest masterpieces of world art: the marble sculpture *David,* commissioned in 1501 by the council of Florence, the paintings which decorate the ceiling of the Sistine Chapel (1508–12), and the plans for much of St. Peter's, Rome.

Mi·chel·son (mīk'l-sən), **Albert Abraham** (1852–1931). U.S. physicist, born in Prussia. He accurately measured the speed of light. He was awarded the Nobel prize for physics (1907).

Mi·chel·son-Mor·ley experiment (mīk'l-sən-mórli) *n.* An experiment performed (1887) in an attempt to detect the motion of the earth through the ether by measuring the difference in velocity of two perpendicular beams of light; no such difference was detected. This important result led to disbelief in the existence of the ether and was later explained by the theory of relativity. [After Albert Abraham MICHELSON and Edward Williams Morley (1838–1923), U.S. chemist.]

Mich·i·gan (míshi-gən). Northern state of the United States, comprising two peninsulas divided by Lake Michigan, and linked by a bridge across the Straits of Mackinac since 1957. The state is predominantly industrial, with motor manufacture, centred on Detroit, the largest city, the chief industry. Other products include iron ore, and oil and gas. French explorers reached the area in the early 17th century. It was occupied by the British (1763–96), became a territory (1805), and was admitted to the Union (1837). Lansing is the capital. **—Mich·i·gan·der** (-gándər) *n.* **—Mich·i·gan·ite** (-gənīt) *n.*

Michigan, Lake. The largest freshwater lake to lie wholly within the territory of the United States, it has an area of 57 757 square kilometres (22,300 square miles) and is the third largest of the Great Lakes of North America. Lake Michigan is a major trade artery, linked via the Illinois Waterway with the Mississippi and Gulf of Mexico. Ocean-going ships from the Atlantic reach it via the St. Lawrence Seaway. The ports of Gary, Chicago, and Milwaukee constitute a major industrial region.

mick (mik) *n.* Also **Mick.** *Slang.* **1.** An Irishman. **2.** A Roman Catholic. In both senses, used derogatorily. [From *Mick,* nickname for *Michael.*]

mick·ey (mícki) *n.* **—take the mickey.** To tease; poke fun at. [20th century : origin obscure.]

Mickey Finn *n.* *Slang.* **1.** An alcoholic drink that is surreptitiously drugged to stupefy, render unconscious, or otherwise incapacitate the drinker. **2.** The drug used for this purpose. Also called "Mickey". [20th century : origin obscure.]

mickey mouse *adj.* **1.** Not serious; childish. **2.** Insubstantial; of little worth: *mickey mouse money.* [After a mouse character in the cartoons of Walt Disney.]

mick·le (mick'l) *adj.* Also **muck·le** (múck'l). *Scottish.* Great. *~adv.* Also **muck·le.** *Scottish.* Greatly. *~n.* *Chiefly Scottish.* Also **muckle** (for sense 2). **1.** A small amount. Used chiefly in the proverb *Many a mickle makes a muckle.* **2.** A large amount: *Many a pickle makes a mickle.* [Middle English *mikell,* from Old Norse *mikill,* replacing Old English *micel,* MUCH.]

Mic·mac (mík-mak) *n., pl.* **-macs** or collectively **Micmac.** **1.** A member of an Algonquian North American Indian people formerly inhabiting the areas that are now Nova Scotia and New Brunswick. **2.** The Algonquian language of this people.

mi·cra. Alternative plural of **micron.**

micro– *comb. form.* Indicates: **1.** The smaller, inner, or more detailed of two contrasting things; for example, **microcosm.** Compare **macro–.** **2.** An instrument or technique for working with small quantities; for example, **microchemistry. 3.** Use of a microscope and related tools; for example, **microscopy. 4.** Abnormally small size; for example, **microcephaly. 5.** Amplification or enlargement; for example, **microphone. 6.** *Symbol* μ One-millionth (10⁻⁶) part of a unit in the metric or related measurement systems; for example, **microampere.** *Note:* Many compounds other than those entered here may be formed with *micro-.* In forming compounds, *micro-* is normally joined to the following word or element without space or hyphen: *micrometer.* However, if the second element begins with a capital letter, it is separated with a hyphen: *micro-America.* If the second element begins with *o,* a hyphen is normally used, but as the compound grows widely familiar, the hyphen may be dropped. An example is the word *microorganism,* which the usage of scientists has established in that form. This prefix is usually pronounced (mīkrō); there is a less frequent variant (mīckrō), which is not shown below. [Middle English, from Latin *mīcro-,* from Greek *mikro-, mikr-,* from *mikros,* small.]

mi·cro·a·nal·y·sis (mīkrō-ə-nál-ə-siss) *n.* *Chemistry.* The analysis of quantities weighing one milligram or less. **—mi·cro·an·a·lyst** (-ánnə-list) *n.* **—mi·cro·an·a·lyt·ic** (-ánnə-líttik), **mi·cro·an·a·lyt·i·cal** (-ánnə-líttik'l) *adj.*

mi·cro·bal·ance (mīkrō-bal-ənss) *n.* A very accurate balance capable of weighing quantities of between a milligram and a microgram.

mi·crobe (mī-krōb) *n.* A minute life form; a microorganism, especially one that causes disease. Not in technical usage. See Usage note at **germ.** [MICRO– + Greek *bios,* life.] **—mi·cro·bi·al** (mī-krōbi-əl), **mi·cro·bic** (mī-krōbik) *adj.*

mi·cro·bi·ol·o·gy (mīkrō-bī-óllə)ji) *n.* The science that deals with microorganisms, and especially their effects on other forms of life. **—mi·cro·bi·o·log·i·cal** (-bī-ə-lójik'l) *adj.* **—mi·cro·bi·o·log·i·cal·ly** *adv.* **—mi·cro·bi·ol·o·gist** (-bī-ólləjist) *n.*

mi·cro·ceph·a·ly (mīkrō-séffəli) *n.* Abnormal smallness of the head, often associated with pathological mental conditions. [Greek *mikrokephalos,* small-headed : MICRO– + -CEPHALOUS.] **—mi·cro·ce·phal·ic** (-si-fál-ik) *n. & adj.* **—mi·cro·ceph·a·lous** (-séffələss) *adj.*

mi·cro·chem·is·try (mīkrō-kémmi-stri) *n.* Chemistry that deals with minute quantities of materials, weighing one milligram or less. Compare **macrochemistry. —mi·cro·chem·i·cal** *adj.*

mi·cro·chip (mīkrō-chip) *n.* A chip of semiconductor material carrying integrated circuits, especially one having logic circuits for computing. **—mi·cro·chipped** (-chipt) *adj.*

mi·cro·cir·cuit (mĭkrō-surkit) *n.* A very small electronic circuit, especially one using small integrated circuits on semiconductor chips. —**mi·cro·cir·cuit·ry** (-súrkitri) *n.*

mi·cro·cli·mate (mĭkrō-klī-mit, -mət) *n.* The climate of a specific place within an area, rather than that of the area as a whole. Compare **macroclimate**. —**mi·cro·cli·mat·ic** (-klī-máttik) *adj.*

mi·cro·cli·ma·tol·o·gy (mĭkrō-klīmə-tólləji) *n.* The scientific study of microclimates. —**mi·cro·cli·ma·to·log·ic** (-tə-lójik) **mi·cro·cli·ma·to·log·i·cal** *adj.*

mi·cro·cline (mĭkrō-klīn) *n.* A mineral of the feldspar group, potassium aluminium silicate KAlSi₃O₈, used in making pottery. [German *Mikroklin* : MICRO- + CLINE.]

mi·cro·coc·cus (mĭkrō-kóckəss) *n., pl.* -cocci (-kók-sī, -kóckī). A bacterium of any of several species of the genus *Micrococcus*, containing gram positive, spherical cells that occur in irregular clusters.

mi·cro·com·pu·ter (mĭkrō-kəm-pewtər ‖ -kom-) *n.* A small computer consisting of a microprocessor and input and output devices such as a visual display unit, usually with external memory.

mi·cro·cop·y (mĭkrō-koppi) *n., pl.* -ies. A greatly reduced photographic copy, usually reproduced by projection.

mi·cro·cosm (mĭkrō-koz'm, mĭkrə-) *n.* 1. A diminutive, representative system more or less analogous to a much larger system in constitution, configuration, or development: *The council meeting is a microcosm of British democracy.* 2. The human race or any specific person, community, or the like regarded as the epitome of the universe. Compare **macrocosm**. [Middle English *microcosme,* from Medieval Latin *mīcro(s)cosmus,* from Greek *mikros kosmos,* small world : MICRO- + COSMOS.] —**mi·cro·cos·mic** (-kózmik), **mi·cro·cos·mi·cal** (-kózmik'l) *adj.*

microcosmic salt *n.* A white solid, ammonium sodium hydrogen phosphate, obtained from human urine and used in bead tests on metal oxides.

mi·cro·crys·tal·line (mĭkrō-kríst'l-īn, -ĭn, -een) *adj.* Designating a solid substance that consists of microscopic crystals.

mi·cro·cyte (mĭkrō-sīt, mĭkrə-) *n.* An abnormally small red blood cell, less than five microns in diameter. [MICRO- + (ERYTHRO)CYTE.]

mi·cro·dot (mĭkrō-dot) *n.* A piece of text reduced in size to a small dot, typically used for secret messages.

mi·cro·e·co·nom·ics (mĭkrō-éekə-nómmiks, -éckə-) *n. Used with a singular verb.* The study of the economics of small-scale systems such as individuals, families, companies, and the production and selling of particular commodities. Compare **macroeconomics**.

mi·cro·e·lec·tron·ics (mĭkrō-i-lek-trónniks, -ee-, -e-) *n. Used with a singular verb.* The branch of electronics that deals with components of miniature size. —**mi·cro·e·lec·tron·ic** *adj.*

mi·cro·fiche (mĭkrō-feesh, -fish) *n., pl.* -fiches or microfiche. A sheet of microfilm, usually measuring 10 by 15 centimetres (4 by 6 inches), capable of accommodating and preserving a considerable number of book pages in reduced form. Also called "fiche".
~*tr.v.* microfiched, -fiching, -fiches. To record on microfiche. [French : MICRO- + *fiche,* slip of paper.]

mi·cro·fil·ar·i·a (mĭkrō-fi-laír-i-ə) *n., pl.* -ariae (-i-ee). A slender larval form of a filaria, often found in the blood of people infected with filariae.

mi·cro·film (mĭkrə-film, mĭkrō-) *n.* 1. A film upon which documents are photographed greatly reduced in size. 2. A reproduction on microfilm.
~*tr.v.* microfilmed, -filming, -films. To reproduce (documents or other materials) on microfilm.

mi·cro·form (mĭkrə-fawrm, mĭkrō-) *n.* Any arrangement of images reduced in size, as on microfilm or microfiche.

mi·cro·ga·mete (mĭkrō-gámmeet, -gə-méet) *n. Biology.* The smaller of a pair of conjugating gametes in protozoans; the male gamete. Compare **macrogamete**.

mi·cro·ga·met·o·cyte (mĭkrō-gə-méetə-sīt) *n.* A cell that divides to produce microgametes in protozoa.

mi·cro·graph (mĭkrō-graaf, -graf) *n.* 1. A photograph or drawing of an object enlarged by a microscope. 2. A device for producing very small writing or engraving. [MICRO- + -GRAPH.]

mi·crog·ra·phy (mĭ-króggrəfi) *n.* 1. The representation, study, or description of microscopic objects. 2. The writing or engraving of very small characters. Compare **macrography**. [MICRO- + -GRAPHY.] —**mi·cro·graph·ic** (mĭkrō-gráffik, mĭkrə-) *adj.*

mi·cro·groove (mĭkrō-grōōv) *n.* A narrow groove of the type used on long-playing records.

mi·cro·hab·i·tat (mĭkrō-hábbi-tat) *n.* The smallest unit of a habitat, as in a clump of grass or a space between rocks.

mi·cro·light (mĭkrō-līt) *n.* A light motorised aircraft, consisting essentially of a wing structure similar to that of a hang-glider with a suspended frame to carry one or two people.

mi·cro·lith (mĭkrō-lith, mĭkrə-) *n. Archaeology.* A small flint that is the remnant of a Stone Age tool or weapon. [MICRO- + -LITH.]

mi·cro·man·ip·u·la·tion (mĭkrō-mə-níppew-láysh'n) *n.* The manipulation of extremely small instruments under a microscope, as in microsurgery. —**mi·cro·man·ip·u·la·tor** (-laytər) *n.*

mi·cro·me·te·or·ite (mĭkrō-méeti-ə-rīt) *n.* A very small meteorite, typically having a diameter of a few micrometres.

mi·cro·me·te·or·ol·o·gy (mĭkrō-méeti-ə-róllaji) *n.* The study of meteorological conditions in a small region, usually a shallow layer up to about 100 metres (110 yards) above ground in which temperature and humidity extremes are found. —**mi·cro·me·te·or·o·log·i·cal** (-rə-lójik'l) *adj.* —**mi·cro·me·te·or·o·lo·gist** (-róllajist) *n.*

mi·crom·e·ter (mī-krómmitər) *n.* Any device for measuring minute distances, especially an instrument (*micrometer gauge*) based on the rotation of a finely threaded screw. [French *micromètre* : MICRO- + -METER.]

micrometer screw *n.* A screw that has a fine, accurately cut thread, used in a micrometer.

mi·cro·me·tre (mĭkrō-meetər) *n.* A unit of length equal to one-millionth (10⁻⁶) of a metre. Also called "micron".

mi·crom·e·try (mī-krómmətri) *n.* Measurement with a micrometer. —**mi·cro·met·ric** (mĭkrō-méttrik), **mi·cro·met·ri·cal** *adj.* —**mi·cro·met·ri·cal·ly** *adv.*

mi·cro·min·ia·tur·ise, mi·cro·min·ia·tur·ize (mĭkrō-mínnəchər-īz, -mín-yəchər-) *tr.v.* -ised, -ising, -ises. To construct or produce very small (electronic) components using integrated circuits. —**mi·cro·min·ia·tur·i·sa·tion** (-ī-záysh'n ‖ *U.S.* -i-) *n.*

mi·cron (mí-kron) *n., pl.* -crons or -cra (-krə). Also **mi·kron**. *Symbol* μ A micrometre. Note that in technical usage *micrometre* is preferred. [New Latin, from Greek, from *mikros,* small.]

Mi·cro·ne·si·a¹ (mĭkrō-neé-zi-ə, -zhi-ə, -zhə, -si-ə, -shi-ə, -shə). A division of the Pacific islands, including Kiribati, the Caroline, Mariana, and Marshall groups and other islands. The Micronesians are people of Australoid and Polynesian stock, with light to dark brown skins and straight or slightly wavy hair. See **Melanesia, Polynesia**.

Micronesia². A country of the west Pacific comprising the Caroline Islands excluding **Palau**. The federation's 600 or so coral or volcanic islands export copra, fish products, and handicrafts, and tourism is increasing. However, most islanders, of Australoid and Polynesian origin, are subsistence farmers. The Spaniards discovered the islands (16th century). They were seized by Japan (1914), and were part of the U.N. Trust Territory of the Pacific Islands administered by the United States (1947–81). The federation is in "free association" with the United States: it is self-governing at home and in foreign affairs, but the United States is responsible for its defence. Area, 701 square kilometres (271 square miles). Population, 110,000. Capital, Palikir (on Pohnpei). See map at **Pacific Ocean**.

Mi·cro·ne·sian (mĭkrō-neé-zi-ən, -zhən, -shən) *adj.* Of or pertaining to Micronesia, its inhabitants, their languages, or their culture.
~*n.* 1. A native or inhabitant of Micronesia. 2. A subfamily of Austronesian languages spoken in Micronesia.

mi·cro·nu·cle·us (mĭkrō-néw-kli-əss ‖ -nōō-) *n., pl.* -clei (-kli-ī) or -uses. The smaller nuclear mass in protozoans, distinguished from the macronucleus in such animals and functioning in sexual reproduction. Compare **macronucleus**.

mi·cro·nu·tri·ent (mĭkrō-néw-tri-ənt ‖ -nōō-) *n.* A substance, such as a vitamin, that in minute amounts is essential to life.

mi·cro·or·gan·ism, mi·cro·or·gan·ism (mĭkrō-órgə-niz'm) *n.* An animal or plant of microscopic size, especially a bacterium or a protozoan.

mi·cro·pa·lae·on·tol·o·gy (mĭkrō-pál-i-on-tólləji, -on-) *n.* The scientific study of microscopic fossils. —**mi·cro·pa·lae·on·to·log·ic** (-tə-lójik), **mi·cro·pa·lae·on·to·log·i·cal** *adj.* —**mi·cro·pa·lae·on·tol·o·gist** (-tólləjist) *n.*

mi·cro·pas·cal (mĭkrō-pass-káa) *n. Symbol* mPa A unit of pressure equal to one thousandth of a pascal.

mi·cro·phone (mĭkrə-fōn) *n.* An instrument that converts sound waves into an electric current or voltage, usually fed into an amplifier, recorder, or broadcast transmitter. [MICRO- + -PHONE.] —**mi·cro·phon·ic** (-fónnik) *adj.*

mi·cro·pho·to·graph (mĭkrō-fótə-graaf, -graf) *n.* 1. A photograph requiring magnification for viewing. 2. A photograph on microfilm. 3. A photomicrograph. —**mi·cro·pho·to·graph·ic** (-gráffik) *adj.* —**mi·cro·pho·tog·ra·phy** (-fə-tóggrəfi) *n.*

mi·cro·phys·ics (mĭkrō-fízziks) *n. Used with a singular verb.* The physics of molecular, atomic, nuclear, and subnuclear systems. —**mi·cro·phys·i·cal** *adj.*

mi·cro·phyte (mĭkrō-fīt, mĭkrə-) *n.* Any plant of microscopic size. [MICRO- + -PHYTE.] —**mi·cro·phyt·ic** (-fíttik) *adj.*

mi·cro·print (mĭkrō-print, mĭkrə-) *n.* The printed or positive reproduction of a microphotograph.

mi·cro·pro·ces·sor (mĭkrō-prō-sessər ‖ -pró-) *n.* A small integrated circuit used as the processor in a minicomputer or microcomputer.

mi·cro·pyle (mĭkrō-pīl, mĭkrə-) *n.* 1. *Botany.* A minute opening in the ovule of a plant, through which the pollen tube usually enters. 2. *Zoology.* A pore in the membrane of the ova of some animals, through which the spermatozoon enters. [MICRO- + Greek *pulē,* gate.] —**mi·cro·py·lar** (-pílər) *adj.*

mi·cro·read·er (mĭkrō-reedər) *n.* An optical device for producing an enlarged image of microfilm, microfiche, or the like.

mi·cro·scope (mĭkrə-skōp) *n.* An optical instrument that uses a combination of lenses to produce magnified images of small objects, especially of objects too small to be seen by the unaided eye. See **simple microscope, compound microscope, electron microscope, X-ray microscope**. [New Latin *microscopium* : MICRO- + -SCOPE.]

mi·cro·scop·ic (mĭkrə-skóppik) *adj.* Also **mi·cro·scop·i·cal** (-skóppik'l). 1. Too small to be seen by the unaided eye but large enough to be studied under a microscope. 2. Exceedingly small; minute: *microscopic changes.* 3. Characterised by or done with extreme attention to detail: *conducted a microscopic investigation.* 4. Of, or pertaining to, or concerned with a microscope. 5. Like or resembling a microscope; having the ability to observe very small objects. 6. *Physics.* Involving or pertaining to the properties of individual atoms or molecules, rather than collections of atoms. In this sense, compare **macroscopic.** —**mi·cro·scop·i·cal·ly** *adv.*

Mi·cro·sco·pi·um (mīkrə-skópi-əm) *n.* A constellation in the Southern Hemisphere. [New Latin, MICROSCOPE.]

mi·cros·co·py (mī-króskəpi) *n.* **1.** Investigation employing a microscope. **2.** The study or use of microscopes. —**mi·cros·co·pist** *n.*

mi·cro·seism (míkrō-sīz'm, míkrə-) *n.* A faint, recurrent tremor of the earth's crust. —**mi·cro·seis·mic** (-síz-mik, sīss-), **mi·cro·seismi·cal** (-síz-mik'l, -síss-) *adj.*

mi·cro·some (míkrō-sōm, míkrə-) *n.* A cell particle of the smallest size, typically consisting of a piece of endoplasmic reticulum to which ribosomes are attached. [German *Mikrosom* : MICRO- + -SOME.] —**mi·cro·so·mal** (-sōm'l), **mi·cro·so·mic** (-sómmik) *adj.*

mi·cro·spo·ran·gi·um (mīkrō-spaw-rán-ji-əm, -spə-) *n.*, *pl.* **-gia** (-ji-ə). A structure or receptacle in which microspores are formed.

mi·cro·spore (míkrō-spawr, míkrə- ‖ -spōr) *n. Botany.* **1.** The smaller of two types of spores produced by heterosporous plants, such as ferns, giving rise to the male gametophyte. Compare **megaspore. 2.** A pollen grain. —**mi·cro·spor·ic** (-spórrik, -spáwrik ‖ -spōrik), **mi·cro·spo·rous** (-spáwrəss ‖ -spōrəss, mī-króspərəss) *adj.*

mi·cro·spo·ro·phyll (míkrō-spáwr-ə-fil, míkrə- ‖ -spōr-) *n.* The structure in ferns and similar plants that bears the microsporangia.

mi·cro·struc·ture (míkrō-strukchər) *n.* Microscopic structure; especially, the structure of a material as viewed under a microscope.

mi·cro·sur·ger·y (míkrō-súrjəri) *n.* Surgery involving intricate operations on relatively inaccessible parts of the body, performed through a microscope using minute instruments. —**mi·cro·sur·geon** *n.* —**mi·cro·sur·gi·cal** *adj.*

mi·cro·tome (míkrō-tōm, míkrə-) *n.* An instrument used to cut samples into very thin sections for microscopic examination.

mi·crot·o·my (mī-króttəmi) *n.* The preparation of specimens by use of a microtome. —**mi·cro·tom·ic** (míkrō-tómmik, míkrə-) *adj.*

mi·cro·tone (míkrō-tōn, míkrə-) *n. Music.* An interval smaller than a half tone.

mi·cro·vil·lus (míkrō-vílləss) *n.*, *pl.* **-vil·li** (-villī). Any of the minute, hairlike structures that project from the surface of absorptive or secretory epithelial cells, such as those of the intestinal tract.

mi·cro·wave (míkrə-wayv, míkrō-) *n.* **1.** Electromagnetic radiation having a wavelength in the approximate range from one millimetre to one metre, the region between infrared and short-wave radio wavelengths. Also used adjectivally: *microwave radiation.* **2.** A microwave oven.

~ *tr.v.* **-microwaved, -waving, -waves.** To cook or heat in a microwave oven.

microwave background *n.* Background microwave radiation throughout the universe; corresponding to black-body radiation at a temperature of 2.7K and thought to be a remnant of the big-bang origin of the universe. Also called "cosmic background".

microwave oven *n.* An oven which heats food by means of microwaves: food is heated as water molecules dissipate the energy they have absorbed from the microwaves. Also called "microwave".

mic·tu·rate (mík-tewr-ayt) *intr.v.* **-rated, -rating, -rates.** To urinate. [Latin *micturīre*, from *mingere* (past participial stem *mict*-), to urinate.] —**mic·tu·ri·tion** (-ísh'n) *n.*

mid¹ (mid) *adj.* **1.** Middle; central. **2.** Being the part in the middle or centre: *in the mid Pacific.* **3.** *Phonetics.* Pronounced with the tongue approximately intermediate between high and low, as in the (u) in *cut* or the (e) in *pet.* Said of vowel sounds.

~ *n. Archaic.* The middle. [Middle English *mid, midde,* Old English *midl.*]

mid² *prep. Chiefly Poetic.* Amid: *mid smoke and flame.*

mid– *prefix.* Indicates a middle part, time, or location; for example, **midship, midway. Note:** Many compounds other than those entered here may be formed with *mid-*. In this dictionary, in forming compounds, *mid-* is normally joined to the following word or element without space or hyphen: *midday.* However, many users prefer the hyphenated form, especially in less standardised compounds: *mid-season.* If the second element begins with a capital letter, it is always separated with a hyphen: *mid-May.* It is always advisable to separate the elements with a hyphen to avoid possible confusion with another form; for example, *mid-den* (the middle of a den) as distinct from the word *midden.* Note that the adjective **mid¹** above is a separate word, though, as with any adjective, it may be joined to another word with a hyphen when used as a unit modifier: *in the mid Pacific,* but *a mid-Pacific island.* [From MID (middle).]

mid. middle.

mid·air (mid-áir, míd-) *n.* A point or region in the middle of the air; space: *floating in midair.*

Mi·das (mí-dass, -dəss). The legendary king of Phrygia to whom Dionysus gave the power of turning to gold all that he touched.

mid-At·lan·tic (míd-ət-lántik) *adj.* **1.** Pertaining to the middle of the Atlantic Ocean. **2.** Adopting U.S. or British speech mannerisms in an attempt to impress people, ingratiate oneself, or integrate: *a mid-Atlantic accent.* **3.** Compromising between styles or tastes prevalent in the United States and Britain.

Mid Atlantic Ridge. Mountain range on the floor of the Atlantic Ocean, stretching from Iceland to the Antarctic Circle. Some of its peaks rise above sea level, forming islands such as the Azores group, Ascension, Iceland, and Tristan da Cunha. See **sea floor spreading, plate tectonics.**

mid·brain (míd-brayn) *n.* **1.** The middle region of the embryonic vertebrate brain, the **mesencephalon** *(see).* **2.** The parts that de-

velop from this region.

mid·course (mid-kórss ‖ -kōrss) *n.* The part of a spacecraft's flight between burnout and the point where final guidance is made.

mid·day (mid-day, -dáy) *n.* The middle of the day; noon.

~ *adj.* Of, pertaining to, or occurring in the middle of the day or at noon: *a midday snack.* [Middle English *midday,* Old English *middæg* : MID (middle) + *dæg,* DAY.]

mid·den (mídd'n) *n.* **1.** A dunghill or refuse heap, especially one near a dwelling. **2.** A **kitchen midden** *(see).* [Middle English *myddung,* from Old Norse *myki-dyngja* (unattested) : *myki-,* muck + *dyngja,* heap (see **dung**).]

mid·dle (mídd'l) *adj. Abbr.* **mid. 1. a.** Equally distant from extremes or limits; central; mean: *the middle point on a line.* **b.** Approximately halfway between two limits: *the middle ground.* **2.** Intermediate; in-between: *the middle piece of cake.* **3.** Medium; moderate: *"He was about the middle height."* (Charles Dickens). **4.** Intervening between an earlier and later period of time; part of a sequence or series: *the middle years.* **5.** *Capital* **M.** Designating a stage in the development of a language or literature between earlier and later stages: *Middle English.* **6.** *Logic.* Designating a term that appears in both premises of a syllogism but not in the conclusion. **7.** *Grammar.* Intermediate between active and passive voice. Said of verb forms in Sanskrit and Greek in which the subject is represented as acting on, for, or with reference to itself. **8.** Of or pertaining to the heartland or silent majority of the designated place: *Middle Britain; Middle England.*

~ *n.* **1.** An area or point equidistant between extremes; the centre: *the middle of a circle.* **2.** Something intermediate between extremes; a mean. **3.** The interior portion: *the middle of the chain.* **4.** The middle part of the human body; the waist. **5.** *Logic.* The **middle term** *(see).* **6.** *Grammar.* The middle voice.

~ *tr.v.* **middled, -dling, -dles. 1.** To place in the middle. **2.** In cricket, to hit (the ball) with the middle of the bat. **3.** *Nautical.* To fold in the middle: *middle the sail.* [Old English *middel*; Adjective sense 8 by analogy with MIDDLE AMERICA senses 1, 2.]

middle age *n.* The time of human life between youth and old age, usually reckoned as the years between 40 and 60.

mid·dle-age spread (mídd'l-áyj) *n.* Also **middle-aged spread.** Thickening of the waistline and a general gain in weight that often takes place in middle age.

mid·dle-aged (mídd'l-áyjd) *adj.* Of or pertaining to middle age.

Middle Ages *n.* **1.** The period in European history between Antiquity and the Renaissance, often dated from A.D. 476, when the last emperor of the Western Roman Empire was deposed, to A.D. 1453, when Constantinople was conquered by the Turks. **2.** The period from about A.D. 1000 to A.D. 1400. Compare **Dark Ages.**

Middle America *n.* **1.** That part of the U.S. middle class thought of as being average in income and education and conservative in values and attitudes. **2.** The American heartland, thought of as being made up of small towns, small cities, and suburbs. **3.** A division of the **Americas.** —**Middle American** *adj.*

mid·dle-brow (mídd'l-brow) *n. Informal.* A person of some education and culture, but whose interests may be considered artistically and intellectually limited or conventional. Compare **highbrow, lowbrow.** —**mid·dle-brow** *adj.*

middle C *n. Music.* The musical note represented by the first ledger line below the treble clef or the first ledger line above the bass clef. It is near the middle of a piano keyboard.

middle class *n. Often plural.* Those in society in an intermediate social and economic position between the working classes and the aristocracy. —**middle-class** (mídd'l-kláass ‖ -kláss) *adj.*

middle common room *n.* In various British universities and colleges, a common room for postgraduate students.

middle distance *n.* **1.** The area between the foreground and background in a painting, drawing, or photograph. **2.** In athletics, a division of competition in racing with events usually ranging from 800 metres to 1500 metres. —**middle-distance** *adj.*

Middle Dutch *n.* Dutch from the mid-12th century to the 15th.

middle ear *n.* The space between the tympanic membrane and the internal ear. It contains the auditory ossicles that convey vibrations to the internal ear. Also called "tympanic cavity", "tympanum". See **ear.**

Middle East *n.* Also **West Asia.** The western subcontinent of Asia. It includes only 5 per cent of the world's land and 4 per cent of its people. The region's northern mountains, enclosing high plateaus, are part of the Alpine-Himalayan system, subject to frequent earthquakes. The stabler tablelands of Arabia and Egypt are slashed by the Great Rift Valley.

The Middle East is the driest of the world's major regions by far. More than 75 per cent of it has less than 250 millimetres (about 10 inches) of rain a year, and is covered by desert, semidesert, or mountain steppe, yet some 60 per cent of its inhabitants rely on farming for a living.

Economically, oil dominates the region, which has half the world's known reserves. It produces more than 30 per cent of world crude oil. The oil states are using their vast wealth to industrialise and diversify their economies against the day when the oil wells run dry. They spend much on irrigation, welfare, and education schemes, interregional aid, and aid to other Third World countries; the Middle East shows the greatest disparity between rich and poor nations. —**Middle Eastern** *adj.*

Middle Empire *n.* The Middle Kingdom of Egypt.

Middle English *n. Abbr.* **M.E., ME., ME** English from the 12th century to the 15th. The five main dialects of Middle English were: Kentish (southeastern), Southern (southwestern), East Midland, West Midland, and Northern. See **Midland.**

Middle French *n.* French from the mid-15th century to the mid-16th.

Middle Greek *n.* Medieval Greek *(see).*

Middle High German *n.* High German from the 11th century to the 16th.

Middle Irish *n.* Irish Gaelic from the 10th century to the 15th.

Middle Island. See **South Island.**

Middle Kingdom *n.* **1.** A kingdom of ancient Egypt lasting from about 2100 to about 1600 B.C. Capitals, Heracleopolis, later Thebes. Also called "Middle Empire". **2. a.** The former Chinese empire, considered by its inhabitants to be the centre of the world. **b.** The original 18 provinces of China. Often called "China Proper".

Middle Low German *n.* Low German from the middle of the 13th century to the 16th.

mid·dle·man (mídd'l-man) *n., pl.* **-men** (-men). **1.** A trader who buys from producers and sells to retailers or consumers. **2.** An intermediary or go-between.

middle management *n.* Middle-ranking executives responsible for day-to-day running of a department.

mid·dle·most (mídd'l-mōst) *adj.* Midmost. [Middle English *middelmast : middel,* MIDDLE + *-mast,* -MOST.]

middle name *n.* **1.** A name that comes between a person's first or Christian name and surname. **2.** *Informal.* A person's most significant character trait: *Carefulness is his middle name.*

mid·dle-of-the-road (mídd'l-əv-thə-rōd) *adj. Abbr.* **M.O.R. 1.** Moderate; not extreme, as in tastes or views. **2.** Designating a type of popular music that is conventional, usually melodic, and has a wide popular appeal.

middle passage *n.* The passage of slave ships from Africa to the West Indies and America during the 16th to the 19th centuries.

Middle Persian *n.* The language of the Sassanians, from the third century A.D. to the seventh.

Mid·dles·brough (mídd'lzbrə). Industrial town and port on the south side of the Tees estuary in northeast England. Its chief products are chemicals, iron, and steel.

Mid·dle·sex (mídd'l-seks). Former county of southeast England. It was absorbed mainly by Greater London in 1965, with small areas passing to Surrey and Hertfordshire.

Middle South Asia. Also **South Asia.** The subcontinent of India. It covers only 3 per cent of the world's land, but has 20 per cent of its people, and is the world's most densely peopled region of comparable size. Its fertile Indus and Ganges plains comprise a vast alluvium-filled trough. To the south, the stable tableland of the Deccan has fertile volcanic soils, but generally, soils are poor. The rising fold mountains of Baluchistan, and the Himalayas, have the highest peaks in the world—more than 30 over 8 600 metres (28,200 feet).

The region is dominated by its monsoon climate, all but parts of the west having a wet season from June to October. Rainfall varies greatly from year to year, much of the region having periodic floods and droughts. Even so, farming is still the majority occupation. Rice is the major food crop, the region producing (and consuming) 25 per cent of the world's output. Important commercial crops include tea, cotton, hemp, and jute. Although less than 7 per cent of the region remains forested, it provides 10 per cent of the world's hardwoods.

The subcontinent has rich mineral resources, including iron ore, bauxite, mica, and chrome, but they are mostly in peninsular India. Pakistan and Bangladesh have sizable gas deposits, and India has oil. However, Middle South Asia will be hard pressed to sustain its population, which could reach nearly 1,400 million by A.D. 2000. Already the region has some of the world's largest cities—more than 15 with well over a million inhabitants. See map at **Asia.**

Middle Stone Age *n.* The Mesolithic Age *(see).*

Middle Temple *n.* One of the four legal societies forming the **Inns of Court** *(see)* in England.

middle term *n. Logic. Abbr.* **M** The term in a syllogism presented in both premises but not appearing in the conclusion.

Mid·dle·ton (mídd'l-tən), **Thomas** (1580–1627). English playwright. His comedies, written between 1604 and 1611, include *A Chaste Maid in Cheapside,* a mirror of contemporary corruption.

mid·dle·weight (mídd'l-wayt) *n.* **1.** A professional boxer weighing between 147 and 160 pounds (66.8 and 72.6 kilograms). **2.** An amateur boxer weighing between 71 and 75 kilograms (157 and 165 pounds).

Middle West. See **Midwest.** **—Middle Western** *adj.* **—Middle Westerner** *n.*

mid·dling (míd-ling, mídd'l-ing) *adj.* Of medium size, quality, or state; mediocre; ordinary. See Synonyms at **average.**
~*adv. Informal.* Fairly; moderately. [Middle English (Scottish) *mydlyn : midde,* MID (middle) + *-LING* (small).] **—mid·dling·ly** *adv.*

mid·dlings (míd-lingz) *pl.n.* **1.** Products that are intermediate in quality, size, price, or grade. **2.** Coarsely ground flour.

Middx Middlesex.

mid·dy[1] (míddi) *n., pl.* **-dies. 1.** *Informal.* A midshipman. **2.** A middy blouse.

middy[2] *n. Australian.* A medium-sized beer glass.

middy blouse *n.* A woman's or child's loose blouse with a sailor collar. Also called "middy".

mid·field (míd-fēeld, -feeld) *n.* In soccer, the area approximately midway between two goalmouths. Also used adjectivally: *a midfield player.*

Mid·gard (míd-gaard). Also **Mid·garth** (míd-gaarth), **Mith·gar·thr** (míth-gaarthər). *Norse Mythology.* The part of the world inhabited by men, imagined as a fortress encircled by a huge serpent, built by the gods around the middle region of the universe. [Old Norse *Midhgardhr.* See mid, yard.]

midge (mij) *n.* **1.** Any of various widely distributed gnatlike flies of the family Chironomidae, particularly common near water, where they form large swarms. **2.** Any of various similar insects, such as any member of the family Ceratopogonidae *(biting midges),* which suck the blood of mammals and birds. **3.** *Informal.* Any small person. [Middle English *migge,* Old English *mycg.*]

midg·et (míjit) *n.* **1.** An extremely small person who is otherwise normally proportioned. **2.** A small or miniature version of something.
~*adj.* **1.** Miniature; diminutive; dwarfed. **2.** Belonging to a type or class much smaller than what is considered standard: *a midget car.* [Diminutive of MIDGE.]

Mid Gla·mor·gan (míd glə-mórgən). From 1994 to 1997 a county of south Wales which had been formed from parts of the former county of Glamorganshire, the Rhymney valley of Monmouthshire and some villages from Breconshire. It is now divided into Unitary Authority areas.

mid·gut (míd-gut) *n.* **1.** The middle section of the digestive tract of vertebrates, which is lined with endoderm and includes the small intestine. Also called "mesenteron". **2.** The middle section of the digestive tract of anthropods.

mid·i (míddi) *n.* A skirt or coat of mid-calf length. [From MIDDLE.] **—mid·i** *adj.*

Mi·di (mée-dee, mee-dée) *n. French.* The south of France.

Mid·i·an·ite (míddi-ə-nīt) *n.* A member of the ancient Arabian tribe of Midian claiming descent from *Midian,* a son of Abraham. Exodus 2:15–22; Judges 6–8. **—Mid·i·an·ite** *adj.*

mid·i·ron (míd-ī-ərn) *n.* An iron golf club that has more loft than a driver and less than a mashie, used for medium fairway shots and long approach shots.

mid·land (míd-lənd) *n.* The middle or interior part of a country or region. **—mid·land** *adj.*

Midland *n.* The dialect of Middle English spoken in the Midlands, which formed the basis of Modern English.

Mid·lands (mídləndz). A region of central England. Imprecisely defined, it roughly corresponds with the Anglo-Saxon kingdom of Mercia, which originally included the present counties of Derbyshire, Nottinghamshire, Staffordshire, northern Leicestershire, and northern Warwickshire. Mercia expanded to include all Leicestershire and Warwickshire, and Northamptonshire, Rutland, east Herefordshire, and Worcestershire. In the broadest sense, the Midlands includes Shropshire, Herefordshire, Worcestershire, and parts of Bedfordshire, Buckinghamshire and Oxfordshire.

mid·life crisis (míd-līf) *n.* A stage in a life, especially a man's life, when the realisation of the approach of middle or old age may lead to emotional upheaval. Sometimes used humorously.

Mid·lo·thi·an (mid-lóthi-ən). Former county of southeast Scotland centred on Edinburgh. Now a Unitary Authority area to the southeast of Edinburgh.

mid·most (míd-mōst) *adj.* **1.** Situated in the exact middle; middlemost. **2.** Situated nearest the middle.
~*adv.* In the middle. [Middle English *midmest,* Old English *midmest : midd,* MID + *-mest,* -MOST.]

mid·night (míd-nīt) *n.* **1.** The middle of the night; specifically, twelve o'clock at night. **2. a.** Intense darkness or gloom. **b.** A period of darkness and gloom.
~*adj.* **1.** Of or pertaining to the middle of the night. **2.** Resembling the middle of the night; dark; gloomy; dreary. **—burn the midnight oil.** See at **oil** *n.* [Middle English *midnight,* Old English *midniht : midd,* MID + *niht,* NIGHT.]

mid·night blue *n.* A very deep blue. **—midnight-blue** *adj.*

midnight sun *n.* The sun as seen at midnight during the summer within the Arctic or Antarctic Circle.

mid-off (míd-óff, -áwf) *n.* In cricket: **1.** A fielding position nearest the bowler on the off side. **2.** A fielder in this position.

mid-on (míd-ón) *n.* In cricket: **1.** A fielding position nearest the bowler on the on side. **2.** A fielder in this position.

mid·point (míd-poynt) *n.* **1.** The point of a line segment or curvilinear arc that divides it into two parts of the same length. **2.** A position midway between two extremes.

Mid·rash (míd-rash, -raash) *n., pl.* **Midrashim** (mid-ráshim, -raáshim, -róshim), **Midrashoth** (míd-rash-ót, -raásh-). Any of a group of Jewish commentaries on the Hebrew Scriptures, written between A.D. 400 and 1200. [Late Hebrew *midhrāsh,* commentary.]

mid·rib (míd-rib) *n.* The central or principal vein of a leaf.

mid·riff (míd-rif) *n.* **1.** A part of the body, the **diaphragm** *(see).* **2.** The middle, outer portion of the front of the human body, extending roughly from just below the breast to the waistline. [Middle English *midrif,* Old English *midhrif : midd,* MID + *hrif,* belly.]

mid·ship (míd-ship) *adj.* Pertaining to the middle of a ship.

mid·ship·man (míd-ship-mən ‖ mid-ship-) *n., pl.* **-men** (-mən). **1.** Formerly a naval cadet on British ships of war whose battle station was amidships or abreast of the mainmast. **2.** An officer ranking below sublieutenant in the Royal and British Commonwealth navies. **3.** Any of various American fishes of the genus *Porichthys,* having several rows of light-producing organs along their bodies. [From earlier *midshipsman* : MIDSHIPS + MAN.]

mid·ships (míd-shipss) *adv. Nautical.* **1.** Amidships. **2.** In the centre position. Said of the helm.
~*n.* The middle part of a ship.

midst (midst, mitst) *n.* **1.** *Archaic.* The middle position or part; the centre. **2.** The condition of being in the interior of, surrounded by, or enveloped in something. Used chiefly in the phrases *in the midst of* and *in our (their, your) midst: in the midst of nature.*
~*prep. Archaic.* Among. [Middle English *middest*, variant of *middes*, from phrases such as *in middes*, variant of *in middan*, dative of *midde*, MID.]

mid·stream (míd-streem, -streém) *n.* The middle of a stream or river.

mid·sum·mer (míd-súmmər, -summər) *n.* **1.** The middle of the summer. **2.** The **summer solstice** (*see*). —**mid·sum·mer** *adj.*

Midsummer's Day. Also **Midsummer Day.** June 24, one of the quarter days in England, Ireland, and Wales, and the feast of Saint John the Baptist.

mid·term (míd-term, -térm) *n.* **1.** The middle of an academic term or a political term of office or a pregnancy. **2. a.** An examination given at the middle of an academic term. **b.** *Plural.* A series of such examinations. —**mid·term** *adj.*

mid·Vic·to·ri·an (míd-vik-táwri-ən ‖ -tóri-) *adj.* Pertaining to, occurring in, or characteristic of the middle period of the reign of Queen Victoria in Great Britain (1837–1901), a period known for rigid social standards.
~*n.* **1.** A person living in the mid-Victorian period. **2.** A person having mid-Victorian ideas.

mid·way (míd-way) *n.* **1.** *U.S.* The area of any fair, carnival, circus, or exposition where side shows and other amusements are located. **2.** *Obsolete.* **a.** The middle of a way or distance. **b.** A middle way or course of action or thought.
~*adv.* (*also* -wáy) **1.** In the middle of a way or distance; halfway. **2.** In an intermediate position: *midway between thrift and meanness.* —**mid·way** *adj.*

Midway Islands. Two small islands surrounded by an atoll in the north Pacific Ocean, annexed by the United States in 1867. There is no indigenous population, but some 2,200 personnel man the U.S. military base there. In the Battle of Midway during World War II (June 1942), U.S. forces, despite heavy losses, won a decisive victory over the Japanese, the turning point of the war in the Pacific.

mid·week (míd-week, -weék) *n.* The middle of the week.
~*adj.* Happening in the middle of the week. —**mid·week** *adv.* —**mid·week·ly** *adj. & adv.*

Mid·west (míd-wést) *n.* Also **Middle West.** A region of north central United States, around the Great Lakes and upper Mississippi valley. Although its limits are ill-defined, it is generally considered to comprise the prairie states of Indiana, Iowa, Ohio, Illinois, Michigan, Minnesota, Missouri, Wisconsin, and Nebraska. Kansas is usually included, and sometimes Ontario peninsula of Canada. A rich farming region, its chief products are maize and pigs. —**Mid·west, Mid·west·ern** *adj.* —**Mid·west·ern·er** *n.*

mid·wick·et (míd-wíckit) *n.* In cricket: **1.** A fielding position towards the boundary on the on side, and between the two batting creases. **2.** A player fielding in this position.

mid·wife (míd-wīf) *n., pl.* -**wives** (-wīvz). One qualified to assist women in childbirth. [Middle English *midwif* : *mid*, with, Old English *mid* + *wif*, WIFE.]

mid·wife·ry (míd-wíffəri, -wíffri, mid-wíffəri, -wíffri ‖ *U.S. also* míd-wīfəri, -wīfri) *n.* The practice of a midwife.

midwife toad *n.* A European toad, *Alytes obstetricans,* the male of which carries the fertilised eggs on its hind legs until they hatch.

mid·win·ter (míd-wíntər) *n.* **1.** The middle of the winter. **2.** The **winter solstice** (*see*).

mid·year (míd-yeer, -yéer, -yer, -yér) *n.* **1.** The middle of the calendar or academic year. **2. a.** An examination in the middle of the academic year. **b.** *Plural.* A series of such examinations. —**mid·year** *adj.*

mien (meen) *n. Literary.* **1.** One's bearing or manner; expression: *a person of noble mien.* **2.** An appearance or aspect: *of fearsome mien.* See Synonyms at **bearing.** [From earlier *meane, mine* (influenced by French *mine*, appearance), short for DEMEAN.]

Mies van der Ro·he (méess ván dər rő-ə, méez, vaán), **Ludwig** (1886–1969). German-born architect in U.S. after 1937. Bauhaus director (1930–33). His steel-frame and glass buildings include the Seagram Building, New York (with Philip Johnson, 1956–59), and the Chicago Federal Center (1963–68).

miff (mif) *n. Informal.* **1.** A petulant, bad-tempered mood; a huff. **2.** A petty quarrel or argument; a tiff.
~*tr.v.* **miffed, miffing, miffs.** To cause (a person) to become offended or annoyed. [Perhaps imitative of an expression of disgust.]

miff·y (míffi) *adj.* -**fier, -fiest.** *Informal.* Easily offended; over-sensitive. —**mif·fi·ness** *n.*

might (mīt) *n.* **1. a.** A tremendous power held by an individual or group: *the whole might of the superpowers.* **b.** Supreme power attributed to a divine being: *the might of God.* **2.** Physical or bodily strength. —See Synonyms at **strength.** —**with might and main.** With all one's strength; with the utmost effort. [Middle English *might,* Old English *miht.*]

might². Past tense of **may.**

might·i·ly (mítili, mít'l-i) *adv.* **1.** In a mighty manner; powerfully. **2.** To a great degree; greatly.

might·y (mítī) *adj.* -**ier, -iest.** **1. a.** Having might; powerful; strong. **b.** Having great emotional or intellectual power: *a mighty intelligence.* **2. a.** Exerting great force; violent: *a mighty blow of his axe.* **b.** Very strong or urgent: *a mighty clamour.* **3.** Awesomely huge: *"the city stood on a mighty hill"* (John Bunyan).
~*adv. Chiefly U.S. Informal.* In a great degree; very; extremely. —**might·i·ness** *n.*

mi·gnon·ette (mín-yə-nét) *n.* **1.** A plant of the genus *Reseda;* especially *R. odorata,* native to the Mediterranean region but widely cultivated for its clusters of fragrant but inconspicuous greenish flowers. **2.** A light, fine pillow lace. [French, feminine of obsolete *mignonnet,* diminutive of *mignon,* dainty, small, MINION.]

mi·graine (mée-grayn, mī-) *n.* **1.** Severe, recurrent headache, usually affecting only one side of the head, characterised by sharp pain and often accompanied by nausea. **2.** An attack of such a headache. [French, from Old French, from Late Latin *hēmicrānia,* pain in half of the head, from Greek *hēmikrania* : HEMI- + *kranion,* CRANIUM.] —**mi·grain·oid** (-oyd), **mi·grain·ous** (-əss) *adj.*

mi·grant (mígrənt) *n.* **1.** A person, animal, bird, or fish that moves from one region to another by chance, instinct, or plan. **2.** An itinerant worker who travels from one area to another in search of work. **3.** *Australian.* An immigrant.
~*adj.* Moving from one place to another; migratory. [Latin *migrāns* (stem *migrant-*), present participle of *migrāre,* to MIGRATE.]

mi·grate (mī-gráyt, mí-grayt) *intr.v.* -**grated, -grating, -grates.** **1.** To move from one country or region and settle in another. **2.** To change location periodically; move seasonally from one region to another. Used of such animals as birds and fish. **3.** *Physics & Chemistry.* To move from one position to another. Used of atoms, molecules, ions, or groups of atoms. [Latin *migrāre.*]

Usage: Migrate, emigrate, and immigrate are sometimes confused. *Migrate* is the neutral term: it can be used with reference to both the place of departure and the destination (*migrate from. . .migrate to*), and can be said of persons, animals, or birds. It often implies a lack of permanent settlement, especially due to seasonal movement. *Emigrate* specifically refers to the place of departure, emphasising movement from that place, and is thus usually followed by *from* (He has emigrated from England), but it is increasingly being used with *to* with the emphasis on the place of destination (He has emigrated to Australia). It is said only of persons, and implies a single move, usually of a permanent character. *Immigrate* specifically refers to the destination, emphasising movement to that place, and is thus usually followed by *to,* but the verb is less commonly used in British English than *emigrate.* It too is said only of persons, and implies a single, and usually permanent move. A complication arises from the use of the noun, *immigrant,* which is frequently followed by *from* (They're immigrants from India), and is now probably more common than *emigrant.*

mi·gra·tion (mī-gráysh'n) *n.* **1.** The action or an act of migrating. **2.** A group migrating together. —**mi·gra·tion·al** *adj.*

mi·gra·to·ry (mī-grə-təri, -tri, mī-gráytəri) *adj.* **1.** Characterised by migration; migrating periodically: *migratory birds.* **2.** Of or relating to a migration. **3.** Roving; nomadic.

mih·rab (mée-rab, -rəb, -raab) *n. Islam.* A niche or similar indication in a mosque used to show the direction of Mecca. [Arabic.]

mi·ka·do (mi-kaádō) *n., pl.* -**dos.** *Often capital* **M.** The emperor of Japan. The title is not used by Japanese people, who use "Tenno". [Japanese, "exalted gate" : *mi* (honorific prefix) + *kado,* gate. Probably originally part of the imperial court.]

mike¹ (mīk) *n. Informal.* A microphone.
~*tr.v.* **miked, miking, mikes.** *Informal.* **1.** To amplify the sound of by means of a microphone. **2.** To attach a microphone to. In both senses, often used with *up.*

mike² *intr.v.* **miked, miking, mikes.** *British Informal.* To avoid work; shirk. [19th century : origin obscure.]

mikron. Variant of **micron.**

mil¹ (mil) *n.* **1.** A unit of length equal to one-thousandth (10⁻³) of an inch. Used chiefly to specify the diameter of wire. **2.** A millilitre. **3.** A unit of angular measurement used in artillery and equal to 1/6400 of a complete revolution. [Short for Latin *mīllēsimus,* thousandth, from *mīlle,* thousand.]

mil. military; militia.

mi·la·dy (mi-láydi) *n., pl.* -**dies.** Also **mi·la·di** *pl.* -**dis. 1.** My lady. A title or form of address formerly used in continental Europe of an English noblewoman or gentlewoman. **2.** A chic or fashionable woman. [French, from English *my lady.*]

milage. Variant of **mileage.**

Mi·lan (mi-lán) *Italian* **Mi·la·no** (mee-laánō). Capital of Milan province and of Lombardy region, northern Italy. At a strategic crossing of the river Olona, it has been a market, industrial, financial, and cultural centre since medieval times. It is now Italy's second city and chief manufacturing centre, its products including textiles, motor vehicles, machinery, aircraft, and clothing. Printing and publishing are also important. The city has three universities, and numerous historic buildings including the cathedral (1386–1813) and La Scala opera house (1778).

Mil·an·ese (míllə-néez ‖ -néess) *n., pl.* **Milanese. 1.** A native or inhabitant of Milan. **2.** The dialect spoken in Milan. **3.** A fine fabric of silk or rayon.
~*adj.* **1.** Of or pertaining to Milan or its people, dialect, culture, or products. **2.** Coated with bread crumbs or flour and fried in oil or butter.

milch (milch) *adj.* Giving milk: *a milch cow.* [Middle English *milche,* Old English *-milce.*]

milch cow *n.* **1.** A cow that produces milk for human consumption. **2.** A source of money or other resources, such as a person or fund, especially one that can be taken for granted: *treated his family as a milch cow.*

mild (mīld) *adj.* **milder, mildest. 1.** Gentle or kind in disposition, manners, or behaviour: *a strong but mild man.* **2.** Moderate in type, degree, effect, or force: *a mild punishment.* **3.** Not very harmful; light: *a mild fever.* **4.** Having no extremes in temperature; temperate: *a mild climate.* **5.** Not sharp, bitter, or strong in taste or smell: *a mild cheese; mild tobacco.*
~*n. British.* A dark draught beer with a low hop content. **—draw it mild.** To moderate one's speech or act calmly. Usually used in the imperative. [Middle English *mild,* Old English *milde.*] **—mild·ly** *adv.* **—mild·ness** *n.*

Mil·den·hall (míldən-hawl). Market town in Suffolk, eastern England, situated on the river Lark. Nearby was found (1942) the "Mildenhall treasure", a hoard of fourth-century Roman silverware, now in the British Museum.

mil·dew (míl-dew || -dōō) *n.* **1.** Any of various plant diseases in which a fungus forms a superficial growth on the plant. See **downy mildew, powdery mildew. 2.** A superficial coating or discolouring of organic materials, such as paint, paper, cloth, leather, and the like, caused by fungi, especially under damp conditions. Compare **mould.**
~*v.* **mildewed, -dewing, -dews.** *—tr.* To affect with mildew. *—intr.* To become affected with mildew. [Middle English *mildew,* Old English *mildēaw,* from Germanic *melith* (unattested), honey + *dawwaz* (unattested), DEW.] **—mil·dew·y** *adj.*

mild steel *n.* A type of steel containing a low amount of carbon (up to 0.25 per cent).

mile (mīl) *n. Abbr.* **m., mi. 1.** A unit of length, equal to 5,280 feet, 1,760 yards, or 1.60934 kilometres, used in most English-speaking countries. Also called "statute mile". **2.** A **nautical mile** *(see).* **3.** Any of various similar units of distance. **4.** A race of a mile. **5. a.** *Informal.* Any relatively great distance. **b.** *Plural.* By a great amount or extent. Used as an intensive: *She's miles better at golf than I am.* **—by a mile.** By a wide margin: *He won by a mile.* [Middle English *mile,* Old English *mīl,* from West Germanic *mīlja* (unattested), from Latin *mīlia, mīllia,* plural of *mīle, mīlle,* thousand.]

mile·age, mil·age (mīlij) *n.* **1.** Total length, extent, or distance measured or expressed in miles. **2.** Total miles covered or travelled in a given time. **3.** The amount of service, use, or wear estimated by miles used or travelled: *This tyre will give very good mileage.* **4.** The number of miles travelled by a motor vehicle on a certain quantity, usually a gallon, of fuel. **5.** *Informal.* The amount of service something has yielded or may yield in the future; usefulness; benefit; advantage: *get full mileage out of a typewriter.* **6.** An allowance for travel expenses established at a specified rate per mile. **7.** Expense per mile, as for the use of a car.

mile·om·e·ter (mī-lómmitər) *n.* A device for indicating the number of miles travelled by a vehicle.

mile·post (mīl-pōst) *n.* **1.** A post on a racetrack marking a point one mile before the winning post. **2.** *Chiefly U.S.* A post set up to indicate distance in miles, as along a road.

mil·er (mīlər) *n.* One trained to or specialising in racing a mile.

mi·les glo·ri·o·sus (mée-layz gláwri-ō-səss || glōri-) *n.,pl.* **milites gloriosi** (mée-li-tayz, -ō-see, -sī) *Latin.* A bragging, swaggering soldier, especially as a stock character in comedy. [After *Miles Gloriosus* ("braggart soldier"), a comedy (*c.* 206 B.C.) by Plautus.]

Mi·le·sian[1] (mī-lée-zi-ən, -zhi-ən, -zhən, -shən) *adj.* Of or pertaining to Miletus or its inhabitants.
~*n.* A native or inhabitant of Miletus.

Milesian[2] *n. Formal.* A native of Ireland; an Irishman.
~*adj.* Of or pertaining to Ireland or its people; Irish. [After *Milesius,* legendary Spanish king whose sons were supposed to have conquered Ireland in about 1300 B.C.]

Miles of Blackfriars (mīlz), **Bernard (James), Baron** (1907–91). British actor and director. He founded the Mermaid Theatre, London, in 1950. He was awarded a life peerage in 1979.

mile·stone (mīl-stōn) *n.* **1.** A stone marker set up on a roadside to indicate the distance in miles to or from a given point. **2.** An important event or turning point in a person's history or career.

Mi·le·tus (mi-léetəss). Ancient Greek seaport of Ionia, west Asia Minor (now Turkey). A centre of learning, Miletus produced the philosophers Thales (*c.* 634–546 B.C.) and Anaximander (*c.* 611–547 B.C.). St. Paul visited it twice (Acts 20, 15; 2 Timothy 4, 20).

mil·foil (míl-foyl) *n.* **1.** A plant, the **yarrow** *(see).* **2.** See **water milfoil.** [Middle English, from Old French, from Latin *millefolium,* "thousand-leafed" (from the fine divisions of the leaves) : *mille,* thousand + *folium,* leaf.]

Mil·ford Ha·ven (mílfərd háyvən). Seaport of Pembrokeshire, southwest Wales. Oil refining and fishing are its main industries.

Milford Haven, 1st Baron. See **Mountbatten, Louis Alexander.**

Mil·haud (mée-ō, mee-ó), **Darius** (1892–1974). French composer. He composed chiefly ballet scores and chamber works, including *Le pauvre Matelot* and *Le Boeuf sur le toit.*

mil·i·ar·i·a (mílli-áir-i-ə) *n. Pathology.* A skin disease caused by an inflammation of the sweat glands and characterised by blebs, redness, and a prickling or burning sensation. Also called "prickly heat", "heat rash". [New Latin *(fēbris) miliaria,* "miliary (fever)", from Latin *mīliārius,* MILIARY.]

mil·i·ar·y (mílli-əri || *U.S.* -erri) *adj.* **1.** Designating a lesion or growth that is very small. **2.** Designating a disease marked by small skin lesions that look like millet seeds. [Latin *mīliārius,* of millet, like millet seeds (as lesions may be), from *milium,* MILLET.]

miliary tuberculosis *n.* An acute form of tuberculosis characterised by very small tubercles in various body organs, caused by the spread of tubercle bacilli through the blood stream.

mi·lieu (méel-yer, meel-yér, -yō̈) *n., pl.* **-lieus** or **-lieux.** Environment or surroundings. [French, environment, midst, from Old French, midst, centre : *mi,* middle, from Latin *medius* + *lieu,* place, from Latin *locus,* place, LOCUS.]

mil·i·tant (mílli-tənt) *adj.* **1.** Fighting or warring. **2.** Aggressive or combative: *a militant mood.* **3.** Vigorously pursuing some cause, especially through a course of confrontation: *militant trade unions.*
~*n.* A militant person; especially, a political activist. [Middle English, from Old French, from Latin *militāns* (stem *militānt-*), present participle of *militāre,* to MILITATE.] **—mil·i·tan·cy** (-tən-si) *n.* **—mil·i·tant·ly** *adv.*

Militant Tendency. A fluid and ill-defined group of political activists on the extreme left of the British Labour movement.

mil·i·tar·i·a (mílli-táir-i-ə) *n. Used with a singular or plural verb.* Items of military equipment and uniform considered as antiques or collectors' pieces. [Latin, neuter plural of *mīlitāris,* MILITARY.]

mil·i·ta·rise, mil·i·ta·rize (míllitə-rīz) *tr.v.* **-rised, -rising, -rises. 1.** To make military; equip or train for war. **2.** To imbue with militarism. **—mil·i·ta·ri·sa·tion** (rī-záysh'n) *n.*

mil·i·ta·rism (míllitə-riz'm) *n.* **1.** The glorification of the ideals of a professional military class. **2.** Predominance of the armed forces in the administration or policy of the state.

mil·i·ta·rist (míllitə-rist) *n.* **1.** One who supports or advocates militarism or warlike policies. **2.** A specialist in military science. **—mil·i·ta·ris·tic** (-rístik) *adj.* **—mil·i·ta·ris·ti·cal·ly** *adv.*

mil·i·tar·y (mílli-təri, -tri || *U.S.* -terri) *adj. Abbr.* **mil. 1.** Of, pertaining to, characteristic of, or performed by a soldier or soldiers; soldierly: *military swagger.* **2.** Characteristic of or befitting the armed forces. **3.** Of or pertaining to war.
~*n., pl.* **military** or **-ies.** *Abbr.* **mil.** Soldiers generally; the armed forces. Preceded by *the*: *ruled by the military.* [French *militaire,* from Latin *mīlitāris,* from *mīles*† (stem *mīlit-*), soldier.] **—mil·i·tar·i·ly** (-tərili, -trili || *U.S.* -térrili) *adv.*

military academy *n.* A college for young trainee officers belonging to, or about to join, the armed forces.

military attaché *n.* An army officer on the official staff of an ambassador, consul general, or minister to a foreign country.

military honours *pl.n.* The ceremonial procedures performed by soldiers on such occasions as state funerals.

military intelligence *n.* **1.** Any information important for its military value. **2.** The branch of the army that procures, analyses, and uses information of military value.

military law *n.* Regulations and rules pertaining to the discipline and administration of the armed forces. Compare **martial law.**

military orchid *n.* A pinkish-purple orchid, *Orchis militaris,* found in Europe and southern England. Also called "soldier orchid".

military police *n. Abbr.* **MP, M.P.** Members of the armed forces assigned to perform internal police duties. **—military policeman** *n.*

mil·i·tate (mílli-tayt) *intr.v.* **-tated, -tating, -tates. 1.** To have force as evidence or influence. Used with *against* or, rarely, *for*: *The facts available to us militate against this interpretation.* **2.** To make less likely or feasible: *factors militating against industrial recovery.* [Latin *mīlitāre,* to serve as a soldier, from *mīles*†, soldier.]

Usage: *Militate* and *mitigate* are not interchangeable in standard English. *Militate* means "provide forceful evidence": *The findings militate against the view that he is innocent. Mitigate* means "lessen in force or intensity": *His apology should mitigate the President's anger.* The words are sometimes confused and *mitigate* is used in the sense of *militate*: *This ought not to mitigate against the decision,* but this is not an acceptable standard usage.

mi·li·tia (mi-líshə) *n. Abbr.* **mil. 1. a.** A citizen army, as distinct from a body of professional soldiers. **b.** The armed citizenry, as distinct from the regular army. **2.** The able-bodied male citizens in a state who are not members of regular armed forces, but who are called to military service in cases of emergency. **3.** The whole body of physically fit male civilians eligible by law for military service. [Original sense, "military organisation", from Latin *mīlitia,* warfare, from *mīles*†, soldier.] **—mi·li·tia·man** *n.*

mil·i·um (míl-i-əm) *n., pl.* **-ia** (-i-ə). *Pathology.* A small, hard, white or yellowish mass just below the surface of the skin, caused by blockage of the secretion of a sebaceous gland. [Middle English, from Latin, millet (the lesions resemble millet seeds).]

milk (milk) *n.* **1. a.** A whitish liquid that is produced by the mammary glands of all mature female mammals after they have given birth and is used for feeding their young until weaned. **b.** The milk of cows, goats, or other animals, used as food by man, or as the principal ingredient of other foods such as butter and cheese. **2.** Any liquid similar to milk in appearance, such as coconut milk, milkweed sap, or plant latex. **3.** Any of various medicinal emulsions or suspensions. **—cry over spilt milk.** To lament what is already past and beyond remedying.
~*v.* **milked, milking, milks.** *—tr.* **1.** To draw milk from the teat or udder of (a female mammal). **2.** To press out, drain off, or remove by or as if by milking: *He milked the information out of him.* **3.** To draw out or extract something from as if by milking: *milk the snake of its venom.* **4.** To obtain money or benefits from for personal gain; exploit: *corrupt officials milking the company's treasury.* *—intr.*

1. To yield or supply milk. **2.** To draw milk from a female mammal. [Middle English *milk*, Old English *milc, meolc*, from Germanic *meluks* (unattested).] **—milk·er** *n.*

milk-and-wa·ter (mílk-ən-wáwtər ‖ *U.S. also* -wóttər) *adj.* Lacking forcefulness; insipid; feeble.

milk bar *n.* A café, or a counter in a café, serving ice cream, non-alcoholic drinks, and light snacks.

milk chocolate *n.* Sweetened chocolate made with milk and other ingredients to give it a creamy taste or appearance.

milk fever *n.* **1.** A mild fever, usually occurring at the beginning of lactation, associated with infection following childbirth. **2.** A disease affecting dairy cows and occasionally sheep or goats, especially soon after giving birth.

milk·fish (mílk-fish) *n., pl.* **-fishes** or collectively **milkfish.** A large fish, *Chanos chanos,* of the South Pacific and Indian oceans, widely used for food. [From its milky colour.]

milk float *n. British.* A small motor vehicle, usually battery-powered, used in delivering milk to houses.

milk glass *n.* An opaque or translucent whitish glass.

milk·ing machine (mílking) *n.* An apparatus fitted with suction devices, used for milking cows mechanically.

milking stool *n.* A low stool with three legs.

milk leg *n. Pathology.* A painful swelling of the leg, occurring in women after childbirth as a result of clotting and inflammation in the femoral veins. Also called "white leg".

milk·maid (mílk-mayd) *n.* A girl or woman who milks cows.

milk·man (mílk-mən, -man) *n., pl.* **-men** (-mən, -men). A man who sells or delivers milk to customers.

milk of magnesia *n.* A trademark for a liquid suspension of magnesium hydroxide, Mg(OH)$_2$, used as an antacid and laxative.

milk pudding *n.* A pudding prepared by cooking rice, semolina, or other grains in sweetened milk.

milk run *n. Informal.* **1.** A military aerial mission that is either of short duration or lacking in danger. **2.** A routine or thoroughly familiar journey, or its route. [From the suggestion that it is as monotonous as the daily delivery of milk.]

milk shake *n.* A beverage made of milk, flavouring, and usually ice cream, shaken or beaten until frothy.

milk·sop (mílk-sop) *n.* A boy or man lacking in courage and manliness; a weakling. [Middle English, sop dipped in milk, hence child fed on this, weakling.] **—milk·sop·py, milk·sop·ping** *adj.*

milk sugar *n.* A constituent of milk, lactose *(see).*

milk thistle *n.* **1.** An annual or biennial herb, *Silybum marianum,* common in lowlands of Britain and Europe, which has an erect grooved stem and red or purple flowers. **2.** Any of a group of plants of the genus *Sonchus;* especially, *S. oleraceus.* In this sense, also called "sow thistle".

milk tooth *n.* Any of the temporary first teeth of a young mammal. Also called "baby tooth".

milk vetch *n.* Any of various plants of the genus *Astragalus,* having compound leaves and clusters of purple, white, or yellowish flowers. [From its supposed ability to increase a goat's yield of milk.]

milk·weed (mílk-weed) *n.* **1.** Any plant of the chiefly North American genus *Asclepias,* most of which have milky juice and pointed pods that split open to release seeds with downy tufts. **2.** Loosely, any of various other plants having milklike juice.

milkweed butterfly *n.* A butterfly, the **monarch** *(see).*

milk·wort (mílk-wurt ‖ -wawrt) *n.* Any plant of the genus *Polygala,* having variously coloured, usually small flowers. [From its supposed ability to increase human lactation.]

milk·y (mílki) *adj.* **-ier, -iest. 1.** Like milk in colour or consistency; opaque-white: *milky glass.* **2.** Filled with, consisting of, or yielding milk or a fluid resembling milk: *a milky kernel of corn.* **3.** Subdued: *a milky character.* **—milk·i·ness** *n.*

Milky Way *n.* **1.** The faint luminous band sometimes observed across the sky, consisting of very large numbers of faint stars visible when the observer looks towards the centre of the Galaxy. **2.** The Galaxy itself, containing the Earth and Solar System. Also called "Galaxy", "Milky Way Galaxy". [Middle English, translation of Latin *Via lactea.*]

mill[1] (mil) *n.* **1.** A building or establishment equipped with machinery for grinding grain into flour or meal. **2.** A device or mechanism, such as rotating millstones, that grinds grain. **3.** A mechanical appliance or machine that reduces a solid or coarse substance into a pulp or minute grains by crushing, grinding, or pressing: *a pepper mill.* **4.** A machine that releases the juice of fruits and vegetables by pressing or grinding: *a cider mill.* **5. a.** Any machine that produces something by the repetition of a simple process, such as a machine for stamping coins. **b.** Any of various machines for shaping, cutting, polishing, or dressing metal surfaces. **6. a.** A building or group of buildings equipped with machinery for processing materials such as wood, hay, textile fibres, and iron ore into finished products, such as paper, fodder, cloth, and steel: *a textile mill.* **b.** Any building or collection of buildings that has machinery for manufacture; a factory. **7.** An agency, institution, or process that operates in a routine way or turns out products in the manner of a factory: *Don't treat university like a degree mill.* **8.** A slow or laborious process: *It took three years for the bill to get through the legislative mill.* **9.** A steel roller bearing a raised design, such as one used for making a die or a banknote printing plate by pressure. **10.** *Slang.* A fist fight. **—go through the mill. 1.** To go through some process, such as training, that is routine and monotonous but necessary. **2.** To go

through a difficult experience, usually having a definite effect on personality or character.

~v. milled, milling, mills. —*tr.* **1.** To grind, pulverise, or break down into smaller particles in a mill. **2.** To transform or process mechanically in a mill. **3.** To shape, polish, dress, or finish in a mill or with a milling tool. **4. a.** To produce a ridge around the edge of (a coin, for example). **b.** To groove or flute the rim of (a coin, for example). **5.** To agitate or stir until foamy. —*intr.* **1.** To move around in churning confusion: *milling around the stage door.* **2.** *Slang.* To fight with the fists; box. **3.** To undergo milling. [Middle English *mille,* Old English *mylen,* from West Germanic *mulīna* (unattested), from Late Latin *molīna,* from *molīnus,* of a mill, from Latin *mola,* millstone.]

mill[2] *n. Abbr.* **M., mi.** A notional monetary unit equal to $^1/_{1000}$ of the dollar of the United States. [Short for Latin *mīllēsimus,* thousandth.]

Mill (mil), **James** (1773–1836). British philosopher and historian. He published a three volume *History of India* (1818), the *Essay on Government* (1820), and *Elements of Political Economy* (1821).

Mill, John Stuart (1806–73). British philosopher, James's son. He wrote *A System of Logic* (1843) and *Principles of Political Economy* (1848). He expressed his utilitarian views in *On Liberty* (1859) and *Utilitarianism* (1863). Mill was a Liberal M.P. (1865–68).

Mil·lais (míllay, mi-láy), **Sir John Everett** (1829–96). English painter, and a founder of the Pre-Raphaelite Brotherhood (1848). His work includes *Christ in the Carpenter's Shop* (1850) and *Order of Release* (1853).

Mil·lay (mi-láy), **Edna St. Vincent** (1892–1950). U.S. poet. Her first volume of verse was *Renascence* (1917). *The Ballad of the Harp Weaver* won her the Pulitzer Prize (1922).

mill·board (míl-bawrd ‖ -bōrd) *n.* A stiff, heavy pasteboard used mainly for book covers. [Alteration of *milled board.*]

mill·dam (míl-dam) *n.* A dam constructed across a stream to raise the water level so the overflow will have sufficient power to turn a mill wheel.

milled (mild) *adj.* **1.** Processed or manufactured in a mill. **2.** Fluted or grooved around the edge, as certain coins are.

mille·feuille (meél-fố-i) *n.* A small pastry consisting of iced layers of puff pastry filled with confectioners' jam, custard or cream. [French, "thousand-leaf".]

mil·le·nar·i·an (milli-naír-i-ən) *adj.* **1.** Of or pertaining to a thousand, especially to a thousand years. **2.** Of, pertaining to, or believing in millenarianism.

~n. One who believes the millennium will occur; an adherent of millenarianism. [Late Latin *mīllēnārius,* MILLENARY.]

mil·le·nar·i·an·ism (milli-naír-i-ə-niz'm) *n.* **1.** In Christianity, the belief in the holy millennium. **2.** Any belief in, doctrine of, or movement aimed at a perfect period or society in the future.

mil·le·nar·y (mi-lénnəri, mílli-nəri ‖ -nerri) *adj.* **1.** Of or pertaining to a thousand; millenarian. **2.** Of or pertaining to millenarianism or the millenarians.

~n., pl. millenaries. 1. a. A sum or total of one thousand, especially a thousand years. **b.** A thousandth anniversary. **2.** A millenarian. [Late Latin *mīllēnārius,* of a thousand, from Latin *mīllēnī,* a thousand each, from *mille,* thousand.]

mil·len·ni·um (mi-lénni-əm) *n., pl.* **-ums** or **-lennia** (-lénni-ə). **1. a.** A span of one thousand years; a millenary. **b.** A thousandth anniversary. **2.** A thousand-year period of holiness either following or preceding the Second Coming of Christ. Revelation 20:1–5. **3.** A hoped-for period of joy, prosperity, and justice. [New Latin (influenced by BIENNIUM) : Latin *mille,* thousand + *annus,* year.] **—mil·len·ni·al** (-əl) *adj.* **—mil·len·ni·al·ist** *n.* **—mil·len·ni·al·ly** *adv.*

milleped, millepede. Variants of **millipede.**

mil·le·pore (mílli-pawr ‖ -pōr) *n.* Any of various reef-building hydrocorals of the genus *Millepora,* of tropical marine waters, forming white or yellowish calcareous formations, and resembling the true corals of the class Anthozoa. [New Latin *Millepora* (genus), "thousand-pored" : Latin *mille,* thousand + *porus,* PORE.]

mill·er (míllər) *n.* **1.** One who works in, operates, or owns a mill for grinding grain. **2.** A milling machine *(see).* **3.** Any of various moths having wings and bodies covered with a powdery substance.

Mil·ler (míllər), **Arthur** (1915–). U.S. playwright. *Death of a Salesman* won the Pulitzer Prize (1949). Other works include *A View from the Bridge* (1955), *The Crucible* (1953), *After the Fall* (1964), *Timebends* (1987), *Broken Glass* (1994).

Miller, Henry (1891–1980). U.S. novelist. His two early novels, *Tropic of Cancer* (1934) and *Tropic of Capricorn* (1935), were published in Paris but banned from the United States until the 1960s because of their frank sexual themes. He also wrote *The Colossus of Maroussi* (1941), and a trilogy, *The Rosy Crucifixion* (1949–60).

mil·ler·ite (míllə-rīt) *n.* A mineral, nickel sulphide, NiS, usually occurring in long slender crystals, and used as a nickel ore. [German *Millerit,* after W.H. *Miller* (1801–80), British mineralogist.]

miller's thumb *n., pl.* **miller's thumbs.** Any of several freshwater fishes of the genus *Cottus,* found in Europe and North America. They have spiny heads and fins, and are mainly bottom dwellers. Also called "bullhead". [Middle English (because of its stocky, thumblike shape). The phrase "miller's thumb" originally referred to the proverbial dishonesty of millers, who gave short weight by tipping the scales with their thumbs.]

mil·les·i·mal (mi-léssim'l) *adj.* **1.** Thousandth. **2.** Consisting of a thousandth, or pertaining to thousandths.

~n. A thousandth. [From Latin *mīllēsimus,* from *mīlle,* thousand.]

mil·let (míllit) *n.* **1.** A grass, *Panicum miliaceum,* cultivated in Asia and Africa for its seed and in Europe and North America for hay. **2.** The white seeds of this plant, widely used as a food grain in Africa and Asia. **3.** Any of several milletlike grasses, such as *Setaria italica,* Italian millet, or their seeds. **4.** A **sorghum** (see). [Middle English *milet,* from Old French, from *mil,* millet, from Latin *milium.*]

Mil·let (mée-ay, -lay, mee-áy, -láy), **Jean François** (1814–75). French painter, whose pictures concentrated on themes of peasant life, as in *The Gleaners* (1857) and *The Angelus* (1859).

mill finish *n.* A smooth surface on various papers, made by machine. Also called "machine finish".

milli– *comb. form. Abbr.* **m** Indicates one-thousandth (10⁻³) of a unit; for example, **millibar, millimetre.** [French, from Latin *mílli-,* from *mílle,* thousand.]

mil·li·ard (mílli-aard) *n. British.* One thousand million; 10⁹. [French, from Old French *miliart,* from *milion,* MILLION.]

mil·li·ar·y (mílli-əri ‖ *U.S.* -erri) *adj.* Pertaining to or marking the distance of an ancient Roman mile, which equalled 1,000 paces. [Latin *mílliárius,* consisting of a thousand, one mile long, from *mílle,* thousand.]

mil·li·bar (mílli-baar) *n. Abbr.* **mb.** A unit of pressure, used especially for measuring the pressure of the atmosphere, equal to one thousandth of a bar. It is equivalent to 100 newtons per square metre.

mil·li·gram, mil·li·gramme (mílli-gram) *n. Abbr.* **mg.** A unit of mass equal to one thousandth of a gram.

Mil·li·kan (míllikən), **Robert Andrews** (1868–1953). U.S. physicist. He was awarded the Nobel prize in physics (1923) for his measurement of the charge of the electron.

mil·li·li·tre (mílli-leetər) *n. Abbr.* **ml.** A unit of volume equal to one thousandth of a litre, or one cubic centimetre.

mil·lime (meel-éem, mee-) *n.* A coin equal to 1/1000 of the dinar of Tunisia. [Perhaps from French *millième,* a thousandth.]

mil·li·me·tre (mílli-meetər) *n. Abbr.* **mm.** A unit of length equal to one-thousandth (10⁻³) of a metre or 0.0394 inch.

mil·li·ner (míllinər) *n.* **1.** A person who makes, trims, designs, or sells women's hats. **2.** *Obsolete.* A seller of ribbons, laces, and other trimmings. [Variant of obsolete *Milaner,* importer of goods, such as women's finery, from MILAN.]

mil·li·ner·y (mílli-nəri, -nri ‖ *U.S.* -nerri) *n.* **1.** Articles, especially women's hats, sold by a milliner. **2.** The profession, business, or shop of a milliner.

mill·ing (mílling) *n.* **1.** The act or process of grinding, especially grain into flour or meal. **2.** The operation of cutting, shaping, finishing, or working metal, cloth, or any other product manufactured in a mill. **3.** The ridges cut on the edges of coins.

milling machine *n.* A machine tool with a rotating cutter acting on a metal workpiece held on a movable table. Also called "miller".

mil·lion (míl-yən) *n., pl.* **million** (for senses 1, 2) or **-lions** (chiefly for sense 3). **1.** The cardinal number written 1,000,000 or 10⁶. **2.** A million monetary units, as of pounds: *He made a million on the stock market.* **3.** *Often plural.* An indefinitely large number: *millions of ants.* **—the millions.** The masses; the common people. [Middle English *milioun,* from Old French *milion,* from Italian *milione,* augmentative of *mille,* thousand, from Latin *mílle.*] **—mil·lion** *adj.*

mil·lion·aire, mil·lion·naire (míl-yə-naír) *n.* **1.** A person whose wealth amounts to a million or more pounds or dollars, or the equivalent in some other currency. **2.** A very wealthy person. [French *millionnaire,* from MILLION.]

mil·lion·air·ess, mil·lion·nair·ess (míl-yə-naír-iss, -ess, -nair-éss) *n.* A female millionaire.

mil·lionth (míl-yənth) *n.* **1.** The ordinal number one million in a series. **2.** Any of a million equal parts. **—mil·lionth** *adj.*

mil·li·pede, mil·le·pede (mílli-peed) *n.* Also **mil·li·ped, mil·le·ped** (-ped). Any crawling, herbivorous arthropod of the class Diplopoda, found throughout the world. They have wormlike bodies with two pairs of legs on each body segment. Compare **centipede.** [Latin *millepeda,* woodlouse, "thousand-feet" : *mílle,* thousand + *pēs* (stem *ped-*), foot.]

mil·li·sec·ond (mílli-sekənd) *n. Abbr.* **ms.** A unit of time equal to one thousandth of a second.

mill·pond (míl-pond) *n.* **1.** The pond or dam from which water is channelled to drive a mill. **2.** Any still stretch of water.

mill·race (míl-rayss) *n.* The fast-moving stream of water that drives a millwheel. Also called "millrun".

mill·run (míl-run) *n.* **1.** A millrace. **2.** The output of a sawmill. **3. a.** A test of the mineral quality or content of a rock or ore by the process of milling. **b.** The mineral yielded by this test.

Mills (milz), **Sir John,** born Lewis Ernest Watts (1908–). British actor. He has had a distinguished career in the theatre, besides giving many noted screen performances, as in *Tunes of Glory* (1960), and *Ryan's Daughter* (1971), which won him an Oscar. He married the playwright Mary Hayley Bell, and their two daughters, Hayley and Juliet, have followed acting careers.

Mills bomb *n. Military.* A high-explosive, oval hand grenade. Also called "Mills grenade". [After Sir William *Mills* (1856–1932), British inventor.]

mill·stone (míl-stōn) *n.* **1.** Either of a pair of cylindrical stones used in a mill for grinding grain. **2.** A heavy weight; a burden, especially a mental burden, such as a responsibility or debt.

mill·stream (míl-streem) *n.* **1.** The water flowing in a millrace. **2.** A stream whose flow is used to run a mill.

mill·wheel (míl-weel, -hweel) *n.* A large wheel, especially one turned by a stream of water, used to work a mill.

mill·wright (míl-rīt) *n.* A person who designs, builds, or repairs mills or mill machinery.

Milne (miln, mil), **A(lan) A(lexander)** (1882–1956). British writer. He wrote for the magazine *Punch* before turning to children's books. His tales of Christopher Robin and his animal friends are told in *Winnie-the-Pooh* (1926) and *The House at Pooh Corner* (1928).

mi·lo (mílō) *n., pl.* **-los.** An early-growing grain sorghum. Some varieties are drought-resistant. Compare **durra, feterita, kaffir corn.** [Sotho *maili.*]

mi·lord (mi-lórd) *n.* My lord. A title or form of address formerly used in continental Europe of an English nobleman or gentleman. [French, from English *my lord.*]

milque·toast (mílk-tōst) *n. U.S.* A person with a meek, timid, and retiring nature. [After Caspar *Milquetoast,* a character in the newspaper cartoon *The Timid Soul,* by H(arold) T(ucker) Webster (1885–1952), from *milk toast,* a bland dish of hot buttered toast in warm milk, often associated with frail persons.]

mil·reis (míl-rayss, mil-ráysh) *n., pl.* **milreis.** A former coin and monetary unit of Portugal and Brazil, worth 1,000 reis. [Portuguese *milréis* : *mil,* thousand, from Latin *mílle* + *réis,* plural of *real,* royal, from Latin *rēgālis,* REGAL.]

milt (milt) *n.* **1.** Fish sperm, including the seminal fluid. **2.** The reproductive glands of male fishes when filled with this fluid. **3.** *Zoology.* The **spleen** (see). *—tr.v.* **milted, milting, milts.** To fertilise (fish roe) with milt. [Sense 1: probably from Middle Dutch *milte,* milt, spleen. Sense 3: Middle English *milte,* Old English *milte.* Both from Germanic *miltjaz* (untested).]

milt·er (míltər) *n.* A male fish that is ready to breed.

Mil·ton (mílton), **John** (1608–74). English poet. In the Civil War he supported Parliament, and wrote an essay in defence of a free press, *Areopagitica* (1644). The essay *The Tenure of Kings and Magistrates* (1649), in defence of the regicides, gained him a post as Cromwell's Latin secretary for foreign affairs. Shortly afterwards he became totally blind. The epic poem, *Paradise Lost,* was published in 10 books in 1667 and in 12-book form in 1674. *Paradise Regained* and *Samson Agonistes* were published in 1671. **—Mil·ton·ic, Mil·to·ni·an** *adj.*

Milton Keynes (keenz). New town and Unitary Authority area, south central England. It was designated a new town to relieve Greater London in 1967. It is the site of the Open University.

Mil·wau·kee (mil-wáwki). The port and largest city of Wisconsin, United States, situated on Lake Michigan. It exports coal and grain from the Midwest via the St. Lawrence Seaway, and produces heavy machinery, electrical equipment, tractors, internal-combustion engines, beer, and tinned meat.

mim (mim) *adj. British Regional.* Old-fashioned in appearance or behaviour; prim. [Perhaps imitative of pursing of the lips.]

mim·bar (mím-baar) *n.* A pulpit in a mosque, with steps on which the preacher stands. [Arabic *minbar.*]

mime (mīm) *n.* **1. a.** A performing art in which characters are mimicked or ideas and moods conveyed by means of facial expressions, gestures, and the like, without the use of words. **b.** A performance or act of mime. **c.** A performer of mime. **2.** *Archaic.* An actor or comedian who specialises in comic mimicry; a buffoon; a clown. **3. a.** A form of ancient Greek and Roman drama in which realistic characters and situations were farcically portrayed and actual persons were mimicked on the stage. **b.** A performance of, or dialogue for, such a comic drama. **c.** An actor in such a drama. *—v.* **mimed, miming, mimes.** *—tr.* **1.** To portray in mime; act out with gestures and facial expressions. **2.** To ridicule by imitation; mimic. *—intr.* **1.** To act as a mimic. **2.** To portray characters and situations by wordless gesture, facial expression, and body movement. [Latin *mīmus,* from Greek *mimos,* imitator.] **—mim·er** *n.*

mim·e·o·graph (mímmi-ə-graf, -graaf) *n. Sometimes capital* **M. 1.** A duplicating machine that makes copies of written, drawn, or typed material from a stencil that is fitted around an inked drum. **2.** A copy made by such a machine. *—v.* **mimeographed, -graphing, -graphs.** *—tr.* To make copies of (a stencil or text) on a mimeograph. **2.** To make (copies) on a mimeograph. *—intr.* To use a mimeograph. [Originally a trademark : from Greek *mimeomai,* first person singular of *mimeisthai,* to imitate + -GRAPH.]

mi·me·sis (mi-mée-siss, mī-) *n.* **1. a.** The imitation or representation of nature or human nature, especially in art and literature. **b.** An instance of such imitation or representation. **2.** *Biology.* Mimicry. **3.** *Medicine.* The appearance, often due to hysteria, of symptoms of a disease not actually present. [Greek *mimēsis,* from *mimeisthai,* to imitate : from *mimos,* imitator.]

mi·met·ic (mi-méttik, mī-) *adj.* **1.** Pertaining to, characteristic of, or showing mimicry. **2. a.** Of or pertaining to an imitation; imitative. **b.** Using imitative means of representation: *a mimetic dance; mimetic gesture.* [Greek *mimētikos,* from *mimeisthai,* to imitate.] **—mi·met·i·cal·ly** *adv.*

mim·ic (mímmik) *tr.v.* **-icked, -icking, -ics. 1.** To copy or imitate closely, especially by reproducing external characteristics such as speech, expression, and gesture; ape. **2.** To copy or imitate so as to ridicule; mock. **3.** To resemble closely; simulate: *an insect mimicking a twig.* **—See Synonyms at imitate.**

—n. **1.** One who imitates: **a.** A performer skilled in mimicking.

b. A person or trained animal that copies or mimics others, especially for entertainment. **c.** An animal that resembles another. **2.** A copy or imitation of some person or object.
~*adj.* **1.** Pertaining to, acting as, resembling, or characteristic of a mimic or mimicry; imitative. **2.** *Literary.* Imitating a person or object, often for amusement; make-believe. [Latin *mīmicus,* imitative, from Greek *mimikos,* from *mimos,* imitator.] **—mim·ick·er** *n.*
mim·ic·ry (mímmikri) *n., pl.* **-ries. 1. a.** The act, practice, or art of mimicking. **b.** An instance of mimicking. **2.** *Biology.* The resemblance, through natural selection, of one organism to another or to a natural object, as a natural aid in concealment. Also called "mimesis".
Mi·mir (mée-meer) *Norse Mythology.* A giant who dwelt by the roots of Yggdrasil, where he guarded the well of wisdom.
mi·mo·sa (mi-mṓ-zə || -sə) *n.* **1.** Any of various mostly tropical plants, shrubs, and trees of the genus *Mimosa,* having ball-like clusters of small flowers, and compound leaves that are often sensitive to touch or light. See **sensitive plant. 2.** Loosely, any of several similar or related plants or trees, such as species of acacia used by florists. [New Latin, from Latin *mīmus,* MIME, from its imitation of animal sensitivity.]
min minute (unit of time).
min. 1. mineralogical; mineralogy. **2.** minimum. **3.** mining.
Min. Minister; Ministry.
mi·na[1] (mī́-nə) *n., pl.* **-nas** or **-nae** (-nee). A varying unit of weight or money, used in ancient Greece and Asia Minor. [Latin, from Greek *mna,* from Akkadian *manū,* designating a unit of weight, from Sumerian *mana.*]
mina[2]. Variant of **myna.**
mi·na·cious (mi-náyshəss) *adj. Formal.* Of a menacing or threatening nature. [Latin *minax* (stem *minac-*), from *minārī,* to menace, from *minae,* threats.] **—mi·na·cious·ness, mi·nac·i·ty** (-nássəti) *n.*
Min·a·mo·to Yor·i·to·mo (mínna-mṓtō yórri-tṓmō) (1148–99). Japanese warrior landlord, the founder of the Shogunate, or *bakufu,* the feudal system by which Japan was ruled until 1867. In 1185, he put down a rebellion by his cousin, Minamoto Yoshinaka, against the emperor, then set up a rival government. He appointed *shugo,* or constables, throughout Japan, and in 1192 he assumed supreme authority as *shogun,* with his capital at Kamakura.
min·a·ret (mínnə-rét, -ret) *n.* A tall, slender tower on a mosque, with one or more projecting balconies from which a muezzin summons the people to prayer. [French, from Spanish *minarete,* from Turkish *minārat,* from Arabic *manārat,* lamp.]
min·a·to·ry (mínnə-təri, mī́nə-, -tri) *adj.* Also **min·a·to·ri·al** (-táwri-əl || -tṓri-əl) *Formal.* Menacing; threatening. [French *minatoire,* from Late Latin *minātōrius,* from Latin *minārī,* to menace. See **minacious.**] **—min·a·to·ri·ly** *adv.*
mince (minss) *v.* **minced, mincing, minces.** *—tr.* **1.** To cut or chop into very small pieces. **2.** To pronounce in an affected way, as with forced elegance and refinement: *He minced his phrases in the presence of his employer.* **3.** To moderate or restrain for the sake of politeness and decorum. Used chiefly in the phrase *not to mince one's words.* *—intr.* **1.** To walk with very short steps or with excessive primness. **2.** To speak in an affected way, as with forced elegance and refinement.
~*n.* Food, especially meat, that is finely chopped; mincemeat. [Middle English *mincen,* from Old French *mincier,* to diminish, from Vulgar Latin *minūtiāre* (unattested), from Late Latin *minūtia,* minutia, from Latin *minuere,* to diminish.] **—minc·er** *n.*
mince·meat (mínss-meet) *n.* **1.** Finely chopped meat. **2.** A mixture of finely chopped dried fruit, spices, and other ingredients, used especially as a pie filling. **—make mincemeat of.** *Slang.* To defeat or destroy utterly, as if by cutting into little pieces.
mince pie *n.* A sweet pie filled with mincemeat.
minc·ing (mín-sing) *adj.* Affectedly refined or dainty. **—minc·ing·ly** *adv.*
mind (mīnd) *n.* **1.** Consciousness considered as residing in the human brain, manifested especially in thought, perception, feeling, will, memory, or imagination. **2.** The totality of conscious and unconscious processes of the brain and central nervous system that directs mental and physical activity. **3. a.** In some philosophical systems a principle of intelligence or consciousness held to pervade reality. **b.** Intelligence or the nonmaterial aspect of being, in contrast to the material: *mind over matter.* **4.** A person's ability to reason as distinguished from emotion or will: *Follow your mind, not your heart.* **5. a.** Intellectual power or ability. **b.** A person considered with reference to intellect: *the greatest mind of the century.* **6. a.** A person's awareness of and attitude to the external world, as shaped by remembered experience: *To my mind, it's impossible.* **b.** Collective memory or attitudes: *the British mind.* **7.** An attitude or emotional state: *left him in a very different mind.* **8.** Opinion or sentiment: *I may change my mind when I hear the facts.* **9.** A desire or purpose. Often used with *good*: *I have a good mind to leave.* **10. a.** Focus of thought; attention; concentration. **b.** Processes of thought and feeling: *preying on her mind.* **11.** Mental balance; sanity: *losing one's mind.* **—blow (someone's) mind.** *Informal.* **1.** To astonish, especially in a pleasurable way. **2.** To give or produce a psychedelic experience to or in. **—bring to mind. 1.** To remember; recollect. **2.** To produce the memory or thought of (a past experience, for example). **—in (one's) mind's eye.** Visualised within one's imagination. **—in** or **of two minds.** Unable to choose; undecided. **—make up (one's) mind.** To decide between alternatives; come to a definite decision or opinion. **—on (one's) mind.** In one's thoughts; especially, worrying one. **—piece of (one's) mind.** *Informal.* One's bluntly expressed opinion; especially, a strongly worded rebuke or condemnation. **—put (one) in mind.** *Informal.* To fill with memories; remind: *The novel put her in mind of her youth.* **—put** or **set (someone's) mind at rest.** To reassure (someone). **—put (someone) in mind of.** To cause to remember or think about; remind of. **—speak (one's) mind.** To speak frankly and in a forthright way.
~*v.* **minded, minding, minds.** *—tr.* **1. a.** To object to; dislike: *Of course I mind your smoking.* **b.** Used in the negative to express willingness or desire: *We don't mind sleeping on the floor.* **c.** Used to express polite requests: *Would you mind asking her?* **2.** To care or be concerned about: *I don't mind who wins.* **3.** To pay attention to the advice or instructions of: *The children minded their mother.* **4.** To make sure: *"And before you let the sun in, mind it wipes its shoes."* (Dylan Thomas). **5. a.** To attend to; heed: *Mind closely what I tell you.* **b.** Used in negative commands to express reassurance: *Don't mind his shouting.* **6.** To be careful about; take heed of or watch out for. **7.** To take care or take charge of; look after. **8.** *Regional.* **a.** To remember or reflect on. **b.** To cause (a person) to remember or reflect on. *—intr.* **1.** To find something objectionable: *Do you mind if I leave now?* **2.** To be concerned or troubled; care: *Nobody minds about what happens to him.* **4.** To be cautious or careful: *Mind as you go down the stairs.* **5.** To get out of the way; shift one's position so as to cease being an obstruction. Usually used in the imperative. **—mind out.** To be careful; beware; pay attention. Usually used in the imperative. **—mind you.** Come to think of it; on the other hand. Used as a mild qualification of a statement: *He seems suitable for the job. Mind you, he's had very little experience.* **—never mind.** *Informal.* Disregard it; it doesn't matter. [Middle English *minde,* Old English *gemynd,* memory, mind, from Germanic *gamundhiz* (unattested).]
Synonyms: *mind, intellect, intelligence, mentality, brains, wits, sense, reason.*
Min·da·nao (míndə-nów). Second largest island of the Republic of the Philippines. Its volcanic, heavily forested mountains include Mount Apo, an active volcano and the country's highest point (2 954 metres; 9,692 feet). The rich volcanic soils produce pineapples, hemp, coffee, rice, and timber. Iron, gold, and coal are mined. The Muslim Moros, the minority since the 1960s, seek self-rule and have resorted to terrorism. Davao is the chief port and city.
mind-bend·ing (mī́nd-bending) *adj. Informal.* **1. a.** Hallucinogenic. **b.** Producing distortions of perception or thought. **2.** Mind-boggling.
mind-bog·gling (mī́nd-boggling) *adj. Informal.* Beyond one's usual experience or mental grasp; overwhelming; stunning.
mind·blow·ing (mī́nd-blō-ing) *adj. Slang.* **1.** Hallucinogenic. **2.** Extremely surprising or exciting.
mind·ed (mī́ndid) *adj.* **1.** Having an intention; disposed; inclined: *I am not minded to answer any of your questions.* **2.** Having a specified kind of mind or tendency. Often used in combination: *evil-minded.* **3.** Having an interest in a specified field. Often used in combination: *arts-minded; ecologically minded.*
mind·er (mī́ndər) *n.* **1.** A childminder. **2.** *U.S.* A babysitter. **3.** *Slang.* A bodyguard or henchman hired by a criminal.
mind-ex·pand·ing (mī́nd-ik-spanding, -ek-) *adj.* Producing intensified or distorted perceptions; psychedelic; hallucinogenic. Said especially of drugs.
mind·ful (mī́ndf'l) *adj.* Attentive; heedful. Used with *of*: *mindful of her responsibilities.* **—mind·ful·ly** *adv.* **—mind·ful·ness** *n.*
mind·less (mī́nd-ləss, -liss) *adj.* **1. a.** Lacking intelligence or good sense; foolish. **b.** Without the need of much mental effort: *a mindless job.* **c.** Without intelligent purpose, meaning, or direction: *mindless violence.* **2.** Giving or showing little attention or care; heedless. Usually used with *of*: *They proceeded, mindless of the dangers.* **—mind·less·ly** *adv.* **—mind·less·ness** *n.*
mind-read·ing (mī́nd-reeding) *n.* **1.** The guessing of what someone is thinking by observing facial expressions and other signs. **2.** The supposed faculty of discerning another's thoughts through extrasensory means of communication; telepathy. **—mind-read·er** *n.*
Mind·szen·ty (mínd-senti), **József** (1892–1975). Hungarian prelate, who became Archbishop of Esztergom and Primate of Hungary after World War II. In 1946 he was made a cardinal. He opposed the Communist regime and in 1948 was jailed for life on a charge of treason. He was freed in 1955, but after suppression of the 1956 uprising he took refuge in the American legation in Budapest. In 1971, the Hungarian government let him go to the Vatican.
mind-your-own-busi·ness (mī́nd-yər-ōn-bíz-nəss, -niss) *n.* A plant, **mother-of-thousands** *(see).*
mine[1] (mīn) *n.* **1. a.** An excavation in the earth for the purpose of extracting free metals, coal, salt, or other minerals. **b.** The site of such an excavation, with its surface buildings, shafts, and equipment. **2.** Any deposit of ore or minerals in the earth or on its surface. **3.** An abundant supply or source of something valuable: *a mine of information.* **4.** *Military.* **a.** A tunnel dug under an enemy emplacement to gain an avenue of attack or to lay explosives. **b.** An explosive device used to destroy enemy personnel, ships, vehicles, or equipment, usually placed just beneath the surface of the ground or sea and designed to be detonated by contact or by a time fuse. **5.** A burrow, tunnel, or gallery made by an insect.
~*v.* **mined, mining, mines.** *—tr.* **1. a.** To extract (ores or minerals) from the earth. **b.** To dig a mine or mines in (the earth) to obtain ores or minerals. **2. a.** To dig under (the earth, or a surface feature);

tunnel under. **b.** To make (a tunnel) by digging. **3.** *Military.* To lay explosive mines in or under. **4.** To attack, damage, or destroy by underhand means; undermine; subvert. **5.** To delve into and make use of; exploit: *mine the archives for information.* —*intr.* **1.** To excavate the earth for the purpose of extracting minerals or ores; work in a mine. **2.** To dig a tunnel or tunnels under the earth; especially, to dig under an enemy emplacement or fortification. **3.** *Military.* To lay explosive mines. [Middle English, from Old French, from Vulgar Latin *mina* (unattested), perhaps from Celtic *meini-*† (unattested), ore.] —**min·a·ble, mine·a·ble** *adj.*

mine² *pron.* Absolute form of *my. Used with a singular or plural verb.* **1.** Belonging to me; my own. Used after a verb: *The green boots are mine.* **2.** The one or ones belonging or pertaining to me: *Mine is the one in the corner.* **3.** *Archaic.* Used to modify: **a.** A following noun beginning with a vowel or *h*: *mine host.* **b.** A preceding noun: *Mother mine.* —**of mine.** Belonging or pertaining to me: *a friend of mine.* [Middle English *min,* Old English *mīn.*]

mine detector *n.* Any of various electromagnetic devices used to locate explosive mines. —**mine detection** *n.*

mine·field (mīn-feeld) *n.* **1.** An area in which explosive mines have been anchored or sunk in water or buried on land. **2.** Anything which is full of hidden dangers: *These negotiations are a minefield.*

mine·lay·er (mīn-lay-ər) *n.* A ship or aircraft equipped for laying explosive underwater mines.

min·er (mīnər) *n.* **1. a.** One who works in a mine. **b.** One who makes his living from extracting minerals from the earth. **2.** A machine for the automatic extraction of minerals, especially of coal. **3.** A member of a military unit engaged in laying explosive mines. **4.** Any of various insects that burrow in leaves, a **leaf miner** *(see).*

min·er·al (mínnərəl, mínrəl) *n.* **1.** Any naturally occurring, homogeneous inorganic substance having a definite chemical composition and characteristic crystalline structure, colour, and hardness. **2.** Any of various natural substances: **a.** An element, such as gold or silver. **b.** A mixture of inorganic compounds, such as bauxite. **c.** An organic derivative, such as coal or petroleum. **3.** Any substance that is neither animal nor vegetable; inorganic matter. **4.** An ore. **5.** *British Informal.* **a.** *Often plural.* Mineral water. **b.** A non-alcoholic carbonated drink, usually with a sweet flavouring.
∼*adj.* **1.** Of or pertaining to minerals: *a mineral deposit; mineral salts.* **2.** Impregnated with minerals: *mineral water.* [Middle English, from Medieval Latin *minerāle* (noun), from *minerālis* (adjective), from Old French *miniere,* from *mine,* MINE.]

min·er·al·ise, min·er·al·ize (mínnərə-līz, mínrə-) *v.* **-ised, -ising, -ises.** —*tr.* **1.** To convert to a mineral substance; petrify. **2.** To transform a metal into a mineral by oxidation. **3.** To impregnate with minerals. —*intr.* To develop or hasten mineral formation. —**min·er·al·i·sa·tion** (-lī-záysh'n ‖ *U.S.* -li-) *n.* —**min·er·al·is·er** *n.*

mineral jelly *n.* **Petrolatum** *(see).*

mineral kingdom *n.* The group of objects and substances that are composed only of inorganic matter. Compare **animal kingdom, plant kingdom.**

min·er·al·o·cor·ti·coid (mínnərəlō-kórti-koyd) *n.* Any corticosteroid hormone that regulates ionic balance and, indirectly, fluid absorption. The main mineralocorticoid is **aldosterone** *(see).*

min·er·al·o·gy (mínnə-rál-əji ‖ -ról-) *n. Abbr.* **min.** The study of minerals, including their distribution, identification, and properties. [MINERA(L) + -LOGY.] —**min·er·a·log·i·cal** (-rə-lójik'l) *adj.* —**min·er·a·log·i·cal·ly** *adv.* —**min·er·al·o·gist** (-ə-jist) *n.*

mineral oil *n.* **1.** Any of various light hydrocarbon oils, especially a distillate of petroleum. **2.** *Chiefly U.S.* **Liquid paraffin** *(see).*

mineral pitch *n.* A bituminous material, **asphalt** *(see).*

mineral tar *n.* A form of bitumen, **maltha** *(see).*

mineral water *n.* Naturally occurring or prepared water that contains dissolved minerals or gases, often used therapeutically.

mineral wax *n.* A hydrocarbon wax, **ozocerite** *(see).*

mineral wool *n.* Any inorganic fibrous material produced by steam blasting and cooling molten silicate or a similar substance. It is used chiefly as an insulator.

Mi·ner·va (mi-nérvə) *Roman Mythology.* The goddess of wisdom, invention, the arts, and martial prowess, identified with the Greek Athena. [Latin.]

min·e·stro·ne (mínni-strṓni ‖ *U.S. also* -strṓn) *n.* A soup of Italian origin containing assorted vegetables, vermicelli, and herbs in a meat or vegetable broth. [Italian, augmentative of *minestra,* from *minestrare,* to serve, dish out, from Latin *ministrāre,* to serve.]

mine·sweep·er (mīn-sweepər) *n.* A ship equipped for destroying, removing, or neutralising explosive marine mines.

Ming (ming). A dynasty which ruled China from 1368 until the Manchu Conquest of 1644. It was founded by a rebel Buddhist monk, Zhu Yuan-zhang who proclaimed himself emperor in 1368. By 1382 he had unified most of China. The arts flourished and periods of foreign trade made the distinctive blue and white porcelain famous abroad. [Mandarin Chinese *míng,* "luminous", "enlightened".] —**Ming** *adj.*

min·gle (míng-g'l) *v.* **-gled, -gling, -gles.** —*tr.* **1.** To mix or bring together (two or more different elements) in close association; combine. **2.** To mix (things) so that the components become united; merge: *"I desired my dust to be mingled with yours"* (Ezra Pound). —*intr.* **1.** To be or become mixed or united. **2.** To mix or pass freely among: *Servants mingled with guests.* —See Synonyms at **mix.** [Middle English *menglen,* frequentative of *mengen,* to mix, Old English *mengan.*] —**min·gler** *n.*

Min·gus, (míng-gəss), **Charles** (1922–79). U.S. jazz musician, composer, and bandleader. Although a virtuoso on the string bass, he was more influential as a composer. His many compositions include *Conversation* (1957) and *Folk Forms No. 1* (*c.*1959).

min·gy (mínji) *adj.* **-gier, -giest.** *British Informal.* **1.** Miserly, stingy; mean: *a mingy father.* **2.** Paltry; inadequate: *a mingy helping of dessert.* [Perhaps MEAN + STINGY.]

min·i (mínni) *n. Informal.* Something distinctively smaller or shorter than other members of its class, especially **1.** A miniskirt. **2.** *Capital* **M.** A trademark for a compact motor car. —**min·i** *adj.*

mini- *comb. form.* Indicates something distinctively smaller or shorter than other members of its class; for example, **minibus, miniskirt.** ***Note:*** Compounds with *mini-* can be formed at will, many such formations being humorous. It is usual to hyphenate less standardised compounds: *a mini-lecture.* Compare **maxi, maxi-.** [Shortening of MINIATURE.]

min·ia·ture (mínni-chər, mín-yə-, -tewr) *n.* **1.** A copy or model that represents or reproduces something in a greatly reduced size. **2. a.** A small painting executed with great detail, often on a surface of ivory or vellum. **b.** A small portrait, picture, or decorative letter on an illuminated manuscript. **c.** The art of making such paintings, portraits, or letters. **3.** Any extremely small representative or example of a class: *These goldfish are miniatures.* —**in miniature.** On a small scale: *The classroom is the real world in miniature.*
∼*adj.* On a small or greatly reduced scale: *miniature furniture.* [Italian *miniatura,* painting (especially the miniature illuminations in medieval manuscripts), from *miniare,* to illuminate, from Latin *miniāre,* to colour with red lead, from *minium,* MINIUM.]

min·ia·tur·ise, min·ia·tur·ize (mínni-chər-īz, mín-yə-, -tewr-) *tr.v.* **-ised, -ising, -ises.** To plan or make on a greatly reduced scale; especially, to make (compact electronic equipment) by using integrated circuits. —**min·ia·tur·i·sa·tion** (-ī-záysh'n ‖ *U.S.* -i-) *n.*

min·ia·tur·ist (mínni-chər-ist, mín-yə-, -tewr-) *n.* An artist who paints miniatures.

mini·bus (mínni-buss) *n.* A high motorised van with rows of seats in the back, capable of transporting small groups of passengers.

min·i·cab (mínni-kab) *n. Chiefly British.* A saloon car used as a taxi and typically summoned by phone.

min·i·com·put·er (mínni-kəm-péwtər, -pewtər ‖ -kom-) *n.* A relatively small digital computer. Compare **mainframe.**

Mi·ni·coy Island (mínni-koy). See **Lakshadweep.**

min·i·é ball (mínni-ay) *n. Often capital* **M.** A conical rifle bullet made in the 19th century and designed with a hollow base that expands when fired to fit the spiral grooves of the bore. [After Captain Claude *Minié* (1814–79), French Army officer, who invented it.]

min·i·fy (mínni-fī) *tr.v.* **-fied, -fying, -fies.** *Rare.* To make smaller or less significant; reduce. [From MINIMUM, after *magnify.*] —**min·i·fi·ca·tion** (-fi-káysh'n) *n.*

min·i·kin (mínnikin) *n. Rare.* A very small or delicate creature.
∼*adj.* **1.** *Obsolete.* Diminutive. **2.** Affectedly dainty; mincing. [Middle Dutch *minneken,* darling, diminutive of *minne,* love.]

min·im (mínnim) *n.* **1.** *Abbr.* **M.** A unit of fluid measure: **a.** In Great Britain, $1/_{20}$ of a scruple or 0.00361 cubic inch. **b.** In the United States, $1/_{60}$ of a fluid dram or 0.00376 cubic inch. **2.** *Music.* A note with a time value of a half a semibreve. Also *U.S.* "half note". **3.** An insignificantly small portion, thing, or person; a jot. **4.** A downward vertical stroke in handwriting. [In music, Middle English *mynym,* from Medieval Latin *minimus,* from Latin, least; other senses, from Latin *minimus,* least. See **minimum.**]

min·i·mal (mínnim'l) *adj.* **1.** Smallest in amount or degree; least possible. **2.** Insignificant or negligible.
∼*n. Mathematics.* In an ordered set, a member that precedes all others. —**min·i·mal·ly** *adv.*

minimal art *n.* A style of abstract painting and sculpture that seeks to obtain an effect of impersonality and restraint by the use of simple geometric shapes and primary colours.

min·i·mal·ist (mínnimə-list) *n.* **1.** A person who champions or produces minimal art. **2. a.** A person who advocates restraint in or the least possible use of something, for example, ornamentation in art or policing in society. **b.** A person who agrees to accept a minimum as a temporary measure. **3.** *Capital* **M. a.** A member of a revolutionary group in Russia during the early 20th century whose policy was the immediate implementation of democracy. **b.** A **Menshevik** *(see).* —**min·i·mal·ist** *adj.* —**minimalism** *n.*

minimal pair *n. Linguistics.* A pair of words or sounds differing in only one very small respect and thereby serving to isolate and identify the phonemes, morphemes, and other minimal linguistic units of a given language. For example, *bang* and *pang* together make up a minimal pair in English.

min·i·max (mínni-maks) *adj. Mathematics.* Of or pertaining to the strategic principle in game theory by which a player selects the strategy to minimise an opponent's greatest possible gain and maximise his own. Compare **maximin.** [*mini*mum + *max*imum.]

min·i·mise, min·i·mize (mínni-mīz) *tr.v.* **-mised, -mising, -mises.** **1.** To reduce to the smallest possible amount, extent, size, or degree. **2.** To represent as having the least degree of importance, value, or size; depreciate. [From MINIMUM.] —**min·i·mi·sa·tion** (-mī-záysh'n ‖ *U.S.* -mi-) *n.* —**min·i·mis·er** *n.*

Usage: Because the traditional senses of this verb relate to an absolute value (the least possible, or lowest), the use of qualifications such as *greatly, somewhat, very much* is criticised. When a qualification needs to be made, an alternative verb, such as *reduce* or *lessen* is preferred, but such usage indicates a continuing shift towards this meaning.

min·i·mum (mínni-məm) *n., pl.* **-mums** or **-ma** (-mə). *Abbr.* **min.** 1. The least possible quantity or degree. 2. The lowest quantity, degree, or number reached or recorded; the lower limit of variation. 3. *Mathematics.* **a.** A number not greater than any other in a finite set of numbers. **b.** A value of a function that is exceeded for any sufficiently small increase or decrease in the function's variables. *~adj. Abbr.* **min.** Of, consisting of, or representing the lowest possible amount or degree permissible or attainable. [Latin, from *minimus,* least, superlative of *minor,* minor.]

minimum lending rate *n.* Until 1981, the lowest rate at which the Bank of England would discount approved bills of exchange.

minimum wage *n.* The lowest wage, determined by law or contract, that an employer may pay an employee.

min·ing (mīning) *n. Abbr.* **min.** 1. The process or business of extracting coal, minerals, or ore from a mine. 2. The process of laying explosive mines.

min·ion (mín-yən) *n.* 1. One who is esteemed; a favourite. 2. **a.** An obsequious follower or dependant; a sycophant. **b.** A subordinate of an individual or organisation: *Civil Service minions.* 3. *Printing.* A size of type, 7-point. *~adj. Rare.* Endearingly dainty; delicate. [French *mignon,* darling, from Old French *mignot,* from Gaulish; akin to Old High German *minna,* love.]

min·i·pill (mínni-pil) *n.* An oral contraceptive that contains only progesterone.

min·i·skirt (mínni-skurt) *n.* A short skirt hemmed several inches above the knees. **—min·i·skirt·ed** *adj.*

min·is·ter (mínnistər) *n.* 1. A person serving as an agent for another by carrying out specified orders or functions. 2. **a.** A person authorised to perform religious functions in a church, especially in a non-Catholic church; a clergyman. **b.** A clergyman officiating at a religious service. 3. A member of a government appointed to head an executive or administrative department of government, in Britain usually under the direction of a Secretary of State. 4. In some countries, a person authorised to represent his government in diplomatic dealings with other governments, usually ranking next below an ambassador. *~v.* **ministered, -tering, -ters.** *—intr.* 1. To attend to the wants and needs of others. Usually followed by *to: Volunteers ministered to the injured.* 2. To exercise clerical functions. *—tr. Archaic.* 1. To administer or dispense: *ministered the Sacrament.* 2. To furnish or provide. [Middle English *ministre,* from Old French, from Latin *minister,* attendant, servant, from *minus,* less.]

min·is·te·ri·al (mínni-stéer-i-əl) *adj.* 1. Of, pertaining to, or characteristic of a minister of religion or of the ministry. 2. **a.** Of or pertaining to a government minister or department. **b.** Of, pertaining to, or representing the government when challenged by the opposition. 3. *Law.* Of or designating a mandatory act or delegated duty admitting of no personal discretion or judgment or requiring no special expertise in its performance. Compare **judicial.** 4. Acting or serving as an agent; instrumental. **—min·is·te·ri·al·ly** *adv.*

minister of state *n.* 1. A government minister who is not head of a department and usually not in the cabinet, who works as an assistant to a senior minister. 2. Any government minister.

Minister of the Crown *n. British.* Any of the senior government ministers, usually but not necessarily in the cabinet, appointed by the Crown on the recommendation of the Prime Minister.

minister plenipotentiary *n.* A diplomatic representative with full authority to speak and act for his government, though lower in rank than an ambassador; a plenipotentiary.

minister resident *n.* A diplomatic agent ranking below a minister plenipotentiary.

min·is·trant (mínnistrənt) *adj.* Serving as a minister. *~n.* One who ministers. [Latin *ministrāns* (stem *ministrant-*), present participle of *ministrāre,* to serve, from *minister,* MINISTER.]

min·is·tra·tion (mínni-stráysh'n) *n.* 1. An act or process of serving or aiding. 2. The act of performing the duties of a minister of religion or aiding. [Latin *ministrātiō* (stem *ministrātiōn-*), from *ministrāre,* to serve, from *minister,* MINISTER.] **—min·is·tra·tive** (-strətiv) *adj.*

min·is·try (mínnistri) *n., pl.* **-tries.** 1. The act of serving; ministration. 2. **a.** The profession, duties, and services of a minister of religion. **b.** Ministers of religion as a group; the clergy. **c.** The period of service of a minister of religion. 3. **a.** A government department presided over by a minister. **b.** The building in which such a department is housed. **c.** The duties, functions, or term of a government minister and his staff. **d.** *Often capital* M. Government ministers as a group. [Middle English *ministerie,* from Latin *ministerium,* functions of a MINISTER.]

Min·i·track (mínni-trak) *n.* A trademark for an electronic measuring system designed to follow the course of satellites and rockets and to correlate radio signals received by a network of ground stations.

min·i·um (mínni-əm) *n. Chemistry.* A lead oxide, **red lead** *(see).* [Middle English, from Latin, cinnabar, red lead, probably of Iberian origin; akin to Basque *arminea,* cinnabar.]

min·i·ver (mínnivər) *n.* 1. A white or light-grey fur of uncertain origin, used as a rich trim on medieval robes. 2. The ermine used in the ceremonial robes of peers. [Middle English, from Anglo-French *menuver,* Old French *menu vair,* small vair : *menu,* small, from Latin *minūtus,* small, MINUTE + *vair,* VAIR.]

min·i·vet (mínni-vet) *n.* Any tropical Asian songbird of the genus *Pericrocotus,* related to the cuckoo shrikes and having a brightly

coloured plumage. [19th century : origin obscure.]

mink (mingk) *n., pl.* **minks** or collectively **mink.** 1. Any of various semiaquatic carnivores of the genus *Mustela,* especially *M. vison* of North America, resembling the weasel and having short ears, a pointed snout, short legs, and partly webbed toes. 2. The soft, thick, lustrous fur of this animal. 3. A coat or stole made of this fur. [Middle English *mynk,* from Scandinavia; akin to Danish *mink*†.]

Min·ne·ap·o·lis (mínni-áppəliss). A city of Minnesota, United States, at the head of navigation on the Mississippi. Adjacent to, and twinned with, St. Paul, it lies in a rich agricultural area, and meat-packaging and flour-milling are its main industries.

Min·nel·li (mi-nélli), **Liza** (1946–). U.S. singer and actress. Daughter of Judy Garland, the Hollywood film actress, and Vincente Minnelli (1910–86), the film director. She has been hailed for her performances in the films *Cabaret* (1972) and *New York, New York* (1977).

min·ne·sing·er (mínni-sing-ər, -zing-) *n.* Any of the German lyric poets and singers in the troubadour tradition who flourished from the 12th to the 14th centuries. [German, "love singer".]

Min·ne·so·ta (mínni-sṓtə). Northernmost state of United States, outside Alaska. Its southern two thirds are prairieland, producing dairy products, meat, and grain. To the north lie reafforested hills, the basis of the state's timber industry. In the eastern mountains beside Lake Superior, exploitation of nickel and copper reserves has superseded the mining of iron ore. Manufacturing is the state's chief activity, yielding processed foods, paper products, machinery, and electronic equipment. With more than 11,000 lakes, tourism is also important. The state was admitted to the Union in 1858. St. Paul on the Mississippi is its capital. **—Min·ne·so·tan** *adj. & n.*

min·now (mínnō) *n., pl.* **minnows** or collectively **-now.** 1. Any of a large number of small, freshwater fishes of the family Cyprinidae; especially, the European species *Phoxinus phoxinus,* widely used as live bait. 2. Any other small, silver-coloured fish. 3. **a.** A small or unimpressive person. **b.** Someone or something that is relatively small in size or status: *The firm was then just a minnow in the car trade.* [Middle English *menow,* Old English *mynwe* (unattested).]

Mi·no·an (mi-nṓ-ən, mī-) *adj.* 1. Of, pertaining to, or designating the advanced Bronze Age culture that flourished in Crete from about 3000 to 1100 B.C. 2. Of, pertaining to, or designating either of two writing systems, **Linear A** and **Linear B** *(both of which see). ~n.* A person living in this Bronze Age culture. [From Greek *Mínōs,* MINOS.]

mi·nor (mīnər) *adj.* 1. Lesser or smaller in amount, extent, quantity, or size. 2. Lesser or relatively low in importance, rank, or stature: *a minor essayist.* 3. Lesser or relatively small in seriousness or danger; requiring comparatively little attention or concern: *minor difficulties; a minor injury.* 4. *Law.* Under legal age; not yet a legal adult. 5. *British.* Designating the junior or younger of two pupils, especially brothers, with the same surname. Used especially in British public schools. 6. *U.S.* Designating or pertaining to an academic subject taken as a subsidiary course. 7. *Logic.* Dealing with a more restricted category; narrower in scope. 8. *Music.* **a.** Designating a **minor scale** *(see).* **b.** Less in distance by a semitone than the corresponding major interval. **c.** Based on a minor scale: *minor key.* 9. Of or pertaining to the minority. *~n.* 1. A person or thing that is lesser in comparison with others of the same class. 2. *Law.* One who has not reached full legal age (in Britain, 18; in some other countries, 21). 3. **a.** *U.S.* An area of specialised study of a degree candidate in a college or university that requires fewer class hours or credits than his major. **b.** One studying a minor: *a chemistry minor.* 4. *Logic.* A **minor premise** or **minor term** *(both of which see).* 5. *Music.* A minor key, scale, or interval. 6. In bell-ringing, a change rung on six bells. 7. *U.S. Sports.* **a.** A **minor league** *(see).* **b.** *Plural.* The minor leagues of a sport, as a group. 8. *Capital* M. A Minorite. *~intr.v.* **minored, -noring, -nors.** *U.S.* To pursue academic studies in a minor subject. Used with *in.* [Middle English, from Latin *minor,* less.]

Mi·nor·ca¹ (mi-nórkə) *n.* A domestic fowl of a breed originating in the Mediterranean region, having white or black plumage.

Minorca². Spanish: **Me·nor·ca** (me-nórkə). Second largest of the Balearic Islands, Spain. Situated in the Mediterranean, it is predominantly low-lying; agriculture, fishing, and tourism are its main industries. Mahón is the chief town and port. **—Minorcan** *adj. & n.*

minor canon *n.* An Anglican clergyman who helps to conduct the daily service at a cathedral but is not a member of its chapter.

Mi·nor·ite (mínə-rīt) *n.* Also **Mi·nor·ist** (-rist) A Franciscan friar, especially one belonging to the order of *Friars Minor.* [From *Friars Minor* (Medieval Latin *Frātrēs Minōrēs*), name given to the order by its founder, Saint Francis of Assisi, as a title of humility.]

mi·nor·i·ty (mī-nórrəti, mi- || -náwrəti) *n., pl.* **-ties.** 1. The smaller in number of two groups which together form a whole; a group of persons or things numbering less than half of a total. Compare **majority.** 2. A racial, religious, political, national, or other group regarded as different from the larger group of which it is part. Also used adjectivally: *minority parties.* 3. The state or period of being under legal age: *an heir still in his minority.* [French *minorité,* from Medieval Latin *minōritās* (stem *minoritāt-*), from Latin *minor,* MINOR.]

minority carrier *n. Electronics.* The carrier that transports the smaller fraction of the current in a semiconductor. Compare **majority carrier.**

minority leader *n. U.S.* The head of the minority party in legislative body. Compare **majority leader.**

minor league *n.* Any league of professional sports clubs, especially baseball, not belonging to the major leagues.

minor-league (mínər-léeg) *adj.* **1.** *Chiefly U.S.* Pertaining or belonging to a minor sports league. **2.** Of subordinate position or secondary importance: *a minor-league politician.* —**mi·nor-lea·guer** *n.*

minor orders *pl.n. Roman Catholic Church.* The former orders of acolyte, exorcist, reader or lector, and doorkeeper.

minor planet *n.* An **asteroid** *(see).*

minor premise *n. Logic.* The premise in a syllogism containing the minor term, which will form the subject of the conclusion.

Minor Prophets *pl.n.* **1.** The Hebrew prophets Hosea, Joel, Amos, Obadiah, Jonah, Micah, Nahum, Habakkuk, Zephaniah, Haggai, Zechariah, and Malachi. **2.** In the Old Testament, the group of books containing their prophecies.

minor scale *n. Music.* A diatonic scale having a minor third between the first and third notes. It has several forms with different intervals above the fifth. Compare **major scale.**

minor suit *n.* In bridge, the suit of clubs or of diamonds, so called because of their lower scoring value.

minor term *n. Logic.* The term in a syllogism that is stated in the minor premise and forms the subject of the conclusion.

Mi·nos (mí-noss, -nəss) *Greek Mythology.* A king of Crete, the son of Zeus and Europa, who ordered the building of the Labyrinth.

Mi·no·taur (mínə-tawr, mínnə-) *Greek Mythology.* The son of Pasiphaë by a sacred bull, having a man's body and a bull's head, slain by Theseus in the Labyrinth. [Middle English, ultimately from Greek *Minōtauros* : MINOS (husband of Pasiphaë) + *tauros*, bull.]

Minsk (minsk). Capital of Belarus. It is a communications, market, and cultural and industrial centre. Its substantial Jewish population (40 per cent) was virtually exterminated by the Germans in World War II.

min·ster (mín-stər) *n. British.* **1.** A monastery church. **2.** Any of certain abbeys or cathedrals, such as those of Beverley or York. [Middle English *minster*, Old English *mynster*, from Vulgar Latin *monisterium* (unattested), variant of Late Latin *monastērium*, MONASTERY.]

min·strel (mín-strəl) *n.* **1.** A medieval musician who travelled from place to place singing and reciting poetry. **2.** *Archaic.* Any lyric poet or musician. **3.** A performer in a minstrel show. [Middle English *ministral*, from Old French *menestral*, entertainer, servant, from Late Latin *ministeriālis*, household officer, from Latin *ministerium*, MINISTRY.]

minstrel show *n.* A variety show in which performers, some with blackened faces, sing, dance, and tell jokes.

min·strel·sy (mín-strəl-si) *n., pl.* **-sies.** **1.** The art or profession of a minstrel. **2.** A troupe of minstrels. **3.** A group of ballads and lyrics sung by minstrels.

mint¹ (mint) *n.* **1.** A place where the coins of a country are manufactured by authority of the government. **2.** An abundant amount or repository, especially of money: *He is worth a mint.* **3.** Anything that may be exploited as a source of money or ideas: *a mint of useful ideas.*
~*tr.v.* **minted, minting, mints. 1.** To produce (money) by stamping metal; coin. **2.** To invent or fabricate (a word, for example).
~*adj.* As if freshly minted; unused: *in mint condition; a mint stamp.* [Middle English *mynt*, Old English *mynet*, money, from West Germanic *munita* (unattested), from Latin *monēta*, money, mint, after the temple of Juno *Monēta* in Rome, where money was minted.]

mint² *n.* **1.** Any of various plants of the genus *Mentha*, characteristically having aromatic foliage and spiked flowers. Many species are cultivated for their leaves, used for flavouring. See **peppermint, spearmint. 2.** Any of various similar or related plants. **3.** A sweet flavoured with mint. [Middle English *minte*, Old English *minte*, from West Germanic *minta* (unattested), from Latin *menta, mentha*, from Greek *minthē*, of Mediterranean origin.] —**mint·y** *adj.*

mint·age (míntij) *n.* **1.** The act or process of minting coins. **2.** Money manufactured in a mint. **3.** The fee paid to a mint by the government. **4.** The impression stamped on a coin.

mint jelly *n.* A clear green jelly, usually made with apples or crab apples, chopped mint, and green vegetable colouring.

mint julep *n.* A tall, frosted drink, popular in the United States, made of bourbon, sugar, crushed mint leaves, and shaved ice.

Min·toff (míntof), **Dom(inic)** (1916–) Maltese prime minister (1955–8 and 1971–84). He helped to reorganise the Maltese Labour Party in 1944 and was elected to the legislative assembly in 1947.

mint sauce *n.* A sauce, traditionally served with roast lamb, made of chopped mint leaves with vinegar and sugar.

min·u·end (mínnew-end) *n.* The quantity or number from which another, the subtrahend, is to be subtracted. [Latin *minuendum*, something to be diminished, neuter gerundive of *minuere*, to lessen.]

min·u·et (mínnew-ét) *n.* **1.** A slow, stately, pattern dance for groups of couples, that originated in 17th-century France. **2.** A piece of music for or in the rhythm of this dance, in ³/₄ time. [French, from obsolete *menuet*, dainty, small, from Old French *menu*, small, from Latin *minūtus*, small, MINUTE.]

mi·nus (mínəss) *prep.* **1.** *Mathematics.* Reduced by the subtraction of; less: *Seven minus four equals three.* **2.** *Informal.* Lacking; deprived of; without.
~*adj.* **1.** Negative or on the negative part of a scale: *a minus value; minus five degrees.* **2.** Designating one subdivision of a grade less

than; slightly less than: *a mark of B minus.* **3.** Of, pertaining to, or involving a loss, deficiency, or disadvantage: *a minus consideration.* **4.** Having a negative electric charge.
~*n.* **1.** A minus sign (–). **2.** A negative quantity. **3.** A loss, deficiency, or disadvantage. **4.** A negative electric charge. [Middle English *mynus*, from Latin *minus*, less, from *minor*, less, minor.]

min·us·cule (mínnə-skewl ‖ mín-yə-, mi-núss-, mī-) *n.* **1.** A small, cursive script developed from uncial between the seventh and ninth centuries A.D. and used in medieval manuscripts. **2.** A letter written in this script. **3.** A lower-case letter. Compare **majuscule.**
~*adj.* **1. a.** Of, pertaining to, or written in minuscule. **b.** Of, pertaining to, or written in lower-case letters. **2.** Said of letters of the alphabet. **3.** Very small; tiny; minute. —See Synonyms at **small.** [French, from Latin *minuscula (littera)*, minuscule (letter), from *minusculus*, diminutive of *minor* (stem *minus-*), less, minor.] —**mi·nus·cu·lar** (mi-núskew-lər) *adj.*

minus sign *n. Mathematics.* The symbol (–) as in $4-2=2$. It is used to indicate subtraction or a negative quantity. Also called "minus". Compare **plus sign.**

min·ute¹ (mínnit) *n.* **1.** *Abbr.* **min** *Symbol* **′ a.** A unit or period of time equal to one-sixtieth of an hour, or to 60 seconds. **b.** A unit of angular measurement equal to one-sixtieth of a degree, or to 60 seconds. Also called "minute of arc". **2.** Any short interval of time; a moment. **3.** A specific point in time. **4.** *Informal.* A distance that can be covered in a minute: *ten minutes from here.* **5.** A note or summary covering points to be remembered; a memorandum. **6.** *Plural.* An official record of proceedings at the meeting of an organisation. —See Synonyms at **moment.**
~*tr.v.* **minuted, -uting, -utes. 1.** To record (a meeting, for example) exactly, as it proceeds. **2.** To record in a memorandum or other notation. **3.** To send a minute to (a person). **4.** To record in the minutes of a meeting. [Middle English, from Old French, from Medieval Latin *minūta*, minute, small note, from Late Latin, from *minūtus*, small, MINUTE.]

mi·nute² (mī-néwt ‖ mi-, -nŏŏt) *adj.* **1.** Exceptionally small; tiny: *minute spores carried by the wind.* **2.** Beneath notice; insignificant; trifling. **3.** Characterised by careful scrutiny and close examination: *her minute and accurate researches.* —See Synonyms at **small.** [Latin *minūtus*, small, from the past participle of *minuere*, to lessen.] —**mi·nute·ness** *n.*

min·ute hand (mínnit) *n.* The long hand on a clock or watch that indicates the minutes.

min·ute·ly¹ (mínnitli) *adj.* At intervals of one minute.
~*adv.* Every minute.

mi·nute·ly² (mī-néwt-li ‖ mi-, -nŏŏt-) *adv.* **1.** With attention to minutiae. **2.** On a very small scale.

min·ute·man (mínnit-man) *n., pl.* **-men** (-men). *Sometimes Capital* **M. 1.** An American militiaman or armed civilian pledged during the War of American Independence to be ready to fight at a minute's notice. **2.** *U.S.* Any militiaman or civilian keen to take up arms. **3.** A U.S. intercontinental ballistic missile.

minute mark *n.* The symbol ′ used to indicate the measurement minutes of arc and also the measurement feet.

minute of arc *n.* A minute (unit of angular measurement).

minute steak *n.* A small, thin steak that can be cooked quickly.

mi·nu·ti·a (mī-néw-shi-ə, mi-, -nŏŏ-, -shə) *n., pl.* **-tiae** (-shi-ee). A small, exact, or trivial detail: *pedantic minutiae.* [Latin *minūtia*, smallness, from *minūtus*, small, MINUTE.]

minx (mingks) *n., pl.* **minxes. 1.** A pert, impudent, or flirtatious woman or girl. **2.** *Archaic.* A prostitute or promiscuous woman. [16th century : origin obscure.]

min·yan (mín-yən, min-ya'an) *n., pl.* **-yans** or **minyanim** (-im). The quorum of ten male Jews aged 13 or older required according to orthodox Jewish law before a religious service can take place. [Hebrew, "number".]

Mi·o·cene (mí-ə-seen, -ō-) *adj. Geology.* Of, belonging to, or characteristic of the geological time and rock series of the fourth epoch of the Tertiary period, characterised by the appearance of primitive apes, whales, and grazing animals.
~*n. Geology.* **1.** The Miocene epoch. Preceded by *the.* **2.** The deposits of this epoch. [Greek *meiōn*, less + -CENE.]

mi·o·sis, my·o·sis (mī-ō-siss) *n., pl.* **-ses** (-seez). *Pathology.* An excessive contraction of the pupil of the eye, often due to the action of drugs. [New Latin : Greek *muein*, to close the eyes + -OSIS.]

mi·ot·ic (mī-óttik) *n.* An agent that causes contraction of the pupil of the eye. [From MIOSIS.] —**mi·ot·ic** *adj.*

Miquelon Island. See **St. Pierre et Miquelon Islands.**

mir (meer) *n.* A prerevolutionary Russian peasant commune. [Russian, commune, peace, world, from Old Church Slavonic *mirŭ*, joy, peace.]

Mi·ra·beau (mírrə-bō, *French* mee-raa-bō), **Honoré Gabriel Riquetti, Comte de** (1749–91). French revolutionary leader. In 1789, he was a delegate to the States-General, where his oratory made him spokesman for the Third Estate. His policy of a constitutional monarchy weakened his influence and in 1790 he entered into secret negotiations with the court.

mi·ra·bi·le dic·tu (mi-ráabi-le dík-tew, -lay, -tŏŏ). *Latin.* Wonderful to relate.

mi·ra·cid·i·um (mír-ə-síddi-əm) *n., pl.* **-ia** (-ə). A ciliated larva of a parasitic fluke in the form in which it hatches from the egg. [New Latin, from Late Latin *miracidion*, diminutive of Greek *meirax* (stem *meirac-*), offspring.]

mir·a·cle (mírrək'l) *n.* **1.** An event that appears unexplainable by the laws of nature and so is held to be supernatural in origin or an act of God. **2.** Broadly, any event that seems exceptionally fortunate: *It was a miracle she escaped unhurt.* **3.** A person, thing, or event that excites admiring awe. **4.** A miracle play. [Middle English, from Old French, from Latin *mīrāculum,* from *mīrārī,* to wonder at, from *mīrus,* wonderful.]

miracle play *n.* A form of religious drama of the Middle Ages in which scenes and events of the Bible or the lives of saints and martyrs were represented. Compare **mystery play.**

mi·rac·u·lous (mi-ráckew-ləss) *adj.* **1.** Of the nature of a miracle. **2.** Caused by or as if by a miracle: *a miraculous cure.* **3.** Having the power to work miracles. [French *miraculeux,* from Medieval Latin *mīrāculōsus,* from Latin *mīrāculum,* MIRACLE.] —**mi·rac·u·lous·ly** *adv.* —**mi·rac·u·lous·ness** *n.*

mir·a·dor (mírrə-dawr, -dór) *n.* A balcony, window, or turret affording a wide view. [Spanish, from *mirar,* to look.]

mi·rage (mírraazh || *chiefly U.S.* mi-ra̋azh) *n.* **1.** An optical phenomenon in which an image, often inverted, is produced as a result of refraction of light by layers of air with differing densities. The commonest form involves an image of the sky, producing the illusion of water. **2.** Something that is illusory or insubstantial like a mirage. [French, from *mirer,* to look at, from Latin *mīrārī,* to wonder at, from *mīrus,* wonder.]

MIRAS mortgage interest relief at source.

mire (mīr) *n.* **1.** An area of wet, soggy, and muddy ground; a bog. **2.** Deep, slimy soil or mud. **3.** A difficult or unpleasant position. ~*v.* **mired, miring, mires.** —*tr.* **1.** To cause to sink or become stuck in mire. **2.** To soil with mud. **3.** To trap or entangle as if in mire. —*intr.* To sink or become stuck in mire. [Middle English, from Old Norse *mȳrr,* a bog, from Germanic; akin to MOSS.] —**mir·i·ness** *n.* —**mir·y** *adj.*

mire·poix (meer-pwa̋a) *n.* A mixture of finely diced vegetables fried in butter, sometimes used as a base for brown sauces and stews. [French, probably in honour of C.P.G.F. de Lévis, Duc de *Mirepoix,* 18th-century French general.]

Mir·i·am (mírri-əm). The sister of Moses. Exodus 15:20.

mirk. Variant of **murk.**

mirky. Variant of **murky.**

Mi·ró (mi-rő), **Joan** (1893–1983). Spanish surrealist painter, born in Catalonia. His style is distinguished by naïve, free-floating forms. He painted a mural at Harvard University and made the ceramic decorations for the UNESCO headquarters in Paris. He donated much of his work to the Joan Miró museum of contemporary art in Barcelona.

mir·ror (mírrər) *n.* **1.** Any surface capable of reflecting sufficient undiffused light to form an image of an object placed in front of it; especially, one of coated glass or polished metal, often mounted in a frame. **2.** Anything that faithfully reflects or gives a true picture of something else: *a mirror of society.* **3.** A **speculum** (*see*) on a bird's wing. ~*tr.v.* **mirrored, -roring, -rors.** To reflect in or as if in a mirror: *mirroring contemporary problems.* [Middle English *mirour,* from Old French *miroir, mirour,* from *mirer,* to look at, from Latin *mīrārī,* to wonder at, from *mīrus,* wonderful.]

mirror carp *n.* A variety of the common carp that has a smooth, shiny body.

mirror image *n.* **1.** An image in or as if in a mirror, showing left and right reversed but otherwise identical to the original. **2.** Something that has the same constituent parts as something else, but has them in reverse order or with inverted values: *Is fascism the mirror image of communism?*

mirror plane *n.* A plane that divides an object or system into two halves that are mirror images of each other.

mirror symmetry *n.* Symmetry such that one half of an object or system is identical to the mirror image of the other half.

mirror twins *pl.n.* Twins whose bodies, including internal organs, are mirror images of each other, such that the heart of one, for example, is located on the right-hand side.

mirror writing *n.* Writing in which both letters and words are reversed, that appears as normal when seen reflected in a mirror.

mirth (murth) *n.* Merriment, gaiety, or enjoyment, especially when expressed in laughter. [Middle English *mirthe,* Old English *myrgth.* See **merry, -th.**] —**mirth·ful** *adj.* —**mirth·less** *adj.*

Synonyms: mirth, merriment, hilarity, glee.

MIRV (murv) *n.* An offensive ballistic-missile system in which a number of warheads aimed at independent targets can be launched by a single booster rocket. [*M*ultiple *I*ndependently targeted *R*e-entry *V*ehicles.]

mir·za (múrzə, meer-za̋a) *n.* In Iran, a respectful title used: **1.** After the name of a prince. **2.** Before the name of a hero, scholar, or high official. [Persian *mīrzā,* short for *mīrzād,* "son of a lord" : *mīr,* prince, from Arabic, *amīr,* prince, EMIR + *zād,* born, from *zādan,* to be born.]

mis-[1] *prefix.* Indicates: **1.** Error or wrongness; for example, **misspell.** **2.** Badness or impropriety; for example, **misbehave, misdeed. 3.** Unsuitableness; for example, **misalliance. 4.** Opposite or lack of; for example, **mistrust. 5.** Failure; for example, **misfire.** [There are two separate developments of *mis-* that became confused in Modern English: 1. Middle English *mis-,* wrong, Old English *mis-,* from Germanic *missa-* (unattested), amiss, divergent, mutual. 2. Middle English *mes-,* bad, wrong, from Old French, from Vulgar Latin *minus-* (unattested), from Latin *minus,* MINUS.]

mis-[2] Variant of **miso-.**

mis·ad·ven·ture (míss-əd-vénchər || -ad-) *n.* **1.** An instance of great misfortune; a disaster. **2.** *Law.* A fatal accident, not due to negligence or criminal intent. —See Synonyms at **misfortune.** [Middle English *misaventure,* from Old French *mesaventure,* from *mesavenir,* to result in misfortune : *mes-,* badly, MIS- + *avenir,* to turn out, from Latin *advenīre,* to come to : *ad,* to + *venīre,* to come.]

mis·ad·vise (míss-əd-víz || -ad-) *tr.v.* **-vised, -vising, -vises.** To advise wrongly.

mis·al·li·ance (míssə-lí-ənss) *n.* An unsuitable alliance, especially in marriage. [French *mésalliance* : *més-,* improper, MIS- + ALLIANCE.]

mis·al·ly (míssə-lí) *tr.v.* **-lied, -lying, -lies.** To ally or unite badly.

mis·an·dry (mi-sándri, -zándri) *n.* Hatred of or hostility towards men; man-hating. [French : MIS- + *-andry,* from Greek *anēr* (stem *andr-*); man.] —**mis·andr·ist** *n. & adj.*

mis·an·thrope (míss'n-thrŏp, mízz'n-) *n.* Also **mis·an·thro·pist** (miss-ánthrəpist, miz-). A person who hates or distrusts humankind. [Greek *misanthrōpos,* hating humankind : MISO- + *anthrōpos,* human.] —**mis·an·throp·ic** (-thróppik) *adj.* —**mis·an·throp·i·cal·ly** *adv.* —**mis·an·thro·py** (miss-ánthrəpi, miz-) *n.*

mis·ap·ply (míssə-plī) *tr.v.* **-plied, -plying, -plies. 1.** To apply wrongly. **2.** To make wrong use of; especially, to misappropriate (funds). —**mis·ap·pli·ca·tion** (míss-áppli-káysh'n) *n.*

mis·ap·pre·hend (míss-áppri-hénd) *tr.v.* **-hended, -hending, -hends.** To fail to interpret correctly; misunderstand. —**mis·ap·pre·hen·sion** (-hénsh'n) *n.*

mis·ap·pro·pri·ate (míssə-prŏpri-ayt) *tr.v.* **-ated, -ating, -ates. 1.** To appropriate (money, funds, or the like) wrongly or dishonestly, especially for one's own use. **2.** To use illegally or wrongly.

mis·be·come (míss-bi-kúm, -bə-) *tr.v.* **-came** (-káym), **-come, -coming, -comes.** To be unsuitable or inappropriate for: *"what I have done that misbecame my place"* (Shakespeare).

mis·be·got·ten (míss-bi-gótt'n, -bə-) *adj.* Also **mis·be·got** (-gót). Begotten in an illegal or disreputable way; especially, illegitimate.

mis·be·have (míss-bi-háyv, -bə-) *v.* **-haved, -having, -haves.** —*intr.* To behave badly. —*tr.* To conduct (oneself) badly.

mis·be·lief (míss-bi-léef, -bə-) *n.* **1.** A wrong or faulty belief; an erroneous opinion. **2.** A heretical or unorthodox religious belief.

mis·be·lieve (míss-bi-léev, -bə-) *intr.v.* **-lieved, -lieving, -lieves.** *Obsolete.* To believe wrongly; hold a false or erroneous opinion.

misc. miscellaneous.

mis·cal·cu·late (míss-kálkew-layt) *v.* **-lated, -lating, -lates.** —*tr.* To calculate wrongly; make a wrong estimate of. —*intr.* To make an error in calculation or judgment. —**mis·cal·cu·la·tion** (-láysh'n) *n.*

mis·call (míss-káwl) *tr.v.* **-called, -calling, -calls. 1.** To call by a wrong or inappropriate name. **2.** *Regional.* To call by a bad name; revile.

mis·car·riage (míss-kárrij, *for sense 2* míss-karrij) *n.* **1. a.** Mismanagement; bad administration: *a miscarriage of justice.* **b.** Failure to attain the right or desired end: *the miscarriage of a hope; a miscarriage of a cargo.* **2.** Premature expulsion of a nonviable foetus from the uterus. In this sense, also called "spontaneous abortion".

mis·car·ry (míss-kárri) *intr.v.* **-ried, -rying, -ries. 1.** To go astray; be lost in transit: *the freight miscarried.* **2.** To go wrong; fail: *a good idea that miscarried.* **3.** To bring forth a foetus prematurely so that it does not survive; abort.

mis·cast (míss-ka̋ast || -ká̋st) *tr.v.* **-cast, -casting, -casts. 1.** To cast in an unsuitable role. **2.** To cast (a role or a theatrical production) inappropriately.

mis·ce·ge·na·tion (míssiji-náysh'n || mi-séji-) *n.* Intermarriage or interbreeding between different races; especially, marriage between white and nonwhite persons. [Latin *miscēre,* to mix + *genus,* race.] —**mis·ce·ge·net·ic** (-néttik) *adj.*

mis·cel·la·ne·a (míssə-láyni-ə) *pl.n.* A conglomeration of various items; especially, a collection of diverse literary works. [Latin *miscellānea,* from the neuter plural of *miscellāneus,* MISCELLANEOUS.]

mis·cel·la·ne·ous (míssə-láyn-i-əss, -yəss) *adj. Abbr.* **misc. 1.** Made up of a variety of parts or ingredients: *a miscellaneous collection.* **2.** Having a variety of characteristics, abilities, or appearances: *miscellaneous opinions.* **3.** Concerned with diverse subjects or aspects: *"various miscellaneous objections . . . against my views"* (Charles Darwin). [Latin *miscellāneus,* from *miscellus,* mixed, from *miscēre,* to mix.] —**mis·cel·la·ne·ous·ly** *adv.* —**mis·cel·la·ne·ous·ness** *n.*

Synonyms: miscellaneous, heterogeneous, motley, mixed, varied, assorted.

mis·cel·la·nist (mi-séllənist || *U.S.* míssə-laynist) *n.* One who compiles or edits a miscellany; a writer of miscellanies.

mis·cel·la·ny (mi-sélloni, *rarely* míss'l-əni || *U.S.* míss'l-ayni) *n., pl.* **-nies. 1.** A collection of various items, parts, or ingredients, especially one composed of diverse literary works. **2.** *Often plural.* A book or other publication containing writings of differing types or on different subjects. [Latin *miscellānea,* MISCELLANEA.]

mis·chance (míss-cha̋anss, -chaanss || -chánss, -chanss) *n.* **1.** An unfortunate occurrence; an unlucky incident. **2.** Bad luck. —See Synonyms at **misfortune.** [Middle English *mischaunce,* from Old French *mescheaunce* : *mes-,* ill, MIS- + *cheaunce,* CHANCE.]

mis·chief (míss-chif || -cheef) *n.* **1.** An act or behaviour that causes discomfiture or annoyance in another: *She's up to some mischief or other again.* **2.** An inclination or tendency to play pranks or cause embarrassment: *full of mischief.* **3.** One that causes minor trouble or a disturbance: *The child was a mischief in school.* **4.** Damage, destruction, or injury caused by a specified person or thing: *Wind wreaked untold mischief upon the crops.* [Middle English *meschief,* from Old French *meschief, meschef,* from *meschever,* to meet with misfortune : *mes-*, amiss, ill, MIS- + *chever*, to "come to a head", happen, from Common Romance *capāre* (unattested), from Latin *caput*, head.]

mis·chie·vous (míss-chivəss || -chéevəss) *adj.* **1.** Causing mischief. **2.** Playfully naughty; teasing: *a mischievous smile.* **3.** Troublesome; irritating: *a mischievous prank.* **4.** Causing harm, injury, or damage: *mischievous lies.* —See Synonyms at **playful.** [MISCHIEF + -OUS.] —**mis·chie·vous·ly** *adv.* —**mis·chie·vous·ness** *n.*

misch metal (mish) *n.* An alloy of cerium and several rare-earth elements. It produces sparks when struck and is used in lighter flints. [Partial translation of German *Mischmetall*, from *mischen*, to mix.]

mis·ci·ble (míssi-b'l) *adj. Chemistry.* Capable of being mixed in all proportions. Said especially of liquids. [Medieval Latin *miscībilis*, from Latin *miscēre*, to mix.] —**mis·ci·bil·i·ty** (-bíllət̄i) *n.*

mis·con·ceive (míss-kən-séev || -kon-) *tr.v.* **-ceived, -ceiving, -ceives.** To interpret in the wrong way; misunderstand. —**mis·con·ceiv·er** *n.*

mis·con·ceived (míss-kən-séevd || -kon-) *adj.* Based on a false understanding; badly thought out.

mis·con·cep·tion (míss-kən-sépsh'n || -kon-) *n.* An incorrect interpretation or understanding; a delusion.

mis·con·duct (míss-kón-dukt, -dəkt) *n.* **1.** Behaviour not conforming to prevailing standards or laws; impropriety; immorality: *professional misconduct.* **2.** Dishonest or bad management, especially by persons entrusted to act on another's behalf; malfeasance. ~*tr.v.* (míss-kən-dúkt || -kon-) **misconducted, -ducting, -ducts.** **1.** To behave (oneself) improperly. **2.** To administer or manage poorly or dishonestly.

mis·con·struc·tion (míss-kən-strúksh'n || -kon-) *n.* **1.** An inaccurate explanation, interpretation, or report; a misunderstanding. **2.** A faulty construction, especially of a sentence or clause.

mis·con·strue (míss-kən-stróō || -kon-, -strēw) *tr.v.* **-strued, -struing, -strues.** To mistake the meaning of; misinterpret; misunderstand.

mis·count (míss-kównt || *West Indies also* -kúngt) *v.* **-counted, -counting, -counts.** —*tr.* To count or estimate incorrectly; miscalculate. —*intr.* To err in counting. ~*n.* (míss-kownt || -kungt). An inaccurate count.

mis·cre·ant (mískri-ənt) *n.* **1.** An evildoer or villain. **2.** *Archaic.* An infidel or heretic. [Middle English *miscreaunt*, heretical, unbelieving, from Old French *mescreant*, present participle of *mescroire*, to disbelieve : *mes-*, MIS- + *croire*, to believe, from Latin *crēdere*.] —**mis·cre·ant** *adj.*

mis·cre·ate (míss-kri-áyt) *tr.v.* **-ated, -ating, -ates.** To make or shape badly. ~*adj.* (-ayt, -ət, -it). *Rare.* Formed unnaturally; deformed. —**mis·cre·a·tion** (-áysh'n) *n.*

mis·cue (míss-kéw) *n.* **1.** In billiards, a stroke that misses or just brushes the ball due to a slip of the cue. **2.** A blunder or mistake. ~*intr.v.* **miscued, -cuing, -cues.** **1.** To make a miscue. **2.** In acting, to miss one's own cue or mistake someone else's cue for one's own.

mis·date (míss-dáyt) *tr.v.* **-dated, -dating, -dates.** To date wrongly or incorrectly.

mis·deal (míss-déel) *v.* **-dealt** (-délt), **-dealing, -deals.** —*tr.* To deal (playing cards) in the wrong order or incorrectly. —*intr.* To deal cards incorrectly. —**mis·deal** *n.* —**mis·deal·er** *n.*

mis·deed (míss-déed, -deed) *n.* A wicked, immoral, or illegal deed.

mis·de·mean·ant (míss-di-méenənt) *n.* One who is guilty of, or has been convicted and sentenced for, a misdemeanour.

mis·de·mean·our, *U.S.* **mis·de·mean·or** (míss-di-méenər) *n.* **1.** A wrong action; a misdeed. **2.** *Law.* Formerly in Britain, an offence of lesser gravity than a felony. Compare **crime, felony.**

mis·di·ag·nose (míss-dĭ-əg-nóz, -nŏss) *tr.v.* **-nosed, -nosing, -noses.** To diagnose incorrectly. —**mis·di·ag·no·sis** *n.*

mis·di·al (míss-dĭ-əl, -dīl) *tr.v.* **-dialled** or *U.S.* **-dialed, -dialling** or *U.S.* **-dialing, -dials.** To dial (a telephone number) incorrectly.

mis·di·rect (míss-di-rékt, -də-, -dīr-) *tr.v.* **-rected, -recting, -rects.** **1.** To instruct incorrectly: *The judge misdirected the jury.* **2. a.** To put a wrong address on. **b.** To give incorrect directions to (someone seeking a location or address). **3.** To direct (energy or an emotion) mistakenly or misguidedly. —**mis·di·rec·tion** (-réksh'n) *n.*

mis·do (míss-dóō) *v.* **-did** (-díd), **-done** (-dún), **-doing, -does** (-dúz). —*tr.* To do wrongly or awkwardly; botch. —*intr. Obsolete.* To do wrong or harm. —**mis·do·er** *n.*

mis·doubt (míss-dówt) *v.* **-doubted, -doubting, -doubts.** *Archaic.* —*tr.* To suspect; fear; feel wary of. —*intr.* To have doubts or be fearful.

mis·em·ploy (míss-im-plóy || -em-) *tr.v.* **-ployed, -ploying, -ploys.** To put to a wrong use; abuse. —**mis·em·ploy·ment** *n.*

mise en scène (méez-on-sáyn, -ON-, -sén) *n.* **1. a.** The properties, scenery, and the like, used to stage a play or a scene in a play. **b.** The arrangement of the performers and of such properties. **2.** An environment; surroundings. [French, "placing on stage".]

mi·ser (mízər) *n.* **1.** One who deprives himself of all but the barest essentials in order to hoard money. **2.** A greedy, stingy, or avaricious person. [Originally, "wretch", from Latin *miser*, wretched.]

mis·er·a·ble (míz-rəb'l, mízzə- || mízh-) *adj.* **1.** Very unhappy; wretched. **2.** Causing or accompanied by wretchedness or other discomfort: *a miserable climate.* **3.** Gloomy; dismal: *a miserable film.* **4.** Unworthy; contemptible: *a miserable fellow.* —See Synonyms at **sad.** [Middle English, from Old French *miserable*, from Latin *miserābilis*, pitiable, from *miserārī*, to have pity, from *miser*, wretched,

unfortunate.] —**mis·er·a·ble·ness** *n.* —**mis·er·a·bly** *adv.*

mi·sère (mi-záir) *n.* In some card games, such as solo whist, an undertaking that a hand will win no tricks. [French, poverty.]

mis·e·re·re (mízzə-raír-i, -réer-i) *n.* **1.** Part of a church seat, a misericord. **2.** A prayer for mercy. [From MISERERE.]

Mis·e·re·re (mízzə-ráir-i, -réer-i) *n.* **1.** The 51st Psalm, which opens with "*Miserere mei Deus*" (Have mercy upon me, O God). **2.** A musical setting of this Psalm. [Latin, imperative of *miserērī*, to have pity, from *miser*, wretched.]

mis·er·i·cord, mis·er·i·corde (mi-zérri-kawrd, *rarely* mízzəri- || *U.S. also* -sérri-) *n.* **1.** In a monastery: **a.** The relaxation of a rule, such as a dispensation from fasting. **b.** A room used by monks granted such a dispensation. **2.** A bracket, sometimes in the form of a carved figure, attached to the underside of a hinged seat in a church stall, against which a standing person may lean. Also called "miserere". **4.** A narrow dagger used in medieval times to deliver the death stroke to one who was seriously wounded, especially a knight. [Middle English, pity, mercy, dagger, from Old French, from Latin *misericordia*, from *misericors*, pitiful : *miserērī*, to have pity + *cors* (stem *cord-*), heart.]

mi·ser·ly (mízərli) *adj.* Characteristic of a miser; tending to hoard money or possessions; extremely mean: *too miserly to leave a tip.* See Synonyms at **stingy.** —**mi·ser·li·ness** *n.*

mis·er·y (mízzəri) *n., pl.* **-ies.** **1.** Prolonged or extreme suffering; a state of great mental, emotional, or physical pain; wretchedness. **2.** A cause or source of suffering or pain, such as an affliction or deprivation. **3.** *British Informal.* One who is constantly depressed or gloomy. [Middle English *miserie*, from Anglo-French, from Latin *miseria*, from *miser*, wretched.]

mis·es·teem (míss-i-stéem, -e-) *tr.v.* **-teemed, -teeming, -teems.** *Formal.* To fail to regard with deserved esteem; disrespect.

mis·es·ti·mate (míss-ésti-mayt) *tr.v.* **-mated, -mating, -mates.** To estimate or appraise inaccurately or wrongly. ~*n.* (-mət, -mit || -mayt). An inaccurate estimate or appraisal.

mis·fea·sance (miss-féez'nss) *n. Law. Rare.* The improper and unlawful execution of some act that in itself is lawful and proper. Compare **malfeasance, nonfeasance.** [Old French *mesfaisance*, from *mesfaire*, to misdo : *mes-*, wrongly, MIS- + *faire*, to do, from Latin *facere*.]

mis·fea·sor (miss-féezər) *n. Law.* One guilty of misfeasance.

mis·fire (míss-fīr) *intr.v.* **-fired, -firing, -fires.** **1.** To fail to explode or ignite when expected, as a gun or internal-combustion engine may. **2.** To fail to achieve the anticipated result: *a scheme that misfired.* —**mis·fire** (-fīr) *n.*

mis·fit (míss-fit, *rarely* -fít) *n.* **1.** Something of the wrong size or shape for its purpose. **2.** A person who is maladjusted or finds it difficult to fit in with people or the immediate environment. ~*v.* (-fít) **misfitted, -fitting, -fits.** *Rare.* —*tr.* To fit poorly. —*intr.* To be of the wrong size or shape.

mis·for·tune (miss-fór-chən, míss-, -chōon, -tewn) *n.* **1.** Bad fortune or ill luck. **2.** An instance of this; a distressing occurrence.

   Synonyms: misfortune, adversity, mishap, mischance, misadventure.

mis·give (miss-gív) *v.* **-gave** (-gáyv), **-given** (-gívv'n), **-giving, -gives.** —*tr.* To arouse suspicion or apprehension in. —*intr.* To be suspicious, apprehensive, or doubtful. [Originally, to suggest doubt (used of the mind) : MIS- (wrongly) + GIVE (in the Middle English sense "to suggest").]

mis·giv·ing (miss-gívving) *n. Often plural.* A feeling of uncertainty or apprehension: *approached the empty house with some misgivings.* See Synonyms at **apprehension, qualm.**

mis·gov·ern (míss-gúvvərn) *tr.v.* **-erned, -erning, -erns.** To govern or administrate inefficiently or badly. —**mis·gov·ern·ment** *n.* —**mis·gov·er·nor** *n.*

mis·guide (míss-gíd) *tr.v.* **-guided, -guiding, -guides.** To give wrong or misleading directions to; lead astray; misdirect. —**mis·guid·ance** *n.* —**mis·guid·er** *n.*

mis·guid·ed (míss-gídid) *adj.* Confused or erring in thought or action; foolish: *a misguided comment.* —**mis·guid·ed·ly** *adv.*

mis·han·dle (míss-hánd'l) *tr.v.* **-dled, -dling, -dles.** To treat or deal with clumsily or inefficiently.

mis·hap (míss-hap, *rarely* -háp) *n.* **1.** Bad luck or misfortune. **2.** An unfortunate accident.

mis·hear (míss-héer) *tr.v.* **-heard** (-hérd), **-hearing, -hears.** To hear wrongly or badly.

Mi·shi·ma (míshimə), **Yukio,** born Kimitake Hiraoka (1925–70). Japanese writer from a samurai family. His stories are often evocations of the imperial past. His novels include *Confessions of a Mask* (1949) and *The Sailor who Fell from Grace with the Sea* (1963). He also did Kabuki and Noh plays.

mis·hit (míss-hít) *n.* In certain games, such as tennis or squash, a faulty or bad hit: *mishits that came off the handle and not the strings.* ~*tr.v.* (-hít) **mishit, -hitting, -hits.** To hit (a ball) faultily or badly.

mish·mash (mísh-mash || mísh-) *n.* A collection or mixture of unrelated things; a hotchpotch. [Reduplication of MASH.]

Mish·nah, Mish·na (mísh-nə, -náá) *n., pl.* **Mish·na·yoth** (-náá-yōt, -nə-yōth). **1.** The first section of the Talmud, consisting of a collection of early oral interpretations of the scriptures as compiled about A.D. 200. **2.** A paragraph from this collection. [Rabbinical Hebrew *mishnāh*, repetition, instruction, from *shānāh*, to repeat.] —**Mish·na·ic** (-náy-ik), **Mish·nic** (mísh-nik), **Mish·ni·cal** *adj.*

mis·in·form (míss-in-fórm) *tr.v.* **-formed, -forming, -forms.** To give wrong or inaccurate information to. —**mis·in·form·ant** (-ənt), **mis·**

in·form·er *n.* —**mis·in·for·ma·tion** (-fər-máysh'n) *n.*

mis·in·ter·pret (míss-in-térprit) *tr.v.* **-preted, -preting, -prets.** 1. To infer inaccurately. 2. To err in understanding. —**mis·in·ter·pre·ta·tion** (-térpri-táysh'n) *n.* —**mis·in·ter·pret·er** *n.*

mis·judge (míss-júj) *v.* **-judged, -judging, -judges.** —*tr.* To make a mistake in one's judgment of. —*intr.* To be wrong in judging. —**mis·judg·ment** *n.*

Miskito. Variant of **Mosquito.**

mis·lay (mis-láy) *tr.v.* **-laid** (-láyd), **-laying, -lays.** 1. To put in a place that is afterwards forgotten; lose. 2. *Rare.* To place or put down incorrectly: *mislay linoleum.* —**mis·lay·er** *n.*

mis·lead (míss-léed) *tr.v.* **-led** (-léd), **-leading, -leads.** 1. To lead or guide in the wrong direction. 2. To lead into error or wrongdoing, whether by accident or design. —See Synonyms at **deceive.**

mis·lead·ing (míss-léeding, miss-) *adj.* Tending to mislead; deceptive. —**mis·lead·ing·ly** *adv.*

mis·like (míss-lík) *tr.v.* **-liked, -liking, -likes.** 1. To disapprove of; dislike. 2. *Archaic.* To be displeasing to.

~*n.* *Rare.* Dislike; disapproval. [Middle English *misliken,* Old English *mislícian* : *mis-,* ill + *lícian,* to LIKE.]

mis·man·age (míss-mánnij) *tr.v.* **-aged, -aging, -ages.** To manage badly or carelessly. —**mis·man·age·ment** *n.*

mis·match (míss-mách) *tr.v.* **-matched, -matching, -matches.** To match unsuitably or inaccurately, especially in marriage. —**mis·match** (míss-mach) *n.*

mis·mate (míss-máyt) *tr.v.* **-mated, -mating, -mates.** *Literary.* To mate or match unsuitably: *Fate mismated them.*

mis·move *n.* A pass in Rugby football that deliberately misses one or more players in the conventional order of three-quarters; for example, from the stand-off half to the outside centre.

mis·name (míss-náym) *tr.v.* **-named, -naming, -names.** To call by a wrong or inappropriate name.

mis·no·mer (míss-nṓmər) *n.* 1. An error in naming a person or place. 2. A name wrongly or unsuitably applied to a person or object. [Middle English, from Anglo-French, from Old French *mesnommer,* to misname : *mes-,* wrongly, MIS- + *nommer,* to name, from Latin *nōmināre,* from *nōmen,* name.]

miso-, mis- *comb. form.* Indicates hating, hatred, or hostility; for example, **misogyny, misandry.** [Greek, from *misein,* to hate, and *misos*†, hatred.]

mi·sog·a·my (mī-sóggəmi, mi-) *n.* Hatred of marriage. [MISO- + -GAMY.] —**mi·sog·a·mist** (-sóggəmist) *n. & adj.*

mi·sog·y·ny (mi-sójəni, mī-) *n.* Hatred of or hostility towards women. [Greek *misogunia* : MISO- + -GYNY.] —**mi·sog·y·nist** (-sójinist) *n. & adj.* —**mi·sog·y·nis·tic** (-sójinístik), **mi·sog·y·nous** (-sójinəss) *adj.*

mi·sol·o·gy (mī-sólləji, mi-) *n.* Hatred of reason, argument, or enlightenment. [Greek *misologia* : MISO- + -LOGY.] —**mi·sol·o·gist** *n.*

mis·o·ne·ism (mísō-née-iz'm, míssō-) *n.* Hatred of change or innovation. [Italian *misoneismo* : MISO- + Greek *neos,* new.] —**mis·o·ne·ist** *n. & adj.*

mis·pick·el (míss-pick'l) *n.* A mineral, **arsenopyrite** *(see).* [German, variant of earlier *Mispûtl, Mispilt*†.]

mis·place (míss-pláyss) *tr.v.* **-placed, -placing, -places.** 1. **a.** To put in a wrong place. **b.** To lose; mislay. 2. To bestow (faith, affection, or confidence, for example) wrongly, as on an improper, unsuitable, or unworthy person or idea: *Your loyalty to that firm is quite misplaced.* —**mis·place·ment** *n.*

mis·play (míss-play) *n.* A mistaken action in a game.

~*tr.v.* (-pláy) **misplayed, -playing, -plays.** To make a misplay of.

mis·plead·ing (miss-pléeding, míss-) *n. Law.* An error in pleading.

mis·print (míss-prínt) *tr.v.* **-printed, -printing, -prints.** To print incorrectly.

~*n.* (miss-print, *rarely* -prínt). An error in printing.

mis·prise, mis·prize (míss-príz) *tr.v.* **-prised, -prising, -prises.** To undervalue; disparage.

mis·pri·sion (míss-prízh'n) *n. Law.* 1. Maladministration of public office. 2. Neglect in reporting a crime: *misprision of treason.* [Middle English, from Anglo-French *mesprisioun,* from *mesprendre* : *mes-,* wrongly, MIS- + *prendre,* to take, from Latin *praehendere,* to grasp, seize.]

mis·pro·nounce (míss-prə-nównss ‖ *West Indies also* -núngss) *tr.v.* **-nounced, -nouncing, -nounces.** To pronounce badly or incorrectly. —**mis·pro·nun·ci·a·tion** (-núnsi-áysh'n.) *n.*

mis·quote (míss-kwót) *tr.v.* **-quoted, -quoting, -quotes.** To quote incorrectly. —**mis·quo·ta·tion** (-kwō-táysh'n) *n.*

mis·read (míss-réed) *tr.v.* **-read** (-réd), **-reading, -reads.** 1. To read inaccurately. 2. To misinterpret: *misread her intentions.*

mis·re·lat·ed participle (míss-ri-láytid, -rə-) *n. Grammar.* A participle that lacks clear connection with the word it modifies. In the sentence *Working at my desk, the sudden noise startled me,* the participle *working* is misrelated because it modifies *me,* not *noise.* Also called "dangling participle".

mis·re·mem·ber (míss-ri-mémbər, -rə-) *tr.v.* **-bered, -bering, -bers.** 1. To recollect incorrectly. 2. *Regional.* To forget.

mis·re·port (míss-ri-pórt, -rə- ‖ -pórt) *tr.v.* **-ported, -porting, -ports.** To report mistakenly or falsely.

~*n.* An inaccurate or wrong report. —**mis·re·port·er** *n.*

mis·rep·re·sent (míss-réppri-zént) *tr.v.* **-sented, -senting, -sents.** 1. To give an incorrect or misleading representation of: *misrepresented the facts of the case.* 2. To serve incorrectly or dishonestly as an official representative of. —**mis·rep·re·sen·ta·tion** (-zen-táysh'n,

-z'n-) *n.* —**mis·rep·re·sen·ta·tive** (-zéntətiv) *adj.* —**mis·rep·re·sent·er** *n.*

mis·rule (míss-róōl ‖ -réwl) *tr.v.* **-ruled, -ruling, -rules.** To rule wrongly, unjustly, or unwisely; misgovern.

~*n.* 1. Misgovernment. 2. Disorder or lawless confusion.

miss¹ (miss) *v.* **missed, missing, misses.** —*tr.* 1. To fail to hit, reach, attain, catch, meet, or otherwise make contact with: *miss the target; missed the bus.* 2. To fail to perceive, understand, or otherwise experience: *missed the subtlety of the argument.* 3. To fail to accomplish or achieve: *You missed catching her by ten minutes; my heart missed a beat.* 4. To fail to be present for or perform: *We don't want to miss a day of work.* 5. **a.** To leave out or omit. Often used with *out: You missed out a name in typing the list.* **b.** To overlook or let go by; let slip: *miss a chance.* 6. To escape or avoid: *missed death by inches.* 7. **a.** To discover the absence or loss of: *I was halfway home before I missed my gloves.* **b.** To feel the lack or loss of; yearn for (what is past or absent): *I miss the good old days.* —*intr.* 1. To fail to hit or otherwise make contact with something: *She fired her final shot and missed again.* 2. To misfire. —**miss out.** *Informal.* To fail to benefit from or achieve something desirable. Often used with *on: She missed out on getting a promotion.*

~*n.* A failure to hit, succeed, or find. —**give (something) a miss.** *Informal.* To pass over something, as by not visiting or attending: *gave the party a miss.* [Middle English *missen,* Old English *missan,* from Germanic *missjan* (unattested); akin to MIS-.]

miss² *n., pl.* **misses.** 1. *Capital* **M.** A title or form of address used when speaking to or of an unmarried woman or girl: **a.** Used before her surname. **b.** Used before her first name, as formerly by servants. 2. A title used in speaking to an unmarried woman or girl, used without her name. 3. An unmarried woman or girl. 4. A title or form of address used by schoolchildren when speaking of or to a schoolmistress. 5. *Capital* **M.** A title given to a young woman representing a town, country, institution, or the like at certain events, especially beauty contests: *Miss Sweden.* 6. *Capital* **M. a.** A title or form of address given to some women who have achieved fame or prominence in certain spheres of activity and who retain their maiden name after marriage. **b.** *Southern U.S.* A respectful title or form of address used with a first name, given to married women. [Short for MISTRESS.]

Usage: In recent years, criticism has been directed, largely from feminist sources, at the twofold titular classification of women into *Miss* and *Mrs.* — a distinction which, unlike the male *Master* and *Mr.,* is not restricted in terms of age. Since *Miss* and *Mrs.* may be seen as defining women solely in terms of their relationship to men, the use of *Ms* has been advocated as a neutral alternative, to be used for or by any woman, regardless of marital status. *Ms* has become increasingly common in written English, especially in letter-writing, where the writer is unsure of the married status of the addressee. In speech, the word has had less success, because of its uncertain pronunciation (miz, although some prefer məz), and is generally only used in a self-conscious or jocular manner.

mis·sal (míss'l) *n.* 1. A book containing all the prayers and responses necessary for celebrating the Roman Catholic Mass throughout the year. 2. Loosely, any prayer book. [Middle English *messel,* from Medieval Latin *missāle,* from *missālis,* pertaining to the mass, from Late Latin *missa,* MASS.]

missel thrush. Variant of mistle thrush.

mis·shape (míss-sháyp, mísh-) *tr.v.* **-shaped, -shaped** or **-shapen** (-sháypən), **-shaping, -shapes.** To shape badly; deform. —**mis·shap·en** *adj.*

mis·sile (míssīl ‖ *chiefly U.S.* míss'l) *n.* 1. Any object or weapon that is fired, thrown, dropped, or otherwise projected at a target; a projectile. 2. **A guided missile** *(see).* 3. **A ballistic missile** *(see).* [Latin *missilis,* from *mittere* (past participle *missus*), to let go, send.]

mis·sile·ry (míssīl-ri ‖ míss'l-) *n.* Also **mis·sil·ry** (míss'l-). 1. The science of making and using guided or ballistic missiles. 2. Missiles collectively.

miss·ing (míssing) *adj.* 1. Not present; absent; lost; lacking. 2. *Military.* Unaccounted for after combat or manoeuvres, and possibly killed or injured.

missing link *n.* 1. A theoretical primate postulated to bridge the evolutionary gap between the anthropoid apes and humans. 2. Something needed to complete a series or solve a mystery.

mis·sion (mísh'n) *n.* 1. **a.** A body of persons sent to a foreign country, especially to conduct negotiations or establish relations. **b.** The business with which such a body of persons is charged. 2. **a.** A body of persons sent to do missionary work in a foreign land. **b.** An establishment of missionaries abroad. **c.** The district assigned to a missionary. **d.** Missionary duty or work. **e.** A missionary building or compound. **f.** An organisation for carrying on missionary work in any territory. 3. *Chiefly U.S.* A permanent diplomatic office in a foreign country. 4. **a.** A journey undertaken to perform an assigned task, such as espionage or exploration. **b.** *Military.* A combat operation assigned to an individual or unit; especially, an air operation against an enemy. 5. A church welfare establishment, especially in a large city: *a seaman's mission.* 6. A church or congregation, especially of a Protestant church, without a resident minister. 7. A series of special religious services to deepen or spread religious faith. 8. An impelling task or duty; a vocation: *a woman with a mission; our company's mission statement.*

~*adj.* 1. Of or pertaining to a mission. 2. *U.S.* In the style of early Spanish missions of the southwestern United States: *mission furniture.*

~*v.* **missioned, -sioning, -sions.** —*tr.* **1.** To send on a mission. **2.** To organise or establish a mission among (a people) or in (a territory). —*intr.* To conduct a religious mission. [French, from Latin *missiō* (stem *missiōn-*), from *mittere* (past participle *missus*), to let go, send.] —**mis·sion·er** *n.*

mis·sion·ar·y (mísh'n-ri, -əri, mísh-nəri || *U.S.* míshə-nerri) *n., pl.* **-ies.** One who is sent on a mission; especially, a person sent to do religious or charitable work in some territory or foreign country. ~*adj.* **1.** Of or pertaining to missions or missionaries. **2.** Engaged in the activities of a mission or missionary. **3.** Tending to propagandise or use insistent persuasion: *missionary fervour.*

missionary position *n.* A conventional position used in heterosexual intercourse in which the partners lie facing one another with the woman underneath. [19th-century missionaries are supposed to have introduced this position to indigenous Polynesians.]

missis. Variant of **missus.**

Mis·sis·sip·pi[1] (míssi-síppi). State of the southern United States on the Gulf of Mexico, bounded by the Mississippi river in the west. All of it is below 250 metres (820 feet), with swamplands along the Mississippi river. Mississippi is the leading state in cotton production, and soya beans, rice, maize, and hay are also important. The state has vast reserves of oil and natural gas, and its manufactures include wood products, clothing, processed foods (including seafood), and chemicals. The first settlers were French (1699), and the area became part of Louisiana. It was British (1763–79), then Spanish, until ceded to the United States (1783). It was admitted to the Union in 1817. Jackson is the capital and largest city.

Mississippi[2]. Chief river of the United States. Rising in the lake region of north Minnesota, it flows 3 780 kilometres (2,348 miles) to the Gulf of Mexico through a delta in south Louisiana. Its many tributaries include the Missouri, Ohio, Arkansas, and Red rivers. The Mississippi-Missouri, 6 212 kilometres (3,860 miles) long, is the world's third longest river after the Nile and Amazon. Its vast basin stretches into Canada and includes or touches 31 U.S. states. St. Louis, Memphis, and New Orleans are its chief ports.

Mis·sis·sip·pi·an (míssi-síppi-ən) *adj.* **1.** *Geology. U.S.* Of, belonging to, or designating the **Lower Carboniferous period** *(see).* **2.** Of or concerned with the state of Mississippi.
~*n.* **1.** *U.S. Geology.* The Mississippian period. Preceded by *the.* **2.** A native or inhabitant of Mississippi.

mis·sive (míssiv) *n. Formal.* A letter or message, especially a formal or official one. Sometimes used humorously.
~*adj.* Sent or dispatched; intended for sending: *letters missive.* [Noun, Middle English phrase *letter missive,* letter sent by superior authority, from Medieval Latin *litterăe missīvae* (plural); adjective, Medieval Latin *missīvus,* from Latin *mittere* (past participle *missus*), to let go, send.]

Mis·so·lon·ghi (míssə-lóng-gi). *Greek* **Mesolóngion.** Port of west central Greece. Situated on the north shore of the Gulf of Pátrai (Patras), it withstood two sieges by the Turks during the Greek War of Independence (1822–23, 1825–26). It was the place of Lord Byron's death (1824).

Missouri[1] (mi-zoŏr-i). State of the central United States, bounded in the east by the Mississippi river. Prairies lie north of the Missouri, with the Great Plains to the west, the rolling hills of the Ozark plateau in the south, and the Mississippi cotton lands to the southeast. The state produces lead, zinc, coal, iron ore, cattle, pigs, maize, soya beans, wheat, and cotton, but is a predominantly manufacturing state, with major transport equipment and food processing industries. The area was under Spanish control (1762–1800), and passed to the United States with the Louisiana Purchase (1803). The Missouri valley became a major pioneer route, St. Louis being known as the "Gateway to the Far West". Missouri became a state in 1821. Jefferson City is its capital.

Missouri[2]. Longest river of the United States. It rises in the Rocky Mountains of Montana and flows 4 130 kilometres (2,565 miles) across the Great Plains to join the Mississippi near St. Louis. Omaha and Kansas City are on its banks. French explorers reached the river in the late 17th century.

mis·spell (míss-spél) *tr.v.* **-spelt** or **-spelled, -spelling, -spells.** To spell incorrectly. —**mis·spell·ing** *n.*

mis·spend (míss-spénd) *tr.v.* **-spent** (-spént), **-spending, -spends.** To spend improperly or extravagantly; squander.

mis·state (míss-stáyt) *tr.v.* **-stated, -stating, -states.** To state wrongly or falsely. —**mis·state·ment** *n.*

mis·step (míss-stép) *n.* **1.** A misplaced or awkward step. **2.** An instance of wrong or improper conduct.

mis·sus (míssiz || míssəss) *n. Informal.* **1.** The mistress of a household. Usually preceded by *the.* **2.** A wife. Usually preceded by *the.*

miss·y (míssi) *n., pl.* **-ies.** *Often capital* **M.** A familiar form of address to a young girl, especially a pert one.

mist (mist) *n.* **1.** A mass of fine droplets of water in the atmosphere, impairing visibility near the ground. Technically, visibility is 1–2 kilometres. **2.** Water vapour condensed on and clouding the appearance of a surface. **3.** Fine drops of any liquid, such as perfume, sprayed into the air. **4.** A colloidal suspension of a liquid in a gas. **5.** Something that dims or conceals sight or judgment. **6.** Something that produces or gives the impression of dimness or obscurity: *lost in the mists of time.*
~*v.* **misted, misting, mists.** —*intr.* To be or become obscured or misty; be blurred or concealed by or as if by a mist. Often used with *up.* —*tr.* To conceal or veil as if with a mist. [Middle English, Old English *mist,* from Germanic.]

mis·tak·a·ble (mi-stáykəb'l) *adj.* Capable of being mistaken or misunderstood. —**mis·tak·a·bly** *adv.*

mis·take (mi-stáyk) *n.* **1.** An error or fault. **2.** A misconception or misunderstanding.
~*v.* **mistook** (-stoŏk), **-taken** (-stáykən), **-taking, -takes.** —*tr.* **1.** To understand wrongly; misinterpret: *"Aziz overrated hospitality, mistaking it for intimacy"* (E.M. Forster). **2.** To recognise or identify incorrectly: *We mistook her for her sister.* **3.** To judge incorrectly: *mistook her own talent.* —*intr.* To make a mistake. [Middle English *mistaken,* from Old Norse *mistaka,* to take in error : *miss-,* wrongly + *taka,* to TAKE.]

mis·tak·en (mi-stáykən) *adj.* **1.** Wrong or incorrect in opinion, understanding, or perception. **2.** Based on error; wrong: *a mistaken view of the situation.* —**mis·tak·en·ly** *adv.* —**mis·tak·en·ness** *n.*

Mis·ter (místər) *n.* **1.** *Abbr.* **Mr.** A title or form of address used when speaking to or of a man. It is usually written in its abbreviated form and placed before a man's surname: *Mr. Jones.* **2.** *Abbr.* **Mr.** A form of address used before the title of a male office-holder: *Mr. Speaker.* **3.** The official term of address for certain naval personnel: **a.** A warrant officer. **b.** In the merchant navy, any officer except for the captain. **4.** *British.* A title or form of address for a male surgeon or consultant, used in preference to *Doctor.* **5.** *Small* **m.** *Informal.* A form of address, without a name, used when speaking to a man. [Weakened form of MASTER.]

mis·ti·gris (místi-gree) *n.* **1.** A blank card that is used in a type of poker. **2.** The type of poker in which this card is used. [French *mistigri*†, jack of clubs, game in which this card is wild.]

mis·time (míss-tīm) *tr.v.* **-timed, -timing, -times.** To time (a stroke or remark, for example) wrongly or inappropriately.

Mis·tin·guett (míss-tang-gét, meéss-, -taN-), stage name of Jeanne Marie Bourgeois (1875–1956). French comedienne. She took her name from Miss Tinguett in the musical comedy, *Miss Helyett.*

mis·tle thrush, mis·sel thrush (míss'l) *n.* A European thrush, *Turdus viscivorus,* with a spotted breast. [Referring to its feeding on mistletoe berries.]

mis·tle·toe (míss'l-tō) *n.* **1.** A Eurasian parasitic shrub, *Viscum album,* having leathery evergreen leaves and waxy white berries. **2.** A mistletoe sprig, used as a Christmas decoration, under which kissing is traditionally permitted. [Middle English *mistilto,* Old English *misteltān* : *mistel,* mistletoe + *tān,* twig, from Germanic *tainaz* (unattested).]

mis·took. Past tense of **mistake.**

mis·tral (místrəl, miss-traál; *French* meess-) *n.* A dry, cold, northerly wind that blows in squalls through the Rhône Valley and nearby areas towards the Mediterranean coast of southern France. [French, from Provençal, from Latin *magistrālis (ventus),* "master (wind)", from *magistrālis,* MAGISTRAL.]

mis·trans·late (míss-traanz-láyt, -tranz-, -traanss-, -transs-) *tr.v.* **-lated, -lating, -lates.** To translate (material, especially in a foreign language) wrongly. —**mis·trans·la·tion** (-láysh'n) *n.*

mis·treat (míss-treét) *tr.v.* **-treated, -treating, -treats.** To handle or treat roughly or wrongly; abuse. See Synonyms at **abuse.** —**mis·treat·ment** *n.*

mis·tress (míss-triss, -trəss) *n.* **1.** A woman in a position of authority, such as the head of a college, household, or estate: *"Thirteen years had seen her mistress of Kellynch Hall"* (Jane Austen). **2.** A woman owning an animal or, formerly, a slave. **3.** A woman who has strong control over something: *mistress of the situation.* **4.** *Often capital* **M.** Any idea or object personified as a woman having control or authority over something: *Britain was once mistress of the seas.* **5.** A woman who has mastered a skill: *a mistress of mechanical engineering.* **6. a.** Especially formerly, a woman who has a continuing sexual relationship with a man to whom she is not married and who often receives financial support from the man. **b.** *Archaic.* A woman loved by a man. **7.** *Capital* **M.** A title or form of address used with a woman's name. Now archaic except in parts of Scotland. **8.** *British.* A female schoolteacher. [Middle English, from Old French *maistresse,* from *maistre,* MASTER.]

mis·tri·al (míss-trī-əl, -trīl) *n. Law.* **1.** A trial that becomes invalid because of a basic error in procedure. **2.** *U.S.* An inconclusive trial, such as one in which the jurors fail to agree on a verdict.

mis·trust (míss-trúst) *n.* Lack of trust; suspicion; doubt.
~*v.* **mistrusted, -trusting, -trusts.** —*tr.* To regard without confidence; be wary or suspicious of. —*intr.* To be wary or doubtful. —See Synonyms at **uncertainty.** —See Usage note at **distrust.** —**mis·trust·ful** *adj.* —**mis·trust·ing·ly** *adv.*

mist·y (místi) *adj.* **-ier, -iest.** **1.** Consisting of or resembling mist: *a misty rain.* **2.** Obscured or clouded by or as if by mist. **3.** Lacking in clarity; vague: *misty ideas.* —**mist·i·ly** *adv.* —**mist·i·ness** *n.*

mis·un·der·stand (míss-undər-stánd) *tr.v.* **-stood** (-stoŏd), **-standing, -stands.** To understand incorrectly; misinterpret.

mis·un·der·stand·ing (míss-undər-stánding) *n.* **1.** A failure to understand correctly. **2.** A disagreement or quarrel.

mis·un·der·stood (míss-undər-stoŏd) *adj.* **1.** Understood wrongly or incorrectly. **2.** Not appreciated or given sympathetic understanding: *Is she a misunderstood genius or merely a crank?*

mis·use (míss-yoōss) *n.* Also **mis·us·age** (-ij). Improper or wrong use; misapplication.
~*tr.v.* (-yoōz) **-used, -using, -uses.** **1.** To use wrongly or incorrectly. **2.** To mistreat or abuse. —See Synonyms at **abuse.** —**mis·us·er** *n.*

mis·val·ue (míss-vál-yoo) *tr.v.* **-ued, -uing, -ues.** To value or estimate incorrectly.

mis·word (miss-wúrd) *tr.v.* **-worded, -wording, -words.** To express incorrectly; word inaccurately.

M.I.T. Massachusetts Institute of Technology.

Mitch·ell (míchəl), **Margaret** (1900–49). U.S. writer. Her only novel, *Gone with the Wind* (1936), won the Pulitzer prize. The film of the same name, a Hollywood epic, was first released in 1939.

mite[1] (mīt) *n.* Any of various small arachnids of the order Acarina (or Acari), some of which are parasitic. They may infest foods and carry disease. [Middle English *mite*, Old English *mīte*, from Germanic *mītōn* (unattested).]

mite[2] *n.* **1. a.** A very small amount of money or contribution. **b.** A **widow's mite** (see). **2.** A coin of very small value, especially a former Flemish coin. **3.** The smallest bit or slightest thing: *not a mite of sympathy.* **4.** Any very small object or creature, especially a child: *Poor wee mite!* [Middle English (originally in the phrase "not worth a mite"), from Middle Dutch *mīte*, probably of same origin as MITE (arachnid).]

Mith·ra·ism (míth-ray-iz'm ‖ -rə-) *n.* A Persian religious cult that flourished in the late Roman Empire, in the first three centuries A.D., rivalling Christianity. See **Mithras.** —**Mith·ra·ic** (-ráy-ik) *adj.* —**Mith·ra·ist** (míth-ray-ist, -ráy- ‖ -rə-) *n. & adj.*

mith·ra·my·cin (míthrə-mī-sin) *n.* An antibiotic that prevents the growth of cancer cells and is used mainly in the treatment of cancer of the testicle.

Mith·ras (míth-rass ‖ -rəss). Also **Mith·ra** (-rə). *Persian Mythology.* The god of light and guardian against evil, often identified with the sun. [Latin, from Greek, from Old Persian *mithra-*, from Sanskrit *Mitra*, Vedic god.]

mith·ri·date (míthrə-dayt) *n.* Formerly, a substance thought to be an antidote against any poison. [Medieval Latin *mithridatum*, from Late Latin, antidote, from Latin, dogtooth violet (used an antidote). See **mithridatism**.]

mith·ri·da·tism (míthrə-dáyt-iz'm) *n.* Tolerance of a poison, acquired by taking gradually larger doses of it. [After *Mithridates* VI, King of Pontus (died 63 B.C.), said to have immunised himself in this manner.] —**mith·ri·dat·ic** (-dáttik, -dáytik) *adj.*

mit·i·cide (mítti-sīd) *n.* An agent that kills mites. —**mit·i·cid·al** (-síd'l) *adj.*

mit·i·gate (mítti-gayt) *v.* **-gated, -gating, -gates.** —*tr.* **1.** To moderate (a quality or condition) in force or intensity; alleviate: *mitigate anger; mitigate heat.* **2.** To serve to lessen the gravity of (an offence); extenuate. —See Synonyms at **relieve.** —See also Usage note at **militate.** [Middle English *mitigaten*, from Latin *mītigāre*, from *mītis*, gentle, mild.] —**mit·i·ga·ble** (-gəb'l) *adj.* —**mit·i·ga·tion** (-gáysh'n) *n.* —**mit·i·ga·tive** (-gətiv, -gaytiv), **mit·i·ga·to·ry** (-gə-tri, -təri, -gáytəri) *adj.* —**mit·i·ga·tor** (-gaytər) *n.*

Mitilíni. See **Mytilene.**

mi·to·chon·dri·on (mīt-ō-kóndri-ən, -ə-) *n., pl.* **-dria.** *Biology.* A microscopic body or organelle found in the cytoplasm of eukaryotic cells, consisting of two sets of membranes. The inner membrane is invaginated, and is the site of energy production by the process of cellular respiration. Also called "chondriosome". [New Latin : Greek *mitos*, thread + *khondrion*, small grain, diminutive of *khondros*.] —**mi·to·chon·dri·al** *adj.*

mit·o·gen (mítta-jen, mī-tō-, -tə-) *n.* An agent that induces mitosis in cells. [MITOSIS + -GEN.] —**mit·o·gen·ic** (-jénnik) *adj.* —**mit·o·gen·ic·i·ty** (-jə-níssəti, -je-) *n.*

mi·to·sis (mī-tō-siss, mi-) *n. Biology.* A type of cell division in which the nucleus divides to produce two daughter cells, each with the same number of chromosomes as the parent cell. Compare **meiosis.** See **anaphase, metaphase, prophase, telophase.** [New Latin : Greek *mitos*, a thread + -OSIS.] —**mi·tot·ic** (-tóttik) *adj.* —**mi·tot·i·cal·ly** *adv.*

mit·rail·leuse (míttrī-érz ‖ méetrə-, -yőz) *n.* An obsolete type of breech-loading machine gun with several barrels. [French, feminine agent-noun from *mitraille*, small shot, from Old French *mistraille*, small money, from *mite*, MITE.]

mi·tral (mítrəl) *adj.* **1.** Of or resembling a mitre. **2.** Pertaining to a mitral valve. [New Latin *mitrālis*, from Latin *mitra*, MITRE.]

mitral valve *n.* The heart valve between the left atrium and the left ventricle that regulates blood flow from the atrium to the ventricle. Also called "bicuspid valve".

mi·tre, *U.S.* **mi·ter** (mītər) *n.* **1.** A tall, pointed hat with two lappets at the back, worn by bishops and abbots. **2. a.** See **mitre joint. b.** The edge of a piece of material to be joined in a mitre joint. **c.** See **mitre square.**
~*v.* **mitred** or *U.S.* **mitered, mitring** or *U.S.* **mitering, mitres** or *U.S.* **miters.** —*tr.* **1.** To appoint as bishop or abbot. **2.** To make join in a mitre joint. **3.** To cut a mitre in. —*intr.* To meet in a mitre joint. [Middle English, from Old French, from Latin *mitra*, from Greek, headband, turban, (in the Septuagint) headdress of the high priest.]

mitre box *n.* **1.** A box open at the ends with sides slotted to guide a saw in cutting mitre joints. **2.** A device for handsaws that may be set to guide cuts at various degrees.

mitre joint *n.* A joint made by bevelling each of two surfaces to be joined, usually at a 45° angle to form a 90° corner.

mitre square *n.* A carpenter's square with a blade set at 45° or at an adjustable angle.

mitt (mit) *n.* **1.** A type of glove that extends over the hand but only partially covers the fingers. **2.** A mitten. **3.** In baseball, a large leather padded mitten of the types worn by catchers and first basemen. **4.** *Slang.* The hand. [Short for MITTEN.]

mit·ten (mítt'n) *n.* **1.** A covering for the hand that encases the thumb separately and the four fingers together. Also called "mitt". **2.** *Slang.* A boxing glove. [Middle English *mytayne*, from Old French *mitaine*, from Vulgar Latin *medietāna* (unattested), "skin-lined glove cut off at the middle", from Latin *medietās*, half, from *medius*, middle.]

Mit·ter·rand (meetə-RON), **François (Maurice Marie)** (1916–96). French president (1981–95). A World War II Resistance fighter, he was elected to the Chamber of Deputies (1946), where he sat except for four years (1959–62) in the Senate. In 1965, as the candidate of the Left, he lost the presidential election to Charles de Gaulle. He lost again to Giscard d'Estaing in 1974, was elected in 1981, and lost to Chirac in 1995.

mit·ti·mus (mítti-məss) *n., pl.* **-muses. 1.** *Law.* A writ committing a person to prison. **2.** *British Archaic.* A dismissal. [Latin, "we send", the first word of such a writ, from *mittere*, to send.]

mitz·vah (míts-və, -vaa) *n., pl.* **mitzvoth** (-vōth, -váwt) or **-vahs.** *Judaism.* **1.** A command enjoined by the Scriptures. **2.** A meritorious act. [Hebrew *miṣwāh*, "(divine) commandment", from *ṣiwwāh*, to command.]

mix (miks) *v.* **mixed, mixing, mixes.** —*tr.* **1. a.** To combine or blend (ingredients or elements) into one mass or mixture so that the constituent parts are indistinguishable: *mix sugar and egg yolks.* **b.** To create or form by adding ingredients together: *mix a cake; mixing purple from red and blue.* **c.** To add (an ingredient or element) to another: *mix flour into the batter.* **2.** To combine; bring together: *mix business and pleasure.* **3.** To consume (different types of drink or food) in succession: *mixed gin and wine and was sick.* **4.** To crossbreed. **5.** To combine (two or more sounds) for broadcasting or recording. —*intr.* **1. a.** To become mixed or blended together. **b.** To be capable of being blended together: *Oil and water do not mix.* **2. a.** To join in socially or get along easily with others: *She does not mix well at parties.* **b.** To associate oneself with a group of people: *mixed with the jet set.* **3.** To be crossbred. —**mix it.** *Slang.* **1.** To start to fight. **2.** To cause trouble.
~*n.* **1.** An act of mixing. **2. a.** A product of mixing; a mixture: *a good mix of people at the party.* **b.** A mixture of ingredients packaged and sold commercially: *a cake mix.* [Back-formation from *mixed, mixt,* from Middle English, from Old French *mixte*, from Latin *miscēre* (past participle *mixtus*), to mix.] —**mix·a·ble** *adj.*
  Synonyms: mix, blend, mingle, coalesce, merge, amalgamate, combine, compound, fuse.

mixed (mikst) *adj.* **1.** Composed of or involving a variety of differing, sometimes conflicting, entities or elements: *mixed feelings; got a mixed reception from the critics; mixed-ability classes.* **2.** Composed of or involving people of different sex, race, or social class: *Is your school single-sex or mixed?* —See Synonyms at **miscellaneous.**

mixed bag *n. Informal.* An assortment or collection of diverse elements.

mixed blessing *n.* An event or situation that has disadvantages as well as its more obvious advantages.

mixed crystal *n. Chemistry.* A crystalline material composed of two or more compounds that have crystallised in a single lattice but have retained their chemical identity.

mixed doubles *n.* A doubles match, as in tennis or badminton, with each team consisting of a male and a female.

mixed economy *n.* An economy with both a significant public sector and a significant private sector. [From the mixture of public and private enterprise in such an economy.]

mixed farming *n.* The farming of both crops and livestock on the same farm.

mixed grill *n.* A dish consisting of a variety of grilled meats, such as lamb chops and bacon.

mixed marriage *n.* A marriage between persons of different races or religions.

mixed metaphor *n.* **1.** A succession of metaphors that produce an incongruous or ludicrous effect, for example: *Her mounting ambition was soon bridled by a wave of opposition.* **2.** The use of such metaphors.

mixed nerve *n.* A nerve containing both sensory and motor nerve fibres.

mixed number *n.* A number, such as 7¼, made up of an integer and a fraction.

mixed-up (míkst-úp) *adj. Informal.* Emotionally confused.

mix·er (míksər) *n.* **1.** One that mixes. **2. a.** A person who mixes socially: *She was a good mixer with people of all ages.* **b.** *U.S.* A social gathering to let people mix socially. **3.** Any device, especially mechanical or electrical, that blends or mixes substances or ingredients. Often used in combination: *a cement-mixer.* **4.** A non-alcoholic drink, such as soda water or ginger ale, used in diluting alcoholic drinks. **5.** *Electronics.* A circuit or device for combining two or more signals or sounds into a single output.

mix·o·lyd·i·an (míksō-líddi-ən) *adj. Music.* Of or designating a mode represented by the white notes of the scale of G on the piano keyboard. [Greek *mixoludios*, half-Lydian : *mixo-*, half + *ludios*, Lydian.]

Mix·tec (méess-tek, méesh-, mísh-) *n., pl.* **-tecs** or collectively **Mixtec. 1.** A member of an American Indian people inhabiting Mexico. **2.** The language of this people. —**Mix·tec** *adj.*

mix·ture (míks-chər, *sometimes* -tewr) *n.* **1.** Something produced by mixing. **2.** Anything consisting of diverse elements. **3.** A fabric made of different kinds of thread or yarn. **4.** The act or process of mixing or of being mixed. **5.** *Chemistry.* Any composition of two or more substances that are not chemically bound to each other. **6.** A liquid medicine containing a combination of different drugs, such as a suspension of a solid in a liquid. **7.** The mixture of air and petrol produced in the carburettor of an internal-combustion engine. **8.** *Plural.* Any of variously coloured and flavoured selections of sweets: *dolly mixtures.* [French, from Latin *mixtūra,* from *miscēre* (past participle *mixtus*), to mix.]

mix up *tr.v.* **1.** To confuse: *I always mix her up with her sister.* **2.** To put into disorder. **3.** To cause to become associated with a group or activity of a usually undesirable nature. Used in the passive with *with*: *got mixed up with a bad crowd.*

mix-up (míks-up) *n.* **1.** A state of confusion; a muddle. **2.** *Informal.* A fight or melee.

Mi-zar (mí-zaar, -zər) *n.* One of the seven stars in the constellation **Ursa Major** *(see).* [Arabic *mi'zar,* veil, cloak.]

Mi-zo-gu-chi (méezō-gōōchi), **Kenji** (1898–1956). Japanese film director. His films, examining the conflict between traditional Japanese values and a modern industrial society, include *Street Sketches* (1925) and *Metropolitan Symphony* (1929). After 1945, he filmed love stories, including *The Love of Actress Sumaku* (1947) and *Red-light District* (1956).

miz-zen, miz-en (mízz'n) *n.* **1.** A fore-and-aft sail set on the mizzen-mast. **2.** A mizzenmast. [Middle English *mesan, meseyn,* from Old French *misaine,* from Italian *mezzana,* mizzen sail, from *mezzano,* middle, from Latin *mediānus,* MEDIAN.] —**miz-zen** *adj.*

miz-zen-mast (mízz'n-maast; *nautical* -məst ‖ -mast) *n.* **1.** The third mast aft on sailing ships carrying three or more masts. **2.** A **jigger mast** *(see).*

miz-zle¹ (mízz'l) *intr.v.* **-zled, -zling, -zles.** *Regional.* To rain in fine, mistlike droplets; drizzle. [Late Middle English *misellen,* perhaps from Middle Dutch *miezelen.*] —**miz-zle** *n.*

mizzle² *intr.v.* **-zled, -zling, -zles.** *British Slang.* To leave suddenly; vanish; decamp. [18th century : origin obscure.]

mk. **1.** mark. **2.** markka.

mks metre-kilogram-second (system of units).

MKSA metre-kilogram-second-ampere (system of units).

mkt. market.

ml millilitre.

ML, M.L. Medieval Latin.

MLD *n.* Minimum lethal dose: the smallest quantity of a drug or other compound that will cause death.

MLF multilateral force (nuclear force).

M.Litt. Master of letters. [Latin *Magister Litterarum.*]

Mlle. Mademoiselle.

Mlles. Mesdemoiselles.

mm millimetre; millimetres.

MM. Messieurs.

m.m. with the necessary changes having been made. [Latin *mutatis mutandis.*]

M.M. Military Medal (in Britain).

Mma-ba-tho (m-mə-baáto). Capital North-West (province), S.A.

Mme. Madame.

Mmes. Mesdames.

mmf, m.m.f. magnetomotive force.

mmHg millimetre of mercury (unit of pressure).

M.Mus. Master of Music.

Mn The symbol for the element manganese.

M.N. Merchant Navy (in Britain).

MND *n.* See **motor neurone.**

mne-mon-ic (ni-mónnik, mni-, nee-) *adj.* Pertaining to, assisting, or designed to assist the memory.
 ~*n.* A device, such as a formula or rhyme, used as an aid in remembering. [Medieval Latin *mnēmonicus,* from Greek *mnēmonikos,* from *mnēmōn,* mindful.] —**mne-mon-i-cal-ly** *adv.*

mne-mon-ics (ni-mónniks, mni-, nee-) *n. Used with a singular verb.* The art or system of improving or developing the memory.

Mne-mos-y-ne (ni-mózzi-nee, mni-, nee-, -móssi-, -ni). *Greek Mythology.* The goddess of memory, mother of the Muses. [Latin, from Greek *mnēmosunē,* memory, from *mnasthai,* to remember.]

Mngr. Monseigneur; Monsignor.

Mo The symbol for the element molybdenum.

mo. month.

m.o., M.O. **1.** mail order. **2.** medical officer. **3.** modus operandi. **4.** money order.

-mo *n. comb. form.* Indicates the specified number of leaves formed by folding a larger sheet of paper; used after numerals or the names of numerals; for example, **duodecimo,** which is generally written "12 mo" and called by printers "twelvemo". [Latin ablative ending of ordinals, after the preposition *in,* in, as in *duodecimo,* from *duodecimus,* twelfth.]

MΩ megohm.

mo-a (mō-ə) *n.* Any of various large, long-necked, flightless birds of the family Dinorthidae, native to New Zealand and now extinct for over a century. [Maori.]

Mo-ab (mō-ab). Ancient kingdom east of the Dead Sea, in an area that is now part of Jordan.

Mo-ab-ite (mō-ə-bīt) *n.* **1.** A descendant of Moab, the son of Lot. Genesis 19:37. **2.** An inhabitant or native of Moab. —**Mo-ab-ite** *adj.*

moan (mōn) *n.* **1.** A low, sustained, mournful sound, usually indicative of sorrow or pain. **2.** Any similar sound: *the moan of the wind.* **3.** *Informal.* A complaint or grievance.
 ~*v.* **moaned, moaning, moans.** —*intr.* **1.** To utter a moan or moans. **2.** To make a sound resembling a moan: *The wind moaned through the trees.* **3.** *Informal.* To grumble; complain. Often used with *at.* —*tr.* **1.** To complain about; bewail: *She moaned her misfortunes to anyone who would listen.* **2.** To utter with a moan or moans. —See Synonyms at **cry.** [Middle English *mone,* complaint, from Old English *mān* (unattested), complaint, from Germanic.]

moat (mōt) *n.* **1.** A wide, deep ditch, usually filled with water, surrounding a medieval town, fortress, or castle as a protection against assault. **2.** A similar, though often smaller, ditch surrounding a more modern building, such as a zoo enclosure.
 ~*tr.v.* **moated, moating, moats.** To surround with or as if with a moat. [Middle English *mote,* originally, "mound", "embankment", from Old French *mote,* *motte,* clod, hill, mound, probably from (unattested) Gaulish *mutt(a)†.*]

mob (mob) *n.* **1.** A large, disorderly crowd or throng; a rabble. **2.** The common people, regarded as ignorant, brutish, or fickle; the masses. Preceded by *the.* **3.** *Informal.* An organised gang of criminals. **4.** *Informal.* Any indiscriminate or loosely associated group of persons or things. **5.** *Australian.* A flock or herd of animals. **6.** *U.S. Slang.* The Mafia. Preceded by *the.*
 ~*tr.v.* **mobbed, mobbing, mobs.** **1.** To crowd around and jostle or annoy, especially in anger or excessive enthusiasm: *The fans mobbed the singer.* **2.** To crowd into (a place): *Crowds mobbed the fairgrounds.* **3.** To attack violently, usually in a crowd or mob; specifically, to surround and attack (a wounded member of one's own species or a member of another species). Used of birds, for example. [Shortening of earlier *mobile,* from Latin *mōbile (vulgus),* "the fickle (crowd)", neuter of *mōbilis,* MOBILE.]

mob-cap (mób-kap) *n.* A large, indoor cap trimmed with frills and ribbons, originally worn by women in the 18th and early 19th centuries. [From earlier *mob,* "negligee", "informal attire", earlier, "slattern", variant of *mab,* short for the name *Mabel.*]

mo-bile (mō-bīl; *rarely* -beel ‖ *chiefly U.S.* -b'l) *adj.* **1.** Capable of moving or of being moved from place to place. See Usage note at **movable.** **2.** Moving quickly from one state to another: *a mobile face.* **3.** Changing or capable of changing one's social status: *This area of London is upwardly mobile.* **4.** Flowing freely; not viscous: *a mobile liquid.* **5. a.** *Military.* Equipped with transport and capable of rapid deployment: *a mobile unit.* **b.** *Informal.* Having one's own means of transport: *no longer mobile since she lost her licence.* **c.** Incorporated in a vehicle and therefore capable of being driven from place to place: *a mobile library.*
 ~*n.* **1.** An ornament or type of sculpture that is suspended and has parts that move, especially in response to air currents. **2.** A **mobile telephone** *(see).* [Old French *mobile,* from Latin *mōbilis,* from the root of *movēre,* to move.] —**mo-bil-i-ty** (mō-bíllǝti, mǝ-) *n.*

-mobile *n. comb. form.* Indicates a specialised kind of vehicle; for example, from AUTOMOBILE.

mobile telephone, mobile phone *n.* A **cellphone** *(see).* Also called "mobile".

mo-bi-lise, mo-bi-lize (mōbi-līz) *v.* **-lised, -lising, -lises.** —*tr.* **1. a.** To make mobile or capable of movement. **b.** To put into circulation. **2.** To assemble, prepare, or put into operation for war or a similar emergency: *mobilise troops.* **3.** To organise or gather together for a purpose. —*intr.* To become prepared for war or a similar emergency. [French *mobiliser.*] —**mo-bi-li-sa-tion** (-lī-záysh'n ‖ *U.S.* -li-) *n.*

Mö-bi-us strip (mérbi-əss, mōbi-, mōbi-) *n.* A one-sided surface that can be formed from a rectangular strip by rotating one end 180° and attaching it to the other end. Also called "Möbius band". Compare **Klein bottle.** [After its inventor August *Möbius* (1790–1868), German mathematician.]

mob-oc-ra-cy (mob-óckrǝ-si) *n., pl.* **-cies.** Political control by a mob. —**mob-o-crat** (móbbǝ-krat) *n.* —**mob-o-crat-ic** (-kráttik), **mob-o-crat-i-cal** *adj.*

mob-ster (móbstǝr) *n. Chiefly U.S.* A gangster.

Mo-bu-tu Sese Seko (mǝ-bōō-tōō, mō-, sésse séckō), born Joseph Désiré Mobutu; also known as Mobutu. (1930–97). President of Zaire (Democratic Republic of Congo). In September 1960, he took control of the Congo in a coup supported by the army. In 1967 he became president of the Congo (which he renamed Zaire). He was overthrown in another coup in 1997.

Mobutu (Sese Seko) Lake. See **Albert, Lake.**

M.O.C. *n. British.* Mother of the chapel: the female leader of the members of a trade union in a particular newspaper office, printing firm, or the like. Compare **F.O.C.**

Moçambique. See **Mozambique.**

moc-ca-sin (mócka-sin) *n.* **1.** A soft flat-soled leather slipper worn by American Indians. **2.** A shoe or slipper resembling an Indian moccasin. **3.** A snake, the **water moccasin** *(see).* [Natick *mohkussin,* from Proto-Algonquian *maxkeseni* (unattested).]

moccasin flower *n.* Any of several orchids of the genus *Cypripedium.* See **lady's slipper.**

mo-cha (móckǝ ‖ *chiefly U.S.* mōkǝ) *n.* **1.** A rich, pungent Arabian coffee. **2.** Coffee of high quality. **3.** A flavouring made of coffee often mixed with chocolate. **4.** A soft, thin glove leather made from goatskin or sheepskin. **5.** Dark olive brown. [Originally exported from *Mocha,* a port of Yemen.] —**mo-cha** *adj.*

mock (mok) *v.* **mocked, mocking, mocks.** —*tr.* **1.** To treat with scorn or contempt; deride; ridicule. **2. a.** To mimic, as when teasing or in derision. **b.** To imitate; counterfeit. **3.** To delude; disappoint. **4.** To defy successfully; thwart: *A small band of defenders mocked the enemy's superior forces.* —*intr.* To express scorn or ridicule.

Often used with *at*: *They mocked at the idea.* —See Synonyms at **ridicule.**
—*n.* **1. a.** An act of mocking. **b.** Mockery; derision. **2.** Something deserving of derision. **3.** Something simulated; an imitation or counterfeit. —**put the mock** or **mocks on.** *Australian Slang.* To thwart the chances of.
—*adj.* Simulated; false; imitation: *a mock battle; mock cream.* [Middle English *mokken, mocquen,* from Old French *mocquer,* to deride, from Vulgar Latin *moccāre* (unattested), probably from a root *mok-,* imitative of laughter.] —**mock·ing·ly** *adv.*

mock·er (móckər) *n.* One that mocks. —**put the mockers on.** *Slang.* To thwart the chances of; stymie.

mock·er·y (móckəri) *n., pl.* **-ies. 1.** Scornful contempt; ridicule; derision. **2.** A derisive or contemptuous act or remark. **3.** An object of scorn or ridicule. **4.** A contemptible, shameful, or impudent imitation; a travesty: *The trial was a mockery of justice.* **5.** Something that is ludicrously futile or unsuitable: *made a mockery of our principles.*

mock-he·ro·ic (mók-hi-rṓ-ik) *n., pl.* **mock-heroics.** A satirical imitation or burlesque of the heroic manner or style. —**mock-he·ro·ic** *adj.* —**mock-he·ro·i·cal·ly** *adv.*

mock·ing·bird (mócking-burd) *n.* Any of several New World birds of the family Mimidae that are noted for their ability to mimic other birds; especially, *Mimus polyglottus,* a grey and white bird of the southern United States.

mock moon *n.* A **paraselene** *(see).*

mock orange *n.* **1.** Any of several deciduous shrubs of the genus *Philadelphus,* having white, usually fragrant, flowers. Also called "syringa". **2.** Any of various other shrubs or trees having flowers or fruit resembling those of the orange.

mock sun *n.* A **parhelion** *(see).*

mock turtle soup *n.* Soup made from calf's head or veal and spiced to taste like real turtle soup.

mock up *tr.v.* To make a mock-up of.

mock-up (mók-up) *n.* **1.** A usually full-sized model of a building, machine, or structure, used for demonstration, study, or testing. **2.** A layout of printed matter.

Moctezuma. See **Montezuma II.**

mod[1] (mod) *n. Sometimes capital* **M.** A member of a group of teenagers which originated in England in the 1960s, noted for its tidy and uniform style of dress, motorscooters, and for its opposition to the **rockers** *(see).*
—*adj.* Characteristic of or pertaining to the mods, especially to their style of dress. [From MODERN.]

mod[2] *n. Sometimes capital* **M.** An annual Gaelic meeting for the holding of literary and musical competitions. [Gaelic *mōd,* assembly, from Old Norse; akin to MOOT.]

mod[3] *Mathematics.* modulus.

MOD, MoD Ministry of Defence (in Britain).

mod. 1. moderate. **2.** *Music.* moderato. **3.** modern.

mo·dal (mṓd'l) *adj.* **1.** Of, pertaining to, or characteristic of a mode. **2.** *Grammar.* Of, pertaining to, or expressing the mood of a verb. **3.** *Music.* Of, pertaining to, characteristic of, or composed in a mode, especially any of the modes typical of medieval church music. **4.** *Philosophy.* Of or pertaining to mode or form as opposed to substance or attributes. **5.** *Logic.* Expressing or characterised by modality. **6.** *Statistics.* Of or pertaining to a statistical mode; most frequent, common, or typical.
—*n.* A modal auxiliary. [Medieval Latin *modālis,* from Latin *modus,* measure, mode.] —**mo·dal·ly** *adv.*

modal auxiliary *n. Grammar.* Any of a set of English verbs, including *can, may, must, ought, shall, will,* and *would,* that are characteristically used with other verbs to express mood or tense. Also called "modal verb".

mo·dal·i·ty (mō-dál-əti, mə-) *n., pl.* **-ties. 1.** The fact, state, or quality of being modal. **2.** A modal quality or attribute of something; a mode. **3.** *Logic.* The classification of propositions on the basis of whether they assert or deny the possibility, impossibility, contingency, or necessity of their content. **4.** *Medicine.* **a.** A method of therapy, usually physical, such as massage. **b.** An apparatus for such a therapy. **5.** Any of the five senses, such as smell or hearing.

modal logic *n.* The logical study of the formal properties of concepts such as necessity, contingency, possibility, or impossibility and the study of the modality of propositions.

mod cons (mód kónz) *pl.n.* Modern conveniences in the home, such as a washing machine, a telephone, or central heating.

mode (mōd) *n.* **1. a.** Manner, way, or method of doing or acting: *"The modern mode of travelling cannot compare with the old mail-coach system in grandeur and power."* (Thomas De Quincey). **b.** A particular form, variety, or manner: *a mode of communication.* **c.** A condition in which a specified operation may be performed: *switched the tape machine to the record mode.* **2.** The current or customary fashion or style. **3.** *Music.* **a.** Any of certain arrangements of the diatonic notes of an octave. The two chief modes in Western music have been the **major** and **minor** *(both of which see).* **b.** Any of several patterned arrangements characteristic of classical Greek and medieval church music. **4.** *Philosophy.* The particular form or manner in which an underlying substance, or some permanent aspect or attribute of it, is manifested. **5.** *Logic.* **a.** The arrangement or order of the propositions in a syllogism according to both quality and quantity. **b.** The modality of a proposition. **6.** *Statistics.* The value or item occurring most frequently in a series of observations or set of statistical data. Also called "norm". **7.** *Ge-*

ology. The mineral composition of a specific sample of igneous rock expressed in percentages of weight. **8.** *Physics.* Any of numerous patterns of vibration or wave motion, as of acoustic or electromagnetic waves, corresponding to resonant frequencies of physical systems. —See Synonyms at **fashion, method.** [French *mode,* fashion, from Latin *modus,* measure, manner, size, harmony, melody.]

mod·el (módd'l) *n.* **1.** A representation, usually smaller but built to scale, of a building or other structure. **2.** A preliminary pattern or representation of an item not yet constructed, serving as the plan from which the finished work, usually larger, will be produced. **3.** A tentative framework of ideas describing something intangible and used as a testing device: *"two conflicting models of generative grammar"* (Noam Chomsky). **4.** A style or design of a product, especially one of a series: *Her car is last year's model.* **5. a.** A person or quality regarded as an example to be imitated or compared: *"in her temper, manners, mind, a model of female excellence"* (Jane Austen). **b.** A pattern, design, or arrangement serving as a basis for imitation: *a constitution on the American model.* **6.** A person or object serving as the subject for an artist or photographer. **7.** A person employed to display clothing, cosmetics, or the like, for prospective buyers or in advertisements. **8.** A figure or object made in clay or wax, for example, especially as used by a sculptor as a preliminary work to copy in a more durable or precious material, such as marble or bronze. **9.** An original garment by a well-known designer. —See Synonyms at **ideal.**
—*v.* **modelled** or *U.S.* **modeled, -elling** or *U.S.* **-eling, -els.** —*tr.* **1.** To make or construct a model of. **2.** To plan, form, or construct according to a particular model or standard. **3. a.** To manipulate or work (a plastic substance): *model clay.* **b.** To make by shaping a plastic substance: *modelled animals in clay.* **4.** To display by wearing or posing with. **5.** In painting and drawing, to give a three-dimensional appearance to, as by shading. —*intr.* **1.** To make a model. **2.** To work as a model: *He models for a living.*
—*adj.* **1.** Serving as or used as a model. **2.** Serving as a standard of excellence; worthy of imitation: *a model husband.* [Obsolete French *modelle,* from Italian *modello,* from Vulgar Latin *modellus* (unattested), from Latin *modulus,* little measure, diminutive of *modus,* measure, rhythm, harmony.] —**mod·el·ler** *n.*

mo·del·lo (mə-déllō, mo-) *n., pl.* **-li** (-lee) or **-los.** A sketch of a proposed larger painting, or a model for a proposed sculpture. [Italian, model.]

mo·dem (mṓ-dem) *n.* A device used in transmitting data between computers along a telephone line. It converts signals from a computer into audio signals and vice versa. [From *mo*dulator *dem*odulator.]

Mo·de·na (mo-dáynə, mə-, móddinə). Capital of Modena province, Emilia-Romagna, north Italy. It is a commercial and industrial centre in a rich agricultural region, and motor vehicles, agricultural machinery and shoes are made there. An Etruscan town, colonised by the Romans (2nd century B.C.) who called it Mutina, it was ruled by the Este family from 1288 to 1859 and has many fine buildings.

mod·er·ate (móddrət, móddrit, móddər-ət, -it) *adj. Abbr.* **mod. 1.** Keeping or kept within reasonable limits; not excessive or extreme: *moderate drinking.* **2.** Not violent; mild; calm: *a moderate climate.* **3. a.** Of medium or average quantity, quality, or extent: *a moderate increase in living standards.* **b.** Of relatively low or below average quantity, quality, or extent: *very moderate prices.* **4.** Opposed to radical or extreme views or measures, especially in politics.
—*n.* One who holds moderate opinions, especially in politics.
—*v.* (móddə-rayt) **moderated, -ating, -ates.** —*tr.* **1.** To make less violent, severe, or extreme. **2.** *Physics.* To reduce the energy of (neutrons), especially by use of a moderator. —*intr.* **1.** To become less violent, severe, or extreme; abate. **2.** To act as a moderator. [Latin *moderātus,* past participle of *moderārī, moderāre,* to reduce, regulate, control; akin to *modus,* MODE.] —**mod·er·ate·ly** *adv.* —**mod·er·ate·ness** *n.* —**mod·er·at·ism** *n.*

moderate breeze *n.* A wind whose speed is 5.5 to 7.9 metres per second (13 to 18 miles per hour); force 4 on the Beaufort scale.

moderate gale *n.* A wind whose speed is 13.9 to 17.1 metres per second (32 to 38 miles per hour); force 7 on the Beaufort Scale.

mod·er·a·tion (móddə-ráysh'n) *n.* **1.** An instance or act of moderating or being moderate. **2.** Freedom from excess or extremes; temperance. —**in moderation.** In moderate amounts or degrees; within reasonable limits.

mod·e·ra·to (móddə-raátō) *adv. Abbr.* **mod.** *Music.* At a moderate tempo; slower than allegretto but faster than andante. Used as a direction. —**mod·e·ra·to** *adj. & n.* [Italian, from Latin *moderātus,* MODERATE.]

mod·er·a·tor (móddə-raytər) *n.* **1. a.** An arbitrator or mediator. **b.** One who presides over a meeting or assembly. **2.** The officer who presides over a synod or general assembly of the Presbyterian Church. **3.** *Physics.* A substance, such as water or graphite, that is used in a nuclear reactor to decrease the speed of fast neutrons, increase the likelihood of fission, and sustain a chain reaction.

mod·ern (módd'n, móddərn) *adj. Abbr.* **mod. 1.** Of, pertaining to, or characteristic of recent times or the present: *modern science; modern dress.* **2.** Up-to-date; modish: *a very modern flat with white walls and high-tech furniture.* **3.** Designating the period of history from about 1450 until the present day. **4.** Characteristic of or done in the style of contemporary art, music, drama, or the like; especially, avant-garde or experimental. **5.** *Capital* **M.** Designating the form of a language that is in current use.
—*n.* **1.** One who lives in modern times. **2.** One who has modern

ideas, standards, or beliefs; especially, an artist, writer, or the like who works in an avant-garde or experimental style. **3.** *Printing.* Any of various typefaces characterised by strongly contrasted heavy and thin parts. [French *moderne,* from Late Latin *modernus,* from *modō,* "just now", originally "to the measure", from *modus,* measure.] —**mod·ern·i·ty** (mo-dérnəti, mə-) *n.* —**mod·ern·ly** *adv.*

modern dance *n.* A style of contemporary dance based on ballet but using much freer and often more expressive bodily movements.

Modern English *n.* English since the early 16th century.

Modern Greek *n.* Greek since the early 16th century, divided into **Dhimotiki** and **Katharevusa** *(both of which see).*

Modern Hebrew *n.* The form of Hebrew, revived from ancient Hebrew, that is now in current use in Israel.

mod·ern·ise, mod·ern·ize (módd'n-īz, móddərn-) *v.* **-ised, -ising, -ises.** —*tr.* To make modern; bring up to date in respect of technology, appearance, style, or character. —*intr.* To accept or adopt modern ways, views, procedures, or styles. —**mod·ern·i·sa·tion** (-ī-záysh'n ‖ *U.S.* -i-) *n.* —**mod·ern·i·ser** *n.*

mod·ern·ism (módd'n-iz'm, móddərn-) *n.* **1. a.** Modern thought, character, or practice. **b.** Sympathy with modern ideas, practices, or standards. **2.** Something, such as a peculiarity of usage or style, that is characteristic of modern times. **3.** *Often capital* **M.** In Christian Churches, any of various movements that attempt to adapt church teachings to take account of modern scientific and philosophical thought; especially, such a movement in the Roman Catholic Church in the late 19th and early 20th centuries. **4.** The theory or practice of modern art, literature, or the like. —**mod·ern·ist** *n. & adj.* —**mod·ern·ist·ic** (-ístik) *adj.*

modern jazz *n.* Any style of jazz developed since the 1940s that is avant-garde or experimental in style, for example bop and free jazz.

modern pentathlon *n.* A pentathlon *(see).*

mod·est (móddist) *adj.* **1.** Having or showing a moderate estimation of one's own talents, abilities, and value. **2.** Having a shy and retiring nature; reserved. **3.** Having a regard for decencies of behaviour or dress. **4.** Quiet and humble in appearance; unpretentious: *a modest house.* **5.** Moderate; not extreme or excessive: *a modest charge.* —See Synonyms at **humble, shy.** [French *modeste,* from Latin *modestus,* "keeping due measure"; akin to *modus,* MODE.] —**mod·est·ly** *adv.*

mod·es·ty (móddisti) *n., pl.* **-ties.** The state or quality of being modest, especially: **1.** Lack of vanity or pretentiousness. **2.** Reserve or propriety in speech, dress, or behaviour.

mod·i·cum (móddi-kəm ‖ *U.S. also* mōdi-) *n., pl.* **-cums** or **-ca** (-kə). A small or moderate amount or quantity. [Latin, short way, short time, from *modicus,* moderate, from *modus,* (due) measure.]

mod·i·fi·ca·tion (móddifi-káysh'n) *n.* **1.** The act of modifying or the condition of being modified. **2.** The result of modifying; a modified form. **3.** A small alteration, adjustment, or limitation. **4.** *Biology.* A physical change in an organism due to environment or activity, but not transmitted to the organism's descendants. —**mod·i·fi·ca·tive** (-kaytiv), **mod·i·fi·ca·to·ry** (-kaytəri, -káytəri) *adj.* —**mod·i·fi·ca·tor** (-kaytər) *n.*

mod·i·fi·er (móddi-fī-ər) *n.* **1.** One that modifies. **2.** *Grammar.* A word, phrase, or clause that limits or qualifies the sense of another word or phrase. Also called "qualifier".

mod·i·fy (móddi-fī) *v.* **-fied, -fying, -fies.** —*tr.* **1.** To change in form or character, usually without fundamental transformation: *"the first tools must have been natural objects only slightly modified"* (V. Gordon Childe). **2.** To make less extreme, severe, or strong: *cannot be persuaded to modify her position in any way.* **3.** *Grammar.* To qualify or limit the meaning of. For example, *"wet"* modifies *"day"* in the phrase *a wet day.* **4.** *Linguistics.* To change (a vowel) by umlaut. —*intr.* To be or become modified. —See Synonyms at **change.** [Middle English *modifien,* to limit, moderate, from Old French *modifier,* from Latin *modificāre : modus,* a measure + *facere,* to do, make.] —**mod·i·fi·a·ble** (-əb'l, -fī-əb'l) *adj.*

Mo·di·glia·ni (mō-dil-yáani, mó-), **Amedeo** (1884–1920). Italian painter and sculptor who settled in Paris (1906), where he concentrated on chiselling heads in stone and painting portraits, mostly of women, in a characteristic elongated style.

mo·dil·lion (mə-díl-yən, mō-) *n. Architecture.* An ornamental bracket used in series under the cornice of the Corinthian, Composite, or Roman Ionic orders. [French *modillon,* from Italian *modiglione,* from Vulgar Latin *mutellio* (stem *mutellion-*), from *mutellus* (unattested), alteration of Latin *mutulus,* projecting block under cornice (Doric order).]

mo·di·o·lus (mə-dī-ə-ləss, mō-) *n., pl.* **-li** (-lī). *Anatomy.* The central, conical, bony shaft of the cochlea. [New Latin, from Latin, hub of a wheel, bucket of a water wheel, diminutive of *modius,* a measure for grain.]

mod·ish (mṓdish) *adj.* Being in or conforming to the prevailing or current fashion; stylish. [From MODE (fashion).] —**mod·ish·ly** *adv.* —**mod·ish·ness** *n.*

mo·diste (mō-déest) *n.* One who produces, designs, or deals in ladies' fashions. [French, from *mode,* MODE (fashion).]

Mo·dred (mṓ-drid, -dred). Also **Mor·dred** (mór-). In Arthurian legend, a knight of the Round Table who led a rebellion against his uncle, King Arthur, and mortally wounded him.

Mods (modz) *pl. n.* The first examination for a B.A. Honours degree in some subjects at Oxford University. Compare **Greats.** [Abbreviation of *(Honour) Moderations,* examinations presided over by a "moderator".]

mod·u·lar (móddewlər) *adj.* **1.** Pertaining to, based on, or made up

of modules: *a modular training scheme; a modular hotel.* **2.** Of or pertaining to a modulus.

mod·u·late (móddew-layt) *v.* **-lated, -lating, -lates.** —*tr.* **1.** To adjust or adapt to a certain measure or proportion; regulate; temper. **2.** To change or vary the pitch, intensity, or tone of: *modulated his voice to a confidential murmur.* **3.** *Electronics.* To vary the frequency, amplitude, phase, or some other characteristic of (a carrier wave). —*intr.* **1.** *Music.* To pass from one key or pitch to another by means of a regular melodic or chord progression. **2.** *Electronics.* To alter the frequency, amplitude, phase, or some other characteristic of a carrier wave. See **modulation.** [Latin *modulārī,* to measure off, set to a measure, play music, from *modulus,* diminutive of *modus,* measure, rhythm.] —**mod·u·la·tive** (-laytiv, -lətiv), **mod·u·la·to·ry** (-lətri, -lətəri, -láytəri) *adj.*

mod·u·la·tion (móddew-láysh'n) *n.* **1.** The act or process of modulating. **2.** *Music.* A passing from one key to another by means of a regular melodic or chord progression. **3. a.** A change in pitch or loudness of the voice; an inflection of the voice. **b.** The use of a particular intonation or inflection of the voice to convey meaning. **4.** *Electronics.* The variation of a property of an electromagnetic wave or signal, such as its amplitude, frequency, or phase, in a manner determined by another wave or signal, especially for the purpose of transferring information from an audible signal, such as the human voice, to a carrier wave suitable for radio or telephonic transmission.

mod·u·la·tor (móddew-laytər) *n.* **1.** One that modulates. **2.** *Electronics.* A device or electric circuit used to modulate a carrier wave. See **modulation.** **3.** *Anatomy.* A receptive sensory end organ, found in light-adapted eyes, which is thought to be related to the discrimination of colour.

mod·ule (móddewl) *n.* **1.** A standard or unit of measurement. **2. a.** *Architecture.* The part of a construction used as a standard to which the rest is proportioned. **b.** A standardised structural component used as a unit, as in a building or item of furniture. **3.** *Electronics.* A self-contained assembly of electronic components and circuitry. **4.** Any of the self-contained, often separable, units that make up a spacecraft. **5.** Any of a set of distinct learning units that make up a course of education or training. [Latin *modulus,* MODULUS.]

mod·u·lus (móddew-ləss) *n., pl.* **-li** (-lī). *Abbr.* **m, M 1.** *Physics.* A constant or coefficient that expresses the degree to which a substance possesses some property; especially, a ratio of the stress on a solid to the strain produced, measuring the elastic properties of the material. See **bulk modulus, rigidity modulus, Young's modulus. 2.** *Mathematics.* **a.** The **absolute value** *(see)* of a complex number, a negative quantity, or a vector. **b.** *Abbr.* **mod** A number or quantity that produces the same remainder when divided into each of two quantities. **c.** The number by which a logarithm in one system must be multiplied to obtain the corresponding logarithm in another system. [New Latin, from Latin, diminutive of *modus,* measure.]

mo·dus op·er·an·di (mṓd-əss óppə-rán-dī, mód-, -dee) *n., pl.* **modi operandi** (-ī, -ee). *Abbr.* **m.o., M.O. 1.** The manner in which something operates. **2.** A person's manner of working. [Latin.]

modus vi·ven·di (vi-vén-dī, -dee) *n., pl.* **modi vivendi** (-ī, -ee). **1.** A way of living. **2.** A practical compromise enabling contending parties to coexist peacefully, either indefinitely or pending a final settlement of their differences. [Latin.]

Moe·so·goth, Moe·so·Goth (mée-sō-goth, -zō-) *n.* A Goth of Moesia, an ancient region corresponding approximately to modern Bulgaria and Serbia.

mo·fette (mō-fét, mo-) *n.* **1.** An opening in the earth from which carbon dioxide and other gases escape, usually marking the last stage of volcanic activity. **2.** The gases escaping from such a fissure. [French, "fetid exhalation", from Italian (Neapolitan dialect) *mofetta,* from *muffa,* mustiness, probably of imitative origin.]

mog (mog) *n.* Also **mog·gy** (móggi) *pl.* **-gies.** *British Informal.* A cat. [20th century : of dialect origin, originally a pet name for a cow.]

Mog·a·dish·u (móggə-díshōō). *Italian* **Mo·ga·di·scio;** *Arabic* **Muq·disho.** Capital and main port of Somalia, on the Indian Ocean. A commercial and financial centre, it exports fruit, livestock, hides, and skins. Founded by the Arabs in the 9th or 10th century, it was sold to Italy (1905), and became the capital of Italian Somaliland.

Mog·a·don (móggə-don) *n.* A trademark for nitrazepam, a hypnotic drug used in the form of pills, usually to treat insomnia.

Mogen David. Variant of **Magen David.**

mo·gul[1] (mṓg'l) *n.* A small mound on a ski slope. [Perhaps from German dialect (Austro-Bavarian) *Mugl.*]

mo·gul[2] (mṓg'l) *n.* **1.** A very rich or powerful person: *an oil mogul.* **2.** A kind of heavy steam locomotive. [From MONGOL.]

Mo·gul (mṓg'l, mō-gul, -gúl, -gōōl). Also **Mo·ghul, Mu·ghal** (mōō-gúl) (for sense 1). **1. a.** One of the followers of Baber, who conquered India in 1526 and founded a Muslim empire that lasted formally until 1857. **b.** A descendant of a follower of Baber. **2.** A Mongol or Mongolian. [Persian and Arabic *mugūl,* MONGOL.] —**Mo·gul** *adj.*

Mo·hács (mṓ-hach). Small industrial town, and important Danube port in southern Hungary near the Croatian border. There the annihilation of a Hungarian army by the Ottoman Turks (1526) resulted in their domination of Hungary for more than 150 years, and paved the way for the Turkish sieges of Vienna. The retreating Turks were defeated at the Second Battle of Mohács (1687).

mo·hair (mṓ-hair) *n.* **1.** The hair of the Angora goat. Also called "angora". **2.** A shiny, heavy, shaggy yarn or fabric made of this hair, often with a mixture of cotton or wool. [Variant (influenced by HAIR) of earlier *moochary, mocayare,* from Italian *moccaiaro,* from Arabic *mukhayyar,* "select", "choice", cloth of goat's hair, from *khayyara,* to choose.] —**mo·hair** *adj.*

Mohammed. See **Muhammad.**

Mohammedan. Variant of **Muhammadan.**

Moharram. Variant of **Muharram.**

Mo·ha·ve (mō-há'avi, mō-) *n., pl.* **-ves** or collectively **Mohave.** Also **Mo·ja·ve** (-há'avi). A member of a Yuman-speaking North American Indian people, formerly living along the Gila and Colorado rivers. —**Mo·ha·ve** *adj.*

Mo·hawk (mō'-hawk) *n., pl.* **-hawks** or collectively **Mohawk.** 1. A member of the Iroquoian-speaking North American Indian people that occupied the territory from the Mohawk river to the St. Lawrence. 2. The language of this people. —**Mo·hawk** *adj.*

Mo·he·gan (mō-hée'gən) *n., pl.* **-gans** or collectively **Mohegan.** A member of an Algonquian-speaking North American Indian people, formerly living in Connecticut. —**Mo·he·gan** *adj.*

Mo·hen·jo-Da·ro (mō-hénjō-da'arō). Ruined ancient city on the Indus river in the Sind province of Pakistan, dating from about 2500 to 1500 B.C.

mo·hi·can (mō-hée-kən, mō-i-) *n.* An unconventional type of hairstyle in which the sides of the head are completely shaved, leaving a central growth of hair from forehead to nape, which may be stiffened into spikes or dyed a different colour. [After the American Indian people.]

Mohican. Variant of **Mahican.**

Mo·ho (mōhō) *n.* The Mohorovicic discontinuity.

Mo·hock (mō-hok) *n.* A member of a band of young aristocrats who terrorised London in the early 18th century. [Variant of MOHAWK.]

Mo·hole (mō-hōl) *n.* A research project, now abandoned, to drill a hole through the ocean floor, through the Mohorovicic discontinuity and into the mantle, to obtain samples of rocks.

Mo·holy-Nagy (mō'hoy-nój), **László** (1895–1946). Hungarian painter and photographer, and a founder of constructivism. He made "photograms" and "space modulators" out of plastic at the Bauhaus in the 1920s. In 1937, he settled in the United States, where his ideas influenced commercial and industrial design.

Mo·ho·ro·vi·čić discontinuity (mō-hə-róvi-chich) *n.* The boundary between the earth's crust and mantle, ranging in depth from about 5 kilometres (3 miles) under ocean basins to 30-35 kilometres (19-22 miles) under continents. Also called "Moho". [After Andrija *Mohorovičić* (1857–1936), Yugoslav geophysicist.]

Mohs scale (mōz) *n.* A scale for determining the relative hardness of a mineral according to its resistance to scratching by one of the following minerals, arranged in order of increasing hardness: 1. talc; 2. gypsum; 3. calcite; 4. fluorite; 5. apatite; 6. orthoclase; 7. quartz; 8. topaz; 9. corundum; 10. diamond. [After Friedrich *Mohs* (1773–1839), German mineralogist who devised it.]

mo·hur (mō-hər || mə-hóor) *n.* 1. A currency unit of Nepal, equal to ½ rupee. 2. A gold coin, formerly used in India, equal to 15 rupees. [Hindi *muhur, muhr,* from Persian *muhr,* a seal.]

moider. Variant of **moither.**

moi·dore (móy-dawr, -dór || -dōr, -dór) *n.* A former Portuguese gold coin. [Earlier *moyodore,* from Portuguese *moeda d'ouro,* "coin of gold" : *moeda,* from Latin *monēta,* MONEY + *d'ouro,* "of gold".]

moi·e·ty (móy-əti) *n., pl.* **-ties.** 1. A half. 2. A part, portion, or share of indefinite size. 3. *Anthropology.* Either of two basic social divisions that make up a people on the basis of unilateral descent. [Middle English *moite, moitie,* from Old French *moite,* from Latin *medietās* (stem *medietāt*-), half, from *medius,* middle.]

moil (moyl) *intr.v.* **moiled, moiling, moils.** To toil or slave. Used chiefly in the phrase *toil and moil.*

~*n. Archaic.* 1. Toil; drudgery. 2. Confusion; turmoil. [Middle English *moillen,* to moisten, smear, from Old French *moillier,* to moisten, paddle in mud, from Vulgar Latin *molliāre* (unattested), from Latin *mollis,* soft.]

Moirae (móyr-ī, -ee) *pl.n.* See **Fates.** [Greek.]

moi·ré (mwá'a-ray || mwáw-, *U.S.* -ráy) *n.* Also **moire** (mwaar || mwawr). 1. Cloth, especially silk, that has a watered or wavy pattern. 2. A watered pattern produced on cloth by engraved rollers. [French, from *moire, mouaire,* from MOHAIR (the fabric originally used for this pattern).] —**moi·ré** *adj.*

moiré pattern *n.* A pattern produced by superimposing a repetitive design, such as a grid, on a slightly displaced design, either the same or different, in order to produce a pattern distinct from its components.

moist (moyst) *adj.* **moister, moistest.** 1. Slightly wet or damp. 2. Filled with moisture. 3. Humid. —See Synonyms at **wet.** [Middle English, from Old French *moiste,* probably from Vulgar Latin *muscidus* (unattested), mouldy, wet, alteration of Latin *mūcidus,* from *mūcus,* mucus.] —**moist·ly** *adv.* —**moist·ness** *n.*

mois·ten (móyss'n || móystən) *v.* **-tened, -tening, -tens.** —*tr.* To make moist. —*intr.* To become moist. —**mois·ten·er** *n.*

mois·ture (móyss-chər) *n.* Diffuse wetness that can be felt as vapour in the atmosphere or as condensed liquid on the surfaces of objects; dampness. [Middle English, from Old French *moistour,* from *moiste,* MOIST.]

mois·tur·ise, mois·tur·ize (móyss-chərīz) *tr.v.* **-ised, -ising, -ises.** To remove dryness from (the skin, for example); add moisture to.

mois·tur·is·er (móyss-chər-īzər) *n.* A cosmetic lotion or cream applied to the skin to soften it and counter dryness.

moi·ther (móythər || míthər) *tr.v.* **-thered, -thering, -thers.** Also **moi·der** (móydər), **-dered, -dering, -ders.** *British Regional.* To confuse,

baffle, or bewilder. Usually used in the passive. [17th century : origin obscure.]

Mojave. Variant of **Mohave.**

Mo·ja·ve Desert (mō-há'avi, mə-). Arid region of southern California, United States. Part of the Great Basin, it has low mountains and broad valleys. Its mineral reserves include iron, potash, gold, and silver. Death Valley National Monument is in the region.

moke (mōk) *n. Slang.* 1. *British.* A donkey. 2. *Australian & N.Z.* An old, broken-down horse. [19th century : origin obscure.]

mo·ko (mōkō) *n., pl.* **-kos.** A Maori pattern of tattoos. [Maori.]

mol *Chemistry.* The symbol for **mole.**

mol. molecular; molecule.

mo·lal (mōlǝl) *adj. Chemistry.* Of or designating a solution containing one mole of solute in 1 000 grams of solvent, usually water. Compare **molar.** [From MOLE (chemistry) + -AL.]

mo·lal·i·ty (mō-lál-əti) *n., pl.* **-ties.** *Chemistry.* The molal concentration of a solute, usually expressed as the number of moles of solute per 1 000 grams of solvent. See **molal.**

mo·lar¹ (mōlər) *adj. Chemistry.* 1. Designating a physical property that is measured for unit amount of substance, usually for one mole: *molar enthalpy.* 2. Of or designating a solution that contains one mole of solute per litre of solution. Compare **molal.** [From MOLE (quantity).]

molar² *n.* A tooth with a broad crown for grinding food, located behind the premolars. A human being has twelve molars, three in each side of the upper and lower jaws.

~*adj.* 1. Of or pertaining to the molar teeth. 2. Capable of grinding. [Latin *molāris* (adjective), from *mola,* millstone.]

mo·lar·i·ty (mō-lárrəti) *n., pl.* **-ties.** *Chemistry.* The molar concentration of a solute, usually expressed as the number of moles of solute per litre of solution. See **molar¹.**

mo·las·ses (mə-lássi, mō-) *n., pl.* **molasses.** 1. A thick uncrystallised syrup produced when raw sugar cane is cut. 2. *U.S.* Black treacle. [Earlier *melasus, malassos,* from Portuguese *melaço,* from Late Latin *mellāceum,* must, from Latin *mel,* honey.]

mold. *U.S.* Variant of **mould.**

Mol·da·v·ia¹ (mol-dáyvi-ə). *Romanian* **Mol·do·va.** The major grain-producing province of Romania, lying between the river Prut and the Carpathian mountains. Founded as a principality in the 14th century, it included Bukovina and Bessarabia, but lost the former to Austria (1775), and the latter to Russia (1812). Following the Crimean War, it united with Walachia (1859) to form modern Romania. See map at **Romania.**

Moldavia². See **Moldova¹.**

Mol·da·vi·an (mol-dáyvi-ən) *n.* 1. A native or inhabitant of Moldavia. 2. The language of Moldavia, a form of Romanian. —**Mol·da·vi·an** *adj.*

Mol·do·va¹ (mól-dōvə). Landlocked republic of eastern Europe, between the rivers Prut and Dnestr, formerly a constituent republic of the U.S.S.R. This, the Moldavian S.S.R., was created (1940) from the Moldavian A.S.S.R. in the Ukraine and part of Bessarabia, the Moldavian territory gained by Russia in 1812 and held by Romania (1918–40). Area, 33 700 square kilometres (13,012 square miles). Population, 4,330,000. Capital, Chisinau. See map at **Commonwealth of Independent States.** —**Mol·do·van** *adj. & n.*

Moldova². See **Moldavia¹.**

mole¹ (mōl) *n.* A small, pigmented growth on the human skin, usually slightly raised and brown, and sometimes hairy. It is a type of **naevus** *(see).* [Middle English *mool, mole,* Old English *māl.*]

mole² *n.* 1. Any of various small, insectivorous, burrowing mammals of the family Talpidae, having thickset bodies with silky light brown to dark grey fur, rudimentary eyes, tough muzzles, and strong forefeet for digging. Most live underground. See **desman, shrew mole.** 2. The pelt of the mole, **moleskin** *(see).* 3. *British.* **a.** An intelligence agent who establishes a cover by working as a legitimate member of a foreign organisation for a period of years, until assigned a mission. **b.** Loosely, any person who works under cover within an organisation, and gives away secret or classified information. [Middle English *molle, mulle, mole,* from Middle Dutch *mol* and Medieval Latin *mulus,* both from an unknown Germanic source.]

mole³ *n.* 1. A massive stone wall used as a breakwater or jetty. 2. The harbour enclosed by such a barrier. [French *môle,* from Medieval Greek *mōlos,* from Latin *mōlēs,* pier, dam, massive structure, mass.]

mole⁴ *n.* A mass or tumour in the uterus, caused by the degeneration or abortive development of a fertilised ovum. [French *môle,* from Latin *mola,* "millstone" (since it is a hardened mass), MOLE (wall, harbour).]

mole⁵ *n. Chemistry.* Symbol **mol.** The basic unit of amount of substance. It is equal to the amount of substance that contains the same number of entities (atoms, ions, molecules, photons, or the like) as there are atoms in 0.012 kilogram of the isotope of carbon with mass number 12. [German *Mol,* short for *Molekulargewicht,* molecular weight.]

mole cricket *n.* Any of various burrowing crickets of the family Gryllotalpidae, with short wings and front legs well adapted for digging and shearing.

mo·lec·u·lar (mə-léckew-lər, mō-, mo-) *adj. Abbr.* **mol.** Pertaining to, consisting of, caused by, or existing between molecules.

molecular beam *n. Physics.* A parallel stream of atoms or molecules, having a low pressure such that the number of collisions between molecules within the beam is negligible. It is used to study atomic and nuclear properties and chemical reactions.

molecular biology *n.* The field of biology in which the structure and development of biological systems are analysed in terms of the physics and chemistry of their molecular constituents, particularly nucleic acids and proteins.

molecular film *n.* A surface film of thickness comparable to that of a single molecule.

molecular formula *n.* A type of chemical formula that indicates the number of each type of atom in each molecule of a compound. Compare **empirical formula, structural formula.**

molecular sieve *n.* A crystalline substance, such as a zeolite, that can absorb large amounts of certain compounds. Molecular sieves are used for producing high vacua, purifying gases, and separating mixtures.

molecular weight *n. Abbr.* **mol. wt.** *Chemistry.* The sum of the atomic weights of a molecule's constituent atoms. Also called "relative molecular mass".

mol·e·cule (mólli-kewl) *n. Abbr.* **mol.** **1.** A stable configuration of atomic nuclei and electrons bound together by electrostatic and electromagnetic forces. It is the simplest structural unit that displays the characteristic physical and chemical properties of a compound. **2.** A small particle; a very tiny bit. [French *molécule,* from New Latin *molecula,* diminutive of Latin *mōlēs,* mass, bulk.]

mole·hill (mól-hil) *n.* A small mound of loose earth thrown up by a burrowing mole. **—make a mountain out of a molehill.** To exaggerate a minor problem.

mole rat *n.* **1.** Any of various burrowing rodents resembling moles, found in Africa and Eurasia. **2.** A rodent, the **bandicoot** *(see).*

mole·skin (mól-skin) *n.* **1.** The short, soft, silky, dark grey fur of the mole. Also called "mole". **2. a.** A heavy-napped cotton twill fabric. **b.** *Plural.* Clothing, especially trousers, of this fabric.

mo·lest (ma-lést, mō-) *tr.v.* **-lested, -lesting, -lests. 1.** To disturb, torment, or annoy. **2. a.** To accost and harass sexually. **b.** To abuse or assault sexually: *He not only accosted her verbally, but molested her as well.* [Middle English *molesten,* to vex, molest, from Old French *molester,* from Latin *molestāre,* to annoy, from *molestus,* troublesome.] **—mo·les·ta·tion** (mō-less-táysh'n, mó-) *n.* **—mo·lest·er** *n.*

Mo·lière (mólli-air ‖ *U.S.* mōl-yaír; *French* mawl-yaír), born Jean-Baptiste Poquelin (1622–73). French dramatist, and founder of high French comedy. His plays include *Les Précieuses ridicules* (1659), *Tartuffe* (1664), *Le Misanthrope* (1666), *L'Avare* (1668), *Le Bourgeois Gentilhomme* (1670), and *Le Malade imaginaire* (1673), which he was taken fatally ill while performing in.

mo·line (ma-lín, mo-, mō-) *adj. Heraldry.* Designating a cross that has arms of equal length with the ends of each slightly broadened and curved back. [Probably from Anglo-French *moliné,* from *molin,* MILL (referring to the curved arms, which resemble those of a windmill).]

moll (mol) *n. Slang.* **1.** A female companion of a thief or gangster. **2.** A prostitute. [From *Moll,* pet form for the name *Mary.*]

mol·li·fy (mólli-fī) *tr.v.* **-fied, -fying, -fies. 1.** To allay (the anger of); placate; calm. **2.** To make gentler; soften or ease: *"with a countenance greatly mollified by the softening influence of tobacco"* (Charles Dickens). **—See Synonyms at pacify.** [Middle English *mollifien,* from Old French *mollifier,* from Latin *mollificāre,* to make soft : *mollis,* soft + *facere,* to make, do.] **—mol·li·fi·a·ble** *adj.* **—mol·li·fi·ca·tion** (-fi-káysh'n) *n.* **—mol·li·fy·ing·ly** *adv.*

mol·lusc, *U.S.* **mol·lusk** (mól-əsk; *rarely* -usk) *n.* Any invertebrate animal of the phylum Mollusca, having a soft body typically protected by a shell. The group includes the snails and slugs, the clams and other bivalves, and the octopuses and squids. [French *mollusque,* from New Latin *Mollusca,* "the soft ones", from Latin *molluscus,* extension of *mollis,* soft.] **—mol·lus·cous** (mo-lúskəss, ma-) *adj.*

mol·lus·can (mo-lúskan, ma-) *adj.* Of or pertaining to the molluscs. **~** *n.* A mollusc.

Moll·wei·de projection (mól-vīdə) *n.* An equal-area map projection using an ellipsoidal shape and having straight lines for parallels of latitude and for the central meridian, other meridians being curved. It is used for representing the whole Earth and often split into sections, with continental areas having their own central meridians. [After Karl *Mollweide* (1774–1825), German mathematician and astronomer.]

mol·ly, mol·lie (mólli) *n., pl.* **-lies.** Any of several tropical and subtropical fishes of the genus *Mollienesia.* The males of some species have sail-like dorsal fins and are bred in aquaria. [New Latin *Mollienesia,* after Comte François N. *Mollien* (1758–1850), French statesman.]

mol·ly·cod·dle (mólli-kodd'l) *n.* A person of weak character who seeks to be pampered and protected. **~** *tr.v.* **mollycoddled, -dling, -dles.** To be overprotective and indulgent towards; spoil by pampering and coddling. See Synonyms at **pamper.** [Slang *molly,* milksop, from *Molly,* pet form of *Mary* + CODDLE.] **—mol·ly·cod·dler** *n.*

Molly Ma·guire (ma-gwír) *n.* **1.** A member of a secret society in Ireland that terrorised law officers attempting to evict tenants in the 1840s. **2.** A member of a secret society of Pennsylvania miners who terrorised mine owners from about 1865 to 1877 in order to secure better working conditions and better pay. [The name refers to the female disguise adopted by members.]

mo·loch (mó-lok) *n.* An Australian ant-eating desert lizard, *Moloch horridus,* with a spiny, yellow and brown body. [After MOLOCH

(alluding to its grotesque appearance).]

Mo·loch (mó-lok ‖ *U.S. also* móllək) *n.* **1.** In the Old Testament, a god of the Ammonites and Phoenicians to whom children were sacrificed by burning. **2.** Anything regarded as demanding a terrible sacrifice. [Late Latin *Moloch,* from Greek *Molokh,* from Hebrew *Molekh.*]

Mol·o·tov (móllə-tov, -tof ‖ *U.S. also* mō̆lə-; *Russian* -təf), **Vyacheslav Mikhailovich,** born Vyacheslav Mikhailovich Skriabin (1890–1986). Soviet politician. He joined the Bolsheviks in 1906 and took the surname Molotov, "the hammer". He helped to found *Pravda* in 1912 and became its acting editor. In 1939 he was made Foreign Secretary and cosigned, with Ribbentrop, the Hitler-Stalin pact. He remained Foreign Minister until 1949 and held office again (1953–56). In 1957, he was expelled with Malenkov from the Central Committee for allegedly having formed an anti-party group. Expelled from CP 1962; reinstated 1984.

Molotov cocktail *n.* A makeshift incendiary bomb made of a breakable container filled with inflammable liquid and provided with a rag wick. [After V.M. MOLOTOV.]

molt *U.S.* Variant of **moult.**

mol·ten (móltən). Archaic past participle of **melt.** **~** *adj.* **1.** Made liquid by heat; melted. Said chiefly of substances, such as metal or rock, that melt at extremely high temperatures. **2.** Brilliantly glowing.

mol·to (mól-tō ‖ *U.S.* mṓl-) *adv. Music.* Very; much. Used with directions: *molto sostenuto.* [Italian, from Latin *multum,* much (adverb), from *multus,* much (adjective).]

Mo·luc·cas (ma-lúckəz). *Bahasa Indonesian.* **Ma·lu·ku; Mo·luk·ken.** Formerly **Spice Islands.** Group of islands in eastern Indonesia. They are hot, humid, and fertile and their cloves, nutmeg, and other spices attracted traders and colonisers. They gained independence from the Dutch (1949) as a province of Indonesia, but the South Moluccans resent rule by Indonesia, and have taken urban guerrilla action. Ambon is the capital. **—Mo·luc·can** *n.* & *adj.*

mol. wt. molecular weight.

mo·ly (mṓli) *n., pl.* **-lies. 1.** In the *Odyssey,* a magic herb with black roots and white flowers, given to Odysseus by Hermes to nullify the spells of Circe. **2.** A plant, the **lily leek** *(see).* [Latin *mōly,* from Greek *mōlu,* akin to Sanskrit *mūlam,* root.]

mo·lyb·de·nite (mo-líbdən-īt, ma-, mō-) *n.* A mineral form of molybdenum sulphide, MoS_2, that is the principal ore of molybdenum.

mo·lyb·de·num (mo-líbdən-əm, ma-, mō-) *n. Symbol* **Mo** A hard, grey, metallic element used to toughen alloy steels and soften tungsten alloy. It is also used in fertilisers, dyes, enamels, and reagents. Atomic number 42, atomic weight 95.94, melting point 2,620°C, boiling point 4,800°C, relative density 10.2, valencies 2, 3, 4, 5. [New Latin, from obsolete *molybdena,* from Latin *molybdaena,* galena, from Greek *molubdaina,* a lead (of a plumb line), from *molubdos,* lead.]

mo·lyb·dic (mo-líbdik, mə-, mō-) *adj.* Of or containing molybdenum. Said especially of a compound containing molybdenum with a high valency.

mo·lyb·dous (mo-líbdəss, mə-, mō-) *adj.* Of or containing molybdenum. Said especially of a compound containing molybdenum with a low valency.

mom (mom) *n. U.S. Informal.* A mother; a mum. [Short for momma, from baby talk.]

Mom·ba·sa (mom-bássə, -báa-sə). Seaport and industrial centre of southeast Kenya. It is the country's chief port, and also handles trade for Uganda and Tanzania.

mo·ment (mṓmənt) *n.* **1.** A brief, indefinite interval of time: *She'll join you in a moment.* **2. a.** A specific point in time: *at that moment.* **b.** The present time: *out at the moment.* **3.** The appropriate or right point in time: *This is the moment to act.* **4. a.** A particular period or event of importance, significance, excellence, enjoyment, or the like: *"Swinburne's entry was for me a great moment."* (Max Beerbohm). **b.** Such a period or event occurring in something that is otherwise unexceptional: *a dull play, but it has its moments.* **5.** Outstanding significance or value; importance: *Your views are of no great moment.* **6.** *Philosophy.* A phase or aspect of a logically developing process; a momentum. **7.** *Physics. Abbr.* **M a.** The product of a quantity, especially a force, and its perpendicular distance from a reference point. **b.** The rotation produced in a body when a force is applied; torque. See **moment of inertia. 8.** *Statistics.* The expected value of a positive integral power of a random variable. The first moment is the mean of the distribution. **—See Synonyms at importance.** [Middle English, from Old French, from Latin *mōmentum,* movement, MOMENTUM.]

Synonyms: moment, minute, instant, second, trice, jiffy, flash.

mo·men·tar·i·ly (mṓmən-trə-li, -tərə- ‖ -térrə-) *adv.* **1.** For only an instant or moment. **2.** *Rare.* Momently. **3.** *U.S. Informal.* Very soon; in just a moment.

mo·men·tar·y (mṓmən-tri, -təri ‖ -terri) *adj.* **1.** Lasting only a brief time. **2.** Occurring or present at every moment: *in momentary fear of being exposed.* **3.** Short-lived; ephemeral. Said of a living creature. **—See Synonyms at transient.** [Latin *mōmentārius,* from *mōmentum,* MOMENT.] **—mo·men·tar·i·ness** *n.*

Usage: Momentary and *momentous* are sometimes confused. *Momentary* refers to shortness of time; *momentous* to level of significance. A *momentary decision* would be one made on the spur of the moment; a *momentous decision* would be a very important one.

mo·ment·ly (mṓmənt-li) *adv.* **1.** Every moment; from moment to moment: *"The throng momently increased."* (Edgar Allan Poe). **2.** For a moment.

moment of inertia *n. Physics.* **1.** A measure of a body's resistance to angular acceleration, equal to: **a.** The product of the mass of a particle and the square of its distance from a reference point or line. **b.** The sum of the products of each mass element of a body multiplied by the square of its distance from an axis. **2.** The sum of the products of each element of an area multiplied by the square of its distance from a coplanar axis.

moment of momentum *n.* **Angular momentum** *(see).*

moment of truth *n.* **1.** A time of crisis or testing, especially one in which the true nature or capabilities of a person or thing are revealed. **2.** In bullfighting, the moment when the matador makes his final sword-thrust.

mo·men·tous (mə-méntəss, mō-) *adj.* Of utmost importance or outstanding significance; having grave implications or consequences: *a momentous decision affecting our future.* See Usage note at **momentary.** —**mo·men·tous·ly** *adv.* —**mo·men·tous·ness** *n.*

mo·men·tum (mə-mén-təm, mō-) *n., pl.* **-ta** (-tə) or **-tums.** **1.** *Physics. Symbol* **p a.** The product of a body's mass and linear velocity. Also called "linear momentum". **b.** See **angular momentum.** **2.** The force of motion, **impetus** *(see).* **3.** Impetus or force gained through movement or progression: *the campaign's momentum.* **4.** *Philosophy.* A moment. [Latin *mōmentum*, motion, movement, from *movimentum* (unattested), from *movēre*, to move.]

mom·ma (mómmə) *n.* Also **mom·mie, mom·my** (mómmi) (for sense 1) *pl.* **-mies.** *Informal.* **1.** *U.S.* A mother; a mummy. **2.** A woman; especially, a large, earthy, usually black, singer. Sometimes considered offensive. [Variant of MAMMA.]

Mo·mus (mṓməss) *n., pl.* **-muses.** **1.** *Greek Mythology.* The god of blame and ridicule. **2.** A fault-finder; a critic of petty details.

Mon (mōn) *n., pl.* **Mons** or collectively **Mon.** **1.** A member of the principal native people of the Pegu region in Burma. **2.** The Mon-Khmer language of this people. —**Mon** *adj.*

Môn. See **Anglesey.**

mon. **1.** monastery. **2.** monetary.

Mon. Monday.

mon–. Variant of **mono–.**

mo·na (mṓnə) *n.* An African monkey, *Cercopithecus monas,* with a dark back and pale underparts. It is a type of guenon. [Portuguese or Spanish, monkey.]

mon·a·chism (mónnəkiz'm) *n.* Monasticism. [Middle English, from Medieval Latin *monachismus,* from Late Greek *monakhismos,* from *monakhos,* MONK.] —**mon·a·chal** (monnək'l) *adj.*

monacid, monacidic. Variants of **monoacid.**

Mon·a·co, Principality of (mónnəkō, mə-naʹakō). Small, independent principality on France's south coast. Business interests, centred at La Condamine, gambling at the Casino at Monte Carlo, and tourism are the main sources of revenue, and spare the Monégasques (who are excluded from the gambling tables) taxation. The Genoese family of Grimaldi have ruled the principality since 1297. At various times under the protection of Spain, Sardinia, and France, its sovereignty was restored in 1861. Area, 1.95 square kilometres (0.75 square mile). Population, 30,000. Capital, Monaco-Ville. See map at **France.** —**Mon·a·can** *adj.* & *n.*

mo·nad (mónnad, mṓ-nad) *n.* **1.** An independent, indivisible, and impenetrable unit of substance viewed as the basic constituent element of physical reality, as in the philosophy of Leibniz. **2.** *Biology.* Any single-celled microscopic organism, especially a flagellate protozoan. Also called "monas". **3.** *Chemistry.* An atom or radical with a valency of 1. [Late Latin *monas* (stem *monad-*), unit, from Greek, from *monos,* single.] —**mo·nad·i·cal** *adj.* —**mo·nad·i·cal·ly** *adv.*

mon·a·del·phous (mónnə-délfəss) *adj. Botany.* **1.** United by the filaments into a single tubelike group. Said of stamens. **2.** Having stamens thus united. Compare **diadelphous.** [MON(O)- + -ADEL-PHOUS.]

mo·nad·ic (mo-náddik, mə-, mō-) *adj.* **1.** Considered or dealt with singly, not comparatively. **2.** *Biology & Chemistry.* Of or pertaining to a monad.

mon·ad·ism (mónnə-diz'm, mṓnə-) *n. Philosophy.* The doctrine, as in the philosophy of Leibniz, that monads are the basic constituent elements of physical reality.

mo·nad·nock (mə-nád-nok) *n.* A mountain or rocky mass that is more resistant and stands isolated above the general level of erosion (peneplain). [After Mt. *Monadnock* in New Hampshire, United States.]

Mon·a·ghan (mónnə-hən, *rarely* -khən, -gən). *Irish* **Contae Mhuineachain.** County in the Republic of Ireland. It lies in the ancient province of Ulster, and is largely agricultural, producing beef and dairy cattle. The county town, Monaghan, produces footwear.

mo·nan·drous (món-ándrəss, mən-) *adj. Botany.* **1.** Of, pertaining to, or characterised by monandry. **2. a.** Designating flowers having a single stamen. **b.** Having flowers bearing a single stamen. [MON(O)- + -ANDROUS.]

mo·nan·dry (món-ándri, mən-, món-andri) *n.* **1.** The custom of having one husband at a time. Compare **polyandry.** **2.** *Botany.* The condition of being monandrous. [MON(O)- + -ANDRY.]

mo·nan·thous (món-ánthəss, mən-) *adj. Botany.* Bearing a single flower. [MON(O)- + Greek *anthos,* flower.]

mon·arch (mónnərk. *Note: a spelling pronunciation* mónnaark *is sometimes heard*) *n.* **1.** A person, such as a king or emperor, who is a head of state, usually by hereditary right and for life, and whose powers vary from those of an absolute ruler to the constitutionally limited powers of a figurehead. **2.** One that surpasses others in power or pre-eminence: *"Mont Blanc is the monarch of the mountains."* (Lord Byron). **3.** A large orange and black butterfly, *Danaus plexippus,* having a wingspread of up to 110 millimetres (4 inches). Also called "milkweed butterfly". [Late Latin *monarcha,* from Greek *monarkhēs* : *mono-,* sole + *-arkhes,* -ARCH.] —**mo·nar·chal** (mo-nárk'l, mə-), **mo·nar·chi·al** (-nárki-əl), **mon·ar·chic** (-nárkik, **mon·ar·chi·cal** (-nárkik'l) *adj.* —**mo·nar·chal·ly, mon·ar·chi·cal·ly** *adv.*

mo·nar·chi·an·ism (mo-nárki-ən-iz'm, mə-) *n.* A Christian heresy of the second and third centuries that denied the doctrine of the Trinity. [Late Latin *monarchiānī,* "the monarchians," from *monarchia,* MONARCHY.] —**mo·nar·chi·an** (mə-nárki-ən) *n.* & *adj.*

mon·ar·chism (món-ər-kiz'm ‖ -aar-) *n.* **1.** The principles of monarchy. **2.** Belief in or advocacy of monarchy. —**mon·ar·chist** (-kist) *n.* & *adj.* —**mon·ar·chis·tic** (-kístik) *adj.*

mon·ar·chy (món-ər-ki ‖ -aar-) *n., pl.* **-chies.** **1.** Government by a monarch. **2.** A state that is ruled by or has a monarch. [Middle English *monarchie,* from Old French, from Late Latin *monarchia,* from Greek *monarkhia,* from *monarkhēs,* MONARCH.]

mo·nas (mónnass, mṓ-nass) *n., pl.* **monades** (mónnə-deez). *Biology.* A monad *(see).* [Late Latin *monas* (stem *monad-*), MONAD.]

mon·as·ter·y (mónnə-stri, -stəri ‖ -sterri) *n., pl.* **-ies.** *Abbr.* **mon.** The residence of a community of persons, especially monks, living under religious vows and usually in seclusion. [Middle English *monasterie,* from Late Latin *monastērium,* from Late Greek *monastērion,* from Greek *monazein,* to live alone, from *monos,* alone.] —**mon·as·te·ri·al** (-steer-i-əl ‖ -sterri-əl) *adj.*

mo·nas·tic (mə-nástik, mo-) *adj.* Also **mo·nas·ti·cal** (-nástik'l). **1.** Pertaining to or characteristic of monasteries or persons living in religious or contemplative seclusion. **2.** Loosely, leading an ascetic or celibate life.
~*n.* A person who lives a monastic life; especially, a monk. [Late Latin *monasticus,* from Late Greek *monastikos,* from Greek *monazein,* to live alone. See **monastery.**] —**mo·nas·ti·cal·ly** *adv.*

mo·nas·ti·cism (mə-násti-siz'm, mo-) *n.* The monastic life or system.

mon·a·tom·ic (mónnə-tómmik) *adj.* **1.** Occurring as single atoms, as, for example, does helium. **2.** Having one replaceable atom or radical. **3.** Univalent. [MON(O)- + ATOMIC.]

mon·au·ral (món-áwrəl, *sometimes* -ówr-əl) *adj.* **1.** Designating sound reception by one ear. **2.** *Electronics.* Monophonic. [MON(O)- + AURAL.] —**mon·au·ral·ly** *adv.*

mon·ax·i·al (món-áksi-əl) *adj.* **Uniaxial** *(see).*

mon·a·zite (mónnə-zīt) *n.* A pale yellow to reddish-brown mineral phosphate of rare-earth metals, chiefly cerium, yttrium, and lanthanum, usually together with thorium. [German *Monazit,* from Greek *monazein,* to live alone (because it is rare). See **monastery.**]

Monck or **Monk** (mungk), **George, 1st Duke of Albemarle** (1608–70). English military commander. Having earlier fought for Charles I, he was commissioned by Cromwell to put down rebellion in Ireland and Scotland in 1652, but in 1660 he led his forces successfully in support of the royalist cause.

Mon·day (mún-di, -day) *n. Abbr.* **Mon., M.** The day of the week following Sunday; the first day of the working week. [Middle English *monday,* Old English *mōnan dæg,* moon's day (translation of Late Latin *lūnae diēs*) : *mōna,* MOON + *dæg,* DAY.]

Monday Club *n.* In Britain, an extreme right-wing grouping within the Conservative Party whose members try to influence official party policy. [From the Club's custom of meeting for lunch on Mondays.]

mon·di·al (móndi-əl) *adj.* Of, pertaining to, or involving the whole world. [French, from ecclesiastical Latin *mundiālis,* from *mundus,* world.]

Mond process *n.* An industrial process for producing nickel by heating the ore in carbon monoxide and decomposing, at a higher temperature, the nickel carbonyl vapour that is produced, in order to yield the metal. [After Ludwig *Mond* (1839–1909), German-born British chemist and industrialist who developed the process.]

Mon·dri·an (móndri-ən, -aan), **Piet** (1872–1944). Dutch painter, influenced by cubism in Paris after 1910. He painted compositions in primary colours of space enclosed by lines and rectangles. He outlined his theories in a book, *Neo-Plasticism* (1920).

monecious. Variant of **monoecious.**

Mo·né·gasque (mónni-gásk, mónnay-) *n.* A citizen of Monaco; a Monacan. [French, from Provençal *Mounegasc,* from *Mounegue,* MONACO.] —**Mo·né·gasque** *adj.*

Mo·nel metal (mo-nél ‖ *U.S.* mṓ-) *n.* A corrosion-resistant alloy of nickel, copper, iron, and manganese. [After Ambrose *Monel,* president of International Nickel Co. (1873–1921).]

Mo·net (mónnay, mo-náy), **Claude** (1840–1926). French painter, and a founder of impressionism. He began to experiment with depicting variations of light and atmosphere from the outset of his career. It was his painting, *Impression: Sunrise* (1873), which gave the impressionists their name.

mon·e·tar·ist (múnni-tə-rist, mónni-) *n.* One who advocates the regulation of the money supply as a method of controlling and stabilising the economy. —**mon·e·tar·ism** *n.* —**mon·e·tar·ist** *adj.*

mon·e·tar·y (múnni-tri, mónni-, -təri ‖ -terri) *adj. Abbr.* **mon.** **1.** Of or pertaining to money. **2.** Of or pertaining to a nation's money supply, interest rates, or the like. —See Synonyms at **financial.** [Late Latin *monētārius,* from Latin *monēta,* MONEY.] —**mon·e·tar·i·ly** *adv.*

mon·e·tise, mon·e·tize (múnni-tīz, mónni-) *tr.v.* **-tised, -tising, -tises. 1.** To make legal tender. **2.** To make into money; mint. [Latin *monēta*, MONEY.] **—mon·e·ti·sa·tion** (-tī-záysh'n ‖ *U.S.* -ti-) *n.*

mon·ey (múnni) *n., pl.* **-eys** or **-ies. 1.** A commodity such as gold or silver that is legally established as an exchangeable equivalent of all other commodities and is used as a measure of their comparative values on the market. **2.** The official currency, as in coins and negotiable paper notes, issued by a government. **3. a.** Assets and property that may be converted into actual currency; wealth: *made her money in the property boom of the 70s.* **b.** *Informal.* Opportunities to acquire wealth: *There's no money in writing.* **c.** Those who own wealth: *married into money.* **4.** Any pecuniary amount of indefinite extent: *put a lot of money into the business; the company is still losing money.* **5.** *Plural. Chiefly Law.* Sums of money: *sued for the return of all moneys paid into the firm.* **6.** Any unspecified amount of currency: *money for groceries.* **—in the money.** *Informal.* **1.** Having won money. **2.** Having plenty of money; rich. **—money for jam** or **old rope.** *Informal.* Profit made with little or no effort; something for nothing. **—put money on.** To place a bet or place one's confidence in. [Middle English *moneye*, from Old French *moneie*, from Latin *monēta*, money, mint, from *Monēta*, epithet of Juno, whose temple in Rome housed the mint.]

Usage: Moneys is the preferred plural form, though *monies* is also to be found. It is used only in referring to the mediums of exchange of different countries, or to forms of currency or particular sums of money in a country.

mon·ey·bags (múnni-bagz) *n., pl.* **moneybags.** *Informal.* A rich or miserly person.

mon·ey·chang·er (múnni-chaynjər) *n.* **1.** A person who exchanges money, as from one currency to another. **2.** *Chiefly U.S.* A machine that holds and dispenses coins.

money cowry *n.* A small shell used as money in certain parts of Africa and the South Pacific. See **cowry.**

mon·eyed, mon·ied (múnnid ‖ múnneed) *adj.* **1.** Having a great deal of money. **2.** Representing or arising from the possession of money: *the triumph of moneyed interests over landed interests.*

mon·ey·er (múnni-ər) *n.* Formerly, a person authorised to coin or mint money. [Middle English *monyer*, from Old French *monier*, from Late Latin *monētārius*, minter, from *monēta*, MONEY.]

mon·ey·grub·ber (múnni-grubbər) *n.* *Informal.* A person who is intent on accumulating money at every opportunity. **—mon·ey·grub·bing** *adj.*

mon·ey·lend·er (múnni-lendər) *n.* One whose business is lending money at an interest rate. **—mon·ey·lend·ing** *n.*

mon·ey·mak·er (múnni-maykər) *n.* **1.** One who accumulates wealth. **2.** An enterprise or product that is actually or potentially profitable. **—mon·ey·mak·ing** *n. & adj.*

money market *n.* The sphere of the financial market dealing in short-term securities and loans, gold, and foreign exchange. Compare **capital market.**

money of account *n. Chiefly U.S.* **Unit of account** *(see).*

money order *n. Abbr.* **m.o., M.O.** An order for the payment of a specific amount of money, usually issued and payable at a bank or post office.

money spider *n.* Any of various spiders of the family Linyphiidae, having a small reddish or black body. [From the belief that the tiny spider brings good luck.]

mon·ey·spin·ner (múnni-spinnər) *n.* *Informal.* Something, such as an idea, project, or business, that is or will be very successful and profitable. [Originally, a name of the money spider, extended to promising or profitable business.] **—mon·ey·spin·ning** *n. & adj.*

money supply *n. Economics.* The total amount of money held by individuals and organisations in a country at a given time, as measured by any of several indicators, specifically (in Britain): **1.** M_1, based on actual currency in circulation plus readily transferrable money in private current or deposit accounts. **2.** M_2, similar to M_1 but including longer-term deposits. **3.** M_3, the most comprehensive, based on all the above plus nonsterling deposits and public-sector deposits.

mon·ey·wort (múnni-wurt ‖ -wawrt) *n.* Any of several plants with rounded, coinlike leaves, such as the Cornish moneywort, *Sibthorpia europaea.* Also called "creeping Jenny", "creeping Charlie".

mon·ger (múng-gər ‖ móng-) *n.* **1.** A dealer in a specified commodity. Usually used in combination: *ironmonger.* **2.** A person promoting something specified and usually undesirable. Used in combination: *scandalmonger, warmonger.*

~*tr.v.* **mongered, -gering, -gers.** To peddle or deal in. [Middle English *mongere*, Old English *mangere*, from *mangian*, to traffic, from Germanic *mangōjan* (unattested), from Latin *mangō*, (fraudulent) dealer.]

mon·go (móng-gō) *n., pl.* **mongo** (móng-gō). A monetary unit, 1/100 of the Mongolian tugrik.

mon·gol (móng-g'l, -gol) *n.* A person affected with **Down's syndrome** *(see).* Not in technical usage. See Usage note at **mongolism.**

Mon·gol (móng-g'l, -gol ‖ -gōl) *n.* **1.** A member of one of the nomadic peoples of Mongolia or a native of Mongolia. **2.** A member of the Mongoloid ethnic group. **3.** The language of Mongolia. **4.** Loosely, the Yuan dynasty of China. [Mongol *Mongol*, perhaps from *mong*, brave.] **—Mon·gol** *adj.*

Mon·go·li·a (mong-gṓl-i-ə, mon-, -yə). Ancient region inhabited by the Mongols, and now comprising the Republic of Mongolia and the Inner Mongolian Autonomous Region of China. In the 13th century, the Mongols under Genghis Khan built one of the world's greatest empires, stretching from China to the Danube, and into Persia. This broke up, his successors establishing the khanate of the Golden Horde in Russia, and the Yuan dynasty in China. See also **Mongolia, Republic of.**

Mongolia, Inner See **Inner Mongolian Autonomous Region.**

Mongolia, Republic of. Formerly **Outer Mongolia.** Republic of east central Asia. It consists of a high plateau, with mountains in the centre, west and north and the Gobi (desert) in the south and east. Much of the terrain is used for pasture, livestock herding (now largely collectivised) being the principal occupation of the seminomadic people. Once the centre of the Mongol empire (1206), it was a province of China (1691-1911 and 1919-21), and then an independent republic, under the protection of the U.S.S.R. Multi-party elections were held in 1990. Area, 1 566 500 square kilometres (604,829 square miles). Population, 2,350,000. Capital, Ulan Bator. See map at **China.**

mon·go·li·an (mong-gṓl-i-ən), mon-, -yən) *adj.* Of, pertaining to, or exhibiting **Down's syndrome** *(see).* Not in technical usage.

Mon·go·li·an (mong-gṓ-i-ən, mon-, -yən). *n.* **1.** A Mongol. **2.** The Mongolic language of Mongolia. **—Mon·go·li·an** *adj.*

Mon·gol·ic (mong-góllik, mon-) *n.* The Altaic subfamily that includes Mongolian and Kalmuck. **—Mon·gol·ic** *adj.*

mon·gol·ism (móng-gə-liz'm) *n. Also capital* **M.** A congenital condition, **Down's syndrome** *(see).* Not in technical usage. [From a supposed resemblance to the features of ethnic Mongoloids.]

Usage: The terms *mongolism* and *mongol* have been replaced in medical usage by *Down's syndrome* and *Down's baby* (or *child*) respectively, and should be avoided as they may give offence.

mon·gol·oid (móng-gə-loyd) *adj.* Characterised by or pertaining to **Down's syndrome** *(see).* Not in technical usage.

Mon·gol·oid (móng-gə-loyd) *adj. Anthropology.* **1.** Of, pertaining to, or designating a major ethnic division of the human species whose members are characterised by yellowish-brown to white skin pigmentation, coarse straight black hair, dark eyes with pronounced epicanthic folds, and prominent cheekbones. This division is considered to include the Chinese, Japanese, Malayans, Mongolians, Siberians, Eskimos, and American Indians. **2.** Characteristic of or like a Mongol.

~*n.* A member of the Mongoloid ethnic division of humanity.

mon·goose (móng-gōōss, múng-, gōōss ‖ *U.S. also* món-) *n., pl.* **-gooses.** Any of various Old World carnivorous mammals of the genus *Herpestes* and related genera, having a slender body and a long tail and notable for the ability to kill poisonous snakes. [Marathi *mangūs*, from Dravidian, akin to Telugu *mangisu*.]

mon·grel (múng-grəl ‖ móng-) *n.* **1.** An animal or plant resulting from various interbreedings; especially, a dog of mixed breed or no definable breed. **2.** A person of mixed racial stock. Used derogatorily or facetiously. **3.** A cross between one thing and another. Also used adjectively: *a mongrel language, half English, half Spanish.* [Probably diminutive of Middle English *mong*, Old English *gemang*, mixture.] **—mon·grel·ism** *n.* **—mon·grel·ly** (-grəli) *adj.*

mon·grel·ise, mon·grel·ize (múng-grəl-īz, móng-) *tr.v.* **-ised, -ising, -ises.** To make mongrel in race, nature, or character. Usually used derogatorily when applied to human beings.

'mongst (mung-st, -kst ‖ mong-) *prep. Poetic.* Amongst.

monied. Variant of **moneyed.**

mon·ies. Alternative plural of **money.**

mon·i·ker, mon·ick·er (mónnikər) *n. Informal.* A personal name or nickname. [19th century : origin obscure.]

mon·i·li·a·sis (mónni-lī-ə-siss, mōni-) *n.* **Candidiasis** *(see).* [New Latin : *Monilia* (genus), from Latin *monile*, necklace (referring to the chain of spores) + -IASIS.]

mo·nil·i·form (mo-nílli-fawrm, mə-, mō-) *adj. Biology.* Resembling a string of beads, as do various fungi, the antennae of certain insects, and the nuclei of some members of the Ciliata. [Latin *monīle*, necklace + -FORM.]

mon·ish (mónnish) *tr.v.* **-ished, -ishing, -ishes.** *Archaic.* To admonish. [Middle English *monisshen*, variant of *monesten*, from Old French *monester*, from Vulgar Latin *monestāre* (unattested), extension of Latin *monēre*, to warn.]

mon·ism (món-iz'm ‖ mṓn-) *n. Philosophy.* A metaphysical theory according to which reality is conceived as consisting of only one basic substance. Compare **dualism, pluralism.** [German *Monismus* : MON(O)- + -ISM.] **—mon·ist** *n. & adj.* **—mo·nis·tic** (mo-nístik, mə- ‖ mō-) *adj.* **—mo·nis·ti·cal·ly** *adv.*

mo·ni·tion (mə-nísh'n, mo-, mō-) *n.* **1.** A warning or intimation of some impending danger. **2. a.** Admonition. **b.** A piece of advice. **3.** A formal order from a bishop or ecclesiastical court to refrain from some particular offence. [Middle English *monicioun*, from Old French *monition*, from Latin *monitiō* (stem *monitiōn-*), from *monēre*, to warn.]

mon·i·tor (mónnitər) *n.* **1.** *Archaic.* One that admonishes, cautions, or reminds. **2.** A pupil who assists a teacher in routine duties. **b.** A senior pupil with various responsibilities such as keeping order in class. **3. a.** Any device used to record, check, or control a process. **b.** A television set in a studio showing images for transmission. **4.** An articulated device holding the rotating nozzle of a water jet, used in mining and fire-fighting. **5.** A heavily ironclad warship of the 19th century with a low, flat deck and one or more gun turrets. **6.** Any carnivorous lizard of the family Varanidae, of tropical and subtropical regions, ranging in length from about 20 centimetres to 3 metres (8 inches to 10 feet). See **Komodo dragon.**

~*v.* **monitored, -toring, -tors.** —*tr.* **1.** To check (the transmission quality of a signal) by means of a receiver or monitor. **2.** To test (a surface) for radiation intensity. **3.** To keep track of by means of an electronic device. **4.** To check by means of a receiver for significant content: *monitor foreign radio broadcasts.* **5.** To scrutinise or check systematically: *carefully monitored the experiment at every stage.* **6.** To keep watch over; supervise: *monitor an examination.* **7.** To direct as a monitor. —*intr.* To act as a monitor. [Latin, one who warns, from *monēre,* to warn.] —**mon·i·tor·i·al** (mónni-táwri-əl ‖ -tŏri-) *adj.* —**mon·i·tress** (-trəss, -triss, -tress) *n.*

mon·i·to·ry (mónni-tri, -təri) *adj.* Conveying an admonition or warning: *a monitory glance.*

~*n., pl.* **monitories.** A letter containing the admonition of a bishop or ecclesiastical court. [Latin *monitōrius,* from *monitor,* MONITOR.]

monk (mungk) *n.* A member of a religious brotherhood living in a monastery, bound by vows such as those of poverty, chastity, and obedience, and devoted to a discipline prescribed by a religious order. [Middle English *munk,* Old English *munuc,* from Late Latin *monachus,* from Late Greek *monakhos,* solitary, monk, from Greek *monos,* alone.]

Monk, Thelonius (1920–82). U.S. black jazz pianist and composer. His spare piano style and unusual harmonic sense made him one of the most influential of modern jazz musicians. His notable compositions include *Round Midnight* (*c.* 1947).

monk·er·y (múngkəri) *n., pl.* **-ies. 1.** Monks or monastic life or practices. Used derogatorily. **2.** A monastery. Used derogatorily.

mon·key (múngki) *n., pl.* **-keys. 1. a.** Any long-tailed primate, including the Old and New World monkeys and the marmosets, but excluding the anthropoid apes and the lemurs, lorises, tree shrews, and tarsiers. **b.** Loosely, any member of the order Primates, apart from the human race. **2.** A mischievous, playful child or young person. Used familiarly: *you cheeky monkey!* **3.** The iron block or ram of a pile driver. **4.** *Slang.* £500. **5.** *Slang.* A person who is mocked, duped, or made to appear a fool. Used chiefly in the phrase *make a monkey out of.* **6.** *Slang.* Drug addiction, regarded as a burdensome affliction: *have a monkey on one's back.* **7.** *Australian Informal.* A sheep.

~*v.* **monkeyed, -keying, -keys.** —*intr. Informal.* To play or fiddle with something idly: *Don't monkey around with my watch.* —*tr.* To imitate or mimic; ape. [16th century : origin obscure.]

monkey bread *n.* The fruit of the **baobab** (*see*).

monkey business *n. Informal.* Mischievous or deceitful behaviour.

mon·key-flow·er (múngki-flowr) *n.* Any of various plants of the genus *Mimulus,* especially *M. luteus,* which has yellow, two-lipped flowers, and is widely cultivated. [From the supposed resemblance of the flower to a monkey's face.]

monkey jacket *n.* **1.** A short, tight-fitting jacket, formerly worn by sailors. **2.** A **mess jacket** (*see*). [From its similarity to the jackets worn by performing monkeys.]

monkey nut *n. British Informal.* A peanut.

monkey pot *n.* **1.** The large, urn-shaped lidded pod of tropical trees of the genus *Lecythis.* **2.** Any tree bearing this type of pod.

monkey puzzle *n.* A coniferous tree, *Araucaria araucana,* native to Chile, having intricately ramifying branches covered with broad, stiff, prickle-tipped leaves. Also called "Chile pine". [Because its branches supposedly make it difficult for a monkey to climb.]

mon·key-shine (múngki-shīn) *n. Usually plural. U.S. Slang.* A playful, mischievous trick. [MONKEY + SHINE (prank).]

monkey suit *n. Slang.* A man's formal dress suit or a full-dress military uniform. [Probably extended from **monkey jacket.**]

monkey wrench *n.* A large wrench with adjustable jaws for turning nuts of varying sizes.

monk·fish (múngk-fish) *n., pl.* **-fishes** or collectively **monkfish. 1.** Any of several raylike sharks of the genus Squatina, having a broad, flat head and body. Also called "angel shark", "angelfish". **2.** Any of various angler fishes of the genus *Lophius.* Also *U.S.* "goosefish". [From the cowled appearance of the head.]

Mon-Khmer (mŏn-kmaír) *n.* A family of languages, including Khmer, spoken in Southeast Asia. —**Mon-Khmer** *adj.*

monk·hood (múngk-hŏod) *n.* **1.** The state or profession of a monk; monasticism. **2.** Monks collectively.

monk·ish (múngkish) *adj.* Of, pertaining to, or characteristic of monks or monasticism. Often used derogatorily.

monk's cloth *n.* A heavy cotton cloth in a coarse basket weave. [Originally used for the habits of monks.]

monk seal *n.* A seal of the nearly extinct genus *Monachus,* formerly much hunted in Mediterranean and Caribbean waters for its fur, which may be grey or yellow with black spots or uniformly brown. [From the cowled appearance of its head.]

monks·hood (múngks-hŏod) *n.* Any of various plants of the genus *Aconitum,* having hooded flowers; especially, *A. napellus,* with purplish flowers. Most species are poisonous. Also called "aconite", "wolfsbane".

Mon·mouth (món-məth, mún-). *Welsh* **Tre·fyn·wy** (tre-vún-wi). Market town in southeast Wales, the county town of Monmouthshire. It is an agricultural and tourist centre.

Monmouth, James Scott, 1st Duke of (1649–85). English pretender to the throne, bastard son of Charles II by Lucy Walter. After 1662 he lived at court, and Charles acknowledged him as his son, creating him duke in 1663. When the Catholic James II succeeded (1685), Monmouth led a rebellion. He was defeated at Sedgemoor, captured, and beheaded.

Mon·mouth·shire (món-məth-shər, mún-, -sheer). *Welsh* **Myn·wy,**

Sir Fyn·wy (mún-wi, sheer vún-wi). Former county of western England, for some purposes, such as censuses, included in Wales. Now a Unitary Authority area of southeast Wales, recreated in 1997 from parts of Gwent but not extending to its historical limits.

Mon·net (mónnay, mo-náy), **Jean (Omer Marie Gabriel)** (1888–1979). French statesman, called the "father of Europe". He was the first president (1952–55) of the European Coal and Steel Community, and laid the plans for the European Economic Community.

mon·o (mónnō) *adj. Electronics.* Monophonic.

~*n., pl.* **monos.** Monophonic sound reproduction.

mono–, mon– *comb. form.* Indicates: **1.** One; single; alone; for example, **monogamy. 2.** The presence of a single atom, radical, or group in a compound; for example, **monohydric.** [Middle English, from Old French, from Latin, from Greek, from *monos,* single, sole, alone.]

mon·o·ac·id (mónnō-ássid) *adj.* Also **mon·o·a·cid·ic** (-ə-síddik, -a-), **mon·ac·id** (món-), **mon·a·cid·ic.** *Chemistry.* Having only one hydroxyl group to react with acids. Said of bases.

mon·o·a·mine (mónnō-ámmin, -ə-méen) *n. Chemistry.* An amine that has only one functional (-NH$_2$) group per molecule.

monoamine oxidase *n. Abbr.* **MAO.** An enzyme that catalyses the oxidation of adrenaline, noradrenaline, and other monoamines. Drugs that inhibit its action are used in the treatment of depression.

mon·o·ba·sic (món-ō-báysik, -ə-) *adj. Chemistry.* **1.** Monoprotic. **2.** Having only one metal ion or positive radical.

mon·o·carp (món-ō-kaarp, -ə-) *n. Botany.* A monocarpic plant. [MONO- + -CARP.]

mon·o·car·pel·lar·y (món-ō-kárpi-ləri, -ə- ‖ -lerri) *adj. Botany.* Consisting of or having only one carpel.

mon·o·car·pic (món-ō-kárpik, -ə-) *adj.* Also **mon·o·car·pous** (-kárpəss). *Botany.* Flowering and bearing fruit only once.

mon·o·cha·si·um (món-ō-káyz-i-əm, -ə- ‖ -kávzh-əm) *n., pl.* **-sia** (-ə). *Botany.* A cyme (*see*) in which each flowering branch gives rise to one other branch only. Compare **dichasium.** —**mon·o·cha·si·al** *adj.* [MONO- + (DI)CHASIUM.]

mon·o·chord (món-ə-kawrd, -ō-) *n.* A musical instrument consisting of a sounding box with one string and a movable bridge, used to study musical notes and intervals. [Middle English *monocorde,* from Old French, from Medieval Latin *monochordum,* from Greek *monokhordon* : MONO- + *khordē,* CHORD.]

mon·o·chro·mat (món-ō-krō-mat, -ə-) *n.* A person who is completely colourblind, perceiving all colours as a single hue. [Back-formation from MONOCHROMATIC.] —**mon·o·chro·ma·tism** (-mə-tiz'm) *n.*

mon·o·chro·mat·ic (món-ə-krə-máttik, -ō-, -krō-) *adj.* Also **mon·o·chro·ic** (-krō-ik). **1.** Having or being in only one colour or shades of one colour. **2.** Having or producing electromagnetic radiation of only one wavelength. **3.** Having a single kinetic energy. Said of a beam of particles. [Greek *monokhrōmatos* : MONO- + *khrōma,* -CHROME.] —**mon·o·chro·mat·i·cal·ly** *adv.*

mon·o·chrome (mónnə-krōm) *n.* **1.** A painting done in different shades of one colour. **2.** The technique of executing such paintings. **3.** A black-and-white photograph.

~*adj.* **1.** Black-and-white. **2.** Having or being in only one colour or shades of one colour. [Medieval Latin *monochrōma,* from Greek *monokhrōmos,* of one colour : MONO- + *khrōma,* -CHROME.] —**mon·o·chro·mic** (-krōmik) *adj.*

mon·o·cle (mónnək'l) *n.* A single lens correcting the vision for one eye. [French, from Late Latin *monoculus,* one-eyed : MONO- + *oculus,* eye.] —**mon·o·cled** (mónnək'ld) *adj.*

mon·o·cline (món-ə-klīn, -ō-) *n.* A geological formation in which all strata are inclined in the same direction. Compare **isocline.** —**mon·o·cli·nal** (-klín'l) *adj.*

mon·o·clin·ic (món-ə-klínnik, -ō-) *adj. Crystallography.* Having three unequal axes, two of which intersect obliquely and are perpendicular to the third. Said of crystals. [MONO- + Greek *-klinēs,* leaning, from *klinein,* to lean.]

mon·o·cli·nous (món-ə-klínəss, -ō-) *adj. Botany.* Having pistils and stamens in the same flower. [New Latin *monoclinus,* monoclinous, "hermaphroditic" : MONO- + Greek *klinē,* couch.]

mon·o·coque (món-ə-kok, -ō- ‖ *U.S.* also -kŏk) *n.* A metal structure, as of an aircraft or racing car, in which the covering absorbs a large part of the stresses to which the body is subjected. [French : MONO- + *coque,* shell, from Latin *coccum,* berry.]

mon·o·cot·y·le·don (món-ə-kótti-léed'n, -ō-) *n.* Also **mon·o·cot** (-kot). *Botany.* Any plant of the Monocotyledonae, one of the two major divisions of angiosperms, characterised by a single embryonic seed leaf that appears at germination. Included among the monocotyledons are such plants as grasses, orchids, and lilies. Compare **dicotyledon.** —**mon·o·cot·y·le·don·ous** (-əss) *adj.*

mo·noc·ra·cy (mo-nóckrə-si, mə-) *n.* Government or rule by a single person; autocracy. [MONO- + -CRACY.]

mon·o·crat (món-ə-krat, -ō-) *n.* One who favours autocracy or monarchy. —**mon·o·crat·ic** (-kráttik) *adj.* —**mon·o·crat·i·cal·ly** *adv.*

mo·noc·u·lar (mo-nóckew-lər, mə-) *adj.* **1.** Having or pertaining to one eye. **2.** Adapted for the use of only one eye. [Late Latin *monoculus,* one-eyed. See **monocle.**]

mon·o·cy·cle (món-ə-sīk'l, -ō-) *n.* A vehicle having a single wheel, a **unicycle** (*see*).

mon·o·cyte (món-ə-sīt, -ō-) *n.* A large white blood cell, having an oval nucleus. It engulfs foreign particles, such as bacteria. [MONO- + -CYTE.] —**mon·o·cyt·ic** (-síttik), **mon·o·cy·toid** (-sítoyd) *adj.*

Mo·nod (mónnō, mo-nó), **Jacques** (1910–76). French molecular biologist, director of the Pasteur Institute in Paris from 1971. He described the process of synthesis of protein in cells, for which he and his collaborators, François Jacob and André Lwoff, were awarded the Nobel prize in physiology or medicine (1965).

mon·o·dac·tyl (món-ə-dák-til, -ō-, -dak-) *n.* An animal having only one claw on each limb. [French *monodactyle*, from Greek *monodaktulos*, one-toed, one-fingered : MONO- + *daktulos*, DACTYL.] —**mon·o·dac·ty·lous** (-dáktiləss) *adj.*

mon·o·dra·ma (món-ə-draamə, -ō- ‖ -drammə) *n.* A dramatic composition for one performer. —**mon·o·dra·mat·ic** (-drə-máttik) *adj.*

mon·o·dy (mónnədi) *n., pl.* **-dies.** **1.** In Greek tragedy, an ode for one voice or actor. **2.** An elegiac verse expressing personal lament. **3.** *Music.* **a.** A style of composition in which one vocal part or melodic line predominates. **b.** A composition in this style. [Late Latin *monōdia*, from Greek *monōidia* : MONO- + *ōidē*, song.] —**mo·nod·ic** (mə-nóddik, mo-), **mo·nod·i·cal** *adj.* —**mo·nod·i·cal·ly** *adv.* —**mon·o·dist** (mónnədist) *n.*

mo·noe·cious, mo·ne·cious (mo-néeshəss, mə-) *adj.* Also **mo·noi·cous** (-nóykəss). **1.** *Botany.* Having male and female reproductive organs in separate flowers on a single plant. Compare **dioecious. 2.** *Zoology.* Hermaphroditic. [New Latin *Monoecia* : MON(O)- + Greek *oikia*, dwelling, from *oikos*, house.] —**mo·noe·cious·ly** *adv.*

mon·o·fil·a·ment (món-ə-fílləmənt, -ō-) *n.* A single filament of yarn or plastic, for example. Also called "monofil".

mo·nog·a·my (mə-nóggə-mi, mo-) *n.* **1. a.** The custom or condition of being married to or having a sexual relationship with only one person at a time. **b.** *Archaic.* The custom of marrying only once during one's lifetime. **2.** *Zoology.* The habit of having only one mate. [French *monogamie*, from Late Latin *monogamia*, from Greek : MONO- + -GAMY.] —**mo·nog·a·mist** *n.* —**mo·nog·a·mous** (-məss) *adj.* —**mo·nog·a·mous·ly** *adv.*

mon·o·gen·e·sis (món-ō-jénnə-siss, -ss-) *n.* **1.** The theory that all living organisms are descended from a single cell. Compare **polygenesis. 2.** Asexual reproduction, as by sporulation. **3.** The development of an ovum into an organism resembling the parent, without metamorphosis. [New Latin : MONO- + -GENESIS.] —**mon·o·gen·ous** (mo-nójənəss, mə-) *adj.* —**mon·o·gen·ous·ly** *adv.*

mon·o·ge·net·ic (món-ō-jə-néttik, -ə-, -je-) *adj.* **1.** Pertaining to or showing monogenesis. **2.** Asexual. **3.** *Geology.* Formed by a single process or from a single source: *a monogenetic range.*

mon·o·gen·ic (món-ō-jénnik, -ə-) *adj.* **1.** Of or regulated by one gene or one of a pair of allelic genes. **2.** Producing offspring mostly of one sex. **3.** Of or pertaining to monogenism. [MONO- + -GENIC.] —**mon·o·gen·i·cal·ly** *adv.*

mo·nog·e·nism (mo-nójən-iz'm, mə-) *n.* The theory that humankind has descended from a single pair of ancestors. Compare **polygenism.** [MONO- + -GEN- + -ISM.] —**mo·nog·e·nist** *n.* —**mo·nog·e·nis·tic** (-ístik) *adj.*

mon·o·glot (món-ō-glot, -ə-). *adj.* Monolingual. —**mon·o·glot** *n.*

mon·o·gram (mónnə-gram) *n.* A design composed of one or more letters, usually the initials of a name, as put on letter paper or linen, for example. [Late Latin *monogramma* : MONO- + -GRAM.] —**mon·o·grammed** (-gramd) *adj.* —**mon·o·gram·mat·ic** (-grə-máttik) *adj.*

mon·o·graph (mónnə-graaf, -graf) *n.* A scholarly book, article, or pamphlet on a specific and usually narrowly limited subject.
~*tr.v.* **monographed, -graphing, -graphs.** To write a monograph on. [MONO- + -GRAPH.] —**mo·nog·ra·pher** (mə-nóggrəfər, mo-) *n.* —**mon·o·graph·ic** (-gráffik) *adj.* —**mon·o·graph·i·cal·ly** *adv.*

mo·nog·y·ny (mo-nójəni, mə-) *n.* The practice or condition of having only one wife at a time. [MONO- + -GYNY.] —**mo·nog·y·nist** *n.* & *adj.* —**mo·nog·y·nous** *adj.*

mon·o·hy·brid (món-ō-hī-brid, -ə-, -hī-) *n.* Hybrid offspring of parents differing in a single characteristic or genetic factor.

mon·o·hy·drate (món-ō-hídrayt, -ə-) *n. Chemistry.* A compound, especially a crystalline salt, that contains one molecule of water per molecule of compound. —**mon·o·hy·drat·ed** (-hī-dráytid, -hídray-tid) *adj.*

mon·o·hy·dric (món-ō-hídrik) *adj. Chemistry.* Containing one hydroxyl radical. [MONO- + HYDRO- + -IC.]

monoicous. Variant of **monoecious.**

mon·o·ki·ni (món-ō-kéeni, -ə-) *n.* A woman's topless swimsuit. [MONO- + -*kini* (from humorous analysis of *bikini* as BI- (two, two-piece) + *kini*).]

mo·nol·a·try (mo-nóllətri, mə-) *n.* The worship of one god to the exclusion of the others but without denying the existence of others. [MONO- + -LATRY.]

mon·o·lay·er (món-ō-lay-ər, -ə-) *n.* **1.** A film of a compound one molecule thick; a monomolecular layer. **2.** A layer one atom thick; a monatomic layer.

mon·o·lin·gual (món-ə-líng-gwəl, -ō- ‖ -gew-əl) *adj.* Speaking, knowing, using, or expressed in only one language.

mon·o·lith (món-ə-lith, -ō-) *n.* **1.** A large block of stone, especially a natural rock buttress or one used in architecture or sculpture. **2.** A column, monument, or the like made from one large block of stone. **3.** Something resembling or suggestive of a monolith, especially in being large, uniform, impersonal, or immovable. [French *monolithe*, from Greek *monolithos* : MONO- + -LITH.]

mon·o·lith·ic (món-ə-líthik, -ō-) *adj.* **1.** Consisting of a monolith or monoliths. **2.** Like a monolith; massive, solid, impersonal, or uniform: *a monolithic bureaucracy.*

monolithic circuit *n. Electronics.* A type of integrated circuit in which all the components are formed in the surface of the chip, with

no added connections. Compare **hybrid circuit.**

mon·o·logue, *U.S.* **mon·o·log** (mónnə-log, *rarely* -lōg) *n.* **1.** A long speech or talk made by one person, often monopolising a conversation. **2. a.** A long speech delivered by an actor; a soliloquy. **b.** Any literary composition in the form of a soliloquy: *dramatic monologue.* [French : MONO- + (DIA)LOGUE.] —**mon·o·log·ic** (-lójik), **mon·o·log·i·cal** *adj.* —**mo·nol·o·gist** (mo-nóllⱥjist, mə- ‖ mónnə-log-ist, -lawg-) *n.*

mon·o·ma·ni·a (món-ə-máyn-i-ə, -ō-, -yə) *n.* **1.** Pathological obsession with one idea. Not in technical usage. See **paranoia. 2.** Intent concentration on, or exaggerated enthusiasm for, a subject or an idea. [New Latin : MONO- + -MANIA.] —**mon·o·ma·ni·ac** (-i-ak, -yak) *n.* —**mon·o·ma·ni·a·cal** (-mə-ní-ak'l) *adj.*

mon·o·mer (mónnə-mər) *n.* Any molecule, usually of a simple structure and of low molecular weight, that can be chemically bound as a unit of a **polymer** (*see*): *Ethylene is a monomer of polyethylene.* [MONO- + Greek *meros*, part.] —**mon·o·mer·ic** (-mérrik) *adj.*

mon·o·me·tal·lic (món-ō-me-tál-ik, -ə-, -mi-) *adj.* **1.** Consisting of or containing one metal. **2.** Pertaining to monometallism.

mo·no·met·al·lism (mo-nóm-métt'l-iz'm, -ə-) *n.* **1.** The use of only one metal, usually gold or silver, as a standard of money. **2.** The economic theory supporting the use of one metallic monetary standard. —**mon·o·met·al·list** *n.*

mo·nom·e·ter (mo-nómmitər, mə-) *n.* A line of verse that consists of only one metrical foot. —**mon·o·met·ric** (món-ō-méttrik, -ə-), **mon·o·met·ri·cal** *adj.*

mo·no·mi·al (mo-nōm-i-əl, mə-) *n.* **1.** *Algebra.* An expression consisting of only one term. **2.** *Biology.* A taxonomic name consisting of a single word. [MON(O)- + (BIN)OMIAL.] —**mo·no·mi·al** *adj.*

mon·o·mo·lec·u·lar (món-ō-mə-léckew-lər, -ə-, -mō-, -mo-) *adj.* **1.** Of or pertaining to a single molecule. **2.** Of or consisting of a layer one molecule thick.

mon·o·mor·phic (món-ō-mór-fik, -ə-) *adj.* Also **monomorphous.** *Zoology.* Having a basic structure remaining unchanged through a series of developmental changes. —**mon·o·mor·phism** *n.*

mon·o·mor·phous (món-ō-mór-fəss, -ə-) *adj.* **1.** *Chemistry.* Existing in only one crystalline form. **2.** Monomorphic.

mon·o·nu·cle·ar (món-ō-néwkli-ər, -ə- ‖ -nŏŏkli-) *adj.* Having only one nucleus. Said of cells.

mon·o·nu·cle·o·sis (món-ō-néwkli-ō-siss ‖ -nŏŏkli-) *n.* **1.** The presence of an abnormally large number of monocytes in the bloodstream. **2. Glandular fever** (*see*). [New Latin : MONO- + NUCLE(US) + -OSIS.]

mon·o·nu·cle·o·tide (món-ō-néw-kli-ə-tīd, -ə-, -ō- ‖ -nŏŏ-) *n. Biochemistry.* A compound consisting of one molecule each of a pentose sugar, phosphoric acid, and a purine or pyrimidine base.

mon·o·pet·al·ous (món-ə-pétt'l-əss, -ə-) *adj.* Having petals united to form one corolla; gamopetalous.

mo·noph·a·gous (mo-nóffəgəss, mə-) *adj.* Eating only one kind of food. Said especially of insects. [MONO- + -PHAGOUS.]

mon·o·pho·bi·a (món-ō-fōb-i-ə, -ə-) *n.* Excessive fear of solitude. [New Latin : MONO- + -PHOBIA.] —**mon·o·pho·bic** (-fōbik) *adj.*

mon·o·phon·ic (món-ə-fónnik, -ō-) *adj.* **1.** *Music.* Of the nature of monophony; having a single melodic line; monodic. **2.** *Electronics.* Designating a system of transmitting, recording, or reproducing sound that uses only one channel to carry or reproduce the sound; monaural.

mo·noph·o·ny (mo-nóffəni, mə-) *n.* Music consisting of a single melodic line, as for example in plainsong. Compare **homophony, polyphony.** [MONO- + -PHONY.]

mon·oph·thong (món-əf-thong ‖ -əp-, -ə) *n.* **1.** A single vowel sound made while the supraglottal speech organs are in a fixed position. **2.** Two written letters representing a single vowel sound; for example, *ea* in *plead* is a monophthong. [Late Greek *monophthongos* : MONO- + *phthongos*†, vowel.] —**mon·oph·thon·gal** (-thóng-g'l) *adj.* —**mon·oph·thon·gal·ly** *adv.*

mon·oph·thong·ise, mon·oph·thong·ize (món-əf-thong-gīz, mə-nóf- ‖ -əp-, -ə-) *v.* **-ised, -ising, -ises.** —*tr.* To make into a monophthong. —*intr.* To become a monophthong. —**mon·oph·thong·i·sa·tion** (-gī-záysh'n ‖ *U.S.* -gi-) *n.*

mon·o·phy·let·ic (món-ō-fī-léttik, -ə-) *adj.* **1.** Of or descended from a single ancestral group of plants or animals. **2.** Belonging to one stock.

Mo·noph·y·site (mo-nóffi-sīt, mə-) *n. Theology.* An adherent of the doctrine, held by Coptic and Syrian Christians, that in the person of Christ there was only one single, divine nature. [Medieval Latin *monophysīta*, from Medieval Greek *monophusitēs* : MONO- + *phusis*, nature.] —**Mo·noph·y·site, Mo·noph·y·sit·ic** (-síttik) *adj.* —**Mo·noph·y·sit·ism** *n.*

mon·o·plane (món-ə-playn, -ō-) *n.* An aircraft with only one pair of wings. Compare **biplane.**

mon·o·ple·gi·a (món-ə-plée-ji-ə, -ō-, -jə) *n.* Paralysis of a single limb or part of the body, such as one side of the face. [MONO- + -PLEGIA.] —**mon·o·ple·gic** (-pléejik ‖ -pléjik) *adj.* & *n.*

mon·o·ploid (món-ə-ployd, -ō-) *adj.* Having a single set of chromosomes; haploid.
~*n.* A monoploid individual or cell. [MONO- + -*ploid*, as in HAPLOID.]

mon·o·pod (món-ə-pod, -ō-) *n.* An adjustable single-legged support for a camera, used in situations where a tripod would be too cumbersome. [MONO- + -POD.]

mon·o·po·di·um (món-o-pōdi-əm, -ō-) *n., pl.* **-dia** (-ə) Also **mon·o·**

pode (-pōd). *Botany*. A main axis of a plant, such as the trunk of certain conifers, that maintains a single line of growth, giving off lateral branches. Compare **sympodium**. [New Latin, from Late Latin *monopodius*, one-footed, from Greek *monopous* (stem *monopod*-) : MONO- + *pous*, foot.] —**mon·o·po·di·al** (-əl) *adj.*

Monopolies and Mergers Commission *n.* In Britain, a public body responsible for determining whether a particular supplier or group of suppliers constitutes a monopoly, and making appropriate recommendations to the government, especially in the case of proposed mergers.

mo·nop·o·lise, mo·nop·o·lize (mə-nóppə-līz) *tr.v.* **-lised, -lising, -lises. 1.** To acquire or maintain a monopoly of. **2.** To dominate or take complete possession of, to the exclusion of others. —**mo·nop·o·li·sa·tion** (-lī-záysh'n || *U.S.* -li-) *n.* —**mo·nop·o·lis·er** *n.*

monopolistic competition *n. Economics.* A situation in commerce that exists when a large number of competitive firms produce products that are similar but are not perfect substitutes, so that one firm can afford to raise its prices relative to the others without necessarily jeopardising its sales. Also called "imperfect competition".

mo·nop·o·ly (mə-nóppə-li) *n., pl.* **-lies. 1.** *Economics.* **a.** Exclusive control by one person, group, or company of the means of producing or selling a commodity or service. Compare **oligopoly**. **b.** Such control that is not exclusive but is sufficient to allow the person or company to control prices. **2.** *Law.* A right granted by a government, giving exclusive control over a specified commercial activity to a single party. **3. a.** A company or group having exclusive control over a commercial activity. **b.** A commodity or service controlled exclusively by one company or group. **4.** Exclusive possession of or control over anything: *You haven't got a monopoly on hardship, you know.* [Latin *monopolium*, from Greek *monopōlion*, sole selling rights : MONO- + *pōlein*, to sell.] —**mo·nop·o·lism** (-liz'm) *n.* —**mo·nop·o·list** *n. & adj.* —**mo·nop·o·lis·tic** (-lístik) *adj.*

Mo·nop·o·ly (mə-nóppəli) *n.* A trademark for a board game in which two to six players advance by throws of dice and attempt to acquire the property marked on the board and put the other players out of business.

monopoly money *n. Informal.* Money, especially in banknotes, that seems like toy money, as, for example, an unfamiliar foreign currency or a currency that has been devalued so as to be almost worthless. [Referring to toy banknotes used in MONOPOLY.]

mon·o·pro·pel·lant (món-ō-prə-péllənt, -ə-) *n.* A rocket propellant in which fuel and oxidiser are combined prior to combustion, such as a mixture of hydrogen peroxide and alcohol.

mon·o·pro·tic (món-ō-prŏtik, -ə-) *adj. Chemistry.* Having only one hydrogen ion to donate to a base in an acid-base reaction; monobasic. [MONO- + PROT(ON) + -IC.]

mo·nop·so·ny (mo-nópsəni, mə-) *n., pl.* **-nies.** A situation in commerce in which the product or service of several sellers is sought by only one buyer. Compare **oligopsony**. [MON(O)- + Greek *opsōnia*, a buying, from *opsōnein*, to buy food (see **opsonin**).]

mon·o·rail (món-ə-rayl, -ō-) *n.* **1.** A railway system in which trains run on a single rail, often an elevated one from which they are suspended. **2.** The track used in such a system.

mon·o·sac·cha·ride (món-ō-sáckə-rīd, -ə-, -rid) *n.* A simple sugar, such as glucose or fructose, that cannot be decomposed by hydrolysis, having the general formula $C_nH_{2n}O_n$. Also called "simple sugar".

mon·o·sep·al·ous (món-ō-séppələss, -ə-) *adj. Botany.* Having sepals united to form a single calyx; gamosepalous.

mon·o·so·di·um glu·ta·mate (món-ə-sŏdi-əm glŏō-tə-mayt, -ō- || gléw-) *n. Abbr.* **MSG.** A white crystalline salt, $NaC_5H_8O_4$, with a taste like meat, used extensively as a food additive. Also called "glutamate", "sodium glutamate".

mon·o·some (món-ə-sōm, -ō-) *n.* An unpaired chromosome, particularly an X chromosome, in an otherwise diploid cell or organism. [MONO- + -SOME (body).] —**mon·o·so·mic** (-sōmik, *rarely* -sóm-mik) *adj.* —**mon·o·so·my** (-sōmi) *n.*

mon·o·sper·mous (món-ō-spérm-əss, -ə-) *adj.* Also **mon·o·sper·mal** (-spérm'l). Having a single seed. Said of certain plants. [MONO- + -SPERMOUS.]

mon·o·stome (món-ə-stōm, -ō-) *adj.* Also **mo·nos·to·mous** (mo-nóstəməss, mə-). **1.** Having one oral sucker only, as do certain flatworms. **2.** Having one mouth or similar opening. [Greek *monostomos*, having one mouth : MONO- + *stoma*, -STOME.]

mon·o·strophe (món-ə-strōf, -ō-; mo-nóstrəfi, mə-) *n.* A poem in which all the stanzas or strophes have the same metrical form. —**mon·o·stroph·ic** (-stróffik) *adj.*

mon·o·sty·lous (món-ə-stīləss, -ə-) *adj. Botany.* Having one style.

mon·o·syl·lab·ic (món-ō-si-lábbik, -ə-) *adj.* **1.** Having only one syllable. **2.** Characterised by or consisting of monosyllables; terse or laconic. —**mon·o·syl·lab·i·cal·ly** *adv.*

mon·o·syl·la·ble (món-ō-síllәb'l, -ə-) *n.* A word or utterance of one syllable. [Late Latin *monosyllabum*, from Greek *monosullabon* : MONO- + *sullabē*, SYLLABLE.]

mon·o·the·ism (món-ō-thee-iz'm, -ə-) *n.* The doctrine or belief that there is only one God. Compare **henotheism**. —**mon·o·the·ist** *n. & adj.* —**mon·o·the·is·tic** (-ístik) *adj.* —**mon·o·the·is·ti·cal·ly** *adv.*

mon·o·tint (món-ə-tint, -ō-) *n.* A picture, a **monochrome** (*see*).

mon·o·tone (mónnə-tōn) *n.* **1.** A succession of sounds or words uttered without changing the pitch of the voice. **2.** *Music.* **a.** A single note that is continuously repeated with different words or time values, as in plainsong. **b.** A chant on a single note. **3.** Sameness, dull repetition, or lack of variety in sound, style, manner, or colour.

—*adj.* Also **mon·o·ton·ic** (-tónnik) (for sense 2). **1.** Of, pertaining to, or characteristic of sounds emitted at a single pitch. **2.** *Mathematics.* Designating sequences of which the successive members either consistently increase or decrease but do not oscillate in relative value. Each member of a *monotone increasing* sequence is greater than or equal to the preceding member; each member of a *monotone decreasing* sequence is less than or equal to the preceding member. See **sequence**. [Greek *monotonos*, having one tone : MONO-, single + *tonos*, TONE.] —**mon·o·ton·i·cal·ly** (-tónni-kli, -k'l-i) *adv.*

mo·not·o·nous (mə-nótt'n-əss) *adj.* **1.** Unvarying in vocal inflection or pitch; sounded in one persistent tone: *a monotonous drone.* **2.** Without variation or variety; boringly dull: *monotonous work.* —See Synonyms at **boring**. [Greek *monotonos* : MONO-, single + *tonos*, TONE.] —**mo·not·o·nous·ly** *adv.* —**mo·not·o·nous·ness** *n.*

mo·not·o·ny (mə-nótt'n-i) *n.* **1.** Uniformity or lack of variation in pitch, intonation, or inflection. **2.** Wearisome sameness; lack of variety. [Greek *monotonia*, from MONOTONOUS.]

mon·o·treme (món-ō-treem, -ə-) *n.* A member of the Monotremata, an order of egg-laying mammals restricted to Australia and New Guinea, and including the platypus and the echidna. [New Latin *Monotremata* : MONO- + Greek *trēma* (stem *trēmat*-), hole.] —**mon·o·tre·ma·tous** (-tréemə-təss, -trémmə-) *adj.*

mon·o·trich·ous (mo-nóttrikəss, mə-) *adj.* Also **mon·o·trich·ic** (món-ō-tríckik, -ə-). Having one flagellum at only one pole or end. Said of certain bacteria. [MONO- + TRICH(O)- + -OUS.]

mon·o·troph·ic (món-ō-tróffik, -ə-, -trŏfik) *adj.* Requiring only one kind of food; monophagous.

mon·o·type (món-ə-tīp, -ō-) *n.* **1.** *Printing.* A single impression from a metal or glass plate of a design or picture. **2.** *Biology.* The sole member of its group, such as a species that also constitutes a genus. —**mon·o·typ·ic** (-típpik) *adj.*

Mon·o·type (món-ə-tīp, -ō-) *n.* A trademark for a typesetting machine operated from a keyboard which activates a unit that casts individual letters from matrices and assembles them.

mon·o·va·lent (món-ō-váylənt, -ə-) *adj. Chemistry.* Possessing a valency of one; univalent. —**mon·o·va·lence, mon·o·va·len·cy** *n.*

mon·ox·ide (mo-nóksīd, mə-) *n.* A compound having only one atom of oxygen. [MON(O)- + OXIDE.]

mon·o·zy·got·ic twin (món-ō-zī-góttik, -ə-) *n.* An **identical twin** (*see*).

Mon·roe (mən-rṓ, mun- || mon-), **James** (1758–1831). U.S. president (1817–25), after whom the **Monroe Doctrine** is named.

Monroe, Marilyn, born Norma Jean Mortenson, also known as Norma Jean Baker (1926–62). U.S. film star. She first came to attention in *The Asphalt Jungle* (1950), and revealed her talent for comedy in *Gentlemen Prefer Blondes* (1953) and *How to Marry a Millionaire* (1953). Her other most notable films were *The Seven Year Itch* (1955), *Bus Stop* (1956), *Some Like It Hot* (1959), and her last film, *The Misfits* (1961), written by her husband Arthur Miller. She died from an overdose of sleeping pills.

Monroe Doctrine *n.* The U.S. policy of opposition to outside interference by Europe in the Americas. [After a foreign policy statement (1823) by President MONROE.]

Mon·ro·vi·a (mon-rṓvi-ə). Capital of Liberia. The country's chief port and industrial centre, it was founded (1822) as a settlement for freed U.S. slaves, and was named after President Monroe.

mons (monz) *n., pl.* **montes** (mónteez). A protuberance of the human body; especially, the mons pubis (or mons veneris), situated over the junctions of the pubic bones at the front of the body. [New Latin, from Latin *mōns* (stem *mont*-), mountain.]

Mons (monz; *French* mawnss). *Flemish* **Ber·gen** (báirkhə). Capital of Hainaut province, Belgium. It has been much fought over, and British forces fought their first major action of World War I here (1914).

Mon·sar·rat (món-sə-rát, -rat), **Nicholas (John Turney)** (1910–79). English novelist. He served in the Royal Navy (1940–6) on convoy runs in the Atlantic, and from his experiences wrote the best seller, *The Cruel Sea* (1951).

Mon·sei·gneur (món-sen-yér, -yŏr) *n., pl.* **Messeigneurs** (máy-). *Abbr.* **Mgr., Mngr., Msgr.** *French.* A title of or form of address for princes and prelates. [French, "my lord".]

Mon·sieur (məss-yér, -yṓ, *weak form* məss-yə || mə-séwr) *n., pl.* **Messieurs** (mayss-, mess-; *also* méssərz). *Abbr.* **M. 1.** A title of courtesy prefixed to the name or nobiliary or professional title of a Frenchman, equivalent to the English "Mr", "Sir", or "my Lord", according to the rank of the man. **2.** A respectful form of address for a Frenchman, used instead of the man's name. [French, "my lord".]

Mon·si·gnor (mon-séen-yər) *n., pl.* **-gnors.** *Italian* **Mon·si·gno·re** (món-seen-yáw-ray) *pl.* **-ri** (-ree). *Abbr.* **Mgr., Mngr., Monsig., Msgr.** A title of or form of address for certain officials of the Roman Catholic Church. [Italian, from French *monseigneur*, MONSEIGNEUR.]

mon·soon (món-sŏōn, mən-) *n.* **1.** A pressure and wind system that influences large climatic regions and reverses seasonally; specifically, the Asiatic monsoon that produces dry and wet seasons in southern and southeastern Asia. **2.** The rain brought by such a system. [Obsolete Dutch *monssoen*, from Portuguese *monção*, from Arabic *mausim*, season, monsoon season.]

mons pu·bis (péwbiss) *n.* See **mons**.

mon·ster (món-stər) *n.* **1.** An imaginary being, such as a cyclops or dragon, made up of elements from various human or animal forms. **2.** An animal or plant having structural defects or deformities. **3.** *Pathology.* A foetus or infant that is grotesquely abnormal.

4. Any very large animal, plant, or object. **5.** One who inspires horror or disgust: *a monster of wickedness.* **6.** *Chiefly U.S. Slang.* One that is highly successful or exercises great influence, especially in a specified field: *The Beatles are monsters of rock music.* ~*adj.* Gigantic; huge. [Middle English *monstre,* from Old French, from Latin *mōnstrum,* prodigy, portent, from *monēre,* to warn.]

mon·ste·ra (món-stéer-ə) *n.* Any plant of the tropical American genus *Monstera,* such as *M. deliciosa,* the Swiss cheese plant, often grown as a house plant for its glossy foliage. [New Latin, perhaps irregularly from Latin *monstrum,* MONSTER.]

mon·strance (món-strənss) *n. Roman Catholic Church.* A receptacle in which the Host is held and exhibited to the congregation. [Middle English, from Old French, from Medieval Latin *mōnstrantia,* from Latin *mōnstrāre,* to show.]

mon·stros·i·ty (món-stróssəti) *n., pl.* **-ties. 1.** One that is monstrous. **2.** The quality or character of being monstrous.

mon·strous (món-strəss) *adj.* **1.** Deviating excessively from the norm in appearance or structure; grotesquely unnatural. **2.** Exceptionally large; enormous: *"Just then flew down a monstrous crow"* (Lewis Carroll). **3.** Hideous; shocking; loathsome: *a monstrous crime.* **4.** Outrageous; disgraceful; indefensible: *a monstrous waste of money.* **5.** Of, pertaining to, or like a fabulous monster: *"Harpies and Hydras, or all the monstrous forms / 'Twixt Africa and Ind"* (Milton). —See Synonyms at **outrageous.** [Middle English from Old French *monstruous,* from Latin *mōnstruōsus,* from *mōnstrum,* MONSTER.] —**mon·strous·ly** *adv.* —**mon·strous·ness** *n.*

mons ve·ne·ris (vénnəriss) *n.* See **mons.**

mon·tage (món-taazh, mon-taázh, mon-) *n.* **1. a.** The art, style, or process of making one pictorial composition from many pictures or designs, closely arranged or superimposed upon each other. **b.** A picture so made. **2.** In films and television: **a.** The technique of producing a rapid sequence of thematically related short scenes or images exhibiting different aspects of the same idea or situation. **b.** A portion of a film or television programme employing such a special effect. **3.** In various other art forms, a sequence using different sensory elements presented at short intervals. [French, "mounting", from *monter,* to MOUNT.]

Mon·taigne (mon-táyn; *French* mon-téñ), **Michel Eyquem, Seigneur de** (1533–92). French essayist. His essays, sceptical, discursive, witty, and lively, are held to be the highest expression of 16th-century French prose.

Mon·tan·a (mon-tánnə, *rarely* -táənə). The fourth largest state of the United States lying in the northwest of the country. The Rockies rely on forestry, tourism, and mining, while the Great Plains to the east produce cattle, oil, gas and coal. Part of the Louisiana Purchase (1803), Montana was admitted to the Union in 1889. The capital is Helena. —**Mon·ta·nan** *adj. & n.*

mon·tane (món-tayn ‖ -táyn) *adj.* Of, growing in, or inhabiting mountain areas. [Latin *montānus,* from *mōns.* See **mons.**]

mon·tan wax (món-tan, -tən) *n.* A hard, white wax obtained from lignite and used in the manufacture of polishes, candles, and insulators. [Latin *montānus,* MONTANE.]

Mont Blanc (món blón). Mountain in France, near the French-Italian border. It is the highest peak (4 807 metres; 15,771 feet) in Europe outside the U.S.S.R. Beneath it runs a road tunnel (12 kilometres; 7.5 miles) opened in 1965.

mont·bre·tia (mon-bréesh-ə, mom-, mont-, -yə) *n.* **1.** A South African plant, *Crocosmia crocosmiiflora,* widely grown as a garden ornamental for its orange-red, funnel-shaped flowers. **2.** Any South African plant of the similar and related genus *Montbretia.* [New Latin, after A.F.E. Coquebert de *Montbret* (died 1801), French botanist.]

mon·te (mónti) *n.* **1.** A game of Spanish origin in which each player bets that one of two cards will be matched by the dealer before the other one. Also called "monte bank". See **three-card monte. 2.** *Australian Informal.* A certainty; a sure thing. [Spanish, "mountain", referring to the pile of unplayed cards, from Latin *mōns* (stem *mont-*), mountain.]

Mon·te Al·ban (mónti al-bán ‖ -ay, *U.S.* aal-baán). A ruined Zapotec city in southwestern Mexico.

Monte Bel·lo Islands (béllō). A formation of uninhabited atolls off Western Australia, used for British nuclear tests (1952, 1956).

Monte Car·lo (kárlō). Seaside resort of Monaco, famous for its casinos, annual motor-car rally, and the Monaco Grand Prix race.

Monte Carlo method *n. Mathematics.* A method of obtaining approximate solutions to problems by statistical sampling. [After a method applied to roulette at the casino in MONTE CARLO.]

Monte Cas·si·no (kə-séenō, ka-). A hill overlooking the town of Cassino, central Italy. Its monastery, founded (*c.* 529) by St. Benedict, was used in World War II by the Nazis as a fortress, dand consequently destroyed by the Allies. It has since been restored.

Mon·te·go Bay (mon-téegō). Seaport and tourist centre in Jamaica. The island's second city and second seaport, it exports agricultural produce.

Mon·te·ne·gro (mónti-néegrō). *Serbo-Croat* **Crna Gora** (chárna gáwra). Constituent republic of Yugoslavia. Lying on the Adriatic, it is predominantly mountainous and agricultural, but does have considerable mineral resources. An ancient state of the Balkans, it was an independent kingdom from 1910 until 1918, when it joined the new Kingdom of Serbs, Croats, and Slovenes, which became Yugoslavia in 1929. With Serbia, it became part of a smaller Yugoslavia in 1992. —**Mon·te·ne·gran** *adj. & n.*

mon·te·ro (mon-taír-ō) *n., pl.* **-ros.** A huntsman's cap with side

flaps. [Spanish, "hunter", from *monte,* forest region, mountain. See **monte.**]

Mon·ter·rey (móntə-ráy). Capital of Nuevo León state, northeast Mexico. The country's third city, it is an important industrial centre with iron and steel and lead works, and textile, glass, and chemical industries. It is also a resort with hot springs.

mon·tes. Plural of **mons.**

Mon·tes·quieu (món-te-skéw, -skew, -skyúr, -skyő), **Charles Louis de Secondat, Baron de la Brède et de** (1689–1755). French jurist and political philosopher, one of the oustanding figures of the early French Enlightenment. He is famous chiefly for two books, the *Persian Letters* (1721), a veiled attack on the monarchy and institutions of the ancien régime, and *The Spirit of the Laws* (1748), a lengthy disquisition on the forms of government.

Mon·tes·so·ri method (món-ti-sáw-ri ‖ -te-, -ső-) *n.* A method of educating young children that stresses development of a child's own initiative and natural abilities, especially through practical play and individual guidance rather than through strict control. Also called "Montessori system". [After Maria *Montessori* (1870–1952), Italian educationalist.]

Mon·te·ver·di (mónti-vaírdi), **Claudio (Giovanni Antonio)** (1567–1643). Italian composer. Throughout his life he wrote madrigals and sacred music, but his great importance is as one of the founders of opera. His operas are remarkable for the rich texture of the orchestral scoring and the dramatic effectiveness of the recitative passages. They include *Orfeo* (1607), *Il ritorno di Ulisse in Patria* (1641), and *L'incoronazione di Poppea* (1642).

Mon·te·vi·de·o (mónti-vi-dáy-ō ‖ -víddi-). Capital of Uruguay since 1828. An important seaport, fishing centre, resort, and railway junction, it was founded (1726) by the Spanish on the Rio de la Plata. The country's only important industrial centre, it has footwear, textiles, soap, food processing, and tanning industries.

Mon·tez (món-tez), **Lola,** born Marie Dolores Eliza Rosanna Gilbert (*c.* 1818–61). Irish dancer, famous for her beauty. She adopted the name Lola Montez when she began to dance, claiming Spanish descent. She had brief affairs with Liszt and Dumas *père* and also, most notoriously, with Ludwig of Bavaria, from 1846 to 1848.

Mon·te·zu·ma II (mónti-zōō-mə, -zéw-), also known as Moctezuma (*c.* 1480–1520). Aztec emperor (*c.* 1502–20), known as Montezuma II to distinguish him from the mid-15th-century ruler of the same name. The Spanish explorer **Cortés** tried to govern through him, but during an Aztec insurrection Montezuma was killed, though whether by the Spanish or the Aztecs it is not certain.

Montezuma's revenge *n.* An attack of diarrhoea experienced by a tourist visiting a tropical country. Used humorously.

Mont·fort (mónt-fərt, -fawrt), **Simon de, Earl of Leicester** (*c.* 1208–65). English baron, born in France, leader of the baronial opposition to Henry III. He and other barons forced Henry to sign the Provisions of Oxford (1258), and after his victory over the king at Lewes (1264) he was the effective ruler of England. He called a parliament in 1265 which included representatives from the boroughs, and is therefore often taken as the first modern parliament.

Mont·gol·fi·er (mont-gólfi-ay, mon-, -ər), **Joseph Michel** (1740–1810) and **Jacques Étienne** (1745–99). French brothers who invented the hot-air balloon in which the first manned flight took place in November 1783.

Mont·gom·er·y (mənt-góm-ri, mont-, mən-, -góm-, -əri). Capital of Alabama, United States. It is a market and industrial centre on the Alabama river. It became the first capital of the Confederate States of America (1861). In the 1950s and 60s it was the centre of the black civil rights movement.

Montgomery, L(ucy) M(aud) (1874–1942). Canadian novelist. Her best-known book is *Anne of Green Gables* (1908).

Montgomery of Alamein, 1st Viscount, born Bernard Law Montgomery (1887–1976). British soldier. He served in India and World War I and was awarded the D.S.O. In 1939 he commanded the Third Division in France; he was made leader of the Fifth Corps after Dunkirk, and at the end of 1941 was given command of the South Eastern Army in England. In command of the Eighth Army in North Africa he halted Rommel's Africa Corps at Alam el-Haifa in August 1942, and in October won victory at El Alamein. Knighted and promoted to general, he led the Allied assault through Normandy in 1944 and in 1945 he became a field marshal and Commander in Chief of the British Army in Germany. From 1951 to 1958 he was Deputy Supreme Allied Commander in Europe.

Mont·gom·er·y·shire (mənt-gúm-ri-shər, mont-, -góm-, -əri-, -sheer). *Welsh* **Sir Dre·fald·wyn, Mald·wyn** (sheer dre-vál-dwin; máldwin). Former county of central Wales, now part of Powys.

month (munth) *n. Abbr.* **m, M, m., M., mo. 1.** Any of the 12 divisions of a year as determined by the Gregorian calendar. Also called "calendar month". **2.** Any period extending from a date in one calendar month to the corresponding date in the following month. **3.** The average period of revolution of the Moon around the Earth determined by using a fixed star as a reference point and equal to 27 days 7 hours 43 minutes 12 seconds. Also called "sidereal month". **4.** The average time between successive new, or full, moons; equal to 29 days 12 hours 44 minutes. Also called "lunar month", "synodic month", "lunation". **5.** One twelfth of a tropical year, totalling 27 days 7 hours 43 minutes 5 seconds. Also called "solar month". —**month of Sundays.** *Informal.* An indefinitely long period of time. [Middle English *moneth,* Old English *mōnath,* from Germanic; akin to MOON.]

Usage: When used before a noun, the singular form is used

along with a hyphen: *a three-month stay in France.* Alternatively, the slightly more formal possessive form may be used, but in this case the hyphen is omitted: *a three months' stay in France.*

Mon·ther·lant (mon-tair-lón), **Henry de** (1896–1972). French novelist and dramatist. His works portray masculine, aristocratic pride in a feminised and democratic society. His plays include *Malatesta* (1946) and *Port-Royal* (1954).

month·ly (múnthli) *adj.* **1.** Occurring, appearing, or coming due every month. **2.** Continuing or lasting for a month.
~*adv.* Once a month; by the month; every month.
~*n., pl.* **monthlies.** **1.** A periodical publication appearing once each month. **2.** *Informal.* A menstrual period.

mon·ti·cule (mónti-kewl) *n.* **1.** A small hill. **2.** A small mound produced by volcanic eruption. [French, from Late Latin *monticulus,* diminutive of Latin *mōns* (stem *mont-*), mountain.]

Mont·martre (mon-mártrə). See **Paris.**

Mont·par·nasse (món-paar-náss). See **Paris.**

Mont·pel·lier (mon-pélli-ay, mont-, -ər). Capital of Hérault département, southern France. It is a centre of the wine trade, and famous for its university (constituted 1289), incorporating a tenth-century medical school.

Mon·tre·al (móntri-áwl ‖ múntri-). *French* **Mont·ré·al** (mon-ray-ál). City in Quebec, southeast Canada. Sited on Montreal island at the confluence of the St. Lawrence and Ottawa rivers, it was founded (1642) as the French settlement of Ville Marie de Montréal, at the foot of Mont Royal. Today it is Canada's largest city and most important port (it lies on the St. Lawrence Seaway), the world's second largest French-speaking city, and an important communications, industrial, trade, and cultural centre.

Mon·treux (mon-trér, -trô). Town in Vaud canton, Switzerland, at the eastern end of Lake Geneva. An important tourist centre, it has an annual television festival. The 13th-century Château de Chillon nearby figures in Byron's *Prisoner of Chillon.*

Mont·ser·rat (mónt-sə-rát, -se-, -rat). British island in the Caribbean Sea, discovered by Columbus (1493), settled by the British. In 1997 the southern half of the island was rendered uninhabitable by eruptions of the Soufrière Hills volcano.

Mont St. Mi·chel (món-san-mee-shél; *French* mon-san-). Rocky islet in Manche département, northwest France. Its principal feature is a Benedictine abbey (708–9), which was used as a prison from the French Revolution until 1863. It is connected to the mainland by a causeway.

mon·u·ment (mónnew-mənt) *n.* **1.** A structure, such as a building, tower, or sculpture, erected as a memorial. **2.** An inscribed stone or other marker placed at a grave or tomb; a tombstone. **3.** A site or building of special historical or archaeological importance, preserved by the government. See **ancient monument, national monument. 4.** A written legal document. **5. a.** An outstanding and enduring achievement viewed as a model for later generations and worthy of lasting fame. **b.** An exceptional example of something: *Her attitude was a monument of selfishness and insensitivity.* [Middle English, from Latin *monumentum,* from *monēre,* to remind, warn.]

mon·u·men·tal (mónnew-mént'l) *adj.* **1.** Of, resembling, or serving as a monument. **2.** Impressively large, sturdy, and enduring. **3.** Of outstanding and lasting significance: *her monumental contribution to the theatre.* **4.** Enormous and astounding: *her monumental stupidity.* **5.** *Fine Arts.* Larger than life-size. —**mon·u·men·tal·ly** *adv.*

Mon·za (mónzə; *Italian* móntsa). City in Lombardy, northern Italy. A centre of the textile industry, it was an important medieval commercial centre. It has a famous motor-racing circuit.

mon·zo·nite (mónzə-nīt, mon-zṓ-) *n.* A coarse-grained igneous rock composed chiefly of plagioclase and orthoclase in approximately equal proportions, with small amounts of other minerals. [French, after Mount *Monzoni* in northeast Italy, where it was discovered.]

moo (moo) *n., pl.* **moos. 1.** The characteristic deep, bellowing sound made by a cow. **2.** Any similar sound.
~*intr.v.* **mooed, mooing, moos.** To make a moo. [Imitative.]

mooch (mooch) *v.* **mooched, mooching, mooches.** Also *chiefly British* **mouch** (mooch). *Slang.* —*intr.* **1.** To dawdle or loiter aimlessly. Often used with *along.* **2.** To sit or wander about in a depressed or apathetic fashion. Often used with *about.* —*tr. Chiefly U.S.* **1.** To obtain by cajolery or begging. **2.** To steal or filch. [Middle English *mowche,* from Old French *muchier,* to hide.] —**mooch·er** *n.*

mood¹ (mood) *n.* **1.** A temporary state of mind or feeling, as evidenced by one's behaviour or the tendency of one's thoughts: *a gloomy mood.* **2.** A prevailing spirit, disposition, or set of attitudes: *The book captures the mood of the Edwardian period.* **3.** A pervading impression on the feelings of an observer: *the sombre mood of the painting.* **4.** A spell of sulking or morose behaviour: *He's in one of his moods.* —**in the mood.** Inclined; disposed. [Middle English *mod,* Old English *mōd,* mind, thought, from Germanic.]
Synonyms: mood, humour, temper.

mood² *n.* **1.** *Grammar.* A class of verb forms used to indicate the speaker's attitude towards either the utterance or the addressee, concerning for example the factuality or likelihood of the action or condition expressed, or types of address such as requests or orders. In English, the indicative mood is usually used for factual statements, the subjunctive mood to indicate doubt, unlikelihood, or wish, and the imperative mood to express a command. Compare **aspect. 2.** *Logic.* Any of the various ways in which a proposition may be constructed. [Alteration (influenced by MOOD¹) of MODE.]

mood·y (moodi) *adj.* **-ier, -iest. 1.** Given to changeable emotional

states; temperamental. **2.** Gloomy; glum; grumpy: *a moody silence.* —**mood·i·ly** *adv.* —**mood·i·ness** *n.*

Moog synthesiser (moog, mōg) *n.* A trademark for an electronic keyboard instrument that is capable of generating a large variety of sounds. Also called "Moog", "synthesiser". [After R.A. *Moog* (1934–). U.S. engineer who invented it.]

moo·lah (moolə) *n. Slang.* Money. [Origin unknown.]

mool·vi, mool·vie (mool-vi, -vee) *n.* A Muslim who is very learned or a doctor of the law. Used especially in India as a title of respect. [Urdu *Mulvī,* from Arabic *mawlawīyah,* judicial.]

moon (moon) *n.* **1.** *Often capital* **M.** The natural satellite of the Earth, visible by reflection of sunlight, having a slightly elliptical orbit, approximately 356 500 kilometres (221,600 miles) distant at perigee and 407 000 kilometres (252,900 miles) at apogee. Its mean diameter is 3 475 kilometres (2,160 miles), its mass approximately one eightieth that of the Earth, and its average period of revolution around the Earth 29 days 12 hours 44 minutes calculated with respect to the Sun. **2.** Any natural satellite orbiting a planet. **3.** The moon as it appears at a particular time in its cycle of phases: *the full moon; a half moon.* **4.** A month, especially a lunar month. **5.** Any disc, globe, or crescent resembling the moon. **6.** Moonlight. —**crying for the moon.** Striving or yearning for something unattainable. —**once in a blue moon.** Never or hardly ever.
~*v.* **mooned, mooning, moons.** —*intr.* **1.** To wander about or pass time languidly and aimlessly. Usually used with *about* or *around.* **2.** To exhibit infatuation by being inattentive or listless. Usually used with *over.* **3.** *Slang.* To expose the buttocks, especially in a public place. Used with the aim of shocking passers-by. —*tr.* To pass (time) idly. Used with *away.* [Middle English *moone, mon,* Old English *mōna,* from Germanic; akin to MONTH.]

moon·beam (moon-beem) *n.* A ray of moonlight.

moon blindness *n.* Recurrent inflammation of horses' eyes, often resulting in blindness. Also called "mooneye". [Formerly attributed to the moon's influence.] —**moon·blind** *adj.*

moon·calf (moon-kaaf ‖ *chiefly U.S.* -kaf) *n.* **1.** A fool from birth; a stupid creature. **2.** An inattentive, daydreaming person. **3.** *Archaic.* A freak. [From the supposed maleficent influence of the Moon on the unborn.]

moon dog *n.* A bright spot on a lunar halo, a **paraselene** *(see).*

moon·eye (moon-ī) *n.* **1.** A silvery freshwater fish, *Hiodon tergisus,* of northern North America. **2.** Moon blindness.

moon·faced (moon-fayst) *adj.* Having a round face.

moon·fish (moon-fish) *n., pl.* **-fishes** or collectively **moonfish. 1.** Any of various fishes of the family Carangidae, having rounded bodies that are silver to yellowish in colour. Also called "dollarfish". **2.** A large marine fish, the **opah** *(see).*

moon·flow·er (moon-flowr) *n.* Any of various white-flowered, often night-blooming plants, such as *Ipomaea alba,* a morning glory.

Moon·ie (mooni) *n.* A member of a religious sect, the Unification Church, founded by Sun Myung Moon. It combines elements of Christian fundamentalism and Buddhism, demands absolute obedience, and has become controversial because of brainwashing techniques it is alleged to use and the way in which it cuts members off from their friends and families. [After S.M. *Moon.*]

moon·light (moon-līt) *n.* The light reflected from the surface of the Moon, principally that originating at the Sun.
~*adj.* **1.** Of moonlight. **2.** Under moonlight.
~*intr.v.* **moonlighted, -lighting, -lights.** *Informal.* To work at a spare-time job, often at night, in addition to one's full-time job. —**moon·light·er** *n.* —**moon·light·ing** *n.*

moonlight flit *n. British Informal.* A hurried departure, usually made at night and with one's possessions, to avoid creditors.

moon·lit (moon-lit) *adj.* Illuminated by the Moon.

moon rat *n.* A large, ratlike, nocturnal, insectivorous mammal, *Echinosorex gymnurus,* of Southeast Asia, having greyish fur and a long snout.

moon·scape (moon-skayp) *n.* **1.** A view or picture of the surface of the moon. **2.** Loosely, any desolate landscape. [MOON + -SCAPE]

moon·seed (moon-seed) *n.* Any of several climbing vines of the genus *Menispermum* or related genera, having red or blackish fruit with crescent-shaped or ring-shaped seeds.

moon·shine (moon-shīn) *n.* **1.** Moonlight. **2.** *Informal.* Foolish or nonsensical talk, thought, or action. **3.** *U.S. Slang.* Whiskey illegally distilled, as at night by moonlight.
~*v.* **moonshined, -shining, -shines.** *U.S.* —*tr.* To distil (alcoholic liquor) illegally. —*intr.* To operate an illegal still. —**moon·shine** *adj.* —**moon·shin·er** *n.*

moon·shot (moon-shot) *n.* A launching of a spacecraft or rocket to the Moon.

moon·stone (moon-stōn) *n.* A mineral valued as a gem for its pearly translucence, commonly **albite, labradorite,** or **orthoclase** *(all of which see).* It is found worldwide.

moon·struck (moon-struk) *adj.* **1.** Dazed or distracted with romantic sentiment; lovelorn. **2.** Afflicted with insanity; crazed; deranged. [From the belief that moonlight inspires romantic love and causes insanity.]

Moon type *n.* A system of printing for the blind that uses embossed letters instead of the raised dots of Braille, requiring less sensitivity of the fingers. [After William *Moon* (1819–94), British inventor.]

moon·wort (moon-wurt ‖ -wawrt) *n.* Any of various ferns of the genus *Botrychium;* especially, *B. lunaria,* having crescent-shaped leaflets. [The leaflets being shaped like the crescent Moon.]

moon·y (mooni) *adj.* **-ier, -iest. 1.** Of or resembling the moon.

2. Dreamy in mood or nature; absent-minded. **—moon·i·ly** *adj.*

moor¹ (moor, mor) *v.* **moored, mooring, moors.** *—tr.* **1.** To secure or make fast (a boat, for example) by means of cables, anchors, or other contrivances. **2.** To fix in place; secure. *—intr.* **1.** To secure a vessel or aircraft. **2.** To be secured, as is a vessel or hot-air balloon. [Middle English *moren*, from Middle Low German *mōren*.]

moor² *n.* A broad tract of open land, often high but poorly drained, often having patches of heath and peat bogs. [Middle English *mor*, Old English *mōr*, from Germanic.]

Moor (moor, mor) *n.* **1.** A member of a Muslim people of mixed Berber and Arab descent, now living chiefly in North Africa. **2.** Any of the Muslims who invaded Spain in the eighth century A.D. and established a civilisation there which lasted until 1492. [Middle English *More*, from Old French, from Latin *Maurus*, from Greek *Mauros*, probably of North African origin.]

moor·age (moor-ij, máwrij) *n.* **1.** A place where a vessel may be moored. **2.** The act of mooring or state of being moored. **3.** A charge for the use of mooring facilities.

moor·cock (moor-kok, mór-) *n.* A male red grouse.

Moore, Bobby, born Robert Frederick Moore (1941–93). English footballer. He played for West Ham United (1958–74). He won a record 108 caps, 90 of them as captain, in full internationals. He was captain when the English team won the World Cup in 1966.

Moore, G(eorge) E(dward) (1873–1958). British philosopher. From 1925 to 1939 he was professor of philosophy at Cambridge University and from 1921 to 1947 he edited the journal *Mind.* His *Principia Ethica* (1903) laid the foundations of much of 20th-century development in epistemology and linguistic analysis.

Moore, Henry (Spencer) (1898–1986). British sculptor. He established his international reputation with his one-man retrospective show at the Museum of Modern Art, New York, in 1946. Moore carved abstract figures in many media.

Moore, Sir John (1761–1809). British general and M.P. (1784–90). A good strategist, he was attempting to cut off a French army in Spain when he had to lead a retreat from Madrid to La Coruña. He was killed in action as his men repulsed a French attack.

Moore, Thomas (1779–1852). Irish-born poet. His Irish lyrics included *Believe Me If All Those Endearing Young Charms.*

moor·fowl (moor-fowl, mór-) *n. Archaic.* The **red grouse** (*see*).

moor·hen (moor-hen, mór-) *n.* **1.** A common, widely distributed water bird, *Gallinula chloropus,* having dark plumage and a red bill and found in ponds and marshes. **2.** A female red grouse.

moor·ing (moor-ing, mór-) *n.* **1. a.** *Usually plural.* Equipment, such as anchors, chains, or lines, for holding fast a vessel. **b.** A permanent anchor for mooring a vessel, with a buoy attached. **2.** A place at which a vessel can be moored. **3.** *Usually plural.* An element providing stability or security: *lost her emotional moorings.*

Moor·ish (moor-ish, mór-) *adj.* **1.** Of or pertaining to the Moors or their culture. **2.** Designating a style of Spanish architecture of the 13th to 16th centuries, characterised by the horseshoe arch and ornate decoration.

Moorish idol *n.* A tropical marine fish, *Zanclus canescens,* with a deeply compressed body marked with black and yellow stripes, a beaklike mouth, and an enlarged dorsal fin.

moor·land (moor-lənd, mór-, *rarely* -land) *n. British.* A tract of moors.

moor·wort (moor-wurt ‖ -wawrt) *n.* A plant, the **bog rosemary** (*see*). [MOOR + WORT.]

moose (mooss) *n., pl.* **moose.** A hoofed mammal, *Alces alces* (or *A. americana*), of the deer family, found in forests of northern North America, and also in Eurasia, where it is called "elk". It has a broad, pendulous muzzle, and the male has large, flat antlers. [Natick *moos,* from Proto-Algonquian *mooswa* (unattested).]

moot (moot) *n.* **1.** In early medieval England, a meeting; especially, a representative meeting of the freemen of a shire. **2.** An imaginary case argued by law students as an exercise.

—tr.v. **mooted, mooting, moots. 1. a.** To offer as a subject for debate; bring up for discussion. **b.** To discuss or debate. **2.** To plead or argue (a case) in a moot court.

—adj. Subject to debate; arguable; unresolved: *a moot point.* [Middle English *mot, moot,* Old English *mōtian* (verb), to converse, *(ge)mōt* moot, assembly, from Germanic; akin to MEET.]

moot court *n.* A mock court where hypothetical cases are tried for the training of law students.

mop¹ (mop) *n.* **1.** A household implement made of absorbent material attached to a handle and used for polishing or washing floors or dishes, for example. **2.** Any loosely tangled bunch or mass: *a mop of hair.*

—tr.v. **mopped, mopping, mops.** To wash, scrub, or wipe with, or as if with, a mop. Often used with *up.* [Middle English *mappe,* perhaps from *mappel,* from Medieval Latin *mappula,* towel, cloth, diminutive of Latin *mappa,* cloth.]

mop² *intr.v.* **mopped, mopping, mops.** *Archaic.* To grimace. Used chiefly in the phrase *mop and mow.*

—n. Archaic. A grimace or dejected expression. [Perhaps imitative of a pout.]

mop·board (móp-bawrd ‖ -bōrd) *n. U.S.* A skirting board.

mope (mōp) *intr.v.* **moped, moping, mopes. 1.** To be gloomy or dejected. **2.** To give oneself up to brooding or sulking.

—n. **1.** A person given to gloomy or dejected moods. **2.** *Plural.* Low spirits; the blues. [Originally, to move as in a daze, perhaps from Middle Dutch *mopen.*] **—mop·er** *n.* **—mop·ing·ly** *adv.* **—mop·ish** *adj.* **—mop·ish·ly** *adv.*

mo·ped (mó-ped) *n.* A light cycle powered by pedals and by a small motor. [Swedish *mo*(tor) *ped*(aler), motor pedals.]

mo·poke (mó-pōk) *n.* Also **more-pork** (mór-pawrk ‖ mōr-pōrk). A small owl, *Ninox novaezeelandiae,* of Australia and New Zealand, having a spotted plumage.

mop·pet (móppit) *n.* A young child; especially, a little girl. [Diminutive of obsolete *moppe,* child, fool, probably of Low German origin, akin to Low German *mops,* fool.]

mop up *tr.v. Military.* To destroy (remaining enemy resistance) after an initial victory. *—intr.v.* To complete a task; finish. **—mop-up** (móp-up) *n.*

mo·quette (mo-két, mō-) *n.* **1.** A heavy fabric with a thick nap, used for upholstery. **2.** A type of carpet with a deep, tufted pile. [French, variant of obsolete *moucade†.*]

mor. morocco (leather).

MOR (ém-ō-áar) *n.* See **middle-of-the-road. —MOR** *adj.*

mo·ra (máwr-ə ‖ mór-ə) *n., pl.* **morae** (-ee) or **-ras. 1.** In quantitative verse, the unit of metrical time equal to the short syllable. **2.** A phonological unit equal to one short-vowelled syllable or half of a long-vowelled syllable. [Latin, "pause".]

mo·raine (mə-ráyn, mo-) *n.* An accumulation of rocks, stones, or other debris carried and deposited by a glacier or ice sheet. *Ground moraine* is taken up by the base of the ice, and deposited over wide areas. *Terminal moraine* is material carried forward by the ice, and deposited as a hummocky ridge at the tip or edge. *Lateral moraine,* carried on the side of a valley glacier, is mostly derived from the valley wall, and is deposited at the sides. *Medial moraine* is the combined adjacent lateral moraines of two valley glaciers below their confluence. [French, from Italian dialect *morena†.*] **—mo·rain·al, mo·rain·ic** *adj.*

mor·al (mórrəl ‖ máwrəl) *adj.* **1.** Of or concerned with the judgment of the goodness or badness of human action and character; pertaining to the discernment of good and evil: *moral philosophy.* **2.** Designed to teach goodness or correctness of character and behaviour; instructive of what is good and bad: *"the highest precepts and the strongest examples of moral and religious endurances"* (Jane Austen). **3.** Being or acting in accordance with standards and precepts of goodness or with established codes of behaviour, especially with regard to sexual conduct. **4.** Arising from conscience or the sense of right and wrong: *a moral obligation.* **5.** Having psychological rather than physical or tangible effects; concerning morale: *moral support.* **6.** Based upon strong likelihood or firm conviction, rather than upon the actual evidence or demonstration of a fact: *a moral certainty.*

—n. **1. a.** The lesson or principle contained in or taught by a fable, story, or event. **b.** This lesson as encapsulated in the concluding sentence of a fable: *Moral: Look before you leap.* **2.** A concisely expressed precept or general truth; a maxim. **3.** *Plural.* Rules or habits of conduct, especially sexual conduct, with reference to standards of right and wrong: *loose morals.* [Middle English, from Old French, from Latin *mōrālis,* from *mōs* (stem *mōr*-) custom.]

Synonyms: moral, ethical, virtuous, righteous.

Usage: Moral and *morale* are sometimes confused in their noun uses. *Moral* has the sense of "lesson, precept", and has a plural form, referring to "rules of proper conduct". *Morale* refers to the degree of confidence or optimism of a person or group, as shown in their behaviour; it has no plural form.

mo·rale (mə-ráal, mo-) *n.* The state of mind or optimistic spirits of an individual or group, as shown in confidence, cheerfulness, and discipline. See Usage at **moral.** [French, feminine of MORAL.]

moral hazard *n. Insurance.* A risk to the insurer resulting from uncertainty about the insured's honesty or discretion.

mor·al·ise, mor·al·ize (mórrəl-īz ‖ máwrəl-) *v.* **-ised, -ising, -ises.** *—tr.* **1.** To derive a moral lesson from (a story, for example); explain in moral terms. **2.** To improve the morals of; reform. *—intr.* **1.** To think about or discuss moral or ethical issues. **2.** To make moral judgements or statements, often in a priggish way. **—mor·al·i·sa·tion** (-ī-záysh'n ‖ *U.S.* -i-) *n.* **—mor·al·is·er** *n.*

mor·al·ism (mórrəl-iz'm ‖ máwrəl-) *n.* **1.** A conventional moral maxim or attitude. **2.** The act or practice of moralising. **3.** The practice of or belief in a system of principles governing conduct, as distinct from a religion.

mor·al·ist (mórrəl-ist ‖ máwrəl-) *n.* **1.** A teacher or student of ethics. **2.** A person who follows a system of moral principles as distinct from an established religion.

mor·al·is·tic (mórrə-lístik ‖ máwrə-) *adj.* Characterised by or given to moralising, especially in a priggish way. **—mor·al·is·ti·cal·ly** *adv.*

mo·ral·i·ty (mə-rál-əti, mo-) *n., pl.* **-ties. 1.** The quality of being moral. **2.** The evaluation of or means of evaluating human conduct, especially: **a.** A set of ideas of right and wrong: *Christian morality.* **b.** A set of customs of a given society, class, or social group which regulate personal and social relationships and prescribe modes of behaviour to facilitate the group's existence or ensure its survival: *middle-class morality.* **3.** Virtuous conduct, especially in compliance with approved codes for sexual behaviour. **4.** A rule or lesson in moral conduct; a moral. **5.** A morality play.

morality play *n.* A play in a genre of the 15th and 16th centuries in which moral instruction was conveyed through allegorically personifying virtues and vices in stories drawn from popular legend.

mor·al·ly (mórrəli ‖ máwrəli) *adv.* **1.** In accordance with accepted rules of conduct; virtuously. **2.** With reference to moral law; ethically. **3.** In all probability; virtually: *morally certain.*

moral philosophy *n.* In philosophy, **ethics** (*see*).

Moral Rearmament *n.* An international movement advocating spiritual revival and the consolidation of morality on conservative Christian principles. It was established in 1938 by Frank Buchman. Also called "Buchmanism", "Oxford Group".

mo·rass (mə-ráss, mo-) *n.* **1.** An area of low-lying, soggy ground; a bog or marsh. **2.** Any difficult or perplexing situation, especially one from which it is difficult to escape. [Dutch *moeras*, variant (influenced by *moer*, moorland) of Middle Dutch *marasch*, from Old French *marasc*, from Germanic; akin to MARSH.]

mor·a·to·ri·um (mórrə-táwri-əm ‖ máwrə-, -tóri-) *n., pl.* **-ums** or **-toria** (-ə). **1.** *Law.* An authorisation to a debtor, such as a bank or nation, permitting temporary suspension of payments. **2.** A deferment or delay of any action. [New Latin, from Late Latin *morātōrius,* MORATORY.]

mor·a·to·ry (mórrə-tri, -təri ‖ máwrə-) *adj.* Authorising delay in payment; postponing: *a moratory contract.* [French *moratoire,* from Late Latin *morātōrius,* from Latin *morārī,* to delay, from *mora,* delay.]

Mo·ra·vi·a (mə-ráyvi-yə, mo-, -i-ə). *Czech* **Mo·ra·va** (mórrava); *German* **Mäh·ren** (maír-ən). Eastern region of the Czech Republic. It is a fertile agricultural area, with major mineral resources and industries. A great Slav empire in the 9th century, Moravia eventually passed to the Habsburgs of Austria (1526), under whom most of its towns became German-speaking. It became part of Czechoslovakia in 1918. In 1938, because of their high proportion of Germans, Hitler annexed parts of Moravia, later making the whole a German "protectorate". After World War II, most of its German-speaking people were expelled. Brno (Brünn) is the chief town.

Mo·ra·via (mo-ráav-yə), **Alberto,** born Alberto Pincherle (1907–90). Italian novelist. His first novel, *The Indifferent Ones* (1929), introduced the continuing theme of his works, the despair and alienation of contemporary life. His best-known works are *The Woman of Rome* (1947), *The Conformist* (1951), and *Two Women* (1957).

Mo·ra·vi·an (mə-ráyvi-ən) *n.* **1.** A native or inhabitant of Moravia. **2.** The Czech dialect spoken in Moravia. **3.** A member of the Moravian Church, a Protestant denomination founded in Saxony in 1722 by Hussite emigrants from Moravia. **—Mo·ra·vi·an** *adj.*

mo·ray (máwray, mo-ráy, mə- ‖ mŏ́ray) *n.* Any of various often voracious, brightly coloured marine eels of the family Muraenidae, of chiefly tropical coastal waters. Also called "moray eel". [Portuguese *moreia,* from Latin *mūrēna,* from Greek *murainá†.*]

Mor·ay (múrri) or **Mor·ay·shire** (-shər, -sheer ‖ -shīr). Former Scottish county. Divided between Highland and Grampian Regions (1974); Unitary Authority area (1996) with Elgin as centre.

Moray, James Stewart or **Stuart, Earl of** (*c.* 1531–70). Regent of Scotland (1567–70), bastard son of King James V, one of the first Scottish noblemen to embrace Protestantism. When Mary married Darnley in 1565, he opposed the marriage and fled to England; in 1566 he returned to Scotland and after Mary's overthrow was appointed regent for James VI. In 1568–69 he gave evidence against Mary, accusing her of complicity in Darnley's murder. He was assassinated by James Hamilton at Linlithgow.

Moray Firth. An arm of the North Sea in east Scotland, containing valuable oil fields. Inverness lies at its head.

mor·bid (mórbid) *adj.* **1. a.** Of, pertaining to, or caused by disease. **b.** Psychologically unhealthy: *a morbid fear of dogs.* **2.** Susceptible to or characterised by preoccupation with unwholesome matters: *a morbid imagination.* **3.** Gruesome; grisly. **4.** *Informal.* Sad; melancholy. [Latin *morbidus,* diseased, from *morbus,* disease.] **—mor·bid·ly** *adv.* **—mor·bid·ness** *n.*

morbid anatomy. The branch of medicine concerned with the anatomy of diseased organs and tissues.

mor·bi·dez·za (mórbi-détsə) *n. Art.* Great delicacy, especially in the painting of flesh tints. [Italian, from *morbido,* delicate, tender. See **morbid**.]

mor·bid·i·ty (mawr-bíddəti) *n., pl.* **-ties**. **1.** The state or quality of being diseased. **2.** The number of cases of a particular disease occurring in a given number of a population. In this sense, also called "morbidity rate". **3.** A concern with morbid matters.

mor·bif·ic (mawr-bíffik) *adj.* Causing or producing disease; pathogenic. [New Latin *morbificus* : Latin *morbus,* disease + *-ficus,* -FIC.]

mor·bil·li (mawr-bíllī) *n.* A disease, **measles** *(see)*. [Latin, plural of *morbillus,* pustule, from *morbus,* disease.]

mor·ceau (máwr-sõ, -sŏ́) *n., pl.* **-ceaux** (-sŏ́). A short literary or musical composition. [French, "morsel".]

mor·da·cious (mawr-dáyshəss) *adj.* **1.** Given to biting; biting. **2.** Caustic; sarcastic. [Latin *mordāx* (stem *mordāc-*), caustic, biting, from *mordēre,* to bite.] **—mor·da·cious·ly** *adv.* **—mor·dac·i·ty** (-dássəti) *n.*

mor·dant (mórd'nt) *adj.* **1. a.** Bitingly sarcastic. **b.** Incisive and trenchant. **2.** Bitingly painful. **3.** Serving to fix colours in dyeing. *~n.* **1.** A reagent, such as alumina or tannic acid, used to fix colouring matter in textiles, leather, or other materials. **2.** A corrosive substance, such as an acid, used to etch treated areas on a surface, especially a printing plate. —See Synonyms at **incisive**. *~tr.v.* **mordanted, -danting, -dants.** To treat with a mordant. [French, from Old French, from the present participle of *mordre,* to bite, from Latin *mordēre.*] **—mor·dan·cy** *n.* **—mor·dant·ly** *adv.*

mor·dent (mórd'nt ‖ *U.S. also* mawr-dént) *n. Music.* A melodic ornament in which a principal note is rapidly interrupted, usually only once, by a note a semitone or full tone above *(upper mordent)* or below *(lower mordent)*. [German, from Italian *mordente,* a grace note, from *mordere,* to bite (in allusion to the sharpness of attack with which it is executed), from Latin *mordēre.*]

Mordred. Variant of **Modred.**

more (mor ‖ mŏr). Comparative of **many** or **much.** *~adj.* **1. a.** Greater in number. **b.** Greater in size, amount, extent, or degree. **2.** Additional; extra: *They need more food.* *~n.* **1.** A greater or additional quantity, number, degree, or amount. Used with *of* and a plural verb: *More of them are coming.* **2.** Something that exceeds or surpasses expectation: *more than necessary.* *~adv.* **1. a.** To a greater extent or degree: *His insults upset her more than his blows did.* **b.** Used to form the comparative of many adjectives and adverbs, especially those of two or more syllables: *more difficult; more intelligently.* **2.** In addition; besides; further; again; longer: *I can't eat a mouthful more.* **—more or less. 1.** About; approximately. **2.** To an undetermined degree. [Middle English *more,* Old English *māra* (adjective), *māre* (adverb and noun).]

More (mor ‖ mŏr), **Sir** or **Saint Thomas** (1478–1535). English statesman, humanist scholar, and writer. His essay *Utopia* (1516) described an ideal form of Commonwealth. He was knighted (1521) and made Lord Chancellor by Henry VIII (1529). After resigning (1532), he refused to subscribe to the Act of Supremacy which made Henry, not the pope, head of the English Church. He was imprisoned in the Tower and beheaded. He was canonised in 1935.

Morea. See **Peloponnese.**

mo·reen (mə-réen, maw-) *n.* A sturdy ribbed fabric of wool or cotton, often with an embossed finish, used for clothing and upholstery. [Perhaps blend of MOIRE and VELVETEEN or SATEEN.]

more·ish, mor·ish (máwrish ‖ mŏrish) *adj. Informal.* Causing one to want more; appetising. Said of food.

mo·rel¹ (mó-rél, mə- ‖ maw-) *n.* Any of various edible mushrooms of the genus *Morchella* and related genera, characterised by a brownish, spongelike cap. [French *morille,* from Dutch *morilje†.*]

morel² *n.* A nightshade; especially, the black nightshade. [Middle English, from Old French *morele,* feminine noun from *morel,* dark brown, from Vulgar Latin *maurellus* (unattested), from Latin *Maurus,* MOOR.]

mo·rel·lo (mə-réllŏ, mo-) *n., pl.* **-los.** A variety of the sour cherry, *Prunus cerasus austera,* having fruit with dark red skin. Also called "morello cherry". [Italian, "dark", from Medieval Latin *morellus,* from Latin *Maurus,* MOOR.]

more·o·ver (mawr-ŏ́vər, máwr- ‖ mŏr-, mŏ́r-) *adv.* Beyond what has been stated; furthermore; besides. See Synonyms at **also.**

morepork. Variant of **mopoke.**

mo·res (máwr-eez, -ayz ‖ mŏr-) *pl.n.* The accepted traditional customs and usages of a particular social group that come to be regarded as essential to its survival and welfare, thence often becoming, through general observance, part of a formalised legal code. [Latin *mōrēs,* plural of *mōs,* custom.]

Moresco. Variant of **Morisco.**

Mo·resque (maw-résk, mə-, mo-) *adj.* Moorish. Said of decoration and architecture. *~n.* An ornament or decoration in Moorish style. [French, from Spanish *Morisco,* MORISCO.]

Mor·gan (mórgən) *n.* A small saddle horse or trotting horse of an American breed. [After Justin *Morgan* (1747–98), owner of the stallion from which the breed is descended.]

Morgan, Sir Henry (*c.*1635–88). Welsh buccaneer and colonial administrator. As commander of the British pirates in the Caribbean, he sacked Puerto Bello (1688) and captured Maracaibo (1669) and Panama (1671). In 1672 he was sent to England as a prisoner for his acts of piracy, but was received as a hero and knighted (1673). He went back to Jamaica as lieutenant governor.

Morgan, J(ohn) P(ierpont) (1837–1913). U.S. industrialist and financier. He founded (1901) the U.S. Steel Corporation, the first billion-dollar corporation in the world.

mor·ga·nat·ic (mórgə-náttik) *adj.* Of, pertaining to, or designating a legal marriage between a woman or man of royal or noble birth and a partner of lower rank, in which agreement is made that any titles or estates of the royal or noble partner will not be shared by the commoner or by any of their offspring. [French or German, from Medieval Latin *matrimonium ad morganaticam,* "marriage for (no dowry but) the morning-gift" (i.e., the husband's token gift to the wife on the morning after the wedding night), from Old High German *morgan,* morning.] **—mor·ga·nat·i·cal·ly** *adv.*

mor·gan·ite (mórgən-īt) *n.* A rosy-pink variety of beryl, valued as a semiprecious gem. [Named in honour of J.P. MORGAN.]

Mor·gan le Fay (mór-gən-lə-fáy, -li-). Also **Mor·gain le Fay** (-gən-, -gayn-). A sorceress, the half sister and enemy of King Arthur.

mor·gen (mórgən, mórkhən) *n., pl.* **morgen** or **-gens**. **1.** A former Dutch and South African unit of land area equal to 0.86 hectare (2.116 acres). **2.** A unit of land area formerly used in Norway, Denmark, and Prussia, equal to about two thirds of an acre. [Dutch, from Middle Dutch *morghen,* morning, that is, "a morning's ploughing".]

morgue (morg) *n.* **1.** A **mortuary** *(see).* **2.** *U.S. Informal.* A reference file or storage room containing old newspapers, cuttings, notebooks, and the like, in a newspaper or magazine office. [French, from *le Morgue†,* the mortuary building in Paris.]

mor·i·bund (mórri-bund) *adj.* **1.** At the point of death; about to die. **2.** Approaching an end; obsolescent: *moribund ideas.* [Latin *moribundus,* from *morī,* to die.] **—mor·i·bun·di·ty** (-búnditi) *n.* **—mor·i·bund·ly** *adv.*

mo·ri·on¹ (máwri-ən ‖ mŏ́ri-, -on) *n.* A crested metal helmet with curved peaks in front and behind, worn by soldiers in the 16th and 17th centuries. [French, from Spanish *morrion,* from *morro,* crown of the head, from Vulgar Latin *murrum*† (unattested), round thing.]

morion² *n.* A variety of smoky quartz, often nearly black. [Manuscript error for Latin *mormorion*†.]

Mo·ris·co (mə-rískō) *n., pl.* **-cos** or **-coes.** Also **Moresco** (-réskō). **1.** A Spanish Moor. **2.** A morris dance.
~*adj.* Also **Moresco.** Moorish. Said of a style of architecture. [Spanish, from *Moro,* Moor, from Latin *Maurus,* MOOR.]

morish. Variant of **moreish.**

Mo·ri·sot (mórri-sō), **Berthe (Marie Pauline)** (1841–95). French impressionist painter. A student of Corot, she is most admired for her graceful paintings of women and children.

mo·ri·tu·ri te sa·lu·ta·mus (mórri-téwr-ī tee sál-yōō-táymɔss, -tóor-, -ee, tay, -ōō-, -taámɔss) *Latin.* We who are about to die salute you. The gladiators' salutation to the Roman emperor.

Mor·mon¹ (mórmən). In the Mormon Church, an American prophet, warrior, and historian of the fourth century A.D., who was revealed to Joseph Smith as the author of a sacred history of the Americas, which Smith translated as the Book of Mormon.

Mormon² *n.* **1.** A member of the Church of Jesus Christ of Latter-day Saints, founded by Joseph Smith in 1830. **2.** A member of any of various sects deriving from Smith's original church that accept the Book of Mormon as the word of God.
~*adj.* Of or pertaining to the Mormons, their religion, or their church. —**Mor·mon·ism** *n.* —**Mor·mon·ist** *adj.*

morn (morn) *n. Poetic.* The morning. —**the morn.** *Scottish.* Tomorrow. [Middle English *morwen, morn,* Old English *morgen.*]

Mor·nay (mor-náy, mór-nay) *n. Sometimes small* **m.** A white sauce flavoured with grated cheese.
~*adj.* Designating a dish prepared with this sauce: *eggs Mornay.* [20th century : origin obscure.]

morn·ing (mórning) *n.* **1.** The first or early part of the day, lasting from midnight to noon or from sunrise to noon. **2.** The hour from daybreak to sunrise; dawn. **3.** The first or early part of anything. [Middle English *morwening,* from *morwen,* MORN (by analogy with EVENING).] —**morn·ing** *adj.*

morning after *n., pl.* **mornings after.** *Informal.* The morning following a night of dissipation, especially drunkenness. Also called the "morning after the night before".

morning-after pill (mórning-aáftər ‖ -áftər) *n.* An oral contraceptive that prevents the implantation of a fertilised egg in the uterus.

morning coat *n.* A tailcoat, usually grey in colour, worn as part of a morning suit.

morning glory *n., pl.* **-ries.** Any of various, usually twining vines of the genus *Ipomoea,* having funnel-shaped, variously coloured flowers that close late in the day.

Morning Prayer *n.* In the Anglican Church, the service of morning worship. Also called "matins".

morn·ings (mórningz) *adv. Informal.* In the mornings; every morning.

morning sickness *n.* Nausea and vomiting upon rising in the morning, often one of the early symptoms of pregnancy. Not in technical usage.

morning star *n.* A planet visible in the east just before sunrise, especially Venus. Compare **evening star.**

morning suit *n.* A suit for a man, worn on formal occasions during the day, such as at weddings, and consisting of a morning coat and grey striped trousers, worn with a top hat.

Mo·ro (máw-rō ‖ mó-) *n., pl.* **-ros** or collectively **Moro. 1.** A member of any of various Muslim Malay peoples of the southern Philippines. **2.** The language of these peoples, of the Malayo-Polynesian family of languages. [Spanish, from Latin *Maurus,* MOOR.] —**Mo·ro id** *adj.*

Moro, Aldo (1916–78). Italian Christian Democratic politician. He was Prime Minister twice (1963–68, 1974–76). In 1978 he was kidnapped and murdered by the Red Brigade.

mo·roc·co (mə-róckō) *n., pl.* **-cos.** *Abbr.* **mor. 1.** A soft, fine leather of goatskin tanned with sumac, made originally in Morocco. It is used chiefly for bookbindings and shoes. **2.** Any imitation of this. Also called "morocco leather".

Mo·roc·co (mə-róckō). *Arabic* **Al Mam·la·ka al Magh·re·bi·a.** Country of northwest Africa, comprising the Atlas mountain ranges, with a fertile plain along the Atlantic, and the Sahara to the southeast. Most of the people are Arab-speaking Muslims, but a third are Muslim Berbers. European penetration begun by Portugal and Spain (15th century) increased in the 19th century, and by 1912 virtually all Morocco was administered by France or Spain, with an international zone at Tangier. Independence came in 1956. In 1976 Morocco occupied the northern two-thirds of the phosphate-rich Spanish Sahara (now Western Sahara), and the rest in 1979. A border dispute with Algeria from 1963, and from 1976, war against the Polisario Front, fighting for an independent Western Sahara, drained Morocco's resources. The economy now relies on agriculture and mining, especially of phosphates, with fishing and tourism. Its area is 710 850 square kilometres (274,461 square miles), but the southern borders are not defined. Population, 27,620,000. Capital, Rabat. —**Mo·roc·can** *adj. & n.*

mo·ron (máw-ron ‖ mó-) *n.* **1.** *Informal.* A remarkably stupid or oafish person. **2.** A mentally subnormal person, having a mental age between 7 and 12 years or an intelligence quotient between 50 and 75. Not in current technical usage. [Greek *mōron,* neuter of *mōros,* foolish.] —**mo·ron·ic** (mə-rónnik, mo-, maw-) *adj.* —**mo·**

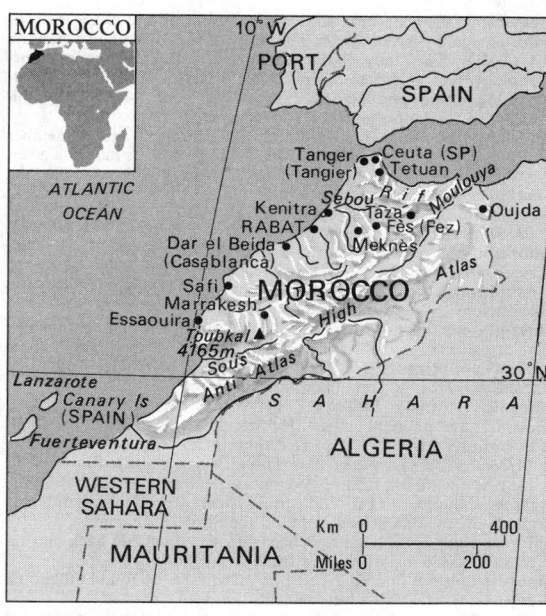

ron·i·cal·ly *adv.* —**mo·ron·ism, mo·ron·i·ty** (mə-rónnəti, mo-, maw-) *n.*

mo·rose (mə-róss ‖ maw-) *adj.* Sullenly melancholy; gloomy; ill-humoured. See Synonyms at **glum.** [Latin *mōrōsus,* captious, fretful, from *mōs* (stem *mōr-*), custom, manner, humour, caprice.] —**mo·rose·ly** *adv.* —**mo·rose·ness** *n.*

morph (morf) *n. Linguistics.* A morpheme, or the phonological representation of a morpheme. [Back-formation from *morpheme.*]

morph–. Variant of **morpho–.**

morph., morphol. morphological; morphology.

–morph *n. comb. form.* Indicates: **1.** A specified form, shape, or structure; for example, **endomorph. 2.** A morpheme; for example, **allomorph.** [Greek *-morphos,* from *morphē,* shape, form.]

mor·phal·lax·is (mórfə-lák-siss) *n., pl.* **-laxes** (-seez). *Biology.* The regeneration of a part by means of structural reorganisation of existing cells with only limited production of new cells, a process observed primarily in invertebrate organisms, such as certain lobsters. [New Latin, "structure exchange" : MORPH(O)- + Greek *allaxis,* exchange, from *allassein,* to exchange, from *allos,* other.]

mor·pheme (mórfeem) *n.* A linguistic unit of relatively stable meaning that cannot be divided into smaller meaningful parts, such as whole words like *god,* word-forming elements like *-ly* as found in *godly,* or grammatical inflections like the plural ending *-s* in *gods.* Morphemes may be abstract units, as when the *-en* in *oxen,* the *-i-* in *mice,* and the *-s* in *girls* are all considered to be identical. [French *morphème,* from Greek *morphē,* form (by analogy with PHONEME).] —**mor·phem·ic** (mor-féemik) *adj.* —**mor·phem·ic·al·ly** *adv.*

mor·phe·mics (mawr-féemiks) *n. With singular verb. Linguistics.* The study of morphemes, their forms, and their functions.

Mor·phe·us (mór-fi-ɔss, -fewss). The god or personification of sleep: *in the arms of Morpheus.* —**Mor·phe·an** *adj.*

mor·phi·a (mórfi-ə) *n.* Morphine. Not in current technical usage. [New Latin : obsolete *morphium,* from MORPHEUS + -IA.]

mor·phic (mórfik) *adj.* Pertaining to form; morphological. [MORPH(O)- + -IC.] —**mor·phi·cal·ly** *adv.*

–morphic, –morphous *adj. comb. form.* Indicates possession of a specified shape or form; for example, **polymorphic, amorphous.** [From -MORPH.]

mor·phine (mórfeen) *n.* A narcotic drug extracted from opium, $C_{17}H_{19}NO_3$, the soluble salts of which are used in medicine to relieve severe and persistent pain. Repeated dosage causes addiction. [French, from MORPHEUS.]

mor·phing (mórfing) *n.* A computer-generated special effect whereby one image (as of a person) metamorphoses smoothly into another (as of an alien). [Perhaps from *(meta)morph(os)ing,* from METAMORPHOSE.]

mor·phin·ism (mór-fi-niz'm, -fee-) *n.* **1.** Morphine addiction. **2.** A chronic condition of poisoning caused by sustained or immoderate dosage of morphine.

morpho–, morph– *comb. form.* Indicates: **1.** A shape, form, or structure; for example, **morphogenesis, morphology. 2.** A morpheme; for example, **morphophonemics.** [German, from Greek, from *morphē,* shape.]

mor·pho·gen·e·sis (mórfō-jénnə-siss) *n.* **1.** Evolutionary development of the structure of an organism or part. **2.** Embryological development of the structure of an organism or part. —**mor·pho·ge·net·ic** (-ji-néttik), **mor·pho·gen·ic** (-jénnik) *adj.*

mor·phol·o·gy (mawr-fóllɔji) *n. Abbr.* **morph., morphol. 1.** The biological study of the form and structure of living organisms. **2.** The structure and form of an organism, excluding its functions. **3.** *Linguistics.* **a.** The form and structure of words in any given language;

1005

especially, the consistent and classifiable forms and changes of inflections and derivations. **b.** The study of such form and structure. **4.** *Geology.* The study of the structure of earth features, **geomorphology** *(see).* [German *Morphologie* : MORPHO- + -LOGY.] **—morpho·log·ic, mor·pho·log·i·cal** (mórfə-lójik'l) *adj.* **—mor·pho·log·i·cal·ly** *adv.* **—mor·phol·o·gist** (-fóllǝjist) *n.*

mor·pho·pho·neme (mórf-ǝ-fōneem, -ō-) *n. Linguistics.* A member of the set of variant phonemes which may be used as part of a given morpheme according to phonological context. For example, the morpheme *electric-* has as its final constituent a morphophoneme consisting of three phonemes, (k), (s), and (sh), as in the words *electrical, electricity, electrician.*

mor·pho·pho·ne·mics (mórfō-fǝ-néemiks, -fō-) *n. Used with a singular verb. Linguistics.* The study of phonological variations within morphemes; the study of morphophonemes. Also called "morphophonology". **—mor·pho·pho·ne·mic** *adj.*

mor·pho·sis (mawr-fō-siss) *n., pl.* **-ses** (-seez). The manner in which an organism or one of its parts changes form or the manner or order of its development. [New Latin, from Greek *morphōsis,* formation, from *morphoun,* to form, from *morphē,* form.]

Mor·ris (mórriss), **William** (1834–96). British craftsman, poet, painter, and political activist. He first made his name in the 1850s as a painter attached to the Pre-Raphaelites, and as a poet, with *The Defence of Guenevere and other Poems,* which appeared in 1858. In 1861 he founded a firm of decorators, dedicated to combating the mass-produced art of the industrial system by producing handmade goods. In 1884 he helped to found the Socialist League.

Morris chair *n.* A large armchair with an adjustable back and removable cushions. [Designed by William MORRIS.]

mor·ris column (mórris || *U.S. also* máwriss) *n.* A round pillar on a pavement, on which advertisements are displayed.

morris dance *n.* An English country dance traditionally performed by men *(morris men)* wearing bright costumes, handkerchiefs, and bells, and often representing a folk tale. Also called "morris". [Middle English *Moreys,* Moorish, from *More,* MOOR.]

Mor·ri·son of Lambeth (mórri-s'n), **Herbert Stanley, Baron** (1888–1965). British politician. He was secretary of the London Labour Party (1915–47) and a member of the London County Council (1922–45). In 1945 he was unofficially deputy prime minister under Attlee and leader of the House of Commons, a post he held until he was appointed Foreign Secretary in 1951. He was awarded a life peerage in 1959.

mor·row (mórrō) *n. Archaic.* **1.** The day following some particular day. Preceded by *the.* **2.** The time immediately subsequent to some particular event. **3.** The morning: *Good morrow!* [Middle English *morwe,* Old English *morgen.*]

morse (morss) *n.* The clasp or fastening, often of gold or silver, on a cope. [Middle English, from Old French *mors,* from Latin *morsus,* bite, clasp, from *mordēre* (past participial stem *mors-*), to bite.]

Morse (morss), **Samuel (Finley Breese)** (1791–1872). U.S. painter and inventor. He is most famous for his refinement of the electric telegraph and earlier telegraph codes (1838).

Morse code *n.* A system of communication in which letters of the alphabet and numbers are represented by patterns of short and long signals, which may be conveyed as sounds, flashes of light, written dots and dashes, or the waving of flags. Also called "Morse", "Morse alphabet". [Invented by Samuel MORSE.]

mor·sel (mórss'l) *n.* **1.** A small piece or bite of food. **2.** A light meal; a snack. **3.** A small piece or amount of anything. [Middle English, from Old French *mors,* a bite, from Latin *morsum,* past participle of *mordēre,* to bite.]

mort[1] (mort) *n.* The note sounded on a hunting horn to announce the death of the hunted animal. [Middle English, from Old French, from Latin *mors* (stem *mort-*), death.]

mort[2] *n. British Regional.* A great number or quantity: *a mort of money.* [Perhaps from northern dialect *murth* (influenced by MORTAL, "extremely"), from Old Norse *mergth,* multitude.]

mort[3] *n.* A salmon two to three years old. [16th century : origin obscure.]

mor·tal (mórt'l) *adj.* **1.** Liable or subject to death. **2.** Of or pertaining to humans as beings who must die. **3.** Of, pertaining to, or accompanying death: *mortal throes.* **4.** Causing death; fatal; deadly: *a mortal wound.* **5.** Fought to the death: *"with victorious Germany and Italy engaged in mortal attack upon us"* (Sir Winston Churchill). **6.** Unrelenting; implacable: *one's mortal enemy.* **7.** Of or like the fear of death; dire; grievous: *in mortal terror.* **8.** *Slang.* Very great; extreme: *"I go there a mortal sight of times"* (Charles Dickens). **9.** *Slang.* Used as an intensive: *There is no mortal reason for us to go.*
~n. A human being.
~adv. *Regional.* Extremely; very: *mortal angry.* [Middle English, from Old French *mortal, mortel,* from Latin *mortālis,* from *mors* (stem *mort-*), death.] **—mor·tal·ly** *adv.*

mor·tal·i·ty (mawr-tál-ǝti) *n., pl.* **-ties.** **1.** The condition of being subject to death. **2. a.** *Archaic.* Death. **b.** The loss of a great many lives. **3.** The frequency or number of deaths in proportion to a population in a given period. Also called "death rate", "mortality rate". **4.** Deadliness. **5.** The quality of being mortal. Said of a sin. **6.** Humankind.

mortality table *n. Insurance.* A table which lists the life expectancies of people according to their age, sex, occupation, and other considerations.

mortal sin *n.* **1.** *Theology.* A sin which totally estranges the soul from the grace of God. Compare **venial sin.** **2.** *Informal.* Any major miscalculation or common error.

mor·tar (mórtǝr) *n.* **1.** A receptacle made of a hard material in which substances are crushed or ground with a pestle. **2.** Any machine in which materials are ground and blended or crushed. **3.** *Military.* A muzzle-loading cannon used to fire shells at low velocities, short ranges, and great angular elevation. Also called "trench mortar". **4.** Any of several similar devices used for various purposes, such as shooting lifelines across a stretch of water. **5.** A mixture of cement or lime with sand and water that is used in building.
~v. **mortared, -taring, -tars.** **—tr.** **1.** To plaster or join with mortar. **2.** To bombard with a mortar; hit with mortar shells. **—intr.** To fire mortars. [Middle English *morter,* partly from Old English *mortere* and partly from Old French *mortier,* both from Latin *mortārium,* a mortar and the substance made in it.]

mor·tar·board (mórtǝr-bawrd || -bōrd) *n.* **1.** A square board with a handle, for holding and carrying mortar. **2.** An academic cap topped by a flat square covered with cloth, usually black and having a tassel on top. Also called "square", "trencher", "trencher cap".

Morte d'Ar·thur, Le (lǝ mórt dárthǝr) *n.* A collection of Arthurian stories compiled and translated from Old French by Sir Thomas Malory, and printed by William Caxton in 1485.

mort·gage (mórgij) *n. Abbr.* **mtg.** *Law.* **1.** A temporary and conditional pledge or conveyance of property to a creditor as security against a debt. **2.** A contract or deed specifying the terms of such a conveyance. **3.** The claim that the mortgagee or creditor has upon property pledged in this manner.
~tr.v. **mortgaged, -gaging, -gages.** **1.** To pledge (property) by mortgage. **2.** *Informal.* To pledge or stake against future success or failure; place an advance liability upon. [Middle English *morgage,* from Old French *mortgage,* "dead pledge" : *mort,* dead, from Latin *mortuus,* from *mors* (stem *mort-*), death + *gage,* GAGE (pledge).]

mort·ga·gee (mórgi-jée) *n.* The holder of a mortgage, usually as security against a loan.

mort·ga·gor (mórgi-jǝr, -jór) *n.* Also **mort·gag·er** (-jǝr). A person who mortgages property.

mor·ti·cian (mawr-tísh'n) *n. U.S.* A funeral director; an undertaker. [MORT(UARY) + -ICIAN.]

mor·ti·fi·ca·tion (mórtifi-káysh'n) *n.* **1.** A feeling of shame, humiliation, or wounded pride. **2.** The cause of such a feeling: *Her sister's imprisonment was a mortification to her.* **3.** The mortifying of the body and appetites. **4.** The death or decay of one part of a living body; necrosis; gangrene.

mor·ti·fy (mórti-fī) *v.* **-fied, -fying, -fies.** **—tr.** **1.** To cause to experience shame, humiliation, or wounded pride; humiliate. **2.** To discipline (one's body and appetites) by self-denial and austerity: *mortify the flesh.* **3.** To cause (a bodily part) to die, as by gangrene. **—intr.** **1.** To practise ascetic discipline or punishment of the body. **2.** To become gangrenous or necrosed, as a part of the body might. **—See Synonyms at degrade.** [Middle English *mortifien,* from Old French *mortifier,* from Late Latin *mortificāre,* to cause to die : *mors* (stem *mort-*), death + *facere,* -FY.] **—mor·ti·fy·ing·ly** *adv.*

Mor·ti·mer (mórtimǝr), **Roger de, 1st Earl of March** (*c.* 1287–1330). English nobleman. He was the lover of Edward II's wife, Isabella, with whom he raised a force to invade England from France (1326). They deposed Edward (1327) and together ruled England until 1330, when Edward III seized power and had Mortimer put to death after trial and conviction by Parliament.

mor·tise, mor·tice (mórtiss) *n.* **1.** A cavity, usually rectangular, in a piece of wood, stone, or other material, cut to receive a similarly shaped projection or **tenon** *(see)* of another piece, to hold the two together. **2.** *Printing.* A hole cut in a plate for the insertion of type.
~tr.v. **mortised** or **morticed, -tising** or **-ticing, -tises** or **-tices.** **1.** To join or fasten securely, as with a mortise and tenon. **2.** To cut or make a mortise in. **3.** *Printing.* **a.** To cut a hole in (a plate) for the insertion of type. **b.** To cut such a hole and insert (type). [Middle English *mortays,* from Old French *mortoise,* from Arabic *murtazz,* fixed in.]

mortise lock *n.* A lock fixed into a mortise in the edge of a door, such that the body of the lock is enclosed. Compare **deadlock, Yale lock.**

mort·main (mórt-mayn) *n. Law.* Perpetual ownership of land by institutions such as churches that cannot transfer or sell them. Also called "dead hand". [Middle English *mortemayne,* from Old French *mortemain,* "dead hand" (that is, institutional possession) : *morte,* feminine of *mort,* dead, from Latin *mortuus,* from *mors* (stem *mort-*), death + *main,* hand, from Latin *manus.*]

Mor·ton (mórt'n), **James Douglas, 4th Earl of** (1516–81). Scottish nobleman. He was appointed Lord High Chancellor to Mary, Queen of Scots (1563). He played a leading role in the murder of David Riccio (1566) and conspired in the plot to murder Darnley. He became Regent after the death of the Earl of Mar (1572). He was removed from power by the Earl of Argyll (1578) and was executed for his part in the murder of Darnley.

mor·tu·ar·y (mórtew-ǝri, -choo- || -erri) *n., pl.* **-ies.** A place where dead bodies are prepared or kept prior to burial or cremation. Also called "morgue".
~adj. Of or pertaining to death or to the burial of the dead. [Middle English *mortuarie,* from Anglo-French, from Late Latin *mortuārium,* from *mortuārius,* of burial, from *mortuus,* dead, from *mors* (stem *mort-*), death.]

mor·u·la (mórrew-lə ‖ mórrə-) *n., pl.* **-lae** (-lee) or **-las.** *Biology.*
1. The spherical mass of embryonic cells formed by cleavage of a fertilised ovum before blastulation. Compare **gastrula. 2.** A spherical mass of developing male gametes occurring especially in certain annelid worms. [New Latin, diminutive of Latin *mōrum*, mulberry.] —**mor·u·lar** (-lər) *adj.*

mor·wong (mór-wong) *n.* An Australasian food fish of the family Cheilodactylidae. [From a native Australian language.]

mos. months.

mo·sa·ic (mə-záy-ik, mō-) *n.* **1. a.** A picture or decorative design made by setting small coloured pieces of glass, stone, or tile in mortar. **b.** The art of process of making such designs. **2.** Anything that resembles a piece of mosaic work: *The stained-glass windows cast light in a mosaic on the church floor.* **3.** Any of several virus diseases of plants, resulting in light and dark areas in the leaves, which often become shrivelled and dwarfed. **4.** A set of overlapping photographs, usually aerial, assembled into a composite picture. **5.** A photosensitive surface in a television camera, consisting of a large number of small sensitive patches on an insulating base. **6.** *Genetics.* An organism containing genetically different types of tissue; a chimera. *~tr.v.* **mosaicked, -icking, -ics.** *Rare.* **1.** To make by mosaic or as if by mosaic. **2.** To adorn with mosaic or as if with mosaic. [Middle English, from Old French *mosaique*, from Italian *mosaico*, from Medieval Latin *mosaicus, musaicus*, irregularly from Late Greek *mouseion*, a mosaic, from *mouseios*, belonging to the Muses, from *Mousa,* Muse.] —**mo·sa·ic** *adj.* —**mo·sa·i·cist** (-i-sist) *n.*

Mo·sa·ic (mō-záy-ik, mə-) *adj.* Also **Mo·sa·i·cal** (mō-záy-i'l, mə-). Of or pertaining to Moses or the laws and writings attributed to him. [New Latin *Mosaicus,* from MOSES.]

mosaic gold *n.* An alloy resembling gold, **ormolu** (*see*).

mo·sa·i·cism (mō-záy-i-siz'm, mə-) *n. Genetics.* The condition in which tissues of genetically different types occur in the same organism. [From MOSAIC.]

Mosaic Law *n.* The ancient law of the Hebrews, traditionally attributed to Moses and contained mainly in the Pentateuch. Also called "Law of Moses".

mo·sa·saur (mṓ-sə-sawr) *n.* Any of various extinct marine lizards of the genus *Mosasaurus* and related genera, which attained a very large size and had paddle-like limbs. [New Latin : *Mosa,* river Meuse (near which fossil remains were found) + *-saurus,* -SAUR.]

mos·cha·tel (móskə-tél) *n.* A plant, *Adoxa moschatellina,* of northern regions, having greenish-white, musk-scented flowers. [French *moscatelle,* from Italian *moscatella,* from *moscato,* MUSK.]

Mos·cow (móss-kō ‖ *U.S. also* -kow). *Russian* **Mos·kva** (mass-kvá·a).· Capital of the Russian Federation, and formerly of the U.S.S.R. Lying on the Moskva river, it is also the communications, economic, and cultural centre of Russia, and accounts for about a quarter of the national industrial output, with metal-working, oil-refining, aircraft, publishing, vehicle, chemical, textile, and clothing plants. Founded in the 12th century, the minor principality of Moscow gradually assumed sovereignty over its neighbours by virtue of its strategic importance at the crossing of major trade routes and as bulwark against the Tatars. By the 15th century it was the capital of the Russian state, and its Grand Duke Ivan IV took the title of tsar in 1547. The capital was transferred to St. Petersburg (1712), but Moscow was reinstated (1918) after the Revolution. It is the site of the Kremlin (citadel) with its many cathedrals, and Red Square with the Lenin Mausoleum and 16th-century cathedral of St. Vassily (Basil). Many times destroyed by fire, as during the French occupation (1812), and rebuilt, the city was heroically defended against the Nazis in World War II (1941). It was the venue for the 1980 Summer Olympics.

Mose·ley (mốzli), **Henry Gwyn-Jeffreys** (1887–1915). English physicist. His research on radioactivity demonstrated the relationship between X-ray spectra and the atomic number of an element and enabled him to formulate (1913) the law that established the atomic number of an element.

Mo·selle[1] (mō-zél, mə-). *German* **Mo·sel** (mố'z'l). River of northwest Europe, flowing 547 kilometres (340 miles) from the Vosges in France to join the Rhine at Koblenz in Germany.

Moselle[2] *n. Also small* **m.** A light, dry white wine produced in the valley of the Moselle river.

Mo·ses (mố-z-iz ‖ -iss). The lawgiver who led the Israelites out of Egypt.

mo·sey (mốzi) *intr.v.* **-seyed, -seying, -seys.** *Chiefly U.S. Informal.* To walk in a leisurely manner; stroll. Often used with *along, down,* or *on down.* [19th century : origin obscure.]

mo·shav (mō-shá'av) *n., pl.* **-shavim** (-sha-véem). An agricultural cooperative settlement in Israel. [Hebrew *moshāb,* "dwelling".]

Mo·shesh (mō-shésh), (1795–1870). Also **Mo·shoe·shoe** (-shôo-shô) or **M·shwe·shwe** (m-shwéshwi). Founder of the Basuto (Sotho) nation (modern Lesotho), and its undisputed chief through many wars with South Africa's white settlers. He was noted especially for his diplomatic skill.

Moslem. Variant of **Muslim.**

Mos·ley (mốzli), **Sir Oswald (Ernald)** (1896–1980). British politician, founder of the British Union of Fascists. He entered the House of Commons as a Conservative in 1918 and switched to the Labour Party in 1924. In 1929 he became a junior minister in the Labour government. He resigned from the government in 1930 when his economic policies to overcome the Depression were rejected. In 1932 he founded the New Party, and a year later the

British Union of Fascists. He married his second wife, Diana Mitford, then Diana Guinness, in 1936 and they were both interned (1940–43) during World War II. Mosley failed in his attempts at a political comeback after the war.

Mo·so·tho (mōō-sốotōō) *n., pl.* **-thos** or collectively **Mosotho.** A member of the Sotho people of Southern Africa, or a citizen of **Lesotho** (*see*). Also called "Basotho", formerly "Basuto".

mosque (mosk) *n.* A Muslim house of worship. Also called "masjid", "musjid". [French *mosquée,* from Italian *moschea,* from Arabic *masjid,* a place of worship, from *sajada,* to bow down.]

mos·qui·to (mə-skéetō, mo-) *n., pl.* **-toes** or **-tos.** Any of various winged insects of the family Culicidae, in which the female of most species is distinguished by a long proboscis for sucking blood. Some species are vectors of diseases such as malaria and yellow fever. [Spanish, diminutive of *mosca,* fly, from Latin *musca.*]

Mos·qui·to (mə-skéetō) *n., pl.* **-tos** or collectively **Mosquito.** Also **Mis·ki·to** (mi-). **1.** A member of a Central American people of mixed native Indian and Negro descent, living on the Atlantic coast of Nicaragua and Honduras. **2.** The language of this people. —**Mos·qui·to** *adj.*

mosquito boat *n.* A motor torpedo boat. [Referring to its speed and small size.]

Mosquito Coast. Also **Miskito Coast** or **Mos·qui·tia** (mi-skéeshə). Sparsely populated banana-growing plain on the Caribbean coast of Nicaragua and Honduras, named after its indigenous Indians. It was discovered (1502) by Columbus, and later became a British protectorate (1678–1860).

mosquito hawk *n.* A bird, the **nighthawk** (*see*).

mosquito net *n.* A fine net used for covering windows and beds to keep out mosquitoes.

moss (moss ‖ mawss) *n.* **1.** Any of various green, usually small bryophyte plants of the class Musci, typically growing in clumps on moist ground or trees, for example. **2.** A patch or covering of such plants. **3.** Any of various other plants that are similar in appearance or manner of growth, such as **club moss, Irish moss,** or **Spanish moss** (*all of which see*). **4.** *Chiefly Scottish.* A peat bog or moor. [Middle English *moss, mos,* Old English *mos.*]

Moss, Stirling (1929–). British racing driver. He was the British champion in 1955 and 1957, and became the number one driver in the Maserati team in 1954. His career lasted from 1947 to 1962, during which time he won 16 Grand Prix races.

moss agate *n.* A semiprecious stone with greenish-brown markings. It is a type of chalcedony.

Mössbauer effect (móss-bow-ər; *German* móss-) *n. Physics.* The emission of gamma rays by excited nuclei in some solids such that the recoil momentum is taken up by the whole lattice rather than by the emitting atom. The resulting gamma rays have a very narrow frequency range and can be used in studying the corresponding gamma-ray absorption in a sample material (*Mössbauer spectroscopy*), giving information about the energies of nuclei and the molecular structure of the sample. [After Rudolf L. *Mössbauer* (born 1929). German physicist.]

moss·bunk·er (móss-bungkər ‖ máwss-) *n.* Also **moss·bank·er** (-bangkər). *U.S.* An inedible fish, the **menhaden** (*see*). [Dutch *marsbanker†.*]

moss campion *n.* A low-growing plant, *Silene acaulis,* of cool regions, having purplish-red flowers and forming dense, cushion-like mats.

moss green *n.* Moderate yellowish to greyish green. —**moss-green** *adj.*

moss·grown (móss-grōn ‖ máwss-) *adj.* **1.** Overgrown with moss. **2.** *Informal.* Old-fashioned; antiquated.

moss·hag, moss-hagg (móss-hag ‖ máwss-) *n. Scottish.* **1.** Ground from which peat has been removed. **2.** A pit in a bog. [MOSS + dialect and Scottish *hag,* gap, pit, from Scandinavian; akin to Old Norse *hogg,* gap, cut, from *hoggva,* to strike, hack, HEW.]

mos·sie (mózzi) *n. Informal.* A mosquito. [By shortening.]

mos·so (móssō ‖ *U.S.* mố-sō) *adv. Music.* With motion or animation. Used as a direction. [Italian, from the past participle of *muovere,* to move, from Latin *movēre.*]

moss pink *n.* A low-growing plant, *Phlox subulata,* forming dense, mosslike mats. It is widely cultivated for its profuse pink or white flowers. Also called "ground pink".

moss rose *n.* A variety of rose, *Rosa centifolia muscosa,* having fragrant pink flowers with a mossy flower stalk and calyx.

moss stitch *n.* A pattern or stitch in knitting consisting of alternate plain and purl stitches on one row, and alternate purl and plain stitches on the next row, giving a minutely chequered fabric with the nubbly texture of moss.

moss·troop·er (móss-trōopər ‖ máwss-) *n.* **1.** A member of a band of raiders operating in the marshy lands on the borders of England and Scotland during the 17th century. **2.** A raider or marauder.

moss·y (móssi ‖ máwssi) *adj.* **-ier, -iest. 1.** Covered with moss or with anything resembling moss. **2.** Resembling moss. —**moss·i·ness** *n.*

most (mōst). **1.** Superlative of **many. 2.** Superlative of **much.** *~adj.* **1.** Greatest in number or quantity. **2.** Largest or greatest in amount, size, or degree. **3.** In the greatest number of instances: *Most fish have fins. ~n.* **1.** The greatest amount, quantity, or degree; the largest part: *Most of the land was fertile.* **2.** The greatest number (of a group or classification); the majority. Used with a plural verb: *Most of her novels have been well received.* —**at (the) most.** Not over; at the

absolute limit: *It's four miles at most.* —**make the most of.** To use as advantageously as possible. —**the most.** *Chiefly U.S. Slang.* A person or thing that produces great excitement or satisfaction.
~*adv.* **1.** In the highest degree, quantity, or extent. Used with many adjectives and adverbs to form the superlative degree: *most honest; most impatiently.* **2.** Very: *a most impressive piece of writing.* **3.** *U.S. Informal & Regional.* Almost: *Most everyone agrees.* [Middle English *most, mest, mast,* Old English *mǣst.*]

Usage: Most has attracted attention on three counts. As an alternative to the adverb *almost,* it is unacceptable in writing or formal speech (*Most everyone agrees*), and is largely restricted to informal American English. As an alternative to the intensifier *very,* it is widely used (*a most amusing experience*), though some stylists object to it, especially in writing, on the grounds that no explicit comparison is involved. As an adverb of degree, it has a standard use (*Those most affected are farmers*), but it is frequently replaced by *mostly* in informal speech.

–most *adj. & adv. suffix.* Indicates the superlative degree; for example, **foremost, innermost.** [Middle English *-most, -mast,* Old English *-mǣst, -mest,* originally an independent superlative suffix, later erroneously regarded as being from the adverb *mǣst,* most.]
most·ly (mōstli) *adv.* **1.** For the most part; almost entirely. **2.** Usually; as a rule. See Usage note at **most.**
mot (mō) *n.* A witticism or short, clever saying; a bon mot. [French, from Old French, from Vulgar Latin *mottum* (unattested), from Latin *muttum,* grunt, from *muttīre,* to mutter.]
M.O.T.[1] Ministry of Transport.
M.O.T.[2] (ém-ō-tée) *n.* **1.** An **M.O.T.** test (*see*). **2.** A certificate awarded after a successful M.O.T. test.
~*tr.v.* **M.O.T.d, M.O.T.ing, M.O.T.s. 1.** To give (a motor vehicle) an M.O.T. test. **2.** To cause (a motor vehicle) to be given an M.O.T. test.
mote[1] (mōt) *n.* A speck, especially of dust. [Middle English *mot, moot,* Old English *mot.*]
mote[2] *intr.v. Archaic.* May; might. [Middle English *moten,* Old English *mōtan,* to be allowed.]
mo·tel (mō-tél, mō-) *n.* A hotel for motorists, usually with blocks of rooms opening directly onto a parking area. [Blend of *motor* + *hotel.*]
mo·tet (mō-tét) *n.* A polyphonic musical composition based on a text of a sacred nature and usually sung without accompaniment. [Middle English, from Old French, from *mot,* phrase, word, MOT.]
moth (moth ‖ mawth) *n., pl.* **moths** (mothss ‖ mothz, *U.S.* also mawthz). **1.** Any of numerous insects of the order Lepidoptera, generally distinguished from butterflies by their nocturnal activity, hairlike or feathery antennae, and stout bodies. **2.** The **clothes moth** (*see*). **3.** The damage caused by the clothes moth. Preceded by *the.* [Middle English *motthe,* Old English *moththe.*]
moth·ball (móth-bawl ‖ máwth-) *n.* **1.** A small disc or ball, originally of camphor but now of naphthalene, stored with clothes to repel moths. **2.** *Plural.* A condition of long storage. Used chiefly in the phrase *put in* or *into mothballs.*
~*tr.v.* **-balled, -balling, -balls. 1.** To preserve with or as if with mothballs: *mothball a battleship.* **2.** To defer (a project) indefinitely; shelve.
moth-eat·en (móth-eet'n ‖ máwth-) *adj.* **1.** Eaten away by moths. **2.** Old and decayed; timeworn: *a moth-eaten phrase.*
moth·er[1] (múthər) *n.* **1.** A female that has borne offspring. **2.** One's own female parent. Often used as a term of address. **3.** A female who has adopted a child or otherwise established a maternal relationship with another person. **4.** A pregnant woman: *When a foetus quickens, the mother begins to feel its movements.* **5.** A woman having some of the responsibilities of a mother: *a house mother; a mother of the chapel.* **6.** Qualities attributed to a mother, such as the capacity to love selflessly: *a man who appealed to the mother in her.* **7.** *Archaic.* An affectionate or familiar form of address for an elderly woman. **8.** *Sometimes capital* **M.** A title of, or form of address for, certain senior nuns: *Mother Abbess.* **9.** A creative or environmental source: *Necessity is the mother of invention.* —**the mother of all** ... *Slang.* Used as a superlative intensifier: *the mother of all battles.*
~*adj.* **1.** Being or resembling a mother: *a mother duck.* **2.** Characteristic of a mother: *mother love.* **3.** Having a maternal relationship: *the mother church.* **4.** Derived from or as if from one's mother; native: *one's mother language.*
~*tr.v.* **mothered, -ering, -ers. 1.** To give birth to; be the mother of. **2.** To create and care for; instigate and carry through. **3.** To watch over, nourish, and protect. **4.** *Informal.* To behave in an overprotective manner towards; coddle: *Stop mothering me — I'm a grown woman!* [Middle English *moder,* Old English *mōdor.*]
mother[2] *n.* A stringy slime composed of yeast cells and bacteria that forms on the surface of fermenting liquids. It is added to wine or cider to start the production of vinegar. Also called "mother of vinegar". [From MOTHER, partly by association with afterbirth.]
Mother Car·ey's chicken (káir-iz) *n.* Any of various petrels, especially the **storm petrel** (*see*). [Perhaps from Latin *Mater Cara,* "Dear Mother", title of the Virgin Mary as patroness of seamen.]
mother country *n.* The country from which the settlers or colonists, or their forebears, of a distant territory or dominion originally came, and to which they still feel a sense of allegiance.
Mother Goose *n.* The imaginary story-teller in *Mother Goose's Tales* or *Melody,* a traditional collection of the main bulk of English nursery rhymes, first published in the 18th century.
mother hen *n.* A person, especially a woman, who is fussy and overprotective.

moth·er·hood (múthər-hŏŏd) *n.* **1.** The state or condition of being a mother. **2.** The feelings or qualities considered characteristic of a mother. **3.** Mothers collectively.
Mother Hub·bard (húbbərd) *n. Also small* **m,** *small* **h.** A woman's long, loose, unbelted dress. [After a character in a nursery rhyme.]
Mothering Sunday *n. British.* The fourth Sunday in Lent, on which mothers traditionally receive posies and other gifts from their children. Also called "Mother's Day". [From the custom of "going a-mothering", visiting parents, on this day.]
moth·er-in-law (múthər-in-law) *n., pl.* **mothers-in-law.** The mother of one's wife or husband.
mother-in-law's tongue *n.* A plant, **sansevieria** (*see*).
moth·er·land (múthər-land) *n.* **1.** The land or country of one's birth. **2.** The native land of one's ancestors.
moth·er·less (múthər-ləss, -liss) *adj.* Without a mother.
~*adv. Australian Informal.* Absolutely; completely.
mother liquor *n. Chemistry.* The liquid remaining after crystals have separated out of a solution.
mother lode *n.* The main lode in a source of ore.
moth·er·ly (múthərli) *adj.* Of, befitting, resembling, or characteristic of a mother; maternal. —**moth·er·li·ness** *n.*
Mother of Parliaments *n.* The British Parliament, which initiated and provided the model for a number of other national parliaments.
moth·er-of-pearl (múthər-əv-pérl) *n.* The pearly, iridescent internal layer of certain mollusc shells, used to make decorative objects. Also called "nacre". —**moth-er-of-pearl** *adj.*
mother-of-thousands (múthər-əv-thówz'ndz) *n.* A European perennial plant, *Helxine soleirolii,* forming dense evergreen mats on walls, for example. Also called "mind-your-own-business", "mother-of-millions".
Mother's Day *n.* **1.** Mothering Sunday. **2.** *U.S.* An annual day of commemoration of mothers and motherhood observed on the second Sunday in May.
mother superior *n., pl.* **mothers superior** or **mother-superiors.** A woman in charge of a female religious community.
mother tongue *n.* **1.** One's native language. **2.** The language from which another has developed.
mother wit *n.* Innate intelligence; common sense.
moth·er·wort (múthər-wurt ‖ -wawrt) *n.* Any of several plants of the genus *Leonurus;* especially, *L. cardiaca,* a weed having clusters of small purple or pink flowers. [Middle English *moderwort* : MOTHER (from its once reputed power to cure diseases of the uterus) + WORT.]
moth mullein *n.* A plant, *Verbascum blattaria,* native to Eurasia, having spikelike clusters of yellow or white flowers.
moth·proof (móth-prōōf ‖ máwth-, -prōōf) *adj.* Resistant to damage by moths.
~*tr.v.* **mothproofed, -proofing, -proofs.** To make resistant to damage by moths.
moth·y (mothi ‖ máwthi) *adj.* **-ier, -iest. Moth-eaten** (*see*).
mo·tif (mō-téef) *n. Also* **mo·tive** (mótiv, mō-téev). **1.** A recurrent thematic element used in the development of an artistic or literary work. **2.** A short significant phrase in a musical composition. **3.** A repeated figure or design in architecture or decoration. [French, from Old French, MOTIVE.]
mo·tile (mō-tīl ‖ *U.S. also* mốt'l) *adj.* Moving or having the power to move spontaneously, as certain spores and microorganisms do. ~*n. Psychology.* A person whose mental imagery chiefly consists of his own bodily motion. [Latin *motus,* motion + -ILE.] —**mo·til·i·ty** (mō-tílləti) *n.*
mo·tion (mósh'n) *n.* **1.** The action or process of change of position. **2.** A meaningful or expressive change in the position of the body or a part of the body; a gesture. **3.** The way in which a body moves; gait. **4.** The ability or power to move. **5.** A prompting from within; an impulse. **6.** *Music.* Melodic ascent or descent of pitch. **7.** *Law.* An application to a court for a ruling. **8.** A formal proposal put to the vote in Parliament or at a meeting or conference. **9.** *Chiefly British.* **a.** The act or process of evacuating the bowels. **b.** Faeces. **10. a.** A mechanical device or piece of machinery that moves or causes motion, as in a watch. **b.** The movement or action of such a device. —**go through the motions of.** To attempt the performance of (a task) without making a serious effort to accomplish it.
~*v.* **motioned, -tioning, -tions.** —*tr.* To signal to or direct by making a gesture. —*intr.* To make a gesture signifying something, such as agreement. [Middle English *mocioun,* from Old French *motion,* from Latin *mōtiō* (stem *mōtiōn-*), from *movēre,* to move.]
mo·tion·less (mósh'n-ləss, -liss) *adj.* Not moving. —**mo·tion·less·ly** *adv.* —**mo·tion·less·ness** *n.*
motion picture *n. Chiefly U.S.* A film (*see*).
motion sickness *n.* Travel sickness (*see*).
motion study *n.* A time and motion study (*see*).
mo·tion-work (mósh'n-wúrk) *n.* The mechanism for moving the hands of a watch or clock.
mo·ti·vate (mốti-vayt) *tr.v.* **-vated, -vating, -vates.** To stimulate to action; provide with an incentive. [From MOTIVE.]
mo·ti·va·tion (mốti-váysh'n) *n.* **1.** The act or process of motivating. **2.** An incentive, inducement, or motive, especially for an act. **3.** *Psychology.* The mental process, function, or instinct that produces and sustains incentive or drive in human and animal behaviour. —**mo·ti·va·tion·al** *adj.*
motivational research *n.* The use of certain techniques borrowed from psychology and sociology, especially by advertisers and mar-

keters, to assess consumer attitudes towards products and services. Also called "motivation research".

mo·tive (mótiv; *also* mō-téev *for sense 2*) *n.* **1.** An emotion, desire, physiological need, or similar impulse acting as an incitement to action. **2.** A motif *(see)*.
~*adj.* **1.** Causing or able to cause motion: *motive power*. **2.** Of, pertaining to, or constituting a motive.
~*tr.v.* **motived, -tiving, -tives.** To provide with an incentive; motivate. [Middle English, from Old French *motif*, from adjective, "causing to move", from Late Latin *mōtīvus*, from Latin *movēre* (past participle *mōtus*), to move.] —**mo·tiv·i·ty** (mō-tívvəti) *n.*

mot juste (mō zhŭst) *n., pl.* **mots justes** *(pronounced as singular)*. The most suitable word or expression. [French, "exact word".]

mot·ley (mótli) *adj.* **1.** Having components of great variety; heterogeneous: *a motley bunch.* **2.** Exhibiting or having many colours; multicoloured. —See Synonyms at **miscellaneous.**
~*n.* **1.** The particoloured professional attire of a court jester. **2.** A heterogeneous mixture or assemblage. **3.** *Obsolete.* A professional jester or clown. —**wear motley. 1.** To play the fool; jest in a frivolous manner. **2.** To be a fool. [Middle English *motteley*, perhaps from Anglo-French *motelé* (unattested), from MOTE (speck).]

mot·mot (mót-mot) *n.* Any of several tropical American birds of the family Momotidae, usually having green and blue plumage. [American Spanish *mot-mot* (imitative).]

mo·to·cross (mót-ō-kross, -ə- ‖ -krawss) *n.* Motorcycle racing, or scrambling, over a hazardous cross-country course. [Alteration of *motor* + *cross*-country.]

mo·to·neu·rone (mótō-néwr-on ‖ -noʹor-) *n. Anatomy. U.S.* A **motor neurone** *(see).* [*Motor* + *neuron*.]

mo·tor (mótər) *n.* **1.** Something that imparts or produces motion, such as a machine or engine. **2.** A device that converts any form of energy into mechanical energy, especially an **internal-combustion engine** *(see),* or an arrangement of coils and magnets that converts electrical energy into mechanical power. **3.** *Informal.* A motorised conveyance; especially, a car.
~*adj.* **1.** Causing or producing motion: *motor power.* **2.** Driven by or having a motor: *a motor scooter.* **3.** Of, pertaining to, or for motor vehicles: *motor oil.* **4.** *Physiology.* **a.** Of, pertaining to, or designating nerves carrying impulses from the nerve centres to the muscles. **b.** Of or pertaining to movements of the muscles: *motor coordination.*
~*v.* **motored, -toring, -tors.** —*intr.* To drive or travel in a motor vehicle. —*tr.* To carry by motor vehicle. [Latin *mōtor*, agent-noun of *movēre* (past participle *mōtus*), to move.]

mo·tor·bike (mótər-bīk) *n.* A motorcycle.

mo·tor·boat (mótər-bōt) *n.* A boat with a propeller driven by an internal-combustion engine.

mo·tor·bus (mótər-buss) *n., pl.* **-buses** or **-busses.** A bus that is powered by an internal-combustion engine or other type of engine.

mo·tor·cade (mótər-kayd) *n. Chiefly U.S.* A procession of cars or other motor vehicles. [*Motor* + caval*cade*.]

motor car *n.* A car.

motor caravan *n.* A motor vehicle having a large caravan-like living-space behind the driver's cab, equipped with beds, a cooker, and other domestic facilities.

mo·tor·cy·cle (mótər-sīk'l) *n.* A vehicle with two wheels in tandem propelled by an internal-combustion engine.
~*intr.v.* **motorcycled, -cycling, -cycles.** To ride on or drive a motorcycle. —**mo·tor·cy·clist** *n.*

motor drive *n.* A system consisting of an electric motor and accessory parts, used to power machinery.

mo·tor·ise, mo·tor·ize (mótər-īz) *tr.v.* **-ised, -ising, -ises. 1.** To equip with a motor or motors. **2.** To supply with motor-driven vehicles in substitution for ones drawn by horses or other animals. **3.** To provide motor-vehicle transport for. —**mo·tor·i·sa·tion** (-ī-záysh'n ‖ *U.S.* -i-) *n.*

mo·tor·ist (mótərist) *n.* One who drives a car.

mo·tor·man (mótər-mən) *n., pl.* **-men** (-mən, -men). *Chiefly U.S.* One who drives an electrically powered train (e.g. a subway).

motor neurone *n.* A nerve cell that conveys impulses away from the brain and spinal cord to muscles or other effector organs. Also *U.S.* "motoneurone".

motor neurone disease *n.* A disease that causes progressive muscular atrophy.

motor scooter *n.* A two-wheeled vehicle with small wheels and a low-powered enclosed engine geared to the rear wheel.

motor vehicle *n.* Any self-propelled, wheeled conveyance that does not run on rails, especially one driven by an internal-combustion engine.

mo·tor·way (mótər-way) *n. British.* A main road designed for fast-moving traffic, usually having two or three lanes in each direction, and uninterrupted by junctions or traffic lights.

Mo·town (mó-town) *n. Sometimes small* **m.** A style of black popular music. [After the trade name of a U.S. record company that specialised in this style from Detroit ("Motortown"), Michigan.]

motte (mot) *n.* A mound on which a castle or fortification is or was sited. [Middle English, from Old French *mote*, mound, MOAT.]

M.O.T. test *n. British.* An annual test of roadworthiness for motor vehicles over a certain age, usually conducted by garages. Also called "M.O.T.". [Ministry of Transport.]

mot·tle (mótt'l) *tr.v.* **-tled, -tling, -tles.** To cover (a surface) with spots or streaks of different shades or colours.
~*n.* **1.** A spot of colour or shading contrasting with the rest of the

surface on which it is found. **2.** A variegated pattern, as on marble. [Probably back-formation from MOTLEY.]

mot·to (móttō) *n., pl.* **-toes** or **-tos. 1.** A brief sentence, phrase, or single word used to express a principle, goal, or ideal, especially when accompanying a coat of arms. **2.** A maxim adopted as a guide to one's conduct. **3.** A quotation prefacing a book or chapter. **4.** A briefly stated sentiment of appropriate character inscribed on or attached to an object. **5.** A proverb or joke contained inside a paper cracker. **6.** *Music.* A recurring theme or motif. —See Synonyms at **saying.** [Italian, "a word", from Gallo-Roman *mottum* (unattested), a sound uttered, from Latin *muttum*, a mutter, grunt, from *muttīre*, to mutter.]

mo·tu pro·pri·o (mótō próprì-ō) *n., pl.* **motu proprios.** An administrative papal bull. [Latin, of (our) own accord.]

moue (moō) *n.* A sulky or disdainful expression; a pout. [French, from Old French, from Germanic, akin to Middle Dutch *mouwe*, pouting lip.]

mou·flon, mouf·flon (moō-flon) *n., pl.* **-flons** or collectively **mou·flon.** A wild sheep, *Ovis musimon,* of Sardinia and Corsica. [French, from Italian *muflone,* from Vulgar Latin *mufro†,* sheep.]

moujik. Variant of **muzhik.**

mou·lage (moō-lä́azh) *n.* **1.** The making of a mould from a mark, such as a footprint, especially for identification. **2.** A mould of this kind. [French, from Old French, from *mouler,* to mould, from *moule, modle,* a mould, from Latin *modulus,* diminutive of *modus,* a measure, manner.]

mould¹, *U.S.* **mold** (mōld) *n.* **1.** A form or matrix for shaping a fluid or plastic substance: *a jelly mould.* **2.** A frame or model around or on which something is formed or shaped. **3.** Something that is made in or shaped on a mould. **4.** The pattern of a mould. **5.** General shape or form: *the oval mould of her face.* **6.** Distinctive shape, character, or type: *in the mould of her ancestors; break the mould of confrontationist politics.* **7.** *Architecture.* A moulding.
~*tr.v.* **moulded, moulding, moulds. 1.** To shape in or on a mould. **2.** To form into a desired shape. **3.** To guide or determine the growth or development of; influence: *mould public opinion.* **4.** To make a mould of or from (sand, for example) prior to casting metal. [Middle English, probably from Old French *modle,* from Latin *modulus,* MODULE.] —**mould·a·bil·i·ty** (mōldə-bílləti) *n.* —**mould·a·ble** *adj.* —**moul·der** *n.*

mould², *U.S.* **mold** *n.* **1.** A rough, variously coloured coating that forms on decaying food, for example, owing to the action of saprophytic fungi. **2.** Any fungus that causes this growth. Compare **mildew.**
~*v.* **moulded, moulding, moulds.** —*intr.* To become mouldy. —*tr.* To cause to become mouldy. [Middle English, probably from obsolete adjective *mould,* past participle of *moul,* to become mouldy, from Old Norse *mugla* (unattested).]

mould³, *U.S.* **mold** *n.* **1.** Loose, friable soil that is rich in humus. **2.** *Poetic.* **a.** The earth; the ground. **b.** The earth of the grave, or the grave itself. [Middle English, Old English *molde,* from Germanic *moldō* (unattested), akin to MEAL.]

mould·board, *U.S.* **mold·board** (mōld-bawrd ‖ -bōrd) *n.* The curved plate of a plough that turns over the furrow.

mould·er, *U.S.* **mold·er** (mōldər) *v.* **-ered, -ering, -ers.** —*intr.* To become dust gradually, by natural decay; crumble. Often used with *away.* —*tr.* To cause to decay or crumble. Often used with *away.* See Synonyms at **decay.** [Perhaps from MOULD (soil).]

mould·ing, *U.S.* **mold·ing** (mōlding) *n.* **1.** *Architecture.* A strip of stone, wood, plaster, or other material, with a shaped section, used as an embellishment on a building, wall, or other surface. Also called "mould". **2.** An object that has been moulded.

moulding board *n.* A board on which dough is kneaded.

mould·y, *U.S.* **mold·y** (mōldi) *adj.* **-ier, -iest. 1.** Covered with or containing mould: *mouldy bread.* **2.** Musty or stale, as from age or decay. **3.** *Slang.* **a.** Unfair. **b.** Boring. **c.** Of poor quality; second-rate. —**mould·i·ness** *n.*

mould·y·warp (mōldi-wawrp) *n.* Also **mold·warp** (mōld-wawrp). *Archaic & Regional.* A mole. [Middle English *moldwarp,* Old English *moldweorp,* "earth-thrower" : MOULD (soil) + *weorpan,* to throw.]

mou·lin (moōlin, moō-láN) *n.* A vertical shaft in a glacier, kept open by falling water and rock debris. [French, "mill", from Old French, from Late Latin *molīnum,* from Latin *molīnus,* of a mill, from *mola,* mill, millstone.]

moult, *U.S.* **molt** (mōlt ‖ molt) *v.* **moulted, moulting, moults.** —*intr.* To shed part or all of an outer covering, such as feathers, fur, or skin, which is replaced periodically by a new growth. —*tr.* To shed or cast off by moulting.
~*n.* **1.** The process of moulting, which occurs in certain mammals, birds, and reptiles. See **ecdysis. 2.** The material cast off during moulting. [Middle English *moute,* Old English *mutian* (unattested), ultimately from Latin *mutāre,* to change; present spelling influenced by -*lt* words such as *fault.*] —**moult·er** *n.*

mound¹ (mownd) *n.* **1.** A pile of earth, gravel, sand, rocks, or debris heaped for protection or concealment. **2.** A natural elevation, such as a small hill. **3.** Any raised mass, as of hay. **4.** *Archaeology.* A **barrow** *(see).* **5.** In baseball, the small elevation where the pitcher stands when pitching.
~*tr.v.* **mounded, mounding, mounds. 1.** To fortify or conceal with a mound. **2.** To heap in a mound. [Originally "enclosing hedge or fence", perhaps from Dutch *mond,* protection, or Old Norse *mund.*]

mound² *n. Heraldry.* An orb or ball of gold representing the earth.

[Middle English, from Old French *monde*, from Latin *mundus*, world.]

Mound Builder *n.* A member of one of the prehistoric North American Indian peoples who built burial and effigy mounds, mainly in the Mississippi valley.

mound-builder (mównd-bíldər) *n.* A bird, the **megapode** (*see*).

mount[1] (mownt) *v.* **mounted, mounting, mounts.** —*tr.* **1.** To climb or ascend. **2.** To get up on; place oneself upon: *mount a horse.* **3.** To get up on in order to copulate. Used of male animals. **4.** To provide with a horse or horses for riding: *The stable mounted all the riders.* **5.** To prepare, place, or fix on or in an appropriate or convenient setting, as for display, study, or use: *mount pictures on cardboard.* **6.** To prepare for display, production, or public viewing: *mount a theatrical performance.* **7.** To place (a specimen) on a microscope slide in preparation for microscopical examination. **8.** *Military.* **a.** To set (guns) in position. **b.** To put in readiness and start to carry out: *mount an attack.* **c.** To be furnished with or carry: *The warship mounted ten guns.* **d.** To post (a guard): *mount sentries.* —*intr.v.* **1.** To go or move upwards. **2.** To get or climb up on a horse or vehicle. **3.** To increase, as in amount, degree, extent, intensity, or number. Often used with *up.* —See Synonyms at **rise.** ~*n.* **1. a.** A horse, other animal, or vehicle on which to ride. **b.** The opportunity to ride a horse, especially in a race. **2.** An object to which another is affixed, such as a piece of cardboard, or on which another is placed for accessibility, display, or use, such as a stamp hinge. **3.** A glass slide on which specimens are placed for microscopy. [Middle English *mounten*, from Old French *monter*, from Vulgar Latin *montáre* (unattested), "to climb a mountain", from Latin *mōns* (stem *mont-*), mountain.] —**mount·a·ble** *adj.* —**mount·ing·ly** *adv.*

mount[2] *n.* **1.** *Abbr.* **mt., Mt.** A mountain or hill. Used chiefly as part of a proper name or in poetry. **2.** In palmistry, any of the seven fleshy cushions around the edges of the palm of the hand. [Middle English *mont, munt*, from Old French *mont* and Old English *munt*, both from Latin *mōns* (stem *mont-*), mountain.]

moun·tain (mówn-tin, -tən || *West Indies also* múng-) *n. Abbr.* **mt., Mt., mtn. 1.** A natural elevation of the earth's surface having considerable mass, generally steep sides, and a height greater than that of a hill. **2. a.** A large heap: *a mountain of ironing.* **b.** A huge quantity. **3.** *Capital* **M.** The extreme revolutionary party of the French Revolution, so called because its members occupied the uppermost seats in the National Convention Hall in 1793. Preceded by *the.* [Middle English *mountaine*, from Old French *montaigne*, from Vulgar Latin *montánea* (unattested), from Latin *montánus*, mountainous, from *mōns* (stem *mont-*), mountain.] —**moun·tain** *adj.*

mountain ash *n.* **1.** Any of various deciduous trees of the genus *Sorbus*, such as *S. aucuparia*, the European mountain ash, having clusters of small white flowers and bright orange-red berries. This species is also called "rowan". **2.** Any of several Australian eucalyptus trees.

mountain devil *n.* A lizard, the **moloch** (*see*).

mountain dew *n. Chiefly U.S. Slang.* Illegally distilled spirits.

moun·tain·eer (mówn-tin-éer, -tən-) *n.* **1.** One who climbs mountains as a sport or hobby. **2.** An inhabitant of a mountainous area. ~*intr.v.* **mountaineered, -eering, -eers.** To climb mountains as a hobby or sport. —**moun·tain·eer·ing** *n.*

mountain goat *n.* Any wild goat of mountainous regions.

mountain laurel *n.* An evergreen shrub, *Kalmia latifolia*, of eastern North America, having leathery, poisonous leaves and clusters of pink or white flowers. Also called "calico bush".

mountain lion *n.* A **puma** (*see*).

moun·tain·ous (mówn-tin-əss, -tən-) *adj.* **1.** Of, pertaining to, or designating a region having many mountains. **2.** Of impressive size or height.

mountain ringlet *n.* Any of several brown butterflies of the genus *Erebia*, found in mountains and northern regions of Eurasia and North America.

mountain sheep *n.* Any wild sheep native to a mountainous area.

mountain sickness *n.* **Altitude sickness** (*see*).

Mountain Standard Time *n. Abbr.* **MST, M.S.T.** Local time in one of the standard time zones of North America, based on the 105th meridian west of Greenwich, seven hours behind Greenwich Mean Time.

Mount·bat·ten, Louis Alexander (mownt-bátt'n), born Prince Louis Alexander of Battenberg; also known as 1st Marquess of Milford Haven (1854–1921). British admiral and first sea lord (1912–14). He became a naturalised British subject when he joined the Royal Navy (1868), and married a granddaughter of Queen Victoria (1884). He subsequently gave up his German titles, changed his surname, and was created a marquess by George V.

Mountbatten of Burma, Louis, 1st Earl (1900–79). British naval officer, son of Prince Louis Mountbatten and great-grandson of Queen Victoria. In 1943 he was appointed Supreme Allied Commander in southeast Asia. He was made a viscount in 1946 and an earl in 1947, when he was appointed Viceroy of India, presiding over the transfer of power to independent India in that year. He stayed in India as Governor-General until 1948. From 1959 to 1965 he was chief of the United Kingdom Defence Staff. He was killed by the Provisional I.R.A. when a bomb detonated by remote control exploded on his yacht.

moun·te·bank (mównti-bangk) *n.* **1.** A hawker of quack medicines and nostrums who attracts customers with stories, jokes, or tricks. **2.** Any charlatan or trickster. [Italian *montambanco, montimbanco,*

"one who climbs on a bench" : *montare,* to mount, (see **mount**[1]) + *in,* in, on, from Latin + *banco, banca,* bench.]

mount·ed (mówntid) *adj.* **1.** Seated upon or riding on a horse, bicycle, or other means of conveyance. **2.** Serving on horseback, or equipped with a horse or horses: *a mounted policeman.* **3.** Fitted into or set in a backing or support: *mounted photographs.*

mount·ing (mównting) *n.* **1.** The act of rising or getting up on something. **2.** That which provides a backing, support, or setting for something else: *a mounting for a gem; a telescope mounting.*

mounting block *n.* A block of stone used as an aid in mounting a horse.

Mount Rush·more National Memorial (rúsh-mawr || -mōr). A tract in the Black Hills, South Dakota, United States. It includes the northeastern side of Mount Rushmore, from which Gutzon Borglum and his son carved (1927–41) gigantic busts of Presidents Washington, Jefferson, Lincoln, and Theodore Roosevelt.

Mount·y, Mount·ie (mównti) *n., pl.* **-ies.** *Informal.* A Royal Canadian Mounted Policeman.

mourn (morn, *rarely* moorn || mōrn) *v.* **mourned, mourning, mourns.** —*intr.* **1.** To express or feel grief or sorrow, especially for someone who has died. **2.** To express public grief for a death by conventional signs; be in mourning. —*tr.* **1.** To feel grief for (a dead person, for example). **b.** To show public signs of grief for (a dead person, for example). **2.** To feel or express regret over; lament: *mourned the abolition of the death penalty.* [Middle English *mournen,* Old English *murnan.*]

Mourne Mountains (morn || mōrn). Mountain range in County Down, southeast Ulster. Slieve Donard (852 metres; 2,796 feet) is the highest point in the province.

mourn·er (mórnər || mōrnər) *n.* One who mourns, especially: **1.** A person attending a funeral out of grief or respect. **2.** Formerly, a person hired to attend a funeral.

mourn·ful (mórn-f'l || mōrn-) *adj.* **1.** Feeling or expressing sorrow or grief. **2.** Arousing or suggesting sorrow or grief: *the mournful sound of the train whistle.* —See Synonyms at **glum.** —**mourn·ful·ly** *adv.* —**mourn·ful·ness** *n.*

mourn·ing (mórn-ing, moorn- || mōrn-) *n.* **1.** The actions or expressions of one who has suffered a bereavement. **2.** The symbols or conventional outward signs of grief for the dead. **3.** The period during which a death is mourned. —**in mourning. 1.** Wearing clothes conventionally expressive of mourning, such as a black tie or armband, or entirely black clothes. **2.** Abiding by appropriate conduct during a period of mourning: *I can't remarry yet—I'm still in mourning for my last husband.* —**mourn·ing·ly** *adv.*

mourning cloak *n. U.S.* The **Camberwell beauty** (*see*).

mourning dove *n.* A wild dove, *Zenaidura macroura,* of North America, noted for its plaintive call and its ability to survive in deserts.

mouse (mowss) *n., pl.* **mice** (mīss). **1. a.** Any of numerous small rodents of the families Muridae and Cricetidae, such as the **house mouse** or the **harvest mouse** (*both of which see*), characteristically having a long, naked or almost hairless tail. **b.** Any of various similar or related animals, such as the **jumping mouse** or the **pocket mouse** (*both of which see*). **2.** *Informal.* **a.** A cowardly or timid person. **b.** *Chiefly U.S.* An affectionate term for a little girl or young woman. **3.** *Slang.* A black eye. **4.** A mousing on a hook. **5.** A **hair mouse** (*see*). **6.** A computer accessory that causes the cursor of a visual display unit to move anywhere on the screen. ~*intr.v.* (*usually* mouz) **moused, mousing, mouses. 1.** To hunt, stalk, or catch mice. **2.** To search furtively for something; prowl. Often used with *about.* [Mouse, mice; Middle English *mous, mys,* Old English *mūs, mȳs.*]

mouse deer *n.* A **chevrotain** (*see*).

mouse-ear (mówss-eer) *n.* Any of various weedy plants of the genus *Cerastium,* having small white flowers. Also called "mouse-ear chickweed".

mous·er (mówzər, mów-sər) *n.* An animal that catches mice, especially a cat.

mouse-tail (mówss-tayl) *n.* Any plant of the genus *Myosurus,* especially *M. minimus,* having a tail-like flower spike.

mouse-trap (mówss-trap) *n.* **1.** A trap for catching mice. **2.** *British. Informal.* Ordinary, low-priced cheese. [Sense 2, as used in such traps.]

mous·ing (mówzing) *n. Nautical.* **1.** A binding around the point and shank of a hook to prevent it from slipping from an eye. **2.** A metal shackle used for the same purpose. [From its mouselike shape.]

mous·sa·ka, mous·a·ka (moō-saáka; *Greek* -sa-káa) *n.* A Greek dish consisting of minced meat, aubergines, and tomatoes covered in cheese sauce. [Greek or Turkish.]

mousse (moōss) *n.* **1.** Any of various chilled desserts made with cream, separated and whipped eggs or gelatine, and flavouring. **2.** A similar dish made from a purée of meat, fish, or shellfish with whipped cream. [French *mousse†*, "froth".]

mousse·line (moōss-léen) *n.* A fine cotton or silk fabric originally made in Mosul, Iraq. [French, MUSLIN.]

Moussorgsky. See **Mussorgsky.**

mous·tache, *U.S.* **mus·tache** (mə-staásh || -stásh, -stósh, *U.S. also* mústash) *n.* **1.** *Sometimes plural.* The hair growing on the upper lip, especially when it is cultivated and groomed. **2.** Something similar to a moustache in appearance and position, especially: **a.** A group of bristles or hairs around the mouth of an animal. **b.** Distinctive colouring or feathers near the beak of a bird. [French, from Italian *mostaccio,* from Greek *mustax* (stem *mustak-*).]

Mous·te·ri·an, Mous·tie·ri·an (mōō-stéer-i-ən) *adj. Archaeology.* Designating or belonging to a Middle Palaeolithic culture following the Acheulian, characterised by the use of flint implements. [French *moustérien, moustiérien,* from *Le Moustier,* village in southwestern France near which archaeological specimens were found.]

mous·y, mous·ey (mów-si || -zi) *adj.* **-ier, -iest. 1.** Of a dull, pale brown colour. Said of hair. **2.** Resembling a mouse in appearance: *a mousy face.* **3.** Shy; retiring; unassertive.

mouth (mowth) *n., pl.* **mouths** (mowthz). **1.** *Anatomy.* **a.** The body opening through which an animal takes in food; the oral cavity. **b.** The system of related organs including the lips, teeth, tongue, and associated parts, with which food is chewed and swallowed and sounds and speech are articulated. **2.** The part of the lips visible on the human face. **3.** A person viewed as a consumer of food: *I've got three mouths to feed at home.* **4.** A pout, grimace, or similar expression. **5. a.** The capacity of speech; a propensity for speaking: *"A fool's mouth is his destruction."* (Proverbs 18:7). **b.** A manner of speech, especially when considered as inappropriate: *a foul mouth.* **c.** *Informal.* Impudent or vulgar talk. **6.** The part of the inner lip of a horse, donkey, or similar animal on which the bit presses, and varying in sensitivity to the bit: *a hard mouth.* **7.** A natural opening, such as the part of a stream or river that empties into a larger body of water, or the entrance to a harbour, canyon, valley, or cave. **8.** The opening through which any container is filled or emptied. **9.** An opening in tools and devices whose function is to hold or grip. **10. a.** An opening in the pipe of an organ. **b.** The opening in the mouthpiece of a flute across which the player blows. **—down in the mouth.** *Informal.* Crestfallen; unhappy. **—give mouth.** To bark. Used of a dog. **—shoot (one's) mouth off.** To speak forcibly but unreliably on a particular subject or issue. **—shut (one's) mouth.** *Informal.* To desist from speaking. Usually used in the imperative.

~*v.* (mouth). **mouthed, mouthing, mouths.** *—tr.* **1.** To utter in a meaninglessly declamatory manner: *mouthing empty compliments.* **2.** To put, take, or move around in the mouth. **3.** To train the mouth of (a horse). *—intr.* **1.** To orate affectedly; declaim; rant. **2.** To grimace. [Middle English *mouth,* Old English *mūth.*]

mouth·brood·er (mówth-brōōdər) *n.* Also **mouth·breed·er** (-breedər). Any of various African cichlid fishes that carry their eggs and young in the mouth.

mouth·ful (moówthfōōl) *n., pl.* **mouthfuls. 1.** The amount of food or other material that can be placed or held in the mouth at one time. **2.** A small amount to be tasted or eaten. **3.** *Informal.* Anything, such as a long name, that is complicated or difficult to pronounce.

mouth organ *n.* Either of two musical instruments, a **harmonica** or a **panpipe** *(both of which see).*

mouth-part, mouth·part (mówth-paart) *n.* Any of the appendages situated around the mouth in arthropods and adapted for feeding; for example, the maxillae and mandibles.

mouth·piece (mówth-peess) *n.* **1.** A part, as of a musical instrument or a telephone, that functions in or near the mouth. **2.** A protective rubber device worn over the teeth by boxers; a gumshield. **3.** *Informal.* One through whom views are expressed, such as a spokesman or newspaper. **4.** *Chiefly U.S. Slang.* A lawyer.

mouth-to-mouth (mówth-tə-mówth) *adj.* Designating a method of artificial respiration in which air is blown forcefully into the lungs of the patient by one whose mouth is placed firmly over the patient's mouth: *mouth-to-mouth resuscitation.*

mouth·wash (mówth-wosh || -wawsh) *n.* An aqueous solution containing an antiseptic or astringent, used for gargling and for cleansing the mouth and teeth.

mouth-wat·er·ing (mówth-wawtəring) *adj.* Appetising; delicious.

mouth·y (mów-thi, -thi) *adj.* **-ier, -iest.** Given to ranting; grandiloquent; bombastic. **—mouth·i·ly** *adv.* **—mouth·i·ness** *n.*

mou·ton (mōōton) *n.* Sheepskin sheared and processed to resemble beaver or seal, and used for garments. [French, "sheep", from Old French *mo(u)ton,* MUTTON.]

mou·ton·née (mōō-to-nay, -tə-, -náy) *adj.* Also **mou·ton·néed** (-náyd). *Geology.* Rounded by glacial action to a shape likened to a sheep's back. Said of a rock formation. See **roche moutonnée.** [French, from *mouton,* sheep.]

mov·a·ble, move·a·ble (mōōvə-b'l) *adj.* **1.** Capable of being moved. **2.** Varying in date from year to year: *a movable holiday.* **3.** *Law.* Of or pertaining to personal property that can be moved, as opposed to real property such as land. **4.** *Printing.* Cast with each character on a separate piece of type.

~*n.* *Usually plural.* **1.** Something that can be moved, especially furniture, as opposed to permanent fixtures. **2.** *Law.* Personal property, as distinguished from real property such as land. **—mov·a·bil·i·ty** (-bíllәti), **mov·a·ble·ness** *n.* **—mov·a·bly** *adv.*

Usage: *Movable* and *mobile* are usually not interchangeable. *Movable* denotes something that has the capability of being moved, usually by some external force (the furniture in a room is *movable*); *mobile* denotes something that can move, usually on account of its own internal characteristics (as with a *mobile crane* or *mobile library*). Occasionally, something may be referred to by either word (as when the tongue is said to be a very *movable* or *mobile* organ), and here the different implications reflect the above distinction.

movable feast *n.* **1.** A religious feast, such as Easter, which varies in date from year to year. **2.** Any event which occurs erratically. Used humorously: *The fire drill is something of a movable feast.*

move (mōōv) *v.* **moved, moving, moves.** *—intr.* **1.** To change in position from one point to another. **2.** To march, as an army or procession does. **3.** To progress in sequence, as in the development of a literary or musical composition. **4.** To follow some specified course: *The Earth moves in orbit around the Sun.* **5. a.** To be transferred from one position to another in a board game. **b.** To transfer a piece in a board game. **6.** To change to or settle in a new place of residence or business. Often used with *in, out,* or *away.* **7.** To be disposed of commercially: *Furs move slowly in summer.* **8.** To change posture or position; stir. **9.** To be disturbed or displaced: *The foliage moved in the breeze; When you kissed me, the earth moved!* **10.** To be put into motion or to turn according to a prescribed motion. Used of machinery. **11.** *Informal.* **a.** To hum with activity; be busy. **b.** To become interesting and exciting. **12.** To initiate some action: *Wait for the election results before we move.* **13. a.** To behave, progress, or proceed as specified: *move towards a solution.* **b.** To change: *The situation hasn't moved.* **14.** To live or be active in a specified environment: *move in diplomatic circles.* **15.** To make a legal submission or a formal motion in parliamentary procedure: *move for an adjournment.* **16.** To evacuate; void. Used of the bowels. *—tr.* **1. a.** To change the place of; shift; remove; displace. **b.** To change the position of: *move one's head.* **c.** To cause to change position: *moved the spectators on.* **d.** To change the course of: *moved the discussion on to more general topics.* **2.** To dislodge from a fixed point of view, especially by persuasion. **3.** To prompt (someone) to some action; actuate: *She was moved to intercede on his behalf.* **4.** To set or maintain in motion. **5.** To set astir; agitate; shake: *The wind moved the blossoms.* **6.** To excite or provoke to the expression of some feeling: *moved to tears.* **7.** To affect deeply. **8.** *Archaic.* To arouse (someone's feelings). **9.** To propose or request in formal parliamentary procedure: *move an adjournment.* **10.** To cause (the bowels) to evacuate. —See Synonyms at **affect.**

~*n.* **1.** An act of moving: *Nobody dared make a move.* **2.** A change of residence or place of business. **3.** In board games: **a.** An act of transferring a piece from one position to another. **b.** The prescribed manner in which a piece may be manoeuvred. **c.** A player's turn to manoeuvre a piece. **4.** One of a series of calculated actions undertaken to achieve some end. —See Synonyms at **affect. —get a move on.** *Informal.* To get started; get going; hurry up. Usually used in the imperative. **—on the move. 1.** In the process of moving about; travelling. **2.** Making progress; advancing; changing. [Middle English *moven,* from Anglo-French *mover,* variant of Old French *moveir,* from Latin *movēre,* to move.]

move·ment (mōōvmənt) *n.* **1. a.** The act or an instance of moving; a change in position. **b.** *Military.* A change in the location of troops, ships, or aircraft for tactical or strategic purposes; a manoeuvre. **2. a.** The activities of a group of people to achieve a specific goal: *the Peace movement.* **b.** A group of people associated through some common aim: *the Labour movement.* **c.** A tendency or trend. **3.** Activity, especially: **a.** Commercial trading. **b.** A change in price of a security or commodity. **4. a.** An evacuation of the bowels. **b.** The faeces so evacuated. **5.** *Fine Arts.* The impression or illusion of motion. **6.** The progression of events in the development of a literary plot. **7.** The rhythmical or metrical structure of a poetic composition. **8.** *Music.* A self-contained component section of a composition. **9.** A mechanism that produces or transmits motion, as do the works of a watch. [Middle English, from Old French, from Medieval Latin *movimentum,* from Latin *movēre,* to move.]

mov·er (mōōvər) *n.* **1.** One that moves: *a beautiful mover on the dance floor.* **2.** One who proposes a motion in a debate.

mov·ie (mōōvi) *n.* *Chiefly U.S. Informal.* **1.** A cinematic film. **2.** A cinema. **3.** *Plural.* **a.** A showing of a film. Preceded by *the.* **b.** The film industry. [Shortened from MOVING PICTURE.]

mov·ing (mōōving) *adj.* **1.** Changing or capable of changing position. **2.** Causing or producing motion. **3.** Pertaining to house or furniture removals: *moving day.* **4.** Affecting the emotions, especially those of sympathy and sorrow: *a moving tale.* **—mov·ing·ly** *adv.* **—mov·ing·ness** *n.*

Synonyms: *moving, stirring, poignant, touching, pathetic, affecting.*

moving average *n.* A form of statistical average obtained by replacing one item in the numerator but keeping the denominator unchanged. It therefore has several successive values.

moving pavement *n.* A device similar to an escalator but running horizontally, used, for example, at airports to help those carrying heavy luggage. Also called "travelator", "walkway".

moving picture *n. U.S.* A cinematic film.

moving staircase *n.* An **escalator** *(see).*

mow[1] (mō) *v.* **mowed, mowed** or **mown** (mōn || mṓ-ən), **mowing, mows.** *—tr.* **1.** To cut down (crops, grass, or similar growth) with a scythe or a mechanical device such as a lawn mower or mowing machine. **2.** To cut such growth from: *mow the lawn.* *—intr.* To mow crops or grass, for example. **—mow down.** To fell in great numbers, as in battle: *mown down by the enemy's guns.* [Mow, mown; Middle English *mowen, mowen,* Old English *māwan, māwen,* from Germanic.] **—mow·er** (mṓ-ər) *n.*

Usage: *Mowed* is the traditionally recommended past participle from, but *mown* is frequently heard in British English (*I have mown the lawn*), less often in American English. *Mown* is the standard form when used before a noun (*A mown lawn looks very nice*) and in compounds (*new-mown*).

mow[2] *n.* **1.** A place for storing hay or crops. **2.** Feed so stored. [Middle English *mough, mow,* stack of hay, Old English *mūga,*

mŭha, mŭwa, from Scandinavian; akin to Old Norse *mŭgi,* crowd.]
mow³ *Archaic.* A grimace.
~*intr.v.* **mowed, mowing, mows.** *Archaic.* To grimace. Used chiefly in the phrase *mop and mow.* [Middle English *mouwe,* from old French. See **moue.**]
mowing machine *n.* A machine for cutting hay, grass, or crops.
mox·i·bus·tion (mŏksi-bŭs-chən) *n.* An Asian method of treating skin irritation and various other disorders by placing down from the leaves of *Artemisia moxa* on the skin and igniting it. [Blend of *(Artemisia)* moxa + combustion.]
Mo·zam·bique, Republic of (mŏ-zəm-beĕk, -zam-). *Portuguese* **Mo·çam·bi·que** (mōō-sum-beĕkə). Formerly **Portuguese East Africa.** Country of Southeast Africa, consisting in the centre and south of a broad coastal plain crossed by the Zambezi, Save, and Limpopo rivers, and plateaux and highlands elsewhere. Some 80 per cent of the people are subsistence farmers producing cassava and maize, but the country is the world's leading exporter of cashew nuts. Transit trade is a vital economic factor, since Mozambique acts as a port for South Africa and Congo (Dem. Rep.) and landlocked Swaziland, Zambia, Malawi, and Zimbabwe. Portuguese colonisation began in 1505. After World War II, African nationalists demanded independence, and set up the Mozambique Liberation Front (Frelimo), which began guerrilla activity in 1964. Led by Samora Machel, it achieved independence as a Marxist one-party state in 1975. Until 1991, there was civil war between the government and a right-wing group, Renamo. Area, 799 380 square kilometres (308,641 square miles). Population, 17,800,000. Capital, Maputo (formerly Lourenço Marques). — **Mo·zam·biqu·an** *n. & adj.*
Mozambique Current *n.* A warm ocean current flowing southwards down the east coast of Southern Africa.
Moz·ar·ab (mŏ-zárrəb) *n.* A member of a group of Spanish Christians who practised a modified form of their religion under the Muslims. [Spanish *Mozárabe,* from Arabic *Musta'rib,* "a would-be Arab", from *'arab,* ARAB.] —**Moz·ar·a·bic** *adj.*
Mo·zart (mŏt-saart), **Wolfgang Amadeus** (1756–91). Austrian composer, one of the most highly gifted and prolific composers in history. Although he began as a child prodigy, both as performer and composer, he had irregular patronage and was often destitute. He wrote most of his greatest works in the last five years of his short life, including his last three symphonies (1788) and the operas *Don Giovanni* (1787) and *Die Zauberflöte* (*The Magic Flute,* 1791). —**Mo·zart·i·an, Mozart·e·an** (mŏt-sárti-ən) *adj. & n.*
mo·zet·ta, Moz·zet·ta (mō-zéttə, mə-‖ *Italian* mo-tséttə) *n.* Roman Catholic Church. A short, hooded cape worn by bishops. [Italian, short for *almozzetta,* irregular diminutive formed from Medieval Latin *almŭtia,* ALMUCE.]
moz·za·rel·la (mótsə-réllə) *n.* A soft, white Italian curd cheese, formerly made from buffalo milk and often used melted in cookery. [Italian, diminutive of *mozza,* "slice", (sliced) cheese, from *mozzare,*

MOZAMBIQUE

to cut off, perhaps from Vulgar Latin *mutiāre* (unattested), from Latin *mutilāre,* to mutilate, cut up, from *mutilus,* cut short.]
mp, m.p. **1.** melting point. **2.** *Music.* mezzo-piano.
MP military police; military policeman
M.P. **1.** Member of Parliament. **2.** Metropolitan Police. **3.** military police; military policeman. **4.** mounted police; mounted policeman.
mpg, m.p.g. miles per gallon.
mph, m.p.h. miles per hour.
M. Phil, M.Ph. Master of Philosophy.
Mpumalanga (m-pŏŏ-maá-lang-ə). New province of South Africa created in 1994 by subdivision of the former Transvaal. Capital: Nelspruit.
Mr., Mr (místər) *n., pl.* **Messrs** (méssərz). A title of courtesy used when speaking to or of a man, preceding the man's surname or office. [Abbreviation of **Mister.**]
M.R. **1.** Master of the Rolls. **2.** motivational research.
M.R.A., MRA Moral Rearmament.
M.R.C. Medical Research Council.
MRI magnetic resonance imaging.
mRNA. messenger RNA.
M.R.Pharm. Member of the Royal Pharmaceutical Society.
Mrs., Mrs (míssiz) *n., pl.* **Mrs.** A title of courtesy used in writing to or of a married woman, preceding the woman's surname or office. [Abbreviation of **mistress.**]
ms **1.** manuscript. **2.** millisecond.
MS **1.** MS., ms, ms. manuscript. **2.** multiple sclerosis.
Ms, Ms. (miz, məz) *n., pl.* **Mses** or **Mss.** A title of courtesy used before a woman's surname or before her first name and surname, without regard to her marital status. See Usage note at **Miss.** [Coined to combine MISS and MRS.]
M.S. **1.** Master of Surgery. **2.** memorial sacrum.
M.Sc. Master of Science.
MSG monosodium glutamate.
m.s.l., M.S.L. mean sea level.
mss, MSS, mss., MSS. manuscripts.
MST, M.S.T. Mountain Standard Time.
Mt(s)., mt(s) mount(s); mountain(s).
m.t., M.T. metric ton.
M.T.B., MTB *British.* motor torpedo boat.
M.Tech. Master of Technology.
mtg. **1.** meeting. **2.** mortgage.
mtn. mountain.
mu (mew ‖ mōō) *n.* The 12th letter in the Greek alphabet, written M, μ. Transliterated in English as *M, m.*
Mu·bar·ak (mōō-báarək), **Muhammad Hosni** (1928–). Egyptian air force officer and politician. He was Vice-President of Egypt 1975–81, and appointed president in 1981. He was twice re-elected uncontested (1987, 1993). Survived an assassination attempt (1995).
muc-. Variant of **muco-.**
much (much) *adj.* **more, most.** Great in quantity, degree, or extent: *Was there much rain?* —**a bit much.** *Informal.* Difficult to accept. ~*pron.* **1.** A large quantity or amount. **2.** Anything remarkable or important: *As a leader, she is not much.* —**make much of.** To pay great attention to. —**think much of.** To esteem highly. ~*adv.* **more** (mor ‖ mōr), **most** (mōst). **1.** To a great degree; to a large extent: *much impressed.* Often used in combination: *much-maligned.* **2.** Often. Used especially in negative sentences: *She doesn't come much these days.* **3.** Just about; almost: *much the same.* —**as much.** Whatever is indicated or implied: *I expected as much.* [Middle English *muche, miche,* shortened from *muchel, michel,* Old English *mycel, micel,* great, large, greatly, much.]
much·ness (múch-nəss, -niss) *n.* **1.** Magnitude; bulk. **2.** Greatness in quantity, number, or degree. —**much of a muchness.** *British.* Barely distinguishable; showing no great variation.
mu·cic acid (méw-sik) *n.* An organic acid, HOOC(CHOH)₄COOH, often derived from milk sugar. [From MUCUS.]
mu·ci·lage (méwssi-lij) *n.* **1.** A sticky substance used as an adhesive. **2.** A gummy substance obtained from plants. [Middle English *muscilage,* from Old French *mucilage,* from Late Latin *mūcilāgō,* musty juice, from Latin *mūcus,* MUCUS.] —**mu·ci·lag·i·nous** *adj.*
mu·cin (méw-sin) *n.* Any of a group of glycoproteins produced by mucous membranes. [MUC(O)- + -IN.]
muck (muk) *n.* **1.** A moist, sticky mixture, especially of mud or filth. **2.** Moist animal dung, especially when mixed with decayed vegetable matter and used as a fertiliser; manure. **3.** Dark, fertile soil containing putrid vegetable matter. **4.** Anything regarded as inferior, filthy, or disgusting. **5.** Earth, rocks, or clay excavated in mining. —**make a muck of.** *Informal.* To botch or mismanage. ~*tr.v.* **mucked, mucking, mucks.** **1.** To fertilise with manure or compost. **2.** *Informal.* To soil or make dirty with or as if with muck. **3. a.** To remove muck or dirt from (a mine or site). **b.** To remove muck from (a stable, for example). Used with *out.* —**muck about.** *Informal.* **1.** To behave badly or in a silly way. **2.** To potter about; do nothing in particular. **3.** To procrastinate. **4.** To cause inconvenience to. —**muck in.** *British Informal.* To participate in a task; do one's share. —**muck up.** *Informal.* **1.** To make dirty or untidy. **2.** To mismanage or interfere with (a plan or project). [Middle English *muk,* from Old Norse *mykr.*] —**muck·i·ly** *adv.* —**muck·y** *adj.*
muck·a·muck (múckə-muck) *n.* Also **muck·et·y·muck** (múckəti-). *U.S. Slang.* A self-important person. Also **"high mucka-muck."**
muck·er (múckər) *n.* **1.** A person who moves waste material in a mine. **2.** *British Slang.* A heavy fall. **3.** *British Slang.* A friend. **4.** *U.S. Slang.* A coarse, vulgar person.

muckle. Variant of **mickle**.

muck·rake (múck-rayk) *intr.v.* **-raked, -raking, -rakes.** To search for and expose scandalous conduct, especially personal, political, or commercial misconduct in public affairs, usually in a sensational manner.
~*n.* A rake used for gathering and spreading muck. [Back-formation from *muckraker,* used in 1906 by Theodore Roosevelt in allusion to the "man with a Muck-rake" in Bunyan's *Pilgrim's Progress.*] —**muck·rak·er** *n.*

muck sweat, muck·sweat (múk-swét, -swet) *n. British Informal.* A state of profuse sweating. [MUCK (soil) + SWEAT.]

muco-, muc– *comb. form.* Indicates mucus or something pertaining to the mucous membrane; for example, **mucoprotein, mucin.** [Latin *mūcus.*]

mu·coid (méw-koyd) *n.* Any of a group of glycoproteins similar to the mucins and found in connective tissue. [MUC(O)- + -OID.] —**mu·coid, mu·coi·dal** (mew-kóyd'l) *adj.*

mu·co·pol·y·sac·cha·ride (méwko-pólli-sácka-rīd) *n.* Any of the polysaccharides that form chemical bonds with water to produce mucilaginous and lubricating fluids and which contain sugar derivatives such as amino acids.

mu·co·pro·tein (méwko-prō-teen, -tee-in) *n.* Any of a group of organic compounds, such as the mucins, that contain proteins and mucopolysaccharides.

mu·co·sa (mew-kō̆-sə, -zə) *n., pl.* **-sae** (-see, -zee) or **-sas.** A mucous membrane. [New Latin *mūcōsa (membrana),* from *mūcōsus,* MUCOUS.] —**mu·co·sal** *adj.*

mu·cous (méw-kəss) *adj.* Also **mu·cose** (-kōss, -kōz). **1.** Producing or secreting mucus. **2.** Pertaining to, consisting of, or resembling mucus. [Latin *mūcōsus,* from *mūcus,* MUCUS.]

mucous membrane *n.* The membrane lining all bodily channels that communicate with the air, such as the respiratory and alimentary tracts, the glands of which secrete mucus.

mu·cro (méwkrō) *n., pl.* **mucrones** (mew-krōneez). *Biology.* A sharp tip of certain plant and animal organs. [New Latin, from Latin *mucrō†,* a sharp point, sword's point.]

mu·cro·nate (méwkrə-nət, -nit, -nayt) *adj. Biology.* Having a mucro. [Latin *mucronātus,* from *mucrō,* a point, MUCRO.] —**mu·cro·na·tion** (-náysh'n) *n.*

mu·cus (méwkəss) *n.* The viscous suspension of mucin, water, cells, and inorganic salts secreted as a protective, lubricant coating by glands in the mucous membrane, or by the external body surface of many animals. [Latin *mūcus, muccus.*]

mud (mud) *n.* **1.** Wet, sticky, soft earth. **2.** *Informal.* Slanderous or defamatory charges: *threw mud at her opponents.* **3. a.** That which is degrading: *My name was dragged in the mud.* **b.** *Informal.* That which is disreputable: *Her name was mud.* —**clear as mud.** Very unclear; confusing.
~*tr.v.* **mudded, mudding, muds.** To soil or bury with or as if with mud. [Middle English *mudde, mode†.*]

mud bath *n.* **1.** An immersion in heated mud, usually rich in supposedly medicinal minerals, for the purpose of curing certain ailments such as rheumatism. **2.** A muddy event or experience, such as a game of Rugby football played in the rain.

mud dauber *n.* Any of several wasps, including those of the genus *Sceliphron,* having long hind legs and a slender abdomen terminating in a bulb. The female lays eggs in paralysed insect larvae, which are placed in a nest of mud.

mud·dle (múdd'l) *v.* **-dled, -dling, -dles.** —*tr.* **1.** To mix confusedly; jumble: *muddled up the two names.* **2.** To mix up (the mind), as with alcohol; confuse or befuddle. **3.** To mismanage or bungle. **4.** To make turbid; muddy. **5.** *U.S.* To stir or mix (a drink) gently. —*intr.* **1.** To act or think in a confused manner. **2.** *Chiefly British.* To progress in an ineffective or disorganised way. Used with *on* or *along.* —**muddle through.** *Chiefly British.* To push on to a successful conclusion in a disorganised way.
~*n.* A confusion, jumble, or mess. [Perhaps from Middle Dutch *moddelen,* to make muddy, from *modde†,* mud.] —**mud·dler** *n.*

mud·dle-head·ed (múdd'l-héddid) *adj.* Mentally confused; stupid; dull. —**mud·dle-head·ed·ness** *n.*

mud·dy (múddi) *adj.* **-dier, -diest. 1.** Covered in, full of, or spattered with mud. **2. a.** Not bright or pure: *muddy blue.* **b.** Not clear; cloudy: *This beer is rather muddy.* **3.** Confused, vague, or obscure, as in expression or meaning: *a muddy style of writing.*
~*tr.v.* **muddied, -dying, -dies. 1.** To make muddy or dirty. **2.** To make dull or cloudy. **3.** To make obscure or confused. —**mud·di·ly** *adv.* —**mud·di·ness** *n.*

Mu·dé·jar, mu·dé·jar (*Spanish* mōō-thékhaar) *n., pl.* **-jares.** Any of the Christianised Moors permitted to remain in Spain after it had been restored to Christian control in the Middle Ages.
~*adj.* Of or pertaining to a type of Moorish architecture of the Middle Ages. [Spanish, from Arabic *mudajjan,* permitted to stay.]

mud·fish (múd-fish) *n., pl.* **-fishes** or collectively **mudfish.** Any of various fishes found in muddy water, such as the **bowfin** *(see).*

mud flat *n.* Land covered at high tide and exposed at low tide.

mud·guard (múd-gaard) *n.* The part of a bicycle, motorbike, or the like, that fits over the back of the wheels as a shield against thrown-up water and mud. Also *U.S.* "fender".

mud·lark (múd-laark) *n.* **1.** A bird, the **magpie lark** *(see).* **2.** *British Slang.* **a.** Formerly, one who scavenged in mudflats. **b.** A street urchin.

mud·pack (múd-pak) *n.* A paste made from a type of mud, spread thickly, especially over the face, for cosmetic purposes.

mud puppy *n.* Any of various aquatic salamanders of the genus *Necturus,* especially *N. maculosus,* of North America, having conspicuous clusters of external gills.

mu·dra (mə-draá) *n.* In Hindu classical dancing, a series of body postures and hand movements enacting a narrative. [Hindi.]

mud·skip·per (múd-skippər) *n.* Any of several species of fishes of the family Gobiidae that are found along the coast of tropical Africa and in the Indo-Pacific region and are noted for their ability to manoeuvre on land and withstand drought.

mud·sling·er (múd-sling-ər) *n. Informal.* One who makes malicious charges against an opponent. —**mud·sling·ing** *n.*

mud·stone (múd-stōn) *n.* A fine-grained, nonfissile rock similar to shale that decomposes into mud when exposed to moisture.

mud·wort (múd-wurt ‖ -wawrt) *n.* Any of various waterweeds of the genus *Limosella,* having creeping runners and small flowers.

muenster. Variant of **münster.**

mues·li (méwzli; *German* müssli) *n.* A food consisting of a mixture of nuts, cereal, dried fruit, honey, and the like, eaten with milk. [Swiss German.]

mu·ez·zin (mōō-ézzin, mew-) *n. Islam.* The crier who calls the faithful to prayer five times a day, usually from a minaret. [Arabic *mu'adhdhin,* active participle of *adhana,* to cause to listen, from *adhina,* to listen.]

muff[1] (muf) *tr.v.* **muffed, muffing, muffs.** *Informal.* **1.** To perform (an act) clumsily; bungle: *muffed the job.* **2.** *Sports.* To fail to execute (a kick, catch, or the like).
~*n. Informal.* **1.** A clumsy or bungling person. **2.** A clumsy or bungled act. [19th century : origin obscure.]

muff[2] *n.* A small cylindrical fur or cloth cover, open at both ends, in which the hands are placed to keep them warm. [Dutch *mof,* from Middle Dutch *moffel,* from Medieval Latin *muffula†.*]

muf·fin (múffin) *n.* **1.** *British.* A small, round, thick, doughy tea cake, usually toasted and served with butter. **2.** A small, cup-shaped bread roll, often sweetened and usually served hot. [Probably from Low German *muffen,* plural of *muffe†,* cake.]

muf·fle[1] (múff'l) *tr.v.* **-fled, -fling, -fles. 1.** To wrap up in a blanket, shawl, or scarf for warmth, protection, or secrecy. **2.** To wrap or pad in order to deaden a sound: *muffled drums.* **3.** To deaden (a sound): *Their hoofbeats were muffled by the sand.* **4.** To make vague or obscure: *a message muffled by excess of detail.*
~*n.* **1.** Anything that muffles. **2.** A kiln or part of a kiln in which pottery can be fired without being exposed to direct flame. [Middle English *muflen,* from Old French *enmoufler,* to "put on a muff or mittens", from *moufle,* mitten, from Medieval Latin *muffula†.*]

muffle[2] *n.* The hairless snout of ruminants and rodents. [French *mufle†.*]

muf·fler (múfflər) *n.* **1.** A heavy scarf worn round the neck for warmth. **2.** Any device that absorbs noise.

muf·ti, Muf·ti[1] (múfti, mōōfti) *n., pl.* **-tis.** A judge who interprets Muslim religious law. [Arabic *muftī,* "one who decides", from *aftā,* to decide (by legal opinion).]

muf·ti[2] (múfti) *n.* Civilian dress, especially when worn by one whose regular clothing is a military or other uniform. [Slang use of MUFTI (judge).]

mug[1] (mug) *n.* **1.** A cylindrical drinking vessel, usually having a handle. **2.** The liquid contained in such a vessel. **3.** The quantity that such a vessel is capable of containing. In this sense, also called "mugful". [Probably from Scandinavian.]

mug[2] *n. Slang.* **1.** The face of a person. **2.** The area of the mouth, chin, and jaw. **3.** A grimace. **4.** *British.* A person who is easily deceived or duped. **5.** *U.S.* A hoodlum; a ruffian. —**a mug's game.** *British Slang.* A foolish and unprofitable activity.
~*v.* **mugged, mugging, mugs.** *Slang.* —*tr.* To waylay and sometimes beat severely, usually with intent to rob. —*intr.* **1.** To grimace; especially, to overact as a performer by means of exaggerated facial expressions. **2.** *British.* To study books, notes, or the like, intensely. —**mug up.** *British Slang.* To study (a subject) intensely. Sometimes used with *on.* [Probably from MUG (vessel), from tankards shaped like grotesque human faces. Sense of "attack" from old slang sense of noun "hoodlum".]

Mu·ga·be (mōō-gaábi), **Robert (Gabriel)** (1924–). Zimbabwean politician. He entered politics in Rhodesia (1960) and helped to found the Zimbabwe African National Union (ZANU) in 1963. From 1964 to 1974 he was detained by the Rhodesian government. In 1976 he became president of ZANU and co-leader, with Joshua Nkomo, of the Patriotic Front which waged war against the ruling white minority in Rhodesia. He became prime minister in April, 1980, after the first one-man-one-vote elections under the new constitution; president (1988), re-elected 1997.

mug·ger[1] (múggər) *n.* One who commits a mugging.

mug·ger[2], **mug·gar, mug·gur** (múggər) *n.* A large crocodile, *Crocodylus palustris,* of southwestern Asia, having an exceptionally broad, wrinkled snout. Also called "marsh crocodile". [Hindi *magar,* from Sanskrit *makara,* a crocodile, from Dravidian.]

mug·ging (múgging) *n. Informal.* An assault, sometimes violent and usually by surprise and with intent to rob.

mug·gins (múgginz) *n. British Slang.* A fool or simpleton.
~*pron.* Oneself. Used in humorous self-deprecation: *Muggins will have to pay, as usual.* [Perhaps from surname *Muggins,* with allusion to MUG (simpleton).]

mug·gy (múggi) *adj.* **-gier, -giest.** Warm and extremely humid. [From dialectal *mug,* fine rain, from Middle English *muggen,* to drizzle, from Old Norse *mugga.*] —**mug·gi·ness** *n.*

Mughal, Mughul. Variants of **Mogul.**

mug·shot (múg-shot) *n.* A photograph of a person's face, especially one of a criminal used for purposes of identification.

mug·wort (múg-wurt ‖ -wawrt) *n.* Any of several plants of the genus *Artemisia;* especially, *A. vulgaris,* native to Eurasia, having clusters of small yellowish-brown flowers. [Middle English *mugwort,* Old English *mucgwyrt : mucg-,* a midge, fly + *wyrt,* WORT.]

mug·wump (múg-wump) *n. U.S. Informal.* A person who acts independently or neutrally, especially in politics. [Natick *mugquomp, mugwomp,* "captain".] —**mug·wump·er·y** *n.*

Mu·ham·mad (mōō-hám-əd). Also **Mo·ham·med** (mō-, mə-, -ed) or **Ma·hom·et** (mə-hómmit) (*c.* 570–632). The prophet and founder of Islam, the son of Abdallah ibn Abd-al-Mutalib of the ruling tribe of Mecca. He was a rich merchant who had a vision in the cave of Mt. Hira telling him to preach true religion. In 622 he fled Mecca, where he made few converts, and set up a theocracy at Yathrib, which was renamed Medina, meaning "city of the prophet". In 630 Muhammad conquered Mecca without a struggle and began to win Arabia to Islam. His teachings are recorded in the Koran.

Mu·ham·ma·dan, Mo·ham·me·dan (mōō-hámmid'n) *adj.* Also **Mo·ham·me·dan** (mō-, mə-), **Ma·hom·e·tan** (mə-hómmitən). Of or pertaining to Muhammad or Islam; Muslim.
~*n.* A follower of Muhammad or believer in Islam; a Muslim. **Mu·ham·ma·dan·ism** (mōō-hámmid'n-iz'm) *n.* Also **Mo·ham·me·dan·ism** (mō-, mə-), **Ma·hom·e·tan·ism** (-hómmitən-). The Muhammadan religion, Islam *(see).*

Mu·ham·mad Re·za Pah·la·vi (mō-hámməd ráyzə páʹaləvi) (1919–80). Shah of Iran (1941–79). His attempts to modernise Iranian society, together with the growth of corruption and the activities of the secret police under his regime, provoked the Islamic reaction culminating in the revolution of 1979 by which he was overthrown.

Mu·har·ram, Mu·har·rum (mōō-hárrəm) *n.* Also **Mo·har·ram** (mō-). **1.** The first month of the Muslim calendar. **2.** A festival held during the first ten days of this month.

Muir (mewr), **Edwin** (1887–1959). British poet, novelist, and literary critic. He was little recognised as a poet until the publication of his *Collected Poems* (1960). By then he had established his reputation more as a critic by the publication of studies such as *The Structure of the Novel* (1928) and *Essays on Literature and Society* (1949).

Muj·i·bur Rah·man (mōōjiboor ráʹamən), also known as Sheik Mujib (1920–75). Bengali politician, the first president of Bangladesh. He was imprisoned twice between 1958 and 1966 by General Ayub Khan for conspiring with the Indian government to secure the independence of East Pakistan. He led the Awami League in its campaign for independence, and after winning the provincial election of 1970, he proclaimed East Pakistan's independence, was arrested, and convicted of treason in 1971. When Indian intervention gained Bangladesh its independence he became prime minister of the provisional government in 1972. He was killed in a coup in 1975, soon after having named himself president with dictatorial powers.

mujik. Variant of **muzhik.**

Mukden. See **Shenyang.**

muk·luk (múk-luk) *n.* **1.** A soft Eskimo boot made of reindeer skin or sealskin. **2.** A boot resembling this. [Eskimo *muklok,* "large seal".]

mu·lat·to (mə-láttō, mōō- ‖ mew-, mōō-) *n., pl.* **-tos** or **-toes.** **1.** A person having one white and one black parent. **2.** Broadly, any person of mixed Caucasian and Negro ancestry.
~*adj.* Of the tawny colour of a mulatto. [Spanish *mulato,* young mule, mulatto, from *mulo,* mule, from Latin *mūlus,* MULE.]

mul·ber·ry (múl-bəri, -bri ‖ *U.S. also* -berri) *n., pl.* **-ries.** **1.** Any of several trees of the genus *Morus,* especially the black mulberry, *M. nigra,* having edible fruit and leaves that are used to feed silkworms. **2.** The sweet, berry-like fruit of any of these trees. **3.** Any of several related or similar trees, such as the **paper mulberry** *(see).* **4.** *Archaic.* Greyish to dark purple. [Middle English *mulberrie, murberie,* Old English *mōrberie : mōr-,* a Germanic borrowing, from Latin *mōrum,* mulberry + Old English *berie,* BERRY.] —**mul·ber·ry** *adj.*

mulch (mulch) *n.* A mixture of straw, earth, leaves, peat, and the like, placed around plants to prevent evaporation of moisture and freezing of roots and to fertilise the soil.
~*tr.v.* **mulched, mulching, mulches.** To cover with a mulch. [Originally "rotten hay", probably extended use of Middle English *mulsh,* soft, yielding, variant of *melsh,* Old English *mel(i)sc, mylsc,* mild, mellow.]

mulct (mulkt) *n.* A fine or similar penalty.
~*tr.v.* **mulcted, mulcting, mulcts.** **1.** To penalise by fining or demanding forfeiture. **2.** To cheat or swindle. [Latin *mulcta, multa,* a fine, of Italic origin.]

Mul·doon (mul-dōōn), **Sir Robert David** (1921–92). New Zealand politician. He became leader of the National Party in 1974, after serving for five years (1967–72) as Minister of Finance. He was prime minister 1975–84.

mule¹ (mewl) *n.* **1.** A sterile hybrid of a male ass and a female horse. Compare **hinny. 2.** Any sterile hybrid, as between a canary and other finches. **3.** *Informal.* A stubborn person. **4.** A type of spinning machine that makes thread or yarn from fibres. Also called "spinning mule". [Middle English *mul,* from Old English *mūl* and Old French *mul,* both from Latin *mūlus,* mule, probably from Mediterranean; akin to Albanian *mušk,* mule.]

mule² *n.* A slipper that has no counter or strap to fit around the heel of the foot. [French, from Latin *mulleus (calceus),* "red (shoe)".]

mu·le·ta (mew-léttə) *n.* A short red cape, suspended from a hollow staff, that is used by the matador to manoeuvre the bull during the **faena** *(see).* [Spanish, crutch, support, "small mule", from *mula,* "she-mule", from Latin *mūla,* feminine of *mūlus,* MULE.]

mu·le·teer (mewli-téer) *n.* A mule driver. [French *muletier,* from *mulet,* diminutive of Old French *mul,* MULE.]

mu·ley (méwli ‖ mōōli, mōōli) *adj.* Hornless. Said of cattle.
~*n., pl.* **muleys.** A hornless animal. [Variant of dialectal *moiley,* from *moil,* hornless, a hornless cow, from Irish *maol,* from Old Irish *máel,* bald, hornless.]

mul·ga (múlgə) *n. Australian.* **1.** Any of various Australian acacias, especially *Acacia aneura,* which grow in the desert. **2.** Scrub consisting of dense growth of acacia. [From a native Australian language.]

mu·li·eb·ri·ty (mewli-ébbrəti) *n. Formal.* **1.** The state or condition of being a woman. **2.** The qualities characteristic of women. [Late Latin *muliebritās,* from Latin *muliebris,* womanly, from *mulier†,* a woman.]

mul·ish (méwlish) *adj.* Characteristic of a mule; stubborn. See Synonyms at **obstinate.** —**mul·ish·ly** *adv.* —**mul·ish·ness** *n.*

mull¹ (mul) *tr.v.* **mulled, mulling, mulls.** To heat and spice (an alcoholic drink such as wine or ale). [17th century : origin obscure.]

mull² *v.* **mulled, mulling, mulls.** —*tr.* To reflect on or consider (a problem) deeply. Often used with *over.* [Middle English *mullen,* to grind, pulverise, from *mul,* dust, from Middle Dutch *mol, mul.*]

mull³ *n.* A soft, thin muslin used in dresses and for trimmings. [Short for *mulmull,* from Hindi *malmal,* from Persian *malmal†.*]

mull⁴ *n.* In Scotland, a promontory. [Middle English; Gaelic *maol.*]

mull⁵ *n.* A moist type of humus that is formed under non-acid conditions and found mingled with mineral soil rather than as a distinct layer. [German, from Danish *muld.*]

Mull (mul). The largest of the Inner Hebrides, western Scotland. The island is mountainous, rising to 966 metres (3,169 feet) at Ben More. Tobermory, the chief town, is also a summer resort.

mul·lah, mul·la (múllər, mōōllə) *n.* A Muslim religious teacher or leader. Sometimes used as a title. [Turkish *mulla* and Persian *mullā,* from Arabic *mawlā,* "master".]

mul·lein (múllin) *n.* Any plant of the genus *Verbascum,* having leaves covered with white, woolly down, and yellow flowers. See **Aaron's rod.** [Middle English *moleyne,* from Old French *moleine,* from Gaulish *melena* (unattested).]

mul·ler (múllər) *n.* **1.** Any of several manual or mechanical devices used for grinding. **2.** A device with a stone or other hard base, used manually or mechanically to grind paints or drugs. [Middle English *molour,* probably from *mullen,* to grind, pulverise. See **mull².**]

Mül·ler·i·an duct (mew-léer-i-ən) *n.* The oviduct of all vertebrates except the jawless fish, which in mammals is differentiated into the Fallopian tubes, womb, and vagina. [After Johannes *Müller* (1801–58), German anatomist.]

mul·let¹ (múllit) *n., pl.* **-lets** or collectively **mullet.** Any of various edible fishes of the families Mugilidae or Mullidae found worldwide in tropical and temperate coastal waters and some freshwater streams; especially, the grey mullets of the genus *Mugil.* See **red mullet.** [Middle English *molet,* from Old French *mulet,* from Latin *mullus,* red mullet, from Greek *mollos.*]

mul·let² *n. Heraldry.* A star having five straight points. [Old French *molette,* rowel on a spur.]

mul·li·gan (múlligən) *n.* **1.** *U.S.* A stew of various meats and vegetables. Also called "mulligan stew". **2.** A second drive from the first tee of a golf course that is permitted without penalty when the first drive is bad. [Probably from the Irish surname *Mulligan.*]

mul·li·ga·taw·ny (múlligə-táwni) *n.* An Indian soup with meat and strongly flavoured with curry. [Tamil *miḷagutaṇṇī(r),* "pepper-water".]

mul·li·grubs (múlli-grubz) *pl.n. Informal.* **1.** A stomach ache; griping of the intestines; colic. **2.** Ill temper or depression. Often used humorously. [Alteration of earlier *mulligrums,* perhaps alteration of MEGRIM.]

mul·li·on (múlli-ən) *n.* A vertical strip dividing the panes of a window or panels of a screen. [Perhaps variant of Middle English *monial,* from Old French *moinel,* from *moien,* MEAN.] —**mul·li·oned** *adj.*

mul·lo·way (múllə-way) *n.* A large Australian marine food fish, *Sciaena antarctica.* [19th century : origin obscure.]

multi- *comb. form.* Indicates: **1.** Many or much; for example, **multicoloured. 2.** More than one; for example, **multiparous. Note:** Many compounds other than those entered here may be formed with *multi-.* In this dictionary, in forming compounds, *multi-* is normally joined to the following word or element without space or hyphen: *multiangular.* However, many users prefer the hyphenated form, especially in less standardised compounds: *multi-company.* The hyphenated form is also used if the second element begins with *i: multi-infection.* In American English the prefix is sometimes pronounced (múltī-); this is not shown in the entries below. [Middle English, from Latin, from *multus,* much.]

mul·ti·ad·dress (múlti-ə-dréss ‖ *U.S.* -áddress) *adj.* Designating a storage system of data-processing computers in which it is possible to store instructions or quantities in more than one position.

mul·ti·cel·lu·lar (múlti-séllewlər) *adj.* Consisting of more than one cell. Said chiefly of metazoans.

mul·ti·col·oured (múlti-kúllərd, -kullərd) *adj.* Having many colours.

mul·ti·cul·tur·al (múlti-kúlchərəl) *adj.* Of or pertaining to a society that includes several different cultures: *a multicultural city.* —**mul·ti·cul·tur·al·ism** *n.*

mul·ti·dis·ci·pli·nar·y (múlti-díssi-plin-əri, -plín-, -plín- ‖ *U.S.* -erri) *adj.* Embracing, or involving contributions from, several distinct academic or other disciplines: *a multidisciplinary approach.*

mul·ti·eth·nic (múlti-éthnik) *adj.* Of or pertaining to a society that includes several different ethnic groups; multicultural.

mul·ti·fac·to·ri·al (múlti-fak-táwr-i-əl ‖ -tŏr-) *adj. Genetics.* Designating inheritance or a characteristic, such as height, that is controlled by two or more genes. See **multiple factor.**

mul·ti·far·i·ous (múlti-faír-i-əss) *adj.* Having great variety; made up of many parts or kinds. [Latin *multifārius* : MULTI- + *-fārius,* doing.] —**mul·ti·far·i·ous·ly** *adv.* —**mul·ti·far·i·ous·ness** *n.*

mul·ti·fid (múlti-fid) *adj. Biology.* Having many clefts forming lobes: *multifid leaves.* [Latin *multifidus* : MULTI- + -FID.]

mul·ti·flo·ra rose (múlti-fláwrə ‖ -flŏrə) *n.* A climbing or sprawling shrub, *Rosa multiflora,* native to Asia, having clusters of small, fragrant flowers. It is the origin of many horticultural varieties. [New Latin *Rosa multiflōra,* "many-flowered rose".]

mul·ti·foil (múlti-foyl) *adj. Architecture.* Having many foils.
~*n.* Any design or object having many foils or scalloped edges.

mul·ti·fold (múlti-fōld) *adj.* Many times doubled; manifold.

mul·ti·form (múlti-fawrm) *adj.* Occurring in or having many forms, shapes, or appearances. [Latin *multiformis* : MULTI- + -FORM.] —**mul·ti·for·mi·ty** (-fórməti) *n.*

mul·ti·grav·i·da (múlti-grávvidə) *n., pl.* **-dae** (-grávvidee). A pregnant woman who has had at least two previous pregnancies. [New Latin : MULTI- + *gravida,* pregnant woman. See **gravid.**]

mul·ti·lat·er·al (múlti-láttrəl, -láttərəl) *adj.* 1. Having many sides. 2. Involving more than two nations or groups: *multilateral disarmament.* —**mul·ti·lat·er·al·ly** *adv.*

mul·ti·lat·er·al·ist (múlti-láttrəl-ist, -láttərəl-) *n.* One who favours multilateral action, especially multilateral nuclear disarmament. Compare **unilateralist.** —**mul·ti·lat·er·al·ist** *adj.*

mul·ti·lin·gual (múlti-líng-gwəl ‖ -gew-əl) *adj.* 1. Capable of speaking or writing in many languages. 2. Written in many languages. 3. Designating a society of various different language groups.

mul·ti·me·di·a (múlti-méedi-ə) *adj.* Including or involving the use of several media of communication, such as films, records, or the like, for the purpose of education or entertainment.

mul·ti·mil·lion·aire (múlti-míl-yə-naír) *n.* A person whose financial assets equal many millions of pounds, dollars, or other currency.

mul·ti·na·tion·al (múlti-násh-ənəl, -nəl) *adj.* 1. Having operations, subsidiaries, or investments in more than one country: *a multinational corporation.* 2. Of, in, or involving several or many countries. ~*n.* A multinational company.

mul·ti·no·mi·al (múlti-nŏmi-əl) *n. Mathematics.* A **polynomial** *(see).* [MULTI- + *bi*nomial.] —**mul·ti·no·mi·al** *adj.*

multinomial theorem *n. Mathematics.* The theorem that establishes the rule for forming the terms of a polynomial expansion. See **binomial theorem, expansion, polynomial.**

mul·tip·a·ra (mul-típpərə) *n., pl.* **-rae** (-ree). A pregnant woman who has borne at least one child; especially, one who is in labour for the second time. [New Latin, feminine of *multiparus,* MULTIPAROUS.]

mul·tip·a·rous (mul-típpərəss) *adj.* 1. Having borne more than one child. 2. Giving birth to more than one offspring at one time. [New Latin *multiparus* : MULTI- + -PAROUS.]

mul·ti·par·tite (múlti-pártīt) *adj.* 1. Having many parts. 2. Multilateral. [Latin *multipartītus* : MULTI- + PARTITE.]

mul·ti·ple (múltip'l) *adj.* Having, pertaining to, or consisting of more than one individual, element, part, or other component; manifold; multiplicate.
~*n. Mathematics.* A quantity into which another quantity may be divided with zero remainder: *4, 6, and 12 are multiples of 2.* A *common multiple* is a quantity into which each of two or more other quantities may be divided with zero remainder: *6, 12, and 24 are common multiples of 2 and 3.* A *lowest common multiple* is the least quantity into which two or more other quantities may be divided with zero remainder: *6 is the lowest common multiple of all common multiples of 2 and 3.* [Old French, from Late Latin *multiplus* : MULTI- + *-plus,* -fold.]

multiple allele *n. Genetics.* A set of three or more alternative forms of a gene at a single locus. Also called "multiple allelomorph".

mul·ti·ple-choice (múltip'l-chóyss) *adj.* Offering a number of solutions from which one correct one is to be chosen: *multiple-choice exam questions.*

multiple factor *n. Genetics.* A combination of genes having a joint or cumulative effect.

multiple fruit *n.* A fruit, such as a pineapple or mulberry, in which the fruits of several flowers are combined into a single structure. Also called "collective fruit".

multiple root *n. Mathematics.* A root *a* of the polynomial equation $f(x) = 0$ in which $(x - a)$ occurs at least twice as a factor of $f(x)$. Also called "root".

multiple sclerosis *n. Abbr.* **MS** A degenerative disease of the central nervous system, in which the sheaths surrounding individual nerve cells of the brain or spinal cord, or both, are damaged causing disorders of speech, vision, and muscle coordination, and partial paralysis.

multiple star *n.* Three or more stars, usually with a common gravitational centre, that appear very close together as one system to the naked eye.

multiple store *n.* Any of a number of shops in different locations owned by the same company, such as a branch of a chain store. Also called "multiple shop".

mul·ti·plet (múlti-plət, -plet, -plit) *n. Physics.* 1. A spectral line having more than one component representing slight variations in energy states characteristic of an atom. 2. Any of several classes or groupings of subatomic particles, such as the nucleon, each member of which has the same set of **quantum numbers** *(see)* except for electric charge. [From MULTIPLE.]

mul·ti·plex (múlti-pleks) *adj.* 1. Multiple; manifold. 2. Designating a simultaneous communication of two or more messages on the same wire or radio channel. Compare **duplex, simplex.** 3. Designating a method of making topographic maps with three cameras arranged to employ stereoscopic principles.
~*v.* **multiplexed, -plexing, -plexes.** —*intr.* To send messages or signals in a multiplex system. —*tr.* To send simultaneously (more than one signal) using one radio frequency. [Latin : MULTI- + *-plex,* -fold.] —**mul·ti·plex·er** *n.*

mul·ti·pli·a·ble (múlti-plī-əb'l ‖ -plí-) *adj.* Also **mul·ti·plic·a·ble** (-plik-, -plík-). Capable of being multiplied.

mul·ti·pli·cand (múltipli-kánd) *n.* The number that is or is to be multiplied by another. [Latin *multiplicandum,* neuter of *multiplicandus,* gerundive of *multiplicāre,* to MULTIPLY.]

mul·tip·li·cate (mul-típli-kət, -kit) *adj. Rare.* Manifold; multiple. [Middle English, from Latin *multiplicātus,* past participle of *multiplicāre,* to MULTIPLY.]

mul·ti·pli·ca·tion (múltipli-káysh'n) *n.* 1. The act of multiplying or the process of being multiplied. 2. The propagation of plants and animals. 3. *Mathematics.* **a.** An operation in which an integer, the multiplicand, is added to itself a specific integral number of times. **b.** The extension of this process to the combination of two real numbers by using laws valid for integers. **c.** Any of certain analogous operations combining expressions other than real numbers. Compare **division.** 4. An increase or build-up achieved by adding. —**mul·ti·pli·ca·tion·al** *adj.*

multiplication sign *n. Mathematics.* Any of various signs, especially ($\times$), placed between multiplicand and multiplier, or operand and operator, as in $a \times b$.

multiplication table *n.* A table listing the products of certain numbers multiplied together, usually the numbers 1 to 12.

mul·ti·pli·ca·tive (múlti-plíckətiv, -pli-kaytiv) *adj.* 1. Tending to multiply or capable of multiplying or increasing. 2. Pertaining to multiplication. —**mul·ti·pli·ca·tive·ly** *adv.*

mul·ti·plic·i·ty (múlti-plíssəti) *n., pl.* **-ties.** 1. The state of being various or manifold. 2. A large number: *a multiplicity of ideas.* 3. *Physics.* **a.** The number of subatomic particles in a **multiplet** *(see).* **b.** The number of levels into which the energy of an atom, molecule, nucleus, or the like can split as a result of coupling between spin angular momentum and orbital angular momentum. [French *multiplicité,* from Latin *multiplicitās,* from *multiplex* (stem *multiplic-*), having many folds, MULTIPLEX.]

mul·ti·pli·er (múlti-plī-ər) *n.* 1. One that multiplies. 2. *Mathematics.* The number by which the multiplicand is multiplied. If 3 is multiplied by 2, 3 is the multiplicand, 2 is the multiplier, and 6 is the product. 3. *Physics.* Any device, such as a phototube, used to enhance or increase an effect. 4. *Economics.* The ratio between an initial increase in investment expenditure and the total income amassed from that first expenditure.

mul·ti·ply (múlti-plī) *v.* **-plied, -plying, -plies.** —*tr.* 1. To increase the amount, number, or degree of; make more numerous. 2. *Mathematics.* To perform multiplication on. —*intr.* 1. To become more in number, amount, or degree. 2. To breed; propagate. 3. *Mathematics.* To perform multiplication. [Middle English *multiplien,* from Old French *multiplier,* from Latin *multiplicāre,* from *multiplex* (stem *multiplic-*), having many folds, MULTIPLEX.]

mul·ti·pur·pose (múlti-púrpəss) *adj.* Having several different purposes: *a multipurpose machine.*

mul·ti·ra·cial (múlti-ráysh'l) *adj.* Of, pertaining to, or composed of people of different races: *a multiracial community.*

mul·ti·se·ri·ate (múlti-séer-i-ət, -ayt) *adj. Botany.* Borne in many whorls or rows. Said of flower parts.

mul·ti·stage (múlti-stayj) *adj.* 1. Functioning by stages. 2. Designating a device, such as a turbine, compressor, or supercharger, that has more than one rotating section.

multistage rocket *n.* A rocket composed of two or more stages, each stage firing in succession. Also called "step rocket".

mul·ti·sto·rey (múlti-stáw-ri ‖ -stŏ-) *adj.* Of or designating a building that has several storeys: *a multistorey car park.*

mul·ti·tude (múlti-tewd ‖ -tŏod) *n.* 1. The condition or quality of being numerous. 2. **a.** A great, indefinite number: *a multitude of sins.* **b.** A huge gathering of people. 3. The masses; the populace. Preceded by *the.* [Middle English, from Old French, from Latin *multitūdō,* a great number, from *multus,* many.]
Synonyms: multitude, host, legion, army, array.

mul·ti·tu·di·nous (múlti-téw-dinəss ‖ -tŏo-) *adj.* 1. Very numerous; existing in great numbers. 2. Consisting of many parts. 3. *Poetic.* Crowded. —**mul·ti·tu·di·nous·ly** *adv.*

mul·ti·va·lent (múlti-váylənt) *adj.* 1. *Chemistry.* Polyvalent. 2. *Biology.* Of or pertaining to homologous chromosomes during meiosis. 3. Having various meanings or values. —**mul·ti·va·lency** *n.*

mul·tum in par·vo (mŏol-tŏom in párvō, múl-, -təm) *n. Latin.* A large amount within a small space or range.

mul·ture (múlchər) *n. British.* Formerly, a fee, usually in the form of a quantity of flour, paid to a miller for grinding one's grain at his mill. [Middle English, from Old French *mo(u)lture,* from Medieval Latin *molitura,* from *molere* (past participial stem *molit-),* to grind.]

mum¹ (mum) *adj.* Not talking; silent: *Keep mum about my mistake.* —**mum's the word.** Used to enjoin or promise silence: *Remember our secret—mum's the word!* [Middle English *mum, mom,* probably from Low German (imitative of closed lips).]

mum² *n. Chiefly British Informal.* A mother. Used chiefly as a term of address.

mum³ *intr.v.* **mummed, mumming, mums.** To act or play in a masque; especially, to act as a mummer. [Middle English *mummen, mommen,* from Old French *momer.*]

Mumbai. See **Bombay.**

mum·ble (múmb'l) *v.* **-bled, -bling, -bles.** —*tr.* 1. To utter indistinctly by lowering the voice or partially closing the mouth. 2. *Rare.* To chew (food) slowly or painfully without or as if without teeth. —*intr.* 1. To speak indistinctly, as by lowering the voice or partially closing the mouth. 2. *Rare.* To chew food slowly or painfully, as if without teeth. —See Synonyms at **mutter.** ~*n.* A low, indistinct sound or speech. [Middle English *momelen,* frequentative of *mom,* inarticulate sound, MUM¹.] —**mum·bler** *n.*

mum·bo jum·bo (múmbō júmbō) *n.* 1. Confusing or meaningless words or actions. 2. Unintelligible or obscure ritual. 3. An object believed to have supernatural powers; a fetish. [Perhaps from the name of a Mandingo idol.]

mum·chance (múm-chaanss ‖ -chanss) *adj. Archaic.* Not speaking; silent. [Originally noun, "dumb show", from Middle Low German *mummenschanze,* masked serenade : *mummen,* from Old French *momer,* from MUM³ + *schanze,* from Old French, CHANCE.]

mu meson *n. Physics.* A particle, the **muon** (*see*). Not in current technical usage.

mum·mer (múmmər) *n.* 1. One who acts or plays in a traditional masque, mime, or the like. 2. *Slang.* An actor. [Middle English *mummar,* from Middle Dutch *mommer,* from Old French *mommeur,* from *momer,* to MUM³.]

mum·mer·y (múmməri) *n., pl.* **-ies.** 1. A performance by mummers. 2. A pretentious or hypocritical show or ceremony.

mum·mi·fy (múmmi-fī) *v.* **-fied, -fying, -fies.** —*tr.* 1. To make into a mummy by embalming and drying. 2. To invest with the appearance or qualities of a mummy: *mummified ideas.* —*intr.* To shrivel or dry up like a mummy. —**mum·mi·fi·ca·tion** (-fi-káysh'n) *n.*

mum·my¹ (múmmi) *n., pl.* **-ies.** 1. The body of a human being or animal embalmed after death, as found in ancient Egyptian tombs. 2. Any withered or shrunken body, living or dead, that resembles a preserved mummy. 3. *British Regional.* A pulp or formless mass. Used in the phrase *beat to a mummy.* 4. A rich brown pigment. [Middle English *mummie,* from Old French *momie,* embalming ointment, mummy, from Medieval Latin *mumia,* from Arabic *mūmīyā,* mummy, bitumen, from *mūm,* wax.]

mummy² *n., pl.* **-ies.** *Informal.* A mother. [Alteration of MAMMY.]

mump¹ (mump) *intr.v.* **mumped, mumping, mumps.** To be silent and moody: *always mumping and moaning.* [Imitative (of closed mouth).]

mump² *v.* **mumped, mumping, mumps.** *Archaic.* —*intr.* To beg. —*tr.* To get by begging. [Perhaps from obsolete Dutch *mompen,* to cheat.]

mumps (mumps) *n. Used with a singular verb.* An acute, contagious viral infection of the salivary glands, especially the parotids, which may spread to the pancreas, brain, or testicles. It is common in children and is characterised by swelling of the area under the lower jaw. [Plural of dialect *mump,* grimace; akin to MUMP (be silent).] —**mump·ish** *adj.*

munch (munch) *v.* **munched, munching, munches.** —*tr.* 1. To chew (food) steadily with a crunching sound. 2. *Slang.* To eat. —*intr.* 1. To chew steadily. Sometimes used with *away, at,* or *on.* 2. *Slang.* To eat. [Middle English *monchen* (imitative).]

Munch (mŏŏngk), **Edvard** (1863–1944). Norwegian painter, etcher, and lithographer. In the 1890s he painted the best-known of his works, the cycle called *Frieze of Life,* which included what has become by far his most famous painting (also produced as a woodcut and a lithograph), *The Scream.*

mun·dane (múndayn, mún-dáyn) *adj.* 1. Unidealised or unelevated; bodily or worldly: *Mundane pleasures undermined those of the spirit.* 2. Ordinary; dull; banal: *lived a dull, mundane existence.* [Middle English *mondeyne,* from Old French *mondain,* from Late Latin *mundānus,* from Latin *mundus,* the world.] —**mun·dane·ly** *adv.* —**mun·dane·ness, mun·dan·i·ty** (mun-dánnəti) *n.*

mung bean (mung, mŏŏng) *n.* A bean, *Phaseolus aureus,* of eastern Asia. It is the source of bean sprouts used in Oriental cookery. [*Mung,* shortened form *mungo,* from Tamil *mūngu,* from Sanskrit *mudga.*]

mun·go (múng-gō) *n.* 1. Recycled wool used for cheap cloth. 2. The cloth produced from such wool. See **shoddy.** [Perhaps from Yorkshire dialect *mong†,* mixture, and Scottish *Mungo,* male forename.]

Mu·nich (méwnik). German **Mün·chen** (múnkhən). Capital of Bavaria, southern Germany. It is the cultural, industrial, and commercial focus of south Germany and a major tourist centre. Its products include machinery, chemicals, instruments, and beer. Founded on the river Isar (1158), Munich became the home of the Wittelsbach family (1255). They made it their capital (1506), from which they ruled Bavaria until 1918, from 1806 as kings. Hitler founded the National Socialist (Nazi) movement in Munich (*c.* 1919). There he

attempted his "beer-hall putsch" (1923) and signed the Munich Agreement (1938). The city was the venue of the 1972 summer Olympic Games. Munich's Oktoberfest, an annual beer festival, is world-famous. See map at **Germany.**

mu·nic·i·pal (mew-níssip'l ‖ méwni-síppl) *adj. Abbr.* **mun.** 1. **a.** Of or pertaining to a city or its government. **b.** Having local self-government: *a municipal borough.* 2. Of or pertaining to the internal affairs of a nation, as distinguished from its international affairs. [Latin *mūnicipālis,* from *mūnicipium,* a franchised city, from *mūniceps,* citizen of a *mūnicipium* (who could perform public offices but not hold magistracies) : *mūnus,* public office + *-ceps,* "-taker", from *capere,* to take.] —**mu·nic·i·pal·ly** *adv.*

mu·nic·i·pal·ise, mu·nic·i·pal·ize (mew-níssip'l-īz) *tr.v.* **-ised, -ising, -ises.** 1. To place under municipal ownership. 2. To make a municipality of a district. —**mu·nic·i·pal·i·sa·tion** (-ī-záysh'n ‖ *U.S.* -i-) *n.*

mu·nic·i·pal·i·ty (mew-níssi-pál-əti) *n., pl.* **-ties.** *Abbr.* **mun.** 1. A city, town, village, borough, or other district having local self-government. 2. A body of officials appointed or elected to manage the affairs of such a community.

mu·nif·i·cence (mew-níffi-sənss) *n.* 1. A disposition to bestow lavish benefits; a generous nature. 2. The lavish bestowal of gifts, entertainment, hospitality, or other benefits.

mu·nif·i·cent (mew-níffi-sənt) *adj.* 1. Extremely liberal in giving; very generous. 2. Showing great generosity: *a munificent gift.* [Latin *mūnificens* (stem *mūnificent-),* from *mūnificus,* "present-making", generous, bountiful : *mūnus,* office, duty, gift + *-ficus,* -FIC.] —**mu·nif·i·cent·ly** *adv.*

mu·ni·ment (méwnimənt) *n.* 1. *Plural. Law.* Documentary evidence of ownership; written proof by which a person defends ownership of property or maintains rights. 2. *Rare.* A means of defence or protection. [Middle English, from Old French, Medieval Latin *mūnimentum,* from Latin, defence, from *mūnīre,* to defend.]

mu·ni·tion (mew-nísh'n) *n. Usually plural.* War material, especially weapons and ammunition. ~*tr.v.* **munitioned, -tioning, -tions.** To supply with munitions. [Originally, "fortification", from French, from Latin *mūnītiō* (stem *mūnītiōn-),* from *mūnīre,* to defend, fortify.] —**mu·ni·tion·er** *n.*

Mun·ro (mun-rṓ), **H(ector) H(ugh),** known as Saki (1870–1916). British short-story writer, born in Burma. His highly original short stories are in a mordant, witty style and often bitter in tone. The first collection, *Reginald,* appeared in 1904. It was followed by *Reginald in Russia* (1910), *The Chronicles of Clovis* (1911), and *Beasts and Super-beasts* (1914). Killed in W.W.I.

Mun·sell scale (múnss'l) *n.* A scale used in specifying colour, based on equal changes in visual hue. [After A.H. *Munsell* (1858–1918), U.S. scientist.]

Mun·ster (múnstər). Province in the southwest Republic of Ireland. A former kingdom, it is the largest Irish province, covering the counties of Clare, Cork, Kerry, Limerick, Tipperary, and Waterford.

mün·ster, mun·ster, muen·ster (mún-stər, mŏŏn-, German mǔn-) *n.* A semisoft, creamy, yellow Alsatian cheese of mild flavour. [After the *Münster* Valley in Alsace.]

munt (mŏŏnt) *n.* Also **mun·tu** (mŏŏntŏŏ). *South African Slang.* A black African. Used derogatorily by whites. [Afrikaans, from Bantu *umuntu,* singular of *abantu,* person, black person.]

munt·jac, munt·jak (múntjak) *n.* Any of several small deer of the genus *Muntiacus,* of southeastern Asia and the East Indies. *M. muntjak* is now widespread in the woods of south central England. Also called "barking deer". [Malay *menjangan,* deer.]

Muntz metal (munts). *n.* A form of brass used for castings and extrusions, consisting of three parts copper and two parts zinc. [After G.F. *Muntz* (1794–1857), British manufacturer.]

mu·on (méw-on) *n. Symbol* μ *Physics.* A subatomic particle in the lepton family, having a mass 207 times that of the electron, a negative electric charge, and a mean lifetime of 2.2×10^{-6} second. Formerly called "mu meson". [From *mu* (Greek letter) + -ON.] —**mu·on·ic** (mew-ónnik) *adj.*

mu·o·ni·um (mew-óni-əm) *n. Physics.* A short-lived entity formed by a muon and its antiparticle attracted together and revolving about a common centre.

mu·rage (méwr-ij) *n.* Formerly, a tax levied to finance the building or repairing of city walls. [Middle English, from Old French, from *mur,* from Latin *murus,* wall.]

mu·ral (méwr-əl) *n.* A picture or decoration, usually a very large one, applied directly to a wall or ceiling. ~*adj.* 1. Of, pertaining to, or resembling a wall. 2. On or affixed to a wall: *a mural painting.* [Old French, from Latin *mūrālis,* from *mūrus,* a wall.] —**mu·ral·ist** *n.*

mur·der (múrdər) *n.* Also *obsolete* **mur·ther** (múrthər). 1. The unlawful, usually premeditated, killing of one human being by another. Compare **homicide, manslaughter.** 2. *Slang.* Something that is very difficult or hazardous or that causes extreme discomfort: *This heat is murder.* —**cry** or **scream blue murder.** *Informal.* To make a loud cry, as in protest or anger. —**get away with murder.** *Informal.* To escape punishment or detection. ~*v.* **murdered, -dering, -ders.** Also *obsolete* **mur·ther.** —*tr.* 1. To kill (a human being) unlawfully. 2. To kill (one or more human beings) brutally or inhumanly. 3. To destroy or put an end to. 4. To mar or spoil by ineptness: *murdering the English language with sloppy speech.* 5. *Slang.* To defeat decisively; trounce: *The new magazine was murdering the competition.* 6. *British Slang.* To consume ravenously: *I could murder a pint.* —*intr.* To commit murder. [Middle English *murther, mordre,* Old English *morthor.*] —**mur·der·er** (-ər), **mur·der·ess** (-ess, -riss) *n.*

mur·der·ous (múrdərəss) *adj.* **1.** Capable of, guilty of, or intending murder: *a murderous rage.* **2.** Characteristic of or involving murder: *a murderous ambush.* **3.** *Informal.* Very difficult or dangerous: *a murderous exam.* —**mur·der·ous·ly** *adv.* —**mur·der·ous·ness** *n.*

Mur·doch (múr-dok), **Dame (Jean) Iris** (1919–). Irish-born British novelist. She was trained as a philosopher and in 1948 was appointed lecturer in philosophy at Oxford University. Her first novel, *Under the Net,* was published in 1954. Among the most popular of her later novels are *The Flight from the Enchanter* (1955), *A Severed Head* (1961), *The Unicorn* (1963), and *The Sea, the Sea* (1978), for which she was awarded the Booker prize.

Murdoch, (Keith) Rupert (1931–). Australian-born newspaper proprietor and media entrepreneur, now an American citizen. In 1971 he became Chairman of News International, a British newspaper group.

mure (mewr) *tr.v.* **mured, muring, mures.** *Rare.* To immure; confine; wall in. [Middle English *muren,* from Old French *murer,* from Late Latin *mūrāre,* to wall in, from Latin *mūrus,* a wall.]

mu·rex (méwr-eks) *n., pl.* **murices** (méwr-i-seez) or **-rexes.** Any of various marine gastropods of the genus *Murex,* with rough, spiny shells, common in warm seas. One species, *M. trunculus,* was the source of the royal dye, Tyrian purple. [New Latin, from Latin *mūrex,* of Mediterranean origin.]

mu·ri·ate (méwr-i-ət, -it, -ayt) *n.* A **chloride** *(see).* Not in current technical usage. [Latin *muria,* brine.]

mu·ri·at·ic acid (méwr-i-áttik) *n.* **Hydrochloric acid** *(see).* Not in current technical usage. [Latin *muriāticus,* from *muria,* brine.]

mu·ri·cate (méwr-i-kayt) *adj.* Also **mu·ri·cat·ed** (-kaytid). Having a roughened surface because of many short spines. [Latin *mūricātus,* murex-shaped, pointed, from MUREX.]

Mu·ri·llo (mewr-rílló, -ríl-yō; *Spanish* moo-rée-yō), **Bartolomé Esteban** (1617–82). Spanish painter. He painted chiefly religious subjects, genre paintings (especially of street urchins and peasant boys), and portraits. In 1660 he helped to found the academy of painting and drawing at Seville and he served as its first president.

mu·rine (méwr-īn, -in, -een) *adj.* **1.** Of or pertaining to a member of the rodent family Muridae, including rats and mice. **2.** Caused, transmitted, or affected by rodents of the family Muridae: *a murine plague.* **3.** Resembling a rat or mouse.
~*n.* A murine rodent. [Latin *mūrinus,* from *mūs* (stem *mūr*-), mouse.]

murk, mirk (murk) *n.* Darkness; gloom.
~*adj. Archaic.* Dark; gloomy. [Middle English *mirke,* from an oblique case of Old English *mirce,* darkness.]

murk·y, mirk·y (múrki) *adj.* **-ier, -iest. 1.** Dark or gloomy: *the murky recesses of the deserted chapel.* **2.** Heavy and thick with, or as if with, smoke, fog, or mist, for example. —See Synonyms at **dark.** —**murk·i·ly** *adv.* —**murk·i·ness** *n.*

mur·mur (múrmər) *n.* **1.** A low, indistinct, and continuous sound or succession of sounds: *the murmur of the waves.* **2.** An indistinct or muttered complaint. **3.** A low utterance: *a murmur of approval.* **4.** *Medicine.* An abnormal sound, usually in the thoracic cavity, originating from the heart or lungs and detectable by the ear or a device such as a stethoscope.
~*v.* **murmured, -muring, -murs.** —*intr.* **1.** To make a low, continuous, and indistinct sound or succession of sounds. **2.** To complain in low mumbling tones; grumble. —*tr.* To say in a low indistinct voice; utter indistinctly. —See Synonyms at **mutter.** [Middle English *murmure,* from Old French, from Latin *murmur,* rumble, murmur.] —**mur·mur·er** *n.* —**mur·mur·ing·ly** *adv.* —**mur·mur·ous** (-əss) *adj.* —**mur·mur·ous·ly** *adv.*

mur·phy (múrfi) *n., pl.* **-phies.** *Slang.* A potato. [From the Irish surname *Murphy* (the potato was a staple Irish food).]

Murphy's Law *n.* An axiom of engineers and scientists: "If anything can go wrong, it will". [20th century : origin obscure.]

mur·ra, mur·rah (múrrə) *n.* A precious substance, variously conjectured to have been jade, fluorite, or porcelain, obtained by the Romans from Parthia to make cups and bowls. [Latin *murr(h)a,* from Late Greek *morria†.*] —**mur·rine, mur·rhine** (múrrīn, múrrin) *adj.*

mur·rain (múrrin, múrrayn) *n.* **1.** Any highly infectious and malignant disease of cattle, such as anthrax. **2.** *Archaic.* Any pestilence or dire disease. [Middle English *moreyne,* from Old French *morine,* from *morir,* to die, from Vulgar Latin *morīre* (unattested), variant of Latin *morī,* to die.]

Mur·ray (múrri). River of southeast Australia. Flowing from the Australian Alps to Lake Alexandrina, it forms, with its tributaries, the country's main river system.

Murray, Sir James (Augustus Henry) (1837–1915). British philologist and lexicographer. He established his reputation by his article on the English language for the *Encyclopaedia Britannica.* His most important work was establishing the framework of the Oxford English Dictionary, of which he was appointed the editor in 1879.

Murray, Lionel (Len), Baron Murray of Epping Forest (1922–). British trade unionist. After studying at the Universities of London and Oxford, he joined the economic department of the Trades Union Congress in 1947, serving as its head from 1954 to 1969. He was Assistant General Secretary of the T.U.C. (1969–73), until becoming General Secretary (1973–84).

mur·rey (múrri) *n. Archaic.* A colour, **mulberry** *(see).* [Middle English *morreye,* from Old French *more,* from Medieval Latin *morātum,* from *morātus,* mulberry-coloured, from Latin *morum,* mulberry.] —**mur·rey** *adj.*

murrhine glass, murrine glass *n.* **1.** Glassware believed to resemble ancient Roman vessels of murra. **2.** Glassware inlaid with precious stones, or with coloured metals and glass. [Latin *murr(h)inus,* from *murr(h)a,* MURRA.]

Mur·ry (múrri), **John Middleton** (1889–1957). British literary critic, husband of Katherine Mansfield. He was editor of the *Athenaeum* and founded his own literary review, the *Adelphi* (1923). During World War II he also edited the pacifist journal, *Peace News.* His volumes of criticism include *The Problem of Style* (1922) and *Keats and Shakespeare* (1925).

murther. *Obsolete.* Variant of **murder.**

mus. 1. museum. **2.** music; musical; musician.

Mus. B., Mus. Bac. Bachelor of Music. [Latin *Musicae Baccalaureus.*]

Mus·ca (múskə) *n.* A constellation in the polar region of the Southern Hemisphere near Apus and Carina. [Latin, "the fly".]

mus·ca·dine (múskə-din, -dīn) *n.* **1.** A musk-flavoured grape used to make wine. Also called "scuppernong". [Variant of MUSCATEL.]

mus·cae vo·li·tan·tes (mússee vólli-tánteez, múskee) *pl.n.* Small motes and threads that seem to move about the field of vision, due to the presence of cell fragments or other defects in the vitreous humour and the lens of the eye. [Latin, "fluttering flies".]

mus·ca·rine (múskə-rin, -reen) *n.* A highly toxic organic compound, $C_8H_{19}O_3N$, related to the cholines, and derived from the mushroom *Amanita muscaria.* [New Latin (*Amanita*) *muscaria,* from Latin *muscārius,* of a fly, from *musca,* a fly.]

mus·cat (múss-kət, -kat) *n.* **1.** Any of various sweet white grapes used for making wine or raisins. **2.** Muscatel. [French, from Provençal *muscat,* "musky" (flavour), from *musc,* MUSK.]

Mus·cat or **Mas·kat** or **Mas·qut** (múss-kət, máss-, -kat). Capital of Oman. Lying on a fine harbour, it was an important port, but it has lately been eclipsed by neighbouring Matrah. Exports include dates, mother-of-pearl, and dried fish, and it has an oil terminal.

Muscat and Oman. See **Oman, Sultanate of.**

mus·ca·tel (múskə-tél) *n.* Also **mus·ca·del** (-dél). **1.** A rich, sweet wine made from muscat grapes. **2.** A muscat grape or raisin. [Middle English *muscadelle,* from Old French *muscadel,* diminutive of MUSCAT.]

mus·cle (múss'l) *n.* **1.** A tissue composed of fibres capable of contracting and relaxing to effect bodily movement. The principal types are **striated muscle** and **smooth muscle,** with **cardiac muscle** *(all of which see)* intermediate between them. **2.** A contractile organ consisting of muscle tissue. **3.** Strength or powerful authority: *Her credentials added muscle to her argument.*
~*v.* **muscled, -cling, -cles.** —*intr. Informal.* To force one's way into a place or situation where one is not wanted. Usually used with *in.* —*tr.* To push (one's way) into a crowded or restricted place or situation: *She muscled her way into the debating chamber.* [French, from Latin *mūsculus,* "little mouse", muscle (from the shape of certain muscles, for example the biceps), from *mūs,* mouse.]

mus·cle-bound (múss'l-bownd) *adj.* **1.** Having stiff, overdeveloped muscles, usually as the result of excessive exercise. **2.** Unable to act flexibly; rigid: *an army too muscle-bound to be effective in a crisis.*

muscle fibre *n.* An elongated, contractile cell having highly striated cytoplasm.

mus·cle·man (múss'l-man) *n., pl.* **-men** (-men). A man with large, highly developed muscles; especially, an aggressive, powerful, or intimidating man.

muscle sense *n.* **Kinaesthesia** *(see).*

mus·co·va·do, mus·ca·va·do (múskə-vaádō) *n.* Unrefined sugar obtained from the juice of sugar cane by evaporation and extraction of the molasses. [Portuguese (*açúcar*) *mascavado,* unrefined or low quality (sugar), from *mascavar,* to adulterate, depreciate, from Vulgar Latin *minuscapāre* (unattested) : *minus,* less, from *minor,* smaller + *capāre* (unattested), to "bring to a head", cause, from Latin *caput,* head.]

mus·co·vite (múss-kə-vīt, -kō-) *n.* A mineral, the most common form of mica, consisting essentially of hydrous potassium aluminium silicate with hydroxyl and fluorine, $KAl_2(AlSi_3O_{10})(OH,F)_2$. It ranges from colourless or pale yellow to grey and brown, has a pearly lustre, and is used as an insulator. Also called "isinglass", "white mica". [Formerly called *Muscovy* glass.]

Mus·co·vite (múss-kə-vīt, -kō-) *n.* **1.** A native or resident of Moscow or of Muscovy. **2.** *Archaic.* A native or resident of Russia. —**Mus·co·vite** *adj.*

Mus·co·vy (múss-kə-vi, -kō-). **1.** The principality of Moscow (12th–16th centuries). **2.** *Archaic.* Russia.

Muscovy duck *n.* A waterfowl, *Cairina moschata,* found wild from Mexico to Brazil, but domesticated around the world for its succulent flesh. It is greenish-black with heavy red wattles. Also called "Muscovy", "musk duck". [Folk etymology from *musk duck* (by mistaken association with MUSCOVY).]

mus·cu·lar (múskew-lər) *adj.* **1.** Pertaining to or consisting of muscle or muscles. **2.** Accomplished with or involving the use of muscle or muscles: *muscular effort.* **3.** Having strong muscles. [Latin *mūsculus,* MUSCLE.] —**mus·cu·lar·i·ty** (-lárrəti) *n.* —**mus·cu·lar·ly** *adv.*

muscular dystrophy *n.* A chronic, noncontagious, congenital disease, in which complete incapacitation follows gradual but irreversible muscular deterioration.

mus·cu·la·ture (múskewlə-chər, -tewr) *n.* The system of muscles of an animal or a body part. [French, from Latin *musculus,* MUSCLE.]

Mus. D., Mus. Doc. Doctor of Music. [Latin *Musicae Doctor.*]

muse (mewz) *v.* **mused, musing, muses.** —*intr.* To ponder or meditate, usually in silence; consider or deliberate at length. Often followed by *over, on,* or *upon: She gazed into the distance, musing on human existence.* —*tr. Archaic.* **1.** To meditate on; consider reflectively: *muse the problem.* **2.** To wonder: *"The maiden paused, musing what this might mean."* (S.T. Coleridge).
~*n. Archaic.* A state of musing or deep meditation. [Middle English *musen,* from Old French *muser,* to muse, dawdle, "sniff around", from *mus,* snout, from Medieval Latin *mūsum.*] —**museful** *adj.* —**muse·ful·ly** *adv.*

Muse (mewz) *n.* **1.** *Greek Mythology.* Any of the nine daughters of Mnemosyne and Zeus, each of whom presided over a different art or science. The Muses are Calliope, Clio, Erato, Euterpe, Melpomene, Polyhymnia, Terpsichore, Thalia, and Urania. **2.** *Small* **m.** The spirit or power regarded as inspiring poets, musicians, and artists; a source of inspiration. Often preceded by *the.* [Middle English, from Old French, from Latin *Mūsa,* from Greek *Mousa.*]

mu·sette (mew-zét) *n.* **1.** A small French bagpipe with a soft sound. **2.** A soft, pastoral tune that imitates the sound of a bagpipe. **3.** A kind of dance performed to such a tune. [Middle English, from Old French, from *muser,* to MUSE, dawdle, play the musette.]

mu·se·um (mew-zée-əm) *n. Abbr.* **mus.** A place or building in which works of artistic, historical, and scientific value are cared for and exhibited. [Latin *mūseum,* library, study, museum, from Greek *mouseion,* "place of the Muses", from *mouseios,* of the Muses, from *Mousa,* a Muse.]

museum piece *n.* **1.** An object of sufficient artistic or historical interest to warrant its inclusion in a museum. **2.** *Informal.* Someone or something considered to be old-fashioned.

Musgrave Ranges. Highland along the border of South Australia with Northern Territory, the highest point being Mount Woodroofe (1 514 metres; 4,970 feet). It is a traditional site of Aborigine reservations.

mush[1] (mush) *n.* **1.** Anything thick, soft, and pulpy in texture. **2.** *Informal.* Maudlin sentimentality. [Probably alteration of MASH.]

mush[2] (mŏŏsh, mush) *interj.* A command given to a team of sledge dogs to start or go faster.
~*intr.v.* **mushed, mushing, mushes.** To travel with a dog sledge.
~*n.* A journey by dog sledge. [Canadian French *mouche!* "run", from *moucher,* to fly, hasten, from French *mouche,* a fly, from Latin *musca.*] —**mush·er** *n.*

mush[3] (mŏŏsh) *n. British Slang.* A human face. [From MUSH[1].]

mush·room (músh-rŏŏm, -rŏŏm) *n.* **1.** Any of various fleshy fruiting bodies produced by fungi of the class Basidiomycetes, characteristically having an umbrella-shaped cap borne on a stalk; especially, any of the edible varieties. **2.** Any of the fungi producing such structures. **3.** Something resembling a mushroom in shape.
~*intr.v.* **mushroomed, -rooming, -rooms.** **1.** To multiply, grow, or expand rapidly: *The demonstration mushroomed into a riot.* **2.** To spread out, flatten, or swell into a mushroom-like shape. **3.** To search for and gather mushrooms. [Middle English *musseroun, muscheron,* from Old French *mousseron, moisseron,* from Gallo-Roman *mussirot†* (unattested), agaric.]

mushroom cloud *n.* The cloud of gas, dust, and the like, rising in the shape of a mushroom, following a nuclear explosion.

mush·y (múshi) *adj.* **-ier, -iest.** **1.** Like mush; soft and pulpy. **2.** *Informal.* Excessively sentimental. —**mush·i·ly** *adv.* —**mush·i·ness** *n.*

mu·sic (méwzik) *n. Abbr.* **mus.** **1.** An art or art form consisting of organised tones that produce a coherent sequence of sounds intended to elicit a pleasurable response in a listener. **2.** Vocal or instrumental sounds having some degree of rhythm, melody, and harmony. **3. a.** A musical composition. **b.** A body of such compositions: *the music of Béla Bartók; French music.* **c.** The written or printed score for a musical composition. **d.** Such scores collectively. **4.** A musical accompaniment. **5.** The study of musicology. **6.** Any aesthetically pleasing or harmonious sound or combination of sounds: *the music of your voice; the music of the wind in the trees.* **7.** *Rare.* A group of musicians: *The Queen's music.* —**face the music.** *Informal.* To accept the consequences, especially of one's own actions. —**music to (someone's) ears.** That which is received with pleasure: *News of her promotion was music to our ears.* [Middle English *musik,* from Old French *musique,* from Latin *mūsica,* from Greek *mousikē (tekhnē),* (art) of the Muses, that is, poetry, literature, and music, for example, from *mousikos,* of the Muses, from *Mousa,* Muse.]

mu·si·cal (méwzik'l) *adj. Abbr.* **mus.** **1.** Of, pertaining to, or capable of producing music: *a musical instrument.* **2.** Characteristic of or resembling music; melodious: *a musical tone of voice.* **3.** Set to or accompanied by music: *a musical revue.* **4.** Devoted to or skilled in music.
~*n.* A musical comedy. —**mu·si·cal·ly** *adv.*

musical chairs *n.* **1.** A game in which the players walk to music around a row of chairs containing one chair fewer than the number of players. When the music stops, the players rush to sit down, and the one left without a chair is ruled out of the game. **2.** *Informal.* A continual temporary rearranging or reshuffling of factors or people in which there is a lot of activity but not much to show for it.

musical comedy *n.* **1.** A play or film in which dialogue is interspersed with songs and dances, usually based upon a rather sketchy plot. **2.** Such plays or films collectively.

musical glasses *pl.n.* An instrument, the **glass harmonica** *(see).*
mu·si·cal·i·ty (méwzi-kál-ət̄i) *n.* **1.** Musical quality. **2.** Skill in the performance of, ability to respond to, or talent for music.

music box *n.* Also **musical box.** A box containing a device, activated by clockwork, which plays tunes when the box is opened.

music centre *n.* A record player, radio, and cassette player combined into one high-fidelity domestic unit.

music drama *n.* **1.** An opera in which the musical and dramatic continuity is sustained, without being interrupted by arias, recitatives, or ensembles, while its text is set to continuously expressive music often based extensively on leitmotifs. **2.** Such operas collectively. See **opera.**

music hall *n. Chiefly British.* **1. a.** Stage entertainment, especially popular in the early 20th century, offering a variety of short acts such as song-and-dance routines, impersonations, and the like. **b.** A theatrical performance of this kind. Also *chiefly U.S.* "vaudeville". **2.** A theatre for such entertainment. —**music-hall** *adj.*

mu·si·cian (mew-zísh'n) *n. Abbr.* **mus.** A person skilled in composing or performing music, especially professionally. [Middle English *musicien,* from Old French, from Latin *mūsica,* MUSIC.] —**mu·si·cian·ly** *adj.* —**mu·si·cian·ship** *n.*

music of the spheres *n.* An inaudible harmony thought by Pythagoras to be produced by the movements of celestial bodies.

mu·si·col·o·gy (méwzi-kólləji) *n.* The historical and scientific study of music. —**mu·si·co·log·i·cal** (-kə-lójik'l) *adj.* —**mu·si·co·log·i·cal·ly** *adv.* —**mu·si·col·o·gist** (-kóllə)ist) *n.*

music paper *n.* Paper, printed with staves, on which music may be written.

music roll *n.* A roll of paper that·is perforated and used in certain mechanical keyboard instruments, such as the player piano.

music stand *n.* A stand that can be raised or lowered, used for holding a musical score.

music therapy *n.* Medical or psychological therapy using music: *"music therapy is the controlled use of music in the treatment, education and training of children and adults suffering from physical, mental or emotional disorders."* (J. Alvin, *Music Therapy.*)

mus·jid (múss-jid) *n.* A **mosque** *(see).*

musk (musk) *n.* **1.** A greasy secretion with a powerful odour, produced in a glandular sac beneath the skin of the abdomen of the male musk deer. It is used in the manufacture of perfumes. **2.** Any similar secretion of certain other vertebrates, such as the otter or civet. **3.** Any synthetic chemical resembling natural musk in odour or use. **4.** The odour of musk or an odour resembling it. **5.** A plant, *Mimulus moschatus,* which resembles a small **monkey flower** *(see),* formerly cultivated for its musky scent. [Middle English *muske,* from Old French *musc,* from Late Latin *muscus,* from Greek *moskhos,* from Persian *mushk,* probably from Sanskrit *muṣka,* testicle, scrotum (from the scrotum-shaped musk bag of a musk deer), "little mouse", from *mūṣ,* mouse.] —**musk, musk·y** *adj.* —**musk·i·ness** *n.*

musk deer *n.* A small, hornless deer, *Moschus moschiferus,* of central and northeastern Asia. The male secretes musk.

musk duck *n.* **1.** A waterfowl, the **Muscovy duck** *(see).* **2.** A waterfowl, *Biziura lobata,* of Australia. The male has a leathery chin lobe, and emits a musky odour during the breeding season.

mus·keg (múss-keg) *n.* Also **mas·keg** (máss-). In Canada, a swamp or bog formed by an accumulation of sphagnum moss, leaves, and decayed matter. [Cree *maskeek,* from Proto-Algonquian *maškyeekwi* (unattested), swamp.]

mus·kel·lunge (músskə-lunj) *n., pl.* **-lunges** or collectively **muskellunge.** Also **mas·ka·longe** (másskə-lonj), **mas·ca·nonge** (másskə-nonj). A large game fish, *Esox masquinongy,* similar to the pike, found in the cooler fresh waters of North America. Also informally called "muskie". [Of Algonquian origin; akin to Algonquian *maskinonge,* "big pike".]

mus·ket (múskit) *n.* A smoothbore shoulder gun used from the late 16th to the 19th century. [French *mousquet,* from Italian *moschetto,* crossbolt, later musket, diminutive of *mosca,* a fly, from Latin *musca.*]

mus·ket·eer (múski-téer) *n.* **1.** Formerly, a soldier armed with a musket; specifically, a member of the French royal household bodyguard in the 17th and 18th centuries. [French *mousquetaire,* from *mousquet,* MUSKET.]

mus·ket·ry (múskitri) *n.* **1.** Muskets collectively. **2.** Musketeers collectively. **3.** The technique of using small arms.

Mus·kho·ge·an, Mus·ko·ge·an (muss-kŏgi-ən) *n.* A North American Indian language family, including Chickasaw, Choctaw, Creek, and Seminole. —**Mus·kho·ge·an, Mus·ko·ge·an** *adj.*

musk mallow *n.* **1.** A plant, *Malva moschata,* native to Europe, having finely divided leaves and pink flowers with a faint scent of musk. **2.** A plant, the **abelmosk** *(see).*

musk·mel·on (músk-mellən) *n.* **1.** Any of several varieties of the melon *Cucumis melo,* such as the cantaloupe, having fruit characterised by a netted rind and flesh with a musky aroma. **2.** The fruit of any of these plants.

musk ox *n.* A large, hoofed mammal, *Ovibos moschatus,* of northern Canada and Greenland, that emits a musky odour. It has a long, dark, shaggy, coat and downward-curving horns.

musk·rat (músk-rat) *n., pl.* **-rats** or collectively **muskrat.** **1.** An aquatic rodent, *Ondatra zibethica,* native to North America, having a brown coat that is widely used as a fur. It has partly webbed hind feet, and musk glands under a broad, flat tail. Also called "musquash". **2.** The fur of this rodent. [MUSK + RAT (possibly influenced by Algonquian (Natick) *musquash,* MUSQUASH).]

musk rose *n.* A prickly shrub, *Rosa moschata,* native to the Mediterranean region, having musk-scented white flowers.

musk thistle *n.* A plant, *Carduus nutans,* that has purple, nodding, brushlike flowers which emit a musky fragrance.

musk tree *n.* Any of various small Australasian trees, especially of the genus *Olearia,* having a musky fragrance.

Mus·lim (mŏŏz-lim, múz-, mŏŏss-) *n.* Also **Mus·lem, Mos·lem** (mŏz-, *also* -lem). **1.** A believer in or adherent of Islam. **2.** A member of the **Nation of Islam** (*see*).
~*adj.* **1.** Of or pertaining to Islam, its adherents, culture, or the like. **2.** Pertaining or belonging to the Nation of Islam. [Arabic *muslim,* "one who surrenders (to God)", active participle of *salama,* to surrender.]

  Usage: Moslem is the form generally preferred in popular journalism and in popular usage. *Muslim* is preferred by scholars, and by English-speaking adherents of Islam. It is considered the only correct form by members of the Nation of Islam (or "Black Muslims"). *Mohammedan* is offensive to many Muslims, because of the implication of worship of the Prophet, which is forbidden by Islam.

Muslim calendar *n.* The lunar calendar used in Muslim countries reckoning time from July 16, A.D. 622, the day after the Hegira, based on a cycle of 30 years, 19 of which have 354 days each and 11 of which are leap years, having 355 days each.

mus·lin (múzlin) *n.* Any of various fine, diaphanous, plain-weave cotton fabrics, used for dresses, or curtains, for example. [French *mousseline,* from Italian *mussolina,* "cloth of Mosul", from Arabic *mūṣlin,* originally made in *Al-Mawṣil,* in Iraq.]

Mus. M. Master of Music. [Latin *Magister Musicae.*]

mus·quash (múss-kwosh ‖ *U.S. also* -kwawsh) *n.* A muskrat. [Algonquian (Natick).]

muss (muss) *tr.v.* **mussed, mussing, musses.** *Chiefly U.S. Informal.* To make messy or untidy; rumple. Often used with *up.*
~*n.* A state of disorder; a mess. [Perhaps variant of MESS.]
—muss·i·ly *adv.* **—muss·y** *adj.*

mus·sel (múss'l) *n.* **1. a.** Any of several marine bivalve molluscs, especially *Mytilus edulis,* having a blue-black shell. **b.** The edible flesh of any of these molluscs. **2.** Any of several freshwater bivalve molluscs of the genera *Anodonta,* and *Unio,* whose shells provide mother-of-pearl. [Middle English, Old English *mus(c)le,* from West Germanic *muskul,* from Latin *mūsculus,* "little mouse", muscle, mussel (from its mouselike shape), from *mūs,* mouse.]

Mus·set (mū-sáy), **(Louis Charles) Alfred de** (1810–57). French poet and dramatist, one of the leading poets of the French Romantic movement. He is most famous for the four poems, *Les Nuits* (1835–37), and for his plays, such as *On ne badine pas avec l'amour* and *Lorenzaccio* (1834).

Mus·so·li·ni (mŏŏssə-léeni ‖ *Italian* mŏ́ŏssō-), **Benito** (1883–1945). Italian politician, founder of the Fascist movement and prime minister and dictator of Italy (1922–45). He founded the first *fascio di combattimento* at Milan (1919) and two years later, when he was elected to parliament, the National Fascist party was formally established. He was invited by King Victor Emmanuel III to form a government in October, 1922. Opposition parties were suppressed and parliamentary government ended by 1928. In the 1930s Mussolini conducted an expansionist foreign policy, invading Ethiopia (1935) and annexing Albania (1939). The Rome-Berlin axis forged during the Spanish Civil War was confirmed by a formal alliance (1939). He brought Italy into World War II on the side of the Axis powers in June, 1940. He was dismissed by the king and arrested in July, 1943, escaped, and headed a puppet Nazi government in north Italy until April, 1945, when he was captured and executed by Italian partisans.

Mus·sorg·sky or **Mous·sorg·sky** (mŏŏ-sórg-ski; *Russian* mŏ́ŏ-sərk-ski), **Modest Petrovich** (1839–81). Russian composer. His works include the opera *Boris Godunov* (first produced 1874), the piano suite *Pictures at an Exhibition* (1874), and many songs.

Mus·sul·man (múss'l-mən) *n., pl.* **-men** (-mən) or **-mans.** *Archaic.* A Muslim. [Turkish *musulmān,* probably from Arabic *mushmūn,* plural of *muslim,* MUSLIM.]

must[1] (must; *weak form* məst) *v.* Used as an auxiliary followed by an infinitive without *to,* or, in reply to a question or suggestion, with the infinitive understood. It can indicate: **1.** Compulsion or obligation: *When duty calls, you must answer.* **2.** Requirement or prerequisite: *You must register in order to vote.* **3.** Probability, expectation, or supposition: *It must be nearly midnight.* **4.** Inevitability or certainty: *To each of us, death must come.* **5. a.** In the first person, insistence or fixed resolve: *I must finish this tonight.* **b.** In the second and third persons, insistence imputed by the speaker to others: *Have another drink, if you must.* **6.** Unpleasant inevitability. Used as a past or historical present: *The rain was coming down and I must lose my umbrella!* **7.** Imminent departure. With *away: We must away!*
~*n.* **1.** A requirement or necessity: *In teaching, patience is a must.* **2.** Something that should without fail be done, seen, or otherwise acted upon: *If you visit Rome, the Vatican is a must.* [Middle English *moste* (past tense), Old English *mōste,* past tense of *mōtan,* to be allowed, from Germanic.]

  Usage: The meanings of *must* are traditionally divided into two major groups: "obligation" and "firm likelihood", or "assumption".

  When *must* refers to obligation, it can often be paraphrased with *have (got) to,* especially if the obligation is being reported rather than imposed: *Passengers must surrender their tickets at the barrier; The notice says that passengers have (got) to give in their tickets to the person at the barrier.* When *must* refers to assumption (*If you haven't eaten since breakfast, you must be hungry*), it cannot

usually be so paraphrased, although there is a tendency in this direction, especially in American English: *Surely you don't mean that! You must be joking/you have to be joking/you've got to be joking.* When *must* refers to obligation, it has two types of negation, which differ in meaning. The contradictory of *I must stop work early* (= "I am obliged to stop work early") is *I must not stop work early* (= "I am obliged not to stop work early"), which means, in effect, *I must work late.* The contrary of *I must stop work early* is *I don't have to/ needn't stop work early* (= "I am not obliged to stop work early").

  When *must* refers to assumption, its negative form is expressed in standard English with *cannot: If you've just eaten a steak, you can't be very hungry.* But in American English, *must not* is frequently used here, too.

must[2] (must) *n.* Mould; mustiness. [Back-formation from MUSTY.]

must[3] (must) *n.* The unfermented or fermenting juice being processed for wine; new wine. [Middle English *must,* Old English *must, moste,* from Latin *mustum,* "new wine", from neuter of *mustus,* new, newborn.]

must[4]. Variant of **musth.**

mustache. *U.S.* Variant of **moustache.**

mus·ta·chi·o (mə-staáshi-ō ‖ -stásh-) *n., pl.* **-chios.** *Often plural.* A moustache, especially a luxuriant one. Usually used humorously. [Spanish *mostaccho* and Italian *mustaccio,* MOUSTACHE.] **—mus·ta·chi·oed** (-ōd) *adj.*

mus·tang (múss-tang) *n.* A wild horse of the North American plains, descended from Spanish stock. [Mexican Spanish *mesten(g)o,* from Spanish, stray (animal), from *mesta,* meeting of owners of stray animals, from Medieval Latin *(animalia) mixta,* wild or stray animals that mixed with and became attached to a grazier's herd, "mixed animals", from Latin *mixtus,* past participle of *miscēre,* to mix.]

mus·tard (mústərd) *n.* **1.** Any of various plants of the genus *Brassica* native to Eurasia, having four-petalled yellow flowers and slender pods. Some species, especially *B. nigra* and *B. alba,* are cultivated for their pungent seeds. **2.** Any of various other plants of the family Cruciferae (or Brassicaceae), such as garlic mustard. **3. a.** Powdered mustard seeds used medicinally, as in mustard plaster. **b.** A condiment consisting of a paste made from powdered mustard seeds mixed with wine, vinegar, or water, and various spices, such as turmeric. **3.** Dark yellow to light olive brown. [Middle English *mustarde,* condiment, later also plant, from Old French *mo(u)starde,* from Common Romance *mosto,* from Latin *mustum,* MUST, "new wine" (because mustard paste was originally made by mixing grape juice with mustard powder).] **—mus·tard** *adj.*

mustard and cress *n.* Seedlings of white mustard and garden cress, eaten together in salads or as a garnish.

mustard gas *n.* An oily, volatile liquid, $(ClCH_2CH_2)_2S$, used in warfare as a gaseous blistering agent. [From its mustard-like odour.]

mustard oil *n.* Any oil obtained from mustard seeds.

mustard plaster *n.* A pastelike mixture of powdered mustard, flour, and water, spread on cloth or paper, and applied in poultice as a counterirritant. Also called "mustard flour", "plaster".

mus·tee (mu-stée, mústee) *n.* Also **mes·tee** (me-stée). **1.** A person one of whose parents is white and the other a quadroon. **2.** Loosely, any person of mixed racial descent. [Spanish *mestizo,* person of mixed parentage.]

mus·ter (mústər) *v.* **-tered, -tering, -ters.** **—***tr.* **1.** To summon or assemble (troops, for example). **2.** To collect or gather. Sometimes used with *up: to muster arguments; muster up courage.* **—***intr.* To assemble or gather: *mustering for inspection.*
~*n.* **1. a.** A gathering, especially of troops, for service, inspection, review, or roll call. **b.** The persons assembled for such a gathering. **2.** The official roll of men in a military or naval unit. Also called "muster roll". **3.** Any gathering or collection. **4.** A flock of peacocks. **—pass muster.** To be acceptable. [Middle English *mostren,* from Old French *mo(u)strer,* from Latin *monstrāre,* to show, indicate (originally by an omen), from *mōnstrum,* an omen, prodigy, probably from *monēre,* to warn.]

musth, must (must) *n.* A condition of frenzied sexual excitement occurring in the males of certain mammals such as the elephant and camel.
~*adj.* Designating a mammal in musth. [Urdu, from Persian *mast,* drunk.]

must·y (músti) *adj.* **-ier, -iest.** **1.** Having a stale or mouldy odour or taste. **2.** Hackneyed; dull; antiquated; stale: *musty views on life.* [Variant (influenced by MUST[3], juice) of obsolete *moisty,* from MOIST.] **—must·i·ly** *adv.* **—must·i·ness** *n.*

mu·ta·ble (méwtə-b'l) *adj.* **1.** Subject to change or alteration. **2.** Prone to frequent change; inconstant; fickle. [Latin *mūtābilis,* from *mūtāre,* to change, MUTATE.] **—mu·ta·bil·i·ty** (-bílləti), **mu·ta·ble·ness** *n.* **—mu·ta·bly** *adv.*

mu·ta·gen (méwtə-jən) *n.* Any agent, including radioactive elements, ultraviolet radiation, and certain chemicals, that causes biological mutation. [MUTA(TION) + -GEN.] **—mu·ta·gen·ic** (-jénnik) *adj.* **—mu·ta·gen·i·cal·ly** *adv.*

mu·tant (méwt'nt) *n. Biology.* **1.** An individual or organism differing from the parental strain or strains as a result of mutation. **2.** A gene that has undergone mutation. [Latin *mūtans* (stem *mūtant-*), changing, participle of *mūtāre,* to change, MUTATE.] **—mu·tant** *adj.*

mu·tate (mew-táyt ‖ méw-tayt) *v.* **-tated, -tating, -tates.** **—***tr.* To cause to undergo alteration, especially by mutation. **—***intr.* To un-

dergo change by mutation. [Latin *mūtāre* (past stem *mutat-*).]
—**mu·ta·tive** (méwtətiv, mew-táytiv) *adj.*

mu·ta·tion (mew-táysh'n) *n.* **1.** The act or process of being altered or changed. **2.** An alteration or change, as in nature, form, or quality. **3.** *Biology.* **a.** Any heritable alteration of the genes or chromosomes of an organism. **b.** A mutant. **4.** *Linguistics.* **a.** The change that is caused in the sound of one vowel by its assimilation to another vowel; especially, umlaut *(see).* **b.** In Celtic languages, a change in the initial consonant of a word or morpheme based upon the phonetic nature of the word preceding it or upon its gender or syntactic function. [Middle English *mutacioun,* from Old French *mutation,* from Latin *mūtātiō* (stem *mūtātiōn-*), from *mūtāre,* to change, MUTATE.] —**mu·ta·tion·al** *adj.* —**mu·ta·tion·al·ly** *adv.*

mu·ta·tis mu·tan·dis (mew-táatiss mew-tándiss, mōō-, -táytiss) *Abbr.* **m.m.** *Latin.* The necessary changes having been made; substituting new terms.

mutch·kin (múchkin) *n. Scottish.* A unit of liquid measure equal to approximately one pint. [Middle English (Scottish) *muchekyn,* from obsolete Dutch *mudseken,* diminutive of *mudde,* bushel, from Latin *modius.*]

mute (mewt) *adj.* **muter, mutest. 1. a.** Refraining from producing speech or vocal sound. **b.** Not expressed in speech in speech or vocal sound: *a mute agreement.* **2. a.** Unable to speak; dumb. **b.** Unable to vocalise, as certain animals are. **3.** *Law.* Refusing, as a defendant, to plead either guilty or not guilty when under arraignment. Used chiefly in the phrase *stand mute.* **4.** *Phonetics.* Not pronounced; silent, as is the *e* in *house.* —See Synonyms at **dumb.** ~*n.* **1.** A person incapable of speech; especially, one both deaf and mute. **2.** *Law.* A defendant who refuses to plead either guilty or not guilty when under arraignment. **3.** *Music.* Any of various devices used to muffle or soften the tone of a musical instrument. **4.** *Phonetics.* **a.** A silent or unpronounced letter. **b.** A plosive; a stop. **5.** One who acts in a dumb show. **6.** Formerly, one hired to mourn at a funeral.
~*tr.v.* **muted, muting, mutes. 1.** To muffle or soften the sound of (a musical instrument, for example). **2.** To soften the tone, colour, shade, or hue of. **3.** To lessen the intensity of: *muted criticism.* [Middle English *muet,* from Old French, diminutive of *mu,* mute, from Latin *mūtus,* silent, dumb.] —**mute·ly** *adv.* —**mute·ness** *n.*

mute[2] *v.* **muted, muting, mutes.** —*tr.* To discharge (faeces). Used of a bird. —*intr.* To discharge faeces. Used of a bird. [Middle English, from Old French *meutir, esmeutir,* from Frankish *smeltjan* (unattested), to SMELT.]

mute swan *n.* A white Eurasian swan, *Cygnus olor,* with an orange bill and a curved neck.

mu·ti·late (méwti-layt) *tr.v.* **-lated, -lating, -lates. 1.** To deprive (a person or animal) of a limb or other essential part. **2.** To render imperfect by damaging or excising a part: *to mutilate books.* [Latin *mutilāre,* to cut off, from *mutilus,* maimed.] —**mu·ti·la·tion** (-láysh'n) *n.* —**mu·ti·la·tive** (-laytiv, -lətiv) *adj.* —**mu·ti·la·tor** *n.*

mu·ti·neer (méwti-neér) *n.* A person, especially a serviceman, who takes part in a mutiny. [Obsolete French *mutinier,* from Old French *mutin,* MUTINY.]

mu·ti·nous (méwtinəss) *adj.* **1.** Pertaining to, engaged in, or disposed towards mutiny. **2.** Rebellious; unruly; disaffected. —See Synonyms at **insubordinate.** [From obsolete *mutine,* MUTINY.] —**mu·ti·nous·ly** *adv.* —**mu·ti·nous·ness** *n.*

mu·ti·ny (méwtini) *n., pl.* **-nies.** Open rebellion against constituted authority; especially, rebellion of sailors or soldiers against superior officers. See Synonyms at **rebellion.**
~*intr.v.* **mutinied, -nying, -nies.** To rebel by engaging in or as if in a mutiny. [From obsolete *mutine,* mutiny, from Old French *mutin,* rebellious, rebellion, from *muete,* revolt, "movement", from Vulgar Latin *movita* (unattested), from Latin *movēre,* to move.]

mut·ism (méwtiz'm) *n.* **1.** The condition of being unable to speak. **2.** *Psychology.* A condition resulting in a refusal to speak.

mutt (mut) *n. Chiefly U.S. Slang.* **1.** A mongrel dog. **2.** A fool. [Shortened from MUTTONHEAD.]

mut·ter (múttər) *v.* **-tered, -tering, -ters.** —*intr.* **1.** To speak indistinctly in low tones. **2.** To complain or grumble morosely. —*tr.* To utter or say in low, indistinct tones.
~*n.* A low, indistinct uttering or utterance, often of discontent. [Middle English *muteren,* akin to Old Norse *mudhla.*] —**mut·ter·er** *n.* —**mut·ter·ing** *n.*
Synonyms: *mutter, mumble, murmur.*

mut·ton (mútt'n) *n.* The flesh of fully grown sheep. —**dead as mutton.** Absolutely dead. —**mutton dressed as lamb.** An old or older person attempting to look young, usually by dressing in an inappropriately youthful style. [Middle English *moto(u)n,* from Old French *moton,* sheep, from Medieval Latin *multō* (stem *multōn-*).]

mutton bird *n. Australian.* Any of various petrels with dark plumage and greyish underparts.

mutton chop *n.* **1.** A thick chop cut from the loin section of mutton. **2.** *Plural.* Side whiskers shaped like chops of meat. Also called "mutton-chop whiskers".

mut·ton·head (mútt'n-hed) *n. Slang.* A stupid person. [From the stupidity of sheep.] —**mutton·head·ed** (-heddid) *adj.*

mu·tu·al (méw-choo-əl, -tew-) *adj.* **1.** Having the same relationship each to the other: *mutual friends.* **2.** Directed and received in equal amount. **3.** Possessed in common: *mutual interests.* [Middle English *mutuall,* from Old French *mutuel,* from Latin *mūtuus,* exchanged, reciprocal, mutual.] —**mu·tu·al·i·ty** (-ál-əti) *n.* —**mu·tu·al·ly** *adv.*

Usage: Mutual is often used in the general sense of "common" (*We all had a mutual interest in getting a decision made*), but this usage is criticised by purists, who feel that the word should be restricted to what only two people do, feel, or represent to each other. Thus, when two people have a *mutual distrust,* each distrusts the other in like manner. As a consequence, in strict usage a phrase such as *a mutual distrust of each other* is felt to be repetitive.

mutual fund *n. U.S.* A unit trust *(see).*

mutual inductance *n. Abbr.* **M** *Physics.* **1.** The ratio expressed by the flux linking one circuit with a neighbouring circuit divided by the current in the neighbouring circuit. **2.** The ratio expressed by the electromotive force induced in a circuit by a neighbouring circuit divided by the corresponding change of current in the neighbouring circuit. See **inductance.**

mutual induction *n. Physics.* Electromagnetic induction in which electromotive force in one circuit is produced by a changing current in a neighbouring circuit.

mutual insurance *n.* An insurance system in which the insured persons become company members, each paying specific amounts into a common fund from which members are entitled to protection and compensation in case of loss.

mu·tu·al·ise, mu·tu·al·ize (méw-choo-ə-līz, -tew-) *tr.v.* **-ised, -ising, -ises. 1.** To make mutual. **2.** To set up or reorganise (a business) as a cooperative.

mu·tu·al·ism (méw-choo-ə-liz'm, -tew-) *n. Biology.* Any association between two or more organisms, in which all benefit. See **symbiosis.**

muu·muu (mōō-mōō) *n.* A long, loose dress that hangs free from the shoulders. [Hawaiian *mu'u mu'u.*]

Muy·bridge (míbrij), **Eadweard,** born Edward James Muggeridge (1830–1904). British photographer. His reputation rests on his experiments in photographing moving objects, especially horses. His *zoöpraxiscope,* patented in 1881, projected animated figures onto a screen and was the forerunner of cinematic photography.

Mu·zak (méwzak) *n.* **1.** A trademark for a system of recorded light music played as a soothing or pleasant background in factories, shops, or airports, for example. **2.** *Small* **m.** Any bland, mediocre background music. Usually used derogatorily.

mu·zhik, mou·jik, mu·jik (mōōzhik; *Russian* mōō-zhéek) *n.* A peasant in tsarist Russia. [Russian *muzhik,* a peasant, diminutive of *muzh,* man, from Old Church Slavonic *mǫzhi.*]

Mu·zo·re·wa (mōōzzə-ráy-wə), **Bishop Abel (Tendekayi)** (1925–). Zimbabwean (formerly Rhodesian) politician, generally considered a moderate voice during the black-white conflict of the 1970s. He was prime minister for some months before the election of Robert Mugabe in 1980.

muz·zle (múzz'l) *n.* **1.** The forward, projecting part of the head, including the jaws and nose, of certain animals. **2.** A leather or wire device fitted over an animal's snout to prevent biting and eating. **3.** The forward, discharging end of the barrel of a firearm.
~*tr.v.* **muzzled, -zling, -zles. 1.** To put a muzzle on (an animal). **2. a.** To restrain (a person) from expressing opinions. **b.** To prevent (views, for example) from being expressed. [Middle English *mosel, musell,* from Old French *musel,* from Gallo-Roman *mūsellum* (unattested), diminutive of Late Latin *mūsum,* snout.] —**muz·zler** *n.*

muz·zle-load·er (múzz'l-lōdər) *n.* A firearm loaded through the muzzle. —**muz·zle-load·ing** *adj.*

muz·zy (múzzi) *adj.* **-zier, -ziest.** *Informal.* **1.** Muddled; confused. **2.** Blurred; indistinct. [18th century : origin obscure.] —**muz·zi·ly** *adv.* —**muz·zi·ness** *n.*

M.V. **1.** motor vessel. **2.** muzzle velocity.

MVD, M.V.D. *n.* Ministry of Internal Affairs (Russian *Ministyerstvo Vnutryennikh Dyel*), a former administrative branch of the Soviet government functioning, from 1946, as a successor to the NKVD. In 1954 the KGB took over the secret police functions of the MVD, and it was disbanded in 1960.

MW, M.W. **1.** medium wave. **2.** megawatt.

my (mī. *There is a weak form* mi, mə, *used in standard speech only in a few set phrases.*) The possessive form of the pronoun *I.* **1.** Used attributively to indicate possession, agency, or reception of an action by the speaker: *my wallet; pursuing my tasks; suffered my first rebuff.* See Usage note at **me.** **2.** Used preceding various forms of polite, affectionate, or familiar address: *my lady; my dear Dr. Mitchell; my good man.* **3.** Used in various interjectional phrases: *My word! My goodness!*
~*interj.* Used as an exclamation of surprise, pleasure, or dismay. [Middle English *my, mi, min,* Old English *mīn.*]

my–. Variant of **myo–.**

my·al·gi·a (mī-ál-ji-ə) *n. Pathology.* Muscular pain. [New Latin : MY(O)- + -ALGIA.] —**my·al·gic** *adj.*

myalgic encephalomyelitis *n. Abbr.* **ME.** A debilitating disorder mainly affecting children and young adults, whose symptoms include exhaustion, muscular weakness and pain, difficulty in walking and in concentration, and impaired short-term memory. The cause is uncertain, and no treatment has proved consistently effective.

my·all[1] (mí-awl) *n.* Any of various Australian acacias with hard wood, used for fences. [From *maiāl,* native Australian name.]

myall[2] *n. Australian.* An Aborigine living in a traditional way, outside white civilisation. [From a native Australian language.]

My·an·mar, Union of. See **Burma.**

myasis. Variant of **myiasis.**

my·as·the·ni·a (mí-əss-théeni-ə, -ass-) *n.* Abnormal muscular weakness or fatigue. [New Latin : MY(O)- + ASTHENIA.] —my·as·then·ic (-thénnik) *adj.*

myc. mycological; mycology.

my·ce·li·um (mī-sée-li-əm) *n., pl.* **-lia** (-li-ə). The vegetative part of a fungus, consisting of a mass of branching, threadlike filaments called hyphae. [New Latin, from Greek *mukēs,* fungus + *-elium,* as in *epithelium.*] —**my·ce·li·al, my·ce·loid** (mí-si-loyd) *adj.*

My·ce·nae (mī-séenee, -séeni). City of ancient Greece, in the northeast Peloponnese. It flourished from *c.* 1600 to 1200 B.C., as a centre of Mycenaean civilisation, and was the seat of king Agamemnon. Excavations begun by Heinrich Schliemann in the late 19th century revealed the noted Lion Gate and treasure-filled tombs.

My·ce·nae·an (mí-si-née-ən) *adj.* Of, pertaining to, or designating the Aegean civilisation that spread its influence from Mycenae to many parts of the Mediterranean region from about 1400 B.C. to 1150 B.C. —**My·ce·nae·an** *n.*

Mycenaean Greek *n.* The early East Greek dialect of the Mycenaeans, attested in documents in Linear B script.

–mycete *n. comb. form.* Indicates a member of a specified class of fungi; for example, **basidiomycete.** [New Latin *-mycetes* (class), from Greek *mukētes,* plural of *mukēs,* fungus.]

my·ce·to·ma (mí-si-tṓ-mə) *n., pl.* **-mas** or **-mata** (-mətə). 1. A chronic fungous infection usually affecting the foot, characterised by nodules that discharge oily pus. 2. A mycetoma nodule. [New Latin : Greek *mukētes,* fungi (see **-mycete**) + -OMA.] —**my·ce·tom·a·tous** (-tómmətəss, -tṓmə-) *adj.*

my·ce·to·zo·an (mī-séeta-zṓ-ən) *n.* A slime mould *(see).* ∼*adj.* Of or pertaining to slime moulds. [New Latin *Mycetozoa,* "fungus-animals" (formerly classed in the animal kingdom) : Greek *mukētes,* fungi (see **-mycete**) + -ZOA.]

–mycin *n. comb. form.* Indicates derivation of a substance from bacteria or fungi; for example, **streptomycin.** [MYC(O)- + -IN.]

myco-, myc– *comb. form.* Indicates fungus; for example, **mycelium, mycology.** [New Latin, from Greek *mukēs,* fungus.]

my·co·bac·te·ri·um (mī́kōbak-téer-i-əm) *n., pl.* **-teria** (-téer-i-ə). Any slender, rod-shaped bacterium of the genus *Mycobacterium,* which includes the bacterium that causes tuberculosis.

mycol. mycological; mycology.

my·col·o·gy (mī-kólləji) *n. Abbr.* **myc., mycol.** 1. The branch of botany that deals with fungi. 2. The fungi native to a region. [New Latin *mycologia* : MYCO- + -LOGY.] —**my·co·log·ic** (mī́kə-lójik), **my·co·log·i·cal** *adj.* —**my·col·o·gist** (-kólləjist) *n.*

my·cor·rhi·za, my·co·rhi·za (mī́kə-rī́zə) *n., pl.* **-zae** (-zee) or **-zas.** *Botany.* The symbiotic association of the mycelium of a fungus with the roots of certain plants, such as conifers or orchids. [New Latin : MYCO- + Greek *rhiza,* a root.] —**my·cor·rhi·zal** *adj.*

my·co·sis (mi-kṓ-siss) *n., pl.* **-ses** (-seez). 1. A fungous growth in the body. 2. A disease caused by a fungous growth. [New Latin : MYC(O)- + -OSIS.]

my·co·tox·in (mī́kō-tóksin) *n.* Any poisonous substance produced by a fungus.

my·dri·a·sis (mi-drī́-ə-siss, mī-) *n.* Prolonged and abnormal dilatation of the pupil of the eye as a result of disease or a drug. [Latin, from Greek *mudriasis†.*]

myd·ri·at·ic (míddri-áttik) *n.* A drug that produces dilatation of the pupils. [From MYDRIASIS.] —**myd·ri·at·ic** *adj.*

myel-, myelo– *comb. form.* Indicates the spinal cord or bone marrow; for example, **myelencephalon, myelitis.** [New Latin, from Greek *muelos,* marrow, from *mus,* muscle.]

my·e·len·ceph·a·lon (mí-ilen-séffə-lon) *n.* The rear part of the embryonic hindbrain from which the medulla oblongata develops. —**my·e·len·ce·phal·ic** (-sə-fál-ik) *adj.*

my·e·lin (mí-i-lin) *n.* Also **my·e·line** (-lin, -leen). 1. A white, fatty material encasing some nerve fibres. Also called "medullary sheath". 2. One of several fatlike substances found in body tissues. [MYEL- + -IN.] —**my·e·lin·ic** (-línnik) *adj.*

my·e·li·nat·ed (mí-ili-naytid) *adj.* Having a myelin sheath; medullated. Said of nerves.

my·e·li·tis (mí-i-lī́tiss) *n.* Inflammation of the spinal column or bone marrow. [New Latin : MYEL- + -ITIS.]

my·e·loid (mí-i-loyd) *adj.* 1. Of, related to, or derived from bone marrow. 2. Of or pertaining to the spinal cord. [MYEL- + -OID.]

my·e·lo·ma (mí-i-lṓ-mə) *n., pl.* **-mas** or **-mata** (-mətə). A malignant tumour of the bone marrow. [New Latin : MYEL- + -OMA.] —**my·e·lo·ma·toid** *adj.*

my·ia·sis (mí-ə-siss, mī-í-ə-siss) *n.* Also **my·a·sis** (mí-ə-siss). *Pathology.* Infestation of human tissue by fly maggots or a disease resulting from it. [New Latin : Greek *muia, mua,* fly + -IASIS.]

my·lo·nite (mílə-nīt) *n.* A fine-grained laminated rock formed along zones of extensive crustal dislocation. [Greek *mulōn,* mill, from *mulē, mulos,* mill, millstone + -ITE.]

my·na, my·nah, mi·na (mínə) *n.* Any of various birds of the family Sturnidae, of southeastern Asia. They are blue-black to dark brown with yellow bills. Certain species can mimic human speech. Also called "myna bird". [Hindi *mainā,* from Sanskrit *madana.*]

myn·heer (mə-néer) *n.* 1. *Often capital* **M.** The Dutch title of courtesy and respect equivalent to the English *sir* or *Mr.* 2. *Informal.* A Dutchman. [Dutch *mynheer,* obsolete variant of *mijnheer,* "my lord" : *mijn,* my, from Middle Dutch *mijni* + *heer,* lord, sir, master, from Middle Dutch.]

myo-, my– *comb. form.* Indicates muscle; for example, **myograph, myasthenia.** [New Latin, from Greek *mus,* muscle.]

my·o·car·di·al infarction (mí-ō-kárdi-əl) *n.* Death of a section of heart muscle that occurs when its blood supply is obstructed by coronary thrombosis, characterised by severe pain in the chest.

my·o·car·di·o·graph (mí-ō-kárdi-ō-graaf, -ə-, -graf) *n.* An instrument for recording graphically the movement of the heart muscle.

my·o·car·di·tis (mī-ō-kaar-dítiss) *n.* Inflammation of the myocardium. [MYOCARD(IUM) + -ITIS.]

my·o·car·di·um (mí-ō-kárdi-əm) *n.* The muscle tissue of the heart. [New Latin : MYO- + Greek *kardia,* heart.] —**my·o·car·di·al** *adj.*

my·o·gen·ic (mí-ō-jénnik) *adj.* Also **my·o·ge·net·ic** (-jə-néttik). 1. Giving rise to muscle tissue. 2. Of muscular origin. [MYO- + -GENIC.]

my·o·glo·bin (mí-ō-glṓbin) *n.* The form of haemoglobin found in muscle fibres, having a greater affinity for oxygen than blood haemoglobin.

my·o·graph (mí-ō-graaf, -ə-, - graf) *n.* An instrument that records muscular contractions by means of tracings *(myograms).* [MYO- + -GRAPH.]

my·ol·o·gy (mī-ólləji) *n.* The scientific study of muscles. —**my·o·log·ic** (mí-ō-lójik) *adj.* —**my·ol·o·gist** (mī-ólləjist) *n.*

my·o·ma (mī-ō-mə) *n., pl.* **-mas** or **-mata** (-mətə). A benign tumour composed of muscle tissue. [MY(O)- + -OMA.] —**my·om·a·tous** (-ómmətəss, -ṓmətəss) *adj.*

my·ope (mí-ōp) *n.* One who has myopia. [French, from Late Latin *myops,* myopic, from Greek *muōps.* See **myopia.**]

my·o·pi·a (mī-ṓpi-ə) *n.* 1. *Pathology.* A visual defect in which distant objects appear blurred because their images are focussed in front of the retina rather than on it; shortsightedness. Compare **hypermetropia.** 2. Mental shortsightedness or lack of discernment in thinking or planning. [New Latin, from Greek *muōpia,* from *muōps,* myopic, "closing or contracting the eyes" : *muein,* to close + *ōps,* eye.] —**my·op·ic** (mī-óppik) *adj.* —**my·op·i·cal·ly** *adv.*

my·o·sin (mí-ə-sin) *n.* A common protein in muscle; with **actin** it forms **actomyosin** *(both of which see).* [Greek *muos,* genitive of *mus,* muscle + -IN.]

myosis. *Pathology.* Variant of **miosis.**

my·o·so·tis (mí-ə-sṓtiss) *n.* Any plant of the genus *Myosotis,* such as the forget-me-not. [New Latin, from Latin *myosotis,* from Greek *muosōtis,* "mouse-ear" (from its furry leaves) : *muos,* genitive of *mus,* mouse + *ous* (stem *ōt-),* ear.]

my·o·to·ni·a (mí-ə-tṓni-ə) *n. Pathology.* Tonic spasm or temporary muscular rigidity. [MYO- + -TONIA.] —**my·o·ton·ic** (-tónnik) *adj.*

Myr·dal (mür-daal), **Gunnar** (1898-1987). Swedish economist and sociologist. He is chiefly famous for *Rich Lands and Poor Lands* (1957), *Asian Drama* (1968), and *The Challenge of World Poverty* (1970). He was awarded the Nobel prize in economics in 1974.

myria– *comb. form.* Indicates: A very large or countless number; for example, **myriapod.** [Greek *murios,* countless, and its plural *murioi,* ten thousand.]

myr·i·ad (mírri-əd) *adj.* 1. Amounting to a very large, indefinite number. 2. Highly varied. ∼*n.* 1. *Archaic.* Ten thousand. 2. A vast number; a great multitude. [Late Latin *mȳrias* (stem *mȳriad-*), from Greek *murias,* from *murios,* countless, and its plural *murioi,* ten thousand.]

myr·i·a·pod (mírri-ə-pod) *n.* Any of a class of arthropods, such as the centipedes, having a distinct head, one pair of antennae, and many segments bearing legs. [New Latin *myriapoda* : MYRIA- + -POD.] —**myr·i·ap·o·dan** (-áppədən) *adj. & n.* —**myr·i·ap·o·dous** (-áppədəss) *adj.*

myr·is·tic acid (mi-ristik, mī-) *n.* An organic compound, $CH_3(CH_2)_{12}COOH$, occurring in animal and vegetable fats. It is used in cosmetics and flavourings. [Greek *muristikos,* fragrant, from *muron,* perfume.]

myrmeco– *comb. form.* Indicates ant; for example, **myrmecophile.** [Greek, from *murmēx,* ant.]

myr·me·col·o·gy (múrmi-kólləji) *n.* The study of ants. [MYRMECO- + -LOGY.] —**myr·me·co·log·i·cal** (-kə-lójik'l) *adj.* —**myr·me·col·o·gist** (-kólləjist) *n.*

myr·me·coph·a·gous (múrmi-kóffəgəss) *adj.* 1. Feeding on ants. 2. Adapted for eating ants. Said, for example, of jaws. [MYRMECO- + -PHAGOUS.]

myr·me·co·phile (múrmi-kō-fīl) *n.* Any organism that habitually shares the nest of an ant colony. [MYRMECO- + -PHILE.] —**myr·me·coph·i·lous** (-kóffiləss) *adj.* —**myr·me·coph·i·ly** (-kóffili) *n.*

myr·mi·don (múrmi-don, -dən) *n.* A faithful follower who carries out orders without question. [After MYRMIDON.]

Myr·mi·don (múrmi-don, -dən) *n.* Any of a legendary Greek warrior people of ancient Thessaly who followed their king Achilles on the expedition against Troy. —**Myr·mi·don** *adj.*

my·rob·a·lan (mī-róbbələn, mi-) *n.* 1. A tree, *Prunus cerasifera,* native to Asia, bearing edible red or yellow fruit. Also called "cherry plum". 2. A tree, the **Indian almond** *(see).* 3. The fruit of either of these trees. [Old French *mirobolan,* from Latin, from Greek *murobalanos :* *muron,* perfume, unguent + *balanos,* acorn, date.]

myrrh (mur) *n.* 1. An aromatic gum resin obtained from several trees and shrubs of the genus *Commiphora,* of India, Arabia, and eastern Africa. It is used in perfume and incense, and was one of the gifts of the Magi to the infant Jesus. 2. Any shrub or tree that exudes such a gum resin. 3. A plant, **sweet cicely** *(see).* [Middle English *myrre,* Old English *myrrha,* from Common Germanic *murra* (unattested), from Latin *myrrha,* from Greek *murrha,* perhaps from Semitic, akin to Arabic *murr.*]

myr·tle (múrt'l) *n.* 1. Any of several evergreen shrubs or trees of the genus *Myrtus;* especially, *M. communis,* an aromatic shrub native to the Mediterranean region. **2.** Any of various other plants or shrubs, such as the **crape myrtle** and the **bog myrtle** *(both of which see).* **3.** *U.S.* A plant, the **periwinkle** *(see).* [Middle English *mirtille,* from Old French, from Medieval Latin *myrtillus,* diminutive of Latin *myrtus,* from Greek *murtos*†.]

my·self (mī-sélf, *also* mi-, mə-) *pron.* A specialised form of the first person singular pronoun. It is used: **1.** As a reflexive pronoun, forming the direct or indirect object of a verb or the object of a preposition: *hurt myself; give myself time; talk to myself.* **2.** For emphasis, after *I*: *I myself wasn't certain.* **3.** As an emphasising substitute: *Myself in debt, I could offer her no assistance.* **4.** Used as an indication of one's real, normal, or healthy condition or identity: *I have not been myself lately.* [Middle English *miself,* alteration of *meself,* Old English *mē selfum* (dative), *mē selfne* (accusative) : *mē,* me + *selfum, selfne,* dative and accusative of *self,* SELF.]

Usage: *Myself* is often heard in everyday speech as part of a compound subject or object, especially in some regional speech (Irish English, for example): *She asked Jane and myself to go to the meeting.* But the usage has attracted criticism, and in formal speech and in writing, the basic form of the pronoun should be used: *She asked Jane and me to go to the meeting.*

my·so·pho·bi·a (mī-sō-fṓbi-ə) *n.* A pathological fear of dirt, contamination, or faeces. [New Latin : Greek *musos,* uncleanness, defilement + -PHOBIA.] **—my·so·pho·bic** *adj.*

My·sore (mī-sór || -sōr). Former name of Karnataka state, southwest India.

mys·ta·gogue (místə-gog) *n.* **1.** In Mediterranean mystery religions, one who prepared candidates for initiation into the mysteries. **2.** A teacher of religious mysteries; a hierophant. **3.** One who holds or spreads mystical doctrines. [Old French, from Latin *mystagogus,* from Greek *mustagōgos* : *mustēs,* an initiate (see **mystery**) + *agōgos,* leader, from *agein,* to lead.] **—mys·ta·gog·ic** (-gójik) *adj.* **—mys·ta·go·gy** (místə-goji, -gōji) *n.*

mys·te·ri·ous (mi-stéer-i-əs) *adj.* **1.** Full of mystery; difficult to explain or account for; of obscure origin: *a mysterious light in the sky.* **2.** Beyond human understanding. Used especially in religious contexts: *the mysterious love of God.* **3.** Implying a mystery. **4.** Enigmatic in manner: *She was given to mysterious silences.* [Old French *mystérieux,* from *mystère,* mystery, from Latin *mystērium,* MYSTERY (riddle).] **—mys·te·ri·ous·ly** *adv.* **—mys·te·ri·ous·ness** *n.*

mys·ter·y¹ (místri, místəri) *n., pl.* **-ies. 1.** Anything that arouses curiosity because it is unexplained, inexplicable, or secret. **2.** The quality or air of being unexplained, secret, or unknown. **3.** A piece of fiction dealing with a mystery, especially a puzzling crime. **4.** The behaviour of someone given to secrecy and intrigue: *"He professed to despise all mystery . . . either in a prince or a minister."* (Jonathan Swift). **5.** *Theology.* A religious truth divinely revealed and unknowable through reason. **6. a.** A Christian rite, such as the Eucharist. **b.** *Often plural.* The elements of the Eucharist. **7.** Any of 15 incidents in the lives of Christ and the Virgin Mary, as commemorated in the 15 divisions of the rosary and considered as subjects of meditation. **8.** A mystery play. **9.** *Often plural.* **a.** Among some ancient Mediterranean peoples, any of certain cults and secret rites to which only initiates were admitted. **b.** The secrets of Freemasonry. [Middle English *misterie, mysterie,* from Latin *mystērium,* from Greek *mustērion,* "secret rites", from *mustēs,* one initiated into secret rites, from *mueîn,* to initiate, from *muein,* to close the eyes or mouth, hence to keep secret (as in religious initiation).]

mystery² *n., pl.* **-ies.** *Archaic.* A trade or occupation. [Middle English *mysterie, misterie,* from Late Latin *misterium,* variant (by association with *mystērium,* secret rites, mystery) of Latin *ministerium,* service, work, occupation, from *minister,* servant.]

mystery play *n.* A medieval drama based on episodes in the life of Christ. Compare **miracle play.** [Old French *mistere, mystere,* from Latin *mystērium,* religious symbol, MYSTERY.]

mystery tour *n.* A pleasurable excursion, such as a coach trip or train journey, to an unknown destination.

mys·tic (místik) *adj.* **1.** Of or pertaining to the religious mysteries of Greece and Rome or to other occult rites. **2.** Mysteriously symbolic; inspiring a sense of mystery and wonder. **3.** Mystical.
∼*n.* One who practises or believes in mysticism or a specified form of mysticism. [Middle English *mistik,* from Latin *mysticus,* from Greek *mustikos,* from *mustēs,* an initiated person. See **mystery¹**.]

mys·ti·cal (místik'l) *adj.* **1.** Characteristic of mystics or of the nature of mysticism. **2.** Believing in or practising mysticism. **3.** Mysterious; enigmatic; symbolic. **4.** *Theology.* **a.** Of a nature or import that by virtue of its divinity surpasses understanding: *the mystical vision of God.* **b.** Spiritually symbolic: *a mystical emblem of the Trinity.* **—mys·ti·cal·ly** *adv.* **—mys·ti·cal·ness** *n.*

mys·ti·cete (místə-seet) *n.* A **whalebone whale** *(see).* [New Latin *mysticetus,* from Greek *mustikētos,* some kind of whale, supposedly a corruption of *ho mus to kētos,* "the mouse, the whale", that is "that whale which is called 'the mouse' " (the semantic development is obscure) : *mus,* mouse + *kētos,* whale (see **cetacean**).]

mys·ti·cism (místi-siz'm) *n.* **1. a.** A spiritual discipline aiming at union with the divine through deep meditation or trancelike contemplation. **b.** The experience of such communion, as described by mystics. **2.** Any belief in the existence of realities beyond perceptual or intellectual apprehension but central to being and directly accessible by intuition. **—mys·ti·cist** *n. & adj.*

mys·ti·fi·ca·tion (místifi-káysh'n) *n.* **1.** The act or an instance of deliberately or wilfully making something obscure or mysterious. **2.** The fact or condition of being mystified; bafflement.

mys·ti·fy (místi-fī) *tr.v.* **-fied, -fying, -fies. 1.** To awe or perplex; bewilder. **2.** To make obscure or difficult to comprehend. —See Synonyms at **puzzle.** [French *mystifier,* irregularly from *mystère,* mystery, from Latin *mystērium,* MYSTERY.] **—mys·ti·fi·er** *n.* **—mys·ti·fy·ing·ly** *adv.*

mys·tique (mi-stéek) *n.* **1.** An attitude of mystical veneration conferring upon an occupation, person, or thing an awesome and mythical status; the special cult of anything: *the mystique of Eastern music.* **2.** A mystical or philosophical conception used as a guide, especially for a doctrine or cult: *Hegelian mystique.* **3.** A rarefied quality that sets a person or thing apart and apparently beyond the understanding of an outsider. [French, from adjective, "mystic", from Latin *mysticus,* MYSTIC.]

myth (mith) *n.* **1. a.** A traditional story originating in a preliterate society, dealing with supernatural beings, ancestors, or heroes that serve as primordial types in a primitive view of the world. **b.** A body of such stories told among a given people; a mythology: *in Norse myth.* **c.** All such stories collectively. **2.** Any real or fictional story, recurring theme, or character type that appeals to the consciousness of a people by embodying its cultural ideals or by expressing commonly felt emotions: *the myth of rebirth.* **3.** An allegorical story. **4.** Any of the fictions or half-truths forming part of the ideology of a society; a notion based more on tradition or convenience than on fact: *the myth of male superiority.* **5.** Any fictitious or imaginary story, explanation, person, or thing. [New Latin *mythus,* from Late Latin *mythos,* tale, myth, from Greek *muthos*†.]

myth·i·cal (míthik'l) *adj.* Also **myth·ic** (míthik). **1.** Having the nature of a myth. **2.** Existing only in myth: *the mythical unicorn.* **3.** Imaginary; fictitious; fancied. **—myth·i·cal·ly** *adv.*

myth·i·cise, myth·i·cize (míthi-sīz) *tr.v.* **-cised, -cising, -cises. 1.** To turn (a person or event) into myth. **2.** To interpret as a myth. **—myth·i·cism** *n.* **—myth·i·cis·er, myth·i·cist** *n.*

myth·mak·er (míth-maykər) *n.* **1.** One who creates a myth. **2.** One who produces false stories or doctrines, especially as propaganda. Used derogatorily: *combating the inventions of the mythmakers.* **—myth·mak·ing** *n. & adj.*

mytho– *comb. form.* Indicates myth; for example, **mythogenesis.**

my·thog·ra·pher (mi-thóggrəfər) *n.* A recorder or narrator of myths. [Greek *muthographos* : MYTH + -GRAPHER.]

myth·o·log·i·cal (míthə-lójik'l) *adj. Abbr.* **myth., mythol.** Also **myth·o·log·ic** (-lójik). **1.** Of, pertaining to, or celebrated in mythology. **2.** Fabulous; imaginary; mythical. **3.** Story-telling. **—myth·o·log·i·cal·ly** *adv.*

my·thol·o·gise, my·thol·o·gize (mi-thóllə-jīz) *v.* **-gised, -gising, -gises.** —*tr.* To convert into myth; mythicise. —*intr.* **1.** To construct or relate a myth. **2.** To interpret or write about myths or mythology. **—my·thol·o·gis·er** *n.*

my·thol·o·gy (mi-thólləji) *n., pl.* **-gies.** *Abbr.* **myth., mythol. 1. a.** A collection of myths, especially about the origin and history of a people and their deities, ancestors, and heroes. **b.** A body of myths, especially mistaken beliefs, concerning some individual, event, or institution. **2.** The field of scholarship dealing with the systematic collection and study of myths. [French *mythologie,* from Late Latin *mȳthologia,* from Greek *muthologia* : *muthos,* MYTH + *-logia,* -LOGY.] **—my·thol·o·gist** *n.*

myth·o·ma·ni·a (mith-ō-máyni-ə, -ə-) *n.* A compulsion to embroider the truth, exaggerate, or tell lies. [MYTH + -MANIA.] **—myth·o·ma·ni·ac** (-máyni-ak) *n. & adj.*

myth·o·poe·ic (míth-ō-pée-ik, -ə-) *adj.* Productive of myths; mythmaking. [Greek *muthopoios,* mythmaker, from *muthopoiein,* to make a myth : *muthos,* MYTH + *poiein,* to make, create.] **—myth·o·poe·ia** (-pée-ə), **myth·o·po·e·sis** (-pō-ée-siss) *n.*

my·thos (mīthoss, míthoss) *n., pl.* **mythoi** (mīthoy, míthoy). **1.** Myth. **2.** Mythology. **3.** The pattern of basic values and historical experiences of a people, characteristically transmitted through the arts. **4.** A deliberately fostered cult; a mystique. [Greek *muthos*†, MYTH.]

Myt·i·le·ne (mitti-léeni). *Modern Greek* **Mit·i·lí·ni. 1.** Ancient port on the island of Lesbos in Greece. **2.** A former name for **Lesbos.**

myxo–, myx– *comb. form.* Indicates mucus or mucus-like material; for example, **myxomycete, myxoma, myxocyte.** [New Latin, from Greek *muxa,* mucus, slime.]

myx·oe·de·ma (mík-si-déemə) *n.* A disease caused by decreased activity of the thyroid gland in adults, and characterised by dry skin, swellings around the lips and nose, mental deterioration, and a subnormal basal metabolic rate. [MYX(O)- + OEDEMA.]

myx·o·ma (mik-sṓ-mə) *n., pl.* **-mas** or **-mata** (-mətə). A benign tumour composed of connective tissue and mucous elements. [New Latin : MYX(O)- + -OMA.] **—myx·om·a·tous** (-sómmətəss) *adj.*

myx·o·ma·to·sis (míksəmə-tṓ-siss) *n., pl.* **-ses** (-seez). A highly infectious, usually fatal, viral disease of rabbits characterised by many skin tumours similar to myxomas. [New Latin : MYXOMA + -OSIS.]

myx·o·my·cete (mík-sō-mī-séet, -sə-) *n.* A **slime mould** *(see).* [New Latin *Myxomycetes* (class) : MYXO- + -MYCETE.]

myx·o·vir·us (mík-sō-vīr-əss, -sə-) *n.* Any of a group of RNA-containing viruses that cause such diseases as influenza and mumps.

M·zi·li·ka·zi (m-zílli-gáazi, -káazi) (*c.* 1800-68). Also **Moselekatze** or **Silkaats.** Founder and chief of the Matabele nation, an offshoot of the Zulu. For nearly half a century his warriors harassed the peoples living in what are now the Transvaal and Zimbabwe.

N

n, N (en) *n., pl.* **n's** or *rare* **ns, N's** or **Ns. 1.** The 14th letter of the modern English alphabet. **2.** Any of the speech sounds represented by this letter.

n, N, n., N. *Note:* As an abbreviation or symbol, *n* may be a small or a capital letter, with or without a full stop. Established forms or those generally preferred precede the definition. When no form is given, all four forms are in general use in that sense. **1. N** Avogadro number. **2. n.** born [Latin *nátus*]. **3. n, N** *Printing.* en. **4. n** nano-. **5. n., N.** *Grammar.* neuter. **6. n.** neutron. **7. N** neutron number. **8. N** newton. **9. N** The symbol for the element nitrogen. **10. n, N, n-** *Chemistry.* normal; normality. **11.** north; northern. **12. n.** note. **13. n.** noun. **14. N.** November. **15. n.** number. **16. n** *Mathematics.* The symbol for an indefinite number.

Na The symbol for the element sodium [Latin *natrium*].

NAACP, N.A.A.C.P. National Association for the Advancement of Colored People (in the United States).

NAA·FI, N.A.A.F.I. (náffi) *n. British.* Navy, Army, and Air Force Institutes: **1.** An organisation that runs canteens and shops for service personnel and their families. **2.** A canteen or shop so run.

naar·tjie, nar·tjie (nárchi, nártzi) *n. South African.* A tangerine or mandarin orange. [Afrikaans, from Tamil *nartei;* akin to Arabic *naranj,* Spanish *naranja.*]

nab (nab) *tr.v.* **nabbed, nabbing, nabs.** *Slang.* **1.** To catch in the act of wrongdoing; arrest. **2.** To grab; snatch. [Variant of dialectal *nap,* to seize, probably from Scandinavian; akin to KIDNAP.]

Nab·a·tae·an, Nab·a·te·an (nábbə-té·ən) *n.* **1.** A member of a northwestern Arab people whose kingdom, centred on Petra, flourished from the fourth century B.C. to the first century A.D. **2.** The Aramaic dialect of this people. **—Nab·a·tae·an** *adj.*

Nab·lus (naáb-ləss, náb-). A city in Samaria, West Bank, under Israeli administration since 1967. It lies near the site of Schechem, a capital of ancient Samaria and an ancient Canaanite city.

na·bob (náy-bob) *n.* **1.** A governor in India under the Mogul Empire. **2.** In the 18th century, an Englishman who returned from India having acquired a fortune. **3.** A man of wealth and prominence. [Portuguese *nababo,* from Urdu, NAWAB.] **—na·bob·er·y** (-əri, nay-bőbbəri), **na·bob·ism** *n.*

Na·bo·kov (nə-bőkof, nábbə-kof), **Vladimir** (1899–1977). Russian-born U.S. novelist. He is best known for his controversial novel *Lolita* (1958). Other novels include *Pale Fire* (1962) and *Ada* (1969).

na·celle (nə-sél) *n.* A separate streamlined enclosure on some aircraft for sheltering the crew or cargo or housing an engine. [French, "small boat", from Late Latin *návicella,* diminutive of *návis,* ship.]

na·cre (náykər) *n.* **Mother-of-pearl** (see). [French, from Old Italian *naccara,* mother-of-pearl, from Arabic *naqqárah,* shell.]

na·cre·ous (náykri-əss) *adj.* **1.** Consisting of mother-of-pearl. **2.** Like mother-of-pearl; pearly.

NAD *n. Biochemistry.* Nicotinamide adenine dinucleotide: a coenzyme that carries hydrogen atoms in electron-transfer reactions.

Na·dar (na-dár, náddaar), **Gaspard Félix Tournachon** (1820–1910). French photographer. Known during his lifetime as a novelist and caricaturist, he is best remembered as a pioneer of photography. He took aerial photographs (1858) from a balloon.

Na·der (náydər), **Ralph** (1934–). U.S. lawyer. A pioneer in the field of consumer protection, he founded the Center for the Study of Responsive Law (1969). His publications include *Unsafe at Any Speed* (1965), and *Who's Poisoning America?* (1981). He was a Green Party candidate for U.S. president in the 1996 election.

NADH *n. Biochemistry.* NAD reduced by the addition of hydrogen.

na·dir (náy-deer, náddeer ‖ -dər) *n.* **1.** A point on the celestial sphere diametrically opposite the zenith. **2.** The point or time of deepest depression, greatest misfortune, or the like; the lowest point. [Middle English, from Old French, from Arabic *nazír assamt : nazír,* opposite + *as-samt,* the ZENITH.]

NADP *n. Biochemistry.* Nicotinamide adenine dinucleotide phosphate: a coenzyme similar in action to NAD.

nae (nay) *adj. Scottish.* No.

~adv. *Scottish.* Not.

nae·vus (née-vəss) *n., pl.* **-vi** (-vī). Also *chiefly U.S.* **nevus.** Any malformation of the skin present at birth, e.g. a strawberry mark or mole; a birthmark. [Latin, birthmark; akin to (*g*)*natus,* born.]

naff (naff) *Slang. adj.* Of poor or disappointing quality; in poor taste: *a naff present.*

~intr.v. **naffed, naffing, naffs.** *Slang.* To go away or cease being an annoyance. Used in the imperative with *off.*

NAF·TA (náf-tə) *n.* The North American Free Trade Agreement between the U.S.A., Canada and Mexico.

nag¹ (nag) *v.* **nagged, nagging, nags.** **—tr. 1.** To pester or annoy by constant scolding, complaining, or urging. **2.** To torment with anxiety, discomfort, or doubt: *nagged by worries.* **—intr. 1.** To scold, complain, or find fault constantly. **2.** To be a continuing source of discomfort, anxiety, or annoyance: *nagging backache.* Often followed by *at: The problem nagged at his mind.* **—See Synonyms at scold.**

~n. A person who habitually nags. [From northern dialect *nag, naeg,* to bite, worry at, nag, perhaps from Old Norse *gnaga,* to bite.] **—nag·ger** *n.* **—nag·ging·ly** *adv.*

nag² *n.* **1. a.** An old or worn-out horse. **b.** *Informal.* Any horse, especially a racehorse, regarded with contempt. **2.** *Archaic.* A small saddle horse or pony. [Middle English *nagget.*]

na·ga·na (nə-gáanə) *n.* Also **n'ga·na.** An often fatal disease of African livestock transmitted by the bite of the tsetse or other flies. [Zulu *u-nakane.*]

Na·ga·sa·ki (naága-saáki, nággə-sácki). A port in west Kyushu, Japan. The city was devastated (August 1945) by an atomic bomb at the end of World War II. Rebuilt, it is now a shipbuilding and steel-making centre.

na·gor (náygawr) *n.* The **reedbuck** (see). [French, name arbitrarily invented by Buffon, based on earlier *nanguer.*]

Na·gor·no-Kar·a·bakh (nə-górnō-karrə-bákh, -bak). Mountainous Autonomous Region in southwestern Azerbaijan, near but not touching the border of Armenia. The population is chiefly Armenian, and possession is disputed between Azerbaijan and Armenia. Area, 4400 square kilometres (1,700 square miles). Population, 177,000.

Nagy (noj), **Imre** (1896–1958). Hungarian politician. Taken prisoner in World War I by the Russians, he later became a Soviet citizen, and when Hungary was overrun by the U.S.S.R., he was installed as a member of the new government. While prime minister (1953–55), he implemented agrarian reforms that won him popularity. In the uprising of 1956 he was again proclaimed prime minister, but was seized by Russian troops and later executed.

Na·hua·tl (naá-waat'l, -waát'l) *n., pl.* **-tls** or collectively **Nahuatl. 1.** A member of a group of Mexican and Central American Indian peoples, including the Aztecs. **2.** The Uto-Aztecan language of the Nahuatl. [Spanish, from Nahuatl, singular of *Nahua,* the Nahuatl people.] **—Na·hua·tl** *adj.*

Na·hum¹ (náy-həm, -əm). A Hebrew prophet of the seventh century B.C. who predicted the fall of Nineveh.

Na·hum² *n.* The book of the Old Testament containing the prophecies of Nahum.

nai·ad (nī-ad ‖ náy-, -əd) *n., pl.* **-ades** (-ə-deez) or **-ads. 1.** *Greek Mythology.* Any of the nymphs living in and presiding over brooks, springs, and fountains. **2.** The aquatic nymph of certain insects, such as the mayfly. **3.** An aquatic plant of the genus *Naias.* [Greek *Naias* (stem *Naiad-*), from *naein,* to flow.]

naif, naïf. Variants of **naive.**

nail (nayl) *n.* **1.** A slim piece of metal, pointed at one end and usually having a flat head at the other, hammered into wood or other materials as a fastener. **2. a.** A fingernail or toenail. **b.** A claw or talon. **3.** Anything resembling a nail in shape, sharpness, or use. **4.** A former measure of length for cloth, equal to 2¼ inches. **—hard as nails. 1.** Callous; harsh; pitiless. **2.** In rugged physical condition; tough. **—hit the nail on the head.** To grasp and express the sense of something exactly and concisely. **—on the nail.** Immediately; without any delay: *paid cash on the nail.*

~tr.v. **nailed, nailing, nails. 1.** To fasten, join, or attach with or as if with nails. **2.** To cover or shut by fastening with nails. Often used with *down* or *up.* **3.** To keep fixed, motionless, or intent: *Fear nailed him to his seat.* **4.** To secure or make sure of, especially by prompt action or concentrated effort; clinch. Often used with *down: nail down the facts.* **5.** To bind to an agreement, promise, or the like. Often used with *down: tried to nail her down to a date.* **6.** *Informal.* To detect and expose: *nail a lie.* **7.** *Informal.* To strike or bring down, especially with something shot or hurled: *nail a bird in flight.* [Middle English *nail,* Old English *nægl.*] **—nail·er** *n.*

nail-bit·ing (náyl-bīting) *n.* Biting of the fingernails, usually as a sign of nervousness or as a habit.

~adj. Causing anxiety or a feeling of suspense: *a nail-biting climax.*

nail bomb *n.* A bomb, usually with gelignite as explosive, and filled with nails.

nail-brush (náyl-brush) *n.* A small brush with short, stiff bristles for cleaning the fingernails or sometimes the toenails.

nail file *n.* A small, flat metal file, or piece of emery board, used for shaping the fingernails or toenails.

nail-head (náyl-hed) *n.* **1.** The broadened or flattened, often circular, end of a nail opposite the point. **2.** An ornamental device resembling the head of a nail.

nail polish *n.* A clear or coloured cosmetic lacquer applied to the fingernails or toenails. Also *chiefly British* "nail varnish", *chiefly U.S.* "nail enamel", "nail lacquer".

nail scissors *pl.n.* Small scissors with short, curved blades for trimming and shaping fingernails or toenails.

nail-set (náyl-set) *n.* A tool for driving a nail into material so that its head is beneath or flush with the surface. Also called "nail-punch".

nain·sook (náyn-sōōk, nán-) *n.* A soft, light cotton material, often with a woven stripe. [Hindi *nainsukh,* "pleasure to the eye" : *nain,* eye + *sukh,* pleasure.]

Nai·paul (nī-pawl), **Sir V(idiadhar) S(urajprasad)** (1932–). West Indian novelist. His novels and reportage concentrate on the subtly destructive effects of Western culture on the Third World, as in *A Bend in the River* (1979). His earlier, more comic novels include *The Suffrage of Elvira* (1958) and *A House for Mr. Biswas* (1961). His later work includes *The Enigma of Arrival* (1987) and *Away in the World* (1994).

nai·ra (nīr-ə) *n., pl.* **naira.** The basic monetary unit of Nigeria, equal to 100 kobo. [Alteration of NIGERIA.]

Nai·ro·bi (nī-rṓbi). The capital of Kenya. Founded (1899) on the Mombasa-Uganda railway, it lies in Kenya's eastern highlands. Nairobi is a major industrial and commercial centre, and is also one of Africa's chief tourist centres, attracting visitors to the Nairobi National Park, a wildlife reserve on the city's outskirts.

na·ive, na·ïve (naa-éev, nī-) *adj.* Also **na·if, na·ïf** (-éef). **1. a.** Lacking worldliness and sophistication; artless; inexperienced. **b.** Simple and credulous as a child; ingenuous. **2.** Lacking critical ability or analytical insight; not subtle or learned. **3.** Untrained or employing unsophisticated or primitive techniques, especially in art. **4.** Not previously exposed to particular experiences, conditions, or information. Said, for example, of a subject in a psychology experiment who has not taken part in one before.
~n. Also **na·if, na·ïf.** A naive person. [French, feminine of *naïf,* from Old French, ingenuous, natural, from Latin *nātīvus,* NATIVE.] **—na·ive·ly** *adv.* **—na·ive·ness** *n.*
Synonyms: *naive, simple, innocent, ingenuous, unsophisticated, natural, unaffected, guileless, artless.*

na·ive·té, na·ïve·té (naa-éev-tay, nī-, -ti) *n.* Also **na·ive·ty** (-éev-ti, -éevə-), **na·ïve·ty** *pl.* **-ties. 1.** The quality of being naive; natural simplicity or artlessness; ingenuousness. **2.** A naive statement or action. [French, ingenuousness, from *naïf,* NAIVE.]

na·ked (náykid) *adj.* **1.** Without clothing or covering on the body; nude. **2.** Without covering; especially, without the usual covering: *a naked flame.* **3.** Devoid of vegetation, trees, or foliage. **4.** Without addition, concealment, disguise, or embellishment: *the naked truth; naked aggression.* **5.** Stripped or bare of something specified; destitute. Used with *of*: *a room naked of furniture.* **6.** Inadequately armed or protected; defenceless; vulnerable: *naked before his enemies.* **7.** *Botany.* **a.** Not encased in ovaries. Said of seeds. **b.** Unprotected by scales. Said of buds. **c.** Lacking a perianth. Said of flowers. **d.** Without leaves or pubescence. Said of branches or stalks. **8.** Lacking protective covering such as scales, fur, feathers, or a shell. **9.** *Physics.* Designating a quark flavour, especially charm or bottom, which is present in an elementary particle unaccompanied by its antiquark. **10.** Unsupported or uncorroborated by authority, evidence, or proof. Chiefly used in legal contexts. [Middle English *naked,* Old English *nacod,* from Germanic.] **—na·ked·ly** *adv.* **—na·ked·ness** *n.*

naked eye *n.* The eye unassisted by an optical instrument.

naked singularity *n.* *Astronomy.* A **singularity** *(see)* that is not surrounded by an event horizon, regarded as a point at which matter may be created and ejected.

Na·ma·qua·land (na-maákwə-land, nə-). Large relatively arid northwestern district of South Africa, noted for its spectacular display of spring wildflowers following the winter rains.

nam·by-pam·by (námbi-pámbi) *adj.* **1.** Weakly sentimental; insipidly affected. **2.** Lacking vigour or decisiveness; spineless.
~n., pl. **namby-pambies. 1.** Insipid, mawkish language or style. **2.** A namby-pamby person. [From *Namby-Pamby,* a satire on the sentimental pastorals of *Ambrose* Philips, by Henry Carey (died 1743).]

name (naym) *n.* **1.** A word or words by which any person or thing is designated and distinguished from others. **2.** A word or words used to describe or evaluate, often disparagingly: *Names will never hurt me.* **3.** Verbal representation or repute as opposed to effective reality: *a democracy in name, a police state in fact.* **4. a.** General reputation: *a bad name.* **b.** A distinguished reputation; renown. **5.** *Informal.* A famous or outstanding person: *a big name in local government.* **6.** At Lloyd's of London, a person whose entire assets can be called upon to meet insurance underwriting losses. **—in the name of. 1.** On behalf of; for the sake of. **2.** By the authority of. **—know (someone) by name.** To have heard of someone but not met him. **—name names.** To reveal the identity of people involved in criminal or otherwise dubious activities. **—the name of the game.** The essential or indispensable part or quality of some activity: *If you're job-hunting, persistence is the name of the game.* **—to (one's) name.** Belonging to one: *not a penny to his name.* **—under the name of.** Using as a name.
~tr.v. **named, naming, names. 1.** To attach a name to. **2.** To identify by name; call by the right name: *name the Stuart Kings of England.* **3.** To mention, specify, or cite by name. **4.** To call by some epithet: *He named them all cowards.* **5.** To nominate or appoint to some duty, office, or honour. **6.** To specify or fix: *name a price.* **7.** *British.* To indicate that (a Member of Parliament) has behaved in an unacceptable way and is required to leave the chamber. Used of the Speaker of the House of Commons. **—name the day.** To arrange to get married, and, usually, to specify a date for the ceremony. **—you name it.** *Informal.* Whatever you can think, say, or imagine: *Writing, acting, digging holes in the road, selling encyclopedias—you name it, he's done it.*
~adj. Informal. Well-known by a name: *name brands.* [Middle English *name,* Old English *nama.*] **—nam·a·ble, name·a·ble** *adj.*
Usage: In British English, a child is named *after* someone. In American English, it is also possible to use *for*: *He was named Fred, for his grandfather.*

name-call·ing (náym-kawling) *n.* Abuse; insulting language.

name day *n. Roman Catholic Church.* The feast day of the saint after whom one is named.

name-drop (náym-drop) *intr.v.* **-dropped, -dropping, -drops.** To show off by implying that one is on intimate terms with famous people, especially by mentioning their names in a familiar fashion. **—name-drop·per** *n.* **—name-drop·ping** *n.*

name·less (náym-ləss, -liss) *adj.* **1.** Having or bearing no name: *nameless stars.* **2.** Unknown by name; obscure: *the nameless dead.* **3. a.** Not designated by name; anonymous: *a nameless benefactor.* **b.** Intentionally left unnamed: *a certain person who shall be nameless.* **4.** Inexpressible; indescribable: *nameless horror.* **—name·less·ly** *adv.* **—name·less·ness** *n.*

name part *n.* A **title role** *(see).*

name·plate (náym-playt) *n.* A small sign, such as a brass plate, fastened to a door or wall of an office or building and showing the occupant's name and sometimes profession.

name·ly (náymli) *adv.* That is to say; to wit; specifically.

name·sake (náym-sayk) *n.* A person or thing with the same name as or deliberately named after another. [From *for the name's sake.*]

name·tape (náym-tayp) *n.* A small strip of cloth sewn or glued to a garment and showing the owner's name.

Na·mib Desert (naá-mib). Extremely dry region running along the coast of Namibia. It is noted for its population of plant and animal species adapted to survive in desert conditions.

Na·mib·i·a (nə-míbbi-ə, naa-). Formerly **South West Africa.** Country of southwest Africa. Rich in minerals, including diamonds, uranium, and copper, it is sparsely populated and mostly too dry for crops. The Namib desert along the Atlantic is one of the harshest in the world, and the Kalahari covers much of the northeast. A German protectorate from 1884, it was occupied by South Africa (1915), which governed it under a League of Nations mandate (1920–46), but refused to accept the U.N. trusteeship that replaced it. In 1971, the International Court of Justice ruled South Africa's presence in Namibia to be illegal. The South West African People's Organisation (SWAPO), recognised by the U.N. as the lawful representative of the Namibian people, began guerrilla activity in 1966. After a 1988 ceasefire South Africa agreed conditionally to withdraw its troops. Free elections held in 1989 were won by SWAPO, and transition to full independence took place in 1990. Area, 826 269 square kilometres (318,252 square miles). Population, 1,580,000. Capital, Windhoek. **—Namibian** *adj. & n.*

Na·mur (na-méwr, nə-; *French* -mür). *Flemish* **Na·men** (naámə). The capital of Namur province, south central Belgium. Owing to its strategic position at the confluence of the Sambre and Meuse rivers, it has been fought over many times.

nan (nan) *n.* Also **nan·na** (nánnə). A grandmother. Used especially by and to children. [From baby talk.]

na·na (naánə) *n. British Informal.* A fool. **—do (one's) nana.** *Australian Informal.* To become extremely angry; lose one's temper. [Probably from BANANA (compare *bananas,* crazy).]

Na·nak (naánək) (1469–1538). Indian spiritual teacher and first Sikh guru. Under Islamic influence he broke away from orthodox Hinduism to preach a monotheistic faith.

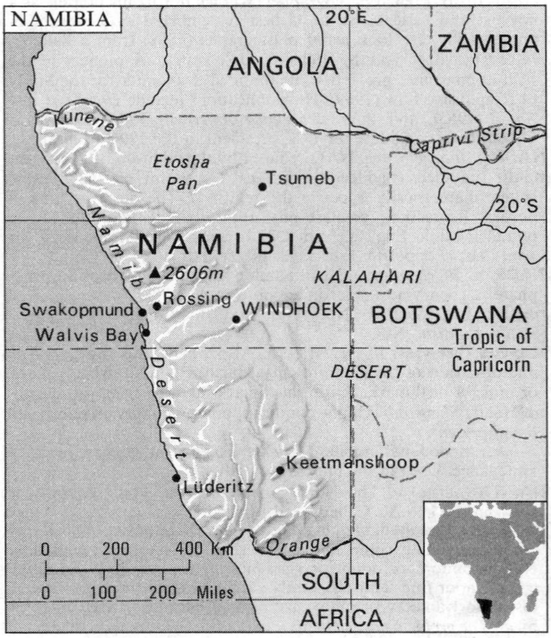
NAMIBIA
20°E
ZAMBIA
ANGOLA
Kunene
Caprivi Strip
Etosha Pan
Tsumeb
20°S
NAMIBIA
Namib Desert
▲2606m
KALAHARI
Rossing
Swakopmund
WINDHOEK
BOTSWANA
Walvis Bay
Tropic of Capricorn
DESERT
Keetmanshoop
Lüderitz
0 200 400 Km
0 100 200 Miles
Orange
SOUTH AFRICA

Na·na Sahib (naánə), born Dandu Panth (c. 1820–60). Indian prince. During the Indian Mutiny (1857) he led a force of rebel sepoys against Delhi, and was responsible for the Cawnpore massacre. Following his defeat (1859), he disappeared.

nan·cy (nán-si) *n., pl.* **-cies.** *Slang.* **1.** An effeminate man. **2.** A male homosexual. Used derogatorily. Also called "nancy boy". [From *Nancy* (woman's name).]

Nan·cy (nán-si; *French* NON-sée). The capital of the Meurthe-et-Moselle département, northeast France. The former seat of the Dukes of Lorraine, it passed to France in 1766. The city is still the economic and cultural focus of Lorraine. Its products include iron and steel, machinery, and textiles.

NAND gate (nand) *n.* A logic gate used in computers in which the output signal is high if any one or more of the input signals is low, and low if all the input signals are high. Also called "NAND circuit". [From *not* AND (that is, the reverse of an AND GATE).]

Nan·jing or **Nan·ching** (nán-jíng). Also **Nan·king** (nán-kíng). The capital of Jiangsu province, east China. Lying on the Chang Jiang (Yangtze) river, it is a former national capital (1368–1421, 1928–37). It is an important cultural and industrial centre.

nan·keen (nang-keén) *n.* Also **nan·kin** (nán-kin, -kín). **1.** A sturdy yellow or buff cotton cloth. **2.** A yellow or buff colour. **3.** *Plural.* Trousers made of nankeen cloth, worn especially in the 19th century. **4.** *Capital* **N.** A kind of Chinese porcelain with a blue-and-white pattern. [Originally imported from NANJING.]

nan·ny (nánni) *n., pl.* **-nies.** A woman employed to look after children in a family; a children's nurse.
~ *adj.* Nannyish: *a nanny state.* [From baby-talk *nana.*] **—nan·ny·ish** *adj.*

nanny goat *n., pl.* **nanny goats.** A female goat. Compare **billy goat.** [From *Nanny,* pet form for *Ann.*]

nano– *comb. form. Abbr.* **n** Indicates: **1.** Extreme smallness; for example, **nanoplankton.** **2.** One thousand-millionth (10⁻⁹) of a specified unit; for example, **nanosecond.** [Latin *nānus,* dwarf, from Greek *nan(n)os.*]

na·no·me·tre (nánnō-meetər, nánnə-) *n.* One thousand-millionth (10⁻⁹) of a metre.

na·no·plank·ton, nan·no·plank·ton (nánnō-plangk-tən, nánnə- || -ton) *n.* Aquatic animal and plant organisms of microscopic size comprising the smallest of the **plankton** *(see).*

na·no·sec·ond (nánnō-sekənd, nánnə-) *n.* One thousand-millionth (10⁻⁹) of a second.

na·no·tech·nol·o·gy (nánnōtek-nóllǝji) *n.* The technology of extreme subminiaturisation, including the hypothetical use of submicroscopic components, tools, or even machines. [NANO-¹ + TECHNOLOGY.]

Nan·sen (nán-sən), **Fridtjof** (1861–1930). Norwegian explorer and politician. He helped to negotiate Norwegian independence (1905), and was awarded the Nobel Peace prize (1922) for his League of Nations work for refugees and Russian famine relief. He took part in Polar and North Atlantic expeditions (1882–1914).

Nansen passport *n.* A passport issued after World War I by the League of Nations to individuals who were stateless. [After Fridtjof NANSEN who, as High Commissioner for Refugees, introduced it.]

Nantes, Edict of (nont) *n.* A decree issued in 1598 by Henry IV of France, granting restricted religious and civil liberties to Huguenots; revoked in 1685 by Louis XIV.

Nan·tuck·et (nan-túckit). A resort island off southeast Massachusetts, northeast United States. It was settled in 1659 and was an Atlantic whaling centre until the 1850s.

Naoi·se (neéshi). *Irish Mythology.* The husband of **Deirdre** *(see).*

nap¹ (nap) *n.* A brief sleep, often during a period other than one's regular sleeping hours.
~ *intr.v.* **napped, napping, naps. 1.** To doze or sleep for a brief period. **2.** *Informal.* To be unaware of imminent danger or trouble. Used chiefly in such phrases as *to be caught napping.* [Middle English *nappen,* to doze, Old English *hnappian.*]

nap² *n.* A dense, soft or fuzzy surface on certain textiles or leathers, usually formed by raising fibres from the underlying material. Compare **pile.**
~ *tr.v.* **napped, napping, naps.** To form or raise a nap on (fabric or leather). [Middle English *noppe,* from Middle Dutch *noppe.*]

nap³ *n.* **1. a.** A card game played for money and resembling whist. Also called "napoleon". **b.** A bid in this game, announcing the intention to win the maximum number (five) of tricks in a hand. **2.** A selection by a tipster of a horse or greyhound that is strongly fancied to win. **—go nap. 1.** To attempt to win all the tricks at nap. **2.** To risk everything on one chance or bet.
~ *tr.v.* **napped, napping, naps.** To tip (a horse or greyhound) as a certain winner in a race. [Shortened from *napoleon.*]

na·palm (náy-paam, -paalm, náppaam) *n.* **1.** An aluminium soap of various fatty acids that when mixed with petrol makes a firm jelly used in flame throwers and incendiary bombs. **2.** The jelly so used in flame throwers and bombs. **3.** A similar incendiary mixture of polystyrene, benzene, and petrol. Also called "napalm-B".
~ *tr.v.* **napalmed, -palming, -palms.** To bombard with napalm. [*Naphthenic* (see **naphthene**) + *palmitic acid.*]

nape (nayp) *n.* The back of the neck. [Middle English, probably akin to Old Frisian *(hals)knap†,* nape.]

Naph·ta·li¹ (náftə-lī). A son of Jacob. Genesis 30:7, 8.

Naphtali² *n.* A tribe of Israel descended from Naphtali. Numbers 1:15, 43.

naph·tha (náf-thə, náp-) *n.* **1.** A colourless flammable liquid, ob-tained from crude petroleum and used as a solvent and cleaning fluid, and as a raw material for petrol. **2.** Any of several volatile hydrocarbon liquids derived from coal tar and other materials and used as solvents. **3.** Petroleum. In this sense, not in current technical usage. [Greek *naphtha†.*]

naph·tha·lene (náf-thə-leen, náp-) *n.* A white crystalline compound, $C_{10}H_8$, derived from coal tar or petroleum, and used to manufacture dyes, moth repellents, explosives, and solvents. [NAPHTHA + *al*cohol + -ENE.]

naph·thene (náf-theen, náp-) *n.* Any of several cycloalkanes and their alkyl derivatives having the general formula C_nH_{2n}, found in various petroleums. [*Naphtha* + -ENE.]

naph·thol (náf-thol, náp- || -thōl) *n.* An organic compound, $C_{10}H_7OH$, occurring in two isomeric forms: **1.** *alpha-naphthol,* colourless or yellow prisms or powder, used in dyes, organic synthesis, and perfumes. **b.** *beta-naphthol,* white lustrous leaflets or powder, used in dyes, insecticides, and in the manufacture of rubber. [*Naphth*alene + -OL (hydroxyl group).]

naph·thyl (náf-thīl, náp-, -thil) *n.* Either of the two forms of the univalent organic radical $C_{10}H_7$-, derived from naphthalene. [*Naphtha* + -YL.]

Napier (náypi-ər), **John** (1550–1617). Scottish mathematician. He is best known for his discovery of natural logarithms (published 1614), and his work on spherical trigonometry.

Na·pier·i·an logarithm (nə-peér-i-ən, nay-) *n.* A **natural logarithm** *(see).*

Napier's bones *n.* A device consisting of a set of graduated rods formerly used for carrying out multiplication and division. [After John NAPIER, who invented the method on which it is based.]

na·pi·form (náypi-fawrm) *adj.* Shaped like a turnip. Said of a root. [Latin *nāpus,* turnip (probably of Mediterranean origin) + -FORM.]

nap·kin (nápkin) *n.* **1.** A square piece of fabric, such as cotton or linen, or a similar piece of soft, absorbent paper, used at table to protect one's clothes or wipe one's lips and fingers. Also called "table napkin". **2.** Any similar cloth or towel. **3.** *Chiefly British.* A nappy. **4.** *U.S.* A **sanitary towel** *(see).* [Middle English *nappekin,* diminutive of *nappe,* tablecloth, from Old French, from Latin *mappa,* napkin, towel.]

Na·ples (náyp'lz). *Italian* **Na·po·li** (naápo-li). The capital of Campania, south central Italy. Founded by Greeks in the sixth century B.C. below Mount Vesuvius, on the Bay of Naples, it became the capital of the kingdom of Naples (1270–1860). Naples is now a major seaport and a cultural, tourist, and industrial centre. It suffered severe earthquake damage in 1980.

Naples yellow *n.* **1.** A permanent yellow pigment consisting of lead antimonate. **2.** A similar pigment consisting of zinc oxide mixed with a yellow colouring matter. **3.** The colour of either of these pigments. [After NAPLES, where it was originally manufactured.]

na·po·le·on (nə-pŏli-ən) *n.* **1.** A rectangular piece of pastry, iced on top, with crisp, flaky layers filled with custard cream. **2.** A former 20-franc gold coin of France. **3.** A card game, **nap** *(see).* [After NAPOLEON I.]

Na·po·le·on I (nə-pŏli-ən), born Napoleon Bonaparte or Buonaparte (1769–1821). Emperor of the French and King of Italy. His victories as French Revolutionary commander in Italy (1796–97) established him as the most brilliant general of his time, and as a skilled politician. Following an abortive attempt to conquer Egypt (1798–99), he deposed the Directory and proclaimed himself First Consul (1799), and later Emperor (1804). His military ascendancy in Europe over the next decade was insufficient to combat the commercial and maritime power of Britain despite his attempted trade embargo, known as the Continental System. After the disastrous Russian campaign (1812–13) an alliance of hostile powers forced him to abdicate (1814). After a brief exile on the island of Elba, he regained power (1815), but was finally defeated at Waterloo, and exiled to St. Helena. His grasp of military technique remains unsurpassed, and his codification of laws, the *Code Napoléon,* still forms the basis of French civil law. **—Na·po·le·on·ic** *adj.*

Napoleon III, born Charles Louis Napoleon Bonaparte (1808–73). Emperor of the French (1852–70). The nephew of Napoleon I, he led Bonapartist opposition to Louis-Philippe, became President of the Second Republic (1848), and later (1852) proclaimed himself Emperor. He instituted reforms and rebuilt Paris. His imperialist adventures in the Crimea (1854–56) and Italy (1859) were successful, but his lack of judgment was shown in the Mexican campaign (1861–67) and culminated in the disastrous Franco-Prussian War and his abdication (1870).

nappe (nap) *n.* **1.** A sheet of water flowing over a dam or similar structure. **2.** *Geology.* A folded sheetlike formation that has been moved from its site of origin by tectonic forces which caused the folding. **3.** *Geometry.* Either of the two parts into which a cone is divided by the vertex. [French *nappe (d'eau),* sheet (of water), from Old French *nappe,* tablecloth, from Latin *mappa,* napkin, towel.]

nap·py¹ (náppi) *n., pl.* **-pies.** A folded piece of towelling or other absorbent or disposable material, worn around a baby's waist and between the legs and used to absorb excreta. Also called "napkin", *U.S* "diaper". [From NAPKIN.]

nap·py² *adj.* **-pier, -piest.** Having a nap; shaggy; fuzzy.

Nar·bonne (naar-bón). *Latin name* **Narbo Martius.** City of southern France. The first Roman colony in Transalpine Gaul, it was later a port until its harbour silted up in the 14th century.

narc, nark (nark) *n. Chiefly U.S. Slang.* A police officer dealing with crimes concerning illegal drugs; a narcotics agent. [Perhaps from Romany *nāk,* nose (influenced by NARCOTIC).]

nar·ce·ine (nár-seen, -si-een) *n.* Also **nar·ce·in** (-sin, -si-in). A white crystalline narcotic, $C_{23}H_{27}O_8N\cdot3H_2O$, obtained from opium. [French *narcéine* : Greek *narkē,* numbness + -INE.]

nar·cis·sism (naar-síss-iz'm, nár-si-) *n.* Also **nar·cism** (nár-siz'm). 1. Excessive admiration of oneself. 2. *Psychoanalysis.* An arresting of development in, or a regression to, the infantile stage of development in which one's own body is the object of erotic interest. [After NARCISSUS.] —**nar·cis·sist** (-sist) *n.* —**nar·cis·sis·tic** (-sístik) *adj.*

nar·cis·sus (naar-síssəss) *n., pl.* -**suses** or -**cissi** (-síssī, -sissee). 1. Any of several widely cultivated plants of the genus *Narcissus,* having narrow, grasslike leaves, and usually white or yellow flowers characterised by a cup-shaped or trumpet-shaped central crown. See **daffodil, jonquil, Chinese sacred lily.** 2. **Pheasant's eye** *(see).* [Latin, from Greek *narkissos,* probably of Mediterranean origin.]

Narcissus. *Greek Mythology.* A youth who, having spurned the love of Echo, pined away in love for his own reflection in a pool of water and was transformed into a flower, the narcissus.

narco– *comb. form.* Indicates: 1. Numbness, sluggishness, or stupor; for example, **narcolepsy.** 2. A narcotic drug; for example, **narcotine.** [Greek *narko-,* from *narkoun,* to benumb, from *narkē,* numbness.]

nar·co·a·nal·y·sis (nárkō-ə-nál-ə-siss) *n.* Psychoanalysis conducted while the patient is in a drug-induced drowsy state.

nar·co·lep·sy (nárkə-lep-si) *n. Pathology.* A condition characterised by sudden and uncontrollable attacks of deep sleep. [NARCO- + -LEPSY.] —**nar·co·lep·tic** (-léptik) *adj.*

nar·co·sis (naar-kō-siss) *n.* Diminished consciousness or complete unconsciousness produced by a drug. Also called "narcotism". [Greek *narkōsis,* a numbing, from *narkoun,* to make numb, from *narkē,* numbness.]

nar·co·syn·the·sis (nárkō-sínthə-siss) *n.* Narcoanalysis directed towards making the patient recall suppressed memories and emotional traumas for later interpretation.

nar·cot·ic (naar-kóttik) *n.* 1. a. Any drug that dulls the senses, induces sleep, and with prolonged use becomes addictive. b. Broadly, any illegal drug. 2. Something that numbs, soothes, or induces a dreamlike or insensitive state.
~*adj.* 1. Inducing sleep or stupor. 2. Of or pertaining to narcotics, their effects, or their use. 3. Of or pertaining to one addicted to a narcotic drug. [Middle English *narkotike,* from Old French *narcotique* (originally an adjective), from Medieval Latin *narcōticus,* from Greek *narkōtikos,* numbing, narcotic, from *narkoun,* to make numb, from *narkē,* numbness.] —**nar·cot·i·cal·ly** *adv.*

nar·co·tine (nárkə-teen, -tin) *n.* An alkaloid, $C_{22}H_{23}NO_7$, obtained from opium and used to relieve coughing, fever, and spasms. [French : *narcotique,* NARCOT(IC) + -INE.]

nar·co·tise, nar·co·tize (nárkə-tīz) *tr.v.* -**tised, -tising, -tises.** 1. To place under the influence of a narcotic. 2. To lull or induce sleep in. 3. To dull; deaden. —**nar·co·ti·sa·tion** (-tī-záysh'n ‖ *U.S.* -ti-) *n.*

nar·co·tism (nárkə-tiz'm) *n.* 1. Addiction to narcotics such as opium, heroin, or morphine. 2. A drugged state; narcosis. [French *narcotisme,* from *narcotique,* NARCOTIC.]

nard (nard) *n.* 1. A plant, **spikenard** *(see).* 2. A balm made from spikenard. [Middle English *narde,* from Latin *nardus,* from Greek *nardos,* from Semitic.]

nar·doo (naar-dōō) *n.* 1. An Australian clover-like fern, *Marsilea drummondii,* found growing in swamps. 2. The spores of this plant, used as a food by the Aborigines. [From a native language.]

nar·es (náir-eez) *pl.n. Singular* -**is** (-iss). The openings in the nasal cavities of vertebrates; nostrils. [Latin *nārēs,* plural of *nāris,* nostril.] —**nar·i·al** (-i-əl) *adj.*

nar·ghi·le, nar·gi·le (nárgi-li, -lay) *n.* An Oriental tobacco pipe, a **hookah** *(see).* [French *narguilé,* from Persian *nārgīleh,* a pipe (whose bowl was originally made of coconut shell), from *nārgīl,* coconut, from Sanskrit *nārikelat†,* coconut.]

nark¹ (nark) *n. British Slang.* An informer, especially one working for the police.
~*v.* **narked, narking, narks.** *British Slang.* —*tr.* To irritate or annoy. —*intr.* To complain; grumble. [Thieves' slang, from Romany *nāk,* nose.]

nark². Variant of **narc.**

Nar·ra·gan·set (nárrə-gán-sit) *n., pl.* -**sets** or collectively **Narraganset.** 1. A member of an Algonquian-speaking North American Indian people that formerly inhabited the area of Rhode Island. 2. The language of this tribe. —**Nar·ra·gan·set** *adj.*

Narragansett Bay. An inlet of the Atlantic Ocean in Rhode Island state, United States. It is known for its resorts and fishing centres.

nar·rate (nə-ráyt, na- ‖ *U.S. also* nárrayt) *v.* -**rated, -rating, -rates.** —*tr.* To give an oral or written account of; tell (a story). —*intr.* To give an account or description; especially, to supply a commentary for a film, television programme, or the like. [Latin *narrāre,* from *gnārus,* knowing.] —**nar·ra·tor** (-ər ‖ nárrətər) *n.*

nar·ra·tion (nə-ráysh'n, na-) *n.* 1. The act or an instance of narrating. 2. Something narrated; a narrative.

nar·ra·tive (nárrətiv) *n.* 1. a. A story or description of actual or fictional events; a narrated account. b. A tendentious narrative: *feminists deconstructing the patriarchal narrative of European history.* 2. The part of a piece of writing that is concerned with the narration of events. 3. The act, technique, or process of narrating.
~*adj.* 1. Consisting of or characterised by the telling of a story or the description of events without analysis: *narrative poetry.* 2. Of or pertaining to narration: *narrative skill.* —**nar·ra·tive·ly** *adv.*

nar·row (nárrō) *adj.* -**rower, -rowest.** 1. Of small or limited width, especially in comparison with length: *a narrow corridor.* 2. a. Limited in area; cramped; confined. b. Limited in scope; restricted: *the enquiry's narrow terms of reference.* 3. Lacking flexibility; rigid in adherence to an idea or way: *narrow principles; a narrow outlook.* 4. *Rare.* Straitened; pinched: *narrow circumstances.* 5. Barely sufficient or successful; precarious: *a narrow margin of victory.* 6. Painstakingly thorough or attentive: *a narrow scrutiny.* 7. *Regional.* Miserly; stingy. 8. *Phonetics.* Tense.
~*v.* **narrowed, -rowing, -rows.** —*tr.* 1. To make narrow or narrower; reduce in width or extent. 2. To limit or restrict. Often used with *down: That narrowed down the possibilities.* —*intr.* To grow less in width or extent; contract.
~*n.* 1. A narrow place or part, such as a pass through mountains or a valley. 2. *Plural.* Any narrow body of water, especially connecting two larger ones. [Middle English *nearwe, narow,* Old English *nearu,* from Germanic.] —**nar·row·ly** *adv.* —**nar·row·ness** *n.*

narrow gauge *n.* A distance between the rails of a railway track that is less than the standard width of 56½ inches. —**nar·row-gauge** (nárrō-gáyj) *adj.*

nar·row-mind·ed (nárrō-míndid) *adj.* Lacking breadth of view, tolerance, or sympathy; bigoted; prejudiced. —**nar·row-mind·ed·ly** *adv.* —**nar·row-mind·ed·ness** *n.*

nar·thex (nár-theks) *n.* 1. A portico or lobby of an early Christian church or basilica, separated from the nave by a railing or screen. 2. Any church entrance hall leading to the nave. [Medieval Greek *narthēx,* "enclosure", originally "casket", "box" (made of hollow stems of giant fennel), from Greek *narthēx,* giant fennel.]

nartjie. Variant of **naartjie.**

Nar·vik (nár-vik, -veek). Ice-free port and tourist centre within the Arctic Circle, Norway.

nar·whal (nár-wəl, -hwəl) *n.* An arctic aquatic mammal, *Monodon monoceros,* having a spotted pelt and (in the male) a spiral tusk several feet long. It is hunted for ivory and oil. [Dutch *narwal,* from Danish *narhval,* from Old Norse *nāhvalr,* "corpse-whale" (so called because with its whitish colour it resembles a floating corpse) : *nār,* corpse + *hvalr,* whale.]

na·ry (náir-i) *adj. Regional.* Not one; no. Usually followed by *a* or *an: Nary a woman remained.* [From *ne'er a,* "never a".]

NAS·A (nássə) *n.* In the United States, the National Aeronautics and Space Administration.

na·sal (náyz'l) *adj.* 1. Of or pertaining to the nose. 2. *Phonetics.* Formed by lowering the soft palate so that most of the air is exhaled through the nose rather than the mouth, as in sounding *m, n,* and *ng* in English or *un, on,* or *en* in French. 3. Characterised by or resembling sounds so formed: *a nasal whine.*
~*n.* 1. *Phonetics.* A nasal sound. 2. A nasal part or bone. 3. The nosepiece of a helmet. [French, from New Latin *nāsālis,* from Latin *nāsus,* nose.] —**na·sal·i·ty** (nay-zál-əti, nə-) *n.* —**na·sal·ly** *adv.*

nasal index *n.* The ratio of the width to the length of the nose, multiplied by 100. It is used in anthropological measurements.

na·sal·ise, na·sal·ize (náyzə-līz) *v.* -**ised, -ising, -ises.** —*tr.* To render nasal. —*intr.* To produce nasal sounds. —**na·sal·i·sa·tion** (-lī-záysh'n ‖ *U.S.* -li-) *n.*

nas·cent (náss'nt, náy-sənt) *adj.* 1. Coming into existence; in the process of emerging. 2. *Chemistry.* Designating or pertaining to a substance that is produced in a highly active form in the reaction mixture: *nascent hydrogen.* [Latin *nāscēns* (stem *nāscent-*), present participle of *nāscī,* to be born.] —**nas·cence** *n.*

nase·ber·ry (náyz-berri, -bəri, -bri) *n., pl.* -**ries.** A tropical tree, **sapodilla** *(see),* or its fruit. [Spanish *néspera* (influenced by BERRY), from Latin *mespila,* MEDLAR.]

Nash (nash), **John** (1752–1835). English architect. He designed much of the area around Regent's Park, as well as Regent Street, and Brighton Pavilion, and remodelled Buckingham Palace. He is also responsible for many of England's finest country houses.

Nash, Ogden (1902–71). U.S. humorist. A regular contributor to the *New Yorker* magazine, he is best known for his epigrammatic verse.

Nash, Paul (1889–1946). British painter. A war artist in both World Wars, he painted many striking war scenes, such as *The Menin Road* (1918) and *Totes Meer* (1941).

Nashe (nash), **Thomas** (1567–1601). English writer. His witty, colourful works include several anti-Puritan pamphlets, a lost dramatic collaboration with Ben Jonson, *The Isle of Dogs* (1597), for which he was imprisoned, and possibly the best of all Elizabethan narrative works, *The Unfortunate Traveller* (1594).

Nash·ville (násh-vil). The capital of Tennessee, United States. Lying on the Cumberland river, it is an important communications, industrial, and commercial centre, with publishing and music industries, and is the home of country-and-western music.

na·si go·reng (náa-si gáw-reng) *n.* A Dutch-Indonesian dish of fried rice mixed with cooked pork, ham, chicken, or seafood, and served with strips of omelette. [Malay, cooked rice (with pork).]

na·si·on (náyzi-ən) *n.* The point at the top of the nose marking the boundary between the nasal bone and the frontal bone of the forehead. [French, from Latin *nāsus,* nose.]

naso– *comb. form.* Indicates nose; for example, **nasofrontal.** [New Latin, from *nāsus,* nose.]

na·so·fron·tal (náyzō-frúnt'l) *adj.* Of or pertaining to the nasal and frontal bones.

na·so·phar·ynx (náyzō-fárringks) *n., pl.* -**pharynges** (-fə-rín-jeez) or

-ynxes. The portion of the pharynx directly behind the nasal cavity and above the soft palate. **—na·so·pha·ryn·ge·al** (-fə-rín-ji-əl, -jəl, fárrin-jée-əl, -jéel) *adj.*

Nas·sau¹ (nássaw). The capital of the Bahamas, on New Providence Island. Tourism, fundamental to the country's economy, is centred here.

Nas·sau² (nássow). Former duchy in western Germany, now incorporated in Hessen and Rhineland Palatinate. Its capital was Wiesbaden. The area is fertile and known for its wines and mineral springs. Branches of the house of Nassau still rule the Netherlands and Luxembourg.

Nas·ser (na͞a-sər, nássər), **Gamal Abdul** (1918–70). Egyptian soldier and statesman. He was President of Egypt (1956–58) and of the United Arab Republic (1958–70). After the war with Israel (1948–49), he led the revolt (1952) under General Neguib that deposed King Farouk. In 1954 he supplanted Neguib as premier. His nationalisation of the Suez Canal (1956) provoked Anglo-French intervention and precipitated an international crisis. He subsequently formed close ties with the U.S.S.R. Despite unsuccessful attempts to form an Arab federation, he did much for Egyptian prosperity.

Nasser, Lake. See **Aswan High Dam.**

nas·tic (nástik) *adj.* Of, pertaining to, or characterised by a tendency in plants to move in a direction determined by an internal stimulus, such as growth movement, rather than an external stimulus. [From Greek *nastos,* pressed down, from *nassein†,* to press.]

na·stur·tium (nə-stúrshəm ‖ na-) *n.* Any of various trailing plants of the genus *Tropaeolum,* having flowers with five broad petals that are usually yellow, orange, or red. Their round pungent leaves and seeds are sometimes used as seasoning. [Latin *nāsturtium,* a kind of cress, originally *nāsitortium* (unattested), "nose-pain" (so called because cress plants such as mustard when eaten cause burning sensations in the nose) : *nāsus,* nose + *tort-,* past stem of *torquēre,* to twist, torture.]

nas·ty (na͞asti ‖ násti) *adj.* **-tier, -tiest.** **1.** Disgusting to see, smell, or touch; filthy; foul. **2.** Morally offensive; indecent. **3.** Malicious; spiteful; mean: *saying nasty things about us.* **4.** Causing discomfort or annoyance; unpleasant; disagreeable: *nasty weather.* **5.** Painful or dangerous; grave: *a nasty accident.*
~*n., pl.* **-nasties.** One that is evil, unpleasant, or offensive. —See Synonyms at **dirty.** [Middle English, *nasty, naxty,* probably akin to Dutch *nestig,* earlier *nistich,* perhaps meaning "fouled like a dirty bird's nest", from *nest,* nest.] **—nas·ti·ly** *adv.* **—nas·ti·ness** *n.*

-nasty *n. comb. form.* Indicates a specified kind of nastic response or change; for example, **epinasty.** [From NASTIC.] **—-nastic** *adj. comb. form.*

nat. **1.** national. **2.** native. **3.** natural.

na·tal (náyt'l) *adj.* **1.** Of or relating to birth; accompanying birth: *natal injuries.* **2.** Of or pertaining to the time or place of one's birth: *a natal star.* [Middle English, from Latin *nātālis,* from *nāscī* (past participle *nātus*), to be born.]

Na·tal (nə-tál ‖ -taál). See **KwaZulu-Natal.**

na·tal·i·ty (nay-tál-əti, nə-) *n., pl.* **-ties.** Birth rate *(see).*

Natal plum *n.* A South African shrub, *Carissa grandiflora,* having forked spines, white flowers, and an edible scarlet berry. [From NATAL, South Africa.]

na·tant (náyt'nt) *adj.* Swimming or floating; especially, floating on the surface. Said, for example, of an aquatic plant. [Latin *natāns* (stem *natant-*), from *natāre,* to swim.]

na·ta·tion (nə-táysh'n, nay-, na-) *n. Formal.* The action or art of swimming. [Latin *natātiō* (stem *natātiōn-*), from *natāre,* to swim.]

na·ta·to·ri·al (náytə-táwri-əl, nátta- ‖ -tóri-) *adj.* Also **na·ta·to·ry** (-tri, -təri, nə-táytəri). Of, pertaining to, or adapted for swimming. [Late Latin *natātōrius,* from Latin *natāre,* to swim.]

Natch·ez (náchiz) *n., pl.* **Natchez. 1.** A member of a Muskhogean-speaking North American Indian people, formerly living in the area of Mississippi. **2.** The language of this tribe. **—Natch·ez** *adj.*

na·tes (náy-teez) *pl.n. Anatomy.* The buttocks *(see).* [Latin *natēs,* plural of *natis,* buttock.]

Na·than (náy-thən, -than). A prophet during the reigns of David and Solomon. II Samuel 12:1–15.

Na·than·ael (nə-thán-yəl). One of the 12 Apostles, usually identified as **Bartholomew.**

nathe·less (náyth-ləss, -liss) *adv.* Also **nath·less** (náth-). *Archaic.* Nevertheless; notwithstanding. [Middle English *nathles,* Old English *nā thē lǣs,* "not less by that" : *nā,* NO + *thē,* by that, instrumental case of *sē,* that + *lǣs,* LESS.]

Na·tick (náytik) *n.* A dialect based on English and the language of the Massachusett tribe spoken in the village of Natick, near the present Natick in Massachusetts, U.S.A. [Origin obscure.]

na·tion (náysh'n) *n.* **1.** A people, usually the inhabitants of a specific territory, who share common customs, origins, history, and frequently language or related languages. **2. a.** An aggregation of people organised under a single government; a country. **b.** The entire people of a country, as distinct from any of the various groups and classes composing it. Preceded by *the: The nation responded in a wonderful show of solidarity.* **3.** The government of a sovereign state: *The Western nations have reacted favourably to the proposal.* **4. a.** A federation or tribe of people, as of black South Africans or North American Indians. **b.** The territory occupied by such a federation or tribe. **—the nations.** In Biblical use, the gentile or heathen peoples: *"And the Lord shall scatter you among the nations."* (Deuteronomy 4:27). [Middle English *nacioun,* from Old French *nacion,*

from Latin *nātiō* (stem *nātiōn-*), "race", "breed", from *nāscī* (past participle *nātus*), to be born.]

Usage: nation, state, country, people, race. Nation primarily signifies a political body rather than a physical territory—the citizens united under one independent government, without close regard for their origins. *State* even more specifically indicates political organisation, generally on a sovereign basis and pertaining to a well-defined area. *Country,* in strict usage, is a geographical term signifying the territory of one nation, but it is often used in the extended sense of *nation. People,* in this context, signifies a group united over a long period by common cultural and social ties, although not necessarily by racial and national bonds. *Race* refers to those recognisable physical traits, stemming from common ancestry, that succeeding generations have in common.

na·tion·al (násh'n'l, násh-n'l) *adj. Abbr.* **nat., natl. 1.** Of, pertaining to, or belonging to a nation as an organised whole. **2.** Characteristic of or peculiar to the people of a nation: *a national trait.* **3.** Occurring, distributed, or recognised nationwide: *a national figure.* **4.** Of or maintained by the government of a nation: *a national park.* **5.** Devoted to one's own nation or its interests; patriotic.
~*n.* **1.** A citizen of a particular nation. **2.** A newspaper distributed to all parts of a nation. **—na·tion·al·ly** *adv.*

national anthem *n.* A hymn or song adopted by a nation and sung or played as an expression of national pride and unity, as on state occasions.

National Assembly *n.* A national legislative body in various countries; especially, the first of the Revolutionary assemblies in France (1789–91).

national assistance *n. British.* The social security benefits that preceded **supplementary benefit** *(see).*

national bank *n.* **1.** A bank associated with national finances and usually owned or controlled by a government. **2.** In the United States, any in a system of Federally chartered, privately owned banks, each required by law to be an investing member of its district Federal Reserve Bank.

national debt *n.* The total amount of money borrowed by a national government.

National Economic Development Council *n. Abbr.* **N.E.D.C.** A British organisation advising government and industry on how to increase economic growth and efficiency.

National Front *n. Abbr.* **N.F.** In Britain, an extreme right-wing political party, best known for its racist policies regarding non-white ethnic minorities.

National Girobank *n.* In Britain, the official registered name of the Post Office banking system, **Giro** *(see).*

National Guard *n.* **1.** In the United States, the military reserve units controlled by each state. **2.** Formerly in France, an armed national force operating intermittently from 1789 to 1871.

National Health Service *n. Abbr.* **NHS.** A comprehensive service providing medical care in the United Kingdom, financed by national insurance and from taxation, in operation since 1948.

national income *n.* The total net value of all goods and services produced within a nation over a specific period of time, usually a year, and representing the sum of wages, profits, rents, interest, and pension payments to residents of the nation. Compare **gross national product.**

national insurance, National Insurance *n.* In the United Kingdom, the insurance system used to help to finance state welfare provisions such as pensions and medical care through regular contributions required from employers and employees.

na·tion·al·ise, na·tion·al·ize (násh'n-ə-līz, náshnə-) *tr.v.* **-ised, -ising, -ises. 1.** To convert (a sector of industry, agriculture, commerce, or public service, together with associated means of production) from private to governmental ownership and control. **2.** To make national in character. **3.** To accept as a citizen or national; naturalise. **—na·tion·al·i·sa·tion** (-lī-záysh'n ‖ U.S. -li-) *n.*

na·tion·al·ism (násh'n-ə-liz'm, náshnə-) *n.* **1.** Pride in and devotion to one's own nation and its interests, especially when excessive. **2.** A strong sense of national identity, often associated with aspirations for national independence or separatism. **—na·tion·al·ist** *adj. & n.* **—na·tion·al·is·tic** (-lístik) *adj.* **—na·tion·al·is·ti·cal·ly** *adv.*

na·tion·al·i·ty (násh'n-ál-əti) *n., pl.* **-ties. 1.** The status of belonging to a particular nation by origin, birth, or naturalisation. **2.** A people having common origins or traditions and constituting or being considered to constitute a nation. **3.** Existence as a politically autonomous entity; the status of a nation. **4.** National character. **5.** A nation or country: *people of different nationalities.*

national monument *n. Chiefly U.S.* A natural landmark or a structure or site of historic interest set aside by a national government and maintained for enjoyment or study by the public.

national park *n.* A tract of land administered by a government-appointed body to preserve its natural character and wildlife.

National Savings Bank. See **Savings Bank.**

national service *n.* In various countries, compulsory military service for a limited period of time.

National Socialism *n.* **Nazism** *(see).*

National Trust *n.* In the United Kingdom, an organisation that aims to preserve places and buildings of aesthetic, cultural, and historical value, for the benefit of the public.

na·tion·hood (náysh'n-ho͞od) *n.* The state of being a nation.

Nation of Islam *n.* An organisation of black Americans who follow the religious practices of Islam and propose segregation of blacks

and whites, with a view to the establishment of a new black nation. Members are known as "Black Muslims".
na·tion-state (náysh'n-stáyt, -stayt) *n.* A state whose people have a sense of national identity based on a common cultural heritage.
na·tion·wide (náysh'n-wīd, -wīd) *adj.* Throughout a whole nation. **—na·tion·wide** *adv.*
na·tive (náytiv) *adj. Abbr.* **nat. 1.** Belonging to one by nature; inborn; innate: *native ability.* **2.** Belonging by birth or origin to a specified country or place: *a native Englishman.* **3.** One's own because of the place or circumstances of one's birth: *our native land.* **4.** Originating, growing, or produced in a certain place; indigenous as opposed to exotic or foreign: *native products.* **5.** Belonging to or characteristic of the original inhabitants of a particular place, especially those of primitive culture: *native customs of Borneo.* **6.** Occurring in nature pure or uncombined with other substances. Said of metallic or other solid elements: *native copper.* **7.** In a natural state; unaffected by artificial influences: *native beauty.* **8.** *Archaic.* Closely related, as by birth or race.
~*n. Abbr.* **nat. 1.** One who is connected with a place by birth or origin. **2.** An established local resident, as distinguished from a visitor or newcomer. **3.** One who is an original inhabitant of a place; especially one belonging to a people of primitive culture originally occupying a country, as distinguished from an invader or settler. **4.** *South African.* Formerly, a black South African. Now considered offensive. **5.** Something, especially an animal or a plant, that originated in a particular place. [Middle English *natif,* from Old French, from Latin *nātīvus,* born, native, from *nāscī* (past participle *nātus*), to be born.] **—na·tive·ly** *adv.* **—na·tive·ness** *n.*
native bear *n. Australian.* The **koala** *(see).*
na·tive-born (náytiv-bórn) *adj.* Belonging to a place by birth.
native peach *n.* A tree, the **quandong** *(see).*
native speaker *n.* One who speaks a particular native language as a first language.
na·tiv·ism (náytiv-iz'm) *n.* **1.** *Philosophy.* The doctrine that the mind produces ideas that are not derived from external sources; the doctrine of innate ideas. **2.** The re-establishment or perpetuation of native cultural traits, especially in opposition to acculturation. **—na·tiv·ist** *n.* **—na·tiv·is·tic** (-ístik) *adj.*
na·tiv·i·ty (nə-tívvəti || *U.S. also* nay-) *n., pl.* **-ties. 1.** Birth, especially the place, conditions, or circumstances of one's birth. **2.** *Capital* **N. a.** The birth of Jesus. **b.** A representation, such as a painting or a play, of this. **c.** Christmas. **3.** *Astrology.* A horoscope based on the time of one's birth. [Middle English *nativite,* from Old French, from Latin *nātīvitās,* from *nātīvus,* born, NATIVE.]
nativity play *n.* A play, especially a short one performed by schoolchildren, based on the gospel accounts of the birth of Christ.
natl. national.
NA·TO (náytō) *n.* The **North Atlantic Treaty Organisation** *(see).*
na·tro·lite (náttrə-līt, náytrə-) *n.* A white zeolite mineral, $Na_2(Al_2Si_3O_{10})\cdot 2H_2O$. [German *Natrolith* : NATRO(N) + -LITE.]
na·tron (náy-trən, -tron) *n.* A mineral form of hydrous sodium carbonate, $Na_2CO_3\cdot 10H_2O$, often found crystallised with other salts. [French, from Spanish *natrón,* from Arabic *naṭrūn,* from Greek *nitron,* NITRE.]
Nat·so·pa, NAT·SO·PA (nát-sṓpə) Formerly, National Society of Operative Printers, Graphical and Media Personnel (in Britain).
nat·ter (náttər) *intr.v.* **-tered, -tering, -ters.** *Chiefly British Informal.* To talk idly about trivial subjects; chatter; gossip.
~*n.* An aimless or trivial conversation; a chat. [19th century (Scottish) : imitative.]
nat·ter·jack (náttər-jak) *n.* A European toad, *Bufo calamita,* with short legs and a yellow stripe down its back. It inflates its body when alarmed. [Perhaps from NATTER (referring to its loud croak) + JACK (chap).]
nat·ty (nátti) *adj.* **-tier, -tiest.** *Informal.* Neat, trim, and smart; spruce; dapper. [Perhaps variant of obsolete *netty,* from Middle English *net,* trim, neat, from Old French *net,* NEAT (tidy).]
nat·u·ral (nách-rəl, náchə-) *adj. Abbr.* **nat. 1.** Present in or produced by nature; not artificial or man-made: *a natural reservoir; natural dyes.* **2.** Pertaining to or concerning physical reality, as opposed to a spiritual, intellectual, or imagined reality: *natural science.* **3.** Pertaining to or produced solely by nature or the expected order of things: *a natural event; natural causes.* **4. a.** Pertaining to or resulting from inherent nature; not acquired empirically: *Self-preservation is an instinct natural to man.* **b.** Distinguished by innate qualities or aptitudes: *a natural leader.* **5.** Free from affectation or artificiality; spontaneous: *She is natural even in awkward company.* **6.** Not altered, treated, or disguised: *natural colouring; a natural landscape.* **7.** Consonant with particular circumstances; expected and accepted: *She saw children as a natural consequence of marriage.* **8.** Based on or in accordance with a supposedly innate sense of what is right and fair: *natural justice.* **9.** In a primitive, unenlightened, or unregenerate state. **10. a.** Illegitimate. Said of offspring. **b.** Related by blood: *They were his natural parents.* **11.** *Music.* **a.** Neither sharp nor flat: *a natural note.* **b.** Having no sharps or flats: *a natural key.* —See Synonyms at **naive, normal, sincere.**
~*n.* **1.** One seeming to have the qualifications necessary for success: *a natural for the job.* **2.** *Music.* **a.** The sign (♮) placed before a note to cancel a preceding sharp or flat. Also *U.S.* "cancel". **b.** A note so affected. **3.** In certain card and dice games, such as pontoon and craps, a combination that wins immediately it is dealt or thrown. [Middle English, from Old French, from Latin *nātūrālis,* from *nātūra,* NATURE.] **—nat·u·ral·ness** *n.*

Usage: There are two ways of forming the opposite of *natural.* The general antonym is *unnatural,* which has a range of applications all to do with being "outside the expected order of things". *Supernatural* and *preternatural* are restricted to contexts where the contrast is between this world and some other miraculous one.
natural childbirth *n.* An approach to childbirth that seeks to avoid the use of anaesthesia and surgical intervention and to ensure the psychological and physiological well-being of the mother through preparation in the form of exercises and relaxation techniques, for example.
natural classification *n.* Classification of animals and plants according to similarities based on supposed descent from a common ancestor.
natural frequency *n. Physics.* The frequency at which a given system will vibrate or oscillate freely.
natural gas *n.* A mixture of hydrocarbon gases found within the Earth, often with petroleum deposits, principally methane together with varying quantities of ethane, propane, butane, and other gases. It is used as a fuel and in the manufacture of organic compounds.
natural gender *n. Grammar.* Gender based upon actual sex or absence of sex of the referent of a noun. Compare **common gender, grammatical gender.**
natural history *n.* **1.** The study of natural objects and organisms, their origins, evolution, interrelationships, and description. **2.** The natural phenomena of a particular region or time.
nat·u·ral·ise, nat·u·ral·ize (nách-rə-līz, náchə-) *v.* **-ised, -ising, -ises.** *—tr.* **1.** To grant full citizenship to (one of foreign birth). **2.** To adopt (something foreign, such as a word or custom) into general use. **3.** To adapt (a plant or animal) to life in a new environment. **4.** To cause to conform to nature; make natural or lifelike. **5.** To explain or account for (a phenomenon) in terms of natural, rather than supernatural causes. *—intr.* To become naturalised or acclimatised; adapt. **—nat·u·ral·i·sa·tion** (-lī-záysh'n || *U.S.* -li-) *n.*
nat·u·ral·ism (nách-rə-liz'm, náchə-) *n.* **1.** Conformity to nature; factual or realistic representation, especially: **a.** In literature, the practice of and belief in presenting a detailed and lifelike account of the circumstances of human life, rather than a conventionalised, fantastic, or symbolic account. **b.** In the visual arts, the practice of and belief in reproducing subjects as exactly as possible. **c.** A movement or school advocating such a practice or belief. **2.** *Philosophy.* The system of thought holding that all phenomena can be explained in terms of natural causes and laws, without attributing moral, spiritual, or supernatural significance to them. **3.** *Theology.* The doctrine that all religious truths are derived from nature and natural causes and not from revelation. **4.** Conduct or thought prompted by natural desires or instincts.
nat·u·ral·ist (nách-rə-list, náchə-) *n.* **1.** One versed in natural history, especially in zoology or botany. **2.** One who believes in and follows the tenets of naturalism.
nat·u·ral·is·tic (nách-rə-lístik, náchə-) *adj.* **1.** Imitating or producing the effect or appearance of nature. **2.** Of, pertaining to, or in accordance with the doctrines of naturalism. **3.** Of or pertaining to natural history.
natural law *n.* **1.** A law of morality thought to derive from an instinctive sense of right and wrong rather than from the legislation of society, for example. **2.** A law of science that ascribes order and regularity to natural phenomena such as tides, for example.
natural logarithm *n. Symbol* **ln** *Mathematics.* A logarithm to the base e (=2.71828 . . .). For example, $\ln 10 = \log_e 10 = 2.30258$. Also called "Napierian logarithm".
nat·u·ral·ly (nách-rə-li, náchə-) *adv.* **1.** In a natural manner. **2.** By nature; inherently. **3. a.** As might be expected in the circumstances. **b.** Without a doubt; of course.
natural number *n. Mathematics.* Any of the set of positive whole numbers; a positive integer.
natural philosophy *n.* The study of nature and the physical universe, especially studies that led historically to the modern science of physics.
natural resources *pl.n.* Material sources of wealth that occur in a natural state, such as forests or minerals.
natural science *n.* A science, such as biology, chemistry, or physics, based on the study of the physical world and its phenomena. **2.** These sciences collectively.
natural selection *n.* The phenomenon that individuals possessing characteristics advantageous for survival in a specific environment constitute an increasing proportion of the population in that environment with each succeeding generation. See **Darwinism.**
natural theology *n.* A theology in which knowledge of God is based on reasoning from natural phenomena, not divine revelation.
natural varnish *n.* **Varnish** *(see).*
natural virtues *pl.n.* The **cardinal virtues** *(see).*
natural wastage *n.* A gradual reduction in the personnel of a company or organisation through retirement, resignation, or death, rather than through enforced redundancies, for example. Also *chiefly U.S.* "attrition".
na·ture (náychər) *n.* **1.** The intrinsic characteristics and qualities of a person or thing: *the essential nature of poetry.* **2.** The order, disposition, and essence of all entities composing the physical universe. **3.** The physical world, usually the outdoors, including all living things and natural phenomena such as fire, snow, and thunder. **4.** Natural scenery: *gaze upon nature.* **5.** *Often capital* **N.** The forces or processes of the physical world, sometimes personified as a fe-

male being: *leave it to Mother Nature.* **6.** The primitive state of existence, untouched and uninfluenced by civilisation or artificiality. **7.** *Theology.* Man's natural state, as distinguished from the state of grace. **8.** Kind; type: *something of that nature.* **9.** The aggregate of a person's instincts, and preferences. **10. a.** A particular kind of individual character or disposition; temperament: *a sweet nature.* **b.** *Literary.* A person or thing characterised by some particular disposition: *"Strange natures made a brotherhood of ill."* (P.B. Shelley). **11.** The natural or real aspect of a person, place, or thing: *her true nature.* **12.** Generally accepted standards of morality or conduct: *thought homosexuality to be against nature.* **13.** Bodily processes and functions, such as urination. Often used euphemistically in the phrase *a call of nature.* —See Synonyms at **disposition, type.** —**by nature.** Because of natural qualities; inherently. —**in** or **of the nature of.** Belonging to the type or category of. [Middle English, from Old French, from Latin *nātūra,* nature, "birth", from *nāscī* (past participle *nātus*), to be born.]

nature study *n.* The observation and study of plants, animals, and natural phenomena, usually nontechnical and informal.

nature trail *n.* A path through a park or in the countryside allowing people to study the flora and fauna as they walk along it.

na·tur·ism (náychə-riz'm) *n.* **Nudism** *(see).*

na·tur·op·a·thy (náychə-róppəthi) *n.* A system of therapy that relies exclusively on natural remedies, such as sunlight, organically grown foods, fresh air, and massage, to treat the sick. [From NATURE + -PATHY.] —**na·tur·o·path** (náychə-rə-path, nə-téwr-ə- || -tóor-) *n.* —**na·tur·o·path·ic** (-páthik) *adj.*

naught (nawt) *n.* **1.** *Archaic.* Nothing. **2.** *Chiefly U.S.* Variant of **nought.** —**set at naught.** To consider as being of little importance. ~*adj.* Worthless; of no value. [Middle English *nauht,* Old English *nāwiht* : *nā,* NO + *wiht,* creature, thing.]

naugh·ty (náwti) *adj.* **-tier, -tiest. 1.** Disobedient; mischievous. Usually said of a child or a child's misdeeds. **2.** Indecent or suggestive of indecency. **3.** *Archaic.* Wicked; evil. [Middle English *nauhty,* from *nauht,* "worthless", NAUGHT.] —**naugh·ti·ly** *adv.* —**naugh·ti·ness** *n.*

Nau·pli·a (náwpli-ə). *Greek* **Návplion** or **Náfplio** (naáf-pli-on). A seaport and capital of Argolis prefecture, Peloponnese, southeast Greece. It was the first capital of independent Greece (1830–34).

nau·pli·us (náw-pli-əss) *n., pl.* **-plii** (-pli-ī). *Zoology.* The microscopic, free-swimming larva of certain crustaceans, having an oval body and three pairs of limbs. [Latin, from Greek *nauplios,* sailor, perhaps variant of *nautilos,* sailor, NAUTILUS.]

Na·u·ru, Republic of (naa-róo, *properly* -óo-róo). Formerly **Pleasant Island.** A state of the central Pacific. Consisting of one coral island, its sole product is phosphates, reserves of which will run out in about 2000. It is a member of the Commonwealth. Area, 21 square kilometres (8 square miles). Population, 10,000. Capital, Yaren. See map at **Pacific Ocean.**

nau·se·a (náw-zi-ə, -si-, -zhi-, -shi- || -zhə, -shə) *n.* **1.** The sensation characterised by a feeling of the need to vomit. **2.** Strong aversion; repugnance; disgust. [Latin, from Greek *nausia,* seasickness, from *naus,* ship.]

nau·se·ate (náw-zi-ayt, -si-, -zhi-, -shi-) *v.* **-ated, -ating, -ates.** —*tr.* **1.** To cause to feel nausea; make queasy. **2.** To cause to feel loathing or disgust; sicken. —*intr.* To feel nausea or queasiness; be queasy. [Latin *nauseāre,* from *nausea,* NAUSEA.] —**nau·se·at·ing·ly** *adv.* —**nau·se·a·tion** (-áysh'n) *n.*

nau·se·ous (náw-zi-əss, -si-, -zhi-, -shi- || -shəss) *adj.* **1.** Causing nausea; sickening. **2.** Repulsive to the mind or senses; very offensive. **3.** Suffering from nausea. —**nau·seous·ly** *adv.* —**nau·se·ous·ness** *n.*

naut. nautical.

nautch (nawch) *n.* A dance form of northern India for girl dancers *(nautch-girls)* accompanied by several musicians and sometimes by a singer. [Hindi *nāc,* from Prakrit *nacca,* dance, from Sanskrit *nṛtya,* from *nṛtyati,* he dances.] —**nautch** *adj.*

nau·ti·cal (náw-tik'l) *adj. Abbr.* **naut.** Of, pertaining to, or characteristic of ships, shipping, seamen, or navigation. [From Latin *nauticus,* from Greek *nautikos,* from *nautēs,* seaman, from *naus,* ship.] —**nau·ti·cal·ly** *adv.*

Usage: *Nautical* is a general term pertaining to sailors, ships, and navigation *nautical miles. Naval* now pertains specifically to the personnel and ships of a navy, or a military sea force.

nautical mile *n. Abbr.* **nm, n.m.** A unit of length used in sea and air navigation: **1.** An international unit equal to 1 852 metres (6,076.103 feet). In this sense, also called "air mile". **2.** A British unit equal to 6,080 feet (1 853 metres). In this sense, formerly called "geographical mile". Compare **sea mile.**

nau·ti·loid (náw-ti-loyd) *n.* A mollusc of the subclass Nautiloidea, which includes the nautiluses and numerous extinct species known only as fossils. [From New Latin *Nautiloidea* : NAUTIL(US) + *-oidea,* from Latin *-oīdēs,* -OID.] —**nau·ti·loid** *adj.*

nau·ti·lus (náw-ti-ləss) *n., pl.* **-luses** or **-li** (-lī). **1.** Any cephalopod mollusc of the genus *Nautilus,* found in the Indian and Pacific oceans, and having a spiral shell with a series of air-filled chambers. See **chambered nautilus. 2.** The **paper nautilus** *(see).* [Latin, from Greek *nautilos,* sailor, from *naus,* ship.]

nav. 1. naval. **2.** navigable. **3.** navigation.

Nav·a·ho (návvə-hō, naávə-) *n., pl.* **-hos** or collectively **Navaho.** Also **Nav·a·jo** (-hō). **1.** A member of a group of Athapascan-speaking North American Indians occupying an extensive reservation in parts of New Mexico, Arizona, and Utah. **2.** The language of this group. [From Spanish, pueblo.] —**Nav·a·ho** *adj.*

na·val (náyv'l) *adj. Abbr.* **nav. 1.** Of or pertaining to the equipment, operations, personnel, or customs of a navy: *a naval officer.* **2.** Having a navy: *a great naval power.* —See Usage note at **nautical.** [Latin *nāvālis,* from *nāvis,* ship.]

naval architect *n.* One who designs ships. —**naval architecture** *n.*

naval dockyard *n.* A dockyard owned by the government for the repair, equipping, or docking of naval ships.

nav·ar (návvaar) *n.* A method of air navigation in which traffic in a pilot's vicinity is observed by ground radar and relayed to the pilot's radarscope. [*Nav*igational + rad*ar.*]

nav·ar·in (návvə-rin, -raN) *n.* A lamb or mutton stew with vegetables. [French.]

Na·varre (nə-vár). *Spanish* **Na·var·ra** (na-bárra). Former kingdom astride the Pyrenees, southwest Europe. Ruled by a Basque dynasty (9th–13th century), it was absorbed by Spain and France (1589). Today, much of it forms the Spanish province of Navarra. —**Na·var·rese** (naávə-réez, návvə-, -reéss) *adj.*

nave[1] (nayv) *n.* The central part of a church, extending from the narthex to the chancel and flanked by aisles. [Medieval Latin *nāvis,* "ship" (referring to the general shape) from Latin.]

nave[2] *n.* The hub of a wheel. [Middle English *nave,* Old English *nafu.*]

na·vel (náyv'l) *n.* **1.** The mark on the abdomen of mammals, where the umbilical cord was attached during gestation; the umbilicus. **2.** A central point; the middle. —**contemplate (one's) navel.** To indulge in introspection. Used humorously. [Middle English *navel,* Old English *nafela.*]

navel orange *n.* A sweet, usually seedless orange having at its apex a navel-like formation enclosing an underdeveloped fruit.

na·vel·wort (náyv'l-wurt || -wawrt) *n.* **1.** A plant, **pennywort** *(see).* **2.** Any plant of the genus *Omphalodes,* having one-sided clusters of usually blue flowers. [From the navel-like depression on its leaves.]

na·vic·u·lar (nə-víckew-lər) *n. Anatomy.* **1.** A comma-shaped bone of the wrist. **2.** The concave bone in front of the anklebone on the instep of the foot. Also called "scaphoid". ~*adj.* Shaped like a boat. [Late Latin *nāviculāris,* "boat-shaped", from Latin *nāvicula,* boat, diminutive of *nāvis,* ship.]

nav·i·ga·ble (návvi-gəb'l) *adj. Abbr.* **nav. 1.** Sufficiently deep or wide to provide passage for ships or boats. **2.** Capable of being steered. Said of sea vessels or aircraft. —**nav·i·ga·bil·i·ty** (-gə-bílləti), **nav·i·ga·ble·ness** *n.* —**nav·i·ga·bly** *adv.*

nav·i·gate (návvi-gayt) *v.* **-gated, -gating, -gates.** —*tr.* **1.** To plan, record, and control the course and position of (a ship or aircraft). **2.** To follow a planned course on, across, or through: *navigate a stream.* **3.** *Informal.* To direct the course of (someone or something) towards some destination. —*intr.* **1.** To control the course of a ship or aircraft. **2.** To voyage over water in a boat or ship; sail. **3.** To guide the driver of a vehicle to a destination, often with the use of maps. [Latin *nāvigāre,* to manage a ship : *nāvis,* ship + *agere,* to drive, conduct.]

nav·i·ga·tion (návvi-gáysh'n) *n. Abbr.* **nav. 1.** The theory and skill of navigating, especially the charting of a course for a ship or aircraft. **2.** The act and practice of navigating. —**nav·i·ga·tion·al** *adj.*

nav·i·ga·tor (návvi-gaytər) *n.* **1.** One who navigates, especially: **a.** One who explores by ship. **b.** A crew member who plots the course of a ship or aircraft. **c.** A person guiding a driver in a car rally. **2.** A device that directs the course of an aircraft or missile.

Nav·ra·ti·lo·va (návrəti-lōvə; *Czech* -lo-vaá), **Martina** (1956–). Czech-born U.S. tennis player. She defected to the United States in 1975. She was Wimbledon singles champion in 1978–79, 1982–87, 1990. She retired after losing the 1994 final.

nav·vy (návvi) *n., pl.* **-vies.** *British Informal.* A labourer, especially one employed in construction or excavation projects. [Slang shortening of NAVIGATOR, humorously applied to labourers who built the navigation canals of England in the 18th and 19th centuries.]

na·vy (náyvi) *n., pl.* **-vies. 1.** All of a nation's warships. **2.** *Often capital* **N.** A nation's entire military organisation for sea warfare and defence, including vessels, personnel, and shore establishments. **3.** *Archaic.* A group of ships; a fleet. **4.** Navy blue. [Middle English *navie,* from Old French, from Vulgar Latin *nāvia* (unattested), fleet, from Latin *nāvis,* ship.] —**na·vy** *adj.*

navy blue *n.* Dark greyish blue. [From the colour of the British naval uniform.] —**na·vy-blue** *adj.*

navy yard *n. U.S.* A **naval dockyard** *(see).*

na·wab (nə-waáb) *n.* **1.** A governor or ruler in India under the Mogul empire. **2.** A title given to eminent Muslims in India. [Urdu *nawwāb,* from Arabic *nuwwāb,* originally plural of *nā'ib,* deputy.]

Nax·os (nák-soss, -səss). The largest island of the Cyclades, in the Aegean Sea, Greece. It was associated, through its wine trade, with Dionysiac cults in ancient times.

nay (nay) *adv.* **1.** No. Now archaic or regional except in recording or expressing a vote. **2.** And moreover. Used to introduce a further, more precise or emphatic expression: *He was ugly, nay, hideous.* ~*n.* **1.** A denial or refusal. **2.** A negative or dissenting vote or voter. —**say (someone) nay.** To deny, refuse, or forbid someone. [Middle English *nay, ney,* from Old Norse *nei* : *ne,* not + *ei,* ever.]

na·ya pai·sa *n.* (nī́-ə pī́-sə), *pl.* **naye paise** (-ay -say). A monetary unit of India, the **paisa** *(see).* [Hindi *nayā paisā,* "new pice".]

Naz·a·rene (názzə-réen, -reen) *n.* **1. a.** A native or inhabitant of Nazareth. **b.** Jesus. Preceded by *the.* **2.** A member of a sect of early Christians of Jewish origin who retained many of the prescribed Jewish observances. [Middle English *Nazaren,* from Late Latin

Nazarēnus, from Greek *Nazarēnos,* from *Nazarat,* NAZARETH.]
—**Naz·a·rene** *adj.*

Naz·a·reth (názzə-rəth). Market town in Galilee, northern Israel. Through its links with Jesus Christ, it has become a place of pilgrimage for Christians and Muslims.

Na·zi (naát-si ‖ nát-) *n., pl.* **-zis.** 1. A member of the National Socialist German Workers' Party, founded in Germany in 1919 and brought to power in 1933 under Adolf Hitler. 2. *Often small.* *n.* An adherent or advocate of policies characteristic of this party; a fascist. [German, phonetic shortening of *Nationalsozialist* National Socialist.] —**Na·zi** *adj.* —**Na·zi·fy** *tr.v.*

Naz·i·rite, Naz·a·rite (názzə-rīt) *n.* In Biblical times, a person, usually a man, who had made a vow to God and was bound to abstain from strong drink and ritual defilement. [From Late Latin *Nazaraeus,* from Hebrew *nāzir,* from *nāzar,* to consecrate oneself.]

Na·zism (naát-siz'm ‖ nát-) *n.* Also **Na·zi·ism** (naát-si-iz'm ‖ nát-). The ideology and practice of the Nazis; especially, the policy of state control of the economy, racist nationalism, and national expansion. Also called "National Socialism".

Nb The symbol for the element niobium.

n.b. 1. *Cricket.* no ball. 2. nota bene.

N.B. 1. New Brunswick. 2. nota bene.

N.B.C. National Broadcasting Corporation (in the United States).

NbE north by east.

N.B.G. *British Informal.* No bloody good.

n-bod·y problem (én-bóddi) *n. Physics.* The problem of determining the motions of *n* bodies moving under the influence of mutual interactions that depend on their distances apart; for example, determining the paths of bodies interacting by gravitational forces. For more than two bodies, there is no complete solution to the problem.

n-butane *n.* A gaseous hydrocarbon, **butane** *(see).*

NbW north by west.

N.C.B. National Coal Board (in Britain).

N.C.C.L. National Council for Civil Liberties (in Britain).

NCO, N.C.O. noncommissioned officer.

Nd The symbol for the element neodymium.

n.d. No date.

Nde·be·le (əndə-bélle) *n., pl.* **-les** or collectively **Ndebele.** 1. A member of a Zulu people or southern Africa, now living chiefly in Northern Province, South Africa and Matabeleland. 2. The Bantu language of this people. Also called "Matabele". [See **Matabele.**] —**Nde·be·le** *adj.*

N'dja·me·na (ən-jaa-máynə). Formerly **Fort La·my** (fór-lə-mée). The capital of Chad. At the confluence of the Chari and Longone rivers, it is a river port on a main caravan route.

né (nay) *adj.* Born. Used after a man's name to indicate an original name. *Michael Caine, né Maurice Micklewhite.* [French, masculine past participle of *naître,* be born.]

Ne The symbol for the element neon.

NE northeast.

Neagh, Lough (nay). Lake in Northern Ireland. With an area of 396 square kilometres (153 square miles), it is the largest freshwater lake in the British Isles.

Ne·an·der·thal (ni-ándər-taal, nay-, -áandər- ‖ -thawl) *adj.* 1. Of or pertaining to Neanderthal man. 2. *Informal.* Crude or reactionary: *a Neanderthal mentality.* —**Ne·an·der·thal** *n.*

Neanderthal man *n.* An extinct species or race of man, *Homo sapiens neanderthalensis,* living during the late Pleistocene age in the Old World, and associated with Middle Palaeolithic tools. [After *Neanderthal,* valley near Düsseldorf in Germany, where remains were found.]

neap (neep) *adj.* Of or pertaining to a neap tide.
~*n.* A neap tide. [Old English *nēp-†,* as in *nēpflōd,* "neap flood".]

Ne·a·pol·i·tan (née-ə-póllitən) *adj.* Of, belonging to, or characteristic of Naples.
~*n.* A native or resident of Naples.

Neapolitan ice cream *n.* Ice cream in brick form, with layers of different colours and flavours.

neap tide *n.* A tide of lowest range, occurring when the sun and moon are in quadrature. Compare **spring tide.**

near (neer) *adv.* **nearer, nearest.** 1. To, at, or within a short distance or interval in space or time: *The day was drawing near.* 2. Almost; nearly. Now rare except when followed by *to,* in the informal phrase *damn near,* or in combination: *came near to winning; damn near killed him; near-extinct.* 3. With or in a close relationship. —**near as dammit.** *Informal.* Varying only in insignificant detail; almost: *It cost £80, near as dammit.*
~*adj.* **nearer, nearest.** 1. Close in time, space, position, or degree: *near neighbours; near equals; the near future.* 2. Closely related by kinship or association; intimate: *near and dear friends.* 3. **a.** Accomplished by a small margin; close; narrow: *a near escape.* **b.** Missed or avoided by a small margin: *a near disaster.* 4. Closely corresponding to or resembling an original: *a near likeness.* 5. **a.** Closer or shorter of two or more. **b.** On the left side, as of a vehicle, animal, or draught team: *the near front wheel; the near hind leg.* 6. *Archaic.* Strictly economical; stingy; parsimonious.
~*prep. Abbr.* **nr.** Close to; within a short distance or time of.
~*v.* **neared, nearing, nears.** —*tr.* To come close or closer to. —*intr.* To draw near or nearer. [Middle English *nere,* Old English *nēar,* comparative adverb of *nēah,* "near".] —**near·ness** *n.*

near·by (néer-bī, -bī) *adj.* Located a short distance away; close at hand; adjacent. —**near·by** *adv.*

Ne·arc·tic (nee-árk-tik ‖ -ár-) *adj.* Of or designating the zoogeographical region that includes the Arctic and temperate areas of North America and also includes Greenland. Compare **Palaearctic.** [NE(O)- + ARCTIC.]

Near East *n.* 1. A region including the countries of the eastern Mediterranean, the Arabian Peninsula, and, sometimes, northeastern Africa. 2. Formerly, the Balkan Peninsula and Turkey. —**Near Eastern** *adj.*

near·ly (néerli) *adv.* 1. Almost but not quite. 2. Closely; intimately: *a matter nearly affecting our interests.* —**not nearly.** Deficient by a long way: *not nearly good enough.*

near point *n.* The closest point to the eye at which an object can be focused without strain. The distance of this point increases with age; for the normal eye it is about 25 centimetres (10 inches).

near·sight·ed (néer-sítid) *adj.* Afflicted with **myopia** *(see);* shortsighted. —**near·sight·ed·ly** *adv.* —**near·sight·ed·ness** *n.*

near thing *n. Informal.* An outcome, such as a victory or disaster, decided by a narrow margin.

neat[1] (neet) *adj.* 1. In good order or clean condition; tidy. 2. Orderly and precise in appearance or procedure; not careless or messy. 3. Skilfully executed; deft; adroit: *a neat turn of phrase.* 4. Simply, precisely, or cleverly worked out or arranged: *a neat idea.* 5. Not diluted or mixed with other substances. Said chiefly of alcoholic drinks. 6. *Rare.* Obtained after all deductions; net: *neat profit.* 7. *Chiefly U.S. Slang.* Appealing: *It would be really neat to go to Paris.* [Old French *net,* from Latin *nitidus,* elegant, shiny, from *nitēre,* to shine.] —**neat·ly** *adv.* —**neat·ness** *n.*

neat[2] *n., pl.* **neat.** *Archaic.* A domestic bovine animal. [Middle English *nete,* Old English *nēat.*]

neath, 'neath (neeth) *prep. Poetic.* Beneath.

neat·herd (néet-herd) *n. Archaic.* A cowherd.

neat's-foot oil *n.* A light, yellow oil obtained from the feet and shinbones of cattle, used chiefly to dress leather.

neb (neb) *n. Chiefly Scottish.* 1. **a.** A beak of a bird. **b.** A nose or snout. 2. A projecting part, especially a nib. [Middle English *neb(b),* Old English *neb(b).*]

Ne·bras·ka (ni-bráskə). State in central United States. Rising from the Missouri prairie lands in the east to the Great Plains and foothills of the Rocky Mountains in the west, it is predominately agricultural, producing cattle, maize, pigs, and wheat. The state also has large oil reserves. Part of the Louisiana Purchase, it was admitted to the Union in 1867. Lincoln is the capital. —**Ne·bras·kan** *adj. & n.*

Neb·u·chad·nez·zar (nébbew-kəd-nézzər, -kad-) *n.* An extremely large wine bottle, equivalent in capacity to 20 standard bottles. [After NEBUCHADNEZZAR II (from the custom of naming very large wine bottles after Old Testament characters).]

Nebuchadnezzar II (*c.*630–562 B.C.). Chaldean King of Babylon. He extended Chaldean power throughout the old Assyrian empire; sacking Jerusalem (586 B.C.), he deported its inhabitants to Babylon.

neb·u·la (nébbew-lə) *n., pl.* **-lae** (-lee) or **-las.** 1. *Astronomy.* **a.** Any diffuse mass of interstellar dust, gas, or both, visible as luminous patches or areas of darkness depending on the way the mass absorbs, scatters, or emits electromagnetic radiation. There are two types: bright nebulae, which include emission and reflection nebulae, and dark nebulae, which are also called absorption nebulae. **b.** A galactic nebula *(see).* 2. *Pathology.* **a.** A cloudy spot on the cornea. **b.** Cloudiness in the urine. 3. *Medicine.* A liquid medication applied by spraying. [New Latin, from Latin, cloud.] —**neb·u·lar** (-lər) *adj.*

nebular hypothesis *n.* A hypothesis put forward by Laplace in 1796 to account for the origin of the Solar System, according to which a rotating nebula cooled and contracted, throwing off rings of matter that contracted into the planets and their moons, while the greater mass of the condensing nebula became the Sun. Compare **planetesimal hypothesis, presolar nebular hypothesis.**

neb·u·lise, neb·u·lize (nébbew-līz) *tr.v.* **-lised, -lising, -lises.** 1. To convert (a liquid) to a fine spray; atomise. 2. To treat with a medicated spray. [From NEBULA.] —**neb·u·li·sa·tion** (-lī-záysh'n ‖ *U.S.* -li-) *n.* —**neb·u·lis·er** *n.*

neb·u·los·i·ty (nébbew-lóssəti) *n., pl.* **-ties.** 1. The quality or condition of being nebulous. 2. A nebula or a mass of material constituting a nebula.

neb·u·lous (nébbew-ləss) *adj.* 1. Cloudy, misty, or hazy. 2. Lacking definite form or limits; unclearly identified or established; vague: *gave an evasive, nebulous answer.* 3. Of or characteristic of a nebula. [Latin *nebulōsus,* from *nebula,* cloud, NEBULA.] —**neb·u·lous·ly** *adv.* —**neb·u·lous·ness** *n.*

nec·es·sar·i·ly (néssə-sərəli, néssi-, -serrəli, -sérrəli) *adv.* 1. As dictated by necessity; of necessity. 2. As a necessary or inevitable consequence: *He isn't necessarily angry just because he won't come.*

nec·es·sar·y (néssə-sori, néssi-, -sri, -serri) *adj.* 1. Needed for the continuing existence or functioning of something; essential; indispensable: *Oxygen is necessary to most living organisms.* 2. Needed to achieve a certain result or effect; requisite: *the necessary tools.* 3. Following unavoidably from conditions, circumstances, or premises; inevitable: *the necessary results of overindulgence.* 4. Required by obligation, compulsion, or convention: *making the necessary apologies.* 5. *Logic.* **a.** Designating a proposition whose denial would be a self-contradiction. **b.** Designating an argument or inference whose denial would lead to a contradiction.
~*n., pl.* **necessaries.** 1. *Often plural.* That which is needed; especially, money or provisions: *the necessaries for the trip.* 2. *Plural.*

Law. Whatever is needed for the maintenance of a dependant, in keeping with his economic and social status. **—the necessary.** *Informal.* Money. [Middle English *necessarie*, from Latin *necessārius*, extension of *necesse*, necessary.]

Synonyms: *necessary, essential, vital, indispensable, requisite, required, prerequisite.*

Usage: In its plural form, a distinction needs to be made between *necessaries* and *necessities. Necessaries* are those things which we need, but which are not absolutely essential. *Necessities* is a much stronger term, referring to those things which are essential—for example, to survive. For some people, the *necessaries* of modern life include the possession of a television set, but few people would consider it a *necessity* of the same order as food or heating.

necessary condition *n. Logic.* A condition for the truth of a proposition or state of affairs that must hold if the proposition is true, but that does *not* guarantee its truth; for example, it is a necessary condition for my car to start that it has not run out of petrol: it is not a **sufficient condition** *(see)* since many other things may be wrong with the car.

ne·ces·si·tar·i·an·ism (ni-séssi-taír-i-ə-niz′m) *n.* Also **nec·es·sar·i·an·ism** (néssə-saír-i-ə-niz′m) The doctrine that events are inevitably determined by preceding causes. **—ne·ces·si·tar·i·an** *adj. & n.*

ne·ces·si·tate (ni-séssi-tayt) *tr.v.* **-tated, -tating, -tates.** 1. To make necessary or unavoidable: *The emergency necessitated a change in plans.* 2. *Chiefly U.S.* To require or compel (someone). Used chiefly in the passive: *He was necessitated to back down.* **—See Synonyms at force.** [Medieval Latin *necessitāre* (past participle *necessitātus*), from Latin *necessitās,* NECESSITY.] **—ne·ces·si·ta·tion** (-táysh′n) *n.*

ne·ces·si·tous (ni-séssitəss) *adj.* Needy; destitute; indigent. [French *nécessiteux,* from Old French *necessite,* NECESSITY.] **—ne·ces·si·tous·ly** *adv.*

ne·ces·si·ty (ni-séssəti) *n., pl.* **-ties.** 1. Something needed for the existence, effectiveness, or success of something; an essential requirement. 2. Something that must inevitably exist or occur, as: **a.** That which is dictated by invariable physical laws or strict social requirements. **b.** That which is dictated by constraining circumstances: *the grim necessities of war.* 3. The state or fact of being indispensable or unavoidable. 4. Pressing or urgent need, such as that arising from poverty, misfortune, or emergency: *Necessity drove him to desperation.* **—of necessity.** As an inevitable consequence; necessarily. **—See Usage note at necessary.** [Middle English *necessite,* from Old French, from Latin *necessitas* (stem *necessitāt-*), from *necesse,* be NECESSARY.]

neck (nek) *n.* 1. The part of the body joining the head to the trunk. 2. **a.** The part of a garment around or near the neck of the wearer. **b.** The neckline of a dress, blouse, or other garment. 3. *Anatomy.* Any relatively narrow portion of a structure, as of a bone or organ, that joins its parts. 4. The part of a tooth between the crown and the root. 5. Any relatively narrow elongation, projection, or connecting part, as: **a.** A peninsula. **b.** A strait. **c.** A pass. **d.** The narrow top part of a bottle, jug, or the like. 6. *Music.* The narrow part along which the strings of a stringed instrument extend to the pegs. 7. *Architecture.* The narrow, upper part of a column, just below the capital. 8. *Geology.* Solidified lava filling the vent of an extinct volcano. 9. *Botany.* The upper, tubular section of an archegonium. 10. **a.** The length of the head and neck of a horse: *winning a race by a neck.* **b.** Any narrow margin by which a competition is won or lost. 11. *Informal.* One's life or personal safety: *risk one's neck; save one's neck.* **—break (one's) neck.** *Informal.* 1. To incur serious physical injury. 2. To make a great effort to accomplish something. **—get it in the neck.** *Informal.* To undergo severe punishment, rebuke, or penalty. **—neck and neck.** Even in a race or contest. **—stick (one's) neck out.** *Informal.* To act boldly, despite the risk of criticism, trouble, or danger.

~intr.v. **necked, necking, necks.** *Slang.* To kiss and caress. [Middle English *necke,* Old English *hnecca.*]

necked (nekt) *adj.* Having a neck or neckline of the specified kind. Used in combination: *a low-necked dress.*

Neck·er (néckər, ne-kaír), **Jacques** (1732–1804). French financier and politician. As a director of the French East India Company (1768), and director of general finance (1777), he introduced reforms and fought corruption. He resigned (1781), was reappointed (1788), and then dismissed and imprisoned. He was subsequently reappointed, but soon resigned and retired to Switzerland (1790).

neck·er·chief (néckər-chif, -cheef) *n.* 1. A kerchief worn around the neck. 2. A triangular piece of coloured cloth worn round the neck as part of a Scout's uniform.

neck·ing (nécking) *n. Architecture.* A moulding or mouldings between the upper part of the shaft of a column and the projecting part of the capital.

neck·lace (néck-ləss, -liss) *n.* 1. An ornament, such as a string of beads or a flexible metal chain or band, worn around the neck. 2. A tyre put round someone's neck and set on fire: *necklace killings.*

neck·let (néck-lət, -lit) *n.* 1. A close-fitting necklace. 2. Something worn about the neck for ornamentation, such as a fur piece.

neck·line (néck-līn) *n.* The line formed by the edge of a garment at or near the neck: *a plunging neckline.*

neck microphone *n.* A small microphone on a loop worn round the neck. Also *U.S.* "lavaliere".

neck of the woods *n. Informal.* A district; a neighbourhood.

neck·tie (nék-tī) *n. Chiefly U.S.* A **tie** (sense 3).

neck·wear (nék-wair) *n.* Articles of dress worn around the neck, such as ties, scarves, and collars.

necro-, necr– *comb. form.* Indicates: 1. Death or the dead; for example, **necrology.** 2. A dead body or dead tissue; for example, **necrobiosis, necropsy.** [New Latin, from Greek *nekros,* corpse.]

nec·ro·bi·o·sis (néckrō-bī-ō̆-siss) *n.* The natural degeneration and death of cells and tissues, as opposed to death from injury or disease and distinguished from death of the entire organism. Compare **gangrene, necrosis.** [New Latin : NECRO- + -BIOSIS.] **—nec·ro·bi·ot·ic** (-óttik) *adj.*

ne·crol·a·try (ne-króllə-tri, ni-) Worship of the dead. [NECRO- + -LATRY.]

ne·crol·o·gy (ne-królləji, ni-) *n., pl.* **-gies.** 1. A list or record of people who have died. 2. The study of the phenomena associated with death. 3. An obituary. [New Latin *necrologium* : NECRO- + -LOGY.] **—nec·ro·log·i·cal** (néckrə-lójik′l) *adj.* **—ne·crol·o·gist** (-królləjist) *n.*

nec·ro·man·cy (néckrō-man-si-, néckrə-) *n.* 1. The art that professes to conjure up the spirits of the dead and commune with them in order to predict the future. 2. Magic, especially black magic or sorcery. See Synonyms at **magic.** [Confusion of: **a.** Late Latin *necromantīa,* from Greek *nekromanteia,* divination by corpses : NECRO- + -MANCY; **b.** Middle English *nigromancie,* from Old French, from Medieval Latin *nigromantia,* black magic : *niger,* black + -MANCY.] **—nec·ro·man·cer** *n.* **—nec·ro·man·tic** (-mántik) *adj.*

ne·croph·a·gous (ne-króffəgəss, ni-) *adj.* Feeding on carrion or corpses. [Greek *nekrophagos* : NECRO- + -PHAGOUS.]

nec·ro·phil·i·a (néckrō-fílli-ə, néckrə-) *n.* Also **ne·croph·i·lism** (ne-króffiliz′m). Sexual attraction to corpses. [NECRO- + -PHILIA.] **—nec·ro·phil·i·ac** (-ak), **nec·ro·phile** (néckrō-fīl, néckrə-) *n.* **—nec·ro·phil·ic** (-fíllik) *adj.*

nec·ro·pho·bi·a (néckrō-fṓbi-ə, néckrə-) *n.* 1. A morbid fear of death. 2. A morbid horror of corpses. [New Latin : NECRO- + -PHOBIA.] **—nec·ro·pho·bic** *adj.*

ne·crop·o·lis (ne-króppə-liss, ni-) *n., pl.* **-lises** or **-leis** (-layss). A cemetery; especially, a large and elaborate one belonging to an ancient city. [Greek *nekropolis* : NECRO- + *polis,* city.]

nec·rop·sy (néck-rop-si) *n., pl.* **-sies.** Also **ne·cros·co·py** (ne-krṓskəpi, ni-) *pl.* **-pies.** An autopsy *(see).* [NECR(O)- + -OPSY.]

ne·crose (ne-krṓss, -krṓz, néckrṓss) *v.* **-crosed, -crosing, -croses.** Also **nec·ro·tise** (néckrə-tīz), **-tised, -tising, -tises.** *—intr.* To be affected with necrosis. *—tr.* To affect with necrosis. [Back-formation from NECROSIS.]

ne·cro·sis (ne-krṓ-siss, ni-) *n., pl.* **-ses** (-seez). 1. The death of living tissue due to disease, injury, or interruption of the blood supply. 2. The death of plant tissue due to injury, frost, or the like. Compare **necrobiosis.** [Late Latin *necrōsis,* from Greek *nekrōsis,* mortification, from *nekroun,* to mortify, from *nekros,* corpse.] **—ne·crot·ic** (-króttik) *adj.*

ne·crot·o·my (ne-króttəmi, ni-) *n., pl.* **-mies.** 1. The dissection of a dead body. 2. Surgical removal of a piece of dead tissue, especially bone. [NECRO- + -TOMY.]

nec·tar (néktər) *n.* 1. A sweet liquid secreted by flowers of various plants and gathered by bees for making honey. 2. **a.** *Greek & Roman Mythology.* The drink of the gods. Compare **ambrosia.** **b.** Any delicious or invigorating drink. [Latin, from Greek *nektar.*] **—nec·tar·ous** *adj.*

nec·tar·ine (néktə-reen, -rin, -réen) *n.* A variety of peach, *Prunus persica nectarina,* having a smooth, waxy skin. [Short for *nectarine peach,* from obsolete *nectarine,* "sweet as nectar", from NECTAR.]

nec·ta·ry (néktəri) *n., pl.* **-ries.** 1. *Botany.* **a.** A glandlike organ, usually at the base of a flower, that secretes nectar. **b.** The part of a flower in which such an organ is contained. 2. *Entomology.* A siphuncle *(see).* Not in current technical usage. [New Latin *nectarium,* from NECTAR.] **—nec·tar·i·al** (nek-táiri-əl) *adj.*

N.E.D.C. National Economic Development Council.

Ned·dy (néddi) 1. A name for a donkey. 2. *Informal.* See **National Economic Development Council.**

Nederland. See **Netherlands.**

née, nee (nay) *adj.* Born. Used when identifying a married woman by her maiden name: *Mrs. Brown neé Jones.* [French, feminine past participle of *naître,* to be born.]

need (need) *n.* 1. A condition or situation in which something necessary or desirable is required or wanted: *in need of water.* 2. A wish or strong desire for something that is lacking: *a need for affection.* 3. Necessity; obligation: *There is no need for you to go.* 4. Something required or wanted; a requisite: *Our needs are modest.* 5. A condition of poverty, emergency, or misfortune.

~v. **needed, needing, needs.** Used as an uninflected auxiliary followed by an infinitive without *to,* indicating obligation or necessity: *He need not come. Need you have been so rude? —tr.* 1. To have need of; require; want urgently. 2. To be obliged or required; have to: *You will need to leave now. —intr.* 1. To be in need or want. 2. *Archaic.* To be necessary. **—See Synonyms at lack.** [Middle English *nede,* Old English *nēd, nēod,* necessity, distress.]

Usage: *Need* is used in two different constructions in standard English. It can be a full verb, taking an *-s* ending in the third person, being followed by an infinitive with *to,* and having a past tense: *He needs to go; he needed to go.* It can also be an auxiliary verb, in which case it has no ending or past tense, and takes an infinitive without *to: He need do it only once, He needn't go just yet, Need they have done it so fast?* The full verb construction is more frequent than the auxiliary use, which tends to be restricted to negative and interrogative sentences: even *He need do it only once* can be interpreted to mean the negative: *He needn't do it more than once.* The auxiliary construction is more commonly used in British than in American English. As always when two closely related constructions are available, there is some uncertainty of usage. Thus, alongside *no-one need go* and *no one needs to go,* you may sometimes hear *no-one needs go;* alongside *need we go* and *do we need to go,* you may hear *do we need go.* See also **use.**

need·ful (néedf'l) *adj. Literary.* Necessary; required.
~n. Whatever is needed, especially money. Preceded by *the: Have you got the needful?* **—need·ful·ly** *adv.* **—need·ful·ness** *n.*

nee·dle (néed'l) *n.* **1.** A small, slender sewing implement, now usually of polished steel, pointed at one end, and having an eye at the other through which a length of thread is passed and held. **2.** Any of various implements similar in appearance and use: **a.** A short, sharp instrument with an eye near the pointed end, used in sewing machines. **b.** A slender, pointed rod used in knitting. **c.** A similar implement, usually shorter, and with a hook at one end, used in crocheting. **3.** A gramophone stylus. **4. a.** Any slender pointer or indicator on a dial, scale, or similar part of a mechanical device. **b.** A **magnetic needle** *(see).* **5.** *Medicine.* **a.** A **hypodermic needle** *(see).* **b.** A slender, sharp-pointed surgical instrument used for sewing up tissues during operations. **6.** A stiff, narrow leaf, as on a conifer. **7.** Any fine, sharp projection, such as a spine of a sea urchin or a crystal. **8.** A sharp, pointed instrument used in engraving. **9.** A beam passed through or under a wall and serving as a usually temporary support. **10.** *Informal.* Hostility or animosity, especially as a result of rivalry: *a lot of needle between the teams.* Also used adjectivally: *a needle match.* **—give (someone) the needle.** *Informal.* To goad or provoke so as to rouse to action.
~v. **needled, -dling, -dles.** *—tr.* **1.** To prick, pierce, or stitch with or as if with a needle. **2.** *Informal.* To goad, provoke, or tease. *—intr.* To sew or do similar work with a needle. [Middle English *nedle,* Old English *nǣdl,* from Germanic.]

nee·dle-bath (néed'l-baath || -bath) *n.* A shower with very fine jets of water which produce a stinging sensation.

needle bearing. A type of roller bearing with long rollers about two to four millimetres in diameter, which bear directly on the shaft.

nee·dle·cord (néed'l-kawrd) *n.* A finely ribbed corduroy fabric.

nee·dle·fish (néed'l-fish) *n., pl.* **-fishes** or collectively **needlefish. 1.** Any of several marine carnivorous fishes of the family Belonidae, having slender bodies and narrow jaws with sharp teeth. **2.** Any of various fishes with projecting jaws, such as the **pipefish** *(see).*

nee·dle·point (néed'l-poynt) *n.* **1.** Decorative needlework on canvas, usually in a diagonal stitch covering the entire surface of the material. See **gros point, petit point. 2.** A type of lace worked on paper patterns with a needle, as distinguished from bobbin lace. Also called "point lace". **—nee·dle·point** *adj.*

need·less (néedliss) *adj.* Not needed or wished for; unnecessary. **—need·less·ly** *adv.* **—need·less·ness** *n.*

needle valve *n.* A valve having a slender point fitting into a conical seat, for accurately regulating the flow of a liquid or gas.

nee·dle·wom·an (néed'l-wŏŏmən) *n., pl.* **-women** (-wimmin). A woman who does needlework, especially a seamstress.

needlewood *n.* An Australian tree, *Hakea leucoptera,* with needle-like leaves and soft wood used mainly for veneers.

nee·dle·work (néed'l-wurk) *n.* Work done with a needle, such as sewing or embroidery. **—nee·dle·work·er** *n.*

need·n't (néed'nt). Contraction of *need not.*

needs (needz) *adv.* Of necessity; necessarily. Used following *must* and preceding a simple infinitive: *He must needs go;* or preceding *must,* with an infinitive understood: *"She shall go, if needs must."* (Robert Browning). [Middle English *nedes,* Old English *nēdes,* "of need", genitive of *nēd,* NEED.]

need-to-know (néed-tə-nṓ) *adj.* Relating to the dissemination to people of only so much information on a subject as they need to know in order to do their job: *details to be revealed on a strictly need-to-know basis.*

need·y (néedi) *adj.* **-ier, -iest.** Being in need; impoverished. **—need·i·ness** *n.*

Né·el temperature (náy-el, -él) *n. Physics.* The characteristic temperature above which a given material changes from an antiferromagnetic state to a ferromagnetic state. Also called "Néel point". [After L. E. F. *Néel* (born 1904), French physicist.]

ne'er (nair). *Poetic.* Contraction of **never.**

ne'er-do-well (náir-dŏŏ-wel) *n.* A worthless, good-for-nothing person; especially, an irresponsible person who never succeeds in any enterprise. **—ne'er-do-well** *adj.*

ne·far·i·ous (ni-fáir-i-əss) *adj.* Evil; infamous: *a nefarious plot.* [Latin *nefārius,* from *nefās,* sin : *ne-,* not + *fās,* divine law, right.] **—ne·far·i·ous·ly** *adv.* **—ne·far·i·ous·ness** *n.*

Nef·er·ti·ti (néffər-teeti), (14th century B.C.). Queen of Egypt. She was the chief wife of Akhenaton. The exquisite limestone bust of Nefertiti (now in the Berlin Museum) has given rise to the tradition that she was one of the most beautiful women in antiquity.

neg. negative.

ne·gate (ni-gáyt, ne-) *tr.v.* **-gated, -gating, -gates. 1.** To render ineffective or invalid; nullify. **2.** To rule out; deny. —See Synonyms at **nullify, neutralise.** [Latin *negāre,* to deny.]

ne·ga·tion (ni-gáysh'n, ne-) *n.* **1.** The act or process of negating. **2.** A denial, contradiction, or negative statement. **3.** The opposite or absence of something regarded as actual, positive, or affirmative: *"Death is nothing more than the negation of life."* (Henry Fielding).

neg·a·tive (néggə-tiv) *adj. Abbr.* **neg. 1.** Expressing, containing, or consisting of a negation, refusal, or denial: *a negative answer.* **2. a.** Lacking the quality of being positive or affirmative: *negative indications of their guilt.* **b.** Being of an opposite nature to that expected or intended: *a negative return on my investments.* **3.** Indicating opposition, indifference, or resistance: *a negative response to an advertising campaign.* **4.** Tending to oppose or disagree with that which is considered positive or constructive: *a negative attitude.* **5.** *Medicine.* Not indicative of the presence of microorganisms, disease, or a specific condition. **6.** *Logic.* Denying agreement between the subject and its predicate. Said of a proposition. **7.** *Mathematics.* Pertaining to or designating: **a.** A quantity less than zero. **b.** The sign (−). **c.** A quantity to be subtracted from another. **d.** A quantity, number, angle, velocity, or direction, in a sense opposite to another of the same magnitude indicated or understood to be positive. **8.** *Physics.* Pertaining to or designating: **a.** Electric charge of the same sign as that of an electron, designated by the symbol (−). **b.** Any body having an excess of electrons. **9.** *Chemistry.* Pertaining to or designating an ion, the anion, that is attracted to a positive electrode. **10.** *Biology.* Indicating resistance to, opposition to, or motion away from a stimulus: *a negative tropism.* **11.** *Optics.* Producing divergent rays. Said of a lens. **12.** Of or pertaining to a photographic negative. Compare **positive.**
~n. **1.** A statement or act indicating or expressing a contradiction, denial, or refusal. **2.** A thing or concept considered to be the counterpart or negation of something positive. **3.** *Grammar.* A word or part of a word, such as *no, not,* or *non-,* that indicates negation. **4.** *Archaic.* The right to veto something. **5.** In photography: **a.** An image in which the light areas of the object rendered appear dark and the dark areas appear light. **b.** A film, plate, or other photographic material containing such an image. **6.** *Mathematics.* A negative quantity. **—in the negative.** In a sense or manner indicating a refusal or denial: *answer in the negative.*
~interj. Chiefly U.S. Used, especially in a military context, to express negation or refusal. Compare **affirmative.**
~tr.v. **negatived, -tiving, -tives. 1.** To refuse to approve or accept; veto or reject. **2. a.** To deny; contradict. **b.** To give a negative sense to. **3.** To demonstrate to be false. **4.** To counteract or neutralise. [Late Latin *negātīvus,* from Latin *negāre,* to NEGATE.] **—neg·a·tive·ly** *adv.* **—neg·a·tive·ness, neg·a·tiv·i·ty** (-tívvəti) *n.*

negative feedback *n.* **1.** A type of **feedback** *(see)* in which an increase in output causes a decrease in input. **2.** Critical or discouraging reactions.

negative prescription *n. Law.* **Prescription** *(see).*

neg·a·tiv·ism (néggəti-viz'm) *n.* **1.** An attitude or system of thought marked by the questioning or denial of traditional beliefs with no attempt to propose alternatives. **2.** The state or tendency of being negative and unconstructive. **3.** *Psychology.* Behaviour characterised by stubborn and unfounded resistance to suggestions, orders, or instructions of others. **—neg·a·tiv·ist** *n.* & *adj.* **—neg·a·tiv·is·tic** (-vístik) *adj.*

ne·ga·tor (ni-gáytər) *n.* A logic gate, a **NOT gate** *(see).*

Neg·ev (néggev) or **Neg·eb** (néggeb). A desert covering the southern half of Israel, bounded in the north by the hills of Judaea. Irrigation projects support numerous agricultural settlements. There are valuable deposits of natural gas and phosphates.

ne·glect (ni-glékt) *tr.v.* **-glected, -glecting, -glects. 1.** To ignore or pay no attention to; disregard: *They neglected his warning.* **2.** To fail to care for or give proper attention to: *She neglected her appearance.* **3.** To fail to do or carry out through carelessness or oversight: *He neglected to make his point.*
~n. **1.** The act or an instance of neglecting something. **2.** The state of being neglected. **3.** Habitual lack of care. [Latin *negligere, neglegere* (past participle stem *neglect-*), "not to choose", not to heed : *neg-,* not + *legere,* to choose.] **—ne·glect·er, ne·glec·tor** *n.*

ne·glect·ful (ni-gléktf'l) *adj.* Tending to neglect; careless; heedless. Often followed by *of: neglectful of responsibilities.* **—ne·glect·ful·ly** *adv.* **—ne·glect·ful·ness** *n.*

neg·li·gee, neg·li·gée, neg·li·gé (néggli-zhay || *U.S.* -zháy) *n.* **1.** A woman's loose dressing gown, often of soft, delicate fabric. **2.** Loosely, any informal or skimpy attire. [French, "casual", "neglected", from *négliger,* to neglect, from Latin *negligere,* NEGLECT.]

neg·li·gence (négglijənss) *n.* **1.** The state or quality of being negligent. **2.** Any negligent act or failure to act. **3.** *Law.* The omission or neglect of any reasonable precaution, care, or action, resulting in accident, injury, or the like.

neg·li·gent (néggli-jənt) *adj.* **1.** Habitually guilty of neglect; lacking in due care or concern. **2.** Careless, especially in a nonchalant or easygoing way. —See Synonyms at **careless.** [Middle English, from Old French, from Latin *negligens* (stem *negligent-*), present participle of *negligere,* to NEGLECT.] **—neg·li·gent·ly** *adv.*

neg·li·gi·ble (négglijə-b'l) *adj.* Not worth considering; trifling: *a negligible amount.* [From Latin *negligere,* to NEGLECT.] **—neg·li·gi·bil·i·ty** (-bílləti), **neg·li·gi·ble·ness** *n.* **—neg·li·gi·bly** *adv.*

ne·go·tia·ble (ni-gṓ-shə-b'l, -shi-ə-, -si-ə-) *adj.* **1.** Capable of being negotiated. **2.** Capable of being legally transferred from one person to another, sometimes after endorsement: *a negotiable document.* **—ne·go·tia·bil·i·ty** (-bílləti) *n.*

ne·go·ti·ant (ni-gṓ-shi-ənt, -si-shənt) *n.* One that negotiates.

ne·go·ti·ate (ni-gṓ-shi-ayt, -si-) *v.* **-ated, -ating, -ates.** *—intr.* To confer with another or others in order to come to terms or reach an agreement. *—tr.* **1.** To arrange, settle, or bring about by conferring or discussing: *negotiate a contract.* **2.** *Finance.* **a.** To transfer title to or ownership of (notes, funds, documents, or similar property) to another person or party in return for value received. **b.** To sell or discount (assets or securities, for example). **3.** To succeed in passing over, accomplishing, or coping with: *negotiate a sharp curve.* [Latin *negōtiārī,* to transact business, from *negōtium,* business, "lack of leisure" : *neg-,* not + *ōtium†,* leisure.] —**ne·go·ti·a·tor** *n.*

ne·go·ti·a·tion (ni-gō-shi-áysh'n, -si-) *n.* An act or the procedure of negotiating.

Ne·gress (née-griss, -gress) *n.* A female Negro. Sometimes considered offensive.

Ne·gril·lo (ni-gríllō, ne-, -grée-ō) *n., pl.* **-los** or **-loes.** A member of a group of diminutive Negroid peoples of Africa, including the Bushmen and the Pygmies. Also called "Negrito". [Spanish, diminutive of NEGRO.]

Ne·gri·to (ni-gréetō, ne-) *n., pl.* **-tos** or **-toes.** **1.** A Negrillo. **2.** Any of various groups of diminutive Negroid people inhabiting parts of Malaysia, the Philippines, and southeastern Asia. [Spanish, diminutive of NEGRO.]

ne·gri·tude (néegri-tewd, néggri- || -tōōd) *n.* **1.** The fact or quality of being a Negro. **2.** An aesthetic and ideological concept affirming the independent validity of black culture. [French *négritude* (coined by Léopold Senghor), from *nègre,* NEGRO.]

Ne·gro (néegrō) *n., pl.* **-groes.** **1.** A member of the Negroid ethnic division of the human species, especially any of various peoples of central and southern Africa. —See Usage note at **black. 2.** A descendant of these or other Negroid peoples. See **Negroid.** [Spanish and Portuguese *negro,* black, from Latin *niger,* black.] —**Ne·gro** *adj.*

Neg·ro, Rio (náy-grō, néggrō). River of South America. Rising in eastern Colombia (where it is known as the Guainía), it flows some 2 250 kilometres (1,400 miles) across Brazil to join the Amazon near Manáus.

Ne·groid (née-groyd) *adj. Anthropology.* Of, pertaining to, characteristic of, or designating a major ethnic division of the human species whose members are characterised by brown to black pigmentation, and often by tightly curled hair, broad nose, and thick lips. This division includes the Negro and other peoples, such as the **Andamanese** and **Melanesian** (*both of which see*). [NEGR(O)- + -OID.] —**Ne·groid** *n.*

ne·gro·phile, ne·gro·phil (néegrō-fīl, néegrə-, -fil) *n. Often capital* **N.** One friendly to blacks and their interests.

ne·gro·pho·bi·a (néegrō-fṓbi-ə, néegrə-) *n. Often capital* **N.** Intense aversion to or fear of blacks. —**ne·gro·phobe** (-fōb) *n.*

ne·gus (néegəss) *n.* A beverage made of wine, hot water, lemon juice, sugar, and nutmeg. [After Colonel Francis *Negus* (died 1732), English soldier who invented it.]

Ne·gus (néegəss) *n.* The title of the emperor of Ethiopia. [Amharic *negŭs,* king.]

Neh. Nehemiah.

Ne·he·mi·ah[1] (née-i-mí-ə, -hi-, -hə-) A Jewish leader and governor of Judah during the Babylonian Captivity (fifth century B.C.).

Nehemiah[2] *n. Abbr.* **Neh.** A book of the Old Testament describing the moral, political, and religious reforms of Nehemiah, and the rebuilding of Jerusalem under his leadership. Also called "Esdras".

Neh·ru (naír-ōō), **Jawaharlal** (1889–1964), also known as Pandit Nehru. Indian politician. Succeeding his father, Pandit Motilal Nehru, as president of the Indian Congress (1929), he took part in the campaign for independence from Britain, and was frequently imprisoned. He became India's first prime minister (1947). The political dynasty was continued by his daughter, Indira Gandhi.

neigh (nay) *intr.v.* **neighed, neighing, neighs. 1.** To utter the cry of a horse. **2.** To utter a sound similar to a horse's cry.
~*n.* The cry of a horse. [Middle English *neien,* Old English *hnǣgan,* from Germanic (imitative).]

neigh·bour, *U.S.* **neigh·bor** (náybər) *n.* **1.** One who lives near or next to another. **2.** A person or thing adjacent to or located near another. **3.** A person like oneself; a fellow human being.
~*adj.* Living or situated near another.
~*v.* **neighboured** or *U.S.* **neighbored, -bouring** or *U.S.* **boring, -bours** or *U.S.* **-bors.** —*tr.* To lie close to; border upon; adjoin. —*intr.* To live or be situated close by. [Middle English *neigh(e)bor,* Old English *nēahgebūr : nēah,* near + *gebūr,* dweller.]

neigh·bour·hood (náybər-hōōd) *n.* **1.** A district, especially one comprising a distinct community in a town or city, often considered in regard to its inhabitants or distinctive characteristics: *a chic neighbourhood.* **2.** The people who live in a particular vicinity. **3.** A range of numbers, prices, or other quantities: *in the neighbourhood of a million dollars.* **4.** *Mathematics.* The set of points surrounding a given point, each of which is at a distance from the given point less than an arbitrary bound.

neigh·bour·ing (náybəring) *adj.* Living or situated close by.

neigh·bour·ly (náybərli) *adj.* Appropriate to, characteristic of, or showing the feelings of a friendly neighbour. —**neigh·bour·li·ness** *n.*

Neis·se (ní-sə). *Polish* **Nysa** (níssə); *Czech* **Nisa.** River of eastern Europe. Rising in Czechoslovakia, it flows 225 kilometres (140 miles) northwards to the Oder river, forming part of the Polish-German border. It is known as the Lusatian Neisse to distinguish it from the Glatzer Neisse, another Oder tributary to the east.

nei·ther (ní-thər, née-) *adj.* Not either; not one and not the other: *Neither shoe fits comfortably.*
~*pron.* Not either one; not the one nor the other: *Neither of them fits.*
~*conj.* **1.** Not either; not in either case. Used with the correlative conjunction *nor: Neither we nor they want it.* **2.** *Archaic.* Nor yet; nor: *"They toil not, neither do they spin."* (Matthew 6:28).
~*adv.* **1.** Also not; not either: *John couldn't understand it, and neither could I.* **2.** *Nonstandard.* In any case; either. Forms a double negative when used for *either* following a negative statement: *I don't like it, neither.* —**neither here nor there.** Of no immediate concern; immaterial. [Middle English *neither, nauther,* Old English *nāhwæther, nōhwæther : nā,* no, not + *hwæther,* which of two.]

Usage: Neither is restricted to a choice of two items, when reference is being made to a preceding list: *Painting and drawing have been suggested, but he is interested in neither.* If the list contains more than two items, *none* is the required form: *Painting, drawing, and sculpture have been suggested, but he is interested in none of them.*

Neither takes a singular verb, even when it is accompanied by plural nouns or pronouns: *Neither motor car has arrived, Neither of them has come, Neither of the houses has been built.* The plural noun or pronoun preceding the verb nonetheless exercises a strong influence, and in informal speech and writing a plural form of the verb is often used loosely: *Neither of the cars have been fixed.*

In the *neither . . . nor* construction, when both elements are singular, the verb is in the singular *(Neither John nor Jim has arrived).* When both are plural, the verb is in the plural *(Neither the cars nor the buses have been fixed).* Purists often insist on a singular verb even in a strongly plural context, but this has come to sound pedantic and stilted.

When the second element in a *neither-nor* construction is a pronoun, the verb agrees with the pronoun: *Neither the boys nor I am interested.* When both elements are pronouns, the agreement is with the one nearer the verb: *Neither he nor I am interested.*

When the construction follows a verb, there is a tendency in informal speech to allow *neither* to precede the verb *(He was neither able to think nor speak),* the lack of stress on the verb making ambiguity unlikely: but this usage is open to criticism in writing, and in formal speech. *He was able neither to think nor to speak* is preferred. See also Usage note at **nor.**

nek (nek) *n. South African.* A narrow ridge connecting two mountains. [Dutch, "neck".]

nek·ton (nék-ton, -tən) *n.* The total population of actively swimming aquatic animals in a sea or lake, including fish, turtles, and whales. Compare **plankton.** [German, from Greek *nēkton,* "swimming thing", neuter of *nēktos,* swimming, from *nēkhein,* to swim.] —**nek·ton·ic** (nek-tónnik) *adj.*

nel·ly (nélli) *n.* —**not on your nelly.** *British Slang.* Emphatically not; absolutely not. [Perhaps from *Nelly* (woman's name).]

nel·son (nél-sən) *n.* In wrestling, any of a variety of holds in which the user places an arm under the opponent's arm and applies pressure with the palm of the hand against the opponent's neck. See also **full nelson, half nelson.** [Probably from surname *Nelson.*]

Nelson[1] (nél-sən). City of South Island, New Zealand. On Tasman Bay, it is a port and a commercial and industrial centre. It is also the centre of the country's only hop-growing district.

Nelson[2]. River in central Manitoba, Canada, flowing from Lake Winnipeg for 640 kilometres (400 miles) into Hudson Bay.

Nelson, Horatio, 1st Viscount (1758–1805). British admiral. Despite the loss of an eye at Calvi (1794), and an arm at Santa Cruz (1797), he was the most successful naval commander of his age. He fought with distinction at Cape St. Vincent (1797) and Copenhagen (1801), and destroyed French power in the eastern Mediterranean at the Battle of the Nile (Aboukir 1798). His destruction of the French fleet, with its Spanish allies, at Trafalgar (1805), secured Britain from invasion at the cost of his own life.

ne·lum·bo (ni-lúmbō) *n., pl.* **-bos.** An aquatic plant of the genus *Nelumbo,* having large, variously coloured flowers. See **lotus.** [New Latin, from Sinhalese *neḷumbu,* lotus, probably of Dravidian origin.]

Ne·man (nyémmən). *Polish* **Niemen;** *German* **Me·mel** (máym'l). River flowing through Russia, Belorussia and Lithuania. It was formerly the western border of the Russian empire.

ne·mat·ic (ni-máttik) *adj. Chemistry.* Pertaining to one of the two types of anisotropic melts characteristic of a liquid crystal in which the molecules are linearly oriented but are not in a planar arrangement. Compare **smectic.** [NEMATO- (referring to the threadlike chains of molecules) + -IC.]

nemato– *comb. form.* Indicates threadlike form; for example, **nematocyst.** [New Latin, from Greek *nēma* (stem *nēmat-*), thread.]

nem·a·to·cyst (némmə-tō-sist, -tə-, ni-máttə-) *n. Zoology.* A stinging organ in various coelenterates, such as jellyfish, which when stimulated puts out a coiled tube that injects the victim with a paralysing poison. [NEMAT(O)- + CYST.] —**nem·a·to·cys·tic** (-sístik) *adj.*

nem·a·tode (némmə-tōd) *n.* Any worm of the phylum Nematoda, having unsegmented, threadlike bodies, many of which, including the hookworm, are parasitic. Also called "nematode worm", "roundworm". [New Latin *Nematoda,* "the threadlike ones" : NEMAT(O)- + -ODE (like).]

Nem·bu·tal (némbew-taal || *U.S.* -tawl) *n.* A trademark for the drug **pentobarbitone sodium** *(see).*

nem con (ném kón) *adv.* Unanimously; without any opposition: *The proposal was adopted nem con.* [Abbreviation of Latin *nemine contradicente,* with no one opposing.]

ne·mer·te·an, ne·mer·ti·an (ni-mérti-ən) *adj.* Also **nem·er·tine** (némmər-tīn). Of, pertaining to, or belonging to the phylum Nemertea (or Nemertina), consisting chiefly of marine worms having soft, cylindrical or flattened bodies, usually brightly coloured, and an evertible proboscis used for catching prey.

~*n.* A worm of this phylum. Also called "proboscis worm", "ribbon worm". [New Latin *Nemertea,* "the Nemertes group", from *Nemertēs,* name of one of the genera in the group, from Greek *Nēmertēs,* name of a Nereid.]

ne·me·sia (ni-méezhə) *n.* Any plant of the genus *Nemesia,* native to southern Africa, several species of which are cultivated as ornamental garden plants for their brightly coloured flowers. [New Latin, from Greek *nemesion,* name of a plant resembling nemesia.]

nem·e·sis (némmi-siss, némmə-) *n., pl.* **-ses** (-seez). **1.** One that inflicts relentless vengeance or destruction. **2.** Retributive justice in its execution or outcome: *invite nemesis.* [From NEMESIS.]

Nemesis *Greek Mythology.* The goddess of retributive justice or vengeance. [Greek, "retribution", from *nemein,* to allot.]

ne·ne (náy-nay) *n.* A goose, *Branta sandvicensis,* of the Hawaiian Islands, now very rare. [Hawaiian *nēnē.*]

nen·u·phar (nénnew-faar) *n.* A water lily. [From Medieval Latin, from Arabic and Persian *nīnūfar, nīlūfar,* from Sanskrit *nīlōtpala* : *nīla,* blue + *utpala,* lotus.]

neo- *comb. form.* Indicates: **1.** A new, revived, or recent form, development, or type; for example, **neologism, neomycin. 2.** A recent formation, modification, or abnormal change; for example, **neoplasm. 3.** The most recent subdivision of a series of geological periods; for example, **Neolithic. Note:** Many compounds other than those entered here may be formed with *neo-.* In this dictionary, in forming compounds, *neo-* is joined to the following word without space or hyphen: *neocolonialism.* Many users, however, prefer the hyphenated form, which should be used if the second element begins with a capital letter, the *N* of *Neo-* being also capitalised: *Neo-Platonism.* (The *N* may be capitalised in other words too: *Neolithic.*) If the second element begins with *o,* again it is separated by a hyphen: *neo-orthodoxy.* [Greek, from *neos,* new.]

ne·o·ars·phen·a·mine (née-ō-aarss-fénnə-meen, -fi-námmin) *n. Medicine.* A yellow powder, $C_{13}H_{13}As_2N_2NaO_4S$, containing arsenic, formerly used in the treatment of syphilis and yaws.

ne·o·clas·si·cism (née-ō-klássi-siz'm) *n.* **1.** A revival of classical aesthetics and forms in art, architecture, music, and literature. **2.** *Usually capital* **N. a.** Such a revival as that which occurred in the 18th and 19th centuries in architecture and art, especially the decorative arts, characterised by order, symmetry, and simplicity of style. **b.** A similar revival that occurred in literature in the late 17th and 18th centuries, characterised by a regard for the classical ideals of reason, form, and restraint. **c.** A movement in music of the late 19th and early 20th centuries that sought to avoid subjective emotionalism and return to the style of the pre-Romantic composers. **—ne·o·clas·sic, ne·o·clas·si·cal** *adj.* **—ne·o·clas·si·cist** *n.*

ne·o·col·on·i·al·ism (née-ō-kə-lṓni-ə-liz'm) *n.* The use by a major power of economic constraints for perpetuating or extending its effective control over a less powerful nation, especially a former colony. **—ne·o·col·on·i·al** *adj.* **—ne·o·col·on·i·al·ist** *n. & adj.*

ne·o·cor·tex (née-ō-kór-teks) *n.* The **neopallium** *(see).*

Ne·o·Dar·win·ism (née-ō-dárwin-iz'm) *n.* The theory that incorporates Darwin's theory of evolution by **natural selection** *(see)* with subsequent discoveries concerning the inheritance and source of genetic variation. See **Darwinism.** Compare **Neo-Lamarckism.** **—Ne·o·Dar·win·i·an** (-daar-wínni-ən) *adj. & n.*

ne·o·dym·i·um (née-ō-dímmi-əm) *n. Symbol* **Nd** A bright, silvery, rare-earth metal element of the lanthanide group found in the minerals monazite and bastnaesite, and used for colouring glass and for doping some glass lasers. Atomic number 60, atomic weight 144.24, melting point 1,024°C, boiling point 3,027°C, relative density 6.80 or 7.004 (depending on allotropic form), valency 3. [New Latin : NEO- + (DI)DYMIUM.]

Ne·o·gae·a (née-ō-jée-ə, -ə-) *n.* An area that is coextensive with the Neotropical region and is considered one of the primary zoogeographic regions. See **Neotropical.** [New Latin : NEO- + Greek *gaia,* earth.] **—Ne·o·gae·an** *adj.*

ne·o·gen·e·sis (née-ō-jénnə-siss) *n. Medicine.* The regeneration of tissue.

ne·o·im·pres·sion·ism, Ne·o·Im·pres·sion·ism (née-ō-im-présh'n-iz'm) *n.* A movement in 19th-century painting that was led by Georges Seurat and characterised by strict and formal composition and meticulous execution using **pointillism** *(see).* **—ne·o·im·pres·sion·ist** *n. & adj.*

Ne·o·La·marck·ism (née-ō-lə-márkiz'm) *n.* The theory that acquired characteristics can be inherited, but that natural selection is also a valid evolutionary principle. See **Lamarckism.** Compare **Neo-Darwinism.** **—Ne·o·La·marck·i·an** (-márki-ən) *adj. & n.*

ne·o·lith (née-ə-lith, -ō-) *n.* A stone implement of the Neolithic Age. [Back-formation from NEOLITHIC.]

Ne·o·lith·ic (née-ə-líthik, -ō-) *adj. Sometimes small* **n.** *Archaeology.* Of or designating the cultural period beginning around 10,000 B.C. in the Middle East and later elsewhere, and characterised by the development of farming and the making of technically advanced, polished, stone implements.

~*n. Archaeology.* The Neolithic period. Preceded by *the.* [NEO- + -LITHIC.]

ne·ol·o·gise, ne·ol·o·gize (nee-óllə-jīz) *intr.v.* **-gised, -gising, -gises.** To coin or use neologisms.

ne·ol·o·gism (nee-óllə-jiz'm) *n.* **1.** A newly coined word, phrase, or expression, or a new meaning for an old word. **2.** The use or formation of new words, phrases, or expressions or of new meanings for old words. [French *néologisme* : NEO- + LOG(O)- + -ISM.] **—ne·ol·**

o·gist *n.* **—ne·ol·o·gis·tic** (-jístik), **ne·ol·o·gis·ti·cal** *adj.*

ne·ol·o·gy (nee-óllaji) *n., pl.* **-gies.** Neologism or an instance of it. [French *néologie* : NEO- + -LOGY.] **—ne·o·log·i·cal** (née-ə-lójik'l) *adj.* **—ne·o·log·i·cal·ly** *adv.*

ne·o·morph (née-ō-mawrf, -ə-) *n.* A biological structure that has not evolved from a similar structure in an ancestor. [NEO- + -MORPH.] **—ne·o·morph·ic** (-mórfik) *adj.*

ne·o·my·cin (née-ō-mí-sin) *n.* An antibiotic drug, $C_{12}H_{26}N_4O_6$, used to treat a wide range of infections, especially those affecting the skin and eyes. [NEO- + -MYCIN.]

ne·on (née-on, -ən) *n. Symbol* **Ne** A rare, inert, gaseous element occurring in the atmosphere to the extent of 18 parts per million, and obtained by fractional distillation of liquid air. It is colourless but glows reddish-orange in an electrical discharge and is used in fluorescent tubes. Atomic number 10, atomic weight 20.183, melting point –248.67°C, boiling point –245.95°C, valency 0.

~*adj.* Illuminated by a tube with neon in it: *a neon sign.* [Greek, "the new (gas)", neuter of *neos,* new.]

ne·o·nate (née-ō-nayt, -ə-) *n.* A newborn child. [New Latin *neonātus* : NEO- + Latin *nātus,* born, from *nascī,* to be born.] **—ne·o·na·tal** (-náyt'l) *adj.*

ne·o·or·tho·dox·y (née-ō-órthə-doksi) *n.* A Protestant movement of the 20th century that aims to revive adherence to certain Reformation doctrines. **—ne·o·or·tho·dox** *adj.*

ne·o·pal·li·um (née-ō-pál-i-əm) *n.* The tissue that makes up most of the cerebral cortex in the brain of mammals. Also "neocortex".

ne·o·phyte (née-ō-fīt, -ə-) *n.* **1.** A recent convert to a religion. **2. a.** A newly ordained Roman Catholic priest. **b.** A novice of a religious order. **3.** A beginner or novice. [Late Latin *neophytus,* from New Testament Greek *neophutos,* "newly planted" : NEO- + *phutos,* "grown", from *phuein,* to bring forth, produce.]

ne·o·plasm (née-ō-plaz'm, -ə-) *n.* Any abnormal new growth of tissue in animals or plants; a benign or malignant tumour. [NEO- + -PLASM.] **—ne·o·plas·tic** *adj.*

Ne·o·Pla·to·nism, Ne·o·pla·to·nism (née-ō-pláyt'n-iz'm) *n.* **1.** A philosophical and religious system developed in Alexandria in the third century A.D., based on the doctrines of Plato and other Greek philosophers, and modified with elements of Oriental mysticism and some Judaic and Christian concepts. **2.** A revival of this system, as in the Middle Ages and Renaissance. **—Ne·o·Pla·ton·ic** (-plə-tónnik) *adj.* **—Ne·o·Pla·to·nist** *n.*

ne·o·prene (née-ō-preen, -ə-) *n.* A synthetic rubber produced by polymerisation of chloroprene and used in waterproof products, adhesives, paints, and rocket fuels. [NEO- + PR(OPYL) + -ENE.]

Ne·o·scho·las·ti·cism (née-ō-skə-lásti-siz'm, -sko-) *n.* A movement to revive the scholasticism of Aquinas by infusing it with modern concepts. **—Ne·o·scho·las·tic** *adj.*

ne·ot·e·ny (ni-óttəni *also* née-ə-teeni) *n.* The retention of larval features in the adult form of an animal. It occurs, for example, in the axolotl, which retains the external gills of the larva. [From German *Neotenie* : NEO- + Greek *teinein,* to extend.]

ne·o·ter·ic (née-ō-térrik, -ə-) *adj.* Of recent origin; new; modern. ~*n.* A modern writer or philosopher. [Late Latin *neōtericus,* from Greek *neōterikos,* "youthful", modern, from *neōteros,* younger, comparative of *neos,* new.]

Ne·o·trop·i·cal (née-ō-tróppik'l) *adj.* Of or designating the zoogeographic region stretching southwards from the tropic of Cancer and including southern Mexico, Central and South America, and the West Indies.

~*n.* The Neotropical region.

ne·o·type (née-ō-tīp) *n.* A plant or animal specimen selected to replace the original **holotype** *(see)* when this has been lost or destroyed.

Ne·o·zo·ic (née-ō-zṓ-ik, -ə-) *adj.* Of or formed in any geological period after the end of the Mesozoic era.

Ne·pal, Kingdom of (ni-páwl, ne-, -páal). State of south central Asia. Lying in the Himalayas, it is a predominantly agricultural country, exporting jute and rice. With massive foreign aid, roads, hydroelectric power, and light industry are being developed. Tourism is important. It is ruled by a hereditary Hindu monarchy. It has been an ally of the United Kingdom since 1850; Nepalese Gurkha battalions still serve in the British army. Area, 147 181 square kilometres (56,820 square miles). Population, 21,130,000. Capital, Kathmandu. See map at **India. —Nep·al·ese** (néppə-léez, néppaw- ‖ -léess) *adj. & n.*

Nep·al·i (ni-páwli, ne-, -páali) *n., pl.* **-lis** or collectively **Nepali. 1.** A native or inhabitant of Nepal. **2.** The central Indic language of Nepal. **—Nep·al·i** *adj.*

ne·pen·the (ni-pénthi) *n.* **1.** A drug, perhaps opium, mentioned in the *Odyssey* as a remedy for grief. **2.** Anything that induces oblivion of sorrow or eases pain. [Greek *nēpenthes (pharmakon),* "grief-banishing (drug)" : *nē-,* not + *penthos,* grief.] **—ne·pen·the·an** (ni-pénthi-ən) *adj.*

ne·per (néepər, náypər) *n. Symbol* **Np.** A unit used for comparing quantities, used especially for telecommunication signal amplitudes. The natural logarithm of the ratio of the quantities is the value in nepers.

neph·e·line (néffi-lin, -leen) *n.* A sodium or potassium aluminium silicate mineral, occurring in igneous rocks, and used in the manufacture of ceramics and enamels. Also called "nephelite". [French *néphéline,* from Greek *nephelē,* cloud (because it becomes cloudy when placed in acid).]

neph·e·lin·ite (néffili-nīt) *n.* An igneous rock consisting chiefly of pyroxene and nepheline.

neph·e·lom·e·ter (néffi-lómmitər) *n.* Any apparatus used to measure the size or concentration of particles in a suspension by the amount of light scattered by the particles. [Greek *nephelē*, cloud + -METER.] —**neph·e·lo·met·ric** (-lō-méttrik) *adj.* —**neph·e·lom·e·try** (-lómmətri) *n.*

neph·ew (névvew, néffew) *n.* The son of one's brother or sister, or of one's brother-in-law or sister-in-law. [Middle English *neveu,* nephew, grandson, from Old French *neveu,* from Latin *nepōs,* nephew, grandson.]

neph·o·graph (néffō-graaf, néffə-, -graf) *n. Meteorology.* A device used for producing photographic records *(nephograms)* of clouds.

ne·phol·o·gy (ni-fólləji, ne-) *n.* The science of clouds. [Greek *nephos,* cloud + -LOGY.] —**neph·o·log·i·cal** (néffə-lójik'l) *adj.* —**ne·phol·o·gist** (-fólləjist) *n.*

neph·o·scope (néffō-skōp, néffə-) *n. Meteorology.* An instrument for observing clouds and measuring their height, speed, and direction of movement.

ne·phral·gi·a (ni-frál-ji-ə, ne-, -jə) *n.* Pain in the kidney, caused by any of various kidney disorders. —**ne·phral·gic** *adj.*

ne·phrec·to·my (ni-fréktəmi, ne-) *n., pl.* **-mies.** The surgical removal of a kidney. [NEPHR(O)- + -ECTOMY.]

ne·phrid·i·um (ni-fríd-i-əm, ne-) *n., pl.* **-ia** (-i-ə) An excretory organ in many invertebrates, consisting basically of a tube through which waste products pass to the exterior. [New Latin : NEPHR(O)- + -IDIUM.] —**ne·phrid·i·al** *adj.*

neph·rite (néffrīt) *n.* A white to dark green variety of jade. [German *Nephrit,* "kidney mineral" (from its supposed power to cure kidney diseases) : NEPHR(O)- + -ITE.]

ne·phrit·ic (ne-fríttik, ni-) *adj.* **1.** Pertaining to the kidneys. **2.** *Pathology.* Of, pertaining to, or affected by nephritis.

ne·phri·tis (ne-frītiss, ni-) *n. Pathology.* Any of various acute or chronic inflammations of the kidneys. Also called "Bright's disease" when chronic. [Late Latin, from Greek : NEPHR(O)- + -ITIS.]

nephro–, nephr– *comb. form.* Indicates the kidney; for example, **nephrogenous, nephritis.** [Greek, from *nephros,* kidney.]

ne·phrog·e·nous (ne-frójinəss, ni-) *adj.* Also **neph·ro·gen·ic** (néffrə-jénnik) Originating in the kidney. [NEPHRO- + -GENOUS.]

neph·ron (néffron) *n.* Any of the excretory units of the kidney, consisting of a tiny, coiled tubule into which urine is filtered from the blood. [German *Nephron,* from Greek *nephros,* kidney.]

ne·phro·sis (ne-frō-siss, ni-) *n.* Any disease of the kidneys, especially when marked by degenerative changes in the renal tubules, as opposed to the inflammation characteristic of nephritis. [New Latin : NEPHR(O)- + -OSIS.] —**ne·phrot·ic** (-fróttik) *adj.*

neph·ros·to·my (ne-fróstəmi, ni-) *n., pl.* **-mies** A surgical operation in which a tube is inserted into a kidney from the skin surface in order to drain the urine from the kidney. [NEPHRO- + -STOMY.]

ne·phrot·o·my (ne-fróttəmi, -ni-) *n., pl.* **-mies.** Surgical incision into the kidney. [New Latin *nephrotomia* : NEPHRO- + -TOMY.]

ne plus ul·tra (née pluss últrə, náy plōoss ōoltraa) *n.* The extreme or utmost point; especially, the point of highest achievement. [Latin, "(sail) no more beyond (this point)", a warning to mariners allegedly inscribed on the Pillars of Hercules.]

nep·o·tism (néppə-tiz'm) *n.* Favouritism shown or patronage granted by persons in high office to relatives. [French *népotisme,* from Italian *nepotismo,* "favouring of nephews" (by 16th-century prelates), from *nepote,* nephew, from Latin *nepōs.*] —**nep·o·tist** *n.* —**nep·o·tis·ti·cal** (-tístik'l) *adj.*

Nep·tune¹ (nép-tewn ‖ -tōon). *Roman Mythology.* The god of the sea, corresponding to the Greek Poseidon. [Latin *Neptūnus†.*]

Neptune² *n. Poetic.* The ocean or sea.

Neptune³ *n.* The eighth planet from the sun, having a sidereal period of revolution around the sun of 164.8 years at a mean distance of 4.5×10^9 kilometres (2.8×10^9 miles), a mean radius of 24 500 kilometres (14,000 miles), and a density 17.2 times that of Earth. —**Nep·tu·ni·an** *adj.*

nep·tu·ni·um (nep-téwni-əm ‖ -tōoni-) *n. Symbol* Np A silvery, metallic, naturally radioactive element, atomic number 93, the first of the transuranium elements, having a number of isotopes with mass numbers from 231 to 241 and half-lives ranging from 7.3 minutes to 2.2 million years. It is found in trace quantities in uranium ores and is produced synthetically by nuclear reactions. [After *Neptune* (planet), since neptunium follows uranium in the periodic table, as Neptune is the next planet after Uranus.]

N.E.R.C. National Environment Research Council (in Britain).

nerd, nurd (nerd) *n. Chiefly U.S. Slang.* An idiotic, foolish, or very unattractive person. [Perhaps from earlier *nert,* alteration of *nut,* or after *Nerd,* a character in *If I Ran the Zoo* (1950), by U.S. children's author Dr. Seuss (Theodor Seuss Geisel, 1904–91).]

Ne·re·id¹ (néer-i-id) *n., pl.* **Nereides** (nə-rée-i-deez, ni-). *Greek Mythology.* Any of the 50 daughters of Nereus; a sea nymph. [Greek *Nēreis,* from *Nēreus,* NEREUS.]

Nereid² *n.* The smaller of the two satellites of the planet Neptune. [From NEREID (nymph); the Nereides were attendants on Neptune.]

ne·re·is (néer-i-iss) *n., pl.* **nereides** (ni-rée-i-deez) Any of several marine worms of the genus *Nereis,* having a long, flat, segmented body and a pair of paddles on each segment. See **ragworm.** [New Latin, from Latin *Nēreis,* NEREID.]

Ne·re·us (néer-i-ōoss, -əss) *Greek Mythology.* A sea god, father of the Nereids.

ne·rit·ic (ne-ríttik, nə-) *adj.* Pertaining to or designating the waters and deposits of a shoreline. See **continental shelf.** [Probably from Latin *nērīta,* sea snail, from Greek *nēritēs,* from *Nēreus,* NEREUS.]

Nernst (nairnst), **Walther Hermann** (1864–1941). German physicist. Best known for his discovery of the third law of thermodynamics, he also carried out important research into free radicals. He received a Nobel prize for chemistry (1920).

Nernst heat theorem *n.* The principle in thermodynamics that changes in entropy tend to zero as the temperature tends to absolute zero. It was an earlier form of the third law of thermodynamics.

Ne·ro (Claudius Caesar) (néer-ō), born Lucius Domitius Ahenobarbus (A.D. 37–68). Roman emperor (A.D. 54–68). He was adopted by the Emperor Claudius, but his early reign was dominated by his mother, Agrippina. He murdered his mother and wife and was rumoured to have started the Great Fire of Rome (A.D. 64) for which the Christians were blamed. His cruelty and irresponsibility provoked revolts throughout the empire which led to his suicide.

ner·o·li (néer-ə-li, nérrə-) *n.* An essential oil distilled from orange flowers and used in perfumery. Also called "neroli oil", "orange flower oil". [Perhaps after Anna Maria de la Trémoille, princess of *Neroli,* who is said to have introduced it into France.]

Ne·ro·ni·an (ni-rōni-ən) *adj.* **1.** Marked by the cruelty, tyranny, or depravity characteristic of the emperor Nero. **2.** Of or pertaining to Nero or his times.

Ne·ru·da (ne-rōo-də), **Pablo,** pen name of Ricardo Eliezer Neftali Reyes Basoalto (1904–73). Chilean poet and diplomat. Though his early works were nihilistic, his later poems reflected the socialist commitment of the Allende government, which he served as ambassador. He was awarded a Nobel prize for literature (1971).

ner·vate (nér-vayt) *adj. Botany.* Having veins. Said of leaves.

ner·va·tion (ner-váysh'n) *n.* A pattern of veins or nerves; venation.

nerve (nérv) *n.* **1:** Any of the bundles of fibres interconnecting the central nervous system and the organs or parts of the body, capable of transmitting both sensory stimuli and motor impulses from one part of the body to another. **2.** A tendon or muscle. Now rare except in the phrase *to strain every nerve.* **3.** The source from which feeling, energy, or dynamic action emanates. **4.** *Usually plural.* The nervous system considered as imparting certain characteristics, such as courage, determination, or endurance. **5. a.** Forcefulness; stamina. **b.** Courage and composure; firm self-control: *lost his nerve at the last minute.* **c.** *Informal.* Brazenness; effrontery: *What a nerve!* **6.** *Plural.* An agitated condition induced by anxiety: *an attack of nerves.* **7.** *Biology.* A vein in an insect's wing. **8.** *Botany.* The midrib or any of the larger veins in a leaf. —See Synonyms at **temerity.** —**get on (someone's) nerves.** To exasperate or irritate someone. —*tr.v.* **nerved, nerving, nerves.** To give strength or courage to (someone, especially oneself). [Latin *nervus,* sinew, nerve.]

nerve block *n.* A method of producing local anaesthesia in a particular part of the body by injecting a local anaesthetic into another part of the body some distance away, in order to block the passage of pain impulses.

nerve cell *n.* Any of the cells of nerve tissue. It consists of a nucleated cell body and cytoplasmic extensions (the dendrites and axons). Also called "neurone".

nerve centre *n.* **1.** A group of nerve cells that perform a specific function. **2.** A source or focus of power or control.

nerve fibre *n.* A threadlike process that is part of a nerve cell; an axon.

nerve gas *n.* Any gas used in chemical warfare that affects the normal functioning of nerves and thereby paralyses the muscles they supply.

nerve impulse *n.* The wavelike progression of electrical activity that marks the transmission of information along a stimulated nerve fibre.

nerve·less (nérv-ləss, -liss) *adj.* **1.** Lacking courage or energy; listless; spiritless. **2.** Undisturbed by danger or upsetting circumstances; confident, courageous, and self-controlled. —**nerve·less·ly** *adv.* —**nerve·less·ness** *n.*

nerve-rack·ing, nerve-wrack·ing (nérv-racking) *adj.* Intensely distressing, irritating, or exhausting.

Ner·vi (náirvi), **Pier Luigi** (1891–1979). Italian architect. His public buildings, such as the UNESCO building in Paris (1953–57), pioneered the decorative use of reinforced concrete.

nerv·ine (nér-veen, -vīn) *adj.* Affecting the nerves; especially, calming nervous excitement.

~*n.* A tonic for nervous disorders.

nerv·ous (nérvəss) *adj.* **1. a.** Agitated, or liable to become agitated, as a result of anxiety; jittery. **b.** Indicating an anxious or agitated condition: *a nervous stammer.* **2.** Spirited or vigorous, especially in style, feeling, or thought: *a nervous, vibrant prose.* **3.** Strung with nerves; containing many delicate nerves. **4. a.** Of or pertaining to the nerves or nervous system. **b.** Stemming from or affecting the nerves or nervous system: *a nervous disorder.* **5. a.** Anxious or afraid: *nervous of heights.* **b.** Producing anxiety; uneasy: *the nervous moments before takeoff.* [Middle English, from Latin *nervōsus,* from *nervus,* sinew, NERVE.] —**nerv·ous·ly** *adv.* —**nerv·ous·ness** *n.*

nervous breakdown *n.* **1.** Neurasthenia *(see).* **2.** Any severe or incapacitating emotional disorder.

nervous exhaustion *n.* Neurasthenia *(see).*

nervous system *n. Anatomy.* A coordinating mechanism in all multicellular animals, except sponges, that regulates internal body functions and responses to external stimuli. In vertebrates it consists of the brain, spinal cord, nerves, ganglia, and parts of receptor and effector organs. See **autonomic nervous system, central ner-**

vous system, peripheral nervous system.

ner·vure (nérvewr, nérv-yər) *n.* **1.** *Botany.* Any of the vascular ridges that form the framework of a leaf. **2.** *Biology.* Any of the thickened ribs of tissue that form the framework of an insect's wing. [French, from Latin *nervus*, NERVE.]

nerv·y (nérvi) *adj.* **-ier, -iest. 1.** *Chiefly British Informal.* Having bad nerves; jumpy; nervous. **2.** *Archaic.* Full of muscular force; sinewy. **3.** Showing or requiring fortitude, energy, or endurance. **4.** *U.S. Informal.* Impudently confident; brazen.

nes·ci·ence (néssi-ənss ‖ *U.S. also* nésh-, néshi-, néesh-) *n.* **1.** *Formal.* Absence of knowledge or awareness; ignorance. **2.** *Rare.* Agnosticism. [Late Latin *nesciēntia*, from *nesciens* (stem *nescient-*), ignorant, from *nescīre*, to be ignorant : *ne-*, not + *scīre*, to know.] **—nes·ci·ent** *adj. & n.*

–ness *n. suffix.* Indicates: **1.** State, quality, or condition of being; for example, *quietness.* **2.** An instance or example of a state, quality, or condition; for example, *kindness.* [Middle English *-ness*, from Old English *-ness, -niss*, of Germanic origin.]

Ness, Loch (ness). A lake of north Scotland. It lies in Glen Mòr, on the Caledonian Canal between Lochend and Fort Augustus. Its depths are supposed to contain the Loch Ness Monster.

Nes·sel·rode (néss'l-rōd) *n.* A frozen dessert, often rum-flavoured, made with chestnuts, preserved oranges, cherries, dried fruits, and cream. [After Count Karl NESSELRODE, whose chef invented it.]

Nesselrode, Karl (Robert), Count (1780–1862). Russian foreign minister (from 1816). He pursued a belligerent policy in the Balkans.

nest (nest) *n.* **1. a.** The structure made by a bird for holding its eggs and young. **b.** The structure or place in which fishes or insects deposit eggs or shelter their young. **c.** Any place where young are reared; a lair. **d.** A number of insects, birds, or other animals occupying such a place; a swarm, brood, or colony: *a nest of hornets.* **2.** A place affording snug seclusion or lodging. **3. a.** A place or environment favouring rapid growth or development of something bad or dangerous; a hotbed: *a nest of rebellion.* **b.** The persons occupying or frequenting such a place. **4.** A set of objects, such as small tables, of graduated size, that can be stacked together, each fitting within the one immediately larger. **5.** A group of weapons in a prepared position: *a nest of missiles.* **—feather (one's) nest.** To exploit one's position in order to procure benefits, especially financial benefits, for oneself.

~v. nested, nesting, nests. *—intr.* **1.** To build or occupy a nest. **2.** To hunt for birds' nests, especially in order to collect the eggs. **3.** To fit together in a stack. *—tr.* **1.** To place in or as if in a nest. **2.** To place within or arrange into a hierarchy, as of mathematical operations. [Middle English *nest*, Old English *nest*.]

nest egg *n.* **1.** An artificial or natural egg placed in a nest to induce a bird to lay. **2.** A sum of money put by as a reserve.

nes·tle (néss'l) *v.* **-tled, -tling, -tles.** *—intr.* **1. a.** To settle snugly and comfortably: *The kittens nestled down lazily among the cushions.* **b.** To lie or be situated in a sheltered or snug position: *The cottage nestled in the wood.* **2.** To draw or press close, especially in an affectionate manner. Often used with *up: She nestled up to him.* **3.** *Archaic.* To nest. *—tr.* **1.** To place or settle as if in a nest: *nestled the baby in my arms.* **2.** To snuggle or press affectionately or contentedly: *nestled his head into her shoulder.* [Middle English *nestlen*, Old English *nestlian*, to make a nest.] **—nes·tler** *n.*

nest·ling (nést-ling, néss-) *n.* **1.** A bird too young and frail to leave its nest. **2.** A young child.

Nes·tor (néss-tawr, -tər). In the Homeric poems, a hero celebrated for his age and wisdom.

Nes·to·ri·an (ne-stáwri-ən) *adj.* Of or designating a church of the East that adheres to the doctrines of Nestorius, a fifth-century Patriarch of Constantinople, asserting that Christ had two distinct natures, divine and human, and that the Virgin Mary should not be called the Mother of God.

~n. A member of this church. **—Nes·to·ri·an·ism** *n.*

net¹ (net) *n.* **1. a.** An openwork material of fibres, cords, wire, or the like, with the threads woven, knotted, or twisted together at regular intervals, forming meshes of varying sizes. **b.** A light mesh fabric, used especially as a curtain or dress material. **2.** Something made of net: **a.** A device for capturing birds, fish, butterflies, or other animals. **b.** A device for excluding birds or insects, especially a **mosquito net** *(see).* **c.** A mesh for holding the hair in place. **3.** *Sports.* **a.** In racket games, a barrier of meshwork cord or rope strung between two posts to divide the playing area in half. **b.** A ball that is hit into such a net. Also called "net ball". **c.** Either of the goals in soccer, hockey, and some other games. **4.** In cricket. **a.** *Usually plural.* A practice area enclosed by netting. **b.** A practice session in such an area. **5.** A meshed network of lines, figures, or fibres. **6.** A situation or circumstance that entraps or is rendered to trap.

~tr.v. netted, netting, nets. 1. To catch or entangle in or as if in a net. **2.** To cover, protect, or surround with or as if with a net. **3.** To hit (a ball) into a net. [Middle English, Old English *net(t)*.]

net², nett *adj.* **1.** *Abbr.* **n. a.** Remaining after all necessary deductions have been made or all losses accounted for: *net profit.* Compare **gross.** **b.** Designating the weight remaining after tare is deducted. **2.** Ultimate; final: *net result; net conclusion.*

~n. *Abbr.* **n.** Total gain; the net amount, as of profit, income, price, or weight.

~tr.v. netted, netting, nets. To bring in as profit or as a final total. [Middle English *net*, neat, clear, plain, from Old French *net*, neat, elegant, from Latin *nitidus*, bright, clear, from *nitēre*, to shine.]

net·ball (nét-bawl) *n.* A team game, usually played by women, which is similar to basketball but in which a player is not allowed to move while holding the ball or to let it touch the ground.

neth·er (néthər) *adj.* Located beneath or below. [Middle English *nether*, Old English *nithera*, lower, from *nither*, down, downwards.]

Neth·er·lands, Kingdom of the (néthərləndz). *Dutch* **Ne·der·land** (náydər-laant). A kingdom of northwest Europe, often known as Holland. A low-lying area, much of it reclaimed from the sea, with 40 per cent of the land below sea-level, it is a heavily agricultural state, but its economy has come to depend increasingly on industry and commerce. Dominated through its history by various European powers, it was, in the 16th century, a leader in European culture, commerce, and colonialism. The Hague is the seat of government. Area, 33 939 square kilometres (13,104 square miles). Population, 15,520,000. Capital, Amsterdam.

Netherlands Antilles. Dutch-administered islands in the Caribbean, in two groups of islands more than 800 kilometres (500 miles) apart. The main group comprises Curaçao (the largest island) and Bonaire, off the coast of Venezuela; to the northeast are Saba, St. Eustatius, and the southern half of Sint Maarten (the northern half is French-owned). Aruba separated from the group in 1986 and is now a self-governing part of the Netherlands realm. Area, 800 square kilometres (308 square miles). Capital, Willemstad (on Curaçao).

neth·er·most (néthər-mōst) *adj.* Farthest down; deepest.

nether world *n.* **1.** The world of the dead; Hades. **2.** Hell. **3.** A place or situation likened to hell. Also called "nether regions".

Ne·to (néttō), **Antonio Agostinho** (1922–79). Angolan politician. After Angola's liberation from Portugal (1975), he became its first president.

net·su·ke (nét-sōoki, -sōokay) *n.* A small toggle of wood or ivory, usually elaborately carved, used in Japan to fasten a purse or other article to a kimono sash. [Japanese.]

nett. Variant of **net** (remaining after deductions).

net·ting (nétting) *n.* **1.** Any openwork fabric or structure of string, wire, or the like. **2.** A piece of this fabric.

net·tle (nétt'l) *n.* **1.** Any plant of the genus *Urtica*, such as *U. dioica*, the stinging nettle, having toothed leaves often covered with hairs that secrete a stinging fluid that affects the skin on contact. **2.** Any of various other stinging or prickly plants. **—grasp the nettle.** To approach a difficulty or task decisively.

~tr.v. nettled, -tling, -tles. 1. To sting with or as if with a nettle. **2.** To irritate; vex. [Middle English *nettle*, Old English *netle, netel(e)*, from Germanic.]

nettle rash *n.* **Urticaria** (see).

net ton *n.* A short **ton** (see).

net·work (nét-wurk) *n.* **1.** An openwork fabric or other structure in which rope, thread, wires, or other materials cross at regular intervals. **2.** Something resembling a net in concept or form, such as: **a.** A system of intersecting lines of communication: *a network of railways.* **b.** Any complex, interconnected group or system: *an espionage network.* **3.** A chain of interconnected radio or television broadcasting stations. **4.** A group or system of electrical components and connecting circuitry designed to function as a unit.

~tr.v. networked, -working, -works. To broadcast over a radio or television network.

net·work·ing (nét-wurking) *n.* The establishing of professional contacts, especially among feminists, at many levels of industry and business for such purposes as disseminating information about jobs or promotions, or offering mutual guidance.

Neu·châ·tel (núr-sha-tél, nō-) A city in northwest Switzerland, capital of the canton of the same name. It lies on the north shore of Lake Neuchâtel. The town is noted for its manufacture of watches, jewellery, and chocolate.

Neu·mann (nóy-man), **(Johann) Balthasar** (1687–1753). Bohemian architect. He designed ornate buildings such as the Vierzehnheiligen church, completed almost 20 years after his death.

Neu·mann (nóy-man), **Johannes von**, known as John (1903–57). Hungarian-born U.S. mathematician. He developed the **game theory** *(see),* and contributed to the mathematical analysis of quantum physics.

neumes, neums (newmz ‖ nōomz) *pl.n.* The signs used in the notation of plainsong during the Middle Ages, surviving today in transcriptions of Gregorian chant. [Middle English, musical phrase sung to a single syllable, from Old French, from Medieval Latin *neuma, neupma*, from Greek *pneuma*, breath.] **—neu·mat·ic** (new-máttik ‖ nōo-) *adj.*

neur. neurological; neurology.

neu·ral (néwr-əl ‖ nóor-) *adj.* **1.** Of or pertaining to the nerves or nervous system. **2.** Of, pertaining to, or located on the same side of the body as the spinal cord; dorsal. [NEUR(O)- + -AL.]

neu·ral·gia (newr-áljə ‖ noor-) *n.* Paroxysmal pain along a nerve. [New Latin : NEUR(O)- + -ALGIA.] **—neu·ral·gic** *adj.*

neu·ras·the·ni·a (néwr-əss-theeni-ə ‖ nóor-) *n.* A condition marked by fatigue, loss of energy and memory, and feelings of inadequacy, once thought to result from exhaustion of the nervous system. Now rare in scientific usage. Also called "nervous breakdown", "nervous exhaustion". [NEUR(O)- + ASTHENIA.] **—neu·ras·then·ic** (-thénnik) *adj.* **—neu·ras·then·i·cal·ly** *adv.*

neu·rax·on (newr-ák-son ‖ nóor-) *n.* A part of a nerve cell, the **axon** *(see).* [New Latin : NEUR(O)- + AXON.]

neu·rec·to·my (newr-éktəmi ‖ nóor-) *n., pl.* **-mies.** Surgical removal of a nerve or part of a nerve. [NEUR(O)- + -ECTOMY.]

NETHERLANDS

neu·ri·tis (newr-ítiss || noor-) *n.* Inflammation of a nerve, causing pain, loss of reflexes, and muscular atrophy. [New Latin : NEUR(O)- + -ITIS.] **—neu·rit·ic** (-íttik) *adj.*

neuro–, neur– *comb. form.* Indicates nerve or nervous system; for example, **neuroblast, neurectomy.** [New Latin, from Greek *neuron*, tendon, nerve.]

neu·ro·blast (newr-ō-blast, -ə- || noor-) *n.* An embryonic cell from which a nerve cell develops. [NEURO- + -BLAST.]

neu·ro·cyte (newr-ō-sīt, -ə- || noor-) *n.* A nerve cell.

neu·ro·en·do·crine system (newr-ō-éndə-krin, -krīn, -kreen || noor-) *n.* The system of nerves and hormones that function together to control certain activities of the body.

neu·ro·fib·ril (newr-ō-fíbril || noor-) *n.* Any of the cytoplasmic threads in the cell body of a neurone, extending into the axon in peripheral nerves.

neu·ro·gen·ic (newr-ō-jénnik, -ə- || noor-) *adj.* **1.** Originating in the nervous system. **2.** Caused by stimulation of the nerves. **3.** Caused by disease of the nervous system. **—neu·ro·gen·i·cal·ly** *adv.*

neu·rog·li·a (newr-óggli-ə, newr-ō-glí-ə || noor-) *n.* The network of branched cells and fibres that supports the nerve cells of the central nervous system. Also called "glia". [New Latin : NEURO- + Medieval Greek *glia*, "glue", tissue.] **—neu·rog·li·al** *adj.*

neu·ro·gram (newr-ō-gram, -ə- || noor-) *n.* An **engram** *(see).* [NEURO- + -GRAM.]

neu·ro·hor·mone (newr-ō-hór-mōn || noor-) *n.* A hormone that is produced within nervous tissue and secreted by specialised nerve cells. An example is oxytocin, produced in the hypothalamus and secreted by the pituitary gland.

neu·ro·hy·po·phy·sis (newr-ō-hī-póffi-siss || noor-) *n.* The posterior part of the pituitary gland. Compare **adenohypophysis.**

neurol. neurological; neurology.

neu·rol·o·gy (newr-ólləji || noor-) *n. Abbr.* **neur., neurol.** The branch of medical science concerned with the nervous system and its disorders. [New Latin *neurologia* : NEURO- + -LOGY.] **—neu·ro·log·i·cal** (newr-ə-lójik'l || noor-) *adj.* **—neu·rol·o·gist** (-ólləjist) *n.*

neu·ro·ma (newr-ō-mə || noor-) *n., pl.* **-mata** (-mətə). A tumour made of nerve tissue. [New Latin : NEUR(O)- + -OMA.]

neu·ro·mus·cu·lar (newr-ō-műs-kewlər || noor-) *adj.* Of, pertaining to, or affecting both nerves and muscles.

neu·rone (newr-ōn || noor-) *n.* Also **neu·ron** (-on). A **nerve cell** *(see).* [Greek *neuron*, sinew, nerve.] **—neu·ron·ic** (newr-ónnik || noor-) *adj.* **—neu·ron·i·cal·ly** *adv.*

neu·ro·pa·thol·o·gy (newr-ō-pə-thólləji || noor-) *n.* The medical study of diseases of the nervous system. **—neu·ro·path·o·log·i·cal** (-páthə-lójik'l) *adj.* **—neu·ro·pa·thol·o·gist** (-pə-thólləjist) *n.*

neu·rop·a·thy (newr-óppathi || noor-) *n.* Any disease or abnormality of the nervous system. [NEURO- + -PATHY.]

neu·ro·phys·i·ol·o·gy (newr-ō-fizzi-ólləji || noor-) *n.* The study of the physical and chemical changes associated with the functioning of the nervous system. **—neu·ro·phys·i·o·log·ical** (-ə-lójik'l) *adj.* **—neu·ro·phys·i·ol·o·gist** (-ólləjist) *n.*

neu·ro·psy·chi·a·try (newr-ō-sī-kī-ətri, -sə- || noor-) *n. Abbr.* **NP** The integrated medical study of both neurological and psychiatric disorders. **—neu·ro·psy·chi·at·ric** (-sīki-áttrik) *adj.* **—neu·ro·psy·chi·a·trist** (-kī-ətrist) *n.*

neu·rop·ter·an (newr-óptərən || noor-) *n.* Any insect of the order Neuroptera, having four net-veined wings, such as the **ant lion** or **lacewing** *(both of which see).* ~*adj.* Of or belonging to the Neuroptera. [New Latin *Neuroptera*, "nerve-winged" : NEURO- + -PTER.] **—neu·rop·ter·ous** *adj.*

neu·ro·sis (newr-ō-siss || noor-) *n., pl.* **-ses** (-seez). Any of various illnesses affecting the mind or emotions, without obvious organic lesion or change, and involving anxiety, depression, phobia, hysteria, or other abnormal patterns of behaviour. Also called "psycho-

neurosis". Compare **psychosis.** [New Latin : NEUR(O)- + -OSIS.]
neu·ro·sur·ger·y (néwr-ō-súrjəri || nóor-) *n.* Surgery of any part of the nervous system. **—neu·ro·sur·geon** *n.* **—neu·ro·sur·gi·cal** *adj.*
neu·rot·ic (newr-óttik || noor-) *adj.* **1.** Of or pertaining to a neurosis: *a neurotic disorder.* **2.** Suffering from neurosis: *a neurotic patient.* **3.** *Informal.* Showing an exaggerated, distorted, or obsessional attitude to the real world: *neurotic about hygiene.*
~*n.* A person suffering from a neurosis. **—neu·rot·i·cal·ly** *adv.*
neu·rot·i·cism (newr-ótti-siz'm || noor-) *n.* A quality of personality characterised by anxiety and a tendency to become neurotic.
neu·rot·o·my (newr-óttəmi || noor-) *n., pl.* **-mies.** The surgical cutting or stretching of a nerve, usually to relieve pain. [NEURO- + -TOMY.]
neu·ro·trans·mit·ter (néwr-ō-transs-míttər, -tranz-, -traanz- || nóor-) *n.* A chemical substance, such as acetylcholine, released from nerve endings and transmitting impulses across a synapse to nerve, muscle, or other cells. Also called "transmitter".
Neus·tri·a (néw-stri-ə || nóō-). The western part of the Frankish kingdom during the Merovingian period (sixth to eighth century). It consisted of the Loire and Seine country and land farther to the north; the chief towns were Soissons and Paris. **—Neus·tri·an** *n. & adj.*
neu·ter (néw-tər || nóō-) *adj. Abbr.* **neut.** **1.** *Grammar.* Neither masculine nor feminine in gender. **2.** Lacking sexual organs or having only nonfunctional ones; specifically: **a.** *Botany.* Having no pistils or stamens; asexual. **b.** *Zoology.* Sexually undeveloped.
~*n.* **1.** *Grammar.* **a.** The neuter gender. **b.** A neuter word. **2. a.** A castrated animal. **b.** A sexually undeveloped or imperfectly developed female insect; a worker. **c.** A plant without stamens or pistils.
~*tr.v.* **neutered, -tering, -ters.** To castrate (an animal). [Middle English *neutre,* from Old French, from Latin *neuter,* neither : *ne-,* not + *uter,* either of two.]
neu·tral (néw-trəl || nóō-) *adj. Abbr.* **neut.** **1.** Not inclining towards or actively taking either side, as in a war or other dispute. **2.** Belonging to neither side or party: *on neutral ground.* **3.** Occupying a middle position; not one thing or the other; indifferent. **4.** Of no sex; sexless; neuter. **5.** *Chemistry.* Of or designating a compound that is neither acidic nor alkaline. **6.** *Physics.* **a.** Of or designating a particle, object, or system that has neither positive nor negative electric charge. **b.** Of or designating a particle, object, or system that has a net electric charge of zero. **7.** Of or pertaining to the state of a mechanical system in which gears are not engaged for transmission of power. **8. Achromatic** *(see).* **9.** *Phonetics.* Designating a vowel that is pronounced with the tongue in a relaxed, middle position, such as the *a* in *around.*
~*n.* **1.** One who takes no side in a dispute. **2. a.** A neutral nation. **b.** A citizen of a neutral nation. **3.** An achromatic colour. **4.** The position of gears in a power system when power cannot be transmitted: *The car is in neutral.* [Latin *neutrālis,* neuter (grammatically), from NEUTER.] **—neu·tral·ly** *adv.*
neu·tral·i·sa·tion (néw-trə-lī-záysh'n || nóō-; *U.S.* -li-) *n.* **1.** The act of neutralising. **2.** *Chemistry.* A reaction between an acid and a base that yields a salt and water.
neu·tral·ise, neu·tral·ize (néw-trə-līz || nóō-) *v.* **-ised, -ising, -ises.** *—tr.* **1.** To make neutral. **2.** To counterbalance or counteract and so render ineffective. **3.** To prohibit warfare in (an area) by signed agreement. **4.** *Chemistry.* **a.** To make (a solution) chemically neutral. **b.** To cause (an acid or base) to undergo neutralisation. *—intr.* To become neutral. **—neu·tral·is·er** *n.*
Synonyms: *neutralise, counteract, negate, nullify.*
neu·tral·ism (néw-trə-liz'm || nóō-) *n.* A political attitude of nonalignment or non-involvement with conflicting alliances. **—neu·tral·ist** *adj. & n.*
neu·tral·i·ty (new-trál-əti || nōō-) *n.* The state or policy of being neutral; especially, nonparticipation in war.
neutral spirits *pl.n. U.S.* Ethanol distilled at or above 190° proof and used frequently in alcoholic beverage blends.
neu·tri·no (new-tréenō || nōō-) *n., pl.* **-nos.** *Physics.* Any of various electrically neutral particles, thought to be massless, belonging to the lepton family. Each is associated with a specific massive lepton; for example, the *electron-type neutrino* or the *muon-type neutrino.* [Italian, diminutive of *neutrone,* neutron, from English NEUTRON.]
neu·tron (néw-tron, *rarely* -trən || nóō-) *n. Symbol* **n** *Physics.* An elementary particle of the baryon family, having almost the same mass as the proton but no electric charge. It is stable when bound in an atomic nucleus, but has a mean lifetime of approximately 15.5 minutes as a free particle. It is present in any atomic nucleus with mass number greater than one. [NEUTR(AL) + -ON.]
neutron bomb *n.* A nuclear weapon that produces a large number of high-energy neutrons but relatively little blast or long-term radioactivity. It is designed to kill people without causing excessive damage or contamination in the target area. Also called "enhanced radiation bomb".
neutron number *n. Symbol* **N** The number of neutrons in the nucleus of a given isotope.
neutron star *n.* A celestial body of great density, formed by the collapse of a star under its own gravity and consisting almost entirely of neutrons. A neutron star has a mass of between 1.5 and 3 times that of the Sun, but might have a radius as small as 100 kilometres.
neu·tro·phil (néw-trə-fil || nóō-) *adj.* Also **neu·tro·phile** (-fīl). Easily stained by neutral dyes. Said of such cells as leucocytes.
~*n.* A phagocytic leucocyte of a type having a lobed nucleus and granular cytoplasm that stains with neutral dyes. [NEUTR(AL) + -PHIL(E).]
Ne·va·da (ni-vaádə, nə-, ne- || -váddə). State in the western United States, lying between California on the west and Utah on the east. Most of the state lies within the desert region known as the Great Basin. Carson City is the capital, but the largest city is Las Vegas. Nevada is a leading supplier of copper, gold, iron ore, and mercury, and oil was discovered there in 1954. The state was admitted to the Union in 1864. **—Ne·vad·an** *adj. & n.*
Ne·va·do del Ruiz (neváathō del rōō-eéss, nəvaádo del rōō-eéss). Volcano in central Colombia, 5 400 metres (17,700 feet) high, that erupted in 1985, claiming the lives of about 23,000 people.
né·vé (névvay, náy-vay) *n.* **1.** The upper part of a glacier, where the snow turns into ice. **2.** A field of snow at the head of a glacier. **3.** The granular snow typically found in such a field. See **firn.** [French dialect (Valais), from Latin *nix* (stem *niv-*), snow.]
nev·er (névvər) *adv.* **1. a.** Not ever; on no occasion: *never tasted venison.* **b.** At no time and under no circumstances whatsoever. Used emphatically: *Do such a thing? Never!* **2. a.** Not at all; in no way: *Never fear; This will never do!* **b.** *Nonstandard.* Not: *I waited but you never arrived.* **—never so.** *Archaic.* Very.
~*interj.* Also **well I never.** Used to express disbelief or amazement. [Middle English *never,* Old English *nǣfre* : *ne,* not + *ǣfre,* ever.]
nev·er·more (névvər-mór || -mór) *adv.* Never again.
nev·er-nev·er (névvər-névvər) *n. British Informal.* The hire-purchase system. Used with *the.*
nev·er-nev·er land *n.* An imaginary and wonderful place; fantasy land. [After *the Neverland,* country in J.M. BARRIE's *Peter Pan* (1904).]
nev·er·the·less (névvər-thə-léss) *adv.* None the less; however.
Nevis. See **St. Kitts-Nevis.**
new (new || nōō) *adj.* **newer, newest.** **1.** Of recent origin; having existed only a short time; lately made, produced, or grown: *a new television series.* **2. a.** Not yet old; fresh; recent. **b.** Used for the first time; not secondhand. **3. a.** Previously existing but recognised, discovered, or encountered lately for the first time: *a new galaxy.* **b.** Not belonging to one's own previous experience: *visiting new places.* **4.** Freshly introduced; unfamiliar; unaccustomed. Used with *to* or *at: I'm new at it.* **5.** Being the latest in a sequence: *the new edition.* **6. a.** Newly entered into a state or position; being so for the first time: *the new rich.* **b.** Changed for the better; refreshed; rejuvenated: *A nap made a new man of him.* **7.** Different and distinct from a former one of the same type: *new neighbours.* **8. a.** Modern; current; fashionable: *a new dance.* **b.** In the most recent form, period, or development of something: *New Latin.* **9.** Novel; unconventional: *a new concept in bathroom accessories.* **10.** Designating crops that are harvested early: *new potatoes.* **11.** Additional; more: *send him some new work.*
~*adv.* Freshly; recently. Used in combination: *new-cut grass.* [Middle English *newe,* Old English *nēowe, nīwe.*] **—new·ness** *n.*
Usage: *new, novel, original. New* is a general term referring to both time and condition. *Novel,* which emphasises condition, is applied to that which is both new and strikingly unusual: *His symphony is not only new* (chronologically), *but novel in its treatment of folk songs. Original* also emphasises state rather than time, and is said of that which is the first of its kind.
New Age *adj.* Pertaining to or designating an alternative model of spiritual values conceived as coming to replace or coexist with the materialistic values of the present age: *"Basically the New Age person is into consciousness-raising, caring and green politics."* (*The Sunday Times.*) **—New Age** *n.*
New·ark (néw-ark || nóō-). City in New Jersey, in the northeast United States, lying on the river Passaic and Newark Bay. It is a major industrial and commercial centre.
new arrival *n. Informal.* A newborn baby.
new·born, new-born (néw-bawrn || nóō-) *adj.* Just born; very recently born: *a newborn baby.*
New Britain. Volcanic island in the southwest Pacific, belonging to Papua New Guinea. It is the largest island in the Bismarck Archipelago. The chief town and port is Rabaul. The island is mountainous with many active volcanoes and hot springs. It was named by the English explorer, William Dampier, who discovered it in 1700.
new broom *n.* A new and enthusiastic person in charge of a job, who attempts to reorganise it and institute changes. [From the proverbial saying *a new broom sweeps clean.*]
New Brunswick. Province in east Canada, lying to the south of Quebec and east of Maine (in the United States). The capital is Fredericton; the two largest cities are Saint John and Moncton. Three-quarters of the province is forested, and timber is the chief industry. About 40 per cent of the population is French-speaking.
New·burg (néw-burg || nóō-) *adj.* **1.** Designating a sauce used for seafood, made from cream, egg yolks, butter, wine, and usually nutmeg. **2.** Cooked or served in this sauce: *lobster Newburg.* [Alteration of *Wenburg,* name of patron for whom sauce was created.]
New Caledonia. Large island in the southwest Pacific Ocean, lying about 1 200 kilometres (750 miles) east of Australia. It has a number of smaller islands as dependencies and is itself an overseas territory belonging to France. Coffee is the main cash crop, but the economic value of the island lies in its rich mineral deposits. It was annexed by France in 1853. See map at **Pacific Ocean.**
New·cas·tle[1] (néw-kaass'l || nóō-, -kass'l). Coastal city and port of New South Wales, in southeast Australia, lying at the mouth of the Hunter River. It is a leading steel-manufacturing centre.

Newcastle disease n. **Fowl pest** (see). [After NEWCASTLE UPON TYNE, where there was an outbreak of it in 1926.]

New·cas·tle-un·der-Lyme (néw-kaass'l-úndər-lîm ‖ nōō-, -kass'l-). Industrial town in Staffordshire, west central England, on the river Lyme. It is important for textiles, bricks, and coalmining.

New·cas·tle up·on Tyne (néw-kaass'l ə-pón tín ‖ nōō-, -kass'l-; *locally* new-káss'l-). City in northeast England, situated on the north bank of the river Tyne. It is the centre of the industrial region known as Tyneside, which, once famous for shipbuilding, is now the centre of new motor manufacturing and electronics industries.

new chum n. *Australian & N.Z. Informal.* A recent immigrant.

New Church n. The **New Jerusalem Church** (see).

New·combe (néw-kəm ‖ nōō-), **John** (1944–). Australian tennis player. He was Wimbledon singles champion (1967, 1970, and 1971), and five times doubles champion (between 1965 and 1974).

new·com·er (néw-kummər ‖ nōō-) n. One who has lately come to a place or situation.

New Commonwealth n. Those countries belonging to the British Commonwealth that have gained independence since 1945. ~*adj.* Of, pertaining to, or coming from these countries. Sometimes used euphemistically to refer to nonwhites.

New Criticism n. A form of literary criticism established in the early 1940s chiefly in the United States, involving a detailed analysis of the literary text's verbal organisation and imagery, and a corresponding rejection of biographical and historical considerations surrounding the composition of the text. —**New Critic** n.

New Deal n. **1.** The programmes and policies for economic recovery and reform, relief, and social security, introduced in the United States during the 1930s by President Franklin D. Roosevelt and his administration. **2.** The period between 1933 and 1940 during which these programmes and policies were developed.

New Delhi. See **Delhi.**

New Economic Policy n. The programme in the U.S.S.R. between 1921 and 1928 whereby concessions were made to capitalism in small industry, the retail trade, and agriculture.

new·el (néw-əl, newl ‖ nōō-) n. **1.** The vertical support at the centre of a winding staircase. **2.** Any of the posts supporting a handrail at the bottom or on the landings of a staircase. Also called "newel post". [Middle English *nowell,* from Old French *nouel,* "kernel", newel, from Latin *nucālis,* nut-shaped, from *nux,* nut.]

New England. The extreme northeasterly states of the United States, settled during the colonial era: Maine, New Hampshire, Vermont, Massachusetts, Rhode Island, and Connecticut.

New English Bible n. *Abbr.* **N.E.B.** A Modern English translation of the Bible and Apocrypha, prepared by an interdenominational panel and published in full in 1970.

new·fan·gled (néw-fáng-g'ld, -fang- ‖ nōō-) adj. **1.** Excessively or needlessly novel: *newfangled ideas.* **2.** *Archaic.* Excessively fond of novelty. Used derogatorily in both senses. [Middle English *newe fangled,* alteration of *newefangel,* fond of new things : NEW + *-fangel,* from Old English *fangol* (unattested), "ready to seize", from *fangen,* past participle of *fōn,* to seize.]

new-fash·ioned (néw-fásh'nd ‖ nōō-) adj. Made according to or following a current fashion.

New Forest. A thickly wooded area, mostly of oak and beech, interspersed with heathland in Hampshire, in south England. The woods were made a royal forest by William I in 1079. Much of its 36 500 hectares (90,000 acres) is open to the public.

New·found·land¹ (néw-fənd-lənd, -land, -lánd, new-fównd-lənd ‖ nōō-; *locally* néw-fənd-lánd). *Abbr.* **N.F., Nfld.** Province in east Canada, comprising the island of Newfoundland (north of the Gulf of St. Lawrence) and the mainland region of Labrador. The capital and largest city is St. John's. For centuries the island has been important for the fishing, but mining is now the leading industry and Newfoundland is Canada's largest supplier of iron.

Newfoundland² n. A dog of a large breed, growing to 71 centimetres (28 inches) at the shoulder, with a broad head and square muzzle, a powerful body, and a dense, usually black coat. [Believed bred in NEWFOUNDLAND, Canada.]

New France. The French possessions in Canada in the colonial era. The name derived from the fur-trading Company of New France, but the region was formally proclaimed the royal province of New France by Louis XIV in 1663. Although French rule in Canada ended with the Peace of Paris in 1763, the feudal, or seigneurial, system instituted in the province by the French monarchy was not abolished formally until 1854.

New·gate (néw-git, -gayt ‖ nōō-). A famous prison in London, demolished in 1902.

New Greek n. *Abbr.* **NGk., N.Gr.** Modern Greek (see).

New Guinea. See **Papua New Guinea.**

New·ham (néw-əm, *sometimes* -ham ‖ nōō-). Borough of Greater London, England, lying north of the river Thames in the eastern part of the city.

New Hampshire. State in the northeast United States, lying between Vermont to the west and Maine to the east. The capital is Concord; the largest cities are Manchester and Nashua. The northern part of the state is noted for the scenic beauty of its lakes and mountains. The industrial centres to the south make the state one of the most heavily industrialised in the Union. One of the original Thirteen Colonies, New Hampshire was a founding member of the United States (1788).

New Haven. City and port in Connecticut, United States. It is famous as the site both of Yale University (since 1716) and of the

world's first commercial telephone exchange (1879).

New Hebrides. See **Vanuatu.**

New High German n. *Abbr.* **N.H.G. German** (see).

Ne Win (náy wín), **U,** born Maung Shu Maung (1911–). Burmese politician. After independence from the United Kingdom, he served as commander in chief (1948–58), then as defence minister and prime minister (1958–60, 1962–74). In 1974 he suspended the constitution and proclaimed himself President. He retired in 1981.

New Ireland. An island in Papua New Guinea.

new·ish (néwish ‖ nōō-) adj. Of fairly recent origin; fairly new.

New Jersey. State in the northeast United States, lying on the coast to the south of New York state and to the east of Pennsylvania. The capital is Trenton. The largest city is Newark. It is one of the most heavily populated and industrialised states. New Jersey was one of the original Thirteen Colonies and a founding member of the United States (1788).

New Jerusalem n. The celestial city; heaven. [From the Apocalypse (Revelation), chapter 21.]

New Jerusalem Church n. The church, founded in 1787, based on the philosophy and teachings of Swedenborg. Also called "New Church". See **Swedenborgianism.**

New Latin n. *Abbr.* **NL, NL., N.L.** The form of Latin in use, especially for scientific nomenclature, since the early Renaissance.

New Learning n. The revived study of the Bible and Greek and Latin classics in the original occurring in the 15th and 16th centuries in Renaissance Europe.

New Left n. A diffuse left-wing movement, especially amongst radical students, that began in many countries in the 1960s. —**New Left·ist** n.

New Look n. **1.** A fashion in women's clothing of the late 1940s characterised by long, full skirts. Preceded by *the.* **2.** *Small* **n,** *small* **l.** *Informal.* Any up-to-date fashion.

new·ly (néw-li ‖ nōō-) adv. **1.** Lately; recently: *newly baked bread.* **2.** In a new or different way: *an old idea newly phrased.*

new·ly-wed (néw-li-wed ‖ nōō-) n. A person recently married.

New·man (néw-mən ‖ nōō-), **John Henry** (1801–90). British poet and priest. As an Anglican he helped to found the Oxford Movement (1833); he later joined the Roman Catholic Church (1845), and was made a cardinal (1879). His best known works are *Apologia pro Vita Sua* (1864) and *The Dream of Gerontius* (1866).

Newman, Paul (1925–). U.S. film actor. Among his films are *Butch Cassidy and The Sundance Kid* (1969) and *The Color of Money* (1986, Oscar). He has also produced and directed films.

New·mar·ket¹ (néw-maarkit ‖ nōō-) n. *Sometimes small* **n. 1.** *British.* A long, close-fitting coat for men and women, worn especially in the late 19th century. Also called "Newmarket coat". **2.** A card game in which players gamble on their chances of duplicating cards on the table. [After NEWMARKET, Suffolk.]

Newmarket². Market town in Suffolk, in east England. It has been a famous racing town since the reign of James I. The course is crossed by the ancient earthwork known as Devil's Dyke. The four main races held annually are the One Thousand Guineas, the Two Thousand Guineas, the Cambridgeshire, and the Cesarewitch.

new maths n. *Used with a singular verb.* A form of mathematics introduced in schools and making use of set theory.

New Mexico. State in the southwest United States, lying to the south of Colorado and to the east of Arizona. The capital is Santa Fe; the largest city is Albuquerque. Most of the state consists of arid desert and forested mountain wilderness. New Mexico is the United States' leading supplier of uranium ore and a major supplier of manganese, potash, salt, and copper. Strong traces of Spanish culture remain: about a third of the population is of mixed Spanish descent, and Spanish is still the dominant language in many parts. New Mexico entered the Union in 1912.

New Model Army n. The British army as reorganized by the Parliamentarians in 1645 during the Civil War.

new moon n. **1.** The phase of the Moon occurring when it passes between the Earth and the Sun and is invisible, or visible only as a narrow crescent at sunset. **2.** The crescent Moon.

New Neth·er·land (néthərlənd). An area of land in the Hudson River Valley granted by Holland to the Dutch West India Company in 1621. The area included New Amsterdam, founded in 1624 on Manhattan Island (later New York City). The region was seized by England in 1664, when it was divided into the two colonies of New York and New Jersey.

New Or·le·ans (órli-ənz, ór-léenz). City in Louisiana, in the southern United States, on the banks of the Mississippi River. It is the largest city in Louisiana and a major port. It is famous for the surviving French flavour of its streetlife and nightlife, for its annual Mardi Gras carnival, and for its jazz and blues tradition, dating from the late 19th century. Andrew Jackson's forces defeated the British at the Battle of New Orleans in 1815.

New Orleans jazz n. The jazz played in New Orleans from 1900 to 1925, characterised by collective improvisation on simple harmonies by a front line of clarinet, trumpet, and trombone.

new penny n., *pl.* **new pence.** A coin of the United Kingdom, a **penny** (see).

New Plymouth. City on the west coast of North Island, New Zealand. It was founded by the New Plymouth Company in 1841 and for some years served as the landing point for settlers to New Zealand. It is now a busy commercial port and the distributing centre for the surrounding dairy-farming region.

New·port¹ (néw-pawrt ‖ nōō-, -pōrt) *Welsh* **Cas·new·ydd-ar-Wysg**

(kass-né-with-aar-wisk). Town in south Wales, lying on the Bristol Channel at the mouth of the river Usk (Wysg). Long an important port serving the west Monmouthshire coalfield, it is now a leading centre for the manufacture of steel.

Newport². Market town on the Isle of Wight, off the coast of southern England. It is situated at the navigable head of the river Medina, and is the island's administrative centre.

Newport News. City in Virginia, in the eastern United States, one of the world's largest shipbuilding and ship-repairing centres.

New·ry (néwr-i ‖ noor-i). Town in southeastern Northern Ireland, in county Down, lying on the river Clanrye and the Newry Canal.

news (newz ‖ nooz) n. *Used with a singular verb.* **1. a.** Information about recent events of general interest, especially as reported by the mass media. Often used in combination: *newsdesk.* **b.** A presentation or broadcast of such information. Also used adjectively: *news bulletin.* **2.** New information about a subject: *What's the news about John's operation?* **3. a.** A person, event, or the like that is a source of interest or provides scope for conversation. **b.** A subject that is given a great deal of coverage by the press, radio, and television: *The government's policies are still news after two years.* **4.** *Capital* **N.** Used as part of the title of certain newspapers: *News of the World.* **—good** (or **bad**) **news.** Something or someone regarded as highly desirable (or undesirable).

news agency n. An organisation that provides news coverage or collects news reports for subscribers, such as newspapers. Also called "press agency".

news·a·gent (néwz-ayjənt ‖ nooz-) n. *British.* A person with a shop that sells newspapers, magazines, stationery, and the like.

news·boy (néwz-boy ‖ nooz-) n. A boy who sells or delivers newspapers.

news·cast (néwz-kaast ‖ nooz-, -kast) n. A radio or television broadcast, often with commentary, of events in the news. [NEWS + (BROAD)CAST.] **—news·cast·er** n. **—news·cast·ing** n.

New Scotland Yard. The official name for **Scotland Yard** (see).

news·flash (néwz-flash) n. A short, usually unscheduled, announcement of news, a **flash** (see).

news·girl (néwz-gurl ‖ nooz-) n. A female newsboy.

news·let·ter (néwz-lettər ‖ nooz-) n. A printed periodical report devoted to news for members of a group such as a society or firm, or for subscribers with a particular common interest.

news·mong·er (néwz-mung-gər ‖ nooz-, -mong-) n. A person who spreads news; a gossip.

New South n. Those U.S. states of the South that were members of the Confederate States of America but were not among the 13 original colonies; especially, Alabama, Arkansas, Mississippi, Tennessee, and Texas.

New South Wales. State in southeastern Australia, bounded on the east by the Pacific Ocean. The capital and largest city is Sydney. The state is economically the most important in Australia, the Sydney-Newcastle-Wollongong complex being the industrial heartland of the country. The leading product is steel.

New Spain. The former Spanish possessions governed from Mexico City, including islands in the West Indies, Central America north of Panama, Mexico, the southwestern United States, and the Philippine Islands.

news·pa·per (néwss-paypər, néwz- ‖ nooz-) n. **1.** A publication, typically issued daily or weekly, printed on folded sheets of paper, and containing news and opinion of current events, feature articles, and usually advertising. Also called "paper". **2.** A newspaper-publishing company. **3.** The paper on which a newspaper has been printed: *wrapped in newspaper.*

news·pa·per·man (néwss-paypər-man, néwz- ‖ nooz-) n., pl. **-men** (-men). *Chiefly U.S.* **1.** The owner or publisher of a newspaper. **2.** A journalist or editor employed by a newspaper.

news·pa·per·wo·man (néwss-paypər-woomən, néwz- ‖ nooz-) n., pl. **-women** (-wimmin). A female newspaperman.

New·speak (néw-speek ‖ noo-) n. Language that consists of or is full of jargon, propaganda, and ambiguities, especially as used by politicians or bureaucrats. [After the bureaucratic language in George ORWELL's novel, *1984.*]

news·print (néwz-print ‖ nooz-) n. **1.** Inexpensive paper made from wood pulp, used chiefly for printing newspapers. **2.** Printing ink: *hands covered in newsprint after reading the paper.*

news·read·er (néwz-reedər ‖ nooz-) n. A person who reads the news on television or the radio; a newscaster.

news·reel (néwz-reel ‖ nooz-) n. A short film that presents current events.

news·room (néwz-room, -room ‖ nooz-) n. A room in a newspaper office or radio or television station where news stories are researched, written, and edited.

news·stand (néwz-stand ‖ nooz-) n. An open booth or stand at which newspapers are sold.

New Style n. *Abbr.* **N.S.** The current method of reckoning the months and days of the year, according to the Gregorian calendar, as distinct from the former style of reckoning according to the Julian calendar.

news vendor n. *Chiefly U.S.* A person who sells newspapers, especially at a newsstand.

news·wor·thy (néwz-wurthi ‖ nooz-) adj. Of sufficient interest or importance to be reported as news.

news·y (néwzi ‖ noozi) adj. **-ier, -iest.** *Informal.* Full of news; informative.

newt (newt ‖ noot) n. Any small amphibian of the genus *Triturus* or related genera, having a long, slender body and tail and short legs. [Middle English, from the phrase *a newt(e),* originally *an ewt(e)* : *an* (indefinite article) + *ewt(e), evete,* EFT.]

new technology n. Technology and technological products developed during and since the 1970s and chiefly characterised by the use of microprocessors.

New Territories. The portion of Hong Kong leased by Great Britain from China in 1898 for 99 years. The area includes most of the former colony's islands and the greater part of its mainland north of Kowloon.

New Test. New Testament.

New Testament n. *Abbr.* **NT, N.T., New Test.** The Gospels, Acts, Pauline and other Epistles, and the Book of Revelation, which together have been viewed by Christians as forming the record of the new dispensation belonging to the Church, as distinct from the Old Testament dispensation shared with Judaism. Together with the Old Testament it makes up the Christian Bible. [Translation of Latin *Novum Testāmentum,* translation of Greek *Kainē Diathēkē,* "new dispensation, covenant, or testament" (Mark 14:24).]

new·ton (néwt'n ‖ noot'n) n. *Abbr.* **N** *Physics.* The SI unit of force, equal to the force required to accelerate a mass of one kilogram one metre per second per second. It is equal to 100,000 dynes. [After Sir Isaac NEWTON.]

New·ton (néwt'n ‖ noot'n), **Sir Isaac** (1642–1727). English mathematician and physicist. He devised calculus independently of Leibniz, and made important discoveries about light. His greatest work, however, is his treatise on gravitation (supposedly inspired by the sight of a falling apple), *Principia Mathematica* (1687).

New·to·ni·an (new-tōni-ən ‖ noo-) adj. Pertaining to or in accordance with the work of Newton, especially that in mechanics and gravitation: *Newtonian physics; a Newtonian explanation.*

Newtonian telescope n. A type of telescope in which light from a distant object is reflected by a large concave mirror onto an angled plane mirror, which directs the light into an eyepiece.

Newton's law of gravitation n. The principle that two bodies attract each other with a force that is directly proportional to the product of the masses and inversely proportional to the square of their distance apart. It is often written in the form $F = G\, m_1 m_2 / d^2$, where G is the gravitational constant.

Newton's laws of motion pl.n. Three laws describing motion, used as the basis for Newtonian mechanics. They are: a body continues in a state of rest or of uniform motion in a straight line unless it is acted on by external forces; the rate of change of momentum of a body is proportional to the external force; any force (*action*) on a system gives rise to an equal and opposite force (*reaction*).

new town n. Any of a number of towns built in Britain since 1946, planned and partly financed by central government as new areas of growth.

new wave n. *Often capital* **N,** *capital* **W. 1.** A movement in the French cinema in the 1960s, led by such directors as Godard and Resnais, that abandoned traditional narrative techniques in favour of greater use of symbolism and abstraction. Also called "Nouvelle Vague". **2.** A form of rock music developed from punk rock in the late 1970s, showing a more sophisticated and commercial approach. **3.** Any cultural movement that is considered to be avant-garde or in reaction against traditional methods, styles, or techniques. [Originally, translation of French *nouvelle vague.*]

New World n. The countries of the Western Hemisphere; North and South America, and adjacent islands.

new year n. **1.** The year about to begin or just begun. **2.** *Capital* **N,** *capital* **Y.** The first day or days of the calendar year. **3. Rosh Hashanah** (see).

New Year's Day n. The first day of the year, as reckoned according to the Gregorian calendar; January 1.

New Year's Eve n. The eve of New Year's Day; December 31.

New York¹. State in the northeast United States, bordering on Canada to the west and north and on Pennsylvania and New Jersey to the south. The capital is Albany; the largest city is New York. The other major cities, Buffalo, Rochester, and Syracuse, lie near the New York State Barge Canal which crosses the central region of the state from east to west. In the regions between New York's many industrial and commercial towns and cities lie rich mixed farming land. The state's origins can be traced to 1664, when England seized from the Dutch the land around the Hudson river known as New Netherland and divided it into the colonies of New York and New Jersey. New York was thus one of the original 13 colonies and was also a founding member of the United States (1787).

New York². Largest city in the United States, lying on the northeast coast, at the mouth of the Hudson river on New York bay. It consists of five boroughs: Manhattan (an island), Queens and Brooklyn (both on Long Island), Richmond (on Staten Island), and the Bronx (on the mainland). The metropolitan area of the city spills over into New Jersey and Connecticut. New York is one of the world's busiest ports. Since the end of World War II the city has gradually replaced London as the world's financial centre, and is the artistic and publishing centre of the United States. Many of its streets, such as Wall Street (finance), Broadway (the theatre), Madison Avenue (advertising), and Fifth Avenue (shopping) have become world famous. New York's population, including large numbers of blacks, Puerto Ricans, and European immigrants, is the most ethnically varied of any American city. It dates from the establishment of New Amsterdam on Manhattan Island in 1624.

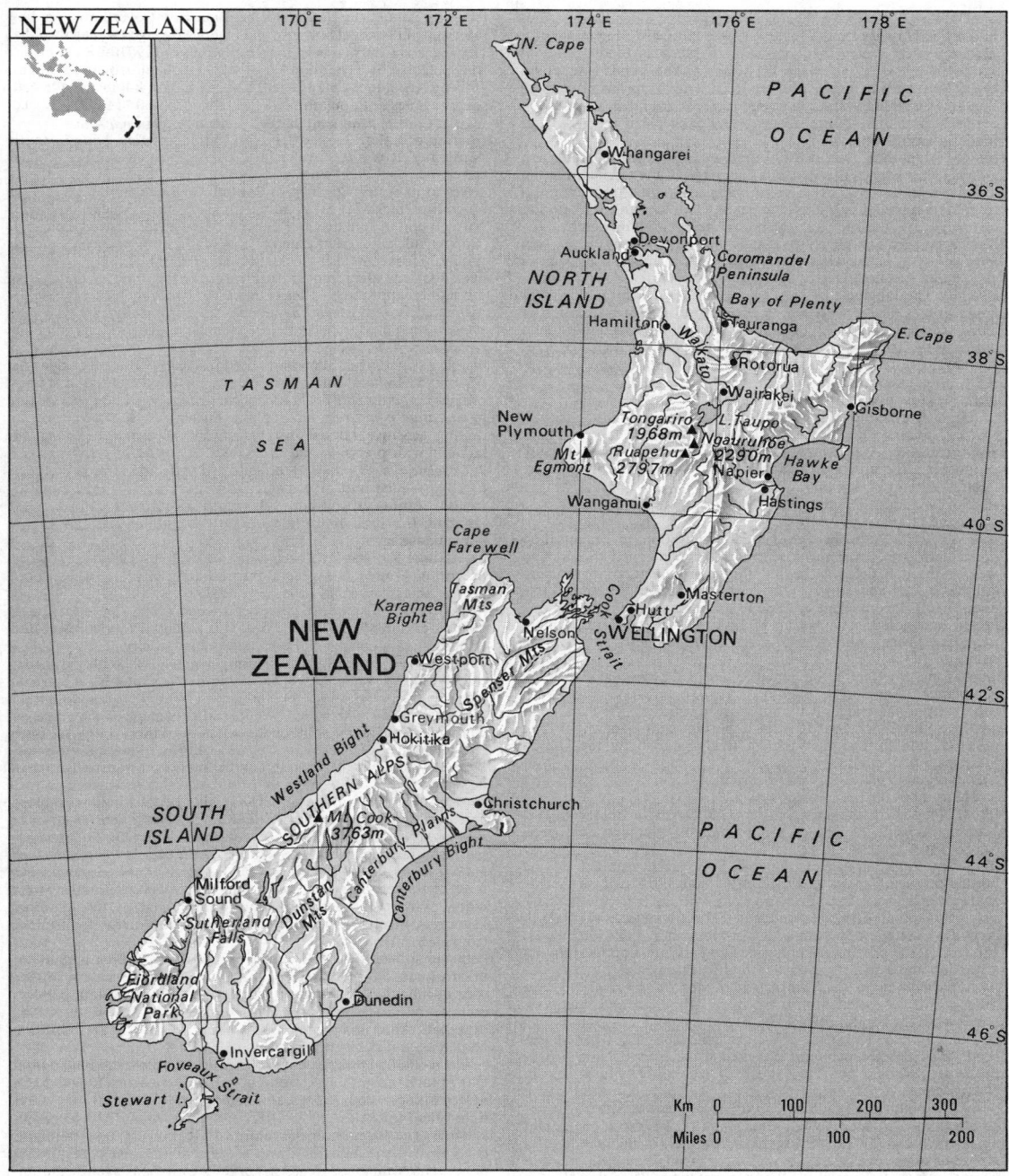

NEW ZEALAND

170°E · 172°E · 174°E · 176°E · 178°E

N. Cape

PACIFIC OCEAN

Whangarei

36°S

Auckland · Devonport

Coromandel Peninsula

NORTH ISLAND

Bay of Plenty

Hamilton · Waikato · Tauranga

E. Cape

38°S

Rotorua

Wairakei

Gisborne

TASMAN SEA

New Plymouth

Tongariro 1968m

L. Taupo

Ngauruhoe 2290m

Mt Egmont

Ruapehu 2797m

Napier

Hawke Bay

Wanganui

Hastings

40°S

Cape Farewell

Tasman Mts

Cook Strait

Masterton

Karamea Bight

Nelson

Hutt

WELLINGTON

NEW ZEALAND

Westport

Spenser Mts

42°S

Greymouth

Hokitika

Westland Bight

SOUTHERN ALPS

Christchurch

PACIFIC OCEAN

SOUTH ISLAND

Mt Cook 3763m

Canterbury Plains

Canterbury Bight

44°S

Milford Sound

Dunstan Mts

Sutherland Falls

Fiordland National Park

Dunedin

46°S

Invercargill

Foveaux Strait

Stewart I.

Km 0 · 100 · 200 · 300
Miles 0 · 100 · 200

New Zea·land (zēēlənd). Independent dominion within the Commonwealth, consisting of two main islands, North Island and South Island, and some smaller islands, lying in the southwest Pacific Ocean southeast of Australia. The islands are poor in natural resources and the mainstay of the country's economy is the export of agricultural products, especially meat and dairy products. The population is predominantly of British stock; the indigenous Maoris make up less than ten per cent of the total. The islands were first settled by Polynesians in the 9th or 10th century. New Zealand became a British colony in 1840, received a large measure of self-government in 1852, and was granted dominion status in 1907. Area, 269 057 square kilometres (103,883 square miles). Population, 3,570,000. Capital, Wellington. —**New Zea·land·er** n.

New Zealand flax n. See **phormium.**

Nex·ø (nég-sö), **Martin Andersen** (1869–1954). Danish novelist. One of Denmark's greatest literary figures, he did not begin his formal education until he was 20. Among his novels are *Pelle the Conqueror* (4 volumes, 1906–10) and *Ditte, the Daughter of Man* (5 volumes, 1917–21), which, like his other works, reflect a Marxist philosophy influenced by a childhood in the slums of Copenhagen.

next (nekst) *adj.* **1.** Nearest in space; adjacent: *the next room.* **2.** Coming directly after in time or sequence; immediately succeeding: *next Monday; the next person on the list.*
~*adv.* **1.** In the time, order, or place immediately following. **2.** On the first subsequent occasion: *when next I write.* —**next to. 1.** Adjacent to; in the closest place to: *the car next to yours.* **2.** Following in order or degree: *Next to drinking he likes sleeping best.* **3.** *Informal.* Almost; practically: *next to impossible.*
~*prep. Archaic.* Next to: *next my skin.*
~*n.* The next person or thing: *The next will be better.* [Middle English *nexte,* Old English *nēahst, nēhst,* superlative of *nēah,* near.]

Usage: In the sense "coming directly after in time or sequence", *next* is generally unambiguous. For example, there is no ambiguity about referring to *next Friday,* if said on Tuesday; but if said on Thursday, a time reference of eight days hence would usually be intended; and if said on Wednesday, there would often be uncertainty as to which of the two Fridays was in question. The use of *this* as a way out of the problem (*this Friday:* the Friday of this week) is thus very common. *Next* and *nearest* are sometimes interchangeable, but not always. *Next* always indicates direct succession in a series. *Nearest,* which does not necessarily imply a sequence, is employed more generally to indicate the closest proximity, as in time, space, or kinship.

next door *adv.* To or in the adjacent house or building. —**next-door** (nĕkst-dór ‖ -dôr) *adj.*

next friend *n. Law.* One who is admitted to court to sue as the representative of a minor or other person under legal disability.

next of kin *n., pl.* **next of kin. 1.** The person most nearly related to one by blood. **2.** *Law.* **a.** The closest relative of a deceased person. **b.** *Used with a plural verb.* Those relatives entitled to the estate of a deceased person in accordance with the statutes of distribution.

nex·us (néksəss) *n., pl.* **nexus** or **-uses. 1.** The bond, link, or tie existing between members of a group or series; a means of connection between things. **2.** A connected series or group. **3.** *Anatomy.* A connection or link. [Latin, from *nectere* (past participle *nexus*), to bind, connect.]

Ney (nay), **Michel, Duc d'Elchingen et Prince de la Moskowa** (1769–1815). French marshal. His command of the rearguard in the retreat from Moscow (1812) saved Napoleon's army from annihilation. He deserted Louis XVIII to rejoin Napoleon in the Waterloo campaign. He was shot for treason by the restored monarchy.

Nez Percé (néz pérss, néss, paúrss; *French* nay pair-sáy) *n., pl.* **Nez Percés** (-iz) or collectively **Nez Percé. 1.** A member of an American Indian people formerly occupying much of the Pacific Northwest. **2.** The language of this people, of the Sahaptin family of languages. [Canadian French, "pierced nose", either translation of Salish *Chopunnish*, "Nez Percé", or from the pierced nose sign whereby the tribe was designated in Salishan sign language, presumably with reference to the custom of wearing ornamental seashells on pierced noses.]

Nfld. Newfoundland.

N.F.U. National Farmers' Union (in Britain).

N.G.A. National Graphical Association (in Britain).

ngai·o (nǐ-ō) *n.* A small tree, *Myoporum laetum*, of New Zealand, producing a useful wood. [Maori.]

n'gana. Variant of **nagana.**

NGC *New General Catalogue of Nebulae and Clusters of Stars*: a catalogue of over 8,000 entries.

NGO *n., pl.* **NGOs.** *Nongovernmental organisation*: an organisation not under direct government control that is concerned with human welfare in such fields as health, the environment, or economics.

ngul·trum (əng-gúltrəm) *n.* The monetary unit of Bhutan, introduced in 1974, equivalent in value to an Indian rupee. [Bhutanese.]

Ngu·ni (əng-gōoni) *n.* A group of languages of the Bantu family, including Swazi, Xhosa, and Zulu, spoken chiefly in southern Africa.

ngwee (əng-gwáy) *n.* A coin equal to ¹/₁₀₀ of the kwacha of Zambia. [Chibemba, "bright".]

Nha Trang (nyaá tráng). City and port in southern Vietnam, lying on the South China Sea. It is an important centre for the fishing industry, and during the Vietnam war was used by the United States as a major military base.

NHS National Health Service (in Britain).

Ni The symbol for the element nickel.

N.I. 1. National Insurance (in Britain). **2.** Northern Ireland.

ni·a·cin (nǐ-ə-sin) *n.* One of the B vitamins, **nicotinic acid** *(see).* [NI(COTINIC) AC(ID) + -IN.]

Ni·ag·a·ra Falls (nǐ-ággərə, -ággrə). Spectacular cataract on the border between Canada and the United States, situated on the Niagara river between Lake Erie and Lake Ontario. The cataract consists of two main falls, the American Falls (51 metres; 167 feet) in New York state and the Canadian, or Horseshoe, Falls (48 metres; 158 feet) in the province of Ontario. The Falls are a popular tourist attraction and a major supplier of hydroelectric energy.

Nia·mey (nyaa-máy). Capital of Niger, lying on the river Niger in the southwest of the country. It is Niger's largest city and chief port. It has been the capital since 1926.

nib (nib) *n.* **1. a.** The point of a quill pen, especially when sharpened. **b.** A tapered penpoint designed to be inserted into a penholder or fountain pen. **2.** A beak or bill, as of a bird; a neb. **3.** Any small, sharp, projecting part. **4.** *Plural.* Crushed cocoa beans. [Probably of Low German origin, variant of NEB.]

nib·ble (nǐbb'l) *v.* **-bled, -bling, -bles.** —*tr.* **1.** To bite at gently and repeatedly. **2. a.** To eat with small, quick bites, in the manner of a mouse or other small creature. **b.** To eat in small amounts: *nibble a biscuit.* —*intr.* **1.** To take small or hesitant bites: *The fish nibbled at the bait.* **2.** To raise petty objections or criticisms; carp. Used with *at.* **3.** To show cautious interest. Used with *at.* —*n.* **1.** A small quantity, especially of food; a bite; a morsel. **2.** An act or instance of nibbling. **3.** *Computing.* Half a **byte** *(see).* [Probably from Low German *nibbeln, knibbeln*, to gnaw, nibble.]

Ni·be·lung (néebə-lŏong) *n., pl.* **-lungs** or **-lungen** (-ən). *Germanic Mythology.* **1.** Any of a race of subterranean dwarfs who possessed a hoard of riches and a magic ring, taken from them by Siegfried. **2.** Any of the followers of Siegfried. **3.** Any of the Burgundian kings in the *Nibelungenlied.* [German, from Middle High German *Nibelungen*, probably corresponding to a tribal name *Nebulones*, perhaps from Old High German *nëbul*, mist.]

Ni·be·lung·en·lied (néebə-lŏong-ən-leet) *n.* A Middle High German epic poem written in the early 13th century by an unknown author, based on the legends of Siegfried and the Burgundian kings.

nib·lick (nǐbblik) *n.* A golf club, a **nine iron** *(see).* [19th century : origin obscure.]

nibs (nibz) *n.* *Used with a singular verb. Informal.* A person who is in authority or who is self-important. Used humorously in the expression *his nibs.* [19th century : akin to earlier (cant) *nabs†* (as in *his nabs,* himself).]

Nic·a·rag·u·a (nickə-rággew-ə, -raágwə). Largest republic on the Central American mainland. It is sparsely populated, and the mainstay of the economy is agriculture—cotton, coffee, rice, sugar, and tobacco. Nicaragua was a Spanish possession until 1821. In 1979 the left-wing Sandinista National Liberation Front overthrew the dictatorship of President Somoza; and from 1982 waged war against the U.S.-backed Contra rebels. In free elections in 1990, the Sandinistas were defeated by a coalition led by Violeta Chamorro, and again in 1996 by Arnoldo Alemán. Area, 120 254 square kilometres (46,430 square miles). Population, 4,240,000. Capital Managua. See map at **Central American States.** —**Nic·a·ra·guan** *adj.* & *n.*

Nicaragua, Lake. Largest lake in Central America, lying in south Nicaragua. It is a freshwater lake, but supports a number of saltwater fish, especially tuna and sharks, which have adapted themselves to its water. See map at **Central American States.**

nic·co·lite (níckə-līt) *n.* A nickel ore, essentially nickel arsenide, NiAs, found in America and Europe. Also called "arsenical nickel", "copper nickel", "kupfernickel". [New Latin *niccolum,* nickel, probably from Swedish *nickel,* NICKEL + -ITE.]

nice (nīss) *adj.* **nicer, nicest. 1.** Pleasing to the mind or the senses; attractive; appealing: *a nice dress.* **2.** Kind; considerate; well-mannered: *a nice person.* Sometimes used ironically: *That's a nice thing to say!* **3.** Morally upright; virtuous: *a nice girl, careful of her reputation.* **4.** Showing refinement or delicacy; proper; seemly: *a nice way of putting it.* Sometimes used ironically: *You have some nice friends!* **5.** *Archaic.* Difficult to please; fastidious; exacting: *"Good company requires only birth, education, and manners, and with regard to education is not very nice."* (Jane Austen). **6. a.** Showing or requiring sensitive critical discernment; subtle: *a nice distinction.* **b.** Done with precision and skill; deft: *a nice bit of craftsmanship.* **7.** *Obsolete.* **a.** Wanton; profligate. **b.** Affectedly modest; coy. **c.** Silly. —**nice and.** Pleasingly: *nice and cosy.* [Middle English, foolish, wanton, shy, from Old French, silly, from Latin *nescius,* ignorant, from *nescire,* to be ignorant : *ne-,* not + *scīre,* to know.] —**nice·ness** *n.*

Usage: Nice has long been criticised by stylists as a "lazy" word in writing — used as a general-purpose term of praise where more precise adjectives could have been used.

Nice (neess). Capital of the *département* of Alpes-Maritimes, France, on the Mediterranean Sea. It is a famous tourist resort and important as a commercial port and industrial city.

nice·ly (nǐss-li) *adv.* **1.** In a pleasing manner. **2.** With precision; exactly: *nicely balanced.* **3.** Satisfactorily; acceptably: *That'll do nicely.*

Ni·cene Creed (nǐ-séen) *n.* **1.** A formal statement of the tenets of Christian faith, and chiefly of the doctrine of the Trinity, set forth by the Council of Nicaea in A.D. 325. **2.** Any of several modifications of this statement, now used in the services of various Christian churches.

ni·ce·ty (nǐ-səti) *n., pl.* **-ties. 1.** The quality of showing or requiring careful and precise treatment; delicacy; subtlety: *the nicety of a diplomatic exchange.* **2.** Delicacy of character or feeling; scrupulousness; fastidiousness. **3.** A subtle point, detail, or distinction: *He left the niceties of spelling to his secretary.* **4.** An elegant or refined characteristic or feature; an amenity: *niceties of dress.* —**to a nicety.** With the utmost care and precision; exactly. [Middle English *nicete,* nicety, foolishness, from Old French *nicete,* foolishness, from *nice,* silly, NICE.]

niche (nich, neesh) *n.* **1.** A recess in a wall for holding a statue or other ornament. **2.** Any steep, shallow recess or concavity, as in a rock or hill. **3.** A situation or activity specially suited to a person's abilities or character. **4.** *Ecology.* **a.** The role and status of an organism within the community it occupies. **b.** The area within a habitat occupied by an organism. ~*tr.v.* **niched, niching, niches.** To place in a niche. [French, from Old French *niche,* "nest", from *nicher,* to nest, from Vulgar Latin *nīdicāre* (unattested), from Latin *nīdus,* nest.]

Nich·o·las I (níckələss) (1796–1855). Russian Tsar (1825–55). A reactionary, he suppressed the reformist Decembrist movement and strengthened the autocracy with the aid of censorship and secret police. His willingness to assist Turkey's Christians against the sultan involved him in the humiliations of the Crimean War (1853–56). The outstanding achievement of his reign was the codification of all existing laws.

Nicholas II (1868–1918). The last Russian Tsar (1894–1917). He pursued a policy of expansionism in the Balkans and Asia. This culminated in Russia's humiliating defeat in the Russo-Japanese War (1904–05), and the 1905 Revolution. Internal difficulties, reverses during World War I, the unpopularity of the court under Rasputin and the Tsarina, and governmental incompetence all helped to precipitate the 1917 Revolution. Forced to abdicate, he and his family were shot by Bolsheviks at Ekaterinburg (Sverdlovsk).

Nicholas, Saint (fourth century A.D.). Patron saint of children, sailors, and Russia. Believed to have been Bishop of Myra, he is attributed with charitable works and miracles; the practice of giving presents on his feast day (6th December) has been transferred to Christmas. He has passed into folklore as "Father Christmas" or "Santa Claus".

Nich·ol·son (níck'l-sən), **Ben** (1894–1982). British painter. He began by specialising in the still life, and progressed to more abstract works.

Nicholson, Jack (1937–). U.S. film actor, with Oscars for *Easy Rider* (1969), *One Flew Over the Cuckoo's Nest* (1976), *Terms of Endearment* (1984), and *As Good as it Gets* (1997).

Ni·chrome (nǐ-krōm) *n.* A trademark for an alloy of nickel, iron, and chromium. It has a high resistance and is used in electrical heating elements.

nick (nik) n. **1.** A shallow notch, cut, or indentation on a surface. **2.** *Printing.* A groove down the side of a piece of type used to ensure that it is correctly placed. **3.** *British Slang.* A prison or police station. **—in good** (or **bad**) **nick.** *Informal.* In good (or bad) working order or condition. **—in the nick of time.** Just at the critical moment; just in time.
~v. **nicked, nicking, nicks.** —*tr.* **1.** To cut a nick or notch in. **2. a.** To make an incision into (a horse's tail) at the root and reset certain muscles to make the horse carry it higher. **b.** To do this to (a horse). **3.** *British Slang.* **a.** To steal. **b.** To arrest. **4.** *U.S. Slang.* To cheat, especially by overcharging. —*intr.* **1.** To mingle or mate together successfully. Used of breeding stock. **2.** *Australian Informal.* To make a hurried or quick departure. Used with *off.* [Middle English *nyke*† (noun).]

nick·el (nick'l) n. **1.** *Symbol* **Ni** A silvery, hard, ductile, ferromagnetic metallic element. It is used in alloys, in corrosion-resistant surfaces and batteries, and for electroplating. Atomic number 28, atomic weight 58.71, melting point 1,555°C, boiling point 2,837°C, relative density 8.902, principal valency 2. **2.** A U.S. coin worth five cents, made of a nickel and copper alloy.
~*tr.v.* **nickelled, -elling, els.** To coat with nickel. [Shortened from German *Kupfernickel,* "copper-demon", an old mining term for niccolite, from which nickel was first extracted (so called because it appeared to contain copper but did not) : *Kupfer,* copper, from Old High German *kupfar,* from Late Latin *cuprum, cyprum,* COPPER + *nickel,* demon, dwarf, from *Nickel,* familiar form of the name *Nikolaus,* NICHOLAS (probably by association with *Nix,* sprite, NIX).]

nickel bloom n. A rare mineral, **annabergite** *(see).*

nick·el·ic (ni-kéllik) adj. Of or containing nickel. Said especially of compounds containing nickel with a valency of 3.

nick·el·if·er·ous (nícka-lífferass) adj. Bearing or containing nickel. Said of ores.

nick·el·o·de·on (nícka-lódi-an) n. *U.S.* **1.** In the early 20th century, a cinema charging an admission price of five cents. **2.** A juke box or player piano. [NICKEL + (MEL)ODEON.]

nick·el·ous (nickalass) adj. Of or containing nickel. Said especially of compounds containing nickel with a valency of 2.

nickel plate n. **1.** A thin layer of nickel on a metal surface, usually formed by electrolysis. **2.** Material or articles with such a layer.

nick·el-plate (nick'l-pláyt) *tr.v.* **-plated, -plating, -plates.** To deposit a thin, even layer of nickel on (a surface of metal or other conducting material), as by the electrolysis of a solution containing nickel.

nickel silver n. A silvery, hard, corrosion-resistant, malleable alloy of copper, zinc, and nickel, used in tableware. Also called "albata" and formerly "German silver".

nick·er[1] (nickar) *intr.v.* **-ered, -ering, -ers.** To neigh quietly. Used of a horse. [Perhaps from NEIGH.] **—nick·er** n.

nicker[2] n. *British Slang.* One pound sterling. [20th century : origin obscure.]

Nick·laus (ník-lowss), **Jack (William)** (1940-). U.S. golfer. He has won 18 major international titles, including six U.S. Masters' championships. He also designs golf courses.

nick-nack. Variant of **knick-knack.**

nick·name (nick-naym) n. **1.** A name added to or replacing the actual name of a person, place, or thing, often used humorously or affectionately and referring to some notable characteristic. **2.** A familiar or shortened form of a proper name.
~*v.* **nicknamed, -naming, -names.** To give a nickname to; call by a nickname. [Middle English *a nekename,* originally *an ekename,* an extra name : *eke,* an addition, Old English *ēaca* + NAME.]

nick point. *U.S.* Variant of **knickpoint.**

Nicobar Islands. See **Andaman and Nicobar Islands.**

Nic·o·de·mus (nícka-déemass). A Pharisee and member of the Sanhedrin who was a secret disciple of Christ and provided his tomb.

Nic·ol prism (nick'l) n. *Physics.* A device for producing or analysing plane-polarised light, consisting of a piece of calcite cut at suitable angles and cemented with Canada balsam. It is used especially in microscopes to identify minerals within a thin slice of rock. Also called "polariser", "polaroid". [After William *Nicol* (1768–1851), British physicist who invented it.]

Nic·ol·son (nick'l-san), **Sir Harold (George)** (1886–1968). British diplomat and writer. An M.P. (1935–45), he published studies of poets, a biography of George V, and diaries and letters. He married the novelist and garden-planner Vita Sackville-West (1892–1962): *The Edwardians* (1930).

Nic·o·si·a (nícka-sée-a). Capital city of Cyprus, lying in the north central part of the island on the flat, arid Mesaoria Plain. It is the country's largest city and the chief trading centre. Since the Turkish invasion of 1974, its northern half has been in Turkish hands.

ni·co·ti·an·a (ni-kōshi-áana, -áyna ‖ -ánna) n. Any of various flowering plants of the genus *Nicotiana,* native to the Americas and Australia, and including ornamental species with fragrant flowers as well as the tobacco plant. [New Latin *herba nicotiana,* "herb of Nicot", after Jean *Nicot,* French ambassador at Lisbon, who, in 1560, sent some tobacco to Catherine de Médicis.]

nic·o·tin·a·mide (nícka-tínna-mīd, -téena-) n. The amide of nicotinic acid, having similar vitamin activity. [NICOTIN(E) + AMIDE.]

nicotinamide adenine dinucleotide n. **NAD** *(see).*

nicotinamide adenine dinucleotide phosphate n. **NADP** *(see).*

nic·o·tine (nícka-teen, -téen) n. A poisonous alkaloid, $C_5H_4NC_4H_7NCH_3$, derived from the tobacco plant, used as an insecticide. [French, earlier *nicotiane,* from NICOTIANA.]

nic·o·tin·ic (nícka-tínnik) adj. **1.** Of or pertaining to nicotine. **2.** Of or pertaining to nicotinic acid.

nicotinic acid n. A member of the vitamin B complex, C_5H_4NCOOH, essential for growth and synthesised for use in treating pellagra. Dietary sources include milk, yeast, and liver. Also called "niacin". [Often obtained by the oxidation of NICOTINE.]

nic·o·tin·ism (nícka-teen-iz'm) n. Nicotine poisoning.

nic·ti·tate (níkti-tayt) *intr.v.* **-tated, -tating, -tates.** Also **nic·tate** (ník-tayt, nik-táyt). To wink or blink. Used in technical contexts. **—nic·ti·ta·tion** (-táysh'n) n.

nictitating membrane n. Also **nictating membrane.** An inner eyelid in birds, reptiles, and some mammals that helps to keep the eye clean.

Nidaros. See **Trondheim.**

nid·der·ing, nid·er·ing (níddaring) n. *Rare.* A cowardly person; a wretch.
~adj. Base; cowardly; vile. [Earlier *nidering,* 16th-century misreading of Middle English *nithing,* Old English *nīthing,* wretch, coward, villain, from Old Norse *nīthingr,* from *nīth,* scorn.]

nid·dle-nod·dle (nídd'l-nodd'l) *intr.v.* **-dled, -dling, -dles.** To nod repeatedly or in a trembling way.
~adj. Nodding; unsteady. [Reduplication of NOD.]

nide (nīd) n. A nest or brood of pheasants. [Latin *nīdus,* nest.]

ni·dic·o·lous (ni-dickalass) adj. Born blind and helpless and therefore requiring a relatively long stay in the nest and protracted parental care for some time. Said of certain birds. [Latin *nīdus,* nest + *colere,* to inhabit.]

ni·dif·u·gous (ni-diffew-gass) adj. Born in a relatively well-developed state and soon able to leave the nest. Said of certain birds. [Latin *nīdus,* nest + *fugere,* to leave, flee.]

nid·i·fy (níddi-fī) *intr.v.* **-fied, -fying, -fies.** Also **nid·i·fi·cate** (níddi-fi-kayt) **-cated, -cating, -cates.** To make a nest. Used of birds. [Latin *nīdificāre* : *nīdus,* nest + *facere,* to make.] **—nid·i·fi·cant** (-kant) adj. **—nid·i·fi·ca·tion** (-fi-káysh'n) n.

nid-nod (nid-nod) v. **-nodded, -nodding, -nods.** —*intr.* To nod repeatedly. —*tr.* To nod (one's head) repeatedly. [Reduplication of NOD.]

ni·dus (ní-dass) n., pl. **-duses** or **-di** (-dī) **1.** A nest; especially one for the eggs of insects or spiders. **2.** A cavity where spores develop. **3.** *Pathology.* The seat of bacterial growth in a living organism; a focus of infection. [Latin *nīdus,* nest.]

niece (neess) n. The daughter of one's brother or sister, or of one's brother-in-law or sister-in-law. [Middle English *nece,* from Anglo-French, Old French *niece,* from Vulgar Latin *neptia* (unattested), from Latin *neptis,* granddaughter, niece.]

Niedersachsen. See **Lower Saxony.**

ni·el·lo (ni-éllō) n., pl. **-elli** (-éllee) or **-los. 1.** Any of several black compounds of sulphur with copper, silver, or lead, used to fill an incised design on the surface of another metal. **2.** A surface or object decorated with niello. **3.** The art or process of ornamenting metal surfaces with niello.
~*tr.v.* **nielloed, -loing, -los.** To decorate or inlay with niello. [Italian, from Medieval Latin *nigellum,* from Latin *nigellus,* blackish, diminutive of *niger,* black.] **—ni·el·list** n.

Niel·sen (néel-san), **Carl (August)** (1865–1931). Danish composer and conductor. His work (especially his six symphonies) experimented with tonality, harmony, and form.

Nie·mey·er (née-mī-ar), **Oscar** (1907-). Brazilian architect. He has had a major influence on South American architecture. His work can be seen in Rio de Janeiro and Brasilia.

Nie·möl·ler (née-möllar), **Martin** (1892–1984). German churchman. A U-boat captain in World War I, he became a Lutheran pastor (1924), and was later sent to a concentration camp (1937) for denouncing Nazism. In 1961 he was appointed one of the six presidents of the World Council of Churches.

Nier·stein·er (néer-shtīnar, -stīnar) n. A white Rhine wine. [After *Nierstein,* city in central Germany.]

Nie·tzsche (néecha), **Friedrich (Wilhelm)** (1844–1900). German philosopher. Rejecting the "slave morality" and values of Christianity in works such as *Also Sprach Zarathustra* (1883–91), he proposed a philosophy asserting the self and the "will to power".

Nie·tzsche·an·ism (née-chi-a-niz'm) n. Also **Nie·tzsche·ism** (néechi-iz'm). **1.** The philosophy of Nietzsche, based upon a distinction between thought and emotion, and emphasising the value of intense emotion in art and life. **2.** Nietzsche's doctrine of the **superman** *(see).* **—Nie·tzsche·an** adj. & n.

nieve (neev) n. *Scottish.* A fist. [Middle English, from Old Norse *hnefi*†.]

niff (nif) n. *British Slang.* A nasty or distasteful smell.
~*intr.v.* **niffed, niffing, niffs.** To have an unpleasant smell; stink. [Of dialect origin; perhaps akin to SNIFF.] **—niff·y** adj.

Nif·lheim, Nif·el·heim (nívv'l-haym) n. *Norse Mythology.* The realm of the dead. [Old Norse *niflheimr,* "home of mist" : *nifl,* mist + *heimr,* home.]

nif·ty (nifti) adj. **-tier, -tiest.** *Informal.* **1.** Stylish or pleasing. **2.** *British.* Nimble; agile. [Perhaps from MAGNIFICENT.]

Ni·ger[1] (níjar; *French* nee-zháir). Independent African republic. The largest nation in West Africa, it is landlocked. Its economy is based on livestock breeding and the export of cotton and groundnuts. Formerly a French possession, it became an independent republic in 1960. Area, 1 267 000 square kilometres (489,191 square miles). Population, 9,470,000. Capital, Niamey. See map, next page.

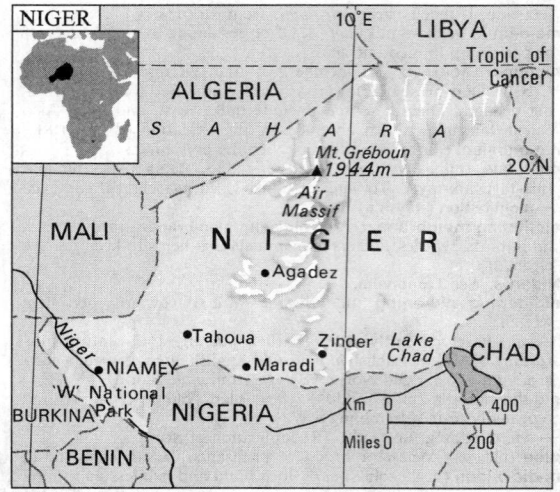

Niger². Third longest river in Africa (4 180 kilometres; 2,600 miles) rising in southwest Guinea on the Fouta Djallon plateau. It follows a roughly semicircular course through Mali, Niger, and Nigeria to the Gulf of Guinea. In Mali it forms a huge inland delta, comprising hundreds of channels and shallow lakes, used for irrigation, especially for rice production. The delta at its mouth, which is the largest in Africa, is an important source of petroleum and palm oil. Most of the Niger is navigable the year round.

Ni·ger-Con·go (níjər-kóng-gō) *n.* A large language family of Africa that includes the Mande, Gur, Kwa, and Bantu languages.

Ni·ge·ri·a (nī-jéer-i-ə), **Federal Republic of.** Independent republic in West Africa, by size the fourteenth largest, but by population the largest, country in Africa. The capital was Lagos, but is now Abuja in the central region of the country. Nigeria is self-sufficient in food and is also Africa's leading petroleum producer. Nigeria gained its independence from Great Britain in 1960, and became a member of the Commonwealth in that year. Recently criticised over human rights. Area, 923 768 square kilometres (356,669 square miles). Population, 115,020,000. **—Ni·ge·ri·an** *adj.* & *n.*

Niger seed *n.* The seed of the African plant **ramtil** (see), used as birdseed. [Probably first found near the NIGER River.]

nig·gard (níggərd) *n.* A stingy, grasping person; a miser. ~*adj.* Parsimonious; niggardly. [Middle English *nigart, niggard,* earlier *nigon,* from *nig,* a miser, from Scandinavian; akin to Swedish dialect *nygg,* from Old Norse *hnöggr,* miserly.]

nig·gard·ly (níggərdli) *adj.* **1.** Unwilling to part with anything; stingy. **2.** Meagre; insufficient. —See Synonyms at **stingy.** **—nig·gard·li·ness** *n.* **—nig·gard·ly** *adv.*

nig·ger (níggər) *n. Slang.* A Negro or member of any dark-skinned people. Used derogatorily. **—a nigger in the woodpile.** *Informal.* Something hidden that obstructs or upsets. [Earlier English dialectal *neeger, neger,* from French *nègre,* from Spanish *negro,* NEGRO.]

nig·gle (níg'l) *v.* **-gled, -gling, -gles.** —*intr.v.* **1.** To be preoccupied with trifles; worry over petty details; fret. **2.** To keep finding fault; complain trivially; carp. —*tr.v.* To annoy or irritate. [Probably from Scandinavian and akin to NIGGARD.] **—nig·gler** *n.*

nig·gling (níggling, níg'l-ing) *adj.* **1.** Excessively concerned with details; fussy. **2.** Persistently nagging; petty. **3.** Showing or requiring close attention to details; exacting: *niggling paperwork.* **—nig·gling·ly** *adv.*

nigh (nī) *adj.* **nigher, nighest** or **next.** *Archaic, Poetic, & Regional.* Close at hand; near. ~*adv. Archaic, Poetic, & Regional.* **1.** Near in time or location: *Night is drawing nigh.* **2.** Nearly; almost. Used with *on* or *onto: nigh on two hours.* ~*prep. Archaic & Regional.* Not far from; near to. [Middle English *neigh,* Old English *nēah.*]

night (nīt) *n.* **1. a.** The period between sunset and sunrise; especially, the hours of darkness. **b.** This period considered as a unit of time: *two nights running.* **c.** This period considered from the viewpoint of its conditions or events: *a starry night.* **2. a.** The period between evening and bedtime: *Tuesday night.* **b.** This period considered from the viewpoint of its activities or events: *a night at the opera.* **c.** This period set aside for a specific purpose or occasion: *Ladies' Night at the club.* **3. a.** The period between bedtime and morning: *spent the night at a friend's.* **b.** One's sleep during this period: *had a bad night.* **4. a.** Darkness: *vanished into the night.* **b.** The onset of darkness. **5.** Any time or condition of gloom, obscurity, ignorance, or sorrow. **—make a night of it.** To spend the evening or most of a night celebrating or in festivity. **—night and day.** Continuously; without stopping. ~*adj.* **1.** Pertaining to the night. **2.** Intended for use at night: *a night key.* **3.** Working or occurring during the night: *night shift; night porter.* [Middle English *niht, night,* Old English *niht, neaht.*]

night blindness *n.* Poor vision in the dark, **nyctalopia** *(see).* **—night·blind** (nīt-blīnd) *adj.*

night-bloom·ing cereus (nīt-blōoming) *n.* Any of several flowering cacti of the genus *Salenicereus* and related genera, having large, fragrant flowers that open at night.

night·cap (nīt-kap) *n.* **1.** A cloth head-covering worn especially in bed. **2.** A drink taken just before bedtime; especially: **a.** A milk drink. **b.** An alcoholic drink.

night·clothes (nīt-klōthz, -klōz) *pl.n.* Clothes, such as pyjamas or a nightdress, worn in bed.

night·club (nīt-klub) *n.* An establishment that stays open late at night and usually provides food, drink, dancing, and entertainment.

night·dress (nīt-dress) *n.* **1.** A loose dress, often long, worn in bed by women. **2.** Nightclothes.

night·fall (nīt-fawl) *n.* The approach of darkness; close of day.

night·gown (nīt-gown) *n.* **1.** A nightdress. **2.** A man's nightshirt.

night·hawk (nīt-hawk) *n.* **1.** Any of several American nightjars of the genus *Chordeiles,* having buff to black mottled feathers. Also called "bullbat", "mosquito hawk". **2.** *Informal.* A night owl.

night heron *n.* Any of several nocturnal herons of the genus *Nycticorax;* especially, *N. nycticorax,* which has black and white plumage and short legs, neck, and bill.

night·ie, night·y (nīti) *n., pl.* **-ies.** *Informal.* A nightdress.

night·in·gale (nīting-gayl) *n.* **1.** A European songbird, *Luscinia megarhyncha,* with brownish plumage, noted for its nocturnal song. **2.** Any of various similar songbirds. [Middle English *nihtyngale,* Old English *nihtegale,* "night-singer" : *niht,* NIGHT + *galan,* to sing.]

Night·in·gale (nīting-gayl), **Florence** (1820–1910). British nurse. Although nursing was not an accepted occupation for upper-class women of her day, she became superintendent of a London hospital (1853). In 1854 she attached herself to the army in the Crimea, and despite strong opposition reformed the medical services. On her return, she became a leading figure in the campaign for improved nursing care. She was the first woman to receive the Order of Merit (1907).

night·jar (nīt-jaar) *n.* Any of various nocturnal birds of the family Caprimulgidae; especially, the common European nightjar, *Caprimulgus europaeus,* having a dull-coloured, mottled plumage. [NIGHT + JAR (make a harsh sound).]

night latch *n.* A spring lock that may be opened from the inside by turning a knob, but from the outside only with a key.

night letter *n. U.S.* A telegram sent at night at a reduced rate.

night·life (nīt-līf) *n.* The entertainment or social activities, as in theatres or clubs, to be found in the evening or at night, especially in a particular area: *the London nightlife.*

night·light (nīt-līt) *n.* A dim light that is left on all night, especially for children or invalids.

night·long (nīt-lóng, -long) *adj.* Lasting through the whole night. ~*adv.* Through the night; all night.

night·ly (nītli) *adj.* **1.** Of or occurring during the night; nocturnal: *nightly prowlings.* **2.** Happening or done every night: *nightly rounds.* ~*adv.* Every night: *He visited her nightly.*

night·mare (nīt-mair) *n.* **1.** A dream arousing feelings of acute fear, dread, or anguish. **2.** An event or condition that evokes feelings of acute anguish or dread: *the nightmare of urban loneliness.* **3.** A demon or spirit formerly thought to plague sleeping people. ~*adj.* Like something in a nightmare; appalling: *a nightmare journey into the unknown.* [Middle English *nihtmare,* female incubus : NIGHT + *mare,* incubus, Old English *mare, mære,* goblin.] **—night·mar·ish** *adj.* **—night·mar·ish·ly** *adv.* **—night·mar·ish·ness** *n.*

night-night (nīt-nīt) *interj. Informal.* Goodnight.

night owl *n.* A person who habitually stays up late and is active at night.

night-rid·er (nīt-rīdər) *n.* Any of a band of mounted and usually masked white men who engaged in nocturnal terrorism in the southern United States after the Civil War. **—night-rid·ing** *n.*

nights (nīts) *adv. Informal.* At night: *He works nights.* [Middle English *nightes,* Old English *nihtes,* adverbial genitive of *niht,* NIGHT.]

night-scent·ed stock (nīt-sentid) *n.* An annual plant, *Matthiola bicornis,* native to Eurasia, whose purple flowers open at night and give out a heavy scent.

night school *n.* Classes or courses, especially of a vocational nature, held in the evening for people who are busy during the day.

night·shade (nīt-shayd) *n.* Any of several plants of the family Solanaceae, many of them having a poisonous juice; especially, the **deadly nightshade** *(see)* and the **bittersweet** *(both of which see).* See **enchanter's nightshade.** [Middle English *nighteschede,* Old English *nihtscada* : probably NIGHT + SHADE (since it was used in folk medicine as a soporific).]

night-shirt (nīt-shurt) *n.* A long, loose shirt worn in bed, especially by men.

night soil *n.* Human faeces collected for use as fertiliser.

night-spot (nīt-spot) *n. Informal.* A nightclub.

night-stick (nīt-stik) *n. U.S.* A policeman's truncheon.

night table *n.* A small table or stand placed at a bedside.

night-tide (nīt-tīd) *n. Chiefly Poetic.* Night-time.

night-time (nīt-tīm) *n.* The time between sunset and sunrise.

night watch *n.* **1.** A guard or watch kept during the night, as on a ship or encampment. **2.** A person who keeps watch at night. **3.** Any of the periods of a watch kept at night.

night watchman *n.* **1.** One who acts as guard during the night. **2.** An inferior batsman in cricket sent in to play out remaining time near the close of day, in order to prevent a better player from being dismissed.

nighty. Variant of **nightie.**

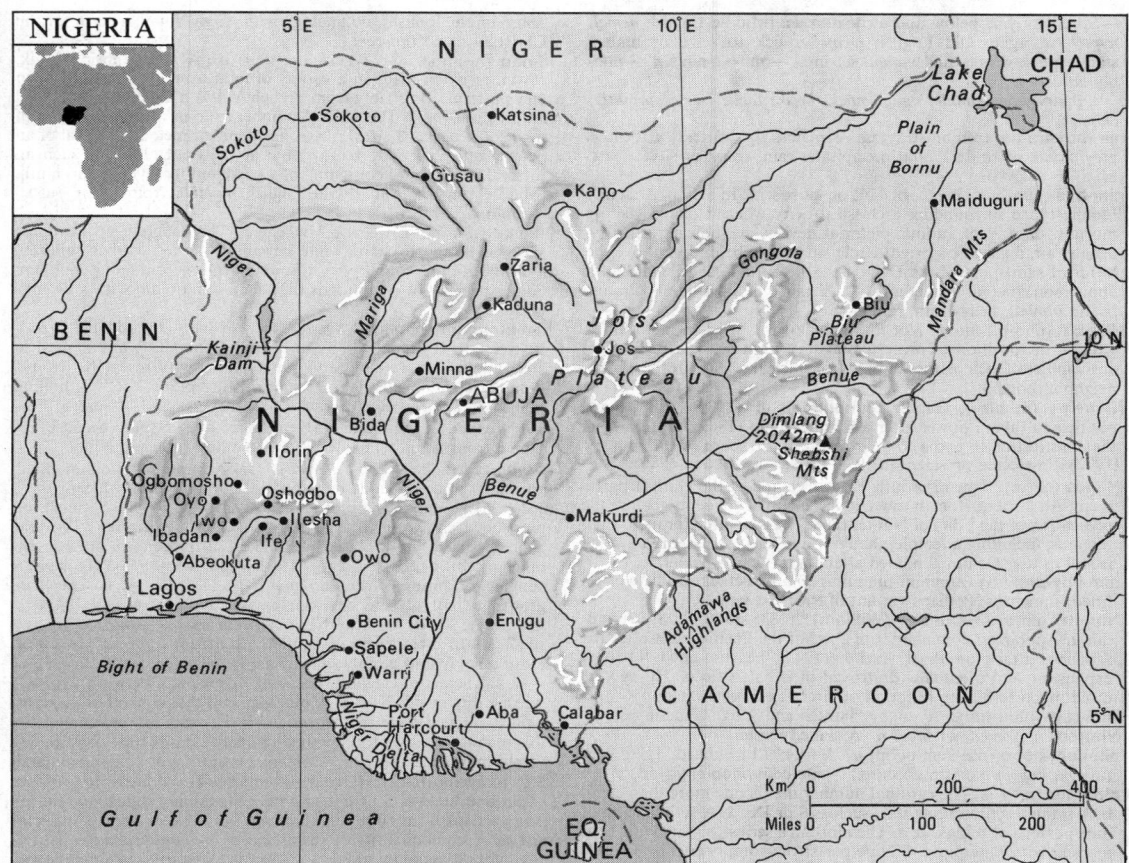

NIGERIA

nig·nog (níg-nog) n. Slang. A stupid person. [From obsolete dialect nigmenog†, fool.]

ni·gres·cence (nī-gréss'nss, ni-) n. 1. The process of becoming black or dark. 2. Blackness or darkness of hair, eyes, or skin. [Latin nigrescens (stem nigrescent-), from nigrescere, to become black, from niger, black.] —ni·gres·cent adj.

nig·ri·fy (níggri-fī) tr.v. -fied, -fying, -fies. Rare. To make black; blacken. [Late Latin nigrificāre : niger, black + facere, to make.]

nig·ri·tude (niggri-tewd, nīgri- ‖ -tood) n. Rare. Blackness. [Late Latin nigritūdō, from niger, black.]

ni·gro·sine (niggrə-seen, nīgrə-, -sin) n. Any of a class of dyes, varying from blue to black, used in the manufacture of inks and for dyeing wood and textiles. [Latin niger, black + -OS(E) + -INE.]

ni·hil (nī-hil, née-, ni-) n. 1. Nothing. 2. A thing of no value. [Latin, shortened from nihilum, nothing.]

ni·hil·ism (nī-i-liz'm, née-, -hi-, ní-hi-) n. 1. A metaphysical doctrine that nothing exists, is knowable, or can be communicated. 2. Philosophy. The rejection of all distinctions in moral value, and a willingness to repudiate all previous theories of morality. 3. The belief that destruction of existing political or social institutions is necessary to ensure future improvement. 4. A doctrine among the Russian intelligentsia of the 1860s and 1870s, advocating terrorism and denying all authority in favour of individualism. [Latin nihil, nothing.] —ni·hil·ist n. —ni·hil·is·tic (-lístik) adj.

ni·hil·i·ty (nī-hílləti, nee-, ni-) n. Non-existence; nothingness. [French nihilité, from Old French, from Medieval Latin nihilitās (stem nihilitāt-), from nihil, nothing.]

nihil ob·stat (ób-stat) n. 1. An attestation by a Roman Catholic censor that a book contains nothing damaging to faith or morals. 2. Official approval, especially of an artistic work. [Latin, "nothing hinders".]

Nihon. See Japan. [Japanese, "Land of the Rising Sun" : ni, the sun + hon, source, origin.]

Ni·jin·sky (ni-jín-ski, -zhín-), Vaslav (1890–1950). Russian ballet dancer. Starting his career with the Imperial Ballet School, St. Petersburg, he later joined Diaghilev's company in Paris, where he performed in such works as Petrushka (1911), and choreographed many ballets, including Le Sacre du Printemps (The Rite of Spring) (1913). Schizophrenia forced him to retire (1919).

Nij·me·gen (nī-maygən; Dutch náy-maykhə). German Nim·we·gen (nī-maygən). City in the east Netherlands, lying on the river Waal near the border with West Germany. It is one of the oldest cities in the Netherlands, having been founded by the Romans.

–nik n. suffix. Informal. Indicates: 1. A person involved with something specified; for example, computernik. 2. A person who has undergone a specified experience; for example, refusenik. 3. A person promoting a specified aim or cause; for example, peacenik.

[Russian -nik (as in SPUTNIK) and Yiddish -nik (agent suffix).]

Ni·ke (níkee). The Greek goddess of victory.

nil (nil) n. Nothing; 0. Used especially in scoring certain games. [Latin, contraction of NIHIL.]

Nile (nīl). River in northeast Africa, the longest in the world, about 6 700 kilometres (4,150 miles) from its remotest source in the highlands south of the equator to the Mediterranean Sea. It drains an area of about 2 850 000 square kilometres (1,000,000 square miles), or about one tenth of Africa. The trunk stream of the Nile is formed at Khartoum by the confluence of the Blue Nile and the White Nile. Only after Aswan, Egypt, site of the last of the river's cataracts, does the floodplain begin to widen. Since 4000 B.C., when the river spawned the rise of the early Egyptian civilisation, the waters of the Nile have supported, by irrigation, almost all of Egypt's agriculture and much of Sudan's.

Nile blue n. Light greenish blue.

Nile green n. Light bluish green.

nil·gai (nílgī) n. A large Indian antelope, Boselaphus tragocamelus, the male of which has a blue-grey coat with white underparts and short horns. The female is tawny brown and lacks horns. [Hindi nīlgāi, "blue cow" : Sanskrit nīla, blue + gāi, go, cow.]

nill (nil) v. nilled, nilling, nills. Archaic. —tr. Not to will; refuse. —intr. To be unwilling. [Middle English nilen, Old English nyllan : ne, not + wyllan, to wish.]

Ni·lo-Ham·ite (nīlō-hámmīt) n. A member of a group of Negroid peoples of eastern Africa.

Ni·lo-Ham·it·ic (nīlō-ha-míttik) n. A former designation for a number of languages that are now considered part of the Nilotic group.

Ni·lo-Sa·har·an (nīlō-sə-haár-ən) n. A large language family of Africa, including Chari-Nile and a number of smaller groups. —Ni·lo-Sa·har·an adj.

Ni·lot·ic (nī-lóttik) adj. 1. Belonging to the Nile or the Nile Valley. 2. Pertaining to a group of peoples in eastern Africa who constitute a distinctive Negroid race, characterised especially by their extreme height. 3. Pertaining to the languages of these peoples. ~n. A group of languages, including Dinka and Masai, considered as a family or as a branch of the Chari-Nile family. [Latin Nīlōticus, from Greek Neilōtikos, from Neilos, the NILE.]

nim¹ (nim) v. nimmed, nimming, nims. Archaic. —tr. 1. To take. 2. To steal; filch. [Middle English nimen, Old English niman.]

nim² n. A game in which two players alternately remove small objects from a collection, usually matchsticks arranged in rows, and attempt to take, or avoid taking, the last one. [20th century : probably special use of archaic NIM.]

nim·ble (nímb'l) adj. -bler, -blest. 1. Quick and agile in movement or action; deft: nimble fingers. 2. a. Quick at devising or understanding: a nimble mind. b. Cleverly contrived: a nimble trick.

—See Synonyms below and at **dexterous.** [Middle English *nemel, nym(b)yl,* agile, Old English *nǣmel,* quick to seize or understand, quick-witted, and *numol,* seizing.] **—nim·ble·ness** *n.* **—nim·bly** *adv.*

Synonyms: *nimble, agile, quick, brisk, facile, spry, sprightly, chipper.*

nim·bo·stra·tus (nímbō-stráytəss, -stráatəss || -stráttəss) *n.* A low, grey cloud, often dark, that precipitates rain, snow, or sleet. [NIMB(US) + STRATUS.]

nim·bus (nímbəss) *n., pl.* **-bi** (-bī) or **-buses.** **1.** In art: **a.** A cloudy luminescence surrounding a classical deity when depicted visiting mortals. **b.** Any of various pictorial devices symbolising sanctity, usually a radiance or a bright circle, appearing behind or above the heads of saints and of the Deity. **2.** A favourable or splendid aura about someone or something. **3.** A rain cloud, a nimbostratus. [Latin *nimbus,* heavy rain, rain cloud.]

NIM·BY (ním-bi) *interj. N*ot *i*n *m*y *b*ack *y*ard; used as a slogan to criticise the position of protesters against an unwanted project or development (such as the dumping of nuclear waste) in their own neighbourhood.

Ni·meir·y (ni-mīr-i), **Gaafar Muhammad al** (1930–). Sudanese politician. Taking power after a military coup (1969), he reformed the constitution to end a 17-year revolt in the south of the country (1972). Re-elected president in 1977, he was deposed in 1985.

Nîmes (neem). Town in south France, capital of the Gard département. An ancient Roman town, it was a Huguenot centre before the revocation of the Edict of Nantes (1685). It is notable for its Roman remains, including a temple, the Pont du Gard, and an arena which is still in use. Denim is named after it (French *de Nîmes).*

nim·i·ny-pim·i·ny (nímmini-pímmini) *adj.* Affectedly delicate or refined; mincing. [Perhaps variant of NAMBY-PAMBY.]

Nim·itz (nímmits), **Chester (William)** (1885–1966). U.S. fleet admiral. Appointed commander in chief of the Pacific Fleet after the Japanese attack on Pearl Harbor (1941), he contained Japanese expansion, and eventually destroyed their battle fleets. His success owed much to his appreciation of aircraft carrier strategy.

Nim·rod[1] (ním-rod). A mighty hunter and king. Genesis 10:8–9.

Nimrod[2] *n. Sometimes small* **n.** A skilled hunter.

nin·com·poop (nín-kəm-pōōp) *n.* A fool; a blockhead. [17th century *nicompoop* : origin obscure.] **—nin·com·poop·er·y** (-əri) *n.*

nine (nīn) *n.* **1. a.** The cardinal number that is one more than eight. **b.** A symbol representing this, such as 9 or IX. **2.** A set made up of nine persons or things. **3. a.** The ninth in a series. **b.** A playing card marked with nine pips. **4.** Nine parts; the components of a whole that has been divided into nine. **5.** A size, as in clothing, designated as nine. **6.** Nine hours after midnight or midday. **—dressed (up) to the nines.** Dressed in one's most formal clothes or very elaborately. [Middle English *ni(gh)en, nyne,* Old English *nigon.*] **—nine** *adj.* **—nine·fold** (nīn-fōld) *adj. & adv.*

nine days' wonder *n.* Something that creates brief interest or excitement.

nine iron *n.* In golf, an iron-headed club with a face slanted at a greater angle than any other iron. Also called "niblick".

nine·pin (nīn-pin) *n.* A skittle.

nine·pins (nīn-pinz) *n. Used with a singular verb.* The game of **skittles** *(see).*

nine·teen (nīn-téen) *n.* **1. a.** The cardinal number that is one more than 18. **b.** A symbol representing this, such as 19 or XIX. **2.** A set made up of 19 persons or things. **3.** The 19th in a series. **4.** A size, as in clothing, designated as 19. **—talk nineteen to the dozen.** To talk very quickly and at length; babble. **—nine·teen** *adj.*

1984, nineteen eight·y-four (nīn-teen áyti-fór || -áyt-ti-, -fōr) *n.* A totalitarian society in which government propaganda and control suppress free speech and create a dehumanised and regimented state. [From the title of George ORWELL's novel *1984,* which depicts a hypothetical totalitarian state.]

nine·teenth (nīn-téenth) *n.* **1.** The ordinal number 19 in a series. **2.** Any of 19 equal parts. **—nine·teenth** *adj. & adv.*

nineteenth hole *n.* A place, especially the club bar, where golfers gather for relaxation after a game. Used humorously.

nine·ti·eth (nīnti-ith, -əth) *n.* **1.** The ordinal number 90 in a series. **2.** Any of 90 equal parts. **—nine·ti·eth** *adj. & adv.*

nine to five *n. Chiefly British.* Usual office hours; working hours. **—nine-to-five** *adj. & adv.*

nine·ty (nīnti) *n., pl.* **-ties.** **1. a.** The cardinal number that is 10 more than 80. **b.** A symbol representing this, such as 90 or XC. **2.** A set made up of 90 persons or things. **3.** The 90th in a series. **4.** A size, as in clothing, designated as 90. **5.** *Plural.* **a.** The range of numbers from 90 to 99, considered as a range of age, price, temperature, or the like. **b.** *Often capital* **N.** The years numbered 90 to 99 in a century. Also used adjectivally: *nineties fashions.* **—nine·ty** *adj.*

Nin·e·veh (nínnivə). Capital of the ancient empire of the Assyrians, lying on the east bank of the river Tigris, opposite the modern Iraqi town of Mosul. It was at the height of its glory during the reigns of Sennacherib (704–681 B.C.) and Assurbanipal (699–626 B.C.). It fell to the combined forces of the Babylonians, Medes, and Scythians in 612 B.C. Excavation has uncovered magnificent remains.

nin·ja (nin-jə) *n., pl.* **-jas** or **-ja.** **1.** A Japanese spy or assassin, especially in feudal times, who was well versed in martial arts. **2.** *Informal.* A martial-arts expert. [Japanese, "practitioner of stealth", from *nin,* to be stealthy or invisible; endure, + *-ja* (from *sha*), person; -er.]

nin·ny (nínni) *n., pl.* **-nies.** A fool; a simpleton. [Perhaps from *innocent* (simple, foolish), on analogy with *Ninny,* familiar form for the Christian name *Innocent.*]

ni·non (née-non, nī-; *French* nee-nóɴ) *n.* A sheer fabric of silk, rayon, or nylon made in a variety of tight, smooth weaves or open lacy patterns. [Probably from French *Ninon,* a nickname for *Anne.*]

ninth (nīnth) *n.* **1.** The ordinal number nine in a series. **2.** Any of nine equal parts. **3.** *Music.* **a.** A harmonic or melodic interval of an octave and a second. **b.** The note at the upper limit of such an interval. **c.** A chord consisting of a triad and its seventh and ninth. [Middle English *nynthe,* Old English *nigotha,* from *nigon,* NINE.] **—ninth** *adj. & adv.*

Ni·o·be (nī-ə-bi, -ō-) *Greek Mythology.* The daughter of Tantalus; she was turned to stone while bewailing the loss of her children.

ni·o·bic (nī-ṓbik, -óbbik) *adj. Chemistry.* Of or containing niobium. Said especially of compounds that contain niobium with a valency of 5.

ni·o·bi·um (nī-ṓbi-əm) *n. Symbol* **Nb** A silvery, soft, ductile, metallic element. It occurs chiefly in columbite-tantalite, and is used in steel alloys, arc welding, and superconductivity research. Atomic number 41, atomic weight 92.906, melting point 2,468°C, boiling point 4,927°C, relative density 8.57, valencies 2, 3, 4, and 5. Formerly called "columbium". [New Latin, after NIOBE (because obtained from tantalite, named after Tantalus, father of Niobe).]

ni·o·bous (nī-ṓbəss) *adj. Chemistry.* Of or containing niobium. Said especially of compounds that contain niobium with a valency of 3.

nip[1] (nip) *v.* **nipped, nipping, nips.** *—tr.* **1. a.** To catch, pinch, or press between two surfaces or points, such as the fingers. **b.** To give a small, sharp bite to. Used of animals. **2.** To remove or sever by pinching, biting, or snipping. Usually used with *off.* **3.** To have a stinging or biting effect on: *nipped by the cold.* **4.** To check in growth or cut off the development of: *nip the scandal before it spreads.* **5.** *Slang.* To steal. Not in current usage. *—intr.* **1.** To give small, sharp bites. Used of animals. **2.** *British Informal.* To go or move quickly and nimbly: *nipped out to the shops.*

~n. **1.** The act of catching, pressing, or pinching between two surfaces; a bite or pinch. **2. a.** A pinch or snip that cuts off or removes a part: *He gave a nip to each corner.* **b.** The small piece removed in this manner. **3. a.** A sharp, stinging quality, as of frosty air. **b.** Severely sharp cold or frost. **4.** *Archaic.* A cutting or stinging remark. **5.** A pungent or sharp flavour; a tang: *the nip of Mexican cooking.* **—nip and tuck.** *U.S.* Neck and neck. [Middle English *nippen, nīpen,* perhaps from Old Norse *hnippa.*]

nip[2] *n.* A small quantity or sip of spirits: *a nip of brandy.*

~v. **nipped, nipping, nips.** *—tr.* To drink (spirits) in small doses: *He had been nipping brandy.* *—intr.* To take a nip or nips of spirits: *He nips all day.* [Short for *nipperkin,* probably from Dutch *nippertje,* a dram, from *nippen,* to sip.] **—nip·per** *n.*

ni·pa (née-pə, nī-) *n.* **1.** A large, distinctive palm, *Nypa fruticans,* of the Philippines and Australia, having long leaves much used for thatching. Also called "nipa palm". **2.** An alcoholic beverage made from the sap of this palm. [Spanish and Portuguese, from Malay *nipah.*]

nip·per (nippər) *n.* **1.** One that nips. **2.** *Plural.* Any of various devices for squeezing or snipping; especially, a small pair of pliers used for electrical work. **3.** The large claw of a crustacean. **4.** *Chiefly British Informal.* A young child.

nip·ping (nípping) *adj.* **1.** Sharp and biting, as cold air might be. **2.** Sarcastic. **—nip·ping·ly** *adv.*

nip·ple (nípp'l) *n.* **1. a.** The small conical protuberance near the centre of the mammary gland in females containing the outlets of the milk ducts. Also called "mamilla". **b.** A corresponding vestigial protuberance on the male chest. **2. a.** A teat on a nursing bottle. **b.** *U.S.* A baby's dummy. **3.** Any of various devices resembling a nipple in appearance or function: **a.** A regulated opening for discharging a liquid, as in a small stopcock. **b.** A pipe coupling threaded at both ends. **c.** A short extension of pipe to which a nozzle can be attached. **4.** A drilled bush screwed into a bearing to enable grease to be forced into the bearing from a grease gun. Also called "grease nipple". **5.** Any natural or geographic body or projection resembling a nipple, such as a mountain crest. [From earlier *neble, nible,* perhaps diminutives of *neb, nib,* a point, beak, NEB.]

nip·ple·wort (nípp'l-wurt || -wawrt) *n.* A plant, *Lapsana communis,* having a milky juice and small, yellow flower heads. [Formerly used in folk medicine to treat breast tumours.]

Nippon. See **Japan.** [Short for *Nippon-koku,* "land of the origin of the sun".] **—Nip·pon·ese** (níppə-néez, -néess) *adj. & n.*

nip·py (níppi) *adj.* **-pier, -piest.** **1.** Sharp or biting; nipping. **2.** *British Informal.* **a.** Active; vigorous; sharp; quick. **b.** Small but having a relatively powerful engine. Said of a motor vehicle. **—nip·pi·ly** *adv.* **—nip·pi·ness** *n.*

NIREX *n. N*uclear *I*ndustry *R*adioactive Waste *Ex*ecutive.

nir·va·na (neer-váanə, nur-) *n.* **1.** *Often capital* **N. a.** *Buddhism.* The state of absolute blessedness, characterised by release from the cycle of reincarnations and attained through the extinction of the self. **b.** *Hinduism.* A similar state in which reunion with Brahma is attained through the suppression of individual existence. **2.** Freedom from the pain and care of the external world; bliss. [Sanskrit *nirvāna,* "extinction (of individual existence)", from *nirvā,* to be extinguished, be blown out : *nir-, nis-*†, out + *vāti,* he blows.]

Ni·san, Nis·san (nī-san, níss'n, nee-sáan) *n.* In the Hebrew calendar, the seventh month of the civil year and the first of the religious year. Formerly called "Abib". [Hebrew *Nīsān,* from Akkadian *Nis-*

sanu, "the first month".]

ni·si (nī-sī) *adj. Law.* Coming into effect at a given date unless cause is shown for modification or nullification: *a decree nisi.* [Latin *nisi,* unless.]

nisi pri·us (prī-əss) *n. Abbr.* **n.p.** *Law.* **1.** In Britain: **a.** A trial of a civil cause before a single judge and a jury in Crown Court. **b.** Formerly, a trial before an assize court. **2.** In the United States: **a.** The court in which a civil action is tried before a judge and jury, as distinguished from an appellate court. **b.** The trial of a civil action before such a court: *cause of nisi prius.* [Medieval Latin, "unless before" (originally the first two words of a writ ordering a sheriff to provide a jury at the Westminster court on a fixed day, *unless* the judges of assize come to the county *before* this day).]

Nis·sen hut (níss'n) *n.* A prefabricated building of corrugated steel in the shape of half a cylinder, used as a military shelter. [After Lieutenant-Colonel Peter N. *Nissen* (1871–1930), British mining engineer.]

ni·sus (nī-səss) *n., pl.* **nisus.** Effort; endeavour; exertion; impulse. [Latin *nīsus,* from the past participle of *nītī,* to strive, endeavour.]

nit[1] (nit) *n.* **1.** The egg of a parasitic insect, such as that of a head louse or body louse. **2.** The young insect. **3.** *Plural.* Infestation with head lice. [Middle English *nite,* Old English *hnitu,* louse egg.] —**nit·ty** *adj.*

nit[2] *n. Chiefly British Informal.* A nitwit.

nit[3] *n.* A unit of luminance equal to 1 candela per square metre. [Latin *nitor,* brightness.]

nit[4] *n. Computing.* A unit of information equal to 1.44 bits. [From Napierian dig*it*.]

nit[5] *n. Australian Informal.* Watch; a lookout: *to keep nit.* [Origin obscure; perhaps akin to NIX (interjection).]

nit-pick·ing (nít-piking) *n. Informal.* Finding fault or arguing over insignificant details. —**nit-pick·ing** *adj.* —**nit-pick·er** *n.*

ni·tra·mine (nítrə-meen) *n.* **Tetryl** *(see).* [NITRO- + AMINE.]

ni·trate (nī-trayt) *n.* **1.** The radical NO_3^- or any compound containing it, as a salt or ester of nitric acid. **2.** Fertiliser consisting of sodium nitrate or potassium nitrate.

~*tr.v.* (*usually* nī-tráyt) **nitrated, -trating, -trates.** To treat with nitric acid or with a nitrate, usually to change an organic compound into a nitrate. [French : NITR(O)- + -ATE.] —**ni·tra·tion** (nī-tráy-sh'n) *n.*

ni·traz·e·pam (nī-trázzə-pam) *n.* A hypnotic drug widely used in the form of pills to induce sleep. A common trademark is Mogadon.

ni·tre, *U.S.* **niter** (nītər) *n.* **1.** **Potassium nitrate** *(see).* **2.** **Sodium nitrate** *(see).* [Middle English, from Old French, from Latin *nitrum,* from Greek *nitron,* of Semitic origin.]

ni·tric (nítrik) *adj.* Of, derived from, or containing nitrogen, especially in a valency state higher than that in a comparable nitrous compound. [French *nitrique* : NITR(O)- + -IC.]

nitric acid *n.* A transparent, colourless to yellowish, fuming, corrosive liquid, HNO_3, a highly reactive oxidising agent, used in the production of fertilisers, explosives, and rocket fuels. Formerly called "aqua fortis".

nitric oxide *n.* A colourless, poisonous gas, NO, produced as an intermediate during the manufacture of nitric acid from ammonia or atmospheric nitrogen.

ni·tride (nī-trīd) *n.* A compound containing nitrogen with another, more electropositive element. [NITR(O)- + -IDE.]

ni·trid·ing (nī-trīding) *n. Metallurgy.* The case-hardening of a ferrous alloy, such as steel, by heating it in ammonia.

ni·tri·fi·ca·tion (nítri-fi-káysh'n) *n.* **1.** The attachment of a nitro group to an organic compound either as an addition or substitution. **2.** The oxidation of ammonium compounds in the soil by nitrifying bacteria, which convert them into nitrates and nitrites.

ni·tri·fy (nítri-fī) *tr.v.* **-fied, -fying, -fies. 1.** To oxidise into nitric acid, nitrous acid, or any nitrate or nitrite, as by the action of nitrifying bacteria. **2.** To treat or combine with nitrogen or compounds containing nitrogen. [French *nitrifier* : NITR(O)- + -FY.] —**ni·tri·fi·er** *n.*

ni·tri·fy·ing bacteria (nítri-fī-ing) *pl.n.* Any of various soil bacteria, such as *Nitrosomonas* and *Nitrobacter,* that oxidise ammonia to nitrite or nitrite to nitrate.

ni·trile (nī-tril, -trīl) *n.* Also **ni·tril** (-tril). Any compound containing trivalent nitrogen, N^{-3}, in a cyanogen group. [NITR(O)- + -ILE.]

ni·trite (nī-trīt) *n.* Any salt or ester of nitrous acid. [NITR(O)- + -ITE.]

nitro-, nitr– *comb. form.* Indicates a compound containing the univalent group NO_2; for example, **nitrobenzene** ($C_6H_5NO_2$), **nitride.** [New Latin, from Latin *nitrum,* from Greek *nitron,* NITRE.]

ni·tro·ben·zene (nítrō-bén-zeen, -ben-zéen) *n.* A poisonous organic compound, $C_6H_5NO_2$, occurring either as bright yellow crystals or as an oily liquid, having the odour of almonds, used in the manufacture of aniline, insulating compounds, and polishes.

ni·tro·cel·lu·lose (nítrō-séllew-lōss, -lōz) *n.* **Cellulose nitrate** *(see).* Not in technical usage.

ni·tro·chlo·ro·form (nítrō-klórrə-fawrm, -kláwrə- ‖ -klórə-) *n.* A poison gas, **chloropicrin** *(see).*

ni·tro·gen (nítrəjən) *n. Symbol* **N** A nonmetallic element constituting nearly four-fifths of the air by volume, occurring as a colourless, odourless, almost inert diatomic gas, N_2, in various minerals and in all proteins. It is used in the manufacture of a wide variety of important compounds, including ammonia, nitric acid, TNT, and fertilisers. Atomic number 7, atomic weight 14.0067, melting point −209.86°C, boiling point −195°C, valencies 3, 5. [French *nitrogène* : NITR(O)- + -GEN.] —**ni·trog·e·nous** (nī-trójinəss) *adj.*

ni·tro·ge·nase (nítrəjə-nayz, -nayss) *n.* An enzyme that takes part in the fixation of atmospheric nitrogen.

nitrogen balance *n.* The difference between the amounts of nitrogen taken into and lost by the body or the soil.

nitrogen cycle *n.* **1.** The cyclic progression of natural chemical reactions to atmospheric nitrogen: the nitrogen either forms organic compounds in rainwater, or is fixed by nitrogen-fixing bacteria; it is then assimilated and metabolised by plants and animals, and returned by decomposition to the soil; here some is recycled as organic compounds by bacteria and fungi, and the remainder is returned to the atmosphere. **2.** The **carbon-nitrogen cycle** *(see).*

nitrogen dioxide *n.* A mildly poisonous brown gas, NO_2, often found in smog and internal-combustion engine exhaust fumes, and synthesised for use as a nitrating agent, catalyst, and oxidising agent. Also called "nitrogen peroxide".

nitrogen fixation *n.* **1.** The conversion of atmospheric nitrogen into nitrogenous compounds by natural agencies or by various industrial processes. **2.** The conversion by certain fungi and soil bacteria of atmospheric nitrogen or inorganic nitrogen compounds into organic compounds assimilable by plants. —**ni·tro·gen-fix·ing** (nítrəjən-fik-sing) *adj.*

ni·trog·en·ise, ni·trog·en·ize (nī-tróji-nīz, nítrəjə-) *tr.v.* **-ising, -ises, -ised.** To combine or treat with nitrogen.

nitrogen mustard *n.* Any of a group of organic compounds resembling mustard gas and having the general formula, RN ($CH_2CH_2CL)_2$, where R is an organic group. They are used in the chemotherapy of cancer.

nitrogen peroxide *n.* **1.** Nitrogen dioxide. **2.** The equilibrium mixture of nitrogen dioxide and dinitrogen tetroxide.

nitrogen tetroxide *n.* A brown liquid, formed by freezing or pressurising nitrogen dioxide, and used as an oxidising, nitrating, and bleaching agent. Also called "dinitrogen tetroxide".

ni·tro·glyc·er·in, ni·tro·glyc·er·ine (nítrō-glíssə-reen, -rin) *n.* A thick, pale yellow liquid, $CH_2NO_3CHNO_3CH_2NO_3$, explosive on concussion or exposure to sudden heat. It is used in the production of dynamite and blasting gelatine, and as a vasodilator in medicine. Also called "trinitroglycerin".

nitro group *n. Chemistry.* The group of atoms $-NO_2$, present in certain types of organic compounds *(nitro compounds).*

ni·tro·hy·dro·chlo·ric acid (nítrō-hídrə-kláwrik, -klórrik ‖ -klórik) *n.* A mixture of acids, **aqua regia** *(see).*

ni·trom·e·ter (nī-trómmitər) *n.* Any device or instrument for measuring the amount of nitrogen in a substance. [NITRO- + METER.]

ni·tro·meth·ane (nítrō-mée-thayn, -méthayn) *n.* An oily, colourless liquid, CH_3NO_2, used in making dyes and resins, in organic synthesis, and as a rocket propellant.

ni·tro·par·af·fin (nítrō-párrə-fin, -feen) *n.* Any of a group of organic compounds formed by replacing one or more of the hydrogen atoms of a paraffin hydrocarbon with the nitro group, NO_2^-, as in nitromethane, CH_3NO_2.

ni·tros·a·mine (nī-trózəmeen, nítrō-sə-méen, -sámmeen) *n.* Any of a group of oily, yellow compounds that contain the divalent group $-NNO$. [Latin *nitrōsus,* full of nitre + AMINE.]

ni·tro·so (nī-trō-sō) *adj.* Designating an organic compound that contains the monovalent group $-NO$. Compare **nitrosyl.** [Latin *nitrōsus,* full of nitre.]

ni·tro·syl (nítrə-sil, nítrō-, -síl) *adj.* Designating an inorganic compound that contains the monovalent group $-NO$. Compare **nitroso.** [Latin *nitrōsus* (see **nitroso**) + -YL.]

ni·trous (nítrəss) *adj.* Of, derived from, or containing nitrogen, especially in a valency state lower than that in a comparable nitric compound. [New Latin *nitrosus,* from Latin *nitrōsus,* full of nitre, from *nitrum,* from Greek *nitron,* NITRE.]

nitrous acid *n.* An unstable inorganic acid, HNO_2, existing in solution only.

nitrous oxide *n.* A colourless inorganic gas, N_2O, used as a mild anaesthetic. Also called "laughing gas".

nit·ty-grit·ty (nítti-grítti) *n. Slang.* The core of a matter; the fundamental truth: *Let's get down to the nitty-gritty.* [Probably based on a reduplication of *grit* in various senses.]

nit·wit (nít-wit) *n. Informal.* A stupid or silly person. [Perhaps NIT + WIT.]

ni·val (nīv'l) *adj. Botany.* Of or growing in or under snow. [Latin *nivālis,* from *nix* (stem *niv-*), snow.]

ni·va·tion (nī-váysh'n) *n.* The weathering of rocks as a result of the alternate freezing and thawing of surrounding snow. [Latin *nix* (stem *niv-*), snow.]

Niv·en (nivv'n), **(James) David (Graham),** né Nevins (1910–83). British actor; portrayer of easy-going, upper-class Englishmen.

niv·e·ous (nívvi-əss) *adj.* Like snow; snow-white. [Latin *niveus,* from *nix* (stem *niv-*), snow.]

nix[1] (niks) *n. Germanic Mythology.* A water sprite, usually in human form or half-human and half-fish. [German *Nix,* from Middle High German *nickes,* from Old High German *nihhus.*]

nix[2] *n. Chiefly U.S. Informal.* Nothing.
~*adv. Chiefly U.S. Informal.* No.
~*interj. U.S. Informal.* Stop! Watch out!
~*tr.v.* **nixed, nixing, nixes.** *U.S. Informal.* To forbid; veto; deny. [German, dialect and colloquial variant of *nichts,* nothing, from Old High German *niwiht,* nothing : *ni,* ne, no + *wiht,* thing, man.]

Nix·ie tube (niksi) *n.* A trademark for a **digitron** *(see).*

Nix·on (niks'n), **Richard (Milhous)** (1913–94). U.S. politician and 37th president. Vice-president from 1953 to 1960, he served as Republican president from 1969 to 1974, during which term he established close ties with China and a measure of détente with the U.S.S.R. Although he increased U.S. commitment in Southeast Asia, he was responsible for the eventual withdrawal of U.S. forces from the area. He became the first U.S. president to resign, when the Watergate scandal linked him with electoral malpractices.

ni·zam (nĭ-zám, -zám, ni-) *n., pl.* **nizam**. A Turkish soldier, especially in the 19th century. [Turkish, from Arabic *niẕām,* government, NIZAM.]

Ni·zam (nĭ-zám, -zaám ‖ ni-) *n.* The title of the former rulers of Hyderabad, India. [Hindi *niẕām(-al-mulk),* "governor (of the empire)", from Arabic *niẕām,* government.]

Nizh·niy·Nov·go·rod (neézhni nov-gərət). Former Gorky or Gorki, a large industrial city in central Russia, at the confluence of the rivers Volga and Oka. Under the Tsarist regime it held historic trade fairs which continued until 1917. The writer, Maxim Gorky, was born here and the city bore his name for 60 years.

Nko·mo (əng-kómó), **Joshua** (1917–). Zimbabwean politician. A trade unionist, be became leader of the ZAPU guerrilla organisation (1961) which, as part of the Patriotic Front, was instrumental in the defeat of the Rhodesian government. In 1980–81 he was a minister under Robert Mugabe, the former head of the rival ZANU. Under the merged ZANU-PF (1988) Nkomo became vice-president (1990) under Mugabe.

Nkru·mah (əng-krōōmə), **Kwame** (1909–72). Ghanaian statesman. His country's first premier (1952–1960), he was instrumental in achieving Ghana's independence from the United Kingdom (1957). He became president (1960), but was deposed and exiled after a military coup (1966).

NKVD, N.K.V.D. *n.* People's Commissariat for Internal Affairs (Russian *Narodny Kommissariat Vnutrennikh Del*): a former administrative branch of the Soviet government corresponding to the later **KGB** *(see).*

n.m., nm 1. nautical mile. 2. nanometre.

NMR nuclear magnetic resonance.

NNE, N.N.E. north-northeast.

NNW, N.N.W. north-northwest.

no¹ (nō) *adv.* 1. Not so; opposed to "yes". Used in expressing refusal, denial, disagreement, or disbelief. 2. Not at all; not by any degree. Used with the comparative: *no better; no more.* 3. *Archaic.* Not.
~*n., pl.* **noes.** 1. A negative response; a denial or refusal: *The proposal produced only noes.* 2. A negative vote or voter. [Middle English *no, na,* Old English *nā : ne,* not + *ā,* ever.]

no² *adj.* 1. Not any; not one; not a: *No biscuits are left.* Also used in the imperative: *No smoking.* 2. Not at all; not close to being: *He is no child.* 3. Hardly any: *got there in no time.* [Middle English *no, na,* Old English *nā,* reduced form of *nān,* NONE.]

No The symbol for the element nobelium.

Nô. Variant of **Noh.**

no. number.

n.o. Not out (in cricket).

no·ac·count (nō-ə-kownt) *adj.* Also **no-count** (nō-kownt). *U.S. Regional.* Worthless; good-for-nothing. —**no-account** *n.*

No·a·chi·an (nō-áyki-ən) *adj.* Also **No·ach·ic** (-áckik, -áykik). Of or relating to Noah or his time: *the Noachian flood.*

No·ah (nō-ə ‖ naw) *n.* The patriarch chosen by God to build the ark in which he, his family, and many animals were saved from the Flood. Genesis 5–9. [Hebrew *Nóah,* "rest".]

nob¹ (nob) *n. Slang.* 1. The head. 2. In cribbage, the jack of the suit turned up by the dealer, scoring one point for the holder: *one for his nob.* [Slang variant of KNOB.]

nob² *n. Chiefly British Slang.* A person of wealth or social standing. [18th century (Scottish *knabb, nab*) : origin obscure.] —**nob·bi·ly** *adv.* —**nob·by** *adj.*

no-ball (nō-báwl) *n. Sports. Abbr.* **n.b.** 1. In cricket, a ball rendered invalid, as by a bowler overstepping the popping crease, and for which the batting side receives one run. 2. In rounders, a ball not delivered according to the rules, as by not being bowled in a continuous underarm action or being bowled too high or too low.
~*interj.* Used by the umpire to indicate a no-ball. —**no-ball** *intr.v.*

nob·ble (nóbb'l) *tr.v.* **-bled, -bling, -bles.** *British Slang.* 1. To disable (a racehorse), especially with drugs. 2. To win over, outdo, or get the better of by devious means: *to nobble a jury by threats or bribery.* 3. To filch or steal. 4. To kidnap. [Perhaps from dialect *knobble,* to knock, beat : KNOB + -LE.] —**nob·bler** *n.*

nob·but (nóbbət) *adv. British Regional.* No more than; only. [NO + BUT.]

No·bel (nō-bél), **Alfred (Bernhard)** (1833–96). Swedish chemist, entrepreneur, and philanthropist. The inventor of dynamite, and developer of nitroglycerin as a high explosive, he was so appalled at the use of explosives in war that he bequeathed the considerable fortune he had amassed to institute the Nobel prizes.

No·bel·ist (nō-béllist) *n.* One who receives a Nobel prize.

no·bel·i·um (nō-beéli-əm, -bélli-) *n.* Symbol **No** A radioactive transuranic element in the actinide series, artificially produced in trace amounts. Atomic number 102, isotopic masses 251–259, of which 259 has the longest half-life. Also called "unnilbium". [After the *Nobel* Institute at Stockholm, where it was discovered.]

Nobel prize *n.* Any of the six prizes awarded annually (since 1901) by the Nobel Foundation for outstanding achievements in the fields of physics, chemistry, physiology or medicine, literature, and (since 1969) economics, and for the promotion of world peace.

No·bi·le (no-beéle), **Umberto** (1885–1978). Italian aeronautical engineer and explorer. He designed several airships, including the semirigid dirigibles, *Roma, Italia,* and *Norge,* in the last of which he flew over the North Pole with Roald Amundsen (1926).

no·bil·i·ar·y (nō-billi-əri ‖ *U.S.* -erri) *adj.* Of or pertaining to the nobility. [French *nobiliaire,* from Latin *nōbilis,* NOBLE.]

nobiliary particle *n.* A preposition occurring as a mark of noble rank before a title or surname; for example, the German *von* and French *de* in *Ulrich von Bertele* and *Guy de Maupassant.*

no·bil·i·ty (nō-billəti) *n., pl.* **-ties.** 1. a. The class comprising nobles, which in Britain consists of dukes, marquesses, earls, viscounts, and barons, together with their female counterparts. b. The state of being a noble. 2. The state or quality of being exalted in character or being morally noble. [Middle English *nobilite,* from Old French, from Latin *nōbilitās* (stem *nōbilitāt-*), from *nōbilis,* NOBLE.]

no·ble (nōb'l) *adj.* **-bler, -blest.** 1. Possessing hereditary rank in a political system or social class usually derived directly or indirectly from a feudalistic stage of a country's development. 2. a. Lofty and exalted in character. b. Proceeding from such a character; showing greatness and magnanimity. 3. Grand, stately, and magnificent in appearance. 4. Of superior quality. 5. Designating an especially corrosion-resistant metal, such as gold.
~*n.* 1. A person of high birth, rank, or title; a nobleman. 2. A former English gold coin. [Middle English, from Old French, from Latin *nōbilis,* knowable, known, famous, noble.] —**no·ble·ness** *n.* —**no·bly** *adv.*

noble art *n. Sports. Chiefly British.* Boxing. Preceded by *the.*

noble gas *n. Chemistry.* An **inert gas** *(see).*

no·ble·man (nōb'l-mən) *n., pl.* **-men** (-mən). A man of noble rank.

noble rot *n.* A fungus, *Botrytis cinerea,* which coats the skins of grapes, resulting in a grape of increased sweetness that is used for making Sauternes and certain Rhine wines. [Translation of German *Edelfäule.*]

noble savage *n.* Primitive man portrayed in Romantic literature as uncorrupted by civilisation.

no·blesse (nō-bléss, nə-) *n.* 1. Noble birth or condition. 2. The nobility; the aristocracy. [Middle English *noblesce, noblesse,* from Old French *noblesse,* from *noble,* NOBLE.]

noblesse o·blige (ō-bleézh) *n.* Benevolent and honourable behaviour considered to be the responsibility of persons of high birth or rank. [French, "nobility obliges".]

no·ble·wom·an (nōb'l-wōōmən) *n., pl.* **-women** (-wimmin). A woman of noble rank.

no·bod·y (nō-bədi, -boddi) *pron.* No person; no one: *Nobody told him what to do.*
~*n., pl.* **nobodies.** A person of no importance, influence, or social position.

Usage: *Nobody* and *no one* take singular verbs and pronoun forms: *Nobody has arrived yet, No one likes his time to be wasted.* Plural pronoun forms are quite often heard in casual speech, but a sentence such as *No one likes their time to be wasted* presents an inappropriate contrast between singular *likes* and plural *their.* However, when short questions (so-called "tag questions") are added to sentences containing *nobody* or *no one,* the use of plural forms is hard to avoid: *Nobody's left me a message, have they?*

no·cent (nō-sənt) *adj. Archaic.* 1. Causing injury; harmful. 2. Guilty of a crime. [Middle English, from Latin *nocēns* (stem *nocent-*), from the present participle of *nocēre,* to harm.]

nock (nok) *n.* 1. The groove at either end of a bow for holding the bowstring. 2. The notch in the end of an arrow that fits on the bowstring.
~*tr.v.* **nocked, nocking, nocks.** 1. To put a notch in (a bow or arrow). 2. To fit (an arrow) to a bowstring. [Middle English *nocke, nokke,* from Middle Dutch *nocke.*]

no-claim discount *n.* A reduction in an insurance premium, especially one on a motor vehicle, in cases where no claims have been made on the policy for a stipulated period. Also called "no-claim bonus", "no-claims bonus".

noc·tam·bu·la·tion (nok-támbew-láysh'n) *n.* Also **noc·tam·bu·lism** (-liz'm). **Somnambulism** *(see).* [NOCT(I)- + AMBULATION.] —**noc·tam·bu·lant** *adj.* —**noc·tam·bu·list** *n.*

nocti-, noct- *comb. form.* Indicates night; for example, *noctambulism.* [New Latin, from Latin *nox* (stem *noct-*), night.]

noc·ti·lu·ca (nókti-lōō-kə, -léw-) *n., pl.* **-cae** (-see). Any of various plantlike, bioluminescent marine organisms of the genus *Noctiluca* which, when grouped in large numbers, make the seas phosphorescent. [New Latin *noctilūca,* moon, lantern : NOCTI- + *lūcere,* to shine.]

noc·ti·lu·cent (nókti-lōō-sənt, -léw-) *adj.* Luminous at night. Said especially of certain high clouds. —**noc·ti·lu·cence** *n.*

noc·tu·id (nóktew-id) *n.* Any night-flying moth of the family Noctuidae, the larvae of which are destructive pests. [New Latin *Noctuidae* (family name) : *Noctua,* generic name, from Latin *noctua,* night owl + -IDAE.] —**noctuid** *adj.*

noc·tule (nóktewl) *n.* Any large, reddish-brown, insectivorous bat of the genus *Nyctalus,* found in Eurasia, Indonesia, and the Philippines. Also called "noctule bat". [French, from Italian *nottola,* from Late Latin *noctula,* diminutive of Latin *noctua,* night owl.]

noc·turn (nókturn) *n. Roman Catholic Church.* Any of the three canonical divisions of the office of **matins** *(see).* [Middle English *nocturne,* from Old French, from Medieval Latin *nocturna,* from the feminine of Latin *nocturnus,* NOCTURNAL.]

noc·tur·nal (nok-túrn'l) *adj.* 1. Of, suitable to, or occurring at night.

2. *Botany.* Having flowers that open during the night. **3.** *Zoology.* Active by night, as certain animals are. Compare **diurnal.** [Late Latin *nocturnālis,* from Latin *nocturnus,* of night, at night, from *nox* (stem *noct-*), night.] **—noc·tur·nal·i·ty** (nŏktur-nál-ət̄i) *n.* **—noc·tur·nal·ly** *adv.*

nocturnal emission *n.* An emission of semen during à **wet dream.**

noc·turne (nŏkturn, nok-túrn) *n.* **1.** *Music.* A romantic composition intended to embody sentiments appropriate to the evening or night; a pensive melody. **2.** A painting of a night scene. [French, "nocturnal", from Latin *nocturnus,* NOCTURNAL.]

noc·u·ous (nŏckew-əss) *adj. Rare.* Harmful; noxious. [Latin *nocuus,* from *nocēre,* to harm.]

nod (nŏd) *v.* **nodded, nodding, nods.** *—intr.* **1.** To lower and raise the head quickly in a gesture of agreement or acknowledgment. **2.** To let the head fall forward when sleepy; doze momentarily. Often used with *off.* **3.** To be careless or momentarily inattentive as if sleepy; lapse: *Even Homer nods.* **4.** To sway, move up and down, or bend, as flowers do in the wind. *—tr.* **1.** To lower and raise (the head) quickly in agreement or acknowledgment. **2.** To express (greetings or approval, for example) by lowering and raising the head: *He nodded his agreement.* **3.** To summon, guide, send, or the like by nodding the head: *He nodded her into the room.* *~n.* **1.** A forward or up-and-down inclination of the head, usually expressive of affirmation or drowsiness. **2.** The nodding motion of anything. **—on the nod.** *Informal.* **1.** Without formal deliberation. **2.** On credit. [Middle English *nodden,* perhaps of Low German origin; akin to Middle High German *notten.*] **—nod·der** *n.*

Nod, Land of. See **Land of Nod.**

no·dal (nŏd'l) *adj.* Of, resembling, or located at a node. **—no·dal·i·ty** (nŏ-dál-ət̄i) *n.*

nod·ding *adj. Botany.* Designating flowers that droop from their stalks, as in the bluebell.

nodding acquaintance *n.* A slight acquaintance with a person or subject.

nod·dle[1] (nŏdd'l) *n. Informal.* The head. Used humorously: *not an idea in his noddle.* [Middle English *nodle†,* back of the head.]

noddle[2] *v.* **-dled, -dling, -dles.** *—intr.* To nod frequently. *—tr.* To nod (the head) briefly. [Frequentative of NOD (verb).]

nod·dy[1] (nŏddi) *n., pl.* **-dies.** **1.** A dunce or fool; a simpleton. **2.** Any tern of the genus *Anous,* that is found in tropical waters and is dark brown with a white head. [From obsolete adjective *noddy,* foolish, "sleepy", "drowsy", probably from NOD (verb). The tern is so named because it is fearless of man and therefore seems stupid.]

noddy[2] *n., pl.* **-dies.** A shot taken during the filming of television interviews, consisting of individual head movements which will be incorporated during editing to provide continuity in the main body of the film. Also called "noddy shot". [From NOD (noun).]

node (nŏd) *n.* **1.** A knob, knot, protuberance, or swelling: *a lymph node.* **2.** *Botany.* The often enlarged point on a stem where a leaf, bud, or other organ diverges from the stem to which it is attached; a joint. **3.** *Physics.* A point or region of minimum or zero amplitude in a periodic system. Compare **antinode.** **4. a.** *Mathematics.* The point at which a continuous curve crosses itself. **b.** The point where lines branch or intersect. **5.** *Astronomy.* **a.** Either of two diametrically opposite points at which the orbit of a planet intersects the ecliptic. The *ascending node* is the point at which the planet moves from the south of the ecliptic to the north, the opposite point being the *descending node.* **b.** Either of two points at which the orbit of a satellite intersects the orbital plane of a planet. **6.** Any central point. [Latin *nōdus,* a knob, knot.]

node of Ran·vi·er (rónvee-ay) *n.* Any of the regions of exposed axon that occur along a myelinated nerve fibre at regular intervals. [After Louis Antoine *Ranvier* (1835–1922), French histologist.]

no·di·cal (nŏdi-k'l, nŏddi-) *adj. Astronomy.* Of or pertaining to the nodes of a heavenly body. [NODE) + -ICAL.]

no·dose (nŏ-dŏss, -dŏss, -dŏz) *adj.* Also **no·dous** (nŏ-dəss). Having nodes or knots: *a nodose branch.* [Latin *nodōsus,* from *nodus,* NODE.] **—no·dos·i·ty** (nŏ-dóssəti) *n.*

nod·ule (nŏddewl) *n.* **1.** A small, knotlike protuberance; a node. **2.** *Anatomy.* A localised swelling. **3.** *Botany.* A small, knoblike outgrowth, such as any of those found on the roots of most leguminous plants. **4.** A small lump of a mineral. [Latin *nōdulus,* diminutive of *nōdus,* a knob, NODE.] **—nod·u·lar** (-ər), **nod·u·lose** (-ŏss, -ŏz), **nod·u·lous** (-əss) *adj.*

no·dus (nŏ-dəss) *n., pl.* **-di** (-dī). A knotty situation, problem, or point; a complication. [Latin *nōdus,* "knot", NODE.]

No·ël (nŏ-él) *n.* **1.** Christmas. **2.** *Small n.* A Christmas carol. [French, from Old French *no(u)el, nael,* from Latin *nātālis (dies),* "birth(day of Christ)", from *nātālis,* of birth, from *nāscī* (past participle *nātus*), to be born.]

No·el-Bak·er (nŏ-əl-báykər), **Philip John, Baron** (1889–1982). British politician. One of the founders of the League of Nations, and subsequently the United Nations Organisation, he was awarded the Nobel peace prize (1959).

no·e·sis (nŏ-ée-siss) *n.* **1.** *Psychology.* The cognitive process; the mental process by which knowledge is gained. **2.** *Philosophy.* The highest knowledge, as of universal forms. [Greek *noēsis,* intelligence, understanding, from *noein,* to perceive, from *nous,* the mind.]

no·et·ic (nŏ-éttik) *adj.* **1.** Of, pertaining to, originating in, or comprehended by the intellect. **2.** Of cognition or rational thought that is comprehended by the intellect alone. [Greek *noētikos,* from *noēsis,* NOESIS.]

no-fault (nŏ-fáwlt ‖ -fólt) *adj.* **1.** Of, pertaining to, or designating a legal action of a type in which blame is not assigned to either party. **2.** *Chiefly U.S.* Of or designating a system of motor-vehicle insurance in which accident victims are compensated by their insurance companies without any assignment of blame.

nog[1] (nŏg) *n.* **1.** A wooden block built into a masonry wall to hold nails that support joinery structures. **2.** A wooden peg or pin. [17th century : origin obscure.]

nog[2] *n.* **1.** Eggnog *(see).* **2.** *British Regional.* A strong beer of a type brewed in East Anglia. [17th century : origin obscure.]

nog·gin (nŏggin) *n.* **1.** A small mug or cup. **2.** A unit of liquid measure equal to one quarter of a pint. **3.** *Informal.* The head. [17th century : origin obscure.]

nog·ging (nŏgging) *n.* **1.** Brickwork used to fill in the boards of a wooden framework. **2.** A short horizontal wooden beam used to strengthen upright posts in the framework of a wall. Also called "nogging piece". [From NOG (wooden block, peg).]

no-go area (nŏ-gŏ) *n.* An area, as in a town, entry to which is barred to certain persons or groups, such as the police or the army.

no-good (nŏ-gŏŏd) *adj. Slang.* Good-for-nothing; contemptible.

Noh, Nō (nŏ) *n. Sometimes small* **n.** The classical drama of Japan, performed with music and dancing in a highly stylised manner by elaborately dressed actors on an almost bare stage. [Japanese *nŏ,* "talent", "ability", from Chinese *néng.*]

no-hoper (nŏ-hŏpər) *n. Informal.* **1.** *British.* A person who appears doomed to failure; a loser. **2.** Anything that appears extremely unpromising, such as a bet, plan, or racehorse. **3. a.** *Chiefly Australian.* An ineffectual or shiftless person. **b.** A socially incompetent or ostracised person.

no-how (nŏ-how) *adv. Nonstandard.* In no way; not at all.

noil (noyl) *n.* A short fibre combed from the long fibres during the preparation of textile yarns. [Probably from Old French *noel,* "small knot (of wool)", from Medieval Latin *nōdellus,* diminutive of Latin *nōdus,* knot, NODE.]

noise (noyz) *n.* **1.** A sound of any kind, especially when loud, confused, indistinct, or disagreeable. **2.** An outcry or clamour: *the noise of the mob.* **3.** General interest or commotion; a stir. **4.** *Physics.* Any electrical disturbance, especially a random and persistent disturbance, that obscures or reduces the clarity or quality of a signal. **5.** *Plural. Informal.* Superficial remarks conveying a specified impression: *made approving noises.* *~v.* **noised, noising, noises.** *—tr.* To spread the rumour or report of. Usually used with *about* or *abroad.* *—intr.* **1.** To talk much or volubly. **2.** *Archaic.* To be noisy; make noise. [Middle English, from Old French *noise, noyse,* from Latin *nausea,* seasickness (with extended senses in popular use, such as "unpleasant situation", "noisy confusion"), from Greek *nausia,* from *naus,* a ship.]

Synonyms: noise, din, racket, uproar, pandemonium, hullabaloo, hubbub, clamour, babel.

noise·less (nóyz-ləss, -liss) *adj.* Creating no noise; silent; quiet. See Synonyms at **still.** **—noise·less·ly** *adv.* **—noise·less·ness** *n.*

noise pollution *n.* Environmental noise of sufficient loudness to be annoying, distracting, or physically harmful.

noi·sette (nwaa-zét, nwə-) *n.* A small round piece of meat, especially loin or fillet of lamb, veal, or pork. *~adj.* Made or flavoured with hazelnuts. [French, diminutive of *noix,* nut.]

noi·some (nóy-səm) *adj. Literary.* **1.** Offensive to the point of arousing disgust; foul and filthy: *a noisome smell.* **2.** Harmful or dangerous. [Middle English *noyesum :* *(a)noy,* vexation, annoyance, from *anoien,* ANNOY + -SOME.] **—noi·some·ly** *adv.* **—noi·some·ness** *n.*

nois·y (nóyzi) *adj.* **-ier, -iest.** **1.** Making a loud noise. **2.** Characterised by noise. **—nois·i·ly** *adv.* **—nois·i·ness** *n.*

No·lan (nŏlən), **Sir Sidney (Robert)** (1917–92). Australian painter. He began his career as an abstract painter, but it was through his landscapes of the Australian outback and figures from Australia's history that he achieved recognition.

no·lens vo·lens (nŏlenz vŏlenz) *adv. Latin.* Willing or not; willy-nilly.

no·li-me-tan·ge·re (nŏli-máy-táng-gəri, -mée-tánjəri) *n.* **1.** A warning or prohibition against meddling, touching, or interfering. **2.** A picture representing Christ appearing to Mary Magdalene after the Resurrection. [Latin, "do not touch me", Christ's warning to Mary Magdalene (Vulgate, John 20:17).]

nol·le pros·e·qui (nólli próssikwī) *n. Law.* A declaration entered in court records that the plaintiff in a civil case or the prosecutor in a criminal case will drop prosecution of all or part of a suit or indictment. [Latin, "to be unwilling to pursue".]

no·lo con·ten·de·re (nŏlŏ kən-téndəri) *n. Law. U.S.* A plea made by the defendant in a criminal action, equivalent to an admission of guilt and subjecting him to punishment but leaving it open to him to deny the alleged facts in other proceedings. [Latin, "I do not wish to contend".]

nom. nominative.

no·ma (nŏmə) *n.* A severe, often gangrenous inflammation of the mouth, occurring especially in a young child after a debilitating disease. [Latin *nomē,* "eating ulcer", from Greek *nomē,* spreading ulcer, "a feeding", "a pasturage".]

no·mad (nŏ-mad, -məd) *n.* **1.** Any of a group of pastoral people having no fixed abode and usually moving from place to place in a search for food and water. **2.** One who has no permanent domicile; a wanderer.

~*adj.* Nomadic. [French *nomade,* from Latin *nomas* (stem *nomad-*), from Greek *nomas,* one that wanders about for pasture; related to *nemein,* to feed or pasture animals.] —**no·mad·ism** *n.*

no·mad·ic (nō-máddik) *adj.* Also **no·mad·i·cal** (-'l). Leading the life of a nomad; wandering; roving. —**no·mad·i·cal·ly** *adv.*

no-man's-land (nō-manz-land) *n.* **1.** Land under dispute by two opposing parties; especially, the field of battle between two opposing entrenched armies. **2.** An unclaimed or unowned piece of land. **3.** Any area of indefiniteness or ambiguity.

nom·arch (nómmaark) *n.* A governor, especially of a nome or nomarchy. [Greek *nomarkhēs* : NOME + -ARCH.]

nom·ar·chy (nómm-aarki, -ərki) *n., pl.* **-ies.** Any of the administrative provinces of modern Greece. [Greek *nomarkhia* : NOME + -ARCHY.]

nom·bril (nómbril) *n. Heraldry.* The point on an escutcheon between the fess point and the base point; the midpoint in the lower half of an escutcheon. [Old French *nombril,* navel, probably alteration of *l'ombril,* the navel.]

nom de guerre (nóm də gaír; *French* NON) *n.* A fictitious name adopted for a particular course of action; a pseudonym. [French, "war name".]

nom de plume (nóm də plōōm) *n.* A pen name. [French, "pen name" —but probably coined in English.]

nome (nōm) *n.* **1.** A province in ancient Egypt. **2.** A nomarchy. [Greek *nomos,* division, district.]

no·men (nōmen) *n., pl.* **-mina** (nómminə, nōminə). The second name of a citizen of ancient Rome, designating gens or patrilinear clan. Compare **cognomen, praenomen.** [Latin, name.]

no·men·cla·tor (nō-mən-klaytər, -men-) *n.* A person or list that assigns names, as in scientific classification. [Latin *nōmenclātor,* "name-caller", a slave who told his master the names of people he met : *nōmen,* name + *-clātor,* caller, from *calāre,* to call.]

no·men·cla·ture (nō-méngkləchər, nə-, nō-mən-klaychər, -mén-). A system of names or terms; a systematic naming in any art, science, or area of activity. [Latin *nōmenclātūra,* from *nōmenclātor,* NOMENCLATOR.] —**no·men·cla·tur·al** (-kláychərəl) *adj.*

nom·i·nal (nómminəl) *adj.* **1. a.** Of, like, or consisting of a name or names. **b.** Bearing a person's name: *nominal shares.* **2.** Existing in name only; not real or actual; theoretical: *the nominal head of the firm.* **3.** Minimal in comparison to the real value: *a nominal sum.* **4.** *Grammar.* Of, like, or functioning as a noun or nouns.

~*n.* A word or phrase that functions as a noun. [Latin *nōminālis,* from *nōmen* (stem *nōmin-*), name.] —**nom·i·nal·ly** *adv.*

nom·i·nal·ism (nómmin'l-izm) *n. Philosophy.* The doctrine that abstract concepts, general terms, or universals have no objective reference but exist only as names. Compare **realism.** —**nom·i·nal·ist** *adj. & n.* —**nom·i·nal·is·tic** (-ístik) *adj.*

nominal value *n.* The stated or par value of a share certificate or bond, as opposed to the actual or market value.

nom·i·nate (nómminayt) *tr.v.* **-nated, -nating, -nates. 1.** To propose by name as a candidate. **2.** To designate or appoint to some office, responsibility, or honour. **3.** To designate; name.

~ *adj.* (-nət, -nit, -nayt). Having a particular name. [Latin *nōmināre,* to name, from *nōmen* (stem *nōmin-*), name.] —**nom·i·na·tor** *n.*

nom·i·na·tion (nómmi-náysh'n) *n.* **1.** The act or an instance of nominating. **2.** The state of being nominated.

nom·i·na·tive (nómmi-nətiv, nóm- ‖ *U.S. for senses 2 and 3 also* -naytiv) *adj. Abbr.* **nom. 1.** *Grammar.* Of or designating the case of the subject of a finite verb (as *We* in *We awoke at dawn*) and of words identified with the subject, such as *women* in *These are the women.* **2.** Having or bearing a person's name. **3. a.** Appointed to office. **b.** Nominated as a candidate to office.

~*n. Abbr.* **nom.** *Grammar.* **1.** The nominative case. **2.** A form or construction in this case. [Noun, Middle English *nominatif (case),* from Old French *(cas) nominatif,* from Latin *nōminātīvus (cāsus),* from *nōmināre,* to NOMINATE.]

nom·i·nee (nómmi-née) *n.* One who is nominated to an office or as a candidate. [NOMIN(ATE) + -EE.]

nomo- *comb. form.* Indicates law, usage, or custom; for example, **nomology.** [Greek *nomos,* usage, law.]

nom·o·gram (nómmə-gram, nōmə-) *n.* Also **nom·o·graph** (-graf). A graph consisting of three coplanar curves, usually parallel straight lines, each graduated for a different variable so that a straight line cutting all three curves intersects the related values of each variable. It is used to represent an equation containing three variables. Also called "alignment chart". [NOMO- + -GRAM.]

no·mo·graph·y (no-móggrəfi, nō-, nə-) *n.* The science of constructing nomograms.

no·mol·o·gy (nō-móllaji, no-) *n.* The science of physical and logical laws. [NOMO- + -LOGY.] —**no·mo·log·i·cal** (nōmə-lójik'l, nómmə-) *adj.* —**no·mol·o·gist** (-móllajist) *n.*

nom·o·thet·ic (nómmə-théttik, nōmə-) *adj.* Also **nom·o·thet·i·cal** ('l). **1.** Lawmaking; legislative. **2.** Of or concerned with the formulation of general or scientific laws. [From obsolete *nomothete,* from Greek *nomothetēs,* legislator : *nomos,* law + *tithēnai,* to put.]

-nomy *n. comb. form.* Indicates the systematisation of knowledge about, or laws governing, a specified field; for example, **astronomy.** [Latin *-nomia,* from Greek; either from agent nouns or adjectives in *-nomos,* from *nemein,* to distribute, manage, or from *nomos,* distribution, law.]

non- *prefix.* Indicates: **1.** Failure or lack; for example, **noncommunication. 2.** Absence of the qualities or characteristics typically associated with; for example, **nonperson. 3.** Not; for example,

nonviable. *Note:* Many compounds other than those entered here may be formed with *non-.* In forming compounds, *non-* in this dictionary is normally joined with the following element without space or hyphen. However, many users prefer the hyphenated form, which is used here only if the second element begins with a vowel, an *n,* or a capital letter: *non-iron, non-nutritive, non-French.* The prefix is pronounced (nón), or occasionally (nún); the latter variant is ignored in the entries below. See also **un-.** [Middle English *non-,* from Old French *non-,* from Latin *nōn,* not.]

nona- *comb. form.* Indicates nine or ninth; for example, **nonagon.** [From Latin *nona,* ninth.]

non-ac·ci·den·tal injury (nón-aksi-dént'l) *n. Abbr.* **NAI, N.A.I.** An injury inflicted deliberately; specifically, a cut, bruise, burn, or fracture inflicted on a child at home, detected by authorities such as health visitors or social workers, and deemed to call for outside investigation or intervention.

non-ad·di·tive (nón-áddi-tiv) *adj. Mathematics.* Having a numerical value that is not equal to the sum of its component parts. —**non·ad·di·tiv·i·ty** (-tívvəti) *n.*

no·nage (nōnij ‖ nónnij) *n.* **1.** The period during which one is legally under age. **2.** A stage of immaturity: *"the bravest achievements were always accomplished in the nonage of a nation"* (Thomas Paine). [Middle English, from Old French : NON- + AGE.]

non·a·ge·nar·i·an (nōnə-ji-naír-i-ən, nónnə-, -jə-) *adj.* **1.** Being ninety years old or between ninety and one hundred years old. **2.** Of or like someone of this age.

~*n.* A person of ninety or between ninety and one hundred years of age. [Latin *nōnāgēnārius,* from *nōnāgēnī,* ninety each, from *nōnāginta,* ninety : *novem,* nine + *-gintā,* ten times.]

non·ag·gres·sion (nónnə-grésh'n) *n.* The avoidance of aggression or hostilities, as between nations. Also used adjectivally: *a nonaggression pact.*

non·a·gon (nónnə-gən, nōnə-, -gon) *n.* A polygon having nine sides and nine angles. [NONA- + -GON.]

non·ag·o·nal (non-ággən'l, nōn-) *adj.* **1.** Having nine sides and nine angles. **2.** Of, pertaining to, or formed in nonagons. —**non·a·gon·al·ly** *adv.*

non·al·co·hol·ic (nón-al-kə-hóllik) *adj.* Containing no alcohol.

non·a·ligned (nón-ə-línd) *adj.* Not in alliance with any power bloc; neutral: *a non-aligned nation.* —**non·a·lign·ment** *n.*

non·a·no·ic acid (nónnə-nō-ik) *n.* A chemical, **pelargonic acid** *(see).* [From *nonane,* a paraffin : NONA- + -ANE (because it is the ninth in the methane series).]

non·ap·pear·ance (nónnə-péer-ənss) *n.* Failure to appear, as in a court of law.

non·bel·lig·er·ent (nón-bə-líjərənt) *n.* A person or a country that takes no part in a war. —**nonbelligerent** *adj.*

nonce[1] (nónss) *n.* The present or particular time or occasion. Used in the phrase *for the nonce.* [Middle English *for the nones, for the nanes,* originally *for then anes,* "for the one (purpose or occasion)" : FOR + *then,* dative singular neuter of THE + *anes,* ONCE.]

nonce[2] *n. Slang.* An imprisoned sex offender. [20th century : origin obscure.]

nonce word *n.* A word invented and used only once, to meet a particular requirement; an example is the word *mileconsuming* in *"the wagon beginning to fall into its slow and mileconsuming clatter"* (William Faulkner).

non·cha·lant (nónshələnt) *adj.* Appearing casually unconcerned; indifferent. See Synonyms at **cool.** [French, from Old French, from *nonchaloir,* to be unconcerned : NON- + *chaloir,* to be interested or concerned, from Latin *calēre,* to be warm.] —**non·cha·lance** *n.* —**non·cha·lant·ly** *adv.*

non·com (nón-kóm) *n. Informal.* A noncommissioned officer.

non·com·bat·ant (nón-kóm-bətənt, -kúm- ‖ *U.S. also* -kəm-bátt'nt) *n.* **1.** A person connected with the armed forces whose duties are other than fighting, such as a chaplain. **2.** A civilian in wartime.

non·com·mis·sioned officer (nón-kə-mísh'nd) *n. Abbr.* **NCO, N.C.O.** A member of the armed forces, such as a sergeant or corporal, appointed to a rank conferring leadership over other men but not holding a commission. Compare **commissioned officer, warrant officer.**

non·com·mit·tal (nón-kə-mítt'l) *adj.* Refusing commitment to any particular course of action or opinion; revealing no preference or purpose. —**non·com·mit·tal·ly** *adv.*

non·com·pli·ance (nón-kəm-plí-ənss ‖ -kom-) *n.* Failure or refusal to comply with something. —**non·com·pli·ant** *adj. & n.*

non compos mentis (nón kóm-poss méntiss, -pəss) *adj.* Not of sound mind, and therefore not responsible for one's actions. [Latin, "not having control of the mind."]

non·con·duc·tor (nón-kən-dúktər ‖ -kon-) *n.* A substance that conducts little or no electricity or heat. —**non·con·duct·ing** *adj.*

non·con·form·ist (nón-kən-fórmist ‖ -kon-) *n.* **1.** One who refuses to be bound by the accepted rules, beliefs, or practices of a group. **2.** *Capital* **N.** A member of a Protestant church that dissents from the Church of England. —**non·con·form·ism** *n.* —**non·con·form·ist** *adj.* —**non·con·form·i·ty** *n.*

non·con·trib·u·to·ry (nón-kən-tríb-bew-təri, -tri ‖ -kóntri-béwtəri) *adj.* **1.** Not requiring contributions. **2.** Designating a pension or insurance scheme in which employees' contributions are paid by the employer. **3.** Not contributing; not making contributions.

non·co·op·er·a·tion (nón-kō-óppə-ráysh'n) *n.* **1.** Failure or refusal to cooperate. **2.** Resistance to government through civil disobedience or refusal to perform civil duties, such as paying taxes. —**non-**

co·op·er·a·tion·ist *n. & adj.* —**non·co·op·er·a·tive** (-óppə-rətiv, -óp- ‖ -raytiv) *adj.* —**non·co·op·er·a·tor** (-raytər) *n.*

non·count·a·ble (nón-kówntəb'l) *adj. Grammar.* Of or designating a noun that refers to an object lacking clearly standardised or defined limits and that is not preceded by the indefinite article; for example, *earth* and *soil* are noncountable nouns, whereas *clod* and *boulder* are not. Some nouns, such as *speed* or *fear*, have both countable and noncountable senses. Compare **countable.**

non·de·nom·i·na·tion·al (nón-di-nómmi-náysh'n'l) *adj.* Not restricted to or associated with a particular religious denomination.

non·de·script (nón-di-skript) *adj.* Lacking in distinctive qualities; without any individual character or form.
~*n.* A person or thing with no outstanding or distinguishing features. [NON- + Latin *dēscriptus*, past participle of *dēscrībere*, DE-SCRIBE.]

non·dis·junc·tion (nón-diss-júngksh'n) *n. Biology.* The failure of homologous chromosomes to move to separate poles during meiosis.

non·dis·tinc·tive (nón-diss-tíngktiv) *adj.* 1. Not distinctive. 2. *Phonetics.* Not helping to distinguish meaning: *The vowel in the words "hit" and "slip" is nondistinctive; only the consonants are differentiated.*

none (nun ‖ *Northern English also* non) *pron.* 1. No one; not one; nobody: *None dared to do it.* 2. Not any; no persons or things of a specified group: *None of my cardigans will go with this new dress.* 3. No part; not any: *none of my business; none of his concern.*
~*adj. Archaic.* Not one; no. Now used only before vowels: *There is none other available.*
~*adv.* In no way; not at all: *We were none the wiser.* [Middle English *nan, none,* Old English *nān : ne,* no + *ān,* one.]

Usage: None may be used with either a singular or a plural verb, depending on the construction in which it appears. Thus when *none* precedes or refers back to a singular noun, the verb is also in the singular: *None of the laundry is clean; Where's the orange juice?* — *There is none* (which is a more formal version of *There isn't any*). A singular verb is also used when *none* can be interpreted as "not one" or "no one": *None of us is to blame.* A plural verb is used when *none* refers back to a plural noun: *Where are the sugar lumps?* — *There are none.* The plural verb is also generally used when the meaning of *none* is "not any of a group of persons or things": *None have been more in need of a pay rise than the nurses.* Problems of usage arise when *none* can be interpreted as either singular or plural: *None of these books is/are helpful.* Purists insist on the singular form in such contexts, but the plural is often used in all styles, when no individualising sense is intended. See also **neither.**

non·e·go (nón-éego, -éggō) *n., pl.* -**gos.** *Philosophy.* All that is not part of the ego or the conscious self.

non·e·lec·tro·lyte (nón-i-léktrə-līt) *n.* A substance that does not ionise in solution or in liquid form and therefore forms solutions or liquids of low conductivity.

non·emp·ty (nón-émpti) *Mathematics.* Designating a set that has at least one member.

non·en·ti·ty (non-éntəti, nən-) *n., pl.* -**ties.** 1. An insignificant person or thing. 2. Non-existence. 3. Something that does not exist, or that exists only in the imagination.

nones (nōnz) *pl.n.* 1. In the ancient Roman calendar, the ninth day before the ides of a month; the seventh of March, May, July, or October, and the fifth day of the other months. 2. *Ecclesiastical.* **a.** The fifth of the seven **canonical hours** *(see).* **b.** The time of day set aside for this prayer, usually the ninth hour after sunrise. [In sense 1, Middle English *nonys, nonas,* from Old French *nones,* from Latin *nōnae,* feminine plural of *nōnus,* ninth. In sense 2, plural of *none,* from Old French *none,* from Late Latin *nōna (hōra),* the ninth hour, from the feminine of Latin *nōnus,* ninth.]

non·es·sen·tial (nón-i-sénsh'l) *adj.* 1. Not essential. 2. *Biochemistry.* Designating amino acids that a particular organism is able to synthesise and that are therefore not essential to its diet.

none·such, non·such (nún-such ‖ nón-) *n.* 1. *Archaic.* A person or thing without equal: *a nonesuch among athletes.* 2. A plant, the **black medick** *(see).* —**none·such** *adj.*

non·et (no-nét) *n. Music.* 1. A composition for nine instruments or voices. 2. A group of nine musicians or performers. [Italian *nonetto,* from *nono,* ninth, from Latin *nōnus.*]

none·the·less, none the less (núnthə-léss ‖ nón-) *adv.* No less; nevertheless; however.

Usage: Nonetheless is now usually written as a single word, especially in American English, but traditionalists generally recommend the form *none the less.*

non·Eu·clid·e·an (nón-yōō-klíddi-ən) *adj.* Designating any of several modern geometries that change or discard one or more of the axioms of Euclid.

non·e·vent (nón-i-vént) *n.* An occurrence which is expected to be interesting or exciting but which fails to take place or to live up to expectations.

non·ex·ist·ence (nón-ig-zístənss ‖ -eg-, -ik-) *n.* 1. The condition of not existing. 2. A thing that does not exist. —**non·ex·ist·ent** *adj.*

non·fea·sance (nón-féez'nss) *n. Law.* Failure to perform some act that is either an official duty or a legal requirement. Compare **malfeasance, misfeasance.** [NON- + obsolete *feasance,* a doing, from Old French *faisance* (see **malfeasance**).]

non·fer·rous (nón-férrəss) *adj.* 1. Not composed of or containing iron. 2. Of or pertaining to metals other than iron.

non·fic·tion (nón-fíksh'n) *n.* Prose works other than fiction. —**non·fic·tion·al** *adj.*

non·flam·ma·ble (nón-flámməb'l) *adj.* Not flammable; not easily set alight. See Usage note at **flammable.**

nong (nong) *n. Australian Slang.* A stupid person; a fool. [Perhaps shortened from earlier *ningnong,* fool. See **nignog.**]

non·gov·ern·men·tal organisation (nón-guvvərn-mént'l) *n.* See NGO.

non·har·mon·ic (nón-haar-mónnik) *adj.* Of or designating a note, such as a grace note, that is not part of the chord with which it is played.

no·nil·lion (nō-níl-yən) *n.* 1. In Britain, the cardinal number represented by the figure 1 followed by 54 zeros; usually written 10^{54}. 2. The cardinal number that is represented by the figure 1 followed by 30 zeros; usually written 10^{30}. In this sense, also *British* "quintillion". [French, from Old French, "the ninth power of a million" : *non-,* nine, ninth + *(m)ilion, (m)illion,* (M)ILLION.] —**no·nil·lion** *adj.*

no·nil·lionth (nō-níl-yənth) *n.* 1. The ordinal number nonillion in a series. 2. Any of a nonillion equal parts. —**no·nil·lionth** *adj.*

non·in·duc·tive (nón-in-dúktiv) *adj. Electricity.* Having low inductance.

non·in·ter·ven·tion (nón-intər-vénsh'n) *n.* Failure or refusal to interfere or intervene in the affairs of another; especially, a deliberate refusal of one nation to intervene in the affairs of another nation or one of its own subdivisions. —**non·in·ter·ven·tion·ist** *n. & adj.*

non·iron (nón-í-ərn ‖ -íɾən) *adj. Chiefly British.* Requiring little or no ironing. Said of garments or fabrics.

non·join·der (nón-jóyndər) *n. Law.* The omission of a party, plaintiff, defendant, or cause of action that should have been included as a necessary part of an action or suit.

non·ju·ror (non-jóor-ər ‖ -awr) *n.* 1. One who refuses to take an oath, as of allegiance. 2. *Capital* N. An Anglican clergyman who refused to swear allegiance to William and Mary in 1689.

non li·cet (nón lí-sit) *adj. Law.* Not allowed; unlawful. [Latin.]

non·lin·e·ar (nón-línni-ər) *adj.* 1. Not in a straight line. 2. *Mathematics.* Occurring as a result of a non-additive operation. —**non·lin·e·ar·i·ty** (-árrəti) *n.*

non li·quet (nón líkwit) *adj. Law.* Unclear. Said of evidence. [Latin.]

non·met·al (nón-métt'l) *n. Chemistry.* Any of a number of elements, such as oxygen or sulphur, that generally occur as negatively charged ions or radicals, form oxides that produce acids, and are poor conductors of heat and of electricity when solid.

non·me·tal·lic (nón-mi-tál-ik) *adj.* 1. Not of metal. 2. *Chemistry.* Of or pertaining to a nonmetal.

non·met·ro·pol·i·tan (nón-méttrə-póllit'n) *adj.* Of or designating an English county that is not one of the six metropolitan counties.

non·mor·al (nón-mórrəl ‖ -máwrəl) *adj.* Unrelated to morals or to ethical considerations; neither moral nor immoral.

non·New·ton·i·an fluid (nón-new-tŏni-ən ‖ -nŏŏ-) *n.* A fluid with a flow behaviour such that the rate of shear is not proportional to the corresponding stress.

non·nu·cle·ar (nón-néw-kli-ər ‖ -nŏŏ-) *adj.* Not possessing, producing, or powered by nuclear energy or nuclear weapons.

no·no (nṓ-nō̄) *n., pl.* -**noes.** *Slang.* 1. Something that is forbidden or unacceptable. 2. Something or someone that is useless or doomed to failure.

non·ob·jec·tive (nón-əb-jéktiv ‖ -ob-) *adj.* Designating a style of art that does not represent objects; abstract.

non ob·stan·te (nón ob-stánti ‖ *U.S. also* -stáantay) *prep. Abbr.* **non obs., non obst.** *Latin.* Notwithstanding.

no-non·sense (nṓ-nón-sənss ‖ -senss) *adj.* 1. Not tolerating extremes of behaviour or taste. 2. Practical; down-to-earth.

non·pa·reil (nón-pə-rəl, -prəl, -ráyl ‖ *U.S.* -rél) *adj.* Without rival; matchless; peerless; unequalled.
~*n.* 1. A person or thing that is unmatched or unequalled; a paragon or nonesuch. 2. *Printing.* Especially formerly, a size of type, 6-point type. [Middle English *nonparaille,* from Old French *nonpareil :* NON- + *pareil,* equal, like, from Vulgar Latin *pariculus* (unattested), diminutive of Latin *pār,* equal.]

non·par·tic·i·pat·ing (nón-paar-tíssi-payting) *adj.* 1. Not participating. 2. *Insurance.* Not giving the right to participate in the profits of a company. —**non·par·tic·i·pa·tor** *n.*

non·par·ti·san (nón-párti-zán, -zan ‖ *U.S.* -zən, -sən) *adj.* 1. Not partisan. 2. Not influenced by, affiliated with, or supporting the interests or policies of any one political party.

non·per·son (nón-pérss'n) *n.* 1. An insipid or unimpressive person. Also called "unperson". 2. An **unperson** (sense 1).

non pla·cet (nón pláss-et, plák) *n.* A negative vote in a church or university assembly, especially at Oxford or Cambridge University. [Latin, "it is not pleasing".]

non·plus (nón-plúss) *n.* A state of perplexity or bafflement preventing action, speech, or thought: *never at a nonplus; reduced to a perfect nonplus.*
~*tr.v.* **nonplussed** or *U.S.* -**plused, nonplussing** or *U.S.* -**plusing, nonplusses** or *U.S.* -**pluses.** To perplex; baffle. [Latin *nōn plūs,* "no more (can be said)" : *nōn,* not + *plūs,* more.]

non pos·su·mus (nón póssew-məss ‖ póssə-) *n. Latin.* A statement indicating an inability to take action on a matter.

non·pro·duc·tive (nón-prə-dúktiv) *adj.* 1. Of or belonging to that part of the labour force that does not directly produce goods, such as clerical personnel. 2. Not yielding what was expected; unproductive. —**non·pro·duc·tive·ly** adv. —**non·pro·duc·tive·ness** n.

non·prof·it·mak·ing (nón-próffit-mayking), **non·profit** (nón-próf-fit) adj. Not set up with the aim of making a profit; not making a profit.

non·pro·lif·e·ra·tion (nón-prə-líffə-ráysh'n, -prō-) n. Limitation of the production or spread of something, especially nuclear weapons. Also used adjectivally: a nonproliferation agreement.

non·pros (nón-próss) tr.v. -prossed, -prossing, -prosses. Law. To enter a judgment of non prosequitur against (a plaintiff).

non pro·se·qui·tur (nón prō-sékwitər) n. Abbr. **non pros.** Law. The judgment entered against a plaintiff who fails to appear in court to prosecute a suit. [Latin, "he does not prosecute".]

non·re·new·a·ble (nón-ri-néw-əb'l, -rə- ‖ -nōō-) adj. Unable to be renewed or extended. 2. Of or designating fuels, especially fossil fuels, that cannot be replaced once exhausted.

non·rep·re·sen·ta·tion·al (nón-réprizen-táysh'n'l) adj. Not representational; especially in art, abstract.

non·res·i·dent (nón-rézzidənt) n. 1. One who does not live or stay at a particular place. 2. One who does not live in the place where he works. —**non·res·i·dence, non·res·i·den·cy** n. —**non·res·i·dent** adj.

non·re·sis·tant (nón-ri-zístənt, -rə-) adj. 1. Not resistant; submissively obedient. 2. Unable to resist illness or infection.
~n. 1. One who believes in complete obedience to authority, even though it may be unjust or arbitrary. 2. One who will not resort to force, even in self-defence. —**non·re·sis·tance** n.

non·re·stric·tive (nón-ri-stríktiv, -rə-) adj. 1. Not restrictive. 2. Grammar. Designating a word, clause, or phrase that is descriptive of but does not limit the basic application of the element it modifies. Compare **restrictive**.

non·re·turn·a·ble (nón-ri-túrnəb'l, -rə-) adj. Designating a bottle or container on which no returnable deposit is paid when purchased.

non·rig·id (nón-ríjid) adj. 1. Not rigid. 2. Designating a lighter-than-air aircraft that holds its shape by gas pressure.

non·sched·uled (nón-shéddewld ‖ U.S. -skéjōold) adj. 1. Operating without fixed flying schedules. Said of certain airlines. 2. Not according to a schedule or plan: a nonscheduled stop at Manchester.

non·se·cre·tor (nón-si-krée'tər) n. A person in whose saliva and other body fluids the A, B, or O antigens determining blood group cannot be detected. Compare **secretor**.

non·sec·tar·i·an (nón-sek-taír-i-ən) adj. Not limited to or associated with any particular religious denomination.

non·sense (nón-sənss ‖ -senss) n. 1. Something that does not make or have sense; especially, behaviour or language that is meaningless or absurd. Also used adjectivally: a nonsense poem. 2. Extravagant foolishness or frivolity. 3. Things of little or no importance or usefulness; trifles: ribbons, laces, and other nonsense. 4. Genetics. A sequence of DNA that is not used as a template for the synthesis of messenger RNA during transcription.
~interj. Used to express rejection or dismissal of an idea or statement. [NON- (not) + SENSE.] —**non·sen·si·cal** (-sén-sik'l) adj. —**non·sen·si·cal·ly** adv.

nonsense verse n. A form of verse dealing with illogical and absurd ideas or characters, and usually employing words invented for humorous effect.

non se·qui·tur (nón sékwitər) n. Abbr. **non seq.** 1. Logic. An inference or conclusion that does not follow from established premises or evidence. 2. A statement that appears to have no relevance to what has just been said. '[Latin, "it does not follow".]

non·skid (nón-skíd) adj. Having a ridged tread or specially treated surface designed to prevent or inhibit skidding. Said of tyres or flooring, for example.

non·smok·er (nón-smókər) n. 1. A person who does not smoke. 2. A carriage or compartment, as in a train, in which smoking is forbidden.

non·spe·ci·fic urethritis (nón-spi-síffik, -spə-) n. Abbr. **NSU.** Inflammation of the urethra, a sexually transmitted infection not caused by gonococcal or other specific infectious agents.

non·stan·dard (nón-stándərd) adj. 1. Varying from or not adhering to a standard. 2. Linguistics. Of or pertaining to usages or varieties of a language that do not conform to those approved by educated native users of the language.

non·start·er (nón-stártər) n. 1. A horse, racing car, or the like that does not compete in a race for which it was entered. 2. Informal. A person, idea, or project regarded as unlikely to succeed and hence not worthy of consideration.

non·stick (nón-stík) adj. Coated with a substance that prevents food adhering during cooking: a nonstick frying pan.

non·stop (nón-stóp) adj. 1. Making or having made no stops: a nonstop flight. 2. Informal. Not relieved by any pause; unceasing. —**non·stop** adv.

non·stri·at·ed (nón-strī-áytid) adj. Having no striations. Said chiefly of certain muscle fibres.

non·strik·er (nón-stríkər) n. 1. Sports. In cricket, the batsman who is not receiving the bowling. 2. A person who does not strike.

nonsuch. Variant of **nonesuch.**

non·suit (nón-séwt, -sōōt) n. Law. A judgment given against a plaintiff when he fails to prosecute his case or to introduce sufficient evidence.
~tr.v. nonsuited, -suiting, -suits. To dismiss the lawsuit of. [Middle English, from Anglo-French no(u)nsuyte : NON- + Old French suite, sieute, SUIT.]

non·sup·port (nón-sə-pórt ‖ -pórt) n. Law. Failure to provide for the maintenance of one's legal dependants.

non·triv·i·al (nón-trívvi-əl) adj. 1. Not trivial. 2. Mathematics. Designating a relationship or expression in which at least one variable is not equal to zero.

non trop·po (nón tróppō, nōn) adv. Music. Moderately. Used to modify a direction: adagio non troppo. [Italian, "not too much".]

non-U (nón-yōō) adj. British Informal. Not belonging or appropriate to upper-class custom, especially in language. Compare **U.**

non·un·ion (nón-yōōn-yən) adj. 1. a. Not belonging to a trade union. b. Not unionised: a non-union shop. 2. Not manufactured or serviced by union labour.
~n. Medicine. Failure of a bone fracture to heal.

non·u·ple (nónnew-p'l) adj. 1. Consisting of nine members; having nine parts or elements; ninefold. 2. Multiplied by nine.
~n. A number or total that is nine times as great as another. [Old French nonuple : non-, nine + -ple, -fold, from Latin -plus.]

non-user (nón-yōōzər) n. One who does not make use of or take something, especially narcotic drugs.

non·vi·a·ble (nón-vī-əb'l) adj. 1. Not capable of living independently after birth. 2. Not workable or practicable.

non·vi·o·lence (nón-vī-ələnss) n. Lack of violence; specifically, a social philosophy based on the rejection of violent means to gain objectives. —**non·vi·o·lent** adj. —**non·vi·o·lent·ly** adv.

non·vol·a·tile (nón-vóllə-tīl ‖ -t'l) adj. Designating or pertaining to a computer memory in which information is retained when the power is switched off.

non·vot·er (nón-vótər) n. A person who does not vote or who has no right to vote. —**non·vot·ing** adj.

non·white, non-white (nón-wīt, -hwīt) n. 1. A person not of the white race. 2. South African. A person not of European descent or not classified as white. —**non·white** adj.

noodle[1] (nōōd'l) n. A thin, usually flat strip of pasta. [German Nudel†.]

noodle[2] n. 1. A fool; a simpleton. 2. Chiefly U.S. Slang. The head. [In sense 1, perhaps blend of NODDLE (head) and NOODLE (food).]

nook (nōōk ‖ nōōk) n. 1. A corner, especially in a room; a recess: They searched for it in every nook and cranny. 2. A quiet, narrow, or secluded spot outdoors. [Middle English noke, nok, perhaps from Scandinavian; akin to Norwegian (dialectal) nok, hook.]

nook·y, nook·ie (nōōki) n. Vulgar Slang. Sexual intercourse. [Perhaps from NOOK (alluding to the pudendum).]

noon (nōōn) n. 1. a. Twelve o'clock in the daytime; midday. b. The time or the point in the Sun's path when it is on the local meridian. 2. The highest point or zenith; the best or brightest part. 3. Archaic. The midpoint: the noon of night. [Middle English none, noon, midday, the hour of the nones (originally 3 p.m.), Old English nōn, "the ninth hour (after sunrise)", from Late Latin nōna (hōra), from the feminine of Latin nōnus, ninth.] —**noon** adj.

noon·day (nōōn-day) n. Noon. —**noon·day** adj.

no one, no-one (nō-wun ‖ Northern England also -won) pron. No person; nobody. See Usage note at **nobody.**

noon·tide (nōōn-tīd) n. Noon. [Middle English nonetyde, Old English nōntīd : nōn, NOON + tīd, TIDE (time).] —**noon·tide** adj.

noose (nōōss) n. 1. A loose loop secured in a rope or cord by means of a slipknot which slides along to tighten it if pulled. 2. A snare or trap. 3. Death by hanging. Preceded by the.
~tr.v. noosed, noosing, nooses. 1. To capture or to hold by or as if by a noose. 2. To make a noose of. [Middle English nose, from Old French nos, nous, from Latin nōdus, a knot.]

no·pal (nṓp'l, nō-pál, -páal) n. 1. Any cactus of the genus Nopalea, found chiefly in Mexico; especially, N. coccinellifera, having erect petals and scarlet flowers. 2. A prickly pear of the genus Opuntia, having yellow or red flowers and purple fruit. [Spanish, from Nahuatl nopalli.]

no-par (nṓ-pár) adj. Without face value; having no par value. Said of share certificates.

nope (nōp) adv. Informal. No. [Alteration of NO (adverb).]

nor[1] (nor; occasional weak form nər) conj. 1. And not; or not; likewise not; not either. Used as a correlative to give continuing negative force: She neither worked nor offered to help. 2. Archaic. Used in place of neither, as the first correlative of a negative pair: Nor grey his beard, nor shambling his gait. [Middle English nor, contraction of nother, nauther, NEITHER.]

Usage: Neither is followed by nor, not by or. When other negative forms are used early in a sentence, the continuation of the negative meaning requires nor when separate clauses are involved (I have no experience of chemistry, nor does the subject interest me). Or may be used when the constructions are within a single clause (I have no experience or interest in chemistry), or share one or more elements (such as she in She will not permit the change, or even consider it), but nor is also available as a more emphatic form in such cases. The use of and with nor is common in informal British English speech (Many didn't go to the cinema, and nor did Joan), but is rare elsewhere. And neither prevails in American English.

nor[2] conj. Regional. Than. [Middle English nor†.]

nor– comb. form. Chemistry. Indicates an unaltered parent compound; for example, **noradrenaline.** [From NORMAL.]

Nor. 1. Norman. 2. north. 3. Norway; Norwegian.

nor·a·dren·a·line, nor·a·dren·a·lin (náwrə-drénnəlin) n. A hormone, $(OH)_2C_6H_3 \cdot CHOH \cdot CH_2NH_2$, secreted by the adrenal medulla and the endings of sympathetic nerves. It is a vasoconstrictor and acts as a transmitter of nerve impulses. Also U.S. "norepinephrine". [NOR- + ADRENALINE.]

Nord·hau·sen acid (nórd-howz'n) *n.* **Fuming sulphuric acid** *(see).* [After *Nordhausen,* a town in Prussian Saxony where it was made.]

Nor·dic (nórdik) *adj. Anthropology.* **1.** Of, pertaining, or belonging to a subdivision of the Caucasoid ethnic group most predominant in Scandinavia. The typical Nordic person is tall, long-headed, blonde, and blue-eyed. **2.** Of or pertaining to cross-country skiing and ski-jumping. Compare **Alpine.**
~*n.* A member of a Nordic people. [French *nordique,* from Old French *nord,* north, from Old English *north.*]

Nord-Ostsee Kanal. See **Kiel Canal.**

nor'easter. *Nautical.* Variant of **northeaster.**

Nor·folk¹ (nór-fək). County in eastern England, bordering on the North Sea. The county town is Norwich. It is a chiefly agricultural county. The eastern portion is notable for the series of shallow lakes and channels known as the Broads.

Norfolk². Largest city in Virginia, eastern United States, lying on the Elizabeth river. It is a major industrial and commercial port and an important military centre.

Norfolk, Thomas Howard, 3rd Duke of (1473–1554). English soldier and politician. He fought at Flodden (1513), and was president of Henry VIII's privy council. He fell from power following the execution of Catherine Howard, his niece and Henry's fifth wife.

Norfolk Island pine *n.* An evergreen tree, *Araucaria excelsa,* native to Norfolk Island in the South Pacific.

Norfolk jacket *n.* A single-breasted men's jacket with a belt, a pocket on each side, and two box pleats in front and back. [Formerly worn for duck hunting in NORFOLK.]

Norfolk plover *n.* A bird, the **stone curlew** *(see).*

NOR gate (nor) *n. Computing.* A logic gate having one output wire and two or more input wires in which there is an output signal only if all the input signals are low. Also called "NOR circuit". Compare **AND gate.** [From NOR, since the gate has a function comparable to the operation of the conjunction *nor* in logic.]

no·ri·a (náwri-ə || nóri-) *n.* A waterwheel with buckets attached to its rim that are used to raise water from a stream, especially for transferral to an irrigation trough. [Spanish, from Arabic *nā'ūrah,* "creaking device", from *na'ara,* to grunt, creak.]

nor·ite (náwrīt) *n.* See **gabbro.** [Norwegian *norit,* "Norwegian rock", from *Norge,* Norway.] —**nor·it·ic** (naw-ríttik) *adj.*

norks (norks) *pl. n. Australian Slang.* A woman's breasts. [Perhaps from *Norco* Co-operative Ltd., a butter manufacturer in New South Wales (alluding to a cow's udders).]

nor·land (nórlənd) *n. Often capital* **N.** *Poetic.* Northland.

norm (norm) *n.* **1.** A standard, model, or pattern regarded as typical for a specific group. **2.** *Mathematics.* **a.** A **mode** *(see).* **b.** An average. **c.** The length of a vector. **3.** *Geology.* The theoretical composition of a standard igneous rock. [Latin *norma,* carpenter's square, pattern.]

norm. normal.

Nor·ma (nórmə) *n.* A constellation in the Southern Hemisphere within the Milky Way near Lupus and Ara.

nor·mal (nórm'l) *adj.* **1.** Conforming, adhering to, or constituting a usual or typical pattern, standard, level, or type; usual; typical: *"Almost all normal people want to be rich without great effort"* (F. Scott Fitzgerald). **2.** *Abbr.* **norm.** *Biology.* **a.** Not affected, immunised, or changed by experimentation. **b.** Functioning or occurring in a natural way. **3.** *Chemistry.* **a.** *Abbr.* **n, N** Designating a solution having one gram equivalent weight of solute per litre of solution. **b.** *Abbr.* **n-** Designating an aliphatic hydrocarbon having a straight and unbranched chain of carbon atoms. **4.** *Abbr.* **norm.** *Geometry.* At right angles; perpendicular. **5.** *Abbr.* **norm.** *Psychology.* Considered average in intelligence, ability, emotional traits, or personality.
~*n. Abbr.* **norm. 1.** Anything that is normal; the standard. **2.** The usual or expected state, form, amount, or degree. **3. a.** Correspondence to a norm. **b.** An average. **4.** *Geometry.* A perpendicular; especially, a perpendicular to a line tangent to a plane curve or to a plane tangent to a space curve. [French, or Late Latin *normālis,* from Latin, made according to the carpenter's square, rectangular, from *norma,* NORM.] —**nor·mal·ly** *adv.*
Synonyms: normal, regular, standard, natural.

nor·mal·cy (nórm'l-si) *n. Chiefly U.S.* Normality.
Usage: This alternative to *normality* is now frequently encountered in formal speech and writing, especially of a technical or semitechnical kind; it continues to attract criticism when used in everyday contexts, where *normality* would be considered the more natural form. *Normalcy* is more common in American English than in British English, but is criticised even in the United States.

normal decane *n. Chemistry.* A **decane** *(see).*

normal distribution *n. Statistics.* A theoretical frequency distribution for a set of variable data, usually represented by a bell-shaped curve symmetrical about the mean. Also called "Gaussian distribution".

nor·mal·ise, nor·mal·ize (nórm'l-īz) *tr.v.* **-ised, -ising, -ises. 1.** To make normal; cause to conform to a standard or norm. **2.** *Metallurgy.* To remove strains and reduce coarse crystalline structures in (steel) by applying heat. **3.** *Mathematics.* To introduce a numerical factor into (an equation) in order to make the area under the graph of the function equal to one, as in quantum mechanics and probability calculations. —**nor·mal·i·sa·tion** (-ī-záysh'n || U.S. -i-) *n.* —**nor·mal·is·er** *n.*

nor·mal·i·ty (nawr-mál-əti) *n.* **1.** The state or fact of being normal. See Usage note at **normalcy. 2.** *Symbol* **N** *Chemistry.* An obsoles-

cent measure of the concentration of a solution equal to the number of gram equivalents of the solute per litre of the solution.

normal pentane *n.* A **pentane** *(see).*

normal school *n.* A school that trains teachers, chiefly of younger children, in countries such as France, the United States, and Canada. [Translation of French *école normale,* originally the name of a school founded as a model for other teacher-training colleges, from Late Latin *normālis,* NORMAL.]

Nor·man (nórmən) *n. Abbr.* **Nor. 1.** A member of a Scandinavian people who conquered Normandy in the tenth century. **2.** A member of the people of Normandy who conquered England in 1066. **3.** A native or inhabitant of Normandy. **4.** A language, Norman French.
~*adj.* **1.** Of or pertaining to Normandy, the Normans, their culture, or their language. **2.** *Architecture.* Designating a variety of Romanesque architecture that was introduced from Normandy into England before the Norman Conquest and flourished until about 1200. [Middle English *Norman,* from Anglo-French, from Old Norse *Northmathr* (stem *Northmann-*), Northman, Scandinavian.]

Norman Conquest *n.* The conquest of England by the Normans under William the Conqueror, beginning in 1066 with the Battle of Hastings.

Nor·man·dy (nórmədi). *French* **Nor·man·die.** Region and former province of northern France, on the English Channel. Major industries include agriculture, cheesemaking (Camembert, Brie), iron ore (at Caen), textiles, shipbuilding, and oil refining. Its major ports are Cherbourg and Le Havre. Viking raids on Normandy began in the ninth century, and it was finally ceded to the Norsemen or Normans (911). After their conquest of England, Normandy passed to England (1106), but was finally recognised to be French territory in 1450. The historic capital of the region is Rouen, where Joan of Arc was burnt at the stake in 1431.

Norman French *n. Abbr.* **N.F.** The dialect of Old French used in medieval Normandy and England. See **Anglo-French.**

nor·ma·tive (nórmətiv) *adj.* **1.** Based upon or prescribing a norm, especially one regarded as a standard of usage in speech and writing: *normative grammar.* **2.** Pertaining to, implying, or establishing a norm or standard: *normative laws.* [French *normatif,* from *norme,* NORM.] —**nor·ma·tive·ly** *adv.* —**nor·ma·tive·ness** *n.*

nor·mo·blast (nórmō-blast) *n.* An immature red blood cell, characterised by abundant haemoglobin and a small nucleus.

nor·mo·ten·sive (nórmō-tén-siv) *adj.* Having, pertaining to, or designating blood pressure that is within the normal range.

Norn¹ (norn) *n., pl.* **Nornir** (nórneer) or **Norns.** *Norse Mythology.* Any of the Fates, Skuld (the Future), Verdandi (the Present), and Urd (the Past). [Old Norse.]

Norn² *n.* An extinct Norse dialect formerly spoken in Orkney and Shetland. [Old Norse *Norrænn,* Norse, from *nordhr,* north.] —**Norn** *adj.*

Norse (norss) *adj. Abbr.* **N. 1.** Of or pertaining to ancient Scandinavia, its people, or their language. **2. a.** Of or pertaining to West Scandinavia (Norway, Iceland, and the Faeroe Islands) or the languages of its inhabitants. **b.** Of or pertaining to Norway, its people, or their language.
~*n., pl.* **Norse.** *Abbr.* **N. 1.** *Used with a plural verb.* **a.** The people of Scandinavia; the Scandinavians. **b.** The people of West Scandinavia; especially, the Norwegians. **c.** The ancient Norwegians. **2.** The Scandinavian or North Germanic branch of Germanic languages; especially, Norwegian. **3.** Any of the West Scandinavian languages or dialects. [Dutch *noor(d)sch,* from *noord,* north, from Middle Dutch *nort.*]

Norse·man (nórss-mən) *n., pl.* **-men** (-mən, -men). Any of the ancient Scandinavians.

north (north) *n. Abbr.* **n, N, n., N., No., Nor. 1. a.** The direction along a meridian to the left of an observer facing in the direction of the earth's rotation; the direction to the left as one faces the rising sun. **b.** The cardinal point on the mariner's compass, located at 0°. **2.** Any area or region lying in this direction. **3.** *Often capital* **N. a.** One of four positions at 90° intervals, that lies in the north, points south, and stands at right angles to east and west. **b.** In games such as bridge or mah-jong, a player who occupies or is said to occupy this position. **4.** *Poetic.* The north wind. —**the North. 1.** The northern or Arctic part of the earth. **2.** The northern part of any country or region, as: **a.** In England, that part of the country lying approximately north of the Humber. **b.** Northern Ireland as distinguished from the Republic of Ireland. **c.** In the United States, the states lying north of Maryland, the Ohio river, and Missouri, and including those that fought for the Union against the Confederacy (or the South) in the Civil War. **3.** The industrialised and technologically advanced nations of the world. Compare **South.**
~*adj.* **1.** To, towards, of, facing, or in the north. **2.** Coming from or originating in the north. Said of a wind. **3.** *Capital* **N.** Officially or conventionally designating the northern part of a country, continent, or other geographical area: *North Korea.*
~*adv.* In, from, or towards the north. [Middle English *north,* Old English *north.*]

North, Frederick, Lord (1732–92). British statesman. A Tory M.P., he became chancellor of the exchequer (1767), and, as a favourite of George III, was appointed prime minister (1770). Britain's loss of the American colonies, for which he bore the ultimate responsibility, led to his resignation.

North, Sir Thomas (*c.*1535–1601). English translator. His best-known work, a vivid, poetic translation of Plutarch's *Lives of*

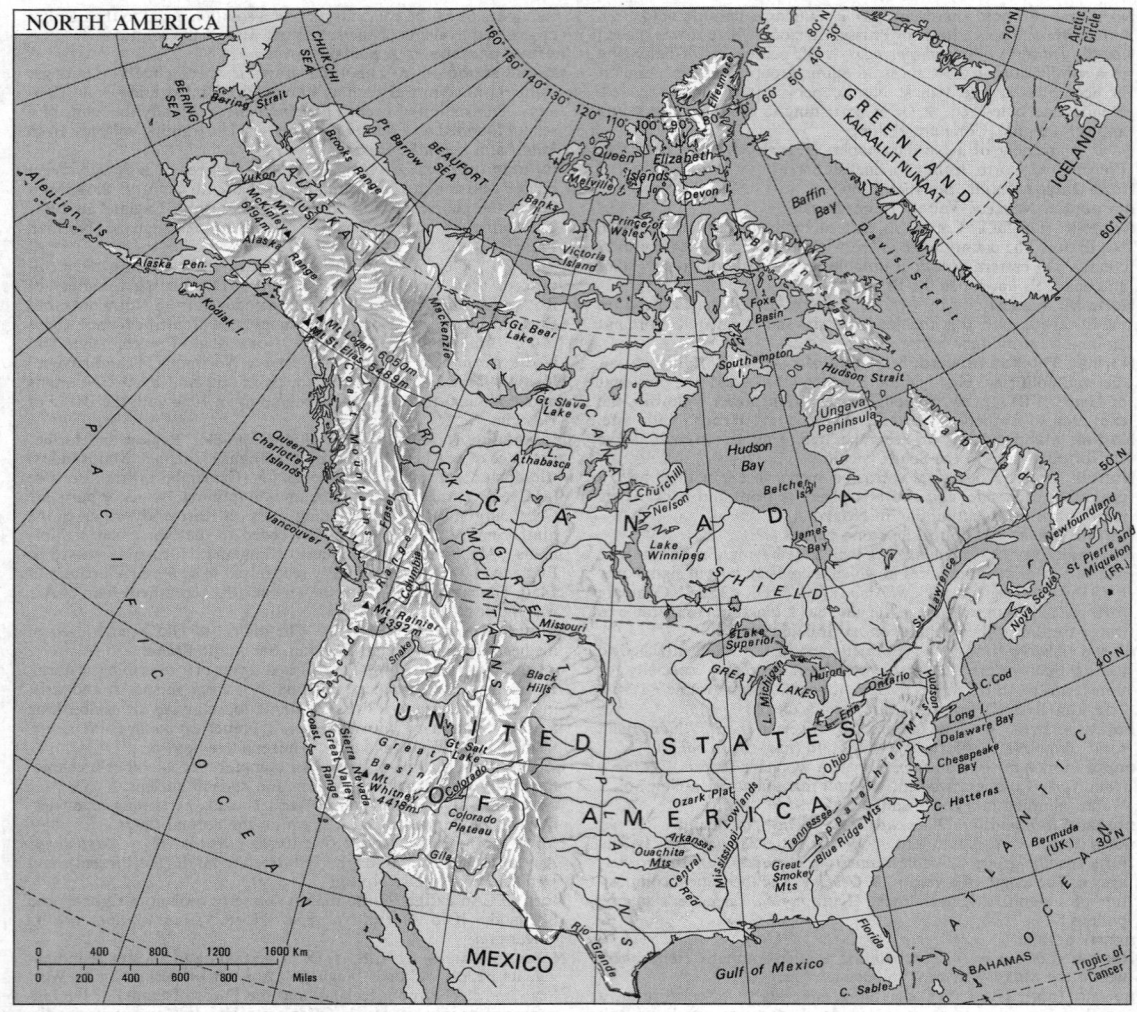

NORTH AMERICA

the Noble Grecians and Romans (1579), was extensively used as source material by Shakespeare.

North America. A division of the **Americas.** It is the world's third largest continent, and it covers about 13 per cent of the earth's land surface and contains about 6 per cent of the world's population.

North·amp·ton (nawr-thámptən, nər-, nórth-hámptən). County town of Northamptonshire, central England, lying on the river Nene. It has long been one of the country's shoemaking centres and today there is also considerable manufacture of machinery.

North·amp·ton·shire (nawr-thámptən-shər, nər-, nórth-hámptən-, -sheer). County in central England. Most of it consists of gently rolling pasture and woods. Iron ore deposits, now largely worked out, led to the siting of iron and steel works at Corby. The county town is Northampton.

North Atlantic Current *n.* An ocean current or drift formed southeast of Newfoundland by the junction of the Gulf Stream and the Labrador Current, and flowing generally northeast across the Atlantic. Also called "North Atlantic Drift".

North Atlantic Treaty Organisation *n. Abbr.* **NATO** (náytō). An alliance for military and naval defence established on April 4, 1949, by countries situated on or near the Atlantic Ocean. The original membership was: Belgium, Canada, Denmark, France (which reduced its links in 1966, and later acquired an independent nuclear deterrent), Iceland, Italy, Luxembourg, the Netherlands, Norway, Portugal, the United Kingdom, and the United States. Greece and Turkey joined in 1952, West Germany in 1955 and Spain in 1982. The French and Spanish forces remain outside NATO's integrated military command. In 1990 the reunified Germany became part of NATO, with some voluntary restrictions. The headquarters of the organisation is in Brussels.

north·bound (nórth-bownd) *adj.* Heading towards or leading towards the north.

north by east *n. Abbr.* **NbE** The direction, or point on a compass, halfway between due north and north-northeast. It is 11° 15′ east of due north. **—north by east** *adv. & adj.*

north by west *n. Abbr.* **NbW** The direction, or point on a compass, halfway between due north and north-northwest. It is 11° 15′ west of due north. **—north by west** *adv. & adj.*

North Carolina. State on the Atlantic coast of the eastern United

States. Since colonial times it has been a tobacco-producing state and it still leads the nation in the production of tobacco, as well as of textiles and furniture. The capital is Raleigh.

north celestial pole *n. Astronomy.* The **North Pole** *(see).*

North·cliffe (nórth-klif), **Alfred Charles William Harmsworth, 1st Viscount** (1865–1922). Irish-born British newspaper proprietor. A pioneer of popular journalism in the United Kingdom, he founded the *Daily Mirror* (1903), and with his brother, Viscount Rothermere, founded the *Daily Mail* (1896).

North Country *n.* The north of England. Preceded by *the.* **—North·coun·try·man** (nórth-kúntrimən) *n.*

North Dakota. State in the north central United States, lying on the border with Canada. It is very rural, its only industries of importance being connected with food processing. The leading products are wheat, cattle, oil, and natural gas. The capital is Bismarck.

north·east (nórth-éest; *nautical* nór-) *n. Abbr.* **NE 1.** The direction, or point on a compass, halfway between north and east. It is 45° east of due north. **2.** Any area or region lying in this direction. **—the Northeast.** In England, that part of the country approximately comprising Northumberland, Durham, and neighbouring areas.

~*adj.* **1.** Situated towards, facing, or in the northeast. **2.** Coming from or originating in the northeast. Said of a wind.

~*adv.* In, from, or towards the northeast. **—north·east·ern** *adj.* **—north·east·ern·er** *n.*

northeast by east *n. Abbr.* **NEbE** The direction, or point on a compass, halfway between northeast and east-northeast. It is 56° 15′ east of due north. **—northeast by east** *adv. & adj.*

northeast by north *n. Abbr.* **NEbN** The direction, or point on a compass, halfway between northeast and north-northeast. It is 33° 45′ east of due north. **—northeast by north** *adv. & adj.*

north·east·er (nórth-éestər; *nautical* nór-) *n.* Also **nor'east·er** (nor-eestər). A storm or gale from the northeast.

north·east·er·ly (nórth-éestərli; *nautical* nór-) *adj.* **1.** Towards or in the northeast. **2.** From the northeast.

~*n., pl.* **northeasterlies.** A storm or wind from the northeast. **—north·east·er·ly** *adv.*

north·east·ward (nórth-éestwərd; *nautical* nór-) *adj.* Situated towards or facing the northeast.

~n. 1. A direction or point towards the northeast. **2.** A region or part situated in or towards the northeast.

~adv. *Chiefly U.S.* Variant of **northeastwards.** **—north·east·ward·ly** *adj. & adv.*

north·east·wards (nórth-éestwərdz) *adv.* Also *chiefly U.S.* **northeastward.** Towards the northeast.

north·er (nórthər) *n. U.S.* A sudden, cold gale from the north, especially around the Gulf of Mexico. The norther may reach a speed of 100 kilometres (about 60 miles) per hour.

north·er·ly (nórthərli) *adj.* **1.** Situated in or towards the north. **2.** From the north. Said of a wind.

~n., pl. northerlies. A storm or wind from the north. **—north·er·ly** *adv.*

north·ern (nórthərn) *adj. Abbr.* **n, n., N, N. 1.** Situated towards, in, or facing the north. **2.** Coming from the north. Said of a wind. **3.** Growing in the north. **4.** *Often capital* **N.** Of, pertaining to, or characteristic of northern regions or the North. **5.** *Astronomy.* North of the celestial equator. [Middle English *northerne,* Old English *northerne.*]

Northern Cape. New province of South Africa, created in 1994, comprising the northern part of the former Cape Province. Capital, Kimberley.

Northern Cross *n.* A cross formed by six stars in the constellation **Cygnus** *(see).*

Northern Crown *n.* A constellation, **Corona Borealis** *(see).*

north·ern·er (nórthərnər) *n.* **1.** A native or inhabitant of the north. **2.** *Often capital* **N.** A native or inhabitant of the north of England or of the northeastern United States.

Northern Hemisphere *n.* The half of the earth lying north of the equator.

Northern Ireland. Province of the United Kingdom consisting of 6 of the counties in the ancient Irish province of Ulster, by which name it is often inaccurately known. Mostly low-lying, it rises to the Sperrin Mountains in the northwest, and the Mourne Mountains in the southeast. Lough Neagh, Ireland's largest lake, is in the centre of the province. Its traditional industries, shipbuilding and linen, have been in decline since World War II. Attempts by successive British governments to revive its economy have been hampered by the state of near civil war that has existed since 1969 between Protestant and Roman Catholic extremists. A joint declaration in 1993 by prime ministers John Major of Great Britain and Albert Reynolds of the Republic of Ireland was designed to pave the way to a political settlement acceptable to both communities, and peace talks from 1996 did eventually lead to the proclamation in April 1998 by P.M. Tony Blair and Taoiseach Bertie Ahern of a peace agreement. Until 1972, when all powers were transferred to Westminster, the province had its own semiautonomous parliament which sat at Stormont near Belfast, the capital and chief port.

northern lights *pl. n.,* The **aurora borealis** *(see).*

north·ern·most (nórthərn-mōst) *adj.* Farthest north.

Northern Province. New province of South Africa, created in 1994 by the subdivision of the former Transvaal. Capital, Pietersburg.

Northern Rhodesia. See **Zambia.**

Northern Territory. Territory in north central Australia, with a coastline along the Timor Sea, the Arafura Sea, and the Gulf of Carpentaria. The chief economic activity is stock-breeding, although exploitation of the region's mineral resources—gold, uranium, bauxite, iron, lead, and zinc—is increasing. The territory was formerly part of New South Wales (1825–63) and South Australia (1863–1911), but since 1911 it has been ruled directly by the Commonwealth of Australia and is now in the process of becoming a fully fledged state. The capital and largest town is Darwin.

North Germanic *n.* A branch of the Germanic group of languages, which includes Danish, Faeroese, Icelandic, Norwegian, and Swedish. See **Germanic.** **—North Germanic** *adj.*

North Holland. Province of the Netherlands, occupying the peninsula between the North Sea and the IJsselmeer. It also includes a number of the West Frisian islands. The capital is Haarlem, the largest city, Amsterdam. A region of low-lying fenland, it is now largely a manufacturing area.

north·ing (nór-thing, -thing) *n.* In navigation: **1.** The difference in latitude between two positions as a result of a movement to the north. **2.** Progress towards the north. **3.** *Astronomy.* A north declination.

North Island. The northern of the two main islands which make up New Zealand. It is the smaller of the two, but the more heavily populated. The main cities are Wellington, the national capital, and Auckland. Most of New Zealand's dairy farming is carried out here.

north·land (nórth-lənd || -land) *n.* **1.** *Often capital* **N.** A region in the north, such as the northern part of the earth or of a country. **2.** *Capital* **N.** Norway and Sweden. **—north·land·er** *n.*

North·man (nórth-mən) *n., pl.* **-men** (-mən, -men). A Norseman.

north-north·east (nórth-nórth-éest; *nautical* nór-nór-) *n. Abbr.* **NNE** The direction, or point on a compass, halfway between due north and northeast. It is 22° 30′ east of due north.

~adj. Situated towards, facing, or in this direction.

~adv. In, from, or towards this direction.

north-north·west (nórth-nórth-wést; *nautical* nór-nór-) *n. Abbr.* **NNW** The direction, or point on a compass, halfway between due north and northwest. It is 22° 30′ west of due north.

~adj. Situated towards, facing, or in this direction.

~adv. In, from, or towards this direction.

North Pole *n.* **1.** The northern end of the earth's axis of rotation.

2. The celestial zenith of this terrestrial point, slightly more than 1 degree from Polaris, the North Star. Also called "north celestial pole". **3.** *Small* **n**, *small* **p.** The north-seeking **magnetic pole** *(see)* of a magnet.

North Rhine-West·pha·li·a (rīn-wést-fáyli-ə). *German* **Nord·rhein-West·fa·len** (nórt-rīn-vest-fáalən). State in western Germany, lying in the lower Rhine basin. It is a very densely populated and extensively industrialised state, the region known as the Ruhr district being the most highly concentrated industrial complex in western Europe. The capital is Düsseldorf.

North Sea. Arm of the Atlantic Ocean, lying between Great Britain and northwest Europe, connected to the English Channel by the Strait of Dover. Long the source of valuable fish, it gained a new economic importance in the late 1960s when large deposits of oil and natural gas were discovered under its sea bed.

North Star *n.* A star, **Polaris** *(see).*

North·um·ber·land (nawr-thúmbərlənd, nər-). County in northeastern England, bordering on Scotland and the North Sea. It is an almost entirely rural county, having lost Newcastle (formerly the county town) and Tynemouth when the former metropolitan county of Tyne and Wear was established in 1974. The county includes the Farne Islands, with their large bird sanctuary. Sheep-farming is the predominant agricultural activity. The county is especially rich in remains of medieval military architecture and the Roman wall is well preserved from Heddon-on-the-Wall to the Cumbria border.

North·um·bri·a (nawr-thúmbri-ə). Kingdom of Anglo-Saxon England, extending from eastern Scotland to the east riding of Yorkshire. It was settled by Angles early in the sixth century and originally consisted of two kingdoms, Bernicia and Deira, which were separated by the river Tees. The two kingdoms were united by Aethelfrith of Bernicia early in the seventh century and shortly thereafter Northumbria became the most powerful kingdom in the country. During the late seventh century the power of Northumbria waned as that of Mercia grew.

North·um·bri·an (nawr-thúmbri-ən) *adj.* **1.** Of or pertaining to Northumbria or its dialect. **2.** Of or pertaining to Northumberland. **~n. 1.** A native of Northumbria or Northumberland. **2. a.** The Old English dialect of Northumbria. **b.** The Modern English dialect of Northumberland.

north·ward (nórthward; *nautical* nórthərd) *adj.* Situated towards, facing, or in the north.

~n. 1. A direction or point towards the north. **2.** A region situated in or towards the north.

~adv. *Chiefly U.S.* Variant of **northwards.** **—north·ward·ly** *adj. & adv.*

north·wards (nórth-wərdz) *adv.* Also *chiefly U.S.* **northward.** Towards the north.

north·west (nórth-wést; *Nautical* nór-) *n. Abbr.* **NW 1.** The direction, or point on a compass, halfway between north and west. It is 45° west of due north. **2.** Any area or region lying in this direction. **—the Northwest.** The northwestern part of England, especially the Lake District and Lancashire.

~adj. 1. To, towards, of, facing, or in the northwest. **2.** Coming from or originating in the northwest. Said of a wind.

~adv. In, from, or towards the northwest. **—north·west·ern** *adj.*

North-West. New province of South Africa, created in 1994 by the subdivision of the former Transvaal. Includes the former homeland of Bophuthatswana. Capital, Mmabatho.

northwest by north *n. Abbr.* **NWbN** The direction, or point on a compass, halfway between northwest and north-northwest. It is 33° 45′ west of due north. **—northwest by north** *adv. & adj.*

northwest by west *n. Abbr.* **NWbW** The direction, or point on a compass, halfway between northwest and west-northwest. It is 56° 15′ west of due north. **—northwest by west** *adv. & adj.*

north·west·er (nórth-wéstər; *nautical* nór-) *n.* Also **nor'west·er** (nor-wéstər). A storm or gale from the north west.

north·west·er·ly (nórth-wéstərli; *nautical* nór-) *adj.* **1.** Towards or in the northwest. **2.** From the northwest.

~n., pl. northwesterlies. A storm or wind from the northwest. **—north·west·er·ly** *adv.*

North-West Frontier Province. Province of northwest Pakistan, bordering on Afghanistan to the north and west. It is a largely mountainous area, with agriculture practised in the fertile valleys. The chief product is wheat. Historically of great importance because of its proximity to the Khyber Pass, the region came under British control in 1849; it remained British until 1947 when the people of the province voted to become part of newly independent Pakistan. The capital is Peshawar.

Northwest Passage. Northern sea route joining the Atlantic and Pacific oceans, through the Canadian Arctic Archipelago and the waters north of Alaska. The first explorations were undertaken by Sir Martin Frobisher (1576–78); proof of the existence of the passage was obtained by the early 19th century, but the first expedition actually to navigate the whole of the route was led by Roald Amundsen (1903–06). The first commercial ship to cross the passage was the U.S. oil tanker, the S.S. *Manhattan* (1969).

Northwest Semitic *n.* A subgroup of the Semitic family of languages, consisting of Canaanite and Aramaic.

Northwest Territories. Territory in northwest Canada, lying between the Yukon to the west and Hudson Bay to the east, and extending north from the borders of the Prairie Provinces to include the Arctic Archipelago. In all, the Territories occupy one-third of

Canada's area. Only the extreme south is outside the permafrost area and the region is sparsely populated, mostly by Indians, Eskimos, and Metis. Fur-trading and fishing are the traditional economic activities of the region, but mining is now by far the most important source of wealth. The capital is Yellowknife.

north·west·ward (nórth-wéstwərd; *nautical* nór-) *adj.* Situated towards, facing, or in the northwest.
~*n.* **1.** A direction or point towards the northwest. **2.** A region or part situated in or towards the northwest.
~*adv. Chiefly U.S.* Variant of **northwestwards. —north·west·ward·ly** *adj. & adv.*

north·west·wards (nórth-wést-wərdz) *adv.* Also *chiefly U.S.* **northwestward.** Towards the northwest.

North Yorkshire. County in northeastern England, created in 1974 from the rural parts of the North Riding of the former county of Yorkshire. It also includes some parts of the former East and West Ridings. The major towns in the county are York (now administratively separate), Harrogate, and Scarborough.

Norw. Norway; Norwegian.

Nor·way, Kingdom of (nór-way). *Norwegian* **Nor·ge** (-gə). Indepen- dent kingdom of northern Europe, occupying the western coastland of the Scandinavian peninsula. Most of the country consists of a mountainous plateau unsuited to agriculture; only about three per cent of the land is cultivated. Fishing, timber, and shipbuilding have traditionally been the mainstays of the economy. Now an industrial country, Norway relies on exports of natural gas and petroleum (discovered in the North Sea in the 1960s), aluminium, iron and steel, chemicals, wood products, and fish, and on shipping. At various times united with Sweden and Denmark from the 14th century, Norway finally gained its independence in 1905. Area, 324 219 square kilometres (125,182 square miles). Population, 4,380,000. Capital, Oslo.

Norway lobster *n.* A slender, edible, European lobster of the genus *Nephrops.*

Norway maple *n.* A tall Eurasian tree, *Acer platanoides,* with pale green, palmately lobed leaves. [First cultivated in NORWAY.]

Norway pout *n.* A small greenish fish, *Trisopterus esmarkii,* found in the northeast Atlantic. It is important in the diet of several food fish, such as cod and haddock. Also called "pout".

Norway rat *n.* The **brown rat** (see).

Norway spruce *n.* A tall evergreen tree, *Picea abies*, of northern regions, growing up to 46 metres (150 feet) in height and having long, dark green needles. It is commonly used as a Christmas tree.

Nor·we·gian (nawr-wéejən) *n. Abbr.* **Nor., Norw. 1.** A native or inhabitant of Norway. **2.** The North Germanic language of the Norwegians. See **Bokmål, Nynorsk.** —**Nor·we·gian** *adj.*

Norwegian elkhound *n.* An **elkhound** *(see).*

nor'west·er (nór-wéstər) *n.* **1.** Variant of **northwester. 2.** A drink of strong spirits. **3.** An oilskin hat, a **sou'wester** *(see).*

Nor·wich (nórrij, nórrich). County town of Norfolk, east central England, lying on the river Wensum just above its confluence with the Yare. An important provincial centre since the rise of the wool trade in the high Middle Ages, Norwich is now a market city and the site of the University of East Anglia (founded 1963).

nos., Nos. numbers.

nose (nōz) *n.* **1.** In humans and other primates, the part of the face bearing the nostrils and containing the organ of smell and the beginning of the respiratory tract. **2.** In many other animals, a similar feature or organ in the face, muzzle, snout, or front end. **3. a.** The sense of smell: *a dog with a good nose.* **b.** The ability to detect or discover, as if by smell: *a nose for a good story.* **4.** An aroma or bouquet, as of wine or tea, for example. **5.** *Informal.* The nose as a symbol of prying: *Keep your nose out of my business.* **6.** Anything that resembles a nose because of shape or position, such as the forward part of an aircraft. **7.** *Slang.* A police informer. —**by a nose.** In horse racing, by the length of a horse's nose, considered as a narrow margin of victory. —**follow (one's) nose. 1.** To go straight ahead. **2.** To be guided by instinct. —**keep (one's) nose clean.** *Informal.* To keep out of trouble. —**lead by the nose.** To control (someone) completely, often humiliatingly, without his perceiving it. —**look down (one's) nose at.** *Informal.* To treat haughtily. —**on the nose.** *Slang.* **1.** *U.S.* Designating a bet on a horse to win. **2.** *Chiefly U.S.* Exactly; precisely. **3.** *Australian.* Bad; foulsmelling. —**pay through the nose.** *Informal.* To pay an exorbitant price. —**put (someone's) nose out of joint.** To displease by supplanting. —**turn up (one's) nose at.** To treat with contempt.

~*v.* **nosed, nosing, noses.** —*tr.* **1.** To find out by or as if by smell. **2.** To touch or examine with the nose; nuzzle. **3.** To steer (a vehicle or one's way) with care to avoid a collision.

~*intr.* **1.** To smell or sniff. **2.** *Informal.* To pry from curiosity or in a meddlesome way. Followed by *around, about,* or *into.* **3.** To move forward slowly and carefully. —**nose out. 1.** To find by persistent searching. **2.** To defeat by a very narrow margin. [Middle English *nose,* Old English *nosu.*]

nose·bag (nōz-bag) *n.* A bag containing feed that fits over a horse's muzzle. Also **U.S.** "feedbag".

nose·band (nōz-band) *n.* The part of a bridle or halter that passes over the animal's nose. Also called "nosepiece".

nose·bleed (nōz-bleed) *n.* A nasal haemorrhage; bleeding from the nose. Also called "epistaxis".

nose cone *n.* The front, usually separable, section of a rocket or guided missile, shaped to offer minimum aerodynamic resistance and often bearing a heat-resistant cladding.

nose dive *n.* **1.** A sudden plunge of an aircraft with its nose towards the earth. **2.** Any sudden, swift, downward plunge or drop.

nose-dive (nōz-dīv) *intr.v.* **-dived** or **U.S. -dove** (-dōv), **-diving, -dives.** To perform a nose dive.

nose·gay (nōz-gay) *n.* A small bunch of flowers. [Middle English : NOSE (fragrance) + *gay,* toy, ornament, from GAY (adjective).]

nose·piece (nōz-peess) *n.* **1.** A piece of armour forming part of a helmet and serving as a guard for the nose. **2.** The bridge of a pair of glasses. **3.** Part of a bridle, a noseband. **4.** The part of a microscope, often rotatable, to which one or more objective lenses are attached.

nose wheel *n.* The landing wheel fitted below the nose of an aircraft.

nosh (nosh) *n. Informal.* Food; a snack or meal.

~*intr.v.* **noshed, noshing, noshes.** *Informal.* To eat. [Yiddish, from *nosherai,* titbits, from Old High German *(h)nascōn,* to gnaw, nibble.]

no-show (nō-shō) *n.* *U.S. Slang.* A traveller who reserves a place, especially on an aircraft, but neither claims nor cancels the reservation before the time of departure.

nosh-up (nósh-up) *n. British Slang.* A large, hearty meal.

no side *n.* In Rugby football, the signal or announcement by the referee that the game has finished.

nos·ing (nōzing) *n.* **1.** The horizontally projecting edge of a stair tread. **2.** A shield covering this edge. **3.** A projecting edge of a moulding.

noso– *comb. form.* Indicates disease; for example, **nosology.** [Greek, from *nosos†,* a disease.]

no·sog·ra·phy (no-sóggrəfi, nō-) *n.* The written systematisation and description of diseases. [New Latin *nosographia* : NOSO- + -GRAPHY.] —**no·sog·ra·pher** *n.* —**no·so·graph·ic** (nóssə-gráffik, nō-sə-), **no·so·graph·i·cal** *adj.*

no·sol·o·gy (no-sólləji, nō-) *n.* The branch of medicine that deals with the naming and classification of diseases. [New Latin *nosologia* : NOSO- + -LOGY.] —**no·so·log·i·cal** (nóssə-lójik'l, nō-sə-) *adj.* —**no·so·log·i·cal·ly** *adv.* —**no·sol·o·gist** (-sólləjist) *n.*

nos·tal·gi·a (no-stál-jə, -ji-ə || nə-; *U.S. also* nō-, -stáal-) *n.* **1.** A wistful or sentimental longing for things, persons, or situations that are past and irrevocable. **2.** Homesickness. [New Latin (translation of German *Heimweh,* homesickness) : Greek *nostos,* a return +

-ALGIA.] —**nos·tal·gic** *adj.* —**nos·tal·gic·al·ly** *adv.*

nos·toc (nóstok) *n.* Any freshwater blue-green alga of the genus *Nostoc,* forming colonies of filaments with a gelatinous covering. [New Latin; coined by Paracelsus as a name for algae that he believed were derived from starlight.]

Nos·tra·da·mus (nóstrə-dáamoss, -dáymoss), born Michel de Nostre-Dame (1503–66). French astrologer and physician. He was court physician to Charles IX, but is best known for his book of prophecies, *Centuries* (1555), written in quatrains.

nos·tril (nóss-trəl, -tril) *n.* Either of the external openings of the nose. [Middle English *nostrill,* Old English *nosthyrl* : *nosu,* NOSE + *thyrl, thyrel,* hole.]

nos·trum (nóstrəm) *n., pl.* **-trums. 1.** A patent medicine, or one in which the ingredients are kept secret; especially, a quack remedy. **2.** A pet scheme for the solution of some problem. [New Latin *nostrum,* "our own" (that is, invented and made by the seller), from Latin, neuter of *noster,* ours.]

nos·y, nos·ey (nōzi) *adj.* **-ier, -iest.** *Informal.* Prying; inquisitive. See Synonyms at **curious.** [From NOSE.] —**nos·i·ly** *adv.* —**nos·i·ness** *n.*

nosy parker *n. Chiefly British Informal.* A person who pries into other people's affairs. [Arbitrary use of surname *Parker.*]

not (not) *adv.* In no way; to no degree. Used to express negation, denial, refusal, disbelief, or prohibition: *Definitely not; I will not go; You may not have any.* In informal speech and writing, *not* is often contracted and suffixed to auxiliary verbs, for example, *aren't, don't.* —**not at all.** You do not need to thank me. Used as a polite reply when one has been thanked. —**not that.** Although it is not to be supposed that: *She denies everything—not that I believe her.* [Middle English *not,* reduced form of *nought,* nothing, not, Old English *nōwiht, nāwiht* : *nō, nā,* no + *wiht,* a man, thing.]

not-. Variant of **noto-.**

no·ta be·ne (nōtə bénni, béeni; *also* nōtaa báynay). *Abbr.* **n.b., N.B.** *Latin.* Note well.

no·ta·bil·i·ty (nōtə-bílləti) *n., pl.* **-ties. 1.** The state or quality of being notable. **2.** A notable or prominent person.

no·ta·ble (nōtəb'l) *adj.* **1.** Worthy of notice; remarkable; striking: *a notable beauty.* **2.** *Archaic & Regional.* Diligent, especially in household management.

~*n.* **1.** A person of note or distinction. **2.** *Often capital* **N.** Any of a council of prominent persons, before the French Revolution, called into assembly by the king at times of emergency. [Middle English, from Old French, from Latin *notābilis,* from *notāre,* to note, from *nota,* a NOTE.] —**no·ta·ble·ness** *n.* —**no·ta·bly** *adv.*

no·tar·i·al (nō-taír-i-əl) *adj.* **1.** Of or pertaining to a notary. **2.** Executed or drawn up by a notary. —**no·tar·i·al·ly** *adv.*

no·ta·rise, no·ta·rize (nōtə-rīz) *tr.v.* **-rised, -rising, -rises.** *Chiefly U.S.* To authenticate or attest as a notary. [From NOTARY.] —**no·ta·ri·sa·tion** (-rī-záysh'n || *U.S.* -ri-) *n.*

no·ta·ry (nōtəri) *n., pl.* **-ries. 1.** A notary public. **2.** *Obsolete.* A clerk; especially, one licensed to draft legal documents. [Middle English *notarie,* "clerk", from Latin *notārius,* "stenographer", from *notārius,* cipher, shorthand character, from *nota,* mark, NOTE.]

notary public *n., pl.* **notaries public.** *Abbr.* **N.P.** A public officer authorised by law to certify documents, take affidavits, and administer oaths. Also called "notary".

no·tate (nō-táyt || *chiefly U.S.* nō-tayt) *tr.v.* **-tated, -tating, -tates.** To represent (music, for example) in notation. [Back-formation from NOTATION.]

no·ta·tion (nō-táysh'n) *n.* **1.** A system of figures or symbols used in specialised fields to represent numbers, quantities, or other facts or values: *musical notation.* **2.** The act or process of using such a system. **3.** *U.S.* A jotting or annotation; a note: *a notation in the margin.* [Latin *notātiō* (stem *notātiōn-*), from *notāre,* to note, from *nota,* a NOTE.] —**no·ta·tion·al** *adj.*

notch (noch) *n.* **1.** A V-shaped cut, especially one used for keeping count. **2.** *U.S.* A narrow pass between mountains. **3.** *Informal.* A level or degree: *She is a notch better than her brother.* **4.** The undercutting of a cliff at high-water level, producing an indentation at its base.

~*tr.v.* **notched, notching, notches. 1.** To cut a notch or notches in. **2.** To record by or as if by making notches: *notched the score on a stick.* **3.** *Informal.* To score. Often used with *up: She notched up three wins in succession.* [Anglo-French *noche†.*]

note (nōt) *n. Abbr.* **n. 1.** *Often plural.* A brief record of something, written down to aid the memory. **2.** A brief written communication. **3.** A formal written diplomatic or official communication. **4.** A commentary to or explanation of a passage in a text, printed in the margin, at the foot of the page, or at the end of the text. **5. a.** A piece of paper currency. **b.** A certificate issued by a government or a bank and sometimes negotiable as money. **c.** A **promissory note** *(see).* **6.** *Music.* **a.** A musical sound of definite pitch. **b.** The symbol of such a note in musical notation, indicating the pitch by its position on the staff and the duration by details of its appearance such as shape. **c.** A key of a piano or similar instrument. **7. a.** The musical call of a bird. **b.** Any expressive vocal sound, such as the cry or call of an animal. **8.** A tone, sign, or suggestion that reveals or characterises a quality, mood, or atmosphere; a mark: *a note of gaiety.* **9.** Importance or consequence: *Nothing of note happened.* **10.** Notice or observation: *We took note of what had happened.* **11.** *Poetic.* A song, melody, or tune. —**compare notes.** To exchange ideas, views, or opinions.

~*tr.v.* **noted, noting, notes. 1.** To observe carefully; notice; perceive. **2.** To write down; make a note of. **3.** To show; indicate. **4.** To make particular mention of; remark. [Middle English *note*, from Old French, from Latin *nota*, mark, sign, cipher, shorthand character.] —**not·er** *n.*

note·book (nṓt-bŏŏk ‖ -bŏŏk) *n.* A small book for writing notes in.

note·case (nṓt-kayss) *n.* A slim flat wallet designed to hold paper money.

not·ed (nṓtid) *adj.* Distinguished by reputation; notable; eminent: *a noted author.* —**not·ed·ly** *adv.* —**not·ed·ness** *n.*

note·let (nṓt-lət, -lit) *n.* A folded card, usually with decorative illustration, for writing short informal letters.

note of hand *n.* A promissory note *(see).*

note·pap·er (nṓt-paypər) *n.* Paper for writing letters on; writing paper.

note row *n. Music.* A tone row *(see).*

note·wor·thy (nṓt-wurthi) *adj.* Deserving recognition; worthy of notice; remarkable: *a noteworthy young talent.* —**note·wor·thi·ly** *adv.* —**note·wor·thi·ness** *n.*

NOT gate (not) *n. Computing.* A logic gate that provides an output signal if the input signal is low and vice versa. Also called "inverter", "negator", "NOT circuit". [From NOT, since the gate's function is comparable to the operation of *not* in logic.]

noth·ing (núth-ing ‖ *Northern England also* nŏth-). *n.* **1.** No thing; not anything. **2.** No significant or notable thing: *There is nothing on television tonight.* **3.** No part; no portion: *Nothing remains of its former glory.* **4.** Insignificance; obscurity: *rising from nothing.* **5.** Absence of anything perceptible; non-existence: *The sound faded into nothing.* **6.** That which has no qualitative value or positive effect: *amount to nothing.* **7.** A zero; a nought. **8.** A person or thing of no consequence or significance. **9.** *Plural.* An affectionate word or remark: *sweet nothings.* —**for nothing.** Free of charge; gratis. —**have (got) nothing on. 1.** To be naked. **2.** To have no social engagements or obligations. **3.** To be markedly inferior in comparison to. —**have (got) nothing on (one).** To have no money on one's person. —**have (got) nothing on (someone).** To have no incriminatory evidence against. —**look like nothing on earth.** To appear ugly or outlandish. —**make nothing of.** To be unable to understand or cope with. —**nothing but.** Only; no other than. —**nothing doing.** *Informal.* **1.** Certainly not. Used as an emphatic refusal. **2.** Nothing of interest happening; not a thing going on. —**nothing for it.** No other course of action is possible. —**nothing like. 1.** Not at all like: *She's nothing like her sister.* **2.** Not nearly: *The blizzard here was nothing like as heavy as it was up north.* —**nothing short of.** No less than; tantamount to. —**nothing to it.** It is quite straightforward.

~*adj. Slang.* Insignificant or unimportant: *a nothing job.*

~*adv.* In no way or degree; not at all: *nothing daunted.* [Middle English *nathing, nothing,* Old English *nāthing, nān thing* : *nān,* NONE + THING.]

noth·ing·ness (núth-ing-nəss, -niss ‖ *Northern England also* nŏth-) *n.* **1.** The condition or quality of being nothing; non-existence. **2.** Empty or featureless space; the void. **3.** Lack of consequence; insignificance. **4.** Something inconsequential or insignificant.

no·tice (nṓtiss) *n.* **1.** The act of observing or regarding with the senses; perception; attention: *That detail escaped my notice.* **2.** Heed or attention paid to another person or thing; especially, respectful attention or consideration: *grateful for the notice you took.* **3.** A formal written announcement, published or displayed for all to see: *a notice of sale.* **4. a.** A formal announcement of purpose, especially of intention to withdraw from an agreement or leave a job: *give two weeks' notice.* **b.** Notification of dismissal from a job. **5.** A printed critical review of a play, book, or other cultural work. **6.** Any announcement of some present or coming event.

~*v.* **noticed, -ticing, -tices.** —*tr.* **1.** To observe; perceive; be aware of: *She did not notice the child in the doorway.* **2.** To consider; take note of; mark: *notice the discrepancy.* **3.** To comment on; mention in passing: *She began her speech by noticing the size of the audience.* **4.** To treat with courteous attention. —*intr. Nonstandard.* To show; be evident: *The stain won't notice.* [Middle English *notyce,* from Old French *notice,* from Latin *nōtitia,* knowledge, acquaintance, from *nōtus,* known, from the past participle of *nōscere,* to get acquainted with.]

no·tice·a·ble (nṓtissəb'l) *adj.* **1.** Readily observed or detected; evident. **2.** Worth noticing; significant. —**no·tice·a·bly** *adv.*

notice board *n. British.* A board on which notices, advertisements, and the like are displayed.

notifiable disease *n.* Any of certain infectious diseases, such as cholera, diphtheria, and tuberculosis, cases of which must be reported to the health authorities.

no·ti·fi·ca·tion (nṓtifi-káysh'n) *n.* **1.** The act or an instance of notifying. **2.** The sign, letter, or other form by which notice is given.

no·ti·fy (nṓti-fī) *tr.v.* **-fied, -fying, -fies. 1.** To give formal notice to; inform. **2.** *Chiefly British.* To give notice or information of (something); make known; proclaim. [Middle English *notifien,* from Old French *notifier,* from Latin *nōtificāre,* to make known : *nōtus,* known, from *nōscere,* to get acquainted with + *facere,* to make.] —**no·ti·fi·a·ble** (-fī-əb'l, -fī-) *adj.* —**no·ti·fi·er** *n.*

no·tion (nṓsh'n) *n.* **1.** A general impression or feeling. **2.** A view; a concept; a theory, especially if subjective or mistaken. **3.** *Rare.* Intention or inclination: *"Men's notion was, not for abolishing punishments, but for making laws just"* (Thomas Carlyle). **4.** *Plural. Chiefly U.S.* Small items for household and clothing use, such as needles, buttons, thread, or ribbons. —See Synonyms at **caprice, idea.**

[Latin *notiō* (stem *notiōn-*), "a becoming acquainted", from *nōscere* (past participle *nōtus*), to get acquainted.]

no·tion·al (nṓsh'n'l) *adj.* **1.** Of, containing, or being a notion or notions; conceived in the mind rather than actual. **2.** *Linguistics.* **a.** Having full lexical meaning, as distinguished from relational meaning. In the phrase *we did the work,* the verb *did* refers to a real activity *(doing* work), and is therefore notional; in the phrase *we did not agree, did* serves merely as a grammatical marker, and is therefore relational. **b.** Conveying an idea directly to the mind; nonsymbolic. —**no·tion·al·ly** *adv.*

noto-, not-[1] *comb. form.* Indicates south or southern; for example, **notornis.** [New Latin, from Greek *notos,* south, south wind.]

noto-, not-[2] *comb. form.* Indicates back or back part; for example, **notochord.** [Greek *nōton,* the back.]

no·to·chord (nṓtə-kawrd) *n.* **1.** A flexible rodlike structure in some lower vertebrates that provides dorsal support; the primitive backbone. **2.** A similar structure in embryos of higher vertebrates, from which the spine develops. [Greek *nōtos,* back + CHORD (cord).]

No·to·gae·a (nṓtə-jée-ə) *n.* A zoogeographical region that includes Australia, New Zealand, and the southwestern Pacific islands. Compare **Arctogaea.** [New Latin, "south realm" : NOTO- + Greek *gaia,* land, earth.] —**No·to·gae·al, No·to·gae·an** *adj.*

no·to·ri·e·ty (nṓtə-rī-əti) *n.* The quality or condition of being notorious. See Synonyms at **fame.**

no·to·ri·ous (nō-táwri-əs, nə- ‖ -tóri-) *adj.* **1.** Known widely and regarded unfavourably; infamous: *A notorious highwayman.* **2.** Generally known and discussed: *notorious facts.* [Medieval Latin *nōtōrius,* from Late Latin, causing to be known, from *nōtus,* known, from the past participle of *nōscere,* to get acquainted.] —**no·to·ri·ous·ly** *adv.* —**no·to·ri·ous·ness** *n.*

no·tor·nis (nō-tórniss) *n.* Any flightless bird, now rare, of the genus *Notornis,* found in New Zealand. See **takahe.** [New Latin, "bird of the south" (that is, New Zealand) : NOT(O)- + Greek *ornis,* bird.]

no·tour bankrupt (nṓtər) *n.* In Scots law, one who has not discharged his debts in the time allowed by the court. [*Notour,* short for NOTORIOUS.]

not proven *adj.* Designating a verdict in Scots law that is returned when there is insufficient evidence available to convict a defendant.

no-trump (nō-trúmp) *n.* Also **no-trumps** (-trúmps). **1.** In bridge and other card games, a declaration to play a hand without a trump suit. **2.** A hand played without a trump suit. —**no-trump** *adj.*

Not·ting·ham (nótting-əm ‖ -həm). Largest city in Nottinghamshire, central England, lying on the river Trent. It has long been a centre for the manufacture of lace and hosiery.

Not·ting·ham·shire (nótting-əm-shər, -sheer ‖ -həm-). County in central England. Most of the land is low-lying and fertile. The rich Nottinghamshire coalfields lie in the west. There are also small oilfields. The county town is Nottingham.

Notts. Nottinghamshire.

not·with·stand·ing (nót-with-stánding, -with-) *prep.* In spite of; regardless of hindrance by: *She left notwithstanding her father's opposition. Her father's opposition notwithstanding, she left.*

~*adv.* All the same; nevertheless: *We proceeded, notwithstanding.*

~*conj.* In spite of the fact that; although. [Middle English *notwithstonding* : NOT + present participle of *withstonden,* to WITHSTAND.]

nou·gat (nōo-gaa ‖ -gət, núggət) *n.* A confection made from a sweet sugar or honey paste into which nuts, almonds, cherries, and the like are mixed. [French *nougat,* from Provençal, from Old Provençal *nogat,* confection of nuts, from Vulgar Latin *nucātum* (unattested), from Latin *nux* (stem *nuc-*), nut.]

nought (nawt) *n.* Also *chiefly U.S.* **naught.** A zero; the figure 0.

noughts and crosses *n. Used with a singular verb.* A game in which two players fill in a figure of nine squares with alternate noughts or crosses. Also *U.S.* "crisscross", "tick-tack-toe".

nou·me·non (nōo-mi-nən, nów-, -mə-, -non) *n., pl.* **-na** (-nə). In the philosophy of Kant: **1.** An object of purely intellectual intuition, as opposed to an object perceived by the senses. **2.** A thing in itself, independent of sensory or intellectual perception of it. Compare **phenomenon.** [German *Noumenon,* from Greek *noumenon,* concept, thought, from *nouein,* to think, apprehend, from *nous,* mind.] —**nou·me·nal** *adj.* —**nou·me·nal·ism** *n.* —**nou·me·nal·ist** *n.* —**nou·me·nal·ly** *adv.*

noun (nown) *n. Abbr.* **n. 1.** A word used to denote or name a person, place, thing, quality, or act. **2. a.** The part of speech of a word that is the subject or object of a verb, object of a preposition, or an appositive. **b.** Any word, phrase, or clause used in this way. [Middle English *nowne,* from Anglo-French *noun,* Old French *non, nom,* from Latin *nōmen,* name.] —**noun, noun·al** *adj.* —**noun·al·ly** *adv.*

nour·ish (núrrish) *tr.v.* **-ished, -ishing, -ishes. 1.** To provide with food or other substances necessary for life and growth. **2.** To foster the development of; promote and sustain: *Freedom nourishes self-respect.* [Middle English *nurishen, norishen,* from Old French *norrir* (stem *norriss-*), from Latin *nūtrīre,* to feed.] —**nour·ish·a·ble** *adj.* —**nour·ish·er** *n.* —**nour·ish·ing·ly** *adv.*

nour·ish·ment (núrrishmənt) *n.* **1. a.** The act of nourishing. **b.** The state of being nourished. **2.** That which supports life and growth in a living organism; food; sustenance. **3.** That which promotes the development or vitality of something.

nous (nowss; *for sense 1 also* nōoss) *n.* **1.** *Philosophy.* Mind; reason; specifically, the principle of divine reason. **2.** *British Informal.* Common sense. [Greek.]

nou·veau riche (nōovō réesh) *n., pl.* **nouveaux riches** *(pronounced as singular).* One who has lately become ostentatiously rich. Usually used derogatorily. [French, "new rich".]

nouvelle cuisine (noo-vél kwi-zéen) *n.* Cuisine minceur by contrast with traditional French cuisine; specifically, cuisine minceur in which vegetables and meat are served together, attractively arranged on the same plate. [French, "new cuisine", a style held to have been invented by the French chef Michel Guérard.]

nou·velle vague (noovel vaág) *n.* The **New Wave** (see). [French.] **Nov.** November.

no·va (nó-və) *n., pl.* **-vae** (-vee) or **-vas.** *Astronomy.* A variable star that suddenly increases in brightness to several times its normal magnitude, and returns to its original appearance over a period from a few weeks to several months or years. Compare **supernova.** [New Latin (stella) nova, "new (star)", from Latin novus, new.]

no·vac·u·lite (nō-vácke-līt) *n.* A very hard, dense, silica-bearing rock used in whetstones. [Latin *novácula,* razor + -ITE.]

No·va Sco·tia (nó-və skósha). Easternmost province of mainland Canada, connected to New Brunswick by the Chignecto Isthmus. It also includes Cape Breton Island. Coalmining and fishing are the chief industries, but the Annapolis Valley is also famous for its apple orchards. It was one of the four original provinces in the Canadian confederation (1867). The capital and largest city is Halifax. —**Nova Sco·tian** *adj. & n.*

no·va·tion (nō-váysh'n) *n. Law.* The substitution of a new obligation for an old one; especially, the transference of a debt. [Late Latin *novātiō* (stem *novātiōn-*), a making new, from Latin *novāre,* to make new, from *novus,* new.]

No·va·ya Zem·lya (nóvə-yə zémli-ə; *Russian* zim-lyá). Largest group of islands in the Eurasian Arctic, lying off the Arctic coast of Russia and belonging to Russia. It consists mainly of two large islands, which are continuations of the Ural and Pai-Khoy mountain systems.

nov·el[1] (nóvv'l) *n.* **1.** A fictional prose narrative of considerable length, typically having a plot that is unfolded by the actions, speech, and thoughts of the characters. **2.** The literary genre represented by this form of narrative. [Italian *(storia) novella,* a short tale, "new story", from feminine of *novello,* new, from Latin *novellus,* NOVEL.]

novel[2] *adj.* Strikingly new, unusual, or different. See Usage note at **new.** [Middle English *novel,* from Old French, from Latin *novellus,* from *novus,* new.] —**nov·el·ly** *adv.*

nov·el·ette (nóvv'l-ét) *n.* **1.** A short novel. **2.** A light romantic or trivial novel, usually short and of little literary merit. **3.** A short, lyrical, instrumental piece (-éttish) *adj.*

nov·el·ise, nov·el·ize (nóvv'l-īz) *tr.v.* **-ised, -ising, -ises. 1.** To turn (facts or a film script, for example) into a novel. **2.** To make novel or new. —**nov·el·i·sa·tion** (-ī-záysh'n || *U.S.* -i-) *n.*

nov·el·ist (nóvv'l-ist) *n.* A writer of novels.

nov·el·is·tic (nóvv'l-ístik) *adj.* Of, pertaining to, or characteristic of novels. —**nov·el·is·ti·cal·ly** *adv.*

no·vel·la (nō-véllə, no-) *n., pl.* **-las** or **-le** (-véllay) **1.** A short prose tale of the type developed by Boccaccio, characterised by epigrammatic terseness. **2.** A short novel. [Italian. See **novel** (narrative).]

No·vel·lo (nə-véllō), Ivor, born David Ivor Davies (1893–1951). British composer, actor-manager, and dramatist. He wrote comedies and musical comedies such as *Glamorous Night* (1935) and *The Dancing Years* (1939), and the patriotic World War I song "Keep the Home Fires Burning".

Nov·els (nóvv'lz) *pl., n. Roman Law.* Amendments made by the Emperor Justinian and his successors to the Justinian Code. [New Latin *novella,* singular of Late Latin *novellae (constitutiōnes),* "new (statutes)", from Latin *novellus,* new, from *novus,* new.]

nov·el·ty (nóvv'lti) *n., pl.* **-ties. 1.** The quality of being novel; newness; originality. **2.** Something that is novel; a new or unusual thing; an innovation. **3.** *Plural.* Small mass-produced articles, such as toys or trinkets. [Middle English *noveltee,* from Old French *novelte,* from *novel,* new, NOVEL.]

No·vem·ber (nō-vémbər, nə-) *n. Abbr.* **Nov., N.** The 11th month of the Gregorian calendar. November has 30 days. [Middle English *Novembre,* from Old French, from Latin *Novembris (mēnsis),* the ninth (month) (of the Roman calendar), from *novem,* nine.]

no·ve·na (nō-vée-nə) *n., pl.* **-nas** or **-nae** (-nee). *Roman Catholic Church.* A recitation of prayers and devotions over a period of time, usually nine consecutive days. [Medieval Latin *novēna,* from Latin *novēnus,* nine each, from *novem,* nine.]

no·ver·cal (nō-vérk'l) *adj. Rare.* Of, pertaining to, or characteristic of a stepmother. [Latin *novercālis,* from *noverca,* a stepmother.]

Nov·go·rod (nóv-gə-rod; *Russian* -rət). City in western Russia, lying on the river Volkhov. It is one of the oldest Russian cities, and during the Middle Ages rose to commercial prosperity owing to its position on one of the major trade routes of eastern Europe. The city's rich architectural heritage was largely destroyed by bombing in World War II, but much has since been restored.

nov·ice (nóvviss) *n.* **1.** A person new to any field or activity; a beginner. **2.** A person who has entered a religious order, but who is on probation before taking final vows. Compare **postulant.** **3.** *Sports.* **a.** A competitor who has not previously won a prize or reached a certain standard. **b.** A racehorse that has yet to win a certain number of races. [Middle English *novyce,* from Old French *novice,* from Medieval Latin *novīcius,* from *novīcius,* extension of *novus,* new.]

no·vi·ti·ate, no·vi·ci·ate (nō-víshi-ət, nə-, -it, -ayt) *n.* **1.** *Ecclesiastical.* **a.** The period of time served by a novice. **b.** A place where

novices live. **c.** A novice. **2.** The state or time of being a beginner. **3.** A beginner. [French *noviciat,* from Medieval Latin *novīciātus,* from *novīcius,* NOVICE.]

No·vo·cain (nó-vo-kayn, -vō-) *n.* A trademark for the anaesthetic **procaine hydrochloride** (see).

No·vo·cas·tri·an (nō-vō-kástri-ən, -və-) *n.* A native or inhabitant of Newcastle. —**No·vo·cas·tri·an** *adj.*

now (now) *adv.* **1.** At the present time. **2.** At once; immediately: *Stop now.* **3.** In the immediate past; very recently. Often preceded by *just: She left just now.* **4.** At this point in a series of events; then: *The ship was now listing to port.* **5.** Nowadays. **6.** In these circumstances; as things are: *Now we won't be able to stay.* **7. a.** Used to introduce a statement or question: *Now, what do you think?* **b.** Used in commands to add emphasis: *Now be a good boy. Hurry up, now!* —**now and again** or **then.** Occasionally.

~*conj.* Since. Often followed by *that: Now that we have eaten, let's go.*

~*n.* The present time or moment: *Now is the time to act.*

~*adj.* **1.** *Informal.* Of the present time; current: *the now generation.* **2.** *Slang.* In tune with the latest trends; with-it.

~*interj.* Used: **1.** To express mild rebuke. **2.** To soothe or placate. [Middle English *nu, now,* Old English *nū.*]

now·a·days (nów-ə-dayz) *adv.* In these days; at the present time. [Middle English *now a dayes,* "on this day" : NOW + *a dayes,* Old English *on dæges* (adverbial genitive) : ON + DAY.]

no way *adv. Informal.* Not at all; absolutely not.

~*interj. Informal.* Used to express emphatic refusal.

no·way (nó-way) *adv.* Also *chiefly U.S.* **no·ways** (nó-wayz). Nowise; certainly not.

no·where (nó-wair, -hwair) *adv.* In, to, or at no place; not anywhere.

~*n.* **1.** No place; a non-existent or insignificant place. **2.** An insignificant or obscure position: *came from nowhere to win the election.*

no·wise (nó-wīz) *adv.* In no way, manner, or degree; not at all. [Middle English *nawyse* : NO + WISE (way).]

now-now (nów-now) *adv. South African Informal.* Very soon; right away. [Afrikaans *nou-nou.*]

nowt (nowt, nōt) *n. British Regional.* Nothing. [Variant of NOUGHT.]

nox·ious (nókshəss) *adj.* Injurious or harmful to health or morals. [Latin *noxius,* from *noxa,* injury, damage.] —**nox·ious·ly** *adv.* —**nox·ious·ness** *n.*

no·yade (nwaa-yaád) *n.* Execution by drowning; especially, that carried out on a large scale at Nantes in France in 1794. [French, from *noyer,* to drown, from Latin *necāre,* from *nex* (stem *nec-*), slaughter.]

noy·au (nwī-ō) *n.* A liqueur consisting of brandy flavoured with the kernels of fruit stones or nuts. [French, kernel, from Vulgar Latin *nucale* (unattested), neuter noun from Late Latin *nucālis,* nutty, from Latin *nux* (stem *nuc-*), nut.]

noz·zle (nózz'l) *n.* A projecting, often adjustable, spout through which gas or liquid is discharged, such as the end of a hose or the pipe in a jet engine or rocket outlet. [Earlier *nosel, nosle,* diminutive of NOSE.]

Np **1.** The symbol for the element neptunium. **2.** neper.

n.p. **1.** new paragraph. **2.** *Law.* nisi prius. **3.** no place of publication.

N.P.A. Newspaper Publishers' Association.

NPN, N.P.N. nonprotein nitrogen.

nr. near.

N.S. **1.** New Style. **2.** not satisfactory or sufficient. **3.** Nova Scotia. **4.** nuclear ship.

n.s.f., N.S.F. not sufficient funds.

N.S.P.C.C. National Society for the Prevention of Cruelty to Children (in Britain).

N.S.W. New South Wales.

-n't *comb. form.* Not.

NT, N.T. **1.** National Trust. **2.** New Testament. **3.** Northern Territory. **4.** no trumps.

nth (enth) *adj.* **1.** Pertaining to an indefinitely large ordinal number: *ten to the nth power.* **2.** Infinitely or indefinitely large or small; most extreme; utmost: *exaggerated to the nth degree.*

n.t.p., N.T.P. normal temperature and pressure (a temperature of 0°C and a pressure of 101.325 kPa).

n-type (én-tīp) *adj. Electronics.* Of or designating a semiconductor or its type of conductivity, in which the bulk of the electric current is carried by electrons. Compare **p-type.** [Negative *type.*]

nu (new || noo) *n.* The thirteenth letter of the Greek alphabet (N, *v*), corresponding to the English *N, n.* Transliterated in English as *N, n.* [Greek *nu,* from a Phoenician word meaning "fish", from a Semitic root *nyn* meaning "to increase" or "to endure".]

nu·ance (new-ónss, néw-onss; *French* nü- || noó-, noō-) *n.* A subtle or slight variation, as in meaning, colour, or quality; a gradation of meaning. [French *nuance,* from Old French, from *nuer,* to show shades of colour (as in clouds), from *nue,* cloud, from Vulgar Latin *nūbe* (unattested), from Latin *nūbēs.*] —**nu·anced** *adj.*

nub (nub) *n.* **1.** A protuberance or knob. **2.** A small lump or piece. **3.** The gist or point: *the nub of a story.* [Variant of *knub,* from Middle Low German *knubbe,* knot on a tree, variant of *knobbe,* KNOB.]

Nu·ba (néwbə || noóbə) *n., pl.* Nuba. **1.** A Nubian. **2.** A member of any of several Nilotic peoples of southern Sudan. **3.** The language spoken by these peoples. —**Nu·ba** *adj.*

nub·bin (núbbin) *n. U.S.* **1.** A small, stunted ear of corn. **2.** Anything stunted or imperfectly developed. [Diminutive of NUB.]

nub·ble (núbb'l) *n.* A small protuberance or lump. [Diminutive of NUB.] —**nub·bly** *adj.*

Nu·bi·a (néw-bi-ə ‖ noo̅-). Ancient state of northeastern Africa, extending at its height from Aswan to Khartoum. By the 20th century B.C. it had come completely under the sway of the Egyptians, although in the 8th and 7th centuries B.C. an independent kingdom of Nubia again asserted itself and Nubian kings conquered Egypt, establishing Dynasty XXV in 712 B.C. In the 6th century A.D. Nubia was joined to Ethiopia, then a Christian kingdom. After Ethiopia fell to the Muslims in the 14th century, Nubia ceased to have a distinctive existence.

Nu·bi·an (néw-bi-ən ‖ noo̅-) *n.* **1.** A native or inhabitant of Nubia. **2.** Any of the languages of Nubia. —**Nu·bi·an** *adj.*

Nubian Desert. An arid wilderness in northeastern Sudan, lying between the river Nile and the Red Sea and merging into the Arabian Desert of eastern Egypt. The desert is largely uninhabited.

nu·bile (néw-bīl ‖ noo̅-, *U.S. also* -b'l) *adj.* **1.** Young and physically attractive. Said of a girl or young woman: *a nubile young girl.* **2.** Ready for marriage; of a marriageable age. Said of a woman. [French *nubile,* from Latin *nūbilis,* marriageable, from *nūbere,* to take a husband.] —**nu·bil·i·ty** (new-bílləti ‖ noo̅-) *n.*

nu·cel·lus (new-séllass ‖ noo̅-) *n., pl.* **-celli** (-séllī). *Botany.* The centre of the ovule of a plant, containing the embryo sac. [New Latin, irregularly from Latin *nucella,* diminutive of *nux* (stem *nuc-*), nut.] —**nu·cel·lar** *adj.*

nucle-. Variant of nucleo-.

nu·cle·ar (néw-kli-ər ‖ noo̅-) *adj.* **1.** *Biology.* Of, pertaining to, or forming a nucleus: *a nuclear membrane.* **2.** *Physics.* Of or concerning atomic nuclei: *nuclear physics.* **3.** Using, armed with, or derived from the energy of atomic nuclei; atomic: *nuclear power plants.* **4.** Of, involving, or possessing atomic or hydrogen bombs: *nuclear war; nuclear nations.*
~ *n.* Nuclear energy (sense 2). [From NUCLEUS.]

nuclear bomb *n.* **1.** An explosive weapon of great destructive power derived from the rapid release of energy in the fission of heavy atomic nuclei, as of uranium-235. **2.** Any bomb deriving its destructive power from the release of nuclear energy. Also called "A-bomb", "atom bomb", "atomic bomb". See **hydrogen bomb.**

nuclear emulsion *n. Physics.* Any of several photographic emulsions used to detect and display the paths of charged elementary particles, especially of charged cosmic-ray particles.

nuclear energy *n. Physics.* **1.** The energy released by a nuclear reaction, especially by fission, fusion, or radioactive decay. **2.** This energy regarded as a source of industrial, commercial, or military power. Also called "atomic energy", "nuclear".

nuclear family *n.* A self-contained family unit consisting of a mother and father and their children. Compare **extended family.**

nuclear fission *n. Physics.* See **fission.**

nu·cle·ar-free zone (néw-kli-ər-frée, -free ‖ noo̅-) *n.* An area in which the siting of nuclear reactors or missiles is banned.

nuclear fuel *n.* A fuel producing power in a nuclear reactor.

nuclear fusion *n. Physics.* See **fusion.**

nuclear isomer *n. Physics.* A type of **isomer** *(see).*

nuclear magnetic resonance *n. Abbr.* **NMR** A technique for measuring the nuclear **magnetic moment** *(see)* of a substance by exposing a sample to a strong magnetic field and high-frequency electromagnetic radiation. It is used, as in spectroscopy, for providing information on the molecular structure of the substance.

nuclear magneton *n. Physics. Symbol* μ_N A unit of the magnetic moment of the nucleon. See **magneton.**

nuclear physics *n. Used with a singular verb.* The scientific study of the forces, reactions, and internal structures of atomic nuclei.

nuclear power *n.* **1.** The electric or motive power produced by a nuclear reactor. **2.** A state that possesses nuclear weapons. Also called "atomic power".

nuclear reaction *n. Physics.* A reaction that alters the energy, composition, or structure of an atomic nucleus. Also called "reaction".

nuclear reactor *n.* Any of several devices in which a **chain reaction** *(see)* is initiated and controlled, with the consequent production of heat, typically used for the generation of power. Neutrons and fusion products are also produced, and reactors are also used for a variety of experimental and medical purposes. Also called "atomic pile", "atomic reactor", "pile", "reactor".

nuclear winter *n.* Harsh climatic conditions of cold and darkness suggested as a likely consequence of nuclear war, and postulated as due to the blocking of the sun's rays by dust and smoke raised into the atmosphere by nuclear explosions.

nu·cle·ase (néw-kli-ayz, -ayss ‖ noo̅-) *n.* Any of several enzymes that hydrolise nucleic acids. [NUCLE(O)- + -ASE.]

nu·cle·ate (newkli-ət, -it, -ayt ‖ noo̅) *adj.* Having a nucleus.
~ *v.* (néw-kli-ayt ‖ noo̅-) **nucleated, -ating, -ates.** —*tr.* To bring together into a nucleus. —*intr.* To form a nucleus. [NUCLE(US) + -ATE.] —**nu·cle·a·tion** (-áysh'n) *n.*

nu·cle·i. Plural of **nucleus.**

nu·cle·ic acid (new-klée-ik, -kláy- ‖ noo̅-) *n.* Any member of either of two groups of complex compounds found in all living cells, and composed of purines, pyrimidines, sugars, and phosphoric acid. See **DNA, RNA.** [NUCLE(O)- + -IC (because found in nucleoproteins).]

nucleo-, nucle- *comb. form.* Indicates: **1.** A nucleus; for example, **nucleon. 2.** Nucleic acid; for example, **nucleoprotein, nucleoside.** [From NUCLEUS.]

nu·cle·o·late (néw-kli-ə-layt ‖ noo̅-) *adj.* Also **nu·cle·o·lat·ed** (-lay-tid). Having a nucleolus or nucleoli. [NUCLEOL(US) + -ATE.]

nu·cle·o·lus (new-kli-ə-ləss, -klée-ə- ‖ noo̅-) *n., pl.* **-li** (-lī). Also **nu·cle·ole** (-ōl). *Biology.* **1.** A small, usually round body composed of protein and RNA in the nucleus of a cell. Also called "plasmosome". **2.** Any discrete, cellular particle resembling a nucleolus, other than a chromosome. [New Latin, from Latin, diminutive of *nucleus,* a kernel, NUCLEUS.] —**nu·cle·o·lar** (-lər) *adj.*

nu·cle·on (néw-kli-on ‖ noo̅-) *n.* A proton or a neutron, especially as part of an atomic nucleus. [NUCLE(O)- + -ON.] —**nu·cle·on·ic** (-ónnik) *adj.*

nu·cle·on·ics (néw-kli-ónniks ‖ noo̅-) *n. Used with a singular verb.* The technology of nuclear energy. [From NUCLEON.]

nucleon number *n. Physics.* **Mass number** *(see).*

nu·cle·o·phile (néw-kli-ō-fīl, -ə- ‖ noo̅-) *n.* A substance whose atoms or molecules behave as an electron pair donor in combining with other atoms or molecules. [NUCLEO- + -PHILE.] —**nu·cle·o·phile, nu·cle·o·phil·ic** (-fillik) *adj.*

nu·cle·o·plasm (néw-kli-ə-plaz'm, -ō- ‖ noo̅-) *n.* The protoplasm of a cell nucleus. Also called "karyoplasm". [NUCLEO- + -PLASM.] —**nu·cle·o·plas·ma·tic** (-plaz-máttik), **nu·cle·o·plas·mic** *adj.*

nu·cle·o·pro·tein (néw-kli-ō-prō-teen, -tee-in ‖ noo̅-) *n.* Any of a group of substances found in all living cells and viruses, and composed of a protein and a nucleic acid.

nu·cle·o·side (néw-kli-ə-sīd ‖ noo̅-) *n.* Any compound made of a sugar and a purine or pyrimidine base without a phosphate group. [NUCLE(O) + -OS(E) + -IDE.]

nu·cle·o·some (néw-kli-ō-sōm, -ə- ‖ noo̅-) *n.* Any of the basic globular subunits of chromatin consisting of DNA and histone. [NUCLEO- + -SOME.] —**nu·cle·o·som·al** (-sōm'l) *adj.*

nu·cle·o·tide (néw-kli-ə-tīd ‖ noo̅-) *n.* Any of various organic compounds consisting of a nucleoside combined with phosphoric acid. [Irregularly from NUCLEO- + -IDE.]

nu·cle·us (néw-kli-əss ‖ noo̅-) *n., pl.* **-clei** (-kli-ī) or *rare* **-cleuses.** **1.** A central thing or part around which other things are grouped; a core: *the nucleus of a city.* **2.** Anything regarded as a basis for future development and growth; a kernel: *the nucleus of a stamp collection.* **3.** *Biology.* A complex, usually spherical, protoplasmic body within a living cell that contains the cell's hereditary material and that controls its metabolism, growth, and reproduction. **4.** *Botany.* The central point of a starch granule. **5.** *Anatomy.* A group of nerve cells or localised mass of grey matter in the brain, where nerve fibres interconnect. **6.** *Physics.* The positively charged central region of an atom, composed of protons and neutrons, and containing almost all of the mass of the atom. See **atomic number, mass number.** **7.** *Chemistry.* A group of atoms chemically bound in a structure resistant to alteration in chemical reactions. **8.** *Astronomy.* **a.** The central portion of the head of a comet. **b.** The central or brightest part of a nebula or of a galaxy. **9.** *Meteorology.* A minute solid particle upon which water vapour molecules accumulate to form a droplet or ice crystal. **10.** *Phonetics.* The most sonorous part of a syllable; especially, a vowel. [Latin, "a nut", "kernel", from *nux* (stem *nuc-*), a nut.]

nu·clide (néw-klīd ‖ noo̅-) *n. Physics.* Any atomic nucleus specified by its atomic number, atomic mass, and energy state. Compare **isotope.** [NUCLE(O)- + -IDE.] —**nu·clid·ic** (new-klíddik ‖ noo̅-) *adj.*

nud·dy (núddi) *Chiefly British Informal. n.* Nudeness; a state of undress. Used in the phrase *in the nuddy.* [From NUDE.]

nude (newd ‖ noo̅d) *adj.* **1.** Without clothing; naked. **b.** Without covering; exposed. **2.** *Law.* Lacking any of various legal requisites, such as evidence: *a nude contract.*
~ *n.* **1.** A nude human figure or a representation of it. **2.** The condition of being nude: *in the nude.* [Latin *nūdus,* nude, bare.] —**nude·ly** *adv.* —**nude·ness** *n.*

nudge (nuj) *tr.v.* **nudged, nudging, nudges. 1.** To push or prod (a person) gently, especially with the elbow and in order to gain attention or give a signal. **2.** To push against (an object) lightly: *The car tyre just nudged the pavement.* **3.** To encourage or compel gradually: *Slowly they nudged her into joining the conspiracy.*
~ *n.* **1.** A gentle push. **2.** An encouragement or incentive. [Perhaps from a Scandinavian word akin to Norwegian dialectal *nugga, nyggja,* to push, rub.]

nudge-nudge, wink-wink (núj-nuj wínk-wínk) *n. Informal.* Sly sexual innuendo or a gesture or expression conveying this: *There was a bit of the old nudge-nudge, wink-wink going on in the office after Sarah kissed her boss at the Christmas party.*
~ *adj. Informal.* Of or designating a leering, smutty, suggestive attitude or reaction: *"Rape is often regarded in a nudge-nudge, wink-wink way"* (The Guardian).
~ *interj. Informal.* Used to show prurience or hint gleefully at sexual matters: *Nudge-nudge, wink-wink, know what I mean?* [Alluding to gestures made when conveying sexual innuendo.]

nudi- *comb. form.* Indicates nakedness or bareness; for example, **nudibranch, nudicaul.** [Latin *nūdus,* NUDE.]

nu·di·branch (néwdi-brangk ‖ noo̅di-) *n.* Any mollusc of the order Nudibranchia; the **sea slug** *(see).* [New Latin *Nudibranchia,* "ones having naked gills" : NUDI- + BRANCHIA.] —**nu·di·bran·chi·an** (-brángki-ən) **nu·di·bran·chi·ate** (-brángki-ət, -it, -ayt) *adj.* —**nu·di·branch** *n.*

nu·di·caul (néw-di-kawl ‖ noo̅-) *adj.* Also **nu·di·cau·lous** (-káwləss). *Botany.* Having no leaves on the stem. [NUDI- + Latin *caulis,* stalk, stem.]

nu·die (néw-di ‖ noo̅-) *n. Slang.* **1.** A **skinflick** *(see).* **2.** A magazine containing pornographic photographs of nudes.

~*adj. Slang.* Characterised by or featuring pornographic nudity: *a nudie film.* [From NUDE.]

nud·ism (néw-diz'm ‖ no͞o-) *n.* The doctrine or practice of living in the nude. Also called "naturism". —**nud·ist** *adj. & n.*

nu·di·ty (néw-dəti ‖ no͞o-) *n., pl.* **-ties.** 1. The quality or state of being nude; bareness; nakedness. 2. *Rare.* A nude figure as represented in painting or sculpture.

nud·nik, nud·nick (no͝od-nik) *n. Chiefly U.S. Slang.* 1. A boring or bothersome person; a pest. 2. A stupid person; a fool. [Yiddish : Russian *nudny,* boring, wearisome + -NIK.]

nuff (nuf) *n. Nonstandard.* Enough. Used chiefly in the phrase *nuff said.*

nu·ée ar·dente (néw-ay aar-dónt; *French* nü-) *n.* A turbulent, incandescent cloud of gas, ash, and rock fragments which flows rapidly over the ground after a violent volcanic eruption, destroying all forms of life in its path within seconds. [French, "burning cloud".]

Nuf·field (núffeeld), **William Richard Morris, 1st Viscount** (1877–1963). British motor-car manufacturer. At his Morris Motor works, in Oxford, he helped to pioneer mass-produced vehicles in Britain from 1912. His philanthropic activities include endowing Nuffield College, Oxford, and the Nuffield Trust and Nuffield Foundation medical and educational bodies.

nu·ga·to·ry (néw-gə-tri, -təri, new-gáytəri ‖ no͞o-) *adj.* 1. Of no value; worthless; trifling: *a nugatory objection.* 2. Having no power; invalid; inoperative: *a nugatory statute.* [Latin *nūgātōrius,* trifling, from *nūgārī,* to jest, trifle, from *nūgae*†, jokes.]

nug·gar (núggər) *n.* A broad-beamed sailing boat used for carrying cargo on the upper Nile. [Arabic *nukkār.*]

nug·get (núggit) *n.* 1. A small lump, especially one of natural gold. 2. A small but valuable portion or unit: *nuggets of information.* [Probably diminutive of dialect *nug*†, lump.] —**nug·get·y** *adj.*

nui·sance (néw-s'nss ‖ no͞o-) *n.* 1. A source of inconvenience, annoyance, or vexation; a bother. 2. *Law.* A use of property or course of conduct that interferes with the legal rights of others by causing damage, annoyance, or inconvenience. [Middle English *nusaunce,* injury, harmful thing, from Old French *nuisance,* from *nuire* (stem *nuis-*), to harm, injure, from Latin *nocēre.*]

nuisance value *n.* The capacity to annoy or frustrate, considered as a useful asset.

Nuits-Saint-Georges (nwée-saN-zhórzh) *n.* A fine red Burgundy wine. [After the town *Nuits-Saint-Georges.*]

N.U.J. National Union of Journalists.

Nu·jo·ma (no͞o-jômə), **Sam (Daniel),** a.k.a. Shafilshuna Nujoma (1929–). Namibian leader, founder and president of SWAPO (1958). Namibian president 1990; re-elected 1994.

nuke (newk ‖ nook) *n. Slang.* A nuclear bomb.
~*tr.v.* **nuked, nuking, nukes.** *Slang.* To attack or destroy with a nuclear bomb.

null (nul) *adj.* 1. Having no legal force; invalid. Often used in the phrase *null and void.* 2. **a.** Of no consequence, effect, or value; insignificant. **b.** Lacking distinctive personality; colourless: *a null face.* 3. Amounting to nothing; lacking; absent; non-existent. 4. *Mathematics.* Of or pertaining to zero magnitude or a set having no members.
~*n.* 1. Zero. 2. An instrumental reading of zero. 3. A letter which has no meaning in a code or cipher. [French *nul, nulle,* "none", from Latin *nūllus* : *ne,* not + *ūllus,* any.]

nul·lah (núllə) *n.* In India, a ravine or watercourse. [Hindi *nālā,* rivulet, ravine, probably from Dravidian.]

nul·la-nul·la (núllə-nullə) *n. Australian.* A hardwood club used by Aborigines. [From a native Australian language.]

Nul·lar·bor Plain (núllər-bawr). Extensive plateau stretching along the Great Australian Bight in southern Australia from Ooldea to the lake district of Western Australia and extending north to the Great Victoria Desert. It is generally flat, with occasional peaks rising 400 metres above sea level.

null hypothesis *n. Statistics.* A hypothesis that is tested against another but is nullified in favour of the alternative, subject to a given level of error.

nul·li·fi·ca·tion (núllifi-káysh'n) *n.* 1. The action of nullifying. 2. *U.S.* The refusal or failure of a U.S. state to recognise or enforce Federal laws within its boundaries. —**nul·li·fi·ca·tion·ist** *n. & adj.*

nul·li·fid·i·an (núlli-fíddi-ən) *n.* A person having no beliefs, especially in religious matters; a sceptic.
~*adj.* Having or characterised by a lack of faith or belief. [Medieval Latin *nullifidius* : Latin *nullus,* no, none + *fidēs,* faith.]

nul·li·fy (núlli-fī) *tr.v.* **-fied, -fying, -fies.** 1. To deprive of legal force; annul; make void: *The court nullified the contract.* 2. To make ineffective or useless. See Synonyms at **neutralise.** [Late Latin *nūllificāre,* to make light of, despise : *nūllus,* none, NULL + *facere,* to make.] —**nul·li·fi·er** *n.*

Synonyms: nullify, negate, abolish, annul, void, invalidate, abrogate, cancel, repeal, revoke, rescind.

nul·lip·a·ra (nu-líppərə) *n.* A woman who has never given birth. [New Latin : Latin *nullus,* no, none + *-para,* from *parere,* to give birth.] —**nul·li·pa·ri·ty** (núlli-párrəti) *n.* —**nul·lip·a·rous** (nu-líppərəss) *adj.*

nul·li·pore (núlli-pawr ‖ -pōr) *n.* Any of several small red seaweeds that secrete calcium carbonate and form encrustations on rocks. [Latin *nullus,* no, none + PORE.]

nul·li·ty (núlləti) *n., pl.* **-ties.** 1. The state or quality of being null: *the nullity of third parties in a two-party parliamentary system.* 2. *Law.*

a. The fact of being null and void. **b.** An act having no legal validity. 3. A nonentity.

num. 1. number. 2. numeral.

Num. Numbers (Old Testament).

N.U.M. National Union of Mineworkers.

numb (num) *adj.* **number** (númmər), **numbest** (númmist). 1. Insensible, as from excessive chill; benumbed: *toes numb with cold.* 2. Stunned or paralysed, as from shock or strong emotion: *numb with grief.* 3. Insensitive or inept. 4. Resembling or of the nature of loss of sensation: *a numb feeling.*
~*v.* **numbed, numbing, numbs.** —*tr.* To make numb; deaden. —*intr.* To become numb. [Middle English *nome(n),* originally "seized with palsy, paralysed", past participle of *nimen,* to take, seize, Old English *niman.*] —**numb·ly** *adv.* —**numb·ness** *n.*

num·bat (núm-bat) *n.* Either of two marsupial mammals, *Myrmecobius fasciatus* or *M. rufus,* native to southern Australia, having a long snout and an extensible tongue for catching termites. [From a native Australian language.]

num·ber (númbər) *n. Abbr.* **n., no., No., num.** 1. *Mathematics.* **a.** A member of the set of positive integers; a member of a series of symbols of unique meaning in a fixed order which may be derived by counting. See **cardinal number, ordinal number. b.** A member of any of the further sets of mathematical objects that may be derived from the positive integers by mathematical induction. See **induction.** Thus, given the positive integers and zero, the operation of addition makes it possible to define the negative integers (those which added to the positive integers produce zero). The integers together with the fractions (of the form m/n, where m and n are integers and n is not zero) form the set of *rational numbers.* The rational numbers together with the *irrational numbers* (those not expressible as quotients of integers, such as $\sqrt{2}$) form the set of *real numbers.* Numbers of the form $a + bi$, where a and b are real numbers and $i^2 = -1$, form the set of *complex numbers,* which is the broadest set commonly used in mathematics. Numbers such as π (pi), that are not expressible as roots of any algebraic equation with rational coefficients, form the set of *transcendental numbers.* See **transfinite number. c.** A symbol used to represent a number; a numeral. 2. *Plural.* The study or processes of arithmetic. 3. **a.** A numeral or series of numerals assigned to or designating a specific person or thing: *a telephone number.* **b.** The person or thing thus designated: *Come in, number three, your time is up.* 4. A specific quantity composed of equal units: *The number of apples in the bowl is ten.* 5. Quantity of units or individuals: *The crowd was small in number.* 6. *Plural.* A large quantity or collection: *Numbers of people visited the fair.* 7. One item in a group or series, as of a journal, considered to be in numerical order: *I saw her article in the latest number of the Herald.* 8. **a.** One of the separate offerings in a programme of music. **b.** *Informal.* A song or piece of instrumental music. **c.** Any self-contained item within a larger piece of music, such as an aria in an opera. 9. *Informal.* A person or thing singled out for some notable characteristic; especially: **a.** A pretty woman. Often considered offensive. **b.** A well-designed garment. **c.** A fast car. 10. *Informal.* A means or circumstance that allows one to gain profit or advantage: *has a nice little number with a generous expense account.* 11. A usually exclusive group of people: *She is one of the duchess's number.* 12. *Usually plural.* Strength or superiority based on quantity: *There's safety in numbers.* 13. *Grammar.* The indication, as by inflection, of the singularity, duality, or plurality of a linguistic form. 14. **a.** *Plural.* Metrical periods or feet; verses: *the melodious numbers of our old poets.* **b.** Measured rhythm in verse. 15. *Plural.* Musical periods or measures. —**a number of.** A considerable, indefinite quantity of. See Usage note below. —**any number of.** A large, indefinite quantity of; numerous. —**by numbers.** 1. *Military.* Step by step, as consecutive numbers are called out. 2. In a mechanical or excessively regulated manner, as when children follow a number code to colour in picture books. —**get** or **have (someone's) number.** *Chiefly U.S. Informal.* To determine (or know) someone's real character or motives. —**(someone's) number is up.** *British Informal.* Used to describe a person who is, or is soon to be, defeated or dead. —**without** or **beyond number.** In a quantity too great to be counted.
~*v.* **numbered, -bering, -bers.** —*tr.* 1. To total in number or amount; add up to. 2. To count or determine the number or amount of. 3. To include in a group or category: *She was numbered among the lost.* 4. To mention one by one; enumerate. 5. To assign a number to. Sometimes used with *off.* 6. To limit or restrict in number: *The days of her life are numbered.* —*intr.* 1. To count or call out numbers: *numbering to ten.* 2. To constitute a group or number: *The applicants numbered in the thousands.* [Middle English *n(o)umbre,* from Old French *nombre,* from Latin *numerus.*] —**num·ber·er** *n.*

Usage: When preceded by *the, number* takes a singular verb: *The number of people now out of work has reached. . .* When preceded by *a,* it takes a plural verb: *A number of people have left the area.*

number crunching *n. Informal.* Complex arithmetical calculations, especially as done by computers.

num·ber·less (númbər-ləss, -liss) *adj.* 1. Innumerable; countless. 2. Not consisting of or concerned with numbers; lacking a number. See Synonyms at **infinite.**

number one *n. Informal.* 1. Oneself: *You think only of number one.* 2. The first or most important. —**num·ber-one** (númbər-wún, wón) *adj.*

number plate *n.* Either of the rectangular metal plates displayed at the front and back of a motor vehicle that bear its registration number. Also called "registration plate".

Num·bers (númbərz) *n. Used with a singular verb. Abbr.* **Num.** The fourth book of the Old Testament, containing the two censuses of the Israelites after the Exodus.

Number Ten *n.* 10 Downing Street, the official London residence of the British prime minister.

number theory *n. Mathematics.* The study of integers and the relationships between them.

numb·fish (núm-fish) *n., pl.* **-fishes** or collectively **numbfish.** A fish, the **electric ray** *(see).*

num·bles (númb'lz) *pl.n. British Archaic.* Entrails, especially of a deer, used for food. Also called "umbles". [Middle English, from Old French *nomble(s),* thigh muscle of deer or other game, from Latin *lumbulus,* diminutive of *lumbus,* loin.]

numbskull. Variant of **numskull.**

num·dah (núm-də, -daa) *n.* Also **num·nah** (-nə). **1.** A coarse felt made in India. **2.** An article made from this felt, especially an embroidered rug. [Urdu *namdā,* from Persian *namad,* carpet.]

nu·men (néw-men ‖ nŏŏ-) *n., pl.* **numina** (-minə). **1.** The presiding divinity or spirit of a place. **2.** The spirit believed by animists to inhabit certain natural objects. **3.** Creative energy regarded as a guiding genius or demon dwelling within one. [Latin *nūmen,* "a nod", hence "command", divine power, deity.]

num·er·a·cy (néw-mərə-si ‖ nŏŏ-) *n.* The condition or quality of being numerate. Compare **literacy.** [NUMER(ATE) + -CY.]

nu·mer·al (néw-mərəl ‖ nŏŏ-) *n. Abbr.* **num.** A symbol, such as a letter, figure, or word used alone or in a group to represent a number. See **Arabic numeral, Roman numeral.**
~adj. Of, pertaining to, or expressing numbers. [Old French *numeral,* from Latin *numerālis,* from Latin *numerus,* NUMBER.] **—nu·mer·al·ly** *adv.*

nu·mer·ar·y (néw-mə-rəri ‖ nŏŏ-, -rerri) *adj.* Of or pertaining to a number or numbers. [Medieval Latin *numerārius,* from Latin *numerus,* NUMBER.]

nu·mer·ate (néw-mə-rət, -rit ‖ nŏŏ-) *adj.* Familiar with the basic principles of mathematics, especially arithmetic.
~tr.v. (-rayt) **numerated, -ating, -ates. 1.** To enumerate; number; reckon. **2.** To read (numerals). [Latin *numerāre,* to number, count, from *numerus,* NUMBER.] **—nu·mer·a·ble** *adj.*

nu·mer·a·tion (néw-mə-ráysh'n ‖ nŏŏ-) *n.* **1.** The act or process of counting by means of reading, writing, or naming numbers. **2.** A system of numbering or of reading numbers. **—nu·mer·a·tive** (-rətiv ‖ -raytiv) *adj.*

nu·mer·a·tor (néw-mə-raytər ‖ nŏŏ-) *n.* **1.** *Mathematics.* **a.** The expression written above the line in a common fraction. Compare **denominator. b.** An expression to be divided by another; the dividend. **2.** One that numbers; an enumerator.

nu·mer·ic (new-mérrik ‖ nŏŏ-) *n.* A number or numeral.
~adj. Variant of **numerical.** [Medieval Latin *numericus,* from Latin *numerus,* NUMBER.]

nu·mer·i·cal (new-mérrik'l ‖ nŏŏ-) *adj.* Also **numeric. 1.** Of or pertaining to a number or series of numbers: *numerical order.* **2.** Designating number or a number: *a numerical symbol.* **3.** Expressed in numbers: *numerical strength.* **4.** Represented by a number or numbers rather than by letter or symbol. [Medieval Latin *numericus,* from Latin *numerus,* NUMBER.] **—nu·mer·i·cal·ly** *adv.*

numerical taxonomy *n.* The branch of taxonomy that assesses quantitatively the relationships between organisms.

numerical value *n. Mathematics.* The absolute value of a number, regardless of sign: *The numerical values of −9 and +9 are equal.*

nu·mer·ol·o·gy (néw-mə-róllǝji ‖ nŏŏ-) *n.* The study of the occult meanings of numbers and of their supposed influence on human fate. [Latin *numerus,* NUMBER + -LOGY.] **—nu·mer·o·log·i·cal** (-rǝ-lójik'l) *adj.* **—nu·mer·o·gist** (-róllǝjist) *n.*

nu·mer·ous (néw-mərəss ‖ nŏŏ-) *adj.* **1.** Consisting of many persons or things: *a numerous collection.* **2.** Many: *numerous books.* [Latin *numerōsus,* from *numerus,* NUMBER.] **—nu·mer·ous·ly** *adv.* **—nu·mer·ous·ness** *n.*

Nu·mid·i·a (new-míddi-ə ‖ nŏŏ-). Ancient country of north Africa, roughly corresponding to modern Algeria. It was part of the Carthaginian empire before the Punic Wars, but with the peace of 201 B.C., Numidia emerged as a separate kingdom under the rule of Masinissa. Its independence lasted until Juba I sided with Pompey in the Roman civil war; after Julius Caesar's victory (46 B.C.), it was absorbed into the Roman empire. **—Nu·mid·i·an** *adj. & n.*

nu·mi·na. Plural of **numen.**

nu·mi·nous (néw-minəss ‖ nŏŏ-) *adj.* **1.** Of or pertaining to a numen. **2.** Spiritually elevated or elevating; mysterious and awe-inspiring.
~n. The presence or revelation of a numen. Used with *the.* [Latin *nūmen* (stem *nūmin-*), NUMEN.]

nu·mis·mat·ics (néw-miz-máttiks ‖ nŏŏ-, -miss-) *n. Used with a singular verb.* The study and collection of money and medals. Also called "numismatology". [From *numismatic* (adjective), from French *numismatique,* from Latin *numisma,* a coin, from Greek *nomisma,* usage, current coin, from *nomizein,* to have in use, from *nomos,* custom.] **—nu·mis·mat·ic** *adj.* **—nu·mis·ma·tist** (new-míz-mətist ‖ nŏŏ-, -miss-) *n.*

num·ma·ry (nûmməri) *adj.* Of or pertaining to coins. [Latin *nummārius,* from *nummus,* coin.]

num·mu·lar (númmewlər) *adj.* Shaped like a coin; circular. [French *nummulaire,* from Latin *nummulus,* diminutive of *nummus,* a coin,

"currency", probably from Greek *nomimos,* customary, legal, from *nomos,* custom.]

num·mu·lite (númmew-līt) *n.* Any extinct protozoan of the family Nummulitidae. They were chiefly marine foraminifers characterised by a coin-shaped shell closely coiled and divided into chambers. [New Latin *Nummulites* (genus name) : Latin *nummulus,* coin (see **nummular**) + *-ites,* -ITE.] **—num·mu·lit·ic** (-líttik) *adj.*

num·nah. Variant of **numdah.**

num·skull, numb·skull (núm-skul) *n.* A stupid person; a blockhead. [NUMB + SKULL.]

nun¹ (nun) *n.* **1.** A woman who belongs to a religious order devoted to religious service or meditation, usually under vows of poverty, chastity, and obedience, as in the Roman Catholic, Anglican, and Orthodox Churches, and in Buddhism. **2.** Any of various birds, especially a pigeon of a domestic breed, having a tuft of feathers on its head. [Middle English *nunne, nun, nonne,* from Old English *nunne* and Old French *nonne,* both from Medieval Latin *nonna,* nun (originally a respectful form of address to old women).]

nun² (nōōn, nŏŏn) *n.* **1.** The 14th letter of the Hebrew alphabet. **2.** The 25th letter of the Arabic alphabet. **3.** The consonant sound represented by either of these letters. [Hebrew and Arabic *nūn,* akin to NU.]

nun·a·tak (núnnə-tak) *n.* An isolated mountain peak or hill that projects through the surface of surrounding glacial ice or snow. [Eskimo.]

nun buoy (nun) *n.* A conical buoy, painted red, marking the right side of a channel leading into a harbour. [From obsolete *nun,* child's spinning top.]

Nunc Di·mit·tis (núngk di-míttis, nŏŏngk) *n.* **1.** The canticle of Simeon, beginning *"Nunc dimittis servum tuum"* ("Now lettest thou thy servant depart"). Luke 2:29–32. **2.** A musical setting of this. **3.** *Small n, small d.* Permission to depart; a dismissal. [Latin.]

nun·ci·a·ture (nún-si-ə-chər, -shi-, -tewr) *n.* The office or term of a nuncio. [Italian *nunciatura,* from *nuncio,* NUNCIO.]

nun·ci·o (nún-si-ō, -shi-) *n., pl.* **-os.** An ambassador from the pope. [Italian, from Latin *nūntius,* messenger.]

nun·cle (núngk'l) *n. Archaic & Regional.* An uncle. [From *an uncle.*]

nun·cu·pa·tive (núng-kew-paytiv, -kéwpətiv) *adj. Law.* Designating a will delivered orally to witnesses rather than written. [Medieval Latin *nūncupātīvus,* from Latin *nūncupāre,* to call by name, name one's heirs : *nōmen,* name + *capere,* to take.]

Nun·ea·ton (nun-éet'n). Manufacturing town in Warwickshire, central England. It was the birthplace of the novelist George Eliot. It derives its name from the local 12th-century nunnery.

nun·ner·y (núnnəri) *n., pl.* **-ies.** A community of nuns or the buildings or buildings in which they live.

N.U.P.E. (néwpi ‖ nŏŏpi) National Union of Public Employees.

nup·tial (núp-sh'l, -ch'l. *Note: the pronunciations* -tew-əl, -tewl *are nonstandard.*) *adj.* **1.** Of or pertaining to marriage or the wedding ceremony. **2.** *Zoology.* Of or at the time of mating: *the nuptial flight of ants.*
~n. Formal. Usually plural. A wedding ceremony. Often used humorously. See Synonyms at **marriage.** [Latin *nuptiālis,* from *nuptiae,* wedding, from *nūbere* (past participle *nuptus*), to take a husband.] **—nup·tial·ly** *adv.*

N.U.R. National Union of Railwaymen.

nurd. Variant of **nerd.**

Nu·rem·berg (néwr-əm-berg ‖ nŏŏr-). *German* **Nürn·berg** (nûrn-bairk). City in Bavaria, southern Germany, lying on the river Pegnitz. It dates from the 11th century. From 1933–38 the Nazis held their annual party congresses there and in 1945–46 it was the site of the trials of the Nazi war criminals.

Nu·re·yev (newr-ráy-ef, néwr-ay-; *Russian* noo-ryáy-if), **Rudolf (Hametovich)** (1938–93). Russian-born ballet dancer and choreographer. With the Kirov Ballet of Leningrad until his defection to the United Kingdom (1961), he joined the Royal Ballet and became the most celebrated male dancer of his generation. His association with Margot Fonteyn was remembered as one of the great partnerships of classical ballet. He took Austrian citizenship in 1982.

nurse (nurss) *n.* **1.** A person trained to care for the sick or disabled. **2.** Especially formerly, a woman employed to take care of another's children; a nursemaid. **3.** A woman employed to suckle children other than her own; a wet nurse. **4.** The state of being nursed: *the baby was put out to nurse.* **5.** That which fosters some quality or condition: *Leisure is the nurse of culture.* **6.** A worker ant or bee that cares for the young in the insect colony. **7.** A mature tree that shields a younger or newly planted tree from the elements.
~v. **nursed, nursing, nurses.** *—tr.* **1.** To feed (a baby or young offspring) at the breast; suckle. **2.** To care for or tend (a child or invalid). **3.** To try to cure or treat: *to nurse a cough.* **4.** To take special care of; foster; cultivate: *She nursed her business through the depression.* **5.** To keep in touch and foster relations with for one's own advantage. **6.** To harbour or bear privately in the mind: *nursing a grudge.* **7.** To hold or clasp carefully or soothingly: *He nursed his bruised knee.* **8.** To sit near, as if taking care of (a fire). **9.** To drink (usually an alcoholic drink) slowly. **10.** In billiards, to keep (the balls) together so as to make a series of cannons. *—intr.* **1.** To take nourishment from the breast; suckle. **2.** To serve as a nurse. [Middle English *norse, nurse,* from Old French *norrice,* from Late Latin *nūtrīcia,* from *nūtrīcius,* adjective of *nūtrix,* a nurse.] **—nurs·er** *n.*

nurse hound *n.* A type of dogfish.

nurse·maid (núrss-mayd) *n.* Also **nurs·er·y·maid** (-ri-, -əri-). A girl or woman employed to take care of children.

nurs·er·y (núrss-ri, -əri) *n., pl.* **-ies.** **1.** A building, room, or area set apart for the use of young children. **2.** A nursery school. **3.** A place where plants are grown for sale, transplanting, or experimentation. **4.** Any place in which something is produced or developed. **5.** In billiards, a series of cannons, or any one of the series, made when the three balls are adjacent to a cushion. In this sense, also called "nursery cannon". [Middle English *norserie*, from *norse*, NURSE.]

nurs·er·y·man (núrss-ri-mən, -əri-) *n., pl.* **-men** (-mən). A man who owns or works in a nursery for plants.

nursery rhyme *n.* A short, traditional rhymed poem or song for children.

nursery school *n.* A school for very young children. Also called "nursery".

nursery slopes *pl.n.* The lower, gentle ski-slopes used by those still learning to ski.

nursery stakes *pl.n. Used with a singular or plural verb.* A horse race for two-year-olds.

nurse shark *n.* Any of various large sharks of the family Orectolobidae, such as *Ginglymostoma cirratum*, a scavenging shark found in the Atlantic. [Middle English *nusse fisshe* (later altered through influence of *nurse*), perhaps from mistaken division of *a nuss* for *an huss* (fish), from *huss†*, shark, dogfish.]

nurs·ing home (núrssing) *n.* **1.** A private hospital or home for convalescent or aged people. **2.** A private maternity hospital.

nursing mother *n.* **1.** A woman who is breastfeeding her child. **2.** A foster mother.

nurs·ling, nurse·ling (núrssling) *n.* **1.** A nursing infant or young animal. **2.** A carefully nurtured person or thing.

nur·ture (núrchər) *n.* **1.** Anything that nourishes; sustenance; food. **2.** The act of promoting development or growth. **3.** *Biology.* The sum of environmental influences and conditions acting upon an organism, and partly determining its structure or behaviour.

~*tr.v.* **nurtured, -turing, -tures.** **1.** To nourish. **2.** To educate or train. **3.** To foster the development of. [Middle English *norture, nurture*, from Old French *nour(e)ture*, from Late Latin *nūtrītūra*, a feeding, from Latin *nūtrīre*, to feed.] —**nur·tur·er** *n.*

N.U.S. **1.** National Union of Seamen. **2.** National Union of Students.

nut (nut) *n.* **1. a.** A hard-shelled, solid-textured, one-seeded fruit that does not split open, such as an acorn or a hazelnut. **b.** Any seed borne in a fruit having a hard shell, such as the peanut or almond. **c.** The kernel of any of these. **2.** *Informal.* Any difficult person, endeavour, or problem. Used chiefly in the phrase *a hard or tough nut to crack.* **3.** *Slang.* The head. **4.** *Slang.* An eccentric, fanciful, or deranged person. **5.** *Slang.* An enthusiast; a buff. **6. a.** A ridge of wood at the top of the fingerboard or neck of stringed instruments, over which the strings pass. **b.** A device at the lower end of the bow of a violin or similar instrument, used for adjusting the hairs. **7.** A small block of metal or wood having a central, threaded hole, designed to fit round and secure a bolt or screw. **8.** Any small piece of a substance, as of coal or butter. **9.** A flat, sweet, round biscuit, usually flavoured with ginger. **10.** *Printing.* An en *(see).* —**do (one's) nut.** *British Slang.* To become very angry. —**off (one's) nut.** *Slang.* Crazy; mad. See **nuts.**

~*intr.v.* **nutted, nutting, nuts.** To gather or search for nuts. [Middle English *note, nute*, Old English *hnutu.*]

N.U.T. National Union of Teachers.

nu·tant (néw-t'nt ‖ nōō-) *adj.* *Botany.* Pointing downwards; drooping. Stalk of flowers. [Latin *nutāns* (stem *nutant-*), present participle of *nutāre*, to nod.]

nu·ta·tion (new-táysh'n ‖ nōō-) *n.* **1.** A nodding of the head. **2.** *Astronomy.* A small periodic motion of the celestial pole of the Earth with respect to the pole of the ecliptic. **3.** *Botany.* A spiral growth movement in the stems of certain plants, especially climbers, caused by differential growth rates in the stem. [Latin *nūtātiō* (stem *nūtātiōn-*), from *nūtāre*, frequentative of *nuere* (unattested), to nod.] —**nu·ta·tion·al** *adj.*

nut-brown (nút-brówn) *n.* Rich reddish brown. —**nut-brown** *adj.*

nut·case (nút-kayss) *n.* *Slang.* A deranged or very stupid person.

nut·crack·er (nút-krackər) *n.* **1.** *Usually plural.* An implement, typically consisting of two levers, used to crack nuts. **2. a.** A bird, *Nucifraga caryocatactes*, of northern Eurasia. **b.** A bird, the nuthatch.

nut-gall (nút-gawl) *n.* A nutlike swelling produced on an oak or other tree by certain parasitic wasps. Also called "gallnut".

nut·hatch (nút-hach) *n.* Any of several small birds of the family Sittidae, having long, sharp bills, and noted for their ability to manoeuvre on tree trunks and branches. Also called "nutcracker". [Middle English *notehache, nuthak*, "nut hatchet" (named from its habit of wedging nuts in bark and hacking them open) : *nute*, NUT + *hache*, axe, hatchet, from Old French, from Medieval Latin *hapia*, from Germanic *hapja* (unattested).]

nut·house (nút-howss) *n.* *Slang.* A mental hospital. Often considered offensive.

nut·let (nút-lət, -lit) *n.* **1.** A small nut. **2.** The stone in certain fruits, such as the peach or cherry. **3.** A hard, one-seeded portion of a schizocarpic fruit, such as the four parts making up fruits of the dead nettle family.

nut·meat (nút-meet) *n.* **1.** A vegetarian food made from nuts. **2.** *U.S.* The edible kernel of a nut.

nut·meg (nút-meg) *n.* **1.** An evergreen tree, *Myristica fragrans*, native to the East Indies and cultivated elsewhere in the tropics.

2. The hard, aromatic seed of this tree, much used as a spice when grated or ground. See **mace.** **3.** Greyish to moderate brown. [Middle English *notemugge, nutemuge*, from Old French *nois muscade*, from Vulgar Latin *nuce muscāta* (unattested), "musky nut" : Latin *nux*, nut + *muscus*, MUSK.] —**nut·meg** *adj.*

nut oil *n.* Oil obtained from nuts such as walnuts and hazelnuts and used in paints and varnishes.

nu·tri·a (néw-tri-ə ‖ nōō-) *n.* **1.** A rodent, the **coypu** *(see).* **2.** The fur of the coypu, often dyed to resemble beaver. **3.** Olive grey. [Spanish *nutr(i)a*, nasalised variant of *lutra*, otter, from Latin *lutra.*] —**nu·tri·a** *adj.*

nu·tri·ent (néw-tri-ənt ‖ nōō-) *n.* Something that nourishes; especially, a nourishing ingredient in a food, or the mineral substances absorbed by the roots of plants.

~*adj.* Having nutritive value, as certain body fluids do. [Latin *nūtriēns* (stem *nūtrient-*), present participle of *nūtrīre*, to nourish.]

nu·tri·ment (néw-tri-mənt ‖ nōō-) *n.* **1.** Anything that nourishes; food. **2.** Anything that aids growth or development. [Latin *nūtrīmentum*, from *nūtrīre*, to nourish.] —**nu·tri·men·tal** (-mént'l) *adj.*

nu·tri·tion (new-trísh'n ‖ nōō-) *n.* **1.** The process of nourishing or being nourished; especially, the interrelated steps by which a living organism assimilates food and uses it for growth and for replacement of tissues. **2.** The study of food value, food intake, and the like. [Old French, from Late Latin *nūtrītiō* (stem *nūtrītiōn-*), from Latin *nūtrīre*, to nourish.] —**nu·tri·tion·al** *adj.* —**nu·tri·tion·al·ly** *adv.*

nu·tri·tion·ist (new-trísh'n-ist ‖ nōō-) *n.* A person who specialises in the study of nutrition.

nu·tri·tious (new-tríshəss ‖ nōō-) *adj.* **1.** Nourishing. **2.** Aiding the growth and development of a living organism. [Latin *nūtrītius*, from *nūtrix*, a nurse.] —**nu·tri·tious·ly** *adv.* —**nu·tri·tious·ness** *n.*

nu·tri·tive (néw-trə-tiv, -tri- ‖ nōō-) *adj.* Promoting nutrition; nourishing.

~*n.* A nutritious food. [Middle English *nutritif*, from Old French, from Late Latin *nūtrītīvus*, from Latin *nūtrīre*, to feed, nourish.] —**nu·tri·tive·ly** *adv.*

nuts (nuts) *pl.n. Vulgar Slang.* The testicles.

~*adj. Slang.* **1.** Crazy; insane. **2.** Extremely fond or enthusiastic: *She's nuts about opera.*

~*interj. Slang.* Used to express contempt, disappointment, defiance, or emphatic refusal. See **nut.** [From NUT. Noun, by comparison in shape; adjective, from phrases such as *off one's nut* (head); interjection, from noun.]

nuts and bolts *pl. n. Informal.* The practical, basic details.

nut·shell (nút-shel) *n.* The shell enclosing the kernel of a nut. —**in a nutshell.** In concise or brief form; epitomised.

nut·ter¹ (núttər) *n.* A person who goes nutting.

nutter² *n. British Slang.* A deranged or eccentric person. [From NUT (mad person).]

nut·ty (nútti) *adj.* **-tier, -tiest.** **1.** Containing or producing many nuts. **2.** Having a flavour or texture like that of nuts. **3.** *Informal.* Deranged; crazy. —**nut·ti·ly** *adv.* —**nut·ti·ness** *n.*

Nuuk (nōōk). Formerly **Godt·håb** (gód-hawb). Capital of Greenland, a port situated on the southwest coast of the country. Founded by the Danes (1721), it is a centre for the fishing of cod and halibut.

nux vom·i·ca (núks vómmikə) *n.* **1.** A tree, *Strychnos nux-vomica*, native to southeastern Asia, having poisonous seeds that are the source of strychnine, brucine, and a medicinal preparation. **2.** A seed of this tree. [Medieval Latin, "emetic nut" : Latin *nux*, nut + *vomica*, from Latin *vomere*, to VOMIT.]

nuz·zle (núzz'l) *v.* **-zled, -zling, -zles.** —*tr.* **1.** To rub or push against gently with or as if with the nose or snout. **2.** To uproot with the snout. —*intr.* **1.** To make rubbing or pressing motions with the nose or snout. **2.** To nestle or cuddle. [Earlier *nousle*, Middle English *noselen*, from *nose*, NOSE.]

NW northwest; northwestern.

NWbN northwest by north.

NWbW northwest by west.

N.W.T. Northwest Territories.

N.Y. New York.

nyaff (nyaf) *n. Scottish Slang.* A boorish or stupid person. [Perhaps akin to dialect *gonoph*, thief, ultimately from Hebrew *gannābh*, thief.]

nya·la (nyáalə) *n., pl.* **-las** or collectively **nyala.** A large spiral-horned antelope, *Tragelaphus angasi*, native to southern Africa. Also called "inyala". [Venda, from Zulu *inxala.*]

Nyan·ja (nyánjə) *n., pl.* **-jas** or collectively **Nyanja.** **1.** A member of a central African people living mainly in Malawi. **2.** The Bantu language of this people, of the Niger-Congo family of languages. —**Nyan·ja** *adj.*

Nyasa, Lake. See Lake **Malawi.**

Nyasaland. See **Malawi.**

nyct-, nycti-, nycto- *comb. form.* Indicates night or darkness; for example, **nyctophobia.**

nyc·ta·lo·pi·a (níktə-lṓpi-ə) *n.* **1.** Vision that is normal in daylight but abnormally weak when the light is dim. In this sense, also called "night blindness". Compare **hemeralopia.** **2.** The inability to see clearly except when the light is dim. Not in technical usage. [Late Latin *nyctalōpia*, from Latin *nyctalops*, night-blind, from Greek *nuktalōps* : *nux* (stem *nukt-*), night + *alaos†*, blind + *ōps*, eye.] —**nyc·ta·lo·pic** (-lṓpik, -lóppik) *adj.*

nyc·ti·nas·ty (níkti-nasti) *n.* The opening and closing of leaves and petals in response to changes of light and temperature. [Greek *nux* (stem *nukt-*), night + -NASTY.] —**nyc·ti·nas·tic** (-nástik) *adj.*

nyc·tit·ro·pism (nik-títtra-piz'm) *n.* The tendency of the leaves or other parts of some plants to change their position at nightfall. [Greek *nux* (stem *nukt-*), night + -TROPISM.] —**nyc·ti·tro·pic** *adj.*

nyc·to·pho·bi·a (ník-tō-fṓbi-ə, -tə-) *n.* An abnormal fear of the dark or of night. —**nyc·to·pho·bic** *adj.*

Nye·re·re (nye-raúr-i. *Note: not* nī-), **Dr. Julius (Kambarage)** (1922–). Tanzanian politician. After campaigning for Tanganyika's independence from the United Kingdom, he became its premier (1961) before taking office as president (1962) of the new independent republic. In 1964, he negotiated union with Zanzibar to form the state of Tanzania. He gave up Tanzania's presidency in 1985 and the leadership of his party in 1990.

ny·lon (nī-lon, *rarely* -lən) *n.* **1.** Any of a family of high-strength, resilient, synthetic materials, the long-chain molecules of which contain the recurring amide group CONH. **2.** Cloth or thread made from nylon. **3.** *Plural.* Women's stockings made of nylon or a similar synthetic fabric. [Coined by the inventors, with -*on* by analogy with forms such as *rayon.*]

nymph (nimf) *n.* **1.** *Greek & Roman Mythology.* Any of numerous female nature spirits, inhabiting and animistically representing features of nature. **2.** *Poetic.* A beautiful young woman. **3.** *Zoology.* Any of the young of insects, such as the mayfly or dragonfly, that undergoes incomplete metamorphosis. Compare **pupa**. [Middle English *nimphe,* from Latin *nympha,* nymph, pupa, from Greek *numphē,* nymph, bride.] —**nymph·al, nym·phe·an** (nímfi-ən ‖ *U.S. also* nim-fée-ən) *adj.*

nym·phae (ním-fee) *pl.n. Singular* **nym·pha** (-fə). *Anatomy.* The **labia minora** (*see*). [New Latin, from Latin, NYMPH.]

nym·pha·lid (nímfəlid) *n.* Any of various medium to large butterflies of the family Nymphalidae. The family includes the admirals, fritillaries, and tortoiseshells. [New Latin *Nymphalidae* (family) : *Nymphalis* (genus), from Latin *nymphālis,* "nymphal", from *nympha,* NYMPH + -IDAE.] —**nym·pha·lid** *adj.*

nym·phet (nímfit, nim-fét) *n.* **1.** A young nymph. **2.** A pubescent or prepubescent girl regarded as sexually desirable to adult men. [Old French *nymphette,* diminutive of *nymphe,* NYMPH.]

nym·pho (nímfō) *n., pl.* -**phos.** *Slang.* A nymphomaniac.

nym·pho·lep·sy (nímfə-lep-si) *n., pl.* -**sies.** A frenzy induced by an obsession for something unattainable. [From NYMPHOLEPT.]

nym·pho·lept (nímfə-lept) *n.* One in a state of nympholepsy. [Greek *numpholēptos,* "caught by nymphs" : *numphē,* NYMPH + *lēptos,* seized.] —**nym·pho·lept, nym·pho·lep·tic** (-léptik) *adj.*

nym·pho·ma·ni·a (nímfə-máyni-ə) *n.* Abnormally strong sexual desire in a heterosexual woman, especially when directed at a large number of men. Compare **satyriasis**. [New Latin : NYMPH + -MANIA.] —**nym·pho·ma·ni·ac** (-ak) *n. & adj.*

Ny·norsk (née-nawrsk, néw-; *Norwegian* nū-) *n.* One of the two officially recognised and mutually intelligible forms of Norwegian, incorporating various dialects. Formerly called "Landsmål". Compare **Bokmål**. [Norwegian, "new Norwegian".]

Ny·os (nee-óss, nyoss), **Lake.** Lake in northern Cameroon. Poisonous gases erupted from it in 1986, killing about 1,500 people.

NYP not yet published.

Nysa. See **Neisse.**

nys·tag·mus (ni-stágməss) *n. Pathology.* A spasmodic, involuntary movement of the eyeball. [New Latin, from Greek *nustagmos,* drowsiness, from *nustazein,* to be sleepy.] —**nys·tag·mic** *adj.*

nys·ta·tin (nísstətin) *n. Medicine.* An antibiotic derived from the bacterium *Streptomyces noursei,* used to treat various fungal infections, especially thrush. [From *New York State* (where it was developed) + -IN.]

N.Z. New Zealand.

o, O (ō) *n., pl.* **o's** or *rare* **os, Os** or **O's. 1.** The 15th letter of the modern English alphabet. **2.** Any of the speech sounds represented by this letter. **3.** A zero: *a phone number with three O's.* **4.** Anything shaped like the letter **O;** a circle.

o, O, o., O. *Note:* As an abbreviation or symbol, *o* may be a small or a capital letter, with or without a full stop. Established forms or those generally preferred precede the definition. When no form is given, all four forms are in general use in that sense. **1. O, O.** ocean. **2. o., O.** octavo. **3. O.** October (unofficial). **4. O, O.** old. **5. o.** only. **6. O, O.** order. **7. O** The symbol for the element oxygen. **8. o.** pint. [Latin *octarius.*] **9. O** A human blood type of the **ABO** group. See **ABO. 10.** The 15th in a series, or the 14th when *J* is omitted.

O (ō) *interj.* **1.** Used before the noun or noun phrase in direct address, especially, as in poetry or prayer, to express earnestness or solemnity: *O my people, what have I done unto thee?* (Micah 6:3). **2.** Variant of **oh.**

Usage: O is used to introduce an invocation, entreaty, or the like, in literary and religious contexts: *O God; O mighty ocean!* It is never followed immediately by a punctuation mark, and it is always capitalised. *Oh* is used to express a reflective pause or a degree of emotion: *Oh, I see.* It is capitalised only when it is the first word in a sentence, and is followed by a comma or, when the emphasis is strong, by an exclamation mark. It may be part of a written sentence, or stand alone. In a few phrases, *Oh* can be replaced by *O,* especially in American English: *O my!; Oh/O dear!*

o' (ə, ō) *prep.* A reduced form of the preposition *of.* Used especially in the phrase *o'clock,* but also found in such terms as *will-o'-the-wisp,* and *man-o'-war,* and in numerous dialects.

O' (ō, ə) *prefix.* Indicates a descendant of. Used in various Irish surnames, for example *O'Connor, O'Malley, O'Reilly.* [Irish *ó,* grandson, descendant, from Old Irish *aue.*]

-o *n., adj., & adv. suffix.* Used to form an informal, abbreviated, or slang variant or word; for example, **ammo, blotto, wino.** [Perhaps from *oh* (interjection), used as humorous suffix.]

-o- *infix.* Used to connect the elements of a compound word, either in the sense of "and", or for the sake of euphony; for example, **Anglo-American; meritocracy.**

oaf (ōf) *n., pl.* **oafs** or *rare* **oaves. 1.** A stupid or clumsy person. **2.** *Obsolete.* A deformed child supposedly substituted for a human one by elves; a changeling. [Earlier *ouph, aufe,* elf, goblin, from Old Norse *alfr.*] —**oaf·ish** *adj.* —**oaf·ish·ly** *adv.* —**oaf·ish·ness** *n.*

O·a·hu (ō-áa-hōō). Third largest island of the U.S. state of Hawaii in the north Pacific. It is the most populous, and highly developed with an economy based on sugar and pineapple plantations and tourism. The important U.S. military installations on the island include Pearl Harbor, attacked by the Japanese (1941). Honolulu is the chief port and state capital.

oak (ōk) *n.* **1.** Any of various deciduous or evergreen trees or shrubs of the genus *Quercus,* having lobed leaves and bearing acorns as fruit. See **cork oak, durmast oak, holm oak. 2.** The durable wood of any of these trees. **3.** Any of various trees or shrubs resembling the oak in some feature, such as the **poison oak** (*see*). **4.** Something made of oak wood, especially a heavy outer door to a set of rooms in an Oxford or Cambridge college. **5.** Any of various brown shades resembling that of oak wood. [Middle English *ok, ook,* Old English *āc,* from Germanic *aik-* (unattested).] —**oak** *adj.*

oak apple *n.* A harmless **gall** on oak trees, caused by the larva of a type of wasp. Also called "oak gall".

oak·en (ṓkən) *adj.* Made of oak wood or a material resembling it.

oak fern *n.* Any of various ferns, especially *Dryopteris linnaeana,* having lobed fronds resembling oak leaves.

Oak·ley (ṓkli), **Annie,** born Phoebe Anne Oakley Mozee (1860–1926). U.S. sharpshooter. She was a star attraction of Buffalo Bill's Wild West Show.

Oak Ridge. City in Tennessee, United States. It was founded (1943) by the U.S. government around the plants set up to produce uranium and plutonium for nuclear bombs.

Oaks (ōks) *n.* Used with a singular verb. A horse race held annually at Epsom for three-year-old fillies. Preceded by *the.* [From the name of an estate near Epsom.]

oa·kum (ṓkəm) *n.* Loose hemp or jute fibre, sometimes treated with tar, creosote, or asphalt. It is used for caulking seams in wooden ships and packing pipe joints. [Middle English *okum,* Old English *ācumba,* "off-combings" : *ā-,* off, away + *-cumba,* from *cemban,* to comb.]

O. & M. organisation and method.

O.A.P. old-age pensioner; old-age pensioner.

oar (or ‖ ōr) *n.* **1.** A long, thin pole, usually wooden, with a blade at one end, used to row and, occasionally, to steer a boat. **2.** A person using an oar; a rower. **3.** An implement for stirring; especially, one used in brewing. —**put (one's) oar in.** To intrude impertinently; meddle. —**rest on (one's) oars.** To stop trying or working; take a rest.

~*v.* **oared, oaring, oars.** —*tr.* **1.** To propel with or as if with oars. **2.** To traverse with or as if with oars: *an hour to oar the strait.* —*intr.* To move forwards by or as if by rowing. [Middle English *oor, or,* Old English *ār,* from Common Germanic *airo* (unattested).] —**oared** *adj.*

oar·fish (ór-fish ‖ ōr-) *n., pl.* -**fishes** or collectively **oarfish.** A marine fish, *Regalecus glesne,* having a slender body up to 8 metres (26 feet) long and a dorsal fin extending the entire body length.

oar·lock (ór-lok ‖ ōr-) *n. U.S.* A **rowlock** (*see*).

oars·man (órz-mən ‖ ōrz-) *n., pl.* -**men** (-mən). A person who rows, especially an expert in rowing; a rower. [*Oar's,* possessive of OAR + MAN.]

oar·weed (ór-weed ‖ ōr-) *n.* Any of various seaweeds of the family

Laminariaceae, such as **kelp** *(see)*. [From dialect *oare*, *ore*, seaweed (from Middle English *ware*, Old English *wār*) + WEED.]

OAS 1. Organisation de L'Armée Secrète: a terrorist organisation of French settlers in Algeria opposed to Algerian independence. 2. Organisation of American States.

o·a·sis (ō-áy-siss) *n., pl.* **-ses** (-seez). 1. A fertile or green area in a desert, resulting from the presence of water. 2. A place or situation preserved from surrounding unpleasantness; a refuge: *The library was an oasis of calm in the noisy building.* [Late Latin *oasis*, from Greek, probably from an Egyptian word akin to Coptic *ouahe*, oasis, "dwelling area".]

oast (ōst) *n.* 1. A kiln for drying hops or malt, or for drying and curing tobacco. 2. An oast-house. [Middle English *ost*, Old English *āst*.]

oast-house (ōst-howss) *n.* A building containing hop-drying kilns, usually having a conical roof.

Oast·ler (ōstlər), **Richard** (1789–1861). British reformer. His campaigning against the exploitation of child labour in factories was instrumental in the introduction of a legal maximum of ten hours work a day for minors (1847).

oat. See **oats.**

oat·cake (ōt-kayk) *n.* A biscuit of baked oatmeal, eaten especially in Scotland and northern England.

oat·en (ōt'n) *adj.* Of, made of, or containing oats, oatmeal, or oat straw: *oaten fodder.*

Oates (ōts), **Joyce Carol** (1938–). U.S. novelist, short-story writer, and poet. Works include: *Them* (U.S. National Book Award, 1969), *On Boxing* (1987), *What I Lived For* (1994).

Oates, Titus (1649–1705). English clergyman and agitator. His allegations of a Roman Catholic conspiracy (the Popish Plot, 1678) to murder Charles II aroused anti-Catholic public hysteria, and led to the arrest and execution of many Catholics and the passing of the 1678 Test Act excluding Catholics from Parliament. Oates was later discredited and imprisoned.

oat grass *n.* 1. Any grass of the genus *Arrhenatherum*; especially, *A. elatius*, common in meadows. 2. Any of several oatlike grasses.

oath (ōth) *n., pl.* **oaths** (ōthz, ōths). 1. A formal statement declaring the truth of a claim or promising to fulfil a pledge, often calling upon God or a sacred object as witness. 2. The words or formula of such a declaration or promise. 3. That which is promised or declared. 4. An irreverent or blasphemous use of the name of God or anything held sacred. 5. Any act or instance of cursing or swearing. —**on** or **under oath.** 1. Bound by an oath. 2. *Law.* Sworn to tell the truth. [Middle English *ooth*, Old English *āth*, from Germanic *aithaz* (unattested).]

oat·meal (ōt-meel) *n.* 1. Meal made from oats; ground oats. 2. A porridge made from rolled or ground oats. 3. Greyish yellow to fawn. —**oat·meal** *adj.*

oats (ōts) *pl.n.* 1. Any of several grasses of the genus *Avena;* especially, *A. sativa*, widely cultivated for its edible seeds. 2. The seeds of *Avena sativa* used as a food and fodder. 3. *Singular. Archaic.* A shepherd's musical pipe made of an oat straw. —**feel (one's) oats.** *U.S. Informal.* 1. To be joyous or frisky. 2. To feel self-satisfied and important, or to act in a way suggesting this. —**get (one's) oats.** *Slang.* To have sexual intercourse. —**off (one's) oats.** *Informal.* To have no appetite for food. —**sow (one's) oats** or **wild oats.** To indulge in adventures and licentiousness during one's youth. [Old English *āte†* (plural *ātan*).] —**oat** *adj.*

O.A.U. Organisation of African Unity. See map for members.

Ob (ob). River of Siberia, Russia, formed by the meeting of the Biya and Katun rivers, which rise in the Altai mountains. It flows north to the Arctic Ocean via the Gulf of Ob and Kara Sea.

ob- *prefix.* Indicates inverse shape or attachment; for example, **obcordate, obovate.** [In borrowed Latin compounds, *ob-* becomes *o-* before *m*, as in **omit,** *oc-* before *c*, as in **occlude,** *of-* before *f*, as in **offend,** *op-* before *p*, as in **oppose.** *Ob-* indicates: 1. To, towards, as in **offer, obvert.** 2. Directed towards in a negative way, against, in opposition to, as in **opponent, obstacle.** 3. Opposite to, before, on, in front of, as in **obsess, obstetric.** 4. On account of, for, as in **obsecrate.** 5. In a certain direction, down, down upon, over, behind, as in **occasion, omit.** 6. Out of, away from, as in **obliterate.** 7. Intensified action, as in **obdurate, obtain.** Latin *ob-*, from the preposition *ob*, to, towards, in front of, on account of, against.]

ob. 1. incidentally [Latin *obiter*]. 2. obiit. 3. oboe.

O.B. *British.* 1. old boy. 2. outside broadcast.

Obad. Obadiah (Old Testament).

O·ba·di·ah[1] (ōbə-dī-ə). A Hebrew prophet.

Obadiah[2] *n. Abbr.* **Obad.** The book in the Old Testament written by Obadiah. Also, in the Douay Bible, "Abdias".

ob·bli·ga·to, ob·li·ga·to (óbbli-gaá-tō) *adj. Music.* Not to be left out; indispensable. Said of an accompaniment that is an integral part of a piece. Compare **ad libitum.**
~*n., pl.* **obbligatos** or **-ti** (-tee). *Music.* An obbligato musical accompaniment. [Italian, past participle of *obbligare*, to obligate, from Latin *obligāre*, to OBLIGE.]

ob·con·ic (ob-kónnik) *adj. Botany.* Also **ob·con·i·cal** (-'l). Cone-shaped, with the tapering end at the point of attachment: *an obconic fruit.*

ob·cor·date (ob-kórdayt) *adj. Botany.* Heart-shaped, with the tapering end at the point of attachment: *an obcordate leaf.*

ob·du·ra·cy (ób-dewr-ə-si ‖ -door-) *n.* The state or quality of being obdurate.

ob·du·rate (ób-dewr-ət, -it, -ayt; -déwr- ‖ -door-) *adj.* 1. Hardened against persuasion or feeling; unyielding; hardhearted: *an obdurate judge.* 2. Hardened against good or moral influence; stubbornly impenitent: *"obdurate conscience of the old sinner"* (Sir Walter Scott). —See Synonyms at **inflexible.** [Middle English *obdurat*, from Latin *obdūrātus*, past participle of *obdūrāre*, to harden : *ob-* (intensive) + *dūrāre*, to harden, from *dūrus*, hard.] —**ob·du·rate·ly** *adv.* —**ob·du·rate·ness** *n.*

O.B.E. 1. Officer (of the Order) of the British Empire. 2. Order of the British Empire.

o·be·ah (ōbi-ə) *n.* Also **o·bi** (ōbi). 1. A form of religious belief, probably of African origin, involving witchcraft or sorcery, and practised especially in the West Indies. 2. A fetish or object used in the practice of obeah. [Of West African origin.]

o·be·di·ence (ō-béedi-ənss, ə-) *n.* 1. **a.** The quality or condition of being obedient. **b.** The act of obeying. 2. A sphere of ecclesiastical authority. 3. A group of persons under such authority. 4. An office or duty in a convent or monastery.

o·be·di·ent (ō-béedi-ənt, ə-) *adj.* 1. Obeying or carrying out a request, command, or the like. 2. Submissive to control; dutiful. [Middle English, from Old French, from Latin *oboediēns* (stem *oboedient-*), present participle of *oboedīre*, to OBEY.] —**o·be·di·ent·ly** *adv.*

Synonyms: obedient, compliant, acquiescent, submissive, docile, amenable, servile, tractable, dutiful.

o·be·di·en·tia·ry (ō-béedi-énshi-əri, ə- ‖ -erri) *n., pl.* **-ries.** A holder of any office subordinate to that of the superior in a convent or monastery. [Medieval Latin *obedientiarius.* See **obedient, -ary.**]

o·bei·sance (ō-báyss'nss, ə- ‖ -béess'nss) *n.* 1. A gesture or movement of the body expressing reverence or respect, such as a bow or curtsy. 2. An attitude associated with this gesture, such as deference or homage. [Middle English *obeisaunce*, from Old French *obeissance*, from *obeissant*, present participle of *obeir*, to OBEY.] —**o·bei·sant** *adj.*

ob·e·lise, ob·e·lize (óbbə-līz) *tr.v.* **-lised, -lising, -lises.** To mark or annotate with an obelus. [Greek *obelizein*, from *obelos*, OBELUS.]

ob·e·lisk (óbbə-lisk, *rarely* ōbə-) *n.* 1. A tall, four-sided shaft of stone, usually monolithic and tapering, that rises to a pyramidal point. 2. A monument in this shape, especially one in ancient Egypt. 3. Anything else in this shape, such as a mountain. 4. *Printing.* The dagger sign (†), used especially as a reference mark. In this dictionary it refers to an etymological footnote indicating that the

O.A.U.

1	Benin		**20**	São Tomé & Principe
2	Botswana	**11** Ghana	**21**	Senegal
3	Burkina	**12** Guinea	**22**	Seychelles
4	Burundi	**13** Guinea-Bissau	**23**	Sierra Leone
5	Cameroon	**14** Ivory Coast	**24**	Swaziland
6	Cape Verde	**15** Lesotho	**25**	Togo
7	Comoros	**16** Liberia	**26**	Uganda
8	Congo	**17** Malawi	**27**	Western Sahara
9	Equatorial Guinea	**18** Mauritius	**28**	Zambia
10	The Gambia	**19** Rwanda	**29**	Zimbabwe

All named and numbered states are O.A.U. members

word or form so marked is of obscure origin. In this sense, also called "obelus", "dagger". [Old French *obelisque,* from Latin *obeliscus,* from Greek *obeliskos,* diminutive of *obelos,* spit, OBELUS.] **—ob·e·lis·cal** (-lísk'l) *adj.* **—ob·e·lis·koid** (-lískoyd) *adj.*

ob·e·lus (óbbə-ləss) *n., pl.* **-li** (-lī). **1.** A mark (— or ÷) used in ancient manuscripts to indicate a doubtful or spurious passage. **2.** *Printing.* An obelisk. [Late Latin *obelus,* from Greek *obelos*†, spit, obelisk, obelus.]

O·ber·am·mer·gau (ṓbər-ámmər-gow). Town in Bavaria, Germany. It is the site of passion plays, held every 10 years since 1634 in thanksgiving for deliverance from the Black Death (1633).

O·ber·on (ṓbər-ən, -on). In medieval folklore, the king of the fairies, husband of Titania. [French, from Old French *Auberon,* of Frankish origin; akin to Old High German *Alberich.*]

o·bese (ō-béess, ə-) *adj.* Extremely fat; unpleasantly overweight. See Synonyms at **fat.** [Latin *obēsus,* "grown fat by eating", from past participle of *obedere,* to eat away : *ob-,* away + *edere,* to eat.] **—o·be·si·ty** (ō-béessəti, ə-), **o·bese·ness** *n.*

o·bey (ō-báy, ə-) *v.* **obeyed, obeying, obeys.** *—tr.* **1.** To carry out or fulfil the command, order, or instruction of. **2.** To carry out or comply with (a command or request). **3.** To act in accordance with (one's own instincts or feelings). *—intr.* To behave obediently. [Middle English *obeien,* from Old French *obeir,* from Latin *oboedīre,* "to listen to" : *ob-,* to, towards + *audīre,* to hear.] **—o·bey·er** *n.*

ob·fus·cate (ób-fəss-kayt, -fuss- || ob-fúss-) *tr.v.* **-cated, -cating, -cates. 1.** To confuse or make obscure; cloud: *His emotions obfuscated his judgment.* **2.** To bewilder or stupefy. **3.** To render indistinct or dim; darken: *The fog obfuscated the shore.* [Late Latin *obfuscāre,* to darken : *ob-* (intensive) + Latin *fuscāre,* to darken, from *fuscus,* dark.] **—ob·fus·ca·tion** (-káysh'n) *n.*

o·bi[1] (ṓbi) *n., pl.* **obis** or **obi.** A wide sash fastened at the back with a large flat bow, worn by women and men in Japan as a part of the traditional dress. [Japanese, "belt", "band", "sash".]

obi[2]**.** Variant of **obeah.**

o·bi·it (ṓbi-it). *Abbr.* **ob.** *Latin.* He (or she) died. Usually followed by the date of death.

o·bit (ṓbit, ō-bít) *n. Informal.* **1.** An obituary. **2.** A memorial service.

o·bi·ter dic·tum (óbbitər dík-təm, ṓbitər) *n., pl.* **obiter dicta** (-tə). **1.** *Law.* An opinion voiced by a judge that has only incidental bearing on the case in question and is therefore not binding. **2.** Any incidental remark or observation; a passing comment. [Latin, "a statement in passing".]

o·bit·u·ar·y (ō-bíttew-əri, ə-, o- || -erri) *n., pl.* **-ies.** *Abbr.* **obit.** A notice of a death, usually with a brief biography of the deceased. [Medieval Latin *obituārius,* (report) of death, from Latin *obitus,* death, from the past participle of *obīre,* to fall, die : *ob-,* down + *īre,* to go.] **—o·bit·u·ar·y** *adj.*

obj. 1. *Grammar.* object; objective. **2.** objection.

ob·ject[1] (əb-jékt || ob-) *v.* **-jected, -jecting, -jects.** *—intr.* **1.** To present a dissenting or opposing argument; raise an objection. Usually followed by *to*: *object to the testimony of a witness.* **2.** To feel adverse to or express disapproval of something. Usually followed by *to*: *object to modern fashion.* *—tr.* To put forward in, or as a reason for, opposition; offer as criticism: *They objected that discipline was lacking.* [Middle English *objecten,* from Latin *objicere, obicere* (past participle *objectus*), to throw against, oppose : *ob-,* towards + *jacere,* to throw.] **—ob·jec·tor** (-ər) *n.*

Synonyms: *object, protest, complain, dissent, demur, remonstrate, expostulate.*

ob·ject[2] (ób-jikt, -jekt) *n.* **1.** Anything perceptible by one or more of the senses, especially something that can be seen and felt; a material thing. **2.** *Philosophy.* Anything intelligible or perceptible by the mind. **3.** A person or thing serving as a focus of attention, curiosity, discussion, feeling, thought, or action; especially, one that evokes ridicule or pity: *an object of contempt.* **4.** The purpose, aim, or goal of a specific action or effort: *the object of the game.* **5.** *Abbr.* **obj.** *Grammar.* **a.** A noun, pronoun, or noun phrase that receives or is affected by the action of a verb within a sentence. In *Mary hit Julia, Julia* is the object of the verb *hit.* **b.** A noun, pronoun, or noun phrase governed by a preposition. In *on television,* the noun *television* is the object of the preposition *on.* —See Synonyms at **intention.** **—no object.** *Informal.* Not an obstacle or hindrance: *Cost is no object.* [Middle English, from Latin *objectus,* "something thrown before or presented to (the mind)", from the past participle of *obicere,* to throw before or against, OBJECT (verb).]

object ball *n.* In billiards and similar games, the ball that the striker hits or intends to hit first with the cue ball.

object glass *n.* A lens in an optical instrument, the objective.

ob·jec·ti·fy (əb-jékti-fī || ob-) *tr.v.* **-fied, -fying, -fies. 1.** To present (someone) as an object; depersonalise: *Pornography objectifies women.* **2.** To impart reality to; externalise or make objective. [From OBJECT (noun).] **—ob·jec·ti·fi·ca·tion** (-fi-káysh'n) *n.*

ob·jec·tion (əb-jéksh'n || ob-) *n. Abbr.* **obj. 1.** An act of objecting. **2.** A statement or other expression offered in opposition. **3.** A reason or cause for expressing opposition or disagreement.

ob·jec·tion·a·ble (əb-jéksh'n-əb'l || ob-) *adj.* Arousing disapproval; offensive: *objectionable behaviour.* See Synonyms at **offensive.** **—ob·jec·tion·a·bil·i·ty** (-ə-bílləti) *n.* **—ob·jec·tion·a·bly** *adv.*

ob·jec·tive (əb-jéktiv || ob-) *adj.* **1.** Of or having to do with a material object as distinguished from a mental concept, idea, or belief. **2.** Having actual existence or reality. **3. a.** Not influenced by emotion, surmise, or personal prejudice. **b.** Based on observable phenomena; presented factually: *an objective appraisal.* **4.** *Medicine.* Designating a symptom or condition perceived as a sign of disease by someone other than the person afflicted. **5.** *Grammar.* **a.** Designating the case of a noun or pronoun serving as the object of a verb or preposition, and sometimes having various other grammatical functions. **b.** Pertaining to a noun or pronoun used in such a case. **6.** Serving as a goal; being the object of a course of action: *an objective point.* —Compare **subjective.** —See Synonyms at **fair.**
~n. **1.** Anything that actually exists, as distinguished from something thought or felt to exist. **2.** Something worked towards or striven for; a goal. **3.** *Abbr.* **obj.** *Grammar.* **a.** The objective case. **b.** A noun or pronoun in the objective case. **4. a.** The lens or lens system in a microscope or telescope that is closest to the object being viewed. **b.** A lens or lens system in a camera or projector that forms the image of the object. Also called "object glass", "object lens". —See Synonyms at **intention.** [Medieval Latin *objectīvus,* from Latin *objectus,* an OBJECT.] **—ob·jec·tive·ly** *adv.* **—ob·jec·tive·ness** *n.*

objective case *n. Grammar.* The case of a noun or pronoun when it is the object of a verb or preposition, or serves various other grammatical functions.

objective complement *n. Grammar.* A noun, noun phrase, or adjective serving as a complement to a verb and qualifying its direct object. In *They elected me president, president* is an objective complement.

objective genitive *n. Grammar.* **1.** The genitive case as indicating the object of a specified action. In the noun phrase *my wounds,* meaning "the wounds inflicted on me", the object *me* is transferred to the genitive case *my.* Compare **subjective genitive. 2.** A noun or pronoun in this case. **—objective genitive** *adj.*

ob·jec·tiv·ism (əb-jéktiv-iz'm, ob-) *n.* **1.** *Philosophy.* Any of several doctrines holding that all reality is objective and external to the mind, and that our perceptions correspond with it. Compare **solipsism. 2.** In art and literature, an emphasis on objective themes or subjects. **—ob·jec·tiv·ist** *n.* **—ob·jec·tiv·is·tic** (-ístik) *adj.*

ob·jec·tiv·i·ty (ób-jek-tívvəti) *n.* **1.** The state, condition, or quality of being objective. **2.** External or material reality.

object language *n.* **1.** A language that is under discussion or being analysed, especially when being discussed in another language, the **metalanguage** *(see).* **2.** A **target language** *(see).*

object lens *n.* A lens in an optical instrument, the objective.

object lesson *n.* A practical illustration of a moral or principle.

object program *n.* A computer program transcribed into machine language by the compiler or assembler from the equivalent source program.

ob·jet d'art (ób-zhay dár) *n., pl.* **objets d'art** *(pronounced as singular).* A usually small artefact valued for its artistic merit. [French, "object of art".]

objet trou·vé (ób-zhay trṓō-vay, trōō-váy) *n., pl.* **objets trouvés** *(pronounced as singular).* An ordinary or commonplace object considered or presented as a work of art. [French, "found object".]

ob·jur·gate (ób-jur-gayt, -jər-) *tr.v.* **-gated, -gating, -gates.** *Rare.* To scold or rebuke sharply; berate. [Latin *objurgāre,* "to bring a lawsuit against", chide : *ob-,* against + *jurgāre,* "to bring a lawsuit", rebuke, from *jūs* (stem *jūr-*), law + *agere,* to act, perform.] **—ob·jur·ga·tion** (-gáysh'n) *n.* **—ob·jur·ga·to·ri·ly** (əb-júrgə-trə-li, ob-, -təri-; ób-jur-gaytərəli) *adv.* **—ob·jur·ga·to·ry** (əb-júrgə-tri, ob-, -təri; óbjur-gaytəri) *adj.*

obl. 1. oblique. **2.** oblong.

ob·lan·ce·o·late (ób-laán-si-ə-lət, -lit, -layt || -lán-) *adj. Botany.* Broader and rounded at the apex, and tapering at the base: *an oblanceolate leaf.*

o·blast (ób-laast, -ləst || -last) *n.* In countries of the former U.S.S.R., a local administrative division. [Russian *oblast',* from Old Church Slavonic : *ob-,* on + *vlast',* power, administration.]

ob·late[1] (óbblayt, ob-láyt, ōb-) *adj.* Designating a spheroid having an equatorial diameter greater than the distance between poles; compressed along or flattened at the poles. Compare **prolate.** [New Latin *oblatus,* "carried towards", stretched, from Latin *oblātus* (past participle of *obferre,* to bring to, offer) : *ob,* to, towards + *-lātus,* "carried".] **—ob·late·ly** *adv.* **—ob·late·ness** *n.*

ob·late[2] (óbblayt) *n.* **1.** A person dedicated to a religious life, but who has not taken formal vows. **2.** *Capital* **O.** *Roman Catholic Church.* A member of any of various religious communities. [Medieval Latin *oblātus,* "one offered (to God)", from Latin, past participle of *obferre,* to offer. See **oblate**[1]**.**] **—ob·late** *adj.*

ob·la·tion (ō-bláysh'n, ə-, o-) *n.* **1.** The act of offering something, such as worship or thanksgiving, to a deity. **2.** *Capital* **O. a.** The act of offering the bread and wine of the Eucharist. **b.** The bread and wine of the Eucharist. **3.** Any charitable offering or gift. [Middle English *oblacioun,* from Old French *oblation,* from Medieval Latin *oblātiō* (stem *oblātiōn-*), from *oblātus,* OBLATE (noun).] **—ob·la·tion·al, ob·la·to·ry** (óbblə-tri, -təri) *adj.*

ob·li·gate (óbbli-gayt) *tr.v.* **-gated, -gating, -gates.** To bind, compel, or constrain by a legal, moral, or social tie.
~adj. **1.** *Biology.* Able to survive in only one kind of environment; obligatory. Said of parasites that cannot live independently of their hosts. Compare **facultative. 2.** Absolutely indispensable; essential. **3.** *Archaic.* Bound or constrained; obliged. [Latin *obligāre,* to OBLIGE.] **—ob·li·ga·ble** (-gəb'l) *adj.* **—ob·li·ga·tor** (-gaytər) *n.*

ob·li·ga·tion (óbbli-gáysh'n) *n.* **1.** The act of binding oneself or being bound by a legal, moral, or social tie. **2. a.** A duty, contract, promise, or any other legal, moral, or social requirement that compels one to follow or avoid a certain course of action. **b.** A course of action imposed by law, society, or conscience by which one is bound or restricted. **3.** The constraining power of a law, promise, contract, or sense of duty. **4.** *Law.* **a.** A legal agreement stipulating a specified payment or action, especially if the agreement also specifies the penalty for failure to comply. **b.** The document containing the terms of such an agreement. **5. a.** Something owed as payment or in return for a special service or favour. **b.** The service or favour for which one is indebted to another. **6.** The state, fact, or condition of being indebted to another for a special service or favour received.

obligato. Variant of **obbligato.**

o·blig·a·to·ry (ə-blíggə-tri, o-, óbbligə-, -təri) *adj.* **1.** Legally or morally constraining; binding. **2.** Of the nature of an obligation; compulsory: *Attendance is obligatory.* **3.** Imposing or recording an obligation: *a bill obligatory.* **4.** *Biology.* Restricted to one mode of life; obligate. **—o·blig·a·to·ri·ly** *adv.*

o·blige (ə-blíj || ō-) *v.* **obliged, obliging, obliges.** *—tr.* **1.** To force or cause to do or refrain from doing something; constrain by physical, legal, social, or moral means. **2.** To make indebted or grateful. Usually used in the passive and with *to*: *They were obliged to him for his hospitality.* **3.** To gratify the wishes of; do a service or favour for: *He obliged us by arriving early.* *—intr.* To do a service or favour; perform a courtesy: *The pianist will oblige with an encore.* —See Synonyms at **force.** [Middle English *obligen,* from Old French *obliger,* from Latin *obligāre,* to tie to : *ob-,* to + *ligāre,* to bind.] **—o·blig·er** *n.*

ob·li·gee (óbbli-jée) *n.* **1.** A person who is under obligation to another. **2.** *Law.* A person to whom another is bound by contract or legal agreement; a creditor. Compare **obligor.**

o·blig·ing (ə-blíjing || ō-) *adj.* Ready to do favours for others; accommodating; helpful; considerate. See Synonyms at **amiable.** **—o·blig·ing·ly** *adv.* **—o·blig·ing·ness** *n.*

ob·li·gor (óbbli-gór, -jór) *n.* *Law.* A person who binds himself to another by contract or legal agreement; a debtor. Compare **obligee.**

o·blique (ō-bléek, ə-, o-) *adj. Abbr.* **obl. 1. a.** Having a slanting or sloping direction, course, or position; inclined. **b.** In geometry, designating lines or planes that are neither parallel nor perpendicular. **2.** Indirect or evasive in execution, meaning, or expression; not straightforward. **3.** Devious, misleading, or dishonest: *oblique answers.* **4.** Not direct in descent; collateral. **5.** *Botany.* Having sides of unequal length or form: *an oblique leaf.* **6.** *Anatomy.* Inclined at an angle; not perpendicular or horizontal: *oblique muscles.* **7.** *Grammar.* Designating any noun case except the nominative or the vocative. **8.** In rhetoric, indirect.

~n. **1.** Something that is oblique, such as a line, direction, or muscle. **2.** *Nautical.* The act of changing course by less than 90°. [Middle English *oblike,* from Latin *oblīquus*†.] **—o·blique·ly** *adv.* **—o·blique·ness** *n.*

oblique angle *n.* An angle that is not a right angle; an acute or obtuse angle. **—o·blique-an·gled** (ə-bléek-áng-g'ld) *adj.*

oblique triangle *n.* A triangle having no right angle.

o·bliq·ui·ty (ō-blíkwəti, ə-, o-) *n., pl.* **-ties. 1.** The state, quality, or condition of being oblique. **2. a.** A deviation from a vertical or horizontal line, plane, position, or direction. **b.** The angle or extent of such a deviation. **3. a.** A mental deviation or aberration. **b.** Immoral conduct. **4.** *Symbol* ϵ *Astronomy.* The angle at which the Earth's axis is tilted from the vertical, equal to the angle between the ecliptic and the celestial equator. It varies regularly between extreme values and the average value also changes with time; at present, it is about 23°27′. [Middle English *obliquitee,* from Old French *obliquite,* from Latin *oblīquitas,* from *oblīquus,* OBLIQUE.] **—o·bliq·ui·tous** *adj.*

o·blit·er·ate (ə-blíttə-rayt, o- || ō-) *tr.v.* **-ated, -ating, -ates. 1.** To do away with completely; destroy so as to leave no trace: *The forest was obliterated by the building of the new town.* **2.** To wipe out, rub off, or obscure (writing or other markings). —See Synonyms at **erase.** [Latin *obliterāre,* "to strike out words", erase : *ob-,* away from + *littera,* letter.] **—o·blit·er·a·tion** (-ráysh'n) *n.* **—o·blit·er·a·tive** (-rətiv, -raytiv) *adj.* **—o·blit·er·a·tor** (-ər) *n.*

o·bliv·i·on (ə-blívvi-ən, o- || ō-) *n.* **1.** The state or condition of being completely forgotten. **2.** Forgetfulness or an instance of forgetting or overlooking. **3.** The state of being completely unaware of oneself or one's surroundings: *drink myself into oblivion.* **4.** *Law.* An official forgetting of offences, or remission of punishment for them; an amnesty. [Middle English, from Old French, from Latin *oblīviō* (stem *oblīviōn-*), from *oblīvīscī,* to forget.]

o·bliv·i·ous (ə-blívvi-əss, o- || ō-) *adj.* **1.** Lacking all memory of something; forgetful. **2.** Unaware or unmindful. —See Synonyms at **forgetful.** **—o·bliv·i·ous·ly** *adv.* **—o·bliv·i·ous·ness** *n.*

Usage: The usual preposition following this word is *of (oblivious of the people around her),* though *to* is sometimes used, especially with inanimate nouns *(oblivious to the difficulties).* Purists have objected to the use of *oblivious* to mean "unaware", but this sense is now both common and widely accepted.

ob·long (ób-long) *adj. Abbr.* **obl. 1.** Having a long dimension, especially having one of two perpendicular dimensions, such as length or width, greater than the other; elongated. **2.** Having the shape of or resembling a rectangle or an ellipse.

~n. An object or figure, such as a rectangle, with an elongated shape. [Middle English *oblonge,* from Latin *oblongus* : *ob-* (intensive) + *longus,* long.]

ob·lo·quy (óbbləkwi) *n., pl.* **-quies. 1.** Abusively detractive language or utterance; condemnation. **2.** Ill repute or discredit suffered by one subjected to such abuse. —See Synonyms at **disgrace.** [Middle English *obloqui,* from Late Latin *obloquium,* from Latin *obloquī,* to speak against, contradict : *ob-,* against + *loquī,* to speak.]

ob·nox·ious (əb-nókshəss, ob-) *adj.* **1.** Highly disagreeable or offensive; odious. **2.** *Obsolete.* Exposed to harm, injury, or evil. **3.** *Obsolete.* Deserving of or liable to censure or punishment; reprehensible. —See Synonyms at **hateful, offensive.** [Latin *obnoxiōsus,* injurious, from *obnoxius,* subject to harm : *ob-,* to + *noxa,* a hurt.] **—ob·nox·ious·ly** *adv.* **—ob·nox·ious·ness** *n.*

ob·nu·bil·ate (ob-néwbi-layt) *tr.v.* **-ated, -ating, -ates.** *Literary.* To darken with or as if with clouds or fog; obscure. [Latin *obnūbilare,* from *nubes,* cloud.] **—ob·nu·bil·ation** (-láysh'n) *n.*

o·boe (ṓbō) *n. Abbr.* **ob. 1.** A slender woodwind musical instrument with a conical tube and a double-reed mouthpiece. It has a range of three octaves, and a penetrating, poignant sound. **2.** A performer on this instrument in an orchestra. **3.** A reed stop in an organ that produces a sound similar to that of an oboe. [Italian, from French *hautbois,* HAUTBOY.] **—o·bo·ist** *n.*

ob·ol (óbb'l, óbbol || ṓb'l) *n.* Also **ob·o·lus** (óbbə-ləss) *pl.* **-li** (-lī). **1.** A silver coin or unit of weight of ancient Greece equal to one sixth of a drachma. **2. a.** Any of various coins, mostly of small value, circulated in medieval Europe. **b.** Any small coin. [Latin, from Greek *obolos,* variant of *obelos,* OBELUS.]

O·bo·te (ō-bṓ-tay, o-, -ti), **(Apollo) Milton** (1924–). Ugandan statesman, first premier (1962), later president. He was opposed to the Bugandan monarchy, which he dismantled (1966). He was ousted by a military coup (see **Amin**) while at the Commonwealth Conference (1971). A counter coup (1980) prepared his re-election as president; but he was again overthrown (1985). He got political asylum in Zambia.

ob·o·vate (ob-ṓvayt, ób-) *adj. Botany.* Egg-shaped in outline, with the narrow end attached to the stalk: *an obovate leaf.*

ob·o·void (ob-ṓvoyd, ób-) *adj. Botany.* Egg-shaped, with the narrow end attached to the stem: *an obovoid fruit.*

O'Bri·en (ō-brī́-ən, ə-), **Conor Cruise** (1917–). Irish politician and journalist. He served as a Labour member of the Irish parliament from 1969 to 1977, when he became a senator until 1979. From 1977 to 1981 he was editor of the *Observer* newspaper.

O'Brien, Edna (1936–). Irish novelist and short-story writer. Her first novel, *The Country Girls,* was published in 1960. Her other works include *A Pagan Place* (1970) and *Time and Tide* (1992).

O'Brien, Flann, pen name of Brian O'Nuallain (1911–66). Irish novelist and humorist. His novels in the English language include *At Swim-Two-Birds* (1939) and *The Third Policeman* (U.K. 1967).

O'Brien, William (1852–1928). Irish politician and journalist. As editor of *United Ireland,* and, from 1883 as an M.P. for the Home Rule party, he was an eloquent advocate of Irish Independence.

O'Brien, William Smith (1803–64). Irish politician and insurgent. Elected to Parliament (1828), he became an active member of the Young Ireland movement, and led the unsuccessful revolution of 1848. He was subsequently arrested and transported to Tasmania.

obs. 1. obscure. **2.** observation. **3.** observatory. **4.** obsolete. **5.** obstetrics.

Obs. observatory.

ob·scene (əb-séen, ob-) *adj.* **1.** Offensive to accepted standards of decency or modesty. **2.** Intended to incite lustful feelings; indecent; lewd. **3.** *Law.* Liable to deprave or corrupt. Said of a publication. **4. a.** Morally repulsive. **b.** Offensive or repulsive to the senses; loathsome. —See Synonyms at **coarse.** [French *obscène* or Latin *obscēnus, obscaenus*†, inauspicious, repulsive.] **—ob·scene·ly** *adv.*

ob·scen·i·ty (əb-sénnəti, ob-) *n., pl.* **-ties. 1.** The quality of being obscene. **2.** Indecency, lewdness, or offensiveness in behaviour, expression, or appearance. **3.** Something obscene, such as a word, act, or expression.

ob·scur·ant (ob-skéwr-ənt, əb-) *n.* **1.** One who opposes intellectual advancement and political reform; an enemy of rationalism. **2.** In German history, an opponent of the Enlightenment in the 18th century. **3.** One who deliberately obscures the truth or fails to give a full explanation. [Latin *obscūrāns* (stem *obscūrant-*), present participle of *obscūrāre,* to darken, from *obscūrus,* dark, OBSCURE.] **—ob·scur·ant** *adj.*

ob·scur·ant·ism (ób-skewr-ránt-iz'm, ob-skéwr-ənt-, əb-) *n.* The principles or practice of obscurants; opposition to enlightenment. **—ob·scur·ant·ist** *n. & adj.*

ob·scure (əb-skéwr, ob-) *adj.* **-scurer, -scurest.** *Abbr.* **obs. 1.** Not clearly expressed; vague or cryptic; difficult: *an obscure text.* **2.** Imperfectly known or understood: *the obscure workings of nature.* **3.** Of undistinguished or humble descent, status, or reputation. **4.** Inconspicuous; unnoticed: *the obscure beginnings of mighty things.* **5.** Out of sight; hidden: *an obscure retreat.* **6. a.** So faintly perceptible as to lack clear delineation; indistinct. **b.** Hardly audible; faint. **c.** *Phonetics.* Having an unstressed neutral sound as represented by the schwa (ə). Said of a vowel. **7. a.** Of sombre hue; dark. **b.** Dingy; dull. **8.** Partially or wholly deficient in light; gloomy. **9.** *Archaic.* Belonging to or inhabiting darkness. —See Synonyms at **dark.**

~tr.v. **obscured, -scuring, -scures. 1.** To darken. **2.** To lessen the glory of; overshadow. **3.** *Phonetics.* To reduce (a vowel) to the neutral unstressed sound represented by the schwa (ə). **4.** To conceal from view; hide. **5.** To obstruct; hinder. **6.** To render unintelligible.

~n. *Poetic.* Darkness; obscurity. [Middle English, from Old

French *obscur,* from Latin *obscūrus.*] **—ob·scure·ly** *adv.* **—ob·scure·ness** *n.*
ob·scu·ri·ty (əb-skéwr-əti, ob-) *n., pl.* **-ties. 1.** Deficiency or absence of light; darkness: *"We wait for light, but behold obscurity."* (Isaiah 59:9). **2. a.** The condition of being unknown: *from obscurity to fame.* **b.** An unknown person. **3. a.** The condition or quality of being imperfectly known or of being difficult to understand: *The origin of the race is lost in obscurity.* **b.** An instance of this. [Old French *obscurité,* from Latin *obscūritās,* from *obscūrus,* OBSCURE.]
ob·se·crate (ób-si-krayt, -se-) *tr.v.* **-crated, -crating, -crates.** *Rare.* To beg for (something) solemnly. [Latin *obsecrāre* (past participle *obsecrātus*), "to entreat in the name of something sacred" : *ob-,* for the sake of + *sacer,* sacred.] **—ob·se·cra·tion** (-kráysh'n) *n.*
ob·se·quent (ób-sikwənt) *adj.* Flowing into another (subsequent) river in the opposite direction from the original (consequent) river. Said of a stream or river. Compare **consequent, subsequent.** [Latin *obsequens* (stem *obsequent-*), present participle of *obsequī,* to yield to : *ob-,* towards, over + *sequī,* to follow.]
ob·se·qui·ous (əb-seékwi-əss, ob-) *adj.* **1.** Displaying ingratiating servility. **2.** *Archaic.* Submissive and obedient; dutiful. [Middle English, from Latin *obsequiōsus,* from *obsequium,* compliance, from *obsequī,* to comply with : *ob-,* to + *sequī,* to follow.] **—ob·se·qui·ous·ly** *adv.* **—ob·se·qui·ous·ness** *n.*
ob·se·quy (ób-si-kwi, -sə-) *n., pl.* **-quies.** *Usually plural.* A funeral rite or ceremony. [Middle English *obsequy,* from Anglo-French *obsequie,* Old French *obseque,* from Medieval Latin *obsequiae* (influenced by *exsequiae,* exequy), from Latin *obsequia,* plural of *obsequium,* compliance, service. See **obsequious.**] **—ob·se·qui·al** (ob-seékwi-əl, əb-) *adj.*
ob·serv·a·ble (əb-zérvəb'l || ob-) *adj.* **1.** Capable of being observed; noticeable; discernible: *observable improvement.* **2.** Deserving or worthy of notice or mention; noteworthy. **3.** Requiring or deserving special notice or observance: *an observable religious holiday.* *~n. Physics.* A physical property, such as mass or temperature, that can be observed or measured directly, as distinguished from a quantity, such as work or entropy, that must be derived from observed quantities. **—ob·serv·a·ble·ness** *n.* **—ob·serv·a·bly** *adv.*
ob·ser·vance (əb-zérv'nss || ob-) *n.* **1.** The act or practice of observing or complying with a law, custom, command, or other prescribed duty. **2.** The act or custom of keeping or celebrating a holiday or other ritual occasion. **3.** A customary rite or ceremony. **4.** The action of watching; observation: *"Consider how much intellect was needed in the architect, and how much observance of nature."* (John Ruskin). **5.** *Roman Catholic Church.* **a.** The rule governing a religious order. **b.** The order itself or the house of such an order. **6.** *Archaic.* Respectful attention: *"He compassed her with sweet observances and worship."* (Alfred Lord Tennyson).

Usage: Both *observance* and *observation* derive from *observe.* *Observance* is the practice of paying attention to laws, customs, holidays, duties, or the like, whereas *observation* is the act of seeing or noticing something.

ob·ser·vant (əb-zérv'nt || ob-) *adj.* **1.** Characterised by or demonstrating an ability to perceive or apprehend quickly and accurately; alert. **2.** Diligent in observing a law, duty, or principle. Usually followed by *of.* [French, from Latin *observāns* (stem *observant-*), present participle of *observāre,* to OBSERVE.] **—ob·ser·vant·ly** *adv.*
ob·ser·va·tion (ób-zər-váysh'n || -sər-) *n. Abbr.* **obs. 1.** The act or faculty of paying attention or noticing, or the fact of being observed; notice. **2.** The act of noting a phenomenon, often with instruments, and recording it for scientific or other purposes. **3.** The result or record of such noting: *a meteorological observation.* **4.** A comment or remark. **5.** *Archaic.* That which is acquired from or based on observing, such as a conclusion or rule. **6.** *Archaic.* Observance. —See Usage note at **observance.** [Middle English, from Latin *observātiō* (stem *observātiōn-*), from *observāre,* to OBSERVE.] **—ob·ser·va·tion·al** *adj.* **—ob·ser·va·tion·al·ly** *adv.*
observation car *n. U.S.* A railway carriage with large windows providing passengers with extensive views of the countryside.
observation post *n. Military.* A position from which observations of enemy movements can be made or guns fired.
ob·ser·va·to·ry (əb-zérvə-tri, -təri || ob-) *n., pl.* **-ries.** *Abbr.* **Obs., obs. 1.** A building designed and equipped for making observations of astronomical, meteorological, or other natural phenomena. **2.** *Chiefly U.S.* A structure overlooking an extensive view. [New Latin *observatorium,* from Latin *observāre,* to OBSERVE.]
ob·serve (əb-zérv || ob-) *v.* **-served, -serving, -serves.** *—tr.* **1.** To perceive; notice; see. **2.** To watch attentively: *observe a child's behaviour.* **3.** To make a systematic or scientific observation of (a natural or other phenomenon): *observe the Moon's orbit.* **4.** To say by way of comment or remark. **5.** To adhere to or abide by (a law, duty, custom, decision, or the like): *observe the terms of a contract.* **6.** To keep or pay tribute to (a holiday, custom, rite, or the like) by celebration, solemnity, or other procedure: *observe an anniversary.* *—intr.* **1.** To take notice. **2.** To say something; make a comment or remark. **3.** To watch or be present without participating actively: *I was invited to the conference to observe.* —See Synonyms at **see.** [Middle English *observen,* from Old French *observer,* from Latin *observāre,* to pay attention to, look to : *ob-,* to + *servāre,* to keep, watch, pay attention.] **—ob·serv·ing·ly** *adv.*

Synonyms: *observe, keep, celebrate, solemnise, commemorate.*

ob·serv·er (əb-zérvər || ob-) *n.* **1.** One that observes. **2. a.** A delegate sent to observe and report on the proceedings of an assembly or meeting, but not to vote or otherwise participate. **b.** One sent to observe and report on the military, political, or administrative conditions in a country or area: *U.N. observers monitored the ceasefire.* **3.** *Military.* **a.** An aircraft crew member who makes observations. **b.** A soldier watching and reporting from an observation post. **4.** *Physics.* One whose observations are made in or referred to a completely specified frame of reference. **5.** *Capital* **O.** Used as part of the title of certain newspapers: *The Surrey Observer.*
ob·sess (əb-séss, ob-) *tr.v.* **-sessed, -sessing, -sesses.** To preoccupy totally; interest to the exclusion of any other object; haunt as a fixed idea. Often used in the passive. [Latin *obsidēre* (past participle *obsessus*), to sit down before, besiege, beset : *ob-,* on + *sedēre,* to sit.]
ob·ses·sion (əb-sésh'n, ob-) *n.* **1. a.** Compulsive preoccupation with a fixed idea or an unwanted feeling or emotion, often with symptoms of anxiety. **b.** A compulsive, often unreasonable, idea or emotion causing such preoccupation. **2.** The act of obsessing or the state of being obsessed. **3.** *Archaic.* The state of being beset or actuated by the devil or an evil spirit. **—ob·ses·sion·al** *adj.*
ob·ses·sive (əb-séss-iv; ob-) *adj.* Characterised by or suffering from obsession: *obsessive gambling.*
~n. One suffering from an obsession or obsessions.
ob·sid·i·an (ob-síddi-ən) *n.* An acid-resistant, lustrous volcanic glass, usually black or banded and displaying curved, shiny surfaces when fractured. [Latin *obsidiānus,* manuscript error for *obsiānus,* from *Obsius,* mentioned by Pliny as the discoverer of a stone similar to obsidian.]
ob·so·lesce (ób-sə-léss, -sō-) *intr.v.* **-lesced, -lescing, -lesced.** To become gradually obsolete. [Back-formation from OBSOLESCENT.]
ob·so·les·cent (ób-sə-léss'nt, -sō-) *adj.* In the process of passing out of use or usefulness; becoming obsolete. See Synonyms at **old.** [Latin *obsolēscēns* (stem *obsolēscent-*), present participle of *obsolēscere,* to grow old, from *obsolēre* (unattested), to be old or in disuse. See **obsolete.**] **—ob·so·les·cence** *n.* **—ob·so·les·cent·ly** *adv.*
ob·so·lete (ób-sə-leet, -leét, -sleet) *adj.* **1.** *Abbr.* **obs.** No longer in use or practice: *an obsolete word.* **2.** No longer used or useful, because of outmoded design or construction, or because of hard wear. **3.** *Biology.* Increasingly vestigial or disappearing in succeeding generations. Said of plant or animal characteristics or organs. —See Synonyms at **old.** [Latin *obsolētus,* from *obsolēre* (unattested), to be old or in use : *ob-,* away from + *solēre*†, to use, be accustomed.] **—ob·so·lete·ly** *adv.* **—ob·so·lete·ness** *n.* **—ob·so·let·ism** *n.*
ob·sta·cle (ób-stək'l) *n.* A person or thing that opposes, stands in the way of, or holds up progress towards some goal. [Middle English, from Old French, from Latin *obstāculum,* from *obstāre,* to hinder : *ob-,* against + *stāre,* to stand.]

Synonyms: *obstacle, obstruction, bar, barrier, block, impediment, hindrance, encumbrance, snag.*

obstacle course *n.* **1.** A series of physical obstacles, such as ladders and water jumps, to be negotiated at speed by soldiers undergoing training or by participants in an obstacle race. **2.** Any unduly demanding or complex activity.
obstacle race *n.* A race in which the participants have to go through, under, or over a number of obstacles.
obstet. obstetric; obstetrics.
ob·stet·ric (ob-stéttrik, əb-) *adj.* Also **ob·stet·ri·cal** (-'l). *Abbr.* **obstet.** Of or pertaining to the profession of obstetrics or to the care of women during and after pregnancy. [New Latin *obstetricus,* from Latin *obstetrīcius,* from *obstetrīx,* midwife, "she who is present", from *obstāre,* to stand before : *ob-,* before + *stāre,* to stand.] **—ob·stet·ri·cal·ly** *adv.*
ob·ste·tri·cian (ób-ste-trísh'n, -stə-, -sti-) *n.* A medical practitioner specialising in obstetrics.
ob·stet·rics (ob-stéttriks, əb-) *n. Used with a singular verb. Abbr.* **obs., obstet.** The branch of medicine concerned with the care of women during pregnancy and childbirth.
ob·sti·na·cy (ób-stinə-si) *n., pl.* **-cies. 1.** The state or quality of being obstinate. **2.** An act or instance of stubbornness.
ob·sti·nate (ób-sti-nət, -nit) *adj.* **1.** Inflexibly and immovably adhering to an attitude, opinion, or course of action; resistant to argument or entreaty. **2.** Difficult to manage, control, or subdue; refractory. **3.** Difficult to alleviate or cure: *an obstinate headache.* —See Synonyms at **contrary.** [Middle English *obstinat,* from Latin *obstinātus,* past participle of *obstināre,* to persist, from *stāre,* to stand.] **—ob·sti·nate·ly** *adv.* **—ob·sti·nate·ness** *n.*

Synonyms: *obstinate, stubborn, headstrong, stiff-necked, pigheaded, mulish, dogged, pertinacious.*

ob·strep·er·ous (əb-streppərəss, ob-) *adj.* Noisily defiant; unruly; boisterously unmanageable. [Latin *obstreperus,* from *obstrepere,* to make noise against : *ob-,* against + *strepere,* to make noise.] **—ob·strep·er·ous·ly** *adv.* **—ob·strep·er·ous·ness** *n.*
ob·struct (əb-strúkt || ob-) *tr.v.* **-structed, -structing, -structs. 1.** To block or fill (a way or passage) with obstacles; make impassable. **2.** To interfere with, impede, or retard. **3.** To hide from view. —See Synonyms at **hinder.** [Latin *obstruere* (past participle *obstructus*) : *ob-,* against + *struere,* to pile up.] **—ob·struct·er, ob·struc·tor** *n.* **—ob·struc·tive** *adj. & n.* **—ob·struc·tive·ly** *adv.* **—ob·struc·tive·ness** *n.*
ob·struc·tion (əb-strúksh'n || ob-) *n.* **1.** A person or thing that gets in the way; an obstacle. **2.** An act or instance of obstructing, or the state of being obstructed. **3.** The causing of delay, or an attempt to cause a delay, in the conduct of business, especially in a legislative body. **4.** *Sports.* The act of impeding another player or competitor in a match or race. **5.** *Medicine.* A blockage in a bodily organ or

passage, especially the intestine. —See Synonyms at **obstacle.**

ob·struc·tion·ist (əb-strúksh'n-ist || ob-) *n.* One who systematically obstructs or interrupts a process; especially, one who impedes the passage of legislation by delaying tactics, such as making long speeches. **—ob·struc·tion·ism** *n.* **—ob·struc·tion·ist** *adj.*

ob·tain (əb-táyn || ob-) *v.* **-tained, -taining, -tains.** *—tr.* **1.** To succeed in gaining possession of (something) as the result of planning or endeavour; get or acquire. **2.** *Archaic.* To reach or arrive at: *"obtain the age of manhood"* (Sir Walter Scott). *—intr.* **1.** To be established, accepted, or customary: *Certain formal customs still obtain today.* **2.** *Archaic.* To win victory; prevail; succeed: *"This, though it failed at present, yet afterwards obtained."* (Jonathan Swift). [Middle English *obteinen,* from Old French *obtenir,* from Latin *obtinēre,* attain : *ob-* (intensive) + *tenēre,* to hold.] **—ob·tain·a·ble** *adj.* **—ob·tain·er** *n.*

ob·tect (əb-tékt, ob-) *adj.* Also **ob·tect·ed** (-id). *Zoology.* Enclosed or covered by a hardened secretion. Said especially of pupae having wings, antennae, and legs enclosed and sealed against the body surface in this way. [Latin *obtectus,* past participle of *obtegere,* to cover up, conceal : *ob-,* down upon, over + *tegere,* to cover.]

ob·test (əb-tést, ob-) *v.* **-tested, -testing, -tests.** *Archaic.* *—tr.* **1.** To supplicate; entreat. **2.** To call (a spirit or power) to witness. **3.** To object or protest. *—intr.* To protest. Sometimes used with *against* or *with.* [Latin *obtestārī,* to call as a witness to, entreat : *ob-,* to + *testārī,* to call as a witness, from *testis,* witness.] **—ob·tes·ta·tion** (ób-tess-táysh'n) *n.*

ob·trude (əb-trōōd, ob- || -tréwd) *v.* **-truded, -truding, -trudes.** *—tr.* **1.** To force (oneself or one's ideas) upon others with undue insistence or without invitation. **2.** To thrust out; push forward; eject. *—intr.* To force oneself upon others or upon their attention. See Synonyms at **intrude.** [Latin *obtrūdere* : *ob-,* against + *trūdere,* to thrust.] **—ob·trud·er** *n.* **—ob·tru·sion** (-trōōzh'n || -tréwzh'n) *n.*

ob·tru·sive (əb-trōō-siv, ob- || -tréw-, -ziv) *adj.* **1.** Projecting; protruding: *an obtrusive rock formation.* **2.** Tending to push self-assertively forward; brashly intrusive. **3.** Undesirably noticeable; unattractively showy. [Latin *obtrūs-,* past participle stem of *obtrūdere,* OBTRUDE.] **—ob·tru·sive·ly** *adv.* **—ob·tru·sive·ness** *n.*

ob·tund (əb-túnd, ob-) *tr.v.* **-tunded, -tunding, -tunds.** *Rare.* To dull or deaden; make less intense. [Middle English *obtunden,* from Latin *obtundere,* to strike against, blunt : *ob-,* against + *tundere,* to beat.] **—ob·tund·ent** *adj. & n.*

ob·tu·rate (ób-tewr-ayt || -tə-) *tr.v.* **-rated, -rating, -rates.** **1.** To close by obstructing or stopping up. **2.** To seal (a gun breech) in order to prevent gas from escaping on firing. [Latin *obturāre*†.] **—ob·tu·ra·tion** (-áysh'n) *n.*

ob·tu·ra·tor (ób-tewr-aytər || -tə-) *n.* **1.** A prosthetic device that closes an opening in the body, especially a denture that closes a defect in the palate. **2.** A device for sealing a gun breech to prevent gas from escaping on firing.

ob·tuse (əb-téwss, ob- || -tōōss) *adj.* **1.** Lacking astuteness or discernment; slow to understand or perceive. **2. a.** Not sharp, pointed, or acute in form; blunt. **b.** Not acute or intense; indistinctly perceived; dull: *an obtuse pain.* **3.** *Botany.* Having a blunt or rounded tip: *an obtuse leaf.* —See Synonyms at **dull, stupid.** [Latin *obtūsus,* past participle of *obtundere,* to blunt, OBTUND.] **—ob·tuse·ly** *adv.* **—ob·tuse·ness** *n.*

obtuse angle *n.* An angle greater than 90° and less than 180°.

ob·verse (ób-verss, -vérss) *adj.* **1.** Facing or turned towards the observer: *the obverse side of a statue.* **2.** *Botany.* Having a narrower base than top; inverse. Said of certain leaves. **3.** Serving as a counterpart or complement.
~n. **1.** The side of a coin, medal, badge, or the like that bears the principal stamp or design; in most coinages, the side bearing the head. Compare **reverse. 2.** A counterpart or complement. **3.** *Logic.* The counterpart of a proposition obtained by exchanging the affirmative for the negative quality of the whole proposition and then negating the predicate. The obverse of *every act is predictable* is *no act is unpredictable.* [Latin *obversus,* past participle of *obvertere,* to turn towards, OBVERT.] **—ob·verse·ly** *adv.*

ob·ver·sion (əb-vérsh'n, ob-, -vérzh'n) *n.* **1.** The process of or condition resulting from obverting something. **2.** *Logic.* Inference of the obverse of a proposition.

ob·vert (ob-vért) *tr.v.* **-verted, -verting, -verts. 1.** *Rare.* To turn so as to present another side or aspect to view. **2.** *Logic.* To subject to obversion, or deduce the obverse of. [Latin *obvertere,* to turn towards : *ob-,* towards + *vertere,* to turn.]

ob·vi·ate (óbvi-ayt) *tr.v.* **-ated, -ating, -ates.** To prevent or dispose of effectively; anticipate so as to render unnecessary. See Synonyms at **prevent.** [Late Latin *obviāre,* "to meet in the way", prevent, from Latin *ob viam,* in the way. See **obvious.**] **—ob·vi·a·tion** (-áysh'n) *n.* **—ob·vi·a·tor** (-ər) *n.*

ob·vi·ous (óbvi-əss) *adj.* **1.** Easily perceived or understood; quite apparent. **2.** *Informal.* Lacking subtlety. **3.** *Archaic.* Standing in the way or in front. —See Synonyms at **evident.** [Latin *obvius,* from *ob viam,* in the way : *ob,* against + *viam,* accusative of *via,* way.] **—ob·vi·ous·ness** *n.*

ob·vi·ous·ly (óbvi-əssli) *adv.* **1.** In an obvious manner. **2.** It is obvious; as is obvious: *He is obviously extremely stupid.*

ob·vo·lute (ób-və-lōōt, -lōōt, -lewt, -léwt) *adj. Botany.* Folded together with overlapping edges. Said of leaves and petals in a bud. [Latin *obvolutus,* past participle of *obvolvere,* to wrap around, surround : *ob-,* over + *volvere,* to roll, wrap.] **—ob·vo·lu·tion** (-lōōsh'n, -léwsh'n) *n.* **—ob·vo·lu·tive** *adj.*

OC Officer Commanding.

oc., Oc. ocean.

o.c. in the work cited [Latin *opere citato*].

O.C. **1.** Officer Commanding. **2.** Old Catholic.

o/c overcharge.

oc·a·ri·na (óckə-réenə) *n. Music.* A small terracotta or plastic wind instrument, used especially in Inca music, with a mouthpiece, finger holes, and an ovoid shape. [Italian, "little goose" (from its shape), diminutive of *oca,* goose, from Vulgar Latin *avica* (unattested), from Latin *avicula,* diminutive of *avis,* bird.]

O'Ca·sey (ō-káyssi, ə-), **Sean** (1884–1964). Irish playwright. Drawing on a childhood spent in the slums of Dublin and on his experiences in the Irish fight for independence he produced three early works: *The Shadow of a Gunman* (1923), *Juno and the Paycock* (1924), and *The Plough and the Stars* (1926). His six volumes of autobiography were published under the title *Mirror in My House* (1956).

occ. **1.** occident; occidental. **2.** occupation.

Occam's razor. Variant of **Ockham's razor.**

occas. occasional; occasionally.

oc·ca·sion (ə-káyzh'n || ō-) *n.* **1. a.** An event or happening. **b.** The time at which an event or happening occurs. **2.** A significant or special event, happening, or celebration. **3.** An appropriate or favourable time; an opportunity. **4.** That which brings on or precipitates an action or event; the immediate cause. **5.** A reason; grounds. **6.** A requirement; a need; a necessity: *"He must buy what he has little occasion for"* (Laurence Sterne). **7.** *Plural. Archaic.* Personal requirements or necessities. **8.** *Plural. Archaic.* Personal affairs or business matters. —See Usage note at **cause. —on occasion.** From time to time; now and then. **—rise to the occasion.** To have the resources to cope with a particular situation.
~tr.v. **occasioned, -sioning, -sions.** To provide occasion for; cause. [Middle English *occasioun,* from Old French *occasion,* from Latin *occāsiō* (stem *occāsiōn-*), "a falling down, happening", from *occīdere* (past participle *occāsus*), to fall down : *ob-,* down + *cadere,* to fall.]

Usage: *Occasion* is followed by different prepositions or particles, depending on its sense. When it means "reason" or "grounds", it is followed by *for* or *to*: *This is an occasion for rejoicing; You have no occasion to object.* When it means "opportunity", it is followed by *to*: *He took the occasion to ask me for advice.* When it means "time of occurrence", it is followed by *of*: *On the occasion of your visit.*

oc·ca·sion·al (ə-káyzh'n'l || ō-) *adj. Abbr.* **occas. 1. a.** Coming irregularly; occurring from time to time: *an occasional visit.* **b.** Infrequent; not habitual: *took an occasional drink.* **2.** Occurring on or created for a special occasion: *occasional verse.* **3.** Designating a cause that is secondary or incidental. **4.** Designed not as part of a set but for use as the occasion requires: *an occasional chair for unexpected guests.* —See Synonyms at **periodic.**

oc·ca·sion·al·ism (ə-káyzh'n'l-iz'm || ō-) *n. Philosophy.* The theory that the connection between mental and bodily processes is the result of divine agency. **—oc·ca·sion·al·ist** *adj. & n.*

oc·ca·sion·al·ly (ə-káyzh'n'l-i, -nəli || ō-) *adv. Abbr.* **occas.** Now and then; from time to time; sometimes.

oc·ci·dent (óksi-dənt || -dent) *n. Abbr.* **occ. 1.** *Literary.* The west; western lands or regions. **2.** *Capital* **O. a.** The Western Hemisphere. **b.** The countries of Europe and the Western Hemisphere. Usually preceded by *the.* Compare **Orient.** [Middle English, from Old French, from Latin *occīdēns* (stem *occident-*), "quarter of the setting sun", west, from present participle of *occīdere,* to fall down, set (of the sun). See **occasion.**]

oc·ci·den·tal (óksi-dént'l) *adj. Abbr.* **occ.** *Often capital* **O.** Of or pertaining to the countries of the Occident, their peoples, or their culture; western.
~n. Usually capital **O.** A native or inhabitant of a western country. **—oc·ci·den·tal·ism** *n.* **—oc·ci·den·tal·ist** *n.*

oc·ci·den·tal·ise, oc·ci·den·tal·ize (óksi-dént'l-īz) *v.* **-ised, -ising, -ises.** *Often capital* **O.** *—tr.* To make occidental in character, outlook, or way of life. *—intr.* To become occidental; adopt occidental ways. **—oc·ci·den·tal·i·sa·tion** (-ī-záysh'n || *U.S.* -i-) *n.*

oc·cip·i·tal (ok-síppit'l) *adj.* Of or pertaining to the back of the head or to the occipital bone: *an occipital fracture.*
~n. The occipital bone. [Old French, from Medieval Latin *occipitālis,* from Latin *occiput* (stem *occipit-*), OCCIPUT.]

occipital bone *n.* A curved, compound bone that forms the lower posterior part of the skull.

occipital lobe *n.* The posterior portion of each cerebral hemisphere, functional in the interpretation of sensory impulses from the eyes.

oc·ci·put (óksi-put, -pət) *n., pl.* **-puts** or **occipita** (ok-síppitə). The back of the skull, especially the occipital area. [Middle English, from Latin : *ob-,* at the back of + *caput,* head.]

oc·clude (ə-klōōd, o- || -kléwd) *v.* **-cluded, -cluding, -cludes.** *—tr.* **1.** To cause to become closed; obstruct: *occlude a larynx.* **2.** To prevent the passage of; shut in, out, or off: *occlude light.* **3.** *Chemistry.* To absorb or adsorb (a substance) in great quantity. **4.** *Meteorology.* To force (air) upwards from the earth's surface, as when a cold front overtakes and undercuts a warm front. **5.** In dentistry, to bring together (the upper and lower teeth) in alignment for chewing. *—intr.* In dentistry, to close so that the cusps fit together. Used of the teeth of the upper and lower jaws. [Latin *occlūdere* : *ob-* (intensive) + *claudere,* to close.] **—oc·clud·ent** *adj.*

occluded front *n. Meteorology.* The air front established when a cold front occludes a warm front. Also called "occlusion".

oc·clu·sion (ə-klōōzh'n, ō- ‖ -klēwzh'n) *n.* **1. a.** An act or the process of occluding. **b.** The state of being occluded. **c.** That which occludes or blocks. **2.** *Meteorology.* **a.** The process of occluding air masses. **b.** An occluded front. **3.** In dentistry, the fit of the teeth when brought together. **4.** *Phonetics.* **a.** The complete closure of the vocal tract at some point. **b.** A speech sound involving a plosive. —**oc·clu·sal** (-klōō-z'l, -s'l ‖ -klēw-) *adj.*

oc·clu·sive (ə-klōō-siv, ō- ‖ -klēw-, -ziv) *adj.* Occluding or tending to occlude.

~*n. Phonetics.* **1.** A closing of the breath passage; a stop. **2.** A nasal consonant.

oc·cult (o-kúlt, ə-, ókult) *adj.* **1.** Of, pertaining to, dealing with, or knowledgeable in supernatural influences, agencies, or phenomena. **2.** Beyond the realm of human comprehension; mysterious; inscrutable. **3.** Available only to the initiated; not divulged; secret: *occult lore.* **4.** *Rare.* Hidden from view; concealed. **5.** *Medicine.* Not immediately obvious.

~*n.* Occult practices or techniques. Usually preceded by *the.*

~*v.* (o-kúlt, ə-) **occulted, -culting, -cults.** —*tr.* **1.** To conceal or cause to disappear from view. **2.** *Astronomy.* To conceal by occultation: *The Moon occulted Mars.* —*intr.* To become concealed or extinguished at regular intervals: *a lighthouse beacon that occults every 45 seconds.* [Latin *occultus,* past participle of *occulere,* to conceal; akin to *celāre,* to hide.] —**oc·cult·ly** *adv.* —**oc·cult·ness** *n.*

oc·cul·ta·tion (ôckul-táysh'n, óck'l-) *n.* **1.** *Astronomy.* **a.** The passage of a celestial body across a line between an observer and another celestial object, as when the Moon moves between Earth and Sun in a solar eclipse. **b.** The disappearance of the further celestial object, or the progressive blocking of light, radio waves, or other radiation from a celestial source during such a passage. **c.** An observational technique for determining the position or radiant structure of a celestial source so occulted: *a lunar occultation of a quasar.* **2.** The act of occulting or the state of being occulted. [Middle English *occultacion,* concealment, from Latin *occultātiō* (stem *occultā-tiōn-*), from *occultāre,* frequentative of *occulere,* to conceal. See occult.]

oc·cult·ism (ôckul-tiz'm, óck'l-, o-kúl-, ə-) *n.* **1.** The study of the supernatural. **2.** A belief in occult powers and the possibility of bringing them under human control. —**oc·cult·ist** *n. & adj.*

oc·cu·pan·cy (ôckewpən-si) *n., pl.* **-cies. 1. a.** The act of taking or holding possession; the act of occupying. **b.** The condition of being occupied. **2.** The period during which one owns, rents, or uses certain premises or land. **3.** The state of being an occupant or tenant. **4.** *Law.* The taking possession of previously unowned property with the intent of obtaining the right to own it.

oc·cu·pant (ôckewpənt) *n.* **1.** One who holds a position or place. **2.** One who has certain legal rights to or control over the premises he occupies; a tenant or owner. **3.** *Law.* One who is the first to take possession of something previously unowned. [French, from the present participle of *occuper,* to OCCUPY.]

oc·cu·pa·tion (ôckew-páysh'n) *n. Abbr.* **occ. 1. a.** An activity that serves as one's regular source of livelihood, such as a profession or a vocation. **b.** An activity engaged in, especially as a means of passing time. **2. a.** The act or process of holding or possessing a place. **b.** The state of being held or possessed. **3. a.** The invasion, conquest, and control of a nation or territory by a foreign military force. **b.** The military government exercising such control. **c.** The period during which such control is in force. [Middle English *occupacioun,* from Old French *occupation,* from Latin *occupātiō* (stem *occupātiōn-*), from *occupāre,* to OCCUPY.]

oc·cu·pa·tion·al (ôckew-páysh'n'l) *adj.* Of, pertaining to, or caused by engagement in a particular occupation: *occupational disease.* —**oc·cu·pa·tion·al·ly** *adv.*

occupational psychology *n.* The study of human behaviour in relation to work, including such aspects as stress and job satisfaction. —**occupational psychologist** *n.*

occupational therapy *n.* Therapy for the physically and mentally ill in which the principal element is some form of productive or creative activity, such as pottery or basket-weaving. —**occupational therapist** *n.*

oc·cu·pi·er (ôckew-pī-ər) *n.* **1.** One that occupies. **2.** *British.* A person who occupies or has possession of a building or piece of land. Usually used in combination: *owner-occupier.*

oc·cu·py (ôckew-pī) *tr.v.* **-pied, -pying, -pies. 1.** To seize possession of and maintain control over (a place or region), as by military conquest or a sit-in, for example. **2.** To fill up; take (time or space): *a lecture that occupied three hours.* **3.** To live in or on, or be a tenant in or of (premises or land). **4.** To hold or fill (an office or position). **5.** To engage, employ, or keep busy (a person or animal). [Middle English *occupien,* from Old French *occuper,* from Latin *occupāre,* to seize : *ob-* (intensive) + *capere,* to take.]

oc·cur (o-kúr ‖ ō-) *intr.v.* **-curred, -curring, -curs. 1.** To take place; come about. **2.** To be found to exist or appear. **3.** To come to mind; suggest itself: *It occurred to me.* —See Synonyms at **happen.** [Latin *occurrere,* to run to meet : *ob-,* towards + *currere,* to run.]

oc·cur·rence (ə-kúrrənss ‖ ō-) *n.* **1.** An act or instance of occurring. **2.** Something that takes place; an incident. —**oc·cur·rent** *adj.*

Synonyms: *occurrence, happening, event, incident, episode.*

OCD Obsessive-Compulsive Disorder.

o·cean (ōsh'n) *n.* **1.** *Abbr.* **O, O., oc., Oc.** The entire body of salt water that covers about 70 per cent of the earth's surface. **2.** *Often*

capital **O.** *Abbr.* **O, O., oc., Oc.** Any of the principal divisions of this body of water, including the Atlantic, Pacific, and Indian oceans, their southern extensions in Antarctica, and the Arctic Ocean. **3.** *Usually plural.* Any great expanse or amount: *oceans of money.* **4.** In classical mythology, the sea encircling the earth. [Middle English *ocean,* from Old French, from Latin *ōceanus,* from Greek *ōkeanos,* OCEANUS.]

o·cean·ar·i·um (ōsh'n-aír-i-əm) *n., pl.* **-iums** or **-ia** (-i-ə). A large aquarium for the study or display of marine life.

ocean basin *n.* A basin (sense 6) (*see*).

O·ce·an·i·a (ō-shi-áyni-ə, -si-, -áani-ə ‖ -ánni-ə). Also **O·ce·an·i·ca** (-ánnikə). The islands of the central, western, and southern Pacific Ocean, taken customarily to include Australia and New Zealand. —**O·ce·an·i·an** *adj. & n.*

o·ce·an·ic (ō-shi-ánnik, -si-) *adj.* **1.** Of or pertaining to the ocean. **2.** Produced by or living in an ocean, especially in the open sea rather than in shallow coastal waters. **3.** Like an ocean in expanse; wide; huge; sweeping.

O·ce·an·ic (ō-shi-ánnik, -si-) *adj.* **1.** Pertaining to a subfamily of the Austronesian language family, comprising Melanesian and Polynesian. **2.** Pertaining to the cultures of the peoples speaking languages in this subfamily. —**O·ce·an·ic** *n.*

O·ce·a·nid (ō-sée-ə-nid) *n., pl.* **-nids** or **Oceanides** (ō-si-ánni-deez). *Greek Mythology.* Any of the ocean nymphs held to be the daughters of Oceanus and Tethys. [Greek *ōkeanis* (stem *ōkeanid-*), from *Ōkeanos,* OCEANUS.]

Ocean Island. Also **Ba·na·ba** (bə-náabə). One of the Gilbert islands (now Kiribati) in the west Pacific. Vast quantities of its valuable phosphate deposits (discovered 1900) were exported before supplies ran out (late 1970s). The Banabans were deported by the Japanese (1942) and accepted resettlement on Rambi, a Fijian island. Accused of gross exploitation, the British Phosphate Commissioners offered them £6.5 million in 1977.

oceanog. oceanography.

o·cean·og·ra·phy (ōsh'n-óggrəfi) *n. Abbr.* **oceanog.** The exploration and scientific study of the ocean and its phenomena. [OCEAN + -GRAPHY.] —**o·cean·og·ra·pher** *n.* —**o·cean·o·graph·ic** (-ə-gráffik), **o·cean·o·graph·i·cal** *adj.*

ocean sunfish *n.* The sunfish (*see*).

O·ce·a·nus (ō-si-áynəss, ō-sée-ə-nəss). *Greek Mythology.* A Titan, the god of the outer sea encircling the earth, and father of the Oceanides and of the river gods.

oc·el·lat·ed (óssil-aytid, ō-sil-, ō-sél-) *adj.* Also **oc·el·late** (-ayt). **1.** Having an ocellus or ocelli. **2.** Resembling an ocellus. **3.** Marked with spots. [Latin *ocellātus,* having little eyes, from *ocellus,* little eye, OCELLUS.] —**oc·el·la·tion** (-áysh'n) *n.*

o·cel·lus (ō-sél-əss) *n., pl.* **-li** (-ī). **1.** A small simple eye, found in many invertebrates. **2.** A marking that resembles an eye. [New Latin, from Latin, diminutive of *oculus,* eye.] —**o·cel·lar** (-ər) *adj.*

oc·e·lot (ō-si-lot, ó-, -lət) *n.* A brush- and forest-dwelling cat, *Felis pardalis,* of the southwestern United States and Central and South America, having a tawny-greyish or yellow coat with black-bordered brown spots. [French, from Nahuatl *ocelotl.*]

och (okh) *interj. Scottish & Irish.* Used to express surprise, regret, or disagreement. [Gaelic, "oh".]

och·e (ocki) *n.* **1.** The line behind which a darts player stands to throw darts at the board. **2.** The place from which a darts player throws darts at the board. —**on the oche.** Standing ready to throw.

och·loc·ra·cy (ok-lóckrə-si) *n., pl.* **-cies.** Government by the masses; mob rule. [French *ochlocratie,* from Greek *okhlokratia* : *okhlos,* mob + *-kratia,* -CRACY.] —**och·lo·crat** (ócklə-krat) *n.* —**och·lo·crat·ic** (-kráttik), **och·lo·crat·i·cal** *adj.* —**och·lo·crat·i·cal·ly** *adv.*

och·lo·pho·bi·a (ôcklə-fṓbi-ə) *n. Psychology.* Abnormal dread of crowds. [New Latin : Greek *okhlos,* crowd + -PHOBIA.] —**och·lo·pho·bic** *adj. & n.*

och·one (o-khṓn) *interj. Scottish & Irish.* Used to express regret or grief. [Gaelic *ochóin,* "oh, alas".]

o·chre, *U.S.* **o·cher** (ṓkər) *n.* **1.** Any of several earthy mineral oxides of iron mingled with varying amounts of clay and sand, occurring in yellow, brown, or red, and used either untreated or processed as pigments. **2.** Moderate orange yellow, from moderate or deep orange to moderate or strong yellow.

~*tr.v.* **ochred** or *U.S.* **ochered, ochring** or *U.S.* **ochering, ochres** or *U.S.* **ochers.** To colour or mark with ochre. [Middle English *oker,* from Old French *ocre,* from Latin *ōchra,* from Greek *ōkhra,* from *ōkhros†,* yellow, pale yellow.] —**o·chre** *adj.* —**o·chre·ous** (ṓkər-əss, ṓkri-), **o·chrey** (ṓkəri, ṓkri) *adj.*

-ock *n. suffix.* Indicates smallness; for example, **hillock.** [Middle English *-oc,* Old English *-oc, -uc.*]

ock·er (óckər) *n. Australian Slang.* An ill-mannered, uncultivated Australian. Compare **Alf, Roy.**

~*adj. Australian Slang.* Rude, uncultivated. [Informal variant of *Oscar;* from the name of such a character in an Australian television series (1973).]

Ock·ham's razor, Oc·cam's razor (óckəmz) *n.* A principle of scientific and philosophical discussion urging the use of the most economical and least complex assumptions, terms, and theories. It is usually formulated as "Entities should not be multiplied unnecessarily". [After William of *Ockham* (c. 1285−c. 1350), English philosopher, + RAZOR (figuratively, as a sharp instrument for cutting away inessentials).]

o'clock (ə-klók ‖ ō-) *adv.* **1.** Of or according to the clock. Used to indicate the time: *three o'clock.* **2.** According to an imaginary clock dial with the observer at the centre and 12 o'clock considered as straight ahead in horizontal position or straight up in vertical position. Used to indicate relative position: *enemy planes at 11 o'clock.* [Reduced from *of the clock.*]

O'Con·nell (ō-kónn'l, ə-), **Daniel,** called the Liberator (1775–1847). Irish politician. He battled (within the constitution) to repeal the laws excluding Roman Catholics from Parliament. Eventually he took his seat (1829), as a Roman Catholic, in the House of Commons. His subsequent campaign for Irish independence was unsuccessful and cost him his legal practice, his fortune, and his health.

o·co·ti·llo (ōkə-téel-yō, ôckə- ‖ *U.S.* -tée-yō) *n., pl.* **-llos.** A succulent, spiny shrub or tree, *Fouquieria splendens,* of Mexico and the southwestern United States, having clusters of tubular scarlet flowers. Also called "candlewood". [Mexican Spanish, diminutive of *ocote,* a Mexican pine, from Nahuatl *ocotl,* torch.]

OCR 1. optical character reader. **2.** optical character recognition.

oc·re·a, och·re·a (ôckri-ə) *n., pl.* **-reae** (-ee). *Botany.* A sheath composed of one or more stipules that enclose the base of a leaf, as in some members of the Polygonaceae. [Latin *ocrea†,* greave, legging.] —oc·re·ate (-ət, -it, -ayt) *adj.*

oct. octavo.

Oct. October.

octa-, oct-. Variants of **octo-.**

oc·ta·chord (ókta-kawrd) *n. Music.* **1.** An eight-stringed instrument. **2.** A sequence of eight notes, especially a scale. [Latin *octachordus,* from Greek *oktakhordos* : OCTA- + CHORD.]

oc·tad (óktad) *n.* A group or series of eight. [Greek *oktas* (stem *oktad-*), number eight, from *oktō,* eight.] —oc·tad·ic (ok-táddik) *adj.*

oc·ta·gon (ókta-gən ‖ *U.S.* -gon) *n.* A polygon with eight sides and eight angles. [Latin *octagōnum,* from Greek *oktagōnon,* from neuter of *oktagōnos,* having eight angles : OCTO- + -GON.]

oc·tag·o·nal (ok-tággən'l) *adj.* **1.** Having eight sides and eight angles. **2.** Of, relating to, or formed in octagons. —oc·tag·o·nal·ly *adv.*

oc·ta·he·dral (ókta-héedrəl) *adj.* **1.** Having eight plane surfaces. **2.** Of, relating to, or formed in octahedrons. —oc·ta·hed·ral·ly *adv.*

oc·ta·he·drite (ókta-héedrīt) *n.* A mineral, **anatase** (*see*). Not in current technical usage. [French *octaédrite,* from *octaèdre,* octahedron (with reference to its octahedral crystals), from Greek *oktaedron,* OCTAHEDRON.]

oc·ta·he·dron (ókta-hée-drən) *n., pl.* **-drons** or **-dra** (-drə). A polyhedron with eight plane surfaces. [Greek *oktaedron* : OCTO- + -HEDRON.]

oc·tal (óktəl) *n.* A number system using the number eight as a base, which is used in computing. Also called "octal notation". [OCTA- + -AL.]

oc·tam·er·ous (ok-támmə-rəss) *adj.* Also oc·tom·er·ous (-tómmə-). *Biology.* Having or consisting of parts arranged in sets of eight. Said especially of flowers having sepals, petals, or other parts arranged in sets of eight. [Greek *oktameres* : OCTO- + -MEROUS.] —oc·tam·er·ism (-riz'm) *n.*

oc·tam·e·ter (ok-támmitər) *n.* A line of verse consisting of eight metrical feet. [OCTO- + METER (after *hexameter*).] —oc·tam·e·ter *adj.*

oc·tane (óktayn) *n.* **1.** Any of various isomeric alkanes with the formula C_8H_{18}. **2.** A colourless, inflammable hydrocarbon, $CH_3(CH_2)_6CH_3$, found in petroleum, and used as a solvent. **3.** Octane number. [OCT(O)- + -ANE.]

oc·tane·di·o·ic acid (óktayn-dī-ō-ik) *n.* A colourless crystalline dicarboxylic derivative of octane, $HOOC(CH_2)_6COOH$, used in the manufacture of synthetic resins and occurring in castor oil and suberin. Also called "suberic acid".

octane number *n.* A numerical measure of the antiknock properties of petrol, based on the percentage by volume of isooctane in a standard reference fuel. For example, a petrol that produces the same degree of knocking as a standard reference fuel containing 80 per cent isooctane has an octane number of 80. Also called "octane rating". Compare **cetane number.**

oc·tan·gu·lar *adj.* Octagonal.

Oc·tans (ók-tanz) *n.* The constellation that includes the south celestial pole. Also called "Octant". [New Latin, from Latin *octāns,* half-quadrant. See **octant.**]

oc·tant (óktənt) *n.* **1.** One eighth of a circle: **a.** A 45° arc. **b.** The area enclosed by two radii at a 45° angle and the intersected arc. **2.** An instrument based on the principle of the sextant, but employing only a 45° angle, used as an aid in navigation. **3.** *Astronomy.* The position of a celestial body when it is separated from another by a 45° angle. **4.** Any one of eight parts into which three-dimensional space is divided by three, usually perpendicular, coordinate planes. **5.** *Capital* **O.** Octans. [Latin *octans* (stem *octant-*), half-quadrant, from *octō,* eight.] —oc·tan·tal (ok-tánt'l) *adj.*

octaroon. Variant of **octoroon.**

oc·ta·va·lent (ókta-váylənt) *adj. Chemistry.* Having a valency of eight.

oc·tave (ók-tiv; *also usually for sense 2 but rarely for other senses,* -tayv) *n.* **1.** *Music.* **a.** The interval of eight diatonic degrees between two notes, one of which has twice as many vibrations per second as the other. **b.** A note that is eight full tones above or below another given note. **c.** Two notes, eight diatonic degrees apart, sounded together, or the consonance that results. **d.** A series of notes in-

cluded within this interval, or the keys of an instrument that produce such a series. **e.** An organ stop that produces notes an octave above those usually produced by the keys played. **2.** *Ecclesiastical.* **a.** The eighth day after a feast day, counting the feast day as one. **b.** The entire period between a feast day and the eighth day following it. **3.** Any group or series of eight. **4. a.** A stanza of eight lines. **b.** An octet in a sonnet. **5.** *Fencing.* A rotating parry.

—*adj.* **1.** Composed of eight elements or parts. **2.** *Music.* Producing tones one octave higher, as an organ stop may. [Middle English, the eighth day (after a festival), from Medieval Latin *octāva (diēs),* from Latin, feminine of *octāvus,* eighth, from *octō,* eight.] —oc·ta·val (ok-táyv'l, óktiv'l) *adj.*

octave coupler *n.* A mechanical device on an organ that automatically connects notes an octave apart to be played simultaneously by pressing the key or pedal for just one note.

Oc·ta·vi·a (ok-táyvi-ə) (64–11 B.C.). Sister of the Roman emperor Augustus. At her brother's behest, she married (40 B.C.) Mark Antony. Though she raised an army and finance for his Armenian campaign, he divorced her (32 B.C.) for Cleopatra. The Porticus Octaviae in Rome was erected to commemorate her.

Octavian. See **Augustus.**

oc·ta·vo (ok-táy-vō ‖ -táa-) *n., pl.* **-vos.** *Abbr.* **o., O., oct. 1.** The page size of a book composed of printer's sheets folded into eight leaves, originally printed on one side of each sheet. **2.** A book composed of pages of this size. Also called "eightvo". Also written *8vo, 8°.* [Latin *(in) octāvō,* "in eighth", ablative of *octāvus,* eighth. See **octave.**] —oc·ta·vo *adj.*

oc·ten·ni·al (ok-ténni-əl) *adj.* **1.** Happening or recurring every eight years. **2.** Lasting eight years. [Late Latin *octennium,* period of eight years : OCT(O)- + Latin *annus,* a year.] —oc·ten·ni·al·ly *adv.*

oc·tet (ok-tét, ók-) *n.* Also oc·tette (for senses 1, 2, 3, 5). **1.** A musical composition written for eight voices or eight instruments. **2.** A group of eight singers or eight instrumentalists. **3.** Any group of eight. **4.** *Chemistry.* A group of eight electrons in the orbital shell of an atom, necessary for stability in the formation of many molecules. **5.** The first eight lines of an Italian sonnet. In this sense, also called "octave". Compare **sestet.** [Italian *ottetto* (influenced by *duet*), from *otto,* eight, from Latin *octō.*]

oc·til·lion (ók-tíl-yən) *n.* **1.** In Great Britain, the cardinal number represented by the figure 1 followed by 48 zeros; usually written 10^{48}. **2.** The cardinal number represented by the figure 1 followed by 27 zeros; usually written 10^{27}. [French : OCT(O)- + (M)ILLION.]

oc·til·lionth (ók-tíl-yənth) *n.* **1.** The ordinal number octillion in a series. **2.** Any of an octillion equal parts. —oc·til·lionth *adj.*

octo-, octa-, oct– *comb. form.* Indicates eight parts or elements; for example, octopus, octameter, octane. [Latin *octō-,* from *octō,* eight; Greek *okta-,* from *oktō,* eight.]

Oc·to·ber (ok-tôbər) *n. Abbr.* **Oct. 1.** The tenth month of the Gregorian calendar. October has 31 days. **2.** *British Archaic.* Ale brewed in this month. [Middle English *octobre,* from Old French, from Latin *Octōber,* "eighth month", from *octō,* eight.]

October Revolution *n.* A part of the **Russian Revolution** (*see*).

Oc·to·brist (ok-tôbrist) *n.* A member of a moderate Russian political party that accepted the reforms outlined in the Imperial Constitutional Manifesto issued by Nicholas II in October, 1905. —Oc·to·brist *adj.*

oc·to·dec·i·mo (ók-tō-déssi-mō ‖ -tə-) *n., pl.* **-mos. 1.** The page size of a book composed of printer's sheets folded into 18 leaves or 36 pages. **2.** A book composed of pages of this size. Also called "eighteenmo". Also written *18mo, 18°.* [Latin *octōdecimō,* ablative of *octōdecimus,* eighteenth, from *octōdecim,* eighteen: OCTO- + *decem,* ten.] —oc·to·dec·i·mo *adj.*

oc·to·ge·nar·i·an (ók-tōji-naír-i-ən, -tə-) *adj.* **1.** Being eighty years old or between eighty and ninety years old. **2.** Of or like someone of this age.

~ *n.* A person who is eighty years old or between eighty and ninety years old. [Latin *octōgēnārius,* containing eighty, from *octōgēni,* eighty each, from *octō,* OCTO- + *-gintā,* "ten times".]

octomerous. Variant of **octamerous.**

oc·to·nar·y (ókta-nəri ‖ -nerri) *adj.* **1.** Of or pertaining to the number eight. **2.** Consisting of eight members or of groups containing eight.

~ *n., pl.* **octonaries.** A group or set of eight. [Latin *octōnārius,* containing eight, from *octōnī,* eight at a time, from *octō,* eight.]

oc·to·ploid (ókta-ployd) *adj. Genetics.* Having eight times the number of haploid chromosomes in a somatic cell nucleus. [OCTO- + -PLOID.]

oc·to·pod (ókta-pod) *n.* Any mollusc of the order Octopoda, such as an octopus, having eight arms and no internal shell. [New Latin *Octopoda,* from Greek *oktōpoda,* neuter plural of *oktōpous* (stem *oktōpod-*), OCTOPUS.]

oc·to·pus (ókta-pəss) *n., pl.* **-puses** or **octopi** (-pī). **1.** Any of numerous carnivorous, marine molluscs of the genus *Octopus* or related genera, found worldwide. It has a saclike body, eight tentacles, each bearing two rows of suckers, a large distinct head, and a strong beaklike mouth. Compare **squid.** **2.** *Informal.* Any powerful and far-reaching organisation or person. [New Latin, from Greek *oktōpous,* eight-footed : OCTO- + *pous,* foot.]

oc·to·roon, oc·ta·roon (ókta-róōn) *n.* The offspring of a white person and a quadroon; one who is one-eighth black. [OCTO- + (QUAD)ROON.]

oc·to·syl·la·ble (ók-tō-síllab'l, -tə-) *n.* **1.** In poetry: **a.** A line of verse containing eight syllables. **b.** A verse with eight syllables in each line. **2.** A word of eight syllables. [Late Latin *octosyllabus*, having eight syllables : OCTO- + *syllaba*, SYLLABLE.] —**oc·to·syl·lab·ic** (-si-lábbik) *adj.*

oc·troi (ók-trwaa ‖ -troy) *n.*, *pl.* **-trois** (-trwaa ‖ -troyz). **1.** A local tax levied on certain items brought into some European cities. **2.** The officials responsible for collecting this tax. **3.** The place where the tax is collected. [French, from Old French, a tax which a city is authorised to levy, from *octroyer*, to grant as a privilege, authorise, from Gallo-Roman *auctōricāre* (unattested), to authorise, from Latin *auctor*, author, originator, from *augēre*, to originate, increase.]

oc·tu·ple (ók-tewp'l ‖ -tōōp'l, ok-téwp'l, -tōōp'l) *adj.* **1.** Consisting of or having eight parts, members, or copies. **2.** Multiplied by eight; eight times as much, as many, or as large.
~*n.* An eightfold amount or number.
~*v.* **octupled, -pling, -ples.** —*tr.* To multiply or increase by eight. —*intr.* To be multiplied eightfold. [Latin *octuplus* : OCTO- + *-plus*, -fold.]

oc·u·lar (óckewlər) *adj.* **1.** Of or pertaining to the eye: *ocular exercises.* **2.** Of or pertaining to the sense of sight: *an ocular aberration.* **3.** Seen by the eye; visual: *ocular proof.*
~*n.* The eyepiece of an optical instrument. [Late Latin *oculāris*, of the eyes, from Latin *oculus*, eye.]

oc·u·lar·ist (óckewlərist) *n.* One who makes artificial eyes.

oc·u·list (óckewlist) *n.* A medical practitioner who treats diseases of the eyes; an ophthalmologist. [French *oculiste*, from Latin *oculus*, eye.]

oc·u·lo·mo·tor (óckew-lō-mṓtər, -lə-) *adj.* **1.** Pertaining to movements of the eyeball. **2.** Pertaining to the oculomotor nerve. [Latin *oculus*, eye + MOTOR.]

oculomotor nerve *n. Anatomy.* The third cranial nerve, which controls the muscles of the eyeballs.

Od, 'Od, Odd (od) *interj. Archaic.* Used in oaths as a euphemism for "God".

OD (ṓ dée) *n. Slang.* A drug overdose.
~*intr. v.* **OD'd** or **ODd, OD'ing** or **ODing, OD's** or **ODs.** *Slang.* To take an overdose of a drug: *He OD'd on barbiturates.*

o.d. on demand.

O.D. 1. officer of the day. **2.** on demand. **3.** overdraft. **4.** overdrawn.

o·da·lisque, o·da·lisk (ṓdə-lisk, óddə-) *n.* A female slave or concubine in a harem. [French, from Turkish *ŏdalik*, chambermaid : *ŏdah*, room + *-lik*, noun suffix.]

odd (od) *adj.* **odder, oddest. 1. a.** Strange, unusual, or peculiar. **b.** Queer or eccentric in conduct. **2. a.** In excess; left over: *odd change.* **b.** Greater than a specified number by a relatively small amount: *twenty odd years ago.* **3. a.** Being one of an incomplete pair or set: *an odd shoe.* **b.** Not matching: *odd socks.* **c.** Remaining after others are paired or grouped: *the odd one out.* **4.** Occasional; irregular; chance: *odd jobs.* **5.** Designating a number or something bearing a number not divisible by two: *1, 3, and 5 are odd numbers.* Compare **even.** —See Synonyms at **strange.** [Middle English *odde*, from Old Norse *oddi*, triangle, point, third, odd number.] —**odd·ly** *adv.* —**odd·ness** *n.*

Usage: Odd is used to express an indefinite, usually small, amount in excess of a specified round number: *60 odd books.* It is not used with precise numbers (as in *63 odd books*), and the hyphen should be used whenever there is a possible ambiguity (as in *60-odd people/60 odd people*). 60 odd never means more than 61–69.

odd·ball (ód-bawl) *n. Informal.* A person marked by eccentric behaviour or attitudes. Also *chiefly British* "odd fish". —**odd·ball** *adj.*

Odd·fel·low (ód-fellō) *n.* A member of the Independent Order of Odd Fellows, a fraternal and benevolent society in Britain.

odd·ish (óddish) *adj.* Somewhat odd; rather peculiar.

odd·i·ty (óddəti) *n.*, *pl.* **-ties. 1.** A person or thing that is odd. **2.** An odd quality, trait, or characteristic; an eccentricity. **3.** The state or quality of being odd; strangeness.

odd-job man (ód-jób-man) *n.* A man who does casual or occasional work for a living, especially odd domestic jobs. Also called "odd-jobber".

odd lot *n.* A quantity that differs from a standard trading unit, especially an amount of stock of fewer than 100 shares.

odd·ment (ód-mənt) *n.* **1.** *Usually plural.* Something left over; a fragment, scrap, or remnant. **2.** An oddity.

odd·pin·nate (ód-pínnayt) *adj. Botany.* Pinnate with a single, unpaired leaflet at the end of the leafstalk.

odds (odz) *pl.n.* **1.** A certain number of points given beforehand to a weaker side in a contest to equalise the chances of all participants. **2.** A ratio expressing the probability of an event or outcome. Used especially of sports contests: *The odds on the champion winning are three to two.* **3.** A ratio expressing the amount by which the stake of one better differs from that of his opposing better: *The bookmaker gave odds of ten to one.* **4.** The likelihood of one thing occurring, rather than another, in any contest or issue of indefinite outcome: *The odds are that she will get the leadership on the first ballot.* **5.** Favourable chance; advantage: *The odds are with me.* **6.** Unfavourable conditions; adversity: *overcame the odds.* **7.** *Chiefly British Informal.* Difference or significance. Used chiefly in phrases such as *it makes no odds* or *what's the odds?* —**at odds.** In disagreement; in conflict. —**over the odds. 1.** More than is agreed on or expected. **2.** Too much; excessive. [Plural of ODD.]

odds and ends *pl.n.* Miscellaneous items, remnants, or pieces.

odds and sods *pl.n. Chiefly British Informal.* Miscellaneous items or people. [ODD (noun) + SOD (person, thing).]

odds-on (ódz-ón ‖ -áwn) *adj.* More likely to win than not; having a good chance of success.

ode (ōd) *n.* **1.** In classical literature, a poem intended to be sung by a chorus at a public festival or as part of a drama. **2.** A lengthy lyrical poem, usually rhymed, often addressed to some praised object, person, or quality, and often characterised by a lofty style. See **Horatian ode, Pindaric ode.** [French, from Old French, from Late Latin *ōda, ōdē*, from Greek *ōidē, aoidē*, song.] —**od·ic** *adj.*

–ode¹ *comb. form.* Indicates a way or path; for example, **electrode.** [Greek *-odos*, from *hodos*, a way.]

–ode² *comb. form.* Indicates resemblance or characteristic nature; for example, **nematode.** [Greek *-ōdēs*, from *eidos*, form, shape.]

O·dels·ting, O·dels·thing (ṓd'lss-ting) *n.* The lower house of the Norwegian parliament. Compare **Lagting.** [Norwegian, from *odel, oda*, from Old Norse *ōthal*, property + *ting*, assembly (see **thing**).]

O·der (ṓdər). *Polish & Czech* **Od·ra** (ódra). River in eastern Europe. Rising in the east Sudeten mountains, Czech Republic, it flows northwards to the Baltic Sea near Szczecin. It is a major trading route, navigable from Ratibor, and north of its confluence with the Neisse, it forms part of the German-Polish border.

O·der-Neis·se Line (ṓdər-nī́-sə) *n.* The border between Poland and Germany, running along the Oder and Neisse rivers. Adopted at the Potsdam conference (August 1945) it was recognised by Poland and East Germany in 1950, and by West Germany in 1970.

O·des·sa or **O·des·a** (ō-déssə). Black Sea port in the Ukraine. It is a major administrative, industrial, cultural, and tourist centre. Kept open all year by ice-breakers, it has a major naval base and fishing and whaling fleets. Founded (14th century) as a Tatar fortress, it was claimed by Lithuanians and Turks, and finally ceded to Russia.

o·de·um (ō-dée-əm, ṓdi-) *n.*, *pl.* **odea.** Also **o·de·on** (ṓdi-ən ‖ *U.S.* -on) *pl.* **-ons.** A building, especially in ancient Greece and Rome, used for public performances of music and poetry. [Latin *ōdēum*, from Greek *ōideion*, from *ōidē*, song, ODE.]

O·din (ṓdin). *Norse Mythology.* The supreme deity and creator of the cosmos and humankind; the god of wisdom, war, art, culture, and the dead, often identified with the Teutonic god Woden. [Old Norse *Ōdhinn*.]

o·di·ous (ṓdi-əss) *adj.* Exciting hatred or repugnance; abhorrent; offensive. See Synonyms at **hateful.** [Middle English, from Old French, from Latin *odiōsus*, from *odium*, ODIUM.] —**o·di·ous·ly** *adv.* —**o·di·ous·ness** *n.*

o·di·um (ṓdi-əm) *n.* **1.** Strong dislike; contempt or aversion. **2.** The disgrace resulting from hateful conduct. —See Synonyms at **disgrace.** [Latin, hatred, from *ōdī*, I hate.]

O·do of Bayeux (ṓdō) (*c.* 1036–97). Bishop of Bayeux. The half-brother of William the Conqueror, he was co-regent of England while William was in Normandy. He was banished (1088) for conspiring against William II, his nephew.

o·dom·e·ter (ō-dómmitər, o-) *n.* An instrument that indicates distance travelled by a vehicle; a mileometer. [French *odomètre*, from Greek *hodometron* : *hodos*, road, journey + *metron*, measure, METER.] —**o·dom·e·try** (-dómmətri) *n.*

–odon *comb. form.* Indicates an animal having teeth of a specified type; for example, **mastodon.** [New Latin, from Greek *odous* (stem *odont*-), tooth.]

–odont *comb. form.* Indicates: **1.** A tooth or teeth of a specified type; for example, **acrodont. 2.** Having a tooth or teeth of a specified type; for example **diphyodont.** [Greek *odous* (stem *odont*-), tooth.]

odonto– *comb. form.* Indicates tooth or teeth; for example, **odontoblast, odontology.** [Greek, from *odous* (stem *odont*-), tooth.]

o·don·to·blast (o-dóntə-blast ‖ ō-) *n.* A tooth cell in the outer surface of dental pulp that produces dentine. [ODONTO- + -BLAST.] —**o·don·to·blas·tic** (-blástik) *adj.*

o·don·to·glos·sum (o-dóntə-glóssəm, ō-) *n.* Any orchid of the genus *Odontoglossum*, having large colourful flowers with a toothlike projection on the lip. [New Latin, "tooth-tongue" : ODONTO- + *glossum*, from Greek *glossa*, tongue.]

o·don·toid (o-dóntoyd ‖ ō-) *adj.* **1.** Resembling a tooth. **2.** Of or pertaining to the odontoid process. [Greek *odontoeidēs* : ODONT(O)- + -OID.]

odontoid process *n. Anatomy.* A small, toothlike projection from the second vertebra of the neck, around which the first vertebra rotates.

o·don·tol·o·gy (ód-on-tólləji ‖ ṓd-) *n.* The study of the anatomy, growth, and diseases of the teeth. [French *odontologie* : ODONTO- + -LOGY.] —**o·don·to·log·i·cal** (o-dóntə-lójik'l ‖ ō-) *adj.* —**o·don·to·log·i·cal·ly** *adv.* —**o·don·tol·o·gist** (-tólləjist) *n.*

o·don·to·phore (o-dóntə-fawr ‖ ō-, -fōr) *n.* A protrusile structure at the base of the mouth of most molluscs, supporting the radula. [ODONTO- + -PHORE.] —**o·don·toph·o·ral** (ód-on-tófferəl ‖ ṓd-), **o·don·toph·o·rine** (-tóffə-rīn, -rin), **o·don·toph·o·rous** (-tóffərəss) *adj.*

o·dor·if·er·ous (ṓdə-rífferəss) *adj.* Having or giving off an odour. [Latin *odōrifer* : ODOUR + -FER.] —**o·dor·if·er·ous·ly** *adv.* —**o·dor·if·er·ous·ness** *n.*

o·dor·im·e·ter (ṓdə-rímmitər) *n.* Also **o·dor·om·e·ter** (-rómmitər). An instrument for measuring the intensity of odours.

o·dor·ous (ṓdərəss) *adj.* Having a distinctive odour, usually, but not necessarily, an unpleasant odour. —**o·dor·ous·ly** *adv.* —**o·dor·**

ous·ness *n.*

o·dour, *U.S.* **o·dor** (ṓdər) *n.* **1.** The property or quality of a thing that affects, stimulates, or is perceived by the sense of smell; its scent. **2.** Any sensation, stimulation, or perception of the sense of smell; a smell. **3.** A strong, pervasive quality. **4.** Esteem; repute. Used chiefly in the phrases *in good odour* and *in bad odour.* —See Synonyms at **smell.** [Middle English, from Anglo-French *odour,* Old French *odor,* from Latin *odor.*] **—o·dour·less** *adj.*

Od's bod·kins (ódz bód-kinz) *interj.* Also **Odd's bod·i·kins** (bóddi-). *Archaic.* Used as an oath. [Euphemism for *"(by) God's body".*]

O·dys·seus (ə-díss-yōōss, o-, ō-, -i-əss). Latin name **U·lys·ses** (yōō-li-seez, yōō-lísseez). *Greek Mythology.* The cunning king of Ithaca, a leader of the Greeks in the Trojan War, whose return home was for ten years frustrated by the god Poseidon.

od·ys·sey (óddi-si) *n.* An extended adventurous wandering. [After ODYSSEY.]

Od·ys·sey (óddi-si) *n.* The second epic of Homer, recounting the wanderings and adventures of Odysseus after the fall of Troy and his eventual return home. [French *Odyssée,* from Latin *Odyssēa,* from Greek *Odusseia,* from *Odusseus,* ODYSSEUS.] **—Od·ys·sey·an** (-sée-ən, -sáy-) *adj.*

Oe oersted.

Oea. See **Tripoli.**

OE, OE., O.E. Old English.

O.E.C.D. *n.* Organisation for Economic Cooperation and Development: an international organisation formed in 1961 to supersede the O.E.E.C., whose aims include the promotion of trade and economic growth and aid to developing countries. The member countries are Australia, Austria, Belgium, Canada, the Czech Republic, Denmark, Finland, France, Germany, Greece, Hungary, Iceland, the Republic of Ireland, Italy, Japan, Republic of Korea, Luxembourg, Mexico, the Netherlands, New Zealand, Norway, Poland, Portugal, Spain, Sweden, Switzerland, Turkey, the United Kingdom and the United States.

OED, O.E.D. Oxford English Dictionary.

oe·de·ma, *U.S.* **e·de·ma** (ee-déemə, i-) *n., pl.* **-mas** or **-mata** (-tə). *Pathology.* An excessive accumulation of serous fluid in the tissues. [Late Latin, from Greek *oidēma,* swelling, from *oidein,* to swell.]

oed·i·pal (éedi-p'l || *U.S. also* éddi-) *adj.* Also **oed·i·pe·an** (-pée-ən). *Sometimes capital* **O.** Of, relating to, or characteristic of the Oedipus complex.

Oed·i·pus (éedi-pəss || *U.S. also* éddi-). *Greek Mythology.* A son of Laius and Jocasta, who was abandoned at birth and who unwittingly killed his father and married his mother.

Oedipus complex *n.* In Freudian psychology: **1.** A boy's feelings, often unconscious, of sexual desire for his mother, usually accompanied by hostility to his father and generally first manifesting itself between the ages of three and five. **2. Electra complex** *(see).*

oeil-de-boeuf (úr-də-búrf, ī-, ö-i-, -böf) *n., pl.* **oeils-de-boeuf** (*pronounced as singular*). A small round or oval window. [French, "bull's eye".]

oe·nol·o·gy, *U.S.* **e·nol·o·gy** (ee-nólləji) *n.* Also **oi·nol·o·gy** (oy-). The study of wines. [Greek *oinos,* wine + -LOGY.] **—oe·no·log·i·cal** (éenə-lójik'l) *adj.* **—oe·nol·o·gist** (-nólləjist) *n.*

oe·no·mel (éen-ō-mel, -ə-) *n.* **1.** A beverage of ancient Greece, consisting of wine and honey. **2.** *Poetic.* A source of strength and sweetness. [Greek *oinomeli* : *oinos,* wine + *meli,* honey.]

o'er. *Poetic.* Contraction of **over.**

oer·sted (ér-sted) *n. Abbr.* **Oe** The centimetre-gram-second electromagnetic unit of magnetic field strength, equal to the magnetic field strength that would cause a unit magnetic pole to experience a force of one dyne in a vacuum. [After Hans Christian OERSTED.]

Oer·sted or **Ør·sted** (ér-sted, -stəd), **Hans Christian** (1777–1851). Danish physicist. Though his discoveries include metallic aluminium and the compressibility of water, he is best known for discovering the magnetic field generated by an electric current.

oe·soph·a·gus, *U.S.* **e·soph·a·gus** (ee-sóffə-gəss, i-) *n., pl.* **-gi** (-gī, -jī). A muscular tube for the passage of food from the pharynx to the stomach; the gullet. [New Latin, from Greek *oisophagos,* of obscure origin; *-phagos,* perhaps from *phagein,* to eat.]

oestr-, oestro-, *U.S.* **estr-, estro-** *comb. form.* Indicates oestrus; for example, **oestrogen.**

oes·tra·di·ol (éestrə-dī-ol || éstrə-, -ōl) *n.* A naturally occurring oestrogen, $C_{18}H_{24}O_2$, produced by the ovarian follicle that can now be made synthetically for treatment of menstrual disorders, menopausal problems, and cancer of the prostate in men. [Irregularly from OESTRIN + DI- + -OL.]

oes·tri·ol (éestri-ol || éstri-, -ōl) *n.* An oestrogenic hormone, $C_{18}H_{24}O_3$, found in the ovaries of mammals, obtained commercially from the urine of pregnant animals and used in treating oestrogen deficiency. [OESTRIN + TRI- + -OL.]

oes·tro·gen (éestrə-jən, éestrō-, -jen || *U.S. also* éstrə-) *n.* Any of several steroid hormones produced chiefly by the ovary and responsible for promoting oestrus and the development and maintenance of female secondary sex characteristics. Compare **androgen.** [OESTRUS + -GEN.] **—oes·tro·gen·ic** (-jénnik) *adj.*

oes·trone (éestrōn || *U.S. also* éstrōn) *n.* An oestrogenic hormone, $C_{18}H_{22}O_2$, found in the mammalian ovary and isolated commercially from the urine of pregnant females for use in treating oestrogen deficiency. Also called "theelin". [OESTRUS + -ONE.]

oes·trous (éestrass || *U.S. also* éstrass) *adj.* **1.** Of or pertaining to oestrus. **2.** On heat. Said of an animal.

oestrous cycle *n.* The series of chemical and physiological changes in female mammals from one period of oestrus to the next.

oes·trus (éestrəss || *U.S. also* éstrəss) *n.* A regularly recurrent period of ovulation and sexual excitement in female mammals other than humans. Also called "heat". [New Latin, from Latin *oestrus,* gadfly, frenzy, from Greek *oistros.*]

oeu·vre (érv-rə, öv-,-r) *n., pl.* **oeuvres** (*pronounced as singular*). *French.* **1.** A work of art. **2.** The sum of an artist's work.

of (ov, *weak form* əv || *chiefly U.S.* uv; *nonstandard weak form, before consonants only,* ə) *prep.* **1.** Derived or coming from; originating at or from: *Jesus of Nazareth; men of the north.* **2. a.** Caused by; resulting from: *of her own free will.* **b.** Owing to; through: *died of tuberculosis.* **3.** Away from; at a distance from: *a mile east of here.* **4.** Used to indicate: **a.** Lack or absence: *free of prejudice.* **b.** Separateness: *regardless of race.* **c.** Removal: *robbed of his dignity; cured of distemper.* **5.** From the total or group comprising; from among: *give of one's time; two of his friends; most of the cases; the third week of March.* **6. a.** Composed or made from: *a dress of silk.* **b.** Constituted by: *a field of three acres.* **7.** Associated with or adhering to: *a man of your religion; the colour of your hair.* **8.** Belonging or connected to: *the coughing of a smoker; the houses of my friends; the rungs of a ladder.* **9.** Possessing; having: *a man of honour.* **10.** Containing or carrying: *a basket of groceries.* **11. a.** That is: *the subject of philosophy.* **b.** Specified as; named or called: *a depth of ten feet; the Garden of Eden; the town of Brighton.* **12.** Centring upon (some object); directed towards: *a love of horses; in search of the escaped prisoner.* **13.** Produced by; issuing from: *the novels of Ernest Hemingway; products of the vine.* **14.** Characterised or identified by: *a year of famine; a painter of distinction.* **15.** Concerning; with reference to; about: *think highly of his proposals; speak of it later.* **16.** Set aside for; having as a purpose; taken up by: *a hall of residence; a day of rest.* **17. a.** *U.S.* Before; until; to. Used in telling the time: *five minutes of two.* **b.** Used in dates: *third of May.* **18.** During or on (a specific time): *of recent years; of an evening.* **19.** As specified: *smelling of lavender.* **20.** *Rare.* By: *beloved of his family.* **21.** Used after an adjective to express a personal judgment on the following noun or noun phrase: *How rude of him to leave!* **22.** Used to indicate a particular relationship, for example: **a.** Between an adjective and a noun or noun phrase, similar to that between a verb and its object: *sure of the facts; capable of stealing.* **b.** A verb and a noun or noun phrase: *She tired of waiting; reminded him of the date.* **c.** A noun and a noun or noun phrase: *made a good job of the car; that rogue of a solicitor.* **d.** An adverb and a noun or noun phrase: *upwind of the smoke.* [Middle English *of,* Old English *of* (preposition and adverb).]

Usage: The normal use of *of* following a noun, to express possession or close relationship, is seen in such phrases as *the crew of the ship; a friend of my mother.* In certain circumstances it is also possible to use the *s* apostrophe forms of the noun following *of*: *a friend of my mother's.* However, the noun in the *of*-phrase must be definite and human. One cannot say *a friend of a mother's,* or *the crew of the ship's.* The noun before the *of*-phrase is usually indefinite *(a friend. . .)*: one is unlikely to hear *the friend of my mother's,* though, in informal English, the use of a demonstrative such as *this* or *that* is common: *I was talking to that friend of my mother's.* The preposition *of* is also used after such verbs as *speak, inform,* and *talk,* as a more formal literary variant of *about*: *I spoke of that to the committee.* After the verb *think,* however, two senses are involved: *think of* means "bring to mind", *think about* means "consider".

o·fay (ō-fay) *n. U.S. Slang.* A white person. Used derogatorily by blacks. [Perhaps Pig Latin, for FOE.]

off (off, awf) *adv.* **1.** At or to a distance from a nearer place; so as to be away: *drive off.* **2.** Distant or away in space or time: *The station is a mile off; The party is a week off.* **3.** So as to be no longer on, attached, or connected: *The electricity was cut off.* **4.** So as to be no longer continuing, operating, or functioning: *turn off the radio.* **5. a.** So as to be completely removed: *Take your clothes off.* **b.** So as to finish, eliminate, or be rid of: *write off a report; kill off the mice.* **6.** So as to be smaller, fewer, or less: *Sales dropped off.* **7.** So as to be away from work or duty: *They took a day off.* **8.** Off-stage. **9.** *Informal.* So as no longer to like: *went right off her.* **10.** Used without a definite independent meaning in many phrasal verbs: *show off; tell off.* **—off and on.** Intermittently: *He slept off and on.* **—off with.** Remove. Used as an imperative interjection: *Off with his head! Off with all of you!*

~adj. **1.** Sour, rotten, bad, or stale. Said of food: *This mince is off.* **2.** Not on, attached, or connected; removed: *with my shoes off.* **3. a.** Not continuing, operating, or functioning: *The oven is off.* **b.** Effecting a disconnection: *the off switch.* **4.** No longer existing or effective; cancelled: *The wedding is off.* **5.** No longer available or on the menu: *Ham is off.* **6. a.** Not up to standard; below a normal or satisfactory level: *Your bowling is off today.* **b.** Characterised by mediocrity or low standards: *an off day.* **7.** In a specified circumstance or condition: *You are better off staying home.* **8. a.** *Informal.* Impolite or unfair; unacceptable: *Arriving so late is a bit off.* **b.** Inconsistent with accuracy or truth; in error: *My guess was slightly off.* **9.** Started on the way; going: *The runners were off.* **10.** Absent or away from work or duty: *He's off every Tuesday.* **11.** On the right-hand side of a vehicle, horse, or team of horses: *The off horse is lame.* **12.** *Nautical.* Seaward; farthest from the shore. **13.** Designating or placed on the off of a cricket field: *the off stump.*

~prep. **1. a.** So as to be removed or distant from (a position of rest or support): *The bird hopped off the branch.* **b.** Taken or subtracted from: *a slice off the joint.* **2.** Away or relieved from: *off duty.*

3. **a.** By consuming: *living off locusts and honey.* **b.** With the means provided by: *living off her pension.* **4. a.** Extending or branching out from: *an artery off the heart.* **b.** Near but not on; slightly away: *off the Market Square.* **5. a.** Deviating from: *off course.* **b.** Not up to the standard of: *off my usual form.* **6. a.** Abstaining from: *He is off the booze.* **b.** *Informal.* No longer liking: *She's right off him.* **7.** Seaward of: *a mile off Land's End.*
~n. **1.** In cricket, the side of the field that is on the right of or behind the right shoulder of a right-handed batsman who is facing the bowling, or on the left of or behind the left shoulder of a left-handed batsman. **2.** The beginning of a horse race. [Middle English *of, off,* of, off, from Old English *of.*]
Usage: The use of *off,* followed by *of* and sometimes by *from, (He stepped off of the pavement; leave off from doing that)* is unacceptable in formal speech and writing, and open to criticism even in informal speech. The use of *off* for *from,* in indicating the notion of "source", should be restricted to informal contexts *(He took the book off me).*
off. office; officer; official.
Of·fa (óffə) (died 796). Anglo-Saxon king of Mercia. Seizing power (757) from his cousin, he dominated much of England south of the Humber. He issued the first Anglo-Saxon coinage, established commercial and diplomatic links with the Frankish empire of Charlemagne, and accepted greater papal control of the English church. After repelling a Welsh invasion, he established the Welsh-Mercian border at the huge earthwork known as Offa's Dyke.
of·fal (óff'l || áwf'l) *n.* **1.** The edible internal organs, such as the heart, liver, or kidneys, of a dead animal. **2.** Dead or decaying matter; putrid flesh. **3.** Refuse; rubbish. [Middle English *offal, ofall,* from Middle Dutch *afval,* "that which falls off", giblets, refuse : *af,* off + *vallen,* to fall.]
Of·fa·ly (óffəli). *Irish* **Uabh Fáilghe.** County of the Republic of Ireland, in the province of Leinster. Tullamore is the county town.
off-bal·ance (óff-bál-ənss, áwf-) *adj.* **1.** Unsteady. **2.** Unprepared: *the remark caught her off-balance.* **—off-bal·ance** *adv.*
off·beat (óff-beet, áwf-) *n. Music.* An unaccented beat in a bar.
~adj. (-bе́et). *Slang.* Not conforming to an ordinary type or pattern; unconventional: *offbeat humour.*
off·break *n.* In cricket, a ball bowled so that it moves from off to leg when it bounces.
off-Broad·way (óff-bráwdway, áwf-) *adj. U.S.* Designating or pertaining to theatrical activity, often experimental and low-cost, presented in theatres outside the Broadway entertainment district of New York City; fringe.
~n. U.S. Theatrical productions presented outside the Broadway entertainment district; fringe theatre. Compare **Broadway.**
off-cen·tre (óff-séntər, áwf-) *adj.* **1.** Not quite central; slightly away from the centre. **2.** Offbeat; eccentric. **—off-cen·tre** *adv.*
off·chance, off chance (óff-chaans) *n.* A remote or slight chance; a hope: *I approached him on the off chance of a loan.*
off-col·our, off colour (óff-kúllər, áwf-) *adj.* **1.** Varying from the usual, expected, or required colour. **2.** Improper; in bad taste: *an off-colour joke.* **3.** *Chiefly British.* Not in good health or spirits.
off-course (óff-kórss, áwf- || -kōrss) *adj.* Pertaining to or designating betting not taking place at a racecourse. **—off course** *adv.*
off·cut (óff-kut, áwf-) *n.* A remnant of a piece of material, such as carpet or wood, left after removing larger pieces of the material for selling.
Of·fen·bach (óff'n-baak), **Jacques,** né Jacob Wiener (1819–80). German-born French cellist and composer of more than 90 pieces, e.g. *Orpheus in the Underworld* (1858).
of·fence, *U.S.* **of·fense** (ə-fénss || ō-; *for sense 4, U.S.* óffenss) *n.* **1.** The act of offending or causing anger, resentment, or displeasure. **2. a.** Any violation or infraction of a moral or social code; a transgression or sin. **b.** A transgression of law; a crime. **3.** Something that offends. **4.** The act of attacking or assaulting. **—give offence.** To cause anger, displeasure, or resentment. **—no offence.** Used to excuse a possibly offensive remark. **—take offence.** To become angered, displeased, or resentful; feel hurt. [Middle English, from Old French, from Latin *offensa,* from the feminine past participle of *offendere,* to OFFEND.]
of·fend (ə-fénd || ō-) *v.* **-fended, -fending, -fends.** *—tr.* **1.** To create or excite anger, resentment, or annoyance in; hurt the feelings of; affront: *Her brusqueness offends many people.* **2.** To be displeasing or disagreeable to: *Onions offend his sense of smell.* **3.** *Obsolete.* **a.** To transgress; violate: *"He hath offended the law"* (Shakespeare). **b.** To cause to sin: *"If thy right eye offend thee, pluck it out."* (Matthew 5:29). *—intr.* **1.** To cause displeasure. **2.** *Archaic.* **a.** To break the law. **b.** To violate a moral or divine law; sin. [Middle English *offenden,* from Old French *offendre,* from Latin *offendere,* to strike against: *of-, ob-,* against + *fendere,* to strike.]
Synonyms: *offend, insult, affront, outrage.*
of·fend·er (ə-féndər || ō-) *n.* **1.** A person who has committed some minor misdemeanour: *sent the offenders to bed early.* **2.** A person who has committed a crime: *a sex offender.*
of·fend·ing (ə-fénding || ō-) *adj.* **1.** Causing offence. **2.** Responsible for some fault or inconvenience: *removed the offending splinter.*
of·fen·sive (ə-fén-siv || ō-) *adj.* **1.** Disagreeable to the senses: *an offensive odour.* **2.** Causing anger, displeasure, or resentment; giving offence; affronting. **3.** Of, pertaining to, or characteristic of an attack; aggressive. —See Synonyms at **hateful.**
~n. **1.** An attitude of attack. Often used with *the.* **2.** An attack or assault, especially a military one. **3.** An aggressive campaign or initiative: *an electoral offensive.* **—of·fen·sive·ly** *adv.* **—of·fen·sive·ness** *n.*
Synonyms: *offensive, insulting, objectionable, obnoxious.*
of·fer (óffər || *chiefly U.S.* áwfər) *v.* **-fered, -fering, -fers.** *—tr.* **1.** To present for acceptance or rejection; proffer. **2.** To put forward for consideration or examination; propose: *offer an opinion.* **3.** To present for sale. **4.** To propose as payment; bid. **5.** To present as an act of worship. Often followed by *up: offer up prayers.* **6.** To exhibit readiness or desire to do; volunteer: *offered to help me.* **7.** To exhibit an intention; attempt: *"ready to shoot me if I should offer to stir"* (Jonathan Swift). **8.** To try to inflict upon: *"He was not afraid of their offering him any harm."* (Herman Melville). **9.** To provide; furnish; afford. **10.** To produce or present (an artistic work): *The theatre offered one new play that season.* **11.** To present; reveal. *—intr.* **1.** To present an offering in worship or devotion. **2.** To make an offer or proposal; especially formerly, to make an offer of marriage. **3.** To present itself; appear; arise: *"This plan was dropped, because of its risk, and because a better offered."* (T.E. Lawrence).
~n. **1.** The act of offering. **2.** Something offered, such as a suggestion, proposal, bid, or recommendation. **3.** *Law.* A proposal which, if accepted, constitutes a legally binding contract. **4.** *Informal.* **a.** A reduction on the normal price of retail goods: *a special offer.* **b.** Goods whose price is thus reduced. **5.** Especially formerly, a proposal of marriage. **6.** *Archaic.* **a.** An attempt; a try: *"imperfect offers and essays"* (Francis Bacon). **b.** A show of intention. **—on offer.** For sale or available. **—under offer.** Having been the object of an offer or bid. Said of property. [Middle English *offeren, offren,* partly (in the sense "to sacrifice") from Old English *offrian,* and partly (in other senses) from Old French *offrir;* both from Latin *offerre* : *ob-,* to + *ferre,* to bring, carry.] **—of·fer·er, of·fer·or** (-ər) *n.*
Synonyms: *offer, proffer, tender, present.*
of·fer·ing (óffər-ing || áwfər-) *n.* **1.** The act of making an offer. **2.** Something that is offered. **3.** A presentation made to a deity as an act of religious worship or sacrifice. **4.** A contribution or gift, especially one made at a religious service. [Middle English *offring,* Old English *offrung,* from *offrian,* to sacrifice, OFFER.]
Of·fer·to·ry (óffər-tri, -təri || áwfər-) *n., pl.* **-ries. 1. a.** One of the principal parts of the Eucharistic liturgy at which bread and wine are offered to God by the celebrant. **b.** A musical setting of the Offertory. **2.** *Small* **o.** A collection of offerings of the congregation. [Old French *offertoire,* from Medieval Latin *offertōrium,* from Latin *offerre,* to OFFER.]
off·hand (óff-hánd, áwf-) *adv.* Without preparation or forethought.
~adj. Also **off·hand·ed** (-hándid). **1.** Said or done offhand. **2.** Inconsiderate; impolite; abrupt. **—off·hand·ed·ly** *adv.* **—off·hand·ed·ness** *n.*
of·fice (óffiss || *chiefly U.S.* áwfiss) *n. Abbr.* **off. 1. a.** A place, such as a building, room, or suite, in which services, clerical work, or professional duties are carried out: *the manager's office; booking office.* **b.** The administrative personnel, executives, or entire staff working in such a place. **2.** A duty or function assigned to or assumed by someone: *"the maternal office was supplied by my aunt"* (Edward Gibbon). **3.** A position of authority, duty, or trust given to a person, as in a government, business, or other organisation: *the office of president.* **4.** *Capital* **O,** *when part of a title.* **a.** A major executive division of the British government, often headed by a cabinet minister. **b.** Any of the branches of the Federal government of the United States ranking just below the departments. **5.** A public position: *take office.* **6.** *Plural. Chiefly British.* Formerly, the parts of a house, such as the laundry and kitchen, in which the servants carried out household work, and often including outbuildings such as the barn. **7.** *Often plural.* An act, usually beneficial, performed for another; a favour: *through the offices of friends.* **8.** *Ecclesiastical.* A ceremony, rite, or service, usually prescribed by liturgy: **a.** *Roman Catholic Church.* The canonical hours. **b.** *Anglican Church.* A prayer service, such as Morning or Evening Prayer. **c.** Any ceremony or service for a special purpose; especially, a rite for the dead. **—in (or out of) office.** In (or out of) government; in (or out of) power. [Middle English, from Old French, from Latin *officium,* performance of duty, from *opificium* (unattested) : *opus,* work + *-ficium,* from *facere,* to do.]
office block *n.* A large, usually modern, building housing a number of offices.
office boy *n.* A boy employed to do minor tasks and to run errands in an office.
of·fice·hold·er (óffiss-hōldər || áwfiss-) *n.* One who holds public office.
office hours *n.* The usual period or periods of the day during which business is conducted or work performed in an office.
of·fi·cer (óffi-sər || *chiefly U.S.* áwfi-) *n. Abbr.* **off. 1. a.** One who holds an office of authority or trust in a business, government, or other institution. **b.** A public or government official: *medical officer; customs officer.* **2. a.** One in a position of authority in the armed forces. **b.** One holding a commission in the armed forces. **3.** One holding authority in the merchant navy, such as a captain, master, mate, chief engineer, or assistant engineer. **4.** A policeman. **5. a.** One elected to an office in a society or club. **b.** A rank above the lowest rank in some honorary societies. **6.** A member of the Order of the British Empire, in the grade below commander.
~tr.v. **officered, -cering, -cers. 1.** To provide with officers; allocate officers to. **2.** To direct or command; act as an officer over. [Middle English, from Anglo-French, Old French *officier,* from

Medieval Latin *officiārius,* "officeholder", from Latin *officium,* OFFICE.]

officer of arms *n. Heraldry.* A herald or pursuivant.

officer of the day *n. Abbr.* **O.D.** A military officer who, for a given day, assumes responsibility for security, order, and the performance of the guard.

of·fi·cial (ə-físh'l ‖ ō-) *adj. Abbr.* **off.** **1.** Of or pertaining to an office or post of authority: *official duties.* **2.** Authorised by a proper authority; authoritative: *official permission.* **3.** Holding office or serving in some public capacity; authorised to perform some special duty: *an official representative.* **4.** Characteristic of or befitting a person of authority: *official behaviour.* **5.** Formal or ceremonial: *an official banquet.* **6.** *Capital* **O.** Of, pertaining to, or designating the wing of both the IRA and Sinn Fein, formed by the split that occurred in those organisations in 1969, that emphasises peaceful political methods of achieving the unification of Ireland. Compare **Provisional. 7.** Designating pharmaceutical products that are recognised and identified in an official publication, such as (in the United Kingdom) the *British Pharmacopoeia.*
~*n. Abbr.* **off.** **1.** One who holds an office or position; especially, one who acts in a subordinate capacity for an organisation, government department, or other institution. **2.** *Capital* **O.** A member of the official IRA or Sinn Fein. [Middle English, an authority, from Old French, from Late Latin *officiālis,* functionary, official, from Latin, of an office or duty, from *officium,* OFFICE.] —**of·fi·cial·ism** *n.* —**of·fi·cial·ly** *adv.*

of·fi·cial·dom (ə-físh'l-dəm ‖ ō-) *n.* Bureaucracy; officials or bureaucrats collectively, especially when considered as rigidly adhering to official regulations, forms, and procedures.

of·fi·cial·ese (ə-físh'l-éez ‖ ō-, -éess) *n.* Language characteristic of official documents or statements, often considered obscure, pretentiously wordy, or formal in style.

Official Receiver *n.* In Britain, a person appointed by the Department of Trade and Industry to act as a **receiver** *(see),* and to manage the estate of a bankrupt temporarily until the appointment of a trustee in bankruptcy.

Official Referee *n. Law.* In England until 1971, a judicial official to whom civil cases were referred, if both parties were willing, for a private trial followed by an award or report to the court. See **referee.**

of·fi·ci·ant (ə-físhi-ənt ‖ ō-) *n.* One who officiates at a religious service or ceremony; a celebrant.

of·fi·ci·ar·y (ə-físhi-əri ‖ ō-, -erri) *n., pl.* **-ies. 1.** A body of officials or officers. **2.** *Rare.* An official or officer.
~*adj.* **1.** Attached to or resulting from an office held. Said of a title. **2.** Having a title resulting from the holding of an office. Said of a dignitary.

of·fi·ci·ate (ə-físhi-ayt ‖ ō-) *intr.v.* **-ated, -ating, -ates. 1.** To perform the duties and functions of an office or position of authority. **2.** To serve as a priest or minister at a religious service. **3.** To take on a particular role, and perform the duties and functions associated with that role, as at a special occasion or ceremony: *officiated as host.* [Medieval Latin *officiāre,* to conduct a religious service, from Latin *officium,* OFFICE (in Late Latin, also "religious service").] —**of·fi·ci·a·tion** (-áysh'n) *n.* —**of·fi·ci·a·tor** (-ər) *n.*

of·fic·i·nal (offi-sín'l, ə-físsin'l ‖ ō-) *adj.* **1.** Designating a drug available without prescription. Compare **magistral. 2.** Designating a plant used in medicine.
~*n.* An officinal drug or plant. [Medieval Latin *officīnālis,* "used or kept in a workshop" (especially a medical laboratory), from Latin *officīna,* workshop, reduction of *opificīna,* workshop, from *opifex,* workman : *opus,* work + *facere,* to do.]

of·fi·cious (ə-físhəss ‖ ō-) *adj.* **1.** Excessively forward in offering one's services or advice to others; intrusive; meddling. **2.** In diplomacy, of a casual nature; not official; unauthorised. **3.** *Obsolete.* Eager to render services or help others. [Latin *officiōsus,* eager to oblige, from *officium,* duty, service, OFFICE.] —**of·fi·cious·ly** *adv.* —**of·fi·cious·ness** *n.*

off·ing (óff-ing, áwf-ing) *n.* **1.** The near immediate future. Used in the phrase *in the offing.* **2.** The part of the sea that is distant yet visible from the shore. **3.** A position at a distance from the shore. [Perhaps from OFF.]

off·ish (óff-ish, áwf-) *adj.* Inclined to be distant and reserved in manner; aloof. —**off·ish·ly** *adv.* —**off·ish·ness** *n.*

off-key, off key (óff-kée, áwf-) *adj.* **1.** Not played or sung in the correct key. **2.** Out of tune. **3.** Discordant; clashing. —**off key** *adv.*

off-licence (óff-líss'nss, áwf-) *n. British.* **1.** A shop or part of a shop or public house selling alcoholic drinks for consumption elsewhere (off the premises). **2.** A licence legally permitting such sales.

off line *adj.* **1.** Not in direct connection with a mainframe computer but controlled by a computer storage device. Said of part of a computer system or a peripheral device. **2.** Switched off. Said of a computer. Compare **on line.**

off-load (óff-lṓd, áwf-, -lṓd) *tr.v.* **-loaded, -loading, -loads. 1.** *Aerospace.* To launch (a guided missile or rocket) with propellant tanks less than fully loaded, for altering the centre of gravity of the projectile. **2.** To unload (a vehicle, especially an aircraft). **3. a.** To shift or delegate (work, for example). **b.** To get rid of (something unwanted): *offloaded her problems onto me.*

off-peak (óff-péek, áwf-) *adj.* **1.** Designating periods of time in which there is least demand for a facility, service, or the like. **2.** Of or pertaining to something offered or existing during off-peak periods: *off-peak prices.*

off-print (óff-print, áwf-) *n.* A reproduction or excerpt of a printed article that was originally contained in a larger publication.
~*tr.v.* **offprinted, -printing, -prints.** To reproduce or reprint (an excerpt). [Translation of German *Abdruck.*]

off-putting (óff-põõtting, áwf-) *adj. Chiefly British Informal.* **1.** Unpleasant; unappealing. **2.** Disconcerting; discouraging.

off-sales (óff-saylz, áwf-) *pl.n.* Sales of alcohol and other drinks at an off-licence.

off-scour·ing (óff-skowr-ing, áwf-) *n.* **1.** *Usually plural.* That which is scoured off; refuse. **2.** A social outcast or misfit.

off-screen (óff-skréen, áwf-) *adj.* **1.** On the soundtrack of a film or television programme only; not seen: *an offscreen commentator.* **2.** In real life; away from the television or cinema screen: *offscreen romances between stars.* —**off-screen** *adv.*

off-season (óff-seez'n, áwf-, -séez'n) *n.* The time of year when there is least demand for something, such as holiday accommodation or other services. —**off-season** *adj. & adv.*

off-set (óff-set, áwf-) *n.* **1.** Something that balances, counteracts, or compensates. **2.** Something deriving or originating but set off from something else. **3.** *Architecture.* A ledge or recess in a wall, formed by a reduction in thickness above. Also called "setoff". **4.** *Botany.* A shoot that develops laterally at the base of a plant, often rooting to form a new plant. **5.** *Geology.* A spur of a range of mountains or hills. **6.** A bend in a pipe or bar to allow it to pass around an obstruction. **7.** *Mining.* A crosscut or drift from a main level. **8.** In surveying, a short distance measured perpendicularly from the main line, used to help in calculating the area of an irregular plot. **9.** *Printing.* **a.** A method of printing whereby the impression or image to be printed is transferred from the inked plate to an intermediate surface, usually a rubber-covered cylinder that transfers the image by rolling onto paper. Also used adjectively: *offset lithography.* **b.** The unintentional or faulty transfer of ink not yet dry from a printed sheet to any surface, such as the next sheet, that is laid over it.
~*v.* (-sét) **offset, -setting, -sets.** —*tr.* **1.** To compensate or cause to compensate for: *offset the loss against tax.* **2.** *Printing.* **a.** To print by offset. **b.** To smear with an offset. **3.** To make or form an offset in (a wall, bar, or pipe). —*intr.* To develop as an offset. —**off-set** *adj.*

off-shoot (óff-shōōt, áwf-) *n.* **1.** Something that branches out or derives its existence or origin from a particular source: *an offshoot of the parent company.* **2.** A branch, descendant, or member of a family or social group. **3.** A lateral shoot from the main stem of a plant.

off-shore (óff-shór, áwf-, -shōr) *adj.* **1.** Moving or directed away from the shore: *an offshore wind.* **2.** Located or occurring at a distance from the shore: *an offshore oil rig.*
~*adv.* **1.** Away from the shore: *The storm moved offshore.* **2.** At a distance from the shore: *a boat moored offshore.*

off-side (óff-síd, áwf-) *adj.* **1.** On the wrong side of the ball when it is played, according to the rules in certain games such as soccer, hockey, or Rugby football; usually, illegally ahead of the ball or puck in the opponent's half or an attacking zone. Said of a player, team, or play in various games. **2.** *Chiefly British.* On the right-hand side of a vehicle, horse, or team of horses.
~*n.* **1.** A situation in a game in which a player is offside. **2.** *Chiefly British.* The right-hand side of a vehicle, horse, or team of horses.

off-spring (óff-spring, áwf-) *n., pl.* **offspring** or *rare* **-springs. 1.** The progeny of a person, animal, or plant. **2.** A result; an outcome; a product. [Middle English *ofspring,* Old English *ofspring* : *of,* from + *springan,* to SPRING.]

off-stage (óff-stáyj, áwf-) *adj.* Located or occurring in the area of a stage not visible to the audience.
~*adv.* Away from the area of a stage visible to the audience.

off-street (óff-stréet, áwf-) *adj.* Away from or not on the street: *off-street parking.*

off-the-cuff (óff-thə-kúf, áwf-) *adj.* Impromptu; not thought up in advance; unprepared. [Referring to notes written on a shirt cuff as reminders for someone delivering a speech.] —**off the cuff** *adv.*

off-the-peg, off the peg (óff-thə-pég, áwf-) *adj. British.* Ready-made: *an off-the-peg dress; off-the-peg ideas.* —**off the peg** *adv.*

off-the-rec·ord, off the record (óff-thə-rék-awrd, áwf- ‖ -ərd) *adj.* Not for publication; not to be repeated. —**off the record** *adv.*

off-the-wall, off the wall (óff-thə-wáwl, áwf-) *adj. U.S. Informal.* Unusual or unconventional; crazy: *off-the-wall notions.* [Perhaps alluding to a ball off the wall in squash or handball, hence unexpected, surprising.] —**off the wall** *adv.*

off-white (óff-wít, áwf-, -hwít) *n.* Greyish or yellowish white. —**off-white** *adj.*

O.F.M. Order of Friars Minor (Franciscans).

O.F.S. Orange Free State.

oft (oft, awft) *adv. Poetic.* Often. Sometimes used in combination: *oft-repeated.* [Middle English, Old English *oft.*]

OFT Office of Fair Trading (in Britain).

of·ten (óff-'n, áwf-, -tən) *adv.* **1.** Frequently; repeatedly; customarily; many times. **2.** Much of the time; in many instances. —**as often as. 1.** As many times as. **2.** Every time that. —**every so often.** Sometimes; fairly regularly. —**more often than not.** More than half the time; in most instances.
~*adj. Archaic.* Repeated; frequent. [Middle English *oftin, often,* variants (before vowels and *h*) of *ofte,* OFT.]

Usage: Many people believe that the *t* in *often* should be pronounced, because it is there in the spelling. The pronunciation (óff-tən) is, however, far less commonly heard. The comparative and superlative forms *oftener* and *oftenest* have achieved some acceptability in standard English; but the compound forms *more often* and *most often* are more regularly used.

of·ten·times (óff-'n-tīmz, áwf-, -tən-) *adv. Archaic*. Also **oft·times** (óff-tīmz, óft-, áwf-, áwft-). Frequently; repeatedly.

OG, O.G. **1.** officer of the guard. **2.** *Philately*. original gum.

Og·a·den, the (óggə-dén || *U.S. also* ō-gaá-dayn). Arid wilderness in southeast Ethiopia, inhabited chiefly by Somali pastoral nomads. Intermittent border warfare between Ethiopia and Somalia culminated in an invasion by Somali forces (1978). A cease-fire was agreed in 1988.

Og·den (óg-dən), **C(harles) K(ay)** (1889–1957). British semanticist. From ideas presented in his book *The Meaning of Meaning* (1923), written in collaboration with I. A. Richards (1893–1979), he developed the concept of Basic English, an international language of 850 essential words and 150 scientific terms.

o·gee (ō-jée, *rarely* ō-jée) *n. Architecture*. **1.** A double curve with the shape of an elongated S. **2.** A moulding having in profile an S-shaped curve. **3.** An arch of two of these curves meeting at a point. In this sense, also called "ogee arch". [Alteration of OGIVE.]

og·ham, o·gam (óggəm || *U.S. also* ō-əm, óg-) *n*. **1. a.** An Ancient British and Irish alphabet used for writing Irish from the fourth or fifth century A.D. to the early seventh century. **b.** A character of this alphabet. **2. a.** An inscription in the ogham alphabet. **b.** A stone inscribed in the ogham alphabet. [Irish *ogham*, from Old Irish *ogom*, said to be named after its mythical inventor *Ogma*†.]

o·give (ō-jīv, *rarely* ō-jīv) *n*. **1.** *Statistics*. **a.** The graphic representation of a frequency distribution, in which every ordinate represents the sum of frequencies in preceding intervals. **b.** A frequency distribution. **2.** *Architecture*. **a.** A diagonal rib of a Gothic vault. **b.** A pointed arch. Also called "ogive curve". [Middle English, from Old French *augive*†.] **—o·gi·val** (ō-jív'l) *adj*.

o·gle (ōg'l || *U.S. also* ógg'l) *v*. **ogled, ogling, ogles.** *—tr*. **1.** To stare at. **2.** To stare at lecherously. *—intr*. To stare in a lecherous manner. —See Synonyms at **gaze**.
~*n*. A stare, especially one that is lecherous. [From Low German *oegeln*, frequentative of *oegen*, to eye, from *oog*, eye.] **—o·gler** *n*.

OG·PU, O.G.P.U. (ōg-pōo) *n*. Unified Government Political Administration (Russian *Obyedinyonnoye Gosudarstvyennoye Politicheskoye Upravlenie*): a former security branch of the Soviet government functioning as a successor to the **Cheka** and corresponding in broad outline to the later **KGB** *(both of which see)*.

o·gre (ōgər) *n*. **1.** A legendary, man-eating giant or monster. **2.** Anyone who is especially cruel, brutish, or hideous. [French *ogre*† (first used by Perrault in *Contes de ma mère l'oye;* 1697).] **—o·gre·ish** (ōgər-ish) *adj*.

o·gress (ō-griss, -gress) *n*. A female ogre.

oh (ō) *interj*. Also *rare* **O**. Used to express strong emotion, such as surprise, fear, anger, or pain.
~*n., pl.* **oh's** or **ohs**. The exclamation *oh* or any occurrence of it. —See Usage note at **O**. [Middle English *o* (expressive formation). The spelling *oh* is not older than 1548.]

ohc, o.h.c. overhead camshaft.

O. Henry (ō-hénri), pen name of William Sydney Porter (1862–1910). U.S. short-story writer, famous for his stories with a "twist in the tail". He wrote more than 300 stories, as collected in *Cabbages and Kings* (1904) and *The Voice of the City* (1908).

OHG Old High German.

O'Higgins (ō-hígginz, ə-; *Spanish* ō-ée-geenss), **Bernardo** (*c.* 1778–1842). Chilean politician and soldier. The illegitimate son of an Irish soldier, he was commander of the Republican army which liberated Chile from Spain (1818). O'Higgins became president, but his social and economic reforms provoked unrest, and he was forced to resign (1823).

O·hi·o¹ (ō-hī-ō). State in the Great Lakes Region of the Middle West, United States. Rich in mineral resources, it is a major coal producing area and one of the main industrial states. Agriculture is also extensive, and large amounts of corn, soya beans, wheat, and dairy goods are produced. Ohio was accepted into the Union in 1803. Capital, Columbus.

Ohio². River of the east central United States. Formed at Pittsburgh (Pennsylvania) by the confluence of the Monongahela and Allegheny rivers, it flows southwest to join the Mississippi at Cairo (Illinois). The river is important for the transportation of bulk cargoes such as coal and gravel.

ohm (ōm) *n. Symbol* Ω The SI unit of electrical resistance equal to that of a conductor in which a current of one ampere is produced by a potential of one volt across its terminals. [After Georg Simon OHM.]

Ohm (ōm), **Georg Simon** (1787–1854). German physicist. Though he made considerable contributions to mathematics and acoustics, he is best known for his work in the field of electrical resistance.

ohm·age (ōmij) *n. Electricity*. Resistance expressed in ohms.

ohm·me·ter (ōm-meetər) *n. Electricity*. An instrument for the direct measurement of the resistance of a conductor in ohms.

OHMS, O.H.M.S. On Her (or His) Majesty's Service.

Ohm's law *n. Physics*. The law stating that the direct electrical current flowing in a conductor is directly proportional to the potential difference between its ends. It is usually formulated as: V = IR, where V is the applied voltage, I is the current, and R (the constant of proportionality) is the resistance of the conductor.

o·ho (ō-hō, ə-) *interj*. Used especially to express ironic surprise or mock astonishment. [Middle English : o + HO.]

–oholic. Variant of **-holic**.

o.h.v., ohv overhead valve.

oi (oy) *interj*. Used to attract attention or express indignation.
~*adj*. Pertaining to or designating a style of popular music of the early 1980s associated with the skinhead movement, and characterised by its aggressiveness, raucousness, and repetitive rhythm. [Variant of HOY.]

–oic *adj. suffix*. Indicates the presence of a carboxyl group or a derivative of it; for example, **decanoic acid**. [Lengthening of -IC (denoting acids).]

oick (oyk) *n. British Slang*. An uncultivated person. [Imitative of uncultivated speech.]

–oid *n. & adj. suffix*. Indicates: **1.** Likeness, resemblance, or similarity to; for example, **anthropoid, crystalloid, planetoid**. **2.** A spurious likeness to; for example, **factoid**. [Latin *-oīdēs*, from Greek *-oeidēs*, of or having the shape or nature of, from *eidos*, form, shape.]

–oidea *pl. n. comb. form*. Indicates an echinoderm belonging to a taxonomic class; for example, **Asteroidea, Crinoidea**. [New Latin, from Latin *-oidēs*, -OID.]

o·id·i·um (ō-íddi-əm) *n., pl.* **-ia**. A spore produced by the fragmentation of a hypha in certain fungi. [New Latin, from Greek *ōion*, egg + *-idion*, diminutive suffix.]

oil (oyl) *n*. **1.** Any of numerous mineral, vegetable, and synthetic substances and animal and vegetable fats, that are generally slippery, combustible, viscous, liquid or liquefiable at room temperatures, soluble in various organic solvents, such as ether, but not in water, and used in a great variety of products, especially lubricants and fuels. **2. a.** Petroleum. **b.** A petroleum derivative, such as a machine oil or lubricant. **3.** Any substance with an oily consistency. **4.** Paraffin used as a domestic fuel. Also used adjectivally: *an oil lamp*. **5. a.** *Often plural*. An oil paint *(see)*. **b.** An oil painting *(see)*. **6.** *Informal*. Insincere flattery. **—burn the midnight oil**. To work hard or study late into the night. **—pour oil on troubled waters**. To bring calm to a difficult situation. **—strike oil**. **1.** To discover crude oil by drilling in the ground for it. **2.** To gain sudden wealth or success. **—the good** or **dinkum oil**. *Australian & N.Z. Informal*. True and useful information.
~*v*. **oiled, oiling, oils.** *—tr*. **1.** To lubricate, supply, cover, or polish with oil. **2.** *Informal*. To bribe. Used chiefly in the phrase *oil someone's palm*. *—intr*. **1.** To load up with or take on fuel oil. **2.** To become oil by melting. [Middle English *oli, oil(e)*, (olive) oil, from Old French, from Latin *oleum*, from Greek *elaion*, from *elaia*, olive.] **—oil** *adj*.

oil beetle *n*. Any of various insects of the family Meloidae, that, when disturbed, exude an oily yellow substance.

oil·bird (óyl-burd) *n*. A nocturnal bird, *Steatornis caripensis*, native to South America and Trinidad, that navigates by echo location and feeds on fruit detected by smell. Also called "guacharo".

oil burner *n*. **1.** A heating unit, furnace, or boiler that burns fuel oil. **2.** A device for spraying fine droplets of fuel oil into an oil burner.

oil cake *n*. The solid residue left after certain oilseeds, such as cottonseed and linseed, have been pressed free of their oil. It is used after grinding as cattle feed or fertiliser.

oil·can (óyl-kan) *n*. A can with a spout for applying lubricating oil.

oil·cloth (óyl-kloth || -klawth) *n*. A fabric treated with clay, oil, and pigments to make it waterproof. It is used as a cover for tables or shelving.

oil colour *n*. An oil paint.

oil·cup (óyl-kup) *n*. A small cup with a tube at the base that feeds oil continuously into a bearing.

oil drum *n*. A metal drum used to transport oil, oil products, or similar liquids.

oil·er (óylər) *n*. **1.** One that oils machinery and engines. **2.** An oil tanker. **3.** An oilcan. **4.** A well that produces oil. **5.** A ship that burns oil.

oil field *n*. An area with reserves of recoverable petroleum, especially one with several oil-producing wells.

oil·fired (óyl-fīrd) *adj*. Designating a furnace, boiler, or heating system that burns oil as a fuel.

oil gland *n*. **1.** Any gland that secretes oil. **2.** *Zoology*. The uropygial gland *(see)*.

oil of cloves *n*. An oil derived from the flowers of the clove and used in microscopy, dentistry, and confectionery.

oil of turpentine *n*. Refined turpentine.

oil of vitriol *n. Chemistry*. Sulphuric acid *(see)*.

oil paint *n*. A paint consisting of a pigment ground in a drying oil, usually linseed, and used in oil painting. Also called "oil", "oil colour".

oil painting *n*. **1.** A picture painted in oil paints. **2.** The art or practice of painting with oil paints.

oil palm *n*. **1.** A tall palm tree, *Elaeis guineensis*, native to tropical Africa, having nutlike fruits that yield a commercially valuable oil. **2.** Any of several other palms yielding oil.

oil·pa·per (óyl-paypər) *n*. Paper that is soaked in oil to make it transparent and water-resistant.

oil rig *n*. An installation at the head of an oil well for drilling for and extracting oil and natural gas from the earth or the sea bed.

oil sand *n. Geology*. **1.** Any stratum or rock formation containing oil. **2.** A stratum of porous sandstone from which petroleum can be extracted through drilled wells.

oil·seed (óyl-seed) *n*. Any seed, such as linseed or rapeseed, from which oil can be extracted in commercially viable quantities.

oil shale *n. Geology.* A black or dark brown shale containing hydrocarbons that yield petroleum by distillation.

oil·skin (óyl-skin) *n.* **1.** Cloth treated with oil so that it is waterproof. **2.** *Often plural.* An outer garment made of this material.

oil slick *n.* A thin film of oil on water; especially, a large patch of oil on the surface of the sea that has leaked from or been discharged by a ship.

oil·stone (óyl-stōn) *n.* A smooth whetstone lubricated with oil, used for fine sharpening.

oil sump *n.* The bottom of the crankcase of an internal-combustion engine that serves as an oil reservoir.

oil varnish *n.* A varnish *(see).*

oil well *n.* A hole dug or drilled in the earth or sea bed from which petroleum flows or is pumped.

oil·y (óyli) *adj.* **-i·er, -i·est. 1.** Of or pertaining to oil. **2.** Impregnated or smeared with oil; greasy. **3.** Excessively suave in action or behaviour; unctuous. **—oil·i·ly** *adv.* **—oil·i·ness** *n.*

oinology. Variant of **oenology.**

oint·ment (óynt-mənt) *n.* Any of numerous viscous or semisolid substances used on the skin as a cosmetic, a soothing agent, or a medicament; an unguent; a salve. [Middle English, variant (influenced by obsolete *oint,* to anoint) of *oinement,* from Old French *oignement,* from Vulgar Latin *unguimentum* (unattested), from Latin *unguentum,* from *unguens* (stem *unguent-*), present participle of *unguere,* to anoint.]

Oir·each·tas (érrəkh-thəss, érrək-) *n.* The parliament of the Republic of Ireland, consisting of the Dáil Eireann (the representative assembly) and the Seanad Eireann (the senate). [Irish, "assembly", "conference", from Old Irish *airech,* nobleman, free man.]

Oisin. See **Ossian.**

Oi·strakh (óy-straak; *Russian* -strəkh), **David (Feodorovich)** (1908–74). Russian violinist. Famous for his interpretations of Russian music, he gave many recitals with his son, Igor (1931–).

O·jib·wa (ō-jíb-way, o-, ə-, -wə) *n., pl.* **-was** or collectively **Ojibwa.** Also **O·jib·way** (-way) *pl.* **-ways** or collectively **Ojibway. 1.** A member of an Algonquian-speaking North American Indian people inhabiting regions of the United States and Canada around Lake Superior. **2.** The Algonquian language spoken by this people. **—O·jib·wa** *adj.*

O.K., OK, o·kay (ō-káy) *n., pl.* **O.K.'s** or **OK's** or **okays.** *Informal.* Approval; endorsement; agreement.
~*tr.v.* **O.K.'d** or **OK'd** or **okayed, O.K.'ing** or **OK'ing** or **okaying, O.K.'s** or **OK's** or **okays.** *Informal.* To approve or endorse; agree to.
~*interj. Informal.* **1.** Used to express approval or agreement. **2.** Used to indicate that the speaker appreciates a point or objection made by another: *O.K. he's clever, but he's very slow.*
~*adj. Informal.* **1.** Satisfactory; all right. **2.** In good condition or health. **3.** *Chiefly U.S.* Used as a term of approval: *an O.K. guy.* [Popularised as a slogan of the O.K. Club, Democratic Party political club of 1840; from *o(ll) k(orrect),* joke spelling of *all correct* + *O(ld) K(inderhook),* nickname of President Martin Van Buren, born at *Kinderhook,* New York.] **—O.K.** *adv.*
Usage: This word, used as a noun or verb *(he gave his O.K., he okayed the agreement),* is restricted to informal speech and writing, and to some forms of official correspondence, especially in business circles. The form *okay* is generally used when there is an inflectional ending, as in *okayed.*

o·ka·pi (ō-káapi) *n., pl.* **-pis** or collectively **okapi.** A ruminant forest mammal, *Okapia johnstoni,* related to the giraffe, but smaller and having a short neck, found in the Congo region in Africa. [Central African name, from Mbuba.]

O'Keeffe (ō-kéef), **Georgia** (1887–1986). U.S. artist; well known for her semi-abstract paintings of flowers and desert landscapes.

O·ke·fe·no·kee Swamp (ōkəfi-nōki). A swamp on the Georgia-Florida border in the southeast United States. It has rich and varied wildlife, and in Georgia is designated the Okefenokee National Wildlife Refuge.

O·kie (óki) *n. U.S. Informal.* An impoverished migrant farm worker; especially, one from Oklahoma forced to leave his farm during the depression of the 1930s. [From **Oklahoma.**]

O·ki·na·wa (ōki-náawə). *Japanese* **Okinawa Gunto.** An island of Japan. The main island of the Ryukyu group, it is 531 kilometres (330 miles) south of the main Japanese chain. Sugar cane, sweet potatoes, and rice are grown and fishing is important. It was occupied by the United States (1945–72). Naha is the capital.

Ok·la·ho·ma (ōklə-hṓmə). State of south central United States drained by the Red and Arkansas rivers. Western Oklahoma is part of the Great Plains. The central and eastern regions are mostly prairie. Cotton was the major crop but has been superseded by wheat. It is a major oil and gas producing state. Explored by the Spanish, it was bought by the United States as part of the Louisiana Purchase (1803) and the eastern section became Indian Territory. Oklahoma was admitted to the Union, as the forty-sixth state, in 1907. Adverse weather conditions and overuse of the land combined to make northwestern Oklahoma part of the Dust Bowl of the 1930s. State capital, Oklahoma City. **—Ok·la·ho·man** *adj. & n.*

Oklahoma City. State capital of Oklahoma, United States. Lying on the North Canadian river, it was founded (1889) during the Oklahoma Land Rush; it grew rapidly, becoming capital in 1910. It is an important livestock market and has grain mills, meat packing, and cotton processing plants. The city is the centre of a vast oil and natural gas field. It houses one of the nation's largest collections of Indian relics.

o·kra (ŏkrə) *n.* **1.** A tall tropical and semitropical plant, *Hibiscus esculentus,* having edible, mucilaginous green pods. Also called "bhindi", "lady's finger". **2.** The edible pods of this plant, used in soups and as a vegetable. **3.** A dish prepared with okra, **gumbo** *(see).* [West African native name *nkruma.*]

-ol¹ *n. suffix. Chemistry.* Indicates alcohol or phenol; for example, **glycerol, naphthol.** [From ALCOHOL.]

-ol². Variant of **-ole.**

O·laf I (ṓləv), also known as **Olav Tryggvassön** (*c.* 969–1000). King of Norway. He was a Viking marauder of England until converted to Christianity. On his accession to the throne (995) he attempted to convert Norway, causing disaffection. He died at the battle of Svolder, leaping into the sea rather than surrender to the Danes.

Olaf II Haraldsson, Saint, also known as Olaf the Stout (*c.* 995–1030). King and patron saint of Norway. On ascending the throne (1015), he continued Olaf I's conversion of Norway to Christianity. Driven from his kingdom (1028) by Canute the Great, he died in battle at Stiklestad. He was canonised in 1031.

O·lav V (ṓ-ləv, -ləf; *Norwegian* ṓo-lav) (1903–91). King of Norway. Grandson of Edward VII of the U.K., he succeeded Haakon VII (1957) and was succeeded by his son Harald V (1937–).

old (ōld) *adj.* **older, oldest. 1. a.** Having lived or existed for a relatively long time; far advanced in years or life: *a feeble old woman.* See Usage note at **elder. 2. a.** Made long ago; in existence for many years; not new: *an old book.* **b.** No longer current or in use: *old magazines.* **c.** In existence long enough to lack freshness; stale: *This bread is a bit old; the same old answers.* **3.** Of or pertaining to a long life or to persons who have had a long life: *a ripe old age.* **4. a.** Having or exhibiting the physical characteristics of advanced life or an aged person: *She had an old face for her years.* **b.** Weak or infirm from, or as if from, age: *feeling very old.* **5.** Having or exhibiting the wisdom of age; mature; sensible: *That child is old for her years.* **6.** Having a specified age: *She was twelve years old.* **7. a.** Belonging to a remote or former period in history; ancient: *old manuscripts.* **b.** Belonging to or being of an earlier time: *his old classmates.* **c.** Previous: *his old job.* **8.** *Usually capital* **O.** *Abbr.* **O, O.** Being the earlier or earliest of two or more related objects, stages, versions, or periods: *the Old Testament; Old High German.* **9.** *Geology.* **a.** Having become slower in flow and less vigorous in action. Said of rivers. **b.** Having become simpler in form and of lower relief. Said of land forms. **10.** Worn or dilapidated through age or use; worn-out: *an old coat.* **11.** Known through long acquaintance or use; long familiar: *an old friend; the old routine.* **12. a.** Dear or cherished, as through long acquaintance. Used as a term of affection or cordiality: *good old Harry.* **b.** *Chiefly British Informal.* Used with certain nouns as a form of address: *Sorry, old chap! Look here, old thing!* **c.** *Chiefly British Informal.* Used with no definite independent meaning to imply some humorous familiarity: *a touch of the old rheumatism.* **13.** Skilled or able through long experience; practised: *He was an old hand at shipbuilding; an old campaigner.* **~***n.* **1.** Former times; yore: *in days of old.* **2.** An individual of a specified age. Used in combination: *a five-year-old.* [Middle English *old, ald,* Old English *eald, ald,* from West Germanic *aldha* (unattested).] **—old·ish** *adj.* **—old·ness** *n.*
Synonyms: old, elderly, aged, venerable, superannuated, archaic, ancient, elder, obsolete, antique, antiquated.

old age pension *n. Abbr.* **OAP.** *British.* A **retirement pension** *(see).* **—old age pen·sion·er** *n.*

Old Bai·ley (báyli) *n.* Popular name for the Central Criminal Court, the Crown Court for the City of London. It is so called because it stands in the thoroughfare called Old Bailey.

old bird *n. British Informal.* One who is cunning, astute, or shrewd.

old boy *n. British.* **1.** A former pupil of a boys' school, especially a private one. **2.** *Informal.* **a.** An old man. **b.** A husband or senior male colleague. **c.** Used as a familiar term of address to a boy, man, or thing personified as a male.

old boy network *n. British.* An unofficial system of mutual help, especially in obtaining jobs, among men who have shared a usually privileged form of schooling, university background, or the like.

Old Bulgarian *n.* Old Church Slavonic. Not in technical usage. **—Old Bulgarian** *adj.*

Old Catholic *n. Abbr.* **O.C. 1.** A member of a Jansenist church originating in Utrecht in the 18th century. **2.** A member of an independent religious organisation formed by a group of German Roman Catholics who refused to accept the doctrine of papal infallibility proclaimed by the first Vatican Council of 1870. **—Old Catholic** *adj.*

Old Church Slavonic *n.* The literary Slavonic language into which the Bible was translated in the 10th or early 11th century. It is still used as the liturgical language of various Slavonic Eastern churches. **—Old Church Slavonic** *adj.*

old country *n.* The native country of an immigrant.

Old Dutch *n.* Dutch from the beginning of the 12th century to the middle of the 13th. **—Old Dutch** *adj.*

old·en (ṓldən) *adj. Archaic & Poetic.* Old; ancient: *in olden times.* See Synonyms at **old.** [Middle English, from *old,* OLD.]

Ol·den·burg (ṓldən-burg), **Claes (Thure)** (1929–). Swedish-born U.S. sculptor. A leading pop artist, he recreated "ordinary environments", as in *The Store* (1960–61), and "soft sculptures" of household objects made from stuffed vinyl and canvas. Since 1976 he has done installations with his wife Coosje Van Bruggen.

Old English n. Abbr. **OE, OE., O.E. 1.** English from the beginning of the 8th century to the middle of the 12th. Also called "Anglo-Saxon". **2.** Printing. **Gothic** (see). **—Old English** adj.

Old English sheepdog n. A large sturdy dog of a breed having a thick, shaggy, bluish-grey and white coat, with hair that hangs over the eyes.

old-e-stab-lished (ŏld-i-stábblisht, -e-) adj. Established for a long time.

oldest profession n. Prostitution. Used euphemistically, preceded by the.

olde-worlde. Variant of **old-world** (quaint). [Pseudo-archaic spelling.]

old-fash-ioned (ŏld-fásh'nd) adj. **1.** Of a style or method formerly in vogue; outdated; antiquated. **2.** Attached to or favouring methods, ideas, or customs of an earlier time: an old-fashioned girl. **3.** Indicating dignified reproach. Used in the phrase an old-fashioned look. **—See Synonyms at old.**

Old French n. French from the 9th century to the middle of the 16th. **—Old French** adj.

Old Frisian n. Frisian from the beginning of the 13th century to the end of the 15th. **—Old Frisian** adj.

old girl n. British. **1.** A former female pupil of a school, especially a private one. **2.** Informal. **a.** An old woman. **b.** A wife, mother, or senior female colleague. **c.** Used as a familiar form of address to a girl, woman, or thing personified as a female.

Old Glory. A nickname for the flag of the United States.

old gold n. Dark yellow, from light olive or olive brown to deep or strong yellow. **—old-gold** adj.

old guard n. **1.** Capital **O**, capital **G.** The imperial guard of Napoleon I. **2.** A group of defenders of an existing or formerly existing cause or principle. **3.** The conservative, often reactionary element of a given class, society, or political group. **4.** Loosely, any group of people who are experienced in or veterans of a given field. [Translation of French Vieille Garde.]

old hand n. One who has had much practice or experience in a particular sphere of activity.

old hat adj. Informal. Behind the times; no longer new; old-fashioned.

Old High German n. Abbr. **OHG** High German from the middle of the 9th century to the end of the 11th. **—Old High German** adj.

Old Icelandic n. Icelandic from the middle of the 12th century to the middle of the 16th. Also called "Old Norse". **—Old Icelandic** adj.

Old Iranian n. Iranian before the Christian era, the principal attested forms being **Avestan** and **Old Persian** (both of which see). **—Old Iranian** adj.

Old Irish n. Irish Gaelic (see), from 725 A.D. to the mid-tenth century. **—Old Irish** adj.

Old Italian n. Italian before the middle of the 16th century. **—Old Italian** adj.

old lady n. **1.** Informal. **a.** One's mother. **b.** One's wife. **2.** A moth, Mormo maura, having dark brown patterned wings.

Old Latin n. Latin from the first texts (sixth century B.C.) up to the second century B.C. **—Old Latin** adj.

old-line (ŏld-lĭn) adj. U.S. **1.** Adhering to conservative or reactionary principles. **2.** Long established; traditional. **—old-lin-er** n.

Old Low German n. Low German from the middle of the 9th century to the middle of the 13th. Also called "Old Saxon". **—Old Low German** adj.

old maid n. **1.** Informal. A woman who is not married, especially an older woman; a spinster. **2.** Informal. A primly fastidious person. **3.** A children's card game. **—old-maid-ish** (ŏld-máydish) adj.

old man n. **1.** Informal. **a.** One's father. **b.** One's husband. **c.** A man in authority. **2.** A plant, the **southernwood** (see). **3.** Australian. An adult male kangaroo.

old man's beard n. Any of various plants having parts suggestive of a beard, such as **traveller's joy** (see).

old master n. **1.** A distinguished European artist of the period from around 1500 to the early 1700s; especially, one of the great painters of this period. **2.** A work created by an old master.

old moon n. A phase of the waning moon; the last quarter.

Old Nick n. Informal. The devil; Satan.

Old Norse n. Abbr. **ON, O.N. 1.** The North Germanic language from which the modern Scandinavian languages are descended. **2.** This language as represented in either of two national literatures: **a. Old Icelandic** (see). **b.** Old Norwegian. **—Old Norse** adj.

Old Norwegian n. Norwegian from the middle of the 12th century to the end of the 14th. Also called "Old Norse". **—Old Norwegian** adj.

Old Persian n. An ancient form of Persian, recorded in cuneiform inscriptions dating from the sixth to the fifth century B.C. **—Old Persian** adj.

Old Prussian n. The Baltic language of the original Prussians, that became extinct in the 18th century. **—Old Prussian** adj.

old rose n. Dark pink to greyish or moderate red. **—old-rose** adj.

Old Russian n. The Russian language from the 11th to the 16th century. It emerged both as a separate East Slavonic vernacular in private letters and as a liturgical and later literary language based on a South Slavonic dialect, **Old Church Slavonic** (see). **—Old Russian** adj.

Old Saxon n. **Old Low German** (see). **—Old Saxon** adj.

old school n. **1.** Any group committed to traditional ideas or practices. **2.** British. One's former school. **—old-school** adj.

old school tie n. British. **1.** A tie that bears the colours of a particular school, especially one that is prestigious. **2.** The unofficial system of mutual assistance found amongst old members of certain schools, especially British public schools.

Old Slavonic n. The language of those Slavonic texts of the 11th, 12th, and 13th centuries which are written in any of the regional versions of **Old Church Slavonic** (see). **—Old Slavonic** adj.

old soldier n. **1.** A long-serving or retired soldier. **2.** Loosely, one who has accumulated much experience; an old hand.

Old South n. The southern states of the original thirteen American colonies; especially, those that later joined the Confederate States of America: Virginia, North and South Carolina, and Georgia.

Old Spanish n. Spanish before the middle of the 16th century. **—Old Spanish** adj.

old Spanish customs pl.n. British Informal. Traditional practices (such as overmanning in industry) that impede progress or impair efficiency, and that may include the taking of bribes. [Origin obscure.]

old squaw n. A marine duck, Clangula hyemalis, with black and white plumage and long upward-pointing tail feathers, that is found in Arctic and North Temperate regions.

old stager n. Informal. A person with great experience; an old hand.

old-ster (ŏld-stər) n. Informal. An old or elderly person.

Old Stone Age n. See **Palaeolithic.**

Old Style n. Abbr. **O.S.** The old method of reckoning dates according to the Julian calendar.

Old Testament n. Abbr. **OT, O.T. 1.** The first of the two main divisions of the Christian Bible, containing the Hebrew Scriptures. Compare **Hebrew Scriptures. 2.** The covenant of God with Israel as distinguished in Christianity from the dispensation of Christ constituting the New Testament. [Middle English, translation of Late Latin Vetus Testāmentum, translation of Greek Palaia Diathēkē, "Old Covenant", designation based on the Pauline distinction between the covenant with Israel and the new covenant of Christ.]

old-time (ŏld-tĭm) adj. Of or pertaining to a time in the past: old-time dancing; old-time music.

old-tim-er (ŏld-tĭmər) n. Informal. **1.** One who has been a resident, member, employee, or the like for a long time. **2.** An old man.

Old Turkic n. Turkic from the seventh century A.D. to the tenth century, attested in documents from various places in Central Asia, and divided into two principal dialects, Turkut and Old Uighur. **—Old Turkic** adj.

Old Uighur n. See **Old Turkic. —Old Uighur** adj.

Ol-du-vai Gorge (ŏl-dōō-vī, -də-). Gorge in northern Tanzania. It contains archaeological sites rich in fossils and palaeolithic implements. Detailed study of the site began in 1931 by Mary and Louis Leakey. One of their most famous discoveries was Homo habilis. Homo erectus remains have also been found there.

Old Welsh n. Welsh before the 12th century. **—Old Welsh** adj.

old-wife (ŏld-wĭf) n., pl. **-wives** (-wīvz). Any of several fishes, such as the **alewife** and the **menhaden** (both of which see).

old wives' tale n. An example of superstitious folklore, usually claiming to explain natural or medical phenomena.

old woman n. Informal. **1.** A wife or mother. **2.** A nervous or fussy person, especially a male.

Old World n. The countries of the Eastern Hemisphere, including Eurasia and Africa, with special reference to Europe.

old-world (ŏld-wûrld) adj. Also **olde-worlde** (ŏldi-wúrldi). **1.** Antique; old-fashioned; quaint. **2.** Often capital **O**, capital **W.** Native or pertaining to the Eastern Hemisphere, or Old World.

Old World monkey n. Any monkey of the family Cercopithecidae, which is widespread throughout the warmer zones of the Eastern Hemisphere and includes the baboons, macaques, and rhesus and colobus monkeys.

Old Year's Night, Auld Year's Night n. Scottish. New Year's Eve.

o-lé (ō-láy) interj. Used to express excited approval, especially in Spanish-speaking countries.
~n. A cry of olé. [Spanish.]

-ole n. suffix. Indicates small, little; for example, **petiole.** [Latin -olus, -ola, -olum, diminutive suffixes.]

o-le-a-ceous (ŏli-áyshəss) adj. Of or pertaining to the Oleaceae, a family of trees and shrubs containing the olive, ash, and lilac.

o-le-ag-i-nous (ŏli-ájinəss) adj. **1.** Of or pertaining to oil. **2.** Oily; unctuous. [French oléagineux, from Latin oleāginus, belonging to the olive tree, from olea, olive, from Greek elaia.] **—o-le-ag-i-nous-ly** adv. **—o-le-ag-i-nous-ness** n.

o-le-an-der (ŏli-ándər ‖ -andər) n. Any poisonous evergreen shrub of the genus Nerium, found in warm climates, especially N. oleander, having fragrant white, pink, or red flowers. [Medieval Latin, alteration of arodandrum, lorandrum, perhaps from a Vulgar Latin deformation of Latin rhododendron, RHODODENDRON.]

o-le-as-ter (ŏli-ástər ‖ -astər) n. A small Eurasian tree, Elaeagnus angustifolia, having silvery leaves and flowers, and olive-like fruit. Also called "wild olive". [Latin, wild olive tree : olea, olive tree, olive, from Greek elaia + -aster, diminutive suffix.]

o-le-ate (ŏli-ayt) n. An ester or salt of oleic acid. [French oléate : OLE(O)- + -ATE.]

o-lec-ra-non (ō-léckrə-nən, ŏli-kráy- ‖ -non) n. Anatomy. The large point on the upper end of the ulna that projects behind the elbow joint and forms the point of the elbow. Also informally called "funny bone". [New Latin, from Greek ōlekranon, "elbow-tip" : ōlenē, elbow + kranion, head, skull.] **—o-lec-ra-nal** (-n'l), **o-le-cra-**

ni·al (-kráyni-əl), **o·le·cra·ni·an** (-kráyni-ən) adj.

o·le·fine (óli-feen, -fin) n. Also **o·le·fin** (-fin). An **alkene** (see). [French (gaz) oléfiant, "oil forming (gas)", ethylene (which forms an oily liquid with chlorine) : OLE(O)- + -fiant, making, from -fier, -FY + -IN.] —**o·le·fin·ic** (-fínnik) adj.

o·le·ic acid (ō-lée-ik) n. An oily liquid occurring in animal and vegetable oils, $CH_3(CH_2)_7CH:CH(CH_2)_7COOH$; cis-9-octadecanoic acid.

o·le·in (óli-in) n. Also **o·le·ine** (-een, -in). A yellow oily liquid, $(C_{17}H_{33}COO)_3C_3H_5$, occurring naturally in most fats and oils, including olive oil. It is used as a textile lubricant. Also called "triolein". [French oléine : OLE(O)- + -IN.]

oleo-, ole- comb. form. Indicates oil or pertaining to oil; for example, **oleoresin, oleomargarine, oleic**. [French olé-, oléo-, from Latin oleo-, from oleum, (olive) oil, from Greek elaion, (olive) oil, olive.]

o·le·o·graph (óli-ə-graaf, -ō-, -graf) n. 1. A chromolithograph printed in imitation of an oil painting. 2. The lacelike pattern formed by a drop of oil on the surface of water. [OLEO- + -GRAPH.] —**o·le·o·gra·pher** (-óggrəfər) n. —**o·le·o·graph·ic** (-gráffik) adj. —**o·le·og·ra·phy** (-óggrəfi) n.

o·le·o·mar·ga·rine (óli-ō-már-jə-rin, -gə-, -reen) n. Also **o·le·o·mar·ga·rin** (-rin). U.S. **Margarine** (see). Also called "oleo".

oleo oil n. An oil obtained from beef fat and used in the manufacture of certain types of margarine.

o·le·o·res·in (óli-ō-rézzin) n. 1. A naturally occurring mixture of an oil and resin, such as the exudate from pine trees. 2. An oil-resin mixture extracted from plants. —**o·le·o·res·in·ous** (-əss) adj.

o·le·um (óli-əm) n., pl. **-lea** (-ə) or **-ums**. A corrosive solution of sulphur trioxide in sulphuric acid. [Latin, OIL.]

O level n. British. 1. Ordinary level: the lower of the two standards of examination formerly taken for the **GCE** (see). 2. a. An examination at this level. b. A certificate awarded for passing such an examination. Compare **A level**.

ol·fac·tion (ol-fáksh'n ‖ ōl-) n. 1. The sense of smell. 2. The action of smelling. [Latin olfacere, to smell. See olfactory.]

ol·fac·to·ry (ol-fák-tri, -təri ‖ ōl-) adj. Of or contributing to the sense of smell: olfactory organ.
~n., pl. **-ries**. A nerve or organ involved in the sense of smell. [Latin olfactōrius (unattested), from olfacere, to smell : olēre, to smell + facere, to make.]

olfactory nerve n. Either of two bundles of nerve fibres, one on each side of the nasal cavity, that conduct chemical indications of smell.

o·lib·a·num (o-líbbənəm, ō-) n. A gum resin, **frankincense** (see). [Middle English, from Medieval Latin, from Arabic al-lubān, "the frankincense", probably from Greek libanos, of Semitic origin, akin to Hebrew lĕbōriā, incense.]

ol·i·garch (ólli-gaark) n. A member of an oligarchy. [Greek oligar-khēs : OLIG(O)- + -arkhēs, -ARCH.]

ol·i·gar·chy (ólli-gaarki) n., pl. **-chies**. 1. a. Government by the few, especially by a small faction of persons or families. b. Those making up such a faction. 2. A state governed by oligarchy: "Greek oligarchies were based on . . . the notion that their members were superior to other men." (Maurice Bowra). —**ol·i·gar·chal** (-gárk'l), **ol·i·gar·chic** (-gárkik), **ol·i·gar·chi·cal** (-kəl) adj.

oligo-, olig- comb. form. Indicates few; for example, **oligopoly, oligosaccharide**. [Greek, from oligos, few, little.]

Ol·i·go·cene (ólligō-seen, o-líg-, -ə-) adj. Of or designating the geological era and deposits of the epoch in the Tertiary period of the Cenozoic era that extended from the Eocene to the Miocene.
~n. 1. The Oligocene epoch. Preceded by the. 2. The deposits of this epoch. [OLIGO- + -CENE.]

ol·i·go·chaete (ólligō-keet) n. Any of various worms of the class Oligochaeta, including the earthworms. [New Latin Oligochaeta : OLIGO- + CHAETA.] —**ol·i·go·chaete** adj. —**ol·i·go·chae·tous** (-kéetəss) adj.

ol·i·go·clase (ólligō-klayz, -klayss) n. One of the plagioclase group of minerals. It is greyish green to yellowish white, and occurs mainly in acid to intermediate igneous rocks. [German Oligoklas : OLIGO- + -CLASE.]

o·li·go·mer (ólligə-mər) n. A molecule consisting of only two, three, or four monomers, that can combine with more monomers to form a polymer. [OLIGO- + -MER.]

ol·i·go·phre·ni·a (ólligō-frèeni-ə) n. Arrested mental development, **mental deficiency** (see). Not in technical usage. [New Latin : OLIGO- + -PHRENIA.] —**ol·i·go·phren·ic** (-frénnik) adj.

ol·i·gop·o·ly (ólli-góppə-li) n., pl. **-lies**. Economics. A market condition in which sellers are so few that the actions of any one of them will materially affect price and hence have a measurable impact upon competitors. Compare **monopoly**. [OLIGO- + (MONO)POLY.] —**ol·i·gop·o·lis·tic** (-lístik) adj.

ol·i·gop·so·ny (ólli-góppsə-ni) n., pl. **-nies**. Economics. A market condition in which purchasers are so few that the actions of any one of them can materially affect price and hence the costs that competitors must pay. Compare **monopsony**. [OLIG(O)- + (MON)OPSONY.] —**ol·i·gop·so·nis·tic** (-nístik) adj.

ol·i·go·sac·cha·ride (ólligō-sáckə-rīd, -rid) n. Any carbohydrate in which a few monosaccharide units are joined together.

ol·i·go·troph·ic (ólligō-tróffik) adj. Poor in plant nutrients and hence plant life, but rich in oxygen. Said of lakes and similar habitats.

ol·i·gu·ri·a (ólli-géwr-i-ə) n. Also **ol·i·gu·re·sis** (-gewr-ée-siss). The

excretion of an abnormally small volume of urine in relation to fluid intake.

o·li·o (óli-ō) n., pl. **-os**. 1. A heavily spiced stew of meat, vegetables, and chickpeas. 2. a. Any mixture or medley; a potpourri. b. A collection of various artistic or literary works or musical pieces; a miscellany. [Modification of Spanish olla, pot, OLLA.]

ol·i·va·ceous (ólli-váyshəss) adj. Olive-green. [OLIV(E) + -ACEOUS.]

ol·i·var·y (óli-vəri ‖ -verri) adj. 1. Shaped like an olive. 2. Anatomy. Of or pertaining to one of the two oval bodies of nervous tissue (olivary bodies) found on either side of the medulla oblongata. In this sense, also called "olive". [Latin olīvārius, from olīva, OLIVE.]

ol·ive (ólliv) n. 1. An Old World semitropical evergreen tree, Olea europaea, having an edible fruit, white flowers, and leathery leaves. 2. The small ovoid fruit of this tree, an important food from the earliest historical times and a source of oil. 3. An olivary. 4. The wood of the olive tree. 5. Yellowish to brownish green. [Middle English, from Old French, from Latin olīva, from Greek elaia.] —**ol·ive** adj.

olive branch n. 1. A branch of an olive tree regarded as an emblem of peace. 2. An offer of peace.

olive drab n. U.S. 1. Greyish olive to dark olive brown or olive grey. 2. a. Cloth of this colour. b. A U.S. army uniform made from such cloth. —**ol·ive-drab** (ólliv-dráb) adj.

olive green n. Greenish yellow. —**ol·ive-green** (ólliv-gréen) adj.

ol·i·ve·nite (o-lívvə-nīt, ə- ‖ ólli-) n. A basic arsenate of copper, $Cu_3As_2O_8\cdot Cu(OH)_2$, brown, olive-green, or grey in colour, found in copper deposits. [German Olivenit : OLIVE + -ITE.]

olive oil n. Oil pressed from olives, used in salad dressings, for cooking, as an ingredient of soaps, and as a skin softener.

Ol·ives, Mount of (óllivz). Hill in west Jordan under Israeli Military Administration. Lying in east Jerusalem, it is the Biblical site of the Garden of Gethsemane and of Christ's ascension.

Olivier (ə-lívvi-ay, o- ‖ ō-), **Laurence (Kerr), Baron Olivier of Brighton** (1907–89). British actor. He established himself as an international star of stage and films before World War II. He directed and starred in film adaptations of Shakespeare's Henry V (1944), Hamlet (1948), Richard III (1955), and Othello (1965). Director, (Royal) National Theatre Company (1961–73).

ol·i·vine (ólli-veen, -véen) n. 1. Any of a group of mineral silicates, all members of which consist of compounds of iron silicate and magnesium silicate in various proportions. They occur in basic and ultrabasic igneous rocks and some metamorphic rocks. Also called "chrysolite". 2. A transparent green variety valued as a gem. Also called "peridot". [German Olivin, chrysolite : OLIVE (because of its colour) + -IN.]

o·lla (óllə, Spanish ól-yə) n. 1. An earthenware pot or jar with a wide mouth. 2. An olla podrida. [Spanish, from Old Spanish, from Latin olla, variant of aulla, jar, pot.]

o·lla po·dri·da (po-dréedə, pə-, Spanish -thréetha) n. 1. A stew of highly seasoned meat and vegetables. 2. Any assorted mixture or miscellany. [Spanish, "rotten pot" : OLLA + podrida, rotten, from Latin putridus, from putrēre, to rot, from puter, decaying, rotten.]

olm (olm, ōlm) n. An unpigmented eel-like salamander, Proteus anguinus, found in underground caves in southeastern Europe. [German.]

o·lo·gy (ólləji) n., pl. **-gies**. Informal. Any of various studies or concepts designated by terms ending in -logy and thereby regarded as generically related. Usually used humorously.

o·lo·ro·so (óllə-rṓ-sō, ṓlə-, -zō) n. A full-bodied, medium-sweet sherry. [Spanish, "fragrant".]

O·lym·pi·a (ə-límpi-ə, ō-). City of ancient Greece situated in the West Peloponnese. It was the scene of the Olympic Games and the site of the temple of Zeus, which contained the statue of Zeus by Phidias, one of the Seven Wonders of the World.

O·lym·pi·ad (ə-límpi-ad, ō-) n. 1. The interval of four years between celebrations of the Olympic Games, by which the ancient Greeks reckoned dates. 2. A celebration of the modern Olympic Games. 3. A regularly held international competition in games such as chess or bridge. [Middle English Olympiade, from Latin Olympias, from Greek Olumpias (stem Olumpiad-), from Olumpia, OLYMPIA.]

O·lym·pi·an (ə-límpi-ən, ō-) adj. 1. Of or pertaining to the greater gods of the ancient Greek pantheon, whose abode was Olympus. 2. a. Majestic in manner. b. Superior to or aloof from mundane affairs.
~n. 1. Any of the 12 major gods inhabiting Olympus. 2. One who exhibits Olympian qualities. 3. A contestant in the Olympic Games.

O·lym·pic (ə-límpik, ō-) adj. Of or belonging to the games held at Olympia or the modern international revival of them.

Olympic Games pl.n. 1. In ancient Greece, a Pan-Hellenic festival of athletic games and contests of choral poetry and dance, first celebrated in 776 B.C., and held every four years until A.D. 393 on the plain of Olympia in honour of the Olympian Zeus. 2. A modern international revival of athletic and sports contests on the model of these ancient games, held every four years. In this sense, also called the "Olympics".

O·lym·pus, Mount (ə-límpəss, ō-). Greek Óros Ólimbos. The highest mountain of Greece (2 917 metres; 9,570 feet). In Greek mythology it is the home of the gods.

Om (ōm) n. In Hindu theology, a sacred syllable that embodies the ultimate, divine principle and is used as a mantra in meditation. [Sanskrit.]

OM. Ostmark.

O.M. Order of Merit.

-oma *n. comb. form.* Indicates tumour; for example, **fibroma, myoma.** [New Latin, from Greek *-ōma,* abstract nominal ending formed from *-o-* stem verbs.]

O·magh (ō-máa, ōmə). Town in Northern Ireland. Lying on the river Strule, it is the county town of Tyrone.

O·man, Sultanate of (ō-máan, -mán). Formerly **Muscat and Oman.** Sultanate located in the southeast of the Arabian peninsula. It is a fertile coastal plain backed by hill ranges and an interior desert plateau. Dates, limes, sugar cane, and cattle are the chief products. Oil is the major source of revenue. Oman has had a close association with Britain since the late 18th century. Area, 309 500 square kilometres (119,500 square miles). Population, 2,300,000. Capital, Muscat.

O·mar Khay·yam (ōmaar kī-ám ‖ -áam) (*c.*1050–1123). Persian poet and mathematician. Though his astronomical observations were instrumental in the reform of the Islamic calendar, he is best known in the West for his *Ruba'iyat* of nearly 500 quatrains expressing wistful, agnostic hedonism, some of which were first translated into English (1859) by Edward Fitzgerald.

o·ma·sum (ō-máy-səm, ə-) *n., pl.* **-sa** (-sə). The third stomach of a ruminant animal, located between the **abomasum** and the **reticulum** (*both of which see*). Also called "manyplies", "psalterium". [Latin *omāsum,* pouch, bullock's tripe, probably from Gaulish.]

om·bre (ómbər) *n.* Also *chiefly U.S.* **om·ber.** A card game played by three players with forty cards, that was popular in Europe during the 17th and 18th centuries. [Spanish *hombre,* "man" (name given to the player who attempts to win the pool), from Latin *homo.*]

om·buds·man (óm-bŏŏdz-mən, -man ‖ -budz-) *n., pl.* **-men** (-men, -mən). In Britain, any of several officials who investigate citizens' complaints of maladministration by government departments (Parliamentary Commissioner for Administration), local authorities or local police authorities (Commissioner for Local Administration), or the National Health Service (Health Service Commissioner). [Swedish, from Old Norse *umbodhsmadhr,* "administration-man, king's representative" : *um,* about + *bodh,* command + *madhr,* (rarely) *mannr,* man.]

Om·dur·man (ómder-máan, -mán). City of the central Sudan. The nation's second city and former capital (1885–98), it is situated on the left bank of the White Nile, opposite Khartoum.

-ome *n. suffix. Biology.* Indicates mass, body, or group; for example, **biome, phyllome.** [Variant of -OMA.]

o·me·ga (ómi-gə, ōmə- ‖ *chiefly U.S.* ō-máygə, -méggə, -méegə) *n.* **1.** The 24th and final letter in the Greek alphabet, written Ω, ω. Transliterated in English as *o* or sometimes as *ō.* **2.** The ending; the last of anything: "*I am Alpha and Omega, the beginning and the ending*" (Revelation 1:8). **3.** *Symbol* Ω⁻ *Physics.* A fundamental particle in the baryon family, having a mass 3,276 times that of the electron, a negative electric charge, and a mean lifetime of 1.5 × 10⁻¹⁰ second. Also called "omega minus". See **particle.** [Greek *ō mega,* "large O" : *ō* + *mega,* neuter of *megas,* large, great.]

om·e·lette (óm-lət, -lit, -let ‖ ómmə-) *n.* Also *chiefly U.S.* **om·e·let.** A dish prepared in a shallow pan, consisting of beaten egg cooked in fat until set, and often having a variety of savoury or sweet fillings. [French *omelette,* from Old French *amelette,* "thin plate",

alteration of *alumette,* variant of *alumelle,* from *lemelle,* from Latin *lāmella,* thin metal plate, diminutive of *lāmina,* plate, layer.]

o·men (ō-men, -mən) *n.* **1.** Any phenomenon supposed to portend good or evil; a prophetic sign. **2.** Prognostication; portent.
~*tr.v.* **omened, omening, omens.** To be an omen of; portend; presage. [Latin *ōmen.*]

o·men·tum (ō-mén-təm, ə-) *n., pl.* **-ta** (-tə). *Anatomy.* Either of two pairs of peritoneal folds. The greater omentum consists of a double fold of peritoneum which covers the stomach and the intestine; the lesser omentum is doubled to link the stomach and duodenum to the liver. [Latin *ōmentum†.*] —**o·men·tal** *adj.*

om·i·cron (ō-mī-krən, -kron ‖ *chiefly U.S.* ómmi-, ōmi-) *n.* The 15th letter in the Greek alphabet, written O, *o.* Transliterated as *o.* [Greek *o mikron,* "small o" : *o* + *mikron,* neuter of *mikros,* small.]

om·i·nous (ómmi-nəss, *rarely* ōmi-) *adj.* **1.** Menacing; threatening: *an ominous silence.* **2.** Being or pertaining to an evil omen; portentous. [Latin *ōminōsus,* from *ōmen* (stem *ōmin-*), OMEN.] —**om·i·nous·ly** *adv.* —**om·i·nous·ness** *n.*

o·mis·sion (ō-mísh'n, ə-) *n.* **1.** The act or an instance of omitting. **2.** The state of being omitted. **3.** Something that is omitted or neglected. [Middle English *omissioun,* from Late Latin *omissiō* (stem *omissiōn-*), from Latin *omittere* (past participle *omissus-*), to OMIT.] —**o·mis·sive** (-míssiv) *adj.*

o·mit (ō-mít, ə-) *tr.v.* **omitted, omitting, omits.** **1.** To leave out; fail to include: *a name omitted from the list.* **2.** To pass over; neglect; fail to do: *omitted to tell her.* [Middle English *omitten,* from Latin *omittere* : *ob-,* away + *mittere,* to send.] —**o·mis·si·ble** (-míssəb'l) *adj.*

om·ma·tid·i·um (ómmə-tíddi-əm) *n., pl.* **-ia** (-ə). *Zoology.* One of the elements, resembling a single simplified eye, that make up the compound eye of arthropods. [New Latin, "small eye" : Greek *omma* (stem *ommat-*), eye + -IDIUM.] —**om·ma·tid·i·al** *adj.*

om·mat·o·phore (o-máttə-fawr, ə- ‖ ō-, -fōr) *n. Zoology.* A movable stalk ending with an eye, as found in snails. [Greek *omma* (stem *ommat-*), eye + -PHORE.] —**om·ma·toph·o·rous** (ommə-tóffərəss) *adj.*

Ommiad. Variant of **Umayyad.**

omni- *comb. form.* Indicates all, everywhere; for example, **omnidirectional, omnirange.** [Latin, from *omnis,* all.]

om·ni·bus (óm-ni-bəss, -buss) *n., pl.* **-buses. 1.** A bus (*see*). **2.** A printed anthology of the works of one author or of writings on a related subject. **3.** A single transmission of a week's broadcasts of a series such as a soap. Also called "omnibus edition".
~*adj.* Including many things or classes; covering many things or situations at once. [French (*voiture*) *omnibus* "(vehicle) for all", and Latin *omnibus* "for all", dative plural of *omnis,* all.]

om·ni·com·pe·tent (óm-ni-kómpitənt) *adj.* Capable of judging or handling all matters. —**om·ni·com·pe·tence** *n.*

om·ni·di·rec·tion·al (óm-ni-di-réksh'n'l, -dīr-) *adj.* Capable of transmitting or receiving signals in all directions.

om·ni·far·i·ous (óm-ni-faír-i-əss) *adj.* Of all sorts and kinds: *omnifarious knowledge.* [Late Latin *omnifarius* : OMNI- + *fārius,* "-doing"; akin to *facere,* to do.] —**om·ni·far·i·ous·ness** *n.*

om·nif·ic (om-níffik) *adj.* Also **om·nif·i·cent** (-níffiss'nt). *Rare.* All-creating. [Medieval Latin *omnificus* : OMNI- + -FIC.]

om·nip·o·tent (om-níppə-tənt) *adj.* **1.** Having a great amount of power, authority, or sway: *omnipotent police.* **2.** All-powerful: *an omnipotent god.*
~*n. Capital* **O.** God. Preceded by *the.* [Middle English, from Old French, from Latin *omnipotēns* : OMNI- + *potēns,* POTENT.] —**om·nip·o·tence** (-təns) *n.*

om·ni·pres·ence (óm-ni-prézz'nss) *n.* The fact of being present everywhere. [Medieval Latin *omnipraesentia,* from *omnipraesēns* : OMNI- + *praesēns,* PRESENT.] —**om·ni·pres·ent** *adj.*

om·ni·range (óm-ni-raynj) *n.* A radio network that provides complete bearing information for aircraft. Also called "omnidirectional radio range".

om·nis·cient (om-níssi-ənt, -níshi-, -nísh-) *adj.* **1.** Having total knowledge; knowing everything. **2.** Having great knowledge.
~*n. Capital* **O.** God. Preceded by *the.* [Latin *omnisciēns* : OMNI- + *sciēns* (stem *scient-*), present participle of *scīre,* to know.] —**om·nis·cience** (-ənss), **om·nis·cien·cy** *n.* —**om·nis·cient·ly** *adv.*

om·ni·um-gath·er·um (óm-ni-əm-gáthərəm) *n.* A miscellaneous collection; a hotchpotch. [Mock Latin formation : Latin *omnium,* of all, genitive plural of *omnis,* all + GATHER.]

om·ni·vore (óm-ni-vawr ‖ -vōr) *n.* An omnivorous animal. [Latin *omnivorus,* OMNIVOROUS.]

om·niv·o·rous (om-nívvərəss) *adj.* **1.** *Zoology.* Eating both animal and vegetable substances. **2.** Eating all kinds of food: *Pigs are omnivorous creatures.* **3.** Taking in everything available, as with the mind: *an omnivorous reader.* [Latin *omnivorus* : OMNI- + -VOROUS.] —**om·niv·o·rous·ly** *adv.* —**om·niv·o·rous·ness** *n.*

OMOV (ómov) *n.* One-man-one-vote; one-member-one-vote.

om·pha·los (ómfə-loss, -ləss) *n., pl.* **-li** (-lī). **1.** In Ancient Greece, a stone at Delphi thought to mark the centre of the earth. **2.** *Formal.* The navel. **3.** A centre. [Greek.]

Omsk (omsk). City of eastern Russia, founded (1716) at the confluence of the Om and Irtysh rivers. It is a major junction on the Trans-Siberian Railway, and an industrial centre.

on (on ‖ awn) *prep.* **1.** Used to indicate: **a.** Position upon and above the surface of; position in contact with and supported by the surface of: *The vase is on the table.* **b.** Contact, as between two surfaces: *mud on trousers; a ring on her finger.* **c.** Location at or along: *a house on the beach.* **d.** Proximity: *a town on the border; on the

brink of extinction. **e.** Attachment to or suspension from: *beads on a string.* **2.** Used to indicate: **a.** Motion towards, against, or onto: *jump on the table; the march on Moscow.* **b.** Direction or tendency as regards: *had a crush on her; an attack on the press.* **c.** Affecting: *hard on her parents; backed out on us.* **d.** A comparison or point of reference: *an improvement on last time.* **3.** Used to indicate: **a.** Occurrence during: *on the third of July.* **b.** The point of time of a specified action: *On entering the room, she saw me.* **c.** The exact moment or point of: *every hour on the hour.* **d.** After a specified process: *on reflection.* **e.** A current occupation: *on her rounds; on duty.* **4.** Used to indicate a connection between an object and a perceptible agent or agency: *I cut my foot on the broken glass; night fell on the town.* **5.** Used to indicate: **a.** A means of support or a sustaining source or agency: *live on bread and water; survives on a small income.* **b.** A means of progress or transmission: *on foot; on the radio.* **6.** Used to indicate: **a.** The state, condition, mode, or process of: *on record; on fire; on the increase.* **b.** The purpose of: *travel on business.* **c.** Availability by means of: *beer on tap; a nurse on call.* **d.** Association with; membership of: *a doctor on the hospital staff; on the board of directors.* **e.** The ground or basis for: *I refused it on principle.* **f.** Addition or repetition: *error on error; 10 per cent on the bill.* **7.** Concerning; about: *a book on astronomy.* **8.** In one's possession; with: *I haven't a penny on me.* **9.** At the expense of: *drinks on the house.* **10.** Indicates regular intake: *on drugs; back on the booze.* **11.** Indicates way or manner. Preceded by *the*: *on the quiet, on the sly.* **12.** Used preceded by an adjective indicating an attitude or characteristic: *keen on tennis; weak on dates.* **13.** *British Informal.* Earning: *You must be on a small fortune in that job.*
~adv. **1.** In or into a position of being attached to or covering something: *Put your clothes on.* **2.** In or into a state or condition of receiving a source of energy, such as electricity: *put the kettle on; turn the radio on.* **3. a.** In the direction of something visible: *looked on while the ship docked.* **b.** With a specified part forward or visible: *edge on.* **4. a.** Towards or at a point lying ahead in space or time; forward: *moved on to the next town.* **b.** At or to a specified point in time or space: *I'll do it later on.* **5.** In a continuous or persistent manner: *She worked on quietly.* **6.** In or at the present position: *stay on; hang on.* **—and so on.** And like the preceding; and so forth. **—on and off.** Intermittently. **—on and on.** Without stopping; continuously. **—on at.** *Informal.* Complaining to or nagging: *She's always on at me.* **—on to.** *Informal.* Having made a discovery about: *We're on to something big.*
~adj. **1. a.** Operating; playing: *The radio is on; Louis Armstrong on trumpet.* **b.** Being supplied. Said especially of electricity, gas, and water. **2.** Taking place or due to take place: *There's a conference on now.* **3.** Onstage or about to go onstage: *You're on after the conjurer.* **4.** Ready to join in some activity: *I'm on for a game.* **5.** Designating or placed on the legside of a cricket pitch: *an on drive.* **—not on.** *Informal.* **1.** Unable to be performed or accomplished: *a good idea, but it's not on.* **2.** Violating accepted standards: *His behaviour just wasn't on.*
~n. In cricket, the side of the cricket pitch that is on the **leg** *(see).* [Middle English *on,* preposition and adverb, Old English *on, an,* from Germanic.]

Usage: To indicate motion to a particular position, the prepositions *on* and *onto* are often interchangeable, though *onto* more strongly conveys movement towards the position: *He jumped on/onto the table. He jumped on the table* means he was already on it and started jumping — or that he jumped down on it from above. If he jumped up, you have to use *onto.* In such contexts, *onto* is written as a single word. When *on* is adverbial, however, it is written separately: *Let us move on to a new topic.* The same is true of *on* and *upon*: *He jumped upon the table; He clambered up on the table.*

-on *n. suffix.* Indicates subatomic particle, unit, or quantum; for example, **electron, photon.** [From (I)ON.]

on·a·ger (ónnə-jər, -gər) *n., pl.* **-gers** or **-gri** (-grī). **1.** A wild ass, *Equus hemionus onager,* of central Asia. **2.** An ancient and medieval stone-propelling siege engine. [Middle English, from Latin *onager,* from Greek *onagros* : *onos,* ass + *agros,* field.]

o·nan·ism (ṓ-nan-iz'm, -nən-) *n.* **1.** Masturbation. **2.** Coitus interruptus. [After *Onan,* son of Judah (Genesis 38:9).] **—o·nan·ist** *n.* **—o·nan·is·tic** (-ístik) *adj.*

O·nas·sis (ō-nássiss, o-, ə-), **Aristotle (Socrates)** (1906–75). Greek entrepreneur. Owning one of the world's largest private commercial fleets, he pioneered the use of oil supertankers.

O.N.C. Ordinary National Certificate: an academic qualification in technical subjects in Britain.

once (wunss || *Northern England also* wonss. *The pronunciation* wunst *is not standard.*) *adv.* **1.** One time only: *once a day.* **2.** At one time in the past; formerly. **3.** At any time; ever: *Once known, never forgotten.* **4.** By one degree: *She is my first cousin once removed.* **—once and for all.** Finally; conclusively.
~n. A single occurrence; one time: *You can go this once.* **—all at once. 1.** All at the same time. **2.** Suddenly. **—at once. 1.** Without delay; immediately. **2.** All together; simultaneously.
~conj. As soon as; if ever; when: *Once he goes, I can clean up.*
~n. One time or occasion: *Once is enough; Please, just for once, be quiet.* [Middle English *ones, anes,* adverbial genitive of *on, an,* ONE.]

once-o·ver (wúnss-ōvər || wónss-) *n. Informal.* **1.** A quick but comprehensive glance or survey. Often preceded by *the.* **2.** A quick beating: *gave him the once-over.*

onc·er (wún-sər || wón-) *n. British Slang.* A one-pound note. [ONCE + -ER.]

onco- *comb. form.* Indicates tumour; for example, **oncogenic, oncology.** [Greek *onkos,* mass.]

on·co·gen·e·sis (óngkō-jénnə-siss) *n.* The formation and development of a tumour.

on·co·gen·ic (óngkō-jénnik) *adj.* Also **on·co·gen·ous** (ong-kójənəss, on-). Producing a tumour or tumours. [ONCO- + -GENIC.]

on·col·o·gy (ong-kólləji, on-) *n.* The scientific study of tumours. [ONCO- + -LOGY.] **—on·co·log·i·cal** (óngkə-lójik'l) *adj.* **—on·col·o·gist** (-kólləjist) *n.*

on·com·ing (ón-kumming || áwn-) *adj.* Coming nearer; approaching: *the oncoming storm.*
~n. An approach; an advance.

on·co·sphere (óngkō-sfeer) *n.* The six-hooked larva of a tapeworm, which, if ingested by an appropriate host, penetrates the intestine wall and invades muscle tissue. Also called "hexacanth". [Greek *onkos,* barb + SPHERE.]

on-cost (ón-kost || áwn-, -kawst) *n.* An overhead cost.

O.N.D. *n. British.* Ordinary National Diploma: an academic qualification in technical subjects in Britain.

ondes Mar·te·not (óND mártə-nō) *pl.n.* A musical instrument that uses electronic vibrations to produce characteristically eerie tones. [French, "Martenot waves", after Maurice *Martenot* (1898–1980), who invented it.]

on dit (óN-dée) *n., pl.* **on dits** (-dée, -déez). *French.* A piece of gossip or hearsay. [Literally, it is said.]

on·do·graph (ón-dō-graaf, -də-, -graf) *n.* An instrument that produces a graphical trace representing an alternating current by measuring the charge imparted to a capacitor at different points in the cycle. [French, from *onde,* wave + -GRAPH.]

on·dom·e·ter (on-dómmitər) *n.* An instrument that measures the frequency of electromagnetic waves, especially in the radio-frequency band. [French *onde,* wave + METER.]

one (wun || *Northern England also* won) *adj.* **1.** Designating a single entity, unit, object, or being; single; individual. Sometimes used in combination: *one-eyed.* **2.** Characterised by unity; of a single kind or nature; undivided: *with one accord; one with my colleagues.* **3.** Designating a person or thing that is contrasted with another or others: *from one end to the other.* **4.** Designating a specified but indefinite thing or time: *He will come one day.* **5. a.** Designating a certain person, especially a person not previously known or mentioned: *One Mr. Jones called for you.* **b.** Designating an indefinite time or occasion: *One Tuesday, he returned.* **6.** *U.S.* A or an. Used informally as a substitute for the indefinite article for emphasis: *That is one fine dog.* **7.** Single in kind; alike or the same. **8.** Being unique in some specified respect: *The one man to leave.*
~n. **1. a.** The first cardinal number; the first positive whole number after zero. **b.** A symbol representing this, such as 1, I, or i. **2.** A size or thing designated as one. **3.** A single person or thing; a unit: *The one in the High street.* **4.** The first in a series. **5.** A banknote or coin having a denomination of one. **6.** One hour after midnight or midday. **7.** *British Informal.* A humorous or jocular person: *You are a one!* **—a right one.** *British Informal.* A fool or nuisance: *We've got a right one here!*
~pron. **1.** A certain person or thing; someone or something. **2.** Any person or thing; anyone or anything: *It's as good as one will get.* **3. a.** Any person representing the same, usually privileged, social class as the speaker: *One does meet intelligent people at Oxford.* **b.** The speaker: *One does so dislike package holidays.* **4.** A single person or thing among persons or things already known or mentioned: *one of the Elizabethans.* **—at one.** In accord or unity. **—in one.** At the first or in a single attempt: *got it in one; downed it in one.* **—one and all.** Everyone. **—one another.** Each other. Used to describe a reciprocal relation or action. **—one by one.** Individually and in succession. **—one up.** *Informal.* In a position of psychological superiority: *one up on the neighbours.* [Middle English *an, on,* Old English *ān.*]

Usage: *One* and *ones* should not be used immediately after a determiner such as *these, those,* or *many. Do you want to buy these books as well as those (books)?* is preferred to *Do you want to buy these books as well as those ones?* However, . . . *as well as those red/nice/inexpensive ones* is perfectly acceptable.

Formal British English is strict about maintaining the use of *one* as a generalising third person pronoun, and sequences such as *One should look after oneself, shouldn't one?* will be heard. American English is more likely to replace such sequences by forms of *he*: *One should ask himself . . . One* is particularly associated with extremely formal speech, where it is often used as a replacement for the first person form even in relation to mundane topics (*One fell off one's horse,* where the meaning is "I fell off my horse"). Because of these associations, the usage is frequently the butt of satire, and nowadays is often avoided, even in formal speech.

-one *n. suffix.* Indicates: **1.** An oxygen-containing or ketone compound; for example, **acetone. 2.** A chemical compound containing oxygen, especially in a carbonyl or similar group; for example, **lactone.** [Greek *-ōnē,* feminine patronymic suffix.]

one-armed bandit (wún-ármd-bándit || wón-) *n. Informal.* A fruit machine, especially one with an arm-like handle that is pulled to set the machine in motion.

one-di·men·sion·al (wún-dī-ménsh'n'l, -di- || wón-) *adj.* Having only one dimension; unidimensional.

O·ne·ga, Lake (on-yáygə). Lake of northwest Russia, Europe's second largest lake, it is drained by the Onega river northwards to the White Sea, and connected by canal to the Baltic Sea and the river Volga. Petrozavodsk is the chief port.

one-horse (wún-hórss || wón-) *adj.* **1.** Drawn by or using only one horse: *a one-horse carriage.* **2.** Contemptibly small, limited, or insignificant: *a one-horse town.* **3.** Describing a contest of which the result is a foregone conclusion: **a one-horse race.**

O·nei·da (ō-nī́də) *n., pl.* **-das** or collectively **Oneida. 1.** A member of one of the five peoples belonging to the league of the Iroquois. **2.** The Iroquoian language of this people. **—O·nei·da** *adj.*

O'Neill (ō-née̍l, ə-), **Eugene (Gladstone)** (1888-1953). U.S. playwright. His best-known works include *Mourning Becomes Electra* (1931), an adaptation of the *Oresteia* of Aeschylus, and *Long Day's Journey Into Night* (1941). He was awarded the Nobel prize for literature (1936).

O'Neill, Terence Marne, Baron (1914–90). Northern Irish politician. Becoming Unionist prime minister of the province in 1963, he was forced to resign (1969) over concessions granted to the Catholic Civil Rights campaign. He was made a life peer (1970).

o·nei·ric (o-nī́r-ik, ə-, ō-) *adj.* Of or pertaining to dreams. [Greek *oneiros,* dream.]

oneiro- *comb. form.* Indicates dreams; for example, **oneirocritic.** [Greek *oneiros,* dream.]

o·nei·ro·crit·ic (o-nī́r-ō-kríttik, ə-, ō-, -ə-) *n.* One who interprets dreams. [Greek *oneirokritikos* : ONEIRO- + CRITIC.] **—o·nei·ro·crit·i·cal** *adj.* **—o·nei·ro·crit·i·cism** (-krítti-siz'm) *n.*

on·ei·rol·o·gy (ón-īr-óllәji, ṓn-) *n.* The art of interpreting dreams. [ONEIRO- + -LOGY.]

o·nei·ro·man·cy (o-nī́r-ə-man-si, ə-, ō-, -ō-) *n.* Divination by dreams. [Greek *oneiros,* dream + -MANCY.] **—o·nei·ro·man·cer** *n.*

one-lin·er (wún-lī́nər || wón-) *n. Chiefly U.S. Informal.* A short, pithy joke or comment.

one-man (wún-mán || wón-) *adj.* Of, pertaining to, consisting of, or performed by one man: *a one-man show.*

one-man band *n.* **1.** A performer, usually a street musician, who plays a number of instruments at once, such as a drum, trumpet, and pair of cymbals, which are fastened to each other and to his body. **2.** A person who single-handedly performs various functions that are more usually performed by a number of people.

one-man, one-vote *n.* Also **OMOV.** A voting system in which each member of a population or membership is entitled to an equal vote in an election.

one·ness (wún-nəss, -niss || wón-) *n.* **1.** The quality or state of being one; singleness: *the infinite oneness of God.* **2.** Singularity; uniqueness. **3.** Undividedness; wholeness. **4.** Sameness of character or nature: *the dull oneness of motorway landscapes.* **5.** Unison; agreement: *oneness of mind and purpose.*

one-night stand (wún-nīt || wón-) *n.* **1.** A performance, by a theatre company for example, in one place on one night only. **2.** *Informal.* **a.** A sexual encounter lasting only one evening or night. **b.** The other person involved in such an encounter.

one-off (wún-óff, -áwf || wón-) *n. British.* One who or that which is highly original or individual, or is not intended to be copied or repeated. Also used adjectivally: *a one-off performance.*

one-piece (wún-péess || wón-) *adj.* Consisting of one piece: *a one-piece bathing costume.*

on·er·ous (ónnə-rəss, ṓnə-) *adj.* **1.** Troublesome or oppressive; burdensome. **2.** *Law.* Entailing obligations that exceed any advantage to the possessor. Said, for example, of a contract. —See Synonyms at **burdensome.** [Middle English, from Old French *onereus,* from Latin *onerōsus,* from *onus* (stem *oner-*), burden.] **—on·er·ous·ly** *adv.* **—on·er·ous·ness** *n.*

one·self (wun-sélf || won-) *pron.* Also **one's self.** A specialised form of the third person singular pronoun **one.** It is used: **1.** As a reflexive pronoun, forming the direct or indirect object of a verb or the object of a preposition: *faith in oneself.* **2.** For emphasis, after *one*: *One must take a certain amount of initiative oneself.* **3.** As an emphasising substitute for *one*: *Oneself is usually to blame.* **4.** As an indication of one's real, normal, or healthy condition or identity: *come to oneself.* **5.** Euphemistically, to indicate one's genitals or private parts: *to expose oneself; to play with oneself.*

one-sid·ed (wún-sī́did || wón-) *adj.* **1. a.** Favouring one side or group; partial; biased: *a one-sided view.* **b.** Laying obligation only on one of the parties: *a one-sided agreement.* **2.** Larger or more developed on one side: *a one-sided pattern.* **3.** With one side stronger or more powerful: *a one-sided contest.* **4.** Existing or occurring on one side only. **—one-sid·ed·ly** *adv.* **—one-sid·ed·ness** *n.*

one-step (wún-step || wón-) *n.* **1.** A ballroom dance resembling the foxtrot and consisting of a series of unbroken rapid steps in $^2/_4$ time. **2.** Music for such a dance.
~*intr.v.* **one-stepped, -stepping, -steps.** To dance the one-step.

one-time (wún-tīm || wón-) *adj.* At or in some past time; former: *a one-time boxing champion.*

one-to-one (wún-tə-wún, -tōō- || wón-, -wón) *adj.* **1.** Allowing the pairing of each member of a class uniquely with a member of another class. **2.** Characterised by pairing and equality between two individuals or groups: *one-to-one discussions.* **3.** *Mathematics.* Pertaining to a correspondence that assigns to each member of one set a unique member of another set. **4.** Characterised by proportional amounts on both sides. **—one to one** *adv.*

one-track (wún-trák || wón-) *adj.* Obsessively limited to a single idea or purpose: *a one-track mind.*

one-up·man·ship (wún-úpmənship || wón-) *n. Informal.* The technique of maintaining a psychological superiority over one's associates or keeping one step ahead of a competitor. [From the phrase *be one up (on),* after GAMESMANSHIP.]

one-way (wún-wáy || wón-) *adj.* **1.** Moving, operating, or permitting movement in one direction only: *a one-way street.* **2.** *U.S.* Providing for travel in one direction only: *a one-way ticket.*

one-woman (wún-wŏŏ-man || wón-) *adj.* Of, pertaining to, consisting of, or performed by one woman: *a one-woman show.*

on·go·ing (ón-gō-ing, -gṓ- || áwn-) *adj.* Progressing or evolving.

on·ion (ún-yən) *n.* **1.** A bulbous plant, *Allium cepa,* cultivated worldwide as a vegetable. **2.** The rounded, edible bulb of the onion plant, composed of tight, concentric layers of succulent white leaf bases, having a pungent odour and taste. **3.** Any of several similar plants of the genus *Allium,* such as the **Welsh onion, shallot,** or **chive** *(all of which see).* **—know (one's) onions.** *British Informal.* To have a thorough and practical knowledge of a certain field.
~*adj.* Of, pertaining to, tasting of, or resembling an onion: *an onion dome; onion flavour.* [Middle English *unyon, oyn(y)oun,* from Anglo-French, Old French *oignon,* from Latin *uniō* (stem *union-*), a dialectal word for a kind of onion, perhaps from *ūniō,* oneness, unity, from *ūnus,* one (perhaps referring to the concentric unity of the layers of an onion).] **—on·ion·y** *adj.*

on·ion·skin (ún-yən-skin) *n.* A thin, strong, translucent paper.

on-line (ón-līn || áwn-) *adj.* **1.** Connected to and controlled by a mainframe computer. Said of a part of a computer system or a peripheral device. **2.** Switched on. Said of a computer. Compare **off-line.**

on·look·er (ón-lŏŏk-ər || áwn-, -lŏŏk-) *n.* One who looks on; a spectator. **—on·look·ing** *adj.* & *n.*

on·ly (ōnli || ṓni) *adj.* **1. a.** Alone in kind or class; sole. **b.** Having no brothers or sisters. Said of a child. **2.** Standing alone by reason of superiority or excellence: *the only place to be.*
~*adv.* **1.** Without anyone or anything else; alone: *Only three survived.* **2. a.** No more than: *He left only an hour ago.* **b.** At least; just: *If you would only come home.* **c.** Merely: *I only work here.* **3.** Exclusively; solely: *I work only here.* **4.** With the specified unexpected result. Used with an infinitive: *They went, only to be turned away.* **—only too.** Extremely: *only too ready to laugh.*
~*conj. Informal.* But; except (that): *I would have rung, only I couldn't remember the number.* [Middle English *only,* Old English *ānlīc* : *ān,* ONE + *-līc,* -LY.]

Usage: It is generally recommended that *only* should be placed before the words it limits, in written English: *I saw only Jane* (and no one else) rather than *I only saw Jane* (I did not speak to her). The tendency to use *only* apart from the limited word, putting it earlier in the sentence, usually before the verb, is widespread in speech: *I only saw Jane, not Jim.* Purists criticise this usage on logical grounds, maintaining that *only* should always go next to the word it limits, or else ambiguity will result. However this construction is rarely ambiguous in speech, because the stress pattern of the sentence indicates clearly which word goes with which: *I* ONLY *saw* JANE (not Jim) as opposed to *I only* SAW *Jane* (I didn't speak to her). Even in the written language, context usually makes it clear which is the intended meaning, but the weight of grammatical tradition, together with the risk of ambiguity, is enough to foster widespread observance of the adjacency rule in formal written English.

The form *not only . . . but also* is a special instance of the general problem affecting the placement of *only.* The two components should be placed before the same word classes in the two parts of the construction: *They recognise not only the theoretical issues but also the practical consequences.* In a speech-influenced style, however, *They not only recognise . . .* will be used.

o.n.o. *British.* or near offer; or nearest offer.

on·o·mas·tic (ón-ə-mástik, -ō-) *adj.* **1.** Of or pertaining to a name or names. **2.** *Formal.* Designating the signature of the nominal author of a document that is copied out in another's handwriting. [Greek *onomastikos,* from *onomazein,* to name, from *onoma,* a name.]

on·o·mas·tics (ón-ə-mástiks, -ō-) *n. Used with a singular verb.* The study of the origins of names, especially the proper names of people and places.

on·o·mat·o·poe·ia (ón-ə-máttə-pée-ə, -ō-, *rarely* o-nómmətə-, ə-) *n.* **1.** The formation of a word that sounds like that to which it refers, as *buzz, crack, cuckoo.* **2.** A word so formed. **3.** The use, especially as a literary device, of words whose sounds suggest a sound referred to or produce some other evocative effect. [Late Latin, from Greek *onomatopoiia,* from *onomatopoiein,* to coin names : *onoma* (stem *onomat-*), name + *poiein,* to make.] **—on·o·mat·o·poe·ic** (-ik), **on·o·mat·o·po·et·ic** (-pō-éttik) *adj.* **—on·o·mat·o·poe·ic·al·ly** *adv.*

On·on·da·ga (ónnən-dáagə || *U.S. also* -dáwgə) *n., pl.* **-gas** or collectively **Onondaga.** A member of a North American Iroquoian-speaking Indian people. **—On·on·da·gan** *adj.*

on·rush (ón-rush || áwn-) *n.* A powerful, forward rush or flow: *the onrush of events.* **—on·rush·ing** (on-rúsh-ing || awn-) *adj.*

on·set (ón-set || áwn-) *n.* **1.** An onslaught; an assault. **2.** A beginning; a start: *the onset of a cold.*

on·shore (ón-shór || áwn-, -shṓr) *adj.* **1.** Towards the shore: *an onshore gale.* **2.** Located or operating on the shore: *an onshore patrol.*
~*adv.* Towards the shore: *The wind shifted onshore.*

on·slaught (ón-slawt || áwn-) *n.* A violent attack. [Earlier *anslaight* (influenced by obsolete English *slaught,* slaughter), from Middle Dutch *aenslag* : *aan,* on + *slag,* a striking.]

on·stage (ón-stáyj || áwn-) *adj.* On the stage; in front of the audience: *onstage action.* **—on·stage** *adv.*

on stream *adj.* In operation or production. Said of industrial products, processes, or equipment.

On·tar·i·o (on-taír-i-ō). Province of eastern Canada. Lying between the Great Lakes in the south, and Hudson Bay and James Bay in the north, it is Canada's wealthiest and most populous province. Its industries include food processing, machinery, engineering, and timber. Hydroelectricity is exported to the United States. Ottawa and Toronto, are the chief cities. Area, 1 068 583 square kilometres (412,582 square miles). Provincial capital, Toronto.

Ontario, Lake. The smallest of the Great Lakes. Lying on the U.S.-Canadian border, it is the most easterly of the Lakes, and receives the entire drainage of the Great Lakes through the Niagara river; it is drained by the St. Lawrence. Its chief cities and ports include Toronto (in Canada), and Rochester (in the United States).

on·to (ón-tōō, *before a word beginning with a consonant* -tə ‖ áwn-, -tōō) *prep.* **1.** On top of; to a position on; upon: *The dog jumped onto the chair.* —See Usage note at **on**. **2.** *Informal.* Having made a discovery about: *I'm onto your schemes.* **3.** In contact with: *get onto the police.* [ON + TO.]

onto– *comb. form.* Indicates being or existence; for example, **ontogeny**. [Greek, from *ōn* (stem *ont-*), present participle of *einai,* to be.]

on·tog·e·ny (on-tójəni) *n., pl.* **-nies.** Also **on·to·ge·ne·sis** (ón-tə-jénnə-siss, -tō-). The course of development of an individual organism. Compare **phylogeny.** [ONTO- + -GENY.] —**on·to·ge·net·ic** (ón-tə-jə-néttik, -tō-) *adj.*

ontological argument *n. Philosophy.* An argument attempting to prove the existence of God through analysis of the nature of the concept of God, as by questioning the ultimate origin of the concept.

on·tol·o·gy (on-tólləji) *n.* The branch of philosophy that deals with the nature of being and first principles. [New Latin *ontologia* : ONTO- + -LOGY.] —**on·to·log·i·cal** (ón-tə-lójik'l, -tō-) *adj.* —**on·to·log·i·cal·ly** *adv.*

o·nus (ṓnəss) *n.* **1.** Anything that is burdensome, especially a responsibility or necessity. **2.** Loosely, stigma or blame. [Latin *onus,* burden.]

on·ward (ón-wərd ‖ áwn-) *adj.* Moving or tending forwards.

on·wards (ón-wərdz ‖ áwn-) *adv.* Also *chiefly U.S.* **onward.** In a direction or towards a position that is ahead in space or time.

–onym *comb. form.* Indicates word or name; for example, **acronym, tautonym.** [Latin *-onymum,* from Greek *-onumon,* from *onuma, onoma,* name.]

–onymy *n. comb. form.* Indicates a set of names or the study of a kind of name, for example, **toponymy.** [Greek *-ōnumia,* from *-ōnumos,* having a (specific) name, from *onuma, onoma,* name.]

on·yx (ónniks, *rarely* ṓ-niks) *n.* **1.** A type of chalcedony that occurs in bands of different colours, usually white with grey or brown. It is used as a gemstone, especially in cameos and intaglios. **2.** Onyx marble. [Middle English *onix,* from Old French, from Latin *onyx,* from Greek *onux,* claw, fingernail, hence onyx (which sometimes has a vein of white on a pink background, like the lunula in a fingernail).]

onyx marble *n.* A banded form of calcite used as an ornamental stone. Also called "onyx", "oriental alabaster".

oo– *comb. form.* Indicates egg or ovum; for example, **oogenesis, oology.** [Greek *ōio-,* from *ōion,* egg.]

o·o·cyst (ṓ-ə-sist) *n.* An encysted form of the zygote that develops in certain sporozoan protozoans, such as the malaria parasite *(Plasmodium).*

o·o·cyte (ṓ-ə-sīt, -ō-) *n.* **1.** A cell of the animal ovary, derived from an oogonium, that undergoes meiosis and produces an ovum. **2.** A female gamete in certain protozoa. [OO- + -CYTE.]

oo·dles (ṓōd'lz) *pl.n. Informal.* A great amount; a lot; lashings. [19th century (U.S.) : origin obscure.]

o·og·a·mous (ō-óggəməss) *adj.* **1.** Characterised by small male gametes and large, less mobile female gametes. **2.** Pertaining to reproduction by oogamy.

o·og·a·my (ō-óggəmi) *n., pl.* **-mies.** Reproduction between oogamous gametes. [OO- + -GAMY.]

o·o·gen·e·sis (ṓ-ə-jénnə-siss) *n. Biology.* The formation, development, and maturation of ova in the ovary from unspecialised precursor cells. [New Latin : OO- + -GENESIS.] —**o·o·ge·net·ic** (-jə-néttik) *adj.*

o·o·go·ni·um (ṓ-ə-gṓ-ni-əm) *n., pl.* **-nia** (-ni-ə) *or* **-ums. 1.** *Biology.* Any of the cells of the animal ovary that develop into oocytes during ovum formation. **2.** *Botany.* A female reproductive structure in certain algae and fungi, containing oospheres. [New Latin : OO- + -GONIUM.] —**o·o·go·ni·al** *adj.*

ooh (ṓō) *interj.* Used to express a sudden thrill of excitement, pleasure, fear, or the like.
~*intr v.* **oohed, oohing, oohs.** To utter "ooh". Used chiefly in the phrase *ooh and ah.*

o·o·lite (ṓ-ə-līt) *n.* **1.** A sedimentary rock, usually a limestone, composed of tiny rounded grains embedded in a fine matrix. **2.** Any of the grains of which such rock is composed. [New Latin *oolites* (translation of German *Rogenstein,* "roe stone") : OO- + -LITE.] —**o·o·lit·ic** (ṓ-ə-líttik) *adj.*

o·ol·o·gy (ō-ólləji) *n.* The study of eggs, especially birds' eggs. [OO- + -LOGY.] —**o·o·log·i·cal** (ṓ-ə-lójik'l) *adj.* —**o·o·log·i·cal·ly** *adv.* —**o·ol·o·gist** *n.*

oo·long (ṓō-long ‖ -lawng) *n.* A dark Chinese tea, from Fujian that is partly fermented before drying. See **black tea.** [Mandarin Chinese *wū lóng,* black dragon.]

oomiak. Variant of **umiak.**

oom·pah (ṓōm-paa, óōm-) *n.* A sound made by a brass instrument, such as a tuba. [Imitative.]

oomph (ṓōmf) *n. Informal.* **1.** Enthusiasm; spirited vigour; drive. **2.** Sex appeal. [Expressive.]

o·o·pho·rec·to·my (ṓ-əfə-réktəmi) *n., pl.* **-mies.** The surgical removal of one or both ovaries. [Greek *ōophoron,* ovary (*ōion,* egg + *-phoros,* bearing) + -ECTOMY.]

o·o·pho·ri·tis (ṓ-əfə-rítiss) *n.* Inflammation of an ovary. Also called "ovaritis". [New Latin : Greek *ōophoron,* ovary + -ITIS.]

o·o·phyte (ṓ-ə-fīt) *n. Botany.* The stage in the alternation of generations of lower plants when sexual organs are developed. [OO- + -PHYTE.] —**o·o·phyt·ic** (ō-fíttik) *adj.*

oops (ṓōpss, óōpss, wóōpss) *interj.* Used to express: **1.** Alarm or apology when dropping something. **2.** The sudden realisation of a mistake or blunder. [Expressive.]

o·o·sperm (ṓ-ə-sperm) *n. Biology.* A fertilised ovum.

o·o·sphere (ṓ-ə-sfeer) *n. Botany.* A nonmotile female gamete or egg, formed in an oogonium and ready for fertilisation. [OO- + -SPHERE.]

o·o·spore (ṓ-ə-spawr ‖ -spōr) *n. Botany.* A thick-walled spore in certain algae and fungi, developed from a fertilised oosphere. —**o·o·spor·ic** (-spórrik, -spáwrik ‖ -spórik), **o·os·po·rous** (-spáwrəss ‖ -spṓrəss) *adj.*

o·o·the·ca (ṓ-ə-théekə) *n., pl.* **-cae** (-see). *Zoology.* The capsule or egg case of certain insects and molluscs. —**o·o·the·cal** *adj.*

ooze¹ (ṓōz) *v.* **oozed, oozing, oozes.** —*intr.* **1.** To flow or leak out slowly, as through small openings. **2.** To disappear or ebb slowly: *His courage oozed away.* **3.** To emit or exude moisture. —*tr.* **1.** To give out; exude. **2.** To emit or radiate in pervasive abundance: *The waiter oozed charm.*
~*n.* **1.** The act of oozing; a gradual flow or leak. **2.** Something that oozes. **3.** An infusion of vegetable matter, as from oak bark, used in tanning. [Middle English *wosen,* from *wose,* juice, Old English *wōs;* akin to Old Norse *vás.*]

ooze² *n.* **1.** Soft, thin mud, especially that found at the bottom of rivers and lakes. **2.** The layer of mudlike sediment covering the floor of oceans and lakes, composed chiefly of remains of microscopic sea animals. **3.** Muddy, boggy ground. [Middle English *wose,* Old English *wāse;* akin to Old Norse *veisa,* puddle.]

ooz·y¹ (ṓōzi) *adj.* **-ier, -iest.** Slowly leaking; dripping: *an oozy packet of ice cream.* —**ooz·i·ly** *adv.* —**ooz·i·ness** *n.*

ooz·y² *adj.* **-ier, -iest.** Of, resembling, or containing ooze: *an oozy riverbed.* —**ooz·i·ness** *n.*

op. 1. operation. **2.** opposite. **3.** optical. **4.** opus. **5.** out of print.

Op. 1. operation. **2.** opus. **3.** out of print.

o.p. 1. opposite prompt (side). **2.** out of print.

O.P. 1. Order of Preachers (in the Dominican order). [Latin *Ordinis Praedicatorum.*] **2.** *Military.* Observation post.

o·pac·i·ty (ə-pássəti, ō-) *n., pl.* **-ties. 1.** The quality or state of being opaque. **2.** Something that is opaque. **3.** *Physics.* The ratio of the amount of light or other radiation falling on a surface to the amount that passes through the surface. [French *opacité,* from Latin *opācitās* from *opācus,* OPAQUE.]

o·pah (ṓpə) *n.* A large, vividly coloured marine fish, *Lampris guttatus,* found in all temperate and tropical seas. Also called "kingfish", "moonfish". [West African name; akin to Ibo *ùbà.*]

o·pal (ṓp'l) *n.* A hydrated amorphous variety of silica, often used as a gem. See **fire opal.** [Latin *opalus,* from Greek *opallios,* from Sanskrit *úpala* (precious) stone, from *úpara,* lower, comparative of *úpa,* under.]

o·pal·esce (ṓp'l-éss) *intr.v.* **-esced, -escing, -esces.** To emit or show an iridescent shimmer of colours. [Back-formation from OPALESCENT.]

o·pal·es·cent (ṓp'l-éss'nt) *adj.* Having or exhibiting a milky iridescence like that of an opal. [OPAL + -ESCENT.] —**o·pal·es·cence** *n.*

o·pal·ine (ṓp'l-īn) *adj.* Opalescent.
~*n.* A whitish opalescent or opaque glass.

o·paque (ə-páyk, ō-) *adj.* **1. a.** Impenetrable by light; neither transparent nor translucent. **b.** Not reflecting light; without lustre; dull: *an opaque finish.* **2.** Impenetrable by any form of radiant energy other than visible light: *opaque to ultraviolet radiation.* **3. a.** Obscure or unintelligible: *an opaque remark.* **b.** Obtuse; dense.
~*n.* Something that is opaque; especially, an opaque pigment used to darken parts of a photographic print or negative. [Middle English *opake,* assimilated to French *opaque,* both from Latin *opācus†,* dark.] —**o·paque** *tr.v.* —**o·paque·ly** *adv.* —**o·paque·ness** *n.*

op art (op) *n. Sometimes capital* O, *capital* A. A form of abstract art that uses geometric shapes, lines, or the like, to create an optical illusion of movement. [*Op,* short for *optical.*]

op. cit. (óp sít) *adv.* In the work cited. [Latin *opere citato*]

O·PEC (ṓ-pek) Organisation of Petroleum Exporting Countries.

o·pen (ṓpən) *adj.* Also *poetic* **ope** (ṓp). **1. a.** Affording unobstructed entrance and exit; not shut or closed: *His mouth was open; an open door.* **b.** Affording unobstructed passage or view; spacious and unenclosed: *open countryside.* **2. a.** Having no protecting or concealing cover; exposed: *an open wound; an open sports car.* **b.** Unconcealed; undisguised; blatant: *an open disregard for manners.* **3.** Not sealed, tied, or folded: *an open package; an open newspaper.* **4. a.** Having small holes; porous. **b.** Having interspersed gaps, spaces, or intervals: *open columns; open fingers.* **c.** Widely spaced or leaded. Said of printed matter. **5. a.** Accessible to all; unrestricted: *an open meeting.* **b.** Having no restrictions with regard to the status or age of a person: *an open competition.* **6. a.** Ready or willing to entertain or consider; susceptible. Used with *to: open to persuasion.* **b.** Unprotected; vulnerable: *open to attack.* **7. a.** Available; obtainable: *The job is still open.* **b.** Available for use; active: *an open account.* **c.** *British.* Not crossed. Said of a cheque. **d.** Available as an option: *two courses open to us.* **8.** Ready to transact business; operating: *When is the zoo open?* **9.** To be considered further; without a definite conclusion: *an open question.* **10. a.** Characterised by lack of pretence; candid; undissembling: *an open nature.* **b.** Free of prejudice; receptive to new ideas and arguments: *an open mind.* **11.** *Music.* **a.** Not stopped by a finger. Said of a string of an instrument such as a guitar. **b.** Not stopped at either end. Said of an organ pipe. **c.** Produced by an unstopped string or hole, or without the use of slides, valves, or keys: *an open note on a trumpet.* **12.** *Phonetics.* **a.** Articulated with the tongue in a low position: *The vowel sound in the word "far" is open.* **b.** Ending in a vowel or diphthong: *an open syllable.* **13. a.** Not frosty; clement: *open weather.* **b.** Not frozen over so as to prevent passage: *open waters.* **14.** *Mathematics.* **a.** Designating or pertaining to an interval that does not contain the end points. **b.** Designating or pertaining to a set in which each point has points in its neighbourhood that also belong to the set. —See Synonyms at **frank**.

~*v.* **opened, opening, opens.** —*tr.* **1.** To cause to become open; release from a closed or fastened position. **2.** To remove obstructions from; clear. **3.** To make or force an opening in: *open an old wound.* **4.** To form spaces or gaps between; spread out: *soldiers opening ranks.* **5. a.** To remove the cover, cork, or lid from; expose: *Open the box.* **b.** To remove the wrapping from; unseal; undo: *opened the parcel.* **6.** To unfold so that the inner parts are displayed; spread out: *a newspaper opened at the sports page.* **7. a.** To begin; initiate; commence: *open a meeting.* **b.** To commence the operation of or start business in: *open an account; open a shop.* **c.** In certain games, such as cricket, or in some card games, to start (a specified action): *He opened the bowling; opened the bidding.* **8.** To permit the use of; make available; especially, to declare ceremonially to be ready for use or action: *The Queen opened Parliament.* **9.** To make more responsive or understanding. **10.** To reveal the secrets of; bare. —*intr.* **1.** To become open or unfastened. **2. a.** To draw apart; separate: *The wound opened under pressure.* **b.** To spread apart; separate. **3.** To extend; unfold: *The gardens opened out onto a stretch of woodland.* **4.** To come into view; become revealed: *The plain opened before us.* **5.** To become receptive or understanding. **6. a.** To begin; commence: *I opened with a bid.* **b.** To begin business or operation: *When does the shop open?* **c.** To give or have the first public performance: *The film opens in March.* **7.** To give access or view. Usually followed by *into* or *onto: The door opens into a passage.* **3.** *Law.* To make preliminary statements in court. Used of counsel. —**open up.** *Informal.* **1.** To speak or act freely and unrestrainedly. **2.** To begin shooting with guns. **3.** To accelerate. **4. a.** To make accessible: *The railway opened up remoter regions.* **b.** To make available (opportunities, for example). **5.** To transform from dull routine: *Amateur dramatics opened up her life.* ~*n.* **1. a.** An unobstructed area of land or water; an opening or clearing. **b.** The outdoors. Preceded by *the.* **2.** An undisguised or unconcealed state. Preceded by *the: The affair was brought into the open.* **3.** A tournament or contest in which both professional and amateur players may participate. [Middle English *open,* Old English *open,* from Germanic *upanaz* (unattested).] —**o·pen·a·ble** *adj.* —**o·pen·ly** *adv.* —**o·pen·ness** *n.*

o·pen-air (ōpən-áir) *adj.* Outdoor: *an open-air concert.*

o·pen-and-shut (ōpən-ənd-shút) *adj.* Presenting no difficulties; easily settled: *an open-and-shut case.*

open book *n.* A person whose mind, motives, or character are easily understood.

o·pen-cast mining (ōpən-kaast ‖ -kast) *n.* A method of mining by excavating the surface of the ground, rather than by sinking shafts underground. Also *U.S.* "strip mining".

open chain *n. Chemistry.* A linear arrangement of atoms in a molecule. Compare **closed chain**.

open circuit *n.* An electrical circuit in which there is no continuous loop, so that no current can flow. Compare **closed circuit**.

open city *n.* A city that is declared demilitarised during a war, thus, under international law, gaining immunity from attack.

open court *n.* A court that is open to the public.

open day *n.* An occasion when an institution, such as a school, may be inspected by the friends or relatives of its members, or by the general public. Also *U.S.* "open house".

open door *n.* **1.** An unhindered opportunity for progress; free access. **2.** Admission to all on equal terms. **3.** A policy whereby a nation opens its foreign and internal trade to nationals of all other nations on equal terms. —**o·pen-door** (‖ -dôr) *adj.*

o·pen-end·ed (ōpən-éndid) *adj.* **1.** Not restrained by definite limits, restrictions, or structure. **2.** Open or adaptable to change. **3.** Having no fixed repayment date: *an open-ended mortgage.* **4.** Inconclusive or indefinite. **5.** Allowing for a spontaneous, unstructured response: *an open-ended question.*

o·pen·er (ōpənər, ōpnər) *n.* **1.** One that opens; especially, a device used to cut open tins or prise off bottle caps. **2.** The player who starts the action in certain games, as: **a.** In cricket, either of a side's first two batsmen. **b.** In poker, one who begins the betting. **3.** *Plural.* In card games such as poker, cards of sufficient value to the holder to open the betting.

o·pen-eyed (ōpən-íd) *adj.* **1.** Having the eyes wide open as in surprise. **2.** Watchful and alert.

o·pen-faced (ōpən-fáyst) *adj.* Having an undisguised or sincere face or expression.

o·pen-hand·ed (ōpən-hándid) *adj.* Giving freely; generous. —**open-hand·ed·ly** *adv.* —**o·pen-hand·ed·ness** *n.*

o·pen-heart (ōpən-hárt) *adj.* Of, pertaining to, or designating surgery in which the heart is exposed while its normal functions in the circulatory system are assumed by external apparatus.

o·pen-heart·ed (ōpən-hártid) *adj.* **1.** Frank. **2.** Kindly.

o·pen-hearth (ōpən-hárth) *adj.* **1.** Designating or pertaining to a reverberatory furnace used in the production of high-quality steel. **2.** Designating steel produced in such a furnace.

open house *n.* **1.** A situation in which friends are always welcome to enjoy the hospitality offered at one's home: *keep open house.* **2.** The extending of hospitality or acceptance to all: *a policy of open house towards refugees.* **3.** *U.S.* An **open day** (see). —**o·pen-house** (ōpən-hówss) *adj.*

o·pen·ing (ōpəning, ōpning) *n.* **1.** The act of becoming open or being made to open. **2.** An open space serving as a passage or gap. **3.** A hole or aperture. **4.** The first period or stage: *The opening of the book was dull.* **5.** The first occasion for or performance of something, such as a play. **6.** A specific pattern or series of initial moves in certain games, especially chess. **7.** A favourable opportunity or chance. **8.** An unfilled job or position; a vacancy. **9.** *Law.* Preliminary remarks made by counsel to the court or jury.

opening time *n.* In Britain, the time at which pubs or bars are open to serve drinks. Compare **closing time**.

open letter *n.* A letter on a subject of general interest, addressed to an individual but intended for general readership, as published in a newspaper for example.

open market *n.* A market in which supply and demand determine prices and where there is no external interference, as from a government.

open marriage *n.* A marriage in which both partners are free to pursue sexual relationships with others.

o·pen-mind·ed (ōpən-míndid) *adj.* Having a mind receptive to new ideas or to reason; free from prejudice or bias. —**o·pen-mind·ed·ly** *adv.* —**o·pen-mind·ed·ness** *n.*

o·pen-mouthed (ōpən-mówthd ‖ -mówtht) *adj.* Having an open mouth; especially, gaping in astonishment.

open order *n. Military.* A formation where there are open spaces between military or naval units; especially, in a ceremonial parade, a formation whereby easier access between ranks of troops is afforded to an inspecting officer.

o·pen-plan (ōpən-plán) *adj.* Having few or no walls or partitions.

open prison *n.* A prison reserved for certain categories of prisoner and designed to allow more freedom of movement than in a conventional prison.

open sandwich *n.* A slice of bread with meat, cheese, salad, or other garnish on top, eaten as a snack.

open season *n.* **1.** A period when hunting or fishing is permitted for a particular game animal or fish. Compare **close season**. **2.** *Informal.* A situation in which criticism is unrestrained.

open secret *n.* Something purporting to be a secret that is in fact widely known.

open ses·a·me (séssəmi, sézzəmi) *n.* An unfailing means of gaining admittance or attaining success. [From the formula used by Ali Baba in the *Arabian Nights* to open the door of the robbers' cave.]

open shop *n.* A business establishment or factory in which workers are employed without regard to union membership. Compare **closed shop, union shop.**

Open University *n.* In Britain, a university whose courses are designed especially for mature students and conducted by such means as television, radio, and correspondence. Preceded by *the.*

open verdict *n.* A verdict of death given by a coroner's jury but with the cause unstated.

o·pen·work (ōpən-wurk) *n.* Ornamental or structural work, as of metal or embroidery, containing numerous openings, usually in set patterns. —**o·pen·work** *adj.*

op·er·a¹ (óppərə, óprə) *n.* **1.** A form of theatrical presentation in which a dramatic performance is set to music. See **grand opera, music drama, operetta. 2. a.** A presentation of this kind. **b.** A work of this kind. **3.** A theatre designed primarily for operas. [Italian, from Latin *opera,* works.]

opera². Alternative plural of **opus**.

op·er·a·ble (óppərə-b'l, óprə-) *adj.* **1.** Capable of being used or operated: *an outmoded but operable motor.* **2.** Capable of being put into practice; practicable: *an operable plan.* **3.** Capable of being treated by surgical operation: *an operable stage of cancer.* —**op·er·a·bil·i·ty** (-bíləti) *n.*

opera buf·fa (boōfə) *n., pl.* **opere buffe** (óppə-ray boō-fay). Also *French* **o·pé·ra bouffe** (boōf). **1.** Comic opera, especially in the 18th century. **2.** A performance of such an opera. [Italian : OPERA + *buffa,* feminine of *buffo,* comic, BUFFO.]

opera cloak *n.* A cloak worn at a formal occasion such as a theatrical performance or a party.

o·pé·ra co·mique (óppərə ko-méek; *French* ō-pay-ra'a) *n., pl.* **opéras comiques** (*pronounced as singular*). **1.** Opera that, in addition to musical solos and ensembles, has dialogue that is spoken rather than sung. **2.** An opera of this type or a performance of it. [French, "comic opera".]

opera glasses *pl. n.* Small, low-powered binoculars for use especially at a theatrical performance.
opera hat *n.* A collapsible top hat.
opera house *n.* A theatre designed chiefly for presenting operas.
op·er·and (óppə-rand || -rənd) *n. Mathematics.* A quantity, variable, or function on which an operation is performed. For example, in d*y*/d*x*, *y* is the operand. See **operator.** [Latin *operandum,* something to be worked upon, neuter gerundive of *operārī,* to work.]
op·er·ant (óppərənt) *adj.* **1.** Operating to produce effects; effective. **2.** *Psychology.* Characterising, pertaining to, or designating a response or behaviour elicited, from a rat for example, by an environment rather than by a specific stimulus and reinforced by rewarding consequences in the environment.
~*n.* **1.** One that operates. **2.** *Psychology.* An instance of operant behaviour. [Latin *operāns* (stem *operānt-*), present participle of *operārī,* to OPERATE.]
opera se·ri·a (sēer-i-ə) *n., pl.* **opere serie** (óppə-ray sēer-i-ay). **1.** Italian opera of a type popular especially in the 17th and 18th centuries, having serious themes and elaborate formal arias. **2.** An opera of this type or a performance of it. [Italian.]
op·er·ate (óppə-rayt) *v.* **-ated, -ating, -ates.** —*intr.* **1.** To function effectively; work: *The system is operating well.* **2. a.** To have an effect or influence. **b.** To bring about a desired or proper effect: *The medicine took some time to operate.* **3.** To perform surgery. **3.** To carry on a military or naval action or campaign. —*tr.* **1.** To run or control the functioning of: *operate a machine.* **2.** To conduct the affairs of; manage: *operate a business.* **3.** To bring about; effect. [Latin *operārī,* to work, from *opus* (stem *oper-*), a work.]
op·er·at·ic (óppə-ráttik) *adj.* **1.** Of, pertaining to, or typical of the opera: *an operatic aria.* **2.** Histrionic or implausible in a way considered characteristic of grand opera. [From OPERA (influenced by DRAMATIC).] **—op·er·at·i·cal·ly** *adv.*
op·er·at·ics (óppə-ráttiks) *pl. n.* Histrionics.
operating table *n.* The table-like structure on which a patient lies during a surgical operation.
operating theatre *n.* The room in which surgical operations are carried out.
op·er·a·tion (óppə-ráysh'n) *n. Abbr.* **op., Op. 1.** The act, process, or way of operating. **2.** The state of being operative or functioning: *in operation.* **3.** A process or series of acts performed to effect a certain purpose or result. **4.** A process or method of productive activity: *the operation of writing.* **5.** *Medicine.* Any procedure for remedying an injury, ailment, or dysfunction in a living body, especially one performed with instruments. **6.** *Mathematics.* A process or action, such as addition, substitution, transposition, or differentiation, performed in a specific sequence and in accordance with specific rules of procedure. **7.** A military or naval action, campaign, or project: *a combined operation.* [Middle English *operacioun,* from Old French *operation,* from Latin *operātiō* (stem *operātiōn-*), from *operārī,* to OPERATE.]
op·er·a·tion·al (óppə-ráysh'n'l) *adj.* **1.** Of or pertaining to an operation or a series of operations. **2.** Of, for, or engaged in military operations. **3.** Serviced and declared fit for proper functioning: *an operational aircraft.* **4.** In use. **—op·er·a·tion·al·ly** *adv.*
op·er·a·tion·al·ism (óppə-ráysh'n'l-iz'm) *n. Philosophy.* The doctrine that the meanings of many scientific concepts are derived from or given by operations performed to investigate the phenomena to which the concepts allegedly refer. **—op·er·a·tion·al·ist** *n.*
operational research *n.* Mathematical or scientific analysis of the systematic efficiency and performance of manpower, machinery, equipment, and policies used in a government, military, or commercial operation, providing quantitative information which may be used in decision-making. Also (*chiefly U.S.*) "operations research", "O.R.".
op·er·a·tive (óppə-rətiv, óppretiv || -raytiv) *adj.* **1.** Exerting influence or force: *operative laws.* **2.** Functioning effectively; efficient. **3.** Significant; relevant: *I said I might go – and "might" is the operative word!* **4.** Engaged in, concerned with, or related to physical or mechanical activity. **5.** Of, pertaining to, or resulting from a surgical operation.
~*n.* **1. a.** A skilled worker, especially in industry. **b.** Broadly, any worker. **2.** *U.S.* **a.** A secret or trusted agent. **b.** A private detective. **—op·er·a·tive·ly** *adv.*
op·er·a·tor (óppə-raytər) *n.* **1.** A person who operates a mechanical device. **2.** A person employed at a telephone exchange or switchboard to connect calls or assist callers. **3.** The owner or director of a business or industrial concern. **4.** A dealer in stocks or commodities. **5.** *Mathematics.* A symbol or symbols standing for a mathematical operation, such as a plus sign representing addition or d/d*x* representing differentiation of the following term or function in an equation. See **operand. 6.** *Informal.* A shrewd and sometimes unscrupulous person who gets what he wants by devious means: *a smooth operator.*
o·per·cu·late (ō-pérkew-lət, -lit, -layt) *adj.* Also **o·per·cu·lat·ed** (-laytid). Having an operculum.
o·per·cu·lum (ō-pérkew-ləm) *n., pl.* **-la** (-lə) or **-lums. 1.** *Biology.* A lid or flap covering an aperture, such as the gill cover in some fishes, the horny flap covering the shell opening in snails or other molluscs, or the lid of a moss capsule. **2. a.** *Anatomy.* Any flap or lid, such as the layer of tissue over an erupting tooth. **b.** A plug of mucus that fills the opening of the womb in a pregnant woman. [Latin, a lid, cover, diminutive formation from *operīre,* to cover.] **—o·per·cu·lar** *adj.* **—o·per·cu·lar·ly** *adv.*
o·pe·re buf·fe. Plural of **opera buffa.**
op·e·ret·ta (óppə-réttə) *n.* A theatrical production that has many of the musical elements of opera, but is lighter and more popular in subject and style, and contains spoken dialogue. Also called "light opera". [Italian, diminutive of OPERA.]
op·er·on (óppə-ron) *n. Genetics.* A cluster of genes in physical proximity to one another, which act together, under the control of a regulator gene outside the operon, to determine the production of a set of functionally related enzymes. [From OPERATE.]
op·er·ose (óppə-rōss, -rōz) *adj. Archaic.* **1.** Involving great labour; laborious. **2.** Industrious; diligent. [Latin *operōsus,* from *opus* (stem *oper-*), work.] **—op·er·ose·ly** *adv.* **—op·er·ose·ness** *n.*
oph·i·cleide (óffi-klīd, ōfi-) *n.* A former musical wind instrument consisting of a long, tapering brass tube bent double and having keys. [French *ophicléïde* : Greek *ophis,* snake (see **ophidian**) + *kleis* (stem *kleid-*), key.]
o·phid·i·an (ō-fíddi-ən) *adj.* Of or pertaining to snakes; snakelike. ~*n.* Any member of the suborder Ophidia or Serpentes; a snake; a serpent. [New Latin *Ophidia,* from Greek *ophis,* snake, serpent.]
oph·i·ol·o·gy (óffi-ólləji, ōfi-) *n.* The scientific study of snakes. [Greek *ophis,* snake (see **ophidian**) + -LOGY.] **—oph·i·o·log·i·cal** (ə-lójik'l) *adj.* **—oph·i·ol·o·gist** (-ólləjist) *n.*
o·phite (ō-fīt, óffīt) *n.* **1.** A mottled-green rock composed of diabase. **2.** Any of various green rocks, such as serpentine. [Latin *ophītes,* from Greek *ophitēs,* serpentine (stone), from *ophis,* serpent.]
o·phit·ic (ō-fíttik, o-) *adj. Mineralogy.* **1.** Of or pertaining to ophite. **2.** Having a structure composed of laths of plagioclase crystals occurring within an individual anhedral pyroxene crystal.
Oph·iu·chus (o-féwkəss, óffi-ōōkəss) *n.* A constellation in the equatorial region near Hercules and Scorpius. [Latin *Ophiūchus,* from Greek *ophioukhos,* "serpent-holder" : *ophis,* snake + *ekhein,* to hold.]
oph·thal·mia (of-thál-mi-ə || op-) *n.* Also **oph·thal·mi·tis** (óf-thal-mī-tiss || óp-). Inflammation of the eye, especially of the conjunctiva. Now used chiefly in compounds. [Middle English *obtalmia,* from Late Latin *ophthalmia,* from Greek *ophthalmos,* eye.]
oph·thal·mic (of-thál-mik || op-) *adj.* **1.** Of or pertaining to the eye or eyes; ocular. **2.** Affected by ophthalmia. [Greek *ophthalmikos,* from *ophthalmos,* eye.]
ophthalmic optician. See **optometrist.**
ophthalmo– *comb. form.* Indicates the eye or eyeball; for example, **ophthalmology, ophthalmoscope.** [Greek, from *ophthalmos,* eye.]
oph·thal·mol·o·gist (óf-thal-mólləjist || óp-) *n. Abbr.* **ophthal.** A medical practitioner specialising in treatment of eye diseases.
oph·thal·mol·o·gy (óf-thal-mólləji || óp-) *n. Abbr.* **ophthal.** The branch of medicine dealing with the anatomy, functions, pathology, and treatment of the eye. [OPHTHALMO- + -LOGY.] **—oph·thal·mo·log·i·cal** (-thál-mə-lójik'l) *adj.* **—oph·thal·mo·log·i·cal·ly** *adv.*
oph·thal·mom·e·ter (óf-thal-mómmitər || óp-) *n.* An optical instrument for measuring astigmatism. Also called "keratometer". [OPHTHALMO- + -METER.] **—oph·thal·mo·met·ric** (of-thál-mə-méttrik || op-), **oph·thal·mo·met·ri·cal** *adj.*
oph·thal·mo·scope (of-thál-mə-skōp || op-) *n.* An instrument consisting essentially of a mirror with a hole and fitted with lenses of different strengths, and used to examine the interior of the eye through the pupil. [OPHTHALMO- + -SCOPE.] **—oph·thal·mo·scop·ic** (-skóppik), **oph·thal·mo·scop·i·cal** *adj.* **—oph·thal·mos·co·py** (óf-thal-móskəpi || óp-) *n.*
O·phuls (ōfəlss; *German* óp-hülss), **Max,** born Max Oppenheimer (1902–57). German-born French film director. Among his ornate, romantic films are *La Ronde* (1950) and *Lola Montes* (1955).
–opia *n. comb. form.* Indicates a specified visual condition or defect; for example, **diplopia, senopia.** [Greek *-ōpia,* from *ōps,* eye.]
o·pi·ate (ōpi-ət, -it, -ayt) *n.* **1.** Any of various sedative narcotic drugs containing opium or one or more of its derivatives. **2.** Any sedative or narcotic drug. **3.** Anything that relaxes or induces sleep or torpor.
~*adj.* **1.** Consisting of or containing opium. **2.** Causing or producing sleep or sedation.
~*tr.v.* (ōpi-ayt) **opiated, -ating, -ates. 1.** To subject to the action of an opiate. **2.** To dull or deaden as if with a narcotic drug. [Medieval Latin *opiātum,* an opiate, from *opiātus,* treated with opium, soporific, from Latin *opium,* OPIUM.]
o·pine (ō-pīn, ə-) *tr.v.* **opined, opining, opines.** *Formal.* To hold or state as an opinion; think. [Old French *opiner,* from Latin *opīnārī,* to think.]
o·pin·ion (ə-pín-yən) *n.* **1.** A belief or conclusion held with confidence, but not substantiated by positive knowledge or proof. **2. a.** An evaluation or judgment based on special knowledge and given by an expert: *a medical opinion.* **b.** A formal statement given by a legal expert of his views on a particular case. **3.** A judgment or estimation of the worth or value of a person or thing: *In my opinion, he is a fool.* **4.** The common, usual, or prevailing feeling or sentiment: *public opinion.* **5.** *Law.* A formal statement by a judge or jury of the legal reasons and principles for the conclusions of the court. **—be of the opinion.** To hold the view. [Middle English, from Old French, from Latin *opīniō* (stem *opiniōn-*), from *opīnārī,* to think.]
Synonyms: *opinion, view, sentiment, feeling, impression, belief, conviction, persuasion, judgment.*
o·pin·ion·at·ed (ə-pín-yə-naytid) *adj.* Holding stubbornly and often unreasonably to one's own opinions. **—o·pin·ion·at·ed·ly** *adv.* **—o·pin·ion·at·ed·ness** *n.*
o·pin·ion·a·tive (ə-pín-yə-naytiv) *adj. Rare.* **1.** Pertaining to or of

the nature of an opinion; based on opinion. **2.** Opinionated.
—**o·pin·ion·a·tive·ly** adv.

opinion poll n. **1. a.** A canvassing of a selected sample group of persons to analyse public opinion on a particular question. **b.** The result of this canvassing.

o·pis·tho·branch (ə-písthə-brangk) n. Any marine gastropod mollusc of the subclass Opisthobranchia, characterised by a shell that is reduced or absent. [New Latin, from Greek opisthen, behind + -BRANCH.]

op·is·thog·na·thous (óppiss-thógnəthəss) adj. Having receding jaws. [Greek opisthen, behind + -GNATHOUS.] —**op·is·thog·na·thism** n.

o·pi·um (ópi-əm) n. **1.** A bitter yellowish-brown drug prepared from the dried juice of unripe seed capsules of the opium poppy, containing many alkaloids such as morphine, noscapine, codeine, and papaverine. It may be chewed and smoked for its narcotic effects and is still used in medicine as an analgesic for severe pain. Habitual use induces strong addiction; excessive use is fatal. **2.** Something that numbs or stupefies. [Middle English, from Latin, from Greek opion, poppy juice, opium, diminutive of opos, juice.]

opium den n. A place where opium is sold and used.

opium poppy n. A poppy plant, Papaver somniferum, originally of Asia Minor, having greyish-green leaves and variously coloured flowers. The juice of its unripe seed capsules is the source of opium.

o·pos·sum (ə-póss'm) n., pl. **-sums** or collectively **opossum**. **1.** Any of various nocturnal, arboreal marsupials of the family Didelphidae, especially Didelphis marsupialis, of the Americas. **2.** Any of several Australian marsupials of the family Phalangeridae, some of which have valuable fur. In both senses, also called "possum". [Algonquian (Powhatan) āpassūm, from Proto-Algonquian waapa'-themwa (unattested), "white beast".]

opossum shrimp n. Any of various shrimplike crustaceans of the order Mysidacea, the females of which carry their eggs and young in a brood pouch.

opp. opposite.

Op·pen·hei·mer (óppən-hīmər), **J(ulius) Robert** (1904–67). U.S. physicist. He led the Los Alamos atomic bomb project (1942–45) but opposed the development of the hydrogen bomb and was eventually dismissed (1953) by the Atomic Energy Commission as a security risk. He won the Fermi award (1963) for his work on the peaceful application of nuclear energy.

op·pi·dan (óppidən) adj. Of or pertaining to a town.
~n. An inhabitant of a town. [Latin oppidānus, town-dweller (outside Rome), from oppidum, town.]

op·po·nent (ə-pónənt) n. One that opposes another or others in a battle, contest, controversy, debate, or game.
~adj. **1.** Acting against an antagonist or an opposing force. **2.** Opposite. **3.** Anatomy. Designating muscles that act to bring two parts into opposing positions. [Latin oppōnēns (stem oppōnent-), present participle of oppōnere, to OPPOSE.] —**op·po·nen·cy** n.
Synonyms: opponent, adversary, antagonist, competitor, rival.

op·por·tune (óppər-tewn, -téwn ‖ -tōōn, -tóōn) adj. **1.** Suited or right for a particular purpose. **2.** Occurring at a time that is fitting or advantageous. [Middle English, from Old French opportun, from Latin opportūnus, seasonable, (originally of wind) "blowing towards the harbour" : ob-, to + portus, harbour.] —**op·por·tune·ly** adv. —**op·por·tune·ness** n.

op·por·tun·ist (óppər-téw-nist, -tew- ‖ -tōō-, -tóō-) n. A person who takes advantage of any opportunity to achieve an end, usually with little or no regard for moral principles. [French opportuniste, from opportunisme, from Italian opportunismo, from opportuno, opportune, from Latin opportūnus, OPPORTUNE.] —**op·por·tun·ism** n. —**op·por·tun·ist** adj.

op·por·tun·is·tic (óppər-tew-nístik ‖ -tōō-) adj. **1.** Opportunist (adj.). **2. a.** Designating a pathogen that can cause disease only in a host with lowered resistance. **b.** Designating a disease caused by an opportunistic pathogen: an opportunistic infection.

op·por·tu·ni·ty (óppər-téw-nəti ‖ -tōō-) n., pl. **-ties.** **1.** A favourable or advantageous combination of circumstances; a suitable occasion or time. **2.** A prospect; a chance: job opportunities. [Middle English opportunite, from Old French, from Latin opportūnitās (stem opportūnitāt-), from opportūnus, OPPORTUNE.]
Usage: Opportunity may be followed by an infinitve form of the verb, introduced by to (She has the opportunity to leave now); a participial form of the verb, introduced by of or for (You have a wonderful opportunity for getting back your job); or a noun phrase, introduced by for (an opportunity for new ideas).

op·pos·a·ble (ə-pōzə-b'l) adj. **1.** Capable of being opposed. **2.** Capable of being placed opposite or in opposition to something. Said especially of the thumb, which can be placed opposite the other digits. —**op·pos·a·bil·i·ty** (-bílləti) n.

op·pose (ə-pōz) v. **-posed, -posing, -poses.** —tr. **1.** To be in contention or conflict with; combat; resist: oppose the enemy force. **2.** To be against; be hostile to: oppose new ideas. **3.** To place in opposition, or be in opposition to; contrast or counterbalance by antithesis. **4.** To place so as to be opposite something else. —intr. To act or be in opposition to something. [French opposer, from Old French, from Latin oppōnere (past participial stem opposit-), to set against : ob-, against + pōnere, to put.] —**op·pos·er** n.
Synonyms: oppose, resist, withstand, combat, contest.

op·po·site (óppə-zit, -sit. The pronunciations -zīt, -sīt are not standard.) adj. Abbr. **op., opp. 1.** Placed or located directly across from something else or from each other; lying in corresponding positions

in relation to an intervening space or object: opposite sides of a building. **2.** Facing the other way; moving or tending away from each other: opposite directions. **3.** Contrary or antithetical in nature or tendency; diametrically opposed; altogether different. **4.** Botany. Growing in pairs on either side of a stem. Said especially of leaves. Compare **alternate.**
~n. **1.** A person or thing that is opposite or contrary to another. **2.** A word that means the opposite of another; an **antonym** (see). **3.** Archaic. An opponent or antagonist.
~adv. In an opposite position or positions: sat opposite at the table.
~prep. **1.** Across from or facing: opposite the bank. **2.** In a complementary dramatic role to: played opposite her. [Middle English, from Old French, from Latin oppositus, from the past participle of oppōnere, to OPPOSE.] —**op·po·site·ly** adv. —**op·po·site·ness** n.
Synonyms: opposite, contrary, antithetical, contradictory.
Usage: As a noun, opposite is followed by of (The opposite of good is bad), though to is sometimes heard in casual speech. As an adjective, the normal predisposition following is to (His ideas on the subject are opposite to mine), though from is also acceptable. As a preposition, opposite can sometimes be followed by to: the house opposite mine; the house opposite to mine.

opposite number n. A person who holds a position which corresponds to that of a specified person, as in an organisation or team; a counterpart.

opposite sex n. Men considered in relation to women, or women considered in relation to men. Preceded by the.

op·po·si·tion (óppə-zísh'n) n. **1.** The act or condition of opposing or of being in conflict; resistance or antagonism. **2. a.** A position or location opposite to or facing another. **b.** Placement in such a position or location. **3.** That which is or serves as an obstacle. **4. a.** Often capital **O.** A political party or organised group opposed to the group, party, or government in power. Preceded by the. **b.** Any person or group hostile to the ideas of another. **5.** Astronomy. **a.** A geometric configuration in which the Earth lies on a straight line between the Sun and a planet. **b.** The position of the exterior planet in this configuration. **6.** Logic. The relation existing between two propositions having an identical subject and predicate but differing in quantity, quality, or both. **7.** Linguistics. Contrast between two phonemes or other elements of a language that have a relationship such that the contrast is significant. [Middle English opposicioun (only in the astronomical sense), from Old French opposition, from Medieval Latin oppositiō (stem oppositiōn-), from Latin, act of opposing, from oppōnere (past participial stem opposit-), to OPPOSE.] —**op·po·si·tion·al** adj. —**op·po·si·tion·ist** n.

op·press (ə-préss ‖ ō-) tr.v. **-pressed, -pressing, -presses. 1.** To subjugate or persecute by unjust or tyrannical use of force or authority. **2.** To weigh heavily upon, especially so as to depress the mind or spirits: Poverty oppressed me. **3.** Obsolete. To overwhelm or crush. [Middle English oppressen, from Old French oppresser, from Medieval Latin oppressāre, frequentative of Latin opprimere (past participle oppressus), to press against : ob-, against + premere, to press.] —**op·pres·sor** n.

op·pres·sion (ə-présh'n ‖ ō-) n. **1.** The act of oppressing, or the state of being oppressed. **2.** That which oppresses or burdens. **3.** A feeling of being heavily weighed down, either mentally or physically; depression; weariness.

op·pres·sive (ə-préssiv ‖ ō-) adj. **1.** Harsh; tyrannical. **2.** Causing a state of physical or mental discomfort or weariness: an oppressive afternoon. —See Synonyms at **burdensome.** [Medieval Latin oppressīvus, from Latin opprimere, to OPPRESS.] —**op·pres·sive·ly** adv. —**op·pres·sive·ness** n.

op·pro·bri·ous (ə-próbri-əss) adj. **1.** Expressing or carrying a sense of disgrace or contemptuous scorn: opprobrious epithets. **2.** Shameful; infamous. [Middle English, from Old French opprobreus, from Late Latin opprobriōsus, from Latin opprobrium, OPPROBRIUM.] —**op·pro·bri·ous·ly** adv.

op·pro·bri·um (ə-próbri-əm) n. **1.** Disgrace inherent in or arising from shameful conduct; ignominy. **2.** Scornful reproach or contempt: a term of opprobrium. **3.** A cause of shame or disgrace. —See Synonyms at **disgrace.** [Latin, "a reproach against", dishonour : ob-, against + probrum, reproach, infamy.]

op·pugn (ə-péwn) tr.v. **-pugned, -pugning, -pugns.** To oppose, contradict, or call into question. [Middle English oppugnen, from Latin oppugnāre, to fight against : ob-, against + pugnāre, to fight.] —**op·pug·nant** (ə-púg-nənt) adj. —**op·pug·nant·ly** adv. —**op·pugn·er** n.

op·sin (óp-sin) n. The protein constituent of **rhodopsin** (see).

-opsis n. comb. form. Indicates view, appearance, or resemblance; for example, coreopsis. [Greek, from opsis, sight, appearance.]

op·son·ic (op-sónnik) adj. Of, pertaining to, or having the effect of opsonin. [OPSON(IN) + -IC.]

opsonic index n. The ratio of the number of bacteria per phagocyte in the blood of a test patient to the number in the blood of a normal individual. It is a measure of the power of a patient's serum to destroy invading bacteria.

op·son·i·fy (op-sónni-fī) tr.v. **-fied, -fying, -fies.** To make (invading bacteria) susceptible to phagocytosis by opsonic action; opsonise. [OPSON(IN) + -FY.] —**op·son·i·fi·ca·tion** (-fi-káysh'n) n.

op·so·nin (ópsənin) n. A substance naturally present in the blood that renders invading bacteria susceptible to phagocytosis. [Latin opsōnium, relish (opsonin being a "relish" enabling the body to "digest" bacteria), indirectly from Greek opsōnein, to buy food or delicacies, from opson†, relish, delicacy.]

op·so·nise, op·so·nize (ópsə-nīz) tr.v. **-nised, -nising, -nises. 1.** To form opsonins in. **2.** To opsonify. [From OPSONIN.] —**op·so·ni·sa·tion** (-nī-záysh'n ‖ *U.S.* -ni-) *n.*

-opsy *n. comb. form.* Indicates an examination; for example, bi-**opsy.** [New Latin *-opsia,* condition of the eyes, examination, from Greek, from *opsis,* sight, appearance.]

opt (opt) *intr.v.* **opted, opting, opts.** To make a choice or decision; indicate a preference. Often used with *for.* [French *opter,* from Latin *optāre.*]

opt. **1.** optative. **2.** optical; optician; optics. **3.** optimum. **4.** optional.

op·ta·tive (op-táytiv, óptətiv) *adj.* **1.** Expressing a wish or choice. **2.** *Abbr.* **opt.** *Grammar.* **a.** Designating a mood of verbs in some languages, such as Greek, used to express a wish. **b.** Designating a statement using a verb in the subjunctive mood to indicate a wish or desire; for example, *Had I the means, I would do it.* ~*n. Abbr.* **opt.** *Grammar.* **1.** The optative mood. **2.** A verb or expression in this mood. [Middle English, from Old French *optatif,* from Late Latin *optātīvus,* from Latin *optāre,* to choose, wish.] —**op·ta·tive·ly** *adv.*

op·tic (óptik) *adj.* **1.** Of or pertaining to the eye or to vision. **2.** Of or pertaining to the science of optics. ~*n.* **1.** An eye. Not in technical usage. **2.** Any of the components of an optical instrument. **3.** *British. Capital* **O.** A trademark for a valved tap fitted to inverted bottles of spirits, especially in public houses, and releasing an exact measure into a glass when pressed. [Old French *optique,* from Medieval Latin *opticus,* from Greek *optikos,* from *optos,* visible.]

op·ti·cal (óptik'l) *adj. Abbr.* **opt.** **1.** Of or pertaining to sight: *an optical illusion.* **2.** Designed to assist sight: *optical instruments.* **3.** Of or pertaining to optics. **4.** Using or depending on light: *an optical character reader.* —**op·ti·cal·ly** *adv.*

optical activity *n. Chemistry.* A property of a substance that enables it to rotate the plane of transmitted polarised light.

optical character reader *n. Abbr.* **OCR** A device for converting printed characters into digital form by optical character recognition. See **optical scanner.**

optical character recognition *n. Abbr.* **OCR** A method of scanning printed characters with an optical device and transforming them into electrical signals, so that the data can be stored magnetically in a computer.

optical fibre *n.* A very thin, typically flexible, optically transparent fibre, as of glass or plastic, through which light can be transmitted by successive internal reflections.

optical glass *n.* Any of various types of clear glass, such as flint and crown glass, having known reproducible optical properties and used in lenses, prisms, and the like.

optical isomer *n. Chemistry.* An **isomer** *(sense 1d).*

optical maser *n. Physics.* A laser, especially one that produces visible radiation. No longer in technical usage.

optical rotation *n. Physics & Chemistry.* Rotation of the plane of polarisation of polarised light by a substance that shows optical activity.

optical scanner *n.* A device for converting printed or illustrated matter into digital form. See **optical character reader.**

optic axis *n.* An optical path through a crystal along which a ray of light can pass without undergoing double refraction.

optic chiasma *n.* The X-shaped structure formed by the two optic nerves when they cross each other on the undersurface of the brain.

optic disc *n.* An area of the retina, the **blind spot** *(see).*

op·ti·cian (op-tísh'n) *n. Abbr.* **opt.** **1.** One who makes lenses and spectacles. **2.** One who sells lenses, spectacles, and other optical instruments. Loosely, an **optometrist** *(see).* [French *opticien,* from Medieval Latin *optica,* OPTICS.]

optic nerve *n.* A motor nerve that connects the retina of the eye with the brain.

op·tics (óptiks) *n. Used with a singular verb. Abbr.* **opt.** *Physics.* The scientific study of light and vision, chiefly the generation, propagation, and detection of electromagnetic radiation having wavelengths greater than X-rays and shorter than microwaves. [Latin *optica,* from Greek *optika,* neuter plural of *optikos,* OPTIC.]

op·ti·mise, op·ti·mize (ópti-mīz) *tr.v.* **-mised, -mising, -mises.** To make the most effective use of. —**op·ti·mi·sa·tion** (-mī-záysh'n ‖ *U.S.* -mi-) *n.*

op·ti·mism (ópti-miz'm) *n.* **1.** A tendency or disposition to expect the best possible outcome, or to dwell upon the most hopeful aspects of a situation. **2.** *Philosophy.* **a.** The doctrine, asserted by Leibniz, that our world is the best of all possible worlds. **b.** The belief that the universe is improving and that good will ultimately triumph over evil. [French, from Latin *optimum,* best, OPTIMUM.]

op·ti·mist (ópti-mist) *n.* **1.** One who habitually or in a particular case expects a favourable outcome. **2.** A believer in philosophical optimism. —**op·ti·mis·tic** (-místik) *adj.* —**op·ti·mis·ti·cal·ly** *adv.*

op·ti·mum (ópti-məm) *n., pl.* **-ma** (-mə) or **-mums.** *Abbr.* **opt.** The best or most favourable condition, degree, or amount for a particular situation. ~*adj.* Also **op·ti·mal** (-m'l). Most favourable or advantageous; best. [Latin, from neuter of *optimus,* best.] —**op·ti·mal·ly** *adv.*

op·tion (ópsh'n) *n.* **1.** The act or an instance of choosing; a choice. **2.** The power or right of choosing; freedom to choose. **3. a.** The exclusive right, usually obtained for a fee, to buy or sell property within a stated time and at a stated price. **b.** A right to buy or sell specific securities or commodities at a stated price within a stated time. **4.** Something chosen or available as a choice. —**keep or leave (one's) options open.** To withhold one's decision; remain uncommitted. —See Synonyms at **choice.** [French, from Latin *optiō* (stem *optiōn-*), choice.]

op·tion·al (ópsh'n'l) *adj. Abbr.* **opt.** Left to choice; not compulsory or automatic. —**op·tion·al·ly** *adv.*

op·tom·e·ter (op-tómmitər) *n.* An instrument used for measuring the refraction of the eye. [Greek *optos,* visible + METER.]

op·tom·e·trist (op-tómmətrist) *n.* One who specialises in optometry. Compare **optician.**

op·tom·e·try (op-tómmitri) *n.* The techniques or profession of examining, measuring, and treating certain visual defects by means of corrective lenses or other methods that do not require the supervision of a doctor. [Greek *optos,* visible.] —**op·to·met·ric** (óptə-méttrik), **op·to·met·ri·cal** *adj.*

opt out *intr.v.* To withdraw; decide against participating; especially: **1.** To opt out of conventional society. **2.** To opt out of all or part of an agreement: *opt out of monetary union.* **3.** To opt out of control by a local or regional authority. Said of a school or hospital. —**opt out** *n.*

op·u·lent (óppwələnt) *adj.* **1.** Having or characterised by great wealth; rich. **2.** Abundant; plentiful; lavish. [Latin *opulentus,* from *opēs,* wealth.] —**op·u·lent·ly** *adv.* —**op·u·lence, op·u·len·cy** *n.*

o·pun·ti·a (o-púnshi-ə, ō-) *n.* Any of various cacti of the genus *Opuntia;* especially, the **prickly pear** *(see).* [New Latin, from Latin, a herb, after *Opus* (stem *Opunt-*), city of Locris, in ancient Greece, where it grew abundantly.]

o·pus (ópəss, óppəss) *n., pl.* **opuses** or **opera** (óppərə, ópərə). *Abbr.* **op., Op.** A creative work; especially, a musical composition. Used with a number to designate the order of a composer's works. [Latin, work.]

o·pus·cule (o-púskewl, ō-) *n.* A small and minor work. [French, from Latin *opusculum,* diminutive of *opus,* work, OPUS.]

Op·us De·i (óppəss dáy-ee) *n.* Official name **Prelature of the Holy Cross and Opus Dei.** An international organisation of Roman Catholic priests and laymen founded in 1928 to foster Christian ideals, especially through the individual's daily work. [Latin, God's work.]

or[1] (or; *occasional weak form* ər) *conj.* Used to indicate: **1. a.** An alternative, usually only before the last term of a series: *hot or cold; this, that, or the other.* **b.** The second of two alternatives, the first being preceded by *either* or *whether: Your answer is either ingenious or wrong; She didn't know whether to laugh or to cry.* **c.** *Archaic.* The first of two alternatives, with the force of *either* or *whether.* **2.** A synonymous or equivalent expression: *acrophobia, or fear of great heights.* **3.** Uncertainty or indefiniteness: *two or three.* [Middle English *or,* contraction of *other,* alteration (influenced by EITHER, WHETHER) of Old English *oththe,* from Common Germanic.]

Usage: When all of the elements connected by *or* are singular, the verb they govern must be singular: *Beer or wine is included in the price.* When all of the elements are plural, the verb is also plural: *Either the cars or the bikes are in need of recall.* When the elements are of different number, the verb generally agrees with the element closest to it: *Either the books or the newspaper is correct; Either the newspaper or the books are correct.* See also **either, neither, nor.**

or[2] *conj. Archaic.* Before. Followed by *ever* or *ere.* ~*prep. Archaic.* Before. [Middle English *ar, or,* Old English *ār,* early, before, from Old Norse.]

or[3] *n. Heraldry.* The metal gold, represented by a white field sprinkled with small dots. ~*adj. Heraldry.* Of gold. Used after the noun: *a bezant or.* [Old French, from Latin *aurum.*]

-or[1] *n. suffix.* Indicates the person or thing performing the action expressed by the root verb; for example, *investor, percolator.* [Middle English *-our, -or,* from Anglo-French *-eour,* Old French *-eor, -eur,* partly from Latin *-or,* and partly from Latin *-ātor* (past participial stem *-āt-* + *-or*).]

Usage: The normal suffix for forming an agent or instrument noun from a verb is *-er (sing-singer),* but *-or* is often used, especially in words which have been borrowed from other languages or in forms derived from Latin: *actor, inspector, percolator.* Occasionally both forms are available, in which case the *-er* ending tends to be used for persons and the *-or* ending for things, as in *converter* ("someone who converts") and *convertor* ("a machine which converts"), but this is not a hard and fast distinction.

-or[2] *n. suffix.* **1.** Used to indicate a state, quality, or activity; for example, **horror, torpor, error. 2.** *U.S.* Variant of **-our.** [Middle English *-or, -our,* from Old French *-eur,* from Latin *-or,* abstract, suffix.]

O.R. *n.* Operational research *(see).*

o·ra. Plural of **os** (mouth).

or·ache (órrich) *n.* Also *chiefly U.S.* **or·ach.** Any of various plants of the genus *Atriplex;* especially, *A. hortensis,* whose edible leaves resemble spinach. [Middle English *arage, orage,* from Anglo-French *arasche,* modification of Vulgar Latin *atrapica* (unattested), variant of Latin *atriplex,* from Greek *atraphaxus†.*]

or·a·cle (órrək'l, órrik'l) *n.* **1.** A shrine consecrated to the worship and consultation of a prophetic god, such as that of Apollo at Delphi. **2.** The priest or other transmitter of prophecies at such a shrine. **3.** A prophecy made known at such a shrine, often in the form of an enigmatic statement or allegory. **4.** Any person or agency considered to be a source of wise counsel or prophecy; an infallible authority or judge. **5.** Any pronouncement or claim considered to be infallible. **6.** *Theology.* A command or revelation from

God. 7. In the Old Testament, the sanctuary of the Temple; the holy of holies. I Kings 6:16, 19–23. 8. *Capital* O. In Britain, a trademark for a viewdata service broadcast by the IBA, providing information on a wide variety of subjects. —**work the oracle.** To achieve one's ends by scheming or manoeuvring. [Middle English, from Old French, from Latin *ōrāculum,* from *ōrāre,* to speak.]

o·rac·u·lar (ə-ráckewlər, o-, ō-) *adj.* 1. Of or pertaining to an oracle. 2. Resembling or characteristic of an oracle: a. Solemnly prophetic: *an oracular warning.* b. Brief and enigmatic; mysterious. [Latin *ōrāculum,* ORACLE.] —**o·rac·u·lar·ly** *adv.*

or·a·cy (áwrə-si, órrə-) *n.* The ability to speak, hear, and understand language, sometimes contrasted with literacy. [Latin *os* (stem *or-*), mouth + -ACY, by analogy with *literacy.*]

o·ral (áw-rəl || ố-, órrəl) *adj.* 1. Spoken, rather than written. 2. a. Of or pertaining to the mouth: *oral hygiene.* b. Designating the surface of an invertebrate animal, such as a jellyfish, on which the mouth is situated. 3. Used in or taken through the mouth: *an oral thermometer; oral vaccine.* 4. Consisting of or using speech: *oral instruction.* 5. *Phonetics.* Designating a speech sound emitted through the mouth only, with the nasal passages closed. 6. In psychoanalysis: a. Of, pertaining to, or designating the first stage of psychosexual development of the infant, when sexual gratification is derived chiefly from stimulation of the mouth parts. b. Designating a personality fixated at this state, characterised by such traits as greediness and dependence. Compare **anal, genital.**
~*n. Often plural.* An academic examination in which the questions and answers are spoken rather than written. [Late Latin *ōrālis,* from Latin *ōs* (stem *ōr-*), the mouth.] —**o·ral·ly** *adv.*

oral contraceptive *n. Medicine.* Any of various hormone compounds in pill form, typically consisting of an oestrogen and a progestogen, used in specific sequence to prevent ovulation and conception. Also informally called the "Pill".

oral history *n.* 1. a. The practice or technique of gathering historical information by interviewing, and usually tape-recording, eyewitnesses of or participants in historical events. b. Broadly, historical information transmitted orally rather than in writing. 2. The information so gathered, or a historical study based on it. —**oral historian** *n.*

or·ange (órrinj, órrənj) *n.* 1. Any of several evergreen trees of the genus *Citrus,* cultivated in tropical and subtropical regions, and having fragrant white flowers and round fruit with a yellowish-red rind and a sectioned, pulpy interior; especially, *C. sinensis,* the sweet orange, and *C. aurantium,* the Seville or sour orange. 2. The fruit of these trees, having a sweetish, acid juice. 3. Any of several plants or trees resembling the orange in some respect, such as the **mock orange** *(see).* 4. Any of a group of colours between red and yellow in hue, of medium lightness and moderate saturation. 5. Orange clothing. 6. An orange object. [Middle English, from Old French *orenge, orange,* from Arabic *nāranj,* from Persian *nārang,* from Sanskrit *nāranga*†, orange, orange tree.] —**or·ange** *adj.* —**or·ange·y, or·ange·ish** *adj.*

Or·ange[1] (órrinj) Also **Or·ange-Nas·sau** (-nássaw). A princely European family who have been rulers of the Netherlands since 1815.

Or·ange[2] (órrinj; *French* o-róɴzh). Town in the Vaucluse département, southeast France. Founded by Charlemagne, it was the seat of the House of Orange, whose descendants still rule the Netherlands.

Orange[3]. South African river, the longest in southern Africa. Rising in the Drakensberg mountains of South Africa and flows 2 093 kilometres (1,300 miles) west to join the Atlantic at Alexander Bay.

or·ange·ade (órrinj-áyd) *n.* A drink, often carbonated, of orange flavoring, sugar, and water. [French : ORANGE + -ADE.]

orange flower oil *n.* An essential oil, **neroli** *(see).*

orange flower water *n.* A solution of neroli in water, used in pharmaceutical preparations and cooking.

Orange Free State. *Afrikaans* **Oranje Vrystaat.** See **Free State.**

Or·ange·man (órrinj-mən, -man) *n., pl.* **-men** (-mən, -men). 1. A member of the Orange Order, a secret society founded in Northern Ireland in 1795 to maintain the political and religious ascendancy of Protestantism. [After William, Prince of *Orange* (William III), the first Protestant king of England.]

Orangeman's Day *n.* July 12, a public holiday in Northern Ireland celebrated by Protestants as the anniversary of the battles of the Boyne (1690) and of Aughrim (1691). Also called "Orange Day".

orange pekoe *n.* A grade of black tea from Sri Lanka or India, consisting of the end buds and their surrounding small leaves.

or·ang·e·ry (órrinj-əri, -ri) *n., pl.* **-ries.** A glass-walled enclosure used, especially formerly, for growing oranges in cool climates, or more commonly nowadays as a greenhouse. [French *orangerie,* from *orange,* from Old French, ORANGE.]

orange stick *n.* A stick of orangewood with tapering ends, used to manicure the fingernails and cuticles.

or·ange-tip (órrinj-tip) *n.* A European butterfly, *Anthocharis cardamines,* having whitish wings tipped with orange.

or·ange·wood (órrinj-wŏŏd) *n.* The fine-grained wood of the orange tree, used in fine woodwork.

o·rang-u·tan (ə-ráng-ōō-tán, aw-, o-, -taán, áw-rangŏŏ-taan, -tan) *n.* Also **o·rang-ou·tang** (-tang). An arboreal anthropoid ape, *Pongo pygmaeus,* of Borneo and Sumatra, having a shaggy reddish-brown coat and very long arms. [Malay *orang hutan* : *ōrang,* man + *hūtan,* forest.]

o·rate (ə-ráyt, aw-, o- || ō-) *intr.v.* **orated, orating, orates.** 1. To speak publicly in a pompous, oratorical manner. 2. To deliver an oration.
~(ór-ayt, -ət, -it) *adj.* Of or pertaining to oracy; especially, of, pertaining to, or designating a preliterate culture that is characterised by oral history (as might be transmitted by griots) rather than by written history. [Back-formation from ORATION.]

o·ra·tion (ə-ráysh'n, aw-, o- || ō-) *n.* 1. A formal address or speech, especially one given on some special occasion such as an academic celebration or funeral. 2. A speech, written out and memorised, as for debating contests. 3. Any high-flown speech. [Latin *ōrātiō* (stem *ōrātiōn-*), from *ōrāre,* to speak.]

or·a·tor (órrətər, órritər) *n.* 1. A person who delivers an oration. 2. A person skilled in the art of public speaking. [Middle English *oratour,* from Old French *orateur,* from Latin *ōrātor,* from *ōrāre,* to speak.] —**or·a·tor·ship** *n.*

or·a·tor·i·cal (órrə-tórrik'l) *adj.* Of or pertaining to an orator, or to oratory. —**or·a·tor·i·cal·ly** *adv.*

or·a·to·ri·o (órrə-táwri-ō || -tṓri-) *n., pl.* **-os.** A musical composition for solo voices, choir, and orchestra, usually telling a sacred story. [Italian, from *Oratorio,* the Oratory of St. Philip Neri at Rome, where famous musical services were held in the 16th century, from Late Latin *ōrātōrium,* ORATORY (chapel).]

or·a·to·ry[1] (órrə-təri, -tri) *n.* 1. The art of public speaking; rhetoric. 2. Rhetorical style or skill, or an instance of it. [Old French *(art) oratoire,* from Latin *(ars) ōrātōria,* (the art) of public speaking, from *ōrātōrius,* of an orator, oratorical, from *ōrātor,* ORATOR.]

oratory[2] *n., pl.* **-ries.** 1. A place for prayer, such as a small private chapel. 2. *Capital* O. A Roman Catholic religious society founded by Saint Philip Neri and consisting of secular priests *(Oratorians).* 3. *Capital* O. Any branch or church of such a society. [Middle English *oratorie,* from Anglo-French, from Late Latin *ōrātōrium (templum),* (place) of prayer, from *ōrātōrius,* of praying, from Latin *ōrāre,* to pray, speak.]

orb (orb) *n.* 1. A sphere or spherical object. 2. An area of endeavour, influence, or activity; a sphere; a province: *the orb of reason.* 3. a. A heavenly body. b. *Archaic.* The Earth. 4. Any of a series of concentric transparent spheres revolving about the Earth, postulated by medieval astronomers as support for the stars and planets. 5. A jewelled globe surmounted by a cross, part of the regalia of a sovereign. 6. *Poetic.* An eye. 7. *Archaic.* A circle or an object of circular form. 8. The orbit of a planet or satellite.
~*v.* **orbed, orbing, orbs.** —*tr.* 1. To shape into a circle or sphere. 2. *Archaic.* To encircle; enclose. —*intr.* To move in an orbit. [Old French *orbe,* from Latin *orbis*†, orb, disc.]

or·bic·u·lar (awr-bíckew-lər) *adj.* Also **or·bic·u·late** (-lət, -lit), **or·bic·u·lat·ed** (-laytid). 1. Orb-shaped; circular or spherical. 2. *Botany.* Circular and flat. Said especially of leaves. 3. Rounded out; complete: *"The household ruin was thus full and orbicular."* (Thomas De Quincey). [Middle English *orbiculer,* from Old French *orbiculaire,* from Late Latin *orbiculāris,* from Latin *orbiculus,* diminutive of *orbis,* ORB.] —**or·bic·u·lar·i·ty** (-lárrəti) *n.* —**or·bic·u·lar·ly** *adv.*

or·bit (órbit) *n.* 1. The path of a celestial body or man-made satellite as it revolves around another body. 2. The path of any body in a field of force surrounding another body; for example, the movement of an atomic electron in relation to a nucleus. 3. a. A range of activity, experience, or knowledge. b. A range of control or influence. 4. Either of two bony cavities in the skull containing an eye and its external structures; an eye socket. 5. The circular area of tissue surrounding the eye of a bird or an insect.
~*v.* **orbited, -biting, -bits.** —*tr.* 1. To put into or cause to move in an orbit: *The first man-made satellite was orbited in 1957.* 2. To revolve around (a centre of attraction). —*intr.* To revolve or move in an orbit. [Latin *orbita,* from *orbitus,* circular, from *orbis,* ORB.]

or·bit·al (órbit'l) *adj.* Of or pertaining to an orbit.
~*n.* 1. *Chemistry.* A region around the nucleus of an atom *(atomic orbital)* or surrounding nuclei in a molecule *(molecular orbital)* containing one electron or a pair of electrons and characterised by a fixed energy. 2. A **ring road** *(see).* —**or·bit·al·ly** *adv.*

orbital decay *n.* The effect of atmospheric drag on an orbiting body, such as an Earth-orbiting satellite, causing eventual re-entry.

orbital velocity *n.* The minimum velocity required to maintain a satellite in orbit around a celestial body.

orc (ork) *n.* 1. Any of several whales; especially, the **killer whale** *(see).* 2. Any of various mythical or fictional monsters. [Old French *orque,* from Latin *orca,* whale, probably from Greek *oruga,* accusative of *orux,* a pickaxe, hence (from its horn), narwhal, from *orussein,* to dig.]

or·ca (ór-kə) *n.* **Orc** (sense 1). [Latin *orca,* ORC.]

Or·cad·i·an (awr-káydi-ən) *n.* A native or inhabitant of the Orkney Islands. [Latin *Orcades,* Orkney Islands.] —**Or·cad·i·an** *adj.*

or·ce·in (órsi-in) *n.* A reddish dye made by oxidising orcinol with hydrogen peroxide in the presence of ammonia and used also as a biological stain and a mild antiseptic.

or·chard (órchərd) *n.* 1. An area of land devoted to the cultivation of fruit or nut trees. 2. The trees cultivated in such an area. [Middle English *orchard,* Old English *ortceard, ortgeard* : Latin *hortus,* a garden + Old English *geard,* YARD.]

or·ches·tra (ór-ki-strə, -ke-, -kə- || awr-késtrə) *n. Abbr.* **orch.** 1. a. A large group of musicians who play together on various musical instruments, usually including strings, woodwinds, brass instruments, and percussion instruments. b. A group of musicians all playing a specified instrument: *a gamelan orchestra.* c. The instruments played by such a group of musicians. 2. An orchestra pit. 3. *Chiefly*

U.S. **a.** The front section of seats nearest the orchestra pit in a theatre; the stalls. **b.** The entire main floor of a theatre. Also called "parquet". **4.** In ancient Greek theatres, a semicircular space in front of the stage on which the chorus danced. [Latin *orchēstra,* from Greek *orkhēstra,* from *orkheisthai,* to dance.] —**or·ches·tral** (awr-késtrəl) *adj.* —**or·ches·tral·ly** *adv.*

orchestra pit *n.* In theatres and concert halls, the area where the musicians sit, immediately in front of and below the stage. Also called "orchestra", "pit".

or·ches·trate (ór-ki-stráyt, -ke-, -kə-) *tr.v.* **-trated, -trating, -trates.** **1. a.** To compose or arrange (music) for performance by an orchestra. **b.** To provide a musical arrangement for. **2.** To arrange, put together, or organise so as to achieve a desired overall effect: *a carefully orchestrated conspiracy.* [French *orchestrer,* from *orchestre,* orchestra, from Latin *orchēstra,* ORCHESTRA.] —**or·ches·tra·tor** *n.*

or·ches·tra·tion (ór-ki-stráysh'n, -ke-, -kə-) *n. Abbr.* **orch. 1.** A musical composition that has been orchestrated. **2.** Arrangement of music for performance by an orchestra. **3.** Arrangement or organisation for a desired overall effect: *the orchestration of a conspiracy.*

or·ches·tri·on (awr-késtri-ən) *n.* Also **or·ches·tri·na** (órki-stréenə). A large mechanical musical instrument, resembling a barrel organ and producing sound in imitation of an orchestra. [*Orchestra* + melod*ion*.]

or·chid (órkid) *n.* **1.** Any of numerous epiphytic or terrestrial plants of the family Orchidaceae, found worldwide, though chiefly in the tropics, and often having brightly coloured flowers of unusual shapes. **2.** The flower of any of these plants, especially one cultivated for ornament or personal adornment. [Latin *orchis* (stem *orchid-*), from Greek *orkhis,* testicle, hence (from the shape of its root) orchid.]`

or·chi·da·ceous (órki-dáyshəss) *adj.* **1.** Of, pertaining to, or characteristic of the orchid family of plants. **2.** Suggesting ostentatious luxury; showy. [New Latin *Orchidaceae* (family); *orchis,* ORCHID + -ACEOUS.]

or·chi·dec·to·my (órki-déktəmi) *n.* Surgical removal of a testicle. [Greek *orkhis* (stem *orkhid-*), testicle + -ECTOMY.]

or·chil (ór-kil, -chil) *n.* Also **ar·chil** (ár-). **1.** Any of several lichens, from which a dye is obtained. **2.** The violet-coloured dyestuff obtained from these lichens. Also called "cudbear". [Middle English, from Old French *orcheil,* perhaps ultimately from Latin *herba urceolāris,* plant used to polish pitchers, from *urceolus,* diminutive of *urceus,* pitcher.]

or·chis (órkiss) *n.* Any orchid of the genus *Orchis,* often having purple flowers. See **fringed orchis.** [New Latin *Orchis,* from Latin, ORCHID.]

or·chi·tis (awr-kítiss) *n.* Inflammation of one or both testicles. [New Latin, from Greek *orkhis,* testicle + -ITIS.]

or·ci·nol (ór-si-nol ‖ -nōl) *n.* A white crystalline compound present in orchil and used as a source of the dye orcein.

OR circuit *n.* A computer logic gate, an **OR gate** *(see).*

Or·cus (órkəss). *Roman Mythology.* **1.** The world of the dead; Hades. **2.** The underworld god Pluto. [Latin *Orcus†.*]

ord. 1. order. **2.** ordinal. **3.** ordinance. **4.** ordinary. **5.** ordnance.

or·dain (awr-dáyn) *v.* **-dained, -daining, -dains.** – *tr.v.* **1. a.** To invest with ministerial or priestly authority; confer holy orders upon. **b.** To authorise as a rabbi. **c.** To authorise as a Buddhist monk. **2. a.** To order by virtue of superior authority. **b.** To decree as part of the order of nature or of the universe. **3.** To prearrange unalterably; predestine: *by fate ordained.* – *intr.v.* To become ordained as a minister, priest, rabbi or Buddhist monk: *He ordained as a rabbi in 1965.* [Middle English *ordeinen,* from Anglo-French *ordeiner,* from Late Latin *ōrdināre,* from Latin, to arrange in order, from *ōrdō* (stem *ōrdin-*), order.] —**or·dain·er** *n.* —**or·dain·ment** *n.*

or·deal (awr-déel ‖ órdeel) *n.* **1. a.** A severely difficult or painful experience that tests character or endurance. **b.** A trying experience. **2.** A former method of legal trial in which the accused was subjected to physically painful or dangerous tests by way of determining guilt or innocence, the result being regarded as a divine judgment. [Middle English *ordal,* Old English *ordāl, ordēl,* from Germanic *uzdailjam* (unattested), "a dealing out", judgment, trial : *uz-* (unattested), out + *dailjan* (unattested), to DEAL.]

ordeal bean *n.* The **Calabar bean** *(see).*

or·der (órdər) *n. Abbr.* **O, O., ord. 1.** A condition of logical or comprehensible arrangement among the separate elements of a group. **2. a.** A condition of methodical or prescribed arrangement among component parts, such that proper functioning or appearance is achieved. **b.** The state, condition, or disposition of a thing: *in good order.* **3. a.** The structures of a given society and the relations defined among individuals and classes constituting it: *the old order.* **b.** The condition in which these structures and relations are maintained and preserved by the rule of law and the police power of the state: *Order was restored after the riot.* **c.** Discipline and good behaviour in any group. **4.** A sequence or arrangement of successive things in time or space. **5.** The established sequence; the customary procedure: *the order of operations.* **6.** A command or direction. **7.** *Military.* **a.** A command given by a superior officer requiring execution of a task or other obedience. **b.** *Plural.* Formal written instructions to report for duty at a stated time and place: *He received his orders to fly to Japan.* **8. a.** A commission or instruction to buy, sell, or supply something. **b.** That which is supplied, bought, or sold. **9. a.** A request for a portion of food by a customer at a restaurant. **b.** The food requested. **10.** *Law.* Any direction or command delivered by a court and entered into the court record, but

not included in the final judgment or verdict. **11. a.** Any of several grades of the Christian ministry: *the order of priesthood.* **b.** *Plural.* The office and rank of an ordained minister or priest. **c.** *Plural.* **Holy orders** *(see).* **12.** A prescribed form of religious service for various occasions. **13.** Any of the nine grades or choirs of angels. See **angel. 14.** An organisation of people united by some common fraternal bond or social aim: **a.** Any of various communities dedicated to a religious life, as through missionary work or monastic contemplation, and often bound by vows of poverty, chastity, and obedience: *the Order of St. Benedict.* **b.** An organisation of knights similarly united: *the Order of the Knights of St. John of Jerusalem.* **15. a.** A group of persons upon whom a government or sovereign has formally conferred honour for unusual service or merit, entitling such persons to wear a special insignia: *the Order of Merit.* **b.** The insignia worn by such persons. **16.** *Usually plural.* A social class: *the lower orders.* **17.** Degree of quality or importance; rank: *poetry of a high order.* **18.** *Architecture.* **a.** Any of several specific styles of classical architecture characterised by the type of column employed, such as **Composite order, Corinthian order, Doric order, Ionic order, Tuscan order** *(all of which see).* **b.** A specific style of architecture: *a cathedral of the Gothic order.* **19.** *Biology.* A taxonomic category of plants and animals ranking above the family and below the class. See **taxonomy. 20.** *Mathematics.* **a.** An indicated number of successive differentiations to be performed on a function, or that have been performed on a derivative. **b.** The number of elements in a finite group. **c.** The number of rows or columns in a determinant or square matrix. Compare **degree. 21.** Approximate size or magnitude: *costing somewhere in the order of a million pounds.* —**call to order. 1.** To request to be quiet and attentive. **2.** To begin (a meeting). —**in order. 1.** Well organised; under control; according to plan. **2.** Permitted or appropriate. **3.** In correct sequence. —**in order that.** So that. —**in order to.** For the purpose of; so that it is possible to. —**keep order.** To ensure the continuation of order or discipline. —**on order.** Requested but not yet delivered. —**out of order. 1.** Not working; broken. **2.** Not following the correct sequence. **3.** Not according to rule or general procedure: *The objection is out of order.* —**to order.** According to the buyer's specifications.

~*v.* **ordered, -dering, -ders.** —*tr.* **1.** To issue a command or instruction to. **2.** To give a command or instruction that (something be done): *The judge ordered a retrial.* **3.** To give an order for; request to be supplied with. **4.** To instruct or force to move to or from a specified locality: *She ordered me out of the house.* **5.** To put in a methodical and systematic arrangement. **6.** To prearrange unalterably; predestine. **7.** *Rare.* To ordain: *He was ordered priest.* —*intr.* To give an order or orders; request that something be done or supplied: *Order now, before prices go up.* —See Synonyms at **command.** —**order about** or **around.** To treat in a domineering way; bully. [Middle English *ordre,* from Old French *ordre,* earlier *ord(e)ne,* from Latin *ōrdō.*] —**or·der·er** *n.*

or·der·ly (órdərli) *adj.* **1.** Having a methodical and systematic arrangement; tidy: *an orderly room.* **2.** Without violence or disruption; peaceful: *an orderly transition of governments.* **3.** *Military.* Of or pertaining to the transmission of military orders.

~*n., pl.* **orderlies. 1.** A male attendant in a hospital. **2.** *Military.* A soldier assigned to attend upon a superior officer and carry orders or messages.

~*adv.* Systematically; regularly. —**or·der·li·ness** *n.*

Synonyms: *orderly, methodical, systematic.*

orderly room *n.* The office used for administration in the barracks of a military unit.

order of magnitude *n. Physics.* **1.** An estimate of size or magnitude expressed as a power of ten: *The Earth's mass is of the order of magnitude of 10^{22} tons, that of the Sun 10^{27} tons.* **2.** A range of values between a specified lower value and an upper value ten times as large: *The masses of the Earth and the Sun differ by five orders of magnitude.*

Order of Merit *n. Abbr.* **O.M.** An honour or title awarded in the United Kingdom for outstanding achievement in any field of endeavour.

Order of Prohibition *n. Law.* See **prohibition** (sense 3).

order of the day *n., pl.* **orders of the day. 1.** The set of commands or instructions issued by a commanding officer to his men. **2.** The list of business to be discussed by a legislative body on a given day. **3.** The prevailing trend or state of affairs.

Order of the Garter *n.* The highest and most exclusive order of knighthood in the United Kingdom, consisting of members of the royal family and a limited number of knights companion who join the order at the specific behest of the sovereign.

order paper *n.* A list giving the order in which questions are to be raised, especially by a legislative body.

or·di·nal (órdin'l) *adj. Abbr.* **ord. 1.** Having a specified position in a numbered series: *an ordinal rank of seventh.* **2.** Pertaining to a biological order.

~*n.* **1.** An ordinal number. **2.** In the Christian Church: **a.** A book of instructions for daily services. **b.** A book of forms for ordination. [Late Latin *ōrdinālis,* from Latin *ōrdō* (stem *ōrdin-*), ORDER.]

ordinal number *n.* A number indicating position in a series or order. The ordinal numbers are first (1st), second (2nd), third (3rd), and so on. Compare **cardinal number.**

or·di·nance (órdinənss) *n. Abbr.* **ord. 1.** An authoritative command or order. **2.** A custom or practice established by long usage. **3.** A religious rite; especially, Holy Communion. **4.** A statute or regulation. [Middle English *ordinaunce*, from Old French *ordenance*, "the art of arranging", from Medieval Latin *ōrdinantia*, from Latin *ōrdināns*, present participle of *ōrdināre*, to put in order, from *ōrdō* (stem *ōrdin-*), ORDER.]

or·di·nand (órdi-nand) *n.* A prospective priest, minister, rabbi, or Buddhist monk; one about to be ordained. [Latin *ordinandus*, gerundive of *ordināre*, to ORDAIN.]

or·di·nar·i·ly (órd-'n-rə-li, -in-, -ri-, -ərə-, -əri- || -érrəli, -érrəli) *adv.* **1.** As a general rule. **2.** In the regular or usual manner: *ordinarily dressed.* **3.** To the usual extent or degree: *ordinarily large profits.*

or·di·nar·y (órd-'n-ri, -in-, -əri || -erri) *adj.* **1.** Commonly encountered; usual: *"a man to be sought for on great emergencies, but ill adapted for ordinary services"* (Anthony Trollope). **2.** Occurring regularly or periodically; normal. **3.** Average in rank or merit; of no exceptional degree or quality; commonplace. **4.** Having immediate rather than delegated jurisdiction, as a judge might. **5.** *Mathematics.* Designating a differential equation containing no more than two variables and derivatives of one with respect to the other. **6.** Designating an academic degree (a pass degree) that is taken or awarded without honours; general. —See Synonyms at **common**. ~*n., pl.* **ordinaries. 1.** A person, object, or situation that is common, normal, or average. **2.** *Law.* A judge or other official with immediate rather than delegated jurisdiction. **3.** In some states of the United States, the judge of a probate court. **4.** *Usually capital* **O.** In the Christian Church: **a.** The part of the Mass that remains unchanged from day to day. Compare **proper. b.** A division of the Divine Office containing the unchangeable parts of the office other than the Psalms. **c.** A cleric, such as the residential bishop of a diocese, with ordinary jurisdiction. **5.** *Heraldry.* Any of the simplest and commonest charges, such as the bend or the cross. **6.** Formerly, a priest or minister who visited condemned prisoners in jail. —**in ordinary.** *British.* Officially employed, especially by the monarchy; having regular rather than temporary or delegated responsibilities: *chaplain in ordinary to the sovereign.* —**out of the ordinary.** Extraordinary or exceptional; unusual; abnormal. [Middle English *ordinarie*, from Latin *ōrdinārius*, from *ōrdō* (stem *ordin-*), ORDER.] —**or·di·nar·i·ness** *n.*

Ordinary level. See **O level.**

ordinary ray *n. Physics.* The ray of light in double refraction that obeys the ordinary laws of refraction. Compare **extraordinary ray.**

ordinary seaman *n. Abbr.* **O.S.** A seaman of the lowest grade in the merchant navy.

ordinary shares *pl.n. Finance. British.* Capital shares in a company that have exclusive claim on the company's net assets and net income after all prior claims have been paid. Compare **preference shares.** Also *U.S.* "common stock", "equity stock".

or·di·nate (órdin-ət, -it) *adj.* Arranged in regular rows, as spots are on an insect's wings. ~*n. Symbol* **y** *Mathematics.* The plane Cartesian coordinate representing the distance from a given point to the x-axis, measured parallel to the y-axis. Compare **abscissa.** [Latin *ōrdināre*, to arrange in order, from *ōrdō* (stem *ōrdin-*), ORDER.]

or·di·na·tion (órdi-náysh'n) *n.* **1.** In the Christian Church: **a.** The ceremony during which a person is admitted to the ministry of a church. **b.** The admission itself. **2.** The analogous ceremony or admission for a rabbi or a Buddhist monk. **3.** Any arrangement or ordering.

ord·nance (órdnənss) *n. Abbr.* **ord., ordn. 1.** Military weapons collectively, together with ammunition and the equipment to keep them in good repair. **2.** Heavy guns; artillery. **3.** The military or government department in charge of military equipment. [Middle English *ordinaunce*, ORDINANCE.]

Ordnance Survey *n. Abbr.* **O.S.** In Britain, the government agency in charge of making and checking maps of Scotland, England, and Wales. [After the *Ordnance* Department of the Army, which originally drew up the maps.]

or·do (ór-dō) *n., pl.* **-dines** (-di-neez). *Roman Catholic Church.* An annual calendar containing instructions for the Mass and office to be celebrated on each day of the year. [Medieval Latin *ōrdō*, from Latin, ORDER.]

or·don·nance (órdənənss; *French* awrdo-náNSS) *n.* **1.** The arrangement of elements in a literary or artistic composition or architectural plan. **2.** In French history: **a.** A royal decree or body of laws on a specific subject. **b.** An order of a criminal court. [French, variant (influenced by *ordonner*, to order) of Old French *ordenance*, ORDINANCE.]

Or·do·vi·ci·an (órdō-vishi-ən) *adj. Geology.* Of, pertaining to, formed in, or designating the second period of the Palaeozoic era, characterised by the appearance of primitive types of fish. ~*n. Geology.* The Ordovician period. Preceded by *the.* [After the *Ordovices*, an ancient Celtic tribe of North Wales.]

or·dure (órdewr || órjər) *n.* **1.** Excrement; dung. **2.** Something considered to be morally offensive. [Middle English, from Old French, from *ord*, dirty, "disgusting", from Latin *horridus*, horrid, from *horrēre*, to shudder.]

ore (or || ōr) *n.* A mineral or aggregate of minerals from which a valuable constituent, especially a metal, can be profitably mined or extracted. [Middle English *oor, or,* Old English *ār*, brass (in sense influenced by Old English *ora†*, unwrought metal, ore).]

ö·re (örə) *n., pl.* **öre.** A coin equal to ¹/₁₀₀ of the krona of Sweden and the krone of Denmark and Norway. [Danish and Norwegian *øre* and Swedish *öre*, from Latin *aureus*, gold coin, from *aurum*, gold.]

o·re·ad (áwri-ad || ôri-) *n. Greek Mythology.* A mountain nymph. [Greek *Oreias* (stem *Oreiad-*), from *oreios*, of a mountain, from *oros*, mountain. See **oro-**.]

o·rec·tic (o-réktik, ə-) *adj.* Of or pertaining to the appetites or desires. [Greek *orektikos*, from *oregein*, to desire.]

o·re·ga·no (órri-ga'anō || *U.S.* ə-réggənō, aw-) *n.* A herb seasoning made from the dried leaves of a species of marjoram, *Origanum vulgare.* [Spanish, marjoram, from Latin *origanum*, Greek *origanon*, oregano, marjoram (probably from a North African language).]

Or·e·gon (órri-gən, -gon || áwri-). Pacific State of the northwest United States containing many areas of great natural beauty. The state is dominated by the Cascade Range, a rugged mountain chain running north to south some 160 kilometres (100 miles) inland. The region was jointly held by Britain and the United States (1818–46) and Oregon Territory was then created (1848). It was admitted to the Union as the 33rd state in 1859. Area, 251 180 square kilometres (96,981 square miles). Capital, Salem.

Oregon fir *n.* The **Douglas fir** (see).

Oregon grape *n.* **1.** An evergreen shrub, *Mahonia aquifolium*, of northwestern North America, having fragrant yellow flowers and small, edible, bluish berries. **2.** The berry of this shrub.

oreide. Variant of **oroide.**

O·res·tes (o-résteez, ə-, aw-). *Greek Mythology.* The son of Agamemnon and Clytemnestra, who, with his sister Electra, avenged his murdered father by slaying his mother and her lover Aegisthus.

Ø·re·sund (ö-rə-sōond). Strait in northern Europe, situated between Sweden and the Danish island of Sjaelland. Connecting the Kattegat with the Baltic Sea, it is an important shipping route.

orfe (orf) *n.* A European freshwater fish, *Idus idus*, with a blue-grey back and a silvery belly. A reddish-gold variety, the golden orfe, is often kept in garden ponds and aquariums. [German and French; akin to Latin *orphus*, Greek *orphos*, sea perch.]

Orff (orf), **Carl** (1895–1982). German composer. The inventor of a system of using percussion instruments, he is best known for *Carmina Burana* (1938), a lively setting of medieval poems.

orfray. Variant of **orphrey.**

org. 1. organic. **2.** organisation; organised.

or·gan (órgən) *n.* **1.** A musical instrument consisting of a keyboard and a number of pipes supplied with wind by means of bellows. Sometimes also called "pipe organ". **2.** Any of various other instruments resembling the organ either in mechanism or sound, such as the electronic organ. **3.** *Biology.* A differentiated part of an organism, adapted for a specific function. **4.** The penis. Used euphemistically. **5.** An institution or medium through which or by means of which some action is performed. **6.** An instrument or vehicle of communication; especially, a periodical publication issued by a political party, business firm, or other group. [Middle English, from Old French *organe*, from Late Latin *organum*, church organ, from Latin, implement, instrument, from Greek *organon*.]

or·ga·na. 1. Alternative plural of **organon. 2.** Alternative plural of **organum.**

or·gan·die (órgəndi) *n.* **-dies.** Also *chiefly U.S.* **or·gan·dy.** A transparent crisp fabric of cotton or silk, used for trimming, curtains, and light clothing. [French *organdi†.*] —**or·gan·die** *adj.*

or·gan·elle (órgə-nél) *n. Biology.* A structure within a cell that is specialised for a particular function; for example, the nucleus and the mitochondria. [New Latin *organella*, diminutive of Latin *organum*, ORGAN.]

or·gan-grind·er (órgən-grīndər) *n.* A street musician who plays a barrel organ.

or·gan·ic (awr-gánnik) *adj. Abbr.* **org. 1.** Of, pertaining to, or affecting an organ of the body. **2.** Of, pertaining to, or derived from living organisms. **3. a.** Using or grown with fertilisers and mulches consisting only of animal or vegetable matter, with no use of chemical fertilisers or pesticides: *organic gardening; organic foods.* **b.** Free from chemical injections or additives: *organic meat.* **c.** Simple, basic, and close to nature: *an organic lifestyle.* **4.** Having properties associated with living organisms. **5.** Likened to an organism in organisation or development; interconnected: *society as an organic whole.* **6. a.** Of or constituting an integral part of something; fundamental; structural. **b.** *Law.* Designating or pertaining to the fundamental or constitutional laws and precepts of a government or organisation. **7.** *Chemistry.* Of or designating carbon compounds. Compare **inorganic.** [Old French *organique*, from Late Latin *organicus*, from Greek *organikos*, serving as an instrument, from *organon*, implement, ORGAN.] —**or·gan·i·cal·ly** *adv.*

organic chemistry *n.* The chemistry of carbon compounds. Compare **inorganic chemistry.**

organic disease *n.* Any disease associated with changes in the structure of an organ or tissue. Compare **functional disease.**

or·gan·i·cism (awr-gánni-siz'm) *n.* **1.** The theory that the total organisation of an organism, rather than the functioning of individual organs, is the principal or exclusive determinant of every life process; holism. **2.** The concept or doctrine that society is analogous to a biological organism, especially in its structure. —**or·gan·i·cist** *n. & adj.* —**or·gan·i·cist** *adj. & n.*

or·gan·i·sa·tion (órgə-nī-záysh'n || -ni-) *n. Abbr.* **org. 1.** The act of organising or the process of being organised. **2.** The state or manner of being organised: *a high degree of organisation.* **3.** Something that has been organised or made into an ordered whole. **4.** Something comprising elements with varied functions that contribute to the whole and to collective functions; an organism. **5.** A number of persons or groups having specific responsibilities and united for some purpose or work. **6.** A business, charity, international agency, or similar corporate concern. **—or·gan·i·sa·tion·al** *adj.* **—or·gan·i·sa·tion·al·ly** *adv.*

Organisation of African Unity *n. Abbr.* **OAU** An association formed (1963) by most independent African states to promote mutual help and cooperation.

Organisation of American States *n. Abbr.* **OAS** An association formed (1948) by the 21 American republics to promote mutual help and cooperation.

or·gan·ise, or·gan·ize (órgə-nīz) *v.* **-ised, -ising, -ises.** *—tr.* **1.** To pull or put together into an orderly, functional, structured whole. **2. a.** To arrange or systematise: *organise one's thoughts before speaking.* **b.** To arrange or compose in a desired pattern. **3.** To arrange systematically for harmonious or united action: *organise a strike.* **4.** To establish as an organisation. **5. a.** To cause (employees) to form or join a trade union. **b.** To induce the employees of (a business or industry) to form or join a union: *organise a department store.* *—intr.* **1.** To develop into or assume an organic structure. **2.** To join or form a trade union or other activist group. [Middle English *organysen,* from Old French *organiser,* from Medieval Latin *organizāre,* from Latin *organum,* instrument, ORGAN.]

or·gan·ised (órgənīzd) *adj.* **1.** Well-ordered and efficient; methodical: *Why can't you get organised?* **2.** Designating criminal activities planned in the manner of a commercial business: *organised crime; organised baseball.* **3.** Unionised: *organised labour.*

or·gan·is·er (órgə-nīzər) *n.* **1.** One who organises or is skilled at organising. **2.** A group of embryonic cells that releases a substance which stimulates differentiation in other embryonic cells.

or·gan·ism (órgə-niz'm) *n.* **1.** Any living individual; any plant or animal. **2.** Any system regarded as analogous to a living body: *the social organism.* **—or·gan·is·mal** (-nízm'l), **or·gan·is·mic** *adj.*

or·gan·ist (órgənist) *n.* One who plays the organ.

organo– *comb. form.* **1.** Indicates organ or organic; for example, **organology. 2.** Indicates carbon compounds; for example, **organometallic, organophosphorus.** [Middle English, from Medieval Latin *organum,* organ of the body, from Latin, implement, ORGAN.]

organ of Cor·ti (kórti) *n.* A sense organ situated on the inner surface of the cochlea in the inner ear that converts sound vibrations into nerve impulses which are then transmitted to the brain. [After Alfonso *Corti* (1822–88), Italian anatomist.]

or·gan·o·gen·e·sis (órgənō-jénni-siss, awr-gánnō-) *n., pl.* **-ses** (-seez). The origin and development of biological organs. [New Latin : ORGANO- + -GENESIS.] **—or·gan·o·ge·net·ic** (-jə-néttik) *adj.* **—or·gan·o·ge·net·i·cal·ly** *adv.*

or·gan·o·lep·tic (órgənō-léptik, awr-gánnō-) *adj.* Pertaining to, affecting, involving, or perceived by a sensory organ. [French *organoleptique* : ORGANO- + Greek *lēptikos,* receptive, from *lēptos,* to be apprehended (by the senses), from *lambanein,* to take, seize, apprehend.] **—or·gan·o·lep·ti·cal·ly** *adv.*

or·gan·ol·o·gy (órgə-nólləji) *n.* The study of plant and animal organs and their functions. [ORGANO- + -LOGY.] **—or·gan·o·log·i·cal** (-nə-lójik'l) *adj.*

or·gan·o·me·tal·lic (órgənō-mi-tál-ik, awr-gánnō-) *adj.* Of, pertaining to, or designating an organic chemical compound that also contains metal atoms.
~n. An organometallic chemical compound.

or·ga·non (órgə-non) *n., pl.* **-na** (-nə) or **-nons.** Also **or·ga·num** (-nəm) *pl.* **-na** (-nə) or **-nums.** *Philosophy.* A set of logical requirements used in scientific investigation or demonstration. [Greek, tool (used as the title of Aristotle's writings on logic).]

or·gan·o·ther·a·py (órgənō-thérrəpi, awr-gánnō-) *n.* The treatment of disease with animal organs or extracts such as insulin and thyroxine. **—or·gan·o·ther·a·peu·tic** (-thérrə-péwtik) *adj.*

or·gan·ot·ro·pism (órgə-nóttrəpiz'm) *n.* Also **or·gan·ot·ro·py** (-nóttrəpi). *Medicine.* The attraction of certain chemical compounds or microorganisms to specific tissues or organs of the body. [ORGANO- + -TROPISM.] **—or·gan·o·trop·ic** (órgənō-tróppik, awr-gánnō-) *adj.* **—or·gan·o·trop·i·cal·ly** *adv.*

or·gan-pipe cactus (órgən-pīp) *n.* A tall, branching cactus, *Pachycereus marginatus,* of Mexico and the southwestern United States.

or·ga·num¹ (órgə-nəm) *n., pl.* **-na** (-nə) or **-nums.** Any of several types of vocal polyphonic music, in two, three, or four parts, of the 9th to the early 13th century. [Medieval Latin, from Late Latin, ORGAN.]

organum². Variant of **organon.**

or·gan·za (awr-gánzə) *n.* A sheer, stiff fabric of silk or synthetic material used for evening dresses or trimming. [Perhaps from *Lorganza,* a trademark.] **—or·gan·za** *adj.*

or·gan·zine (órgən-zeen, awr-gán-) *n.* **1.** A thread of raw silk, usually used as a warp thread. **2.** A fabric made of this thread. [French *organsin,* from Italian *organzino*†.]

or·gasm (ór-gaz'm) *n.* **1.** The climax of sexual excitement, marked by ejaculation of semen in the male and by the release of tumescence in erectile organs of both sexes. **2.** Loosely, any onrush of intense excitement. [French *orgasme,* from Greek *orgasmos,* from *organ,* to swell (with lust), be excited.] **—or·gas·mic** (awr-gázmik), **or·gas·tic** *adj.*

OR gate (or) *n. Electronics.* A computer logic gate that has one output and two or more inputs, and gives an output signal for any input signal or combination of input signals. Also called "OR circuit". [From its similarity to the function of the conjunction *or* in logic.]

or·geat (ór<u>zh</u>aa) *n.* **1.** A sweet flavouring of orange and almond used in cocktails and food. **2.** A drink containing this flavouring. [French, from Old French, from Old Provençal *orjat,* from *orge,* barley, from Latin *hordeum.*]

or·gi·as·tic (órji-ástik) *adj.* Of, pertaining to, or characteristic of an orgy. [Greek *orgiastikos,* from *orgiazein,* to hold secret rites, from *orgia,* secret rites, ORGY.]

or·gy (órji) *n., pl.* **-gies. 1.** A revel involving unrestrained indulgence, especially sexual excesses. **2.** Excessive indulgence in any specified activity: *an orgy of reading.* **3.** *Often plural.* A secret rite in the cults of Demeter, Dionysus, or other Greek or Mediterranean deities, typically involving frenzied singing, dancing, drinking, and sexual activity. [Originally in the plural *orgies,* from Old French, from Latin *orgia,* from Greek.]

or·i·bi (órribi) *n., pl.* **-bis** or collectively **oribi.** Any of several small, brownish African antelopes of the genus *Ourebia,* especially *O. ourebia,* the male of which has straight, ridged horns. [Afrikaans, said to be from a Hottentot word meaning "antelope".]

o·ri·el (áwri-əl || órri-, ṓri-) *n.* A projecting bay window, usually in an upper storey, supported from below with corbels or brackets. Also called "oriel window". [Middle English *oriole, oriel,* from Old French *oriol,* from Medieval Latin *oriolum*†, upper chamber.]

o·ri·ent (áwri-ənt || órri-, ṓri-, -ent) *n.* **1.** The east; eastern lands or regions. **2.** *Capital* **O. a.** The Eastern Hemisphere. **b.** The countries of Asia, especially of eastern Asia, and the Eastern Hemisphere. Usually preceded by *the.* Compare **Occident. c.** In ancient times, the lands and regions east of the Mediterranean. **3. a.** The lustre characteristic of a pearl of high quality. **b.** A pearl having this lustre.
~adj. Also **oriental** (for sense 2). **1.** *Poetic.* Eastern; oriental. **2.** Having exceptional quality and lustre. Said of pearls and gems. **3.** *Archaic.* Rising; ascending: *"The orient moon"* (P.B. Shelley).
~v. (-ent) **oriented, -enting, -ents.** *Chiefly U.S.* To orientate. See Usage note at **orientate.** [Middle English, from Old French, from Latin *oriēns* (stem *orient-*), rising, rising sun, east, from *orīrī,* to rise.]

o·ri·en·tal (áwri-ént'l || órri-, ṓri-) *adj.* **1.** Eastern. **2.** *Usually capital* **O.** Pertaining to the countries or regions of the Orient or to their peoples, languages, or culture. **3.** *Capital* **O.** *Ecology.* Of or designating the zoographical region that includes tropical Asia and the adjacent islands of the Malay Archipelago. **4.** Variant of **orient** (sense 2). **5.** Pertaining to or designating precious varieties of corundum: *an oriental ruby.*
~n. Usually capital **O.** An inhabitant or native of the Orient, or the descendant of one. **—o·ri·en·tal·ly** *adv.*

oriental alabaster *n.* A mineral, **onyx marble** *(see).*

oriental amethyst *n.* A type of **amethyst** *(see).*

o·ri·en·tal·ise, o·ri·en·tal·ize (áwri-ént'l-īz || órri-, ṓri-) *v.* **-ised, ising, ises.** *Often capital* **O.** *—tr.* To make oriental in character, lifestyle, or appearance. *—intr.* To become oriental; adopt oriental qualities. **—o·ri·en·tal·i·sa·tion** (-ī-záysh'n || *U.S.* -i-).

O·ri·en·tal·ism (áwri-ént'l-iz'm || órri-, ṓri-) *n. Often small* **o. 1.** A quality, mannerism, or custom peculiar to or characteristic of the Orient. **2.** Scholarly knowledge of eastern cultures, languages, and peoples. **3.** A prejudiced or patronising attitude towards or a policy of discrimination against Eastern people and cultures. **—O·ri·en·tal·ist** *n. & adj.*

Oriental poppy *n.* A plant, *Papaver orientale,* native to western Asia and widely cultivated for its brilliant scarlet flowers.

Oriental rug *n.* A type of rug made by hand in the Orient.

o·ri·en·tate (áwri-en-tayt, -ən- || órri-, ṓri-, -én-) *v.* **-tated, -tating, -tates.** Also *chiefly U.S.* **orient.** *—tr.* **1.** To place in a particular relation to the points of the compass: *orientate the swimming pool north and south.* **2.** To cause (especially a church or grave) to face east; locate or place so as to face east. **3.** To align or position with respect to a reference system. **4.** To discover the bearings of. Often used reflexively: *She orientated herself by a familiar landmark.* **5.** To cause to become familiar with or adjusted to facts or circumstances. *—intr.* **1.** To turn towards the east. **2.** To become adjusted or aligned. [Back-formation from ORIENTATION.]

Usage: There is some free variation between *orient* and *orientate* in modern English. *Orient* tends to be used much more in American English. *Orientate* is used more in British English, especially as an intransitive verb (*orientating towards the east*) and in forms that can function adjectivally (*It's orientated correctly; He is very work-orientated*).

o·ri·en·tat·ed (áwri-en-taytid, -ən- || órri-, ṓri-) *adj.* Directed or inclined towards; favouring. Used in combination: *career-orientated.*

o·ri·en·ta·tion (áwri-en-táysh'n, -ən- || órri-, ṓri-) *n.* **1.** The act of orientating or the state of being orientated. **2.** Location or position relative to the points of the compass. **3.** *Architecture.* The location of a church so that its longitudinal axis is from west to east and its main altar at the eastern end. **4.** The line or direction followed in the course of a trend, movement, or development. **5.** An adjustment or adaptation to a new environment, situation, custom, or set of ideas. **6.** *Psychology.* Individual awareness of the outside world in its relation to the self. **7.** Introductory instruction concerning a new situation. [Probably ORIENT (verb) + -ATION.]

or·i·en·teer·ing (áwri-en-teér-ing, -ən- || órri-, ṓri-) *n.* A cross-country race in which the competitors have to work out the route by means of a compass and map and report to checkpoints on the way. [Swedish *orientering,* orientation.]

or·i·fice (órri-fiss || áwri-) *n.* A mouth or vent; an aperture or cavity. [Old French, from Late Latin *ōrificium* : Latin *ōs* (stem *ōr-*), mouth + *facere,* to make.]

or·i·flamme, aur·i·flamme (órri-flam ‖ áwri-) *n.* **1.** The red flag of the Abbey of St. Denis, used as a standard by the early kings of France. **2.** Any inspiring standard or symbol. [Middle English *oriflamble*, from Old French *oriflambe*, from Medieval Latin *auriflamma* : Latin *aurum*, gold + *flamma*, FLAME.]

orig. original; originally.

o·ri·ga·mi (órri-gáami, áwri-) *n.* **1.** The art or process, originating in Japan, of folding paper into shapes resembling flowers, birds, or other objects. **2.** A decorative pattern made in this way. Compare **kirigami.** [Japanese : *ori*, a folding + *-gami*, from *kami*, paper.]

o·ri·ga·num (órri-gáanəm ‖ *U.S.* ə-ríggənəm) *n.* Also **o·ri·gan** (órrigən). Any plant of the genus *Origanum*; especially, wild marjoram. See **marjoram.** [Middle English, from Old French, from Latin *origanum*, from Greek *origanon.*]

Or·i·gen (órri-jen) (*c.* 185–*c.* 254). Christian writer and teacher, and one of the Greek Fathers of the Church. His many works include the *Hexapla* (interpretations of Old Testament texts), and *Contra Celsum*, a defence of Christianity against the attacks of the philosopher Celsus.

or·i·gin (órri-jin) *n.* **1.** That from which anything derives its existence; a source or cause. **2.** *Often plural.* Parentage; ancestry; derivation. **3.** A coming into being. **4.** *Anatomy.* **a.** The point of attachment of a muscle that remains fixed when the muscle contracts. **b.** The beginning of a nerve or blood vessel, especially when it arises from a larger nerve or blood vessel. **5.** *Mathematics.* The point of intersection of coordinate axes, from which measurements are made. See **Cartesian coordinate system.** [Middle English *origyne*, from Latin *orīgō* (stem *orīgin-*), from *orīrī*, to rise.]
    Synonyms: origin, inception, source, root.

o·rig·i·nal (ə-ríjin'l, o-) *adj. Abbr.* **orig. 1.** Of or pertaining to the beginning of something; initial; first. **2.** Fresh and unusual; not imitative; strikingly new. **3.** Able to think of and present new ideas; creative; inventive. **4.** Designating that from which a copy, reproduction, or translation is made. —See Usage note at **new.** —*n. Abbr.* **orig. 1.** The primary form of anything from which varieties arise: *Later models retained many features of the original.* **2.** An authentic work of art, literature, or the like, as distinguished from a copy or reproduction. **3.** One that is the model for an artistic or literary work. **4.** One having an unusual turn of mind or pattern of behaviour. **5.** *Informal.* A peculiar or eccentric person. [Middle English, from Old French, from Latin *orīginālis*, from *orīgō*, ORIGIN.]

o·rig·i·nal·i·ty (ə-riji-nál-əti, o-) *n., pl.* **-ties. 1.** The quality of being original. **2.** The capacity to act or think independently. **3.** Something original.

o·rig·i·nal·ly (ə-ríj-inəli, o-, -nəli) *adv. Abbr.* **orig. 1.** With reference to origin. **2.** At first. **3.** In a highly distinctive manner.

original sin *n. Theology.* **1.** The tendency to evil inherent in human beings as a result of Adam's first act of disobedience. **2.** The state of deprivation from grace resulting from Adam's sinful disobedience.

o·rig·i·nate (ə-riji-nayt, o-) *v.* **-nated, -nating, -nates.** —*tr.* To bring into being; create; invent. —*intr.* **1.** To come into being; start; spring. **2.** *Chiefly U.S.* To begin a journey from a specified starting point. Used of forms of transport. —**o·rig·i·na·tion** (-náysh'n) *n.* —**o·rig·i·na·tive** (-nətiv, -naytiv) *adj.* —**o·rig·i·na·tive·ly** *adv.* —**o·rig·i·na·tor** *n.*

O·ri·no·co (óri-nṓkō). Third-largest river of northeastern South America. It flows through southern Venezuela from the Brazilian border to the Colombian border, forms part of the border between Venezuela and Colombia, and then flows northeastwards across Venezuela to empty into the Atlantic. It has a length of about 2 575 kilometres (1,600 miles). [Spanish and Portuguese, from an Amerindian language "coiling snake".] —**O·ri·no·can** (-nṓkən) *adj. & n.*

o·ri·ole (áwri-ōl ‖ óri-) *n.* **1.** Any of various Old World birds of the family Oriolidae, of which the males are characteristically bright yellow and black. **2.** Any of various New World birds of the family Icteridae, of which the males are black and orange or yellow. See **Baltimore oriole.** [French *oriol*, from Old French, from Medieval Latin *oriolus*, "golden (bird)", variant of Latin *aureolus*, diminutive of *aureus*, golden, from *aurum*, gold.]

O·ri·on¹ (ə-rí-ən, o-, aw-). *Greek Mythology.* A giant hunter, pursuer of the Pleiades and lover of Eos, killed by Artemis.

Orion² *n.* A constellation in the celestial equator near Gemini and Taurus, containing the stars Betelgeuse and Rigel.

or·i·son (órriz'n) *n. Poetic.* A prayer. [Middle English, from Old French, from Latin *ōrātiō* (stem *oration-*), ORATION.]

Ork·ney (órk-ni) *n.* A type of cheese resembling Cheddar but with a flakier texture, made in the Orkney Islands.

Orkney Islands. Also **Ork·neys** (órk-niz). Group of 70 islands off northern Scotland, which belonged to Norway until 1471. Formerly a county, now officially an Island Authority area, the islands are used as a base for the North Sea oil industry. Principal islands are Mainland (Pomona), Hoy, and Sanday; Kirkwall is the chief town.

Or·lan·do (awr-lándō), **Vittorio Emmanuele** (1860–1952). Italian politician. Elected prime minister (1917), he resigned (1919) after failing to convince the Allies of Italian claims to Austrian territory.

orle (orl) *n. Heraldry.* An inner border not quite touching the edge of a shield. [French *orle, ourle,* from *ourler,* to edge, hem, from Vulgar Latin *orulāre* (unattested), from *orula* (unattested), diminutive of Latin *ora,* edge, border.]

Or·le·an·ist (awr-lée-ənist, órli-) *n.* A supporter of the Orléans branch of the French royal family, descended from the Duke of

Orléans, younger brother of Louis XIV.

Or·lé·ans (awr-lée-ənz, órli-; *French* -lay-ón). City in north central France. A royal residence since the seventh century, it is the capital of the Loiret département. Joan of Arc raised the English siege here (1429) in the Hundred Years' War; its cathedral was destroyed (1568) by the Huguenots, who were themselves massacred here on St. Bartholomew's Day, 1572.

Or·lé·ans (awrlay-óN), **Charles, Duc d'** (1391–1465). French general and poet. Captured by the English at Agincourt (1415), he spent the next quarter of a century as a prisoner in England and spent much of this time writing poetry in English. His son became Louis XII of France.

Orléans, Louis Philippe Joseph, Duc d', known as Philippe Égalité (1747–93). French politician. He was a radical revolutionary, despite being a member of the royal family. He voted for the execution of his cousin, Louis XVI, but was himself executed for treason. His son, Louis Philippe, became king.

Or·lon (ór-lon) *n.* A trademark for a synthetic acrylic fibre that is used alone or with other fibres in a variety of fabrics. —**or·lon** *adj.*

or·lop (ór-lop) *n. Nautical.* The lowest deck of a ship, especially a warship. Also called "orlop deck". [Middle English *overlop,* deck of a single-decker covering the hold, from Middle Low German *overlōp,* "a leaping over" : *over,* over + *lōpen,* to leap.]

Or·lov (awr-lóf; *Russian* aar-), **Grigory Grigoryevich, Count** (1734–83). Russian politician. A lover of Catherine the Great, he engineered, with his brother Alexei (1737–1808), the coup (1762) which brought Catherine to power. As adviser to the empress, he unsuccessfully supported reforms such as emancipation of the serfs.

Or·mazd, Or·muzd (órməzd). The chief deity of Zoroastrianism, the creator of the world, the source of light, and the embodiment of good. Also called "Ahura Mazda". Compare **Ahriman.** [Persian *Ormazd,* from Avestan *Ahura-Mazda,* "wise spirit" : *ahura,* spirit + *mazdā,* wise.]

or·mer (órmər) *n.* **1.** Any of various abalones; especially, an edible species, *Haliotis tuberculata,* found chiefly in the Channel Islands. **2.** The shell of this mollusc. Also called "sea ear". [Channel Islands French, from French *ormier,* short for *oreille-de-mer,* "sea-ear", from Latin *auris maris* : *auris,* ear + *maris,* genitive of *mare,* sea.]

or·mo·lu (ór-mə-lōō, -mṓ-, -lew, -lü) *n.* **1.** Any of several copper and tin or zinc alloys resembling gold in appearance and used to decorate furniture, mouldings, architectural ornamentations, and jewellery. Also called "mosaic gold". **2.** An imitation of gold. **3.** Formerly, gold or gold leaf used for gilding. [French *or moulu,* "ground gold" : *or,* gold, from Latin *aurum* + *moulu,* past participle of *moudre,* to grind, from Latin *molere.*]

or·na·ment (órnə-mənt) *n.* **1.** Anything that decorates or adorns; an embellishment. **2.** Decorations or adornments collectively. **3.** A small object used as a decoration, such as a porcelain figure. **4.** A person considered as a source of pride, honour, or credit because of personality, talent, or skill: *He is an ornament to his profession.* **5.** *Music.* A group of notes that embellishes or decorates a melody. —*tr.v.* (-mént) **ornamented, -menting, -ments. 1.** To furnish with ornaments. **2.** To be an ornament to. [Middle English, from Old French *ornement,* from Latin *ōrnāmentum,* from *ōrnāre,* to adorn.] —**or·na·ment·er** (-mentər) *n.*

or·na·men·tal (órnə-mént'l) *adj.* Of, pertaining to, or serving as an ornament; especially, decorative but inessential. —*n.* Something that is ornamental; especially, a plant grown for its beauty. —**or·na·men·tal·ly** *adv.*

or·na·men·ta·tion (órnə-men-táysh'n) *n.* **1. a.** The act, process, or result of ornamenting. **b.** The state of being ornamented. **2.** That which ornaments. **3.** Ornaments collectively.

or·nate (awr-náyt, ór-nayt) *adj.* **1.** Elaborately and heavily ornamented; excessively decorated. **2.** Showy or florid in style or manner; flowery. [Middle English *ornat,* from Latin *ōrnātus,* past participle of *ōrnāre,* to adorn.] —**or·nate·ly** *adv.* —**or·nate·ness** *n.*
    Synonyms: ornate, florid, flamboyant, lavish, gaudy, showy.

or·ner·y (órnəri) *adj.* **-ier, -iest.** *U.S. Informal.* **1.** Having an ugly disposition; specifically, stubborn and mean-spirited. **2.** Deceitful; unfair; treacherous: *an ornery fraud.* **3.** Ordinary. [Variant of ORDINARY.] —**or·ner·i·ness** *n.*

or·ni·thine (órni-theen) *n.* An amino acid, $C_5H_{12}N_2O_{12}$, produced in the liver during the formation of urea. [ORNITH(O)- (representing *ornithuric acid,* secreted in urine of birds and reptiles) + -INE.]

ornitho–, ornith– *comb. form.* Indicates a bird or birds; for example, **ornithology.** [New Latin, from Greek, from *ornis* (stem *ornith-*), bird.]

or·ni·thol·o·gy (órni-thóllǝji) *n. Abbr.* **ornith., ornithol.** The scientific study of birds. [New Latin *ornithologia* : ORNITHO- + -LOGY.] —**or·ni·tho·log·i·cal** (-thǝ-lójik'l) *adj.* —**or·ni·tho·log·i·cal·ly** *adv.* —**or·ni·thol·o·gist** (-thóllǝjist) *n.*

or·ni·thop·ter (órni-thoptər) *n.* An aircraft supported in the air and propelled by wing movements. Also called "orthopter". [ORNITHO- + -PTER.]

or·ni·tho·rhyn·chus (órnithō-ríngkǝss) *n.* The **duck-billed platypus** (see). [New Latin, from ORNITHO- + Greek *rhunkos,* bill.]

or·ni·tho·sis (órni-thṓ-siss) *n.* A contagious virus disease of the psittacosis group that infects poultry and other birds, and is transmissible to humans. [New Latin : ORNITH(O)- + -OSIS.] —**or·ni·thot·ic** (-thóttik) *adj.*

oro–¹ *comb. form.* Indicates a mountain; for example, **orology.** [Greek *orost,* mountain.]

oro–² *comb. form.* Indicates a mouth; for example, **oropharynx.** [Latin *ōs* (stem *or-*), mouth.]

o·rog·e·ny (o-rójəni, aw-) *n.* The process of mountain formation, especially by folding and faulting of the earth's crust. Also called "orogenesis". [ORO-¹ + -GENY.] **—or·o·gen·ic** (áw-rə-jénnik, ó-, -rō- ‖ ó-) *adj.* **—or·o·gen·i·cal·ly** *adv.*

o·rog·ra·phy (o-róggrəfi, aw- ‖ ó-) *n.* The study of the physical geography of mountains and mountain ranges. [ORO-¹ + -GRAPHY.] **—or·o·graph·ic** (áw-rə-gráffik, ó-, -rō- ‖ ó-), **or·o·graph·i·cal** *adj.* **—or·o·graph·i·cal·ly** *adv.*

o·ro·ide (áw-rō-īd, ó- ‖ ó-) *n.* Also **o·re·ide** (-ri-). An inexpensive alloy of copper, zinc, and tin, used in imitation gold jewellery. [French *oréide : or,* gold, from Latin *aurum,* gold + *-éide,* -OID.] **—o·ro·ide, o·re·ide** *adj.*

o·rol·o·gy (o-rólləji, aw- ‖ ó-) *n.* The study of mountains. [ORO-¹ + -LOGY.] **—or·o·log·i·cal** (áw-rə-lójik'l, ó-, -rō- ‖ ó-) *adj.* **—o·ro·log·i·cal·ly** *adv.* **—o·rol·o·gist** *n.*

o·rom·e·ter (o-rómmitər, aw- ‖ ó-) *n.* An instrument that indicates height above sea level using barometric means.

O·ron·tes (o-rón-teez, ə-, aw-). River of southwestern Asia. Rising in the Lebanon, it flows 370 kilometres (230 miles) mainly northwards through Syria and Turkey to join the Mediterranean near Samandag. Though unnavigable, it is used extensively for irrigation.

o·ro·tund (ó-rō-tund, áw-, -ə ‖ ó-) *adj.* **1.** Full in sound; sonorous: *spoke in orotund tones.* **2.** Pompous and bombastic: *orotund talk.* [Latin *ōre rotundō,* "with round mouth" : *ōs* (stem *ōr-*), mouth + *rotundus,* rounded, ROTUND.] **—o·ro·tun·di·ty** (-túndəti) *n.*

or·phan (órf'n) *n.* **1.** A child whose parents are dead. **2.** *Chiefly U.S.* A child who has lost one parent by death.
~adj. 1. Being an orphan. **2.** For orphans: *an orphan home.*
~ tr.v. orphaned, -phaning, -phans. To deprive (a child) of both parents, or *chiefly U.S.* one parent, by death. [Latin *orphanus,* from Greek *orphanos,* orphaned.] **—or·phan·hood** *n.*

or·phan·age (órf'n-ij) *n.* **1.** An institution for the care and protection of orphans and abandoned children. **2.** The state or condition of being an orphan.

or·phar·i·on (awr-fárri-on) *n.* A large, lutelike musical instrument popular in the 17th century. [Blend of *Orpheus* +*Arion* (legendary Greek musicians).]

Or·phe·an (awr-fée-ən ‖ órfi-ən) *adj.* **1.** Of or pertaining to Orpheus. **2.** Beautiful; entrancing. Said of sounds.

Or·pheus (ór-fewss ‖ -fi-əss). *Greek Mythology.* Poet and musician who ventured into Hades to retrieve his wife Eurydice. The poems on which Orphism is based were ascribed to him.

Or·phic (órfik) *adj.* **1.** Of or ascribed to Orpheus; Orphean: *the Orphic poems; Orphic mysteries.* **2.** Of, pertaining to, or characteristic of the dogmas, mysteries, and philosophical principles set forth in the poems ascribed to Orpheus. **3.** *Sometimes small* **o.** Mystic or occult in nature; esoteric. [Latin *Orphicus,* from Greek *Orphikos,* from ORPHEUS.] **—Or·phi·cal·ly** *adv.*

Or·phism (órfiz'm) *n.* **1.** An ancient Greek mystery religion arising in the sixth century B.C. from a synthesis of pre-Hellenic beliefs with the cult of Dionysus **Zagreus** *(see).* **2.** An early form of cubism using geometric shapes and vivid colours. [French *orphisme,* from *Orphée,* from Greek *Orpheus,* ORPHEUS.] **—Or·phist** *n. & adj.*

or·phrey (órfri) *n., pl.* **-phreys.** Also **or·fray** *pl.* **-frays. 1.** A band of elaborate embroidery decorating the front of certain ecclesiastical vestments. **2.** Any elaborate embroidery, especially when worked in gold. [Middle English *orfrey, orphreis* (taken as plural), from Old French *orfreis,* from Medieval Latin *aurifrigium* : Latin *aurum,* gold + *Phrygium,* neuter of *Phrygius,* embroidered, PHRYGIAN.]

or·pi·ment (órpimənt) *n.* A mineral, arsenic trisulphide, As₂S₃, used as a lemon-yellow pigment in tanning and linoleum manufacture. [Middle English, from Old French, from Latin *auripigmentum : aurum,* gold + *pigmentum,* PIGMENT.]

or·pine (órpīn) *n.* Any of several plants of the genus *Sedum;* especially, *S. telephium,* native to Eurasia, having clusters of reddish-purple flowers. Also *British* "livelong". [Middle English *orpin,* from Old French *orpine,* short for *orpiment,* ORPIMENT, probably after the yellow flowers of one species.]

Or·ping·ton (órpingtən) *n.* A domestic fowl of a breed having a large body, a single comb, and unfeathered legs, such as the buff Orpington. [After *Orpington,* Kent, where the breed originated.]

or·re·ry (órrəri) *n., pl.* **-ries.** A mechanical model of the Solar System. [After Charles Boyle (1676–1731), 4th Earl of *Orrery,* for whom one was made.]

or·ris (órriss) *n.* **1.** Any of several species of iris having a fragrant rootstock; especially, *Iris florentina.* **2.** Orrisroot. [Probably unexplained variant of IRIS.]

or·ris·root (órriss-rōot ‖ -rŏot) *n.* The fragrant rootstock of the orris, used in perfumes and cosmetics.

Or·si·ni (awr-séeni). An aristocratic family of medieval Italy. Originating in Rome, they supported the Papal (or Guelph) faction against the Imperial (or Ghibelline) faction. The family included two popes—Celestine III (reigned 1191–98), and Nicholas III (reigned 1277–80).

or·tan·ique (órtə-néek) *n.* A fruit produced by crossing an orange with a tangerine. [From *orange* + *tangerine* + *unique.*]

Or·te·ga Sa·a·ved·ra (ortáygə saa-váydrə), **Daniel** (1945–). Nicaraguan politician, president of Nicaragua 1985–90.

Ortega y Gas·set (awr-táygə i ga-sét), **José** (1883–1955). Spanish philosopher. He is best known for his neo-Kantian doctrines of

individualism and will-power, as expounded in such works as *The Revolt of the Masses* (1929).

Or·te·li·us (awr-táyli-əss), **Abraham** (1527–98). Flemish geographer. A careful scholar and an extensive traveller, he published his *Theatrum Orbis Terrarum* (1570), which appeared in 40 editions and is regarded as the first modern atlas. He was appointed Cartographer Royal of Spain (1575).

orth. orthopaedic; orthopaedics.

or·thi·con (órthi-kon) *n.* A television camera tube that uses a low-energy electron beam to scan a photoactive mosaic. Also called "image orthicon". [ORTH(O)- + ICON(OSCOPE).]

or·tho (órthō) *adj. Chemistry & Physics.* **1.** Of, pertaining to, or designating adjacent positions in a benzene ring. Used in combination, often italicised: *orthodichlorobenzene.* **2.** Of, pertaining to, or designating the most highly hydrated form of an acid. Used in combination: *orthophosphoric acid.* **3.** Of, pertaining to, or designating the form of a diatonic molecule in which the nuclear spins are parallel. Used in combination: *orthohydrogen.* Compare **meta, para, pyro.** [From ORTHO-.]

ortho-, orth– *comb. form.* Indicates: **1.** Straight or upright; for example, **orthotropic. 2.** *Mathematics.* Perpendicular to or at right angles; for example, **orthorhombic. 3.** Correct or standard; for example, **orthography. 4.** *Medicine.* Correction of maladjustments or deformities; for example, **orthopaedics.** [Middle English, from Old French, from Latin, from Greek *orthos,* straight, correct, right, upright.]

or·tho·bo·ric acid (órthō-báw-rik, -bó- ‖ -bó̌-) *n. Chemistry.* **Boric acid** *(see).*

or·tho·cen·tre (órthō-sentər) *n.* The point of intersection of the three altitudes of a triangle.

or·tho·ce·phal·ic (órthō-si-fál-ik) *adj.* Also **or·tho·ceph·a·lous** (-séffələss). Having a ratio of skull height to skull length between 0.70 and 0.75. [ORTHO-, correct + -CEPHALIC.] **—or·tho·ceph·a·ly** (-séffəli) *n.*

or·tho·chro·mat·ic (ór-thō-krō-máttik-, -thə-, -krə-) *adj.* **1.** Of, having, or reproducing the colours of nature accurately. **2.** Of or pertaining to a film, plate, or emulsion that renders all colours, except red, in tones of grey approximating to the relative brilliance of these colours. Compare **panchromatic. —or·tho·chro·mat·ic·al·ly** *adv.* **—or·tho·chro·ma·tism** (-krō̌mətiz'm) *n.*

or·tho·clase (órthō-klayss, -klayz) *n.* A **potassium feldspar** *(see),* essentially potassium aluminium silicate, KAlSi₃O₈, characterised by a monoclinic crystalline structure and found in igneous, metamorphic, and sedimentary rocks. [German *Orthoklas* : ORTHO- + -CLASE.]

or·tho·don·tics (ór-thō-dóntiks, -thə-) *n.* The dental speciality and practice of correcting abnormally aligned or positioned teeth. Also called "orthodontia". [ORTH(O)- + -ODONT + -ICS.] **—or·tho·don·tic** *adj.* **—or·tho·don·tist** *n.*

or·tho·dox (órthə-doks) *adj.* **1. a.** Adhering to a commonly accepted, customary, or traditional practice or belief. **b.** Broadly, conventional in outlook or behaviour. **2.** Adhering to the accepted or traditional and established faith, especially in religion. Compare **heterodox. 3.** Adhering to the Christian faith as expressed in the early Christian ecumenical creeds. **4.** *Capital* **O. a.** Of, pertaining to, or designating any of the churches of the Eastern Orthodox Church. **b.** Of, pertaining to, or designating Orthodox Judaism. [Old French *orthodoxe,* from Late Latin *orthodoxus,* from Greek *orthodoxos,* having the right opinion : ORTHO- + *doxa,* opinion, from *dokein,* to think.] **—or·tho·dox·ly** *adv.*

Orthodox Church *n.* The **Eastern Orthodox Church** *(see).*

Orthodox Judaism *n.* The branch of the Jewish faith that adheres to the Mosaic Law as interpreted in the Talmud, and considers it binding in modern as well as ancient times. Compare **Conservative Judaism, Reform Judaism.**

orthodox sleep *n.* The major part of sleep, during which no dreaming occurs and the body and brain are in a state of very low activity. Compare **paradoxical sleep.**

or·tho·dox·y (órthə-doksi) *n., pl.* **-ies. 1.** The quality or state of being orthodox. **2.** Orthodox practice, custom, or belief.

or·tho·e·py (órthō-eppi, -éppi, awr-thō̌-ipi) *n.* **1.** The study of the pronunciation of words. **2.** The customary pronunciation of words. [New Latin *orthoepia,* from Greek *orthoepeia* : ORTHO- + *epos,* word.] **—or·thō·ep·ic** (-éppik), **or·tho·ep·i·cal** *adj.* **—or·tho·e·pist** (órthō-eppist, -éppist, awr-thō̌-ipist) *n.*

or·tho·gen·e·sis (órthō-jénni-siss) *n.* **1.** *Biology.* The theory that evolutionary change is predetermined by the constitution of germ plasm and independent of external factors. **2.** *Anthropology.* The theory that all cultures pass through sequential periods in the same order. [New Latin : ORTHO- + -GENESIS.] **—or·tho·ge·net·ic** (jə-néttik) *adj.* **—or·tho·ge·net·i·cal·ly** *adv.*

or·tho·gen·ic (ór-thō-jénnik, -thə-) *adj.* **1.** In psychiatry, pertaining to the correction or treatment of mental and emotional abnormalities in children. **2.** Of or pertaining to orthogenesis. [ORTHO- + -GENIC.]

or·thog·na·thous (awr-thóg-nəthəss) *adj.* Also **or·thog·nath·ic** (órthəg-náthik). Having the lower jaw correctly aligned with the upper so that it does not protrude or recede. [ORTHO- + -GNATHOUS.] **—or·thog·na·thism** (-thóg-nəthiz'm), **or·thog·na·thy** *n.*

or·thog·o·nal (awr-thóggən'l) *adj. Mathematics.* **1.** Pertaining to or composed of right angles. **2. a.** Having a defined scalar product of zero. Said of two vectors. **b.** Having a defined product of zero. Said of two functions. **c.** Of or designating a matrix that is equal to the inverse of its transpose. [Greek *orthogōnios* : ORTHO- + *gōnia*, angle.] —**or·thog·o·nal·ly** *adv.*

orthogonal projection *n.* The two-dimensional graphic representation of an object formed by the perpendicular intersections of lines drawn from points on the object to a plane of projection. Also called "orthographic projection".

or·tho·graph·ic (órthə-gráffik) *adj.* Also **or·tho·graph·i·cal** (-gráffik'l). **1.** Of or pertaining to orthography. **2.** Spelt correctly. **3.** *Mathematics.* Having perpendicular lines. —**or·tho·graph·i·cal·ly** *adv.*

or·thog·ra·phy (awr-thóggrəfi) *n., pl.* **-phies. 1.** The art or study of correct spelling according to established usage. **2.** The aspect of language study concerned with letters and their sequences in words. **3.** Any method of representing the sounds of language by literal symbols. [Middle English *ortografie*, from Old French, from Latin *orthographia*, from Greek : ORTHO- + -GRAPHY.] —**or·thog·ra·pher, or·thog·ra·phist** *n.*

or·tho·hy·dro·gen (órthō-hídrəjən) *n.* A form of hydrogen in which the two nuclei in each molecule have parallel spins; one of two possible forms of molecular hydrogen, constituting 75 per cent of hydrogen at room temperature. Compare **parahydrogen.**

or·tho·pae·dics, *U.S.* **or·tho·pe·dics** (ór-thə-péediks, -thō-) *n. Abbr.* **orth.** *Used with a singular verb.* The surgical or manipulative treatment of disorders of the skeletal system and associated muscles. [French *orthopédie* : ORTHO- + Greek *paideia*, education, from *pais* (stem *paid*-), child.] —**or·tho·pae·dic** *adj.* —**or·tho·pae·di·cal·ly** *adv.* —**or·tho·pae·dist** *n.*

or·tho·psy·chi·a·try (órthō-sī-kí-ətri, -si-) *n.* The prevention and early treatment of mental disorders, especially in the young. —**or·tho·psy·chi·at·ric** (-sī-ki-áttrik), **or·tho·psy·chi·at·ri·cal** *adj.* —**or·tho·psy·chi·a·trist** (-sī-kí-ətrist, -si-) *n.*

or·thop·ter (ór-thoptər) *n.* An aircraft, an **ornithopter** *(see).* [ORTHO- + -PTER.]

or·thop·ter·an (awr-thóptə-rən) *n.* Also **or·thop·ter·on** (-rən, -ron) *pl.* **-era.** Any insect of the order Orthoptera, characterised by membranous, folded hind wings covered by leathery, narrow fore wings, and including the locusts, cockroaches, crickets, and grasshoppers. [New Latin *Orthoptera* (order), "straight-wings" : ORTHO- + *-ptera,* from *-pterus,* -PTEROUS.] —**or·thop·ter·al, or·thop·ter·an, or·thop·ter·ous** *adj.*

or·thop·tics (awr-thóptiks) *n. Used with a singular verb.* The practice of using eye exercises and other nonsurgical methods to correct abnormalities of vision. [ORTH(O)- + OPTICS.] —**or·thop·tist** *n.*

or·tho·rhom·bic (órthō-rómbik) *adj.* Of, pertaining to, or designating a crystalline structure of three mutually perpendicular axes of different length.

or·tho·scope (ór-thō-skōp, -thə-) *n.* Formerly, an instrument for examining the eye through a layer of water that compensates for the curvature of the cornea. [ORTHO- + -SCOPE.]

or·tho·scop·ic (ór-thō-skóppik, -thə-) *adj.* **1.** Having or pertaining to normal vision. **2.** Pertaining to the use of the orthoscope.

or·thos·ti·chous (awr-thóstikəss) *adj. Biology.* Characterised by parallel arrangement in a vertical row. Said especially of leaves. [ORTHO- + Greek *stikhos,* a row.] —**or·thos·ti·chy** *n.*

or·thot·ics (awr-thóttiks) *n. Used with a singular verb.* The branch of orthopaedics concerned with the use of mechanical devices to support or correct weakened or deformed joints. [From *orthotic* : ORTH(O)- + -OTIC.] —**or·thot·ic** *adj.* —**or·tho·tist** *n.*

or·tho·trop·ic (ór-thō-tróppik, -thə-) *adj.* Tending to grow or form along a vertical axis. Said especially of plant parts. [ORTHO- + -TROPIC.] —**or·tho·trop·i·cal·ly** *adv.* —**or·thot·ro·pism** (awr-thóttrə-piz'm) *n.*

or·tho·tro·pous (awr-thóttrəpəss) *adj. Botany.* Growing straight, so that the micropyle is at the side opposite the stalk. Said of an ovule. [ORTHO- + -TROPOUS.]

or·to·lan (órtə-lən) *n.* **1.** A small, brownish bird, *Emberiza hortulana,* of Europe and Asia, eaten as a delicacy. **2.** Loosely, any of several American birds, such as the bobolink. [French, from Provençal, gardener, from Latin *hortolānus,* from *hortulus,* diminutive of *hortus,* garden.]

orts (orts) *n. Sometimes singular. Archaic & Regional.* Small scraps or leavings of food after a meal is completed. [Middle English, probably from Middle Dutch *orte,* contraction of *oor aete,* leftover, "out eat" : *oor-,* out + *eten,* to eat.]

Or·vie·to¹ (órvi-áytō). Town of west central Italy. Thought to be near the site of the Etruscan city of Volsinii, it has many Etruscan remains. Its most notable building is its cathedral.

Orvieto² *n.* A light, white Italian wine produced in the area around Orvieto.

Or·well (ór-wel, -wəl), **George,** pen name of Eric Arthur Blair (1903–50). British writer. Despite his prosperous background, he became a socialist and lived amongst low-paid workers and tramps as recorded in *Down and Out in Paris and London* (1933). Disillusioned with communism while fighting the Nationalists in the Spanish Civil War, he attacked totalitarianism in novels such as *Animal Farm* (1945) and *1984* (1949). —**Or·well·i·an** (-wélli-ən) *adj.*

Or·well·ism (ór-wel-iz'm, -wəl-) *n.* The dubious use of propaganda; specifically, the distortion and manipulation of news or history by governments or official agencies in order to influence public opinion. [After George ORWELL, referring especially to the description of such practices in his novel *1984.*]

–ory¹ *n. suffix.* Indicates: **1.** A place for; for example, **conserva-**

tory, observatory. **2.** Something used as; for example, **accessory, directory.** [Middle English *-orie,* from Anglo-French *-orie* or Old French *-orie, -oire,* from Latin *-ōrium, -ōria,* from *-ōrius,* adjective suffix.]

–ory² *adj. suffix.* Indicates characterisation by, possession of the nature of, or tendency towards; for example, **compensatory.** [Middle English *-orie,* Anglo-French, Old French *-oire, -orie,* from Latin *-ōrius,* adjective suffix.]

o·ryx (órriks ‖ ő-riks, áw-) *n., pl.* **oryxes** or **oryx.** Any of several antelopes of the genus *Oryx,* of Africa and Arabia, having long, straight horns. [Latin, from Greek *orux,* pickaxe, spike, hence (from the sharp horns) gazelle, perhaps from *orussein,* to dig.]

os¹ (oss ‖ ōss) *n., pl.* **ora** (áwrə ‖ ōrə). *Anatomy.* A mouth or opening. [Latin *ōs* (stem *ōr*-), mouth.]

os² (oss) *n., pl.* **ossa** (óssə). *Anatomy.* A bone. [Latin *os* (stem *oss*-), bone.]

os³ (ōss) *n., pl.* **osar** (ő-saar). *Geology.* An **esker** *(see).* [Swedish *ås,* ridge, from Old Norse *āss.*]

Os The symbol for the element osmium.

o.s., o/s out of stock.

O.S. 1. Old Series. **2.** Old Style. **3.** ordinary seaman. **4.** Ordnance Survey (in Britain).

OSA, O.S.A. Order of St. Augustine.

O·sage (ō-sáyj, ő-sayj) *n., pl.* **Osages** or collectively **Osage. 1.** A member of a Siouan-speaking North American Indian people, formerly inhabiting the region between the Missouri and Arkansas rivers. **2.** The Siouan language of this people. —**O·sage** *adj.*

O·sa·ka (ō-sáakə). Port of southern Japan. Situated on the Yodo delta, it is the centre of the Osaka Bay conurbation of southwest Honshu, and the country's second most important industrial and commercial city. Among its historic buildings are Imperial palaces and ancient Buddhist temples.

OSB, O.S.B. Order of St. Benedict.

Os·borne (óz-bawrn, -bərn), **John (James)** (1929–94). British playwright. His first major play, *Look Back in Anger* (1956), heralded a revolution in British postwar theatre, with naturalistic, politically and socially conscious plays coming to dominate serious drama.

Os·can (óskən) *n.* **1.** A member of an ancient people of Campania. **2.** The Italic language of this people.
~*adj.* Of or pertaining to the Oscans or their language.

Os·car (óskər) *n.* An **Academy Award** *(see).* [Apparently humorously named after a remark made by an official when he first saw it, that it looked like his uncle Oscar.]

os·cil·late (óssi-layt) *v.* **-lated, -lating, -lates.** —*intr.* **1.** To swing back and forth with a steady uninterrupted rhythm. **2.** To waver between two or more thoughts or courses of action; vacillate. **3.** *Physics.* To move or change between alternate extremes, usually in a regular way with a definable period. Said of vibrating objects, systems, waves, and the like. —*tr.* To cause to oscillate. —See Synonyms at **swing.** [Latin *ōscillāre,* from *ōscillum,* a swing, originally a mask of Bacchus hung from a tree in a vineyard to swing in the wind (as a charm), diminutive of *ōs,* face, mouth.] —**os·cil·la·tor** *n.* —**os·cil·la·to·ry** (óssi-lə-təri, -tri, -laytəri, -láytəri) *adj.*

os·cil·la·tion (óssi-láysh'n) *n.* **1.** The state or act of oscillating. **2.** A single cycle in which a system changes to one extreme state, then to the other extreme, and back to its original state; a period.

os·cil·lo·gram (o-sílla-gram, ə-) *n.* **1.** The graph traced by an oscillograph. **2.** An instantaneous oscilloscope trace or photograph of such a trace. [OSCILLO(GRAPH) + -GRAM.]

os·cil·lo·graph (o-sílla-graaf, ə-, -graf) *n.* A device that records oscillations as a continuous graph of variation in a quantity with time. [French *oscillographe* : OSCILL(ATION) + -GRAPH.] —**os·cil·log·ra·phy** (óssi-lóggrəfi) *n.*

os·cil·lo·scope (o-sílla-skōp, ə-) *n.* An electronic instrument that produces an almost instantaneous graph of the change of some quantity with time (or some other variable) by deflection of a narrow beam of electrons focused onto a fluorescent screen. The varying quantity is converted into an electrical signal used to deflect the electrons in a vertical direction, with repeated scanning in the horizontal direction by a periodic deflecting potential, thus producing a trace on the screen. [OSCILL(ATION) + -SCOPE (used especially for displaying oscillating signals).] —**os·cil·lo·scop·ic** (-skóppik) *adj.*

os·cine (óssīn, óssin) *adj.* Of or pertaining to the Oscines, a large suborder of the passerine birds that includes most songbirds. [New Latin *Oscines,* from Latin *oscinēs,* plural of *oscen,* a singing bird used for augury.] —**os·cine** *n.*

os·ci·tan·cy (óssi-tən-si) *n., pl.* **-cies.** Also **os·ci·tance** (-tənss). **1.** The act of yawning. **2.** The state of being drowsy or inattentive; dullness. [Latin *ōscitāns,* present participle of *ōscitāre,* to gape : *ōs,* mouth + *citāre,* to move.] —**os·ci·tant** *adj.*

Os·co-Um·bri·an (óskō-úmbri-ən) *n.* A subdivision of the Italic languages, including Oscan and Umbrian. —**Os·co-Um·bri·an** *adj.*

os·cu·lant (óskewlənt) *adj. Biology.* **1.** Intermediate in characteristics between two similar or related taxonomic groups. **2.** Closely adhering or joined; embracing. [Latin *ōsculāns* (stem *ōsculant*-), present participle of *ōsculārī,* to OSCULATE.]

os·cu·late (óskew-layt) *v.* **-lated, -lating, -lates.** —*tr.* To kiss. Usually used humorously. —*intr.* **1.** To kiss. Usually used humorously. **2.** *Biology.* To have characteristics intermediate between those of two similar or related taxonomic groups. **3.** In geometry, to touch at a single point without crossing. Used of two curves or surfaces. [Latin *ōsculārī,* from *ōsculum,* kiss, OSCULUM.]

os·cu·la·tion (óskew-láysh'n) *n.* **1. a.** The act of osculating. **b.** A kiss. **2.** In geometry: **a.** A point at which two figures touch. **b.** A **tacnode** (*see*). —**os·cu·la·to·ry** (-lə-təri, -tri, laytəri, -láytəri) *adj.*

os·cu·lum (óskew-ləm) *n., pl.* **-la** (-lə). Also **os·cule** (óskewl). *Zoology.* An opening; especially, the opening in a sponge for expelling water. [New Latin, from Latin *ōsculum,* little mouth, kiss, diminutive of *ōs,* mouth.] —**os·cu·lar** *adj.*

-ose[1] *adj. suffix.* Indicates possession of or similarity to; for example, **bellicose, grandiose.** [Middle English, from Latin *-ōsus.* See **-ous.**]

-ose[2] *n. suffix. Chemistry.* Indicates: **1.** A carbohydrate; for example, **fructose, lactose. 2.** A product of protein hydrolysis; for example, **proteose.** [From GLUCOSE.]

o·si·er (ṓ-zi-ər, -zhər, -zhi-ər) *n.* **1.** Any of several willows having long, rodlike twigs used in basketry; especially, *Salix viminalis* and *S. purpurea,* both native to Eurasia. **2.** A twig of such a willow. **3.** Any of various similar trees. [Middle English, from Old French, from Medieval Latin *ausēriat†,* willow bed.] —**o·si·er** *adj.*

O·si·ris (ō-sír-iss, o-). *Egyptian Mythology.* A god who was ruler and judge in the underworld, brother and consort of Isis. He is identified with the Nile, and his annual death and resurrection symbolised the self-renewing fertility of nature. —**O·si·ri·an** *adj.*

-osis *n. suffix.* Indicates: **1.** A condition or process; for example, **metamorphosis, osmosis. 2.** A diseased or abnormal condition; for example, **tuberculosis, neurosis. 3.** An increase or formation of; for example, **sclerosis, leucocytosis.** [Middle English, from Latin, from Greek *-ōsis,* abstract noun suffix formed from *o*-stem verbs.]

Os·lo (óz-lō, óss-; *Norwegian* ṓoss-loō). Capital of Norway. An ice-free port at the head of Oslo Fjord, it was founded (1050) by Harold III and became the nation's capital in 1299. Following destruction by fire, it was rebuilt in 1624 when it was renamed Christiania, reverting to its former name in 1925.

Os·man I (oz-maán, oss-, ōss-, ózmən), also known as Othman I (1259–1326). Founder of the Ottoman dynasty that ruled Turkey after 1290. He raised a conquering army of Muslim Turks that held sway over most of northwestern Asia Minor.

Os·man·li (oz-mánli, oss-, -maánli) *n., pl.* **-lis. 1.** An Ottoman Turk. **2.** Ottoman Turkish (*see*). **3.** The Turkish language when written in Arabic script, as it was until 1930.
~*adj.* Ottoman. [Turkish : *Osman,* Osman I + *-li,* adjectival suffix.]

os·mat·ic (oz-máttik) *adj.* Also **os·mic** (ózmik). Having or characterised by a sense of smell. [Greek *osmē,* smell + -AT(E) + -IC.]

os·mic (ózmik) *adj.* Of, pertaining to, or containing osmium. Said especially of compounds containing osmium with a high valency. [From OSMIUM.]

os·mi·rid·i·um (ózmi-ríddi-əm) *n.* A natural alloy of osmium and iridium, used in needles, pen nibs, electric-switch contacts, and other small items subject to wear. Also called "iridosmine". [German : OSM(IUM)- + IRIDIUM.]

os·mi·um (ózmi-əm) *n. Symbol* **Os** A bluish-white, hard, metallic element, found in small amounts in osmiridium and platinum ores. It has the highest measured density of any element. It is used as a platinum hardener, in making pen points and instrument pivots, and also as a catalyst in cortisone synthesis. Atomic number 76, atomic weight 190.2, melting point 3,000°C, boiling point 5,000°C, relative density 22.57, valencies 2, 3, 4, 8. [New Latin, from Greek *osmē,* smell (from the smell of osmium tetroxide).]

os·mom·e·ter (oz-mómmitər, oss-) *n.* Any of various instruments or pieces of apparatus used to measure osmotic pressures. [OSMO(SIS) + METER.] —**os·mo·met·ric** (óz-mə-méttrik, óss-) *adj.* —**os·mo·met·ri·cal·ly** *adv.* —**os·mom·e·try** (-mómmətri) *n.*

os·mo·reg·u·la·tion (óz-mō-réggew-láysh'n, óss-) *n.* The maintenance in the body of a living animal of the correct proportions of water and salts. [OSMO(SIS) + REGULATION.] —**os·mo·reg·u·la·to·ry** (-lə-tri, -təri, -láytəri) *adj.*

os·mose (oz-mṓss, óss-, -mōz, -mōz) *v.* **-mosed, -mosing, -moses.** —*intr.* To undergo or diffuse by osmosis. —*tr.* To subject to osmosis. [From OSMOSIS, taken to be the common element of *exosmose* and *endosmose,* obsolete forms of EXOSMOSIS and ENDOSMOSIS.]

os·mo·sis (oz-mṓ-siss, oss-) *n.* **1.** The diffusion of solvent through a semipermeable membrane until there is an equal concentration of solution on either side of the membrane. **2.** The tendency to diffuse in such a manner. **3.** *Informal.* Any gradual, often unconscious, process of assimilation or absorption that resembles this diffusion: *learning a language by osmosis.* [Earlier *osmose,* from Greek *ōsmos,* action of pushing, from *ōthein,* to push.] —**os·mot·ic** (-móttik) *adj.* —**os·mot·i·cal·ly** *adv.*

osmotic pressure *n. Symbol* **Π.** The pressure developed across a membrane as a result of osmosis. For a given solution it is the pressure required to prevent osmosis from the solution to a pure solvent, such as water. [Greek *ōsmos* (stem *ōsmot-*), OSMOSIS.]

os·mous (ózməss) *adj.* Also **os·mi·ous** (ózmi-əss). Of, pertaining to, or containing osmium. Said especially of compounds containing osmium with a low valency.

os·mun·da (oz-múndə) *n.* Also **os·mund** (ózmənd). Any fern of the genus *Osmunda,* having erect, compound fronds and, in some species, fibrous roots used as a potting medium for cultivated plants. [Middle English, from Old French *osmundet†.*]

os·prey (óss-pri, -pray) *n., pl.* **-preys. 1.** A fish-eating hawk, *Pandion haliaetus,* having plumage that is dark on the back and white below. Also *chiefly U.S.* "fish eagle", "fish hawk", "ossifrage". **2.** A deco-

rative feather formerly used to trim women's hats. [Middle English *ospray,* from Old French *ospreit* (unattested), from Vulgar Latin *avispreda* (unattested), from Latin *avis praedae,* "bird of prey" : *avis,* bird, + *praeda,* prey. The Old French form and meaning are influenced by Old French *osfraie,* from Latin *ossifraga,* OSSIFRAGE.]

os·sa. Plural of **os** (bone).

Os·sa, Mount (óssə). Mountain in the Duana range of central Tasmania, it is, at 1 617 metres (5,305 feet), the island's highest point.

os·se·in (óssi-in) *n.* The protein residue of bone after acid dissolution, used in gelatine and glue. [OSSE(OUS) + -IN.]

os·se·ous (óssi-əss) *adj.* Composed of, containing, or resembling bone; bony. [Latin *osseus,* from *os,* bone.] —**os·se·ous·ly** *adv.*

Os·set (óssit) *n.* Also **Os·sete** (ósseet). A member of a people of Iranian origin living in Ossetia, a region of the former U.S.S.R., straddling the Caucasus mountains. —**Os·se·tian** (o-seésh'n) *n. & adj.*

Os·set·ic (o-séttik) *n.* The Iranian language of the Ossets.
~*adj.* Of or pertaining to the Ossets, their country, or their languages.

os·si·a (óssi-ə) *conj. Music.* Or else. Used as a direction to the performer to designate an alternative section or passage. [Italian, from *o sia,* "or let it be".]

Os·si·an (óssi-ən ‖ ósh'n) (*c.* third century A.D.). Legendary Irish warrior-poet. He occurs in the Fianna cycle of ballads under the name of Oisin. —**Os·si·an·ic** (-ánnik) *adj.*

os·si·cle (óssik'l) *n. Anatomy.* A small bone; especially, any of the three sound-conducting bones, malleus, incus, and stapes, of the inner ear. [Latin *ossiculum,* diminutive of *os,* bone.] —**os·sic·u·lar** (o-sickew-lər, ossik-) *adj.* —**os·sic·u·late** (-lət, -lit) *adj.*

os·si·fi·ca·tion (óssifi-káysh'n) *n.* **1.** The natural process of bone formation. Also called "osteogenesis". **2. a.** The abnormal hardening or calcification of soft tissue into a bonelike material. **b.** A mass or deposit of such material. **3.** The process of becoming or state of being set in a rigidly conventional pattern, as of behaviour, habits, or beliefs. —**os·sif·i·ca·to·ry** (-káytəri, -kə-təri, -tri ‖ o-síffikə-) *adj.*

os·si·frage (óssi-frij, -frayj) *n. Archaic.* Either of two hawks, the **osprey** or the **lammergeier** (*both of which see*). [Latin (*avis*) *ossifraga,* "bone-breaking (bird)", lammergeier (which is said to drop its prey from a height to break the bones), from *ossifragus,* bonebreaking : *os* (stem *oss-*), bone + *frangere,* to break.]

os·si·fy (óssi-fī) *v.* **-fied, -fying, -fies.** —*intr.* **1.** To change into bone; become bony. **2.** To become set in a rigidly conventional pattern of behaviour or attitude. —*tr.* **1.** To make or form bone in or of; convert (a membrane or cartilage, for example) into bone. **2.** To mould into a rigidly conventional pattern of behaviour or attitude. [Latin *os* (stem *oss-*), bone + -FY.] —**os·sif·ic** (o-síffik) *adj.*

os·so buc·co, os·so bu·co (óssō bŏŏkō) *n.* A dish of Italian origin, consisting of shin of veal braised with tomatoes, wine, and spices. [Italian, marrow bone.]

os·su·ar·y (óssew-əri ‖ *U.S.* -erri; *also* óshōō-) *n., pl.* **-ies.** A container or receptacle, such as an urn or vault, for holding the bones of the dead. [Late Latin *ossuārium,* from *ossuārius,* of bones, from *ossu,* variant of *os* (stem *oss-*), bone.]

os·te·al (ósti-əl) *adj.* **1.** Bony; osseous. **2.** Pertaining to bone or to the skeleton. [OSTE(O)- + -AL.]

os·te·ich·thy·es (ósti-íkthi-eez) *n.* A class of fish having an endoskeleton made of bone, an air bladder or lungs, and gills covered by an operculum. Also called "bony fish".

os·te·i·tis (ósti-ítiss) *n.* Inflammation of bone or bony tissue. [New Latin : OSTE(O)- + -ITIS.]

Os·tend (oss-ténd). *Flemish* **Oos·tende** (ōst-éndə); *French* **Os·tende** (-tónd). Seaport of northwest Belgium. Lying in the West Flanders province, it is the country's third port, the base of its fishing fleet, and the terminal of a ferry service across the English Channel to Dover.

os·ten·si·ble (o-stén-səb'l) *adj.* Given or appearing as such, especially in a false or pretended way; seeming; apparent: *His ostensible purpose was charity, his real goal popularity.* [French, from Medieval Latin *ostensibilis,* from Latin *ostendere,* to show : *ob-,* before + *tendere,* to stretch.] —**os·ten·si·bly** *adv.*

os·ten·sive (o-stén-siv) *adj.* **1. a.** Ostensible; apparent. **b.** Indicating meaning by a direct example of the term being defined. Said of a definition. **2.** Obviously or manifestly demonstrative. [Late Latin *ostensīvus,* from Latin *ostensus,* past participle of *ostendere,* to show. See **ostensible.**] —**os·ten·sive·ly** *adv.*

os·ten·so·ri·um (óss-tən-sáwri-əm, -ten- ‖ -sóri-) *n., pl.* **-soria** (-sáwri-ə ‖ -sóri-). Also **os·ten·so·ry** (o-stén-səri) *pl.* **-ries.** *Roman Catholic Church.* A receptacle in which the Host is exposed for adoration; a monstrance. [Medieval Latin *ostensōrium,* from Latin *ostendere,* to show. See **ostensible.**]

os·ten·ta·tion (óss-ten-táysh'n, -tən-) *n.* **1.** Pretentious, gaudy, or showy display, often meant to impress others. **2.** *Archaic.* An act of showing; an exhibition. [Middle English *ostentacioun,* from Old French *ostentation,* from Latin *ostentātiō* (stem *ostentātiōn-*), from *ostentāre,* frequentative of *ostendere.* See **ostensible.**]

os·ten·ta·tious (óss-ten-táyshəss, -tən-) *adj.* Characterised by or given to ostentation; showy; pretentious. See Synonyms at **ornate.** —**os·ten·ta·tious·ly** *adv.*

osteo-, oste- *comb. form.* Indicates bone or bones; for example, **osteomyelitis, osteoid.** [Greek, from *osteon,* bone.]

osteo. osteopath; osteopathy.

os·te·o·ar·thri·tis (ósti-ō-aar-thrítiss) *n.* Degenerative joint disease due to destruction of joint cartilage, characterised by pain and impaired mobility of the affected joint.

os·te·o·blast (ósti-ō-blast, -ə-) *n.* A cell from which bone develops. [OSTEO- + -BLAST.] **—os·te·o·blas·tic** (-blástik) *adj.*

os·te·oc·la·sis (ósti-óckləsiss) *n.* **1.** Surgical fracture of a bone, performed to correct a deformity. **2.** The dissolution and resorption of bony tissue. [New Latin : OSTEO- + Greek *klasis*, breakage (see -clase).]

os·te·o·clast (ósti-ō-klast, -ə-) *n.* **1.** An instrument used in surgical osteoclasis. **2.** A large multinuclear cell that resorbs bony tissue in osteoclasis. [OSTEO- + -CLAST.] **—os·te·o·clas·tic** (-klástik) *adj.*

os·te·o·cra·ni·um (ósti-ō-kráyni-əm) *n.* The ossified embryonic cranium, as distinguished from the **chondrocranium** (*see*). **—os·te·o·cra·ni·al** *adj.*

os·te·o·cyte (ósti-ə-sīt) *n.* A bone cell. [OSTEO- + -CYTE.]

os·te·o·gen·e·sis (ósti-ō-jénnəsiss) *n.* Ossification (*see*).

os·te·oid (ósti-oyd) *adj.* Resembling bone. [OSTE(O)- + -OID.]

os·te·ol·o·gy (ósti-ólləji) *n.* **1.** The anatomical study of bones. **2.** The bone structure or system of an animal. [Greek *osteologia* : OSTEO- + -LOGY.] **—os·te·o·log·i·cal** (-ə-lójik'l) *adj.* **—os·te·ol·o·gist** (-ólləjist) *n.*

os·te·o·ma (ósti-ó-mə) *n., pl.* **-mas** or **-mata** (-mətə). A benign bony tumour. [OSTEO- + -OMA.]

os·te·o·ma·la·ci·a (ósti-ō-mə-láyshi-ə, -láyshə) *n.* Softening of the bones because of a deficiency of vitamin D or of calcium. [New Latin : OSTEO- + *malacia*, softness, from Greek *malakia*, from *malakos*, soft.]

os·te·o·my·e·li·tis (ósti-ō-mí-ə-lítiss) *n.* Inflammation of the bone marrow due to infection.

os·te·o·path (ósti-ə-path) *n.* Also *rare* **os·te·op·a·thist** (ósti-óppəthist). *Abbr.* **osteo** (-ō). One who practises osteopathy.

os·te·op·a·thy (ósti-óppəthi) *n. Abbr.* **osteo.** A medical therapy relying on manipulative techniques, based on the theory that many diseases are caused or exacerbated by displacement of bones, especially those of the spine, from their correct positions. [OSTEO- + -PATHY.] **—os·te·o·path·ic** (ósti-ə-páthik) *adj.* **—os·te·o·path·i·cal·ly** *adv.*

os·te·o·phyte (ósti-ə-fīt) *n.* A small abnormal bony outgrowth, occurring, for example, in osteoarthritis. [OSTEO- + -PHYTE.] **—os·te·o·phyt·ic** (-fíttik) *adj.*

os·te·o·plas·tic (ósti-ə-plastik) *adj.* **1.** *Medicine.* Of or pertaining to osteoplasty. **2.** *Physiology.* Pertaining to or functioning in bone formation.

os·te·o·plas·ty (ósti-ə-plasti) *n., pl.* **-ties.** The surgical repair or alteration of bone. [OSTEO- + -PLASTY.]

os·te·o·por·o·sis (ósti-ō-pawr-ó-siss ‖ -pōr-) *n.* Brittleness and porosity of the bones, resulting in a liability to fracture. It is common in the elderly.

os·te·o·sar·co·ma (ósti-ō-saar-kómə) *n.* A malignant bone tumour.

os·te·ot·o·my (ósti-óttəmi) *n., pl.* **-mies.** The surgical division or sectioning of bone. [OSTEO- + -TOMY.] **—os·te·ot·o·mist** *n.*

Österreich. See **Austria.**

os·ti·ar·y (ósti-əri ‖ *U.S.* -erri) *n., pl.* **-ies.** *Archaic.* A doorkeeper at a church. [Latin *ōstiārius*, doorkeeper, from *ōstium*, an opening, from *ōs*, mouth.]

os·ti·na·to (ósti-naátō) *n., pl.* **-tos.** *Music.* A short melody or phrase that is constantly repeated in the same pitch. [Italian, "stubborn", from Latin *obstinātus*, OBSTINATE.]

os·ti·ole (ósti-ōl) *n. Biology.* A small opening or pore, such as that in the fruiting body of certain fungi. [Latin *ōstiolum*, diminutive of *ōstium*, OSTIUM.] **—os·ti·o·lar** (-ōlər, -ələr) *adj.*

os·ti·um (óss-ti-əm) *n., pl.* **-tia** (-ti-ə). *Biology.* A small opening, such as any of the openings in a sponge, through which water enters the body of the organ or organism. [Latin *ōstium*, river mouth, opening, from *ōs*, mouth.]

os·tler, hos·tler (ósslə) *n.* One who takes charge of horses, as at an inn; a stableman. [16th century contraction of HOSTELLER.]

Ost·mark (óst-maark) *n. Abbr.* **OM.** See **mark²**.

Ost·po·li·tik (óst-polli-teek) *n.* **1.** Formerly, a policy of the West German government designed to improve and ultimately normalise trade and diplomatic relations with the Communist countries of eastern Europe. **2.** A similar policy on the part of any other Western country. [German, East politics.]

os·tra·cise, os·tra·cize (óstrə-sīz) *tr.v.* **-cised, -cising, -cises. 1.** To banish or exclude from a group; shut out; shun. **2.** To banish by ostracism, as in ancient Greece. [Greek *ostrakizein*, from *ostrakon*, shell, shard (see **ostracon**).]

os·tra·cism (óstrə-siz'm) *n.* **1.** Banishment or exclusion from a group; disgrace. **2.** In Athens and other city states of ancient Greece, the temporary banishment by popular vote of a citizen considered dangerous to the state. **3.** The act of ostracising. **4.** The state or condition of being ostracised. [French *ostracisme*, from Greek *ostrakismos*, from *ostrakizein*, to OSTRACIZE.]

os·tra·cod (óstrə-kod) *n.* Any of various minute, chiefly freshwater crustaceans of the order Ostracoda, having a bivalved carapace. [New Latin *ostracoda*, from Greek *ostrakōdēs*, testaceous, from *ostrakon*, shell.]

os·tra·con (óstrə-kon) *n.* A fragment of pottery used in ancient Athens when voting for the ostracism of a citizen. [Greek *ostrakon*, potsherd.]

os·trich (óss-trich, -trij ‖ áwss-) *n., pl.* **-triches** or collectively **ostrich. 1.** A large, flightless African bird, *Struthio camelus*, characterised by a long, bare neck and legs, two-toed feet, and plumage

often used for decoration and brushes. **2.** *U.S.* A similar bird, the **rhea** (*see*). **3.** One who refuses to accept reality or heed a serious danger, and is therefore thought to emulate the ostrich's alleged habit of burying its head in the sand to escape danger. [Middle English *ostriche*, from Old French *ostrusce*, from Vulgar Latin *avis-trūthius* (unattested) : Latin *avis*, bird + Late Latin *strūthiō*, ostrich, from Greek *struthiōn* (see **struthious**).]

ostrich fern *n.* A fern, *Matteuccia struthiopteris*, of northern temperate regions, having long, plumelike fronds.

Os·tro·goth (óss-trə-goth, -trō-) *n.* A member of a tribe of eastern Goths that conquered and ruled Italy from A.D. 493 to 555. [Late Latin *Ostrogothis* : *ostro-*, eastward + *Gothus*, GOTH.] **—Os·tro·goth·ic** (-góthik) *adj.*

Os·trov·sky (o-strófsk-yi), **Alexandr Nikolayevich** (1823–86). Russian dramatist. Often regarded in his homeland as the greatest Russian playwright, he wrote more than 50 plays, of which the best known is *The Storm* (1860).

Os·ty·ak, Os·ti·ak (ósti-ak) *n.* **1.** A member of a Finno-Ugric people inhabiting western Siberia. **2.** The Ugric language spoken by this people. **—Os·ty·ak** *adj.*

Oś·wię·cim (osh-fi-ént-shim). *German* **Ausch·witz** (ówsh-vits). Town of southern Poland. Situated at the confluence of the Iola and Vistula rivers, it lies near the site of the Auschwitz-Birkenau extermination camp, where, between 1942 and 1945, some 4,000,000 people, mostly German and east European Jews, were systematically put to death by the Nazis.

ot-. Variant of **oto-**.

o·tal·gi·a (ō-tál-ji-ə, -jə) *n. Medicine.* Earache. [OTO- + -ALGIA.]

OTC, O.T.C. Officers' Training Corps. **2.** over-the-counter.

oth·er (úthər) *adj.* **1. a.** Being or designating the remaining one of two or more: *the other ear.* **b.** Being or designating the remaining ones of several. Used before a plural noun: *His other books are still in storage.* **2.** Different from that or those implied or specified: *Any other person would tell the truth; Call me some other time.* **3. a.** Of a different character or quality. Used with *than: other than meets the eye.* **b.** Besides; apart from. Used with *than: Nobody other than Peter could have got away with it.* **4.** Of a different time or era either future or past: *other centuries; other generations.* **5.** Additional; extra: *I have no other shoes.* **6.** Opposite; contrary; reverse: *the other side.* **7.** Alternate; second: *every other day.* **8.** Recent but unspecified. Used in phrases such as *the other day* and *the other morning.* ~*pron.* **1. a.** The remaining one of two or more: *One took a taxi, the other walked home.* **b.** *Plural.* The remaining ones of several: *After her departure the others resumed the discussion.* **2. a.** A different person or thing: *I don't want this toy, I want the other.* **b.** An additional person or thing: *How many others will come later?* **3.** *Plural.* People who do not share the attributes, experience, or views of the speaker or those he represents: *Others may disagree.* **—or other.** Used with *some* to refer to some unknown person or thing: *Some poet or other said that beauty is truth.* ~*adv.* **1.** Differently; in another way: *She never performs other than perfectly.* **2.** Otherwise; in other respects: *I felt a bit queasy, but other than that I was not carsick.* **—no other.** *Archaic.* No differently; nothing else: *She could do no other.* [Middle English *other*, Old English *ōther*.]

Usage: Other than may be used both in adjectival and adverbial constructions, as in *books other than fiction; perform other than efficiently.* It is also used as a conjunction (*I said nothing, other than to remark that...*), but many people prefer the use of *apart from* or (especially in American English) *aside from* in such constructions. In negative constructions, when *other* precedes the noun, *than* is recommended in formal usage, though *but* is more common informally: *I have no other shoes than/but these.* The same variation takes place in formal sentences such as *She could do no other than/but leave.*

o·ther-di·rec·ted (úthər-dī-réktid, -di-) *adj.* Guided by the values of one's peers or of society at large rather than by independent personal principles: *an other-directed personality.* Compare **inner-directed, tradition-directed. —o·ther-di·rect·ed·ness** *n.*

oth·er·ness (úthər-nəss, -niss) *n.* The quality or condition of being different, distinct, or unusual.

other ranks *pl.n.* British. People in the armed forces other than commissioned officers.

oth·er·wise (úthər-wīz) *adv.* **1.** In another way; differently: *She thought otherwise.* **2.** Under other circumstances: *Otherwise I might have helped.* **3.** In other respects: *an otherwise logical mind.* ~*conj.* If not: *Get going, otherwise they'll catch you.* ~*adj.* **1.** Other than supposed; different: *The evidence is otherwise.* **2.** Other: *be otherwise than happy.* [Middle English *otherwise*, Old English *(on) ōthre wīsan*, (in) another manner : *ōther*, OTHER + *wīse*, way, -WISE.]

oth·er·world·ly (úthər-wúrldli) *adj.* **1.** Of, pertaining to, or characteristic of another world, especially a mystical or transcendental world. **2.** Devoted to the world of the mind; concerned with intellectual or imaginative things, rather than with practical realities; absent-minded or impractical. **—oth·er·world·li·ness** *n.*

Othman¹. *Poetic.* Variant of **Ottoman.**

Othman². See **Osman I.**

o·tic (ótik, óttik) *adj.* Of, pertaining to, or located near the ear; auricular. [Greek *ōtikos*, from *ous* (stem *ōt*-), ear.]

–otic *adj. suffix.* Indicates: **1.** Affected with or by; for example, **sclerotic. 2.** Having a specific disease; for example, **epizootic. 3.** Producing or causing; for example, **narcotic.** [Old French *-otique* and Latin *-ōticus,* from Greek *-ōtikos,* adjectival suffix formed from *-o-* stem verbs and *-ōt-* stem nouns.]

o·ti·ose (ōti-ōss, ōshi-, -ōz) *adj.* **1.** Having no real use; purposeless. **2.** Having a lazy nature; indolent. [Latin *ōtiōsus,* from *ōtium*†, leisure. See also **negotiate.**] **—o·ti·ose·ly** *adv.* **—o·ti·os·i·ty** (-ossəti) *n.*

O·tis (ōtiss), **Elisha Graves** (1811–61). U.S. inventor, best known for inventing the safety lift (1852), which he demonstrated (1854) by severing the cable of a lift in which he was travelling.

o·ti·tis (ō-títiss) *n.* Inflammation of the ear; especially, *otitis media,* inflammation of the middle ear causing pain and impaired hearing. [New Latin : OT(O)- + -ITIS.] **—o·tit·ic** (ō-títtik) *adj.*

oto-, ot- *comb. form.* Indicates the ear; for example, **otology.** [New Latin, from Greek *ous* (stem *ōt-*), ear.]

o·to·cyst (ōtō-sist, ōtə-) *n.* **1.** The structure in the skull of a vertebrate embryo that develops into the inner ear in the adult. **2.** An organ of balance, the **statocyst** *(see).* **—o·to·cys·tic** (-sístik) *adj.*

otol. otology.

o·to·lar·yn·gol·o·gy (ōtō-lárring-góllaji, ōtə-) *n.* The branch of medicine concerned with diseases of the ear and throat. [OTO- + LARYNGO- + -LOGY.] **—o·to·lar·yn·go·log·i·cal** (-gə-lójik'l, -lə-ríng-) *adj.* **—o·to·lar·yn·gol·o·gist** (-gólləjist) *n.*

o·to·lith (ōtō-lith, ōtə-) *n.* Any of many minute calcareous particles found in the inner ear of certain vertebrates and in the statocysts of numerous invertebrates. [French *otolithe* : OTO- + -LITH.]

o·tol·o·gy (ō-tólləji) *n. Abbr.* **otol.** The anatomy, physiology, and pathology of the ear. **—o·to·log·i·cal** (ōtə-lójik'l) *adj.* **—o·tol·o·gist** (ō-tólləjist) *n.* [OTO- + -LOGY.]

o·to·rhi·no·lar·yn·gol·o·gy (ōtō-rīnō-lárring-góllaji, ōtə-) *n.* The branch of medicine concerned with diseases of the ear, nose, and throat. [OTO- + RHINO- + LARYNGO- + -LOGY.] **—o·to·rhi·no·lar·yn·go·log·i·cal** (-gəlójik'l) *adj.* **—o·to·rhi·no·lar·yn·gol·o·gist** *n.*

o·to·scope (ōtə-skōp, ōtō-) *n.* An instrument for examining the eardrum and the passage in the outer ear leading to it. [OTO- + -SCOPE.] **—o·to·scop·ic** (-skóppik) *n.*

ottar. Variant of **attar.**

O.T.T. Over the top.

ot·ta·va (o-táavə, ō-) *n. Music.* An octave. [Italian.]

ottava ri·ma (réemə) *n.* A stanza form perfected by the poets Ariosto and Tasso, consisting of eight lines of eleven syllables each in iambic pentameter and having a rhyme pattern *ababbcc.* [Italian, "eighth rhyme".]

Ot·ta·wa¹ (óttə-wə ‖ -waa, -waw) *n., pl.* **-was** or collectively **Ottawa. 1.** A member of a North American Indian people, originally inhabiting the region of the Ottawa river in Ontario, Canada. **2.** The Ojibwa dialect of this people, of the Algonquian family of languages. **—Ot·ta·wa** *adj.*

Ottawa². Capital of Canada. Founded (1827) as Bytown on the Ottawa river, in the southeast of the country, it became the capital in 1867. The industrial development along the Ottawa valley, of which the city is the centre, rests mainly on sawmilling and timber. One third of the population is French-speaking.

Ottawa. River of eastern Canada. The principal tributary of the St. Lawrence, it rises in the Laurentian plateau of western Quebec and flows 1 120 kilometres (696 miles) west to join the St. Lawrence west of Montreal.

ot·ter (óttər) *n., pl.* **-ters** or collectively **otter. 1.** Any of various aquatic, carnivorous mammals of the family Mustelidae, such as *Lutra lutra,* the Eurasian otter, having webbed feet and dense, dark brown fur. **2.** The fur of any of these animals. [Middle English *oter,* Old English *otor.*] **—ot·ter** *adj.*

ot·ter·hound (óttər-hownd) *n.* A dog of a breed formerly used to hunt otters. It is a good swimmer, strongly built with a large head and long drooping ears.

otter shrew *n.* Any of various small, otter-like, semiaquatic mammals of the family Potamogalidae, of west and central Africa.

otto. Variant of **attar.**

Ot·to I (óttō), also called Otto the Great (912–973). King of Germany (936–73); first Holy Roman Emperor (962–73).

Otto, Nikolaus August (1832–91). German engineer. His invention of the internal-combustion engine (1876) facilitated the development of the motor car.

Otto cycle *n.* A cycle of changes in a heat engine in which heat is produced and lost at constant volume, approximately applicable to a four-stroke petrol engine. [After N. A. OTTO.]

ot·to·man (óttə-mən, óttō-) *n., pl.* **-mans. 1. a.** An upholstered sofa or divan without arms or a back. **b.** An upholstered low seat or cushioned footstool. **2.** A heavy silk or rayon fabric with a corded texture, usually used for coats and trimmings. [French *ottomane,* feminine of OTTOMAN.]

Ot·to·man (óttə-mən, óttō-) *n., pl.* **-mans.** *Poetic* **Oth·man** (óth-mən, -maan). **1.** A Turk of the Ottoman Empire. **2.** A Turk belonging to the tribe or family of **Osman I** *(see).*

~adj. 1. Of or pertaining to the Turks; Turkish. **2.** Of or pertaining to the Ottoman Empire and the dynasty founded by Osman I. [French, from Medieval Latin *Ottomānus,* from Arabic *Othmānī,* Turkish, from *Othmān,* Osman I. See **Osmanli.**]

Ottoman Empire *n.* An empire of the east Mediterranean. Spanning over six hundred years (1300–1922), it started as a small enclave of Osmanli Turks, replaced the Byzantine Empire in Asia Minor, and during the 16th and 17th centuries included the Levant, Mesopotamia, much of North Africa, and southeast Europe to the borders of Austria. By the end of World War I it had lost all its possessions outside Turkey, where it was finally overthrown by revolution.

Ottoman Turkish *n.* The form of Turkish used by the Ottoman Turks. Also called "Osmanli". **—Ottoman Turkish** *adj.*

ou *n., pl.* **ous** (ōss, ōz). *South African Informal.* Any male person; a fellow; a guy. [Afrikaans, probably from Dutch *ouwe,* old person.]

O.U. **1.** Open University. **2.** Oxford University.

oua·ba·in (waá-baa-in, -bayn, waa-báy-in) *n.* A white poisonous glucoside, $C_{29}H_{44}O_{12} \cdot 8H_2O$, extracted from the seeds of the African trees *Strophanthus gratus* and *Acokanthera ouabaio.* It is used as a heart stimulant, and by some African peoples as a dart poison. [French *ouaba(io),* from Somali *wabayo.*]

Oua·ga·dou·gou (waágə-dōo-gōō, wággə-). Capital of the republic of Upper Volta. Founded in the 11th century, in the heart of the country, it was once the centre of the Mossi empire.

ou·bli·ette (ōobli-ét) *n.* A dungeon with a trapdoor in the ceiling as its only means of entrance or exit. [French, from *oublier,* to forget, from Old French *oblider,* from Vulgar Latin *oblītāre* (unattested), from Latin *oblīviscī* (past participle *oblītus*), to forget.]

ouch¹ (owch) *interj.* **1.** Used to express sudden pain. **2.** Used to express embarrassment, as on realising an error one has made. **3.** Used to express pretended distaste, as on hearing a poor joke.

ouch² *n. Archaic.* **1.** A setting for a precious stone. **2.** A brooch or ornament set with jewels. [Middle English *ouche,* from the phrase *an ouche,* mistaken division of *a nouche,* from Old French *nouche,* brooch, from Frankish *nuskja.*]

oud (ōod) *n.* A musical instrument of northern Africa and southwest Asia resembling a lute. [Arabic *'ūd,* "wood".]

Ou·de·naar·de (ōodə-naárdə). *French* **Au·de·narde** (ōdə-nárd). Town in East Flanders province, western Belgium. Here, in 1708, during the War of the Spanish Succession, an allied army led by Eugene of Savoy and Marlborough defeated the French.

ought¹ (awt) *v.* Used as an auxiliary followed by an infinitive with *to.* It can indicate: **1.** Obligation or duty: *You ought to work harder than that.* **2.** Expediency or prudence: *You ought to wear a raincoat in this weather.* **3.** Desirability: *You ought to have been there, it was great fun.* **4.** Probability or likelihood: *She ought to have it finished by next week.* [Middle English *aghten, oughten,* to be obliged to, owe, from *aghte, oughte,* possessed, owned, Old English *āhte,* first and third singular past indicative of *āgan,* to possess.]

Usage: As an auxiliary verb, *ought to* has no inflections, and may be negated using *not* or *n't: You ought not/oughtn't to go.* It does not itself take an auxiliary form, though in casual (and especially jocular) use such constructions as *You didn't ought to go* will be heard. An emphatic form, *did ought,* is also common in regional speech: *You did ought to go, you know.* In negative and question forms, *to* is sometimes omitted (*You oughtn't go; Ought she go?*), as it may be in cases where the main verb is not present, being understood from the context: *Are you going to visit her? We ought (to).* *Ought to* is often felt to be awkward in question forms, *should* being used instead. In negative questions, there are three possibilities: *Oughtn't we to go?, Ought we not to go?,* and the formal *Ought not we to go?*

ought² Variant of **aught.**

ought³ *n. Nonstandard.* Nothing; zero; nought. [Perhaps mistaken division (*an ought* for *a nought*).]

Oui·ja (wée-jə ‖ -ji) *n.* A trademark for a board with the alphabet and other symbols on it, and a planchette or movable pointer that is thought, when touched with the fingers of several people, to move in such a way as to spell out spiritualistic and telepathic messages on the board. [French *oui,* yes + German *ja,* yes.]

ounce¹ (ownss) *n. Abbr.* **oz. 1. a.** A unit of mass or weight in avoirdupois measure equivalent to one sixteenth of a pound avoirdupois. It is equal to 28.349 grams. **b.** A unit of mass or weight in Troy measure equivalent to one twelfth of a Troy pound. It is equal to 31.103 grams. **c.** A unit of mass or weight in apothecaries' measure equal to one twelfth of an apothecaries' pound. It is identical to the Troy ounce. **2.** A **fluid ounce** *(see).* **3.** A very small quantity or portion. [Middle English *unce,* from Old French, from Latin *uncia,* a twelfth, ounce, from *ūnus,* unit, one.]

ounce² *n.* The **snow leopard** *(see).* [Middle English *once,* from Old French, variant of *lonce* (the *l* being taken as the definite article), from Latin *lynx* (stem *lync-*), lynx, from Greek *lunx.*]

our (owr, ar, ów-ər). The possessive form of the pronoun *we.* Used attributively to indicate possession, agency, or reception: *our house; our victory; our defeat.* [Middle English *ure, oure,* Old English *ūre.*]

-our, *U.S.* **-or,** *suffix.* Indicates a state, quality, or activity; for example, **fervour, candour, behaviour.** [Old French *-or, -ur* or Latin *-or* (genitive *-oris*).]

Our Father *n.* The **Lord's Prayer** *(see).* [From the opening words.]

Our Lady. See **Mary.**

ours (owrz, arz, ów-ərz). Possessive pronoun, absolute form of *our.* **1.** Belonging to us; for us; our own: *The house is ours.* **2.** The one or ones belonging or pertaining to us: *They couldn't find their hats so they took ours; Ours is the best.* **—of ours.** Belonging or pertaining to us: *a friend of ours.* [Middle English *ures, oures* from *ure, oure,* OUR.]

our·self (owr-sélf, aar-) *pron.* Myself or ourselves collectively. A specialised form corresponding to *ourselves,* but used only in regal or formal proclamations or editorial comments with the formal *we* understood as singular.

our·selves (owr-sélvz, aar-) *pron.* A specialised form of the first person plural pronoun. It is used: **1.** As a reflexive pronoun, forming the direct or indirect object of a verb, or the object of a preposition: *We injured ourselves; gave ourselves time; talked among ourselves.* **2.** For emphasis, after *we*: *We ourselves are excluded from the contract.* **3.** As an emphasising substitute: *The Smiths and ourselves are in trouble; She invited only Tom and ourselves; Ourselves in debt, we couldn't help you.* **4.** As an indication of (our) normal, real, or healthy condition or identity: *We have not been ourselves lately.*

-ous *adj. suffix.* Indicates: **1.** Possessing, having, or full of; for example, **cancerous, joyous. 2.** *Chemistry.* Occurring with a valency that is lower than that in a comparable *-ic* system; for example, **ferrous, osmous.** Compare **-ic.** [Middle English, from Old French *-os, -us, -eus, -eux,* from Latin *-ōsus, -us,* adjectival suffixes.]

Ouse (o͞oz). Any of four rivers of England: **1.** The **Great Ouse** *(see).* **2.** The **Yorkshire Ouse.** Formed by the rivers Swale and Ure, it flows 100 kilometres (60 miles) to join the river Trent, forming the Humber estuary on the northeast coast. **3.** The **Ouse.** Rising in the South Downs, it flows 48 kilometres (30 miles) across Sussex to enter the English Channel at Newhaven. **4.** The **Little Ouse.** Rising in the Gog Magog hills of Suffolk, it flows north and west across Norfolk to join the Great Ouse at the Cambridgeshire border.

ousel. Variant of **ouzel.**

oust (owst) *tr.v.* **ousted, ousting, ousts. 1.** To eject from a position or place; force out; displace. **2.** *Law.* To deprive of land or property. [Anglo-French *ouster,* from Latin *obstāre,* to hinder : *ob-*, off, against + *stāre,* to stand.]

oust·er (ówstər) *n.* **1.** One that ousts. **2.** *Law.* **a.** The act of forcing someone out of possession or occupancy of material property to which he is entitled. Also used adjectivally: *an ouster injunction.* **b.** Illegal or wrongful dispossession. **3.** *Chiefly U.S.* **a.** The act of ousting. **b.** The state of being ousted. [Anglo-French, substantive use of the infinitive *ouster,* to OUST.]

out (owt) *adv.* **1.** Away or forth from inside: *go out of the office.* **2. a.** Away from the centre or middle: *The troops fanned out.* **b.** Away from somewhere considered as central: *They live out at Harlow.* **3.** Away from a normal or usual place: *stepped out for a minute.* **4.** Away from the coast: *The tide goes out at three o'clock.* **5.** From inside a building or shelter into the open air; outside: *The girl went out to play.* **6.** From within a container or source: *drain the water out.* **7. a.** To exhaustion or depletion: *The supplies have run out.* **b.** Into extinction or imperceptibility: *The fire has gone out; rub out a mistake.* **8. a.** To a finish or conclusion: *Hear me out.* **b.** Completely: *We fitted out the kitchen.* **9.** Into being or evident existence: *The new car models have come out.* **10.** Into view: *The moon came out.* **11.** Without inhibition; boldly: *Speak out.* **12.** Into possession of another or others; into distribution: *giving out free passes.* **13.** Into disuse or an unfashionable status: *Knee-length hems have gone out.* **14.** So as to be unconscious or asleep: *went out like a light; knocked him out.* **15. a.** So as to be a rough representation: *sketch out.* **b.** So as to embellish or complete a rough representation or version: *type out; fill out the details.* **16.** So as to project: *Stuck out her tongue.* **17.** From a state of harmony to one of discord: *I was very put out; We fell out.* **18.** On strike: *The workers came out over pay and conditions.* **19.** *Informal.* Around; existing: *She's the best saxophone player out.* **20.** *Sports.* Incorrectly positioned, or beyond some limit as defined by the rules: *He kept serving out.* **21.** *British.* So as to be part of, or received into, adult society, especially high society: *a debutante coming out the year after next.* **—out of. 1.** From among: *one out of thousands.* **2.** Past the boundaries or limits of: *The eagle soared out of sight.* **3.** *Informal.* Based in or with headquarters in: *She works out of the branch office.* **4.** From: *made out of wood.* **5.** Because of; owing to: *They did it out of malice.* **6.** Born of; foaled by. **7.** In or into a condition of no longer having: *We're out of coffee; tricked out of her savings.* **8.** Away from a usual place, state, or condition: *moving out of publishing; getting out of control.* **—out of here.** Away; going; gone: *Let's get out of here!; Do that again and I'm out of here!* **—out of it.** Isolated; excluded; left out.
~*adj.* **1. a.** Outside: *She is out in the garden.* **b.** Away; not in the usual or expected place: *He is out at Harlow; I'm afraid she's out.* **2.** Exhausted; depleted: *Our supplies are out.* **3.** Extinct; extinguished; imperceptible: *The fire is out.* **4.** Finished; concluded: *before the week is out.* **5. a.** In existence: *My new book is out.* **b.** In view; evident: *The daffodils are out.* **6.** No longer fashionable or in use: *Those hairstyles are out.* **7.** Unconscious or asleep: *She's out for a good few hours.* **8.** Away from the courtroom, considering a verdict: *The jury is out.* **9.** On strike: *All our members are out.* **10.** *Sports.* Not in the correct position, or beyond some limit as defined by the rules: *That last ball was out.* **11.** No longer taking part in the game, or part of the game: *Yorkshire were out for 250.* **12.** Excluded, especially from power or control: *After the 1945 election, the Conservatives were out.* **13.** *Informal.* Not allowed; prohibited: *Smoking in here is out.* **14.** Inaccurate: *Your calculations were two millimetres out.* **15.** To be sent away: *out mail.* **16.** Determined and desirous: *out to get you; out for your blood.* **17.** *Chiefly U.S. Informal.* Without an amount (of money) possessed previously: *I am out ten dollars.* **18.** Not available for use or consideration: *Catching a taxi is out, because we haven't the money.* **19.** Bare or threadbare: *My jacket is out at the elbow.* **—out with it.** Used to demand that suppressed information be revealed. **—want out.** *Informal.* To wish to leave, escape, or be let out.
~*prep.* Through; forth from: *I looked out the window.*
~*n.* **1.** A means of escape: *The window was my only out.* **2.** In baseball: **a.** Any play in which a batter or base runner is dismissed. **b.** The player dismissed in such a play. **3.** *Chiefly U.S.* A person or thing that is out; especially, one who is out of power. **4.** *Printing.* A word or other part of a manuscript omitted from the printed copy.
~*v.* **outed, outing, outs.** *—intr.* To be disclosed or revealed; come out: *Truth will out.* *—tr.* **1.** To put (a person or thing) out. **2.** *British Slang.* To knock unconscious. **3.** *Informal.* To disclose or reveal the truth about; specifically, to oblige to come out as a homosexual.
~*interj.* **1.** Used to demand the departure of a person or animal, as from a room or car, for example. **2.** Used by radio operators to indicate the end of transmission. **3.** Used in games such as tennis to declare a shot or ball out. [Middle English *out,* Old English *ūt.*]

out- *prefix.* Indicates: **1.** To a surpassing or greater degree; for example, **outplay, outshoot, outwork. 2.** Situated outside or externally; for example, **outboard, outhouse. 3.** Emerging or coming forth; for example, **outburst, outgrowth.** ***Note:*** Many compounds other than those entered here may be formed with *out-*. In forming compounds, *out-* is normally joined with the following element without space or hyphen: **outlive.** However, in formations (usually nonce words) in which the second element begins with a capital, the hyphen is used: *That jailbreaker could out-Houdini Houdini himself.* The separate word *out* also appears in a few phrases that are hyphenated. Those entered here are: **out-and-out, out-group, out-of-bounds, out-of-date, out-of-door(s), out-of-phase, out-of-pocket, out-of-the-way, out-relief,** and **out-tray.**

out·age (ówtij) *n. Chiefly U.S.* **1.** A quantity or portion of something lacking after delivery or storage. **2.** A temporary suspension of operation, especially of electric power. [OUT + -AGE.]

out-and-out (ówt'nd-ówt, ówt'n-) *adj.* Complete; thoroughgoing: *an out-and-out swindler.* **—out-and-out** *adv.*

out·back (ówt-bak) *n.* The remote and underdeveloped areas of a given country; especially, the inland bush country of Australia. Also used adjectivally: *outback life.* **—out·back·er** *n.*

out·bal·ance (ówt-bál-ənss) *tr.v.* **-anced, -ancing, -ances.** To be more important than; outweigh.

out·bid (ówt-bíd) *tr.v.* **-bid, -bidding, -bids.** To bid higher than another.

out·board (ówt-bawrd || -bōrd) *adj.* **1.** *Nautical.* **a.** Situated outside the hull of a vessel. **b.** Being away from the centre line of the hull of a ship. **2.** *Aeronautics.* Situated towards or nearer the end of a wing.
~*n.* **1.** An outboard motor. **2.** A boat with an outboard motor. **—out·board** *adv.*

outboard motor *n.* A detachable engine mounted on the stern of a boat, or on outboard brackets.

out·bound (ówt-bownd) *adj.* Outward bound; heading away.

out·brave (ówt-bráyv) *tr.v.* **-braved, -braving, -braves. 1.** To be braver than. **2.** To face or stand up to defiantly.

out·break (ówt-brayk) *n.* A sudden occurrence; an eruption: *an outbreak of arrests; an outbreak of measles.*

out·breed (ówt-bre͞ed, -breed) *v.* **-bred** (-bréd, -bred), **-breeding, -breeds.** *—tr.* To subject to outbreeding. *—intr.* To produce offspring by outbreeding.

out·breed·ing (ówt-bre͞eding, -breeding) *n.* **1.** The breeding of distantly related or unrelated stocks of animals. **2.** *Anthropology.* The bearing of children by parents from different groups, often as a consequence of taboos against marriage within the group.

out·build·ing (ówt-bilding) *n.* A smaller ancillary building detached from a main building.

out·burst (ówt-burst) *n.* A sudden, violent outpouring; an energetic display, as of activity or passion: *an outburst of spite.*

out·cast (ówt-kaast || -kast) *n.* One that has been excluded from a society or system; one that has been rejected. **—out·cast** *adj.*

out·caste (ówt-kaast || -kast) *n.* **1.** A Hindu who has been expelled from or has abandoned his caste. **2.** One who has no caste. **—out·caste** *adj.*

out·class (ówt-klaass || -kláss) *tr.v.* **-classed, -classing, -classes.** To surpass or defeat decisively, so as to appear of a higher class.

out·come (ówt-kum) *n.* A result or consequence. See Synonyms at **effect.**

out·crop (ówt-krop) *n.* **1.** A portion of bedrock or other stratum protruding through the soil level. **2.** An emergence or outbreak.
~*intr.v.* (-króp) **outcropped, -cropping, -crops.** *Geology.* To protrude above the soil. Used of rock formations.

out·cross (ówt-króss || -kráwss) *v.* **-crossed, -crossing, -crosses.** *—tr.* To breed (animals that belong to different strains of the same breed). *—intr.* To breed. Used of animals belonging to different strains of the same breed.
~*n.* (ówt-kross || -krawss). **1.** The process of outcrossing. **2.** An offspring produced by outcrossing.

out·cry (ówt-krī) *n., pl.* **-cries. 1.** A strong protest or objection: *public outcry over the government cuts.* **2.** A loud cry or clamour.

out·date (ówt-dáyt) *tr.v.* **-dated, -dating, -dates.** To replace or make obsolete, antiquated, or old-fashioned.

out·dat·ed (ówt-dáytid) *adj.* Out-of-date; antiquated.

out·dis·tance (ówt-dístənss) *tr.v.* **-tanced, -tancing, -tances. 1.** To outrun, especially in a long-distance race. **2.** To surpass by a wide margin, especially through superior skill or endurance.

out·do (ówt-do͞o) *tr.v.* **-did** (-díd), **-done** (-dún), **-doing, -does** (-dúz). To exceed in performance; surpass. See Synonyms at **excel.**

out·door (ówt-dór || -dṓr) *adj.* Also **out-of-door** (-əv-). Located in, done in, or suited to the open air.

out·doors (ówt-dórz || -dṓrz) *adv.* Also **out-of-doors** (-əv-). In or into the open; outside a house or shelter: *go outdoors for fresh air.*
~*n.* Also **out-of-doors.** The open air; an area away from human habitation.

out·er (ówtər) *adj.* **1.** Located on the outside; external. **2.** Farther from the centre or middle.

outer ear *n.* The **external ear** *(see).*

Outer Hebrides. See **Hebrides.**

Outer Mongolia. See **Mongolian People's Republic.**

out·er·most (ówtər-mōst) *adj.* Most distant from the centre or inside; farthest out; outmost.

outer planet *n.* Any of the planets Jupiter, Saturn, Uranus, Neptune, or Pluto, whose orbit is beyond the asteroid belt. Compare **inner planet.**

outer space *n.* Space beyond the Earth's atmosphere. Not in technical usage.

out·face (ówt-fáyss) *tr.v.* **-faced, -facing, -faces. 1.** To overcome with a bold or self-assured look; stare down. **2.** To defy; resist.

out·fall (ówt-fawl) *n.* The point where or mouth from which a sewer, drain, or stream discharges.

out·field (ówt-feeld) *n.* **1.** The outer part of a cricket field; the part farthest from the wicket. Compare **infield. 2. a.** The grass-covered playing area extending outwards from a baseball diamond, divided into right, centre, and left fields. Compare **infield. b.** The members of a baseball team playing in the outfield. **—out·field·er** *n.*

out·fit (ówt-fit) *n.* **1.** A set of tools or equipment for a specialised purpose: *a mountain-climber's outfit; a welder's outfit.* **2.** A set of clothing: *appear at the dance in an elegant outfit.* **3.** *Informal.* An association of persons, especially a military unit or a business organisation. **4.** The act of equipping or fitting out. **~v. outfitted, -fitting, -fits.** *—tr.* To provide with an outfit: *This shop outfits skiers.* *—intr.* To acquire an outfit: *We outfitted a week before departing.*

out·fit·ter (ówt-fittər) *n.* **1.** A shop, often slightly old-fashioned, that sells men's clothes. **2.** One who sells or provides outfits.

out·flank (ówt-flángk) *tr.v.* **-flanked, -flanking, -flanks. 1.** To manoeuvre around and behind the flank of (an opposing force). **2.** To gain a tactical advantage over.

out·flow (ówt-flō) *n.* **1.** The act of flowing out. **2.** Something that flows out. **3.** The amount flowing out.

out·fox (ówt-fóks) *tr.v.* **-foxed, -foxing, -foxes.** To outwit; be more cunning than.

out·gas (ówt-gáss, -gass) *v.* **-gassed, -gassing, -gasses.** *Physics.* *—tr.* To remove adsorbed gas from (a solid or liquid) by heating. *—intr.* To release gas.

out·go (ówt-gố) *tr.v.* **-went** (-wént), **-gone** (-gón ‖ -gáwn, -gáan), **-going, -goes** (-gốz). To exceed; surpass. **~n.** (ówt-gō) *pl.* **outgoes. 1.** Something that goes out, especially expenditure or cost. **2.** The act of going out.

out·go·ing (ówt-gō-ing, -gố-) *adj.* **1. a.** Departing; going out: *an outgoing steamship.* **b.** Retiring or leaving: *the outgoing president.* **2.** Friendly; sociable; extroverted: *an outgoing personality.*

out·go·ings (ówt-gō-ingz) *pl.n.* Regular and unavoidable expenses, such as payment of rent.

out·group (ówt-grōōp) *n.* A group of people excluded from or not belonging to an **in-group** *(see).*

out·grow (ówt-grố) *tr.v.* **-grew** (-grōō), **-grown** (-grốn), **-growing, -grows. 1.** To grow too large for: *She outgrew her new suit.* **2.** To lose or discard in the course of maturation: *We outgrew our youthful idealism.* **3.** To surpass in growth: *He has outgrown his father.*

out·growth (ówt-grōth) *n.* **1.** That which grows out of something; an offshoot: *an outgrowth of new buds on a branch.* **2.** The act or process of growing out. **3.** A result or consequence: *Inflation is an outgrowth of war.*

out·guess (ówt-géss) *tr.v.* **-guessed, -guessing, -guesses. 1.** To anticipate correctly the actions of. **2.** To gain the advantage over by cleverness or forethought; outwit.

out·gun (ówt-gún) *tr.v.* **-gunned, -gunning, -guns. 1.** To have more guns than. **2.** To outshoot. **3.** *Informal.* To outdo; surpass.

out·haul (ówt-hawl) *n.* *Nautical.* A rope used to extend a sail along a spar or boom.

out·Her·od (ówt-hérrəd) *tr.v.* **-oded, -oding, -ods.** To outdo in evil or surpass in cruelty. Used chiefly in the phrase *out-Herod Herod.* [The phrase *out-Herod Herod* is from Shakespeare's *Hamlet,* Act III, scene 2.]

out·house (ówt-howss) *n.* **1.** An outbuilding. **2.** *U.S.* An outside lavatory.

out·ing (ówting) *n.* **1.** An excursion or pleasure trip: *an outing to the zoo.* **2.** A walk outdoors; an airing. **3.** An appearance in an outdoor competition, such as a horse race.

out·jock·ey (ówt-jócki) *tr.v.* **-eyed, -eying, -eys.** To get the better of, especially by trickery.

out·land (ówt-land, -lənd) *n.* **1.** *Plural.* The outlying areas of a country; the provinces. **2.** *Archaic.* A foreign land. [Middle English *outland,* Old English *ūtland : ūt,* OUT + *land,* LAND.] **—out·land** *adj.* **—out·land·er** *n.*

out·land·ish (ówt-lándish) *adj.* **1.** Conspicuously unconventional; bizarre; absurd. **2.** Strikingly foreign; unfamiliar. **3.** Geographically remote from the familiar world. **4.** *Archaic.* Of foreign origin; not native. **—See** Synonyms at **strange.** [Middle English *outlandish,* Old English *ūtlandisc :* OUTLAND + -ISH.] **—out·land·ish·ly** *adv.* **—out·land·ish·ness** *n.*

out·last (ówt-laást ‖ -lást) *tr.v.* **-lasted, -lasting, -lasts.** To endure or live longer than.

out·law (ówt-law) *n.* **1.** A habitual criminal. **2.** *Law.* Formerly, a person excluded from normal legal protection and rights. **3.** A wild or vicious animal. **~tr.v. outlawed, -lawing, -laws. 1.** To declare illegal. **2.** To ban. **3.** To deprive of the protection of the law. [Middle English *outlawe, outlage,* Old English *ūtlaga,* from Old Norse *ūtlagi,* from *ūtlagr,* outlawed : *ūt,* out + *lög,* law.]

out·law·ry (ówt-lawri) *n., pl.* **-ries. 1.** The act or process of outlawing someone or something. **2.** The state of being outlawed. **3.** Defiance of the law. [Middle English *outlagerie,* from Anglo-French *utlagerie,* from Middle English *outlage,* an OUTLAW.]

out·lay (ówt-lay) *n.* **1.** The spending or disbursing of money. **2.** The amount spent. **—See** Synonyms at **price. ~tr.v.** (-láy) **outlaid** (-láyd), **-laying, -lays.** To spend (money).

out·let (ówt-let, -lit) *n.* **1.** A passage for escape or exit, such as an air vent, drain, or river mouth. **2. a.** A means of fulfilling potential or channelling energies or abilities: *"There is now scarcely any outlet for energy in this country except business."* (John Stuart Mill). **b.** A means of satisfying a drive, urge, or desire; emotional gratification. **c.** A means of achieving self-expression. **3. a.** A commercial market for goods or services. **b.** A shop that sells the goods of a particular manufacturer or wholesaler. **4.** A point at which an electric current is taken from a circuit; especially, a wall socket.

out·li·er (ówt-lī-ər) *n.* **1.** A portion of anything that exists or lies apart from the main body or system to which it belongs. **2.** One whose home lies at some appreciable distance from his place of work. **3.** *Geology.* An area of younger rocks surrounded by older.

out·line (ówt-līn) *n.* **1. a.** A line described in the plane of vision by the outer boundary of any object or figure. **b.** *Plural.* Contours delineating such a figure; lineaments. **c.** Contour; shape. **2.** A drawing or style of drawing in which objects are delineated in contours without shading. **3. a.** A general description or schematic summary. **b.** An abstract. **c.** A schematic synopsis of a written work. **d.** A preliminary draft or plan. **4.** *Plural.* The salient characteristics or general principles of a given subject; the gist: *They agreed on the main outlines, but quibbled over particulars.* **—See** Synonyms at **form. ~tr.v. outlined, -lining, -lines. 1.** To draw the outline of. **2.** To display or accentuate the outline of. **3.** To give the main points of; summarise.

out·live (ówt-lív) *tr.v.* **-lived, -living, -lives. 1.** To live beyond or longer than; outlast. **2.** To live through; survive.

out·look (ówt-lŏŏk ‖ -lōōk) *n.* **1.** A point of view or attitude. **2.** Probable or expected outcome. **3.** The act of looking out. **4. a.** A place where something can be viewed. **b.** The view seen from such a place. **—See** Synonyms at **prospect.**

out·ly·ing (ówt-lī-ing) *adj.* Comparatively distant or remote from a centre or middle.

out·ma·noeu·vre (ówt-mə-nōōvər ‖ -néwvər) *tr.v.* **-vred, -vring, -vres.** To gain the advantage over by adroitness or skill.

out·mod·ed (ówt-mōdid) *adj.* **1.** Not in fashion. **2.** No longer usable or practical; obsolete: *an outmoded technique.* **—out·mod·ed·ly** *adv.* **—out·mod·ed·ness** *n.*

out·most (ówt-mōst) *adj.* Farthest out; outermost.

out·num·ber (ówt-númbər) *tr.v.* **-bered, -bering, -bers.** To exceed the number of; be more numerous than.

out-of-body experience (ówtəv-bóddi) *n.* The experience of seeming to see one's own body and its surroundings as if outside it, which may be associated with an altered state of consciousness and/or being near death from illness or injury.

out of bounds, out-of-bounds (ówtəv-bównds) *adj.* Beyond certain prescribed limits; barred. **—out of bounds** *adv.*

out-of-date (ówtəv-dáyt) *adj.* Outmoded; old-fashioned.

out-of-door. Variant of **outdoor.**

out-of-doors. Variant of **outdoors.**

out-of-phase (ówtəv-fáyz) *adj.* Designating or pertaining to two or more waves, alternating signals, or other periodically varying quantities for which the maximum and minimum values of each quantity occur at different times.

out of pocket *adj.* Also **out-of-pocket** (ówtəv-póckit) (for sense 3). **1.** Having suffered financial loss: *That deal left me out of pocket.* **2.** Lacking readily available money. **3.** Directly paid for in cash rather than charged to an expense account or bought on credit: *out-of-pocket expenses.*

out-of-the-way (ówtəv-thə-wáy) *adj.* **1.** Distant; remote; secluded. **2.** Out of the ordinary; unusual.

out·pa·tient (ówt-paysh'nt) *n.* A patient who receives treatment at a hospital or clinic without being hospitalised.

out·per·form (ówt-pər-fórm) *tr.v.* **-formed, -forming, -forms.** To do better than, usually in every respect.

out·play (ówt-pláy) *tr.v.* **-played, -playing, -plays.** To surpass (one's opponent) in playing some game.

out·point (ówt-póynt) *tr.v.* **1.** To score a greater number of points than. **2.** *Nautical.* To sail nearer to the direction of the wind than (another vessel).

out·post (ówt-pōst) *n.* **1.** A detachment of troops stationed at a distance from a main unit of forces. **2.** The station occupied by such troops. **3. a.** Any outlying settlement. **b.** Anything regarded as an outlying settlement or representative: *The country club is the last outpost of 19th-century civilisation.*

out·pour (ówt-pór ‖ -pōr) *tr.v.* **-poured, -pouring, -pours.** To pour out. **~n.** (-pawr ‖ -pōr). A rapid outflow; an outpouring. **—out·pour·er** *n.*

out·pour·ing (ówt-pawring ‖ -pōring) *n.* **1.** The act or an instance of pouring out: *an outpouring of love.* **2.** Something that pours out or is poured out; an outflow: *an outpouring of lava.*

out·put (ówt-pòot) *n.* **1.** The act of producing; production. **2.** The amount of something produced or manufactured during a given span of time. **3.** The material or substance produced in a process. **4.** The power or energy delivered by a motor or machine. **5.** The energy, power, or work produced by a technical system. **6.** *Computing.* **a.** The data produced by a computer from a specific input. **b.** The form in which the data is delivered: *paper-tape output.* **c.** A device used in producing output. **7.** *Electronics.* **a.** The voltage or current produced by a component or circuit. **b.** The terminal or point in a circuit from which this voltage or current is taken.
~ *tr.v.* **-output** or **outputted, -putting, -puts.** To produce (an output). Used of a factory, machine, or electronic device, for example.

out·rage (ówt-rayj, *rarely* -rij) *n.* **1.** An act of extreme violence or viciousness. **2.** Any act grossly offensive to decency, morality, or good taste. **3.** A severe insult or offence to one's integrity or pride: *"I have only had insults and outrage from her."* (W.M. Thackeray). **4.** A strong feeling of resentful anger.
~*tr.v.* **outraged, -raging, -rages.** **1.** To offend or enrage. Often used in the passive. **2.** To commit an outrage upon. **3.** *Archaic.* To rape. —See Synonyms at **offend.** [Middle English, excess, from Old French, "excess", atrocity, from *outre,* beyond. See **outré.**]

out·ra·geous (ówt-ráyjəss, owt-) *adj.* **1. a.** Being an outrage; grossly offensive; heinous. **b.** Disgraceful; shameful. **2.** Having no regard for the conventions of morality, decency, or good taste; shocking. **3.** Extravagant; immoderate; extreme: *She spends an outrageous amount on clothes.* **4.** Violent or unrestrained in temperament or behaviour. **—out·ra·geous·ly** *adv.* **—out·ra·geous·ness** *n.*

out·rank (ówt-rángk) *tr.v.* **-ranked, -ranking, -ranked.** **1.** To be of a higher rank than. **2.** To be more important than; take precedence over.

ou·tré (óo-tray, oo-tráy) *adj.* Deviating from what is usual or proper; eccentric. [French, past participle of *outrer,* to pass beyond, go to excess, from *outre,* beyond, from Old French, from Latin *ultrā,* beyond, further.]

out·reach (ówt-réech) *v.* **-reached, -reaching, -reaches.** *—tr.* **1.** To reach further than; surpass in reach. **2.** To go beyond; surpass. **3.** To extend (something) outward. *—intr.* To reach out.
~ *n.* (-reech). **1.** An act or programme of reaching out; specifically, of reaching out a helping hand to those in need. **2.** The extent of a reach.

out-re·lief (ówt-ri-leef) *n. British.* Formerly, financial assistance given to the poor who were not living in the workhouse.

out·ride[1] (ówt-ríd) *tr.v.* **-rode** (-ród), **-ridden** (-ridd'n), **-riding, -rides.** To ride faster, further, or better than; outstrip.

out·ride[2] (ówt-rīd) *n.* In verse, an unstressed syllable or cluster of syllables within a given metrical unit that is omitted from the scansion pattern in sprung rhythm. [Coined by Gerard Manley HOPKINS.]

out·rid·er (ówt-rīdər) *n.* **1.** A mounted attendant who rides in front of or beside a carriage. **2.** A person who precedes any procession or vehicle to clear the way and ensure easy progress. **3.** A person who patrols and reconnoitres ahead of a party of explorers, raiders, or the like; a scout. **4.** Any guide or escort. **5.** *U.S.* A herdsman or cowboy supervising cattle, usually at some distance from the farmhouse or central camp. **6.** Either of the two small balancing wheels attached by projecting spars to the back wheel of a child's bicycle.

out·rig·ger (ówt-riggər) *n.* **1. a.** In seagoing canoes of the South Pacific and Indian oceans and similar craft, a float attached to laterally projecting spars so as to ride parallel to the length of the craft on either side as a means of preventing it from capsizing. **b.** Any vessel fitted with such a float. **2.** Any frame extending laterally beyond the main structure of a vessel, vehicle, aircraft, building, or machine, to stabilise the structure or support an extending part. **3.** In rowing, a **rigger** *(see).* **—out·rigged** *adj.*

out·right (ówt-rít) *adv.* **1.** Without reservation or qualification; openly. **2.** Entirely; utterly; wholly. **3.** Without delay; straightaway: *kill outright.*
~*adj.* (ówt-rīt). **1.** Without reservation; unqualified: *an outright gift.* **2. a.** Complete; total: *the outright cost.* **b.** Thoroughgoing; out-and-out: *outright cruelty.* **3.** Straightforward; forthright: *an outright speech.* **4.** *Archaic.* Directed straight on; moving straight onwards: *"an even, outright, but imperceptible speed"* (R.L. Stevenson).

out·run (ówt-rún) *tr.v.* **-ran** (-rán), **-run, -running, -runs.** **1.** To run faster than. **2.** To escape from: *outrun one's creditors.* **3.** To go beyond or exceed (some limit): *Her ingenuity outran her intelligence.*

out·sell (ówt-sél) *tr.v.* **-sold** (-sóld), **-selling, -sells.** **1.** To surpass in amount sold. **2.** To outdo in selling.

out·set (ówt-set) *n.* **1.** The beginning; the start; the commencement. **2.** An initial stage, as of an activity.

out·shine (ówt-shín) *v.* **-shone** (-shón ‖ -shón), **-shining, -shines.** *—tr.* **1.** To shine more brightly than. **2.** To surpass (a rival). *—intr.* To shine forth.

out·shoot (ówt-shóot) *v.* **-shot** (-shót), **-shooting, -shoots.** *—tr.* **1.** To shoot better than. **2.** To extend beyond. *—intr.* To protrude or project.
~*n.* (-shoot). **1.** A protuberance, projection, or outgrowth. **2.** A flowing or gushing forth.

out·side (ówt-síd) *n.* **1.** The part or parts that face out; the outer surface; the exterior. **2. a.** The part or side of an object that is presented to the viewer; the external aspect. **b.** The superficial or obvious aspect of something. **3.** The space beyond a boundary or limit. **4. a.** An outer or external position: *The car door opens only from the outside.* **b.** Anything considered as external or most exposed; for example, the part of a pavement or path nearest the road. **5.** A player whose position is nearest the edge of the field. **—at the outside.** At the utmost limit; at the most: *We'll be leaving in ten days at the outside.* **—on the outside.** In society at large, as opposed to some enclosed community.
~*adj.* **1.** Acting, occurring, originating, or existing at a place beyond certain limits; outer; foreign: *outside assistance.* **2.** Of, restricted to, or situated on the outside of an enclosure or boundary; external: *outside environs; an outside door lock.* **3.** Extreme; uttermost: *The cost exceeded even my outside estimate.* **4.** Slight; slim: *an outside possibility.* **5.** Not part of a group; not a member: *an outside delegate.* **6.** *Sports.* Occupying a position near the specified edge of a playing field. Said of a player. **7.** Designating a curve that is less tight or that covers a greater distance than other concentric curves within it: *the outside track.*
~*adv.* **1.** On or into the outside. **2.** Outdoors. **3.** *Slang.* Out of prison. **—outside of.** *Chiefly U.S.* Outside: *She has few interests outside of her work.*
~*prep.* **1.** On or to the outer side of. **2.** Beyond the limits of. **3.** With the exception of; except: *no info outside the figures given.*
Usage: As a preposition, *outside* (like *inside*) is sometimes followed by *of,* but this is criticised in formal speech or writing: *Don't mention this outside of these four walls.* In writing, this usage is somewhat more common in American English.

outside broadcast *n. Abbr.* **O.B.** A radio or television broadcast made from outside a studio. Also used adjectivally: *outside-broadcast cameras.*

outside centre *n.* **1.** In Rugby football, a player occupying a position outside the scrum, just beyond the inside centre. **2.** The position of any such player.

outside half *n. British.* In Rugby football, a **stand-off half** *(see).*

out·sid·er (ówt-sídər) *n.* **1. a.** A person who is excluded from some particular party, association, or set. **b.** One who is isolated or detached from the activities or concerns of the community in which he lives. **2.** A contestant in a race, especially a horse race, considered to have little chance of winning.

outside world *n.* Society at large as opposed to some private or enclosed community, such as that of an institution: *leaving prison for the outside world.*

out·size (ówt-sīz, -síz) *n.* **1.** A very large size. **2.** A garment designed to fit a very large person. **—out·size, out·sized** *adj.*

out·skirts (ówt-skurts) *pl.n.* The parts or regions remote from a central district; peripheral areas: *the outskirts of the city.*

out·smart (ówt-smárt) *tr.v.* **-smarted, -smarting, -smarts.** To gain the advantage over by cunning; outwit.

out·span (ówt-spán) *v.* **-spanned, -spanning, -spans.** *South African.* *—intr.* **1.** To take off a yoke or harness from an animal. **2.** To pitch camp. Used especially of travellers by ox wagon. **3.** To interrupt a journey to rest. *—tr.* To unharness or unyoke (an animal).
~*n.* (-span). *South African.* **1.** An act of outspanning. **2.** A time or a place set aside for outspanning. **3.** Grazing land. [Partial translation of Afrikaans *uitspan* : *uit,* OUT + *spannen,* to stretch, hitch.]

out·spo·ken (ówt-spókən) *adj.* **1.** Spoken without reserve; candid. **2.** Frank and unsparing in speech. —See Synonyms at **frank.** **—out·spo·ken·ly** *adv.* **—out·spo·ken·ness** *n.*

out·spread (ówt-spréd) *v.* **-spread, -spreading, -spreads.** *—intr.* To spread out; stretch. *—tr.* To cause to spread out.
~*n.* (-spred). **1.** The act of spreading out. **2.** Extent.
~*adj.* (-spréd). Spread out; extended.

out·stand (ówt-stánd) *intr.v.* **-stood** (-stóod), **-standing, -stands.** **1.** To stand out plainly; be outstanding. **2.** *Nautical.* To set sail; put out to sea.

out·stand·ing (ówt-stánding; *also, particularly in sense 1,* -standing) *adj.* **1.** Standing out; projecting upwards or outwards. **2.** Standing out among others of its kind; prominent; salient. **3.** Superior to others of its kind; distinguished; excellent. **4.** Still in existence; not settled or resolved: *outstanding debts; a long outstanding problem.*

out·stare (ówt-stáir) *tr.v.* **-stared, -staring, -stares.** To stare longer than (a person or animal staring back into one's eyes), such that one's adversary is the first to look away.

out·sta·tion (ówt-staysh'n) *n.* A remote station or post.

out·stay (ówt-stáy) *tr.v.* **-stayed, -staying, -stays.** **1.** To stay longer than. **2.** To stay beyond (a certain limit); overstay: *We outstayed our welcome.*

out·stretch (ówt-stréch) *tr.v.* **-stretched, -stretching, -stretches.** **1.** To stretch out; extend. **2.** To stretch beyond.

out·strip (ówt-stríp) *tr.v.* **-stripped, -stripping, -strips.** **1.** To run faster than and leave behind; outrun. **2.** To exceed in growth, skill, or achievement; surpass. —See Synonyms at **excel.**

out·swing·er (ówt-swing-ər) *n.* In cricket, a bowled ball that moves in the air from leg to off. Compare **inswinger.**

out·take (ówt-tayk) *n.* A series of frames cut and discarded from the finished version of a film.

out·tray (ówt-tray) *n.* A tray or shallow basket usually on an office desk, in which are placed outgoing letters and messages and work that has been dealt with for filing. Compare **in-tray.**

out·turn (ówt-turn) *n. Rare.* **1.** Output. **2.** Outcome: *"But whether the outturn would have been very different is quite another question"* (*The Guardian*).

out·ward (ówt-wərd) *adj.* **1.** Of, pertaining to, or moving towards the outside or exterior; outer. **2.** Pertaining to the physical self, as distinguished from the mind or spirit: *The ascetics have no interest in the outward being.* **3.** Easily perceptible, especially to sight; evident: *Her outward manner remained composed.* **4.** Purely external; superficial. **5.** Towards or sailing towards a destination away from home or a home port. Said of a voyage or a ship. ~*adv.* Chiefly *U.S.* Outwards. ~*n.* **1.** The outside; the exterior. **2.** Outward appearance. [Middle English *outward,* Old English *ūtanweard* : *ūtan,* outside, from *ūt,* OUT + *-weard,* -WARD.] —**out·ward·ness** *n.*

out·ward·ly (ówtwərdli) *adv.* **1.** According to external appearance, usually as distinct from the real state of affairs: *She remained outwardly composed at the news, but her mind was reeling.* **2.** From, to, or on the outside; externally.

out·wards (ówt-wərdz) *adv.* Also chiefly *U.S.* **outward.** Towards the outside; away from a central point.

out·wear (ówt-wáir) *tr.v.* **-wore** (-wór ‖ -wòr), **-worn** (-wórn ‖ -wórn), **-wearing, -wears. 1.** To wear out; exhaust by using. **2.** To last longer than; outlast. **3.** To outgrow or outlive: *ethics outworn by a changing society.*

out·weigh (ówt-wáy) *tr.v.* **-weighed, -weighing, -weighs. 1.** To weigh more than. **2. a.** To be more significant, important, or influential than. **b.** To be preferred to; prevail over.

out·wit (owt-wít) *tr.v.* **-witted, -witting, -wits. 1.** To surpass in cleverness or cunning; fool. **2.** *Archaic.* To surpass in intelligence. —See Synonyms at **deceive.**

out·with (ówt-wíth, -wíth) *prep. Scottish.* Outside.

out·work (ówt-wúrk) *tr.v.* **-worked, -working, -works. 1.** To work better or faster than. **2.** To work out to a finish; complete. ~*n.* (-wurk). **1.** Work done outside a factory or shop; paid work done at home. **2.** *Often plural. Military.* A trench or fortification beyond the main defences. —**out·work·er** *n.*

ou·zel, ou·sel (óoz'l) *n.* **1.** A bird, the **ring ouzel** (*see*). **2.** *Archaic.* A blackbird. **3.** The water ouzel or **dipper** (*see*). [Middle English *ousel,* Old English *ōsle.*]

ou·zo (óozō) *n., pl.* **-zos.** An aniseed-flavoured Greek liqueur. [Modern Greek *ouzon†*.]

o·va. Plural of **ovum.**

o·val (óv'l) *adj.* **1.** Resembling an ellipse in shape; ellipsoidal or elliptical. **2.** Resembling an egg in shape. ~*n.* **1.** An oval form or figure. **2.** An oval track or sports field, as for horse racing or athletic events. [Medieval Latin *ōvālis,* from Latin *ōvum,* egg.] —**o·val·ly** *adv.* —**o·val·ness** *n.*

O·val, The (óv'l). A cricket ground in south London. Second in importance only to Lords as a centre of the game, it is the headquarters of the Surrey County Cricket Club. Traditionally, the final test match of an English series is played here.

Oval Office *n.* The U.S. president: *a statement from the Oval Office.* [From the president's oval-shaped office in the White House.]

O·vam·bo (ō-vám-bō, -vaám-) *n., pl.* **-bos** or collectively **Ovambo. 1.** A member of a southern African people of mixed Hottentot and Negroid descent, living chiefly in northern Namibia. **2.** The Bantu language of this people, of the Niger-Congo family of languages. —**O·vam·bo** *adj.*

o·va·ri·ec·to·my (ō-vàir-i-éktəmi) *n., pl.* **-mies.** Surgical excision of an ovary. [OVAR(Y) + -ECTOMY.]

o·va·ri·ot·o·my (ō-vàir-i-óttəmi) *n., pl.* **-mies. 1.** Ovariectomy. **2.** Surgical incision into an ovary to remove a tumour. [New Latin *ovariotomia* : OVAR(Y) + *-tomia,* -TOMY.]

o·va·ri·tis (òvə-rítiss) *n. Medicine.* **Oophoritis** (*see*). [New Latin : OVAR(Y) + -ITIS.]

o·va·ry (óvəri) *n., pl.* **-ries. 1.** *Zoology.* Either of a pair of female reproductive glands that produce ova. **2.** *Botany.* The part of a pistil containing the ovules. [New Latin *ovarium,* from Latin *ōvum,* egg.] —**o·var·i·al** (ō-váir-i-əl), **o·var·i·an** (ō-váir-i-ən) *adj.*

o·vate (ó-vayt, -vət, -vit) *adj.* **1.** Oval; egg-shaped. **2.** *Botany.* Broad and rounded at the base and tapering towards the end: *an ovate leaf.* [Latin *ōvātus,* egg-shaped, from *ōvum,* egg.] —**o·vate·ly** *adv.*

o·va·tion (ō-váysh'n, ə-) *n.* **1.** Enthusiastic and prolonged applause. **2.** A show of public homage or welcome. **3.** An ancient Roman victory ceremony of lesser importance than a triumph. [Latin *ovātiō* (stem *ovātiōn-*), from *ovāre,* to rejoice, from imitative base *eu-.*]

ov·en (úvv'n ‖ óv'n) *n.* **1.** A chamber or enclosed compartment in which food is heated, baked, or roasted. **2.** A similar device, usually refractory-lined, in which ceramics are fired, metals heat-treated, or objects dried. [Middle English *oven,* Old English *ofen.*]

ov·en·bird (úvv'n-burd) *n.* **1.** Any of various South American birds of the family Furnariidae that build intricate clay nests having a concealed entrance passage. **2.** A thrushlike North American warbler, *Seiurus aurocapillus,* having a shrill call, and characteristically building a domed nest on the ground. [From its nest, shaped like a Dutch oven.]

oven·proof (úvv'n-proof ‖ óv'n-, -proóf) *adj.* Not harmed by heating in an oven; able to withstand the heat of an oven without cracking. Compare **flameproof.**

oven·read·y (úvv'n-réddi) *adj.* Ready for immediate roasting or cooking in an oven; especially, plucked, gutted, and trussed: *an oven-ready chicken.*

oven·ware (úvv'n-wair) *n.* Plates, dishes, and pots made of oven-proof material.

o·ver (óvər) *prep.* Also *poetic* **o'er** (or, ó-ər ‖ òr). **1.** In or at a position above or higher than: *a sign over the door.* **2. a.** Above and across from one end or side to the other: *a leap over the fence.* **b.** Down the side of or across and down the other side: *jump over the cliff.* **3.** On the other side of: *a village over the border.* **4.** Upon the surface of: *a coat of varnish over the woodwork.* **5.** Covering all

or various parts of; through the extent of: *The rash spread over her body.* **6.** So as to cover or close: *A rock slid over the cave entrance.* **7.** Up to the top of or higher than the level or height of: *water over one's knees.* **8.** Through the period or duration of: *records maintained over two years.* **9.** Until or beyond the end of: *stay over the holidays.* **10.** More than, in degree, quantity, or extent: *over ten miles.* **11.** In preference to: *respected over all others.* **12.** In a position to rule or control: *preside over the meeting.* **13.** Upon; directed towards: *her power over animals.* **14.** While occupied with, engaged in, or partaking of: *a chat over coffee.* **15.** With reference to; concerning: *an argument over methods.* **16.** By means of; by the agency of: *Don't tell me over the phone.* **17.** Recovered from; past the effects of: *over the worst.* —**be all over.** To be excessively affectionate towards or attentive to. —**over and above.** In addition to. ~*adv.* Also *poetic* **o'er. 1.** Above the top or surface. **2. a.** Across to another or opposite side. **b.** Across the edge or brim of a vessel: *The water boiled over.* **3. a.** Across a distance in a particular direction or place: *over in America.* **b.** To another specified place or position: *Move your chair over here.* **4.** Throughout an entire area or region: *wander all over.* **5.** To a different opinion or allegiance: *win someone over.* **6. a.** To a different person, condition, or title: *sign over land.* **b.** So as to be exchanged: *change over.* **7.** So as to be completely enclosed or covered: *The river froze over.* **8.** Through, from beginning to end: *Think the problem over; look this over.* **9. a.** From an upright position: *The book fell over.* **b.** From an upward position to an inverted or reversed position: *turn the book over.* **c.** Overleaf. **10.** *Chiefly U.S.* Another time; again: *Count your cards over.* **11.** In repetition: *ten times over.* **12.** In addition or excess; in surplus: *three pounds left over.* **13.** *Chiefly U.S.* Beyond or until a specified time: *stay a day over.* —**all over.** Typically; characteristically: *That's her all over.* —**over against. 1.** As opposed to; contrasted with. **2.** Opposite; in front of. ~*adj.* **1.** Completely finished; done; past: *The war is over.* **2.** Having gone across or to the other side. **3. a.** Upper; higher. **b.** External; outer. **4.** In excess or addition; in surplus: *My estimate was fifty pounds over.* ~*n.* **1.** Something remaining or extra. **2.** In cricket: **a.** A series of six balls bowled from one end of the pitch. **b.** The play occurring during this spell of bowling. ~*tr.v.* **overed, overing, overs.** *Rare.* To go or pass over. ~*interj.* **1.** Used in radio conversations to mark the end of a transmission by one speaker. **2.** In cricket, used by an umpire to signal the change of bowling ends between overs. [Middle English *over,* Old English *ofer.*]

over- *prefix.* Indicates: **1.** Superiority of rank or power; for example, **overseer. 2.** Location above, outside, or across; for example, **overhead. 3.** Passage beyond or above a limit or boundary; for example, **overshoot. 4.** Movement or transference to a lower or inferior position; for example, **overturn. 5.** Quantity in excess of what is normal, agreed, or desirable; for example, **overheat, overreact.** *Note:* Many compounds other than those entered here may be formed with *over-.* In forming compounds, *over-* is joined with the following element without space or a hyphen: **overrule.** —See Usage note at **overly.** [Middle English *over-,* Old English *ofer-,* from *ofer,* OVER.]

o·ver·a·bun·dance (óvər-ə-búndənss) *n.* Prodigally lavish abundance; excessive profusion. —**o·ver·a·bun·dant** *adj.*

o·ver·a·chieve (óvər-ə-chéev) *intr.v.* **-achieved, -achieving, -achieves.** To perform better than expected or justified. —**o·ver·a·chiev·er** *n.* —**o·ver·a·chieve·ment** *n.*

o·ver·act (óvər-ákt) *v.* **-acted, -acting, -acts.** —*tr.* To act (a part) with unnecessary exaggeration. —*intr.* To exaggerate a role; overact a dramatic part.

o·ver·age (óvər-áyj) *adj.* Above the proper or required age.

o·ver·all (óvər-awl) *adj.* **1.** From one end to the other. **2.** Including everything; comprehensive. ~*adv.* (-áwl). **1.** From one end to the other: *it measures 12 metres overall.* **2.** Generally; on the whole. ~*n.* (-awl). *British.* A loose-fitting protective outer garment; a smock.

o·ver·alls (óvər-awlz) *pl.n.* Loose-fitting, coarse trousers with a bib front and shoulder straps, worn over clothing as protection from dirt and wear.

o·ver·arch (óvər-árch) *tr.v.* **-arched, -arching, -arches.** To form an arch over. —**o·ver·arch·ing** *adj.*

o·ver·arm (óvər-aarm) *adj. Sports.* Executed with the arm raised above the shoulder: *an overarm throw.* —**o·ver·arm** *adv.*

o·ver·awe (óvər-áw) *tr.v.* **-awed, -awing, -awes.** To subdue by inspiring awe; overcome with awe.

o·ver·bal·ance (óvər-bál-ənss) *v.* **-anced, -ancing, -ances.** —*tr.* **1.** To throw off balance. **2.** To have greater weight or importance than. —*intr.* To lose one's balance; tip over. ~*n.* (-bal-). Something that overbalances; an excess of weight or quantity.

o·ver·bear (óvər-báir) *v.* **-bore** (-bór ‖ -bòr), **-borne** (-bórn ‖ -bòrn), **-bearing, -bears.** —*tr.* **1.** To crush or press down upon with physical force. **2.** To prevail over, as if by superior weight or force; dominate. —*intr.* To bear too much fruit or offspring.

o·ver·bear·ing (óvər-báir-ing) *adj.* **1.** Domineering; arrogant: *"the overbearing character and insulting manners of the English people"* (Jawaharlal Nehru). **2.** Overwhelming in power or significance; predominant. —See Synonyms at **dictatorial.** —**o·ver·bear·ing·ly** *adv.*

o·ver·bid (ōvər-bíd) v. **-bid, -bid, -bidding, -bids.** —tr. **1.** To outbid (a person) for something. **2.** To bid unjustifiably high for (something). —intr. **1.** To bid higher than the actual value of something. **2.** In bridge and similar card games, to bid higher than is warranted by the value of one's hand.
~n. (ōvər-bid). **1.** A bid that is higher than another bid. **2.** A bid that is too high.

o·ver·bite (ōvər-bīt) n. In dentistry, the condition in which the front upper incisor and canine teeth project over the lower.

o·ver·blouse (ōvər-blowz) n. A blouse designed to be worn over a skirt or trousers, instead of tucked in.

o·ver·blow (ōvər-blō) tr.v. **-blew** (-blōo), **-blown** (-blōn), **-blowing, -blows.** To blow (a wind instrument) so as to produce a harmonic instead of a fundamental note.

o·ver·blown (ōvər-blōn) adj. **1.** Exaggerated; overdone. **2.** Pompous; conceited. **3.** Past the stage of full bloom. **4.** Blown past or over.

o·ver·board (ōvər-bawrd ‖ -bōrd) adv. Over the side of a boat or ship into the water. **—go overboard.** Informal. **1.** To show wild enthusiasm. **2.** To react in an exaggerated or extreme way. **—throw overboard.** To get rid of; abandon.

o·ver·book (ōvər-bōōk ‖ -bōōk) v. **-booked, -booking, -books.** —tr. To make more bookings for seats or accommodation on or in (an aeroplane or hotel, for example) than there are places available. —intr. To overbook places, as in an aeroplane or hotel.

o·ver·build (ōvər-bíld) tr.v. **-built, -building, -builds. 1.** To build on top of. **2.** To build more buildings in (an area) than is justified or necessary. **3.** To build with excessive size or elaboration.

o·ver·bur·den (ōvər-búrd'n) tr.v. **-dened, -dening, -dens. 1.** To burden with too much weight. **2.** To burden with too much work, worry, or responsibility.
~n. (-burd'n). **1.** Geology. **a.** Material overlying a useful mineral deposit. **b.** Unconsolidated material covering solid rock or bedrock. **2.** Archaeology. A sterile stratum overlying a stratum bearing traces of the culture being studied.

o·ver·buy (ōvər-bī) v. **-bought** (-báwt), **-buying, -buys.** —tr. **1.** To buy in excessive amounts. **2.** Finance. To buy (stocks and shares) on margin in excess of one's ability to provide further security if prices drop. —intr. To buy goods beyond one's means.

o·ver·call (ōvər-káwl) tr.v. **-called, -calling, -calls. 1.** To overbid. **2.** In bridge, to bid higher than (one's opponent) when one's partner has not bid.
~n. (-kawl). **1.** An overbid. **2.** In bridge, an instance of overcalling.

o·ver·cap·i·tal·ise, o·ver·cap·i·tal·ize (ōvər-káppit'l-īz) tr.v. **-ised, -ising, -ises. 1.** To provide an excess amount of capital for (a business enterprise). **2.** To estimate the value of (property) too highly. **3.** To place an unlawfully or unreasonably high value on the nominal capital of (a company). **—o·ver·cap·i·tal·i·sa·tion** (-ī-záysh'n ‖ U.S. -i-) n.

o·ver·cast (ōvər-kaast, -káast ‖ -kast, -kást) adj. **1. a.** Covered or obscured, as with clouds. **b.** Meteorology. Designating the sky when more than 95 per cent of it is covered with cloud. **2.** Gloomy; dark; melancholy. **3.** Sewn with long, overlying stitches in order to prevent unravelling, as at the edges of fabric.
~n. (ōvər-kaast ‖ -kast). **1.** A covering, as of clouds. **2.** In mining, an arch or support for a passage over another passage. **3.** A fishing cast falling beyond the point intended. **4.** An overcast stitch or seam. In this sense, also called "overcasting".
~tr.v. **overcasted, -casting, -casts. 1.** To make cloudy or gloomy. **2.** In fishing, to cast beyond the (intended point). **3.** To sew with an overcast stitch.

o·ver·charge (ōvər-chárj) v. **-charged, -charging, -charges.** —tr. **1.** To charge (a customer) too high a price for something. **2.** To fill too full; overload. **3.** To supply (a battery) with too much charge or too high a current, so as to damage the electrodes. **4.** To exaggerate. —intr. To charge too high a price.
~n. (-chaarj). **1.** Abbr. o/c An excessive charge or price. **2.** A load or burden that is too full or heavy.

o·ver·cloud (ōvər-klówd) v. **-clouded, -clouding, -clouds.** —tr. **1.** To cover with clouds. **2.** To make dark and gloomy. —intr. To become cloudy.

o·ver·coat (ōvər-kōt) n. A heavy coat worn in cold weather.

o·ver·come (ōvər-kúm) v. **-came** (-káym), **-come, -coming, -comes.** —tr. **1.** To defeat in competition or conflict; conquer. **2.** To surmount; prevail over. **3.** To overpower, as with emotion; affect deeply; cause to break down. —intr. To surmount opposition; be victorious. **—See Synonyms at defeat.** [Middle English overcomen, Old English ofercuman : ofer, OVER + cuman, to COME.]

o·ver·com·pen·sate (ōvər-kóm-pən-sayt, -pen-) v. **-sated, -sating, -sates.** —intr. **1.** To pay or make excessive compensation. **2.** To show overcompensation. —tr. To compensate excessively. **—o·ver·com·pen·sa·to·ry** (-kóm-pən-sáy-təri, -pen-, -say-, -sə-, -tri) adj. **o·ver·com·pen·sa·tion** (ōvər-kóm-pən-sáysh'n, -pen-) n. The exertion of effort in excess of that needed to compensate for a physical or psychological characteristic or defect.

o·ver·crop (ōvər-króp) tr.v. **-cropped, -cropping, -crops.** To exhaust the fertility of (land) by overcultivation.

o·ver·crowd (ōvər-krówd) tr.v. **-crowded, -crowding, -crowds.** To put too much or too many in (one place). **—o·ver·crowd·ed** adj.

o·ver·de·vel·op (ōvər-di-véllǝp) tr.v. **-oped, -oping, -ops. 1.** To develop to excess: muscles overdeveloped by weightlifting. **2.** In photog-

raphy, to process (a plate or film) too long or in too concentrated a solution. **—o·ver·de·vel·op·ment** n.

o·ver·do (ōvər-dōo) tr.v. **-did** (-díd), **-done** (-dún), **-doing, -does** (-dúz). **1.** To do, use, or stress to excess; carry too far. **2.** To wear out the strength of; overtax. **3.** To cook too much or too long.

o·ver·dose (ōvər-dōss) v. **-dosed, -dosing, -doses.** —intr. To commit or attempt to commit suicide by taking a lethal dose of a drug. —tr. To give too large a dose to.
~n. (-dōss). A lethal or excessive dose, especially of a drug or drugs.

o·ver·draft (ōvər-draaft ‖ -draft) n. **1.** The act of overdrawing an account. **2.** Abbr. O.D. The amount overdrawn.

o·ver·draught (ōvər-draaft ‖ -draft) n. **1.** A current of air made to pass over the fuel in a furnace. **2. a.** A series of flues in a kiln designed to force air down from the top. **b.** The air so forced.

o·ver·draw (ōvər-dráw) v. **-drew** (-drōo), **-drawn** (-dráwn), **-drawing, -draws.** —tr. **1.** To draw on (an account) in excess of credit. **2.** To pull back too far: overdraw a bow. **3.** To spoil the effect of by exaggeration in telling or describing. —intr. To draw on a bank account in excess of credit. **—be overdrawn.** To have drawn money from a bank account in excess of credit.

o·ver·dress (ōvər-dréss) intr.v. **-dressed, -dressing, -dresses.** To dress in a more formal or elaborate manner than is desirable in a given situation.
~n. A skirted garment, such as a pinafore, worn over other outer clothing.

o·ver·drive (ōvər-drív) n. A gearing mechanism in a motor vehicle that reduces the power output required to maintain driving speed in a specific range by increasing the ratio of drive shaft to engine speed. **—go into overdrive.** To redouble one's energies or act with even greater speed or intensity, as if switching to the highest possible gear.
~tr.v. (-drív) **overdrove** (-dróv), **-driven** (-drívv'n), **-driving, -drives. 1.** To drive (a vehicle) too far or too long. **2.** To push (oneself) too far; overwork.

o·ver·dub (ōvər-dúb) tr.v. **-dubbed, -dubbing, -dubs. 1.** To add the sound of (a voice or instrument) to a recording more than once, so that the sound is doubled, tripled, and so on. **2.** To add in (new sounds) to a recording.
~n. (-dub). An act or instance of overdubbing sounds.

o·ver·due (ōvər-déw ‖ -dōo) adj. **1.** Being unpaid after becoming due. **2.** Past the due time of arrival; expected or required but not yet come. **—See Synonyms at tardy.**

o·ver·es·ti·mate (ōvər-ésti-mayt) tr.v. **-mated, -mating, -mates. 1.** To estimate too highly. **2.** To esteem too greatly.
~n. (-mət, -mit). An estimate or estimation that is excessively high. **—o·ver·es·ti·ma·tion** (-máysh'n) n.

o·ver·ex·ert (ōvər-ig-zért, -eg- ‖ -ik-) tr.v. **-erted, -erting, -erts.** To exert too much; overtax; strain. **—o·ver·ex·er·tion** n.

o·ver·ex·pose (ōvər-ik-spóz, -ek-) tr.v. **-posed, -posing, -poses. 1.** To expose too long or too much. **2.** To expose (a photographic film or plate) too long or with too much light. **—o·ver·ex·po·sure** n.

o·ver·ex·tend (ōvər-ik-sténd, -ek-) tr.v. **-tended, -tending, -tends.** To expand or disperse (one's defences or finances, for example) beyond a safe or reasonable limit. **—o·ver·ex·ten·sion** n.

o·ver·fall (ōvər-fawl) n. **1.** A turbulent expanse of water caused by currents running over a submerged ridge or by the meeting of underwater currents. **2.** A device that releases or drains excess water from a canal, lock, or the like.

o·ver·flow (ōvər-flō) v. **-flowed, -flowing, -flows.** —intr. **1.** To flow or run over the top, brim, or banks. **2.** To be filled beyond capacity, as a container or waterway may be. **3.** To have a boundless supply; be superabundant: overflowing with gratitude. —tr. **1. a.** To flow over (the banks or a brim, for example). **b.** To flow over the top, brim, or banks of. **2.** To spread over or cover; flood. **3.** To cause to fill beyond capacity.
~n. (ōvər-flō). **1.** The act of overflowing. **2. a.** The liquid substance which flows over. **b.** The amount of such liquid. **3.** An outlet or vent through which excess liquid may escape.

o·ver·fly (ōvər-flí) tr.v. **-flew** (-flō), **-flown** (-flōn), **-flying, -flies. 1.** To fly over, or fly an aircraft over: The helicopter accidentally overflew enemy territory. **2.** To fly beyond; fly an aircraft beyond: The pilot overflew the runway. **—over·flight** (-flīt) n.

o·ver·gar·ment (ōvər-gaarmənt) n. An outer garment.

o·ver·glaze (ōvər-glayz) n. A second coat of glaze on pottery.
~adj. Applied to a glazed surface. Said especially of a colour, design, or painting.
~tr.v. (-gláyz, -glayz) **overglazed, -glazing, -glazes.** To apply an overglaze to.

o·ver·graze (ōvər-gráyz) v. **-grazed, -grazing, -grazes.** —tr. To destroy or seriously damage (grass cover or pasture land) by allowing animals to graze for too long a period. —intr. To overgraze grass cover or pastureland.

o·ver·ground (ōvər-grownd, -grównd) adj. Above the surface of the ground: an overground extension of the railway.

o·ver·grow (ōvər-grō) v. **-grew** (-grōo), **-grown, -growing, -grows.** —tr. **1.** To grow and spread across (an area). Often used in the passive: a pathway overgrown with weeds. **2.** To cause the growth or spread of vegetation across: We overgrew the old paddock with ferns. **3.** To choke and replace (a weaker plant). **4.** To grow too large for. —intr. To grow beyond normal size.

o·ver·grown (ōvər-grōn) adj. Grown too large for one's age; oversized: *That overgrown bully needs cutting down to size.*

o·ver·growth (ōvər-grōth) *n.* **1.** A growth over or upon something. **2.** Excessively abundant or luxuriant growth.

o·ver·hand (ōvər-hand) *adj.* **1.** Sewn with stitches drawing two edges together, with each stitch passing over the seam formed by the edges. **2.** *Chiefly U.S.* Thrown, struck, or executed with the hand above the level of the shoulder. ~*adv.* In an overhand manner. ~*n.* **1.** An overhand stitch or seam. **2.** *Chiefly U.S.* An overhand throw, stroke, or delivery. ~*tr.v.* **overhanded, -handing, -hands.** To sew with an overhand seam or stitches.

overhand knot *n.* A knot formed by making a loop in a piece of cord and pulling one end through it. Also called "single knot".

o·ver·hang (ōvər-hăng) *v.* **-hung** (-hŭng), **-hanging, -hangs.** —*tr.* **1.** To project or extend beyond. **2.** To hang over or above. **3.** To threaten or menace; loom over. **4.** To ornament with hangings. —*intr.* To hang or project over something. ~*n.* (-hăng). **1.** A projecting part of something, such as an architectural structure or rock formation. **2.** The amount of projection: *an overhang of six inches.* **3.** The length of the wing of a biplane or other multiplane that projects beyond the tip of the wing above or below it.

o·ver·haul (ōvər-hawl, -hawl) *tr.v.* **-hauled, -hauling, -hauls.** **1. a.** To examine or go over carefully, searching for defects to be repaired. **b.** To dismantle in order to make repairs. **c.** To make all needed repairs on; fix; renovate. **2.** *Nautical.* To slacken (a line) or release and separate the blocks of (a tackle). **3.** To catch up with; overtake. ~*n.* (-hawl). A comprehensive repair job; a renovation.

o·ver·head (ōvər-hed, -hed) *adj.* **1.** Located, functioning, or performed above the level of the head: *an overhead light.* **2.** Of or pertaining to the operating expenses of a business concern. ~*n.* (-hed). **1.** *Usually plural.* The incidental operating expenses of a business, including the costs of rent, rates, electricity, and interior decoration, but excluding labour and materials. **2.** The top surface in an enclosed space of a ship. ~*adv.* (-hed). Over or above the level of the head: *look overhead.*

overhead camshaft *n. Abbr.* **ohc, o.h.c.** A camshaft in an internal-combustion engine that is situated above the valves and acts directly onto their stems or onto rocker arms.

overhead valve *n. Abbr.* **ohv, o.h.v.** An internal-combustion engine valve that is situated in the cylinder head above the piston. Also used adjectivally: *an overhead-valve engine.* Compare **side-valve.**

o·ver·hear (ōvər-heer) *tr.v.* **-heard** (-herd), **-hearing, -hears.** To happen to hear (something spoken or someone speaking) without being addressed intentionally by the speaker. —**o·ver·hear·er** *n.*

o·ver·heat (ōvər-heet) *v.* **-heated, -heating, -heats.** —*tr.* **1.** To heat too much. **2.** To cause to become angry or excited: *overheated by a sharp exchange of insults.* **3.** *Economics.* To overstimulate (the economy), particularly by generating a level of demand so high that it cannot be met by the suppliers. —*intr.* To become overheated.

o·ver·in·dulge (ōvər-in-dŭlj) *v.* **-dulged, -dulging, -dulges.** —*tr.* To indulge excessively; gratify too much or unwisely. —*intr.* To indulge in something to excess. —**o·ver·in·dul·gence** *n.* —**o·ver·in·dul·gent** *adj.* —**o·ver·in·dul·gent·ly** *adv.*

o·ver·is·sue (ōvər-ĭssew, -ĭshōō, -ĭssew, -ĭshōō) *tr.v.* **-sued, -suing, -sues.** To issue more than the necessary, sensible, or authorised amount of (shares or banknotes, for example). ~*n.* Shares, banknotes, or the like so issued.

o·ver·joyed (ōvər-jóyd) *adj.* Filled with joy; delighted.

o·ver·kill (ōvər-kil) *n. Informal.* **1.** Destructive capacity, especially that of nuclear weapons, exceeding the amount needed to defeat an enemy. **2.** Any greatly excessive action or response: *government overkill in dealing with dissent.*

o·ver·lad·en (ōvər-lāyd'n) *adj.* Overloaded; overburdened.

o·ver·land (ōvər-land, -land) *adj.* **1.** Across land; proceeding over land: *an overland flight.* **2.** By land, rather than by sea or air: *an overland journey.* ~*v.* **overlanded, -landing, -lands.** *Australian.* —*tr.* To drive (livestock) overland for long distances, especially through remote areas such as the outback. —*intr.* To overland livestock. —**o·ver·land** *adv.* —**o·ver·land·er** *n.*

o·ver·lap (ōvər-lăp) *v.* **-lapped, -lapping, -laps.** —*tr.* **1.** To lie or extend adjacent to and partly over, thereby covering part of. **2.** To have an area, time span, interest, or other dimension or aspect in common with; coincide partly with. —*intr.* **1.** To lie adjacent to and partly cover something. **2.** To coincide partly: *Their duties overlap.* ~*n.* (-lăp). **1.** A part or portion that overlaps or is overlapped. **2.** The amount thus overlapping. **3.** An instance of overlapping.

o·ver·lay (ōvər-lāy) *tr.v.* **-laid, -laying, -lays.** **1.** To lay or spread over or upon. **2. a.** To cover or decorate the surface of: *overlay wood with silver.* **b.** To embellish superficially: *a simple tune overlaid with ornate harmonies.* **3.** *Printing.* To put an overlay upon. ~*n.* (-lāy). **1.** Something that is laid over or covers something else. **2.** A layer of decoration, such as gold leaf or wood veneer, applied to a surface. **3.** *Printing.* A piece of paper or other material used on a press, cylinder, or plate to even out the pressure. **4.** A transparent sheet containing graphic matter, such as labels or coloured areas, placed on illustrative matter to be incorporated into it.

Usage: Overlay and overlie have similar senses, but are not usually interchangeable. *Overlay* applies mainly to the act of superimposing one thing on another, as when a carpenter *overlays* plywood with veneer. The past tense is *overlaid.* Overlie applies when one thing is seen to lie over or rest upon another, as when warm air *overlies* cold air. The past tense is *overlain.*

o·ver·leaf (ōvər-leef) *adv.* On the other side of the page; especially, on the reverse side of a right-hand page.

o·ver·leap (ōvər-leep) *tr.v.* **-leapt** (-lept), or **-leaped, -leaping, -leaps.** **1.** To leap across or over. **2.** *Archaic & U.S.* To pass over; omit; ignore: *The report overleaps all but the most essential points.*

o·ver·lie (ōvər-lī) *tr.v.* **-lay, -lain, -lying, -lies.** **1.** To lie over or upon. **2.** To smother by lying upon (an infant or other newborn creature). —See Usage note at **overlay.**

o·ver·load (ōvər-lōd) *tr.v.* **-loaded, -loading, -loads.** To load too heavily. ~*n.* (-lōd). An excessive load.

o·ver·long (ōvər-lóng ‖ -lawng) *adj.* Too long. —**o·ver·long** *adv.*

o·ver·look (ōvər-lŏŏk ‖ -lŏŏk) *tr.v.* **-looked, -looking, -looks.** **1.** To look over or at from a higher place. **2.** To rise above, especially so as to afford a view over: *The tower overlooks the sea.* **3.** To fail to notice or consider; miss. **4.** To ignore deliberately or indulgently; disregard. **5.** To look over; examine. **6.** To watch over; supervise; oversee. **7.** To cast a spell or the evil eye upon; bewitch. ~*n.* (-lŏŏk). *U.S.* **1.** An elevated place that affords an extensive view. **2.** An act or instance of overlooking something.

o·ver·lord (ōvər-lawrd) *n.* **1.** A lord having power or sway over another or other lords. **2.** One who is in a position of supremacy or domination over others: *science overlords.* —**o·ver·lord·ship** *n.*

o·ver·ly (ōvərli) *adv. Chiefly U.S.* To an excessive degree; too: *This hotel seems not to be overly clean.*

Usage: The use of this word as an intensifying adverb is common in American English (*She has been overly cautious about the problem*), but it has attracted criticism as an unnecessary development, the same sense already being expressed by the prefix *over-* (as in *overcautious*). The usage has as yet had little impact on British English.

o·ver·man (ōvər-man, -mən) *n., pl.* **-men** (-men, -mən). **1.** A man having authority over others; especially, an overseer or foreman. **2.** The Nietzschean Superman. ~*tr.v.* (-mán). **overmanned, -manning, -mans.** To provide with more workers than are needed. —**o·ver·man·ning** *n.*

o·ver·mas·ter (ōvər-máastər ‖ -mástər) *tr.v.* **-tered, -tering, -ters.** To overpower; overcome. —**o·ver·mas·ter·ing** *adj.* —**o·ver·mas·ter·ing·ly** *adv.*

o·ver·match (ōvər-mách) *tr.v.* **-matched, -matching, -matches.** *Chiefly U.S.* **1.** To be more than the match of; exceed. **2.** To match with a superior opponent. ~*n.* (-mach). *Chiefly U.S.* A contest in which one opponent is distinctly superior.

o·ver·much (ōvər-múch, -much) *adj.* Too much; excessive. ~*adv.* **1.** In too great a degree. **2.** Very much. Usually used in the negative: *I don't care for her overmuch.* ~*n.* An excessive amount.

o·ver·night (ōvər-nīt, -nīt) *adj.* **1.** Lasting for, extending over, or remaining during a night: *an overnight journey.* **2.** For use over a single night or for a short journey. **3.** Sudden; meteoric: *an overnight success.* ~*adv.* **1.** During or for the length of the night. **2.** In or as if in the course of one night; suddenly: *The situation changed overnight.* **3.** On the preceding night or evening.

overnight bag *n.* A bag containing articles for an overnight stay, such as toilet articles and night clothes.

o·ver·pass (ōvər-paass ‖ -pass) *n.* A passage, bridge, or flyover that crosses above another path or roadway. ~*tr.v.* (-páass ‖ -páss) **overpassed, -passing, -passes.** **1.** To pass over or across; traverse. **2.** To go beyond; exceed; surpass. **3.** *Chiefly U.S.* To overlook; disregard.

o·ver·pay (ōvər-páy) *v.* **-paid, -paying, -pays.** —*tr.* **1.** To pay (someone) too much. **2.** To pay (an amount) in excess of a sum due. —*intr.* To pay too much. —**o·ver·pay·ment** *n.*

o·ver·pitch (ōvər-pích) *v.* **-pitched, -pitching, -pitched.** —*tr.* In cricket, to bowl (a ball) so that it pitches too close to the stumps making it relatively easy to hit. —*intr.* To overpitch a ball.

o·ver·play (ōvər-pláy) *tr.v.* **-played, -playing, -plays.** **1.** To play (a dramatic role) in an exaggerated manner; overact. **2.** To overestimate the strength of (one's holding or position) and thus contribute to one's own defeat. Used chiefly in the phrase *overplay one's hand.* **3.** To exaggerate; invest with too much importance.

o·ver·plus (ōvər-pluss) *n.* An amount in excess of need.

o·ver·pow·er (ōvər-pówr, -pów-ər) *tr.v.* **-ered, -ering, -ers.** **1.** To overcome or vanquish by superior force; subdue. **2.** To affect so strongly as to make helpless or ineffective; overwhelm. **3.** To furnish with excessive mechanical power.

o·ver·pow·er·ing (ōvər-pówr-ing, -pów-ər-) *adj.* So strong or intense as to overpower; overwhelming. —**o·ver·pow·er·ing·ly** *adv.*

o·ver·price (ōvər-príss) *tr.v.* **-priced, -pricing, -prices.** To put too high a price on. —**o·ver·pric·ing** *n.*

o·ver·print (ōvər-prínt, -print) *tr.v.* **-printed, -printing, -prints.** To imprint over something already printed; especially, to print over (printed images) with another colour. ~*n.* (-print). **1.** A mark or impression made by overprinting. **2. a.** A mark or words printed over a postage stamp. **b.** A stamp so marked.

o·ver·pro·duce (ōvər-prə-déwss ‖ -dōóss) *v.* **-duced, -ducing,**

-duces. —*tr.* To produce too much of; produce more than is needed or can be sold. —*intr.* To overproduce a commodity or article. —**o·ver·pro·duc·tion** (-dúksh'n) *n.*

o·ver·pro·tect (ōvər-prə-tékt ‖ -prō-) *tr.v.* **-tected, -tecting, -tects.** 1. To protect more than is necessary or advisable. 2. To shelter (someone, especially a child) excessively from the hard physical and social realities of the outside world, thereby distorting or stunting emotional development. —**o·ver·pro·tec·tion** *n.*

o·ver·rate (ōvər-ráyt) *tr.v.* **-rated, -rating, -rates.** 1. To rate or assess too highly. 2. To overestimate the merits of. —**o·ver·rat·ed** *adj.*

o·ver·reach (ōvər-réech) *v.* **-reached, -reaching, -reaches.** —*tr.* 1. To reach or extend over or beyond. 2. To miss by reaching too far or attempting too much: *overreach a goal.* 3. To defeat (oneself) by going too far, doing or trying to gain too much, or by being too cunning. 4. *Chiefly U.S.* To get the better of; trick; outwit. —*intr.* 1. To reach or go too far. 2. To outwit others; cheat. 3. To strike the front part of a hind foot against the rear or side part of a forefoot or foreleg. Used of horses. —**o·ver·reach·er** *n.*

o·ver·re·act (ōvər-ri-áct, -ree-) *intr.v.* To react to a situation with excessive force or vehemence. **o·ver·re·ac·tion** *n.*

o·ver·ride (ōvər-rīd) *tr.v.* **-rode** (-rōd), **-ridden** (-rídd'n), **-riding, -rides.** 1. To declare null and void; set aside. 2. To ride (a horse) too hard. 3. To trample upon. 4. To prevail over; conquer; supplant. 5. To ride across. 6. To extend over or overlap.

o·ver·rid·er (ōvər-rīdər) *n.* Either of a pair of short, vertical, metal or rubber attachments to a motor-vehicle bumper that prevent the bumper interlocking with that of another vehicle.

o·ver·rid·ing (ōvər-rīding) *adj.* Having the superior claim; prior to all others: *of overriding importance.* —**o·ver·rid·ing·ly** *adv.*

o·ver·ripe (ōvər-rīp) *adj.* 1. More than ripe; too ripe. 2. Jaded; decadent. —**o·ver·ripe·ness** *n.*

o·ver·rule (ōvər-rōol) *tr.v.* **-ruled, -ruling, -rules.** 1. **a.** To disallow the arguments of or rule against (a person), especially by virtue of higher authority. **b.** To decide or rule against (an argument, action, or decision). **c.** To declare null and void; invalidate; reverse. 2. To dominate by strong influence; prevail over.

o·ver·run (ōvər-rún) *v.* **-ran** (-rán), **-run, -running, -runs.** —*tr.* 1. To attack and defeat conclusively: *The troops overran the town.* 2. To spread or swarm over destructively: *Slugs overran the garden.* 3. To spread swiftly throughout: *The new fashion overran the country.* 4. To overflow: *The river overran its banks.* 5. To run or extend beyond: *Her speech has overrun the time limit.* 6. *Archaic.* To run faster than. 7. *Printing.* **a.** To rearrange or move (set type or pictures) from one column, line, or page to another. **b.** To print (a job order) in a quantity larger than that ordered. —*intr.* 1. To run over; overflow. 2. To go beyond the normal or desired limit. 3. To run with a closed throttle, as a motor vehicle engine does, such that the engine speed is controlled by the rotation of the wheels, and thus by such factors as the incline of the road.

~*n.* (-run). 1. An instance or act of overrunning. 2. The amount by which something overruns.

o·ver·score (ōvər-skór ‖ -skōr) *tr.v.* **-scored, -scoring, -scores.** To cross out by drawing a line or lines over or through.

o·ver·seas (ōvər-séez) *adv.* Beyond the sea; abroad.

~*adj.* Also *rare* **o·ver·sea** (-sée). Pertaining to or situated in areas across the sea: *overseas students; an overseas posting.*

~*n. Informal. Used with a singular verb.* Overseas countries collectively.

o·ver·see (ōvər-sée) *tr.v.* **-saw** (-sáw), **-seen, -seeing, -sees.** 1. To watch over and direct; supervise. 2. *Archaic.* To scrutinise; inspect. —See Synonyms at **conduct.**

o·ver·se·er (ōvər-seer, -see-ər) *n.* 1. One who keeps watch over and directs the work of others, especially labourers. 2. A supervisor or superintendent.

o·ver·sell (ōvər-sél) *tr.v.* **-sold** (-sóld), **-selling, -sells.** 1. To contract to sell more of (a commodity) than can be delivered within the terms of a contract. 2. To be too aggressive in selling (something). 3. To present with excessive or unwarranted enthusiasm.

o·ver·set (ōvər-sét) *v.* **-set, -setting, -sets.** —*tr.* 1. To tip over; overturn. 2. To throw into a confused or disturbed state; upset. 3. *Printing.* To set too much (printed matter) for a given space. ~*n.* (-set). 1. *Printing.* An excess of set type. 2. An upset.

o·ver·sew (ōvər-sō, -sō) *tr.v.* **-sewed, -sewn** or **-sewed, -sewing, -sews.** To sew over (raw edges of fabric) to prevent fraying.

o·ver·sexed (ōvər-sékst) *adj.* Having a sexual drive or interest that is judged to be excessive.

o·ver·shad·ow (ōvər-sháddō) *tr.v.* **-owed, -owing, -ows.** 1. **a.** To cast a shadow over. **b.** To cast gloom and despondency on. 2. To make insignificant by comparison; dominate.

o·ver·shoe (ōvər-shōo) *n.* An article of footwear worn over shoes as protection from water, snow, or cold.

o·ver·shoot (ōvər-shōot) *v.* **-shot** (-shót), **-shooting, -shoots.** —*tr.* 1. To shoot or pass over or beyond. 2. To miss by or as if by shooting, hitting, or propelling something too far. 3. **a.** To fly beyond or past (a specific location): *The plane overshot the runway.* **b.** To fly (an aircraft) beyond or past a specific location. 4. To go beyond; exceed. —*intr.* To shoot or go too far.

o·ver·shot (ōvər-shot) *adj.* 1. Having an upper part projecting beyond the lower, especially when excessive or abnormal: *an overshot jaw.* 2. Designating a water wheel or mill in which the flowing water feeds and drives the wheel from the top.

o·ver·side (ōvər-sīd, -sīd) *adv.* Over the side of a ship into another boat or into the water.

o·ver·sight (ōvər-sīt) *n.* 1. An unintentional omission or mistake. 2. Watchful care or management; supervision.

o·ver·sim·pli·fy (ōvər-símpli-fī) *tr.v.* **-fied, -fying, -fies.** To distort by presenting in too simple a form. —**o·ver·sim·pli·fi·ca·tion** (fi-káysh'n) *n.*

o·ver·size (ōvər-síz, -sīz) *adj.* Also **o·ver·sized** (ōvər-sízd). Larger in size than usual or necessary.

~*n.* (ōvər-síz). 1. An unusually large size. 2. An article made in an unusually large size.

o·ver·skirt (ōvər-skurt) *n.* An outer skirt, especially a shorter one worn draped over another skirt.

o·ver·sleep (ōvər-sléep) *tr.v.* **-slept** (-slépt), **-sleeping, -sleeps.** To sleep beyond one's usual or planned time for waking.

o·ver·spend (ōvər-spénd) *v.* **-spent** (-spént), **-spending, -spends.** —*intr.* To spend more than is prudent or necessary. —*tr.* 1. To spend in excess of: *overspend one's income.* 2. To exhaust. Used chiefly in the past participle: *overspent with worry.*

~*n.* The act or an instance of overspending.

o·ver·spill (ōvər-spil) *n. British.* An overflow or excess; especially, an overflow of people from one area to another. Also used adjectivally: *an overspill estate.*

~*intr.v.* (-spíl) **overspilt** (-spílt) or **-spilled, -spilling, -spills.** To overflow, especially as a growing town or a population might.

o·ver·state (ōvər-stáyt) *tr.v.* **-stated, -stating, -states.** To state in exaggerated terms. —**o·ver·state·ment** *n.*

o·ver·stay (ōvər-stáy) *tr.v.* **-stayed, -staying, -stays.** To stay beyond (set limits or expected duration): *She overstayed her welcome.*

o·ver·steer (ōvər-steer) *intr.v.* **-steered, -steering, -steers.** To turn, or have a tendency to turn, more sharply than is usual or is intended by the driver turning the wheel. Used of a motor vehicle. ~*n.* (-steer). 1. An instance of oversteering. 2. A tendency to oversteer.

o·ver·step (ōvər-stép) *tr.v.* **-stepped, -stepping, -steps.** To go beyond (a limit): *overstep the bounds of taste.*

o·ver·stock (ōvər-stók) *tr.v.* **-stocked, -stocking, -stocks.** 1. To supply with too much of (a commodity). 2. To stock too much of (a commodity).

~*n.* (-stok). An excessive supply.

o·ver·strung (ōvər-strung *for sense 1; for sense 2,* -strúng) *adj.* 1. Being or designating a piano having strings on two levels crossing diagonally. 2. Tense and strained; highly strung.

o·ver·stuff (ōvər-stúf) *tr.v.* **-stuffed, -stuffing, -stuffs.** 1. To stuff too much into. 2. To upholster overall and thickly.

o·ver·sub·scribe (ōvər-səb-skríb ‖ -sub-) *tr.v.* **-scribed, -scribing, -scribes.** To subscribe for (something) in excess of available supply or accommodation: *The opera season was oversubscribed.* —**o·ver·sub·scrip·tion** (-skrípsh'n) *n.*

o·ver·sup·ply (ōvər-sə-plí, -plī) *n., pl.* **-plies.** A supply in excess of what is required.

~*tr.v.* (-plī) **oversupplied, -plying, -plies.** To supply in excess.

o·vert (ō-vert, ō-vért) *adj.* Open and observable; not concealed or hidden. [Middle English, from Old French, from the past participle of *ovrir,* to open, from Vulgar Latin *operīre* (unattested), from Latin *aperīre.*] —**o·vert·ly** *adv.*

o·ver·take (ōvər-táyk) *tr.v.* **-took** (-tŏok), **-taken** (-táykən), **-taking, -takes.** 1. **a.** To move past and take up a position in front of. **b.** To pass or surpass after catching up with. 2. To catch up with; draw even or level with. 3. To come upon unexpectedly; take by surprise: *Night overtook us.*

o·ver·task (ōvər-táask ‖ -tásk) *tr.v.* **-tasked, -tasking, -tasks.** 1. To give too demanding a task to. 2. To be too demanding a task for; strain to exhaustion.

o·ver·tax (ōvər-táks) *tr.v.* **-taxed, -taxing, -taxes.** 1. To impose an excessive tax or taxes on. 2. To subject to an excessive burden or strain. —**o·ver·tax·a·tion** (-tak-sáysh'n) *n.* —**o·ver·tax·ing** *adj.*

o·ver·the·count·er (ōvər-thə-kówntər) *adj.* 1. *Abbr.* **OTC, O.T.C.** Capable of being sold legally without a prescription. Said of certain drugs or medicines. 2. Not listed or available on an officially recognised stock exchange but traded in direct negotiation between buyers and sellers. Said of securities. Compare **under-the-counter.** —**over the counter** *adv.*

o·ver·throw (ōvər-thrō) *tr.v.* **-threw** (-thrōo ‖ -thréw), **-thrown** (-thrōn ‖ -thrō-ən), **-throwing, -throws.** 1. To throw over; overturn. 2. To bring about the downfall or destruction of, especially by force or concerted action: *a plot to overthrow the government.*

~*n.* (-thrō). 1. An instance of overthrowing. 2. Downfall; destruction. 3. In cricket: **a.** A throw by a fielder that goes beyond the wicket. **b.** A run made as a result of an overthrow.

o·ver·thrust (ōvər-thrust) *n. Geology.* A fault caused by the movement of rocks on the upper surface of a gently inclined fault plane over the rocks on the lower surface. Compare **underthrust.**

o·ver·time (ōvər-tīm) *n.* 1. Time spent at a job in addition to regular working hours. Also used adjectivally: *overtime payments.* 2. Pay given for such extra work. 3. *Sports. U.S.* Extra time.

~*adv.* Beyond the established time limit, especially that of the normal working day: *The staff worked overtime.*

~*tr.v.* (-tīm) **overtimed, -timing, -times.** To exceed the desired time limit for: *overtime a photographic exposure.*

o·ver·tone (ōvər-tōn) *n.* 1. In music and acoustics, a **harmonic** (see) other than the fundamental. 2. *Often plural.* An implication or hint: *praise with overtones of envy.* [Translation of German *Oberton.*]

o·ver·top (ōvər-tóp) *tr.v.* **-topped, -topping, -tops.** 1. To extend or rise over or beyond the top of; tower above. **2.** To be superior to; surpass in importance; override.

o·ver·trick (ṓvər-trik) *n.* In card games, a trick won in excess of contract or game.

o·ver·trump (ṓvər-trúmp, -trump) *v.* **-trumped, -trumping, -trumps.** *—tr.* To trump with a higher trump card than any played on the same trick. *—intr.* To play a trump higher than one previously played on a trick.

o·ver·ture (ṓvər-tewr, -chər) *n.* **1.** *Music.* **a.** An instrumental composition intended especially as an introduction to an opera, oratorio, or other extended musical work. **b.** A similar orchestral work, such as one written as introductory music to a play, or as a concert piece. **2.** Any introductory section or part, as of a poem. **3.** *Often plural.* An act, offer, or proposal that indicates readiness to undertake a course of action or to open a relationship. Used chiefly in the phrase *make overtures to.* **4.** In the Presbyterian Church: **a.** The submitting of a proposal by the highest church court to the presbyteries for their judgment on it preceding formal decision by the court. **b.** A proposal thus submitted.

—tr.v. **overtured, -turing, -tures. 1.** To present as an overture or proposal. **2.** To present or offer an overture to. **3.** To introduce with an overture or prelude. [Middle English, from Old French, from Vulgar Latin *opertūra* (unattested), from Latin *apertūra,* an opening, from *aperīre* (past participle *apertus*), to open.]

o·ver·turn (ṓvər-túrn) *v.* **-turned, -turning, -turns.** *—tr.* **1.** To cause to turn over or capsize; upset. **2.** To overthrow; defeat. **3.** To negate; nullify: *overturn a decision.* *—intr.* To turn over or capsize; become upset. *—***o·ver·turn** (ṓvər-turn) *n.*

o·ver·use (ṓvər-yōōz) *tr.v.* **-used, -using, -uses.** To use to excess. *—n.* (-yōōss). Excessive use.

o·ver·val·ue (ṓvər-vál-yōō) *tr.v.* **-ued, -uing, -ues.** To place too high a value on.

o·ver·view (ṓvər-vew) *n.* **1.** A broad, comprehensive view. **2.** A general survey or inspection.

o·ver·ween·ing (ṓvər-wéening) *adj.* **1.** Presumptuously arrogant; overbearing. **2.** Excessive; immoderate: *overweening ambition.* [Middle English, "having an excessively high opinion of oneself" : OVER- + WEEN + -ING.] *—***o·ver·ween·ing·ly** *adv.*

o·ver·weigh (ṓvər-wáy) *tr.v.* **-weighed, -weighing, -weighs. 1.** To weigh down excessively; overburden. **2.** To have more weight than; outweigh; overbalance.

o·ver·weight (ṓvər-wáyt) *adj.* Weighing more than is normal, necessary, or allowed.

—n. (-wayt). **1.** More weight than is normal, necessary, or allowed; an excess of weight. **2.** *Archaic.* Greater weight; preponderance. *—tr.v.* (-wáyt) **overweighted, -weighting, -weights. 1.** To weigh down too heavily; overload. **2.** To give too much emphasis, importance, or consideration to.

o·ver·whelm (ṓvər-wélm, -hwélm) *tr.v.* **-whelmed, -whelming, -whelms. 1.** To overcome completely, either physically or emotionally; overpower: *quite overwhelmed by all this praise.* **2.** To surge over and submerge; engulf. **3.** To turn over; upset; overthrow.

o·ver·whelm·ing (ṓvər-wélming, -hwélming) *adj.* Overpowering in effect or strength: *overwhelming news; an overwhelming majority.* *—***o·ver·whelm·ing·ly** *adv.*

o·ver·wind (ṓvər-wīnd) *tr.v.* **-wound, -winding, -winds.** To wind (a watch, for example) beyond the correct limit.

o·ver·win·ter (ṓvər-wintər) *v.* **-wintered, -wintering, -winters.** *—intr.* **1.** To spend the winter in a specified place. **2.** To survive winter in a particular form or in a particular place. *—tr.* To preserve through the winter.

o·ver·work (ṓvər-wúrk) *v.* **-worked, -working, -works.** *—tr.* **1.** To force to work too hard or long. **2.** To use or rework too often or to excess: *overwork a metaphor.* *—intr.* To work too long or hard. *—n.* Excessive work; work that is too hard or lasts too long.

o·ver·write (ṓvər-rīt) *v.* **-wrote** (-rṓt), **-written** (-rítt'n), **-writing, -writes.** *—tr.* **1. a.** To write (something) over other writing. **b.** To write something over (other writing). **2.** To write (a text) or write about (a subject) in an excessively flowery, mannered, or prolix style. *—intr.* **1.** To write at unnecessarily great length. **2.** To write in an inappropriately ornate or fulsome style.

o·ver·wrought (ṓvər-ráwt) *adj.* **1.** Excessively nervous or excited; agitated; strained. **2.** Extremely elaborate or ornate; overdone.

O·vett (ō-vét), **Steven Michael James** (1955–). British middle distance runner. In the 1980s he set three world records at 1500 metres and two at 1 mile. He was Olympic champion at 800 metres in 1980.

ovi-, ovo– *comb. form.* Indicates egg or ovum; for example, **ovoviviparous, oviduct.** [Latin *ōvi-, ōvo-,* from *ōvum,* egg.]

Ov·id (óvvid, ṓvid), born Publius Ovidius Naso (43 B.C.–A.D. 18). Roman poet. His work includes *Metamorphoses,* an urbane treatment of several legends. He also wrote many love poems.

o·vi·duct (ṓvi-dukt, óvvi-) *n.* *Zoology.* A tube through which ova leave an ovary. In mammals it is called the **Fallopian tube** (*see*). [New Latin *oviductus* : OVI- + DUCT.] *—***o·vi·duc·tal** (-dúkt'l) *adj.*

o·vif·er·ous (ō-víffərəss) *adj.* Bearing or producing ova or eggs. [OVI- + -FEROUS.]

o·vi·form (ṓvi-fawrm) *adj.* Egg-shaped. [OVI- + -FORM.]

o·vine (ō-vīn) *adj.* Of, pertaining to, or resembling a sheep; sheeplike. [Late Latin *ovīnus,* from *ovis,* sheep.]

o·vip·a·rous (ō-víppərəss) *adj.* Producing eggs that hatch outside the body. Compare **ovoviviparous, viviparous.** [Latin *ōviparus* :

OVI- + -PAROUS.] *—***o·vi·par·i·ty** (ṓvi-párrəti) *n.* *—***o·vip·a·rous·ly** *adv.*

o·vi·pos·it (ṓvi-pózzit) *intr.v.* **-ited, -iting, -its.** To lay eggs, especially with an ovipositor. *—***o·vi·po·si·tion** (-pə-zísh'n) *n.*

o·vi·pos·i·tor (ṓvi-pózzitər) *n.* **1.** A tubular structure, consisting of a pair of valves extending near the rear of the abdomen, with which most insects lay eggs. **2.** An egg-laying organ in certain fish, which is an extension of the edge of the genital opening.

o·vi·sac (ṓvi-sak) *n.* *Biology.* An egg-containing capsule, such as a **Graafian follicle** or an **ootheca** (*both of which see*).

ovo–. Variant of **ovi-.**

o·void (ṓvoyd) *adj.* Also **o·voi·dal** (ō-vóyd'l). **1.** Egg-shaped. **2.** *Botany.* Egg-shaped, and having the broader end nearest the point of attachment. Said of leaves or fruits, for example.

—n. Something egg-shaped. [French *ovoïde* : OV(I)- + -OID.]

o·vo·lo (ṓvə-lō) *n., pl.* **-li** (-lee). *Architecture.* A rounded convex moulding, often a quarter section of a circle or ellipse. Also called "thumb". [Italian, diminutive of *ovo,* egg, from Latin *ōvum.*]

ov·on·ic (ō-vónnik) *adj.* Designating a phenomenon or device based on the Ovshinsky effect.

—n. An Ovshinsky device. [Blend of Ov*shinsky* + electr*onic.*]

o·vo·tes·tis (ṓvō-téss-tiss) *n., pl.* **-tes** (-teez). *Zoology.* The hermaphroditic reproductive organ of some gastropods.

o·vo·vi·vip·a·rous (ṓvō-vī-víppərəss, -vi-) *adj.* Producing eggs that hatch within the female's body, as do some fishes and reptiles. Compare **oviparous, viviparous.** [New Latin *ovoviviparus* : OVO- + *viviparus,* VIVIPAROUS.] *—***o·vo·vi·vi·par·i·ty** (-vī-vi-párrəti), **o·vo·vi·vip·a·rous·ness** *n.* *—***o·vo·vi·vip·a·rous·ly** *adv.*

Ov·shin·sky device (ov-shín-ski) *n.* An electronic device using the Ovshinsky effect. Also called "ovonic", "ovonic device".

Ovshinsky effect *n.* *Electronics.* An effect that occurs in certain glasses containing selenium and tellurium. When a suitable voltage is applied across a thin film of this material its resistance falls rapidly, enabling devices incorporating these glasses to be used as switches. [After S.R. *Ovshinsky* (born 1923), U.S. inventor.]

o·vu·late (óvvew-layt, ṓ-vew-) *intr.v.* **-lated, -lating, -lates.** *Biology.* **1.** To produce ova. **2.** To discharge ova. [New Latin *ovulum,* OVULE.] *—***o·vu·la·tion** (-láysh'n) *n.*

o·vule (óvvewl, ṓ-vewl) *n.* **1.** *Botany.* A female reproductive structure consisting of the integuments, nucellus, and embryo sac which after fertilisation becomes a seed. **2.** *Zoology.* An immature ovum. [French, from New Latin *ovulum,* diminutive of Latin *ōvum,* egg.] *—***o·vu·lar** (óvvew-lər, ṓ-vew-), **o·vu·lar·y** (óvvew-ləri, ṓ-vew- ‖ *U.S.* -lerri) *adj.*

o·vum (ṓvəm) *n., pl.* **ova** (ṓvə). The unfertilised female reproductive cell of animals; an egg cell. [New Latin, from Latin *ōvum,* egg.]

owe (ō) *v.* **owed, owing, owes.** *—tr.* **1.** To be indebted to the amount of; have to pay or repay: *She owes me five pounds.* **2.** To be morally obliged to; have an obligation to render or offer: *I owe you an apology.* **3.** To be in debt to. **4. a.** To be indebted or obliged for: *I owe a lot to my friends.* **b.** To be indebted or obliged for being the cause of: *He owes his success to his mother.* **5.** To bear (a certain feeling) towards a person: *She owes them a grudge.* *—intr.* To be in debt: *She owes for everything she has.* [Middle English *owen,* to possess, owe, Old English *āgan,* to possess.]

Ow·en (ṓ-in), **David (Anthony Llewellyn), Baron** (1938–). British politician. A Labour M.P., he became Foreign Secretary (1977–79), but left the party in 1981 to cofound the SDP and become the leader of it (1983–87) and its non-Lib-Dem rump (1988–90).

Owen, Robert (1771–1858). British philanthropist. After establishing the mill community of New Lanark (where he was manager and later owner) as a cooperative (1800), he started similar ventures in the United States and Ireland.

Owen, Wilfred (1893–1918). British poet, who served in World War I. His poems describe the nightmarish conditions in which soldiers lived and died; among his most famous poems is "Anthem for Doomed Youth". He was killed a week before the armistice.

Owen Falls. Waterfall in southeast Uganda. Lying on the White Nile, 3.2 kilometres (2 miles) from Lake Victoria, it became (1954) the site of a dam which provides hydro-electric power for Uganda and Kenya, and irrigation for Sudan and Egypt.

Ow·ens (ṓ-inz), **Jesse,** born James Cleveland Owens (1913–80). U.S. athlete. In 1935/36 he broke six world records in sprinting, hurdling, and long jump; the new records stood for 20 years. His greatest triumph came at the 1936 Olympics in Germany, when his success as a black athlete embarrassed the Nazi government.

ow·ing (ṓ-ing) *adj.* Still to be paid; due; owed. *—***owing to.** Because of; on account of. See Usage note at **due.**

owl (owl) *n.* **1.** Any of various often nocturnal birds of prey of the order Strigiformes, having hooked and feathered talons, short necks, large heads with short, hooked beaks, and large forward-facing eyes. **2.** Any of various breeds of domestic pigeon resembling owls. **3.** A solemn, wise-looking person. [Middle English *owle,* Old English *ūle.*]

owl·et (ów-lit, -let, -lət) *n.* A young owl.

owl·ish (ówlish) *adj.* Resembling an owl, especially in seeming solemn and wise. *—***owl·ish·ly** *adv.* *—***owl·ish·ness** *n.*

owl-light (ówl-līt) *n.* *Poetic.* Twilight; dusk.

own (ōn) *adj.* Of or belonging to oneself or itself; individual; particular. Used to intensify the fact of possession and usually preceded by a possessive pronoun: *My own book.* Sometimes used to indicate oneself as the sole agent of the action expressed by the verb: *She made her own bed while I made the rest.*

~*n.* That which belongs to one: *It is my own.* —**come into (one's) own. 1.** To obtain possession of what belongs to one. **2.** To reach one's deserved level; fulfil one's potential. **3.** To obtain rightful recognition. —**hold (one's) own.** To maintain one's place in spite of attack or criticism. —**of (one's) own.** Belonging completely to oneself alone. —**on (one's) own. 1.** Alone; without company; by oneself. **2.** Without help; through one's own unaided efforts. **3.** Completely independent; responsible for oneself.

~*v.* **owned, owning, owns.** —*tr.* **1.** To have or possess: *She owns the shop.* **2.** To acknowledge or admit: *"I own myself a debtor to the world for two items."* (Lawrence Sterne). —*intr.* To confess or acknowledge: *She owned to being annoyed.* —See Synonyms at **acknowledge.** —**own up.** To confess fully and openly. Sometimes used with *to.* [Middle English *owen,* Old English *āgen.*]

own·er (ṓnər) *n.* A person who owns or possesses; especially, the person having legal ownership.

owner-occupier *n. Chiefly British.* Someone who is the freeholder or long-leaseholder of the property he lives in. [Because he is held to *own* the property he *occupies.*]

own·er·ship (ṓnər-ship) *n.* **1.** The state or fact of being an owner. **2.** Legal right to possession; proprietorship; dominion.

own goal *n. British.* **1.** A goal scored, typically inadvertently, by a player against his own team rather than against the opposing team. **2.** *Informal.* A ploy that rebounds upon its perpetrator, typically to ludicrous effect.

owt. *Northern English.* Variant of **aught**[1].

ox (oks) *n., pl.* **oxen** (ŏks'n). **1.** An adult castrated bull of the genus *Bos.* **2.** Any bovine mammal. [Middle English *ox,* Old English *oxa.*]

ox-. **1.** Variant of **oxa-.** **2.** Variant of **oxo-.**

oxa–, ox– *comb. form. Chemistry.* Indicates the presence of oxygen atoms, especially when replacing carbon; for example, **oxalic acid.** [From OXYGEN.]

ox·a·late (ŏksə-layt) *n.* Any salt or ester of oxalic acid.
~*tr.v.* **oxalated, -lating, -lates.** To treat (a specimen) with an oxalate or oxalic acid. [French : *oxalique,* OXALIC ACID + -ATE.]

ox·al·ic acid (ok-sál-ik) *n.* A poisonous, crystalline organic acid, $HOOCCOOH·2H_2O$, used as a cleansing agent for motor-vehicle radiators and for metals in general, as a laundry bleach, and in textile finishing and cleaning. Also called "ethanedioic acid". [French *oxalique,* from Latin *oxalis,* wood sorrel, OXALIS.]

ox·a·lis (ŏksəliss, ok-sál-iss) *n.* Any plant of the genus *Oxalis,* having clover-like leaves and pink, yellow, or white flowers. See **wood sorrel.** [New Latin, from Latin, from Greek, from *oxus,* "sharp", sour.]

ox·a·zine (ŏksə-zeen) *n.* A heterocyclic chemical compound, C_4H_5NO, that exists in 13 isomeric forms. [OXY- + AZINE.]

ox·blood (ŏks-blud) *n.* Dark or deep red to medium reddish brown. Also called "oxblood". —**ox·blood red** *adj.*

ox·bow (ŏks-bō) *n.* **1.** A U-shaped piece of wood that fits under and around the neck of an ox, with its upper ends attached to the bar of the yoke. **2.** A U-shaped bend in a river. **3.** The land within such a bend of a river. **4.** A lake formed from a U-shaped bend in a river. In this sense, also called "oxbow lake". —**ox·bow** *adj.*

Ox·bridge (ŏks-brij) *n.* The universities of Oxford and Cambridge, especially considered as representing traditional academic and social excellence, privilege, and exclusiveness.
~*adj.* Of or pertaining to Oxbridge: *Oxbridge philosophers; Oxbridge snobbery.* [*Ox*ford + Cam*bridge.*]

ox·eye (ŏks-ī) *n.* **1.** Any of various Eurasian plants of the genus *Buphthalmum,* having daisy-like flowers with yellow rays and dark centres. **2.** A round or oval dormer window.

oxeye daisy *n.* A perennial plant, *Chrysanthemum leucanthemum,* having daisy-like flowers with white rays and yellow centres.

ox·fence (ŏks-fenss) *n.* **1.** A strong fence for containing cattle. **2.** A fence used as an obstacle in showjumping, steeplechasing, and the like, consisting of a hedge, a railing or railings, and usually a ditch. Also called "oxer".

Ox·ford[1] (ŏks-fərd). City in southern central England. The county town of Oxfordshire, it lies between the river Thames (known locally as the Isis) and its tributary, the Cherwell. Its university (1249) has been, and still is, one of the world's most important places of learning; its historic buildings dominate the city centre. Cowley, the industrial suburb, has grown around the Morris motor-car works.

Oxford[2] *n. Sometimes small* o. **1.** A stout, low shoe that laces over the instep. **2.** A cotton cloth of a tight basket weave, used primarily for men's shirts. **3.** A sheep, the Oxford Down. [After OXFORD.]

Oxford bags *pl. n.* Trousers with extremely wide legs, originally fashionable in the 1920s.

Oxford blue *n.* **1.** Dark, deep blue. **2.** A sportswoman or sportsman who has been awarded a **blue** *(see)* by Oxford University. —**Oxford blue** *adj.*

Oxford Down *n.* A large sheep of an English breed, having a dark brown face and legs and short wool. Also called "Oxford".

Oxford English *n.* A style of English pronunciation, similar to **received pronunciation,** thought to be used at Oxford University and often considered to be affected. Also called "Oxford accent".

Oxford frame *n.* A picture frame whose sides cross and project outwards at the corners.

Oxford grey *n.* Dark grey. —**Oxford grey** *adj.*

Oxford Group *n.* See **Moral Rearmament.**

Oxford Movement *n.* A movement within the Church of England that originated at Oxford University in 1833. It sought to link the

Anglican Church more closely to the Roman Catholic Church. See **Tractarianism.**

Ox·ford·shire (ŏks-fərd-sheer, -shər). *Abbr.* **Oxon.** County of southern central England. An agricultural valley rising to the Cotswolds in the west and the Chilterns in the south, it is drained by the river Thames. Dairy and sheep farming are important, and the major industrial centre is Cowley. The county town is Oxford.

ox·hide (ŏks-hīd) *n.* Leather made from the hide of an ox. —**ox·hide** *adj.*

ox·i·dant (ŏksidənt) *n.* A chemical reagent that oxidises. Also called "oxidiser".

ox·i·dase (ŏksi-dayz, -dayss) *n.* Any of various plant or animal enzymes that act as oxidants. [OXID(ATION) + -ASE.] —**ox·i·da·sic** (-dáy-zik, -sik) *adj.*

ox·i·da·tion (ŏksi-dáysh'n) *n. Chemistry.* The process of oxidising or a chemical reaction in which something is oxidised. Compare **reduction.** [French, from *oxyder,* to oxidise.] —**ox·i·da·tive** (-daytiv) *adj.* —**ox·i·da·tive·ly** *adv.*

ox·i·da·tion-re·duc·tion (ŏksi-dáysh'n-ri-dúksh'n) *n.* A chemical reaction in which an atom or molecule loses electrons to another atom or molecule. Also called "redox".

oxidative phosphorylation *n. Biochemistry.* A vital process of intracellular respiration, occurring within the mitochondria of the cell, and responsible for most **A.T.P.** *(see)* formation.

ox·ide (ŏks-īd) *n.* A binary compound of an element or radical with oxygen. [French, from *oxygène,* OXYGEN.] —**ox·id·ic** (ok-síddik) *adj.*

ox·i·dise, ox·i·dize (ŏksi-dīz) *v.* **-dised, -dising, -dises.** Also **ox·i·date** (-dayt) **-dated, -dating, -dates.** —*tr.* **1.** *Chemistry.* **2.** To add oxygen to (a compound), as in combustion reactions. **b.** To remove hydrogen from (a compound), as in dehydrogenation reactions. **c.** To remove electrons from (a compound, ion, or group), as in the change of ferrous ions (Fe^{2+}) to ferric ions (Fe^{3+}). **2.** To coat with oxide. —*intr.* **1.** *Chemistry.* To undergo oxidation; gain oxygen or lose hydrogen or electrons. Used of chemical compounds. **2.** To become coated with oxide. —**ox·i·dis·a·ble** *adj.* —**ox·i·di·sa·tion** (-dī-záysh'n ‖ *U.S.* -di-) *n.*

ox·i·dis·er (ŏksi-dīzər) *n.* Any substance that oxidises or induces oxidisation; especially, the oxidant in a rocket fuel.

ox·i·dis·ing agent (ŏksi-dīzing) *n. Chemistry.* A substance, such as oxygen or hydrogen peroxide, that oxidises another substance and is itself reduced in doing so. Compare **reducing agent.**

ox·ime (ŏks-eem) *n.* Any of a group of chemical compounds, used in chemical analysis, that have the general formula RR'C:NOH. If R and R' are both organic groups the compound is called a *ketoxime;* if R' is an organic group and R is a hydrogen atom it is an *aldoxime.* [OXO- + -*ime* representing -IMIDE.]

ox·lip (ŏks-lip) *n.* **1.** A Eurasian plant, *Primula elatior,* very similar to the primrose with flowers borne in clusters. **2.** A hybrid plant, the *false oxlip,* a cross between primroses and cowslips and having darker yellow flowers than the true oxlip. [Old English *oxanslyppe : oxan,* genitive of *ox,* OX + *slyppe, slypa,* sticky substance, dung.]

oxo–, ox– *comb. form. Chemistry.* Indicates a compound containing oxygen linked to another atom by a double bond; for example, **oxopropanoic acid.** [From OXYGEN.]

Oxon. 1. Of Oxford (University). Used in degree titles: *B.A. Oxon.* **2.** Oxfordshire.

Ox·o·ni·an (ok-sṓni-ən) *adj.* Of, pertaining to, or characteristic of Oxford or Oxford University.
~*n.* **1.** A student, graduate, or member of Oxford University. **2.** A native or inhabitant of Oxford. [Medieval Latin *Oxōnia,* Oxford, from Old English *Ox(e)naford,* OXFORD.]

ox·o·ni·um (ok-sṓni-əm) *adj.* **1.** Designating an ion with the general formula R_3O, where R is either a hydrogen atom or an organic group. **2.** Designating a compound formed from this ion: *an oxonium salt.* [OXO- + -ON(E) + -IUM.]

ox·peck·er (ŏks-peckər) *n.* Either of two African birds, *Buphagus africanus* or *B. erythrorhynchus,* that feed upon ticks on the hides of animals. Also called "rhinoceros bird", "tick bird".

ox·tail (ŏks-tayl) *n.* The tail of an ox, as used in soups and stews.

ox·ter (ŏkstər) *n. Northern British.* An armpit. [Old English *ōxta, ōhsta;* akin to Latin *axilla.*]

ox·tongue, ox-tongue (ŏks-tung ‖ -tong) *n.* **1.** The tongue of an ox used as food. **2.** Either of two plants, *Picris echioides* or *P. hieracioides,* having tongue-shaped, hairy leaves and yellow flowers.

Oxus. See **Amudar'ya.**

ox·y (ŏksi) *adj.* **1.** Containing or mixed with oxygen. Often used in combination: *oxyhydrogen.* **2.** *Chemistry.* Combined with oxygen or containing oxygen in chemical combination. Used in combination: *oxyacide; oxyhaemoglobin.* See **oxo-.**

oxy– *comb. form.* Indicates something sharp; for example, **oxycephaly.** [Greek *oxus,* sharp.]

ox·y·a·cet·y·lene (ŏksi-ə-sétti-leen, -lin) *adj.* Containing a mixture of acetylene and oxygen, at a flame temperature of 3,300°C.

ox·y·ac·id (ŏksi-ássid) *n.* An acid, such as sulphuric acid or nitric acid, that contains oxygen in its molecule. Also called "oxygen acid".

ox·y·ceph·a·ly (ŏksi-séffəli) *n.* A congenital abnormality in which the skull assumes a conical shape. [OXY-, sharp + *-cephaly,* from -CEPHALIC.] —**ox·y·ce·phal·ic** (-si-fál-ik), **ox·y·ceph·a·lous** (-séffələss) *adj.*

ox·y·gen (ŏksijən) *n. Symbol* **O** A colourless, odourless, tasteless gaseous element constituting 21 per cent of the earth's atmosphere by volume, from which the pure liquid form is obtained by fractional distillation. It combines with most elements, is essential for plant and animal respiration, and is required for nearly all combustion and combustive processes. Atomic number 8, atomic weight 15.9994, melting point –218.4°C, boiling point –183.0°C, gas density at 0°C 1.429 kilograms per cubic metre, valency 2. [French *oxygène*, "acid-former" : OXY-, sharp (here, "acid") + -GEN.] **—ox·y·gen·ic** (óksi-jénnik), **ox·yg·e·nous** (ok-síjənəss) *adj.* **—ox·y·gen·i·cal·ly** *adv.*

oxygen acid *n.* An oxyacid.

ox·y·gen·ate (ók-sijə-nayt, ok-síjə-) *tr.v.* **-ated, -ating, -ates.** Also **ox·y·gen·ise** (-nīz), **-ised, -ising, -ises.** To treat, combine, or infuse with oxygen. **—ox·y·gen·a·tion** (-náysh'n) *n.*

oxygen debt *n.* The condition that exists in cells when insufficient oxygen is available for oxidation of foodstuffs to produce the energy required by the cells (for example, for strenuous exercise).

oxygen mask *n.* A device covering the mouth and nose of a patient through which oxygen is supplied from a tank or other source.

oxygen tent *n.* A transparent canopy placed over the head and shoulders of a patient for administering oxygen to aid respiration.

ox·y·hae·mo·glo·bin (óksi-héemə-glôbin, -glôbin) *n.* A bright red chemical complex of haemoglobin and oxygen, that transports oxygen from the lungs to the tissues via the blood.

ox·y·hy·dro·gen blowpipe (óksi-hídrəjən) *n.* A torch that burns a mixture of hydrogen and oxygen for welding. Also called "oxyhydrogen burner".

ox·y·mo·ron (óksi-máwr-on ‖ -môr-) *n., pl.* **-mora** (-máwr-ə ‖ -môr-) or **-morons.** A rhetorical figure in which an epigrammatic effect is created by the conjunction of incongruous or contradictory terms; for example, *a mournful optimist.* [Greek *oxumōron*, a clever remark, more pointedly witty for seeming stupid, neuter of *oxumōros*, "sharp-foolish" : OXY-, sharp + *mōros*, stupid, foolish.]

oxy·salt (óksi-sawlt) *n.* A salt of an oxyacid.

ox·y·sul·phide (óksi-súl-fīd) *n.* Chemistry. A compound consisting of sulphur and oxygen, combined with a metal or positive radical, in which part of the sulphur has been replaced by oxygen.

ox·y·tet·ra·cy·cline (óksi-téttrə-sí-klin, -kleen) *n.* An antibiotic, $C_{22}H_{24}N_2O_9 \cdot 2H_2O$, derived from the mould *Streptomyces rimosus*, and used to treat bacterial infection in humans and animals. A trademark is "Terramycin".

ox·y·to·cic (óksi-tô-sik) *adj.* Hastening the process of childbirth, especially by inducing contraction of the uterine muscle. **~***n.* An oxytocic drug or agent. [OXY-, sharp + Greek *tokos*, childbirth, from *tiktein*, to bear + -IC.]

ox·y·to·cin (óksi-tô-sin) *n.* A pituitary hormone that increases contraction of the uterus during childbirth and stimulates the flow of milk. [See **oxytocic**.]

ox·y·tone (óksi-tōn) *adj.* In ancient Greek grammar, of or designating a word that has an acute accent on the last syllable. **~***n.* An oxytone word. [Greek *oxutonos* : OXY-, sharp + *tonos*, TONE.] **—ox·y·ton·ic** (-tónnik) *adj.*

ox·y·u·ri·a·sis (ók-si-yoor-í-ə-siss) *n.* A disease, **enterobiasis** (see). [OXY- + URO- (urinary tract) + -IASIS.]

o·yez (ō-yess, -yez, ō-yéss, -yéz, -yáy) *interj.* Also **O·yes** (ō-yess, ō-yéss). Used three times in succession to order attention and silence, as by a public crier, or to open a court of law. **~***n.* Also **o·yes** *pl.* **oyesses** (ō-yessiz). *Archaic.* The cry "oyez": *"Fame with her loud'st Oyes cries 'This is he!' "* (Shakespeare). [Middle English *oyes!* from Anglo-French *oyez!*, hear ye!, imperative plural of *oyer*, Old French *oïr*, to hear, from Latin *audīre*.]

O·yo Empire (ō-yō) *n.* West African empire existing from the 17th to the 19th century. The modern city of Oyo is the capital of Oyo province, southwest Nigeria.

oys·ter (óystər) *n.* **1. a.** Any of several bivalve molluscs of the genus *Ostrea*, chiefly of shallow marine waters, having an irregularly shaped shell. **b.** The soft, edible flesh of any such mollusc, valued as a delicacy. **2.** Any of various similar or related bivalve molluscs, such as the **pearl oyster** (see). **3.** An oval-shaped piece of muscle,

regarded as a delicacy, found in the hollow of the pelvic bone of a fowl. **4. a.** Any special delicacy. **b.** A source of complete fulfilment, affording every possible chance of personal advancement and satisfaction. Often used in the phrase *The world is (one's) oyster.* **5.** *Slang.* A quiet, reserved person. **6.** A colour, oyster white. **~***intr.v.* **oystered, -tering, -ters.** To gather, dredge for, or breed oysters. [Middle English *oistre*, from Old French, from Latin *ostrea*, from Greek *ostreon*.] **—oys·ter** *adj.*

oyster bed *n.* A place where oysters breed or are raised. Also called "oyster bank", "oyster park".

oys·ter·catch·er (óystər-kachər) *n.* Any of several shore birds of the genus *Haematopus*, especially *H. ostralogus*, having black and white plumage and a long orange-red bill.

oyster crab *n.* A small crab, *Pinnotheres ostreum*, that lives inside the shells of living oysters.

oyster mushroom *n.* A basidiomycete fungus, *Pleurotus ostreatus*, having a shell-shaped edible cap.

oyster pink *n.* Pale greyish pink. **—oyster pink** *adj.*

oyster plant *n.* **1.** A coastal plant, *Mertensia maritima*, having fleshy, grey, oyster-flavoured leaves and small blue flowers. **2.** A vegetable, **salsify** (see).

oyster white *n.* Pale yellowish green to light grey. Also called "oyster". **—oyster white** *adj.*

oz ounce; ounces.

Oz (oz). *Informal.* Australia. [From the first syllable of *Australia*.]

O·zark Plateau (ō-zaark). Also **Ozark Mountains.** Highland of the south central United States. Lying between the Arkansas river to the south and west, the Missouri to the north and the Mississippi to the east.

o·zo·ce·rite (ōzō-séer-īt) *n.* Also **o·zo·ke·rite** (-kéer-, ō-zôkər-, o-, ə-, -it). A yellow-brown to black or green mineral hydrocarbon wax, used in making electrical insulation, lubricants, and inks. Also called "earth wax", "mineral wax". [German *Ozokerit* : Greek *ozein*, to smell + *kēros*, wax + -ITE.]

o·zone (ō-zōn, ō-zôn) *n.* **1.** A blue, gaseous allotrope of oxygen, O_3, derived or formed naturally from diatomic oxygen by electric discharge or exposure to ultraviolet radiation. It is an unstable, powerfully bleaching, poisonous, oxidising agent, with a pungent, irritating odour, used to purify and deodorise air, to sterilise water, and as a bleach. **2.** *Informal.* Fresh, pure, invigorating air, especially that found at the seaside. [German *Ozon*, from Greek *ozōn*, present participle of *ozein*, to smell, reek.] **—o·zon·ic** (ō-zónnik, -zônik), **o·zo·nous** (ō-zōnəss, ō-zônəss) *adj.*

o·zone-friend·ly (ō-zōn-fréndli) *adj.* Referring to manufactured products, such as aerosols, that do not contain CFCs or other chemicals harmful to the ozone layer.

ozone hole *n.* An area of depletion in the ozone layer, especially over Antarctica, largely caused by industrial gases, and posing a threat to the well-being of the planet and its inhabitants.

ozone layer *n.* The ozonosphere.

o·zo·nide (ō-zō-nīd, ō-zə-) *n.* **1.** Any of various often explosive chemicals formed by attachment of ozone to the double bond of an unsaturated compound and used in analytical chemistry to locate such bonds.

o·zo·nise, o·zo·nize (ōzō-nīz) *tr.v.* **-nised, -nising, -nises. 1.** To treat or impregnate with ozone. **2.** To convert (oxygen) to ozone. **—o·zo·ni·sa·tion** (-ni-záysh'n ‖ *U.S.* -ni-) *n.* **—o·zo·nis·er** *n.*

o·zo·nol·y·sis (ōzō-nólla-siss) *n. Chemistry.* A method of treating an organic compound with ozone to locate a double bond by the formation of an ozonide. [OZON(E) + -o- + -LYSIS.]

o·zo·no·sphere (ō-zōnə-sfeer, -zónnə-) *n.* **1.** A region of the upper atmosphere, between 15 and 30 kilometres (10 and 20 miles) in altitude, containing the greatest concentration of ozone, which absorbs solar ultraviolet radiation in a wavelength range not screened by other atmospheric components. **2.** A region of the atmosphere, between 10 and 50 kilometres (6 and 30 miles) in altitude, which contains a relatively high concentration of ozone. In both senses, also called "ozone layer". [OZON(E) + -o- + -SPHERE.] **—o·zo·no·spher·ic** (-sférrik ‖ -sféer-ik), **o·zo·no·spher·i·cal** *adj.*

P

p, P (pee) *n., pl.* **p's,** or *rare* **ps, Ps** or **P's. 1.** The sixteenth letter of the modern English alphabet. **2.** Any of the speech sounds represented by this letter. **—mind (one's) p's and q's.** To take care to observe polite social conventions in one's speech and manner.

p, P, p., P. *Note:* As an abbreviation or symbol, *p* may be a small or a capital letter, with or without a full stop. Established forms or those generally preferred precede the definition. When no form is given, all four forms are in general use in that sense. **1. p** *Physics.* momentum. **2. p.** page. **3. P** *Physics.* parity. **4. p.** part. **5. p.** participle. **6. p.** past. **7. p.** *Chess.* pawn. **8. p.** penny; pence. See Usage note at **penny. 9. p.** per. **10. p.** peseta. **11. p.** peso. **12. P** The symbol for the element phosphorus. **13. p, p.** *Music.* piano (a direction). **14. p** *Physics.* pico-. **15. p.** pint. **16. p.** pipe. **17. p.** pole. **18. p.** population. **19. p.,** P. **20. P** *Physics.* pressure. **21. P.** priest. **22. p., P.** prince. **23. p.** pro. **24. p** proton. **25. p.** purl. **26. P** The medieval Roman numeral for 400. **27.** The 16th in a series.

pa[1] (paa) *n. Informal.* Papa; father. [Short for PAPA.]

pa[2], pah (paa) *n.* A Maori village, originally a fortified village. [Maori *pā.*]

Pa The symbol for the element protactinium.

Pa. Pennsylvania.

p.a. per annum.

P.A. 1. personal assistant. **2.** power of attorney. **3.** press agent. **4.** Press Association. **5.** public-address system. **6.** publicity agent. **7.** Publishers' Association. **8.** purchasing agent.

P/A power of attorney.

P. & O. Peninsular and Oriental Shipping Company.

pab·u·lum (pábbewləm) *n., pl.* **-lums.** *Formal.* **1.** Any substance that gives nourishment; food. **2.** Insipid intellectual nourishment. [Latin *pābulum,* food, fodder.]

PABX private automatic branch (telephone) exchange.

pa·ca (páaka, páckə) *n.* Either of two species of tailless, nocturnal, tropical American rodent, especially *Cuniculus paca,* having a large head and brown fur with three to five lines of white spots running down each side. [Portuguese and Spanish, from Tupi *páca.*]

pace[1] (payss) *n.* **1.** A step made in walking; a stride. **2.** The distance spanned by a step or stride; specifically: **a.** A unit of length equal to 30 inches (76 centimetres). **b.** *Military.* 30 inches (76 centimetres) at quick time or 36 inches (91.5 centimetres) at double time. Called in full "regulation pace". **c.** A length measured from the point at which the heel of one foot is raised to the point at which it is set down again after an intervening step by the other foot; about 1.5 metres or 5 feet. **3. a.** The rate of speed at which a person, animal, or group walks or runs. **b.** The rate of speed at which any activity or movement proceeds. **c.** Great speed or intensity of activity: *couldn't keep up with the pace.* **d.** In cricket, the fastest type of bowling. Also used adjectivally: *a pace bowler.* **4.** A manner of walking or running: *set out at a jaunty pace.* **5. a.** A gait of a horse in which both feet on one side leave and return to the ground together. **b.** Any of the gaits of a horse or other quadruped, such as the walk, trot, canter, or gallop. **—keep pace with.** To advance at the same speed as. **—put (someone) through his paces.** To test (someone's) abilities; require (someone) to demonstrate his skills. **—set the pace. 1.** To go at a speed that other competitors attempt to match or surpass. **2.** To behave or perform in a way that others try to emulate. **—stand** or **stay the pace.** To be able to keep up with others.
~*v.* **paced, pacing, paces.** —*tr.* **1.** To walk or stride back and forth across, as in agitation or distress. **2.** To measure by counting the number of steps needed to cover a distance. Often used with *out.* **3.** To set or regulate the rate of speed for. **4.** To train (a horse) in a particular gait, especially the pace. —*intr.* **1.** To walk with long, deliberate steps. **2.** To go at the pace. Used of a horse or rider. [Middle English *pas,* from Old French, from Latin *passus,* a step, "a stretch of the leg", from *pandere* (past participle *passus*), to stretch.]

pa·ce[2] (páa-chay, páy-si) *prep.* With the permission of; with deference to. Used to express polite, or ironically polite, disagreement: *I have not, pace my detractors, entered into any "deals".* [Latin *pāce,* ablative of *pāx,* peace.] **—pa·ce** *adv.*

pace·mak·er (páyss-maykər) *n.* **1. a.** One who sets the pace in a race. **b.** A pacer. **2.** A leader in any field. **3. a.** *Physiology.* The sinoatrial node *(see).* **b.** *Medicine.* Any of several usually miniaturised electronic devices, surgically implanted in the body, used to regulate, or to aid in the regulation of, the heartbeat. **—pace·mak·ing** *n. & adj.*

pac·er (páy-sər) *n.* **1.** A horse trained to pace. **2.** A pacemaker.

pace·set·ter (páyss-settər) *n.* A pacemaker (senses 1 and 2). **—pace·set·ting** *adj.*

pace·way (páyss-way) *n. Australian.* A racecourse used for trotting and pacing races.

pacha. Variant of **pasha.**

pa·chi·si (pə-cheézi, paa-) *n.* **1.** An ancient game of India similar to backgammon but using cowry shells instead of dice. **2. Parcheesi** *(see).* [Hindi *pacīsī,* from *pacīs,* twenty-five (the highest throw) : Sanskrit *pañca,* five + *vimsati,* twenty.]

pachouli. Variant of **patchouli.**

pach·y·derm (pácki-derm) *n.* Any of various large, thick-skinned, hoofed mammals, such as the elephant or hippopotamus. [French *pachyderme,* from Greek *pakhudermos,* thick-skinned : *pakhus,* thick + *derma,* skin, -DERM.] **—pach·y·der·ma·tous** (-dérmətəss), **pach·y·der·mous** (-dérməss) *adj.*

pach·y·tene (pácki-teen) *n. Biology.* The third stage of prophase in **meiosis** *(see)* during which the chromosomes coil up and shorten, the individual chromatids become visible, and crossing over may occur. [Greek *pakhus,* thick + *taina,* band.]

Pacif. Pacific.

pa·cif·ic (pə-síffik) *adj.* Also **pa·cif·i·cal** (-'l). **1.** Tending to diminish or put an end to conflict; appeasing; calming. **2.** Of a peaceful nature; tranquil; serene. [French *pacifique,* from Latin *pācificus* : *pāx* (stem *pāc-*), peace + *-ficus,* -FIC.] **—pa·cif·i·cal·ly** *adv.*

Pa·cif·ic (pə-síffik) *n. Abbr.* **Pac., Pacif.** The Pacific Ocean. Preceded by *the.*
~*adj. Abbr.* **Pac., Pacif.** Of or in the Pacific Ocean.

pac·i·fi·ca·tion (pássifi-káysh'n) *n.* **1.** Placation; appeasement. **2.** The act or process of pacifying or bringing about a state of peace. **3.** *Often capital* P. A peace treaty: *the Pacification of Ghent.* **4.** The reduction or elimination of insurgent or terrorist activity in an area. [French, from Latin *pācificātiō* (stem *pācificātiōn-*), "peacemaking"; see **pacify.**] **—pa·cif·i·ca·tor** (-kaytər) *n.* **—pa·cif·i·ca·to·ry** (pə-siffi-kə-tri, -təri, -kaytəri, pássifi-kaytəri, -káytəri) *adj.*

Pacific Islands, U.N. Trust Territory of the. Area of the northwest Pacific Ocean including the Caroline, Marshall, and Mariana groups excluding Guam, with more than 2,000 islands overall. Captured from Germany by Japan (1914), it was made a Japanese mandate by the Treaty of Versailles (1919). The United States captured the islands (1944), and they were under U.S. administration as a United Nations Trust Territory (1947–78). Separate constitutional governments were then set up. The Caroline Islands, excluding Palau, form the Federated States of Micronesia, a republic in "free association" with the United States. The Marshall Islands have the same status. The Northern Marianas (the Mariana Islands except Guam) form a "commonwealth" of the United States. Guam remains an "unincorporated territory" of the United States. The Trusteeship agreement ended when Palau became a republic (1994).

Pacific Ocean. Largest of the world's oceans. It is larger than the world's entire land area and is deepest at Challenger Deep in the Marianas Trench (11 033 metres; 36,197 feet). To the south and west are coral and volcanic islands, while the ocean floor is scattered with volcanic mountains. See map, pages 1110–1111.

Pacific Standard Time *n. Abbr.* **PST, P.s.t., P.S.T.** Time in one of the standard time zones of North America, equal to the local time at the 120th meridian west of Greenwich, eight hours behind Greenwich Mean Time. Also called "Pacific Time".

pac·i·fi·er (pássi-fɪ-ər) *n.* **1.** One that pacifies. **2.** *U.S.* A baby's dummy or teething ring.

pac·i·fism (pássi-fiz'm) *n.* **1.** The belief that disputes between nations should and can be settled peacefully. **2. a.** Opposition to war or violence as a means of resolving disputes. **b.** Such opposition demonstrated by refusal to participate in military action. [French *pacifisme,* from *pacifique,* PACIFIC.] **—pac·i·fis·tic** (-fístik) *adj.*

pac·i·fist (pássifist) *n.* **1.** A person who supports or advocates pacifism. **2.** A person who refuses to do military service on the grounds of his belief in pacifism. **—pac·i·fist** *adj.*

pac·i·fy (pássi-fɪ) *tr.v.* **-fied, -fying, -fies. 1.** To ease the anger or agitation of; restore calm to; appease. **2.** To establish peace in; end war, fighting, or violence in. [Middle English *pacifien,* from Old French *pacifier,* from Latin *pācificāre* : *pax* (stem *pāc-*), peace + *facere,* to make.]

Synonyms: pacify, placate, mollify, conciliate, appease, quieten.

pack[1] (pak) *n. Abbr.* **pk. 1.** A collection of items tied up or wrapped; a bundle. **2.** A container made to be carried on the back of a person or an animal, such as: **a.** A knapsack or rucksack. **b.** A parachute prepared for use. **3.** The amount of something, such as food, that is processed and packaged at one time or in one season. **4.** *Chiefly U.S.* A small package containing a standard number of identical or similar items: *a pack of matches.* Also used in combination: *a six-pack.* **5. a.** A complete set of related items: *a pack of cards.* **b.** A set of films to be inserted together into a camera. **c.** A large amount; a lot. Usually used derogatorily, in the phrase *a pack of lies.* **6. a.** A group of animals, such as dogs or wolves, that run and hunt together. **b.** A gang or band of people: *a pack of thugs.* **c.** A group of aircraft, ships, or vehicles moving in or as if in formation. **d.** An organised local unit of Cub Scouts or Brownies. **7.** In Rugby football, the forwards in a team. **8.** *Medicine.* **a.** The swathing of a patient in hot, cold, wet, or dry sheets or blankets.

b. The sheets or blankets so used. **c.** A material, such as gauze, therapeutically inserted into a body cavity or wound. **9.** An **ice pack** *(see)*. **10.** See **face pack**. **11. Pack ice** *(see)*. **12.** *Computing.* A pile of punched computer cards. **—go to the pack.** *Australian & N.Z. Informal.* **1.** To become depraved or degenerate. **2.** To collapse or break down.
~v. packed, packing, packs. —tr. 1. To fold, roll, or combine into a bundle; wrap up. **2. a.** To put into a receptacle for transporting or storing: *pack one's belongings.* **b.** To fill up with items: *pack one's trunk.* **c.** To load (an animal) with a pack. **3.** To process and put into containers in order to preserve, transport, or sell. **4. a.** To bring together (persons or things) closely; crowd together. **b.** To fill up tight; cram. Often used with *out: The theatre was packed out.* **5.** *Medicine.* To wrap (a patient) in a pack. **6.** To wrap tightly for protection or insert packing into to prevent leakage: *pack a valve stem.* **7.** To press together; compact firmly: *clay and straw packed into bricks.* **8.** *Informal.* **a.** To be capable of delivering: *pack a hard punch.* **b.** *Chiefly U.S.* To carry: *pack a pistol.* **9.** To send away, especially peremptorily. Used with *off* or *away.* **—intr. 1.** To place one's belongings in boxes, suitcases, or the like for transporting or storing. **2.** To be susceptible of compact storage: *Dishes pack more easily than glasses.* **3.** To crowd together; cram. **4.** To become compacted; form lumps or masses: *Rain caused the loose soil to pack.* **5.** To depart abruptly. Sometimes used with *off* or *away.* **—pack down.** In Rugby football, to form a scrum. **—pack in.** *Informal.* **1.** To stop doing or end (an activity); give up. **2.** To stop seeing or going out with (a girlfriend or boyfriend); give up. **—pack (one's) bags.** To prepare to depart. **—pack up.** *Informal.* **1.** To stop an activity; especially, to stop work. **2.** To break down; cease functioning. Used of a car or other machine, for example. **—send packing.** To dismiss (a person) abruptly.
~adj. Used or suitable for carrying loads: *a pack animal.* [Middle English *pak, pack,* from Middle Low German and Middle Dutch *pak†.*] **—pack·a·bil·i·ty** *n.* **—pack·a·ble** *adj.*
pack² *tr.v.* **packed, packing, packs.** To put one's own supporters on (a jury or committee, for example) to ensure decisions favourable to oneself. [Probably from obsolete *pact v.,* from PACT.]
pack·age (páckij) *n. Abbr.* **pkg. 1.** A wrapped or boxed object; a parcel or bundle containing one or more objects. **2.** A container in which something is packed for storage or transporting. **3.** A package deal. **4.** A comprehensive arrangement; especially, an undertaking to provide together all the various goods, products, and services required by a customer. **5.** A set of programs designed to operate a computer for some specified purpose: *a bought-ledger package.*
~tr.v. packaged, -aging, -ages. 1. To place in a package; make a package of. **2.** To design or make wrappers or containers for (goods). **3.** To put together or produce in a comprehensive package. [PACK (bundle) + -AGE.]
package deal *n.* A proposition or offer made up of several items, each of which must be accepted.
package holiday *n.* A holiday arranged by a company at a fixed price, including travel and accommodation.
pack·ag·er (páckijər) *n.* **1.** A person who makes up packages. **2.** A person or company producing finished products, especially books or television programmes, on another's behalf.
package store *n. U.S.* An off-licence.
pack·ag·ing (páckijing) *n.* **1.** The act, process, industry, art, or style of packing. **2.** Material used for making packages. **3.** The manner in which something, such as an idea or proposal, is presented. **4.** The occupation or activities of a packager.
packaging company *n.* A packager.
pack·drill (pák-dril) *n.* A military punishment that involves marching while carrying a full pack of equipment.
packed (pakt) *adj.* Also **packed-out** (pákt-ówt). *Informal.* Very crowded or full: *a packed auditorium.*
packed cell volume *n.* The volume of erythrocytes in the blood, given as a fraction of the blood's total volume. Also called "haematocrit".
packed lunch *n.* Food, such as sandwiches and fruit, packed and carried to be eaten at work or at school, for example.
pack·er (páckər) *n.* One that packs; specifically, one whose occupation is the processing and packing of wholesale goods, usually meat products.
Packer, Joy, born Joy Petersen (1905–77). South African author. Among her best-known works are *Valley of the Vines* (1955) and *Nor the Moon by Night* (1957).
pack·et (páckit) *n.* **1.** *Abbr.* **pkt. a.** A small container or a wrapping of cardboard, paper, or the like with or without its contents. **b.** A small package or bundle. **2.** *Slang.* A large sum of money: *It must have cost a packet.* **3.** A boat, usually a coastal or river steamer, that plies a regular route, carrying passengers, goods, and mail. In this sense, also called "packet boat". **—catch** or **cop** or **stop a packet.** *British Slang.* To undergo an injury, punishment, or other unpleasant experience. [PACK (bundle) + -ET.]
pack·horse (pák-hawrss) *n.* A horse used to carry loads.
pack ice *n.* Floating masses of ice on the sea, usually with channels *(leads)* between. Also called "pack".
pack·ing (pácking) *n.* **1.** The act or process of one that packs; especially, the processing and packaging of food products. **2.** Material used to cushion or fill gaps to protect fragile objects. **3.** A material used to prevent leakage or seepage, as around a pipe joint. **4. a.** The

application of a medical pack. **b.** The material used to pack a wound.
packing box *n.* A **stuffing box** *(see).*
packing case *n.* A large wooden box or crate, used for moving large objects or a large number of objects.
packing fraction *n. Physics.* The quotient of the algebraic difference between the isotopic mass and the mass number of a nuclide, divided by its mass number, often interpreted as a measure of stability. For most nuclides, a negative or small positive value indicates relatively high stability. [From the presumed manner in which neutrons and protons are packed in the atomic nucleus.]
pack·ing-nee·dle (pácking-need'l) *n.* A large needle used for sewing up packages.
pack rat *n.* Any of various large western North American rodents of the genus *Neotoma,* that collect in their nests a great variety of small objects.
pack·sack (pák-sak) *n. U.S.* A rucksack.
pack·sad·dle (pák-sadd'l) *n.* A saddle for a pack animal on which loads can be secured.
pack·thread (pák-thred) *n.* A strong two-ply or three-ply twine for sewing or tying up packages or bundles.
pact (pakt) *n.* **1.** A formal agreement, as between nations; a treaty. **2.** A compact; a bargain. [Middle English, from Old French, from Latin *pactum,* from *pasciscī* (past participle *pactus*), to agree.]
pad¹ (pad) *n.* **1. a.** A thin, cushion-like mass of soft material used as filling, to give shape, or for protection against jarring, scraping, or other injury. **b.** A piece of soft but resilient material worn in certain sports to protect various parts of the body. **2.** A flexible saddle made without a frame. **An ink pad** *(see).* **4.** A number of sheets of paper of the same size stacked one on top of the other and glued together at one end, such as a notepad or writing pad. **5.** The broad, floating leaf of an aquatic plant, such as the water lily. **6. a.** The cushion-like flesh on the underpart of the toes and feet of many animals. **b.** The foot of any of these animals. **7.** The fleshy underside of the end of a finger or toe: *the pad of the thumb.* **8.** A **launching pad** *(see).* **9.** *Slang.* **a.** *Chiefly U.S.* A home, apartment, or room. **b.** *U.S.* A bed.
~tr.v. padded, padding, pads. 1. To line or stuff with soft material. **2.** To lengthen (something written or spoken) with extraneous material. Often used with *out.* [Dutch or Low German; akin to Flemish *pad,* probably to Lithuanian *pādas,* "sole of the foot".]
pad² *v.* **padded, padding, pads. —intr. 1.** To go about on foot, especially slowly. **2.** To move or walk about making a soft, dull sound: *padded barefoot over the rug.* **—tr.** To go along (a route) on foot, especially slowly and solemnly.
~n. 1. A muffled sound resembling that of soft footsteps. **2.** *Archaic.* A horse with a plodding gait. **3.** *British Archaic.* A road or path. [16th century (noun) : cant, from Dutch or Low German *pad,* PATH, and *padden* (verb).]
pa·dauk (pə-dówk, -dáwk) *n.* Also **pa·douk** (-dóok). **1.** Any of various tropical trees of the genus *Pterocarpus,* having reddish wood with a mottled or striped grain. **2.** The wood of any of these trees, used for decorative cabinetwork. See **amboyna.** [Native Burmese name.]
pad·ded cell (páddid) *n.* A room with soft, padded walls, as in a mental hospital, used for violent patients.
pad·ding (pádding) *n.* **1.** Any soft material used to pad something. **2.** Matter added to a speech or written work to make it longer.
pad·dle¹ (pádd'l) *n.* **1.** A wooden implement having a blade at one end, or sometimes at both ends, used without a rowlock to propel a canoe or small boat. **2.** Any of various implements resembling this, such as: **a.** An iron tool for stirring molten ore in a furnace. **b.** A tool with a shovel-like blade used to mix materials in glassmaking. **c.** A pallet with which to mix and shape clay. **d.** A narrow board used to beat clothes when washing them by hand. **e.** *U.S.* A flattened board used to administer corporal punishment. **f.** A light wooden racket used in playing table tennis. **3.** A board of a paddle wheel. **4.** *Usually plural.* A panel on the gate of a lock or on a sluice gate that controls the flow or level of water. **5.** A flipper or flattened appendage of certain animals. **6.** The act or an instance of paddling.
~v. paddled, -dling, -dles. —intr. 1. To propel a boat, canoe, or the like with a paddle. **2.** To row slowly and gently. **3.** To move through water by means of repeated short strokes of the limbs. **—tr. 1.** To propel (a canoe, for example) with a paddle or paddles. **2.** To convey, as in a boat or canoe propelled by paddles: *paddle the supplies across.* **3.** *U.S.* To beat with a paddle. **4.** To stir or shape (material) with a paddle. [Middle English *padell†.*] **—pad·dler** *n.*
paddle² *intr.v.* **-dled, -dling, -dles. 1. a.** To walk in shallow water. **b.** To dabble about in shallow water; splash gently with the hands or feet. **2.** To move with a waddling motion; toddle.
~n. The act or an instance of paddling. [Of Dutch origin.]
paddle boat *n.* A steamship propelled through the water by paddle wheels on each side or by one paddle wheel astern.
pad·dle·fish (pádd'l-fish) *n., pl.* **-fishes** or collectively **paddlefish.** Any of various large fishes of the family Polyodontidae having an elongated, paddle-shaped snout.
paddle wheel *n.* A steam-driven wheel with boards or paddles affixed around its circumference, used to propel a ship.
pad·dock¹ (páddok) *n.* **1.** A fenced area, usually near a stable, used chiefly for grazing horses. **2. a.** An enclosure at a racecourse where the horses are assembled, saddled, and paraded before each race. **b.** In motor racing, an area near the racetrack where the cars assem-

PACIFIC OCEAN

ble before a race. **3.** *Australian & N.Z.* Any piece of fenced-in land. ~*tr.v.* **paddocked, -docking, -docks.** To confine in a paddock. [Variant of dialectal *parrock,* Middle English *parrok,* Old English *pearruc,* from West Germanic *parruk* (unattested), perhaps from Medieval Latin *parricus†.* See also **park.**]

paddock² *n. Archaic & Regional.* A frog or toad. [Middle English *paddok,* from *pad, pade,* toad, from Old Norse *padda†,* toad.]

pad·dy¹ (páddi) *n., pl.* **-dies. 1.** A specially irrigated or flooded field where rice is grown. Also called "paddy field". **2.** Rice, especially in the husk, whether gathered or still in the field. [Malay *pādi.*]

paddy² *n., pl.* **-dies.** *British Informal.* A display of bad temper; a paddywhack. [From PADDY. See **paddy whack.**]

Pad·dy (páddi) *n. Often small* **p.** *Informal.* An Irishman. Often considered offensive. [Pet form for *Patrick,* a common Irish name.]

paddy wagon *n. U.S. Slang.* A police van. [From PADDY.]

pad·dy·whack, pad·di·wack (páddi-wak, hwak) *n. British Informal.* **1.** A rage or display of bad temper. **2.** A beating or spanking. [PADDY (alluding to the supposedly hot temper of the Irish) + WHACK.]

pad·e·mel·on, pad·dy·mel·on (páddi-mellən) *n.* A small Australian wallaby of the genus *Thylogale,* inhabiting scrubland. Also called "scrub wallaby". [From a native Australian language.]

Pa·de·rew·ski (páddə-réfski), **Ignace Jan** (1860–1941). Polish pianist, composer, and politician. Famous for his interpretations of Chopin, he studied and taught at the Warsaw Conservatoire and taught at the Strasbourg Conservatoire before his performing debut in Vienna (1887). During World War I he organised the Polish Army in France and in 1919 became for 10 months the first prime minister of a newly independent Poland.

Pa·di·shah (páadi-shaa) *n.* **1.** Formerly, a title of a shah of Iran.

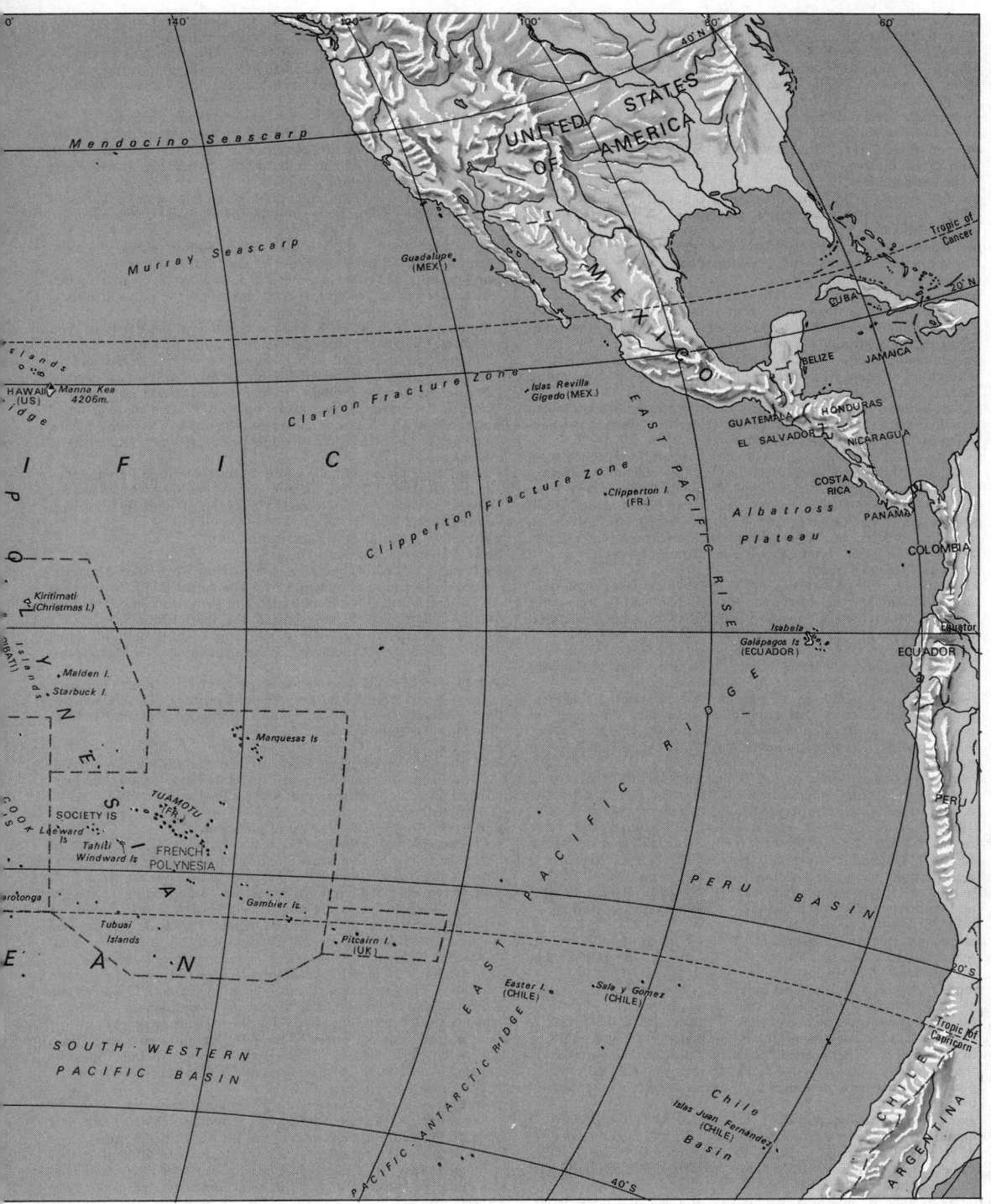

2. Formerly, a title of the sultan of Turkey. [Persian *pādshāh,* from Middle Persian *pātakh-shāh : pati,* master + *shāh,* SHAH.]

pad·lock (pád-lok) *n.* A detachable lock, usually with a U-shaped bar hinged at one end, designed to be passed through the staple of a hasp or a link in a chain, and then snapped shut.
~*tr.v.* **padlocked, -locking, -locks.** To lock up with or as if with a padlock. [Middle English *padlok : pad†,* padlock + *lok,* LOCK.]

padouk. Variant of **padauk.**

pa·dre (paá-dri, -dray) *n.* **1.** Father. Used as a title of address for a priest in Italy, Spain, Portugal, and Latin America. **2.** *Informal.* A military chaplain. **3.** *Chiefly British Informal.* A clergyman. [Spanish, Portuguese, and Italian, father, from Latin *pater* (stem *patr-*).]

pa·dro·ne (pə-drŏ-ni, pa-, -nay) *n., pl.* **-nes** (-niz) or *Italian* **padroni** (-nee). **1.** *Italian.* **a.** A master or patron. **b.** An owner or manager of an inn; a proprietor. **2.** In the United States, a person who exploits Italian immigrant labour. [Italian, from Latin *patrōnus,* protector, PATRON.] —**pa·dro·nism** *n.*

pad·saw (pád-saw) *n.* A small narrow saw with a blade supported at one end only, used for cutting small curved holes. Also called "keyhole saw". [PAD, perhaps short for PADLOCK + SAW.]

Pad·u·a (páddew-ə, paádoo-ə). *Italian* **Pa·do·va** (paádova). Capital city of Padua province, Veneto region, northeast Italy. Situated on the river Bacchiglione, it became an important cultural centre during the late Middle Ages. It has superb architectural and artistic works by Giotto and Donatello, while Galileo taught at the university (*c.* 1600).

pad·u·a·soy (páddew-ə-soy) *n.* **1.** A rich, heavy silk fabric with a corded effect. **2.** A hanging or garment made of this fabric. [Variant (taken as *Padua say,* serge of Padua) of French *pou-de-soie,* from earlier *poult-de-soie†.*]

pae·an, *U.S.* **pe·an** (pée-ən) *n.* **1.** A song of joyful praise or exultation. **2.** Any fervent expression of joy or praise: *a paean to liberty.* **3.** An ancient Greek hymn of thanksgiving to a god, especially to Apollo. [Latin *paeān*, from Doric Greek *paian, paiōn*, war cry, hymn of praise to Apollo, from *Paian†*, title of Apollo as physician of the gods, ultimately from a cultic cry.]

paederast. Variant of **pederast.**

pae·di·a·trics (péedi-áttriks) *n. Used with a singular verb.* The branch of medicine that deals with the care of babies and children and their diseases. [PAEDO- + -IATRICS.] —**pae·di·a·tric** *adj.* —**pae·di·a·tric·ian** (-ə-tríshʹn) *n.*

paedo-, paed– *comb. form.* Also *chiefly U.S.* **pedo-, ped-.** Indicates child; for example, **paediatrics, paedology.** [Greek *pais* (stem *paid-*), child.]

pae·do·gen·e·sis (péedō-jénni-siss) *n.* Reproduction of young during the larval or preadult stage, occurring chiefly in insects. —**pae·do·ge·net·ic** (-jə-néttik) *adj.*

pae·dol·o·gy (pee-dólləji) *n.* The study of the behaviour and development of children. [PAEDO- + -LOGY.] —**pae·do·log·ic** (péedə-lójik), **pae·do·log·ic·al** *adj.* —**pae·do·log·i·cal·ly** *adv.* —**pae·dol·o·gist** (pee-dólləjist) *n.*

pae·do·mor·pho·sis (pée-də-mórfə-siss, -dō-, -mawr-fó-siss) *n.* Evolutionary change in which primitive or embryonic structures appear in adult animals.

pae·do·phil·i·a (pée-də-fílli-ə, -dō-) *n.* Sexual attraction of adults, usually men, to children of either sex. [PAEDO- + -PHILIA.] —**pae·do·phile** (-fīl), **pae·do·phil·i·ac** (-fílli-ak) *n. & adj.*

pa·e·lla (pī-éllə; *Spanish* pa-él-ya) *n.* A saffron-flavoured Spanish dish made with varying combinations of rice, vegetables, chicken, and seafood. [Catalan, "frying pan", from Old French *paelle*, from Latin *patella*, diminutive of *patina*, pan, from Greek *patanē*, dish.]

pae·on (pée-ən) *n. Greek & Latin Prosody.* A metrical foot having one long syllable and three short syllables occurring in random order. [Latin *paeōn*, from Greek *paiōn*, variant of PAEAN.]

paeony. Variant of **peony.**

Pá·ez (paʹa-ess), **José Antonio** (1790–1873).Venezuelan revolutionary. With Bolívar, he overthrew Spanish rule (1823). Removing Venezuela from the confederation of Greater Colombia, he became its first president (1831–35, 1839–43) and dictator (1861–63).

pa·gan (páygən) *n.* **1.** A person who is not a Christian, Muslim, or Jew, although possibly having another faith; a heathen. **2.** One who has no religion. **3.** Formerly, any non-Christian.
—adj. **1.** Of or pertaining to pagans. **2.** Not religious; heathen. [Middle English, from Late Latin *pāgānus*, civilian ("heathen" in patristic writers), from Latin *pāgānus*, country-dweller, from *pāgus*, village, country.] —**pa·gan·dom** (-dəm) *n.* —**pa·gan·ish** *adj.* —**pa·gan·ism** *n.*

Pa·gan (paa-gaʹan). Now named Bagan City on the Ayeyarwady river, central Burma (Myanmar). Founded in *c.*A.D. 849, it was the capital of the Pagan dynasty (11th–13th century). Many of their 5,000 Buddhist temples, pagodas, and monasteries still exist, despite capture of the city by the Mongols (1287), sacking by the Shans (1299), and a severe earthquake (1975). The city remains a centre of pilgrimage, and an important architectural site.

Pa·ga·ni·ni (pággə-néeni), **Niccolò** (1782–1840). Italian violinist and composer. His works include six violin concertos and many other virtuoso violin pieces.

pa·gan·ise, pa·gan·ize (páygə-nīz) *v.* **-ised, -ising, -ises.** *—tr.* To make pagan. *—intr.* To become pagan. —**pa·gan·i·sa·tion** (-nī-záyshʹn ‖ *U.S.* -ni-) *n.*

page¹ (payj) *n.* **1.** In medieval times: **a.** A boy attending a knight, as the first stage of training for knighthood. **b.** A youth in ceremonial employment to a person of rank or in attendance at court. **2.** A boy employed to run errands, carry messages, or act as a guide, as in a hotel or club. Also called "pageboy". **3.** A boy who attends on the bride at a wedding. Also called "pageboy". **4.** *U.S.* A young person who acts as a messenger in Congress or certain other legislative bodies.
—tr.v. **paged, paging, pages. 1.** To summon or call (a person) by name, especially over a public address system or a signalling device. **2.** To attend as a page. [Middle English, from Old French, from Italian *paggio*, probably from Greek *paidion*, child, diminutive of *pais* (stem *paid-*), child, boy.]

page² *n. Abbr.* **p.,** *pl.* **pp. 1. a.** One side of a leaf of a book, letter, newspaper, manuscript, or the like. **b.** An entire leaf: *tear out a page.* **2.** The writing or printing on one side of a leaf. **3.** *Printing.* The type set for printing a page. **4.** A noteworthy or memorable event: *a new page in history.* **5.** *Plural.* A source or record of knowledge: *in the pages of science.* **b.** An extract or passage: *pages from Johnson.* **6.** An amount of viewdata displayed as a unit on a television or other screen. **7.** A unit of data in a computer memory that can be accessed or changed in a single operation.
—tr.v. **paged, paging, pages. 1.** To number the pages of; paginate. **2.** *Computing.* To call and connect to (a terminal). **3.** To call up and display a page of (viewdata) on a screen. [French, from Latin *pāgina*, page.]

pag·eant (pájənt) *n.* **1.** An elaborate public dramatic presentation, usually depicting some historical or traditional event. **2.** *Archaic.* **a.** A scene of a medieval mystery play. **b.** A portable platform on which mystery plays were presented. **3.** Any spectacular and colourful display or procession. **4.** Colourful display; pomp. [Middle English *pagyn*, from Medieval Latin *pāgina*, scene of a play, from Latin, PAGE.]

pag·eant·ry (pájəntri) *n., pl.* **-ries. 1.** Pageants and their presentation. **2.** Grand display; pomp. **3.** Empty or flashy display.

page·boy, page-boy (páyj-boy) *n.* **1.** A page who runs errands or attends a bride. **2.** A woman's hairstyle, reaching to the neck at the back and gradually curving up the sides to the forehead, with the ends curled under.

Pa·get's disease (pájits) *n.* **1.** A chronic disease affecting the elderly and characterised by thickening and deformation of the bones. **2.** An inflammatory condition of the nipple, associated with underlying cancer of the milk ducts. [After Sir James *Paget* (1814–99), British pathologist.]

pag·i·nal (pájin'l, páyjin'l) *adj.* **1.** Of, pertaining to, or consisting of pages. **2.** Page for page: *paginal facsimile.* [Late Latin *pāginālis*, from Latin *pāgina,* PAGE.]

pag·i·nate (páji-nayt, páyji-) *tr.v.* **-nated, -nating, -nates.** To number the pages of; page. Compare **foliate.** [Latin *pāgina,* PAGE.]

pag·i·na·tion (páji-náyshʹn, páyji-) *n.* **1.** The system by which pages are numbered. **2.** The arrangement and number of pages in a book, as noted in a catalogue or bibliography.

pa·go·da (pə-gódə) *n.* **1.** A religious building of the Far East, typically: **a.** An ornate pyramidal Hindu temple. **b.** A many-storeyed Buddhist tower, erected as a memorial or shrine. **2.** A structure, such as a garden pavilion, built in imitation of an Eastern pagoda. [Portuguese *pagode,* probably from Persian *butkada* : *but,* idol + *kada,* temple; altered by association with Prakrit *bhagodī,* holy.]

pagoda tree *n.* A Chinese deciduous tree, *Sophora japonica,* having pinnate leaves and clusters of white, pealike flowers. [Referring to its shape.]

Pa·go Pa·go (paʹang-gō paʹang-gō). Formerly **Pan·go Pan·go.** Harbour and town of Tutuila Island, and the capital of American Samoa. It was a U.S. naval base (1878–1951), particularly important during World War II.

pah¹ *interj.* Used to express contempt.

pah². Variant of **pa** (Maori village).

Pa·hang (pə-húng, háng). Longest river in Peninsular Malaysia. Navigable for most of its length (436 kilometres; 271 miles), it rises in the northwest, flows southwards, and then turns eastwards near Mengkarak through Pahang State to the South China Sea.

pah·la·vi (paʹaləvi) *n., pl.* **-vis.** A gold coin of Iran, not part of the official currency of the country. [Persian *pahlawī,* after MOHAMMED REZA PAHLAVI.]

Pah·la·vi (paʹaləvi) *n.* Also **Peh·le·vi** (páyləvi). The Iranian language used in Persia from the third to the ninth century. [Persian *pahlawī,* from *Pahlaw,* from Middle Persian, from Old Persian *Parthava,* PARTHIA.] —**Pah·la·vi** *adj.*

paid. Past tense and past participle of **pay.**

pail (payl) *n.* **1.** A bucket, especially one made of metal or wood. **2.** The amount contained in a pail. [Middle English *payle,* Old English *pægel†,* small measure, gill; Middle English form influenced by Old French *paelle,* pan; see **paella.**]

paillasse. *Chiefly U.S.* Variant of **palliasse.**

pail·lette (pal-yét, pálli-ét; *French* pa-yét) *n.* **1.** A small piece of metal or foil, used in enamel painting. **2.** A spangle used to ornament a dress or costume. [French, diminutive of *paille,* straw.]

pain (payn) *n.* **1.** An unpleasant sensation, occurring in varying degrees of severity, especially as a consequence of injury, disease, or emotional disorder. **2.** Suffering or distress. **3.** *Plural.* The physical distress accompanying certain physiological processes such as labour or teething. **4.** *Plural.* Great care or effort: *take pains with one's work.* **5.** *Informal.* An irritating or tiresome person or thing; a nuisance. In this sense, also called "pain in the neck". —**at pains.** Making great efforts: *at pains to be early.* —**on pain of.** Subject to the penalty of (some specified punishment, such as death).
—v. **pained, paining, pains.** *—tr.* **1.** To hurt or injure; cause pain to. **2.** To cause distress to or irritate. *—intr.* To hurt. [Middle English *paine,* from Old French *peine,* from Latin *poena,* penalty, from Greek *poinē,* penalty.]

pain barrier *n.* **1.** An experience of temporary acute pain that affects runners at a certain point in a long-distance run (such as a marathon), and must be endured until it passes if the run is to be completed. **2.** An experience of temporary acute discomfort that accompanies a process and must be surmounted if the process is to be completed successfully: *"The pain barrier of real work"* (The *Spectator*).

Paine (payn), **Thomas** (1737–1809). British radical author. After his arrival in America (1774), he wrote the pamphlet *Common Sense* (1776) arguing for American independence from Britain. After the War of Independence, he returned to Britain (1787) and published *The Rights of Man* (1791–92) defending the French Revolution. Accused of treason, he fled to France, but offended Robespierre and was imprisoned for 11 months (1793-94), during which time he continued writing his *Age of Reason,* a manifesto in favour of deism.

pained (paynd) *adj.* Showing or expressing irritation, boredom, or emotional distress.

pain·ful (páynf'l) *adj.* **1.** Causing pain; hurtful. **2.** Full of pain; distressing; hurting. **3.** Requiring care and labour; irksome: *a painful task.* **4.** *Informal.* Irritating; infuriating. —**pain·ful·ly** *adv.*

pain·kill·er (páyn-killər) *n.* Something, such as a drug, that relieves pain. —**pain·kill·ing** *adj.*

pain·less (páyn-ləss, -liss) *adj.* Free from pain, complication, or distress; not troublesome. —**pain·less·ly** *adv.* —**pain·less·ness** *n.*

pains·tak·ing (páynz-tayking) *adj.* Taking or involving great pains; careful and diligent. —**pains·tak·ing·ly** *adv.*

paint (paynt) *n.* **1. a.** A liquid mixture, usually of a solid pigment in a liquid vehicle such as oil or water, used as a decorative or protective coating. **b.** The thin dry film formed by such a mixture applied to a surface. **c.** The solid pigment before it is mixed with a liquid vehicle. **2. a.** A cosmetic, especially one that colours, such as rouge. **b. Greasepaint** *(see).* **3.** *Medicine.* A liquid containing analgesics, antiseptics, or other healing agents, applied to the skin or mucous membranes. **4.** An act or instance of painting. **5.** *U.S.* A piebald horse.
~v. **painted, painting, paints.** *—tr.* **1.** To make (a picture) with paints. **2. a.** To represent in a picture with paints. **b.** To portray vividly to the imagination, as with words or music. **3.** To coat or decorate with paint: *paint a house.* **4.** To apply cosmetics to. **5.** To apply medicine to; swab: *paint a wound.* *—intr.* **1.** To practise the art of painting pictures. **2.** To cover something with paint. **3.** To serve as a surface to be coated with paint: *These nonporous surfaces paint badly with a brush and should be sprayed.* [Middle English *peynten,* to paint, from Old French *peindre* (past participle *peint*), from Latin *pingere.*]
paint·box (páynt-boks) *n.* A box containing dry paints.
paint·brush (páynt-brush) *n.* A brush for applying paint.
paint·ed (páyntid) *adj.* **1.** Represented in paint. **2.** Covered or adorned with paint. **3.** Excessively made up with cosmetics. **4.** Having no reality; false; pretended: *painted expressions.*
painted lady *n..* A widely distributed butterfly, *Vanessa cardui,* having brown, black, and orange markings.
paint·er[1] (páyntər) *n.* A person who paints, either as an artist or as a workman.
painter[2] *n. Nautical.* A rope attached to the bow of a boat, used for tying up. [Middle English *paynter,* perhaps from Old French *pentoir,* clothesline, from *pendre,* to hang, from Latin *pendēre.*]
paint·er·ly (páyntərli) *adj.* **1.** Of, pertaining to, or characteristic of a painter; artistic. **2. a.** Having qualities unique to the art of painting as distinguished from other visual arts. **b.** Designating a style of painting marked by openness of form, with shapes distinguished by variations of colour rather than by outline or contour: *the painterly style of Titian.* Compare **linear.**
paint·ing (páynting) **1.** The process, art, or occupation of coating surfaces with paint, for either functional or artistic effect. **2.** An artistic composition, picture, or design done in paint.
pair (pair) *n., pl.* **pairs** or *informal* **pair.** *Abbr.* **pr. 1.** Two corresponding persons or items, similar in form or function and matched or associated: *a pair of shoes.* **2.** One object composed of two joined, similar parts, dependent upon each other: *a pair of pliers.* **3. a.** Two persons joined together in marriage, engagement, or a similar relationship. **b.** Two persons having something in common and considered together: *a pair of dancers.* **c.** Two mated animals. **d.** Two animals joined together in work. **4.** Two playing cards of the same denomination. **5. a.** Two members of a parliament or similar body with opposing opinions who agree to abstain from voting on some issues so as to allow for occasional absences at votes. **b.** A member taking part in such an arrangement. **6.** A member of a pair: *lost the pair to this earring.* **7.** A pair-oar. **8.** *Chemistry.* An **electron pair** *(see).* —See Synonyms at **couple.**
~v. **paired, pairing, pairs.** *—tr.* **1.** To arrange in sets of two; couple. **2.** To join in a pair; mate. Sometimes followed by *off.* **3.** To provide a partner for. *—intr.* **1.** To form a pair or pairs. Often followed by *off.* **2.** To join in marriage; mate. **3.** To form a pair in a voting body. [Middle English *paire,* from Old French, from Latin *paria,* equal things, from the neuter plural of *pār,* equal.]
Usage: *Pair* can be followed by a verb in the singular or the plural, depending on the intended meaning. The singular is used when *pair* emphasises the unity of the components: *This pair of shoes is not for sale.* The plural is used when the components are considered as individuals: *The pair are working together more harmoniously now.* When following a numeral (other than *one*), the plural is standard (*six pairs of shoes*), though the singular is used informally. See also Usage note at **couple.**
pair bond *n.* The mutual attraction that binds a female and a male animal of the same species. It occurs particularly among birds and may last for one or more breeding seasons or for a lifetime. **—pair-bond·ed** (pair-bóndid) *adj.* **—pair bonding** *n.*
paired (paird) *adj.* Existing in a pair; consisting of a linked pair, especially a left and right pair.
pair-oar (pair-awr) *n.* A boat rowed by two people, each with one oar, sitting one behind the other. Also called "pair".
pair production *n. Physics.* The simultaneous creation of a positron and electron from a high-energy gamma ray in a very strong electric field, especially in that of an atomic nucleus.
pair royal *n.* In some card games, three cards of the same denomination forming a set.
pai·sa (pī́-sə, -saa) *n., pl.* **paise** (-say) (for sense 1) or **paisa** (for sense 2). **1.** A coin equal to 1/100 of the rupee of India. Also called "naya paisa". **2.** A coin equal to 1/100 of the rupee of Pakistan or 1/100 of the taka of Bangladesh. [Hindi *paisā,* PICE.]
pais·ley (páyzli) *adj. Sometimes capital* **P. 1.** Made of a soft wool fabric with a woven or printed, colourful, intricate pattern of abstract, curved shapes, ultimately derived from the palmette motif of Persian rugs. **2.** Marked with such a pattern.
~n., pl. **paisleys. 1.** A shawl or other article of clothing made of paisley fabric. **2.** A paisley pattern. [Originally popular in shawls made in PAISLEY.]
Pais·ley (páyzli). Industrial burgh and port of Scotland. Situated on the White Cart Water west-southwest of Glasgow, it became famous in the 19th century for its shawls based on cashmere Indian designs, to which it has given its name.
Paisley, Ian (1926–). Ulster politician. Ordained a Baptist minister (1946), he founded the Free Presbyterian Church of Ulster (1951), and as an M.P. both in the Northern Irish Parliament (1970–72) and in the House of Commons, London (1970–85, 1986–) he has adopted a militant Protestant and Unionist position. Also an M.E.P. (1979–). **—Pais·ley·ite** *n. & adj.*
Pai·ute, Pi·ute (pī́-oot, pī-yoót) *n., pl.* **-utes** or collectively **Paiute. 1.** A member of either of two distinct North American Indian peoples, the Northern Paiute and the Southern Paiute, belonging to the Shoshonean subfamily of the Uto-Aztecan language family. They formerly lived in the southwestern United States. **2.** The language of either of these peoples. **—Pai·ute** *adj.*
pajamas. *U.S.* Variant of **pyjamas.**
pak choi (pák chóy; *Chinese* baák) A plant, the **Chinese cabbage** *(see).* [Cantonese *paak ts'oi,* "white vegetable".]
pa·ke·ha (paáki-haa) *n. N.Z.* A white person as opposed to a Maori. [Maori.]
Pa·ki·stan, Islamic Republic of (paáki-staán, pácki-, -stán). Country of southern Asia, formerly West Pakistan. It was originally created from Indian territory as a Muslim state (1947) by the efforts of Jinah and the Muslim League. It was formerly in two separate parts, but East Pakistan separated in 1971 to become Bangladesh. Pakistan has suffered with the loss of East Pakistan, a source of jute (formerly the country's chief export), and relations with India are generally poor. Pakistan remains chiefly agricultural, rice, leather, and cotton being the main exports. However, industry is expanding, and cotton (yarn and cloth) and carpets account for a third of exports. Money sent home by expatriates is an important source of income. With considerable uranium reserves, Pakistan has an extensive nuclear programme. General Muhammad Zia al-Huq took power in a military coup (1977), deposing prime minister Zulfikar Ali Bhutto. In 1982 stricter Muslim laws were introduced. After Zia's death in 1988, elections brought his daughter Benazir Bhutto to power as prime minister. She was dismissed (1990), re-elected (1993), dismissed for alleged corruption (1996). Millions of Afghan refugees in the country posed severe problems. Area, 796 095 square kilometres (307,374 square miles). Population, 134,150,000. Capital, Islamabad. See map, next page. **—Pa·ki·stan·i** *adj. & n.*
pal (pal) *n. Informal.* A friend; a chum.
~intr.v. **palled, palling, pals.** *Informal.* To associate as pals. **—pal up.** *Informal.* To make friends. [Romany *pal, phal,* from *phrall,* from Sanskrit *bhrātar-,* brother.] **pal·ly** *adj.*
PAL *n.* Phase alternation line: a system of colour-television broadcasting used on the continent of Europe.
pal·ace (pál-iss, -əss) *n.* **1.** The official residence of royalty. **2.** The official residence of a high dignitary, such as a bishop or archbishop. **3. a.** Any large or splendid residence. **b.** Any large, often gaudy and ornate building used for entertainment, exhibitions, and the like. [Middle English *palais,* from Old French, from Latin *palātium,* from *Palātium,* the PALATINE Hill or the house built there by the emperor Augustus.]
palace revolution *n.* **1.** A usually peaceful overthrow of a sovereign or head of state effected by persons already in power. **2.** Any takeover of power or higher position in the hierarchy of an organisation.
pal·a·din (pál-ədin) *n.* **1.** Any of the 12 peers of Charlemagne's court. **2.** A paragon of chivalry; a heroic champion. [French, from Italian *paladino,* from Latin *palātīnus,* PALATINE.]
Pal·ae·arc·tic (pál-i-árktik, páyl-, -ártik) *adj.* Of or designating the zoogeographical region that covers the whole of Europe and Asia, Africa north of the Sahara, and the Himalayas. Compare **Nearctic.** [PALAE(O)- + ARCTIC.]
pal·ae·eth·nol·o·gy (pál-i-eth-nólləji, páyl-) *n.* The ethnology of early humankind. [PALAE(O)- + ETHNOLOGY.] **—pal·ae·eth·no·log·ic** (-éthnə-lójik), **pal·ae·eth·no·log·i·cal** *adj.* **—pal·ae·eth·nol·o·gist** (-nólləjist) *n.*
palaeo–, palae-, *U.S.* **paleo–, pale–** *comb. form.* Indicates ancient or prehistoric; for example, **palaeography, palae-ethnology.** [Greek *palaio-,* from *palaois,* ancient, from *palai,* long ago.]
pal·ae·o·an·thro·pol·o·gy (pál-i-ō-ánthrə-pólləji, páyl-) *n.* The study of humanlike creatures more primitive than *Homo sapiens.* **—pal·ae·o·an·thro·po·log·ic** (-ánthrəpə-lójik), **pal·ae·o·an·thro·po·log·i·cal** *adj.* **—pal·ae·o·an·thro·pol·o·gist** (-pólləjist) *n.*
pal·ae·o·bot·any (pál-i-ō-bóttən-i, páyl-) *n.* The study of plant fossils and ancient vegetation. **—pal·ae·o·bo·tan·ic** (-bə-tánnik, -bo-), **pal·ae·o·bo·tan·i·cal** *adj.* **—pal·ae·o·bot·a·nist** (-bóttənist) *n.*
Pal·ae·o·cene (pál-i-ə-seen, páyl-, -ō-) *adj. Geology.* Of, belonging to, or designating the geological time or rock series of the first epoch of the Tertiary period, preceding the Eocene and characterised by the appearance of placental mammals.
~n. Geology. **1.** The Palaeocene epoch. Preceded by *the.* **2.** The deposits of this epoch. Preceded by *the.* [PALAEO- + -CENE.]
pal·ae·og·ra·phy (pál-i-óggrəfi, páyl-) *n.* **1.** The study and scholarly interpretation of ancient written documents. Compare **epigraphy. 2.** The documents so studied. **—pal·ae·og·ra·pher** *n.* **—pal·ae·o·graph·ic** (-ə-gráffik), **pal·ae·o·graph·i·cal** *adj.*
pal·ae·o·lith (pál-i-ə-lith, páyl-, -ō-) *n.* A stone implement of the Palaeolithic period. [PALAEO- + -LITH.]
Pal·ae·o·lith·ic (pál-i-ə-líthik, páyl-, -ō-) *adj. Sometimes small* **p.** Of, belonging to, or designating the cultural period beginning with the

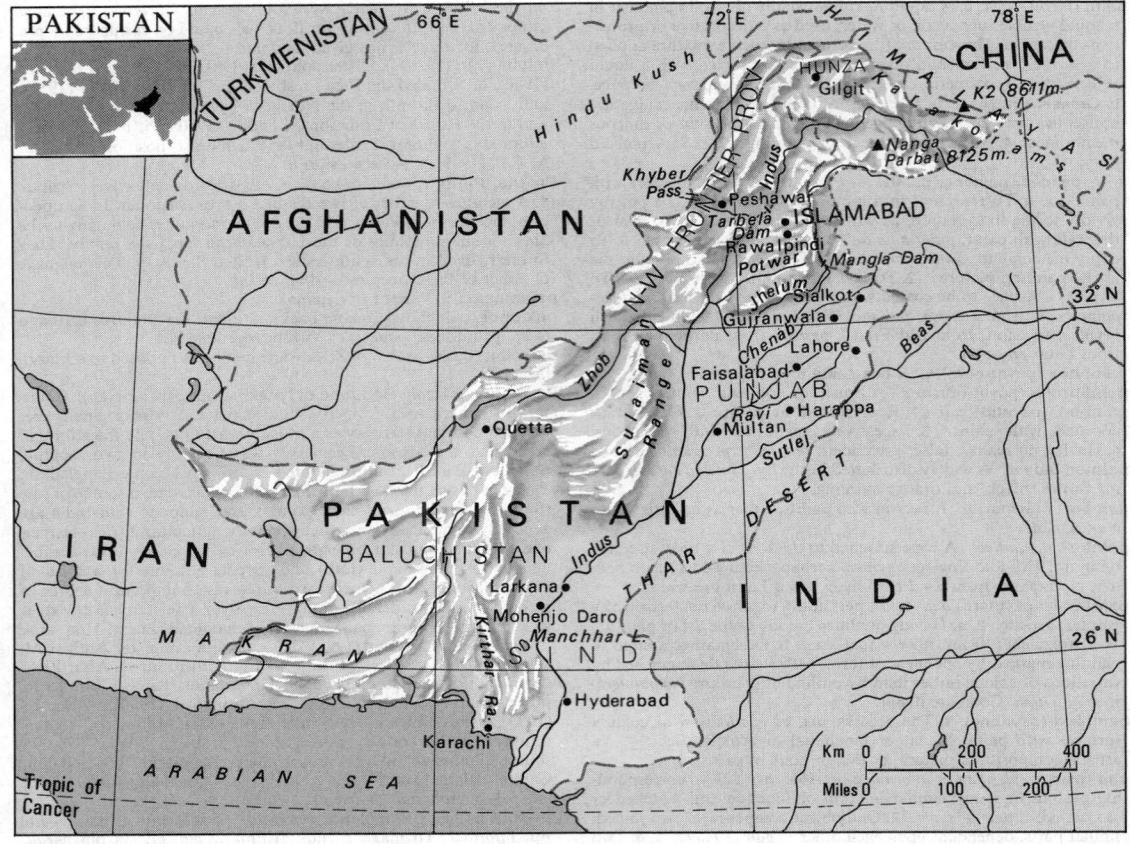

earliest chipped stone tools, about 2.5 to 3 million years ago, until the beginning of the Mesolithic, about 12,000 years ago.
~*n. Archaeology.* The Palaeolithic period. Preceded by *the.* Also called the "Old Stone Age".

pal·ae·o·mag·net·ism (pál-i-ō-mág-nit-iz'm, páyl-, -nət-) *n.* The study of the residual magnetism in rocks in order to try to reconstruct the configuration of the continents in the geological past.

pal·ae·on·tol·o·gy (pál-i-on-tólləji, páyl-) *n.* **1.** The study of fossils and ancient life forms. **2.** Palaeozoology. [PALAE(O)- + ONTO- + -LOGY.] —**pal·ae·on·to·log·ic** (-ónta-lójik), **pal·ae·on·to·log·i·cal** *adj.* —**pal·ae·on·tol·o·gist** (-tólləjist) *n.*

Pal·ae·o·zo·ic (pál-i-ə-zṓ-ik, páyl-, -ō-) *adj. Geology.* Of, belonging to, or designating the era of geological time between the Precambrian and Mesozoic eras, including the Cambrian, Ordovician, Silurian, Devonian, Carboniferous, and Permian periods, and which is characterised by the appearance of marine invertebrates, primitive fishes, land plants, and primitive reptiles.
~*n.* The Palaeozoic period. Preceded by *the.* [PALAEO- + -ZOIC.]

pal·ae·o·zo·ol·o·gy (pál-i-ō-zṓo-ólləji, páyl-, -zō-) *n.* The study of animal fossils and ancient animal life. —**pal·ae·o·zo·o·log·i·cal** (-zṓo-ə-lójik'l, -zō-) *adj.* —**pal·ae·o·zo·ol·o·gist** *n.*

pa·laes·tra, *U.S.* **pa·les·tra** (pə-léess-trə, -léss-) *n., pl.* **-trae** (-tree) or **-tras.** In ancient Greece, a public place for training in and practising wrestling and athletics. [Greek *palaistra,* from *palaein,* to wrestle.]

pal·ais (pál-ay) *n., pl.* **palais** (-ayz). A public dance hall. Also called "palais de danse". [French, "palace".]

pal·an·quin, pal·an·keen (pál-ən-kéen) *n.* An east Asian covered litter, carried on poles on the shoulders of four men. [Portuguese *palanquim,* from Javanese *pĕlangki,* from Sanskrit *palyaṇka, paryaṅka,* bed : *pari,* around + *añcati,* he bends.]

pal·at·a·ble (pál-ətə-b'l) *adj.* **1.** Acceptable to the taste; sufficiently agreeable in flavour to be eaten. **2.** Acceptable to the mind or sensibilities; agreeable: *a palatable suggestion.* [From PALATE.] —**pal·at·a·bil·i·ty** (-bílləti), **pal·at·a·ble·ness** *n.* —**pal·at·a·bly** *adv.*

pal·a·tal (pál-ət'l, pə-láyt'l) *adj.* **1.** Of or pertaining to the palate. **2.** *Phonetics.* Produced with the front of the tongue against the hard palate, as is the *y* in *young.*
~*n.* A palatal sound. —**pal·a·tal·ly** *adv.*

pal·a·tal·ise, pal·a·tal·ize (pál-ət'l-īz) *v.* **-ised, -ising, -ises.** *Phonetics.* —*tr.* To pronounce with a palatal quality. —*intr.* To develop a palatal quality. Said of a phoneme considered diachronically, for example. —**pal·a·tal·i·sa·tion** (-ī-záysh'n ‖ *U.S.* -i-) *n.*

pal·ate (pál-ət, -it) *n.* **1.** The roof of the mouth in vertebrates which separates the mouth from the nasal cavity and consists of a bony front, the *hard palate,* backed by the fleshy *soft palate.* **2.** The projection from the lower lip of a lipped flower. **3.** The sense of taste:

delicacies pleasing to the most refined palate. [Middle English, from Latin *palātum,* perhaps from Etruscan.]

pa·la·tial (pə-láysh'l) *adj.* **1.** Of or suitable for a palace: *the palatial gardens.* **2.** Of the nature of a palace; spacious and ornate. [Latin *palātium,* PALACE.] —**pa·la·tial·ly** *adv.*

pa·lat·i·nate (pə-látti-nayt, -nət, -nit) *n.* The territory or jurisdiction of a palatine, especially: **1.** The **Palatinate** (*see*). **2.** Any of the English counties palatine (Durham, Lancaster, Chester, and Ely), whose lords in the Middle Ages had royal powers. **3.** Any of the American palatine colonies (Maine, Maryland, and Carolina), whose proprietors had royal prerogatives. [Medieval Latin *palātīnātus,* from *palātīnus,* a PALATINE.]

Pa·lat·i·nate (pə-látti-nət, -nit). Either of two former regions of western Germany. *Lower* or *Rhineland* or *Rhenish Palatinate,* often called the "Palatinate", lay in what are now Rheinland-Pfalz, Hessen, and Baden-Württemberg. *Upper Palatinate* lay in what is now northeast Bavaria. They were ruled by counts palatine, who became electors of the Holy Roman Emperor (1356), and were then known as electors palatine.

pal·a·tine[1] (pál-ə-tīn) *n.* **1. a.** A soldier of the palace guard of the Roman emperors formed in the time of Diocletian. **b.** A soldier of a major division of the Roman army formed in the time of Constantine. **2.** Used as a title of various administrative officials of the late Roman and Byzantine Empires. **3.** A count delegated with royal powers, as: **a.** An imperial minister or emissary in the Carolingian Empire. **b.** A minor imperial official in the late Holy Roman Empire. **c.** A ruler of either of the German **Palatinates** (*see*); an elector palatine. **d.** The lord of an English palatinate. **e.** The senior proprietor of a colonial American palatinate.
~*adj.* **1.** Belonging to or fit for a palace. **2.** Pertaining to or designating a palatine or palatinate. [Latin *palātīnus,* from *palātium,* a PALACE.]

pal·a·tine[2] (pálə-téen) *n.* A fur cape and hood worn by women. [French; introduced about 1676 by Anne de Gonzague, Princess *Palatine.*]

pal·a·tine[3] (pál-ə-tīn) *adj.* **1.** Of or pertaining to the palate. **2.** Designating either of the two bones that make up the hard palate.
~*n.* Either of these bones.

Pal·a·tine[1] (pál-ə-tīn) *adj.* Of or pertaining to the Palatinate.
~*n.* **1.** A ruler of the Palatinate (the Rhineland Palatinate); an Elector Palatine. **2.** A native or resident of the Palatinate.

Palatine[2]. The chief of the seven hills of Rome.
~*adj.* Designating this hill or situated on it.

Palau, Republic of (pə-lów). Formerly Belau or Belew. Four volcanic islands and numerous islets in the Caroline group, in the west Pacific Ocean. When the Caroline group opted to become part of the Federated States of Micronesia (1978), Palau broke away. Formerly part of the UN Trust Territory of the Pacific, Palau became an independent republic in 1994. The people, who are largely Micronesians, live mainly by fishing and farming. Area, 508 square kilometres (196 square miles). Population, 17,000. Capital, Koror. See map at **Pacific Ocean.** (pp. 1110–11).

pa·lav·er (pə-laávər || -lávvər) *n.* **1.** *Informal.* **a.** Confused or pointless chatter or fuss. **b.** A tiresome and lengthy procedure: *such a palaver to get through customs.* **c.** Talk intended to charm or beguile. **2.** Formerly, a parley between European explorers and representatives of local populations, especially in Africa.
~*v.* **palavered, -ering, -ers.** —*tr.* To flatter or cajole. —*intr. Informal.* To chatter confusedly and at length. [Portuguese *palavra,* word, speech, from Late Latin *parabola,* speech, PARABLE.]

pale¹ (payl) *n.* **1.** A stake or pointed stick; a picket. **2. a.** A boundary. **b.** *Archaic.* A fence enclosing an area. **3.** The area enclosed by a fence or boundary. **4.** *Heraldry.* A wide vertical stripe in the middle of a shield. **—beyond the pale.** Irrevocably unacceptable or unreasonable. **—the (English** or **Irish) Pale.** The medieval dominions of the English in Ireland.
~*tr.v.* **paled, paling, pales.** To enclose with pales; fence in. [Middle English, pointed stake, boundary, from Old French *pal,* stake, from Latin *pālus.*]

pale² *adj.* **paler, palest. 1.** Whitish in complexion; pallid; wan. **2.** Of a low intensity of colour; light. **3.** Designating a colour having high lightness and low saturation. Compare **deep. 4.** Of a low intensity of light; dim; faint. **5.** Feeble; weak; inferior.
~*v.* **paled, paling, pales.** —*tr.* To cause to turn pale. —*intr.* **1.** To become pale; blanch. **2.** To decrease in relative importance; be outshone; diminish. [Middle English, from Old French, from Latin *pallidus,* from *pallēre,* to be pale.] **—pale·ly** *adv.* **—pale·ness** *n.*

pa·le·a (páy-li-ə) *n., pl.* **-leae** (-li-ee). Also **pale** (payl). *Botany.* A small, chafflike bract partly enclosing the flower of a grass spikelet. [New Latin, from Latin, chaff.]

pale·face (páyl-fayss) *n.* A white person. A term said to have been used by North American Indians.

paleo–, pale–. *U.S.* Variant of **palaeo-.**

Pa·ler·mo (pə-laír-mō, -lér-). Capital of Sicily and Palermo province. Situated on the Tyrrhenian Sea at the foot of Mount Pellegrino, it is the chief port for Sicily.

Pal·es·tine (pál-ə-stīn, -i-, -e-). Historic region of southwest Asia, sometimes called the Holy Land. Situated on the eastern Mediterranean coast, it covers Israel and territories of Jordan and Egypt. Its many rulers have included the Hebrews, Egyptians, Romans, Byzantines, Arabs, and Turks. The area west of the Jordan was awarded to Britain under a League of Nations mandate (1920). Britain supported Jewish claims to a separate homeland, and in 1948 it was divided by the United Nations between two separate states, Israel and Jordan. However, the Arabs refused to recognise the newly created Israel and immediately attacked it. Arab-Israeli military conflict has been frequent ever since. Israel occupied Jordanian territory west of the Jordan (1967), and the Palestine Liberation Organisation (formed 1964) continued to fight for the creation of a Palestinian homeland for Arabs. In 1993 Israel and the PLO signed a declaration of principle on Palestinian self-rule. **—Pal·es·tin·i·an** (pál-ə-stínni-ən, -i-, -e-) *adj. & n.*

palestra. *U.S.* Variant of **palaestra.**

Pa·les·tri·na (pál-ess-treénə, -iss-, -əss-), **Giovanni Pierluigi da** (*c.* 1525–94). Italian composer. His works include over 100 masses, 179 motets, and several magnificats, litanies, and madrigals. He was a master of polyphony and counterpoint.

pale·tot (pál-tō) *n.* **1.** Especially formerly, a loose cloak or coat. **2.** A 19th-century woman's fitted jacket. [French.]

pal·ette (pál-ət, -et, -it) *n.* Also **pallet** (senses 1, 2). **1.** A board, typically with a hole for the thumb, upon which an artist mixes colours. **2.** The range of colours used in a particular painting or class of paintings, or by a particular artist: *a limited palette.* **3.** A **pallette** *(see).* [French, from Old French, flat board, diminutive of *pale,* shovel, from Latin *pāla,* spade, shovel.]

palette knife *n.* A knife with a thin, flexible blade, as used in cookery and by artists for mixing, scraping, or applying paint.

pal·frey (páwl-fri || pól-) *n., pl.* **-freys.** *Archaic.* A woman's saddle horse. [Middle English, from Old French *palefrei,* from Medieval Latin *palafrēdus,* from Late Latin *paraverēdus,* extra post horse : Greek *para,* beside + Latin *verēdus,* post horse, of Gaulish origin.]

Pa·li (paáli) *n.* An ancient Indic language, surviving in the scriptures of Theravada Buddhism. [Sanskrit *pāli-bhāsā* : *pāli,* canon (of scriptures) + *bhāsa,* language.] **—Pa·li** *adj.*

pal·i·mon·y (pál-i-məni) *n. Informal.* Alimony or maintenance that is demanded by a person who has lived with another person for some years without being married to her or him. [PAL + ALIMONY.]

pal·imp·sest (pál-imp-sest || pə-límp-) *n.* A manuscript, typically of vellum or parchment, that has been written upon several times, often with remnants of earlier, imperfectly erased writing still visible. Remnants of this kind are a major source for the recovery of lost literary works of classical antiquity. [Latin *palimpsēstus,* from Greek *palimpsēstos,* rubbed again : *palin,* again + *-psēstos,* "scraped", from *psēn,* to rub, scrape.] **—pal·imp·sest** *adj.*

pal·in·drome (pál-in-drōm) *n.* A word or sequence of words which reads the same backwards or forwards, letter by letter, as *A man, a plan, a canal, Panama!* [Greek *palindromos,* running back again:*palin,* again + *dromos,* a running.] **—pal·in·drom·ic** (-drómmik, -drōmik) *adj.*

pal·ing (páyling) *n.* **1.** Any of a row of upright, pointed sticks forming a fence; a pale; a picket. **2.** Pointed sticks used in making fences; pales. **3.** A fence made of pales or pickets.

pal·in·gen·e·sis (pál-in-jénni-siss) *n., pl.* **-ses** (-seez). **1.** The doctrine of transmigration of souls; metempsychosis. **2.** *Biology.* **Recapitulation** *(see).* [Greek *palin,* again + GENESIS.] **—pal·in·ge·net·ic** (-jə-néttik) *adj.* **—pal·in·ge·net·i·cal·ly** *adv.*

pal·i·node (pál-i-nōd) *n.* **1.** A poem in which the poet recants something said in a previous poem. **2.** Any formal statement of recantation. [Late Latin *palinōdia,* from Greek *palinōidia* : *palin,* again + *ōidē,* song.]

pal·i·sade (pál-i-sáyd) *n.* **1.** A fence of pales forming a defence barrier or fortification. **2.** Any of the pales of such a fence. **3.** *Botany.* The upper part of the mesophyll tissue of a leaf consisting of closely packed cylindrical cells and forming the main photosynthesising area of the plant. **4.** *Plural. U.S.* A line of lofty, steep cliffs, usually along a river.
~*tr.v.* **palisaded, -sading, -sades.** To equip or fortify with a palisade. [French *palissade,* from Provençal *palissada,* from *palissa,* a pale, from Vulgar Latin *pālicea,* from Latin *pālus,* stake.]

pall¹ (pawl) *n.* **1.** A cover for a coffin, bier, or tomb, often made of black, purple, or white velvet. **2.** A coffin, especially one being borne to a grave or tomb. **3. a.** Any covering that darkens or obscures: *a pall of smoke over the city.* **b.** A gloomy or oppressive atmosphere: *Defeat cast a pall over the homecoming of the troops.* **4.** *Ecclesiastical.* **a.** A linen cloth, or a square of cardboard faced with cloth, used to cover the chalice. **b.** A vestment, the **pallium** *(see).* **5.** *Heraldry.* A Y-shaped charge on a shield.
~*tr.v.* **palled, palling, palls.** To cover with or as if with a pall. [Middle English *pal,* Old English *pæll,* from Latin *pallium,* a cover, cloak, PALLIUM.]

pall² *v.* **palled, palling, palls.** —*intr.* **1.** To become insipid, boring, or wearisome. Often used with *on.* **2.** To have a dulling, wearisome, or unpleasant effect. Often used with *on.* **3.** To become cloyed or satiated. —*tr.* To cloy; satiate. [Middle English *pallen,* aphetic variant of *appallen,* to APPAL.]

Pal·la·di·an¹ (pə-láydi-ən) *adj.* **1.** Of, pertaining to, or characteristic of Athena, the Greek goddess of wisdom. **2.** *Literary.* Of, pertaining to, or characterised by wisdom or study. [Latin *palladius,* of Pallas, from Greek *palladios,* from *Pallas* (stem *Pallad-*), goddess of wisdom, PALLAS (Athena).]

Palladian² *adj. Architecture.* **1.** In or designating the Renaissance style of Andrea Palladio. **2.** In or designating a mid-18th-century style derived from that of Palladio, especially in Britain.

Pal·la·dio (pə-laádi-ō; *Italian* pal-), **Andrea,** born Andrea di Pietro (1508–80). Italian architect. The founder of modern Italian architecture, he developed a style based on the classical style of ancient Rome, breaking with the ornate Italian Renaissance style. His works include the Villa Rotonda and the Palazzo Chiericati.

pal·la·di·um¹ (pə-láydi-əm) *n. Symbol* **Pd** A soft, ductile, steel-white, tarnish-resistant, metallic element occurring with platinum, especially in gold, nickel, and copper ores. It is used as a catalyst in hydrogenation, as a purifying filter for hydrogen, and is alloyed for electric contacts, jewellery, nonmagnetic watch parts, and surgical instruments. Atomic number 46, atomic weight 106.4, melting point 1 555°C, boiling point 3 167°C, relative density 12.02 (20°C), valency 2, 3, 4. [New Latin, from the asteroid PALLAS, discovered (1802) just before the element.] **—pal·lad·ic, pal·la·dous** *adj.*

pal·la·di·um² *n., pl.* **-dia** (-láydi-ə) or **-ums. 1.** A sacred object held to have the power to preserve a city or state possessing it. **2.** A safeguard, especially one viewed as a guarantee of the integrity of social institutions: *the right to free speech, palladium of democracy.* [Latin, from Greek *Palladion,* the statue of Pallas Athena that assured the safety of Troy as long as it remained within the city, from *Pallas* (stem *Pallad-*), PALLAS (Athena).]

Pal·las (pál-əss, -ass) *n.* The second-largest asteroid of the Solar System, approximately 450 kilometres (300 miles) in diameter. [Discovered by Peter S. *Pallas* (died 1811), German naturalist.]

Pallas Athena, Pallas Athene. The goddess **Athena** *(see).*

pall·bear·er (páwl-bair-ər) *n.* Any of the persons carrying or attending the coffin at a funeral. [Originally, one who held up the corners of the pall covering the coffin.] **—pall·bear·ing** *n. & adj.*

pal·let¹ (pál-it, -ət) *n.* **1.** A machine part that converts reciprocating motion to rotary motion, or vice versa, such as a click or pawl for controlling the motion of a ratchet wheel in a watch escapement. **2.** The lip or projection of a pawl for engaging the teeth on a ratchet wheel. **3.** A wooden, paddle-like potter's tool for mixing and shaping clay. **4.** A tool used for printing or gilding letters on book bindings or taking up and applying gold leaf. **5.** A portable platform for storing or moving cargo or freight, especially by fork-lift truck. **6.** A painter's palette. **7.** A valve in the wind chest of an organ, connected to a key which when depressed admits air to a groove beneath the pipes corresponding to the key. [French PALETTE.]

pallet² *n.* A narrow, hard bed or straw-filled mattress. [Middle English *pailet,* from Anglo-French *paillete,* bundle of straw, from *paille,* straw, from Latin *palea,* chaff.]

pal·let·is·a·tion (pál-i-tī-záysh'n, -ə- || *U.S.* -ti-) *n.* The process of converting a warehouse, factory, or the like, to enable all goods to be moved on pallets by fork-lift truck.

pal·lette, pal·ette (pál-it, -ət, pə-lét) *n.* A plate that protects the armpit on a suit of armour. [Variant of PALETTE (thin board).]

pal·li·asse (pál-i-ass, -áss) *n.* Also *chiefly U.S.* **pail·lasse** (pal-yáss). A thin mattress filled usually with straw or sawdust. [French, from Italian *pagliaccio,* from Vulgar Latin *paleaceum* (unattested), from Latin *palea,* chaff, straw.]

pal·li·ate (pál-i-ayt) *tr.v.* **-ated, -ating, -ates. 1.** To make (an offence or crime) seem less serious; extenuate; excuse. **2.** To make less severe, without curing; reduce the pain or intensity of; mitigate; alleviate. [Late Latin *palliāre,* to cloak, from Latin *pallium,* cloak, PALLIUM.] **—pal·li·a·tion** (-i-áysh'n) *n.*

pal·li·a·tive (pál-i-ətiv || -aytiv) *adj.* Tending or serving to palliate. ~*n.* Something that palliates. **—pal·li·a·tive·ly** *adv.*

pal·lid (pál-id) *adj.* **1.** Having an abnormally pale or wan complexion. **2.** Lacking colour or brightness. **3.** Lacking in radiance or vitality; dull; lifeless: *a pallid performance.* [Latin *pallidus,* from *pallēre,* to be pale.] **—pal·lid·ly** *adv.* **—pal·lid·ness** *n.*

pal·li·um (pál-i-əm) *n., pl.* **-liums** or **-lia** (-i-ə). **1.** A large rectangular cloth worn as a cloak in ancient Rome. **2.** A woollen shoulder-band with two pendants hanging from it at the front and back, worn by the pope and conferred by him on archbishops and sometimes on bishops. Also called "pall". **3.** *Zoology.* An outer layer or covering, such as the mantle of a mollusc or the cerebral cortex. [Latin *pallium*†.]

pall-mall (pál-mál, pél-mél) *n.* **1.** A 17th-century game in which a boxwood ball was struck with a mallet to drive it through an iron ring suspended at the end of an alley. **2.** The alley in which this game was played. [Obsolete French *palle-maille,* from Italian *pallamaglio* : *palla, balla,* ball, from Middle High German *balle* + *maglio,* mallet, from Latin *malleus.*]

pal·lor (pál-ər) *n.* Extreme or unnatural paleness: *a ghostly pallor.* [Latin, from *pallēre,* to be pale.]

palm¹ (paam || polm, paalm) *n.* **1.** The inner surface of the hand, extending from the wrist to the base of the fingers. **2.** The similar part of the forefoot of a quadruped. **3.** A unit of length equal to either the width, about 75 to 100 millimetres (3 to 4 inches), or the length, about 175 to 200 centimetres (7 to 10 inches) of the hand. **4.** The part of a glove or mitten that covers the palm of the hand. **5.** A metal shield worn by sailmakers over the palm of the hand and used to force a needle through heavy canvas. **6.** The blade of an oar or paddle. **7.** The flattened part of the antlers of certain animals, such as the moose. **—cross (someone's) palm.** To pay, tip, or bribe (someone). **—grease the palm of.** To bribe. **—in the palm of (someone's) hand.** Completely subject to someone's will; ready to carry out someone's wishes.

~*tr.v.* **palmed, palming, palms. 1.** To conceal in the palm of the hand, as in cheating at dice or cards or in a sleight-of-hand trick. **2.** To pick up furtively. **—palm off. 1.** To dispose of or pass off by deception. **2.** To satisfy in a spurious or deceitful way: *tried to palm me off with some silly excuse.* **3.** To rid oneself of. Used with *on*: *palms off all his boring friends on her.* [Middle English *paume,* from Old French, from Latin *palma,* palm of the hand, palm tree.]

palm² *n.* **1.** Any of various chiefly tropical evergreen trees or shrubs of the family Palmae, characteristically having unbranched trunks with a crown of large pinnate or palmate leaves. **2.** A leaf or frond of a palm tree, carried as an emblem of victory, success, or joy. **3.** Triumph; victory. **4.** A small metallic representation of a palm leaf on certain military decorations indicating that they have been awarded a second time. **—bear** or **carry off the palm.** To win the prize in a given contest; be the victor. [Middle English *palme,* Old English *palm,* from Latin *palma,* PALM, hence (from the resemblance of its leaves to the outspread human hand) palm tree.]

Pal·ma (de Mallorca) (paámə, pál-mə; *Spanish* pál-ma). Capital and seaport of the Balearic Islands, Spain. Situated on the island of Majorca, it exports wine and agricultural produce and has become an important tourist and commercial centre.

pal·mar (pál-mər || paál-, pól-) *adj.* Of, pertaining to, or corresponding to the palm of the hand or an animal's paw: *palmar folds.* [New Latin *palmaris,* from Latin *palma,* PALM (hand).]

pal·ma·ry (pál-məri || paál-, pól-) *adj. Rare.* Worthy to receive the palm; outstanding; superior. [Latin *palmārius,* deserving of the palm of victory, from *palma,* PALM (tree).]

Palmas, Las. See **Las Palmas.**

pal·mate (pál-mayt, -mət, -mit || paál-, pól-) *adj.* Also **pal·mat·ed** (-máytid, -maytid). **1.** Resembling a hand with the fingers extended: *palmate antlers; palmate coral.* **2.** *Botany.* Having leaflets or lobes radiating or diverging from one point: *a palmate leaf.* **3.** *Zoology.* Having webbed toes, as on the feet of many water birds. [Latin *palmātus,* from *palma,* PALM (hand).] **—pal·mate·ly** *adv.*

pal·ma·tion (pal-máysh'n || paal-, pol-) *n.* **1.** The state of being palmate. **2. a.** A palmate structure or form. **b.** A division or part of a palmate structure.

Palm Beach. Seaside resort of southeast Florida, situated on a barrier beach between the Atlantic Ocean and Lake Worth.

palm civet *n.* Any of several arboreal mammals of the family Viverridae, of Africa and Asia, having long tails and grey or brown fur.

palm·er (paámər || pól-mər, paál-) *n.* In medieval Europe, a pilgrim who carried a palm branch as a token of having visited the Holy Land. [Middle English *palmere,* from Medieval Latin *palmārius,* from *palma,* PALM (branch).]

Palm·er·ston (paámər-stən), **Henry John Temple, 3rd Viscount** (1784–1865). British Whig statesman. Entering Parliament as a Tory (1807) he was secretary of war (1809–28) before joining the Whigs. As foreign secretary (1830–34, 1835–41, 1846–51) he helped to secure Belgian independence and worked against the increase of Russian influence in the east. As prime minister (1855–58, 1859–65), he nearly took Britain into the American Civil War on the side of the South, defeated the Sepoy revolt in the Indian Mutiny (1857–58), and spoke out for Italian nationalism. Popular with the people, he made many enemies among other ministers and abroad through his outspoken assertiveness.

palm·er·worm (paámər-wurm || pól-mər-, paál-) *n.* Any of several caterpillars that injure fruit trees by feeding upon their leaves.

pal·mette (pal-mét) *n.* A stylised palm leaf used as a decorative element, notably in Persian rugs and in classical mouldings, reliefs, frescoes, and vase paintings. [French, diminutive of *palme,* palm, from Latin *palma,* PALM.]

pal·met·to (pal-méttō) *n., pl.* **-tos** or **-toes.** Any of several small, mostly tropical palms having fan-shaped leaves; especially, *Sabal palmetto,* of the southern United States. This species is also called "cabbage palmetto". [Spanish *palmito,* diminutive of *palma,* palm, from Latin, PALM.]

palm·ist (paám-ist || pólm-, paálm-) *n.* Also **palm·is·ter** (-ər). One who practises palmistry. [Back-formation from PALMISTRY.]

palm·is·try (paá-mi-stri || pól-, paál-) *n.* The practice or art of telling fortunes from the lines, marks, and patterns on the palms of the hands; chiromancy. [Middle English *pawmestrie* : *paume,* PALM + an obscure element not corresponding to *-ist* + *-ry.*]

pal·mi·tate (pál-mi-tayt || pól-, paál-) *n. Chemistry.* An ester or salt of palmitic acid. [PALMIT(IN) + -ATE.]

pal·mit·ic acid (pal-míttik || pol-, paal-) A common saturated fatty acid, $CH_3(CH_2)_{14}COOH$, occurring in many natural oils and fats, and used in making soaps. [From PALMITIN.]

pal·mi·tin (pál-mitin || pól-, paál-) *n.* The glyceryl ester, $C_3H_5(OOCC_{15}H_{31})_3$, of palmitic acid, found in palm oil and animal fats, and used to manufacture soap. Also called "tripalmitin". [French *palmitine,* perhaps from *palmite,* pith of the palm tree, from *palme,* palm, from Latin *palma,* PALM.]

palm-kernel oil (paám-kern'l || pólm-, paálm-) *n.* **1.** A hard, white oil obtained from the kernel or endosperm of seeds of the West African palm, *Elaeis guineensis.* **2.** Any oil extracted from the kernels of other palms.

palm oil *n.* **1.** A yellowish fatty oil obtained from the pericarp of the fruits of the West African palm, *Elaeis guineensis,* and used in the manufacture of margarine, cooking fats, chocolates, and cosmetics. **2.** Oil obtained from the pericarp of any other palm fruits.

Palm Springs. Spa resort in California, United States, situated at the west end of the Coachella Valley.

palm sugar *n.* Sugar made from the sap of various palm trees.

Palm Sunday *n.* The Sunday before Easter, commemorating Christ's entry into Jerusalem, when palm branches were strewn before him.

palm wine *n.* An alcoholic drink made from the fermented sap of a palm and consumed especially in West Africa.

palm·y (paámi || pólmi, paálmi) *adj.* **-ier, -iest. 1.** Of or pertaining to palm trees. **2.** Covered with palm trees. **3.** Prosperous; flourishing: *palmy days.*

pal·my·ra (pal-mír-ə) *n.* A tall palm, *Borassus flabellifer,* of tropical Asia, having large, fanlike leaves used for matting. Also called "palmyra palm". [Variant of earlier *palmeira,* from Portuguese, palm tree, from *palma,* palm, from Latin, PALM.]

Pal·my·ra (pal-mír-ə). Biblical name **Tad·mor** (tád-mawr). City of ancient Syria. On the trade route between the Roman and Parthian Empires, in the third century A.D. it was capital of an empire that included Egypt, Syria, and Asia Minor. It was destroyed by the Romans (A.D. 273) and conquered by Muslims (A.D. 634).

pa·lo·lo worm (pə-lólō) *n.* Any of several edible polychaete worms of the families Eunicidae and Vereidae living in reefs of the south Pacific, which come to the surface to reproduce twice a year. [Samoan and Tongan native name.]

Pal·o·mar, Mount (pál-ə-maar). Peak in California, United States. Rising to a height of 1 871 metres (6,140 feet), it is the site of an observatory, having one of the world's largest reflecting telescopes, 508 centimetres (200 inches) in diameter.

pal·o·mi·no (pál-ə-méenō) *n., pl.* **-nos.** A horse of a type having a golden or tan coat and a white or cream-coloured mane and tail. [American Spanish, from Spanish, dove-coloured, from Latin *palumbīnus,* pertaining to ring doves, from *palumbes,* ring dove.]

pa·loo·ka (pə-lóokə) *n. U.S. Slang.* An incompetent or easily defeated sports player, especially a boxer. [20th century origin.]

palp (palp) *n. Zoology.* **1.** Either of two elongated sensory organs, usually near the mouth, in invertebrate organisms such as crustaceans and insects. Also called "palpus". **2.** Either of two sensory organs extending from the heads of certain molluscs and annelids. **3.** A **pedipalp** *(see).* [French *palpe,* from Latin *palpus,* a touching.]

pal·pa·ble (pál-pəb'l) *adj.* **1.** Capable of being handled, touched, or felt; tangible. **2.** Easily perceived; obvious: *a palpable fraud.* **3.** *Medicine.* Perceptible by palpation: *a palpable tumour.* —See Synonyms at **perceptible.** [Middle English, from Late Latin *palpābilis,* from Latin *palpāre,* to touch.] **—pal·pa·bil·i·ty** (-pə-bílləti) *n.* **—pal·pa·bly** *adv.*

pal·pate¹ (pal-páyt, pál-payt) *tr.v.* **-pated, -pating, -pates.** *Medicine.* To examine or explore by touching (an organ or area of the body) as a diagnostic aid. [Latin *palpāre,* to touch.] **—pal·pa·tion** (-páysh'n) *n.* **—pal·pa·tor** *n.*

pal·pate² (pál-payt) *adj. Zoology.* Having a palp or palps.

pal·pe·bral (pálpibrəl || pal-péebrəl, -pébbrəl) *adj.* Of or pertaining to the eyelids. [Late Latin *palpebrālis,* from Latin *palpebra,* eyelid.]

pal·pe·brate (pál-pi-brayt || pal-pée-, -pé-) *adj.* Having eyelids. ~*intr.v.* **palpebrated, -brating, -brates.** To blink or wink, especially rapidly and involuntarily.

pal·pi·tant (pálpitənt) *adj.* Palpitating; quivering. [Latin *palpitāns* (stem *palpitānt-*), present participle of *palpitāre*, to PALPITATE.]

pal·pi·tate (pál-pi-tayt) *intr.v.* **-tated, -tating, -tates.** **1.** To shake; quiver; flutter. **2.** To beat more quickly than normal; throb. Used especially of the heart. —See Synonyms at **pulsate.** [Latin *palpitāre*, to palpitate, frequentative of *palpāre*, to touch.] —**pal·pi·tat·ing·ly** *adv.*

pal·pi·ta·tion (pál-pi-táysh'n) *n.* **1.** A trembling or shaking. **2.** Irregular, rapid beating or pulsation of the heart.

pal·pus (pál-pəss) *n., pl.* **-pi** (-pī). *Zoology.* A palp.

pals·grave (páwlz-grayv) *n.* Formerly, a count palatine, especially one of the Counts Palatine of the Rhine or Electors Palatine. [Dutch *paltsgrave*, from Middle Dutch : *palts*, palatine, ultimately from Vulgar Latin *palāntius* (unattested), variant of *palātīnus*, PALATINE + *grave*, count, from Middle Dutch.]

pal·sied (páwl-zid ‖ ṕól-) *adj.* **1.** *Medicine.* Afflicted with palsy. **2.** Trembling; shaking.

pal·stave (páwl-stayv) *n. Archaeology.* A type of celt (axe), resembling a chisel, usually made of bronze with a tongue that slots into a handle. [From Danish *paalstav*, from Old Norse *pálstavr* : *páll*, hoe, from Latin *palus*, stake + *stafr*, STAFF.]

pal·sy (páwl-zi ‖ ṕól-) *n., pl.* **-sies. 1.** Paralysis. **2.** A condition marked by loss of power to feel or to control movement in any part of the body. **3. a.** A weakening or debilitating influence. **b.** An enfeebled condition or debilitated state thought to result from such an influence. **4.** A fit of some strong emotion marked by an inability to act: *"a little palsy of indignation."* (Anthony Burgess).
—*tr.v.* **palsied, -sying, -sies. 1. a.** To paralyse. **b.** To deprive of strength: *palsied blows.* **2.** To make helpless, as with fear. [Middle English *palesie*, from Old French *paralisie*, from Vulgar Latin *paralisia* (unattested), from Latin *paralysis*, PARALYSIS.]

pal·ter (páwl-tər ‖ ṕól-) *intr.v.* **-tered, -tering, -ters. 1.** To talk or act insincerely; equivocate. **2.** To be capricious; trifle. **3.** To use trickery in bargaining. [16th century : origin obscure.]

pal·try (páwl-tri ‖ ṕól-) *adj.* **-trier, -triest. 1.** Petty; trifling; insignificant. **2.** Worthless; contemptible. —See Synonyms at **trivial.** [Dialectal *paltry*, feeble, from *palt, pelt†*, rags, rubbish.] —**pal·tri·ly** *adv.* —**pal·tri·ness** *n.*

pa·lu·dal (pə-léw-d'l, -lóo-, pál-yŏod'l) *adj.* **1.** Of or pertaining to a swamp; marshy. **2.** Malarial. [From Latin *palūs* (stem *palūd-*), marsh.]

pal·u·dism (pál-yŏo-diz'm) *n.* A disease, **malaria** *(see).* [From Latin *palūs* (stem *palūd-*), marsh.]

pal·y¹ (páyli) *adj. Archaic.* Pale.

pal·y² *adj. Heraldry.* Designating a shield or heraldic charge that is vertically striped. [From Old French *palé*, from *pal*, PALE (stake).]

pal·y·nol·o·gy (pál-i-nóllǝji) *n.* The scientific study of living and fossil spores and pollen. Also called "pollen analysis". [From Greek *palunein*, to sprinkle + -LOGY.]

pam (pam) *n.* The jack of clubs and highest trump in certain variations of the card game **loo** *(see).* [Gamblers' slang, shortened from French *pamphile*, apparently from Latin name *Pamphilus*, from Greek *pamphilos*, "loved by all" : *pan*, all, PAN- + *philos*, beloved.]

pam. pamphlet.

pa·mir (pǝ-méer) *n.* Sparse grassland on the high plateaux of Central Asia.

Pa·mir (pǝ-méer) Also **Pamirs** (-meerz) or **Pamir Knot.** Mountain complex lying mainly in Tajikistan, but also reaching into China, Jammu and Kashmir, Pakistan, and Afghanistan.

pam·pas (pám-pǝz) *pl.n. Singular* **-pa** (-pǝ). A nearly treeless grassland area of South America, chiefly in east central Argentina and Uruguay. [Plural of American Spanish *pampa*, from Aymara and Quechua, plain.]

pam·pas grass (pámpǝss) *n.* Any of several tall grasses of the genus *Cortaderia*, native to South America; especially, *C. argentea* which is widely cultivated for its creamy-white, long, fluffy panicles.

pam·pe·an (pámpi-ǝn, pam-pée-ǝn) *adj.* Of or pertaining to the pampas or the Indian people who inhabit them.
—*n. Capital* **P.** An Indian of the pampas.

pam·per (pámpǝr) *tr.v.* **-pered, -pering, -pers. 1.** To treat with excessive indulgence; spoil; coddle. **2.** *Archaic.* To indulge with rich food; glut. [Middle English *pamperen*, frequentative of obsolete *pamp*, probably of Low German origin, akin to Flemish *pamperen*.] —**pam·per·er** *n.*

Synonyms: *pamper, indulge, spoil, coddle, mollycoddle, baby.*

pam·pe·ro (pam-páir-ō ‖ *U.S.* paam-) *n., pl.* **-ros.** A strong, cold, southwest wind that blows across the pampas. [American Spanish, "pampean", from *pampa*, PAMPAS.]

pam·phlet (pám-flit, -flǝt) *n. Abbr.* **pam., pamph., pph. 1.** An unbound printed work, usually informative and with a paper cover. **2.** A short essay or treatise, usually on a current topic, published without a binding. [Middle English *pamflet*, from *Pamflet*, familiar name of *Pamphilus*, a popular short amatory Latin poem of the 12th century.] —**pam·phlet·ar·y** (-fli-tǝri, -tri ‖ *U.S.* -terri) *adj.*

pam·phlet·eer (pámf-li-téer, -lǝ-) *n.* A writer of pamphlets or other short works that take a partisan stand on an issue.
—*intr.v.* **pamphleteered, -eering, -eers.** To write, issue, or publish pamphlets.

Pam·phy·li·a (pam-fílli-ǝ). An ancient region of southern Asia Minor that became a Roman province.

Pam·phyl·i·an (pam-fílli-ǝn) *n.* The ancient Greek dialect of Pamphylia, belonging to Arcado-Cyprian.

Pam·plo·na (pam-plónǝ). Capital of Navarra Province, northern Spain. Situated in the Basque region at the foot of the Pyrenees, it is

famous for the Fiesta de San Fermín when bulls are let loose in the streets among crowds of revellers.

pan¹ (pan) *n.* **1. a.** A shallow, wide, open container, usually of metal and often without a lid, used for holding liquids, cooking, and other domestic purposes: *a milk pan.* **b.** The quantity a pan will hold. **2.** Any vessel similar in form, such as: **a.** An open, metal dish used to separate gold or other metal from gravel, earth, or other waste, by washing. **b.** Either of the receptacles on a balance or pair of scales. **c.** A vessel used for boiling and evaporating liquids. **d.** *British.* The bowl of a lavatory. **3.** See **dustpan. 3. a.** A basin or depression in the earth, often containing mud or water. **b.** A natural or artificial basin used to obtain salt by evaporating brine. **4.** A piece of drift ice that has broken off a larger floe. **5.** A **hardpan** *(see).* **6.** In flintlocks, the small cavity in the lock used to hold powder. **7.** *Slang.* The face. **8.** The steel top of an oil drum used as a musical instrument in a steel band.
—*v.* **panned, panning, pans.** —*tr.* **1.** To wash (gravel, sand, or other sediments) in a pan for precious metal. **2.** *Informal.* To criticise harshly. **3.** *Slang.* To beat (someone) up. —*intr.* **1.** To wash gravel, sand, or other sediments in a pan. **2.** To yield gold as a result of washing in a pan. —**pan out.** *Informal.* To work out; turn out: *Let's see how things pan out.* [Middle English *panne*, Old English *panne*, from West Germanic *panna* (unattested), perhaps from Latin *patina*, from Greek *patanē*, pan, dish.]

pan² (pan, paan) *n.* **1.** The leaf of the betel palm. **2.** A preparation of this leaf with betel nuts and lime, used for chewing in Asia. [Hindi *pān*, from Sanskrit *parṇá*, feather, leaf.]

pan³ (pan) *v.* **panned, panning, pans.** —*intr.* To move a film or television camera to follow a moving object or take in a larger scene. —*tr.* To move (a camera) in such a manner.
—*n.* An act or the process of panning with a camera. [Short for PANORAMA.]

Pan (pan). *Greek Mythology.* The god of woods, fields, and flocks, portrayed with a human torso with goat's legs, horns, and ears.

pan- *comb. form.* Indicates: **1.** All; entirely; for example, **panacea, panorama. 2.** *Capital* **P. a.** Of, involving, or comprising all; for example, **Pan-Arabism. b.** The aspiration for the political union of a specified group: **Pan-Africanism.** [Greek, from *pas* (neuter *pan*), all.]

pan·a·ce·a (pánnǝ-séer, -sée-ǝ). *n.* A remedy for all diseases, evils, or difficulties; a cure-all. [Latin *panacēa*, from Greek *panakeia*, from *panakēs*, all-healing : PAN- + *akos*, cure.] —**pan·a·ce·an** *adj.*

pa·nache (pǝ-násh, pa-, -náash) *n.* **1.** A dashing or stylish manner: *leapt upon the platform with panache.* **2.** A bunch of feathers or a plume, especially on a helmet. [French, from Italian *pennachio*, from Late Latin *pinnāculum*, diminutive of Latin *pinna*, feather.]

pa·na·da (pǝ-na´adǝ) *n.* A thick mixture of flour or breadcrumbs combined with milk, stock, or water, used for soups, for thickening sauces, or as a base for souffles. [Spanish, from *pan*, bread, from Latin *pānis*, bread.]

Pan·a·ma, Isthmus of (pánnǝ-ma´a, -maa). Formerly **Isthmus of Darién.** Strip of land that joins North and South America. Situated between the Pacific Ocean and the Caribbean Sea, it is about 644 kilometres (400 miles) long and at its minimum 50 kilometres (30 miles) wide.

Panama, Republic of. Country of Central America. In the Isthmus of Panama, it has central volcanic mountains and narrow coastal lowlands. Discovered by Columbus (1502), it was settled by the Spaniards, gaining independence from Spain as part of Colombia in 1819, and full independence in 1903. The Panama Canal, built in the Panama Canal Zone by the United States, opened in 1914, and has dominated the country's economy. The country's chief foreign exchange earner is the canal, followed by petroleum products (made from imported oil), bananas, sugar, and shrimps. Area, 75 650 square kilometres (29,209 square miles). Population, 2,670,000. Capital, Panamá City. See map at **Central American States.** —**Pan·a·ma·ni·an** (-máyni-ǝn) *adj. & n.*

Panama Canal. Canal crossing the Isthmus of Panama, joining the Pacific and Atlantic Oceans. 82 kilometres (51 miles) long, it was begun by the French in 1881 but later abandoned (1889). In 1903, the United States backed a successful Panamanian revolt against Colombian rule and gained construction rights for the canal, which opened in 1914. A treaty ratified in 1978 provided for U.S. administration of the canal until the end of 1999.

Panama Canal Zone. Land, about 8 kilometres (5 miles) on each side of the Panama Canal, leased to the United States in 1903, when the canal was built. According to a treaty ratified in 1978, Panama assumed territorial jurisdiction in 1979.

Pa·na·má City (pánnǝ-ma´a). Capital of the Republic of Panama. Situated on the Pacific coast, it was founded in 1519, and became capital of Panama on independence (1903).

Panama hat *n. Often small* **p.** A natural-coloured, hand-plaited hat made from leaves of the jipijapa plant of South and Central America. Also called "panama".

Pan-A·mer·i·can (pánnǝ-mérrikǝn) *adj.* Of or pertaining to North, South, and Central America collectively.

pan·a·tel·la, pan·a·tel·a (pánnǝ-téllǝ) *n.* A long, slender cigar. [Spanish, from American Spanish, a long thin biscuit, from Italian *panatella*, from *panata*, PANADA.]

Pan·ath·e·nae·a (pan-áthi-née-ǝ) *n.* The main, annual civic and religious festival of ancient Athens, held in honour of Athena. [New Latin, from Greek *panathēnaia* : PAN- + *athēnaia*, from *Athēna*, Athena.] —**pan·ath·e·na·ic** (-náy-ik) *adj.*

Pan·a·vis·ion (pánnə-vizh'n) *n.* A trademark for a method of wide-screen film projection that superseded CinemaScope because of its improved anamorphic lens.

pan-broil (pán-broyl) *tr.v.* **-broiled, -broiling, -broils.** *U.S.* To fry in a heavy pan using little or no fat.

pan·cake (pán-kayk) *n.* **1.** A very thin flat cake made of batter that is fried on both sides until brown and usually rolled up with a savoury or sweet filling inside. **2.** *U.S.* A thin, fluffy cake made of sweetened batter, fried or baked on a griddle. Also called "griddle cake". **3.** A flat cake or a stick of compressed make-up. *~v.* **pancaked, -caking, -cakes.** *—intr.* To make a pancake landing. *—tr.* To cause to make a pancake landing.

Pancake Day *n.* A day on which pancakes are traditionally eaten, Shrove Tuesday.

pancake landing *n.* An irregular or emergency landing in which an aircraft drops flat to the ground from a low altitude.

pan-chax (pán-chaks) *n.* Any of various small, brightly coloured Old World tropical fishes of the genus *Aplocheilus* and related genera, often kept in home aquariums. [New Latin *Panchax†*, former generic name.]

pan-cha-yat (pun-chī́-ət) *n.* In India, a village council. [Hindi, from Sanskrit *pancha,* five (originally the number of members forming such a council).]

Pan-chen Lama (páanchən) *n.* One of Tibet's two Grand Lamas, the other being the Dalai Lama. See **Lamaism.** [From the Tibetan title *Pan-chen-rin-po-che,* "great jewel (among the) scholars".]

pan-chro-mat-ic (pán-krō-máttik, -krə-) *adj.* Sensitive to all colours: *panchromatic film.* **—pan-chro-ma-tism** (pan-krŏmə-tiz'm) *n.*

pan-cre-as (páng-kri-əss, -ass) *n. Anatomy.* A long, soft, irregularly shaped gland lying near the stomach. It secretes pancreatic juice into the duodenum and contains the islets of Langerhans, which produce insulin. [Greek *pankreas,* "all-flesh", pancreas : PAN- + *kreas,* flesh.] **—pan-cre-at-ic** (-áttik) *adj.*

pancreatic juice *n.* A clear, alkaline secretion of the pancreas containing enzymes that aid in the digestion of proteins, carbohydrates, and fats.

pan-cre-a-tin (páng-kri-ətin ‖ pan-krée-) *n.* A mixture of enzymes extracted from the pancreases of cattle or pigs and used as a digestive aid. [From Greek *pankreas* (stem *pankreat-*), PANCREAS + -IN.]

pan-da (pándə) *n.* **1.** A chiefly herbivorous, bearlike mammal, *Ailuropoda melanoleuca,* of the bamboo forests in the mountains of China and Tibet, having woolly fur with distinctive black and white markings. Also called "giant panda". **2.** A small, raccoon-like mammal, *Ailurus fulgens,* of Nepal and China, having reddish fur and a long, ringed tail. Also called "lesser panda". [French, perhaps from a native Nepalese word.]

panda car *n.* In Britain, a police patrol car. [Alluding to the markings, similar to these of a panda.]

pan-da-nus (pan-dáynəss) *n.* Any of various palmlike trees and shrubs of the genus *Pandanus,* of southeastern Asia, having large buttress roots and a crown of narrow leaves. Also called "screw pine". [New Latin, from Malay *pandan.*] **—pan-da-na-ceous** (pándə-náyshəss) *adj.*

Pan-de-an pipe (pan-dée-ən). **Panpipes** *(see).*

pan-dect (pán-dekt) *n.* **1.** A comprehensive digest or complete treatise of a subject. **2.** *Plural.* Any complete body of laws; a legal code. **3.** *Plural. Capital* **P.** A digest of Roman civil law, compiled for the emperor Justinian in the sixth century A.D., and part of the **Corpus Juris Civilis** *(see).* Also called the "Digest". [Late Latin *Pandectēs,* the Corpus Juris Civilis, from Latin, book containing everything, from Greek *pandektēs,* all-receiving : PAN- + *dektēs,* receiver, from *dekheisthai,* to receive.]

pan-dem-ic (pan-démmik, pán-) *adj.* **1.** Widespread; general; universal. **2.** Epidemic over an especially wide geographical area. *~n.* A pandemic disease. [From Late Latin *pandēmus,* from Greek *pandēmos,* of all the people : PAN- + *dēmos,* people.]

pan-de-mo-ni-um (pándi-mŏni-əm) *n.* **1.** Any place characterised by great confusion, uproar, and noise. **2.** Wild uproar, noise, or chaos. **—**See Synonyms at **noise.** [From *Pandæmonium,* capital of Hell in Milton's *Paradise Lost* : PAN- + Greek *daimōn,* demon, spirit, deity.] **—pan-de-mo-ni-ac** (-ak) *adj.*

pan-der (pándər) *n.* Also **pan-der-er** (pándərər) **1.** A go-between in sexual intrigues; a pimp; a procurer. **2.** One who caters to the lower tastes and desires of others or exploits their weaknesses. *~v.* **pandered, -dering, -ders.** *—tr. Archaic.* To act as a pander for. *—intr.* To satisfy another's whims, tastes, or desires, especially when these are considered to be in some way inferior. Used with *to.* [From *Pandare,* character in Chaucer's *Troilus and Criseyde,* who procures Criseyde's love for Troilus; name taken from *Pandaro* (in Boccaccio's *Filostrata*), *Pandarus* (in the *Aeneid*), *Pandaros* (in the *Iliad*).] **—pan-der-ism** *n.*

pandit. Variant of **pundit.**

P & O Peninsular and Oriental (Steamship Company).

Pan-do-ra's box (pan-dáw-rəz ‖ -dŏ) *n.* **1.** *Greek Mythology.* The box that contained all the ills of mankind, opened by Pandora who was sent by Zeus as a punishment for Prometheus' theft of fire. Only hope was left in the box. **2.** Any source of great suffering or troubles, especially one that does not appear to be so at first.

pan-dore (pan-dawr ‖ -dŏr) *n.* An ancient musical instrument, a **bandore** *(see).* [From Italian *pandora,* from Late Latin, from Greek *pandoura,* three-stringed lute.]

pan-dow-dy (pan-dówdi) *n., pl.* **-dies.** *U.S.* Sliced apples baked with sugar and spices in a deep dish, with a thick crust on top. [19th century : origin obscure.]

p. & p. *British.* postage and packing.

pan-du-rate (pándewr-ayt) *n.* Also **pan-du-ri-form** (pan-déwr-i-fawrm ‖ -dóor-). *Botany.* Resembling a violin in shape. Said of leaves. [New Latin *panduratus,* from Late Latin *pandūra,* three-stringed lute, PANDORE.]

pan-dy (pándi) *n., pl.* **-dies.** *Archaic.* A stroke on the hand with a leather strap, as a punishment. *~tr.v.* **pandied, -dying, -dies.** *Archaic.* To slap on the hand. [Latin *pande (manum),* extend (the hand), order given to the pupil about to be punished, from imperative of *pandere,* stretch out, extend.]

pan-dy-bat (pándi-bat) *n. Chiefly Irish.* A leather strap formerly used for hitting boys on the hand as a punishment in schools.

pane (payn) *n.* **1.** Any of the divisions of a window or door, filled with glass. **2.** A single sheet of glass used in such a division. **3.** A panel of a door, wall, or other surface. **4.** Any of the flat surfaces or facets of an object, such as a bolt, having many sides. **5. a.** A rectangular division of a sheet of stamps. **b.** A sheet of stamps with such divisions. [Middle English *pane, pan,* piece of cloth, section, from Old French *pan,* from Latin *pannus,* rag.]

pan-e-gyr-ic (pán-i-jirrik, -ə- ‖ -jī́r-ik) *n.* **1.** A formal eulogistic composition intended as a public compliment. **2.** Elaborate praise; an encomium. [French *panégyrique,* from Latin *panēgyricus,* from Greek *(logos) panēgurikos,* "(speech) for a public festival", from *panēguris,* general assembly, public festival : PAN- + *ēguris,* variant of *agora,* assembly.] **—pan-e-gyr-i-cal** *adj.* **—pan-e-gyr-i-cal-ly** *adv.*

pan-e-gy-rise, pan-e-gy-rize (pán-i-ji-rīz, -ə-) *v.* **-rised, -rising, -rises.** *—intr.* To eulogise. *—tr.* To compose or deliver a panegyric. [From Greek *panēgurizein;* see **panegyric, -ise.**] **—pan-e-gy-rist** (-jírrist, -jirrist ‖ -jī́r-ist) *n.*

pan-el (pánn'l) *n.* **1.** A flat, usually rectangular piece forming a part of a surface in which it is set, and being raised, recessed, or framed. **2.** A distinct section of the body of a motor vehicle. **3.** A vertical section of fabric, as in a skirt; a gore. **4. a.** A thin wooden board, used as a surface for oil painting. **b.** A painting on such a board. **5. a.** A board having switches to control parts of an electrical device. **b.** An **instrument panel** *(see).* **6. a.** Formerly in Britain, a list of patients entitled to medical treatment through the national health insurance scheme. **b.** A list of doctors available to such patients. **7. a.** The complete list of persons summoned for jury duty. **b.** Those persons selected from the list to compose a jury. **c.** A jury. **8. a.** A group of people gathered to plan or discuss an issue, answer questions, judge a contest, or to act as a team on a radio or television quiz programme. **b.** A discussion by such a group. **9.** *Law.* In Scotland, a person or persons standing trial. *~tr.v.* **panelled** or *U.S.* **-eled, -elling** or *U.S.* **-eling, -els.** **1.** To cover or furnish with panels. **2.** To decorate with panels. **3.** To separate into panels. **4.** To select or empanel (a jury). [Middle English, from Old French, piece of parchment on which names of a jury were written, from Vulgar Latin *panellus* (unattested), diminutive of Latin *pannus,* rag, cloth.]

panel beater *n.* One who beats out the panels of dented and crumpled motor-vehicle bodies.

panel heating *n.* A form of space heating in which heated panels are concealed in walls or ceilings. The panels are heated either by hot-water pipes or by electricity.

pan-el-ling (pánn'l-ing) *n.* **1.** A section of panels or a panelled wall. **2.** Panels collectively.

pan-el-list (pánn'l-ist) *n.* A member of a panel, especially a radio or television panel.

panel pin *n.* A small nail with a narrow head, used mainly for attaching plywood or hardboard panels to a frame.

panel saw *n.* A small hand saw used for cutting panelling.

pan-et-to-ne (pán-i-tŏ́-ni, -e-, -ə-, -nay) *n., pl.* **-nes** or *Italian* **-ni** (-nee). An Italian yeast cake, made with candied fruit peels and raisins, and eaten especially at Christmas. [Italian, from *panetto,* diminutive of *pane,* bread, from Latin *panis.*]

pang (pang) *n.* **1.** A sudden, sharp spasm of pain. **2.** A sudden, sharp feeling of emotional distress. [16th century : variant of earlier *prange,* of Germanic origin; akin to Middle Low German *prange,* a pinching.]

pan-ga (páng-gə) *n.* A broad-bladed African knife, similar to a machete, used as a tool or weapon. [From an East African name.]

Pan-gae-a (pán-jée-ə) *n. Geology.* The single supercontinent into which all the world's landmass is thought to have been grouped before it began breaking up some 200 million years ago. [20th century : from Greek, "all earth" : PAN- + *gaia,* earth.]

pan-gen-e-sis (pán-jénni-siss) *n. Biology.* The discredited hypothesis that every somatic cell generates self-representative hereditary materials that enter the bloodstream and eventually coalesce in reproductive cells, making possible the inheritance of hereditary characteristics. [PAN- + -GENESIS.] **—pan-ge-net-ic** (-jə-néttik) *adj.* **—pan-ge-net-i-cal-ly** *adv.*

Pan-Ger-man-ism (pán-jérməniz'm) *n.* A political movement, prominent especially in the 19th century, advocating the union of all German-speaking peoples. [French *Pangermanisme* (translation of German *Alldeutschtum*) : PAN- + *Germanisme,* Germanism.] **—Pan-Ger-man-ist** *n.*

pan-go-lin (pang-gŏ́lin, páng-gə-lin) *n.* Any of several long-tailed, scale-covered mammals of the genus *Manis,* of tropical Africa and Asia, having a long snout and a sticky tongue with which it catches and eats ants. Also called "scaly anteater". [Malay *pĕngguling,* from *guling,* to roll (referring to its habit of rolling itself up).]

Pango Pango. See **Pago Pago.**

pan·han·dle[1] (pán-hand'l) *intr.v.* **-dled, -dling, -dles.** *U.S. Informal.* To beg, especially on the streets. [Perhaps back-formation from *panhandler,* person who begs with a pan.] **—pan·han·dler** *n.*

pan·han·dle[2] *n.* **1.** The handle of a pan. **2.** *Often capital* **P.** *Chiefly U.S.* A narrow strip of territory projecting from a larger, broader area to which it belongs in such a way that its borders, as drawn on a map, appear to outline the handle of a pan.

Pan-Hel·len·ic, Pan·hel·len·ic (pán-he-lénnik, -hi-, -le̅énik) *adj.* Of or pertaining to all Greek peoples or a movement to unify them.

pan·ic (pánnik) *n.* **1.** A sudden, overpowering feeling of terror or anxiety. **2.** An outbreak of such a feeling, often affecting many people at once, usually leading to irrational or foolish behaviour. Also used adjectivally: *panic reactions.* —See Synonyms at **fear.** **—press** or **push the panic button.** *Informal.* To react to an emergency by taking hasty action.
∼*v.* **panicked, -icking, -ics.** —*tr.* To affect with panic. —*intr.* To be affected with panic. —See Synonyms at **frighten.** [Originally adjectival, from French *panique,* from Greek *panikos,* of Pan (who would arouse terror in lonely places).] **—pan·ick·y** *adj.*

panic grass *n.* Any of numerous grasses of the genus *Panicum,* many of which are grown for grain and fodder. [Middle English *panyk,* from Latin *pānicum*†.]

pan·i·cle (pánnik'l) *n. Botany.* **1.** A branched raceme in which each branch bears a further raceme. **2.** Loosely, any branched racemose inflorescence. [Latin *pānicula,* diminutive of *pānus,* tuft, from Greek *pēnos,* web.] **—pan·i·cled** *adj.*

pan·ic-strick·en (pánnik-strickən) *adj.* Also **pan·ic-struck** (pánnik-struk). Overcome by panic; terrified.

pa·nic·u·late (pə-níckew-lət, -lit, -layt) *adj.* Also **pa·nic·u·lat·ed** (-laytid). *Botany.* Growing or arranged in a panicle. [New Latin *paniculatus,* from Latin *pānicula,* PANICLE.] **—pa·nic·u·late·ly** *adv.*

Panjabi. Variant of **Punjabi.**

pan·jan·drum (pan-jándrəm) *n.* A pompous and pretentious person who has an exaggerated idea of his own importance. Used humorously, often as a mock title. [From the *Grand Panjandrum,* character in a nonsense story by Samuel Foote (1720–1777), English playwright.]

Pank·hurst (pángk-hurst), **Emmeline Goulden** (1858–1928). British suffragette. Founder of the Women's Social and Political Union (1903) she fought, with violence when she considered it necessary, for women's suffrage. Frequently imprisoned, she went on hunger strikes and was force-fed. Her daughters, Dame Christabel (Harriette) (1880–1958) and Sylvia (Estelle) (1882–1960), supported her, the former becoming leader of the suffragette movement before turning to preaching and the latter becoming a pacifist, socialist, and internationalist.

pan·mix·is (pan-míksiss) *n. Genetics.* Random mating within an interbreeding population. [New Latin, from Greek : PAN- + *mixis,* act of mating.]

pan·nage (pánnij) *n. Archaic.* **1.** Food or pasturage for pigs, especially in a forest. **2.** The right to pasture pigs in a forest or a fee paid to obtain this right. [Middle English, from Old French *pannage, pasnage,* from Medieval Latin *pastionaticum,* from Latin *pastiō* (stem *pastiōn-*), pasture, from *pascere,* to feed.]

panne (pan) *n.* A velvet-like fabric with a flattened pile and a very high lustre. [French, from Old French, fur lining, from Latin *penna, pinna,* feather.]

pan·ni·er (pánni-ər) *n.* **1.** A large wicker basket, especially: **a.** Either of a pair of baskets carried on either side of a pack animal. **b.** A basket carried on a person's back. **2.** A container on the rear of a bicycle or motorcycle, often one of a pair. **3. a.** A framework of wire, bone, or other material formerly used to expand a woman's skirt at the hips. **b.** A part of a skirt or overskirt looped up around the hips so as to reveal the underskirt. [Middle English *panier,* from Old French, from Latin *pānārium,* breadbasket, from *pānis,* bread.] **—pan·ni·ered** *adj.*

pan·ni·kin (pánnikin) *n. British.* A small saucepan or metal cup. [Diminutive of PAN.]

Pan·no·ni·a (pa-nṓni-ə, pə-). An ancient Roman province in central Europe occupying parts of modern Hungary, Slovenia and Croatia.

pa·no·cha (pə-nṓ-chə) *n.* Also **pa·no·che** (-chee). A coarse grade of Mexican sugar. [Mexican Spanish, diminutive of Spanish *pan,* bread, from Latin *pānis.*]

pan·o·ply (pánnəpli) *n., pl.* **-plies.** **1.** The complete arms and armour of a warrior. **2.** Any imposing array that covers or protects. [Greek *panoplia,* full suit of armour : PAN- + *hoplon*†, weapon.]

pan·op·tic (pan-óptik) *adj.* Also **pan·op·ti·cal** (-'l) Showing or seeing every part or aspect in one view. [From Greek *panoptēs,* all-seeing : PAN- + *optos,* visible.]

pan·o·ram·a (pánnə-raámə || -rámmə) *n.* **1.** An unlimited view of all visible objects over a wide area. **2.** A comprehensive picture of a chain of events or a specific subject: *a panorama of ancient history.* **3.** A picture or series of pictures exhibited a part at a time by being unrolled and passed before the spectator, thus representing a continuous scene. [PAN- + Greek *horāma,* sight, from *horān,* to see.] **—pan·o·ram·ic** (-rámmik) *adj.* **—pan·o·ram·i·cal·ly** *adv.*

panoramic sight *n.* An artillery sight that gives a view over a wide area.

pan·pipes (pán-pīps) *pl.n. Sometimes capital* **P.** *Sometimes singular.* A primitive wind instrument consisting of a series of pipes or reeds of graduated length bound together, and played by blowing across the top open ends. Also called "mouth organ", "Pandean pipes" "Pan's pipes", "syrinx". [PAN + PIPE.]

pan·sy (pánzi) *n., pl.* **-sies.** **1.** Any plant of the genus Viola, especially *V. wittrockiana,* the garden pansy, having rounded, velvety petals of various colours. See **wild pansy.** **2.** Deep to strong violet. **3.** *Slang.* A homosexual or very effeminate male. Used derogatorily. [Fanciful formation from French *pensée,* "thought", from the feminine past participle of *penser,* to think.]

pant (pant) *v.* **panted, panting, pants.** —*intr.* **1.** To breathe rapidly in short gasps, as after exertion. **2.** To give off or emit smoke, steam, or the like in loud puffs. **3.** To pulsate rapidly; throb. **4.** To yearn frantically: *"my spirit began to burn and pant"* (R.D. Blackmore). —*tr.* To utter hurriedly or breathlessly.
∼*n.* **1.** The act of panting. **2.** A short, laboured breath; a gasp. **3.** A short, loud puff, as of steam from an engine. **4.** A throb; a pulsation. [Middle English *panten,* from Anglo-French *panter,* from Old French *pantaisier,* from Vulgar Latin *phantasiāre* (unattested), to fantasise, have nightmares, gasp with horror, from Latin *phantasia,* an apparition, fantasy, from Greek, from *phantazein,* to make visible, from *phainein,* to show.] **—pant·ing·ly** *adv.*

Pan·ta·gru·el·i·an (pántə-groo-élli-ən) *n.* Characteristic of or appropriate to Rabelais' character Pantagruel, noted for his ebullient, often coarse, humour and huge appetite. **—Pan·ta·gru·el·ism** (-gro͞o-ə-liz'm) *n.*

pan·ta·lets, pan·ta·lettes (pántə-léts) *pl.n.* **1.** Long underdrawers, trimmed with ruffles extending below the skirt, worn by women in the mid-19th century. **2.** A pair of frills to be attached to the legs of such underdrawers. [Diminutive of PANTALOON.]

pan·ta·loon (pántə-lo͞on || -lo͞on) *n.* **1.** *Plural.* **a.** Formerly, men's tight trousers extending from waist to ankle. **b.** *Archaic.* Trousers of any kind. **2.** *Capital* **P.** A character in the commedia dell'arte, portrayed as a foolish old man with slippers and tight trousers. [French *pantalon,* from Italian *pantalone,* originally a nickname for Venetian characters in Italian comedies, from *Pantaleone,* a saint once popular in Venice.]

pan·tech·ni·con (pan-tékni-kən || -kon) *n. British.* **1.** A large van or lorry, especially one used for furniture removals. **2.** *Archaic.* A furniture warehouse. [Originally the name of a 19th-century bazaar in London where artistic things were sold : PAN- + Greek *tekhnikon,* neuter of *tekhnikos,* artistic, from *tekhnē,* art skill.]

pan·the·ism (pán-thee-iz'm, -thi-) *n.* **1.** The doctrine that God is, or is in, everything and that the various forces and workings of nature are modes or manifestations of his existence. **2.** Belief in and worship of all gods. Compare **deism, theism.** **—pan·the·ist** *n.* **—pan·the·is·tic** (-ístik), **pan·the·is·ti·cal** *adj.*

pan·the·on (pánthi-ən, pan-the̅e-ən || -on) *n.* **1.** *Capital* **P.** A circular temple in Rome, completed in 25 B.C., and dedicated to all the gods. **2.** Any temple dedicated to all gods. **3.** All the gods of a people. **4.** A public building commemorating and dedicated to the great or revered figures of a nation. **5.** The most eminent figures in the history of a particular field: *the philosophers' pantheon.* [Middle English *Panteon,* the Pantheon, from Latin *Panthēon,* from Greek *pantheion* : PAN- + *theos,* god.]

pan·ther (pánthər) *n.* **1.** The leopard, *Panthera pardus,* especially in its black, unspotted form. **2.** *U.S.* Any of several similar or related animals, such as the puma or jaguar. [Middle English *panter,* from Old French *pantere,* from Latin *panthēra,* from Greek *panthēr*†.]

pant·ies (pántiz) *pl.n. Singular* **pan·tie, pan·ty.** *Informal.* A pair of women's or children's underpants. [From PANTS.]

pan·ti·hose, pan·ty·hose (pánti-hōz) *pl.n. Chiefly U.S. & South African.* A pair of woman's tights. [PANTIES + HOSE.]

pan·tile (pán-tīl) *n.* An S-curved roofing tile, laid so the down curve of one tile overlaps the up curve of the next one. [PAN + TILE (i.e., "dish-tile", from the concave shape).]

pan·ti·soc·ra·cy (pánt-i-sóckrə-si, -ī-) *n.* A utopian society in which everyone is equal and everyone rules. [PANT(O)- + ISOCRACY.]

pan·to (pántō) *n., pl.* **-tos.** *British Informal.* A pantomime.

panto–, pant– *comb. form.* Indicates all; for example, **pantisocracy, pantomorphic.** [From Greek *pas* (stem *pant-*), all.]

pan·tof·fle, pan·to·fle (pan-tóff'l) *n.* Also **pantoufle** (-to͞of'l). *Archaic.* A slipper. [Middle English *pantufle,* from Old French *pantoufle,* from Old Italian *pantofola,* perhaps from Medieval Greek *pantophellos,* "all cork" (of which medieval slippers were made) : *pas* (stem *pant-*), PAN-+ *phellos*†, cork, cork oak.]

pan·to·graph (pánt-ə-graf, -graaf, -ō-) *n.* **1.** An instrument for copying a picture or diagram to any desired scale, consisting of styluses for tracing and copying, mounted on four jointed rods in the form of a parallelogram with extended sides. **2.** Any similarly linked framework, used as an extensible support or contact, as on the framework that collects current from overhead cables in an electric locomotive. [French *pantographe* : PANTO- + -GRAPH.]

pan·to·mime (pántə-mīm) *n.* **1.** *British.* A kind of musical play performed at Christmas time, usually based on fairy stories, and characterised by topical jokes, extravagant sets, and having specific conventions, especially farcical, deriving from the commedia dell'arte. **2. a.** A genre of theatrical performance invented in Rome in the reign of Augustus, in which one actor played all the parts in mime, with music and singing in the background. **b.** The actor in this genre. **c.** Any of various revivals or derivatives of this genre. **3.** Acting that consists mostly of gesture. **4.** *Archaic & U.S.* **Mime** *(see).* **5.** *Informal.* A ridiculous or confused situation.
∼*v.* **pantomimed, -miming, -mimes.** *Rare.* —*tr.* To represent by mime. —*intr.* To express oneself in mime. [Latin *pantomīmus,* "the

complete mime" : PANTO- + *mimos,* MIME.] **—pan·to·mim·ic** (-mímmik), **pan·to·mim·i·cal** *adj.* **—pan·to·mim·ist** (-mīmist) *n.*

pan·to·then·ic acid (pántə-thénnik) *n.* A component of the vitamin B complex, $C_9H_{17}NO_5$, common in liver but found in all living tissue. [Greek *pantothen,* from all sides, from *pan,* all. See **pan-**.]

pan·toum (pan-tóom) *n.* A verse form consisting of quatrains in which the second and fourth lines are repeated as the first and third lines of the following quatrain, and in which the final line of the poem repeats the opening line. [French, from Malay *pantūn.*]

pan·try (pántri) *n., pl.* **-tries.** A small room or cupboard, usually off a kitchen, where food, china, and the like are stored. [Middle English *pantrie,* from Old French *paneterie,* bread closet, from *panetier,* servant in charge of the bread, from *pan,* bread, from Latin *pānis.*]

pants (pants) *pl.n.* **1.** Underpants. **2.** *Chiefly U.S.* Trousers. **—the pants off.** *Informal.* Thoroughly. Used in phrases like *scare the pants off someone.* **—with (one's) pants down.** Unprepared or in an awkward situation. [Short for *pantaloons,* plural of PANTALOON.]

pant·suit (pánt-sewt, -sóot) *n.* Also **pants suit.** *Chiefly U.S.* A trouser suit.

Pan·zer (pánzər; *German* -tsər) *adj.* Of, pertaining to, or designating the fast armoured mechanical units of the German army, especially during World War II: *a Panzer division.*
~n. **1.** An armoured tank in a Panzer unit. **2.** *Plural.* Panzer troops. [German *Panzer,* armour, from Middle High German *Panzier,* from Old French *pancier,* body-armour, from *panse,* body, from Vulgar Latin *pantica* (unattested), variant of Latin *pantex,* paunch.]

Pao·loz·zi (pow-lótsi), **Sir Edouardo Luigi** (1924–). British sculptor. In the 1940s in Paris he became influenced by dada and surrealism, particularly in his early collages. In the 1950s his sculptures, such as *St Sebastian no. 2,* were animals, figures, or heads made using old machine parts cast in bronze. His 1960s work included brightly coloured metal sculptures such as *The City of the Circle and the Square* (1963–66).

pap[1] (pap) *n.* **1.** *Archaic & Regional.* A teat or nipple. **2.** Something resembling a nipple. [Middle English *pappe,* from Scandinavian (imitative of sucking).]

pap[2] *n.* **1.** Soft or semiliquid food, as for infants. **2.** Something lacking real value or substance; drivel. [Middle English *pape,* probably from Latin *pappa,* baby talk for food.]

pa·pa (pə-paá || *chiefly U.S.* paápə) *n.* Father. Used, especially formally, by children. [French, from Old French, from Late Latin, from Greek *pap(p)as.*]

pa·pa·cy (páypə-si) *n., pl.* **-cies. 1.** The office and jurisdiction of a pope. **2.** The period of time during which a pope is in office. **3.** The system of church government headed by the pope. [Middle English *papacie,* from Medieval Latin *pāpātia,* from Late Latin *pāpa,* POPE.]

pa·pa·in (pə-páy-in, -pī-) *n.* An enzyme capable of digesting protein, obtained from the unripe fruit of the papaya and used as a meat tenderiser, and in medicine as a protein digestant. [From PAPAYA.]

pa·pal (páyp'l) *adj.* **1.** Of, pertaining to, or issued by the pope: *a papal bull.* **2.** Of or pertaining to the papacy: *papal succession.* **3.** Of or pertaining to the Roman Catholic Church. [Middle English, from Old French, from Medieval Latin *pāpālis,* from Late Latin *pāpa,* POPE.] **—pa·pal·ly** *adv.*

Papal States. Former states of central Italy, under papal sovereignty (756–1870). They were originally given by Pepin the Short to Pope Stephen II and confirmed in this by Charlemagne (774). Varying in size over time owing to political struggles, the papal possessions were reduced after the Austro-Italian war (1859) and in 1870 Italian troops occupied Rome. The papacy did not recognise this loss of power until the Lateran Treaty (1929), when the Vatican City was created as a separate state.

pa·pa·raz·zo (páppə-rát-sō) *n., pl.* **-raz·zi** (-see). A reporter or photographer, especially a freelance one, who doggedly searches for sensational stories about, or takes candid pictures of, celebrities for magazines and newspapers. [Italian, probably from French *paperassier,* scribbler, from *paperasse,* scrap paper, from *papier,* paper, from Old French, PAPER.]

pa·pav·er·ine (pə-páyvə-rin, -reen || -pávvə-) *n.* Also **pa·pav·er·in** (-rin). A nonaddictive opium derivative, $C_{20}H_{21}NO_4$, used medicinally as an antispasmodic to treat such conditions as colic and asthma. [From New Latin *Papaver* (genus name), from Latin *papāver,* POPPY.]

pa·paw, paw·paw (páw-paw, pə-páw) *n.* **1.** A papaya. **2.** A tree, *Asimina triloba,* of central North America, having small, fleshy, edible fruit. **3.** The fruit of this tree. Also called "custard apple". [Probably from Spanish *papaya,* PAPAYA.]

pa·pa·ya (pə-pī-ə) *n.* **1.** An evergreen tropical American tree, *Carica papaya,* bearing large, yellow, edible fruit. **2.** The fruit of this tree. Also called "pawpaw". [Spanish, from Cariban.]

Pa·pe·e·te (paá-pi-áyti, pə-páyti, -peéti). See **Tahiti.**

Pa·pen (paápən), **Franz von** (1879–1969). German politician. He served Hitler as vice-chancellor (1933–34) and as a diplomat. Although acquitted at the Nuremberg Trials, he was imprisoned for three years to undergo denazification.

pa·per (páypər) *n.* **1.** A thin sheet material made of cellulose pulp, derived mainly from wood, rags, and certain grasses, processed into flexible leaves or rolls by deposit from an aqueous suspension, and used chiefly for writing, printing, drawing, wrapping, and covering walls. **2.** A single sheet or leaf of this material. **3.** One or more sheets of this material, bearing writing or printing, such as: **a.** An official document. **b.** An essay, treatise, or scholarly dissertation. **c.** An examination, report, essay, or similar exercise by a student. **d.** A newspaper. **3.** *Sometimes capital* **P.** In Britain, either of two documents issued by the government discussing potential legislation, a **Green Paper** or **White Paper** *(both of which see).* **4.** *Plural.* A collection of letters, diaries, and other writings, especially those produced by one person. **5.** *Plural.* Documents establishing the identity of the bearer. **6.** *Plural.* **Ship's papers** *(see).* **7.** A negotiable document, such as a cheque or letter of credit. **8.** *Slang.* A free ticket to a theatre. **9.** *Plural.* Cigarette papers. **—on paper. 1.** In writing or print. **2.** In theory, as distinguished from actual performance or fact: *good on paper, but poor in reality.*
~tr.v. **papered, -pering, -pers. 1.** To wrap or cover in paper. **2.** To supply with paper. **3.** To cover with wallpaper. **4.** *Slang.* To fill (a theatre, for example) by issuing free passes: *paper the house.*
~adj. **1.** Made of or in the form of paper: *paper money.* **2.** Resembling paper in thinness or flimsiness. **3.** Existing only in printed or written form; notional; theoretical: *paper profits.* [Middle English *papir,* from Old French *papier,* from Latin *papȳrus,* paper, from Greek *papuros,* PAPYRUS.] **—pa·per·er** *n.* **—pa·per·y** *adj.*

pa·per·back (páypər-bak) *n.* A book or edition having a flexible paper binding and selling relatively cheaply.
~tr.v. **paperbacked, -backing, -backs.** To publish in paperback form. **—pa·per·back** *adj.* **—pa·per·back·er** *n.*

pa·per·board (páypər-bawrd || -bōrd) *n.* Pasteboard.

pa·per·bound (páypər-bownd) *adj.* Bound in paper; paperback.

pa·per·bark tree (páypər-baark) *n.* Any of various Australian trees of the genus *Melaleuca,* having papery bark shed in thin layers.

pa·per·boy (páypər-boy) *n.* A boy who delivers newspapers.

paper chase *n.* A cross-country run in which a trail of paper is left by one or more runners for the rest of the field to follow.

pa·per·clip (páypər-klip) *n.* A clip, usually a piece of bent wire, for holding sheets of paper together.

paper cup (páypər kup) *n.* A disposable drinking vessel that resembles a glass or mug in shape and is made of a waterproof substance resembling paper.

pa·per·girl (páypər-gurl) *n.* A girl who delivers newspapers.

pa·per·hang·er (páypər-hang-ər) *n.* One whose occupation is decorating walls with wallpaper. **—pa·per·hang·ing** *n.*

pa·per·knife (páypər-nīf) *n., pl.* **-knives** (-nīvz). A thin, blunt knife used for opening sealed envelopes, slitting uncut pages of books, and creasing paper.

pa·per·less (páypər-ləss, -liss) *adj.* Using information technology, as in the form of computers and word processors, to the extent that documentation on paper is not necessary: *a paperless office.*

paper mulberry *n.* A tree, *Broussonetia papyrifera,* native to Asia, having bark that can be processed into a paper-like fabric. See **tapa.**

paper nautilus *n.* A marine cephalopod mollusc of the genus *Argonauta,* having a paper-thin spiral shell. Also called "argonaut".

paper tape *n.* Paper in a long narrow strip with rows of holes punched across it, different combinations of holes representing different characters. It is used in telex machines, computers, and similar devices in which information is represented digitally.

paper tiger *n.* A person, nation, or thing that appears strong, invincible, and threatening but is in fact weak and often ineffectual.

pa·per·weight (páypər-wayt) *n.* A small heavy object, often decorative, placed on top of loose papers to keep them in place.

pa·per·work (páypər-wurk) *n.* Work, such as clerical work, involving the handling of reports, letters, forms, and the like.

pap·e·terie (páppətri || *French* pap-treé) *n.* A box used to hold paper and other writing materials. [French, stationery box, from *papier,* paper, from Old French, PAPER.]

Pa·pia·men·to (páp-yə-méntō) *n.* The Portuguese- and Spanish-based creole language of the Netherlands Antilles. [Papiamento, from *papia,* talk.]

pa·pi·er-mâ·ché (páppi-ay-máshay, -maáshay || *U.S. also* páypər-, -mə-sháy) *n.* A material made from paper pulp or shreds of paper mixed with glue or paste, that can be moulded into various shapes when wet and that becomes hard and suitable for varnishing when dry. [French, "chewed paper".] **—pa·pier-mâ·ché** *adj.*

pa·pil·la (pə-píllə) *n., pl.* **-pillae** (-píllee). Any small, nipple-like projection, such as a protuberance on the top of the tongue, at the root of a hair, or at the base of a developing tooth. [New Latin, from Latin, nipple, diminutive of *papula,* pimple.] **—pa·pil·lar·y** (pə-píl-ləri || *U.S.* páppi-lerri) *adj.* **—pa·pil·late** (pə-píl-ayt, páppil-, -ət, -it), **pa·pil·lose** (pə-píl-ōss, páppil-, -ōz) *adj.*

pap·il·lo·ma (páppi-lṓ-mə) *n., pl.* **-mata** (-mətə) or **-mas.** A small, benign epithelial tumour, usually occurring on the surface of a mucous membrane or the skin, such as a wart or corn. [PAPILL(A) + -OMA.] **—pap·il·lo·ma·tous** *adj.*

pap·il·lon (páppi-lon) *n.* A dog of a small breed with large, forward-facing ears and a long, fine coat that is white with coloured patches. [French, "butterfly" (referring to the appearance of the ears), ultimately from Latin *pāpiliō* (stem *pāpiliōn-*).]

pap·il·lote (páppi-lōt) *n.* **1.** A paper frill used to decorate the bone end of a cooked chop or cutlet. **2.** Greaseproof paper or foil in which some foods are cooked. [French, from *papillon,* butterfly.]

pa·pist (páypist) *n.* A Roman Catholic. Usually used derogatorily. [French *papiste,* from *pape,* POPE.] **—pa·pis·ti·cal** (pay-pístik'l, pə-) *adj.* **—pa·pi·stry** (páypistri) *n.*

pa·poose, pap·poose (pə-póoss, pa-) *n.* Also **pap·poose.** A North American Indian infant or young child. [Algonquian *papoos.*]

pap·pus (páppəss) *n., pl.* **pappi** (páppī). A tuft of bristles, found on seeds of certain plants, such as dandelions and thistles, that aid dispersal. [Latin, from Greek *pappos,* grandfather, hence pappus.] —**pap·pose** (páppōss), **pap·pous** (páppəss) *adj.*

pap·py¹ (páppi) *adj.* **-pier, -piest.** Of or like pap; mushy; pulpy.

pappy² *n., pl.* **-pies.** *U.S. Informal.* Father. [Diminutive of PAPA.]

pa·pri·ka (pápprikə, pə-préekə, pa-) *n.* A mild, powdered seasoning made from sweet red peppers. [Hungarian, from Serbian, from *papar,* pepper, from Greek *peperi,* PEPPER.] —**pap·ri·ka** *adj.*

Pap test (pap) *n.* A test in which a smear of a bodily secretion, especially from the cervix or vagina, is fixed and examined for the presence of abnormal cells to detect cancer in an early stage. Also called "Pap smear", "Papanicolaou's test", "smear test". [Invented by George *Papanicolaou* (1883–1962), U.S. scientist.]

Pap·u·an (páp-oo-ən, páap-, -yoo-) *n.* **1.** A native or inhabitant of Papua New Guinea. **2.** A member of a subgroup of an Oceanic Negroid people of Melanesia. **3.** Any of numerous languages of Papua New Guinea. —**Pap·u·an** *adj.*

Pa·pu·a New Guinea, Independent State of (páp-oo-ə-, páap-, -yoo-). Country in the southwest Pacific. A member of the Commonwealth, it consists of eastern New Guinea, the Bismarck Archipelago, Bougainville, and other islands. Formerly an Australian territory, it gained independence in 1975 and exports copper, coffee, cocoa, timber, and copra. Area, 462 841 square kilometres (178,704 square miles). Population, 4,400,000. Capital, Port Moresby.

pap·ule (páppewl) *n.* Also **pap·u·la** (páppew-lə) *pl.* **-lae** (-lee). A small, inflammatory, congested spot on the skin; a pimple. [Latin *papula,* pimple.] —**pap·u·lar, pap·u·lif·er·ous** (-líffərəss) *adj.*

pap·y·rol·o·gy (páppi-róllǝji) *n.* The study of ancient papyri. [From Greek *papuros,* PAPYRUS + -LOGY.] —**pap·y·ro·log·i·cal** (-rə-lójik'l) *adj.* —**pap·y·rol·o·gist** (-róllǝjist) *n.*

pa·py·rus (pə-pīr-əss) *n., pl.* **-ri** (-pīr-ī) or **-ruses.** **1.** A tall aquatic reedlike plant, *Cyperus papyrus,* of southern Europe and northern Africa. **2.** A kind of paper made from the pith stems of this plant, used by the ancient Egyptians, Greeks, and Romans as a writing material. **3.** A document written on this paper. [Middle English *papirus,* paper, from Latin *papȳrus,* from Greek *papuros†.*]

par (par) *n.* **1.** An accepted average; a normal standard: *up to par.* **2.** An equality of status, level, or value; an equal footing: *on a par.* **3.** *Finance.* **a.** The established face value of a monetary unit expressed in terms of a monetary unit of another country using the same metal standard. **b.** A condition of equality between the face value of a stock, bond, or other negotiable instrument and its current market value: *sell at par.* **4.** In golf, the number of strokes considered necessary to complete a hole or course in expert play. —*adj.* **1.** Equal to the standard; normal. Used chiefly in the phrase *par for the course.* **2.** *Finance.* Of or pertaining to face value. [Latin *par,* equal.]

par. 1. paragraph. **2.** parallel. **3.** parenthesis. **4.** parish.

pa·ra¹ (párrə) *n. Informal.* **1.** A paratrooper. **2.** A paragraph.

pa·ra² (páarə) *n.* A monetary unit equal to ¹/₁₀₀ of the dinar of Yugoslavia. [Serbo-Croatian, from Turkish, from Persian *parāh,* "piece".]

par·a³ (párrə) *adj. Chemistry & Physics.* **1.** Of, pertaining to, or designating positions in a benzene ring separated by two carbon atoms. Used in combination: *para-dichlorobenzene.* Also written italic *p-*: *p-dichlorobenzene.* **2.** Of, pertaining to, or designating a polymer of a chemical compound. Used in combination: *paraformaldehyde.* **3.** Of, pertaining to, or designating a form of a diatomic molecule in which the nuclear spins are antiparallel. Used in combination: *parahydrogen.* Compare **ortho, meta.** [Independent use of PARA- (chemical prefix).]

para-¹, par- *comb. form.* Indicates: **1.** Alongside; for example,

paragenesis. 2. Near or beside; for example, **parathyroid gland. 3.** Beyond; over and above; for example, **paralinguistics, paranormal. 4.** Incorrect; abnormal; for example, **paraesthesia. 5.** Resembling or similar to; for example, **paramilitary, paratyphoid fever. 6.** Subsidiary or auxiliary to; for example **paramedical. 7.** Isomeric to or polymeric to; for example, **paraldehyde.** [In borrowed Greek compounds, *para-* indicates: 1. Beside, to the side of, alongside, as in **paradigm, Paraclete.** 2. Beyond, as in **paradox.** 3. Wrongly, harmfully, unfavourably, as in **paralysis.** 4. Among, as in **parallax.** *Para-* is the preverbal form of the preposition *para,* beside, for.]

para-² *comb. form.* Indicates something that protects or stops; for example, **parachute, parasol.** [French, from Italian, from *parare,* to defend, from Latin *parāre,* to make ready.]

par·a·min·o·sal·i·cyl·ic acid (párrə-ə-mīnō-sál-i-síllik, -méénō-) *n. Abbr.* **PAS, PASA** A drug, chemically similar to aspirin, used in the treatment of tuberculosis, usually in combination with isoniazid or streptomycin.

pa·rab·a·sis (pə-rábbə-siss) *n., pl.* **-ses** (-seez). In ancient Greek comedies, an address by the chorus to the audience. [Greek, a stepping forward (to address the audience), from *parabainein,* go forward : PARA- + *bainein,* to go.]

par·a·bi·o·sis (párrə-bī-ō-siss) *n. Biology.* The natural or artificial fusion of two organisms, as in the development of Siamese twins or the experimental joining of animals for research.

par·a·blast (párrə-blast) *n.* The food yolk of a meroblastic egg. [PARA- (resembling) + -BLAST.] —**par·a·blas·tic** (-blásstik) *adj.*

par·a·ble (párrəb'l) *n.* A simple story illustrating a moral or religious lesson, especially one told by Jesus in the Gospels. [Middle English, from Old French *parabole,* from Late Latin *parabola,* from Greek *parabolē,* juxtaposition, comparison, parable, from *paraballein,* to set beside : PARA- *para,* beside + *ballein,* to throw.]

pa·rab·o·la (pə-rábbələ) *n. Geometry.* A plane curve formed by the locus of points equidistant from a fixed line and a fixed point not on the line. It is a conic section with an eccentricity of 1, formed by a plane intersecting a conical surface parallel to the axis of the cone. [New Latin, from Greek *parabolē,* juxtaposition, parallelism (see **parable**); referring to the parallelism of the plane section containing the parabola and an element in the conical surface.]

par·a·bol·ic (párrə-bóllik) *adj.* Also **par·a·bol·i·cal** (-'l). **1.** Of or like a parable. **2.** Of or having the form of a parabola. **3.** Of or having the form of a paraboloid; generated by a parabola: *a parabolic antenna.* —**par·a·bol·i·cal·ly** *adv.*

pa·rab·o·loid (pə-rábbə-loyd) *n. Geometry.* A surface having sections that are parabolas; especially, one in which the sections parallel to two coordinate axes are parabolas, the sections parallel to the other axis being either an ellipse or circle (an *elliptic paraboloid*), or a hyperbola (a *hyperbolic paraboloid*). [PARABOL(A) + -OID.] —**pa·rab·o·loi·dal** (-lóyd'l) *adj.*

paraboloid of revolution *n. Geometry.* An elliptic paraboloid formed by revolving a parabola about its own axis.

Par·a·cel·sus (párrə-sél-səss), **Philippus Aureolus,** born Theophrastus Bombastus von Hohenheim (*c.* 1493–1541). Swiss physician. He improved pharmacy, encouraged scientific experiments, and generally revolutionised European medicine.

pa·ra·ce·ta·mol (párrə-séetə-mol, -séttə-) *n.* A drug that relieves pain and reduces fever, commonly used as an alternative to aspirin. [From *para-acetylaminophenol.*]

pa·rach·ro·nism (pə-ráckrə-niz'm) *n.* An error made in a chronology, especially by giving too late a date. Compare **prochronism.** [PARA- (incorrect) + Greek *khronos,* time + -ISM, perhaps by analogy with *anachronism.*]

par·a·chute (párrə-shōōt) *n.* **1.** An apparatus used to retard free fall from an aircraft, consisting of a canopy attached by cords to a

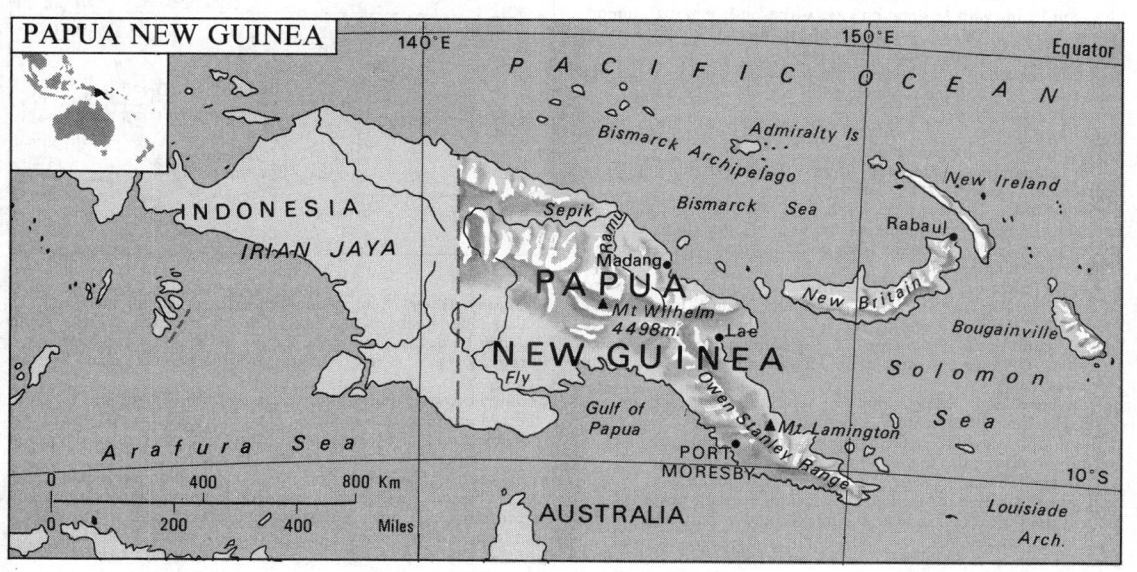

PAPUA NEW GUINEA

140°E · 150°E · Equator · PACIFIC OCEAN · Bismarck Archipelago · Admiralty Is · New Ireland · Bismarck Sea · Rabaul · INDONESIA · IRIAN JAYA · Sepik · Madang · PAPUA · New Britain · Mt Wilhelm 4498m · Lae · Bougainville · NEW GUINEA · Solomon Sea · Fly · Gulf of Papua · Owen Stanley Range · Mt Lamington · PORT MORESBY · 10°S · Arafura Sea · AUSTRALIA · Louisiade Arch. · 0 400 800 Km · 0 200 400 Miles

harness and worn or stored folded until deployed in descent. **2.** Any of various similar unpowered devices for retarding free-speeding or free-falling motion, as for example on some jets. **3.** A membranous, winglike extension between the limbs of flying squirrels and certain lizards; a patagium.

~*v.* **parachuted, -chuting, -chutes.** —*tr.* To drop (supplies, for example) by means of a parachute. —*intr.* To descend by means of a parachute. [French PARA- (protecting) + *chute,* fall, CHUTE.] —**par·a·chut·ist** *n.*

Par·a·clete (párrə-kleet) *n.* **1.** The Holy Ghost as an advocate or counsellor. **2.** *Small* **p.** An advocate. [Middle English *Paraclit,* from Old French *Paraclet,* from Late Latin *Paraclētus,* from Greek *Paraklētos,* "the Comforter", advocate, "one called to help", from *parakalein,* to call to help : PARA- (alongside) + *kalein,* to call.]

pa·rade (pə-ráyd) *n.* **1. a.** A public procession on some festive or ceremonial occasion. **b.** The occasion or action of making such a procession. The event itself, or the persons involved: *the Easter parade.* **2. a.** A ceremonial inspection of troops. **b.** The troops taking part in such an inspection. **c.** The place of assembly for an inspection of troops. Also called "parade ground". **3.** A continuous succession, as of persons or things on display or being reviewed: *a parade of fashions.* **4.** In fencing, a parry. **5.** An ostentatious show; a pompous display: *make a parade of humanitarian zeal.* **6.** A public square or a promenade. —**on parade. 1.** Being displayed or reviewed. **2.** Behaving ostentatiously.

~*v.* **paraded, -rading, -rades.** —*tr.* **1.** *Military.* **a.** To assemble (troops) for a formal display or inspection. **b.** To cause (troops, for example) to go on a ceremonial march. **2.** To march or walk through or around. **3.** To exhibit ostentatiously; flaunt. —*intr.* **1.** *Military.* To assemble for a formal inspection. **2.** To take part in a parade. **3.** To promenade in a public place. Used with *through* or *along.* —See Synonyms at **show.** [French, from Italian *parata,* from Vulgar Latin *parāta* (unattested), "a making ready", from Latin *parāre,* to prepare.] —**pa·rad·er** *n.*

par·a·digm (párrə-dīm ‖ -dim) *n.* **1.** A list of all the inflectional forms of a word taken as an illustrative example of the conjugation or declension to which it belongs. **2.** Any example or model used as a standard. **3.** In the philosophy of science, the prevailing scientific framework of theories and concepts within which a scientist works. [Late Latin *paradīgma,* from Greek *paradeigma,* model, from *para-deiknunai,* to compare, exhibit : PARA-, (alongside) + *deiknunai,* to show.] —**par·a·dig·mat·ic** (-dig-máttik, -dīg-) *adj.*

par·a·dise (párrə-dīss ‖ *U.S. also* -dīz) *n.* **1.** *Often capital* **P.** The Garden of Eden. **2.** *Theology.* **a.** Heaven, the abode of righteous souls after death. **b.** An intermediate resting place for righteous souls awaiting the Resurrection. **3.** The Muslim heaven, regarded as a garden of sensual delights and pleasures. **4.** Any place of ideal beauty or loveliness. **5.** A state of delight. [Middle English *paradis,* from Old French, from Late Latin *paradīsus,* from Greek *paradeisos,* garden, park, paradise, from Avestan *pairi-daēza,* circumvallation, walled-in park : *pairi,* around + *daēza,* wall.] —**par·a·di·si·a·cal** (párrədi-sī-ik'l, -zī-), **par·a·di·sa·i·cal** (-sáy-ik'l, -záy-) *adj.* —**par·a·di·si·a·cal·ly, par·a·di·sa·i·cal·ly** *adv.*

par·a·dos (párrə-doss) *n.* A bank of earth, especially one backing a trench, that gives protection from the rear. [French : PARA- (protect) + *dos,* back, from Latin *dorsum.*]

par·a·dox (párrə-doks) *n., pl.* **-doxes. 1. a.** A seemingly absurd, contradictory statement that may nonetheless be true. **b.** A self-contradictory statement such as *I'm telling you the truth when I say I'm a liar.* **2.** A person, situation, or action exhibiting inexplicable or contradictory aspects. **3.** An assertion that is essentially self-contradictory, although perhaps based on a valid deduction from acceptable premises. **4.** A statement contrary to received opinion. [Latin *paradoxum,* from Greek *paradoxon,* from *paradoxos,* incredible, conflicting with expectation : PARA- (beyond) + *doxa,* opinion, from *dokein,* to think.] —**par·a·dox·i·cal** (-dóksik'l) *adj.* —**par·a·dox·i·cal·ly** *adv.* —**par·a·dox·i·cal·ness** *n.*

paradoxical sleep *n.* A stage of sleep characterised by **rapid eye movement** *(see)* and increased electrical activity of the brain. Compare **orthodox sleep.**

par·a·drop (párrə-drop) *n. Military.* The delivery of supplies or personnel to a place by parachute.

~*tr.v.* **paradropped, -dropping, -drops.** To deliver (something) by parachute. [PARA(CHUTE) + DROP.]

par·aes·the·sia (párress-théezi-ə) *n.* An abnormal sensation of prickling, tingling, or itching of the skin. [Latin, from Greek : PARA- (incorrect) + *aisthēsia,* from *aisthēsis,* sensation.] —**par·aes·thet·ic** (-théttik) *adj.*

par·af·fin (párrə-fin, -feen, -fín, -féen) *n.* **1.** A liquid mixture of hydrocarbons obtained from petroleum and boiling in the range 150–300°C, used as a heating fuel and as a fuel for aircraft. Also called "paraffin oil", "kerosene". **2.** See **paraffin wax. 3.** See **liquid paraffin. 4.** A type of hydrocarbon, an **alkane** *(see).* Not in current technical usage.

~*tr.v.* **paraffined, -fining, -fins.** To saturate, impregnate, or coat with paraffin. [19th century : German, from Latin *parum,* (too) little + *affinis,* related, referring to its chemical inertia and lack of affinity to other substances.] —**par·af·fin·ic** (-fínnik) *adj.*

Usage: The term *kerosene* is used in the United States. In Britain, *paraffin* is used for the domestic fuel for portable heaters; *kerosene* is used in certain industrial contexts, and in particular for the fuel for jet aircraft.

paraffin wax *n.* A white or colourless waxy solid mixture of hydro-

carbons obtained from petroleum and used to make candles, wax paper, lubricants, and sealing materials.

par·a·form·al·de·hyde (párrəfawr-mál-di-hīd) *n.* A white solid polymer of formaldehyde, (HCHO)$_n$, where *n* is at least 6, used as a disinfectant, a fumigant, and a fungicide. Also called "paraform".

par·a·gen·e·sis (párrə-jénni-siss) *n.* Also **par·a·ge·ne·sia** (-ji-néezi-ə). *Geology.* The successive order in which a formation of associated minerals is generated. [PARA- (alongside) + -GENESIS.] —**par·a·ge·netic** (-ji-néttik) *adj.*

par·a·go·ge (párrə-gōji) *n.* Also **par·a·gogue** (-gog). The addition of a sound or syllable to the end of a word; for example, the addition of *-st* to *again* to make *against.* [Late Latin, from Greek *paragōgē,* alteration, derivation, from *paragein,* lead past, change : PARA- (beyond) + *agein,* to lead.] —**par·a·gog·ic** (-gójik) *adj.*

par·a·gon (párrə-gən ‖ -gon) *n.* **1.** A model or pattern of excellence or perfection of a kind; a peerless example: *paragon of virtue.* **2. a.** An unflawed diamond weighing at least 100 carats. **b.** A very large spherical pearl. **3.** *Printing.* A type size of 20 points.

~*tr.v.* **paragoned, -goning, -gons.** *Archaic.* **1.** To compare. **2.** To match; equal. [Obsolete French, from Italian *paragone,* comparison, touchstone, from Medieval Greek *parakonē,* whetstone, from Greek *parakonan,* to sharpen against, to compare : *para,* alongside + *akonan,* to sharpen, from *akonē,* whetstone, from *akē,* point.]

par·a·graph (párrə-graaf, -graf) *n. Abbr.* **par., para. 1.** A distinct division of a written work or composition that expresses some thought or point relevant to the whole but is complete in itself and usually marked by beginning on a separate, indented line and/or by special spacing. **2.** A mark (¶) used to indicate where a new paragraph should begin or to serve as a reference mark. **3.** A brief article, notice, or announcement, as in a newspaper.

~*tr.v.* **paragraphed, -graphing, -graphs.** *Abbr.* **par. 1.** To divide or arrange in paragraphs. **2.** To express or put in a paragraph. [Medieval Latin *paragraphus,* sign marking a new section of writing, from Greek *paragraphos,* line to mark exchange in dialogue, from *para-graphein,* to write beside : PARA- (beside) + *graphein,* to write.] —**par·a·graph·ic** (-gráffik), **par·a·graph·i·cal** *adj.*

par·a·graph·i·a (párrə-graf-i-ə, -graaf-) *n. Psychiatry.* The writing of words or letters other than those intended or an inability to express ideas in writing, often resulting from certain disorders of the brain. [New Latin : PARA- (abnormal) + *-graphia,* "writing"; see **-graph.**]

Par·a·guay, Republic of (párrə-gwī, -gwĭ ‖ *chiefly U.S.* -gway). *Spanish* **República del Paraguay.** Landlocked South American country. It is divided by the river Paraguay, with fertile lowlands and hills to the east, and the infertile Gran Chaco region to the west. The eastern more populous area produces cattle, oilseeds, sugar cane, and cotton. Area, 406 752 square kilometres (157,048 square miles). Population, 4,960,000. Capital, Asunción. —**Par·a·guay·an** (-gwī-ən ‖ -gwáy-) *adj. & n.*

Paraguay, River. South American river, 2 550 kilometres (1,585 miles) long. Rising in the Mato Grosso of Brazil, it flows south through Paraguay, joining the Paraná at the Argentine border.

Paraguay tea *n.* A tree, **maté** *(see),* or the beverage made from its leaves.

par·a·hy·dro·gen (párrə-hídrəjən) *n.* A form of hydrogen in which the two nuclei in each molecule have antiparallel spins; one of two possible forms of hydrogen, constituting 25 per cent of the gas at room temperature. Compare **orthohydrogen.**

par·a·keet, par·ra·keet (párrə-keet, -kéet) *n.* Also **par·a·quet** (-ket). Any of various small parrots, usually having long, tapering tails and a predominantly green plumage. [Old French *paroquet,* perhaps a pet form of *Pierre,* from Latin *Petrus,* (the name, Peter).]

par·al·de·hyde (pə-rál-di-hīd, pa-) *n.* A colourless aromatic liquid polymer, $C_6H_{12}O_3$, of acetaldehyde, used as a solvent and as a sedative. [PAR(A)- + (ACET)ALDEHYDE.]

par·a·lin·guis·tic (párrə-ling-gwístik) *adj.* Of or pertaining to nonlinguistic features of verbal communication such as gestures or intonation.

par·a·lin·guis·tics (párrə-ling-gwístiks) *n. Used with a singular verb.* The study of the paralinguistic features of verbal communication.

par·a·li·pom·e·na (párrə-lī-pómminə, -li-) *pl.n.* The books of Chronicles in the Douay Bible. [Middle English, from Late Latin, from Greek, "things omitted" (that is, not covered in Kings), from *paraleipein,* to omit: PARA- (to one side) + *leipein,* to leave.]

par·a·lip·sis, par·a·leip·sis (párrə-líp-siss) *n., pl.* **-ses.** A rhetorical device used to emphasise a statement by first saying that one will not speak of the subject in question and then speaking of it, for example, *to say nothing of her former accomplishments, which include winning the championship and 3 medals.* [Late Latin, from Greek, "a leaving aside", from *paraleipein.* See **paralipomena.**]

par·al·lax (párrə-laks) *n.* **1.** An apparent change in the position of an object when the observer changes position. **2.** *Astronomy.* **a.** Change in the observed position of a star or other celestial body resulting from motion of the earth. **b.** A measure of this effect; the angle subtended at the body by a line joining two extreme positions of observation. **c.** The distance of a celestial body as determined in this way. See **diurnal parallax, annual parallax, secular parallax.** [French *parallaxe,* from New Latin *parallaxis,* from Greek, change, from *parallassein,* to change, alternate : PARA- + *allassein,* to change, exchange, from *allos,* other.] **—par·al·lac·tic** (-láktik) *adj.*

par·al·lel (párrə-lel) *adj. Abbr.* **par. 1.** Being an equal distance apart at every point. **2.** *Geometry.* **a.** Designating two or more equidistant coplanar lines that do not intersect. Compare **skew. b.** Designating two or more planes that do not intersect. **c.** Designating a line and a plane that do not intersect. **d.** Designating curves or surfaces that are everywhere equidistant. **e.** Designating two or more vectors that have parallel lines of action and act in the same direction. Compare **antiparallel. 3. a.** Having comparable parts, analogous aspects, or readily recognised similarities. **b.** Having the same tendency or direction. **4.** *Grammar.* Containing or characterised by corresponding syntactical forms or constructions. **5.** *Music.* Moving consistently by the same intervals. Said of two or more melodies. **6.** Designating or pertaining to a system of computer operation in which two or more users use the system at the same time by **time sharing** *(see).* Compare **serial. 7.** *Electricity.* Designating a circuit or part of a circuit connected in parallel.
~*adv.* In a parallel relationship or manner.
~*n. Abbr.* **par. 1.** A surface or line that is equidistant from another. **2.** *Mathematics.* One of a set of parallel geometric figures, usually lines. **3. a.** Anything that closely resembles or is analogous to something else. **b.** A comparison indicating likeness or analogy. **4.** The condition of being parallel; near similarity or exact agreement in particulars. **5.** *Geography.* Any of the imaginary lines joining places of equal latitude, encircling the earth parallel to the equator. **6.** *Printing.* A sign (||), usually indicating material referred to in a note or reference. **7.** *Electricity.* A configuration of two or more two-terminal components connected between two points in a circuit with one terminal of each connected to each of the two points. Used chiefly in the phrase *in parallel.* See **series circuit.**
~*tr.v.* **paralleled, -leling, -lels. 1.** To make or place parallel to. **2.** To be or extend parallel to. **3.** To be similar or analogous to. **4.** To be or provide an equal or match for. **5.** To show to be analogous; compare or liken. [Latin *parallēlus,* from Greek *parallēlos* : *para,* beside + *allēlōn,* of one another, from *allos,* other.]

parallel bars *pl.n.* A gymnastic apparatus, consisting of two horizontal bars supported on posts, often at different heights.

par·al·lel·e·pi·ped, par·al·lel·o·pi·ped (párrə-lellə-pī-ped, -le-léppi-, -pid) *n. Geometry.* A solid with six faces, each a parallelogram, having opposite pairs of faces congruent. [Greek *parallēlepipedon* : *parallēlos,* PARALLEL + *epipedon,* plane surface, from *epipedos,* level : *epi,* on + *pedon,* ground.]

par·al·lel·ism (párrə-lel-iz'm) *n.* **1.** The state or position of being parallel; a parallel relationship. **2.** Likeness, correspondence, or similarity in aspect, course, or tendency. **3. a.** The use of corresponding syntactical forms or literary devices. **b.** An instance of this. **4.** *Philosophy.* The doctrine that to every mental change there corresponds a concomitant, but causally unconnected, physical alteration.

par·al·lel·o·gram (párrə-léllə-gram) *n.* A four-sided plane figure with both pairs of opposite sides parallel. [Late Latin *parallēlogrammum,* from Greek *parallēlogrammon,* from *parallēlogrammos,* bounded by parallel lines : *parallēlos,* PARALLEL + *grammē,* line.]

parallelogram rule *n. Mathematics & Physics.* A rule for adding two vectors or vector quantities, such as forces or velocities, by forming a parallelogram in which two adjacent sides represent the vectors; their resultant is then indicated by the diagonal of the parallelogram through the point of intersection of the vectors.

parallel turn *n.* In skiing, a turn executed by shifting and dropping one's weight, keeping both skis parallel.

pa·ral·o·gism (pə-rál-ə-jiz'm) *n. Logic.* Fallacious or illogical reasoning; especially, a faulty argument of whose fallacy the reasoner is not aware. [French *paralogisme,* from Late Latin *paralogismus,* from Greek *paralogismos,* from *paralogos,* unexpected, beyond calculation : PARA- + *logos,* word.] **—pa·ral·o·gist** *n.* **—pa·ral·o·gis·tic** (-jístik) *adj.*

par·a·lyse, *U.S.* **par·a·lyze** (párrə-līz) *tr.v.* **-lysed, -lysing, -lyses. 1.** To affect with paralysis; cause to be paralytic. **2.** To make helpless or unable to move, as through emotion or fear. **3.** To impair the progress or functioning of; make inoperative or powerless. [From French *paralyser,* from *paralysie,* paralysis.] **—par·a·ly·sa·tion** (-záysh'n) *n.* **—par·a·lys·er** *n.*

pa·ral·y·sis (pə-rál-ə-siss) *n., pl.* **-ses** (-seez). **1.** Loss or impairment of the ability to move or have sensation in a bodily part as a result of injury to or disease of its muscles or nerve supply. **2.** Partial or complete inability to move or function; stoppage or impairment of activity. [Latin, from Greek *paralusis,* from *paraluein,* to loosen, disable : *para,* "unfavourably" + *luein,* to release.]

paralysis ag·i·tans (ájitanz) *n.* **Parkinson's disease** *(see).* [New Latin, "shaking palsy".]

par·a·lyt·ic (párrə-líttik) *adj.* **1.** Affected with paralysis; paralysed. **2.** Of or pertaining to paralysis. **3.** *British Slang.* Very drunk.
~*n.* A person suffering from paralysis. [Middle English, from Old French *paralytique,* from Latin *paralyticus,* from Greek *paralutikos,* from *paralusis,* PARALYSIS.] **—par·a·lyt·i·cal·ly** *adv.*

par·a·mag·net (párrə-magnit) *n.* A paramagnetic substance.

par·a·mag·net·ism (párrə-mág-nit-iz'm, -nət) *n. Physics.* A type of magnetism occurring in substances with a positive magnetic susceptibility. It is caused by unpaired electron orbitals in the atoms which result in each atom having a dipole moment. An applied magnetic field tends to align these dipoles in such a way that for small fields and high temperatures the induced field is proportional to the applied field. Below the Curie point certain paramagnetic materials exhibit ferromagnetism. **—par·a·mag·net·ic** (-mag-néttik) *adj.* **—par·a·mag·net·ical·ly** *adv.*

Par·a·mar·i·bo (párrə-márri-bō). Capital and port of Surinam. It was founded by the French (1540), settled by the British (1630) and later taken over by the Dutch. Exports include bauxite and coffee.

paramatta. Variant of **parramatta.**

par·a·me·ci·um (párrə-meé-si-əm || -shi-) *n., pl.* **-cia** (-si-ə) or **-ums.** Any of various ciliate protozoans of the genus *Paramecium,* usually oval and having an oral groove for feeding. [New Latin, from Greek *paramēkēs,* oblong : PARA, (alongside) + *mēkos,* length.]

par·a·med·ic (párrə-méddik) *n.* A **—paramedical.**

par·a·med·i·cal (párrə-méddik'l) *adj.* Of or designating auxiliary medical personnel, such as radiographers, laboratory technicians, and physiotherapists, or their work. **par·a·med·i·cal** *n.*

par·a·ment (párrəmənt) *n., pl.* **-ments** or **paramenta** (párrə-méntə). An ecclesiastical vestment or hanging. [Middle English, from Medieval Latin *parāmentum,* from *parāre,* to decorate, prepare.]

pa·ram·e·ter (pə-rámmitər) *n.* **1.** A variable or an arbitrary constant appearing in a mathematical expression, each value of which restricts or determines the specific form of the expression. **2.** *Usually plural. Informal.* Loosely: **a.** A fixed constraint or boundary: *keep within the parameters of our budget.* **b.** A characteristic and defining feature or factor; a touchstone: *one of the parameters of democracy.* [New Latin : PARA- (alongside) + -METER.] **—par·a·met·ric** (párrə-méttrik) *adj.* **—par·a·met·ri·cal·ly** *adv.*

Usage: Using *parameter* in its fairly recent nonmathematical sense ("any defining or limiting factor") has attracted criticism on the grounds that it sounds pretentious. In general it is better to use one of the older, simpler words, such as *limit* or *constraint.*

par·a·mil·i·tar·y (párrə-mílli-təri, -tri || *U.S.* -terri) *adj.* **1.** Designating a group of people organised on a military pattern, especially as an auxiliary military force. **2.** Of or pertaining to such forces.

par·am·ne·si·a (párram-neézi-ə) *n. Psychology.* A distortion of memory in which fantasy and experience are confused. [PAR(A)- (resembling) + AMNESIA.]

pa·ra·mo (párrə-mō) *n., pl.* **-mos.** A high, treeless plain of tropical South America. [American Spanish, from Spanish *paramo*†, a wasteland.]

par·a·morph (párrə-mawrf) *n.* A mineral crystal formed or affected by paramorphism. [PARA- (subsidiary to) + -MORPH.]

par·a·mor·phism (párrə-mórf-iz'm) *n.* Structural alteration of a mineral without change of chemical composition. Also called "metastasis". **—par·a·mor·phic, par·a·mor·phous** *adj.*

par·a·mount (párrə-mownt) *adj.* **1.** Of chief concern or significance; primary; foremost: *of paramount importance.* **2.** Supreme in rank, power, or authority. —See Synonyms at **dominant.**
~*n. Rare.* A person of the highest power or authority; a supreme ruler. [Anglo-French *paramont,* "superior" (used of feudal overlordship) : Old French *par,* by, from Latin *per* + *amont,* above : *a,* to, from Latin *ad* + *mont,* mountain, from Latin *mōns* (stem *mont-*).] **—par·a·mount·cy** (-si) *n.* **—par·a·mount·ly** *adv.*

par·a·mour (párrə-moor) *n.* **1.** A lover, of either sex; especially, the lover of someone who is married. **2.** *Archaic.* A sweetheart. [Middle English, originally an adverb, "by way of love", from Old French *par amour* : *par,* by, from Latin *per* + *amour,* love, from Latin *amor,* from *amāre,* to love.]

Pa·ra·ná (párra-naá). Second-largest river in South America. Formed by the confluence of the rivers Grande and Paranaíba in southeast Brazil, it flows southwest for 2 900 kilometres (1,800 miles) through Paraguay, to join the river Uruguay at the Plata Estuary. It is important for navigation.

pa·rang (paá-rang) *n.* A short, heavy, straight-edged knife used in Malaysia and Indonesia as a tool and weapon. [Malay.]

par·a·noi·a (párrə-nóy-ə) *n.* **1.** A nondegenerative, limited, usually chronic psychosis characterised by delusions of persecution, defended by the afflicted with apparent logic and reason. **2.** Loosely, unwarranted fear or distrust of people or situations. [New Latin, from Greek, madness, from *paranoos*, demented : PARA- (beyond) + *nous*, mind.] **—par·a·noi·ac** (-ak) *adj. & n.*

par·a·noid (párrə-noyd) *adj.* **1.** Pertaining to, characteristic of, or suffering from paranoia: *a paranoid delusion.* **2.** Suggestive of paranoia; showing unreasonable distrust, suspicion, or an exaggerated sense of one's own importance.
~n. One afflicted with paranoia.

paranoid schizophrenia *n.* A type of schizophrenia resembling paranoia and characterised chiefly by delusions and hallucinations.

par·a·nor·mal (párrə-nórm'l) *adj.* Not within the range of normal experience or scientifically explainable phenomena. **—par·a·nor·mal·ly** *adv.*

par·an·thro·pus (pa-ránthrəpəss) *n., pl.* **-puses.** An extinct anthropoid ape of the genus *Paranthropus* (later renamed as a species of *Australopithecus),* known from remains found in South Africa. [New Latin : PAR(A)- (resembling) + Greek *anthrōpos,* man.]

par·a·pet (párrə-pit, -pet) *n.* **1.** A low, protective wall or railing along the edge of a roof, balcony, or similar structure. **2.** An earth or stone embankment protecting soldiers from enemy fire. **—stick one's head above the parapet.** To put oneself into an exposed or high-profile position. —See Synonyms at **bulwark.** [French, from Italian *parapetto,* chest-high wall : PARA- (protecting) + *petto,* chest, from Latin *pectus.*] **—par·a·pet·ed** (párrə-pettid) *adj.*

par·aph (párrəf, pə-ráf) *n.* A flourish made after or below a signature, originally to prevent forgery. [French *parafe, paraphe,* from Old French *paraffe,* from Medieval Latin *paraphus,* from *paragraphus,* PARAGRAPH.]

par·a·pher·na·lia (párrəfər-náyli-ə) *n. Sometimes used with a plural verb.* **1.** Personal belongings. **2.** The articles used in some activity; equipment; gear: *drug paraphernalia.* **3.** Formerly, a married woman's personal property exclusive of her dowry. **4.** The accompanying problems or procedures involved in any project: *all the paraphernalia of moving.* [Medieval Latin *paraphernālia* (in sense 3), from Greek *parapherna* : PARA- (beyond) + *phernē,* dowry.]

par·a·phrase (párrə-frayz) *n.* **1.** A restatement of a text or passage in another form or other words, often to clarify meaning. **2.** The making of paraphrases, often used as a teaching device.
~v. **paraphrased, -phrasing, -phrases.** *—tr.* To express in a paraphrase. *—intr.* To compose a paraphrase. [French, from Latin *paraphrasis,* from Greek, from *paraphrazein,* to paraphrase : PARA- (alongside) + *phrazein,* to show.] **—par·a·phras·tic** (-frástik) *adj.*

pa·raph·y·sis (pə-ráffə-siss) *n., pl.* **-ses** (-seez). Any of the sterile filaments found among the sexual organs of certain fungi, algae, and mosses. [PARA- (subsidiary to) + Greek *phusis,* nature.]

par·a·ple·gia (párrə-pleéjə, -pleéji-ə) *n.* Complete paralysis of the lower body, including both legs, caused by injury to or disease of the spinal cord. [New Latin, from Greek *paraplēgia,* a stroke on one side, from *paraplēssein,* to strike on one side : PARA- (alongside) + *plēssein,* to strike.] **—par·a·ple·gic** (-pleéjik) *adj. & n.*

par·a·po·di·um (párrə-pṓdi-əm) *n.,* **-dia** (-ə). Any of the lateral appendages of polychaete worms, which occur in pairs and are used in locomotion and respiration. [New Latin : PARA- + *-podium* (footlike part). See **podium.**]

par·a·psy·chol·o·gy (párrə-sī-kólləji) *n.* The study of phenomena such as telepathy, clairvoyance, and psychokinesis that are not explainable by known natural laws. **—par·a·psy·cho·log·i·cal** (-kə-lójik'l) *adj.* **—par·a·psy·chol·o·gist** (-kólləjist) *n.*

Par·a·quat (párrə-kwot, -kwat) *n.* A trademark for a poisonous, yellow, water-soluble solid used in solution as a weedkiller.

paraquet. Variant of **parakeet.**

Pa·rá rubber (pə-raá, paárə) *n.* Rubber obtained from various tropical South American trees of the genus *Hevea,* especially *H. brasiliensis.*

par·a·sang (párrə-sang) *n.* An ancient Persian unit of distance, usually estimated at about $5^1/_2$ kilometres ($3^1/_2$ miles). [Latin *parasanga,* from Greek *parasangēs,* from Iranian, akin to Persian *farsang*†.]

par·a·se·le·ne (párrəsi-leé-ni) *n., pl.* **-nae** (-nee). A luminous spot on a lunar halo. Also called "mock moon", "moon dog". [New Latin : PARA- (resembling) + Greek *selēnē,* moon.] **—par·a·se·le·nic** (-lénnik) *adj.*

pa·ra·shah (párrə-shaa, paárə-) *n., pl.* **-shoth** (-shōt) or **-shioth** (-shi-ōt). Any of the portions of the Torah read on the Sabbath and on festivals in the synagogue. [Hebrew, "explanation".]

Par·a·shu·ra·ma (párrə-shoō-raámə) *n. Hinduism.* See **Rama.**

par·a·site (párrə-sīt) *n.* **1.** *Biology.* Any organism that grows, feeds, and is sheltered on or in a different organism while contributing nothing to the survival of its host. **2.** A person who habitually takes advantage of the generosity of others without making any useful return. **3.** In ancient Greece, one who was given free meals in return for his witty or cheeky conversation. [Old French, from Latin *parasītus,* from Greek *parasitos,* originally "fellow guest", later "parasite" : PARA- (beside) + *sitos,* grain, food.]

par·a·sit·ic (párrə-síttik) *adj.* Also **par·a·sit·i·cal** (-'l). **1.** Of, pertaining to, or characteristic of a parasite. **2.** Caused by a parasite, as certain diseases are. **—par·a·sit·i·cal·ly** *adv.*

par·a·sit·i·cide (párrə-sítti-sīd) *n.* Something used to destroy parasites. [From PARASIT(E) + -CIDE.] **—par·a·sit·i·cide, par·a·sit·i·ci·dal** (-sīd'l), **par·a·sit·i·cid·ic** (-síddik) *adj.* **—par·a·sit·i·ci·dal·ly** *adv.*

par·a·sit·ise, par·a·sit·ize (párrə-si-tīz, -sī-) *tr.v.* **ised, -ising, -ises.** To live on (a host) as a parasite.

par·a·sit·ism (párrə-sī-tiz'm) *n.* **1.** The characteristic behaviour or mode of existence of a parasite. **2.** A diseased condition resulting from parasitic infestation.

par·a·si·tol·o·gy (párrə-sī-tólləji) *n.* The scientific study of parasites. [From PARASIT(E) + -LOGY.] **—par·a·si·to·log·i·cal** (-sītə-lójik'l) *adj.* **—par·a·si·tol·o·gist** (-tólləjist) *n.*

par·a·sol (párrə-sol, -sól) *n.* A light, usually small umbrella carried, especially by women, for protection from the sun. [French, from Italian *parasole* : PARA- (protecting) + *sole,* sun, from Latin *sōl.*]

par·a·su·i·cide (párrə-soō-i-sīd, -séw-) *n.* **1. a.** An attempt to kill oneself that is not motivated by a genuine wish to die. **b.** The making of such attempts. **2.** A person who makes such an attempt.

par·a·sym·pa·thet·ic nervous system (párrə-símpə-théttik) *n. Anatomy.* The part of the autonomic nervous system originating in the central and back parts of the brain and in the lower part of the spinal cord that inhibits or opposes the physiological effects of the sympathetic nervous system, as in tending to stimulate digestive secretions, slowing the heart, and dilating blood vessels.

par·a·syn·the·sis (párrə-sínthi-siss) *n. Grammar.* The formation of words by a combination of compounding and adding an affix, as in the formation of the word *freemasonry* from *free* plus *mason* plus *-ry,* rather than from *free* plus *masonry.* **—par·a·syn·thet·ic** (-sin-théttik) *adj.*

par·a·tax·is (párrə-táksiss) *n.* The coordination of grammatical elements such as phrases or clauses, without the use of coordinating elements such as conjunctions, as in *It was cold; the snows came.* Compare **asyndeton, hypotaxis.** [Greek, from *paratassein,* to arrange side by side : PARA- (beside) + *tassein,* to arrange.] **—par·a·tac·tic** (-táktik), **par·a·tac·ti·cal** *adj.* **—par·a·tac·ti·cal·ly** *adv.*

par·a·thi·on (párrə-thī́-on) *n.* A highly poisonous liquid insecticide, $(C_2H_5O)_2P(S)OC_6H_4NO_2$. [PARA- + *thio(phosphate)* + -ON.]

par·a·thy·roid (párrə-thī́r-oyd) *adj.* **1.** Situated close to the thyroid gland. **2.** Of of pertaining to the parathyroid gland.
~n. The parathyroid gland.

parathyroid gland *n.* Any of four small kidney-shaped glands that lie in pairs near or within the lateral lobes of the thyroid gland and secrete parathyroid hormone.

parathyroid hormone *n.* A hormone, synthesised and secreted by the parathyroid glands, that raises the level of calcium in the blood. Deficiency results in tetany. Also called "parathormone".

par·a·troop·er (párrə-troōpər) *n.* A member of the paratroops.

par·a·troops (párrə-troōpss) *pl.n.* Infantry, trained and equipped to carry out parachute missions. [PARA(CHUTE) + TROOPS.] **—pa·ra·troop** *adj.*

par·a·ty·phoid (párrə-tī́foyd) *adj.* **1.** Resembling typhoid fever. **2.** Of or pertaining to paratyphoid fever.
~n. Paratyphoid fever.

paratyphoid fever *n.* An acute intestinal disease, similar to typhoid fever but less severe and caused by any of three bacteria of the genus *Salmonella.* Also called "paratyphoid".

par·a·vane (párrə-vayn) *n. Nautical.* A device equipped with sharp teeth and towed alongside a ship to cut the mooring cables of submerged mines. [PARA- (alongside) + VANE.]

par a·vion (par a-vyóɴ) *adv. French.* By aeroplane. Used as a label or notation on letters or articles sent by air mail.

par·boil (pár-boyl) *tr.v.* **-boiled, -boiling, -boils. 1.** To cook partially by boiling for a brief period. **2.** To subject to intense, often uncomfortable heat. [Middle English *parboilen,* "to boil thoroughly", later (by influence of PART) to parboil, from Old French *parbo(u)illir,* from Late Latin *perbullīre* : Latin *per,* thoroughly + *bullīre,* to boil.]

par·buck·le (pár-buck'l) *n.* **1.** A rope sling for rolling cylindrical objects up or down an inclined plane. **2.** A sling for raising or lowering a heavy object vertically.
~tr.v. **parbuckled, -ling, -les.** To raise or lower with a parbuckle. [Alteration (influenced by BUCKLE) of earlier *parbunkle*†.]

Par·cae (pár-see, -kī) *pl.n.* The three **Fates** *(see).* [Latin.]

par·cel (párss'l) *n.* **1.** Something wrapped up or packaged; a package. **2.** A portion or plot of land, usually a division of a larger area. **3.** A quantity of merchandise offered for sale. **4.** A group or company; a bunch. **5.** A distinct, often essential part of something. Used chiefly in the phrase *part and parcel.*
~tr.v. **parcelled,** or *U.S.* **-celed, -celling** or *U.S.* **-celing, -cels. 1.** To divide into portions or allotments and distribute. Usually followed by *out.* **2.** To make into a parcel or parcels; wrap; package. Sometimes followed by *up.* **3.** *Nautical.* To wind protective strips of canvas round (rope). [Middle English *parcelle,* from Old French, from Vulgar Latin *particella* (unattested), from Latin *particula,* portion, particle, diminutive of *pars* (stem *part-*), part.]

par·ce·nar·y (pár-si-nəri || *U.S.* -nerri) *n., pl.* **-ies.** *Law.* **Coparcenary** *(see).* [Anglo-French *parcenarie,* from Old French *parçonerie,* from *parçonier,* partner, PARCENER.]

par·ce·ner (pár-sənər) *n. Law.* A **coparcener** *(see).* [Anglo-French, from Old French *parçonier,* partner, from Vulgar Latin *partiōnārius* (unattested), from Latin *partītiō,* partition, from *partīre,* to divide, from *pars* (stem *part-*), part.]

parch (parch) *v.* **parched, parching, parches.** *—tr.* **1.** To make very dry, especially by the action of heat. **2.** To make thirsty. Usually used in the passive: *I'm parched.* **3.** To dry or roast (corn, peas, or the like) by exposing to heat. *—intr.* **1.** To become very dry: *The fields will soon parch in this heat.* **2.** To become thirsty. —See Synonyms at **burn.** [Middle English *parchen*†.]

Par·chee·si (paar-cheé-si, -zi) *n.* A trademark for a board game based on the ancient game of **pachisi** *(see).*

parch·ment (párchmənt) *n.* **1.** The skin of a sheep or goat, prepared for writing or painting upon. **2.** A written text or drawing on a sheet of this material. **3.** Stiff, durable paper made in imitation of this material. [Middle English *perchement, parchemin,* from Old French *parchemin, parcamin,* from Vulgar Latin *particamīnum* (unattested), blend of Latin *Parthica (pellis),* "Parthian (leather)", and *pergamīna,* parchment, from Greek *pergamēnē,* from *Pergamēnos,* of Pergamun, from *Pergamon,* Pergamum in western Turkey (where it was first used as a substitute for papyrus).]

par·close (pár-klōz) *n.* A railing dividing a chapel or altar from the main body of a church. [Middle English, from Old French *parclos(e),* from past participle of *parclore,* to close off. See **per-, close.**]

pard (pard) *n. Archaic.* A leopard or other large cat. [Middle English *parde,* from Old French, from Latin *pardus,* from Greek *pardos,* from an Oriental source. See also **leopard.**]

par·da·lote (párdə-lōt) *n.* The **diamond bird** *(see).* [New Latin *pardalotus,* from Greek *pardalōtos,* having a leopard's spots, from *pardos* (stem *pardal-*), leopard.]

pard·ner (párdnər) *n. U.S. Regional.* A friend or partner. [Variant of PARTNER.]

par·don (párd'n) *tr.v.* **-doned, -doning, -dons. 1.** To release (a person) from punishment; forgive. **2.** To pass over (an offence) without punishment. **3.** To make courteous allowance for; to excuse: *Pardon me, but I must go.* —See Synonyms at **forgive.**
—*n.* **1. a.** The act of forgiving. **b.** Forgiveness; courteous overlooking or allowance. **2.** *Law.* **a.** The exemption of a convicted person from the penalties of an offence or crime by the power of the executor of the laws. **b.** The official document or warrant declaring such an exemption. **3.** Formerly, a papal indulgence.
—*interj.* Used as a polite or conventional apology for causing inconvenience, or as a request for spoken words to be repeated. [Middle English *pardonen,* from Old French *pardoner,* to give, pardon, from Late Latin *perdōnāre,* to give wholeheartedly : *per,* thoroughly + *dōnāre,* to give, from *dōnum,* gift.] **—par·don·a·ble** *adj.* **—par·don·a·bly** *adv.*

par·don·er (párd'n-ər) *n.* **1.** One who pardons. **2.** A medieval ecclesiastic authorised to raise money for religious works by granting papal indulgences to contributors.

pare (pair) *tr.v.* **pared, paring, pares. 1.** To remove the outer covering or skin of (a fruit or vegetable) by peeling with a knife or similar instrument. **2.** To remove the edges of (toenails, for example). **3.** To remove by or as if by cutting, clipping, or shaving. Used with *off* or *away: paring off lemon rind.* **4.** To lessen or diminish bit by bit; whittle away. Used with *off* or *down: paring expenditure down to a minimum.* [Middle English *paren,* from Old French *parer,* to prepare, from Latin *parāre.*]

Pa·ré (pa-ráy), **Ambroise** (*c.* 1510–90). French surgeon and pioneer of modern surgery. As an army surgeon he abandoned the cauterisation of amputated limbs with red-hot irons and boiling oil in favour of ligatures to tie off arteries.

par·e·gor·ic (párrə-górrik ‖ -gáwrik) *n.* Camphorated tincture of opium, formerly taken internally for the relief of diarrhoea and intestinal pain. [Late Latin *parēgoricus,* from Greek *parēgorikos,* from *parēgoros,* encouraging, soothing, addressing : PARA- (beside), alongside + *agora,* assembly.]

pa·rei·ra (pə-ráirə) *n.* A drug prepared from the root of a South American plant, *Chondrodendron tomentosum,* used as a diuretic and tonic. [From Portuguese *parreira brava,* "wild vine".]

pa·ren·chy·ma (pə-réngkimə) *n.* **1.** *Anatomy.* The tissue characteristic of an organ, as distinguished from connective tissue. **2.** *Botany.* Tissue composed of soft, unspecialised, thin-walled cells. **3.** *Zoology.* A loose connective tissue occurring in flatworms and related invertebrates. [New Latin, from Greek *parenkhuma,* visceral flesh, from *parenkhein,* to pour in beside (from the belief that the tissues of the organs were poured in by their blood vessels) : PARA- (beside) + *en,* in + *khein,* to pour.] **—pa·ren·chy·mal, par·en·chym·a·tous** (párren-kímmətəss) *adj.* **—par·en·chym·a·tous·ly** *adv.*

par·ent (páir-ənt) *n.* **1.** A father or mother. **2.** A forefather; an ancestor; a progenitor. **3.** Any organism that produces or generates another. **4.** A guardian; a protector. **5.** The source or cause of something; the origin. **6.** *Physics & Chemistry.* A nucleus, atom, ion, or molecule that breaks up or changes to give a different nucleus, atom, or the like (the daughter). Also used adjectivally: *a parent ion.* [Middle English, from Old French, from Latin *parēns* stem *parent-*), from the present participle of *parere,* to give birth.] **—pa·ren·tal** (pə-rént'l) *adj.* **—pa·ren·tal·ly** *adv.* **—par·ent·hood** *n.*

par·ent·age (páir-əntij) *n.* **1.** Descent or derivation from parents or ancestors; lineage; ancestry. **2.** Derivation from a source; origin or cause. **3.** The state or relationship of being a parent.

parental generation *n.* A generation from which a genetic experiment begins. Compare **filial generation.**

par·en·ter·al (pə-réntərəl, pa-) *adj.* **1.** Located outside the alimentary canal. **2.** Taken into the body or administered in a manner other than through the digestive tract, as by intravenous or intramuscular injection. [PAR(A)- + ENTER(O)- + -AL.]

pa·ren·the·sis (pə-rén-thə-siss, -thi-) *n., pl.* **-ses** (-seez). *Abbr.* **par., paren. 1.** Either or both of the upright curved lines, (or), used to mark off explanatory or qualifying remarks in writing or printing. Also called "bracket", "round bracket". **2.** *Mathematics.* Such a mark used as one of a pair to enclose a sum, product, or other expression considered or treated as a collective entity in a mathematical operation. **3.** A qualifying or amplifying phrase occurring within a sentence in such a way as to form an interpolation independent of the surrounding syntactical structure; for example, in the sentence: *It was the best film —and I go to a lot —I have seen in a long time,* the words *and I go to a lot* constitute a parenthesis. **4.** An interruption of continuity; an interval; an interlude. [Late Latin, from Greek, "a putting in beside", from *parentithenai,* to insert : PARA- + *en,* in + *tithenai,* to put.]

pa·ren·the·sise, pa·ren·the·size (pə-rén-thə-sīz, -thi-) *tr.v.* **-sised, -sising, -sises. 1.** To insert as a parenthesis. **2.** To place between parenthetical marks. **3.** To insert a parenthesis or parentheses into.

par·en·thet·i·cal (párrən-théttik'l) *adj.* Also **par·en·thet·ic** (-théttik). **1.** Contained, or as if contained, in parentheses; qualifying or explanatory: *a parenthetical remark.* **2.** Using or containing parentheses. **—par·en·thet·i·cal·ly** *adv.*

par·ent·ing (páir-ənt-ing) *n.* The bringing up of children by or as by a parent.

pa·rer·gon (pa-rérg-ən, pə-, -ráirg-, -on) *n., pl.* **-ga.** *Formal.* Work done apart from one's main, primary, or professional work. [Latin, from Greek : PARA- + *ergon,* work.]

pa·re·sis (pə-reé-siss, pa-, párrə-siss) *n. Pathology.* **1.** Slight or partial paralysis. **2.** General paralysis. See **general paralysis of the insane.** [New Latin, from Greek, act of letting go, from *parienai,* to loose, let fall : PARA- (beside) + *hienai,* to throw.] **—pa·ret·ic** (-réttik) *n. & adj.* **—pa·ret·i·cal·ly** *adv.*

pa·re·u (paa-ráy-ōō) *n.* A rectangular piece of cloth worn in Polynesia as a wraparound skirt or loincloth. [Tahitian.]

pa·re·ve (paárəvə) *adj.* Also **par·ve** (párvə). *Judaism.* Designating or pertaining to foods that are prepared without meat, milk, or their derivatives, and that therefore may be eaten with meat or dairy dishes. [Yiddish *parev*†.]

par ex·cel·lence (paár éksə-lonss, -lónss) *adv.* To the highest degree or epitome of something; pre-eminently. [French "by (way of) pre-eminence".]

par·fait (paar-fáy) *n.* **1.** A dessert made of cream, eggs, sugar, and flavouring frozen together. **2.** A dessert made of several layers of different flavours of ice cream garnished and served in a tall glass. [French, from *parfait,* perfect, from Latin *perfectus,* PERFECT.]

par·get (párjit) *n.* **1.** Plaster, roughcast, or any similar mixture used to coat walls or line chimneys. **2.** Ornamental plasterwork. **3.** A cement mixture used to waterproof outer walls.
—*tr.v.* **pargetted** or *U.S.* **-geted, -getting,** or *U.S.* **-geting, -gets.** To cover or adorn with parget. [Middle English *pargetten,* from Old French *parjeter,* to throw onto a surface : *par,* onto, from Latin *per* + *jeter,* to throw. See **jet** (stream).] **—par·get·ing** *n.*

par·he·lic circle (paar-heélik) *n.* A type of halo consisting of a large circle of white light lying parallel to the horizon and passing through the Sun. It is formed by reflection of sunlight by ice crystals in the atmosphere. Also called "parhelic ring". See **anthelion.**

par·he·li·on (paar-heéli-ən, -on) *n., pl.* **-helia** (-heéli-ə). *Meteorology.* A bright spot sometimes appearing to either side of the sun, often on a luminous ring or halo. Also called "mock sun", "sundog". [Latin *parēlion,* from Greek : PARA- (beside, beyond) + *hēlios,* sun.] **—par·he·lic** (-heélik, -héllik), **par·he·li·a·cal** (párhi-lī́-ək'l) *adj.*

pa·ri·ah (pə-rī́-ə, párri-ə) *n.* **1.** A social outcast. **2.** Formerly, a member of a low caste of agricultural and domestic workers in southern India and Burma. [Tamil *paṛaiyan,* drummer, from *paṛai,* drum (the pariahs having been originally a caste of drummers).]

pariah dog *n.* A **pye dog** *(see).*

Par·i·an (páir-i-ən) *adv.* **1.** Of or pertaining to the island of Paros or its inhabitants. **2.** Designating a type of white marble highly valued in ancient times for making statues. **3.** Designating a fine white porcelain.
—*n.* **1.** A native or inhabitant of Paros. **2.** Parian marble. **3.** Parian porcelain.

pa·ri·es (páir-i-eez) *n., pl.* **parietes** (pə-rī́-i-teez). *Biology.* The wall of an organ. [New Latin, from Latin *pariēs*†, wall of a room.]

pa·ri·e·tal (pə-rī́-it'l) *adj.* **1.** *Biology.* Pertaining to or forming the wall of a hollow structure. **2.** *Anatomy.* Of or pertaining to either of the parietal bones. **3.** *Botany.* Attached to the ovary wall. Said of the ovules or placenta in certain plants. [French *pariétal,* from Late Latin *parietālis,* from Latin *pariēs* (stem *pariet-*), PARIES.]

parietal bone *n. Anatomy.* Either of two large, irregularly quadrilateral bones, between the frontal and occipital bones, that together form the sides and top of the skull.

parietal lobe *n. Anatomy.* The division of each hemisphere of the brain that lies beneath each parietal bone.

par·i·mu·tu·el (párri-méwchoo-əl) *n., pl.* **pari-mutuels.** *Chiefly U.S.* A system of betting on races, or a machine that records bets under that system, a **totalisator** *(see).* [French *pari mutuel,* mutual stake.]

par·ing (páir-ing) *n. Often plural.* That which has been pared off or removed.

pa·ri pas·su (párri pássōō, paári paássōō) *adv. Latin.* With equal pace, speed, or progress; side by side: *proceed pari passu.*

Par·is¹ (párriss). *Greek Mythology.* The prince of Troy whose abduction of Helen provoked the Trojan War.

Par·is² (párriss ‖ *French* pa-reé). Capital of France and of the Paris département. It is situated on the river Seine in the north of the country and is the administrative, cultural, and commercial centre of France. Capital of France since A.D. 987, it has witnessed many revolutions, including the French Revolution of 1789, and was occupied by the Germans during World War II. Its architecture includes the churches Nôtre Dame and Sacré Cœur, the Eiffel Tower, the art galleries of the Louvre and the Jeu de Paume, and the Centre Pompidou. **—Pa·ris·i·an** (pə-rízzi-ən, -rízh'n) *adj. & n.*

Paris, Treaty of *n.* **1.** A treaty (1763) between Great Britain, France, and Spain that ended their participation in the Seven

Years' War. **2.** A treaty (1783) between Great Britain and the United States that ended the War of American Independence. In this sense, also called "Treaty of Versailles".

Paris Commune *n.* **1.** The revolutionary committee that governed Paris from 1789 to 1795. **2.** The revolutionary government of Paris from March 18 to May 28, 1871. Also called the "Commune".

Paris green *n.* A poisonous emerald-green powder, $(CuO)_3As_2O_3 \cdot Cu(Cu_2H_3O_2)_2$ used as a pigment, insecticide, and wood preservative. [After PARIS, where it was once made.]

par·ish (párrish) *n. Abbr.* **par.** **1.** In the Anglican, Roman Catholic, and some other churches, an administrative part of a diocese that has its own church. **2.** In England, a political division of a county for local civil government, usually corresponding to the ecclesiastical parish. **3.** Members of an ecclesiastical parish collectively; the community of parishioners. **—on the parish.** Formerly, receiving money or other welfare assistance, paid for and administered by the parish. [Middle English *paroche, parisshe,* from Old French *paroisse,* from Late Latin *parochia,* from Late Greek *paroikia,* from *paroikos,* Christian, from Greek, "neighbour", "sojourner", "stranger" : *para,* near, beside + *oikos,* house.]

parish clerk *n.* In the Church of England, a layperson appointed to lead the congregation in their part in church services and to help the parson with the administration of church business. The position may be amalgamated with that of **sexton** *(see).*

parish council *n.* In Britain, a civil body that administers the affairs of a parish.

pa·rish·ion·er (pə-rísh'n-ər) *n.* A member of a parish. [Middle English *parisshoner,* perhaps from Old French *paroissien,* from *paroisse,* PARISH.]

par·ish-pump (párrish-púmp) *adj.* Of or designating an idea or outlook that is blinkered or parochial.

parish register *n.* The record of births, deaths, and marriages occurring in a parish.

par·i·son (párri-sən) *n.* A mass of glass, roughly rounded after removal from the furnace and prior to being blown or shaped. [From French *paraison,* from *parer,* to prepare.]

par·i·ty¹ (párrəti) *n., pl.* **-ties.** **1.** Equality, as in amount, status, or value. **2.** Equivalence, correspondence, or resemblance. **3.** *Finance.* **a.** The equivalent in value of a sum of money expressed in terms of a different currency, at a fixed, official rate of exchange. **b.** The equivalence in value between coins of a different metal established at a fixed ratio. **c.** Equality of prices of goods or securities in two different markets. **4.** *Mathematics & Computing.* The comparative odd-even relationship between two integers. If both are odd, or both even, they are said to have the same parity; if one is odd and one even, they have different parity. Also used adjectivally: *a parity error.* **5.** *Symbol* P *Physics.* **a.** An intrinsic symmetry property of elementary particles that is characterised by the behaviour of the wave function of such particles under reflection through the origin of spatial coordinates. **b.** A quantum number, either $+1$ (even) or -1 (odd), that mathematically describes this property. [Latin *paritās* (stem *paritāt-*), from *pār,* equal.]

parity² *n.* **1.** The condition of having borne offspring. **2.** The number of children borne by one woman. [From -PAR(OUS) + -ITY.]

park (park) *n. Abbr.* **pk.** **1.** A tract of land set aside for public use, such as: **a.** An expanse of enclosed grounds, sometimes landscaped, for recreational use within or adjoining a town or city. **b.** An enclosed area of land in which wild animals are kept: *a deer park* **c.** An extensive tract of land kept in its natural state: *a national park.* **2. a.** *U.S.* A stadium or enclosed playing field: *a ball park.* **b.** *British Slang.* A soccer pitch. **3.** A country estate, especially when including extensive gardens, woods, or the like. **4.** *Military.* **a.** An area where vehicles and artillery are stored and serviced. **b.** The materiel kept in such an area.

~ *v.* **parked, parking, parks.** —*tr.* **1. a.** To put or leave (a car or other vehicle) for a time in a certain location, such as a garage or at the side of the road. **b.** To put on hold or in a queue: *Your call has been parked.* **2.** To place (a spacecraft) in a temporary orbit, a *parking orbit.* **3.** *Informal.* To place, put, set, or leave somewhere: *Park your coats on this chair.* **4.** *Military.* To assemble (artillery or other equipment) in order. —*intr.* To park a vehicle. [Middle English, from Old French *parc,* enclosure, from Medieval Latin *parricus†.* See **paddock.**]

Park (park), **Chung Hee** (1917–79). President of South Korea (1963–79). Having fought as a general in the South Korean army, he came to power in a military coup (1961), became president, and later established martial law and assumed dictatorial powers (1972), ostensibly to resist invasion by North Korea. He was assassinated.

par·ka (párkə) *n.* **1.** A hooded fur jacket worn as an outer garment by Eskimos. **2.** A similar garment of warm cloth, worn for sports or outdoor work. [Aleutian, skin, from Russian, pelt of a reindeer, from Samoyed.]

Par·ker (párkər), **Charlie,** known as **Bird** (1920–55). U.S. jazz musician. His brilliant technique as an alto saxophonist made him a legend in his own time, and influenced the next generation of musicians.

Parker, Dorothy (Rothschild) (1893–1967). U.S. comic writer, poet, and critic. She was drama critic for *Vanity Fair* (1917–20) and book critic for the *New Yorker* (1927–33). She was noted for her satirical humour as in the short stories *Here Lies* (1939).

parkin (párkin) *n.* A spicy, ginger-flavoured cake, popular especially in Northern England.

park·ing lot (párking) *n. U.S.* A car park *(see).*

parking meter *n.* A coin-operated meter monitoring the length of

time that a car has been parked adjacent to it.

parking ticket *n.* A legal summons issued for a violation of parking regulations. Also called "ticket".

Par·kin·son's disease (párkin-sənz) *n.* A progressive neurological disease of the later years, characterised by muscular tremor, slowing of movement, partial facial paralysis, peculiarity of gait and posture, and weakness. Also called "parkinsonism", "paralysis agitans", "shaking palsy". [After James *Parkinson* (1755–1824), English surgeon.]

Par·kin·son's Law *n.* A satirical observation propounded as an economic law: "Work expands to fill the time available for its completion." [After C. Northcote *Parkinson* (1909–93), British writer.]

park·land (párk-land) *n.* **1.** A stretch of land set aside for public use, or enclosed as a park. **2.** Such stretches of land collectively.

park·way (párk-way) *n. Chiefly U.S.* A wide road, often having a middle strip planted with flower or shrubs.

park·y (párki) *adj.* **-ier, -iest.** *British Informal.* Chilly; cold. Said of weather. [19th century : perhaps from PERKY.]

parl. parliamentary.

Parl. Parliament.

par·lance (párlənss) *n.* **1.** A particular manner of speaking; a specified or personal language, style, or idiom: *legal parlance.* **2.** *Archaic.* Conversation, especially a parley or debate. [Old French, from *parler,* to speak, from Medieval Latin *parabolāre,* to PARLEY.]

par·lan·do (paar-lán-dō ‖ *U.S.* -laán) Also **par·lan·te** (-tay). *adv. Music.* To be sung in a style suggestive of speech. Used as a direction. [Italian, from *parlare,* to speak, from Medieval Latin *parabolāre,* to PARLEY.] **—par·lan·do** *adj.*

par·lay (pár-li, -lay) *tr.v.* **-layed, -laying, -lays.** *U.S.* **1.** To bet (an original wager and its winnings) on a subsequent event, as in a race or contest. **2.** To manoeuvre (an asset) to great advantage: *She parlayed her physical attributes into a film career.*

~ *n. U.S.* A bet comprising the sum of an original wager plus its winnings, or a series of bets made in such a manner. [French *paroli,* a bet of this kind in faro, from Italian (Neapolitan), from *paro,* like, from Latin *pār,* equal.]

par·ley (párli) *n., pl.* **-leys.** A discussion or conference, especially between enemies over terms of truce or other matters.

~ *v.* **parleyed, -leying, -leys.** —*intr.v.* To discuss, confer, or debate, as with an enemy or over a disagreement. —*tr.* To speak or converse in (a foreign language). Often used humorously. [French *parlée,* from the past participle of *parler,* to talk, from Old French, from Medieval Latin *parabolāre,* to talk, from Late Latin *parabola,* discourse, PARABLE.]

par·lia·ment (párlə-mənt, párli-, párli-ə-) *n.* **1.** A national representative body having supreme legislative powers within the state. **2.** *Capital* P. **a.** *Abbr.* **Parl.** In Britain, the highest legislative body, made up of the sovereign, the **House of Lords** and the **House of Commons,** *(both of which see).* **b.** The people composing such a body at any one time. **c.** Any of various equivalent bodies in other countries, as in most Commonwealth countries. **d.** The lower house or chamber of such a body. [Middle English, from Old French *parlement,* from *parler,* to talk. See **parley.**]

par·lia·men·tar·i·an (párlə-men-taír-i-ən, párli-, párli-ə-, -mən-) *n.* **1.** One who is expert in parliamentary procedures, rules, or debate. **2.** *Capital* P. A supporter of Parliament, as opposed to the king, during the English Civil War; a Roundhead. **3.** Broadly, a member of a parliament.

~*adj.* Of or pertaining to the Long Parliament or to the Roundheads. **—par·lia·men·tar·i·an·ism** *n.*

par·lia·men·ta·ry (párlə-mén-təri, párli-, párli-ə-, -tri) *adj. Abbr.* **parl.** *Often capital* P. **1.** Of, pertaining to, or resembling Parliament or a parliament. **2.** Proceeding from, passed, or decreed by Parliament or a parliament. **3.** In accordance with the rules and customs of Parliament or a parliament: *Parliamentary procedure.* **4.** Having a parliament. **5.** Of or supporting Parliament during the English Civil War.

Parliamentary Commissioner for Administration *n.* In Britain, the **ombudsman** *(see).*

Parliamentary Undersecretary *n.* See **undersecretary.**

par·lour, *U.S.* **par·lor** (párlər) *n.* **1.** A room in a private home formerly reserved for the entertainment of visitors. **2.** A small room affording intimacy, such as: **a.** In a hotel, club, or the like, a room reserved for guests who desire a greater degree of privacy. **b.** In a monastery or convent, a room for receiving visitors and where conversation is permitted. **3.** *Chiefly U.S.* A room equipped and furnished for some special function or business: *a beauty parlour.*

~*adj.* Designating one who puts foward ideas, often extreme or radical, from a position of safety, and who never takes any action to promote them: *a parlour socialist.* [Middle English *parlour,* from Old French *parleur,* room used for conversation, from *parler,* to talk. See **parley.**]

parlour car *n. U.S.* A railway coach for day travel fitted with indicidual reserved seats.

parlour game *n.* A game, especially a word-game, played indoors.

parlour maid *n.* A female servant employed to wait at table during meals.

par·lous (párləss) *adj. Archaic.* **1.** Perilous; dangerous. **2.** Shrewd; cunning.

~*adv.* Extremely; very. [Middle English, variant of *perilous,* from *peril,* PERIL.] **—par·lous·ly** *adv.*

Par·ma (pármə) City of Emilia Romagna, capital of Parma province, north Italy. Situated on the river Parma and near the Apennine Mountains, it was a cultural centre in the Middle Ages.

Parma violet n. A violet, *Viola odorata sempervirens,* cultivated for its fragrant lavender flowers.

Par·men·i·des (paar-ménni-deez). (*c.* 515– *c.* 450 B.C.). Greek philosopher. The greatest of the Eleatic school, he believed that reality is unchanging, permanent, and part of the world of being, of which all that can be said is that it is. He greatly influenced Plato.

Par·me·san (pármi-zan, -zən, -zán) n. A hard, dry Italian cheese made from skim milk and usually served grated as a garnish. *~adj.* Of or from Parma. [French, from Italian *parmigiano,* of Parma.]

Par·mi·gia·ni·no (pármi-ja-néenō) (1503–40). Italian painter and etcher. His work is characterised by elongation of form and includes the *Madonna of the Long Neck* and his *Vision of St. Jerome.*

par·mi·gia·na (pármi-jáanə) adj. Prepared with parmesan cheese: *veal parmigiana.* [Italian, feminine of *parmigiano,* Parmesan.]

Par·nas·si·an[1] (paar-nássi-ən) adj. Of, pertaining to, or symbolically associated with Mount Parnassus or with the world of poetry.

Parnassian[2] n. A member of a school of late 19th-century French poets whose work is characterised by detachment and emphasis on metrical form. [*Le Parnasse contemporain,* (1866), was the name of the group's first collection of poems.] —**Par·nas·si·an** adj.

Par·nas·sus, Mount (paar-nássəss). *Greek* **Par·na·ssós** (párna-sóss). Greek mountain, 2 457 metres (8,061 feet). Situated to the north of the Gulf of Corinth, it was held sacred in ancient times to Dionysus and Apollo. The oracle of Delphi was, and the modern town is, on its south side.

Par·nell (paar-nél), **Charles Stewart.** (1846–91). Irish politician and nationalist. He was president of the Irish National Land League (1879) and was imprisoned for his obstructive behaviour in the House of Commons (1881). He fought for Irish Home Rule in Parliament and supported the unsuccessful Home Rule Bill of Gladstone.

pa·ro·chi·al (pə-rōki-əl) adj. 1. Of, supported by, or located in a parish. 2. Restricted to a narrow scope; provincial: *parochial views.* [Middle English *parochiel,* from Old French *parochial,* from Late Latin *parochiālis,* from *parochia,* PARISH.] —**pa·ro·chi·al·ism** n. —**pa·ro·chi·al·i·ty** (-ál-əti) n. —**pa·ro·chi·al·ly** adv.

par·o·dy (párrədi) n., pl. **-dies.** 1. A literary, musical, or artistic work that broadly mimics characteristics of another work or a style and holds it up to ridicule. 2. The genre or the compositon of such works; satirical mimicry. 3. That which so unconvincingly attempts to be or imitate someone or something that it becomes an unintentional mockery; a travesty: *The trial was a parody of justice.* —See Synonyms at caricature.

~tr.v. **parodied, -dying, -dies.** To make a parody of. See Synonyms at **imitate.** [Latin *parōdia,* from Greek *parōidia,* "mock-song", burlesque poem : PARA- (beside, "quasi-") + *ōidē,* song.] —**pa·rod·ic** (pə-róddik), **pa·rod·i·cal** adj. —**par·o·dist** (párrədist) n.

pa·rol (pə-rōl) n. Law. An oral utterance; word of mouth. Now used only in the phrase *by parol.*

~adj. Law. Given by word of mouth; not written: *give parol evidence.* Compare **documentary.** [French *parole,* "word", from Old French, from Vulgar Latin *paraula* (unattested), variant of Late Latin *parabola,* discourse, PARABLE.]

pa·role (pə-rōl) n. 1. Law. a. The release of a prisoner before his term has expired, on condition of continued good behaviour. b. The duration of such conditional release. Used in the phrase *on parole.* 2. A password used by a military officer of the day or an officer on guard. 3. Word of honour; especially, a promise given by a prisoner to observe the conditions of his parole. 4. Linguistics. Language as actually used, or as realised in the actual speech and writing of a speech community, as opposed to its **langue** *(see).* Compare **performance.** —**on parole.** 1. Free from prison, subject to certain conditions, as a result of parole. 2. Informal. Permitted a second chance, under close inspection, following an initial failure.

~tr.v. **paroled, -roling, -roles.** To release (a prisoner) on parole. [French, word of honour, "word", PAROL.] —**pa·ro·lee** (pə-rō-lée, párrō-) n.

par·o·no·ma·sia (párrə-nō-máy-zi-ə ‖ -zhə) n. A play on words; especially, a **pun** *(see).* [Latin, from Greek, from *paronomazein,* to call by a different name, to name besides : PARA- + *onomazein,* to name, from *onoma,* name.] —**par·o·no·mas·tic** (-mástik) adj. —**par·o·no·mas·ti·cal·ly** adv.

par·o·nym (párrənim) n. A paronymous word. [Greek *parōnumon,* from *parōnumos,* PARONYMOUS.] —**par·o·nym·ic** (-nímmik) adj.

pa·ron·y·mous (pə-rónniməss) adj. Allied by derivation from the same root; having the same stem; cognate; for example, *beautiful* and *beauteous.* [Greek *parōnumos,* derivative : PARA- (beside) + *onuma, onoma,* name.] —**pa·ron·y·mous·ly** adv.

Pá·ros (paír-oss, párross). Greek island in the Aegean Sea. Situated in the Cyclades group to the south of the Greek mainland, it is famous for its white translucent marble, used in sculpture.

pa·rot·id gland (pə-róttid) n. Either of the largest of the paired salivary glands, located below and in front of each ear. Also called "parotid". [From Greek *parōtis* (stem *parotid-*) "(tumour) near the ear" : PARA- (beside) + *ōt-,* stem of *ous,* ear.]

par·o·ti·tis (párrə-títiss) n. Also **pa·rot·i·di·tis** (pə-rótti-dítiss). Inflammation of the parotid glands, as in mumps. [PAROT(ID) + -ITIS.] —**par·o·tit·ic** (-títtik) adj.

-parous adj. comb. form. Indicates giving birth to or bearing; for example, **multiparous.** [Latin *-parus,* from *parere,* to give birth to.]

pa·rou·si·a (pə-rōō-si-ə, -rów-, -zi-ə) n. The **Second Coming** *(see).*

[Greek, "presence" : PARA- + *ousia,* being, from *einai,* to be.]

par·ox·ysm (párrək-siz'm) n. 1. A sudden outburst of emotion or action: *a paroxysm of laughter.* 2. Pathology. a. A crisis in or recurrent intensification of a disease. b. A spasm or fit; a convulsion. [French *paroxysme,* from Greek *paroxusmos,* irritation, exasperation, paroxysm, from *paroxunein,* to stimulate, irritate : PARA- (intensifier) + *oxunein,* to sharpen, goad, from *oxus,* sharp.] —**par·ox·ys·mal** (-sízm'l) adj. —**par·ox·ys·mal·ly** adv.

par·ox·y·tone (pə-rók-si-tōn, pa-) adj. In ancient Greek grammar, of or designating a word that has an acute accent on the penultimate syllable.

~n. A paroxytone word. [Greek *paroxutonos* : PARA- (beside) + *oxutonos,* OXYTONE.]

par·quet (pár-kay, -ki) n. 1. a. Parquetry. b. A floor of parquetry. 2. U.S. The stalls of a theatre, the **orchestra** *(see).*

~tr.v. **parqueted** (-kayd), **-queting** (-kay-ing), **-quets** (-kayz). 1. To furnish (a room) with a floor of parquetry. 2. To cover (a floor) with parquetry.

~adj. Made of parquetry: *a parquet floor.* [French, Old French, small enclosure, diminutive of *parc,* enclosure, PARK.]

par·quet·ry (párkitri) n., pl. **-ries.** Wood, often of contrasting colours, worked into an inlaid mosaic, used especially for floors. [French *parqueterie,* from *parquet,* theatre floor, PARQUET.]

parr (par) n., pl. **parrs** or collectively **parr.** A young salmon during the first two years of its life when it lives in fresh water. [18th century : origin obscure.]

Parr (par), **Catherine** (1512–48). Sixth wife of Henry VIII. The daughter of Sir Thomas Parr of Kendal, her marriage with Henry (1543) was her third.

parrakeet. Variant of **parakeet.**

par·ra·mat·ta, par·a·mat·ta (párrə-máttə) n. A light dress fabric made of a mixture of wool and cotton or silk. [After PARRAMATTA, where it was made.]

Par·ra·mat·ta (párrə-máttə). City of New South Wales, Australia. Situated on the Parramatta river, it is now a suburb of Sydney. It is the second oldest European settlement in Australia (founded 1790).

par·rel, par·ral (párrəl) n. Nautical. A sliding loop of rope or chain to which a running yard or gaff is fastened, permitting movement of the yard up and down the mast. [Middle English *perell,* from *parail,* equipment, aphetic variant of APPAREL.]

par·ri·cide (párri-sīd) n. 1. One who murders his father or mother or other near relative. 2. The act of committing such a murder. [Latin *parricīda* (the perpetrator) and *parricīdium* (the crime) : *parri-†,* "kin" + -CIDE.] —**par·ri·cid·al** (-sīd'l) adj.

par·rot (párrət) n. 1. Any of numerous tropical and semitropical birds of the order Psittaciformes, characterised by short, hooked bills, brightly coloured plumage, and, in some species, the ability to mimic human speech or other sounds. 2. One who mindlessly imitates the words or actions of another.

~tr.v. **parroted, -roting, -rots.** To repeat or imitate without meaning or understanding. [Dialectal French *perrot,* from Old French *perroquet,* variant of *paroquet,* PARAKEET.] —**par·rot·ry** n.

parrot-fashion (párrət-fash'n) adv. Mechanically and without true understanding: *She learnt her notes parrot-fashion.*

parrot fever n. A virus disease, **psittacosis** *(see).*

par·rot·fish (párrət-fish) n., pl. **-fishes** or collectively **parrotfish.** Any of various brightly coloured tropical marine fishes of the family Scaridae, having jaws resembling a parrot's beak.

par·ry (párri) v. **-ried, -rying, -ries.** —*tr.* 1. To deflect or ward off (a fencing thrust or sword, for example). 2. To avoid, counter, or turn aside: *parried her questions.* —*intr.* To deflect or ward off a blow.

~n., pl. **parries.** 1. An act of deflecting or warding off a blow, especially in fencing. 2. An evasive answer or action; an evasion. [French *Parez,* "Parry"! (in fencing), imperative of *parer,* to defend, parry, from Italian *parare,* from Latin *parāre,* to prepare.]

Par·ry (párri), **Sir (Charles) (Hubert) Hastings** (1848–1918). British composer. He was the director of the Royal College of Music; his works include the oratorios *Judith, Job* (1892), and *King Sa* (1894), and the choral song *Jerusalem* (1916).

parse (parz ‖ parss) v. **parsed, parsing, parses.** —*tr.* Grammar. 1. To break (a sentence) down into component parts of speech with an explanation of the form, function, and syntactical relationship of each part. 2. To describe (a word) by stating part of speech, form, and syntactical relationships in a sentence. —*intr.* To admit to being parsed: *His sentences do not parse easily.* [From Latin *pars,* part (in phrase *pars ōrātiōnis,* part of speech).] —**pars·er** n.

par·sec (pár-sek) n. Symbol **pc** A unit of length, used in astronomy, based on the distance from earth at which stellar parallax is one second of arc. It is equal to 3.2616 light-years or 3.0857×10^{13} kilometres. [PAR(ALLAX) + SEC(OND).]

Par·see, Par·si (pár-see, -sée) n. A member of a Zoroastrian religious sect, originally from Persia and now based mainly in western India. [Persian *Pārsī,* a Persian, from *Pārs,* Persia, from Old Persian *Pārsa,* PERSIA.] —**Par·see** adj. —**Par·see·ism** n.

Parsi·fal. See Percival.

par·si·mo·ni·ous (pár-si-mōni-əss) adj. Marked by parsimony. See Synonyms at **stingy.** —**par·si·mo·ni·ous·ly** adv.

par·si·mo·ny (pár-si-məni ‖ U.S. -mōni) n. 1. Unusual or excessive frugality, especially with regard to money; extreme economy. 2. Meanness; stinginess. [Middle English *parcimony,* from Latin *parsimōnia,* from *parcere* (past participle *parsus*), to spare.]

pars·ley (párssli) n. 1. A widely cultivated herb, *Petroselinum crispum,* native to the Mediterranean region, having much-divided, curled leaves that are used as a garnish and for seasoning. **2.** Any of various superficially similar plants, such as **cow parsley** *(see).* [Middle English *persely, peresil,* from Old English *petersilie* and Old French *persil, perresil,* both from Late Latin *petrosīlium,* from Latin *petroselīnum,* from Greek *petroselinon,* rock parsley : *petra,* rock + *selinon,* parsley, CELERY.]

pars·nip (párssnip) *n.* **1.** A strong-scented plant, *Pastinaca sativa,* cultivated for its long, white, edible root. **2.** The root of this plant. [Middle English *pasnepe* (influenced by *nepe,* turnip), from Old French *pasnaie,* from Latin *pastināca,* parsnip, carrot, from *pastinum*†, a kind of two-pronged dibble.]

par·son (párss'n) *n.* **1.** In the Church of England, a clergyman with full legal control of a parish under ecclesiastical law. **2.** Loosely, any clergyman. [Middle English *persone,* parish priest, from Old French, person, parson, from Medieval Latin *persōna (ecclēsiae),* "PERSON (of the church)".]

par·son·age (párss'n-ij) *n.* The official residence of a parson.

parson bird *n.* The **tui** *(see).* [Referring to the white tuft at the throat, which resembles a clerical collar.]

parson's nose *n.* The fatty end part of the rump of a cooked fowl. Also called "pope's nose".

part (part) *n. Abbr.* **p., pt. 1. a.** A portion, division, or segment of a whole; a piece: *a book in three parts.* **b.** An essential constituent; a vital element of the whole. **2.** Any of several equal portions or fractions into which a whole may be divided: *a drink of two parts gin and one part vermouth.* **3.** *Mathematics.* An aliquot part. **4. a.** An organ, member, or other division of an animal or plant. **b.** *Plural.* See **private parts. 5.** A component that can be separated from a system: *a machine part.* **6. a.** A role given to an actor to play. **b.** The words of the role as spoken. **c.** These words written down. **7.** One's proper or expected share in responsibility or obligation; a duty: *It was not my part to give advice.* **8.** *Usually plural.* Ability; talent: *a man of many parts.* **9.** *Usually plural.* A region, land, or territory: *foreign parts.* **10.** *U.S.* A hair **parting** *(see).* **11.** *Music.* **a.** Any of the melodic lines in concerted music or in harmony. **b.** The individual score for it. **—for (one's) part.** So far as one is concerned. **—for the most part.** To the greater extent; generally; mostly. **—in good part.** With good grace: *to take a joke in good part.* **—in part.** To some extent; partly. **—on the part of.** By, felt by, or done by. **—play a part. 1.** To act in a dissembling or deceitful manner. **2.** To be significant or of use. Used with *in: played a part in the revival of folk music.* **—take part.** To join in; participate. Usually used with *in: He took part in the celebration.* **—take (someone's) part.** To side with someone in a disagreement; support: *He took her part in the argument.*

~v. **parted, parting, parts.** *—tr.* **1.** To divide or break into separate pieces, portions, sections, or the like: *parted the bread.* **2.** To separate by or as if by coming between; put or keep apart: *parted the boxers.* **3.** To comb (the hair) away from a dividing line on the scalp. **4.** *Informal.* To cause to abandon or leave: *He won't be parted from the television.* *—intr.* **1.** To divide or break; come apart: *The curtain parted in the middle.* **2.** To go away from one another; separate: *parted as friends.* **3.** To separate into ways going in different directions: *The road parts in the forest.* **4.** To leave; depart. Usually used with *from.* **5.** To die. Used euphemistically. —See Synonyms at **separate. —part with.** To give up; relinquish.

~adv. Partially; in part: *part yellow, part green.*

~adj. Abbr. **p., pt.** Not full or complete; partial: *a part owner.* [Middle English, from Old French, from Latin *pars* (stem *part-*).]

part. 1. participle. 2. particular.

par·take (paar-táyk) *v.* **-took** (-tŏŏk || -tōōk), **-taken, -taking, -takes.** *—intr.* **1.** To take part or have a share; participate. Used with *in: partake in the festivities.* **2.** To take or be given part or portion. Usually used with *of: He partook of his mother's cake.* **3.** To have some quality or characteristic; show evidence. Used with *of: a nature that partook of the ferocity of the lion.* *—tr. Archaic.* To take or have part of; share. —See Synonyms at **share.** [Back-formation from *partaker,* from *part taker.*] **—par·tak·er** *n.*

par·tan (párt'n) *n. Scottish.* A crab. [Middle English of Celtic origin.]

part and parcel *n.* A basic part or essential function.

part·ed (pártid) *adj.* **1.** Separated or divided into parts; cleft. **2.** Kept apart; separated: *parted fingers.* **3.** *Botany.* Cleft almost to the base, so as to have distinct divisions or lobes; partite. **4.** *Archaic.* Deceased.

par·terre (paar-táir) *n.* A flower garden having the beds and paths arranged to form a pattern. [French, from Old French, from *par terre,* on the ground : *par,* on, from Latin *per* + *terre,* ground, from Latin *terra.*]

part exchange *n.* The system or an instance of paying for an object partly in money and partly by another object, often a second-hand object of the same type.

par·the·no·car·py (párthinō-kaarpi, paar-thēenō-) *n. Botany.* The production of fruit without fertilisation or seed production. [Greek *parthenos*†, virgin + *-carpy,* from CARPOUS.]

par·the·no·gen·e·sis (párthinō-jénni-siss) *n.* **1.** *Biology.* Reproduction of organisms in which an unfertilised egg cell develops into an individual genetically identical to its parents. **2.** Human reproduction without apparent participation of the male; virgin birth. [New Latin : Greek *parthenos*†, virgin + -GENESIS.] **—par·the·no·ge·net·ic** (-jə-néttik) *adj.* **—par·the·no·ge·net·i·cal·ly** *adv.*

Par·the·non (pártha-non, -nan) *n.* A temple dedicated to Athena on the Acropolis at Athens, built (447–32 B.C.). The Elgin Marbles formed an outside frieze.

Par·thi·a (párthi-ə). Ancient region south of the Caspian Sea. Approximating to Khorasan in modern northeast Iran, it was part of the Persian Empire, but from 250 B.C. established and expanded its own empire to control the area between the rivers Euphrates and Indus. It was eventually overthrown by the Sassanian Persians (A.D. 226). **—Par·thi·an** *n. & adj.*

Parthian shot *n.* A remark, comment, or the like, directed in or as if in retreat, in simulation of the Parthian archers who shot at the enemy while feigning flight. Also called "parting shot".

par·tial (pársh'l) *adj.* **1.** Of, pertaining to, or affecting only part; not total; incomplete: *a partial truth.* **2.** Favouring one person or side over another or others; biased; prejudiced. **3.** Having a particular liking for someone or something; especially fond. Usually used with *to: very partial to fat Turkish cigarettes and strawberries.* **4.** *Mathematics.* Of, designating, or pertaining to operations or sequences of operations, such as differentiation and integration, when applied to only one of several variables in a function at a time.

~n. **1.** In music and acoustics, a **harmonic** *(see).* **2.** *Mathematics.* A partial derivative. [Middle English *parcial,* from Old French *partial,* from Late Latin *partiālis,* from Latin *pars* (stem *part-*), PART.] **—par·tial·ness** *n.*

partial derivative *n. Mathematics.* The derivative with respect to a single variable of a function of two or more variables, regarding other variables as constants. Also called "partial".

partial eclipse *n.* An eclipse in which a celestial body is only partly obscured.

partial fraction *n.* Any of a set of fractions having an algebraic sum equal to a specified fraction, usually a ratio of polynomials.

par·ti·al·i·ty (párshi-ál-əti) *n., pl.* **-ties. 1.** The state or condition of being partial. **2.** Favourable prejudice or bias. **3.** A special fondness; a predilection: *a partiality for antiques.*

par·tial·ly (pársh'l-i) *adv.* **1.** In part; to a certain degree; partly. See Usage note at **partly. 2.** *Archaic.* **a.** In a prejudiced or biased manner. **b.** With special favour or fondness towards something or someone; with partiality.

partial pressure *n.* The individual pressure of one gas in a mixture of gases, equal to the pressure that the gas would exert if no other components were present. See **Dalton's Law.**

partial product *n. Mathematics.* A number formed in long multiplication by multiplying one number by a digit of the multiplier.

partial tone *n.* In music and acoustics, a **harmonic** *(see).*

par·ti·ble (pártəb'l) *adj.* Capable of being parted, divided, or separated; divisible. Said of estates or property. [Late Latin *partībilis,* from Latin *partīrī,* to divide, from *pars* (stem *part-*), PART.]

par·tic·i·pant (paar-tíssipənt || pər-) *n.* One who participates or takes part in something.

~adj. Participating; taking part.

par·tic·i·pate (paar-tíssi-payt || pər-) *intr.v.* **-pated, -pating, -pates.** To take part; join or share with others. Usually used with *in.* See Synonyms at **share.** [Latin *participāre,* from *particeps,* a partaker : *pars* (stem *part-*), PART + *-ceps,* "-taking".] **—par·tic·i·pance** (-pənss) *n.* **—par·tic·i·pa·tor** (-paytər) *n.*

par·tic·i·pa·tion (paar-tíssi-páysh'n || pər-) *n.* **1.** The act of participating: *participation in a game.* **2.** A taking part or sharing, such as sharing in a company's profits or influencing its decision-making: *worker participation.*

par·ti·ci·ple (párti-sipp'l, pártsip'l || paar-tissip'l) *n. Abbr.* **p., part.** *Grammar.* A nonfinite form of a verb that is used with an auxiliary verb to indicate certain tenses, and that can also function independently as an adjective; for example, in the expressions *a glowing coal* and *a beaten dog, glowing* and *beaten* are participles. See **misrelated participle, past participle, present participle.** [Middle English, from Old French *participle, participe,* from Latin *participium,* from *particeps,* partaker (translation of Greek *metokhē*). See **participate.**] **—par·ti·cip·i·al** (-síppi-əl) *adj.* **—par·ti·cip·i·al·ly** *adv.*

par·ti·cle (pártik'l) *n.* **1.** A very small piece or part; a speck: *a particle of dust.* **2.** A very small amount, trace, or degree: *not a particle of doubt.* **3.** *Physics.* **a.** A body whose spatial extent and internal motion and structure, if any, are negligible. **b.** Any very small constituent of matter. **c.** An **elementary particle** *(see).* **4.** *Grammar.* **a.** In various languages, such as ancient Greek, any of a class of forms, such as prepositions or conjunctions, consisting of a single word that has no inflection. **b.** A suffix or prefix, such as *-ness* or *in-.* **5.** *Archaic.* A small division or section of something written, such as a clause of a document. **6. a.** A small piece of a consecrated Host. **b.** Any of the smaller, individual Hosts. [Middle English, from Latin *particula,* diminutive of *pars* (stem *part-*), PART.]

particle accelerator *n. Physics.* An **accelerator** *(see).*

par·ti-col·oured (párti-kullərd) *adj.* Having different parts or sections coloured differently; pied. [Middle English *party,* particoloured, from Old French *parti,* striped, from the past participle of *partir,* to divide, from Latin *partīre,* from *pars* (stem *part-*), PART.]

par·tic·u·lar (pər-tíckew-lər, -tík-yə-) *adj. Abbr.* **part. 1.** Of, belonging to, or associated with a single person, group, thing, or category; not general or universal: *his particular beliefs.* **2.** Separate and distinct from others; specific: *I wanted a particular hat.* **3.** Worthy of note; exceptional; special: *of particular interest.* **4. a.** Especially or excessively attentive to or concerned with details or niceties; fussy: *particular about his dress.* **b.** Detailed; full: *a particular account of the events.* **5.** *Logic.* Encompassing some, but not all, of a class or group; restricted. Said of a proposition. *Some snakes are venomous*

is a particular proposition. Compare **universal.** **6.** *Mathematics.* Designating a solution of a differential equation that is distinguished from the general representation of the set of all solutions by virtue of not involving arbitrary constants.
~n. **1.** An individual item, fact, or detail: *correct in every particular.* **2.** *Plural.* Items or details of information or news: *Tell us the particulars of your trip to China.* **3.** *Logic.* A particular proposition. **—in particular.** Particularly; especially. [Middle English *particuler,* concerned with details, from Old French, from Late Latin *particulāris,* from Latin *particula,* detail, PARTICLE.]

par·tic·u·lar·ise, par·tic·u·lar·ize (pər-tíckew-lə-rīz, -tík-yə-) *v.* **-ised, -ising, -ises.** *—tr.* **1.** To state or enumerate in detail; itemise. **2.** To mention or treat individually; specify; single out. *—intr.* To give particulars. **—par·tic·u·lar·i·sa·tion** (-rī-záysh'n || *U.S.* -ri-) *n.* **—par·tic·u·lar·is·er** *n.*

par·tic·u·lar·ism (pər-tíckew-lə-riz'm, -tík-yə-) *n.* **1.** Exclusive adherence to or interest in one's own group, party, sect, or nation. **2.** A policy of allowing each state in a nation or federation to act independently. **3.** *Theology.* The belief that divine grace is reserved for a select group of people rather than for everyone. **—par·tic·u·lar·ist** *n.* **—par·tic·u·lar·is·tic** (-rístik) *adj.*

par·tic·u·lar·i·ty (pər-tíckew-lárrəti, -tík-yə-) *n., pl.* **-ties. 1.** The quality, or state, of being particular rather than general. **2.** Exactitude of detail, especially in description: *characters delineated with great particularity.* **3.** Attention to or concern with details; fastidiousness: *showed some particularity regarding his choice of friends.* **4.** A specific point or detail; a particular. **5.** *Rare.* An individual characteristic; a peculiarity.

par·tic·u·lar·ly (pər-tíckew-lər-li, -tík-yə-) *adv.* **1.** To a great degree; especially: *I particularly wanted to go for a walk.* **2.** With particular reference or emphasis; specifically: *Any colour will do, but I was thinking of blue particularly.* **3.** In a particular manner; severally; individually. **4.** With regard to particulars; in detail.

par·tic·u·late (paar-tíckew-lət, -lit, -layt) *adj.* **1.** Of, pertaining to, or formed of separate particles. **2.** *Genetics.* Designating the type of inheritance proposed by Gregor Mendel, in which characteristics are determined by discrete particles (genes). See **Mendel's laws.**

part·ing (párting) *n.* **1.** The act or process of separating or dividing. **2.** A division or separation: *the parting of the ways.* **3.** A departure or leave-taking. **4.** *British.* The line on the head where the hair is parted. Also *U.S.* "part". **5.** The act or time of a person's dying. Used euphemistically.
~adj. **1.** Given, received, or done at a departure or leave-taking: *a parting kiss.* **2.** *Literary.* Going away; leaving; departing. **3.** Dividing; separating.

parting shot *n.* A **Parthian shot** *(see).*

par·ti pris (párti prée) *n., pl.* **partis pris** (*pronounced as singular*). *French.* An opinion or decision already arrived at; a prejudice. ["Side taken".]

par·ti·san[1], par·ti·zan (párti-zán, -zan || -z'n, -s'n) *n.* **1.** A militant supporter of a party, cause, faction, person, or idea: *vociferous battle between partisans of the rival theories.* **2.** A member of a detached, often unofficially organised body of fighters who attack or harass an enemy within occupied territory; a guerrilla.
~adj. **1.** Of, pertaining to, or characteristic of a partisan or partisans. **2.** Favouring or supporting a single party or cause: *partisan politics.* [French, from Tuscan Italian *partigiano,* from *parte,* part, from Latin *pars* (stem *part-*), PART.] **—par·ti·san·ship** *n.*

par·ti·san[2], par·ti·zan (pártiz'n) *n.* A weapon, resembling a pike, having a long shaft surmounted by a blade with broad, projecting cutting edges, used chiefly in the 16th and 17th centuries. [Obsolete French *partizane,* from obsolete Italian *partesana,* "weapon used by a supporter", variant of (Tuscan) *partigiano,* PARTISAN (supporter).]

par·ti·ta (paar-téetə) *n. Music.* A set of related instrumental pieces, such as a series of variations or a suite. [Italian, from the feminine past participle of *partire.* See **partite.**]

par·tite (pár-tīt) *adj.* **1.** Divided into parts; parted. Often used in combination: *tripartite.* **2.** *Botany.* Parted. [Latin *partītus,* past participle of *partīre,* to divide, from *pars* (stem *part-*), PART.]

par·ti·tion (paar-tísh'n || pər-) *n.* **1. a.** The act or process of dividing something into parts. **b.** The state of being so divided. **2.** Something that separates, such as a thin wall dividing a larger area. **3.** A part or section into which something has been divided. **4.** *Mathematics.* **a.** An expression of a positive integer as a sum of positive integers. **b.** The decomposition of a set into a family of mutually exclusive sets. **5.** *Logic.* The analysis of a class into its component parts. **6.** *Chemistry.* The distribution of a substance between two different phases, as between two solvents. **7.** *Law.* A division of real property among joint owners or tenants.
~tr.v. **partitioned, -tioning, -tions. 1. a.** To divide into parts, pieces, or sections: *The island was partitioned.* **b.** *Law.* To divide (property) among several owners. **2.** To divide or separate by means of a partition. Often used with *off: partition an alcove off.* [Middle English *particioun,* from Old French *partition,* from Latin *partītiō* (stem *partītiōn-*) from *partīre,* to divide. See **partite.**] **—par·ti·tion·er** *n.* **—par·ti·tion·ist** *n.* **—par·ti·tion·ment** *n.*

par·ti·tive (pártitiv) *adj.* **1.** Serving to divide something into parts. **2.** *Grammar.* Indicating a part as distinct from a whole. The phrase *some of the coffee* is a partitive construction. In certain inflected languages, such constructions are put into the genitive case.
~n. Grammar. **1.** A partitive word, such as *many* or *less.* **2.** A partitive construction or case. [Medieval Latin *partītīvus,* from Latin, from *partīre,* to divide. See **partite.**] **—par·ti·tive·ly** *adv.*

part·let (párt-lit, -lət) *n.* A woman's garment worn especially in the 16th century, consisting of a covering for the neck and shoulders, and having a band or ruffle at the neck. [Middle English *patelet,* from Old French *patelete,* band of cloth, diminutive of *patte,* paw, band. See **patten.**]

part·ly (pártli) *adv.* In part; in some degree; not completely.
Usage: *Partly* and *partially* are not usually interchangeable. *Partly* has the wider application, being used primarily when the emphasis is on the part as opposed to the whole of some physical thing *(a partly finished jigsaw),* or when the meaning is "to some extent" *(He is partly to blame). Partially* indirectly emphasises the whole of a condition or state, and generally means "to a limited degree" *(The move was partially successful).*

part·ner (pártnər) *n.* **1.** A person associated with another or others in some activity of common interest, especially: **a.** A member of a business partnership. **b.** A spouse or lover. **c.** Either of two persons dancing together. **d.** Either of a pair or a team in a game or sport, such as bridge or tennis. **2.** *Usually plural. Nautical.* A wooden framework used to strengthen a ship's deck at the point where a mast or other structure passes through it.
~tr.v. **partnered, -nering, -ners. 1.** To make a partner of. **2.** To bring together as partners. **3.** To be the partner of. [Middle English *partener,* variant of *parcener,* from Anglo-French, PARCENER.]
Synonyms: *partner, colleague, ally, confederate, accomplice, associate.*

part·ner·ship (pártnər-ship) *n.* **1.** The state of being a partner; an association of partners. **2. a.** A contract entered into by two or more persons in which each agrees to share the labour and expenses in a joint business enterprise. **b.** The people involved in such a partnership. **c.** The relationship between these people.

part of speech *n. Grammar.* Any of a group of traditional classifications of words according to their functions in context. The chief ones are **noun, pronoun, verb, adjective, adverb, preposition, conjunction,** and **interjection** *(all of which see).* In addition, an **article** *(see),* is sometimes considered as belonging to this classification.

par·ton (pár-ton) *n.* A hypothetical elementary particle, such as a quark, suggested as a constituent of nucleons. [PART + -ON.]

par·took. Past tense of **partake.**

par·tridge (pártrij) *n., pl.* **-tridges** or collectively **partridge. 1.** Any of several plump-bodied Old World game birds, especially of the genera *Perdix* and *Alectoris.* **2.** *U.S.* Any of several similar or related birds. [Middle English *partrich,* from Old French *perdriz,* from Latin *perdix,* from Greek.]

par·tridge·ber·ry (pártrij-berri) *n., pl.* **-ries. 1.** A creeping, woody, evergreen plant, *Mitchella repens,* of eastern North America, having small white flowers and scarlet berries. Also called "twinberry". **2.** The fruit of this plant.

partridge wood *n.* The hard, durable, reddish-brown wood of a tropical American tree, *Andira inermis,* used for construction work and furniture. [Referring to its colour and striping.]

part song *n.* A song for three or more voice parts; especially, a short, unaccompanied piece for a choir.

part-time (párt-tīm) *adj.* For or during less than the customary time: *a part-time job.* **—part-time** *adv.* **—part-tim·er** *n.*

par·tu·ri·ent (paar-téwr-i-ənt || -tóor-) *adj.* **1.** About to bring forth young; being in labour. **2.** Of or pertaining to giving birth. **3.** About to produce or come forth with something, such as an idea or discovery. [Latin *parturiēns* (stem *parturient-*), present participle of *parturīre,* to be in labour, from *parere* (future participle *parturus*), to bear.] **—par·tu·ri·en·cy** *n.*

par·tu·ri·tion (pártewr-ísh'n) *n.* The act of giving birth; childbirth. [Late Latin *parturītiō* (stem *parturitiōn-*), from Latin *parturīre,* to be in labour. See **parturient.**]

part·work (párt-wurk) *n. British.* A series of magazines on a particular subject, issued in regular instalments, that builds up into a whole unit or book.

par·ty (párti) *n., pl.* **-ties. 1. a.** A social gathering for pleasure, amusement, or the like: *a cocktail party.* **b.** A group of persons gathered together to participate in some activity: *a sailing party.* **2.** *Sometimes capital* **P.** A permanent political group organised to promote and support its principles and candidates for public office: *the Labour Party.* **3.** *Law.* **a.** A person or group that has entered into a contract. **b.** A person or group involved in legal proceedings. **4.** A participant or accessory: *I won't be party to this corruption.* **5.** *Informal.* A person. Used humorously: *collapse of stout party!*
~adj. **1.** Of or appropriate to a social gathering or party: *a party dress; the party spirit.* **2.** Of, pertaining to, or supporting a political party. **3.** *Heraldry.* Divided into two parts. Said of a shield. [Middle English *partie,* part, party, from Old French, from the past participle of *partir,* to divide, from Latin *partīre.* See **partite.**]

party line *n.* **1.** A telephone line shared by two or more subscribers. **2.** The official policies, attitudes to particular issues, and principles of a political party to which loyal members are expected to adhere; especially, such policies, attitudes, and principles regarded as dogmatic. **—par·ty-line** (párti-līn) *adj.*

party politics *n.* Politics conducted merely for the sake of one's political party rather than for a greater cause, such as the good of the country. **—par·ty-po·lit·i·cal** (pártipə-líttik'l) *adj.*

par·ty-poop·er (párti-pōopər) *n. Chiefly U.S. Slang.* One who declines to participate enthusiastically at a social gathering.

party wall *n. Law.* A wall built on the boundary line of adjoining properties and shared by two owners or tenants.

pa·rure (pə-róor, -réwr) *n.* A set of matched jewellery or other ornaments. [French, adornment, from Old French, from *parer,* to prepare, adorn, from Latin *parāre,* to prepare.]

par value *n.* The value imprinted on a share certificate or bond which provides the basis for interest, dividend, or share of capital; face value.

Par·va·ti (paar-vaʹatee). *Hinduism.* The wife of Siva.

parve. Variant of **pareve.**

par·ve·nu (párvə-new ‖ -nōō) *n.* A person who has risen above his socioeconomic class without the background or qualifications for his new status, and is thought to be an upstart. [French, from the past participle of *parvenir,* to arrive, from Latin *parvenīre,* to come through : *per,* through + *venīre,* to come.] —**par·ve·nu** *adj.*

par·vis, par·vice (párviss) *n.* **1.** An enclosed courtyard or space in front of a palace or church. **2.** A portico or colonnade in front of a church. [Middle English *parvys,* from Old French *parvis,* from Late Latin *paradīsus,* enclosed garden, PARADISE.]

Parzival. See **Percival.**

pas (paa) *n., pl.* **pas** (paaz, *or as singular*). **1.** A dance step or series of steps. **2.** A dance. **3.** The right to go before; precedence. [French, from Latin *passus,* step, from the past participle of *pandere,* to stretch out.]

PAS, PASA para-aminosalicyclic acid.

Pas·a·de·na (pássə-deénə). City of southern California, United States. Situated northeast of Los Angeles, it is a holiday resort and has a specialised electronics industry.

pas·cal (pass-kál, -kaʹal, pásskʹl) *n. Symbol* **Pa** An SI unit of pressure equal to a pressure of one newton per square metre. [After Blaise PASCAL.]

Pas·cal (pass-kál, -kaʹal, páskʹl) *n.* A high-level computing language used for dealing with alphabetic data, and widely used as a teaching language. [After Blaise PASCAL.]

Pas·cal (pass-kál), **Blaise** (1623–62). French mathematician, philosopher, and scientist. He invented a calculating machine, discovered that the pressure in a fluid is everywhere equal (leading to the invention of the hydraulic press and the barometer), and investigated the mathematical theory of probability and the differential calculus. After religious revelations (1654) he became a Jansenist; his posthumously published *Pensées* (1670) is a study of Christian beliefs, human nature, and the inadequacy of reason.

Pascal's triangle *n.* A triangular array of numbers in which each number is the sum of the two neighbouring numbers in the row above. [After Blaise PASCAL who devised it.]

pas·chal (páskʹl, páskʹl) *adj.* Of or pertaining to the Passover or to Easter. [Middle English *paskal,* from Old French *pascal,* from Late Latin *paschālis,* from *pascha,* Passover, Easter, from Late Greek *paska,* from Hebrew *pesah,* PESACH.]

paschal lamb *n.* **1.** A lamb eaten at the feast of the Passover. **2.** *Capital P, capital L.* Jesus Christ.

pas de deux (də dö̌) *pl.* **pas de deux.** A ballet figure or dance for two persons. [French, "step for two".]

pa·se (páa-say) *n.* In bullfighting, a presentation and movement of the cape by the matador to attract, deceive, and direct the charge-of the bull. Also called "pass". [Spanish, "a passing", "pass", from *pasar,* to pass, from Vulgar Latin *passāre.* See **pass.**]

pasela. Variant of **bonsella.**

pash (pash) *n. Informal.* An infatuation. [Shortened from *passion.*]

pa·sha, pa·cha (páa-shə, pá-, pə-sháa) *n.* **1.** Formerly, a high official, especially a provincial governor, in the Ottoman Empire and various Islamic kingdoms. **2.** *Capital P.* A mode of address for or title of such an official or a person considered worthy of equal respect. When used as a title, it is placed after the surname: *Glubb Pasha.* [Turkish, probably from *baş,* chief.]

pa·sha·lik, pa·sha·lic (páashə-lik) *n.* The jurisdiction of or territory presided over by a pasha. [Turkish.]

Pash·to (púsh-tō, pásh-) *n.* **1.** An Iranian language, one of the two official languages of Afghanistan. **2.** A speaker of this language. Also called "Pushtu," "Afghan". [Persian *pashtu,* from Afghan *pashtó,* from Old Persian *parshtā-,* "one who asks".] —**Pash·to** *adj.*

Pa·siph·a·ë (pa-siffi-ee, pə-). *Greek Mythology.* The wife of Minos and mother, by a white bull, of the Minotaur.

Pas·more (páss-mawr, páass-), **(Edwin John) Victor** (1908–). British artist, founder of the London "Euston Road School" (1937). His early work shows the influence of cubism and fauvism, but after 1947 he produced colourful abstracts.

pa·so do·ble (páassō dȯblay, pássō) *n., pl.* **paso dobles.** **1.** A Latin-American ballroom dance in duple time. **2.** A piece of music to which a paso doble is danced. [Spanish, "double step".] —**pa·so do·ble** *intr.v.*

Pa·so·li·ni (pássō-léeni; *Italian* páazō-), **Pier Paolo** (1922–75). Italian film director and writer. His films, frequently concerned with religion and Marxism, include *The Gospel According to St Matthew* (1964), *Theorem* (1968), and the sordid *Salo or the 120 days of Sodom* (1975). His murder was never solved.

pasque·flow·er (pásk-flowr, -páask) *n.* Any of several plants of the genus *Anemone;* especially the Eurasian species *A. pulsatilla,* having large purple white flowers and plumed fruit. [Earlier *passe-flower* (influenced by Old French *pasque,* Easter), from Old French *passefleur : passer,* to PASS (surpass) + *fleur, flor,* FLOWER.]

pas·qui·nade (páskwi-náyd) *n.* A lampoon; especially, one posted in a public place.

—*tr.v.* **pasquinaded, -ading, -ades.** To ridicule with a pasquinade. [French, from Italian *pasquinata,* from *Pasquino,* nickname of an ancient statue in Rome on which lampoons were posted in the 16th century.] —**pas·qui·nad·er** *n.*

pass (paass ‖ pass) *v.* **passed, passing, passes.** —*intr.* **1.** To move on or ahead; proceed: *The path was too narrow for us to pass.* **2.** To run; extend: *The river passes through our land.* **3.** To carry on despite obstacles: *pass through difficult years.* **4.** To catch up with and move past; overtake: *The sports car passed on the right.* **5.** To move past in time; elapse: *The days passed quickly.* **6.** To be transferred from one to another; circulate: *The wine passed round the table.* **7.** To be communicated or exchanged: *Abusive language passed between the two candidates.* **8.** To be transferred or conveyed to another by a will, deed, or the like: *The title passed to the eldest son.* **9.** To undergo transition from one condition, form, quality, or characteristic to another: *Daylight passed into darkness; joy passed into anger.* **10.** To come to an end; be terminated; subside: *His anger passed suddenly.* **11.** To cease to exist; die. Used euphemistically. **12.** To happen; take place: *What passed during the morning?* **13.** To be allowed to happen without notice or challenge: *Let their rude remarks pass.* **14.** To gain success in a test or examination by reaching the required standard: *Every pupil passed.* **15.** To be accepted as something different. Often used with *as* or *for:* "*would have his Noise and Laughter pass for Wit*" (William Wycherly). **16.** To be approved or adopted: *The motion to adjourn passed.* **17.** *Law.* **a.** To pronounce an opinion, judgment, or sentence. Used with *on* or *upon.* **b.** *Chiefly U.S.* To sit in judicial or legal investigation. Used with *on* or *upon:* A *jury passed on that issue.* **b.** To pronounce an opinion, judgment, or sentence. Used with *on* or *upon.* **18.** *Sports.* To hit, throw, or kick a ball, for example, to a teammate. **19.** In fencing, to thrust or lunge. **20. a.** In card games, to forgo one's turn to play or bid. **b.** In quizzes, board games, and similar contests, to miss a question or round of play by declining to attempt an answer or by opting to forgo one's turn. **21.** *Informal.* To decline an offer: "*Who's for another beer?*" "*I'll pass*". —*tr.* **1.** To go by without stopping; leave behind: *passed him on the final bend.* **2. a.** *Rare.* To go by without paying attention to; let go unmentioned. **b.** *Chiefly U.S.* To fail to pay (a dividend). **3.** To go beyond; exceed: *The returns passed all expectations.* **4.** To go across; go through: *pass enemy lines.* **5. a.** To gain success in (a test or examination) by reaching the required standard: *He passed every test.* **b.** To officially allow to pass a test, examination, or the like: *The instructor passed all the candidates.* **6. a.** To cause to move: *passed his hand over the fabric.* **b.** To cause to move into a specified position: *pass a cable round a cylinder.* **c.** To cause to move as part of a process: *pass liquid through a filter.* **7.** To cause to go by: *pass soldiers in review.* **8.** To allow to go by or elapse; spend: *passed the winter in Venice.* **9. a.** To cause to be transferred from one to another; circulate: *pass the news quickly.* **b.** To hand over to someone else: *pass the bread.* **c.** To circulate (money) fraudulently: *pass counterfeit banknotes.* **d.** *Law.* To transfer title or ownership of. **10.** *Sports.* To throw, hit, or kick (a ball, for example) to a teammate. **11.** To cross over; issue from: *No secrets pass her lips.* **12.** To discharge; void (bodily waste). **13. a.** To approve; adopt: *Parliament passed the bill.* **b.** To be sanctioned, ratified, or approved by: *The bill passed the House of Commons.* **14.** To pronounce; utter: *pass judgment.* **15.** To go past without noticing. Used with *by: passed them by.* —**bring to pass.** *Archaic.* To cause to happen. —**come to pass.** *Archaic.* To happen. —**pass away. 1.** To go away in time; end; terminate. **2.** To die. Used euphemistically. **3.** To spend or while away (time). —**pass off. 1.** To offer, sell, or put into circulation (an imitation of something) as genuine. **2.** To stop gradually: *The pain eventually passed off.* **3.** To take place or occur in a specified way: *passed off very well.* **4.** To consider superficially: *passed off the remark.* —**pass on. 1.** To transmit or convey. **2.** To move on. **3.** To die. Used euphemistically. —**pass out. 1.** To distribute. **2.** *Informal.* To faint. **3.** *British.* To finish a military course. —**pass over. 1.** To leave out; overlook; disregard. **2.** To die. Used euphemistically. —**pass up.** *Informal.* To reject; let go by: *pass up an opportunity.*

—*n.* **1.** The act of passing; passage. **2.** A way through or on which one can move or travel; especially, one in the form of a narrow gap between mountain peaks. **3. a.** A permit, ticket, or authorisation to come and go at will, as at restricted premises. **b.** A free ticket entitling one to use certain forms of public transport for a stated period of time. **c.** A ticket or card entitling one to admission to a usually specified place: *A backstage pass.* **d.** Written leave of absence from military duty. **e.** In South Africa, a **reference book** (see). **4.** A sweep or run by an aircraft over an area or target. **5.** A condition or situation, often critical in nature; a predicament: *This has come to a sorry pass.* **6.** A sexual invitation or overture: *He made passes at pretty girls.* **7.** A motion of the hand or the waving of a wand in conjuring. **8.** *Sports.* A transfer of a ball, for example, by hitting, kicking, or throwing between teammates. **b.** In fencing, a lunge or thrust. **10. a.** In card games, a refusal to bid, draw, bet, or play. **b.** In quizzes, board games, and similar contests, a refusal to attempt an answer or play. **11.** In bullfighting, a positioning or flourishing of the cape; a pase. —**See Synonyms at way.**

~*interj.* Used in card games, quizzes, and the like to indicate a refusal to bid, answer, attempt a play, or the like. [Middle English *passen,* to proceed, from Old French *passer,* from Vulgar Latin *passāre* (unattested), from Latin *passus,* step, pace, stride, from the past participle of *pandere,* to stretch out.]

Usage: Passed is the spelling used for the forms of the verb *pass* (past tense and past participle): *He passed/has passed the examina-*

tion. For all other uses (adjective, adverb, preposition), the spelling is *past.* The forms can have different meanings: *Passed examinations are better than failed ones, Past examinations can be forgotten.*

pass. 1. passenger. 2. passive.

pass·a·ble (paáss-əb'l || páss-) *adj.* 1. a. Capable of being passed: *a passable law.* b. Capable of being traversed, or crossed, as a road or stream may be. 2. Acceptable for general circulation: *passable currency.* 3. Satisfactory but not outstanding. —**pass·a·ble·ness** *n.* —**pass·a·bly** *adv.*

pas·sa·ca·glia (pássə-kaál-yə, -kál-) *n.* 1. A 17th- and 18th-century musical form consisting of continuous variations on a ground bass in slow triple time. 2. A dance to this music. Compare **chaconne.** [Italian, from Spanish *passacalle* : *pasar,* to pass, from (unattested) Vulgar Latin *passāre* (see **pass**) + *calle,* street, from Latin *callis*†, path.]

pas·sage[1] (pássij) *n.* 1. The act or process of passing: a. A movement from one place to another; a going by, through, over, or across; a transit: *the passage of trains.* b. The process of elapsing: *the passage of time.* c. The process of passing from one state, condition, or stage to another; transition. d. The enactment into law of a legislative measure. 2. A journey, especially one by air or water. 3. a. The right to travel on something, especially a ship: *book a passage.* b. The price paid for this: *worked his passage.* 4. The right, permission, or power to come and go freely. 5. a. A channel or duct through, over, or along which something may pass: *the nasal passages.* b. A path, corridor or the like. 6 a. An exchange of words, arguments, or vows between two persons. b. An exchange of blows. Used in the phrase *passage at arms.* 7. A segment of a literary work: *a passage from Gibbon.* 8. *Music.* a. A segment of a composition. b. A section of a composition lacking melodic or developmental value but allowing the performer an opportunity to attempt some virtuoso playing; especially, rapid scales and arpeggios. 9. *Medicine.* An emptying of the bowels. —See Synonyms at **way.** [Middle English, from Old French, from *passer,* to PASS.]

passage[2] *v.* **-saged, -saging, -sages.** —*intr.* 1. To move sideways in response to pressure applied by the rider to the other side. Used of a horse. 2. To cause a horse to move in this way. Used of a rider. —*tr.* To cause (a horse) to passage. —**pas·sage** *n.*

passage hawk *n.* A young falcon or hawk that is captured while it is migrating.

pas·sage·way (pássij-way) *n.* A corridor.

pas·sant (páss'nt) *adj. Heraldry.* Designating a beast facing and walking towards the viewer's right with one front leg raised: *a lion passant.* [Middle English, from Old French, from the present participle of *passer,* to PASS.]

pass·book (paáss-bŏŏk || páss-, -bōōk) *n.* 1. A small book held by a depositor, as with a building society, in which deposits and withdrawals are recorded. 2. A book in which a merchant records credit sales. 3. In South Africa, a **reference book** *(see).*

Pass·chen·daele (pásh'n-dayl). Village in Flanders, west Belgium. It was the site of the third Battle of Ypres (1917) in World War I, a British offensive resulting in the loss of 245,000 British troops.

pass degree *n.* A degree given by a college or university, indicating that a candidate has reached a standard entitling him to a degree but not an honours degree.

pas·sé (pássay, paássay, pa-sáy) *adj.* 1. Out-of-date; no longer current or in fashion. 2. Past the prime; faded; aged. [French, past participle of *passer,* to pass, from Old French, to PASS.]

passe·men·terie (pass-méntri, *French* -MON-trée) *n.* Ornamental trimming for a garment, such as braid, lace, or metallic beads. [French, from *passement,* from *passer,* from Old French, to PASS.]

pas·sen·ger (pássinjər) *n. Abbr.* **pass.** 1. A person who travels in a train, aeroplane, ship, bus, or other conveyance, without participating in its operation. 2. *British Informal.* A member, as of a team, who fails to contribute sufficient effort towards the work or enterprise undertaken. 3. *Archaic.* A wayfarer or traveller.
~*adj.* Of or for passengers rather than goods: *a passenger train.* [Middle English *passyngere, passager,* from Old French *passager,* (adjective), passing, from *passage,* PASSAGE.]

passenger pigeon *n.* An extinct migratory bird, *Ectopistes migratorius,* abundant in North America until the late 19th century.

passe-par·tout (páss paar-tōō, paáss-, -pər, -tōō) *n.* 1. Something enabling one to pass or go everywhere; especially, a master key. 2. a. A mounting for a picture in which coloured tape forms the frame. b. The tape so used. 3. A mat used in mounting a picture. [French, "pass everywhere".]

passe·pied (paáss-pyáy, páss-) *n.* 1. A dance, originating in France, that resembles the minuet and became popular in England towards the end of the 17th century. 2. A piece of music for this dance. [French, "pass-foot".]

pas·ser-by (paáss-ər-bī || páss-) *n., pl.* **passers-by** (-ərz-bī). A person who passes by, often by chance and on foot.

pas·ser·ine (pássə-rīn, -reen) *n.* A bird of the order Passeriformes, which includes perching birds and songbirds such as the jays, blackbirds, finches, warblers, and sparrows. More than half of all known birds belong to this order. [Latin *passerīnus,* from *passer*†, sparrow.] —**pas·ser·ine** *adj.*

pas seul (sōl) *n.* A dance or ballet figure performed by one person. [French, "step by oneself".]

pas·si·ble (pássib'l) *adj.* Capable of suffering; sensitive. [Middle English, from Old French, from Medieval Latin *passibilis,* from Latin *patī* (past participle *passus*), to suffer.] —**pas·si·bil·i·ty** (-bílləti) *n.*

pas·sim (pássim) *adv.* Throughout; frequently. Used in textual annotation to indicate that the word or passage occurs frequently in the work cited. [Latin *passim,* here and there, everywhere, scattered about, adverbial formation from *pandere,* to spread out, scatter.]

pass·ing (paáss-ing || páss-) *adj.* 1. Of brief duration; transitory: *a passing fancy.* 2. Cursory; superficial; casual: *a passing glance.* 3. *Archaic.* Very; great: " *'Tis a passing shame.*" (Shakespeare).
~*adv. Archaic.* Very; surpassingly: *passing rich.*
~*n.* 1. The act of one that passes or the state of having passed. 2. A place where or a means by which one can pass. 3. Death. Used euphemistically. —**in passing.** Casually or briefly, in the course of speaking about or doing something else: *mentioned in passing.*

passing bell *n.* A **death knell** *(see).*

passing note *n. Music.* A note that is not part of a particular melodic sequence but is placed between two notes or chords to provide a smooth transition from one to the other.

passing shot *n.* In tennis, a shot that is hit beyond the reach of an opponent at the net.

pas·sion (pásh'n) *n.* 1. Any powerful emotion or appetite, such as love, joy, hatred, anger, or greed. 2. a. Ardent adoring love. b. Strong sexual desire; lust. c. The object of such love or desire. 3. a. Boundless enthusiasm: *a passion for travelling.* b. The object of such enthusiasm. 4. An abandoned display of emotion, especially of anger: *a passion of remorse.* 5. *Archaic.* Passivity, as opposed to action. 6. *Archaic.* Martyrdom. 7. *Capital* **P.** a. The sufferings of Christ in the period following the Last Supper and including the Crucifixion. b. A narrative of this (as in any of the Gospels), or a musical setting or serial pictorial representation of it. —See Synonyms below and at **feeling.** [Middle English, from Old French, from Late Latin *passiō* (stem *passiōn-*), (translation of Greek *pathos*), suffering, from Latin *patī* (past participle *passus*), to suffer.] —**pas·sion·less** *adj.* —**pas·sion·less·ly** *adv.*
Synonyms: *passion, fervour, enthusiasm, zeal, ardour.*

pas·sion·al (pásh'n'l) *adj.* Of or pertaining to passion.
~*n.* A book relating the sufferings of saints and martyrs.

pas·sion·ate (pásh'n-ət, -it) *adj.* 1. Capable of or having intense feelings. 2. Easily angered; bad-tempered. 3. Amorous; lustful. 4. Showing or expressing strong emotion; ardent: *a passionate speech against injustice.* 5. Arising from or marked by passion: *a passionate rage.* —**pas·sion·ate·ly** *adv.*

pas·sion·flow·er (pásh'n-flowr) *n.* Any of various chiefly tropical American vines of the genus *Passiflora,* usually having large, showy flowers. Some species bear edible fruit. See **granadilla.** [From the imagined resemblance of its parts to aspects of Christ's Passion such as the crown of thorns, the nails, and the cross.]

passion fruit *n.* The edible fruit of the passionflower. Also called "granadilla".

Passion play *n.* A play representing the Passion of Christ.

Passion Sunday *n.* The last Sunday but one before Easter.

Pas·sion·tide (pásh'n-tīd) *n.* The fortnight between Passion Sunday and Easter.

Passion Week *n.* 1. The week between Passion Sunday and Palm Sunday. 2. See **Holy Week.**

pas·sive (pássiv) *adj.* 1. Receiving or subjected to an action without responding or initiating an action in return. 2. Accepting without objection or resistance; submissive; compliant: *passive obedience.* 3. Not participating, acting, or operating; inert. 4. *Finance.* Designating certain bonds or shares that do not bear interest. 5. *Abbr.* **pass.** *Grammar.* Designating a verb form or voice used to indicate that the grammatical subject is the object of the action or the effect of the verb; for example, in the sentence *They were impressed by his manner,* the verb *were impressed* is in the passive voice. 6. *Chemistry.* Rendered inactive. Said of metals that form a protective coating that prevents further reaction. 7. *Electronics.* a. Having no source of power. b. Not amplifying or controlling a signal. 8. Designating or relating to an aerial, satellite, or other device that receives or reflects radio waves, without emitting them. Compare **active.** —See Synonyms at **inactive.**
~*n. Abbr.* **pass.** *Grammar.* 1. The passive voice. 2. A verb or construction in this voice. [Middle English, from Latin *passīvus,* capable of suffering, from *patī* (past participle *passus*), to suffer.] —**pas·sive·ly** *adv.* —**pas·sive·ness, pas·siv·i·ty** (pa-sívvəti, pə-) *n.*

passive euthanasia *n.* Euthanasia effected by the withholding of treatment that would prolong the patient's life.

passive resistance *n.* Resistance to authority or law by nonviolent methods, such as refusal to comply or peaceful demonstrations.

passive smoking *n.* The inhaling of the smoke from the cigarettes, cigars, or pipes of others, regarded as a health hazard.

pas·siv·ism (pássiviz'm) *n.* 1. Passive character or behaviour. 2. The theory and practice of passive resistance. —**pas·siv·ist** *n.*

pass·key (paáss-kee || páss-) *n.* Any of various kinds of keys, such as a **master key** or **skeleton key** *(both of which see).*

pass laws *pl.n.* In South Africa, the laws and by-laws regulating black people's rights of movement and domicile. See **reference book.**

Pass·o·ver (paáss-ōvər || páss-) *n. Judaism.* A festival beginning on the evening of the 14th of Nisan and traditionally celebrated for eight days. It commemorates the escape of the Jews from Egypt. Exodus 12. Also called "Pesach", "Pesah". See **Seder.** [From the phrase *pass over,* translation of Hebrew *pesaḥ,* PESACH.]

pass·port (paáss-pawrt || páss-, -pōrt) *n.* 1. An official document issued by a government that certifies the identity and citizenship of an individual and grants him permission to travel abroad. 2. A permit issued by a foreign country allowing one to transport goods or to travel through that country. **3.** An official document issued to a ship, especially a neutral merchant ship in time of war, authorising it to leave port, or to enter certain waters freely. **4.** Anything that enables one to be admitted or accepted: *His wit was his passport into high society.* [French *passeport,* safe-conduct, permission to pass through a port : *passer,* to PASS + PORT.]

pas·sus (pássəss) *n., pl.* **passus** or **-suses.** A section or division of a story, poem, or the like, especially in medieval literature. [Latin, a stretch, section, from past participle of *pandere,* to stretch.]

pass·word (paàss-wurd || páss-) *n.* A secret word or phrase that certifies the speaker's identity, membership, or right to be admitted.

past (paast || past) *adj.* **1.** No longer current; gone by; finished. **2.** Having existed or occurred in, or belonging to, an earlier time; bygone: *past events.* **3.** Just gone by or elapsed: *in the past month.* **4.** Having served formerly in some official capacity: *a past president.* **5.** *Grammar.* Of, pertaining to, or designating a verb tense or form used to express an action, event, or condition completed or begun prior to the time it is expressed.
—*n.* **1. a.** The time before the present. Preceded by *the*: *in the past.* **b.** That which has occurred in the past: *came to terms with the past.* **2. a.** Former background, career, experiences, and activities: *a distinguished past.* **b.** A former period of someone's life kept secret, especially so that his or her reputation may be maintained: *a man with a past.* **3.** *Grammar.* **a.** The past tense. **b.** A verb form in the past tense.
—*adv.* **1.** Earlier than the present time; ago: *forty years past.* **2.** So as to pass by or go beyond: *He waved as he walked past.*
—*prep.* **1.** Beyond in time; later than; after: *It is past midnight.* **2. a.** Beyond in position: *the lake past the meadow.* **b.** Moving beyond: *drove past the wreckage.* **3.** Beyond the power, scope, extent, or influence of: *The problem is past understanding.* **4.** Beyond the number or amount of: *The child couldn't count past 20.* **—past it.** Unable to do those things which one could do in the past; no longer capable. **—would not put it past (someone).** To regard someone as having such competence, or of being of such a nature, as to be capable of a particular action or achievement. [Middle English *passed, past,* from the past participle of *passen,* to PASS.]

pas·ta (pástə || *chiefly U.S.* paàstə) *n.* **1.** Paste or dough made of flour and water, used dried, as in macaroni, or fresh, as in ravioli. **2.** A prepared dish of pasta. [Italian, from Late Latin, PASTE.]

paste[1] (payst) *n.* **1.** A smooth viscous adhesive, such as flour and water or starch and water, used to join light materials, such as paper and cloth. **2.** Any similar soft, smooth, thick mixture. Often used in combination: *toothpaste.* **3.** A smooth dough of water, flour, and butter or other shortening, used in making pastry. **4.** A food that has been pounded until it is reduced to a smooth, creamy mass: *anchovy paste.* **5.** A sweet, doughy confection: *almond paste.* **6.** Moistened clay used in making porcelain or pottery. **7. a.** A hard, brilliant glass used in making artificial gems. **b.** A gem made of this glass. In this sense, also called "strass".
—*tr.v.* **pasted, pasting, pastes.** **1.** To cause to adhere by applying paste. **2.** To cover with something to which paste has been applied: *He pasted the wall with posters.* [Middle English, from Old French, from Late Latin *pasta,* dough, paste, from Greek *pastē,* barley porridge, from *pastos,* sprinkled, from *passein,* to sprinkle.]

paste[2] *tr.v.* **pasted, pasting, pastes.** *Slang.* To punch, beat, or hit. [Alteration of BASTE (to beat).]

paste·board (páyst-bawrd || -bōrd) *n.* **1.** A thin, firm board made of sheets of paper pasted together or of pressed paper pulp, used especially to make book covers. **2.** *Slang.* **a.** A ticket. **b.** A playing card. **c.** A visiting card.
—*adj.* **1.** Made of pasteboard. **2.** Weak and pliable; flimsy. **3.** Fake; counterfeit.

pas·tel (pást'l, pa-stél) *n.* **1.** A picture or sketch drawn with crayons made of ground and mixed pigment, chalk, water, and gum. **2. a.** The dried paste used to make such crayons. **b.** A crayon of this material. **3.** The art or process of drawing with such crayons. **4.** A soft, delicate hue; a light tint. **5.** A sketchy or brief prose work. [French, from Italian *pastello,* from Late Latin *pastellus,* woad dye, crayon, diminutive of *pasta,* PASTE (referring to the paste of decocted woad twigs).] **—pas·tel** —*adj.* **—pas·tel·ist, pas·tel·list** *n.*

pas·tern (páss-tern, -tərn) *n.* **1.** The part of a horse's foot between the fetlock and hoof. **2.** The bone comprising this part. In this sense, also called "pastern bone". **3.** A comparable part of the leg of a dog or other quadruped. [Middle English *pastron,* a horse's hobble, hence the part of the leg to which it is attached, from Old French *pasturon,* variant of *pasture,* a hobble, from Late Latin *pāstōria,* a sheep's hobble, from *pāstor,* PASTOR.]

Pas·ter·nak (pástər-nak; *Russian* pəsteer-nák), **Boris (Leonidovich)** (1890–1960). Russian author and translator. His *Dr. Zhivago* (1957), a novel of disillusionment with the Russian Revolution was banned by the Soviet authorities. Expelled by the Soviet Writers' Union (1958), he was forced to refuse the Nobel prize.

paste-up (páyst-up) *n.* **1.** Any composition of light, flat objects pasted on a sheet of paper or other backing; a collage. **2.** *Printing.* A layout of type proofs, artwork, or both, exactly positioned and prepared for making a printing plate. Also *U.S.* "mechanical".

Pas·teur (pa-stőr), **Louis** (1822–95). French microbiologist and chemist. The founder of modern microbiology, he became professor at the Sorbonne (1867) and discovered that microorganisms in the air were responsible for fermentation in beer and milk. In investigating ways of excluding these organisms, he developed the process of pasteurisation. He also developed vaccines for anthrax, rabies, and chicken cholera.

pas·teur·i·sa·tion (paàss-tər-ī-záysh'n, páss-, -chər, -tewr- || *U.S.* -i-) *n.* The process of destroying most disease-producing microorganisms and limiting fermentation in milk, beer, and other liquids by application of heat. [Invented by Louis PASTEUR.]

pas·teur·ise, pas·teur·ize (paàss-tər-īz, páss-, -chər-, -tewr-) *tr.v.* **-ised, -ising, -ises.** To subject (a liquid, especially milk) to pasteurisation. **—pas·teur·is·er** *n.*

Pasteur treatment *n.* A rabies treatment in which the growth of antibodies is stimulated during the incubation of the disease by increasingly strong inoculations of the attenuated rabies virus. Also called "pasteurism". [After Louis PASTEUR.]

pas·tic·cio (pa-stích-ō, -steéch-) *n., pl.* **-ci** (-ee). A work, especially of music, produced by borrowing fragments or motifs from various sources; a potpourri. [Italian, "pasty", "hotchpotch", from Medieval Latin *pastīcius,* pasty, from Late Latin *pasta,* PASTE.]

pas·tiche (pa-steésh, páss-teesh) *n.* **1.** A dramatic, literary, or musical piece openly imitating the previous work of another artist, often with satirical intent. **2.** A hotchpotch; a pasticcio. [French, from Italian *pasticcio,* PASTICCIO.]

pas·tille (páss-til, -teel, -t'l, pa-steél) *n.* Also **pas·til** (-til, -t'l). **1.** A small medicated or flavoured tablet; a lozenge. **2.** A tablet containing aromatic substances, burned to fumigate or deodorise the air. **3.** A paste or pastel for making crayons. **4.** A pastel crayon. [French, from Latin *pāstillus,* roll, diminutive of *pānis,* bread.]

pas·time (paàss-tīm || páss-) *n.* An activity that occupies one's time pleasantly; something that interests, amuses, or diverts.

pas·ti·na (pa-steénə) *n.* Tiny pieces of macaroni, usually cooked in soups or used as baby food. [Italian, diminutive of *pasta,* pasta, from Late Latin, PASTE.]

pas·tis (pa-steéss) *n.* An alcoholic drink flavoured with anise. [French *pastis*†.]

past master *n. Abbr.* **P.M.** **1.** One who has formerly held the position of master in an organisation such as a lodge or club. **2.** A person thoroughly experienced and skilled in a particular craft.

pas·tor (paàss-tər || páss-) *n.* **1.** A Christian minister in the capacity of having spiritual charge over a congregation or other group. **2.** *Rare.* A shepherd. **3.** A starling, *Sturnus roseus,* of south Europe and Asia, having a pink and black plumage. In this sense, also called "rosy pastor". [Middle English *pastour,* from Old French, from Latin *pāstor,* shepherd, from *pāscere* (past participle *pāstus*), to graze, feed. Sense 1 arises from a recurrent Biblical metaphor, seen in Psalms 23:1, John 10:11 and 21:15.]

pas·tor·al (paàss-tərəl, páss-) *adj.* **1.** Of or pertaining to shepherds, herdsmen, and others directly involved in animal husbandry. **2.** Used for pasture. Said of land. **3. a.** Of or pertaining to the country or country life; rural. **b.** Having the qualities of idealised country life, such as charming simplicity and a leisurely, carefree pace. **4.** Of or designating an artistic work that portrays country life in this way. **5.** Designating a branch of theology dealing with the relations between religious truth and spiritual needs or clerical duties. **6.** Of or pertaining to a pastor or his duties. —See Synonyms at **rural.**
—*n.* **1.** A literary or other artistic work that portrays rural life, usually in an idealised manner. **2.** A letter from a pastor such as a bishop, to those in his care. **3.** *Music.* A pastorale. [Middle English, from Latin *pāstōrālis,* from *pāstor,* shepherd, PASTOR.] **—pas·tor·al·ism** *n.* **—pas·tor·al·ly** *adv.*

pas·to·rale (pástə-raàl, -raàli || -rál) *n., pl.* **-rali** (-raàlee) or **-rales.** *Music.* **1.** An opera or other vocal composition based on a rural theme or subject. **2.** An instrumental composition with a tender melody in a moderately slow rhythm, suggestive of idyllic rural life. Also called "pastoral". [Italian, from *pastorale,* pastoral, from Latin *pāstōrālis,* PASTORAL.]

pas·tor·al·ist (paàss-tərə-list, trə- || páss-) *n.* **1.** *Australian.* A sheep farmer or cattle farmer. **2.** *Rare.* One who writes pastorals.

pastoral staff *n.* A **crosier** *(see).*

pas·tor·ate (paàstə-rət, -rit || pástə-) *n.* **1.** The office, rank, or jurisdiction of a pastor. **2.** A pastor's term of office with one congregation. **3.** A body of pastors; pastors collectively.

past participle *n. Abbr.* **pp., p.p.** A verb form indicating past or completed action or time. It is used as a verbal adjective in phrases such as *finished work, baked beans,* and with auxiliaries to form the passive voice or perfect and pluperfect tenses in constructions such as *The work was finished.* Also called "perfect participle".

past perfect *adj.* Designating a verb tense, the **pluperfect** *(see).*
—*n.* **1.** The pluperfect tense. **2.** A verb in this tense.

pas·tra·mi (pə-straàmi) *n.* A highly seasoned smoked beef, usually cut from the breast or shoulder. [Yiddish, from Romanian *pastramă,* from *păstra*†, to preserve.]

pas·try (páystri) *n., pl.* **-tries.** **1.** A baked paste, of any of various kinds, made from flour, water, and shortening, sometimes with egg yolk, used for the crusts of pies, tarts, and the like. **2.** Baked foods collectively, such as pies or tarts, made with this paste. **3.** An individual cake or turnover made of flaky pastry, usually topped with icing, and having a sweet filling. [From PASTE.]

past tense *n.* A verb tense used to express an action, event, or condition that occurred or began in the past. For example, in *While she was sewing, he read aloud,* the verbs *was sewing* and *read* are in the past tense.

pas·tur·age (paàss-chər-ij, -tewr- || páss-) *n.* **1.** The grass or other vegetation eaten by grazing animals. **2. a.** Land covered with such grass or vegetation. **b.** A particular piece of such land. **c.** The right to graze cattle on such land. **3.** The business of grazing cattle.

pas·ture (paàss-chər, -tewr || páss-) *n.* **1.** The grass or other vegetation eaten as food by grazing animals. **2. a.** Land on which such vegetation grows. **b.** A particular piece of such land.
~v. **pastured, -turing, -tures.** *—tr.* **1.** To herd (animals) into a pasture to graze. **2.** To provide (animals) with pasturage. Used of land. **3.** To feed on (vegetation). Used of animals. **4.** To use (land) for animals to graze on. *—intr.* To graze in a pasture. [Middle English, from Old French, from Late Latin *pāstūra,* from Latin *pāscere* (past participle *pāstus*), to pasture, feed.] **—pas·tur·a·ble** *adj.* **—pas·tur·er** *n.*

past·y[1] (páysti) *adj.* **-ier, -iest. 1.** Resembling paste in colour or consistency. **2.** Pale and lifeless-looking. Said of the face or complexion. **—past·i·ness** (páysti-nəss, -niss) *n.*

pas·ty[2] (pásti, paásti) *n., pl.* **-ties.** *Chiefly British.* A pie consisting of an envelope of pastry with a filling of seasoned meat and sometimes vegetables, or of jam or fruit. [Middle English *pastee,* from Old French *paste,* from noun, dough, PASTE.]

past·y[3] (páysti) *n., pl.* **-ies.** Either of the patches used by a striptease performer to conceal her nipples. [From PASTE (to stick).]

PA system *n.* A **public-address system** *(see).*

pat[1] (pat) *v.* **patted, patting, pats.** *—tr.* **1. a.** To tap gently with the open hand or with something flat. **b.** To tap or stroke lightly as a gesture of affection. **2.** To mould by tapping gently with the hands or a flat implement. *—intr.* **1.** To run or walk with a tapping sound. **2.** To hit something or against something gently or lightly.
~n. **1.** A light stroke or tap. **2.** The sound made by such a stroke or tap, or by light footsteps. **3.** A small mass of something, shaped by or as if by patting: *a pat of butter.* **—pat on the back.** *Informal.* A compliment, especially when intended as an encouragement. [Middle English *patte* (probably imitative).]

pat[2] *adj.* **1.** Timely; opportune; fitting: *a pat answer.* **2.** Needing no change; exactly right. **3.** Glib; somewhat insincere: *Her reply was too pat to be convincing.*
~adv. Informal. **1.** Without changing position; steadfastly. **2.** Perfectly; precisely; aptly. **—have off pat.** *Informal.* To know or have memorised completely. **—stand pat.** *Chiefly U.S. Informal.* **1.** To refuse to change one's position or opinion. **2.** To decline to draw more cards to a poker hand. [Probably "with a hitting stroke", from PAT (to tap).] **—pat·ly** *adv.* **—pat·ness** *n.*

pat[3] *n.* **—on (one's) pat.** *Australian Slang.* One one's own; alone. [Rhyming slang, short for *Pat Malone.*]

Pat *n. Informal.* An Irishman. [Short for *Patrick,* a very common Christian name in Ireland.]

pat. patent; patented.

pa·ta·gi·um (pə-táy-ji-əm) *n., pl.* **-gia** (-ji-ə). *Zoology.* **1.** A thin membrane extending between the fore and hind limb to form a wing or winglike extension, as in bats and flying squirrels. **2.** An expandable, membranous fold of skin between the wing and body of a bird. [New Latin, from Latin, gold edging on a woman's tunic, from Greek *patageion* (unattested), "clattering gold braid", from *patagos,* a clatter (imitative).]

Pat·a·go·ni·a (páttə-gṓni-ə). Region of South America in Argentina and Chile. Extending southwards from the Río Colorado to the Straits of Magellan, it is a cool, semiarid plateau at the foot of the Andes. The chief occupation is the raising of sheep, and its mineral wealth includes oil, iron ore, and coal. **—Pat·a·go·ni·an** *adj. & n.*

pat·ball (pát-bawl) *n. Informal.* A game, especially tennis, when played at an unexpectedly low level of competence.

patch (pach) *n.* **1.** A small piece of material affixed to another, larger piece to conceal or reinforce a weakened or worn area. **2. a.** Any small piece of cloth used for patchwork. **b.** *Military.* A small cloth badge affixed to a sleeve or lapel to indicate the unit to which one belongs. **3.** A dressing or bandage applied to protect a wound or sore, or to allow a substance to pass through the skin into the body. **4.** A small pad or shield of cloth worn over an injured eye or to conceal a missing eye. **5.** A **beauty spot** *(see).* **6. a.** A small piece of land. **b.** *U.S.* The produce grown on such a piece of land: *a patch of beans.* **7.** *Informal.* A district for which a policeman, or a group of policemen, is responsible. **8.** A small part or section of a surface that differs from or contrasts with the whole: *The flowers made white patches against the grass.* **9.** A discoloured area on the skin or mucous membrane. **10.** A small piece or part of anything: "*that little patch of blue which prisoners call the sky*" (Oscar Wilde). **11.** A period of experience of a specified type: *went through a bad patch after the divorce.* **—not a patch on.** *Informal.* Not comparable to; not nearly as good as.
~tr.v. **patched, patching, patches. 1. a.** To put a patch or patches on, especially when mending clothes. **b.** To be a patch for or on. Used of material. **2. a.** To make by sewing scraps of material together: *patch a quilt.* **b.** To make by piecing various elements together, especially hastily: *They patched a plan together.* **3.** To mend, repair, or put together, especially hastily, clumsily, or poorly: *patching old costumes for the tour.* **4.** *Electronics & Computing.* To join up (circuits) temporarily by a connected board into which plugs may be fitted. **—patch up.** To settle; make up: *They patched up their quarrel.* [Middle English *pacche,* perhaps variant of *peche,* from Old French *pece, pieche,* PIECE.] **—patch·a·ble** *adj.* **—patch·er** *n.*

patch board *n. Electronics.* A **plugboard** *(see).*

patch·ou·li, pach·oo·li (páchōōli, pə-chṓōli) *n., pl.* **-lis.** Also **patch·ou·ly** *pl.* **-lies. 1.** Any of several Asiatic trees of the genus *Pogostemon,* especially *P. patchouly* and *P. cablin,* having leaves that yield a fragrant oil used in the manufacture of perfumes. **2.** A perfume made from this oil. [Tamil *paccilai* : *paccu,* green + *ilai,* leaf.]

patch pocket *n.* A pocket consisting of a patch of material sewn onto the outside of a garment, as on a shirt or a pair of jeans, rather than inset through a slit in the fabric.

patch test *n.* A test for allergic sensitivity made by applying a suspected allergen to the skin in a small surgical pad.

patch·work (pách-wurk) *n.* **1.** Needlework consisting of various coloured patches of material sewn together, as in a quilt. **2.** A collection of miscellaneous or incongruous parts; a jumble: *a patchwork of outmoded theories.*

patch·y (páchi) *adj.* **-ier, -iest. 1.** Made up of or marked by patches: *a patchy pair of trousers.* **2.** Uneven in quality or performance: *patchy work.* **—patch·i·ly** *adv.* **—patch·i·ness** *n.*

patd. patented.

pate (payt) *n.* **1.** The head; especially, the top of the head: *a bald pate.* **2.** The brains; the intellect. [Middle English *pate*†.]

pâte (paat) *n.* Paste used in making porcelain and pottery. [French, patty, paste, from Old French *paste,* PASTE.]

pâ·té (páttay, pátti, *French* paa-táy) *n.* **1.** A firm meat paste often made with liver. **2.** A firm paste made of other ingredients, such as fish or vegetables. **3.** A small pastry filled with meat or fish. [French *paté(e),* from Old French *pasté(e),* from *paste,* PASTE.]

pâté de foie gras (də fwaá graá) *n.* A rich paste made from livers of specially fattened geese, usually flavoured with truffles. Also called "foie gras". [French, "pâté of fat liver".]

pa·tel·la (pə-téllə) *n., pl.* **-tellae** (-téllee). **1. a.** A flat, triangular bone located at the front of the knee joint. Also called "kneecap". **b.** *Biology.* Any dish-shaped formation. **2.** An ancient Roman pan or dish. [Latin, diminutive of *patina,* plate. See **paten.**] **—pa·tel·lar, pa·tel·late** (-tél-ət, -it, -ayt) *adj.*

pa·tel·li·form (pə-télli-fawrm) *adj.* Shaped like a pan, dish, or cup: *the patelliform shell of the limpet.* [New Latin *patelliformis* : PATELL(A) + -FORM.]

pat·en, pat·in (pátt'n) *n.* **1.** A plate, especially one used to hold the Eucharistic bread. **2.** A thin disc of metal. [Middle English *paten, pat(e)yn,* from Old French *patene,* from Latin *patina,* dish, pan, from Greek *patanē.*]

pa·ten·cy (páyt'n-si) *n.* **1.** The state or quality of being obvious. **2.** The state of being open.

pa·tent (páyt'nt, pátt'nt. *Note. Although the pronunciation* (páyt'nt) *is the general one in Britain,* (pátt'nt) *is preferred for the technical senses 1–3.) n. Abbr.* **pat. 1. a.** A grant made by a government to an inventor, assuring him the sole right to make, use, and sell his invention for a certain period of time. **b.** The official document certifying such a grant, **letters patent** *(see).* **2.** Something that is protected by such a grant. **3. a.** In the United States, a grant made by a government to an individual, conveying to him fee-simple title to public lands. **b.** The official document of such a grant. **c.** The land so granted. **4.** A sign or piece of evidence that one is entitled to possess something or has a certain quality, for example: *a patent of respectability.*
~adj. (for senses 2, 3, 6, 7, 8 usually páyt'nt) **1.** Open to general inspection; unsealed. Used chiefly in the phrase *letters patent.* **2.** Obvious; plain: *His insincerity was patent.* **3.** *Informal.* Ingenious; well-thought-out; well-constructed. **4.** *Abbr.* **pat.** Protected by a patent. **5.** *Abbr.* **pat.** Of, pertaining to, or dealing in patents: *patent law.* **6.** *Biology.* Spreading open; expanded. **7.** *Anatomy.* Open; unobstructed. Said of vessels, ducts, and other hollow parts. **8.** Ground and polished on both sides of the glass.
~tr.v. **patented, -enting, -ents.** *Abbr.* **pat. 1.** To obtain a patent on. **2.** To grant a patent to. [As noun, Middle English *(letters) patente,* letters patent, from Old French *(lettres) patentes,* from Medieval Latin *(litterae) patentes,* "open letter or document", from *patentes,* plural of *patens,* open, from the present participle of *patēre,* to be open.] **—pa·tent·a·bil·i·ty** (-ə-bílləti) *n.* **—pa·tent·a·ble** *adj.*

pa·tent·ee (páyt'n-teé, pátt'n-) *n.* A person who has been granted a patent.

patent leather (páyt'nt) *n.* **1.** Black leather finished to a hard, glossy surface. **2.** Any of several synthetic materials having a similar appearance. [Made by a once-patented process.]

patent log (*usually* páyt'nt) *n. Nautical.* A torpedo-shaped instrument with rotary fins that is dragged from the stern of a vessel to measure the speed or distance travelled. Also called "screw log", "taffrail log".

pa·tent·ly (páyt'nt-li, *rarely* pátt'nt-) *adv.* Obviously; clearly; plainly.

patent medicine *n.* (*usually* páyt'nt) A drug or other medical preparation that is protected by a patent and can be bought without a prescription. Not in technical usage.

Patent Office (*usually* pátt'nt) *n.* A government department in which claims for patents are studied and patents are issued and recorded.

pat·en·tor (páyt'n-tər, pátt'n-, -tór) *n.* One that grants a patent.

patent right (pátt'nt, páyt'nt) *n.* The right granted by a patent; especially, the right to have exclusive manufacture and sale of an invention.

pa·ter (páytər) *n. British.* Father. Usually used humorously. [Latin.]

Pater, Walter (Horatio) (1839–94). British critic and essayist. A humanist and believer in "art for art's sake". His works include *Imaginary Portraits* (1887) and *Plato and Platonism* (1893).

pa·ter·fa·mil·i·as (páytər-fə-mílli-ass, páttər-) *n., pl.* **patresfamilias** (páytreez-, páttreez-). The father of a family considered as head of the household. [Latin : *pater,* father + *familiās,* archaic genitive of *familia,* FAMILY.]

pa·ter·nal (pə-térn'l) *adj.* **1.** Of, pertaining to, or characteristic of a father; fatherly. **2.** Received or inherited from one's father. **3.** Related through one's father. [Medieval Latin *paternālis,* from Latin *paternus,* fatherly, from *pater,* father.] **—pa·ter·nal·ly** *adv.*

pa·ter·nal·ism (pə-térn'l-iz'm) *n.* A policy or practice of managing or governing people in a fatherly manner, especially by providing for their needs without giving them responsibility. **—pa·ter·nal·is·tic** (-ístik) *adj.* **—pa·ter·nal·is·ti·cal·ly** *adv.*

pa·ter·ni·ty (pə-térnəti) *n.* **1.** The fact or condition of being a father; fatherhood. **2.** Descent on a father's side; paternal descent. **3.** Authorship; origin. Also used adjectivally: *paternity leave; paternity suit.* [Old French *paternite,* from Late Latin *paternitās* (stem *paternitāt-*), from Latin *paternus,* fatherly, PATERNAL.]

pa·ter·nos·ter (páttər-nóstər) *n.* **1.** *Often capital* **P.** The **Lord's Prayer** *(see),* especially when recited in Latin. **2.** Any of the large beads on a rosary, on which the Lord's Prayer is said. **3.** A sequence of words spoken as a prayer or as a magic formula. **4.** A type of lift in which open compartments move continuously in a looped chain, passing each floor slowly enough for users to enter or alight. **5.** A weighted fishing line having several jointed attachments for hooks connected by beadlike swivels. [Latin *pater noster,* "our father".]

path (paath || path) *n., pl.* **paths** (paat͟hz || pat͟hz, paaths, paths). **1.** A trodden track or way. **2.** Any surface track or way. **3.** A way that allows forward movement: *clear a path through the forest.* **4.** The route or course along which something moves: *the path of a hurricane.* **5.** A course of action or conduct: *the path of righteousness.* —See Synonyms at **way.** [Middle English *path,* Old English *pæth.*] **—path·less** (-ləss, -liss) *adj.*

path. pathological; pathology.

-path *n. suffix.* Indicates: **1.** One who practises a specified type of alternative medicine; for example **naturopath. 2.** One who suffers from a specified disease; for example **psychopath.** [Sense 1, back-formation from -PATHY. Sense 2, from Greek *-pathēs,* -sufferer, from *pathos,* suffering, PATHOS.] **—-path·ic** *adj. suffix.*

Pa·than (pə-taán) *n.* A member of a Pashto-speaking tribal people of Indo-Iranian stock and Muslim religion, living chiefly in northwest Pakistan and Afghanistan. [Hindi *Paṭhan,* from Afghan *Pë-ṣtana,* plural of *Pëṣtūn,* an Afghan, from *pashtó,* the Afghan language. See **Pashto.**]

pa·thet·ic (pə-théttik) *adj.* **1.** Of, pertaining to, expressing, or arousing pity, sympathy, or tenderness; full of pathos: *the ragged children made a pathetic sight.* **2.** *Informal.* Inadequate: *a pathetic attempt.* **3.** *Informal.* Of little interest or worth; feeble; useless. —See Synonyms at **moving.** [French *pathétique,* from Late Latin *pathēticus,* from Greek *pathētikos,* from *pathētos,* liable to suffer, from *pathos,* passion, suffering.] **—pa·thet·i·cal·ly** *adv.*

Synonyms: *pathetic, pitiful, regrettable, lamentable.*

pathetic fallacy *n.* The attribution of human emotions or characteristics to inanimate things, as in romantic literature.

path·find·er (paáth-fīndər || páth-) *n.* **1.** One who discovers a way through or into unexplored regions. **2.** An aircraft of pilot who finds a target area and marks it by flares or other signalling devices. **2.** A radar system or radio beacon used for navigation or homing.

patho- *comb. form.* Indicates disease or suffering; for example, **pathogen.** [New Latin, from Greek *pathos,* emotion, suffering.]

path·o·gen (páthə-jen, -jən) *n.* Also **path·o·gene** (-jeen). Any agent that causes disease, especially a microorganism such as a bacterium or fungus. [PATHO- + -GEN.]

path·o·gen·e·sis (páthə-jenni-siss) *n.* Also **pa·thog·e·ny** (pə-thójəni). The origin and development of a diseased or morbid condition. [New Latin : PATHO- + -GENESIS.]

path·o·gen·ic (páthə-jénnik) *adj.* Also **path·o·ge·net·ic** (páthō-jə-néttik, -je-). Capable of causing disease: *pathogenic bacteria.* **—path·o·gen·i·ci·ty** (-je-níssəti) *n.*

path·og·no·mon·ic (páthəg-nə-mónnik, pə-thóg-) *adj.* Distinctive or characteristic of a particular disease. Said of signs and symptoms. [From Greek *pathognōmonikos,* "indicating a disease" : PATH- + *gnōmonikos,* from *gnōmōn,* indicator, judge.]

pathol. pathological; pathology.

path·o·log·i·cal (páthə-lójik'l) *adj.* Also **path·o·log·ic** (-lójik). *Abbr.* **path., pathol. 1.** Of or pertaining to pathology. **2.** Pertaining to or caused by disease. **3.** Unhealthy or compulsive in behaviour: *a pathological liar.* **—path·o·log·i·cal·ly** *adv.*

pa·thol·o·gy (pə-thólləji) *n., pl.* **-gies.** *Abbr.* **path., pathol. 1.** The scientific study of the nature of disease, its causes, processes, development, and consequences. **2.** The anatomical or functional manifestations of disease, or of a particular disease, for example changes in organs and tissues. [New Latin *pathologia* and Old French *pathologie,* from Greek *pathologia,* study of passions : PATHO- + -LOGY.] **—pa·thol·o·gist** *n.*

pa·thos (páythoss) *n.* **1.** A quality, or the evocation of such a quality in art or literature, that arouses feelings of pity, sympathy, tenderness, or sorrow in another: *the pathos of their parting.* **2.** A feeling of sympathy or pity. [Greek, passion, suffering.]

Usage: *Pathos* (and *pathetic*) are general terms to do with the sense of "feeling pity or sympathy". *Bathos* (and *bathetic*) are quite different in meaning and more restricted in application, referring to the sudden intrusion of something banal or ordinary in an elevated or high-flown context, producing a sense of anticlimax.

path·way (paáth-way || páth-) *n.* **1.** A path. **2.** *Chemistry.* A particular chain of reactions leading to a given product.

-pathy *n. comb. form.* Indicates: **1.** Feeling; perception; for example, **telepathy. 2. a.** Disease; a diseased condition; for example, **neuropathy. b.** A system of treating disease; for example, **homeopathy.** [Latin *-pathia,* from Greek *-patheia,* from *pathos,* PATHOS.]

pa·tience (páysh'nss) *n.* **1.** The capacity of calm, uncomplaining endurance, or perseverance: *"This is the story of what a woman's patience can endure."* (Wilkie Collins). **2.** Tolerant understanding: *had no patience with fools.* **3.** The capacity to put up with delay and wait for the right moment. **4.** *Chiefly British.* Any of various card games played by one person in which the cards have to be matched up in certain combinations. Also *U.S.* "solitaire".

Synonyms: *patience, resignation, forbearance.*

pa·tient (páysh'nt) *adj.* **1.** Sharing or marked by patience. **2.** Capable of bearing affliction with calmness.

~n. **1.** A person or animal receiving medical treatment. **2.** One who is the recipient of an action. [Middle English *pacient,* from Old French *patient,* from Latin *patiēns* (stem *patient-*), from the present participle of *patī,* to suffer.] **—pa·tient·ly** *adv.*

patin. Variant of **paten.**

pat·i·na (páttinə) *n.* **1.** A thin layer of corrosion, usually brown or green, that appears on copper or copper alloys, such as bronze, as a result of natural or artificial oxidation. Compare **verdigris. 2.** The sheen produced by age and use on a surface. **3.** Any surface appearance. [Italian, originally, "a mixture prepared in a bowl and used to coat calfskins", from Latin *patina,* shallow dish, plate. See **paten.**]

pa·tine (pa-teén) *tr.v.* **-tined, -tinihg, -tines.** *Rare.* To coat with a patina. [French, *patine,* from Old French *patene,* from Latin PATINA.]

pat·i·o (pátti-ō || paáti-) *n., pl.* **-os. 1.** An inner, roofless courtyard. **2.** A usually paved area for dining or relaxation adjacent to a house or flat. [Spanish, courtyard.]

pa·tis·se·rie (pə-teéssəri, pa-) *n.* **1.** A bakery specialising in rich, fancy cakes and pastries. **2.** Such cakes and pastries. [French *pâtisserie,* from Old French, "pastry", from *pâtissier,* pastry cook, from *pastitz* (unattested), pasty, from Vulgar Latin *pastīcium* (unattested), from Late Latin *pasta,* dough, PASTE.]

Pat·more (pát-mawr), **Coventry (Kersey Dighton)** (1823–96). British poet and critic. His works include *The Angel in the House* (1854–63), a poetic treatment of married love. Associated with the Pre-Raphaelite Brotherhood, he became a Catholic (1864) after his first wife died.

Pat·mos, Pát·mos (pát-moss). Greek island of the Dodecanese group, in the southeastern Aegean Sea. It is where Saint John the Divine is reputed to have written the Book of Revelation.

Pat·na (pát-nə; *Hindi* pút-). Capital city of Bihar State, India. Situated on the Ganges, it is on the former site of Pataliputra, capital of the Maghda Kingdom (5th century B.C.) and the Maurya and Gupta Empire. It is now the centre of a rice-growing area.

Patna rice *n.* A type of rice having long grains, used chiefly in savoury dishes. [After PATNA.]

pat·ois (pátwaa; *French* pa-twá) *n., pl.* **patois** (-z, *or as singular).* **1.** Any regional French or Swiss dialect. **2.** A West Indian French Creole, such as that spoken in St. Lucia. **3.** Any English Creole, especially Jamaican Creole. **4.** Any regional dialect. **5.** Illiterate or substandard speech. **6.** The special jargon of a group; cant. [French, perhaps from Old French *patoier,* to handle roughly, from *patte,* paw.]

Pa·ton (páyt'n), **Alan** (1903–88). South African novelist. He rose to international fame with *Cry, the Beloved Country* (1948), an indictment of South Africa's racial policies. His other books include *Debbie Go Home* (1961) and *The Long View* (1968). He was national president of the Liberal Party (1953–68).

Pat·ras (páttrəss, pə-tráss). Port of western Greece. Situated on the east side of the Gulf of Patras in the north Peloponnese. It was a starting place for the Greek War of Independence (1821).

pat·res·fa·mil·i·as. Plural of **paterfamilias.**

patri- *prefix.* Indicates father; for example, **patriclinous.** [Latin *pater,* father, and Greek *patēr,* father.]

pa·tri·al (páytri-əl) *n. British.* Until 1983, a citizen of the United Kingdom who had the right to British nationality by virtue of birth, adoption, naturalisation, or registration in the United Kingdom; through being the child or grandchild of a patrial; or through being resident, with a certain status, in the United Kingdom for at least five years. **—pa·tri·a·li·ty** (-əl-iti).

pa·tri·arch (páytri-aark || páttri-) *n.* **1.** The paternal leader of a family or tribe. Compare **matriarch. 2.** In the Old Testament: **a.** Any of the progenitors of the human race before the Flood, from Adam to Noah. **b.** Abraham, Isaac, Jacob, or any of Jacob's 12 sons, the eponymous progenitors of the 12 tribes of Israel: *"and Jacob begat the twelve patriarchs"* (Acts 7:8). **3.** In the early Christian church, any of the bishops of Rome, Constantinople, Jerusalem, Antioch, and Alexandria. **4.** *Roman Catholic Church.* **a.** A bishop who holds the highest episcopal rank after the pope. **b.** The pope himself. **5.** In the Eastern Orthodox Church: **a.** The bishop of Alexandria, Antioch, Constantinople, Jerusalem, Moscow, Serbia, or Romania. **b.** The bishop of Constantinople, as leader of the Greek Orthodox Church. Also called "ecumenical patriarch". **6.** A high dignitary of the Mormon priesthood, empowered to invoke blessings. Also called "evangelist". **7.** A man regarded as the founder or original head of an enterprise, organisation, or tradition. **9.** A very old and venerable man; an elder. **10.** The most venerable specimen in a group: *patriarch of the herd.* **11.** Loosely, any man holding a powerful or authoritative position in a conventional hierarchy who insists on being heard, respected, and obeyed. Often used derogatorily. [Middle English *patriarke,* from Old French *patriarche,* from Late Latin *patriarcha,* from Greek *patriarkhēs* : *patria,* lineage, family, from *patēr,* father + -ARCH.]

pa·tri·ar·chal (páytri-árk'l || páttri-) *adj.* Also **pa·tri·ar·chic** (-árkik). **1.** Pertaining to or characteristic of a patriarch; venerable; dignified. **2.** Of or pertaining to a patriarchy: *a patriarchal social system.* **3.** Ruled by a patriarch: *a patriarchal see.* **—pa·tri·ar·chal·ly** *adv.* **—pa·tri·ar·chal·ism** *n.*

patriarchal cross *n.* A Latin cross having two horizontal bars, of which the upper is the shorter.

pa·tri·ar·chate (páytri-aark-ət, -ayt, -it || páttri-) *n.* **1.** The territory, residence, rule, or rank of a patriarch. **2.** A patriarchy.

pa·tri·ar·chy (páytri-aarki || páttri-) *n., pl.* **-chies. 1.** A system of social organisation in which descent and succession are traced through the male line. **2.** The rule of a people or family by men. **3.** A society or social system founded by men and serving their interests alone, so that they retain and inherit power, wealth, privileges, and opportunities that most women do not.

pa·tri·cian (pə-trísh'n) *n.* **1.** A member of one of the noble families of the Roman Republic, which before the third century B.C. had exclusive rights to the Senate and the magistracies. Compare **plebeian. 2.** A dignity or title conferred by the Byzantine emperors. **3.** A member of the hereditary ruling class in the medieval free cities of Italy and Germany. **4.** A member of an aristocracy. **5.** A person of notably superior upbringing, manners, and tastes. [Middle English *patricion,* from Old French *patricien,* from Latin *patricius,* (nobleman) of senatorial rank, from *patres,* "fathers", senators, from *pater,* father.] **—pa·tri·cian** *adj.* **—pa·tri·cian·ly** *adv.*

pa·tri·ci·ate (pə-tríshi-ət, -ayt, -it) *n.* **1.** The rank of patrician. **2.** Patricians as a class; nobility; aristocracy. [Latin *patriciātus,* from *patricius,* PATRICIAN.]

pat·ri·cide (páttri-sīd) *n.* **1.** The act of murdering one's father. **2.** One who murders his father. [Late Latin *patricīdium* (crime) and Latin *patricīda* (killer) : PATRI- + -CIDE.] **—pat·ri·cid·al** (-sīd'l) *adj.*

Pat·rick (páttrik) **Saint** (*c.* 385–460). Patron saint of Ireland. Probably born in south Wales, he was kidnapped by pirates and taken to Ireland, escaping after six years to France where he was ordained as a bishop (*c.* 430). Returning to Ireland as a Christian missionary (*c.* 432), he established a see at Armagh (454).

pat·ri·cli·nous (páttri-klīnəss) *adj.* Also **pat·ro·cli·nous** (páttrō-, páttrə-), **pat·ro·cli·nal** (-klīn'l). Mainly derived from the male line. Said of plants and animals. Compare **matriclinous.** [PATRI- + *-clinous,* from Greek *-klinēs,* leaning, from *klinein,* to lean.]

pat·ri·lin·e·al (páttri-línni-əl) *adj.* Relating to, based on, or tracing descent through the male line. Compare **matrilineal.**

pat·ri·lo·cal (páttri-lōk'l) *adj. Anthropology.* Pertaining to the custom in some primitive societies of living in the home territory of a husband's family or tribe.

pat·ri·mo·ny (páttri-məni || *U.S.* -mōni) *n., pl.* **-nies. 1.** An inheritance from a father or other ancestor. **2.** A legacy; a heritage. **3.** An endowment or estate belonging to a church. [Middle English *patrimoine,* from Old French, from Latin *patrimōnium,* from *pater,* father.] **—pat·ri·mo·ni·al** (-mōni-əl) *adj.* **—pat·ri·mo·ni·al·ly** *adv.*

pa·tri·ot (páytri-ət, páttri-) *n.* A person who loves, supports, and defends his country. [Old French *patriote,* compatriot, from Late Latin *patriōta,* from Greek *patriōtēs,* from *patris,* fatherland, from *patēr,* father.] **—pa·tri·ot·ic** (-óttik) *adj.* **—pa·tri·ot·i·cal·ly** *adv.* **—pa·tri·ot·ism** *n.*

Pa·tri·ot (páytri-ət) *n.* A trade name for a U.S.-made, ground-to-air, anti-missile system.

pa·tris·tic (pə-trístik, pa-) *adj.* Also **pa·tris·ti·cal** (-'l). **1.** Of or pertaining to patristics. **2.** *Biology.* Designating similarity between different types of plants or animals due to common ancestry. [PATR(I)- + -IST + -IC.] **—pa·tris·ti·cal·ly** *adv.*

pa·tris·tics *n. Used with a singular verb.* The study of the teachings and lives of the fathers of the early Christian church. Also called "patrology".

pa·trol (pə-trōl) *n.* **1.** The action of moving about an area for purposes of observation or security. **2.** A person or group of persons who carry out such an action. **3. a.** A military unit sent out on a reconnaissance mission. **b.** One or more vehicles, boats, ships, or aircraft assigned to guard or reconnoitre a given area. **4.** A small group, usually six, of Scouts or Guides, a division of a troop or company.

~v. **patrolled, -trolling, -trols.** *—tr.* To engage in a patrol of. *—intr.* To engage in a patrol. [French *patrouiller,* from Old French *patouiller,* to paw or paddle around in mud: *patte,* paw (see **patten**) + *-ouiller,* imitative verb suffix.] **—pa·trol·ler** *n.*

patrol car *n.* A police car that patrols an area and is usually in radio contact with headquarters.

pa·trol·man (pə-trōl-man, -mən) *n., pl.* **-men** (-men, -mən). **1.** *British.* A person employed by a motoring organisation to patrol a given area and go to the assistance of motorists who are in trouble. **2.** *Chiefly U.S.* A policeman or guard who patrols an assigned area.

pa·trol·o·gy (pə-tróllәji) *n.* **1.** Patristics. **2.** A collection of the writings of the fathers of the early Christian church. [17th century : from Greek *patēr* (stem *patr-*), father + -LOGY.] **—pat·ro·log·i·cal** (páttrə-lójik'l) *adj.* **—pa·trol·o·gist** *n.*

patrol wagon *n. U.S.* A police van used to convey prisoners.

pa·tron (páytrən; *rarely* páttrən) *n.* **1.** Anyone who supports, protects, or champions; a benefactor: *a patron of the arts.* **2.** A regular customer. **3.** One who has the right to present a clergyman to an ecclesiastical benefice. **4.** In ancient Rome: **a.** The former owner of a freed slave who retained certain rights over him. **b.** The protector of a client. **5.** A patron saint. [Middle English *patroun,* from Old French *patron,* from Medieval Latin *patrōnus,* patron, patron saint, from Latin, defender, advocate, from *pater,* father.] **—pa·tron·al** (pə-trōn'l, pa- || *chiefly U.S.* páytrən'l) *adj.*

pat·ron·age (páttrənij; *rarely* páytrənij) *n.* **1.** Support, encouragement, or championship from a patron. **2.** A patronising manner. **3.** The trade given to a commercial establishment by its customers. **4.** Customers or patrons collectively; clientele. **5.** The power or action of distributing governmental or political positions. **6.** The positions so distributed. **7.** The right to present a clergyman to an ecclesiastical benefice.

pa·tron·ess (páytrə-niss, páttrə-, -ness) *n.* A female patron.

pat·ron·ise, pat·ron·ize (páttrə-nīz || *chiefly U.S.* páytrə-) *tr.v.* **-ised, -ising, -ises. 1.** To act as a patron to; support. **2.** To go to regularly as a customer. **3.** To treat in an offensively condescending manner. **—pat·ron·is·er** *n.* **—pat·ron·is·ing·ly** *adv.*

patron saint *n.* The guardian saint of any nation, place, craft, activity, class, or person. Also called "patron".

pat·ro·nym·ic (páttrə-nímmik) *n.* A name derived from the first name of one's father or a paternal ancestor; especially, one formed by a suffix or prefix, as in *Johnson,* the son of John. In the Russian formula *Anton Pavlovich Chekhov, Pavlovich* (son of Pavel, "Paul") is a patronymic while *Chekhov* is a true surname. Compare **metronymic.** [Late Latin *patronymicum,* from *patrōnymicus,* "derived from the name of a father", from Greek *patrōnumia,* patronymic : PATR(I)- + *onuma,* name.] **—pat·ro·nym·i·cal·ly** *adv.*

pa·troon (pə-trōōn) *n. U.S.* Formerly, a member of the Dutch West India Company who was granted proprietary and manorial rights in New York and New Jersey. [Dutch, from French *patron,* patron, from Old French, PATRON.]

pat·sy (pátsi) *n., pl.* **-sies.** *Chiefly U.S. Slang.* A person who is cheated, victimised, or made the butt of a joke. [20th century : origin obsure.]

pat·tée (páttay, pátti) *adj.* Having triangular arms that become wider towards the ends. Said of a cross. Often used after the noun: *a cross pattée.* [French *patte,* paw.]

pat·ten (pátt'n) *n.* A wooden sandal, shoe, or clog; especially, a wooden overshoe raised on a wooden or metal support. [Middle English *patin,* from Old French *patin,* from *patte,* a paw, hoof, from Vulgar Latin *patta*† (unattested).]

pat·ter¹ (páttər) *v.* **-tered, -tering, -ters.** *—intr.* **1.** To make a quick succession of light, soft taps: *Rain pattered on the roof.* **2.** To move with quick, light, soft steps. *—tr.* To cause to patter.

~n. A succession of quick, light, tapping sounds. [Frequentative of PAT (tap lightly).]

patter² *v.* **-tered, -tering, -ters.** *—intr.* **1.** To chatter glibly and rapidly. **2.** To mumble prayers in a mechanical manner. *—tr.* To utter in a glib, rapid, or mechanical manner.

~n. **1.** Glib, rehearsed, rapid speech, as of an auctioneer, salesman, or comedian. **2.** The jargon of a particular group; cant. **3.** Meaningless talk; chatter. **4.** Rapid speech inserted into a song. [Middle English *patren, patern,* from Latin *pater(noster),* PATER(NOSTER), from the mechanical recitation of the prayer.] **—pat·ter·er** *n.*

pat·tern (páttərn) *n.* **1.** A plan, diagram, or model to be followed in making things: *a dress pattern.* **2.** A representative sample; a specimen. **3. a.** An archetype. **b.** An ideal worthy of imitation: *a pattern of womanly virtues.* **4. a.** Any artistic or decorative design: *a paisley pattern.* **b.** A design of natural or accidental origin: *the pattern of ice crystals on a windowpane.* **5.** A recurrent set of features or characteristics: *behavioural patterns.* **6.** Form and style in an artistic work or body of artistic works. **7. a.** The arrangement of identically aimed rifle shots upon a target. **b.** The distribution and spread of shot from a shotgun. **8.** A shape, usually wooden, embedded in sand to make a mould for metal casting.

~tr.v. **patterned, -terning, -terns. 1.** To make, mould, or design by following a pattern. Usually used with *on, upon,* or *after.* **2.** To cover or ornament with a design or pattern. [Alteration of Middle English *patron,* from Old French, from Medieval Latin *patrōnus,* patron, (hence) "something to be imitated", pattern. See **patron.**]

Pat·ti (pátti), **Adelina** (1843–1919). Spanish-born Italian soprano. She had a voice remarkable for its range, timbre, and flexibility.

Pat·ton (pátt'n), **George Smith, Jr.** (1885–1945). U.S. general. A graduate from West Point (1909), during World War II he commanded the Seventh Army during the Sicilian campaign (1943) and led the Third Army in Europe, breaking through the German defences in Normandy and crossing France (1944) to reach eventually the Czech border (1945).

pat·ty (pátti) *n., pl.* **-ties. 1.** A small pie. **2.** *Chiefly U.S.* A small, oval, flattened cake of chopped or minced food. [French *pâté,* small pie, from Old French *paste,* from *paste,* PASTE.]

pat·u·lous (páttew-ləss) *adj.* Also **pat·u·lent** (-lənt). *Botany.* Spreading or expanded: *patulous branches.* [Latin *patulus,* from *patēre,* to be open.] **—pat·u·lous·ly** *adv.* **—pat·u·lous·ness** *n.*

Pau (pō). Town in southwest France. Capital of the Pyrénées-Atlantiques département, it is a popular resort and produces textiles and leather. It was the seat of the kings of Navarre.

P.A.U. Pan American Union.

pau·a (pów-ə) *n.* A New Zealand abalone, *Haliotis iris,* having edible flesh and an ornamental shell used for decoration. [Maori.]

pau·ci·ty (páwssəti) *n.* 1. Smallness of number; fewness. 2. Smallness of quantity; a scarcity. [Middle English *paucite,* from Old French, from Latin *paucitās* (stem *paucitāt-*), from *paucus,* few.]

Paul VI (pawl), born Giovanni Battista Montini (1897–1978). Italian pope (1963–78). He reconvened the second Vatican Council, worked for reform within the Vatican, and reiterated the teachings of his church on contraception in the encyclical *Humanae Vitae* (On Human Life) (1968).

Paul, Saint (*c.* A.D. 5–67), also known as Saul of Tarsus, The Apostle to the Gentiles. Originally an anti-Christian, he had a vision on the road to Damascus that led to his conversion; his life and doctrines are set forth in the Acts of the Apostles and his epistles.

paul·dron (páwldrən) *n.* Either of two metal plates in a suit of armour designed to protect the shoulder. [French *espauleron,* from Old French *espaule (épaule),* shoulder. See epaulette.]

Pau·li (pówli), **Wolfgang** (1900–58). U.S. physicist. Born in Vienna, he was educated at Munich and Copenhagen and in 1925 formulated his **exclusion principle** of quantum theory. He was awarded the Nobel prize for physics (1945).

Pauli exclusion principle *n. Physics.* The **exclusion principle** *(see).* [After Wolfgang PAULI.]

Paul·ine (páwlīn) *adj.* Of or pertaining to St. Paul, his writings, or his teachings and the theological doctrines derived from them. —**Paul·in·ism** *n.* —**Paul·in·ist** *n.*

Pau·ling (páwling), **Linus Carl** (1901–94). U.S. biochemist. For his work on the nature of chemical bonding he received the Nobel prize for chemistry (1954). For his views against nuclear weapons, detailed in *No More War* (1958), he received the Nobel peace prize (1962). He also got the 1971 International Lenin peace prize.

Paul Jones *n.* A dance in which partners are changed at a given signal. [After John Paul JONES.]

pau·low·ni·a (paw-lóni-ə) *n.* Any of several trees of the genus *Paulownia,* native to the Orient, having large, heart-shaped leaves and clusters of purplish or white flowers. [New Latin, after Anna *Paulovna* (died 1865), Russian princess.]

paunch (pawnch) *n.* The belly; especially, a pot-belly: *"His hands clasped themselves over his capacious paunch."* (Virginia Woolf). —*tr.v.* **paunched, paunching, paunches.** To disembowel (an animal). [Middle English *paunche,* from Anglo-French, from Old French *pance,* from Latin *pantex†* (stem *pantic-*). —**paunch·i·ness** *n.* —**paunch·y** *adj.*

pau·per (páwpər) *n.* 1. One who is extremely poor. 2. Formerly, one who lived on public charity. —**pau·per·ism** *n.* —*tr.v.* **paupered, -pering, -pers.** To pauperise. [Latin, poor.]

pau·per·ise, pau·per·ize (páwpə-rīz) *tr.v.* **-ised, -ising, -ises.** To make a pauper of; impoverish. —**pau·per·i·sa·tion** (-rī-záysh'n ‖ U.S. -rĭ-) *n.*

pau·piette (pō-pyét, paw-) *n.* A thin slice of meat wrapped round a savoury filling. [French, from Old French *poupe,* fleshy part, from Latin *pulpa,* PULP.]

pause (pawz) *intr.v.* **paused, pausing, pauses.** 1. To cease or suspend activity for a time: *She paused to listen.* 2. To linger; tarry: *pausing for a while at the café.* 3. To hesitate: *He paused before accepting the task.* —*n.* 1. A hiatus in action or activity; a temporary respite. 2. A delay or suspended reaction, as from uncertainty; a hesitation: *After a pause, the audience burst into cheers.* 3. A break, stop, or rest in speaking or reading for a calculated purpose or effect: *a pause to let the words sink in.* 4. **a.** *Music.* A sign indicating a fermata. **b.** *Prosody.* A measured break or rest; a caesura. 5. A reason for hesitation. Usually used in the phrase *give someone pause.* [Middle English, a pause, from Old French, from Latin *pausa,* from Greek *pausis,* a stoping, from *pauein,* to stop.]

pav (pav) *n. Australian Informal.* A dessert, **pavlova** *(see).*

pa·vane, pa·van (pə-váan, -ván, pávv'n) *n.* Also **pa·vin** (pávvin). 1. A slow, stately court dance introduced into England in the 16th century. 2. A piece of music for this dance. [Old French *pavane,* from Old Spanish *pavana,* from Old Italian *(danza) pavanna,* "(dance) of Padua", dialectal variant of *padovana,* feminine of *padovano,* of Padua, from *Padova,* PADUA.]

Pa·va·rot·ti (pávvə-rótti), **Luciano** (1935–). Italian tenor. He sang in a local choir before winning a singing competition in Emilia-Romagna when aged 25. He made his debut at La Scala (1965), and now specialises in Verdi and Puccini.

pave (payv) *tr.v.* **paved, paving, paves.** 1. To cover with any hard, smooth surface that will bear traffic. 2. To cover uniformly, as if with a pavement. 3. To be or compose the pavement of. [Middle English *paven,* from Old French *paver,* from Latin *pavīre,* to strike, stamp.] —**pav·er** *n.*

pa·vé (pávvay) *n.* 1. A setting of precious stones placed together so closely that no metal shows: *a brooch in pavé.* 2. A paved surface. [French, from the past participle of *paver,* to PAVE.]

pave·ment (páyvmənt) *n.* 1. *Chiefly British.* A paved footway along the side of a road. Also *U.S.* "sidewalk". 2. A natural rock pavement resulting from weathering, glacial action, or wind erosion. 3. *U.S.* A hard, paved surface; especially, a roadway. 4. The material of which a pavement is made.

pavement artist *n.* 1. One who draws in chalks or crayons on the pavement in order to obtain money from passers-by. 2. One who executes and sells paintings and drawings, especially portraits of passers-by, in the street.

Pa·via (páavi-ə). Capital city of Pavia province, Lombardy, north Italy. Situated on the river Ticino, it was a centre of romanesque art

in the 12th and 13th centuries, and is where St. Augustine is buried. It is now an agricultural centre.

pav·id (pávvid) *adj. Literary.* Fearful; frightened; timid. [Latin *pavidus,* from *pavēre,* to fear.]

pa·vil·ion (pə-víl-yən) *n.* 1. *British.* A building at the edge of a cricket pitch or other sports ground where players may change and rest. 2. An ornate tent, especially of the kind used by knights in medieval Europe. 3. **a.** A temporary, often open structure, used at parks or fairs for amusement or shelter. **b.** A display stand at an exhibition. 4. A building or other structure connected to a larger building; an annexe. 5. Any of a group of related buildings forming a complex, as of a hospital. 6. A part of a building that is higher than the rest and usually ornate. 7. The surface of a brilliant-cut gem that slants outwards from girdle to culet. —*tr.v.* **pavilioned, -ioning, -ions.** 1. To shelter in or as if in a pavilion. 2. To provide with a pavilion or pavilions. [Middle English *pavilon,* from Old French *paveillon,* from Latin *pāpiliō†* (stem *pāpiliōn-*), butterfly, tent (from its resemblance to a butterfly's wings).]

pav·ing (páyving) *n.* 1. A pavement. 2. Material used to pave surfaces. Also used adjectively: *a paving stone.*

pav·iour, *U.S.* **pav·ior** (páyv-yər) *n.* 1. A person who puts down paving. 2. Material or tools used for paving. [Middle English *pavier,* from *paven,* PAVE.]

pav·is, pav·ise (pávviss) *n.* A medieval shield large enough to protect the whole body. [Middle English, from Old French *pavais,* from Old Italian *pavese,* "of Pavia", from PAVIA, where pavises were first made.]

Pav·lov (páv-lov; *Russian* -ləf), **Ivan Petrovich** (1849–1936). Russian physiologist and experimental psychologist. For his research on the nature of digestion he received the Nobel prize for physiology or medicine (1904). He is best known for his work on conditioned reflexes in animals.

pav·lov·a (pav-lóvə) *n.* A meringue cake topped with fruit and whipped cream, popular especially in Australia and New Zealand. [After Anna PAVLOVA.]

Pav·lo·va (páv-lóvə; *Russian* pávləvə), **Anna** (1881–1931). Russian ballerina. Making her debut in 1899, she worked with Diaghilev in 1909 and from 1914 toured the world with her own company. Her most famous roles were in *Swan Lake* and *Les Sylphides.*

Pav·lo·vi·an (pav-lóvi-ən) *adj.* 1. Of or pertaining to Pavlov or his theories. 2. Loosely, automatic; mechanical: *a Pavlovian response.*

Pa·vo (páavō) *n.* A constellation in the Southern Hemisphere near Apus and Indus. [Latin *pāvō,* peacock (probably imitative), obscurely related to Greek *taōs,* a peacock. See also peacock.]

pav·o·nine (pávvə-nīn) *adj.* 1. Of or like a peacock. 2. Resembling a peacock's tail in colour, design, or iridescence. [Latin *pāvōnīnus,* from *pāvō,* peacock. See peacock.]

paw (paw) *n.* 1. The nailed or clawed foot of an animal. 2. *Informal.* A human hand, especially one that is large, clumsy, or dirty. —*v.* **pawed, pawing, paws.** —*tr.* 1. To strike with the paw or paws. 2. To strike with a repeated scraping motion: *"His black charger pawed the straw"* (W.M. Thackeray). 3. To handle clumsily, rudely, or with amorous intent; caress awkwardly. —*intr.* 1. To scrape the ground with the forefeet: *The horse pawed restlessly.* 2. To make clumsy, grasping motions with the hands. [Middle English *pawe, powe,* from Old French *poue,* from Germanic *pauta* (unattested).] —**paw·er** *n.*

paw·ky (páwki) *adj.* **-ier, -iest.** *British Regional.* 1. Dryly humorous. 2. Shrewd; astute. [Northern English and Scottish dialect *pawk†,* a trick.] —**paw·ki·ly** *adv.* —**paw·ki·ness** *n.*

pawl (pawl) *n.* A hinged or pivoted device adapted to fit into a notch of a ratchet wheel to impart forward or prevent backward motion. Also called "detent". [Dutch *pal,* possibly from Latin *pālus,* stake.]

pawn¹ (pawn) *n.* 1. Something given as security for a loan; a pledge. 2. The condition of being held as a pledge against the payment of a loan: *jewels in pawn.* 3. A person serving as security; a hostage. 4. The act of pawning. —*tr.v.* **pawned, pawning, pawns.** 1. To give or deposit as security for the payment of money borrowed. 2. To risk; hazard; stake: *pawn one's honour.* [Middle English *paun,* from Old French *pan, pand,* security, from West Germanic *panda* (unattested).] —**pawn·a·ble** *adj.* —**pawn·age** *n.* —**pawn·er, pawn·or** (-ər) *n.*

pawn² (pawn) *n. Abbr.* **P** A chessman of the lowest value, allowed to move one square at a time (or two squares for the first move) and capture on a one-space diagonal forward move. 2. A person or thing used to further the purposes of another. [Middle English *poun, pawne,* from Old French *poon, peon,* from Medieval Latin *pedō* (stem *pedōn-*), a foot soldier, from Latin *pēs* (stem *ped-*), foot.]

pawn·bro·ker (páwn-brōkər) *n.* One who lends money at interest in exchange for personal property left with him as security. —**pawn·bro·king** *n.*

Paw·nee (paw-née) *n., pl.* **-nees** or collectively **Pawnee.** 1. A member of a confederation of four North American Plains Indian peoples. 2. The language of this confederation.

pawn·shop (páwn-shop) *n.* The shop of a pawnbroker.

pawpaw. Variant of **papaw.**

pax (paks) *interj. British Slang.* Used to express a request for a truce, especially among schoolchildren. [Latin, peace.]

PAX, P.A.X. private automatic (telephone) exchange.

Pax·ton (pákstən), **Sir Joseph** (1801–65). British architect and landscape gardener. While working as chief gardener to the Duke of Devonshire he submitted the winning design for the Crystal Palace to house the Great Exhibition of 1851. He used a greenhouse he had designed as his model, producing one of the earliest examples of prefabricated construction, built of iron and glass.

pay¹ (pay) *v.* **paid** or **payed** (for sense 10), **paying, pays.** *—tr.* **1.** To remunerate or recompense for goods or services rendered. **2.** To give (money) in exchange for goods or services. Often used with *out.* **3.** To give the indicated amount of (money owed); discharge (a debt or obligation): *pay taxes.* **4.** To yield as recompense or return: *This job pays little.* **5.** To undergo; subject oneself to: *pay the penalty.* **6.** To bear the cost of: *He paid my way through university.* **7.** To afford an advantage to; profit: *It paid him to be generous.* **8.** To give or bestow: *pay compliments; pay attention.* **9.** To make (a visit or call). **10.** *Nautical.* To let out (a rope or cable) gradually. Used with *out.* *—intr.* **1.** To make payment. **2.** To discharge a debt or obligation. **3.** To be profitable or worthwhile. **—pay back. 1.** To return borrowed money to. **2.** To avenge oneself on; retaliate against: *paid him back for the unjust treatment he had received.* **3.** To extend hospitality, for example, in like manner to: *paid her back for her kindness.* **—pay (one's) way.** To contribute one's own share; pay for oneself. **—pay up.** To pay the full amount demanded.
~adj. **1.** Requiring payment to operate: *a pay telephone, pay television.* **2.** Yielding valuable metal in mining: *pay stratum.*
~n. **1.** The act of paying or the state of being paid. **2.** Money given in return for work done; a salary; wages. **3.** Paid employment; hire: *the men in our pay.* **4. a.** Recompense or reward: *His thanks were pay enough.* **b.** Retribution or punishment. **5.** *Rare.* A person considered with regard to his credit or willingness to pay. [Middle English *payen,* from Old French *paier,* from Medieval Latin *pācāre,* to satisfy, pay, from Latin, to pacify, from *pāx* (stem *pāc-*), peace.]

pay² *tr.v.* **payed** or **paid, paying, pays.** *Nautical.* To coat or cover (seams of a ship, for example) with waterproof materials such as tar or asphalt. [Old French *peier,* from Latin *picāre,* to pitch, to tar, from *pix* (stem *pic-*), pitch.]

pay·a·ble (páy-əb'l) *adj.* **1.** Requiring payment on a certain date; due. **2.** That can or may be paid. **3.** Capable of producing profit: *a payable business venture.* **—pay·a·bly** *adv.*

pay bed *n.* A bed in a British National Health Service hospital paid for by the user, who is treated as a private patient.

pay claim *n.* A demand for an increase in wages or salary.

pay·day (páy-day) *n.* The day on which wages are paid.

pay dirt *n.* *U.S.* **1.** Earth, ore, or gravel with enough metal content to make mining profitable. **2.** Something useful or profitable.

P.A.Y.E. *n.* Pay as you earn: a system of tax collection in Britain in which an employee's income tax is deducted from his pay by his employer and paid directly to the government.

payed. *Nautical.* Alternative past tense and past participle of **pay.**

pay·ee (pay-ée) *n.* A person to whom money is paid.

pay·er (páy-ər) *n.* **1.** A person who pays. **2.** A person named as responsible for paying a bill or note.

pay·ing guest (pay-ing) *n.* *Abbr.* **P.G.** A lodger or boarder.

pay·load (páy-lōd) *n.* **1.** The revenue-producing part of a cargo. **2.** *Aerospace.* **a.** The passengers, mail, bombs, or cargo in an aircraft. **b.** The warhead of a missile. **c.** In rockets and satellites, the data-collecting and transmitting equipment. **d.** In manned spacecraft, the personnel, life-support systems, and equipment necessary to accomplish missions.

pay·mas·ter (páy-maastər || -mastər) *n.* *Abbr.* **pm.** An official or employee in charge of paying wages and salaries.

pay·ment (páymənt) *n.* *Abbr.* **payt., pt. 1.** The act of paying or state of being paid. **2.** That which is paid; compensation; recompense. **3.** One's due, reward, or punishment; a requital.

pay·nim (páynim) *n.* *Archaic.* Any non-Christian, especially a Muslim. [Middle English *painim,* from Old French *paienime,* from Late Latin *pāgānismus,* heathendom, from *pāgānus,* PAGAN.]

pay off *tr.v.* **1. a.** To pay the full amount owed on (a debt). **b.** To get revenge on. **2.** To pay the wages due to and discharge (an employee). **3.** *Informal.* To bribe. *—intr.v.* **1.** To give full return; be profitable: *The effort pays off in the long run.* **2.** *Nautical.* To turn to leeward. Used of a vessel.

pay·off (páy-off, -awff) *n.* **1. a.** Full payment of a salary or wages. **b.** The time of payment. **2.** *Informal.* A final settlement or reckoning; the climax of a narrative, especially of a joke, or of a sequence of events. **3.** Final retribution or revenge. **4.** *Informal.* A bribe.

pay·o·la (pay-ṓlə) *n.* *U.S. Slang.* **1.** Bribery; especially, the bribing of disc jockeys to promote records. **2.** Such a bribe. [PAY + *-ola* (as in *Victrola,* U.S. trademark for a former type of gramophone).]

pay packet *n.* *British.* An envelope containing an employee's wages or salary, as cash or a cheque. Also *U.S.* "pay envelope".

pay·phone (páy-fōn) *n.* A coin-operated telephone. Also called "call box", *U.S.* "pay station".

pay·roll (páy-rōl) *n.* **1.** A list of employees receiving wages, with the amounts due to each. **2.** The total sum of money to be paid out to employees at a given time.

pay·sage (pay-zaázh) *n.* A representation of a rural scene in art; a landscape. [French, landscape, from *pays,* country, Old French *païs,* from Vulgar Latin *pagensis* (unattested), from Latin *pāgus,* rural district.] **—pay·sa·gist** *n.*

payt. payment.

Paz (pass || paz, paass, paaz), **Octavio** (1914–98). Mexican poet. He was a diplomat and served as Mexican ambassador to India in the 1960s. His poetry includes the ten-volume *Sun Stone* (1957) and his *Collected Poems* (written 1957–87) were published in Spanish and English in 1988. His prose work includes *Tiempo Nublado* (1984). He was awarded the Nobel prize for literature in 1990.

Pb The symbol for the element lead [Latin *plumbum.*].

P.B. 1. British Pharmacopoeia. **2.** prayer book.

PBX, P.B.X. private branch (telephone) exchange.

pc 1. parsec. **2.** Also **pc.** piece. **3.** Also **pc.** price.

p.c. 1. after meals [Latin *post cibum.*]. **2.** per cent. **3.** petty cash. **4.** postcard.

P.C. 1. Parish Council; Parish Councillor. **2.** Past Commander. **3.** Personal computer. **4.** Police Constable. **5.** Political correctness; politically correct. **6.** Post Commander. **7.** Privy Council; Privy Councillor.

p/c, P/C 1. petty cash. **2.** prices current.

Pd The symbol for the element palladium.

pd. paid.

p.d. 1. per diem. **2.** potential difference.

P.D. 1. per diem. **2.** *U.S.* Police Department.

P.D.S.A. People's Dispensary for Sick Animals (in Britain).

PE 1. physical education. **2.** potential energy. **3.** printers' error. **4.** probable error.

pea (pee) *n.* **1.** A climbing annual legume, *Pisum sativum,* grown in all temperate zones, and having compound leaves, small white flowers, and edible seeds in a green, elongated pod. **2.** Any of the rounded green seeds of the pea, cooked and eaten as a vegetable. **3.** *Plural.* The unopened pods of the pea plant. **4.** Any of several plants of the genus *Lathyrus,* such as the **sweet pea** *(see).* See **chickpea, cowpea. 5.** *Australian Informal.* One that seems likely to succeed or win. Preceded by *the.* [Taken as singular of earlier *pease,* Middle English *pese,* Old English *pise,* from Late Latin *pīsa,* from Latin, plural of *pīsum,* pea, from Greek *pison*†, a pea.]

peace (peess) *n.* **1.** The absence of war or other hostilities. **2.** An agreement or treaty to end hostilities: *the Peace of Westphalia.* **3.** Freedom from quarrels and disagreement; harmonious relations: *They made peace with each other.* **4.** Public security; law and order: *disturbing the peace.* **5.** Calm; serenity: *peace of mind.* **—at peace. 1.** In a state of tranquillity; serene. **2.** Free from strife. **—hold** or **keep (one's) peace.** To be silent. **—keep the peace.** To maintain or observe law and order. **—make (one's) peace with.** To be reconciled with; renew friendly relations with. [Middle English *pes, pais,* from Old French, from Latin *pāx* (stem *pāc-*).]

Peace (peess). River in British Columbia, Canada, flowing 1 520 kilometres (945 miles) from the Rocky Mountains through wheat-growing areas into the Slave river at Lake Athabaska.

peace·a·ble (peésəb'l) *adj.* **1.** Inclined or disposed to peace; promoting calm: *They met in a peaceable spirit.* **2.** Peaceful; undisturbed. **—peace·a·ble·ness** *n.* **—peace·a·bly** *adv.*

Peace Corps *n.* An organisation set up by the U.S. government in 1961 that trains and sends volunteers abroad to work with people of developing countries on projects for technological, agricultural, and educational improvement.

peace·ful (peéssf'l) *adj.* **1.** Undisturbed by strife, turmoil, or disagreement; tranquil. **2.** Opposed to strife; peaceable. **3.** Of or characteristic of a condition of peace. —See Synonyms at **calm.** **—peace·ful·ly** *adv.* **—peace·ful·ness** *n.*

peace·mak·er (peéss-maykər) *n.* One who makes peace, especially by settling the disputes of others. **—peace·mak·ing** *n.* & *adj.*

peace offering *n.* **1.** Any offering made to an adversary in the interests of peace or reconciliation. **2.** An offering made to God in thanksgiving; especially, a sacrificial offering as prescribed by Levitical law. Leviticus 3:2–6.

peace pipe *n.* A **calumet** *(see).*

peace·time (peéss-tīm) *n.* A time of no war. **—peace·time** *adj.*

peach¹ (peech) *n.* **1.** A small tree, *Prunus persica,* native to China but widely cultivated throughout the temperate zones, having pink flowers and edible fruit. **2.** The soft, juicy, single-seeded fruit of this tree, having white or yellow flesh and downy, red-tinted, yellow skin. **3.** Yellowish pink to light orange. **4.** *Informal.* **a.** Any especially admirable or pleasing person or thing. **b.** A pretty girl.
~adj. Of the colour peach. [Middle English *peche,* from Old French, from Late Latin *persica,* from Latin, plural of *persicum (mālum),* "Persian (apple)", from *Persicus,* PERSIAN.]

peach² *v.* **peached, peaching, peaches.** *—intr. Informal.* To inform on someone. *—tr. Obsolete.* To inform against. [Middle English *pechen,* aphetic variant of *impechen,* IMPEACH.]

peach·blow (peéch-blō) *n.* A purplish-pink monochrome glaze used on Chinese porcelain. Also called "peachbloom".

peach Melba *n.* Also *French* **pêche Melba** (pesh). A dessert consisting of peach halves, ice cream, and raspberry sauce. [After Dame Nellie MELBA.]

peach·y (peéchi) *adj.* **-ier, -iest. 1.** Like a peach, especially in colour or texture. **2.** *U.S. Informal.* Splendid; fine. **—peach·i·ness** *n.*

pea·cock (peé-kok) *n.* **1. a.** A male peafowl of the genus *Pavo,* distinguished by its crested head, brilliant blue or green feathers, and long tail feathers that are marked with eyelike, iridescent spots and can be spread in a fanlike form. **b.** Loosely, a female peafowl of the genus *Pavo.* **2.** A glossy, greenish-black peafowl, *Afropavo congensis,* from the forests of central Africa, having white plumes on the head. Also called "Congo peacock". **3.** A common butterfly, *Inachis* (or *Nymphalis*) *io,* with red, brown, and black wings each bearing a bright, bluish-purple eyespot. **4.** A vain person given to self-display; a dandy.
~intr.v. **peacocked, -cocking, -cocks.** To strut about like a peacock; exhibit oneself in a vain way. [Middle English *pecok, pocok* : Old English *pēa,* peafowl, from Latin *pāvō,* peacock, obscurely re-

lated to Greek *taōs*†, peacock + *cok*, COCK.] —**pea·cock·ish, pea·cock·y** *adj.*

Peacock, Thomas Love (1785–1866). British novelist and poet. In the service of the East India Company (1819–56), he wrote seven novels, most of them satirical, attacking intellectual fashions and caricaturing the poets of the Romantic school, including his friend Shelley. His works include *Headlong Hall* (1816), *Crotchet Castle* (1831), and *Gryll Grange* (1860).

peacock blue *n.* Light to moderate greenish blue. —**pea·cock-blue** (pée·kok-blōō ‖ -blēw) *adj.*

pea crab *n.* Any of various small, globular crabs of the genus *Pinnotheres,* the females of which live as commensals within the shells of oysters and similar molluscs.

pea·fowl (pée-fowl) *n., pl.* -**fowls** or collectively **peafowl.** Any of three large pheasants, *Pavo cristatus,* of India and Ceylon, *P. muticus,* of southeastern Asia, or *Afropavo congensis,* of central Africa. [*Peacock* + *fowl.*]

peag, peage (peeg) *n.* North American Indian money, **wampum** (*see*). [Narraganset *wampompeag,* WAMPUM.]

pea green *n.* Moderate yellowish green. —**pea-green** (pée-gréen) *adj.*

pea·hen (pée-hen) *n.* The female peafowl.

pea jacket *n.* A short, double-breasted coat of heavy navy-blue wool, worn by sailors. Also called "pea coat". [Probably from Dutch *pijjakker* : *pij,* a kind of coarse cloth, from Middle Dutch *pīe*† + *jekker,* a jacket.]

peak[1] (peek) *n. Abbr.* **pk.** 1. A tapering, projecting point; a pointed extremity: *peak of a cap; peak of a roof.* 2. **a.** The pointed summit of a mountain. **b.** The mountain itself: *High Peak.* 3. **a.** The point of a beard. **b.** A **widow's peak** (*see*). 4. The point of greatest development, value, or intensity; height; maximum: *at the peak of her fame.* 5. *Physics.* The highest value attained by a varying quantity: *a current peak.* 6. *Nautical.* **a.** The narrow portion of a ship's hull at the bow or stern. **b.** The upper after corner of a fore-and-aft sail. **c.** The outermost end of a gaff. —See Synonyms at **summit.** ~*v.* **peaked, peaking, peaks.** —*tr.* 1. *Nautical.* To raise (a gaff) above the horizontal. 2. To raise (the blade of an oar) to a vertical position. 3. To bring to a peak, head, or maximum. —*intr.* 1. To be formed into a peak or peaks: *Beat the egg whites until they peak.* 2. To achieve a maximum of development, value, or intensity. ~*adj.* Approaching or constituting the maximum: *peak efficiency; peak viewing time.* [Perhaps back-formation from *peaked,* variant of dialect *picked,* pointed, from PICK (tool).]

peak[2] *intr.v.* **peaked, peaking, peaks.** *Rare.* To become sickly, emaciated, or pale. [16th century : origin obscure.]

Peak District. Plateau region mainly in Derbyshire, central England. Peak national park encompasses the southern Pennines and is crossed by rivers such as the Wye and Dove,which have cut gorges and caves in the limestone rock and produced potholes. Its maximum height is at Kinder Scout, 636 metres (2,088 feet).

Peake (peek), **Mervyn (Laurence)** (1911–68). British author and illustrator, born and partly educated in China. He is best known for his trilogy of Gothic fantasies *Titus Groan* (1946), *Gormenghast* (1950), and *Titus Alone* (1959). He also illustrated editions of *The Rime of the Ancient Mariner* (1943) and *Alice in Wonderland* (1946).

peaked (peekt) *adj.* Ending in a peak; pointed.

peak·y (pééki) *adj.* Having a sickly, pale or pinched appearance.

peal (peel) *n.* 1. A ringing of a set of bells; especially, a change or set of changes, rung on bells. 2. A set of bells tuned to each other; a chime; a carillon. 3. A loud burst of noise or series of noises, as of laughter or thunder. ~*v.* **pealed, pealing, peals.** —*intr.* To sound in a peal; ring: *The bells pealed out.* —*tr.* To utter loudly and sonorously. [Middle English *pele,* summons to church by bell, short for *appel,* an appeal, from *appelen,* to APPEAL.]

pean. Variant of **paean.**

pea·nut (pée-nut) *n.* 1. A vine, *Arachis hypogaea,* native to tropical America and widely cultivated in semitropical regions. It has yellow flowers on stalks that bend over and grow into the soil so that the seed pods ripen underground. 2. The edible, nutlike, oily seed of this vine, used for food and as a source of oil. Also called "goober", "groundnut", "monkey nut". 3. *Plural. Slang.* A very small amount of money; a trifling sum: *Clothes were being sold for peanuts at the jumble sale.* 4. *U.S. Slang.* A small or insignificant person.

peanut butter *n.* A paste made from roasted ground peanuts.

peanut oil *n.* The oil pressed from peanuts, used for cooking, in soaps, and as a pharmaceutical vehicle.

pear (pair) *n.* 1. A widely cultivated tree, *Pyrus communis,* having glossy leaves, white flowers, and edible fruit. 2. The gritty-textured fruit of this tree, spherical at the apex and tapering towards the base. [Middle English *pere,* Old English *peru, pere,* from Latin *pirus,* pear tree, *pirum,* pear; akin to Greek *apios,* pear tree.]

pearl[1] (perl) *n.* 1. A smooth, lustrous, variously coloured deposit, chiefly calcium carbonate, formed around a grain of sand or other foreign matter in the shells of certain molluscs and valued as a gem. 2. Mother-of-pearl; nacre. 3. A person or object likened to a pearl in beauty or value. 4. *Printing.* A type size, 5 points. 5. *Plural.* A string of pearls. 6. A bluish or greyish white. ~*v.* **pearled, pearling, pearls.** —*tr.* 1. To decorate or cover with or as with pearls. 2. To make into the shape or colour of pearls. —*intr.* 1. To dive or fish for pearls or pearl-bearing molluscs. 2. To form beads resembling pearls. ~*adj.* 1. Made of or containing pearl. 2. Having the shape or col-

our of pearls or mother of pearl. [Middle English *perle,* from Old French, from Vulgar Latin *per(nu)la* (unattested), diminutive of Latin *perna,* leg; ham, sea-mussel (from its ham-shaped peduncle).]

pearl[2]. Variant of **purl** (embroidery).

Pearl. See **Zhujiang** (river).

pearl ash *n. Chemistry.* **Potassium carbonate** (*see*).

pearl barley *n.* Barley rubbed into small, rounded grains, used in stews and soups.

pearl diver *n.* A person who dives in search of molluscs containing pearls. Also called "pearler".

pearl·er (pérlər) *n.* 1. A pearl diver. 2. A boat engaged in searching for pearls. 3. Variant of **purler.**

pearl fish *n.* Any of various fishes of the family Carapidae, especially of the genus *Fierasfer,* that shelter inside sea cucumbers or occasionally pearl shells.

pearl grey *n.* Light bluish grey. —**pearl-grey** (pérl-gráy) *adj.*

Pearl Harbor. Inlet of the Pacific Ocean on Oahu Island, Hawaii, United States. Site of a U.S. naval base, it was the object of a surprise attack by the Japanese Air Force on December 7, 1941, which precipitated the United States into World War II.

pearl·ised, pearl·ized (pérlīzd) *adj.* Having a pearly finish: *pearlised nail varnish.*

pearl·ite (pérlīt) *n.* 1. A mixture of ferrite and cementite forming distinct layers or bands in slowly cooled carbon steels. 2. Variant of **perlite.** [French *perlite,* from *perle,* a soft gelatinous capsule, from Old French, PEARL + -ITE.]

pearl millet *n.* A tropical grass, *Pennisetum typhoideum,* having long, bulrush-like flowering spikes and whitish seeds that are used as food in the Old World.

pearl oyster *n.* Any of several bivalve marine molluscs of the genus *Pinctada* and related genera, of tropical waters. *P. margaritifera* is a major commercial source of pearls.

pearlwort (pérl-wurt ‖ -wawrt) *n.* Any of various short, tufted plants of the genus *Sagina* bearing tiny white or green flowers.

pearl·y (pérli) *adj.* **-ier, -iest.** 1. Resembling pearls: *pearly teeth.* 2. Covered or decorated with pearls or mother-of-pearl. ~*n.* A pearly king or queen. 2. **a.** *Plural.* The traditional costume worn by a pearly king or queen. **b.** A pearl button.

pearly everlasting *n.* A plant, *Anaphalis margaritacea,* having woolly, grey-green foliage and whitish, long-lasting flowers.

Pearly Gates *pl.n.* 1. *Informal.* The gateway to heaven. 2. *Small p, small g. British Slang.* The teeth.

pearly king *n.* A London costermonger wearing a ceremonial costume elaborately decorated with pearl buttons.

pearly nautilus *n.* The **chambered nautilus** (*see*).

pearly queen *n.* The wife of a pearly king, who wears a costume decorated in similar fashion.

pear-main (paír-mayn, pér-) *n.* Any of several varieties of red-skinned apple. [Middle English *parmayn,* a kind of pear, from Old French *parmain,* from Vulgar Latin *parmānus* (unattested), of PARMA.]

pear oil *n.* A solvent, **amyl acetate** (*see*).

Pears (peerz), **Sir Peter (Neville Luard)** (1910–86). British tenor. He joined Sadler's Wells (1943) and sang the title role in *Peter Grimes,* written by his partner Benjamin Britten. A founder with Britten of the Aldeburgh Festival (1948), he had several roles created for him, including Aschenbach in *Death in Venice* (1974).

Pearse (peerss), **Patrick (Henry)** (1879–1916). Irish nationalist, poet, and teacher. A leader of the Gaelic revival, particularly in schools, and of the Irish Republican Brotherhood, he commanded the rebels in the Easter Rising (1916), becoming president of the provisional government in an independent Irish republic. After the defeat of the insurgents, he was court-martialled and shot.

Pear·son (péerss'n), **Lester (Bowles)** (1897–1972). Canadian Liberal prime minster (1963–68). He represented Canada at the United Nations, became chairman of NATO (1951), and received the Nobel peace prize (1957) for his key role in the negotiation of a solution to the Suez crisis (1956).

Pear·y (péer-i), **Robert (Edwin)** (1856–1920). U.S. rear-admiral and explorer. Making a total of eight Arctic voyages, on his last he claimed to be the first man to reach the North Pole (1909).

Peary Land. Peninsula of northern Greenland. At its northernmost point, Cape Morris Jessup, it is 710 kilometres (440 miles) from the North Pole and is the world's most northerly point of land. A mountainous region, it was first explored by Robert Peary (1892).

peas·ant (pézz'nt) *n.* 1. A member of the class comprising small farmers and tenants and labourers on the land where these constitute the main labour force in agriculture. 2. A countryman; a rustic. 3. *Informal.* An uncouth, crude, or ill-bred person; a boor. [Middle English *paissaunt,* from Old French *paisant,* from *païs,* country, from Medieval Latin *pāgēnsis,* "inhabitant of a district", rustic, peasant, from Latin *pāgus,* a district, canton, rural area.]

peas·ant·ry (pézz'ntri) *n.* 1. The social class constituted by peasants. 2. **a.** The condition or rank of a peasant. **b.** Conduct or manners thought to be characteristic of peasants.

pease (peez) *n., pl.* **pease** or **peasen** (-'n). *Obsolete.* A pea.

pease-cod, peas-cod (péez-kod) *n. Archaic.* The pod of the pea. [Middle English *pesecod* : *pese,* PEA + COD (pod).]

pease pudding *n. Chiefly British.* A purée made from boiled dried peas. [*Pease,* Old English *pise* (plural *pisan*), PEA.]

pea-shoot·er (pée-shōōtər) *n.* A toy consisting of a small tube through which dried peas or other pellets are blown at a target.

pea soup *n.* A purée or soup made of dried or fresh peas.

pea·soup·er (pée-sŏopər, -sŏopər) *n. Chiefly British Informal.* A dense yellow fog.

peat (peet) *n.* Partially decomposed, compacted vegetable matter, usually mosses or sedges, found in bogs and fens, and used as fertiliser and fuel. [Middle English *pete,* from Medieval Latin *peta,* probably from Celtic, akin to Medieval Latin *pecia, petia,* PIECE.] —**peat·y** *adj.*

peat bog *n.* A bog *(see).*

peat moss *n.* 1. Any moss, especially of the genus *Sphagnum,* growing in fens. 2. The partly decomposed remains of such mosses, used as a mulch and plant food. Also called "bog moss".

peau de soie (pŏ́ də swáá) *n.* A smooth, satiny fabric of silk or rayon. [French, "skin of silk".]

pea·vey (péevi) *n., pl.* **-veys.** Also **pea·vy** *pl.* **-vies.** *U.S.* A wooden lever with a metal point and a hinged hook near the end, used by lumberjacks to handle logs. [After Joseph *Peavey,* U.S. blacksmith, to whom its invention (about 1870) has been attributed.]

peb·ble (pébb'l) *n.* 1. a. A small stone eroded smooth. b. *Geology.* A rock fragment larger than a gravel and smaller than a cobble, having a diameter of 4 to 64 millimetre (0.16 to 2.5 inches). 2. a. Clear, colourless quartz; rock crystal. b. A lens made of such quartz. 3. A crinkled surface, as on leather or paper. 4. *Australian Informal.* An obstinate or intractable person or animal. ~*adj.* Designating a spectacle lens that is thick and has high powers of magnification. ~*tr.v.* **pebbled, -bling, -bles.** 1. To pave or pelt with pebbles. 2. To impart an irregularly rough, grainy surface to (leather or paper). [Middle English *pibbil, puble,* Old English *papol(stān)* : *papol-,* pebble (probably imitative) + *stān,* STONE.] —**peb·bly** *adj.*

pebble-dash (pébb'l-dash) *n. British.* Mortar in which small pebbles are embedded, used as a finish for outside walls. ~**pebbledashed, -dashing, -dashes.** —*tr.v. British.* To cover with pebbledash.

pe·can (pi-kán, -káan, pée-kan) *n.* 1. A tree, *Carya illinoensis,* of the southern United States, having deeply furrowed bark and edible nuts. 2. The smooth, thin-shelled, oval nut of the pecan. [Earlier *paccan,* from Algonquian, akin to Ojibwa *pagân,* hard-shell nut, Abnaki *pagann,* Cree *pakan.*]

pec·ca·ble (pécka-b'l) *adj.* Liable to sin. [Old French, from Latin *peccāre,* to sin. See **peccant.**] —**pec·ca·bil·i·ty** (-bíllɘti) *n.*

pec·ca·dil·lo (pécka-díllō) *n., pl.* **-loes** or **-los.** A small sin or fault. [Spanish *pecadillo,* diminutive of *pecado,* sin, from Latin *peccātum,* from *peccāre,* to sin. See **peccant.**]

pec·cant (péckɘnt) *adj.* 1. Sinful; guilty. 2. Violating a rule or accepted practice; erring; faulty. [Latin *peccāns* (stem *peccant-*), present participle of *peccāre,* to sin, stumble.] —**pec·can·cy** *n.* —**pec·cant·ly** *adv.*

pec·ca·ry (péckɘri) *n., pl.* **-ries.** Either of two piglike, hoofed mammals, *Tayassu angulatus* or *T. pecari,* of southern North America, Central America, and South America, having dense, long, dark bristles. [Spanish *pecari,* from Carib *pakira.*]

pec·ca·vi (pe-káavee, -káyvī) *n., pl.* **-vis.** A confession of sin. [Latin, "I have sinned".]

pêche Melba *n. French.* A dessert; peach Melba *(see).*

Pe·chen·ga (pɘ-chéngɘ). *Finnish* **Pet·sa·mo** (pét-sɘmō). Port on the Barents Sea, northwest Russia. Ice-free, it has a large fishing fleet, and is the centre of a strategic mining region. The area was part of Finland from 1920 to 1944.

Pe·cho·ra (pɘ-chórɘ). River of European Russia. It rises in the Ural Mountains, and flows northwards for 1 790 kilometres (1,112 miles) to the Barents Sea, passing through the important Pechora coal basin.

peck¹ (pek) *v.* **pecked, pecking, pecks.** —*tr.* 1. To strike with a beak or some sharp-pointed instrument. 2. To make (a hole, for example) by striking repeatedly with the beak or a pointed instrument. 3. To grasp and pick up with the beak: *The bird pecked insects from the log.* 4. *Informal.* To kiss briefly and casually: *He pecked her on the cheek.* —*intr.* 1. To make strokes with the beak or something pointed like a beak: *the noise of birds pecking outside.* 2. To eat in small, sparing bits; nibble. Used with *at: pecking at her food.* 3. To criticise repeatedly; nag; carp. Used with *at.* ~*n.* 1. A stroke or light blow with the beak. 2. A mark or hole made by such a stroke. 3. *Informal.* A light, quick kiss. [Middle English *pecken,* probably from Middle Low German *pekken†.*]

peck² *n. Abbr.* **pk., pk** 1. a. A unit of volume or capacity in the British Imperial System, used in dry measure, equal to 9.092 litres (554.84 cubic inches). b. A unit of volume or capacity in the U.S. system, used in dry measure, equal to 7.571 litres (537.605 cubic inches). 2. A container holding or measuring this amount. 3. *Informal.* A great deal: *a peck of troubles.* [Middle English, from Anglo-French *pek†.*]

peck·er (péckɘr) *n.* 1. One who or that which pecks. 2. *British Slang.* Courage; mettle; pluck. Used chiefly in the phrase *keep one's pecker up.* 3. *U.S. Vulgar Slang.* The penis.

pecking order *n.* 1. A hierarchy within certain flocks of birds, especially poultry, according to which each member submits to pecking and domination by the stronger or more aggressive members, and has the privilege of pecking and dominating the weaker members. Also called "peck order". 2. Any supposedly similar hierarchy, as in a human group. [Translation of German *Hackordnung.*]

Peck·in·pah (péckin-paa), **(David) Sam(uel)** (1925–84). U.S. film director. He began by working for television on such serials as *Gunsmoke.* His often violent films, several of which are westerns,

include *The Wild Bunch* (1969), *Straw Dogs* (1971), *The Getaway* (1972), *Cross of Iron* (1977), and *Convoy* (1978).

peck·ish (péckish) *adj. Informal.* 1. *Chiefly British.* Somewhat hungry. 2. *U.S.* Peevish; irritable.

Peck·snidf·i·an (pek-snítfi-ɘn) *adj.* Addicted to fatuous and hypocritical talk of benevolence and other virtues. [After Seth *Pecksniff,* a character in Dickens' novel *Martin Chuzzlewit* (1844).]

pec·o·ri·no (péckɘ-réenō) *n.* A hard, pale yellow Italian cheese made from ewe's milk. [Italian (adjective), of ewes, from *pecora,* sheep, from Latin, cattle, plural of *pecu* (stem *pecor-*) herd, cattle.]

Pe·cos (páykɘss). River of southern United States. It flows 1 180 kilometres (735 miles) across New Mexico and Texas, to join the Rio Grande.

pecs (peks) *pl.n. Informal.* Pectorals; pectoral muscles.

Pécs (paakh). *German* **Fünf·kir·chen** (fünf-keerkhɘn). Industrial city of southwest Hungary, lying at the centre of the country's main coalmining region.

pec·tase (pék-tayz, -tayss) *n.* An enzyme found in certain fruits that catalyses the conversion of pectins to pectic acids.

pec·tate (pék-tayt) *n.* A salt or ester of pectic acid.

pec·ten (péktin) *n., pl.* **-tens** or **-tines** (-eez). *Zoology.* 1. Any body structure or organ resembling a comb, such as the ridged part of the eye of reptiles and birds. 2. A scallop of the genus *Pecten.* [New Latin, from Latin, comb.]

pec·tic acid (péktik) *n. Chemistry.* Any of several colloidal substances, essentially complex organic acids, derived from the sugar galactose. [French *pectique.* See **pectin.**]

pec·tin (péktin) *n.* Any of a group of complex colloidal substances of high molecular weight found in ripe fruits, such as apples, and used to form a gel when heated with sugar, as in jam-making. [French *pectine,* from *pectique,* from Greek *pēktikos,* coagulating, from *pēktos,* coagulated, from *pēgnunai,* to coagulate.] —**pec·tic,** **pec·tin·ous** *adj.*

pec·tin·ase (pékti-nayz, -nayss) *n.* A plant enzyme that catalyses the hydrolysis of pectin.

pec·ti·nate (pékti-nayt) *adj.* Also **pec·ti·nat·ed** (-naytid). Shaped like a comb; comblike. [Latin *pecten* (stem *pectin-*), comb, PECTEN + -ATE.] —**pec·ti·na·tion** (-náysh'n) *n.*

pec·to·ral (péktɘrɘl) *adj.* 1. *Anatomy.* Pertaining to the breast or chest: *a pectoral muscle.* 2. Worn on the chest or breast: *a pectoral cross.* ~*n.* 1. A chest muscle or organ. 2. A pectoral fin. 3. A medicine for chest diseases. 4. An ornament or decoration worn on the chest. [Middle English, from Old French, of or worn on the chest, from Latin *pectorālis,* from *pectus* (stem *pector-*), breast.]

pectoral fin *n.* Either of the anterior pair of fins attached to the pectoral girdle of fishes. Also called "pectoral".

pectoral girdle *n. Zoology.* A skeletal structure in vertebrates, attached to and supporting the forelimbs or fins. Also called "pectoral arch", and, chiefly in humans, "shoulder girdle".

pec·u·late (péckew-layt) *v.* **-lated, -lating, -lates.** —*tr.* To embezzle or take for one's own use. —*intr.* To steal money or goods entrusted to one. [Latin *pecūlārī,* to embezzle, from *pecūlium,* "wealth in cattle", private property, from *pecu,* cattle.] —**pec·u·la·tion** (-láysh'n) *n.* —**pec·u·la·tor** *n.*

pe·cu·li·ar (pi-kéwli-ɘr, pɘ-) *adj.* 1. Unusual or eccentric; strange; queer. 2. Calling for special consideration or attention; distinct and particular. 3. a. Exclusive; unique: *the peculiar attributes of beauty.* b. Belonging distinctively or especially to one person, group, or kind: *he spoke with an accent peculiar to his native county.* —See Synonyms at **characteristic, strange.** ~*n.* 1. *British.* A church or parish under the jurisdiction of a diocese different from that in which it lies. 2. *Rare.* Some privilege or property that belongs exclusively to one. 3. *Printing.* A special sort *(see).* [Middle English *peculier,* from Latin *pecūliāris,* individual, peculiar, of private property, from *pecūlium,* "wealth in cattle", private property, from *pecu,* cattle, wealth.] —**pe·cu·liar·ly** *adv.*

pe·cu·li·ar·i·ty (pi-kéwli-árrɘti) *n., pl.* **-ties.** 1. The quality or state of being peculiar. 2. a. A notable or distinctive feature or characteristic. b. An eccentricity; an idiosyncrasy; a quirk.

Peculiar People *pl.n. Sometimes small* p, *small* p. An evangelical Protestant denomination founded in 1838, the members of which believe in divine healing.

pe·cu·ni·ar·y (pi-kéwni-ɘri ‖ -erri) *adj.* 1. Consisting of or pertaining to money: *a pecuniary loss; pecuniary motives.* 2. Requiring the payment of money: *a pecuniary offence.* —See Synonyms at **financial.** [Latin *pecūniārius,* from *pecūnia,* "wealth in cattle", property, money, from *pecu,* cattle.]

ped-. 1. Variant of **paed-.** 2. Variant of **pedo-** (soil).

-ped, -pede *n. comb. form.* Indicates foot or feet; for example, *biped, centipede.* [Latin *pēs* (stem *ped-*), foot.]

ped·a·gog·ic (péddɘ-gójik, -gōjik, -góggik) Also **ped·a·gog·i·cal** (-'l) *adj.* 1. Of, pertaining to, or characteristic of teaching. 2. Characterised by pedantic formality. —**ped·a·gog·i·cal·ly** *adv.*

ped·a·gog·ics (péddɘ-gójikss, -gōjikss, -góggiks) *n. Used with a singular verb.* The art of teaching; education; pedagogy.

ped·a·gogue (péddɘ-gog) *n.* 1. A schoolteacher; an educator. 2. One who instructs in a pedantic or dogmatic manner. [Middle English *pedagoge,* from Old French *pedagogue,* from Latin *paedagōgus,* from Greek *paidagōgos,* teacher, trainer (of boys) : *paid-,* PEDO- + *agōgos,* leader, from *agein,* to lead.] —**ped·a·gogu·ish** *adj.*

ped·a·go·gy (péddɘ-goji, -gōji, -goggi) *n.* 1. The art or profession of teaching. 2. Preparatory training or instruction.

ped·al (pédd'l) *n.* **1. a.** A lever operated by the foot on various musical instruments, such as the piano, organ, or harp. **b.** Any of various electronic devices used to modify the signal from an electronic instrument, especially a guitar. **2.** A pedal point. **3.** A lever worked by the foot in a machine, such as a motor vehicle, bicycle, or sewing machine. —*adj.* (in sense 1 also péed'l) **1.** Pertaining to a foot or footlike part: *the pedal extremities.* **2.** *Music.* Pertaining to a pedal. —*v.* **pedalled** or *U.S.* **pedaled, pedalling** or *U.S.* **-aling, -als.** —*intr.* **1.** To use or operate a pedal or pedals. **2.** To ride a bicycle. —*tr.* To operate the pedals of. [French *pédale,* from Italian *pedale,* (organ) pedal, from Latin *pedālis,* of the foot, from *pēs,* foot.] —**ped·al·ler** *n.*

pedal bin *n.* A small bin, typically for kitchen refuse, the lid of which is raised and lowered by a foot pedal.

ped·al·board (pedd'l-bawrd) *n.* A bank of foot-operated keys, as on an organ.

pe·dal·fer (pi-dál-fər) *n. Geology.* Soil rich in aluminium and iron and deficient in carbonates, characteristic of humid, high-temperature regions with forest cover. Compare **pedocal.** [PED(O)-(soil) + AL(UM) + Latin *ferrum,* iron.]

ped·a·lo (pédd'l-ō) *n., pl.* **-los** or **-loes.** A small pleasure boat propelled by paddle wheels operated by pedals. [From PEDAL.]

pedal point *n. Music.* A note, usually in the bass and on the tonic or the dominant, sustained through harmonic changes in the other parts. Also called "pedal".

pedal pushers *pl.n.* Calf-length women's and girls' slacks, originally worn for cycling.

ped·ant (pédd'nt) *n.* **1.** One who pays undue attention to book learning and formal rules or details without having a true insight or understanding. **2.** One who exhibits his learning ostentatiously. **3.** *Archaic.* A schoolmaster; a pedagogue. [French, from Italian *pedante,* apparently from *peda-* as in PEDAGOGUE + -ANT.] —**pe·dan·tic** (pi-dántik, pe-), **pe·dan·ti·cal** *adj.* —**pe·dan·ti·cal·ly** *adv.*

ped·ant·ry (pédd'ntri) *n., pl.* **-ries. 1.** Excessive attention to detail or rules in learning or teaching. **2. a.** The habit of mind or manner characteristic of a pedant. **b.** An instance of pedantic behaviour.

ped·ate (péddayt) *adj.* **1.** *Zoology.* Having feet. **2.** Resembling or functioning as a foot or feet: *pedate appendages.* **3.** *Botany.* Having radiating lobes or divisions, with the lateral lobes cleft or divided: *a pedate leaf.* [Latin *pedātus,* from *pēs* (stem *ped-*), foot.]

ped·dle (pédd'l) *v.* **-dled, -dling, -dles.** —*tr.* **1.** To travel about selling (wares); peddling *goods from door to door.* **2.** To sell (narcotic drugs, for example), especially in small quantities. **3.** To try to spread or circulate (ideas or opinions). —*intr.* To travel about selling wares. [Back-formation from PEDLAR.]

ped·dler (péddlər) *n.* **1.** One who peddles, especially narcotic drugs. **2.** *U.S.* Variant of **pedlar.**

ped·er·ast, paed·er·ast (pédde-rast) *n.* One who practises pederasty. [Back-formation from PEDERASTY.]

ped·er·ast·y (pédde-rasti) *n.* Homosexual relations, especially between a male adult and a boy or young man. [New Latin *paederastia,* from Greek *paiderastia : pais* (stem *paid-*), boy + *erastēs,* lover (from *eros,* sexual love, EROS.]

pe·des. Plural of **pes.**

ped·es·tal (péddist'l) *n.* **1.** An architectural support or base, as for a column or statue. **2.** Either of the supports for a kneehole desk, usually consisting of a set of drawers. **3.** Any support or foundation. —**put on a pedestal.** To treat with exaggerated regard, ignoring imperfections. —*tr.v.* **pedestalled** or *U.S.* **pedestaled, -talling** or *U.S.* **-taling, -tals.** To place on or provide with a pedestal. [Old French *piedestal,* from Old Italian *piedestallo,* from *pie di stallo,* "foot of a stall" : *pie,* foot, from Latin *pēs* + *di,* of, + *stallo,* stall.]

pe·des·tri·an (pi-déstri-ən) *n.* A person travelling on foot; a walker, especially in town and cities. —*adj.* **1.** Of, suitable for, pertaining to, or designed for pedestrians: *pedestrian traffic.* **2.** Going or performed on foot: *a pedestrian journey.* **3.** Commonplace; undistinguished; ordinary. [Latin *pedester,* going on foot, hence prosaic, from *pedes,* one who goes on foot, from *pēs* (stem *ped-*), a foot.] —**pe·des·tri·an·ism** *n.*

pedestrian crossing *n. British.* A place where pedestrians have priority over traffic when crossing the road. Also *U.S.* "crosswalk". See **pelican crossing, zebra crossing.**

pedestrian precinct *n.* An area in a town reserved for pedestrians and closed to vehicular traffic.

pedi- *comb. form.* Indicates foot; for example, **pediform.** [Latin, from *pēs* (stem *ped-*), foot.]

pediatrician. *U.S.* Variant of **paediatrician.**

ped·i·cel (péddi-sel, -səl) *n.* **1.** *Biology.* A small stalk, part, or organ, especially one serving as a support. **2.** *Botany.* **a.** Any of several small stalks bearing a single flower in an inflorescence. **b.** A support for a fern sporangium or moss capsule. **3.** The second segment of an insect's antenna. [New Latin *pedicellus,* diminutive of Latin *pediculus,* little foot, pedicel, from *pēs,* a foot.]

ped·i·cel·late (péddi-séll-ət, -it, -ayt) *adj.* Also **ped·i·cel·lar** (-ər). Having or supported by a pedicel.

ped·i·cle (péddik'l) *n.* A pedicel.

pe·dic·u·lar (pi-dickewlər, pe-) *adj.* Of, or caused by lice. [Latin *pedicularis,* from *pediculus,* louse, diminutive of *pedis,* louse.]

pe·dic·u·late (pi-dickew-lət, pe-, -lit, -layt) *adj.* Of or pertaining to marine fish of the order Pediculati (or Lophiiformes), which includes the anglerfish.

—*n.* A fish of this order. [New Latin *Pediculati,* "little-footed ones" (from the shape of their pectoral fins), from Latin *pedículus,* little foot. See **pedicel.**]

pe·dic·u·lo·sis (pi-dickew-lō-siss, pe-) *n.* Infestation with lice. [New Latin : Latin *pedículus,* louse (see **pedicular**) + -OSIS.] —**pe·dic·u·lous** (-ləss) *adj.*

ped·i·cure (péddi-kewr) *n.* **1. a.** Cosmetic care of the feet and toenails. **b.** A single cosmetic treatment of the feet and toenails. **2.** A chiropodist. —*tr.v.* **pedicured, -curing, -cures.** To give a pedicure to. [French *pédicure :* PEDI- + Latin *cūrāre,* to take care of, from *cūra,* care.] —**ped·i·cur·ist** *n.*

ped·i·form (péddi-fawrm) *adj.* Shaped like a foot. [French *pédiforme :* PEDI- + -FORM.]

ped·i·gree (péddi-gree) *n.* **1.** Recorded ancestry; lineage: *The young man's pedigree was impeccable.* **2.** A list of ancestors; a family tree. **3.** The recorded descent of a purebred animal. Also used adjectivally: *a pedigree cow.* **4.** A source or derivation. [Middle English *pedegru,* from Old French *pie de grue,* "crane's foot", from the three-line, claw-shaped mark formerly used to show the succession in a pedigree : *pie,* foot, from Latin *pēs* + *de,* of + *grue,* crane, from Latin *grūs.*] —**ped·i·greed** *adj.*

ped·i·ment (péddi-mənt) *n.* **1.** A wide, low-pitched gable surmounting the facade of a building in the Grecian style. **2.** A similar or derivative element used widely in architecture and decoration. **3.** A sloping rock surface, usually covered with alluvium, found in desert areas at the base of mountains. [Variant of earlier *perement,* probably variant (influenced by PEDI-) of PYRAMID.] —**ped·i·men·tal** (-mént'l) *adj.* —**ped·i·ment·ed** (-mentid, -məntid) *adj.*

ped·i·palp (péddi-palp) *n.* Either of the second pair of appendages in arachnids that are attached to the head and may be adapted as sensory organs, as in spiders, or as claws, as in scorpions. Also called "palp". [New Latin *pedipalpus.* See **pedi-, palp.**]

ped·lar (péddlər) *n.* Also *chiefly U.S.* **ped·dler, ped·ler.** One who peddles for a living; a hawker. [Middle English *pedlere,* earlier *pedder,* from *ped†,* wicker basket, pannier.]

pedo–¹, ped– *comb. form.* Indicates soil; for example, **pedalfer, pedocal.** [Greek *pedon,* earth, soil.]

pedo–². *Chiefly U.S.* Variant of **paedo-.**

ped·o·cal (péd-ō-kal, -ə-) *n. Geology.* A lime-rich soil of cool, semi-arid, and arid regions. Compare **pedalfer.** [PEDO- (soil) + Latin *calx,* lime, limestone, from Greek *khalix,* pebble, small stone.] —**ped·o·cal·ic** (-kálik) *adj.*

pe·dol·o·gy (pi-dóllə-ji, pe-) *n.* The scientific study of soils, their origins, characteristics, and uses. Compare **agrology.** [PEDO- (soil) + -LOGY.] —**ped·o·log·ic** (péddə-lójik), **ped·o·log·i·cal** *adj.* —**ped·o·log·i·cal·ly** *adv.* —**pe·dol·o·gist** (-dólləjist) *n.*

pe·dom·e·ter (pi-dómmitər) *n.* An instrument that gauges the approximate distance travelled on foot by registering the number of steps taken. [French *pédomètre :* pedo-, variant of PEDI- + -METER.]

pe·dun·cle (pi-dúngk'l ‖ *U.S.* also pée-dungk'l) *n.* **1.** *Botany.* The main stalk of an inflorescence, or a stalk or stem bearing a solitary flower. **2.** *Zoology.* A stalklike structure in various invertebrate animals. **3.** *Anatomy.* A stalklike bundle of fibres, especially of nerve fibres, connecting different parts of the central nervous system. [New Latin *pedunculus,* diminutive of Latin *pēs* (stem *ped-*), a foot.] —**pe·dun·cu·lar** *adj.*

pe·dun·cu·late (pi-dúngkew-lət, pe-, -lit, -layt) *adj.* Also **pe·dun·cu·lat·ed** (-laytid). Having or supported by a peduncle.

pedunculate oak *n.* The common or English oak, *Quercus robur,* having acorns borne on long peduncles. See **oak.**

pee (pee) *intr.v.* **peed, peeing, pees.** *Slang.* To urinate. —*n. Slang.* **1.** Urine. **2.** A act of urinating. [Euphemistic abbreviation, from *p* in PISS.]

Pee·bles (peeb'lz). Former county town of Peeblesshire, Scotland. Situated on the river Tweed, it is an agricultural centre and important for the manufacture of woollen goods.

Pee·bles·shire (peéb'lz-shər, -sheer, -shīr). Also **Tweed·dale.** Former county of southeast Scotland, now part of Borders.

peek (peek) *intr.v.* **peeked, peeking, peeks. 1.** To glance quickly. **2.** To look or peer furtively, as from a place of concealment. —*n.* A furtive or brief look. [Middle English *piken†.*]

peek·a·boo (péek-ə-bōō, -bōō) *n. Chiefly U.S.* A child's game, **peep-bo** (*see*). —*adj.* Having a pattern of small holes. Said of a garment or fabric. [PEEK + BOO; akin to Dutch *kiekeboe.*]

peel¹ (peel) *n.* The skin or rind of certain fruits, such as the orange or apple. —*v.* **peeled, peeling, peels.** —*tr.* **1.** To strip or cut away the skin, rind, or bark from; pare. **2.** To strip away; pull off (an outer covering). **3.** To put (another player's ball) through a hoop in croquet. —*intr.* **1.** To lose or shed skin, bark, or other covering. **2.** To come off in thin strips or pieces, as bark, skin, or paint may. **3.** *Slang.* To remove one's clothes; undress. Often used with *off.* —**peel off. 1.** To leave flight formation in order to land or make a dive. Used of an aircraft. [Middle English *pelen,* from Old French *peler,* to peel, remove hair from, from Latin *pilāre,* to plunder, "pile up (booty)", from *pīa,* "pile", PILLAR.]

peel² *n.* **1.** A long-handled, shovel-like tool used by bakers to move bread or pastries into and out of an oven. **2.** Formerly, a T-shaped pole, used by printers for hanging freshly printed sheets of paper to dry. [Middle English *pele,* from Old French, shovel, from Latin *pāla,* spade.]

peel³ *n.* Any of several fortified houses or towers constructed in the border area between Scotland and England in the 16th century. [Middle English *pel(e)*, castle, small tower, (originally) palisade, from Anglo-French, from Latin *pālus,* stake.]

Peel (peel). Seaport of the Isle of Man, western Europe. Situated on the west coast, its chief industries are tourism and fishing.

Peel, Sir Robert (1788–1850). British Conservative prime minister (1834–35, 1841–46). Entering Parliament as a Tory (1809), he served as secretary for Ireland (1812–18) and was Home Secretary (1822–27, 1828–30), during which time he reorganised and consolidated the London police as the Metropolitan Police (1829) and helped to pass the Catholic Emancipation Act (1829). After the passing of the parliamentary Reform Bill (1832), he outlined the reforming programme of the emergent Conservative Party with the Tamworth Manifesto (1834). Following the split between the traditional protectionist Tories and the new Conservatives over free trade and the repeal of the Corn Laws (1846) his government fell, after which he gave his support to the Whigs.

peel·er¹ (péelər) *n.* **1.** A person or device that peels; especially, a kitchen implement for peeling the rind or skin from a fruit or vegetable. **2.** *U.S. Slang.* A striptease artist.

peeler² *n. British Slang.* A policeman. Not in current usage. [After Sir Robert Peel.]

pee·lie-wal·ly (péeli-wál-i) *adj. Scottish.* Pale and insipid-looking. [Perhaps reduplication of obsolete *wally,* faded, from *wallow,* to fade, Old English *walwian.*]

peel·ing (péeling) *n.* A piece or strip that has been peeled off, as of skin, bark, or rind.

peen (peen) *n.* The end of a hammerhead opposite the flat striking surface, often wedge-shaped or ball-shaped and used for chipping, indenting, and metalworking.

~*tr.v.* **peened, peening, peens.** To hammer, bend, or shape with a peen. [*Peen, pane,* perhaps from French *panne,* from Dutch *pen,* from Latin *pinna,* point.]

Pee·ne·mün·de (páynə-mündə). Fishing village in northern Germany. Situated on the Isle of Usedom on the Baltic coast, it was a centre for the development of guided missiles prior to and during World War II, producing the V1 flying bomb and the V2 rocket.

peep¹ (peep) *n.* **1.** A weak, shrill sound or utterance, like that of a young bird. **2.** Any slight sound or utterance: *I don't want to hear a peep out of you.* **3.** Any of various small North American sandpipers.

~*intr.v.* **peeped, peeping, peeps.** **1.** To utter short, soft, high-pitched sounds, like those of a baby bird. **2.** To speak in a thin, high-pitched voice. [Middle English *pepen* (imitative).]

peep² *v.* **peeped, peeping, peeps.** —*intr.* **1.** To look furtively; steal a quick glance. **2.** To peer through a small opening or from behind something: *"She stretched herself up on tiptoe, and peeped over the edge of the mushroom."* (Lewis Carroll). **3.** To become visible gradually, as though emerging from a hiding place: *At dawn the sun peeped over the horizon.* —*tr.* To cause to emerge or become partly visible.

~*n.* **1.** A quick or furtive look; a glance. **2.** A first glimpse or first appearance: *the peep of dawn.* [Middle English *pepen,* alteration of *piken,* PEEK.]

peep-bo (péep-bō) *n.* A child's game in which a person repeatedly covers and exposes his face to the cry of "peep-bo". Also called "bo-peep", chiefly *U.S.* "peekaboo".

peep·er¹ (péepər) *n.* A creature that peeps.

peeper² *n.* **1.** Someone who looks furtively. **2.** *Slang.* An eye.

peep·hole (péep-hōl) *n.* A small hole or crevice through which one may peep.

peeping Tom *n.* A man who derives sexual gratification from pruriently and secretly spying on the intimate behaviour of others; a voyeur. [From the story of *Peeping Tom* of Coventry, a tailor who was the sole person to peep at the naked Lady Godiva (and was struck blind).]

peep·show (péep-shō) *n.* An exhibition of pictures or objects, especially of an erotic nature, viewed through a small hole or magnifying glass. Also called "raree show".

peep sight *n.* A rear sight of a firearm consisting of an adjustable eyepiece with a small opening through which the front sight and the target are aligned.

peep-toe (péep-tó) *adj.* Also **peep-toed** (-tód). Cut away to reveal the big toe or part of the toes. Said of a shoe.

pee·pul, pi·pal (péep'l) *n.* A fig tree, *Ficus religiosa,* of India, regarded as sacred by Buddhists. According to Buddhist tradition, this is the tree under which the Buddha attained enlightenment. Also called "bo tree". [Hindi *pīpal,* from Sanskrit *pippala.*]

peer¹ (peer) *intr.v.* **peered, peering, peers.** **1.** To look intently, searchingly, or with difficulty: *We peered through the mist.* **2.** To be partially visible; show: *The moon peered from behind a cloud.* —See Synonyms at **gaze.** [Perhaps contraction of APPEAR.]

peer² *n.* **1. a.** A nobleman. **b.** A member of the British peerage; a duke, marquis, earl, viscount, or baron. **2.** A person who has equal standing with another, as in rank, class, or age. **3.** *Archaic.* A companion; a fellow. [Middle English *peer(e),* from Old French *per,* equal, one's equal, (hence) nobleman, from Latin *pār,* equal.]

peer·age (péer-ij) *n.* **1.** The rank or title of a peer. **2.** The body of peers. **3.** A book listing peers and their families.

peer·ess (péer-iss, -ess) *n.* **1.** A woman who holds a life peerage. **2.** The wife or widow of a peer.

peer group *n.* Those of the same age and status as an individual.

peer·less (péer-ləss, -liss) *adj.* Without peer; unmatched; unequalled. —**peer·less·ly** *adv.* —**peer·less·ness** *n.*

peer of the realm *n., pl.* **peers of the realm.** *British.* A hereditary peer who has the right to sit in the House of Lords on his majority.

peeve (peev) *tr.v.* **peeved, peeving, peeves.** *Informal.* To annoy or make resentful; vex.

~*n. Informal.* **1.** A vexation; a grievance: *a pet peeve.* **2.** A resentful mood: *be in a peeve.* [Back-formation from PEEVISH.]

pee·ver (péevər) *n. Scottish Regional.* **1.** A tile, stone, or the like used in the game of hopscotch. **2.** *Plural.* The game of hopscotch itself. [Origin obscure.]

pee·vish (péevish) *adj.* **1.** Querulous; discontented; fretful. **2.** Ill-tempered. **3.** Contrary; fractious. [Middle English *pevisht.*] —**pee·vish·ly** *adv.* —**pee·vish·ness** *n.*

pee·wee (pée-wee) *n. U.S.* **1.** *Informal.* Any relatively or unusually small person or thing. **2.** Variant of **pewee.** [Whimsical formation based on WEE.] —**pee·wee** *adj.*

pee·wit, pe·wit (pée-wit) *n.* A bird, the **lapwing** (see). [Imitative of its call.]

peg (peg) *n.* **1.** A small cylindrical or tapered pin, as of wood, used to fasten things, such as floorboards, to mark a point, such as a boundary, or to plug a hole, such as the vent of a barrel. **2.** A similar pin forming a projection that may be used as a support, as for hanging clothes on. **3.** Any of the pins of a stringed musical instrument that are turned to tighten or slacken the strings so as to regulate their pitch. **4.** An implement fitted with a pointed prong or claw for tearing or catching. **5.** A degree or notch, especially in estimation. **6.** *Chiefly British.* A small alcoholic drink, especially brandy or whisky and soda. **7.** A pretext or occasion for: *a peg to hang one's grievances upon.* **8.** A **clothes peg** (see). **9.** *Informal.* A wooden leg. **10.** In croquet, a coloured post that players must hit in order to proceed. —**take (someone) down a peg.** To reduce the pride of; humble. —**off the peg.** *Chiefly British.* Bought ready to wear. Said of a garment. —**a square peg in a round hole.** A misfit.

~*v.* **pegged, pegging, pegs.** —*tr.* **1. a.** To put or insert a peg into. **b.** To provide (a barrel) with a vent and peg. **c.** To pierce or strike with or as with a peg. **2.** To designate or mark by means of pegs: *pegging the score in a cribbage game.* **3.** *Finance.* **a.** To stabilise or fix the prices of (securities, stocks, or the like) so as to minimise fluctuation. **b.** To fix levels of (prices, wages or the like), as by government legislation. **4.** To aim and throw (a missile, such as a stone or a ball) at or to a person or target. —*intr.* To proceed doggedly and steadily; hammer away; persist. Often followed by *away: pegging steadily away until the work's done.* —**peg out.** *Informal.* **1.** To become exhausted; collapse. **2.** *Informal.* To die. **3.** In croquet: **a.** To win a game by hitting the peg. **b.** To cause (an opponent's ball) to strike the peg. **4.** To score the winning point in cribbage. [Middle English *pegge,* probably from Middle Dutch.]

Peg·a·sus¹ (péggə-səss). *Greek Mythology.* The winged steed that caused Hippocrene, the fountain of the Muses on Helicon, to well forth with a stroke of his hoof; the mount of Bellerophon. [Latin, from Greek *Pegasos,* from *pēgē,* spring.]

Pegasus² *n.* A constellation in the Northern Hemisphere near Aquarius and Andromeda.

peg·board (pég-bawrd ‖ -bôrd) *n.* **1.** A board for playing games such as cribbage, having holes into which pegs are inserted, either as part of a game or to keep score. **2.** Hardboard having rows of small holes into which hooks or pegs may be inserted.

peg leg *n. Informal.* An artificial leg, especially one made of wood.

peg·ma·tite (pég-mə-tīt) *n. Geology.* A very coarse-grained igneous rock, sometimes rich in rare elements such as uranium, tungsten, and tantalum. Most pegmatites are granite. [French : Greek *pēgma* (stem *pēgmat-*), framework, from *pēgnunai,* to fasten + -ITE.] —**peg·ma·tit·ic** (-títtik) *adj.*

peg top *n.* A wooden spinning top, tapering to a usually metal point on which it rotates.

Pé·guy (pay-gée), **Charles (Pierre)** (1873–1914). French poet, nationalist, and publisher. He founded the journal *Cahiers de la quinzaine* (1900–14) in which he published his own work and that of other writers. Combining this with socialist and Catholic views, he also wrote *Notre Jeunesse* (1910), *Le Mystère de la charité de Jeanne d'Arc* (1910), and *Eve* (1913).

Pehlevi. Variant of **Pahlavi.**

P.E.I. Prince Edward Island.

pei·gnoir (páyn-waar, payn-waár, pen-) *n.* A woman's loose-fitting dressing gown; a negligee. [French, "garment worn while combing the hair", from Old French *peigner,* to comb the hair, from Latin *pectināre,* from *pecten* (stem *pectin-*), comb.]

Pei·ping. See **Beijing.**

Peirce (perss), **Charles (Sanders)** (1839–1914). U.S. philosopher and logician. He founded pragmatism as a reaction against "useless" metaphysical speculation and theorising. He was also a pioneer in the development of modern formal logic, inspired by the algebraic laws and methods of De Morgan and Boole.

pej·o·rate (péjə-rayt) *tr.v.* **-ated, -ating, -ates.** To diminish in quality, status, or worth. [Back-formation from PEJORATIVE.]

pej·o·ra·tion (péjə-ráysh'n) *n.* **1.** The process or condition of worsening or degenerating. **2.** *Linguistics.* The process by which the semantic status of a word changes for the worse, over a period of time. For example, *egregious,* which formerly meant "distinguished," " has come to mean "conspicuously bad". Compare **amelioration.** [Medieval Latin *pējōrātiō* (stem *pējōrātiōn-*), from Late Latin *pējōrāre,* to become or make worse, from Latin *pējor,* worse.]

pe·jor·a·tive (pi-jórrətiv, pə-, péejə-rətiv ‖ -raytiv, *U.S. also* péjə-) *adj.* **1.** Tending to make or become worse. **2.** Expressing disapproval.
~*n.* A pejorative word. —**pe·jor·a·tive·ly** *adv.*

pek·an (péckən) *n.* A mammal, the **fisher** (*see*). [Canadian French *pékan,* of Algonquian origin, akin to Abnaki *pékané.*]

peke (peek) *n. Informal.* A Pekingese dog.

Pe·kin (pee-kín, péekin) *n.* A large white duck of an Oriental breed, widely reared in the United States for food. [French *pékin,* from *Pékin,* Peking (Beijing).]

Peking. See **Beijing.**

Pe·king·ese (péeking-éez ‖ -éess *for senses* 1, 2.) *n., pl.* **Pekingese.** Also **Pe·kin·ese** (péekin-). **1.** A resident or native of Peking (Beijing), China. **2.** The Chinese dialect of Peking (Beijing). **3.** A toy dog of a breed developed in China, having a flat nose, long hair, and short, bowed forelegs. —**Pe·king·ese** *adj.*

Peking man *n.* An early form of man whose fossil remains were found at Zhoukoudian (Choukoutien) near Beijing (Peking). The remains are classified as *Homo erectus,* but were formerly classified as *Sinanthropus pekinensis* or *Pithecanthropus pekinensis.*

pe·koe (péekō) *n.* A high-quality variety of black tea made from the leaves around the buds. [Chinese (Amoy) *peh ho : peh,* white + *ho,* down (referring to the downy appearance of the young leaves).]

pel·age (péllij) *n.* The coat of a mammal, consisting of hair, fur, wool, or other soft covering, as distinct from bare skin. [French, from Old French *pel,* poil, hair, from Latin *pilus.*]

Pe·la·gi·an·ism (pe-láyji-ə-niz'm, pi-) *n.* The theological doctrine propounded by Pelagius, and condemned as heresy by the Roman Catholic Church in A.D. 417. Included in its tenets were denial of original sin and affirmation of man's ability to be righteous by the exercise of free will. —**Pe·la·gi·an** *adj. & n.*

pe·lag·ic (pe-lájik, pi) *adj.* Of, pertaining to, or living in open oceans or seas rather than waters adjacent to land or inland waters. See **plankton, nekton.** [Latin *pelagicus,* from Greek *pelagikos,* from *pelagos,* sea.]

Pe·la·gi·us (pe-láyji-əss, pi-). (*c.* A.D. 360– *c.* 420). British heretical theologian. Settling in Rome (*c.* 380), he rejected St. Augustine's teachings on predestination and original sin, and in the heretical doctrine of Pelagianism proclaimed the free will of man to do good or evil. He was condemned by Pope Innocent I (417) and by the Council of Ephesus (431).

pel·ar·gon·ic acid (péllaar-gónnik, -gónik) *n.* A colourless or yellow oil, $CH_3(CH_2)_7COOH$, used as a petrol additive and in the manufacture of lacquers, plastics, and pharmaceuticals. Also called "nonanoic acid". [Obtained from the leaves of PELARGONIUM.]

pel·ar·go·ni·um (péllaar-gṓni-əm) *n.* Any of various plants and shrubs of the genus *Pelargonium,* which includes the geraniums. [New Latin, from Greek *pelargos,* a stork (from the long, beak-shaped capsules of the plants).]

Pe·las·gi·an (pe-láz-gi-ən, pi-, -ji-) *n.* A member of a people living in the region of the Aegean Sea before the coming of the Greeks. [Greek *Pelasgoi,* native name of unknown origin probably altered by folk etymology as if to mean "sea people", from *pelagos,* sea.] —**Pe·las·gi·an, Pe·las·gic** *adj.*

Pe·lé (péllay), born Edson Arantes do Nascimento (1940–). Brazilian footballer. One of the world's greatest inside forwards, he helped to win the World Cup for Brazil in 1958, 1962, and 1970. Playing for Santos (1955–74) and the New York Cosmos (1975–77), he scored more than 1,200 goals.

Pe·lée, Mount (pə-lay). Volcano on the West Indian island of Martinique. Its eruption (1902), with clouds of incandescent gas, destroyed the town of St. Pierre. —**Pe·lé·an** *adj.*

pel·er·ine (péllə-reen ‖ *U.S. also* -rin, -réen) *n.* A woman's cape, usually short, with points descending in front. [French *pèlerine,* from the feminine of *pèlerin,* a pilgrim, from Late Latin *pelegrīnus,* PILGRIM.]

pelf (pelf) *n.* Wealth or riches, especially when dishonestly acquired. [Middle English, booty, from Old French *pelfre.* See **pilfer.**]

pel·ham (péllam) *n.* A horse's bit, combining a curb and a snaffle. [Probably from the surname *Pelham.*]

pel·i·can (péllikən) *n.* Any of various large, web-footed birds of the genus *Pelecanus,* of tropical and warm regions, having under the lower bill a large pouch used for catching and holding fish. [Middle English *pelican,* Old French *pelican,* from Late Latin *pelicānus,* from Greek *pelekan, pelekinos,* from *pelekus,* an axe (probably from the shape of its bill), akin to Sanskrit *parasu,* an axe, probably of Mesopotamian origin.]

pelican crossing *n.* A pedestrian crossing where traffic lights are operated by the person wishing to cross the road. [Irregularly from *pedestrian light controlled crossing.*]

pe·lisse (pe-léess, pi-, pə-) *n.* **1.** A long cloak or outer robe, usually of fur or with a fur lining. **2.** A woman's loose, light cloak, often with openings for the arms. [French, from Medieval Latin *pellicia,* leather garment, cloak, from Latin *pellicius,* made of skin, from *pellis,* skin.]

pe·lite (péelīt) *n.* Any rock composed of fine fragments, of such components as clay, quartz particles, or rock flour. [Greek *pēlos†,* clay + -ITE.] —**pe·lit·ic** (pi-líttik) *adj.*

Pel·la (péllə). Ancient city of Greece. Capital of Macedonia, under Philip II (382–336 B.C.), it was the birthplace of his son Alexander the Great (356 B.C.).

pel·la·gra (pe-láygrə, pi-, pə-, -lággrə ‖ *U.S. also* -laágrə) *n.* A chronic disease caused by niacin deficiency, and characterised by skin eruptions, digestive and nervous disturbances, and eventual mental deterioration. [Italian : *pelle,* skin, from Latin *pellis* + Greek *agra,* seizure.] —**pel·lag·rous** *adj.*

pel·lag·rin (pe-láygrin, pi-, pə-, -lággrin ‖ -laágrin) *n.* A person afflicted with pellagra. [From PELLAGRA.]

pel·let (péllit) *n.* **1.** A small, solid or densely packed ball or mass, as of bread, wax, or medicine. **2.** A bullet or piece of small shot. **3.** A stone ball, used as a catapult missile or as a primitive cannonball. **4.** A hard mass of undigestible food that is regurgitated by certain birds, especially birds of prey.
~*tr.v.* **pelleted, -leting, -lets. 1.** To make or form into pellets. **2.** To strike with pellets. [Middle English *pelet,* from Old French *pelote,* from Vulgar Latin *pilotta* (unattested), diminutive of Latin *pila,* ball, PILL.]

pel·li·cle (péllik'l) *n.* **1.** A thin skin or film, such as an organic membrane or a liquid film. **2.** A rigid outer layer of cytoplasm in certain single-celled organisms such as the euglenas. **3.** The thin outer covering of a mushroom cap. [Old French *pellicule,* from Medieval Latin *pellicula,* from Latin, diminutive of *pellis,* skin.] —**pel·lic·u·lar** (pe-lickewlər, pi-, pə-) *adj.*

pel·li·to·ry (pélli-təri, -tri) *n., pl.* **-ries. 1.** Any of various plants of the genus *Parietaria,* that grow on walls, rocks, and the like, and have clusters of small flowers arising at the leaf bases. **2.** A small plant, *Anacyclus pyrethrum,* of the Mediterranean region, containing a volatile oil once used for the relief of toothache and facial neuralgia. [Sense 1, altered from Middle English *peritorie, paritorie,* from Old French *paritaire,* from Late Latin *parietāria (herba),* "herb of the wall", from *parietārius,* belonging to walls, from Latin *pariēs* (stem *pariet-*), wall. See **paries.** Sense 2, altered from earlier *peletre,* Middle English *peletre, peretre,* from Latin *pyrethrum,* PYRETHRUM.]

pell-mell (pél-mél) *adv.* **1.** In a jumbled, confused manner; helter-skelter. **2.** In frantic, disorderly haste; headlong. [French *pêle-mêle,* Old French *pesle mesle, mesle mesle,* reduplications of *mesle,* imperative of *mesler,* to mix, from Vulgar Latin *misculāre* (unattested), from Latin *miscēre.*] —**pell-mell** *adj. & n.*

pel·lu·cid (pe-léw-sid, pi-, -lōo-) *adj.* **1.** Admitting the passage of light; transparent; translucent. **2.** Transparently clear in style or meaning: *pellucid prose.* [Latin *pellūcidus,* from *pellūcēre, perlūcēre,* to shine through : *per,* through + *lūcēre,* to shine.] —**pel·lu·cid·i·ty** (péllew-síddəti), **pel·lu·cid·ness** *n.* —**pel·lu·cid·ly** *adv.*

Pel·man·ism (pélməniz'm) *n.* **1.** A system of training the memory. **2.** *Often small* **p.** A game in which playing cards are placed face down and the players try to turn up matching pairs. [Proprietary term, after the *Pelman* Institute, London.]

pel·met (pélmit) *n.* A piece of board or draped material fixed above a window or door to hide a curtain rail. [Probably from French *palmette,* PALMETTE (referring to ornamental palm-leaf design on cornice moulding).]

Pel·o·pon·nese (pélləpə-neess, -néess ‖ -neez). Also **Pel·o·pon·ne·sus** (-néessəss). Peninsula of southern Greece, known as Morea in the Middle Ages. Joined to the mainland by the Isthmus of Corinth, it is largely mountainous with fertile coastal lowlands in the west and north. Ruled by Sparta until the fourth century B.C., it has many ruins, and produces currants, wine, and olives. —**Pel·o·pon·ne·sian** (-néesh'n, -néezh'n) *adj.*

Peloponnesian War *n.* A war between Athens and Sparta with their allies (431–404 B.C.) that was won by Sparta.

pe·lo·ri·a (pe-láw-ri-ə, pi-, pə- ‖ -lṓ-) *n. Botany.* Unusual regularity in the form of a flower or other structure that is normally irregular. [New Latin, from Greek *pelōros,* monstrous, from *pelōr,* monster, prodigy.] —**pe·lor·ic** (-láwrik, -lórrik) *adj.*

pe·lo·rus (pi-láwrəss ‖ -lṓrəss) *n., pl.* **-ruses.** A fixed compass card on which bearings relative to the ship's heading are taken. [Perhaps after *Pelorus,* pilot of Hannibal.]

pe·lo·ta (pə-lóttə, pe-, -lṓtə) *n.* **1.** A fast game popular in the Basque country and Spanish America in which players hit a ball with a scoop-shaped wicker racket against any of three walls of a court. **2.** The ball used in this game. [Spanish, ball, augmentative of *pella,* from Latin *pila,* ball.]

pelt¹ (pelt) *n.* **1. a.** The skin of an animal with the fur or hair still on it. **b.** A stripped animal skin ready for tanning. **2.** An animal hide, especially one used as a garment. [Middle English, perhaps back-formation from PELTRY.]

pelt² *v.* **pelted, pelting, pelts.** —*tr.* **1.** To strike or assail repeatedly with or as with blows or missiles; throw things at; bombard. **2.** To cast, hurl, or throw (missiles). —*intr.* **1.** To beat or strike heavily and repeatedly. **2.** To move at a fast speed. **3.** To pour with rain. Often used with *down.*
~*n.* **1.** A sharp blow; a whack. **2.** A rapid pace; speed. Used chiefly in the phrase *at full pelt.* [Middle English *pelten,* perhaps from Latin *pultāre.*] —**pelt·er** *n.*

pel·tast (péltast) *n.* In ancient Greece, a foot soldier who carried a spear and small leather shield. [Latin *peltasta,* from Greek *peltastēs,* from *peltē,* small shield.]

pel·tate (péltayt) *adj. Botany.* Having the leaf stalk attached near the centre of the surface, rather than at or near the margin. [New Latin *peltatus,* "having a shield", from Latin *pelta,* small light shield, from Greek *peltē.*] —**pel·tate·ly** *adv.*

Pel·ti·er effect (pélti-ay) *n.* The generation of heat at either of the two junctions of a thermocouple when it is passing current. Compare **Seebeck effect.** [After Jean *Peltier* (1785–1845), French physicist.]

Peltier element *n.* An electronic device consisting of metal strips that alternate with strips of n-type and p-type semiconductor so that when a current is passed heat is absorbed from one set of metallic strips and emitted from the other set, as a result of the Peltier effect. [After Jean *Peltier.*]

pel·try (péltri) *n.* Undressed pelts collectively. [Middle English, from Old French *peleterie,* from *peletier,* furrier, from *pel,* skin, from Latin *pellis.*]

pel·vic (pélvik) *adj.* Of, in, near, or pertaining to the pelvis.

pelvic fin *n.* Either of a pair of lateral hind fins of fishes, attached to the pelvic girdle. Also called "ventral fin".

pelvic girdle *n.* The skeletal structure of bone or cartilage by which the hind limbs or analogous parts are supported and joined to the vertebral column. Also called "pelvic arch", and in humans "hip girdle".

pel·vis (pél-viss) *n., pl.* **-vises** or **-ves** (-veez). *Anatomy.* **1.** A basin-shaped skeletal structure, composed of the innominate bones on the sides, the pubis in front, and the sacrum and coccyx behind. **2.** The **renal pelvis** *(see).* [New Latin, from Latin *pēlvis,* basin.]

Pem·broke¹ (pémbrŏŏk ‖ -brŏk) *n.* A Welsh corgi of a breed characterised by a short tail and pointed ears. [After PEMBROKE.]

Pem·broke² (pém-brŏŏk, -brək ‖ -brŏk). Seaport in southwest Wales. Situated on Milford Haven, it has a medieval castle where Henry VII was born.

Pem·broke·shire (pém-brŏŏk-shər, -brək-, -sheer ‖ -brŏk-). County of southwest Wales, part of Dyfed (1975–96), now a Unitary Authority area. Its coast is a national park, and tourism and dairy farming are important. Its county town is Haverfordwest.

pem·mi·can, pem·i·can (pémmikən) *n.* **1.** A food originally prepared by North American Indians from lean, dried strips of meat pounded into paste, mixed with fat and berries, and pressed into small cakes. **2.** A similar food made chiefly from beef, dried fruit, and suet, used as emergency rations. [Cree *pimikân,* from *pimii,* grease, fat.]

pem·phi·gus (pémfigəss, pem-fígəss) *n.* Any of several acute or chronic skin diseases characterised by itching blisters. The variety *pemphigus vulgaris* is a serious disease that spreads from the mucous membranes to large areas of skin. [New Latin, from Greek *pemphix* (stem *pemphig-*), drop, pustule, of imitative origin.]

pen¹ (pen) *n.* **1.** An instrument for writing or drawing with ink: **a.** Formerly, one made from a large quill with the nib split and sharpened. **b.** A tapering metal device with a split point, fitted to a metal, plastic, or wooden holder. It may be dipped in ink or supplied by a reservoir within the holder. **c.** A penholder and its pen together. See **ball-point pen, fountain pen. 2.** A writing instrument viewed as the writer's weapon or means of expression of ideas or opinions. **3.** A writer or author: *a hired pen.* **4.** A style of writing: *a witty pen.* **5.** The chitinous internal shell of a squid.
—tr.v. **penned, penning, pens.** To write or compose with a pen. [Middle English *penne,* from Old French *penne,* feather, pen, from Latin *penna,* feather (in Late Latin, also "pen").] **—pen·ner** *n.*

pen² *n.* **1.** A fenced enclosure for animals. **2.** The animals kept in such an enclosure. **3.** Any of various other enclosures, such as a bullpen or a playpen. **4.** A repair dock for submarines. **5.** In Jamaica: **a.** A farm where livestock is bred. **b.** A country estate. *—tr.v.* **penned, penning, pens.** To confine in or as if in a pen. [Middle English *pen,* from Old English *penn.*]

pen³ *n.* A female swan. Compare **cob.** [Origin obscure.]

pen⁴ *n.* *U.S. Slang.* A penitentiary. [Short for PENITENTIARY.]

pen., *Pen.* peninsula.

P.E.N. (pen) *n.* International Association of Poets, Playwrights, Editors, Essayists, and Novelists.

pe·nal (péen'l) *adj.* **1.** Of or pertaining to punishment, especially for breaking the law. **2.** Subject to punishment; legally punishable: *a penal offence.* **3.** Prescribing or enumerating punishments or penalties for offences: *penal laws.* **4.** Serving as or constituting a means or place of punishment: *penal servitude.* [Middle English, from Old French, from Latin *poenālis,* from *poena,* penalty.] **—pe·nal·ly** *adv.*

penal code *n.* The body of laws relating to crimes and offences and the penalties for their commission.

pe·nal·ise, pe·nal·ize (péen'l-īz ‖ *U.S. also* pénn'l-) *tr.v.* **-ised, -ising, ises. 1.** To subject to a penalty, especially for infringement of a law or official regulation. **2.** To impose a handicap on; place at a disadvantage. **3.** To make punishable by a penalty. *—See Synonyms at* **punish. —pe·nal·i·sa·tion** (-ī-záysh'n ‖ *U.S.* -i-) *n.*

pen·al·ty (pénn'lti) *n., pl.* **-ties. 1.** A punishment established by law or authority for a crime or offence. **2.** Something, especially a sum of money, required as a forfeit for an offence or a failure to fulfil a contract or obligation. **3.** The disadvantage or painful consequences resulting from an action or condition. **4.** *Sports.* A handicap or loss of advantage imposed on a team or competitor for infraction of a rule. **5.** *Often plural.* In contract bridge, points scored by the opponents when the declarer fails to make his bid. [Anglo-French *penalte* (unattested), from Medieval Latin *poenālitās* (stem *poenālitāt-*), from Latin *poenālis,* PENAL.]

penalty area *n.* In soccer, the area in front of the goal where the goalkeeper may handle the ball and where a penalty kick may be awarded. Also called "penalty box".

penalty box *n.* **1.** In soccer, the penalty area. **2.** In ice hockey, the enclosure where penalised players sit.

penalty kick *n.* **1.** In soccer, a direct free kick at the goal awarded following a foul committed in the penalty area of the defending team and taken from the penalty spot, with only the goalkeeper in defence. **2.** In Rugby football, a kick awarded against a team for an infringement, such as a player's being offside.

penalty rate *n.* *Australian.* A special rate paid to people working outside the normal hours; overtime rate.

penalty spot *n.* In soccer, a mark 11 metres (12 yards) from the goalmouth from which a penalty kick is taken.

pen·ance (pénnənss) *n.* **1.** An act of self-mortification or devotion performed by way of demonstrating contrition for sin. **2.** *Ecclesiastical.* **a.** A sacrament that includes contrition, confession to a priest, acceptance of punishment, and absolution. **b.** A punishment imposed as a condition of absolution. **3.** A feeling of sorrow for one's wrongdoing or sin. **—do penance.** To show repentance by undergoing imposed or voluntary punishment. [Middle English *penaunce,* from Old French *penance,* from Latin *paenitentia,* penitence, from *paenitēns,* PENITENT.]

Penang and **Pinang.** See **George Town.**

pe·na·tes (pe-naátayz, pi-, pə-, -náyteez) *pl.n.* The Roman gods of the household, tutelary deities of the home and of the state, whose cult was closely connected and often identified with that of the **lares** *(see).* [Latin *Penātēs,* household gods, akin to *penus†,* the interior of a house (compare **penetrate**).]

pence (penss). *British.* Alternative plural of **penny.** Often used in combination: **twopence.** See Usage note at **penny.**

pen·cel, pen·sil (pén-s'l, -sil) *n.* A narrow flag, streamer, or pennon, especially one carried at the top of a lance or spear. [Middle English, from Anglo-French, contracted from Old French *penoncel,* diminutive of *penon,* PENNON.]

pen·chant (pón-shon, pénchənt) *n.* A strong inclination; a definite and continued liking. [French, from the present participle of *pencher,* to incline, from Vulgar Latin *pendicāre* (unattested), from Latin *pendēre,* to hang.]

pen·cil (pén-s'l, -sil) *n.* **1.** A narrow, generally cylindrical implement for writing, drawing, or marking, consisting of a thin rod of graphite, crayon, or similar substance encased in wood or held in a plastic or metal mechanical device. **2.** Something shaped or used like a pencil; especially, a narrow medicated or cosmetic stick: *a styptic pencil; an eyebrow pencil.* **3. a.** *Archaic.* An artist's brush, especially a fine one. **b.** An artist's style or technique in drawing or delineating. **c.** Descriptive skill. **4.** A narrow cone or cylinder of rays, especially light rays, forming a beam of small diameter. **5.** *Mathematics.* A family of geometrical figures that share a common property, such as all straight lines in a plane that pass through a fixed point.
~tr.v. **pencilled** or *U.S.* **penciled, -cilling** or *U.S.* **-ciling, -cils. 1.** To write or produce by using a pencil: *pencil a note.* **2.** To mark, shade, or colour with or as if with a pencil. **—pencil in.** To enter on note down provisionally in a diary, timetable, or the like. [Middle English *pensel, pencel,* from Old French *pincel,* from Vulgar Latin *pēnicellus* (unattested), from Latin *pēnicillus,* a brush, pencil, "small tail", diminutive of *pēnis,* tail.] **—pen·cil·ler** *n.*

pencil sharpener *n.* A device consisting of blade within a case used for giving a sharp point to a pencil.

pend (pend) *intr.v.* **pended, pending, pends. 1.** To wait for a decision or judgment. **2.** *Regional.* To hang; depend. [Latin *pendere,* to suspend, hang.]

pen·dant, pen·dent (péndənt) *n.* **1.** Something suspended from something else; especially, an ornament or piece of jewellery attached to a necklace or bracelet. **2.** A hanging lamp or chandelier. **3.** A sculptured ornament suspended from a vaulted Gothic roof or ceiling. **4. a.** Either of a matched pair; a parallel or companion piece. **b.** An additional thing or part that supplements or complements another; a complement. **5.** A short rope hanging from a mast or spar with an eye at its lower end to which fittings may be attached. **6.** *Nautical.* A **pennant** *(see).*
~adj. Variant of **pendent.** [Middle English *pendaunt,* from Old French *pendant,* from the present participle of *pendre,* to hang, from Vulgar Latin *pendere* (unattested), to hang, variant of Latin *pendēre,* to hang.]

pen·dent, pen·dant (péndənt) *adj.* **1.** Hanging down; dangling; suspended. **2.** Projecting; jutting; overhanging. **3.** Awaiting settlement; undecided; pending.
~n. Variant of **pendant.** [Middle English *penda(u)nt,* from Old French *pendant,* hanging. See **pendant.**] **—pen·dent·ly** *adv.*

pen·den·te li·te (pen-dénti líti) *adj. Law.* While a lawsuit is pending; during litigation. [Latin, "with litigation pending".]

pen·den·tive (pen-déntiv) *n. Architecture.* An overhanging, triangular section of vaulting between the rim of a dome and each adjacent pair of the arches that support it. [French *pendentif,* "overhanging feature", from Latin *pendēns* (stem *pendent-*), present participle of *pendēre,* to hang.]

Pen·de·rec·ki (péndə-rétski), **Krzysztof** (1933–). Polish experimental composer. Receiving wide acclaim for his *Passion and Death of our Lord Jesus Christ according to St. Luke* (1966), he developed his own musical notation, abandoning normal tempos and employing unconventional sounds. Other works include *Threnody to the Victims of Hiroshima* (1961), two operas *The Devils of Loudun* (1969), and *Paradise Lost* (1977–78), a flute concerto (1992–93), and a violin concerto (1995).

pend·ing (pénding) *adj.* **1.** Not yet dealt with, decided, or settled; awaiting conclusion or confirmation. **2.** Impending; imminent.
~prep. **1.** While in process of; during. **2.** While awaiting; until.

[Anglicised form of French *pendant,* from Old French, "hanging" (after Latin *pendēns* (stem *pendent-*), hanging, pending).]

pen·drag·on (pen-drággən) *n.* The supreme war leader of the post-Roman Celts of England and Wales. [Middle English, from Welsh : *pen,* chief, head, from Celtic *gwenno-* (unattested) + *dragon,* standard, from Latin *dracō,* cohort's standard, DRAGON.] — **pen·drag·on·ship** *n.*

pen·du·lar (péndewlər) *adj.* Of or resembling the motion of a pendulum; swinging back and forth.

pen·du·lous (péndewləss) *adj.* **1.** Hanging loosely. **2.** *Rare.* Wavering; undecided. [Latin *pendulus,* from *pendēre,* to hang.] — **pen·du·lous·ly** *adv.* — **pen·du·lous·ness** *n.*

pen·du·lum (péndewləm) *n.* **1. a.** A mass suspended from a fixed low-friction support at the end of a relatively light thread so that it is free to swing in a vertical plane under the influence of gravitational force only. Also called "simple pendulum". **b.** Any of several related, freely swinging configurations differing in mass distribution, suspension, and possible modes of motion. Also called "compound pendulum". **2.** Any such object used to regulate the movement of various devices, especially clocks. **3.** Something that swings back and forth from one course, opinion, or condition to another: *the pendulum of public opinion.* [New Latin, from Latin, neuter of *pendulus,* PENDULOUS.]

Pe·nel·o·pe (pi-nélləpi, pə-). In the *Odyssey,* the wife of Odysseus and mother of Telemachus, celebrated for her constancy.

pe·ne·plain, pe·ne·plane (péeni-playn, -pláyn) *n. Geology.* A nearly flat land surface representing an advanced stage of erosion. [Latin *paene, pēne,* almost + PLAIN.] — **pe·ne·pla·na·tion** (-plə-náysh'n) *n.*

pe·nes. Alternative plural of **penis.**

pen·e·tra·li·a (penni-tráyli-ə) *pl.n.* **1.** The innermost parts of a building; especially, the sanctuary of a temple. **2.** Innermost or hidden parts; recesses: *the penetralia of the soul.* [Latin *penetrālia,* plural of *penetrāle,* innermost part, from *penetrālis,* inner, interior, from *penetrāre,* to PENETRATE.]

pen·e·trance (pénnitrənss) *n. Genetics.* **Expression** *(see).* [From PENETRANT.]

pen·e·trant (pénnitrənt) *adj.* Penetrating; piercing.
~*n.* Something that penetrates or is capable of penetrating. [Latin *penetrāns* (stem *penetrant-*), present participle of *penetrāre,* to PENETRATE.]

pen·e·trate (pénni-trayt) *v.* **-trated, -trating, -trates.** —*tr.* **1. a.** To enter or force a way into; pierce: *penetrated the enemy's territory.* **b.** To insert the penis into the vagina or anus of. **2. a.** To enter into and permeate: *The smell penetrated the entire building.* **b.** To cause to be permeated or diffused; steep. **3.** To grasp the inner significance of; understand: *penetrate a mystery.* **4.** To see through. **5.** To affect deeply, as by piercing the consciousness or emotions. **6.** To infiltrate: *The spy penetrated the enemy's intelligence service.* —*intr.* **1.** To pierce or enter into something; make a way in or through something. **2.** To gain admittance or access. **3.** To gain insight into something. [Latin *penetrāre,* from *penitus,* deeply, from *penus†,* the interior of a house.] — **pen·e·tra·bil·i·ty** (-trə-bílləti) *n.* — **pen·e·tra·ble** (-trəbj'l) *adj.* — **pen·e·tra·bly** *adv.* — **pen·e·tra·tor** (-traytər) *n.* — **pen·e·tra·tive** *adj.*

pen·e·trat·ing (pénni-trayting) *adj.* **1.** Able or seeming to penetrate: *a penetrating wind.* **2.** Keenly perceptive or understanding: *penetrating insight.* — **pen·e·trat·ing·ly** *adv.*

pen·e·tra·tion (penni-tráysh'n) *n.* **1.** The act or process of piercing or penetrating something. **2.** The power or ability to penetrate. **3.** The extent to which a person or thing penetrates, especially: **a.** The extent to which an incursion or infiltration by a hostile force is successful. **b.** The depth reached by a projectile after hitting its target. **c.** In ball games, the depth to which the ball is sent into an opponent's playing area. **4.** Understanding; insight.

pen·e·trom·e·ter (penni-trómmitər) *n.* **1.** A device for measuring the penetrating power of X-rays. **2.** A device for measuring the penetrability of semisolids. [PENETR(ATION) + -METER.]

pen friend *n.* A person with whom one corresponds regularly and forms a friendship, usually without meeting. Also called "pen pal".

pen·guin (péng-gwin) *n.* **1.** Any of various flightless marine birds of the family Spheniscidae, of cool regions of the Southern Hemisphere. They have scalelike, barbless feathers, flipper-like wings, and webbed feet. See **Adélie penguin, emperor penguin. 2.** *Obsolete.* The great auk. [16th century : origin obscure.]

-penia *n. comb. form.* Indicates lack or deficiency; for example, *leukopenia.* [New Latin, from Greek *penia,* poverty, lack.]

pen·i·cil·la·mine (penni-síllə-meen) *n.* A drug that is a chelating agent and is used to treat poisoning by various metals and also severe rheumatoid arthritis.

pen·i·cil·late (penni-síl-ət, -it, -ayt) *adj.* Having or resembling a tuft or brush of fine hairs, such as those on caterpillars and certain grasses. [Latin *pēnicillus,* brush, PENCIL + -ATE.] — **pen·i·cil·late·ly** *adv.* — **pen·i·cil·lus** (-si-láysh'n) *n.*

pen·i·cil·lin (penni-síllin) *n.* Any of several isomeric antibiotic compounds obtained from penicillium moulds, especially *Penicillium notatum* and *P. chrysogenum,* or produced biosynthetically, and used to treat a wide variety of bacterial infections. [New Latin *penicillium,* PENICILLIUM.]

pen·i·cil·li·um (penni-sílli-əm) *n., pl.* **-liums** or **-lia** (-sílli-ə). Any of various moulds of the genus *Penicillium,* having a characteristic blue-green colour, and producing tufts of fine filaments. They grow on decaying fruits and ripening cheese, and are used in the production of penicillin and in making cheese. [New Latin, from Latin *pēnicillus,* brush, PENCIL.]

penile (péenīl) *adj.* Of or relating to the penis. [New Latin *penilis.*]

pen·ill (péenihl) *n., pl.* **penillion** (pi-nílli-ən; *Welsh* pe-níhl-yon). **1.** A form of improvised Welsh poetry sung in accompaniment to a tune played on a harp, especially at eisteddfods. **2.** A stanza of such poetry. [Welsh, verse, stanza.]

pen·in·su·la (pi-nín-sewlə, pə-, pe-, -shŏŏlə) *n. Abbr.* **pen., Pen.** A long projection of land into water. Compare **cape.** [Latin *pēninsula* : *paene,* almost + *īnsula,* an island.]

pen·in·su·lar (pi-nín-sew-lər, pə-, -shŏŏ-) *adj.* Of, pertaining to, or resembling a peninsula.
~*n.* An inhabitant of a peninsula.

Pen·in·su·lar War (pi-nín-sew-lər, pə-, -shŏŏ-). The part of the Napoleonic Wars fought against France in the Peninsula (Spain and Portugal) from 1808-14 by Britain, Portugal, and Spain.

pe·nis (pée-niss) *n., pl.* **-nises** or **-nes** (-neez). **1.** *Anatomy.* The male organ of copulation in higher vertebrates, and of urinary excretion in mammals. **2.** Any of various copulatory organs in males of lower animals. [Latin *pēnis,* tail, penis.]

penis envy *n.* **1.** In Freudian psychology, an emotional and sexual drive in women supposedly originating when a girl perceives her genitalia as a lack or castration. **2.** Loosely, a supposed envy in women of men's power, status, and dominance in society.

pen·i·tent (pénnitənt) *adj.* Feeling or expressing remorse for one's misdeeds or sins.
~*n.* **1.** One who is penitent. **2.** A person performing penance under the direction of a confessor. [Middle English, from Old French, from Latin *paenitēns* (stem *paenitent-*), present participle of *paenitēre,* to repent.] — **pen·i·tence** *n.* — **pen·i·tent·ly** *adv.*

pen·i·ten·tial (penni-ténsh'l) *adj.* **1.** Of, pertaining to, or expressing penitence. **2.** Pertaining to or of the nature of penance.
~*n.* **1.** A book or set of church rules concerning the sacrament of penance. **2.** A penitent. — **pen·i·ten·tial·ly** *adv.*

pen·i·ten·tia·ry (penni-tén-shəri, -shi-əri ‖ *U.S.* -erri) *n., pl.* **-ries. 1.** *Roman Catholic Church.* A tribunal of the Roman Curia, presided over by a cardinal designated in this office as the Grand Penitentiary, having jurisdiction in matters relating to penance, dispensations, and papal absolutions. **2.** *U.S.* A prison, especially one for those convicted of serious crimes.
~*adj.* **1.** Of or for the purpose of penance; penitential. **2.** Pertaining to or used for punishment or reform of wrongdoers. **3.** *U.S.* Resulting in or punishable by imprisonment in a penitentiary: *a penitentiary offence.* [Middle English *penitenciary,* penance officer, from Medieval Latin *penitentiārius,* from Latin *paenitentia,* repentance, from *paenitēns,* (stem *paenitent-*) PENITENT.]

pen·knife (pén-nīf) *n., pl.* **-knives** (-nīvz). A small pocketknife, usually with one or more blades that fold into the handle, originally used to make or sharpen quill pens.

pen·man (pén-mən) *n., pl.* **-men** (-mən). **1.** An author; a writer. **2.** An expert in penmanship. **3.** A copyist; a scribe.

pen·man·ship (pén-mən-ship) *n.* The art, skill, style, or manner of handwriting; calligraphy.

Penn (pen), **William** (1644–1718). English Quaker. Converted to Quakerism (1667), he was imprisoned in the Tower of London for his views (1668). In 1681 he was given a charter in Pennsylvania by the Crown in lieu of a debt to his late father, and proceeded to establish a colony practising religious toleration (1682).

pen·na (pénnə) *n., pl.* **pennae** (pénnee). Any of the larger feathers forming the visible plumage of a bird, as distinguished from the down feathers. [Latin, feather.] — **pen·na·ceous** (pe-náyshəss) *adj.*

pen name *n.* A literary pseudonym.

pen·nant (pénnənt) *n.* **1.** *Nautical.* A long, narrow, relatively small flag, often triangular, used for signalling or for identification. Also called "pendant". **2.** Any similar flag; a pennon. **3.** *U.S. & Austrialian.* A flag used as an emblem or one awarded to the winner of a contest. [Blend of PENDANT and PENNON.]

pen·nate (pénnayt) *adj.* Also **pen·nat·ed** (-aytid). Feathered or winged. [Latin *pennātus,* winged, from *penna,* feather, wing.]

pen·ni (pénni) *n., pl.* **-nis** or **pennia** (-ə). A coin equal to ¹/₁₀₀ of the markka of Finland. [Finnish, perhaps from Middle Low German *pennige,* from West Germanic *panninga* (unattested).]

pen·ni·less (pénni-ləss, -liss, -less) *adj.* Entirely without money; very poor. — **pen·ni·less·ly** *adv.* — **pen·ni·less·ness** *n.*

Pen·nines (pénnīnz). Also **Pennine Chain.** Range of hills in north England. Extending from the Cheviot Hills in the north to the Vale of Trent in the south, its maximum height is at Cross Fell, 893 metres (2,930 feet). Its Pennine Way is used by walkers, and tourism and sheepfarming are important.

pen·ni·nite (pénni-nīt) *n.* A bluish-green form of **chlorite** *(see).* [German *Pennin,* Pennine Alps along the Swiss-Italian border (where it was discovered) + -ITE.]

pen·non (pénnən) *n.* **1.** A long, narrow banner or streamer, often forked or triangular in shape, borne upon a lance. **2.** A pointed or tapering banner or flag flown by a boat. **3.** Any banner, flag, or pennant. **4.** *Poetic.* A pinion; a wing. [Middle English, from Old French *penon,* augmentative of *penne,* feather, wing, from Latin *penna.*] — **pen·noned** *adj.*

pen·non·cel, pen·on·cel, pen·non·celle (pénnən-sel) *n.* A small pennon, flag, or streamer borne upon a lance. [Middle English *penoncelle,* from Old French *penoncel,* diminutive of *penon,* PENNON.]

penn'orth. Variant of **pennyworth.**

Penn·syl·va·ni·a (pén-sil-váyni-ə). State of northeast United States. It was established as a colony (1682) by the Quaker William Penn, who aimed to promote religious toleration. Its many industrial towns include the capital Harrisburg, Pittsburgh, and Philadelphia, and agriculture and dairy farming are important.

Pennsylvania Dutch n. 1. *Used with a plural verb.* The descendants of German and Swiss immigrants who settled in Pennsylvania in the 17th and 18th centuries. 2. German as spoken by this group. Also called "Pennsylvania German".

Penn·syl·va·ni·an (pén-sil-váyni-ən) adj. 1. Of or pertaining to the state of Pennsylvania. 2. *Geology. U.S.* Of, belonging to, or designating the Upper Carboniferous period.
—n. 1. A native or inhabitant of Pennsylvania. 2. *Geology. U.S.* The Upper Carboniferous period. Preceded by *the*.

pen·ny (pénni) n., pl. **-nies** or **pence** (penss) for senses 1, 3). 1. **a.** *Abbr.* **p.** A coin of the United Kingdom equal to ¹/₁₀₀ of a pound. Also called "new penny". **b.** *Abbr.* **d.** Formerly, a coin of the United Kingdom equal to ¹/₂₄₀ of a pound, or ¹/₁₂ of a shilling. **c.** A coin of the Republic of Ireland and of various dependent territories of the United Kingdom. 2. *Abbr.* **p.** *U.S. & Canadian.* A coin worth one **cent** *(see)*. 3. Any of various coins of small denomination. 4. A sum of money: *that must have cost a pretty penny.* —**pennies from heaven.** Unexpected good fortune. —**spend a penny.** *British.* To urinate. Used euphemistically. —**the penny drops.** Comprehension or realisation occurs, usually suddenly. —**turn an honest penny.** To earn money by honest work. —**two** or **ten a penny.** Very common and hence without much value. [Middle English *penny,* Old English *penig, penning,* from West Germanic *panninga* (unattested); probably akin to PAWN (security).]

Usage: The change to decimal currency in 1971 had several linguistic consequences for British English, to which the community is still reacting. Chief among these is the question of how to pronounce the conventional abbreviation *p,* as in *10p.* Immediately following decimalisation, the pronunciation "tenpence" was ambiguous, as it was unclear whether this would have meant ten "old" as opposed to "new" pence. (For a while, the forms *old pence* and *new pence* were used, but these have now largely died out as people have become familiar with the new system.) The abbreviation *p,* pronounced (pee), came to be used as an alternative, and it quickly became the dominant form. However, many people find the abbreviated form unpleasant, and prefer the form *pence,* even in cases where the old singular form, *penny,* would have been used. There is now a trend for *pence* to be used in more formal styles, and *p* to be used informally. When used in isolation *pence* is pronounced (penss). In combination, it used to be pronounced (-pənss), for example *tenpence* (ténpənss). Since decimalisation this pronunciation has been giving way to (-pénss) even in combination: thus *tenpence* is pronounced (tén-pénss) —and may be written *ten pence.*

-penny adj. comb. form. Indicates costing or worth the specified number of pennies; for example, **tenpenny.**

pen·ny-a·lin·er (pénni-ə-línər) n. A hack writer, especially a journalist.

penny black n. *Often capital* **P,** *capital* **B.** Any of a set of postage stamps, costing one penny and bearing the head of Queen Victoria on a black background, that were the first adhesive stamps issued.

pen·ny·cress (pénni-kress) n. Any of several plants of the genus *Thlaspi,* native to Europe, and characteristically having small, winged seed pods; especially, *T. arvense,* which grows as a weed on waste ground. [Perhaps variant of *penny grass,* from its round, flat pods.]

pen·ny-dread·ful (pénni-drédf'l) n. *Informal.* A piece of cheap, sensational popular fiction, such as a book or magazine.

pen·ny-far·thing (pénni-fárthing) n. An early bicycle with a very large front wheel driven directly by pedals, and a small back wheel. [Alluding to the relative size of the wheels.]

penny-pinch·ing (pénni-pinching) adj. *Informal.* Very mean or stingy with money. —**pen·ny-pinch·ing** n.

pen·ny·roy·al (pénni-róy-əl) n. A Eurasian plant, *Mentha pulegium,* having hairy leaves and small lilac-blue flowers. It yields a useful aromatic oil. [Variant of Middle English *puliol real,* from Anglo-French : Old French *poliol,* pennyroyal, from Latin *pūlegium†,* fleabane + *real, roial,* ROYAL.]

pen·ny·weight (pénni-wayt) n. *Abbr.* **dwt., pwt.** A unit of troy weight equal to 24 grains, ¹/₂₀ of a troy ounce or approximately 1.555 grams.

penny whistle n. A type of metal flageolet having six fingerholes. Also called "tin whistle".

pen·ny-wise (pénni-wíz) adj. Careful, often overcareful, in dealing with small sums of money or small matters. —**penny-wise, pound-foolish.** Careful with small sums but wasteful with large sums of money.

pen·ny·wort (pénni-wurt ‖ -wawrt) n. Any of several plants having rounded leaves suggestive of pennies, such as: 1. A Eurasian plant, *Umbilicus rupestris* (or *Cotyledon umbilicus*), having thick, rounded leaves and yellowish-green, bell-shaped flowers. This species is also called "navelwort". 2. A small, prostrate plant, *Hydrocotyle vulgaris,* having tiny pink flowers.

pen·ny·worth (pénni-wurth, -wərth, pénnərth) n. Also **penn'orth** (pénnərth). 1. As much as a penny will buy. 2. A small amount; a modicum. 3. A bargain.

pe·nol·o·gy, poe·nol·o·gy (pee-nólləji) n. The theory and practice of prison management and criminal treatment and rehabilitation. Compare **criminology.** [Latin *poena,* penalty, from Greek *poinē* +

-LOGY.] —**pe·no·log·i·cal** (péenə-lójik'l) adj. —**pe·no·log·i·cal·ly** adv. —**pe·nol·o·gist** (-nóllǝjist) n.

penoncel. Variant of **pennoncel.**

pen pal n. A pen friend *(see).*

pen-push·er (pén-pŏoshǝr) n. *Informal.* 1. Someone who deals with a large amount of paperwork, especially a clerk or other office worker. 2. A writer. —**pen-push·ing** n. & adj.

pensil. Variant of **pencel.**

pen·sile (pén-síl) adj. 1. Hanging down loosely; suspended: *a pensile nest.* 2. Building a hanging nest. Said of birds. [Latin *pēnsilis,* from *pendēre* (past participle *pēnsus),* to hang.] —**pen·sile·ness, pen·sil·i·ty** (pen-sílti) n.

pen·sion¹ (pénsh'n) n. A sum of money paid regularly by a government, company, patron, or the like as, for example, a retirement or injury benefit, in return for a service or by way of patronage.
—tr.v. **pensioned, -sioning, -sions.** 1. To grant a pension to. 2. To retire or dismiss with a pension. Usually used with *off.* [Middle English *pensioun,* from Old French *pension,* from Medieval Latin *pēnsiō* (stem *pēnsiōn-),* from Latin, payment, from *pendere* (past participle *pēnsus),* to weigh, pay.]

pen·sion² (pónss-yon, ponss-yón) n. A boarding house or small hotel in some continental countries, especially France. —**en pension.** *Chiefly British.* 1. Designating the system of hotel charges at a fixed rate per day or a longer period, inclusive of meals: *en pension terms.* 2. At such a rate or under such a system: *living en pension.* [French, boarding house, boarding school, originally "payment for the board and education of a child", extended use of Old French *pension,* payment, PENSION (grant).]

pen·sion·a·ble (pénsh'n-əb'l) adj. 1. Entitling one to receive a pension: *pensionable age.* 2. Conferring the right to a pension: *a pensionable job.*

pen·sion·ar·y (pénsh'n-əri, -ri ‖ -erri) adj. 1. Constituting a pension. 2. Receiving a pension. 3. Mercenary; venal.
—n., pl. **pensionaries.** 1. A pensioner. 2. A hireling.

pen·sion·er (pénsh'n-ər) n. 1. One who receives a pension; especially, one who receives a government retirement pension. 2. One who is dependent on the bounty of another.

pension fund n. A fund contributed to by employers and usually also employees to provide retirement and widows' pensions for employees.

pen·sive (pén-siv) adj. 1. Deeply or seriously thoughtful. 2. Suggesting or expressing deep, often melancholy thoughtfulness. [Middle English *pensif,* from Old French, from *penser,* to think, from Latin *pēnsāre,* frequentative of *pendere* (past participle *pēnsus),* to weigh.] —**pen·sive·ly** adv. —**pen·sive·ness** n.
Synonyms: pensive, contemplative, reflective, meditative.

penstemon. *Chiefly U.S.* Variant of **pentstemon.**

pen·stock (pén-stok) n. 1. A sluice or gate used to control a flow of water. 2. A pipe or conduit used to carry water to a waterwheel or turbine. [PEN (enclosure) + STOCK.]

pent (pent). Alternative past tense and past participle of **pen.**
~adj. *Poetic.* Pent-up.

penta–, pent– comb. form. Indicates five; for example, **pentameter, pentangular.** [Greek, from *pente,* five.]

pen·ta·chlo·ro·phe·nol (péntə-kláwrə-féenol, klórrə- ‖ -klōrə-, -nōl) n. A compound, C_6Cl_5OH, used in solution as a fungicide and wood preservative.

pen·ta·chord (péntə-kawrd) n. *Music.* 1. An instrument with five strings. 2. A series of five notes in a diatonic scale.

pen·ta·cle (péntək'l) n. A five-pointed star, often thought to have magical or mystical significance, formed by five straight lines connecting the vertices of a pentagon and enclosing another pentagon in the completed figure. Also called "pentagram", "pentangle". [Medieval Latin *pentaculum* (unattested) : Greek *penta-,* PENTA- + *-culum,* diminutive suffix.]

pen·tad (péntad) n. 1. A group or series of five members. 2. A five-year period. [Greek *pentas* (stem *pentad-),* from *pente,* five.]

pen·ta·dac·tyl (péntə-dáktil) adj. Also **pen·ta·dac·ty·late** (-ayt, -ət, -it). Having five fingers or toes on each hand or foot. [Latin *pentadactylus,* from Greek *pentadaktulos* : PENTA- + *daktulos,* finger, DACTYL.]

pen·ta·gon (péntə-gən ‖ U.S. -gon) n. A polygon having five sides and five angles. —**the Pentagon.** The U.S. Department of Defense; the U.S. military command. [Latin *pentagōnum,* from Greek *pentagōnon* : PENTA- + -GON.]

pen·tag·o·nal (pen-tággən'l) adj. 1. Having five sides and five angles. 2. Of or formed in pentagons. —**pen·tag·o·nal·ly** adv.

pen·ta·he·dron (péntə-hée-drən) n., pl. **-drons** or **-dra** (-drə). A polyhedron having five plane surfaces. [New Latin : PENTA- + -HEDRON.] —**pen·ta·he·dral** adj.

pen·tam·er·ous (pen-támmərəss) adj. 1. Having or divided into five similar parts. 2. *Botany.* Having flower parts, such as petals, sepals, and stamens, in sets of five. [New Latin *pentamerus* : PENTA- + -MEROUS.] —**pen·tam·er·ism** n.

pen·tam·e·ter (pen-támmitər) n. 1. A line of verse composed of five metrical feet; especially, a line of classical verse having a set metrical pattern consisting of four dactyls and two stressed feet. 2. English verse composed in iambic pentameter. [Latin, from Greek *pentametros* : PENTA- + -METER.] —**pen·tam·e·ter** adj.

pen·tane (pén-tayn) n. Any of three isomeric alkanes, C_5H_{12}: 1. *Normal pentane.* A colourless flammable liquid used as an anaesthetic, solvent, and in the manufacture of artificial ice. 2. *Isopentane.* A colourless flammable liquid used as a solvent and in the manufacture of polystyrene foam. **3.** *Neopentane.* A colourless gas used in the manufacture of synthetic rubber. [PENT(A)- + -ANE.]

pen·tan·gu·lar (pen-táng-gewlər) *adj.* Having five angles.

pen·ta·no·ic acid (pèntə-nō-ik) *n.* A colourless liquid, $CH_3(CH_2)_3COOH$, used in making perfumes, flavourings, and pharmaceuticals. Also called "valeric acid". [PENTAN(E) + -OIC.]

pen·ta·prism (pèntə-priz'm) *n.* A prism with a pentagonal cross-section, used especially in single-lens reflex cameras to deflect an image through the lens to the viewfinder.

pen·ta·quine (pèntə-kween, -kwin) *n.* A drug used in the treatment of malaria. [PENTA- + QUIN(OLINE).]

pen·tar·chy (pèntaarki) *n., pl.* **-chies. 1.** Government by five rulers. **2.** A body of five rulers governing jointly. **3.** A country governed by five joint rulers. **4.** An association or federation of five governments, each ruled by a different leader. [Greek *pentarkhia* : PENTA- + -ARCHY.] **—pen·tar·chi·cal** (pen-tárkik'l) *adj.*

pen·ta·stich (pèntə-stik) *n.* A poem, strophe, or stanza containing five lines. [Late Greek *pentastikhos,* of five verses : PENTA- + *stikhos,* -STICH.]

Pen·ta·teuch (pèntə-tewk ‖ -tōōk) *n.* The first five books of the Old Testament: Genesis, Exodus, Leviticus, Numbers, and Deuteronomy. [Late Latin *Pentateuchus,* from ecclesiastical Greek *Pentateukhos* : PENTA- + *teukhos,* a tool, case for papyrus rolls, scroll.] **—Pen·ta·teuch·al** (-téwk'l ‖ -tōōk'l) *adj.*

pen·tath·lon (pen-táth-lən, -lon) *n.* An athletic contest consisting of five events for each participant. Originating in the ancient Olympics, it was revived in the modern Olympics as the *modern pentathlon,* and consists of running, riding, swimming, fencing, and pistol shooting. [Greek : PENT(A)- + *athlon,* contest (see **athlete**).] **—pen·tath·lete** *n.*

pen·ta·tom·ic (pèntə-tómmik) *adj. Chemistry.* Designating a molecule that contains five atoms.

pen·ta·ton·ic scale (pèntə-tónnik) *n.* Any of various five-note musical scales, especially one composed of the first, second, third, fifth, and sixth notes of a diatonic scale.

pen·ta·va·lent (pèntə-váylənt) *adj. Chemistry.* Having a valency of 5; quinquevalent.

Pen·te·cost (pènti-kost ‖ -kawst) *n.* **1.** A festival of the Christian Church occurring on the seventh Sunday after Easter, to celebrate the descent of the Holy Ghost upon the disciples. Also called "Whit", "Whit Sunday". **2.** A Jewish festival, **Shavuot** *(see).* [Middle English *Pentecost,* Old English *Pentecosten,* from Late Latin *Pentēcostē,* from Greek *pentēkostē (hēmera),* the fiftieth day (after the Resurrection), Pentecost, from *pentēkostos,* fiftieth, from *pentēkonta,* fifty : *pente,* five + *-konta,* "ten times".]

Pen·te·cos·tal (pènti-kóst'l ‖ -kàwst'l) *adj.* **1.** Of, pertaining to, or occurring at Pentecost. **2.** Of, pertaining to, or designating any of various Christian religious congregations that seek to be filled with the Holy Ghost, in emulation of the disciples at Pentecost. **—Pen·te·cos·tal** *n.* **—Pen·te·cos·tal·ism** *n.*

pen·tene (pènteen) *n.* A colourless flammable alkene, C_5H_{10}, occurring in several isomeric forms. Formerly called "amylene". [PENT(A)- + -ENE.]

pent·house (pènt-howss) *n.* **1. a.** A maisonette or flat situated on the roof of a building. **b.** A residence, often with a terrace, comprising the top floor of a block of flats. **c.** A structure housing machinery on the roof of a building. **2.** A shed or sloping roof attached to the side of a building or wall. [Alteration (assimilated to HOUSE) of Middle English *pentis,* from Old French *appentis,* from Medieval Latin *appenticium,* appendage, from Latin *appendix,* from *appendēre,* to append : *ad,* on + *pendēre,* to suspend, hang.]

pen·ti·men·to (pènti-méntō) *n.* **1.** The emergence in a painting of an underlying image, for example, an earlier painting, part of a painting, or original draft, that shows through the final picture, usually when the top layer of paint has become transparent with age. **2.** Such an underlying image. [Italian, "repentance", correction.]

Pent·land Firth (pèntlənd). Strait, 32 kilometres (20 miles) long, separating north Scotland from the Orkney Islands. Despite its strong currents, it is a major shipping route.

pent·land·ite (pèntlən-dīt) *n.* The principal ore of nickel, a light-brown nickel iron sulphide. [French; discovered by Joseph B. *Pentland* (died 1873), Irish scientist.]

pen·to·bar·bi·tone sodium (pènt-ō-bárbi-tōn, -ə-) *n.* A white crystalline or powdery barbiturate, $C_{11}H_{17}N_2NaO_3$, used as a sedative. Also called "sodium pentobarbital".

pen·tode (pèntōd) *n.* An electronic valve with five electrodes. In addition to a cathode and an anode it has a control grid, a screen grid, and a suppressor grid situated between the screen and the anode. [PENTA- + Greek *hodos,* way.]

pen·to·san (pènt-ə-san, -ō-) *n.* Any of a group of complex carbohydrates (hemicelluloses) such as xylan and araban, with the general formula $(C_5H_8O_4)n.,$ found with cellulose in many woody plants and yielding pentoses on hydrolysis. [PENTOS(E) + -AN.]

pen·tose (pén-tōss, -tōz) *n.* A sugar having five carbon atoms per molecule. [PENT(A)- + -OSE.]

pent·ox·ide (pent-ók-sīd) *n.* An oxide having five atoms of oxygen in the molecule. [PENT(A)- + OXIDE.]

pent·ste·mon (pent-stéemən, -stémmən, pèntstimən) *n.* Also *chiefly U.S.* **pen·ste·mon** (pen-). Any of numerous plants of the North American genus *Penstemon,* having four fertile stamens and one bearded sterile stamen. [New Latin, irregularly from PENTA- + Greek *stēmōn,* warp (here representing "stamen").]

pent-up (pènt-úp) *adj.* Not given expression; repressed: *pent-up anger.*

pen·tyl (pén-tīl, -til) *n. Chemistry.* The univalent organic radical C_5H_{11}, occurring in several isomeric forms in many organic compounds. Formerly called "amyl". [PENT(A)- + -YL.]

pentyl acetate *n.* A colourless combustible liquid, $CH_3COOC_5H_{11}$, used as a paint solvent and in flavourings, photographic films, and the extraction of penicillin.

pen·tyl·ene·tet·ra·zol (pèntileen-téttrə-zol ‖ -zōl) *n.* A drug, $C_6H_{10}N_4$, used as a stimulant of the central nervous system.

pe·nult (pe-núlt, pi-, pə-, pénult ‖ pée-) *n.* The next to the last syllable in a word. Also called "penultima". [Latin *paenultimus,* last but one : *paene, pēne*†, almost + *ultimus,* farthest away, last, from *uls,* beyond.]

pe·nul·ti·mate (pe-núlti-mət, pi-, pə, -mit) *adj.* **1.** Next to last. **2.** Of or pertaining to the penult of a word: *penultimate stress.*
~*n.* **1.** The next to the last. **2.** The penult. [Latin *paenultimus,* PENULT.]

pe·num·bra (pi-núm-brə, pe-, pə-) *n., pl.* **-brae** (-bree) or **-bras. 1.** A partial shadow between regions of complete shadow (umbra) and complete illumination occurring, for example, on parts of the earth from which a partial eclipse may be observed. **2.** *Astronomy.* The partly darkened fringe around a sunspot. [New Latin : Latin *paene, pēne*†, almost + UMBRA.] **—pe·num·bral, pe·num·brous** *adj.*

pe·nu·ri·ous (pi-néwr-i-əss, pe-, pə- ‖ -nóor-) *adj.* **1.** Miserly; stingy. **2.** Poverty-stricken; needy. **3.** Yielding little; barren: *a penurious land.* [Medieval Latin *'pēnūriōsus,* from *pēnūria,* PENURY.] **—pe·nu·ri·ous·ly** *adv.* **—pe·nu·ri·ous·ness** *n.*

pen·u·ry (pènnewr-i) *n.* **1.** Extreme want or poverty; destitution. **2.** Extreme dearth; barrenness; insufficiency. [Middle English, from Latin *paenūria, pēnūria*†, want, scarcity.]

Pe·nu·ti·an (pi-néw-ti-ən, -sh'n ‖ -nōō-) *n.* A family or phylum of North American Indian languages of Pacific coastal areas from California to British Columbia.

Pen·zance (pen-zánss, pən-; *locally* -záness). Seaside resort in Cornwall, southwest England. A port for early crops from the Scilly Isles, its other industries include tourism and fishing.

pe·on (pée-ən, -on; *Spanish* pay-ón; *also for sense 2* pewn) *n., pl.* **peons** or **peones** (pay-ōneez). **1. a.** An unskilled labourer or farm worker of Latin America or the southwestern United States. **b.** Formerly, such a worker bound in servitude to a creditor. **2.** A native Indian or Ceylonese messenger, servant, or foot soldier. **3.** Any menial worker; a drudge. [Spanish *peon,* Portuguese *peão* and French *pion,* all from Medieval Latin *pedo* (stem *pedōn*-), a foot soldier, from Latin *pēs* (stem *ped*-), a foot.]

pe·on·age (pée-ənij) *n.* Also **pe·on·ism** (-əniz'm). **1.** The condition of being a peon. **2.** A system by which debtors are bound in servitude to their creditors until the debts are paid.

pe·o·ny, pae·o·ny (pée-erni, pée-əni) *n., pl.* **-nies.** Any of various garden plants of the genus *Paeonia,* having large yellow, pink, red, white, or creamy globular flowers. [Middle English *pione,* Old English *peonie,* from Latin *peōnia,* from Greek *paiōniā,* supposedly discovered by *Paiōn,* physician (of the gods). See **paean**.]

peo·ple (péep'l) *n., pl.* **people** or **peoples** (for senses 1, 2). **1.** A body of persons living in the same country under one national government; a nationality. **2.** A body of persons sharing a common religion, culture, language, or inherited condition of life. **3.** *Plural.* Persons in general; men, women, and children; human individuals collectively. **4.** *Plural.* The mass of ordinary persons; the populace. Usually preceded by *the.* **5.** *Usually plural.* **a.** The citizens of a nation, state, or other political unit. **b.** In certain forms of Marxist ideology, the proletariat: *a people's court.* **6.** *Plural.* Persons subordinate to or loyal to a ruler, superior, or employer. **7.** *Plural.* **a.** Family, relatives, or ancestors. **b.** Visitors; guests: *We're having people for dinner tonight.* **8.** *Plural.* Persons with regard to some characteristic, or considered as a group: *working people; young people.* **9.** *Plural.* Human beings considered as distinct from lower animals or inanimate things. **10.** *Plural.* A race or kind of beings distinct from human beings: *the little people.* **—See Usage note at nation.**
~*tr.v.* **peopled, -pling, -ples.** To furnish with a population; populate. [Middle English *peple, poeple,* from Old French *pueple, pople,* from Latin *populus.*] **—peo·pler** (péeplər) *n.*
Usage: **People** is the usual word for a group of human beings, considered collectively and without differentiation: *Several people were in the room.* **Persons** is more restricted in use: it tends to be found in more formal and impersonal contexts, and is therefore typical of written rather than spoken English, particularly administrative and official English. In its singular form, *person* takes a singular pronoun (*If a person has an interest in politics, he will . . .*), though a plural form *(they)* is sometimes used in informal speech.

people's front *n.* A political coalition, a **popular front** *(see).*

People's Republic of China. See **China**.

pep (pep) *n. Informal.* Energy; high spirits; vim.
~*tr.v.* **pepped, pepping, peps.** *Informal.* To bring energy or liveliness to; invigorate. Usually followed by *up.* [Short for PEPPER.] **—pep·py** (péppi) *adj.* **—pep·pi·ness** *n.*

PEP (pep) *n.* A **Personal Equity Plan** *(see).*

Pep·in the Short (péppin), also known as Pepin III (c. 715–768). King of the Franks (751–768). The father of Charlemagne, he came to the defence of Pope Stephen II against the king of the Lombards, Aistulf (754), and established the core territory of the Papal States.

pep·los (pèpp-ləss, -loss) *n., pl.* **-loses.** Also **pep·lus** (-ləss). A loose outer robe worn by women in ancient Greece. Also called "peplum". [Greek *peplos*†.]

pep·lum (péppləm) *n., pl.* **-lums. 1.** A short overskirt or ruffle attached at the waistline. **2.** A peplos. [Latin, from *peplus*, PEPLOS.]

pe·po (péepō) *n., pl.* **-pos.** The fruit of any of various related plants, such as the cucumber and melon, having a hard rind, fleshy pulp, and numerous seeds. [Latin, melon, from Greek *pepōn*.]

pep·per (péppər) *n.* **1.** A woody vine, *Piper nigrum,* of the East Indies, having small, berry-like fruit. **2.** The dried, blackish fruit of this plant, used as a pungent condiment. When ground whole, it is called *black pepper,* and with the shell removed, *white pepper.* **3.** Any of several other plants of the genus *Piper,* such as cubeb, betel, and kava. **4.** Any of several varieties of a tropical plant, *Capsicum annuum* (or *C. frutescens*). **5.** The podlike fruit of any of these plants, varying in size, shape, colour, and degree of pungency. The milder types include the **sweet pepper** and **pimiento** *(both of which see),* and the more pungent types include the **chilli** *(see).* **6.** Any of various condiments made from the more pungent varieties of *C. annuum* (or *C. frutescens*), such as **cayenne pepper, chilli pepper,** and **paprika** *(all of which see).* In this sense, also called "hot pepper".

~*tr.v.* **peppered, -pering, pers. 1.** To season or sprinkle with pepper. **2.** To sprinkle liberally; dot. **3.** To pelt or shower with small missiles. **4.** To punish. **5.** To make (a speech or article, for example) lively and vivid as with wit or invective. [Middle English *peper,* Old English *pipor,* from Latin *piper,* from Greek *peperi,* from Sanskrit *pippalī,* berry.]

pep·per-and-salt (péppər-ənd-sáwlt ‖ -sólt) *adj.* Having a close mixture of black and white or brown and white. Said of hair or fabrics.

pep·per·corn (péppər-kawrn) *n.* **1.** A dried berry of the pepper vine *Piper nigrum.* **2.** Any small or insignificant thing.

peppercorn rent *n.* A nominal rent. [Referring to a peppercorn as representing a trifling sum.]

pep·pered moth (péppərd) *n.* A European moth, *Biston betularia,* that exists in two distinct forms, a black and white speckled form predominating in rural regions, and a black or melanic form that flourishes in industrial areas. See **pigmentation.**

pepper mill *n.* A small utensil for grinding peppercorns.

pep·per·mint (péppər-mint) *n.* **1.** A plant, *Mentha piperita,* having small purple or white flowers and downy leaves that yield a pungent oil. **2.** The oil from this plant, or a preparation made from it, used as flavouring. **3.** A sweet with this flavouring.

pep·pe·ro·ni (peppə-rōni) *n.* A variety of highly seasoned Italian salami. [Italian, *peperone,* chilli, from *pepere,* pepper.]

pepper pot *n.* **1.** A container with small holes in the top for sprinkling ground pepper. Also called "pepperbox". **2.** A thick West Indian stew of meat or fish, vegetables, and condiments.

pepper tree *n.* Any of several trees of the genus *Schinus;* especially, *S. molle,* native to South America, having yellowish-white flowers and red ornamental fruits with seeds that are used as a condiment.

pep·per·wort (péppər-wurt ‖ -wawrt) *n.* Any of several plants of the genus *Lepidium,* having small white flowers and winged, pungent fruits. Also *U.S.* "peppergrass".

pep·per·y (péppəri) *adj.* **1.** Of, like, or containing pepper; sharp or pungent in flavour. **2.** Vigorously sharp-tempered in disposition and manner: *a peppery general.* **3.** Sharp and stinging in style or content: *a peppery speech.* **—pep·per·i·ness** *n.*

pep pill *n. Informal.* Any tablet or capsule containing an ingredient that stimulates the central nervous system; especially, any of the amphetamines.

pep·sin, pep·sine (pépsin) *n.* **1.** A digestive enzyme found in gastric juice that catalyses the breakdown of protein to peptides. **2.** A substance containing this enzyme, obtained from the stomachs of pigs and used as a digestive aid. [German *Pepsin,* from Greek *pepsis,* digestion, from *peptein,* to digest, cook.]

pep·sin·o·gen (pep-sínnəjən) *n.* An inert substance found in the cells of the gastric mucosa that is converted to pepsin during digestion by the action of hydrochloric acid. [PEPSIN + -GEN.]

pep talk *n.* A speech of exhortation delivered by a leader, as to team members or staff.

pep·tic (péptik) *adj.* **1. a.** Of or assisting digestion: *peptic secretion.* **b.** Induced by or associated with the action of digestive secretions. **2.** Of or involving pepsin. **3.** Capable of digesting.

~*n.* A digestive agent. [Latin *pepticus,* from Greek *peptikos,* from *peptein,* to digest.]

peptic ulcer *n.* An ulcer of the mucous membrane, especially of the stomach or oesophagus, caused by the action of digestive secretions.

pep·ti·dase (pépti-dayz, -dayss) *n.* An enzyme that hydrolyses peptides, releasing amino acids. [PEPTID(E) + -ASE.]

pep·tide (pép-tīd) *n.* Also **pep·tid** (-tid). Any of various natural or synthetic compounds containing two or more amino acids linked by the carboxyl group of one amino acid and the amino group of another. [PEPT(ONE) + -IDE.]

peptide bond *n.* The chemical bond, —CO·NH=CHCONHCH=, between the organic acid groups and amino groups of neighbouring amino acids, constituting the primary linkage of all protein structures.

pep·tise, pep·tize (pép-tīz) *tr.v.* **-tised, -tising, -tises. 1.** To increase the dispersion of a colloidal solution, by the addition of an electrolyte. **2.** To liquefy (a colloidal gel) to form a sol, by the addition of an electrolyte. [Greek *peptein,* to digest + -ISE.] **—pep·ti·sa·tion** (-tī-záysh'n ‖ *U.S.* -ti-) *n.*

pep·tone (péptōn) *n.* Any of various protein compounds obtained by acid or enzyme hydrolysis of natural protein and used as nutrients and culture media. [German *Pepton,* from Greek *pepton,* from *peptein,* to digest, cook.] **—pep·ton·ic** (pep-tónnik) *adj.*

pep·to·nise, pep·to·nize (péptə-nīz) *tr.v.* **-nised, -nising, -nises. 1.** To convert (protein) into a peptone. **2.** To dissolve (food) by means of a proteolytic enzyme. **3.** To combine with peptone. **—pep·to·ni·sa·tion** (-nī-záysh'n ‖ *U.S.* -ni-) *n.*

Pepys (peeps) **Samuel** (1633-1703). English diarist. His diary, a detailed account of everyday life, includes descriptions of the Great Fire of London and the Great Plague.

Pe·quot (pée-kwot) *n., pl.* **-quots** or collectively **Pequot. 1.** A member of an Algonquian-speaking North American Indian people formerly living in southern New England. **2.** The language of this tribe. **—Pe·quot** *adj.*

per (per, *weak form* pər) *prep. Abbr.* **p. 1.** Through; by means of: *per bearer.* Used in business. **2.** To, for, or by each; for every: *40 miles per gallon.* **3.** According to; by the. Often used with *as: as per instructions.* **—as per usual.** As usual. Used humorously. [Latin.]

PER Professional and Executive Register (in Britain).

per– prefix. Chemistry. Indicates: **1.** A compound that includes an element in its highest oxidation state; for example, **perchloric acid. 2.** A compound that includes the peroxy group in its structure; for example, **hydrogen peroxide. 3.** A complete substitution or addition in an organic compound; for example, **perchloroethylene.** [Latin, from preposition *per,* through, by, away. In borrowed Latin compounds, *per-* indicates: 1. Through, as in **percolate.** 2. Throughout, to the end, as in **perennial, perorate.** 3. Thoroughly, completely, as in **perfect, perceive.** 4. Away, as in **perdition, peregrine.** 5. Destruction, as in **perfidy, perjure.** 6. Intensified action, as in **perfervid, perform.**]

per. 1. period. **2.** person.

per·ac·id (per-ássid) *n.* **1.** Any acid containing the peroxy group. **2.** An inorganic acid, such as perchloric acid, containing the largest proportion of oxygen in a series of related acids.

per·ad·ven·ture (pərəd-vénchər, pér-əd-, pérrəd-) *adv. Archaic.* Perhaps; perchance; it may be.

~*n. Archaic.* Uncertainty; doubt: *beyond peradventure.* [Middle English *per aventure* : Old French *per,* by + *aventure,* ADVENTURE.]

Pe·rak (páir-ə, péer-ə, *also* pi-rák). State in the west of peninsular Malaysia. It has rich tin deposits and produces sugar, rubber, rice, and coconuts. Ipoh is the capital.

per·am·bu·late (pə-rámbew-layt) *v.* **-lated, -lating, -lates.** *Formal.* —*tr.* To traverse, especially in order to inspect. —*intr.* To walk about; roam; stroll. [Latin *perambulāre* : *per-,* through + *ambulāre,* to walk, AMBULATE.] **—per·am·bu·la·to·ry** (pə-rámb-yōōlə-təri, -tri) *adj.* **—per·am·bu·la·tion** (-láysh'n) *n.*

per·am·bu·la·tor (pə-rámbew-laytər) *n. Chiefly British Formal.* A **pram** *(see).*

per an·num (ánnəm) *adv. Abbr.* **p.a., per an., per ann.** By the year; annually. [Latin.]

per·bo·rate (pər-báwr-ayt, pér- ‖ -bŏr-) *n.* A salt containing the radical BO₃, formed from a borate and hydrogen peroxide.

per·cale (pər-káyl, -ká·al) *n.* An opaque cotton fabric used to make sheets and clothing. [French, from Persian *pargālah*†.]

per·ca·line (pérkə-leen, -lin) *n.* A glazed fine cotton fabric used for linings. [French, from PERCALE.]

per cap·i·ta (káppitə) *adv.* Per person: *income per capita.* [Latin, "by heads".] **—per capita** *adj.*

per·ceive (pər-séev) *tr.v.* **-ceived, -ceiving, -ceives. 1.** To become aware of directly through any of the senses; especially, to see or hear. **2.** To take notice of; observe; detect. **3. a.** To become aware of in one's mind; achieve understanding of; apprehend. **b.** To regard rightly or wrongly as doing or being what is stated: *They were widely perceived to be threatening us; their perceived threats to us.* — See Synonyms at **see.** [Middle English *perceiven,* from Old French *perceivre,* from Latin *percipere,* "to seize wholly", "see all the way through" : *per-,* thoroughly + *capere,* to seize.] **—per·ceiv·a·ble** *adj.* **—per·ceiv·a·bly** *adv.*

per·ceived noise decibel (pər-séevd) *n. Abbr.* **PNdB.** A unit used to measure perceived noise levels by comparing them with the level of sound pressure of a reference sound that is judged to be of equal level by a normal listener.

per cent, per·cent (pər-sént) *adv. Abbr.* **p.c., pct.** *Symbol* **%** Per hundred; for or out of each hundred. Used to indicate that the preceding number is a percentage: *A quarter of ten is 25 per cent.* ~*n.* **1.** A hundredth part; a percentage part. **2.** *Plural.* Securities yielding a specified rate of interest: *the six per cents.* [Short for Latin *per centum,* by the hundred : *per,* by + *centum,* hundred.]

Usage: Per cent and percentage are both used to express quantity with relation to a whole. *Per cent* is always used in a specific sense, with a number: *60 per cent of the population agreed. Percentage* is never preceded by a number, and is generally qualified by a term indicating size *(A large percentage agreed).* It is also often used loosely in the sense of "a certain proportion" *(A percentage of the population objected),* but this has attracted criticism. The construction of the verb following is governed by the number of the noun used with *per cent/percentage: A large percentage of the patients are . . . , A large percentage of the population is . . .*

per·cent·age (pər-séntij) *n.* **1.** A fraction or ratio with 100 fixed and understood as the denominator. It is formed by multiplying a decimal equivalent of a fraction by 100. For example, 0.98 equals a percentage of 98. **2. a.** A specified proportion or share in relation to the whole: *in a high percentage of cases*. **b.** *Informal*. A certain proportion: *A percentage of the electorate never votes*. **3.** An allowance, commission, or the like that varies in proportion to a larger sum, such as total sales: *work for a percentage*. **4.** *Informal*. Advantage; gain.

per·cen·tile (pər-sént-īl) *n. Statistics*. A number scale of 100 equal divisions of a range of a set of statistical data, that indicates the value below which that percentage of the data lies. For example, a score higher than 97 per cent in an examination is in the 97th percentile. [From PER CENT.]

per·cept (pér-sept) *n.* **1.** The object of perception. **2.** An impression in the mind of something perceived by the senses, viewed as the basic component in the formation of concepts. [Back-formation from PERCEPTION.]

per·cep·ti·ble (pər-sép-tə-b'l, -ti-) *adj.* Capable of being perceived; discernible by the senses or mind. —**per·cep·ti·bil·i·ty** (-bíllǝti) *n.* —**per·cep·ti·bly** *adv.*

> **Synonyms:** perceptible, palpable, appreciable, noticeable, discernible.

per·cep·tion (pər-sépsh'n) *n.* **1.** The process, act, or faculty of perceiving. **2.** The effect or product of perceiving. **3.** The awareness of the external world, or some aspect of it, through physical sensations and the interpretation of these by the mind. **4.** Any insight, intuition, or knowledge gained by perceiving. **5.** The ability or capacity to gain insight by perceiving. [Latin *perceptiō* (stem *perceptiōn-*), from *percipere* (past participle *perceptus*), to PERCEIVE.] —**per·cep·tion·al** *adj.*

per·cep·tive (pər-séptiv) *adj.* **1.** Of or pertaining to perception. **2. a.** Having the ability to perceive; keen in discernment. **b.** Marked by discernment and understanding; sensitive. —**per·cep·tive·ly** *adv.* —**per·cep·tiv·i·ty** (pér-sep-tívvǝti) *n.*

per·cep·tu·al (pər-séptew-ǝl) *adj.* Of, based on, or involving perception. —**per·cep·tu·al·ly** *adv.*

Perceval. See **Percival**.

Per·ce·val (pérsiv'l), **Spencer** (1762–1812). British prime minister (1809–12). He was assassinated in the lobby of the House of Commons by a bankrupt Liverpool broker.

perch¹ (perch) *n.* **1.** A rod or branch serving as a roost for a bird. **2. a.** A place for resting or sitting, especially one that is high. **b.** A secure position. **3.** A pole used in acrobatics. **4. a.** A unit of length, the **rod** (*see*). **b.** One square rod of land. **5.** A unit of cubic measure used in stonework, usually 16.5 feet by 1 foot by 1.5 feet, or 24.75 cubic feet. **6.** A frame on which cloth is laid for examination of quality. **7.** A pole connecting the front and back axles in a wagon, carriage, or the like.

~*v.* **perched, perching, perches.** —*intr.* **1.** To alight or rest on a perch; roost. **2.** To stand, sit, rest, or be situated on some elevated place or position: *The child perched on the window sill*. —*tr.* **1.** To place on or as on a perch. **2.** To lay (cloth) on a perch in order to examine it. [Middle English *perche*, from Old French, from Latin *pertica*, stick, from Italic root *pert-* (unattested), pole.]

perch² *n., pl.* **-es** or collectively **perch. 1.** Any of various freshwater fishes of the genus *Perca*, especially either of two edible species, *P. fluviatilis*, of Europe and *P. flavescens*, of North America. **2.** Any of various related or similar fishes, such as the **pike perch** (*see*). [Middle English *perche*, from Old French, from Latin *perca*, from Greek *perkē*.]

per·chance (pər-cháanss, pér- || -chánss) *adv. Archaic*. Perhaps; possibly. [Middle English *perchaunce*, from Old French *per chance, par chance* : *per, par*, by, + CHANCE.]

Per·che·ron (pérshǝ-ron || pérchǝ-) *n.* A large draught horse of a breed developed in France. [French, from *Percheron*, a native of *le Perche*, district south of Normandy.]

perch·ing (pérching) *adj.* Having feet especially adapted for grasping a perch. Said of certain birds.

per·chlo·ric acid (pər-klórrik, pér-, -kláwr-ik || -klór-) *n.* A clear, colourless, hygroscopic liquid, $HClO_4$, explosively unstable under some conditions.

per·chlor·o·eth·yl·ene (pər-kláwr-ō-éthi-leen, pér- || -klór-) *n.* A colourless, nonflammable organic solvent, $Cl_2C{:}CCl_2$, used in dry-cleaning solutions and to dissolve a variety of waxes, tars, rubbers, and gums. Also called "tetrachloroethylene".

per·cip·i·ent (pər-síppi-ǝnt) *adj.* Having the power of perceiving; especially, perceiving keenly and readily. ~*n.* One that perceives. [Latin *percipiēns* (stem *percipient-*), present participle of *percipere*, to PERCEIVE.] —**per·cip·i·ence** *n.*

Per·ci·val, Per·ce·val (pérssiv'l). Also **Par·si·fal, Par·zi·val** (pársif'l). In Arthurian legend, a naive and virtuous young knight who is eventually granted a sight of the Holy Grail.

per·coid (pér-koyd) *n.* Also **per·coi·de·an** (per-kóydi-ǝn). Any member of the Percoidea, a large suborder of fishes that includes the perches, sunfishes, and groupers. [New Latin *Percoidea* : Latin *perca*, PERCH (fish) + -OID.] —**per·coid, per·coi·de·an** *adj.*

per·co·late (pérkǝ-layt) *v.* **-lated, -lating, -lates.** —*tr.* **1.** To cause (liquid, powder, or small particles) to pass through a porous substance or small holes; filter; sift. **2.** To pass or ooze through: *Water percolated the sand*. **3.** To make (coffee, for example) in a percolator. —*intr.* **1.** To drain or seep through a porous substance or filter. **2.** To become lively or active. **3.** *Informal*. To pass along gradually: *The news percolated down to me*. ~*n.* (-lǝt, -lit, -layt). A liquid that has been percolated. [Latin *percōlāre* : *per-*, through + *cōlāre*, to filter, strain, from *cōlum*,

sieve.] —**per·co·la·tion** (-láysh'n) *n.*

per·co·la·tor (pérkǝ-laytǝr. *Note: the pronunciation* pérkew-laytǝr *is not standard.*) *n.* A type of coffeepot in which hot water passes through ground coffee beans; especially, one in which boiling water is forced repeatedly up through a centre tube to filter through a small perforated container of ground coffee.

per con·tra (kóntrǝ) *adv. Latin*. On the contrary.

per·cuss (pər-kúss) *tr.v.* **-cussed, -cussing, -cusses.** To strike or tap firmly, as in medical practice: *percuss a patient's chest*. [Latin *percutere* (past participle *percussus*), to strike hard : *per-* (intensive) + *quatere*, to strike.]

per·cus·sion (pər-kúsh'n) *n.* **1.** The striking together of two bodies, especially when noise is produced. **2.** The sound, vibration, or shock caused by such a striking together. **3.** The act of detonating a percussion cap in a firearm. **4.** A method of medical diagnosis in which various areas of the body, especially the chest, back, and abdomen, are tapped to determine by resonance the condition of internal organs. **5. a.** Musical percussion instruments collectively. **b.** The section of an orchestra consisting of these instruments. [Latin *percussiō* (stem *percussiōn-*), from *percutere*, to PERCUSS.]

percussion cap *n.* A thin metal cap containing gunpowder or some other detonator that explodes on being struck.

percussion instrument *n.* A musical instrument in which sound is produced by striking, such as a drum, xylophone, or cymbal.

per·cus·sion·ist (pər-kúsh'n-ist) *n.* One who plays percussion instruments.

per·cus·sive (pər-kússiv) *adj.* Of, pertaining to, or characterised by percussion. —**per·cus·sive·ly** *adv.* —**per·cus·sive·ness** *n.*

per·cu·ta·ne·ous (pér-kew-táyni-ǝss) *adj.* Passed, done, or effected through or by means of the skin. —**per·cu·ta·ne·ous·ly** *adv.*

Per·cy (pér-si), **Sir Henry**, also called Hotspur (1364–1403). English soldier. He plotted with his father, the Earl of Northumberland, to overthrow Henry IV. He was killed in battle at Shrewsbury.

Percy, Bishop Thomas (1729–1811). English antiquary and poet. The Bishop of Dromore from 1782, his chief work is *The Reliques of Ancient English Poetry* (1765), a selection of medieval ballads and songs, which stimulated the Romantic revival.

per di·em (dī-em, dée-) *adv. Abbr.* **p.d., P.D.** Per day. ~*n. Abbr.* **p.d., P.D.** An allowance for daily expenses. ~*adj. Abbr.* **p.d., P.D.** Reckoned on a daily basis: *per diem costs*. [Latin, "by the day".]

per·di·tion (pər-dísh'n) *n.* **1. a.** The loss of the soul; eternal damnation. **b.** Hell. **2.** *Archaic*. Utter loss or ruin. [Middle English *perdicioun*, from Late Latin *perditiō* (stem *perditiōn-*), from Latin *perdere* (past participle *perditus*), to throw away, destroy, lose : *per-*, away + *dare*, to give.]

per·du, per·due (pér-dew, per-déw || -dōō, -dǒō) *adj.* Concealed; hidden. Used chiefly in the phrase *lie perdu*. ~*n. Obsolete*. A soldier sent on a dangerous mission. [French, "lost", from the past participle of *perdre*, to lose, from Latin *perdere*. See perdition.]

per·du·ra·ble (pər-déwr-ǝb'l || -dóor-) *adj.* Extremely durable; permanent. [Middle English, from Old French, from Late Latin *perdūrābilis*, from Latin *perdūrāre*, "to last throughout", endure : *per-*, throughout + *dūrāre*, to last.] —**per·du·ra·bil·i·ty** (-ǝ-bílləti) *n.* —**per·du·ra·bly** *adv.*

père (pair) *n. French*. Father. Used after a proper name to distinguish a father from a son who has the same name: *Dumas père*. Compare **fils**.

Père David's deer *n.* A large reddish-grey Chinese deer, *Elaphurus davidianus*, that survives only in captivity. [After Père Armand David (1826–1900), French missionary.]

per·e·gri·nate (pérrigri-nayt) *v.* **-nated, -nating, -nates.** —*intr.* To journey or travel from place to place usually for a long time and over great distances. —*tr.* To travel through or over. In both senses, often used humorously. [Latin *peregrīnārī*, to travel in foreign lands, from *peregrīnus*, foreign. See peregrine.] —**per·e·gri·na·tion** (-náysh'n) *n.* —**per·e·gri·na·tor** *n.*

per·e·grine (pérri-grin, -green || -grīn) *adj. Archaic.* **1.** Foreign; alien. **2.** Roving or wandering; migratory. ~*n.* The peregrine falcon. [Medieval Latin *peregrīnus*, from Latin, a foreigner, stranger, from *pereger*, being abroad : *per-*, away, + *ager*, land, field.]

peregrine falcon *n.* A widely distributed bird of prey, *Falco peregrinus*, having grey and white plumage, formerly much used in falconry. Also called "peregrine". [Middle English, translation of Medieval Latin *falco peregrinus*, "pilgrim falcon"; so named because young peregrines were caught in passage ("pilgrimage") from their breeding place, rather than taken from the nest.]

Per·el·man (pérrǝlmǝn), **S(idney) J(oseph)** (1904–79). U.S. humorist. Beginning as a cartoonist, he became a scriptwriter on Marx Brothers films. He wrote a lot for the *New Yorker*.

per·emp·to·ry (pǝ-rémp-tǝri, pérrǝmp-, -tri) *adj.* **1.** Overbearing; imperious: *a peremptory manner*. **2.** Having the nature of or expressing command; urgent: *"a bell began to toll with a peremptory clang."* (Thomas Hardy). **3.** Not admitting denial or refusal; imperative: *a peremptory command*. **4.** *Law*. Precluding further debate or action: *a peremptory decree*. [Late Latin *peremptōrius*, "precluding debate", decisive, from *perimere* (past participle *peremptus*), to take away completely : *per-*, completely + *emere*, to obtain.] —**per·emp·to·ri·ly** *adv.* —**per·emp·to·ri·ness** *n.*

peremptory challenge *n. Law.* The right of a defendant in a criminal trial to object to a certain number of proposed jurors.

pe·ren·nate (pérri-nayt, pə-rénnayt) *intr.v.* **-nated, -nating, -nates.** *Rare.* To survive from one growing season to the next, often with a period of reduced or arrested growth between seasons. Used of plants. [Latin *perennātus,* past participle of *perennāre,* to survive, continue : PER- (through) + *-ennāre,* from *annus,* year.]

per·en·ni·al (pə-rénni-əl) *adj.* **1.** Lasting or active through the year or through many years: *the perennial snowcaps of the Alps.* **2. a.** Lasting an indefinitely long time; everlasting; perpetual: *perennial happiness.* **b.** Appearing again and again; continually recurring. **3.** *Botany.* Having a life span of more than two years. Compare **annual, biennial.** —See Synonyms at **continual.**
~n. Botany. A perennial plant. [Latin *perennis* : *per-,* throughout + *annus,* year.] **—per·en·ni·al·ly** *adv.*

Pe·res (pe-réz), **Shimon** (1923–). Israeli politician, prime minister (1984–86, 1995–96). He was Minister of Defence (1974–77), and acting prime minister (1977). In 1984 he won a general election without an overall majority, and formed a government of national unity with the outgoing prime minister, Yitzhak Shamir. He became foreign minister in 1993. He shared the 1994 Nobel peace prize with Yasser Arafat and Yitzhak Rabin.

pe·res·troi·ka (pírri-stróykə, pérri-) *n. Russian.* Restructuring, a policy of social and economic reform introduced by Mikhail Gorbachev in the Soviet Union and associated with *glasnost.* In a speech of January 1987 he declared that *perestroika* would entail creating efficient machinery for progress; encouraging initiative, self-management and open criticism in public life; and an end to "the domineering style of management and administration by decree" in the national economy. [Russian *perestroika,* reconstruction: *pere-,* again + *stroĭ,* structure + *-ka,* noun suffix.]

Pe·rez de Cue·llar (pérress day kwéll-yaar, pérrəss də kwáy-aar), **Javier** (1920–). Peruvian diplomat. He was Secretary General of the United Nations from 1982 to 1991.

per·fect (pér-fikt || -fekt) *adj. Abbr.* **perf. 1.** Lacking nothing essential to the whole; complete of its nature or kind. **2.** In a state of undiminished or highest excellence; without defect; flawless. **3.** Highly skilled or talented in a certain field or area. **4. a.** Faithfully reproducing an original; accurate; exact: *a perfect reproduction of a painting.* **b.** Corresponding in every respect to an ideal or conventionally recognised standard: *the perfect host.* **c.** Precise; correct: *perfect pitch; perfect timing.* **5.** Complete; thorough; utter: *a perfect fool.* **6.** Pure; undiluted; unmixed: *perfect red.* **7.** Excellent and delightful in all respects: *a perfect day.* **8.** *Botany.* Having both stamens and pistils in the same flower; monoclinous. **9.** *Grammar.* Of, pertaining to, or designating a verb form expressing action completed prior to a fixed point of reference in time. English verbs have three perfect tenses: the present (or simple) perfect, the pluperfect (or past perfect), and the future perfect. **10.** Of, pertaining to, or designating a number or quantity equal to an integral power of another number or quantity: *4, 9, and 16 are perfect squares.* **11.** *Music.* **a.** Designating the three basic intervals of the octave, fourth, and fifth. **b.** Designating a cadence in which the final chord has its root in both bass and soprano. **12.** Designating a gas that obeys the ideal gas laws.
~n. Abbr. **perf.** *Grammar.* **1.** The perfect tense. **2.** A verb or verb form in this tense.
~tr.v. (*usually* pər-fékt) **perfected, -fecting, -fects. 1.** To bring to perfection or completion. **2.** To improve. **3.** To complete the printing of (a sheet) by printing the reverse side. [Middle English *perfit, parfit,* from Old French *parfit,* from Latin *perfectus,* finished, complete, excellent, from past participle of *perficere,* to complete : *per-,* completely + *facere,* to do.] **—per·fect·er** *n.* **—per·fect·ness** *n.*
Usage: In its absolute senses, it is not possible to use comparative and superlative forms with *perfect* in standard English. However, in the more general sense of "excellent", these forms are often used loosely: *That's one of the most perfect specimens I've ever seen.*

perfect binding *n.* A common method of binding sheets of paper without sewing, as in making paperback books, in which each cut sheet (page) is glued by one edge onto a stiff backing. **—per·fect-bound** (pérfikt-bównd) *adj.*

per·fect·i·ble (pər-féktəb'l) *adj.* Capable of becoming or being made perfect. **—per·fect·i·bil·i·ty** (-bílləti) *n.*

per·fec·tion (pər-féksh'n) *n.* **1.** The state or quality of being perfect. **2.** The process or act of perfecting: *Perfection of the plan took years.* **3.** A person or thing that perfectly embodies something: *Her pastry is culinary perfection.* **4.** An instance or quality of excellence. **—to perfection** Perfectly: *cooked to perfection.*

per·fec·tion·ism (pər-féksh'n-iz'm) *n.* **1.** A belief that moral or spiritual perfection can be achieved by man in this life. **2.** A propensity for setting extremely high standards and being displeased with anything less. **—per·fec·tion·ist** *n. & adj.*

per·fec·tive (pər-féktiv) *adj.* **1.** Tending towards perfection. **2.** *Grammar.* Of or designating a verb in the perfective aspect.
~n. Grammar. **1.** The perfective aspect. **2.** A verb in the perfective aspect. **—per·fec·tive·ly** *adv.* **—per·fec·tive·ness, per·fec·tiv·i·ty** (pérfek-tívviti) *n.*

perfective aspect *n.* An aspect of verbs that expresses a completed action as distinct from a continuing or not necessarily completed action. Compare **imperfective aspect.** See **aspect.**

per·fect·ly (pér-fikt-li || -fekt-) *adv.* **1.** In a perfect manner or to a perfect degree. **2.** Completely; fully; wholly: *perfectly ridiculous.*

perfect number *n.* A number that is equal to the sum of its integral factors, for example 28, whose divisors are 1,2,4,7, and 14. The first four perfect numbers are 6, 28, 496, and 8,128.

per·fec·to (pər-féktō) *n., pl.* **-tos.** A cigar of standard length, thick in the centre and tapering at each end. [Spanish, perfect, from Latin *perfectus,* PERFECT.]

perfect pitch *n.* **Absolute pitch** *(see).*

perfect rhyme *n.* The commonest English rhyme, having identity in sound for the last accented vowel and any final consonants or syllables but with variation in the preceding consonant, as *great, late; rider, wider.* Also called "full rhyme", "true rhyme".

perfect square *n.* An integer that is the square of an integer.

per·fer·vid (pər-férvid) *adj. Literary.* Impassioned; zealous; extravagantly eager. [New Latin *perfervidus* : *per-* (intensifier) + Latin *fervidus,* FERVID.] **—per·fer·vid·ly** *adv.* **—per·fer·vid·ness** *n.*

per·fi·dy (pérfidi) *n., pl.* **-dies.** Deliberate breach of faith; calculated violation of trust; treachery. [Latin *perfidia,* from *perfidus,* treacherous : *per-* (destruction) + *fidēs,* faith.] **—per·fid·i·ous** (pər-fíd-di-əss) *adj.* **—per·fid·i·ous·ly** *adv.*

per·fo·li·ate (pər-fōli-ət, per-, -it, -ayt) *adj.* Designating a leaf that completely clasps the stem and is apparently pierced by it. [New Latin *perfoliatus,* "pierced through the leaf" : Latin *per-,* through + *foliātus,* "leaved", FOLIATE.] **—per·fo·li·a·tion** (-áysh'n) *n.*

per·fo·rate (pérfə-rayt) *tr.v.* **-rated, -rating, -rates. 1.** To pierce, punch, or bore a hole or holes in. **2.** To pierce or stamp (a sheet of paper, for example) with rows of holes, such as those between postage stamps, to allow easy separation.
~adj. (-rit, -rət, -rayt). Having a perforation or perforations. [Latin *perforāre* : *per-,* through + *forāre,* to bore.] **—per·fo·ra·ble** (-rəb'l) *adj.* **—per·fo·ra·tive** (-rətiv, -raytiv), **per·fo·ra·to·ry** (-rə-tri, -təri) *adj.* **—per·fo·ra·tor** (-raytər) *n.*

per·fo·ra·tion (pérfə-ráysh'n) *n.* **1.** The act of perforating, or state of being perforated. **2.** A hole or series or set of holes punched or bored through something. **3.** In stamp-collecting: **a.** Any of the small holes, or the set of such holes, punched between or around individual stamps on a sheet or roll for the purpose of easy separation. **b.** The method of dividing sheets or rolls of stamps in this way. Compare **roulette. 4.** The series of ridges and indentations along the edge of an object, especially a postage stamp, that has been detached, by tearing, along a perforated line.

per·force (pər-fórss, per- || -fōrss) *adv.* By necessity; willy-nilly. [Middle English *par force,* from Old French : *par,* by, + FORCE.]

per·form (pər-fórm) *v.* **-formed, -forming, -forms.** *—tr.* **1.** To begin and carry through to completion; do: *perform an operation.* **2.** To take action in accordance with the requirements of; fulfil (a promise or duty, for example.) **3. a.** To enact (a feat or role) before an audience. **b.** To give a public presentation of (a piece of music, for example). *—intr.* **1.** To carry out a particular activity; function, especially in a specified way: *My car performs badly on wet roads.* **2.** To fulfil an obligation or requirement; accomplish something as promised or expected. **3.** To portray a role or demonstrate some skill before an audience. **4.** To present a dramatic or musical work or other entertainment before an audience. [Middle English *performen,* from Anglo-French *parformer,* variant of Old French *parfornir* (assimilated to *forme,* FORM) : *par-* (intensifier), from Latin *per-* + *fornir,* to FURNISH.] **—per·form·a·ble** *adj.* **—per·form·er** *n.*
Synonyms: *perform, execute, accomplish, achieve, effect, fulfil, discharge.*

per·form·ance (pər-fórmənss) *n.* **1.** The act of performing, or the state of being performed. **2.** The act or style of performing a work or role before an audience. **3. a.** The way in which someone or something functions. **b.** Excellence in functioning. Also used adjectivally: *a high-performance car.* **4.** A presentation, especially a theatrical one, before an audience. **5.** Something performed; an accomplishment; a deed. **6.** *Informal.* An instance of bad behaviour, such as a display of temper, usually in public. **7.** *Informal.* Something involving effort or difficulty: *Moving house was quite a performance.* **8.** *Linguistics.* The spoken and written utterances collectively of an individual user of language, as opposed to his linguistic **competence** *(see).* Compare **parole.**

performance poetry *n.* Poetry written to be declaimed in public performance. **—performance poet** *n.*

performance test *n.* A psychological test that requires only nonverbal responses, used, for example, to test the intellectual ability of children with speech problems.

per·form·ing arts (pər-fórming) *pl.n.* Those arts, such as drama and music, which are realised in performance rather than directly by the creative artist.

per·fume (pérfewm || *U.S. also* pər-féwm) *n.* **1.** A volatile liquid, distilled from flowers or prepared synthetically, that emits and diffuses a fragrant odour. **2.** Any agreeable scent or odour.
~tr.v. (pər-féwm, per-, pérfewm) **perfumed, -fuming, -fumes.** To impregnate with fragrance; impart a pleasant odour to. [French *parfum,* probably from obsolete Italian *parfumare,* to smoke through : *par-,* through, from Latin *per-* + *fumare,* to smoke, from Latin *fūmāre,* from *fūmus,* smoke.]

per·fum·er (pər-féwmər, per-) *n.* A maker or seller of perfumes.

per·fum·er·y (pər-féwməri, per-) *n., pl.* **-ies. 1.** Perfumes in general. **2.** An establishment that specialises in making or selling perfume. **3.** The art of making perfume.

per·func·to·ry (pər-fúngk-təri, -tri) *adj.* Done or acting routinely and with little interest or care. See Synonyms at **superficial.** [Late Latin *perfunctōrius,* from Latin *perfungī* (past participle *perfunctus*), "to get through with" : *per-,* completely + *fungī,* to perform.] **—per·func·to·ri·ly** *adv.* **—per·func·to·ri·ness** *n.*

per·fuse (pər-féwz) *tr.v.* **-fused, -fusing, -fuses. 1.** To coat, suffuse, or permeate with liquid, colour, or light. **2.** To pour or diffuse (a liquid) over or through something. [Latin *perfundere* (past participle *perfusus*), to pour over or through : *per-*, through + *fundere*, to pour.] —**per·fu·sive** (-féw-siv, -ziv) *adj.*

per·go·la (pérgələ || pər-gṓlə) *n.* An arbour or passageway with a roof of trelliswork on which climbing plants grow. [Italian, from Latin *pergula*, projecting roof, from *pergere*, to proceed.]

per·haps (pər-háps, praps) *adv.* Possibly; maybe; it may be that. [PER (by) + plural of HAP (chance).]

pe·ri (péer-i) *n.* **1.** In Persian mythology, a beautiful fairy. **2.** A fairy-like being. [Persian *pāri*; akin to Avestan *pairika*, witch.]

peri– *prefix.* Indicates: **1.** About, around, encircling, or enclosing; for example, **periotic, periscope. 2.** Close at hand, adjacent, or near; for example, **perihelion.** [Latin, from Greek, from *peri*, about, near, around.]

per·i·anth (pérri-anth) *n. Botany.* The outer organs of a flower, consisting of the calyx and corolla (the sepals and petals), or of either of these if the other is absent. [French *périanthe*, from New Latin *perianthium* : PERI- + ANTH(O)- + -IUM.]

per·i·apt (pérri-apt) *n.* An amulet or charm worn as protection against harm and disease. [Old French *periapte*, from Greek *periapton*, from *periaptos*, appended, from *periaptein*, to hang or fasten around : *peri-*, PERI- + *haptein*, to fasten (see **synapse**).]

per·i·blem (pérri-blem) *n. Botany.* A zone of tissue in the apical meristem of a root that develops into the cortex. [German, from Greek *periblēma*, protection, from *periballein*, to throw around : *peri-*, PERI- + *ballein*, to throw.]

per·i·car·di·tis (pérrikaar-dítiss) *n.* Inflammation of the pericardium. [New Latin : PERICARD(IUM) + -ITIS.]

per·i·car·di·um (pérri-kár-di-əm) *n., pl.* **-dia** (-di-ə). The membranous sac enclosing the heart. [New Latin, from Greek *perikardion*, from *perikardios*, around the heart : PERI- + *kardia*, heart.] —**per·i·car·di·ac** (-ak), **per·i·car·di·al** *adj.*

per·i·carp (pérri-kaarp) *n. Botany.* The casing of the seed or seeds within a fruit, developed from the ovary wall. [New Latin *pericarpium*, from Greek *perikarpion*, pod, shell : *peri-*, PERI- + -CARP.] —**per·i·car·pi·al** (-kárpi-əl) *adj.*

per·i·chon·dri·um (pérri-kón-dri-əm) *n., pl.* **-dria** (-dri-ə). *Anatomy.* The fibrous membrane covering the surface of cartilage except at joint endings. [New Latin : PERI- + CHONDR(O)- + -IUM.] —**per·i·chon·dri·al** *adj.*

per·i·clase (pérri-klayss, -klayz) *n.* A mineral form of magnesium oxide, MgO, usually occurring in isomeric crystals or grains. [German *Periklas*, from New Latin *periclasia*, "perfect cleavage" : PERI (around, hence above others, exceedingly) + -CLASE.]

Per·i·cles (pérri-kleez) (*c.* 495–429 B.C.). Athenian statesman and general. A great democrat and skilled orator, he controlled Athenian affairs during the city's most glorious era. He fostered cultural life, encouraging Sophocles and Phidias among others, and also ordered the building of the Parthenon. —**Per·i·cle·an** (perri-kleé-ən) *adj.*

per·i·cli·nal (pérri-klín'l) *adj.* **1.** Of or pertaining to a pericline. **2.** *Botany.* **a.** Designating a line of cell division parallel to the surface of the organ, as found in a meristem. **b.** Having tissue of one origin completely enclosed by tissue of a different origin.

per·i·cline (pérri-klīn) *n.* **1.** A variety of albite occurring as elongated white crystals. **2.** A formation of stratified rock shaped like a dome or basin in which the slopes follow the direction of folding. Also called "dome". [Greek *periklinēs*, sloping on all sides : *peri-*, PERI- + *klinein*, to slope, lean.]

per·i·cra·ni·um (pérri-kráy-ni-əm) *n., pl.* **-nia** (-ni-ə). *Anatomy.* The external **periosteum** *(see)* that covers the outer surface of the skull. [New Latin, from Greek *perikranion*, from *perikranios*, around the skull : PERI- + *kranion*, CRANIUM.] —**per·i·cra·ni·al** *adj.*

per·i·cy·cle (pérri-sīk'l) *n. Botany.* The outermost layer of the stele of a plant, usually though not always consisting of a layer of cells. [French *péricycle*, from Greek *perikuklos*, spherical : *peri-*, PERI- + *kuklos*, CYCLE.] —**per·i·cy·clic** (-síklik, -sícklik) *adj.*

per·i·cyn·thi·on (pérri-sínthi-ən) *n.* The point at which a spacecraft or other body in orbit round the Moon is nearest to the Moon: the **apolune, perilune.** [PERI- + *-cynthion*, from CYNTHIA (the Moon).]

per·i·derm (pérri-derm) *n. Botany.* An outer layer of tissue of plant roots and stems, consisting of the bark and the layer of growing tissue beneath the bark. [New Latin *peridermis* : PERI- + -DERM.] —**per·i·der·mal** (-dérm'l), **per·i·der·mic** (-dérmik) *adj.*

pe·rid·i·um (pə-ríd-i-əm) *n., pl.* **-ridia** (-i-ə). The covering of the spore-bearing organ in many fungi. [New Latin, from Greek *pēridion*, diminutive of *pēra*†, leather bag.] —**pe·rid·i·al** *adj.*

per·i·dot (pérri-dot || -dōt) *n.* A transparent, pale green variety of **olivine** *(see).* [French *péridot*, from Old French *peritot*†.] —**per·i·dot·ic** (-dóttik || -dṓtik) *adj.*

per·i·do·tite (pérri-dṓtit || *U.S. also* pə-ríddə-tīt) *n.* Any of a group of igneous rocks composed mainly of olivine and various pyroxenes and amphiboles. [French *péridotite*, from *péridot*, PERIDOT.]

per·i·gee (pérri-jee) *n.* The point nearest the Earth in the orbit of the Moon, a spacecraft or any other body. Compare **apogee.** [French *périgée*, from New Latin *perigeum*, from Greek *perigeion*, from *perigeios*, near the Earth : *peri-*, PERI- + *gē*, the Earth.] —**per·i·ge·an** *adj.*

per·i·gla·cial (pérri-gláy-sh'l, -si-əl) *adj.* Designating a region around a glacier.

per·i·gon (pérri-gən || -gon) *n.* An angle of 360°; a round angle. [PERI- + -GON.]

Pér·i·gueux (*French* perri-gő). Town in southwest France. Situated on the river Isle, it is capital of the Dordogne département.

pe·rig·y·nous (pə-ríjinəss) *adj. Botany.* **1.** Having sepals, petals, and stamens around the edge of a flat or cuplike receptacle containing the ovary. **2.** Designating flower parts arranged in this way: *perigynous stamens.* [New Latin *perigynus* : PERI- + -GYNOUS.] —**pe·rig·y·ny** (pə-ríjini) *n.*

per·i·he·li·on (pérri-heéli-ən) *n., pl.* **-helia** (-heéli-ə). The point nearest the Sun in the orbit of a planet or other body. Compare **aphelion.** [New Latin : PERI- + Greek *hēlios*, sun.]

per·il (pérrəl, pérril) *n.* **1.** A condition of imminent danger; exposure to the risk of harm or loss. **2.** Something that endangers; a serious risk. —**at (one's) peril.** At the risk of danger or punishment. —See Synonyms at **danger.**

~*tr.v.* **perilled** or *U.S.* **periled, -illing** or *U.S.* **-iling, -ils.** *Rare.* To expose to danger or the chance of injury; imperil. [Middle English, from Old French, from Latin *perīculum*, trial, danger.] —**per·il·ous** *adj.* —**per·il·ous·ly** *adv.*

per·i·lune (pérri-lo͞on || -lewn) *n.* The point in the orbit of a body, such as a spacecraft, round the Moon that is nearest to the Moon. Compare **apolune, pericynthion.** [PERI- + Latin *lūna*, Moon, by analogy with *perigee.*]

per·i·lymph (pérri-limf) *n.* The fluid surrounding the structures of the internal ear in vertebrates.

pe·rim·e·ter (pə-rímmitər, pi-, pe-) *n.* **1.** *Mathematics.* **a.** A closed curve bounding a plane area. **b.** The length of such a boundary. **2.** Any outer boundary, such as the edge of a playing field or a fortified strip protecting a military position. **3.** A diagnostic instrument used to measure the extent of a person's field of vision. [French *périmètre*, from Latin *perimetros*, from Greek : *peri-*, PERI- + -METER.] —**per·i·met·ric** (pérri-méttrik), **per·i·met·ri·cal** *adj.* —**per·i·met·ri·cal·ly** *adv.*

per·i·morph (pérri-mawrf) *n.* A mineral that encloses a different mineral. Compare **endomorph.** [PERI- + -MORPH.] —**per·i·mor·phic** (-mórfik), **per·i·mor·phous** *adj.* —**per·i·mor·phism** *n.*

per·i·my·si·um (pérri-mízzi-əm) *n., pl.* **-mysia** (-mízzi-ə). A sheath of connective tissue enveloping bundles of muscle fibres. [New Latin : PERI- + Greek *mus*, muscle.]

per·i·na·tal (pérri-náyt'l) *adj.* Of, pertaining to, or occurring in the period from approximately three months before to one month after birth: *perinatal mortality.*

per·i·neph·ri·um (pérri-néf-ri-əm) *n., pl.* **-ria** (-ri-ə). The connective and fatty tissue surrounding the kidney. [New Latin, from Greek *perinephros*, fat around the kidney : *peri-*, PERI- + *nephros*, kidney.] —**per·i·neph·ral, per·i·neph·ri·al, per·i·neph·ric** *adj.*

per·i·ne·um (pérri-neé-əm) *n., pl.* **-nea** (-neé-ə). **1.** The portion of the body in the pelvis occupied by the urogenital passages and the rectum. **2.** The region between the scrotum and the anus in males, and between the posterior vulva junction and the anus in females. [New Latin, from Late Latin *perinaion*, from Greek : *peri-*, PERI- + *inan*†, to excrete.] —**per·i·ne·al** *adj.*

per·i·neu·ri·um (pérri-néwr-i-əm || -no͝or-) *n., pl.* **-neuria** (-i-ə). A sheath of connective tissue enclosing a bundle of nerve fibres. [New Latin : PERI- + NEUR(O)- + -IUM.] —**per·i·neu·ri·al** *adj.*

pe·ri·od (peér-i-əd) *n. Abbr.* **per. 1.** An interval of time characterised by the occurrence of certain conditions or events: *slack periods.* **2.** An interval of time characterised by the prevalence of a specified culture, ideology, or technology: *artefacts of the pre-Columbian period.* **3.** A unit of geological time, longer than an epoch and shorter than an era. **4.** An interval regarded as a distinct evolutionary or developmental phase; a stage: *Picasso's blue period.* **5.** Any of various arbitrary temporal units, especially: **a.** A division of time allotted for teaching a class. **b.** A division of the playing time of a game. **6.** *Physics.* The time interval between two successive occurrences of any recurrent event or cycle; the reciprocal of frequency. **7.** An instance or occurrence of menstruation. **8.** A point or portion of time at which something is ended; a completion; a conclusion. **9.** The full pause at the end of a spoken sentence. **10.** *Chiefly U.S.* A **full stop** *(see).* **11. a.** In formal literary composition, a sentence of several carefully balanced clauses. **b.** *Plural.* Rhetorical language. **12.** A metrical unit of Greek verse consisting of two or more cola. **13.** *Music.* A group of two or more phrases within a composition, made up of eight or sixteen measures and terminating with a cadence. **14.** *Mathematics.* **a.** The smallest interval in the range of the independent variable required for a periodic function to begin another cycle. **b.** A group of digits separated by commas in a written number. **c.** The number of digits that repeat in a repeating decimal. For example, $^1/_7 = 0.142857142857\ldots$ has a six-digit period. **15.** *Astronomy.* **a.** The time taken for a heavenly body to complete one orbit or one rotation on its axis. **b.** The interval between two maximum emissions from a variable star. **16.** *Chemistry.* Any of the horizontal rows of elements in the periodic table. Compare **group.**

~*adv. Chiefly U.S.* Used to add finality and emphasis to a preceding statement: *I'm going, period!*

~*adj.* Of, belonging to, or representing a particular historical age or time: *a period piece; period furniture.* [Middle English *paryode*, from Old French *periode*, from Late Latin *periodus*, period of time, from Latin, sentence, from Greek *periodos*, circuit : *peri-* PERI- + *hodos*, way.]

per·i·o·date (per-ī́-ə-dayt, pər-) *n.* A salt or ester of a periodic acid.

pe·ri·od·ic (peér-i-óddik) *adj.* Also **pe·ri·od·i·cal** (-'l). **1.** Having periods or repeated cycles. **2.** Happening or appearing at regular intervals. **3.** Taking place now and then; intermittent. [French *périodique,* from Latin *periodicus,* from Greek *periodikos,* from *periodos,* PERIOD.] **—pe·ri·od·i·cal·ly** *adv.*

***Synonyms:** periodic, sporadic, intermittent, occasional, fitful.*

per·i·od·ic acid (pér-ī-óddik) *n.* Any of several acids that contain more oxygen than iodic acid, especially HIO_4 and H_5IO_6.

pe·ri·od·i·cal (peér-i-óddik'l) *n.* A publication issued at regular intervals, usually of a week or longer.
~adj. **1.** Of, pertaining to, or designating such a publication. **2.** Variant of **periodic.**

periodic function *n.* A mathematical function, such as sin *x* or cos *x,* whose value is repeated at regular invervals.

pe·ri·o·dic·i·ty (peér-i-ə-díssəti) *n.* The quality of being periodic; recurrence at regular intervals.

periodic law *n. Chemistry.* The principle that the properties of the elements recur periodically with increasing atomic number.

periodic system *n.* The classification of the chemical elements on the basis of the periodic law.

periodic table *n. Chemistry.* A tabular arrangement of the elements according to their atomic number.

per·i·o·don·tal (pérri-ə-dónt'l, -ō-) *adj.* Of or designating tissue and structures surrounding and supporting the teeth. [PERI- + ODONT(O)- + -AL.]

per·i·o·don·tics (pérri-ə-dóntiks, -ō-) *n. Used with a singular verb.* Also **per·i·o·don·tia** (-dónshə). The branch of dentistry dealing with periodontal disease. [New Latin *periodontium,* periodontal tissue : PERI- + ODONT(O)- + -IUM.] **—per·i·o·don·tic** *adj.* **—per·i·o·don·tist** *n.*

per·i·os·te·um (pérri-óss-i-əm) *n., pl.* **-tea** (-ti-ə). A fibrous membrane covering all bones, except at points of articulation. [New Latin, from Late Latin *periosteon,* from Greek, from *periosteos,* around the bones : *peri-,* PERI- + *osteon,* bone.] **—per·i·os·te·al, per·i·os·te·ous** *adj.*

per·i·os·ti·tis (pérri-oss-títiss) *n.* Inflammation of the periosteum. **—per·i·os·tit·ic** (-títtik) *adj.*

per·i·o·tic (pérri-ōtik, -óttik) *adj.* **1.** Situated around the ear. **2.** Of or designating the bones immediately around the inner ear. [PERI- + OTIC.]

per·i·pa·tet·ic (pérripə-téttik) *adj.* **1.** Walking about from place to place in the pursuit of one's business; itinerant. **2.** Carried on while walking or moving from place to place: *a peripatetic conversation.* **3.** *British.* Employed in a number of places and travelling between them; especially, working in more than one school: *a peripatetic music teacher.* [From PERIPATETIC.]

Per·i·pa·tet·ic (pérripə-téttik) *adj.* Of or pertaining to the philosophy or methods of teaching of Aristotle, who conducted discussions while walking about in the Lyceum of ancient Athens.
~n. **1.** A member of Aristotle's school. **2.** A follower of the philosophy of Aristotle; an Aristotelian. [Middle English, from Old French *peripatetique,* from Latin *peripatēticus,* from Greek *peripatētikos,* from *peripatein,* to walk about while teaching : *peri-,* PERI- + *patein,* to tread, walk.]

per·i·pe·te·ia (pérripə-tí-ə, -teé-ə) *n.* Also **pe·rip·e·ty** (pə-ríppəti). An abrupt or unexpected change in a course of events or situation, especially in a drama or literary work. [Greek, from *peripiptein,* to change suddenly, "fall around" : *peri-,* PERI- + *piptein,* to fall.]

pe·riph·er·al (pə-ríffərəl, -riffrəl) *adj.* Also **per·i·pher·ic** (pérri-férrik). **1.** Pertaining to, located on, or constituting the periphery. **2.** Not of central importance; minor or incidental.
~n. Computing. A peripheral device. **—pe·riph·er·al·ly** *adv.*

peripheral device *n.* A device used to feed information into or extract information from a computer, such as a keyboard, printer, or magnetic tape unit, or a device outside the main store in which information is stored. Also called "peripheral", "peripheral unit".

peripheral nervous system *n.* The part of the nervous system comprising the cranial nerves, the spinal nerves, and the autonomic nervous system.

peripheral vision *n. Antatomy.* Vision in which images fall upon parts of the retina outside the macula lutea.

pe·riph·er·y (pə-ríff-əri, pe-) *n., pl.* **-ies. 1. a.** The outermost part or region within a precise boundary. **b.** The region or area immediately beyond a precise boundary. **c.** Broadly, an area forming an imprecise boundary; the fringe or edge of something, especially of a social group. **2.** *Mathematics.* **a.** A **perimeter** *(see).* **b.** The surface of a solid. **3.** *Anatomy.* A region in which nerves end. [Middle English *peripherie,* from Late Latin *peripherīa,* from Greek *periphereia,* from *peripherēs,* carrying around, from *peripherein,* to carry around : *peri-,* PERI- + *pherein,* to carry.]

pe·riph·ra·sis (pə-ríffrə-siss, pe-) *n., pl.* **-ses** (-seez). **1.** The use of indirect or roundabout methods of expression. **2.** An indirect expression; a circumlocution. [Latin, from Greek, from *periphrazein,* to express in a roundabout way : *peri-,* PERI- + *phrazein,* to say.]

per·i·phras·tic (pérri-frástik) *adj.* **1.** Of or characterised by periphrasis. **2.** *Grammar.* Constructed by using an auxiliary word rather than an inflected form; for example, the phrases *the word of his father* and *his father did say* are periphrastic, while *his father's word* and *his father said* are inflected. **—per·i·phras·ti·cal·ly** *adv.*

pe·rip·ter·al (pə-ríptərəl, pe-) *adj. Architecture.* Built with a row of columns on all sides. [Latin *peripteros,* from Greek, "flying around" : *peri-,* PERI- + *pteron,* wing.]

pe·rique (pə-reék) *n.* A strongly flavoured, black tobacco grown in Louisiana and used in various blends. [Louisiania French, said to be after *Périque,* nickname of *Pierre* Chenet, planter who introduced tobacco-growing in Louisiana.]

per·i·sarc (pérri-saark) *n. Zoology.* A horny external covering that encloses the colonies of certain hydrozoans. [PERI- + Greek *sarx* (stem *sark-*), flesh.] **—per·i·sar·cal** (-sárk'l), **per·i·sar·cous** *adj.*

per·i·scope (pérri-skōp) *n.* Any of various optical instruments that contain reflecting elements, such as mirrors and prisms, to permit observation from a position displaced from a direct line of sight, as from a submerged submarine or a trench below ground level. [PERI- + -SCOPE.] **—per·i·scop·ic** (-skóppik) *adj.*

per·ish (pérrish) *v.* **-ished, -ishing, -ishes.** *—intr.* **1.** To die, especially in a violent or untimely manner. **2.** To pass from existence; die out or away. **3.** To decay; rot away. *—tr.* To destroy or rot away; cause to perish. [Middle English *perisshen,* from Old French *perir* (present stem *periss-*), from Latin *perīre,* to pass away : *per-,* away + *īre,* to go.]

per·ish·a·ble (pérrishə-b'l) *adj.* Liable to perish, decay, or spoil.
~n. Plural. Perishable foodstuffs. **—per·ish·a·bil·i·ty** (-bílləti), **perish·a·ble·ness** *n.* **—per·ish·a·bly** *adv.*

per·ished (pérrisht) *adj. Informal.* **1.** Debilitated or extremely distressed because of cold. **2.** Feeling extremely cold; frozen.

per·ish·er (pérrishər) *n. British Informal.* An annoying young person or child; a rascal.

per·ish·ing (pérrishing) *adj. Informal.* **1.** Unpleasantly or distressingly cold; freezing: *It's perishing outside.* **2.** Damned; confounded: *Stop that perishing dog barking.*
~adv. Informal. Very. Used as an intensive. **—per·ish·ing·ly** *adv.*

per·i·sperm (pérri-sperm) *n. Botany.* The nutritive tissue in the seeds of many plants that is derived from the nucellus and deposited outside the embryo sac.

pe·ris·so·dac·tyl (pə-ríssō-dák-til, -t'l) *adj. Zoology.* **1.** Having an odd number of toes. **2.** Of or designating certain hoofed mammals, such as horses and rhinoceroses, of the order Perissodactyla, that have an odd number of toes.
~n. Zoology. A hoofed mammal of this order. [Greek *perissodaktulos* : *perissos,* excessive, uneven, from *peri-,* PERI- (around, hence beyond) + *daktulos,* DACTYL.] **—pe·ris·so·dac·ty·lous** *adj.*

per·i·stal·sis (pérri-stál-siss || -stáwl-) *n., pl.* **-ses** (-seez). Involuntary wavelike muscular contractions that propel contained matter along tubular organs, as in the alimentary canal. [New Latin, from *peristalticus,* of peristalsis, from Greek *peristaltikos,* compressing around, from *peristellein,* to wrap around : *peri-,* PERI- + *stellein,* to place, set.] **—per·i·stal·tic** *adj.*

per·i·stome (pérri-stōm) *n.* **1.** *Botany.* A circular row of toothlike appendages surrounding the mouth of a moss capsule. **2.** *Zoology.* The area around the mouth in certain invertebrates. [New Latin *peristoma* : PERI- + -STOME.] **—per·i·sto·mal** (-stōm'l), **per·i·sto·mi·al** (-stōmi-əl) *adj.*

per·i·style (pérri-stīl) *n. Architecture.* **1.** A series of columns surrounding a temple or other structure, or enclosing a court. **2.** A court enclosed by such columns. [French *péristyle,* from Latin *peristȳlum,* from Greek *peristulon,* from *peristulos,* surrounded by columns : *peri-,* PERI- + *stulos,* pillar.] **—per·i·sty·lar** (-stīlər) *adj.*

per·i·the·ci·um (pérri-theé-si-əm, -shi-) *n., pl.* **-cia** (-si-ə). A flask-shaped fruiting body in certain fungi, containing ascospores. [New Latin : PERI- + Greek *thēkion,* diminutive of *thēkē,* a case, chest.]

per·i·to·ne·um (pérri-tə-neé-əm, -tō-) *n., pl.* **-nea** (-neé-ə). The membrane lining the walls of the abdominal cavity and covering the viscera. [Late Latin *peritonēum,* from Greek *peritonaion,* neuter of *peritonaios,* stretched across, from *peritonos,* stretched around or over : *peri-,* PERI- + *tenein,* to stretch.] **—per·i·to·ne·al** *adj.*

per·i·to·ni·tis (pérri-tə-nītiss, -tō-) *n.* Inflammation of the peritoneum. [New Latin : PERITON(EUM) + -ITIS.]

pe·rit·ri·cha (pə-ríttrikə) *pl.n. Singular* **per·i·trich** (pérri-trik). **1.** Bell-shaped or tubular microorganisms of the order Peritrichida, characterised by a wide oral opening surrounded by cilia. **2.** Bacteria entirely covered with cilia. [New Latin : PERI- + Greek *thrix* (stem *trikh-*), hair.] **—pe·rit·ri·chous** *adj.*

per·i·wig (pérri-wig) *n.* A wig or peruke. [Earlier *perwyke,* from Old French *perruque,* PERUKE.]

per·i·win·kle[1] (pérri-wingk'l) *n.* A **winkle** *(see).* [16th century : origin obscure.]

periwinkle[2] *n.* **1.** Any of several trailing, evergreen plants of the genus *Vinca;* especially, *V. minor,* having blue flowers. Also *U.S.* "myrtle". **2.** Light purplish-blue. Also called "periwinkle blue". [Variant (influenced by PERIWINKLE, snail) of Middle English *pervenke,* from Old French *pervenche,* from Latin *pervinca,* shortening of *vincapervinca†.*] **—per·i·win·kle** *adj.*

per·jure (pérjər) *tr.v.* **-jured, -juring, -jures.** To render (oneself) guilty of perjury by deliberately giving false evidence or testifying falsely under oath. [Middle English *perjuren,* from Old French *perjurer,* from Latin *perjūrāre* : *per-* (destruction) + *jūrāre,* to swear.] **—per·jur·er** *n.*

per·ju·ry (pérjəri) *n., pl.* **-ries. 1.** *Law.* The deliberate, wilful giving of false, misleading, or incomplete evidence or testimony by a witness under oath in a judicial proceeding, whether given in a court or by affidavit. **2.** Any violation of an oath or promise. [Middle English *perjurie,* from Anglo-French *parjurie,* from Latin *perjūrium,* from *perjūrus,* perjured, from *perjūrāre,* to PERJURE.] **—per·ju·ri·ous** (pər-jóor-i-əss, per-) *adj.* **—per·ju·ri·ous·ly** *adv.*

perk[1] (perk) *v.* **perked, perking, perks.** *—intr.* **1.** To stick up or jut out jauntily, as a dog's ears might. Often used with *up.* **2.** To regain one's animation or good spirits. Used with *up.* *—tr.* **1.** To raise smartly and quickly. **2.** To make vigorous and lively again; cheer. Often used with *up.* **3.** To make more attractive, trim, or smart in appearance. Often used with *up.* [Middle English *perken,* perhaps from Anglo-French *perquer,* to perch, from *perque,* rod, from Latin *pertica.* See **perch** (roost).]

perk² *n.* **1.** A payment or profit received in addition to a regular wage or salary, especially one received regularly or expected as one's due. **2.** Any extra benefit received through one's employment. Also formally called "perquisite". —See Synonyms at **right.** [Shortened from PERQUISITE.]

perk³ *v.* **perked, perking, perks.** —*intr.* To percolate. Used of coffee. —*tr.* To cause (coffee) to percolate. [Shortened from PERCOLATE.]

Per·kin's mauve (pérkinz) *n.* A dye, mauveine *(see).* [After Sir William *Perkin* (1838–1907), British chemist who developed it.]

perk·y (pérki) *adj.* **-ier, -iest. 1.** Cheerful and brisk; jaunty. **2.** Assertive and confident. —**perk·i·ly** *adv.* —**perk·i·ness** *n.*

per·lite, pearlite (pérlīt) *n.* A natural volcanic glass similar to obsidian but having distinctive concentric cracks and a relatively high water content. In a fluffy heat-expanded form it is used as a lightweight aggregate in plaster and concrete and in thermal and acoustic insulation. [French. See **pearl, -ite.**] —**per·lit·ic** (pər-líttik) *adj.*

perm¹ (perm) *n.* **1.** A treatment producing long-lasting artificial waves in the hair through any of various processes, especially by applying chemicals to the hair while wet, winding it on rollers, and drying with heat. **2.** The hairstyle produced by such treatment. See **cold wave.** Also called "permanent wave", *U.S.* "permanent". —*tr.v.* **permed, perming, perms.** To give a perm to. [Shortened from PERMANENT WAVE.]

perm² *tr.v.* **permed, perming, perms.** To make a selection and combination of (matches and their results) on a football-pools' coupon; make a permutation of. —*n.* A **permutation** *(see),* on a football-pools' coupon. [Shortened from PERMUTATION.]

Perm (perm ‖ *Russian* pyairm). City and region of Russia, just west of the Urals, situated on the river Kama.

perm. permanent.

per·ma·frost (pérmə-frost ‖ -frawst) *n.* Permanently frozen rock, soil, and subsoil continuous in polar regions and occurring locally in perennially frigid areas. [PERMA(NENT) + FROST.]

Perm·al·loy (perm-ál-oy ‖ pérmə-loy) *n.* A trademark for any of several alloys of nickel and iron, often with small amounts of other elements, having exceptionally high magnetic permeability.

per·ma·nence (pérmənənss) *n.* The condition or quality of being permanent.

per·ma·nen·cy (pérmənən-si) *n., pl.* **-cies. 1.** Permanence. **2.** Someone or something permanent.

per·ma·nent (pérmənənt) *adj. Abbr.* **perm. 1.** Fixed and changeless; lasting or meant to last indefinitely. **2. a.** Not expected to change for a long or indefinite period: *my permanent address.* **b.** *Often capital* **P.** Designating a high-ranking member of a government department whose position is not affected by changes in the government: *Permanent Secretary to the Treasury.* —*n. U.S.* A perm for the hair. [Middle English, from Old French, from Latin *permanēns* (stem *permanent-*), present participle of *permanēre,* to remain throughout : *per-,* throughout + *manēre,* to remain.] —**per·ma·nent·ly** *adv.*

permanent magnet *n.* A material that retains induced magnetic properties after it is removed from a magnetic field; a ferromagnet.

Permanent Under Secretary *n.* An **Under Secretary** *(see).*

permanent wave *n.* A hairstyle or hair treatment, a perm *(see).*

permanent way *n. British.* The rails, sleepers, and roadbed of a railway track.

per·man·ga·nate (pər-máng-gə-nayt, -nit, -nət) *n.* Any of the salts of permanganic acid, all of which are strong oxidising agents. [PERMANGAN(IC ACID) + -ATE.]

permanganate of potash *n.* **Potassium permanganate** *(see).*

per·man·gan·ic acid (pérmang-gánnik) *n.* An unstable inorganic acid, $HMnO_4$, existing as a strongly oxidising, aqueous solution.

per·me·a·bil·i·ty (pérmi-ə-bíllati) *n.* **1.** The property or condition of being permeable. **2.** *Physics.* **Magnetic permeability** *(see).* **3.** The rate of diffusion of a pressurised gas through a porous material.

per·me·a·ble (pérmi-əb'l) *adj.* Capable of being permeated. [Late Latin *permeābilis,* from Latin *permeāre,* to PERMEATE.] —**per·me·a·bly** *adv.*

per·me·ance (pérmi-ənss) *n.* **1.** The act of permeating. **2.** A measure of the ability of a magnetic circuit to conduct magnetic flux; the reciprocal of **reluctance** *(see).* [Latin *permeāns,* present participle of *permeāre,* to PERMEATE.]

per·me·ate (pérmi-ayt) *v.* **-ated, -ating, -ates.** —*tr.* **1.** To spread or flow throughout; pervade. **2.** To pass through the openings or interstices of: *liquid permeating a membrane.* —*intr.* To spread; penetrate; diffuse. [Latin *permeāre : per-,* through + *meāre,* to go, pass.] —**per·me·ant** (-ənt), **per·me·a·tive** (-ətiv, -aytiv) *adj.* —**per·me·a·tion** (-áysh'n) *n.*

per men·sem (mén-sem) *adv. Latin.* By the month or for each month.

Per·mi·an (pérmi-ən) *adj.* Of, belonging to, or designating the geological time, system of rocks, and sedimentary deposits of the sixth and last period of the Palaeozoic era. —*n. Geology.* The Permian period. Preceded by *the.* [After *Perm,* former Russian province (see **PERM**), where the rock strata were first identified.]

per mill, per mil (mil) *adv.* By the thousand; per thousand. [*mill, mil,* from Latin *mille,* a thousand.]

per·mis·si·ble (pər-míssə-b'l) *adj.* That can be permitted, tolerated, or accepted; allowable: *maximum permissible dosage.* —**per·mis·si·bil·i·ty** (-bílləti), **per·mis·si·ble·ness** *n.* —**per·mis·si·bly** *adv.*

per·mis·sion (pər-mísh'n) *n.* **1.** The act of permitting. **2.** Consent, especially formal consent; leave; authorisation. [Middle English, from Old French, from Latin *permissiō* (stem *permissiōn-*), from *permittere* (past participle *permissus*), to PERMIT.]

per·mis·sive (pər-míssiv) *adj.* **1.** Granting permission; allowing. **2.** Permitting discretion, as distinct from prescriptive. **3.** Lenient, tolerant, or liberal, especially when based on or reflecting a belief that there should be as few restraints as possible in matters of sexual morality. **4.** *Archaic.* Not forbidden; permitted. —**per·mis·sive·ly** *adv.* —**per·mis·sive·ness** *n.*

per·mit (pər-mít) *v.* **-mitted, -mitting, -mits.** —*tr.* **1.** To allow (something); consent to; tolerate. **2.** To give permission to; authorise. **3. a.** To afford opportunity for; make possible. **b.** To allow as possible; admit of. —*intr.* To afford opportunity; allow. —**permit of.** To allow as a possibility; permit. —*n.* (pérmit ‖ *U.S. also* pər-mít). **1.** Permission; leave. **2.** A document or certificate giving permission to do something; a licence; a warrant. [Latin *permittere : per-,* through + *mittere,* to let go, send.] —**per·mit·ter** *n.*

Usage: Permit may be followed by *of* when it means "admit; be open to the possibility": *The wording permits (of) only one interpretation.* The use of this construction in the general sense of "allow" is considered nonstandard: the sentence *The law does not permit of their doing that* would in standard English be *The law does not permit their doing that* or *The law does not permit them to do that.*

per·mit·tiv·i·ty (pérmi-tívvəti) *n., pl.* **-ties.** *Physics.* **1.** A measure of the ability of a medium to transmit an electric field, expressed as the ratio of its electric displacement to the intensity of the field at some point. Also called "absolute permittivity". See **electric constant. 2.** The ratio of electric flux density produced by an electric field in a medium to that produced in a vacuum by the same field. Also called "relative permittivity", "dielectric constant". [From PERMIT.]

per·mu·ta·tion (pérmew-táysh'n) *n.* **1.** A complete change; a transformation. **2.** The act of changing the arrangement or order of a given set of objects in a group. **3.** *Mathematics.* An ordered arrangement of all or some of the elements of a set. **4.** Broadly, any of the variations possible in a given situation: *permutations of our original plan.* **5.** A particular selection and combination of matches and their results, made on a football-pools' coupon. In this sense, also called "perm". —**per·mu·ta·tion·al** *adj.*

per·mute (pər-méwt) *tr.v.* **-muted, -muting, -mutes. 1.** To change the order of. **2.** *Mathematics.* To subject to permutation. [Middle English *permuten,* from Old French *permuter,* from Latin *permūtāre : per-,* completely + *mūtāre,* to change.] —**per·mut·a·ble** *adj.*

per·ni·cious (pər-níshəss) *adj.* **1. a.** Tending to cause death or serious injury; deadly. **b.** Causing great harm; destructive; ruinous. **2.** Causing moral injury; evil: *a pernicious philosophy.* [Latin *perniciōsus,* from *perniciēs,* destruction : *per-,* completely + *nex* (stem *nec-*), death.] —**per·ni·cious·ly** *adv.* —**per·ni·cious·ness** *n.*

pernicious anaemia *n.* A severe anaemia associated with failure to absorb vitamin B_{12}.

per·nick·e·ty (pər-níckəti) *adj.* Also *U.S.* **per·snick·e·ty** (-sníckəti) *Informal.* **1.** Fussy; very strict in matters of detail. **2.** Involving or showing minute attention to detail. [19th century (Scottish) : origin obscure.]

Pe·rón (pe-rón), **Juan (Domingo)** (1895–1974). Argentinian soldier and politician, president (1946–55, 1973–74). As vice-president (1944) in a right-wing military government he developed a personal following among urban workers. Imprisoned by democrats in 1945, he was released following street demonstrations in his favour, and was elected president in 1946. While restricting civil liberties he carried out social reforms. His second wife, (Maria) Eva (Duarte de) Perón (1919–52), known as Evita, won popularity for her charitable works. Perón was overthrown by the army in 1955, but returned from exile to become president again in 1973. He was succeeded by his third wife, María Estela (Martínez de) Perón (1931–), known as Isabelita, who was ousted by the army in 1976.

per·o·ne·al (pérrə-née-əl) *adj. Anatomy.* Of or pertaining to the fibula or to the outer portion of the leg. [New Latin *peroneus,* of the fibula, from *perone,* fibula, from Greek *peronē,* "pin, buckle".]

per·o·rate (pérrə-rayt) *intr.v.* **-rated, -rating, -rates. 1.** To make a peroration. **2.** To speak at great length, often in an inflated, pompous manner; declaim. [Latin *perōrāre,* to harangue at length : *per-,* thoroughly, to the end + *ōrāre,* to orate.]

per·o·ra·tion (pérrə-ráysh'n) *n.* The concluding part of a speech or written discourse, usually consisting of a formal recapitulation.

per·ox·i·dase (pə-róksi-dayss, -dayz) *n.* An enzyme found in most plant cells and some animal cells that catalyses peroxide oxidation reactions. [PEROXID(E) + -ASE.]

per·ox·ide (pə-rók-sīd) *n. Chemistry.* **1. Hydrogen peroxide** *(see).* **2.** Any compound containing oxygen that yields hydrogen peroxide with an acid, such as sodium peroxide, Na_2O_2. —*tr.v.* **peroxided, -iding, -ides. 1.** To treat with peroxide. **2.** To bleach (hair) with hydrogen peroxide.

peroxide blonde *n.* A person, usually a woman, having hair dyed or bleached with or as if with hydrogen peroxide.

peroxy–, peroxo– *comb. form.* Indicates the presence of the perox-

ide group in a chemical compound; for example, **peroxysulphuric acid.**
per·oxy·sul·phu·ric acid (pə-róksi-sul-féwr-ik) *n.* A white unstable crystalline acid, H_2SO_5, used as an oxidising agent. Also called "Caro's acid", "persulphuric acid".
per·pend (pər-pénd) *v.* **-pended, -pending, -pends.** *Archaic.* —*tr.* To wonder about; ponder. —*intr.* To wonder; reflect. [Latin *perpendere,* to consider carefully : *per-,* thoroughly + *pendere,* to consider, weigh.]
per·pen·dic·u·lar (pér-pən-díckew-lər || -pen-) *adj.* **1.** *Mathematics.* Intersecting at or forming right angles. **2.** At right angles to the horizontal; vertical. **3.** Vertical or very steep; precipitous, as a cliff face or mountainside might be. **4.** *Often capital* **P.** Designating a style of English Gothic architecture of the 14th–16th centuries, characterised by emphasis of the vertical element and especially by vertical lines in window tracery. —See Synonyms at **vertical.**
~*n.* **1.** A line or plane perpendicular to a given line or plane. **2.** A perpendicular position. **3.** A device, such as a plumb line, used in marking the vertical from a given point. **4.** A vertical or nearly vertical line or plane. [Middle English *perpendiculer,* from Old French, from Latin *perpendiculārius,* from *perpendiculum,* plumb line : *per-,* thoroughly + *pendēre,* to hang + *-culum,* instrumental suffix.] —**per·pen·dic·u·lar·i·ty** (-lárrəti) *n.*
per·pe·trate (pér-pi-trayt, -pə-) *tr.v.* **-trated, -trating, -trates.** **1.** To be guilty of; commit: *perpetrate a crime.* **2.** To carry out; perform (an act, especially one considered outrageous or bad): *perpetrate a practical joke.* [Latin *perpetrāre,* to accomplish : *per-,* completely + *patrāre,* to do, "perform in the capacity of a father", from *pater,* father.] —**per·pe·tra·tion** (-tráysh'n) *n.* —**per·pe·tra·tor** (-ər) *n.*
per·pet·u·al (pər-péchoo-əl, -péttew-) *adj.* **1.** Lasting for eternity. **2.** Lasting for an indefinitely long time. **3.** Having effect or having tenure for an unlimited duration or for a complete lifetime: *a treaty of perpetual friendship.* **4.** Ceaselessly repeated or continuing without interruption: *perpetual nagging.* **5.** Flowering throughout the growing season. —See Synonyms at **continual.**
~*n.* A plant that flowers throughout the growing season. [Middle English *perpetuel,* from Old French, from Latin *perpetuālis,* from *perpetuus,* continuous, permanent, from *perpes* (stem *perpet-*), throughout, uninterrupted : *per-,* thoroughly + *petere,* to go towards.] —**per·pet·u·al·ly** *adv.* —**per·pet·u·al·ness** *n.*
perpetual calendar *n.* A chart or mechanical device that indicates the day of the week corresponding to any given date over a period of many years.
perpetual motion *n.* The hypothetical continuous and perpetual operation of an isolated mechanical device or other closed system, without loss of energy and without an external energy source.
per·pet·u·ate (pər-péchoo-ayt, -péttew-) *tr.v.* **-ated, -ating, -ates.** **1.** To make perpetual. **2.** To prolong the existence or memory of: *a myth perpetuated by repetition.* [Latin *perpetuāre,* from *perpetuus,* PERPETUAL.] —**per·pet·u·a·tion** (-áysh'n), **per·pet·u·ance** (-ənss) *n.* —**per·pet·u·a·tor** (-aytər) *n.*
per·pe·tu·i·ty (pér-pə-téw-əti || -tóo-) *n., pl.* **-ties.** **1.** The quality, state, or condition of being perpetual: *"The perpetuity of the Church was an article of faith."* (Morris West). **2.** Time without end; eternity. **3.** *Law.* **a.** The condition of an estate that is limited so as to be inalienable either perpetually or longer than the period determined by law. **b.** An estate so limited. **4.** *Finance.* An annuity payable indefinitely. —**in perpetuity.** For ever.
Per·pi·gnan (páir-peen-yoN, pér-, -yóN). Town in southern France, capital of Pyrénées-Orientales département. Situated on the river Têt, it is a tourist and agricultural centre.
per·plex (pər-pléks) *tr.v.* **-plexed, -plexing, -plexes.** **1.** To fill with uncertainty or bewilderment; confuse or puzzle. **2.** To make confusedly intricate; complicate: *Her explanation only perplexed the matter even more.* —See Synonyms at **puzzle.** [From obsolete adjective *perplex,* involved, perplexed, from Latin *perplexus,* intricate : *per-,* thoroughly + *plectere* (past participle *plexus*), to weave, entwine.] —**per·plex·ed·ly** (-pléksid-li, -plékst-) *adv.*
per·plex·i·ty (pər-pléksəti) *n., pl.* **-ties.** **1.** The state or condition of being perplexed or puzzled; bewilderment. **2.** The state or condition of being intricate or complicated: *the perplexity of life in the 20th century.* **3.** Something that perplexes.
per pro·cu·ra·ti·o·nem (prókewr-áyshi-ónem, próckewr-, -aáti-) *prep. Abbr.* **per pro, per proc., p.p.** *Latin.* On behalf of.
per·qui·site (pérkwizit) *n.* **1.** *Formal.* A **perk** *(see).* **2.** A tip; a gratuity. **3.** Something claimed as an exclusive right: *the perquisite of the upper classes.* —See Synonyms at **right.** [Middle English, from Medieval Latin *perquīsītum,* acquisition, perquisite, from the past participle of Latin *perquīrere,* to search for : *per-,* thoroughly + *quaerere,* to seek.]
Per·rault (pérrō, pe-rō), **Charles** (1628–1703). French writer. His *Tales of Mother Goose* (*c.* 1697) includes Tom Thumb, Puss in Boots, and Sleeping Beauty.
per·ron (pérrən) *n.* **1.** A platform at the entrance of a large building or a church. **2.** A flight of steps leading to such a platform. [Middle English, from Old French, from Vulgar Latin *petro* (stem *petron-*) (unattested), augmentative of *petra,* stone.]
per·ry (pérri) *n., pl.* **-ries.** A fermented alcoholic beverage made from pears. [Middle English *pereye,* from Old French *pere,* from Vulgar Latin *pirātum* (unattested), from Latin *pirum,* PEAR.]
Per·ry (pérri), **Fred(erick John)** (1909–95). British tennis player. He won the Wimbledon men's singles title in three consecutive years (1934–36), a record surpassed only by Björn Borg, and was the world singles table-tennis champion in 1929.
Pers. Persia; Persian.
per·salt (pér-sawlt || -solt) *n.* A salt of a peracid.
per se (sáy, sée) *adv.* In or by itself; as such; intrinsically. [Latin *per sē* : *per,* by, PER + *sē* (accusative), self.]
per·se·cute (pér-si-kewt) *tr.v.* **-cuted, -cuting, -cutes.** **1.** To oppress or harass with ill-treatment; especially, to subject to severe penalties because of political or religious dissent. **2.** To annoy persistently; bother. [Middle English, from Old French *persecuter,* back-formation from *persecuteur,* pursuer, from Late Latin *persecutor,* from Latin *persequī* (past participle *persecūtus*), to pursue : *per-,* throughout, to the end + *sequī,* to follow.] —**per·se·cu·tive, per·se·cu·to·ry** (-kewtəri, -kéwtəri || *U.S. also* -kew-tawri, -tōri) *adj.* —**per·se·cu·tor** (-kewtər) *n.*
per·se·cu·tion (pér-si-kéwsh'n) *n.* **1.** The act or practice of persecuting. **2.** The state or condition of being persecuted. **3.** A period during which people are persecuted. —**per·se·cu·tion·al** *adj.*
persecution complex *n.* A psychological delusion that other people feel hostility towards one or are attempting to victimise one.
Per·se·id (pér-si-id) *n., pl.* **-ids** or **Per·se·i·des** (pər-sée-i-deez, per-). *Astronomy.* Any of a shower of meteors that appears to originate in the vicinity of the constellation Perseus during August. [New Latin *Perseïdes,* plural of *Perseis,* daughter of PERSEUS.]
Per·seph·o·ne (per-séffəni, pər-). *Greek Mythology.* The wife of Hades and queen of the underworld; identified with Proserpina.
Per·se·us[1] (pér-sewss || -si-əss, -sóoss). *Greek Mythology.* The son of Zeus and Danae who slew Medusa and rescued Andromeda.
Perseus[2] *n.* A constellation in the Northern Hemisphere near Andromeda and Auriga.
per·se·ver·ance (pér-si-véer-ənss) *n.* **1.** The holding to a course of action, belief, or purpose without giving way; steadfastness. **2.** The Calvinistic doctrine that those who have been chosen by God will continue in a state of grace to the end and will finally be saved.
Synonyms: *perseverance, persistence, tenacity, steadfastness.*
per·sev·er·a·tion (pər-sévvə-ráysh'n) *n. Psychology.* **1.** Continued or repetitive activity or actions; specifically: **a.** The uncontrollable repetition of a word, phrase, or gesture. **b.** The spontaneous recurrence of a thought, image, phrase, or tune in the mind. **2.** The retention in new and inappropriate circumstances of a form of behaviour or a working pattern from other circumstances.
per·se·vere (pér-si-véer) *intr.v.* **-vered, -vering, -veres.** To persist in or remain constant to a purpose, idea, or task in the face of obstacles or discouragement. [Middle English *perseveren,* from Old French *perseverer,* from Latin *persevērāre,* from *persevērus,* very serious : *per-* (intensifier) + *sevērus,* serious, severe.] —**per·se·ver·ing·ly** *adv.*
Per·shing (pér-shing, -zhing), **John J(oseph)** (1860–1948). U.S. general. He commanded the U.S. Expeditionary Force sent to Europe in 1917, and later became U.S. chief of staff (1921–24).
Per·shing II missile (pérshing) *n.* A U.S. short-range ballistic missile armed with one nuclear warhead.
Persia. *Abbr.* **Pers.** See **Iran.**
Per·sian (pér-sh'n || -zh'n) *adj. Abbr.* **Pers.** Of or pertaining to Persia or Iran, its people, languages, or culture.
~*n.* **1.** A native or inhabitant of ancient or modern Persia or modern Iran. **2.** The Iranian language of the Persians, of the West Iranian group of Indo-European languages, in any of its several historical forms, Old Persian, Avestan, Pahlavi, Middle Persian, and modern Iranian.
Persian cat *n.* A domestic cat of a breed having long, silky fur.
Persian Gulf. See The **Gulf.**
Persian lamb *n.* **1.** The lamb of the karakul sheep of Asia. **2.** The glossy, loosely curled fur obtained from such a lamb, usually when it is three or four days old. In this sense, also called "caracul".
per·si·car·i·a (pér-si-káir-i-ə) *n.* Any of various plants of the genus *Polygonum* having spikes of pink or white flowers. Common persicaria, *P. persicaria,* is also called "redshank". [New Latin, from Latin *persicum,* peach.]
per·si·flage (pér-si-flaazh, páir-, -flaazh) *n.* **1.** A light, bantering style in writing or speaking. **2.** Idle, good-natured banter. [French, from *persifler,* to banter : *per-* (intensive), from Latin + *siffler,* to whistle, hiss, boo, from Vulgar Latin *sīfilāre* (unattested), from Latin *sībilāre.*]
per·sim·mon (per-símmən, pər-) *n.* **1.** Any of various chiefly tropical trees of the genus *Diospyros,* such as the Chinese persimmon *D. Kaki,* having orange-red fruit that is edible only when completely ripe. **2.** The fruit of any of these trees. [Of Algonquian origin; akin to Cree *pasiminan,* dried fruit, Delaware *pasĭmĕnan.*]
per·sist (pər-síst || -zíst) *intr.v.* **-sisted, -sisting, -sists.** **1.** To hold firmly and steadfastly to some purpose, state, belief, or course of action, despite obstacles, warnings, or setbacks. **2.** To continue in existence; last: *The pain persisted for several months.* [Latin *persistere* : *per-* (intensive) + *sistere,* to stand firm.]
per·sist·ence (pər-síss-tənss || -zíss-) *n.* Also **per·sis·ten·cy** (-tən-si). **1.** The act of persisting. **2.** The quality of being persistent; perseverance; tenacity. **3.** The continuance of an effect after the cause is removed: *persistence of vision.* —See Synonyms at **perseverance.**
per·sist·ent (pər-síss-tənt || -zíss-) *adj.* **1.** Refusing to give up or let go; persevering obstinately. **2.** Insistently repetitive or continuous. **3.** Continuing to exist, often in spite of action designed to prevent this; enduring: *a persistent rumour; a persistent superconducting current.* **4.** *Botany.* Lasting past maturity without falling off. Said of certain leaves or flowers. **5.** *Zoology.* **a.** Retained permanently,

rather than disappearing in an early stage of development: *the persistent gills of axolotls.* **b.** Continuing to grow after the normal period of growth. [Back-formation from *persistence,* or PERSIST + -ENT.] **—per·sist·ent·ly** *adv.*

per·son (pérss'n) *n. Abbr.* **per.** **1.** A living human being, especially as distinguished from an animal or thing. **2.** A human being considered without reference to his or her sex. See **-person.** **3.** The composite of characteristics that make up an individual personality. **4. a.** The living body of a human being. **b.** The body together with its clothing: *a pistol concealed about his person.* **c.** The penis. Used in the phrase *expose one's person.* **5.** *Archaic.* Guise; character. **6.** Physique and general appearance. **7.** *Law.* A human being or organisation with legal rights and duties. **8.** *Theology.* The separate individualities of the Father, Son, and Holy Spirit, as distinguished from the essence of the Godhead that unites them. **9.** *Grammar.* **a.** Any of three groups of pronoun forms with corresponding verb inflections that distinguish between the speaker (first person), the individual addressed (second person), and the individual or thing spoken of (third person). **b.** Any of the different forms or inflections expressing these distinctions. **—in person.** Physically present. —See Usage note at **people.** [Middle English *persone, person,* from Old French *persone,* from Latin *persōna,* mask (especially one worn by an actor), hence the character played by an actor, probably from Etruscan *phersu,* mask.]

-person *n. suffix.* Indicates are holding a specified position or doing a specified job, for example, **salesperson, chairperson.**

Usage: In recent years titles or job descriptions in which a person's sex is explicitly represented (such as *chairman, barman*) have attracted the criticism of those concerned with the status of women's rights in society. It is argued that such suffixes as *-man* symbolise the biases of a male-dominated society and should be avoided where possible. Consequently the neutral *-person* form has come to be increasingly used, especially in American English.

per·so·na (pər-sṓ-nə, per- || -naa) *n., pl.* **-nae** (-nee, -nī) (for sense 1) or **-nas** (for senses 2, 3). **1.** A character in a dramatic or literary work. **2.** *Psychology.* The role that a person assumes in order to display his conscious intentions to himself and to others. Compare **anima.** **3.** A person's public image. [Latin *persōna,* mask, PERSON.]

per·son·a·ble (pérss'n-əb'l) *adj.* Pleasing in appearance or personality; attractive. **—per·son·a·ble·ness** *n.*

per·son·age (pérss'n-ij) *n.* **1. a.** A person. **b.** A person of distinction. **2.** A historical or fictional character. [Middle English, from Old French, from *persone,* PERSON.]

per·so·na gra·ta (per-sṓ-nə graá-tə, pər- || *U.S. also* gráttə) *n., pl.* **personae gratae** (-nee -tee, -nī -tī). A person who is acceptable; especially, a diplomat who is fully acceptable to a foreign government. [Latin, "an acceptable person".] **—per·so·na gra·ta** *adj.*

per·son·al (pérss-'n'l, -n'l) *adj.* **1.** Of or pertaining to a particular person; private; one's own: *personal affairs.* **2.** Characterised by or involving action on the part of a particular person, rather than of a representative: *a personal appearance; took a personal interest in the case.* **3.** Done to or for or directed towards a particular person: *a personal favour.* **4. a.** Concerning or referring to a person's individual character and his intimate affairs or interests, especially in a critical or hostile manner: *an uncalled-for, highly personal remark.* **b.** Making or tending to make personal remarks: *He always becomes personal in an argument.* **5.** Of or pertaining to the body or physical being: *personal cleanliness.* **6.** Pertaining to or having the nature of a person or self-conscious being: *a personal God.* **7.** *Law.* Pertaining to a person's movable property: *personal effects.* Compare **real.** **8.** *Grammar.* Of or pertaining to grammatical person.

personal assistant *n. Abbr.* **P.A.** A person who assists an executive, usually in a secretarial capacity.

personal column *n.* The section of a newspaper or magazine containing brief classified advertisements, announcements, and especially private messages.

personal equation *n.* **1.** The tendency of a person, based on his individual characteristics, to subjectivity or error. **2.** The resulting variation in observation, judgment, and reasoning. **3.** The allowance or correction made for such variation.

Personal Equity Plan *n.* A scheme that enables individuals to invest in shares and unit trusts without incurring capital gains or income tax liability. Also called "PEP".

per·son·al·ise, per·son·al·ize (pérss-nəl-īz, -'n'l-) *tr.v.* **-ised, -ising, -ises.** **1.** To endow with personal or human qualities; personify. **2.** To have printed or marked with one's initials or name: *personalised stationery.*

per·son·al·i·ty (pér-sə-nál-əti) *n., pl.* **-ties.** **1.** The state or quality of being a person. **2. a.** The dynamic character, self, or psyche that constitutes and animates the individual person and makes his experience of life unique. **b.** A person as the embodiment of distinctive traits of mind and behaviour. **3.** The pattern of collective behavioural, temperamental, emotional, and mental traits of an individual. **4.** The distinctive qualities of an individual; especially, those distinguishing personal characteristics that make one socially appealing. **5. a.** A person of prominence or notoriety; a celebrity: *personalities in the news.* **b.** A person with an amusing or striking turn of mind; a character. **6.** *Plural.* Remarks of a personal nature, especially when offensive. **7.** The characteristics of a place or situation that give it a distinctive quality. —See Synonyms at **disposition.** [Middle English *personalite,* from Old French, from Late Latin *persōnālitās* (stem *persōnālitāt-*), from Latin *persōnālis,* personal, from *persōna,* PERSON.]

per·son·al·ly (pérss-nəli, -'n'l-i) *adv.* **1.** In person; without the intervention of another. **2.** As far as oneself is concerned: *Personally, I don't care how much it costs.* **3.** As a person: *I admire his skill but dislike him personally.* **4.** As applying to oneself, and usually as a criticism: *Don't take his remarks personally.*

personal organiser *n.* A ring binder, typically of compact format, including removable pages that serve as a diary and often other removable pages (such as calendars, timetables, and maps) that give supplementary information. [From the claim that using such a ring binder will help you to organise your life more efficiently.]

personal pronoun *n.* A pronoun indicating speaker, person spoken to, or person or thing spoken about. The personal pronouns in the subject form in current English are: *I, we, you, he, she, it, they.*

personal property *n. Law.* Temporary or movable property as distinguished from real property.

per·son·al·ty (pérss-'n'l-ti, -nəl-) *n., pl.* **-ties.** *Law.* Personal property. [Anglo-French *personalté,* from Late Latin *persōnālitās,* PERSONALITY.]

persona non grata (*see* **persona grata**; non, nōn) *n., pl.* **personae non gratae.** *Abbr.* **p.n.g.** A person who is not acceptable or welcome; especially, a diplomat not acceptable to a foreign government. [Latin, "unacceptable person".] **—persona non grata** *adj.*

per·son·ate¹ (pér-sə-nayt) *tr.v.* **-ated, -ating, -ates.** **1.** To impersonate (a character); play the role or portray the part of. **2.** To endow with personal qualities; personify. **3.** *Law.* To assume the identity of (a person) with intent to deceive. [From PERSON.] **—per·son·a·tion** (-náysh'n) *n.* **—per·son·a·tive** (-nətiv, -naytiv) *adj.* **—per·son·a·tor** (-naytər) *n.*

per·son·ate² (pér-sə-nayt, -nət, -nit) *adj. Botany.* Designating a corolla having the upper lip arched and the lower lip protruding so that the throat is nearly closed. [Latin *persōnātus,* masked, from *persōna,* mask, PERSON.]

per·son·i·fi·ca·tion (pər-sónnifi-káysh'n, per-) *n.* **1.** The personifying of something abstract or inanimate, as: **a.** A rhetorical figure of speech in which objects or abstractions are endowed with human qualities or are represented as possessing human form, as in *Hunger sat shivering on the road* or *Flowers danced about the lawn.* **b.** The artistic representation of an abstract quality or idea as a person. **2.** A person or thing exemplifying to a remarkable degree a specified quality or idea; an embodiment: *a personification of bigotry.*

per·son·i·fy (pər-sónni-fī, per-) *tr.v.* **-fied, -fying, -fies.** **1.** To think of or represent (an object or abstraction) as having personality or the qualities, thoughts, or movements of a living human being. **2.** To represent (an object or abstraction) by a human figure. **3.** To represent (an abstract quality or idea): *He personifies evil.* **4.** To be the embodiment or perfect example of: *She personified liberalism.* [French *personnifier,* from *personne,* person, from Old French *persone,* PERSON.] **—per·son·i·fi·er** *n.*

per·son·nel (pér-sə-nél) *n.* **1.** The body of persons employed by or active in an organisation, business, or service: *military personnel.* **2.** The administrative division of an organisation concerned with the recruitment and well-being of its personnel. [French, from Old French *personal,* personal, from Late Latin *persōnālis,* from Latin *persōna,* mask, PERSON.]

per·spec·tive (pər-spéktiv) *n.* **1.** Any of various techniques for representing three-dimensional objects and depth relationships on a two-dimensional surface. *Linear perspective* renders depth by using actual or suggested lines that intersect in the background to delimit relative size from background to foreground. *Aerial* or *atmospheric perspective* renders depth by changes of form, size, tone, and colour with recession of objects from the picture plane. **2.** Any picture representing objects in this way. **3.** A view or vista. **4.** The appearance of objects in depth as perceived by normal binocular vision. **5. a.** The relationship of aspects of a subject to one another and to a whole: *a perspective of history.* **b.** Any of such aspects. **6.** Subjective evaluation of the relative significance of facts or things; one's personal point of view. **7.** An objective and well-balanced evaluation or point of view: *get things in perspective.* [Middle English, from Medieval Latin *perspectīva (ars),* optics, from Late Latin *perspectīvus,* of a view, from Latin *perspicere* (past participle *perspectus*), to see through or into, inspect : *per-* (intensive) + *specere,* to look.] **—per·spec·tive** *adj.* **—per·spec·tive·ly** *adv.*

per·spec·tiv·ism (pər-spéktiv-iz'm) *n. Sometimes capital* **P.** *Philosophy.* The doctrine that reality can be accurately understood only from several different points of view.

Per·spex (pér-speks) *n.* A trademark for a clear acrylic plastic used as a substitute for glass.

per·spi·ca·cious (pér-spi-káyshəss) *adj.* Acutely discerning, perceptive, or understanding. [Latin *perspicāx,* clear-sighted, from *perspicere,* to see through. See **perspective.**] **—per·spi·ca·cious·ly** *adv.* **—per·spi·cac·i·ty** (pér-spi-kássəti), **per·spi·ca·cious·ness** *n.*

per·spi·cu·i·ty (pér-spi-kéw-əti) *n.* **1.** The quality of being perspicuous; clarity of expression or exposition. **2.** Perspicacity.

per·spic·u·ous (pər-spíckew-əss, per-) *adj.* Clearly expressed or presented; easy to understand; lucid. [Latin *perspicuus,* from *perspicere,* to see through. See **perspective.**] **—per·spic·u·ous·ly** *adv.* **—per·spic·u·ous·ness** *n.*

per·spi·ra·tion (pér-spə-ráysh'n, -spi-) *n.* **1.** The salty moisture excreted through the pores of the skin by the sweat glands; sweat. **2.** The act of perspiring. **—per·spir·a·to·ry** (-spír-ə-tri, -təri) *adj.*

per·spire (pər-spír) *v.* **-spired, -spiring, -spires.** *—intr.* To excrete perspiration through the pores of the skin. *—tr.* To expel through external pores; exude. [French *perspirer,* from Old French, from

Latin *perspīrāre*, breathe through : *per-*, through + *spīrāre*, to blow, breathe.]

per·suade (pər-swáyd) *tr.v.* **-suaded, -suading, -suades. 1.** To induce (someone) to follow a course of action, as by argument, reasoning, or entreaty: *persuaded him to part with his money.* Sometimes used with *into*: *She would not be persuaded into leaving.* **2.** To make (someone or oneself) believe something; convince: *persuaded me that she was right.* [Latin *persuādēre* : *per-* (intensive) + *suādēre*, to persuade, urge.] **—per·suad·a·ble** *adj.* **—per·suad·er** *n.*
Synonyms: persuade, induce, prevail on, convince.

per·sua·si·ble (pər-swáy-zəb'l, -səb'l) *adj.* That can be persuaded; persuadable. **—per·sua·si·bil·i·ty** (-zə-bíllati) *n.*

per·sua·sion (pər-swáyzh'n) *n.* **1. a.** The act of persuading or attempting to persuade. **b.** The state of being persuaded. **2.** The ability or power to persuade. **3.** A strong conviction or belief. **4. a.** A body of religious beliefs; a religion: *worshippers of various persuasions.* **b.** Those who adhere to such beliefs; a sect. **5.** Any grouping or faction. **—See Synonyms at opinion.** [Latin *persuāsiō* (stem *persuāsiōn-*), from *persuādēre*, to PERSUADE.]

per·sua·sive (pər-swáy-siv, -ziv) *adj.* Tending or having the power to persuade: *a persuasive argument.* **—per·sua·sive·ly** *adv.* **—per·sua·sive·ness** *n.*

per·sul·phu·ric acid (pér-sul-féwr-ik) *n.* **Peroxysulphuric acid** *(see).*

pert (pert) *adj.* **perter, pertest. 1.** Impudently bold; saucy: *a pert little girl.* **2.** High-spirited; vivacious: *a pert old lady.* **3.** Jaunty: *a pert little hat.* [Middle English, short for Old French *apert*, straightforward, open, from Latin *aperīre* (past participle *apertus*), to open, and from Old French *aspert*, from Latin *expertus*, EXPERT.] **—pert·ly** *adv.* **—pert·ness** *n.*

pert. pertaining.

per·tain (pər-táyn, per-) *intr.v.* **-tained, -taining, -tains. 1.** To have reference; relate: *evidence pertaining to the accident.* **2.** To belong as an adjunct or accessory: *the farm and all the lands which pertain to it.* **3.** To be fitting or suitable. [Middle English *partenen*, from Old French *partenir*, from Latin *pertinēre*, to relate to, reach to : *per-*, to, thoroughly + *tenēre*, to hold.]

Perth[1] (perth). City in east Scotland, situated on the river Tay. A former capital of Scotland, it is where James I was murdered (1437) and where John Knox preached against idolatry (1559).

Perth[2]. Capital of Western Australia. Situated on the Swan river, it was founded in 1829, and expanded with the discovery of gold at Kalgoorlie in the 1890s. It is now a commercial and cultural centre, and a market centre for agricultural products.

Perth·shire (pérth-shər, -sheer, -shīr). Largely mountainous former county of Scotland, from 1975 to 1996 incorporated into Central and Tayside Region and now part of Perthshire and Kinross Unitary Authority area.

per·ti·na·cious (pérti-náyshəss) *adj.* **1.** Holding firmly or tenaciously to some purpose, belief, or opinion. **2.** Stubbornly or perversely persistent. **—See Synonyms at obstinate.** [Latin *pertināx* : *per-*, thoroughly, completely + *tenāx*, tenacious, from *tenēre*, to hold.] **—per·ti·na·cious·ly** *adv.* **—per·ti·na·cious·ness** *n.*

per·ti·nac·i·ty (pérti-nássəti) *n.* The quality or state of being pertinacious.

per·ti·nent (pérti-nənt) *adj.* Having a clear connection with a specific matter; apposite. See Synonyms at **relevant.** [Middle English, from Old French, from Latin *pertinēns* (stem *pertinent-*), present participle of *pertinēre*, to reach, concern, PERTAIN.] **—per·ti·nence** (-nənss), **per·ti·nen·cy** *n.* **—per·ti·nent·ly** *adv.*

per·turb (pər-túrb, per-) *tr.v.* **-turbed, -turbing, -turbs. 1.** To disturb greatly; make uneasy or anxious. **2.** To throw into great disorder. **3.** *Physics.* To cause perturbation to (an electron or celestial body). [Middle English *perturben*, from Old French *perturber*, from Latin *perturbāre* : *per-*, thoroughly + *turbāre*, to throw into disorder, from *turba*, confusion, probably from Greek *turbē*, disorder.]

per·tur·ba·tion (pér-tər-báysh'n, -tur-) *n.* **1. a.** The act of perturbing. **b.** The state or condition of being perturbed; agitation. **2.** Something that perturbs. **3.** *Physics.* Variation in a designated orbit, as of an electron or planet, resulting from the influence of one or more external bodies.

per·tus·sis (pər-tússiss) *n.* **Whooping cough** *(see).* [New Latin : Latin *per-* (intensive) + *tussis*, a cough, TUSSIS.] **—per·tus·sal** *adj.*

Pe·ru (pə-róō). Republic of western South America. It rises from the Pacific Ocean to the Andes, 6 768 metres (22,205 feet) at Mt. Huascaran, descending again to the forested Amazon Basin. Conquered by the Spanish (1533), who destroyed its Inca civilisation, it regained its independence in 1824 and lost its southern territories to Chile in the War of the Pacific (1879–83). It has considerable mineral resources, including copper, iron, silver, zinc, and oil, while its agricultural products include maize, cotton, sugar, and coffee. Fishing and livestock are also important, and industrial production is expanding rapidly. Area, 1 285 216 square kilometres (496,225 square miles). Population, 23,950,000. Capital, Lima.

Pe·ru·gia (pə-róō-jə, pe-, -ji-ə). Capital of mountainous Perugia province, Umbria, central Italy. It is an agricultural trade centre and its products include furniture, glassware, and chocolates.

Pe·ru·gi·no (pérroo-jéenō), born Pietro di Cristoforo Vannucci (*c.* 1445–1523). Italian painter, born near Perugia (from which his name derives). His outstanding works include a fresco in the Sistine Chapel, *Christ giving the Keys to St. Peter.*

pe·ruke (pə-róōk, pe-) *n.* A wig, especially one of a type worn by men in the 17th and 18th centuries; a periwig. [French *perruque*,

from Italian *parrucca, perrucca*†, head of hair, wig.]

pe·rus·al (pə-róoz'l, pe-) *n.* The act or an instance of perusing.

pe·ruse (pə-róoz, pe-) *tr.v.* **-rused, -rusing, -ruses. 1.** To read or examine, especially with great care. **2.** To read, especially in a casual or leisurely fashion. [Middle English *perusen*, to use up, perhaps from Anglo-Latin *perusāre* (unattested) : *per-* (intensive) + Vulgar Latin *usāre* (unattested), to USE.] **—pe·rus·er** *n.*

Pe·rutz (pə-róots), **Max Ferdinand** (1914–). British chemist, of Austrian birth. He used the technique of X-ray diffraction to discover the structure of haemoglobin. In 1962 he shared the Nobel prize for this work, with John Kendrew (1917–97).

Pe·ru·vi·an (pə-róŏvi-ən, pe-) *adj.* Of or pertaining to Peru, its inhabitants, or their culture.
~*n.* A native or inhabitant of Peru. [New Latin *Peruvia*, Peru + -AN.]

Peruvian bark *n.* A medicinal bark, **cinchona** *(see).*

perv (perv) *n.* **1.** *Slang.* A pervert. **2.** *Australian Slang.* A glance that is sexually inviting or suggestive.
~*intr.v.* **perved, perving, pervs.** *Australian Slang.* To glance or stare in a sexually suggestive manner. [Shortened from PERVERT.]

per·vade (pər-váyd, per-) *tr.v.* **-vaded, -vading, -vades.** To spread right through; be present throughout; permeate: *"A marvellous stillness pervaded the world."* (Joseph Conrad). [Latin *pervādere* : *per-*, through + *vādere*, to go.] **—per·va·sion** (-váyzh'n) *n.*

per·va·sive (pər-váy-siv, per- || -ziv) *adj.* Having the quality of pervading or tendency to pervade. [Latin *pervāsus*, past participle of *pervādere*, to PERVADE.] **—per·va·sive·ly** *adv.* **—per·va·sive·ness** *n.*

per·verse (pər-vérss, per-) *adj.* **1. a.** Having a disposition to oppose and contradict. **b.** Characterised by or arising from such a disposition. **2.** Directed away from what is right or good; perverted. **3.** Obstinately persisting in an error or fault; wrongly self-willed or stubborn. **4.** Irritable; peevish. **—See Synonyms at contrary.** [Middle English *pervers*, from Old French, from Latin *pervertere* (past participle *perversus*), to PERVERT.] **—per·verse·ly** *adv.* **—per·verse·ness** *n.*

per·ver·sion (pər-vérsh'n, per- || -vérzh'n) *n.* **1.** The act of perverting or the state of being perverted. **2.** A sexual practice or act considered abnormal. **3.** An incorrect interpretation or perverted form. **—per·ver·sive** (-vér-siv || -ziv) *adj.*

per·ver·si·ty (pər-vérss-əti, per-) *n., pl.* **-ties. 1.** The quality or state of being perverse. **2.** An instance of being perverse.

per·vert (pər-vért, per-) *tr.v.* **-verted, -verting, -verts. 1. a.** To cause to turn from what is considered morally right; corrupt. **b.** To cause to deviate from what is natural or normal. **2.** To employ for a wrong or improper purpose; misuse. **3.** To interpret incorrectly; distort; misconstrue. **4.** To bring to a worse condition; debase.
~*n.* (pér-vert). One who practises sexual perversion. [Middle English *perverten*, from Old French *pervertir*, from Latin *pervertere*, to turn the wrong way, turn around : *per-*, completely + *vertere*, to turn.] **—per·vert·er** *n.* **—per·vert·i·ble** *adj.*

per·vert·ed (pər-vér·tid, per-) *adj.* **1.** Deviating greatly from what is considered proper and correct: *a perverted idea of justice.* **2.** Of, pertaining to, or practising sexual perversion. **—per·vert·ed·ly** *adv.*

per·vi·ous (pér·vi-əss) *adj.* **1.** Allowing passage or entrance; permeable: *material pervious to water.* **2.** Open to arguments, ideas, or change. [Latin *pervius* : *per-*, through + *via*, way, road.] **—per·vi·ous·ly** *adv.* **—per·vi·ous·ness** *n.*

pes (payz, peez ‖ payss) *n., pl.* **pedes** (péd-eez, -ayz). *Biology.* A foot or footlike part, especially: **1.** The human foot. **2.** The corresponding part in other higher vertebrates. [New Latin, from Latin *pēs*, foot.]

Pe·sach, Pe·sah (páy-saakh) *n.* Passover *(see).* [Hebrew *pesaḥ*, a passing over, from *pāsaḥ*, to pass over.]

Pe·sca·ra (pess-ká·ərə). Seaport of Italy, capital of Pescara province. Situated on the Adriatic coast, it is a resort.

pe·se·ta (pə-sáytə, pe-) *n. Abbr.* **p., pta. 1.** The basic monetary unit of Spain, equal to 100 centimos. **2.** A coin worth one peseta. [Spanish, diminutive of PESO.]

pe·se·wa (péssə-wə, -waa) *n., pl.* **pesewa** or **pesewas.** A monetary unit equal to $^1/_{100}$ of the cedi of Ghana.

Pe·sha·war (pə-shaa·wər, pe-, -shaw-). Strategic city in north Pakistan. At 18 kilometres (11 miles) from the eastern end of the Khyber Pass, it has long been a major trading centre for central Asia.

pes·ky (péski) *adj.* **-kier, -kiest.** *Chiefly U.S. Informal.* Troublesome; annoying: *a pesky mosquito.* [Probably irregularly from PEST.] **—pes·ki·ly** *adv.* **—pes·ki·ness** *n.*

pe·so (páy-sō ‖ péssō) *n., pl.* **-sos.** *Abbr.* **p. 1. a.** The basic monetary unit of Argentina, Bolivia, Chile, Colombia, Cuba, the Dominican Republic, Mexico, and the Philippines, equal to 100 centavos. **b.** The basic monetary unit of Uruguay, equal to 100 centesimos. **2.** A coin or note worth one peso. [Spanish, "weight", from Latin *pēnsum*, from *pendere* (past participle *pēnsus*), to weigh.]

pes·sa·ry (péssəri) *n., pl.* **-ries.** *Medicine.* **1.** Any of various contraceptive or supportive devices placed and worn in the vagina. **2.** A medicated vaginal suppository. [Middle English *pessarie*, from Medieval Latin *pessārium*, from Late Latin *pessum, pessus*, from Greek *pessos*, pessary, oval stone for games.]

pes·si·mism (péssi-miz'm ‖ pézzi-) *n.* **1.** A tendency to take the gloomiest and least hopeful possible view of a situation. **2.** The doctrine or belief that this is the worst of all possible worlds and that all things ultimately tend towards evil. **3.** The doctrine or belief that the evil in the world outweighs the good. [French *pessimisme*, from Latin *pessimus*, worst.] **—pes·si·mist** *n.* **—pes·si·mis·tic** (-místik) *adj.* **—pes·si·mis·ti·cal·ly** *adv.*

pest (pest) *n.* **1.** An annoying person or thing; a nuisance. **2.** An injurious plant or animal, especially one harmful to man, crops, or livestock. **3.** *Archaic.* A pestilence. [French *peste*, from Latin *pestis†*, plague.]

Pes·ta·loz·zi (pèstə-lótsi), **Johann Heinrich** (1746–1827). Swiss educationalist. He opened homes and schools for poor children, and in works such as *How Gertrude Teaches Her Children* (1801) described his theory that a child should be taught to think, rather than to learn by rote.

pes·ter (péstər) *tr.v.* **-tered, -tering, -ters.** To harass with petty annoyances or repeated demands; bother. See Synonyms at **harass.** [Probably from Old French *empestrer*, to tie up (an animal), impede, from Vulgar Latin *impastōriāre* (unattested) : *in*, on, in + *pastōria* (unattested), the tying up of an animal, from Late Latin *pāstūra*, PASTURE; influenced by PEST.] **—pes·ter·er** *n.*

pest·house (pést-howss) *n.* Formerly, a hospital for patients suffering from plague or some other infectious disease; a lazaretto.

pes·ti·cide (pésti-sīd) *n.* Any chemical that is used to kill pests, especially insects and rodents. [From PEST + -CIDE.] **—pes·ti·cid·al** (-síd'l) *adj.*

pes·tif·er·ous (pess-tíffərəss) *adj.* **1.** Producing or breeding infectious disease. **2.** Infected with or contaminated by an epidemic disease. **3.** Morally evil or corrupting; pernicious. **4.** *Informal.* Irritating; annoying. [Middle English, from Latin *pestiferus* : *pestis*, PEST + -FEROUS.] **—pes·tif·er·ous·ly** *adv.*

pes·ti·lence (péstilənss) *n.* **1.** Any usually fatal epidemic disease, especially bubonic plague. **2.** An epidemic of such a disease. **3.** A pernicious, evil influence or agent.

pes·ti·lent (péstilənt) *adj.* **1.** Tending to cause death; deadly; fatal. **2.** Infected or contaminated with a contagious disease. **3.** Morally, socially, or politically harmful; pernicious. **4.** Extremely irritating or annoying. [Middle English, from Latin *pestilēns* (stem *pestilent-*), from *pestis*, plague, PEST.]

pes·ti·len·tial (pésti-lénsh'l) *adj.* **1.** Of or pertaining to pestilence. **2.** Tending to cause epidemic disease; pestiferous. **3.** Pernicious or troublesome; pestilent.

pes·tle (péss'l; *also* pést'l) *n.* **1.** A club-shaped hand tool for grinding or mashing substances in a mortar. **2.** A large bar moved vertically to stamp or pound, as in a press or mill.
~v. **pestled, -tling, -tles.** *—tr.* To pound, grind, or mash with a pestle. *—intr.* To use a pestle. [Middle English *pestel*, from Old French, from Latin *pistillum.*]

pet¹ (pet) *n.* **1.** A tame animal kept for amusement or companionship. **2.** Any object of the affections. **3.** A person especially loved or indulged; a favourite: *teacher's pet.*
~adj. **1.** Kept as a pet: *a pet cat.* **2.** Of or pertaining to pets: *pet food.* **3.** Especially cherished or indulged; favourite: *a pet daughter.*
~v. **petted, petting, pets.** *—tr.* **1.** To treat or regard as a pet; indulge or pamper. **2.** To stroke or caress gently. **3.** To fondle or

caress in an erotic way. *—intr.* To fondle and caress in an erotic way. [16th century (Scottish and northern English dialect) : origin obscure.] **—pet·ter** *n.*

pet² *n.* A fit of bad temper or pique.
~intr.v. **petted, petting, pets.** To be sulky and peevish. [16th century : origin obscure.]

pet. petroleum.

Pé·tain (pe-tán), **Henri Philippe (Omer)** (1856–1951). French military leader. As a general in World War I, he became a national hero for successfully defending Verdun (1916). Appointed head of state in 1940, he accepted the terms of surrender to Germany, and headed the pro-German government of unoccupied Vichy France until 1942. After the Liberation he was condemned to death, a sentence later commuted to life imprisonment.

pet·al (pét'l) *n. Botany.* A separate, often brightly coloured segment of a corolla. Compare **sepal.** [New Latin *petalum*, from Greek *petalon*, leaf.] **—pet·alled** *adj.*

-petal *adj. comb. form.* Indicates a moving towards or seeking; for example, **centripetal.** [New Latin *-petus*, from Latin *petere*, to seek.]

pet·al·if·er·ous (pétt'l-iffərəss) *adj.* Bearing petals. [From PETAL + -FEROUS.]

pet·al·o·dy (pétt'l-ōdi) *n.* A condition in some plants where the stamens or other floral parts take on the appearance and function of petals. [Greek *petalōdēs*, leaflike, from *petalon*, leaf, PETAL.] **—pet·al·o·dic** (-óddik) *adj.*

pet·al·oid (pétt'l-oyd) *adj.* Resembling a petal; petal-like.

pet·al·ous (pétt'l-əss) *adj.* Having petals; petalled.

pé·tanque (pay-tóNk) *n.* A type of **boules** *(see),* played especially in southern France. [Provençal, from *ped tanco*, (with the) foot fixed (to the ground or spot).]

pe·tard (pe-tárd, pi-) *n.* **1.** Formerly, a small bell-shaped bomb used to breach a gate or wall. **2.** A firework that explodes with a loud noise. **—hoist with (one's) own petard.** Suffering harm as a result of one's own cleverness or scheming. [French *pétard*, from *péter*, to break wind, from *pet*, a fart, from Latin *pēditum*, from *pēdere*, to break wind.]

pet·cock (pét-kok) *n.* A small valve or tap used to drain or reduce pressure from pipes, radiators, and boilers. [Perhaps PET(TY) + COCK.]

pe·te·chi·a (pi-téeki-ə, pe- ‖ *U.S. also* -tècki-ə) *n., pl.* **-chiae** (-ee). A small spot on a body surface, such as the skin or mucous membrane, caused by a minute haemorrhage. [New Latin, from Italian *petecchia†*, skin spot.] **—pe·te·chi·al** *adj.* **—pe·te·chi·ate** (-ət, -it, -ayt) *adj.*

pe·ter¹ (péetər) *intr.v.* **-tered, -tering, -ters. 1.** To diminish gradually. Usually used with *out.* **2.** *Chiefly U.S.* To become exhausted. Used with *out: all petered out.* [U.S. mining slang, *peter†*.]

peter² *n. Slang.* **1.** A prison cell. **2.** A safe or strongbox. [Perhaps from the name *Peter.*]

peter³ *n.* In bridge and other card games, a conventional sequence of play designed to indicate to one's partner the strength of one's hand in a particular suit. It usually involves playing a high card and then a low card in that suit.
~intr.v. **-tered, -tering, -ters.** To play a peter. [From PETER (verb), to give out, diminish gradually.]

Pe·ter (péetər) *n.* Either of the two books of the New Testament attributed to St. Peter.

Peter I, known as Peter the Great (1672–1725). Tsar of Russia (1682–1725) who turned his country into a major European power. From 1682 he ruled jointly with his half-brother Ivan V, under the regency of Ivan's elder sister, Sophia. Effectively sole ruler from 1689, Peter campaigned against the Turks and Persians, and led Russia, Poland, and Denmark to victory over Sweden in the Battle of Poltava (1709). Extending Russian territory around the Baltic and Caspian shores, he also founded the Russian navy and St. Petersburg (1703), and reformed the administration of the state.

Peter, Saint, called "Simon Peter" (died *c.* A.D. 67). The chief of the Apostles; traditionally regarded as first Bishop of Rome. [Greek *petros*, stone, rock, translation of Aramaic *Kēphā*, surname conferred upon the Apostle by Jesus: "*thou art Peter, and upon this rock I will build my church*" (Matthew 16:18).]

Pe·ter·bor·ough (péetər-brə, -bərə, -burrə). City and Unitary Authority area, eastern England, situated on the river Nene. Catherine of Aragon is buried in its 12th-century cathedral. It was made a new town (1967), is an agricultural centre, and produces bricks and diesel engines.

Pe·ter·head (péetər-héd). Port in Aberdeenshire in northeast Scotland. The Old Pretender landed there in 1715. It is a service centre for the North Sea oil industry. Its industries include fishing, engineering, and the quarrying of granite.

Pe·ter·loo massacre (péetər-lóo) *n.* The violent dispersing (with fatalities) by cavalry of a meeting of English radicals in Manchester on August 16, 1819. The incident became a symbol of repression. [After St. Peter's Fields (in Manchester) + (WATER)LOO.]

pe·ter·man (péetər-mən) *n., pl.* **-men** (-mən, -men). *British Slang.* A criminal who specialises in opening safes.

Peter Pan *n.* **1.** A man who clings to his childhood and remains emotionally or psychologically a boy; a chronically immature man. **2.** A man who looks much younger than he is. [After the central character in J.M. Barrie's play, *Peter Pan* (1904).]

Peter principle *n.* The principle that in a hierarchy, a person competent for certain tasks will be promoted to others he is less able to fulfil, and will thus find his own level of incompetence. [From *The*

Peter Principle (1969), book by L. Peter and R. Hull.]

pe·ter·sham (péetər-shəm) *n.* **1.** A thick woollen fabric. **2.** An overcoat made of such a fabric. **3.** A stiff, ribbed silk braid. [After Viscount *Petersham* (died 1851), British army officer.]

Pe·ter·son (péetər-s'n), **Oscar (Emmanuel)** (1925–). Canadian jazz pianist and composer. His style is noted for its technical accomplishment. His compositions include the ballet *Africa Suite* (1993).

Peter's pence *n.* Also **Peter pence. 1.** A tax, originally of one penny per household, paid in medieval England to the Papal See. **2.** An annual voluntary contribution made by Roman Catholics towards the expenses of the Holy See. [From St. PETER, as symbolising the papacy.]

pet·i·o·lar (pétti-ólər) *adj. Biology.* Of, pertaining to, or growing on a petiole.

pet·i·o·late (pétti-ə-layt ‖ *U.S. also* -ó-lət) *adj.* Also **pet·i·o·lat·ed** (-laytid). *Biology.* Having a petiole.

pet·i·ole (pétti-ōl) *n.* **1.** *Botany.* The stalk by which a leaf is attached to a stem; a leafstalk. **2.** *Zoology.* The slender, stalklike connection between the thorax and abdomen in certain insects. [New Latin *petiolus,* from Late Latin *petiolus, peciolus,* small foot, fruit stalk, irregularly from Latin *pediculus,* diminutive of *pēs* (stem *ped-*), foot.]

pet·i·o·lule (pétti-ō-lewl, péeti-, -ō-, -lōol) *n. Botany.* The stalk of a leaflet in a compound leaf. [New Latin *petiolulus,* diminutive of *petiolus,* PETIOLE.]

pet·it, pet·ty (pétti) *adj. Law.* Lesser; minor. [Middle English, from Old French *petit,* "small", perhaps from Gallo-Roman (unattested) *pittitto-* (perhaps imitative of children's speech).]

Pe·tit (pə-tée), **Roland** (1924–). French dancer and choreographer. An innovator in contemporary ballet, he has introduced both realism and fantasy in works that include *The Strolling Players* (1945), *Carmen* (1949), and the film *Daddy Long Legs* (1954).

pe·tit bour·geois (pétti bóor-zhwáa, pə-tée) *n., pl.* **petits bourgeois.** Also **petty bourgeois.** A member of the petite bourgeoisie, often considered as narrow-minded, conservative, and self-righteous. **—pe·tit-bour·geois** *adj.*

pe·tite (pə-téet) *adj.* Small, slender, and trim. Said of a girl or woman. [French, feminine of PETIT.]

petite bourgeoisie *n.* Also **petty bourgeoisie.** The class that includes small businessmen, skilled manual workers, and low-ranking white-collar staff; the lower middle classes.

pet·it four (pétti fóor, pə-tée fór ‖ fôr) *n., pl.* **petits fours** or **petit fours** (-z, *or pronounced as singular*). A small, rich biscuit or cake, often decorated and eaten at tea or after a meal. [French, small cake, from *four,* oven.]

pe·ti·tion (pi-tísh'n, pə-) *n.* **1.** A written document bearing many signatures, requesting action on a particular issue from those in authority. **2.** A solemn supplication or request to a superior authority; an entreaty. **3.** *Law.* **a.** A formal written application asking a court for a specific judicial action: *a petition for appeal.* **b.** The act of making such a request. **c.** That which is asked for in any such request.
~*v.* **petitioned, -tioning, -tions.** *—tr.* **1.** To address a petition to. **2.** To ask for by petition; request formally. *—intr.* To make a request or entreaty. Often followed by *for: petition for retrial.* [Middle English *peticioun,* from Old French *petition,* from Latin *petītiō* (stem *petītiōn-*), attack, solicitation, from *petere* (past participle *petītus*), to seek, demand.] **—pe·ti·tion·ar·y** (-əri) *adj.* **—pe·ti·tion·er** *n.*

pe·ti·ti·o prin·ci·pi·i (pi-tíshiō prin-síppi-ī, -kíppi-) *n. Logic.* The fallacy of assuming in the premise of an argument that which one wishes to prove in the conclusion; begging the question. [Medieval Latin, "postulation of the beginning".]

pet·it juror (pétti) *n.* A member of a petit jury.

pet·it jury (pétti) *n.* A jury of 12 persons that sits at civil and criminal trials. Also called "trial jury". Compare **grand jury.**

pet·it larceny (pétti) *n.* In the United States and formerly in Britain, theft of objects whose value is below a certain designated figure. Compare **grand larceny.**

pe·tit maître (pə-tée méttr) *n.* A dandy. [French, "small master".]

pet·it mal (pétti mál ‖ *U.S. also* máal) *n. Pathology.* A mild form of epilepsy characterised by frequent but transient lapses of consciousness and only rare spasms or falling. Compare **grand mal.** [French, "small illness".]

pet·it point (pétti póynt; *French* pə-tée pwáN) *n.* **1.** A small stitch used in needlepoint. **2.** Needlepoint done with such a stitch. Compare **gros point.** [French, "small point".]

pe·tits pois (pə-tée pwáa, pétti) *pl.n.* Small tender green peas. [French, small peas.]

Pet·ra (péttrə, péetrə). Ancient ruined city of southwest Jordan. It was capital of the Nabataeans, prospering as an important East-West trading post from the fourth century B.C. until its capture by the Romans (A.D. 106). It was rediscovered in 1812.

Pet·rarch (péttraark; *also* péetraark), born Francesco Petrarca (1304–74). Italian poet and scholar who, with Dante and Boccaccio, instituted the literary Renaissance in Italy. A Florentine by birth, his works unite classical scholarship with Christian belief in the spirit of humanism. He is especially remembered for his love sonnets dedicated to Laura. **—Pet·rarch·an** (pe-trárkən, pi-) *adj.*

Petrarchan sonnet *n.* A sonnet in a form of Italian origin comprising an octave with the rhyme pattern *abbaabba,* and a sestet of various rhyme patterns such as *cdccdc* or *cdecde.*

pet·rel (péttrəl) *n.* Any of various sea birds of the order Procellariiformes, especially the **storm petrel** (see). [Variant of earlier *pitteral†.*]

Pe·tri dish (péetri) *n.* A shallow dish with a loose-fitting cover, used especially to culture microorganisms for research. [After Julius R. *Petri* (died 1921), German bacteriologist.]

Pe·trie (péetri), **Sir (William Matthew) Flinders** (1853–1942). British archaeologist. He is especially known for his excavations in Egypt which began with work on the pyramids at Giza in 1880. His published works include *Methods and Aims of Archaeology* (1904).

pet·ri·fac·tion (péttri-fáksh'n) *n.* Also **pet·ri·fi·ca·tion** (-fi-káysh'n). **1. a.** The process of petrifying; the conversion of organic matter into stone or a stony substance. **b.** Something resulting from this process. **2.** The state of being petrified, as by fear. [From PETRIFY (by analogy with, for example, STUPEFACTION).]

pet·ri·fy (péttri-fī) *v.* **-fied, -fying, -fies.** *—tr.* **1.** To convert (wood or other organic matter) into stone or a stony substance by structural impregnation with dissolved minerals. **2.** To cause to become stiff or stonelike; deaden. **3.** To stun or paralyse with terror. *—intr.* To become stony, especially by mineral replacement of organic matter. [French *petrifier* : Latin *petra,* stone, from Greek + *facere,* to make.]

Pe·trine (péetrīn) *adj.* **1.** Of or pertaining to St. Peter. **2.** Of or pertaining to the pope considered as a successor of St. Peter.

petro– *comb. form.* Indicates: **1.** Rock or stone; for example, **petrology. 2.** Petroleum; for example, **petrochemistry.** [Greek *petros,* stone and *petra,* rock.]

pet·ro·chem·i·cal (péttrō-kémmik'l) *n.* · Any chemical derived from petroleum or natural gas. **—pet·ro·chem·i·cal** *adj.*

pet·ro·chem·is·try (péttrō-kémmistri) *n.* The chemistry of petroleum and its derivatives.

pet·ro·dol·lar (péttrō-dollər) *n.* A dollar earned by an oil-producing country from its exports, especially as part of a reserve to be invested abroad.

pet·ro·glyph (péttrə-glif, péttrō-) *n.* A usually prehistoric carving or line drawing on rock. **—pet·ro·glyph·ic** (-gliffik) *adj.*

Petrograd. See **St. Petersburg.**

pe·trog·ra·phy (pi-tróggrə-fi, pi-) *n.* The description and classification of rocks. [PETRO- + -GRAPHY.] **—pe·trog·ra·pher** (-fər) *n.* **—pet·ro·graph·ic** (péttrə-gráffik), **pet·ro·graph·i·cal** *adj.* **—pet·ro·graph·i·cal·ly** *adv.*

pet·rol (péttrəl) *n. Chiefly British.* A volatile mixture of flammable liquid hydrocarbons derived from crude petroleum and used principally as a fuel for internal-combustion engines and as an illuminant, thinner, and solvent. As a fuel it usually contains antiknock compounds and corrosion inhibitors. Also *U.S.* "gasoline". [French *pétrole* (in the phrase *essence de pétrole*), from Old French *petrole,* from Medieval Latin *petroleum,* PETROLEUM.]

pet·ro·la·tum (péttrə-láytəm, péttrō-, -láatəm) *n.* A colourless to amber gelatinous semisolid, obtained from petroleum, consisting of various alkanes and alkenes, and used in lubricants and medicinal ointments. Also called "petroleum jelly". [New Latin, from Medieval Latin *petroleum,* PETROLEUM.]

petrol bomb *n.* A bottle containing petrol, stoppered by a wick, and thrown as a weapon when the wick is lit.

pe·tro·le·um (pi-tróli-əm, pə-) *n. Abbr.* **pet.** A natural, yellow-to-black, thick, flammable liquid hydrocarbon mixture found principally beneath the earth's surface and processed for fractions including natural gas, petrol, naphtha, kerosene, fuel and lubricating oils, paraffin wax, asphalt, and a wide variety of derivative products. Also called "crude oil", "rock oil". [Medieval Latin : PETRO- + *oleum,* oil.]

petroleum ether *n.* A volatile mixture of the higher alkane liquids obtained as a fraction of petroleum distillation and used as a solvent.

petroleum jelly *n.* Petrolatum.

pe·trol·ic (pi-tróllik, pə-) *adj.* Derived from petroleum.

pe·trol·o·gy (pi-tróllǝji, pə-, pe-) *n.* The study of the origin, composition, structure, and alteration of rocks. [PETRO- + -LOGY.] **—pet·ro·log·ic** (péttrə-lójik), **pet·ro·log·i·cal** *adj.* **—pet·ro·log·i·cal·ly** *adv.* **—pe·trol·o·gist** (-tróllǝjist) *n.*

petrol station *n. British.* A **filling station** (see).

pet·ro·nel (péttrə-nel) *n.* A firearm or large pistol used by cavalry soldiers in the 16th and 17th centuries. [French *petrinal,* variant of *poitrinal* (noun), from adjective, "of the chest" (the butt end was designed to rest on the chest while firing), from *poitrine,* chest, from Vulgar Latin *pectorina* (unattested), from Latin *pectus,* chest.]

pe·tro·sal (pe-tróss'l, pə-) *adj.* Also **pet·rous** (péttrəss). *Anatomy.* Pertaining to or located near the portion of the temporal bone that surrounds the inner ear. [Latin *petrōsus,* PETROUS.]

pet·rous (péttrəss) *adj.* **1.** Of, pertaining to, or resembling rock; stony; hard. **2.** *Anatomy.* Variant of **petrosal.** [Latin *petrōsus,* rocky, from *petra,* rock, from Greek.]

pet·ti·coat (pétti-kōt) *n.* **1.** An item of woman's underwear, made of a light fabric and having the form either of a skirt or of a dress or slip. **2.** *Slang.* A woman or girl.
~*adj.* **1.** Female; feminine. **2.** Of or by women: *petticoat government.* [Middle English *petycote* : PETTY + COAT.]

pet·ti·fog (pétti-fog ‖ -fawg) *intr.v.* **-fogged, -fogging, -fogs.** To act like a pettifogger. [Back-formation from PETTIFOGGER.]

pet·ti·fog·ger (pétti-foggər ‖ -fawgər) *n.* **1.** An unscrupulous lawyer. **2.** A person who pays excessive attention to small details; an extremely fussy person; a quibbler. [PETTY + *fogger,* unscrupulous dealer, perhaps after *Fugger,* 15th-16th century family of merchants in Augsburg, Germany.]

pet·tish (péttish) *adj.* Ill-tempered; peevish; petulant. [Probably from PET (ill temper).] —**pet·tish·ly** adv. —**pet·tish·ness** n.

pet·ti·toes (pétti-tōz) pl.n. Pig's trotters considered as food. [16th century (originally, offal), from Old French petite oie, "little goose", giblets of a goose; assimilated to petty toes.]

pet·ty (pétti) adj. **-tier, -tiest. 1.** Small, trivial, or insignificant in quantity or quality: petty grievances. **2.** Having or showing a contemptibly narrow-minded and ungenerous nature: a petty outlook. **3.** Of subordinate or inferior rank. **4.** Law. Variant of **petit.** —See Synonyms at **trivial.** [Middle English pety, small, variant of petit, PETIT.] —**pet·ti·ly** adv. —**pet·ti·ness** n.

petty bourgeois. Variant of **petit bourgeois.**

petty bourgeoisie. Variant of **petite bourgeoisie.**

petty cash n. Abbr. p.c., p/c, P/C A small fund of money for incidental expenses, as in an office. Also U.S. "float".

petty officer n. Abbr. P.O., p.o. A naval noncommissioned officer ranking between a chief petty officer and a leading seaman, and equivalent in rank to a sergeant in the army.

petty sessions n. Used with a singular verb. **1.** A magistrate's court. **2.** A sitting of a magistrate's court.

pet·u·lant (péttew-lənt ‖ péchoo-) adj. Unreasonably irritable or ill-tempered; peevish. [French pétulant, saucy, from Latin petulāns (stem petulant-), present participle of petulāre (unattested), to jab at, frequentative of petere, to attack.] —**pet·u·lance, pet·u·lan·cy** n. —**pet·u·lant·ly** adv.

pe·tu·ni·a (pi-téwn-iə, pə- ‖ -tōon-) n. Any of various widely cultivated plants of the genus Petunia, native to tropical America, having funnel-shaped flowers in various shades. [New Latin, from obsolete French petun, tobacco, from Tupi petyn, petyma.]

pe·tun·tse, pe·tun·tze (pi-túnt-si, pə-, -tōont-, -say) n. A variety of feldspar sometimes mixed with kaolin in Chinese porcelain. [Chinese bái dùn zi, "white heap".]

Pev·en·sey (pévv'nzi). Village in East Sussex, southeast England. Now situated inland as a result of the retreating sea, it is where William the Conqueror landed in 1066. It is one of the Cinque Ports and has the remains of a Norman castle and Roman fort.

Pevs·ner (pévz-nər), **Antoine** (1886–1962). Russian sculptor and painter, a pioneer of constructivism. He initiated the movement with The Realist Manifesto (1920), written jointly with his brother Naum Gabo. Pevsner moved to Paris in 1923 after the movement's abstract tendencies fell out of favour with the Bolshevik authorities.

Pevsner, Sir Nikolaus (Bernhard Leon) (1902–83). British writer on architecture, born in Germany. He held professorial chairs in fine art at Cambridge, Oxford, and London and is known for his standard survey The Buildings of England (50 vols, 1951–74).

pew (pew) n. **1.** A bench for the congregation in a church. **2.** A small enclosure or box of seats in a church, especially one formerly reserved for a particular family or group of regular churchgoers. **3.** British Informal. A seat or chair. Used chiefly in the phrase take a pew. [Middle English pewe, puwe, from Old French puie, raised seat, balcony, from Latin podia, plural of podium, podium, balcony, from Greek podion, small foot, base, supporting structure, diminutive of pous (stem pod-), foot.]

pewit. Variant of **peewit.**

pew·ter (péwtər) n. **1.** Any of numerous silver-grey alloys of tin with various amounts of antimony, copper, and lead, formerly used widely for fine kitchen utensils and tableware. **2.** Pewter articles collectively. [Middle English pewtre, from Old French peutre, peautre, variant of peltre, tin, from (unattested) Vulgar Latin peltrum†.] —**pew·ter** adj.

pe·yo·te (pay-ōti) n. **1.** A cactus, **mescal** (see). **2.** A hallucinatory drug derived from the tubercles of this cactus. [Mexican Spanish, from Nahuatl.]

pf. 1. pfennig. **2.** preferred.

pfen·nig (fénnig; German pfénnikh) n., pl. **-nigs** or **pfennige** (-ə). Abbr. **pf., pfg.** A coin equal to $^1/_{100}$ of the Deutschmark of Germany. [German Pfennig, from Old High German pfenning, from West Germanic panninga (unattested). See also **penny, penni.**]

pfg. pfennig.

PG adj. In Britain, designating a rating for films, equivalent to the former "A" rating, containing some scenes that may be unsuitable for young children. [parental guidance.]

Pg. Portugal; Portuguese.

P.G. 1. paying guest. **2.** postgraduate.

PGA Professional Golfers' Association.

pH n. Chemistry. A measure of the acidity or alkalinity of a solution calculated as the common logarithm of the reciprocal of the hydrogen ion concentration in moles per cubic decimetre of solution and numerically equal to 7 for neutral solutions. pH increases with increasing alkalinity and decreases with increasing acidity. [potential of Hydrogen.]

ph. phase.

Phae·drus (féedrəss) (first century A.D.). A Thracian-born freedman of the emperor Augustus, author of a collection of fables based on those attributed to Aesop.

phae·ton (fáyt'n, fáy-ət'n) n. A light, open, four-wheeled carriage, usually drawn by a pair of horses. [French phaéton, after Phaéton, French form of Phaethon, son of Helios who attempted to drive the chariot of the sun.]

phage (fayj) n. A **bacteriophage** (see).

–phage n. comb. form. Indicates something that eats or destroys; for example, **bacteriophage.** [Greek -phagos, from phagein, to eat.]

phag·e·dae·na, phag·e·de·na (fáji-déenə) n. An ulcer of the skin and subcutaneous tissues that spreads rapidly and causes sloughing off of the skin. [Latin, from Greek phagedaina, from phagein, to consume, eat.]

phago– comb. form. Indicates eating or destroying; for example, **phagocyte.** [Greek, from phagein, to eat.]

phag·o·cyte (fág-ə-sīt, -ō-) n. Physiology. A cell such as a leucocyte that engulfs and digests cells, microorganisms, or other foreign bodies in the bloodstream and tissues. [PHAGO- + -CYTE.] —**phag·o·cyt·ic** (-síttik) adj.

phag·o·cy·to·sis (fág-ə-sī-tō-siss, -ō-) n. Physiology. The envelopment and digestion of bacteria or other foreign bodies by phagocytes. [New Latin : PHAGOCYT(E) + -OSIS.]

–phagous adj. comb. form. Indicates eating or tending to eat; for example, **phyllophagous.** [Latin -phagus, from Greek -phagos, eating, from phagein, to eat.]

–phagy, –phagia n. comb. form. Indicates an eating or consumption; for example, **cytophagy, dysphagia.** [Greek -phagia, from phagein, to eat.]

pha·lan·ge·al (fa-lán-ji-əl, fə-, fál-ən-jée-əl ‖ fáyl-) adj. Anatomy. Of or pertaining to a phalanx or phalanges.

pha·lan·ger (fə-lánjər) n. Any of various small, arboreal marsupials of the family Phalangeridae, of Australia and adjacent islands, having a long tail and dense, woolly fur. [New Latin, from PHALANX, "toe bone" (with reference to the peculiar structure of the second and third toes of its hind feet).]

pha·lan·ges (fa-lánjeez, fə- ‖ U.S. also fay-) pl.n. Singular **phalanx** or **pha·lange** (fál-anj ‖ U.S. fáyl-, fə-lánj). Anatomy. The bones of the fingers or toes.

phal·an·ster·y (fál-ən-stri, -stəri ‖ -sterri) n., pl. **-ies. 1.** A community of the followers of Charles **Fourier** (see). Also called "phalanx". **2.** The buildings of such a community. [French Phalanstère : phalange, phalanx, from New Latin phalanx, PHALANX + monastère, monastery, from Late Latin monastērium, MONASTERY.] —**phal·an·ste·ri·an** (-stéer-i-ən) n. & adj. —**phal·an·ste·ri·an·ism** n.

pha·lanx (fál-angks ‖ chiefly U.S. fáyl-) n., pl. **-lanxes** or **phalanges** (fa-lánjeez, fə- ‖ fay-). **1.** An ancient Greek formation of infantry carrying overlapping shields and long spears, perfected by Philip II of Macedon and used by Alexander the Great. **2.** Any close-knit or compact body of people. **3.** A phalanstery. **4.** Anatomy. Singular of **phalanges.** [Latin, from Greek, wooden beam, finger bone, line of battle.]

phal·a·rope (fál-ə-rōp) n. Any of several wading birds of the family Phalaropodidae, having lobed toes that enable them to swim. [French, from New Latin phalaropus : Greek phalaris, coot (which has a white patch on the head), from phalaros, having a white spot + -pus, from Greek pous, foot.]

phal·lic (fál-ik) adj. **1.** Of, pertaining to, or resembling a phallus. **2.** Of or pertaining to the cult of the phallus as an embodiment of generative power. [Greek phallikos, from phallos, PHALLUS.]

phal·lo·cen·tric (fál-ō-séntrik, -ə-) adj. Dominated by men or male preoccupations and interests.

phal·lo·crat (fál-ə-krat, -ō-) n. One who believes in male superiority; a male chauvinist. —**phal·lo·crat·ic** (-kráttik) adj.

phal·lus (fál-əss) n., pl. **phalli** (-ī) or **-luses. 1.** A representation of the penis and testes as an embodiment of generative power. **2. a.** The penis. **b.** The sexually undifferentiated tissue in the embryo that becomes the penis or clitoris. [Late Latin phallus, penis, from Greek phallos.]

–phane n. comb. form. Indicates resemblance or similarity to a specified material; for example, **cellophane.** [Greek -phanēs, appearing, shining, from phainesthai, to appear.]

phan·er·o·crys·tal·line (fánnərō-krístə-līn, -lin) adj. Designating igneous or metamorphic rocks having a crystalline structure in which the crystals are visible to the naked eye. [Greek phaneros, visible + CRYSTALLINE.]

phan·er·o·gam (fánnər-ə-gam, -ō-) n. Botany. A plant that produces flowers and true seeds; a spermatophyte. No longer in technical usage. Compare **cryptogam.** [New Latin phanerogamus, "one having visible reproductive parts" : Greek phaneros, visible, from phainein, to show + -GAMOUS.] —**phan·er·o·gam·ic** (-gámmik), **phan·er·o·ga·mous** (fánn-rō-ggəməss) adj.

phan·er·o·phyte (fánnərō-fīt, fə-nérrə-) n. A perennial plant that bears its dormant buds well above soil level. [Greek phaneros, visible + -PHYTE.]

phan·tasm (fán-taz'm) n. **1.** Something apparently seen but having no physical reality; a phantom. **2.** An illusory mental image. **3.** In Platonic philosophy, objective reality as perceived and distorted by the five senses. [Middle English fantasme, from Old French, from Latin phantasma, apparition, spectre, from Greek, from phantazein, to make visible, from phainein, to show.] —**phan·tas·mal** (fan-táz'm'l), **phan·tas·mic** (-tázmik) adj.

phan·tas·ma·go·ri·a (fán-tazmə-górri-ə, fan-tázmə-, -gáwri- ‖ -gōri-) n. **1.** A fantastic sequence of haphazardly associative imagery, as seen in dreams or fever. **2.** Any scene of constant and bewildering change. [Originally, the name of an early 19th-century magic-lantern show producing optical illusions, from PHANTASM + an obscure second element.] —**phan·tas·ma·go·ric** (-górrik ‖ -gáwrik), **phan·tas·ma·go·ri·cal** adj.

phantasy. Variant of **fantasy.**

phan·tom (fántəm) n. **1.** Something apparently seen, heard, or sensed, but having no physical reality; a ghost; a spectre. **2.** An image that appears only in the mind.

~adj. **1.** Unreal; ghostlike. **2.** Pathology. Designating an organ, structure, or condition that does not exist but appears to from various signs and symptoms. [Middle English *fantosme, fantome,* from Old French, from Latin *phantasma,* PHANTASM.]

phantom limb *n.* The sensation that a limb or part of a limb still exists after it has been amputated, usually because pain appears to come from the amputated part.

phantom pregnancy *n.* A condition in which symptoms of pregnancy, such as an enlarged abdomen, occur in a nonpregnant woman. Caused by the secretion of pituitary hormones, it is usually the result of an emotional disorder. Also called "pseudocyesis".

-phany *n. comb. form.* Indicates a manifestation or sudden appearance; for example, **epiphany.** [Greek *-phania,* from *phainein,* to show.]

Phar·aoh (fair-ō) *n. Often small* p. 1. A king of ancient Egypt. 2. A tyrant. [Late Latin *Pharaō,* from Greek *Pharaō,* transcription of Hebrew *Par'ōh,* from an Egyptian word meaning "great house".] **—Phar·a·on·ic** (-ay-ónnik) *adj.*

pharaoh ant *n.* A small reddish ant, *Monomorium pharaonis,* originally of tropical countries but now a pest of heated buildings in temperate regions.

Phar·i·sa·ic (fárri-sáy-ik ‖ -záy-) *adj.* 1. Of or pertaining to the Pharisees. 2. *Small* p. Variant of **pharisaical.**

phar·i·sa·i·cal (fárri-sáy-ik'l ‖ -záy-) *adj.* Also **pharisaic.** Hypocritically self-righteous and censorious. **—phar·i·sa·i·cal·ly** *adv.* **—phar·i·sa·i·cal·ness** *n.*

phar·i·sa·ism (fárri-say-iz'm) *n.* Also **phar·i·see·ism** (-see-). 1. Hypocritical observance of the letter of religious or moral law without regard for the spirit; sanctimoniousness. 2. *Capital* P. The doctrines and practices of the Pharisees.

phar·i·see (fárri-see) *n.* 1. *Capital* P. A member of an ancient Jewish sect that emphasised strict interpretation and observance of the Mosaic law in both its oral and written form. Compare **Sadducee.** 2. A hypocritically self-righteous person. [Middle English *pharise,* Old English *farise,* from Late Latin *pharisaeus,* from Greek *pharisaios,* from Aramaic *perīshayyā,* plural of *perīsh,* "separated".]

phar·ma·ceu·ti·cal (fármə-séwtik'l, -sŏotik'l,) *adj.* Also **phar·ma·ceu·tic** (farmə-séwtik, -sŏotik). Of or pertaining to pharmacy or pharmacists.

~n. A pharmaceutical product or preparation. [Late Latin *pharmaceuticus,* from Greek *pharmakeutikos,* from *pharmakeutēs,* pharmacist, from *pharmakeuein,* to give drugs, from *pharmakon,* drug. See pharmaco-.] **—phar·ma·ceu·ti·cal·ly** *adv.*

phar·ma·ceu·tics (fármə-séwtiks, -sŏotiks) *n.* 1. *Used with a singular verb.* Pharmacy. 2. *Used with a plural verb.* Pharmaceutical remedies.

phar·ma·cist (fármə-sist) *n.* A person trained in pharmacy.

pharmaco- *comb. form.* Indicates drugs; for example, **pharmacology.** [Greek *pharmakon†,* drug, poison, potion.]

phar·ma·cog·no·sy (fármə-kóg-nə-si) *n.* The branch of pharmacology dealing with crude natural drugs. [PHARMACO- + Greek *-gnōsia,* knowledge, from -GNOSIS.] **—phar·ma·cog·no·sist** *n.* **—phar·ma·cog·nos·tic** (-kog-nóstik) *adj.*

phar·ma·col·o·gy (fármə-kóllǝji) *n.* The science of drugs, including their composition, uses, and effects. [PHARMACO- + -LOGY.] **—phar·ma·co·log·i·cal** (-kə-lójik'l), *adj.* **—phar·ma·co·log·i·cal·ly** *adv.* **—phar·ma·col·o·gist** (-kóllǝjist) *n.*

phar·ma·co·poe·ia, phar·ma·co·pe·ia (fármə-kə-pée-ə, -kō-) *n.* 1. A book containing an official list of medicinal drugs together with articles on their preparation and use. 2. The range of drugs used in medicine. [New Latin, from Greek *pharmakopoiia,* preparation of drugs, from *pharmakopoios,* preparing drugs : PHARMACO- + *-poios,* "making", from *poiein,* to make.] **—phar·ma·co·poe·ial** (-əl) *adj.* **—phar·ma·co·poe·ist** (-ist) *n.*

phar·ma·cy (fármə-si) *n., pl.* cies. 1. The science of preparing and dispensing drugs. 2. A place where drugs are prepared; a dispensary. [Middle English *farmacie,* from Old French, from Late Latin *pharmacia,* from Greek *pharmakeia,* from *pharmakon,* drug.]

pha·ros (fair-oss) *n. Literary.* A lighthouse. [From *Pharos,* formerly an island in the bay of Alexandria, celebrated in antiquity for its lighthouse.]

pha·ryn·ge·al (fárrin-jée-əl, fə-rínji-əl, fa-) *adj.* Also **pha·ryn·gal** (fə-ríng-g'l, fa-). Of, pertaining to, located in, going to, or coming from the pharynx: *pharyngeal air-stream mechanism.*

~n. Also **pha·ryn·gal.** A speech sound produced in the pharynx. [New Latin *pharyngeus,* from *pharynx,* PHARYNX.]

phar·yn·gi·tis (fárrin-jí-tiss) *n.* Inflammation of the pharynx. [New Latin : PHARYNG(O)- + -ITIS.]

pharyngo-, pharyng- *comb. form.* Indicates pharynx; for example, **pharyngoscope, pharyngitis.** [New Latin, from Greek *pharungo-,* from *pharunx,* PHARYNX.]

phar·yn·gol·o·gy (fárrin-góllə-ji, fárrin-) *n.* The medical study of the pharynx and its diseases. [PHARYNGO- + -LOGY.] **—phar·yn·go·log·i·cal** (-gə-lójik'l) *adj.* **—phar·yn·gol·o·gist** (-jist) *n.*

pha·ryn·go·scope (fə-ríng-gə-skōp, fa-, -gō-) *n.* An instrument used in examining the pharynx. [PHARYNGO- + -SCOPE.] **—phar·yn·gos·co·py** (fárring-góskəpi, fárrin-) *n.*

phar·yn·got·o·my (fárring-góttəmi, fárrin-) *n., pl.* -mies. A surgical incision of the pharynx. [PHARYNGO- + -TOMY.]

phar·ynx (fárringks) *n., pl.* **pharynges** (fə-rínjeez, fa-) or **pharynxes.** The section of the digestive tract that extends from the nasal cavities and mouth to the oesophagus. [New Latin, from Greek *pharunx,* throat, pharynx.]

phase (fayz) *n. Abbr.* ph. 1. Any one of a sequence of distinct apparent forms. 2. A distinct stage of development: *The war fell into*

three clear phases. 3. A temporary manner, attitude, or pattern of behaviour: *a passing phase.* 4. *Astronomy.* Any of the cyclically recurring apparent forms of the Moon or a planet. 5. *Physics.* **a.** A particular stage in a periodic process or phenomenon. **b.** The fraction of a complete cycle elapsed as measured from a given reference point and often expressed as an angle. 6. *Chemistry.* A discrete homogeneous part of a material system that is mechanically separable from the rest, as is ice from water. 7. *Biology.* A characteristic form or appearance that occurs in a cycle or that distinguishes some individuals of a group. 8. *Biology.* A stage in cell division. **—in** (or **out of) phase.** *Physics.* Reaching (or not reaching) corresponding phases at the same time, as two waves might.

~tr.v. phased, phasing, phases. 1. To plan or carry out systematically by phases: *a phased withdrawal of troops.* 2. To bring into harmony or efficient joint functioning. Often used with *with: phase one process with another.* **—phase in.** To introduce slowly by one stage at a time. **—phase out.** To eliminate or withdraw slowly by one stage at a time. [Back-formation from *phases* (plural), from New Latin *phasis,* from Greek, appearance, phase of the Moon, from *phainein,* to show.] **—pha·sic** (fáyzik) *adj.*

phase-contrast microscope (fáyz-kón-traast ‖ -trast) *n.* A microscope that renders differences in the phase of light transmitted or reflected by a specimen as variations in contrast. Also called "phase microscope".

phase modulation *n.* In telecommunications, the variation of the phase of a carrier wave by an amount proportional to the amplitude of a modulating signal.

phase rule *n.* A rule stating that the number of degrees of freedom in a material system at equilibrium is equal to the number of components minus the number of phases plus the constant 2. For example, the system of water vapour, water, and ice has zero degrees of freedom, since three phases of one component coexist.

-phasia *n. comb. form.* Indicates a specified type of speech disorder; for example, **dysphasia.** [New Latin, from Greek, speech, from *phasis,* utterance, from *phanai,* to say, speak.]

phat·ic (fáttik) *adj.* Designating utterances that assert or cement a friendly social relationship rather than conveying specific thoughts or ideas. Much conversation about the weather, for example, is merely phatic. [From the term *phatic communion,* coined by B. Malinowski : Greek *phatos,* spoken, from *phanai,* to speak.]

Ph.D. Doctor of Philosophy [Latin *Philosophiae Doctor*].

pheas·ant (fézz'nt) *n., pl.* -ants or collectively **pheasant.** Any of various game birds of the family Phasianidae, native to the Old World, characteristically having long tails and, in the males of many species, brilliantly coloured plumage. [Middle English *fesaunt, fesant,* from Old French *fesan, faisan,* from Latin *phasiānus,* from Greek *phasianos,* "the Phasian (bird)", of the river Phasis in the Caucasus, from *Phāsis,* the river Phasis.]

pheasant's eye *n.* 1. Any of various plants of the genus *Adonis;* especially *A. annua,* which has small scarlet flowers and finely divided leaves. 2. A narcissus, *Narcissus poeticus,* having white petals and a shallow, red-rimmed, yellow corona. In this sense, also called "narcissus".

phel·lem (fél-əm, -em) *n. Botany.* Cork cambium *(see).* [Greek *phellos,* cork + *-em,* as in PHLOEM.]

phel·lo·derm (fél-ō-derm, -ə-) *n.* The soft cortex tissue that forms on the inner side of the phellogen of some trees. [Greek *phellos,* cork + -DERM.] **—phel·lo·der·mal** (-dérm'l) *adj.*

phel·lo·gen (fél-ō-jen, -ə-jən) *n.* A tissue in woody plants, from which cork and phelloderm develop. [Greek *phellos,* cork + -GEN.] **—phel·lo·ge·net·ic** (-jə-néttik, -je-), **phel·lo·gen·ic** (-jénnik) *adj.*

phe·nac·e·tin (fi-nássə-tin, fe-) *n.* An analgesic drug, **acetophenetidin** *(see).* [PHEN(O)- + ACET(O)- + -IN.]

phen·a·cite (fénnə-sīt) *n.* A rare natural beryllium silicate, coloured yellow, brown, or pale rose, occurring as vitreous crystals sometimes used as gems. [Greek *phenax†* (stem *phenak-*), an impostor (from its resemblance to quartz).]

phe·nan·threne (fi-nán-threen, fe-) *n.* A colourless crystalline compound, $C_{14}H_{10}$, obtained by fractional distillation of coal-tar oils and used in dyes, drugs, and explosives. [PHEN(O)- + ANTHR(A-C)ENE.]

phen·ar·sa·zine chloride (fin-ár-sə-zeen, fen-) *n.* A highly poisonous yellow crystalline compound, $C_{12}H_9AsClN$, used as a poison gas and sometimes with tear gas.

phen·a·zine (fénnə-zeen) *n.* A yellow crystalline compound, $C_6H_4N_2C_6H_4$, used in the manufacture of dyes.

phe·net·ic (fi-néttik) *adj. Biology.* Of, pertaining to, or designating a system of classification based on observed similarities and differences between organisms rather than on their supposed evolutionary relationships. [*Phenotype* + *genetic.*]

phen·e·tole (fénni-tōl) *n.* A colourless, oily, phenyl ether, $C_6H_5OC_2H_5.$

phenix. *U.S.* Variant of **phoenix.**

pheno-, phen- *comb. form. Chemistry.* Indicates: 1. Showing or displaying; for example, **phenocryst.** 2. A compound derived from, containing, or related to benzene; for example, **phenol, phenothiazine.** [Greek *phainein,* to show. Sense 2 is from French *(acide) phénique,* an early name for phenol, from Greek *phainein* (so named because it was originally extracted from illuminating gas).]

phe·no·bar·bi·tone (féen-ō-bárbi-tōn, -ə-) *n.* Also **phe·no·bar·bi·tal** (-t'l). A white, shiny, crystalline compound, $C_{12}H_{12}N_2O_3$, used in medicine as a sedative, for treating insomnia, and as a hypnotic.

phe·no·cop·y (féen-ō-koppi, -ə-) *n., pl.* -ies. *Genetics.* 1. An environmentally induced phenotypic variation that closely resembles a genetically determined character. **2.** A characteristic or organism existing as such a variation. [PHENO(TYPE) + COPY.]

phe·no·cryst (féen-ō-krist, fén-, -ə-) *n.* A conspicuous crystal embedded in a finer-grained groundmass giving a porphyritic texture. [PHENO- + CRYST(AL).] —**phe·no·crys·tic** (-krístik) *adj.*

phe·nol (féen-ol ‖ -ōl) *n. Chemistry.* **1.** A caustic, poisonous, white, crystalline compound, C_6H_5OH, derived from benzene and used in various resins, plastics, disinfectants, and pharmaceuticals. Also called "carbolic acid". **2.** Any of a class of aromatic organic compounds having at least one hydroxyl group attached directly to the benzene ring. [PHEN(O)- + -OL.] —**phe·no·lic** (fi-nóllik, fee ‖ nō-lik) *adj.*

phenolic resin *n.* Any of various synthetic thermosetting resins, obtained by the reaction of phenols with simple aldehydes and used to make moulded products and as coatings and adhesives.

phe·nol·o·gy (fi-nóllə-ji) *n.* The study of periodic biological phenomena, such as flowering, breeding, and migration, especially as related to climate. [PHENO(MENON) + -LOGY.] —**phe·no·log·i·cal** (féenə-lójik'l) *adj.* —**phe·nol·o·gist** (-jist) *n.*

phe·nol·phthal·ein (féen-ol-tháyl-een, -fthál-, -thál-, -i-in ‖ -ōl-) *n.* A pale yellow crystalline powder, $(C_6H_4OH)_2C_2O_2C_6H_4$, used as an acid-base indicator, in making dyes, and as a cathartic.

phe·nom·e·nal (fi-nómmin'l) *adj.* **1.** Of or pertaining to a phenomenon or phenomena. **2.** Extraordinary; outstanding; remarkable. **3.** *Philosophy.* Known or derived through the senses, rather than through the mind. —**phe·nom·e·nal·ly** *adv.*

phe·nom·e·nal·ism (fi-nómmin'l-iz'm) *n. Philosophy.* The doctrine that the sole objects of knowledge are perceptual experiences. —**phe·nom·e·nal·ist** *n.* —**phe·nom·e·nal·is·tic** (-ístik) *adj.* —**phe·nom·e·nal·is·ti·cal·ly** *adv.*

phe·nom·e·nol·o·gy (fi-nómmi-nóllə-ji) *n.* **1.** The study of all possible appearances in human experience, during which considerations of objective reality and of purely subjective response are temporarily left out of account. **2.** A philosophical movement based on such study, originated by Edmund Husserl about 1905. [German *Phänomenologie* : PHENOMENO(N) + -LOGY.] —**phe·nom·e·no·log·i·cal** (-nə-lójik'l) *adj.* —**phe·nom·e·no·log·i·cal·ly** *adv.* —**phe·nom·e·nol·o·gist** (-nóllə-jist) *n.*

phe·nom·e·non (fi-nómmi-nən ‖ *U.S.* -non) *n., pl.* **-na** (-nə) or **-nons** (for sense 2). **1.** Any occurrence or fact that is directly perceptible by the senses. **2. a.** An unusual, significant, or unaccountable fact or occurrence; a marvel. **b.** A person outstanding for some extreme quality or achievement: *"I thought Mr. Barkis a phenomenon of respectability."* (Charles Dickens). **3.** *Philosophy.* That which appears real to the senses, regardless of whether its underlying existence is proved or its nature understood. Compare **noumenon**. **4.** *Physics.* An observable event. [Late Latin *phaenomenon*, from Greek *phainomenon*, from *phainomenos*, present participle of *phainesthai*, to appear, from *phainein*, to show.]

phe·no·thi·a·zine (féenō-thí-ə-zeen) *n.* A greenish organic compound, $C_{12}H_9NS$, used in insecticides, anthelmintics, and dyes.

phe·no·type (féen-ō-tīp, -ə-) *n. Genetics.* **1.** The environmentally and genetically determined observable appearance of an organism. Compare **genotype**. **2.** An individual or group of organisms exhibiting a particular phenotype. [German *Phänotypus* : PHENO- + TYPE.] —**phe·no·typ·ic** (-típpik), **phe·no·typ·i·cal** *adj.* —**phe·no·typ·i·cal·ly** *adv.*

phen·ox·ide (fi-nók-sīd, fe-) *n.* Any of various salts of phenol containing the ion C_6H_5O.

phen·yl (féen-īl, fén-, -'l) *adj. Chemistry.* Designating, containing, or combined with the group C_6H_5, derived from benzene. Usually used in combination: *phenylalanine*. [PHEN(O)- + -YL.] —**phe·nyl·ic** (fi-níllik, fe-) *adj.*

phen·yl·al·a·nine (féenīl-ál-ə-neen, fénn'l-) *n.* A natural amino acid, $C_6H_5CH_2CH(NH_2)COOH$, that occurs as a constituent of many proteins and is extracted for use as a dietary supplement. It is normally converted to tyrosine in the body; a failure in this reaction causes phenylketonuria.

phen·yl·ene (fénn'l-een) *n.* An organic radical, C_6H_4, derived from benzene by removal of two hydrogen atoms.

phenylene blue *n.* **Indamine** *(see).*

phe·nyl·ke·to·nu·ri·a (féenīl-kee-tō-néwr-i-ə, fénn'l-, -tə- ‖ -nóor-) *n.* A congenital defect of protein metabolism that causes excessive accumulation of phenylalanine in the blood and leads to mental retardation unless detected and remedied. [New Latin : PHENYL + KETONE + -URIA.] —**phe·nyl·ke·to·nu·ric** *adj. & n.*

phe·nyl·thi·o·car·bam·ide (féenīl-thí-ō-kárbə-mīd, fénn'l-) *n. Abbr.* **PTC** A crystalline compound, $C_7H_8N_2S$, the taste of which is determined by a pair of genes. If one or both genes are dominant the compound is bitter to the taster, if neither is dominant it is tasteless. Also called "phenylthiourea".

pher·o·mone (férrə-mōn) *n.* A substance that is externally secreted by certain animals and induces a behavioural or physiological response in other animals of the same species. [Greek *pherein*, to bear + *hormone*.] —**pher·o·mo·nal** (-mōn'l) *adj.*

phew (few) *interj.* Used to express relief, fatigue, surprise, or disgust.

phi (fī) *n.* The 21st letter in the Greek alphabet, written Φ, φ. Transliterated in English as *ph*, or *f* in modern Greek names. [Greek.]

phi·al (fí-əl) *n.* A small bottle, or a **vial** *(see).* [Middle English *fiole*, from Old French, from Old Provençal *fiola*, from Latin *phiala*, vessel, saucer, from Greek *phialē*†, broad vessel.]

Phi Beta Kappa *n.* **1.** A fraternity of American university students and graduates whose members are chosen on the basis of high academic standing. It is the oldest fraternity in the United States (founded 1776). **2.** A member of this fraternity. [From the initials of the Greek phrase *philosophia biou kubernētēs*, "philosophy the guide of life" (motto of the society).]

Phi·di·as (fí-di-ass, fíddi-) (*c.* 500 – *c.* 430 B.C.). Athenian sculptor, considered by his contemporaries the greatest in Greece. He supervised work on the Parthenon, and his statue of Zeus at Olympia was listed as one of the Seven Wonders of the World.

phil. philosopher; philosophical; philosophy.

Phil. **1.** Philippians (New Testament). **2.** Philippines.

phil–. Variant of **philo–.**

Phil·a·del·phi·a (fíllə-délfi-ə) City in Pennsylvania, United States, situated on the Delaware river. It was founded in 1681 by William Penn. Its industries include textiles and oil refining, and its port exports grain and timber. The signing of the Declaration of Independence (1776) and the drafting of the U.S. Constitution (1787) both took place here.

Philadelphia lawyer *n. U.S.* A lawyer of great ingenuity in the discovery and manipulation of subtle legalisms.

phil·a·del·phus (fíllə-délfəss) *n. Botany.* the **mock orange** *(see).*

Phi·lae (fí-lee). Submerged island in the river Nile, southeast Egypt. It is the former site of ancient ruins, most of which were removed to the island of Agilkia before the completion of the Aswan High Dam.

phi·lan·der (fi-lándər) *intr.v.* **-dered, -dering, -ders.** To engage in love affairs frivolously or casually; flirt. Used of a man. [From *Philander*, a traditional literary name for a lover, mistakenly adopted from Greek *philandros*, "loving men", "loving one's husband" : PHIL(O)- + *anēr* (stem *andr-*), man.] —**phi·lan·der·er** *n.*

phil·an·throp·ic (fíl-ən-thróppik, -an-) *adj.* Also **phil·an·throp·i·cal.** Showing, engaged in, or practising philanthropy: *a philanthropic gesture; a philanthropic institution.* —**phil·an·throp·i·cal·ly** *adv.*

phi·lan·thro·py (fi-lánthrə-pi) *n., pl.* **-pies.** **1.** The effort or wish to increase the well-being of humanity, as by charitable works. **2.** Love of humanity in general. **3.** An action or institution designed to promote human welfare. [Late Latin *philanthrōpia*, from Greek *philanthrōpia*, benevolence, from *philanthrōpos*, "lover of mankind" : PHIL(O)- + *anthrōpos*, man.] —**phi·lan·thro·pist** (-pist) *n.*

phi·lat·e·ly (fi-láttə-li) *n.* The collection and study of postage stamps, postmarks, and related materials; stamp-collecting. [French *philatélie* : PHILO- + Greek *atelēs*, tax-free (here used as a rendering of the old postmark *franc de port*, "carriage-free"; see **frank**) : A- (without) + *telos*, charge.] —**phil·a·tel·ic** (fíllə-téllik) *adj.* —**phil·a·tel·i·cal·ly** *adv.* —**phi·lat·e·list** (-list) *n.*

–phile, –phil *n. comb. form.* Indicates one having a strong affinity or fondness for; for example, **Anglophile.** [French *-phile* or New Latin *-philus*, from Greek *-philos*, beloved, dear, loving.]

Philem. Philemon (New Testament).

Phi·le·mon¹ (fī-lée-mən, fi-, -mon). A friend and convert of St. Paul.

Philemon² *n. Abbr.* **Philem.** A book of the New Testament, a short epistle to Philemon by St. Paul.

phil·har·mon·ic (fíl-aar-mónnik, -ər-, -haar-) *adj. Often capital* **P.** Devoted to or appreciative of music. Used chiefly in the names of symphony orchestras, choirs, or musical societies.

~*n. Often capital* **P.** A symphony orchestra or choir, or the group that supports it. [French *philharmonique*, from Italian *filarmonico* : *fil-*, PHILO- + *armonico*, harmonic.]

phil·hel·lene (fíl-hélleen) *n.* Also **phil·hel·len·ist** (-héllənist). **1.** One who admires Greece or the Greeks. **2.** Formerly, one who advocated the national independence of Greece. [Greek *philellēn* : PHIL(O)- + HELLENE.] —**phil·hel·len·ic** (-he-léenik) *adj.* —**phil·hel·len·ism** (-hélləniz'm) *n.*

–philia *n. comb. form.* Indicates: **1.** Tendency towards; for example, **haemophilia.** **2.** Abnormal attraction to; for example, **necrophilia.** [New Latin, from Greek *philia*, friendship, from *philos*, loving.] —**philiac** *n. & adj. comb. form.*

–philic. Variant of **–philous.**

Phil·ip II¹ (fíllip) (*c.* 382 – 336 B.C.). King of Macedonia (359 – 336) and father of Alexander the Great. He created a powerful army which finally defeated a Greek coalition at Chaeronea (338), and achieved a peace settlement in which all the states except Sparta took part.

Philip II² (1527–98). King of Spain (1556–98). A devout Catholic, he married Mary I of England (1554) to seal an alliance in defence of the Netherlands. From his father, Charles V, he acquired the kingdom of Naples and Sicily (1554) and the duchy of Milan (1540), the Low Countries (1555), and territories in the Americas (1556). When Charles abdicated in 1556, Philip was left a huge empire which he tried to maintain through a series of costly wars. In 1588, he launched the ill-fated Armada against England.

Philip, Prince, Duke of Edinburgh (1921–). Husband of Queen Elizabeth II. He was born in Corfu but educated mainly in Britain. He served in the Royal Navy in World War II and took up British citizenship in 1947. He was created Duke of Edinburgh on the eve of his wedding to Elizabeth later that year. In 1956 he introduced the Duke of Edinburgh's Award Scheme to encourage the leisure activities of young people between 14 and 25 years of age.

Philip, Saint¹. One of the Apostles; said to have spread the Gospel in Asia Minor. Matthew 10:3; Acts 1:13.

Philip, Saint². Called "the Evangelist". Christian leader of the first century A.D.

Phi·lip·pi (fílli-pī, fi-líppī). Ancient town in Macedonia, Greece; the scene of the defeat of Brutus and Cassius by Mark Antony and Octavian (42 B.C.). —**Phi·lip·pi·an** (fi-líppi-ən) *n. & adj.*

Phi·lip·pi·ans (fi-líppi-ənz) *n.* Used with a singular verb. *Abbr.* **Phil.** A book of the New Testament, the epistle of Saint Paul to the Christians of Philippi.

Phi·lip·pic (fi-líppik) *n.* **1.** Any of the orations of Demosthenes against Philip of Macedon in the fourth century B.C. **2.** Any of the orations of Cicero against Mark Antony in 44 B.C. **3.** *Small* **p.** Any verbal denunciation characterised by invective.

Philippine mahogany *n.* Any of various Philippine hardwood trees of the genus *Shorea* and related genera.

Phil·ip·pines, Republic of the (filli-peenz, *rarely* -pīnz ‖ peénz). Country in southeast Asia of over 7,000 islands, most uninhabited. The largest islands are Luzon and Mindanao. The country is mountainous and heavily forested, and relies on agriculture, but manufacturing is expanding. Coconut products, copper, sugar, and forest products are the chief exports. The islands were colonised by the Spaniards, transferred to the United States (1898) following the Spanish-American war, and, after Japanese occupation in World War II, granted independence (1946). Ferdinand Marcos, elected president in 1965, became president with dictatorial powers in 1976; but was replaced by Corazon Aquino after elections (1986), and she by Fidel Ramos (1992). Area, 300 000 square kilometres (115,831 square miles). Population, 71,900,000. Capital, Manila. —**Phil·ip·pine** (filli-peen, *rarely* -pīn) *adj.*

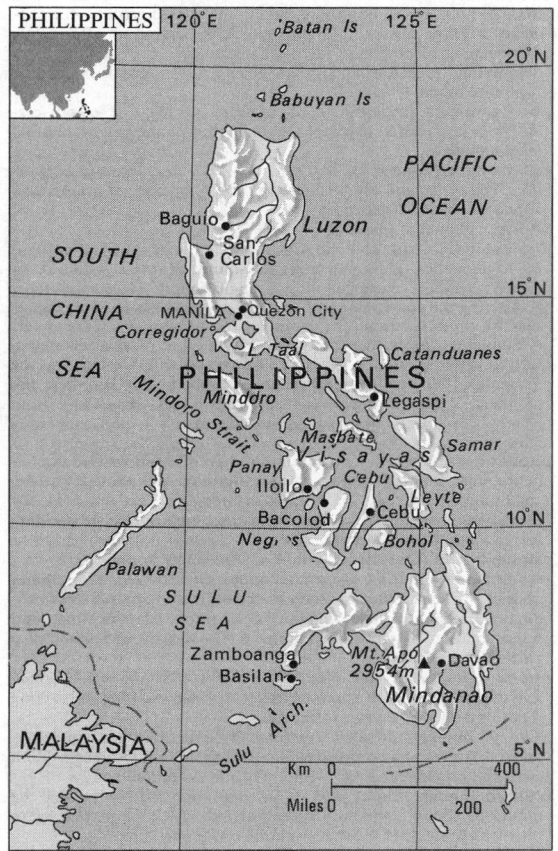

Philippine Sea. Region of the west Pacific Ocean. Situated immediately to the east of the Philippines, it reaches its maximum depth in the Philippines Trench (10 540 metres; 34,578 feet).

Phi·lis·tine (filliss-tīn ‖ *U.S.* -teen, -tin, *also* fi-líss-) *n.* **1.** A member of the warlike people of ancient Philistia in southwestern Palestine. **2.** *Usually small* **p.** A boorish and uncultured person, especially one who is proud of his ignorance and actively antagonistic to intellectual or artistic matters.

—*adj.* **1.** Of or pertaining to the ancient Philistines. **2.** *Sometimes small* **p.** Lacking in or hostile to culture: *philistine cuts in arts spending.* [Middle English, from Late Latin *Philistīnus,* from Late Greek *Philistinos,* from Hebrew *Pelishtī,* Philistia, from *pelesheth,* "land of the Philistines".] —**Phi·lis·tin·ism** (-tin-iz'm) *n.*

Phillips Screw *n.* A trademark for a screw with a cross-shaped groove in its head, used with a matching screwdriver.

phil·lu·me·ny (fi-léwmə-ni, -lóōmə-) *n.* The collection and study of matchbox labels. [PHILO- + Latin *lumen,* light + -Y.] —**phil·lu·men·ist** *n.*

Phi·lo (fī-lō), **Judaeus** (died *c.* A.D. 50). Jewish philosopher and historian. The author of many treatises, he is especially known for trying to interpret the Scriptures in terms of Greek philosophy.

philo-, phil-. Indicates love; for example, **philology, philanthropy.** [New Latin, from Greek, from *philos,* loving.]

phil·o·den·dron (fíllə-dén-drən) *n., pl.* **-drons** or **-dra** (-drə). Any of various climbing tropical American plants of the genus *Philodendron,* many of which are cultivated as house plants for their heart-shaped, glossy green leaves. [New Latin, from Greek, from *philodendros,* "tree-loving" : PHILO- + *dendron,* tree.]

phi·lol·o·gy (fi-lóllə-ji) *n. Abbr.* **philol. 1.** The study of language; especially, **historical linguistics** (*see*). **2.** *Archaic.* Literary study or classical scholarship. [French *philologie,* from Old French, from Latin *philologia,* love of learning, from Greek : PHILO- + -LOGY.] —**phil·o·log·i·cal** (fíllə-lójik'l) *adj.* —**phil·o·log·i·cal·ly** *adv.* —**phi·lol·o·gist** (-jist), **phi·lol·o·ger** (-jər) *n.*

Phil·o·mel (fíl-ə-mel, -ō-) *n.* Also **Phil·o·me·la¹** (-meélə ‖ -máylə). *Poetic.* The nightingale personified. [From PHILOMELA.]

Phil·o·me·la² (fíllə-meélə ‖ máylə). *Greek Mythology.* A princess of Athens who, after being raped and having her tongue cut out by Tereus, king of Thrace, was turned into either a swallow or a nightingale.

phil·o·pro·gen·i·tive (fíllō-prō-jénnətiv) *adj.* **1.** Producing many offspring; prolific. **2.** Loving one's own offspring or children in general. **3.** Of or pertaining to love of children. —**phil·o·pro·gen·i·tive·ly** *adv.* —**phil·o·pro·gen·i·tive·ness** *n.*

philos. philosopher; philosophical; philosophy.

phi·los·o·pher (fi-lóssəfər) *n.* **1.** *Abbr.* **phil., philos.** A student of or specialist in philosophy. **2.** A person who lives and thinks according to a particular philosophy. **3.** A writer or thinker whose intellectual or ideological theories are used as the basis of a policy, cult, or school of thought: *the philosopher of monetarism.* **4.** A person who remains calm and rational even under the most trying of circumstances. **5.** *Archaic.* An alchemist. [Middle English *philosophre,* from Old French *philosophe,* from Latin *philosophus,* from Greek *philosophos* "loving wisdom" : PHILO- + *sophos,* wise.]

philosophers' stone, philosopher's stone *n.* **1.** In alchemy: **a.** The substance held to have the power of transmuting baser metals into gold. **b.** The **elixir** (*see*). **2.** Anything, such as a principle or idea, thought capable of effecting spiritual or other regeneration.

phil·o·soph·i·cal (fíllə-sóffik'l) *adj.* Also **phil·o·soph·ic** (-sóffik). *Abbr.* **phil., philos. 1.** Of, pertaining to, or based on a system of philosophy. **2.** Characteristic of or befitting a philosopher; enlightened; wise. **3.** Serene and stoical in the face of difficulties. —**phil·o·soph·i·cal·ly** *adv.*

phi·los·o·phise, phi·los·o·phize (fi-lóssə-fīz) *v.* **-phised, -phising, -phises.** —*intr.* **1.** To talk or speculate in a philosophical manner. **2.** To indulge in moralistic and often superficial reasoning. —*tr.* **1.** To make (a theory or view) philosophical. **2.** To explain (an event, decision, or the like) in a philosophical way. —**phi·los·o·phis·er** *n.*

phi·los·o·phy (fi-lóssəfi) *n., pl.* **-phies.** *Abbr.* **phil., philos. 1. a.** Love and pursuit of wisdom by intellectual means. **b.** The investigation of causes and laws underlying reality. **c.** A particular system of philosophical inquiry or demonstration. **2.** Inquiry into the nature of things based on logical reasoning rather than empirical methods. **3.** The critique and analysis of fundamental beliefs as they come to be conceptualised and formulated. **4.** Formerly, the investigation of natural phenomena and its systematisation in theory and experiment, as in alchemy, astrology, or astronomy: *natural philosophy.* **5.** All the disciplines presented in university curricula of science and the liberal arts, except medicine, law, and theology: *Doctor of Philosophy.* **6.** The science comprising logic, ethics, aesthetics, metaphysics, and epistemology. **7.** The general principles underlying a particular branch of study, field of activity, or approach to practical problems: *the philosophy of history; monetarist philosophy.* **8.** The system of values by which one lives. **9.** The calmness and detachment thought to befit a philosopher. [Middle English *philosophie,* from Old French, from Latin *philosophia,* from Greek, from *philosophos,* "loving wisdom." See **philosopher.**]

–philous, –philic *adj. comb. form.* Indicates a love of or attraction to something; for example, **photophilous, lyophilic.** [Greek *philos,* beloved, dear, loving.]

phil·tre, *U.S.* **phil·ter** (filtər) *n.* **1.** A love potion. **2.** Any magic potion or charm. [French *philtre,* from Latin *philtrum,* from Greek *philtron,* "love charm," from *philein,* to love, from *philos,* beloved.]

phi·mo·sis (fī-mō-siss) *n.* Abnormal narrowing of the opening of the foreskin, which prevents its being drawn back over the tip of the penis. [New Latin, from Greek, a muzzling, from *phimos,* muzzle.]

phiz (fiz) *n.* Also **phiz·og** (fízzog) *Slang.* A face or facial expression. Not in current usage. [Alteration and shortening of PHYSIOGNOMY.]

Phiz. See Hablot Knight **Browne.**

phle·bi·tis (fli-bītiss, flee-) *n. Pathology.* Inflammation of a vein. [PHLEB(O)- + -ITIS.] —**phle·bit·ic** (-bíttik) *adj.*

phlebo-, phleb- *comb. form.* Indicates a vein; for example, **phlebotomy, phlebitis.** [Greek, from *phleps†* (stem *phleb-*), vein.]

phle·bot·o·mise, phle·bot·o·mize (fli-bóttəmīz, flee-, fle-) *tr.v.* **-mised, -mising, -mises.** *Medicine.* To perform a phlebotomy on.

phle·bot·o·my (fli-bóttə-mi, flee-, fle-) *n., pl.* **-mies.** *Medicine.* The therapeutic practice of opening a vein to draw blood. Also called "venesection". [Middle English *flebotomye,* from Old French *flebotomie,* from Late Latin *phlebotomia,* from Greek, "blood-letting" : PHLEBO- + -TOMY.] —**phleb·o·tom·ic** (flébbə-tómmik, fleébə-), **phleb·o·tom·i·cal** *adj.* —**phle·bot·o·mist** (-mist) *n.*

Phleg·e·thon (fléggə-thən, -thon). *Greek Mythology.* A river of fire, one of the six rivers of Hades. [Greek, from *phlegethein*, to blaze, from *phlegein*, to burn.]

phlegm (flem) *n.* **1.** *Physiology.* Thick mucus secreted by the respiratory mucosa. **2.** One of the four humours of ancient physiology. **3.** Sluggishness of temperament. **4.** Calm self-possession; equanimity. [Middle English *fleume*, from Old French, from Late Latin *phlegma*, body moisture, from Greek, flame, inflammation, phlegm, from *phlegein*, to burn.] —**phlegm·y** (flémmi) *adj.*

phleg·mat·ic (fleg-máttik) *adj.* Having or suggesting a calm, unexcitable temperament; unemotional. [Middle English from Old French from Late Latin *phlegmaticus*, from Greek *phlegmatikos*, having phlegm, from *phlegma* (stem *phlegmat*-), PHLEGM.]

phlo·em (flṓ-em) *n.* *Botany.* The nutrient-conducting tissue of vascular plants, consisting of sieve tubes and other cellular material. Also called "bast". Compare **xylem.** [German *Phloem*, from Greek *phloios, phloos,* bark.]

phlo·gis·tic (flo-jístik, flǝ- ‖ flṓ-) *adj.* **1.** Of or pertaining to phlogiston. **2.** *Medicine.* Of or pertaining to inflammation or fever.

phlo·gis·ton (flo-jíss-tǝn, flǝ-, -ton ‖ flṓ-) *n.* A hypothetical substance formerly thought to be a volatile constituent of all combustible substances released in combustion. [New Latin, from Greek, from *phlogistos*, "inflammable", from *phlogizein*, to set on fire, from *phlox* (stem *phlog*-), flame, from *phlegein*, to burn.]

phlog·o·pite (flógga-pīt) *n.* A yellow to dark-brown mica, $KMg_3AlSi_3O_{10}(Oh)_2$, used in insulation. [German *Phlogopit*, from Greek *phlogōpos*, "fiery-looking" : *phlox* (stem *phlog*-), flame (see **phlogiston**) + *ōps*, eye.]

phlox (floks) *n., pl.* **phlox** or **phloxes.** Any plant of the genus *Phlox*, chiefly native to North America but widely cultivated, having lance-shaped leaves and clusters of white, red, or purple flowers. [New Latin, from Latin, a flower, from Greek, wallflower, flame, from *phlegein*, to burn.]

phlyc·te·na, phlyc·tae·na (flik-tée-nǝ) *n., pl.* **-nae** (-nee). *Medicine.* A small blister; a vesicle. [New Latin, from Greek *phluktaina*, blister, from *phluein, phluzein*, to boil over.]

Phnom Penh (pnóm pén, nóm, pǝ-nóm). Capital of Cambodia (Kampuchea). Situated at the head of the Mekong Delta, it was a loyalist stronghold during the civil war (1970–75) but suffered greatly, with most of its population being dispersed after its fall to the Khmer Rouge (1976). It was a thriving port and a cultural and commercial centre, producing textiles, shipping, and dried fish.

-phobe *n. comb. form.* Indicates one that fears, often irrationally, or is averse to or lacks an affinity for something specified; for example, **xenophobe.** [Greek *-phobos*, fearing, from *phobos*, fear, flight.]

pho·bi·a (fṓb-i-ǝ) *n.* **1.** A persistent, abnormal, or irrational fear of something specified. **2.** Any strong fear, dislike, or aversion. [New Latin, independent use of *-phobia*, -PHOBIA.] —**pho·bic** (-ik) *adj.*

-phobia *n. comb. form.* Indicates persistent, irrational, abnormal, or intense fear; for example, **hypnophobia.** [New Latin, from Late Latin, from Greek, from *phobos*, fear, flight.]

-phobic *adj. comb. form.* Indicates: **1.** Having an abnormal fear or dread of; for example, **arachnophobic.** **2.** Lacking an affinity for; for example, **lyophobic.** [-PHOBIA + -IC.]

Pho·bos (fṓb-oss, fṓb-) *n.* *Astronomy.* The larger and inner of the two satellites of the planet Mars.

phoe·be (féebi) *n.* Any of several small dull-coloured North American birds of the genus *Sayornis*. [Imitative of its call.]

Phoe·be¹ (féebi). *Greek Mythology.* The goddess Artemis. [Greek *Phoibē*, from *phoibos*, shining.]

Phoe·be² (féebi) *n.* **1.** *Poetic.* The moon. **2.** *Astronomy.* The ninth, smallest, and outermost of the major satellites of Saturn. [From PHOEBE.]

Phoe·bus (féebǝss). *Greek Mythology.* Apollo, the god of the sun. [Greek *phoibos*, radiant.]

Phoe·ni·cia (fi-néesh-ǝ, -nísh-, -i-ǝ). Ancient name for the coastal areas of modern Syria and Lebanon. It was settled by a Semitic people descended from the Canaanites who established a trading empire (*c.* 1200 B.C.) along the Mediterranean. Its chief colony was at Carthage, North Africa, with others in Spain, Cyprus, and Sicily, and its chief towns were Sidon and Tyre.

Phoe·ni·cian (fi-néesh-'n, -nísh-, -i-ǝ) *n.* **1.** A native, inhabitant, or subject of ancient Phoenicia. **2.** The Northwest Semitic language of ancient Phoenicia. [Middle English *Phenicien*, from Old French, from Latin *Phoenīcius*, from Greek *phoinix*, PHOENIX, also a Phoenician (the association is unexplained).] —**Phoe·ni·cian** *adj.*

phoe·nix (féeniks) *n.* **1.** A mythological bird that consumed itself by fire after 500 years, and rose renewed from its ashes. **2.** A person or thing that has been restored to a new existence from destruction, downfall, or ruin. **3.** A person or thing of unsurpassed excellence or beauty; a paragon. [Middle English *fenix*, from Old French, from Latin *phoenix*, from Greek *phoinix*, purple, Phoenician.]

Phoenix¹. Town in Arizona, United States. Situated on the river Salt, it is in a dairy and citrus fruit region, is a health resort, and produces textiles, aircraft, steel, and aluminium.

Phoenix². *n. Astronomy.* A constellation in the Southern Hemisphere near Tucana and Sculptor.

Phoenix Islands. See **Kiribati.**

phon (fon) *n.* A unit of loudness equal to the number of decibels a sound is above a reference tone having a frequency of 1000 hertz and a given root-mean-square sound pressure. [Greek *phōnē*, sound.]

phon. phonetic; phonetics; phonology.

pho·nate (fō-náyt ‖ *U.S.* fṓ-nayt) *v.* **-nated, -nating, -nates.** —*intr.*

To utter vocal sounds; vocalise. —*tr.* To utter (a sound). [PHON(O)- + -ATE.] —**pho·na·tion** (-náysh'n) *n.* —**pho·nat·o·ry** (fṓnǝ-tǝri, -tri, fō-náy- ‖ *U.S.* -tawri, -tōri) *adj.*

phone¹ (fōn) *n.* *Linguistics.* Any individual sound as realised in speech. [Greek *phōnē*, sound, voice.]

phone² *n.* A telephone. ~*v.* **phoned, phoning, phones.** —*intr.* To telephone. —*tr.* **1.** To telephone (someone). **2.** To impart (information or news, for example) by telephone. [Short for TELEPHONE.] *Usage:* This form of *telephone*, a word in its own right, is not usually preceded by an apostrophe ('phone) in written English.

-phone *n. comb. form.* Indicates: **1.** A sound or sound-emitting device; for example, **radiophone. 2.** A speaker of a specified language; for example, **Anglophone.** ~*adj. comb. form.* Indicates speaking a specified language; for example, **Francophone.** [Greek *phōnē*, sound, voice.]

phone-in (fōn-in) *n.* A live radio or television programme in which listeners or viewers telephone the studio to answer quiz questions, respond to charity appeals, or put questions and views to the presenter or a guest for discussion.

pho·neme (fōn-eem) *n.* *Linguistics.* Any of the classes of speech sounds in a given language or accent that can affect the meaning or distinguish words one from another. The initial consonant sounds in *leaf* and *reef* belong to different phonemes (l) and (r) respectively, since these words are distinct in meaning. [French *phonème*, from Greek *phōnēma*, an utterance, from *phōnein*; See **phonetic.**]

pho·ne·mic (fǝ-néemik, fō-) *adj.* Also **pho·ne·mat·ic** (fōni-máttik, fónni-) **1.** Of, pertaining to, or having the characteristics of a phoneme. **2.** Of or pertaining to phonemics. **3.** Serving to differentiate the meaning of otherwise identical utterances. **4.** Pertaining to or designating speech sounds that belong to different phonemes. —**pho·ne·mi·cal·ly** *adv.*

pho·ne·mi·cise, pho·ne·mi·cize (fǝ-néemi-sīz, fō-) *tr.v.* **-cised, -cising, -cises.** To analyse (speech sounds) into phonemes. —**pho·ne·mi·ci·sa·tion** *n.*

pho·ne·mics (fǝ-néemiks, fō-) *n.* Used with a singular verb. *Linguistics.* The study and establishment of the phonemes of a language. —**pho·ne·mi·cist** (-néemi-sist) *n.*

phonet. phonetic; phonetics.

pho·net·ic (fǝ-néttik, fō-) *adj. Abbr.* **phon., phonet. 1.** Of or pertaining to phonetics. **2.** Representing the sounds of speech with a set of distinct symbols, each denoting a single sound: *phonetic spelling.* **3.** Altering the conventional spelling of a word so as to better represent its pronunciation; for example, the spelling *kwik* for *quick.* **4.** Employing more than the minimum number of symbols necessary to differentiate the meaning of utterances. **5.** Designating the distinction between any speech sounds, whether or not these are phonemes. [New Latin *phoneticus*, from Greek *phōnētikos*, from *phōnein*, to sound, from *phōnē*, sound, voice.] —**pho·net·i·cal·ly** *adv.*

phonetic alphabet *n.* **1.** A standardised set of symbols used in phonetic transcription. See **International Phonetic Alphabet. 2.** In telecommunications, any of various systems of code words for identifying letters in voice communication, such as *Charlie* standing for *C, Foxtrot* for *F,* and the like.

pho·ne·ti·cian (fō-néesh'n, fónni-) *n.* An expert in phonetics.

pho·net·ics (fǝ-néttiks, fō-) *n.* Used with a singular verb. *Abbr.* **phon., phonet. 1.** The science or study of the sounds of speech, their production, reception, combination, description, classification, and representation by written symbols. **2.** The system of sounds of a particular language.

pho·ney (fṓni) *adj.* **-nier, niest.** Also *chiefly U.S.* **pho·ny.** *Informal.* **1.** Not genuine or real; spurious; fake: *a phoney painting.* **2.** Having a false manner or image; insincere. ~*n., pl.* **phoneys** or **-nies.** *Informal.* **1.** Something not genuine; a fake. **2.** A person who projects false feelings or a false image. [20th century : origin obscure.] —**pho·ni·ly** *adv.* —**pho·ni·ness** *n.*

phon·ic (fónnik, fṓnik) *adj.* **1.** Of, pertaining to, or having the nature of sound, especially speech sound. **2.** Of or pertaining to phonics. [PHON(O)- + -IC.] —**phon·i·cal·ly** *adv.*

phon·ics (fónniks) *n.* Used with a singular verb. **1.** The study or science of sound; acoustics. Not in current technical usage. **2.** A method of teaching reading and pronunciation by training learners to recognise the phonetic value of letters and syllables.

phono-, phon- *comb. form.* Indicates sound or a voice; for example, **phonology.** [Greek *phōnē*, sound, voice.]

pho·no·gram (fṓnǝ-gram) *n.* A character, symbol, or sequence of symbols, as in a phonetic alphabet, representing a word or phoneme in speech. [PHONO- + -GRAM.] —**pho·no·gram·ic, pho·no·gram·mic** (-grámmik) *adj.* —**pho·no·gram·i·cal·ly, pho·no·gram·mi·cal·ly** *adv.*

pho·no·graph (fṓnǝ-graaf, -graf) *n.* **1.** An early machine for recording and reproducing sounds using a wax cylinder. **2.** *U.S.* A gramophone (*see*). [PHONO- + -GRAPH.] —**pho·no·graph·ic** (-gráffik) *adj.* —**pho·no·graph·i·cal·ly** *adv.*

pho·nog·ra·phy (fǝ-nóggrǝ-fi, fō-) *n.* **1.** The science or practice of transcribing speech by means of symbols representing elements of sound; phonetic transcription. **2.** Any system of writing or shorthand based on phonetic transcription. [PHONO- + -GRAPHY.] —**pho·nog·ra·pher** (-fǝr) *n.* —**pho·nog·ra·phist** (-fist) *n.*

pho·no·lite (fṓn-ǝ-līt, -ō-) *n.* A volcanic rock composed principally of orthoclase and nepheline. Also called "clinkstone". [French,

from German *Phonolith* : PHONO- + -LITH (it clinks when struck).]
—**pho·no·lit·ic** (-líttik) *adj.*

pho·nol·o·gy (fə-nólləji, fō-) *n. Abbr.* phon., phonol. 1. The study of the sound system of a language or of two or more related languages. 2. The sound system of a given language. [PHONO- + -LOGY.] —**pho·no·log·i·cal** (fŏnə-lójik'l, fónnə-) *adj.* —**pho·no·log·i·cal·ly** *adv.* —**pho·nol·o·gist** (-jist) *n.*

pho·nom·e·ter (fə-nómmitər, fo-, fō-) *n.* A device that measures the intensity of sound, usually calibrated in phons. [PHONO- + -METER.] —**pho·no·met·ric** (fŏnə-méttrik, fónnə-), **pho·no·met·ri·cal** *adj.*

pho·non (fŏn-on) *n. Physics.* The quantum of thermal energy in a crystal lattice, used especially in mathematical models to calculate vibrational properties of solids. There are two types of phonon: *acoustic,* corresponding to longitudinal motion of the lattice points, and *optic,* corresponding to transverse motion. [PHON(O)- + -ON.]

pho·no·re·cep·tion (fŏnō-ri-sép-sh'n) *n.* Perception of or response to sound waves. —**pho·no·re·cep·tor** (-tər) *n.*

pho·no·scope (fŏn-ə-skōp, -ō-) *n.* A device that produces a visible display of the mechanical properties of a sounding body, especially of musical instruments. [PHONO- + -SCOPE.]

pho·no·type (fŏn-ə-tīp, -ō-) *n.* 1. A phonetic symbol used in printing. 2. Text printed in phonetic symbols. —**pho·no·typ·ic** (-típpik), **pho·no·typ·i·cal** *adj.* —**pho·no·typ·i·cal·ly** *adv.*

pho·no·typ·y (fŏn-ə-tīpi, -ō-) *n.* The practice of transcribing speech sounds by means of phonetic symbols. —**pho·no·typ·ist** *n.*

phony. *Chiefly U.S.* Variant of **phoney.**

-phony *n. comb. form.* Indicates sound of a specified kind; for example, **telephony.** [Greek *-phōnia,* from *phōnē,* sound.]

phoo·ey (fōō-i) *interj.* Used as an exclamation of disgust, disbelief, disappointment, or contempt. [Imitative.]

-phore *n. comb. form.* Indicates a bearer or producer of; for example, **semaphore.** [Greek *-phoros,* bearing, from *pherein,* to bear.]

-phoresis *n. comb. form.* Indicates transmission; for example, **electrophoresis.** [Greek *phorēsis,* a bearing, from *phorein,* frequentative of *pherein,* to bear.]

phor·mi·um (fáwr-mi-əm) *n.* A genus of perennial plants, grown chiefly for their long, stiff, bladelike leaves; especially, *P. tenax* (New Zealand flax), often used as a border plant.

-phorous *adj. comb. form.* Indicates bearing or producing; for example, **gonophorous.** [Greek *-phoros,* from *pherein,* to bear.]

phos– *comb. form.* Indicates the presence of light; for example, **phosgene.** [Greek *phōs,* light.]

phos·gene (fóss-jeen, fóz-) *n.* A colourless volatile liquid or gas, $COCl_2$, used as a poison gas and in making glass, dyes, resins, and plastics. Also called "carbonyl chloride". [PHOS- (from the former method of obtaining the compound by exposure to sunlight) + *-gene,* variant of -GEN.]

phos·ge·nite (fózji-nīt) *n.* A rare fluorescent secondary mineral, $Pb_2(Cl_2CO_3)$, occurring as white, yellow, or grey tetragonal crystals. [German *Phosgenit* : PHOSGENE + -ITE.]

phosph–. Variant of **phospho–.**

phos·pha·gen (fósfə-jen) *n.* Phosphocreatine. [PHOSPHA(TE) + -gen.]

phos·pha·tase (fósfə-tayz, -tayss) *n.* Any of numerous enzymes that catalyse the hydrolysis of phosphoric acid esters to phosphate ions. [PHOSPHAT(E) + -ASE.]

phos·phate (fóss-fayt, *rarely* -fət, -fit) *n.* 1. *Chemistry.* Any salt or ester of phosphoric acid containing mainly pentavalent phosphorus and oxygen. 2. A fertiliser containing phosphorous compounds. [French *phosphat,* from *phosphore,* phosphorus, from New Latin *phosphorus,* PHOSPHORUS.] —**phos·phat·ic** (foss-fáttik, fóss-) *adj.*

phosphate rock *n.* Any of various sedimentary rocks composed largely of apatite, or guano deposits, both of which are used as fertiliser and as a source of phosphorous compounds.

phos·pha·tide (fósfə-tīd) *n.* A phospholipid.

phos·pha·tise, phos·pha·tize (fósfə-tīz) *v.* -tised, -tising, -tises. —*tr.* 1. To change into a phosphate or phosphates. 2. To treat with phosphate or phosphoric acid. —*intr.* To change into or become a phosphate. —**phos·pha·ti·sa·tion** (-tī-záysh'n ‖ *U.S.* -ti-) *n.*

phos·pha·tu·ri·a (fósfə-téwr-i-ə ‖ -tóor-) *n.* A condition in which excessive phosphates are discharged in the urine. [New Latin : PHOSPHAT(E) + -URIA.] —**phos·pha·tu·ric** (-ik) *adj.*

phos·phene (fóss-feen) *n.* A luminous visual sensation experienced when the eyeball is pressed. [PHOS- + Greek *phainein,* to show.]

phos·phide (fóss-fīd) *n.* A compound of phosphorus and a more electropositive element. [PHOSPH(O)- + -IDE.]

phos·phine (fóss-feen) *n.* 1. A colourless, spontaneously flammable poisonous gas, PH_3, having a garlic-like smell and is used as a doping agent for solid-state components. 2. A synthetic yellow dye. [PHOSPH(O)- + -INE.]

phos·phite (fóss-fīt) *n.* Any salt of phosphorous acid.

phospho–, phosph– *comb. form.* Indicates the presence of phosphorus; for example, **phosphocreatine.** [French, from *phosphore,* phosphorus, from New Latin *phosphorus,* PHOSPHORUS.]

phos·pho·cre·a·tine (fóss-fō-kree-ə-teen, -fə-) *n.* Also **phos·pho·cre·a·tin** (-tin). An organic compound, $C_4H_{10}N_3O_5P$, found in vertebrate tissues, capable of providing physiological energy as in muscular contraction. Also called "phosphagen".

phos·pho·lip·id (fóss-fə-líppid, -fō-) *n.* Any of a group of compound lipids consisting of phosphoric acid, fatty acids, and a nitrogenous base, forming an important part of cell membranes. Also called "phosphatide".

phos·pho·ni·um (foss-fóni-əm, fóss-) *n.* A univalent radical, PH_4, derived from phosphine. [PHOSPH(O)- + (AMM)ONIUM.]

phos·pho·pro·tein (fóss-fō-prṓ-teen, -fə-, -tee-in) *n.* Any of a group of proteins, containing chemically bound phosphoric acid.

phos·phor (fóss-fər ‖ -fawr) *n.* 1. Any substance that can be stimulated to emit light by incident radiation. 2. Something exhibiting phosphorescence. [French *phosphore,* from New Latin *phosphorus,* PHOSPHORUS.]

phosphor bronze *n.* A hard, strong, corrosion-resistant bronze containing up to 0.5 per cent phosphorus and used in electric switches, springs, and chains.

phos·pho·resce (fósfə-réss) *intr.v.* -resced, -rescing, -resces. To exhibit phosphorescence. [Back-formation from *phosphorescent* : PHOSPHOR + -ESCENT.]

phos·pho·res·cence (fósfə-réss'nss) *n.* Persistent emission of light following exposure to and removal of incident radiation. Compare **fluorescence, bioluminescence.** [From PHOSPHOR.] —**phos·pho·res·cent** *adj.* —**phos·pho·res·cent·ly** *adv.*

phos·phor·ic (foss-fórrik, fóss- ‖ -fáwrik; *U.S. also* fósfərik) *adj.* Of, pertaining to, or containing phosphorus, especially in a valency state higher than that of a comparable phosphorous compound.

phosphoric acid *n.* A clear colourless liquid, H_3PO_4, used in fertilisers, soaps and detergents, food flavouring, and pharmaceuticals.

phos·pho·rism (fósfər-iz'm) *n.* Chronic phosphorus poisoning from ingestion or inhalation. [PHOSPHOR(US) + -ISM.]

phos·pho·rite (fósfər-īt) *n.* 1. A fibrous variety of **apatite** *(see).* 2. A concretionary mass of rock consisting predominantly of calcium phosphate. [PHOSPHOR(US) + -ITE.]

phos·pho·rous (fósfərəss ‖ *U.S. also* foss-fáwrəss, -fórəss) *adj.* Of or containing phosphorus, especially in the trivalent state.

phosphorous acid *n. Chemistry.* A white or yellowish hygroscopic crystalline solid, H_3PO_3, used as a reducing agent and to produce phosphite salts.

phos·pho·rus (fósfərəss) *n.* 1. *Symbol* P A highly reactive, poisonous, nonmetallic element occurring naturally in phosphates, especially apatite, and existing in three allotropic forms, white (sometimes yellow), red, and black. It is an essential constituent of living cells and, depending on the allotropic form, is used in safety matches, pyrotechnics, incendiary shells, fertilisers, glass, and steel. Atomic number 15, atomic weight 30.9738, melting point (white) 44.1°C, boiling point 280°C, relative density (white) 1.83, valencies 3, 5. 2. Any phosphorescent substance. [New Latin, from Greek *phōsphoros,* "light-bearing" (so named from the fact that white phosphorus is phosphorescent in air) : PHOS- + -PHOROUS.]

phosphorus pentoxide *n.* A white solid, P_2O_5, produced by burning phosphorus. It has an affinity for water, with which it forms phosphoric acid.

phos·pho·ryl·ase (foss-fórri-layz, fósfəri-, -layss) *n. Biochemistry.* Any of a group of enzymes that catalyse the production of glucose-1-phosphate from glycogen. [PHOSPHOR(US) + -YL + -ASE.]

phos·pho·ryl·ate (foss-fórri-layt, fósfəri-) *tr.v.* -ated, -ating, -ates. To change (an organic substance) into an organic phosphate. [PHOSPHOR(US) + -YL + -ATE.] —**phos·pho·ryl·a·tion** (-láysh'n) *n.*

phos·sy jaw (fóssi) *n. Informal.* Degeneration of the bone of the lower jaw caused by prolonged exposure to phosphorus fumes. [*phossy,* shortened from PHOSPHORUS.]

phot (fōt, fot) *n. Physics.* A unit of illumination equal to one **lumen** *(see)* per square centimetre. [Greek *phōs* (stem *phōt-*), light.]

pho·tic (fṓtik) *adj.* 1. Of or pertaining to light. 2. *Biology.* Pertaining to the production of light by organisms. 3. Pertaining to or designating the upper zone or region of a body of water, into which sunlight penetrates. [PHOT(O)- + -IC.]

pho·to (fṓtō) *n., pl.* -tos. *Informal.* A photograph.

photo–, phot– *comb. form.* Indicates: 1. Light; for example, **photosynthesis, photic.** 2. Photographic; for example, **photomontage.** [Greek *phōs* (stem *phōt-*), light.]

pho·to·ac·tin·ic (fṓtō-ak-tínnik) *adj.* Able to emit actinic radiation.

pho·to·ac·tive (fṓtō-áktiv) *adj.* 1. Capable of responding to photoelectric stimulation. 2. Capable of responding to light by chemical reaction. —**pho·to·ac·tiv·i·ty** (-ak-tívvəti) *n.*

pho·to·au·to·troph·ic (fṓtō-áwt-ə-tróffik, -ō-, -trófik) *adj. Biology.* Capable of using light as a source of energy in the synthesis of food from inorganic materials.

pho·to·bi·ot·ic (fṓtō-bī-óttik) *adj. Biology.* Depending on light for the continuance of life and growth.

pho·to·call (fṓtō-kawl) *n.* The appearance of a person or people on some special occasion to enable the press to take photographs of them. Also called "photo opportunity".

pho·to·cath·ode (fṓtō-káthōd) *n.* A cathode that emits electrons when it is illuminated.

pho·to·cell (fṓtō-sel) *n. Electronics.* A photoelectric cell *(see).*

pho·to·chem·is·try (fṓtō-kémmistri) *n.* The chemistry of the interactions of radiant energy and chemical systems. —**pho·to·chem·i·cal** (-kémmik'l) *adj.*

pho·to·chro·mic (fṓtō-krṓmic) *adj.* 1. Of or designating a substance exhibiting photochromism. 2. Of or pertaining to transparent materials containing compounds exhibiting photochromism.

pho·to·chro·mism (fṓtō-krṓmiz'm) *n.* The ability of certain compound materials, especially treated plastics, to darken or change colour when exposed to visible or near ultraviolet light and to revert to their original transparency or colour when the light source is removed.

pho·to·chron·o·graph (fṓtō-krónnə-graaf, -graf) *n.* A device for measuring small intervals of time by the length of a trace made by a light beam on a moving photographic film. —**pho·to·chron·og·ra·phy** n.

pho·to·com·pose (fōtō-kəm-pōz ‖ -kom-) tr.v. **-posed, -posing, -poses.** To prepare (written or graphic matter) for printing by photocomposition; filmset; photoset. —**pho·to·com·pos·er** n.

pho·to·com·po·si·tion (fōtō-kómpə-zísh'n) n. The projection of the image of type characters, by photomechanical or electronic means, onto photographic film, which is used to prepare printing plates. Also called "filmsetting", "phototypesetting".

pho·to·con·duc·tiv·i·ty (fōtō-kón-duk-tívvəti) n. Physics. The increase in electrical conductivity of certain semiconductors when exposed to light. —**pho·to·con·duc·tive** (-kən-dúktiv ‖ -kon-) adj. —**pho·to·con·duc·tion** n.

pho·to·cop·i·er (fōtō-koppi-ər, -kóppi-) n. A device for photographically reproducing written, printed, or graphic material.

pho·to·cop·y (fōtō-koppi; as verb also -kóppi) tr.v. **-copied, -copying, -copies.** To make a photographic reproduction of (printed, written, or graphic material). —n., pl. **photocopies.** A photographic reproduction.

pho·to·cur·rent (fōtō-kurrənt) n. Physics. An electric current produced by illumination of a photoelectric material.

pho·to·dis·in·te·gra·tion (fōtō-diss-inti-gráysh'n) n. Physics. Nuclear disintegration or transformation caused by absorption of gamma rays, or other high-energy radiation.

pho·to·dy·nam·ic (fōtō-dī-námmik) adj. Biology. Of or pertaining to the effect of light on organisms. —**pho·to·dy·nam·ics** n.

pho·to·e·las·tic·i·ty (fōtō-ée-lass-tíssəti, -i-) n. Physics. The effect of distortion of a solid on its optical properties; especially, the production of double refraction in crystals by applied stress. —**pho·to·e·las·tic** adj.

pho·to·e·lec·tric (fōtō-i-léktrik) adj. Also **pho·to·e·lec·tri·cal** (-'l). Of or pertaining to electric effects, such as increased electrical conduction, caused by illumination. —**pho·to·e·lec·tri·cal·ly** adv. —**pho·to·e·lec·tric·i·ty** (-lek-tríssəti, -éllek-, -éelek-) n.

photoelectric cell n. An electronic device having an electrical output that varies in response to incident radiation, especially to visible light. Also called "electric eye", "magic eye", "photocell".

photoelectric effect n. Physics. The ejection of electrons from a substance by incident electromagnetic radiation, especially by visible and ultraviolet light.

pho·to·e·lec·tron (fōtō-i-lék-tron) n. Physics. An electron released or ejected from a substance by the photoelectric effect.

pho·to·e·mis·sion (fōtō-i-mísh'n) n. Physics. The emission of photoelectrons, especially from metallic surfaces.

pho·to·en·grave (fōtō-in-gráyv, -en-) tr.v. **-graved, -graving, -graves.** To reproduce by photoengraving. —**pho·to·en·grav·er** n.

pho·to·en·grav·ing (fōtō-in-gráyving, -en-) n. **1.** The process of reproducing graphic or printed material by transferring the image photomechanically to a plate or other surface in etched relief for printing. **2.** A plate prepared by this method. **3.** A reproduction made by this method.

photo finish n. **1.** The end of a race in which the leading contestants cross the finishing line so close together that the winner must be determined by a photograph taken at the moment of crossing. **2.** Informal. Any extremely close finish or result.

Pho·to·fit (fōtō-fit) n. A trademark for a system of, or the equipment for, creating a picture of the face of a criminal suspect, missing person, or the like. The process involves combining photographs of individual facial features into a composite portrait, on the basis of a description. Compare **Identikit.**

pho·to·flash (fōtō-flash) n. In photography, a **flashbulb** (see).

pho·to·flood (fōtō-flud) n. A reusable electric lamp that produces a bright continuous light for photographic illumination.

pho·to·fluor·og·ra·phy (fōtō-floo-ə-róggrəfi, -floor-) n. Medicine. The process of taking photographs (photofluorograms) of fluoroscopic images. [PHOTO- + FLUORO- + -GRAPHY.] —**pho·to·fluor·o·graph·ic** (-rə-gráffik) adj.

photog. photograph; photographer; photography.

pho·to·gel·a·tine process (fōtō-jéllə-tin) n. In photography, **collotype** (see).

pho·to·gene (fōt-ō-jeen, -ə-) n. Physiology. A retinal **afterimage** (see). [PHOTO- + -gene, variant of -GEN.]

pho·to·gen·ic (fōt-ə-jénnik, -ō-, rarely -jéenik) adj. **1.** Having a physical appearance, especially facial characteristics, that photographs well. **2.** Biology. Producing or emitting light; phosphorescent. **3.** Rare. Caused or produced by light. [PHOTO- + -GENIC.] —**pho·to·gen·i·cal·ly** adv.

pho·to·ge·ol·o·gy (fōtō-jee-ólləji, -ji-) n. The study of geology and geological phenomena by means of aerial and satellite photography.

pho·to·gram (fōtə-gram) n. **1.** A shadowy image produced without a camera by placing an object in contact with film or photosensitive paper and exposing to light. **2.** Archaic. A photograph. [PHOTO- + -GRAM.]

pho·to·gram·me·try (fōt-ō-grámmətri, -ə-) n. **1.** The process of making maps or scale drawings by aerial or other photography. **2.** The process of making precise measurements by the use of photography. [PHOTOGRAM + -METRY.] —**pho·to·gram·met·ric** (-grə-méttrik) adj. —**pho·to·gram·me·trist** (-grámmətrist) n.

pho·to·graph (fōtə-graaf, -graf) n. Abbr. **photog.** An image, especially a positive print, recorded by a camera and reproduced on a photosensitive surface. —v. **photographed, -graphing, -graphs.** —tr. To take a photo-

graph of. —intr. **1.** To practise photography. **2.** To appear in photographs in a specified way: She photographs well. [PHOTO- + -GRAPH.]

pho·tog·ra·pher (fə-tóggrəfər) Abbr. **photog.** A person who takes photographs, especially as a profession.

pho·to·graph·ic (fōtə-gráffik) adj. Also **pho·to·graph·i·cal** (-'l). **1.** Of, pertaining to, or produced by photography. **2.** Used in photography: a photographic lens. **3.** Resembling a photograph; especially, representing or simulating something with great accuracy and fidelity of detail. **4.** Capable of retaining facts or forming accurate and lasting impressions, often after reading or seeing something for only a short time: had a photographic memory. —**pho·to·graph·i·cal·ly** adv.

photographic magnitude n. The magnitude of a star as measured from a photographic plate, taking into account the difference in colour sensitivity between the emulsion and the eye.

pho·tog·ra·phy (fə-tóggrəfi) n. Abbr. **photog.** **1.** The process of creating optical images on photosensitive surfaces. **2.** The art, practice, or occupation of taking and printing photographs, slides, or films. [PHOTO- + -GRAPHY.]

pho·to·gra·vure (fōt-ə-grə-véwr, -ō-) n. **1.** The process of printing from an intaglio plate on which an image has been engraved by means of photography. **2.** A picture or reproduction, or graphic material generally, produced by this process.

pho·to·he·li·o·graph (fōtō-héeli-ə-graaf, -graf) n. A refracting telescope equipped to photograph the sun.

pho·to·i·on·i·sa·tion (fōtō-ī-ən-ī-záysh'n ‖ U.S. -i-) n. The ionisation of an atom or molecule as a result of exposure to radiation. See **ionising radiation.**

pho·to·jour·nal·ism (fōtō-júrn'l-iz'm) n. Journalism making extensive use of photographs rather than written material as a means of reporting news. —**pho·to·jour·nal·ist** n.

pho·to·ki·ne·sis (fōtō-kī-née-siss, -ki-) n. Biology. Movement as a response to light. —**pho·to·ki·net·ic** (-néttik) adj.

pho·to·lith·o·graph (fōt-ō-líth-ə-graaf, -ə-, -líth-, -ō-, -graf) tr.v. **-graphed, -graphing, -graphs.** To reproduce by means of photolithography. —n. A picture made by photolithography. —**pho·to·li·thog·ra·pher** (-li-thóggrəfər) n.

pho·to·li·thog·ra·phy (fōtō-li-thóggrəfi, -lī-) n. **1.** A planographic printing process using plates prepared by photographic means. Also "photolith". **2.** Electronics. A technique for making printed circuits, integrated circuits, and the like by photographically reproducing a pattern for electroplating, etching, or diffusion. —**pho·to·lith·o·graph·ic** (-líthə-gráffik) adj.

pho·to·lu·mi·nes·cence (fōtō-lōomi-néss'nss, -léwmi-) n. **Luminescence** (see) produced by infrared radiation, visible light, or ultraviolet radiation. —**pho·to·lu·mi·nes·cent** adj.

pho·tol·y·sis (fō-tóllə-siss) n. Chemical decomposition induced by light or other radiant energy. [New Latin : PHOTO- + -LYSIS.] —**pho·to·lyt·ic** (fōt-ə-líttik, -ō-) adj.

photom. photometry.

pho·to·map (fōt-ō-map, -ə-) n. A map made by superimposing orientating data on an aerial photograph.

pho·to·me·chan·i·cal (fōtō-mi-kánnik'l) adj. Of, pertaining to, or designating any of various methods by which plates are prepared for printing by means of photography. —n. A piece of artwork or paste-up of typeset material that is ready to be processed into a printing plate by photographic means. —**pho·to·me·chan·i·cal·ly** adv.

pho·tom·e·ter (fō-tómmitər) n. An instrument for measuring a property of light, especially luminous intensity or flux. [PHOTO- + -METER.]

pho·tom·e·try (fō-tómmitri) n. Abbr. **photom.** Physics. The measurement of the properties of light, especially of luminous intensity. [PHOTO- + -METRY.] —**pho·to·met·ric** (fōt-ə-méttrik, -ō-), **pho·to·met·ri·cal** adj. —**pho·tom·e·trist** (-tómmətrist) n.

pho·to·mi·cro·graph (fōtō-míkrə-graaf, -míkrō-, -graf) n. A photograph made through a microscope. Compare **microphotograph.** —tr.v. **photomicrographed, -graphing, -graphs.** To photograph through a microscope. —**pho·to·mi·cro·graph·ic** (-gráffik) adj. —**pho·to·mi·crog·ra·pher** (-mī-króggrəfər) n. —**pho·to·mi·crog·ra·phy** (-mī-króggrəfi) n.

pho·to·mon·tage (fōtō-món-ta'azh) n. **1.** A technique of making a composite picture by assembling several photographs or pieces of photographs, often in combination with other types of graphic material. **2.** A composite picture produced by this technique.

pho·to·mul·ti·pli·er (fōtō-múlti-plī-ər) n. A device for detecting and measuring electromagnetic radiation, consisting of a photocathode to detect the radiation and an electron multiplier to amplify it and produce a detectable electric signal.

pho·to·mur·al (fōtō-méwr-əl) n. A mural made from a very much enlarged photograph or a montage of photographs.

pho·ton (fō-ton) n. Physics. The quantum of electromagnetic energy, generally regarded as a discrete, stable **elementary particle** (see) having zero mass, no electric charge, and carrying angular and linear momentum. [PHOT(O)- + -ON.] —**pho·ton·ic** (-tónnik) adj.

pho·to·nas·ty (fōtō-nasti) n. Botany A nastic movement in which the stimulus is light. [PHOTO- + -NASTY.] —**pho·to·nas·tic** adj.

pho·to·neu·tron (fōtō-néw-tron ‖ -nŏŏ-) n. A neutron produced by an atomic nucleus as a result of a photodisintegration.

pho·to·nu·cle·ar (fōtō-néwkli-ər ‖ -nŏŏkli-) adj. Physics. Of, pertaining to, or designating a nuclear reaction induced by photons.

pho·to·off·set (fṓtō-óff-set, -áwf-) *n.* **Offset printing** *(see).*

pho·to op·por·tun·i·ty *n.* A **photocall** *(see).*

pho·to·pe·ri·od (fṓtō-péer-i-əd) *n. Biology.* The relative exposure of an organism to daylight as a proportion of the total day, considered especially with regard to the effect on growth and functioning. —**pho·to·pe·ri·od·ic** (-óddik), **pho·to·pe·ri·od·i·cal** *adj.* —**pho·to·pe·ri·od·ism** (-əd-iz'm) *n.*

pho·toph·i·lous (fō-tóffiləss) *adj.* Also **pho·to·phil·ic** (fṓt-ə-fíllik, -ō-) *Biology.* Growing or functioning best in strong light. [PHOTO- + -PHILOUS.] —**pho·toph·i·ly** (-tóffili) *n.*

pho·to·pho·bi·a (fṓt-ō-fṓbi-ə, -ə-) *n.* **1.** Abnormal sensitivity, especially of the eyes, to light. **2.** *Psychology.* An abnormal dread of or aversion to sunlight or well-lit places. [PHOTO- + -PHOBIA.] —**pho·to·pho·bic** (-fṓbik) *adj.*

pho·to·pi·a (fō-tṓpi-ə) *n.* Daylight vision with eyes adapted to normal bright light. [New Latin : PHOT(O)- + -OPIA.] —**pho·to·pic** (-tóppik, -tṓpik) *adj.*

pho·to·pol·y·mer (fṓtō-póllimər) *n.* Any polymeric material that is sensitive to light.

pho·to·re·al·ism (fṓtō-réer-liz'm, -rée-ə-) *n.* A style of painting that attempts to imitate the effects of still photography, especially by painting in very fine detail and using commonplace subject matter. —**pho·to·re·al·ist** *n.*

pho·to·re·cep·tion (fṓtō-ri-sép-sh'n, -rə-) *n. Biology.* The detection or perception of visible light; vision; sight. —**pho·to·re·cep·tive** (-tiv) *adj.*

pho·to·re·cep·tor (fṓtō-ri-séptər, -rə-) *n.* A photoreceptive nerve and the cell or organ that it serves.

pho·to·re·con·nais·sance (fṓtō-ri-kónni-s'nss, -rə- ‖ -z'nss) *n. Military.* Photographic aerial reconnaissance.

pho·to·sen·si·tise, pho·to·sen·si·tize (fṓtō-sén-sə-tīz) *tr.v.* **-tised, -tising, -tises.** To make (an organism or substance) sensitive to light. —**pho·to·sen·si·ti·sa·tion** (-tī-záysh'n ‖ U.S. -ti-) *n.*

pho·to·sen·si·tive (fṓtō-sén-sətiv) *adj.* Sensitive to light. —**pho·to·sen·si·tiv·i·ty** (-sə-tívvəti) *n.*

pho·to·set (fṓtō-set) *tr.v.* **-set, -setting, -sets.** *Printing.* To photocompose.

pho·to·sphere (fṓt-ə-sfeer, -ō-) *n.* The surface of a star, especially of the Sun. —**pho·to·spher·ic** (-sférrik ‖ -sféer-ik) *adj.*

Pho·to·stat (fṓt-ō-stat, -ə-) *n.* **1.** A trademark used for a device used to make quick, directly readable negative or positive photographic copies of written, printed, or graphic material. **2.** *Sometimes small* **p.** A copy made by Photostat.
~*tr.v.* **Photostatted** or *U.S.* **-stated, -statting** or *U.S.* **-stating, -stats.** *Often small* **p.** To make a copy by Photostat. [PHOTO- + -STAT.] —**Pho·to·stat·ter** *n.* —**Pho·to·stat·ic** (-státtik) *adj.*

pho·to·syn·the·sis (fṓtō-síntha-siss) *n.* **1.** The process by which chlorophyll-containing cells in green plants convert incident light to chemical energy and synthesise organic compounds from inorganic compounds, especially carbohydrates from carbon dioxide and water, with the simultaneous release of oxygen. **2.** A similar process occurring in certain bacteria. —**pho·to·syn·thet·ic** (-sin-théttik) *adj.* —**pho·to·syn·thet·i·cal·ly** *adv.*

pho·to·syn·the·sise, pho·to·syn·the·size (fṓtō-síntha-sīz) *v.* **-sised, -sising, -sises.** —*tr.* To synthesise by the process of photosynthesis. —*intr.* To perform the process of photosynthesis.

pho·to·tax·is (fṓtō-táksiss) *n.* Also **pho·to·tax·y** (-taksi). *Biology.* The movement of an organism in response to a source of light. [PHOTO- + -TAXIS.] —**pho·to·tac·tic** (-táktik) *adj.*

pho·to·tel·e·graph (fṓtō-télli-graaf, -graf) *tr.v.* **-graphed, -graphing, -graphs.** To transmit (printed or other graphic material) by facsimile *(see).* —**pho·to·te·leg·ra·phy** (-ti-léggrəfi) *n.* —**pho·to·tel·e·graph·ic** (-gráffik), **pho·to·tel·e·graph·i·cal** *adj.* —**pho·to·tel·e·graph·i·cal·ly** *adv.*

pho·to·ther·a·py (fṓtō-thérrəpi) *n.* The treatment of disease, especially certain skin conditions, with light, including infrared and ultraviolet radiation. Also called "phototherapeutics".

pho·tot·o·nus (fō-tóttənəss) *n. Biology.* Sensitivity of an organism caused by exposure to light. [PHOTO- + TONUS.] —**pho·to·ton·ic** (fṓt-ō-tónnik, -ə-) *adj.*

pho·to·tran·sis·tor (fṓtō-tran-síss-tər, -traan-, -zíss-) *n. Electronics.* A transistor having highly photosensitive electrical characteristics.

pho·tot·ro·pism (fṓtō-trṓp-iz'm, fō-tóttrəp-) *n.* Also **pho·tot·ro·py** (-i). *Botany.* Growth or movement of a plant part in response to a source of light. [PHOTO- + -TROPISM.] —**pho·to·trop·ic** (-tróppik, -trṓpik) *adj.* —**pho·to·trop·i·cal·ly** *adv.*

pho·to·tube (fṓtō-tewb ‖ -tōōb) *n. Electronics.* An electron tube with a photocathode.

pho·to·type·set·ter (fṓtō-típ-settər) *n.* Any of various machines used in photocomposition.

pho·to·type·set·ting (fṓtō-típ-setting) *n. Printing.* **Photocomposition** *(see).*

pho·to·vol·ta·ic (fṓtō-vol-táy-ik ‖ -vōl-) *adj. Electronics.* Capable of producing a voltage when exposed to radiant energy, especially visible light.

photovoltaic effect *n.* The difference in potential produced when electromagnetic radiation falls on a thin film of one solid deposited on the surface of another solid, especially when those solids are semiconductors.

pho·to·zin·co·graph (fṓtō-zíngkə-graaf, -graf) *tr.v.* **-graphed, -graphing, -graphs.** To make (a print) by photozincography.
~*n.* A print produced by photozincography.

pho·to·zin·cog·ra·phy (fṓtō-zing-kóggrəfi) *n.* A photoengraving

process in which sensitised zinc plates are used.

phras·al (fráyz'l) *adj.* Of, pertaining to, or consisting of a phrase or phrases. —**phras·al·ly** *adv.*

phrasal verb *n. Grammar.* A verb combined with an adverb or preposition or both, that functions as a unit and usually means more than the sum of its parts; thus, *give in*, "to yield", *hang back*, "to hesitate", or *put up with* "to tolerate" are phrasal verbs.

phrase (frayz) *n. Abbr.* **phr.** **1.** Any sequence of words intended to have meaning. **2.** A brief, apt, and cogent expression, such as *at a stroke.* **3.** A particular or characteristic style of verbal expression. **4.** *Grammar.* A group of two or more words in sequence that form a syntactic unit or group of syntactic units, but, especially in English, not containing a finite verb. **5.** A series of dance movements forming a unit in a choreographic pattern. **6.** *Music.* A segment of a composition constituting a more or less distinctive melody, usually consisting of about four bars and ending in a cadence.
~*tr.v.* **phrased, phrasing, phrases.** **1.** To express in words: *a tactfully phrased reply.* **2.** To pace or mark off (something read aloud or spoken) by pauses. **3.** *Music.* To divide (a passage) into phrases. [Latin *phrasis*, from Greek, speech, style of speech, from *phrazein*, to show, explain.]

phrase book *n.* A book, often pocket-sized, that gives common and useful expressions in a foreign language with their translations.

phrase marker *n. Linguistics.* The representation of a sentence's grammatical structure, usually by a tree diagram.

phra·se·o·gram (fráyzi-ə-gram, -ō-) *n.* A symbol, such as one used in shorthand, that denotes a particular phrase.

phra·se·o·graph (fráyzi-ə-graaf, -ō-, -graf) *n.* A phrase having a phraseogram. —**phra·se·o·graph·ic** (-gráffik) *adj.*

phra·se·ol·o·gist (fráyzi-ólləjist) *n.* A person who uses epigrammatic phrases or a particular phraseology.

phra·se·ol·o·gy (fráyzi-ólləji) *n., pl.* **-gies.** **1.** The way in which words and phrases are used in speech or writing; style. **2.** The characteristic mode of expression used by a particular person or group; parlance: *nautical phraseology.* [New Latin *phraseologia* : PHRASE + -LOGY.] —**phra·se·o·log·i·cal** (-ə-lójik'l) *adj.*

phras·ing (fráyzing) *n.* **1.** The manner in which an expression is phrased; wording. **2.** *Music.* **a.** The division of a passage into phrases. **b.** The manner in which phrases are rendered or interpreted as in a performance.

phra·try (fráytri) *n., pl.* **-tries.** **1.** In ancient Greece, a subdivision of a tribe or phyle, being originally a kinship group and surviving in classical Athens as a division in the political and military organisation of the state. **2.** *Anthropology.* An exogamous subdivision of the tribe, comprising two or more related clans. [Greek *phratria*, from *phratēr*, fellow clan member.] —**phra·tric** (fráytrik) *adj.*

Phraya. See **Chao Praya.**

phre·at·ic (free-áttik) *adj. Geology.* Of, pertaining to, or designating **ground water** *(see).* [Greek *phrear* (stem *phreat-*), a well.]

-phrenia *n. comb. form.* Indicates mental disorder; for example, **schizophrenia.** [Greek *phrēn*, mind.]

phren·ic (frénnik ‖ fréenik) *adj.* **1.** *Archaic.* Of or pertaining to the mind. **2.** *Anatomy.* Of or pertaining to the diaphragm: *the phrenic nerve.* [New Latin *phrenicus* : PHREN(O)- + -IC.]

phre·ni·tis (fri-nítiss, fre-) *n. Pathology.* **1.** **Encephalitis** *(see).* **2.** Inflammation of the diaphragm. **3.** Frenzy; delirium. [Late Latin *phrenītis*, from Greek *phrenitis* : *phrēn*, diaphragm, mind + -ITIS.] —**phre·nit·ic** (-níttik) *adj.*

phreno-, phren- *comb. form.* Indicates: **1.** The mind; for example, **phrenology.** **2.** The diaphragm; for example, **phrenic.** [Greek *phrēn*, diaphragm, mind.]

phre·nol·o·gy (frénnə-lójik ‖ freénə-) *n. Abbr.* **phrenol.** The now discredited practice of studying character and mental capacity from the shape and irregularities of the skull. [PHRENO- + -LOGY.] —**phren·o·log·i·cal** (-ə-lójik ‖ freénə-), **phren·o·log·i·cal·ly** *adv.* —**phre·nol·o·gist** (-nóllə-jist) *n.*

Phryg·i·a (friji-ə). Former kingdom of western and central Asia Minor. It reached the peak of its prosperity in the eighth century B.C.

Phryg·i·an (friji-ən) *adj.* **1.** Of or pertaining to Phrygia or its people, language, and culture. **2.** *Music.* **a.** Of or designating a mode of the ancient Greeks. **b.** Of or designating an authentic church mode with tonic E and dominant C.
~*n.* **1.** A native or inhabitant of Phrygia. **2.** The Indo-European language of the Phrygians.

Phrygian cap *n.* A soft cap with a forward-curving peak, represented in ancient Greek art as part of the attire worn by Phrygians. Compare **liberty cap.**

PHS Public Health Service (in the United States).

phthal·ein (tháy-leen, fthál-, thál-, -i-in) *n.* Any of a group of chemical compounds formed by a combination of phthalic anhydride with a phenol, from which certain synthetic dyes are derived. [PHTHAL(IC) + -EIN.]

phthal·ic (thál-ik, fthál-, tháyl-) *adj. Chemistry.* **1.** Of, pertaining to, or derived from naphthalene. **2.** Pertaining to phthalic acid. [Short for *naphthalic* : (NA)PHTH(A) + AL(COHOL) + -IC.]

phthalic acid *n.* A colourless, crystalline organic acid, $C_6H_4(COOH)_2$, prepared from naphthalene and used in the synthesis of dyes, perfumes, and other organic compounds.

phthalic anhydride *n.* A white, crystalline compound, $C_6H_4(CO)_2O$, used in the manufacture of phthaleins and other dyes, resins, plasticisers, and insecticides.

phthal·in (thál-in, fthál-, tháyl-) *n.* Any of various colourless compounds derived from the reduction of phthaleins.

phthal·o·cy·a·nine (thál-ō-sī-ə-neen, fthál-, tháyl-) *n.* Any of several stable, light-fast, blue or green organic pigments derived from the basic compound $(C_6H_4C_2N)_4N_4$, and used in enamels, printing inks, linoleum, and plastics. [PHTHAL(IC) + CYANINE.]

phthi·ri·a·sis (thi-rī-ə-siss ‖ *U.S. also* thī-) *n. Pathology.* Infestation with lice; pediculosis. [Latin *phthiriasis*, from Greek *phtheiriasis* : *phtheir*, louse + -IASIS.]

phthis·ic (tízzik, thī-sik, fthī-) *n. Archaic.* **1. Phthisis** *(see).* **2. Asthma** *(see).* [From Middle English *ptisike*, from Old French *tisique*, from Latin *phthisicus*, from Greek *phthisikos*, consumptive, from *phthisis*, PHTHISIS.] —**phthis·ic, phthis·i·cal** *adj.*

phthi·sis (thī-siss, fthī-, tī-) *n.* Also *archaic* **phthis·ic** (-sik, tízzik). *Pathology.* **1. Tuberculosis** *(see)* of the lungs. **2.** Wasting away or emaciation and atrophy of the body or part of the body. [Latin, from Greek, from Greek *phthinein*, *phthien*, to decay, waste away.]

phut (fut) *n.* A heavy, dull sound, as of impact with an inflatable object. —**go phut.** *Informal.* To collapse or fail. [Hindi *phatnā*, burst, collapse (imitative).]

phyco– *comb. form.* Indicates algae; for example, **phycology.** [Greek *phukos†*, seaweed.]

phy·col·o·gy (fī-kóllə-ji) *n.* The branch of botany concerned with the study of algae. [PHYCO- + -LOGY.] —**phy·co·log·i·cal** (fīkə-lójik'l) *adj.* —**phy·col·o·gist** (-kóllə-jist) *n.*

phy·co·my·cete (fīkō-mī-seet, -mī-séet) *n. Botany.* Any of various filamentous aquatic fungi, including certain moulds and mildews. [New Latin *phycomycetes* : PHYCO- + -MYCETE.] —**phy·co·my·ce·tous** (-séetəss) *adj.*

phy·la. Plural of **phylum.**

phy·lac·ter·y (fi-láktəri) *n., pl.* **-ies. 1.** *Judaism.* Either of two small leather boxes, each containing strips of parchment inscribed with quotations from the Hebrew Scriptures. One is strapped to the forehead and the other to the left arm by religiously observant Jewish men during morning worship, except on Sabbath and holidays. **2.** *Literary.* **a.** An amulet **b.** A reminder. [Middle English *filakterie*, from Late Latin *phylactērium*, from Greek *phulaktērion*, safeguard, from *phulaktēr*, guard, from *phulax* (stem *phulak-*), guard.]

phy·lax·is (fi-lák-siss) *n.* Inhibiting of infection by the body. [Greek *phulaxis*, "a guarding", from *phulassein*, to guard.] —**phy·lac·tic** (-tik) *adj.*

phy·le (fī-li) *n., pl.* **-lae** (-lee). A large grouping of citizens, based on kinship, constituting the largest political subdivision of an ancient Greek city-state. [Greek *phulē*, tribe.] —**phy·lic** *adj.*

phy·let·ic (fī-léttik) *adj. Biology.* Of, pertaining to, or reflecting the phylogeny or evolutionary development of an organism. [New Latin *phylesis*, a genus development, from Greek *phulon*, tribe, class, race.] —**phy·let·i·cal·ly** *adv.*

–phyll *n. comb. form.* Indicates leaf; for example, **chlorophyll.** [Greek *phullon*, leaf.]

phyl·lite (fíl-īt) *n.* A metamorphic rock, similar to slate but often having a wavy, silky lustre, and a distinctive cleavage. [PHYLL(O)- + -ITE.]

phyllo–, phyll– *comb. form.* Indicates leaf; for example, **phylloclade.** [New Latin, from Greek *phullon*, leaf.]

phyl·lo·clade (fíl-ō-klayd, -ə-) *n.* Also **phyl·lo·clad** (-klad). *Botany.* A **cladophyll** *(see).* [New Latin *phyllocladium* : PHYLLO- + Greek *klados*, a branch.]

phyl·lode (fíl-ōd) *n. Botany.* Also **phyl·lo·di·um** (fi-lódi-əm) *pl.* **-dia** (-ə). A flattened leafstalk that performs the functions of a leaf. [New Latin *phyllodium*, from Greek *phullōdēs*, like a leaf : PHYLL(O)- + -ODE (like).] —**phyl·lo·di·al** *adj.*

phyl·loid (fíl-oyd) *adj. Botany.* Resembling a leaf; leaflike. [New Latin *phylloides* : PHYLL(O)- + -OID.]

phyl·lome (fíl-ōm) *n. Botany.* A leaf, or a plant structure that functions as a leaf. [PHYLL(O)- + -OME.] —**phyl·lom·ic** (fí-lómik, -lómmik) *adj.*

phyl·loph·a·gous (fi-lóffəgəss) *adj. Zoology.* Feeding on leaves. [PHYLLO- + -PHAGOUS.]

phyl·lo·pod (fíllə-pod) *n.* Any of various crustaceans of the order Phyllopoda, having swimming and respiratory appendages that resemble leaves.
~*adj.* Also **phyl·lop·o·dous** (fi-lóppədəss). **1.** Possessing leaflike feet. **2.** Of or pertaining to the phyllopods. [New Latin *phyllopoda*, "leaf-footed" : PHYLLO- + -POD.] —**phyl·lop·o·dan** (fi-lóppədən) *adj. & n.*

phyl·lo·qui·none (fíllō-kwi-nōn) *n.* A form of **vitamin K** *(see)*, occurring in plants.

phyl·lo·tax·y (fíllə-taksi) *n.* Also **phyl·lo·tax·is** (-táksiss). *Botany.* **1.** The arrangement of leaves on a stem. **2.** The principles governing leaf arrangement. [New Latin : PHYLLO- + -TAXIS.] —**phyl·lo·tac·tic** (-táktik), **phyl·lo·tac·ti·cal** *adj.*

–phyllous *adj. comb. form.* Indicates a specified kind or number of leaves; for example, **heterophyllous.** [New Latin -*phyllus*, from Greek *phullon*, leaf.]

phyl·lox·e·ra (fillok-séer-ə, fi-lóksər-ə) *n., pl.* **-rae** (-ee) or **-ras.** Any of several small insects of the genus *Phylloxera*; especially, *P. vitifoliae*, a species very destructive of grape crops. [New Latin : PHYLLO- + Greek *xēros*, dry.] —**phyl·lox·e·ran** *adj. & n.*

phy·log·e·ny (fī-lójəni) *n., pl.* **-nies.** Also **phy·lo·gen·e·sis** (fīlō-jénnə-siss), *pl.* **-ses** (-seez). *Biology.* The evolutionary development of a species, genus, or other taxonomic rank. Compare **ontogeny.** [Greek *phulē*, tribe, clan, and *phulon*, tribe, race + -GENY.] —**phy·lo·ge·net·ic** (-jə-néttik), **phy·lo·gen·ic** (-jénnik) *adj.* —**phy·lo·ge·net·i·cal·ly** *adv.*

phy·lum (fī-ləm) *n., pl.* **-la** (-lə). **1.** *Biology.* A taxonomic division of the animal kingdom or, less commonly, the plant kingdom, directly above a class in size. **2.** *Linguistics.* A large division of related families of languages or linguistic stocks, especially of the New World. [New Latin, from Greek *phulon*, tribe, class, race.]

phys. 1. physical. **2.** physician. **3.** physicist; physics. **4.** physiological; physiology.

phys·i·at·rics (fízzi-áttriks) *n. Used with a singular verb. U.S.* **Physiotherapy** *(see).* [PHYS(IO)- + -IATRICS.] —**phys·i·at·ric, phys·i·at·ri·cal** *adj.* —**phys·i·at·rist** (-áttrist) *n.*

phys·ic (fízzik) *n. Archaic.* **1.** Any medicine or drug. **2.** A cathartic. **3.** The art of healing or profession of medicine. **4.** Physics.
~*tr.v.* **physicked, -icking, -ics.** *Archaic.* **1.** To treat with or as if with medicine. **2.** To act upon as a cathartic; purge. [Middle English *fisike*, from Old French *fisique*, from Latin *physica*, natural medicine or science, physics, from Greek *phusikē*, from *phusikos*, natural, from *phusis*, nature, from *phuein*, to bring forth, make grow.]

phys·i·cal (fízzik'l) *adj. Abbr.* **phys. 1.** Of or pertaining to the body, as distinguished from the mind or spirit; bodily; corporeal: *physical strength.* **2.** Of or pertaining to material things: *physical environment.* **3.** Of or pertaining to matter and energy or the sciences dealing with them, especially physics. **4. a.** Highly conscious of or communicating through one's body. **b.** Involving a great deal of physical contact: *a physical game, with a lot of hard tackles.*
~*n. U.S.* A physical examination. [Middle English *phisycal*, from Medieval Latin *physicālis*, medicinal, from Latin *physica*, natural medicine. See physic.] —**phys·i·cal·ly** *adv.*

physical anthropology *n.* The science of human evolutionary biology, genetic development, racial variation, and classification. Also called "somatology". Compare **cultural anthropology.**

physical chemistry *n.* The scientific analysis of the properties and behaviour of chemical systems primarily by physical theory and technique as, for example, the thermodynamic analysis of macroscopic chemical phenomena.

physical education *n. Abbr.* **PE.** Education, training, and practice in physical exercise, team games, gymnastics, and the like, especially as part of a school curriculum.

physical examination *n.* A medical examination to detect illness or dysfunction and, especially, to determine physical fitness for a particular activity or service. Also *British* "medical", *U.S.* "physical".

physical geography *n.* The study of the natural features of the Earth's surface, including land forms, oceans, seas, soils, the atmosphere, and the distribution of fauna and flora. Also called "physiography".

phys·i·cal·ism (fízzik'l-iz'm) *n. Philosophy.* The doctrine that all phenomena can be described in terms of time and space, and consequently that any meaningful statement other than an analytic and tautologous one, can in principle be reduced to an empirically verifiable physical statement. —**phys·i·cal·ist** (-istik) *adj.* —**phys·i·cal·is·tic** (-istik) *adj.*

physical jerks *pl.n. British Informal.* Physical exercises.

physical medicine *n.* The branch of medicine that treats physical disabilities, such as those resulting from rheumatism or polio.

physical quantity *n. Physics.* A **quantity** *(see).*

physical science *n.* Any of the sciences, such as physics, chemistry, astronomy, and geology, that analyses the nature and properties of energy and nonliving matter. Compare **life science.**

physical therapy *n. U.S.* **Physiotherapy** *(see).*

phy·si·cian (fi-zísh'n) *n. Abbr.* **phys. 1.** A person qualified to practise medicine, especially in areas other than surgery; a medical doctor. **2.** *Archaic.* Any person who heals or exerts a healing influence. [Middle English *fisicien*, from Old French, from *fisique*, PHYSIC.]

phys·i·cist (fízzi-sist) *n. Abbr.* **phys.** A scientist who specialises in physics.

phys·i·co·chem·i·cal (fízzikō-kémmik'l) *adj.* Of or pertaining to physical chemistry or the physical and chemical aspects of a phenomenon. [*Physico-*, "physics and", + CHEMICAL.]

phys·ics (fízziks) *n. Abbr.* **phys. 1.** *Used with a singular verb.* The science of matter and energy and of interactions between the two. It is based on mathematics and grouped in traditional fields such as acoustics, optics, mechanics, thermodynamics, and electromagnetism. In modern physics, relativity and quantum theory are used and other areas of study include atomic and nuclear physics, cryogenics, solid-state physics, particle physics, and astrophysics. **2.** *Used with a plural verb.* Physical properties, interactions, processes, or laws: *the physics of supersonic flight.* **3.** *Used with a singular verb. Archaic.* The study of the natural or material world and phenomena; natural science or natural philosophy. [Plural of PHYSIC (translation of Latin plural *physica*, natural science).]

physio–, phys– *comb. form.* Indicates: **1.** Natural or nature; for example, **physiography. 2.** Physical; for example, **physiotherapy.** [Greek *phusio-*, from *phusis*, nature, from *phuein*, to make grow.]

phys·i·og·no·my (fízzi-ónnə-mi ‖ -óg-nə-) *n., pl.* **-mies. 1.** The art or practice of judging human character from facial features. **2.** Facial features, especially when regarded as revealing character. **3.** The aspect and character of an inanimate or abstract entity: *the physiognomy of the Midlands.* [Learned respelling of Middle English *fysnamye*, *phisnomye*, from Old French *phizonomie*, from Medieval Latin *physionomia*, from Late Greek *phusiognōmia*, short for Greek *phusiognōmonia* : PHYSIO- + *gnōmōn*, "judge", "interpreter".] —**phys·i·og·nom·ic** (-ə-nómmik ‖ -əg-), **phys·i·og·nom·i·cal** *adj.* —**phys·i·og·nom·i·cal·ly** *adv.* —**phys·i·og·no·mist** (-mist) *n.*

phys·i·og·ra·phy (fízzi-óggrə-fi) *n.* **Physical geography** *(see).* [PHYSIO- + -GRAPHY.] —**phys·i·og·ra·pher** (-fər) *n.* —**phys·i·o·graph·ic** (-ə-gráffik), **phys·i·o·graph·i·cal** *adj.* —**phys·i·o·graph·i·cal·ly** *adv.*

phys·i·o·log·i·cal (fízzi-ə-lójik'l) *adj.* **1.** Of or pertaining to physiology. **2.** In accordance with or characteristic of the normal functioning of a living organism. —**phys·i·o·log·i·cal·ly** *adv.*

physiological saline *n.* A salt solution, **saline** *(see).*

phys·i·ol·o·gy (fízzi-óllə-ji) *n. Abbr.* **phys., physiol. 1.** The biological science of essential and characteristic life processes, activities, and functions. **2.** All the vital processes of an organism, organ, or tissue. [Latin *physiologia,* from Greek *phusiologia,* study of nature : PHYSIO- + -LOGY.] —**phys·i·ol·o·gist** *n.*

phys·i·o·ther·a·py (fízzi-ō-thérrə-pi) *n. Medicine.* The study or practice of the therapeutic use of physical methods or agents, such as remedial exercises, massage, or infrared and ultraviolet rays. Also *U.S.* "physical therapy", "physiatrics". —**phys·i·o·ther·a·peu·tic** (-péwtik) *adj.* —**phys·i·o·ther·a·pist** *n.*

phy·sique (fi-zéek) *n.* The body, considered with reference to its proportions, muscular development, and appearance: *a muscular physique.* [French, from adjective, "physical", from Latin *physicus,* natural, from Greek *phusikos;* see **physic.**]

phy·so·clis·tous (fī-sō-klístəss) *adj.* Having an air bladder that is not joined to the alimentary canal, as in certain fishes. [Greek *phusa,* bladder + *-clistous,* from Greek *kleistos,* closed.]

phy·so·stig·mine (fī-sō-stíg-meen) *n.* A colourless or pink alkaloid, $C_{15}H_{21}N_3O_2$, extracted from the Calabar bean, and used especially in eyedrops to restrict the size of the pupil and to relieve pressure in the eyeball. Also called "eserine". [New Latin *Physostigma* (genus of the Calabar bean) : Greek *phusa,* bellows, bladder + STIGMA.]

phy·sos·to·mous (fī-sóstəməss) *adj.* Having a connecting tube between the air bladder and a part of the alimentary canal, as in certain fishes. [Greek *phusa,* bellows, bladder + -STOME + -OUS.]

-phyte *n. comb. form. Botany.* Indicates a plant with a specified character or habitat; for example, **xerophyte.** [Greek *phuton,* plant, from *phuein,* to make grow.]

phyto-, phyt- *comb. form.* Indicates plant or plant life; for example, **phytogenesis.** [New Latin, from Greek *phuto-,* from *phuton,* plant, from *phuein,* to make grow.]

phy·to·gen·e·sis (fītō-jénnə-siss) *n.* Also **phy·tog·e·ny** (fī-tójəni). The origin and evolutionary development of plants. [PHYTO- + -GENESIS.] —**phy·to·ge·net·ic** (-jə-néttik) *adj.* —**phy·to·ge·net·i·cal·ly** *adv.*

phy·to·gen·ic (fītō-jénnik) *adj.* Also **phy·tog·e·nous** (fī-tójənəss). Having a plant origin, as coal has. [PHYTO- + -GENIC.]

phy·to·ge·og·ra·phy (fītō-ji-óggrə-fi) *n.* The study of the distribution of plants. —**phy·to·ge·og·ra·pher** (-fər) *n.* —**phy·to·ge·o·graph·i·cal** (-jée-ə-gráffik'l), **phy·to·ge·o·graph·ic** *adj.*

phy·tog·ra·phy (fī-tóggrəfi) *n.* The science of plant description; descriptive botany. [PHYTO- + -GRAPHY.]

phy·to·hor·mone (fītō-hór-mōn) *n.* A **growth substance** *(see).*

phy·to·lite (fīt-ō-līt, -ə-) *n.* Also **phy·to·lith** (-lith). A fossil plant. [PHYTO- + -LITE.]

phy·tol·o·gy (fī-tóllə-ji) *n.* The study of plants; botany. [New Latin *phytologia* : PHYTO- + -LOGY.] —**phy·to·log·ic** (fītə-lójik), **phy·to·log·i·cal** *adj.*

phy·ton (fī-ton) *n.* A segment of a plant sufficiently large to be able to grow independently if given appropriate conditions. [New Latin, from Greek *phuton,* plant, from *phuein,* to make grow.] —**phy·ton·ic** (fī-tónnik) *adj.*

phy·to·pa·thol·o·gy (fītō-pə-thóllə-ji) *n.* The study of the origin, nature, and prevention of plant diseases. —**phy·to·path·o·log·i·cal** *adj.* —**phy·to·pa·thol·o·gist** (-jist) *n.*

phy·toph·a·gous (fī-tóffə-gəss) *adj.* Feeding on plants, including shrubs and trees. Said especially of certain insects. [PHYTO- + -PHAGOUS.] —**phy·toph·a·gy** (-ji) *n.*

phy·to·plank·ton (fīt-ō-plángk-tən, -ə-) *n.* Minute, floating aquatic plants. —**phy·to·plank·ton·ic** (-tónnik) *adj.*

phy·to·so·ci·ol·o·gy (fītō-sō-si-óllə-ji ‖ -shi-) *n.* The branch of ecology that deals with the characteristics, relationships, and distribution of associated plants. —**phy·to·so·ci·o·log·i·cal** (-ə-lójik'l) *adj.* —**phy·to·so·ci·o·log·i·cal·ly** *adv.* —**phy·to·so·ci·ol·o·gist** (-jist) *n.*

phy·to·tox·ic (fītō-tóksik) *adj.* Poisonous to plants. —**phy·to·tox·ic·i·ty** (-tok-síssəti) *n.*

phy·to·tox·in *n.* Any poison, such as curare or strychnine, that is derived from a plant.

phy·to·tron (fītō-tron) *n.* A building, often divided into many compartments, in which plants can be grown under controlled conditions. [PHYTO- + -TRON.]

pi¹ (pī) *n., pl.* **pis. 1.** The 16th letter in the Greek alphabet, written Π, π. Transliterated in English as *P, p.* **2.** *Symbol* π *Mathematics.* A transcendental number, approximately 3.14159, representing the ratio of the circumference to the diameter of a circle and appearing as a constant in a wide range of mathematical problems. [Greek. The mathematical sense is from the first letter of Greek *periphireia,* PERIPHERY, and *perimetros,* PERIMETER.]

pi² *Chiefly U.S.* Variant of **pie** (printing).

pi³ *adj. British Informal.* Pious; sanctimonious. [Shortening.]

pi·a (pí-ə, píе-ə) *n. Anatomy.* The pia mater. —**pi·al** *adj.*

pi·ac·u·lar (pī-áckewlər) *adj.* In the Christian Church: **1.** Making expiation or atonement for a sacrilege: *piacular sacrifice.* **2.** Requiring expiation; wicked; blameworthy. [Latin *piāculāris,* from *piāculum,* sin offering, propitiatory sacrifice, from *piāre,* to appease, atone for, from *pius,* pious.]

Piaf (pée-af, p-yaff), **Edith,** born Edith Giovanna Gassion (1915–63). French cabaret singer. Her songs include *Milord, La vie en rose,* and *Non, je ne regrette rien,* which became a personal anthem.

pi·affe (pi-áf) *intr.v.* **piaffed, piaffing, piaffes.** In dressage, to perform the piaffer. [French *piaffer,* to strut.]

pi·af·fer (pi-áffər) *n.* A dressage movement in which a horse trots very slowly or on the spot with high action of the legs. [French, from *piaffer,* to strut.]

Pia·get (pee-á-zhay, -áa-), **Jean** (1896–1980). Swiss child psychologist. He studied the development of intellectual awareness through the successive stages of childhood, systematically observing changes in such conceptions as justice and guilt.

pi·a ma·ter (pī-ə máytər, pée-ə máatər) *n. Anatomy.* The fine vascular membrane that envelops the brain and spinal cord under the arachnoid membrane and the dura mater. Also called "pia". [Medieval Latin (translation of Arabic *al'umm ragīgah,* "tender mother").]

pi·an·ism (péer-niz'm, pée-ə-, pi-ánniz'm) *n.* Technique, artistry, or execution in piano playing.

pi·a·nis·si·mo (pée-ə-níssi-mō, peer-, pée-aa-) *adv. Abbr.* **pp, pp.** *Music.* Very softly or quietly. Used as a direction. ~*n., pl.* **pianissimos.** *Music.* A part of a composition that is to be played pianissimo. [Italian, superlative of PIANO (softly).] —**pi·a·nis·si·mo** *adj.*

pi·an·ist (péer-nist, pée-ə-, pi-ánnist) *n.* One who plays the piano.

pi·a·nis·tic (péer-nístik, pée-ə-) *adj.* **1.** Of or pertaining to the piano. **2.** Well-adapted to the piano. —**pi·a·nis·ti·cal·ly** *adv.*

pi·an·o¹ (p-yánnō, -yáanō, pi-ánnō, -áanō) *n., pl.* **-os.** A musical instrument with a manual keyboard actuating hammers that strike wire strings set vertically in an upright frame or horizontally in a roughly triangular frame, producing sounds that may be softened or sustained by means of pedals. [Italian, short for PIANOFORTE.]

pi·a·no² (p-yáanō, pi-áanō) *adv. Abbr.* **p, p.** *Music.* Softly; quietly. Used as a direction. ~*n., pl.* **pianos.** *Music.* A passage to be played softly. [Italian, from Late Latin *plānus,* smooth, from Latin, even.] —**pi·a·no** *adj.*

piano accordion *n.* An accordion that has a piano-like keyboard played by the right hand.

pi·an·o·for·te (p-yánnō-fórt-i, -yáanō-, pi·áanō-, -fawrti ‖ *U.S. also* -fawrt, -fōrt) *n.* A piano. [Italian, from *piano e forte,* soft and loud.]

Pi·a·no·la (peer-nōlə, pée-ə-, p-ya-) *n.* A trademark for a mechanical piano that plays music automatically according to the perforations on a paper roll by means of pedal-operated bellows.

piano player *n.* **1.** A pianist. **2.** Any of various automatic devices for playing a piano.

piano trio *n.* **1.** An instrumental ensemble for playing chamber music, consisting of a piano, violin, and cello. **2.** A piece of music written for such an ensemble.

pi·as·sa·va (pée-ə-sáavə) *n.* Also **pi·as·sa·ba** (-sáabə). **1.** Either of two Brazilian palm trees, *Attalea funifera* or *Leopoldinia piassaba,* from which a strong, coarse fibre is obtained. **2.** The fibre of either of these trees, used for making ropes, brushes, and brooms. [Portuguese *piassaba,* from Tupi *piaçába.*]

pi·as·ter, pi·as·tre (pi-ástər, pée-astər) *n.* **1.** A coin equal to $1/100$ of the pound of Egypt, Lebanon, Sudan, and Syria. **2.** The basic monetary unit of the former South Vietnam, equal to 100 cents. **3.** Formerly, a Spanish dollar; a piece of eight. [French *piastre,* from Italian *piastra (d'argento),* plate (of silver), from Latin *emplastra, emplastrum,* PLASTER.]

pi·az·za (pi-átsə, -ádzə, -áatsə, -áazə ‖ *U.S.* -ázzə, -áazə) *n., pl.* **-zas** (for all senses) or **piazze** (-átsay, -áatsay) (for sense 1). **1.** A public square in an Italian town. **2.** *British.* A roofed and arcaded passageway; a colonnade. **3.** *U.S.* A verandah; a porch. [Italian, from Latin *platea,* broad street, courtyard, from Greek *plateia,* from *platus,* broad, flat.]

pi·broch (pée-brok, -brokḥ) *n.* A series of variations on a traditional dirge or martial theme for the highland bagpipes. [Scottish Gaelic *piobaireachd,* pipe music, from *piobair,* piper, from *píob,* pipe.]

pi·ca¹ (píkə) *n.* **1.** A printer's unit of type size, equal to 12 points or about 0.42 centimetres ($1/6$ inch). **2.** An equivalent unit of composition measurement used in determining the dimensions of lines, illustrations, or printed pages. **3.** A size of letters in typewriting, having 10 characters to the inch, the equivalent of 12-point printing type. [Probably from Anglo-Latin *pīca,* PIE (church almanac).]

pica² *n.* A craving for unnatural food such as mud or cloth, as occurs occasionally in hysteria and pregnancy. [New Latin, from Latin *pīca,* magpie (from its omnivorous nature).]

pic·a·dor (píckə-dawr; *Spanish* péeka-thór) *n., pl.* **-dors** or **-dores** (-tháwrayss). A horseman in a bullfight who lances the bull's neck muscles so that it will tend to keep its head low for the subsequent stages. [Spanish, from *picar,* to prick, pierce. See **picaro.**]

Pic·ar·dy (píckərdi). *French* **Picardie.** Region and former province of northern France, now mainly in the Somme département. Stretching from the English Channel along the rivers Somme and Oise, its main industries are agriculture and the production of textiles. It was the scene of heavy fighting during both World Wars.

pic·a·resque (píckə-résk ‖ *U.S. also* péekə-) *adj.* **1.** Of or involving clever rogues or adventurers. **2.** Of, pertaining to, or characteristic of the *picaresque novel,* in which the rogue-hero and his escapades are depicted episodically with broad realism and satire. [French, from Spanish *picaresco,* from *picaro,* rogue, PICARO.]

pic·a·ro (píckə-rō, péekə-) *n., pl.* **-ros** (-rōz; *Spanish* -rōss). An adventurer; a rogue. [Spanish, "rogue", from *picar,* to wound lightly, "to prick", from Vulgar Latin *piccāre* (unattested), to pick, from *piccus* (unattested), woodpecker, from Latin *pīcus.*]

pic·a·roon (píckə-ro͞on) *n.* **1. a.** A pirate. **b.** A rogue or thief. **2.** A pirate ship.

~intr.v. **picarooned, -rooning, -roons.** To act as a pirate. [Spanish *picarón,* augmentative of *picaro,* PICARO.]

Pi·cas·so (pi-kássō || *U.S. also* -kaá-sō), **Pablo (Ruiz y),** (1881–1973). Spanish painter, perhaps the most prolific and versatile artist of this century. Among his many works are *Les Demoiselles d'Avignon* (1907) and *Guernica* (1937).

pic·a·yune (píckə-yo͞on || *U.S.* pícki-) *adj. U.S.* **1.** Of little value or importance; paltry. **2.** *Informal.* Petty; mean.

~n. **1.** A Spanish-American coin, a half real, formerly used in parts of the southern United States. **2.** In the United States, a five-cent piece. **3.** *Chiefly U.S. Informal.* Something of very small value; a trifle: *not worth a picayune.* [French *picaillon,* small copper coin, from Provençal *picaioun*†.]

pic·ca·lil·li (píckə-lílli) *n., pl.* **-lis.** A pickled relish made of various chopped vegetables, mustard, and hot spices. [Perhaps blend of PICKLE and CHILLI.]

pic·ca·nin (píckə-nin) *n. Chiefly South African Informal.* A black African child. [Shortened from PICCANINNY.]

pic·ca·nin·ny (píckə-ninni) *n., pl.* **-nies.** Also *chiefly U.S.* **pick·a·nin·ny.** A small black or Aboriginal child. Often considered offensive.

~adj. Very small; tiny. [Originally West Indian, from Spanish *pequeño,* small, or Portuguese *pequenino,* little one, from *pequeno,* small.]

pic·co·lo¹ (píckə-lō) *n., pl.* **-los.** A small flute pitched an octave above a regular flute. [Shortened from *piccolo flute,* from PICCOLO (adjective).]

piccolo² *adj.* Designating a musical instrument considerably smaller than the usual size: *a piccolo trumpet; a piccolo concertina.* [Italian *piccolo*†, small.]

pice (pīss) *n., pl.* **pice.** An Indian coin of low value, a **paisa** *(see).*

pi·ce·ous (pī-si-əss) *adj.* **1.** Of, pertaining to, or resembling pitch. **2.** Glossy black in colour. [Latin *piceus,* from *pix* (stem *pic-*), pitch.]

pich·i·ci·e·go (píchi-see-áygō) *n.* Also **pich·i·ci·a·go** (-áygō, -aágō) *pl.* **-gos. 1.** An extremely small armadillo, *Chlamyphorus truncatus,* of Argentina, having pale-pink armour and white hair. **2.** A similar South American armadillo, *Burmeisteria retusa,* having yellow-brown armour and whitish hair. [Spanish, perhaps from Guarani *pichey,* armadillo + Spanish *ciego,* blind, from Latin *caecus.*]

pick¹ (pik) *v.* **picked, picking, picks.** *—tr.* **1.** To select from or as if from a group: *picked the best.* **2. a.** To pull or pluck off: *pick an apple.* **b.** To gather in by picking: *pick cotton.* **c.** To gather the harvest from: *picked a field.* **3. a.** To remove the outer covering of; pluck: *pick a chicken clean of feathers.* **b.** To tear off bit by bit: *pick meat from the bones.* **4. a.** To probe (the teeth or nose, for example) to remove extraneous matter. **b.** To scratch or try to remove (a spot, for example) with the fingernails. **5.** To untangle and isolate (threads) as in weaving. **6.** To break up, pierce, or dig by means of a sharp, pointed instrument, such as a pick. **7.** To make (a hole) with a sharp instrument. **8.** To seek and discover (a flaw): *He picked holes in their argument.* **9.** To take up (food) with the beak; peck: *The parrot picked its seed.* **10. a.** To steal the contents of (a person's pocket). **b.** To steal (money, for example) from a person's pocket. **11.** To open (a lock) without the use of the key. **12.** To make (one's way) carefully: *picked her way through the mud.* **13.** To provoke: *pick a fight.* **14.** To pluck the strings of (a musical instrument). *—intr.* **1.** To decide with care or forethought: *pick and choose.* **2.** To work with a pick. **3.** To harvest or gather fruit, crops, or the like. **4.** To eat food sparingly and without apparent appetite: *just picked at his meal.* —See Synonyms at **choose.** **—pick at.** *Informal.* To find fault with or make petty criticisms about; nag: *She picks at him day and night.* **—pick off.** To shoot after singling out: *I picked the ducks off one by one.* **—pick on. 1.** To tease or bully. **2.** To select, especially for something unpleasant. **—pick out. 1. a.** To discern from the surroundings; distinguish: *At last we managed to pick out his face in the crowd.* **b.** To cause to stand out by the use of a different colour; distinguish from a background: *pick out the design in green.* **c.** To distinguish or select from a mass of detail. **2.** To play (music) slowly by or as if by ear: *He managed to pick out the tune.* **—pick over.** To sort out or examine item by item, especially in order to select the best.

~n. **1.** The act of picking, especially with a pointed instrument. **2.** The act of selecting or choosing; choice: *Take your pick.* **3.** That which is selected or regarded as the most desirable; the best or choicest one: *the pick of the crop.* **4.** The amount or quantity of a crop that is picked by hand. **5.** *Printing.* **a.** A particle of dirt or paper caught in type or a printing plate, and causing a mark or smudge on the printed sheet. **b.** The mark so produced. [Middle English *piken,* to pierce, probably from Old French *piquer,* to prick, pick, from Vulgar Latin *piccāre* (unattested), to prick, pierce.]

pick² *n.* **1.** A tool for breaking hard surfaces, consisting of a curved bar sharpened at one or both ends and fitted to a long handle. **2.** Anything used for picking, such as an ice pick or a toothpick. **3.** *Music.* A **plectrum** *(see).* [Middle English *pik,* probably a variant of PIKE (pole).]

pick³ *n.* **1.** A weft thread in weaving. **2.** A passage or throw of the shuttle in a loom.

~tr.v. **picked, picking, picks. 1.** To throw (a shuttle) across the loom. **2.** *Archaic.* To cast; pitch: *"as high as I could pick my lance"* (Shakespeare). [Middle English *pykken,* to throw (a shuttle), to cast, variant of *picchen,* to PITCH.]

pickaback. Variant of **piggyback.**

pickaninny. *Chiefly U.S.* Variant of **piccaninny.**

pick·axe (pík-aks) *n.* A pick, usually with a point at one end of the head and chisel edge at the other.

~v. **pickaxed, -axing, -axes.** *—intr.* To use a pickaxe. *—tr.* To use a pickaxe on. [Alteration (influenced by AXE) of Middle English *pikois, pikeis,* pickaxe, from Old French *picois,* from *pic,* pickaxe, perhaps from *piquer,* to prick. See **picket.**]

picked (pikt) *adj.* Chosen by careful selection.

pick·er¹ (píckər) *n.* **1.** One that picks; especially, a machine or person that harvests crops or gathers fruit. **2.** A machine that separates and cleans the fibres of wool, cotton, or the like.

picker² *n.* In weaving, the part of a loom that throws the shuttle across it.

pick·er·el (píckrəl, píckərəl) *n., pl.* **-els** or collectively **pickerel.** A young pike. [Middle English *pikerel,* diminutive of *pik, pike,* PIKE (fish).]

pick·et (píckit) *n.* **1. a.** A person or persons stationed outside a place of employment, usually during a strike, to express grievance or protest and discourage entry by nonstriking employees or customers. **b.** A person or persons present outside any building to protest. **2.** A pointed stake driven into the ground to support a fence, secure a tent, tether animals, mark points in surveying or, when pointed at the top, serve as part of a defensive barrier. **3.** *Military.* A detachment of one or more soldiers positioned in front of their lines to give advance warning of enemy approach.

~v. **picketed, -eting, -ets.** *—tr.* **1.** To enclose, secure, tether, mark out, or fortify with pickets. **2.** *Military.* **a.** To post as a picket. **b.** To guard with a picket. **3.** To post a picket or act as a picket at (a place of work, for example) during a strike or demonstration. *—intr.* To act or serve as a picket. [French *piquet,* from *piquer,* to prick, from *pic,* PICK (tool).] **—pick·et·er** *n.*

picket fence *n.* A fence of pointed, upright pickets.

picket line *n.* A line or procession of people picketing a place of business or otherwise staging a public protest.

Pick·ford (pík-fərd), **Mary,** born Gladys Mary Smith (1893–1979). U.S. star of the silent screen, born in Canada. Known as "America's Sweetheart", her films included *Pollyanna* (1919).

pick·in (píckin) *n. West African.* A small child. Also *West Indian* "pickney" [Variant of PICCANINNY, or from Portuguese *pequeno,* small.]

pick·ings (píckingz) *pl.n.* Something that is or may be picked, as: **a.** Leftovers. **b.** Profits, spoils, or a share of spoils.

pick·le (píck'l) *n.* **1. a.** *Often plural.* Any edible product, especially vegetables or fruit, that has been preserved and flavoured in a solution of brine or vinegar. **b.** A relish containing such vegetables or fruit. **c.** *Chiefly U.S.* A cucumber thus preserved and flavoured. **2.** A solution of brine or vinegar, often spiced, for preserving and flavouring food. **3.** An acid or other chemical solution used as a bath to remove scale and oxides from the surface of metals before plating or finishing. **4.** *Informal.* A troublesome, embarrassing, or difficult situation. **5.** *British Informal.* A naughty child.

~tr.v. **pickled, -ling, -les. 1.** To preserve or flavour in a solution of brine or vinegar. **2.** To treat (metal) in a chemical bath. [Middle English *pekille,* from Middle Dutch and Middle Low German *pekel*†.]

pick·led (píck'ld) *adj.* **1.** Preserved in or treated with pickle. **2.** *Informal.* Drunk.

pick·lock (pík-lok) *n.* **1.** A person who picks locks; especially, a thief. **2.** An instrument for picking a lock.

pick-me-up (pík-mee-up, -mi-) *n. Informal.* A drink, often alcoholic, taken as a stimulant or restorative.

pick·pock·et (pík-pockit) *n.* One who steals from pockets or handbags.

pick up *tr.v.* **1.** To take up or gather up by hand: *pick up your toys.* **2.** To take on (passengers, freight, survivors, hitchhikers, or the like). **3.** *Informal.* **a.** To go and fetch; collect: *pick the kids up from school.* **b.** To get or acquire without deliberate planning: *pick up a bargain.* **c.** To acquire (skill, knowledge, or understanding) over a period of time. **4.** To bring by chance or intent within sight or hearing: *picked up a foreign station.* **5.** To gain or recover (speed). **6.** *Informal.* To take into custody; arrest: *The coastguard picked up five smugglers.* **7.** To accept the responsibility of paying: *pick up the bill.* **8.** *Slang.* To make casual acquaintance with, usually in anticipation of sexual relations. *—intr.v. Informal.* To improve in condition or activity: *Sales will pick up next autumn.*

pick-up, pick·up (pík-up) *n.* **1. a.** The action or process of picking up: *the pick-up and delivery of farm produce.* **b.** Capacity for acceleration: *a sports car with good pick-up.* **c.** *Informal.* An improvement in condition or activity: *a pick-up in sales.* **2.** *Informal.* **a.** A place where passengers, freight, or the like are picked up. Also used adjectivally: *a pick-up point.* **b.** Passengers, freight, or the like to be picked up. **3.** *Slang.* A stranger with whom casual acquaintance is made, usually in anticipation of sexual relations. Often used derogatorily. **4.** A light truck with an open body and low sides used for making light deliveries. Also called "pick-up truck". **5. a.** *Electronics.* A device that converts the oscillations of a gramophone needle into electrical impulses for subsequent conversion into sound. **b.** A device on an electric guitar that converts the vibrations of the strings into electric signals for subsequent amplification and

conversion into sound. See **crystal pickup, magnetic pickup. 6.** In radio and television: **a.** The reception of waves for conversion to electrical impulses. **b.** The apparatus used for such reception.
~adj. Designating a musical group formed at short notice for a specific performance, as opposed an established one.
Pick·wick·i·an (pik-wícki-ən) *adj.* **1.** Characterised by simplicity and benevolence. **2.** Understood or meant in a sense other than the obvious or literal one. Said of words or their sense. [After Mr. *Pickwick* in Dickens' *The Pickwick Papers* (1837).]
pick·y (pícki) *adj.* **-ier, -iest.** *Informal.* Excessively meticulous; fussy.
pic·nic (pík-nik) *n.* **1. a.** A meal taken to be eaten in the open air on an excursion to the seaside or the country, for example. **b.** An excursion or outing in which food is taken to be eaten in the open air. **c.** Any informal or makeshift meal eaten in the open air. **2.** *Slang.* An easy task or pleasant experience: *Teaching's no picnic.*
~intr.v. **picnicked, -nicking, -nics.** To go on or participate in a picnic. [French *piquenique,* perhaps a reduplication (influenced by obsolete French *nique,* a trifle) of *piquer,* to pick, peck, from Old French. See **picket.**] **—pic·nick·er** *n.*
pico– *comb. form. Symbol* **p** Indicates one million millionth, 10^{-12}; for example, *picosecond.* [Spanish *pico,* small quantity, peak, from *picar,* to prick. See **picaro.**]
Pi·co del·la Mi·ran·do·la (péekō déllə mi-rándələ), **Giovanni, Conte** (1463–94). Italian humanist and philosopher. He tried to reconcile Christianity, Platonism, and Hebrew philosophy, but attracted papal censure.
pic·o·line (píckə-leen, pīkə-, -lin) *n.* Any of three isomeric liquid methylpyridine bases, C_6H_7N, derived from coal tar, horse urine, and bone oil and used as an industrial solvent. [Latin *pix* (stem *pic-*), pitch + -OL + -INE.]
pi·cot (pée-kō, pee-kṓ, pi-) *n.* A small embroidered loop forming an ornamental edging, as on ribbons, handkerchiefs, or hems.
~tr.v. **picoted** (-kōd, -kṓd), **-coting** (-kō-ing, -kṓ-), **-cots** (-kōz, -kṓz). To trim with edging. [French, "small point", diminutive of *pic,* peak, point, prick, from *piquer,* to prick. See **picket.**]
pic·o·tee (píckə-tée) *n.* A carnation of a type having pale petals bordered by a darker colour. [French *picoté,* furnished with points, from *picoter,* to mark with points or pricks, from PICOT.]
pic·rate (píckrayt) *n.* A salt or ester of picric acid. [PICR(O)- + -ATE.]
pic·ric acid (píckrik) *n.* A poisonous, explosive yellow crystalline solid, $C_6H_2(NO_2)_3OH$, used in explosives, dyes, and antiseptics. Also called "trinitrophenol". [PICR(O)- + -IC.]
pic·rite (píckrīt) *n.* A coarse-grained igneous rock consisting of olivine and augite with small quantities of plagioclase feldspar. [PICRO- (containing magnesium) + -ITE.]
picro– *comb. form.* Indicates something bitter; for example, **picrotoxin.** [Greek *pikro-,* from *pikros,* bitter.]
pic·ro·tox·in (píckrə-tóksin, píckrō-) *n.* A bitter powder, $C_{30}H_{34}O_{13}$, used as a stimulant and antidote for barbiturate poisoning.
Pict (pikt) *n.* A member of an ancient northern British people. They came into conflict with the Britons, and later made raids on Roman garrisons. By about A.D. 900, they had effectively disappeared, having been assimilated with the Scots. [Middle English, from Late Latin *Pictī* (plural), probably alteration of the indigenous name by folk etymology, as if to mean "the painted (i.e. tattooed) people", from *pictus,* past participle of *pingere,* to paint.]
Pict·ish (píktish) *adj.* Of or pertaining to the Picts or their language.
~n. The language of the Picts, extinct by the tenth century, and known chiefly from place names.
pic·to·graph (pík-tə-graaf, -tō-, -graf) *n.* Also **pic·to·gram** (-gram). **1.** A picture representing a word or idea; a hieroglyph. **2.** A record in hieroglyphic symbols. **3.** A pictorial representation of numerical data or relationships as by charts, symbols, or the like. [Latin *pictus,* past participle of *pingere,* to paint + -GRAPH.] **—pic·to·graph·ic** (-gráffik) *adj.* **—pic·to·graph·i·cal·ly** *adv.* **—pic·tog·ra·phy** (pik-tóggrəfi) *n.*
Pic·tor (píktər) *n.* A constellation in the Southern Hemisphere near Columba and Dorado. [Latin, painter, from *pingere* (past participle *pictus*), to paint.]
pic·to·ri·al (pik-táwri-əl || -tōri-) *adj.* **1.** Pertaining to, characterised by, or composed of pictures. **2.** Of or pertaining to painting, drawing, or etching. **3.** Represented in a picture. **4.** Having vivid imagery; graphic: *pictorial prose.* **5.** Illustrated by pictures.
~n. An illustrated periodical. [Late Latin *pictōrius,* from Latin *pictor,* painter. See **Pictor.**] **—pic·to·ri·al·ly** *adv.*
pic·ture (pík-chər) *n.* **1. a.** A visual representation or image painted, drawn, photographed, or otherwise rendered on a surface. Also used adjectivally: *a picture postcard.* **b.** An image in the mind: *a vivid picture of the attack.* **2.** Any visible image, especially one on a flat surface: *the picture reflected in the lake.* **3.** A vivid or realistic verbal description: *a Shakespearean picture of guilt.* **4.** A person or object that bears a striking resemblance to another: *the picture of her mother.* **5.** A person, object, or scene that typifies or embodies an emotion, state of mind, or mood: *a picture of embarrassment.* **6.** The circumstances of an event or time considered as a scene; a situation: *Their defeat changed the picture.* **7.** A cinematic film. **8.** *Plural. British.* **a.** A cinema. **b.** A showing of a film at a cinema. **9.** Someone or something that is very beautiful: *She looked a picture in her new dress.* **—in the picture.** Apprised of the relevant facts; informed. **—out of the picture. 1.** Irrelevant. **2.** No longer in contention; too far behind to be capable of victory.
~tr.v. **pictured, -turing, -tures. 1.** To make a visible representation or picture of. **2.** To form a mental image of; visualise: *I can't picture her as a nurse.* **3.** To describe vividly in words; make a verbal picture of: *pictured her heroism glowingly.* [Middle English, from Latin *pictūra,* from *pingere* (past participle *pictus*), to paint.]
picture card *n.* A **court card** *(see).*
picture hat *n.* A wide-brimmed hat, often highly decorated, originally worn by women in the 18th century.
picture palace *n. British.* A cinema. Not in current usage.
pic·tur·esque (pík-chə-résk) *adj.* **1.** Constituting or suggesting a striking or attractive picture; suitable for a picture: *the picturesque emerald hills of Ireland.* **2.** Striking or interesting in an unusual way; irregularly or quaintly attractive. **3.** Strikingly expressive or vivid: *picturesque language.* [Alteration (influenced by PICTURE) of French *pittoresque,* from Italian *pittoresco,* from *pittore,* painter, from Latin *pictor,* from *pingere* (past participle *pictus*), to paint.] **—pic·tur·esque·ly** *adv.* **—pic·tur·esque·ness** *n.*
picture tube *n.* A **television tube** *(see).*
picture window *n.* A large window, usually of a single sheet of glass, giving out on to an attractive view.
picture writing *n.* **1.** The recording of events using pictures or symbols, such as in early hieroglyphs. **2.** A writing system that uses pictographs.
pic·ul (píck'l) *n.* Any of various units of weight used in the Far East; especially, a Chinese unit equal to about 60 kilograms (133 pounds). [Malay *pīkul,* a man's load.]
pid·dle (pídd'l) *intr.v.* **-dled, -dling, -dles. 1.** To spend time aimlessly; diddle. **2.** *Informal.* To urinate. [Perhaps from PEDDLE. In sense 2, perhaps blend of PISS + PUDDLE.]
pid·dling (pídd'l-ing, píddling) *adj. Informal.* Beneath consideration; trifling; trivial.
pid·dock (píddək) *n.* Any of various marine bivalve molluscs of the family Pholadidae, capable of boring into wood, rock, and other materials. [18th century : origin obscure.]
pidg·in (píjin) *n.* A simplified form of speech, usually a mixture of two or more languages, that has a rudimentary grammar and vocabulary and is used for communication between groups speaking different languages. Compare **creolised language.** [From PIDGIN ENGLISH.] **—pidg·in** *adj.*
pidgin English *n. Somtimes capital* **P.** A pidgin based on English and used originally as a trade language in Far Eastern ports. [A pidgin rendering of *business English.*]
pie[1] (pī) *n.* A baked food consisting of a shell of pastry and a filling of fruit, meat, cheese, or other ingredients, usually covered with a pastry crust. [Middle English *pie,* perhaps "magpie" (comparing the mixture in a pie to the various items a magpie might collect).]
pie[2] *n. Archaic.* A bird, the **magpie** *(see).* [Middle English, from Old French, from Latin *pīca.*]
pie[3] *n.* A former monetary unit of India and Pakistan. [Hindi *pā'ī,* from Sanskrit *pādikā,* quarter, from *pāda,* foot, leg, quarter.]
pie[4] *n.* An almanac of services used in the English church before the Reformation. [Medieval Latin *pīca,* almanac, PICA.]
pie[5] *n.* Also *chiefly U.S.* **pi'** *pl.* **pis. 1.** *Printing.* Type that has been jumbled or thrown together at random. **2.** Any jumble or disorder: *An army without ranks will go to pie.*
~v. **pied, pieing, pies.** Also **pi, pied, piing, pies.** *Printing. —tr.* To jumble or mix up (type). *—intr.* To become jumbled.
pie·bald (pī-bawld) *adj.* Spotted or patched, especially in black and white: *a piebald horse.*
~n. A piebald animal, especially a horse. Compare **skewbald.** [PIE (magpie) + BALD.]
piece (peess) *n.* **1.** A thing considered as a unit or element of a larger quantity or class; a portion: *a piece of string.* **2.** A portion or part that has been separated from a whole: *a piece of cake.* **3. a.** An object that is one member of a group or class: *a piece of furniture.* **b.** Such an object considered as particularly fine, valuable, or rare: *a collector's piece.* **4.** An artistic, musical, or literary work or composition. **5.** An instance; a specimen: *a piece of folly.* **6.** *Informal.* One's fully expressed opinion; one's mind: *speak one's piece.* **7.** A coin or counter: *a ten-pence piece.* **8.** In various board games, any of the counters or men used in playing. **9.** In chess, any of the figures other than a pawn. **10.** A firearm, especially a rifle. **11.** A person, especially a woman, considered in terms of sexual attractiveness. Usually considered offensive. **12.** *Scottish.* A sandwich or slice of buttered bread. **13.** *U.S. Regional.* A short or manageable distance. **—a piece of (one's) mind.** *Informal.* Frank or aggressive criticism or censure. **—go to pieces. 1.** To break into small pieces; fall apart. **2.** *Informal.* To lose mental and emotional self-control; break down. **—a nasty piece of work.** *British Informal.* A cruel or unpleasant person. **—of a piece. 1.** Belonging to the same kind or class. **2.** Internally consistent and predictable; forming a coherent whole.
~tr.v. **pieced, piecing, pieces. 1. a.** To mend or put together by joining or uniting the pieces of: *He pieced together the vase.* **b.** To combine the parts or pieces of in such a way as to be able to understand or draw conclusions from: *tried to piece the story together.* **2.** To join (broken threads) when spinning. **—piece out. 1.** To eke out; cause to last. **2.** To increase by adding a piece to. [Middle English, from Anglo-French, Old French *pece,* from Medieval Latin *pecia, petia,* from Gaulish *pettia*† (unattested).]
pièce de ré·sis·tance (p-yéss də ráyzi-stóNss, rézzi-) *n.* **1.** The principal dish of a meal. **2.** The most outstanding item or event in a group or series, especially in a series of artistic works. [French.]

piece goods *pl.n.* Fabrics made and sold in standard lengths.

piece-meal (peess-meel) *adv.* **1.** Piece by piece; gradually: *articles acquired piecemeal.* **2.** In pieces; apart.
—adj. Accomplished or made piece by piece or in separate stages; fragmentary. [Middle English *pecemele* : *pece*, PIECE + *-mele*, by a certain measure, Old English *mælum*, dative plural of *mæl*, a point of time. See **meal**.]

piece of cake *n. Informal.* Something that is very easy to perform, obtain, operate, or the like.

piece of eight *n., pl.* **pieces of eight.** An obsolete Spanish silver coin.

piece rate *n.* A fixed rate of payment per number of products turned out.

piece-work (peess-wurk) *n.* Work paid for according to the number of items produced. **—piece-work-er** *n.*

pie chart *n.* A circular chart having radii dividing the circle into sectors proportional to the relative size of the quantities represented. Also called "pie graph". [From PIE (pastry).]

Pieck (peek), **Wilhelm** (1876–1960). German communist statesman, president of the German Democratic Republic (1949–60).

pie-crust (pi-krust) *n.* The baked pastry of a pie.
—adj. Designating a piece of furniture with an ornamental moulding like the edge of a piecrust.

pied (pid) *adj.* Patchy in colour; splotched; piebald. [Middle English, from PIE (magpie), from its piebald colouring.]

pied-à-terre (p-yéd-aa-taír, p-yáyd-, p-yáyt-) *n., pl.* **pieds-à-terre** (*pronounced as singular*). *French.* A secondary or temporary lodging: *a small pied-à-terre in the city.* [French, "foot to the ground".]

pied-mont (péed-mont) *adj. Geology.* Formed or lying at the foot of a mountain or mountain range: *a piedmont plain.*
—n. Geology. A piedmont area or region. [French, from Italian *piémonte,* PIEDMONT.]

Pied-mont (péed-mont, p-yéd-, -mənt). *Italian.* **Pie-mon-te** (p-ye-móntay). Autonomous region of northwest Italy. It includes part of the Alps and Po valley, and Asti, Novara, and Torino are among its provinces. It formed the heartland of modern Italy during the Risorgimento (from 1814), and its capital, Turin, was Italy's first national capital. **—Pied-mon-tese** (eez) *n. & adj.*

Pied Piper *n.* **1.** In German legend, a piper who rid the town of Hamelin of its rats by leading them away with his music. When he was refused due payment he led away the children of the town as well. Also called "Pied Piper of Hamelin". **2.** *Often small* **p.** A person who lures away others to follow him.

pied wagtail *n.* A British subspecies of the white wagtail (*Motacilla alba*), *Motacilla alba yarrellii*, having black and white plumage and a long black tail. Also called "water wagtail".

pie-eyed (pi-id) *adj. British Slang.* Drunk.

pie graph *n.* A pie chart (*see*).

pie in the sky *n. Informal.* False expectation; unwarranted hope. **—pie-in-the-sky** *adj.*

pie-man (pi-mən) *n., pl.* **-men** (-mən, -men). *British Archaic.* A person who sells pies.

pier (peer) *n.* **1. a.** A platform extending from a shore over water and supported by piles or pillars, used to secure, protect, and provide access to ships or boats. **b.** Such a structure supporting various buildings used predominantly for entertainment. **2.** A supporting structure at the junction of connecting spans of a bridge. **3.** *Architecture.* Any of various vertical supporting structures, especially: **a.** A pillar, rectangular in cross-section, supporting an arch or roof. **b.** The portion of a wall between windows or openings. **c.** A reinforcing structure that projects from a wall; a buttress. [Middle English *per, pere,* from Anglo-Latin *pera†*.]

pierce (peerss) *tr.v.* **pierced, piercing, pierces. 1.** To cut or pass through or into, with or as if with a sharp instrument; stab; penetrate. **2.** To make a hole or opening in; perforate. **3.** To make a way through: *The path pierced the wilderness.* **4. a.** To sound sharply through: *His shout pierced the din.* **b.** To shine through: *His torch pierced the darkness.* **5.** To succeed in discerning or understanding: *He pierced the heart of the mystery.* **6.** To affect penetratingly; move deeply; transfix: *pierced by anguish.*
—intr. To penetrate into or through something: *The rocket pierced through space.* [Middle English *percen,* from Old French *percer, percier,* from Vulgar Latin *pertusiāre* (unattested), from Latin *pertundere* (past participle *pertūsus*), to pierce through : *per,* through + *tundere,* to thrust.] **—pierc-er** *n.* **—pierc-ing-ly** *adv.*

pierced (peerst) *adj.* Designating an ear having a tiny hole made in the lobe to hold an earring.

pier glass *n.* A long mirror formerly hung on the portion of wall (pier) between windows.

Pi-e-ri-an (pi-éer-i-ən, -érri) *adj.* Of or pertaining to the Muses or to artistic inspiration. [After the PIERIAN SPRING.]

Pierian Spring. 1. *Greek Mythology.* A fountain in Pieria in ancient Macedonia, sacred to the Muses. **2.** A source of inspiration, especially to artists and poets.

Pie-ro del-la Fran-ces-ca (p-yáir-ō délla fran-chéska) (*c.* 1420–92). Italian painter of the Renaissance. His mature works include a fresco cycle, *The Story of the True Cross* (1452–66), Arezzo.

Pier-rot (péer-ō; *French* p-ye-rô) *n.* **1.** A stock male character in traditional French pantomime having a whitened face and floppy white clothing. **2.** *Small* **p.** A clown, doll, or the like similarly dressed and made up. [French, diminutive of *Pierre,* from Latin *Petrūs,* (the name Peter).]

pier table *n.* A table designed to stand between windows, under a pier glass.

pi-e-tà (pée-ay-taa) *n. Often capital* **P.** A painting, drawing, or sculpture of the Virgin Mary holding and mourning over the dead body of Jesus. [Italian, "pity", from Latin *pietās,* PIETY.]

Pie-ter-mar-itz-burg (péetər-márrits-burg). Capital of KwaZulu-Natal province, South Africa. Founded (1838) by the Boers.

pi-e-tism (pi-ə-tiz'm) *n.* **1.** Piety. **2.** Affected or exaggerated piety. **3.** *Capital* **P.** A reforming movement in the German Lutheran Church during the 17th and 18th centuries, which strove to renew the devotional ideal in the Protestant religion. [German *Pietismus,* from Latin *pietās,* PIETY.] **—pi-e-tist** *n.* **—pi-e-tis-tic** (-tístik), **pi-e-tis-ti-cal** *adj.* **—pi-e-tis-ti-cal-ly** *adv.*

pi-e-ty (pi-əti) *n., pl.* **-ties. 1.** Religious devotion and reverence to God. **2.** Devotion and reverence to parents and family. **3.** A pious act or thought. **4.** The state or quality of being pious. [French *piété,* from Latin *pietās* (stem *pietāt-*), from *pius,* PIOUS.]

piezo— *comb. form.* Indicates pressure; for example, **piezometer.** [Greek *piezein,* to squeeze, press.]

pi-e-zo-e-lec-tric crystal (pi-éezō-i-léktrik, péezō-, pee-étsō-) *n.* Any of certain crystals lacking a centre of symmetry, such as quartz, that when subjected to stress produces a **potential difference** (*see*) between its two stressed surfaces.

pi-e-zo-e-lec-tric-i-ty (pi-éezō-éllek-tríssəti, péezō-, pee-étsō-, -i-lek- || -trízzəti) *n.* The generation of electricity or of electric polarity in dielectric crystals subjected to mechanical stress, and, conversely, the generation of stress in such crystals subjected to an applied voltage. Also called "piezoelectric effect". **—pi-e-zo-e-lec-tric** (-i-léktrik), **pi-e-zo-e-lec-tri-cal** *adj.* **—pi-e-zo-e-lec-tri-cal-ly** *adv.*

pi-e-zom-e-ter (pi-eez-ómmitər, péez-, pée-ets-) *n.* Any instrument for measuring pressure, especially high pressure. [PIEZO- + -METER.] **—pi-e-zo-met-ric** (-ə-méttrik, -ō-), **pi-e-zo-met-ri-cal** *adj.* **—pi-e-zom-e-try** (-ómmətri) *n.*

pif-fle (píff'l) *intr.v.* **-fled, -fling, -fles.** *Informal.* To talk or act in a feeble or futile way.
—n. Informal. Foolish or futile talk or ideas; nonsense. [Imitative.]

pif-fling (piffling) *adj.* Futile and trivial; silly.

pig (pig) *n.* **1.** Any of several mammals of the family Suidae, having short legs, cloven hoofs, bristly hair, and a cartilaginous snout used for digging; especially, the domesticated pig, *Sus scrofa.* **2.** The edible parts of a pig; pork. **3.** *Informal.* A person regarded as being unpleasantly dirty, piglike, greedy, or gross. **4.** See **guinea pig. 5. a.** An oblong block of metal, chiefly iron or lead, poured from a smelting furnace. **b.** A mould in which such metal is cast. **c. Pig iron** (*see*). **6.** *Slang.* A policeman. Used derogatorily. **7.** *British Informal.* A tedious or difficult thing. **8.** *Regional.* A segment of an orange, apple, or other fruit. **—a pig in a poke.** Something that is obtained without first being inspected, or whose value is unknown. **—make a pig of (oneself).** To be greedy or self-indulgent.
—v. **pigged, pigging, pigs.** *—intr.* **1.** To give birth to pigs; farrow. **2.** To act in a greedy, dirty or piggish way. *—tr. Informal.* To eat (food) greedily; gobble. **—pig it.** To live in a piglike way. [Middle English *pigge,* probably from Old English *picga†* (unattested).]

pig bed *n.* A bed of sand in which pigs of iron are cast.

pi-geon (píj-ən, -in) *n.* **1.** Any of various birds of the widely distributed family Columbidae, characteristically having deepchested bodies, small heads, and short legs; especially, *Columba livia* or any of its domesticated varieties. This species is also called "rock dove". **2.** *Slang.* One who is easily swindled; a dupe. **3.** *British Informal.* Responsibility; affair: *It's not my pigeon.* [Middle English *pijon,* from Old French, young bird, pigeon, from Late Latin *pīpiō* (stem *pīpiōn-*), squab, young chirping bird, from *pīpīre,* to chirp.]

pigeon chest *n.* A chest deformity marked by a projecting sternum, such as may occur as the result of rickets. Also called "chicken breast". **—pi-geon-chest-ed** *adj.*

pi-geon-heart-ed (píj-ən-hártid, -in-) *adj.* Lacking courage; cowardly.

pi-geon-hole (píj-ən-hōl, -in-) *n.* **1.** The small hole or holes for nesting, in a pigeon loft. **2.** A small compartment or recess for holding papers; a cubbyhole. **3.** *Informal.* A category or classification.
—tr.v. **pigeonholed, -holing, -holes. 1.** To place or file in a pigeonhole. **2.** To classify mentally; categorise. **3.** To put aside and ignore; shelve.

pigeon pea *n.* **Dhal** (*see*).

pi-geon-toed (píj-ən-tōd, -in-) *adj.* Having the toes turned inwards.

pi-geon-wing (píj-ən-wing, -in-) *n.* A dance step performed by jumping and clapping the feet together. [Probably a translation of French *ailes de pigeon,* a ballet term for a leap in which the dancer's legs imitate the motion of a bird's wings.]

pig-ger-y (píggəri) *n., pl.* **-ies. 1.** A place where pigs are kept. **2.** Greediness or slovenliness; piggishness. [PIG + -ERY.]

pig-gin (píggin) *n.* A small wooden bucket with one stave projecting above the rim for use as a handle. Also called "pipkin". [16th century : origin obscure.]

pig-gish (píggish) *adj.* **1.** Like a pig; greedy; dirty. **2.** *British Informal.* Stubborn; pig-headed. **—pig-gish-ly** *adv.* **—pig-gish-ness** *n.*

Pig-gott (píggət), **Lester (Keith)** (1935–). British jockey. He won the Derby a record nine times, the Ascot Gold Cup 11 times, and rode more than 5,000 winners. He won his thirtieth Classic victory in the 2000 Guineas at Newmarket in 1992 and retired in 1995.

pig-gy (piggi) *n., pl.* **-gies.** A little pig. Used especially by children.
—adj. **piggier, -giest.** Piggish.

pig-gy-back (píggi-bak) *n.* Also **pick-a-back** (píckə-). **1.** A ride on the shoulders or back of another person. **2.** A method of transporting vehicles by loading them onto another vehicle such as a train or a specially designed lorry.

~*tr.v.* **piggybacked, -backing, -backs.** Also **pick·a·back.** To carry or transport by piggyback.

~*adj.* Of, pertaining to, or designating a piggyback. **2.** *Informal.* Of or pertaining to a method of transplant surgery in which the new organ is initially supported by the existing organ, which is left in the body until the transplant has established itself: *a piggyback heart transplant.* —**pig·gy·back** *adv.*

piggy bank *n.* A child's receptacle for holding money, often shaped like a pig, and having a slot into which coins are inserted.

pig·head·ed (píg-héddid) *adj.* Stubborn, especially in a stupid or belligerent way. See Synonyms at **obstinate.** —**pig·head·ed·ly** *adv.* —**pig·head·ed·ness** *n.*

pig iron *n.* Crude iron cast in blocks or pigs. Also called "pig".

pig·jump (píg-jump) *intr.v.* **-jumped, -jumping, -jumps.** *Australian & N.Z.* To kick out with the hind legs, keeping the front legs rigid and on the ground. Used of a horse.

pig Latin *n.* A coded jargon in which the initial consonant of each word is transposed to the end of that word with *-ay* (ay) added to form a new syllable, as *igpay atinlay* for *pig Latin.*

pig·let (píg-lət, -lit) *n.* A young pig.

pig·ment (píg-mənt) *n.* **1.** Any substance or matter used as colouring. **2.** Dry colouring matter, usually an insoluble powder to be mixed with a vehicle to produce paint and similar products. **3.** *Biology.* A substance, such as chlorophyll or haemoglobin, that produces a characteristic colour in plant or animal tissue.

~*tr.v.* (also pig·mént) **pigmented, -menting, -ments.** To colour with pigment. [Latin *pigmentum,* from *pingere,* to paint.] —**pig·men·tar·y** (-əri ‖ -erri) *adj.*

pig·men·ta·tion (píg-mən-táysh'n, -men-) *n. Biology.* **1.** Coloration of tissues by pigment. **2.** Deposition of pigment by cells.

pigment cell *n.* A **chromatophore** *(see).*

pigmy. Variant of **pygmy.**

Pigmy. Variant of **Pygmy.**

pig·nut (píg-nut) *n.* **1.** Either of two trees, *Carya glabra* or *C. ovalis,* of the eastern United States, bearing nuts with slightly bitter kernels. **2.** The nut of either of these trees. **3.** A plant, the **earthnut** *(see),* or its tuberous root.

pig·root (píg-rōot) *intr.v.* **-rooted, -rooting, -roots.** *Australian & N.Z.* To pigjump.

pig's ear *n.* **1.** A large, sweet, flaky biscuit, shaped like a cloverleaf. **2.** *Informal.* A messy or clumsy performance of a task: *You've made a right pig's ear of these accounts.*

pig's fry *n.* The offal, such as the heart and liver, of a pig, fried together and eaten.

pig·skin (píg-skin) *n.* **1.** The skin of a pig. **2.** Leather made from this. —**pig·skin** *adj.*

pig·stick (píg-stik) *intr.v.* **-sticked, -sticking, -sticks.** To hunt wild boar on horseback with a spear. —**pig·stick·er** *n.* —**pig·stick·ing** *n.*

pig·sty (píg-stī) *n., pl.* **-sties.** **1.** A shelter or pen where pigs are kept. **2.** *Chiefly British.* A filthy or very untidy place. Also *U.S.* "pigpen".

pig·swill (pig-swil) *n.* **1.** Leftover food or other edible matter used to feed pigs. Also called "pig's wash". **2.** *Informal.* Extremely poorquality food.

pig·tail (píg-tayl) *n.* **1.** A plait of hair that hangs down behind the head. **2.** Either of a pair of similar plaits at the sides of the head. **3.** A twisted roll of tobacco. —**pig·tailed** *adj.*

pig·weed (píg-weed) *n.* **1.** A coarse weed, *Amaranthus retroflexus,* having hairy leaves and spikes of green flowers. Also called "redroot". **2.** *U.S.* A plant, **fat hen** *(see).*

pi·ka (píkə, péekə) *n.* Any of several small, tailless, harelike mammals of the genus *Ochotona,* of the mountains of North America and Eurasia. Also called "cony". [Tungus (East Siberia) *piika.*]

pike¹ (pīk) *n.* **1.** A weapon consisting of a long wooden shaft with a pointed steel or iron head, formerly used by infantry. **2.** Any spike or sharp point, such as the tip of a spear.

~*tr.v.* **piked, piking, pikes.** To pierce or kill with a pike. [Middle English, Old English *pīc†,* prick, point.]

pike² *n., pl.* **pikes** or collectively **pike. 1.** A freshwater game and food fish, *Esox lucius,* of the Northern Hemisphere, having a long snout and sometimes attaining a length of over 1½ metres (four feet). **2.** Any of various similar or related fishes. [Middle English, perhaps from PIKE (spike), referring to the shape of its jaw.]

pike³ *n.* A turnpike *(see).* [Short for TURNPIKE.]

pike⁴ *n. Chiefly British Regional.* A mountain or hill peak. [Middle English, akin to Norwegian dialectal *pīk†.*]

pike·let (pík-lət, -lit) *n.* **1.** *British Regional.* A small, flat crumpet. **2.** *Australian & N.Z.* A small, flat drop scone. [West Midlands dialect, shortened from Welsh *bara pyglyd,* pitchy bread.]

pike·man (pík-mən) *n., pl.* **-men** (-mən). **1.** The keeper of a turnpike. **2.** Formerly, a soldier armed with a pike.

pike·perch (pík-perch) *n., pl.* **-perches** or collectively **pikeperch.** Any of various fishes related to the perches and resembling the pike, such as the **walleye** *(see).*

pik·er (píkər) *n. Informal.* A timid, cautious person, often mean and petty, who tends to back out of situations or shirk work. [Middle English, perhaps special use from PIKE (weapon).]

pike·staff (pík-staaf ‖ -staf) *n., pl.* **-staffs** or **-staves** (-stayvz). **1.** The shaft of a pike. **2.** A walking stick tipped with a metal spike. [PIKE (point) + STAFF.]

pi·lar (pílər) *adj.* Of or covered with hair. [New Latin *pilaris,* from Latin *pilus,* a hair.]

pi·las·ter (pi-lástər) *n. Architecture.* A rectangular column with a capital and base, set into a wall to ornament it. [Old French *pilastre,* from Italian *pilastro,* from Medieval Latin *pilastrum,* from Latin *pīla,* PILLAR.]

Pi·late (pílət), **Pontius** (First century A.D.). Roman governor of Judaea (A.D. 26–36). He ordered Christ's crucifixion (allegedly with some reluctance). He is referred to by the Jewish authors Josephus and Philo, who both allude to his political insensitivity.

pi·lau, pi·law (pi-lów, -law) *n.* Also **pi·laf, pi·laff** (píl-af, pi-láf, pee- ‖ *Chiefly U.S.* -láaf). A dish consisting of rice cooked in a spicy seasoned stock, often with meat, shellfish, or vegetables. Also used adjectively: *pilau rice.* [Turkish *pilāw,* from Persian *pilāw* from Osmanli *pilau†,* "rice porridge".]

pil·chard (pílchərd) *n.* Any of various small marine fishes related to the herrings; especially, a commercially important edible species, *Sardina pilchardus,* of European waters. [16th century : *pilcher†.*]

pile¹ (pīl) *n.* **1.** A quantity of objects stacked, thrown, or having fallen together in a heap; a mound. **2.** *Often plural. Informal.* A large accumulation or quantity: *piles of trouble.* **3.** *Informal.* A large sum of money; a fortune. **4.** A funeral pyre. **5.** *Informal.* A very large building or complex of buildings. **6.** *Physics.* A **nuclear reactor** *(see).* **7.** *Electricity.* A **voltaic pile** *(see).*

~*v.* **piled, piling, piles.** —*tr.* **1.** To set or stack in a pile or heap. Sometimes used with *up.* **2.** To load with a pile: *He piled the table with books.* —*intr.* **1.** To become or form a heap or pile. Often used with *up.* **2.** *Informal.* To move in a disorderly mass or group. Used with *in, on, off,* or *out: pile out of a car.* —**pile it on.** *Informal.* To exaggerate. [Middle English, from Old French, heap, heap of stone, from Latin *pīla,* PILLAR.]

pile² *n.* **1.** A heavy beam of timber, concrete, or steel, driven into the earth as a foundation or support for a structure. **2.** *Heraldry.* A wedge-shaped charge, usually pointing downwards.

~*tr.v.* **piled, piling, piles. 1.** To drive piles into. **2.** To support or provide with piles. [Middle English *pile,* pointed shaft, stake, Old English *pīl,* from West Germanic *pīla* (unattested), from Latin *pīlum,* heavy javelin, pestle.]

pile³ *n.* **1. a.** Cut or uncut loops of yarn forming the surface of certain fabrics, such as velvet, plush, and carpeting. Compare **nap. b.** Any such filament or loop of yarn. **2.** The surface so formed. **3.** Soft, fine hair, fur, or wool. [Middle English, probably from Anglo-French *pyle,* from Latin *pilus,* hair.] —**piled** *adj.*

pi·le·at·ed (píli-aytid, pílli-) *adj.* Also **pi·le·ate** (-ət, -it, -ayt). **1.** *Botany.* Having a pileus. **2.** *Zoology.* Having a crest, as certain birds do. [Latin *pīleātus,* from PILEUS.]

pile-driv·er (píl-drīvər) *n.* **1.** A machine that drives piles (beams) into the earth by means of a steam hammer or by raising a weight between guideposts and dropping it on the head of the pile. **2.** *Informal.* A powerful punch or kick.

pi·le·ous (píli-əss, pílli-) *adj. Biology.* Hairy. [Latin *pilus,* hair.]

piles (pīlz) *pl.n.* **Haemorrhoids** *(see).* Not in technical usage. [Plural of *pile,* from Latin *pila,* ball. See **pill.**]

pi·le·um (píli-əm, pílli-) *n., pl.* **pilea** (-ə). *Zoology.* The top of a bird's head, extending from the base of the bill to the nape. [New Latin, from Latin *pīleus,* felt cap, PILEUS.]

pile up *intr.v. Informal.* To crash; collide. Used especially of motor vehicles. —*tr. Informal.* To cause to crash or collide.

pile-up (píl-up) *n. Informal.* A collision involving several motor vehicles.

pi·le·us (píli-əss, pílli-) *n., pl.* **pilei** (-ī). **1.** *Botany.* The umbrella-like cap of the reproductive body of certain fungi, such as mushrooms. **2.** A round, brimless skullcap worn in ancient Rome. [New Latin, from Latin *pīleus, pilleus,* felt cap.]

pile·wort (píl-wurt ‖ -wawrt) *n.* The **lesser celandine** *(see).*

pil·fer (pílfər) *v.* **-fered, -fering, -fers.** —*tr.* To steal (a small amount or inexpensive item); filch. —*intr.* To steal or filch. —See Synonyms at **rob.** [Middle English, from Anglo-French, Old French *pelfrer,* to rob, despoil, from *pelfre†,* booty.] —**pil·fer·age** (-ij) *n.* —**pil·fer·er** *n.*

pil·grim (píl-grim) *n.* **1.** A religious devotee who journeys to a shrine or sacred place. **2.** One who embarks on a quest for some end conceived as sacred. **3.** Any traveller. **4.** *Capital* P. A Pilgrim Father. [Middle English *pelegrim,* from Old French *peligrin,* from Late Latin *pelegrīnus,* alteration of Latin *peregrīnus,* PEREGRINE.]

pil·grim·age (pílgrim-ij) *n.* **1.** A journey to a sacred place or shrine. **2.** Any long journey or search, especially one of exalted purpose or moral significance.

~*intr.v.* **pilgrimaged, -aging, -ages.** To go on a pilgrimage.

Pilgrim Father *n. pl.* **Pilgrim Fathers.** A member of the group of English Puritans that founded the colony of Plymouth in New England in 1620. Also called "Pilgrim".

pi·lif·er·ous (pī-líffərəss, pi-) *adj.* **1.** *Botany.* Designating the outermost layer of cells, in the region behind a root apex, that are elongated to form root hairs. **2.** Bearing or terminating in a hair or hairs. [Latin *pilus,* hair + -FEROUS.]

pil·i·form (píli-fawrm, pílli-) *adj. Botany.* Resembling a hair. [Latin *pilus,* hair + -FORM.]

pil·ing (píl-ing) *n.* **1.** The act of driving building piles into the earth. **2.** Building piles collectively. **3.** A structure composed of piles.

Pil·i·pi·no (pilli-péenō) *n.* The national language of the Philippines, based primarily on Tagalog, and having many Spanish and local dialectal elements. [Tagalog, from *pilipino,* Filipino, from Philippine Spanish, FILIPINO.]

pill¹ (pil) *n.* **1.** A small pellet or tablet of medicine, sometimes coated, taken by swallowing whole or chewing. **2.** *Sometimes capital* **P.** *Informal.* An oral contraceptive. Usually preceded by *the.* **3.** *Slang.* Something considered to resemble a pill, such as a tennis ball. **4.** Anything distasteful or unpleasant, but necessary: *a bitter pill to swallow.* **5.** *Slang.* An insipid or ill-natured person.
~*v.* **pilled, pilling, pills.** —*tr.* **1.** To dose with pills. **2.** To make into pills. —*intr.* To form small balls resembling pills: *a jumper that pills.* [Middle Dutch *pile,* probably from Latin *pilula,* diminutive of *pila*†, ball.]

pill² *v.* **pilled, pilling, pills.** —*tr.* **1.** *Archaic.* To pillage (people or a place). **2.** *Archaic & Regional.* To peel. —*intr. Archaic.* To pillage. [Middle English *pillen,* perhaps from Old English *pylan,* from Latin *pilāre,* from *pilus,* hair; influenced by Old French *piller,* to plunder.]

pil·lage (píllij) *v.* **-laged, -laging, -lages.** —*tr.* **1.** To rob (people or a place) of goods by violent seizure; plunder. **2.** To take as spoils. —*intr.* To take spoils by robbery and violence.
~*n.* **1.** The act of pillaging. **2.** Something pillaged; spoils. [Middle English, from Old French, from *piller,* to tear up, maltreat, plunder, from *pille,* dialectal variant of *peille,* rag, cloth, probably from Latin *pilleus,* felt cap.] **—pil·lag·er** *n.*

pil·lar (píllər) *n.* **1.** *Architecture.* A slender, freestanding, vertical support; a column. **2.** Any similar structure used for decoration. **3.** Someone or something similar in function or shape: *a pillar of strength; a pillar of flame.* **4.** One who occupies a central or responsible position: *a pillar of the state.* **—from pillar to post.** From one place or situation to another; hither and thither.
~*tr.v.* **pillared, -laring, -lars.** To support or decorate with a pillar or pillars. [Middle English *piler, piller,* from Old French *pilier,* from Vulgar Latin *pīlāre* (unattested), extension of Latin *pīla*†, pillar.]

pillar box *n. British.* A bright red, pillar-shaped public postbox.

pil·lar-box red (píllər-boks) *n.* Bright red; scarlet. **—pillar-box red** *adj.*

Pillars of Hercules. Two peaks, Gibraltar and Jebel Musa, one on each side of the Strait of Gibraltar, at the entrance to the Mediterranean Sea.

pill·box (píl-boks) *n.* **1.** A small box for pills usually having a shallow, cylindrical shape. **2.** A woman's small, round hat. **3.** A roofed concrete emplacement for a machine gun or other weapon.

pil·lion (píl-yən) *n.* A pad or cushion for a passenger behind the saddle on a motorcycle, scooter, or horse. Also used adjectivally: *a pillion passenger.*
~*adv.* On a pillion: *ride pillion.* [Scottish Gaelic *pillean,* diminutive of *peall,* covering, cushion, from Latin *pellis,* skin, hide.]

pil·li·winks (pílli-wingks) *n.* A medieval instrument of torture for squeezing the fingers and thumbs. [Middle English *pyrewinkes*†.]

pill·ock (píllək) *n. British slang.* A person, especially a man or boy, who is foolish or whom one dislikes. [English regional *pillick, pilluck* penis, from Scandinavian.]

pil·lo·ry (pílləri) *n., pl.* **-ries.** **1.** A wooden framework with holes for the head and hands, in which offenders were formerly locked to be exposed to public scorn as punishment. **2.** Public humiliation or exposure to scorn.
~*tr.v.* **pilloried, -rying, -ries.** **1.** To put in a pillory as punishment. **2.** To expose to public ridicule and abuse. [Middle English, from Anglo-Latin *pillorium,* from Old French *pilori,* probably from Provençal *espilori*†.]

pil·low (píllō) *n.* **1.** A cushion for the head, used especially during sleep, consisting of a cloth case stuffed with something soft, such as down, feathers, or foam rubber. **2.** Something similar in function or shape: *a pillow of moss.* **3.** The pad on which bobbin lace is made.
~*tr.v.* **pillowed, -lowing, -lows.** **1.** To rest (one's head) on or as if on a pillow. **2.** To act as a pillow for. [Middle English *pilwe,* Old English *pyle, pylu,* from Latin *pulvīnus*†, pillow.] **—pil·low·y** *adj.*

pillow block *n. Engineering.* A block that encloses and supports a journal or shaft; a bearing.

pil·low·case (píllō-kayss) *n.* A removable covering for a pillow, usually of cotton or linen. Also called "pillowslip".

pill·wort (píl-wurt ‖ -wawrt) *n.* An aquatic Eurasian fern, *Pilularia globulifera,* with pill-like spore-producing bodies.

pi·lo·car·pine (pīlō-kár-peen) *n.* Also **pi·lo·car·pin** (-pin). A poisonous alkaloid, $C_{11}H_{16}N_2O_2$, obtained from the leaves of the jaborandi tree and used to increase the secretion of various glands, and, as eye drops, to constrict the pupil. [From New Latin *Pilocarpus,* genus of the jaborandi : Greek *pilos,* felt + -CARPOUS.]

pi·lose (pī-lōz, -ōss) *adj.* Covered with fine, soft hair. [Latin *pilōsus,* from *pilus,* a hair.]

pi·lot (pīlət) *n.* **1.** One who operates or is licensed to operate an aircraft or spacecraft in flight. **2. a.** One who is licensed to take charge of and steer a ship into and out of port or through dangerous waters, though not himself belonging to the ship's crew. **b.** The helmsman of a ship. **3.** One who guides or directs a course of action for others. **4.** The part of a tool, device, or machine that leads or guides the whole. **5.** A **pilot light** *(see).* **6.** Something that serves as a test, trial, or model, such as a television programme produced as a prototype of a series being considered for transmission.
~*tr.v.* **piloted, -loting, -lots.** **1.** To serve as the pilot of. **2.** To steer, or control the course of.
~*adj.* **1.** Serving as a tentative model for future experiment or development: *a pilot film; a pilot study.* **2.** Serving or leading as a guide: *a pilot beacon.* [French *pilote,* from Italian *pilota,* alteration of obsolete *pedota,* from Medieval Greek *pēdōtēs* (unattested), from Greek *pēda,* plural of *pēdon,* rudder, steering oar.]

pi·lot·age (pīlətij) *n.* **1.** *Nautical.* **a.** The technique or act of piloting. **b.** The fee paid to a pilot. **2.** Navigation of an aircraft by visual identification of landmarks.

pilot balloon *n.* A small balloon used to determine wind velocity.

pilot cell *n.* A storage battery cell tested to determine the condition of the entire battery.

pilot cloth *n.* A thick, dark, blue cloth used for seamen's coats and similar garments.

pilot engine *n.* A locomotive engine sent ahead of a train to check the track for safety.

pilot fish *n.* A marine fish, *Naucrates ductor,* that often swims in company with larger fishes, especially sharks.

pi·lot·house (pīlət-howss) *n.* A **wheelhouse** *(see).*

pi·lot·ing (pīləting) *n.* **1.** The occupation or service of a pilot. **2.** *Nautical.* Coastal navigation by reference to landmarks, buoys, soundings, and the like. See **celestial navigation.**

pilot lamp *n.* A small electric lamp wired to light in response to specified conditions in an electric circuit. Also called "pilot light".

pilot light *n.* **1.** A small gas flame that is kept burning constantly in order to ignite a gas burner, as in a cooker, or the main burner, as in a boiler. Also called "pilot". **2.** A pilot lamp.

pilot officer *n.* The lowest-ranking commissioned officer in the Royal Air Force and various other air forces, ranking below a flying officer and equivalent in rank to a second lieutenant in the Army or a midshipman in the Navy.

pilot plant *n.* A small version of an industrial plant built to provide experience and design data for the full-scale plant.

pilot whale *n.* Any of several small, dark-coloured whales of the genus *Globicephala.* Also called "blackfish".

pils·ner, pil·sen·er (pílz-nər, pílss-) *n.* A strong, pale lager. [After *Pilsen* (PLZEŇ), Czech Republic, where is was originally brewed.]

Pilt·down man (pílt-down) *n.* A species of early man, *Eoanthropus dawsoni,* postulated from bones found in an early Pleistocene gravel bed in 1912, and proved in 1953 to have been a forgery based on the artificial modification and juxtaposition of the cranium of a modern man and the mandible of an orang-utan. [After the site near *Piltdown* Common, Sussex, identified by Charles Dawson (died 1916), English lawyer and amateur palaeontologist.]

pil·ule (píl-yōōl) *n.* A pill, especially a little pill. [French, from Latin *pilula,* diminutive of *pila,* ball. See **pill.**] **—pil·u·lar** (píl-lew-lər) *adj.*

Pi·ma (péemə) *n., pl.* **-mas** or collectively **Pima.** **1.** A member of a North American Indian people living in southern Arizona and northern Mexico. **2.** The Uto-Aztecan language of this people. **—Pi·man** *adj.*

pi·men·to (pi-méntō) *n., pl.* **-tos.** **1.** A tree, the **allspice** *(see),* or its berries. **2.** The **pimiento** *(see).* [Spanish *pimiento,* pepper, from Late Latin *pigmenta,* plural of *pigmentum,* plant juice, PIGMENT.]

pi·mien·to (pi-méntō, -mi-éntō) *n., pl.* **-tos.** Also **pi·men·to.** **1.** A **sweet pepper** *(see).* **2.** The mild, ripe, red fruit of certain sweet peppers, used in salads, cookery, and as stuffing for green olives. Also called "red pepper". [Spanish, pepper, allspice, PIMENTO.]

pimp (pimp) *n.* **1.** A man who solicits clients for a prostitute or brothel. **2.** A man who procures prostitutes for a client or patron; a pander. **3.** *Australian & N.Z. Slang.* A person who betrays secrets; an informer or telltale.
~*intr.v.* **pimped, pimping, pimps.** **1.** To serve as a pimp. **2.** *Australian & N.Z. Slang.* To betray secrets or be a telltale. Often used with *on.* [19th century : origin obscure.]

pim·per·nel (pímpər-nel, -n'l) *n.* **1.** Any plant of the genus *Anagallis,* especially the scarlet pimpernel, *A. arvensis,* whose small, red, starlike flowers close in bad weather. Also called "poor man's weatherglass", "shepherd's weatherglass". **2.** Any of various similar or related plants, such as the yellow pimpernel, *Lysimachia nemorum.* [Middle English *pympernele,* from Old French *pimpernelle,* from Vulgar Latin *piperīnella* (unattested), from Latin *piper,* PEPPER.]

pim·ple (pímp'l) *n.* A small swelling of the skin, sometimes containing pus; a papule or pustule. [Middle English *pinple,* nasalised form from Old English *pipliant*†, to break out in pimples.] **—pim·pled, pim·ply** *adj.*

pin (pin) *n.* **1.** A short, straight, stiff piece of wire with a blunt head and a sharp point, used especially for fastening. **2.** Anything resembling a pin in shape or use, such as a hairpin or safety pin. **3.** An ornament, brooch, or badge, especially a thin one, fastened to the clothing by means of a pin. **4.** Something of little or no value: *"I would not care a pin."* (Shakespeare). **5.** A slender, cylindrical piece of wood or metal for holding or fastening parts together, or serving as a support for suspending one thing from another, such as: **a.** A thin rod for securing the ends of fractured bones. **b.** A peg for fixing the crown to the root of a tooth. **c.** See **cotter pin.** **6.** *Nautical.* **a.** See **belaying pin.** **b.** See **thole pin.** **7.** *Music.* Any of the pegs securing the strings, and regulating their tension, on a stringed instrument. **8.** The part of a key stem entering a lock. **9.** The safety clasp in a hand grenade, whose removal releases the spring that activates the detonation process. **10.** See **rolling pin.** **11.** Any of the wooden clubs at which the ball is aimed in various bowling games. **12.** In golf, the pole bearing a pennant to mark a hole. **13.** In chess: **a.** The act of pinning an opponent's piece. **b.** The position of a piece when pinned. **14.** In wrestling, a hold that prevents one's opponent from moving, especially one pressing both his shoulders

to the ground. **15.** A small beer cask holding 20.5 litres (4.5 gallons). **16.** *Plural. Informal.* The legs: *steady on his pins.*
~*tr.v.* **pinned, pinning, pins. 1.** To fasten or secure with or as if with a pin or pins. **2. a.** To transfix. **b.** To place in a position of trusting dependence. Used with *on* or *to: He pinned his faith on an absurdity.* **3. a.** In wrestling, to secure (one's opponent) in an immobilising hold, especially when pressing both his shoulders to the ground. **b.** To hold fast; immobilise: *He was pinned under the wreckage.* **4.** *Informal.* To attribute (a wrongdoing or crime). Used with *on: The murder was pinned on the wrong man.* **5.** In chess, to prevent the moving of (a piece) without exposing a more valuable piece to capture. **—pin down. 1.** To oblige (someone) to make a definite response or commitment. **2.** To specify clearly; locate precisely: *I had a feeling of sadness but couldn't pin down its cause.* ~*adj.* Having a grain suggestive of the heads of pins: *pin leather.* [Middle English *pin*, peg, Old English *pinn*, probably from Latin *pinna*, quill.]

pi·ña cloth (péen-yə) *n.* A soft, sheer fabric made from the fibres of pineapple leaves. [Spanish *piña*, pineapple, pinecone, from Latin *pīnea*, from *pīnus*, PINE.]

pi·ña co·la·da (péen-yə kə-láadə, ko-, kō-) *n.* A cocktail consisting of dark rum, pineapple juice, and coconut milk or syrup. [Spanish, "strained pineapple".]

pin·a·fore (pínnə-fawr ‖ -fōr) *n.* A sleeveless garment like an apron, usually with a bib, worn over clothing in order to protect it. [PIN (verb) + AFORE (originally pinned on dress).]

pinafore dress *n.* A sleeveless, collarless dress designed to be worn over a jumper or blouse.

Pi·nang (pə-náng, pe-). State of Peninsular Malaysia. It is made up of Pinang Island at the north end of the Strait of Malacca, and Province Wellesley on the mainland, and produces coconuts, rice, and rubber. George Town, the capital, is also called Pinang.

pi·nas·ter (pī-nástər) *n.* A pine tree, *Pinus pinaster,* native to the Mediterranean region, having large cones and a characteristic pyramidal form. Also called "maritime pine", "cluster pine". [Latin *pīnaster,* a wild pine : *pīnus,* PIN(E) + -ASTER.]

pin·ball (pín-bawl) *n.* A game played on a board or machine in which the player operates a plunger to shoot a ball down a slanted surface having obstacles and targets; especially, a slot-machine game in which a player propels a number of small steel balls, one at a time, into a slanted area containing electronic devices that, when touched by the ball, register points for the contestant. Also used adjectivally: *a pinball machine.*

pince-nez (pánss-náy, pínss-, -nay) *n., pl.* **pince-nez** (*pronounced as singular*). Glasses, without arms or side pieces, that are held in position by being clipped to the bridge of the nose. [French, "pinch-nose" : *pincer,* to PINCH + *nez,* nose, from Latin *nāsus.*]

pin·cer (pín-sər) *n.* Anything resembling the grasping parts of pincers.

pincer movement *n.* Also **pincers movement.** A military manoeuvre in which the enemy is attacked from two flanks with the aim of encirclement.

pin·cers (pín-sərz) *pl.n.* **1.** A grasping tool having a pair of jaws and handles pivoted together to work in opposition. **2.** The articulated, prehensile claws of certain arthropods, such as the lobster. [Middle English *pynsour,* a pincer, from Old French *pinceour* (unattested), from *pincier,* to PINCH.]

pinch (pinch) *v.* **pinched, pinching, pinches.** —*tr.* **1.** To squeeze between the thumb and a finger, the jaws of a tool, or other edges. **2.** To squeeze or bind (a part of the body) in such a way as to cause discomfort or pain: *The shoes pinch my toes.* **3.** To nip, wither, or shrivel: *buds pinched by the frost.* **4.** To cause to become thin or tired-looking, as from lack of food, emotional stress, or the like: *Her face was pinched with grief.* **5.** To give an inadequate supply to; stint: *The children were pinched of food.* **6.** *Informal.* To steal. **7.** *Slang.* To arrest. **8.** To move by means of a pinch bar. **9.** *Nautical.* To head (a boat) too close into the wind. **10.** To cause to have very little money. Usually used in the passive: *very pinched for cash at the moment.* **11.** To cut off the tips of (buds or shoots). Usually used with *back* or *down.* —*intr.* **1.** To press, squeeze, or bind painfully: *This collar pinches.* **2.** To be miserly or excessively frugal. **3.** *Nautical.* To sail too close to the wind. **4.** To become narrow and then give out altogether. Used of a vein of ore.
~*n.* **1.** The act or an instance of pinching. **2. a.** An amount of something that can be held between thumb and forefinger: *a pinch of rosemary.* **b.** A very small amount. **3.** A painful, difficult, or straitened circumstance: *to feel the pinch.* **4.** *Slang.* A theft or robbery. **5.** *Slang.* An arrest or police raid. **—at a pinch.** In extreme circumstances; if unavoidable. [Middle English *pinchen,* to pinch, prick, from Old North French *pinchier* (unattested), variant of Old French *pincier,* from Gallo-Roman *pinctiare, punctiare* (unattested), from Latin *pungere* (past participle *punctus*), to prick.]

pinch bar *n.* A crowbar with a pointed projection at one end.

pinch·beck (pínch-bek) *n.* **1.** An alloy of zinc and copper used as imitation gold. **2.** A cheap imitation.
~ *adj.* **1.** Made of pinchbeck. **2.** Imitation; spurious. [Invented by Christopher *Pinchbeck* (c. 1670–1732), English watchmaker.]

pinch·cock (pínch-kok) *n.* A clamp used to regulate or close a flexible tube, especially in laboratory apparatus.

pinch effect *n. Physics.* The radial constriction of a **plasma** (see), caused by the interaction of its internal electric currents and its self-generated magnetic field.

pinch·pen·ny (pínch-penni) *n., pl.* **-nies.** A mean or niggardly person; a miser.

~*adj.* Miserly; mean.

pin curl *n.* A coiled strand of hair, usually damp, secured with a hairclip and combed into a wave or curl when dry.

pin·cush·ion (pín-kōōsh'n) *n.* A small, firm cushion in which pins are stuck when not in use.

Pin·dar (pín-dər, -daar) (c. 518–438 B.C.). Greek poet. He is remembered especially for his *Odes.*

Pin·dar·ic (pin-dárrik) *adj.* **1.** Pertaining to or characteristic of the poetic style of Pindar. **2.** Of or characteristic of a Pindaric ode.
~*n.* *Often plural.* A Pindaric ode.

Pindaric ode *n.* **1.** An ode in the form developed by Pindar, consisting of a series of triads formed by the strophe, antistrophe, and epode. **2.** An ode based on an adaptation of this form, with irregular stanzas and rhyme schemes, especially as practised by English poets of the 17th and 18th centuries.

pine[1] (pīn) *n.* **1.** Any of various evergreen trees of the genus *Pinus,* having needle-shaped leaves in clusters and bearing cones. Many are valued for shade and ornament and for their wood and resinous sap, which yields turpentine and pine tar. **2.** Loosely, any coniferous tree, especially of the family Pinaceae, such as the cedar, spruce, or fir. **3.** The wood of any of these trees. **4.** Any of various similar but unrelated plants, such as the screw pine or ground pine. [Middle English *pine,* from Old English *pīn* and Old French *pin,* from Latin *pīnus.*]

pine[2] *v.* **pined, pining, pines.** —*intr.* **1.** To suffer intense longing or yearning. Usually used with *for: pining for home.* **2.** To wither or waste away from longing or grief. Usually used with *away.* —*tr. Archaic.* To grieve or mourn for. —See Synonyms at **yearn.**
~*n. Archaic.* Intense longing or grief. [Middle English *pinen,* Old English *pīnian,* torture, from *pīne* (unattested), torture, from Latin *poena,* penalty, from Greek *poinē,* punishment.] **—pin·y, pin·ey** *adj.*

pin·e·al (pínni-əl, pī-née-əl) *adj.* Pertaining to the pineal body. [French *pinéal,* from Latin *pīnea,* pine cone, from *pīneus,* of the pine, from *pīnus,* PINE.]

pineal body *n.* A small glandlike structure in the brain of vertebrates. In animals it secretes melatonin but its functions in humans are uncertain. Also called "pineal gland", "epiphysis".

pineal eye *n.* An extension of the pineal body that forms an eyelike protuberance on the head in certain reptiles and primitive cartilaginous fish.

pine·ap·ple (pín-app'l) *n.* **1.** A tropical American plant, *Ananas comosus,* having large, swordlike leaves and a large, fleshy, edible fruit consisting of the flowers fused into a compound whole with a terminal tuft of leaves. **2.** The fruit of this plant. **3.** *Slang.* A small hand grenade. [Originally "pine cone" (from the resemblance of the fruit to a pine cone), Middle English *pinappel* : PINE + APPLE.]

pineapple weed *n.* A low-growing annual plant, *Matricaria matricarioides,* having greenish-yellow, rayless flower heads and a smell of pineapple when crushed.

pine cone *n.* The woody conical reproductive structure of a pine tree.

pine marten *n.* An arboreal musteline mammal, *Martes martes,* found in woods, especially pine woods, of northern Europe.

pi·nene (pín-een) *n.* Either of two isomeric terpene liquids, $C_{10}H_{16}$, that are the main constituents of oil or spirits of turpentine. [PIN(E) + -ENE.]

pine needle *n.* The needle-shaped leaf of a pine tree.

pine nut *n.* The edible seed of certain pines.

Pi·ne·ro (pi-néer-ō), **Sir Arthur Wing** (1855–1934). British playwright. Abandoning a career in law, he won fame as a writer of immensely popular farces, such as *Dandy Dick* (1887). His later plays include *The Second Mrs Tanqueray* (1893).

pin·er·y (pínəri) *n., pl.* **-ies. 1.** A hothouse or plantation for the cultivation of pineapples. **2.** A forest of pine trees.

pine tar *n.* A viscous or semisolid brown to black substance produced by the destructive distillation of pine wood and used in roofing preparations, paints and varnishes, and as an antiseptic.

pi·ne·tum (pī-née-təm) *n., pl.* **-ta** (-tə). An area planted with pine trees or related conifers, especially for botanical study. [Latin *pīnētum,* pine-wood, from *pīnus,* PINE.]

piney. Variant of **piny.**

pin·feath·er (pín-fethər) *n.* In birds, a growing feather still enclosed in its horny sheath; especially, one just emerging through the skin.

pin·fold (pín-fōld) *n.* A pound for stray animals, such as sheep.
~*tr.v.* **pinfolded, -folding, -folds.** To confine in or as if in a pinfold. [Middle English *pyn(de)fold,* Old English *pundfald* : *pund-,* POUND (enclosure) + *fald,* FOLD.]

ping (ping) *n.* A brief, high-pitched sound, such as that made by a bullet striking metal.
~*intr.v.* **pinged, pinging, pings.** To produce a ping. [Imitative.]

pin·go (píng-gō) *n.* A mound of gravel or earth occurring in arctic regions when water trapped in the ground by permafrost freezes and expands. [Eskimo.]

Ping-Pong (píng-pong) *n.* **1.** A trademark for table-tennis equipment. **2.** *Small* **p,** *small* **p.** The game of table tennis.

pin·guid (píng-gwid) *adj.* **1.** Oily, greasy, or fatty. **2.** Designating soil that is rich and fertile. [Latin *pinguis,* fat + -ID.] **—pin·guid·i·ty** (-gwíddəti) *n.*

pin·head (pín-hed) *n.* **1.** The head of a pin. **2.** Anything small, trifling, or insignificant. **3.** *Slang.* A stupid person. **—pin·head·ed** (-héddid) *adj.*

pin·hole (pín-hōl) *n.* A tiny puncture made by or as if by a pin.

pinhole camera *n.* A camera having a pinhole instead of a lens.

pin·ion[1] (pín-yən) *n.* **1.** A bird's wing. **2.** The outer rear edge of a bird's wing, containing the primary feathers. **3.** A primary feather of a bird.

~tr.v. **pinioned, -ioning, -ions. 1. a.** To remove or bind the wing feathers of (a bird) to prevent flight. **b.** To cut or bind (the wings of a bird). **2.** To restrain or immobilise (a person) by binding the arms. **3.** To fix in one place; make fast: *He jabbed with his fork and pinioned a piece of meat.* [Middle English *pynyon,* from Old French *pignon,* from Vulgar Latin *pinniō,* stem *pinniōn-* (unattested), augmentative of Latin *pinna, penna,* a feather, wing.]

pinion² *n.* A small cogwheel that engages or is engaged by a larger cogwheel or a rack. [French *pignon,* alteration of obsolete *pignol,* from Vulgar Latin *pīneolus,* from Latin *pīnea,* pine cone, from *pīnus,* PINE.]

pin·ite (pín-īt, pī́n-) *n.* A hydrous, usually amorphous mineral silicate of aluminium and potassium. [German *Pinit;* found at *Pini,* mine in Saxony.]

pink¹ (pingk) *n.* **1.** Any of various plants of the genus *Dianthus,* often cultivated for their fragrant flowers. **2.** Any of various similar plants of other genera. **3.** A flower of any of these plants. **4.** The highest degree of excellence or perfection: *He is in the pink of condition.* **5.** Any of a group of colours pale reddish in hue, of medium to high lightness, and low to moderate saturation. **6. a.** Any object of this colour. **b.** Pink clothing. **7.** *British.* **a.** The scarlet coat of a huntsman. **b.** A huntsman wearing a scarlet coat. **8.** *Slang.* A person half-heartedly Communist or left-wing. Used derogatorily.

~adj. **pinker, pinkest. 1.** Of the colour pink. **2.** *British.* Designating the scarlet coat worn by a huntsman. **3.** *Slang.* Half-heartedly or mildly left-wing or Communist. Used derogatorily. [Perhaps short for obsolete *pink eye,* "small eye" (from the shape of the flower), from obsolete Dutch *pinck oog(en),* "small eye(s)", (also) conjunctivitis : *pin(c)k*†, small, the little finger + *oog,* eye.] **—pink·ish** *adj.* **—pink·ness** *n.* **—pink·y** *adj.*

pink² *tr.v.* **pinked, pinking, pinks. 1.** To stab lightly with a pointed weapon; prick. **2.** To decorate with a perforated pattern. **3.** To cut with pinking shears. [Middle English *pynken,* probably of Low German origin; akin to Low German *pinken*†, to peck.]

pink³ *n.* Also **pink·ie** (píngki), **pink·y,** *pl.* **-ies.** *Nautical.* A sailing vessel with a narrow stern. [Middle English *pynk,* from Middle Dutch *pin(c)ke*†.]

pink⁴ *intr.v.* **pinked, pinking, pinks.** To knock because of faulty combustion. Used of a car engine. [Imitative.]

pink elephants *pl.n.* Hallucinations resulting from excessive consumption of alcohol. Used humorously.

Pink·er·ton (píngkərtən), **Allan** (1819–84). U.S. detective, born in Scotland. In 1850 he founded in Chicago Pinkerton's National Detective Agency, later the most famous in the United States.

pink·eye (píngk-ī) *n.* Acute contagious conjunctivitis, with inflamed eyelids and eyeballs. Not in technical usage. [See **pink** (colour).]

pink gin *n.* A drink made from gin, water, and angostura bitters.

pink·ie (píngki) *n.* Also **pink·y,** *pl.* **-ies.** *Chiefly Scottish & U.S. Informal.* **1.** The little finger. **2.** Variant of **pink** (sailing vessel). [Dutch *pinkje,* diminutive of *pink,* little finger, from obsolete *pin(c)k*†.]

pinking shears *pl.n.* Sewing scissors with notched or serrated blades. They are used to finish edges of cloth with a scalloped or zigzag pattern, for decoration or to prevent fraying.

pink·o (píngkō) *n., pl.* **-os** or **-oes.** *Chiefly U.S.* A person regarded as mildly left-wing or Communist. Used derogatorily. **—pink·o** *adj.*

Pink·ster, Pinx·ster (píngkstər) *n. U.S. Regional.* Whit Sunday or Whitsuntide. [Dutch, PENTECOST.]

pin money *n.* **1.** Money for incidental expenses, for example money given by a man to his wife or his daughter for her personal expenses. **2.** Extra money, earned for example from part-time work, that does not contribute to the family budget or household expenses, or is spent on non-essential items. [Originally, a small sum for buying hat-pins or hairpins.]

pin·na (pínnə) *n., pl.* **pinnae** (pínnee) or **-nas. 1.** *Botany.* Any of the leaflets of a pinnate leaf. **2.** *Zoology.* A feather, wing, fin, or similar appendage. **3.** *Anatomy.* The external part of the ear; the auricle. [Latin *pinna, penna,* wing, feather.] **—pin·nal** *adj.*

pin·nace (pín-əss, -iss) *n. Nautical.* **1.** A small sailing boat formerly used as a tender for merchant and war vessels. **2.** Any small ship or ship's boat. [French *pinace,* from Old Spanish *pinaza* or Italian *pinaccia,* from (unattested) Vulgar Latin *pīnācea (nāvis),* "(ship) of pine-wood", from Latin *pīnus,* pine tree.]

pin·na·cle (pínnək'l) *n.* **1.** *Architecture.* A small turret or spire on a roof or buttress. **2.** Any tall, pointed formation, such as a mountain peak. **3.** The highest point; the summit; the acme: *the pinnacle of achievement.* —See Synonyms at **summit.**

~tr.v. **pinnacled, -cling, -cles. 1.** To furnish with a pinnacle. **2.** To place on or as if on a pinnacle. [Middle English *pin(n)acle,* from Old French, from Late Latin *pinnāculum,* "little wing," from Latin *pinna,* feather, wing.]

pin·nate (pín-ayt, -ət, -it) *adj.* Also **pin·nat·ed** (pi-náytid, pínnaytid). **1.** Resembling a feather; pennate. **2.** *Botany.* Having leaflets, lobes, or divisions in a feather-like arrangement on each side of a common axis, as many compound leaves do. [Latin *pinnātus,* feathered, from *pinna,* feather.] **—pin·nate·ly** *adv.*

pin·nat·i·fid (pi-nátti-fid, -náyti-) *adj. Botany.* Having pinnately cleft lobes or divisions reaching over halfway to the midrib. Said of certain leaves. [Latin *pinnātus,* PINNATE + -FID.] **—pin·nat·i·fid·ly** *adv.*

pin·nat·i·sect (pi-nátti-sekt, -náyti-) *adj. Botany.* Divided nearly to the midrib. Said of certain leaves. [PINNATI- + -SECT.]

pin·ni·ped (pínni-ped) *adj.* Also **pin·ni·pe·di·an** (-peédi-ən). *Zoology.* Of or belonging to the Pinnipedia, an order of aquatic mammals that includes the seals, walruses, and similar animals having finlike flippers for locomotion.

~n. A mammal belonging to this order. [Latin *pinna,* feather, wing, PINNA + -PED.]

pin·nule (pínnewl) *n.* Also **pin·nu·la** (pínnew-lə) *pl.* **-lae** (-lee). **1.** *Botany.* Any of the lobes of a leaflet of a pinnately compound leaf. **2.** *Zoology.* A feather-like or plumelike organ or part, such as a small fin, or any of the appendages of a crinoid. [New Latin *pinnula,* from Latin, diminutive of *pinna, penna,* feather, wing, fin.] **—pin·nu·lar** (-lər) *adj.*

PIN number (pin) *n.* A personal identification number, as required for various banking transactions. [From *P(ersonal) I(dentification) N(umber)* plus a redundant *number.*]

pin·ny (pínni) *n., pl.* **-nies.** *Informal.* A pinafore or apron.

Pi·no·chet (U·gar·te) (peénō-shay; *Spanish* -chét), **Augusto** (1915–). Chilean general. He led the group of officers who, in 1973, overthrew the elected government of Salvador Allende. President 1974–90, he directed a notoriously brutal junta. He resigned as commander-in-chief of the army in 1998 and took up a lifelong post in the senate.

pi·noch·le, pi·noc·le, pe·nuch·le (peé-nuck'l, -nock'l) *n.* **1.** A game of cards, played chiefly in the United States, for two to four persons, played with a special pack of 48 cards, with points being scored by taking tricks and forming certain combinations. **2.** The combination of the queen of spades and jack of diamonds in this game. [19th century : origin obscure.]

pi·not noir (peénō nwar) *n.* A variety of black grape used for making Champagne and red Burgundy wine. [French, "black pinot" : *pinot,* variant of *pineau,* diminutive of *pin,* pine (tree); comparing the shape of its grape clusters to pine cones.]

pin·point (pín-poynt) *n.* **1.** An extremely small thing; a particle; a bit: *a pinpoint of light.* **2.** A tiny or insignificant spot: *the pinpoint of ground upon which we stand.* **3.** *Military.* **a.** A point on a map indicating a strictly defined target. **b.** A precisely identified and limited target. **4.** The sharp tip of a pin.

~tr.v. **pinpointed, -pointing, -points. 1. a.** To locate and identify precisely: *Our radar pinpointed the planes.* **b.** To define or delimit precisely. **2.** *Military.* To take precise aim at: *pinpoint a target.*

~adj. **1.** Characterised by meticulous precision: *He spots flaws with pinpoint accuracy.* **2.** Minuscule; tiny: *pinpoint creatures.*

pin·prick (pín-prik) *n.* **1.** A slight puncture made by or as if by a pin. **2.** An insignificant wound. **3.** A minor annoyance.

~v. **pinpricked, -pricking, -pricks.** *—tr.* To puncture with or as if with a pin. *—intr.* To make a slight puncture with a pin.

pins and needles *n. Used with a singular or plural verb.* A tingling felt in a part of the body numbed from lack of circulation.

pin·scher (pínshər) *n.* See **Doberman pinscher.**

pin·stripe (pín-strīp) *n.* **1.** A thin stripe on a fabric. **2.** A kind of fabric with thin stripes, often used for men's suits. Also used adjectivally: *a pinstripe suit.*

pint (pīnt) *n. Abbr.* **p., pt., o. 1. a.** A unit of volume or capacity, used in liquid measure, equal to one eighth of a gallon, in Britain 0.568 litre (20 fluid ounces), and in the United States 0.473 litre (16 fluid ounces). **b.** A unit of volume or capacity used in dry measure in the United States, equal to one half of a quart or 0.5506 litre. **2.** A container such as a milk bottle having such a capacity, or the amount of a substance that can be contained in it. **3.** *British Informal.* **a.** A pint of beer. **b.** A drink of beer in a pub. [Middle English *pinte,* from Old French, probably from Medieval Latin *pincta,* "painted mark (on a measuring container)", from Vulgar Latin *pinctus* (unattested), painted. See **pinto.**]

pint·a¹ (pī́ntə) *n. Informal.* A pint of milk. [From pronunciation of *pint of,* as in CUPPA and in the slogan, "Drinka pinta milka day".]

pin·ta² (pín-tə, -taa; *Spanish* peén-) *n.* A contagious skin disease prevalent in tropical America, caused by spirochaete microorganisms, and characterised by extreme thickening and localised discoloration of the skin. [American Spanish, from Spanish, painted mark, from the feminine of Vulgar Latin *pinctus* (unattested), painted. See **pinto.**]

pin·ta·de·ra (píntə-daír-ə) *n.* A decorative seal or stamp, of the Neolithic period and early American cultures, usually made of terracotta and thought to have been used for applying pigment to the skin. [Spanish, instrument for painting, from *pintar,* to PAINT.]

pin·tail (pín-tayl) *n., pl.* **-tails** or collectively **pintail.** A duck, *Anas acuta,* of the Northern Hemisphere, having grey, brown, and white plumage and a sharply pointed tail in the male.

Pin·ter (píntər), **Harold** (1930–). British playwright, actor, and director. His plays, which include *The Birthday Party* (1958), *The Caretaker* (1960) and *The Homecoming* (1965), are known for their elusive dialogue and atmosphere of menace. **—Pin·ter·esque** (-ésk) *adj.*

pin·tle (pínt'l) *n.* An upright pin or bolt used as a pivot; specifically: **1.** *Nautical.* The pin on which a rudder turns. **2.** The pin on a gun carriage. **3.** A pin or bolt on the back of a towing vehicle to which a towed vehicle is attached. [Middle English *pintel,* "penis", Old English *pintel*†.]

pin·to (píntō) *n., pl.* **-tos** or **-toes.** *U.S.* Any horse with irregular spots or markings.

~adj. U.S. Irregularly marked; piebald. [American Spanish, from obsolete Spanish, "painted", "spotted", from Vulgar Latin *pinctus* (unattested), variant of Latin *pictus,* past participle of Latin *pingere,*

to paint.]

pint-size (pīnt-sīz) *adj.* Also **pint·sized** (-sīzd). *Informal.* Of small dimensions; diminutive.

pin-up (pín-up) *n.* **1.** A picture to be pinned up on a wall; especially, a photograph of a sexually attractive person or a nude or partially dressed person. **2.** A person considered as a suitable model for such a picture. **3.** A photograph of a celebrity.
~adj. U.S. Designed to be attached to a wall: *a pin-up lamp.*

pin·wheel (pín-weel, -hweel) *n.* **1.** A firework, a small **catherine wheel** *(see).* **2.** A cogwheel with a circle of pins at right angles to its face, used as a tripping device. **3.** *U.S.* A toy, a **windmill** *(see).*

pin·work (pín-wurk) *n.* The fine stitches raised in needlepoint lace from the surface of a motif.

pin·worm (pín-wurm) *n.* A small nematode worm, *Enterobius vermicularis,* that infects the human intestines and rectum, especially in children. Also called "threadworm".

pin wrench *n.* A wrench having a projection designed to fit a hole in the object to be turned.

pinx·it (píngksit) *n. Abbr.* **pinx.** *Latin.* He or she painted (this). Formerly used as part of the painter's signature on a painting.

Pinxter. Variant of **Pinkster.**

pin·yin (pín-yín) *n.* A system of transliteration of Chinese characters into Roman characters, introduced in China in 1957. [Chinese, "spell sound".]

pi·o·let (peé-ə-lay, -láy) *n.* A kind of ice axe. [French, diminutive of French dialectal *piola,* small axe, ultimately from Old Provençal *apcha, apia,* axe, from Germanic; akin to Old High German *happa,* sickle.]

pi·on (pī-on) *n. Symbol* π *Physics.* Any of three elementary particles in the meson family, *pi zero, pi minus,* and *pi plus,* having zero spin, negative parity, and 0, + 1, and − 1 times the charge of the electron respectively. The pi zero has a lifetime of 9×10^{-16} second and decays into photons, while the two pions have lifetimes of about 2.5×10^{-8} and decay into leptons. They are exchanged between particles in the strong remaining interaction. Also called "pi meson". [Shortened from PI MESON.]

pi·o·neer (pī-ə-neér) *n.* **1.** One who ventures into unknown or unclaimed territory to settle. Also used adjectivally: *a pioneer spirit.* **2.** An innovator in a particular field: *a pioneer in aviation.* Also used adjectivally: *pioneer research.* **3.** A military engineer employed in the construction and fortification of roads, bridges, or the like, and the maintenance of communication lines. **4.** *Ecology.* A plant species that is one of the first to establish itself in a previously barren environment.
~v. **pioneered, -neering, -neers.** *—tr.* **1.** To initiate or participate in the development of: *men who pioneered the submarine.* **2. a.** To explore or open up (a region). **b.** To be a pioneer to (travellers, for example); conduct. *—intr.* To act as a pioneer. [French *pionnier,* from Old French *peon(n)ier,* originally "a foot soldier sent out to clear the way", from *pion, peon,* foot soldier. See **peon.**]

pi·ous (pī-əss) *adj.* **1.** Having or showing reverence and earnest compliance in the observance of religion; devout. **2. a.** Marked by conspicuous devoutness. **b.** Marked by false devoutness; solemnly hypocritical. **3.** Not secular; devotional: *pious readings.* **4.** Professing or exhibiting a strict, traditional sense of virtue and morality; high-minded: *the pious instructions of his parents.* **5.** Well-intentioned but having little likelihood of being realised. Used chiefly in the phrase *a pious hope.* **6.** *Archaic.* Having filial reverence; dutiful. [Latin *pius.*] **—pi·ous·ly** *adv.* **—pi·ous·ness** *n.*

pip[1] (pip) *n.* **1.** The seed of a fleshy fruit, such as an apple or orange. **2.** A rootstock of certain flowering plants, especially lily of the valley. **3.** *U.S. Informal.* Something remarkable of its kind: *a pip of a plan.* [Shortened from PIPPIN.]

pip[2] *tr.v.* **pipped, pipping, pips.** *British Slang.* **1.** To strike with a gunshot; hit. **2.** To defeat, especially at the last moment: *He was pipped at the post.* **3.** To blackball. [Perhaps from PIP (dot on dice, hence, "small ball").]

pip[3] *n.* **1.** A dot indicating a unit of numerical value on playing cards, dice, or dominoes. **2.** *British Informal.* A shoulder insignia indicating the rank of certain officers in the British Army. **3.** A radar signal. **4.** Any of the segments found on the surface of a pineapple. [16th century : *peepe*†.]

pip[4] *v.* **pipped, pipping, pips.** *—tr.* To break through (an eggshell) in hatching. *—intr.* To peep or chirp, as a young bird does.
~n. A short, high-pitched signal, especially one of a series constituting a time signal in a radio transmission. [Variant of PEEP (peek) and PEEP (cheep).]

pip[5] *n.* **1. a.** A disease of birds, characterised by a thick mucous discharge that forms a crust in the mouth and throat. **b.** The crust symptomatic of this disease. **2.** *British Slang.* A bad mood or depression. Preceded by *the*: *She gives me the pip.* [Middle English *pippe,* from Middle Dutch, phlegm, mucus, from West Germanic *pipit* (unattested), probably from Vulgar Latin *pīppīta,* (earlier) *pītīta* (both unattested), alterations of Latin *pītuīta,* phlegm.]

pi·pa (peépə) *n.* A South American toad, *Pipa pipa,* the female of which carries her fertilised eggs on her back, where they develop in pits in the skin. Also called "Surinam toad". [Surinam dialect *pipá* (feminine), *pipál* (masculine), of African origin.]

pip·age (pīpij) *n.* **1.** The transmission of liquids through pipes. **2.** The charge for such transmission. **3.** Pipes; piping.

pipal. Variant of **peepul.**

pipe (pīp) *n.* **1. a.** Any hollow cylinder or tubular conveyance for a fluid or gas. **b.** A section or piece of such a tube. **2. a.** An instrument for smoking, consisting of a tube of wood or clay with a mouthpiece at one end and a small bowl at the other. **b.** The amount of tobacco or other substance to fill the bowl of a smoking pipe; a pipeful. **3. a.** *Biology.* A tubular part or organ. **b.** *Plural. Informal.* The human respiratory system or vocal cords. **4.** *Abbr.* **p. a.** A wine cask having a capacity of 105 gallons (457 litres). **b.** This volume as a unit of liquid measure. **5.** *Abbr.* **p.** *Music.* **a.** A tubular wind instrument, such as a flute. **b.** Any of the tubes in an organ. **c.** *Plural.* A small wind instrument, consisting of tubes of different lengths bound together: *pipes of Pan.* **d.** *Plural.* A set of bagpipes. **e.** A primitive type of flute that was played with one hand while the other beat a drum or tabor. **6.** *Archaic.* The sound of the voice, especially as used in singing or acting. **7.** A birdcall. **8. a.** *Nautical.* A kind of whistle used for signalling crew members: *a boatswain's pipe.* **b.** The sound this pipe makes. **9.** *Mining.* **a.** A vertical, cylindrical vein of ore. **b.** Any of the vertical veins of eruptive origin in which diamonds are found in South Africa. **10.** *Geology.* An eruptive passageway opening into the crater of a volcano. **11.** A cone-shaped cavity in a steel ingot, formed during cooling by unequal contraction. **—put that in your pipe and smoke it.** That is the situation whether you like it or not.
~v. **piped, piping, pipes.** *—tr.* **1. a.** To convey (liquid or gas) by means of pipes. **b.** To supply or convey as if by means of a pipe. **2.** To provide or connect with pipes. **3. a.** To play (a tune) on a pipe or pipes: *"Piper, pipe that song again."* (William Blake). **b.** To lead by playing on pipes. **4.** *Nautical.* To call (crew members, for example) by sounding the boatswain's pipe. **5.** To utter in a shrill, reedy tone. **6.** To furnish (a garment or fabric) with piping. **7. a.** To force (icing, for example) through a tube or forcing bag fitted with a nozzle to make a decorative pattern. **b.** To make (a decorative pattern) in this way. *—intr.* **1.** To play on a pipe. **2.** To speak shrilly; make a shrill sound. **3.** To chirp or whistle, as a bird does. **4.** *Nautical.* To call on a boatswain's pipe. **5.** In metallurgy, to develop conical cavities. **—pipe down.** *Informal.* To stop talking; be quiet. **—pipe up.** To speak up, especially in a small, shrill voice. [Middle English *pipe,* Old English *pīpe,* from Common Germanic *pīpa* (unattested), from Common Romance *pīpa* (unattested), from Latin *pīpāre,* to chirp.] **—pipe·ful** *n.* **—pip·y** *adj.*

pipe·clay (pīp-klay) *n.* A fine white clay used in making tobacco pipes and pottery, in calico printing, and in whitening leather.

pipe cleaner *n.* A pliant, tufted piece of wire used for cleaning the stem of a tobacco pipe.

piped music *n.* Prerecorded background music as played continuously in supermarkets, airports, or the like.

pipe dream *n.* A wishful, fantastic notion or hope. [From the fantasies induced by opium.]

pipe·fish (pīp-fish) *n., pl.* **-fishes** or collectively **pipefish.** Any of various slim, elongated marine or freshwater fishes of the family Syngnathidae, characterised by a tubelike snout and an external covering of bony plates. Also called "needlefish".

pipe·fit·ting (pīp-fitting) *n.* **1. a.** The act or work of joining pipes together. **b.** A branch of the plumbing trade that deals specifically with the installation and repair of piping systems. **2.** A section of pipe used to join two or more pipes together.

pipe·line (pīp-līn) *n.* **1.** A long pipe, often buried underground, for the conveyance of water, gas, or petroleum products. **2.** A channel by which information of a generally secret or confidential nature is transmitted. **3.** A line of communication or route of supply: *a new pipeline for medical supplies.* **—in the pipeline.** On the way to being accomplished or realised: *a promotion in the pipeline.*
~tr.v. **pipelined, -lining, -lines.** **1.** To convey by means of a pipeline. **2.** To lay a pipeline through.

pipe organ *n.* A musical instrument, an **organ** *(see).*

pip·er (pīpər) *n.* One who plays a pipe or the bagpipes.

Pip·er (pīpər), **John (Egerton Christmas)** (1903–92). British painter and writer. He also designed stage sets, as well as stained-glass windows for Coventry Cathedral.

pi·per·a·zine (pi-pérrə-zeen, pī-, -zin) *n.* A colourless crystalline compound, $C_4H_{10}N_2$, used to inhibit corrosion, in insecticides, and as an anthelmintic. [PIPER(INE) + AZ(O)- + -INE.]

pip·er·ine (píppər-een, -īn, -in) *n.* A crystalline alkaloid, $C_{17}H_{19}NO_3$, extracted from black pepper, and used as flavouring and as an insecticide. [Latin *piper,* PEPPER + -INE.]

pi·per·o·nal (pi-pérrə-n'l, pī-, píppərō-, -nal) *n.* A white powder, $C_8H_6O_3$, having a floral odour, used as flavouring and in perfume. Also called "heliotropin". [PIPER(INE) + -ON(E) + -AL.]

pipe·stone (pīp-stōn) *n.* A heat-hardened compacted red clay used by American Indians for making tobacco pipes.

pi·pette, pi·pet (pi-pét || *chiefly U.S.* pī-) *n. Chemistry.* Any of variously shaped glass tubes, open at both ends, usually calibrated, and used especially to transfer small volumes of liquid from one container to another. [French, diminutive of *pipe,* PIPE.]

pipe·wort (pīp-wurt || -wawrt) *n.* An aquatic plant, *Ericocaulon septangulare,* having submerged, narrow, translucent leaves and small greyish flowers in a flat, button-like cluster.

pipe wrench *n.* A wrench with two serrated jaws, one adjustable, used for gripping and turning pipes. Compare **Stillson wrench.**

pip·ing (pīping) *n.* **1.** A system of pipes, such as one used in plumbing. **2.** *Music.* **a.** The act of playing on a pipe. **b.** The music produced by a pipe. **3.** A shrill, high-pitched sound. **4.** A rounded strip of cloth, sometimes covering a cord, used for trimming the seams and edges of garments or furniture covers. **5.** Rounded strands produced by forcing a substance such as icing through a

tube or forcing bag with a nozzle, used to decorate food.
~adj. **1.** Playing on a pipe. **2.** Making a high-pitched sound with little resonance, as does a pipe.
~adv. Used as an intensive: *piping hot.*

pip·i·strelle (píppi-strél) *n.* Any small bat of the genus *Pipistrellus*, especially *P. pipistrellus.* [French, from Italian *pipistrello, vipistrello,* ultimately from Latin *vespertilio,* bat, from *vesper,* evening.]

pip·it (píppit) *n.* Any of various widely distributed songbirds of the genus *Anthus,* characteristically having brownish upper plumage and a light, streaked breast. The meadow pipit, *A. pratensis,* was formerly also called "titlark". [Imitative of its note.]

pip·kin (píp-kin) *n.* **1.** A small earthenware or metal cooking pot. **2.** A **piggin** *(see).* [16th century : origin obscure.]

pip·pin (píppin) *n.* **1.** Any of several varieties of eating apple. **2.** *Informal.* An admired person or thing. Not in current usage. [Middle English *pepin, pipin,* seed, seedling apple, from Old French *pepin,* from Romance stem *pipp-* (suggestive of a small seed).]

pipsqueak (píp-skweek) *n.* A small or insignificant person. Used derogatorily. [Originally a name given to a small artillery shell used by the Germans in World War I : PIP (dot) + SQUEAK.]

pi·quant (peék-ənt, -ON, -aant || *U.S. also* píkwənt) *adj.* **1.** Pleasantly pungent in taste or odour; spicy. **2.** Interesting yet having a disconcerting or troubling effect: *a piquant reversal of roles.* **3.** *Archaic.* Causing hurt pride or feelings; stinging: *a piquant answer.* [Old French, present participle of *piquer,* to pierce, prick, PIQUE.] **—pi·quan·cy** (-ən-si) *n.* **—pi·quant·ly** *adv.*

pique (peek) *n.* A feeling of resentment or vexation arising from wounded pride or vanity: *an old man's fit of pique.*
~tr.v. **piqued, piquing, piques. 1.** To cause to feel resentment or vexation; injure the pride of: *piqued by her snub.* **2.** To provoke; arouse: *The portrait piqued my curiosity.* **3.** To pride (oneself). Used with *on* or *upon*: *piqued themselves on their style.* [Old French, "a pricking", from *piquer,* to prick, from Vulgar Latin *piccāre* (unattested), perhaps from Latin *pīcus,* magpie, woodpecker.]

pi·qué (peé-kay || *U.S. also* pi-káy) *n.* A tightly woven fabric with various raised patterns, produced especially by a double warp. [French, "quilting", from *piquer,* to backstitch (as in quilting), to prick, PIQUE.]

pi·quet (pi-két, -káy) *n.* A card game for two people, played with a pack from which all cards below the seven (aces being high) are removed. [French, of obscure origin.]

pi·ra·cy (pír-ə-si) *n., pl.* **-cies. 1.** Robbery committed at sea. **2.** Any illegal act, such as kidnapping, committed at sea or in the air. **3.** The unauthorised use or reproduction of copyright material.

Pi·rae·us (pīr-eé-əss). *Greek* **Pi·re·evs** or **Pi·rai·évs** (pee-re-éffs). Port of Athens, Greece, situated on the Saronic Gulf. It is the main industrial part of the city.

pi·ra·gua (pi-raág-wə, -rág-) *n.* **1.** A canoe made by hollowing out a tree trunk; a dugout. **2.** A flat-bottomed sailing boat with two masts. [Spanish, from Carib *piraguas.*]

Pi·ran·del·lo (pírrən-déllō, peér-ən-), **Luigi** (1867–1936). Italian playwright, novelist, and short-story writer. His work examines the relativity of truth and the elusiveness of identity, as in *Six Characters in Search of an Author* (1921) and *Henry IV* (1922). Pirandello won the Nobel prize for literature in 1934.

Pi·ra·ne·si (peér-ə-náy-zi, -si), **Giovanni Battista** (1720–78). Italian artist, known for his architectural etchings. His studies of Rome and its ruins contributed to the emergence of neoclassicism.

pi·ra·nha (pi-raán-ə, -yə) *n.* Any of several tropical American freshwater fishes of the genus *Serrasalmus.* They are voraciously carnivorous and often attack and destroy living animals. [Portuguese, from Tupi, variant of *piraya,* scissors.]

pi·ra·ru·cu (pi-raárə-kōō) *n.* A fish, the **arapaima** *(see).* [Portuguese *pirarucú,* from Tupi *pirá-rucú,* "red fish" : *pirá,* fish + *(u)rucú,* red.]

pi·rate (pír-ət, -it) *n.* **1.** One who robs at sea or plunders the land near the sea without commission from a sovereign nation. **2.** A ship used for this purpose. **3.** One who operates without proper authorisation, especially: **a.** One who makes use of or reproduces the work, especially copyright material, of another, without permission or illicitly: *a video pirate.* **b.** One who broadcasts on an unauthorised radio wavelength. Also used adjectivally: *a pirate radio station.*
~v. **pirated, -rating, -rates.** *—tr.* **1.** To attack and rob (a ship at sea). **2.** To seize (goods) by piracy. **3.** To make use of or reproduce (another's work) illicitly. *—intr.* To act as a pirate. [Middle English, from Latin *pīrāta,* from Greek *peiratēs,* "attacker", from *peiran,* to attempt, attack, from *peira,* an attempt.] **—pi·rate, pi·rat·ic** (pīr-áttik), **pi·rat·i·cal** *adj.* **—pi·rat·i·cal·ly** *adv.*

pi·rog (pi-rōg) *n., pl.* **-rogen** (-ən), **-roghi** (-ee) or **-rogi.** A large Russian pastry made of dough with various stuffings of meat, fish, rice, eggs, and vegetables. [Russian, probably from *pir,* feast.]

pi·rogue (pi-rōg) *n.* A canoe made from a hollowed tree trunk; a piragua. [French, from Spanish *piragua,* PIRAGUA.]

pir·ou·ette (pírroo-ét) *n.* In ballet, a full turn of the body on the tip of the toe or on the ball of the foot.
~intr.v. **pirouetted, -etting, -ettes.** To execute a pirouette. [French, from Old French *pirouet*†, a spinning top.]

pi·rozh·ki, pi·rosh·ki (pi-rózh-ki, -rósh-) *pl.n. Singular* **pi·rozh·ok** (pírrə-zhók). Small Russian pastries made with various fillings. [Russian, small pocket of pastry, diminutive of PIROG.]

Pi·sa (peé-zə; *Italian* -sa). Capital of Pisa province, Tuscany, Italy. Situated on the river Arno near the Ligurian Sea, it was a commercial and artistic centre (12th and 13th centuries); its many historical monuments include its leaning Romanesque bell tower.

pis al·ler (peéz-állay || *U.S.* -a-láy) *n. French.* A course of action adopted for want of a better alternative. [French, "worst to go".]

Pi·sa·nel·lo (peé-zə-néllō; *Italian* -sa-), born Antonio Pisano; also called Vittore Pisano (*c.*1395–*c.*1455). Italian artist and medallist. In his own day he was celebrated for his medallions; he is especially admired today for his sketches of the natural world.

Pi·sa·no (pee-zaá-nō, -saá-), **Andrea,** born Andrea da Pontedera (*c.* 1290–*c.*1348). Italian sculptor and architect. He worked mainly in Florence where he executed the bronze door of the Baptistery.

pis·ca·ry (pískəri) *n., pl.* **-ries. 1.** *Law.* The right to fish. Used chiefly in the phrase *common of piscary,* meaning the right to fish in waters belonging to another. **2.** A place in which to fish. [Middle English *piscairie,* from Medieval Latin *piscāria,* right to fish, from Latin, neuter plural of *piscārius,* of fish or fishing, from *piscis,* fish.]

pis·ca·to·ri·al (pískə-táwri-əl || -tōri-) *adj.* Also **pis·ca·to·ry** (-tri, -təri) **1.** Of or pertaining to fish, fishermen, or fishing. **2.** Involved in or devoted to fishing. [Latin *piscātōrius,* of fish or fishing, from *piscātor,* fisherman, from *piscārī,* to fish, from *piscis,* fish.] **—pis·ca·to·ri·al·ly** *adv.*

Pi·sces (pí-seez, písk-eez, píss-) *n.* **1.** A constellation in the equatorial region of the Northern Hemisphere near Aries and Pegasus. **2. a.** The 12th sign of the **zodiac** *(see).* Also called the "Fish", the "Fishes". **b.** One born under this sign. **3.** A taxonomic group that includes the cartilaginous and bony fishes. [Middle English, from Medieval Latin, "the Fishes", from plural of Latin *piscis,* fish.] **—Pi·sce·an** *n. & adj.*

pisci– *comb. form.* Indicates fish; for example, **pisciform.** [From Latin *piscis,* fish.]

pi·sci·cul·ture (píssi-kulchər || píski-, pí-si-) *n.* The breeding, hatching, and rearing of fish under controlled conditions. **—pi·sci·cul·tur·al** (-kúlchərəl) *adj.* **—pi·sci·cul·tur·ist** (-kúlchərist) *n.*

pi·sci·form (píssi-fawrm || píski-, pí-si-) *adj.* Having the shape of a fish. [PISCI- + -FORM.]

pi·sci·na (pi-seé-nə, -sí-, -sheé-) *n., pl.* **-nae** (-nee) or **-nas.** *Ecclesiastical.* A stone basin with a drain for carrying away the water used in ceremonial ablutions. Also called "sacrarium". [Medieval Latin, from Latin, fish tank, from *piscis,* fish.] **—pis·ci·nal** *adj.*

pi·scine (píss-īn || písk-, píss-, -in, -een) *adj.* Of, pertaining to, or typical of a fish. [Medieval Latin *piscīnus,* from *piscis,* fish.]

Pi·scis Aus·tri·nus (pí-siss oss-trínəss, píssiss, awss-) *n.* A constellation in the Southern Hemisphere near Aquarius and Grus. [New Latin, "(the) Southern Fish".]

pish (pish) *interj.* Used to express disdain.

pi·shogue (pi-shōg) *n. Irish.* **1.** Black magic; sorcery; witchcraft. **2.** An evil spell; an incantation. [Irish *piseog,* witchcraft.]

pi·si·form (píssi-fawrm, pí-si-) *adj.* Suggestive of a pea in size or shape; pealike.
~n. Anatomy. A small bone at the junction of the ulna and the wrist. [Latin *pīsum,* PEA + -FORM.]

pis·mire (píss-mīr, píz-) *n.* An ant. [Middle English *pissemyre,* from *pisse,* PISS (from the urinous smell of an anthill) + obsolete *mire,* ant, probably from Scandinavian; akin to Danish *myre,* ant.]

pi·so·lite (pí-sō-līt, -sə-) *n. Geology.* A concretionary limestone composed of globules more than 2 millimetres in diameter. [New Latin *pisolithus,* "pea stone" : Greek *pisos, pison,* PEA + -LITE.] **—pi·so·lit·ic** (-líttik) *adj.*

piss (piss) *v.* **pissed, pissing, pisses.** *—intr.* **1.** *Vulgar.* To urinate. **2.** *Vulgar Slang.* To rain. Often used with *down.* *—tr. Vulgar.* **1.** To discharge (blood, for example) with the urine. **2.** To wet or soak with urine. **—piss about** or **around.** *Vulgar Slang.* To behave in a silly or time-wasting fashion. **—piss off.** *Vulgar Slang.* **1.** To annoy, irritate, or anger. **2.** To go, depart, or leave. **—piss on** or **over.** *Vulgar Slang.* To defeat or vanquish utterly.
~n. Vulgar. **1.** Urine. **2.** An act of urinating. **—take the piss out of.** *Vulgar Slang.* To make fun of.
~interj. Vulgar Slang. Used to express anger, frustration, or disappointment. [Middle English, from Old French *pisser,* from Vulgar Latin *pisare* (unattested), of imitative origin.]

Pis·sar·ro (pi-saárō), **Camille** (1830–1903). French impressionist painter. He took part in all eight impressionist exhibitions (1874–86), chiefly producing rural scenes.

piss artist *n. British Vulgar Slang.* **1.** A person who is known to drink alcohol and who often behaves in a high-spirited or buffoonish way. **2.** A very incompetent or unreliable person.

pissed (pist) *adj.* **1.** *British Vulgar Slang.* Drunk; intoxicated. **2.** *U.S. Slang.* Annoyed; irritated.

pis·soir (piss-waar, pee-swaár) *n. French.* A public urinal.

piss-up (píss-up) *n. British Vulgar Slang.* A drinking bout, especially one involving a group of people.

pis·ta·chi·o (piss-táshi-ō, -taáshi-, -táchi-) *n., pl.* **-os.** Also **pis·tache** (-tásh). **1.** A tree, *Pistacia vera,* of the Mediterranean region and western Asia, bearing small hard-shelled nuts. **2.** The nut of this tree, having an edible, oily, green kernel. Also called "pistachio nut". **3.** Moderate to light yellowish green. [Italian *pistaccio,* from Latin *pistācium,* from Greek *pistakion,* pistachio nut, from *pistakē,* pistachio tree, from Persian *pistah*†.]

pis·ta·reen (pístə-reén) *n.* A small silver coin used in America and the West Indies during the 18th century. [Probably altered from Spanish *peseta,* PESETA.]

piste (peest) *n.* **1.** A ski slope or run of densely packed snow. **2.** The area in which a fencing bout takes place. [French, racetrack.]

pis·til (pístil) *n. Botany.* The female reproductive organ of a flower,

including the stigma, style, and ovary. [French *pistil,* from Latin *pistillum,* PESTLE.]
pis·til·late (pístil-ayt, -ət, -it) *adj. Botany.* **1.** Having a pistil or pistils. **2.** Bearing pistils but no stamens: *pistillate flowers.*
pis·tol (píst'l) *n.* A firearm designed to be held and fired with one hand. **—hold a pistol to (someone's) head.** To bring overwhelming pressure to bear on (someone) to comply with one's wishes.
~tr.v. **pistolled** or *U.S.* **-oled, -tolling,** or *U.S.* **-toling, -tols.** To shoot with a pistol. [French *pistole,* from German *Pistole,* from Czech *pištala,* "pipe", akin to Russian *pischal,* shepherd's pipe.]
pis·tole (pi-stōl, pístōl) *n.* An obsolete gold coin, used in various European countries until the late 19th century. [French, variant of *pistolet,* perhaps "small pistol" (originally a name given in jest to Spanish coins which were smaller than French coins, as a pistol is smaller than a harquebus), from *pistole,* PISTOL.]
pis·to·leer (pístə-léer) *n.* Formerly, a soldier armed with a pistol.
pistol grip *n.* **1.** The grip of a pistol, shaped to fit the hand. **2.** A similar grip sometimes used on a rifle or other firearm. **3.** A grip used on certain tools, such as a saw, shaped to fit the hand.
pis·tol-whip (píst'l-wip, -hwip) *tr.v.* **-whipped, -whipping, -whips.** *Chiefly U.S.* To beat with a pistol.
pis·ton (pístən) *n.* **1.** A solid cylinder or disc that fits into a larger cylinder and moves back and forth under fluid pressure, as in a reciprocating engine, or displaces or compresses fluids, as in pumps and compressors. **2.** *Music.* A valve mechanism in brass instruments for altering pitch. [French, from Old French, from Old Italian *pistone, pestone,* augmentative of *pestello,* PESTLE.]
piston ring *n.* An adjustable split metal ring that fits round a piston and closes the gap between the piston and cylinder wall.
piston rod *n.* A **connecting rod** *(see)* that is attached to a piston.
pit[1] (pit) *n.* **1.** A relatively deep hole in the ground. **2. a.** An area excavated for minerals. Often used in combination: *a chalkpit.* **b.** A coal mine. **c.** The shaft of a coal mine. **3.** A trap consisting of a concealed hole in the ground; a pitfall. **4.** Hell. Preceded by *the.* **5.** An enclosed space, often one dug in the ground, in which animals, such as dogs or gamecocks, are placed for fighting. Often used in combination: *a cockpit.* **6. a.** The lowest surface of a body, organ, or part: *the pit of the stomach.* **b.** A small indentation in the skin left by disease or injury; a pockmark. **7. a.** An **orchestra pit** *(see).* **b.** *Chiefly British.* The ground floor of a theatre. **c.** Those who sit in this area. **8.** *U.S.* The section of an exchange where trading in a specific commodity is carried on. **9.** *Botany.* A thin-walled area in the wall of lignified plant cells. **10.** A box sunk into a sports ground and filled with sand or other material to cushion the fall of athletes taking part, for example, in the long jump or the triple jump. **11. a.** A sunken area in a garage floor from which mechanics may inspect or work on the underside of vehicles. **b.** *Often plural.* A place beside a motor-racing track where cars or motorcycles may be serviced during a race. **12.** *Plural. Slang.* The most wretched or disagreeable place or condition. Preceded by *the.* —See Synonyms at **hole.**
~v. **pitted, pitting, pits.** *—tr.* **1.** To make cavities, depressions, or scars in: *"the mountain was pitted with deep craters"* (Muriel Spark). **2.** To place in contest against another; set in direct opposition: *"a man pitted in conflict against the sea"* (D.H. Lawrence). **3.** To put, bury, or store in a pit. *—intr.* **1.** To become marked with small pits. **2.** To retain an impression after being indented, as by a fingernail. Used of skin. [Middle English *pitt,* Old English *pytt,* from West Germanic *putti* (unattested), from Latin *puteus,* a pit, well.]
pit[2] *n. Chiefly U.S.* The single, central kernel of certain fruits, such as a peach or cherry; a stone.
~tr.v. Chiefly U.S. **pitted, pitting, pits.** To extract pits from (fruit). [Perhaps from Dutch, from Middle Dutch *pit(te),* from West Germanic *pithan* (unattested), PITH.]
pi·ta[1] (péetə) *n.* Any of several plants of the genus *Agave,* that yield a strong fibre. Also called "istle", "ixtle". [Spanish, from Quechua.]
pita[2]. Variant of **pitta.**
pit·a·pat (píttə-pát, -pat) *intr.v.* **-patted, -patting, -pats. 1.** To move with quick, tapping steps. **2.** To make a repeated tapping sound.
~n. A series of quick steps, taps, or beats.
~adv. With a rapid tapping sound. [Imitative.]
pit bull *n.* A dog that is or resembles a kind of bull terrier and is noted for its feisty fighting spirit. Also called "pitbull terrier". [Perhaps from a dogfight *pit.*]
Pit·cairn Islands (pít-kairn). Small group of volcanic islands in the south Pacific Ocean. The largest, Pitcairn Island, was settled by nine fleeing mutineers of the *Bounty* (1790) together with some Tahitians. It is a British Overseas Territory. See map at **Pacific Ocean.**
pitch[1] (pich) *n.* **1.** Any of various thick, dark, sticky substances obtained from the distillation residue of coal tar, wood tar, or petroleum, and used for waterproofing, roofing, caulking, and paving. **2.** Any of various natural bitumens, such as mineral pitch or asphalt, having similar uses. **3.** A resin derived from the sap of various coniferous trees, such as the pines.
~tr.v. **pitched, pitching, pitches.** To smear or cover with or as if with pitch. [Middle English *pich,* Old English *pic,* from Latin *pix* (stem *pic-*).] **—pitch·i·ness** *n.* **—pitch·y** *adj.*
pitch[2] *v.* **pitched, pitching, pitches.** *—tr.* **1.** To throw, usually forcefully, in a specific direction. **2. a.** In cricket, to bowl (a ball) so that it lands in a specified place. **b.** In baseball, to be the pitcher of (a game or a strike, for example). **3.** To put up or in position; establish: *pitch a tent.* **4.** To set firmly; implant; embed: *pitched the cricket stumps in the ground.* **5. a.** To fix the level of: *pitch one's expectations high.* **b.** To set the character and course of: *He pitched his speech to the party line.* **6.** To set at a specified pitch of music or sound. **7.** In card games, to lead (a card), thus establishing the trump suit. **8.** In golf, to strike (a ball) with great elevation and backspin so as to minimise movement on landing. **9.** To tell. Used chiefly in the phrase *pitch someone a yarn.* *—intr.* **1.** To land on the ground at a specified place: *The ball pitched near the wicket.* **2.** In baseball, to play in the position of pitcher. **3.** To plunge; fall, especially forwards: *He pitched over the railing.* **4.** To stumble around; lurch. **5.** To dip bow and stern alternately. Used of a ship or an aircraft. Compare **roll. 6.** To slope downwards: *The hill pitched steeply.* **7.** To set up living quarters; encamp; settle. **—pitch for.** *Informal.* To try to obtain something, especially through persuasion; *pitching for more business.* **—pitch in.** *Informal.* **1.** To set to work vigorously. **2.** To join forces with others; help; cooperate. **—pitch into.** *Informal.* To attack verbally or physically; assault. **—pitch on.** *Informal.* To choose.
~n. **1.** An act or instance of pitching. **2. a.** In cricket, the spot where a bowled ball lands. **b.** In baseball, a throw of the ball by the pitcher for action by the batter. **3. a.** The playing area in certain ball games such as football or hockey. **b.** In cricket, the rectangular area between the wickets, 22 yards by 10 feet. In this sense, also called "wicket". **4.** *Nautical.* The alternate dip and rise of a craft's bow and stern. **5. a.** Any steep downward slant. **b.** The degree of such a slant. **6.** *Architecture.* **a.** The angle of a roof. **b.** The highest point of a structure: *the pitch of an arch.* **7.** A point or stage of development or intensity, especially an extreme point: *reached a pitch of excitement.* **8.** The subjective quality of a complex sound, dependent on frequency, loudness, and intensity, and often measured as the frequency of a pure note of a given intensity judged equivalent to the complex sound by a normal ear. **9.** *Music.* **a.** The relative position of a note in a scale, as determined by its frequency. **b.** Any of various standards that establish a frequency for each musical note, used in the tuning of instruments: *high pitch, low pitch.* See **concert pitch. 10. a.** The distance travelled by a screw in a single revolution. **b.** The distance between two corresponding points on adjacent screw threads or gear teeth. **c.** The distance between two corresponding points on a helix. **11.** The distance a propeller would travel in an ideal medium during one complete revolution, measured parallel to the shaft of the propeller. **12. a.** *Slang.* A set talk designed to persuade: *sales pitch.* **b.** The place or stand of a vendor, hawker, or the like. **13.** A card game, **all fours** *(see).* **14.** In golf, a shot that is pitched. In this sense, also called "pitch shot". **—queer (someone's) pitch.** *Informal.* To spoil the chances or plans of. [Middle English *picchen,* to pierce, fix, set, throw, Old English *picc(e)an* (unattested), to prick, thrust, peculiar causative of *pician* (unattested), PICK (prick).]
pitch accent *n. Linguistics.* **Tonic accent** *(see).*
pitch-and-toss (pích-ən-tóss || -táwss) *n.* A game in which the player who comes closest to hitting a mark with a coin is entitled to toss all the other coins, and keep those that land heads up.
pitch-black (pích-blák) *adj.* Extremely dark or black.
pitch·blende (pích-blend) *n.* The principal ore of uranium, a brownish-black mineral of uranium dioxide with small amounts of uranium decay products. It is the chief source of radium. Also called "uraninite". [German *Pechblende* : *Pech,* pitch (from its black colour), from Latin *pix* + BLENDE.]
pitch circle *n.* An imaginary circle passing through the teeth of a gearwheel, having a radius that would enable it to touch but not overlap a similar circle on a mating gear.
pitch-dark (pích-dárk) *adj.* Extremely dark.
pitched battle *n.* **1.** A battle fought in close contact by troops whose formation and tactics have been carefully planned. **2.** Any fierce combat or dispute.
pitched roof *n.* A roof that is not flat.
pitch·er[1] (píchər) *n.* **1.** One that pitches. **2.** In baseball, the player who throws the ball from the mound to the batter. **3.** In golf, an iron club with a sharply inclined head.
pitcher[2] *n.* **1. a.** A large vessel for liquids made of clay, earthenware, or the like, and usually having two handles and a spout for pouring. **b.** Any large jug. **2.** *Botany.* A juglike part, such as the leaf of a pitcher plant. [Middle English *picher,* from Old French *pichier, bichier,* from Frankish *bikari* (unattested), BEAKER.]
pitcher plant *n.* Any of various insectivorous plants of the genera *Sarracenia, Heliamphora, Darlingtonia, Nepenthes,* and *Cephalotus,* having leaves modified to form juglike organs that trap insects.
pitch·fork (pích-fawrk) *n.* A large fork with sharp, widely spaced prongs for lifting and pitching hay.
~tr.v. **pitchforked, -forking, -forks. 1.** To lift or toss with a pitchfork. **2.** To force or thrust into a place or position very suddenly. [Middle English *pychforke,* alteration of *pikforke* (through wrong association with *picchen,* to toss, PITCH) : probably PICK + FORK.]
pitch·man (pích-mən) *n., pl.* **-men** (-mən). *U.S. Informal.* A pedlar or vendor of small wares, especially one with a colourful sales talk.
pitch pine *n.* **1.** Any of various American pine trees yielding pitch or turpentine, such as *Pinus rigida* of eastern North America. **2.** The wood of any of these trees.
pitch pipe *n. Music.* A small pipe that, when sounded, gives the standard pitch for a piece of music or for tuning an instrument.
pitch·stone (pích-stōn) *n.* Any of various glassy volcanic rocks dis-

tinguished by their dark lustre and relatively high water content. [Translation of German *Pechstein*.]

pit·e·ous (pítti-əss) *adj.* **1.** Arousing pity; pathetic. **2.** *Archaic.* Pitying; compassionate. —See Usage note at **pitiable.** [Middle English *piteus, pitous,* from Old French *piteus,* from *pite,* PITY.] —**pit·e·ous·ly** *adv.* —**pit·e·ous·ness** *n.*

pit·fall (pít-fawl) *n.* **1.** A trap made by digging a hole in the ground and concealing its opening. **2.** Any danger or difficulty that is not easily anticipated or avoided.

pith (pith) *n.* **1.** *Botany.* The soft, spongelike substance in the centre of stems and branches of most vascular plants. Also called "medulla". **2.** The white fibrous tissue between the rind and the pulp in such fruits as oranges and grapefruits. **3.** The essential or central part of anything; the essence; the gist. **4.** Force; strength; vigour. —*tr.v.* **pithed, pithing, piths.** **1.** To remove the pith from (a plant stem). **2.** To sever or destroy the spinal cord of (a laboratory animal), usually by means of a needle inserted into the vertebral canal. **3.** To kill (animals) by cutting the spinal cord. [Middle English *pithe,* Old English *pitha,* from West Germanic *pithon†* (unattested). See also **pit** (stone of fruit).]

pit·head (pít-hed) *n.* The top of a mine shaft, especially of a coal mine, including the hoisting gear and ancillary buildings.

pith·e·can·thro·pus (píthi-kan-thrŏ-pəss, -kánthrə-) *n., pl.* **-pi** (-pī). A member of the former genus *Pithecanthropus,* thought to indicate the existence of a primate between man and ape. It is now reclassified as *Homo erectus.* See **Java man, Peking man.** [New Latin : Greek *pithēkos†,* ape + -ANTHROPUS.] —**pith·e·can·thro·poid** *adj.*

pith helmet *n.* A light sun hat made from dried pith; a topi.

pith·os (píth-os) *n., pl.* **-thoi** (-oy). *Archaeology.* A large jar used for storing goods such as oil or grain. [Greek.]

pith·y (píthi) *adj.* **-ier, -iest.** **1.** Consisting of or resembling pith. **2.** Precisely meaningful; cogent and terse. —See Synonyms at **concise.** —**pith·i·ly** *adv.* —**pith·i·ness** *n.*

pit·i·a·ble (pítti-əb'l) *adj.* **1.** Arousing or deserving of pity or compassion. **2.** Arousing disdainful pity; paltry; despicable. —**pit·i·a·ble·ness** *n.* —**pit·i·a·bly** *adv.*

Usage: Pitiable, pitiful, and *piteous* are often interchangeable. However, *pitiable* tends to be used in contexts where the wretchedness of a condition is being emphasised *(the pitiable circumstances those people live in); pitiful* often introduces a sense of "contemptible" *(they earn a pitiful wage); piteous* stresses the arousal of compassionate feelings *(a piteous sight).*

pit·i·ful (pítti'l) *adj.* **1.** Arousing pity; pathetic. **2.** So inferior or insignificant as to be contemptible; mean; paltry. **3.** *Archaic.* Filled with pity or compassion. —See Synonyms at **pathetic.** —See Usage note at **pitiable.** —**pit·i·ful·ly** *adv.* —**pit·i·ful·ness** *n.*

pit·i·less (pítti-ləss, -liss) *adj.* Having no pity; without mercy. See Synonyms at **cruel.** —**pit·i·less·ly** *adv.* —**pit·i·less·ness** *n.*

Pit·man (pít-mən), **Sir Isaac** (1813–97). British inventor of the Pitman shorthand system (1837). It was based on the sound rather than the written appearance of words.

pi·ton (pée-ton; *French* pee-tón) *n.* A metal spike fitted at one end with an eye or ring through which to pass a rope, used in mountain climbing. [French, from Old French, "nail", from Romance root *pitt-,* pointed thing.]

Pi·tot-stat·ic tube (péetō-státtik ‖ pee-tō-) *n.* A device consisting of a Pitot tube and a static tube combined to measure simultaneously total and static pressure in a fluid stream. It can be used in aircraft to determine relative wind speed.

Pi·tot tube (péetō ‖ *U.S.* pée-tō) *n.* A device used to measure the total pressure of a fluid stream. It is essentially a tube attached to a manometer at one end with its other end pointing upstream. [After Henri *Pitot* (1695–1771), French physicist.]

pit pony *n.* A small horse or pony, formerly used in coal mines for haulage.

pit-saw (pít-saw) *n.* A large saw for cutting logs, hand-operated by two men, one of whom stands on the log and the other in a pit underneath.

Pitt (pit), **William, 1st Earl of Chatham,** also known as Pitt the Elder (1708–78). British statesman and orator. He became an M.P. in 1735, and was associated with the Whig faction, opposing Robert Walpole. He was Paymaster General (1746–55) and Secretary of State (1756–57, 1757–61) for much of the Seven Years' War. In 1766–68 he formed an all-party ministry that failed to cope with the crisis in the American colonies, and he resigned through ill health.

Pitt, William, also known as Pitt the Younger (1759–1806). British statesman and prime minister (1783–1801, 1804–06). The son of William Pitt the Elder, he became an M.P. in 1781 and as Chancellor of the Exchequer (1782–83) began a lifelong rivalry with Charles James Fox. He became at 24 the youngest prime minister in British history. His India Act (1784) and Canada Act (1791) laid the basis of future colonial administration. In response to Irish unrest, he accomplished the Act of Union between Ireland and Britain (1800). The Napoleonic wars dominated Pitt's second ministry. He negotiated an alliance with Russia and Austria which collapsed after Napoleon's victory at Austerlitz (1805).

pit·ta, pi·ta (pítta, péeta) *n.* A flat, oval, slightly leavened kind of bread, which can be slit open to take a filling, originally from Greece and the Middle East. [Modern Greek.]

pit·tance (pítt'nss) *n.* **1.** A meagre allowance of money: *She lives on a pittance.* **2.** A very small salary or remuneration. **3.** A small amount or portion of anything. [Middle English *pitaunce,* from Old French *pitance,* from Medieval Latin *pittantia,* from Vulgar Latin

pietantia (unattested), pious donation, portion (of food) given to monastics, from *pietārī,* to be charitable, from Latin *pietās,* piety, from *pius,* pious.]

pit·ter-pat·ter (pítta-pattər, -páttər) *n.* A rapid series of light, tapping sounds.
—*intr.v.* **-tered, -tering, -ters.** To move with or make a pitter-patter: *rain pitter-pattered on the roof.*
—*adv.* With a series of light, tapping sounds. [Imitative.]

Pitts·burgh (píts-burg). City in southwest Pennsylvania. Situated at the confluence of the Allegheny, Monongahela, and Ohio rivers, it is the U.S.A.'s largest inland river port. It produces coal and steel.

pi·tu·i·tar·y (pi-téw-i-tri, -təri ‖ -tōō-, -terri) *n., pl.* **-ies.** **1.** *Anatomy.* The pituitary gland. **2.** *Medicine.* An extract from the anterior or posterior lobes of the pituitary gland, prepared for therapeutic use.
—*adj.* **1.** Of or pertaining to the pituitary gland. **2.** *Archaic.* Of or secreting phlegm or mucus; mucous. [Latin *pītuītārius,* from *pītuīta,* phlegm.]

pituitary gland *n. Anatomy.* A small, oval endocrine gland attached to the base of the vertebrate brain, the secretions of which control the other endocrine glands and influence growth, metabolism, and maturation. Also called "hypophysis", "pituitary body".

pit·u·ri (píchəri) *n.* An Australian shrub, *Duboisia hopwoodii,* the leaves of which yield a narcotic. [From a native Australian name.]

pit viper *n.* Any of various venomous snakes of the family Crotalidae, such as the copperhead or rattlesnake, characterised by a small pit on each side of the head.

pit·y (pítti) *n., pl.* **-ies.** **1. a.** Sorrow or grief aroused by the misfortune of another; compassion for another's suffering. **b.** Concern or regret for one considered inferior or less favoured; condescending sympathy. **2.** A regrettable or disagreeable fact or necessity. —**for pity's sake.** Used to express angry frustration or an embittered plea: *Go away, for pity's sake!* —**more's the pity.** Regrettably; so much the worse: *I didn't see it, more's the pity.* —**take pity on.** To attempt to alleviate the misfortune of.
—*v.* **pitied, pitying, pities.** —*tr.* To feel pity for. —*intr. Archaic.* To feel pity. [Middle English *pite,* from Old French *pit(i)e,* from Late Latin *pietās* (stem *pietāt-*), compassion, extended sense of Latin *pietās,* piety, from *pius,* pious.] —**pit·y·ing·ly** *adv.*

Synonyms: pity, compassion, commiseration, sympathy, condolence.

pit·y·ri·a·sis (pítti-rí-ə-siss) *n.* Any of various skin diseases of humans and animals, characterised by epidermal shedding of flaky scales. [Greek *pituriasis,* from *pituron†,* grain husk, dandruff.]

più (pew) *adv. Music.* More. Used in directions to performers, as in *più forte,* more loudly. [Italian, from Latin *plūs,* more.]

Pi·us V, Saint, born Michele Ghislieri (1504–72). Pope (1566–72). He supported the Inquisition and encouraged the suppression of Protestantism in France and the Netherlands. In 1570 he excommunicated Elizabeth I of England. He was canonised in 1712.

Pius XII, born Eugenio Pacelli (1876–1958). Italian pope (1939–58). As Papal Secretary of State he negotiated the concordat with Nazi Germany (1933). During World War II he believed the best way to achieve peace was to maintain formal relations with all the belligerents but he was much criticised for not speaking out against the persecution of the Jews.

Piute. Variant of **Paiute.**

piv·ot (pívvət) *n.* **1.** A short rod or pointed shaft on which a related part rotates or swings; a fulcrum. **2.** A person or thing that chiefly determines the course or effect of something; the essential component. **3.** A person who helps to keep the order and direction of wheeling troops. **4.** The act of turning on or as if on a pivot.
—*v.* **pivoted, -oting, -ots.** —*tr.* To mount on, attach by, or furnish with a pivot or pivots. —*intr.* To turn on or as if on a pivot: *It all pivots on her decision.* [French, of obscure origin.]

pi·vo·tal *adj.* **1.** Of, pertaining to, or being a pivot. **2.** Of vital importance; crucial. —**pi·vot·al·ly** *adv.*

pix¹ (piks) *pl.n. Informal.* Photographs or films. [Abbreviation of pictures.]

pix². Variant of **pyx.**

pix·el (píks-el) *n.* An element of a computer graphics display on a VDU. [From PIX + *element.*]

pix·ie, pix·y (píksi) *n., pl.* **-ies.** A fairy-like or elfin creature. [17th century : origin obscure.]

pix·i·lat·ed, pix·il·lat·ed (píksi-laytid) *adj.* **1.** Behaving as if led by pixies; bemused; whimsical; eccentric. **2.** *Slang.* Drunk. [From *pixy-led,* altered after past participles such as TITILLATED.]

Pi·zar·ro (pi-záa-rō; *Spanish* pee-thá-), **Francisco** (1475–1541). Spanish conquistador. In 1530 with some 180 men he crossed the Andes and in 1532 reached the heart of the Inca empire. He captured and killed its emperor, Atahualpa, at Cajamarca, and entered Cuzco in 1533. Within two years he subdued the whole empire and founded Lima as his capital (1535).

pizz. *Music.* pizzicato.

piz·za (péet-sə) *n.* A baked dish of Italian origin consisting of a shallow breadlike crust typically covered with a spiced mixture of tomatoes and cheese, and sometimes other ingredients, such as anchovies, meat, or olives. [Italian.]

piz·zazz, pe·zazz (pi-záz, pə-) *n. Slang.* Flamboyance; zest or flair. [Imitative.]

piz·ze·ri·a (péetsə-rée-ə) *n.* A place where pizzas are made, sold, and eaten. [Italian, from PIZZA.]

piz·zi·ca·to (pítsi-káatō) *adv. Abbr.* **pizz.** *Music.* Played by plucking rather than bowing the strings of an instrument, such as a violin.

~*n., pl.* **pizzicatos** or **-ti.** A passage or note played in this manner. [Italian, past participle of *pizzicare,* to pluck, pinch, from *pizzare,* to prick, pinch, from Old Italian *pizza,* a point, edge, from Gallo-Roman *pīnts-, pīts-* (unattested). See also **pinch.**] —**piz·zi·ca·to** *adj.*
piz·zle (pízz'l) *n.* The penis of an animal, especially that of a bull. [Earlier *peezel,* from Low German *pēsel,* diminutive of Middle Low German *pēse,* sinew, penis, perhaps an early borrowing of Latin *pēniculus,* diminutive of *pēnis,* PENIS.]
PK psychokinesis.
pk. **1.** pack. **2.** park. **3.** peak. **4.** peck.
pkg. package.
pkt. packet.
pl. **1.** place. **2.** plate. **3.** plural.
Pl. Place (used in street names).
P.L.A. Port of London Authority.
PL/1 *n.* A high-level symbolic language designed for programming computers. [*Program Language Number 1.*]
plac·a·ble (pláck-əb'l, *rarely* pláyk-) *adj. Rare.* Easily calmed or pacified; tolerant. [Middle English, agreeable, from Old French, placable, from Latin *plācābilis,* from *plācāre,* to calm, appease.] —**plac·a·bil·i·ty** (-ə-bíllәti) *n.* —**plac·a·bly** *adv.*
plac·ard (plák-aard, -ərd) *n.* **1.** A printed or written announcement for display in a public place; a poster: *demonstrators carrying placards with slogans.* **2.** A nameplate, as on the door of a house.
~*tr.v.* **placarded, -arding, -ards.** **1.** To announce or advertise (a message or product) on a placard. **2.** To post placards on or in. **3.** To display as a placard. [Middle English *placquart,* plate, breastplate, from Old French *plaquart,* from *plaquier,* to plaster, from Middle Dutch *placken*†, to patch, paste. See also **plaque.**] —**plac·ard·er** *n.*
pla·cate (plə-káyt, *rarely* play- || *U.S.* pláy-kayt, plá-) *tr.v.* **-cated, -cating, -cates.** To allay the anger of, especially by making concessions; appease. See Synonyms at **pacify.** [Latin *plācāre,* to calm, appease.] —**pla·cat·er** *n.* —**pla·ca·tion** (-káysh'n) *n.* —**pla·ca·to·ry** (-əri), **pla·ca·tive** (plə-káytiv, pláckətiv) *adj.*
place (playss) *n.* **1.** A portion of space; an area with definite or indefinite boundaries. **2.** Such an area, for example a building, set aside for a specified activity: *a place of worship.* **3.** A definite location, especially: **a.** A house, flat, or other residence: *My place or yours?* **b.** A business establishment or office. **c.** A particular town or city. **4.** *Usually capital* **P.** *Abbr.* **Pl.** A public square or street with houses in a town. **5. a.** A space for one person to sit or stand, for example as a passenger or spectator. **b.** A setting for one person at a table. **6.** A position regarded as belonging to someone or something else; stead: *I was chosen in his place.* **7.** A particular point that one has reached; especially, a point up to which one has read in a book: *I lost my place.* **8.** A position figuratively occupied by a thing, group, or activity in a larger complex; an existing function; a role: *the place of trade unions in society.* **9.** Proper or customary location or order: *Everything is in place.* **10. a.** A social status entailing a certain mode of behaviour: *the days when servants knew their place.* **b.** An appropriate right or duty: *It's not my place to criticise.* **c.** A location or situation requiring a particular mode of behaviour: *This is not the place for flippancy.* **11. a.** A position of eminence: *a place in history.* **b.** A position as a member of a selective body, for example as an employee of a firm or member of a team: *She's got a place at Oxford.* **12. a.** A relative position in a series, especially in a series classified according to achievement: *went up to third place in the hit parade.* **b.** *British.* A position as one of the first three (or, sometimes, four) horses to finish a race, and especially as either the second or third horse. **c.** A specified stage in a list of points to be made, as in an argument: *In the first place, they have no right to protest.* **13.** *Abbr.* **pl.** The position of a number in relation to other numbers in a series. See **decimal place.** —**all over the place.** In confusion or disarray. —**give place to.** **1.** To make space or room for. **2.** To be superseded by. —**go places.** *Informal.* To enjoy increasing success. —**in place of.** Instead of. —**know (one's) place.** To be aware of one's position of inferiority and act accordingly. —**out of place.** **1.** Inappropriate. **2.** In the wrong place. —**put (someone) in his place.** To cause (someone who is arrogant or conceited) to be humbled. —**take (one's) place.** To take up a usual or specified position: *took his place at the front.* —**take place.** To occur; happen.
~*v.* **placed, placing, places.** —*tr.* **1.** To put in a specified position; set. **2.** To put in a specified relation or order: *Place the words in alphabetical order.* **3.** To arrange for (a person or thing) to receive appropriate treatment, especially: **a.** To find accommodation or employment for. **b.** To invest (money). **c.** To lay (an order or bet, for example). **d.** To find a publisher for (a book). **e.** To have (an advertisement, for example) displayed or published. **4.** To appoint to a post: *placed in a key position.* **5.** To rank in an order or sequence: *I'd place him second best.* **6.** To put, lay, or fix: *placed emphasis on her appearance.* **7.** To recollect clearly the circumstances or context of: *I can't place him now.* **8.** To adjust (one's speaking or singing voice) for the best possible effects. **9.** To declare the position of (a horse, runner, or other contestant), especially amongst the first three finishes of a race. —*intr. U.S.* To arrive among the first three finishers in a race; especially, to finish in second place. [Middle English, space, locality, from Old French, from Latin *platea,* "broad street", space, from Greek *plateia (hodos),* "broad(way)", from feminine of *platus,* broad.]
Place (playss), **Francis** (1771–1854). British radical. A prosperous London tailor, he fought for trade union rights. He helped to draft the People's Charter (1838) from which Chartism was born.
pla·ce·bo (plə-sée-bō, pla-; *in sense 1 also* -cháy-) *n., pl.* **-bos** or **-boes.** **1.** *Roman Catholic Church.* The service or office of vespers for the dead. **2. a.** *Medicine.* A substance containing no active drug given to a patient who thinks he is ill who believes it to be an active drug, to humour him or to effect a cure *(the placebo effect)* by changing his psychological attitude by this deception. **b.** An inactive substance used as a control in an experiment. **3.** Anything lacking intrinsic remedial value, done or given to humour another. [Medieval Latin, from the first word of the first antiphon of the service, *Placēbo (Dominō in rēgiōne vivōrum),* "I shall please (the Lord in the land of the living)", from *placēre,* to please.]
place card *n.* A card that bears a name indicating where a person must sit at a dinner table.
place kick *n.* In Rugby or American football, a kick made when the ball is propped up in a fixed position on the ground. —**place-kick** (pláyss-kik) *v.* —**place-kick·er** *n.*
place·man (pláyss-mən) *n., pl.* **-men** (-mən). *Chiefly British.* A person appointed to an office as a reward for loyalty rather than merit, especially one who will serve the interests of the appointer.
place mat *n.* A protective table mat, often decorative, on which dishes and plates are placed at mealtimes.
place·ment (pláyss-mənt) *n.* **1. a.** The act of placing or arranging. **b.** The state of being placed or arranged. **2.** The act or business of finding jobs, lodgings, or other positions for applicants. **3.** In racket games such as tennis or squash, the act or practice of accurately placing the ball in parts of the court.
pla·cen·ta (plə-sén-tə) *n., pl.* **-tas** or **-tae** (-tee). **1.** *Anatomy.* A vascular, membranous organ that develops in female mammals during pregnancy and provides the foetus with nutrients and removes waste products via the umbilical cord. Following birth, the placenta is expelled as part of the afterbirth. **2.** *Botany.* **a.** The part of the ovary to which the ovules are attached. **b.** In nonflowering plants, the tissue that bears the spore cases. [Latin, flat cake, from Greek *plakoenta,* accusative of *plakoeis, plakous,* flat, flat cake, from *plax* (stem *plak-*), flat surface.]
pla·cen·tal (plə-sént'l, pla-) *adj.* Also **pla·cen·tate** (-séntayt). Having a placenta. Said especially of animals.
plac·en·ta·tion (pláss-en-táysh'n, -'n-) *n.* **1.** *Zoology.* **a.** The formation of a placenta. **b.** The type or structure of a placenta. **2.** *Botany.* The way in which the placenta is arranged in or attached to the ovary.
plac·er (plássər) *n.* **1.** A glacial or alluvial deposit of sand or gravel containing deposits of heavy minerals such as gold, platinum, and diamonds. **2.** A place where such a deposit is washed to extract its mineral content. [American Spanish, "shoal", from *plaza,* place, from Latin *platea,* "broad road", PLACE.]
placer mining *n.* The obtaining of minerals from placers by washing or dredging. —**placer miner** *n.*
plac·id (plássid) *adj.* Having a calm appearance or temperament; not easily excited or upset. See Synonyms at **calm.** [French, from Latin *placidus,* pleasing, gentle, from *placēre,* to please.] —**pla·cid·i·ty** (pla-síddəti, plə-), **plac·id·ness** *n.* —**plac·id·ly** *adv.*
plack·et (pláckit) *n.* A slit in a dress, blouse, or skirt to make the garment easy to put on or take off or to give access to a pocket. [Earlier *plackerd,* dress, petticoat, originally, "breastplate", variant of PLACARD.]
plac·oid (pláckoyd) *adj. Zoology.* Platelike, as the hard, toothlike scales of sharks, skates, and rays are. [Greek *plax* (stem *plak-*), flat surface, plate + -OID.]
pla·fond (plə-fón, pla-, -FÓN) *n.* A ceiling, especially one that is decorated, as with paintings. [French, from *plat,* flat + *fond,* bottom.]
pla·gal (pláyg'l) *adj. Music.* **1.** Designating a medieval mode having a range from the fourth below to the fifth above its final note. **2.** Designating a cadence with the subdominant chord immediately preceding the tonic chord. Compare **authentic.** [Medieval Latin *plagālis,* from *plaga,* plagal mode, from *plagius,* plagal, from Medieval Greek *plagios (ēkhos),* plagal (mode), from Greek *plagios,* placed sideways, oblique, from *plagos,* side.]
plage (plaazh) *n. Astronomy.* A **flocculus** *(see).*
pla·gia·rise, pla·gia·rize (pláyj-ə-rīz, -i-ə-) *v.* **-rised, -rising, -rises.** —*tr.* **1.** To steal and use (the ideas or writings of another) as one's own. **2.** To appropriate passages or ideas from (another) to use as one's own. —*intr.* To take and use as one's own the writings or ideas of another. [From PLAGIARY.] —**pla·gia·ris·er** *n.*
pla·gia·rism (pláyj-ə-riz'm, -i-ə-) *n.* **1.** The act of plagiarising. **2.** That which is plagiarised. [From PLAGIARY.] —**pla·gia·rist** *n.* —**pla·gia·ris·tic** (-rístik) *adj.*
pla·gia·ry (pláyj-əri, -i-əri || -i-erri) *n., pl.* **-ries.** *Archaic.* **1.** Plagiarism. **2.** A plagiarist. [Originally "kidnapper", from Latin *plagiārius,* from *plagium,* kidnapping, from *plaga,* net.]
plagio– *comb. form.* Indicates a slanting or inclining; for example, **plagiotropism.** [Greek *plagios,* placed sideways, oblique, from *plagos,* side.]
pla·gi·o·clase (pláyji-ō-klayz, pláji-, -ə-, -klayss) *n.* Any of a common rock-forming series of triclinic feldspars consisting of mixtures of sodium and calcium aluminium silicates. Also called "plagioclase feldspar". [German *Plagioklas* : PLAGIO- + -CLASE.] —**pla·gi·o·clas·tic** (-klástik) *adj.*
pla·gi·o·cli·max (pláyji-ō-klī-maks, pláji-, -ə-) *n. Ecology.* A stable plant community that, because of environmental factors such as grazing pressure, cannot develop into a natural climax.

pla·gi·ot·ro·pism (pláyji-ō-trŏp-iz'm, pláji-, -ə-, -óttrəp-) *n. Biology.* A tendency, especially in lateral roots, to grow at an oblique angle to the direction of the stimulus. [PLAGIO- + -TROPISM.] —**pla·gi·o·trop·ic** (-tróppik, -trŏpik) *adj.* —**pla·gi·o·trop·i·cal·ly** *adv.*

plague (playg) *n.* **1.** A highly infectious, usually fatal, epidemic disease, especially bubonic plague. **2.** A sudden influx, as of destructive or harmful insects: *a plague of locusts.* **3.** *Informal.* Any cause for annoyance; a nuisance: *the plague of their chatter.* **4.** A disaster or affliction, or calamity, especially one seen as a punishment. —**a plague on.** *Archaic.* Used as a curse: *A plague on your good deeds!* —*tr.v.* **plagued, plaguing, plagues. 1.** To harass, pester, or annoy: *plagued their parents with silly questions.* **2.** To afflict with or as if with plague or any other evil. —See Synonyms at **harass.** [Middle English, a blow, calamity, malignant disease, from Old French, from Late Latin *plāga,* from Latin, a stroke, wound, probably from Greek *plaga, plēgē,* stroke.] —**plagu·er** *n.*

pla·guy, pla·guey (pláygi) *adj.* Irritating; bothersome. —**pla·gui·ly** (-li) *adv.*

plaice (playss) *n., pl.* **plaices** or collectively **plaice. 1.** An edible marine flatfish, *Pleuronectes platessa,* of western European waters. **2.** *U.S.* Any related flatfish, such as *Hippoglossoides platessoides* of North American Atlantic waters. [Middle English, from Old French *plaïs, plaiz,* from Late Latin *platessa,* "flatfish".]

plaid (plad ‖ playd) *n.* **1.** A long, rectangular piece of woollen cloth of a tartan or checked pattern worn over one shoulder as part of Scottish Highland costume. **2.** Cloth with a tartan or checked pattern. —*adj.* **1.** Made of plaid. **2.** Having a tartan or checked pattern. [Scottish Gaelic *plaide†.*]

Plaid Cymru (plīd kŏomri) *n.* The Welsh Nationalist party. It is dedicated to the cause of autonomy for Wales and the promotion of the Welsh language. [Welsh, party of Wales.]

plain (playn) *adj.* **plainer, plainest. 1.** Free from obstructions; open to view; clear: *plain sight.* **2.** *Rare.* Having no visible elevation or depression; flat; level. **3.** Easily understood; clearly evident; obvious to the mind: *make one's intention plain.* **4.** Uncomplicated; easily done; simple: *plain needlework.* **5.** Straightforward; frank; candid: *plain speaking.* **6. a.** Not mixed with other substances; pure: *plain water.* **b.** Containing no raising agents: *plain flour.* **7. a.** Common in rank or station; ordinary: *a plain man.* **b.** Without affectation or pretension. **8.** Not ruled; without lines. Said of paper. **9.** Not rich or elaborate: *plain food.* **10.** With little ornamentation or decoration: *a plain dress.* **11.** Not dyed, twilled, or patterned: *a plain fabric.* **12.** Not beautiful or handsome; unattractive: *a plain face.* **13.** Sheer; utter; unqualified: *plain stupidity.* **14.** Not in code: *a plain message.* **15.** Designating the basic, simple knitting stitch. —See Synonyms at **evident.** —*n.* **1.** An extensive, level, treeless land region, such as a valley floor or a plateau summit. **2.** In knitting, plain stitch. —*adv.* In a clear or obvious manner: *plain stupid.* [Middle English, from Old French, from Latin *plānus,* flat, clear.] —**plain·ly** *adv.* —**plain·ness** *n.*

plain-chant (pláyn-chaant ‖ -chant) *n.* Plainsong. [French, from Medieval Latin *cantus plānus,* PLAINSONG.]

plain chocolate *n.* A dark, bitter chocolate made without milk. Compare **milk chocolate.**

plain clothes *pl.n.* Ordinary, civilian clothes as opposed to uniform, especially police uniform. —**plain-clothes** (pláyn-klōthz, -klōz) *adj.*

plain-laid (pláyn-layd) *adj.* Designating a rope made of three strands laid together with a right-hand twist.

plain sailing *n.* **1.** Easy sailing over a direct course. **2.** Easy, unimpeded progress. [Alteration of PLANE SAILING (navigation using PLANE ANGLES).]

Plains Indian *n.* A member of any of the North American Indian peoples that once inhabited the Great Plains of North America.

plains·man (pláynz-mən) *n., pl.* **-men** (-mən, -men). An inhabitant or settler of a plains region, especially the prairie regions of the United States.

plain·song (pláyn-song ‖ -sawng) *n. Music.* **1. Gregorian chant** *(see).* **2.** Any medieval liturgical music without strict meter and traditionally sung without accompaniment. Also called "plainchant". [Translation of Medieval Latin *cantus plānus.*]

plain-spo·ken (pláyn-spōkən, -spŏkən) *adj.* Blunt; frank.

plain stitch *n.* In knitting, the basic, simple stitch, producing either a flat surface, as in stocking stitch, or a ribbed surface, as in garter stitch. Compare **purl stitch.**

plaint (playnt) *n.* **1.** *Archaic & Poetic.* **a.** A complaint. **b.** An utterance of grief or sorrow; a lamentation. **2.** *Law.* A statement of grievance submitted to a court as a request for redress. [Middle English *pleinte, plaint,* from Old French *plainte,* from Latin *planctus,* past participle of *plangere,* to strike (one's breast), lament.]

plain·tiff (pláyntif) *n. Law.* The party that institutes a suit in a court. Compare **defendant.** [Middle English *plaintif,* from Old French, from adjective *plaintif,* PLAINTIVE.]

plain·tive (pláyntiv) *adj.* Expressing restrained sorrow; mournful; melancholy: *the plaintive sound of wind in the trees.* [Middle English *pleintif,* from Old French *plaintif,* from *plainte,* lamentation, PLAINT.] —**plain·tive·ly** *adv.* —**plain·tive·ness** *n.*

plain vanilla *adj.* Of the plainest, most straightforward kind; nofrills. Used typically in financial circles: "a plain vanilla dollar put" (*Risk* magazine). [From the notion that *vanilla* is the plainest,

most ordinary ice cream.]

plain weave *n.* A weave in which the filling threads and the warp threads interlace alternately, forming a checked pattern. Also called "taffeta weave".

plait (plat ‖ playt) *n.* **1.** A length of interwoven strands, especially of hair. **2.** A pleat. —*tr.v.* **plaited, plaiting, plaits. 1.** To interweave (hair, grass, thread, or the like) into a plait. **2.** To make by plaiting. [Middle English, fold, crease, from Old French *pleit,* from Vulgar Latin *plic(i)tus* (unattested), from Latin *plicitus,* variant past participle of *plicāre,* to fold.] —**plait·er** *n.*

plan (plan) *n.* **1.** Any detailed scheme, programme, or method worked out beforehand for the accomplishment of an object: *a plan of attack.* **2.** A proposed or tentative project or course of action: *Do you have any plans for the evening?* **3.** A systematic arrangement of details; an outline or sketch: *the plan of a story.* **4.** A drawing or diagram made to scale showing the structure or arrangement of something: *a town plan; the plan of a building.* **5.** In rendering perspective, one of several imaginary planes perpendicular to the line of vision between the viewer and the object being depicted. —*v.* **planned, planning, plans.** —*tr.* **1.** To formulate a scheme or programme for the accomplishment or attainment of: *plan a campaign.* **2.** To have as a specified aim or purpose; intend: *They plan to go to the beach.* **3.** To draw or make a graphic representation of. —*intr.* To make a plan. Often used with *on* or *for.* [French, as "level ground", "plane", from Latin *plānum,* from *plānus,* flat; as "ground plan", "map", altered from *plant* (in sense influenced by Italian *pianta,* ground plan or design), from *planter,* to plant, from Latin *plantāre.* See **plant.**]

pla·nar (pláyn-ər ‖ -aar) *adj.* **1.** Of, pertaining to, or situated in a plane. **2.** Flat: *a planar surface.* [Late Latin *plānāris,* from Latin *plānum,* level surface, from *plānus,* flat, PLAIN.] —**pla·nar·i·ty** (play-nárrəti, plə-) *n.*

pla·nar·i·an (plə-naír-i-ən) *n.* Any of various flatworms of the order Tricladida, having broad, ciliated bodies and a three-branched digestive cavity. [New Latin *Planaria* (genus), from Latin *plānus,* flat.]

planar process *n.* A method of manufacturing semiconductor devices in which impurities are diffused through holes etched into an oxide layer formed on a silicon substrate, producing a diffused junction.

pla·na·tion (play-náysh'n, plə-) *n.* Lateral erosion, as of a valley, by a running stream. [From PLANE (level surface).]

planch·et (plánchit) *n.* A flat disc of metal ready for stamping as a coin; a coin blank. [Diminutive of *planch,* board, Middle English *plaunche,* from Old French *planche,* from Latin *planca.* See **plank.**]

plan·chette (plaan-shét, plON-) *n.* A small triangular board with a pointer supported by two casters and a vertical pencil which is said to spell out messages from the spirit world when the operator's fingers are placed lightly upon it. [French, diminutive of Old French *planche,* board. See **planchet.**]

Planck (plangk), **Max (Karl Ernst Ludwig)** (1858–1947). German physicist. While professor at the university of Berlin (1889–1928) he originated the quantum theory (1900); he was awarded the Nobel prize (1918), and his theory was applied by Einstein, Bohr, and others to transform 20th-century physics.

Planck's constant *n. Symbol h Physics.* The constant of proportionality relating the quantum of energy that can be possessed by radiation to the frequency of that radiation. Its value is approximately 6.6262×10^{-34} joule seconds. [After Max PLANCK.]

Planck's formula *n.* The formula, put forward by Planck, by which the distribution of energy in **black-body radiation** (see) over a narrow frequency range is expressed as a function of frequency and temperature.

plane¹ (playn) *n.* **1.** *Geometry.* A surface containing all the straight lines connecting any two points on it. **2.** Any flat or level surface. **3.** A level of development, existence, or achievement. **4.** An aeroplane or hydroplane. **5.** *Aeronautics.* A supporting surface of an aircraft; an aerofoil or wing. —*adj.* **1.** *Geometry.* Designating a figure lying in a plane: *a plane curve.* **2.** Flat. —See Synonyms at **level.** [Latin *plānum,* a flat surface, from *plānus,* flat.] —**plane·ness** *n.*

plane² *n.* **1.** A carpenter's tool with an adjustable blade for smoothing and levelling wood. **2.** A flat, trowel-shaped tool for smoothing the surface of clay, sand, or plaster in a mould. —*v.* **planed, planing, planes.** —*tr.* **1.** To smooth or finish with or as if with a plane. **2.** To remove with a plane. Used with *off* or *away.* —*intr.* **1.** To work with a plane. **2.** To act as a plane. [Middle English, from French *plane, plaine,* from Late Latin *plāna,* from *plānāre,* to plane, from *plānus,* level.]

plane³ *intr.v.* **planed, planing, planes. 1.** To rise partly out of the water, as a hydroplane does at high speeds. **2.** To soar or glide. [French *planer,* to soar (with wings stretched on a level), from *plan,* a level surface, from Latin *plānum,* from *plānus,* flat.]

plane⁴ *n.* The **plane tree** (see).

plane angle *n.* An angle formed by two straight lines in a plane.

plane geometry *n.* The geometry of planar figures.

plane polarisation *n.* A form of polarisation of electromagnetic radiation in which the waves are restricted to vibration in one plane.

plan·er (pláynər) *n.* **1.** One that planes. **2.** A machine tool for smoothing and planing the surfaces of wood or metal. **3.** *Printing.* A smooth block of wood used to level a forme of type.

plane sailing *n.* **1.** The calculation of the position of a ship on the basis that it is sailing on a plane and not the curved surface of the earth. **2.** See **plain sailing.**
plan·et (plánnit) *n.* **1.** A nonluminous celestial body illuminated by light from a star, such as the Sun, around which it revolves. In the **Solar System** *(see)* there are nine known major planets: Mercury, Venus, Earth, Mars, Jupiter, Saturn, Uranus, Neptune, and Pluto. **2.** In ancient astronomy, any of the seven celestial bodies (Mercury, Venus, the Moon, the Sun, Mars, Jupiter, and Saturn) visible to the naked eye and thought to revolve about a fixed Earth. **3.** *Astrology.* Any of the seven revolving celestial bodies that in conjunction with the stars are supposed to influence human affairs and personalities. [Middle English *planete,* from Old French, from Late Latin *planēta,* from Greek *planēs, planētēs,* plural of *planētos,* wandering planet, from *planasthai,* to wander.]
plane table *n.* A portable surveying instrument consisting essentially of a drawing board and a ruler mounted on a tripod and used to sight and map topographical details.
plan·e·tar·i·um (plánni-taír-i-əm) *n., pl.* **-iums** or **-ia** (-i-ə). **1.** An apparatus or model representing the Solar System. **2.** A device for projecting images of celestial bodies in their courses, on the inner surface of a hemispherical dome. **3.** A building or room containing such a device, with seats for an audience. [PLANET + -ARIUM.]
plan·e·tar·y (plánni-tri, -təri || -terri) *adj.* **1.** Of, pertaining to, or resembling the physical or orbital characteristics of a planet or the planets. **2.** Terrestrial; mundane; earthly. **3.** Wandering; erratic: *planetary life.* **4.** Designating or pertaining to a **gear train** *(see),* consisting of a central gear with an internal ring gear and one or more pinions.
planetary nebula *n.* Any of several objects in the Galaxy, each consisting of a hot, blue-white, central star surrounded by an envelope of expanding gas. See **Ring Nebula.**
plan·e·tes·i·mal (plánni-téssim'l || -tézzim'l) *n. Astronomy.* **1.** Any of the innumerable small bodies consisting of interstellar dust, thought to have been present in the presolar medium. **2.** In the planetesimal hypothesis, any of the innumerable small bodies thought to have been formed from gaseous solar material. [PLANET + (INFINIT)ESIMAL.] **—plan·e·tes·i·mal** *adj.*
planetesimal hypothesis *n.* The hypothesis put forward by T.C. Chamberlain and F.R. Moulton in 1906 to account for the formation of the planets in the Solar System. It states that gas drawn off from the young Sun and another star as they passed close to each other condensed into planetesimals, which then by gravitational aggregation and accretion formed the planets. Compare **nebular hypothesis, presolar nebular hypothesis.**
plan·e·toid (plánnitoyd) *n. Astronomy.* An **asteroid** *(see).* **—plan·e·toi·dal** *adj.*
plane tree *n.* Any of several trees of the genus *Platanus,* having ball-shaped fruit clusters, large leaves with pointed lobes, and, usually, outer bark that flakes off in patches. Also called "plane", "platan". See **London plane.** [*Plane,* from Middle English, from Old French, from Latin *platanus,* from Greek *platanos,* from *platus,* broad (from its broad leaves).]
planet wheel *n.* Any of the small gear wheels in an **epicyclic train** *(see).*
plan·gent (plánjənt) *adj.* **1.** Striking with a reverberating sound, as waves do against the shore. **2. a.** Loud and resounding, as is the sound of bells. **b.** Expressing sadness; plaintive: *plangent strains.* [Latin *plangens* (stem *plangent-*), present participle of *plangere,* to strike (one's breast).] **—plan·gen·cy** *n.* **—plan·gent·ly** *adv.*
plani–. Variant of **plano–.**
pla·nim·e·ter (pla-nímmitər, plə- || play-) *n.* An instrument that measures the area of a plane figure as a mechanically coupled pointer traverses the figure's perimeter. [French *planimètre* : PLANI- + -METER.] **—plan·i·met·ric** (plánni-méttrik || pláyni-), **pla·ni·met·ri·cal** *adj.* **—pla·ni·met·ri·cal·ly** *adv.* **—pla·nim·e·try** (-nímmətri) *n.*
plan·ish (plánnish) *tr.v.* **-ished, -ishing, -ishes.** To flatten, smooth, toughen, or polish (metal) by rolling or hammering. [French *planir* (present stem *planiss-*), to make level, from *plan,* level, from Latin *plānus.*] **—plan·ish·er** *n.*
pla·ni·sphere (plánni-sfeer, pláyni-) *n.* **1.** A representation of a sphere or part of a sphere on a plane surface. **2.** *Astronomy.* A polar projection of the celestial sphere on a chart equipped with an adjustable overlay to show the stars visible at a particular time and place. [Middle English *planispherie,* from Medieval Latin *plānisphaerium* : PLANI- + -SPHERE.] **—pla·ni·spher·ic** (-sférrik) *adj.*
plank (plangk) *n.* **1.** A long piece of timber cut thicker than a board. **2. a.** *Chiefly U.S.* Any of the policies of a political platform. **b.** Loosely, anything that supports a position: *the chief plank in their argument.* **—walk the plank.** To be forced, as by pirates, to walk down a plank extended over the side of a ship so as to drown. *~tr.v.* **planked, planking, planks. 1.** To furnish, lay, or cover with planks. **2.** To put or set down emphatically or with force. **3.** *U.S.* To bake or grill and serve (fish or meat) on a plank. **4.** *Informal.* To pay at once. Usually used with *down* or *out.* [Middle English *plank(e),* from Old North French *planke,* from Latin *planca.*]
plank·ing (plángking) *n.* Planks considered collectively.
plank-sheer (plángk-sheer) *n.* A horizontal timber forming the outer edge of the upper deck of a wooden ship. Also called "covering board". [Altered (by association with PLANK and SHEER) from earlier *planshire,* Middle English *plancher,* from Old French *planchier,* from *planche,* plank, from Latin *planca.*]
plank·ton (plángk-tən, -ton) *n. Biology.* Plant and animal organisms, generally microscopic, that float or drift in great numbers in fresh or salt water. Compare **nekton.** [German, from Greek, "wanderer", neuter of *planktos,* wandering, from *plazesthai,* to wander, drift.] **—plank·ton·ic** (-tónnik) *adj.*
plan·ner (plánnər) *n.* One who plans; especially, an official responsible for planning architectural development and the use of land.
plan·ning (plánning) *n.* The making of plans, especially for future building and land use. Also used adjectivally: *planning department.*
planning permission *n.* Permission from a local or government authority to build on a site, or to alter a building or its use.
plano–, plani– *comb. form.* Indicates flatness; for example, **planometer, planimeter.** [Latin *plānus,* flat.]
pla·nog·ra·phy (plə-nóggrəfi, pla-, play-) *n.* A process for printing from a smooth surface, such as lithography or offset. [PLANO- + -GRAPHY.] **—pla·no·graph** (pláyn-ə-graaf, -ō-, -graf) *tr.v.* **—pla·no·graph·ic** (pláyn-ə-gráffik, -ō-) *adj.* **—pla·no·graph·i·cal·ly** *adv.*
pla·nom·e·ter (pla-nómmitər, plə- || play-) *n.* A flat metal plate for gauging the accuracy of a plane surface in precision metalworking; a surface plate. [PLANO- + -METER.] **—plan·o·met·ric** (plán-ō-méttrik, pláyn-, -ə-) *adj.* **—pla·nom·e·try** (-nómmətri) *n.*
plant (plaant || plant) *n.* **1.** Any organism that characteristically has cellulose cell walls, grows by synthesising inorganic substances, lacks the power of locomotion, and lacks specialised sensory organs and nervous tissue. **2.** A plant having no permanent woody stem; a herb, as distinguished from a tree or shrub. ***Note:*** In this dictionary, *plant* is used in this sense rather than the word *herb,* to avoid confusion with the medicinal and cookery senses of the latter term. **3. a.** Equipment, including machinery, tools, instruments, and fixtures, and the buildings containing them, necessary for any industrial or manufacturing operation. **b.** A factory or other place where industrial processes are carried out. **4.** *U.S.* The buildings, equipment, and fixtures of any institution. **5.** *Informal.* A person secretly placed amongst others in order to observe, spy on, or mislead them. **6.** *Informal.* **a.** A misleading piece of evidence placed so as to be discovered. **b.** Something, especially stolen goods, fraudulently placed so as to incriminate a person. **7.** *Slang.* A scheming trick; a swindle. **8.** In snooker, a situation in which a red ball can be potted by being hit by another red ball that has been hit by the cue ball. *~tr.v.* **planted, planting, plants. 1.** To place or set (seeds, roots, cuttings, or young plants) in the ground to grow. **2. a.** To furnish or supply (a plot of land) with plants or seeds. **b.** To stock (water) with fish or spawn. **c.** To introduce (an animal) into an area. **3.** To fix or set firmly in position: *He planted both feet on the ground.* **4.** To establish or set up; found: *plant a colony.* **5.** To implant (an idea, sentiment, or the like) in the mind; introduce and establish firmly. **6.** *Informal.* **a.** To place or station (a person) for the purposes of observation, spying, misleading, or the like: *Detectives were planted all over the store.* **b.** To place (something) for the purpose of deception: *plant false evidence.* **7.** *U.S. Informal.* To hide by burying. **8.** *Slang.* To deliver (a blow or punch). [Middle English *plante,* from Old French and Old English, from Latin *planta,* shoot, from *plantāre,* to plant, "drive in with the sole of the foot", from *planta,* sole of the foot.] **—plant·a·ble** *adj.*
Plan·tag·e·net (plan-tájə-nət, -táj-, -nit) *n.* A family and, especially, a line of English kings from Henry II to Richard III (1154–1485) who succeeded the Norman monarchs and descended from Queen Matilda's marriage to Geoffrey, Count of Anjou. The line includes the Angevin, Lancastrian, and Yorkist kings, and ended with the accession of the Tudors. [Middle English, from Old French, sprig of broom (from an insignia in the crest of the Counts of Anjou) : Latin *planta,* sprig + *genista,* broom.] **—Plan·tag·e·net** *adj.*
plan·tain[1] (plántin, plaántin) *n.* Any of various plants of the genus *Plantago*; especially, *P. major,* a weed with a rosette of broad leaves and a spike of small, greenish flowers. See **ribgrass.** [Middle English, from Old French, from Latin *plantāgō* (stem *plantagin-*), from *planta,* sole of the foot (from its broad leaves).]
plan·tain[2] *n.* **1.** A large tropical plant, *Musa paradisiaca,* resembling the banana and bearing similar fruit. **2.** The green-skinned, starchy fruit of this plant, used as a staple food in tropical regions. [Spanish *plántano,* plane tree, from Medieval Latin *plantanus,* variant of Latin *platanus,* PLANE TREE.]
plantain lily *n.* Any of several plants of the genus *Hosta,* native to Asia, widely cultivated for their broad leaves and white, blue, or lilac flowers. Also called "hosta", "day lily".
plan·tar (plánt-ər || -aar) *adj.* Of, pertaining to, or located on the sole of the foot. [Latin *plantāris,* from *planta,* sole of the foot.]
plan·ta·tion (plan-táysh'n, plaan-) *n.* **1.** An area under cultivation. **2.** A group of cultivated trees or plants. **3.** A large estate or farm on which crops such as cotton, tobacco, or sugar are grown and harvested. **4.** Formerly, a newly established colony or settlement.
plant community *n.* A distinct group of plants that grow in the same habitat and are to some extent dependent on each other.
plant·er (plaánt-ər || plánt-) *n.* **1. a.** One who plants. **b.** A machine or tool for planting or sowing seeds. **2.** The owner or manager of a plantation. **3.** An early settler or colonist. **4.** A decorative container for house plants.
plan·ti·grade (plánti-grayd) *adj. Zoology.* Walking with the entire lower surface of the foot on the ground, as humans and bears do. *~n.* A plantigrade animal. Compare **digitigrade.** [French, from New Latin *plantigradus* : Latin *planta,* sole of the foot + -GRADE.]
plant kingdom *n.* One of the main divisions of the living world, comprising the algae, bryophytes, pteridophytes, and seed plants, and usually the fungi. Compare **animal kingdom, mineral kingdom.**

plant louse *n.* An **aphid** *(see).*
plants·man (plaántss-mən, -man || plánt-) *n., pl.* **-men** (-mən). A skilled or keen gardener.
plan·u·la (plánnew-lə) *n., pl.* **-lae** (-lee). The free-swimming, ciliated larva of a coelenterate. [New Latin, from Latin, little plane (from the flatness of the larva), from *plānus,* flat, level.] **—plan·u·lar** *adj.*
plaque (plak, plaak) *n.* **1.** A flat plate, slab, or disc that is ornamented or engraved for mounting, as on a wall for decoration or on a monument for information. **2.** A small pin or brooch worn as an ornament or a badge of membership. **3.** *Pathology.* A small, disc-shaped formation or growth; a patch. **4. Dental plaque** *(see).* **5.** In bacteriology, a clear area in a colony of bacterial cells caused by the localised destruction of bacteria by a bacteriophage. [French, from Old French, metal plate, coin, from Middle Dutch *placke,* from *placken*†, to patch, paste. See also **placard.**]
plash[1] (plash) *n.* **1.** A light splash. **2.** The sound of such a splash. ~*v.* **plashed, plashing, plashes.** *—tr.* To spatter (liquid) about; splash. *—intr.* To splash lightly. [Perhaps from Dutch *plassen,* from Middle Dutch *plasschen* (imitative).]
plash[2] *tr.v.* **plashed, plashing, plashes.** To interweave (branches, for example); pleach. [Middle English, from Old French *plassier,* from Latin *plectere,* to plait.]
plash·y (pláshi) *adj.* **-ier, -iest. 1.** Marshy; wet. **2.** Plashing or splashing.
-plasia, -plasy *n. comb. form.* Indicates growth or change; for example, **hypoplasia, heteroplasy.** [New Latin, from Greek *plasis,* moulding, from *plassein,* to mould.]
plasm (plázz'm) *n.* **1.** See **germ plasm. 2.** Plasma.
-plasm *n. comb. form. Biology.* Indicates the material characteristically forming cells; for example, **protoplasm.** [From PLASMA.]
plas·ma (plázmə) *n.* Also **plasm** (plázz'm). **1. a.** *Physiology.* The clear, yellowish fluid portion of blood, lymph, or intramuscular fluid in which cells are suspended. **b.** *Medicine.* Cell-free, sterilised **blood plasma** *(see),* used in transfusions. **2.** Protoplasm or cytoplasm. **3. Whey** *(see).* **4.** *Physics.* An electrically neutral, highly ionised gas composed of ions, electrons, and neutral particles. [New Latin, extended use of Late Latin *plasma,* a form, mould, from Greek, from *plassein,* to mould.] **—plas·mat·ic** (plaz-máttik), **plasmic** (plázmik) *adj.*
plasma engine *n.* A hypothetical engine for use in space that generates thrust by emitting a jet of plasma.
plas·ma·gel (plázmə-jel) *n. Biology.* A jelly-like state of cytoplasm, characteristically occurring in the periphery of the cell.
plas·ma·gene (plázmə-jeen) *n. Genetics.* A self-reproducing hereditary structure in cell cytoplasm that functions in a manner analogous to, but independent of, chromosomal genes. **—plas·ma·gen·ic** (-jénnik, -jéenik) *adj.*
plasma membrane *n. Biology.* The semipermeable membrane that encloses the cytoplasm of a cell.
plas·ma·pher·e·sis (plázmə-férrə-siss) *n.* The method of obtaining quantities of plasma, rather than whole blood, from donors for the purpose of transfusion. [New Latin, from PLASMA + Greek *aphesis,* a removal, from *aphairein,* to take away: *apo,* off, away + *hairein,* to take.]
plas·ma·sol (plázmə-sol || -sōl, *U.S. also* -sawl) *n. Biology.* A state of cytoplasm that is more liquid than plasmagel and is found in the interior of the cell. [PLASMA + SOL (colloid).]
plas·min (plázmin) *n. Biochemistry.* A proteolytic enzyme in plasma that dissolves fibrin in blood clots. Also called "fibrinolysin". [PLASM(O)- + -IN.]
plasmo–, plasm– *comb. form.* Indicates plasma or resemblance to plasma; for example, **plasmolysis, plasmin.** [New Latin PLASMA.]
plas·mo·des·ma (pláz-mə-déz-mə, -mō-) *n., pl.* **-mata** (-mətə). Also **plas·mo·desm** (-dezz'm). *Biology.* A strand of living cytoplasm connecting two plant cells that are otherwise functionally separate. [New Latin : PLASMO- + Greek *desma,* a bond, from *dein,* to bind.]
plas·mo·di·um (plaz-mṓdi-əm) *n., pl.* **-dia** (-ə). **1.** Any protozoan of the genus *Plasmodium,* which includes the parasites that cause malaria. **2.** A naked, multinucleate mass of protoplasm such as that characteristic of the vegetative phase of the slime moulds. [New Latin : PLASMO- + -ODE + -IUM.]
plas·mo·lyse, *U.S.* **plas·mo·lyze** (plázmə-līz) *v.* **-lysed, -lysing, -lyses.** *—tr.* To subject to plasmolysis. *—intr.* To undergo plasmolysis. [Back-formation from PLASMOLYSIS.]
plas·mol·y·sis (plaz-móllə-siss) *n. Biology.* Shrinkage or contraction of the protoplasm in a plant or bacterial cell, caused by loss of water through osmosis. [PLASMO- + -LYSIS.] **—plas·mo·lyt·ic** (plázmə-líttik) *adj.* **—plas·mo·lyt·i·cal·ly** *adv.*
plas·mo·some (plázmə-sōm) *n. Biology.* A **nucleolus** *(see).*
-plast *n. comb. form.* Indicates an organised unit of living matter; for example, **protoplast.** [Greek *plastos,* moulded. See **plastic.**]
plas·ter (plaástər || plástər) *n.* **1.** A mixture of lime, sand, and water, sometimes with hair or other fibre added, that hardens to a smooth solid and is used for coating walls and ceilings. **2.** A **sticking plaster** *(see).* **3. Plaster of Paris** *(see).* **4.** A pastelike mixture applied to a part of the body for healing or cosmetic purposes. **5.** A **mustard plaster** *(see).*
~*tr.v.* **plastered, -tering, -ters. 1.** To cover, coat, or repair with plaster or similar material. **2.** To cover by or as if by pasting; especially, to cover conspicuously or to excess. **3.** To apply a plaster to. **4.** To cause to adhere to another surface: *"His hair was plastered to his forehead."* (William Golding). **5.** To make smooth by applying a sticky substance. Used with *down*: *plastered down with hair oil.* **6.** *Slang.* To inflict injury, damage, or defeat on: *plastered by the bombers.* [Middle English *plaster,* Old English *plaster,* from Medieval Latin *plastrum,* short for Latin *emplastrum,* from Greek *emplastron, emplaston,* salve, from *emplastos,* past participle of *emplassein,* to daub on, plaster : *em-, en,* in + *plassein,* to mould, plaster.] **—plas·ter·er** *n.*
plas·ter·board (plaástər-bawrd || plástər-, -bōrd) *n.* A thin, rigid board or sheet of layers of fibreboard or paper, with a plaster core, used to cover walls and ceilings.
plaster cast *n.* **1.** A mould or cast of a piece of sculpture or other object made with plaster of Paris. **2.** *Medicine.* A **cast** *(see).*
plas·tered (plaástərd || plástərd) *adj. Slang.* Drunk.
plas·ter·ing (plaást-ər-ing, -ring || plást-) *n.* **1.** A layer or coating of plaster. **2.** *Informal.* A heavy defeat.
plaster of Paris *n.* Any of a group of gypsum cements, essentially hemihydrated calcium sulphate, $2CaSO_4{\cdot}H_2O$, a white powder that forms a paste when mixed with water and hardens into a solid. It is used in making small moulded articles and in surgical casts. Also called "plaster". [Middle English; originally made in *Paris.*]
plaster saint *n. Informal.* A deceptively pious and upright person.
plas·tic (plástik, plaástik) *adj.* **1.** Capable of being shaped or formed; pliable: *Clay is a plastic substance.* **2.** Pertaining to or dealing with shaping or modelling: *the plastic arts.* **3.** Giving form or shape to a substance. **4.** Easily influenced; impressionable. **5.** Made of a plastic or plastics: *a plastic garden hose.* **6.** *Informal.* Synthetic or artificial in taste or appearance: *plastic food.* **7.** *Physics.* Capable of undergoing continuous deformation without breaking or returning to the original size. Said of solids. **8.** *Biology.* Capable of changing or developing tissue; formative. Said of cells and tissues. —See Synonyms at **flexible.**
~*n.* **1.** Any of various materials based on polymerised organic compounds, often with additives such as pigments, fillers, or plasticisers. They can be moulded, extruded, or cast into various shapes and coatings, or drawn into filaments used as textile fibres. **2.** Plastic money. [French *plastique,* from Latin *plasticus,* from Greek *plastikos,* fit for moulding, from *plastos,* moulded, from *plassein,* to mould.] **—plas·ti·cal·ly** *adv.* **—plas·tic·i·ty** (plass-tíssəti, plaass-) *n.*
-plastic *adj. comb. form.* Indicates a forming or growing; for example, **cytoplastic.** [Greek *plastikos,* fit for moulding, PLASTIC.]
plastic bullet *n.* A cylindrical piece of plastic, about 10 centimetres (4 inches) long, intended to be fired low among members of a disorderly crowd to disperse it.
plastic explosive *n.* A type of high explosive in the form of a mouldable jelly, used with a detonator.
Plas·ti·cine (pláss-tə-seen, plaáss-, -ti-) *n.* A trademark for a putty-like modelling material used especially by children.
plas·ti·cise, plas·ti·cize (plásti-sīz, plaásti-) *v.* **-cised, -cising, -cises.** *—tr.* To make plastic. *—intr.* To become plastic.
plas·ti·cis·er (plásti-sīzər, plaásti-) *n.* Any of various substances added to plastics or other materials to keep them soft or pliable.
plastic money *n.* Credit cards. Used humorously.
plastic surgery *n.* Cosmetic or remedial surgery to remodel, repair, or restore injured or defective tissue or body parts. **—plastic surgeon** *n.*
plas·tid (plástid, plaástid) *n. Biology.* Any of several specialised cytoplasmic structures occurring in plant cells and in some plantlike organisms, and having various physiological functions. [German *Plastid, Plastiden* (plural), from Greek *plastides,* feminine plural of *plastēs,* moulder, sculptor, from *plastos,* moulded, from *plassein,* to mould.] **—plas·tid·i·al** (plass-tíddi-əl, plaass-) *adj.*
plas·tron (pláss-trən, -tron) *n.* **1.** A breastplate worn under a coat of mail. **2.** A protective breastplate worn by fencers. **3.** A trimming on the front of a bodice. **4.** The front of a man's dress shirt. **5.** *Zoology.* The ventral surface of the shell of a turtle or tortoise. **6.** *Anatomy.* The breastbone together with the cartilages associated with it. [Old French, from Old Italian *piastrone,* augmentative of *piastra,* "metal plate", from Latin *emplastra, emplastrum,* PLASTER.] **—plas·tral** (-trəl) *adj.*
-plasty *n. comb. form.* Indicates plastic surgery; for example, **dermatoplasty.** [Greek *-plastia,* from *plastos,* moulded. See **plastic.**]
-plasy. Variant of **-plasia.**
plat[1] (plat) *tr.v.* **platted, platting, plats.** *Regional.* To plait or braid. ~*n. Regional.* A plait. [Middle English *platen,* variant of *plaiten,* to PLAIT.]
plat[2] **1.** *Archaic.* A small area of ground; a patch. **2.** *U.S.* A chart, plan, or the like, especially one showing the proposed design of a town or group of buildings. [Variant of PLOT.]
plat. 1. platform. **2.** platoon.
Pla·ta, Rí·o de la (plaátə, rée-ō dellə). *English* **River Plate** (playt). Estuary in South America, formed by the confluence of the rivers Paraná and Uruguay. It proceeds into the Atlantic Ocean.
plat·an (plátt'n) *n.* A **plane tree** *(see).* [Middle English, from Latin *platanus,* PLANE TREE.]
plat·an·na (plát-ánnə) *n. South African.* See **xenopus.**
plate (playt) *n.* **1. a.** A shallow dish in which food is served or from which it is eaten. **b.** The contents of such a dish. **c.** The amount a plate will hold; a plateful. **d.** *U.S.* A whole course served on such a dish. **2.** *U.S.* Food and service for one person at a meal: *dinner at a set price per plate.* **3. a.** Household utensils covered with a thin layer of precious metal, such as gold or silver. **b.** Articles, in a church for example, made of gold and silver. **4.** A dish passed among a congregation for the collection of offerings. **5.** A smooth, flat, relatively thin, rigid body of uniform thickness. **6. a.** A sheet of

hammered, rolled, or cast metal. **b.** A very thin plated coat or layer of metal. **c.** Metal or metal objects coated with such a layer. **7. a.** A flat piece of metal forming part of a machine: *a boiler plate.* **b.** A flat piece of metal on which something is engraved. **c.** A number plate on a motor vehicle. **8. a.** A thin piece of metal used for armour. **b.** Armour made of this. **9.** *Abbr.* **pl.** *Printing.* **a.** A sheet of metal, plastic, rubber, paperboard, or other material converted into a printing surface, such as an electrotype or stereotype. **b.** A print of a woodcut, lithograph, or other engraved material, especially when reproduced in a book. **c.** A full-page book illustration, often in colour and printed on paper different from that used on the text pages. **10.** *Abbr.* **pl.** *Photography.* A light-sensitive sheet of glass or metal upon which an image can be recorded. **11.** A **dental plate** *(see).* **12.** *Architecture.* In wood-frame construction, a horizontal member, capping the exterior wall studs, upon which the roof rafters rest. **13.** In baseball, a flat piece of heavy rubber set in the ground that is used to define the place over which the ball must be thrown by a pitcher for a strike. Also called "home plate". **14.** *Sports.* **a.** A dish, cup, or other trophy offered as a prize. **b.** A contest, especially a horse race, offering such a prize. **15.** *Anatomy & Zoology.* **a.** A thin, flat layer or scale. **b.** A platelike part or organ. **16.** *Electronics.* **a.** An electrode, as in a storage battery or capacitor. **b.** *U.S.* The anode in a thermionic valve. **17.** Any of the regions of the earth's crust. See **plate tectonics. —on a plate.** So as to be easily available or taken without effort. **—on (one's) plate.** *Informal.* Requiring one's attention: *I've a lot on my plate just now.*
~tr.v. **plated, plating, plates. 1.** To coat or cover with a thin layer of metal. **2.** To armour. **3.** *Printing.* To make a stereotype or electrotype from. **4.** To give a glossy finish to (paper) by pressing between metal sheets or rollers. [Middle English, from Old French, from feminine of *plat,* flat, from Vulgar Latin *plattus* (unattested), from Greek *platus,* broad, flat.]

pla·teau (pla-tō, plə-, pláttō) *n., pl.* **-teaus** or **-teaux** (-z). **1.** An elevated and comparatively level expanse of land; tableland. **2.** A relatively stable or quiescent period or state; a levelling off: *a plateau of business activity.* **3.** A flat region on a graph. [French, from Old French *platel,* a flat piece, from *plat,* flat, from Vulgar Latin *plattus* (unattested), from Greek *platus,* broad, flat.]

plat·ed (pláytid) *adj.* **1.** Coated with a thin layer of metal. Often used in combination: *gold-plated.* **2.** Covered or furnished with plates or sheets of metal. Often used in combination: *armour-plated.* **3.** Knitted with two kinds of wool, one on the face and one on the back.

plate·ful (pláyt-fōōl) *n., pl.* **-fuls. 1.** The amount of food or other substance that a plate will hold. **2.** A generous portion of food.

plate glass *n.* Rolled and polished flat glass containing few impurities, used for mirrors and windows.

plate·lay·er (pláyt-lay-ər) *n. British.* A person who lays and maintains railway track.

plate·let (pláyt-lət, -lit) *n.* An irregular-shaped disc, smaller than a red blood cell, that is found in the blood of vertebrates and promotes coagulation. Also called "blood platelet", "thrombocyte". [Diminutive of PLATE.]

plate·mark (pláyt-maark) *n.* A mark on metal, a **hallmark** *(see).*

plat·en (plátt'n) *n.* **1.** A flat plate in a printing press that serves to position the paper and hold it against the inked type. **2.** The roller on a typewriter against which the keys strike. [Earlier *plattin,* from Old French *platine,* from *plate,* PLATE.]

plat·er (pláytər) *n.* **1.** One that plates. **2.** *Slang.* An inferior racehorse.

plate tectonics *n.* **1.** The theory that the earth's crust is composed of a series of rigid plates and that movement of these plates in relation to each other is responsible for all the features of the earth's surface. **2.** The study of the earth's crust based on this theory.

plat·form (plát-fawrm) *n. Abbr.* **plat. 1.** A floor or horizontal surface raised above the level of the adjacent area, especially: **a.** A stage for public speaking. **b.** A raised area alongside the tracks in a railway station where passengers may alight from or board trains. **2.** An area in certain buses reserved for the conductor, next to the seating area. **3.** A thick raised sole or heel on certain types of shoes and boots. Also used adjectivally: *platform soles.* **4.** The declared policies with which a political figure or group makes an appeal to an electorate. [French, "ground plan", from Old French, "flat form" : feminine of *plat,* flat (see **plateau**) + *forme,* FORM.]

platform balance *n.* An equal-arm balance having two flat platforms above the beam and frequently using a sliding rider instead of weights.

platform scale *n.* A weighing instrument consisting of a platform coupled to an automatic system of levers and adjustable weights, designed to move a pointer over a scale.

Plath (plath), **Sylvia** (1932–63). U.S. poet. She made her reputation with *The Colossus* (1960). In 1963 she committed suicide, and her posthumous collection *Ariel* (1965) contains poems of anguish. She wrote one novel, *The Bell Jar* (1963).

plat·ing (pláyting) *n.* **1.** A thin layer or coating of metal, such as gold or silver. **2.** A covering or layer of metal sheets or plates.

pla·tin·ic (plə-tínnik) *adj. Chemistry.* Of, pertaining to, or containing platinum. Said especially of compounds containing platinum with a valency of 4. [PLATIN- + -IC.]

plat·i·nise, plat·i·nize (plátti-nīz) *tr.v.* **-nised, -nising, -nises.** To coat with platinum, as by electroplating or vacuum evaporation. [PLATIN(I)- + -IZE.]

plat·i·nised (plátti-nīzd) *adj.* Coated or treated with platinum; especially, coated with finely divided platinum: *platinised asbestos.*

platino-, platin-, platini- *comb. form.* Indicates the presence or characteristics of platinum: for example, **platinotype, platinoid.**

plat·i·noid (plátti-noyd) *adj.* Like platinum.
~n. **1.** An alloy of copper, nickel, tungsten, and zinc, formerly used in electric coils. **2.** Any metal resembling platinum chemically, especially osmium, iridium, or palladium. [PLATIN(O)- + -OID.]

plat·i·no·type (pláttinō-tīp) *n.* **1.** A process formerly used for making photographic prints, using a finely precipitated platinum salt and an iron salt in the sensitising solution to produce photographic prints in platinum black. **2.** A photographic print produced by this process. [PLATINO- + -TYPE.]

plat·i·nous (pláttinəss) *adj. Chemistry.* Of, pertaining to, or containing platinum. Said especially of compounds containing platinum with a valency of 2.

plat·i·num (pláttinəm) *n.* **1.** *Symbol* **Pt** A silver-white metallic element occurring worldwide, usually mixed with other metals such as iridium, osmium, or gold. It is ductile and malleable, does not oxidise in air, and is used in electrical components, jewellery, dentistry, electroplating, and as a catalyst. Atomic number 78, atomic weight 195.09, melting point 1773.5°C, boiling point 3827°C, relative density 21.45, valencies 2, 4. **2.** Medium to light bluish grey. [New Latin, from Spanish *platina,* PLATINA.]

platinum black *n.* A fine black powder of metallic platinum, used as a catalyst and as a gas absorbent.

platinum blonde *n.* **1.** A very light silver-blond hair colour. **2.** A person having hair of this colour. See Usage note at **blond. —platinum blonde** *adj.*

platinum metals *pl.n.* The group of chemically related elements ruthenium, osmium, rhodium, iridium, palladium, and platinum.

plat·i·tude (plátti-tewd || -tōōd) *n.* **1.** A trite, unoriginal, sententious remark or statement. **2.** Lack of originality; triteness. [French, "flatness", from *plat,* flat, from Old French, from Vulgar Latin *plattus* (unattested), from Greek *platus,* broad, flat.] **—plat·i·tud·i·nise** (-téwd-i-nīz || -tōōd-) *intr.v.* **—plat·i·tu·di·nous** (-téwd-inəss || -tōōd-) *adj.*

Pla·to (pláytō) (*c.* 428–347 B.C.). Greek philosopher, a major influence on Western thought. An Athenian aristocrat, he became a devoted admirer of Socrates. In about 386 he founded the Academy, where he taught and wrote for much of the rest of his life. Plato presented his philosophy in the form of dramatic *Dialogues* in which Socrates conducts the discussions, as in *The Republic,* where he proposes a system for educating rulers as "philosopher kings".

Pla·ton·ic (plə-tónnik || *U.S. also* play-) *adj.* Also **Pla·ton·i·cal** (-'l). **1.** Of, pertaining to, or characteristic of Plato or his philosophy. **2. a.** *Often small* **p.** Transcending physical desire and tending towards the purely spiritual or ideal: *platonic love.* **b.** *Small* **p.** Intimate, but not indulging in sexual intimacy: *a platonic relationship.* [Latin *Platonicus,* from Greek *Platōn,* Plato.] **—Pla·ton·i·cal·ly** *adv.*

Pla·to·nise, Pla·to·nize (pláytə-nīz) *v.* **-nised, -nising, -nises.** *—intr.* To adopt or adhere to the philosophy of Plato. *—tr.* To explain in accordance with Platonic philosophy.

Pla·to·nism (pláyt'n-iz'm) *n.* The philosophy of Plato, especially the view that asserts that the phenomena of the world are an imperfect and transitory copy of a transcendent world of archetypal forms. **—Pla·to·nist** *n.*

pla·toon (plə-tōōn) *n. Abbr.* **plat. 1.** A subdivision of a military company divided into squads or sections. **2.** A body of persons working together. [French *peloton,* "little ball", group of soldiers, from Old French *pelote,* from Vulgar Latin *pilotta* (unattested), diminutive of Latin *pila,* ball. See **pill.**]

Platt·deutsch (plát-doych) *n.* The Low German vernacular of northern Germany. [German, from Dutch *platduits* : *plat,* flat, low, clear, from Middle Dutch, from Old French, flat (see **platitude**) + *Duitsch,* German, from Middle Dutch *duutsch.*]

plat·te·land (pláttə-lant) *n. South African.* Rural districts; country areas. [Afrikaans, "flat land".] **—plat·te·land·er** (-landər) *n.*

plat·ter (pláttər) *n.* **1. a.** A large, shallow, often wooden dish or plate, used especially for serving food. **b.** A meal served on such a dish. **2.** *Chiefly U.S. Slang.* A gramophone record. [Middle English *plater,* from Anglo-French, from Old French *plate,* PLATE.]

plat·y¹ (pláyti) *adj.* **-ier, -iest.** Designating soil or minerals occurring in flaky layers.

platy² (plátti) *n., pl.* **platy, platys,** or **platies.** Any of several small freshwater fishes of the genus *Xiphophorus,* of southern North America; especially, *X. maculatus,* a colourful aquarium fish. Also called "platyfish". [New Latin *Platypoecilus,* "flat and colourful" (Greek *poikilos,* variegated), from Greek *platus,* broad, flat.]

platy- *comb. form.* Indicates flatness; for example, **platyhelminth.** [Greek *platus,* broad, flat.]

plat·y·hel·minth (plátti-hélminth) *n. Zoology.* Any of various parasitic and nonparasitic worms of the phylum Platyhelminthes, such as a tapeworm or a planarian, characteristically having a flattened body. Also called "flatworm". [PLATY- + Greek *helmis* (stem *helminth-*), parasitic worm.] **—plat·y·hel·min·thic** (-hel-mínthik) *adj.*

plat·y·pus (plátti-pəss || -pōōss) *n., pl.* **-puses.** The **duck-billed platypus** *(see).* [New Latin, from Greek *platupous,* "flat-footed" : PLATY- + *pous,* foot.]

plat·yr·rhine (plátti-rīn) *adj.* Also **plat·yr·rhin·i·an** (plátti-rínni-ən). **1.** *Anthropology.* Having a broad, flat nose. **2.** *Zoology.* Of or designating the New World monkeys, many of which are characterised by widely separated nostrils.
~n. Also **plat·yr·rhin·i·an.** A platyrrhine person or monkey. [New

Latin *Platyrrhina*, "flat-nosed ones", from *platyrrhinus*, flat-nosed, from Greek *platurrhis, platurrhinos* : PLATY- + Greek *rhis* (stem *rhin-*), nose (see **rhino-**).]

plau·dit (pláwdit) *n. Usually plural.* Enthusiastic approbation or praise; especially, critical approval. [Originally "an appeal for applause", from Latin *plaudite*, imperative of *plaudere*, to applaud.]

plau·si·ble (pláwz-ə-b'l, -i-) *adj.* **1.** Seemingly or apparently valid, likely, or acceptable: *a plausible excuse.* **2.** Giving a deceptive impression of truth, acceptability, or reliability; specious. [Originally "deserving applause", acceptable, from Latin *plausibilis*, from *plaudere* (past participle *plausus*), to applaud, acclaim.] **—plau·si·bil·i·ty** (-bílləti), **plau·si·ble·ness** *n.* **—plau·si·bly** *adv.*

plau·sive (pláw-siv, -ziv) *adj.* **1.** Showing or expressing praise or approbation; applauding. **2.** *Obsolete.* Plausible. [Latin *plaudere*, to applaud.]

Plau·tus (pláwtəss), **Titus Maccius** (*c.* 254–184 B.C.). Roman comic dramatist. Twenty-one of his comedies survive, all adapted from Greek sources to which he added his own earthy Roman humour. His imitators included Shakespeare and Molière.

play (play) *v.* **played, playing, plays.** *—intr.* **1.** To occupy oneself in amusing or diverting activities; especially, to engage in childish games. **2. a.** To take part in a game. **b.** To participate in a betting game; gamble. **3.** To act in jest or sport. **4.** To deal or behave carelessly or indifferently; toy; trifle. Usually used with *with.* **5.** To allow a specified type of play. Used of a sports ground: *the court is playing slow.* **6. a.** To act or behave in a specified way: *play fair.* **b.** *Informal.* To cooperate: *I asked them but they won't play.* **7.** To act or perform, especially in a dramatic production. **8.** To perform on a musical instrument. **9.** To emit sound or be sounded in performance: *The band is playing.* **10.** To be performed or shown, as in a theatre or cinema: *Othello is playing next week.* **11.** To move or seem to move quickly, lightly, or irregularly: *The breeze played on the water.* **12.** To function or operate uninterruptedly; especially, to discharge a steady stream: *The fountains played in the courtyard.* **13.** To move or operate freely within a bounded space, as machine parts do. *—tr.* **1. a.** To perform or act (a role or part) in a dramatic performance. **b.** To assume the role of; act as: *play Iago.* **2.** To put on or perform (a drama or other theatrical work) on or as if on the stage. **3.** To put on or produce a theatrical, musical, or other performance in (a specified place): *played Bristol last week.* **4.** To pretend to be; mimic the activities of: *The boys played cowboys and Indians.* **5.** To participate in (a game or sport). **6.** To compete against in a game or sport. **7. a.** To occupy or work at (a position) in a game: *He plays goalkeeper.* **b.** To employ the position of in a game: *play Russell at centre forward.* **c.** To use or move (a card, piece, or the like) in a game: *play the ace.* **d.** To make (a shot or stroke), as in tennis: *played a forehand.* **8.** To perform or put into effect, especially as a trick or deception: *play a joke on someone.* **9.** To use or manipulate (two or more competitors, for example) for one's own interests: *play them against each other.* **10. a.** To bet or wager. **b.** To make a wager on. **11. a.** To perform on (a musical instrument): *play the guitar.* **b.** To perform (music) on an instrument or instruments. **12.** To cause (a record or record player, for example) to emit recorded sounds. **13.** To discharge, set off, or cause to operate in or as if in a continuous stream: *play a hose on a fire.* **14.** To cause to move rapidly, lightly, or irregularly: *play lights over the dance floor.* **15.** In angling, to exhaust (a hooked fish) by allowing it to pull on the line. **—play about** or **around. 1.** To act in a silly or frivolous way, often so as to annoy: *Stop playing about and tell me!* **—play along.** To deceive or give a false impression to. **—play along with.** To cooperate with a plan or person, for example, especially out of self-interest. **—play at.** To participate in or engage in half-heartedly or frivolously. **—play down.** To minimise the importance of; make little of: *play down one's failings.* **—play down to.** To act or behave in a condescending manner towards. **—play on.** Also **play upon** (for sense 1). **1.** To take advantage of (another's attitudes or feelings) for one's own interests. **2.** In cricket, to allow the ball to hit the wicket after hitting it. Used of a batsman. **—play (oneself) in.** To introduce or accustom (oneself) gradually to a new situation. **—play out. 1.** To do or play until completed; finish. **2.** To accompany the departure of with music. **—play up.** *Informal.* **1.** To emphasise or publicise: *play up one's conquests.* **2.** To act or behave in a way so as to cause irritation or discomfort. **3.** To engage in an activity wholeheartedly. **—play up to.** *Informal.* **1.** To support (another actor) in a performance. **2.** To try to ingratiate oneself with.

∼n. **1. a.** A dramatic work written for performance on the stage; a drama. **b.** The performance of such a work. **2.** Activity engaged in for enjoyment or recreation, especially as a childish pastime. **3.** Fun or jesting: *done in play.* **4. a.** The act of carrying on or engaging in a game or sport. **b.** The manner or way of playing a game or sport. **5.** A manner or method of dealing with people generally. Used especially in the phrases *foul play* and *fair play.* **6.** A turn, move or action in a game: *It's your play.* **7.** Participation in betting; gambling. **8.** *Sports.* The condition of a ball, puck, or similar object in active or legitimate use or motion during a game. Used in the phrases *in play* and *out of play.* **9.** Action, motion, or use: *the play of the imagination.* **10.** Quick, often irregular movement or action, especially of light or colour: *the play of the light.* **11.** Movement or space or scope for movement: *give the rope more play.* **—bring** or **call into play.** To cause to operate; activate. **—make a play for.** *Informal.* To attempt to attract or obtain by using art, wiles, or skill. **—make great play with.** To exploit enthusiastically. [As verb, Middle English *playen*, from Old English *plegan*; as noun, Middle English *pley, play*, Old English *plega.*] **—play·a·ble** (pláy-əb'l) *adj.*

pla·ya (plī-ə) *n. U.S.* **1.** An inland drainage basin, surrounded by sheets of saline or alkaline crust and containing a shallow lake. **2.** The lake in such a basin. [Spanish, "shore", from Medieval Latin *plagia*, from Greek, sides, neuter plural of *plagios.* See **plagio-**.]

play-act (pláy-akt) *intr.v.* **-acted, -acting, -acts. 1.** To play a pretended role; make believe. **2.** To behave in an overdramatic or artificial manner. **—play-acting** *n.* **—play-actor** *n.*

play back *tr.v.* To replay (a recording). *—intr.* **1.** In cricket, to step back in order to hit the ball. **2.** To replay a recording.

play·back (pláy-bak) *n.* **1.** The act or process of replaying a newly made record or tape. **2.** A method of or apparatus for reproducing sound recordings.

play·bill (pláy-bil) *n.* **1.** A poster announcing a theatrical performance. **2.** *U.S.* A programme for a theatrical performance.

play·boy (pláy-boy) *n.* A wealthy, often suave, carefree man, especially one who regularly indulges in the pleasures of nightclubs, sports, and female company.

play·er (pláy-ər) *n.* **1.** One who participates in a game or sport, especially professionally. **2.** One who performs in theatrical roles; an actor. **3.** One who plays a musical instrument. **4.** The mechanism actuating a player piano. **5.** An apparatus for reproducing recorded sound: *a cassette player.* **6.** A gambler. **7.** A trifler.

Player, Gary (Jim) (1935–). South African professional golfer, winner of numerous international tournaments.

player piano *n.* A mechanically operated piano that uses a perforated paper roll to actuate the keys.

play·ful (pláyf'l) *adj.* **1.** Full of fun and good spirits; frolicsome; sportive: *a playful kitten.* **2.** Humorous; jesting: *a playful comment.* **—play·ful·ly** *adv.* **—play·ful·ness** *n.*

Synonyms: *playful, mischievous, impish, waggish, frivolous.*

play·go·er (pláy-gō-ər) *n.* One who regularly attends the theatre.

play·ground (pláy-grownd) *n.* **1.** An outdoor area set aside for recreation and play, as in a school; especially, one containing seesaws, swings, and the like. **2.** Broadly, any area in which one may enjoy oneself: *The Riviera is a millionaire's playground.*

play·group (pláy-grōōp) *n.* A supervised gathering of children of preschool age where they can engage in games and other activities.

play·house (pláy-howss) *n.* **1.** A theatre. **2.** A small house for children to play in. **3.** *U.S.* A child's toy house; a doll's house.

playing card *n.* Any of a pack of cards with a design designating its value in the colour of one of the four **suits** *(see)*, and used in various card games.

playing field *n.* A field for games such as cricket and soccer.

play·mate (pláy-mayt) *n.* A companion in play or recreation.

play off *tr.v.* **1.** To use or manipulate (two or more competitors) especially for one's own interests: *She played her two suitors off against each other.* **2.** *Sports.* To establish the winner of (a tie) by playing an additional game or series of games. *—intr.v. Sports.* To participate or meet in a play-off.

play-off (pláy-off, -awff) *n. Sports.* **1.** A final game or series of games played to break a tie. **2.** *U.S.* A series of games played to determine a championship.

play·pen (pláy-pen) *n.* A portable enclosure in which a baby or young child can be left to play.

play·room (pláy-rōōm, -rŏŏm) *n.* A room designed or set aside for recreation or playing.

play·school (pláy-skōōl) *n.* Educational activities based on play for preschool children.

play·suit (pláy-sewt, -sōōt) *n.* A garment designed for a young child to play in.

play·thing (pláy-thing) *n.* **1.** Something to play with; a toy. **2.** One treated as a toy: *a plaything of fate.*

play·time (pláy-tīm) *n.* Time devoted to recreation, especially as a break from school lessons.

play·wright (pláy-rīt) *n.* One who writes plays; a dramatist.

pla·za (plaázə, plázzə) *n.* A public square or similar open area, especially in towns or cities of Spanish-speaking countries. [Spanish, from Vulgar Latin *plattea* (unattested), variant of Latin *platea*, broad street. See **place.**]

plc, PLC, p.l.c., P.L.C. public limited company.

plea (plee) *n.* **1.** An appeal or entreaty: *a plea for leniency.* **2.** An excuse; a pretext: *"Necessity, the tyrant's plea"* (Milton). **3.** *Law.* **a.** In civil cases, a defendant's answer to the declaration made by the plaintiff. **b.** In criminal law, the answer of the accused to a charge or indictment. **c.** Formerly, an action or suit. [Middle English *plai(d), plee*, a lawsuit, pleading, from Anglo-French *plai, ple*, Old French *plaid*, legal action, agreement, decree, from Medieval Latin *placitum*, from Latin, "something agreeable", opinion, decision, from the neuter of *placitus*, pleasing, agreeable, from the past participle of *placēre*, to please.]

plea bargaining *n.* The practice, especially between defending and prosecuting counsel, of reaching agreement over the charge on which the defendant should stand trial, normally resulting in the defendant pleading guilty to a less serious offence than that with which he could otherwise be charged (and would be so charged, were he to plead not guilty).

pleach (pleech || playch) *tr.v.* **pleached, pleaching, pleaches.** To plait or interlace (branches or twigs, for example), especially in making a hedge or an arbour. [Middle English *plechen*, from Old

North French *plechier,* from Latin *plectere* (past participle *plexus*), to weave, plait.]

plead (pleed) *v.* **pleaded** or *Chiefly U.S. & Scottish* **pled** (pled), **pleading, pleads.** *—intr.* **1.** To appeal earnestly; implore; beg: *pleaded with her to stay.* **2.** To argue or offer persuasive reasons for or against something. **3.** To furnish or provide an argument or appeal: *His misfortunes plead for him.* **4.** *Law.* **a.** To put forward a plea of a specified nature in a court of law: *plead guilty.* **b.** To enter an answer or pleading on behalf of a defendant or as part of the prosecution in a law action. **c.** To address a court as a lawyer or advocate. *—tr.* **1.** To assert or put forward as defence, vindication, or excuse; submit as a plea: *plead illness.* **2.** To present as an answer to a charge, indictment, or declaration made against one. **3. a.** *Law.* To argue or present (a case) in a court of law. **b.** To present the arguments for (a cause). [Middle English *pleden,* from Anglo-French, from Old French *plaidier.* See **plea.**] **—plead·a·ble** *adj.* **—plead·er** *n.*

plead·ing (pleéding) *n.* **1. a.** The act of entreating or making a plea. **b.** A plea or entreaty thus made. **2.** *Law.* **a.** The art or procedure of one who acts as an advocate in a law court. **b.** The act or technique of drawing up or presenting pleas in legal cases. **c.** A formal statement, generally written, propounding the cause of action or the defence of a legal case. **d.** *Plural.* The consecutive statements, allegations, and counterallegations made in turn by plaintiff and defendant, or prosecutor and accused, until a single issue is reached upon which the trial may be held. **—plead·ing·ly** *adv.*

pleas·ance (plézz'nss) *n. Archaic.* **1.** A secluded, landscaped area, such as the garden of a mansion. **2.** Pleasure or a source of pleasure. [Old French *(maison de) plaisance,* "(house of) pleasure", from *plaisant,* PLEASANT.]

pleas·ant (plézz'nt) *adj.* **1.** Giving or affording pleasure or enjoyment; agreeable. **2.** Pleasing in manner, appearance, or other personal qualities. **3.** Fair and comfortable. **4.** *Obsolete.* Merry; lively. —See Synonyms at **amiable.** [Middle English *plesaunt,* from Old French *plaisant,* from the present participle of *plaisir,* to PLEASE.] **—pleas·ant·ly** *adv.* **—pleas·ant·ness** *n.*

pleas·ant·ry (plézz'ntri) *n., pl.* **-ries.** **1.** A jesting, entertaining, or humorous remark or action: *exchanged pleasantries.* **2.** Pleasingly humorous style or manner in conversation or at social occasions. [French *plaisanterie,* from *plaisant,* PLEASANT.]

please (pleez) *v.* **pleased, pleasing, pleases.** *—tr.* **1.** To give enjoyment, pleasure, or satisfaction to; make glad or contented. **2.** *Formal.* To be the will or desire of. Used impersonally with *it: May it please you to accept our gifts.* *—intr.* **1.** To give satisfaction or pleasure; be agreeable. **2.** To have the will or desire; wish: *Do whatever you please.* **—be pleased to.** *Formal.* To be willing to; agree to: *He was pleased to grant me an audience.* **—please (oneself).** To do or act as one likes. **—if you please.** **1.** If it is your will, desire, or pleasure. **2.** If you can believe or imagine it. Used as an ironical expression of indignation or surprise.

~interj. Used: **1.** To indicate a polite request. **2.** To express an earnest wish or protest. [Middle English *plaisen, plesen,* from Old French *plaisir,* from Latin *placēre.*]

Usage: The usual intensive accompanying *pleased* in British English is *very;* In American English, *very much* is also used, and often preferred. The usual prepositions following *pleased* are *with (He was pleased with my work), about (He was pleased about my new job),* and *at (He was pleased at seeing me win). Over* is sometimes used informally instead of *about* and *at,* but is open to criticism.

pleas·ing (pleézing) *adj.* Giving pleasure or enjoyment; agreeable; gratifying. **—pleas·ing·ly** *adv.* **—pleas·ing·ness** *n.*

pleas·ur·a·ble (plézh-ərəb'l, -rəb'l) *adj.* Agreeable; gratifying. **—pleas·ur·a·ble·ness** *n.* **—pleas·ur·a·bly** *adv.*

pleas·ure (plézhər) *n.* **1. a.** An enjoyable sensation or emotion; *got pleasure from swimming.* **b.** Satisfaction; delight: *I'll do it with pleasure.* **2.** A source of enjoyment, gratification, or delight. **3.** Amusement, diversion, or worldly enjoyment: *"Pleasure . . . is a safer guide than either right or duty."* (Samuel Butler). Also used adjectivally: *a pleasure cruise.* **4.** Sensual gratification or indulgence. **5.** One's preference, wish, or choice: *What is your pleasure?*

~v. **pleasured, -uring, -ures.** *—tr.* **1.** *Archaic.* To give pleasure or enjoyment to; please; gratify. **2.** To gratify sexually. Used euphemistically. *—intr. Archaic.* To take pleasure; delight. Often used with *in.* [Middle English *plesure,* (earlier) *plesir,* from Old French *plaisir,* noun use of *plaisir,* to PLEASE.]

Synonyms: *pleasure, enjoyment, delight, joy.*

pleasure principle *n.* In psychoanalysis, the drive to seek immediate gratification of instinctual needs and to reduce pain. [Translation of German *Lustprinzip.*]

pleat (pleet) *n.* A fold in cloth or other material, made by doubling the material upon itself and then pressing or stitching into place.

~tr.v. **pleated, pleating, pleats.** To press or arrange in pleats. [Middle English, variant of PLAIT.]

pleb (pleb) *n. Informal.* A person of the lower classes; a plebeian. Used derogatorily. [Short for PLEBEIAN.] **—pleb·by** (plébbi) *adj.*

plebe (pleeb) *n.* A freshman at the U.S. Military or Naval Academy. [Short for PLEBEIAN.]

ple·be·ian (pli-beé-ən) *adj.* **1.** Of or pertaining to the Roman plebs. In this sense, compare **patrician.** **2.** Of, belonging to, or characteristic of common people. **3.** Crude; vulgar; low: *plebeian tastes.*

~n. **1.** A member of the Roman plebs. **2.** A member of the lower classes. **3.** Someone who is vulgar or coarse. [Latin *plēbēius,* from *plēbs,* common people.] **—ple·be·ian·ism** *n.*

pleb·i·scite (plébbi-sīt, -sit) *n.* **1.** A direct vote in which the entire electorate of a country, region, or other political unit is invited to accept or refuse the measure, programme, or government of the person or party initiating the consultation. **2.** Such a vote whereby a population exercises the right of national self-determination. Compare **referendum.** [French *plébiscite,* from Latin *plēbiscītum,* people's decree : *plēbi,* genitive of *plēbs,* common people + *scītum,* decree, from *sciscere* (past participle *scītus*), to approve, decree, "to seek to know", from *scīre,* to know.]

plebs (plebz) *n.* **1.** The common people of ancient Rome. **2.** The common people; the populace. [Latin *plēbs.*]

plec·tog·nath (plék-tog-nath, -təg-) *n.* Any of various tropical marine fishes of the order Tetraodontiformes (or Plectognathi), which includes the triggerfishes, puffers, trunkfishes, and others. [New Latin *Plectognathi,* "ones having twisted jaws" (from their ankylosed jaws) : Greek *plektos,* past participle of *plekein,* to weave, twist + *-gnathi,* plural of *-gnathus,* -GNATHOUS.] **—plec·tog·nath** *adj.*

plec·trum (plék-trəm) *n., pl.* **-trums** or **-tra** (-trə). Also **plec·tron** (-trən ‖ -tron). A small, thin, flexible piece of metal, plastic, bone, or other material, used to pluck the strings of certain musical instruments, such as the guitar or lute. Also called "pick". [Latin, from Greek *plēktron,* from *plēssein* (stem *plek-*), to strike + *-tron,* instrumental suffix.]

pled. Alternative past tense and past participle of **plead.**

pledge (plej) *n.* **1.** A formal promise to do something, such as the performance of an obligation or duty, or to refrain from doing something. **2. a.** Something given or held as security to guarantee payment of a debt or fulfilment of an obligation. **b.** The condition of something thus given or held: *put an article in pledge.* **3.** Something, such as an item of personal property, put in pawn. **4.** Something given as a token or sign. **5.** The act of drinking to someone; a toast. **—take the pledge.** To make a solemn vow to abstain from drinking alcoholic drinks.

~tr.v. **pledged, pledging, pledges.** **1.** To offer or guarantee by a solemn promise. **2.** To bind or secure by or as if by a pledge. **3.** To deposit as security; pawn. **4.** To drink a toast to. —See Synonyms at **devote.** [Middle English *pleg(g)e,* from Old French *plege,* from Late Latin *plebium,* from *plebire,* to pledge, probably from Frankish *plegan* (unattested), to guarantee (influenced by Latin *praebēre,* to offer).]

pledg·ee (pléj-eé) *n.* **1.** A person to whom something is pledged. **2.** A person with whom something is deposited as a pledge.

pledg·er (pléjər) *n.* One who makes or gives a pledge.

pledg·or, pledge·or (pléj-ór) *n.* A person who deposits property as a pledge.

-plegia *n. comb. form. Medicine.* Indicates a form of paralysis; for example, **paraplegia.** [New Latin, from Greek *plēgē,* a stroke, blow, from *plēssein* (stem *plēg-*), to strike.] **—plegic** *adj. comb. form.*

Plei·ad[1] (plī-əd, pleé-) *n., pl.* **Pleiades** (-eez). *Sometimes small* **p.** A group of seven illustrious persons. [French *Pléiade,* the name adopted by Ronsard (*c.* 1553) to designate himself and his six most eminent companions among the poets of the "brigade", in allusion to a group of Alexandrian poets named after the PLEIADES.]

Pleiad[2]**, Pleiade** *n. Greek Mythology.* Any of the Pleiades.

Pleiad[3]**, Pleiade** *n. Astronomy.* Any of the stars in the Pleiades.

Plei·a·des[1] (plī-ədeez, pleé-) *pl.n. Greek Mythology.* The seven daughters of Atlas and Pleione (Maia, Electra, Celaeno, Taygeta, Merope, Alcyone, and Sterope), who were changed into stars.

Pleiades[2] *pl.n. Astronomy.* An open star cluster in the constellation Taurus, consisting of several hundred stars, of which six or seven are visible to the naked eye. Also called the "Seven Sisters".

pleio-. Variant of **pleo-.**

Pleiocene. Variant of **Pliocene.**

plei·ot·ro·pism (plī-óttrə-piz'm) *n.* Also **plei·ot·ro·py** (-óttrəpi). *Genetics.* The control or determination of more than one characteristic or function by a single gene. [Greek *ple(i)ōn,* more + -TROPISM.] **—plei·o·trop·ic** (plī-ə-tróppik) *adj.* **—plei·o·trop·i·cal·ly** *adv.*

Pleis·to·cene (plī-stə-seen, -stō-) *adj. Geology.* Of, belonging to, or designating the geological time, rock series, and sedimentary deposits of the earlier of the two epochs of the Quaternary period, characterised by the alternate appearance and recession of northern glaciation and the appearance of the progenitors of man.

~n. Geology. The Pleistocene epoch or system of deposits. Preceded by *the.* [Greek *pleistos,* most + -CENE.]

ple·na·ry (pleén-əri, plén-) *adj.* **1.** Complete in all aspects or essentials; full; absolute: *plenary powers.* **2.** Fully attended by all qualified members: *a plenary session.*

~n. A plenary session or meeting of an organisation; a plenum. [Late Latin *plēnārius,* from Latin *plēnus,* full.] **—ple·na·ri·ly** *adv.* **—ple·na·ri·ness** *n.*

plenary indulgence *n. Roman Catholic Church.* An indulgence that remits the full temporal punishment incurred by a sinner.

plen·i·po·ten·ti·ar·y (plénnipə-tén-shəri, -shi-əri ‖ *U.S. also* -shi-erri) *adj.* **1.** Invested with or conferring full powers. **2.** Absolute; full: *plenipotentiary power.*

~n., pl. **plenipotentiaries.** A person, especially an ambassador or diplomat, fully authorised to represent a government. [Medieval Latin *plēnipotentiārius,* from Late Latin *plēnipotens* : Latin *plēnus,* full + *potens,* POTENT.]

plen·i·tude (plénni-tewd ‖ -to͞od) *n.* **1.** Abundance; copiousness. **2.** The condition of being full, ample, or complete. [Middle English, fullness, from Old French, from Latin *plēnitūdō,* from *plēnus,* full.]

plen·te·ous (plénti-əss) *adj.* **1.** Abundant; copious. **2.** Producing or yielding in abundance. [Middle English *plenti(v)ous*, from Old French *plentiveus*, from *plentif*, abundant, from *plente(t)*, PLENTY.] —**plen·te·ous·ly** *adv.* —**plen·te·ous·ness** *n.*

plen·ti·ful (pléntí'f'l) *adj.* **1.** Existing in great quantity or ample supply. **2.** Providing or producing an abundance: *a plentiful harvest.* —**plen·ti·ful·ly** *adv.* —**plen·ti·ful·ness** *n.*

plen·ty (pléntí) *n.* **1.** A full or wholly adequate amount or supply; as much as one could want: *plenty of time.* **2.** A large quantity or amount; abundance: *goods in plenty.* **3.** A condition of general abundance or prosperity: *peace and plenty.*

~*adj.* Plentiful; abundant. Always used after the noun or pronoun: *That's plenty.*

~*adv.* Chiefly *U.S. Informal.* Sufficiently; quite: *It's plenty hot.* [Middle English *plent(i)e*, *plentet*, from Old French *plente(t)*, from Latin *plēnitās* (stem *plēnitat*), from *plēnus*, full.]

ple·num (pléen-əm ‖ plén-) *n.*, *pl.* **-nums** or **plena** (-ə). **1. a.** A condition in which air or other gas, in an enclosure, is at a pressure greater than that outside the enclosure. **b.** An enclosure in which such a condition exists. **2.** In the philosophy of the Stoics, the whole of space regarded as being filled with matter. **3.** An assembly or meeting with all members present. **4.** Fullness. [Latin, neuter of *plēnus*, full.] —**ple·num** *adj.*

pleo-, pleio-, plio- *comb. form.* Indicates more; for example, **pleomorphism**, **pleiotropism**, **Pliocene**. [Greek *pleiōn*, *pleōn*, more.]

ple·och·ro·ism (pli-óckrō-iz'm) *n.* The property possessed by some crystals of exhibiting different colours when viewed along different axes. Compare **dichroism**. [PLEO- + -CHRO(OUS) + -ISM.] —**ple·o·chro·ic** (-plee-ə-krṓ-ik) *adj.*

ple·o·mor·phism, plei·o·mor·phism (plée-ə-mórf-iz'm, -ō-) *n.* **1.** *Chemistry.* Polymorphism *(see).* **2.** *Biology.* The occurrence of two or more structural forms during a life cycle, especially of certain plants. [PLEO- + -MORPH + -ISM.] —**ple·o·mor·phic** (-mórfik) *adj.*

ple·o·nasm (plée-ə-naz'm) *n.* **1.** The use of more words than are required to express an idea; redundancy. **2.** An instance of this. **3.** A superfluous word or phrase. [Late Latin *pleonasmus*, from Greek *pleonasmos*, "superabundance", from *pleonazein*, to be more than enough, from *ple(i)ōn*, more.] —**ple·o·nas·tic** (-nástik) *adj.* —**ple·o·nas·ti·cal·ly** *adv.*

ple·o·pod (plée-ə-pod) *n. Zoology.* An appendage of crustaceans, a **swimmeret** *(see).* [PLEO- + -POD.]

ple·si·o·sau·rus (plée-si-ə-sáwrəss, -ō- ‖ -zi-) *n.*, *pl.* **-sauri** (-sáwrī). Also **ple·si·o·saur** (-sawr). A large, long-necked marine reptile of the extinct suborder Plesiosauria, common in Europe and North America during the Mesozoic era. [New Latin, from Greek *plēsios*, near + -SAURUS.]·

plessor. *Medicine.* Variant of **plexor.**

pleth·o·ra (pléthərə) *n.* **1.** A superabundance; an excess. **2.** An excess of blood in the circulatory system or in one organ or area. [Late Latin *plēthōra*, from Greek *plēthōra*, *plēthōrē*, fullness, from *plēthein*, to be full.]

ple·thor·ic (ple-thórrik, pli- ‖ -tháwrik, pléthərik) *adj.* **1. a.** Excessive in quantity; superabundant: *plethoric wealth.* **b.** Inflated in style; turgid: *plethoric prose.* **2.** Characterised by an overabundance of blood. —**ple·thor·i·cal·ly** *adv.*

ple·thys·mo·graph (plə-thíz-mə-graf, ple-, -thiss-, -graaf) *n.* An instrument used to measure changes in the volume of fluid in a part of the body, such as a limb, caused by fluctuations in blood pressure. [Greek *plēthusmos*, enlargement + -GRAPH.] —**ple·thys·mog·ra·phy** (pléthiz-móggrəfi, pléthiss-) *n.*

pleu·ra¹ (plóor-ə ‖ pléwr-ə) *n.*, *pl.* **pleurae** (-ee). *Anatomy.* Either of two membranous sacs, each of which lines one side of the thoracic cavity and envelops the contiguous lung, reducing the friction of respiratory movements to a minimum. [Medieval Latin, from Greek *pleura*†, side, rib.] —**pleu·ral** *adj.*

pleu·ra². Plural of **pleuron.**

pleu·ri·sy (plóor-ə-si, -i- ‖ pléwr-) *n. Pathology.* Inflammation of the pleura, characterised by pain in the chest or side that becomes worse on deep breathing or coughing. [Middle English *pleresye*, *pluresy*, from Old French *pleurisie*, from Late Latin *pleurisis*, for Latin *pleurītis*, from Greek *pleuritis*, from *pleura*†, side, rib.] —**pleu·rit·ic** (plóor-ríttik ‖ pléwr-) *adj.*

pleuro-, pleur- *comb. form.* Indicates: **1.** The side; for example, **pleurodont.** **2.** The pleura; for example, **pleuropneumonia.** [New Latin, from Greek *pleura*†, side, rib.]

pleu·ro·dont (plóor-ə-dont ‖ pléwr-) *adj. Zoology.* **1.** Having the teeth attached by their sides to the inner side of the jaw, as in some lizards. **2.** Attached in this way: *pleurodont teeth.*

~*n.* An animal with pleurodont teeth. [PLEUR(O)- + -ODONT.]

pleu·ron (plóor-on ‖ pléwr-) *n.*, *pl.* **pleura** (-ə) *Zoology.* Either of the two lateral parts of the cuticle covering each of the body segments of arthropods. [New Latin, from Greek *pleuron*, *pleura*†, rib, side.]

pleu·ro·pneu·mo·nia (plóor-ō-new-mṓni-ə ‖ pléwr-, -nṓo-) *n. Pathology.* Pneumonia aggravated by pleurisy.

pleu·ro·pneu·mo·ni·a-like organism (plóor-ō-new-mṓni-ə-līk ‖ pléwr-, -nṓo-) *n. Abbr.* **PPLO** Any of a group of tiny, nonmotile, bacteria-like organisms formerly thought to cause a disease resembling pneumonia but now known to be harmless.

pleu·rot·o·my (ploor-róttəmi ‖ plew-) *n.*, *pl.* **-mies.** Surgical incision into the pleura. [PLEURO- + -TOMY.]

pleus·ton (plṓo-stən, -ston ‖ pléw-) *n.* Plants, such as algae, that float upon the surface of bodies of fresh water. [Greek *pleusis,*

sailing, from *plein*, to sail + (PLANK)TON.] —**pleus·ton·ic** (plṓo-stónnik ‖ pléw-) *adj.*

plex·i·form (plék-si-fawrm) *adj.* Similar to or having the form of a plexus; complicated in structure. [PLEX(US) + -FORM.]

Plex·i·glas (plék-si-glaass ‖ -glass) *n. U.S.* A trademark for a light, permanently transparent, weather-resistant thermoplastic form of polymethyl methacrylate.

plex·im·e·ter (plek-símmítər) *n. Medicine.* A small, thin plate held against the body and struck with a plexor in the technique of **percussion** *(see).* [PLEX(OR) + -METER.] —**plex·i·met·ric** (pléksi-méttrik) *adj.* —**plex·im·e·try** (plek-símmətri) *n.*

plex·or (pléksər) *n.* Also **ples·sor** (pléssər). *Medicine.* A small, rubber-headed hammer used with a pleximeter, in diagnosis by **percussion** *(see)* and also in testing nervous reflexes. [Greek *plēxis*, stroke, from *plēssein*, to strike.]

plex·us (pléksəss) *n.*, *pl.* **plexus** or **-uses.** **1.** *Anatomy.* A structure in the form of a network, especially of nerves, blood vessels, or lymphatics: *the solar plexus.* **2.** Any interlacing of parts; a network. [New Latin, from Latin, network, from *plexus*, past participle of *plectere*, to plait.]

pli·a·ble (plí-əb'l) *adj.* **1.** Easily bent or shaped; flexible. **2. a.** Receptive to change; adaptable. **b.** Easily influenced, persuaded, or swayed; tractable. —See Synonyms at **flexible.** —**pli·a·bil·i·ty** (-ə-bílləti), **pli·a·ble·ness** *n.* —**pli·a·bly** *adv.*

pli·an·cy (plí-ən-si) *n.* The quality or condition of being pliant.

pli·ant (plí-ənt) *adj.* **1.** Easily bent or flexed; supple; limber. **2.** Easily altered or modified to fit conditions; adaptable. **3.** Yielding readily to influence or domination; docile; compliant. —See Synonyms at **flexible.** [Middle English, from Old French, present participle of *plier*, to bend, fold, from Latin *plicāre*, to fold.] —**pli·ant·ly** *adv.* —**pli·ant·ness** *n.*

pli·ca (plíkə) *n.*, *pl.* **plicae** (plí-see). **1.** *Zoology & Anatomy.* A fold or ridge as of skin, membrane, or shell. **2.** A matted and encrusted state of the hair, resulting from dirt and vermin. [Medieval Latin, a fold, plait, from Latin *plicāre*, to fold.] —**pli·cal** (plí'l) *adj.*

pli·cate (plí-kayt) *adj.* Also **pli·cat·ed** (-id). Arranged in folds like those of a fan; pleated: *plicate leaves.* [Latin *plicātus*, past participle of *plicāre*, to fold.] —**pli·cate·ly** *adv.* —**pli·cate·ness** *n.*

pli·ca·tion (plī-káysh'n) *n.* Also **plic·a·ture** (plícka-chər, -tewr). **1. a.** The act or process of folding. **b.** The state of being folded. **2.** A fold. **3.** A surgical technique in which folds are sutured in the walls of a hollow organ to reduce its size.

pli·é (plée-ay) *n.* A movement in ballet in which the knees are bent while the back remains straight and the feet remain flat on the floor. [French, from past participle of *plier*, to bend.]

pli·er (plí-ər) *n.* One who plies (a trade).

pli·ers (plí-ərz) *pl.n.* Any of variously shaped tools having a pair of pivoted jaws, used for holding, bending, or cutting.

plight¹ (plīt) *n.* A condition or situation of difficulty or adversity. See Synonyms at **predicament.** [Middle English *plit*, from Anglo-French, Old French *pleit*, *ploit*, "a fold", from Vulgar Latin *plicitum* (unattested), from Latin *plicitus*, past participle of *plicāre*, to fold.]

plight² *tr.v.* **plighted, plighting, plights.** *Archaic.* **1.** To promise or bind by a solemn pledge; especially, to betroth. **2.** To give or pledge (one's word or oath, for example): *plight one's troth.*

~*n. Archaic.* **1.** A solemn pledge, as of faith. **2.** An engagement. [Middle English, Old English *pliht* (noun), peril.] —**plight·er** *n.*

plim·soll, plim·sole (plím-səl ‖ -sōl) *n. British.* A light rubber-soled cloth shoe, worn especially as a sports shoe. Also called "gymshoe", and, in southwest England and in Wales, "dap". [Probably because the rubber rim resembles a PLIMSOLL LINE.]

Plimsoll line *n.* Any of a set of lines on the hull of a merchant ship to indicate the depth to which it may be legally loaded under specific conditions. Also called "load line", "Plimsoll mark". [After Samuel *Plimsoll* (1824–98), Member of Parliament who supported the British Merchant Shipping Act (1876).]

plink (plingk) *n.* A light tinkling sound.

~*v.* **plinked, plinking, plinks.** —*intr.* To produce a plink. —*tr.* To cause to plink.

plinth (plinth) *n.* **1.** A block or slab upon which a pedestal, column, or statue is placed. **2.** The base block at the intersection of the skirting board and the vertical frame round a doorway. **3.** A continuous course of stones supporting a wall. Also called "plinth course". **4.** A square base, as on a vase. [French *plinthe*, from Latin *plinthus*, from Greek *plinthos*†, brick, square stone block.]

Plin·y¹ (plínni), Latin name Gaius Plinius Secundus; also known as Pliny the Elder (A.D. 23–79). Roman writer and administrator. He is remembered chiefly for his encyclopedic *Natural History.*

Pliny². Latin name Gaius Plinius Caecilius Secundus; also known as Pliny the Younger (*c.* A.D. 61–113). Roman politician and writer, the nephew of Pliny the Elder. His correspondence provides much valuable information about Roman life, and includes a letter from Bithynia which gives one of the first accounts of the early Christians.

plio-. Variant of **pleo-.**

Pli·o·cene (plí-ə-seen, -ō-) *adj. Geology.* Of, belonging to, or designating the geological time, rock series, and sedimentary deposits of the last of the five epochs of the Tertiary period, characterised by the appearance of distinctly modern plants and animals.

~*n. Geology.* The Pliocene epoch or system of deposits. Preceded by the. [Greek *pleiōn*, more + -CENE.] —**Pli·o·cen·ic** (-sénnik, -séenik) *adj.*

plis·sé (plée-say ‖ *U.S.* pli-sáy) *n.* **1.** A puckered texture of cloth created by treating fabric with a caustic soda. **2.** Fabric having such a texture. [French, past participle of *plisser,* to fold, pleat.]

PLO Palestine Liberation Organisation.

plod (plod) *v.* **plodded, plodding, plods.** —*intr.* **1.** To move or walk heavily or laboriously; trudge. **2.** To work or act perseveringly or monotonously; drudge. Used with *at, on,* or *upon.* —*tr.* To make (one's way) or trudge heavily and slowly along or over.
~*n.* **1.** The act of moving or walking heavily and slowly. **2. a.** A laborious journey. **b.** A laborious piece of work. **3.** The sound made by a heavy step. [16th century : imitative] **—plod·ding·ly** *adv.*

plod·der (plóddər) *n.* One who moves or, especially, works steadily but laboriously and unimaginatively.

plodge (ploj) *intr.v.* **plodged, plodging, plodges.** *Northeastern English.* To wade or paddle, especially in the sea.
~*n. Northeastern English.* An act of wading or paddling. [Akin to PLOD, perhaps influenced by PLUNGE; imitative.]

-ploid *adj. & n. comb. form. Biology.* Indicates a specified multiple of a set of chromosomes; for example, **polyploid.** [Greek *-ploos,* -fold + -OID.] **—-ploidy** *n. comb. form.*

plonk¹ (plongk) *v.* **plonked, plonking, plonks.** *Informal* —*tr.* **1.** To fling down or drop heavily or abruptly. Often used with *down*: *He plonked the goods down on the counter.* **2.** To play (the piano, for example) badly. —*intr.* **1.** To fall or be dropped heavily or abruptly. **2.** To play a piano or other instrument badly.
~*n.* **1.** An abrupt or heavy fall or drop. **2.** The sound made by this. [Variant of PLUNK.] **—plonk** *adv.*

plonk² *n. Informal.* Wine of indifferent quality. [Originally Australian slang, probably from French *(vin) blanc,* white (wine).]

plonk·o (plóngk-ō) *n., pl.* **-os.** Also **plonk·ie** (-i). *Australian Informal.* An alcoholic, especially one addicted to cheap wine; a wino. [PLONK (wine) + -O.]

plop (plop) *v.* **plopped, plopping, plops.** —*intr.* To fall or move with a sound like that of an object falling into water without splashing. —*tr.* To drop or move so as to make such a sound.
~*n.* A plopping sound or movement. [19th century : imitative.] **—plop** *adv.*

plo·sion (plṓzh'n) *n. Phonetics.* The sudden release of breath in the articulation of a plosive. Also called "explosion". Compare **implosion.** [From EXPLOSION.]

plo·sive (plṓ-siv, -ziv) *adj. Phonetics.* Designating a speech sound whose articulation requires, at some stage, the complete closure of both the nasal and the oral passage, as in the sound of (p) in *top.*
~*n. Phonetics.* A plosive speech sound. Also called "explosive". [French, from *explosif,* EXPLOSIVE.]

plot (plot) *n.* **1.** A small piece of ground, generally used for a specific purpose. **2. a.** A graphic representation, as on a chart. **b.** Something located on a graph. **c.** *U.S.* A ground plan, as for a building; a chart; a diagram. **3.** A plan of the main series of events or an outline of the action of a story, drama, or the like. **4.** A secret plan, usually to accomplish a hostile or illegal purpose; a scheme. —See Synonyms at **conspiracy. —the plot thickens.** Matters are becoming more complex, often with intriguing or sinister overtones.
~*v.* **plotted, plotting, plots.** —*tr.* **1. a.** To represent graphically, as on a chart: *plot a ship's course.* **b.** To make a plan or map of. **2.** To prearrange secretly or deviously: *plot an assassination.* **3.** To conceive and arrange the action and incidents of: *plot a novel.* **4. a.** To locate (points or other figures) on a graph mathematically by means of coordinates. **b.** To draw (a curve) connecting points on a graph. —*intr.* To devise secretly; conspire. [In the sense "a piece of ground" (and hence the extended senses "plan", "diagram"), Middle English *plot(te),* Old English *plot*†. In the sense "secret plan", from *complot,* from Old French *complote*†.] **—plot·ter** *n.*

Plo·ti·nus (plō-tínəss, plo-) (*c.* A.D. 205–270). Greek philosopher. He initiated Neo-Platonism, developing Plato's teaching along mystic lines which suggests some knowledge of Oriental philosophy.

plough (plow) *n.* Also *chiefly U.S.* **plow. 1.** A farm implement consisting of a heavy blade or blades at the end of a beam, usually pulled by a draught animal or tractor and used for breaking up and turning over soil in preparation for sowing. **2.** Any implement with a similar function, such as a snowplough. **3.** Ploughed land. **4.** *British Slang.* Failure in an examination. **—put** or **set (one's) hand to the plough.** To start a piece of work. **—the Plough.** *Astronomy.* A group of seven bright stars forming part of the constellation Ursa Major. Also called "Charles' Wain", *U.S.* "Big Dipper".
~*v.* **ploughed, ploughing, ploughs.** Also *Chiefly U.S.* **plow, plowed, plowing, plows.** —*tr.* **1. a.** To break and turn over (earth) with a plough. **b.** To dig in (stubble, for example) with a plough. **2. a.** To form (a furrow, for example) with a plough. **b.** To make or form with driving force: *ploughed his way through the crowd.* **3.** To make furrows or indentations in. **4.** To cut through (water): *plough the high seas.* **5.** *British Slang.* To fail (a candidate) in an examination. —*intr.* **1.** To break and turn up earth with a plough. **2.** To admit of being ploughed: *Rocky earth ploughs poorly.* **3.** To move or progress in the manner of a plough. Usually used with *through.* **4.** To proceed laboriously; plod. **5.** *British Slang.* To fail an examination. **—plough back.** To reinvest (earnings or profits) in one's business. **—plough into.** *Informal.* **1.** To strike with force. **2.** To undertake (a task, for example) with eagerness and vigour. [Middle English *plou, plogh,* Old English *plōg, plōh,* from late Germanic *plōgaz* (unattested), of Italic origin.] **—plough·er** *n.*

plough·boy (plów-boy) *n.* **1.** A boy who leads or guides a team of animals in ploughing. **2.** A country boy.

plough·land (plów-land) *n.* **1.** In medieval England, a unit of land area roughly equivalent to the area capable of being ploughed by a team of eight oxen in a single year. **2.** Land under cultivation or suitable for cultivation.

plough·man (plów-mən) *n., pl.* **-men** (-mən, -men). **1.** A person who ploughs. **2.** A farmer or rustic.

ploughman's lunch *n.* In Britain, a meal, usually lunch, that is typically taken in a pub. It consists of French bread or a roll, butter, British cheese, and pickle. The name is meant to suggest traditional peasant fare.

ploughman's spikenard *n.* A European plant, *Inula conyza,* having clusters of yellowish flower heads. Also called "fleawort".

plough·share (plów-shair) *n.* The cutting blade of a plough; a share.

plov·er (plúvvər || *U.S. also* plṓvər) *n., pl.* **-ers** or collectively **plover. 1.** Any of various widely distributed wading birds of the family Charadriidae, including the lapwing, having rounded bodies, short tails, and short bills. **2.** Any of various similar or related birds. [Middle English, from Old French *plovier,* from Vulgar Latin *pluviārius, ploviārius* (unattested), "rain-bird" (reason for naming obscure), from Latin *pluvia,* rain, from *pluere,* to rain.]

ploy (ploy) *n.* **1.** A tactic or stratagem, as in a conversation or game, to obtain an advantage. **2.** An activity; an occupation or amusement. [18th century (Scottish) : origin obscure.]

P.L.P. Parliamentary Labour Party (in Britain).

P.L.R. Public Lending Right.

plu. plural.

pluck (pluk) *v.* **plucked, plucking, plucks.** —*tr.* **1.** To detach by grasping and pulling abruptly with the fingers; pick: *pluck a flower.* **2.** To pull out the hair or feathers of: *pluck a chicken.* **3.** To give an abrupt pull to; tug at: *pluck a sleeve.* **4.** *Music.* To sound (the strings of an instrument) by pulling and releasing them with the fingers or a plectrum. **5.** *Slang.* To rob or swindle. —*intr.* To give an abrupt pull; tug. Used with *at.* **—pluck up.** To gather, raise, or summon up (one's courage, for example).
~*n.* **1.** The act of plucking; a tug; a snatch. **2.** Resourceful courage and daring in the face of difficulties; spirit. **3.** The heart, liver, windpipe, and lungs of a slaughtered animal. [Middle English *plukken,* Old English *pluccian,* from West Germanic *plukkōn* (unattested), from Vulgar Latin *piluccāre* (unattested), to remove the hair, pluck, irregularly from *pilus,* hair.] **—pluck·er** *n.*

pluck·y (plúcki) *adj.* **-ier, -iest.** Having or showing courage or spirited resourcefulness in trying circumstances. See Synonyms at **brave. —pluck·i·ly** *adv.* **—pluck·i·ness** *n.*

plug (plug) *n.* **1.** An object, such as a cork, rubber disc, or wad of cloth, used to stop a hole or gap. **2. a.** A fitting, with metal prongs for insertion in a fixed socket, used to connect an appliance to a power supply. **3.** A **spark plug** *(see).* **4. a.** A flat cake of pressed or twisted tobacco. **b.** A portion of chewing tobacco. **5.** *Geology.* A mass of igneous rock filling the opening, or vent, of a volcano. **6.** *Informal.* A favourable public mention, as of a commercial product, especially on television or radio. **7.** *U.S. Slang.* Something inferior, useless, or defective; especially, an old, worn-out horse.
~ *v.* **plugged, plugging, plugs.** —*tr.* **1.** To fill (a hole) tightly with or as if with a plug or stopper; stop up. **2.** To use as a plug: *plugged a cork in a bottle.* **3.** To connect (an electrical appliance) to a socket. Used with *into.* **4.** *Slang.* **a.** To hit with a bullet; shoot. **b.** To hit with the fist; punch. **5.** *Informal.* **a.** To make favourable public mention of (a product, for example). **b.** To advertise or publicise (a song, for example) by constant repetition or mention. —*intr.* **1.** To function by being connected to an electrical socket. Used with *into.* **2.** *Informal.* To work doggedly and persistently at some activity. Often used with *away* or *along*: *plug away at homework.* **3.** *Slang.* To fire bullets. [Middle Dutch *plugge*†.] **—plug·ger** *n.*

plug·board (plúg-bawrd || -bōrd) *n. Electronics.* A board containing a number of sockets used for patching circuits. Also called "patch board".

plug hat *n. U.S. Slang.* A man's stiff silk hat. [Probably because the head fits into it like a plug.]

plug·hole (plúg-hōl) *n.* The main drainage hole in a bath, basin, or other fixture into which a plug fits.

plug in *intr.v.* **1.** To work by being plugged into a socket. Used of an electrical appliance. **2.** *Chiefly U.S. Slang.* To become aware of or in touch with something: *It's time to face facts and plug in to the real world.* —*tr.v.* To cause to be plugged in.

plug-in (plúg-in) *adj.* Designating an appliance that works by being plugged in to an electrical power source.
~*n.* A plug-in appliance or piece of equipment.

plug-ug·ly (plúg-úggli) *n., pl.* **-lies.** *U.S. Slang.* A gangster or ruffian.
~*adj.* Very ugly. [After the *plug-ugly* gangs in 19th-century New York, whose members wore PLUG HAT(S).]

plum¹ (plum) *n.* **1.** Any of several shrubs or small trees of the genus *Prunus;* especially, *P. domestica,* bearing smooth-skinned, fleshy, edible fruit with a single hard-shelled seed. **2.** The fruit of any of these trees. **3. a.** Any of several trees bearing plumlike fruit. **b.** The fruit of such a tree. **4.** A raisin, when added to a pudding or cake. **5.** Dark purple to deep reddish purple. **6.** *Informal.* Something that is the best of its kind or that is especially desirable, such as a good position. Also used adjectivally: *a plum job.* [Middle English *plum(me), plowme,* Old English *plūme,* from West Germanic, from Latin *prūnum.* See **prune.**]

plum². *Informal.* Variant of **plumb.**

plum·age (plṓō-mij || pléw-) *n.* **1.** The feathers of a bird. **2.** Feathers used ornamentally. **3.** Elaborate dress; finery. [Middle English, from Old French, from *plume*, PLUME.]

plu·mate (plōo-mayt, -mət, -mit) *adj. Biology.* Resembling or possessing a plume or feather. [Latin *plūmātus*, feathered, from *plūma*, a feather.]

plumb (plum) *n.* **1.** A weight suspended from the end of a line, used to determine water depth or to establish a true vertical. **2.** The truly vertical position of a freely suspended plumb line. **—out of** or **off plumb.** Not vertical.
~*adj.* Also **plum** (for sense 2). **1.** Exactly vertical. **2.** *Chiefly U.S. Informal.* Utter; sheer: *a plumb fool.* —See Synonyms at **vertical.**
~*adv.* Also **plum** (for sense 2). **1.** In a vertical or perpendicular line. **2.** *Chiefly U.S. Informal.* Utterly; completely: *plumb tired.*
~*v.* **plumbed, plumbing, plumbs.** —*tr.* **1.** To test the alignment or angle of with a plumb line. **2.** To straighten or make perpendicular. Usually used with *up.* **3.** To determine the depth of; sound. **4.** To reach or experience (the lowest point or worst extreme of something). **5.** To examine closely; probe into. **6.** To connect to a water supply or drain; fit as part of the plumbing system. Often used with *in: She plumbed in the washing machine.* —*intr.* **1.** To be connected to a water supply or drain. Usually used with *in: That washing machine will plumb in easily.* **2.** To work as a plumber. [Middle English *plumbe, plombe,* from Old French *plombe,* from Latin *plumbum,* lead.] **—plumb·a·ble** *adj.*

plum·ba·go (plum-báygō) *n., pl.* **-gos. 1.** Graphite. **2.** Any plant of the genus *Plumbago,* the **leadwort** *(see).* [Latin *plumbāgō,* lead ore, leadwort, from *plumbum,* lead.]

plumb bob *n.* A usually conical piece of metal attached to the end of a plumb line. Also called "plummet".

plumb·er (plúmmər) *n.* A workman who installs and repairs pipes and plumbing fixtures for water and drainage. [Middle English *plummer,* from Old French *plommier,* from Late Latin *plumbārius,* lead worker, from Latin *plumbum,* lead.]

plumber's helper *n.* A device having a large suction cup at the end of a handle, used to clear drains; a plunger.

plumber's snake *n.* A plumber's tool, a **snake** *(see).*

plumb·er·y (plúmməri) *n., pl.* **-ies.** *Rare.* **1.** A plumber's workshop or place of business. **2.** A plumber's work; plumbing.

plum·bic (plúmbik) *adj. Chemistry.* Of, pertaining to, or containing lead. Said especially of compounds that contain lead with a valency of 4. [From Latin *plumbum,* lead.]

plum·bi·con (plúmbi-kon) *n. Electronics.* A type of television camera tube in which the optical image is detected by a semiconducting lead oxide layer. [From Latin *plumbum,* lead + ICON.]

plumb·ing (plúmming) *n.* **1.** The pipes, fixtures, and other apparatus of a water or sewage system. **2.** The work or trade of a plumber. **3.** The act of using a plumb line.

plum·bism (plúmbiz'm) *n.* **Lead poisoning** *(see).*

plumb line *n.* **1.** A line from which a weight is suspended to determine verticality or depth. **2.** A line regarded as directed exactly towards the earth's centre of gravity.

plum·bous (plúmbəss) *adj.* Of, pertaining to, or containing lead. Said especially of compounds that contain lead with a valency of 2. [Late Latin *plumbōsus,* full of lead, from *plumbum,* lead.]

plumb rule *n.* A narrow strip of wood with a plumb line and bob attached, used to test for a true vertical.

plum cake *n.* A kind of rich cake containing raisins, currants, and often other dried fruit.

plum duff *n.* A boiled suet pudding made with raisins or currants.

plume (plōom ‖ plewm) *n.* **1.** A feather, especially one that is large and ornamental. **2.** A large feather or cluster of feathers worn as an ornament or symbol of rank, as on a helmet. **3.** A token of honour or achievement. **4.** A feather-like structure, form, or object: *a plume of smoke.* **5.** *Biology.* A feathery structure, such as the cluster of fine hairs on certain fruits and seeds.
~*tr.v.* **plumed, pluming, plumes. 1.** To decorate, cover, or supply with or as if with plumes. **2.** To smooth (itself or its feathers); preen. Used of a bird. **3.** To pride or congratulate (oneself). Used with *on* or *upon.* [Middle English, from Old French, from Latin *plūma.*] **—plum·y** *adj.*

plume·let (plōom-lət, -lit ‖ plewm-) *n.* A small plume.

plum·met (plúmmit) *n.* **1.** A plumb bob *(see).* **2.** Anything that weighs down or oppresses.
~*intr.v.* **plummeted, -meting, -mets.** To drop straight down; plunge. [Middle English *plomet,* from Old French *plombet,* ball of lead, diminutive of *plomb,* lead, from Latin *plumbum.*]

plum·my (plúmmi) *adj.* **-mier, -miest. 1.** Made of, resembling, or full of plums. **2.** Having or designating a deep, rich voice and exaggerated articulation, often considered upper-class or over-refined. **3.** *Informal.* Desirable; good: *a plummy job.*

plu·mose (plōo-mōss, -mōz ‖ plew-) *adj.* **1.** Having plumes or feathers; feathered. **2.** Resembling a feather or plume; feathery. [Latin *plūmōsus,* from *plūma,* a feather.] **—plu·mose·ly** *adv.* **—plu·mos·i·ty** (plōo-móssəti ‖ plew-) *n.*

plump¹ (plump) *adj.* **plumper, plumpest. 1. a.** Overweight in an attractive way. **b.** Well-rounded and full in form: *plump cheeks.* **2.** Abundant; ample: *a plump reward.* —See Synonyms at **fat.**
~*v.* **plumped, plumping, plumps.** —*tr.* To make full or well-rounded. Often used with *up: plump up a pillow.* —*intr.* To become rounded or full. Often used with *up.* [Middle English, from Middle Dutch, from Middle Low German *plomp, plump,* thick, blunt, dull, probably akin to *plumpen,* to PLUMP.] **—plump·ish** *adj.* **—plump·ly** *adv.* **—plump·ness** *n.*

plump² *v.* **plumped, plumping, plumps.** —*intr.* **1.** To drop abruptly or heavily: *plump into a chair.* **2. a.** To make one choice out of several possibilities. **b.** To vote for or choose only one, in a situation in which more than one could have been chosen. In both senses, used with *for.* **3.** To give all one's support or praise. Used with *for.* —*tr.* **1.** To drop or throw down heavily or abruptly: *plump an ice cube into a glass.* **2.** To utter or say abruptly. Used with *out* or *in.*
~*n.* **1.** A heavy or abrupt fall or collision. **2.** The sound of this.
~*adj.* Blunt; direct.
~*adv.* **1.** With a heavy or abrupt impact. **2.** Straight down. **3.** Without qualification; bluntly. [Middle English, from Middle Low German *plumpen,* to plunge into water (probably imitative).]

plum pudding *n.* Christmas pudding *(see).*

plum tomato *n.* A variety of tomato that produces long, oval fruits, which are often tinned.

plu·mule (plōo-mewl ‖ plew-) *n.* **1.** A down feather. **2.** *Botany.* The rudimentary bud of a plant embryo, which becomes the shoot of the seedling. [Latin *plūmula,* diminutive of *plūma,* feather.] **—plu·mu·lose** (-ōss, -ōz) *adj.*

plun·der (plúndər) *v.* **-dered, -dering, -ders.** —*tr.* **1.** To rob (a person or place) of goods by force, especially in time of war; pillage; loot. **2.** To seize wrongfully or by force; steal. —*intr.* To take booty; rob; pillage. —See Synonyms at **rob.**
~*n.* **1.** Property stolen by fraud or force; booty. **2.** The act or practice of plundering. [Middle Dutch *plunderen* or Frisian *plunderje,* "to rob (of household goods)", akin to Middle Dutch *plunde, plunnet†,* household goods, clothes.] **—plun·der·a·ble** *adj.* **—plun·der·er** *n.* **—plun·der·ous** *adj.*

plun·der·age (plúndərij) *n.* **1.** The act of plundering; pillage. **2.** *Maritime Law.* **a.** The embezzling of goods on board a ship. **b.** The goods so acquired.

plunge (plunj) *v.* **plunged, plunging, plunges.** —*tr.* **1.** To thrust or throw forcefully into a substance or place: *Plunge the lobsters into boiling salted water.* **2.** To cast suddenly or violently into a specified state or situation: *The room was plunged into darkness.* —*intr.* **1.** To throw oneself into a substance or place. **2.** To throw oneself earnestly or wholeheartedly into a specified state or activity. **3.** To enter violently or speedily. **4.** To descend steeply; fall precipitously, as a road or cliff might. **5.** To move forwards and downwards violently. **6.** *Informal.* To speculate or gamble extravagantly.
~*n.* **1.** An act or instance of plunging. **2. a.** A place or area for diving or plunging, as a swimming pool. **b.** A swim; a dip. **—take the plunge. 1.** To take a decisive, difficult step. **2.** *Informal.* To get married. [Middle English *plungen, plongen,* from Old French *plonger, plungier,* from Vulgar Latin *plumbicāre* (unattested), to sound with a plumb, from Latin *plumbum,* lead.]

plunge bath *n.* A bath deep enough to jump or plunge into.

plung·er (plúnjər) *n.* **1.** One that plunges. **2.** A part that operates with a repeated thrusting or plunging movement, such as a piston. **3.** A device consisting of a rubber suction cup attached to the end of a stick, used to clean out clogged drains and pipes.

plunging fire *n.* Gunfire that reaches its target at an almost perpendicular angle, as from guns situated at a higher level than the target.

plunging neckline *n.* A neckline of a garment cut very low and having a very steep U- or V-shape.

plunk (plungk) *v.* **plunked, plunking, plunks.** *Informal.* —*tr.* **1.** To strum or pluck (the strings of a musical instrument or the instrument itself). **2.** To throw or place heavily or abruptly. Used with *down: plunk one's money down.* —*intr.* **1.** To emit a hollow, twanging sound. **2.** To drop or fall abruptly or heavily; plump.
~*n. Informal.* **1.** A short, hollow, twanging sound. **2.** *Chiefly U.S.* A heavy blow or stroke.
~*adv. Informal.* **1.** With a short, hollow thud. **2.** Exactly; precisely: *plunk in the centre.* [Imitative.] **—plunk·er** *n.*

plu·per·fect (plōo-pér-fikt ‖ plew-, -fekt) *adj. Abbr.* **plup., plupf.** *Grammar.* Of or designating a verb tense used to express action completed prior to a stated or implied past time.
~*n.* **1.** The pluperfect tense, formed in English with the past participle of a verb and one or more auxiliaries; for example, in the sentence *He had gone by the time we arrived, had gone* is in the pluperfect. **2.** A verb or form in this tense. Also called "past perfect". [New Latin *plūsperfectum,* contracted from Latin *(tempus praeteritum) plūs quam perfectum,* "(past tense) more than perfect" (translation of Greek *khronos hupersuntelikos*) : Latin *plūs,* more + *quam,* than + *perfectus,* PERFECT (tense).]

plu·ral (plóor-əl ‖ pléwr-) *adj. Abbr.* **pl., plu., plur. 1.** Of or composed of more than one member, set, or kind. **2.** Of or relating to a grammatical form that designates more than one of the things or persons stated. Compare **dual, singular.**
~*n. Grammar.* **1.** The plural number or form. **2.** A word or word element in this form. [Middle English *plurel, plural,* from Old French *plurel,* from Latin *plūrālis,* from *plūs* (stem *plūr-*), more.] **—plu·ral·ly** *adv.*

plu·ral·ise, plu·ral·ize (plóor-ə-līz ‖ pléwr-) *v.* **-ised, -ising, -ises.** —*tr.* **1.** To make plural. **2.** To express in the plural. —*intr.* **1.** To become plural. **2.** To hold more than one position or ecclesiastical benefice at one time. **—plu·ral·i·sa·tion** (-lī-záysh'n ‖ *U.S.* -li-) *n.*

plu·ral·ism (plóor-ə-liz'm ‖ pléwr-) *n.* **1.** The condition of being plural. **2.** A condition of society in which numerous ethnic, religious, or cultural groups remain distinct but coexist within one nation. **3.** The belief that political power should not be wielded by central government alone, but shared by regional councils and organisations. **4.** The holding by one person of more than one position or office, especially two or more ecclesiastical benefices, at one time. **5.** *Philosophy.* **a.** The doctrine that reality is composed of many ultimate substances. **b.** The belief that no single explanatory system or view of reality can account for all the phenomena of life. Compare **monism, dualism.**

plu·ral·ist (ploŏr-ə-list ‖ plé̄wr-) *n.* **1.** A person who holds more than one office, especially two or more ecclesiastical benefices, at one time. **2.** One who adheres to philosophical pluralism. **3.** One who advocates cultural pluralism. —**plu·ral·is·tic** (-lísstik) *adj.*

plu·ral·i·ty (ploor-rál-əti ‖ plew-) *n., pl.* **-ties.** *Abbr.* **plur. 1.** The state or fact of being plural. **2.** A large number or amount; a multitude. **3.** *Ecclesiastical.* **a.** Pluralism. **b.** The offices or benefices held by a pluralist. **4.** *U.S.* A **relative majority** *(see).* **5.** The larger or greater part of anything.

plural marriage *n.* Marriage to more than one partner at the same time or during one period; polygamy.

pluri- *comb. form.* Indicates more than one or many; for example, **pluricellular.** [Latin *plūs* (stem *plūr-*), more, *plures* (plural), several.]

plus (pluss) *prep.* **1.** Added to. **2.** Increased by; along with: *earnings plus dividends.*

~*adj.* **1.** Involving or pertaining to addition. **b.** Positive, as on a scale; more than zero. **2.** Added or extra: *a plus benefit.* **3.** *Informal.* Increased to a further degree: *personality plus.* **4.** Slightly more than: *a mark of C plus.* **5.** *Electricity.* Positive.

~*conj.* What is more; in addition.

~*n., pl.* **pluses** or **plusses. 1.** The plus sign (+). **2.** A positive quantity. **3.** A favourable factor: *Clear weather was a plus for the trip.* [Latin *plūs,* more.]

Usage: Within a sentence, *plus* can be a preposition (like *together with*) rather than a conjunction, and therefore a following verb may be singular or plural depending on the number of the subject: *Their strength plus their spirit makes them very strong. Their resources plus their determination make them very strong.*

plus fours *pl.n.* Loose knickerbockers bagging below the knees, traditionally worn by men for golf. [From the phrase *plus four inches,* the length added to ordinary knickerbockers to make them overhang the knees.]

plush (plush) *n.* A fabric of silk, rayon, cotton, or other material, having a thick, deep pile.

~*adj.* **1.** Made of or covered with plush. **2.** *Informal.* Ostentatiously luxurious, as in furnishings. [From obsolete French *pluche,* from Old French *p(e)luche,* from *peluch(i)er,* to pluck, from Vulgar Latin *pilūccāre* (unattested), "to remove the hair," irregularly from *pilus,* hair.] —**plush·ly** *adv.*

plush·y (plúshi) *adj.* **-ier, -iest. 1.** Resembling plush in texture. **2.** *Informal.* Plush; luxurious: *a plushy office.* —**plush·i·ly** *adv.* —**plush·i·ness** *n.*

plus-mi·nus (plúss-mînəss, -mīnəss) *adv.* Chiefly *South African.* Approximately, more or less: *at plus-minus 6.30 a.m.* [Probably from the arithmetical sign (±).]

plus sign *n.* The symbol (+), as in *2 + 2 = 4,* used to indicate addition or a positive quantity. Also called "plus". Compare **minus sign.**

plus twos *pl.n.* Trousers similar to, but less wide than, plus fours.

Plu·tarch (ploŏ-taark ‖ plé̄w-), (*c.* A.D. 46–120). Greek historian. He wrote the *Parallel Lives,* a collection of biographies which Shakespeare used in his Roman plays.

Plu·to¹ (ploŏtō ‖ plé̄wtō). *Roman Mythology.* The god of the dead and ruler of the underworld, identified with the Greek Hades. [Latin, from Greek *Ploutōn,* "rich one", from *ploutos,* wealth.]

Pluto² *n.* The ninth and farthest planet from the Sun, having a sidereal period of revolution about the Sun of 248.4 years, 4.5 thousand million kilometres (2.8 thousand million miles) distant from the Earth at perihelion and 7.4 thousand million kilometres (4.6 thousand million miles) at aphelion, and a diameter approximately one fifth that of the Earth. [After PLUTO (god).]

plu·toc·ra·cy (ploŏ-tóckrə-si ‖ plew-) *n., pl.* **-cies. 1.** Government by the wealthy. **2.** A wealthy class that controls a government. **3.** A government or state in which the wealthy rule. [Greek *ploutokratia* : *ploutos,* wealth + -CRACY.] —**plu·to·crat** (ploŏ-tə-krat, -tō-) *n.* —**plu·to·crat·ic** (-kráttik) *adj.* —**plu·to·crat·i·cal·ly** *adv.*

plu·ton (ploŏ-ton ‖ plé̄w-) *n.* Igneous rock formed beneath the surface of the earth by consolidation of magma. [Probably back-formation from PLUTONIC.]

Plu·to·ni·an (ploŏ-tôni-ən ‖ plew-) *adj.* Also **Plu·ton·ic** (-tónnik). **1.** Of or pertaining to Pluto or the underworld. **2.** Of or pertaining to the planet Pluto.

plu·ton·ic (ploŏ-tónnik ‖ plew-) *adj.* *Geology.* Of deep igneous or magmatic origin: *plutonic water.* [From PLUTO (referring to the infernal regions).]

plu·to·ni·um (ploŏ-tôni-əm ‖ plew-) *n.* *Symbol* **Pu** A naturally radioactive, silvery, metallic transuranic element, occurring in uranium ores and produced artificially by neutron bombardment of uranium, having fifteen isotopes with masses ranging from 232 to 246 and half-lives from 20 minutes to 76 million years. It is a radiological poison, specifically absorbed by bone marrow, and is used, especially the highly fissionable isotope Plutonium-239, as a reactor fuel and in nuclear weapons. Atomic number 94, melting point 639.5°C, boiling point 3,226.8°C, relative density 19.8, valencies 3, 4, 5, 6. [Discovered shortly after NEPTUNIUM, and named by analogy after the planet PLUTO (beyond the planet Neptune).]

plu·vi·al (ploŏ-vi-əl ‖ plé̄w-) *adj.* **1.** Of or pertaining to rain; rainy. **2.** *Geology.* Caused by rain.

~*n.* A period of prolonged rain causing geological change. [Latin *pluviālis,* from *pluvia,* rain. See **pluvious.**]

pluvio- *comb. form.* Indicates rain; for example, **pluviometer.** [Latin *pluvia,* rain. See **pluvious.**]

plu·vi·om·e·ter (ploŏ-vi-ómmitər ‖ plé̄w-) *n.* A device for measuring rainfall, a **rain gauge** *(see).* [French *pluviomètre* : PLUVIO- + -METER.] —**plu·vi·o·met·ric** (-ō-méttrik, -ə-), **plu·vi·o·met·ri·cal** *adj.* —**plu·vi·om·e·try** (-ómmətri) *n.*

plu·vi·ous (ploŏ-vi-əss ‖ plé̄w-) *adj.* Also **plu·vi·ose** (-ōss, -ōz). Characterised by heavy rainfall; rainy. [Middle English *pluvyous,* from Latin *pluviōsus,* from *pluvia,* rain, from *pluvius,* rainy, from *pluvere,* to rain.] —**plu·vi·os·i·ty** (-vi-óssiti) *n.*

ply¹ (plī) *tr.v.* **plied, plying, plies.** *Rare.* **1.** To join together, as by moulding or twisting. **2.** To double over (cloth, for example).

~*n., pl.* **plies. 1.** A layer, as of doubled-over cloth or of paper. **2.** Any of the sheets of wood glued together to form plywood. **3.** Any of the strands twisted together to make yarn, rope, or thread. Used in combination to indicate a specified number of strands, twists, or folds: *three-ply.* **4.** *Rare.* A bias; an inclination. [Middle English *plien,* from Old French *plier,* from Latin *plicāre,* to fold.]

ply² *v.* **plied, plying, plies.** —*tr.* **1.** To use diligently as a tool or weapon; wield: *plies an axe.* **2.** To engage in (a trade, for example); practise diligently. **3.** To traverse or sail over regularly: *plied the coastal routes.* **4.** To continue supplying or offering to: *plying her guests with food.* **5.** To assail vigorously. —*intr.* **1.** To traverse a route or course regularly: *A boat plies between the islands.* **2.** To perform or work diligently or regularly: *plied at the weaver's trade; ply for hire.* **3.** *Nautical.* To work against the wind by a zigzag course; tack. [Middle English *(ap)plien,* to employ, APPLY.]

Plym·outh¹ (plímməth). Port and Unitary Authority area, southwest England. On Plymouth Sound between the Plym and Tamar estuaries, it has long been important as a naval station. Sir Francis Drake sailed from here to fight the Spanish Armada and it was the last port of call for the *Mayflower* before she sailed to America (1620). Since 1914 Plymouth has comprised the three towns of Plymouth, Stonehouse, and Devonport.

Plymouth². Town in Massachusetts, United States, southeast of Boston on Plymouth Bay. It was the landing point for the Pilgrim Fathers of the *Mayflower* (1620). Tourism, fishing, and electronics are important.

Plymouth Brethren *n.* A strict puritanical Protestant sect founded in 1830 in Plymouth, England.

ply·wood (plī-wood) *n.* A structural material made of thin layers of wood glued tightly together, usually with the grains of adjoining layers at right angles to each other. [PLY (layer) + WOOD.]

Pl·zeň (*Czech* p'lzeň). *German* **Pil·sen** (pílz'n). Capital of West Bohemia, Czech Republic. Situated on the river Berounka, it is most famous for its pilsner beer, brewed since the Middle Ages.

Pm The symbol for the element promethium.

pm. **1.** paymaster. **2.** premium.

p.m. **1.** post meridiem. **2.** post-mortem. **3.** post-mortem examination.

P.M. **1.** past master. **2.** postmaster; postmistress. **3.** post meridiem. **4.** post-mortem examination. **5.** prime minister. **6.** provost marshal.

PMBX private manual branch (telephone) exchange.

P.M.G. **1.** Paymaster general. **2.** postmaster general.

PMT *n.* **1.** Premenstrual tension. **2.** A photomechanical transfer.

p.n., **P/N** promissory note.

PNdB Perceived noise decibel.

pneum. pneumatic.

pneu·ma (néwmə ‖ noŏmə) *n.* The soul or vital spirit. [Greek *pneuma,* blast of wind, breath, divine inspiration, spirit.]

pneu·mat·ic (new-máttik ‖ noŏ-) *adj.* *Abbr.* **pneum. 1.** Of or pertaining to air or other gases. **2.** Of or pertaining to pneumatics. **3.** Run by or using compressed air: *a pneumatic drill.* **4.** Filled with air, especially compressed air: *a pneumatic tyre.* **5.** Having air cavities, as do the bones of many birds. **6.** Having or pertaining to shapely, full breasts: *"Uncorseted, her friendly bust/Gives promise of pneumatic bliss."* (T.S. Eliot). **7.** Of or pertaining to the pneuma; spiritual.

~*n.* A pneumatic tyre. [French *pneumatique,* from Latin *pneumaticus,* from Greek *pneumatikos,* from *pneuma* (stem *pneumat-*), wind, spirit.] —**pneu·mat·i·cal·ly** *adv.* —**pneu·ma·tic·i·ty** (néw-mə-tissəti ‖ noŏ-) *n.*

pneu·mat·ics (new-máttiks ‖ noŏ-) *n.* *Used with a singular verb.* The study of the mechanical properties of air and other gases.

pneumatic trough *n.* *Chemistry.* A flat dish filled with water or other liquid, used in laboratory experiments for collecting gases by displacement of liquid from an inverted container.

pneumato- *comb. form.* Indicates: **1.** Air; for example, **pneumatophore. 2.** Breath or breathing; for example, **pneumatometer. 3.** Spirit or spirits; for example, **pneumatology.** [Greek *pneuma* (stem *pneumat-*), blast of wind, breath, spirit.]

pneu·ma·tol·o·gy (néw-mə-tólləji ‖ noŏ-) *n.* **1.** The doctrine or study of spiritual beings and phenomena; especially, the belief in spirits intervening between man and God. **2.** The Christian doctrine of the Holy Ghost. **3.** *Archaic.* Psychology. [New Latin *pneumatologia* : PNEUMATO- + -LOGY.] —**pneu·ma·to·log·ic** (-tə-lójik), **pneu·ma·to·log·i·cal** *adj.* —**pneu·ma·tol·o·gist** (-tólləjist) *n.*

pneu·ma·tom·e·ter (new-mə-tómmitər ‖ nŏŏ-) *n.* A device for measuring the pressure of inspiration or expiration in the lungs. [PNEUMATO- + -METER.] —**pneu·ma·tom·e·try** (-tómmətri) *n.*

pneu·mat·o·phore (new-máttə-fawr ‖ nŏŏ-, -fôr) *n.* **1.** *Zoology.* A gas-filled sac serving as a float in certain colonial organisms, such as the Portuguese man-of-war. **2.** *Botany.* A specialised root in certain aquatic plants, such as the mangrove, that grows upwards and through which exchange of respiratory gases occurs.

pneumo-, pneum- *comb. form.* Indicates: **1.** The lung or respiratory organs; for example, **pneumograph. 2.** Air or gas; for example, **pneumothorax.** [Greek *pneuma*, wind, breath, spirit.]

pneu·mo·ba·cil·lus (new-mō-bə-sílləss ‖ nŏŏ-) *n., pl.* **-cilli** (-síllī). A rod-shaped bacterium, *Klebsiella pneumoniae,* associated with respiratory infections, especially pneumonia.

pneu·mo·coc·cus (new-mə-kóckəss, -ō- ‖ nŏŏ-) *n., pl.* **-cocci** (-kók-sī). A spherical bacterium, *Streptococcus pneumoniae,* that causes pneumonia. —**pneu·mo·coc·cal** *adj.*

pneu·mo·co·ni·o·sis (new-mō-kŏni-ō-siss ‖ nŏŏ-) *n.* Also **pneu·mo·no·co·ni·o·sis** (-mōnō-). Any lung disease caused by prolonged inhalation of mineral or metallic dusts, characterised by breathlessness and coughing. [New Latin : PNEUMO- + Greek *konia, konis,* dust + -OSIS.]

pneu·mo·gas·tric (new-mō-gástrik ‖ nŏŏ-) *adj.* **1.** Of or involving the lungs and the stomach. **2.** Relating to or designating the vagus nerve. In this sense, not in current technical usage.

pneu·mo·graph (new-mō-graf, -mə-, -graaf ‖ nŏŏ-) *n.* A device for recording chest movements during respiration. [PNEUMO- + -GRAPH.] —**pneu·mo·graph·ic** (-gráffik) *adj.*

pneu·mo·nec·to·my (new-mə-néktəmi ‖ nŏŏ-) *n., pl.* **-mies.** Also **pneu·mec·to·my** Surgical removal of a lung or of lung tissue. [Greek *pneumōn,* lung (see **pneumonic**) + -ECTOMY.]

pneu·mo·nia (new-mŏni-ə ‖ nŏŏ-) *n.* A disease marked by inflammation of one lung (*single pneumonia*) or both (*double pneumonia*), which become nonfunctional owing to the presence of pus in the air sacs, and caused by viruses, bacteria, and physical and chemical agents. [New Latin, from Greek, from *pneumōn,* lung, from *pneuma,* breath.]

pneu·mon·ic (new-mónnik ‖ nŏŏ-) *adj.* **1.** Pertaining to, affected by, or similar to pneumonia. **2.** Of, affecting, or pertaining to the lungs; pulmonary. [New Latin *pneumonicus,* from Greek *pneumonikos,* of the lungs, from *pneumōn,* lung.]

pneu·mon·it·is (new-mə-nítiss) *n.* Inflammation of the lungs that is restricted to the walls of the air sacs. [PNEUMON- + -ITIS.]

pneu·mo·tho·rax (new-mō-tháwr-aks, -mə- ‖ nŏŏ-, -thôr-) *n.* Accumulation of air or gas in the pleural cavity, occurring as a result of disease or injury, or formerly induced to collapse the lung in the treatment of tuberculosis and other lung diseases.

p.n.g. persona non grata.

p-n junction (pée-én) *n. Electronics.* A junction between a p-type and an n-type semiconducting region, used in rectifiers and in transistors. [*P-n,* abbreviation of *Positive-negative.*]

Po¹ The symbol for the element polonium.

Po² (pō). Italy's longest river, 652 kilometres (405 miles). Rising in the western Alps, it flows eastwards to a delta on the Adriatic Sea.

p.o. 1. petty officer. **2.** post office.

P.O. 1. Personnel Officer. **2.** petty officer. **3.** postal order. **4.** post office.

poach¹ (pōch) *tr.v.* **poached, poaching, poaches.** To cook gently in a boiling or simmering liquid: *fish poached in wine.* [Middle English *pochen,* from Old French *poch(i)er* (originally of shelled eggs, to cook so that the whites form pockets), from *poche,* pocket, from Frankish *pokka* (unattested).]

poach² *v.* **poached, poaching, poaches.** —*intr.* **1.** To trespass on another's property in order to take fish or game. **2.** To take fish or game in a forbidden area. **3.** To take, acquire, or appropriate something or someone by devious or unfair means. **4.** To become muddy or broken up from being trampled. Used of land. —*tr.* **1.** To trespass on (another's property) for fishing or hunting. **2.** To take (fish or game) illegally. **3.** To take, acquire, or appropriate (something or someone) by devious or unfair means: *was accused of poaching staff from a rival company.* **4.** In tennis and similar games, to play (a shot that should have been taken by one's partner). **5.** To make (land) muddy or broken up by trampling. [Earlier *poche,* perhaps from French *pocher,* to pocket. See **poach** (cookery).]

poach·er¹ (pṓchər) *n.* A vessel or dish designed for the poaching of food, such as eggs or fish.

poacher² *n.* A person who poaches on the property of another.

po·chard (pṓchərd) *n.* Any of various diving ducks of the genera *Aythya* and *Netta;* especially, *A. ferina,* of Europe, the male of which has grey and black plumage and a reddish head.

pock (pok) *n.* **1.** A pustule caused by smallpox or a similar eruptive disease. **2.** A mark or scar left in the skin by such a pustule; a pockmark. [Middle English *pokke,* Old English *pocc,* from Germanic.] —**pock·y** *adj.*

pock·et (póckit) *n.* **1. a.** A small, flat pouch or pouchlike piece of material sewn into a garment and used to carry small articles. **b.** A piece of material sewn onto the outside of a garment with the top edge open. **2. a.** A small sack or bag. **b.** *Chiefly South African.* A sack, used as a rough measure, in which commodities such as potatoes or sugar are sold in bulk. **3.** Any receptacle, cavity, or opening similar in shape or purpose to a garment pocket, such as a compartment on the inside of a car door, or a receptacle on the back of an aeroplane seat or inside a suitcase. **4.** Supply of money; financial

means. **5.** *Mining.* **a.** A small cavity in the earth containing ore. **b.** A small body or accumulation of ore. **6.** Any of the pouchlike receptacles at the corners and sides of a billiard table. **7.** In Australian Rules football, a side position at either end of the field. **8.** A small, isolated or protected area or group. **9.** An air pocket (*see*). —See Synonyms at **hole.** —**in** (or **out) of pocket.** Having gained (or lost) money. —**in (one's) pocket.** Under one's influence or control. —**line (one's) pockets.** To profit dishonestly by one's position. —**put (one's) hand in (one's) pocket.** To pay for something or donate money.

~*adj.* **1.** Suitable for or capable of being carried in one's pocket: *a pocket edition.* **2.** Small; miniature.

~*tr.v.* **pocketed, -eting, -ets. 1.** To place in or as if in one's pocket. **2.** To take possession of for oneself, especially dishonestly. **3.** To accept or tolerate (an insult, for example). **4.** To suppress or conceal: *He pocketed his pride.* **5.** *U.S.* To prevent (a bill) from becoming law by delaying its signing until the adjournment of the legislative body. Used of the U.S. president. See **pocket veto. 6.** In billiards, snooker, and similar games, to hit (a ball) directly or indirectly into a pocket. [Middle English *poket,* from Anglo-French *poket(e),* diminutive of *poke, poque,* bag, POKE.] —**pock·et·a·ble** *adj.* —**pock·et·er** *n.*

pocket battleship *n.* A small battleship built to conform with limitations on size and armament established by treaty.

pocket billiards *n.* The game of **pool** (*see*).

pock·et·book (póckit-bŏŏk ‖ -bŏŏk) *n.* **1. a.** A small notebook. **b.** A pocket-sized folder or case used to hold money and papers. **2.** *U.S.* A handbag. **3.** *U.S.* A pocket-sized, usually paperbound book.

pocket borough *n.* A borough in England, prior to the Reform Act of 1832, whose representation was controlled by a single person or family. Compare **rotten borough.**

pock·et·ful (póckit-fŏŏl) *n., pl.* **-fuls** or **pocketsful.** As much as a pocket will hold.

pocket gopher *n.* A **gopher** (*see*).

pocket handkerchief. 1. A small handkerchief kept in a garment pocket. **2.** Something small and square or rectangular, such as a tiny garden or lawn.

pock·et·knife (póckit-nīf) *n., pl.* **-knives** (-nīvz). A small knife with a blade or blades folding into the handle.

pocket money *n.* **1.** Money given at regular intervals to a child, usually by the parents. **2.** Money for incidental or minor expenses.

pocket mouse *n.* Any of various small, North American burrowing rodents of the genus *Perognathus,* having external cheek pouches.

pocket veto *n.* In the United States: **1.** The president's indirect veto of a bill presented to him within ten days of Congressional adjournment, by his retaining the bill unsigned until Congress adjourns. **2.** A similar action exercised by a state governor or other chief executive.

pock·mark (pók-maark) *n.* **1.** A pitlike scar left on the skin by smallpox or another eruptive disease. **2.** A pit or scar on a surface. —*tr.v.* **pockmarked, -marking, -marks.** To disfigure with pockmarks. —**pock·marked** *adj.*

po·co (pṓkō) *adv. Music.* Somewhat; a little. Used as a direction: *poco adagio.* [Italian, little, from Latin *paucus,* little, few.]

po·co a po·co (pṓkō-a-pṓkō, -aa-) *adv. Music.* Gradually; little by little. Used as a direction: *poco a poco diminuendo.* [Italian.]

po·co·cu·ran·te (pṓkō-kewr-ránti, -kŏŏ-) *adj.* Indifferent; unconcerned; apathetic.

~*n.* One who does not care; an unconcerned person. [Italian, "little caring".] —**po·co·cu·ran·tism** *n.*

pod¹ (pod) *n.* **1.** *Botany.* **a.** The long, two-valved fruit of a leguminous plant, such as the pea, which contains several seeds and usually dries and splits open when ripe. **b.** The seed case of such a fruit. **c.** Any of several similar fruits. **2.** A podlike protective covering. **3.** *Aeronautics.* A streamlined housing that encloses engines, machine guns, or fuel, carried externally on aircraft.

~*v.* **podded, podding, pods.** —*intr.* **1.** To bear or produce pods. **2.** To expand or swell like a pod. —*tr.* To remove (seeds, peas, beans, or the like) from a pod. [17th century : back formation from dialect *podware†,* crops, bagged vegetables.]

pod² *n.* **1.** A school of seals or whales. **2.** A small flock of birds. [19th century (U.S.) : origin obscure.]

pod³ *n.* **1.** The lengthways groove in certain boring tools, such as augers. **2.** The socket for holding the bit in a boring tool. [16th century : perhaps variant of PAD (cushion).]

–pod, –pode *n. comb. form.* Indicates a specified kind or number of feet; for example, **cephalopod, tripod.** [New Latin *-podius, -poda,* from Greek *pous* (stem *pod-*), foot.] —**-podous** *adj. comb. form.*

po·dag·ra (pə-dággrə, pō-, po-, póddəgrə) *n. Pathology.* Gout, especially of the big toe. [Middle English, from Latin, from Greek, "trap for the feet", foot disease, gout : *pous* (stem *pod-*), foot + *agra, agrē,* seizure.] —**po·dag·ral, po·dag·ric** *adj.*

pod·dy (póddi) *n. pl.* **-dies.** *Australian.* A calf requiring to be handfed.

~*adj. Australian.* Requiring to be handfed. Said especially of a lamb or calf. [From adjective, fat, from dialect *pod,* fat protruding belly, special use of POD (seed vessel).]

po·des·ta (po-désta, pō- ‖ *Italian* pódess-taá) *n.* **1.** A governor appointed by Frederick Barbarossa to rule over one or more of the Lombard cities. **2.** The chief magistrate or officer in any of the republics of medieval Italy. **3.** Under the Fascist regime in Italy, the chief magistrate or mayor in any of the Italian communes except Rome and Naples. **4.** A subordinate magistrate or judge in some modern Italian towns. [Italian *podestà, potestà,* from Latin *potestās* (stem *potestāt-*), power, magistrate, from *potis,* able.]

Pod·go·ri·ca (pód-go-ritsa). Also, from 1946 to 1992, **Ti·to·grad** (teéto-grad). Capital of Montenegro, southern Yugoslavia. It was almost completely rebuilt after suffering severe damage in World War II.

Pod·gor·ny (pod-górni, *Russian* pud-), **Nikolai Viktorovich** (1903–83). Soviet politician. He became president of the U.S.S.R. (1965) but resigned (1977) when displaced by Brezhnev.

podg·y (póji) *adj.* **-ier, -iest.** Also *chiefly U.S.* **pudg·y** (púji). Short and plump; chubby. See Synonyms at **fat.** **—podg·i·ly** *adv.* **—podg·i·ness** *n.*

po·di·um (pṓ-di-əm) *n., pl.* **-dia** (-di-ə) or **-ums. 1.** An elevated platform, as for an orchestral conductor or lecturer; a dais. **2.** *Architecture.* A low wall serving as foundation. **3.** A wall circling the arena of an ancient amphitheatre. **4.** *Zoology.* Any structure resembling or functioning as a foot. [Latin, raised platform, balcony, from Greek *podion,* "small foot", base, from *pous* (stem *pod-*), foot.]

-podium *n. comb. form.* Indicates a part that resembles a foot; for example, **monopodium.** [New Latin, from Greek *podion,* "small foot", from *pous,* foot.]

pod·o·phyl·lin (póddō-fíllin) *n.* A bitter-tasting resin obtained from the dried root of the **May apple** *(see),* and used as a laxative. [New Latin *podophyllum,* "(plant with) footlike leaves" : Greek *pous* (stem *pod-*), foot + *phullon,* a leaf + -IN.]

pod·zol (pód-zol) *n.* Also **pod·sol** (-sol). A leached soil formed mainly in cool, humid climates. [Russian, "ash ground" : *pod,* bottom, ground + *zola,* ashes.] **—pod·zol·ic** (pod-zóllik) *adj.*

pod·zo·lise, pod·zo·lize (pód-zo-līz) *v.* **-lised, lising, lises.** Also **pod·so·lise** (-so-) *—tr.* To make (soil) acidic by leaching out bases; form into a podzol. *—intr.* To become acidic by leaching; become a podzol. Used of soil. **—pod·zol·i·sa·tion** (-lī-záysh'n || *U.S.* -li-) *n.*

Poe (pō), **Edgar Allan** (1809–49). U.S. author. His macabre stories and poems, such as *The Fall of the House of Usher* (1839) and *Ligeia* (1840), had widespread influence, especially on Baudelaire and Mallarmé in France.

P.O.E. 1. port of embarkation. **2.** port of entry.

po·em (pṓ-im, -əm, -em) *n.* **1.** A composition designed to convey a vivid and imaginative sense of experience, characterised by the use of condensed language, chosen for its sound and suggestive power as well as its meaning, and by the use of such literary techniques as structured metre, natural cadences, rhyme, and imagery. **2.** Any composition in verse rather than in prose. **3.** Any literary composition written with an intensity of language or conscious use of stylistic devices more characteristic of poetry than of prose: *a prose poem.* **4.** Any creation, object, or experience thought to embody the lyrical beauty or structural perfection characteristic of poetry. [French *poème* or Latin *poēma,* from Greek *poiēma, poēma,* "created thing", work, poem, from *poiein,* to make, create.]

po·e·sy (pṓ-i-zi, -e- || -si) *n., pl.* **-sies.** *Archaic.* **1.** Poetry. **2. a.** The art or practice of composing poems. **b.** The inspiration involved in composing poetry. **3.** Poems collectively. [Middle English *poesie,* from Old French, from Common Romance *poēsia* (unattested), variant of Latin *poēsis,* from Greek *po(i)ēsis,* "a making", "creation", poetry, from *poiein,* to make, create.]

po·et (pṓ-it, -et) *n.* **1.** A writer of poems. **2.** One who is especially gifted in the perception and expression of the beautiful or lyrical. [Middle English *poete,* from Old French, from Latin *poēta,* from Greek *poiētēs,* "maker", poet, from *poiein,* to make, create.]

Synonyms: *poet, bard, versifier, rhymer, rhymester, poetaster.*

po·et·as·ter (pṓ-i-táss-tər, -ə- || -táyss-) *n.* An inferior poet. See Synonyms at **poet.** [New Latin : Latin *poēt(a),* POET + -ASTER.]

po·et·ess (pṓ-i-tiss, -ə-, -tess) *n.* A female poet. Sometimes considered demeaning. See Usage note at **-ess.**

po·et·ic (pō-éttik) *adj.* Also **po·et·i·cal** (-'l). **1.** Of or pertaining to poetry. **2.** Having a quality or style characteristic of poetry: *poetic diction.* **3.** Suitable as a subject for poetry: *a poetic love affair.* **4.** Of, pertaining to, or befitting a poet: *poetic insight.* **5.** Having or showing the sensitivity or insight of a poet. **6.** Characterised by romantic imagery: *a poetic account.* [From French *póetique,* from Latin *poēticus,* from Greek *poiētikos,* inventive, ingenious, from *poiētēs,* "maker", POET.]

po·et·i·cal (pō-éttik'l) *adj.* **1.** Variant of **poetic. 2.** Fancifully depicted or embellished; idealised. **—po·et·i·cal·ly** *adv.*

po·et·i·cise, po·et·i·cize (pō-étti-sīz) *tr.v.* **-ised, -ising, -ises.** To give a poetic quality to.

po·et·i·cism (pō-étti-siz'm) *n.* A poetic term or expression that has become no longer vivid or evocative.

poetic justice *n.* An outcome whereby a person receives his just deserts in a manner peculiarly or ironically appropriate.

poetic licence *n.* The deviation made, especially by an artist or writer, from conventional form or fact to achieve a desired effect.

po·et·ics (pō-éttiks) *n. Used with a singular verb.* **1.** Literary criticism that deals with the nature, forms, and laws of poetry. **2.** A treatise on or study of poetry or aesthetics. **3.** Poetic utterances or feelings.

po·et·ise, po·et·ize (pṓ-i-tīz, -ə-) *v.* **-ised, -ising, -ises.** *—intr.* To write or express oneself in poetry. *—tr.* To give poetic expression to. **—po·et·is·er** *n.*

poet laureate *n., pl.* **poets laureate** or **poet laureates. 1.** A poet appointed for life by the British sovereign to compose poems for state occasions, who is a member of the Royal Household. **2.** A poet appointed for a fixed term to a somewhat analogous position by the U.S. government.

po·et·ry (pṓ-i-tri-, -ə- || póytri) *n.* **1.** The art or work of a poet. **2. a.** Poems regarded as forming a division of literature. **b.** The poetic works of a given author, group, nation, or genre. **3.** Any piece of literature written in metre; verse. **4.** Prose that resembles a poem, as in form, sound, or other qualities. **5.** The essence of or characteristic quality possessed by a poem or poems. **6.** A quality that suggests poetry, as in grace, beauty, or harmony: *the poetry of dance movements.* [Middle English, from Medieval Latin *poētria,* from Latin *poēta,* POET.]

po-faced (pṓ-fáyst) *adj.* Having a neutral or stern expession. [*Po,* variant (after French pronunciation) of POT.]

pogge (pog) *n.* A marine European fish, *Agonus cataphractus,* with a body covering of bony plates, a large broad head, and a long tapering tail. [17th century : origin obscure.]

po·go·ni·a (pə-gṓni-ə) *n.* Any of various small terrestrial orchids of the genus *Pogonia,* of the North Temperate Zone, having pink or whitish flowers. [New Latin, "bearded plant" (from the yellow hair covering the lip of its flower), from Greek *pōgōn*†, beard.]

po·go stick (pṓgō) *n.* A strong stick with footrests and a heavy spring set into the bottom end, propelled along the ground by hopping. [20th century : origin obscure.]

po·grom (póg-rəm, -rom, pə-gróm) *n.* An organised and often officially encouraged massacre or persecution of a minority group, especially a Jewish community. [Russian, "like thunder", devastation : *po-,* like, from *po,* at, by, next to + *grom,* thunder.]

po·hu·tu·ka·wa (pō-hṓōtə-kaʼa-wə) *n.* A New Zealand tree, *Metrosideros excelas,* with red flowers and hard, heavy red wood used for marine timber work. [Maori.]

poi (poy, pṓ-i) *n.* A Hawaiian food made from taro root cooked, pounded to a paste, and fermented. [Hawaiian.]

-poiesis *n. comb. form.* Indicates making, creating, or producing; for example, **haematopoiesis.** [From Greek *poiēsis,* a making, creation, from *poiein,* to make.] **—-poietic** *adj. comb. form.*

poign·ant (póyn-yənt, -ənt, *also* póyg-nənt) *adj.* **1.** Appealing to the emotions; affecting; touching: *poignant sentiment.* **2.** Piercing; incisive: *poignant criticism.* **3.** Keenly distressing to the mind: *poignant anxiety.* **4.** Relevant; to the point: *"Her illustrations were apposite and poignant."* (Charles Lamb). **5.** Agreeably intense or stimulating: *poignant delight.* **6. a.** *Archaic.* Sharp or sour to the taste; piquant. **b.** Sharp or pungent to the smell: *a poignant perfume.* —See Synonyms at **moving.** [Middle English *poynaunt, pugnaunt,* pointed, sharp, from Old French *puignant,* present participle of *poindre,* from Latin *pungere,* to prick, pierce.] **—poign·an·cy, poign·ance** *n.* **—poign·ant·ly** *adv.*

poi·ki·lo·therm (póykil-ə-therm, -ō-) *n. Zoology.* A poikilothermic organism, such as a fish or reptile. [Greek *poikilos,* various, variant + -THERM.]

poi·ki·lo·ther·mic (póykil-ə-thérmik, -ō-) *adj.* Also **poi·ki·lo·ther·mal** (-thérm'l). *Zoology.* Having a body temperature that varies with the external environment; cold-blooded. Compare **homoiothermic. —poi·ki·lo·ther·mism, poi·ki·lo·ther·my** *n.*

poi·lu (pwaa-lṓō, *French* -lǘ) *n., pl.* **-lus** (*pronounced as singular, or* -z). *World War I Slang.* A French front-line soldier. [French, "hirsute", hence (slang) pugnacious, from *poil,* hair, from Latin *pilus.*]

Poin·ca·ré (pwaɴka-ráy), **Jules Henri** (1854–1912). French mathematician. He made a distinguished contribution to experimental physics and theoretical astronomy, as well as pure and applied mathematics, anticipating Einstein's work on relativity.

Poincaré, Raymond Nicolas Laudry (1860–1934). French politician. A cousin of Jules Henri Poincaré, he held office as ninth president of the Republic (1913–20) and served for three terms as prime minister (1912–13, 1922–24, and 1926–29).

poin·ci·an·a (póyn-si-áanə || *U.S.* -ánnə) *n.* **1.** Any of various tropical trees of the genus *Poinciana,* having large orange or red flowers. **2.** A related tree, the **royal poinciana** *(see).* [New Latin, after M. de *Poinci,* 17th-century governor of French Antilles.]

poin·set·ti·a (poyn-sétti-ə) *n.* A tropical American shrub, *Euphorbia pulcherrima,* having petal-like, usually scarlet, bracts beneath yellow flowers, widely grown as a house plant. [New Latin; discovered by J.R. *Poinsett* (1799–1851), U.S. minister to Mexico.]

point (poynt) *n. Abbr.* **pt. 1.** The sharp or tapered end of something: *the point of a knife.* **2.** Something that has a sharp or tapered end, such as a knife or needle. **3.** A tapering extension of land projecting into water; a promontory; a cape. **4.** A mark formed by or as if by the sharp end of something. **5.** A mark or dot used in printing or writing. **6.** A mark used in punctuation; especially, a full stop. **7.** See **decimal point. 8.** *Phonetics.* A diacritical mark used to differentiate or modify vowels and consonants, such as a **vowel point** *(see).* **9.** Any of the protruding marks used in certain methods, such as Braille, of writing and printing for the blind. **10.** *Geometry.* A dimensionless geometric object having no property but position. **11.** A position, place, or situation; a spot: *a good point to begin.* **12.** A specified degree, condition, or limit in a scale, course, or the like: *a melting point.* **13. a.** One of the 32 equal divisions marked at the circumference of a mariner's compass card that indicate direction. **b.** The distance or interval of 11 degrees, 15 minutes between any two adjacent markings. **14.** Any distinct condition or degree: *the point of no return.* **15.** A specific moment in time: *At this point she left.* **16.** A crucial situation in a course of events. **17.** An important, essential, or primary factor: *missed the whole point.* **18.** A purpose, goal, advantage, or reason: *can't see any point in continuing.*

19. The major idea or essential part of a concept or narrative: *get to the point of the story.* **20.** A significant, outstanding, or effective idea, argument, or suggestion: *made some excellent points.* **21.** A separate or individual item or element; a detail: *several points worth noting.* **22. a.** A striking or distinctive characteristic or quality: *his good points.* **b.** A quality or characteristic that is important or distinctive; especially, a standard characteristic used to judge an animal. **c.** *Plural.* The extremities of a horse, dog, or the like: *a bay pony with white points.* **23.** A single unit, as in counting, rating, or measuring. **24.** *U.S.* A unit of credit used in marking academic achievement. **25.** A unit of scoring or counting in a game or sport: *won the match on points.* **26.** The stiff and attentive stance taken by a hunting dog. **27.** *Electricity.* **a.** An electrical contact, especially one in the distributor of a car engine or crystal set. **b.** *Chiefly British.* A **power point** *(see).* **28.** *Finance.* A unit of value used to quote or state the current prices of stocks, commodities, or the like. **29.** A unit equal to .0001 used in calculating a rate of exchange in U.S. dollars: *The pound gained three points against the dollar.* **30.** *Printing.* A unit of type size equal to 0.01384 inch, or approximately $^1/_{72}$ of an inch. **31.** A jeweller's unit of mass equal to 2 milligrammes or 0.01 carat. **32. a.** Needlepoint. **b.** Bobbin lace. **33.** *Often plural.* **a.** A device consisting of two sections of railway track and the accompanying apparatus, used to transfer trains from one track to another. **b.** The junction of railway tracks at such a device. **34.** A ribbon or cord with a metal tag at the end, used to fasten clothing in the 16th and 17th centuries. **35.** In cricket: **a.** The position of a fielder on the off side straight out from the batsman, as if at the point of his bat. **b.** A fielder in this position. **36.** In boxing, the top of the chin, as a spot for delivering a blow. **37.** In backgammon, any of the tapered divisions of the board. **38.** A small body of troops that goes ahead of or behind the main force to reconnoitre. **39.** An aggressive stance or stroke made holding a bayonet. **40.** The act of pointing. **—beside the point.** Having nothing to do with the subject; irrelevant. **—in point.** By way of example. Used chiefly in the phrase *a case in point.* **—in point of fact.** As a matter of fact. **—make a point of.** To take special care or pains to. **—make (one's) point.** To prove oneself successfully to be right. **—not to put too fine a point on it.** To speak frankly or bluntly. **—on the point of.** At the moment immediately prior to; about to: *on the point of surrendering.* **—off the point.** Away from the subject in question. **—score points off.** To make points at the expense of (someone). **—stretch a point. 1.** To make an exception. **2.** To exaggerate. **—to the point.** Relevant; apposite. **—up to a point.** To some extent but not entirely: *You are right up to a point.*

~*v.* **pointed, pointing, points.** —*tr.* **1.** To direct or aim: *point a weapon.* **2.** To cause to head: *pointed us in the right direction.* **3.** To indicate the position or direction of: *point the way.* **4.** To sharpen (a pencil, for example); provide with a point. **5.** To separate with a decimal point. Used with *off.* **6.** To mark with a point or full stop; punctuate. **7.** To mark (a consonant) with a vowel point. **8.** To give emphasis to (a remark, for example); stress. Often used with *up.* **9.** To indicate the presence and position of (game) by standing immobile and directing the muzzle towards it. **10.** To fill and finish the joints of (brickwork, for example) with cement or mortar. —*intr.* **1.** To direct attention or indicate position with or as if with the finger. Usually used with *at* or *to.* **2.** To turn the mind or thought in a particular direction: *The facts all point to one conclusion.* **3.** To be turned or faced in a given direction; aim. **4.** To perform the action of a hunting dog scenting game and gazing towards it fixedly. **5.** *Nautical.* To sail close to the wind. **—point out.** To call attention to; indicate. [Middle English *poynt,* from Old French *point,* a prick, dot, small particle, and *pointe,* pointed end or tip, respectively from Latin *punctum* and *puncta* from the neuter and feminine of *punctus,* past participle of *pungere,* to pierce, prick.]

point-blank (póynt-blángk) *adj.* **1.** Aimed straight at the mark or target; especially, aimed straight without allowing for the drop in a projectile's course: *a point-blank shot.* **2. a.** So close to a target that a weapon may be aimed directly at it. **b.** Close enough so that missing the target is unlikely or impossible: *point-blank range.* **3.** Straightforward; blunt: *a point-blank accusation.*

~*adv.* **1.** With a straight aim; directly; straight: *The policeman fired point-blank.* **2.** Without hesitation, deliberation, or equivocation: *answer point-blank.* [Probably POINT (verb) + BLANK (white centre spot of a target).]

point d'ap·pui (pwáɴ da-pwée) *n., pl.* **points d'appui** (*pronounced as singular*). **1.** *Military.* Formerly, a secure position or base serving as a support for operations in the field. **2.** A base or support. [French, point of support.]

point defect *n. Crystallography.* A defect in a crystal lattice occurring at a single lattice point; a vacancy or an interstitial.

point-de·vice (póynt-di-víss) *adj. Archaic.* Scrupulously correct or neat; precise. [Middle English *at point devis,* probably from Anglo-French *à point devis* (unattested), "arranged to (the) point" : *à point,* to perfection + *devis,* "divided", arranged, from Latin *divisus,* past participle of *dīvidere,* to divide.] **—point-de·vice** *adv.*

point duty *n.* In Britain, the duty of a traffic warden or constable stationed at a junction, roundabout, or the like, to regulate traffic.

pointe (poynt) *n.* In ballet, the tip of the toes. [French.]

point·ed (póyntid) *adj.* **1.** Having an end coming to a point. **2.** Sharp; cutting: *a pointed question.* **3.** Obviously directed at or making reference to a particular target: *pointed wit.* **4.** Clearly evident or conspicuous; emphasised; marked: *a pointed lack of interest.* **5.** Characterised by the use of a pointed crown, as in Gothic architecture: *a pointed arch.* **—point·ed·ly** *adv.* **—point·ed·ness** *n.*

point·er (póyntər) *n.* **1.** One that sharpens, directs, indicates, or points. **2.** A scale indicator on a watch, balance, or other measuring instrument. **3.** A long, tapered stick for indicating objects on a chart, blackboard, or the like. **4.** A hunting dog of a breed having a short-haired coat that is usually white with black or brownish spots. **5.** *Informal.* A suggestion; a hint; a piece of advice. **—the Pointers.** In the constellation of the Plough, the two stars which align with the Pole Star and can be used to indicate north.

poin·til·lism (pwáɴtee-iz'm, póyn–, -til-) *n.* A method of painting exemplified by Seurat and his followers in late 19th-century France consisting of the juxtaposition of dots of primary colours which blend in the viewer's eye from a distance, giving brighter secondary colours. Compare **divisionism.** [French *pointillisme,* from *pointiller,* to paint small dots, from *pointille,* small point or dot, from Italian *puntiglio,* diminutive of *punto,* point, dot, from Latin *punctum,* from the neuter past participle of *pungere,* to pierce, prick.] **—poin·til·list** *n.* & *adj.* **—poin·til·lis·tic** (-ístik) *adj.*

point·ing (póynting) *n.* **1.** Cement or mortar used to fill up cracks or spaces in joints, as in brickwork. **2.** A method of marking psalms to indicate how irregular lines are to be chanted.

point lace *n.* A type of handmade lace, **needlepoint** *(see).*

point·less (póynt-ləss, -liss) *adj.* **1.** Meaningless; irrelevant: *a pointless remark.* **2.** Ineffectual; futile: *It would be pointless to complain.* **—point·less·ly** *adv.* **—point·less·ness** *n.*

point of honour *n., pl.* **points of honour.** A matter that affects one's honour or reputation.

point of inflection *n. Mathematics.* A stationary point on a curve at which the tangent to the curve changes from rotating in one direction to rotating in the other, as the curve passes through the point.

point of no return *n.* A stage or point reached in a course of action after which turning back or stopping is no longer possible.

point of order *n.* A question as to whether that which is being discussed is in order or allowed by the rules.

point of reference *n.* A **reference** *(see).*

point-of-sale (póynt-əv-sáyl) *adj.* Of, provided for, or situated at the place where purchases are made: *point-of-sale advertising.*

point of view *n.* **1.** The position from which something is observed or considered; a standpoint. **2.** A manner of viewing things; an attitude.

points·man (póynts-mən) *n., pl.* **-men** (-mən, -men). A person who operates the points on a railway line. Also *U.S.* "switchman".

point source *n. Optics.* A source of light or other radiation that can be regarded as having negligible size.

point system *n.* **1.** *Printing.* A system of measurement by the **point** *(see).* **2.** Any system of printing or writing for the blind that uses an alphabet of raised symbols or dots that correspond to letters, such as Braille. **3.** A system of evaluating and averaging achievement, as in education, by awarding numerical units or points.

point-to-point (póynt-tə-póynt) *n.* A cross-country or steeplechase race over a course marked by flags, often organised by a recognised hunt club or other body.

poise¹ (poyz) *v.* **poised, poising, poises.** —*tr.* **1.** To carry or hold in equilibrium; balance. **2.** To hold steady or raised, as in readiness: *with hands poised.* —*intr.* To be balanced or held in suspension; hover: *poise on the brink.*

~*n.* **1.** The state or condition of being balanced or held in equilibrium; stability; balance. **2.** Freedom from awkwardness or embarrassment; assurance; composure. **3.** The bearing or deportment of the head or body; mien. **4.** A state or condition of hovering or being suspended. [Middle English *poisen, peisen,* to weigh, from Old French *poiser, peser,* from Vulgar Latin *pēsāre* (unattested), variant of Latin *pensāre,* frequentative of *pendere,* to weigh.]

poise² (pwaaz) *n.* A centimetre-gram-second unit of dynamic viscosity equal to one dyne-second per square centimetre. [French, after Jean Louis Marie *Poiseuille* (1799–1869), French physician.]

poised (poyzd) *adj.* **1.** Assured; composed. **2.** Held balanced or steady in readiness: *stood poised for the jump.*

poi·son (póyz'n) *n.* **1.** Any substance that causes injury, illness, or death, especially by chemical means. **2.** Anything that is destructive, corruptive, or fatal: *the poison of her criticism.* **3.** A substance that inhibits or retards a chemical reaction or deactivates a catalyst. **4.** A substance in a nuclear reactor that absorbs neutrons without undergoing fission, thereby slowing down the chain reaction.

~*tr.v.* **poisoned, -soning, -sons. 1.** To give poison to; kill or harm with poison. **2.** To put poison on or into: *poison a cup.* **3. a.** To pollute: *Fumes poisoned the air.* **b.** To have a harmful influence on; corrupt, ruin, taint, or embitter: *Jealousy poisoned their friendship.* **4.** To inhibit or retard (a chemical or nuclear reaction).

~*adj.* Poisonous. [Middle English *poysoun,* potion, poisonous drink, from Old French *poison,* from Latin *pōtiō* (stem *pōtiōn-*), from *pōtāre,* to drink.] **—poi·son·er** *n.*

poison gas *n.* Any lethal or crippling vapour such as phosgene or chlorine, used in warfare.

poison hemlock *n. U.S.* A poisonous plant, **hemlock** *(see).*

poison ivy *n.* A North American shrub or vine, *Rhus radicans,* having leaflets in groups of three, small green flowers, and whitish berries, causing a rash on contact.

poi·son·ous (póyz'n-əss) *adj.* **1. a.** Capable of harming or killing by or as if by poison. **b.** Broadly, toxic or venomous. **2.** Containing a poison. **3.** Marked by apparent ill will; malicious: *a poisonous glance.* **4.** *Informal.* Objectionable; unpleasant. **—poi·son·ous·ly** *adv.* **—poi·son·ous·ness** *n.*

poison-pen letter (póyz'n-pén) n. A letter or note, usually anonymous, containing abusive or malicious information about the recipient or a third party.

Pois·son distribution (pwásson, pwaa-són) n. Statistics. A probability distribution used to describe the occurrence of events in a large number of independent repeated trials. [After S.D. Poisson (1781–1840), French mathematician.]

Poi·tiers (pwáat-yay, pwaat-yáy). Capital of Vienne département, west France. It was the capital of the former province of Poitou and the site of many battles, including the defeat of the French (under John II) by the English (under Edward the Black Prince) in 1356. An agricultural centre, it also produces chemicals and electrical equipment.

poke¹ (pōk) v. poked, poking, pokes. —tr. 1. To push or jab, as with a finger or arm; prod. 2. To make (a hole or pathway, for example) by or as if by prodding, thrusting, or poking. 3. To cause to project; stick: A seal poked its head out of the water. 4. To stir (a fire) by prodding the wood or coal with a poker or stick. 5. To strike; punch. 6. Slang. To have sexual intercourse with. —intr. 1. To make thrusts or jabs with a stick, poker, or the like. Used with at. 2. To pry or meddle; intrude: poking into another's business. 3. To search or look in a curious manner: poking around in the drawer. 4. To thrust forward; appear; protrude: His head poked from under the blankets. 5. Chiefly U.S. To live or proceed in a slow or lazy manner; dawdle; potter. Often used with along. ~n. 1. A push, thrust, or jab. 2. A punch or blow with the fist. 3. U.S. A person who moves slowly or aimlessly; a dawdler. [Middle English poken, from Middle Dutch and Middle Low German poken, to strike, thrust (probably imitative).]

poke² n. 1. A large bonnet having a projecting brim at the front, worn especially in the 18th and 19th centuries. Also called "poke bonnet". 2. The brim of such a bonnet. [From POKE (to thrust).]

poke³ n. Chiefly Regional. A sack or bag. [Middle English, from Old North French poque, variant of Old French poche, pocket, from Frankish pokka (unattested), bag.]

pok·er¹ (pōkər) n. One that pokes; specifically, a metal rod used to stir a fire.

poker² n. Any of various card games played by two or more players who bet on the value of their hands. [19th century: origin obscure.]

poker face n. A face lacking any interpretable expression. [From the impassive face of an expert poker player.] —pok·er·faced (pōkər-fáyst, -fayst) adj.

poker machine n. Australian. A fruit machine. Also informally called "pokie".

pok·y, poke·y (pōki) adj. -ier, -iest. Informal. 1. Small and cramped: a poky flat. 2. U.S. Dawdling; dull; slow. ~n. Chiefly U.S. Slang. Variant of pokey. [From POKE, to thrust, (hence, slang) to confine.]

Po·lack (pō-lak || U.S. -laak) n. 1. Chiefly U.S. Slang. A person of Polish descent or birth. Used derogatorily. 2. Obsolete. A native of Poland; a Pole. [Polish Polak.] —Po·lack adj.

Po·land (pōlənd). Polish Pol·ska (pól-ska). Country in eastern Europe. It is largely an undulating plain rising to the Carpathian Mountains in the south, and is crossed by the rivers Vistula and Warta. Becoming a united state in the 10th century, it was a great power during the 15th and 16th centuries but was partitioned in 1772, 1793, and 1795, after which it disappeared until reformed in 1918. Occupied by the Germans (1939–45), it came under Communist rule in 1948. Poland is largely an agricultural country, although industry has grown considerably since World War II. Economic troubles led to riots over the price of food in 1970, 1976, and 1980–81, culminating in strikes, the declaration of martial law, and the suppression of the free trade union, Solidarity. In 1983 martial law was lifted. Early in 1988 austerity measures led to unrest. A new government negotiated an agreement with Solidarity on trade union

pluralism and democratic elections. Solidarity received massive support in the elections, in which Poland's first non-Communist government for more than 40 years won power. Area, 312 677 square kilometres (120,725 square miles). Population, 38,620,000. Capital, Warsaw.

Po·lan·ski (pə-lánski), **Roman** (1933–). Polish-born film director. His films, such as Rosemary's Baby (1968), Chinatown (1974), and Tess (1980), are notable for their brooding menace and black humour.

po·lar (pōlər) adj. 1. a. Of, pertaining to, or designating a pole. b. Measured from or referred to a pole or poles: polar diameter. 2. Pertaining to, connected with, or located near the North Pole or South Pole. 3. Occupying or characterised by opposite extremes. 4. Serving as a guide, as a polestar or a pole of the Earth might. 5. Central or pivotal. [New Latin polāris, from Latin polus, POLE.]

polar angle n. The angle formed by the polar axis and the radius vector in a polar coordinate system.

polar axis n. The fixed reference axis from which the polar angle is measured in a polar coordinate system.

polar bear n. A large, white-furred bear, Thalarctos maritimus, of Arctic regions.

polar body n. Genetics. A minute cell produced and ultimately discarded in the development of an ovum, containing little or no cytoplasm but having one of the nuclei derived from the first or second meiotic division of the oocyte.

polar cap n. 1. a. A high-altitude icecap. b. The polar regions of ice. 2. Astronomy. Any differentiated polar region of a planet.

polar circle n. The **Arctic Circle** or **Antarctic Circle** (both of which see).

polar coordinate n. Either of two coordinates, the radius vector or the polar angle, that together can be used to specify the position of any point in a plane.

polar distance n. Astronomy. The angular distance between the celestial pole and the point to be measured on the celestial sphere.

po·lar·im·e·ter (pōlə-rímmitər) n. An instrument used to measure the rotation of the plane of polarisation of polarised light, or the degree of polarisation of light passing through an optically active compound or sample. —po·lar·i·met·ric (-ri-méttrik) adj. —po·lar·im·e·try (-rímmətri) n.

Po·lar·is (pō-láariss, pə-, -lárriss) n. 1. A star of the second magnitude in the constellation Ursa Minor, almost at the north celestial pole. Also called "North Star", "Pole Star". 2. A U.S. Navy intermediate range surface-to-surface ballistic missile. [New Latin (Stella) Polāris, polar (star).]

po·lar·i·sa·tion (pōlə-rī-záysh'n || U.S. -ri-) n. 1. The uniform and nonrandom elliptical, circular, or linear variation of a wave characteristic, especially of vibrational orientation, in light or other radiation. 2. The partial or complete polar separation of positive and negative electric charge in a nuclear, atomic, molecular, or chemical system. 3. A concentration, as of groups, forces, or interests, about two conflicting or contrasting positions.

po·lar·i·scope (pō-lárri-skōp, pə-) n. An instrument for ascertaining, measuring, or exhibiting the properties of polarised light, or for studying the interactions of polarised light with optically transparent media.

po·lar·ise, po·lar·ize (pōlə-rīz) v. -ised, -ising, -ises. —tr. 1. To induce polarisation in; impart polarity to. 2. To cause to concentrate about two conflicting or contrasting positions. —intr. To become polarised. —po·lar·is·a·ble adj. —po·lar·is·er n.

po·lar·i·ty (pō-lárrəti, pə-) n., pl. -ties. 1. Intrinsic separation into contrasting or opposite poles; intrinsic polar alignment or orientation, especially with respect to a physical property: magnetic polarity. 2. The possession or manifestation of two opposing attributes, tendencies, or principles: political polarity. 3. A specified polar extreme: an electric terminal with positive polarity.

po·lar·og·ra·phy (pōlə-róggrəfi) n. An electrochemical method of quantitative or qualitative analysis based on the relationship between an increasing current passing through the solution being analysed and the increasing voltage used to produce the current. [From POLAR(ISATION) + -GRAPHY.] —po·lar·o·graph·ic (pō-lárrə-gráffik, pə-) adj. —po·lar·o·graph·i·cal·ly adv.

Po·lar·oid (pōlə-royd) n. 1. A trademark for a specially treated, transparent plastic capable of polarising light passing through it, used in sunglasses and other glare-reducing optical devices. 2. a. A trademark for a type of camera that develops the film and produces prints within a few seconds of taking the photograph. b. A photograph taken with such a camera.

Polar Regions pl.n. The land and water areas surrounding the North and South poles.

pol·der (pōl-dər, pól-) n. An area of low-lying land, especially in the Netherlands, that has been reclaimed from a body of water and is protected by dykes. [Middle Dutch polre, poldert.]

pole¹ (pōl) n. Abbr. p. 1. Either axial extremity of any axis through a sphere. 2. Either of the regions contiguous to the extremities of the earth's rotational axis, the **North Pole** or the **South Pole** (both of which see). 3. Physics. See **magnetic pole**. 4. Electricity. Either of two oppositely charged terminals, as in an electric cell or battery. 5. Astronomy. See **celestial pole**. 6. Biology. a. A structurally or physiologically distinct region at either axial extremity of a nucleus, cell, or organism. b. Either end of the spindle formed in a cell during mitosis or meiosis. 7. Either of two antithetical ideas, propensities, forces, or positions. 8. Any fixed point of reference. 9. Geometry. The origin in a polar coordinate system; the polar angle vertex. —**poles apart**. Having very different opinions, views,

POLAND

tastes, or the like. [Middle English, from Latin *polus*, from Greek *polos*, axis of the sphere, firmament.]

pole² *n.* **1.** A long, relatively slender, and generally rounded piece of wood or other material. **2.** The long, tapering, wooden shaft extending up from the front axle of a vehicle to the collars of the animals drawing it; a tongue. **3. a.** A unit of length, a **rod** *(see)*. **b.** A unit of area equal to a square rod (30¼ square yards). **4.** *Nautical.* A small or light spar. **5.** In horseracing or motor racing, the starting position nearest the inner rail on the inside lane. **—under bare poles.** *Nautical.* Having no sails up. Said of a sailing vessel. **—up the pole.** *Informal.* **a.** Crazy; mad. **b.** Misguided or mistaken.
~*v.* **poled, poling, poles.** —*tr.* **1.** To propel with a pole. **2.** To support (plants) with a pole. **3.** To strike, poke, or stir with a pole. **4.** To stir (molten metal) with a green pole that introduces carbon and deoxidises the substance by reacting with the oxygen. —*intr.* **1.** To propel a boat, raft, or the like with a pole. **2.** To use ski poles to gain speed or turn. [Middle English *po(o)le*, Old English *pāl*, from Germanic, from Latin *pālus*, stake.]

Pole (pōl) *n.* A native or inhabitant of Poland.

pole·axe (pṓl-aks) *n.* **1.** A battle-axe used in the Middle Ages, consisting of an axe, or an axe, hammer, and pick combination, with a long shaft. **2.** An axe having a hammer face opposite the blade, used to slaughter cattle.
~*tr.v.* **poleaxed, -axing, -axes.** To strike or fell with or as if with a poleaxe. [Middle English *pollax* : POLL (head) + AXE.]

pole·cat (pṓl-kat) *n.* **1.** A carnivorous mammal, *Mustela putorius*, of Europe, Asia, and northern Africa, having dark brown or black fur. It emits a foul-smelling fluid when alarmed. **2.** Any of several similar or related animals, especially the ferret in Britain or the skunk in the United States. [Middle English *polcat* : *pol-*† (meaning unknown) + CAT.]

pole horse *n.* A horse harnessed to the pole, or tongue, of a vehicle. Also called "poler".

po·lem·ic (pə-lémmik, po-, pō-) *n.* **1. a.** A controversy or argument, especially one that is a refutation of or an attack upon a particular opinion, doctrine, or the like. **b.** Loosely, any virulent criticism. **2.** A person engaged in or inclined to controversy, argument, or refutation.
~*adj.* Also **po·lem·i·cal** (-'l). Of, pertaining to, or given to controversy, argument, or refutation. [Medieval Latin *polemicus*, controversialist, from Greek *polemikos*, of war, hostile, opposed, from *polemos*†, war.] **—po·lem·i·cal·ly** *adv.*

po·lem·i·cist (pə-lémmi-sist, po-, pō-) *n.* Also **pol·e·mist** (-lémmist, póllimist). A person who writes or is skilled in polemics. **—po·lem·i·cise, pol·e·mise** *intr.v.*

po·lem·ics (pə-lémmiks, po-, pō-) *n.* *Used with a singular verb.* The art or practice of argument or controversy, especially in support of or against a doctrine or belief.

pol·e·mol·o·gy (pól-i-móllәji, -e-, -ə-) *n.* The study of wars and conflicts between nations. [Greek *polemos*, war + -LOGY.] **—pol·e·mo·log·i·cal** (-mə-lójik'l) *adj.* **—pol·e·mol·o·gist** *n.*

po·len·ta (pō-léntə, pə-) *n.* A thick porridge made from maize and eaten especially in Italy. [Italian, from Latin, pearl barley.]

pol·er (pṓlər) *n.* **1.** One that propels, supports, conveys, or strikes with a pole. **2.** A pole horse.

Pole Star (pṓl-staar) *n.* **1.** A star, **Polaris** *(see)*. **2.** *Small* **p**, *small* **s.** A guiding principle.

pole vault *n.* *Sports.* A field event in which the contestant jumps or vaults over a high crossbar with the aid of a long flexible pole.

pole-vault (pṓl-vawlt || -volt) *intr.v.* **-vaulted, -vaulting, -vaults.** *Sports.* To perform or compete in the pole vault. **—pole-vault·er** *n.*

poleyn (pṓlayn) *n.* A piece of armour protecting the knee.

po·lice (pə-léess || pō-, pṓleess) *n., pl.* **police. 1. a.** The government department established to maintain order, enforce the law, and prevent and detect crime. **b.** An official civil force, or body of persons, established and maintained for this purpose; a police force. **c.** *Used with a plural verb.* The members of such a force collectively. **2. a.** Any group of persons resembling the police force of a community in organisation or function: *military police.* **b.** *Used with a plural verb.* The members of such a group. **3.** *Archaic.* The regulation and control of the affairs of a community, especially with respect to the maintenance of order, law, health, morals, safety, and other matters affecting general welfare.
~*tr.v.* **policed, -licing, -lices. 1.** To regulate, control, or keep in order with or as if with police. **2.** *U.S.* To make (a military area) neat in appearance. [Originally "policy", "government organisation", from French, from Late Latin *polītia*, administration of the commonwealth, from Latin *polītīa*, the state, from Greek *politeia*, polity, citizenship, from *politēs*, citizen, from *polis*, city.]

police court *Law.* **1.** Formerly, a magistrate's court. **2.** Formerly in Scotland, a district court.

police dog *n.* A dog, especially a German shepherd, trained to aid the police.

police force *n.* A body of persons trained in methods of law enforcement and crime prevention and detection, and given authority to maintain the peace, safety, and order of the community.

po·lice·man (pə-léess-mən, pléess-) *n., pl.* **-men** (-mən). A male member of a police force.

police officer *n.* A policeman or policewoman.

police state *n.* A country or other political unit in which the government exercises rigid and repressive controls over social, economic, and political life, especially by means of a secret police force.

police station *n.* The headquarters of a unit of a police force where those under arrest are first charged.

po·lice·wom·an (pə-léess-wŏŏmən, pléess-) *n., pl.* **-women** (-wimmin). *Abbr.* **P.W.** A female member of a police force.

pol·i·cy¹ (pól-ə-si, -i-) *n., pl.* **-cies. 1.** Any overall plan or course of action adopted, as by a government, political party, or business organisation, designed to influence and determine immediate and long-term decisions or actions: *foreign policy; company personnel policy.* **2. a.** A course of action, guiding principle, or procedure considered to be expedient, prudent, or advantageous: *Honesty is the best policy.* **b.** Prudence, shrewdness, or sagacity in practical matters. **3.** *Scottish.* The park surrounding a country seat or large house. [Middle English *policye*, polity, commonwealth, policy, from Old French *policie*, from Latin *polītīa*, state, from Greek *politeia*, citizenship, from *politēs*, citizen, from *polis*, city.]

policy² *n., pl.* **-cies.** A written contract or certificate of insurance. [French *police*, from Provençal *poliss(i)a* or Italian *polizza*, probably from Medieval Latin *apodixa*, from Latin *apodīxis*, from Greek *apodeixis*, "a showing or making known", proof, from *apodeiknunai*, to show off, make known : *apo*, off, from + *deiknunai*, to show.]

pol·i·cy·hol·der (pól-ə-si-hōldər, -i-) *n.* A person or organisation that holds an insurance policy.

po·li·o·my·e·li·tis (pṓ-li-ō-mī́-ə-lītiss) *n.* An infectious viral disease occurring mainly in children and in its severest form attacking the central nervous system and producing paralysis, muscular atrophy, and often deformity. Also called "infantile paralysis", "polio". [Greek *polios*, grey + MYELITIS.]

po·lis (pól-iss) *n., pl.* **-leis** (-īss || -ayss) A city-state of ancient Greece. [Greek *polis*, city.]

pol·ish (póllish) *v.* **-ished, -ishing, -ishes.** —*tr.* **1.** To make smooth and shiny by abrasion or chemical action. **2.** To free from coarseness; make elegant; refine: *polish one's manners.* **3.** To remove flaws from; perfect or complete: *polish one's piano technique.* —*intr.* **1.** To become smooth or shiny by or as if by rubbing. **2.** To become perfect or refined. **—polish off.** *Informal.* **1.** To complete or finish quickly: *polish off a meal.* **2.** To eliminate or dispose of: *He polished off his enemies.* **—polish up.** To improve by study or practice. Often used with *on*: *polish up your singing.*
~*n.* **1.** Smoothness or shininess of surface or finish. **2.** A substance applied to smooth, colour, or shine a surface: *shoe polish.* **3.** The act or process of polishing. **4.** Elegance of style or manners; refinement. [Middle English *polisshen*, from Old French *polir* (present stem *poliss-*), from Latin *polīre.*] **—pol·ish·er** *n.*

Po·lish (pṓlish) *adj.* *Abbr.* **Pol.** Of or pertaining to Poland, its inhabitants, or their language or culture.
~*n.* *Abbr.* **Pol. 1.** The West Slavonic language that is the major language of Poland. **2.** *Used with a plural verb.* The people of Poland. [From POLE.]

pol·ished (póllisht) *adj.* **1.** Refined; elegant; cultured. **2.** Impeccable; accomplished; flawless. **3.** Having the husk removed. Said of grains of rice. **3.** Having no imperfections or errors; flawless.

Pol·it·bu·ro (póllit-bewr-ō, pə-lít-) *n., pl.* **-ros.** The chief political and executive committee of a Communist party, as in the former U.S.S.R. [Russian *Polit(icheskoe) Buro*, political bureau.]

po·lite (pə-lī́t || pō-) *adj.* **-liter, -litest. 1.** Marked by consideration for others, correct manners, or tact; courteous. **2.** Refined; elegant; cultivated: *polite society.* [Middle English *polyt*, polished, smoothed, from Latin *polītus*, past participle of Latin *polīre*, to POLISH.] **—po·lite·ly** *adv.* **—po·lite·ness** *n.*
Synonyms: *polite, civil, courteous, genteel.*

pol·i·tesse (pólli-téss) *n.* Courteous formality; politeness. [French, from Italian *politezza, pulitezza*, cleanliness, from *pulīto*, "polished", clean, from Latin *polītus*, past participle of *polīre*, to POLISH.]

pol·i·tic (pól-ətik, -itik) *adj.* **1.** Artful; ingenious; shrewd: *a politic diplomat.* **2.** Using, displaying, or proceeding from policy; prudent; judicious: *a politic decision.* **3.** Crafty; unscrupulous; cunning. **4.** Political. Now archaic except in the phrase *the body politic.* [Middle English *polytyk*, "political", pursuing a policy, prudent, from Old French *politique*, from Latin *polīticus*, from Greek *politikos*, of a citizen, from *politēs*, citizen, from *polis*, city.] **—pol·i·tic·ly** *adv.*

po·lit·i·cal (pə-líttik'l || pō-) *adj.* **1.** Of or pertaining to the study, structure, or affairs of government or the state, especially in regard to civil policy-making rather than military, legal, or administrative matters. **2.** Having a definite or organised policy or structure of government. **3.** Of or pertaining to policies or parties within a state: *strong political views.* **4.** Of or pertaining to the citizens of a state: *political rights.* **5.** Of or pertaining to the security of the government or state: *a political offence.* **6.** Very interested or active in politics: *I'm not a political person, I'm afraid.* **7.** Having or influenced by partisan interests; not neutral, objective, or unbiased: *The English legal system must never become a political institution.* **8.** Arising from or influenced by partisan or selfish factors, rather than the merits of the case: *a purely political decision; His promotion must have been political.* **—po·lit·i·cal·ly** *adv.*

political animal *n.* **1.** A person who is skilled or experienced in the art of political subterfuge and who uses it to advance his personal interests or career. **2.** A person who is extremely interested or involved in politics. **3.** Any person, or human beings in general, considered as being unavoidably influenced by politics.

political asylum *n.* The protection offered by a state to a foreigner who has left or wishes to leave his own country for political reasons.

political economy *n.* The science of economics. Not in current usage.

politically correct *adj. Abbr.* **P.C.** Conforming to a dogmatic political ideology, favouring the suppression of anything that smacks of racism, sexism, homophobia, Eurocentrism, and other objects of its adherents' disapproval. —**political correctness** *n.*

political prisoner *n.* A person imprisoned for any act a state considers hostile, especially the expression of views in conflict with its ideology, or for any offence it may consider to endanger its security. Compare **prisoner of conscience.**

political science *n.* The study of government and of political institutions. —**political scientist** *n.*

pol·i·ti·cian (pólli-tísh'n) *n.* **1. a.** One who is actively involved in politics, especially party politics. **b.** One who holds or seeks a political office. **2.** One skilled or experienced in the science or administration of government. **3.** One skilled at or given to scheming.

po·lit·i·cise, po·lit·i·cize (pə-lítti-sīz || pō-) *v.* **-cised, -cising, -cises.** —*intr.* To engage in or discuss politics. —*tr.* To make political in character or awareness. —**po·lit·i·ci·sa·tion** (-sī-záysh'n) *n.*

pol·i·tick·ing (pólli-ticking) *n.* **1.** Involvement in politics, especially for one's personal advantage. **2.** Canvassing for votes.

po·lit·i·co (pə-líttikō) *n., pl.* **-cos.** *Informal.* A politician or political agitator. Often used derogatorily. [Italian and Spanish, "political", from Latin *polīticus,* POLITIC.]

pol·i·tics (pól-ə-tiks, -i-) *n. Usually used with a singular verb (1–5).* **1.** The art or science of power and government. **2.** The policies, goals, or affairs of a government or state or of the groups or parties within it. **3. a.** The conducting of or engaging in political affairs, often professionally. **b.** The business, activities, or profession of a person so involved. **4.** The methods or tactics involved in managing a state or government. **5. a.** The scheming and manoeuvring for power and personal advantage that occurs within a given group: *office politics.* **b.** A political aspect inherent in a given situation or sphere: *sexual politics.* **6.** *Used with a plural verb.* Opinions or principles dealing with political subjects: *Her politics are conservative.*

pol·i·ty (pólləti) *n., pl.* **-ties. 1.** The form of government of a nation, state, church, or organisation. **2.** Any organised society, such as a nation, having one specific form of government. **3.** The supervision of public affairs. **4.** The condition of having a government or being politically organised. [From Latin *polītia,* POLICY.]

pol·ka (pólkə, pōlkə) *n.* **1.** A lively dance consisting of three steps and a skip, originating in Bohemia, performed by couples in duple time. **2.** A piece of music for this dance. [French and German, from Czech *pulka,* half-step, from *pul,* half.] —**pol·ka** *intr.v.*

pol·ka dot (pólkə, pōlkə, pōkə) *n.* **1.** Any of a number of dots or round spots forming a pattern on cloth. **2.** A pattern or fabric marked with such dots. [Perhaps a respelling of *poke a dot.*]

poll (pōl) *n.* **1.** The casting and registering of votes in an election. **2.** The number of votes cast or recorded. **3.** A tax required for voting, a **poll tax** *(see).* **4.** A list or record of persons, especially for taxing or voting purposes. **5. a.** Any sampling of opinion on an issue in a given group: *took a poll of the class.* **b.** An **opinion poll** *(see).* **6.** The head, especially the top of the head where hair grows. **7.** The blunt or broad end of a hammer, axe, or other similar tool. —**go to the polls.** To vote. Used of a country or electorate. ~*v.* **polled, polling, polls.** —*tr.* **1.** To receive (a specified number of votes). **2.** To register (a person), especially for voting purposes. **3.** To receive or record the votes of. **4.** To cast (a vote or ballot). **5.** To canvass (a person, area, or sample group of persons) to survey general opinion. **6.** To cut off or trim (hair, horns, or wool, for example). **7.** To trim or cut off the hair, wool, branches, or horns of: *poll sheep; polled sheep.* —*intr.* To vote in an election. [Middle English *pol, polle,* head (whence the Modern English senses of "counting by heads", "registering of votes"), of Low German origin perhaps akin to Middle Low German *polle*†.] —**poll·er** *n.*

pol·lack, pol·lock (pólløk) *n., pl.* **-lacks** or collectively **pollack.** A marine food and game fish, *Pollachius pollachius,* related to the cod, occurring chiefly in northern Atlantic waters. [17th century : from Scottish *podlock*†.]

pol·lard (pól-ərd || -aard) *n.* **1.** A tree whose top branches have been cut back to the trunk so that it may produce a dense growth of new shoots. **2.** An animal that no longer has its horns. ~ *tr.v.* **pollarded, -larding, -lards.** To make a pollard. [From POLL.]

pol·len (póllən) *n. Botany.* The fine, powder-like material produced by the anthers of flowering plants and by the male cones of conifers, which contains the male gametes and functions as the male element in fertilisation. [New Latin, from Latin, flour, dust.]

pollen analysis *n.* **Palynology** *(see).*

pollen count *n.* The average number of pollen grains in a cubic yard or other standard volume of air over a 24-hour period at a particular time and place, used to estimate the possible severity of hay-fever attacks.

pollen tube *n. Botany.* The slender tube that grows from a grain of pollen down the style of a pollinated plant to the ovule, and conveys male gametes which fertilise the egg cell.

pol·lex (pólleks) *n., pl.* **pollices** (pólli-seez). The innermost forelimb digit; the thumb. [Latin, thumb.] —**pol·li·cal** *adj.*

pollin-, pollini- *comb. form.* Indicates pollen; for example, **pollinosis, polliniferous.** [New Latin *pollen* (stem *pollin-*), POLLEN.]

pol·li·nate, pol·len·ate (pólli-nayt) *tr.v.* **-nated, -nating, -nates.** *Botany.* To convey or transfer pollen from an anther or male cone to a stigma or female cone of (a plant or flower) in the process of fertilisation. [New Latin *pollen* (stem *pollin-*), POLLEN.] —**pol·li·na·tion** (-náysh'n) *n.* —**pol·li·na·tor** *n.*

pol·lin·ic (po-línnik, pə-) *adj. Botany.* Of or pertaining to pollen.

pol·li·nif·er·ous, pol·len·if·er·ous (pólli-níffərəss) *adj.* **1.** Producing or yielding pollen. **2.** Adapted for carrying pollen, as a bee's legs are. [POLLINI- + -FEROUS.]

pol·lin·i·um (po-lín-i-əm, pə-) *n., pl.* **-ia** (-i-ə). *Botany.* A mass of agglutinated pollen grains, found in the flowers of most orchids and milkweeds. [New Latin : POLLIN- + -IUM.]

pol·li·no·sis, pol·len·o·sis (pólli-nṓ-siss) *n. Pathology.* Allergic reaction to pollen, as in disorders such as hay fever or asthma. [New Latin : POLLIN- + -OSIS.]

pol·li·wog, pol·ly·wog (pólli-wog) *n. U.S.* An immature frog or toad; a tadpole. [Middle English *polwygle* : *pol, polle,* POLL (head) + *wiglen, wigelen,* to WIGGLE.]

pollock. Variant of **pollack.**

Pol·lock (póllək), **Jackson** (1912–56). U.S. artist. After early surrealist work, he turned to the technique of action painting, throwing or dripping paint onto a very large canvas.

poll·ster (pōlstər) *n.* A person who conducts opinion polls.

poll tax *n.* **1.** A former tax levied, especially in the United States, on persons rather than on property, often as a requirement for voting. Also called "poll". **2.** *British.* The **community charge** *(see).*

pol·lut·ant (pə-lōō-t'nt, -léw-) *n.* Anything that pollutes; especially, any gaseous, chemical, or organic waste that contaminates air, soil, or water.

pol·lute (pə-lōōt, -léwt) *tr.v.* **-luted, -luting, -lutes. 1.** To contaminate (the environment) with harmful or poisonous substances. **2.** To render morally impure; corrupt. **3.** To make ceremonially impure; profane; desecrate. [Middle English *polluten,* from Latin *polluere* (past part. stem *pollut-*).] —**pol·lut·er** *n.* —**pol·lu·tive** *adj.*

pol·lu·tion (pə-lōō-sh'n, -léw-) *n.* **1.** The act or process of polluting or the state of being polluted. **2.** The contamination of soil, water, or the atmosphere by the discharge of noxious substances. **3.** Broadly, any public nuisance attributable to a particular cause: *noise pollution.*

Pol·lux[1] (pólləks) *Greek Mythology.* One of the twin sons of Zeus and Leda. See **Castor and Pollux.**

Pollux[2] *n. Astronomy.* A first-magnitude star in the constellation Gemini. [After the mythical twin POLLUX.]

Pol·ly (pólli) *n.* A name for a parrot.

Pol·ly·an·na (pólli-ánnə) *n.* A foolishly or blindly optimistic person. [After the title character in *Pollyanna* (1913), novel by U.S. writer Eleanor Porter (1868–1920).]

po·lo (pōlō) *n.* **1.** A game of Oriental origin played by two teams of three or four players on horseback, equipped with long-handled mallets for driving a small wooden ball through the opponents' goal. **2.** Any similar game, such as water polo. [Balti *polo,* "ball", akin to Tibetan *bo-lo.*] —**po·lo·ist** *n.*

Po·lo (pōlō), **Marco** (*c.* 1254–1324). Venetian traveller. His father Niccolò and uncle Maffeo had already made one successful trading expedition to the court of the Mongol Emperor Kublai Khan in China before they took Marco with them in 1271. He entered Kublai's diplomatic service and undertook missions to all parts of the Mongol Empire before returning to Venice in 1295. His memoirs were long the West's chief source of knowledge of the Orient.

pol·o·naise (póllə-nayz || pōlə-) *n.* **1.** A stately, marchlike dance in triple time, consisting mainly of a promenade of couples. **2.** A piece of music for this dance. **3.** A woman's dress of the 18th century, having a fitted bodice and draped cutaway skirt, worn over an elaborate underskirt. [French, from the feminine of *polonais,* Polish, from Medieval Latin *Polōnia,* Poland.]

polo neck *n.* **1.** A soft, high, continuous collar worn turned down so as to fit closely about the neck. **2.** A sweater having such a collar. —**polo-neck** *adj.*

po·lo·ni·um (pə-lōni-əm) *n. Symbol* **Po** A naturally radioactive metallic element, occurring in minute quantities as a product of radium disintegration and produced by bombarding bismuth with neutrons. It has many isotopes ranging in mass number from 193 to 218, of which polonium-210, with a half-life of 134.8 days, is the most readily available. Atomic number 84, melting point 254°C, boiling point 962°C, relative density 9.32, valencies 2, 4, 6. [Latin *Polōnia,* Poland, country of one of its discoverers, Marie Curie.]

po·lo·ny (pə-lōni) *n., pl.* **-nies.** *British.* A large, lightly seasoned sausage made chiefly from pork, usually eaten cold and sliced in salads or sandwiches. Also called "Bologna". [Probably from *Bologna (sausage).*]

Pol Pot (pol pót), also called Saloth Sar (1926–98). Cambodian military leader and prime minister. He joined the anti-French forces under Ho Chi Minh and led the pro-Communist Chinese-backed Khmer Rouge guerrillas against the Kampuchean government. His brutal regime as prime minister (1976–79) resulted in at least two million deaths. He announced his retirement as leader of the Khmer Rouge in 1985.

Polska. See **Poland.**

pol·ter·geist (póltər-gīst, pōltər-) *n.* A noisy, mischievous spirit that manifests itself by slamming doors, moving objects, and the like. [German *Poltergeist* : *poltern,* to make noises, rattle, knock, from Middle High German *boldern, buldern* + German *Geist,* ghost, from Old High German *geist.*]

pol·troon (pol-trōōn) *n.* A base coward. Not in current usage. [French *poltron,* from Italian *poltrone,* perhaps augmentative of *poltro,* lazy person.] —**pol·troon·er·y** *n.*

pol·y (pólli) *n., pl.* **polys.** *Informal.* A polytechnic.

poly– *comb. form.* Indicates: **1.** More than one, many, or much; for example, **polygamy. 2.** More than usual; abnormal or excessive; for example, **polydipsia. 3.** A polymer; for example, **polythene, polyester.** [Greek *polus*, much, many.]

pol·y·a·del·phous (pólli-ə-délfəss) *adj. Botany.* Having or designating stamens arranged in three or more groups by means of their united stalks or filaments. Said of flowers. [POLY- + Greek *adelphos*, brother + -OUS.]

pol·y·am·ide (pólli-ám-īd, -id) *n. Chemistry.* A polymer containing repeated amide linkages, as in various kinds of nylon.

pol·y·a·mine (pólli-áymeen) *n.* Any of a group of organic compounds that contain two or more amino groups.

pol·y·an·dry (pólli-andri) *n.* **1.** The state or practice of having more than one husband at a single time. **2.** *Botany.* The condition in flowers of having an indefinite number of stamens. **3.** The practice of a female animal's mating with more than one male during a single breeding season. [Greek *poluandria*, from *poluandros* : POLY- + -ANDROUS.] —**pol·y·an·drous** (-ándrəss) *adj.*

pol·y·an·thus (pólli-ánthəss) *n., pl.* **-thuses.** Any of a group of hybrid garden primroses, especially *Primula polyantha*, having clusters of variously coloured flowers. [New Latin, from Greek *poluanthos*, "having many flowers" : POLY- + -ANTHOUS.]

polyanthus narcissus *n.* A bulbous plant, *Narcissus tazetta*, native to Eurasia, having clusters of fragrant white or yellow flowers.

pol·y·a·tom·ic (pólli-ə-tómmik) *adj. Chemistry.* Having three or more atoms as constituents. Said especially of molecules.

pol·y·ba·sic (pólli-báy-sik) *adj. Chemistry.* Polyprotic.

pol·y·ba·site (pólli-báy-sīt, pə-líbbə-) *n.* A black mineral with a metallic lustre, containing silver, copper, antimony, arsenic, and sulphur, essentially $(Ag,Cu)_{16}(Sb,As)_2S_{11}$, often found in veins of silver. [German *Polybasit* : POLY- + BAS(IS) + -ITE.]

Po·ly·bi·us (po-líbbi-əs(s), pə-) (*c.*201–120 B.C.). Greek historian. His 40-volume history of Rome in the second and third centuries B.C. has mostly been lost.

pol·y·car·bon·ate (pólli-kárbə-nayt, -nit, -nət) *n.* Any of a class of clear, strong polyester resins, made from phosgene and dihydric phenols, and used in moulded articles.

pol·y·car·pel·lar·y (pólli-kaar-péllǝri ‖ *U.S.* -kárpə-lerri) *adj.* Having or consisting of many carpels. [POLY- + CARPEL + -ARY.]

pol·y·car·pic (pólli-kárpik) *adj. Botany.* Also **pol·y·car·pous** (-pəss) (for sense 1). **1.** Having fruit with two or more carpels. **2.** Producing flowers and fruit several times in one season. [POLY- + -CARPOUS.] —**pol·y·car·py** *n.*

pol·y·cen·trism (pólli-séntriz'm) *n.* The principle or advocacy, especially in Communism, of more than one possible dogma or political centre. —**pol·y·cen·trist** *n. & adj.*

pol·y·chaete (pólli-keet) *n.* Any of various marine worms of the class Polychaeta, including the lugworms, bristleworms, and ragworms, having paired, flattened, bristle-tipped organs of locomotion. [New Latin *Polychaeta*, from Greek *polukhaitēs*, with much hair : POLY + *khaitē*, long hair, CHAETA.] —**pol·y·chaete, pol·y·chae·tous** (-kéetəss) *adj.*

pol·y·chro·mat·ic (pólli-krō-máttik, -krə-) *adj.* Also **pol·y·chro·mic** (-krómik), **pol·y·chro·mous** (-króməss). **1.** Having many colours or manifesting changes of colour. **2.** *Physics.* Having a mixture of wavelengths. Said of light and other electromagnetic radiation. **3.** *Physics.* Having a mixture of energies. Said of streams of particles. —**pol·y·chro·ma·tism** (-krómə-tiz'm) *n.*

pol·y·chro·mat·o·phil·i·a (pólli-krō-máttə-fílli-ə, -krómətə-) *n.* Also **pol·y·chro·mo·phil·i·a** (-krómə-). Susceptibility to staining with more than one type of dye, as seen in diseased red blood cells. [POLY- + CHROMATO- + -PHILIA.] —**pol·y·chro·mat·o·phil·ic** *adj.*

pol·y·chrome (pólli-krōm) *adj.* **1.** Having many or various changing colours; polychromatic. **2.** Made or decorated in many or various colours.
~*n.* An object having or decorated in many colours. [Greek *polukhrōmos* : POLY- + -CHROME.]

pol·y·chro·my (pólli-krōmi) *n.* The art of employing many colours in decoration, especially as used in ancient architecture or pottery.

pol·y·con·ic projection (pólli-kónnik) *n. Geography.* A conic map projection having distances between meridians along every parallel of latitude equal to those distances on a globe. The central geographical meridian is a straight line and the others are curved, while the parallels are arcs of circles.

pol·y·cot·ton (pólli-kótt'n) *n.* A textile composed of a mixture of cotton and polyester fibres.

pol·y·cot·y·le·don (pólli-kótti-léed'n) *n. Botany.* A plant having several cotyledons. —**pol·y·cot·y·le·don·ous** *adj.*

pol·y·cy·clic (pólli-síklik, -sícklik) *adj. Chemistry.* Of or designating a compound with molecules that contain three or more rings of atoms.

pol·y·cy·thae·mi·a (pólli-sī-théemi-ə) *n. Pathology.* A condition marked by an abnormally large number of red cells in the blood. [POLY- + CYT(O)- + -HAEMIA.]

pol·y·dac·tyl (pólli-dáktil) *adj.* Also **pol·y·dac·ty·lous** (-əss). Having more than the normal number of fingers or toes.
~*n.* A polydactyl person or animal. [Greek *poludaktulos* : POLY- + DACTYL.] —**pol·y·dac·tyl·ism, pol·y·dac·ty·ly** *n.*

pol·y·dem·ic (pólli-démmik) *adj. Ecology.* Occurring in or inhabiting two or more regions. [POLY- + (EN)DEMIC.]

pol·y·dip·si·a (pólli-dípsi-ə) *n.* Excessive or abnormal thirst. [New Latin : POLY- + Greek *dipsa*, thirst.] —**pol·y·dip·sic** *adj.*

pol·y·em·bry·o·ny (pólli-émbri-əni, -em-brī-əni) *n. Biology.* The development of more than one embryo from a single egg or ovule, as occurs in the development of identical twins. [POLY- + Late Latin *embryō* (stem *embryōn*-) + -Y.] —**pol·y·em·bry·on·ic** (-émbri-ónnik) *adj.*

pol·y·es·ter (pólli-éstər) *n. Chemistry.* Any of numerous synthetic resins, produced chiefly by reaction of dibasic acids with dihydric alcohols. Reinforced polyester resins are light, strong, and weather-resistant, and are used in boat hulls, swimming pools, waterproof fibres, adhesives, and moulded parts. [POLY(MER) + ESTER.] —**pol·y·es·ter·i·fi·ca·tion** (-ifi-káysh'n) *n.*

pol·y·eth·ene (pólli-étheen) *n.* A synthetic material, **polythene** *(see)*. Also called "polyethylene".

pol·y·ether (pólli-éethər) *n.* Any of a large number of synthetic polymeric materials containing C-O-C linkages, as in the epoxy resins.

po·lyg·a·la (pə-líggələ) *n.* A plant, the **milkwort** *(see).* [New Latin *Polygala*, from Latin, from Greek *polugalon* : POLY- + *gala*, milk.]

po·lyg·a·mist (pə-líggəmist) *n.* One who practises polygamy.

po·lyg·a·my (pə-líggəmi) *n.* **1.** The state or practice of having more than one spouse at any one time, especially more than one wife, or in the case of animals, more than one female mate. **2. a.** The condition of having both hermaphrodite and unisexual flowers on the same plant. **b.** The condition of having hermaphrodite and unisexual flowers on different plants of the same species. [Old French *polygamie*, from Late Latin *polygamia*, from Greek *polugamia* : POLY- + -GAMY.] —**po·lyg·a·mous** *adj.* —**po·lyg·a·mous·ly** *adv.*

pol·y·gene (pólli-jeen) *n.* Any of a set of cooperating genes, each producing a small quantitative effect on a single characteristic.

pol·y·gen·e·sis (pólli-jénni-siss) *n.* The derivation of a species or type from more than one ancestor. Compare **monogenesis.** —**pol·y·ge·net·ic** (-jə-néttik), **pol·y·gen·ic** (-jénnik) *adj.*

pol·y·glot (pólli-glot) *adj.* Speaking, writing, written in, or composed of several languages.
~*n.* **1.** A person with a reading, writing, or speaking knowledge of several languages. **2.** A book, especially the Bible, containing versions of the same text in different languages. **3.** A mixture or confusion of languages. [French *polyglotte*, from Greek *poluglōttos* : POLY- + *glōtta*, *glōssa*, tongue.] —**pol·y·glot·ism, pol·y·glot·tism** *n.*

pol·y·gon (pólli-gən ‖ -gon) *n.* A closed plane figure bounded by three or more line segments. [Late Latin *polygōnum*, from Greek *polugōnon*, from *polugōnos*, "having many angles" : POLY- + -GON.] —**po·lyg·o·nal** (pə-líggən'l) *adj.* —**po·lyg·o·nal·ly** *adv.*

po·lyg·o·num (pə-líggənəm) *n.* Any of numerous plants of the widely distributed genus *Polygonum*, including knotgrass and bistort, characterised by stems with knotlike joints and heads of small pink or white flowers. [New Latin, from Greek *polugonon*, knotgrass : POLY- + *gonu*, knee.]

pol·y·graph (pólli-graaf, -graf) *n.* **1.** An instrument that simultaneously records changes in such physiological processes as heartbeat, blood pressure, and respiration, and is sometimes used in lie detection. **2.** A device that produces simultaneous copies of matter written, printed, or drawn. **3.** An author who is prolific or who writes many varying works. [Greek *polugraphos*, "writing a lot" : POLY- + -GRAPH.] —**po·lyg·ra·pher** (pə-líggrəfər) *n.* —**pol·y·graph·ic** (-gráffik) *adj.*

po·lyg·y·ny (pə-líjəni) *n.* **1.** The condition or practice of having more than one wife or female mate at a single time. **2.** The condition in flowers of having many styles. [POLY- + Greek *gunē*, woman.] —**po·lyg·y·nous** *adj.*

pol·y·he·dral angle (pólli-héedrəl). *Geometry.* A configuration formed by three or more planes having intersections that form a common vertex. Compare **solid angle.**

pol·y·he·dron (pólli-hée-drən, -hé-) *n., pl.* **-drons** or **-dra** (-drə). *Geometry.* A solid bounded by polygons. [New Latin, from Greek *poluedron*, neuter of *poluedros*, having many sides or seats : POLY- + -HEDRON.] —**pol·y·he·dral** *adj.*

pol·y·his·tor (pólli-hístər) *n.* A polymath. [Greek *poluistōr* : POLY- + *histōr*, learned.] —**pol·y·his·tor·ic** (-hiss-tórrik ‖ -táwrik) *adj.*

pol·y·hy·dric (pólli-hídrik) *adj.* Also **pol·y·hy·drox·y** (pólli-hī-dróksi). *Chemistry.* Containing at least two hydroxyl groups.

Pol·y·hym·ni·a (pólli-hím-ni-ə). *Greek Mythology.* The Muse of sacred song, poetry, and mime. [Latin, from Greek *Polumnia*, from *polumnos*, abounding in songs : POLY- + *humnos*, HYMN.]

pol·y·mas·ti·gote (pólli-másti-gōt) *adj. Zoology.* Having a tuftlike arrangement of flagella. [POLY- + Greek *mastix*† (stem *mastig*-), whip + -ATE.]

pol·y·math (pólli-math) *n.* A person of great or varied learning. [Greek *polumathēs* : POLY- + *math*, stem of *manthanein*, to learn.] —**pol·y·math, pol·y·math·ic** (-máthik) *adj.*

pol·y·mer (póllimər) *n. Chemistry.* A substance formed by linkage of numerous natural and synthetic compounds of usually high molecular weight of two or more repeated units. [From POLYMERIC.]

pol·y·mer·ic (pólli-mérrik) *adj. Chemistry.* Of, pertaining to, or consisting of a polymer. [Greek *polumerēs*, having many parts : POLY- + -MEROUS.] —**pol·y·mer·i·cal·ly** *adv.* —**po·lym·er·ism** (pə-límmə-riz'm, póllimə-) *n.*

pol·y·mer·ise, pol·y·mer·ize (póllimə-rīz, pə-límmə-) *v.* **-ised, -ising, -ises.** *Chemistry.* —*tr.* To cause (a chemical compound) to form a polymer. —*intr.* To react to form a polymer. Used of compounds. —**pol·y·mer·i·sa·tion** (-rī-záysh'n ‖ *U.S.* -ri-) *n.*

po·lym·er·ous (pə-límmərəss) *adj. Biology.* Consisting of numerous parts. [POLY- + -MEROUS.]

pol·y·me·thyl methacrylate (pólli-méethīl, -méthil) *n.* A clear synthetic material used extensively as a substitute for plate glass.

pol·y·morph (pólli-mawrf) *n.* **1.** *Biology.* An organism characterised by polymorphism. **2.** *Chemistry.* A specific crystalline form of a compound or mineral that can crystallise in different forms. **3.** Any of a group of white blood cells that have a lobed nucleus and granular cytoplasm. Also called "polymorphonuclear leucocyte". [From *polymorphous,* having many forms, from Greek *polumorphos* : POLY- + -MORPHOUS.]

pol·y·mor·phism (pólli-mórfiz'm) *n.* **1.** *Biology.* The occurrence of different forms, stages, or colour types in organisms of the same species. **2.** *Chemistry.* Crystallisation of a compound or mineral in at least two distinct forms. **—pol·y·mor·phic** (-mórfik), **pol·y·mor·phous** *adj.*

pol·y·myx·in (pólli-míksin) *n. Medicine.* Any of various mainly toxic antibiotics derived from strains of the soil bacterium *Bacillus polymixa* and used to treat a variety of infections. [New Latin *(Bacillus) polymixa* : POLY- + MYX(O)- + -IN.]

Pol·y·ne·sia (pólli-néezh-ə, -i-ə, -néezi-ə, -néeshə). A division of the Pacific islands, including New Zealand and the many smaller islands in the southern and central Pacific. The smaller islands are mostly coral islands and the larger ones volcanic. See also **Melanesia, Micronesia.** See map at **Pacific Ocean.**

Pol·y·ne·sian (pólli-née-zh'n, -zhi-ən, -zi-ən, -sh'n) *adj.* Of or pertaining to Polynesia, its inhabitants, culture, or languages.
~*n.* **1.** A member of the native peoples of Polynesia, including the Hawaiians, Maoris, Samoans, and Tahitians. **2.** A subfamily of Austronesian languages spoken in Polynesia.

pol·y·neu·ri·tis (pólli-newr-rítiss, -new- || -noor-, -noō-) *n.* Any disorder involving inflammation of all the peripheral nerves.

pol·y·no·mi·al (pólli-nōmi-əl) *adj.* Of, pertaining to, or consisting of more than two names or terms.
~*n.* **1.** *Biology.* A taxonomic name consisting of more than two terms. **2.** *Mathematics.* **a.** An algebraic function of two or more summed terms, each term consisting of a constant multiplier and one or more variables raised, in general, to integral powers. For example, the general form of a polynomial of degree n in a single real variable x is $a_0x^n + a_1x^{n-1} + \ldots + a_{n-1}x + a_n$ where $a_0, a_1, \ldots, a_n$ are real numbers with $a_0 \neq 0$ and n is a positive integer. **b.** Any mathematical expression of two or more terms. Also called "multinomial". [POLY- + (BI)NOMIAL.]

pol·y·nu·cle·o·tide (pólli-néw-kli-ə-tīd || -noō-) *n.* A compound consisting of a chain of linked nucleotides, such as the nucleic acids DNA and RNA.

po·lyn·ya (póllin-yaa, -yáa) *n.* A large area of open water surrounded by sea ice. [Russian *polyn'ya,* from *polyi,* open.]

pol·y·on·y·mous (pólli-ónniməss) *adj.* Having or called by several different names. [POLY- + -ONYM + -OUS.]

pol·yp (póllip) *n.* **1.** *Zoology.* A coelenterate having a cylindrical body and an oral opening usually surrounded by tentacles, such as a hydra or coral. Compare **medusa. 2.** *Pathology.* A growth protruding from the mucous lining of an organ, such as the nose. In this sense, also called "polypus". [French *polype,* from Latin *polypus,* from Greek *polupous,* "many-footed" : POLY- + *pous,* foot.] **—pol·yp·oid** *adj.*

pol·y·par·y (pólli-pəri || *U.S.* -perri) *n., pl.* **-ies.** Also **pol·y·par·i·um** (-páir-i-əm) *pl.* **-ia** *Zoology.* The common framework and base of a polyp colony, especially of coral. [From POLYP.]

pol·y·pep·tide (pólli-péptīd) *n. Biochemistry.* A **peptide** *(see)* containing between 10 and 100 amino acids.

pol·y·pet·al·ous (pólli-pétt'l-əss) *adj. Botany.* Having distinctly separate petals: *a polypetalous corolla.*

pol·y·pha·gi·a (pólli-fáy-ə, -ji-ə) *n.* An excessive or pathological desire to eat. [New Latin, from Greek *poluphagia,* from *poluphagos,* eating much, POLYPHAGOUS.] **—pol·y·pha·gi·an** *adj.*

po·lyph·a·gous (pə-líffəgəss) *adj. Zoology.* Feeding on or utilising a variety of foods. [Greek *poluphagos,* eating much : POLY- + -PHA-GOUS.]

pol·y·phase (pólli-fayz) *adj. Electricity.* Having, using, or pertaining to two or more alternating electrical signals with the same amplitudes but different phases; multiphase.

Pol·y·phe·mus (pólli-féeməss) *n. Greek Mythology.* The Cyclops who confined Odysseus and his companions in a cave until Odysseus blinded him and escaped.

pol·y·phone (pólli-fōn) *n. Phonetics.* A written character or combination of characters having two or more phonetic values, such as the letter *c* in *cake* and *certain.* [POLY- + -PHONE.]

pol·y·phon·ic (pólli-fónnik) *adj.* **1.** *Music.* **a.** Of or pertaining to polyphony. **b.** Of or designating an instrument that can sound more than one note at a time. **2.** Having many voices. **3.** *Phonetics.* Of or pertaining to a polyphone. **—pol·y·phon·i·cal·ly** *adv.*

polyphonic prose *n.* Prose that has a distinct rhythmic pattern and uses poetic devices so as to give the effect of verse, especially when read aloud.

po·lyph·o·ny (pə-líffəni, po-) *n., pl.* **-nies. 1.** The simultaneous combination of two or more independent melodic parts, especially when in close harmonic relationship; counterpoint. Compare **homophony, monophony. 2.** A style of composition, or a piece of music, incorporating polyphony. **3.** The representation of two or more sounds by one written character, such as the *c* in *cake* and *certain.* [Greek *poluphōnia,* variety of tones, from *poluphōnos,* having many tones : POLY- + *phōnē,* sound, PHONE.] **—po·lyph·o·nous** *adj.* **—po·lyph·o·nous·ly** *adv.*

pol·y·phy·let·ic (pólli-fī-léttik) *adj. Biology.* Pertaining to or charac-

terised by development from more than one ancestral type. **—pol·y·phy·let·i·cal·ly** *adv.*

pol·y·phy·o·dont (pólli-fí-ə-dont) *adj.* Having many sets of teeth that develop and are shed in succession. [New Latin, "producing many teeth", from Greek *poluphuēs* (POLY- + *-phuēs,* from *phuein,* to bring forth) + -ODONT.]

pol·y·ploid (pólli-ployd) *adj. Genetics.* Having more than twice the normal haploid chromosome number.
~*n. Genetics.* An organism with more than two sets of chromosomes. [POLY- + -PLOID.] **—pol·y·ploi·dic** (-plóydik) *adj.* **—pol·y·ploi·dy** (-ploydi) *n.*

pol·yp·noe·a (po-lípni-ə, pə-, póllip-née-ə) *n.* Very rapid breathing; panting. [New Latin : POLY- + Greek *pnoia,* breathing, from *pnein,* to breathe.] **—pol·yp·no·e·ic** *adj.*

pol·y·pod (pólli-pod) *adj.* Also **po·lyp·o·dous** (pə-líppədəss). Having numerous legs. Said of insect larvae and similar organisms.
~*n.* A polypod animal or organism. [Greek *polypous* (stem *polypod*-), "many-footed" : POLY- + *pous,* foot.]

pol·y·po·dy (pólli-pədi, -pōdi) *n., pl.* **-dies.** Any of various ferns of the widely distributed genus *Polypodium,* having simple or compound fronds and creeping rootstocks. Also called "wall fern". [Middle English *polypodie,* from Latin *polypodium,* from Greek *polupodion,* diminutive of *polupous,* POLYPOD.]

pol·y·pore (pólli-pawr || -pōr). A **pore fungus** *(see).*

pol·y·pro·pyl·ene (pólli-prōpi-leen) *n.* A synthetic, strong, polymeric material made from propene and used extensively in making moulded articles, such as kitchenware, toys, and chairs. Also called "polypropene".

pol·y·pro·tic (pólli-prōtik) *adj. Chemistry.* Designating an acid with two or more replaceable hydrogen atoms in each molecule; polybasic. [POLY- + PROT(ON) + -IC.]

pol·yp·tych (pólliptik) *n.* A decorated altarpiece or panel having four or more hinged sections which can be folded together. [Greek *poluptukhos,* having many folds : POLY- + *ptukhē,* a fold, from *ptussein†,* to fold.]

pol·y·pus (pólli-pəss) *n., pl.* **-pi** (-pī) or **-puses.** *Pathology.* A **polyp** *(see).* [Latin, POLYP.]

pol·y·rhyth·mic (pólli-ríthmik) *adj. Music.* Designating a composition or performer that has or uses several different rhythms, as for different parts, simultaneously. **—pol·y·rhythm** (-rith'm) *n.*

pol·y·sac·cha·ride (pólli-sáckə-rīd) *n.* Also **pol·y·sac·cha·rose** (-rōz, -rōss). A carbohydrate consisting of a group of nine or more monosaccharides joined by glycosidic bonds, such as starch and cellulose.

pol·y·se·my (pólli-seemi, pə-líssəmi) *n.* The quality or condition of an individual word having several different meanings at a given time. **—pol·y·se·mous** (pólli-séeməss, pə-líssəməss) *adj.*

pol·y·sep·al·ous (pólli-sépp'l-əss) *adj. Botany.* Having distinctly separated sepals.

pol·y·some (pólli-sōm) *n.* A structure in the cytoplasm of cells that consists of a group of ribosomes associated with messenger RNA. Also called "polyribosome". [POLY- + -SOME.]

pol·y·so·mic (pólli-sōmik) *adj. Genetics.* Having an excess number of one or more chromosomes, but not all. [POLY- + (CHROMO)-SOM(E) + -IC.] **—pol·y·so·my** (pólli-sōmi) *n.*

pol·y·sper·my (pólli-spermi) *n.* The entry of several sperms into an ovum during fertilisation. **—pol·y·sper·mic** (-spérmik) *adj.*

po·lys·ti·chous (pə-lístikəss, po-) *adj.* Arranged in two or more series or rows. Said especially of leaves on a stem.

pol·y·sty·rene (pólli-stīr-een) *n.* A polymeric form of styrene used either as a hard, rigid plastic for moulded articles, or as a white, light, expanded foam for packing and thermal insulation.

pol·y·sul·phide (pólli-súlfīd) *n. Chemistry.* A sulphur compound containing at least two sulphur atoms linked together per molecule.

pol·y·syl·lab·ic (pólli-si-lábbik) *adj.* **1.** Having more than three syllables. **2.** Characterised by words having more than three syllables. **—pol·y·syl·lab·i·cal·ly** *adv.*

pol·y·syl·la·ble (pólli-sillab'l) *n.* A polysyllabic word. [Medieval Latin *polysyllaba,* feminine of *polysyllabus,* polysyllabic, from Greek *polusullabos* : POLY- + *sullabē,* SYLLABLE.] **—pol·y·syl·lab·i·cism** (-si-lábbi-siz'm), **pol·y·syl·la·bism** (-sílləbiz'm) *n.*

pol·y·syn·de·ton (pólli-síndi-tən || -ton) *n.* The repetition of connectives or conjunctions in close succession for rhetorical effect, as in the phrase *here and there and everywhere.* [Late Greek *polusundeton,* from *polusundetos,* using many connectives : Greek, POLY- + *sundetos,* bound together (see **syndetic**).]

pol·y·syn·thet·ic (pólli-sin-théttik) *adj. Linguistics.* Designating a language, such as Eskimo, in which many of the elements of a sentence or phrase are combined into one word and do not exist separately; holophrastic. Compare **synthetic.**

pol·y·tech·nic (pólli-ték-nik) *adj.* **1.** Pertaining to technical training. **2.** Pertaining to or dealing with many arts or sciences.
~*n.* In Britain, a college of higher education teaching technical and vocational subjects and applied sciences up to degree level, generally called "university" since 1992. [French *polytechnique,* from Greek *polutekhnos,* skilled in many arts : POLY- + *tekhnē,* art.]

pol·y·tene (pólli-teen) *adj. Genetics.* Designating a chromosome in which the chromatids have remained unseparated after duplicating, resulting in a very large chromosome with conspicuous transverse bands.

pol·y·tet·ra·fluor·o·eth·y·lene (pólli-téttrə-floˊor-ō-éthi-leen) *n. Abbr.* **PTFE** A waxy, opaque-white, thermoplastic resin $(-C_2F_4)n,$ thermally stable, resistant to acids, alkalis, and oxidising agents, and having an extremely low coefficient of friction. It is used as a low-friction coating, especially for nonstick pans and for chemical-resistant gaskets, seals, and hoses. A trademark is "Teflon".

pol·y·the·ism (pólli-thee-iz'm, -thée-) *n.* The worship of or belief in more than one god. [French *polythéisme*, from Greek *polutheos*, believing in many gods : POLY- + *theos*, god.] —**pol·y·the·ist** *n.* —**pol·y·the·is·tic** (-thee-ístik) *adj.*

pol·y·thene (pólli-theen) *n.* Any of various synthetic polymeric materials made from ethene and used in moulded articles, pipes, coatings, and textiles. There are two main forms: *low-density polythene*, which is soft and flexible, and *high-density polythene*, which is harder and rigid. Also called "polyethylene", "polyethene". [Shortened from *polyethylene*.]

po·lyt·o·cous (pǝ-líttǝkǝss, po-) *adj. Biology.* Producing many offspring or ova at a single time. [Greek *polutokos*, bearing numerous offspring : POLY- + *tokos*, offspring, from *tiktein*, to beget.]

pol·y·ton·al·i·ty (pólli-tō-nál-ǝti) *n. Music.* The use or occurrence of two or more keys simultaneously in a composition. —**pol·y·ton·al** (-tōn'l) *adj.* —**pol·y·ton·al·ly** *adv.*

pol·y·troph·ic (pólli-tróffik ‖ -trôfik) *adj.* **1.** *Biology.* Obtaining nourishment from various types of organic material. **2.** *Pathology.* Characterised by or pertaining to excessive nutrition. [Greek *polytrophos*, well-fed : POLY- + *trephein*, to feed.]

pol·y·typ·ic (pólli-típpik) *adj.* Also **pol·y·typ·i·cal** (-'l). Existing in, having, or involving many different forms or types.

pol·y·un·sat·u·rat·ed (pólli-un-sáchǝ-raytid, -sáchoor-, -sáttewr-) *adj.* Of, pertaining to, or containing long chains of carbon atoms with numbers of double carbon-carbon linkages. Said especially of natural fats and oils used in margarines and cooking oils.

pol·y·ure·thane (pólli-yóor-ǝ-thayn; *also, wrongly,* -theen) *n.* Also **pol·y·ure·than** (-than). Any of various thermoplastic or thermosetting resins, of varying flexibility, used in paints, varnishes, adhesives, foams, and electrical insulation. Also called "urethane".

pol·y·u·ri·a (pólli-yóor-i-ǝ) *n. Pathology.* Excessive passage of urine, as in diabetes. [POLY- + -URIA.] —**pol·y·u·ric** *adj.*

pol·y·va·lent (pólli-váylǝnt) *adj.* **1.** *Microbiology.* Containing, sensitive to, or interacting with more than one kind of antigen, antibody, toxin, or microorganism. **2.** *Chemistry.* **a.** Having more than one valency. **b.** Having a valency of 3 or higher; multivalent. [POLY- + *valent*, from VALENCE.] —**pol·y·va·lence, pol·y·va·len·cy** *n.*

pol·y·vi·nyl (pólli-vín'l, -vínil) *adj.* Designating any of a group of polymerised thermoplastic vinyl compounds, such as PVC.

polyvinyl acetate *n. Abbr.* **PVA.** A common, clear, thermoplastic resin used in paints and adhesives.

polyvinyl chloride *n.* See **PVC.**

pol·y·zo·an (pólli-zō-ǝn) *n.* Any aquatic invertebrate animal of the phylum Polyzoa (or Bryozoa), consisting of a colony of polyp-like individuals. Also called "bryozoan". [New Latin *Polyzoa* : POLY- + -ZOA.] —**pol·y·zo·an** *adj.*

pol·y·zo·ar·i·um (pólli-zō-áir-i-ǝm) *n., pl.* **-aria** (-i-ǝ). Also **pol·y·zo·a·ry** (-zō-ǝri) *pl.* **-ries.** *Zoology.* A polyzoan colony or its supporting skeletal structure. [POLY- + -ZO(A) + -ARIUM.] —**pol·y·zo·ar·i·al** (-zō-áir-i-ǝl) *adj.*

pol·y·zo·ic (pólli-zō-ik) *adj. Biology.* **1.** Forming or consisting of a colony of zooids. **2.** Having many sporozoites. [POLY- + -ZOIC.]

pom (pom) *n. Australian & N.Z. Slang.* A British person; a pommy.

pom·ace (púmmiss) *n.* **1.** The pulpy residue remaining after the juice has been pressed from apples or other fruit. **2.** Any similar pulpy material, such as that remaining after the extraction of oil from nuts, seeds, or fish. [Middle English, from Medieval Latin *pōmācium*, cider, from Latin *pōmum*, apple.]

po·ma·ceous (po-máyshǝss, pō-) *adj.* **1.** Of, pertaining to, or characteristic of apples. **2.** Of, pertaining to, or bearing pomes. [New Latin *pomaceus* : Latin *pōmum*, apple (see POMACE) + -ACEOUS.]

po·made (po-maád, pǝ-, -máyd ‖ pō-) *n.* A perfumed ointment applied to the hair. Also called "pomatum".
~*tr.v.* **pomaded, -mading, -mades.** To apply pomade to. [French *pommade*, from Italian *pomata*, hair ointment (originally applescented), from *pomo*, apple, from Latin *pōmum*.]

po·man·der (pō-mándǝr, pǝ- ‖ pṓ-mandǝr) *n.* **1.** A mixture of aromatic substances carried in an apple-shaped container, formerly regarded as a protection against infection and now used to perfume rooms, wardrobes, or the like. **2.** A case or box for holding this mixture. [Middle English, variant of Old French *pome d'embre*, from Medieval Latin *pōmum de ambra*, "apple" or "ball of amber" : *pōmum*, apple, POME + *de*, of + *ambra*, AMBER.]

Pom·bal (pom-bál), **Sebastião José de Carvalho e Melo, Marquês de** (1699–1782). Portuguese statesman. As chief minister during most of the reign of King Joseph (1750–77), he was both a ruthless despot and a social and economic reformer.

pom·be (pómbay) *n. East African.* An alcoholic drink made from grain, especially from millet. [Swahili.]

pome (pōm) *n. Botany.* A fleshy fruit in which the ovary and seeds are enclosed in an enlarged receptacle, such as the apple, pear, or quince. [Middle English, from Old French *pomme, pome,* apple, from Vulgar Latin *pōma* (unattested), from Latin *pōmum*.]

pome-gran·ate (pómmi-grannit, pómmǝ-, póm- ‖ U.S. *also* púm-) *n.* **1.** A semitropical shrub or small tree, *Punica granatum*, native to Asia, and widely cultivated for its edible fruit. **2.** The fruit of this tree, having a tough, reddish rind, and containing many seeds enclosed in a juicy red pulp with a mildly acid flavour. [Middle English *poumgarnei, pomegranard,* from Old French *pome grenate* :

pome, apple, POME + *grenate,* having many seeds, from Latin *grānātus,* from *grānum,* grain.]

pom·e·lo (pómmi-lō, púmmi-) *n., pl.* **-los.** The **grapefruit** or **shaddock** (*both of which see*). [19th century : origin obscure.]

Pom·e·ran·i·a (pómmǝ-ráyni-ǝ). Former region of central Europe, now absorbed into eastern Germany and Poland (1945). It extends from the Baltic Sea to the river Vistula in a low-lying plain.

Pom·er·a·ni·an (pómmǝ-ráyni-ǝn) *adj.* Of or relating to Pomerania or its people.
~*n.* **1.** A native or inhabitant of Pomerania. **2.** A toy dog of a breed having long, silky hair and a small body.

pom·fret cake (púm-frit, póm-) *n.* A soft, round, flat, liquorice sweet. Also called "pomfret", "Pontefract cake". [From *Pomfret*, earlier form of PONTEFRACT, where it was originally made.]

pom·i·cul·ture (pómmi-kulchǝr ‖ U.S. pṓmi-) *n.* The cultivation of fruit. [Latin *pōmum*, fruit, POME + CULTURE.]

po·mif·er·ous (po-míffǝrǝss, pō-) *adj. Botany.* Bearing pomes. [Latin *pōmifer*, fruit-bearing : *pōmum*, fruit, POME + -FER.]

pom·mel (púmm'l, pómm'l) *n.* **1.** A knob on the hilt of a sword or other weapon. **2.** The raised front part of a saddle; a saddlebow. ~*tr.v.* **pommelled** or *U.S.* **pommeled, -melling** or *U.S.* **-meling, -mels.** To beat; pummel. [Middle English *pomel*, from Old French, from Vulgar Latin *pōmellum* (unattested), rounded knob, diminutive of Latin *pōmum*, fruit, apple, POME.]

pom·my, pom·mie (pómmi) *n., pl.* **-mies.** *n. Sometimes capital* **P.** *Australian & N.Z. Slang.* A British person. Often used derogatorily. [20th century : origin obscure.]

po·mol·o·gy (po-móllǝji) *n.* The scientific study and cultivation of fruit. [New Latin *pomologia* : Latin *pōmum*, fruit, POME + -LOGY.] —**po·mo·log·i·cal** (pómmǝ-lójik'l ‖ U.S. pṓmǝ-) *adj.* —**po·mo·log·i·cal·ly** *adv.* —**po·mol·o·gist** (-móllǝjist) *n.*

Pomona. See **Mainland.**

pomp (pomp) *n.* **1.** Dignified or magnificent display; splendour. **2.** Vain or ostentatious display. [Middle English, from Old French *pompe,* from Latin *pompa,* from Greek *pompē,* "a sending", solemn procession, from *pempein*, to send.]

pom·pa·dour (póm-pǝ-door, pón-, -dawr ‖ -dōr) *n.* **1.** A woman's hairstyle, popular in the 18th century, formed by sweeping the hair straight up from the forehead, into a high, turned-back roll. **2.** A man's hair style with the hair brushed up from the forehead. [Invented by the Marquise de POMPADOUR.]

Pom·pa·dour (póm-pǝ-door, pón-, -dawr ‖ -dōr), **Marquise de,** also known as Madame de Pompadour; born Jeanne Antoinette Poisson (1721–64). Mistress of King Louis XV of France. She was popularly blamed for engineering France's alliance with Austria, which led to the disastrous Seven Years' War (1756–63).

pom·pa·no (póm-pǝ-nō, púm-) *n., pl.* **-nos** or collectively **pompano.** Any of several marine food fishes of the genus *Trachinotus*; especially, *T. glancus*, of tropical and temperate Atlantic waters. [Spanish *pámpano*†.]

Pom·pei·i (pom-páy-ee). Ancient city of Campania, southern Italy. Situated on the Gulf of Naples, it was buried by the eruption of Mt. Vesuvius (A.D. 79). Since its rediscovery (1748), excavations have provided an invaluable insight into ancient Roman life.

Pom·pey (pómpi), *also called* Pompey the Great; Latin name Gnaeus Pompeius Magnus (106–48 B.C.). Roman general and statesman. He suppressed the slave revolt led by Spartacus and campaigned on the Empire's eastern frontiers. He joined Julius Caesar and Crassus to form a ruling triumvirate in 60 B.C. He broke with Caesar in 50 B.C. but was defeated by him at Pharsala in 48 B.C. and fled to Egypt, where he was murdered.

Pom·pi·dou (pómpi-dōō; *French* PON-pee-dṓō), **Georges (Jean Raymond)** (1911–74). French statesman and president. He served as adviser (1944–46) and personal assistant (1958–59) to de Gaulle, helping to draft the constitution of the Fifth Republic. He was prime minister four times and helped to negotiate a settlement between France and the Algerians (1961) and to defuse the student revolt (1968). He succeeded de Gaulle as president (1969–74).

pompom[1] *n.* Also **pom·pon** (póm-pon). **1.** A tuft or ball of wool, feathers, or other material worn as a decoration, especially on a hat. **2.** A small, button-like flower of certain chrysanthemums and dahlias. [French *pompon*†.]

pom·pom[2] (póm-pom) *n.* **1.** In World War I, a variety of large machine gun using one-pound shells. **2.** In World War II, an automatic, rapid-fire, antiaircraft cannon. [Imitative.]

pom·pous (pómpǝss) *adj.* **1.** Characterised by an exaggerated show of dignity or self-importance; pretentious. **2.** Self-important in speech or manner. **3.** *Archaic.* Characterised by pomp or stately display; ceremonious. [Middle English, from Old French *pompeux,* from Late Latin *pompōsus,* from Latin *pompa,* POMP.] —**pom·pos·i·ty** (pom-póssǝti) *n.* —**pom·pous·ly** *adv.* —**pom·pous·ness** *n.*

'pon (pon). *Archaic.* Contraction of **upon.**

ponce (ponss) *n. Chiefly British.* **1.** A man who lives off the earnings of a prostitute; a pimp. **2.** *Slang.* A flashy, showy, and often effeminate man. Used derogatorily.
~ *intr.v.* **ponced, poncing, ponces.** *Chiefly British.* **1.** To be a ponce. **2.** *Slang.* **a.** To act in a flashy, showy, and often effeminate manner. Usually used with *about* or *around*. **b.** To do something in an ostentatious, inefficient, or frivolous manner. Usually used with *about* or *around*. [Perhaps from POUNCE.]

Ponce de Le·ón (pónss dǝ lée-ǝn; *Spanish* pón-thay the-lay-ón), **Juan** (1460–1521). Spanish explorer. He sailed with Columbus on his second voyage (1493–94) and started the settlement of Puerto

Rico in 1508, becoming its governor (1509–12). He discovered Florida in 1513, but when starting a settlement there in 1521 he was killed in a skirmish with the local inhabitants.

pon·cey, pon·cy (pón-si) *adj. Slang.* Characteristic of a ponce; especially, flashy or showy. Used derogatorily.

pon·cho (pónchō) *n., pl.* **-chos. 1.** A blanket-like cloak having a hole in the centre for the head, worn originally in South America. **2.** A similar garment worn instead of a jacket or coat, or as a shawl. [American Spanish, from Araucanian *pontho*, woollen fabric.]

pond (pond) *n.* A still body of water, smaller than a lake, often of artificial construction.

~v. ponded, -ponding, ponds. —*intr.* To form a pond. —*tr.* To confine in, or as if in, a pond; dam up. [Middle English *ponde, pounde,* enclosure, Old English *pund-.*]

pon·der (póndər) *v.* **-dered, -dering, -ders.** —*tr.* To weigh mentally; consider carefully. —*intr.* To meditate; deliberate; reflect. Often used with *on* or *upon.* [Middle English *ponderen,* from Old French *ponderer,* from Latin *ponderāre,* to weigh, ponder, from *pondus* (stem *ponder-*), weight.] —**pon·der·er** *n.*

pon·der·a·ble (póndərə-b'l) *adj.* Capable of being weighed or assessed; appreciable.

~n. A factor or consideration that can be assessed. —**pon·der·a·bil·i·ty** (-bílləti) *n.*

pon·der·ous (póndər-əss) *adj.* **1.** Having great weight; massive; huge. **2.** Graceless or unwieldy from weight. **3.** Lacking fluency; laboured; dull: *a ponderous speech.* —See Synonyms at **heavy.** [Middle English, from Old French *pondereux,* from Latin *ponderōsus,* from *pondus* (stem *ponder-*), weight.] —**pon·der·ous·ly** *adv.* —**pon·der·os·i·ty** (-óssəti) *n.,* —**pon·der·ous·ness** *n.*

Pon·di·cher·ry (póndi-chérri, -shérri). Union Territory of southeast India. On the Coromandel Coast, it was a former French territory (founded 1674), reverting to Indian control in 1954.

pond lily *n.* The **water lily** *(see).*

Pon·do (póndō) *n., pl.* **-dos** or collectively **Pondo.** A member of a Xhosa-speaking black people of southern Africa, living chiefly in Pondoland in Transkei. —**Pon·do** *adj.*

pon·dok (pón-dok) *n.* Also **pon·dok·kie** (pon-dócki). *South African.* **1.** A crude or roughly built hut or shelter; a shack. **2.** A very small or dilapidated house. [Afrikaans, perhaps from Malay, hut, or from Hottentot, hut.]

pond scum *n.* Any of various freshwater algae that form a usually greenish scum on the surface of stagnant water.

pond skater *n.* Any water insect of the family Gerridae, having a slender body and long legs used to skim across the water's surface. Also called "skater", "water strider".

pond·weed (pónd-weed) *n.* **1.** Any of various submerged or floating aquatic plants of the genus *Potamogeton.* **2.** Any of various similar plants, such as **Canadian pondweed** *(see).*

pone (pōn, póni) *n.* In card games, the player on the dealer's right or, in two-handed games, the dealer's opponent. [Latin, "play!", from second-person singular imperative of *ponere,* to put, place.]

pong (pong) *n. British Informal.* An unpleasant smell; a stink.

~intr.v. ponged, ponging, pongs. *British Informal.* To give off an unpleasant smell; stink. [20th century : origin obscure.] —**pong·y** (póng-gi) *adj.*

pon·gee (pónjee, pon-jée) *n.* **1.** A soft, thin undyed cloth of Chinese or Indian silk with a knotty weave. **2.** A synthetic fabric resembling this. [Mandarin Chinese *běn zhī,* "homemade" : *běn,* own, self + *zhī,* weave.]

pon·gid (póng-gid, pónjid) *n.* Any primate of the family Pongidae; an **anthropoid ape** *(see).*

~adj. Of or pertaining to the family Pongidae. [New Latin *Pongidae,* from *Pongo* (genus), from Congolese *mpongo,* ape.]

pon·go (póng-gō) *n., pl.* **-gos.** *British Military Slang.* A serviceman, especially one in the army. [From PONG.]

pon·iard (pón-yərd, -yaard) *n.* A dagger.

~tr.v. poniarded, -iarding, -iards. To stab with a poniard. [French *poignard,* from *poing,* fist, from Old French, from Latin *pugnus.*]

pons (ponz) *n., pl.* **pontes** (pónteez). *Anatomy.* **1.** Any slender tissue joining two parts of an organ. **2.** The **pons varolii.** [Latin *pōns,* bridge.]

pons as·i·no·rum (ássi-náwrəm ‖ -nórəm) *n.* **1.** A proposition in the first book of Euclid, stating that the angles opposite the equal sides of an isosceles triangle are equal. **2.** A problem difficult for beginners. [Latin, "asses' bridge" (the fifth proposition of Euclid mentioned in sense 1, supposedly very difficult to "cross"): *pōns,* PONS + *asinōrum,* genitive plural of *asinus,* ASS.]

pons va·ro·li·i (və-rōli-ī) *n.* A band of nerve fibres in the brain connecting the medulla oblongata and the mesencephalon below the cerebellum. Also called "pons". [New Latin, "bridge of Varoli", after Constanzo *Varoli* (1542–75), Italian surgeon and anatomist.]

pont (pont) *n. South African.* A flat-bottomed ferryboat, moved by a cable, rope, or chain attached at both sides of a river bank. [Afrikaans, from Dutch, ferryboat, PUNT.]

Pon·ta Del·ga·da (pónta del-gaádə). Largest city of the Azores, situated on São Miguel Island. It is a tourist centre and fuelling point for shipping.

Pon·te·fract (pónti-frakt; *formerly* púm-frit). Town in west Yorkshire, northern England. Britain's first parliamentary election by secret ballot was held here in 1872. Important for coalmining (once) and (still) for liquorice sweets and pomfret cakes.

Pontefract cake *n.* A **pomfret cake** *(see).*

Pon·tic (póntik) *adj.* Of or pertaining to the Black Sea region.

[Latin *Ponticus,* from Greek *Pontikos,* from *Pontos,* PONTUS.]

pon·ti·fex (pónti-feks) *n., pl.* **pontifices** (pon-tíffi-seez). **1.** In ancient Rome, a member of the Pontifical College, the highest college of priests, headed by the *Pontifex Maximus.* **2.** A pontiff. [Latin, probably from Etruscan, reshaped by folk etymology as if to mean "bridge-maker".]

pon·tiff (póntif) *n.* **1. a.** The pope. **b.** *Archaic.* A bishop. **2.** A pontifex. [French *pontif,* from Latin *pontifex,* PONTIFEX.]

pon·tif·i·cal (pon-tíffik'l) *adj.* **1.** Pertaining to, characteristic of, or suitable for a pope or bishop. **2.** Having the dignity, pomp, or authority of a pontiff. **3.** Pompously authoritative.

~n. 1. *Plural.* The vestments and insignia of a pontiff. **2.** A book of ceremonies and rites for a bishop. [Latin *pontificālis,* from *pontifex,* PONTIFEX.] —**pon·tif·i·cal·ly** *adv.*

pon·tif·i·cate (pon-tíffi-kət, -kit, -kayt) *n.* The office or term of office of a pontiff.

~intr.v. (-kayt) pontificated, -cating, -cates. 1. To serve as a pontiff. **2.** To speak or behave with pompous authority. [Latin *pontificātus,* from *pontifex,* PONTIFEX.]

pon·ti·fy (pónti-fī) *intr.v.* **-fied, -fying, -fies.** To speak or behave with pompous authority; pontificate.

pon·til (póntil) *n.* A glassmaker's tool, a **punty** *(see).* [French, perhaps from Italian *puntello,* diminutive of *punto,* point, from Latin *punctum,* from the neuter past participle of *pungere,* to prick.]

pon·tine (póntīn) *adj.* **1.** Of or pertaining to bridges. **2.** Pertaining to the **pons varolii** *(see).* [Latin *pōns* (stem *pont-*), bridge.]

Pontine Marshes. Reclaimed area in south Latium, central Italy. Drainage was completed in the 1930s, destroying malarial breeding grounds and providing rich agricultural land.

Pontius Pilate. See **Pilate.**

Pont l'É·vêque (pón lay-vék) *n.* A soft-centred square French cheese made of whole cows' milk. [After *Pont L'Évêque,* town in northern France.]

pon·to·nier (pónta-néer) *n. Military.* A person in charge of pontoons or engaged in the construction of pontoon bridges. [French *pontonnier,* from *ponton,* PONTOON.]

pon·toon[1] (pon-tōōn, pón-) *n.* **1. a.** A flat-bottomed boat or other structure used to support a floating bridge. **b.** A floating structure serving as a dock. **2.** A float on a seaplane. [French *ponton,* floating bridge, from Old French, from Latin *pontō* (stem *pontōn-*), boat bridge, from *pōns,* bridge.]

pontoon[2] *n.* **1.** A card game in which the aim is to hold cards that have a score higher than those of the banker, but no higher than 21. **2.** A winning hand in this game, consisting of an ace and a court card or ten, that adds up to exactly 21. Also called "vingt-et-un", "twenty-one". [Probably from French *vingt-et-un,* twenty-one.]

pontoon bridge *n.* A temporary floating bridge using pontoons for support. Also called "bateau bridge".

Pon·tus (póntəss). Ancient kingdom in northeast Asia Minor. Situated on the south shore of the Black Sea, it reached its peak under Mithridates VI but declined after his defeat by Pompey (c.65 B.C).

Pon·ty·pool (pónt-i-pōōl, *Welsh* -ə-). Town in southeast Wales. Situated on the South Wales coalfield, it began smelting iron ore in 1577 and was an early centre for the manufacture of tinplate.

Pon·ty·pridd (pónt-i-preéth, *Welsh* -ə-). Town in south Wales. Important for coalmining (once) and light engineering (still).

po·ny (póni) *n., pl.* **-nies. 1.** A horse of any of several small breeds, not over 14.2 hands high. **2.** *Informal.* A racehorse. **3.** *U.S.* A translation or summary used as an aid in studying or examinations; a **crib** *(see).* **4.** Anything small for its kind, such as a liqueur glass. **5.** *British Slang.* The sum of 25 pounds.

~intr.v. ponied, -nying, -nies. *U.S. Slang.* To pay money owed or due. Used with *up.* [Earlier *powny,* probably from obsolete French *poulenet,* diminutive of *poulain,* from Late Latin *pullāmen,* from Latin *pullus,* foal.]

pony express *n.* In the United States, a postal system using relays of ponies; specifically, the system in operation from St. Joseph, Missouri, to Sacramento, California (1860–61).

po·ny·tail (póni-tayl) *n.* A hairstyle, as for girls or women, in which the hair is clasped at the back so as to hang down like a tail.

pony trekking *n.* The practice or pastime of riding cross-country on ponies.

poo (pōō) *n. Informal.* Faeces. Used by or to young children.

~intr.v. pooed, pooing, poos. *Informal.* To defecate. Used by or to young children. [Imitative.]

pooch (pōōch) *n. Chiefly U.S. Informal.* A dog. [20th century : origin obscure.]

pood (pōōd) *n.* A former Russian weight equivalent to about 16.4 kilograms (36 pounds). [Russian *pud,* from Old Norse *pund,* POUND.]

poo·dle (pōōd'l) *n.* A dog of any of various breeds originally developed in Europe as hunting dogs, having thick, curly hair, and ranging in size from the fairly large standard poodle to the very small toy poodle. [German *Pudel(hund),* "poodle (dog)", probably from Low German *(pudeln,* to splash), "splashing dog" (because the poodle was originally trained as a water dog); akin to Old English *pudd,* ditch. See **puddle.**]

poof, pouffe, pouf (pōōf, pŏŏf) *n.* Also **poove** (pōōv), **puff.** *British Slang.* **1.** A male homosexual. Used derogatorily. **2.** An effeminate or weak man. [19th century : perhaps akin to PUFF (noun), in the sense "braggart".] —**poof·y, poov·ey** *adj.*

poof·ter, poof·tah (pōōf-tər, pŏŏf-) *n. British Slang.* A poof. Also called "woofter".

pooh (pōō) *interj.* Used to express disdain or disgust. [Imitative.]

Pooh-Bah (pōō-baä) *n.* A pompous, ostentatious official; especially, one who, holding many offices, fulfils none of them. [After the Lord-High-Everything-Else in W.S. Gilbert's *Mikado* (1885).]

pooh-pooh (pōō-pōō) *tr.v.* **-poohed, -poohing, -poohs.** *Informal.* To express contempt or disdain for; dismiss or make light of. [Reduplication of POOH.]

pool¹ (pōōl) *n.* **1.** A small body of still water; a small pond. **2.** A puddle of any liquid. **3.** A deep place in a river or stream. **4.** A **swimming pool** (*see*). **5.** An underground reservoir, as of oil or gas. [Middle English, Old English *pōl,* from West Germanic *pōla-, pōl-* (unattested).]

pool² *n.* **1.** In certain gambling games, the total amount staked by all players. **2. a.** A supply of people with certain skills, material resources, or the like that can be drawn on: *a typing pool.* **b.** Any grouping of resources for the common advantage of the participants: *a car pool.* **3.** *Finance. Chiefly U.S.* **a.** A mutual fund established by a group of shareholders for speculating in or manipulating prices of securities. **b.** The persons or parties participating in such a combination. **4. a.** An agreement between competing business concerns to establish controls over production, market, and prices for common profit. **b.** The group of concerns participating in such an agreement. **5.** In fencing, a match in which each member of a team fences successively with each member of an opposing team. **6.** Any of several games played on a six-pocket billiard table, usually with 15 object balls and a cue ball. Also called "pocket billiards". Compare **billiards.**
~*v.* **pooled, pooling, pools.** —*tr.* To combine (money, funds, or interests) into a common stock for mutual benefit. —*intr.* To join or form a pool. [French *poule,* stakes, target (as in *jeu de la poule,* "game of the hen"), hen, from Late Latin *pullus,* hen, from Latin, young of an animal.]

Poole (pōōl). Coastal resort and Unitary Authority area, southwest England. It was once an important port, but today relies on such industries as pottery, chemicals, boatbuilding, and tourism.

pool·room (pōōl-rōōm, -rōōm) *n. U.S.* A commercial establishment or room for the playing of pool or billiards.

pools (pōōlz) *pl.n. Informal.* The **football pools** (*see*).

pool table *n.* A six-pocket billiard table on which pool is played.

poon (pōōn) *n.* **1.** Any of several trees of the genus *Calophyllum,* of southern and eastern Asia, having light, hard wood used for masts and spars. **2.** The wood or medicinal oil obtained from any of these trees. [Singhalese *pūna,* probably from Tamil *punnai.*]

Poo·na (pōōnə). See **Pune.**

poop¹ (pōōp) *n. Nautical.* **1.** The superstructure at the stern of a ship. **2.** The **poop deck.**
~*tr.v.* **pooped, pooping, poops.** *Nautical.* **1.** To break over the stern of (a ship). Used of waves. **2.** To be subjected to the breaking of (waves). Used of a ship or ship's stern. [Middle English, from Old French *poupe,* from Latin *puppis†.*]

poop² *tr.v.* **pooped, pooping, poops.** *U.S. Slang.* To cause to become fatigued or exhausted; tire. Usually used in the passive.
—**poop out.** *U.S.* To give up because of exhaustion: *poop out of the race.* [20th century : origin obscure.]

poop³ *n. U.S. Slang.* Inside information. [20th century : origin obscure.]

poop deck *n. Nautical.* The deck at the stern of a ship built above the main deck. Also called "poop".

poor (poor, por ‖ pōr) *adj.* **poorer, poorest. 1. a.** Having little or no wealth and few or no possessions; poverty-stricken. **b.** *Law.* Dependent on charity or public funds; destitute. **c.** Wanting or lacking in financial or other resources: *an area poor in timber and coal.* **2. a.** Lacking in mental or moral quality; ignoble: *a poor loser; a poor spirit.* **b.** Inferior; inadequate; inefficient: *a poor memory.* **3. a.** Lacking desirable elements or constituents: *Poor soil leads to poor milk.* **b.** Bad or ill; weak: *poor health.* **4. a.** Lacking in value or quality; trivial: *a poor exchange.* **b.** Lacking in quantity: *poor attendance.* **5. a.** Humble: *in my poor opinion.* **b.** Needing or deserving pity; pitiable: *poor old Sarah, in trouble again.* [Middle English *povere, poure,* from Old French *povre,* from Latin *pauper.*] —**poor·ness** *n.*

poor box *n.* A box, especially in a church, for collecting charitable donations.

poor·house (poor-howss, pór- ‖ pōr-) *n.* Formerly, an establishment maintained at public expense as a place for the accommodation and sometimes employment of paupers; a workhouse.

poori. Variant of **puri.**

poor law *n.* Formerly, a law or system of laws providing for public relief and support of the poor.

poor·ly (poor-li, pór- ‖ pōr-) *adv.* In a poor manner.
~*adj.* In poor health; ailing; ill: *Emily's feeling poorly.* See Synonyms at **sick.**

poor man's weatherglass *n.* A plant, the scarlet pimpernel. See **pimpernel.** [So called because its blossoms open only in fair weather.]

poor relation *n.* Something thought of as inferior when compared with a similar thing or class of things; something overshadowed by or receiving less attention than another.

poor white *n.* A member of a socially deprived, exploited, and poverty-stricken class of white farmers and labourers, especially in the American South and South Africa. Often used derogatorily.

poove. Variant of **poof.**

pop¹ (pop) *v.* **popped, popping, pops.** —*intr.* **1.** To make a short, light, explosive sound. **2.** To burst open with such a sound. **3.** To move quickly or unexpectedly; appear abruptly: *pop round to the shops; she popped up from nowhere.* **4.** To open wide suddenly so as to protrude: *His eyes popped with interest.* **5.** In baseball, to hit a short high fly ball that can be caught by an infielder. **6.** To shoot a pistol or other firearm. —*tr.* **1.** To cause to make a sharp bursting sound: *beer bottles being popped open.* **2.** To cause to burst open or explode with such a sound. **3.** To put or thrust quickly or suddenly: *She popped the crisp into her mouth.* **4.** To fire (a pistol or other firearm). **5.** To fire at; shoot. **6.** *British Informal.* To pawn: *He popped all the silver.* **7.** *Slang.* To take or swallow (drugs in pill form), usually habitually. —**pop off.** *Informal.* **1.** To leave abruptly or hurriedly. **2.** To die. **3.** *U.S.* To speak in a burst of vehement anger.
~*n.* **1.** A sudden, light, explosive sound. **2.** A shot with a firearm. **3.** *Informal.* A non-alcoholic, flavoured, carbonated drink, such as lemonade. —**in pop.** *British Informal.* In pawn; pawned.
~*adv.* **1.** With a popping sound. **2.** Abruptly or unexpectedly. [Middle English *poppen* (imitative).]

pop² *n.* **1.** A father. **2.** An old man. In both senses, used as a familiar term of address. [Short for *poppa,* variant of PAPA.]

pop³ *n.* Pop music (*see*).
~*adj.* **1.** Of, pertaining to, or specialising in pop. **2.** Of, pertaining to, or suggestive of pop art. [Short for POPULAR.]

Pop *n.* A club and debating society at Eton College.

pop. **1.** popular. **2.** population.

pop art *n.* A form of art that depicts objects of everyday life and adapts techniques of commercial art, such as comic strips.

pop-corn (póp-kawrn) *n.* **1.** A variety of maize, *Zea mays everta,* having hard kernels that burst when heated to form white, irregularly shaped puffs. **2.** The edible, popped kernels of popcorn. [Contraction of *popped corn.*]

pope¹ (pōp) *n.* **1.** *Often capital* **P.** The bishop of Rome and head of the Roman Catholic Church on earth, and considered by Catholics to be, by apostolic succession from St. Peter, the vicar of Christ on earth. **2.** *Eastern Orthodox Church.* **a.** A priest. **b.** The patriarch of Alexandria. **3.** The head of the Coptic Church in Egypt. **4.** Any figure considered to have unquestioned authority: *the pope of surrealism.* [Middle English, Old English *pāpa,* from Late Latin, from Greek *pappas,* title of bishops, PAPA.]

pope² *n.* A fish, the ruffe (*see*). [From POPE (prelate).]

Pope, Alexander (1688–1744). English poet. He is best known for the famous satirical, mock-epic poems *The Rape of the Lock* (1712; 1714) and *The Dunciad* (1728; 1743). He also wrote philosophical poems such as *An Essay on Man* (1733–34), and edited Shakespeare and translated Homer.

pope·dom (pōp-dəm) *n.* The office, jurisdiction, or tenure of a pope; the papacy.

pop·er·y (pōp-əri) *n.* The doctrines, practices, and rituals of the Roman Catholic Church. Used derogatorily.

pope's nose *n.* The **parson's nose** (*see*).

pop-eyed (póp-īd) *adj.* **1.** Having bulging eyes. **2.** Amazed; astonished: *popeyed at the spectacle.*

pop·gun (póp-gun) *n.* A toy gun that operates by compressed air, firing corks or pellets with a popping noise.

pop·in·jay (póppin-jay) *n.* **1.** A vain, supercilious person; a fop. **2.** *Archaic.* A parrot. [Middle English *papejay, papengay,* parrot, from Old French *papegai,* from Spanish *papagayo,* from Arabic *babaghā.*]

pop·ish (pōpish) *adj.* Of or pertaining to the popes or the Roman Catholic Church. Used derogatorily. —**pop·ish·ly** *adv.* —**pop·ish·ness** *n.*

Popish Plot *n.* See Titus **Oates.**

pop·lar (póppler) *n.* **1.** Any of several fast-growing deciduous trees of the genus *Populus,* having triangular leaves and soft, light wood. See **aspen, cottonwood, Lombardy poplar. 2.** The wood of any of these trees. **3.** Loosely, the **tulip tree** (*see*). [Middle English *poplere,* from Anglo-French, Old French *poplier,* earlier *pople,* from Latin *pōpulus.*]

pop·lin (pópplin) *n.* A light, ribbed fabric of silk, rayon, wool, or cotton, used in making clothing and upholstery. [Obsolete French *papeline,* from Italian *papalina,* feminine of *papalino,* papal, from Medieval Latin *papalis,* from Late Latin *papa,* POPE (the fabric was first made at the papal town of Avignon).]

pop·lit·e·al (pop-lítti-əl, póppli-tée-əl) *adj.* Of or pertaining to the part of the leg behind the knee joint. [New Latin *popliteus,* from Latin *poples†* (stem *poplit-*), the hollow of the knee.]

pop music *n.* Modern music, often electrically amplified, typically using simple melodies and strong rhythms and having a broad, popular appeal, especially to young people. Also called "pop".

Po·po·ca·te·petl, Mount (póppə-kátta-pétt'l; *Spanish* -ka-táy-pett'l). Dormant volcano in central Mexico. It is 5 452 metres (17,887 feet) high.

pop·o·ver (póp-ōvər) *n.* A very light, puffy, hollow muffin of American origin, made with eggs, milk, and flour. [So called because it pops up over the rim of the baking tin.]

pop·pa·dom, pop·pa·dum (póppədəm) *n.* A thin, round, savoury Indian biscuit, usually fried in oil and served with curry. [Tamil *pappatam,* probably from *parappu,* "lentil", "pulse" + *atam,* "something cooked".]

pop·per (póppər) *n.* **1.** One that pops. **2.** A **press-stud** *(see).* **3.** *Slang.* A drug, **amyl nitrite** *(see),* inhaled for sensual gratification. **4.** *Chiefly U.S.* A basket or pan in which popcorn is popped.

Pop·per (póppər). **Sir Karl (Raimund)** (1902–94). British philosopher, born in Austria. He proposed that any theory, to qualify as a scientific theory, must in principle be falsifiable. His best-known works are *The Logic of Scientific Discovery* (1934), *The Open Society and its Enemies* (1945), and *The Poverty of Historicism* (1957). **—Pop·per·i·an** (po-péer-i-ən) *adj.*

pop·pet (póppit) *n.* **1.** A poppet valve. **2.** *Nautical.* **a.** A small wooden strip on the gunwale of a boat that forms or supports the oarlocks. **b.** Any of the beams of a launching cradle supporting a ship's hull. **3.** *Chiefly British.* A sweet, endearing person, animal, or child; a darling. [Middle English *popet,* child, doll, PUPPET.]

poppet valve *n.* An intake or exhaust valve, operated by springs and cams, that opens by axial motion. Also called "poppet".

pop·ping crease (pópping) *n.* In cricket, a line four feet in front of the wicket and parallel with the bowling crease at which the batsman stands when receiving a ball and behind which he must keep his bat or foot to avoid being stumped. Also called "batting crease".

pop·ple (pópp'l) *intr.v.* **-pled, -pling, -ples.** To move in a tossing, bubbling, or rippling manner, as choppy water does.
~*n.* **1.** Choppy or bubbling water. **2.** The sound made by boiling liquid. [Middle English *poplen,* from Middle Dutch *popelen*†, quiver (imitative).]

pop·py (póppi) *n., pl.* **-pies.** **1.** Any of numerous plants of the genus *Papaver,* of temperate regions, having conspicuous red, orange, or white flowers, and a milky white juice. See **opium poppy.** **2.** Any of several similar or related plants, such as the **California poppy** and the **horned poppy** *(both of which see).* **3.** The narcotic extracted from the opium poppy. **4.** Vivid red to reddish orange. **5.** An artificial poppy worn on Remembrance Sunday and days leading up to it. [Middle English *popi,* Old English *popig, popaeg,* altered from Vulgar Latin *papāvum* (unattested), variant of Latin *papāver*†.]

pop·py·cock (póppi-kok) *n.* Senseless talk; nonsense. [Dutch dialect *pappekak,* "soft dung" : *pap,* soft food, pap, from Middle Dutch *pappe,* probably from Latin *pappa,* father, food + *kak,* dung, from *kakken,* to defecate, from Latin *cacāre.*]

Poppy Day *n.* **Remembrance Sunday** *(see).* [From the custom of wearing artificial poppies, after the *Flanders poppy,* flower chosen to commemorate the casualties of the World Wars.]

pop·py·head (póppi-hed) *n.* **1.** The seed capsule of a poppy. **2.** An ornamental carving on the top end of a church bench or pew.

pop-shop (póp-shop) *n. British Informal.* A pawnshop.

Pop·si·cle (pópsik'l) *n. U.S.* A trademark for an ice lolly.

pop·sy, pop·sie (pópsi) *n., pl.* **-sies.** *British Informal.* **1.** A young, pretty woman. **2.** A girlfriend. [Irregularly from POPPET + -Y.]

pop·u·lace (póppew-ləss, -liss) *n.* **1.** The common people; the masses. **2.** A population. [French, from Italian *popolaccio,* rabble, from *popolo,* the people, from Latin *populus.*]

pop·u·lar (póppewlər) *adj. Abbr.* **pop.** **1.** Widely liked or appreciated by the public. **2. a.** Liked by friends, associates, or acquaintances; sought after for company. **b.** Liked or appreciated by an individual or group: *Cats are not popular with me.* **3.** Of, representing, or carried on by the common people or the people at large: *a popular uprising.* **4.** Fit for or reflecting the taste and intelligence of the broad mass of people: *a popular newspaper.* **5.** Accepted by, originating with, or prevalent among the people in general: *a popular misunderstanding.* **6.** Suited or appealing to ordinary people, as by being within their financial means: *popular prices.* [Latin *populāris,* of the people, from *populus,* people.] **—pop·u·lar·ly** *adv.*

popular front *n.* Any of various political coalitions formed in European countries during the 1930s, as an alliance of democratic, left-wing, and revolutionary parties having common interests in the struggle against reaction and fascism.

pop·u·lar·ise, pop·u·lar·ize (póppewlə-rīz) *tr.v.* **-ised, -ising, -ises.** To make popular; especially, to cause to become readily intelligible to the layman: *a programme popularising science.* **—pop·u·lar·i·sa·tion** (-rī-zaysh'n || *U.S.* -ri-) *n.* **—pop·u·lar·is·er** *n.*

pop·u·lar·i·ty (póppew-lárrəti) *n.* The quality or state of being popular, especially of being widely admired or sought after.

popular music *n.* Light music, typically being melodic and emotionally evocative, and having a broad, popular appeal.

pop·u·late (póppew-layt) *tr.v.* **-lated, -lating, -lates.** **1.** To supply with inhabitants, as by colonisation; fill with people. **2.** To inhabit or become inhabitants of. **3.** *Physics & Chemistry.* To cause (quantum states or energy levels) to be occupied. [Medieval Latin *populāre,* to people, from Latin *populus,* people.]

pop·u·la·tion (póppew-láysh'n) *n. Abbr.* **p., pop.** **1. a.** All the people inhabiting a specified area. **b.** The total number of such people. **2.** The total number of inhabitants of a particular race, class, or group in a specified area. **3.** The act or process of furnishing with inhabitants. **4.** *Ecology.* All the organisms that constitute a specific interbreeding group, especially a species, inhabiting a specified habitat. **5.** *Statistics.* The entire set of individuals, items, or scores from which a sample is drawn. Also called "universe". **6.** *Astronomy.* Either of two classes to which stars can be assigned according to their age, distribution, and content of metal: *population I,* which contains young, luminous, metal-rich stars found in the spiral arms of galaxies; and *population II,* which contains older, metal-deficient stars found in the Galactic halo.

population density *n.* The number of people, plants, or animals in a given unit area.

population explosion *n.* A sudden sharp increase in population caused by a rise in the birth rate or a decline in the death rate, or both. [Late Latin *populātiō,* from Latin *populus,* people.]

population inversion *n. Physics.* A condition in which the usual or unexcited energy level of atoms in laser material is less heavily populated than a higher level, making stimulated emission and laser action possible.

pop·u·lism (póppew-liz'm) *n.* **1.** A political philosophy directed to the needs of the common people and advocating a more equitable distribution of wealth and power. **2.** A style of political or personal conduct displaying identification with the interests, attitudes, or activities of the common people.

pop·u·list (póppewlist) *n.* **1.** An advocate of populism. **2.** *Capital* **P.** A member of a U.S. political party, *the Populist Party* or *People's Party,* formed in 1892 to represent agrarian interests and disappearing in the early years of the 20th century.
~*adj.* Pertaining to or characteristic of populism or its advocates.

pop·u·lous (póppewləss) *adj.* Containing many people or inhabitants; thickly settled or populated. [Middle English *populus,* from Latin *populōsus,* from *populus,* people.] **—pop·u·lous·ly** *adv.* **—pop·u·lous·ness** *n.*

pop-up (póp-up) *adj.* **1.** Having a mechanism that springs upwards or makes an object spring upwards: *a pop-up toaster.* **2.** Designating a book having paper or pages cut and folded in such a way that, when opened, pictures of figures and objects spring up.

por·bea·gle (pór-beeg'l) *n.* A shark, *Lamna nasus,* of temperate Atlantic waters. Also called "mackerel shark". [Cornish *porghbugel*†.]

por·ce·lain (pórss-lin, pór-sə-, -layn || pṓrss-, pṓr-sə-) *n.* **1.** A hard, white, translucent ceramic made by firing a pure clay and glazing with variously coloured fusible materials; china. Also used adjectivally: *a porcelain vase.* **2.** An object or objects collectively made of this material. [French *porcelaine,* from Old French *pourcelaine,* from Italian *porcellana,* "of a sow", hence cowry shell, hence porcelain (from the resemblance of the shell to a sow's vulva), from *porcella,* diminutive of *porca,* sow, from Latin, feminine of *porcus,* swine.] **—por·ce·la·ne·ous** (-sə-láyni-əss) *adj.*

porcelain clay *n.* **Kaolin** *(see).*

porcelain enamel *n.* A silicate glass fired on metal. Also called "vitreous enamel".

porch (porch || pōrch) *n.* **1.** A covered platform, usually having a separate roof, at an entrance to a house. **2.** *U.S.* An open or enclosed gallery or room attached to the outside of a building; a verandah. **3.** *Archaic.* A portico or covered walk. **—the Porch.** Zeno's Stoic school of philosophy, so named from the portico in Athens where he instructed his pupils. [Middle English *porche,* from Old French, from Latin *porticus,* PORTICO.]

por·cine (pór-sīn) *adj.* Of, pertaining to, or resembling a pig. [Latin *porcīnus,* from *porcus,* pig.]

por·cu·pine (pórkew-pīn) *n.* Any of various rodents, especially of the genera *Hystrix* and *Erethizon,* characteristically covered with long, sharp quills or spines. [Middle English *porkepin,* from Old French *porc espin,* "spiny pig", from Vulgar Latin *porcospīnus* (unattested) : Latin *porcus,* pig + *spīna,* thorn.]

porcupine fish *n.* Any of various spiny tropical marine fishes of the family Diodontidae; especially, *Diodon holocanthus,* capable of inflating itself when attacked.

porcupine grass *n.* Any of various Australian grasses of the genus *Triodia.* See **spinifex.**

pore[1] (por || pōr) *intr.v.* **pored, poring, pores.** **1.** To read or study carefully and attentively. Usually used with *over*: *pore over a book.* **2.** To meditate deeply; ponder. Usually used with *over.* **3.** *Rare.* To gaze steadily or earnestly. [Middle English *pouren*†.]

pore[2] *n.* **1.** A minute orifice, such as one in the skin of an animal, serving as an outlet for perspiration, or in a plant leaf or stem, serving as a means of absorption and transpiration. **2.** Any minute surface opening or passageway, as in a rock. [Middle English, from Old French, from Latin *porus,* from Greek *poros,* passage.]

pore fungus *n.* Any fungus having a crustlike fruiting body with a pitted or porous surface. Also called "polypore".

por·gy (pórgi) *n., pl.* **-gies** or collectively **porgy.** **1.** Any of various North American marine fishes of the family Sparidae. **2.** Any of several similar or related fishes. [18th century : **origin obscure.**]

po·rif·er·an (pə-riffərən, paw-) *n.* Any animal of the phylum Porifera, which includes the sponges. [New Latin *Porifera,* neuter plural of *porifer,* bearing pores : Latin *porus,* PORE + -FER.] **—po·rif·er·al, po·rif·er·an** *adj.*

po·rif·er·ous (pə-riffərəss, paw-) *adj.* **1.** Having pores. **2.** *Zoology.* Of or pertaining to the phylum Porifera, which includes the sponges. [From PORE + -FEROUS.]

pork (pork || pōrk) *n.* The flesh of a pig used as food. [Middle English, from Old French *porc,* pig, from Latin *porcus.*]

pork barrel *n. U.S. Slang.* A government project or appropriation benefiting a specific area and constituents.

pork·er (pórkər || pṓrkər) *n.* **1.** A fattened young pig. **2.** *Informal.* One who resembles a pig, as in being fat and greedy.

pork·ling (pórk-ling || pṓrk-) *n.* A young or small pig.

pork pie *n.* A thick-crusted pie filled with minced pork and usually served cold.

pork·pie hat (pórk-pī || pṓrk-) *n.* A man's hat having a low, flat crown and a brim that can be turned up or down. [From a fancied reemblance.]

pork·y (pórki || pṓrki) *adj.* **1.** Pertaining to or resembling pork: *a porky flavour.* **2.** *Informal.* Fat or fleshy. **—pork·i·ness** *n.*

porn (pórn) *n. Slang.* Pornography.
—*adj. Slang.* Also **por·no** (pórnō). Pornographic.
por·nog·ra·phy (pawr-nóggrəfi) *n.* **1.** Written, graphic, or other material intended solely to excite feelings of sexual lust, and usually considered obscene. **2.** The trade in or production of such material. **3.** Any activity, or representations of it, considered obscene or offensive: *the pornography of violence.* [Greek *pornographos,* writing about prostitutes : *pornē,* harlot, prostitute + -GRAPH.] —**por·nog·ra·pher** *n.* —**por·no·graph·ic** (pórnə-gráffik) *adj.*
por·o·mer·ic (páw-rə-mérrik ‖ pō-) *adj.* Permeable to water vapour. Said of synthetic materials used in making shoes, for example.
— *n.* A poromeric material. [PORE + -MER + -IC.]
po·ros·i·ty (paw-róssəti, pə- ‖ pō-) *n., pl.* **-ties. 1.** The state or property of being porous. **2.** *Geology.* A measure of this property, equal to the volume of air in a rock divided by the total volume. **3.** A structure or part that is porous. [Middle English, from Medieval Latin *porōsitās* (stem *porōsitāt-*), from *porōsus,* POROUS.]
po·rous (páwr-əss ‖ pōr-) *adj.* **1.** Having or full of pores. **2.** Admitting the passage of gas or liquid through pores or interstices. [Middle English, from Medieval Latin *porōsus,* from Latin *porus,* PORE.] —**po·rous·ly** *adv.* —**po·rous·ness** *n.*
porous pot *n. Chemistry.* A plate or container of porous fireclay, used to separate electrolytes in a cell or to support a semipermeable membrane.
por·phyr·i·a (pawr-fírri-ə) *n.* A hereditary disease involving disturbance in the metabolism of porphyrins and producing symptoms of mental confusion, neuritis, and abdominal pain. [New Latin, from PORPHYRIN, which colours the faeces of porphyria patients.]
por·phy·rin (pórfi-rin) *n. Biochemistry.* Any of various nitrogen-containing, heterocyclic organic compounds occurring widely in plant and animal tissues and providing the foundation structure for haemoglobin, chlorophyll, and certain enzymes. [Greek *porphura,* PURPLE (from its colour).]
por·phy·ry (pórf-iri, -əri) *n., pl.* **-ries.** *Geology.* Igneous rock containing relatively large conspicuous crystals, especially feldspar, in a fine-grained matrix. [Middle English *porfurie,* red or purple stone, from Medieval Latin *porphyrium,* from Latin *porphyrītēs,* purple-coloured stone, from Greek *porphurītēs,* from *porphura,* PURPLE.] —**por·phy·rit·ic** (-i-ríttik), **por·phy·rit·i·cal** *adj.*
por·poise (pórpəss) *n., pl.* **-poises** or collectively **porpoise. 1.** Any of several gregarious aquatic mammals of the genus *Phocaena* and related genera, of oceanic waters, characteristically having a blunt snout and a triangular dorsal fin. **2.** Broadly, any of several related mammals, such as the **dolphin** (*see*). [Middle English *porpoys,* from Old French *porpois,* from Vulgar Latin *porcopiscis* (unattested) : Latin *porcus,* a pig + *piscis,* fish.]
por·ridge (pórrij) *n.* **1.** Oatmeal or similar ground grain, cooked in milk or water and often eaten at breakfast. **2.** *British Slang.* A prison sentence; time in prison. —**do porridge.** *British Slang.* To serve a sentence in prison. [Variant (influenced by Middle English *porray,* a pottage) of POTTAGE.]
por·rin·ger (pórrinjər) *n.* A shallow cup or bowl with a handle. [Alteration of *pottinger,* Middle English *potinger, poteger,* from Old French *potager,* from *potage,* POTTAGE.]
port¹ (port ‖ pōrt) *n. Abbr.* **pt. 1. a.** A town having a harbour for ships taking on or discharging cargoes. **b.** A place on a waterway that provides a harbour for a nearby town. **2.** A place of shelter; a haven. **3.** A **port of entry** (*see*). [Middle English, from Old English and Old French, both from Latin *portus,* house door, port.]
port² *n.* The left-hand side of a ship or aircraft when facing forwards. Compare **starboard.**
—*adj.* On the left-hand side.
—*tr.v.* **ported, porting, ports.** To turn or shift (the helm of a vessel) to the left. [17th century : probably referring to the side of a ship usually facing the port.]
port³ *n.* **1.** *Nautical.* **a.** An opening in the side of a ship used for access. **b.** A porthole. **2.** An opening for a gun to be fired through, as in a tank or wall. **3.** An opening, as in a cylinder or valve face, for the passage of steam or fluid. **4.** *Scottish.* A gateway or portal, as to a town. **5.** A point at which data can be input or output for a computer. [Middle English, opening, from Old French *porte,* gate, door, from Latin *porta.*]
port⁴ *n.* **1.** A rich, sweet fortified wine of Portugal. **2.** Any of various similar wines produced in other countries. [Short for *Oporto,* port in northwest Portugal (Portuguese *o porto,* "the port"), from which it was shipped.]
port⁵ *tr.v.* **ported, porting, ports.** *Military.* To carry (a rifle, sword, or other weapon) diagonally across the body, with the muzzle or blade near the left shoulder.
—*n.* **1.** *Military.* The position of a rifle or other weapon when ported. **2.** The manner in which a person carries himself; bearing. [Middle English, "a bearing", from Old French, from *porter,* to bear, from Latin *portāre.*]
Port. Portugal; Portuguese.
port·a·ble (pór-təb'l ‖ pōr-) *adj.* **1.** Capable of being carried. **2.** Easily carried or moved. **3.** *Archaic.* Endurable; bearable.
—*n.* Something that is portable, such as a light typewriter. [Middle English, from Old French, from Late Latin *portābilis,* from Latin *portāre,* to carry.] —**port·a·bil·i·ty** (-tə-bílləti), **port·a·ble·ness** *n.* —**port·a·bly** *adv.*
Port Adelaide. Chief port of South Australia, serving Adelaide.
port·age (pórt-ij ‖ pōrt-, pawr-tá*a̱zh*) *n.* **1. a.** The act or process of carrying; transport. **b.** The cost of such transporting. **2. a.** The car-

rying of boats and supplies overland between two waterways. **b.** A place, track, or route used in such transporting.
—*v.* **portaged, -aging, -ages.** —*tr.* To transport by portage. —*intr.* To carry boats and supplies overland. [Middle English, from Old French, from Medieval Latin *portāgium,* from Latin *portāre,* to carry.]
por·tal (pórt'l ‖ pōrt'l) *n.* **1.** A doorway, entrance, or gate; especially, one that is large and imposing. **2.** *Often plural.* Any entrance or means of entrance: *portals of knowledge.*
—*adj.* Of or pertaining to the portal vein. [Middle English, from Old French, from Medieval Latin *portāle,* a city gate, porch, from *portālis,* of a gate, from Latin *porta,* a gate.]
portal system *n.* A vein or group of veins that terminates at both ends in a capillary bed, such as the *hepatic portal system.*
por·tal-to-por·tal (pórt'l-tə-pórt'l ‖ pōrt'l-tə-pōrt'l) *adj. Chiefly U.S.* Of or based on the time spent on an employer's property, from the moment of arrival to that of departure: *portal-to-portal pay.*
portal vein *n. Anatomy.* A vein that conducts blood from one organ to another organ other than the heart.
por·ta·men·to (pór-tə-mén-tō ‖ pōr-) *n., pl.* **-ti** (-tee). *Music.* A smooth, uninterrupted glide in passing from one tone to another, especially with the voice or a bowed string instrument. [Italian, "a carrying", from *portare,* to carry, from Latin *portāre.*]
Port Arthur. See **Lüda.**
por·ta·tive (pór-tətiv ‖ pōr-) *adj.* **1.** Portable. **2.** Of or pertaining to carrying. [Middle English *portatif,* from Old French, from Latin *portāre,* to carry.]
Port-au-Prince (pórt-ō-prínss; French -pránss). Capital of Haiti, West Indies. It is the country's chief port and commercial centre.
Port Blair (blair). Administrative centre and main port of the Andaman and Nicobar Islands, lying on South Andaman Island.
port·cul·lis (pórt-kúlliss ‖ pōrt-) *n.* A sliding grille of iron or wood suspended in the gateway of a fortified place in such a way that it can be quickly lowered in case of attack. [Middle English *porculis, port colice,* from Old French *porte coleïce : porte,* gate, from Latin *porta* + *coleïce,* feminine of *couleïs,* sliding, from *couler,* to slide, from Latin *colāre,* to strain, from *cōlum,* sieve.]
Porte (port ‖ pōrt) *n.* The government or court of the Ottoman Empire. [French (*la Sublime*) *Porte,* "(the High) Gate" (translation of Turkish *Bab-i Ali*), from Old French *porte,* gate, PORT.]
porte-co·chère, porte-co·chere (pórt-ko-shaír ‖ pōrt-, -kō-) *n.* **1.** A supported roof projecting from an entrance to a building, such as a hotel, providing shelter for those getting in and out of vehicles. **2.** Formerly, a carriage entrance leading into a courtyard. [French *porte cochère,* "coach-door" : Old French *porte,* gate, PORT + *cochère,* for coaches, from *coche,* COACH.]
Port Elizabeth. Seaport and industrial centre in Eastern Cape Province, Republic of South Africa. It was settled by the British in 1799. Its industries include vehicle assembly and fruit canning.
por·tend (pawr-ténd ‖ pōr-) *tr.v.* **-tended, -tending, -tends.** To serve as an omen or warning of; presage. See Synonyms at **foretell.** [Middle English *portenden,* from Latin *portendere: por-,* variant of PRO- + *tendere,* to stretch.]
por·tent (pór-tent ‖ pōr-) *n.* **1.** An indication of something momentous or calamitous about to occur; an omen. **2.** Prophetic or threatening significance: *a vision of dire portent.* **3.** Something amazing or miraculous; a marvel. [Latin *portentum,* from *portendere* (past participle *portentus*), to PORTEND.]
por·ten·tous (pawr-téntəss ‖ pōr-) *adj.* **1.** Marked by pompousness; pretentiously weighty. **2.** Full of unspecifiable significance; exciting wonder and awe; prodigious: *a portentous monster.* **3.** Of the nature of or constituting a portent; foreboding; ominous. —**por·ten·tous·ly** *adv.* —**por·ten·tous·ness** *n.*
por·ter¹ (pórt-ər ‖ pōrt-) *n.* **1. a.** A person employed to carry luggage, as at a hotel or railway station. **b.** A person who accompanies an expedition of explorers or mountaineers and carries equipment and supplies; a bearer. **2.** *U.S.* A railway employee who waits on passengers. [Middle English *portour,* from Old French *porteur,* from Late Latin *portātor,* from Latin *portāre,* to carry.]
porter² *n. Chiefly British.* **1.** A gatekeeper; a doorman, especially in a large building. **2.** A person in charge of the entrance and entrance hall of a building such as a college, who deals with enquiries and often has caretaking responsibilities. **3.** *Roman Catholic Church.* Formerly, an ordinand in the lowest of the minor orders. [Middle English, from Old French *portier,* from Late Latin *portārius,* from Latin *porta,* a gate.]
porter³ *n.* A dark beer resembling light stout, made from malt browned by drying at a high temperature. [Shortened from *porter's beer* or *ale* (originally brewed especially for porters).]
Por·ter (pórt-ər ‖ pōrt-), **Cole** (1893–1964). U.S. composer. He wrote the music and lyrics for musical comedies such as *High Society* and *Kiss Me Kate.* Among his popular songs is "Night and Day".
Porter, Katherine Anne (1890–1980). U.S. writer. Her volumes of shorts stories include *Flowering Judas* (1930) and *Pale Horse, Pale Rider* (1939). Her only novel is *Ship of Fools* (1962).
por·ter·age (pór-tərij ‖ pōr-) *n.* **1.** The carrying of parcels or goods as done by porters. **2.** The charge for this.
por·ter·house (pór-tər-howss ‖ pōr-) *n.* **1.** In 19th-century America, an alehouse or chophouse. **2.** A cut of beef taken from the chump end of the sirloin, having a T-bone and a piece of fillet. In this sense also called "**porterhouse steak**". [PORTER (beer) + HOUSE.]
port·fo·li·o (pórt-fóli-ō ‖ pōrt-) *n., pl.* **-os. 1.** A portable case used for holding loose sheets of paper, drawings, maps, and the like.

b. Such a case used for holding official documents such as those of a government ministry, or for samples of an artist's work. **2.** The office, post, or responsibility of a cabinet member or minister of state. **3. a.** An itemised list of the investments, securities, and other financial assets owned by a bank, investment organisation, or other investor. **b.** The investments and assets so listed. [Italian *portafoglio* : *portare*, to carry, from Latin *portāre* + *foglio*, leaf, sheet, from Latin *folium*.]

Port Glasgow. Town in west central Scotland. It is situated on the river Clyde estuary to the west of Glasgow. Its industries include shipbuilding and engineering.

Port Har·court (hár-kərt, -kawrt). Deepwater port in southeast Nigeria. It is the centre of the country's oil industry.

port·hole (pórt-hōl ‖ pōr-) *n.* **1.** A small, usually circular window in a ship's side. **2.** An opening in a fortified wall; an embrasure.

por·ti·co (pór-tikō ‖ pōr-) *n., pl.* **-coes** or **-cos.** A porch or walkway with a roof supported by columns, often leading to the entrance of a building. [Italian, from Latin *porticus,* porch, from *porta,* a gate.] **—por·ti·coed** *adj.*

por·ti·ère, por·ti·ere (pór-ti-aír ‖ pōr-) *n.* A heavy curtain hung across a doorway. [French *portière,* from *porte,* door, from Old French, gate, PORT.]

por·tion (pór-sh'n ‖ pōr-) *n.* **1.** A section or quantity within a larger thing; a part of a whole. **2.** A part separated from a whole. **3.** A part that is allotted to a person or group, such as: **a.** The amount of food or of a specific dish, served to one person at a meal; a helping. **b.** The part of an estate received by an heir. **4.** *Archaic.* A woman's dowry. **5.** *Archaic.* One's allotment of human destiny; one's lot or fate: *Liars will have their portion in Hell.* ~*tr.v.* **portioned, -tioning, -tions. 1.** To divide into parts or shares for distribution; parcel out. Usually used with *out.* **2.** *Archaic.* To provide with a share, inheritance, or dowry. [Middle English, from Old French, from Latin *portiō* (stem *portiōn-*).] **—por·tion·a·ble** *adj.* **—por·tion·er** *n.* **—por·tion·less** *adj.*

Port Jackson. Also **Sydney Harbour.** Inlet of the Pacific Ocean in New South Wales, Australia. The fine harbour is spanned by Sydney Harbour Bridge (opened 1932), the world's second longest steel arch bridge, with a span of 503 metres (1,652 feet).

Port·land (pórt-lənd, pōrt-). Deepwater port and largest city in Oregon, United States. It is a major exporter of wood, grain, and fruit.

Portland, Isle of. Peninsula in Dorset, south England, connected to the mainland by Chesil Bank. Its limestone quarries have provided the stone for such buildings as St. Paul's Cathedral, London.

Portland, William Henry Cavendish Bentinck, 3rd Duke of (1738–1809). British statesman. He was twice prime minister, first as a Whig (1783) and later as a Tory (1807–09).

Portland cement *n.* A hydraulic cement made by heating a mixture of limestone and clay in a kiln and pulverising the resultant clinker. [It resembles *Portland stone,* quarried at the Isle of PORTLAND.]

Port Laoi·se or **Port Laoighi·se** (leésha). County town of Laois, Leinster province, Republic of Ireland. It is a market town, and its industries include malting and flour milling.

Port Lou·is (lōō-iss, lōō-i). Capital and seaport of Mauritius. Founded in 1735 by the French, it exports sugar and rum.

port·ly (pórtli ‖ pōrtli) *adj.* **-lier, -liest. 1.** Being stout and corpulent and having a dignified bearing. Said especially of an adult man. **2.** *Archaic.* Stately; majestic; imposing. —See Synonyms at **fat.** [From PORT (bearing).] **—port·li·ness** *n.*

port·man·teau (pórt-mán-tō ‖ pōrt-) *n., pl.* **-teaus** or **-teaux** (-tōz). *Chiefly British.* A large suitcase that opens into two hinged compartments. [French *portemanteau,* from Old French, "coat-carrier" : *porter,* to carry, from Latin *portāre* + MANTEAU.]

portmanteau word *n.* A word formed by merging the sounds and meanings of two different words; a blend; for example, *chortle,* from *chuckle* and *snort.* ["You see, it's like a *portmanteau . . .* there are two meanings packed up in one word." (Lewis Carroll).]

Port·mei·ri·on (pórt-mír-i-ən, -maír-; *Welsh* -yon). Resort in north Wales, near Porthmadog. Begun in 1926 by Sir Clough Williams-Ellis (1883–1979), it resembles the Italian village of Portofino.

Port Mo·res·by (mórz-bi ‖ mōrz-). Capital of Papua New Guinea. It is a major commercial centre and port.

port of call *n.* **1.** A port where ships dock in the course of voyages to load or unload cargo, obtain supplies, or undergo repairs. **2.** A stopping-place on a journey; a place visited.

port of entry *n. Abbr.* **P.O.E.** A place where travellers or goods may officially enter or leave a country. Also called "port".

Port of Spain. Capital and chief port of Trinidad and Tobago, West Indies. It is situated on Trinidad, on the Gulf of Paria.

Por·to No·vo (pórtō nṓvō). Capital and chief port of Benin, West Africa. It was an important centre of the slave trade and the capital of a native kingdom during the 19th century.

por·trait (pór-trit, -trət, -trayt ‖ pōr-) *n.* **1.** A painting, photograph, or other visual likeness, usually of a person; especially one showing the face. **2.** A verbal picture or description, especially of a person. **3.** Any close likeness of one thing to another. [French, from Old French, from the past participle of *portraire,* PORTRAY.]

por·trait·ist (pór-trətist ‖ pōr-) *n.* A person who makes portraits, especially a painter or photographer.

por·trai·ture (pór-tri-chər, -trə-, -tewr ‖ pōr-) *n.* **1.** The practice or art of making portraits. **2.** A portrait. **3.** Portraits collectively.

por·tray (pawr-tráy ‖ pōr-) *tr.v.* **-trayed, -traying, -trays. 1.** To depict or represent pictorially; make a picture of. **2.** To depict or describe in words. **3.** To represent dramatically, as on the stage. [Middle

English *portraien,* from Old French *portraire,* from Latin *prōtrahere,* to draw forth, reveal (in Medieval Latin, also "to portray") : *prō,* forth + *trahere,* to draw.] **—por·tray·a·ble** *adj.* **—por·tray·er** *n.*

por·tray·al (pawr-tráy-əl ‖ pōr-) *n.* **1.** The act or process of depicting or portraying. **2.** A representation or description.

por·tress (pór-triss, -trəss, -tress ‖ pōr-) *n.* A female doorkeeper or porter, especially in a convent.

Port Sa·id (saá-eed, sīd). City in northeast Egypt, on the Mediterranean coast. It was founded in 1859 at the entrance to the new Suez Canal. Its main industry is the fuelling and servicing of ships.

Port Sa·lut (pór-sə-lōō, -sa-; *French* -sa-lü) *n.* A mild, semihard fermented French cheese, made originally by Trappist monks.

Ports·mouth (pórts-məth ‖ pōrts-). City and Unitary Authority area, southern England. It is situated on Portsea Island at the entrance to Portsmouth Harbour and is Britain's main naval base.

Port Stanley. Also **Stanley.** Capital of the Falkland Islands, lying on East Falkland island. It is the islands' only town and chief port.

Port Su·dan. Chief port of Sudan, on the Red Sea. It was founded in 1907 as the terminus of the railway to the Nile valley.

Port Tal·bot (táwl-bət ‖ tól-, tál-). Town in south Wales, situated at the mouth of the river Avon on Swansea Bay. Its many steelworks were affected by cutbacks in the late 1970s.

Por·tu·gal (pór-tew-g'l, -choo- ‖ pōr-). *Abbr.* **Port.** Republic of southwest Europe, situated on the Iberian peninsula; in ancient times the Roman province of Lusitania. Its coastal plain rises to mountains in the north and east. It is one of western Europe's poorer countries, but manufacturing is expanding, and in 1979 provided nearly as many jobs as farming. Textiles and clothing, chemicals, cork, wine, wood, fish, and fruit are the main exports. There are rich mineral resources, including tungsten, copper, and uranium. Tourism is important in the economy, as is the money sent home by overseas workers. Portugal became a kingdom in the 12th century, and during the 15th century established an empire as a result of exploring Africa, discovering Brazil, and finding the sea route to India. It was ruled by Spain (1580–1640), invaded by France (1807), and in 1910 became a republic later ruled by the fascist dictator Salazar. A peaceful military coup (1974) overthrew Salazar's successor, Marcello Caetano, and 1975 saw the return to democratic civilian rule. Madeira and the Azores are integral parts of Portugal, but its African territories achieved independence in the 1970s. Area, 92 270 square kilometres (35,626 square miles). Population, 9,810,000. Capital, Lisbon.

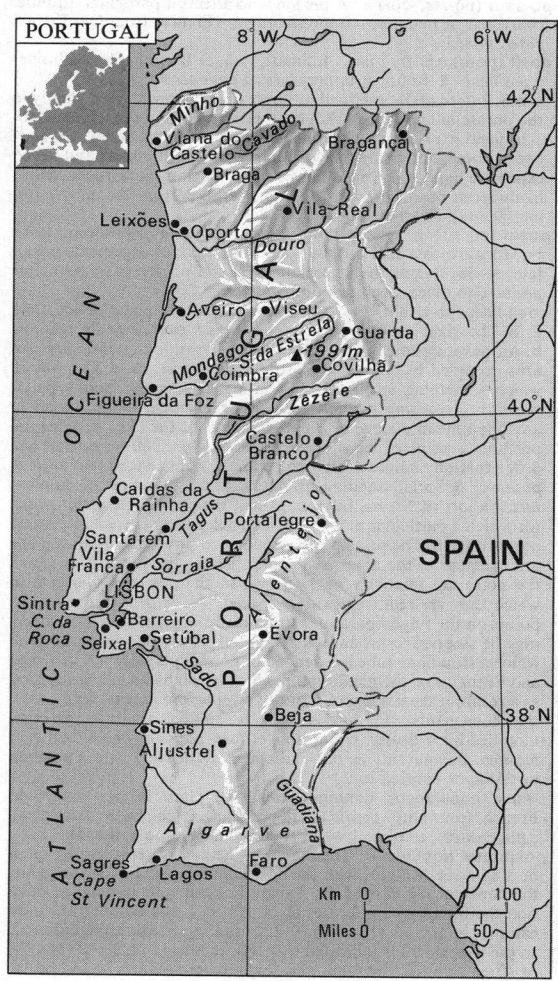

Por·tu·guese (pór-tew-géez, -choo- || pŏr-, -géess) *adj. Abbr.* **Pg., Port.** Of or pertaining to Portugal, its people, culture, or language. *~n., pl.* **Portuguese.** *Abbr.* **Pg., Port. 1.** A native or inhabitant of Portugal. **2.** The Romance language of Portugal, Brazil, and various former Portuguese territories.
Portuguese East Africa. See **Mozambique.**
Portuguese Guinea. See **Guinea-Bissau, Republic of.**
Portuguese man-of-war *n.* A complex, colonial hydrozoan organism of the genus *Physalia,* of warm seas, having a bluish, bladder-like float from which are suspended numerous long, stinging tentacles capable of inflicting severe injury.
Portuguese West Africa. See **Angola.**
por·tu·lac·a (pór-tew-láckə, -choo-, -láykə || pŏr-) *n.* Any plant of the genus *Portulaca,* having fleshy stems and leaves; especially, *P. grandiflora,* cultivated for its showy flowers that open only in sunlight. This species is also called "rose moss". See **purslane.** [New Latin, from Latin *portulāca,* purslane, from *portula,* diminutive of *porta,* gate, from the gatelike covering on its capsule.]
pos. 1. position. **2.** positive.
pose[1] (pōz) *v.* **posed, posing, poses.** *—intr.* **1.** To assume or hold a particular position or posture, as in sitting for a portrait. **2.** To affect a particular mental attitude or play a part, usually in order to impress. **3.** To represent oneself in a given character or as other than what one is: *He posed as a vicar in order to enter people's houses.* *—tr.* **1.** To place (a model, for example) in a specific position. **2.** To propound or assert; put forward: *pose a problem.*
~n. **1.** A bodily attitude or position, especially one assumed for an artist or photographer. **2.** An affected attitude of mind or body. [Middle English *posen,* from Old French *poser,* from Late Latin *pausāre,* to cease, from Latin *pausa,* a pause, from Greek *pausis,* from *pauein,* to pause; confused in some senses with Latin *pōnere* (past participle *positus*), to place.]
pose[2] *tr.v.* **posed, posing, poses.** *Rare.* To puzzle or confuse with a difficult question or problem. [Short for *appose,* Middle English *apposen, opposen,* to confront with objections, from Old French *opposer,* to OPPOSE.]
Po·sei·don (pə-sī́d'n, po-). *Greek Mythology.* The god of the sea, earthquakes, and horses; brother of Zeus; identified with the Roman god Neptune. [Latin, from Greek *Poseidōn*†.]
Posen. See **Poznán.**
pos·er[1] (pṓzər) *n.* A person who poses.
poser[2] *n.* A baffling question or problem.
po·seur (pō-zér, -zŏr) *n.* A person who affects a particular attitude, character, or manner to impress others. [French, from Old French *poser,* POSE.]
posh (posh) *adj. Informal.* **1.** Smart, rich, or fashionable; exclusive: *a posh car.* **2.** Refined; upper-class: *a posh accent.*
~adv. Informal. In a refined or upper-class manner. Used chiefly in the phrase *to talk posh.* [19th century : origin obscure. One unsubstantiated explanation cites the acronym for "port (side) out, starboard home", referring to accommodation on the shady and hence expensive side of ships sailing between England and India. More likely from obsolete *posh,* a dandy, perhaps from Romany *pāšh,* half(penny), small change.]
pos·it (pózzit) *tr.v.* **-ited, -iting, -its. 1.** To place in position. **2.** To put forward as a fact or truth or for the sake of argument; postulate. —See Synonyms at **presume.** [Latin *pōnere* (past participle *positus*), to place. See **position.**]
po·si·tion (pə-zísh'n || pō-) *n. Abbr.* **pos. 1.** A place or location. **2. a.** The right or appropriate place: *The guns were in position.* **b.** An advantageous place: *manoeuvre for position.* **c.** *Military.* An area occupied by troops for a strategic purpose. **3. a.** The way in which something is placed. **b.** The arrangement of bodily parts; posture: *a standing position.* **c.** The arrangement of the pieces at any one time in a game of chess, draughts, or the like. **4.** A mental posture; a point of view: *the government's position on foreign aid.* **5.** A situation or state relative to certain circumstances: *in a difficult position.* **6.** Social standing or status; rank. **7.** A post of employment; a job. **8.** *Sports.* In team games, the part of the playing-area for which a particular player is responsible. **9. a.** The act or process of positing. **b.** The principle or proposition posited. **10.** *Music.* The arrangement of the notes in a chord, either *close position,* in which the notes are relatively near to one another, or *open position,* in which they are relatively widely spaced. **11.** *Music.* **a.** Any of the points on the fingerboard of a string instrument, at which the string may be stopped to produce a true note. **b.** Any of seven lengths to which a trombone tube is extended in normal playing. **12.** In Greek and Latin verse, the condition in which a syllable is metrically long as a result of the placing of a short vowel before at least two successive consonants. **13.** *Finance.* The holding of securities or commodities by a dealer, either above *(long position)* or below *(short position)* the quantity he has undertaken to deliver. **—in a position to.** Able or entitled to.
~tr.v. **positioned, -tioning, -tions.** To place in position. [Old French, from Latin *positiō* (stem *positiōn-*), from *pōnere* (past participle *positus*), to place.] **—po·si·tion·al** *adj.* **—po·si·tion·er** *n.*
positional notation *n.* The common method of representing numbers by a set of digits, with the position of a digit in a string giving the power of the base of the system. For example, in decimal notation the number 12 indicates $(1 \times 10) + 2$; the number 212 indicates $(2 \times 10^2) + (1 \times 10) + 2$. In binary notation the base is 2, so the decimal 12 is indicated by 1100; that is, $(1 \times 2^3) + (1 \times 2^2) + (0 \times 2) + 0$. The same number in octal notation would be 14; that is, $(1 \times 8) + 4$.
pos·i·tive (pózə-tiv, -i-) *adj. Abbr.* **pos. 1.** Characterised by or displaying certainty, acceptance, or affirmation: *a positive answer.* **2.** Measured or moving in a direction of increase, progress, improvement, or forward motion. **3.** Explicitly or openly expressed or laid down: *a positive demand.* **4.** Admitting of no doubt; irrefutable. **5.** Determined or settled in opinion or assertion; confident; sure: *a positive manner.* **6.** Overconfident; dogmatic. **7.** Constructive rather than censorious or destructive; helpful or beneficial: *positive criticism.* **8.** Concerned with matters of fact rather than value; descriptive and empirical: *positive economics.* **9.** Composed of or characterised by the presence, rather than the absence, of particular qualities or attributes; real: *a positive benefit.* **10.** Without relation to or comparison with anything else; absolute. **11.** *Informal.* Used as an intensive: *She is a positive angel.* **12.** *Mathematics.* Pertaining to or designating: **a.** A quantity greater than zero. **b.** The sign (+). **c.** A quantity, number, angle, or direction opposite to another designated as negative. **13.** *Physics.* Pertaining to or designating electric charge of a sign opposite to that of an electron. **14.** *Medicine.* **a.** Indicating the presence of a particular disease, condition, or organism: *a positive Wassermann test.* **b.** Indicating the presence of the **Rh factor** *(see).* **15.** *Biology.* Indicating or characterised by response or motion towards the source of a stimulus: *positive tropism.* Compare **negative. 16.** In photography, having the areas of light and dark in their original and normal relationship, or having natural colours, as in a print made from a negative. **17.** *Grammar.* Expressing or involving the simple, uncompared degree of comparison of adjectives or adverbs. Compare **comparative, superlative. 18.** Driven by or generating power directly through intermediate parts having little or no play: *positive drive.* **19.** Designating a lens or mirror capable of converging a beam of radiation.
~n. **1.** That which is positive. **2.** *Philosophy.* That which is given or perceptible to the senses. **3.** *Mathematics.* A quantity greater than zero. **4.** *Physics.* A positive electric charge. **5.** In photography, an image in which the lights and darks or colours appear as they do in nature. **6.** *Grammar.* **a.** The positive degree of an adjective or adverb. **b.** An adjective or adverb expressing the positive degree; for example, the simple form *bright* as opposed to the forms *brighter* or *brightest.* [Middle English, from Old French *positif,* from Latin *positīvus,* arbitrarily laid down, dogmatic, from *pōnere* (past participle *positus*), to place.] **—pos·i·tive·ness** *n.*
positive discrimination *n.* Discrimination designed to remedy previous injustices or to make up for an existing discriminatory state of affairs; especially, the treating of a person or social group more favourably because of some disadvantage possessed, such as being physically handicapped or being a member of a racial minority.
positive feedback *n.* A type of **feedback** *(see)* in which an increase in output causes an increase in input.
pos·i·tive·ly (pózə-tiv-li, -i-) *adv.* **1.** In a positive manner. **2.** *Informal.* Used as an intensive: *Silly?—She's positively certifiable.*
positive prescription *n. Law.* **Prescription** *(see).*
positive vetting *n.* A form of thorough security checking, performed by the Ministry of Defence, on any civil servants likely to be handling confidential or politically sensitive information.
pos·i·tiv·ism (pózə-tiv-iz'm, -i-) *n.* **1. a.** A philosophical doctrine contending that sense perceptions are the only admissible basis of human knowledge and precise thought. **b.** A philosophical system based upon this doctrine; especially, the system of Auguste **Comte** *(see),* designed to supersede theology and metaphysics, and depending on a hierarchy of the sciences, beginning with mathematics and culminating in sociology. **2.** The application of positivism in logic, epistemology, and ethics. See **logical positivism. 3.** Dogmatic certainty, as in speculation and argument. **—pos·i·tiv·ist** *n.* **—pos·i·tiv·is·tic** (-vísstik) *adj.*
pos·i·tron (pózzi-tron) *n. Symbol* e^+ The **antiparticle** *(see)* of the electron. Also called "antielectron". [POSI(TIVE) + (ELEC)TRON.]
pos·i·tron·i·um (pózzi-trṓni-əm) *n. Physics.* A short-lived entity formed when electron and a positron are bound together in a configuration resembling the hydrogen atom. [From POSITRON.]
po·sol·o·gy (pə-sólləji, po-) *n.* The branch of medicine concerned with the science of the dosage of drugs and other agents. [French *posologie,* from Greek *posos,* how much.]
poss. 1. possession. **2.** possessive. **3.** possible; possibly.
pos·se (póssi) *n.* **1.** *U.S.* A posse comitatus. **2.** *U.S.* Any body of armed men with legal authority. **3.** *Informal.* Any large body of people, usually with a shared purpose. **—in posse.** *Law.* Possible; potential. [Short for POSSE COMITATUS.]
posse com·i·ta·tus (kómmi-taátəss, -táytəss) *n. U.S.* A body of men that a sheriff or other peace officer is empowered to summon to aid in maintaining peace or capturing a criminal, for example. Also called "posse". [Medieval Latin *posse comitātūs,* "force of the county" : *posse,* power, from Latin, to be able, have power (see **potent**) + *comitātūs,* genitive of *comitātus,* COUNTY.]
pos·sess (pə-zéss || pō-) *tr.v.* **-sessed, -sessing, -sesses. 1.** To have as property; own. **2.** To have as a quality, characteristic, or other attribute. **3.** To acquire mastery of or have knowledge of: *possess valuable data.* **4.** To gain or exert influence or control over; dominate: *Fury possessed him.* **5.** *Rare.* To control or maintain (one's nature) in a particular state or condition: *Possess your heart in patience.* **6.** To have sexual intercourse with. Used of a man. **7.** *Archaic.* To gain or seize. [Middle English *possessen,* from Old French *possesser,* from Latin *possīdere* (past participle *possessus*), "to sit as

master", take possession of : *posse,* to be able + *sīdere,* to sit down and from Latin *possidēre* (past participle *possessus*), to own, possess : *posse,* to be able + *sedēre,* to sit.] **—pos·ses·sor** *n.*

pos·sessed (pə-zést || pō-) *adj.* **1.** Owning, having, or mastering something such as property or knowledge. Used with *of: possessed of vital secrets; possessed of a sharp tongue.* **2.** Influenced or controlled by a strong emotion or idea, by or as if by an evil spirit or other force. Often used with *by* or *with: possessed with an urge to kill; a man possessed.* **3.** *Rare.* Self-possessed; calm or collected.

pos·ses·sion (pə-zésh'n || pō-) *n.* **1.** The act or fact of possessing. **2.** The state of being possessed. **3.** *Abbr.* **poss.** That which is owned or possessed. **4.** *Plural.* Wealth or property. **5.** *Abbr.* **poss.** *Law.* Actual control, holding, or occupancy with, or without, rightful ownership. **6.** Any territory subject to foreign control. **7.** Self-control. **8.** The state of being dominated by, or as if by, evil spirits or by a strong emotion or idea. **9.** *Sports.* Control of the ball, puck, or the like. —See Synonyms at **assets.**

pos·ses·sive (pə-zéssiv || pō-) *adj. Abbr.* **poss. 1.** Of or pertaining to ownership or possession. **2.** Having or manifesting a desire to control or dominate: *a possessive husband.* **3.** *Grammar.* Of, pertaining to, or designating a noun or pronoun case that expresses belonging or a similar relation.

~n. Abbr. **poss.** *Grammar.* **1.** The possessive case. **2.** A possessive form or construction. **—pos·ses·ive·ly** *adv.* **—pos·ses·sive·ness** *n.*

possessive adjective *n. Grammar.* A pronominal adjective expressing possession. In the sentences *This is my duty* and *It is their fate,* the possessive adjectives are *my* and *their.*

possessive pronoun *n. Grammar.* Any of several pronouns expressing possession and capable of replacing noun phrases. In current English, they are: *mine, his, hers, its, ours, yours, theirs, whose.*

pos·ses·so·ry (pə-zéssəri) *adj.* **1.** Of, pertaining to, or having possession. **2.** *Law.* Depending on or arising from possession.

pos·set (póssit) *n.* A spiced drink of hot sweetened milk curdled with wine or ale. [Middle English *poshet, poshot*†.]

pos·si·bil·i·ty (póssə-bílləti, póssi-) *n., pl.* **-ties. 1.** The fact or state of being possible. **2.** Something possible. **3.** A contestant or candidate capable of winning or being chosen. **4.** *Plural.* Capacity for favourable development; potential: *The possibilities of microtechnology are unlimited.*

pos·si·ble (póss-əb'l, -ib'l) *adj. Abbr.* **poss. 1.** Capable of happening, existing, or being true without contradicting proven facts, laws, or circumstances. **2.** Capable of occurring or being done without offence to character, nature, or custom; suitable or acceptable: *the only possible answer.* **3.** Capable of favourable development; potential. **4.** That may or may not occur; of uncertain likelihood.

~n. A possibility; especially, a candidate or contestant who has a strong chance of being selected or achieving success. [Middle English, from Old French, from Latin *possibilis,* from *posse,* to be able.]

Synonyms: *possible, practical, workable, practicable, feasible, viable.*

pos·si·bly (póss-əbli, -ibli) *adv.* **1.** Perhaps; maybe. **2.** In any way at all; under any circumstances: *She can't possibly have said that.*

pos·sum (póss'm) *n., pl.* **-sums** or (for sense 1) collectively **possum. 1.** A marsupial, the **opossum** *(see).* **2.** *Australian & N.Z.* A **phalanger** *(see).* **—play possum.** To pretend to be dead, asleep, or unaware in order to deceive an opponent.

Pos·sum (póssem) *n.* A trademark for a device that enables paralysed patients to operate such instruments as typewriters by means of blowing or extremely light touch.

post[1] (pōst) *n.* **1.** A long piece of wood, metal, or other material set upright in the ground to serve as a marker or support. **2.** Anything resembling this. **3.** The starting or finishing point at a racecourse, usually marked by a pole. **4.** *Informal.* A goal post.

~tr.v. **posted, posting, posts. 1. a.** To place (an announcement), as by sticking or pinning in public view. Sometimes used with *up.* **b.** To cover (a wall, for example) with posters; placard. Often used with *over.* **2.** To announce by or as if by posters: *post banns.* **3.** To denounce publicly. **4.** To publish (a name, especially of a missing ship) on a list. [Middle English *post,* Old English *post,* from West Germanic *posta* (unattested), from Latin *postis.*]

post[2] *n.* **1.** A military base where troops are stationed. **2.** The grounds and buildings of a military base. **3.** *Military. British.* Either of two bugle calls, *first post* or *last post,* sounded in the evening as a signal to retire to quarters. **4.** An assigned position or station, as of a guard or sentry. **5.** A position of employment; especially, an appointed public office. **6.** A place to which anyone is assigned for duty or work. **7.** A **trading post** *(see).*

~tr.v. **posted, posting, posts. 1.** To assign to a position or station: *post a sentry.* **2.** To appoint to a naval or military command. **3.** To appoint or assign (someone) to a position or job in a distant location: *was posted to Libya as consul.* [French *poste,* from Old Italian *posto,* from Vulgar Latin *postum* (unattested), contraction of Latin *positum,* neuter past participle of *pōnere,* to place.]

post[3] *n.* **1. a.** Letters, parcels, and other material collected, handled, and delivered by the Post Office or some other delivery system; mail. **b.** The system of delivering such items; the postal system. **2. a.** A particular delivery or collection of postal material: *missed the second post.* **b.** Postal material from or for a specific person or organisation: *He opened her post.* **3. a.** A postbox; a letter box. **b.** A post office. **4.** *Capital* **P.** Used as part of the title of certain newspapers: *The Sunday Post.* **5. a.** Formerly, any of a series of relay stations along a fixed route, furnishing fresh riders and horses for the delivery of mail on horseback. **b.** A rider on such a mail route; a courier. **—by return of post.** By the next post in the opposite direction.

~v. **posted, posting, posts.** *—intr.* **1.** To travel in stages or relays. **2.** *Archaic.* To travel quickly; speed or hasten. **3.** To bob up and down in the saddle in rhythm with a horse's trotting gait. *—tr.* **1.** To send (a letter, package, or the like) by post. **2.** To inform of the latest news. Usually used in the passive: *keep me posted.* **3.** To send by mail in a system of relays on horseback. **4.** In bookkeeping: **a.** To transfer (an item or items) to a ledger. **b.** To make the necessary entries in (a ledger).

~adv. **1.** By post. **2.** By post horse. **3.** With great speed; rapidly. [French *poste,* from Italian *posta,* from Vulgar Latin *posta* (unattested), contraction of Latin *posita,* feminine past participle of *pōnere,* to place.]

post- *prefix.* Indicates: **1.** After in time; later; subsequent to; for example, **postdate, postgraduate. 2.** After in position; behind; posterior to; for example, **postfix, postaxial.** ***Note:*** Many compounds other than those entered here may be formed with *post-.* In forming compounds, *post-* is now usually joined with the following element without space or hyphen: *postwar.* However, if the second element begins with a *t* or a capital letter, it is separated with a hyphen: *post-traumatic, post-Victorian.* Compounds made up of the Latin word *post* and another Latin form are hyphenated. Those entered here are **post-bellum, post-mortem,** and **post-obit.** [Latin, from *post,* behind, after.]

post·age (pōstij) *n.* The charge for delivering an item of post.

postage stamp *n.* A small printed, usually adhesive, label issued by a government and sold in various denominations to be affixed to items of mail as evidence of the payment of postage.

post·al (pōst'l) *adj.* **1.** Of or pertaining to post or the Post Office. **2.** Sent or delivered by post: *a postal ballot.* **—post·al·ly** *adv.*

postal order *n.* A **money order** *(see),* bought from and only payable at a post office.

post·ax·i·al (pōst-áksi-əl) *adj. Anatomy.* Located behind an axis of the body, especially behind the fibula or the ulna.

post·bag (pōst-bag) *n.* **1.** The usually large amount of post from the public received by a public figure, a radio or television programme, or other institution or person. **2.** A **mailbag** *(see).*

post-bel·lum (pōst-bélləm) *adj.* Of, during, or designating the period after a war, especially the American Civil War. [Latin *post,* after + *bellum,* war.]

post·box (pōst-boks) *n.* A box, usually metal and set into a wall, or a freestanding **pillar box** *(see),* into which outgoing post is put for collection by a postal service. Also called "letter box".

post·boy (pōst-boy) *n.* **1.** A boy or man who carries or delivers post in offices. **2.** A postilion.

post·card (pōst-kaard) *n. Abbr.* **p.c.** A card, often bearing a picture on one side, with space for an address, postage stamp, and short message. Also called "card".

post·ca·va (pōst-kaávə, -káyvə) *n. Anatomy.* The inferior **vena cava** *(see).* **—post·ca·val** *adj.*

post chaise *n.* A closed, four-wheeled, horse-drawn carriage, formerly used to transport post and passengers. Also called "chaise". [POST (mail) + CHAISE.]

post·code (pōst-kōd) *n.* In the United Kingdom, a combination of letters and figures, that specifies the location of a postal address, and is used in the automatic sorting of post by the Post Office. Also called "postal code", *U.S.* "zip code".

post·con·cil·i·ar (pōst-kən-silli-ər || -kon-) *adj.* Designating, pertaining to, or characteristic of the Roman Catholic Church since the Second Vatican Council (1962–65).

post·date (pōst-dáyt) *tr.v.* **-dated, -dating, -dates. 1.** To put a date on (a cheque, letter, or document) that is later than the actual date. **2.** To occur later than; follow in time.

post·di·lu·vi·an (pōst-di-lōōvi-ən || -léwvi-) *adj.* Also **post·di·lu·vi·al** (-əl). Existing or occurring after the biblical Flood.

~n. A person or thing living after the biblical Flood.

post·doc·tor·al (pōst-dóktərəl) *adj.* Of, pertaining to, designating, or engaged in academic study beyond a doctoral degree.

post·er (pōstər) *n.* **1. a.** A large printed placard, bill, or announcement, often illustrated, posted to advertise or publicise something. **b.** An illustration, picture, reproduction of a painting, or the like, on a large sheet of paper, often used to decorate the wall of a room. **2.** One who posts bills or notices.

poster art *n.* An art form characteristically used in advertising or decorative posters.

poste res·tante (pōst réstoNt, ri-stóNt) *n.* **1.** Used on an item such as a letter to indicate that it should be held at a particular post office until claimed by the addressee. **2.** The department of a post office dealing with such post. Also *U.S.* "general delivery". [French, "remaining mail" : *poste,* POST (mail) + *restante,* from *rester,* to REST.]

pos·te·ri·or (po-steér-i-ər || pō-) *adj.* **1.** Located behind a part or towards the rear of a structure. **2.** *Zoology & Anatomy.* Pertaining to the caudal (hind) end of the body in an animal or the dorsal (back) side in man. **3.** *Botany.* Next to or nearest the main stem or axis. Said of flowers and buds. **4.** Coming after in order; following. **5.** Following in time; later; subsequent. Compare **anterior.**

~n. The buttocks. Used humorously or euphemistically. [Latin, comparative of *posterus,* coming after, next, from *post,* after.] — **pos·te·ri·or·i·ty** (po-steér-i-órriti || pō-) *n.* **—pos·te·ri·or·ly** *adv.*

pos·ter·i·ty (po-stérrəti || pō-) *n.* **1.** Future generations. **2.** All of a person's descendants. [Middle English *posterite,* from Old French *posterite,* from Latin *posteritās* (stem *posteritāt-*), from *posterus,* next. See **posterior.**]

pos·tern (póss-tərn, póss-, -tern) *n.* A small, usually private, rear gate, especially one in a fort or castle.
~*adj.* Situated at the back or side. [Middle English *posterne,* from Old French, variant of *posterle,* from Late Latin *posterula,* diminutive of *postera,* back door, from the feminine of *posterus,* coming after. See **posterior.**]

poster paint *n.* Opaque watercolour paint in bright colours. Also called "poster colour".

post exchange *n. Often capital* P, *capital* E. *Abbr.* **PX** *U.S.* A shop or set of shops on a military base for the sale of tax-free merchandise and services to military personnel and their families.

post·ex·il·i·an (póst-ig-zíll-i-ən ‖ -eg-, -ek-síll-) *adj.* Also **post·ex·il·ic** (-ik). Of, pertaining to, or designating the period of Jewish history following the Babylonian captivity (after 586 B.C.).

post·fix (póst-fíks) *tr.v.* **-fixed, -fixing, -fixes.** To add at the end of something; suffix.
~*n.* (póst-fiks). A suffix. —**post·fix·al** (-fíks'l), **post·fix·i·al** *adj.*

post-free *adj.* Free of postal charges or with postage prepaid. —**post-free** *adv.*

post·gla·ci·al (póst-gláy-si-əl, -sh'l) *adj. Geology.* Pertaining to or occurring during the time following a glacial period.

post·grad·u·ate (póst-gráddew-ət, -it) *adj. Abbr.* **P.G.** Of, pertaining to, designating, or pursuing advanced study beyond the level of a bachelor's or equivalent degree.
~*n.* A person engaged in such study.

post-haste (póst-háyst) *adv.* With great speed; hastily; rapidly.
~*n. Archaic.* Great speed; rapidity. [Originally *post, haste,* a direction on letters : POST (courier) + HASTE (imperative).]

post hoc er·go prop·ter hoc (póst hók érgő próptər hók) *n. Latin.* The fallacy of assuming or arguing that because one event or situation comes after another, it must in some way be the result of it. ["After this, therefore on account of this".]

post horn *n.* A simple horn formerly blown to announce the arrival of a coach, especially a mail coach.

post horse *n.* Formerly, a horse kept at inns and post houses to be used by post riders or hired by travellers.

post house *n.* A public house or inn where post horses were kept.

post·hu·mous (póstewməss) *adj.* **1.** Occurring or continuing after one's death: *a posthumous award; posthumous fame.* **2.** Published after the author's death: *a posthumous book.* **3.** Born after the death of the father: *a posthumous child.* [Latin *posthumus,* "last", alteration (influenced by *humus,* earth, and taken as "after burial") of *postumus,* superlative of *posterus,* coming after, next. See **posterior.**]
—**post·hu·mous·ly** *adv.* —**post·hu·mous·ness** *n.*

post·hyp·not·ic suggestion (póst-hip-nóttik) *n.* A suggestion made to a hypnotised person specifying an action to be performed in a subsequent waking state.

pos·tiche (po-stéesh, pósteesh ‖ *U.S. also* paw-) *adj.* **1.** Added superfluously or inappropriately. Said especially of architectural ornamentation. **2.** Artificial; false.
~*n.* **1.** Something false; a sham. **2.** A small hairpiece. [French, from Italian *posticcio,* fake, counterfeit, from *posto,* added, placed, from Latin *positus,* past participle of *pōnere,* to place.]

pos·til·i·on, pos·til·li·on (po-stilli-ən, -stíl-yən ‖ pō-) *n.* A person who rides the near (left-hand) horse of the leading pair to guide a team of horses drawing a coach. [French *postillon,* from Italian *postiglione,* from *posta,* POST (mail).]

post·im·pres·sion·ism, post·im·pres·sion·ism (póst-im-présh'n-iz'm) *n. Often capital* P. A school of painting in France in the late 19th century, exemplified by artists such as Cézanne, Gauguin, and van Gogh, who rejected the objective naturalism of impressionism and used form and colour in freer and more individually subjective ways. —**post·im·pres·sion·ist** *n. & adj.* —**post·im·pres·sion·is·tic** (-ístik) *adj.*

post·ing (pósting) *n.* An appointment to a job or post, especially to a military or public position, or to one overseas.

post·lude (póst-lōōd, -lewd) *n.* **1. a.** An organ voluntary played at the end of a church service. **b.** A concluding piece of music. **2.** A final chapter or phase. [POST- + (PRE)LUDE.]

post·man (póst-mən) *n., pl.* **-men.** (-mən) A man employed by the Post Office to collect and deliver post. Also *chiefly U.S.* "mailman".

post·mark (póst-maark) *n.* An official mark printed over the stamp on an item of post; especially, one that cancels the stamp and records the date and place of posting.
~*tr.v.* **postmarked, -marking, -marks.** To stamp with a postmark.

post·mas·ter (póst-maastər ‖ -mastər) *n.* An official in charge of a local post office. —**post·mas·ter·ship** *n.*

postmaster general *n., pl.* **postmasters general.** *Abbr.* **P.M.G.** The executive head of certain national postal services.

post·me·rid·i·an (póst-mə-ríddi-ən) *adj.* Of, pertaining to, or taking place in the afternoon.

post me·rid·i·em (póst mə-ríddi-əm, -em) *adv. Abbr.* **p.m.** After noon. Used chiefly in the abbreviated form to specify the hour: *10.30 p.m.* [Latin *post merīdiem,* after midday : *post,* after + *merīdiem,* accusative of *merīdiēs,* midday, noon (see **meridian**).]

post·mil·le·nar·i·an (póst-mílli-naír-i-ən) *adj.* Of or pertaining to postmillennialism.
~*n.* A person who believes in postmillennialism. Compare **premillenarian.** —**post·mil·le·nar·i·an·ism** *n.*

post·mil·len·ni·al (póst-mi-lénni-əl) *adj.* Happening or existing after the millennium.

post·mil·len·ni·al·ism (póst-mi-lénni-əl-iz'm) *n.* The doctrine that Christ's second coming will follow the millennium. Also called "postmillenarianism". Compare **premillennialism.** —**post·mil·len·ni·al·ist** *n.*

post·mis·tress (póst-miss-triss, -trəss) *n. Abbr.* **P.M.** A woman in charge of a local post office.

post·mod·ern·ism, post·mod·ern·ism (póst-móddərniz'm) *n.* Either of two trends in art, literature, and architecture, which largely reject the theories and practices of modernism. One of the trends reverts to more traditional, formal, even classical approaches; the other seeks to go beyond art, form, and meaning altogether, and favours works which are anarchic, outrageous, or transitory.

post·mor·tem (póst-mór-tem, -təm) *adj. Abbr.* **p.m. 1.** Occurring or done after death. **2.** Of or pertaining to a post-mortem examination.
~*n.* **1.** A post-mortem examination, especially an **autopsy** *(see).* **2.** *Informal.* An analysis or review of some completed event, especially of a failure or defeat. [Latin, after death.]

post·na·sal (póst-náyz'l) *adj.* At the rear part of the nasal cavity.

postnasal drip *n.* The chronic secretion of mucus from the posterior nasal cavities, resulting in congestion and coughing.

post·na·tal (póst-náyt'l) *adj.* Of or occurring during the period immediately after birth. —**post·na·tal·ly** *adv.*

postnatal depression *n.* A period of depression and anxiety experienced by a mother after having given birth, sometimes manifested by aggression towards the baby.

post·nup·tial (póst-núp-sh'l, -ch'l) *adj.* Happening after marriage. —**post·nup·tial·ly** *adv.*

post·o·bit (póst-óbit, -óbbit) *adj.* Also **post·o·bit·u·ar·y** (póst-ə-bittew-əri ‖ -erri) Coming into effect after a person's death.
~*n.* A bond given by a borrower promising to repay a debt after the death of a person from whose estate he expects to inherit. Also called "post-obit bond". [Latin *post obitum,* after death : *post,* after + *obitum,* accusative of *obitus,* death (see **obituary**).]

post office *n. Abbr.* **P.O., p.o. 1.** *Capital* P, *capital* O. The public department responsible for all postal services, and, in many countries, for telecommunications as well. **2.** Any local office where post is received, sorted, and delivered, stamps and other postal matter are sold, and certain financial business is conducted.

post office box *n. Abbr.* **P.O.B., P.O. box.** A private rented box, pigeonhole, or the like in a post office, to which post can be addressed and delivered, and where it is kept until collected.

post·op·er·a·tive (póst-ópp-ərətiv, -rətiv ‖ -əraytiv) *adj.* Of, administered, or occurring in the period shortly after surgery. —**post·op·er·a·tive·ly** *adv.*

post·or·bi·tal (póst-órbit'l) *adj. Anatomy.* Located behind the eye or eye socket: *a postorbital bone.*

post·paid (póst-páyd) *adj. Abbr.* **p.p., ppd.** With the postage paid in advance.

post·par·tum (póst-pártəm) *adj.* Of or occurring in the period shortly after childbirth. [Latin *post partum,* after birth : *post,* after + *partum,* accusative of *partus,* a bringing forth, from the past participle of *parere,* to bear.]

post·pone (pə-spōn, póst-pōn) *tr.v.* **-poned, -poning, -pones. 1.** To delay until a future time; put off. **2.** *Rare.* To place after in importance; subordinate. [Latin *postpōnere,* to place after : *post,* after + *pōnere,* to put, place.] —**post·pon·a·ble** *adj.* —**post·pone·ment** *n.* —**post·pon·er** *n.*

post·po·si·tion (póst-pə-zísh'n) *n. Grammar.* **1.** The placing of a word or particle after the word which it modifies or to which it is grammatically related. **2.** A word or particle so placed. In *what for?* and *homewards, for* and *-wards* are postpositions. [French, from Old French *postposer,* to place after, from Latin *postpōnere,* POSTPONE.] —**post·po·si·tion·al** *adj.* —**post·po·si·tion·al·ly** *adv.*

post·pos·i·tive (póst-póz-ə-tiv, -i-) *adj. Grammar.* Of, pertaining to, or designating a word or particle characterised by postposition: *a postpositive adjective.* Compare **prepositive.**
~*n.* A postpositive word or particle. [Late Latin *postpositīvus,* from Latin *postpōnere* (past participle *postpositus*), to place after, POSTPONE.] —**post·pos·i·tive·ly** *adv.*

post·pran·di·al (póst-prándi-əl) *adj.* Following or after any meal, especially dinner. Often used humorously.

post·script (póst-skript) *n. Abbr.* **p.s., P.S. 1.** A message appended at the end of a letter after the writer's signature. **2.** Additional information appended to a book, article, or the like. [Latin *postscriptum,* from *postscrībere* (past participle *postscriptus*), to write after : *post,* after + *scrībere,* to write.]

post·trau·mat·ic (póst-traw-máttik, -trow-) *adj.* Following trauma or resulting from it: *post-traumatic amnesia; post-traumatic stress.*

pos·tu·lant (póstewlənt) *n.* **1.** A person submitting a request or application; a petitioner. **2.** A candidate for admission into a religious order. Compare **novice.** [French, from Latin *postulāns* (stem *postulānt-*), present participle of *postulāre,* to demand, POSTULATE.] —**pos·tu·lan·cy, pos·tu·lant·ship** *n.*

pos·tu·late (póstew-layt) *tr.v.* **-lated, -lating, -lates. 1.** To make claim for; demand. **2.** To put forward for consideration as true or real with no proof: *He postulated the presence of ghosts to explain the strange noises.* **3.** To assume as a premise or axiom; take for granted, especially in a mathematical or logical proof or theorem. **4.** To appoint or promote (a person) provisionally, subject to higher authorisation. —See Synonyms at **presume.**

~*n.* (-lit, -lət, -layt). **1.** Something assumed as being self-evident or generally accepted, as used as a basis for an argument. **2.** A fundamental element; a basic principle. **3.** *Logic & Mathematics.* An axiom. **4.** A requirement; a prerequisite. [Latin *postulāre*, to request, demand.] —**pos·tu·la·tion** (-láysh'n) *n.*

pos·tu·la·tor (póstew-laytər) *n.* **1.** One who postulates. **2.** *Roman Catholic Church.* A church official who presents a plea for canonisation or beatification. [Medieval Latin. See **postulate**.]

pos·ture (póss-chər, -tewr) *n.* **1.** A position or attitude of the body or of bodily parts: *a sitting posture.* **2.** A characteristic way of bearing one's body, especially the trunk and head; carriage: *learning good posture.* **3.** A pose; a particular bodily position, such as one assumed by an artist's model. **4.** The arrangement of the parts of any object. **5.** The present condition or tendency of something: *the military posture of a nation.* **6.** A frame of mind affecting one's behaviour; an overall attitude: *a posture of tolerance.* **7.** An exaggerated or unnatural attitude or mode of behaviour; a pose.
~*v.* **postured, -turing, -tures.** —*intr.* To assume an exaggerated or unnatural pose or mental attitude; pose for effect. —*tr.* To put in a posture; position. [French, from Italian *postura,* from Latin *positūra,* position, from *pōnere* (past participle *positus*), to place.] —**pos·tur·al** *adj.* —**pos·tur·er, pos·tur·ist** *n.*

post·vo·cal·ic (pōst-vō-kál-ik) *adj.* Designating a consonant or consonantal sound directly following a vowel.

post·war (pōst-wáwr) *adj.* Occurring after a particular war.

post·wom·an (pōst-wōomən) *n., pl.* **-women** (-wimmin). A female postman.

po·sy (pōzi) *n., pl.* **-sies. 1.** A flower or small bunch of flowers. **2.** *Archaic.* A brief verse or sentimental phrase, especially when inscribed on a trinket. [Variant of POESY.]

pot¹ (pot) *n.* **1. a.** Any of various usually domestic containers made of metal, glass, or pottery, such as a short, cylindrical vessel for holding jam, a rounded juglike vessel for liquid tea or coffee, or a round, fairly deep cooking vessel with a handle. **b.** Such a vessel and its contents: *a pot of soup; a pot of tea.* **c.** The amount that such a vessel will hold. **2. a.** A large drinking cup; a tankard. **b.** A drink, usually of beer, contained in such a cup. **3.** An artistic or decorative ceramic vessel of any size or shape. **4. a.** A flowerpot. **b.** Something resembling a domestic pot in appearance or function, such as a chimney pot or chamber pot. **5.** A vessel, usually gold, silver, or silverplate, awarded as a sports prize. **6.** A trap for fish, crustaceans, or eels, consisting of a wicker or wire basket: *a lobster pot.* **7.** In gambling card games, the total amount staked by all the players in one hand. **8.** *U.S. Informal.* A common fund to which the members of a group contribute and upon which they draw for certain stated purposes. **9.** *Informal.* **a.** *Plural.* A great deal; a large amount: *pots of money.* **b.** A large amount of money: *made a pot.* **10.** *Informal.* A **pot-belly** (see). **11.** In billiards, snooker, and similar games, a shot intended to send a ball into a pocket. **12.** *Informal.* A **pot shot** (see). —**go to pot.** *Informal.* To deteriorate.
~*v.* **potted, potting, pots.** —*tr.* **1.** To place or plant in a pot: *pot a plant.* **2.** To preserve (food) in a pot. **3.** To cook in a pot. **4.** To shoot (game) for food rather than for sport. **5.** *Informal.* To shoot with a pot shot. **6.** *Informal.* To win or capture; bag. **7.** In billiards, snooker, and similar games, to hit (a ball) directly or indirectly into a pocket. **8.** *Informal.* To make (a child) sit on a potty. —*intr. Informal.* To take a pot shot. [Middle English, Old English *pott,* from Vulgar Latin *pottus* (attested only in Late Latin).]

pot² *n. Chiefly Northern British.* A pothole.

pot³ *n. Informal.* **Cannabis** (see). [Perhaps shortened from Mexican Spanish *potiguaya†.*]

pot. potential.

po·ta·ble (pōtə-b'l) *n. Often plural.* Drinkable liquid.
~*adj.* Fit to drink. [French, from Late Latin *pōtābilis,* from Latin *pōtāre,* to drink.] —**po·ta·bil·i·ty** (-bílləti), **po·ta·ble·ness** *n.*

po·tage (po-táazh) *n. French.* A thick soup. [Old French, contents of a pot, from *pot,* POT.]

po·tam·ic (pə-támmik, po-) *adj.* Of or pertaining to rivers. [Greek *potamos,* river.]

po·ta·mol·o·gy (póttə-mólləji) *n.* The scientific study of rivers. [Greek *potamos,* river + -LOGY.]

pot·ash (póttash) *n.* **1.** Potassium carbonate. **2.** Potassium hydroxide. **3.** Any of several compounds containing potassium, especially soluble compounds, such as potassium oxide, potassium chloride, and various potassium sulphates, used chiefly in fertilisers. [Singular of earlier *pot ashes* (translation of obsolete Dutch *potasschen*) : POT + plural of ASH (so called because first obtained by evaporating the lye of wood ashes in iron pots).]

potash feldspar *n.* Potassium feldspar *(see).*

potash muriate *n. Chemistry.* Potassium chloride *(see).*

po·tas·si·um (pə-tássi-əm) *n. Symbol* **K** A soft, silver-white, light, highly or explosively reactive metallic element obtained by electrolysis of its common hydroxide and found in, or converted to, a wide variety of salts used in fertilisers and soaps. Atomic number 19, atomic weight 39.102, melting point 63.2°C, boiling point 765.5°C, relative density 0.856, valency 1. [New Latin, from *potassa,* potassium monoxide, from English POTASH.] —**po·tas·sic** *adj.*

potassium-argon dating *n.* A method of dating rocks and minerals by measuring the isotope argon-40 in the sample, present as a result of the radioactive decay of the naturally occurring isotope potassium-40. The technique can be used for ages up to 10^{10} years.

potassium bitartrate *n.* A white crystalline solid or powder, $KHC_4H_4O_6$, used in baking powder, in the tinning of metals, and as a component of laxatives. Also called "cream of tartar".

potassium bromide *n.* A white crystalline solid or powder, KBr, used as a sedative, in photographic emulsion, and in spectroscopy. Also called "bromide".

potassium carbonate *n.* A transparent, white, deliquescent, granular powder, K_2CO_3, used in making glass, pigments, ceramics, and soaps. Also called "pearl ash", "potash".

potassium chlorate *n.* A moderately poisonous crystalline compound, $KClO_3$, used as an oxidising agent, bleach, and disinfectant, and in making explosives, matches, and fireworks.

potassium chloride *n.* A colourless crystalline solid or powder, KCl, used in fertilisers and in the preparation of potassium compounds. Also called "potassium muriate", "potash muriate".

potassium cyanide *n.* A poisonous white compound, KCN, used in extracting gold and silver from ores, electroplating, photography, and as a fumigant and insecticide. Also called "cyanide".

potassium dichromate *n.* A bright yellowish-red crystalline compound, $K_2Cr_2O_7$, used as an oxidising agent, and in pyrotechnics, explosives, and safety matches.

potassium feldspar *n.* Any member of the feldspar group of minerals that comprises silicates of aluminium and potassium. Orthoclase and microcline are the most common members of the group. Also called "potash feldspar".

potassium hydroxide *n.* A caustic deliquescent solid, KOH, used as a bleach and in detergents and soaps, matches, and many potassium compounds. Also called "caustic potash", "lye".

potassium nitrate *n.* A transparent or white crystalline compound, KNO_3, used to pickle meat and in explosives, matches, rocket propellants, and fertilisers. Also called "nitre", "saltpetre".

potassium permanganate *n.* A dark purple crystalline compound, $KMnO_4$, used as an oxidising agent, disinfectant, and in deodorisers and dyes. Also called "permanganate of potash", "purple salt".

potassium sulphate *n.* A colourless or white crystalline compound, K_2SO_4, used in medicine, glassmaking, fertilisers, and as a reagent in analytical chemistry.

po·ta·tion (pō-táysh'n, pə-) *n. Formal.* **1.** The act of drinking. **2.** A drink, especially an alcoholic drink. [Middle English *potacioun,* from Old French *potation,* from Latin *pōtātiō* (stem *pōtātiōn-*), drinking, from *pōtāre,* to drink.]

po·ta·to (pə-táytō) *n., pl.* **-toes. 1.** A plant, *Solanum tuberosum,* native to South America and widely cultivated for its starchy, edible tubers. **2.** A tuber of this plant, which is cooked and eaten as a vegetable. Also called "Irish potato", "white potato". **3.** Any of several similar plants; especially, the **sweet potato** *(see).* [Spanish *patata,* from Taino *batata.*]

potato beetle *n.* The **Colorado beetle** *(see).*

potato chip *n.* **1.** *Australian, N.Z., & U.S.* A crisp. **2.** *British.* A chip.

po·ta·to·ry (pōtə-təri, -tri) *adj. Formal.* Of, pertaining to, or given to drinking. [Latin *pōtātōrius,* from *pōtāre,* to drink.]

pot-au-feu (pót-ō-fér; *French* -fő) *n.* A thick French soup in which meat and vegetables are simmered, sometimes with rice or pasta. [French, "pot on the fire".]

pot-bel·ly (pót-belli, -bélli) *n., pl.* **-lies. 1.** A protruding abdominal region; a fat, rounded stomach. Also informally called "pot". **2.** A person having a pot-belly. —**pot·bel·lied** *adj.*

pot-belly stove *n. Chiefly U.S.* A short rounded stove in which wood or coal is burned. Also called "pot-bellied stove".

pot-boil·er (pót-boylər) *n.* A literary or artistic work of poor quality, produced as quickly as possible for profit. [So called because the income enables one to keep a cooking pot on the boil, that is, sustains the necessities of life.]

pot-bound (pót-bownd) *adj.* Designating a pot plant whose roots no longer have enough space in the flowerpot to grow, and whose growth above the surface is consequently poor or retarded.

pot-boy (pót-boy) *n. Chiefly British.* Formerly, a boy or man working in an inn or a public house serving customers and doing chores.

po·teen (po-téen, -chéen) *n.* Also **po·theen** (po-théen). Irish whiskey that is distilled unlawfully. [Irish Gaelic *poitín,* small pot, whiskey made in a private still, diminutive of *pota,* POT.]

Po·tem·kin (pə-témkin; *Russian* pət-yómkin), **Grigory Alexandrovich, Prince** (1739–91). Russian soldier and statesman. He became Catherine II's lover and lifelong favourite. He built up the Black Sea Fleet, annexed the Crimea, and campaigned against the Turks (1787–91).

po·ten·cy (pōt'n-si) *n., pl.* **-cies.** Also **po·tence** (pōt'nss) **1.** The quality or state of being potent. **2.** Inherent capacity for growth and development; potentiality. —See Synonyms at **strength.**

po·tent (pōt'nt) *adj.* **1.** Possessing inner or physical strength; powerful. **2.** Capable of commanding attention; able to convince: *potent arguments.* **3.** Having great control or authority. **4.** Capable of causing strong physiological or chemical effects, as medicines or alcoholic drinks might. **5.** Able to achieve sexual penetration of the female and to father children. Said of a male. [Middle English (Scottish), from Latin *potēns* (stem *potent-*), present participle of Old Latin *potēre* (unattested) (superseded by *posse*), to be able, have power.] —**po·tent·ly** *adv.* —**po·tent·ness** *n.*

po·ten·tate (pōt'n-tayt) *n.* **1.** One who has the power and position to rule over others; a monarch. **2.** One who dominates or leads any group or endeavour: *an industrial potentate.* [Middle English *poten-*

tat, from Old French, from Late Latin *potentātus*, from Latin, power, rule, from *potēns*, POTENT.]

po·ten·tial (pə-ténsh'l, pō-) *adj. Abbr.* **pot. 1.** Possible but not yet realised; capable of being but not yet in existence; latent: *"Every admirer is a potential enemy."* (Cyril Connolly). See Synonyms at **latent. 2.** *Grammar.* Expressing possibility, capability, or power. Said of a verb or verb form: *the potential subjunctive.*
~*n. Abbr.* **pot. 1.** The inherent ability or capacity for growth, development, or coming into being: *Women have a potential for political influence that has never been realised.* **2.** The ability to succeed; unrealised talent: *She has great potential.* **3.** *Grammar.* A potential verb form. **4.** *Physics.* The work required to bring a unit electric charge, magnetic pole, or mass from an infinitely distant position to a designated point in a static electric, magnetic, or gravitational field, respectively. **5.** *Electricity.* The potential energy of a unit charge at any point in an electric circuit measured with respect to a specified reference point in the circuit or to earth; voltage. [Middle English *potencial*, from Old French, from Late Latin *potentiālis*, powerful, from *potentia*, latent power, from Latin, potency, from *potēns*, POTENT.] —**po·ten·tial·ly** *adv.*

potential difference *n. Symbol* **V** The difference in electrical potential between two points in a circuit or other system; the work done in moving unit electric charge from one point to the other.

potential energy *n.* The energy of a particle or system of particles derived from position, rather than motion, with respect to a specified reference state taken as zero energy. Compare **kinetic energy.**

po·ten·ti·al·i·ty (pə-ténshi-ál-əti, pō-) *n., pl.* -ties. **1.** Inherent capacity for growth, development, or coming into existence. **2.** Something possessing this capacity.

po·ten·ti·ate (pə-ténshi-ayt, pō-) *tr.v.* -ated, -ating, -ates. **1.** To make possible or effective. **2.** To increase (the effectiveness) of two drugs, hormones, or the like by administering them in combination. [POTENCY + -ATE, by analogy with *substantiate.*] —**po·ten·ti·a·tion** (-áysh'n) *n.*

po·ten·til·la (pŏt'n-tíllə) *n.* Any of numerous plants or shrubs of the genus *Potentilla*, of the North Temperate Zone. See **cinquefoil.** [New Latin, from Medieval Latin, garden valerian, from Latin *potēns*, POTENT.]

po·ten·ti·om·e·ter (pə-ténshi-ómmitər, pō-) *n. Electricity.* **1.** An instrument for measuring an unknown voltage or potential difference by comparison with a standard voltage. **2.** Any three-terminal resistor with an adjustable centre connection, widely used for volume control in radio and television receivers.

pot·head (pót-hed) *n. Slang.* A person who habitually smokes cannabis.

poth·er (póthər) *n.* **1.** A commotion; a disturbance. **2.** A state of nervous activity; fuss. **3.** A choking cloud of smoke or dust.
~*v.* **pothered, -ering, -ers.** —*tr.* To make confused; trouble; worry. —*intr.* To be overly concerned with trifles; fuss. [16th century : origin obscure.]

pot·herb (pót-herb ‖ *U.S. also* -erb) *n.* Any plant whose leaves, stems, or flowers are cooked and eaten or used as seasoning.

pot·hole (pót-hōl) *n.* **1.** A deep hole or pit, especially in a road surface. **2.** A hole in the rocky bed of a stream, formed by the grinding effect of pebbles whirled round by eddies. **3.** Loosely, a vertical cave system, especially in the Pennines of northern England.
~*intr.v.* **potholed, -holing, -holes.** To explore underground caves, especially vertical cave systems, as a hobby or sport. —**pot·hol·er** *n.* —**pot·hol·ing** *n.*

pot·hook (pót-hŏŏk ‖ -hōŏk) *n.* **1.** A bent or hooked piece of iron for hanging a pot or kettle over an open fire. **2.** A curved iron rod with a hooked end used for lifting hot pots, irons, or stove lids. **3.** A curved, S-shaped mark made by children learning to write.

pot·house (pót-howss) *n. British Archaic.* A small, rough public house or tavern. Used derogatively.

pot·hunt·er (pót-huntər) *n.* **1.** One who hunts game for food, ignoring the rules of sport. **2.** One who participates in contests simply to win prizes. —**pot·hunt·ing** *adj. & n.*

po·tiche (po-téesh) *n.* A vase or jar with a round or polygonal body tapering at the neck and having a removable cover. [French, from *pot*, POT.]

po·tion (pósh'n) *n.* A liquid drink or dose, especially of medicinal, magic, or poisonous content. [Middle English *pocioun*, from Old French *potion*, from Latin *pōtiō* (stem *pōtiōn-*), from *pōtāre* (alternative past participle *pōtus*), to drink.]

Po·ti·phar (pótti-fər, -faar) *n.* Pharaoh's chief officer, who purchased Joseph as a slave. Genesis 39:1–20.

pot·latch (pót-lach) *n.* A ceremonial feast among North American Indians living on the Pacific coast of Washington, British Columbia, and Alaska, at the end of which the host distributes valuable gifts or destroys property to show that he can afford to do so. [Chinook, from Nootka *patlatsh*, giving, gift.]

pot luck *n.* Whatever food happens to be available. —**take pot luck. 1.** To take whatever food is offered. **2.** To choose at random.

pot marigold *n.* A plant, *Calendula officinalis*, native to southern Europe, often grown for its showy yellow or orange flowers, the dried florets of which were formerly used for seasoning.

pot marjoram *n.* **Marjoram** *(see).*

Po·to·mac (pə-tŏmək) *n.* River in the eastern United States. Rising in the Allegheny Mountains of West Virginia, it flows 462 kilometres (287 miles) to the Atlantic Ocean at Chesapeake Bay. Washington D.C. stands at its highest navigable point.

po·to·roo (pŏtə-rŏŏ) *n., pl.* -roos. *Australian.* A **kangaroo rat** *(see).* [From a native Australian name.]

pot·pie (pót-pī) *n.* A mixture of meat or poultry and vegetables covered with a pastry crust and baked in a deep dish.

pot plant *n.* **1.** A cultivated plant grown in a flowerpot; especially, one used as a house plant. **2.** *Informal.* A cannabis plant.

pot·pour·ri (pó-pŏŏrri ‖ *U.S.* -pŏŏ-rée) *n., pl.* -ris. **1.** A combination of various incongruous elements. **2.** A miscellaneous anthology or collection. **3.** A mixture of dried flower petals and spices, kept in a jar and used to scent the air. [French *pot pourri* (translation of Spanish OLLA PODRIDA) : POT + *pourri*, rotten, from the past participle of *pourrir*, to rot, from Vulgar Latin *putrīre* (unattested), variant of Latin *putrēre*, from *puter*, rotten.]

pot-roast, pot roast (pót-rōst) *n.* A piece of meat, usually beef, that is browned and then cooked until tender, often with vegetables, in a covered pot.
~*tr.v.* **pot-roasted, -roasting, -roasts.** To cook (meat) in this way.

Pots·dam (póts-dam). City in eastern Germany, on the river Havel. It was the administrative capital of the Prussian province of Brandenburg, and the location of the Potsdam Conference (1945).

pot·sherd (pót-sherd) *n.* Also **pot·shard** (-shard). A fragment of broken pottery, as found in an archaeological excavation. Also called "shard", "sherd". [Middle English : POT + SHARD.]

pot shot *n.* **1.** A shot aimed to kill, without regard for sporting rules. **2. a.** A random shot. **b.** A shot fired at an animal or person within easy range. [Referring to shots fired by a hunter who kills game only for his pot.]

pot still *n.* A still used in whisky-making, in which the mash is heated directly.

pot·stone (pót-stōn) *n.* An impure variety of soapstone once used to make cooking vessels.

pot·ta·ble (póttə-b'l) *adj.* Designating a ball in billiards, snooker, or similar games that can be potted relatively easily.

pot·tage (póttij) *n.* **1.** A thick soup or stew of vegetables and sometimes meat. **2.** *Archaic.* Porridge. [Middle English *potage*, from Old French, *potage*, POTAGE.]

pot·ted (póttid) *adj.* **1. a.** Placed in a pot. **b.** Grown in a pot, as a plant. **2.** Preserved in a pot or jar. **3.** *Chiefly British Informal.* Shortened or summarised often in a crude or superficial way: *a potted history of the Church.* **4.** *Chiefly U.S. Slang.* Intoxicated.

pot·ter¹ (póttər) *n.* A person who makes earthenware pots, dishes, or other vessels. [Middle English, Old English *pottere*, from POT.]

potter² *v.* -tered, -tering, -ters. Also *chiefly U.S.* **put·ter** (púttər). —*intr.* **1.** To occupy oneself aimlessly; tinker about. Usually used with *about.* **2.** To move about or do things slowly or feebly. Often used with *about.* —*tr.* To waste (especially time) in idling. Used with *away.* [Frequentative of dialect *pote*, to poke, from Old English *potian*, to thrust.] —**pot·ter·er** *n.*

Pot·ter (póttər), **(Helen) Beatrix** (1866–1943). British writer and illustrator of children's books. *The Tale of Peter Rabbit* (1902) was the first in a series of perennially popular works.

Potter, Stephen (1900–69). British writer. He is remembered chiefly for his humorous books offering advice on outwitting and outshining other people. These include *Gamesmanship* (1947), *Lifemanship* (1950), and *One-Upmanship* (1952).

Pot·ter·ies, The (póttəriz). Trent Valley region of Staffordshire, north-central England. Situated around Stoke-on-Trent, it includes the towns of Burslem, Hanley, Longton, Fenton, and Tunstall. Josiah Wedgwood founded his pottery here (1769). It became the centre of the English pottery industry in the 19th century.

pot·ter's clay (póttərz) *n.* A clay suitable for making pottery or for modelling, low in iron content. Also called "potter's earth".

potter's wheel *n.* A revolving, horizontal disc, operated electrically or by treadle, upon which clay is shaped manually.

potter wasp *n.* Any of various wasps of the genus *Eumenes*, characteristically building pot-shaped nests of clay.

pot·ter·y (póttəri) *n., pl.* -ies. **1.** Ware, such as vases, pots, bowls, or plates, made of stoneware, earthenware or porcelain. **2.** The craft or occupation of a potter. **3.** The establishment in which this craft is pursued. [Middle English, from Old French *poterie*, from *potier*, POTTER.]

potting shed *n.* A garden shed in which plants can be grown and protected from harsh weather before being planted outside.

pot·tle (pótt'l) *n.* **1.** A pot or drinking vessel with a two-quart capacity. **2.** The liquid contained in such a vessel. **3.** An old liquid measure equal to about two quarts. **4.** A small basket of strawberries. [Middle English *potel*, from Old French, diminutive of POT.]

pot·to (póttō) *n., pl.* -tos. **1.** Any of several small African primates of the genera *Perodicticus* and *Arctocebus*; especially *P. potto*, having woolly fur. **2.** The **kinkajou** *(see).* [Probably from Guinea dialect; akin to Wolof *pata*, a tailless monkey.]

Pott's disease *n.* Tuberculosis of the spine often resulting in deformity. [After Percivall *Pott* (1714–88), British surgeon.]

pot·ty¹ (pótti) *adj.* -tier, -tiest. *Chiefly British Informal.* **1.** Somewhat silly or crazy; foolish. **2.** Of little importance; trivial. [Perhaps from the phrase *to go to pot*, to deteriorate, from POT (liquor).]

potty² *n., pl.* -ties. A child's chamber pot.

pot·ty-trained (pótti-traynd) *adj. Informal.* Designating a child who has learnt to use a potty or lavatory; toilet-trained.

pot-wal·lop·er (pót-wollopər, -wóllapər) *n.* Also **pot-wal·ler** (-wollər, -wáwlər). In some English boroughs before 1832, a man entitled to vote as a result of having his own fireplace. [Literally, "pot-boiler", from POT + dialect *wallop, wall,* to boil, from Old English *weallan,* to boil.]

pouch (powch) *n.* **1.** A small flexible receptacle; a bag. **2.** A small bag of leather or other relatively nonporous material for carrying loose pipe tobacco. **3.** *Archaic.* A purse for small coins. **4.** A leather bag for carrying powder or small-arms ammunition. **5.** A bag for mail, especially one for diplomatic dispatches. **6.** Anything resembling a bag in shape: *He had pouches under his eyes.* **7.** *Zoology.* A saclike structure, such as the cheek pockets of the hamster, or the external abdominal pocket in which marsupials carry their young. **8.** *Anatomy.* A small saclike structure occurring as an outgrowth of a larger structure. **9.** *Scottish.* A pocket.
~*v.* **pouched, pouching, pouches.** —*tr.* **1.** To place in or as if in a pouch; pocket: *He pouched all the money.* **2.** To cause to resemble a pouch in shape. **3.** To swallow. Used of certain birds and fishes. —*intr.* To assume the form of a pouch or pouchlike cavity. [Middle English *pouche,* from Old French *po(u)che,* from Frankish *pokka* (unattested).] **—pouch·y** *adj.*

pouffe, pouf (pōōf) *n.* **1. a.** A large, firm cushion used as a seat. **b.** A small, soft, backless couch. **2.** A woman's hairstyle popular in the 18th century, characterised by high rolled puffs. **3.** Any part of a dress or other garment gathered into a puff. **4.** A rounded soft pad used to stiffen or give body to puffs in the hair, or puffs in a garment. **5.** Variant of **poof.** [French (imitative).]

pou·lard, pou·larde (pōō-laard ‖ *U.S.* pōō-lárd) *n.* A young hen that has been spayed for fattening. Compare **capon.** [French *poularde,* from Old French *pollarde,* from *polle, poule,* hen, from Vulgar Latin *pulla* (unattested), from Latin *pullus,* young of an animal.]

Pou·lenc (pōō-langk; *French* pōō-láNk), **Francis** (1899–1963). French composer, member of Les Six. His works range from song cycles like *Le Bestiaire* (1919) to the operas *Les Mamelles de Tirésias* (1947) and *Dialogue des Carmélites* (1957).

poult (pōlt ‖ polt) *n.* A young domestic fowl or related bird. [Middle English *pult,* short for *polet, poulet,* pullet, from Old French *poulet,* diminutive of *poule,* hen, chicken. See **poulard.**]

poul·ter·er (pōl-tərər ‖ pól-) *n.* A poultry dealer. [Middle English *poulter,* poulterer, from Old French *pouletier,* from *poulet,* POULT.]

poul·tice (pōl-tiss ‖ pól-) *n.* A moist, soft mass of bread, meal, kaolin, or other adhesive substance, usually heated, spread on cloth, and applied to warm, moisten, or stimulate an aching or inflamed part of the body. Also called "cataplasm". [Earlier *pultes* (taken as singular), from Medieval Latin *pultēs,* pulp, thick paste, from Latin, plural of *puls* (stem *pult-*), pap, possibly from Greek *poltos,* porridge.] **—poul·tice** *tr.v.*

poul·try (pōl-tri ‖ pól-) *n.* Domestic birds, such as chickens, turkeys, ducks, or geese. [Middle English *pultrie,* from Old French *pouleterie,* from *pouletier,* POULTERER.]

pounce[1] (pownss; *West Indian also* pungss) *v.* **pounced, pouncing, pounces.** —*intr.* **1.** To spring or swoop with intent to seize someone or something. Used with *on, upon,* or *at.* **2.** To attack suddenly and unexpectedly. —*tr. Rare.* To seize with or as if with talons.
~*n.* **1.** The act of pouncing. **2.** The talon or claw of a bird of prey. [Middle English, talon, claw (hence verb, to seize), probably variant of *punson,* PUNCHEON.] **—pounc·er** *n.*

pounce[2] *n.* **1.** A fine powder formerly used to seal the porous surfaces of paper and parchment and prepare them for writing on. **2.** A fine powder, such as pulverised charcoal, dusted over a stencil to transfer a design to an underlying surface.
~*tr.v.* **pounced, pouncing, pounces.** **1.** To sprinkle, smooth, or treat with pounce. **2.** To transfer (a stencilled design) with pounce. [French *ponce,* from Vulgar Latin *pōmex* (unattested), variant of Latin *pūmex,* PUMICE.] **—pounc·er** *n.*

pounce[3] *tr.v.* **pounced, pouncing, pounces.** To ornament (metal, for example) by perforating from the back with a pointed implement. [Middle English *pounsen,* variant of *pounsonen,* from Old French *poinçonner,* to prick, stamp, from *poinçon,* pointed tool. See **punch, puncheon.**]

pounce box *n.* A small box with a perforated top, formerly used to sprinkle sand or pounce on writing paper to dry the ink.

poun·cet box (pówn-sit, -sət) *n.* A small perfume box with a perforated top. [Perhaps from *pounced box* (perforated box).]

pound[1] (pound; *West Indies also* pungd) *n., pl.* **pound** or **pounds.** **1.** *Abbr.* **lb a.** A unit of mass in the avoirdupois system equal to 7,000 grains and divided into 16 ounces. It is equivalent to 0.453592 kilogram. Also called "pound avoirdupois". **b.** A unit of weight in the troy system equal to 5,760 grains and divided into 12 ounces. It is equal to 0.373242 kilogram. Also called "pound troy". **c.** A unit of weight in the apothecaries' system equal to 5,760 grains or one pound troy. **2.** A unit of weight differing in various countries and times, especially one equal to half a kilogram. **3.** A British unit of force equal to the weight of a standard one-pound mass where the local acceleration of gravity is 32.174 feet per second per second. Also called "pound force". **4.** *Symbol* **£ a.** The basic monetary unit of the United Kingdom, equal to 100 new pence; before 1971 it was equal to 20 shillings or 240 old pence. Also called "pound sterling". **b.** The basic monetary unit of various dependent territories of the United Kingdom, equal to 100 pence. **c.** The Irish **punt** *(see).* **5. a.** The basic monetary unit of Lebanon, Sudan, Syria, and Egypt, equal to 100 piastres. **b.** The basic monetary unit of Cyprus and Malta, equal to 1,000 mils. **c.** Formerly, the basic monetary unit of Israel, equal to 100 agorot. It is now worth 1/10 of the shekel. **6.** A former monetary unit of Scotland before the Union, usually worth a small fraction of the pound sterling. Also called "pound Scots". **7.** A coin or note worth one pound. [Middle English *po(u)nd,* Old English *pund,* from Latin *pondō* (a weight of 12 ounces).]

pound[2] *v.* **pounded, pounding, pounds.** —*tr.* **1.** To strike or hammer with a heavy blow or blows. **2.** To drive (something) in or out with repeated blows; hammer. **3.** To beat to a powder or pulp; pulverise or crush. **4.** To instil by persistent and emphatic repetition: *pound knowledge into their heads.* **5.** To assault with heavy gunfire. —*intr.* **1.** To strike vigorous, repeated blows. Often used with *on* or *at: He pounded on the table.* **2.** To move along heavily and noisily. **3.** To pulsate rapidly and heavily: *Her heart pounded.* **4.** To work or move laboriously: *a ship pounding through heavy seas.* **5.** To assault an enemy position with heavy gunfire. Often used with *away at.* **6.** To do something in a vigorous attacking way: *pounded away at the typewriters.* **—pound out.** To produce something by or as if by pounding: *pounding out his new novel.*
~*n.* **1.** A heavy blow. **2.** The sound of a heavy blow; a thump. **3.** The act of pounding. [Alteration (with unhistorical *d*) of earlier *p(o)unne,* Middle English *pounen,* Old English *pūnian*†.]

pound[3] *n.* **1.** A public enclosure for the confinement of stray livestock or dogs. **2.** A place in which impounded property is held until redeemed. **3.** An enclosure in which animals or fish are trapped or kept. **4.** A place of confinement for lawbreakers. **5.** A stretch of canal between two adjoining locks.
~*tr.v.* **pounded, pounding, pounds.** To impound. [Middle English *pound,* Old English *pund-,* as in *pundfald;* compare PINFOLD.]

Pound, Ezra (Loomis) (1885–1972). U.S. poet. He was instrumental in establishing the modernist movement in poetry. As a result of his pro-Fascist stance during World War II, he was confined to a mental hospital in the United States until 1958, when he returned to Italy. His best-known work is the unfinished sequence of poems, the *Cantos* (1925–60).

pound·age (pówndij) *n.* **1.** A tax or commission based on value per pound (sterling). **2.** A rate or charge based on weight in pounds. **3.** Weight measured in pounds.

pound·al (pównd'l) *n. Abbr.* **pdl.** A unit of force in the foot-pound-second system of measurement, equal to the force required to accelerate a standard one-pound mass one foot per second per second. [*pound* quint*al.*]

pound cake *n.* A rich cake containing eggs and originally made with a pound each of flour, butter, and sugar.

pound·er (pówndər) *n.* **1. a.** Something weighing a pound. **b.** Something weighing a specified number of pounds. Used in combination: *a quarter-pounder.* **2.** A gun firing shells that weigh a specified number of pounds. Used in combination: *an eighteen-pounder.* **3. a.** Something costing a pound. **b.** Something worth a specified number of pounds. Used in combination: *a five-pounder.*

pound-fool·ish (pównd-fōōlish) *adj.* Unwise in dealing with large sums of money or important matters. See **penny-wise.**

pound of flesh *n.* Something owed and harshly insisted upon. [From Antonio's debt in Shakespeare's *Merchant of Venice.*]

pour (por ‖ pōr) *v.* **poured, pouring, pours.** —*tr.* **1.** To make (a fluid or granular solid) stream or flow. **2.** To send forth, produce, express, or utter copiously, as if in a stream or flood. **—pour out.** To give unrestrained expression to: *poured out his tale of woe.* —*intr.* **1.** To stream or flow continuously or profusely. **2.** To rain hard or heavily. **3.** To go forth or stream in large numbers or quantities. **4.** To fill cups with tea, coffee, or the like: *Will you pour?*
~*n.* A pouring or flowing forth; especially, a downpour of rain. [Middle English *pouren*†.] **—pour·er** *n.*

pour·boire (poor-bwaar, pōōr-bwár) *n.* Money given as a gratuity; a tip. [French, "for drinking".]

pour·par·ler (poor-párlay ‖ -paar-láy) *n.* Conversation or discussion preliminary to negotiation. [French, "for speaking".]

pour point *n.* The lowest temperature at which an oil or other liquid will pour when cooled under given conditions.

pousse-ca·fé (pōōss-ka-fáy) *n.* **1.** A brandy or liqueur served after dinner with coffee. **2.** *Chiefly U.S.* A drink consisting of several layers of liqueurs. [French, "coffee pusher".]

pous·sette (pōō-sét) *n.* A country-dance figure in which a couple or couples join hands and dance round one another. [French, from *pousse,* a push, from *pousser,* to push, from Old French, from Latin *pulsāre,* frequentative of *pellere,* to push, beat.] **—pous·sette** *intr.v.*

pous·sin (pōō-sáN) *n.* A young chicken, five to six weeks old and weighing about one and a half pounds, reared for eating. [French.]

Poussin, Nicolas (1594–1665). French painter. His landscapes and historical and religious subjects are considered some of the finest examples of the classical style.

pout[1] (powt) *v.* **pouted, pouting, pouts.** —*intr.* **1.** To protrude the lips in an expression of displeasure or sulkiness. **2.** To show displeasure or disappointment; sulk. **3.** To project or protrude: *His lips pouted in expectation of a kiss.* —*tr.* **1.** To push out or protrude (the lips). **2.** To utter or express with a pout.
~*n.* **1.** A protrusion of the lips, especially as an expression of sullen or childish discontent. **2.** *Sometimes plural.* A fit of petulant sulkiness. [Middle English *pouten,* perhaps from Old English *pūtian* (unattested), to swell, be inflated, from Germanic.]

pout[2] *n., pl.* **pout** or **pouts.** **1.** Any of various European food fishes related to the cod; especially, the **bib** or the **Norway pout** *(both of which see).* **2.** Any of various other fishes, such as the **eelpout** *(see).* [Middle English *poute* (unattested), Old English *-pūte* (as in *ælepūte,* eelpout), from Germanic; akin to POUT (expression).]

pout·er (pówtər) *n.* **1.** Any of a breed of pigeons capable of distending the crop until the breast becomes puffed out. **2.** One who pouts.

pov·er·ty (póvvǝrti) *n.* **1. a.** The state or condition of being poor; lack of the means of providing material needs or comforts. **b.** The renunciation by religious persons of the right to personal property. **2.** Lack of something necessary or desirable; insufficiency; paucity: *a poverty of talent.* **3.** Deficiency in amount; scantiness: *the poverty of his vocabulary.* **4.** Unproductiveness; infertility: *the poverty of the soil.* [Middle English *poverte*, from Old French, from Latin *paupertās* (stem *paupertāt-*), from *pauper*, poor.]

poverty line *n.* A level of income that is considered a minimum for a decent standard of living.

poverty trap *n.* A situation in which a person's net income will fall through taxation or loss of benefits if his gross income increases.

pow (pow) *n.* The sound of a blow, collision, or explosion. ~*interj.* Used to imitate the sound of a blow, collision, or explosion. [Imitative.]

POW, P.O.W. prisoner of war.

pow·an (pów-ǝn) *n.* Any of various related freshwater fishes; especially, the whitefish *Coregonus clupeoides*, found in Scottish lakes. Also called "lake herring". [Scottish variant of POLLAN.]

pow·der (pówdǝr) *n.* **1.** A substance consisting of ground, pulverised, or otherwise finely dispersed solid particles. **2.** Any of various preparations in this form, such as certain medicines, and detergents; especially, a flesh-coloured cosmetic powder used on the face to give a matt complexion. **3. a.** An explosive mixture, **gunpowder** *(see).* **b.** Any of various similar explosive substances. **4.** Powder snow. —**keep (one's) powder dry.** To wait for a suitable opportunity to deal with an opponent. ~*v.* **powdered, -dering, -ders.** —*tr.* **1.** To reduce to powder; pulverise. **2.** To dust or cover with or as if with powder; apply powder or small specks or particles to. —*intr.* **1.** To become pulverised; turn to powder. **2.** To use powder as a cosmetic. [Middle English *poudre*, from Old French, from Latin *pulvis* (stem *pulver-*).] —**pow·der·er** *n.*

powder blue *n.* Moderate to pale blue. [The colour of powdered smalt.] —**pow·der-blue** (pówdǝr-blōō) *adj.*

pow·dered (pówdǝrd) *adj.* Produced in the form of a powder.

powder flask *n.* A small flask or similar receptacle formerly used for carrying gunpowder.

powder horn *n.* A container consisting of an animal's horn capped at the open end, formerly used to carry gunpowder.

powder keg *n.* **1.** A barrel for holding gunpowder or other explosives. **2.** A potentially explosive thing or situation.

powder magazine *n.* A storage place for gunpowder.

powder metallurgy *n.* The technology of powdered metals, especially the production and use of metallic powders for making objects by pressure and heating.

powder puff *n.* A soft pad for applying cosmetic or talcum powder.

powder room *n.* A public lavatory for women.

powder snow *n.* Loose, dry snow on the ground, making an ideal skiing surface. Also called "powder".

pow·der·y (pówdǝri) *adj.* **1.** Composed of or similar to powder. **2.** Dusted or covered with or as if with powder. **3.** Easily made into powder; friable.

powdery mildew *n.* **1.** Any of various plant diseases caused by fungi of the family Erysiphaceae and resulting in a white, powdery growth appearing mostly on the upper surface of leaves. **2.** Any of the fungi causing such a disease.

Pow·ell (pów-ǝl, pó-, -il), **Anthony (Dymoke)** (1905–). British novelist. His 12-volume novel cycle *A Dance to the Music of Time* is a social satire of 20th-century Britain portraying Nicholas Jenkins and his upper-middle-class friends.

Powell, (John) Enoch (1912–98). British politician. He became a Conservative M.P. in 1950. His controversial views on immigration and his opposition to membership of the European Community cost him his place in the Shadow Cabinet. He left the Conservative Party, and was Ulster Unionist Coalition M.P. for South Down 1974–87. —**Pow·el·lism** *n.* —**Pow·el·lite** *n. & adj.*

pow·er (pów-ǝr, powr) *n.* **1.** The ability or capacity to act or perform effectively. **2.** *Often plural.* **a.** A specific capacity, faculty, or aptitude: *his powers of concentration.* **b.** Natural abilities or capacities: *at the height of her powers.* **3.** Strength or force exerted or capable of being exerted; might. **4. a.** The ability or official capacity to exercise control; authority. **b.** A right; a prerogative. **5.** A person, group, or nation having great influence or control over others. **6.** The might of a nation, political organisation, or similar group. **7.** Forcefulness; effectiveness. **8.** *Informal.* A large number or amount: *a power of good.* **9.** *Physics.* The rate at which work is done, mathematically expressed as the first derivative of work with respect to time and commonly measured in units such as the watt and horsepower. **10. a.** The ability to do work; energy. **b.** The capacity to make machines and other physical systems operate, or to generate light and heat: *wave power.* **c.** Electrical or mechanical energy as opposed to unaided human energy. Also used adjectivally: *power tools; a power saw; a power loom.* **11.** *Mathematics.* **a.** The product of a quantity multiplied by itself a specified number of times. **b.** Loosely, an **exponent** *(see).* **c.** The number of elements in a finite set. **12.** *Optics.* A measure of the **magnification** *(see)* of an optical instrument, such as a microscope or telescope. **13.** *Plural.* **a.** Deities; supernatural spirits. **b.** In medieval angelology, the sixth group of angels in the hierarchical order of nine. See **angel.** **14.** *Archaic.* An armed force. —See Synonyms at **strength.** —**the powers that be.** The authorities; those in power. ~ *tr. v.* **powered, -ering, -ers.** To supply with power, especially

mechanical power: *steam-powered* ; *nuclear-powered.* ~*adj.* Designating or pertaining to a mechanical device in which the force or torque applied by an operator is amplified by an engine: *power brakes; power steering.* [Middle English *pouer*, from Old French *poeir, povoir*, from *poeir*, to be able, from Old Latin *potēre* (unattested) (superseded by *posse*).]

power base *n.* A position that allows a person or group to build up and consolidate power, usually through the support of a committed following: *used the Young Turks of the party as his power base.*

pow·er·boat (pów-ǝr-bōt, pówr-) *n.* A motorboat *(see).*

power broker *n.* One who exerts influence over those in power, especially by promising or withdrawing the support of his followers. —**pow·er·brok·ing** *n.*

power cut *n.* An interruption in the supply of electricity to a particular area.

power dive *n.* A downward plunge of an aircraft accelerated by both gravity and engine power. —**pow·er-dive** (pów-ǝr-dīv, pówr-) *v.*

power drill *n.* **1.** A portable electric drill. **2.** A large drilling machine having a vertical, motorised drill set in a table stand.

pow·er·ful (pów-ǝr-f'l, pówr-) *adj.* **1.** Having or capable of exerting power. **2.** Strong in effect. **3.** *Chiefly U.S. Regional.* Great: *It did a powerful lot of good.* —**pow·er·ful·ly** *adv.* —**pow·er·ful·ness** *n.*

pow·er·house (pów-ǝr-howss, pówr-) *n.* **1.** A power station. **2.** A person or group having great strength or contributing greatly to the activity of a body: *the nation's intellectual powerhouse.*

pow·er·less (pów-ǝr-lǝss, pówr-, -liss) *adj.* **1.** Lacking strength or power; helpless; ineffectual. **2.** Lacking legal or other authority. —**pow·er·less·ly** *adv.* —**pow·er·less·ness** *n.*

power of appointment *n. Law.* A power, granted by deed or will, giving a person the authority to assign an estate, or an interest in it, to any person *(general power)* or to a person from a particular group *(special power).*

power of attorney *n. Abbr.* **P/A, P.A.** *Law.* A legal instrument authorising one to act as another's attorney, legal representative, or agent; legal authority to act on behalf of another. Also called "procuration".

power pack *n. Electronics.* A compact, often portable, device that converts supply current to direct or alternating current as required by specific equipment.

power plant *n.* **1.** All the equipment, including structural members, that constitutes a unit power source: *the power plant of a lorry.* **2.** A complex of structures, machinery, and associated equipment for generating power, especially electric power.

power point *n.* A device into which an electric plug can be inserted in order to connect it with a circuit. Also called "point".

power politics *n.* Used with a singular verb. International diplomacy in which each nation uses or threatens to use military or economic power to further its own interests. [Translation of German *Machtpolitik*.]

power series *n. Mathematics.* A sum of successively higher integral powers of a variable or combination of variables, each multiplied by a constant coefficient.

power-shar·ing (pów-ǝr-shair-ing, pówr-) *n.* A system whereby minority parties or interests exercise some measure of political power in cooperation with the majority. —**power-shar·ing** *adj.*

power shovel *n.* A large, usually mobile machine having a boom, a dipper stick, and a bucket for excavating.

power station *n.* A building housing equipment for generating electricity.

pow-wow (pów-wow) *n.* **1. a.** A conference or meeting with or of North American Indians. **b.** *Informal.* Any conference or gathering for discussion. **2.** Among some North American Indians, a medicine man. **3.** A North American Indian ceremony in which incantations and dancing are used to invoke divine aid in hunting, in battle, or against disease. ~*intr.v.* **powwowed, -wowing, -wows.** To hold a powwow. [Algonquian; akin to Narraganset *powwaw*, magician.]

Pow·ys (pów-iss, pó-). Inland mountainous county of central Wales, created in 1974 from Radnorshire, Breconshire, and Montgomeryshire, which survived the local government reorganisation of 1996, albeit with some boundary changes, as a Unitary Authority area.

Powys, John Cowper (1872–1963). British author. His brothers Theodore Francis (1875–1953) and Llewelyn (1884–1939) were also writers. John Cowper wrote poetry and long, mystical novels set in the West Country, such as *A Glastonbury Romance* (1932).

pox (poks) *n.* **1.** Any disease characterised by purulent skin eruptions, such as chicken pox or smallpox. **2.** Syphilis. —**a pox on (someone** or **something).** *Archaic.* Used to wish misfortune and calamity on someone or something. [Alteration of *pocks*, plural of POCK (mark).]

Poz·nań (póz-nan; *Polish* -nañ). *German* **Pos·en** (pó'z'n). Capital of Poznań Province in west Poland, situated on the river Warta. It was the residence of the Polish kings until 1296. During World War II, it was occupied by Germany and badly damaged. In 1956, it was the scene of severe rioting over economic and political problems.

poz·zuo·la·na (pót-swǝ-láanǝ) *n.* Also **poz·zo·la·na** (pót-sǝ-). **1.** A siliceous volcanic ash used to produce hydraulic cement. **2.** Any artificially produced substance resembling this ash. [Italian *pozzolana*, "of Pozzuoli," town near Vesuvius.] —**poz·zuo·la·nic** *adj.*

pp *Music.* pianissimo.

pp. **1.** pages. **2.** past participle. **3.** *Music.* pianissimo.

p.p. 1. parcel post. 2. parish priest. 3. past participle. 4. per procurationem. 5. postpaid.

P.P. 1. parish priest. 2. postpaid.

ppd. 1. postpaid. 2. prepaid.

pph. pamphlet.

P.P.S. 1. Parliamentary Private Secretary. 2. additional postscript. [Latin *post postscriptum*].

p.q. previous question.

P.Q. Province of Quebec.

Pr The symbol for the element praseodymium.

PR public relations.

pr. 1. pair. 2. present. 3. price. 4. printing. 5. pronoun.

Pr. 1. priest. 2. prince. 3. Provençal.

P.R. 1. proportional representation. 2. public relations. 3. Puerto Rico.

praam, pram (praam, pram) *n.* 1. A flat-bottomed boat used especially in the Baltic as a barge. 2. *Chiefly British.* A small dinghy having a flat, snub-nosed bow. [Dutch, from Middle Dutch *praem,* from Old Slavonic *pramŭ.*]

prac·ti·ca·ble (práktikǝ-b'l) *adj.* 1. Capable of being effected, done, or executed; feasible. 2. Capable of being used for a specified purpose: *a practicable way of entry.* —See Synonyms at **possible.** —See Usage note at **practical.** [French *practicable,* from *pratiquer,* to PRACTISE.] —**prac·ti·ca·bil·i·ty** (-bílloti) *n.* —**prac·ti·ca·bly** *adv.*

prac·ti·cal (práktik'l) *adj.* 1. Of, pertaining to, governed by, or acquired through practice or action, rather than theory, speculation, or ideals. 2. Manifested in or involving practice. 3. Actually engaged in some work or occupation. 4. Capable of being used or put into effect. 5. a. Functioning well in actual use; suitable for its purpose: *Season tickets are very practical.* b. Designed to serve a purpose without elaboration: *practical low-heeled shoes.* 6. Concerned with the production or operation of something useful: *Woodworking is a practical art.* 7. Level-headed, efficient, and down-to-earth. 8. Being actually so in almost every respect; virtual: *a practical disaster.* —See Synonyms at **possible.**

~*n.* An examination testing a student's practical ability in a subject: *a chemistry practical.* [Late Latin *practicus,* practical, from Greek *praktikos,* from *praktos,* to be done, from *prattein, prassein,* to practise.] —**prac·ti·cal·i·ty** (prákti-kál-ǝti), **prac·ti·cal·ness** *n.*

Usage: Practical and *practicable* are sometimes confused. A *practical* solution to a problem is one of proven effectiveness; a *practicable* solution is one that is capable of being put into effect, though it may not necessarily solve the problem. There may be several *practicable* suggestions for dealing with a situation, but not all of these may be *practical* ones. *Practicable* is not used of people, and thus lacks the sense of down-to-earth efficiency which is apparent in such contexts as *John is a very practical person.* In contemporary usage, *practical* seems to be taking over some of the senses of *practicable,* but the trend is open to criticism.

practical joke *n.* A mischievous trick played on a person especially to cause him or her to feel embarrassment or indignity.

prac·ti·cal·ly (práktikli) *adv.* 1. In a way that is practical. 2. In every important respect; virtually. 3. Almost.

Usage: Practically is now widely used in such senses as "in effect": *The species is practically extinct;* and "nearly": *He had practically finished eating when I arrived.* These uses are often criticised on the grounds that, as the events in question have not taken place "in practice", the word *practically* is inappropriate.

practical nurse *n.* *U.S.* A professional nurse who is trained but not registered. Compare **registered nurse.**

prac·tice (práktiss) *n.* 1. A habitual or customary action or way of doing something: *make a practice of being punctual.* 2. a. Repeated performance of an activity in order to learn or perfect a skill. b. *Archaic.* The skill so learned or perfected. c. The condition of being skilled through repeated performance: *He is out of practice at golf.* 3. The act or process of doing something; a performance. 4. The exercise of an occupation or profession, such as medicine or law: *set up in practice as a solicitor.* 5. The business of a professional person, such as a solicitor or doctor: *How large is the practice?* 6. *Plural.* Habitual actions or acts, especially when they are objectionable, questionable, or unacceptable. 7. The methods of procedure used in a court of law. 8. *Archaic.* a. The act of tricking. b. A stratagem; a trick. —See Synonyms at **habit.** [Middle English *practisen,* from Old French *practiser, pratiquer,* from Medieval Latin *practicāre,* from Late Latin *practicus,* PRACTICAL.]

Usage: Both the noun and the verb are usually spelt with a *c* in American English. In British English, only the noun has a *c;* the verb has an *s.* Confusion sometimes arises when the noun and past participle are used adjectivally: *a practice match* but *a practised tennis-player.*

prac·tise, *U.S.* **prac·tice** (práktiss) *v.* **-tised, -tising, -tises.** —*tr.* 1. To do or perform habitually or customarily; make a habit of. 2. To exercise or perform repeatedly in order to acquire or polish a skill: *practise a dance step.* 3. *Chiefly U.S.* To give lessons or repeated instructions to; drill: *to practise students in handwriting.* 4. To work at, especially as a profession: *practise law.* 5. To carry out in action; act in accordance with: *practise one's religion.* 6. To take advantage of; impose upon. Used with *on* or *upon.* —*intr.* 1. To do or perform something habitually or repeatedly. 2. To do something repeatedly in order to acquire or polish a skill. 3. To work at a profession. See Usage at **practice.**

prac·tised (práktist) *adj.* 1. Proficient; skilled; expert. 2. Acquired or brought to perfection by practice.

prac·tis·ing (prákti-sing) *adj.* 1. Actively professing and adhering to the beliefs, way of life, or principles of: *a practising Christian.* 2. Actively employed as or engaged in the profession of: *She is both a novelist and a practising barrister.*

prac·ti·tion·er (prak-tísh'n-ǝr) *n.* One who practises an occupation, profession, or technique: *a medical practitioner.* [From earlier *practician,* from obsolete French *practicien,* from *pra(c)tique,* practice, from Late Latin *practicus,* PRACTICAL.]

prae-. Variant of **pre-.**

prae·di·al, pre·dial (préedi-ǝl) *adj.* 1. Pertaining to land or its products. 2. Attached to or arising from land or landed property: *praedial serfs.* [Medieval Latin *praediālis,* of an estate, from Latin *praedium,* estate, from *praes,* surety.]

praefect. Variant of **prefect.**

prae·mu·ni·re (préemew-nír-i) *n.* *Law.* 1. Formerly in Britain, the offence of appealing to or obeying a foreign court or authority, such as that of the Pope, thus challenging the supremacy of the Crown. 2. The writ charging this offence. 3. The penalty for this offence. [Middle English, from Medieval Latin *praemūnīre (facias),* "that you warn (someone to appear)" (words in the writ), from Latin *praemūnīre,* to fortify (meaning influenced by *praemonēre,* to forewarn) : *prae,* before + *mūnīre,* to fortify.]

prae·no·men (prée-nōmǝn) *n., pl.* **-nomina** (-nómminǝ || -nóminǝ) or **-nomens.** In ancient Rome, any first or personal name. Compare **cognomen, nomen.** [Latin *praenōmen* : *prae,* before + *nōmen,* name.] —**prae·nom·i·nal** (-nómmin'l) *adj.*

prae·tor (prée-tǝr, -tawr) *n.* A high elected magistrate of the Roman Republic, ranking below the consuls. [Latin *praetor,* "leader", "chief", from *praeīre,* to go before : *prae-,* in front of + *īre,* to go.] —**prae·tor·ship** *n.*

prae·to·ri·an (pree-táwri-ǝn, pri- || -tóri-) *adj.* 1. Of or pertaining to a praetor or the praetorship. 2. *Capital* **P.** Of, pertaining to, or characteristic of the Praetorian Guard.

~*n.* 1. An ex-praetor. 2. *Capital* **P.** A member of the Praetorian Guard or of a group having comparable position and power.

Prae·to·ri·an Guard (pree-táwri-ǝn, pri-) *n.* 1. The elite guard of the Roman emperors, usually numbering about 5,000 men, whose notoriously bribable allegiance on many occasions determined the imperial succession. 2. A member of this guard. [Originally the bodyguard of a praetor under the Roman Republic.]

Prae·to·ri·us (pri-táwri-ǝss; *German* pre-tōri-ooss), **Michael,** born Michael Schultheiss; also known as Michael Schulz (1571–1621). German composer. His *Syntagma Musicum* (1615–19) is an account of the musical theory and musical instruments employed in his time.

prag·mat·ic (prag-máttik) *adj.* Also **prag·mat·i·cal** (-'l) 1. a. Dealing with facts or actual occurrences; based on or dealing with immediate circumstances rather than theoretical considerations; practical. b. Active rather than contemplative. 2. Pertaining to the study of events and historical phenomena with emphasis on their practical outcome. 3. Of or pertaining to pragmatism. 4. Of or pertaining to the affairs of a state. 5. *Rare.* Interfering; bossy.

~*n.* 1. A pragmatic sanction. 2. *Rare.* A meddler; a busybody. [Latin *pragmaticus,* skilled in affairs, from Greek *pragmatikos,* from *pragma* (stem *pragmat-*), deed, affair, from *prattein,* to do.] —**prag·mat·i·cal·ly** *adv.*

prag·mat·ics (prag-máttiks) *n.* Usually used with a singular verb. The branch of semiotics concerned with the relations between signs or expressions and their users.

pragmatic sanction *n.* An edict issued by a sovereign that becomes part of the fundamental law of the land.

prag·ma·tism (prágmǝ-tiz'm) *n.* 1. *Philosophy.* The theory, developed by Charles S. Peirce and William James, that the meaning of a proposition or course of action lies in its observable consequences, and that the sum of these consequences constitutes its meaning. 2. A method or tendency in the conduct of political affairs characterised by the rejection of theory and precedent, and by the use of practical means and expedients. 3. A pragmatic outlook or way of behaving. —**prag·ma·tist** *n.* —**prag·ma·tis·tic** (-tístik) *adj.*

Prague (praag). *Czechoslovakian* **Pra·ha** (práaha) Capital of the Czech Republic, lying on the river Vltava in central Bohemia. It became the capital of newly independent Czechoslovakia in 1918. In 1968 Soviet forces entered the city following the "Prague Spring", a period in which the city had become the focus of the movement for greater economic and political freedom led by Alexander Dubček. Prague is the leading Czech industrial centre.

prai·rie (práir-i) *n.* An extensive area of flat or rolling temperate grassland, especially in central North America. [French, from Old French *praerie,* from Vulgar Latin *prātāria* (unattested), from Latin *prātum†,* meadow.]

prairie chicken *n.* Either of two grouse, *Tympanuchus cupido* or *T. pallidicinctus,* of western North America, having deep-chested bodies and mottled brownish plumage. Also called "prairie hen".

prairie dog *n.* Any of several burrowing rodents of the genus *Cynomys,* of west-central North America. They have yellowish fur, a barklike call, and live in large communities.

prairie oyster *n.* 1. A raw egg immersed in a liquid, usually Worcester sauce or vinegar, and swallowed whole, especially as a remedy for a hangover. 2. *U.S. Regional & Canadian.* A testicle of a calf, cooked and served as food.

Prairie Provinces. Region of west central Canada: the provinces of Manitoba, Alberta, and Saskatchewan.

prairie schooner *n.* A canvas-covered wagon used by pioneers crossing the North American prairies.

prairie wolf *n.* The **coyote** (see).

praise (prayz) *n.* **1.** An expression of warm approval or admiration; strong commendation. **2.** The glorification and extolling of a deity, ruler, or hero. **3.** *Archaic.* A reason for praise; merit. —**praise be.** Used to express gratitude or relief. —**sing the praises of.** To praise highly and publicly.
~*tr.v.* **praised, praising, praises. 1.** To express warm approval of or admiration for; commend; applaud. **2.** To extol or exalt; worship. [Middle English *preisen*, from Old French *presier*, to prize, praise, from Late Latin *pretiāre*, from Latin *pretium*, price.] —**prais·er** *n.*
   Synonyms: praise, acclaim, commend, extol, laud.

praise·wor·thy (práyz-wurthi) *adj.* Meriting praise; highly commendable. —**praise·wor·thi·ly** *adv.* —**praise·wor·thi·ness** *n.*

Pra·krit (praá-krit) *n.* **1.** Any of the vernacular languages of India, as opposed to the literary language, **Sanskrit** *(see).* **2.** Any of the various ancient Indic languages on which the modern vernaculars are based. [Sanskrit *prākrta*, vulgar, vernacular : *pra-*, before + *krta*, made, from *kr*, to make.] —**Pra·krit·ic** (-kríttik) *adj.*

pra·line (praá-leen ‖ práy-, *U.S. also* práw-) *n.* A crisp confection or sweet made of nut kernels stirred in boiling sugar syrup until brown. It is often crushed and used as a flavouring. [French, invented by the cook of César de Choiseul, Count du Plessis-*Praslin*, French field-marshal (1598–1675).]

prall·tril·ler (praál-trillər) *n. Music.* A melodic detail or embellishment, consisting of a mordent (a rapid alteration of two notes), using the auxiliary note above the principal note. Also called "inverted mordent". [German *Pralltriller*, "elastic trill" : *prallen*, to rebound (akin to Middle High German *prellen*†) + *triller*, trill, from Italian *trillo*, TRILL.]

pram¹ (pram) *n.* A small carriage for babies and children consisting of a cot and a supporting structure on four, or sometimes three, wheels, which can be pushed. Also called "perambulator", *U.S.* "baby carriage". [Shortened from PERAMBULATOR.]

pram². Variant of **praam.**

prance (praanss ‖ pranss) *intr.v.* **pranced, prancing, prances. 1. a.** To spring forward on the hind legs. Used of a horse. **b.** To move with a succession of such springs or bounds. **2.** To ride a horse that moves in this way. **3.** To walk or move about in a lively manner; spring; strut.
~*n.* An act of prancing. [Middle English *praunce*†.] —**pranc·er** *n.* —**pranc·ing·ly** *adv.*

pran·di·al (prándi-əl) *adj.* Of or relating to a meal, especially dinner. [Latin *prandium*, late breakfast.] —**pran·di·al·ly** *adv.*

prang (prang) *n. Informal.* **1.** A crash, accident, or collision, especially in an aircraft or car. **2.** The destruction of a target by bombing.
~*v.* **pranged, pranging, prangs.** *Informal.* —*tr.* **1.** To crash or damage in a collision. **2.** To bomb. —*intr.* To crash an aircraft or other vehicle. [Imitative.]

prank¹ (prangk) *n.* A mischievous trick; a practical joke. [16th century : origin obscure.]

prank² *v.* **pranked, pranking, pranks.** —*tr.* To decorate or dress ostentatiously or gaudily. —*intr.* To make an ostentatious display. [Akin to Dutch *pronk*†, finery and *pronken*†, to strut.]

prank·ster (prángkstər) *n.* One who plays tricks or pranks.

pra·se·o·dym·i·um (práy-zi-o-dímmi-əm, -si-) *n. Symbol* **Pr** A soft, yellow, malleable, ductile rare-earth element that develops a characteristic green tarnish in air. It occurs naturally with other rare earths in monazite and is used to colour glass yellow, as a core material for carbon arcs, and in metallic alloys. Atomic number 59, atomic weight 140.907, melting point 935°C, boiling point 3,127°C, relative density 6.64, valencies 3, 4. [New Latin, contraction of *praseodidymium* : Greek *prasios*, leek-green, from *prason*, leek + DIDYMIUM.]

prat (prat) *n.* **1.** *British Informal.* A stupidly pretentious or incompetent person. **2.** *Archaic & Vulgar.* The buttocks. [Perhaps imitative of the sound of spanking.]

prate (prayt) *v.* **prated, prating, prates.** —*intr.* To talk idly and at great length; chatter. —*tr.* To utter idly or to little purpose.
~*n.* Empty, foolish, or trivial talk. [Middle English *praten*, akin to Middle Dutch and Middle Low German *prāten* (perhaps imitative).] —**prat·er** *n.* —**prat·ing·ly** *adv.*

prat·fall (prát-fawl) *n. Chiefly U.S.* **1.** An embarrassing mistake or failure. **2.** A fall on the buttocks. [PRAT + FALL.]

prat·in·cole (prátting-kōl, práyting-) *n.* Any of several swallow-like Old World birds of the genus *Glareola* and related genera, having brown and black plumage. [New Latin *pratincola*, "meadow-dweller" : Latin *prātum*, meadow (see **prairie**) + *incola*, inhabitant.]

pra·tique (prátteek, pra-téek) *n. Nautical.* Clearance granted to a ship to proceed into port after compliance with quarantine or health regulations. [French, PRACTICE.]

prat·tle (pratt'l) *v.* **-tled, -tling, -tles.** —*intr.* To talk idly or meaninglessly; babble. —*tr.* To utter in a childish or silly way.
~*n.* Childish or meaningless sounds; babble. [Frequentative of PRATE (akin to Low German *prateln*).] —**prat·tler** *n.*

prawn (prawn) *n.* Any of various edible marine crustaceans of the genus *Palaemon* and related genera, closely related to and resembling the shrimps.
~*intr.v.* **prawned, prawning, prawns.** To fish for prawns. [Middle

English *prayne*†.] —**prawn·er** *n.*

prax·i·ol·o·gy, prax·e·ol·o·gy (práksi-óllǝji) *n.* The study of human conduct. [From PRAXIS + -LOGY.]

prax·is (práks-iss) *n., pl.* **-es** (-eez). **1.** Practical application or exercise of a branch of learning. **2.** Habitual or established practice; custom. [Medieval Latin, from Greek, doing, action, from *prattein*, *prassein*, to do.]

Prax·it·e·les (prak-sítti-leez) (mid-fourth century B.C.). Athenian sculptor. His few surviving works include *Hermes carrying Dionysus*, discovered at Olympia (1877).

pray (pray) *v.* **prayed, praying, prays.** —*intr.* **1.** To utter or address prayer to a god or some other object of worship. **2.** To make a fervent request; plead; beg. —*tr.* **1.** To say a prayer or prayers to. **2.** To ask (someone) imploringly; beseech. Often used to introduce an entreaty or question: *Pray, be careful.* **3.** To make a devout or earnest request for: *I pray your indulgence.* **4.** To move or bring by prayer or entreaty. [Middle English *preyen*, from Old French *preier*, from Latin *precārī*, to entreat, from *prex* (stem *prec-*), prayer.]

pray·er¹ (práy-ǝr) *n.* One who prays.

prayer² (prair) *n.* **1. a.** The practice of addressing God in words or through meditation, as in praise, gratitude, sorrow, or intercession. **b.** An instance of this. **c.** A specially worded form used in addressing God. **d.** A petition or act of devotion to any object of worship. **2.** *Sometimes capital* **P.** A religious service in which praying predominates: *morning prayer.* **3. a.** Any fervent request. **b.** The thing so requested: *His safe arrival was their prayer.* **4.** *Slang.* The slightest chance of achieving something: *you haven't a prayer!* [Middle English *preyere*, from Old French *preiere*, from Medieval Latin *precāria*, written petition, prayer, from Latin, feminine of *precārius*, obtained by entreaty, from *precārī*, to entreat, PRAY.]

prayer beads *pl.n.* A string of beads for keeping count of the prayers one is saying; a rosary.

prayer book *n.* **1.** A book containing prayers and other forms of worship. **2.** *Usually capital* **P,** *capital* **B.** *Abbr.* **P.B.** The Book of Common Prayer.

prayer·ful (prair-f'l) *adj.* **1.** Inclined to pray frequently; devout. **2.** Characterized by or conducive to prayer. —**prayer·ful·ly** *adv.* —**prayer·ful·ness** *n.*

prayer mat *n.* A small mat or carpet knelt on by Muslims when praying. Also called "prayer rug".

prayer meeting *n.* An evangelical service, especially one held on a weekday evening, in which the laity participate by singing, praying, or testifying.

prayer shawl *n.* A large, lightweight shawl worn, especially by Jews, during prayer. See **tallith.**

prayer wheel *n.* A cylinder inscribed with or containing written prayers and revolved on an axis, used especially by the Buddhists of Tibet.

praying mantis *n.* A green or brownish predatory insect, *Mantis religiosa*, that while at rest, folds its front legs, appearing to be at prayer.

P.R.B. Pre-Raphaelite Brotherhood.

pre– *prefix.* Indicates: **1.** An earlier or prior time; for example, **prearrange, pre-Columbian. 2.** Preliminary or preparatory work or activity; for example, **preschool. 3.** A location in front or anterior; for example, **preaxial.** *Note:* Many compounds other than those entered here may be formed with *pre-*. In this dictionary, *pre-* is normally joined with the following element without space or hyphen: *prearrange.* However, many users prefer the hyphenated form, especially if the second element begins with a capital letter: *pre-Christian*, or the letter *e: pre-eminent.* [Middle English, from Old French, from Latin *prae-*, from *prae*, before, in front. In Latin compounds, *prae-* indicates: 1. Before in time, as in **prescient.** 2. Before in position, in front, as in **premorse.** 3. Before in degree or importance, superior, exceeding, as in **preponderate.** 4. Intensifying action, as in **prepotent.**]

preach (preech) *v.* **preached, preaching, preaches.** —*tr.* **1.** To expound upon in writing or speech; especially, to urge acceptance of or compliance with (specified religious or moral principles). **2.** To deliver (a sermon, lengthy advice, or the like). —*intr.* **1.** To deliver a sermon. **2.** To give religious or moral instruction, especially in a drawn-out, tiresome manner. [Middle English *prechen*, from Old French *prechier*, from Late Latin *praedīcāre*, from Latin, to proclaim : *prae*, before + *dīcāre*, to say.]

preach·er (préechər) *n.* **1.** A Protestant clergyman; a minister. **2.** One who preaches.

preach·i·fy (préechi-fī) *intr.v.* **-fied, -fying, -fies.** *Informal.* To preach tediously and didactically. —**preach·i·fi·ca·tion** (-fi-káysh'n) *n.*

preach·ment (préechmǝnt) *n.* **1.** The act of preaching. **2.** A tiresome or unwelcome moral lecture; tedious sermonising.

preach·y (préechi) *adj.* **-ier, -iest.** *Chiefly U.S. Informal.* Inclined to preach.

pre·ad·am·ite (prée-áddǝmīt) *n.* **1.** One supposed to have been in existence before Adam (traditionally thought to have been the first man, created by God). **2.** One who holds that there were people in existence before Adam. [PRE- + ADAM + -ITE.] —**pre·ad·am·ite** *adj.*

pre·ad·ap·ta·tion (prée-áddap-táysh'n, -áddǝp-) *n.* The condition of an organism or group of organisms of having one or more characteristics that would be advantageous, and therefore enhance its chances of survival, in a changed environment.

pre·ad·o·les·cence (prée-áddǝ-léss'nss) *n.* The period between childhood and adolescence, often designated as between the ages of ten and twelve. —**pre·ad·o·les·cent** n. & adj.

pre·am·ble (prée-ámb'l, prée-amb'l) n. 1. A preliminary statement; especially, the introduction to a formal document, explaining its purpose. 2. An introductory occurrence or fact; a preliminary. [Middle English, from Old French preambule, from Medieval Latin praeambulum, from Late Latin praeambulus, walking in front : prae, in front + ambulāre, to walk.] —**pre·am·bu·lar·y** (pree-ámbew-ləri || U.S. -lerri) adj.

pre·am·pli·fi·er (prée-ámplifī-ər) n. An electronic circuit or device that detects and sufficiently amplifies weak signals, especially from a radio receiver, for subsequent amplification stages. Also informally called "preamp".

pre·ar·range (prée-ə-ráynj) tr.v. -ranged, -ranging, -ranges. To arrange in advance. —**pre·ar·range·ment** n.

pre·a·tom·ic (prée-ə-tómmik) adj. Of or pertaining to the period preceding the use of atomic energy.

pre·au·di·ence (prée-áwdi-ənss) n. In Britain, the right of certain lawyers belonging to various ranks to be heard before others, when there is no particular order in which business is to be heard in court. The Attorney-General and the Solicitor-General take precedence in most matters, followed by Queen's Counsel and then junior barristers (in the order in which they were called to the bar).

pre·ax·i·al (prée-áksi-əl) adj. Anatomically positioned in front of a body axis. —**pre·ax·i·al·ly** adv.

preb·end (prébbənd) n. 1. A clergyman's stipend, drawn from a special endowment belonging to his cathedral or church. 2. The property or tithe providing the endowment for such a stipend. 3. The clergyman who receives such a stipend; a prebendary. [Middle English prebende, from Old French, from Medieval Latin praebenda, from Late Latin, from Latin, "things to be given", from praebēre, to grant : prae, forth + habēre, to hold, offer.] —**pre·ben·dal** (pri-bénd'l) adj.

preb·en·dar·y (prébbən-dəri, -dri || -derri) n., pl. -ies. 1. A clergyman who receives a prebend. 2. In the Anglican Church, a clergyman holding the honorary title of prebend without a stipend.

prec. preceding.

Pre·cam·bri·an, Pre·cam·bri·an (prée-kámbri-ən) adj. Of, belonging to, or designating the oldest and largest division of geological time, preceding the Cambrian, often subdivided into the Archaeozoic and Proterozoic eras, and characterised by the appearance of primitive forms of life.
~n. The Precambrian era. Preceded by the.

pre·can·cel (prée-kánss'l) tr.v. -celled or U.S. -celed, -celling or U.S. -celing, -cels. To cancel a postage stamp before posting.
~n. A precancelled stamp or envelope.

pre·can·cer·ous (prée-kán-sərəss) adj. Designating a growth that is not malignant but will become so if left untreated.

pre·car·i·ous (pri-kaír-i-əss, prə-) adj. 1. Dangerously lacking in security or stability. 2. Subject to chance or unknown conditions. 3. Based upon uncertain or unproved premises: a precarious argument. 4. Archaic. Dependent on the will or favour of another. [Latin precārius, dependent on prayer, from precārī, to entreat, from prex (stem prec-), entreaty, prayer.] —**pre·car·i·ous·ly** adv.

pre·cast (prée-káast || -kást) tr.v. -cast, -casting, -casts. To form (concrete or other building materials) into structurally useful shapes, typically blocks, before use. —**pre·cast** adj.

prec·a·to·ry (préckə-təri, -tri || pri-káy-, prə-) adj. Also **prec·a·tive** (-tiv). Relating to or expressing entreaty or supplication. [Late Latin precātōrius, from precārī, to entreat. See precarious.]

pre·cau·tion (pri-káwsh'n, prə-) n. 1. An action taken in advance to protect against possible failure or danger; a safeguard. 2. Caution practised in advance; forethought; circumspection. [French précaution, from Late Latin praecautiō, from Latin praecavēre, to guard against before : prae, before + cavēre, to guard against.]

pre·cau·tion·ar·y (pri-káwsh'n-əri, prə-, -ri || -erri) adj. Also **pre·cau·tion·al** (-'l). 1. Of or constituting a precaution. 2. Advising or exercising precaution.

pre·cau·tious (pri-káwshəss, prə-) adj. Exercising precaution. —**pre·cau·tious·ly** adv. —**pre·cau·tious·ness** n.

pre·cede (pri-séed, prée-) v. -ceded, -ceding, -cedes. —tr. 1. To come before in time; exist or occur prior to. 2. To come before in order or rank; surpass; outrank. 3. To be or go in a position in front of or in advance of. 4. To preface; introduce: precede a speech with an anecdote. —intr. To exist or go before. [Middle English preceden, from Old French preceder, from Latin praecēdere : prae, before + cēdere, to go.]

pre·ced·ence (préssi-d'nss, préessi-, prée-sée-, pri-) n. Also **pre·ced·en·cy** (-i). 1. The act or state of preceding. 2. Priority in importance, position, rank, or the like. 3. A ceremonial order of rank, observed especially on formal occasions.

Usage: The preposition that follows the phrases take/have precedence is over (less often of, which tends to be more formal). One also gives precedence to. The noun precedent may be followed by of (the precedent of staying for a year) or for (there is no precedent for doing that). The adjective , when used after a verb, is followed by to (His statement was precedent to mine).

prec·e·dent (préssi-dənt, préessi-) n. 1. An act or instance that may be used as an example in dealing with or justifying subsequent similar cases. 2. Law. A judicial decision that may be used as a standard in subsequent similar cases.
~adj. (pri-séed'nt; rarely préssidənt). Preceding; prior. —See Usage note at precedence. [Middle English, from Old French, from

Latin praecēdēns, present participle of praecēdere, PRECEDE.] —**prec·e·dent·ed** (-dentid) adj. —**prec·e·dent·ly** (pri-séed'ntli) adv.

prec·e·den·tial (préssi-dénsh'l, préessi-) adj. 1. Of, pertaining to, or serving as a precedent. 2. Having precedence.

pre·ced·ing (pri-séeding, prée-) adj. Abbr. **prec.** Existing or coming before in time, place, rank, or sequence; previous.

pre·cen·tor (pri-séntər, prée-) n. 1. One who directs the singing of the congregation or choir in a church. 2. In some cathedrals, a member of the clergy who is in charge of music. [Late Latin, from Latin praecinere, to sing before : prae, before + canere, to sing.] —**pre·cen·to·ri·al** (prée-sen-táwri-əl || -tóri-) adj. —**pre·cen·tor·ship** n.

pre·cept (prée-sept) n. 1. A rule or principle imposing a particular standard of action or conduct. 2. Law. An order or direction from one official to another as: a. A writ or warrant. b. British. A written order from a sheriff with instructions for holding an election. 3. British. An order from a county council to a rating authority for the levying of rates. [Middle English, from Latin praeceptum, from praecipere (past participle praeceptus), to take beforehand, warn, teach : prae, before + capere, to take.]

pre·cep·tive (pri-séptiv) adj. 1. Of or expressing a precept. 2. Giving precepts; didactic. —**pre·cep·tive·ly** adv.

pre·cep·tor (pri-séptər || prée-septər) n. A teacher; an instructor. [Middle English preceptur, from Latin praeceptor, teacher, from praecipere, to teach. See precept.] —**pre·cep·to·ri·al** (prée-sep-táw-ri-əl || -tóri-) adj. —**pre·cep·to·ri·al·ly** adv. —**pre·cep·tor·ship** n.

pre·cep·to·ry (pri-séptəri) n., pl. -ries. In the Order of the Knights Templars: 1. A subordinate community. 2. The buildings of such a community.

pre·cep·tress (pri-sép-trəss, -triss) n. A female preceptor.

pre·cess (pri-séss, prée-) intr.v. -cessed, -cessing, -cesses. Physics & Astronomy. To move in or be subjected to precession. [Back-formation from PRECESSION.]

pre·ces·sion (pri-sésh'n, prée-) n. 1. The act or state of preceding; precedence. 2. Physics. A complex motion executed by a rotating body in which the axis or rotation changes orientation when the body is subject to an applied torque. A torque of constant magnitude will cause the axis to describe a conical locus at a constant angular velocity. 3. Astronomy. Precession of the equinoxes. [New Latin praecessiō, from Medieval Latin praecessiō (stem praecession-), a going forward, from Latin praecēdere (past participle praecessus), PRECEDE.] —**pre·ces·sion·al** adj.

precession of the equinoxes n. Astronomy. A slow westward shift of the equinoctial points along the plane of the ecliptic at a rate of 50.27 seconds of arc per year, resulting from precession of the Earth's axis of rotation.

pre·cinct (prée-singkt) n. 1. Usually plural. a. A place or enclosure marked off by definite limits, especially one that surrounds a church, cathedral, or the like. b. A boundary. 2. Plural. Neighbourhood; environs. 3. A part of a town designed for a specified purpose: a shopping precinct. 4. U.S. In a town or city: a. A district to be patrolled by the police. b. An electoral district. [Middle English precincte, from Medieval Latin praecinctum, "enclosure", from Latin praecingere (past participle praecinctus), to gird about : prae, before, around + cingere, to gird.]

pre·ci·os·i·ty (préshi-óssəti, préssi-) n., pl. -ties. Extreme meticulousness or overrefinement, as in language. [Middle English preciousite, from Old French precieusite, (stem preciōsitāt-) from Latin pretiōsitās, from pretiōsus PRECIOUS.]

pre·cious (préshəss) adj. 1. Of high cost or worth; valuable: precious metal. 2. Highly esteemed; cherished. 3. Dear; beloved. 4. Affectedly dainty or overrefined. 5. Informal. a. Arrant; thoroughgoing. b. Used as an intensive to express anger or irritation: Take your precious books, for all I care! —See Synonyms at costly.
~n. One who is precious; a darling.
~adv. Used as an intensive: precious little to eat! [Middle English, from Old French precieus, precios, from Latin pretiōsus, from pretium, price.] —**pre·cious·ly** adv. —**pre·cious·ness** n.

precious stone n. Any of various minerals, such as diamond, ruby, or sapphire, valued for their rarity or appearance.

prec·i·pice (préss-i-piss, -ə-) n. 1. An extremely steep, high face of a cliff or mass of rock. 2. The brink of a dangerous situation. [Old French, from Latin praecipitium, from praecipitāre, to throw headlong. See precipitate.]

pre·cip·i·ta·ble (pri-síppitəb'l) adj. Capable of being precipitated. [From PRECIPITATE.]

pre·cip·i·tant (pri-síppitənt) adj. 1. Rushing or falling headlong. 2. Impulsive in thought or action; rash. 3. Abrupt or unexpected; sudden. —See Usage note at precipitate.
~n. Any substance that causes precipitation. [French précipitant, from Latin praecipitāns, present participle of praecipitāre, to throw headlong, PRECIPITATE.] —**pre·cip·i·tance, pre·cip·i·tan·cy** n. —**pre·cip·i·tant·ly** adv.

pre·cip·i·tate (pri-síppi-tayt, prə-) v. -tated, -tating, -tates. —tr. 1. To throw from or as from a great height; hurl downwards. 2. To cause to happen before anticipated or required. 3. Meteorology. To cause (water vapour) to condense as rain, snow, dew, frost, sleet, or hail. 4. Chemistry. To cause (a solid substance) to be separated from a solution. —intr. 1. Meteorology. To condense and fall. 2. Chemistry. To be separated from a solution as a precipitate. 3. To fall headlong. —See Synonyms at speed.
~adj. (-tət, -tit || -tayt). 1. Speeding headlong; moving rapidly and heedlessly. 2. Acting with excessive haste or impulse; lacking due

deliberation. **3.** Occurring suddenly or unexpectedly. —See Synonyms at **reckless.**
~*n.* (-tayt, -tət, -tit). *Chemistry.* A solid or solid phase separated from a solution, usually as a suspension of particles, which may subsequently settle. [Latin *praecipitāre,* to throw headlong, from *praeceps,* headlong : *prae,* in front + *caput,* head.] —**pre·cip·i·tate·ly** *adv.* —**pre·cip·i·tate·ness** *n.* —**pre·cip·i·ta·tive** (-tətiv, -taytiv) *adj.* —**pre·cip·i·ta·tor** (-taytər) *n.*
Usage: *Precipitate, precipitant,* and *precipitous,* and their corresponding adverbs, are sometimes confused. *Precipitate* and *precipitant* apply primarily to rash, overhasty human actions: *That was a very precipitate remark; He acted precipitantly when he resigned. Precipitous* is used primarily of physical steepness: *The precipitous west face of the mountain.*

pre·cip·i·ta·tion (pri-síppi-táysh'n, prə-) *n.* **1. a.** The act of precipitating. **b.** The state of being precipitated. **2.** Abrupt or impulsive haste. **3.** *Meteorology.* **a.** Deposition of water droplets or ice particles condensed from atmospheric water vapour as rain, snow, dew, frost, sleet, or hail. **b.** The quantity of such substances falling in a specific area within a specific period. **4.** *Chemistry.* The production of a precipitate.

pre·cip·i·tin (pri-síppitin, prə-) *n. Biochemistry.* An antibody that reacts with an antigen to form a precipitate. [PRECIPIT(ATE) + -IN.]

pre·cip·i·tous (pri-síppitəss, prə-) *adj.* **1.** Like a precipice; extremely steep. **2.** Having several precipices. **3.** *Nonstandard.* Precipitate. —See Usage note at **precipitate.** [French *précipiteux,* from Old French, from Latin *praecipitium,* PRECIPICE.] —**pre·cip·i·tous·ly** *adv.* —**pre·cip·i·tous·ness** *n.*

pré·cis (práy-see; *rarely* préssee || *U.S. also* pray-sée) *n., pl.* **précis** (-z). A concise summary of the essential facts or statements of a book, article, or other text; an abstract.
~*tr.v.* **précised** (-seed), **-cising** (-see-ing), **-cises** (-seez). To make a précis of. [French *précis,* "precise", from Old French *precis,* PRECISE.]

pre·cise (pri-síss, prə-) *adj.* **1.** Clearly expressed or delineated; distinct; definite: *precise ideas.* **2.** Of or producing great exactness or accuracy: *a precise measurement; precise instruments.* **3.** Exactly corresponding to what is indicated; correct: *the precise amount of seasoning.* **4.** Strictly distinguished from others; very: *at that precise moment.* **5.** Strictly correct in manners, behaviour, or the like: *precise in his dress.* [Old French *precis,* from Latin *praecīsus,* shortened, from *praecīdere,* to cut off in front, shorten : *prae,* in front + *caedere,* to cut.] —**pre·cise·ly** *adv.* —**pre·cise·ness** *n.*

pre·ci·sian (pri-sízh'n, prə-) *n.* A person who is strict and precise in adherence to established rules, forms, or standards; especially, one who is strict in matters of religion or morality. [From PRECISE.] —**pre·ci·sian·ism** *n.*

pre·ci·sion (pri-sízh'n, prə-) *n.* The state or quality of being precise.
~*adj.* Precise in nature, action, or performance: *a precision tool; precision handling.* [French *précision,* from Latin *praecīsiō* (stem *praecīsiōn-*), act of cutting, from *praecīdere,* to cut off in front, abridge. See **precise.**] —**pre·ci·sion·ist** *n.*

pre·clin·i·cal (prée-klínnik'l) *adj.* **1.** Occurring in the early stages of a disease, before diagnosis is possible. **2.** Preparing for, or pertaining to the studies that prepare for, the study of medicine.

pre·clude (pri-klóod || -kléwd) *tr.v.* **-cluded, -cluding, -cludes. 1.** To make impossible or impracticable by previous action; prevent. **2.** To bar or prevent (a person) from something; debar. —See Synonyms at **prevent.** [Latin *praeclūdere* : *prae,* in front + *claudere,* to close.] —**pre·clu·sion** (-klóozh'n || -kléwzh'n) *n.* —**pre·clu·sive** (-klóo-siv || -kléw-, -ziv) *adj.* —**pre·clu·sive·ly** *adv.*

pre·co·cial (pri-kósh'l, prə-) *adj.* Covered with down and capable of moving about when first hatched. Said of birds. Compare **altricial.** [New Latin *praecoces,* precocial birds, from Latin *praecox,* PRECOCIOUS.]

pre·co·cious (pri-kóshəss, prə-) *adj.* **1. a.** Characterised by unusually early development or maturity, especially in mental aptitude. **b.** Aping the manners and speech of adults: *a precocious brat.* **2.** Manifesting or characterised by premature or unusually early development. **3.** *Botany.* Blossoming before the leaves sprout. [Latin *praecox,* "ripening before its time", from *praecoquere,* to cook or ripen before : *prae,* before + *coquere,* to cook, ripen.] —**pre·co·cious·ly** *adv.* —**pre·co·cious·ness, pre·coc·i·ty** (-kóssəti) *n.*

pre·cog·ni·tion (prée-kog-nísh'n) *n.* **1.** Knowledge of something in advance of its occurrence. **2.** In Scots law, an unsworn statement given by a witness in advance of a trial. [Late Latin *praecognitiō,* from Latin *praecognōscere* (past participle *praecognitus*), to know before : *prae,* before + *cognōscere,* to know (see **cognition**).] —**pre·cog·ni·tive** (prée-kóg-nitiv) *adj.*

pre-Co·lum·bi·an (prée-kə-lúmbi-ən) *adj.* Of, relating to, or originating in the Americas before the voyages of Columbus.

pre·con·ceive (prée-kən-séev || -kon-) *tr.v.* **-ceived, -ceiving, -ceives.** To form an opinion or conception of (a matter) beforehand, without knowledge or experience: *preconceived ideas.*

pre·con·cep·tion (prée-kən-sépsh'n || -kon-) *n.* **1.** An opinion or conception formed in advance of actual knowledge. **2.** A prejudice.

pre·con·di·tion (prée-kən-dísh'n || -kon-) *n.* A condition that must exist or be established before something can occur or be considered; a prerequisite.
~*tr.v.* **preconditioned, -tioning, -tions.** To condition, train, or accustom in advance.

pre·co·nise, pre·co·nize (prée-kən-īz) *tr.v.* **-nised, -nising, -nises. 1.** To command or announce in public. **2.** To call or summon in public. **3.** *Roman Catholic Church.* To publicly approve the nomination of (a new bishop). Used of the pope. [Middle English, from Medieval Latin *praeconizare,* from *praeco* (stem *praecon-*), herald.] —**pre·co·ni·sa·tion** (-ī-záysh'n || *U.S.* -i-) *n.*

pre·con·scious (prée-kónshəss) *adj.* **1. a.** *Psychology.* Of or designating mental contents capable of being recalled although not present in the conscious mind. **b.** Designating the part of the mind held to be the region of such contents. **2.** Before the development of consciousness. —See Usage note at **conscious.** —**pre·con·scious·ly** *adv.*

pre·con·tract (prée-kón-trakt) *n.* An agreement or contract, as of marriage, entered into beforehand.
~*v.* (-kən-trákt || -kon-) **precontracted, -tracting, -tracts.** —*tr.* **1.** To engage (a person) in a contract of marriage by previous agreement. **2.** To establish previously by contract. —*intr.* To enter into a contract beforehand.

pre·cook (prée-kóok || -kóok) *tr.v.* **-cooked, -cooking, -cooks.** To cook in advance, or cook partially before final cooking.

pre·crit·i·cal (prée-kríttik'l) *adj.* Prior to the occurrence of a critical condition.

pre·cur·sor (pri-kúrssər, prée-) *n.* **1.** One that precedes and indicates or announces someone or something to come; a forerunner; a harbinger. **2.** One that precedes another; a predecessor. **3.** A substance that is converted into another substance during a chemical or biochemical reaction. [Latin *praecursor,* from *praecurrere,* to run before : *prae,* before + *currere,* to run.]

pre·cur·so·ry (pri-kúrss-əri, prée-) *adj.* Also **pre·cur·sive** (-iv). **1.** Preceding in the manner of a precursor; preliminary; introductory. **2.** Suggesting or indicating something to follow; premonitory.

pred. predicate.

pre·da·cious, pre·da·ceous (pri-dáyshəss, pre-) *adj.* Living by seizing or taking prey; predatory. Said of such animals as lions and hawks. [Latin *praedārī,* to plunder. See **predatory.**] —**pre·da·cious·ness, pre·dac·i·ty** (-dássəti) *n.*

pre·date (prée-dáyt) *tr.v.* **-dated, -dating, -dates. 1.** To mark or designate with an earlier date than the actual one. **2.** To precede in time; antedate.

pre·da·tion (pri-dáysh'n, pre-) *n.* **1.** The act or practice of plundering or marauding. **2.** A feeding relationship in an ecological community in which one species of animal (the predator) captures, kills, and eats another (the prey). [Latin *praedātiō* (stem *praedātiōn-*), from *praedārī,* to plunder. See **predatory.**]

pred·a·tor (préddə-tər || -tawr) *n.* One that is predatory; especially, an animal that lives by preying upon others. [Latin *praedātor,* from *praedārī,* to plunder. See **predatory.**]

pred·a·to·ry (préddə-tri, -təri) *adj.* **1.** Of, pertaining to, or characterised by plundering, pillaging, or marauding: *a predatory war.* **2.** Preying on other animals; predacious. **3.** *Informal.* Addicted to or characterised by a tendency to exploit or destroy others for one's own gain. [Latin *praedātōrius* from *praedārī,* to plunder, from *praeda,* booty.] —**pred·a·to·ri·ly** *adv.* —**pred·a·to·ri·ness** *n.*

pre·de·cease (prée-di-séess, -də-) *tr.v.* **-ceased, -ceasing, -ceases.** To die before (some other person). —**pre·de·cease** *n.*

pred·e·ces·sor (prée-di-sessər, -séssər || *chiefly U.S.* préddə-) *n.* **1.** One who precedes another in time, especially in an office or position. **2.** Something that has been succeeded by another. **3.** An ancestor or forefather. [Middle English *predecessour,* from Old French *predecesseur,* from Late Latin *praedecessor* : Latin *prae,* before + *dēcessor,* one who leaves, from *dēcessus,* past participle of *dēcēdere,* to die, go away : *dē,* away + *cēdere,* to go.]

pre·del·la (pri-déllə) *n., pl.* **delle** (-dèllay). **1. a.** An altar platform. **b.** Ornamentation on the front side of this platform. **2. a.** A raised shelf at the back of the altar. **b.** Ornamentation on the front side of this shelf. [Italian, stool, step, perhaps from Old High German *bret,* board.]

pre·des·ti·nar·i·an (prée-desti-náir-i-ən, pree-désti-, pri-) *adj.* **1.** Of or pertaining to predestination. **2.** Believing in or based on the doctrine of predestination.
~*n.* One who believes in the doctrine of predestination. —**pre·des·ti·nar·i·an·ism** *n.*

pre·des·ti·nate (prée-désti-nayt, pri-) *tr.v.* **-nated, -nating, -nates. 1.** To destine or determine in advance; foreordain. **2.** *Theology.* To predestine.
~*adj.* (-nət, -nit, -nayt). Foreordained; predestined. [Middle English *predestinaten,* from Latin *praedestināre,* PREDESTINE.]

pre·des·ti·na·tion (prée-desti-náysh'n, pree-désti-, pri-) *n.* **1.** The act of predestining, or the condition of being predestined. **2.** *Theology.* **a.** The act whereby God is believed to have foreordained all things. **b.** The doctrine that God has foreordained all things, especially the salvation, or damnation, of individual souls. **3.** Destiny.

pre·des·tine (prée-déstin, pri-) *tr.v.* **-tined, -tining, -tines. 1.** To fix upon, decide, or decree in advance; foreordain. **2.** *Theology.* To foreordain by divine will or decree; predestinate. [Middle English *predestinen,* from Old French *predestiner,* from Latin *praedestināre* : *prae,* before + *dēstināre,* to determine, DESTINE.]

pre·de·ter·mi·nate (prée-di-térmi-nət, -nit, -nayt) *adj.* Determined or established beforehand.

pre·de·ter·mine (prée-di-términ) *tr.v.* **-mined, -mining, -mines. 1.** To determine, decide, or establish in advance. **2.** To influence or sway towards an action or opinion; give a tendency to beforehand; predispose. [Late Latin *praedētermināre* : *prae,* before + *dētermināre,* DETERMINE.] —**pre·de·ter·mi·na·tion** (-áysh'n) *n.* —**pre·de·ter·mi·na·tive** (-ətiv || -aytiv) *adj.* —**pre·de·ter·min·er** *n.*

predial. Variant of **praedial.**

pred·i·ca·ble (préddi-kəb'l) *adj.* Capable of being stated or predicated.
~n. **1.** Something that can be predicated; a quality or attribute. **2.** *Logic.* Any of five general attributes of the Aristotelian class, *genus, species, property, difference,* and *accident,* designating the peculiar relation that a predicate bears to its subject, regardless of the quantity or quality of a proposition. [Medieval Latin *praedicābilis,* from Late Latin *praedicāre,* to proclaim, PREDICATE.] **—pred·i·ca·bil·i·ty** (-kə-bílləti), **pred·i·ca·ble·ness** *n.*

pre·dic·a·ment (pri-díckə-mənt, prə- *for senses 1, 2;* préddikə- *for sense 3*) *n.* **1.** A troublesome, embarrassing, or ludicrous situation. **2.** *Archaic.* A specified state or condition. **3.** *Logic.* A state or classification of existence. [Middle English, from Late Latin *praedicāmentum* (translation of Greek *katēgoria,* category), something predicated, condition (especially an unpleasant one), from *praedicāre,* to proclaim, PREDICATE.] **—pre·dic·a·men·tal** (-mént'l) *adj.* **—pre·dic·a·men·tal·ly** *adv.*
Synonyms: *predicament, plight, dilemma, quandary.*

pred·i·cant (préddikənt) *adj.* Concerned with preaching.
~n. A member of a religious order dedicated to preaching. [Latin *praedicāns* (stem *praedicānt-*), present participle of *praedicāre,* to speak in public. See **predicate.**]

pred·i·cate (préddi-kayt) *v.* **-cated, -cating, -cates.** *—tr.* **1.** To base or establish (a concept, statement, or action). Used with *on* or *upon*: *He predicates his argument on these facts.* **2.** *Logic.* **a.** To state or affirm as an attribute or quality of: *predicate aggressiveness of mankind.* **b.** To make (a term or expression) the predicate of a proposition. **3.** To carry the connotation of; imply. **4.** To proclaim; assert; declare. *—intr.* To make a statement or assertion.
~n. (-kət, -kit, -kayt; *also* prédi-). *Abbr.* **pred. 1.** *Grammar.* The part of a sentence or clause that expresses something about the subject. It regularly consists of a verb and may include objects, modifiers, or complements of the verb; for example in the simple sentences: *The house is white* and *The man hit the dog;* the words *is white* and *hit the dog* are predicates. **2.** *Logic.* Whatever is stated about the subject of a proposition.
~adj. (-kət, -kit, -kayt). **1.** *Grammar.* Of or belonging to the predicate of a sentence or clause. **2.** Predicated; stated. [Late Latin *praedicāre,* to proclaim, from Latin : *prae,* in front of, in public + *dicāre,* to say.] **—pred·i·ca·tion** (-káysh'n) *n.*

predicate calculus *n.* The branch of symbolic logic dealing not only with relations between propositions as a whole, but also with their internal structure, especially the relation between subject and predicate. Symbols are used to represent the subject and predicate of the proposition and the existential or universal quantifier is used to denote whether the proposition is universal or particular in its application. Compare **propositional calculus.**

pre·dic·a·tive (pri-díckətiv, prə- || préddi-kaytiv) *adj. Grammar.* Pertaining to or designating an adjective, noun, or construction that follows certain verbs, typically copula verbs, and applies directly to the subject of the verb. For example, in the sentence *The young girl is ill, ill* is a predicative adjective. Compare **attributive.**
~n. Grammar. A predicative word or construction, especially an adjective. **—pre·dic·a·tive·ly** *adv.* **—pre·dic·a·tive·ness** *n.*

pred·i·ca·to·ry (préddi-kaytəri, -káytəri || *U.S.* -kə-tawri, -tōri) *adj.* Of, pertaining to, or characteristic of preaching or a preacher. [Late Latin *praedicātōrius,* from *praedicāre,* to proclaim, PREDICATE.]

pre·dict (pri-díkt, prə-) *v.* **-dicted, -dicting, -dicts.** *—tr.* To state, tell about, or make known in advance, especially on the basis of special knowledge; foretell: *predict the weather.* *—intr.* To foretell what will happen; prophesy. —See Synonyms at **foretell.** [Latin *praedīcere* (past participle *praedictus*), to foretell : *prae,* before + *dīcere,* to tell, say.]

pre·dict·a·ble (pri-díkt-əb'l, prə-) *n.* **1.** That may be predicted or anticipated. **2.** Having no element of originality: *predictable opinions.* **—pre·dict·a·bil·i·ty** (-ə-bílləti) *n.* **—pre·dict·a·bly** *adv.*

pre·dic·tion (pri-díksh'n, prə-) *n.* **1.** The act of foretelling or predicting. **2.** Something foretold or predicted; a prophecy. **—pre·dic·tive** (-díktiv) *adj.* **—pre·dic·tive·ly** *adv.* **—pre·dic·tive·ness** *n.*

pre·dic·tor (pri-díktər, prə-) *n.* **1.** One that predicts. **2.** An instrument that enables an anti-aircraft gun to track enemy aircraft.

pre·di·gest (prée-dī-jést, -di-) *tr.v.* **-gested, -gesting, -gests.** To subject (food) to a partial artificial process to assist with digestion. **—pre·di·ges·tion** (-jéss-chən, -jésh-) *n.*

pred·i·kant (préddi-kant, práydi-) *n.* In South Africa, a minister of the Dutch Reformed Church. [Dutch, from Latin *praedicāns* (stem *praedicant-*). See **predicant.**]

pre·di·lec·tion (prée-di-léksh'n || *chiefly U.S.* préddə-) *n.* A preference or partiality; a predisposition. [French *prédilection,* from Medieval Latin *praedīligere,* to prefer : Latin *prae,* before + *dīligere,* to love, choose (see **diligent**).]

pre·dis·pose (prée-diss-pōz) *tr.v.* **-posed, -posing, -poses. 1.** To make (someone) inclined to something in advance; put into a certain frame of mind for something: *His good manners predispose people to like him.* **2.** To make susceptible or liable. **3.** *Archaic.* To settle or dispose of in advance. **—pre·dis·pos·al** *n.*

pre·dis·po·si·tion (prée-dispə-zísh'n) *n.* **1.** The state of being predisposed; a tendency or inclination. **2.** Susceptibility to a particular type of disease.

pred·ni·sone (préd-ni-sōn) *n.* A synthetic corticosteroid drug, similar to cortisone, used to treat rheumatic, inflammatory, and allergic conditions. [Apparently *pre*gnant + *d*iene + corti*sone.*]

pre·dom·i·nant (pri-dómminənt, prə-) *adj.* **1.** Having greatest ascendancy, importance, influence, authority, or force. **2.** Most common or conspicuous; prevailing: *the predominant colour was red.* —See Synonyms at **dominant.** [Old French, from Medieval Latin *praedomināns* (stem *praedominant-*), present participle of *praedominārī,* PREDOMINATE.] **—pre·dom·i·nance, pre·dom·i·nan·cy** *n.* **—pre·dom·i·nant·ly** *adv.*

pre·dom·i·nate (pri-dómmi-nayt, prə-) *v.* **-nated, -nating, -nates.** *—intr.* **1.** To be of greater power, importance, or quantity; be most important or outstanding. **2.** To have authority, power, or controlling influence; prevail. Often used with *over.* *—tr. Rare.* To dominate or prevail over. [Latin *praedominārī,* to subdue beforehand : *prae,* before + *dominārī,* to DOMINATE.] **—pre·dom·i·nate·ly** (-nət-li, -nit-) *adv.* **—pre·dom·i·nat·ing·ly** *adv.* **—pre·dom·i·na·tion** (-náysh'n) *n.* **—pre·dom·i·na·tor** (-naytər) *n.*

pre·ec·lamp·si·a (prée-ik-lámpsi-ə, -ek-) *n.* A condition affecting pregnant women, marked by high blood pressure, swelling of the ankles, and the presence of protein in the urine.

pre·em·i·nent (prée-émmi-nənt, pri- || -nent) *adj.* Superior to all others; outstanding. See Synonyms at **dominant.** [Late Latin *praeēminēns* (stem *praeēminent-*), from Latin, present participle of *praeēminēre,* to excel : *prae,* in front of + *ēminēre,* to stand out (see **eminent**).] **—pre·em·i·nence** *n.* **—pre·em·i·nent·ly** *adv.*

pre·empt (prée-émpt, pri-) *v.* **-empted, -empting, -empts.** *—tr.* **1. a.** To stop (a person) doing something by taking advance action. **b.** To take advance action to counteract (a plan, for example). **2.** To exercise one's right to buy (property, for example) before others. **3.** To seize; take over. **4.** *Chiefly U.S.* To settle on (public land) so as to obtain the right to buy before others. *—intr.* In bridge, to make a pre-emptive bid. [Back-formation from PRE-EMPTION.] **—pre·emp·tor** (-ər, -awr) *n.* **—pre·emp·to·ry** (-əri) *adj.*

pre·emp·tion (prée-émpsh'n, pri-) *n.* **1.** An act or instance of pre-empting. **2. a.** The right to purchase something before others. **b.** A purchase made using such a right. [Medieval Latin *praeemptiō* (stem *praeemptiōn-*), from *praeemere,* to buy beforehand : *prae,* before + *emere,* to buy.]

pre·emp·tive (prée-émptiv, pri-) *adj.* **1.** Of, pertaining to, or characteristic of pre-emption. **2.** Designed to anticipate and frustrate opposition: *a pre-emptive strike against the enemy.* **3.** Designating or characteristic of a high bid in bridge that is intended to prevent the opposing players from bidding. **—pre·emp·tive·ly** *adv.*

preen (preen) *v.* **preened, preening, preens.** *—tr.* **1.** To smooth or clean (feathers) with the bill. Used of a bird. **2.** To adorn or trim (oneself) carefully; primp. **3.** To take pride or satisfaction in (oneself). Used with *on*: *preening themselves on having won another victory.* *—intr.* **1.** To dress up; primp. **2.** To smooth or clean feathers with the bill. Used of a bird. [Middle English *preinen, proinen, prunen,* perhaps a variant of PRUNE, influenced by dialect *preen*†, to pierce.] **—preen·er** *n.*

pre·ex·il·i·an (prée-ig-zílli-ən, -eg-, -ek-, -sílli-) *adj.* Also **pre·ex·il·ic** (-zíllik, -síllik). Pertaining to the history of the Jewish people prior to their exile in Babylonia at the end of the sixth century B.C.

pre·ex·ist (prée-ig-zíst, -eg- || -ik-) *v.* **-isted, -isting, -ists.** *—intr.* To exist before. *—tr.* To exist before (something): *dinosaurs that preexisted mammals.* **—pre·ex·ist·ence** *n.* **—pre·ex·ist·ent** *adj.*

pref. 1. preface; prefatory. **2.** preference; preferred. **3.** prefix.

pre·fab (prée-fab || -fáb) *n.* A prefabricated part or building.

pre·fab·ri·cate (prée-fábbri-kayt) *tr.v.* **-cated, -cating, -cates. 1.** To construct or manufacture in advance. **2.** To produce standard sections of (a house, for example) that can be easily assembled. **—pre·fab·ri·ca·tion** (-káysh'n) *n.* **—pre·fab·ri·ca·tor** (-kaytər) *n.*

pref·ace (préf-əss, -iss) *n. Abbr.* **pref. 1. a.** A statement or essay, usually by the author, introducing a book and explaining its scope, intention, or background. **b.** The introductory section of a speech. **2.** Anything introductory or preliminary. **3.** *Usually capital* **P.** A thanksgiving prayer ending with the Sanctus and introducing the Eucharistic prayer of the Roman Catholic Mass.
~tr.v. **prefaced, -acing, -aces. 1.** To introduce by or provide with a preliminary statement or essay. **2.** To serve as an introduction to. [Middle English, from Old French, from Medieval Latin *prefātia,* alteration of Latin *praefātiō,* a saying beforehand, from *praefārī,* to say beforehand : *prae,* before + *fārī,* to speak.] **—pref·ac·er** *n.*

pref·a·to·ry (préffə-təri, -tri) *adj.* Also **pref·a·to·ri·al** (-táwri-əl || -tōri-) *Abbr.* **pref.** Of the nature of, or serving as, an introductory statement or essay; preliminary. [Latin *prefātiō,* PREFACE.] **—pref·a·to·ri·ly** *adv.*

pre·fect (prée-fekt) *n.* Also **prae·fect** (for senses 1, 3). **1.** Any of several high military or civil officials, such as magistrates or administrators, of ancient Rome. **2. a.** In some countries, such as France or Italy, a high-ranking administrative official in the provinces. **b.** The chief of police in Paris. **3.** *Roman Catholic Church.* A cardinal presiding over a congregation of the Curia. **4.** In some schools, a senior pupil authorised with a limited disciplinary power over other pupils. [Middle English, from Old French, from Latin *praefectus,* overseer, chief, from the past participle of *praeficere,* to place at the head of : *prae,* before + *facere,* to do.]

prefect apostolic *n., pl.* **prefects apostolic.** A Roman Catholic priest with broad jurisdiction in an area where no bishop has been appointed.

pre·fec·ture (prée-fek-tewr, -choor, -chər) *n.* **1. a.** The office or authority of a prefect. **b.** The district under the control of a prefect. **2.** The residence or offices of a prefect. **—pre·fec·tur·al** *adj.*

pre·fer (pri-fér, prə- || *West Indies also* préffər) *tr.v.* **-ferred, -ferring,**

-fers. **1.** To choose rather than another or others as better or more to one's taste; value more highly; like better: *prefer to walk; prefers cider to beer.* **2.** *Law.* To give priority or precedence to (a creditor). **3.** *Law.* To enter, prosecute, or offer for consideration or resolution before a legal body: *He preferred charges against her for theft.* **4.** To promote. [Middle English *preferren,* from Old French *preferer,* from Latin *praeferre,* to hold or set before : *prae,* before + *ferre,* to bear.] **—pre·fer·rer** *n.*

Usage: When the object of *prefer* is an infinitive the construction following is introduced by *rather than*: *I prefer to ride rather than to walk.* It is possible to omit the second *to* (. . . *to ride rather than walk*), but it is not acceptable in standard English to omit *rather.* In all other constructions, *prefer* is followed by *to*: *I prefer riding to walking; I prefer whisky to gin. Than* can never be used in such constructions, though *rather than* is sometimes heard in informal speech (*I prefer whisky rather than gin*). In such cases, stricter usage prefers the *to* construction, or an alternative containing *have* (*I would rather have whisky than gin*) or *instead of* (*I would rather have whisky instead of gin*).

pref·er·a·ble (préf-rəb'l, préffə- || pri-fér-əb'l, prə-) *adj.* More desirable or worthy; preferred. **—pref·er·a·bil·i·ty** (-rə-billəti || -ə-), **pref·er·a·ble·ness** *n.* **—pref·er·a·bly** *adv.*

pref·er·ence (préf-rənss, préffə-) *n. Abbr.* **pref. 1. a.** The selecting of someone or something over another or others. **b.** Someone or something so chosen. **2.** The state of being better liked or more highly valued. **3.** *Law.* **a.** The paying of one or more creditors by an insolvent debtor before, or to the exclusion of, other creditors. **b.** The right to be so paid. **4.** The granting of precedence or advantage to one over all others, as to one country or group of countries in levying duties. —See Synonyms at **choice.** [French *préférence,* from Medieval Latin *praeferentia,* from Latin *praeferēns,* present participle of *praeferre,* PREFER.]

preference shares *pl.n. British.* Shares with a fixed rate of dividend, that entitle their holders to priority of payment, over those who hold ordinary shares. Also *U.S.* "preferred stock". Compare **ordinary shares.**

pref·er·en·tial (préffə-rénsh'l) *adj.* **1.** Of, having, providing, or obtaining advantage or preference: *The old patients receive preferential treatment.* **2.** Manifesting or originating from partiality or preference, as in international trade: *preferential tariff rates.* **—pref·er·en·tial·ism** *n.* **—pref·er·en·tial·ist** *n.* **—pref·er·en·tial·ly** *adv.*

preferential voting *n.* A system of voting in which the voter indicates his choices in order of preference.

pre·fer·ment (pri-férmənt, prə-) *n.* **1.** The act of advancing to a higher position or office; promotion. **2.** A position, appointment, or rank giving advancement. [Middle English *preferrement,* from *preferren,* PREFER.]

pre·fig·u·ra·tion (preé-fíggə-ráysh'n || *chiefly U.S.* -fíggew-) *n.* **1.** The act of representing, suggesting, or imagining in advance. **2.** Something that prefigures. **—pre·fig·ur·a·tive** (-rətiv) *adj.* **—pre·fig·ur·a·tive·ly** *adv.* **—pre·fig·ur·a·tive·ness** *n.*

pre·fig·ure (preé-fíggər, pri- || *chiefly U.S.* -fíggewr) *tr.v.* **-ured, -uring, -ures. 1.** To suggest, indicate, or represent by an antecedent form or model; presage; foreshadow: *The art and theories of Cézanne prefigured the cubist school of art.* **2.** To imagine or picture to oneself in advance. [Middle English *prefiguren,* from Late Latin *praefigūrāre,* to shape beforehand : *prae,* before + *figūrāre,* to shape, from *figūra,* FIGURE.] **—pre·fig·ure·ment** *n.*

pre·fix (preé-fiks, -fíks) *tr.v.* **-fixed, -fixing, -fixes. 1.** To put or fix something before. **2.** To add as a prefix.
~*n.* (preé-fiks; *rarely* préffiks). **1.** *Abbr.* **pref.** *Grammar.* An affix put before a word that changes or modifies the meaning; for example, in the word *disbelieve, dis-* is a prefix. See **combining form. 2.** A title placed before a person's name. [New Latin *praefixum,* a prefix, from Latin *praefīgere* (past participle *praefīxus*), to fix before : *prae,* before + *fīgere,* to fix.] **—pre·fix·al** *adj.* **—pre·fix·al·ly** *adv.*

pre·for·ma·tion (preé-fawr-máysh'n) *n.* **1.** The act of shaping or forming in advance; prior formation. **2.** *Biology.* A now invalidated biological theory that all parts of a future organism exist completely formed in the germ cell and develop only by increasing in size. **—pre·for·ma·tion·ism** *n.*

pre·fron·tal lobe (preé-frúnt'l) *n.* The part of each cerebral hemisphere of the brain situated in front of the frontal lobe.

prefrontal lobotomy *n.* A surgical operation, a **leucotomy** *(see).*

preg·gers (préggərz) *adj. Chiefly British Informal.* Pregnant.

preg·na·ble (prég-nəb'l) *adj.* Vulnerable to seizure or capture, as a fort. [Earlier *preignable,* Middle English *prenable,* from Old French, from *prendre,* to take, capture, from Latin *prehendere.*] **—preg·na·bil·i·ty** (-nə-billəti) *n.*

preg·nan·cy (prég-nən-si) *n., pl.* **-cies. 1.** The condition of being pregnant. **2.** The period of being pregnant.

preg·nant (prég-nənt) *adj.* **1.** Carrying a developing foetus within the uterus. **2.** Creative; inventive. **3.** Fraught with implications: *a pregnant silence.* **4. a.** Abounding; profuse. **b.** Filled; charged; fraught: *pregnant with meaning.* **5.** Producing results; fruitful; momentous: *a pregnant decision.* [Middle English, from Latin *praegnāns* (stem *praegnānt-*), variant of *praegnās,* probably *prae,* before + *gnascī,* be born.] **—preg·nant·ly** *adv.*

pre·heat (preé-heét) *tr.v.* **-heated, -heating, -heats.** To heat beforehand: *preheat the oven for 30 minutes.*

pre·hen·sile (pri-hén-sīl, preé- || *U.S.* -s'l) *adj.* Adapted for seizing or holding, especially by wrapping around an object: *a prehensile tail.* [French *préhensile,* from Latin *prehendere* (past participle *prehensus*), to seize.] **—pre·hen·sil·i·ty** (preé-hen-sílləti) *n.*

pre·hen·sion (pri-hénsh'n) *n. Formal.* **1.** The act of grasping or seizing. **2. a.** Apprehension by the senses. **b.** Understanding. [Latin *prehensiō* (stem *prehensiōn-*), from *prehendere* (past participle *prehensus*), to seize.]

pre·his·tor·ic (preé-hiss-tórrik, -iss- || -táwrik) *adj.* Also **pre·his·tor·i·cal** (-'l) **1.** Of, pertaining to, or belonging to the era before recorded history. **2.** Very old-fashioned or out-of-date. Used humorously. **—pre·his·tor·i·cal·ly** *adv.*

pre·his·to·ry (preé-hístri, -hístəri) *n.* **1.** The history of mankind in the period before written or recorded history, investigated by archaeology. **2.** The study of this. **3.** The history of the earlier stages of an event or incident. **—pre·his·to·ri·an** (preé-hiss-táwri-ən, -iss- || -tōri-) *n.*

pre·ig·ni·tion (preé-ig-nísh'n) *n.* The ignition of fuel in an internal-combustion engine before the spark passes through the fuel.

pre·judge (preé-júj) *tr.v.* **-judged, -judging, -judges.** To judge beforehand without adequate evidence. [French *préjuger,* from Latin *praejūdicāre* : *prae,* before + *jūdicāre,* to judge, from *jūdex,* JUDGE.] **—pre·judg·er** *n.* **—pre·judg·ment, pre·judge·ment** *n.*

prej·u·dice (préj-ōō-diss, -ə-) *n.* **1. a.** An adverse judgment or opinion formed beforehand or without knowledge or examination of the facts. **b.** A preconceived preference or idea; a bias. **2.** The act or state of holding unreasonable preconceived judgments or convictions. **3.** Irrational suspicion or hatred of a particular group, race, or religion. **4.** Detriment or injury caused to a person by the preconceived and unfavourable conviction of another or others. Now rare except in the phrases *in* or *to the prejudice of.* **—without prejudice.** *Law.* Without affecting any right or claim.
~*tr.v.* **prejudiced, -dicing, -dices. 1.** To cause (a person) to judge prematurely and irrationally; bias. **2.** To affect injuriously or detrimentally by some judgment or act. [Middle English, from Old French, from Latin *praejūdicium* : *prae,* before + *jūdicium,* judgment, from *jūdex,* JUDGE.]

prej·u·di·cial (préj-ōō-dísh'l, -ə-) *adj.* Causing or of the nature of prejudice; detrimental. **—prej·u·di·cial·ly** *adv.*

prel·a·cy (préllə-si) *n., pl.* **-cies. 1. a.** The office or station of a prelate. **b.** Prelates collectively. Also called "prelature". **2.** Church government administered by prelates. Often used derogatorily. In this sense, also called "prelatism".

prel·ate (prél-ət, -it) *n.* A bishop or an abbot, or one having a similar status in the church. [Middle English *prelat,* from Old French, from Medieval Latin *praelātus,* from Latin (past participle of *praeferre,* to bear before, prefer) : *prae,* before + *-lātus,* "carried".] **—pre·lat·ic** (pri-láttik) *adj.*

prelate nul·li·us (núl-i-əss, nōōl-, nōōl-) *n.* A Roman Catholic prelate, usually a titular bishop, who has jurisdiction over a territory not in a diocese but subject directly to the Holy See. [PRELATE + Latin *nūllius,* of nobody, from *nūllus,* NULL.]

pre·lect (pri-lékt) *intr.v.* **-lected, -lecting, -lects.** To lecture or discourse in public. [Latin *praelegere* (past participle *praelectus*) : *prae,* in front of, in public + *legere,* to read.] **—pre·lec·tion** *n.* **—pre·lec·tor** *n.*

pre·li·ba·tion (preé-lī-báysh'n) *n. Rare.* A foretaste. [Latin *praelībātiō* (stem *praelībātiōn-*), from *praelībāre,* to taste beforehand : *prae,* before + *lībāre,* to taste.]

pre·lim·i·nar·y (pri-límmin-ri, prə-, -əri, -lím-nəri || -erri) *adj.* Prior to or preparing for the main matter, action, or business; introductory; prefatory.
~*n., pl.* **preliminaries. 1.** Something, such as a statement or action, that is antecedent or preparatory. **2. a.** An academic test or examination that is preparatory to one that is longer, more complex, or more important. **b.** *Sports.* An early qualifying stage of a competition: *got through the preliminaries but was knocked out in the first round.* **3.** *Plural. Printing.* Material that precedes the actual text of a book, such as the title pages, preface, or dedication. Also informally called "prelims". [French *préliminaire,* from Medieval Latin *praelīmināris* : *prae,* before + *līmināris,* of a threshold, from *līmen,* threshold, lintel (see **limen**).] **—pre·lim·i·nar·i·ly** *adv.*

pre·lims (pri-límz, preé-limz) *pl.n. Informal.* **1.** Preliminary examinations. **2.** Material that precedes the actual text of a book; preliminaries.

pre·lit·er·ate (preé-líttər-ət, -it) *adj.* Of or pertaining to any culture not having a written language.

prel·ude (préllewd || *U.S. also* práy-lōōd, preé-) *n.* **1.** That which precedes or introduces a performance, event, or action. **2.** *Music.* A piece or movement serving as an introduction to a musical composition, as: **a.** An independent piece of moderate length that precedes a fugue. **b.** The opening section of a **suite** *(see).* **c.** The overture to an opera or oratorio, or a similar piece played before one of the acts of an opera. **d.** A piece played before a church service; an introductory voluntary. **3.** *Music.* A short composition in a free style, usually for piano or orchestra.
~*v.* **preluded, -luding, -ludes.** —*tr.* **1.** To serve as a prelude to. **2.** To introduce with or as if with a prelude. —*intr.* To serve as a prelude or introduction. [Old French, from Medieval Latin *praelūdium,* from Latin *praelūdere,* to play beforehand : *prae,* before + *lūdere,* to play, from *lūdus,* game.] **—pre·lud·er** *n.* **—pre·lu·di·al** (pri-lōōdi-əl, pre-, -léwdi-) *adj.*

prem. premium.

pre·mar·i·tal (preé-márrit'l, pri-) *adj.* Occurring before marriage: *premarital sex.*

pre·ma·ture (prémmə-tewr, preémə-, -téwr, -choor, -chóor, -chər ||

-toor, -toór) *adj.* **1.** Occurring, growing, or existing prior to the customary, correct, or assigned time; uncommonly or unexpectedly early: *a premature end.* **2.** Too hurried or impulsive. **3.** Born or occurring after a gestation period of less than the normal time: *a premature baby.* [Latin *praemātūrus* : *prae*, before + *mātūrus*, ripe, MATURE.] —**pre·ma·ture·ly** *adv.* —**pre·ma·ture·ness, pre·ma·tu·ri·ty** (-téwr-əti, -choor- ‖ -toór-) *n.*

pre·max·il·la (prée-mak-síllə) *n., pl.* **-maxillae** (-síllee). Either of two bones located in front of and between the maxillary bones in the upper jaw of vertebrates. —**pre·max·il·lar·y** (-sílləri ‖ *U.S.* -máksi-lerri) *adj.*

pre·med (prée-méd) *n. Informal.* Premedication.

pre·med·i·ca·tion (pree-méddi-káysh'n) *n.* Drugs, including a sedative, administered before a general anaesthetic to prepare a patient for surgery.

pre·med·i·tate (prée-méddi-tayt, pri-) *v.* **-tated, -tating, -tates.** —*tr.* To plan, arrange, or plot (a deed or events) in advance. —*intr.* To meditate or deliberate beforehand. [Latin *praemeditāri* : *prae*, before + *meditāri*, MEDITATE.] —**pre·med·i·ta·tive** (-tətiv, -taytiv) *adj.* —**pre·med·i·ta·tor** (-taytər) *n.*

pre·med·i·tat·ed (prée-méddi-taytid, pri-) *adj.* Characterised by deliberate purpose, previous consideration, and some degree of planning. —**pre·med·i·tat·ed·ly** *adv.*

pre·med·i·ta·tion (pree-méddi-táysh'n, pri-, prée-) *n.* **1.** The act of speculating, arranging, or plotting in advance. **2.** *Law.* The contemplation and plotting of a crime in advance, showing intent to commit the crime.

pre·men·stru·al tension (prée-ménstrew-əl) *n. Abbr.* **P.M.T.** A group of symptoms including emotional disturbance, fatigue, irritability, and sometimes depression that affects some women for up to about a week before menstruation. It is associated with retention of water and salts in the tissues.

pre·mier (prém-yər, -i-ər ‖ *U.S.* pri-méer, préemi-ər) *adj.* **1.** First in status or importance; chief. **2.** First to occur or exist; earliest.
~ *n.* **1.** The head of government in some countries, as, for example a **prime minister** (*see*). **2.** The chief executive of a Canadian province or an Australian state. [Middle English *primier*, from Old French *premier*, first, chief, from Latin *prīmārius*, of the first rank, from *prīmus*, first.] —**pre·mier·ship** *n.*

prem·i·ere (prémmi-air, -ər ‖ *U.S.* pri-méer, prim-yáir) *n.* **1.** The first public presentation of a film, play, or other performance. **2.** The leading lady of a theatre company.
~ *v.* **premiered, -miering, -mieres.** —*tr.* To present the first public performance of. —*intr.* To have its first public presentation. [French, feminine of *premier*, first, chief, PREMIER.]

Premier League *n.* The top division of English football. Also called "Premier Division", "Premiership".

pre·mil·le·nar·i·an (prée-mílli-naír-i-ən) *adj.* Of or pertaining to premillennialism.
~ *n.* A person who believes in premillennialism. Compare **postmil·lenarian.**

pre·mil·len·ni·al (prée-mi-lénni-əl) *adj.* Of or happening before the millennium.

pre·mil·len·ni·al·ism (prée-mi-lénni-əl-iz'm) *n.* The belief that Christ's second coming will immediately precede the millennium. Compare **postmillennialism.** —**pre·mil·len·ni·al·ist** *n.*

Prem·in·ger (prémminjər), **Otto (Ludwig)** (1906-86). Austrian-born U.S. film director. Among his most successful films are *Laura* (1944) and *Anatomy of a Murder* (1959).

prem·ise (prémmiss) *n.* Also **prem·iss** (for sense 1). **1. a.** A proposition upon which an argument is based or from which a conclusion is drawn. **b.** *Logic.* One of the first two propositions (major or minor) of a syllogism, from which the conclusion is drawn. **2.** *Plural. Law.* **a.** In a document, matter previously referred to; the aforesaid. **b.** The preliminary or explanatory statements or facts of a document, as in a conveyance or deed. **3.** *Plural.* **a.** Land and the buildings upon it. **b.** A building or part of a building. —**on** (or off) the **premises.** Inside (or outside) a building, shop, restaurant or the like together with its adjoining grounds.
~ *v.* (prémmiss, pri-míz). **premised, -ising, -ises.** —*tr.* **1.** To state in advance as introduction or explanation. **2.** To state or assume in an argument. —*intr.* To make a premise. [Middle English *premisse*, from Old French, from Medieval Latin *praemissa* (*prōpositiō*), "(proposition) put before", from Latin *praemissus*, past participle of *praemittere*, to send ahead : *prae*, before + *mittere*, to send.]

pre·mi·um (préemi-əm) *n., pl.* **-ums.** *Abbr.* **pm., prem. 1.** A prize awarded for a particular act. **2.** Something offered free or at a reduced price, as an inducement to buy. **3.** A sum of money or bonus paid in addition to a regular price, salary, or other amount. **4.** *U.S.* The amount paid, often in addition to the interest, to obtain a loan. **5.** The amount paid or payable, often in instalments, for an insurance policy. **6.** The amount at which something is valued above its par or nominal value, as money or securities. **7.** Payment for training in a trade or profession. **8.** An unusual or high value: *put a premium on honesty and hard work.* —See Synonyms at **bonus.** —**at a premium. 1.** Above par or an average. **2.** In great demand; more valuable than usual.
~ *adj.* Of high quality. [Latin *praemium*, profit from booty, "that which is obtained before others" : *prae*, before + *emere*, to take.]

Premium Bond *n.* In Britain, a bond that can be bought from the government, that, while earning no interest, entitles the holder to the chance of a monthly cash prize. Also officially called "Premium Savings Bond".

pre·mo·lar (prée-mólər) *n.* Any of eight bicuspid teeth located in pairs on each side of the upper and lower jaws, behind the canines and in front of the molars. —**pre·mo·lar** *adj.*

pre·mo·ni·tion (prémmə-nísh'n, préemə-) *n.* **1.** A warning in advance; a forewarning. **2.** A presentiment of the future; a foreboding. [Old French, from Late Latin *praemonitiō* (stem *praemonitiōn*-), from Latin *praemonēre*, to warn beforehand : *prae*, before + *monēre*, to warn.] —**pre·mon·i·to·ri·ly** (pri-mónni-trəli, -tərili) *adv.* —**pre·mon·i·to·ry** *adj.*

pre·morse (pri-mórss) *adj. Biology.* Abruptly truncated, as though bitten or broken off: *premorse leaves.* [Latin *praemorsus*, past participle of *praemordēre*, to bite off in front : *prae*, in front + *mordēre*, to bite.]

pre·mu·ni·tion (prée-mew-nísh'n) *n.* Relative immunity to severe infection as a result of inducing an active low-grade infection. [Latin *praemūnitiō* (stem *praemūnitiōn*-), fortification beforehand, from *praemūnīre*, to fortify beforehand : *prae*, before + *mūnīre*, to fortify.] —**pre·mune** (-méwn) *adj.*

pre·na·tal (prée-náyt'l) *adj.* Existing or taking place prior to birth; preceding birth. —**pre·na·tal·ly** *adv.*

prenatal diagnosis *n.* Examination of a pregnant woman in order to discover genetic, developmental, or other abnormalities in the foetus. Techniques used include **amniocentesis** and **foetoscopy** (*both of which see*).

pren·tice (préntiss) *n. Archaic.* An apprentice.
~ *adj. Archaic.* **1.** Of or pertaining to an apprentice. **2.** Inexperienced; unskilled.

prentice piece *n.* Formerly, a piece of work done by an apprentice at the end of his indenture to show that he had mastered his craft.

pre·oc·cu·pan·cy (prée-óckewpən-si, pri-) *n.* **1.** The act or right of taking possession before others; preoccupation. **2.** The state of being preoccupied or engrossed.

pre·oc·cu·pa·tion (pree-óckew-páysh'n, pri-, prée-) *n.* **1.** The state of being preoccupied; absorption of the attention or intellect. **2.** Something that preoccupies or engrosses the mind. **3.** Possession or occupation in advance; preoccupancy.

pre·oc·cu·pied (pree-óckew-pīd, pri-, prée-) *adj.* **1. a.** Absorbed in thought; engrossed. **b.** Excessively concerned with something; distracted. **2.** Formerly or already occupied. **3.** Already used and therefore unavailable for further use. Said of taxonomic names.

pre·oc·cu·py (pree-óckew-pī, pri-, prée-) *tr.v.* **-pied, -pying, -pies. 1.** To occupy completely the mind or attention of; engross. **2.** To occupy or take possession of in advance or before another. [Latin *praeoccupāre* : *prae*, before + *occupāre*, to OCCUPY.]

pre·or·dain (prée-awr-dáyn) *tr.v.* **-dained, -daining, -dains.** To appoint, decree, or ordain in advance; foreordain. —**pre·or·dain·ment, pre·or·di·na·tion** (-di-náysh'n) *n.*

prep (prep) *adj. Informal.* Preparatory: *a prep school.*
~ *n. Informal.* **1.** The preparing of lessons; homework. **2.** Time set aside for this.

prep. 1. preparation; preparatory. **2.** preposition.

pre·pack (prée-pák) *tr.v.* **-packed, -packing, -packs.** To wrap or pack (products) before marketing them.

prep·a·ra·tion (préppə-ráysh'n) *n. Abbr.* **prep. 1.** The act or process of preparing. **2.** The state of being made ready beforehand; readiness. **3.** *Usually plural.* Preliminary measures that serve to make ready for something: *preparations for the wedding reception.* **4.** A substance, such as a medicine, prepared for a particular purpose. **5.** *Music.* **a.** The anticipation of a dissonant note by means of its introduction as a consonant note in the preceding chord. **b.** The note so used. **6. a.** Homework, especially at a boarding school. **b.** Time set aside for this.

pre·par·a·tive (pri-párrətiv, prə-) *adj.* Serving or tending to prepare or make ready; preparatory.
~ *n.* That which prepares for something following. —**pre·par·a·tive·ly** *adv.*

pre·par·a·to·ry (pri-párrə-tri, prə-, -təri) *adj. Abbr.* **prep. 1.** Serving to make ready or prepare. **2.** Preliminary; introductory. **3.** Occupied in or pertaining to preparation. —**preparatory to.** In preparing for. —**pre·par·a·to·ri·ly** *adv.*

preparatory school *n.* Also *Informal* **prep school. 1.** In Britain, a school, usually private, for pupils up to the age of 13, attended in preparation for public schools. **2.** In the United States, a secondary school, usually private, preparing pupils for university.

pre·pare (pri-paír, prə-) *v.* **-pared, -paring, -pares.** —*tr.* **1.** To make ready for a specified purpose or for some act, event, or experience: *prepared the fish for cooking; wasn't prepared for the shock.* **2. a.** To put together or make by combining various elements or ingredients; manufacture; compound. **b.** To subject to a treatment or process: *prepare fruit by boiling with sugar.* **c.** To compose (a speech, for example) for subsequent use. **3.** To fit out; equip: *The troops were prepared for service in the Arctic.* **4.** *Music.* To lead up to and soften (a dissonance or its impact) by means of preparation. —*intr.* To put things or oneself in readiness; get ready. [Middle English *preparen*, from Old French *preparer*, from Latin *praeparāre*, to prepare in advance : *prae*, before + *parāre*, to prepare.] —**pre·par·ed·ly** (-paírd-li, -paír-id-) *adv.* —**pre·par·er** *n.*

pre·pared (pri-paírd, prə-) *adj.* **1.** Made ready. **2.** Willing: *Both sides were prepared to meet.*

pre·par·ed·ness (pri-paír-id-nəss, prə-, -paírd-, -niss) *n.* The state of being prepared; especially, military readiness for war.

pre·pay (prée-páy) *tr.v.* **-paid, -paying, -pays.** To pay or pay for beforehand. —**pre·pay·ment** *n.*

pre·pense (pri-pénss) *adj. Law.* Contemplated in advance; premeditated. Used chiefly in the phrase *malice prepense.* [Variant of obsolete *prepensed, purpensed,* from Middle English *purpensen,* think of in advance, from Old French *pourpenser,* to premeditate : *pour,* forth, before, from Latin *prō-* + *penser,* think, from Latin *pensāre,* frequentative of *pendere,* to weigh.] —**pre·pense·ly** *adv.*

pre·pon·der·ant (pri-póndərənt, prə-) *adj.* Being superior, as in power, or importance; predominant. —See Synonyms at **dominant.** —**pre·pon·der·ance, pre·pon·der·an·cy** *n.* —**pre·pon·der·ant·ly** *adv.*

pre·pon·der·ate (pri-póndə-rayt, prə-) *intr.v.* **-ated, -ating, -ates.** 1. To exceed something else in weight. 2. To be greater, as in power, force, quantity, or importance; predominate. 3. *Archaic.* To be weighed down, as one end of a balance. [Latin *praeponderāre* : *prae,* in front of, exceeding + *ponderāre,* to weigh, from *pondus* (stem *ponder-*), weight.] —**pre·pon·der·at·ing·ly** *adv.* —**pre·pon·der·a·tion** (-ráysh'n) *n.*

prep·o·si·tion (préppə-zísh'n) *n. Abbr.* **prep.** *Grammar.* 1. In some languages, a word that indicates the relation of a substantive to a verb, an adjective, or another substantive. Some English prepositions are *at, by, in, to, from,* and *with.* 2. Any word or construction of similar function, such as *with regard to* or *concerning.* [Middle English *preposicioun,* from Latin *praepositiō* (translation of Greek *prothesis*), from *praepōnere* (past participle *praepositus*), to place in front : *prae,* in front + *pōnere,* to place.]

pre·po·si·tion·al (prépə-zísh'n'l) *adj.* 1. Pertaining to, composed of, or used as a preposition. 2. Designating, pertaining to, or inflected in the prepositional. ~*n.* 1. The grammatical case in certain Indo-European languages, such as Russian, that is used only as the object of prepositions. 2. A form or construction in this case. —**pre·po·si·tion·al·ly** *adv.*

prepositional phrase *n. Grammar.* A phrase consisting of a preposition and the noun it governs and having adjectival or adverbial value; for example, in the phrases *a dress of wool* and *written in haste,* the prepositional phrases are *of wool* (adjectival value) and *in haste* (adverbial value).

pre·pos·i·tive (pri-pózzətiv, prée-) *adj. Grammar.* Put before; prefixed: *a prepositive adjective.* Compare **postpositive.** ~*n. Grammar.* A word or particle put before another word. [Late Latin *praepositīvus,* from *praepōnere* (past participle *praepositus*), to place in front. See **preposition.**] —**pre·pos·i·tive·ly** *adv.*

pre·pos·sess (préepə-zéss) *tr.v.* **-sessed, -sessing, -sesses.** 1. To preoccupy the mind of to the exclusion of other thoughts or feelings. 2. To influence beforehand for or against someone or something; prejudice; bias. 3. To impress favourably in advance.

pre·pos·sess·ing (préepə-zéssing) *adj.* Impressing favourably; pleasing. —**pre·pos·sess·ing·ly** *adv.* —**pre·pos·sess·ing·ness** *n.*

pre·pos·ses·sion (préepə-zésh'n) *n.* 1. A preconception or prejudice. 2. The state of being preoccupied with thoughts, opinions, or feelings, especially ones that are favourable.

pre·pos·ter·ous (pri-póstrəss, prə-, -póstərəss) *adj.* Contrary to nature, reason, or common sense; absurd. See Synonyms at **foolish.** [Latin *praeposterus,* "inverted", perverted, absurd : *prae-,* before + *posterus,* coming after, following, next, from *post,* after.] —**pre·pos·ter·ous·ly** *adv.* —**pre·pos·ter·ous·ness** *n.*

pre·po·ten·cy (prée-pōt'n-si, pri-) *n.* 1. The state or condition of being prepotent; predominance. 2. *Genetics.* The capacity of one parent to transmit more characteristics to the offspring than the other parent. 3. *Botany.* The capacity of some pollen to cause fertilisation more readily than pollen from another source.

pre·po·tent (prée-pōt'nt, pri-) *adj.* Also **pre·po·ten·tial** (-pə-ténsh'l, -pō-). 1. Greater in power, influence, or force; predominant. 2. *Genetics.* Showing prepotency. [Middle English, from Latin *praepotēns* (stem *praepotent-*), present participle of *praeposse,* to be very powerful : *prae-* (intensifier) + *posse,* to be able or powerful.] —**pre·po·tent·ly** *adv.*

prep·py, prep·pie (préppi) *n., pl.* **-pies.** *U.S. Informal.* A student or graduate of the U.S. preparatory school system. ~*adj. U.S. Informal.* Of, pertaining to, or being a preppy; especially, having the conservative tastes and values or dressing in the neat, casual style, characteristic of a preppy.

pre·print *n.* A printing or copy of a book, report, document, or the like, issued in advance of general publication or distribution. ~*tr.v.* **preprinted, -printing, -prints.** To print and issue in advance of general publication.

prep school *n. Informal.* A **preparatory school** (*see*).

pre·puce (prée-pewss) *n.* 1. The **foreskin** (*see*). 2. A structure corresponding to the foreskin covering the glans of the clitoris. [Middle English, from Old French, from Latin *praepūtium.*] —**pre·pu·tial** (-péwsh'l, pri-) *adj.*

pre·quel (preekwəl) *n.* A film, book, or the like that is made or written after another which is about the same subject, but that relates events that occurred prior to those related in the previous film, book, or the like. [PRE- or PRE(VIOUS) + (SE)QUEL.]

Pre-Raph·a·el·ite (prée-ráf-ə-līt, -ráffi-, -ráffay- ‖ *U.S. also* -ráyffi-, -ráafi-) *n.* A painter or writer belonging to or influenced by the Pre-Raphaelite Brotherhood, a society founded in 1848 by Rossetti and others to advance the style and spirit of Italian painting before Raphael. —**Pre-Raph·a·el·it·ism** *n.* —**Pre-Raph·a·el·ite** *adj.*

pre·re·cord (prée-ri-kórd, -rə-) *tr.v.* **-corded, -cording, -cords.** To record beforehand; especially, to record (a broadcast) in advance of transmission.

pre·re·cord·ed (prée-ri-kórdid, -rə-) *adj.* 1. Recorded beforehand: *prerecorded laughter.* 2. Bearing a commercial recording; not blank: *prerecorded tapes.*

pre·req·ui·site (prée-rékwizit, pri-) *adj.* Required as a prior condition to something. See Synonyms at **necessary.** ~*n.* That which is prerequisite.

Usage: As a noun, *prerequisite* is followed by *of* or *for,* and occasionally by *to: Hard work is a prerequisite for success.* As an adjective, it is followed by *to: Hard work is prerequisite to success.*

pre·rog·a·tive (pri-róggətiv, prə-) *n.* 1. **a.** An exclusive right or privilege held by a person or group, especially a hereditary or official right. **b.** See **Royal Prerogative.** 2. Any characteristically exclusive right or privilege. 3. A natural advantage making one superior: *Thinking is one of man's prerogatives.* —See Synonyms at **right.** ~*adj.* Of, arising from, or exercising a prerogative. [Middle English, from Old French, from Latin *praerogātīva (centuria),* "(century) chosen to vote first", from *praerogātīvus,* asked to vote first, from *praerogāre,* to ask before others : *prae-,* before + *rogāre,* to ask.]

pres. 1. present (time). 2. president.

Pres. President.

pres·age (préssij) *n.* 1. An indication or warning of a future occurrence; an omen; a portent. 2. A feeling or intuition of what is going to occur; a presentiment; a foreboding. 3. *Rare.* A prediction. ~*v.* **pre·sage** (préssij, pri-sáyj) **presaged, -saging, -sages.** —*tr.* 1. To indicate or warn of in advance; portend. 2. To have a presentiment of. 3. To foretell or predict. —*intr.* To make or utter a prediction. —See Synonyms at **foretell.** [Middle English, from Latin *praesāgium,* foreboding, from *praesāgīre,* to perceive beforehand : *prae-,* before + *sāgīre,* to perceive.] —**pre·sage·ful** (pri-sáyj-f'l) *adj.*

pres·by·o·pi·a (préz-bi-ṓpi-ə ‖ préss-) *n.* The inability of the eye to focus sharply on nearby objects, resulting from hardening of the lens with advancing age; longsightedness. [New Latin : Greek *presbus,* old man + -OPIA.] —**pres·by·op·ic** (-óppik) *adj.*

pres·by·ter (préz-bi-tər ‖ préss-) *n.* 1. In the early Christian church, an elder of the congregation. 2. In various hierarchical churches, a priest. 3. In the Presbyterian Church: **a.** A teaching elder. **b.** A ruling elder. [Late Latin, an elder, from Greek *presbuteros,* a priest, "older", comparative of *presbus,* old man.]

pres·byt·er·ate (prez-bíttər-ət, -it, -ayt ‖ press-) *n.* 1. The office of a presbyter. 2. The body or order of presbyters.

pres·by·te·ri·al (préz-bi-téer-i-əl ‖ préss-) *adj.* Of or pertaining to a presbyter or the presbytery. —**pres·by·te·ri·al·ly** *adv.*

pres·by·te·ri·an (préz-bi-téer-i-ən ‖ préss-) *adj.* 1. Of or pertaining to ecclesiastical government by presbyters. 2. *Capital* P. Of or pertaining to a Presbyterian Church. ~*n. Capital* P. A member or adherent of a Presbyterian Church. —**pres·by·te·ri·an·ism** *n.*

Presbyterian Church *n.* Any of various Protestant churches governed by presbyters and traditionally Calvinist in doctrine. In England, the Presbyterian Church became part of the **United Reformed Church** (*see*), in 1972.

pres·by·ter·y (préz-bi-tri, -təri ‖ préss-, *U.S.* -terri) *n., pl.* **-ies.** 1. In the Presbyterian Church: **a.** A court composed of the ministers and representative elders of a particular locality. **b.** The district represented by this court. 2. Presbyters collectively. 3. Government of a church by presbyters. 4. The section of the church east of the choir where the main altar is situated; a sanctuary. 5. *Roman Catholic Church.* The residence of a priest. [Middle English *presbytory,* from Late Latin *presbyterium,* a council of presbyters, from Greek *presbuterion,* from *presbuteros,* priest, PRESBYTER.]

pre·school (prée-skṓl) *adj.* Of or pertaining to children below the age at which they begin full-time education. —**pre·school·er** *n.*

pre·sci·ence (préssi-ənss, préshi- ‖ prée-si-) *n.* Knowledge of actions or events before they occur; foreknowledge; foresight. —**pre·sci·ent** (-ənt) *adj.* —**pre·sci·ent·ly** *adv.*

pre·scind (pri-sínd, prée-) *v.* **-scinded, -scinding, -scinds.** —*tr.* To separate or divide, especially so as to consider individually. Used with *from.* —*intr.* To withdraw one's attention. Used with *from.* [Latin *praescindere,* to cut off in front : *prae-,* in front + *scindere,* to cut off.]

pre·scribe (pri-skríb, prə-) *v.* **-scribed, -scribing, -scribes.** —*tr.* 1. To set down as a rule or guide; ordain; enjoin. 2. *Medicine.* To order or recommend the use of (a drug, treatment, or the like). —*intr.* 1. To establish rules, laws, or directions. 2. *Medicine.* To order or recommend a remedy or treatment. 3. *Law.* To assert a right or title to something on the grounds of prescription. [Middle English *prescriben,* to hold by right of prescription, from Medieval Latin *prescrībere,* to claim by such right, from Latin *praescrībere,* to write at the beginning, prescribe : *prae-,* before, in front + *scrībere,* to write.] —**pre·scrib·er** *n.*

pre·script (prée-skript) *n.* Something prescribed, especially a rule or regulation of conduct. ~*adj.* (prée-skript, pri-skrípt). Established as a rule; set down; prescribed. [Latin *praescriptum,* from *praescrībere* (past participle *praescriptus*), PRESCRIBE.]

pre·scrip·ti·ble (pri-skrípt-əb'l) *adj.* Capable of, subject to, or derived from prescription. —**pre·scrip·ti·bil·i·ty** (-ə-bílləti) *n.*

pre·scrip·tion (pri-skrípsh'n, prə-) *n.* 1. **a.** The act of prescribing. **b.** That which is prescribed. 2. *Medicine.* **a.** A written instruction by a doctor for the preparation and administration of a medicine. **b.** A prescribed medicine. **c.** An ophthalmologist's or optometrist's written instruction for the grinding of corrective lenses. **3.** A formula directing the preparation or correction of anything. **4.** *Law.* **a.** The process of acquiring title to property by reason of uninterrupted possession of specified duration. Also called "positive prescription". **b.** The limitation of time beyond which an action, debt, or crime is no longer valid or enforceable. Also called "negative prescription". [Middle English *prescripcion,* from Old French *prescription,* from Latin *praescriptiō* (stem *praescriptiōn-*), a writing in front, from *praescrībere,* PRESCRIBE.]

prescription charge *n.* In Britain, a tax levied as a charge for each medicine or appliance supplied under the National Health Service.

pre·scrip·tive (pri-skríptiv, prə-) *adj.* **1.** Sanctioned or authorised by long-standing custom or usage. **2.** Making or giving injunctions, directions, laws, or rules. **3.** *Law.* Acquired by or based upon uninterrupted possession. **4.** *Linguistics.* Of or designating a grammar that seeks to lay down rules for the usage of language, as opposed to just describing it. Compare **descriptive.** **—pre·scrip·tive·ly** *adv.*

pre·scrip·tiv·ism (pri-skríptiv-iz'm, prə-) *n.* **1.** *Philosophy.* The doctrine that ethical propositions prescribe a course of action or a code of morality and are not true or false. Compare **emotivism, descriptivism.** **2.** *Linguistics.* The doctrine that a grammar should be prescriptive.

pres·ence (prézz'nss) *n.* **1.** The state or fact of being present. **2.** Immediate proximity in time or space. **3. a.** The area immediately surrounding a great personage, especially a sovereign granting an audience. **b.** A great or imposing person. **4.** A person's manner of carrying himself; bearing. **5.** A person or thing, especially a supernatural being, that is felt to be present. **6.** A person or body of persons present in a given place; especially, military personnel protecting a national interest. **7.** Charismatic bearing or authority, as in an actor. —See Synonyms at **bearing.**

presence of mind *n.* Ability to think and act efficiently, especially when under pressure.

pre·sen·ile dementia (prée-séen-īl || -sén-) *n.* Any of several conditions, especially **Alzheimer's disease** *(see),* characterised by deterioration of mental abilities in young or middle-aged people.

pre·se·nil·i·ty (prée-si-nílləti, -sə-) *n.* Reduction of mental or physical abilities, normally associated with age, occurring in young or middle-aged people. **—pre·se·nile** *adj.*

pres·ent[1] (prézz'nt) *n.* **1.** A moment or period in time designated as being intermediate between past and future; now. **2.** *Abbr.* **pr., pres.** *Grammar.* **a.** The present tense. **b.** A verb form in the present tense. **3.** *Plural. Law.* The document or instrument in question: *be it known by these presents.*
~*adj.* **1.** Being, pertaining to, existing, or occurring at a moment or period in time considered as the present: *present events.* **2.** At hand; nearby; in the vicinity. **3.** Existing or occurring within; contained in. **4.** *Abbr.* **pr., pres.** *Grammar.* Designating a verb tense or form that expresses current time. **5.** *Obsolete.* Readily available; immediate. [Middle English, from Old French, from Latin *praesēns* (stem *praesent-*), present participle of *praeesse,* to be before one, be present : *prae-,* in front of + *esse,* to be.]

pre·sent[2] (pri-zént, prə-) *v.* **-sented, -senting, -sents.** *—tr.* **1.** To introduce, especially with formal ceremony: *She was presented to the king.* **2. a.** To bring before the public: *present a play.* **b.** *British.* To act as a presenter on (a radio or television programme). **3. a.** To hand over or give, especially as a gift or award: *presented a huge bill; presented the cheque to the winner.* **b.** To hand over or give to, especially formally: *presented him with a gold watch.* **4.** To offer to the view or mind; show: *presented a sharp contrast.* **5. a.** To constitute or entail: *This presents a challenge to us all.* **b.** To face; confront: *presented me with a dilemma.* **6.** To offer for consideration: *An idea presented itself.* **7. a.** To point or aim (a weapon). **b.** To salute with (a weapon). Used chiefly in the phrase *present arms.* **8.** To recommend (a clergyman) for a benefice. **9.** *Law.* **a.** To offer to a legislature or court for consideration. **b.** To bring a charge or accusation against. **10.** To represent or depict in a particular manner: *He presented himself to us as a benefactor.* *—intr.* **1.** To be directed towards the neck of the womb and vagina during labour. Used of part of an unborn child. **2.** To present oneself: *The patient presented with various symptoms.* **3.** To present itself; manifest: *The disease can present in various ways.* —See Synonyms at **offer.** **—present (oneself).** To arrive or appear.
~*n.* **pres·ent** (prézz'nt). A gift. [Middle English *presenten,* from Old French *presenter,* from Latin *praesentāre,* from *praesēns,* PRESENT (adjective).]

pre·sent·a·ble (pri-zént-əb'l, prə-) *adj.* **1.** Fit to be given, displayed, or offered. **2.** Of decent enough appearance to be fit for introduction to others. **—pre·sent·a·bil·i·ty** (-ə-bílləti), **pre·sent·a·ble·ness** *n.* **—pre·sent·a·bly** *adv.*

pres·en·ta·tion (prézz'n-táysh'n || *chiefly U.S.* prée-zen-, -z'n-) *n.* **1. a.** The act of presenting or offering someone or something, as for acceptance or approval. **b.** The state of being presented. **c.** The manner or style in which someone or something is presented; especially, the way in which a commercial product is promoted through design, packaging, and advertising. **2.** A performance, as of a play. **3. a.** A formal ceremony at which something, such as an award or prize, is presented. **b.** Something that is presented. Also used adjectivally: *a presentation copy of a book.* **4.** A formal introduction, such as at court. **5.** The act or right of nominating a clergyman to a benefice. **6.** The process of offering for consideration. **7.** *Medicine.* The position of the foetus in the uterus at birth, with respect to the neck of the uterus. **—pres·en·ta·tion·al** *adj.*

pre·sent·a·tive (pri-zéntətiv, prə-) *adj.* **1.** Having the capacity or function of bringing an idea or image to mind. **2.** *Philosophy.* **a.** Perceived or capable of being perceived directly rather than through association. **b.** Having the ability to so perceive. **3.** Capable of nominating or of being nominated to an ecclesiastical benefice. **—pre·sent·a·tive·ness** *n.*

pres·ent-day (prézz'nt-dáy) *adj.* Current.

pres·en·tee (prézz'n-tée) *n. U.S.* **1.** A person who is presented. **2.** A person to whom something is given.

pre·sent·er (pri-zéntər, prə-) *n.* **1.** One who presents. **2.** *British.* One who introduces a radio or television programme.

pre·sen·tient (pri-sén-shi-ənt, -sh'nt || -zén-) *adj.* Having a presentiment or presentiments. [Latin *praesentiēns* (stem *praesentient-*), present participle of *praesentīre,* to have a presentiment. See **presentiment.**]

pre·sen·ti·ment (pri-zénti-mənt, -sénti-) *n.* A sense of something about to occur; a premonition. See Synonyms at **apprehension.** [Obsolete French, from Old French *presentir,* to have a presentiment, from Latin *praesentīre,* to perceive beforehand : *prae-,* before + *sentīre,* to perceive.]

pres·ent·ly (prézz'ntli) *adv.* **1.** In a short time; soon; directly: *She will arrive presently.* **2.** *U.S.* At this time or period; now: *He is presently staying with us.* **3.** *Archaic.* Immediately.
Usage: In American English, *presently* is being increasingly used to mean "at this time, now", a trend which has attracted a good deal of criticism. This usage has so far had little influence on British English, where the meaning of "in a short time, soon", is standard.

pre·sent·ment (pri-zént-mənt, prə-) *n.* **1.** The act of presenting; presentation. **2.** Something presented, such as a picture or exhibition. **3.** *Law.* **a.** The act of submitting or presenting a formal statement of a legal matter to a court or authorised person. **b.** A report written by a jury or a similar body. **4.** *Finance.* The presenting of a bill or note for payment.

present participle *n. Grammar.* A participle expressing present action, in English formed by the infinitive plus *-ing* and used: **1.** To express present action in relation to the time indicated by the finite verb in its clause. **2.** To form certain compound tenses of the verb. **3.** To function as a verbal adjective.

present perfect *n. Grammar.* **1.** The verb tense expressing action completed at the present time. This tense is formed in English by combining the present tense of *have* with a past participle; for example in the sentence: *He has spoken,* the words *has spoken* constitute the present perfect. **2.** A verb in this tense.

present tense *n. Grammar.* The verb tense expressing action in the present time or habitual action in the past and future; for example, in the sentence *She drinks her coffee quickly,* the verb *drinks* is in the present tense.

pre·serv·a·tive (pri-zérvətiv, prə-) *n.* Something that preserves; especially a chemical to inhibit food decay. **—pre·serv·a·tive** *adj.*

pre·serve (pri-zérv, prə-) *v.* **-served, -serving, -serves.** *—tr.* **1.** To protect from injury, peril, or other adversity; maintain in safety. **2. a.** To keep in a good, healthy condition: *moisturising cream preserves the skin.* **b.** To keep or maintain in an unchanged form: *Her name will be preserved.* **3.** To keep or maintain intact. **4. a.** To prepare (food) so as to prevent decomposition, as by bottling or salting. **b.** To prepare (fruit, for example) by boiling with sugar, so as to prevent decomposition or make jam. **5.** To prevent (organic bodies) from decaying or spoiling. **6.** To keep or protect (game or fish) for one's private hunting or fishing. *—intr.* **1.** To prepare fruit or other foods for storage. **2.** To maintain a private area stocked with game or fish. —See Synonyms at **defend.**
~*n.* **1.** Something that acts to preserve; a preservative. **2.** *Often plural.* Fruit that has been preserved by boiling with sugar, especially for use as jam. **3.** An area maintained: **a.** For the protection of wildlife. **b.** *U.S.* For natural resources. **4.** Something considered to be the special domain or sphere of certain persons: *Ancient Greek is the preserve of scholars.* [Middle English *preserven,* from Old French *preserver,* from Medieval Latin *praeservāre,* "to guard beforehand" : Latin *prae-,* before + *servāre,* to keep, guard.] **—pre·serv·a·bil·i·ty** (-ə-bílləti) *n.* **—pre·serv·a·ble** *adj.* **—pres·er·va·tion** (prézzər-váysh'n) *n.* **—pre·serv·er** *n.*

pre·set (prée-sét) *tr.v.* **-set, -setting, -sets.** To set (controls, for example) in advance.

pre·shrunk (prée-shrúngk) *adj.* Shrunk during manufacture to minimise subsequent shrinkage.

pre·side (pri-zíd, prə-) *intr.v.* **-sided, -siding, -sides.** **1.** To occupy a place of authority, as, for example, a chairman or president. **2.** To possess or exercise authority or control. **3.** *Music.* To be the featured instrumental performer: *presided at the piano.* [French *presider,* from Latin *praesidēre,* "to sit in front of", superintend : *prae-,* before + *sedēre,* to sit.] **—pre·sid·er** *n.*

pres·i·den·cy (prézzi-dən-si || -den-) *n., pl.* **-cies.** The office, function, or term of a president.

pres·i·dent (prézzi-dənt || -dent) *n. Abbr.* **p., P., pres., Pres.** **1.** One appointed or elected to preside over an organised body of people, such as an assembly or meeting. **2.** *Often capital* **P.** The chief executive of a republic. **3.** *Sometimes capital* **P. a.** *U.S.* The chief officer of a branch of government. **b.** *U.S.* The chief executive officer of a business corporation. **c.** The chief officer of a society, club, university college, or any similar body. [Middle English, from Old French, from Latin *praesidēns* (stem *praesident-*), present participle

of *praesidēre,* PRESIDE.] —**pres·i·den·tial** (-dénsh'l) *adj.* —**pres·i·den·tial·ly** *adv.* —**pres·i·dent·ship** *n.*
pres·i·dent-e·lect (prézzi-dənt-i-lékt || -dent-, -ə-) *n.* A person who has been elected president but has not yet begun his term of office.
pre·sid·i·o (pri-seédi-ō, -síddi-, -zíddi-) *n., pl.* **-os.** A garrison; a military post, especially in a country under Spanish control. [Spanish, from Latin *praesidium,* garrison, fortification, from *praesidēre,* "to sit in front of", guard, PRESIDE.]
pre·sid·i·um (pri-síddi-əm, -zíddi-) *n.* **1.** Any of various permanent executive committees in Communist countries having power to act for a larger governing body. **2.** *Capital* **P.** A committee of the Supreme Soviet, headed by the premier, and constituting the highest policy-making body of the former U.S.S.R. [Russian *prezidium,* from Latin *praesidium.* See **presidio.**]
pre·sig·ni·fy (preé-síg-ni-fī) *tr.v.* **-fied, -fying, -fies.** To betoken or signify beforehand; prefigure; foreshadow.
Pres·ley (prézli), **Elvis (Aaron)** (1935–77). U.S. rock and roll singer. Following his first popular record success, *Heartbreak Hotel* (1956), he embarked on a career that was to encompass over thirty films and the sale of over 150 million copies of his records.
presolar nebular hypothesis *n.* A theory put forward to account for the origin of the Sun and the Solar System in which gas and dust from the interstellar medium contracted under the influence of gravity to form a nebula. The dust particles in the nebula became centres of accretion for matter, forming planetismals which in turn coalesced and accreted matter to form the bodies in the Solar System. Compare **planetismal, primitive solar-nebula hypothesis.**
press[1] (press) *v.* **pressed, pressing, presses.** —*tr.* **1. a.** To exert steady weight or force against; bear down on: *The wrestler pressed his opponent down.* **b.** To apply pressure to or push, as with a finger: *pressed the button.* **2. a.** To squeeze the juice or other contents from. **b.** To extract (juice, for example) by squeezing or compressing. **3. a.** To apply steady force to, so as to make compact, reshape, or flatten: *pressed flowers.* **b.** To smooth, flatten, or shape (clothing) using steam or steady pressure from an iron. **4.** To clasp or embrace closely. **5.** To seek to influence as by insistent arguments; entreat insistently. **6.** To attempt to force to action; urge on; spur. **7.** To place in trying or constraining circumstances; distress; harass: *pressed by lack of money; pressed for time.* **8.** To lay stress upon; emphasise: *pressed her point.* **9.** To advance or carry on vigorously: *pressed his attack.* **10.** To put forward importunately or insistently: *They pressed their claim.* **11.** To manufacture (a record) from a mould or matrix. **12.** To lift (a weight) first to the shoulders and then above the head. Used of a weightlifter. —*intr.* **1.** To exert force or pressure. **2.** To weigh heavily, as on the mind. **3.** To advance eagerly; push forward: *Let's press on with the next course.* **4.** To require haste; be urgent. **5.** To press clothes or other material. **6.** To assemble closely and in large numbers; crowd. **7.** To employ urgent persuasion or entreaty; ask earnestly or persistently. —See Synonyms at **urge.**
~n. **1.** Any of various machines or devices that apply pressure. Often used in combination: *a winepress.* **2.** Any of various machines used for printing; a **printing press** *(see).* **3. a.** A place or establishment where matter is printed. **b.** *Often capital* **P.** A printing or publishing firm: *The Nonesuch Press.* **4.** The method, art, or business of printing. **5. a.** The news media as a whole; especially, the newspapers. Preceded by *the.* Also used adjectivally: *a press release.* **b.** The people involved in the news media; especially, reporters and photographers. Preceded by *the.* **c.** The material dealt with in the news media; especially, reviews or editorial comment: *The new play received a bad press.* **6.** The act of gathering in large numbers or of pushing forward. **7.** A large gathering; a throng. **8. a.** The act of applying pressure. **b.** The state of being pressed. **9.** The haste or urgency of business or affairs. **10.** The set of proper creases in a garment or fabric, formed by ironing. **11.** An upright cupboard or case used for storing clothing, books, or other articles. **12.** In weightlifting, the act of pressing a weight. —**at** or **in press.** Being printed. —**go to press.** To start printing or being printed. [Middle English *pressen,* from Old French *presser,* from Latin *pressāre,* frequentative of *premere* (past participle *pressus*), to press.]
press[2] *tr.v.* **pressed, pressing, presses. 1.** To force into military service; impress. **2.** To use in a manner different from the usual or intended. Used chiefly in the phrase *press into service.*
~n. Conscription or impressment into service, especially into the navy. [Alteration (by association with PRESS, to apply pressure, compel) of earlier *prest,* to give money to (recruits), from Middle English *prest,* money given to recruits, from Old French, "loan", from *prester,* to lend, from Latin *praestāre,* to place something at someone's disposal, furnish : *prae-,* PRE- + *stāre,* to stand.]
press agent *n. Abbr.* **P.A.** A person employed to arrange advertising and favourable publicity for an actor, theatre, or the like.
press agency *n.* A **news agency** *(see).*
press box *n.* A section reserved for reporters, as in a stadium.
press conference *n.* An interview held for news reporters and photographers by a politician or other public figure.
press·er (préssər) *n.* **1.** A person who presses clothes. **2.** Any of various devices that apply pressure to a product in manufacturing.
press gallery *n.* An area above the ground floor reserved for the press, as in a parliament.
press gang *n.* A company under an officer with the task of pressing men into military, especially naval, service.
press-gang (préss-gang) *tr.v.* **-ganged, -ganging, -gangs. 1.** To press into military service. **2.** To force (a person) to do something unwillingly.
press·ing (préssing) *adj.* **1.** Demanding immediate attention; urgent: *a pressing need.* **2.** Importunate; insistent: *a pressing invitation.* —See Synonyms at **urgent.**
~n. **1.** A series of gramophone records produced at one time. **2.** Any of these records. —**press·ing·ly** *adv.*
press·man (préss-mən, -man) *n., pl.* **-men** (-mən, -men). **1.** A printing press operator. **2.** *British.* A journalist.
press·mark (préss-maark) *n.* A mark in or on a book indicating where it should be placed in a library.
press officer *n.* A person employed by an organisation to liaise with and answer enquiries from the press.
press of sail *n. Nautical.* The greatest amount of sail that a ship can carry safely. Also called "press of canvas".
pres·sor (préss-ər, -awr) *n.* An agent that increases blood pressure. [Latin *premere* (stem *press-*), to PRESS.] —**pres·sor** *adj.*
press release *n.* An announcement or official account of an event, performance, or other news or publicity item issued to the press.
press·room (préss-rōōm, -rŏŏm) *n.* The room in a printing or newspaper publishing establishment that contains the presses.
press secretary *n.* A person who manages the public affairs and press conferences of a public figure.
press-stud (préss-stud) *n.* A small metal or plastic fastener for clothes, that works by having its two parts pushed together. Also *chiefly U.S.* "snap fastener".
press-up (préss-up) *n.* A physical exercise performed by lying with the face and palms to the floor and pushing the body up and down with the arms. Also *U.S.* "push-up".
pres·sure (préshər) *n.* **1. a.** The act of pressing. **b.** The condition of being pressed. **2.** The application of continuous force by one body upon another that it is touching; compression. **3. a.** *Abbr.* **p** *Physics.* Force applied over a surface, measured as force per unit of area. It is measured in pascals, pounds per square inch, or the like. **b.** *Meteorology.* See **atmospheric pressure. 4.** A constraining influence upon the mind or will, as, for example, a moral force: *brought pressure to bear upon the government.* **5.** Urgent claims or demand; harassment: *working under pressure.* **6.** A burdensome, distressing, or weighty condition; oppression, as of grief. **7.** *Obsolete.* A mark made by application of force or weight; an impression.
~tr.v. **pressured, -suring, -sures.** To bring pressure upon (a person), as by influence or persuasion. [Middle English, from Latin *pressūra,* from *premere,* to PRESS.]
pressure cabin *n.* A pressurised section of an aircraft.
pressure cooker *n.* **1.** An airtight metal pot that uses steam under pressure at high temperature to cook food quickly. **2.** A situation in which one is under a lot of pressure.
pressure gauge *n.* **1.** A device for measuring fluid pressure. **2.** A device for measuring the pressure of explosions.
pressure group *n.* Any group that exerts pressure on legislators and public opinion to advance or protect its interests.
pressure point *n.* Any of several places on the skin where an artery lies over a bone, and where pressure may be applied to stop bleeding from a wound beyond that point.
pressure ridge *n.* A ridge of floating ice formed as two ice floes push against each other.
pressure sore *n.* A **bed sore** *(see).*
pressure suit *n.* A garment that is worn in high-altitude aircraft or in spacecraft to compensate for low-pressure conditions. Compare **G-suit.**
pressure system *n.* Any system of high or low atmospheric pressure, such as a depression or anticyclone.
pres·sur·ise, pres·sur·ize (préshər-īz) *tr.v.* **-ised, -ising, -ises. 1.** To coerce (a person) with pressure, especially into a course of action. **2.** To maintain normal air pressure in (an enclosure, such as an aircraft or submarine). **3.** To put (gas or liquid) under a greater than normal pressure. —**pres·sur·i·sa·tion** (-ī-záysh'n || *U.S.* -i-) *n.*
press·work (préss-wurk) *n.* **1.** The directing or running of a printing press. **2.** The matter printed by a printing press.
Pres·tel (préss-tel) *n.* A trademark for a system operated by British Telecom for transmitting a wide variety of computer-stored information over the telephone system in viewdata form, and allowing viewers to return information to the computer.
pres·ti·dig·i·ta·tion (présti-díji-táysh'n) *n.* Manual skill and dexterity in the execution of tricks; sleight of hand. [French, from *prestidigitateur,* juggler, from *preste,* nimble, from Latin *praestus* (see **presto**) + Latin *digitus,* finger.] —**pres·ti·dig·i·ta·tor** (-taytər) *n.*
pres·tige (press-teézh, préss- || -teéj) *n.* **1.** Prominence or influential status achieved through success, renown, or wealth. **2.** The power to command admiration in a group.
~adj. Possessing or conferring prestige. [French, originally "illusion brought on by magic", phantasmagoria, from Latin *praestigiae,* "juggler's tricks", illusions, alteration of *praestrigiae* (unattested), from *praestringere,* to bind up, dazzle, blind : *prae-,* before + *stringere,* to bind, tighten.] —**pres·tig·ious** (-tíj-əss, -tíji- || -teéji-) *adj.* —**pres·tig·ious·ly** *adv.* —**pres·tig·ious·ness** *n.*
pres·tis·si·mo (press-tíssimō) *adv. Music.* At as fast a tempo as possible. Used as a direction.
~n., pl. **prestissimos.** *Music.* A section or passage to be played in this manner. [Italian, superlative of PRESTO.] —**pres·tis·si·mo** *adj.*
pres·to (préstō) *adv.* **1.** *Music.* In rapid tempo. Used as a direction. **2.** Suddenly; at once. Used chiefly in the phrase *hey presto.*
~n., pl. **prestos.** *Music.* A section or passage to be played presto.

[Italian, from Latin *praestus,* ready, from *praestō*†, at hand.] **—pres·to** *adj.*

Pres·ton (préstən). County town of Lancashire, northwest England. Situated on the river Ribble, it is a port and has textile and engineering industries. Cromwell defeated the Royalists here in 1648.

Pres·ton·pans (préstən-pánz). Town in East Lothian, east central Scotland. It was the site of the defeat of the English by the Jacobites under Charles Edward Stuart (Bonnie Prince Charlie) (1745).

pre·stress (prée-stréss) *tr.v.* **-stressed, -stressing, -stresses.** To subject (material) to stress before applying a load, so as to counterbalance applied stresses under loaded conditions.

prestressed concrete *n.* Reinforced concrete in which the reinforcing wires or bars have been subjected to stress before forming the concrete, so as to strengthen the material under load.

Prest·wick (prést-wik). Town in Scotland. Situated on the Firth of Clyde, it is famous for its golf course. Scotland's international airport is located here.

pre·sum·a·ble (pri-zéwm-əb'l, prə-, -zóom- || -zhóom-) *adj.* Capable of being presumed or taken for granted; reasonable as a supposition; probable. **—pre·sum·a·bly** *adv.*

pre·sume (pri-zéwm, prə-, -zóom || -zhóom) *v.* **-sumed, -suming, -sumes.** *—tr.* **1.** To take for granted; assume. **2.** *Law.* To take as being proved in the absence of contrary evidence. **3.** To engage oneself in, without authority or permission; venture; dare. Often used with an infinitive. *—intr.* **1.** To act overconfidently; take liberties. **2.** To take unwarranted advantage of something. Used with *on* or *upon*: *presumed upon her kindness.* —See Synonyms at **conjecture.** [Middle English *presumen,* from Old French *presumer,* from Late Latin *praesūmere,* to venture, from Latin, "to take in advance", presuppose, foresee, assume : *prae-,* before + *sūmere,* to take.] **—pre·sum·ed·ly** (-idli) *adv.* **—pre·sum·er** *n.*

Synonyms: *presume, suppose, postulate, assume, posit.*

pre·sump·tion (pri-zúmpsh'n, prə-) *n.* **1.** Behaviour or language that is boldly arrogant or offensive; effrontery. **2.** The act of presuming or accepting as true. **3.** Acceptance or belief based on reasonable evidence; an assumption or supposition. **4.** A condition or basis for accepting or presuming. **5.** *Law.* An inference as to the truth of an allegation or proposition, based on probable reasoning, in the absence of, or prior to, actual proof or disproof. [Middle English *presumpcion,* from Old French, from Latin *praesumptiō* (stem *praesumptiōn-*), from *praesūmere,* PRESUME.]

pre·sump·tive (pri-zúmptiv, prə-) *adj.* **1.** Providing a reasonable basis for belief or acceptance. **2.** Founded on probability or presumption: *an heir presumptive.* **3.** *Zoology.* Designating a cell or cells of an embryo that differentiate into a particular structure or organ. **—pre·sump·tive·ly** *adv.*

pre·sump·tu·ous (pri-zúmp-tew-əss, prə-, -choo-, -chəss, -shəss) *adj.* **1.** Excessively forward or bold, especially because of excessive self-confidence; arrogant. **2.** *Obsolete.* Presumptive. [Middle English, from Old French *presumptueux,* from Late Latin *praesumptuōsus,* audacious, from *praesumptiō,* audacity, PRESUMPTION.] **—pre·sump·tu·ous·ly** *adv.* **—pre·sump·tu·ous·ness** *n.*

pre·sup·pose (prée-sə-póz) *tr.v.* **-posed, -posing, -poses.** **1.** To assume or suppose in advance; take for granted. **2.** To require or involve necessarily as an antecedent condition: *Intelligent speaking presupposes intelligent thinking.* [Middle English *presupposen,* from Old French *presupposer,* from Medieval Latin *praesuppōnere* : *prae-,* before + *suppōnere,* to SUPPOSE.] **—pre·sup·po·si·tion** (-suppə-zísh'n) *n.*

pret. preterite.

pre·tax (prée-táks) *adj.* Before taxation.

pre·tence, *U.S.* **pre·tense** (pri-ténss, prə- || *U.S. also* prée-tenss) *n.* **1.** The act of pretending; a false appearance or action intended to deceive. **2.** A false or studied show of something; an affectation. **3.** A false reason or excuse; a pretext. **4.** Something imagined or pretended; a piece of make-believe. **5.** A mere show without reality; an outward appearance. Used with *at*: *There was some pretence at negotiating.* **6.** A right asserted with or without foundation; a claim. **7.** Ostentation; pretentiousness. [Middle English, from Anglo-French *pretense,* from Medieval Latin *praetensa* (unattested), from Latin *pretendere,* to PRETEND.]

Usage: *Pretence* has the general meaning, derived from the verb *pretend,* of "act of pretending": *He made a pretence of doing his homework. Pretension* is a more specific term meaning "unsupported claim": *He has pretensions to being a writer.* Occasionally, *pretence* is used in place of the latter, but careful writers prefer to distinguish the two.

pre·tend (pri-ténd, prə-) *v.* **-tended, -tending, -tends.** *—tr.* **1.** To affect; feign. **2.** To claim or allege insincerely or falsely; profess: *She pretended to be simple.* **3.** To represent fictitiously in play; make believe: *You pretend to be Romeo.* **4.** *Informal.* To take upon oneself; venture: *I won't pretend to tell you, a novelist, how to write.* *—intr.* **1.** To feign an action, character, or the like, as in play. **2.** To put forward a claim. Used with *to*: *pretended to the throne.*
~adj. Informal. Imaginary; taken as such, especially for the purposes of a game: *pretend money.* [Middle English *pretenden,* from Latin *praetendere,* "to stretch forth", hold out as a pretext, assert : *prae-,* before + *tendere,* to stretch.]

Synonyms: *pretend, feign, dissemble, fake, simulate.*

pre·tend·ed (pri-téndid, prə-) *adj.* **1.** Falsely asserted or alleged: *pretended loyalty.* **2.** False; untrue; feigned. **—pre·tend·ed·ly** *adv.*

pre·tend·er (pri-téndər, prə-) *n.* **1.** One who simulates, pretends, or alleges falsely; a hypocrite or dissembler. **2. a.** One who sets forth a claim. **b.** A claimant to a throne. **3.** *Capital* **P.** In British history: **a.** James Edward **Stuart** *(see),* the Old Pretender. **b.** Charles Edward **Stuart** *(see),* the Young Pretender.

pre·ten·sion (pri-ténsh'n, prə-) *n.* **1.** A specious allegation; a pretext. **2.** An asserted, but usually unproved, claim to something, such as a privilege, right, or other position of distinction or importance. **3.** An asserted but unsupported claim, as to some merit or skill: *no pretensions to being a chess player.* See Usage note at **pretence. 4.** Pretentiousness; ostentation; display.

pre·ten·tious (pri-ténshəss, prə-) *adj.* **1. a.** Claiming or demanding a position of distinction or merit, especially when unjustified: *a pretentious play.* **b.** Affecting or adopting any mannerism, habit, style of dress, or the like, simply for the sake of appearance. **2.** Making an extravagant outer show; ostentatious. **—pre·ten·tious·ly** *adv.* **—pre·ten·tious·ness** *n.*

pret·er·ite, pret·er·it (préttrit, préttərit) *adj. Abbr.* **pret., pt.** *Grammar.* Designating the verb tense that expresses or describes a past or completed action or condition; for example, in the sentence *Mary bought cakes, bought* is in the preterite tense.
~n. Abbr. **pret., pt.** *Grammar.* **1.** The verb form expressing or describing a past or completed action or condition; the past tense. **2.** A verb in this form. [Middle English, past, past tense, from Old French, from Latin *praeteritus,* gone by, past, past participle of *praeterīre,* to go by, pass : *praeter,* beyond, comparative of *prae-,* before + *īre,* to go.]

pret·er·i·tion (préttə-rísh'n) *n.* **1.** The act of passing by, disregarding, or omitting. **2.** In Roman Law, the neglect of a testator to mention a legal heir or heirs in his will. **3.** *Theology.* The passing over of the non-elect by God. [Late Latin *praeteritiō* (stem *praeteritiōn-*), from Latin *praeterīre,* to go by, pass over. See **preterite.**]

pre·ter·i·tive (pri-térrətiv, prə-) *adj. Grammar.* Designating a verb limited to a past tense or past tenses.

pre·ter·mit (préetər-mít) *tr.v.* **-mitted, -mitting, -mits.** *Formal.* **1.** To disregard intentionally, or allow to pass unnoticed or unmentioned. **2.** To fail to do or include; omit; neglect. **3.** To desist from temporarily. [Latin *praetermittere,* to let go by : *praeter,* beyond (see **preterite**) + *mittere,* to let go.] **—pre·ter·mis·sion** (-mísh'n) *n.* **—pre·ter·mit·ter** *n.*

pre·ter·nat·u·ral (préetər-nách-rəl, -náchoo-, -náchə-) *adj.* **1.** Out of or beyond the normal course of nature; differing from the natural; abnormal **2.** Transcending the natural or material order, often connoting divinity; supernatural. [Medieval Latin *praeternātūrālis,* from Latin *praeter nātūram,* beyond nature : *praeter,* beyond + accusative of *nātūra,* NATURE.] **—pre·ter·nat·u·ral·ism** *n.* **—pre·ter·nat·u·ral·ly** *adv.* **—pre·ter·nat·u·ral·ness** *n.*

pre·text (prée-tekst) *n.* An ostensible or professed purpose.
~tr.v. **pretexted, -texting, -texts.** To allege as an excuse: *"I shall pretext a catastrophe."* (Aldous Huxley). [Latin *praetextus,* outward show, pretence, from past participle of *praetexere,* to weave in front, cloak, disguise, pretend : *prae-,* before + *texere,* to weave.]

Pre·to·ri·a (pri-táwri-ə, prə- || -tóri-). Administrative capital of the Republic of South Africa. Founded in 1855, its industries include steel making and food processing.

Pre·to·ri·a-Wit·wa·ters·rand-Ver·ee·nig·ing (pri-táwri-ə-wit-wáwtərz-rand-fə-reéni-king) *Abbr.* **PWV.** New province created in 1974 out of part of the former Transvaal. It was later renamed Gauteng.

Pre·to·ri·us (pri-táwri-əss, prə- || -tóri-; *Afrikaans* -üss), **Andries Wilhelmus Jacobus** (1799–1853). Afrikaner politician and soldier. Leading the Great Trek to the Natal, he defeated the Zulus (1838), then, seeking independence from the British, trekked on to the Transvaal. Following the Boer victory (1848), he secured independence for the area as a republic, and for the Orange Free State. His son, Marthinus Wessel Pretorius (1819–1901), was president of both states, and was leader of the Boers in the first Boer War (1880–81).

pret·ti·fy (príttī-fī) *tr.v.* **-fied, -fying, -fies.** To make pretty, especially in a superficial or insubstantial way. Often used derogatorily. **—pret·ti·fi·ca·tion** (-fi-káysh'n) *n.* **—pret·ti·fi·er** *n.*

pret·ty (prítti) *adj.* **-tier, -tiest.** **1.** Pleasing or attractive to the eye or ear, especially in a graceful or delicate way: *a pretty girl; a pretty tune.* **2.** Excellent; fine; good. Often used ironically: *That's a pretty mess you've got us into!* **3.** *Archaic.* Gallant; fine. **4.** Effeminate; foppish: *a pretty boy.* **5.** *Informal.* Considerable in size or extent: *a pretty fortune.* —See Synonyms at **beautiful.**
~adv. Informal. **1.** To a fair degree; somewhat; moderately: *He is a pretty good student.* **2.** Very; extremely: *a pretty good judge of character.* **—sitting pretty.** *Informal.* In favourable circumstances; in a good position.
~n., pl. **pretties.** *Informal.* One that is pleasing or pretty.
~tr.v. **prettied, -tying, -ties.** *Informal.* To make pretty. Used with *up*: *pretty up the house.* [Middle English *prety, praty,* clever, skilfully made, fine, Old English *prættig,* cunning, tricky, from *prætt,* trick, wile, craft, from West Germanic *pratt-*† (unattested).] **—pret·ti·ly** *adv.* **—pret·ti·ness** *n.*

pretty-pretty (prítti-pritti) *adj.* Pretty in a contrived way.

pret·zel (préts'l) *n.* A glazed, salted biscuit, usually baked in the form of a loose knot or stick. [German *Pretzel, Brezel,* from Old High German *brezitella,* from Medieval Latin *brachiatellum* (unattested), diminutive of *brachītum* (unattested), "armlet", hence a ring-shaped cake, from Latin *bracchium,* arm, from Greek *brakhiōn.*]

pre·vail (pri-váyl, prə-) *intr.v.* **-vailed, -vailing, -vails.** **1.** To be greater in strength or influence; triumph or win a victory. Often used with *over* or *against*: *Let common sense prevail over passions.* **2.** To be most common or frequent; be predominant. **3.** To be in force, use, or effect; be current. **4.** To use persuasion or inducement successfully. Used with *on, upon,* or *with.* —See Synonyms at **persuade.** [Middle English *prevayllen,* from Latin *praevalēre,* to be more powerful : *prae-,* before, beyond + *valēre,* to be strong.] **—pre·vail·er** *n.*

pre·vail·ing (pri-váyling, prə-) *adj.* **1.** Most frequent or common; predominant. **2.** Generally current; widespread; prevalent. **3.** To be met with at a given time: *the prevailing circumstances.* **—pre·vail·ing·ly** *adv.* **—pre·vailing·ness** *n.*

Synonyms: *prevailing, prevalent, current, rife.*

prev·a·lent (prévvələnt) *adj.* **1.** Widely or commonly occurring. **2.** Generally accepted or practised. See Synonyms at **common, prevailing.** [Latin *praevalēns* (stem *praevalent-*), present participle of *praevalēre,* to PREVAIL.] **—prev·a·lence** *n.* **—prev·a·lent·ly** *adv.*

pre·var·i·cate (pri-várri-kayt, prə-) *intr.v.* **-cated, -cating, -cates. 1.** To stray from or evade the truth; equivocate. **2.** To speak or act evasively; quibble. [Latin *praevāricārī,* to walk crookedly, deviate from one's course, collude : *prae-,* before, beyond + *vāricāre,* to straddle, from *vāricus,* straddling, from *vārus,* stretched, bent, knock-kneed (see **varus**).] **—pre·var·i·ca·tion** (-káysh'n) *n.* **—pre·var·i·ca·tor** (-kaytər) *n.*

pre·ven·i·ent (pri-véeni-ənt, prée-, prə-) *adj.* **1.** Antecedent; previous; preceding. **2.** Expectant; anticipatory. **3.** Seeking or tending to prevent. [Latin *praeveniēns* (stem *praevenient-*), present participle of *praevenīre,* to come before, precede, anticipate : *prae-,* before + *venīre,* to come.] **—pre·ven·i·ent·ly** *adv.*

pre·vent (pri-vént, prə-; *for sense 4,* prée-) *v.* **-vented, -venting, -vents.** *—tr.* **1.** To keep from happening, as by some prior action; avert; thwart. **2.** To keep (someone) from doing something; hinder; impede. Often used with *from.* **3.** *Archaic.* To anticipate or counter in advance. **4.** *Archaic.* To come before; precede. *—intr.* To be an obstacle: *There will be a picnic, if nothing prevents.* [Middle English *preventen,* to anticipate, from Latin *praevenīre,* to come before, anticipate : *prae-,* before + *venīre,* to come.] **—pre·vent·a·bil·i·ty** (-ə-bílləti), **pre·vent·i·bil·i·ty** *n.* **—pre·vent·a·ble, pre·vent·i·ble** *adj.* **—pre·vent·er** *n.*

Synonyms: *prevent, preclude, obviate, forestall.*

Usage: When *prevent* is followed by the *-ing* form of a verb, formal English requires that any preceding noun be in the possessive case: *He prevented Jean's leaving.* Less formally, the noun may be used without any possessive marker and followed by *from*: *He prevented Jean from leaving.* A construction lacking both *from* and the possessive ending is sometimes used, especially in British English, but attracts criticism: *He prevented Jean leaving.*

pre·ven·tion (pri-vénsh'n, prə-) *n.* **1.** The act of preventing. **2.** A hindrance; an obstacle.

pre·ven·tive (pri-vént-iv, prə-) *adj.* Also **pre·ven·ta·tive** (-ətiv). **1.** Designed or used to prevent or hinder; acting as an obstacle; precautionary. **2.** *Medicine.* Thwarting or warding off illness or disease; prophylactic. **3.** In Britain, designating the branch of Customs that is concerned with intercepting smuggling.

~n. Also **pre·ven·ta·tive. 1.** Something that prevents; an obstacle. **2.** A contraceptive. **3.** *Medicine.* Something used to ward off illness. **—pre·ven·tive·ly** *adv.* **—pre·ven·tive·ness** *n.*

Pré·vert (pray-váir), **Jacques** (1900–77). French poet and screenplay writer. His poetry, which is surrealist, exuberant, and humorous, deals in the main with Parisian low life. His film-scripts include *Les Enfants du Paradis* (1944).

pre·view (prée-vew, -véw) *n.* Also *U.S.* **pre·vue** (for sense 1). **1.** An advance showing of a film, an art exhibition, or some other event to an invited audience, prior to public presentation. **2.** Broadly, any advance viewing or exhibition.

~v. **previewed, -viewing, -views.** Also *U.S.* **pre·vue, -vued, -vuing, -vues.** *—tr.* To view or exhibit in advance. *—intr.* To be shown or exhibited in advance.

Prev·in (prévvin), **André (George)** , born Andreas Ludwig Priwin (1929–). German-born U.S. conductor, arranger, and composer. Winner of four Academy Awards for his film scores, he later gained recognition in the world of classical music. He was principal conductor of the London Symphony Orchestra (1969–79) and the Los Angeles Philharmonic Orchestra (1986–88), and was appointed Conductor Laureate of the London Symphony Orchestra in 1992.

pre·vi·ous (préev-yəss, -i-əss) *adj.* **1.** Existing or occurring prior to something else in time or order; antecedent. **2.** *Informal.* Premature; hasty. **—previous to.** Prior to; before. [Latin *praevius,* going before, leading the way : *prae-,* before + *via,* way.] **—pre·vi·ous·ly** *adv.* **—pre·vi·ous·ness** *n.*

previous question *n. Abbr.* **p.q.** In parliamentary procedure, a motion to not take a vote on the issue being debated, which, if carried, ends the debate, but if defeated, means that an immediate vote on the issue must be taken. Compare **closure.**

pre·vise (pri-vī́z, prée-) *tr.v.* **-vised, -vising, -vises.** *Rare.* **1.** To foresee. **2.** To notify in advance. [Latin *praevidēre* (stem *praevīs-*) : *prae-,* before + *vidēre,* to see.] **—pre·vi·sion** (-vízh'n) *n.* **—pre·vi·sion·al** *adj.*

pre·vo·cal·ic (prée-vō-kál-ik, -və-) *adj. Phonetics.* Preceding a vowel.

pre·war (prée-wáwr) *adj.* Existing or occurring before a particular war.

prex·y (préksi) *n., pl.* **-ies.** *U.S. Slang.* A president, especially of a college or university. [Shortened variant of PRESIDENT.]

prey (pray) *n.* **1.** Any creature hunted or caught for food; a quarry. **2.** One that can be damaged or hurt; a victim: *The district fell prey to the developers.* **3.** *Archaic.* Something taken by violence; booty.

~intr.v. **preyed, preying, preys. 1.** To hunt, catch, or eat as prey. **2.** To victimise someone or make a profit at someone's expense. **3.** To plunder or pillage. **4.** To exert a grave or harmful effect: *Remorse preyed upon his mind.* [Middle English *preye,* from Old French *preie,* from Latin *praeda,* booty, prey.] **—prey·er** *n.*

Pri·am (prī́-əm, -am). *Greek Mythology.* King of Troy, the father of Paris and Hector, killed when his city fell to the Greeks.

pri·ap·ic (prī-áppik, -áypik) *adj.* Also **pri·a·pe·an** (prī́-ə-pée-ən). Phallic. [From PRIAPUS.]

pri·a·pism (prī́-əp-iz'm) *n.* Persistent, usually painful, erection of the penis, especially as a consequence of disease or a neurological disorder. [French, *priapisme,* from Late Latin *priāpismus,* from Greek *priapismos,* from *priapizein,* "to act like Priapus", be lewd, from *Priapos,* PRIAPUS.]

pri·a·pus (prī-áypəss) *n.* **1.** *Capital* **P.** The Graeco-Roman god of procreation, guardian of gardens and vineyards, and personification of the erect phallus. **2.** An image of the god Priapus, such as a statuette with a large, erect penis. [Latin, from Greek *Priapos*†.]

Prib·i·lof Islands (príb-bi-loff). Also **Fur Seal Islands.** Group of volcanic islands lying in the central Bering Sea, the breeding ground of the Alaska fur seal and an internationally recognised seal reserve.

price (prīss) *n. Abbr.* **pr. 1.** The sum of money or goods asked or given for something. **2.** The cost at which something is obtained: *Victory must be achieved at any price.* **3.** The cost of bribing someone. **4.** A reward offered for the capture or killing of a person. **5.** *Archaic.* Value or worth. **6.** Betting odds. **—at a price.** At considerable cost. **—what price.** *Chiefly British.* Used in questions to indicate: **1.** The unlikelihood of something specified taking place: *What price inflation coming down?* **2.** A disparaging attitude to something specified: *What price United's performance?*

~tr.v. **priced, pricing, prices. 1.** To fix or establish a price for: *shoes priced at nineteen pounds.* **2.** To find out the price of: *spent the day pricing dresses.* [Middle English *pris,* price, value, praise, from Old French, from Latin *pretium,* price, value, reward.]

Synonyms: *price, charge, fee, cost, expense, expenditure, outlay.*

price index *n.* A number relating prices of a group of commodities to their prices during a particular base period.

price·less (prī́ss-ləss, -liss) *adj.* **1.** Of inestimable worth; invaluable. **2.** Highly amusing, absurd, or odd. —See Synonyms at **costly.**

price support *n. Economics.* A system of maintaining a minimum price for certain goods, especially agricultural products of the European Union, whereby the Union or a government undertakes to buy them if the market price falls below an agreed level.

price tag *n.* **1.** A label attached to a piece of merchandise indicating its price. **2.** The cost of something: *Success carried a high price tag.*

price war *n.* A situation in which suppliers in the same market cut their prices in a competitive battle to increase their sales.

pri·cey (prī́-si) *adj.* **-ier, -iest.** *Informal.* Expensive.

prick (prik) *n.* **1. a.** The act of piercing or pricking. **b.** The sensation of being pierced or pricked. **2.** Any painful or stinging feeling or reflection: *the pricks of remorse.* **3.** A small mark or puncture made by a pointed object. **4.** A pointed object, such as a goad, thorn, or the like. **5. a.** *Vulgar.* A penis. **b.** *Vulgar Slang.* A foolish or disagreeable person. **—kick against the pricks.** To hurt or torment oneself by futile resistance.

~v. **pricked, pricking, pricks.** *—tr.* **1. a.** To puncture lightly. **b.** To puncture so as to cause injury. **2.** To sting with a mental or emotional pang. **3.** *Archaic.* To incite; impel: *"My duty pricks me on"* (Shakespeare). **4.** To mark or delineate on a surface by means of small punctures: *prick a pattern.* **5.** *Nautical.* To measure with dividers on a chart. **6.** To cause to rise sharply or stiffly. Used chiefly with *up*: *The dog pricked up his ears.* **7.** To transplant (seedlings) prior to a final planting. Used chiefly with *out* or *off.* *—intr.* **1.** To pierce or puncture something. **2.** To feel a stinging or pricking sensation. **3.** *Archaic.* To ride at a gallop. [Middle English *prik(ke),* Old English *prica,* pricked mark, puncture, from West Germanic *prikk-* (unattested).]

prick·er (príckər) *n.* **1.** Anything, such as a tool, that pricks. **2.** *U.S.* A prickle or thorn.

prick·et (príckit) *n.* **1. a.** A small spike for holding a candle upright. **b.** A candlestick having such a spike. **2.** A male deer before his antlers branch. [Middle English *priket,* from *prik,* PRICK.]

prick·le (prick'l) *n.* **1.** A small, sharp point arising from the epidermis of a branch, leaf, or other plant structure, and containing no woody or vascular tissue. **2.** A spine, as on a hedgehog. **3.** A prickling or tingling sensation.

~v. **prickled, -ling, -les.** *—tr.* **1.** To prick, as with a thorn. **2.** To cause a tingling sensation in. *—intr.* **1.** To feel or cause a tingling or pricking. **2.** To rise or stand up like prickles. [Middle English *prikle, prikel,* from Old English *pricel(s),* from West Germanic *prikkil-* (unattested), diminutive of *prikk-,* PRICK.]

prick·ly (prickli, prick'l-i) *adj.* **-lier, -liest. 1.** Having prickles or sharp spines. **2.** Tingling; smarting; stinging. **3. a.** Touchy; irritable. **b.** Causing irritation: *a prickly problem.* **—prick·li·ness** *n.*

prickly heat *n.* A noncontagious skin complaint, **miliaria** *(see).*

prickly pear *n.* **1.** Any of various cacti of the genus *Opuntia,* having bristly flattened or cylindrical joints, showy, usually yellow flowers, and ovoid, sometimes edible fruit. See **cholla, nopal. 2.** The fruit of any of these plants.

prickly poppy *n.* Any of various plants of the genus *Argemone,* chiefly of tropical America, having large yellow or white flowers and prickly leaves, stems and pods.

pride (prīd) *n.* **1.** A sense of one's own proper dignity or value; self-respect. **2.** Pleasure or satisfaction taken in one's work, achievements, or possessions: *took pride in her garden.* **3. a.** A cause or source of pride: *These men were their country's pride.* **b.** The best representative or member of a group, class, or the like: *She was the pride of the three sisters.* **c.** The most successful or thriving condition; the prime: *the flush and pride of youth.* **4. a.** An excessively high opinion of oneself; conceit; arrogance. **b.** In traditional Christianity, the consideration or personification of this condition as the first of the seven deadly sins. **5. a.** Mettle or spirit in horses. **b.** *Archaic.* The state of sexual desire or heat, especially in female animals; rut. **6.** A company of lions. —See Synonyms at **flock.** **—pride of place.** The best or most important position. —*v.* **prided, priding, prides.** —*tr.* To esteem (oneself) for. Used with *on* or *upon: I pride myself on this garden.* —*intr. Rare.* To indulge in self-esteem; glory. [Middle English *pride, prude, prute,* Old English *prȳte, prȳde,* from *prūt, prūd,* PROUD.] **—pride·ful** *adj.* **—pride·ful·ly** *adv.* **—pride·ful·ness** *n.*

Pride, Thomas (died 1658). English colonel in the Parliamentary army. In 1648 he led his regiment to Parliament and expelled about 150 Presbyterian and Royalist members who were opposed to the condemnation of Charles I ("Pride's Purge"); he was one of the signatories of Charles' death warrant.

prie–dieu (prēed-yér, -yō) *n., pl.* **-dieus** or **-dieux** (-z). A low desk with space for a book above and with a footpiece below for kneeling in prayer. [French *prie-Dieu,* "pray God".]

pri·er, pry·er (prī-ər) *n.* One who pries.

priest (prēest) *n.* **1.** *Abbr.* **P., Pr.** In the Roman Catholic, Eastern Orthodox, Anglican, Armenian, and separated Catholic hierarchies, an ordained minister ranking below a bishop but above a deacon and having authority to pronounce absolution and administer sacraments. **2.** A minister in a non-Christian religion. —*tr.v.* **priested, priesting, priests.** *Archaic.* To ordain or admit to the priesthood. [Middle English *pre(e)st, preost,* from Old English *prēost,* from Vulgar Latin *prester* (unattested), contracted from Late Latin *presbyter,* from Greek *presbuteros,* "elder", comparative of *presbus,* old man.]

priest·craft (prēest-kraaft ‖ -kraft) *n.* The art and practice of being a priest; especially, priests' influence on or involvement in secular affairs and issues. Used derogatorily.

priest·ess (prēess-tiss, -tess, -téss) *n.* A female priest in a non-Christian religion.

priest·hood (prēest-hood) *n.* **1.** The character, office, or vocation of a priest. **2.** The clergy.

Priest·ley (prēestli), **J(ohn) B(oynton)** (1894–1984). British author. His robust and perceptive novels, including *The Good Companions* (1929), enjoyed great popularity, as did his plays. These include *Laburnum Grove* (1933), a social comedy, and *Dangerous Corner* (1932), an examination of the nature of time and perception.

Priestley, Joseph (1733–1804). British scientist. He is best known for his work on the isolation of gases, and for the discovery of oxygen (1774). As a Presbyterian minister, he influenced the Unitarian movement.

priest·ly (prēest-li) *adj.* **-lier, -liest.** Of, pertaining to, or befitting a priest or priests. **—priest·li·ness** *n.*

priest·rid·den (prēest-ridd'n) *adj.* Dominated or heavily influenced by priests. Used derogatorily.

priest's hole (prēests-hōl) *n.* Also **priest-hole** (prēest-). Formerly in Britain, a hiding-place used to conceal and protect Roman Catholic priests.

prig (prig) *n.* **1.** A person regarded as overprecise, affectedly arrogant, smug, or narrow-minded. **2.** *Archaic.* A coxcomb. **3.** *British Slang.* A petty thief or pickpocket. Not in current usage. —*tr.v.* **prigged, prigging, prigs.** *British Slang.* To steal or pilfer. Not in current usage. [16th century (cant, "tinker") : origin obscure.] **—prig·ger·y** (priggəri) *n.* **—prig·gish** *adj.* **—prig·gish·ly** *adv.*

prim (prim) *adj.* **primmer, primmest. 1.** Precise, neat, or trim. **2.** Excessively formal or strict in matters of convention or morality. —*v.* **primmed, primming, prims.** *tr.* To fix (the face or mouth) in a prim expression. —*intr.* To assume a prim expression. [Old French *prin, prime,* very fine, excellent, from Latin *prīmus,* first, PRIME.] **—prim·ly** *adv.* **—prim·ness** *n.*

prim. 1. primary. **2.** primitive.

pri·ma ballerina (prēemə) *n., pl.* **prima ballerinas.** The leading female dancer in a ballet company. Compare **ballerina.** [Italian, "first ballerina".]

pri·ma·cy (prīmə-si) *n., pl.* **-cies. 1.** The state or condition of being first or foremost. **2.** The office or province of an ecclesiastical primate. [Middle English, from Medieval Latin *prīmātia,* from *prīmās,* PRIMATE.]

pri·ma don·na (prēemə dónnə ‖ *U.S. also* primmə) *n., pl.* **prima donnas. 1.** The leading female soloist in an opera company. **2.** A temperamental and conceited person. [Italian, "first lady".]

primaeval. Variant of **primeval.**

pri·ma fa·cie (prīmə fáy-shee, -shi-ee, -see, -si-ee ‖ *chiefly U.S.* -shə) *adv.* At first sight; before closer inspection. [Latin.] **—pri·ma·fa·cie** *adj.*

prima-facie evidence *n. Law.* Evidence that would, if uncontested, establish a fact or raise a presumption of a fact.

pri·mal (prīm'l) *adj.* **1.** Being first in time; original; archetypal. **2.** Primitive in character. **3.** Of first importance; primary. —*n.* A reliving of a painful experience, often dating from an earlier period of one's life, which may be evoked for therapeutic purposes, as in primal therapy. —*v.* **primalled, -malling, -mals.** —*intr.* To experience a primal. —*tr.* To cause or help to primal. [Medieval Latin *prīmālis,* from Latin *prīmus,* first.]

primal scream *n.* A scream that may be emitted during or as if during a primal.

primal therapy *n.* A form of psychotherapy in which attempts are made to make patients relive painful earlier experiences, as of infancy and sometimes birth, the reliving of which with full intensity is held to produce permanent positive physical and psychological changes. **—primal therapist** *n.*

pri·ma·ri·ly (prīm-rəli, -ərəli ‖ prī-mérrəli, prī-, *U.S. also* prī-merrəli) *adv.* **1.** At first; originally. **2.** Chiefly; principally.

pri·ma·ry (prīm-əri ‖ -erri) *adj. Abbr.* **prim. 1.** Occurring first in time, development, or sequence; earliest; original: *primary source.* **2.** Of or designating education for children up to the age of 11. **3.** Of or standing first in a list, series, or sequence: *primary negotiations.* **4.** First or best in degree, quality, or importance: *a primary consideration.* **5.** *Geology.* **a.** Of, pertaining to, or designating the earliest periods of geological development up to and including the Palaeozoic era; Precambrian. Not in current technical usage. **b.** Designating features of a rock that developed at the time of formation. **6. a.** Of or designating a fundamental or basic part of an organised whole: *Word play is a primary element in Shakespeare's language.* **b.** Of or designating certain basic, natural industries, such as fishing or forestry, or their products. **7.** Immediate; direct: *a primary effect.* **8.** Of or pertaining to the basic colours from which all other colours may be derived. See **primary colour. 9.** *Linguistics.* **a.** Having a word root or other linguistic element as a basis that cannot be further analysed or broken down. Said of the derivation of a word or word element. **b.** Referring to present or future time. Said of the various present and future tenses in Latin, Greek, and Sanskrit. **10.** *Electricity.* Of, pertaining to, or designating an inducting current, circuit, or coil. **11.** Of, pertaining to, or designating the main flight feathers projecting along the outer edge of a bird's wing. **12.** *Chemistry.* **a.** Pertaining to the replacement of one of several atoms or radicals in a compound by another atom or radical. **b.** Having a carbon atom attached solely to one other carbon atom in a molecule. **13.** Of, pertaining to, or designating plant growth derived solely from apical meristems present in the embryo. —*n., pl.* **primaries.** *Abbr.* **prim. 1. a.** One that is first in time, order, or sequence. **b.** One that is first or best in degree, quality, or importance. **c.** One that is fundamental or basic. **2.** A primary colour. **3.** Any of the main flight feathers projecting along the outer edge of a bird's wing. **4.** An inducting electric current, circuit, or coil. **5.** *Astronomy.* A celestial body, especially a star, to which the orbit of a satellite, or secondary, is referred. **6.** A *cosmic ray (see).* **7.** In the United States: **a.** A meeting of the registered voters of a political party for the purpose of nominating candidates and for choosing delegates to their party convention. **b.** A preliminary election in which the registered voters of a political party nominate candidates for office. [Middle English, from Latin *prīmārius,* of the first rank, chief, basic, from *prīmus,* first.]

primary accent *n.* The strongest stress or accent in a word; for example, in the word *typical,* the first syllable carries the primary accent. Also called "primary stress". Compare **secondary accent, tertiary accent.**

primary cell *n.* A cell in which an irreversible chemical reaction generates electricity. Also called "galvanic cell", "voltaic cell". Compare **secondary cell.**

primary coil *n.* An electrically conducting coil, as in a transformer, that carries an inducting current. Also called "primary winding".

primary colour *n.* A colour belonging to any of three groups, each of which is regarded as generating all colours. These groups are: **1.** *Additive, physiological,* or *light* primaries—red, green, and blue. Lights of red, green, and blue wavelengths may be mixed to produce all colours. **2.** *Subtractive* or *colorant* primaries—magenta, yellow, and cyan. Substances that reflect light of one of these wavelengths and absorb (subtract) other wavelengths may be mixed to produce all colours. **3.** *Psychological* primaries—red, yellow, green, and blue, plus the achromatic pair black and white. All colours may be subjectively conceived as mixtures of these.

primary group *n.* In sociology, a group of people in regular personal and social contact, such as a family or team of workers. Compare **secondary group.**

primary radiation *n.* Cosmic radiation as it enters the Earth's atmosphere.

primary school *n.* A school for children between the ages of 5 or 6 and 11.

pri·mate (prī-mət, -mit, -mayt *for sense 1;* -mayt *for sense 2) n.* **1.** A bishop of highest rank in a province or country, such as the Archbishop of Canterbury who is the *Primate of all England.* **2.** Any member of the order Primates, which includes the monkeys, apes, and humans, typically having dexterous hands and feet, binocular vision, and a well-developed brain. —*adj.* Of, pertaining to, or belonging to the order Primates. [Middle English *primat,* from Old French, from Medieval Latin *prīmās* (stem *prīmāt-*), archbishop, from Latin "of the first rank", chief, leader, from *prīmus,* first.] **—pri·ma·tial** (prī-máysh'l) *adj.*

prime (prīm) *adj.* **1.** First in excellence, quality, or value: *prime beef.* **2.** First in degree or rank; chief: *Money was his prime motive.* **3.** First or early in time, order, or sequence. **4.** *Mathematics.* Designating a prime number. —See Synonyms at **chief.**
∼*n.* **1.** The earliest or first part, such as the break of day or the season of spring. **2.** *Mathematics.* A prime number. **3.** The age of maximum physical health and intellectual vigour: *the prime of life.* **4.** The period or phase of ideal or peak condition. **5.** In fencing, the first of eight positions of thrust and parry. **6.** A mark (′) written above and to the right of a letter in order to distinguish it from the same letter already in use or to designate a related quantity or thing, such as feet, minutes of angle, or minutes of time. **7.** In religious observance: **a.** The second of the seven **canonical hours** *(see).* **b.** *Rare.* The time of day set aside for this prayer, usually about 6:00 a.m. **8.** *Music.* **a.** The tonic or keynote of a scale. **b.** A zero interval between notes.
∼*v.* **primed, priming, primes.** —*tr.* **1.** To make ready; prepare. **2.** To prepare (a gun, mine, or grenade) for firing by inserting a charge of gunpowder or a primer or by releasing the safety pin. **3.** To prepare for operation, as by pouring water into a pump or petrol into a carburettor. **4.** To prepare (a surface) for painting by covering with size, primer, or an undercoat. **5.** To prepare with information. **6.** To fortify: *primed him with brandy.* —*intr.* To prepare someone or something for future action or operation. [Middle English, from Old French, feminine of *prin,* from Latin *prīmus,* first; the canonical hour derives from Old English *prīm,* from Latin *prīma (hōra),* first (hour), from the feminine of *prīmus.*] **—prime·ly** *adv.* **—prime·ness** *n.*

prime meridian *n.* The zero meridian, (0°), from which longitude east and west is measured and which passes through Greenwich.

prime minister *n. Abbr.* **P.M. 1.** A chief minister appointed by a ruler. **2.** *Often capital* **P,** *capital* **M.** In some countries, such as Britain, the chief minister who leads the government. **—prime ministership, prime ministry** *n.*

prime mover *n.* **1.** The initial force, such as electricity, wind, or gravity, that engages or moves a machine. **2.** That which is regarded as the initial source of energy directed towards a goal. **3.** Any machine or mechanism that converts natural energy into work. **4.** In Aristotelian philosophy, the self-moved being that causes all motion.

prime number *n.* A number divisible by only itself and one.

prim·er[1] (prīmər ‖ *chiefly U.S.* prímmər) *n.* **1.** A school textbook. **2.** A book that covers the basic elements of any subject: *a primer of Freudian psychology.* [Middle English, from Anglo-French, from Medieval Latin *prīmārium (manuāle),* "basic handbook", from Latin *prīmārius,* basic, PRIMARY.]

prim·er[2] (prīmər) *n.* **1.** A cap or tube containing a small amount of explosive used to detonate the main explosive charge of a firearm or mine. **2.** Someone or something that primes or causes to be primed. **3.** An undercoat of paint or size applied to prepare a surface, as for painting. [From PRIME (verb).]

prime rate *n.* The lowest rate of interest on bank loans at any given time and place, offered to preferred borrowers.

pri·me·ro (pri-maír-ō) *n.* A gambling card game, popular in Elizabethan England. [Alteration of Spanish *primera,* feminine of *primero,* "first", from Latin *prīmarius,* principal, from *prīmus,* first.]

prime time *n.* The hours, usually during the evening, when television attracts its largest audience, so that companies can charge high rates for advertising. Also used adjectivally: *a prime-time slot.*

pri·me·val, pri·mae·val (prī-méev'l) *adj.* Belonging to the first or earliest age: *the primeval swamp.* [Latin *prīmaevus,* in the first period of life : *prīmus,* first + *aevum,* age.] **—pri·me·val·ly** *adv.*

prime vertical *n. Astronomy.* The great circle that passes through an observer's zenith at right angles to the celestial meridian and intersects the horizon at the east and west points.

prim·i·grav·i·da (prími-grávvi-də) *n., pl.* **-das** or **-dae** (-dee). *Medicine.* A woman who is pregnant for the first time. [New Latin, from Latin *prima,* first (feminine) + *gravida,* GRAVID.]

prim·ing (prīming) *n.* **1.** The explosive used to ignite a charge. **2.** A preliminary coat of paint or size applied to a surface.

pri·mip·a·ra (prī-míppə-rə) *n., pl.* **-aras** or **-arae** (-ree). *Medicine.* A woman who has borne only one child. [Latin : *prīmus,* first + *-para,* feminine of *-parus,* -PAROUS.] **—pri·mi·par·i·ty** (prīmi-párrəti) *n.* **—pri·mip·a·rous** (-rəss) *adj.*

prim·i·tive (prímmə-tiv, prímmi-) *adj. Abbr.* **prim. 1.** Of or pertaining to an earliest or original stage or state: *the primitive Church.* **2.** Characterised by simplicity or crudity; unsophisticated: *primitive weapons.* **3.** Of or pertaining to early stages in the evolution of human culture: *primitive societies.* **4.** *Linguistics.* Serving as the basis for derived or inflected forms: *"Pick" is the primitive word from which "picket" is derived.* **5.** *Mathematics.* Any form in geometry or algebra from which another form is derived. **6. a.** Of or pertaining to late medieval or pre-Renaissance European painters. **b.** Loosely, of or pertaining to any unsophisticated painting. **c.** Of or designating one who paints in a primitive style. **7.** *Geology.* Of or pertaining to rocks formed by the first solidification of the earth's crust. **8.** *Biology.* Occurring in or characteristic of an early stage of development or evolution.
∼*n.* **1.** A person belonging to a primitive society. **2.** Someone or something at a low or early stage of development. **3. a.** One belonging to an early stage in the development of a culture or artistic trend; especially, a painter of the pre-Renaissance period. **b.** An artist having a primitive style. **c.** A work by a primitive painter. **4.** *Linguistics.* A word or word element from which another word or inflected form of the word is derived. Compare **derivative.** [Middle English *primitif,* from Old French, from Latin *prīmitīvus,* first of its kind, from *prīmitus,* at first, in the first place, from *prīmus,* first.] **—prim·i·tive·ly** *adv.* **—prim·i·tive·ness, prim·i·tiv·i·ty** (-tívvəti) *n.*

primitive solar-nebula hypothesis *n.* A theory of the origin of the Solar System that combines elements of the **nebular hypothesis** and the **planetismal hypothesis** (*both of which see*). It states that dust and gas condensed from galactic matter, forming a *presolar medium* which contracted under its own gravity and eventually led to the formation of the Sun and planetismals, which in turn accreted further matter to form the planets, their satellites, and the rest of the bodies in the Solar System.

prim·i·tiv·ism (prímmə-tiv-iz'm, prímmi-) *n.* **1.** The state or quality of being primitive. **2.** A belief that modern civilisation would benefit by a return to or consideration of primitive culture, customs, or ideas. **3.** The style of primitive painters. **—prim·i·tiv·ist** *adj. & n.* **—prim·i·tiv·is·tic** (-ístik) *adj.*

Primitive Methodism *n.* A form of Methodism characterised by evangelical fervour, that broke away from the official church early in the 19th century and was readmitted in 1932. **—Primitive Methodist** *adj. & n.*

pri·mo (prée-mō) *n., pl.* **-mos** or **-mi** (-mee). *Music.* The principal part in a duet or ensemble composition. [Italian, "first", from Latin *prīmus.*] **—pri·mo** *adj.*

Pri·mo de Ri·ve·ra (préemō day ri-váir-ə), **Miguel** (1870–1930). Spanish general and politician. He seized power (1923) and established a military directorate to run the country. Political dissent and ill-health forced his resignation (1930). His son José Antonio (1903–36) founded the Falangist movement, and was executed by the republicans in the Civil War.

pri·mo·gen·i·tor (prī-mō-jénnitər, -mə-) *n.* The earliest ancestor or forefather. [Medieval Latin : Latin *prīmus,* first + GENITOR.]

pri·mo·gen·i·ture (prī-mō-jénni-chər, -mə-, -choor, -tewr) *n.* **1.** The state or condition of being the first-born or eldest child. **2.** *Law.* The right of the eldest child, especially the eldest son, to inherit the entire estate of one or both parents. Compare **ultimogeniture.** [Medieval Latin *prīmōgenitūra* : Latin *prīmus,* first + *genitūra,* birth, from *gignere* (stem *genit-*), to beget.] **—pri·mo·gen·i·tar·y** (-tri, -təri ‖ -terri), **pri·mo·gen·i·tal** *adj.*

pri·mor·di·al (prī-mórdi-əl, prī-) *adj.* **1.** Happening at, belonging to, or characteristic of the beginning of time or history. **2.** Fundamental; seeming to have always existed: *primordial images in myths.* **3.** *Biology.* Belonging to or characteristic of the earliest stage of development of an organism or part.
∼*n.* A basic principle. [Middle English, from Late Latin *prīmōrdiālis,* from Latin *prīmōrdium,* origin, from *prīmōrdius,* original : *prīmus,* first + *ordīrī,* to begin.] **—pri·mor·di·al·ly** *adv.*

primordial soup *n.* The suspension of organic molecules thought to have been the origin of life. Compare **spontaneous generation, abiogenesis.**

pri·mor·di·um (prī-mórdi-əm, prī-) *n., pl.* **-dia** (-ə). An organ or part in its earliest stage of development. [Latin, "origin". See **primordial.**]

primp (primp) *v.* **primped, primping, primps.** —*tr.* To neaten (one's hair, for example) with considerable attention to detail. —*intr.* To primp oneself. [Dialectal variant of PRIM.]

prim·rose (prím-rōz) *n.* **1.** Any of various plants of the genus *Primula*; especially, *P. vulgaris,* which has single, pale yellow flowers on long, hairy stalks. See **bird's eye primrose. 2.** See **evening primrose. 3.** Pale yellow. [Middle English *primerose,* from Old French, from Medieval Latin *prīma rosa,* "first (or earliest) rose" : Latin *prīma,* feminine of *prīmus,* first + *rosa,* ROSE.] **—prim·rose** *adj.*

primrose path *n.* A life of ease or pleasure, especially at the risk of eventual ruin.

prim·u·la (prímmewlə) *n.* Any plant of the genus *Primula,* which includes the primrose, cowslip, oxlip, and polyanthus. [Medieval Latin, feminine noun from *primulus,* diminutive of *primus,* first.]

pri·mum mo·bi·le (prī-məm mōbi-li, prée-, -lay) *n.* **1.** In medieval astronomy, the tenth and outermost concentric sphere of the universe, thought to revolve around the Earth from east to west in 24 hours and believed to cause the other nine spheres to revolve with it. **2.** A prime mover. [Medieval Latin, "first moving (thing)", a translation of Arabic *al-muharrik al-awwal.*]

pri·mus (prīməss) *n., pl.* **-muses.** The first-ranking bishop of the Scottish Episcopal Church. [Medieval Latin *prīmus,* from Latin, first.]

Pri·mus (prīməss) *n.* A trademark for a small, portable, oil-burning cooking stove.

pri·mus in·ter pa·res (prī-məss íntər párreez) *n. Latin.* The first among equals.

prin. 1. principal. **2.** principle.

prince (prinss) *n.* **1.** *Archaic.* A hereditary ruler; a king. **2.** *Abbr.* **P., Pr.** The ruler of a principality or a small state. **3.** *Abbr.* **P., Pr.** A male member of a royal family; especially, in Britain, the son or grandson of a monarch. **4.** *Abbr.* **P., Pr.** A nobleman of varying status in different countries. **5.** An outstanding man: *John Wesley was the prince of preachers.* [Middle English, from Old French, from Latin *princeps* (stem *princip-*), first in rank, sovereign, ruler : *prīmus,* first + *cipere,* variant of *capere,* to take.] **—prince·dom** *n.*

Prince Albert *n. U.S.* A man's long, double-breasted frock coat. [Popularised by Prince *Albert* Edward, later EDWARD VII.]

prince consort *n.* A prince who is the husband of a sovereign queen.

Prince Edward Island. Island province of southeast Canada, situated in the Gulf of St. Lawrence and separated from the mainland by the Northumberland Strait.
prince·ling (prínss-ling) *n.* Also **prince·let** (-lət, -lit). A prince of minor status or importance.
prince·ly (prínss-li) *adj.* **-lier, -liest. 1.** Of or befitting a prince. **2.** Sumptuous; lavish. **—prince·li·ness** *n.* **—prince·ly** *adv.*
Prince of Darkness. A name for **Satan.**
Prince of Peace. A name for **Christ.**
Prince of the Church *n.* A cardinal in the Roman Catholic Church.
Prince of Wales *n.* **1.** A title given to the eldest son of a British sovereign. **2.** A male holding this title.
prince regent *n.* A prince who rules the country, as during the absence or incapacity of a sovereign.
prince royal *n.* The eldest son of a sovereign.
prince's-feath·er (prínssiz-féthər) *n.* An annual plant, *Amaranthus hypochondriacus,* having dense, feathery, red flower clusters.
prin·cess (prin-séss, prín-; *before a name,* prín-sess, -səss, -siss) *n.* **1.** *Archaic.* A hereditary female ruler; a queen. **2.** The female ruler of a principality. **3.** A female member of a royal family other than the monarch; especially, in Britain, the daughter or grand-daughter of a monarch. **4.** A noblewoman of varying rank in different countries. **5.** The wife of a prince. **6.** Any woman thought of as having the status or qualities of a princess.
~*adj.* Designed to hang in smooth, close-fitting, unbroken lines from shoulder to flared hem: *a princess dress.* [Middle English *princesse,* from Old French, feminine of PRINCE.]
princess royal *n.* The eldest daughter of a sovereign.
Prince·ton (prínss-tən). University town in west central New Jersey, United States. It is the site of the defeat of the British under James Grant and Lord Cornwallis by George Washington's forces (1777).
prin·ci·pal (prín-sip'l) *adj. Abbr.* **prin.** First, highest, or foremost in importance, rank, worth, or degree; chief. See Synonyms at **chief.**
~*n. Abbr.* **prin. 1.** One who holds a position of presiding rank; especially, the head of a college, school, or the like. **2.** A main participant in a given situation. **3.** A person having a leading or starring role in a dramatic work. **4.** *Finance.* **a.** The capital or main body of an estate or financial holding, as distinguished from the interest or revenue from it. **b.** A sum of money owed as a debt, upon which interest is calculated. **5.** *Law.* **a.** A person who empowers another to act as his representative. **b.** The person having prime responsibility for an obligation, as distinguished from one who acts as surety or as an endorser. **c.** One who commits or is an accomplice to a crime. **6.** The main truss or rafter that supports and gives form to a roof. **7.** Either of the participants in a duel. **8.** *Capital* **P.** An administrative officer of the British government service in the grade between Assistant Secretary and Senior Executive Officer. **9.** *Music.* **a.** A player leading any of the instrumental groupings in an orchestra. **b.** An organ stop, the four-foot diapason. [Middle English, from Old French, from Latin *principālis,* first, original, hence overseer, ruler, from *princeps,* first one in rank, chief, PRINCE.] **—prin·ci·pal·ly** (-sipli, -sip'l-i) *adv.*
Usage: *Principal* and *principle* are often confused in spelling, but they have no senses in common. *Principal* is both an adjective and a noun, with senses to do with "leading, chief": *the principal violinist; the principal of the college. Principle* is only a noun, pertaining to basic truths, laws, or rules: *the principle of self-government.*
principal axis *n.* **1.** An imaginary line that passes through the centres of curvature of a system of lenses or mirrors. **2.** Any of the three mutually perpendicular axes about which the moment of inertia of a body is a maximum.
principal boy *n.* The leading young male character in a pantomime, played by a woman. Compare **dame.**
principal focus *n.* A **focal point** *(see).*
prin·ci·pal·i·ty (prín-si-pál-əti) *n., pl.* **-ties. 1.** A territory ruled by a prince or from which a prince derives his title. **2.** The position, authority, or jurisdiction of a prince; sovereignty. **3.** *Plural.* In medieval angelology, one of the nine orders of angels. See **angel. —the Principality.** Wales as source of the title "Prince of Wales".
principal parts *pl.n.* In traditional grammars of inflected languages, the primary forms of a verb from which all other forms may be derived. In English, the principal parts are generally considered to be the present infinitive *(play, eat),* the past tense *(played, ate),* the past participle *(played, eaten),* and the present participle *(playing, eating).* **Note:** In this dictionary, all inflected forms of defined verbs are given. For regular verbs, this includes, in addition to the principal parts, the third-person singular form *(plays, eats),* which is listed following the present participle.
prin·cip·i·um (prin-síppi-əm) *n., pl.* **-ia** (-ə). A principle, especially one that is basic. [Latin, basis, origin, PRINCIPLE.]
prin·ci·ple (prín-sip'l) *n. Abbr.* **prin. 1.** A basic truth, law, or assumption: *the principles of democracy.* **2. a.** A rule or standard, especially of good behaviour. **b.** Moral or ethical standards or judgments collectively. **3.** A fixed or predetermined policy or mode of action: *acting on the principle of every man for himself.* **4.** A basic, or essential, quality or element determining intrinsic nature or characteristic behaviour. **5.** A scientific rule or law concerning, for example: **a.** Natural phenomena: *the principle of relativity.* **b.** Mechanical processes: *the principle of jet propulsion.* **6.** A basic source; an origin. **7.** A constituent imparting a distinctive character. **—in principle.** With regard to the idea or proposal in itself, rather than the practicalities: *In principle I'd love to come, but I'm afraid I'm too ill.* —See Usage note at **principal.** [Middle English, origin, commencement, hence fundamental quality or truth, modification of Old French *principe,* from Latin *principium,* from *princeps,* first. See **prince.**]
prin·ci·pled (prín-sip'ld) *adj.* Motivated by or based on moral, ethical or theoretical principles.
prink (pringk) *v.* **prinked, prinking, prinks.** *—tr.* To adorn (oneself) in a showy manner. *—intr.* To primp. [Probably alteration of PRANK (adorn).] **—prink·er** *n.*
print (print) *n.* **1.** A mark or impression made in or upon a surface by pressure: *the print of footsteps in the sand.* **2. a.** A device or implement, such as a stamp, die, or seal, used to press markings on or into a surface. **b.** Something formed or marked by such a device: *a print of butter.* **3. a.** Lettering or other impressions produced in ink from type by a printing press or other means. **b.** Matter, such as newspaper publications, produced by such a process. **c.** The state or form of matter so produced. **d.** A newspaper or periodical. **4.** A design or picture transferred from an engraved plate, wood block, lithographic stone, or other medium. **5.** A photographic image transferred to paper or a similar surface, usually from a negative. **6.** A fabric or garment with a dyed pattern that has been pressed onto it. **7.** A fingerprint. **—in print. 1.** In printed or published form. **2.** Still offered for sale by the publisher: *books in print.* **—out of print.** No longer offered for sale by the publisher.
~*v.* **printed, printing, prints.** *—tr.* **1.** To press (a mark or design, for example) onto or into a surface. **2.** To make an impression on or in (a surface) with a stamp, seal, die, or similar device. **3.** To press (a stamp or similar device) onto or into a surface to leave a marking. **4.** To produce by means of pressed type on a paper surface, with or as if with a printing press. **5.** To offer in printed form; publish. **6.** To write in unjoined characters similar to those commonly used in print. **7.** To impress firmly in the mind or memory. **8.** To produce (a positive photograph) by passing light through a negative onto sensitised paper. *—intr.* **1.** To work as a printer. **2.** To write in unjoined characters similar to those commonly used in print. **3.** To produce or receive an impression, marking, or image. **4.** To produce a book, newspaper, or the like, by printing. [Middle English *pri(e)nte, pre(i)nte,* from Old French *preinte,* from the past participle of *preindre,* to press, from Latin *premere.*]
print·a·ble (príntəb'l) *adj.* **1.** Capable of being printed or of producing a print. **2.** Regarded as fit for publication.
printed circuit *n.* An electronic circuit in which the conducting connections are formed by depositing a metal, such as copper, in predetermined patterns on an insulating substrate. Other materials, especially semiconductors, may also be deposited to form various electronic components.
print·er (príntər) *n.* **1.** A person who operates a printing press. **2.** A typesetter. **3.** Loosely, a person involved in the business of printing. **4.** One that prints. **5.** The part of a word processor or computer that produces printed matter.
printer's devil *n.* An apprentice in a printing establishment.
print·er·y (príntəri) *n., pl.* **-ies.** *U.S.* **1.** A place where typographic printing is done. **2.** A factory where fabrics are printed.
print·ing (prínting) *n. Abbr.* **pr., print., ptg. 1.** The process, art, or business of producing printed material by means of inked type and a printing press or by similar means. **2. a.** The act of one that prints. **b.** Matter that is printed. **3.** All the copies of a book or other publication that are printed at one time. Compare **edition. 4.** Written unjoined characters resembling those appearing in print.
printing office *n.* An establishment where printed material is produced, especially one that is officially authorised.
printing press *n.* A machine that transfers lettering or images by the contact of various forms of inked surface with paper or similar material fed into it. Also called "press". See **flat-bed press, rotary press, web press.**
print out *intr.v.* To print as a computer function; produce print-out. *—tr.v.* To produce (information) as print-out.
print-out (print-owt) *n.* The printed output of a computer.
print run *n.* The number of copies printed during a continuous operation of a printing press.
print shop *n.* A printers' workplace.
pri·on (prée-on) *n.* A pathogen that causes such spongiform encephalopathies as scrapie and CJD, has been alleged to cause BSE, and been called a protein particle without nucleic acid. [From *pr(otinaceous)* + *i(nfectious)* + *-on,* as in *(cod)on.*] **—pri·on·ic** *adj.*
pri·or[1] (prí-ər) *adj.* **1.** Preceding in time or order: *a prior commitment.* **2.** Preceding in importance or value: *a prior consideration.* **—prior to.** Before; earlier than. [Latin. See **prior** (cleric).]
prior[2] *n.* **1.** A monk in charge of a priory, or ranking next under the abbot of an abbey. **2.** One of the ruling magistrates of the medieval Italian republic of Florence. [Middle English *pri(o)ur,* from Old English and Old French *prior,* both from Medieval Latin *prior,* from Late Latin, superior officer, administrator, from Latin, former, superior.] **—pri·or·ate** (-ət, -it) *n.* **—pri·or·ship** *n.*
pri·or·ess (prí-ər-iss, -ess) *n.* A nun at the head of a priory or ranking next below an abbess in an abbey. [Middle English *prioresse,* from Old French, feminine of PRIOR.]
pri·or·i·ty (prī-órrəti || *U.S. also* -áwrəti) *n., pl.* **-ties. 1.** Precedence, especially as established by order of importance or urgency. Also used adjectivally: *priority booking.* **2. a.** An established right to precedence. **b.** Anything which has or claims precedence: *Accuracy was not one of her priorities.* **c.** The right of a vehicle to proceed rather than give way to other traffic. **3.** A preceding or coming

earlier in time. [Middle English *priorite,* from Old French, from Medieval Latin *priōritās* (stem *priōritāt-),* from Latin *prior,* PRIOR.] **—pri·or·i·tise, pri·or·i·tize** *v.*

pri·or·y (prī́-əri) *n., pl.* **-ies.** A monastery or convent governed by a prior or prioress. [Middle English *priorie,* from Anglo-French, from Medieval Latin *priōria,* from PRIOR.]

Pri·pet (preépit). *Russian* **Pri·pyat** (pri-pyát). River in eastern Europe. Rising near the Polish border in northwest Ukraine, it flows 800 kilometres (500 miles) generally eastwards through the Pripet Marshes to join the river Dnepr near Kiev.

prise, prize (prīz) *tr.v.* **prised, prising, prises.** To move, open, or force with or as if with a lever.

~n. Leverage. [Middle English *prisen* (verb, from noun), from Old French *prise,* lever, instrument for forcing, from past participle of *prendre,* from Latin *prehendere,* to seize.]

prism (prízz'm) *n.* **1.** *Mathematics.* A polyhedron having parallel, congruent polygons as bases and parallelograms as sides. **2.** A homogeneous transparent solid, usually with triangular bases and rectangular sides, used to produce or analyse a continuous spectrum. **3.** A crystalline solid having three or more similar faces parallel to a single axis. [Late Latin *prisma,* from Greek, "a thing sawn", prism, from *priein†,* to saw.]

pris·mat·ic (priz-máttik) *adj.* Also **pris·mat·i·cal** (-'l). **1.** Of, pertaining to, or resembling a prism. **2.** Refracting light as a prism does. **3.** Multicoloured; iridescent. **—pris·mat·i·cal·ly** *adv.*

pris·ma·toid (prízmə-toyd) *n. Mathematics.* A polyhedron having all vertices lying in one of two parallel planes. [New Latin *prismatoides* : Greek *prisma* (stem *prismat-*), PRISM + -OID.] **—pris·ma·toi·dal** (-tóyd'l) *adj.*

pris·moid (príz-moyd) *n.* A prismatoid whose bases and sides are equal in number and whose faces are parallelograms or trapezoids. [French *prismoïde* : *prisme,* prism, from Late Latin *prisma,* PRISM + -OID.] **—pris·moi·dal** *adj.*

pris·on (prízz'n) *n.* **1.** A place where persons convicted or accused of crimes are confined; a jail. **2.** Any place or condition of forced confinement or constraint. **3.** Imprisonment.

~tr.v. **prisoned, -oning, -ons.** *Rare.* To imprison. [Middle English *priso(u)n, prisun,* from Old French *prison,* "seizure, imprisonment", from Latin *pre(n)siō,* contraction from *prehensiō* (stem *prehensiōn-*), from *prehendere,* to seize.]

pris·on·er (príz-nər, prízz'n-ər) *n.* **1.** A person held in custody, captivity, or a condition of forcible restraint, especially while awaiting trial or serving a prison sentence. **2.** One deprived of freedom of action or expression: *a prisoner of fate.*

prisoner of conscience *n.* A person imprisoned for political or religious views. Compare **political prisoner.**

prisoner of war *n. Abbr.* **POW, P.O.W.** A person, especially a member of the armed services, taken captive by or surrendering to enemy forces during wartime.

pris·sy (príssi) *adj.* **-sier, -siest.** Finicky, fussy, and prudish. [Blend of PRIM and SISSY.] **—pris·si·ly** *adv.* **—pris·si·ness** *n.*

pris·tine (príss-teen, -tīn || *U.S. also* pri-steén) *adj.* **1.** Of, pertaining to, or typical of the earliest time or condition; primitive or original. **2. a.** Remaining in a pure state; uncorrupted. **b.** Loosely, not soiled; fresh; clean. [Latin *prīstinus,* original.]

prith·ee (prí-thi, -thee || *chiefly U.S.* -thee) *interj. Archaic.* Please; I pray thee. [Earlier *preythe,* from (I) *pray thee.*]

priv. private.

pri·va·cy (prívvə-si, prívə-) *n., pl.* **-cies. 1.** The condition of being secluded or isolated from the view of, or from contact with, others. **2.** Concealment; secrecy.

pri·vate (prī́-vət, -vit) *adj. Abbr.* **priv., pvt. 1.** Secluded from the sight, presence, or intrusion of others: *a private bathroom.* **2. a.** Of or confined to one person; personal: *private opinions.* **b.** Exclusive to a small group, usually a pair: *a private joke.* **3.** Not available for public use, control, or participation: *a private club.* **4.** Belonging to a particular person or persons, as opposed to the public or the government: *private property.* **5.** Not holding an official or public position. **6.** Not public; intimate; secret: *private tragedy.*

~n. **1.** *Abbr.* **Pvt.** A serviceman of the lowest rank in many armies, marine corps, and civilian organisations, ranking below lance-corporal in the British army. **2.** *Plural. Informal.* The genitals. **—in private.** Secretly; confidentially. [Middle English *privat,* from Latin *prīvātus,* not belonging to the state, not in public life, deprived of office, from the past participle of *prīvāre,* to deprive, release, from *prīvus,* single, individual, deprived of.] **—pri·vate·ly** *adv.* **—pri·vate·ness** *n.*

private bill *n.* A bill put before a legislative body, dealing with the affairs of an individual or organisation, such as a local authority, rather than with national matters.

private carrier *n.* A carrier by land, water, or air, such as an airline company, which reserves the right to decide whether it will carry particular passengers or goods. Compare **common carrier.**

private detective *n.* A privately employed detective as distinguished from one belonging to a public police force. Also informally called "private eye".

private enterprise *n.* **1.** Business activities unregulated by state ownership or control; privately owned business in general. **2.** A privately owned business enterprise, especially one in a system of free enterprise or laissez-faire capitalism. **3.** Loosely, capitalism.

pri·va·teer (prīvə-teér) *n.* **1.** A ship privately owned and manned but authorised by a government during wartime to attack enemy vessels. **2.** The commander or any crew member of such a ship.

~intr.v. **privateered, -teering, -teers.** To sail or serve as a privateer. [From PRIVATE (adjective) by analogy with *volunteer.*]

private income *n.* An income derived from trusts, investments, or the like, rather than from employment.

private law *n.* The branch of law which deals with or affects the rights of, and the relations between, private individuals. Compare **public law.**

private limited company *n. Finance.* A limited liability company whose shares are distributed privately rather than by public subscription and can be transferred only under special conditions. Compare **public limited company.**

private member *n.* A member of the British Parliament who does not hold office in the government or in his party.

private member's bill *n.* In Britain, a bill presented to Parliament sponsored by a private member rather than the government.

private parts *pl.n.* The genitals. Used euphemistically.

private patient *n. Chiefly British.* A patient who meets the costs of medical treatment either by direct payment or through private insurance rather than through the National Health Service.

private practice *n. Chiefly British.* Medical practice, or a business based upon it, in which treatment is given and paid for by private arrangement rather than through the National Health Service.

private school *n.* A school run and supported by private individuals or by a charity or other body rather than by a government or public agency, and usually charging fees. See **public school.**

private sector *n.* The section of a state's economy that is under the control of privately owned enterprises, rather than of government departments or public corporations. Compare **public sector.**

pri·va·tion (prī-váysh'n) *n.* **1. a.** Lack of the basic necessities or comforts of life. **b.** The condition resulting from such lack. **2.** An act, condition, or result of deprivation or loss. [Middle English *privacion,* from Old French *privation,* from Latin *prīvātiō* (stem *prīvātiōn-*), from *prīvāre,* to deprive. See **private.**]

pri·vat·ise, pri·vat·ize (prī́-vət-īz, -vit-) *v.* **-ised, -ising, -ises.** *—tr.* To transfer or sell (public assets, such as national industries) to private ownership. *—intr.* To transfer public assets to private ownership. **—pri·vat·i·sa·tion** (-ī-záysh'n || *U.S.* -i-) *n.*

priv·a·tive (prívvətiv, prī-váytiv) *adj.* **1.** Causing deprivation, lack, or loss. **2.** *Grammar.* Altering the meaning of a term from positive to negative.

~n. Grammar. A privative prefix or suffix, such as *a-, non-, un-,* or *-less.* [Latin *prīvātīvus,* from *prīvāre,* to deprive. See **private.**] **—priv·a·tive·ly** *adv.*

priv·et (prívvit) *n.* Any of several trees or shrubs of the genus *Ligustrum,* having pointed leaves, clusters of white tubular flowers, and black to purple berries; especially *L. ovalifolium* which is widely planted as hedging. [16th century : origin obscure.]

privet hawk *n.* A large hawk moth, *Sphinx ligustri,* the larvae of which feed mostly on privet and lilac.

priv·i·lege (prívvilij) *n.* **1. a.** A special advantage, immunity, permission, right, or benefit granted to or enjoyed by an individual, race, sex, class, or caste. **b.** Such a right or advantage held as a result of status or rank, and exercised to the exclusion or detriment of others. **2.** The principle of granting and maintaining privileges: *a society based on privilege.* **3.** Any of the basic rights to which a nation's citizen is entitled by the constitution. **4.** The rights and immunities of members of Parliament enjoyed by virtue of their position, such as immunity from libel charges based on allegations made within the legislative chambers. **5.** The right extended to or claimed by priests, lawyers, and certain public officials to withhold confidential information from the police or tribunals. **6.** The right of the press to publish defamatory material when reporting court or parliamentary proceedings in which such material is presented. **7.** *U.S. Finance.* Any option to buy or sell a stock, including **put, call, spread,** and **straddle** *(all of which see).* —See Synonyms at **right.**

~tr.v. **privileged, -leging, -leges. 1.** To grant a privilege to. **2.** To free or exempt. Used with *from.* [Middle English, from Old French, from Latin *prīvilēgium,* law affecting an individual, prerogative : *prīvus,* single, individual + *lēx* (stem *lēg-*), law.]

priv·i·leged (prívvilijd) *adj.* **1.** Enjoying a privilege or having privileges: *a privileged childhood.* **2.** Protected against any action for defamation: *a privileged remark.* **3.** Protected against demands for publication or access: *privileged information.*

priv·i·ty (prívvəti) *n., pl.* **-ties. 1.** Knowledge of something private or secret shared between individuals, especially with the implication of approval or consent. **2.** *Law.* **a.** A relationship between parties that is held to be sufficiently close and direct to support a legal claim on behalf of or against another person with whom this relationship exists. **b.** A successive or mutual interest in or relationship to the same property. [Middle English *privete, privite,* a secret, privacy, from Old French, from Medieval Latin *prīvitās* (stem *prīvitāt-*), from Latin *prīvus,* single, private.]

priv·y (prívvi) *adj.* **-ier, -iest. 1.** Sharing in or having knowledge of something private or secret. Used with *to*: *privy to another's thoughts and desires.* **2.** *Rare.* Belonging or proper to a person (such as the British sovereign) in his private rather than his official capacity: *Privy Council.* **3.** *Archaic.* Concealed; secret.

~n., pl. **privies. 1. a.** *Archaic & U.S.* A lavatory. **b.** An outhouse. **2.** *Law.* Any of the parties having an interest in the same matter. [Middle English *prive,* secret, private, acquainted with, from Old French *prive,* from Latin *prīvātus,* PRIVATE.] **—priv·i·ly** *adv.*

Privy Council *n. Abbr.* **P.C. 1.** A council of the British sovereign that now consists of all current and former cabinet ministers and certain senior legal and ecclesiastical officials in private capacity and others appointed as a high honour, membership being for life. In certain cases its Judicial Committee acts as a supreme appellate court in the Commonwealth. **2.** A similar council in various other countries which serves as an advisory body to the head of state. **—Privy Councillor** *n.*

Privy Purse *n. Sometimes small* **p**, *small* **p**. **1.** The sum of money assigned to the British sovereign, or any of various other sovereigns, for the private expenses of the royal household. **2.** The official in charge of the private expenses of the British royal household. Also officially called "Keeper of the Privy Purse".

Privy Seal *n.* In Britain, a royal seal attached to certain documents as proof that they are issued by royal authority.

prix fixe (prée fiks, féeks) *n., pl.* **prix fixes** *(pronounced as singular).* **1.** A **table d'hôte** *(see).* **2.** The price at which a table d'hôte meal is offered. Compare **à la carte**. [French, "fixed price".]

prize[1] (prīz) *n.* **1.** Something offered or won as an award for achieving superiority or excellence in competition with others. **2.** Something offered for winning in a raffle, lottery, or other game of chance. **3.** Anything worth striving for or aspiring to.

~adj. **1.** Offered or given as a prize: *a prize cup.* **2.** Given a prize, or likely to win a prize: *a prize cow.* **3.** Worthy of a prize; first-class. Often used ironically: *a prize idiot.*

~tr.v. **prized, prizing, prizes. 1.** To value highly; esteem, cherish, or treasure. **2.** *Rare.* To estimate the worth of; appraise; evaluate. —See Synonyms at **appreciate**. [Middle English *pris* (noun), variant of PRICE; verb, Middle English, from Old French *preisier* (stem *pris-*), to PRAISE.]

prize[2] *n.* **1.** Something seized by force or taken as booty; especially, an enemy ship and cargo captured at sea during wartime. **2.** Something valuable taken from another. **3.** The act of seizing; capture. [Middle English *pris(e),* from Old French *prise,* from Vulgar Latin *pre(n)sa* (unattested), "something seized", from the past participle of Latin *pre(he)ndere,* to seize.]

prize.[3] Variant of **prise**.

prize court *n. Law.* A court authorised to determine and allocate claimants' shares to goods seized at sea during wartime.

prize fight *n.* A match fought between professional boxers for money. **—prize fighter** *n.* **—prize fighting** *n.*

prize money *n.* **1.** Money constituting a prize or prizes. **2.** Money representing a part of the value of ships or property captured at sea, formerly allocated for division between the captors.

prize ring *n.* **1.** The platform enclosed by ropes in which contending boxers meet. **2.** Professional boxing. Preceded by *the.*

p.r.n. *Medicine.* as the situation demands [Latin *pro re nata.*]

pro[1] (prō) *n., pl.* **pros.** *Abbr.* **p. 1.** An argument in favour of something; an affirmative consideration. Used chiefly in the phrase *pros and cons.* **2.** One who supports a proposal or takes the affirmative side in debate.

~prep. In favour of.

~adv. In favour of something; affirmatively.

~adj. Favouring. [Middle English, from Latin *prō,* for.]

pro[2] *n., pl.* **pros.** *Informal.* **1.** A professional, especially in sports. **2.** An expert in any field of endeavour. **3.** A prostitute.

~adj. Informal. Professional: *pro football.* [Short for PROFESSIONAL.]

pro-[1] *prefix.* Indicates: **1.** Favour or support; for example, **prorevolutionary. 2.** Acting as; for example, **proconsul, properdin.** ***Note:*** Many compounds other than those entered here may be formed with *pro-*. In this dictionary, when forming compounds, *pro-* is normally joined with the following element without space or hyphen: *profascist.* However, many users prefer the hyphenated form, especially when the second element begins with a capital letter: *pro-American.* It is also preferable to use the hyphen when the second element begins with *o* or when forming the compound brings together three or more vowels that would be confusing to read: *pro-aesthetic.* [In borrowed Latin compounds, *prō-* indicates: 1. Forwards, forth, in public, as in **project, proclaim.** 2. Forwards and downwards, as in **profligate.** 3. Away, as in **prodigal.** 4. In front of, before, as in **prohibit.** 5. Anterior, before, in anticipation of, as in **provide.** 6. Onwards, forwards, as in **progress.** 7. Extending out, as in **prolong.** 8. Substituting for, acting as, as in **pronominal.** 9. On behalf of, for, as in **prosit.** 10. Intensified action, as in **promiscuous.** Latin *prō-*, from *prō,* before, in front of, according to, for.]

pro-[2] *prefix.* Indicates before in time or position, or forwards; for example, **prophage, procarp, procephalic.** [Greek *pro,* before, in front of, forward.]

P.R.O. 1. Public Records Office. **2.** public relations officer.

pro·a (prṓ-ə) *n.* A swift Malayan sailing boat with a triangular sail and a single outrigger. [Earlier *parao, prau,* from Malay *pĕrāhū,* probably from Marathi *pạḍāv.*]

pro·ac·tive (prō-áktiv) *adj.* Anticipating events by taking the initiative, rather than just reacting to them passively. Opposite **reactive** (sense 1). [Probably Greek PRO-[2] + ACTIVE, though perhaps influenced by Latin PRO-[2] (senses 5, 6).] **—pro·ac·tive·ly** *adv.*

pro-am (prṓ-ám) *adj. Chiefly U.S.* Of, pertaining to, or designating a sports competition in which both professional and amateur players take part. [*pro*fessional + *am*ateur.]

pro and con *adj.* Also **pro and contra.** For and against.

~prep. For and against. See **pro.** [Latin *pro,* for + *contra,* against.]

prob·a·bi·lism (próbbəb'l-iz'm) *n.* **1.** *Philosophy.* The doctrine that probability is a sufficient basis for belief and action, since certainty in knowledge is unattainable. **2.** *Roman Catholic Church.* A principle that when there is doubt as to the moral rectitude of an action, that opinion which favours liberty may be followed, provided that it is theologically probable, even though the contrary may be equally, or even more, probable. **—prob·a·bi·list** *n.* **—prob·a·bi·lis·tic** (-ístik) *adj.*

prob·a·bil·i·ty (próbbə-bílləti) *n., pl.* **-ties. 1.** The quality or condition of being probable; likelihood. **2.** A probable situation, condition, or event. **3.** *Statistics.* A number expressing the likelihood of occurrence of a specific event, such as the ratio of the number of experimental results that would produce the event to the total number of results considered possible. If the probability is 1 the event is certain to happen, if it is 0 it is certain not to happen. **—in all probability.** Most probably; very likely.

probability density function *n. Statistics.* A function that enables the probability for any value or interval within a range to be determined and formulas for parameters to be established. Also called "density", "density function".

probability theory *n.* A branch of mathematics dealing with the statistical evaluation of the probability of random occurrences.

prob·a·ble (próbbəb'l) *adj. Abbr.* **prob. 1.** Likely to happen or to be true. **2.** Relatively or most likely but not certain; plausible. **3.** *Theology.* Of or pertaining to moral opinions and actions for the lawfulness of which intrinsic reasons or extrinsic authority may be adduced; possible; provable.

~n. Informal. A candidate or competitor who is likely to be selected or successful. [Middle English, from Old French, from Latin *probābilis,* provable, laudable, from *probāre,* to approve, PROVE.]

probable cause *n. Law.* Reasonable grounds for belief that an accused person is guilty as charged and that accordingly further legal action is justified.

prob·a·bly (próbbəbli; *informally also* prób-bli, próbbli, próbbəli) *adv. Abbr.* **prob.** Most likely; very likely; presumably.

pro·band (prṓ-band) *n.* In genealogical or medical surveys, the ancestor or member of a family adopted as the starting point for a study. [Latin *probandus,* gerundive of *probāre,* to test.]

pro·bang (prṓ-bang) *n.* A flexible rod used in surgery to displace foreign bodies stuck in the oesophagus. [Alteration (influenced by PROBE) of earlier *provang* (so named by the inventor).]

pro·bate (prṓ-bayt, -bət, -bit) *adj. U.S.* Of or pertaining to a probate court or its action.

~n. **1.** Legal establishment of the validity of a will. **2.** A document certifying such validity. **3.** *Chiefly U.S.* The right to validate wills.

~tr.v. **probated, -bating, -bates.** *U.S.* To establish the validity of (a will). [Middle English *probat,* from Latin *probātum,* something proved, from *probāre,* to examine, demonstrate as good, PROVE.]

probate court *n. U.S.* A court limited to the jurisdiction of probating wills and administering estates.

pro·ba·tion (prə-báysh'n, prō-). *n.* **1.** A trial period in which a person's fitness for membership of a working or social group is tested. **2.** *Law.* The action of suspending the sentence of one convicted of an offence and granting provisional freedom, under the supervision of a probation officer, on the promise of good behaviour. **3.** *Chiefly U.S.* A trial period in which a student is permitted to redeem poor results or bad conduct. **4.** The status of a person on probation. **5.** The act or process of testing or being tested. [Middle English *probacioun,* from Old French *probation,* from Latin *probātiō* (stem *probātiōn-*), from *probāre,* to try, PROVE.] **—pro·ba·tion·al, pro·ba·tion·ar·y** (-ri, -əri || -erri) *adj.* **—pro·ba·tion·al·ly** *adv.*

pro·ba·tion·er (prə-báysh'n-ər, prō-) *n.* A person on probation prior to membership of a body.

probation officer *n.* A social worker who under the direction of a court supervises and gives support to an offender on probation.

pro·ba·tive (prṓbə-tiv) *adj.* Also **pro·ba·to·ry** (-tri, -təri, prə-báytəri, prō-). **1.** Serving to test, try, or prove. **2.** Furnishing evidence or proof. [Middle English *probatiffe,* from Latin *probātīvus,* of proof, from *probāre,* to try, PROVE.]

probe (prōb) *n.* **1.** Any object or device used to investigate an unknown configuration or condition. **2.** A slender, flexible instrument used to explore a wound or body cavity. **3.** The act of exploring or searching with the aid of such an instrument. **4.** An investigation into the nature of something; especially, an investigation conducted by a legislative committee into corrupt practices. Used especially in journalism. **5.** *Electronics.* An electrical lead attached to a measuring or detecting instrument, used for testing circuits. **6.** Loosely, any act of examining or testing. **7.** A **space probe** *(see).*

~v. **probed, probing, probes.** *—tr.* **1.** To explore with a probe. **2.** To test or examine: *probed their defences; probing her motives.* **3.** To investigate (a matter, especially a public scandal) thoroughly; delve into. *—intr.* To conduct an exploratory investigation; search. [Medieval Latin *proba,* examination, from Late Latin, proof, test, from Latin *probāre,* to test, PROVE.] **—prob·er** *n.*

pro·bi·ty (prṓbəti) *n.* Complete and confirmed integrity; uprightness. See Synonyms at **honesty.** [Old French *probité,* from Latin *probitās* (stem *probitāt-*), goodness, honesty, from *probus,* good, honest, virtuous.]

prob·lem (prób-ləm, -lem, -lim) *n. Abbr.* **prob. 1.** A question or situation that presents uncertainty, perplexity, or difficulty. **2.** A person who is difficult to deal with. **3.** A question put forward for consideration, discussion, or solution.

~adj. **1.** Difficult to deal with or handle: *a problem child.* **2.** Dealing with a social or moral problem: *a problem play.* [Middle English *probleme,* from Old French, from Latin *problēma,* from Greek *problēma,* "thing thrown forward", projection, obstacle, problem, from

proballein, to throw forward : *pro-*, forward + *ballein*, to throw.]

prob·lem·at·i·cal (prób-lə-máttik'l, -li-, -le-) *adj.* Also **prob·lem·at·ic** (-máttik). **1.** Posing a problem; difficult to solve. **2.** Open to doubt; debatable. —**prob·lem·at·i·cal·ly** *adv.*

pro·bos·cid·i·an (prō-boss-íddi-ən) *n.* Also **pro·bos·ci·de·an** (-íddi-ən, -i-dée-ən). An animal belonging to the Proboscidea, an order of mammals that is characterised by a trunk or proboscis and includes the elephant. —**pro·bos·cid·i·an** *adj.*

pro·bos·cis (prō-bóssiss, prə-) *n.*, *pl.* **-cises** or **-boscides** (-bóssideez). **1.** A long, flexible snout or trunk, such as that of an elephant. **2.** A slender, tubular feeding and sucking structure of some insects. **3.** A human nose, especially a prominent one. Used humorously. [Latin, from Greek *proboskis* : *pro-*, in front + *boskein*, to feed.]

proboscis monkey *n.* A monkey, *Nasalis larvatus*, native to the forests of Borneo, the male of which has a large, long nose.

proboscis worm *n.* A marine worm, the **nemertean** *(see).*

proc. 1. proceedings. **2.** process.

pro·caine hydrochloride (prō'kayn) *n.* A white crystalline powder, $C_{13}H_{20}O_2N_2 \cdot HCl$, used as a local anaesthetic in medicine and dentistry. A trademark is "Novocain". Also called *informal* "procaine". [PRO- (in place of) + (CO-)CAINE.]

pro·cam·bi·um (prō-kámbi-əm) *n. Botany.* A layer of meristematic tissue from which the vascular tissue is formed. [PRO- (before) + CAMBIUM.] —**pro·cam·bi·al** *adj.*

pro·carp (prō'kaarp) *n. Botany.* A specialised female reproductive organ in certain algae. [New Latin *procarpium* : PRO- (before) + -CARP.]

procaryote. Variant of **prokaryote.**

pro·ca·the·dral (prō-kə-théedrəl) *n.* A church functioning as the cathedral church of a diocese.

pro·ce·dur·al (prə-séejər-əl, prō-, -séed-yər-) *adj.* Of or pertaining to procedure, especially of a court of law or parliamentary body.

pro·ce·dure (prə-séejər, prō-, -séed-yər) *n.* **1.** A manner of proceeding; a way of performing or effecting something. **2.** An act composed of steps; a course of action. **3.** A set of established forms or methods for conducting the affairs of a business, legislative body, or court of law. [French *procédure*, from Old French, from *proceder*, PROCEED.]

pro·ceed (prō-séed, prə-) *intr.v.* **-ceeded, -ceeding, -ceeds. 1. a.** To go forwards or onwards, especially after an interruption; continue. **b.** To resume speaking. **2.** To undertake and carry on some action or process. **3.** To move on in an orderly manner. **4. a.** To come into being; arise. **b.** To issue forth; originate. Used of the Holy Spirit. **c.** To come out; emerge: *cries proceeding from next door.* **5.** To institute and conduct a legal action. Used with *against.* [Middle English *proceden*, from Old French *proceder*, from Latin *prōcēdere* : *prō-*, forward + *cēdere*, to go.] —**pro·ceed·er** *n.*

pro·ceed·ing (prō-séeding, prə-) *n.* **1.** A course of action; a procedure. **2.** A continuing of an action. **3.** *Plural.* A sequence of events occurring at a particular place or time. **4.** *Plural. Abbr.* **proc.** A record of business carried on by a society or other organisation; minutes. **5.** *Law.* **a.** *Plural.* Litigation. **b.** The instituting or conducting of litigation.

pro·ceeds (prō'seedz) *pl.n.* The amount of money derived from a commercial or fund-raising venture; profits; yield.

pro·ce·phal·ic (prō'se-fál-ik, -ke-, -sə-) *adj. Anatomy.* Pertaining or belonging to the front of the head. [PRO- (in front) + -CEPHALIC.]

proc·ess¹ (prō'sess, -siss ‖ *chiefly U.S.* próss-ess, -əss) *n. Abbr.* **proc. 1.** A system of operations in the production of something. **2.** A series of actions, changes, or functions that bring about an end or result: *the peace process.* **3.** The course or passage of time. **4.** Ongoing movement; progression. **5.** *Law.* **a.** A summons or writ ordering a defendant to appear in court. **b.** The total set or number of summonses or writs issued in a particular proceeding. **c.** The entire course of a judicial proceeding. **6.** *Biology.* A part extending or projecting from an organ or organism; an appendage. **7.** Any of various photomechanical or photoengraving methods.

~*tr.v.* **processed, -essing, -esses. 1.** To put through the steps of a prescribed procedure. **2.** To prepare, treat, or convert by subjecting to some special process: *processed cheese; to process film.* **3.** *Law.* To serve with a summons or writ. **4.** To institute legal proceedings against; prosecute. **5.** *Computing.* To subject (numbers, text, or other data) to modification by program.

~*adj. Abbr.* **proc. 1.** *Chiefly U.S.* Prepared or converted by a special treatment. **2.** Made by or used in photomechanical or photoengraving methods: *a process print.* [Middle English *proces(se)*, from Old French *proces*, from Latin *prōcessus*, from the past participle of *prōcēdere*, to PROCEED.]

proc·ess² (prō-séss, prō-) *intr.v.* **-cessed, -cessing, -cesses.** *Rare.* To move along or go in or as if in a procession. [Back-formation from PROCESSION.]

pro·ces·sion (prə-sésh'n) *n.* **1.** The act of proceeding, moving along, or issuing forth. **2. a.** A group of persons, vehicles, or objects moving along in an orderly and formal manner, usually in a long line. **b.** The movement of such a group. **3.** Any continuous and orderly course: *the procession of the seasons.*

~*intr.v.* **processioned, -sioning, -sions.** *Rare.* To form or go in a procession. [Middle English, from Old French, from Late Latin *prōcessiō* (stem *prōcessiōn-*), religious procession, from Latin, a marching forward, from *prōcēdere*, to PROCEED.]

pro·ces·sion·al (prə-sésh'n 'l) *adj.* Of, pertaining to, or suitable for a procession.

~*n.* **1.** A book containing the ritual observed during a religious procession. **2.** A hymn sung when the clergy enter a church at the beginning of the service. **3.** Any music intended to be played or sung during a procession. —**pro·ces·sion·al·ly** *adv.*

pro·ces·sor (prō-sess-ər, -siss- ‖ *chiefly U.S.* pró-) *n.* **1.** One who processes. **2.** The **central processing unit** *(see)* of a computer.

process printing *n.* Printing from multiple, usually four, halftone images, each inked with a different colour such that the composite impression will reproduce the colours of the original.

pro·cess-serv·er (prō-sess-sérvər, -siss- ‖ pró-) *n.* A sheriff's officer who delivers summonses or writs.

pro·cès-ver·bal (prō-sáy-vair-bál, -ba'al) *n.*, *pl.* **-baux** (-bó). **1.** An official record of diplomatic negotiations. **2.** In France, a detailed official record of a legal charge or other proceedings. [French, "verbal proceedings", originally referring to evidence delivered orally by illiterate subaltern police officers.]

pro·chron·ism (prōkrən-iz'm, próckrən-) *n.* An anachronism consisting in assigning something too early a date. Compare **parachronism.** [PRO- + Greek *khronos*, time + -ISM.]

pro·claim (prə-kláym, prō-) *tr.v.* **-claimed, -claiming, -claims. 1.** To announce officially and publicly; declare. **2.** To indicate unmistakably; make plain. **3.** To praise; extol. [Middle English *procla(y)men*, from Old French *proclamer*, from Latin *prōclāmāre* : *prō-*, forward, forth + *clāmāre*, to cry out.] —**pro·claim·er** *n.*

proc·la·ma·tion (próckla-máysh'n) *n.* **1.** The act of proclaiming. **2.** Something proclaimed; especially, an official public announcement.

pro·clit·ic (prō-klíttik, prō-) *adj. Linguistics.* Forming an accentual unit with the following word and thus having no independent accent. Compare **enclitic.**

~*n.* A proclitic word. [New Latin *procliticus*, formed by analogy with Late Latin *encliticus*, ENCLITIC : Greek *pro-*, forward + *klinein*, to lean.]

pro·cliv·i·ty (prō-klívvəti, prə-) *n.*, *pl.* **-ties.** A natural propensity or inclination; a predisposition. [Latin *prōclīvitās*, from *prōclīvus*, sloping forward : *prō-*, forward + *clīvus*, slope, hill.]

pro·con·sul (prō-kón-s'l) *n.* **1.** A provincial governor of consular rank in ancient Rome. **2.** A high administrator in any of various territories of the European colonial empires. [Middle English, from Latin, combined from *prō consule*, (one acting) for a consul : *prō-*, for + CONSUL.] —**pro·con·su·lar** (-sew-lər ‖ -sə-) *adj.* —**pro·con·su·late** (-sew-lət, -lit ‖ -sə-) *n.*

pro·cras·ti·nate (prō-krásti-nayt, prə-) *v.* **-nated, -nating, -nates.** —*intr.* To put off doing something until a future time. —*tr.* *Rare.* To postpone or delay needlessly. [Latin *prōcrāstināre*, "to put forward to tomorrow" : *prō-*, forward + *crāstinus*, of tomorrow, from *crās†*, tomorrow.] —**pro·cras·ti·na·tion** (-náysh'n) *n.* —**pro·cras·ti·na·tor** (-naytər) *n.*

pro·cre·ate (prō-kri-ayt, -áyt) *v.* **-ated, -ating, -ates.** —*tr.* **1.** To beget (offspring). **2.** To produce or create; originate. —*intr.* To beget offspring; reproduce. [Latin *prōcreāre* : *prō-*, forward, forth + *creāre*, to CREATE.] —**pro·cre·ant** (-ənt) *adj.* —**pro·cre·a·tion** (-áysh'n) *n.* —**pro·cre·a·tor** (-ər) *n.*

pro·cre·a·tive (prō-kri-aytiv, -áytiv) *adj.* **1.** Capable of reproducing; generative. **2.** Of or directed towards procreation: *procreative instinct.*

pro·crus·te·an (prō-krústi-ən, prə-) *adj.* Producing or designed to produce conformity by ruthless or arbitrary means. [After *Procrustes*, from Greek *Prokroustēs*, "stretcher", name of legendary robber who stretched or shortened captives to fit an iron bed.]

procrustean bed *n. Often capital* P. An arbitrary standard to which exact conformity is forced.

pro·cryp·tic (prō-kríptik) *adj. Zoology.* Having a pattern or coloration adapted for natural camouflage. [Probably PRO(TECT) + CRYPTIC.]

procto-, proct- *comb. form.* Indicates rectum or anus; for example, **proctology.** [Greek *prōktos*, anus.]

proc·tol·o·gy (prok-tólləji) *n.* The physiology and pathology of the rectum and anus. [PROCTO- + -LOGY.] —**proc·to·log·ic** (próktə-lójik), **proc·to·log·i·cal** *adj.* —**proc·to·log·i·cal·ly** *adv.* —**proc·tol·o·gist** (-tólləjist) *n.*

proc·tor (próktər) *n.* **1.** In certain universities and schools, an official responsible for discipline and for invigilating at examinations. **2.** An agent or representative, especially one hired to collect tithes or to conduct a court case on another's behalf. **3.** In the Church of England, an elected clerical member of a synod.

~*v.* **proctored, -toring, -tors.** *U.S.* To serve as proctor at (an examination). —*intr.* To serve as a proctor. [Middle English *proc(u)tour*, agent, deputy, contraction of *procuratour*, PROCURATOR.] —**proc·to·ri·al** (prok-táwri-əl ‖ -tóri-) *adj.*

proc·to·scope (próktə-skōp) *n.* An instrument for examining the rectum. [PROCTO- + -SCOPE.] —**proc·to·scop·ic** (-skóppik) *adj.* —**proc·tos·co·py** (prok-tóskəpi) *n.*

pro·cum·bent (prō-kúmbənt) *adj.* **1.** *Botany.* Trailing along the ground; prostrate: *a procumbent vine.* **2.** Lying face down; prone. [Latin *prōcumbens* (stem *prōcumbent-*), present participle of *prōcumbere*, to fall forward, bend down : *prō-*, forward, down + *-cumbere*, to lie down.]

proc·u·ra·tion (próckewr-áysh'n) *n* **1.** The act or process of procuring or being procured. **2.** *Law.* The criminal act of procuring women for purposes of prostitution. **3.** *Law.* **a.** The appointment or duties of an agent or legal representative. **b.** The document certifying such appointment or duties. **c.** **Power of attorney** *(see).*

proc·u·ra·tor (prók-yŏŏ-raytər, próckewr-aytər) *n.* **1.** An agent having power of attorney. **2.** A Roman official acting as a financial agent of the emperor or as the administrator of a minor province. [Middle English *procuratour,* from Old French, from Latin *prōcūrātor,* from *prōcūrāre,* to take care of, PROCURE.] **—proc·u·ra·to·ri·al** (-ə-táwri-əl || -tōri-), **proc·u·ra·to·ry** (-ətri, -ətəri, -áytəri) *adj.*

procurator fiscal *n.* In Scotland, an official who serves as coroner and public prosecutor. Also called "fiscal".

pro·cure (prə-kéwr, prō-) *v.* **-cured, -curing, -cures.** *—tr.* **1.** To obtain; acquire. **2.** To bring about; effect: *procure a solution.* **3.** To obtain (a child or woman) to serve as a prostitute. *—intr.* To obtain girls or women to serve as prostitutes. [Middle English *procuren,* to take care of, gain, obtain, from Old French *procurer,* from Late Latin *prōcūrāre,* to obtain, from Latin, to take care of, manage for someone else : *prō-,* for, on behalf of + *cūrāre,* to take care of.] **—pro·cure·ment** *n.*

pro·cur·er (prə-kéwr-ər, prō-) *n.* **1.** One who procures. **2.** A pander.

pro·cur·ess (prə-kéwr-iss, prō-, próckewr-, -ess) *n.* A female procurer.

Pro·cy·on (prṓ-si-ən || -on) *n.* A double star in the constellation Canis Minor. [Latin, from Greek *Prokuōn,* "before the dog star" : *pro-,* before + *kuōn,* dog.]

prod (prod) *tr.v.* **prodded, prodding, prods. 1.** To jab or poke, as with a pointed instrument. **2.** To rouse to action; urge; goad.
∼n. **1.** The act or an instance of prodding. **2.** Anything pointed used to prod; a goad. **3.** An incitement or reminder; a stimulus. [16th century : perhaps imitative.] **—prod·der** *n.*

Prod *n. Informal.* Also **Prod·dy, Prod·die** (próddi) *pl.* **-dies.** A Protestant. Used derogatorily. **—Prod, Prod·dy** *adj.*

prod·i·gal (próddig'l) *adj.* **1.** Recklessly wasteful; extravagant. **2.** Extremely generous. **3.** Profuse; lavish: *prodigal praise.*
∼n. A person given to luxury or extravagance; a spendthrift or profligate. [Latin *prōdigus,* from *prōdigere,* to drive away, squander : *prōd-,* variant of *prō-,* forth, away + *agere,* to drive.] **—prod·i·gal·ly** *adv.*

prod·i·gal·i·ty (próddi-gál-əti) *n., pl.* **-ties. 1.** Extravagant wastefulness. **2.** Profuse generosity. **3.** Extreme abundance; lavishness.

pro·di·gious (prə-díjəss) *adj.* **1.** Impressively great in size, force, or extent; enormous. **2.** Extraordinary; marvellous. **3.** *Obsolete.* Portentous; ominous. [Latin *prōdigiōsus,* from *prōdigium,* omen, portent, PRODIGY.] **—pro·di·gious·ly** *adv.* **—pro·di·gious·ness** *n.*

prod·i·gy (próddiji) *n., pl.* **-gies. 1.** A person with exceptional talents or powers: *a child prodigy.* **2.** An act, object, or event so extraordinary or rare as to inspire wonder; a marvel. **3.** *Archaic.* An omen or portent. [Latin *prōdigium,* prophetic sign, marvel.]

pro·drome (prṓ-drōm) *n.* An early symptom of a disease, often different in nature from the later symptoms. [French, from Greek *prodromos,* precursor : *pro-,* forward + *dromos,* running.] **—pro·dro·mal** (prō-drṓm'l), **pro·drom·ic** (prō-drómmik) *adj.*

pro·duce (prə-déwss || prō-, -dŏŏss) *v.* **-duced, -ducing, -duces.** *—tr.* **1.** To bring forth; yield. **2.** To create by mental or physical effort. **3.** To manufacture. **4. a.** To cause to occur or exist; give rise to. **b.** To give birth to. **5.** To bring forward; exhibit. **6.** *British.* To interpret and supervise the acting and artistic design of (a play, for example). **7.** To sponsor and present to the public: *produce a film.* **8.** In geometry, to extend (an area or volume) or lengthen (a line). *—intr.* To make or yield the customary product or products.
∼n. (pród-yōōss || -ōōss, *chiefly U.S.* prṓd-) *Abbr.* **prod.** Something produced; a product; especially, agricultural products collectively. [Latin *prōdūcere,* to lead or bring forth : *prō-,* forward + *dūcere,* to lead.] **—pro·duc·i·ble** *adj.*

pro·duc·er (prə-déw-sər || prō-, -dŏŏ-) *n.* **1.** One that produces. **2.** *Economics.* A person or organisation that grows or manufactures goods or provides services for sale. **3. a.** A person who arranges the finance, hiring of actors, and other practical business in the making of a cinematic film or the staging of a play. Compare **director. b.** *British.* The person who supervises and instructs the actors or participants in a radio or television production, and is responsible for the overall artistic interpretation. **4.** A furnace that manufactures producer gas. **5.** *Ecology.* Any organism that is the first stage in a food chain, such as bacteria or green plants, building up foods from and feeding on inorganic matter. Compare **consumer.**

producer gas *n.* A gas used as fuel, generated by passing air with steam over burning coke or coal, to yield a combustible mixture of nitrogen, carbon monoxide, and hydrogen. Also called "air gas".

prod·uct (pród-ukt, -əkt) *n. Abbr.* **prod. 1. a.** Anything produced by human or mechanical effort or by a natural process. **b.** An article considered as merchandise: *redesign the product.* **c.** Marketable goods collectively: *What the company needs is product.* **d.** A person who has undergone a specified type of training or education: *a grammar school product.* **2.** A direct result; a consequence. **3.** *Chemistry.* A substance produced by a chemical change. **4.** *Mathematics.* **a.** The result obtained by performing multiplication. **b.** A **scalar product** *(see).* **c.** A **vector product** *(see).* [Latin *prōductum,* from the past participle of *prōdūcere,* to PRODUCE.]

pro·duc·tion (prə-dúksh'n || prō-) *n.* **1.** The act or process of producing. **2.** *Economics.* The creation of value or wealth by producing goods and services. **3.** Something produced; a product. **4. a.** The total number of products; output. **b.** The rate at which products are produced. **5. a.** *British.* The artistic supervision and interpretation of a stage play or other live public entertainment. **b.** A public performance or showing of such an entertainment. **c.** A version of a play or similar work with a particular interpretation and staging: *a new production of Fidelio.* **6.** Mass production. Also used adjectivally: *a production model.* **7.** *Informal.* **a.** A great effort. **b.** An unnecessarily complicated procedure; a fuss. **—pro·duc·tion·al** *adj.*

production line *n.* **1.** An **assembly line** *(see).* **2.** A method of mass-producing goods using a continuous flow of components, which are assembled on a moving conveyor. **3.** Any system or institution whose products or graduates emerge regularly and systematically and have standardised characteristics. **—pro·duc·tion-line** (prə-dúksh'n-līn || prō-) *adj.*

pro·duc·tive (prə-dúktiv || prō-) *adj.* **1.** Producing or capable of producing. **2.** Producing abundantly; fertile; prolific. **3.** Yielding favourable or useful results; constructive. **4.** *Economics.* Of or involved in the creation of goods and services to produce wealth or value. **5.** Resulting in. Used with *of*: *difficulties productive of dispute.* **—pro·duc·tive·ly** *adv.* **pro·duc·tive·ness** *n.*

pro·duc·tiv·i·ty (pród-uk-tívvəti, prṓd-, ək-) *n.* **1.** Productiveness. **2.** Rate or efficiency of production; specifically, productivity of labour measured by the output produced in a given time or by the time required to produce a given output.

product liability *n.* Legal responsibility on the part of a manufacturer, as opposed to a retailer, to ensure that a product is safe or good quality, and fit for its purpose.

pro·em (prṓ-em) *n.* A short introduction; a preface. [Middle English *proheme,* from Old French *pro(h)eme,* from Latin *prooemium,* from Greek *prooimion,* prelude : *pro-,* before + *oimē,* song, from *oimos,* way, path.] **—pro·e·mi·al** (prō-éemi-əl) *adj.*

prof., Prof. professor.

prof·a·na·tion (próffə-náysh'n) *n.* The act or an instance of profaning; desecration.

pro·fane (prə-fáyn, prō-) *adj.* **1.** Showing contempt or irreverence towards God or sacred things; blasphemous. **2.** Nonreligious in subject matter, form, or use; secular: *sacred and profane music.* **3.** Not initiated into the mysteries of ritual. **4.** Vulgar; coarse.
∼tr.v. **profaned, -faning, -fanes. 1.** To treat with irreverence. **2.** To put to an improper, unworthy, or degrading use; abuse. [Middle English *prophane,* from Old French, from Medieval Latin *prophānus,* variant of Latin *profānus,* "before (i.e., outside) the temple", hence not sacred, secular, impious : *prō-,* before + *fānum,* temple.] **—pro·fan·a·to·ry** (-fánnə-tri, -təri) *adj.* **—pro·fane·ly** *adv.* **—pro·fane·ness** *n.* **—pro·fan·er** *n.*
Synonyms: *profane, blasphemous, sacrilegious.*

pro·fan·i·ty (prə-fánnəti, prō-) *n., pl.* **-ties. 1.** The condition or quality of being profane. **2. a.** Abusive, vulgar, or irreverent language. **b.** The use or an instance of such language.

pro·fess (prə-féss, prō-) *v.* **-fessed, -fessing, -fesses.** *—tr.* **1.** To affirm openly; declare or claim. **2.** To make a pretence of. **3.** To claim skill in or knowledge of. **4.** To affirm belief in: *profess Catholicism.* **5.** To receive into a religious order. *—intr.* **1.** To make an open affirmation. **2.** To take the vows of a religious order. [Latin *prōfitērī* (past participle *prōfessus*), to declare publicly : *prō-,* forth, in public + *fatērī,* to acknowledge, confess.]

pro·fessed (prə-fést, prō-) *adj.* **1.** According to one's own admission; self-confessed: *a professed hedonist.* **2.** Self-proclaimed but pretended. **3.** Belonging to a profession. **4.** Having taken the vows of a religious order. **—pro·fess·ed·ly** (-féssid-li) *adv.*

pro·fes·sion (prə-fésh'n || prō-) *n.* **1.** An occupation or vocation requiring training, as in law, theology, or the sciences. **2.** The body of qualified persons of any specific occupation or field. **3.** The act or an instance of professing; a declaration; a claim. **4.** An avowal of faith in a religion, especially on first being accepted into it. **5.** The taking of vows by a person joining a religious order. [Middle English, vow made on entering a religious order, from Old French, from Latin *professiō* (stem *professiōn-*), declaration, confession, from *profitērī,* PROFESS.]

pro·fes·sion·al (prə-fésh'n'l || prō-) *adj.* **1.** Of, pertaining to, engaged in, or suitable for a profession. **2.** Engaged in a specific activity as a source of livelihood. **3.** Performed by persons receiving pay. **4.** Having great skill or experience in a particular field or activity.
∼n. Abbr. **pro., Pro. 1.** A person following a profession. **2.** One who earns his livelihood as a sportsman, either playing or coaching. **3.** One who has an assured competence in a particular field or occupation. **—pro·fes·sion·al·ly** *adv.*

professional foul *n. Sports.* In team games, a deliberate foul, usually committed when the opposing team seems certain of scoring.

pro·fes·sion·al·ism (prə-fésh'n'l-iz'm || prō-) *n.* **1.** Professional status, methods, character, or standards. **2.** The use of professional players in organised sports.

pro·fes·sor (prə-féssər || prō-) *n.* **1.** *Abbr.* **prof., Prof. a.** A tutor of the highest rank in a university or comparable institution. **b.** *U.S.* A teacher or instructor. **2.** One who professes. [Middle English *professour,* from Latin *professor,* from *profitērī,* PROFESS.] **—pro·fes·so·ri·al** (próf-ə-sáwri-əl, -i-, -e- || -sōri-) *adj.* **—pro·fes·so·ri·al·ly** *adv.* **—pro·fes·sor·ship** (-ship) *n.*

prof·fer (próffər) *tr.v.* **-fered, -fering, -fers.** To offer; tender. See Synonyms at **offer.**
∼n. The act of proffering; an offer. [Middle English *profren,* from Old French *p(o)roffrir* : *por-,* from Latin *prō-,* forth + *offrir,* to offer, from Latin *offerre,* "to carry towards" : *ob-,* to, towards + *ferre,* to carry.] **—prof·fer·er** *n.*

pro·fi·cien·cy (prə-físh'n-si || prō-) *n., pl.* **-cies.** The state or quality of being proficient; skill; competence.

pro·fi·cient (prə-físh'nt || prō-) *adj.* Performing in a given art, skill, or branch of learning with expert correctness and facility; adept. ~*n. Rare.* An adept; an expert. [Latin *prōficiens* (stem *prōficient-*), present participle of *prōficere,* to make progress. See **profit.**] **—pro·fi·cient·ly** *adv.*

***Synonyms:** proficient, adept, skilled, skilful.*

pro·file (prṓ-fīl; *old-fashioned* -feel) *n.* **1. a.** A side view of an object or structure, especially of a human head. **b.** A representation of an object or structure seen from the side. **2.** An outline of any object. **3.** A biographical essay presenting the subject's most noteworthy characteristics and achievements. **4. a.** A graph or table representing numerically the extent to which a person or thing shows various tested characteristics: *an organisational profile.* **b.** The characteristics represented. **5. a.** A vertical section of the soil at any point of the earth's surface down to the parent rock, showing the different horizons. **b.** A graphical representation of this section. Also called "soil profile". **6. a.** A vertical section of the earth's crust at any point showing the different layers of rock. **b.** A graphical representation of this section. —See Synonyms at **form.**

~*tr.v.* **profiled, -filing, -files. 1.** To draw or shape a profile of. **2.** To write or produce a profile of. [Italian *profilo,* from *profilare,* to draw in outline : *pro-,* forward + *filare,* to spin, draw a line, from Late Latin *fīlāre,* to spin, from Latin *fīlum,* thread, string.]

prof·it (próffit) *n.* **1.** An advantageous gain or return; a benefit. **2.** The return received on a business undertaking after all operating expenses have been met. **3.** *Economics.* The prospect of such return considered as the chief motivation in all activity in a capitalist economy. **4.** *Often plural.* **a.** The return received on an investment after all charges have been paid. **b.** The rate of increase in the net worth of a business enterprise in a given accounting period. **c.** Income received from investments or property. **d.** The amount received for a commodity or service in excess of the original cost.

~*v.* **profited, -iting, -its.** —*intr.* **1.** To make a gain or profit. **2.** To be advantageous; benefit. —*tr.* To be beneficial to. [Middle English, from Old French, from Latin *prōfectus,* advance, progress, success, profit, from the past participle of *prōficere,* to go forward, accomplish, be advantageous : *prō-,* for + *facere,* to do, make.]

prof·it·a·ble (próffit-əb'l) *adj.* **1.** Beneficial; advantageous. **2.** Yielding a financial profit. **—prof·it·a·bil·i·ty** (-ə-bílləti), **prof·it·a·ble·ness** *n.* **—prof·it·a·bly** *adv.*

profit and loss *n.* An account showing net and gross profit or loss over a given period. **—prof·it-and-loss** (próffit-ənd-lóss) *adj.*

prof·i·teer (próffi-téer) *n.* One who makes excessive profits on commodities in short supply.

~*intr.v.* **profiteered, -teering, -teers.** To act as a profiteer.

prof·i·te·role (próffitə-rṓl, prə-fíttə-, -rōl) *n.* A small, round case of choux pastry usually filled with cream and served with a chocolate sauce. [Fench, diminutive of *profit,* PROFIT.]

prof·it-shar·ing (próffit-shair-ing) *n.* A system by which employees receive a share of the profits of a business enterprise. **—prof·it-shar·ing** *adj.*

prof·li·gate (próffli-gət, -git || -gayt) *adj.* **1.** Given over to dissipation; dissolute. **2.** Recklessly wasteful; wildly extravagant.

~*n.* A profligate person; a wastrel. [Latin *prōflīgātus,* from the past participle of *prōflīgāre,* to strike down, destroy, ruin : *prō-,* forward, down + *flīgere,* to strike.] **—prof·li·ga·cy** (-gə-si) *n.*

pro for·ma (prō fórmə) *adv. Latin.* As a matter of, or according to, form. **—pro for·ma** *adj.*

pro·found (prə-fównd || prō-; *West Indian also* -fúngd) *adj.* **-er, -est. 1.** Situated at, extending to, or coming from a great depth; deep. **2.** Coming as if from the depths of one's being: *profound contempt.* **3.** Thoroughgoing; far-reaching. **4.** Penetrating beyond what is superficial or obvious: *a profound thinker.* **5.** Unqualified; absolute; complete. [Middle English *profounde,* from Old French *profond, profund,* from Latin *profundus* : *prō-,* before + *fundus,* bottom.] **—pro·found·ly** *adv.* **—pro·found·ness** *n.*

pro·fun·di·ty (prə-fúndəti || prō-) *n., pl.* **-ties. 1.** Great depth. **2.** Depth of intellect, feeling, or meaning. **3.** Something profound or abstruse. [Middle English *profundite,* from Old French, from Late Latin *profunditās* (stem *profunditāt-*), from *profundus,* deep, PROFOUND.]

pro·fuse (prə-féwss || prō-) *adj.* **1.** Plentiful; overflowing. **2.** Giving or given freely and abundantly; extravagant. Usually used with *in* or *with*: *profuse in his compliments.* [Middle English, from Latin *prōfūsus,* from the past participle of *prōfundere,* to pour forth : *prō-,* forth + *fundere,* to pour.] **—pro·fuse·ly** *adv.* **—pro·fuse·ness** *n.*

pro·fu·sion (prə-féwzh'n || prō-) *n.* **1.** The state of being profuse; abundance. **2.** Lavish or unrestrained expense; extravagance. **3.** A profuse outpouring or display.

prog[1] (prog) *n. British Informal.* A proctor. —*tr.v.* **progged, progging, progs.** *British Informal.* To subject to a proctor's authority. [Shortening.]

prog[2] *n. British Informal.* A programme. [Shortening.]

prog. 1. programme. **2.** progress; progressive.

pro·gen·i·tive (prō-jénnətiv) *adj.* Capable of producing offspring; fertile. [Middle English. See **progenitor.**]

pro·gen·i·tor (prō-jénnitər, prə-) *n.* **1.** A direct ancestor. **2.** An originator of a line of descent. **3.** Any founder or precursor of a trend or tradition. [Middle English *progenitour,* from Old French *progeniteur,* from Latin *prōgenitor,* from *prōgenitus,* past participle of *prōgignere,* to beget : *prō-,* forth + *gignere,* to beget.]

prog·e·ny (prójəni) *n., pl.* **-nies. 1.** Children or descendants; offspring. **2.** A result of creative effort; a product. [Middle English *progenie,* from Old French, from Latin *prōgeniēs,* descent, descendants, from *prōgignere,* to beget. See **progenitor.**]

pro·ges·ta·tion·al (prṓ-jess-táysh'n'l) *adj.* **1.** Preceding gestation. **2.** Preceding ovulation.

pro·ges·ter·one (prō-jéstə-rōn, prə-) *n.* A female hormone, $C_{21}H_{30}O_2$, secreted by the corpus luteum of the ovary prior to ovulation, which prepares the uterus for implantation of a fertilised ovum. [PRO- (acting for) + GES(TATION) + STER(OL) + -ONE.]

pro·ges·to·gen (prō-jéstə-jən, -jen) *n.* Any substance having an action like progesterone. [PROGEST(ERONE) + -GEN.]

pro·glot·tid (prō-glót-id) *n., pl.* **-tids.** Also **pro·glot·tis** (-iss) *pl.* **-tides** (-i-deez). Any of the segments of a tapeworm. [New Latin *proglottis* (stem *proglottid-*), from Greek *proglōssis,* tip of the tongue (from its shape) : *pro-,* before + *glōssa, glōtta,* tongue.] **—pro·glot·tic, pro·glot·ti·de·an** (-i-dée-ən, prṓ-glot-; *also* prṓ-glo-tíddi-ən) *adj.*

prog·na·thous (prog-náy-thəss, próg-nə-) *adj.* Also **prog·nath·ic** (-náthik). Having one or both jaws projecting forward to a considerable degree. [PRO- (in front, projecting) + -GNATHOUS.] **—prog·na·thism** (próg-nə-thiz'm) *n.*

prog·no·sis (prog-nṓ-siss) *n., pl.* **-ses** (-seez). **1. a.** A prediction of the probable course and outcome of a disease. **b.** The likelihood of recovery from a disease. **2.** Any forecast or prediction. [Late Latin, from Greek *prognōsis,* from *progignōskein,* to foreknow, predict : *pro-,* before + *gignōskein,* to know.]

prog·nos·tic (prog-nóstik, prəg-) *adj.* **1.** Of, pertaining to, or acting as a prognosis. **2.** Predicting; foretelling.

~*n.* **1.** A sign or omen of some future happening. **2.** A symptom indicating the future course of a disease. [Medieval Latin *prognōsticus,* from Greek *prognōstikos,* from *progignōskein,* to predict. See **prognosis.**]

prog·nos·ti·cate (prog-nósti-kayt, prəg-) *tr.v.* **-cated, -cating, -cates. 1.** To predict, using present indications as a guide. **2.** To foreshadow; portend. [Medieval Latin *prognōsticāre,* from *prognōsticus,* PROGNOSTIC.] **—prog·nos·ti·ca·tor** (-kaytər) *n.* **—prog·nos·ti·ca·tion** (-káysh'n) *n.*

pro·gram (prṓ-gram || -grəm) *n.* **1.** A set of instructions, written in a suitable programming language, that are fed into a computer to enable it to perform logical or arithmetical operations on data. **2.** *U.S.* Variant of **programme.**

~*v.* **programmed** or *U.S.* **programed, -gramming** or *U.S.* **-graming, -grams.** —*tr.* **1.** To supply (a computer) with a program or programs. **2.** To organise or convert (data) into a program. **3.** *U.S.* Variant of **programme.** —*intr.* To write a computer program. **—pro·gram·ma·ble** (-əb'l, prō-grám-) *adj.*

pro·gramme, *U.S.* **pro·gram** (prṓ-gram || -grəm) *n.* **1. a.** A listing of the order of events and other pertinent information for some public presentation. **b.** A booklet containing such information sold at concerts, plays, and similar events. **2.** The presentation itself. **3.** A radio or television show. **4.** Any organised list or schedule of procedures or activities. **5.** A schedule of projects to be carried out: *a building programme.* **6.** A syllabus.

~*tr.v.* **programmed** or *U.S.* **programed, -gramming** or *U.S.* **-graming, -grammes** or *U.S.* **-grams. 1.** To include or schedule in a programme. **2.** To design (a plan, for example) as a definite programme. **3.** To cause (a machine, animal, or person) to follow a set procedure; control or direct the behaviour of. [French *programme,* from Late Latin *programma,* public notice, from Greek, from *prographein,* to set forth as a public notice : *pro-,* before + *graphein,* to write.] **—pro·gram·mat·ic** (-grə-máttik) *adj.*

pro·grammed learning (prṓ-gramd || -grəmd) *n.* A system of instruction, relying largely on textbooks or machines and requiring minimal supervision by teachers.

programme music *n.* Music intended to convey ideas or suggest the episodes of a story. Compare **absolute music.**

pro·gram·mer, pro·gram·er (prṓ-grammər || -grəmmər) *n.* **1.** One who prepares a computer program. **2.** A person who schedules radio or television programmes.

pro·gram·ming language (prṓ-gram-ing || -grəm-) *n.* Any of various coded systems of words and symbols used to write instructions to a computer in familiar notation rather than directly in a machine code. See **high-level language, low-level language.**

pro·gress (prṓ-gress || *chiefly U.S.* pró-, -grəss) *n.* **1.** Movement towards a goal. **2.** Development; unfolding. **3.** Steady improvement, as of a society or civilisation: *a believer in progress.* **4.** *Chiefly British.* A state journey made by a sovereign through the realm. **—in progress.** Under way; currently being done or made.

~*intr.v.* (prə-gréss, prō-) **-gressed, -gressing, -gresses. 1.** To advance; proceed. **2.** To advance towards a more desirable form or condition. [Middle English *progresse,* from Latin *prōgressus,* from past participle of *prōgredī,* to go forward : *prō-,* forward + *gradī,* to step, go.]

progress chaser *n.* A person whose task is to encourage or exhort those working on a project and to monitor their output, to ensure that progress is maintained.

pro·gres·sion (prə-grésh'n, prō-) *n.* **1.** The act of or an instance of progressing. **2. a.** A sequence, as of events. **b.** The movement from one item in such a sequence to the next. **3.** *Mathematics.* A series of numbers or quantities, each derived from the one preceding by some consistent operation. See **arithmetic progression, geometric progression. 4.** *Music.* A succession of notes or chords or the modulation from one to the next. —See Synonyms at **series.** **—pro·gres·sion·al** *adj.*

pro·gres·sion·ism (prə-grésh'n-iz'm, prō-) *n.* The doctrine that society or nature has progressed, is progressing, or ought to progress towards a higher and more desirable state. **—pro·gres·sion·ist** *n.*

pro·gres·sive (prə-gréssiv, prō-) *adj.* **1.** Moving forward; ongoing; advancing. **2.** Proceeding in steps; continuing steadily by increments. **3. a.** Believing in or striving for constant improvement or new advances. **b.** Characterised by an advance over the established forms; very modern: *progressive rock music.* **c.** Promoting or favouring political and social reform. **4.** *Capital* **P.** Of or belonging to a Progressive Party. **5.** Of, designating, pertaining to, or influenced by a theory of education characterised by emphasis on the individual needs and capacities of each child and informality of curriculum. **6.** Of or denoting a tax or tax system in which the rate of taxation increases as the taxable amount increases. **7.** *Pathology.* Continuously spreading or increasing in severity. **8.** *Grammar.* Designating a verb form or aspect that expresses an action or condition in progress; continuous. In English, it is formed by adding the suffix *-ing* to the root verb form.
∼n. **1.** A person who favours or strives for advances or reform in politics, education, or other fields. **2.** *Capital* **P.** One who belongs to a Progressive Party. **3. a.** The progressive form of a verb. **b.** A verb in this form. **—pro·gres·sive·ly** *adv.* **—pro·gres·sive·ness** *n.*

Progressive Party *n.* **1.** A South African political party existing between 1959 and 1975, having broadly liberal policies. **2.** Any of three U.S. political parties, formed in 1912 (under the leadership of Theodore Roosevelt), 1924, and 1948 respectively.

Progressive Reform Party *n.* A South African political party formed in 1975 by the merging of the Progressive Party with the *Reform Party,* a group of former members of the **United Party** *(see).*

pro·gres·siv·ism (prə-gréssiv-iz'm, prō-) *n.* The doctrines and practice of political or educational progressives.

pro·hib·it (prə-híbbit, prō-) *tr.v.* **-ited, -iting, -its. 1.** To forbid by authority. **2.** To prevent or debar. [Middle English *prohibiten,* from Latin *prōhibēre,* to hold in front, hinder, hold back : *prō-,* in front + *habēre,* to hold.]
Usage: The usual preposition following this verb is *from (The law prohibits you from doing that),* but the following constructions are also used: *The law prohibits doing that; The law prohibits your doing that.* The construction *The law prohibits you doing that* is also found but is not acceptable.

pro·hi·bi·tion (prṓ-i-bísh'n, -hi-) *n.* **1.** The act of prohibiting or state of being prohibited. **2.** A law, order, or decree that forbids something. **3.** *Law.* An order from the High Court forbidding a lower court or tribunal from deciding a particular case. In this sense, also officially called "Order of Prohibition". **4. a.** The forbidding by law of the manufacture, transportation, sale, and possession of alcoholic drinks. **b.** *Capital* **P.** The period (1920–33) during which such a law was in force in the United States.

pro·hi·bi·tion·ist (prṓ-i-bísh'n-ist, -hi-) *n.* **1.** One in favour of banning the manufacture and sale of alcoholic drinks. **2.** A member of a party in the United States that advocated the Prohibition.

pro·hib·i·tive (prə-híbbitiv, prō-) *adj.* Also **pro·hib·i·to·ry** (-híbbi-tri, -təri). **1.** Prohibiting or likely to prohibit. **2.** Preventing or discouraging something, such as purchase or use: *prohibitive costs.* **—pro·hib·i·tive·ly** *adv.*

proj·ect (prój-ekt, -ikt ‖ prṓj-) *n.* **1.** A plan or proposal. **2.** An undertaking requiring concerted effort. **3.** A research undertaking or plan.
∼v. **pro·ject** (prə-jékt, prō-), **-jected, -jecting, -jects.** *—tr.* **1.** To thrust outwards or forwards. Compare **retroject. 2.** To throw forwards; hurl; impel. **3.** To transport in one's imagination. **4.** *Psychology.* To externalise and attribute (an emotion, for example) to someone or something else. Used with *onto.* **5.** To direct (one's voice) so as to be heard clearly at a distance. **6.** To form a plan or intention for; intend. Used especially in the past participle: *my projected tour of Wales.* **7. a.** To cause (an image) to appear upon a surface. **b.** To cast (light or shadow). **8.** To produce a projection of. **9. a.** To use as a basis for estimates or predictions: *If you project these figures to next year, you will see that prices should rise.* **b.** To estimate; predict: *projected a ten per cent rise.* **10.** To convey or represent vividly to an audience: *projects himself poorly.* *—intr.* **1.** To extend forwards or out; protrude. **2.** To direct one's voice so as to be heard clearly at a distance. [Middle English *proiecte,* from Latin *prōjectum,* a projecting, projection, from the past participle of *prō(j)icere,* to throw forth : *prō,* forth + *jacere,* to throw.]

pro·jec·tile (prə-jék-tīl, prō-, prój-ik-, -ek- ‖ *chiefly U.S.* -t'l) *n.* **1.** A fired, thrown, or otherwise projected object, such as a bullet, having no capacity for self-propulsion. **2.** A self-propelling missile, such as a rocket.
∼adj. (*always* -jék-). **1.** Capable of being impelled or hurled forwards. **2.** Driving forwards; impelling. **3.** *Zoology.* Capable of being thrust outwards; protrusile. [New Latin *prōjectilis,* from Latin *prō(j)icere,* to throw forth, PROJECT.]

pro·jec·tion (prə-jéksh'n, prō-) *n.* **1.** The act of projecting or state of being projected. **2.** Something that thrusts outwards; a protuberance. **3.** A plan for an anticipated course of action. **4.** A prediction made after all available information has been examined. **5. a.** The process of projecting a filmed image onto a screen or other viewing surface. **b.** The image so projected. **6.** The image of a geometric figure produced by a coordinate mapping. **7.** A system of intersecting lines, such as the grid of a map, on which part or all of the globe or the celestial sphere may be represented as a plane surface. See **map projection. 8.** *Psychology.* The naive or unconscious attribution of one's own feelings, attitudes, or desires to others. **—pro·jec·tion·al** *adj.*

pro·jec·tion·ist (prə-jéksh'n-ist, prō-) *n.* **1.** One who operates a film projector. **2.** A map-maker.

pro·jec·tive (prə-jéktiv, prō-) *adj. Mathematics.* **1.** Pertaining to or made by projection. **2.** Extending outwards; projecting. **3.** Designating a property of a geometric figure that does not vary when the figure undergoes projection. **—pro·jec·tive·ly** *adv.*

projective geometry *n.* The study of geometric properties that are invariant under projection.

projective test *n.* A psychological test in which a subject's responses to relatively unstructured standard stimuli, such as a series of abstract patterns or incomplete sentences, are analysed to obtain information about the personality or sometimes intelligence.

pro·jec·tor (prə-jéktər, prō-) *n.* **1.** A machine for projecting an image onto a screen. **2.** A device for projecting a beam of light. **3.** One who devises plans or projects.

pro·kar·y·ote, pro·car·y·ote (prō-kárri-ōt) *n.* Any organism in which the genetic material is not bounded by a nuclear membrane but exists free in the cytoplasm. Prokaryotes consist mainly of the bacteria and blue-green algae. Compare **eukaryote.** [PRO- + KARYO- + *-ote,* as in *zygote.*] **—pro·kar·y·o·tic** (-óttik) *adj.*

Pro·kof·i·ev (prə-kóffi-ef), **Sergei Sergeyevich** (1891–1953). Russian composer. He wrote seven symphonies, several operas, ballets, and concertos. His glittering, inventive compositions include the opera *The Love of Three Oranges.* In 1948 his works were denounced as undemocratic by the Soviet government.

pro·lac·tin (prō-láktin) *n.* A pituitary hormone that, in mammals, stimulates and controls the secretion of milk, and stimulates the production of progesterone by the corpus luteum in the ovary. Also called "luteotrophic hormone". [PRO- (forth) + LACT(O)- + -IN.]

pro·la·mine (prṓ-ləm-in, prō-lám-, -een) *n.* Also **pro·la·min** (-in). Any of a class of simple proteins found in wheat, rye, and other grains. [PROL(INE) + AM(MONIA) + -INE.]

pro·lapse (prō-láps, prṓ-láps) *intr.v.* **-lapsed, -lapsing, -lapses.** *Medicine.* To fall or slip out of place.
∼n. Also **pro·lap·sus** (prō-lápsəss). *Medicine.* The falling down or slipping out of place of an organ or part, such as the uterus. [Late Latin *prōlapsus,* a falling, from Latin, past participle of *prōlābī,* to fall or slip down : *prō-,* forward, down + *lābī,* to fall, slip.]

pro·late (prṓ-layt, prō-láyt) *adj.* Designating the shape of a solid, especially of a spheroid, having its polar axis longer than its equatorial diameter; cigar-shaped. Compare **oblate.** [Latin *prōlātus,* stretched out (used as past participle of *prōferre,* to bring forward, stretch out) : *prō-,* forth + *-lātus,* "carried".] **—pro·late·ly** *adv.* **—pro·late·ness** *n.*

pro·la·tive (prō-láy-tiv, prṓlə-) *adj. Grammar.* Serving to extend or complete predication, as an infinitive verb does when joined without *to* to an auxiliary verb. For example, the word *hope* in *we must hope* is a prolative verb or infinitive. [PROLAT(E) + -IVE.]

prole (prōl) *n. Informal.* A member of the working class; a proletarian. Used derogatorily. [Shortened from PROLETARIAN; popularised by George Orwell's novel *1984.*]

pro·leg (prṓ-leg) *n.* Any of the stubby limbs on the abdominal segments of insect larvae. [PRO- (for, serving as) + LEG.]

pro·le·gom·e·non (prṓ-le-gómmi-nən, -li-, -non) *n., pl.* **-na** (-nə). A critical introduction, usually to a scholarly text. [Greek, from the present passive participle of *prolegein,* to say beforehand : *pro-,* before + *legein,* to say.] **—pro·le·gom·e·nous** *adj.*

pro·lep·sis (prō-lépsiss, -lép-) *n., pl.* **-ses** (-seez). **1.** The rhetorical device of anticipating and answering an objection or argument before one's opponent has put it forward. **2.** The use of a descriptive word in anticipation of the act or circumstances that would make it applicable. In the sentence *That gambler is a dead man: Sam Sneak has sworn to get him,* the use of the adjective *dead* indicates a prolepsis. [Late Latin, rhetorical anticipation, from Greek *prolēpsis,* from *prolambanein,* to take beforehand, anticipate : *prō-,* before + *lambanein,* to take.] **—pro·lep·tic** (-tik), **pro·lep·ti·cal** *adj.*

pro·le·tar·i·an (prṓ-li-táir-i-ən, -le-, -lə-) *adj.* Of, pertaining to, or characteristic of the proletariat.
∼n. A member of the proletariat. [Latin *prōlētārius,* Roman citizen of the lowest class (who serves the state only by producing offspring), from *prōlēs,* offspring.] **—pro·le·tar·i·an·ism** *n.*

pro·le·tar·i·at (prō-li-táir-i-ət, -le-, -lə-, -at) *n.* **1. a.** The class of industrial wage earners who, possessing neither capital nor means of production, must earn their living by manual labour. **b.** The poorest class of working people. **2.** In ancient Rome, the people who possessed no property, constituting the lowest class of citizens. [French *prolétariat,* from Latin *prōlētārius,* PROLETARIAN.]

pro·lif·er·ate (prō-líffə-rayt, prə-) *v.* **-ated, -ating, -ates.** *—intr.* **1.** To reproduce or produce new growth or parts rapidly and repeatedly: *cells proliferating.* **2.** To increase or spread at a rapid rate. *—tr.* To cause to grow or increase rapidly. [French *prolifère,* from Medieval Latin *prōlifer,* producing offspring, PROLIFEROUS.] **—pro·lif·er·a·tion** (-ráysh'n) *n.* **—pro·lif·er·a·tive** (-rətiv, -raytiv) *adj.*

pro·lif·er·ous (prō-líffərəss, prə-) *adj.* **1.** *Biology.* Reproducing freely by means of buds and side branches. **2.** *Botany.* Freely producing buds or offshoots, sometimes from abnormal places. [Medieval Latin *prōlifer,* producing offspring : Latin *prōlēs,* offspring + -FEROUS.]

pro·lif·ic (prō-líffik, prə-) *adj.* **1.** Producing offspring or fruit in great abundance; fertile. **2.** Producing abundant works or results.

[Medieval Latin *prōlificus* : Latin *prōlēs,* offspring + *-ficus,* from *facere,* to make.] —**pro·lif·i·cal·ly** *adv.*

pro·line (prō-leen, -lin) *n.* An amino acid, $C_5H_9O_2N$, found in proteins. [German *Prolin* : P(YR)ROL(E) + -INE.]

pro·lix (prō-liks, prō-liks) *adj.* **1.** Wordy and tedious. **2.** Tending to speak or write at great length; long-winded. [Middle English, from Old French *prolixe,* from Latin *prōlixus,* "poured forth", extended, abundant : *prō,* forth + *-lixus,* from *liquēre,* to be liquid.] —**pro·lix·i·ty** (prō-líksəti, prə-) *n.* —**pro·lix·ly** *adv.*

pro·loc·u·tor (prō-lóckewtər) *n.* A presiding officer or chairman, especially of the lower house of a convocation in the Anglican Church. [Middle English, from Latin *prōlocūtor,* "one who speaks out", advocate, from *prōloquī,* to speak out, plead : *prō-,* forth + *loquī,* to speak.]

pro·logue, *U.S.* **pro·log** (prō-log, *rarely* -lōg || *U.S. also* -lawg) *n.* **1.** The lines introducing a discourse or play. **2.** The character or actor who delivers these lines. **3.** An introductory act or event.
~*tr.v.* **prologued** or *U.S.* **prologed, -loguing** or *U.S.* **-loging, -logues** or *U.S.* **-logs.** To add a prologue to. [Middle English *prolog,* from Old French *prolog(u)e,* from Latin *prologus,* from Greek *prologos,* (speaker of) a prologue, : *pro-,* before + *legein,* to speak.]

pro·logu·ise, pro·logu·ize (prō-lo-gīz; *rarely* prō-, -lō- || *U.S. also* -law-) *intr.v.* **-ised, -ising, -ises.** Also *U.S.* **pro·log·ize** (*sometimes* -jīz). To write or deliver a prologue. —**pro·logu·is·er** *n.*

pro·long (prō-lóng, prə- || *U.S. also* -láwng) *tr.v.* **-longed, -longing, -longs.** Also **pro·lon·gate** (prō-long-gayt, prə- || *chiefly U.S.* prə-lóng-gayt, prō-, -láwng-), **-gated, -gating, -gates. 1.** To lengthen in duration; protract. **2.** To lengthen in extent. [Middle English *prolongen,* from Old French *prolonguer,* from Late Latin *prōlongāre* : Latin *prō-,* out, extending + *longus,* LONG.] —**pro·lon·ga·tion** (prō-long-gáysh'n, prō- || -lawng-) *n.*
Synonyms: *prolong, protract, extend.*

pro·lu·sion (prō-lōō-zh'n, prə-, -lēw-) *n.* **1.** A preliminary exercise in writing. **2.** An essay written as a preface to a more detailed work. [Latin *prōlūsiō* (stem *prōlūsiōn-*), from *prōlūdere* (past participle *prōlūsus*), to play or practise beforehand : *prō-,* before + *lūdere,* to play.] —**pro·lu·so·ry** (-sə-ri, -zə-) *adj.*

prom (prom) *n.* **1.** *British Informal.* **a.** A promenade. **b.** A promenade concert. **2.** *U.S.* A ball or formal dance held for a high-school or college class. [Short for PROMENADE.]

prom. promontory.

prom·e·nade (prómmə-naád, -naad; -náyd *for noun sense 4 and intransitive verb sense 2*) *n.* **1.** A leisurely walk, especially one taken in a public place as a social activity. **2.** A public place for such walking, especially along the seafront. In this sense, also informally called "prom". **3. a.** A formal ball. **b.** A formal march by the guests at the opening of a ball. **4.** A march executed between the figures of a square dance or country dance.
~*v.* **promenaded, -nading, -nades.** —*intr.* **1.** To go on a leisurely walk. **2.** To execute a promenade in square or country dancing. —*tr.* **1.** To take a promenade along or through. **2.** To take or display on or as if on a promenade. [French, from *se promener,* to take a walk, from Late Latin *prōmināre,* to drive forward : *prō-,* forward + *mināre,* to drive, from Latin *minārī,* to threaten, from *minae,* threats.]

promenade concert *n. Chiefly British.* A concert in which part of the audience stands rather than sits. Also informally called "prom".

promenade deck *n.* The upper deck or a section of the upper deck on a passenger ship where the passengers can promenade.

prom·e·nad·er (prómmə-naádər; *for sense 1 also* -náydər) *n.* **1.** One who promenades. **2.** One attending a promenade concert.

Pro·me·the·an (prə-meéthi-ən, prō-) *adj.* **1.** Pertaining to or suggestive of Prometheus. **2.** Boldly creative; life-bringing.
~*n.* One who is Promethean in manner or actions.

Pro·me·theus (prə-meé-thewss, prō, -thi-əss || -thōōss). *Greek Mythology.* A Titan who stole fire from the gods to give to humankind and was punished by being chained to a rock where a vulture gnawed at his liver.

pro·me·thi·um (prə-meéthi-əm, prō-) *n. Symbol* **Pm** A radioactive rare-earth element prepared by fission of uranium or by neutron bombardment of neodymium, having 14 isotopes with mass numbers ranging from 140 to 154, and used as a source of beta rays. Atomic number 61, melting point 1,080°C, boiling point 2,460°C, valency 3. [New Latin, after PROMETHEUS (referring to the fire of a nuclear furnace).]

prom·i·nence (prómmi-nənss) *n.* Also **prom·i·nen·cy** (-nən-si). **1.** The condition or quality of being prominent. **2.** Something that is prominent; a projection. **3.** Emphasis or importance. **4.** *Astronomy.* A tonguelike cloud of luminous gas rising from the sun's surface, visible as part of the corona during a total solar eclipse.

prom·i·nent (prómminənt) *adj.* **1.** Immediately noticeable; conspicuous. **2.** Widely known; eminent. **3.** Projecting outwards; protuberant. [Latin *prōminēns* (stem *prōminent-*), present participle of *prōminēre,* to jut out, project : *prō-,* forth + *-minēre,* to jut.] —**prom·i·nent·ly** *adv.*

prom·is·cu·i·ty (próssmiss-kéw-əti || prō-miss-) *n., pl.* **-ties. 1.** The state or character of being promiscuous. **2.** Promiscuous sexual intercourse. **3.** An indiscriminate mixture; a hotchpotch.

pro·mis·cu·ous (prə-mískew-əss || prō-) *adj.* **1.** Characterised by casual association with many sexual partners. **2.** Consisting of diverse and unrelated parts or individuals; confused. **3.** Lacking standards of selection; indiscriminate. **4.** Casual; random. [Latin *prōmiscuus,* mixed : *prō-* (intensifier), thoroughly + *miscēre,* to

mix.] —**pro·mis·cu·ous·ly** *adv.* —**pro·mis·cu·ous·ness** *n.*

prom·ise (prómmiss) *n.* **1.** A declaration giving assurance that one will or will not do something; a vow. **2.** Something which one has undertaken to give or perform. **3.** Indication of future excellence or success: *a child with great promise.*
~*v.* **promised, -ising, -ises.** —*tr.* **1.** To pledge or offer assurance. Followed by an infinitive or clause. **2.** To make a promise of; pledge oneself to give. **3.** To afford a basis for expecting: *That clear sky promises a hot afternoon.* —*intr.* **1.** To make a promise. **2.** To afford a basis for expectation. Often used with *well* or *fair.* [Middle English *promys(se),* from Latin *prōmissum,* from the neuter past participle of *prōmittere,* "to send forth", promise : *prō-,* forth + *mittere,* to let go, send.] —**prom·is·er** *n.*

Promised Land *n.* **1.** The land of Canaan, promised to Abraham and his descendants. Genesis 12:7. **2.** *Small* **p.,** *small* **l.** Any place or time of anticipated happiness.

prom·is·ee (prómmiss-eé) *n. Law.* An individual to whom a promise is made.

prom·is·ing (prómmiss-ing) *adj.* Likely to develop in a desirable or successful way. —**prom·is·ing·ly** *adv.*

prom·i·sor (prómmiss-ór) *n. Law.* An individual who makes a promise.

prom·is·so·ry (prómmiss-əri, prə-míss-) *adj.* **1.** Containing, involving, or having the nature of a promise. **2.** *Insurance.* Of or designating the preliminary undertakings or guarantees indicating how the provisions of an insurance contract will be carried out after it is signed. [Medieval Latin *prōmissōrius,* from Latin *prōmissor,* one who promises, from *prōmittere,* to PROMISE.]

promissory note *n. Abbr.* **p.n., P/N** A written promise to pay or repay a specified sum of money at a stated time or on demand. Also called "note", "note of hand".

prom·mer (prómmər) *n. British Informal.* One attending a promenade concert. [From PROM.]

pro·mo (prōmō) *n. Informal.* An advertising or publicity campaign. Also used adjectivally: *promo material.* [Shortened from PROMOTION or PROMOTIONAL.]

prom·on·to·ry (prómmən-tri, -təri) *n., pl.* **-ries.** *Abbr.* **prom. 1.** A high ridge of land or rock jutting out into a sea or other expanse of water. **2.** *Anatomy.* A projecting bodily part. [Medieval Latin *prōmontōrium,* alteration of Latin *prōmunturium* : probably from *prō-,* forward + *mōns* (stem *mont-*), mountain.]

pro·mote (prə-mōt || prō-) *tr.v.* **-moted, -moting, -motes. 1. a.** To raise to a more important or responsible job or rank. **b.** *Chiefly U.S.* To advance (a student) to the next, higher course or class. **2.** To contribute to the progress or growth of; further. **3.** To urge the adoption of; advocate. **4.** To attempt to sell or popularise by advertising or by securing financial support. —See Synonyms at **advance.** [Middle English *promoten,* from Latin *prōmovēre* (past participle *prōmōtus*), to move forward, advance : *prō-,* forward, onwards + *movēre,* to move.]

pro·mot·er (prə-mōtər || prō-) *n.* **1.** An active supporter; an advocate. **2.** A finance and publicity organiser, as of a boxing match. **3.** *Chemistry.* A substance added to a catalyst in small amounts to increase its activity.

Promoter of the Faith *n. Roman Catholic Church.* The official name for a **devil's advocate** (see).

pro·mo·tion (prə-mōsh'n || prō-) *n.* **1.** The act of promoting. **2.** An advancement in rank or responsibility. **3.** Encouragement; furtherance. **4. a.** Advertising or other publicity. **b.** An advertising or publicity campaign. —**pro·mo·tion·al** *adj.* —**pro·mo·tion·al·ly** *adv.*

pro·mo·tive (prə-mōtiv || prō-) *adj.* Tending to promote.

prompt (prompt) *adj.* **1.** On time; punctual. **2.** Done without delay. **3.** Ready for action; quick to respond.
~*adv.* Exactly on time: *Come at two o'clock prompt.*
~*tr.v.* **prompted, prompting, prompts. 1.** To press into action; incite. **2.** To give rise to; inspire. **3.** To assist with a reminder; remind. **4.** In theatrical productions, to give a cue to (a performer who has forgotten his lines).
~*n.* **1. a.** The act of prompting or giving a cue. **b.** The information suggested; a reminder or cue. **2.** A theatrical prompter. **3.** *Finance.* **a.** A prompt note. **b.** The time limit stipulated in a prompt note. [Middle English, from Old French, from Latin *promptus,* "brought to light", "visible", hence, at hand, ready, prompt, from the past participle of *prōmere,* to bring forth, make manifest : *prō-,* forth + *emere,* to take.] —**prompt·i·tude, prompt·ness** *n.* —**prompt·ly** *adv.*

prompt·book (prómpt-bŏŏk- || -bōŏk) *n.* An annotated script used by a theatre prompter.

prompt·er (prómptər) *n.* **1.** One who prompts. **2.** One who gives cues to actors.

prompt neutron *n.* A neutron instantaneously emitted (within 10^{-8} second) in nuclear fission. Compare **delayed neutron.**

prompt note *n.* A notice sent to the purchaser of goods reminding him of the amount due to the seller and the date on which it is due. Also called "prompt".

prompt side *n. Abbr.* **P.S.** The side of the stage on which the prompter sits: in Britain, to the left of an actor facing the audience, in the United States, to the right.

prom·ul·gate (próm-'l-gayt, -mul- || prō-, *U.S. also* prō-múl-) *tr.v.* **-gated, -gating, -gates. 1.** To make known (a decree, law, or doctrine) by public declaration; announce officially. **2.** To put (a law) into effect by formal public announcement. [Latin *prōmulgāre* : *prō-,* forth + *mulgēre,* to milk, cause to emerge.] —**prom·ul·ga·tion** (-gáysh'n) *n.* —**prom·ul·ga·tor** (-gaytər) *n.*

pro·my·ce·li·um (prō-mī-séeli-əm) n., pl. **-lia** (-ə). Botany. A germ tube produced by certain fungal spores.

pron. 1. pronominal; pronoun. **2.** pronounced; pronunciation.

pro·nate (prō-náyt, prónayt) v. **-nated, -nating, -nates.** —tr. v. To turn (the palm of the hand or inner surface of a limb) downwards or backwards. —intr. v. To become pronated. [Late Latin prōnāre, to bend forward, from Latin prōnus, PRONE.] —**pro·na·tion** (-náysh'n) n.

pro·na·tor (prō-náytər ‖ U.S. prō-naytər) n. An arm or limb muscle that effects pronation.

prone (prōn) adj. **1.** Lying with the front or face downwards; prostrate. **2.** Tending or liable: prone to mischief. Often used in combination: accident-prone. [Middle English, from Latin prōnus, "bending" or "leaning forward".] —**prone·ly** adv. —**prone·ness** n.

Usage: prone, supine, prostrate. Prone always means lying face downwards. Supine also means lying down, but always on one's back. Prostrate can mean lying down in either position, and suggests placing oneself, being thrown, or collapsing into this position..

pro·neph·ros (prō-néf-ross, prō-, -rəss) n., pl. **-roi** (-roy) or **-ra** (-rə). A primitive kidney that disappears early in the embryonic development of higher vertebrates. [New Latin : Greek pro-, before + nephros, kidney.] —**pro·neph·ric** (-rik) adj.

prong (prong ‖ U.S. also prawng) n. **1.** A sharply pointed part of a tool or instrument, such as a tine of a fork. **2.** Any sharply pointed projection. **3.** Anything that can be used in combination with something else to attack an enemy or tackle a problem, such as a unit of troops or a policy: the three prongs of our attack on inflation. —tr.v. **pronged, pronging, prongs.** To pierce with a prong. [Middle English pronge, prange, forked instrument; perhaps akin to Middle Low German prange, pinching instrument, from Germanic prang- (unattested), pinch.]

pronged (prongd ‖ prawngd) adj. **1.** Having a specified number of prongs. **2.** Coming from a specified number of directions at once.

prong·horn (próng-hawrn ‖ práwng-) n., pl. **-horns** or collectively **pronghorn.** A small deer, Antilocapra americana, resembling an antelope and having small forked horns, found on North American plains. Also called "prongbuck," "pronghorn antelope".

pro·nom·i·nal (prō-nómmin'l, prə-) adj. Abbr. **pron., pronom. 1.** Of, pertaining to, or functioning as a pronoun. **2.** Resembling a pronoun, as by specifying a person, place, or thing, while functioning primarily as another part of speech. His in his choice is a pronominal adjective. [Late Latin prōnōminālis, from Latin prōnōmen, PRONOUN.] —**pro·nom·i·nal·ly** adv.

pro·nom·i·nal·ise, pro·nom·i·nal·ize (prō-nómmin'l-z, prə-) tr.v. **-ised, -ising, -ises.** To treat as or make into a pronoun. —**pro·nom·i·nal·i·sa·tion** (-ī-záysh'n ‖ U.S. -i-) n.

pro·noun (prṓ-nown ‖ West Indies also -nung) n. Abbr. **pron., pr.** Any of a class of words that function as substitutes for nouns or noun phrases and denote persons or things asked for, previously specified, or understood from the context. [Middle English pronom, from Latin prōnōmen : prō-, in place of + nōmen, name.]

pro·nounce (prə-nównss ‖ prō-; West Indies also -núngss) v. **-nounced, -nouncing, -nounces.** —tr. **1. a.** To articulate (a word or speech sound). **b.** To articulate in the approved manner. **2.** To transcribe (a word) in phonetic symbols. **3.** To state officially and formally; declare. **4.** To declare to be in a specified condition: The doctor pronounced the victim dead. **5.** To deliver (a verdict or opinion, for example). —intr. **1.** To declare one's opinion or make a pronouncement. Used with on. **2.** To articulate words. [Middle English pronuncen, pronouncen, from Old French prononcier, from Latin prōnūntiāre, to speak in public, declare : prō-, forth, in public + nuntiāre, to declare, from nuntius, message, messenger.] —**pro·nounce·a·ble** adj. —**pro·nounc·er** n.

pro·nounced (prə-nównst ‖ prō-; West Indies also -núngst) adj. Abbr. **pron. 1.** Spoken; voiced. **2.** Distinct; strongly marked. —**pro·nounced·ly** (-nównst-li, -nówn-sid) adv. —**pro·nounced·ness** n.

pro·nounce·ment (prə-nównss-mənt ‖ prō-; West Indies also -núngss-) n. **1.** A formal declaration. **2.** An authoritative statement.

pron·to (próntō) adv. Informal. Without delay; quickly. [Spanish, from Latin promptus, PROMPT.]

pro·nu·cle·us (prō-néw-kli-əss, prō- ‖ -nṓṓ-) n., pl. **-clei** (-ī). The haploid nucleus of a sperm or egg prior to fusion of the nuclei in fertilisation. —**pro·nu·cle·ar** adj.

pro·nun·ci·a·men·to (prə-nún-si-ə-méntō ‖ prō-, -nṓṓn-, -thi-) n., pl. **-tos. 1.** An edict or proclamation, especially when announcing a coup d'état. **2.** Any authoritarian pronouncement. [Spanish.]

pro·nun·ci·a·tion (prə-nún-si-áysh'n ‖ prō-, -nówn-) n. Abbr. **pron. 1.** The act or manner or an instance of articulating speech. **2.** The approved manner of pronouncing a particular word or sound. **3.** A phonetic transcription of a word. —**pro·nun·ci·a·tion·al** adj.

pro·oes·trus (prō-éess-trəss, prō- ‖ U.S. -éss-) n. The period of the oestrous cycle immediately before oestrus.

proof (prṓof ‖ prṓof) n. **1.** The evidence establishing the validity of a given assertion. **2.** Conclusive demonstration of something. **3.** The testing or validation of something by experiment or trial. **4.** Archaic. Proven impenetrability. **5.** Law. The evidence used to determine the verdict or judgment in a case. **6.** In Scots law, trial before a judge rather than a jury. **7.** The validation of a proposition by application of specified rules, as of induction or deduction, to assumptions, axioms, and sequentially derived conclusions. **8.** The strength of an alcoholic drink with reference to **proof spirit** (see). **9.** Printing. A trial sheet of printed material that is checked against the original version and on which corrections are made. Also called

"proof sheet". **10.** In engraving, a trial impression of a plate, stone, or block. **11.** In photography, a trial print.

~adj. **1.** Fully or successfully resistant; impervious. Used with against or in combination: proof against fire; waterproof. **2.** Of standard alcoholic strength. **3.** Used in proving or making corrections. ~v. **proofed, proofing, proofs.** —tr. **1.** To make or run off (a printed or engraved proof). **2.** To proofread (copy). **3.** To make resistant or impervious. —intr. To proofread. [Middle English pre(o)ve, prof, prove, from Old French pre(o)ve, from Late Latin proba, from Latin probāre, to test, PROVE.]

proof·read (prṓof-reed ‖ prṓof-) v. **-read** (-red), **-reading, -reads.** —tr. To read (copy or a printer's proof) against the original typescript, printed version, or manuscript in order to check that they are correct. —intr. To correct a printer's proof while reading against the original version. —**proof·read·er** n.

proof spirit n. An alcohol-water mixture or an alcoholic drink containing 49.28 per cent ethanol by weight or 57.1 per cent by volume and having a relative density of 0.92 at 15.56°C (60°F). In the United States, proof spirit contains 50 per cent ethanol by volume at 15.56°C (60°F).

prop[1] (prop) n. **1.** Anything used to support or shore something up. **2.** A person or thing serving as a support or stay. **3. a.** In Rugby football, either of the two forwards who play on the left or right of the front row of the scrum. **b.** The position of such a player. In both senses, also called "prop forward". —tr.v. **propped, propping, props. 1.** To keep from falling; support, especially by means of a rigid object. Often used with up. **2.** To lean or rest for support. Usually used with against. [Middle English proppe, probably from Middle Dutch proppe†, vine-prop, stopper.]

prop[2] n. A stage **property** (see).

prop[3] n. Informal. A propeller.

prop- comb. form. Chemistry. Indicates derivation from propionic acid; for example, propane. [From PROPIONIC (ACID).]

prop. 1. proper; properly. **2.** property. **3.** proposition. **4.** proprietary; proprietor.

pro·pae·deu·tic (prō-pee-déw-tik ‖ -pi-, -dṓṓ-) adj. Providing introductory instruction. ~n. Often plural. Preparatory instruction. [Greek propaideuein, to teach beforehand : pro-, before + paideuein, to rear or educate, from pais (stem paid-), child.]

prop·a·ga·ble (próppəgəb'l) adj. Capable of being propagated.

prop·a·gan·da (próppə-gándə) n. **1.** The systematic propagation or discrediting of a given doctrine or cause by circulating polemical material, such as posters or leaflets. **2.** Material disseminated by the champions or opponents of a doctrine or course. [From PROPAGANDA FIDE.] —**prop·a·gan·dism** n. —**prop·a·gan·dist** n. —**prop·a·gan·dis·tic** (-gan-dístik) adj. —**prop·a·gan·dis·ti·cal·ly** adv.

Prop·a·gan·da Fi·de (próppə-gándə féeday) n. Roman Catholic Church. The Congregation of the Roman Curia that has authority in the matters of preaching the gospel and of administering Church missions. Also called "Propaganda." [Italian, short for the New Latin title Sacra Congregatio de Propaganda Fide, Sacred Congregation for Propagating the Faith, from Latin prōpāgandus, gerundive of prōpāgāre, to PROPAGATE.]

prop·a·gan·dise, prop·a·gan·dize (próppə-gánd-īz) v. **-dised, -dising, -dises.** —tr. **1.** To spread (a doctrine or opinion) by means of propaganda. **2.** To subject (a person or group of persons) to propaganda. —intr. To spread propaganda.

prop·a·gate (próppə-gayt) v. **-gated, -gating, -gates.** —tr. **1.** To cause (animals) to breed. **2.** To breed (offspring). **3.** To multiply (plants) by cuttings, graftings, or the like. **4.** To transmit (characteristics) from one generation to another. **5.** To make known; promote or spread. **6.** Physics. To cause (a wave, for example) to move through a medium; transmit. —intr. **1.** Physics. To move through a medium. **2.** To breed or multiply. [Latin prōpāgāre, to propagate (plants) by means of slips, from prōpāgo, prōpāgēs, slip, shoot, offspring : prō, forth + pāgo, from pangere, to layer.] —**prop·a·ga·tive** (-gətiv, -gaytiv) adj.

prop·a·ga·tion (próppə-gáysh'n) n. **1.** Increase or spread, as by natural reproduction. **2.** Dissemination, as of a belief: propagation of the Gospel. —**prop·a·ga·tion·al** adj.

prop·a·ga·tor (próppə-gaytər) n. One that propagates; especially, a tray with a clear glass or plastic cover containing soil in which seeds or cuttings are raised.

prop·a·gule (próppə-gewl) n. A plant structure, such as a bud, bulb, or tuber, that becomes detached from the parent plant and develops into a new individual. [From PROPAGATE + -ULE.]

pro·pane (prṓ-payn) n. A colourless alkane gas, C_3H_8, found in natural gas and petroleum, and used as fuel. [PROP- + -ANE.]

pro·pane-di·ol (prō-payn-dī-ol ‖ -ōl) n. Chemistry. **Propylene glycol** (see).

pro·pa·no·ic ac·id (prōpə-nṓ-ik) n. Chemistry. **Propionic acid** (see). [PROPANE + -IC.]

pro·pa·nol (prōpə-nol ‖ -nōl) n. A colourless, liquid alcohol that occurs in two isomeric forms, 1-propanol, $CH_3CH_2CH_2OH$, and 2-propanol, $CH_3CHOHCH_3$. Both forms are used as solvents. Also called "propyl alcohol". [PROPAN(E) + -OL.]

pro·pa·none (prōpə-nōn) n. Chemistry. An organic ketone, **acetone** (see).

pro·par·ox·y·tone (prō-pə-róksi-tōn, -pa-, -tən) adj. Having an acute accent on the antepenult in Classical Greek. ~n. A proparoxytone word. [Greek proparoxutonos : pro-, before + PAROXYTONE.] —**pro·par·ox·y·ton·ic** (-tónnik) adj.

pro pa·tri·a (prō páttri-ə, pa'atri-, -aa). *Latin.* For one's country.

pro·pel (prə-pél ‖ prō-) *tr.v.* **-pelled, -pelling, -pels.** To cause to move or sustain in motion. [Middle English *propellen*, from Latin *prōpellere* : *prō*, forward + *pellere*, to drive.]

pro·pel·lant, pro·pel·lent (prə-péllənt ‖ prō-) *n.* 1. Something that propels or provides thrust, such as an explosive charge or a rocket fuel. 2. The gas used in a domestic aerosol spray. ~*adj.* Serving to propel; propelling.

pro·pel·ler (prə-péllər ‖ prō-) *n.* Any of various related simple machines for propelling aircraft or boats, especially one having radiating blades mounted on a revolving power-driven shaft. Also called "screw", "screw propeller".

propeller shaft *n.* 1. The shaft that drives a propeller. 2. The shaft in a motor vehicle that transmits power from the gearbox to the differential. Also called "prop shaft".

pro·pel·ling pencil (prə-pélling ‖ prō-) *n.* A pencil in which the lead can be retracted, extended, or replaced.

pro·pe·nal (prōpi-nal) *n. Chemistry.* An organic aldehyde, **acrolein** (*see*).

pro·pend (prō-pénd, prə-) *intr.v.* **-pended, -pending, -pends.** *Archaic.* To have a propensity towards. [Latin *prōpendēre*, to hang forward or downwards, be inclined or favourable : *prō-*, forward, down + *pendēre*, to hang.]

pro·pene (prō-peen) *n.* A colourless, flammable alkene gas, C_3H_6, obtained by cracking petroleum and used in organic synthesis. Also called "propylene".

pro·pe·no·ic acid (prō-pee-nō-ik, -pi-) *n. Chemistry.* An organic acid, **acrylic acid** (*see*).

pro·pen·si·ty (prə-pén-səti, prō-) *n., pl.* **-ties.** An innate inclination; a tendency; a bent. [From archaic *propense*, inclined, from Latin *prōpensus*, past participle of *prōpendēre*, to be inclined or favourable, PROPEND.]

prop·er (próppər) *adj. Abbr.* **prop.** 1. Suitable; fitting; appropriate: *the proper moment.* 2. Out-and-out; thorough: *a proper rascal.* 3. Worthy of the name: *take one's medicine like a proper man.* 4. Meeting a requisite standard of competence or validity. 5. a. Within the strict limitation of the term. Used after the noun: *France proper.* b. Rigorously correct; exact. 6. Characteristically belonging to the being or thing in question. Used after the noun and with *to*: *an optical effect proper to fluids.* 7. a. Seemly; decorous in behaviour. b. Displaying exaggerated propriety or gentility. 8. *Mathematics.* Designating a subset of a given set when the latter has at least one element not in the subset. 9. *Ecclesiastical.* Belonging to the proper of the day. —See Synonyms at **fit.** ~*adv.* Thoroughly: *He got told off good and proper.* ~*n. Sometimes capital* **P.** *Ecclesiastical.* 1. The parts of the Mass or Divine Office that vary according to the particular day or feast. 2. An office to be said on an appointed day or feast. Compare **ordinary.** [Middle English *propre*, one's own, distinctive, correct, proper, from Old French, from Latin *proprius*, one's own, personal, particular.] —**prop·er·ly** (*informally also* próppli) *adv.* —**prop·er·ness** *n.*

proper adjective *n.* An adjective formed from a proper noun.

pro·per·din (prō-pérdin) *n.* A natural protein in human blood serum that helps provide immunity to Gram-negative bacteria and viruses. Not in technical usage. [Perhaps PRO- (acting as) + Latin *perdere*, "to give away", squander, hence, to destroy : *per-*, away, to destruction + *dare*, to give + -IN.]

proper fraction *n.* 1. A numerical fraction in which the numerator is less than the denominator; a common fraction that is less than one. 2. A polynomial fraction in which the numerator is of lower degree than the denominator. Compare **improper fraction.**

proper motion *n. Astronomy.* The component of a star's motion in space, relative to the sun, that is perpendicular to the line of sight.

proper noun *n.* A noun designating by name a being or thing without a limiting modifier. Also called "proper name". Compare **common noun.**

prop·er·tied (próppər-tid ‖ -teed) *adj.* Owning land or securities as a principal source of revenue.

prop·er·ty (próppərti) *n., pl.* **-ties.** *Abbr.* **prop.** 1. The right of possession, use, and disposal of something; ownership. 2. A possession, or possessions collectively. 3. Something tangible or intangible to which its owner has legal title. 4. A piece of land, such as that on which a house stands or that used for farming. 5. Any article, except costumes and scenery, used on the set or stage of a film, play, or musical. Also called "prop". 6. a. A characteristic trait or peculiarity. b. A special capability or power; a virtue. c. A quality serving to define or describe an object or substance. d. A characteristic attribute possessed by all members of a class. e. *Logic.* A predicable that is common and peculiar to the whole of a species and is necessarily predicated of its essence without being part of that essence. —See Synonyms at **asset, quality.** [Middle English *propriete*, from Old French *propr(i)ete*, from Latin *proprietās* (stem *proprietāt-*), ownership, peculiarity, from *proprius*, own, particular, PROPER.]

prop forward *n.* A player in Rugby football, a **prop** (*see*).

pro·phage (prō-fayj) *n.* A noninfectious association between a bacterial virus and a bacterium, in which the viral chromosomes link with the bacterial chromosomes but do not cause disruption of the bacterial cell or promote replication of the virus itself. [PRO- (before) + -PHAGE.]

pro·phase (prō-fayz) *n. Biology.* The first stage in cell division in meiosis and mitosis, during which chromosomes become visible and the nuclear membrane begins to disintegrate. See **diakinesis, diplotene, leptotene, pachytene, zygotene.**

proph·e·cy (próffə-si, próffi-) *n., pl.* **-cies.** 1. A prediction. 2. a. The inspired utterance of a prophet, viewed as a declaration of divine will. b. Such a revelation transmitted orally or in writing. c. The quality or activity of receiving and transmitting such relevations. [Middle English *propheci(e), prophesye*, from Old French *profecie, prophecie*, from Latin *prophētīa*, from Greek *prophēteia*, from *prophētēs*, PROPHET.]

Usage: Prophecy and *prophesy* are sometimes confused in spelling. *Prophecy* is the noun; *prophesy* the verb. Their pronunciations are also different.

proph·e·sy (próffi-sī, próffə-) *v.* **-sied, -sying, -sies.** —*tr.* 1. To reveal by divine inspiration. 2. To predict. 3. To prefigure; foreshow. —*intr.* 1. To reveal the will of God. 2. To predict the future. 3. To speak as a prophet. —See Synonyms at **foretell.** —See Usage note at **prophecy,** [Middle English *prophecien*, from Old French *prophecier*, from *prophecie*, PROPHECY.] —**proph·e·si·er** *n.*

proph·et (próffit) *n.* 1. A person who speaks by divine inspiration or as the interpreter through whom divine will is expressed. 2. One who predicts the future. 3. The chief spokesman of a cause. —**the Prophet.** 1. *Islam.* Muhammad. 2. In the Mormon Church, Joseph Smith. —**the Prophets.** The prophetic writings of the Hebrew Scriptures; the second main division of the Old Testament. [Middle English *prophet(e), profete*, from Old French, from Latin *prophēta*, from Greek *prophētēs*, "one who speaks beforehand" : *pro-*, before + *-phētēs*, "speaker", from *phanai*, to say.]

proph·et·ess (próffit-iss, -ess) *n.* A female prophet.

pro·phet·ic (prə-féttik, prō-) *adj.* Also **pro·phet·i·cal** (-'l). 1. Of or belonging to a prophet or prophecy. 2. Of the nature of prophecy. —**pro·phet·i·cal·ly** *adv.* —**pro·phet·i·cal·ness** *n.*

pro·phy·lac·tic (próffi-láktik ‖ *chiefly U.S.* prōfi-) *adj.* Acting to defend against or prevent something, especially disease; protective. ~*n.* 1. A prophylactic medicine, device, or measure. 2. Something intended as a precaution. 3. *Chiefly U.S.* Any contraceptive device, especially a condom. [Greek *prophulaktikos*, from *prophulassein*, to stand on guard before (a place), take precautions against : *pro-*, before + *phulassein*, to guard, protect, from *phulax*, a guard.] —**pro·phy·lac·ti·cal·ly** *adv.*

pro·phy·lax·is (próffi-lák-siss ‖ *chiefly U.S.* prōfi-) *n., pl.* **-laxes** (-seez). The prevention of or protective treatment for disease. [New Latin, from Greek *prophulaktikos*, PROPHYLACTIC.]

pro·pin·qui·ty (prə-pingkwəti, prō-, pro-) *n.* 1. Nearness in place or time; proximity. 2. Kinship. 3. Similarity in nature. [Middle English *propinquite*, from Latin *propinquitās* (stem *propinquitāt-*), from *propinquus*, near.]

pro·pi·o·nate (prōpi-ə-nayt) *n.* A salt or ester of propionic acid. [PROPION(IC ACID) + -ATE.]

pro·pi·on·ic acid (prōpi-ónnik) *n.* A fatty acid, $CH_3CH_2CO_2H$, prepared synthetically and used in a salt form as a mould inhibitor in bread. Also called "propanoic acid". [French *propionique* : Greek *pro-*, before, first (because this acid is first in order among the fatty acids) + *piōn*, fat + -IC.]

pro·pi·ti·ate (prə-píshi-ayt, prō-) *tr.v.* **-ated, -ating, -ates.** To conciliate (an offended power); appease. [Latin *propitiāre*, from *propitius*, PROPITIOUS.] —**pro·pi·ti·a·ble** *adj.* —**pro·pi·ti·at·ing·ly** *adv.* —**pro·pi·ti·a·tive** (-ətiv, -aytiv) *adj.* —**pro·pi·ti·a·tor** (-aytər) *n.*

pro·pi·ti·a·tion (prə-pishi-áysh'n, prō-) *n.* 1. The act of propitiating. 2. Something that propitiates; especially, an offering to a god.

pro·pi·ti·a·to·ry (prə-pishi-ətri, prō-, -pish-, -ətəri) *adj.* Of or offered in propitiation; conciliatory. ~*n., pl.* **propitiatories.** In ancient Jewish ceremony, the **mercy seat** (*see*). —**pro·pi·ti·a·to·ri·ly** *adv.*

pro·pi·tious (prə-píshəss ‖ prō-) *adj.* 1. Presenting favourable circumstances; auspicious. 2. Kindly; gracious. —See Synonyms at **favourable.** [Middle English *propycyous*, from Old French *propicius*, from Latin *propitius*, favourable, kind.] —**pro·pi·tious·ly** *adv.* —**pro·pi·tious·ness** *n.*

prop·jet (próp-jet) *n.* A **turboprop** (*see*).

prop·o·lis (próppəliss) *n.* A resinous substance used by bees in making their hives. [Latin, from Greek, suburb, hence (unexplained sense development) bee glue : *pro-*, before, beyond + *polis*, city.]

pro·po·nent (prə-pōnənt ‖ prō-) *n.* 1. One who argues in support of something; an advocate. 2. *Law.* A person who applies for probate of a will. [Latin *prōpōnēns* (stem *prōpōnent-*), present participle of *prōpōnere*, to PROPOSE.]

pro·por·tion (prə-pór-sh'n ‖ prō-, -pór-) *n.* 1. A part considered in relation to the whole. 2. A relationship between things or parts of things with respect to comparative magnitude, quantity, or degree. 3. A relationship between quantities, such that if one varies, another varies in a manner dependent on the first; a ratio. 4. Harmonious relationship; symmetry. 5. *Usually plural.* Dimensions; size: *He has the proportions of a giant.* 6. *Mathematics.* A relationship of equality between two ratios. Four quantities, *a, b, c, d,* are said to be in proportion if $a/b = c/d$. ~*tr.v.* **proportioned, -tioning, -tions.** 1. To adjust so that proper relations between parts are attained. 2. To adjust in degree, quantity, or other measure, in relation to something else. [Middle English *proporcioun*, from Old French *proporcion*, from Latin *prōportiō* (stem *prōportiōn-*) (translation of Greek *analogia*, analogy), from the phrase *prō portiōne*, "for the share of", proportionally : *prō*, for + *portiō*, share, portion.] —**pro·por·tion·a·ble** *adj.* —**pro·por·tion·a·**

bly *adv.* —**pro·por·tion·er** *n.* —**pro·por·tion·ment** *n.*
Synonyms: *proportion, harmony, symmetry, balance.*
pro·por·tion·al (prə-pór-sh'n'l ‖ prō-, -pór-) *adj.* **1.** Forming a relationship with other parts or quantities; being in proportion. **2.** Properly related in size or other measurable characteristics. **3.** *Mathematics.* Having a constant ratio.
~*n.* Any of the quantities in a mathematical proportion. —**pro·por·tion·al·i·ty** (-sh'n-ál-ə-ti) *n.* —**pro·por·tion·al·ly** *adv.*
proportional representation *n. Abbr.* **P.R.** Representation of all parties in an elective body in proportion to their share of the total vote cast in an election. Compare **first-past-the-post.**
pro·por·tion·ate (prə-pór-sh'n-ət, -it ‖ prō-, -pór-, -ayt) *adj.* Being in due proportion; proportional.
~*tr.v.* (-ayt) **proportionated, -ating, -ates.** To make proportionate. —**pro·por·tion·ate·ly** (-ət-li, -it- ‖ -ayt-) *adv.* —**pro·por·tion·ate·ness** *n.*
pro·pos·al (prə-pṓz'l ‖ prō-) *n.* **1.** The act of proposing. **2.** A plan or scheme that is proposed; a suggestion. **3.** An offer of marriage.
pro·pose (prə-pṓz ‖ prō-) *v.* **-posed, -posing, -poses.** —*tr.* **1.** To put forward for consideration, discussion, or adoption: *propose new methods.* **2.** To present or nominate (a person) for a position, office, or membership. **3.** To offer (a toast). **4.** To purpose; intend. —*intr.* To form or make a proposal, especially of marriage. [Middle English *proposen,* from Old French *proposer,* from Latin *prōpōnere* (past participle *prōpositus*), to put or set forth, declare, propound : *prō,* forward + *pōnere,* to place.] —**pro·pos·er** *n.*
prop·o·si·tion (próppə-zísh'n) *n. Abbr.* **prop. 1.** A plan or scheme suggested for consideration or acceptance. **2.** *Informal.* A matter or person requiring special handling. **3.** A suggested business offer, arrangement, or the like. **4.** A subject for discussion or analysis, as in a debate. **5.** *Logic.* **a.** A statement in which the subject is affirmed or denied by the predicate and can or is shown to be true or false. **b.** A statement containing only logical constants and having a fixed truth-value. **6.** *Informal.* An offer of sexual intercourse.
~*tr.v.* **propositioned, -tioning, -tions.** *Informal.* To propose a private bargain to; especially, to make an offer of sexual intercourse to. [Middle English *proposicioun,* from Old French *proposition,* from Latin *prōpositiō* (stem *prōpositiōn-*), from *prōpōnere,* PROPOSE.] —**prop·o·si·tion·al** (-'l) *adj.* —**prop·o·si·tion·al·ly** *adv.*
propositional calculus *n.* The branch of symbolic logic dealing with the relationships formed between propositions by such connectives as *and, or,* and *if* as opposed to their internal structure. Compare **predicate calculus.**
propositional function *n. Logic.* An expression having the form of a proposition, but containing undefined symbols for the substantive elements. It becomes a proposition when appropriate values are assigned to the symbols.
pro·pos·i·tus (prə-pózzi-təss, prō-) *n., pl.* **-ti** (-tī). *Law.* One from whom a line of descent is traced. [New Latin, specialised use of the past participle of Latin *prōpōnere,* to place before, PROPOSE.]
pro·pound (prə-pównd, prō- ‖ *West Indies also* -pungd) *tr.v.* **-pounded, -pounding, -pounds. 1.** To put forward for consideration; set forth. **2.** *Law.* To present (a will) before the proper authority to obtain probate. [Alteration of earlier *propoune,* Middle English (Scottish) *proponen,* from Latin *prōpōnere,* to PROPOSE.] —**pro·pound·er** *n.*
propr. proprietor.
pro·prae·tor (prṓ-prée-tər, prō-) *n.* A Roman official appointed, usually immediately after holding the praetorship, to be the chief administrator of a province. [Latin, from *prō praetōre,* (one acting) for a praetor : *prō,* for + PRAETOR.] —**pro·prae·to·ri·al** (-táwri-əl ‖ -tóri-), **pro·prae·to·ri·an** *adj.*
pro·pri·e·tar·y (prə-prī-ə-tri, -təri ‖ prō-, -terri) *adj. Abbr.* **prop., pty. 1.** Of or pertaining to a proprietor or to proprietors collectively. **2.** Exclusively owned; private. **3.** Befitting an owner: *a proprietary air.* **4.** Owned by a private individual or corporation under a trademark or patent. **5.** *Medicine.* Of or designating a medical preparation or agent made and distributed under a trade name.
~*n., pl.* **proprietaries.** *Abbr.* **prop., pty. 1.** A proprietor. **2.** A group of proprietors. **3.** Ownership; proprietorship. **4.** Formerly, the governor of a proprietary American colony. **5.** A proprietary medicine or agent. [Late Latin *proprietārius,* from Latin *proprietās,* property, PROPRIETY.] —**pro·pri·e·tar·i·ly** *adv.*
proprietary colony *n.* Any of certain early North American colonies, such as Carolina and Pennsylvania, that were granted by the Crown in the 17th century to one or more Lords Proprietary, who had full governing rights.
pro·pri·e·tor (prə-prī-ə-tər ‖ prō-) *n. Abbr.* **prop., propr. 1.** A person who has legal title to something; an owner. **2. a.** The owner or owner-manager of a business or other institution. **b.** *British.* The publisher of a newspaper or magazine. [Alteration of PROPRIETARY (noun).] —**pro·pri·e·to·ri·al** (-táwri-əl ‖ -tóri-) *adj.* —**pro·pri·e·to·ri·al·ly** *adv.* —**pro·pri·e·tor·ship** *n.* —**pro·pri·e·tress** *n.*
pro·pri·e·ty (prə-prī-əti ‖ prō-) *n., pl.* **-ties. 1.** The quality of being fitting or proper; appropriateness. **2. a.** Conformity to prevailing customs and usages. **b.** *Plural.* The usages and customs considered to be correct in polite society. Preceded by *the.* —See Synonyms at **etiquette.** [Middle English *propriete,* ownership, one's own nature, idiosyncrasy, from Old French, from Latin *proprietās* (stem *proprietāt-*), from *proprius,* PROPER.]
pro·pri·o·cep·tor (próppri-ō-séptər, -ə-) *n.* A sensory receptor, chiefly in muscles, tendons, and joints, that responds to stimuli

arising within the organism. [Latin *proprius,* one's own + (RE)CEPTOR.] —**pro·pri·o·cep·tive** *adj.*
prop root *n.* A root growing from above ground into the soil and helping to support the plant stem, as in maize.
prop shaft *n.* A **propeller shaft** *(see).*
prop·to·sis (prop-tṓ-siss) *n., pl.* **-ses** (-seez). Forward displacement of an organ, such as the eyeball. [Late Latin, from Greek *proptōsis,* a falling forward, from *propiptein,* to fall forward : *pro-,* forward + *piptein,* to fall.]
pro·pul·sion (prə-púl-sh'n ‖ prō-) *n.* **1.** The process of driving or propelling. **2.** A driving or propelling force. [Medieval Latin *prōpulsiō* (stem *prōpulsiōn-*), from Latin *prōpellere* (past participle *prōpulsus*), to drive forward, PROPEL.] —**pro·pul·sive, pro·pul·so·ry** (-səri) *adj.*
pro·pyl (prṓ-pil, -pīl) *n. Chemistry.* A univalent organic radical with composition C_3H_7, derived from propane. [PROP- + -YL.]
prop·y·lae·um (próppi-lée-əm, prō-pī-) *n., pl.* **-laea** (-lée-ə). *Architecture.* An entrance or vestibule to a temple or group of buildings. Also called "propylon". [Latin, from Greek *propulaion : pro-,* before + *pulē,* gate.]
propyl alcohol *n. Chemistry.* **Propanol** *(see).*
pro·pyl·ene (prṓpi-leen) *n. Chemistry.* **Propene** *(see).* [PROPYL + -ENE.]
propylene glycol *n.* A colourless viscous hygroscopic liquid, $CH_3CH(OH)CH_2OH$, used in antifreeze solutions, in hydraulic fluids, and as a solvent. Also called "propanediol".
pro ra·ta (prṓ ráatə; *old-fashioned* ráytə ‖ *U.S. also* ráttə) *adj.* In proportion. [Latin *pro rata (parte),* according to the calculated (share).] —**pro ra·ta** *adv.*
pro·rate (prṓ-ráyt, -rayt) *v.* **-rated, -rating, -rates.** *U.S.* —*tr.* To divide, distribute, or assess proportionately. —*intr.* To settle affairs on the basis of proportional distribution. [From PRO RATA.] —**pro·rat·a·ble** (-ráytəb'l) *adj.* —**pro·ra·tion** (-ráysh'n) *n.*
pro·rogue (prə-rṓg, prō-) *tr.v.* **-rogued, -roguing, -rogues.** To discontinue the sessions of (a parliament or similar body) for a period of time. [Middle English *prorogen,* from Old French *prorog(u)er,* from Latin *prōrogāre,* "to ask publicly (for an extension of one's term of office)", prolong, defer : *prō-,* forward, in public + *rogāre,* to ask.] —**pro·ro·ga·tion** (prṓ-rə-gáysh'n, prórrə-) *n.*
pros- *prefix.* Indicates: **1.** Near, to, or towards; for example, **prosenchyma. 2.** In front; for example, **prosencephalon.** [Greek, from *pros,* near, at, towards, to.]
pro·sa·ic (prṓ-záy-ik, prə-) *adj.* **1.** Of or like prose; not poetic. **2. a.** Matter-of-fact; straightforward. **b.** Lacking in imagination and spirit; dull; ordinary. [Late Latin *prōsaicus,* from Latin *prōsa,* PROSE.] —**pro·sa·i·cal·ly** *adv.* —**pro·sa·ic·ness** *n.*
pro·sa·ism (prṓ-zay-iz'm) *n.* **1.** A quality or style that is prosaic. **2.** A prosaic expression, phrase, or word.
pro·sce·ni·um (prə-séeni-əm, prō-) *n., pl.* **-nia** (-ə). **1.** In a modern theatre, the area located between the curtain and the orchestra. **2.** In an ancient theatre, the stage, located between the background and the orchestra. [Latin, from Greek *proskēnion : pro-,* before + *skēnē,* "tent", stage-building used as background (see **scene**).]
proscenium arch *n.* In a traditional theatre, the arch over the front of and framing the stage.
pro·sciut·to (prō-shṓo-tō, pro-) *n., pl.* **-ti** (-ti). A type of spiced Italian ham. [Italian, from *pro-,* beforehand, PRE- + *asciutto,* dried.]
pro·scribe (prō-skrīb, prə-) *tr.v.* **-scribed, -scribing, -scribes. 1.** To denounce or condemn; specifically, to outlaw or banish. **2.** To prohibit; forbid. **3.** In ancient Rome, to publish the name of (a person) as outlawed and confiscate his property. [Latin *prōscrībere,* to publish in writing, proscribe : *prō-,* in front, publicly + *scrībere,* to write.] —**pro·scrib·er** *n.*
pro·scrip·tion (prō-skríp-sh'n, prə-) *n.* **1.** The act of proscribing; prohibition. **2.** The condition of being proscribed. —**pro·scrip·tive** *adj.* —**pro·scrip·tive·ly** *adv.*
prose (prṓz) *n.* **1.** Ordinary speech or writing, as distinguished from verse. **2.** Commonplace expression or quality. **3.** A piece of English prose to be translated into another language as an exercise. **4.** *Roman Catholic Church.* Formerly, a hymn of irregular metre sung after the gradual at Mass.
~*adj.* Written in prose.
~*v.* **prosed, prosing, proses.** —*tr.* To make into prose. —*intr.* **1.** To write prose. **2.** To speak or write in a dull, tiresome style. [Middle English, from Old French, from Latin *prōsa (ōrātiō),* "straightforward discourse", from *prōsus, prorsus,* straightforward, direct, from *prōversus,* past participle of *prōvertere,* to turn forward : *prō-,* forward + *vertere,* to turn.]
pros·e·cute (próssi-kewt) *v.* **-cuted, -cuting, -cutes.** —*tr.* **1.** To pursue or persist in so as to complete. **2.** To carry on (a trade, for example); practise. **3. a.** To initiate legal or criminal court action against. **b.** To seek to obtain or enforce by legal action. —*intr.* **1.** To initiate and conduct legal proceedings. **2.** To act as prosecutor. [Middle English *prosecuten,* to follow, from Latin *prōsequī* (past participle *prōsecūtus*), to follow up or forward : *prō-,* forward + *sequī,* to follow.]
prosecuting attorney *n. U.S.* An attorney empowered to prosecute cases on behalf of a government and the people.
pros·e·cu·tion (próssi-kéwsh'n) *n.* **1. a.** The act of prosecuting. **b.** The state of being prosecuted. **2.** The institution and carrying out of a legal proceeding. **3.** The lawyers who act on behalf of the Crown or State in criminal proceedings. **4.** The act or process of carrying out or continuing something.

pros·e·cu·tor (próssi-kewtər) *n.* **1.** One who prosecutes. **2.** One who initiates and carries out a legal action, especially criminal proceedings. **3.** *Law.* The barrister or advocate conducting the prosecution in criminal proceedings. Also called "public prosecutor".

pros·e·lyte (próssi-līt, próssə-) *n.* A convert to a religion or doctrine, especially a recent convert.
~*v.* Variant of **proselytise.** [Middle English *proselite,* from Late Latin *prosēlytus,* from Greek *prosēlutos,* "one who comes to a place", stranger, religious convert.] **—pros·e·lyt·er** *n.*

pros·e·lyt·ise, pros·e·lyt·ize (próssi-lit-īz, próssə-) *v.* **-ised, -ising, -ises.** Also **proselyte, -lyted, -lyting, -lytes.** *—intr.* **1.** To make proselytes. **2.** Loosely, to promote or speak enthusiastically on behalf of a cause. **3.** *Archaic.* To become a proselyte; convert. *—tr.* **1.** To convert from one belief or faith to another. **2.** Loosely, to try to win (a person) to a cause one espouses. **—pros·e·lyt·i·sa·tion** (-ī-záysh'n || *U.S.* -i-) *n.* **—pros·e·lyt·is·er** *n.*

pros·e·lyt·ism (próssi-lit-iz'm, próssə- || -līt-) *n.* **1.** The practice of proselytising. **2.** The state of being a proselyte; conversion. **—pros·e·lyt·i·cal** (-líttik'l) *adj.* **—pros·e·lyt·ist** (-lit-ist || -līt-) *n.*

pros·en·ceph·a·lon (próss-en-séff'l-on, -kéff'l-, -ən) *n. Anatomy.* The **forebrain** *(see).* [New Latin : PROS- (before, in front) + ENCEPHALON.] **—pros·en·ce·phal·ic** (-si-fál-ik, -ki-) *adj.*

pros·en·chy·ma (pross-éngkimə) *n. Botany.* Tissue consisting of elongated cells with tapering ends, occurring in supporting and conducting tissue. [New Latin : PROS- (near, towards) + (PAR)ENCHYMA.] **—pros·en·chym·a·tous** (-eng-kímmətəss) *adj.*

prose poem *n.* A short work, often a single paragraph, written as prose but employing poetic techniques and imagery.

Pro·ser·pi·na (prə-sérpinə, pro- || prō-, -zérpinə). Also **Pros·er·pine** (próssər-pīn). *Roman Mythology.* The wife of Pluto and daughter of Jupiter and Ceres; the goddess of the underworld, corresponding to the Greek Persephone.

pro·sim·i·an (prō-símmi-ən) *adj.* Of or belonging to the Prosimii, a primitive suborder of primates that includes the lemurs, lorises, and tarsiers. [New Latin *Prosimii* : *pro-,* before + Latin *simia,* ape, from *simus,* snub-nosed, from Greek *simos* (see **simian**).] **—pro·sim·i·an** *n.*

pro·sit (prṓ-zit, -sit, prōst) *interj.* Your health! Used as a drinking toast. [German, from Latin, "may it be advantageous".]

pros·o·dist (próss-ədist || próz, prṓz-) *n.* A specialist in prosody.

pros·o·dy (próssədi || próz-ədi, prṓz-) *n. pl.* **-dies.** *Abbr.* **pros. 1.** The science of versification, covering such aspects as metrical, rhythmical, and stanzaic forms. **2.** A particular system of versification. [Middle English *prosodye,* from Latin *prosōdia,* tone or accent of a syllable, from Greek *prosōidia,* accompanied song, modulation of voice, pronunciation, diacritical mark : *pros-,* to, in addition to + *ōidē,* song, lay, ode.] **—pro·sod·ic** (prə-sóddik, prō- || -zóddik) *adj.* **—pro·sod·i·cal·ly** *adv.*

pro·so·po·poe·ia, pro·so·po·pe·ia (próss-ə-pə-peé-ə, -ō- || *U.S. also* prə-sō-, prō-) *n.* In rhetoric: **1.** The impersonation of an absent or imaginary speaker. **2.** Personification, as of abstractions or inanimate objects. [Latin *prosopopoiia,* from Greek *prosōpopoiia,* dramatisation : *prosōpon,* face, mask, dramatic character : *pros,* towards + stem *op-,* to see + *poiein,* to make.] **—pro·so·po·poe·ial** *adj.*

pros·pect (próspekt) *n.* **1. a.** Something expected; a possibility. **b.** Expectation: *no prospect of a job.* **2.** *Plural.* Chances for success, especially with regard to wealth or social position. **3. a.** A potential customer. **b.** A candidate deemed likely to succeed. **4.** The direction in which an object, such as a building, faces. **5.** An extensive or distant view or scene presented to the eye: *a pleasant prospect.* **6.** The act of surveying or examining. **7.** In mining: **a.** The location or probable location of a mineral deposit. **b.** An actual or probable deposit. **c.** The mineral yield obtained by working an ore.
~*v.* (prə-spékt, próspekt) **prospected, -pecting, -pects.** *—tr.* To explore (a region) for gold or other mineral deposits. *—intr.* To explore for mineral deposits. Often used with *for.* [Middle English *prospecte,* from Latin *prōspectus,* distant view, vista, from the past participle of *prōspicere,* to look forward, foresee : *prō-,* forward + *specere,* to look.]
Synonyms: *prospect, outlook, expectation.*

pro·spec·tive (prə-spéktiv, pro- || prō-) *adj.* **1.** Being in prospect; likely to become: *the prospective bridegroom.* **2.** Looking forward in time; characterised by foresight. **—pro·spec·tive·ly** *adj.*

pros·pec·tor (prə-spéktər, pro- || próspektər) *n.* One who explores an area for natural deposits, such as gold or oil.

pro·spec·tus (prə-spéktəss || prō-) *n.* **1.** A formal summary of a proposed commercial, literary, or other venture. **2.** A brochure published by an institution, such as a school or university, giving such details as facilities and charges. [Latin, PROSPECT.]

pros·per (próspər) *v.* **-pered, -pering, -pers.** *—intr.* To be fortunate or successful; thrive. *—tr. Archaic.* To cause to be successful. [Middle English *prosperen,* from Old French *prosperer,* from Latin *prosperāre,* to make fortunate, from *prosperus,* fortunate.]

pros·per·i·ty (pross-pérrəti, prəss-) *n., pl.* **-ties.** The condition of being prosperous and having good fortune or financial success.

pros·per·ous (próspross, próspərəss) *adj.* **1.** Having success; flourishing. **2.** Affluent; well-to-do. **3.** Propitious; favourable. **—pros·per·ous·ly** *adv.* **—pros·per·ous·ness** *n.*

Prost (prōst), **Alain** (1955–). French motor racing driver, who won a record 51 Formula One Grand Prix races between 1970 and 1993, and was world champion in 1985, 1986, 1989 and 1993.

pros·ta·glan·din (próstə-glándin) *n.* Any of various substances composed of fatty acids and having hormone-like activity, found especially in mammals. [From *prostate gland* + -IN.]

pros·tate (próss-tayt; *rarely* -tit) *n.* A gland in male mammals that secretes a liquid that forms a part of the semen. Also called "prostate gland". [New Latin *prostata,* from Greek *prostatēs,* "stander before (the bladder)", from *proïstanai,* to cause to stand in front : *pro-,* in front + *histanai,* to cause to stand.] **—pros·tate, pros·tat·ic** (pross-táttik) *adj.*

pros·ta·tec·to·my (próstə-téktəmi) *n., pl.* **-mies.** The surgical removal of all or part of the prostate. [PROSTAT(E) + -ECTOMY.]

pros·ta·ti·tis (próstə-tītiss) *n.* Inflammation of the prostate.

pros·the·sis (pross-theé-siss, próss-thə-) *n., pl.* **-ses** (-seez). **1.** The artificial replacement of a limb, tooth, or other body part. **2.** An artificial device used in such replacement. **3.** *Linguistics.* Variant of **prothesis.** [Late Latin, addition of a letter or syllable, from Greek, attachment, addition, from *prostithenai,* to put to, add : *pros-,* in addition + *tithenai,* to place, put.] **—pros·thet·ic** (-théttik) *adj.* **—pros·thet·i·cal·ly** *adv.*

prosthetic group *n. Biochemistry.* The nonpeptide part of a conjugated protein, such as the haem group in haemoglobin.

pros·thet·ics (pross-théttiks) *n. Used with a singular verb.* Prosthetic surgery. **—pros·the·tist** (-theé-tist, próss-thə-) *n.*

pros·tho·don·tics (próss-thə-dóntiks, -thō-) *n. Used with a singular verb.* Also **pros·tho·don·ti·a** (-dón-shə, -shi-ə). Prosthetic dentistry. [From PROSTH(ESIS) + -ODONT + -ICS.] **—pros·tho·don·tist** *n.*

pros·ti·tute (prósti-tewt || -tōōt) *n.* **1.** One who solicits and accepts payment for sexual services, especially a woman or girl who accepts payment from men, or a man or boy who engages in homosexual practices for payment. **2.** One who sells or degrades his abilities or name for money or an unworthy cause.
~*tr.v.* **prostituted, -tuting, -tutes. 1.** To offer (oneself or another) for sexual hire. **2.** To degrade (oneself or one's talents) for money or an unworthy cause. [Latin *prōstitūta,* from the past participle of *prōstituere,* to expose publicly, prostitute : *prō-,* forth, in public + *statuere,* to set, place, from *stare* (past participle *status*), to stand.] **—pros·ti·tu·tor** (-ər) *n.*

pros·ti·tu·tion (prósti-téwsh'n || -tōōsh'n) *n.* **1.** The act or practice of prostituting. **2.** The act of offering or devoting one's talents to an unworthy use or cause.

pros·trate (pro-stráyt, prə- || *chiefly U.S.* próstrayt) *tr.v.* **-trated, -trating, -trates. 1.** To make (oneself) bow or kneel down in humility or adoration. **2.** To throw down flat. **3. a.** To make very weak or exhausted; overcome. **b.** To cause to be submissive; overthrow.
~*adj.* (próss-trayt; *rarely* -trət, -trit). **1.** Lying face down, as in submission. **2.** Lying down full-length. **3. a.** Physically or emotionally exhausted; incapacitated. **b.** Overthrown or defeated. **4.** *Botany.* Growing along the ground. —See Usage Note at **prone.** [Middle English *prostrat* (adjective), from Latin *prōstrātus,* past participle of *prōsternere,* to throw down, prostrate : *prō-,* down before + *sternere,* to stretch out, cast down.] **—pros·tra·tor** (-ər) *n.*

pros·tra·tion (pro-stráysh'n, prə-) *n.* **1. a.** The act of prostrating oneself. **b.** The state of being prostrate. **2.** Total exhaustion.

pro·style (prṓ-stīl) *adj. Architecture.* Having a row of columns across the front only, as in some Greek temples.
~*n.* A prostyle building or portico. [Latin *prostylos,* from Greek *prostulos,* having pillars in front : *pro-,* in front + *stulos,* pillar.]

pros·y (prṓzi) *adj.* **-ier, -iest. 1.** Matter-of-fact; dry; prosaic. **2.** Dull; commonplace. **—pros·i·ly** *adv.* **—pros·i·ness** *n.*

prot-. Variant of **proto-.**

Prot. 1. Protectorate. **2.** Protestant.

pro·tac·tin·i·um (prṓtak-tínni-əm) *n. Symbol* **Pa** A rare radioactive element chemically similar to uranium, having 12 known isotopes, the most common of which is protactinium 231 with a half-life of 32,480 years. Atomic number 91, melting point about 1,600°C, relative density 15.37, valency 4 or 5. [New Latin : PROT(O)- + ACTINIUM (because it disintegrates into actinium).]

pro·tag·o·nist (prō-tággənist, prə-) *n.* **1. a.** The leading character in Greek drama. **b.** The leading character in any play, novel, or other literary work. **2.** Any leading or principal figure; especially, one who initiates a political policy. [Greek *prōtagōnistēs* : PROT(O)- + *agōnistēs,* actor, from *agōnizesthai,* to contend, from *agōnia,* a contest, from *agōn,* gathering, contest, from *agein,* to lead.]
Usage: Traditionally, *protagonist* has the sense of "leader" or (in literary works) "leading character". It is therefore considered improper to use a phrase such as *chief protagonist* (for it contains a redundant word) or to use the word in the plural, when only one literary work is being referred to. However, the word is extending its meaning, and is now often used in the sense of "leader in a matter of importance", as well as in the sense of "partisan" or "champion": *She was a staunch protagonist of the liberation movement.* See also **antagonist.**

Pro·tag·o·ras of Abdera (prō-tággə-rass, prə-, -rəss) (*c.* 490–*c.* 421 B.C.). Greek philosopher. He is said to have coined the maxim, "Man is the measure of all things."

pro·ta·mine (prṓtə-meen, -min) *n.* Also **pro·ta·min** (-min). Any of the group of the simplest proteins that are highly basic, soluble in water, not coagulated by heat, and yield only amino acids, chiefly arginine, upon hydrolysis. [PROT(O)- + -AMINE.]

pro·tan·drous (prō-tándrəss) *adj.* Also **pro·tan·dric** (-tándrik). Having male gametes that mature before the female gametes. Said of certain plants and hermaphrodite animals. Compare **protogynous.** [PROTO- + -ANDROUS.] **—pro·tan·dry** (-tándri) *n.*

pro·ta·no·pi·a (prṓtə-nṓpi-ə) *n.* A form of partial colourblindness in which perception of red is defective, and reds, yellows, and greens are confused. [New Latin : PROT(O)- + AN- (without) + -OPIA.] **—pro·ta·nope** (-nōp) *n.* **—pro·ta·nop·ic** (-nóppik) *adj.*

prot·a·sis (próttə-siss) *n.* **1.** *Grammar.* A subordinate clause expressing the condition in a conditional sentence. Compare **apodosis.** **2.** The introductory part of a classical drama. [Late Latin, proposition, from Greek, "a stretching forward", proposition, premise, from *proteinein,* to stretch forward, offer, propose : *prō-,* before + *teinein,* to stretch.]

pro·te·a (prṓti-ə) *n.* Any shrub of the southern African genus *Protea,* having showy, conelike flower heads. [New Latin, from PROTEUS (referring to the many different forms of the shrub).]

pro·te·an (prō-tée-ən, prṓti-) *adj.* Readily taking on different characters or forms; changeable. [From PROTEUS.]

pro·te·ase (prṓti-ayz, -ayss) *n.* An enzyme that catalyses the hydrolytic breakdown of proteins. Also called "proteolytic enzyme". [PROTE(IN) + -ASE.]

pro·tect (prə-tékt, prō-) *tr.v.* **-tected, -tecting, -tects.** **1.** To keep from harm, attack, or injury; guard. **2.** *Economics.* To help (domestic industry) by imposing tariffs on imported goods. **3.** *Commerce.* To assure payment of (drafts or notes, for example) by setting aside funds in advance. —See Synonyms at **defend.** [Latin *prōtegere* (past participle *prōtectus*), to cover in front, protect : *prō-,* in front + *tegere,* to cover.] **—pro·tect·ing·ly** *adv.*

pro·tec·tion (prə-téksh'n, prō-) *n.* **1.** The act of protecting. **2.** The condition of being protected. **3.** One that protects. **4.** A document, such as a passport, guaranteeing safe conduct to travellers. **5.** *Economics.* A tariff system protecting domestic industries from foreign competition. **6.** *Informal.* **a.** Money extorted by racketeers in exchange for a promise of freedom from molestation. Also called "protection money". **b.** Freedom from molestation obtained in this way. **—pro·tec·tion·al** *adj.*

pro·tec·tion·ism (prə-téksh'n-iz'm, prō-) *n. Economics.* The theory, policy, or system of protecting domestic industries from foreign competition. **—pro·tec·tion·ist** *n. & adj.*

pro·tec·tive (prə-téktiv, prō-) *adj.* **1.** Adapted or intended to afford protection. **2.** Of, pertaining to, or designed to protect domestic industries from foreign competition: *a protective tariff.* **3.** Showing or expressing often undue concern over the safety or welfare of others: *too protective towards him.* **—pro·tec·tive** *n.* **—pro·tec·tive·ly** *adv.* **—pro·tec·tive·ness** *n.*

protective colouring *n. Zoology.* **1.** Colour and markings of an animal that help it to appear inconspicuous in its surroundings so that it is less likely to be seen by predators; camouflage. **2. Batesian mimicry** *(see).*

pro·tec·tor (prə-téktər, prō-) *n.* **1.** A person who protects; a guardian. **2.** *Usually capital* **P.** Formerly, a title given to one who ruled during the absence, minority, or illness of the monarch. **—pro·tec·tor·al** *adj.* **—pro·tec·tor·ship** *n.*

pro·tec·tor·ate (prə-téktər-ət, prō-, téktr-, -it) *n. Abbr.* **Prot.** **1.** A relationship of protection and partial control assumed by a superior power over a dependent country or region. **2.** The protected country or region. **3.** *Capital* **P.** **a.** The government, office, or term of a protector. **b.** The government of England under Oliver Cromwell (1653–58) and his son Richard (1658–59).

pro·tec·to·ry (prə-téktəri, prō-) *n., pl.* **-ries.** Formerly, an institution run by the Roman Catholic Church providing for the welfare of destitute children.

pro·té·gé (prót-ə-zhay, prṓt-, -e-, -ay- || *U.S. also* -zháy) *n. Feminine* **pro·té·gée.** One whose welfare, training, or career is promoted by an influential person. [French, from the past participle of *protéger,* to PROTECT.]

pro·te·id (prṓ-tee-id, -teed) *n.* A protein. Not in technical usage.

pro·tein (prṓ-teen, -tee-in) *n.* **1.** Any of a group of complex nitrogenous organic compounds of high molecular weight that contain amino acids as their basic structural units and that occur in all living matter and are essential for the growth and repair of animal tissue. Foods containing a high proportion of protein include meat, eggs, and cheese. **2.** The nutritional value provided by food containing any or a combination of these compounds: *You need more protein.* [French *protéine,* "primary substance (to the body)", from Late Greek *proteios,* primary, from Greek *prōtos,* first.] **—pro·tein·a·ceous** (-áyshəss; *also* -tin-), **pro·tein·ic** (-téenik), **pro·tei·nous** *adj.*

pro·tein·ase (prṓ-teen-ayz, -tee-in-, -ayss) *n.* A protease that hydrolyses proteins into polypeptides.

pro·tein·ate (prṓ-teen-ayt, -tee-in-) *n.* A protein compound.

pro·tein·u·ri·a (prṓ-teen-yóor-i-ə, -tee-in-) *n. Pathology.* **Albuminuria** *(see).*

pro tem (prō tém) *adv.* Pro tempore. **—pro tem** *adj.*

pro tem·po·re (prō témpəri) *adv. Abbr.* **p.t.** For the time being; temporarily. [Latin.] **—pro tem·po·re** *adj.*

proteo– *comb. form.* Indicates protein; for example, **proteolysis.**

pro·te·o·clas·tic (prṓti-ō-kástik) *adj.* Of, pertaining to, or causing proteolysis; proteolytic. [PROTEO- + -CLASTIC.]

pro·te·ol·y·sis (prṓti-óllə-siss) *n.* The breaking down of proteins into simpler, soluble substances, as in digestion. [PROTEO- + -LYSIS.] **—pro·te·o·lyt·ic** (-ə-líttik) *adj.*

proteolytic enzyme *n.* **Protease** *(see).*

pro·te·ose (prṓti-ōz, -ōss) *n.* Any of several water-soluble substances created as a product of partial digestion of protein. Also *U.S.* "albumose". [PROTE(O)- + -OSE.]

Prot·er·o·zo·ic (próttər-ō-zṓ-ik, prṓtər-, -ə-) *adj. Geology.* Of, belonging to, or designating the geological time and deposits of the Precambrian era between the Archaeozoic era and the Cambrian period of the Palaeozoic era.
~*n. Geology.* The Proterozoic period. Preceded by *the.* [Greek *proteros,* earlier, anterior + -ZOIC.]

pro·test (prə-tést, prō- || prṓ-test) *v.* **-tested, -testing, -tests.** *—tr.* **1.** To promise or affirm with earnest solemnity: *The accused protested innocence.* **2.** *Law.* To declare (a bill of exchange or promissory note) dishonoured or refused. **3.** *Literary.* To proclaim or make known. **4.** *U.S.* To object to, especially in a formal statement. *—intr.* **1. a.** To express strong objection, disagreement, or annoyance. Used with *about, against,* or *at.* **b.** To hold a rally or meeting to voice disapproval or objection. **2.** To make an earnest avowal or affirmation. —See Synonyms at **object.**
~*n.* (prṓ-test). **1.** A formal declaration of disapproval or objection issued by a concerned party. **2.** Any individual or collective gesture or display of objection or disapproval. Also used adjectivally: *a protest song.* **3.** *Law.* **a.** A formal statement drawn up by a notary for a creditor, declaring that the debtor has refused to accept or honour a bill of exchange or promissory note. **b.** A formal declaration made by a taxpayer, stating that the tax demanded is illegal or excessive and reserving the right to contest it. **4.** A formal written statement by the master of a ship giving the circumstances and details of a disaster, injury, or the like, that occurred at sea. **5.** *Sports.* A formal objection lodged against a player or other competitor. **—under protest.** Against one's will; expressing disagreement or objections. [Middle English *protesten,* from Old French *protester,* from Latin *prōtestārī,* to declare in public, testify, protest : *prō-,* forth, in public + *testārī,* to be a witness, make a will, from *testis,* a witness, will.] **—pro·test·er** *n.* **—pro·test·ing·ly** *adv.*

prot·es·tant (próttistənt; *also* prə-téstənt, prō-) *n. Rare.* One who makes a declaration or protest. **—prot·es·tant** *adj.*

Prot·es·tant (próttistənt) *n. Abbr.* **Prot.** **1.** A member of any of the Christian churches, such as the Anglican, Baptist, Methodist, or Presbyterian, descending from those that seceded from the Church of Rome at the time of the Reformation, denying the universal authority of the Pope and emphasising the principle of justification by faith. **2.** Any of those who adhered to the doctrine of Luther and, in 1529, protested against the decree of the Diet of Spires commanding submission to the authority of Rome.
~*adj.* Of or pertaining to Protestants or Protestantism. [Latin *prōtestāns* (stem *prōtestānt-*), present participle of *prōtestārī,* to PROTEST.]

Protestant Episcopal Church *n.* The autonomous branch of the Anglican Communion in the United States. Also called "Episcopal Church".

Prot·es·tant·ism (próttistənt-iz'm) *n.* **1.** Adherence to a Protestant church. **2.** The religion fostered by the Protestant movement. **3.** Protestants or the Protestant churches collectively.

pro·tes·ta·tion (prṓt-ess-táysh'n, prótt-, -iss-) *n.* **1.** An emphatic declaration. **2.** A strong or formal expression of dissent.

Pro·teus (prṓ-tewss,-ti-əss || -tōoss). *Greek Mythology.* A sea god who could change his shape at will.

pro·tha·la·mi·on (prṓthə-láymi-ən || -on) *n., pl.* **-mia** (-ə). Also **pro·tha·la·mi·um** (-əm) *pl.* **-mia** (-ə). A song or ode in celebration of a wedding; an epithalamium. [Coined by Edmund Spenser : PRO- (before) + Greek *epithalamion,* EPITHALAMIUM.]

pro·thal·lus (prō-thál-əss, prō-) *n., pl.* **–li** (-ī). Also **pro·thal·li·um** (-i-əm) *pl.* **-lia** (-i-ə). *Botany.* A small, flat mass of tissue, produced by a germinating spore of certain pteridophytes and gymnosperms, that bears sexual organs. [New Latin : Greek *pro-,* in front of, before + *thallos,* a shoot.] **—pro·thal·li·al** *adj.*

proth·e·sis (próthə-siss) *n., pl.* **-ses** (-seez). Also **pros·the·sis** (for sense 1). **1.** *Linguistics.* The addition of a phoneme at the beginning of a word to ease pronunciation or to form a new word. **2.** In the Eastern Orthodox Church, the preparation of the Eucharistic elements for consecration. [Greek, from *protithenai,* to put before : *pro-,* before + *tithenai,* to put, place.] **—pro·thet·ic** (prə-théttik, prō-) *adj.* **—pro·thet·i·cal·ly** *adv.*

proth·o·no·tar·y (prṓth-ə-nōtəri, -ō-, prō-thónnə-tri, -təri || -terri) *n., pl.* **-ies.** Also **pro·to·no·tar·y** (prṓt-, -tónnə-). **1.** Formerly, the principal clerk in certain courts of law. **2.** *Roman Catholic Church.* One of a college of twelve ecclesiastics charged with the registry of important pontifical proceedings. **3.** *Archaic.* A chief scribe. [Middle English *prothonotarie,* from Late Latin *prōtonotārius* : PROTO- + *notārius,* "of shorthand", secretary, from *nota,* mark, shorthand character.] **—pro·tho·no·tar·i·al** (-táir-i-əl) *adj.*

pro·tho·rax (prṓ-tháw-raks, prō- || -thṓ-) *n., pl.* **-axes** or **-thoraces** (-rə-seez). The anterior division of the thorax of an insect, bearing the first pair of legs. **—pro·tho·rac·ic** (prṓ-thaw-rássik || -thə-) *adj.*

pro·throm·bin (prō-thrómbin, prō-) *n.* A plasma protein that is converted into thrombin during blood coagulation.

pro·tist (prṓtist) *n. Biology.* Any of the single-celled organisms of the kingdom Protista, which includes protozoans, bacteria, fungi, some algae, and other forms not readily classified as either plants or animals. [New Latin *Protista,* "simplest organisms", from Greek *prōtista,* neuter plural of *prōtistos,* the very first, primal, from *prōtos,* first.] **—pro·tist·an** *adj. & n.* **—pro·tis·tol·o·gy** (prṓtiss-tólləji) *n.*

pro·ti·um (prṓ-ti-əm || *U.S. also* -shi-) *n.* The most abundant isotope of hydrogen, H_1, with atomic mass 1. [New Latin : PROT(O)- + -IUM.]

proto–, prot– *comb. form.* Indicates: **1.** The earliest form or the first in rank or time; for example, **protium, protoplast, prototype.**

2. *Capital* **P.** The earliest form of a language as reconstructed by comparative linguistics; for example, **Proto-Germanic. 3.** *Chemistry.* The member of a series that has the least amount of a specified element or radical; for example, **protoporphyrin.** [Greek *prōtos*, first.]

pro·to·col (prṓ-tə-kol, -tō- ‖ -kōl) *n.* **1. a.** The forms of ceremony, precedence, and etiquette observed by diplomats and heads of state. **b.** Any rules or code of behaviour or etiquette. **2.** The first copy of a treaty or other document prior to its ratification. **3.** Any official record of a transaction or negotiations, especially one that is used as a preliminary draft for a document, such as a treaty. **4.** The official formulae annexed to a charter, papal bull, or the like. —See Synonyms at **etiquette.**
~*v.* **protocolled** or *U.S.* **-coled, -colling** or *U.S.* **-coling, -cols.** —*intr.* To form or issue protocols. —*tr.* To record or embody in a protocol. [Earlier Scottish *prothocoll*, from Old French *prothocole*, from Medieval Latin *protocollum*, from Late Greek *prōtokollon*, first sheet glued to binding of a book, bearing a table of contents : PROTO- + *kolla*, glue.] —**pro·to·col·ar** (-kóllər), **pro·to·col·a·ry** (-kólləri), **pro·to·col·ic** (-kóllik) *adj.*

Pro·to-Ger·man·ic (prṓtō-jer-mánnik) *n.* The hypothetical prehistoric language that was the ancestor of the Germanic languages.
pro·tog·y·nous (prō-tójinəss) *adj.* Having female gametes that mature before the male gametes. Said of certain plants and hermaphrodite animals. Compare **protandrous.** [PROTO- + -GYNOUS.] —**pro·tog·y·ny** *n.*

pro·to·his·to·ry (prṓtō-hístri, -hístəri) *n.* The study of human culture, or a particular instance of it, just prior to its earliest recorded history. —**pro·to·his·tor·ic** (-hiss-tórrik ‖ -táwrik) *adj.*

pro·to·hu·man (prṓtō-héwmən) *n.* A member of any of several species of prehistoric primates resembling modern man but more primitive in development. —**pro·to·hu·man** *adj.*

Pro·to-In·do-Eur·o·pe·an (prṓtō-índō-yoor-ə-pée-ən) *n.* The hypothetical, reconstructed ancestor of the Indo-European languages.
pro·to·lan·guage (prṓtō-lang-gwij) *n. Linguistics.* A language that is reconstructed by comparative linguistics as the hypothetical ancestor of another existing language or group of languages. Compare **Ursprache.**

pro·to·lith·ic (prṓ-tō-líthik, -tə-) *adj.* Of, pertaining to, or characteristic of the very beginning of the Stone Age; eolithic. [PROTO- + -LITHIC.]

pro·to·mar·tyr (prṓtō-maartər) *n.* **1.** The first Christian martyr, Saint Stephen. **2.** The first martyr in a cause.
pro·to·mor·phic (prṓ-tō-mórfik, -tə-) *adj.* Primitive in structure or form. [PROTO- + -MORPHIC.]

pro·ton (prṓ-ton) *n. Symbol* **p** *Physics.* A stable, positively charged elementary particle in the baryon family having a mass 1,836 times that of the electron. It is a constituent of all atomic nuclei. See **neutron, particle.** [Greek *prōton*, neuter of *prōtos*, first.] —**pro·ton·ic** (prō-tónnik) *adj.*

pro·to·ne·ma (prṓtə-née'mə) *n., pl.* **-nemata** (-née'mətə, -némmətə). *Botany.* A green, threadlike structure that arises on germination of a moss spore, and that eventually develops into a mature plant. [PROTO- + Greek *nēma*, thread.] —**pro·to·ne·mal** (-née'm'l), **pro·to·ne·ma·tal** (-née'mət'l, -némmət'l) *adj.*

proton number *n.* **Atomic number** *(see).*
protonotary. Variant of **prothonotary.**
proton synchrotron *n. Physics.* A ring-shaped **synchrotron** *(see)* that uses a frequency modulated accelerating voltage to accelerate protons to energies of the order of 10^9 electronvolts. Also called "proton accelerator".

pro·to·path·ic (prṓtə-páthik) *adj.* Of, pertaining to, or designating the cutaneous sensory reception of gross pressure, pain, heat, or cold. Compare **epicritic.** [Medieval Greek *prōtopathēs*, affected first, from Greek *prōtopathein*, to feel or be affected first : PROTO- + *paskhein*, to feel, experience.] —**pro·top·a·thy** (prō-tóppəthi) *n.*

pro·to·plasm (prṓ-tə-plaz'm, -tō-) *n.* A complex, jelly-like colloidal substance constituting the living matter of plant and animal cells, and performing the basic life functions. See **cytoplasm, nucleoplasm.** [German *Protoplasma* : PROTO- + -PLASM.] —**pro·to·plas·mic** (-plázmik), **pro·to·plas·mal** (-plázm'l), **pro·to·plas·mat·ic** (-plaz-máttik) *adj.*

pro·to·plast (prṓ-tə-plast, -tō-) *n.* **1.** *Biology.* The protoplasm and plasma membrane of a plant or bacterial cell after the cell wall has been removed. **2.** *Rare.* A prototype. [Old French *protoplaste*, from Late Latin *prōtoplastus*, "first formed", from Greek *prōtoplastos* : PROTO- + -PLAST.] —**pro·to·plas·tic** (-plástik) *adj.*

pro·to·por·phy·rin (prṓtō-pórfərin) *n.* A metal-free porphyrin, $C_{34}H_{34}N_4O_4$, which, with iron, forms haem.
Pro·to-Sem·i·tic (prṓtō-si-míttik, -se-, -sə-) *n.* The hypothetical common ancestor of the Asiatic (Eastern) branch of Hamito-Semitic, from which Arabic, Canaanite, Aramaic, Ethiopic, and Ugaritic are descended.

pro·to·star (prṓtō-staar) *n.* A mass of gas and dust in interstellar space that is thought to contract to form a star.
pro·to·stele (prṓ-tō-steel, -tə-, -stéelee) *n. Botany.* A type of stele commonly found in roots that lacks pith and has a solid core of xylem. —**pro·to·ste·lic** (-stéelik) *adj.*

pro·to·troph·ic (prṓtə-tróffik, -trṓfik) *adj.* Obtaining nourishment by the assimilation of inorganic materials. Said of plants and bacteria. [PROTO- + -TROPH(Y) + -IC.] —**pro·tot·roph·y** (prō-tóttrəfi) *n.* **pro·to·troph** (prṓtə-trof) *n.*

pro·to·type (prṓ-tə-típ, -tō-) *n.* **1.** An original type, form, or in-

stance that serves as a model on which later stages are based or judged. **2.** An early and typical example. **3.** *Biology.* A primitive or ancestral form or species. [French, from Greek *prōtotupon*, original form, archetype, from neuter of *prōtotupos*, "in the first form", original : PROTO- + -TYPE.] —**pro·to·typ·al** (-típ'l), **pro·to·typ·ic** (-típpik), **pro·to·typ·i·cal** *adj.*

pro·to·xy·lem (prṓtə-zī-lem, -tō-, -ləm) *n. Botany.* The first type of xylem that is formed from the procambium. Compare **metaxylem.**
pro·to·zo·an (prṓ-tə-zṓ-ən, -tō-) *n., pl.* **-zoans** or **-zoa** (-zṓ-ə). Also **pro·to·zo·on** (-on). One of the single-celled, usually microscopic organisms of the phylum or subkingdom Protozoa, which includes the most primitive forms of animal life. [New Latin *Protozoa* : PROTO- + -ZOAN.] —**pro·to·zo·an, pro·to·zo·ic** (-zṓ-ik) *adj.*

pro·to·zo·ol·o·gy (prṓ-tə-zō-óllə̄ji, -tō-, -zoo-) *n.* The biological study of protozoans. —**pro·to·zo·o·log·i·cal** (-zṓ-ə-lójik'l, -zṓō-) *adj.* —**pro·to·zo·ol·o·gist** (-óllə̄jist) *n.*

pro·tract (prə-trákt, prō-) *tr.v.* **-tracted, -tracting, -tracts. 1.** To draw out or lengthen in time; prolong, especially unnecessarily. **2.** In surveying, to draw to scale by means of a scale and protractor; plot. **3.** *Anatomy.* To extend or protrude. —See Synonyms at **prolong.** [Latin *prōtrahere* (past participle *prōtractus*), to drag out, lengthen : *prō-*, out, extending + *trahere*, to drag, pull.] —**pro·tract·ed·ly** *adv.* —**pro·tract·ed·ness** *n.* —**pro·trac·tive** *adj.*

pro·trac·tile (prə-trák-tīl, prō- ‖ *U.S.* -til, -t'l) *adj.* Also **pro·tract·i·ble** (-təb'l). *Zoology.* Capable of being protracted; extensible. —**pro·trac·til·i·ty** (-trak-tíllati) *n.*

pro·trac·tion (prə-tráksh'n, prō-) *n.* **1. a.** The act of protracting. **b.** The state of being protracted. **2.** A drawing made to scale. **3.** The irregular lengthening of a normally short syllable.

pro·trac·tor (prə-tráktər, prō-) *n.* **1.** A semicircular instrument for measuring and constructing angles. **2.** An adjustable pattern used by tailors. **3.** A surgical instrument for removing foreign objects, especially bullets, from the body.

pro·trude (prə-trṓod, prō- ‖ -tréwd) *v.* **-truded, -truding, -trudes.** —*tr.* To push or thrust outwards. —*intr.* To jut out; project. [Latin *prōtrūdere* : *prō-*, forth + *trūdere*, to thrust.] —**pro·trud·ent** (-'nt) *adj.*

pro·tru·sile (prə-trṓo-sīl, prō- ‖ -tréw-, *U.S.* -sil, -s'l) *adj.* Also **pro·tru·si·ble** (-sib'l). Capable of being thrust outwards, as the tongue is. [PROTRUS(ION) + -ILE.] —**pro·tru·sil·i·ty** (prṓ-trṓo-síllati ‖ -trew-) *n.*

pro·tru·sion (prə-trṓo-zh'n, prō- ‖ -tréw-) *n.* **1. a.** The act of protruding. **b.** The state of being protruded. **2.** Something that protrudes.

pro·tru·sive (prə-trṓo-siv, prō- ‖ -tréw-, -ziv) *adj.* **1.** Tending to protrude; protruding. **2.** Unduly or disagreeably conspicuous; obtrusive. —**pro·tru·sive·ly** *adv.* —**pro·tru·sive·ness** *n.*

pro·tu·ber·ance (prə-téw-bərənss, prō- ‖ -tṓo-) *n.* Also **pro·tu·ber·an·cy** (-i) *pl.* **-cies. 1.** That which protrudes; a bulge or knob. **2.** The condition of being protuberant.

pro·tu·ber·ant (prə-téw-bərənt, prō- ‖ -tṓo-. *The popular pronunciation* prə-trṓobərənt *reflects a nonstandard blending of this word with* **protrudent**) *adj.* Swelling outwards; bulging. [Late Latin *prōtūberāns* (stem *prōtūberānt-*), present participle of *prōtūberāre*, to PROTUBERATE.] —**pro·tu·ber·ant·ly** *adv.*

pro·tu·ber·ate (prə-téw-bə-rayt, prō- ‖ -tṓo-) *intr.v.* **-ated, -ating, -ates.** *Rare.* To swell or bulge out. [Late Latin *prōtūberāre* : *prō-*, forth, outwards + *tūber*, swelling, bump.] —**pro·tu·ber·a·tion** (ráysh'n) *n.*

proud (prowd) *adj.* **prouder, proudest. 1.** Feeling pleasurable satisfaction over an attribute or act by which one's stature is measured. **2.** Occasioning pride; gratifying: *a proud moment.* **3.** Marked by exacting or constraining self-respect: *too proud to accept charity.* **4.** Having excessive self-esteem; haughty; arrogant. **5.** Of great dignity; honoured: *a proud name.* **6.** Majestic; magnificent. **7.** Occasioned by pride, expressing pride: *a proud smile.* **8.** Spirited or excited. Said of animals: *a proud mare.* **9.** Projecting slightly from a surrounding surface; not flush: *the sockets are proud of the wall.* ~*adv.* So as to project slightly from a surface. —**do (someone) proud.** To be very generous towards; especially, to entertain on a lavish scale. [Middle English *proud*, late Old English *prūt, prūd*, from Old French *prod, prud*, good, gallant, brave, from Late Latin *prōde*, advantageous, from Latin *prōdesse*, to be beneficial : *prōd-*, variant of *prō-*, for + *esse*, to be. Sense 9 and adverb : 16th century, "overgrown, swollen".] —**proud·ly** *adv.* —**proud·ness** *n.*

Synonyms: proud, arrogant, haughty, disdainful, supercilious.
proud flesh *n. Pathology.* The swollen flesh around a healing wound. [Middle English, from PROUD (swollen).]

Prou·dhon (prṓoDON, prṓo-dón), **Pierre Joseph** (1809–65). French political theorist and economist. Best-known for his theory that "all property is theft" in his *Qu'est-ce que la propriété* (1840).

Proust (prṓost), **Joseph-Louis** (1754–1826). French chemist. He discovered that compounds contain fixed proportions of elements by weight: the law of definite proportions.

Proust, Marcel (1871–1922). French novelist. His masterpiece was the 12-volume *A la recherche du temps perdu* (published 1913–27), strongly autobiographical in theme, and an exploration of memory and perception. —**Prous·ti·an** (prṓosti-ən) *adj. & n.*

proust·ite (prṓostīt) *n.* A red silver ore, Ag_3AsS_3, occurring in hexagonal crystals often in association with other silver-bearing minerals. [After Joseph-Louis PROUST.]

Prout (prowt), **William** (1785–1850). British chemist and physician. *Prout's Hypothesis* showed that all atomic weights are multiples of that of hydrogen and he also discovered that gastric juices in the stomach contain hydrochloric acid.

prov. **1.** province; provincial. **2.** provisional.

Prov. **1.** Provençal. **2.** Proverbs (Old Testament). **3.** Provost.

prove (prŏŏv) *v.* **proved, proved** or **proven** (prŏŏv'n. *There is also a spelling pronunciation* prōv'n), **proving, proves.** —*tr.* **1.** To establish the truth or validity of by presentation of argument or evidence. **2.** *Law.* To establish the authenticity of (a will). **3.** To determine the quality of by testing or scientific experiment. **4.** *Mathematics.* **a.** To validate (a hypothesis or proposition) by a proof. **b.** To verify (the result of a calculation). **5.** *Printing.* To make a sample impression of (type). **6.** *Archaic.* To experience: *"And we will all the pleasures prove"* (Christopher Marlowe). —*intr.* **1.** To turn out: *"a very agreeable companion may . . . prove a very improper . . . friend"* (Lord Chesterfield). **2.** To rise to the desired degree before baking. Used of dough. —See Synonyms at **confirm.** [Middle English *proven,* to put to test, prove, from Old French *prover,* from Latin *probāre,* to test, demonstrate as good, from *probus,* good, virtuous.] —**prov·a·bil·i·ty** (prŏŏvə-bíllәti), **prov·a·ble·ness** *n.* —**prov·a·ble** *adj.* —**prov·a·bly** *adv.* —**prov·er** *n.*

Usage: *Proved* is the preferred past participle form of this verb in British English: *He has proved his point. Proven* is less often used, and tends to be found in formal (especially legal) contexts. But it is the preferred form in American English, and is normal in both American and British English when used adjectivally before a noun.

prov·en (prŏŏv'n; prṓv'n) *adj.* Having been put to the test and shown to be valid: *proven ability.* See **not proven.** —**prov·en·ly** *adv.*

prov·e·nance (próvvə-nәnss || *U.S. also* -naanss) *n.* The place of origin; derivation. [French, from *provenant,* present participle of *provenir,* to come forth, originate, from Latin *prōvenīre* : *prō-,* forth + *venīre,* to come.]

Pro·ven·çal (próv-oN-saál, -'n- || *U.S. also* prōv-, prə-vénss'l) *n. Abbr.* **Prov., Pr.** **1.** A native or inhabitant of Provence, France. **2.** The Romance language of Provence, especially the literary language of the troubadours. —**Pro·ven·çal** *adj.*

Pro·vence (pro-vóNss, prō-, -vaánss). Region and former province of southeast France. It extends from the Alps westwards to the Rhône valley and from the Mediterranean northwards to the former province of Dauphiné, and is a distinct cultural region with its own language, Provençal, in which the medieval troubadours composed their love lyrics. Tourism is important, especially along the Riviera, and wine and fruit are the chief products.

prov·en·der (próvvindər) *n.* **1.** Dry food, such as hay, used as fodder for livestock. **2.** *Informal.* Food or provisions. [Middle English *provendre,* from Old French *provend(r)e,* from Medieval Latin *prōbenda,* fodder, alteration of Late Latin *praebenda,* support, subsistence, pension, "things to be supplied", from *praebendus,* gerundive of *prae(hi)bēre,* to hold forth, supply : *prae-,* before + *habēre,* to hold.]

pro·ve·ni·ence (prə-veén-i-ənss, prō-, -yənss) *n.* A source or origin of something. [Latin *prōveniēns* (stem *prōvenient-*), present participle of *prōvenīre,* to come forth. See **provenance.**]

pro·ven·tric·u·lus (prṓ-ven-tríckew-ləss) *n., pl.* **-li** (-lī). *Zoology.* **1.** The glandular part of the stomach anterior to the gizzard in birds. **2.** The thick-walled, muscular stomach of insects and crustaceans. Also called "gizzard". [New Latin : PRO- (in front of) + Latin *ventriculus,* stomach, gizzard, VENTRICLE.] —**pro·ven·tric·u·lar** (-lər) *adj.*

prov·erb (próvverb) *n.* **1.** A short, pithy saying in frequent and widespread use, expressing a well-known truth or fact. **2.** A person or thing recognised as a typical example; one that is proverbial. —See Synonyms at **saying.**

~*tr.v.* **proverbed, -erbing, -erbs.** **1.** To give the character of a proverb to. **2.** To make into a proverb. [Middle English *proverbe,* from Old French, from Latin *prōverbium,* "set of words put forth" : *prō-,* forth + *verbum,* word.]

pro·ver·bi·al (prə-vérbi-əl, pro- || prō-) *adj.* **1.** Of the nature of a proverb. **2.** Expressed in a proverb or proverbs. **3.** Widely referred to, as if the subject of a proverb; well known. —**pro·ver·bi·al·ly** *adv.*

Prov·erbs (próvverbz) *n. Used with a singular verb. Abbr.* **Prov.** A book of the Old Testament.

pro·vide (prə-vīd || prō-) *v.* **-vided, -viding, -vides.** —*tr.* **1.** To furnish; supply: *You can provide the drinks.* **2.** To give; afford: *the delay provided an opportunity to reflect.* **3.** To set down as a stipulation: *The contract provides that in case of injury you will be excused.* **4.** *Ecclesiastical.* Formerly, to appoint to a an ecclesiastical benefice, especially when the benefice has not yet become vacant. **5.** *Rare.* To make ready; prepare. —*intr.* **1.** To take measures in preparation. Used with *for* or *against.* **2.** To supply means of subsistence. Used with *for.* **3.** To make a stipulation or condition: *The will doesn't provide for such a contingency.* [Middle English *providen,* to foresee, make provision, from Latin *prōvidēre* : *prō-,* beforehand, in anticipation of + *vidēre,* to see.] —**pro·vid·er** *n.*

pro·vid·ed (prə-vīdid || prō-) *conj.* On the condition; if and only if. Often followed by *that*: *She will go, provided that I stay behind.*

Usage: When a requirement is explicitly set forth, the standard construction is *provided that* (or simply *provided*): *You may leave, provided that you have finished the job.* The use of *providing* is common in informal speech, but attracts criticism in written English.

prov·i·dence (próvvi-dənss || -denss) *n.* **1.** Care or preparation in advance; foresight. **2.** Prudent management; economy. **3.** The care, guardianship, and control exercised by a deity. **4.** *Capital* **P.** God, especially when viewed as a guardian and protector.

Providence. Seaport and capital of Rhode Island in the United States, situated where the Providence river joins Narragansett Bay. Its industries include jewellery, printing, and textiles.

prov·i·dent (próvvi-dənt || -dent) *adj.* **1.** Providing for future needs or events; showing foresight. **2.** Frugal; economical. [Middle English, from Latin *prōvidēns* (stem *prōvident-*), present participle of *prōvidēre,* to foresee, PROVIDE.] —**prov·i·dent·ly** *adv.*

prov·i·den·tial (próvvi-dénsh'l) *adj.* **1.** Of or resulting from divine providence. **2.** Happening as if through divine intervention; fortunate; opportune. —**prov·i·den·tial·ly** *adv.*

provident society *n.* A **friendly society** *(see).*

pro·vid·ing (prə-vīding || prō-) *conj.* On the condition; provided. Sometimes followed by *that.* See Usage note at **provided.**

prov·ince (próvvinss) *n. Abbr.* **prov.** **1.** A territory governed as an administrative or political unit of a country or empire, such as Saskatchewan in Canada. **2.** Any of various lands outside Italy conquered by the Romans and administered by them as self-contained units. **3.** An ecclesiastical division of territory under the jurisdiction of an archbishop. **4.** *Plural.* Areas of a country situated away from the capital or national cultural centre. Preceded by *the.* **5.** A comprehensive area of knowledge, activity, or interest. **6.** The range of one's proper duties and functions; scope; jurisdiction. **7.** *Ecology.* A subdivision of a **region** *(see).* —**the Province.** The Province of Northern Ireland. [Middle English *provynce,* from Old French *province,* from Latin *provincia*†.]

pro·vin·cial (prə-vínsh'l || prō-) *adj.* **1.** *Abbr.* **prov.** Of or pertaining to a province. **2.** Of or supposedly characteristic of people from the provinces; not fashionable or sophisticated. **3.** Limited in perspective; narrow and self-centred.

~*n.* **1.** A native or inhabitant of the provinces. **2.** A person who has supposedly provincial ideas or habits. —**pro·vin·cial·ism, pro·vin·ci·al·i·ty** (-vínshi-ál-əti) *n.* —**pro·vin·cial·ly** *adv.*

proving ground *n.* A place for testing new devices or theories.

pro·vi·rus (prṓ-vīr-əss) *n.* A virus that does not cause lysis and has become part of the host cell, and is transmitted from one cell generation to the next in the chromosome.

pro·vi·sion (prə-vízh'n || prō-) *n.* **1.** The act of supplying or fitting out. **2.** That which is provided. **3.** A preparatory measure: *make provision for our distinguished guest.* **4.** *Plural.* A stock of necessary supplies, especially food. **5.** A stipulation or qualification; especially, a clause in a document or agreement. **6.** The appointment of an ecclesiastical clergyman to a benefice before it is vacant.

~*tr.v.* **provisioned, -sioning, -sions.** To supply with provisions. [Middle English, foresight, precaution, from Old French, from Latin *prōvīsiō* (stem *prōvīsiōn-*), from *prōvīsus,* past participle of *prōvidēre,* to PROVIDE.] —**pro·vi·sion·er** *n.*

pro·vi·sion·al (prə-vízh'n-'l || prō-) *adj.* Also **pro·vi·sion·ar·y** (-əri || -erri) (for sense 1). **1.** *Abbr.* **prov.** Provided for the time being, pending permanent arrangements: *a provisional plan.* See Synonyms at **transient.** **2.** *Capital* **P.** Of, pertaining to, or designating the wing of both the Irish Republican Army and Sinn Fein formed by the split in those organisations, that emphasises the use of terrorist methods to achieve the unification of Ireland. Compare **Official.**

~*n.* **1.** A stamp that is issued temporarily by a post office until the normal issue is available. **2.** *Capital* **P.** A member of the Provisional Irish Republican Army or Sinn Fein. —**pro·vi·sion·al·ly** *adv.*

provisional licence *n.* A licence issued for a fixed period to a person who is learning to drive a motor vehicle, with certain restrictions, for example not allowing the holder to drive a car alone.

pro·vi·so (prə-vīzō, prō-) *n., pl.* **-sos** or **-soes.** **1.** A clause in a document making a qualification, condition, or restriction. **2.** Any condition or stipulation. [Middle English, from Medieval Latin *prōvīsō (quod),* provided (that), from *prōvīsus,* past participle of *prōvidēre,* to PROVIDE.]

pro·vi·so·ry (prə-vīzəri || prō-) *adj.* Depending on a proviso; conditional. —**pro·vi·so·ri·ly** *adv.*

pro·vi·ta·min (prṓ-víttə-min, prō-, -vītə-) *n.* A substance, such as carotene (provitamin A), that is converted into a vitamin in animal bodies.

Pro·vo (prōvō) *n., pl.* **-vos.** Also *locally* **Pro·vie** (prōvee). A member of the Provisional IRA or Sinn Fein. [Shortened from PROVISIONAL (*IRA* or *Sinn Fein*).] —**Pro·vo** *adj.*

prov·o·ca·tion (próvvə-káysh'n) *n.* **1.** The act of provoking or inciting. **2.** Something that provokes; a cause of irritation. **3.** *Law.* Action by one person that causes another person to lose self-control and kill the doer, not amounting to a defence but reducing the gravity of the crime from murder to manslaughter.

pro·voc·a·tive (prə-vóckətiv || prō-) *adj.* Tending to arouse or excite a response, especially anger, curiosity, or sexual interest. —**pro·voc·a·tive·ly** *adv.* —**pro·voc·a·tive·ness** *n.*

pro·voke (prə-vṓk || prō-) *tr.v.* **-voked, -voking, -vokes.** **1.** To incite to anger or resentment. **2.** To stir or incite to action; arouse. **3.** To bring on by inciting. —See Synonyms at **annoy.** [Middle English *provoken,* from Old French *provoquer,* from Latin *prōvocāre,* to call forth, challenge : *prō-,* forth + *vocāre,* to call.] —**pro·vok·ing·ly** *adv.*

Synonyms: *provoke, incite, excite, stimulate, arouse, rouse, stir.*

pro·vo·lo·ne (provo-lṓnay) *n.* A hard Italian curd cheese.

prov·ost (próvvəst || *U.S. also* prṓ-vost, -vəst) *n. Abbr.* **prov.** **1.** The chief officer of a Scottish burgh. **2. a.** In the Anglican Church, the highest official in certain cathedrals, especially one of the modern foundations. **b.** In the Roman Catholic Church, the head of a cathedral chapter. **3.** The head of certain colleges at Cambridge and Oxford. [Middle English *provost,* from Old English *profost* and Old

French *provost,* both from Medieval Latin *prōpositus, praepositus,* from Latin *praepositus,* "(one) placed before (others)", president, superintendent, from the past participle of *praepōnere,* to place before or over : *prae-,* before + *pōnere,* to place.] **—prov·ost·ship** *n.*

pro·vost court (prə-vṓ || *U.S.* prṓvō) *n.* A military court for the trial of minor offences committed in occupied hostile territories.

pro·vost guard (prə-vṓ || *U.S.* prṓvō) *n. Chiefly U.S.* A detail of soldiers on police duty under a provost marshal.

pro·vost marshal (prə-vṓ || *U.S.* prṓvō) *n. Abbr.* **P.M.** The head of military police.

prow (prow) *n.* **1.** The painted front part of a ship's hull; the bow. **2.** A similar projecting part of anything. [French *pro(u)e,* probably from Italian dialect *prua,* from Latin *prōra,* from Greek *prōira.*]

prow·ess (prów-iss, -ess) *n.* **1.** Outstanding skill or ability. **2.** Outstanding strength, courage, or daring, especially in battle. [Middle English *prowesse,* from Old French *proesse,* from *prou,* variant of *prod, prud,* gallant, brave, PROUD.]

prowl (prowl) *v.* **prowled, prowling, prowls.** *—tr.* To roam through stealthily, as if in search of prey or plunder. *—intr.* To move around furtively or with predatory intent.

~n. An act of prowling: *on the prowl.* [Middle English *prollen*†.]

prowl car *n. U.S.* A police patrol car.

prowl·er (prówl-ər) *n.* One who prowls; especially, a man who prowls at night, intent on theft, voyeurism, or sexual molestation.

prox. proximo.

prox·i·mal (próksim'l) *adj.* **1.** Nearest; proximate. **2.** *Biology.* Near the central part of the body or a point of attachment or origin: *the proximal end of a bone.* Compare **distal.** [Latin *proximus,* nearest, next, PROXIMATE.] **—prox·i·mal·ly** *adv.*

prox·i·mate (próksi-mət, -mit) *adj.* **1.** Closely related in space, time, or order; nearest; next. **2.** Approximate. [Latin *proximātus,* past participle of *proximāre,* to come near, from *proximus,* nearest.] **—prox·i·mate·ly** *adv.*

prox·i·me ac·ces·sit (próksi-mi ak-séssit, -may, ək-) *n.* **1.** One who has second place after the winner of an academic prize or distinction. **2.** A second prize. [Latin, "(he) came very near".]

prox·im·i·ty (prok-símməti) *n.* The state, quality, or fact of being near or next in space or time; closeness. [Old French *proximite,* from Latin *proximitās,* from *proximus,* nearest. See **proximate.**]

proximity fuse *n.* An electronic device for detonating a projectile as it approaches a target, as in antiaircraft shells. Also "VT fuse".

prox·i·mo (próksi-mō) *adv. Abbr.* **prox.** *Archaic.* Of or in the following month: *on the 15th proximo.* Compare **ultimo, instant.** [Latin *proximō (mense),* in the next (month), ablative of *proximus,* nearest, next. See **proximate.**]

prox·y (próksi) *n., pl.* **-ies. 1.** A person authorised to act for another; an agent or substitute. **2.** The authority to act for another. **3.** The written authorisation for such action. **—by proxy.** By means of an intermediary. [Middle English *procusie, proxcy,* contractions of *procuracie,* from Anglo-French, from Medieval Latin *prōcūrātia,* from Latin *prōcūrātiō,* a caring for, from *prōcūrātus,* past participle of *prōcūrāre,* to take care of, PROCURE.]

Pro·zac (prṓzak) *n.* **1.** A trademark for the SSRI antidepressant fluoxetine hydrochloride. **2.** A dose (e.g. a tablet) of Prozac.

prude (prōōd || prewd) *n.* A person who is over-concerned with being or seeming to be proper or modest, especially with regard to sex. [French, short for Old French *pr(e)udefemme,* virtuous woman, "fine thing of a woman" : *preu,* virtuous, variant of *prod, prud* (see **proud**) + *de,* of + *femme,* woman.] **—prud·er·y** (-əri) *n.*

pru·dence (prṓōd'nss || préwd'nss) *n.* **1.** The state, quality, or fact of being prudent or sensible. **2.** Careful management; economy.

pru·dent (prṓōd'nt || préwd'nt) *adj.* **1.** Wise in handling practical matters; exercising good judgment or common sense. **2.** Careful with regard to one's own interests; provident. **3.** Careful about one's conduct; circumspect; discreet. [Middle English, from Old French, from Latin *prūdēns* (stem *prūdent-*), foreseeing, wise, contraction of *prōvidēns,* PROVIDENT.] **—pru·dent·ly** *adv.*

pru·den·tial (prōō-dénsh'l || prew-) *adj.* **1.** Arising from or characterised by prudence. **2.** Exercising prudence, good judgment, or common sense. **—pru·den·tial·ly** *adv.*

Prud·hoe Bay (prúddō, prṓōdō). Inlet of the Arctic Ocean, north Alaska, United States. Oil was discovered here (1968), and it is connected to Valdez on the south coast by the trans-Alaska pipeline.

prud·ish (prṓōd-ish || préwd-) *adj.* Having an excessive regard for propriety, modesty, or morality, especially that of others; prim. **—prud·ish·ly** *adv.* **—prud·ish·ness** *n.*

pru·i·nose (prṓō-i-nōz, -nōss || préw-) *adj. Botany.* Having a white, powdery covering or bloom. [Latin *pruīnōsus,* covered with frost, from *pruīna,* hoarfrost.]

prune¹ (prōōn || prewn) *n.* **1.** The partially dried fruit of any of several varieties of the common plum, *Prunus domestica.* **2.** *Chiefly British Informal.* A foolish or ineffectual person. [Middle English *prun(n)e,* from Old French *prune,* from Vulgar Latin *prūna* (unattested), from Latin, plural of *prūnum,* plum; akin to Greek *proumnon,* from an unknown source in Asia Minor.]

prune² *v.* **pruned, pruning, prunes.** *—tr.* **1.** To cut off or remove dead or living parts or branches of (a plant, shrub, or tree) to improve shape or growth. **2.** To remove or cut out as superfluous. **3.** To remove superfluous material from; cut down: *prune the budget.* *—intr.* To remove branches or parts from a plant. [Middle English *prouynen,* from Old French *pro(o)ignier,* from Vulgar Latin *prōrotundiāre* (unattested), to cut roundedly in front : Latin *prō-,* in front + *rotundus,* round, circular.] **—prun·er** *n.*

pru·nel·la (prōō-néllə || prew-) *n.* Also **pru·nel·lo** (-néllō). A strong, heavy fabric of worsted twill, used chiefly for shoe uppers, clerical robes, and academic gowns. [French *prunelle,* "sloe", here perhaps "sloe-coloured stuff". See **prunelle.**]

pru·nelle (prōō-nél || prew-) *n.* A green, sloe-flavoured French liqueur. [French, "sloe", diminutive of *prune,* plum.]

pru·ri·ent (próor-i-ənt || préwr-) *adj.* **1.** Obsessively interested in improper matters, especially those of a sexual nature. **2.** Characterised by or arousing such interest: *prurient thoughts.* [Latin *prūriēns* (stem *prūrient-*), present participle of *prūrīre,* to itch, be lascivious.] **—pru·ri·ence, pru·ri·en·cy** *n.* **—pru·ri·ent·ly** *adv.*

pru·ri·go (proor-rīgō, prōō- || prew-) *n.* A chronic, inflammatory skin disease characterised by eruption and severe itching. [Latin, an itching, from *prūrīre,* to itch.] **—pru·rig·i·nous** (-ríjinəss) *adj.*

pru·ri·tus (proor-rītəss, prōō- || prew-) *n. Pathology.* **1.** Severe itching, usually of undamaged skin. **2.** Any condition characterised by this. [Latin, from *prūrīre,* to itch.] **—pru·rit·ic** (-ríttik) *adj.*

Prus·sia (prúshə). Former north German state, now chiefly in Germany, Poland, and countries of the former U.S.S.R. Bordering the Baltic Sea, it was established in the 13th century by the victory of the Teutonic Knights over the heathen Prussians. It became a hereditary duchy in 1525, and united with the Mark of Brandenburg in 1618. It became the Kingdom of Prussia in 1701 and under Frederick the Great took Silesia and parts of Poland. Prussia gained further territories at the Congress of Vienna (1815) and expanded under Bismarck to form the North German Confederation (1867) and the German Empire (1871). After World War I it became a republic much reduced in size (1918) and was dissolved completely (1946–47) after World War II by the Allies. Berlin was the capital.

Prus·sian (prúsh'n) *adj.* **1.** *Abbr.* **Prus., Pruss.** Of or pertaining to Prussia, its people, or their language and culture. **2.** Similar to or suggestive of the Junkers and the military class of Prussia, especially in being sternly disciplined.

~n. **1.** Any of the western Balts inhabiting the region between the Vistula and the Neman in ancient times. **2.** A Baltic inhabitant of Prussia. **3.** A German inhabitant of Prussia. **4.** See **Old Prussian.**

Prussian blue *n.* **1.** An insoluble dark blue pigment and dye, ferric ferrocyanide or one of its modifications. **2. Iron blue** *(see).* **3.** Moderate to deep greenish blue. [Discovered in Berlin (1704) by H. de Diesbach, a maker of artist's colours.] **—Prus·sian blue** *adj.*

Prus·sian·ise, Prus·sian·ize (prúsh'n-īz) *tr.v.* **-ised, -ising, -ises.** To make Prussian in character or organisation, as by imposing rigid discipline. **—Prus·sian·i·sa·tion** (-ī-záysh'n || *U.S.* -i-) *n.*

prus·si·ate (prúshi-ət, prússi-, -it, -ayt) *n. Chemistry.* **1.** A ferrocyanide or ferricyanide. **2.** A salt of hydrocyanic acid; a cyanide. [French : from *(acide) prussique,* PRUSSIC (ACID) + -ATE.]

prus·sic acid (prússik) *n. Chemistry.* **Hydrocyanic acid** *(see).* [French *acide prussique,* because obtained from Prussian blue.]

pry¹ (prī) *intr.v.* **pried, prying, pries.** To look or enquire closely, curiously, or inquisitively, especially in a furtive manner. Often used with *into.*

~n., pl. **pries. 1.** An act of prying. **2.** A too-inquisitive person. [Middle English *prien,* perhaps related to PEER.] **—pry·ing·ly** *adv.*

pry² *tr.v.* **pried, prying, pries.** *U.S.* To prise, as with a lever. [From PRISE, mistaken for third person singular, as if *pries.*]

pryer. Variant of **prier.**

Prynne (prin), **William** (1600–69). English political agitator. A Puritan, he was imprisoned (1633) and had his ears cut off for his pamphlet, *Historiomastix,* an attack on the theatre which insulted the Queen. He was later branded on both cheeks for pamphleteering, and again imprisoned (1650) for writings attacking the Commonwealth.

Prze·wal·ski's horse (pshi-vál-skiz, pshe-, shə- || -skeez) *n.* A Mongolian wild horse with an erect mane, *Equus przewalskii* (or *E. caballus przewalskii*), now an endangered species. [After N.M. *Przewalski* (1839–88), Russian explorer who discovered it.]

Ps. Psalm; Psalms (Old Testament).

p.s. 1. passenger steamer. **2.** postscript.

P.S. 1. permanent secretary. **2.** Police Sergeant. **3.** postscript. **4.** private secretary. **5.** prompt side. **6.** passenger steamer.

Psa. Psalm; Psalms (Old Testament).

psalm (saam || solm, saalm) *n.* **1.** A sacred song; a hymn. **2.** *Usually capital* **P.** *Abbr.* **Ps., Psa.** Any of the sacred songs or hymns collected in the Old Testament Book of Psalms.

~tr.v. **psalmed, psalming, psalms.** To sing of or celebrate in psalms. [Middle English *(p)salm,* Old English *(p)sealm,* from Late Latin *psalmus,* from Greek *psalmos,* song sung to the harp, psalm (translation of Hebrew *mizmōr,* song, psalm), from *psallein,* to pluck, play the harp.]

psalm·ist (saam-ist || sólm-, saalm-) *n.* A writer or composer of psalms. **—the Psalmist.** King David, to whom many of the scriptural psalms are traditionally attributed.

psalm·o·dy (saa-mədi, sál- || sól-, saal-) *n., pl.* **-dies. 1.** The singing of psalms in divine worship. **2.** The composition or arranging of psalms for singing. **3.** A collection of psalms. [Middle English *psalmodie,* from Late Latin *psalmōdia,* from Late Greek, from Greek, singing to the harp : *psalmos,* PSALM + *ōidē,* song, ode.] **—psalm·o·dist** *n.*

Psalms (saamz || solmz, saalmz). *Abbr.* **Ps., Psa.** A book of the Old Testament, the Book of Psalms, containing 150 songs.

Psal·ter (sáwl-tər || sól-) *n. Often small* **p. 1.** A book containing the Book of Psalms or a particular version of it in liturgical use. **2.** A musical setting for the Psalms. **3.** The Psalms. [Middle English *(p)salter, sauter,* from Old English *(p)saltere* and Old French *(p)sautier,* both from Late Latin *psalterium,* early Christian transference of Greek *psaltērion,* psalm, song, PSALTERY.]

psal·te·ri·um (sawl-téer-i-əm ‖ sol-) *n., pl.* **-teria** (-téer-i-ə). The third division of the stomach of ruminants, the **omasum** *(see).* [New Latin, from Late Latin, PSALTER (when slit open its folds fall apart like the leaves of a book).] —**psal·te·ri·al** *adj.*

psal·ter·y (sáwl-təri ‖ sól-) *n., pl.* **-ies.** An ancient, stringed musical instrument played by plucking the strings with the fingers or a plectrum. [Middle English *(p)salterie, sautre,* from Old French *(p)salterie, sauter(i)e,* from Latin *psaltērium,* from Greek *psaltērion,* from *psallein,* to pluck, play upon a stringed instrument.]

psam·mite (sámmīt) *n.* Metamorphosed arenaceous rock. [French : Greek *psammos,* sand + -ITE.] —**psam·mit·ic** (sam-íttik) *adj.*

pse·phite (sée-fīt) *n.* A rock consisting of relatively large fragments embedded in a finer matrix. [French, from Greek *psēphos,* pebble.] —**pse·phit·ic** (see-fíttik) *adj.*

pse·phol·o·gy (si-fóllə-ji, se-) *n.* The study of electoral systems and voting trends and behaviour. [Greek *psēphos,* pebble, vote (from the use of pebbles to cast votes in ancient Greece) + -LOGY.] —**pseph·o·log·i·cal** (séefə-lójik'l, séffə-) *adj.* —**pse·phol·o·gist** *n.*

pseud (sewd, sóod) *n. Chiefly British Informal.* A pretentious, superficial, or affected person. [Shortened from PSEUDO.] —**pseud** *adj.*

pseud. pseudonym.

pseud·ax·is (sew-dáksiss, soó-) *n. Botany.* A **sympodium** *(see).* [PSEUD(O)- + AXIS.] —**pseud·ax·i·al** *adj.*

pseud·e·pig·ra·pha (séw-di-píggrə-fə, soó-) *pl. n. Sometimes capital* **P. 1.** Spurious writings; specifically, writings falsely attributed to Biblical characters or times. **2.** A body of Jewish religious texts written between 200 B.C. and A.D. 200 and spuriously ascribed to various prophets and kings of Hebrew Scriptures. [Greek, neuter plural of *pseudepigraphos,* falsely ascribed : PSEUDO- + *epigraphein,* to ascribe : *epi,* on, upon + *graphein,* to write.] —**pseud·e·pig·ra·phal** (-f'l), **pseud·ep·i·graph·ic** (-deppi-gráffik), **pseud·ep·i·graph·i·cal, pseud·e·pig·ra·phous** (-píggrə-fəss) *adj.*

pseu·do (séw-dō, soó-) *adj.* False or counterfeit; fake. [Middle English, from PSEUDO-.]

pseudo-, pseud- *comb. form.* Indicates— **1.** Inauthenticity; sham; for example, **pseudoscience. 2.** Deceptive similarity; for example, **pseudopodium.** *Note:* Many compounds other than those entered here may be formed with *pseudo-.* In this dictionary in forming compounds, *pseudo-* is normally joined with the following element without a space or hyphen: *pseudoscience.* However, many users prefer the hyphenated form, and it is used here if the second element begins with a capital letter: *pseudo-Americanism.* The hyphen is also better if the second element begins with *o* or if the compound brings together three or more vowels that would be confusing to read (as in *pseudo-oolite).* [Middle English, from Late Latin, from Greek *pseudēs,* false, from *pseudein†,* to lie.]

pseu·do·carp (séw-dō-kaarp, soó-, -də-) *n. Botany.* A fruit, such as the pear, apple, or strawberry, that contains fleshy tissue developed from floral parts as well as the ovary. Also called "accessory fruit". [PSEUDO- + -CARP.] —**pseu·do·car·pous** (-kárpəss) *adj.*

pseu·do·cy·e·sis (séw-dō-sī-ée-siss, soó-, -də-) *n.* **Phantom pregnancy** *(see).*

pseu·do·her·maph·ro·dit·ism (séw-dō-her-máffrə-dī-tiz'm, soó-, -də-) *n.* An abnormal condition, present at birth, in which the external genital organs resemble those of the opposite sex.

pseu·do·morph (séw-dō-mawrf, soó-, -də-) *n.* **1.** A false, deceptive, or irregular form. **2.** *Mineralogy.* A mineral having the crystalline form of another mineral rather than that normally characteristic of its composition. [PSEUDO- + -MORPH.] —**pseu·do·mor·phic** (-mórfik), **pseu·do·mor·phous** (-mórfəss) *adj.* —**pseu·do·mor·phism** (-mórf-iz'm) *n.*

pseu·do·nym (séw-də-nim, soó- ‖ -dō-) *n. Abbr.* **pseud.** A fictitious name, especially one assumed by an author. [French *pseudonyme,* from Greek *pseudōnumon,* neuter of *pseudōnumos* : PSEUD(O)- + -ONYM.] —**pseu·don·y·mous** (sew-dónniməss, soó-) *adj.*

pseu·do·po·di·um (séw-də-pódi-əm, soó-, -dō-) *n., pl.* **-dia** (-ə). Also **pseu·do·pod** (-pod). A temporary protrusion of the cytoplasm of a cell, in organisms such as the amoeba, as a means of locomotion and of surrounding and ingesting food. [PSEUDO + PODIUM.]

pseu·do·sci·ence (séw-dō-sī-ənss, soó-) *n.* An unscientific or trivially scientific theory, methodology, or activity that appears to be or is presented as scientific. —**pseu·do·sci·en·tif·ic** (-ən-tíffik) *adj.* —**pseu·do·sci·en·tist** *n.*

pseud·y (séw-di, soó-) *adj.* **-ier, -iest.** *Informal.* Pretentious or insincere. [From PSEUD.] —**pseud·i·ness** *n.*

psf, p.s.f. pounds per square foot.

pshaw (pshə, pshaw, shaw) *interj.* Used to indicate impatience, irritation, disapproval, or disbelief.

psi (psī ‖ sī) *n.* The 23rd letter in the Greek alphabet, written Ψ, ψ. Transliterated in English as *ps.* [Late Greek, from Greek *psei,* originally (in the alphabet used at Athens) written ΦΣ.]

psi, p.s.i. pounds per square inch.

psi·lo·cy·bin (sī-lə-síbin, sī-, -lō-) *n.* A phosphate, $C_{12}H_{17}N_2O_4P$, that is the hallucinogen in the fungus *Psilocybe mexicana.* [New Latin *Psilocybe,* from Greek *psīlos,* bald + *kubē,* head (referring to its appearance) + -IN.]

psi·lom·e·lane (sī-lómmilayn) *n.* A black, hydrated oxide ore of

manganese. [Greek *psilos,* mere + *melas* (stem *melan-*), black.]

psi·lo·phyte (sī-lō-fīt, -lə-) *n.* Any of a group of simple vascular plants, the Psilophyta, that appeared early in the Palaeozoic era and were the first of the land plants.

psi particle *n.* An elementary particle in the meson family, believed to consist of a charmed quark and its antiquark, the discovery of which led to the concept of charm in physics. Also called "J particle", "J psi particle". [Greek *psi* (arbitrary designation).]

psit·ta·cine (sítta-sīn, -sin) *adj.* Of, pertaining to, or characteristic of parrots. [Latin *psittacīnus,* from *psittacus,* parrot, from Greek *psittakos†.*]

psit·ta·co·sis (sítta-kó-siss) *n.* A virus disease of parrots and related birds, communicable to human beings, in whom it produces high fever, nosebleeds, and complications similar to pneumonia. Also called "parrot fever". [New Latin : Latin *psittacus,* parrot (see **psittacine**) + -OSIS.] —**psit·ta·cot·ic** (-kóttik, -kótik) *adj.*

pso·as (só-ass, -əss) *n. Anatomy.* Either of two hip muscles, *psoas major,* which flexes the hip joint, and *psoas minor,* a slender muscle that is often absent. [Greek, accusative plural of *psoa,* interpreted as singular.]

pso·ri·a·sis (so-rí-ə-siss, saw-, sə-) *n.* A chronic, noncontagious skin disease characterised by inflammation and red, scaly patches. [New Latin, from Greek *psōriasis,* from *psōrian,* to have the itch, from *psōra,* itch, from *psēn,* to rub, scratch.] —**pso·ri·at·ic** (sáw-ri-áttik, só- ‖ sō-) *adj.*

pst, psst (pst) *interj.* Used as a whisper to attract somebody's attention, especially without others noticing.

PST, P.S.T. Pacific Standard Time.

P.S.V. public service vehicle (in Britain).

psych, psyche (sīk) *tr.v.* **psyched, psyching, psychs.** *Informal.* **1.** To put (a person, especially oneself) into the right psychological frame of mind, as for a performance or competition. Usually used with *up.* **2.** To undermine the confidence of by using psychological tactics. Often used with *out: She psyched out her opponent by insults.*

psych. psychological; psychologist; psychology.

psy·che (sī-ki, -kee) *n.* **1.** The soul or spirit, as distinguished from the body. **2.** *Psychiatry.* The mind functioning as the centre of thought, feeling, and behaviour, and consciously or unconsciously adjusting and relating the body to its social and physical environment. [Latin, from Greek *psukhē,* breath, life, soul.]

Psy·che (sī-ki, -kee). *Classical Mythology.* A maiden loved by Eros and united with him after Aphrodite's jealousy was overcome. She became the personification of the soul.

psy·che·del·i·a (síki-deelia, -délli-) *pl.n.* **1.** The world of psychedelic drugs, those who take them, and the effects produced by them. **2.** The music, art, books, or other artefacts that deal with or are supposed to suggest or evoke psychedelic experiences. [PSYCHE-DELIC + -IA.]

psy·che·del·ic (síki-déllik) *adj.* **1.** Of, pertaining to, or generating hallucinations, distortions of perception, and, occasionally, states resembling psychosis: *psychedelic drugs.* **2.** Producing an effect similar to the effects of psychedelic drugs: *psychedelic art.*
~ *n.* A psychedelic drug. [From PSYCHE (mind) + Greek *dēlos,* clear, visible.]

psy·chi·a·trist (sī-kí-ə-trist, si-, sə-) *n.* A doctor specially trained to practise psychiatry.

psy·chi·a·try (sī-kí-ə-tri, si-, sə-) *n.* The medical study, diagnosis, treatment, and prevention of mental or emotional disorders. [PSYCH(O)- + -IATRY.] —**psy·chi·at·ric** (sī-ki-áttrik), **psy·chi·at·ri·cal** *adj.* —**psy·chi·at·ri·cal·ly** *adv.*

psy·chic (sīkik) *adj.* Also **psy·chi·cal** (-'l). **1.** Of or pertaining to the human mind or psyche. **2. a.** Of or pertaining to extraordinary, especially extrasensory and nonphysical, mental processes or forces, such as extrasensory perception and telepathy. **b.** Proceeding from or produced by such processes or forces. **c.** Designating a person who is especially responsive to such processes or forces.
~ *n.* **1.** A psychic person. **2.** A medium. [Greek *psukhikos,* from *psukhē,* soul, life, PSYCHE.] —**psy·chi·cal·ly** *adv.*

psy·chics (sīkiks) *n. Used with a singular verb.* The analysis, examination, and study of psychic phenomena.

psy·cho (síkō) *n., pl.* **-chos.** *Slang.* A psychopath or psychotic. —**psy·cho** *adj.*

psycho-, psych- *comb. form.* Indicates the mind or mental processes; as, **psychology.** [Greek *psukhē,* breath, life, PSYCHE.]

psy·cho·a·cous·tics (síkō-ə-kóostiks) *n. Used with a singular verb.* The study of sound in relation to its reception, both physiological and psychological.

psy·cho·ac·tive (síkō-áktiv) *adj.* Having an effect on the mind.

psy·cho·an·a·lyse, psy·cho·an·a·lyze (síkō-ánnə-līz) *tr.v.* **-lysed, -lysing, -lyses.** To analyse and treat by psychoanalysis. [Back-formation from PSYCHOANALYSIS.]

psy·cho·a·nal·y·sis (síkō-ə-nál-ə-siss) *n.* **1.** A method of psychotherapy originated by Sigmund Freud, based on the exploration of unconscious mental processes as manifested in dreams and disturbed relationships with others. Its aim is to reveal repressed anxieties and overcome the effects of bad experiences in early childhood, typically using the technique of free association. **2.** A technique of research into human behaviour and mental processes using the methods and theories of psychoanalysis. **3.** A th... human psychology, based on the findings of psych... cerning the structure of the mind and the effect... mental processes on behaviour. —**psy·cho·an·a·lys**

—**psy·cho·an·a·lyt·ic** (-ánnə-líttik), **psy·cho·an·a·lyt·i·cal** *adj.* —**psy·cho·an·a·lyt·i·cal·ly** *adv.*

psy·cho·bab·ble (síkō-babb^ᵘl) *n.* Psychotherapeutic jargon. [Coined in 1975 by R.D. Rosen, author of *Psychobabble.*]

psy·cho·bi·ol·o·gy (síkō-bī-óllaji) *n.* The study of the interactions between mental and biological processes as they affect personality.

psy·cho·chem·i·cal (síkō-kémmik'l) *adj.* Causing psychological changes or mental disorders.
~*n.* A psychochemical substance, such as a drug or gas.

psy·cho·dra·ma (síkō-draamə, -draámə ‖ *U.S. also* -drámmə) *n.* **1.** A psychotherapeutic and analytic technique in which individuals spontaneously play out roles based on their personal histories. **2.** A psychological drama. —**psy·cho·dra·mat·ic** (-drə-máttik) *adj.*

psy·cho·dy·nam·ics (síkō-dī-námmiks) *n. Used with a singular verb.* **1.** The interaction of various mental or emotional processes, especially when they are considered as constituents of a system of interrelated forces. **2.** Behavioural analysis in terms of motives or drives. —**psy·cho·dy·nam·ic** *adj.*

psy·cho·gen·e·sis (síkō-jénnə-siss) *n.* **1. a.** The origin and development of psychological processes, personality, or behaviour. **b.** The origin of the soul. **2.** The psychological or mental, as opposed to the physiological or physical, origin of something. —**psy·cho·ge·net·ic** (-jə-néttik) *adj.* —**psy·cho·ge·net·i·cal·ly** *adv.*

psy·cho·gen·ic (síkō-jénnik) *adj.* Having a psychological rather than physiological origin. Said of certain disorders. [PSYCHO- + -GENIC.] —**psy·cho·gen·i·cal·ly** *adv.*

psy·cho·geri·at·rics (síkō-jérri-áttriks) *n.* The psychiatry of the mental disorders of old people. —**psycho·ger·i·at·ric** *adj.*

psy·chog·no·sis (sī-kog-nō-siss) *n. Rare.* The study of the psyche. [PSYCHO- + -GNOSIS.] —**psy·chog·nos·tic** (-nóstik) *adj.*

psy·cho·his·to·ry (síkō-hístəri) *n.* The study of individual and collective psychology as it influences and is affected by the historical process: *the psychohistory of the Nazi holocaust.* —**psy·cho·his·tor·i·cal** (-his-tórrik'l) *adj.* —**psy·cho·his·tor·i·cal·ly** *adv.*

psy·cho·ki·ne·sis (síkō-kī-née-siss, -ki-) *n.* **1.** *Abbr.* **PK** In parapsychology, the production of motion, especially in inanimate and remote objects, by the exercise of psychic powers. **2.** *Psychiatry.* Uninhibited, maniacal motor response. [PSYCHO- + -KINESIS.] —**psy·cho·ki·net·ic** (-kī-néttik, -ki-) *adj.*

psychol. psychological; psychologist; psychology.

psy·cho·lin·guis·tics (síkō-ling-gwístiks) *n. Used with a singular verb.* A branch of linguistics concerned with the mental and psychological aspects of language and speech, such as, for example, the childhood acquisition of language. —**psy·cho·lin·guist** (-ling-gwist) *n.* —**psy·cho·lin·guis·tic** *adj.*

psy·cho·log·i·cal (síkə-lójik'l) *adj. Also rare* **psy·cho·log·ic.** *Abbr.* **psych., psychol.** **1.** Of or pertaining to psychology. **2.** Of, pertaining to, or derived from the mind or emotions: *Your fear of water is purely psychological—you're a perfectly good swimmer.* **3.** Capable of influencing the mind or emotions. —**psy·cho·log·i·cal·ly** *adv.*

psychological moment *n.* The time when the mental state of a person is most likely to produce the desired response.

psychological warfare *n.* The use of tactics in warfare designed to undermine the courage, loyalty, or morale of the enemy.

psy·chol·o·gise, psy·chol·o·gize (sī-kóllə-jīz) *v.* -**gised, -gising, -gises.** —*tr.* To explain (behaviour) in terms of psychology. —*intr.* To investigate behaviour using psychological concepts.

psy·chol·o·gism (sī-kóllə-jiz'm) *n.* The application or use, often spurious, of psychological theories to interpret or explain phenomena in other sciences or in the arts, as in history or literature.

psy·chol·o·gist (sī-kóllajist) *n. Abbr.* **psych., psychol.** A person trained to perform psychological research or therapy.

psy·chol·o·gy (sī-kóllaji) *n., pl.* -**gies.** *Abbr.* **psych., psychol.** **1.** The science concerned with understanding and explaining mental processes and behaviour. **2.** The emotional and behavioural characteristics of an individual, group, or activity: *the psychology of war.* **3.** Subtle tactical action or argument: *She used poor psychology on her employer.* [New Latin *psychologia* : PSYCHO- + -LOGY.]

psy·cho·met·rics (síkō-ə-méttriks, -ō-) *n. Used with a singular verb.* **1.** The measurement of psychological variables, such as intelligence, aptitude, or emotional disturbance. **2.** The mathematical, especially statistical, design of psychological tests and measures. —**psy·cho·met·ric, psy·cho·met·ri·cal** *adj.* —**psy·cho·met·ri·cal·ly** *adv.* —**psy·cho·me·tri·cian** (-me-tríshʼn, -mə- ‖ sī-kómmə-), **psy·chom·e·trist** (sī-kómmə-trist) *n.*

psy·chom·e·try (sī-kómmətri) *n.* **1.** Psychometrics. **2.** In parapsychology, the supposed ability to divine facts about events, objects, or people, through proximity to them or through touching them. [PSYCHO- + -METRY.]

psy·cho·mo·tor (síkō-mōtər) *adj.* Of or pertaining to muscular activity associated with mental processes.

psy·cho·neu·ro·sis (síkō-newr-rō-siss ‖ -noor-, -new-, -nōō-) *n., pl.* -**ses** (-seez). *Psychology.* Neurosis (see). —**psy·cho·neu·rot·ic** (-rót-tik) *adj. & n.*

psy·cho·path (sík-ə-path, -ō-) *n.* A person with a personality disorder, especially one manifested in aggressively antisocial behaviour, amoral attitudes, and continually fluctuating moods. [From PSYCHOPATHY.] —**psy·cho·path·ic** (-páthik) *adj.*

psy·cho·pa·thol·o·gy (síkō-pə-thóllə-ji) *n.* The study of pathological mental disorders. —**psy·cho·path·o·log·ic** (-pátha-lójik), **psy·cho·path·o·log·i·cal** *adj.* —**psy·cho·pa·thol·o·gist** (-thóllə-jist) *n.*

psy·chop·a·thy (sī-kóppəthi) *n.* A mental disorder or disease. [PSYCHO- + -PATHY.]

psy·cho·phar·ma·col·o·gy (síkō-fármə-kóllə-ji) *n.* A branch of pharmacology concerned with the study and use of drugs that affect the mind. —**psy·cho·phar·ma·co·log·i·cal** (-kə-lójik'l) *adj.* —**psy·cho·phar·ma·col·o·gist** (-kóllə-jist) *n.*

psy·cho·phys·ics (síkō-fízziks) *n. Used with a singular verb.* The psychological study of relationships between physical stimuli and sensory responses. —**psy·cho·phys·i·cal** *adj.* —**psy·cho·phys·i·cal·ly** *adv.* —**psy·cho·phys·i·cist** (-fízzi-sist) *n.*

psy·cho·phys·i·ol·o·gy (síkō-fízzi-óllaji) *n.* The study of correlations between mental processes and physiology. —**psy·cho·phys·i·o·log·i·cal** (-ə-lójik'l) *adj.* —**psy·cho·phys·i·o·log·i·cal·ly** *adv.*

psy·cho·pro·phy·lax·is (síkō-próffi-láksiss ‖ *chiefly U.S.* -prófi-) *n.* The use of psychological conditioning to prepare a woman for natural childbirth. —**psy·cho·pro·phy·lac·tic** (-láktik) *adj.*

psy·cho·sex·u·al (síkō-sék-sew-əl, -shoo-, -shwəl) *adj.* Of or pertaining to the psychological aspects of sex or the mental processes relating to it. —**psy·cho·sex·u·al·i·ty** (-ál-əti) *n.*

psy·cho·sis (sī-kō-siss) *n., pl.* -**ses** (-seez). Any severe mental disorder, with or without organic damage, characterised by deterioration of normal intellectual and social functioning and by partial or complete withdrawal from reality. Compare **neurosis.** [New Latin : PSYCH(O)- + -OSIS.]

psy·cho·so·mat·ic (síkō-sə-máttik, -sō-) *adj.* Of or pertaining to phenomena that exhibit an interaction of the physiological and the psychological, especially disorders, such as high blood pressure, that may be initiated or aggravated by mental stress.

psy·cho·sur·ger·y (síkō-súrj-əri) *n.* Brain surgery when used to treat mental disorders. —**psy·cho·sur·gi·cal** (-ik'l) *adj.*

psy·cho·tech·nics (síkō-ték-niks) *n. Used with a singular verb. Chiefly U.S.* The practical or technological use of psychology, as in analysis of social or industrial problems. —**psy·cho·tech·ni·cal** *adj.* —**psy·cho·tech·ni·cian** (-tek-níshʼn) *n.*

psy·cho·ther·a·py (sík-ō-thérrə-pi, -ə-) *n.* **1.** Treatment of emotional and psychosomatic disorders based on the application of psychological knowledge, rather than exclusively on the use of drugs, surgery, or other physical treatment. **2.** Psychotherapy using depth psychology, by contrast with behaviour therapy. —**psy·cho·ther·a·peu·tic** (-péwtik) *adj.* —**psy·cho·ther·a·pist** (-pist) *n.*

psy·chot·ic (sī-kóttik) *n.* One suffering from a psychosis. [From PSYCHOSIS.] —**psy·chot·ic** *adj.* —**psy·chot·i·cal·ly** *adv.*

psy·chot·o·mi·met·ic (sī-kóttō-mi-méttik, -mī-) *adj.* Designating a drug, such as LSD, that is capable of causing psychosis or psychotic symptoms.
~*n.* A psychotomimetic drug. [PSYCHOT(IC) + MIMETIC.]

psy·cho·trop·ic (síkō-tróppik, -trōpik) *adj.* Affecting the moods or mental processes. Said of a drug. [PSYCHO- + -TROPIC.] —**psy·cho·trop·ic** *n.* —**psy·cho·trop·ic·al·ly** *adv.*

psychro– *comb. form.* Indicates cold; for example, **psychrometer.** [Greek *psukhros†,* cold.]

psy·chrom·e·ter (sī-krómmitər) *n.* A hygrometer that uses the difference in readings between two thermometers, one having a wet bulb ventilated to cause evaporation and the other having a dry bulb, as a measure of atmospheric moisture. Also called "wet-and-dry-bulb thermometer". [PSYCHRO- + -METER.]

psy·chro·phil·ic (sík-rō-fíllik, -rə-) *adj. Biology.* Thriving at relatively low temperatures, usually between 0 and 25°C. Said of certain bacteria. Compare **mesophilic, thermophilic.** [PSYCHRO- + -PHIL(E) + -IC.]

psyl·la (síllə) *n. Also* **psyl·lid** (síllid). Any of various plant lice of the family Chermidae (or Psyllidae), especially *Psylla mali,* a pest that infests apple trees. [Greek *psulla,* flea.]

Pt The symbol for the element platinum.

pt. **1.** part. **2.** payment. **3.** pint. **4.** point. **5.** port. **6.** preterite.

p.t. **1.** past tense. **2.** pro tempore.

P.T. **1.** Pacific Time. **2.** physical therapy. **3.** physical training. **4.** postal telegraph. **5.** purchase tax (formerly, in Britain).

pta. peseta.

P.T.A. **1.** Parent-Teacher Association. **2.** passenger transport authority (in Britain).

Ptah (ptaa, taa) *n.* In ancient Egypt, the creator god and the god of Memphis, represented in the form of a mummy.

ptar·mi·gan (tármigən) *n., pl.* -**gans** or collectively **ptarmigan.** A game bird, *Lagopus mutus,* of the grouse family, inhabiting arctic and subarctic regions of the Northern Hemisphere. It has feathered feet and plumage that is brownish-grey in summer, grey in autumn, and white in winter. [Alteration (by pseudo-learned association with Greek *pteron,* wing) of Scottish Gaelic *tarmachan,* diminutive of *tarmach†.*]

Pte. private (in the British and various other armies).

–pter *n. comb. form.* Indicates wings or winglike parts; for example, **ornithopter.** [New Latin *-ptera,* from Greek *-pteros,* -PTEROUS.]

pter·i·dol·o·gy (térri-dóllə-ji) *n.* The study of ferns. [Greek *pteris* (stem *pterid-*), fern, from *pteron,* feather + -LOGY.] —**pter·i·do·log·i·cal** (-də-lójik'l) *adj.* —**pter·i·dol·o·gist** (-dóllə-jist) *n.*

pter·id·o·phyte (térri-dō-fīt, -də-; *also* te-ríddə-, tə-) *n. Botany.* Any plant of the division Pteridophyta, including the ferns and horsetails, that reproduces by spores and has vascular tissue. [New Latin *Pteridophyta* : Greek *pteris,* fern (see **pteridology**) + -PHYTE.] —**pter·id·o·phyt·ic** (-fíttik), **pter·i·doph·y·tous** (-dóffitəss) *adj.*

pter·i·do·sperm (térri-dō-sperm, -də-; *also* te-rídda-, tə-) *n.* The seed fern (see).

ptero– *comb. form.* Indicates feather, wing, or winglike part; for example, **pterodactyl.** [Greek *pteron,* feather, wing.]

pter·o·dac·tyl (térrə-dáktil, térrō-) *n.* Any of various extinct flying reptiles of the family Pterodactylidae. See **pterosaur.** [New Latin *Pterodactylus,* "wing-finger" : PTERO- + DACTYL.]

pter·o·pod (térrə-pod, térrō-) *n.* Any of various small marine gastropod molluscs of the order Pteropoda, that swim with winglike expanded lobes of the foot. Also called "sea butterfly". [New Latin *Pteropoda,* "wing-footed ones", from Greek *pteropous,* wing-footed : PTERO- + *-pous,* -POD.] **—pter·o·pod** *adj.*

pter·o·saur (térrə-sawr, térrō-) *n.* Any of various extinct flying reptiles of the order Pterosauria, including the pterodactyls, of the Jurassic and Cretaceous periods, characterised by wings consisting of a flap of skin supported by the very long fourth digit on each front limb. [New Latin *Pterosauria,* "winged lizards" : PTERO- + -sauria, plural of -SAURUS.]

–pterous, –pteran *adj. comb. form.* Indicates a specified number or kind of wings; for example, **dipterous.** [Greek *-pteros,* -winged, from *pteron,* feather, wing.]

pter·y·goid (térrig-oyd) *adj. Anatomy.* Of or designating either of two processes in the skull attached to the body of the sphenoid bone.
~*n. Anatomy.* Either of these processes. Also called "pterygoid process". [Greek *pterugoeidēs* : *pterux,* wing, from *pteron,* feather, wing + -OID.]

PTFE polytetrafluoroethylene.

ptg. printing.

ptis·an (tízz'n, ti-zán) *n.* A **tisane** *(see).* [Middle English *tisan,* peeled barley, barley water, from Old French, from Medieval Latin *tisana,* variant of Latin *ptisana,* from Greek *ptisanē,* from *ptissein,* to peel, crush.]

P.T.O, p.t.o. please turn over.

Ptol·e·ma·ic (tóllə-máy-ik) *adj.* **1.** Of or pertaining to the astronomer Ptolemy. **2.** Of or pertaining to the Ptolemies or to Egypt during their rule, 323 B.C. to 30 B.C.

Ptolemaic system *n.* The astronomical system of Ptolemy, having the Earth at the centre of the universe, with the Moon, planets, and the stars revolving about it.

Ptol·e·ma·ist (tóllə-máy-ist) *n.* An adherent of or believer in the astronomical system of Ptolemy.

Ptol·e·my (tólləmi), Ptolemy, Claudius Ptolemaeus (*c.* A.D. 90 – *c.* 168). Graeco-Egyptian mathematician and geographer. His work, preserved at the Great Library in Alexandria, was translated into Arabic, spread across the Islamic world, and was reintroduced to Europe, where it had a great influence on medieval and Renaissance scholars. His *Geographike hyphegesis* inspired Columbus.

Ptolemy I Soter (*c.* 367– *c.* 284 B.C.). Macedonian soldier, king, and historian. One of Alexander the Great's generals, he became governor of Egypt after his death, and eventually (305) proclaimed himself king, founding the Ptolemaic dynasty. He founded the Library at Alexandria, and recorded Alexander's campaigns.

Ptolemy XIII Theos Philopator (63–47 B.C.). King of Egypt. Following his succession to the throne (51 B.C.) with his sister and wife, Cleopatra, he exiled her (48 B.C.) to Syria. Julius Caesar, however, supported the reinstatement of Cleopatra, and Ptolemy was killed in the subsequent civil war.

pto·maine, pto·main (tō-mayn, tō-máyn, tə-) *n.* Any of various basic nitrogenous materials, some poisonous, produced by the putrefaction and decomposition of protein. [French *ptomaïne,* from Italian *ptomaina,* from Greek *ptōma,* "fall, fallen body", corpse, from *piptein,* to fall.]

ptomaine poisoning *n.* Food poisoning. Ptomaines were formerly erroneously considered a cause of all food poisoning.

pto·sis (tō-siss) *n.* Abnormal and permanent lowering of an organ; especially, drooping of the upper eyelid caused by muscle failure. [New Latin, from Greek *ptōsis,* fall, from *piptein,* to fall.] **—pto·tic** (tōtik, tóttik) *adj.*

pts. **1.** parts. **2.** payments. **3.** pints. **4.** points. **5.** ports.

pty. proprietary.

pty·a·lin (tí-ə-lin) *n.* A salivary enzyme in humans and some other animals that hydrolyses starch into dextrins and ultimately maltose. [Greek *ptualon,* saliva, from *ptuein,* to spit + -IN.]

pty·a·lism (tí-ə-liz'm) *n.* Excessive flow of saliva. [Greek *ptualon,* saliva. See **ptyalin.**]

p-type (pée-tīp) *adj. Electronics.* Of or designating a semiconductor or its type of conductivity, in which the majority of carriers are holes rather than electrons. Compare **n-type.** [Positive *type.*]

Pu The symbol for the element plutonium.

pub (pub) *n. Chiefly British.* A place where alcoholic drinks are sold under licence to be consumed on or off the premises, and which often also provides light meals. Also used adjectivally: *a pub lunch.*
~*intr.v.* **pubbed, pubbing, pubs.** To have a drink in a pub. Used chiefly in the phrase *go pubbing.* [Short for PUBLIC HOUSE.]

pub. **1.** public. **2.** publication. **3.** published; publisher; publishing.

pub crawl —*n. Slang.* A round of drinking in several pubs in succession. **—pub-crawl** (púb-krawl) *intr.v.* **—pub-crawl·er** *n.*

pube (pewb) *n. Informal.* A pubic hair. [Short for *pubic hair.*]

pu·ber·ty (péwbar-ti) *n.* The stage of maturation in early adolescence in which the individual becomes physiologically capable of sexual reproduction and the secondary sexual characteristics appear. [Middle English *puberte,* from Latin *pūbertās* (stem *pūbertāt-*), from *pūber,* adult.] **—pu·ber·al, pu·ber·tal** (-t'l) *adj.*

pu·ber·u·lent (pew-bérrew-lənt ‖ -bérrə-) *adj.* Also **pu·ber·u·lous** (-ləss). *Biology.* Covered with minute hairs or very fine down; finely pubescent. [Latin *pūber,* grown up, adult, (of plants) downy.]

pu·bes (péw-beez). Plural of **pubis.**
~*n., pl.* **pubes.** *Anatomy.* The pubic region. [Latin *pūbēs.*]

pu·bes·cence (pew-béss'nss) *n.* **1.** The attainment or onset of puberty. **2. a.** A covering of soft down or short hairs, as on certain plants and insects. **b.** The state of being pubescent.

pu·bes·cent (pew-béss'nt) *adj.* **1.** Reaching or having reached puberty. **2.** Covered with short hairs or soft down. [French, from Latin *pūbēscens* (stem *pūbēscent-*), present participle of *pūbēscere,* to reach puberty, from *pūber,* adult.]

pu·bic (péwbik) *adj.* Of, pertaining to, or in the region of the lower part of the abdomen, the pubis, or the pubes. [From PUBES.]

pu·bis (péw-biss) *n., pl.* **-bes** (-beez). The forward portion of either of the hipbones, at the juncture forming the front arch of the pelvis. [New Latin *(os) pubis,* bone of the groin, from Latin *pūbis,* genitive of *pūbēs,* PUBES.]

publ. **1.** publication. **2.** published; publisher.

pub·lic (púbblik) *adj. Abbr.* **pub. 1.** Of, concerning, or affecting the community or the people as a whole: *public affairs.* **2.** Maintained for or open to be used by the whole community. **3.** Participated in or able to be attended by the whole community: *public worship.* **4.** Connected with or acting on behalf of the people, community, or government, rather than concerned with private matters or interests: *public office.* **5. a.** Open to the knowledge or judgment of all: *a public scandal.* **b.** Known or recognised by many people: *a public figure.* **—go public. 1.** To offer shares for sale to the public, especially for the first time. Used of a private company. **2.** To appeal directly to the public, as by means of the media, instead of going through the usual internal channels or complaints procedures. **—make public.** To cause to be known by several or many people or the people at large.
~*n. Abbr.* **pub. 1.** The community or the people as a whole. **2.** A group of people sharing a common specified interest: *the reading public.* **3.** Admirers or followers, especially of a famous person. [Middle English *publique, publyk,* from Old French *public, publique,* from Latin *pūblicus,* alteration of *poplicus,* from *populus,* people.] **—pub·lic·ness** *n.*

pub·lic-ad·dress system (púbblik-ə-dréss) *n. Abbr.* **PA** An electronic amplification apparatus installed and used for broadcasting in public areas. Also called "PA system".

pub·li·can (púbbli-kən) *n.* **1.** *Chiefly British.* The keeper of a public house; a tavernkeeper. **2.** A collector of public taxes or tolls in the ancient Roman Empire. [Middle English, from Old French *publicain,* from Latin *pūblicānus,* contractor for public revenues, from *pūblicum,* public revenue, from *pūblicus,* PUBLIC.]

pub·li·ca·tion (púbbli-káysh'n) *n. Abbr.* **pub., publ. 1.** The act or process of publishing printed matter. **2.** Any printed material offered for sale or distribution, such as a book or periodical. **3.** The communication of information to the public. **4.** *Law.* The act of making defamatory information public. [Middle English *publicatioun,* from Old French, from Late Latin *pūblicātiō* (stem *pūblicātiōn-*), from *pūblicāre,* to make public, from Latin *pūblicus,* PUBLIC.]

public company *n.* A **public limited company** *(see).*

public convenience *n. Chiefly British.* A lavatory that is available for use by the general public. Also called "convenience".

public corporation *n.* In Britain, a state-owned organisation responsible for the management of a nationalised industry.

public defender *n.* In the United States, a lawyer or staff of lawyers, usually publicly appointed, having responsibility for the legal defence of those unable to afford or obtain legal assistance.

public domain *n.* **1.** The status of publications, products, and processes that are not protected under patent or copyright. **2.** *U.S.* Land owned and controlled by the state or federal government.

public enemy *n.* A person, usually a criminal, who is considered to be especially dangerous to the community.

public gallery *n.* A gallery in a parliament or council chamber where the public may sit and listen to proceedings.

public house *n. Chiefly British.* A pub.

pub·li·cise, pub·li·cize (púbbli-sīz) *tr.v.* **-cised, -cising, -cises.** To give publicity to; bring to public attention; advertise.

pub·li·cist (púbbli-sist) *n.* A person who publicises something or someone; especially, a press or publicity agent.

pub·lic·i·ty (pub-líssəti, pəb-) *n.* **1.** Information that concerns a person, group, event, or product and is disseminated through various forms of the media to attract public notice. **2.** Public interest, notice, or notoriety achieved by the spreading of such information. **3.** The act, process, or occupation of disseminating information to gain public interest. **4.** The condition of being public. [French *publicité,* from *public,* PUBLIC.]

public law *n.* **1.** The branch of law dealing with the state or government and the way it relates to individuals or other governments. Compare **private law. 2.** A law affecting the public.

public lending right *n. Abbr.* **P.L.R.** The right of an author to receive royalties when his books are lent by a public library.

public library *n.* A noncommercial library for the use of the general public, usually supported by public funds.

public limited company *n. Finance. Abbr.* **PLC, p.l.c., P.L.C.** A limited liability company whose shares are made available for subscription by the public rather than distributed privately, and can be transferred freely on the open market. Also called "public company". Compare **private limited company.**

pub·lic·ly (púbblikli) *adv.* **1.** In a public manner; not privately; openly. **2.** By or with consent of the public.

public nuisance *n.* **1.** *Law.* An illegal act that causes harm to the community at large rather than to a particular individual. **2.** *Informal.* A person who is considered to be obnoxious by many people.

public opinion *n.* The views of the public, especially on a matter of public concern or interest.

public prosecutor *n.* **1.** A government official who prosecutes criminal actions on behalf of the state or community. **2.** A prosecutor (*see*).

public relations *n. Usually used with a singular verb. Abbr.* **PR, P.R. 1.** The methods and activities employed by an individual, organisation, or government to promote a favourable relationship and good image with the public. **2.** The degree of success achieved in such a relationship. **3.** The staff employed to promote such a relationship. **4.** The art or science of establishing such a relationship.

public school *n.* **1.** In Britain, a private, independent, secondary, fee-paying school at which the pupils usually board. Compare **comprehensive, grammar school, secondary modern school. 2.** Loosely, any school maintained by the state.

public sector *n.* The section of the economy that is under the control of government departments or public corporations, including nationalised industries, national and local government, welfare, and education. Compare **private sector.** —**public-sector** *adj.*

public servant *n.* A person who holds a government position by election or by appointment.

public service *n.* **1.** Employment within a governmental system, especially within the civil service. **2.** A service performed for the benefit of the public. Also used adjectivally.

public speaking *n.* The art or process of making speeches before an audience. —**public speaker** *n.*

pub·lic-spir·i·ted (púbblik-spírritid) *adj.* Motivated by or showing active devotion to the good of the community; concerned for the public welfare. —**pub·lic-spir·it·ed·ness** *n.*

public utility *n.* **1.** An industrial organisation that provides an essential service or commodity, such as water, electricity, transport, or communication, to the public, and is usually under state ownership or control. Also called "public utility company". **2.** *Usually plural. Finance.* Shares issued by such a company.

public works *pl.n.* Construction projects, such as motorways or dams, financed by public funds and constructed by a government for the benefit or use of the general public.

pub·lish (púbblish) *v.* **-lished, -lishing, -lishes.** —*tr.* **1.** To prepare and issue (printed material) for public distribution or sale. **2.** To bring to the public attention; announce. —*intr.* **1.** To issue a publication. **2.** To be the author of a published work. [Middle English *publishen,* from Old French *publier* (stem *publiss-*), from Latin *pūblicāre,* to make public, from *pūblicus,* PUBLIC.] —**pub·lish·a·ble** *adj.*

pub·lish·er (púbblishər) *n. Abbr.* **pub., publ.** A person or company engaged in publishing printed material.

pub·lish·ing (púbblishing) *n.* The business, people, or work involved in the publication of books, periodicals, and the like.

Puc·ci·ni (poŏ-chéeni, poŏ-), **Giacomo** (1858–1924). Italian composer. A major composer of the verismo movement, he wrote in a style that is especially noted for its lyrical qualities. His enormously popular works include *La Bohème* (1896), *Tosca* (1900), *Madame Butterfly* (1904), and the unfinished *Turandot.*

puce (pewss) *n.* Deep red to dark greyish purple. [French *(couleur) puce,* "flea (colour)", from Latin *pūlex,* flea.] —**puce** *adj.*

puck (puk) *n.* A hard rubber disc used in ice hockey as the playing and scoring medium. [19th century : origin obscure.]

Puck *n.* In English folklore, a mischievous sprite. Also called "Robin Goodfellow". [Middle English *p(o)uke,* Old English *pūca†.*]

pucka. Variant of **pukka.**

puck·er (púckər) *v.* **-ered, -ering, -ers.** —*tr.* To gather into small wrinkles or folds. —*intr.* To become contracted and wrinkled. —*n.* A wrinkle or wrinkled part, as in tightly stitched cloth. [Originally "to form a pocket", perhaps from POCKET.]

puck·ish (púckish) *adj.* Mischievous; impish: *a puckish grin.* [From PUCK.] —**puck·ish·ly** *adv.* —**puck·ish·ness** *n.*

pud·ding (poŏdding) *n.* **1. a.** A sweet dessert, usually containing flour or a cereal product, that has been boiled, steamed, or baked. **b.** A savoury dish baked in suet pastry, with a pudding-like consistency. **c.** Any mixture with a soft, pudding- or porridge-like consistency. **2.** A sausage-like preparation made with minced meat or various other ingredients stuffed into a bag or skin and boiled. **3.** The sweet course of a meal. —**in the pudding club.** *Informal.* Pregnant. [Middle English, from Old French *boudin,* from Vulgar Latin *botellīnus* (unattested), diminutive of Latin *botellus,* sausage.]

pudding stone *n.* A rock, a **conglomerate** (*see*).

pud·dle (púdd'l) *n.* **1.** A small pool of water, especially one formed by rain. **2.** A small pool of any liquid. **3.** A tempered paste of wet clay and sand used as waterproofing. —*v.* **puddled, -dling, -dles.** —*tr.* **1.** To make muddy. **2.** To work (clay or sand) into a thick, watertight paste. **3.** *Metallurgy.* To process (impure metal) by puddling. —*intr.* **1.** To splash or paddle in or as if in a puddle. Used with *about.* **2.** To dabble or fuss in a disorganised fashion: *always puddling about with his papers but never gets his desk cleared.* [Middle English *podel, pothel,* diminutive of Old English *pudd†,* ditch.] —**pud·dly** (púdd'l-i, púddli) *adj.*

pud·dler (púdd'l-ər, púddlər) *n.* **1.** One who puddles iron or clay. **2.** One who puddles about.

pud·dling (púdd'l-ing, púddling) *n.* **1.** *Metallurgy.* The purification of impure metal, especially pig iron, by agitation of a molten bath of the metal in an oxidising atmosphere. **2.** Compaction of wet clay

or a similar material to make a watertight paste.

pu·den·cy (péwd'n-si) *n.* Modesty; shame; prudishness. [Late Latin *pudēntia,* shame, from Latin *pudēns* (stem *pudent-*), present participle of *pudēre,* to feel shame.]

pu·den·dum (pew-dén-dəm) *n., pl.* **-da** (-də). *Often plural.* The human external genital organs, especially a woman's. [New Latin, from Late Latin *pudenda,* gerundive of *pudēre,* to be ashamed.] —**pu·den·dal** *adj.*

pudgy. Variant of **podgy.**

pueb·lo (pwéb-lō, poŏ-éb-) *n., pl.* **-los. 1.** A community dwelling, up to five storeys high, built of stone or adobe by Indian tribes of the southwestern United States. **2.** *Capital* P. A member of a tribe, such as the Hopi or Zuñi, inhabiting such dwellings. **3.** An Indian village of the southwestern United States. [Spanish, "people", "population", from Latin *populus,* people.]

puer·ile (péwr-īl ‖ péw-ər-, *chiefly U.S.* -il) *adj.* **1.** Immature; childish. **2.** Pertaining to childhood. [French *puéril,* from Latin *puerīlis,* from *puer,* child, boy.] —**puer·ile·ly** *adv.* —**puer·ile·ness** *n.*

puer·il·ism (péwr-il-iz'm ‖ péw-ər-) *n. Psychiatry.* Infantile or childish behaviour exhibited by an adult suffering from a mental illness. [PUERILE + -ISM.]

puer·il·i·ty (pewr-rílləti, péwr- ‖ péw-ə-) *n., pl.* **-ties. 1.** The condition of being puerile. **2.** A childish action, idea, or utterance.

pu·er·per·al (pew-érpərəl) *adj. Medicine.* Connected with, resulting from, or following childbirth. [Latin *puerperus,* bearing young : *puer,* child + -PAROUS.]

puerperal fever *n.* Infection of the womb and of the bloodstream following childbirth. Also called "childbed fever".

pu·er·pe·ri·um (péwr-péer-i-əm, péw-ər-) *n.* The approximate six-week period after childbirth to return of normal uterine size. [Latin, childbirth, from *puerperus,* PUERPERAL.]

Puer·to Ri·co, Commonwealth of (pwér-tō reekō, pwaír-, -tə). Caribbean island. Self-governing but associated with the United States, it is largely mountainous and densely populated. Its chief industries include textiles, chemicals, the breeding of cattle, and sugar production. Large-scale emigration to the United States (1940s and 1950s) has declined and there is a small independence movement. Area, 8 897 square kilometres (3,434 square miles). Population, 3,594,000. Capital, San Juan. —**Puer·to Ri·can** *adj. & n.*

puff (puf) *n.* **1. a.** A short, forceful exhalation of breath. **b.** A short, sudden gust of wind. **c.** A brief, sudden emission of air, vapour, or smoke. **d.** A short, sibilant sound produced by a puff. **2.** An amount of vapour, smoke, or similar material released in a puff. **3.** An act of drawing in and expelling the breath, as in smoking tobacco. **4.** *Rare.* A swelling or rounded protuberance. **5.** A light, flaky pastry. **6.** See **powder puff. 7.** A soft roll of hair forming part of a hairstyle. **8.** A portion of fabric that is gathered at the edges and full in shape. **9.** An extravagantly flattering recommendation of a book, play, or the like, especially in a newspaper. **10.** Variant of **pouffe. 11.** *U.S.* An eiderdown. **12.** *Genetics.* A swelling seen in certain areas of giant chromosomes. —*v.* **puffed, puffing, puffs.** —*intr.* **1.** To blow in puffs. **2.** To come forth in a puff or puffs. **3.** To breathe forcefully and rapidly; pant. **4.** To emit or move while emitting puffs of smoke, vapour, or the like: *The train puffed.* **5.** To take puffs on a cigarette, pipe, or cigar. **6.** To swell or seem to swell, as with air or pride. Often used with *up* or *out.* —*tr.* **1.** To emit or give forth in a puff or puffs. **2.** To impel with puffs. **3.** To smoke (a cigar, for example). **4.** To inflate or distend. **5.** To fill with pride or conceit. Used with *out* or *up: all puffed up by her recent success.* **6.** To publicise with exaggerated praise. **7.** To cause to be out of breath. Usually used in the passive with *out.* [Middle English *puffen,* Old English *puffan* (unattested), imitative.] —**puff·i·ly** *adv.* —**puff·i·ness** *n.*

puff-ad·der (púff-addər) *n.* A venomous African viper, *Bitis arietans,* having crescent-shaped yellowish markings. [South African Dutch and Afrikaans *pofadder* : *pof,* puff + ADDER; so called because it inflates its body when aroused.]

puff·ball (púff-bawl) *n.* Any of various fungi of the genus *Lycoper-*

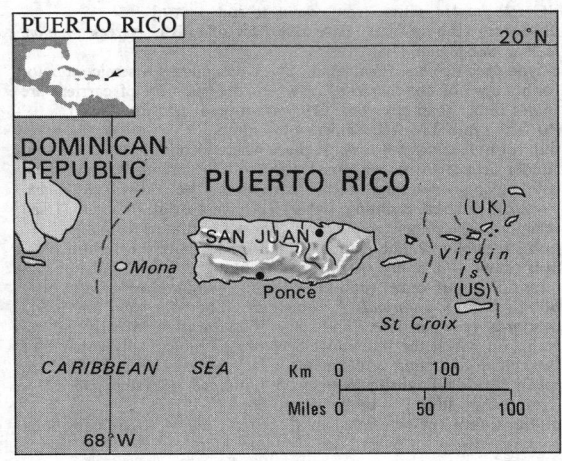

don and related genera, having a ball-shaped fruiting body that, when broken open, releases the enclosed spores in puffs of dust.
puffed sleeve (puft) *n.* A short sleeve, gathered at both ends so that it stands out from the shoulder. Also called "puff sleeve".
puff·er (púffər) *n.* **1.** One that puffs. **2.** Any of various marine fishes of the family Tetraodontidae, that are capable of swelling up. Also called "blowfish", "swellfish".
puff·e·ry (púffəri) *n.* Exaggerated praise or recommendation.
puf·fin (púffin) *n.* Any of several sea birds of the genera *Fratercula* and *Lunda,* of northern regions, characteristically having black and white plumage and a vertically flattened, brightly coloured bill. Also called "sea parrot". [Middle English *poffo(u)n, pophyn*†.]
puff pastry *n.* Dough that is rolled and folded in layers, and that expands in baking to form a rich, light, flaky pastry.
puf·fy (púffi) *adj.* **puffier, puffiest. 1.** Swollen or bloated: *puffy eyes after a night spent crying.* **2.** Breathless.
pug[1] (pug) *n.* A small dog of a breed originating in China, having a snub nose, wrinkled face, square body, short smooth hair, and a curled tail. [16th century : perhaps of Dutch origin.]
pug[2] *n.* **1.** Clay ground and kneaded with water into a plastic consistency for forming bricks or pottery. **2.** A machine for grinding and mixing clay.
~*tr.v.* **pugged, pugging, pugs. 1.** To knead (clay) with water. **2.** To fill in with clay or mortar. **3.** To cover or pack with clay, mortar, sawdust, or felt in order to soundproof. [16th century : origin obscure.]
pug[3] *n.* A footprint, track, or trail, especially of an animal.
~*tr.v.* **pugged, pugging, pugs.** To track by pugs. [Hindi *pag,* probably from Sanskrit *padakaḥ,* foot, from *pada.*]
pug[4] *n. Slang.* A boxer. [Shortened from PUGILIST.]
pug·gree, pug·ree (púggri) *n.* Also **pug·ga·ree, pug·a·ree,** (púggəri). A band or scarf wrapped around the crown of a hat. [Hindi *pagṛī,* from Sanskrit *parikara;* akin to Arabic *pairikara,* turban.]
pu·gi·lism (péwjil-iz'm) *n.* The skill or practice of fighting with the fists; boxing. [Latin *pugil,* fighter, from *pugnus,* fist.]
pu·gi·list (péwjil-ist) *n.* One who fights with the fists; especially, a professional boxer. **—pu·gi·lis·tic** (-ístik) *adj.*
Pu·gin (péwjin), **Augustus Welby Northmore** (1812–52). British architect. A convert to Roman Catholicism and a leader of the Gothic Revival movement, which he advocated in his book *Contrasts* (1836), he designed many Catholic churches and cathedrals. He also collaborated with Barry on the Houses of Parliament.
pug·na·cious (pug-náyshəss) *adj.* Eager to fight; having a quarrelsome disposition. See Synonyms at **belligerent.** [Latin *pugnāx* (stem *pugnāc-*), fond of fighting, from *pugnāre,* to fight, from *pugnus,* fist.] **—pug·na·cious·ly** *adv.* **—pug·na·cious·ness, pug·nac·i·ty** (-nássəti) *n.*
pug nose *n.* A short nose that is flattened and turned up at the end. [Probably from PUG (dog).] **—pug-nosed** (púg-nōzd) *adj.*
puis·ne (péwni) *adj. Law.* Lower in rank; junior.
~*n. Law.* One of lesser rank; especially, an associate judge. [Old French, "born afterwards". See **puny.**]
puis·sance (pwée-SONSS, -SÓNSS, *for sense 1; for sense 2, also* péw-i-s'nss, pwíss'nss) *n.* **1.** An equestrian competition testing a horse's ability to jump heights. **2.** *Archaic & Poetic.* Power; potency; might.
puis·sant (pwée-SONT, -SÓNT, péw-i-s'nt, pwíss'nt) *adj. Archaic & Poetic.* Mighty; powerful; potent. [Middle English *puissaunt,* from Old French, from Gallo-Roman *possiantem* (unattested), from Latin *posse,* to be powerful.] **—puis·sant·ly** *adv.*
puke (pewk) *v.* **puked, puking, pukes.** *Slang.* *—intr.* To vomit. Sometimes used with *up.* *—tr.* To vomit (something) up.
~*n. Slang.* **1.** Vomit. **2.** The act of vomiting. [16th century.]
puk·ka, puck·a (púckə) *adj.* **1.** Genuine; authentic. **2.** Superior; first-class. **3.** Correct; right and proper. [Hindi *pakkā,* cooked, ripe, firm, from Sanskrit *pakva.*]
pul (pōol) *n., pl.* **puls** or **puli** (-i, -ee). A coin of Afghanistan, equal to 1/100 of the afghani. [Persian, from Turkish, possibly from Late Greek *phollis,* bellows, money bag, from Latin *follis.*]
pu·la (pōo-laa, -lə) *n., pl.* **-la** or **-las.** The standard monetary unit of Botswana, introduced in 1976. [Tswana, "rain".]
Pu·la (pōo-lə, -laa). *Italian* **Po·la** (pō-la). Town in Croatia. Situated on the Istrian peninsula on the Adriatic coast, it was an Austrian naval base (1815–1918) before passing to Italy (1919) and finally Yugoslavia (1947). It has many historical remains, notably the massive Roman stadium.
pul·chri·tude (púlkri-tewd ‖ -tōod) *n. Literary.* Physical beauty. [Middle English *pulcritude,* from Latin *pulchritūdō,* from *pulcher*†, beautiful.] **—pul·chri·tu·di·nous** (-téwdi-nəss ‖ -tōodi-) *adj.*
pule (pewl) *intr.v.* **puled, puling, pules.** To whine; fret. [Earlier *pewle, peule,* probably from French *piauler* (imitative).] **—pul·er** *n.*
pu·li[1] (pōol-i, péwl-, -ee) *n., pl.* **-lis** or **pulik** (-ik). A long-haired sheepdog of a Hungarian breed. Also called "Hungarian puli". [Hungarian.]
pu·li[2]. Alternative plural of **pul.**
Pu·lit·zer prize (pōol-itsər, *also* péwl-) *n.* Any of several awards established by the U.S. publisher Joseph Pulitzer (1847–1911) and conferred annually in the United States for accomplishments in U.S. journalism, literature, and music.
pull (pōol) *v.* **pulled, pulling, pulls.** *—tr.* **1.** To apply force to so as to cause or tend to cause motion towards the source of the force. **2.** To remove from a fixed position; extract: *pull teeth.* Usually used with *away, off,* or *out.* **3.** To tug at; jerk or tweak. **4.** To rip or tear; rend. **5.** To stretch (toffee, for example) repeatedly. **6.** To strain (a muscle, for example) injuriously. **7.** *Informal.* To attract; draw. **8.** *Informal.* To perform or bring about successfully. Often used with *off*: *You'll never pull off a bank robbery.* **9.** *Slang.* To draw out (a knife or gun) in readiness for use. **10.** In cricket, to strike (a ball) aggressively from the off to the leg side by forcing it across the line of the body. **11.** In golf or baseball, to hit (a ball) in the direction one is facing when the swing is carried through, as to the left of a right-handed player. **12. a.** To operate (an oar) in rowing. **b.** To transport or propel by rowing. **c.** To be rowed by: *That boat pulls six oars.* **13.** To rein in (a horse) to keep it from winning a race. **14.** *Printing.* To produce (a print or impression) from type. **15.** To remove the feathers from (a bird); pluck. *—intr.* **1. a.** To exert force in pulling something. **b.** To tug or jerk. Used with *at.* **2. a.** To move: *The bus pulled away from the kerb.* **b.** To move in a vehicle: *She pulled away from the kerb.* **3.** To drink or inhale deeply. Often used with *at* or *on.* **4.** To row a boat. **5.** To strain repeatedly at the bit. Used of a horse. **—pull about.** To subject to rough physical treatment. **—pull a fast one.** *Informal.* To use a sly or underhand trick to gain advantage. **—pull ahead.** To move in front by going faster. **—pull apart** or **to pieces. 1.** To separate the parts of forcefully. **2.** To criticise severely or unfairly. **—pull down.** To dismantle or demolish (a building or structure). **—pull for.** To hope or cheer for the success of. **—pull round, pull through** *(see below).* **— pull (oneself) together.** To regain one's composure. **—pull together.** To make a joint effort; cooperate.
~*n.* **1.** The action or process of pulling or being pulled. **2.** Force exerted in pulling, or required to overcome resistance in pulling. **3.** Any sustained effort: *a long pull across the mountains.* **4.** Something used for pulling, such as a knob on a drawer. **5.** A deep inhalation or swallow, as on a cigar or of a drink. **6.** *Informal.* A means of gaining special advantage; influence: *She has pull with the boss.* **7.** *Informal.* Ability to draw or attract; popular appeal. **8.** A stroke or hit that pulls the ball in cricket, golf, or baseball. **9.** A spell or period of rowing. **10.** The act of reining in a horse, especially when racing. **11.** *Printing.* A print or impression. **12.** The force required to draw back the trigger of a firearm or a bow. [Middle English *pullen,* to pull, pluck, Old English *pullian*†.] **—pull·er** *n.*
pull·back (pōol-bak) *n.* **1.** The act or process of pulling or moving something back; especially, an orderly withdrawal of troops. **2.** Any device for holding or drawing something back.
pul·let (pōollit) *n.* A young hen, especially of the common domestic fowl, usually less than one year old. [Middle English *polet, pulet,* from Old French *poulet, pollet,* diminutive of *poul,* cock, *poule,* hen, from Latin *pullus,* young of an animal, chick.]
pul·ley (pōolli) *n., pl.* **-leys. 1.** A simple machine used to change the direction and point of application of a pulling force, especially for lifting weights, consisting essentially of a wheel with a grooved rim in which a pulled rope or chain is run. **2.** A wheel turned by or driving a belt. [Middle English *po(u)ley,* from Old French *po(u)lie,* from Vulgar Latin *polidium* (unattested), probably from Late Greek *polidion* (unattested), diminutive of Greek *polos,* pole, pivot.]
pull in *intr.v.* **1.** To stop at a station. Used of a train. **2. a.** To stop in a lay-by, at a motorway café, or the like. **b.** To move over to or stop at the side of the road. Used of a motor vehicle or a driver. *—tr.v.* **1.** *Chiefly British.* To catch or arrest (a criminal or suspect). **2.** To make or earn (a profit or sum of money). **3.** To attract (a crowd).
pull-in (pōol-in) *n. British.* A café at the side of the road.
Pull·man (pōolmən) *n.* A well-furnished railway carriage, usually with individual sleeping compartments. Also called "Pullman car". [After George M. *Pullman* (1831–97), U.S. industrialist.]
pul·lo·rum disease (pōo-láwr-əm ‖ pə-, -lór-) *n.* A severe contagious diarrhoea of young poultry, caused by the bacterium *Salmonella pullorum.* [Latin *pullorum,* genitive plural of *pullus,* young animal, PULLET.]
pull out *intr.v.* **1.** To depart from a station. Used of a train. **2. a.** To move from a stationary position at the side of a road. Used of a vehicle. **b.** To move out of a lane of traffic in order to pass another vehicle. **3.** To withdraw from a situation or commitment. **4.** *Military.* To withdraw from a site of battle. **5.** To change from a dive into level flight. *—tr.v.* To withdraw (troops) from a battle.
pull·out (pōol-owt) *n.* **1.** A withdrawal, especially of troops. **2.** *Aeronautics.* The change from a dive into level flight. **3.** Something designed to be pulled out, such as a leaflet in a book or magazine. **—pull-out** *adj.*
pull over *intr.v.* **1.** To bring a vehicle to a stop at the side of a road. **2.** To move to the side of the road in order to stop or to allow faster vehicles to pass.
pull·o·ver (pōol-ōvər) *n.* A garment, such as a sweater, that is put on by being drawn over the head. **—pull·o·ver** *adj.*
pull-tab (pōol-tab) *n.* A **tab** *(see)* on a can of drink.
pull through *intr.v.* Also **pull round.** To recover from an illness or setback. *—tr.v.* To cause to recover from an illness or setback.
pull·through (pōol-thrōo) *n.* Something designed to be pulled through; specifically, a long soft brush or piece of material for cleaning the inside of a wind instrument such as a saxophone.
pul·lu·late (púllew-layt) *intr.v.* **-lated, -lating, -lates. 1.** To put forth sprouts or buds; germinate. **2.** To breed rapidly or abundantly. **3.** To teem; swarm. [Latin *pullulāre,* to grow, sprout, from *pullulus,* diminutive of *pullus,* young animal, PULLET.] **—pul·lu·la·tion** (-láysh'n) *n.* **—pul·lu·la·tive** (-lətiv, -laytiv) *adj.*
pull up *intr.v.* **1.** To come to a halt. Used of a vehicle. **2.** To move to a place or position that is level or ahead, as in a race. Used with

with. —*tr.v.* **1.** To bring (a vehicle, horse, or the like) to a halt. **2.** To reprimand or scold. **3.** To stop (a person who is doing something wrong, making mistakes, or the like).

pull-up (po͝ol-up) *n.* An exercise for strengthening the arms, performed by hanging by the hands from an overhead bar and pulling the body upwards until the chin is even with or above the bar.

pul·mo·nar·y (púl-mənri, po͝ol-, -mənəri || -mə-nerri) *adj.* **1.** Of or pertaining to the lungs. **2.** Having lungs or lunglike organs. [Latin *pulmōnārius,* from *pulmō,* (stem *pulmōn-*), lung.]

pulmonary artery *n.* An artery in which deoxygenated blood travels directly from the right ventricle of the heart to the lungs.

pulmonary vein *n.* A vein in which oxygenated blood travels directly from the lungs to the left atrium of the heart.

pul·mo·nate (púl-mə-nət, po͝ol-, -nit, -nayt) *adj.* **1.** Having lungs or lunglike organs. **2.** Pertaining to the Pulmonata, an order of gastropods including snails and slugs, in which the mantle cavity is modified to function as a lung.
~*n.* A pulmonate mollusc. [Latin *pulmōnātus,* from *pulmō,* lung. See **pulmonary.**]

pul·mon·ic (pul-mónnik, po͝ol-) *adj.* Pulmonary.

pulp (pulp) *n.* **1.** A soft, moist, shapeless mass of matter. **2.** The soft, juicy part of fruit. **3.** A mass of pressed vegetable matter; *apple pulp.* **4.** A mixture of cellulose material, such as wood, paper, and rags, ground up and moistened to make paper. **5.** The soft inner structure of a tooth, consisting of nerve and blood vessels. **6.** In mining, a mixture of powdered ore and water. **7.** Magazines and books collectively, that contain sensational or pornographic subject matter and are characteristically printed on rough, unfinished paper. Also used adjectivally: *pulp fiction.* **—reduce (someone) to pulp.** To cause (someone) to be incapable of thought or action, as through fear, shock, or the like.
~*v.* **pulped, pulping, pulps.** —*tr.* **1.** To reduce to pulp. **2.** To remove the pulp from (fruit). —*intr.* To be reduced to a pulp. [Latin *pulpa*†, solid flesh, pulp.] **—pulp·ous, pulp·y** *adj.*

pul·pit (po͝ol-pit || púl-) *n.* **1.** An elevated platform, lectern, or stand used in preaching or conducting a religious service. **2.** Any similar raised platform, such as one used by harpooners in a whaling boat. **3. a.** The clergy collectively. Preceded by *the.* **b.** The profession of preaching the Christian message. **4.** Any medium of communication through which a person expresses an opinion, especially regularly. [Middle English, from Latin *pulpitum*†, scaffold, platform.]

pulp·wood (púlp-wo͝od) *n.* Soft wood, such as spruce or pine, used in making paper.

pul·que (po͝ol-ki, po͝ol-, -kay) *n.* An alcoholic milky drink made in Mexico from various species of agave. [Mexican Spanish; perhaps akin to Nahuatl *poliuhqui, puliuhqui,* decomposed, spoilt.]

pul·sar (púl-saar) *n. Astronomy.* Any of numerous small, dense stars that emit regular pulses of radiation, usually radio waves, as a result of their rapid rotation. [From *puls*ating *star.*]

pul·sate (pul-sáyt || *chiefly U.S.* púl-sayt) *intr.v.* **-sated, -sating, -sates.** **1.** To expand and contract rhythmically; throb. **2.** To quiver. [Latin *pulsāre,* frequentative of *pellere* (past participle *pulsus*), to push, beat, strike.] **—pul·sa·tive** (púl-sətiv, pul-sáytiv) *adj.*
***Synonyms:** pulsate, beat, palpitate, throb.*

pul·sa·tile (púl-sə-tīl || *U.S.* -til) *adj.* Pulsating; vibrating. [Medieval Latin *pulsātilis,* from Latin *pulsāre,* to PULSATE.]

pul·sa·ting star (pul-sáyting || *chiefly U.S.* púl-sayting) *n.* A star that periodically becomes brighter as its outer layers expand and contract.

pul·sa·tion (pul-sáysh'n) *n.* **1.** The act of pulsating. **2.** A single beat, throb, or vibration.

pul·sa·tor (pul-sáytər) *n.* A pulsating device or machine, such as a pump.

pul·sa·to·ry (púl-sə-tri, -təri, pul-sáytəri) *adj.* Having rhythmical vibration or movement; pulsating.

pulse¹ (puls) *n.* **1.** *Physiology.* The rhythmical throbbing of arteries produced by the regular contractions of the heart. **2.** Any regular beating rhythm. **3.** A single throb or beat. **4.** *Physics & Electronics.* A transient amplification or intensification of a characteristic of a system, especially of a wave characteristic, followed by return to equilibrium or steady state: *a signal pulse; a beam pulse.* **5.** The perceptible emotions or sentiments of a group: *the pulse of the electorate.* **6.** *Informal.* Energy; vitality: *the pulse of the party.*
~*intr.v.* **pulsed, pulsing, pulses.** To throb or vibrate; pulsate. [Middle English *pous, puls,* from Old French *pous, pols,* from Latin *pulsus,* beating, striking, from the past participle of *pellere,* to push, beat, strike.] **—pulse·less** *adj.*

pulse² *n.* **1.** The edible seeds of certain pod-bearing plants, such as lentils. **2.** A plant yielding such seeds. [Middle English *pols, puls,* from Old French *po(u)ls,* porridge, from Latin *puls,* pottage made of meal and pulse, possibly from Greek *poltos,* porridge.]

pulse-height analyser (púlss-hīt) *n.* An electronic device that sorts signal pulses into predetermined ranges of amplitude.

pulse·jet (púlss-jet) *n.* A type of ramjet in which air intake and combustion occur intermittently, producing rapid periodic bursts of thrust.

pulse modulation *n. Electronics.* Modulation by coded variation of the amplitude or other characteristic of wave pulses.

pul·sim·e·ter (pul-símmitər) *n.* Also **pul·som·e·ter** (-sómmitər). *Medicine.* An instrument that measures the frequency or strength of the pulse. [PULSE + -METER.]

pul·som·e·ter (pul-sómmitər) *n.* **1.** A pump for raising water by the pulsed condensation of steam. **2.** Variant of **pulsimeter.** [PULSE + -METER.]

pul·ver·a·ble (púl-vrəb'l, -vərəb'l) *adj.* Capable of being pulverised.

pul·ver·ise, pul·ver·ize (púlvə-rīz) *v.* **-ised, -ising, -ises.** —*tr.* **1.** To pound, crush, or grind to a powder or dust. **2.** To demolish, defeat, or destroy. —*intr.* To be ground or reduced to powder or dust. [Old French *pulveriser,* from Late Latin *pulverizāre,* from Latin *pulvis* (stem *pulver-*), dust.] **—pul·ver·is·a·ble** *adj.* **—pul·ver·i·sa·tion** (-rī-záysh'n || *U.S.* -ri-) *n.* **—pul·ver·is·er** *n.*

pul·ver·u·lent (pul-vérrewlənt) *adj.* **1.** Made of, covered with, or crumbling to fine powder or dust. **2.** Powdery; dusty; crumbly. [Latin *pulverulentus,* dusty, from *pulvis,* dust. See **pulverise.**]

pul·vil·lus (pul-víl-əss) *n., pl.* **-li** (-ī). Any of the soft, cushion-like pads between the claws of an insect's foot. [Latin, diminutive of *pulvīnus*†, cushion.]

pul·vi·nate (púlvi-nayt) *adj.* Also **pul·vi·nat·ed** (-naytid). **1.** Having a convex face. Said of a frieze. **2.** *Botany.* Having a swelling at the base. Said of a leafstalk. [Latin *pulvīnātus,* from PULVINUS.]

pul·vi·nus (pul-vī-nəss) *n., pl.* **-ni** (nī). *Botany.* A swelling at the base of a leafstalk, which, through changes in turgor, can alter the position of the leaf. [Latin *pulvīnus*†, cushion.]

pu·ma (péwmə) *n.* A large American wild cat, *Panthera concolor* (or *Felis concolor*), resembling a short-legged lioness. Also called "cougar", "mountain lion". [Spanish, from Quechua.]

pum·ice (púmmiss) *n.* A porous, lightweight volcanic rock with the same composition as rhyolite, often used as an abrasive. Also called "pumice stone".
~*tr.v.* **pumiced, -icing, -ices.** To clean, polish, or smooth with pumice. [Middle English *pomys,* from Old French *pomis,* from Latin *pūmex.*] **—pu·mi·ceous** (pew-míshəss) *adj.* **—pum·ic·er** *n.*

pum·mel (púmm'l) *tr.v.* **-melled** or *U.S.* **-meled, -melling** or *U.S.* **-meling, -mels.** To beat or hit with or as if with the fists. [From POMMEL (originally, to beat with the pommel of a sword).]

pump¹ (pump) *n.* A machine or device for transferring a liquid or gas from a source or container through tubes or pipes to another container or receiver.
~*v.* **pumped, pumping, pumps.** —*tr.* **1.** To raise or cause to flow by means of a pump. **2.** To inflate with gas by means of a pump. Often used with *up.* **3.** To remove the water from. Often used with *out.* **4.** To cause to operate with the up-and-down motion of a pump handle. **5.** To propel, eject, or insert with a pump. **6.** *Physics.* To supply (a laser) with sufficient energy to achieve population inversion. **7.** *Informal.* **a.** To question closely or persistently for information. **b.** To gain or force (information) from a person by persistent questioning: *They pumped the truth from him.* **8. a.** To fill with a steady stream of something, such as bullets or information. **b.** To supply or fill somebody or something with (a steady flow of something): *pumped money into the project.* —*intr.* **1.** To operate a pump. **2.** To raise or move gas or liquid with a pump. **3.** To gush or flow, especially in regular spurts. **4.** To move up and down in the manner of a pump handle. [Middle English *pumpe, pompe* (nautical use), from Middle Low German *pumpe* or Middle Dutch *pompe,* probably imitative.] **—pump·er** *n.*

pump² *n.* **1.** A low-heeled woman's shoe with no fastenings. **2.** A light shoe used for dancing and certain sports. [16th century.]

pum·per·nick·el (púmpə-nick'l, po͝ompər-) *n.* A dark, sourish bread made from whole, coarsely ground rye. [German *Pumpernickel* : early New High German *Pumpern,* a fart (imitative) + *Nickel,* "devil", general pejorative (see **nickel**); so named from being hard to digest.]

pump gun *n.* A gun or rifle that may be reloaded by means of a sliding magazine under the barrel.

pump·kin (púmp-kin, púm- || púng-) *n.* **1.** A coarse, trailing vine, *Cucurbita pepo,* cultivated for its fruit. **2.** The large, round fruit of this vine, with thick, orange-yellow rind, orange, pulpy flesh, and many seeds. **3.** Either of two similar vines, *C. maxima* or *C. moschata,* bearing large, pumpkin-like squashes. [Variant (influenced by -KIN) of earlier *pumpion, pompon,* from Old French *popon, pompon,* from Latin *pepō,* from Greek *pepōn,* a large melon (edible only when ripe), from *pepōn,* ripe, from *peptein,* to cook, ripen.]

pun¹ (pun) *n.* A play on words, sometimes on different senses of the same word and sometimes on the similar sense or sound of different words; for example, the words of the dying Mercutio in *Romeo and Juliet:* "ask for me tomorrow, and you shall find me a grave man".
~*intr.v.* **punned, punning, puns.** To make a pun or puns. [Probably short for obsolete *pundigrion,* perhaps a fanciful alteration of Italian *puntiglio,* "fine point", diminutive of *punto,* POINT.] **—pun·ning·ly** *adv.*

pun² *tr.v.* **punned, punning, puns.** *British Regional.* To pack down (rubble or earth) by ramming and pounding it. [Dialect variant of POUND (verb).]

pu·na (po͞onə) *n.* **1.** A high, dry, bleak plateau within the Andes of Bolivia or Peru, sparsely covered with coarse grasses and stunted shrubs. **2.** The vegetation of a puna. [Quechua.]

punch¹ (punch) *n.* **1.** A tool for making holes in a material: *a leather punch.* **2.** A tool for forcing a pin, bolt, or rivet in or out of a hole. **3.** A tool for stamping a design on a surface. **4.** A **countersink** *(see).* **5.** A device for punching cards *(card punch)* or paper tape *(tape punch)* for use in a computer.
~*v.* **punched, punching, punches.** —*tr.* To use a punch on. —*intr.* To use a punch. [Short for PUNCHEON (punching tool).]

punch² *tr.v.* **punched, punching, punches.** **1.** To hit with a sharp blow of the fist. **2.** To poke or prod with a stick. **3.** *Western U.S.* To herd (cattle), especially as a profession.

~*n.* **1.** A blow with the fist. **2.** *Informal.* Vigour or forcefulness: *His writing lacks punch.* **—pull (one's) punches.** *Informal.* **1.** To hold back deliberately from giving full force to one's blows. **2.** To lessen deliberately the full impact of one's words; especially, to not be outspoken in one's criticism. [Middle English *punchen,* variant of *pounsen,* POUNCE (to perforate).] **—punch·er** *n.*

punch³ *n.* A mixed drink consisting of fruit juices, water, sugar, spices, or the like, usually with a wine or spirit base, and often hot. [Perhaps from Hindi *pānch,* from Sanskrit *pañca,* five (originally prepared with five ingredients).]

Punch *n.* The quarrelsome hook-nosed husband of Judy in the comic puppet show, *Punch and Judy.* **—pleased as Punch.** Highly pleased; gratified. [Short for PUNCHINELLO.]

punch·bag (púnch-bag) *n.* Also *U.S.* **punching bag.** A large, heavy, stuffed bag, usually of canvas, suspended from above and designed to be punched with the fists for exercise or boxing training.

punch·ball (púnch-bawl) *n.* **1.** A small inflated bag or ball, usually of leather, either suspended from above or supported on a springy pole and designed to be punched with the fists for exercise or boxing training. **2.** A punchbag.

punch·bowl (púnch-bōl) *n.* A large bowl from which punch or other drinks may be served by means of a ladle.

punch-drunk (púnch-drúngk, -drungk) *adj.* **1.** Suffering from the effects of repeated blows on the head. **2.** Acting in a dazed manner.

punched card (puncht) *n.* Also **punch card.** A card punched with holes or notches to represent letters and numbers or with a pattern of holes to represent related data, for use in a computer.

punched tape *n.* Also **punch tape.** Paper tape in which holes are punched to represent data to be processed by a computer.

pun·cheon¹ (púnchən) *n.* **1.** A short, wooden upright used in structural framing. **2.** A piece of broad, heavy timber, roughly dressed, with one face finished flat. **3.** A punching, perforating, or stamping tool, especially one used by a goldsmith. [Middle English *ponchon, pons(y)on,* a sharp tool, from Old French *po(i)nchon, poinçon,* from Vulgar Latin *punctiō* (unattested), from *punctiāre* (unattested), to pierce, prick, from Latin *pungere* (past participle *punctus*), to prick.]

puncheon² *n.* **1.** A cask with a capacity of between 320 and 550 litres (70 and 120 gallons). **2.** This specific volume of liquid used as a measure. [Old French *po(i)nçon, po(i)nchon*†.]

Pun·chi·nel·lo (púnchi-néllō) *n., pl.* **-los** or **-loes.** **1.** The short, fat, comic-looking character in an Italian puppet show and probable prototype of the English Punch. **2.** A person thought to resemble this puppet. [Variant of earlier *policinello,* from Italian dialect (Neapolitan) *polecenella,* perhaps diminutive of *polecena,* young turkey cock (from the puppet's beaklike nose), from *pulcino,* chicken, from Late Latin *pullicenus,* diminutive of Latin *pullus,* PULLET.]

punch line *n.* The line or part of a joke or humorous story that gives the point of the whole and causes amusement.

punch press *n.* A power press fitted with punches and dies for cutting, forming, or imprinting metal, plastic, or the like.

punch-up (púnch-up) *n.* *Chiefly British Slang.* A fist fight.

punch·y (púnchi) *adj.* **-ier, -iest.** *Informal.* **1.** Having force, vigour, or zest: *a punchy advert.* **2.** Punch-drunk. **—punch·i·ly** *adv.*

punc·tate (púngk-tayt) *adj.* Also **punc·tat·ed** (-táytid || -taytid). Having tiny spots, points, or depressions. [New Latin *punctatus,* from Latin *punctum,* pricked mark, POINT.] **—punc·ta·tion** (-táysh'n) *n.*

punc·til·i·o (pungk-tílli-ō) *n., pl.* **-tilios.** **1.** Precise observance of formalities or etiquette. **2.** A fine or petty point of etiquette. [Italian *puntiglio,* "fine point", diminutive of *punto,* POINT.]

punc·til·i·ous (pungk-tílli-əss) *adj.* **1.** Attentive to the finer points of etiquette and formal conduct. **2.** Showing attention to detail; precise; scrupulous. —See Synonyms at **meticulous.** [French *pointilleux,* from *pointille,* "fine point", from Italian. See **punctilio.**] **—punc·til·i·ous·ly** *adv.* **—punc·til·i·ous·ness** *n.*

punc·tu·al (púngk-tew-əl, -choo-, -cho͞ol) *adj.* **1. a.** Acting or arriving exactly at the time appointed; prompt. **b.** Always observant of or keeping to appointed times. **2.** Paid or accomplished at or by the appointed time. **3.** *Archaic.* Precise; exact. **4.** Confined to or being a point in space. [Middle English, from Medieval Latin *punctuālis,* "to the point", from Latin *punctum,* pricked mark, POINT.] **—punc·tu·al·i·ty** (-ál-əti), **punc·tu·al·ness** *n.* **—punc·tu·al·ly** *adv.*

punc·tu·ate (púngk-tew-ayt, -choo-) *v.* **-ated, -ating, -ates.** —*tr.* **1.** To provide (a text) with punctuation marks. **2.** To interrupt periodically. **3.** To stress; emphasise. —*intr.* To use punctuation. [Medieval Latin *punctuāre,* to mark with a point, punctuate, from Latin *punctum,* pricked mark, point, from the past participle of *pungere,* to prick, pierce.] **—punc·tu·a·tive** (-aytiv) *adj.* **—punc·tu·a·tor** (-aytər) *n.*

punc·tu·a·tion (púngk-tew-áysh'n, -choo-) *n.* **1.** The use of standard marks and signs in writing and printing to separate words into sentences, clauses, and phrases, as in order to clarify meaning, give intonation, or provide emphasis. **2.** The marks so used. **3.** An act or instance of punctuating. **—punc·tu·a·tion·al** *adj.*

punctuation mark *n.* Any of a set of marks or signs used to punctuate texts; for example, the comma (,) or the full stop (.).

punc·ture (púngk-chər) *v.* **-tured, -turing, -tures.** —*tr.* **1.** To pierce with a pointed object. **2.** To make (a hole) by piercing. **3.** To cause to collapse by piercing. **4.** To depreciate; deflate: *She punctured his ego.* —*intr.* To be pierced or punctured.

~*n.* **1.** An act or instance of puncturing. **2.** A hole or depression made by a sharp object; especially, a hole in a pneumatic tyre. [Middle English, from Latin *punctūra,* a pricking, puncture, from *pungere* (past participle *punctus*), to prick.] **—punc·tur·a·ble** *adj.*

pun·dit (púndit) *n.* Also **pan·dit** (for sense 1). **1.** A Brahmanic scholar, learned in Sanskrit and in Hindu philosophy, religion, and law. **2.** A learned person or a person who claims to be an expert. [Hindi *paṇḍit,* from Sanskrit *paṇḍita,* a learned man, from Dravidian (akin to Telegu *paṇḍa,* wisdom).] **—pun·dit·ry** (-ri) *n.*

Pune. Formerly **Poona.** City of central western India. Situated in the western Ghats, Maharashtra state, it was captured by the British in 1817. Mild in climate, it became and remains a resort town and military centre. It also has cotton and paper mills.

pung (pung) *n.* *U.S.* A low box sleigh drawn by one horse. [Shortened from *tom-pong, tow-pong,* of Algonquian origin, akin to TOBOGGAN.]

pun·gent (púnjənt) *adj.* **1.** Having a sharp, acid taste or smell. **2.** Penetrating; biting; caustic: *pungent satire.* **3.** *Biology.* Pointed: *a pungent leaf.* [Latin *pungēns* (stem *pungent-*), present participle of *pungere,* to prick, sting.] **—pun·gen·cy** *n.* **—pun·gent·ly** *adv.*

Pu·nic (péwnik) *adj.* **1.** Of or pertaining to ancient Carthage or its people. **2.** Having the characteristic of treachery attributed to the Carthaginians by the Romans: *Punic faith.*

~*n.* The West Semitic language of ancient Carthage, a dialect of Phoenician. [Latin *Pūnicus,* earlier *Poenicus,* from *Poenus,* a Carthaginian, from Greek *Phoinix,* Phoenician.]

Punic Wars *pl.n.* Three wars waged by Rome against Carthage (264–241 B.C., 218–201 B.C., and 149–146 B.C.) in which Rome finally defeated Carthage and annexed its territory.

pun·ish (púnnish) *v.* **-ished, -ishing, -ishes.** —*tr.* **1.** To subject (a person) to a penalty, such as imprisonment, a fine, or a beating, for a crime, fault, offence, or misbehaviour. **2.** To inflict a penalty on a criminal or wrongdoer for (a crime or offence, for example). **3.** To handle roughly; injure; hurt. **4.** *Informal.* To deplete (a stock or supply) heavily. —*intr.* To give punishment. [Middle English *punissen, punyschen,* from Old French *punir* (stem *puniss-*), from Latin *pūnīre, poenīre,* from *poena,* penalty, punishment, from Greek *poinē.*] **—pun·ish·er** *n.* **—pun·ish·ing·ly** *adv.*

Synonyms: *punish, chastise, discipline, castigate, penalise.*

pun·ish·a·ble (púnnish-əb'l) *adj.* Liable to or deserving punishment.

pun·ish·ment (púnnish-mənt) *n.* **1. a.** An act of punishing. **b.** The condition of being punished. **2.** A penalty imposed for wrongdoing, as for a crime or offence. **3.** *Informal.* Rough handling.

pu·ni·tive (péwnətiv) *adj.* Inflicting or aiming to inflict punishment; punishing. [French *punitif,* from Medieval Latin *pūnītīvus,* from Latin *pūnīre* (past participle *punītus*), PUNISH.] **—pu·ni·tive·ly** *adv.* **—pu·ni·tive·ness** *n.*

Pun·jab or **Pan·jab** (pún-jaáb, -jaab; *also* po͝on- || *U.S. also* -jáb). Region of the northwest Indian subcontinent. It was ruled by the Sikhs until annexation by the British (1849) and was divided along religious lines in 1947. West Punjab passed to Pakistan, and is now the province of Punjab, East Punjab remaining Indian. East Punjab was further divided (1966) into linguistic areas to form the present Indian states of Punjab and Haryana.

Pun·ja·bi (pún-jaábi, pun-, *also* po͝on-, po͝on- || *U.S. also* -jábbi) *n.* Also **Pan·ja·bi** (for sense 2). **1.** A native or inhabitant of the Punjab. **2.** The Indic language spoken in the Punjab, belonging to the Indo-European family. **—Pun·jab·i** *adj.*

punk¹ (pungk) *n.* **1.** A youth culture that developed in Britain in the late 1970s among fans of punk rock, characterised by a rejection of middle-class values and standard pop culture, and the adoption of a deliberately aggressive and outrageous personal appearance, often involving startling make-up and hairstyles, and leather clothing. **2.** A young person belonging to this culture. **3.** Punk rock. [Shortened from *punk rock(er).*]

punk² (pungk) *n.* **1.** Dry, decayed wood, used as tinder. **2.** Any of various substances that smoulder when ignited, used to light fireworks. **3. a.** An object of little value or poor quality. **b.** Such objects collectively; rubbish. **4.** *Slang.* Any disreputable or worthless person. **5.** *Chiefly U.S. Slang.* **a.** A young ruffian or petty criminal. **b.** An inexperienced or callow youth.

~*adj. Slang.* Of poor quality; worthless. [18th century.]

punk³ *n.* **1.** *Archaic.* A passive homosexual; a catamite. **2.** A prostitute. [16th century : origin obscure.]

pun·ka, pun·kah (púngkə) *n.* A fan used especially in India, made of a palm frond or strip of cloth hung from the ceiling and moved manually or by machine. [Hindi *pankhā,* from Sanskrit *pakṣaka,* fan, from *pakṣa,* shoulder, wing.]

punk rock *n.* A type of rock music that developed in the late 1970s, characterised by a spirit of aggression and defiance embodied typically in loud, raucous singing, offensive lyrics, and driving rhythms. [PUNK (worthless, rotten) + ROCK (music).] **—punk rocker** *n.*

pun·net (púnnit) *n.* *British.* A small, square basket used for holding soft fruit. [Perhaps diminutive of dialect *pun,* POUND (weight).]

pun·ster (pún-stər) *n.* A maker of puns.

punt¹ (punt) *n.* An open, flat-bottomed boat with squared ends, propelled by a long pole and used in shallow waters.

~*v.* **punted, punting, punts.** —*tr.* **1.** To propel (a boat) with a pole. **2.** To carry in a punt. —*intr.* **1.** To propel a punt. **2.** To travel in a punt as a leisure activity. [Middle Low German *punte, punto,* ferryboat, from Latin *pontō,* a Gaulish vessel, apparently from *pōns* (stem *pont-*), bridge.] **—punt·er** *n.*

punt² (punt) *n.* In soccer, Rugby football, American football, or similar games, a kick in which the ball is dropped from the hands and kicked before it touches the ground.

~*v.* **punted, punting, punts.** —*tr.* To propel (a ball) by means of a punt. —*intr.* To execute a punt. [Probably from dialectal *bunt, punt*†, to push, kick.]

punt³ (punt) *intr.v.* **punted, punting, punts.** **1.** In gambling games such as roulette or faro, to lay a bet against the bank. **2. a.** To gamble; bet. **b.** To bet on a horse race. [French *ponter,* from *ponte,* bet against the banker, from Spanish *punto,* "point", "ace", from Latin *punctum,* POINT.]

punt[4] (poont) *n.* **1.** The basic monetary unit of the Republic of Ireland, equal to 100 pence. **2.** A coin worth one punt. Also called "pound".

Pun·ta A·re·nas (pŏontə aráy-nass). The world's southernmost city, lying on the Strait of Magellan in Chile. It is an oil port, with military and naval installations, and a tourist centre.

punt·er (púntər) *n.* **1.** A person who punts. **2.** *British* **a.** *Informal.* A person who places a bet. **b.** *Slang.* A female prostitute's male client. **c.** *Informal.* A member of the general public; especially, one who is an actual or potential customer or supporter.

pun·ty (púnti) *n., pl.* **-ties.** In glassmaking, an iron rod on which molten glass is handled. Also called "pontil". [Variant of PONTIL.]

pu·ny (péwni) *adj.* **-nier, -niest. 1.** Of inferior size, strength, or significance; weak. **2.** Feeble; ineffectual: *a puny attempt.* [Phonetic spelling of PUISNE, from Old French "born afterwards" : *puis,* afterwards, from Vulgar Latin *postius* (unattested), comparative of Latin *post,* after + *ne,* born, from Latin *nātus,* past participle of *nāscī,* to be born.] **—pu·ni·ly** *adv.* **—pu·ni·ness** *n.*

pup (pup) *n.* **1.** A young dog; a puppy. **2.** The young of certain other animals, such as the seal. **3.** *British Informal.* An insolent person. **4.** *Informal.* An object or item that turns out to be worthless or inferior. Used chiefly in such phrases as *buy a pup* or *be sold a pup.* **—in pup.** Pregnant. Said of a bitch.
~*intr.v.* **pupped, pupping, pups.** To give birth to pups. [Back-formation from PUPPY.]

pu·pa (péw-pə) *n., pl.* **-pae** (-pee) or **-pas.** The nonmobile stage in the metamorphosis of many insects, following the larval stage and preceding the adult form, during which many internal changes occur. Compare **nymph.** [New Latin *pupa,* from Latin *pūpa,* girl, doll, feminine of *pūpus,* boy.] **—pu·pal** *adj.*

pu·pate (pew-páyt || *U.S.* péw-payt) *intr.v.* **-pated, -pating, -pates.** To become a pupa. **—pu·pa·tion** (pew-páysh'n) *n.*

pu·pil[1] (péw-p'l, -pil) *n.* **1.** A student under the direct supervision of a teacher. **2.** *Law.* **a.** A minor under the supervision of a guardian. **b.** A trainee barrister. [Middle English *pupille,* orphan, ward, (hence) pupil, from Old French, from Latin *pūpillus,* diminutive of *pūpus,* boy.]

pupil[2] *n.* The apparently black circular aperture in the centre of the iris of the eye through which light passes to the retina. [Middle English *pupilla* and Old French *pupille,* both from Latin *pūpilla,* "little orphan girl", pupil (by analogy with Greek *korē,* little girl, doll, pupil of the eye, originally referring to the miniature reflections that can be seen by looking closely at another's eye), feminine of *pūpillus,* PUPIL.]

pu·pil·lage, *U.S.* **pu·pil·age** (péwpilij) *n.* **1.** The state or period of being a pupil. **2. a.** The practical training received by an inexperienced barrister in the chambers of an experienced barrister. **b.** The period of time spent in such training.

pu·pil·lar·y[1], pu·pi·lar·y (péwpi-lәri || -lerri) *adj.* Of or pertaining to a ward or a student.

pupillary[2], pupilary *adj.* Of or affecting the pupil of the eye.

pu·pip·a·rous (pew-píppәrәss) *adj.* Producing well-developed young that are ready to pupate. [PUPA + -PAROUS.]

pup·pet (púppit) *n.* **1.** A small figure of a person or animal, having jointed parts animated from above by strings or wires; a marionette. **2.** A similar figure having a cloth body and hollow head, designed to be fitted over and manipulated by the hand or finger. **3.** A toy representing a human figure; a doll. **4.** A person or group whose behaviour is determined by the will of others.
~*adj.* **1.** Of or pertaining to puppets. **2.** Sponsored and controlled by another or others while professing autonomy: *a puppet state.* [Middle English *popet, popette,* small child, doll, from Old French *poupette,* diminutive of *poupe* (unattested), doll, from Vulgar Latin *puppa* (unattested), doll, from Latin *pūpa. See* **pupa.**]

pup·pet·eer (púppi-teér) *n.* A person who operates and entertains with puppets or marionettes.

pup·pet·ry (púppitri) *n., pl.* **-ries. 1.** The art of making puppets and presenting puppet shows. **2.** The actions of puppets. **3.** Stilted or artificial dramatic performance.

Pup·pis (púppiss) *n.* A constellation in the Southern Hemisphere near Canis Major and Pyxis. [Latin "ship", from *puppis,* POOP[1].]

pup·py (púppi) *n., pl.* **-pies. 1.** A young dog; a pup. **2.** A conceited or inexperienced youth. [Middle English *popi,* from Old French *po(u)pee,* doll, toy, plaything, from Vulgar Latin *puppa* (unattested). See **puppet.**] **—pup·py·ish** *adj.*

puppy fat *n.* The fatty tissue or fat appearance of a child or adolescent. It usually becomes less noticeable with age.

puppy love *n.* Adolescent love or infatuation.

pup tent *n.* A **shelter tent** *(see).*

Pur·beck marble (púr-bek) *n.* A nonmarine marble, used in architecture and sculpture on account of its high gloss. [After Isle of *Purbeck,* Dorset, the peninsula where it is quarried.]

pur·blind (púr-blīnd) *adj.* **1.** Having poor vision; nearly or partly blind. **2.** Slow in understanding or discernment; dull. [Middle English *pur(e)blind,* originally "totally blind" : PURE (completely) + BLIND.] **—pur·blind·ly** *adv.* **—pur·blind·ness** *n.*

Pur·cell (púr-s'l, -sel; *also* -sél), **Henry** (1659–95). English composer. As organist at Westminster Abbey and Composer in Ordinary to the Chapel Royal, he was the leading musical figure of Restoration England.

pur·chas·a·ble (púr-chәss-әb'l, -chiss-) *adj.* **1.** Capable of being bought. **2.** Capable of being bribed; venal. **—pur·chas·a·bil·i·ty** (-ә-bíllәti) *n.*

pur·chase (púr-chәss, -chiss) *tr.v.* **-chased, -chasing, -chases. 1.** To obtain in exchange for money or its equivalent; buy. **2.** To acquire by effort; earn. **3.** *Law.* To acquire (property) legally by means other than inheritance. **4.** To raise, haul, or hold with a mechanical device such as a lever or wrench.
~*n.* **1.** That which is bought. **2. a.** The act of buying. **b.** Acquisition through the payment of money or its equivalent. **3.** *Law.* **a.** The acquisition of property other than by inheritance. **b.** Annual rent or income, especially from land. **4.** A grip applied manually or mechanically to move something or prevent it from slipping. **5.** A tackle, lever, or other device used to obtain mechanical advantage. **6.** A position, as of a lever or one's feet, affording means to move or secure a weight. **7.** Any means of increasing power, influence, or advantage. [Middle English *po(u)rchasen,* from Old French *po(u)rchacier, purchacier,* to pursue, seek to obtain : *po(u)r-,* for, from Latin *prō* + *chacier,* to CHASE.] **—pur·chas·er** *n.*

purchase tax *n.* Formerly, a tax in Britain on certain consumer goods, especially non-essential, luxury items. It was replaced in 1973 by value-added tax.

purchasing agent *n. Abbr.* **P.A.** A person acting as another's agent in making purchases.

purchasing power *n.* **1.** The ability of a person or group to purchase, generally measured by income. **2.** The value of a particular monetary unit in terms of the goods or services it will buy.

pur·dah (púr-daa, -dә) *n.* **1.** A curtain used to screen Hindu or Muslim women from men or strangers, especially in India. **2.** In India, the system of secluding women, especially of high rank, from public view. **3.** Seclusion or ostracism resulting from embarrassment or disgrace. Used humorously: *After his blunder, he was in purdah for weeks.* [Hindi *pardā,* screen, veil, from Persian *pardah*†.]

pure (pewr) *adj.* **purer, purest. 1.** Having a homogeneous or uniform composition; not mixed: *pure oxygen.* **2.** Free from adulterants or impurities; full-strength: *pure chocolate.* **3.** Free from dirt, defilement, or pollution; clean. **4.** Free from foreign elements: *keeping the language pure.* **5.** Containing nothing inappropriate or extraneous: *a pure production of Hamlet.* **6. a.** Complete: *by pure chance.* **b.** Thorough; utter: *pure folly.* **7.** Free or relatively free from taint, sin, or faults. **8.** Chaste; virgin. **9.** Of unmixed blood or ancestry. **10.** *Genetics.* Breeding true to parental type; homozygous: *a pure line.* **11.** *Music.* Free from discordant qualities. **12.** *Phonetics.* Articulated with a single unchanging speech sound; monophthongal: *a pure vowel.* **13.** Theoretical rather than applied: *pure science.* **14.** *Philosophy.* Free from empirical elements: *pure reason.* [Middle English *pur, pure,* from Old French *pur* (feminine *pure*), from Latin *pūrus,* clean.] **—pure·ness** *n.*

pure·bred (péwr-bréd) *adj.* Of a strain established through breeding many generations of unmixed stock. **—pure·bred** (-bred) *n.*

pu·rée (péwr-ay; *rarely* póor- || *U.S.* pew-ráy, -rée) *tr.v.* **-réed, -réeing, -rées.** To convert (vegetables or fruit, for example) to a semisolid state, as by cooking and pressing through a strainer.
~*n.* Food so prepared. [French, from Old French *purer,* to purify, strain, from Latin *pūrāre,* to purify, from *pūrus,* PURE.]

Pure Land Buddhism *n.* A form of Buddhism widely followed in Japan, which teaches salvation through faith in, and the calling on the name of, the Buddha Amida. Also called "Jodo".

pure·ly (péwrli) *adv.* **1.** In a pure manner. **2.** Innocently; chastely. **3.** Totally; entirely: *purely by chance.*

pur·fle (púrf'l) *tr.v.* **-fled, -fling, -fles.** To finish or decorate the border or edge of (a table or violin, for example).
~*n.* Also **pur·fling** (púrfling). An ornamental border or edging. [Middle English *purfilen,* from Old French *porfiler,* to weave, from Vulgar Latin *prōfīlāre* (unattested), to draw in outline : Latin *prō,* forth, out + *fīlum,* thread.]

pur·ga·tion (pur-gáysh'n) *n.* The act of purging or purifying.

pur·ga·tive (púrgәtiv) *adj.* Tending to cleanse or purge.
~*n. Medicine.* A purgative agent, a **laxative** *(see).*

pur·ga·to·ri·al (púrgә-táwri-әl || -tōri-) *adj.* **1.** Serving to purify of sin; expiatory. **2.** Of, pertaining to, or resembling purgatory.

pur·ga·to·ry (púrgә-tri, -tәri) *n., pl.* **-ries. 1.** *Roman Catholic Church.* A state in which the souls of those who have died in grace must expiate venial sins. **2.** Any place or condition of expiation, suffering, or remorse.
~*adj.* Tending to cleanse or purge. [Middle English *purgatorie,* from Medieval Latin *purgātōrium,* from Late Latin *purgātōrius,* from Latin *purgāre,* to PURGE.]

purge (purj) *v.* **purged, purging, purges.** —*tr.* **1. a.** To free from impurities; purify. **b.** To remove (impurities and other elements) by or as if by cleansing. **2.** To rid of sin, guilt, or defilement. **3.** *Law.* **a.** To clear (a person) of a charge or imputation. **b.** To atone for (an offence) by being punished. **4.** To rid (a nation, political party, or other group) of persons considered to be undesirable. **5.** *Medicine.* **a.** To cause evacuation of (the bowels). **b.** To induce evacuation of the bowels in (a patient). —*intr.* **1.** To become pure or clean. **2.** To undergo or cause an emptying of the bowels.
~*n.* **1.** The act or process of purging. **2.** That which purges; especially, a medicinal purgative. **3.** The purging of dissidents and others considered undesirable from a government, political party, or the like. [Middle English *purgen,* from Old French *purger,* from

Latin *purgāre, pūrigāre* (unattested), to cleanse : *pūrus,* PURE + *agere,* to lead.] **—purg·er** *n.*

pu·ri (po͝or-i) *n.* A light, flat wheat cake of northern Indian origin, usually deep-fried in fat. [Hindi, from Sanskrit *purah,* cake.]

Pu·ri (po͝o-ree). Also **Jagannath** or **Juggernaut.** Seaport in Orissa, east central India. It is a major centre of pilgrimage for Hindus.

pu·ri·fi·ca·tor (péwr-i-fi-kaytər) *n.* A cloth used to clean the chalice and paten and the lips and fingers of the celebrant at the Eucharist.

pu·ri·fy (péwr-i-fli) *v.* **-fied, -fying, -fies.** *—tr.* **1.** To rid of impurities; cleanse. **2.** To rid of foreign or objectionable elements. **3.** To free from sin, guilt, or other defilement. *—intr.* To become clean or pure. [Middle English *purifien,* from Old French *purifier,* from Latin *pūrificāre,* to make pure : *pūrus,* PURE + *facere,* to make.] **—pu·ri·fi·ca·tion** (-fi-káysh'n) *n.* **—pu·rif·i·ca·to·ry** (-fi-kaytəri, -káytəri, -fickətri) *adj.* **—pu·ri·fi·er** *n.*

Pu·rim (péwr-im, po͝or-; *Hebrew* po͝o-reém) *n. Judaism.* A holiday in the month of Adar, celebrating the deliverance of the Jews from the threatened massacre by Haman. Esther 9:20–22. [Hebrew *pūrīm,* plural of *pūr,* lot (from the lots cast by Haman to determine the day of destruction of the Jews), from Akkadian *pūru,* stone.]

pu·rine (péwr-een, -in) *n.* **1.** A colourless crystalline compound, $C_5H_4N_4$, used in organic synthesis and metabolism studies. **2.** Any of a group of naturally occurring organic compounds derived from or having molecular structures related to purine, including uric acid, adenine, guanine, and caffeine. [German *Purin* : blend of Latin *pūrus,* PURE + New Latin *uricus,* URIC (ACID) (in which it is found) + -INE.]

pur·ism (péwr-iz'm) *n.* Strict observance of or insistence upon traditional correctness, especially of language. [French *purisme,* from *pur,* PURE.]

pur·ist (péwr-ist) *n.* One who practises or urges strict correctness, especially in the use of words. **—pu·ris·ti·cal** (pewr-rístik'l) *adj.* **—pu·ris·ti·cal·ly** *adv.*

pu·ris·tic *adj.* **1.** Characterised by purism. **2.** *Capital* **P.** Of or pertaining to Katharevousa.
∼n. Capital **P.** A variety of Modern Greek **Katharevousa** *(see).*

Pu·ri·tan (péwr-i-tən) *n.* **1.** A member of a group of English Protestants who, in the 16th and 17th centuries, after the Reformation, sought further simplification of the ceremonies and creeds of the Church of England and strict religious discipline. **2.** *Small* **p.** One who lives in accordance with the precepts of the Puritans; especially, one who regards luxury or pleasure as sinful.
∼adj. **1.** Of or pertaining to the Puritans or Puritanism. **2.** *Small* **p.** Characteristic of a puritan; puritanical. [Late Latin *pūritās,* purity, from *pūrus,* PURE, by analogy with *Catharan,* CATHAR.]

pu·ri·tan·i·cal (péwr-i-tánnik'l) *adj.* Also **pu·ri·tan·ic** (-tánnik). **1.** Rigorous in religious observance; marked by stern morality. **2.** *Capital* **P.** Of, pertaining to, or characteristic of the Puritans. Used derogatorily. **—pu·ri·tan·i·cal·ly** *adv.* **—pu·ri·tan·i·cal·ness** *n.*

Pu·ri·tan·ism (péwr-i-tən-iz'm) *n.* **1.** The practices and doctrines of the Puritans. **2.** *Small* **p.** Scrupulous moral rigour; especially, hostility to social pleasures and indulgences.

pu·ri·ty (péwr-əti) *n.* **1.** The quality or condition of being pure. **2.** *Physics.* The proportion of a single-frequency spectral component in a mixture of achromatic and spectral colours. [Middle English, from Old French *pureté*; assimilated to Late Latin *pūritās* (stem *pūritāt-*), from Latin *pūrus,* PURE.]

purl[1] (purl) *intr.v.* **purled, purling, purls.** To flow or ripple with a murmuring sound. Used chiefly of water.
∼n. The motion or sound made by rippling water. [16th century : probably imitative; akin to Norwegian *purla*†.]

purl[2] *v.* **purled, purling, purls.** Also **pearl** (for transitive sense 2 and intransitive sense 2). *—tr.* **1.** To knit with a purl stitch. **2.** To edge or finish with lace or embroidery. *—intr.* **1.** To do knitting with a purl stitch. **2.** To edge or finish with lace or embroidery.
∼n. Also **pearl** (for senses 2 and 3). *Abbr.* **p. 1.** The inversion of a knit stitch; a purl stitch. **2.** A decorative edging of lace or embroidery. **3.** Gold or silver wire used in embroidery. [Earlier *pirl*†; perhaps akin to PURL (ripple).]

pur·ler (púrlər) *n.* Also **pear·ler** (for sense 2). *Informal.* **1.** *British.* **a.** A blow throwing one forwards. **b.** A headlong fall. Used chiefly in the phrases *come a purler* or *take a purler.* **2.** *Australian.* One that is outstanding or excellent.

pur·lieu (púr-lew ‖ -lo͞o) *n.* **1.** Any outlying or neighbouring area; specifically, in former times, land beyond the perimeter of a forest but still partly subject to hunting laws. **2.** *Plural.* Outskirts; environs. **3.** A place that one frequents. [Middle English *purlewe,* perhaps alteration of Anglo-French *puralée,* perambulation, from the past participle of Old French *poraler, puraler,* to traverse : *por,* through, from Latin *prō,* forth + *aler,* to go, probably from Vulgar Latin *amlāre* (unattested), from Latin *ambulāre,* to walk.]

pur·lin, pur·line (púrlin) *n.* Any of several horizontal timbers supporting the rafters of a roof. [Middle English *purly(o)n*†.]

pur·loin (púr-loyn, pur-lóyn ‖ pər-) *v.* **-loined, -loining, -loins.** *—tr.* To steal; filch. *—intr.* To commit theft. [Middle English *purloynen,* to remove, from Anglo-French *purloigner,* "to put far away" : Old French *pur-,* away, from Latin *prō-,* away + *loign,* far, from Latin *longē,* far, from *longus,* long.] **—pur·loin·er** *n.*

purl stitch *n.* An inverted plain stitch in knitting. Also called "purl".

pur·ple (púrp'l) *n.* **1.** Any of a group of colours with a hue between that of violet and red. **2.** Cloth of this colour, formerly worn as a symbol of royalty or high office. **3.** A pigment or dyeing agent used to produce such cloth. **4.** Imperial, royal, or other high rank. **5.** The cloth worn by or the rank or office of a cardinal or bishop.
∼adj. **1.** Of the colour purple. **2.** Royal or imperial; regal. **3.** Elaborate and ornate: *purple prose.*
∼v. **purpled, -pling, -ples.** *—tr.* To make purple. *—intr.* To become purple. [Middle English *purpel, purpyl,* Old English *purple,* altered by dissimilation from *purpuran,* of purple, from *purpura,* purple cloth, from Latin, purple. See **purpura.**]

purple emperor *n.* A Eurasian butterfly, *Apatura iris,* having a purple sheen on the upper side of the wing in the male.

purple gallinule *n.* **1.** A dark, bluish-purple waterfowl, *Porphyrio porphyrio,* resembling a large moorhen. **2.** A similar American bird, *Porphyrula martinica,* with a blue-purple breast and green back.

purple heart *n.* Also **pur·ple·heart** (púrp'l-haart) (for senses 1, 2). **1.** Any of several tropical American trees of the genus *Peltogyne,* valued for their decorative wood. **2.** The purplish heartwood of any of these trees. **3.** *Chiefly British Informal.* A purple, heart-shaped amphetamine tablet containing the drug Drinamyl.

Purple Heart *n.* The U.S. Armed Forces medal awarded to servicemen and servicewomen wounded in action.

purple loosestrife *n.* A marsh plant, *Lythrum salicaria,* having long spikes of purple flowers.

purple patch *n.* **1.** An extravagant, florid, or ornate passage of literary writing. **2.** Broadly, any brief performance that is unusually stylish or effective. Also called "purple passage".

purple salt *n. Chemistry.* **Potassium permanganate** *(see).*

purple sprouting broccoli *n.* See **broccoli.**

pur·plish (púrplish, púrp'l-ish) *adj.* Having a somewhat purple tint.

pur·port (pər-pórt, pur-, púr-pərt, -pawrt ‖ -pōrt; -pōrt) *tr.v.* **-ported, -porting, -ports.** **1.** To contain the claim or profession (to be or do something). **2.** To have or give the appearance, often falsely, of being, professing, or intending. —See Synonyms at **mean.**
∼n. (púr-pawrt, -pərt ‖ -pōrt). **1.** The apparent meaning; the import or significance. **2.** The purpose or intention. —See Synonyms at **meaning.** [Middle English *purporten,* to imply, from Old French *porporter,* to embody, contain, from Medieval Latin *prōportāre,* to carry forth : Latin *prō,* forth + *portāre,* to carry.] **—pur·port·ed·ly** (pər-pórt-id-li, pur- ‖ -pōrt-) *adv.*

pur·pose (púrpəss) *n.* **1.** The object towards which one strives or for which something exists; a goal; an aim. **2.** A result or effect that is intended or desired. **3.** Determination; resolution. **4.** The matter at hand; the point at issue: *Let's return to the purpose.* —See Synonyms at **intention.** **—on purpose.** Deliberately.
∼tr.v. **purposed, -posing, -poses.** To intend or resolve to perform or accomplish. [Middle English *porpos, purpos,* from Old French, from *porposer, purposer,* to design, intend, from Latin *prōpōnere* (past participle *prōpositus*), to put forward, PROPOSE.]

pur·pose-built (púrpəss-bílt) *adj.* Built specifically for the purpose being served: *a purpose-built ski-resort.*

pur·pose·ful (púrpəss-f'l) *adj.* **1.** Having a purpose; intentional. **2.** Having or manifesting purpose; determined. —See Usage note at **purposely.** **—pur·pose·ful·ly** *adv.* **—pur·pose·ful·ness** *n.*

pur·pose·less (púrpəss-ləss, -liss) *adj.* Without any purpose; aimless; pointless. **—pur·pose·less·ly** *adv.* **—pur·pose·less·ness** *n.*

pur·pose·ly (púrpəss-li) *adv.* **1.** With a particular purpose in mind. **2.** On purpose; intentionally.

Usage: *Purposely, purposefully,* and *purposively* are sometimes confused. Of the three, *purposely* is the most general term, meaning "deliberately, on purpose". *Purposefully* adds the nuance of "acting in a determined way", and *purposively* adds the nuance of "acting so as to achieve a particular end". Some contexts allow all three words, but usually a distinction is maintained: *He purposely left the room, so I could sleep* and *He purposefully left the room, to fetch the papers. Purposively* tends to be restricted to psychological or behavioural description: *This organism acts purposively.*

pur·pos·ive (púrpəss-iv) *adj.* **1.** Having or serving a purpose. **2.** Purposeful as opposed to aimless or random. —See Usage note at **purposely.** **—pur·pos·ive·ly** *adv.* **—pur·pos·ive·ness** *n.*

pur·pu·ra (púrpewr-ə) *n.* A skin rash made up of small purple spots caused by subcutaneous bleeding. [Latin, from Greek *porphura,* purple (dye), shellfish from which it was obtained, from Semitic.]

pur·pure (púrpewr) *n. Heraldry.* The colour purple. [Old English and Old French *purpre,* from Latin *purpura.* See **purpura.**] **—pur·pure** *adj.*

pur·pur·in (púrpewr-in) *n.* A red crystalline derivative of anthraquinone, $C_{14}H_5O_2(OH)_3$, used as a stain in biology. [Latin *purpura,* purple (see **purpura**) + -IN.]

purr (pur) *n.* **1.** The characteristic softly vibrant sound of a cat, understood to express pleasure or contentment. **2.** Any similar sound, such as the idling of a well-tuned motor car.
∼v. **purred, purring, purrs.** *—intr.* To emit a purr. *—tr.* To utter or express by means of a purr: *purred their approval.* [Imitative.]

purse (purss) *n.* **1.** A small bag or pouch for carrying money, especially coins. **2.** *U.S.* A woman's handbag. **3.** Anything that resembles a bag or pouch. **4.** Available wealth or resources; money. **5.** A sum of money collected as a present or offered as a prize.
∼tr.v. **pursed, pursing, purses.** To gather or contract (the lips or brow) into wrinkles or folds; pucker. [Middle English *purs,* Old English *purs,* from Late Latin *bursa,* bag, oxhide, from Greek *bursa,* leather, hide.]

purs·er (púrssər) *n.* The officer in charge of money matters and welfare of passengers on a ship. [Middle English, from *purs,* PURSE.]

purse seine (sayn) *n.* A fishing seine that is pursed or drawn into the shape of a bag to enclose the catch.
purse strings *pl.n.* **1.** The strings that tighten and close the opening of an old-fashioned purse. **2.** Control of finance or money supply.
purs·lane (púrss-lin, -layn) *n.* **1.** A trailing weed, *Lythrum portula* (or *Peplis portula*), having small yellow flowers, reddish stems, and fleshy leaves that are sometimes used in salads. Also called "water purslane". **2.** Any of various similar but unrelated plants, such as sea purslane. [Middle English *purcelan, purslane,* from Old French *porcelaine,* cowrie shell, from Late Latin *porcillāgo,* from Latin *porcil(l)āca, portulāca.*]
pur·su·ance (pər-séw-ənss, -sŏŏ- || -shŏŏ-) *n.* The carrying out or putting into effect of a plan, idea, or the like.
pur·su·ant (pər-séw-ənt, -sŏŏ- || -shŏŏ-) *adj.* Proceeding from and conformable to; in accordance with. Used with *to.*
∼*adv.* Also **pur·su·ant·ly.** Accordingly; consequently. [Middle English *poursuiant,* from Old French, present participle of *poursuivre,* PURSUE.]
pur·sue (pər-séw, -sŏŏ || -shŏŏ) *v.* **-sued, -suing, -sues.** —*tr.* **1.** To follow in an effort to overtake or capture; chase. **2.** To strive to gain or accomplish. **3.** To proceed along the course of; follow: *pursue the original plan.* **4.** To carry further; advance: *pursued the argument.* **5.** To be engaged in (a vocation or hobby, for example). **6.** To follow closely; harass. —*intr.* **1.** To chase; follow. **2.** To continue; carry on. [Middle English *pursuen,* from Anglo-French *pursuer,* from Old French *po(u)rsuivre, po(u)rsuir,* from Vulgar Latin *prōsequere* (unattested), from Latin *prōsequī*: *prō-,* forth, onward + *sequī,* to follow.] —**pur·su·a·ble** *adj.* —**pur·su·er** *n.*
pur·suit (pər-séwt, -sŏŏt || -shŏŏt) *n.* **1.** The act or an instance of chasing or pursuing. **2.** The act of striving: *pursuit of success.* **3.** An activity engaged in: *academic pursuits.* **4.** A cycling race, usually on a circular track, in which two riders or teams, beginning some distance apart, attempt to overtake each other. [Middle English *pursu(i)te,* from Old French *poursuite,* from *poursuivre,* PURSUE.]
pur·sui·vant (púr-si-vənt, -swi-) *n.* **1.** In the British Colleges of Heralds, an officer ranking below a herald. **2.** *Archaic.* A follower, messenger, or attendant. [Middle English *pursevant,* from Old French *pours(u)ivant,* follower, from the present participle of *poursuivre,* PURSUE.]
pur·sy (púrssi || pússi) *adj.* **-sier, -siest.** **1.** Short of wind. **2.** Fat; corpulent. [Middle English *pursy, pursive,* from Anglo-French *porsif,* Old French *polsif,* from *polser,* to wheeze, be short of breath, from Latin *pulsāre,* to pulse. See **pulsate.**] —**purs·i·ness** *n.*
pur·te·nance (púrtinənss) *n. Archaic.* An animal's viscera or inner organs, especially the heart, liver, and lungs. [Middle English *purtenaunce,* "appurtenance", "accessory", alteration of Old French *partenance,* pertinence, from PERTINENT.]
pu·ru·lence (péwr-ŏŏ-lənss, -rew-) *n.* **1.** The condition of discharging or containing pus. **2.** Pus.
pu·ru·lent (péwr-ŏŏ-lənt, -rew-) *adj.* Containing or discharging pus. [Latin *pūrulentus* : *pūs* (stem *pūr-*), pus + -ULENT.] —**pu·ru·lent·ly** *adv.*
pur·vey (pər-váy, pur- || *U.S. also* púr-vay) *tr.v.* **-veyed, -veying, -veys.** To supply (food or information, for example); furnish. [Middle English *purveien, porveien,* from Old French *porveeir, porveioir,* from Latin *prōvidēre,* to foresee, PROVIDE.]
pur·vey·ance (pər-váy-ənss, pur-) *n.* The act of procuring supplies.
pur·vey·or (pər-váy-ər, pur-) *n.* **1.** A person who furnishes provisions, especially food. **2.** A distributor; a dispenser.
pur·view (púr-vew) *n.* **1.** The extent or range of function, power, or competence; scope. **2.** Range of vision, comprehension, or experience; outlook. **3.** *Law.* The body, scope, or limit of a statute. [Middle English *purveu, purvewe,* proviso, provisional clause, from Anglo-French *purveu,* "(it is) provided" (word used to introduce a proviso), from Old French *porveu,* past participle of *porveeir,* to provide, PURVEY.]
pus (puss) *n.* A viscous, yellowish-white fluid formed in infected tissue, consisting chiefly of leucocytes, cellular debris, and liquefied tissue elements. [Latin *pūs.*]
Pu·san (pŏŏ-sán). Seaport in southeast Korea. Capital of South Kyongsang province, it is the nearest point on the Asiatic mainland to Japan and was a United Nations supply base during the Korean War. It is a commercial and industrial centre.
Pu·sey (péwzi), **Edward Bouverie** (1800–82). British theologian. A member of the Oxford Movement, he advocated a revival of ceremony and Catholicism in the Anglican church. —**Pu·sey·ism** (-iz'm) *n.* —**Pu·sey·ite** (-īt) *n.*
push (pŏŏsh) *v.* **pushed, pushing, pushes.** —*tr.* **1.** To exert force against (an object) to move it away. **2.** To move by exerting force in this manner; thrust; shove. **3.** To force (an enemy or opposing team) to move back or retreat: *pushed the tank battalion back.* **4.** To force (one's way): *He pushed his way through the crowd.* **5.** To urge on or encourage, especially in a forceful way: *They push us hard at school.* **6.** *Informal.* To bear hard upon; press: *pushed for time.* **7.** To extend or enlarge: *push civilisation past the frontier.* **8.** *Informal.* **a.** To promote or market (a product). **b.** To sell (a narcotic) illegally. **c.** To advocate or seek support for: *push the idea.* **9.** *Sports.* To hit (a ball) with a slow, precise stroke, rather than with a sharp rap or swinging stroke. —*intr.* **1.** To exert outward force against something. **2.** To advance despite difficulty or opposition; press forward. **3.** To expend great or vigorous effort, especially to bring about or obtain something. Oten used with *for*: *pushing for an enquiry.* —**push along.** *Informal.* To depart; set out. —**push off.** **1.** *Informal.* **a.** To depart; set out. **b.** To go away or withdraw hastily. Often used in the imperative. **2.** To cause (a boat, for example) to begin to move. —**push on.** To continue. —**push (someone) about** or **around.** *Informal.* To bully someone or order him about. —**push through.** To force the acceptance or adoption of (a bill or amendment, for example).
∼*n.* **1.** The act of pushing; a thrust. **2.** A vigorous or insistent effort towards an end. **3.** A provocation to action; a stimulus. **4.** *Informal.* Persevering energy; enterprise. **5.** A struggle; a strain: *It'll be a push but we can do it.* **6.** *Australian Informal.* A group of people; a clique. —**at a push.** With some difficulty. —**give (someone) the push.** *Informal.* **1.** To dismiss (someone) from a job. **2.** To end an emotional relationship with (someone). [Middle English *posshen, pusshen,* from Old French *polser, poulser,* to push, beat, from Latin *pulsāre,* frequentative of *pellere* (past participle *pulsus*), to push, beat.]
push·ball (pŏŏsh-bawl) *n.* **1.** A game, played chiefly in the United States, in which two opposing teams attempt to push a heavy ball, 1.83 metres (six feet) in diameter, across a goal. **2.** The ball so used.
push-bike (pŏŏsh-bīk) *n. Informal.* A bicycle operated solely by pedalling, as distinct from a motorised bicycle.
push button *n.* A small button that activates an electric circuit.
push-but·ton (pŏŏsh-butt'n) *adj.* Operated by or as if by push buttons: *push-button warfare.*
push·cart (pŏŏsh-kaart) *n.* A light cart pushed by hand; a barrow.
push·chair (pŏŏsh-chair) *n.* A light, folding, four-wheeled chair for wheeling small children about.
push·er (pŏŏshər) *n.* **1.** One that pushes. **2.** An energetically ambitious person. **3.** *Informal.* A person who sells drugs illegally. **4.** A utensil, used by a child, for pushing food onto a spoon or fork.
push·ing (pŏŏshing) *adj.* **1.** Energetic; enterprising. **2.** Aggressive; forward; presumptuous.
∼*adv. Informal.* Almost; nearly: *pushing 40.* —**push·ing·ly** *adv.*
Push·kin (pŏŏsh-kin), **Alexandr Sergeyevich** (1799–1837). Russian poet. He wrote the verse novel *Eugene Onegin* (1825–31), the play *Boris Godunov* (1831), and many narrative and lyrical poems and short stories, all considered classics of their genre. He is regarded as the founder of the Russian literary language.
push·o·ver (pŏŏsh-ōvər) *n. Informal.* **1.** Anything easily accomplished. **2.** A person or group easily defeated or taken advantage of.
push-pull (pŏŏsh-pŏŏl) *adj.* Designating an arrangement of two identical electronic devices that act 180° out of phase with each other in order to minimise distortion.
push·rod (pŏŏsh-rod) *n.* Also **push rod.** A rod moved by a cam to operate the valves in an internal-combustion engine.
push-start (pŏŏsh-staart) *n.* A method of starting a motor vehicle by pushing it, then putting it into gear, so that the engine turns.
∼*tr.v.* (*also* -stárt) **push-started, -starting, -starts.** To start (a motor vehicle) in this way.
Push·tu (púsh-tŏŏ, -tŏŏ; *also* pŏŏsh-) *n.* An Iranian language, **Pashto** *(see).*
push-up (pŏŏsh-up) *n. U.S.* A **press-up** *(see).*
push·y (pŏŏshi) *adj.* **-ier, -iest.** *Informal.* Disagreeably forward or aggressive. —**push·i·ly** *adv.* —**push·i·ness** *n.*
pu·sil·lan·i·mous (péw-si-lánniməss, -zi-) *adj.* Lacking courage; cowardly. [Late Latin *pūsillanimis* : Latin *pūsillus,* very small, weak, from *pūsus,* boy + *animus,* mind, soul.] —**pu·sil·la·nim·i·ty** (-lə-nímməti) *n.* —**pu·sil·lan·i·mous·ly** *adv.*
puss[1] (pŏŏss) *n. Informal.* **1.** A cat. **2.** A girl or young woman. Used affectionately. **3.** *Archaic.* A hare. [Probably from Middle Low German *pūs*†.]
puss[2] *n. Slang.* **1.** The mouth. **2.** The face. [Irish *bus,* lip, mouth, from Old Irish, lip.]
puss moth *n.* A Eurasian moth, *Cerura vinula,* the caterpillar of which has a forked tail and prominent eyespots at the anterior end to alarm predators. [From PUSS (cat), referring to its furry body.]
puss·y[1] (pŏŏssi) *n., pl.* **-ies.** **1.** *Informal.* A cat. **2.** *Vulgar Slang.* **a.** The female genitals. **b.** Women collectively, considered as sexual objects. [See **puss** (cat).]
pus·sy[2] (pússi) *adj.* **-sier, -siest.** Resembling or containing pus.
puss·y·foot (pŏŏssi-fŏŏt) *intr.v.* **-footed, -footing, -foots.** **1.** To move stealthily or cautiously. **2.** *Informal.* To act or proceed cautiously or timidly to avoid committing oneself.
pussy willow *n.* **1.** A North American shrub or small tree, *Salix discolor,* having silky, pale grey catkins. **2.** Any of several similar willows.
pus·tu·lant (pústewlənt) *adj.* Causing pustules to form.
∼*n.* An agent that produces pustules.
pus·tu·late (pústew-layt) *v.* **-lated, -lating, -lates.** —*tr.* To cause (tissue) to form pustules. —*intr.* To form pustules.
∼*adj.* (-lət, -lit, -layt). Covered with pustules.
pus·tu·la·tion (pústew-láysh'n) *n.* **1.** The formation or appearance of pustules. **2.** A pustule.
pus·tule (pústewl) *n.* **1.** A slight, inflamed raised area of the skin filled with pus. **2.** Any small swelling similar to a blister or pimple. [Middle English, from Old French, from Latin *pustula,* a blister.] —**pus·tu·lar** (-ər) *adj.*
pusz·ta (pŏŏsh-tə) *n.* Temperate grassland on the plains of Hungary. [Hungarian.]
put (pŏŏt) *v.* **put, putting, puts.** —*tr.* **1.** To place in a specified location; set: *put the cat out; put words into her mouth.* **2.** To cause to be in a specified condition: *put one's room in order; She put his mind at rest.* **3.** To cause to undergo something; subject: *was put to*

death. **4.** To assign; attribute: *put a false interpretation on events; put the blame on his wife.* **5.** To estimate. Used with *at*: *He put the time at five o'clock.* **6.** To impose: *put a tax on cigarettes; put an end to his agony.* **7.** To bet; wager (a stake). **8.** To hurl with an overhand pushing motion: *put the shot.* **9.** To bring up for consideration or judgment: *The committee put the question.* **10.** To express; state: *putting it bluntly.* **11.** To render in a specified language or literary form: *put prose into verse.* **12.** To adapt: *lyrics put to music.* **13.** To urge or force to some action: *put an outlaw to flight.* **14.** To apply: *We must put our minds to it.* **15.** To impart; invest: *put some effort into it.* **16.** To cause to penetrate. Used with *through*: *put her hand through the window.* —*intr.* To proceed: *The ship put into the harbour.* **—put about.** **1.** *Nautical.* **a.** To change direction; go from one tack to another. **b.** To cause (a ship) to put about. **2.** To spread (a rumour or news, for example). **—put across.** **1.** To state so as to be understood or accepted. **2.** To convey (an impression): *She puts across an image of haughtiness.* **3.** To project or give a specified impression of (oneself): *He put himself across rather feebly at the interview.* **—put aside** or **by.** **1.** To save for later use; reserve. **2.** To abandon; discard. **—put away.** **1.** To save or keep in reserve. **2.** *Informal.* To confine in an institution, such as a mental hospital. **3.** To consume (food or drink), especially in large quantities. **—put back.** **1.** To postpone for or until a specified time: *The meeting is being put back for 24 hours.* **2.** To cause delay or disruption to. **—put forth.** **1.** To grow: *The plant put forth leaves.* **2.** To offer for consideration. **—put forward.** **1.** To propose (an idea, for example). **2.** To nominate, as for a position of authority. **—put in.** **1.** *Nautical.* To enter a port or harbour. **2.** To insert; interject. **3.** To submit (a form, for example). **4.** To apply or enter: *put in for the job.* **5.** To devote or contribute (work, time, or money, for example). **6. a.** To cause (a political party, for example) to be elected. **b.** In cricket, to make (the opposing team) bat. **—put it about.** **1.** To spread information or rumour. **2.** *Slang.* To be sexually promiscuous. **—put one across** or **over on.** *Informal.* To trick or deceive (someone), especially into believing a claim or excuse. **—put out.** **1.** To extinguish: *put out a fire.* **2.** *Nautical.* To leave, as from a port: *The ship put out to sea.* **3.** To blind (eyes), as by poking. **4.** To publish. **5.** To inconvenience: *I was put out by her late arrival.* **6.** To confuse; disconcert. **7.** To dislocate: *put his back out.* **—put over.** **1.** To communicate or put across. **2.** *U.S.* To achieve. **—put through.** **1. a.** To connect (a caller) by telephone. **b.** To make (a telephone call). **2.** To carry to a successful termination. **—put upon.** To impose on; take advantage of. Used in the passive: *He was put upon by his friends.*

~*n.* **1.** An act of putting the shot. **2.** *Finance.* An option to sell a stipulated amount of stock or securities within a stated time and at a fixed price. Compare **call, straddle.**

~*adj. Informal.* Fixed; stationary: *Stay put.* [Middle English *put(t)en* (unattested), Old English *pūtian*†, to push, thrust.]

pu·ta·men (pew-táy-men, -mən) *n., pl.* **-tamina** (-támminə). *Botany.* A hard, shell-like covering, such as that enclosing the kernel of a peach. [New Latin, from Latin *putāmen,* clippings, prunings, shells, from *putāre,* to prune, cut.] **—pu·tam·i·nous** (pew-támminəss) *adj.*

pu·ta·tive (péw-tətiv, pew-táytiv) *adj.* Generally regarded as such; supposed; reputed: *his putative mother.* [Middle English, from Old French *putatif,* from Late Latin *putātīvus,* from Latin *putāre,* to compute, consider.] **—pu·ta·tive·ly** *adv.*

put down *tr.v.* **1. a.** To write down; record. **b.** To record a promise or arrangement made by (someone): *Put her down for Tuesday.* **c.** To record or have recorded on a list. **d.** To list or table on an agenda: *put down a motion on overseas aid.* **2.** To repress; defeat. **3.** *Informal.* To express rejection or criticism of. **4.** To kill (an animal) mercifully. **5.** To attribute or ascribe: *Put it down to inexperience.* **6.** To regard or estimate: *I'd put her down for a liar.* **7.** To land (an aircraft). **8.** To stop reading (a book, for example). —*intr.v.* To land. Used of an aircraft.

put-down (po͝ot-down) *n. Slang.* A dismissal or rejection, especially in the form of a critical or slighting remark.

put·log (pút-log, po͝ot- || *U.S. also* -lawg) *n.* Also **put·lock** (-lok). Any of the short pieces of timber that support a scaffolding floor. [17th century : origin obscure.]

put off *tr.v.* **1.** To delay or postpone (a meeting, for example). **2.** To avoid meeting (a person) by giving an excuse. **3.** To annoy by distracting. **4.** To cause (someone) to feel dislike for (someone or something). **5.** To disconcert; make apprehensive.

put-off (po͝ot-off, -awf) *n. Chiefly U.S.* A pretext for inaction.

put on *tr.v.* **1.** To clothe oneself with; don. **2.** To apply or activate: *put on the brake.* **3.** To present; perform: *put on a play.* **4.** To assume affectedly: *put on a funny accent.* **5.** To switch on (an electrical appliance). **6. a.** To increase in: *put on weight.* **b.** To add: *put on ten runs after tea.* **7.** To cause to be connected, as on the telephone. **8.** *U.S.* To tease or mislead (someone).

put-on (po͝ot-on || -awn) *adj.* Pretended; feigned.

~*n. U.S. Informal.* **1.** The act of teasing or misleading someone, especially for amusement. **2.** Something intended as a hoax or joke.

put-put (pút-put) *n. Slang.* **1.** A small engine. **2.** The noise made by such an engine. **3.** A boat or vehicle operated by such an engine. Also used adjectivally: *a put-put engine.*

~*intr.v.* **put-putted, -putting, -puts.** **1.** To make the sound of a put-put engine. **2.** To travel in or on, or as if in or on, a put-put boat or vehicle. [Imitative.]

pu·tre·fac·tion (péwtri-fáksh'n) *n.* **1.** The partial decomposition of organic matter by microorganisms, producing foul-smelling matter. **2.** Putrefied matter. **3.** The condition of being putrefied. [Middle English *putrefaccioun,* from Late Latin *putrefactiō* (stem *putrefactiōn-*), from Latin *putrefacere,* PUTREFY.] **—pu·tre·fac·tive** (péwtri-fáktiv), **pu·tre·fa·cient** (-fáysh'nt) *adj.*

pu·tre·fy (péwtri-fī) *v.* **-fied, -fying, -fies.** —*tr.* **1.** To decompose (something); cause to decay. **2.** To make gangrenous. —*intr.* **1.** To decompose. **2.** To become gangrenous. **—**See Synonyms at **decay.** [Middle English *putrefien,* from Old French *putrefier,* from Latin *putrefacere* : *puter,* rotten + *facere,* to make.]

pu·tres·cence (pew-tréss'nss) *n.* **1.** A putrescent character or condition. **2.** Putrid matter.

pu·tres·cent (pew-tréss'nt) *adj.* **1.** Becoming putrid; putrefying. **2.** Of or pertaining to putrefaction. [Latin *putrēscens,* present participle of *putrēscere* (stem *putrēscent-*), to grow rotten, inceptive of *putrēre,* to be rotten, from *puter,* rotten.]

pu·tres·ci·ble (pew-tréssə-b'l) *adj.* Subject to putrefaction. [French, from Late Latin *putrēscibilis,* from Latin *putrēscere,* to grow rotten. See **putrescent.**] **—pu·tres·ci·bil·i·ty** (-bílləti) *n.*

pu·tres·cine (pew-tréss-een, -in) *n.* A colourless amine, $NH_2(CH_2)_4NH_2$, occurring in putrefying animal substances; 1,4-diaminobutane. [Latin *putrēscere,* become rotten (see **putrescent**) + -INE.]

pu·trid (péwtrid) *adj.* **1.** In a decomposed, foul-smelling state; rotten. **2.** Proceeding from or displaying putrefaction. **3.** Corrupt; morally rotten. **4.** *Slang.* Extremely objectionable or worthless; vile. [Latin *putridus,* from *putrēre,* to be rotten. See **putrescent.**] **—pu·trid·i·ty** (pew-tríddəti), **pu·trid·ness** *n.* **—pu·trid·ly** *adv.*

putsch (po͝och) *n. Sometimes capital* **P.** A sudden attempt by a group to overthrow a government. [German, from Swiss German, a thrust (imitative).]

putt (put) *n.* In golf, a light stroke made on the putting green in an effort to place the ball into the hole.

~*v.* **putted, putting, putts.** —*tr.* To hit (the ball) with such a stroke on the green. —*intr.* To putt the ball. [Variant of PUT.]

put·tee (pútti || pu-tée) *n.* Also **put·ty** *pl.* **-ties.** **1.** A strip of cloth wound spirally around the leg from ankle to knee, for covering and protection. **2.** A rectangular canvas legging with small straps and buckles, covering the lower leg between mid-calf and ankle. [Hindi *paṭṭī,* from Sanskrit *paṭṭikā,* from *paṭṭa*†, cloth band.]

put·ter[1] (púttər) *n.* **1.** In golf, a short, stiff-shafted club used for putting. **2.** A golfer who is putting.

put·ter[2] (po͝otər) *n.* **1.** One that puts. **2.** A shot-putter.

putter[3]. *U.S.* Variant of **potter.**

putting green *n.* **1.** In golf, the area at the end of a fairway in which the hole is placed, having turf more closely mown than the rest of the course. **2.** An area for practising putting.

put·to (po͝ot-ō) *n., pl.* **-ti** (-ee, -i). A figure of a small boy or cherub in painting, sculpture, and ornamentation.

put·ty (pútti) *n., pl.* **-ties.** **1.** A doughlike cement made by mixing whiting and linseed oil, used to fill holes in woodwork and secure panes of glass. **2.** Any substance with a similar consistency or function. **3.** A fine lime cement used as a finishing coat on plaster. **4.** Yellowish or light greyish brown. **5.** A person or group that is very compliant, impressionable, or easily influenced: *His accomplices were putty in his hands.*

~*tr.v.* **puttied, -tying, -ties.** To fill cover, or secure with putty. [French *potée,* from Old French, contents of a pot, a potful, from *pot,* a pot, from Middle Low German, from Vulgar Latin *pottus* (attested only in Late Latin).]

put up *tr.v.* **1.** To erect; build. **2.** To preserve, as in glass jars: *put up jam.* **3.** To nominate. **4.** To provide (funds) in advance. **5.** To provide lodgings for: *put someone up for the night.* **6.** To incite to some action: *put someone up to a prank.* **7.** To raise and arrange (long hair) in a style. **8.** To offer (property) for sale. **9.** To offer or show (resistance, for example), especially when hard-pressed: *put up a fight.* **10.** To raise or increase: *put up the price.* **11.** *Archaic.* To sheath (a sword). —*intr.v.* **1.** To stay in lodgings. **2.** To stand as a candidate. **—put up with.** To endure patiently; tolerate.

put-up (po͝ot-up, -úp) *adj. Informal.* Planned or prearranged secretly. Used chiefly in the phrase *a put-up job.*

puy (pwee) *n.* A small extinct volcanic cone. [French.]

puz·zle (puzz'l) *v.* **-zled, -zling, -zles.** —*tr.* **1.** To cause uncertainty and indecision in; perplex. **2.** To clarify or solve (something confusing) by reasoning or study. Used with *out*: *He puzzled out the significance of her statement.* —*intr.* To ponder a problem in an effort to solve or understand it. Often used with *over* or *about.*

~*n.* **1.** One that puzzles. **2.** A toy, game, testing device, or the like, that tests ingenuity. See **jigsaw puzzle.** **3.** The condition of being perplexed; bewilderment. [16th century : origin obscure.] **—puz·zle·ment** (-mənt) *n.* **—puz·zler** (púzzlər, púzz'l-ər) *n.*

Synonyms: *puzzle, perplex, mystify, bewilder, confound, baffle.*

PVC *n.* Polyvinyl chloride: a common thermoplastic resin used in a wide variety of manufactured products, including raincoats, garden hoses, gramophone records, and floor tiles.

pvt., Pvt. private.

P.W. policewoman (in Britain).

P.W.D. Public Works Department.

pwt. pennyweight.

PWV. Pretoria-Witwatersrand-Vereeniging.

PX *U.S.* post exchange; Post Exchange.

py-. Variant of **pyo-.**

py·a (pyaa, pi-áa) *n.* A coin equal to 1/100 of the kyat of Burma. [Burmese.]

py·ae·mi·a (pī-éemi-ə) *n.* Blood poisoning due to the presence of pus-forming bacteria. [New Latin : PY(O)- + -AEMIA.] **—py·ae·mic** *adj.*

pyc·nid·i·um (pik-níddi-əm) *n., pl.* **-nidia** (-ə). *Botany.* A rounded or flask-shaped asexual fruiting body containing spores. It occurs in certain fungi. [New Latin : Greek *puknos,* thick + *-idium,* Latin diminutive suffix, from Greek *-idion.*] **—pyc·nid·i·al** *adj.*

pyc·nom·e·ter (pik-nómmitər) *n.* A standard vessel used in measuring the relative density of materials. [Greek *puknos,* thick, dense + METER.]

pye dog (pī) *n.* A stray, untamed domestic dog in Asia. Also called "pariah dog". [Hindi *pāhī,* pariah, outsider.]

py·e·li·tis (pī-ə-lī-tiss) *n.* Inflammation of the pelvis of the kidney, usually caused by bacterial infection. [New Latin *pyelo-,* pelvis, from Greek *puelos,* basin + -ITIS.] **—py·e·lit·ic** (-líttik) *adj.*

py·e·log·ra·phy (pī-ə-lóggrəfi) *n.* Examination of the kidneys by means of X-ray pictures *(pyelograms).* [New Latin *pyelo-,* pelvis (see **pyelitis**) + -GRAPHY.] **—py·e·lo·graph·ic** (-lə-gráffik) *adj.*

py·e·lo·ne·phri·tis (pī-ə-lō-ni-frītiss, -ne-) *n.* Inflammation of both the kidney and the pelvis of the ureter. [New Latin *pyelo-,* pelvis (see **pyelitis**) + NEPHRITIS.]

py·gid·i·um (pī-jíddi-əm) *n., pl.* **-gidia** (-ē-ə). The posterior body region of certain invertebrates. [New Latin, from Greek *pugidion,* diminutive of *pugē†,* rump.] **—py·gid·i·al** *adj.*

Pyg·ma·li·on (pig-máyli-ən, -máyl-yən). *Greek Mythology.* A king of Cyprus who carved and then fell in love with a statue of a woman, which Aphrodite brought to life as Galatea.

pyg·my, pig·my (píg-mi) *n., pl.* **-mies.** An individual of unusually small size or significance.
~*adj.* **1.** Unusually or atypically small. **2.** Of little importance or stature. [Middle English *pigmie,* from Latin *pygmaeus,* dwarfish, from Greek *pugmaios,* from *pugmē,* fist, the length from the elbow to the knuckles.] **—pyg·mae·an, pyg·me·an** (pig-mée-ən) *adj.*

Pyg·my, Pig·my (píg-mi) *n., pl.* **-mies. 1.** A member of any of several African and Asian peoples with a hereditary stature of from four to five feet. **2.** In Greek legend, a member of a race of dwarfs.
~*adj.* Of or pertaining to the Pygmies.

pygmy chimpanzee *n.* An African anthropoid ape, *Pan paniscus,* related to though smaller than the chimpanzee but said to display more cooperative social behaviour and an even greater capacity to learn, or imitate, sign language. Also called "bonobo".

py·ja·mas, *U.S.* **pa·ja·mas** (pi-jáaməz, pə- ‖ *U.S. also* -jámməz) *pl.n.* **1.** A loose-fitting garment consisting of trousers and a jacket, worn especially for sleeping. **2.** Loose-fitting trousers worn in the Orient. [Hindi *pāejāma* : Persian *pāī,* leg, foot, from Middle Persian + *jāmah†,* garment.] **—py·ja·ma** (-jáamə ‖ -jámmə) *adj.*

pyk·nic (pík-nik) *adj. Anthropology.* Characterised by short, stocky, and powerful stature; endomorphic. [Greek *puknos,* thick, dense.] **—pyk·nic** *n.*

py·lon (pī-lən ‖ -lon) *n.* **1.** A steel tower supporting high-tension electric cables forming part of the grid system. **2.** *Aeronautics.* A tall tower used to guide pilots, especially as a marker for the turning point in a race. **3.** A large structure marking an entrance or approach; specifically, a monumental gateway in the form of a pair of truncated pyramids serving as the entrance to an ancient Egyptian temple. **4.** A streamlined casing for attaching an external engine pod or fuel tank to the body of an aircraft. [Greek *pulōn,* gateway, from *pulē,* a gate.]

py·lo·rus (pī-láw-rəss ‖ pi-, -ló-) *n., pl.* **-ri** (-rī). The passage connecting the stomach and the duodenum. [Late Latin *pylōrus,* from Greek *pulóros,* "a gatekeeper" : *pulē,* a gate + *ouros,* watcher, from *horan,* to see.] **—py·lor·ic** (-lórrik, -láwrik ‖ -lórik) *adj.*

Pym (pim), **John** (1584–1643). English politician. A Somerset squire, he became a leading Parliamentary opponent of Charles I, moving the bills of impeachment against his advisers. Charles' attempts to arrest him (1642) in the House of Commons precipitated the Civil War, in which his coordination of military activity earned him the title "King" Pym.

pyo-, py- *comb. form.* Indicates pus; for example, **pyorrhoea, pyaemia.** [Greek *puon,* pus.]

py·o·der·ma (pí-ō-dérmə) *n.* Any skin disease in which pus is produced. [New Latin : PYO- + -DERMA.] **—py·o·der·mic** *adj.*

py·o·gen·e·sis (pí-ō-jénnə-siss) *n. Pathology.* Pyosis. [PYO- + -GENESIS.] **—py·o·gen·ic** (-jénnik) *adj.*

Pyong·yang (pyóng-yáng). *Japanese* **Heijo.** Capital of North Korea. Situated on the river Taedong, it was rebuilt after its destruction by U.S. bombing during the Korean War (1950–53). In a coal and iron region, its industries include heavy engineering and textiles.

py·or·rhoe·a (pí-ə-réer, -rée-ə) *n.* **1.** A discharge of pus. **2.** Inflammation of the gum and tooth sockets leading to loosening of the teeth. [New Latin : PYO- + -RRHEA.] **—py·or·rhoe·al** *adj.*

py·o·sis (pī-ó-siss) *n.* The formation of pus. Also called "pyogenesis". [New Latin, from Greek *puōsis,* from PY(O)- + -OSIS.]

pyr-. Variant of **pyro-.**

py·ra·can·tha (pīr-ə-kánthə) *n.* A shrub of the genus *Pyracantha,* the **fire thorn** *(see).* [New Latin, from Greek *purakantha,* name of a shrub : PYR(O)- + Greek *akantha,* thorn.]

pyr·a·lid (pírrə-lid) *n.* Also **py·ral·i·did** (pi-rál-i-did). Any of various small or medium-sized moths of the large, widely distributed family Pyralididae. [New Latin *pyralididae,* from *pyralis* (genus), from Greek *puralis,* fabulous insect supposed to live in fire, from *pur,* fire.] **—pyr·a·lid** *adj.*

pyr·a·mid (pírrə-mid) *n.* **1.** In geometry, a polyhedron with a polyg-

onal base and triangular faces meeting in a common vertex. **2.** Anything having such a shape or structure. **3. a.** A massive monument found especially in Egypt, having a rectangular base and four triangular faces culminating in a single apex, and serving as a tomb or temple. **b.** A similar New World monument, as among the Mayas. **4.** *Plural.* A game similar to billiards played with 15 coloured balls and a cue ball. **5.** *Anatomy.* Any of various approximately pyramidal structures, as in the medulla of the kidney.
~*v.* **pyramided, -miding, -mids.** —*tr.* **1.** To place or build in the shape of a pyramid. **2.** To build (an argument or thesis, for example) progressively from a basic general premise. **3.** *Finance. U.S.* To speculate in (securities or property) by making a series of buying and selling transactions in which paper profits are used as margin for making further purchases. —*intr.* **1.** To assume the shape of a pyramid. **2.** To increase rapidly and on a widening base. **3.** *Finance. U.S.* To pyramid securities or property. [Latin *pyramis* (stem *pyramid-*), from Greek *puramis†.*] **—py·ram·i·dal** (pi-rámmid'l), **pyr·a·mid·ic** (pírrə-míddik), **pyr·a·mid·i·cal** *adj.* **—py·ram·i·dal·ly** (pi-rámmid'l-i) *adv.*

pyr·a·mid·ing (pírrə-midding) *n. Finance.* A system of business organisation in which a holding company controls subsidiary companies which are themselves holding companies, thereby achieving a concentration of power by means of limited capital ownership.

pyramid selling *n.* A system of selling in which one person with the right to sell certain goods sells part of this right or part of a consignment to others, who repeat this procedure, with only those at the bottom end of this pyramidal structure actually selling the goods.

py·ran (pír-an, -án) *n.* An unsaturated ring compound, C_5H_5O, having two double bonds and, depending on the position of these, two isomers. [PYR(O)- + -AN.]

py·ra·nom·e·ter (pīr-ə-nómmitər) *n.* A solarimeter *(see).* [Greek *pur,* fire + *ano,* up + -METER.]

py·rar·gy·rite (pīr-rárji-rīt, pī-) *n.* A deep red to black silver ore with the composition Ag_3SbS_3. Also called "ruby silver". [German *Pyrargyrit* : PYR(O)- + Greek *arguros,* silver + -ITE.]

py·ra·zole (pír-ə-zōl) *n.* A crystalline ring compound, $C_3H_4N_2$, consisting of a five-membered ring having two double bonds. [PYR(O)- + AZOLE.]

pyre (pīr) *n.* A heap of combustible material, especially one for burning a corpse as a funeral rite. [Latin *pyra,* from Greek *pura,* from *pur,* fire.]

py·rene[1] (pír-een, -réen) *n.* The one-seeded stone of certain single fruits. [New Latin *pyrena,* from Greek *purēn.*]

py·rene[2] (pír-een) *n.* A tetracyclic hydrocarbon, $C_{16}H_{10}$, obtained from coal tar. [PYR(O)- + -ENE.]

Pyrenean mountain dog *n.* A dog of an ancient breed originating in central Europe, typically having a large, powerful body with a coat of thick, fine, white hair.

Pyr·e·nees (pírrə-néez). *French* **Pyrénées;** *Spanish* **Pirineos.** Mountain range in southwest Europe, separating France from the Iberian Peninsula. It rises to 3 404 metres (11,168 feet) at Pico de Aneto, and includes the Principality of Andorra. **—Pyr·e·ne·an** (pírrə-née-ən) *adj.*

py·re·noid (pīr-rée-noyd, pīr-ə-) *n.* Any of the protein granules of certain algae and some other lower plants in which starch is formed. [PYREN(E) (fruit stone; from the shape of its nucleus) + -OID.]

py·re·thrin (pīr-réeth-rin, pī- ‖ *U.S. also* -réth-) *n.* Either of two viscous liquid esters, $C_{21}H_{28}O_3$ or $C_{22}H_{28}O_5$, that are extracted from pyrethrum flowers and used as insecticides. See **cinerin.** [French *pyréthrine* : PYRETHR(UM) + -IN.]

py·re·thrum (pīr-rée-thrəm, pī- ‖ *U.S. also* -réth-) *n.* **1.** Any of various Old World plants of the genus *Chrysanthemum* (or *Tanacetum*) having showy, daisy-like flowers; especially, *C. cinerariaefolium,* widely cultivated as a source of insecticide. **2.** An insecticide prepared from the dried flowers of pyrethrum plants. **3.** A medicinal preparation made from the root of a related plant, *Anacyclus pyrethrum,* used to stimulate the flow of saliva. In this sense, also called "pyrethrum root". [Latin, from Greek *purethron,* feverfew, from *puretos,* fever, from *pur,* fire.]

py·ret·ic (pīr-réttik, pī-, pi-) *adj.* Characterised or affected by fever; feverish. [New Latin *pyreticus,* from Greek *puretikos,* from *puretos,* fever, from *pur,* fire.]

Py·rex (pír-eks) *n.* A trademark for any of various types of heat- and chemical-resistant glass used for ovenware and tableware.

py·rex·i·a (pīr-réksi-ə, pī-, pi-) *n.* Fever. [New Latin, from Greek *purexis,* from *puressein,* to have a fever, from *puretos,* fever. See **pyretic.**] **—py·rex·i·al, py·rex·ic** *adj.*

pyr·he·li·om·e·ter (pīr-héeli-ómmitər, pər-) *n.* Any of various devices that measure all or restricted components of solar radiation. [PYR(O)- + HELIO- + -METER.]

pyr·i·dine (pírri-deen) *n.* A flammable, colourless or yellowish liquid base, C_5H_5N, used to synthesise vitamins and drugs, as a solvent, and as a denaturant for alcohol. [PYR(O)- + -ID + -INE.] **—py·rid·ic** (pīr-riddik, pī-, pi-) *adj.*

pyr·i·dox·ine (pírri-dók-seen, -sin) *n.* Also **pyr·i·dox·in** (-sin). A pyridine derivative, $C_8H_{11}O_3N$, occurring in plant and animal tissues and active in various metabolic processes. Also called "vitamin B_6". [PYRID(INE) + OX- + -INE.]

pyr·i·form (pírri-fawrm) *adj.* Pear-shaped: *a pyriform organ.* [New Latin *pyriformis* : Medieval Latin *pyrum,* variant of Latin *pirum,* PEAR + -I- + -FORM.]

py·rim·i·dine (pīr-rímmi-deen, pī-, pi-) *n.* **1.** A liquid and crystalline organic base, $C_4H_4N_2$. **2.** Any of several basic compounds, such as uracil, cytosine, or thymine, having a molecular structure similar to pyrimidine and found in living matter as a nucleotide component. [German *Pyrimidin,* variant of PYRIDINE.]

py·rite (pír-īt) *n.* A yellow to brown, widely occurring mineral sulphide, FeS$_2$, used as an iron ore and to produce sulphur dioxide for sulphuric acid. Also called "fool's gold", "iron pyrites". [Latin *pyrītēs,* PYRITES.] —**py·rit·ic** (pī-ríttik, pī-), **py·rit·i·cal** *adj.*

py·ri·tes (pī-rīteez, pī-, pi-, pə-) *n., pl.* **pyrites.** Any of various natural metallic sulphides. [Latin *pyrītēs,* flint, pyrite, from Greek *puritēs (lithos),* "fire (stone)", from *puritēs,* of fire, from *pur,* fire.]

py·ro (pír-ō) *adj. Chemistry.* Of, pertaining to, or designating an acid derived from an anhydride and having a water content intermediate between those of the ortho and meta acids. Used in combination: **pyrosulphuric acid.** Compare meta, ortho.

pyro-, pyr- *comb. form.* Indicates: **1.** Fire or heat; for example, **pyrotechnic. 2.** Resulting from or by the action of fire or heat; for example, **pyrography. 3.** A mineral that changes its properties when heat is applied; for example **pyromorphite. 4.** *Chemistry.* A new substance obtained by heating another substance; for example **pyrophosphoric acid.** [Greek *pur,* fire.]

py·ro·cat·e·chol (pír-ō-kátti-chol, -ə-, -kol ‖ -chōl, -kōl) *n.* A colourless, crystalline organic compound, C$_6$H$_4$(OH)$_2$, used as an antiseptic and photographic developer. [PYRO- + CATECH(U) + -OL.]

py·ro·cel·lu·lose (pír-ō-séllew-lōz, -ə-, -lōss) *n.* A cellulose nitrate used as a component of smokeless powder.

py·ro·chem·i·cal (pír-ō-kémmik'l, -ə-) *adj.* Of or designating high-temperature chemical activity. —**py·ro·chem·i·cal·ly** *adv.*

py·ro·clas·tic (pír-ō-klástik, -ə-) *adj.* Made up of fragments ejected from a volcano. Said of a rock. [PYRO- + -CLAST + -IC.]

py·ro·e·lec·tric (pír-ō-i-léktrik, -ə-) *adj.* Exhibiting or pertaining to pyroelectricity.

~*n.* A pyroelectric material.

py·ro·e·lec·tric·i·ty (pír-ō-éllek-tríssəti, -i-lék-, -ée-lek- ‖ -trízzəti) *n.* The polarisation of electric charge in a crystal by change of temperature.

py·ro·gal·lol (pír-ō-gál-ol, -ə- ‖ -ōl) *n.* A white, lustrous crystalline compound, C$_6$H$_3$(OH)$_3$, used as a photographic developer and to treat skin diseases; 1,2,3-trihydroxybenzene. Also called "pyrogallic acid". [PYRO- + GALL(IC) + -OL (hydroxyl group).] —**py·ro·gal·lic** *adj.*

py·ro·gen (pír-ə-jen, -ō-, -jən) *n.* A substance that produces fever. [PYRO- + -GEN.]

py·ro·gen·ic (pír-ə-jénnik, -ō-) *adj.* Also **py·rog·e·nous** (pīr-rójənəss, pī-). **1.** Producing or produced by fever. **2.** Caused by or generating heat. **3.** *Geology.* Igneous.

py·rog·ra·phy (pīr-róggrəfi, pī-) *n.* **1.** The art or process of producing designs on wood, leather, or other material by using heated tools or a fine flame. **2.** A design made by this process. [PYRO- + -GRAPHY.] —**py·ro·graph** (pír-ə-graaf, -ō-, -graf) *n.* —**py·rog·ra·pher** (-róggrəfər) *n.* —**py·ro·graph·ic** (-gráffik) *adj.*

py·ro·lig·ne·ous (pír-ō-líg-ni-əss, -ə-) *adj.* Made by the destructive distillation of wood.

pyroligneous acid *n.* A mixture of methanol, acetic acid, acetone, various tars, and related products from wood distillation, used in meat smoking. Also called "wood vinegar".

py·ro·lu·site (pír-ō-lōo-sīt, -ə-, -léw-) *n.* A soft, black to dark grey ore of manganese, consisting essentially of manganese dioxide. [German *Pyrolusit* : PYRO- + Greek *lousis,* a washing, from *louein,* to wash + -ITE (it is used in purifying glass).]

py·ro·lyse, py·ro·lyze (pír-ə-līz, -ō-) *tr.v.* **-lysed, -lysing, -lyses.** To subject (something) to pyrolysis. [PYRO- + -LYSE.]

py·rol·y·sis (pīr-rólə-siss, pī-) *n.* Chemical change caused by heat. [PYRO- + -LYSIS.] —**py·ro·lyt·ic** (pír-ə-líttik, -ō-) *adj.*

py·ro·man·cy (pír-ə-man-si, -ō-) *n.* Divination by fire or flames. [Middle English *piromance,* from Old French *pyromancie,* from Late Latin *pyromantīa,* from Greek *puromanteia* : PYRO- + -MANCY.] —**py·ro·man·tic** (-mántik) *adj.*

py·ro·ma·ni·a (pír-ə-máyn-i-ə, -ō-, -máyn-yə) *n.* The uncontrollable impulse to start fires. [PYRO- + -MANIA.] —**py·ro·ma·ni·ac** (-i-ak) *adj. & n.* —**py·ro·ma·ni·a·cal** (-mə-nī-ək'l) *adj.*

py·ro·met·al·lur·gy (pír-ō-mi-tál-ər-ji, -ə-, -me-, -métt'l-urji) *n.* Metallurgy that depends on the action of heat, involving such processes as smelting.

py·rom·e·ter (pīr-rómmitər, pī-) *n.* An electrical thermometer used for measuring high temperatures. [PYRO- + -METER.] —**py·ro·met·ric** (pír-ə-méttrik, -ō-), **py·ro·met·ri·cal** *adj.* —**py·rom·e·try** (-rómmətri) *n.*

py·ro·mor·phite (pír-ə-mórfīt, -ō-) *n.* A lead ore (PbCl)Pb$_4$(PO$_4$)$_3$, occurring in green, brown, or yellow crystals. [German *Pyromorphit* : PYRO- + MORPH(O)- + -ITE.]

py·rone (pír-ōn) *n. Chemistry.* A type of organic compound having a six-membered ring formed by five carbon atoms and one oxygen atom. [PYR(O)- + -ONE.]

py·rope (pír-ōp) *n.* A deep-red garnet, Mg$_3$Al$_2$Si$_3$O$_{12}$, used as a gem. [Middle English *pirope,* from Old French, from Latin *pyrōpus,* gold bronze, fiery garnet, from Greek *purōpos,* "fiery-eyed" : PYR(O)- + Greek *ōps,* eye.]

py·ro·phor·ic (pír-ə-fórrik, -ō- ‖ -fáwrik) *adj.* **1.** Spontaneously igniting in air. **2.** Producing sparks by friction. [Greek *purophoros,* "fire-bearing" : PYRO- + -PHOROUS.]

py·ro·phos·phate (pír-ō-fóss-fayt, -ə-) *n.* A salt of pyrophosphoric acid.

py·ro·phos·phor·ic acid (pír-ə-foss-fórrik, -ə- ‖ -fáwrik; U.S. also

-fósfərik) *n.* A syrupy viscous liquid, H$_4$P$_2$O$_7$, used as a catalyst and in organic chemical manufacture. [PYRO- + PHOSPHORIC (it is made by heating a phosphoric acid).]

py·ro·phyl·lite (pír-ō-fíl-īt, -ə-, -róffi-līt) *n.* A silvery white or pale-green mineral, hydrous aluminium silicate, Al$_2$Si$_4$O$_{10}$(OH)$_2$, occurring naturally in soft, compact masses. [German *Pyrophyllit* : PYRO- + PHYLL(O)- + -ITE (its foliations spread when heated).]

py·ro·sis (pīr-rō-siss, pī-) *n. Chiefly U.S.* Heartburn. [Greek *purōsis,* a burning, from *puroun,* to burn, from *pur,* fire.]

py·ro·stat (pír-ə-stat, -ō-) *n.* **1.** An automatic sensing device that activates an alarm or extinguisher in the event of fire. **2.** A high-temperature thermostat. [PYRO- + -STAT.]

py·ro·sul·phate (pír-ō-súl-fayt, -ə-) *n.* A salt of pyrosulphuric acid. [PYROSULPH(URIC ACID) + -ATE (salt).]

py·ro·sul·phu·ric acid (pír-ō-sul-féwr-ik, -ə-) *n.* A heavy, oily, colourless to dark-brown liquid, H$_2$S$_2$O$_7$, produced by adding sulphur trioxide to concentrated sulphuric acid and used in petroleum refining and explosives.

py·ro·tech·nic (pír-ə-ték-nik, -ō-) *adj.* Also **py·ro·tech·ni·cal** (-'l). **1.** Of or pertaining to fireworks. **2.** Resembling fireworks; brilliant: *a pyrotechnic wit.* [PYRO- + Greek *tekhnikos,* of art or skill. See technical.] —**py·ro·tech·ni·cal·ly** *adv.*

py·ro·tech·nics (pír-ə-ték-niks, -ō-) *n.* Also **py·ro·tech·ny** (-tek-ni) (for sense 1). **1.** *Used with a singular verb.* The art of manufacturing or setting off fireworks. **2.** *Used with a singular or plural verb.* A fireworks display. **3.** *Used with a singular or plural verb.* A brilliant display, as of rhetoric or wit, or of virtuosity in the performing arts. —**py·ro·tech·nist** *n.*

py·rox·ene (pír-rókseen, pī-) *n.* Any of a group of crystalline mineral silicates common in igneous and metamorphic rocks and containing two metallic oxides, usually magnesium, iron, calcium, or sodium. [French *pyroxène,* "stranger to fire" (i.e., foreign substance in igneous rocks) : PYRO- + Greek *xenos,* stranger.] —**py·rox·en·ic** (pír-ok-sénnik) *adj.*

pyr·rhic[1] (pírrik) *n.* A Greek metrical foot composed of two short syllables. [Latin, from Greek *(pous) purrhikhios,* pyrrhic (foot), from *purrhikhē,* PYRRHIC (dance).] —**pyr·rhic** *adj.*

pyrrhic[2] *n.* An ancient Greek war dance imitative of actual fighting. [Latin, from Greek *purrhikhē,* traditionally supposed to be from *Purrhikhos,* the name of its inventor.] —**pyr·rhic** *adj.*

Pyrrhic victory A victory involving great losses on the victor's part. [After *Pyrrhus,* (c. 318–272 B.C.), King of Epirus, whose tactical victories against the Romans failed to avert his defeat.]

Pyr·rhon·ism (pírrən-iz'm) *n.* **1.** The sceptical philosophy of Pyrrho of Elis (c. 360–270 B.C.); especially, the doctrine that nothing can be known as absolutely certain. **2.** Loosely, scepticism or philosophic doubt. —**Pyr·rhon·ist** *n.*

pyr·rho·tite (pírrə-tīt, pírrō-) *n.* Also **pyr·rho·tine** (-tīn). A brownish-bronze weakly magnetic mineral iron sulphide. When it contains nickel, it is a nickel ore, and is used for making sulphuric acid. Also called "magnetic pyrites". [German *Pyrrhotin,* from Greek *purrhotēs,* redness, from *purrhos,* fiery, red, from *pur,* fire.]

pyr·role (pírrōl, *also* pi-rōl) *n.* A yellowish or brown oil, C$_4$H$_5$N, with an odour similar to chloroform and used to manufacture a wide variety of drugs. Also called "azole". [Greek *purrhos,* red, tawny, from *pur,* fire + -OLE.] —**pyr·rol·ic** (pi-róllik, -rōlik) *adj.*

pyr·rol·i·dine (pi-rólli-deen, -rōli-, -din) *n.* A colourless heterocyclic base, C$_4$H$_9$N$_1$, made synthetically by the hydrogenation of pyrrole and occurring in tobacco leaves. [PYRROLE + -IDE + -INE.]

py·ru·vic acid (pīr-rōō-vik, pī- ‖ -réw-) *n.* A colourless liquid, CH$_3$COCOOH, formed as a fundamental intermediate in protein and carbohydrate metabolism. [PYR(O)- + Latin *ūva,* grape.]

Py·thag·o·ras (pī-thággə-rass, -rəss ‖ U.S. pi-) (c. 580–c. 500 B.C.). Greek philosopher, theologian, and mathematician. The school he founded in southern Italy taught spiritual growth through asceticism and the study of musical harmony and geometry. Though his famous theorem was known previously, he was the first to prove its universal validity. His insight into the relationship between numbers and the perceived universe gives him claim to be the first true mathematician.

Pythagoras' theorem *n.* The theorem that in a right-angled triangle the square of the length of the hypotenuse is equal to the sum of the squares of the lengths of the other two sides.

Py·thag·o·re·an·ism (pī-thággə-réer-niz'm, -rée-ə- ‖ U.S. pi-) *n.* The philosophy of Pythagoras, chiefly distinguished by its description of reality in terms of arithmetical relationships and the doctrine of the transmigration of souls. —**Py·thag·o·re·an** (pī-thággə-réern, -rée-ən ‖ U.S. pi-) *n. & adj.*

Pyth·e·as (píthi-ass, -əss) (fourth century B.C.). Greek navigator. Based in Marseilles, he passed through the Straits of Gibraltar and explored the Atlantic coasts of Europe, Britain, and possibly Iceland. His voyages are described by Strabo (c. 60 B.C.–A.D. 21).

Pyth·i·a (píthi-ə) *n.* The oracular priestess of Apollo at Delphi.

Pyth·i·an (píthi-ən) *adj.* **1.** Of or pertaining to Delphi, the temple of Apollo at Delphi, or its oracle. **2.** Of or pertaining to the Pythian games. [Latin *Pythius,* from Greek *Puthios,* from *Puthō, Puthōn,* ancient name of Delphi, after the serpent PYTHON.] —**Pyth·ic** *adj.*

Pythian games *pl.n.* In ancient Greece, a pan-Hellenic athletics festival held every four years at Delphi in honour of Apollo.

py·thon (píth'n ‖ U.S. *also* pī-thon) *n.* Any of various large, nonvenomous Old World snakes of the family Pythonidae, that coil around and crush their prey. [After PYTHON.]

Py·thon (píth'n ‖ U.S. *also* pī-thon) *n. Greek Mythology.* A dragon or serpent that was the tutelary demon of the oracular cult at Delphi until killed and expropriated by Apollo.

Py·thon·esque *adj.* Designating, displaying, or pertaining to a style of humour characterised by bizarre and far-fetched imaginative associations, brutal or outrageous visual jokes, and zany behaviour. [After the B.B.C. television series, *Monty Python's Flying Circus.*]

py·tho·ness (pīthə-ness,-niss) *n.* **1.** Pythia. **2.** A prophetess. [Middle English *phitonesse*, from Old French *phitonise, pithonise*, from Late Latin *pŷthōnissa*, from Greek *Puthōn*, PYTHON.]

py·thon·ic (pī-thónnik) *adj.* **1.** Of, pertaining to, or resembling a python. **2.** Of or like an oracle; prophetic.

py·u·ri·a (pī-yoor-i-ə) *n.* The abnormal condition of pus in the urine. [New Latin : PY(O)- + -URIA.]

pyx, pix (piks) *n.* **1.** *Roman Catholic Church.* **a.** A container in which the Eucharist is carried. **b.** A container in which supplies of wafers for the Eucharist are kept. **2.** A chest in the British mint in which specimen coins are placed to await assay. [Middle English *pyxe*, from Latin *pyxis*, box, from Greek *puxis*, box.]

pyx·id·i·um (pik-síddi-əm) *n., pl.* **-idia** (-ə). *Botany.* A seed capsule having a circular lid that falls off to release the seeds. Also called "pyxis". [New Latin, from Greek *puxidion*, diminutive of *puxis*, PYXIS.]

pyx·is (pík-siss) *n., pl.* **pyxides** (-si-deez). *Botany.* A pyxidium.

Pyxis *n.* A constellation in the Southern Hemisphere, near Antlia and Puppis. [New Latin *Pyxis (nautica)*, "the Mariner's Compass", from Greek *puxis*, box, PYXIS.]

q, Q (kew) *n., pl.* **q's** or *rare* **qs, Qs,** or **Q's. 1.** The 17th letter of the modern English alphabet. **2.** Any of the speech sounds represented by this letter.

q, Q, q., Q. *Note:* As an abbreviation or symbol, *q* may be a small or a capital letter, with or without a full stop. Established forms or those generally preferred precede the definition. When no form is given, all four forms are in general use in that sense. **1.** q. quart. **2.** q. quarter. **3.** q. quarterly. **4.** q., Q. quarto. **5.** Q *Chess.* queen. **6.** Q. Queen. **7.** q. query. **8.** q. question. **9.** Q quetzal. **10.** q. quintal. **11.** q. quire. **12.** *Physics.* heat. **13.** The 17th in a series; 16th when *J* is omitted.

Qaddafi, Moammar al-. See Moammar al-**Gaddafi.**

Qah·re·man·shahr (kaari-man-shár). See Ker-män-shäh.

q and a question and answer.

Qandahar. See Kandahar.

Qa·tar, State of (ka-taár). Independent country, bordering the Gulf. It consists of the peninsula of Qatar which is mainly desert. Its economy is primarily based on large resources of onshore and offshore oil and gas. Qatar was a British protectorate from 1916 until 1971. Area, 11 437 square kilometres (4,416 square miles). Population, 560,000. Capital, Doha. See map at **Gulf States.**

QB *Chess.* queen's bishop.

Q.B. Queen's Bench.

QBP *Chess.* queen's bishop's pawn.

Q.C. Queen's Counsel.

Q.E.D. which was to be demonstrated or proved. Used to indicate that an incontrovertible conclusion has been reached. [Latin *quod erat demonstrandum.*]

Q.E.F. which was to be done. [Latin *quod erat faciendum.*]

Q factor *n.* **1.** A measure of the efficiency of a resonant circuit given by $(I/R) (L/C)^{1/2}$, where R is the resistance, L the inductance, and C the capitance of the circuit. Also called "quality factor". **2.** The heat released in a nuclear reaction, usually expressed in electronvolts. Also called "Q value". [Sense 2, *Q* (heat) + FACTOR.]

Q fever *n.* A disease of livestock caused by the rickettsia, *Coxiella burnettii*, that can be transmitted to humans and causes severe headaches and pneumonia. [From Queensland, Australia, where it was first identified.]

qilin. Variant of **kylin.**

Qin. See Ch'in.

Qing. See Ch'ing.

Qing·hai or **Ch'ing-hai** or **Tsing·hai** (chíng-hí). Province in northwestern China, named after one of the largest salt lakes in China, Qinghai Hu, which is also known by its Mongol name, Koko Nor, meaning "Blue Sea".

QKt *Chess.* queen's knight.

QKtP *Chess.* queen's knight's pawn.

ql. quintal.

Q.M. quartermaster.

Q.M.G. Quartermaster General.

qn. question.

Qom (kom, kawm, khawm). Also **Qum** or **Kum.** City in central Iran, on the main route connecting the capital Tehran with southern Iran. It is an important holy city for Shiite Muslims and pilgrims flock to visit the tomb of Fatima, sister of Imam Riza.

qoph (koff, kŏof, kawf, kŏf) *n.* The 19th letter of the Hebrew alphabet. [Hebrew *qōph*, from a Northwest Semitic word meaning "eye of a needle".]

QP *Chess.* queen's pawn.

q. pl. as much as you please. [Latin *quantum placet.*]

qq. questions.

Qq. quartos.

qq.v. which (things) see. [New Latin *quae vide.*]

QR *Chess.* queen's rook.

qr. 1. quarter. **2.** quarterly. **3.** quire.

QRP *Chess.* queen's rook's pawn.

q.s. as much as suffices. [Latin *quantum sufficit.*]

Q-ship (kéw-ship) *n.* A merchant ship carrying concealed guns as a trap for unsuspecting enemy ships. [From *Q*, perhaps representing *query.*]

QSO *Astronomy.* quasi-stellar object.

QSRS *Astronomy.* quasi-stellar radio source.

qt. 1. quantity. **2.** quart.

q.t. *n. Informal.* Quiet. Used in the phrase *on the q.t.*

qto. quarto.

qty. quantity.

qu. 1. queen. **2.** query. **3.** question.

qua (kway, kwaa) *prep.* By virtue of being; as; in the capacity of. [Latin *quā*, ablative singular feminine of *quī*, who.]

quack¹ (kwak) *n.* The characteristic harsh, rasping call of a duck. *—intr.v.* **quacked, quacking, quacks.** To emit a quack. [Imitative; compare Dutch *kwakken* and German *quacken.*]

quack² *n.* **1.** An untrained person who pretends to have medical knowledge. **2.** *Informal.* A doctor or surgeon. **3.** A charlatan; a mountebank. Also used adjectivally: *quack remedies.* *—v.* **quacked, quacking, quaks.** *—intr.* To act as a quack. *—tr.* To offer or advertise (a cure, for example) in extravagant terms. [Shortened from QUACKSALVER.] *—***quack·er·y** *n.*

quack·sal·ver (kwák-sal-vər) *n. Archaic.* A quack; a charlatan. [Dutch *quacksalver* : probably from obsolete *quacken*, to chatter + *salf*, SALVE.]

quad¹ (kwod) *n. Informal.* A quadrangle.

quad² *n. Printing.* A piece of type metal lower than the raised typeface, used for filling spaces and blank lines. Formerly called "quadrat".

quad³ *n. Informal.* A **quadruplet** *(see).*

quad. 1. quadrangle. **2.** quadrant. **3.** quadrilateral.

quadr-. Variant of **quadri-.**

quad·ran·gle (kwód-rang-g'l) *n. Abbr.* **quad. 1.** In geometry, a plane figure consisting of four points, no three of which are collinear, connected by straight lines. **2. a.** A rectangular area surrounded on all four sides by buildings: *an Oxford college quadrangle.* **b.** The buildings bordering this area. [Middle English, from Old French, from Late Latin *quadr(i)angulum*, from Latin *quadr(i)angulus*, having four angles : QUADR(I)- + *angulus*, ANGLE.] *—***quad·rang·u·lar** (kwod-ráng-gew-lər) *adj.*

quad·rant (kwódrənt) *n. Abbr.* **quad. 1.** In geometry: **a.** A circular arc subtending a central angle of 90°; a quarter of the circumference of a circle. **b.** The plane area bounded by two perpendicular radii and the arc they subtend. **c.** Any of the four areas into which a plane is divided by the reference axes in a coordinate system, designated *first, second, third,* and *fourth*, counting clockwise from the area in which both coordinates are positive. **2.** Anything, such as a machine part, that is shaped like a quarter circle. **3.** An early instrument for measuring altitudes, consisting of a graduated arc with a movable radius for measuring angles. [Middle English, quarter of a day, from Latin *quadrāns* (stem *quadrant-*), fourth part, quarter; akin to *quattuor*, four.]

quad·ra·phon·ic (kwódrə-fónnik) *adj.* Of, pertaining to, or reproduced by a high-fidelity sound system with equipment for the reproduction of sound from four separate channels. Compare **stereophonic.** [Irregularly from QUADR(I)- + PHONIC.] *—***quad·ra·phon·ics, quad·raph·o·ny** (kwod-ráffəni, kwód-) *n.*

quad·rat (kwódrət) *n.* **1.** *Printing.* A quad (type metal). Not in current technical usage. **2. a.** A square or rectangular area of vegetation, usually one square metre, selected at random for study of its plants, which are regarded as typical of the surrounding area. **b.** A rectangular frame used to mark out such an area. [Middle English, variant of QUADRATE.]

quad·rate (kwód-rət, -rit, -rayt) *adj.* **1.** *Zoology.* Of, pertaining to, or designating a bone or cartilaginous structure of the skull, joining the upper and lower jaws in birds, fish, reptiles, and amphibians. **2.** *Archaic.* Square or rectangular.

~n. **1.** A quadrate bone. **2.** An approximately square or cubic area, space, or object.
~intr.v. (kwo-dráyt, kwə- ‖ *U.S.* kwód-rayt) **quadrated, -rating, -rates.** To correspond; agree; square. Often used with *with.* [Middle English, square, from Latin *quadrātus,* past participle of *quadrāre,* to make square, from *quadrus,* a square.]

quad·rat·ic (kwo-dráttik, kwə-) *adj.* Of, pertaining to, or containing equations whose terms are of the second degree or less. [From QUADRATE.] **—quad·rat·ic** *n.*

quadratic equation *n.* An equation of the second degree, having the general form $ax^2 + bx + c = 0$, where *a, b,* and *c* are constants.

quadratic formula *n.* The formula $x = [-b \pm \sqrt{(b^2 - 4ac)}]/2a$, used to calculate the roots of a quadratic equation.

quad·rat·ics (kwo-dráttiks, kwə-, kwó-) *n. Used with a singular verb.* The algebra of quadratic equations.

quad·ra·ture (kwódrə-chər, -tewr) *n.* **1.** The process of making something square. **2.** *Mathematics.* The process of constructing a square equal in area to a given surface. **3.** *Astronomy.* Any configuration in which the angular separation of two celestial bodies, as measured from a third, is 90°. **4.** *Electronics.* The state in which two alternating signals of the same frequency differ in phase by 90°.

quad·ren·ni·al (kwo-drénni-əl, kwó-) *adj.* **1.** Happening once in four years. **2.** Lasting for four years.
~n. An event occurring every four years. **—quad·ren·ni·al·ly** *adv.*

quad·ren·ni·um (kwo-drénni-əm, kwó-) *n., pl.* **-ums** or **-nia** (-ə). A period of four years. [Latin *quadr(i)ennium* : QUADR(I)- + *annus,* year.]

quadri-, quadr– *comb. form.* Indicates four; for example, **quadriceps, quadric.** [Latin; akin to *quattuor,* four.]

quad·ric (kwódrik) *adj.* Of, pertaining to, or designating geometric surfaces that are defined by quadratic equations. [QUADR(I)- + -IC.]

quad·ri·cen·ten·ni·al (kwódri-sen-ténni-əl) *n. Chiefly U.S.* A 400th anniversary. **—quad·ri·cen·ten·ni·al** *adj.*

quad·ri·ceps (kwódri-seps) *n., pl.* **quadriceps** or **-cepses** (-sepsiz). The large four-part extensor muscle at the front of the thigh. [New Latin : QUADRI- + (BI)CEPS.] **—quad·ri·cip·i·tal** (-síppit'l) *adj.*

quad·ri·ga (kwo-dréegə, kwə-, -drīgə) *n.* In classical times, a chariot drawn by four horses.

quad·ri·lat·er·al (kwódri-láttrəl, -láttərəl) *n. Abbr.* **quad.** In geometry, a four-sided polygon.
~adj. Abbr. **quad.** Having four sides.

qua·drille¹ (kwə-dríl, kwo-, *rarely* kə-) *n.* **1.** A dance of French origin composed of five figures and performed by four or more couples. **2.** A piece of music for this dance in ⁶/₈ and ²/₄ time. [French, originally "one of the four divisions of an army, group of knights at a tournament", from Spanish *cuadrilla,* diminutive of *cuadra,* "square", from Latin *quadra.*]

quadrille² *n.* A card game popular during the 18th century, played by four people with a pack of 40 cards. [French, perhaps from Spanish *cuartillo,* from *cuarto,* fourth, from Latin *quārtus;* assimilated to QUADRILLE (above).]

quad·ril·li·on (kwó-dríl-iən, kwo-, kwə-) *n.* **1.** *British.* The cardinal number represented by 1 followed by 24 zeros, usually written 10^{24}. **2.** The cardinal number represented by 1 followed by 15 zeros, usually written 10^{15}. [French : QUADR(I)- + -(M)ILLION.] **—quad·ril·li·on** *adj.* **—quad·ril·li·onth** *n. & adj.*

quad·ri·no·mi·al (kwódri-nṓmi-əl) *n.* A polynomial with four terms. [QUADRI- + -nomial (as in *binomial*).]

quad·ri·par·tite (kwódri-pártīt) *adj.* **1.** Consisting of or divided into four parts. **2.** Involving four participants.

quad·ri·ple·gi·a (kwódri-plée-jə, -ji-ə) *n. Medicine.* Paralysis of all four limbs. Also called "tetraplegia". [QUADRI- + -PLEGIA.] **—quad·ri·ple·gic** (-pléejik) *adj. & n.*

quad·ri·va·lent (kwódri-váylənt) *adj. Chemistry.* **1.** Having four valencies. **2.** *Rare.* Having a valency of four; tetravalent. **—quad·ri·va·lence, quad·ri·va·len·cy** *n.*

quad·riv·i·um (kwo-drívvi-əm) *n., pl.* **-ia** (-ə). The higher division of the seven liberal arts in the Middle Ages, composed of geometry, astronomy, arithmetic, and music. Compare **trivium.** [Late Latin, from Latin, "place where four ways meet" : QUADRI- + *via,* way.]

quad·roon (kwo-drṓon, kwə-) *n.* A person having one Negro grandparent. [Spanish *cuarterón,* from *cuarto,* quarter, from Latin *quārtus.*]

quad·ru·ma·nous (kwo-drṓomə-nəss) *adj.* Also **quad·ru·ma·nal** (-n'l). Having four feet with thumb-like first digits, as do primates other than humans. [New Latin *quadrumana* (noun), neuter plural of *quadrumanus* : *quadru-,* variant of QUADRI- + *manus,* hand.]

quad·ru·ped (kwódrṓo-ped, *rarely* -pid) *n.* A four-footed animal.
~adj. Four-footed. [Latin *quadrupēs* : *quadru-,* variant of QUADRI- + -PED.] **—quad·ru·pe·dal** (-pédd'l, kwo-drṓopid'l) *adj.*

quad·ru·ple (kwóddrṓo'l, kwo-drṓop'l, kwə- ‖ -dréwp'l, *also* -drúpp'l) *adj.* **1.** Consisting of or having four parts, members, or copies. **2.** Multiplied by four; four times as much, as many, or as large. **3.** *Music.* Having four beats to the measure: *quadruple time.*
~n. A fourfold amount.
~v. **quadrupled, -pling, -ples.** *—tr.* To multiply or increase by four; quadruplicate. *—intr.* To be multiplied fourfold. [French, from Latin *quadruplus* : *quadru-,* variant of QUADRI- + *plus,* -fold.]

quad·ru·plet (kwóddrṓo-plit, -plet, -plət, kwo-drṓo- ‖ -dréw-, *also* -drú-) *n.* **1.** A group or combination of four associated by common properties or behaviour. **2.** Any of four offspring born in a single birth. In this sense, also informally called "quad".

quad·ru·pli·cate (kwo-drṓopli-kət, -kit, -kayt) *adj.* **1.** Multiplied by four; quadruple. **2.** Fourth in a group or set of four.
~n. **1.** Any of a set of four. **2.** A set of four copies.
~v. (-kayt) **quadruplicated, -cating, -cates.** *—tr.* To multiply by four. *—intr.* To become quadruplicated. [Latin *quadruplicātus,* past participle of *quadruplicāre,* to multiply by four, from *quadruplex,* fourfold : *quadru-,* variant of QUADRI- + *-plex,* -fold.] **—quad·ru·pli·cate·ly** *adv.* **—quad·ru·pli·ca·tion** (-káysh'n) *n.*

quad·ru·plic·i·ty (kwóddrṓo-plíssəti) *n.* The state of being quadruple or of being multiplied by four. [Latin *quadruplex,* fourfold. See **quadruplicate.**]

quaes·tor (kwéest-ər, -awr ‖ *U.S. also* kwést-) *n.* Any of various public officials in ancient Rome responsible for finance or administration in various areas of government. [Middle English *questor,* from Latin *quaestor,* from *quaerere* (past participial stem *quaesit-*), to seek, ask.] **—quaes·to·ri·al** (kwee-stáwri-əl ‖ kwe-, -stóri-) *adj.* **—quaes·tor·ship** *n.*

quaff (kwoff, kwaaf ‖ kwaf) *v.* **quaffed, quaffing, quaffs.** *—tr.* To drink deeply. *—intr.* To take a long, deep draught.
~n. A long, deep draught. [Perhaps imitative.] **—quaff·er** *n.*

quag·ga (kwággə ‖ kwáagə; *South African* kwákhə) *n.* A zebra-like mammal, *Equus quagga,* of southern Africa, that has been extinct since the late 19th century. [Obsolete Afrikaans, from Khoisan *qua-ha* (imitative).]

quag·gy (kwóggi, kwággi) *adj.* **-gier, -giest. 1.** Like a marsh; soggy. **2.** Soft; flabby. [From *quag,* marshy place; akin to dialect *quag,* to tremble, shake (imitative).]

quag·mire (kwóg-mīr, kwág-) *n.* **1.** A bog or swamp. Also called "quag". **2.** A difficult or precarious situation from which extrication is almost impossible. [From *quag* (see QUAGGY) + MIRE.]

qua·hog (kwáw-hog, kwáa-, káw- ‖ *U.S. also* kṓ-, -hawg) *n.* An edible clam, *Venus mercenaria,* having a hard, rounded shell. [Narraganset *poquaûhock.*]

quaich, quaigh (kwaykh) *n.* A two-handled Scottish drinking cup of varying size. [Scottish Gaelic *cuach,* from Old Irish *cūach,* from Latin *caucus,* drinking cup, from Greek *kauka, kaukion.*]

Quai d'Or·say (káy dór-say, dawr-sáy). Quay on the left bank of the river Seine in Paris, which has given its name to the French Ministry of Foreign Affairs located there.

quail¹ (kwayl) *n., pl.* **quails** or collectively **quail. 1.** Any of various small partridge-like Old World birds of the family Phasianidae; especially, *Coturnix coturnix,* having mottled brown plumage and a distinctive cry. **2.** Any of various similar or related New World birds, such as the **bobwhite** *(see).* [Middle English *quaille,* from Old French, from Medieval Latin *coacula* (imitative of its cry).]

quail² *intr.v.* **quailed, quailing, quails.** To lose courage; recoil in fear; cower. See Synonyms at **recoil.** [Middle English *quailen†,* to decline, fail, give way.]

quaint (kwaynt) *adj.* **quainter, quaintest. 1.** Agreeably curious, especially in an old-fashioned way: *a quaint little old cottage.* **2.** Unfamiliar or unusual in character; odd; strange: *what quaint manners you have.* **3.** Inappropriate; illogical: *They fought the war out of a quaint sense of honour.* —See Synonyms at **strange.** [Middle English *queinte, cointe,* clever, skilfully made, from Old French *cointe,* expert, elegant, from Latin *cognitus,* past participle of *cognōscere,* to be acquainted with : *com-,* with + *gnōscere,* to know.] **—quaint·ly** *adv.* **—quaint·ness** *n.*

quake (kwayk) *intr.v.* **quaked, quaking, quakes. 1.** To shake or tremble with instability or shock: *The ground quaked.* **2.** To shiver or tremble, as with cold or strong emotion: *quaking with rage.* —See Synonyms at **shake.**
~n. **1.** An instance of quaking; a shake. **2.** *Informal.* An earthquake. [Middle English *quaken,* Old English *cwacian,* from Germanic *kwei-* (unattested), to shake.] **—quak·i·ly** *adv.* **—quak·y** *adj.*

Quak·er (kwáykər) *n.* A member of the **Religious Society of Friends** *(see).* Not used officially by the Friends. [From QUAKE, probably in allusion to the admonition of George Fox, founder of the Society, to "tremble at the word of the Lord".] **—Quak·er** *adj.* **—Quak·er·ism** *n.* **—Quak·er·ly** *adj. & adv.*

quaking aspen *n.* A tree, the **aspen** *(see).*

quaking grass *n.* Any of several grass species of the genus *Briza,* having delicate, spreading panicles with ovoid spikelets. [Referring to its motion in wind.]

qual·i·fi·ca·tion (kwóllifi-káysh'n) *n.* **1.** Any quality, accomplishment, or ability that makes a person suitable for a particular position or task. **2.** A degree, diploma, or other evidence of successful completion of a course of study or training: *left school without any qualifications.* **3.** A condition or circumstance that must be met or complied with. **4.** A restriction or modification: *an offer with a number of qualifications.*

qual·i·fied (kwólli-fīd) *adj.* **1.** Having the appropriate qualifications for an office, position, or task. **2.** Limited, restricted, or modified: *gave qualified approval.* **—qual·i·fied·ly** (-fīd-li ‖ -fī-idli) *adv.*

qual·i·fi·er (kwólli-fī-ər) *n.* **1.** One that qualifies or has qualified: *Five qualifiers proceeded to the final.* **2.** A preliminary round or heat in a contest of selection process. **3.** *Grammar.* A modifier *(see).*

qual·i·fy (kwólli-fī) *v.* **-fied, -fying, -fies.** *—tr.* **1.** To describe by enumerating the characteristics or qualities of; characterise. **2.** To make competent or suitable for an office, position, or task. **3.** To authorise to work or act legally. **4.** To modify, limit, or restrict, as by giving exceptions. **5.** To make less harsh or severe; moderate. **6.** *Grammar.* To modify the meaning of (a word or phrase). *—intr.* **1.** To be or to become qualified. **2.** To reach the later or final stages of a contest or selection process by succeeding in earlier rounds. [French *qualifier,* from Medieval Latin *quālificāre,* to attribute a quality to : Latin *quālis,* of what kind + *facere,* to make.]

qual·i·ta·tive (kwólli-tətiv, -taytiv) *adj.* Of, pertaining to, or concerning quality or qualities: *A purely qualitative assessment, taking no account of number or size.* [Late Latin *quālitātivus,* from Latin *quālitās,* QUALITY.] —**qual·i·ta·tive·ly** *adv.*

qualitative analysis *n.* Chemical determination of the constituents of a substance without regard to quantity. Compare **quantitative analysis.**

Qua·li·täts·wein (kwólli-táyts-vīn; *German* kvál-ee-) *n.* **1.** A designation awarded to a wine produced in Germany, officially testifying to its quality and its origin in any of several specified regions. **2.** A wine thus endorsed. [German, "quality wine".]

qual·i·ty (kwólləti) *n., pl.* **-ties.** *Abbr.* **qlty. 1.** A characteristic or attribute of something; a property; a feature: *Her worst quality is her impatience.* **2.** The natural or essential character of something: *the hard quality of mahogany.* **3.** Degree or grade of excellence: *goods of low quality.* **4.** Excellence; superiority. **5.** *Archaic.* **a.** High social position. **b.** People of high social position. Preceded by *the.* **6.** *Music.* Timbre, as determined by overtones. **7.** *Phonetics.* The character of a vowel sound determined by the size and shape of the oral cavity and the amount of resonance with which the sound is produced. **8.** *Logic.* The positive or negative character of a proposition. **9.** *Informal.* A newspaper or magazine of a relatively high intellectual standard, and usually having a relatively low circulation.

~*adj.* High in quality; excellent: *quality goods; quality entertainment; quality time.* [Middle English *qualite,* from Old French, from Latin *quālitās* (stem *quālitāt-*), from *quālis,* what kind.]

Synonyms: *quality, property, attribute, character, trait.*

quality factor *n.* The **Q factor** *(see).*

quality of life *n.* The degree of emotional, intellectual, or cultural satisfaction in one's everyday life, as distinct from the degree of material comfort. Compare **standard of living.**

qualm (kwaam, kwawm || kwaalm) *n.* **1.** *Often plural.* A feeling of misgiving, uneasiness, or doubt, especially over a matter of conscience. **2.** A sudden feeling of sickness, faintness, or nausea. [16th century : origin obscure.] —**qualm·ish** *adj.* —**qualm·ish·ly** *adv.*

Synonyms: *qualm, scruple, compunction, misgiving, reservation.*

quamash. Variant of **camass.**

quan·da·ry (kwóndəri || kwóndri) *n., pl.* **-ries.** A state of uncertainty or perplexity; a dilemma. See Synonyms at **predicament.** [16th century : origin obscure.]

quan·dong, quan·dang (kwón-dong) *n.* **1.** A shrubby Australian tree, *Santalum acuminatus* which, yields an edible fruit containing an edible seed. Also called "native peach". **2.** An Australian tree the brush quandong, *Elaeocarpus grandis,* producing straw-coloured, easily worked timber. [From a native Australian language.]

quan·go (kwáng-gō) *n., pl.* **-gos.** A *qu*asi-*a*utonomous *n*ational *g*overnment (or *n*ongovernmental) *o*rganisation: any of numerous government-sponsored agencies or authorities with independent powers.

quant (kwont) *n.* A long pole used manually to propel a flat-bottomed boat, such as a punt, over shallow waterways. [Perhaps from Latin *contus,* from Greek *kontos,* pole for propelling a boat.] —**quant** *v.*

Quant (kwont), **Mary** (1934–). British fashion designer. She opened her first boutique in 1957 with her husband, Alexander Plunket Greene, and by the 1960s had become one of the world's most influential designers. She was awarded the O.B.E. in 1966.

quan·ta. Plural of **quantum.**

quan·tal (kwónt'l) *adj. Physics.* **1.** Of or pertaining to a quantum or a quantised system. **2.** Existing in only one of two possible states.

quan·ta·some (kwóntə-sōm) *n. Botany.* Any of the small particles occurring on the surface of the membranes of chloroplasts on which are thought to be the functional units of photosynthesis. [Probably from Latin *quanta,* "how many", plural of QUANTUM + -SOME.]

quan·tic (kwóntik) *n. Mathematics.* A homogeneous polynomial having two or more variables, as in $x^3 + x^2y + y^2x + y^3$. See **quadric, cubic, quartic.** [Latin *quantus,* how much + -IC.]

quan·ti·fi·er (kwónti-fī-ər) *n.* **1.** One that quantifies. **2.** *Grammar.* A modifier indicating range, quantity, or application, such as *many* or *four.* **3.** *Logic.* An operator, or its symbol, indicating range, quantity, or application; especially, a *universal quantifier,* which indicates that every object of the kind specified is being referred to, and an *existential quantifier,* which indicates that at least one such object does actually exist.

quan·ti·fy (kwónti-fī) *tr.v.* **-fied, -fying, -fies. 1.** To determine or express the quantity of: *One cannot quantify the value of a human life.* **2.** *Logic.* To limit the quantity of (a term or proposition) by prefixing a quantifier such as *all, some,* or *none.* [Medieval Latin *quantificāre* : *quantus,* how great + *facere,* to make.] —**quan·ti·fi·a·ble** (-fī-əb'l || -fī-əb'l) *adj.* —**quan·ti·fi·ca·tion** (-fi-káysh'n) *n.*

quan·tise, quan·tize (kwónt-īz) *tr.v.* **-tised, -tising, -tises.** *Physics.* **1.** To limit the possible values of (a magnitude or quantity) to a set of discrete values by quantum mechanical rules. **2.** To replace the dynamic variables of (a system) by the corresponding quantum mechanical operators in order to calculate the behaviour of the system. [QUANT(UM) + -ISE.] —**quan·ti·sa·tion** (-ī-záysh'n || *U.S.* -i-) *n.*

quan·ti·ta·tive (kwónti-tətiv, -taytiv) *adj.* **1. a.** Expressed or capable of expression as a quantity. **b.** Of, pertaining to, or susceptible of measurement. **c.** Pertaining to or based upon duration of sound rather than stress. Said especially of classical verse. [Medieval Latin *quantitātivus,* from Latin *quantitās,* QUANTITY.] —**quan·ti·ta·tive·ly** *adv.*

quantitative analysis *n.* Chemical determination of the amounts or proportions of constituents in a substance. Compare **qualitative analysis.**

quan·ti·ty (kwóntəti) *n., pl.* **-ties.** *Abbr.* **qt., qty. 1. a.** A number or amount of anything, either specified or indefinite. **b.** A considerable amount or number. **2.** The measurable, countable, or comparable property or aspect of a thing. **3.** Anything serving as the object of a mathematical operation. **4.** *Phonetics.* The length of a vowel or consonant sound expressed in terms of the time needed to produce it. **5.** *Logic.* The exact character of a proposition in respect of its universality, singularity, or particularity. **6.** *Physics.* An attribute that can be measured and assigned a value of a certain number of units. In this sense, also called "physical quantity". [Middle English *quantite,* from Old French, from Latin *quantitās* (stem *quantitāt-*), from *quantus,* how great.]

quantity surveyor *n.* A person who estimates, usually as a profession, the amounts and overall cost of the materials and labour needed in the construction of a building.

quan·tum (kwón-təm) *n., pl.* **-ta** (-tə). **1.** The quantity or amount of something. **2.** A specific portion of something. **3.** Something that may be counted or measured. **4.** *Physics.* A discrete, indivisible amount of some quantity, especially energy or angular momentum, by which a given system may change in any process. [Latin, neuter of *quantus,* how great.]

quantum chromodynamics *n. Physics.* **Chromodynamics** *(see).*

quantum electrodynamics *n. Physics.* The quantum-mechanical theory of the properties and interactions of charged elementary particles with each other and with electromagnetic radiation.

quantum gravitation *n. Physics.* A theory of gravitation in which interactions are caused by the exchange of particles (gravitons).

quantum jump *n.* **1.** *Physics.* The transition of an atomic or molecular system from one discrete energy level to another. It usually occurs with absorption or emission of radiation having energy equal to the difference between the two levels. **2.** Any abrupt change or step from one level or category to a quite different one, especially in knowledge or information. Also called "quantum leap".

quantum mechanics *n. Mathematics & Physics.* A formulation of the early ideas arising from quantum theory. It is used to interpret atomic and nuclear phenomena. See **wave mechanics, matrix mechanics, black-body radiation.**

quantum number *n. Physics.* Any of a set of real numbers that individually characterise the properties and collectively specify the state of a particle or of a system which is quantised.

quantum state *n. Physics.* Any one of the possible states of a system described by quantum theory.

quantum statistics *n. Physics.* The use of statistics to determine the properties of large numbers of particles by calculating the distribution of the particles over possible quantum states. See **Fermi-Dirac statistics, Bose-Einstein statistics.**

quantum theory *n.* A mathematical theory of physical systems that was developed to account for several physical phenomena that could not be explained by classical mechanics. It postulates that a system can gain or lose energy only in discrete amounts (quanta). Further developments led to the theory of **wave-particle duality** *(see)* and were formalised in quantum mechanics.

quar. 1. quarter. **2.** quarterly.

quar·an·tine (kwórrən-teen, *rarely* -tīn || *U.S. also* kwáwrən-) *n.* **1. a.** A period of time, originally lasting 40 days, during which a vehicle, a person, an animal, or goods suspected of carrying a contagious disease are detained at their port of entry under enforced isolation to prevent disease from entering a country. **b.** A place for such detention. **2.** Enforced isolation or restriction of free movement imposed to prevent a contagious disease from spreading. **3.** Any enforced isolation.

~*tr.v.* **quarantined, -tining, -tines. 1.** To place in quarantine. **2.** To isolate politically or economically. [Italian *quarantina,* period of forty days, from *quaranta,* forty, from Latin *quadrāgintā.*]

quark[1] (kwaark, kwawrk) *n. Physics.* Any of a hypothetical set of fermions having electric charges of magnitude one-third or two-thirds that of the electron, proposed (together with their antiparticles) as the fundamental units of baryons and mesons. [Coined by Murray GELL-MANN from a line in James Joyce's *Finnegans Wake,* "three quarks for Muster Mark!".]

quark[2] (kwaark, kfaark) *n.* A low-fat, soft cheese made of skimmed milk and often served mixed with fruit.

quar·rel[1] (kwórrəl || kwáwrəl) *n.* **1.** An angry dispute; a disagreement; an argument. **2.** A cause for dispute or argument: *We have no quarrel with the findings.*

~*intr.v.* **quarrelled** or *U.S.* **quarreled, -relling** or *U.S.* **-reling, -rels. 1.** To engage in a quarrel; argue angrily. **2.** To disagree; differ. **3.** To find fault with something; complain. —See Synonyms at **argue.** [Middle English, (cause for) complaint, from Old French, from Latin *querēla,* from *querī,* to complain.] —**quar·rel·ler** *n.*

quarrel[2] *n.* **1.** A bolt for a crossbow. **2.** A small diamond-shaped or square pane of glass in a latticed window. [Middle English *quarel,* from Old French, from Vulgar Latin *quadrellus* (unattested), diminutive of Late Latin *quadrus,* square.]

quar·rel·some (kwórrəl-səm || kwáwrəl-) *adj.* Characterised by quarrelling or tending to quarrel. See Synonyms at **belligerent.**

quar·ri·on (kwórri-ən) *n.* A parrot, the **cockatiel** *(see).* [Probably from an Australian native name.]

quar·ry[1] (kwórri || kwáwri) *n., pl.* **-ries. 1.** A bird or other animal that is hunted, or such animals collectively; prey; game. **2.** Any object of pursuit. [Middle English *querre,* entrails of a beast given to the hounds, from Anglo-French, Old French *cuiree,* variant of *co(u)ree,* from Vulgar Latin *corāta,* viscera, from Latin *cor,* heart.]

quarry[2] *n., pl.* **-ries. 1.** An open excavation or pit from which stone is obtained by digging, cutting, or blasting. **2.** A source from which material, such as information, can be extracted.

~v. **quarried, -rying, -ries.** *—tr.* **1.** To cut, dig, blast, or otherwise obtain (stone) from a quarry. **2.** To obtain (information) by long, careful searching. **3.** To use (land) as a quarry. *—intr.* To obtain material from or as if from a quarry. [Middle English *quarey, quarere,* from Old French *quarriere,* from *quarre* (unattested), "square stone", from Latin *quadrus,* square.] **—quar·ri·er** *n.*

quarry[3] *n., pl.* **-ries. 1.** A square or diamond shape. **2.** A pane of glass of this shape. [Variant of QUARREL (bolt).]

quart[1] (kwawrt || kawrt) *n. Abbr.* **q., qt.** A unit of liquid measure equal to two pints or a quarter of a gallon, and equivalent: **1.** In the British imperial system, to 1.136 litres. **2.** In the U.S. customary system, to 0.946 litres. [Middle English, from Old French *quarte, quārta,* feminine of Latin *quārtus,* fourth.]

quart[2] (kart) *n.* In card games like piquet, a sequence of four cards in one suit. [French *quarte,* fourth, QUARTE.]

quar·tan (kwáwrt'n) *adj.* Occurring every fourth day, counting inclusively, or every 72 hours. Said of a fever.

~n. A recurrent malarial fever, occurring every 72 hours. Also called "quartan malaria". [Middle English *quarteyne,* from Old French *quartaine,* from Latin *quārtāna (fēbris),* "quartan fever", from *quārtānus,* of the fourth, from *quārtus,* fourth.]

quarte, quart (kart) *n.* The fourth regular position in fencing. [French, "fourth", "quart", from Old French. See **quart.**]

quar·ter (kwáwtər || kwáwrtər, káwtər) *n. Abbr.* **q., qr., quar. 1.** Any of four equal parts of something. **2. a.** A period of fifteen minutes. **b.** The point on a clock's face marking either 15 minutes after or 15 minutes before an hour. Also called "quarter-hour". **3.** A coin equal to one fourth of the dollar of the United States and Canada. **4. a.** One fourth of a year; three months. **b.** *U.S.* An academic term lasting for approximately three months. **5.** *Astronomy.* **a.** One-fourth of the period of the Moon's revolution around the Earth. **b.** Either of two of the visible phases of the Moon: the *first quarter,* from new moon until it approaches fullness; and the *third quarter,* from after fullness until it has disappeared in the sunrise. **6.** *Sports. Chiefly U.S.* Any of four equal periods of playing time into which some games are divided. **7.** A fourth of any of various units of weight or measure, as of a yard, a mile, a pound, or a hundredweight. **8.** *British.* A measure of grain equal to approximately eight bushels. **9. a.** Any of the four major divisions of the compass: north, south, east, or west. **b.** A fourth of the distance between any two of the 32 divisions of the compass. **10. a.** The general direction on either side of a ship located 45 degrees off the stern. **b.** Any of the four major divisions of the horizon as determined by the four points of the compass. **c.** Any region or area of the earth thought of as falling in such a specified division. **11. a.** The upper portion of the aft side of a ship, usually between the aftermost mast and the stern. **b.** The part of a yard between the slings and the yardarm. **12.** *Heraldry.* Any of four divisions of a shield. **13.** Any of the four limbs of a carcass of an animal, usually including the adjoining parts. **14.** Either side of a horse's hoof. **15.** The part of the side of a shoe between the heel and the vamp. **16.** *Plural.* A place of residence; specifically, the buildings or barracks housing military personnel. **17.** *Usually plural.* A proper or assigned station or place, as for officers and crew on a warship. **18.** A district or section, as of a city, especially characterised by a specified group of people or activity: *the Latin quarter.* **19.** *Often plural.* An unnamed person or group of persons considered as a source of something, such as help or information: *got help from the highest quarters; no news from that quarter.* **20.** Mercy or clemency, especially when shown to an enemy: *gave no quarter.*

~v. **quartered, -tering, -ters.** *—tr.* **1. a.** To cut or otherwise divide into four equal or equivalent parts. **b.** To quartersaw (a log). **2.** To divide or separate into a number of parts. **3.** Formerly, to cut or dismember (a human body) into four parts: *hung, drawn, and quartered.* **4.** *Heraldry.* **a.** To divide (a shield) into four equal areas with vertical and horizontal lines. **b.** To place (a charge) in a quarter or quarters. **5. a.** To mark or place (holes, for example) a fourth of a circle apart. **b.** To fix (one machine part) at right angles to its connecting part. **6.** To provide (soldiers, for example) with lodgings. **7.** To traverse (an area of ground) laterally back and forth while slowly moving forward. Used especially of hunting dogs. *—intr.* **1.** To take up or be assigned lodgings. **2.** To traverse an area of ground by ranging over it from side to side.

~adj. **1.** Being one of four equal or equivalent parts. **2.** Being a fourth of a standard or usual value. [Middle English, from Old French *quartier,* from Latin *quārtārius, from quārtus,* fourth.]

quar·ter·age (kwáwtərij) *n.* A monetary allowance, wage, or payment made or received quarterly.

quar·ter·bound (kwáwtər-bównd) *adj.* Bound in leather or similar material only along the spine and adjoining part of the boards.

quarter day *n.* Any of the four days of the year regarded as the beginning of a new season or quarter, when most quarterly payments are due. In England, Wales, and Ireland, these days are Lady Day, Midsummer Day, Michaelmas, and Christmas; in Scotland they are Candlemas, Whit Sunday, Martinmas, and Lammas.

quar·ter·deck (kwáwtər-dek) *n.* The after part of the upper deck of a sailing ship, usually reserved for officers.

quar·ter·fi·nal (kwáwtər-fīn'l) *n.* In a competition or tournament, any of four matches constituting a round or stage whose winners go on to play in the semifinal round. **—quar·ter·fi·nal** *adj.*

quarter horse *n.* A strong saddle horse of a breed developed in the western United States. [Formerly trained for races of up to a quarter of a mile.]

quar·ter·ing (kwáwtəring) *n. Heraldry.* **1.** The combining of different coats of arms on one shield, thereby showing the uniting of different families. **2.** *Plural.* The coats of arms so displayed.

quar·ter·light (kwáwtər-līt) *n. British.* A small triangular window in the front of a car, next to the main side window.

quar·ter·ly (kwáwtərli) *adj. Abbr.* **q., qr., quar. 1.** Occurring or appearing at regular intervals of three months: *a quarterly magazine; a quarterly payment.* **2.** Having four sections. Said of a heraldic shield.

~n., pl. **quarterlies.** *Abbr.* **q., qr., quar.** A publication issued regularly every three months. **—quar·ter·ly** *adv.*

quar·ter·mas·ter (kwáwtər-maastər || -mastər) *n. Abbr.* **Q.M. 1.** A military officer responsible for the food, clothing, and equipment of troops. **2.** A naval petty officer responsible for the steering of a ship, and other navigational duties. [From QUARTER (residence).]

Quartermaster General *n. Abbr.* **Q.M.G.** A military officer in charge of the branch of the army that deals with food, clothing, equipment, and other supplies.

quar·tern (kwáwt'n || kwáwtərn) *n.* **1.** A fourth of something. **2.** *British.* A loaf weighing about four pounds. [Middle English *quarteron,* from Old French, from *quartier,* QUARTER.]

quarter note *n. Music. Chiefly U.S.* A note, the **crotchet** *(see).*

quar·ter-phase (kwáwtər-fayz) *adj. Electronics.* Two-phase.

quar·ter·saw (kwáwtər-saw) *tr.v.* **-sawed, -sawed** or **-sawn, -sawing, -saws.** To saw (a log) into quarters lengthways along its axis.

quarter sessions *n. Law.* Formerly in Britain, a court held at least four times a year to try offences and hear appeals. In 1972 it was abolished and its jurisdiction transferred to the crown courts.

quar·ter·staff (kwáwtər-staaf || -staf) *n., pl.* **-staves** (-stayvz). A long wooden staff, formerly used as a weapon.

quarter tone *n. Music.* Half a **semitone** *(see).*

quar·tet, quar·tette (kwáwr-tét, káwr-) *n.* **1.** A musical composition for: **a.** Four singers. **b.** Four instruments, especially stringed instruments. **2.** A group of four performing musicians. **3.** Any set of four persons or things. [French *quartette,* Italian *quartetto,* diminutive of *quarto,* fourth, from Latin *quārto.* See **quarto.**]

quar·tic (kwáwrtik || káwrtik) *adj. Mathematics.* Of or pertaining to the fourth degree; biquadratic.

~n. Mathematics. An algebraic equation of the fourth degree. Also called "biquadratic". [From Latin *quārtus,* fourth.]

quar·tile (kwáwr-tīl || káwr-, *U.S.* -t'l) *n. Statistics.* One of three values that mark the division of a **frequency distribution** *(see)* into four parts, each containing a quarter of the whole group of items under consideration. [Medieval Latin *quārtīlis,* of a quartile, from Latin *quārtus,* fourth. See **quarto.**] **—quar·tile** *adj.*

quar·to (kwáwrtō) *n., pl.* **-tos.** *Abbr.* **q., Q., qto. 1.** The page size obtained by folding a whole sheet into four leaves. **2.** A book composed of pages of this size or folded in this way. Also written *4to, 4°.* **3.** A size of paper, 8 by 10 inches (203 by 256 millimetres). [Latin *(in) quārto,* in quarter, from *quārtus,* fourth.] **—quar·to** *adj.*

quartz (kwáwrts || káwrts) *n.* **1.** A hard, crystalline, vitreous mineral form of silicon dioxide, SiO_2, found worldwide in such varieties as agate, chalcedony, chert, flint, opal, and rock crystal. It may be clear and transparent (as in rock crystal) or any of various colours, such as purple (as in amethyst) or yellow (as in citrine). **2.** Quartz glass.

~adj. **1.** Made of quartz. **2.** Designating a timepiece that is regulated by electronic circuitry using a small quartz crystal to operate its mechanism and produce a high degree of accuracy. [From German *Quarz,* from Middle High German *quarz,* from old West Slavonic *kwardy,* hard.]

quartz crystal *n.* A small crystal of quartz accurately cut along certain axes so that it can be vibrated at a particular frequency, used for its piezoelectric properties to produce an electrical signal of constant known frequency.

quartz glass *n.* A pure silica glass, highly transparent to ultraviolet radiations.

quartz·if·er·ous (kwáwrts-íffərəss) *adj.* Containing quartz.

quartz-i·o·dine lamp (kwáwrts-ī-ə-deen || *U.S. also* -əd'n, -ə-dīn) *n.* A type of lamp, used especially for car headlights, having a quartz envelope containing inert gas with a small amount of iodine vapour and a tungsten filament. The iodine vapour improves the brightness of the lamp. Also called "quartz-iodide lamp".

quartz·ite (kwáwrts-īt) *n.* A metamorphic rock resulting from the recrystallisation of sandstone.

qua·sar (kwáy-zaar, -saar) *n. Astronomy.* A member of any of several classes of starlike objects having exceptionally large red shifts that are often emitters of radio frequency as well as visible radiation and have apparently immense speeds, energies, and distances from Earth. Also called "quasi-stellar object". [*Quasi* stell*ar.*]

quash (kwosh) *tr.v.* **quashed, quashing, quashes. 1.** *Law.* To set aside or annul. **2.** To put down or suppress forcibly and completely. [Middle English *quassen,* from Old French *quasser, casser,* from Late Latin *cassāre,* from Latin *cassus,* empty, void.]

qua·si (kwáy-zī, kwáa-, kwá-, -sī, -zi) *adv.* To some degree; almost or somewhat. Usually used in combination: *quasi-scientific litera-ture.*

~adj. Resembling but not being something specified. Used in combination: *a quasi-victory.* [Latin *quasi,* as if : *quam,* than, how, as + *sī,* if.]

Qua·si·mo·do (kwa͡azi-mṓdō; *Italian* kwa-ze͡emodo), **Salvatore** (1901–68). Italian poet. Though his earlier work drew on an idyllic childhood in Sicily, his postwar writing, such as *Il falso e vero verde* (1956), reflects concern over social issues. He was awarded the Nobel prize in 1959.

qua·si-stel·lar object (kwáyzĭ-stéllər, kwa͡azĭ-) *n. Abbr.* **QSO** A quasar.

quasi-stellar radio source *n. Abbr.* **QSRS** *Astronomy.* A quasi-stellar object which is only detected by its radio emission. Not in technical usage.

quas·sia (kwŏsha) *n.* **1. a.** A tree, *Quassia amara,* of tropical America, having bright scarlet flowers. **b.** The wood or bark of this tree. **2.** A bitter substance obtained from the wood and bark of this tree and related trees, used in medicine and as an insecticide. [New Latin, after Graman *Quassi,* 18th-century native of Surinam, who discovered its medicinal properties.]

qua·ter·nar·y (kwə-térnəri, kwo- ‖ *U.S. also* kwóttər-nerri) *adj.* **1.** Consisting of four; in fours. **2.** *Chemistry.* **a.** Designating a compound having four groups connected to a nitrogen or phosphorus atom. **b.** Designating a compound consisting of four different atoms or radicals.

~n., pl. quaternaries. 1. The number four. **2.** A set of four objects. [Middle English, set of four, from Latin *quaternārius,* consisting of four each, from *quaternī,* four each, from *quater,* four times.]

Qua·ter·nar·y (kwə-térnəri, kwo- ‖ *U.S. also* kwóttər-nerri) *adj. Geology.* Of, belonging to, or designating the geological time and system of rocks, and sedimentary deposits of the second period of the Cenozoic era, from the end of the Tertiary (two million years ago) to the present, characterised by the appearance and development of human beings, and including the Pleistocene and Holocene epochs.

~n. *Geology.* The Quaternary period or system of deposits. Preceded by *the.* [From QUATERNARY (fourth).]

quaternary ammonium compound *n. Chemistry.* Any of a class of compounds containing an ion NR_4^+, where R is an organic group or a hydrogen atom.

qua·ter·ni·on (kwə-térni-ən, kwo-) *n.* **1.** A set of four persons or items. **2.** *Mathematics.* An element of a system of four dimensional vectors obeying laws similar to those of complex numbers. [Middle English, from Late Latin *quaterniō* (stem *quaterniōn-*), from Latin *quaternī,* four each. See **quaternary.**]

quat·rain (kwóttrayn ‖ kwo-tráyn) *n.* A stanza of verse having four lines that often rhyme alternately. [French, from Old French, from *quatre,* four, from Latin *quattuor.*]

quat·re·foil (káttrə-foyl, káttər-) *n.* **1.** A figure of a flower with four petals or a leaf with four leaflets, especially in heraldry. **2.** *Architecture.* An ornament or tracery with four foils or lobes. **3.** *Geometry.* A curve that has four lobes. [Middle English *quaterfoile,* set of four leaves : *quater-,* four, from Old French *quatre* + FOIL (leaf).]

quat·tro·cen·to (kwóttrō-chéntō, kwáttrō-) *n.* The 15th-century period of Italian art and literature. [Italian, short for *(mil)quattro cento,* "(one thousand) four hundred".]

qua·ver (kwáyvər) *v.* **-vered, -vering, -vers.** **—intr. 1.** To quiver, as from weakness or emotion; tremble. Used especially of the voice. **2.** To speak in a quivering voice. **3.** To produce a trill on a musical instrument or in singing. **—tr.** To utter or sing in a trilling or trembling voice.

~n. 1. *Music.* A note having an eighth of the time value of a whole note. Also *U.S.* "eighth note". **2.** A quivering sound. **3.** A trill. [Middle English *quaveren,* frequentative of obsolete *quaven* (imitative), to tremble, from Germanic; akin to Low German *quabbeln,* to tremble.] **—qua·ver·ing·ly** *adv.* **—qua·ver·y** *adj.*

quay (kee) *n.* A wharf or reinforced bank, such as one that juts out from a harbour, where ships are loaded or unloaded. [Earlier *key,* Middle English *key, kay,* from Old French *chai, cay,* from Gaulish *caio,* rampart, retaining wall.]

quay·age (kée-ij) *n.* **1.** A charge for the use of a quay. **2.** The space available for or on quays. **3.** Quays collectively.

quay·side (kée-sīd) *n.* The area alongside or forming a quay. **—quay·side** *adj.*

quean (kween) *n.* **1.** *Scottish.* A young woman, especially one who is not married. **2.** *Archaic.* An impudent or disreputable woman; especially, a prostitute. [Middle English *quen(e),* Old English *cwene,* woman, wife, from Germanic.]

quea·sy (kwéezi) *adj.* **-sier, -siest. 1.** Nauseated or easily nauseated. **2.** Causing nausea or sickness: *queasy food.* **3. a.** Causing uneasiness. **b.** Uneasy; troubled. **4.** Easily troubled: *a queasy conscience.* [Middle English *coysy, qwesye,* perhaps originally "wounded", from Anglo-French, Old French *coisi* (unattested), akin to *coisier,* to injure.] **—quea·si·ly** *adv.* **—quea·si·ness** *n.*

Que·bec¹ (kwi-bék). *French* **Qué·bec** (kay-bék). Capital of Quebec province, Canada, situated at the confluence of the St. Lawrence and St. Charles rivers in the southeast of the country. A picturesque city, it is the hub of French Canadian culture. It is chiefly a distribution and manufacturing centre with a wide range of industries including timber, printing, textiles, shipbuilding, and iron and steel production. Tourism is also important.

Quebec². Largest province in Canada, in the east of the country. Most of it is part of the Laurentian (or Canadian) Shield, a plateau

of hard rock which was scoured by ice sheets and glaciers and is now rich in minerals and timber. Between this block and the Appalachian Mountains in the south lies the valley of the St. Lawrence river. Montreal is at the centre of this rich agricultural strip, which provides cereals and dairy products. Originally a French colony known as New France or Canada (1534–1763), the province still retains French language and customs, and there is a strong separatist movement. Capital, Quebec.

que·bra·cho (ki-bra͡achō, kay-) *n., pl.* **-chos. 1.** Any of several South American trees having very hard wood; especially, *Aspidosperma quebracho,* the bark of which is used in medicine, and trees of the species *Schinopsis,* whose barks yield tannin. **2.** The bark or wood of any of these trees. [American Spanish, variant of *quiebrahacha,* "axe-breaker" : *quiebra,* from *quebrar,* to break + *hacha,* axe.]

Quech·ua (kéch-wə, -waa ‖ kéchoo-ə, ke-cho͡o-) *n., pl.* **-uas** or collectively **Quechua.** Also **Quich·ua** (kích-), **Kech·ua. 1.** A member of a South American Indian people originally constituting the ruling class of the Incan Empire. **2.** The language of this people, still spoken by other Indian peoples of Peru, Ecuador, Bolivia, Chile, and Argentina. [Spanish, from Quechua *kkechúwa,* "plunderer", "robber".] **—Quech·uan** *n. & adj.*

queen (kween) *n. Abbr.* **qu. 1.** A female monarch or ruler. **2.** The wife or widow of a king. **3.** A woman, or a thing personified as a woman, who is eminent or supreme in a specified field or area: *a beauty queen; the queen of my heart.* **4.** *Abbr.* **Q** The most powerful piece in chess, able to move in any direction in a straight or diagonal line. **5.** A playing card bearing the figure of a queen, next above the jack and below the king in each suit. **6.** The fertile, fully developed female in a colony of social bees, ants, or termites. **7.** *Slang.* **a.** One who is showily effeminate: *a drag queen.* **b.** A male homosexual. Used derogatorily.

~v. queened, queening, queens. —tr. 1. To make (a woman) a queen. **2.** *Chess.* To convert (a pawn) into a queen, when it has reached the far end of the board. **—intr.** To reign as queen. **—queen it.** *Slang.* To act or behave in a showy, effeminate manner. [Middle English *qu(e)ene,* Old English *cwēn,* woman, wife, queen, from Germanic.] **—queenship** *n.*

Queen Anne *n.* The style of English architecture (characterised by classical decoration and red brickwork) and furniture (characterised especially by fine upholstery and wood inlays) typical of the reign of Queen Anne (1702–14). Often used adjectivally.

Queen Anne's lace *n.* A widely distributed plant, *Daucus carota,* native to Eurasia, having finely divided leaves and flat clusters of small white flowers. Also called "wild carrot".

Queen Anne's War *n.* See **War of the Spanish Succession.**

queen cake *n.* A small sponge cake often iced or containing currants and sometimes baked in the shape of a heart.

Queen Charlotte Islands. Group of islands off the coast of British Columbia, western Canada. Logging and fishing are the main occupations and the native Indians are renowned for their canoe building. Masset in the north of Graham Island is the chief town.

queen consort *n.* The wife of a reigning king.

queen dowager *n.* The widow of a king.

Queen Elizabeth Islands. Also (until 1954) **Par·ry Islands** (párri). The northern part of the Arctic Archipelago, which forms part of the Northwest Territories of Canada. The islands possess rich oil deposits, exploited since the early 1960s.

queen·ly (kwéenli) *adj.* **-lier, -liest. 1.** Of or resembling a queen. **2.** Pertaining to or befitting a queen. **—queen·li·ness** *n.*

queen mother *n.* A dowager queen who is the mother of the reigning monarch.

queen of puddings *n.* A sweet pudding consisting of a moist jam and breadcrumb mixture topped with meringue.

Queen of the May *n.* A May Queen *(see).*

queen post *n.* Either of two upright supporting posts set vertically between the rafters and the tie beam at equal distances from the apex of a roof. Compare **king post.**

Queens (kweenz). Borough of New York City, in the United States at the western end of Long Island, and coextensive with Queen's County.

Queen's Bench *n. Abbr.* **Q.B.** One of the divisions of the English High Court of Justice. Also called "King's Bench" during the reign of a king.

Queens·ber·ry Rules (kwéenz-bri, -bəri ‖ -berri) *pl. n.* **1.** A boxing code of fair play developed in 1867 by the eighth Marquis of Queensberry. **2.** Broadly, any set of rules that prescribe fair play.

Queen's Counsel *n. Abbr.* **Q.C.** A member of a group of pre-eminent barristers nominally appointed to serve as counsel to the British Crown. Also called "King's Counsel" during the reign of a king.

Queen's County. See **Leix.**

Queen's English *n.* British English as traditionally spoken by the middle and upper-middle classes, especially in the south of England, considered to be a standard of correctness. Also called "King's English" during the reign of a king.

queen's evidence *n.* Evidence given for the crown by an accused person against an accomplice in a British legal proceeding. Also called "king's evidence" during the reign of a king.

Queen's highway *n.* In Britain, any public road. Also called "King's highway" during the reign of a king.

Queens·land (kwéenz-lənd, -land. *Note: in Australia usually* -land). Second largest state in Australia, in the northeast of the country. It includes the adjacent islands in the Pacific Ocean and the Gulf of

Carpentaria. The Great Barrier Reef runs along its eastern coastline, and the coastal plains give way to the high peaks of the Great Dividing Range. There are grasslands on the western hills and vast plains further west. Agriculture and manufacturing are both economically important, and there is also considerable mineral wealth, including copper, coal, gold, bauxite, uranium, oil, and gas. The first settlement, in 1824, was a penal colony. Brisbane is the capital city.

queen's metal n. A form of britannia metal containing a small amount of zinc.

Queen's Regulations n. The military laws governing discipline, punishment, and the code of conduct of members of the armed forces. Also called "King's Regulations" during the reign of a king.

Queen's shilling n. See **King's shilling**.

Queen's speech n. In Britain, the **Speech from the Throne** (see).

queen truss n. A building truss having queen posts.

queer (kweer) adj. **queerer, queerest. 1.** Deviating from the expected or normal; strange: a queer situation. **2.** Odd or unconventional in behaviour; eccentric. **3.** Arousing suspicion. **4.** Slang. Fake; counterfeit. **5.** Unwell; queasy. **6.** Informal. Homosexual. Often used derogatorily. —See Synonyms at **strange.**
~n. Informal. A homosexual, especially a male one. Used derogatorily. **2.** Counterfeit money.
~tr.v. **queered, queering, queers.** Informal. **1.** To ruin or spoil. **2.** To put into a bad position. [Perhaps from German quer, perverse, cross, from Middle High German twerch, querch, from Old High German twerh, dwerah. See thwart.] —**queer·ly** adv. —**queer·ness** n.

Queer Street n. Chiefly British. Difficulties, especially financial ones.

que·le·a (kweéli-ə) n. A small African finch, Quelea quelea, with brown plumage and a red bill, that is a serious pest of grain crops. [New Latin, perhaps from Medieval Latin qualea, QUAIL.]

quell (kwel) tr.v. **quelled, quelling, quells. 1.** To put down forcibly; suppress: quelled the riot. **2.** To pacify; calm: quelled her fears. [Middle English quellen, to kill, destroy, Old English cwellan, from Germanic.]

Quemoy. See **Jinmen.**

quench (kwench) tr.v. **quenched, quenching, quenches. 1.** To put out; extinguish. **2.** To suppress; stifle; put down. **3.** To slake; satisfy. **4.** To cool (hot metal) by thrusting into water or other liquid. **5.** To reduce (sparking or oscillation) in an electronic circuit. **6.** To suppress (luminescence, fluorescence, or electrical discharge, for example) by adding a deactivating agent. [Middle English quenchen, Old English ācwencan.] —**quench·a·ble** adj. —**quench·er** n.

Que·neau (kə-nō'), **Raymond** (1903–79). French novelist and poet. His bizarre, erudite humour, full of puns and surrealism, cloaked a profound pessimism. Notable among his works are Le Chien-dent (1933) and Zazie dans le Métro (1959).

que·nelle (kə-nél', ki-) n. A dumpling, especially of pounded fish, bound with eggs and poached in stock or water. [French.]

quer·ce·tin (kwérssi-tin) n. A yellow, powdered crystalline compound, $C_{15}H_{10}O_7$, synthesised or occurring as a glycoside in the rind and bark of numerous plants, and used medicinally to treat abnormal capillary fragility. [Latin quercētum, oak forest, from quercus, oak.]

que·rist (kwéer-ist) n. Rare. A questioner; an enquirer. [Latin quaerere, to seek, ask.]

quern (kwern) n. **1.** A hand-turned grain mill consisting of two stone wheels, one resting upon the other. **2.** A small hand mill for grinding spices. [Middle English querne, Old English cweorn, from Germanic.]

quer·u·lous (kwérroō-ləss, kwérrew-) adj. **1.** Given to complaining or fretting; peevish. **2.** Expressing a complaint or grievance; grumbling; fretful. [Latin querulus, from querī, to complain.] —**quer·u·lous·ly** adv. —**quer·u·lous·ness** n.

que·ry (kwéer-i) n., pl. **-ries. 1.** A question; an inquiry. **2.** A doubt in the mind. **3.** Abbr. **q., qu.** A notation, usually (?), calling attention to an item to question its validity or accuracy.
~tr.v. **queried, -rying, -ries. 1.** To express doubt or uncertainty about; question. **2.** Chiefly U.S. To put a question to (a person). **3.** To mark with a query, as to question validity or accuracy. —See Synonyms at **ask.** [Variant (influenced by ENQUIRY) of earlier quaere, from Latin, imperative of quaerere, to seek, ask.]

quest (kwest) n. **1.** The act or an instance of seeking or pursuing something; a search. **2.** In medieval romance, an expedition undertaken by a knight in order to perform some prescribed feat: the quest for the Holy Grail. —**in quest of.** In pursuit of; seeking.
~v. **quested, questing, quests.** —intr. **1.** To make a search; go on a quest. **2.** To search for game. Used of a hunting dog. —tr. Archaic. To seek; search for. [Middle English queste, from Old French, from Vulgar Latin quaesita (unattested), from Latin, feminine past participle of quaerere, to seek.] —**quest·er** n.

ques·tion (kwéss-chən, kwésh-, also kwést-yən) n. Abbr. **q., qn., qu. 1.** An expression of enquiry that invites or calls for a reply; an interrogative sentence, phrase, or gesture. **2.** A subject or point open to controversy; an unsettled issue. **3.** A matter or problem, especially one conditioned by or considered in terms of a specified factor: a question of ethics. **4.** A point or subject under discussion or being considered. **5.** A proposition brought up for consideration by an assembly. **6.** Uncertainty; doubt. **7.** Possibility; chance: no question of my giving in. —**beg the question. 1.** To presuppose the conclusion in one's argument. **2.** To equivocate. —**call into ques-**

tion. To cast doubt upon. —**out of the question.** Not worth considering; impossible. —**pop the question.** Informal. To propose marriage.
~v. **questioned, -tioning, -tions.** —tr. **1.** To put a question to. **2.** To interrogate (a witness or suspect, for example). **3.** To express doubt about; dispute. —intr. To ask questions. —See Synonyms at **ask.** [Middle English, from Old French, from Latin quaestiō (stem quaestiōn-), from quaerere (past participle quaestus), to seek, ask.] —**ques·tion·er** n. —**ques·tion·ing·ly** adv.

ques·tion·a·ble (kwéss-chən-əb'l, kwésh-) adj. **1.** Open to doubt; uncertain; problematic. **2.** Of dubious morality or respectability. —See Synonyms at **doubtful.** —**ques·tion·a·bil·i·ty** (-əbílliti), **ques·tion·a·ble·ness** n. —**ques·tion·a·bly** adv.

question mark n. **1.** A punctuation symbol (?) written, in English, at the end of a sentence or phrase to indicate a direct question. Also called "interrogation mark", "interrogation point", "interrogative". **2. a.** This symbol used to indicate uncertainty, as in dating a museum specimen, for example: (?10th century). **b.** Informal. An unknown factor; a situation of doubt or insecurity.

ques·tion·mas·ter (kwéss-chən-maass-tər, kwésh- ‖ -mass-) n. British. One who chairs a quiz game, as on the radio or television.

ques·tion·naire (kwéss-chə-naír, kwésh-, késs-, kwést-yən-, kést-) n. A printed form containing a set of questions, especially one used for gathering information from people, as in a survey. [French, from questionner, to question, from question, QUESTION.]

question time n. In Britain, a period during a parliamentary session when questions may be put to certain ministers concerning matters for which they are responsible.

Quet·ta (kwéttə). Capital city of Baluchistan province in Pakistan, situated on the main route north to Afghanistan via the Bolan Pass. It is an important trade centre.

quet·zal (kwét-s'l, két- ‖ ket-saál, -sál) n., pl. **-zals** or **-zales** (-saálayss, -ayz). **1.** A Central American bird, Pharomacrus mocino, having brilliant bronze-green and red plumage and, in the male, long flowing tail feathers. **2.** Abbr. **Q a.** The basic monetary unit of Guatemala, equal to 100 centavos. **b.** A coin worth one quetzal. [American Spanish, from Nahuatl quetzalli, tail feather.]

Quet·zal·co·a·tl (kéts'l-kō-átt'l, -áat'l). A god of the Toltecs and Aztecs, represented as a plumed serpent.

queue (kew) n. **1.** A line or file of people or vehicles waiting to do something, such as board a bus, or to receive attention in turn, as at a shop counter. **2.** A long plait of real or artificial hair worn hanging down the back of the neck; a pigtail. —**jump the queue.** To do something or receive attention before one's turn has come.
~intr.v. **queued, queuing, queues.** To wait in a queue. Often used with up. [French, tail, line, from Old French coe, cue, from Latin cauda, tail.]

queue-jump·ing (kéw-jumping) n. The practice or an act of making sure one does something or receives attention before one's turn has come. —**queue-jump·er** n. —**queue-jump·ing** adj.

Que·zon City (káy-son, -zon ‖ U.S. -sawn). City adjoining Manila on the island of Luzon, in the Philippines. It was the country's capital from 1948 to1976.

quib·ble (kwíbb'l) intr.v. **-bled, -bling, -bles. 1.** To make exaggerated distinctions or raise objections to unimportant details: quibbling over trivialities. **2.** Archaic. To make a pun.
~n. **1.** A petty distinction or minor objection. **2.** Archaic. A pun. [From obsolete quib, pun, perhaps from Latin quibus, dative and ablative plural of quī, who, which (used in legal documents and hence associated with quips and quibbles).]

quiche (keesh) n. A small savoury tart consisting of beaten eggs with cheese, bacon, or other ingredients baked in an unsweetened pastry shell. [French, probably from German (dialectal) Küche, diminutive of Kuchen, cake, from Old High German kuocho.]

quick (kwik) adj. **quicker, quickest. 1.** Moving or functioning rapidly and energetically; speedy: a quick worker. **2.** Occupying a brief space of time: a quick chat over lunch. **3.** Understanding, thinking, or learning with speed and dexterity; intellectually sharp. **4.** Perceiving with speed and sensitivity; alert; keen. **5.** Done or occurring in a relatively short time; prompt; immediate. **6.** Hasty or sharp in reacting: quick to attack her opponents. **7.** Archaic. Pregnant. Used especially in the phrase quick with child. **8.** Archaic. Alive. —See Synonyms at **fast, nimble.**
~n. **1.** Sensitive or raw exposed flesh, as under the fingernails. **2.** The most personal and sensitive area of the emotions: cut to the quick. **3.** The vital core of a thing; the essence. Used chiefly in the phrase the quick of the matter. **4.** British. Quickset.
~adv. Quickly; promptly.
~interj. Used to urge quick action or response. [Middle English qui(c)ke, swift, living, alive, Old English cwic(u), living, alive, from Germanic.] —**quick·ness** n. —**quick·ly** adv.
Usage: Quick is occasionally used as an adverb in informal speech (especially in the imperative: Come quick!), but quickly is the preferred form in formal speech and writing. See also **slow.**

quick assets pl. n. Liquid assets, including cash on hand and assets readily convertible to cash.

quick-change (kwik-cháynj) adj. Of or designating an actor, entertainer, or other performer, who must quickly change costume on a number of occasions during the performance.

quick·en (kwickən) v. **-ened, -ening, -ens.** —tr. **1.** To make more rapid; speed up; accelerate. **2.** To make alive; vitalise. **3.** To excite and stimulate; stir. —intr. **1.** To become more rapid. **2.** To show life; come or return to life: "and the weak spirit quickens" (T.S.

Eliot). **3. a.** To reach the stage of pregnancy when the foetus can be felt to move. Used of the mother. **b.** To make these first movements, thus showing signs of life. Used of a foetus. —See Synonyms at **speed.** —**quick·en·er** n.

quick-fire (kwĭk-fīr) adj. Suggesting rapid gunfire: quick-fire questions.

quick fix n. Informal. A quick and simple solution that may well not last. [Perhaps from **fix** n. (senses 4, 5).]

quick-freeze (kwĭk-frēez) tr.v. **-froze** (-frōz), **-frozen** (-frōz'n), **-freezing, -freezes.** To freeze (food) by a process sufficiently rapid to retain natural flavour, nutritional value, or other properties.

quick·ie (kwĭcki) n. Informal. Something made, done, or consumed rapidly or hastily.

quick·lime (kwĭk-līm) n. Chemistry. **Calcium oxide** (see). [So called because it is the first substance produced by heating limestone.]

quick march n. A march done in quick time, especially by soldiers. ~interj. Used as a command for such a march.

quick·sand (kwĭk-sand) n. A bed of loose sand and mud mixed with water forming a soft, shifting mass that yields easily to pressure and may suck down any denser object resting on its surface.

quick·set (kwĭk-set) n. Chiefly British. **1. a.** Cuttings or slips of a plant suitable for hedges. **b.** A single slip or cutting of such a plant. **2.** A hedge consisting of such plants. —**quick·set** adj.

quick·sil·ver (kwĭk-sĭlvər) n. The element **mercury** (see). ~adj. Unpredictable; mercurial. [Middle English quicksilver, Old English cwicseolfor (translation of Latin argentum vivum) : QUICK, "living" + SILVER.]

quick·step (kwĭk-step) n. A fast ballroom dance. —**quick·step** intr.v.

quick-tem·pered (kwĭk-témpərd) adj. Easily aroused to anger.

quick time n. A military marching pace of 120 steps per minute.

quick-wit·ted (kwĭk-wĭttid) adj. Showing mental alertness or agility: a quick-witted reply. See Synonyms at **shrewd, intelligent.** —**quick-wit·ted·ly** adv. —**quick-wit·ted·ness** n.

quid¹ (kwĭd) n., pl. **quid** or rare **quids.** British Informal. A pound sterling. —**quids** in. Informal. In a good or advantageous position, especially for making money; in the black. [Probably from Latin quid, something, perhaps alluding to QUID PRO QUO; compare French quibus, "wherewithal".]

quid² n. A cut of something to be chewed, such as tobacco. [Dialect variant of CUD.]

quid·di·ty (kwĭddəti) n., pl. **-ties. 1.** The real nature of a thing; the essence. **2.** A hairsplitting distinction; a quibble. [Medieval Latin quidditās, from Latin quid, what, something, anything.]

quid·nunc (kwĭd-nungk) n. Archaic. A busybody; a gossip. [Latin quid nunc?, "What now?".]

quid pro quo (kwĭd prō kwō) n., pl. **quid pro quos.** An equal exchange or substitution. [Latin, "something for something".]

qui·es·cent (kwī-éss'nt) adj. **1.** Inactive or still; dormant. **2.** Medicine. Designating a disease that is in an inactive or undetectable phase. —See Synonyms at **latent.** [Latin quiēscēns (stem quiēscent-), present participle of quiēscere, to be QUIET.] —**qui·es·cence** n. —**qui·es·cent·ly** adv.

qui·et (kwī-ət) adj. **-eter, -etest. 1.** Making no noise; silent. **2.** Free of noise; hushed. **3.** Calm and unmoving; still. **4.** Free from disturbance and agitation; untroubled. **5.** Restful; soothing. **6.** Characterised by tranquillity; serene; peaceful. **7.** Not showy or brash; restrained; unobtrusive. **8.** Private; unnoticed: a quiet word; quiet anger. —**keep quiet about.** To let no one know about; say nothing about. —See Synonyms at **calm, still.** ~n. The quality or condition of being quiet; silence; tranquillity; repose. —**on the quiet.** Secretly; surreptitiously. ~v. **quieted, -eting, -ets.** —tr. To quieten. —intr. To be quietened. [Middle English, from Old French, from Latin quiētus, from the past participle of quiēscere, to be quiet, be at rest, from quiēs, quiet.] —**qui·et·ly** adv. —**qui·et·ness** n.

qui·et·en (kwī-ət'n) v. **-ened, -ening, -ens.** —tr. **1.** To cause to become silent or at rest; soothe or silence. **2.** To calm or allay (fears, for example). —intr. To become quiet. Usually used with down: The child had been crying but soon quietened down. —See Synonyms at **pacify.** [QUIET + -EN.] —**qui·et·en·er** n.

qui·et·ism (kwī-ət-ĭz'm) n. **1.** A form of Christian mysticism requiring passive contemplation and the joyful surrender of the will. **2.** A state of quietness and passivity. —**qui·et·ist** adj. & n. —**qui·et·is·tic** (-ĭstik) adj. —**qui·et·is·tic·al·ly** adv.

quiet sun n. Astronomy. The Sun at a time when there is very little sunspot activity.

qui·e·tude (kwī-i-tewd, -ə- ‖ -tōōd) n. A condition of tranquillity. [Medieval Latin quiētūdō, from Latin quiētus, QUIET.]

qui·e·tus (kwī-áy-təss, -ée-) n. **1.** Something that serves to suppress, check, or eliminate. **2.** Release from life; death. **3.** Anything that kills or eliminates; a deathblow. **4.** A final discharge, as of a duty or debt. [Medieval Latin quiētus (est), "(he is) discharged", from Latin quiētus, at rest, released, QUIET.]

quiff (kwĭf) n. British. **1.** A tuft of hair brushed up to a peak over the forehead and sometimes lacquered. **2.** A strand or curl of hair that falls on the forehead. [20th century; akin to coif.]

quill (kwĭl) n. **1.** The hollow, stemlike main shaft of a feather. Also called "calamus". **2.** Any of the larger wing or tail feathers of a bird. Also called "quill feather". **3.** A writing pen made from such a feather. Also called "quill pen". **4.** A plectrum for a stringed musical instrument of the clavichord type. **5.** A toothpick made from the stem of a feather. **6.** Any of the sharp hollow spines of a

porcupine or hedgehog. **7.** A musical pipe having a hollow stem. **8.** A spindle or bobbin, originally a length of reed or cane, around which yarn is wound in weaving. **9.** A small roll of dried bark, especially cinnamon. **10.** In machinery, a hollow shaft that rotates on a solid shaft when gears are engaged. ~v. **quilled, quilling, quills.** —intr. To wind thread or yarn onto a quill. —tr. To make or press small ridges in (fabric). [Middle English quil(le), akin to Middle Low German quiele†.]

Quil·ler-Couch (kwĭllar-kōōch), **Sir Arthur (Thomas)** (1863–1944). British critic and writer, best known as the editor of the Oxford Book of English Verse (1900) (under the pen-name "Q").

quil·let (kwĭllit) n. Archaic. A verbal nicety or subtlety; a quibble. [Perhaps short for obsolete quillity, variant of QUIDDITY.]

quilt (kwĭlt) n. **1.** A bed coverlet or blanket made of two layers of fabric with a layer of cotton, wool, feathers, or down in between, all stitched firmly together, usually in a crisscross design. **2.** A duvet. **3.** Any thick cover of protective material. ~v. **quilted, quilting, quilts.** —tr. **1.** To make into a quilt by stitching together (layers of fabric). **2.** To make like a quilt: quilt a skirt. **3.** To pad and stitch ornamentally. **4.** To sew up between layers of fabric. —intr. **1.** To make a quilt. **2.** To do quilted needlework. [Middle English quilte, from Old French cuilte, from Latin culcita, sack filled with feathers, mattress.]

quilt·ing (kwĭlting) n. **1.** Material used to make quilts. **2.** Quilted material.

quim (kwĭm) n. British Vulgar Slang. A woman's genitals. [16th century : origin obscure.]

Quim·per (kaɴ-paír, kám-). Administrative centre of the Finistère département in Brittany, northwestern France. It is famous for its pottery and fine Gothic cathedral.

quin (kwĭn) n. British. A **quintuplet** (see).

quin– comb. form. Indicates cinchona or cinchona bark; for example, quinidine. [Spanish quina, cinchona bark, short for quinaquina, perhaps from Quechua.]

qui·na·ry (kwīnəri) adj. **1.** Of, pertaining to, or based on the number five. **2.** Consisting of five things or parts. [Latin quinārius, from quinī, five each, distributive of quinque, five.]

qui·nate (kwīnayt) adj. Arranged in groups of five: quinate leaflets. [Latin quinī, five each.]

quince (kwĭnss) n. **1.** A tree, Cydonia oblonga, native to Asia, having white flowers and apple-like fruit. **2.** The aromatic, many-seeded fruit of this tree, edible only when cooked. [Middle English quynce, plural of quyn, quince, from Old French c(o)oin, from Latin cotōneum, cydōneum (mālum), "Cydonian (apple)", from Greek kudōnion, from Kudōnia, Cydonia, ancient capital of Crete.]

quin·cen·te·nar·y (kwĭn-sen-téen-əri, -tén-) n., pl. **-naries.** Also chiefly U.S. **quin·cen·ten·ni·al** (-ténni-əl). **1.** A five-hundredth anniversary. **2.** A celebration of this. [Irregularly from Latin quinque, five + CENTENARY.] —**quin·cen·te·nar·y, quin·cen·ten·ni·al** adj.

quin·cunx (kwĭn-kungks) n. An arrangement of five objects, with one at each corner of a rectangle and one at the centre, as in the five on a dice. [Latin quincunx (stem quincunc-), five twelfths of a Roman coin (as denoted by five dots or dashes so arranged) : quinque, five + uncia, a twelfth part.] —**quin·cun·cial** (kwĭn-kúnsh'l) adj. —**quin·cun·cial·ly** adv.

quin·dec·a·gon (kwĭn-déckə-gən, kwĭn- ‖ -gon) n. Geometry. A polygon having 15 sides and 15 angles. [Irregularly from Latin quindecim, fifteen + -GON.] —**quin·dec·a·gon·al** (-di-kággən'l) adj. —**quin·dec·a·gon·al·ly** adv.

quin·de·cen·ni·al (kwĭn-di-sénni-əl, -de-) adj. **1.** Occurring once every 15 years. **2.** Lasting 15 years. [Latin quindecim, fifteen + annus, year.] —**quin·de·cen·ni·al·ly** adv.

quin·i·dine (kwĭnni-deen) n. A colourless crystalline alkaloid, $C_{20}H_{24}N_2O_2$, resembling quinine and used in treating certain heart disorders and malaria. [QUIN- + -ID(E) + -INE.]

qui·nine (kwi-néen, kwĭnneen ‖ U.S. kwī-nīn, kwi-) n. **1.** A bitter, colourless, amorphous powder or crystalline alkaloid, $C_{20}H_{24}N_2O_2 \cdot 3H_2O$, derived from certain cinchona barks and used to treat malaria, though now largely replaced by less toxic drugs. **2.** Any of various compounds or salts of this alkaloid. [QUIN- + -INE.]

quin·oid (kwĭn-oyd) n. Chemistry. A substance resembling quinone in structure or physical properties. [QUIN(ONE) + -OID.]

qui·noi·dine (kwi-nóy-deen, -din) n. A brownish-black mixture of alkaloids remaining after extraction of crystalline alkaloids from cinchona bark, used as a quinine substitute. [QUIN- + -OID + -INE.]

quin·o·line (kwĭnnə-leen, -lin) n. An aromatic organic base, C_9H_7N, having a pungent tarlike odour, synthesised or obtained from coal tar, and used as a preservative and in making antiseptics and dyes. [QUIN- + -OL + -INE.]

qui·none (kwi-nṓn, kwĭn-ōn) n. Chemistry. Any of a class of aromatic compounds found widely in plants; especially, the yellow crystalline form $C_6H_4O_2$, used in making dyes, in tanning hides, and in photography. [QUIN- + -ONE.]

quin·o·noid (kwĭnnə-noyd, kwi-nṓn-oyd) adj. Chemistry. Of, containing, or resembling quinone, in structure or properties.

quin·qua·ge·nar·i·an (kwĭng-kwə-ji-naír-i-ən) n. A person fifty years old, or between fifty and sixty years of age. ~adj. Of or characteristic of a fifty-year-old. [Latin quinquāgēnārius, consisting of fifty, from quinquāgēnī, fifty each, from quinquāginta, fifty.]

Quin·qua·ges·i·ma (kwĭng-kwə-jéssimə) n. The Sunday before the beginning of Lent; the first day of Shrovetide. Also called "Quinquagesima Sunday". [Medieval Latin *quinquāgēsima*, from Latin, fiftieth, from *quinquāginta*, fifty.]

quinque– *comb. form.* Indicates five; for example, **quinquefoliate.** [Latin *quinque*, five.]

quin·que·fo·li·ate (kwíng-kwi-fṓli-ət, -ĭt, -ayt) *adj. Botany.* Having five leaves, leaflets, or leaflike parts. [QUINQUE- + Latin *folium*, leaf, FOIL.]

quin·quen·ni·al (kwing-kwénni-əl, kwĭn-) *adj.* 1. Happening once every five years. 2. Lasting for five years. —*n.* 1. A fifth anniversary. 2. A period of five years. —**quin·quen·ni·al·ly** *adv.*

quin·quen·ni·um (kwing-kwénni-əm, kwĭn-) *n., pl.* -**ums** or -**quennia.** A period of five years. [Latin : QUINQUE- + *annus*, year.]

quin·que·va·lent (kwing-kwi-váylənt) *adj. Chemistry.* Pentavalent. —**quin·que·va·lence** *n.*

quin·sy (kwínzi) *n.* Acute inflammation of the tonsils and surrounding tissue, leading to the formation of an abscess. [Middle English *quinesye*, from Old French *quinencie*, from Medieval Latin *quinancia*, from Greek *kunanchē*, dog quinsy, sore throat : *kuōn*, hound + *ankhein*, to strangle.]

quint (kĭnt, kwĭnt) *n.* In piquet and similar games, a sequence of five cards of the same suit in one hand. [French, from Latin *quinta*, feminine of *quintus*, fifth.]

quin·tain (kwíntĭn) *n.* 1. A post, or a target mounted on a post, to be tilted at especially by horsemen. 2. The exercise of tilting. [Middle English *quintaine*, from Old French, from Latin *quintāna via*, the fifth street in a Roman camp, supposedly used for military exercises, from *quintānus*, fifth in rank, from *quintus*, fifth.]

quin·tal (kwínt'l) *n. Abbr.* **q., ql.** 1. A unit of mass in the metric system equal to 100 kilograms (220 pounds). 2. A short hundredweight, 100 pounds (45.36 kilograms). [Middle English, from Old French, from Medieval Latin *quintāle*, from Arabic *qintār*, KANTAR.]

quin·tar (keen-tár) *n.* A monetary unit, equal to $^1/_{100}$ of the lek of Albania. [Albanian *qintar*.]

quinte (kaNt) *n.* In fencing, the fifth in a series of eight parrying positions. [Old French, fifth.]

quin·tes·sence (kwin-téss'nss) *n.* 1. The pure, highly concentrated essence of something. 2. The purest or most typical example; the embodiment: *Her manners were the quintessence of courtesy.* 3. In ancient and medieval philosophy, the fifth and highest essence (after the four elements of earth, air, fire, and water), thought to be the substance of the heavenly bodies and latent in all things. [Middle English, from Old French *quinte essence*, from Medieval Latin *quinta essentia* (translation of Greek *pemptē ousia*, fifth essence) : Latin *quinta*, feminine of *quintus*, fifth + *essentia*, ESSENCE.]

quin·tes·sen·tial (kwĭnti-sénsh'l) *adj.* 1. Being most typical; expressing the essence of the thing or person specified. 2. Having the nature of a quintessence; pure and concentrated in nature. —**quin·tes·sen·tial·ly** *adv.*

quin·tet, quin·tette (kwin-tét, kwĭn-) *n.* 1. A group of five persons or things; especially, a group of five musicians. 2. A musical composition for five voices or instruments. [French *quintette*, from Italian *quintetto*, from *quinto*, fifth, from Latin *quintus*.]

quin·tile (kwín-tīl) *n.* 1. *Astrology.* The aspect of planets distant from each other by 72° or a fifth of the zodiac. 2. *Statistics.* The portion of a frequency distribution containing a fifth of the total sample. [Latin *quintus*, fifth.]

quin·til·li·on (kwin-tíl-yən, kwĭn-) *n.* 1. *British.* The cardinal number represented by 1 followed by 30 zeros, usually written 10^{30}. 2. The cardinal number represented by 1 followed by 18 zeros, usually written 10^{18}, equivalent to the British trillion. [Latin *quintus*, fifth + (M)ILLION.] —**quin·til·li·on** *adj.* —**quin·til·li·onth** *n.* & *adj.*

quin·tu·ple (kwín-tew-p'l, kwĭn-téw- ‖ -tṓo-, -tṓo-, *also* -tupp'l) *adj.* 1. Consisting of or having five parts, members, or copies. 2. Multiplied by five; five times as much, as many, or as large. —*n.* A fivefold amount or number. —*v.* **quintupled, -pling, -ples.** —*tr.* To multiply or increase by five. —*intr.* To be multiplied fivefold. [French, from Late Latin *quintuplex* : Latin *quintus*, fifth + -*plex*, -fold.]

quin·tu·plet (kwín-tew-plit, -plĕt; kwin-téw- ‖ -túpplət) *n.* 1. A group or combination of five associated by common properties or behaviour. 2. Any of five offspring born in a single birth. In this sense, also called "quin". [From QUINTUPLE.]

quin·tu·pli·cate (kwin-téw-pli-kət, -kĭt, -kayt ‖ -tṓo-) *adj.* 1. Multiplied by five; fivefold. 2. Being the fifth of a set of copies. —*n.* 1. Any of a set of five copies. 2. A set of five copies. —*tr.v.* (-kayt) **quintuplicated, -cating, -cates.** 1. To make five copies of. 2. To multiply by five. [Late Latin *quintuplicātus*, from *quintuplicāre*, to make fivefold, from *quintuplex*, QUINTUPLE.]

quip (kwĭp) *n.* 1. A brief, witty remark delivered offhand. 2. A cleverly sarcastic remark; a verbal thrust; a gibe. 3. A quibble. —See Synonyms at **joke.** —*intr.v.* **quipped, quipping, quips.** To make a quip or quips. [Earlier *quippy*, perhaps from Latin *quippe*, indeed, certainly (often used ironically), from *quid*, what.]

qui·pu, quip·pu (kée-pṓo) *n.* A device consisting of variously coloured and knotted cords attached to a base rope, used by the Incas of Peru for calculating and recording. [Spanish *quipo*, from Quechua *quipu*.]

quire¹ (kwīr) *n. Abbr.* **q., qr.** 1. A set of 24 or sometimes 25 sheets of paper of the same size and stock; $^1/_{20}$ ream. 2. 4 sheets of paper folded to form 8 leaves, or 16 pages. 3. A set of all leaves required for a book before binding. —*tr.v.* **quired, quiring, quires.** To fold or arrange in quires. [Middle English, from Old French *quaer*, set of four sheets, from Vulgar Latin *quaternum* (unattested), from Latin *quaternī*, set of four, from *quater*, four.]

quire² *n. Archaic.* A **choir** (see).

Quir·i·nal (kwírrĭn'l). One of Rome's seven hills, the site of the Quirinal Palace, the residence of the head of state of Italy since 1870.

quirk (kwurk) *n.* 1. A peculiarity of behaviour; an oddity; a whim. 2. An unpredictable or unaccountable act or event: *a quirk of fate.* 3. a. A sudden sharp turn or twist. b. A flourish in handwriting, drawing, or music. 4. An equivocation; a quibble; a subterfuge. 5. A quip. 6. *Architecture.* A lengthways groove on a moulding. —See Synonyms at **eccentricity.** [16th century : origin obscure.] —**quirk·i·ly** *adv.* —**quirk·i·ness** *n.* —**quirk·y** *adj.*

quis·ling (kwízling) *n.* A traitor who serves as the puppet of the enemy occupying his country. [After Vidkun QUISLING.]

Quis·ling (kwiz-ling; *Norwegian* kvíss-), **Vidkun,** (Abraham Lauritz Jonsson) (1887–1945). Norwegian politician. Forming the fascist National Union Party (1933), he went on to become minister president (1942) under the Nazi occupation. Following the Axis surrender (1945), he was tried and executed for treason.

quit (kwĭt) *v.* **quitted** or *chiefly U.S.* **quit, quitting, quits.** —*tr.* 1. To end one's involvement with; leave abruptly: *"You and I are on the point of quitting the theatre of our exploits"* (Lord Nelson). 2. To give up; relinquish; put aside. 3. To leave; depart from 4. *Chiefly U.S.* To discontinue; cease; stop. 5. *Archaic.* To rid oneself of by paying: *quit a debt.* 6. *Archaic.* To conduct or acquit (oneself). —*intr.* 1. To cease to perform. 2. To give up as in defeat; stop. 3. To leave rented premises: *notice to quit.* 4. To leave a job. —*adj.* Absolved of a duty or obligation; free; released. Often used with *of.* [Middle English *quiten*, to set free, release, from Old French *quiter*, from Medieval Latin *quiētāre*, to set free, quit, discharge, from Latin *quiētus*, freed, QUIET.]

Usage: Quitted and quit are both used as past tense and past participle forms of this verb. *Quit* is standard in American English (*She quit her job*). In British usage, *quitted* is often used, but is slowly being replaced by *quit*, which is nowadays the more common variant. Many British speakers dislike the use of *quit* in the general sense of "stop" (*She has quit smoking*) because of its American overtones and would never allow it in formal contexts.

quit·claim (kwĭt-klaym) *n. Law.* The transfer of a title, right, or claim to another. —*tr.v.* **quitclaimed, -claiming, -claims.** To renounce all claim to (a possession or right). [Middle English *quiteclaimen* (verb), from Old French *quiteclamer*, "to declare free" : *quite*, free, QUIT + *clamer*, to CLAIM.]

quite (kwīt) *adv.* 1. To the greatest extent; entirely; completely: *quite alone; not quite finished.* 2. Actually; truly; really: *quite different.* 3. a. Somewhat; fairly: *quite easy.* b. To only a limited degree: *I quite liked it, but felt it could have been better.* —**quite a** or **an.** 1. Considerable. Used to qualify an indefinite noun: *quite a few; quite a gap.* 2. *Informal.* Exceptional; extraordinary; impressive: *quite an establishment.* —**quite something.** *Informal.* Something extraordinary or impressive. —*interj.* Also **quite so.** Used to indicate agreement. [Middle English, from adjective, "free", rid of, from Old French, from Latin *quiētus*, freed, QUIET.]

Usage: Many people have objected to the "weaker" senses of *quite*, where the word means "rather, somewhat" (*It's quite warm today*), preferring to restrict it to the more positive senses of "entirely" (*quite certain*) and "actually" (*quite ill*). However, the weaker sense is very widely used, especially in informal speech. Nowadays, it is felt to be somewhat pedantic to criticise a phrase such as *quite all right* as containing a redundancy, or a phrase such as *quite similar* as containing a contradiction, and this kind of use will often be heard even in formal speech. *Quite a(n)*, indicating indefinite quantity, is generally acceptable (*Quite a large number stayed away*); but when indicating extraordinary quality (*quite a show*), it is informal.

Qui·to (kéetō). Capital city of Ecuador and capital of Pichincha province. It is an educational, cultural, manufacturing, and political centre and was the northern capital of the Inca empire.

quit·rent (kwĭt-rent) *n.* Formerly, a rent paid by a freeman in lieu of services required of him by feudal custom.

quits (kwĭts) *adj.* Even with someone by payment or requital. —**call it quits.** To agree that something, such as a dispute or debt, is settled on both sides. [Middle English, "discharged", "paid up", from Medieval Latin *quittus*, QUIT.]

quit·tance (kwĭtt'nss) *n.* 1. Release from a debt, obligation, or penalty. 2. A document or receipt certifying such a release. 3. Something given as requital or recompense; repayment. [Middle English *quitance*, from Old French, from *quiter*, to free, discharge a debt, QUIT.]

quit·ter (kwĭttər) *n. Informal.* One who gives up easily.

quit·tor (kwĭttər) *n.* An inflammation of the hoof cartilage of horses and other solid-hoofed animals, characterised by degeneration of hoof tissue, formation of a slough, and fistulous sores. [Middle English *quiture*, perhaps from Old French, decoction, from Latin *coctūra*, from *coquere* (past participle *coctus*), to cook.]

quiv·er¹ (kwívvər) *v.* **-ered, -ering, -ers.** —*intr.* To shake with a slight rapid motion; tremble; vibrate. —*tr.* To cause to quiver. —See Synonyms at **shake.**

~*n.* The act or motion of quivering. [Middle English *quiveren,* from QUIVER (nimble).]

quiver² *n.* **1.** A portable case for arrows. **2.** A case full of arrows. [Middle English, from Anglo-French *quiveir* (unattested), Old French *cuivre,* from West Germanic.]

quiver³ *adj. Obsolete.* Nimble; brisk. [Middle English *quiver,* Old English *cwifer-.*]

quiv·er·ful (kwívvər-fŏŏl) *n., pl.* **-fuls. 1.** The amount held by a quiver. **2.** A large number; a sizeable quantity. Often used in the phrase *a quiverful of children.*

qui vive (kēe vēev) *n.* Alert watchfulness or vigilance. Used chiefly in the phrase *on the qui vive.* [French, "(Long) live who?" (a sentinel's challenge demanding to know the allegiance of the person approaching).]

quix·ot·ic (kwik-sóttik) *adj.* Also **quix·ot·i·cal** (-'l). Caught up in the romance of noble deeds or unreachable ideals; romantic, absent-minded, and unpractical. [After DON QUIXOTE.] —**quix·ot·i·cal·ly** *adv.* —**quix·o·tism** (kwíksət-iz'm) *n.*

quiz (kwiz) *tr.v.* **quizzed, quizzing, quizzes. 1.** To question closely or repeatedly; interrogate. **2.** To test the knowledge of by posing questions. **3.** *Archaic.* To poke fun at; mock. **4.** *Archaic.* To look at questioningly or mockingly, especially through a quizzing glass. ~*n., pl.* **quizzes. 1.** A short oral or written test of knowledge. **2.** A competition in which the knowledge of the contestants is tested by questioning, especially as an entertainment, as on a radio or television programme. Also used adjectivally: *a quiz show.* **3.** A questioning or inquiry. **4.** *Archaic.* **a.** A practical joke. **b.** An eccentric person. [18th century : origin obscure.] —**quiz·zer** *n.*

quiz·zi·cal (kwízzik'l) *adj.* **1.** Suggesting humorous or ironical puzzlement; questioning. **2.** Teasing; mocking: *"his face wore a somewhat quizzical, almost impertinent air"* (Lawrence Durrell). —**quiz·zi·cal·i·ty** (kwízzi-kál-əti) *n.* —**quiz·zi·cal·ly** *adv.*

quiz·zing glass (kwízzing) *n.* A small monocle.

Qum. See Qom.

Qum·rān (kōōm-raán, -rán). Village on the northwest coast of the Dead Sea in the part of Jordan occupied by Israel in 1967, thought to be the city of Salt mentioned in Joshua 15:62. It includes Khirbat Qumrān, ruins left by a community of Essenes, a Jewish sect, which flourished there from the mid-second century B.C. until A.D. 68, when it was finally destroyed by Vespasian's army. Remains of the sect's library, the Dead Sea Scrolls, were first found by local shepherds in 1947 in caves at Qumrān.

quod (kwod) *n. British Slang.* Prison. [17th century : origin obscure.]

quod·li·bet (kwódli-bet) *n.* **1.** A theological or philosophical argument, especially done as an exercise. **2.** A musical medley. [Middle English, scholastic debate, disputation, from Medieval Latin *quodlibetum,* from Latin *quodlibet,* what you please : *quod,* what + *libet,* it pleases, from *libēre,* to please.]

quoin, coign (koyn, kwoyn) *n.* **1. a.** An exterior angle of a wall or other masonry. **b.** A stone serving to form such an angle; a cornerstone. **2.** A keystone. **3.** *Printing.* A wedge-shaped block used to lock type in a chase. **4.** A wedge used to raise the level of a gun. ~*tr.v.* **quoined, quoining, quoins.** To provide, secure, or raise with a quoin or quoins. [Variant of COIN (corner).]

quoit (koyt, kwoyt) *n.* A flat ring of iron or rope used in the game of quoits. ~*tr.v.* **quoited, quoiting, quoits.** To throw in the manner of a quoit. [Middle English *coite†.*]

quoits (koyts, kwoyts) *n. Used with a singular verb.* A game in which quoits are thrown at a stake, with points awarded for encircling it.

quok·ka (kwóckə) *n.* A small rare wallaby, *Setonix brachyurus,* occurring mainly on the islands off the coast of Western Australia. [From a native Australian language.]

quon·dam (kwón-dam, -dəm) *adj.* That once was; former: *a quondam friend.* [Latin, formerly, from *quom,* when.]

quo·rate (kwáw-rayt, -rət, -rit ‖ kwŏ-) *adj.* Constituting or having a quorum. [QUOR(UM) + -ATE.]

quo·rum (kwáw-rəm ‖ kwŏ-) *n.* The minimum number of officers or members of a committee, organisation, or assembly, usually a majority, who must be present for the valid transaction of business. [Middle English, a quorum of justices of the peace, from Latin texts of commissions reading, for example, *quorum vos . . . duos esse volumus,* "of whom we wish that you be . . . two", genitive plural of *quī,* who.]

quot. quotation.

quo·ta (kwŏtə) *n.* **1.** A share, as of goods to be distributed or work to be done, assigned to a group or to each member of a group; an allotment. **2.** A stipulated number, proportion, or amount, as of persons who may be admitted or of goods that may be imported: *import quotas.* [Medieval Latin, from Latin, feminine of *quotus,* of what number. See **quote.**]

quot·a·ble (kwŏt-əb'l) *adj.* Suitable for or worth quoting. —**quot·a·bil·i·ty** (-ə-bílləti) *n.* —**quot·a·bly** *adv.*

quo·ta·tion (kwŏ-táysh'n, kwə-) *n. Abbr.* **quot. 1.** The act of quoting. **2.** A passage that is quoted. **3.** An estimate of costs or prices: *She gave me a quotation for painting the house.* **4.** *Commerce.* **a.** The quoting of current prices and bids for shares and goods. **b.** The prices or bids cited. **5.** Registration given by the Stock Exchange to a company, allowing the company's shares and stock to be dealt in on the Stock Exchange. —**quo·ta·tion·al** *adj.* —**quo·ta·tion·al·ly** *adv.*

quotation mark *n.* Either of a pair of punctuation marks used to mark the beginning and end of a passage attributed to another and repeated word for word. They appear in the form (" ") (double quotation marks) or (' ') (single quotation marks). Also called "inverted comma", informally "quote".

quote (kwŏt) *v.* **quoted, quoting, quotes.** —*tr.* **1.** To repeat or copy the words of (another), usually with acknowledgement of the source. **2.** To cite or refer to for illustration or proof. **3.** To state (a price) for securities, goods, or services. —*intr.* **1.** To give a quotation, as from a book. **2.** To be registered on the Stock Exchange, as a company whose shares and stocks may be dealt in. ~*n. Informal.* **1.** A quotation. **2.** A quotation mark. [Middle English, to mark (chapters, references, or the like) with numbers, from Medieval Latin *quotāre,* from Latin *quotus,* of what number, from *quot,* how many.] —**quot·er** *n.*

quoth (kwŏth) *tr.v. Archaic.* Uttered; said. Used only in the first and third persons, with the subject following: *"Quoth the raven 'Nevermore!'."* (Edgar Allen Poe). [Middle English *quoth,* Old English *cwæth,* he said, from *cwethan,* to say.]

quo·tha (kwŏthə) *interj. Archaic.* Used to express surprise or sarcasm, after quoting the word or phrase of another. [Contraction of *quoth he.*]

quo·tid·i·an (kwŏ-tíddi-ən, kwo-) *adj.* **1.** Recurring daily. Said particularly of attacks of malaria. **2.** Everyday; commonplace. [Middle English *cotidien,* from Old French, from Latin *quotīdiānus,* from *quotīdiē,* each day : *quot,* how many, as many as + *diēs,* day.]

quo·tient (kwŏsh'nt) *n.* **1.** The quantity resulting from division of one quantity by another; the number of times one quantity must be multiplied to make up another. **2.** *Informal.* The rate or proportion of some specified quality: *a high anxiety quotient amongst those with dangerous occupations.* [Middle English *quocient,* from Latin *quotiēns,* how many times, from *quot,* how many.]

Qur'an. Variant of **Koran.**

q.v. Which see. Used to indicate a cross-reference. [Latin, *quod vide.*]

Q value *n. Physics.* The **Q factor** (see).

Qwa·qwa In South Africa, the tribal homeland for the South Sotho people.

r, R (ar) *n., pl.* **r's** or *rare* **rs, Rs** or **R's. 1.** The 18th letter of the modern English alphabet. **2.** Any of the speech sounds it represents.
r, R, r-, R. *Note:* As an abbreviation or symbol, *r* may be a small or a capital letter, with or without a full stop. Established forms or those generally preferred precede the definition. When no form is given, all four forms are in general use in that sense. **1.** R *Chemistry.* gas constant. **2. R.** rabbi. **3.** R *Chemistry.* radical. **4.** r, R radius. **5.** r., R. railway. **6.** R rand. **7.** r. range. **8.** r. rare. **9.** R, R. Réaumur (scale). **10.** R. rector. **11.** R. regiment. **12.** R. Regina. **13.** R., r. registered (trademark). **14.** R. regius. **15.** R. Republican (party) (in the United States). **16.** r, R resistance (electricity). **17.** R *Ecclesiastical.* response. **18.** r. retired. **19.** R. Rex. **20.** r., R. right. **21.** r., R. river. **22.** r., R. road. **23.** r. rod (unit of length). **24.** R röntgen (unit of radiation). **25.** R rook (chess). **26.** r., R. rouble. **27.** R. royal. **28.** r. rubber (card games). **29.** r, r. *Sports.* run. **30.** r., R. rupee. **31.** Rydberg constant. **32.** The 18th in a series; 17th when *J* is omitted.
Ra (ra). Also **Re** (ray). The sun god, the supreme deity of the ancient Egyptians, represented as a man usually with the head of a hawk crowned with a solar disc and uraeus. [Egyptian *ra'*.]
Ra The symbol for the element radium.
R.A. 1. rear admiral. **2.** *Astronomy.* right ascension. **3.** Royal Academy; Royal Academician. **4.** Royal Artillery.
R.A.A.F. Royal Australian Air Force.
Ra·bat (rə-baát). Capital of Morocco, on the Atlantic Ocean at the mouth of the Bou Regreg river. There have been settlements here since ancient times, and it was a Muslim fortress (*c.* A.D. 700).
rabato. Variant of **rebato.**
Ra·baul (raa-bówl, rə-). Port in the northeast of the island of New Britain, Papua New Guinea. The town is surrounded by active volcanoes and was severely damaged by eruptions in 1937.
Rabbah Ammon, Rabbath Ammon. See **Amman.**
rab·bet (rábbit) *n.* Also **re·bate** (réé-bayt, rábbit). **1.** A cut or groove along or near the edge of a piece of wood that allows another piece to fit into it to form a joint. **2.** A joint made in this manner.
~*v.* **rabbeted, -beting, -bets.** *—tr.* **1.** To cut a rabbet in. **2.** To join by a rabbet. *—intr.* To be joined by a rabbet. [Middle English *rabet,* from Old French *rabat,* a beating down, from *rabattre,* to beat down, reduce : *re-,* back + *abattre,* to beat down : *a-,* from Latin *ad-,* to + *battre,* to beat, from Latin *battuere.*]
rab·bi (ráb-ī) *n., pl.* **-bis.** Also **rab·bin** (rábbin). **1.** *Abbr.* **R.** The ordained spiritual leader of a Jewish congregation. **2.** Formerly, a person authorised to interpret Jewish law. [Hebrew *rabbī,* my master : *rabh,* great one + *-ī,* my.]
rab·bin·ate (rábbin-ayt) *n.* The office or function of a rabbi.
Rab·bin·ic (ra-bínnik, rə-) *n.* The Hebrew language as used in the learned writings of the rabbis of the medieval period.
rab·bin·i·cal (ra-bínnik'l, rə-) *adj.* Also **rab·bin·ic** (-bínnik). Of, pertaining to, or characteristic of rabbis, or their views, learning, writings, or language. **—rab·bin·i·cal·ly** *adv.*
rab·bin·ism (rábbin-iz'm) *n.* Rabbinical teachings and traditions.
rab·bin·ist (rábbin-ist) *n.* A strict observer of the Talmud and of rabbinical traditions. **—rab·bin·is·tic** (-ístik).
rab·bit (rábbit) *n., pl.* **-bits** or collectively **rabbit. 1.** Any of various long-eared, short-tailed, burrowing mammals of the family Leporidae, such as the commonly domesticated Old World species *Oryctolagus cuniculus.* **2.** *U.S.* Loosely, a hare. **3.** The fur of a rabbit or hare. **4.** *Informal.* One who plays a particular game or sport badly.
~*intr.v.* **rabbited, -biting, -bits. 1.** To hunt rabbits. **2.** *Slang.* To talk at length, usually trivially and often rapidly. Often used with *on.* [Middle English *rabet,* probably from Old French; akin to Walloon *robete,* diminutive of Flemish *robbe†.*] **—rab·bit·er** *n.*
rabbit fever *n.* A disease, tularaemia *(see).*
rab·bit·fish (rábbit-fish) *n., pl.* **-fishes** or collectivly **rabbitfish. 1.** A fish, the **chimaera** *(see);* especially, the species *Chimaera monstrosa,* of European seas. Also called "ratfish". **2.** Any fish of the family Siganidae, of tropical Indo-Pacific waters.
rabbit punch *n.* A chopping blow to the back of the neck.
rab·ble¹ (ráb'l) *n.* **1.** A tumultuous mob. **2.** A group of persons regarded with contempt: *a rabble of poor aristocrats.* **3.** The lower classes. Used derogatorily, preceded by *the.* [Middle English *rabble†.*]
rabble² *n.* Also **rab·bler** (rábblər). *Metallurgy.* **1.** An iron bar with one end bent like a rake, used to stir and skim molten iron in puddling. **2.** Any of various similar tools or mechanically operated devices used in roasting or refining furnaces.
~*tr.v.* **rabbled, -bling, -bles.** *Metallurgy.* To stir or skim (molten iron) with a rabble. [French *râble,* fire shovel, from Old French *roable,* from Medieval Latin *rotabulum,* from Latin *rutābulum,* from *ruere†* (past participle *rutus*), to rake up.]
rab·ble-rous·er (ráb'l-rowzər) *n.* One who incites a crowd to action or violence; a demagogue.
Ra·be·lais (rábbə-lay, ráb-ǁ-láy), **François** (*c.* 1494–1553). French humanist and satirist. A Franciscan, then a Benedictine monk, he studied medicine at Montpellier. His satirical tales attacked medi-

eval scholasticism and superstition: the most popular are *Pantagruel* (1532) and *Gargantua* (1534). Despite his religious sincerity, his works are full of high-spirited vulgarity.
Rab·e·lai·si·an (rábbə-láyzi-ən ǁ *U.S. also* -láyzh'n) *adj.* Pertaining to or characteristic of the works of Rabelais.
ra·bi (rúbbi) *n.* **1.** In India and Pakistan, a crop that is harvested at the beginning of spring. Compare **kharif. 2.** In north India, the cool dry or winter season. [Urdu, spring crop, from Arabic *rabī',* spring.]
Ra·bi (rúbbi, ráabi) *n.* Also **Ra·bi·a** (rə-béé-ə). Either the third or the fourth month of the Muslim calendar. [Arabic *rabī',* spring.]
Ra·bi (ráabi), **Isidor Isaac** (1898–1988). Austrian-born U.S. physicist. He is particularly noted for his work on magnetic forces within the atom. He was awarded the Nobel prize for physics (1944).
rab·id (rábbid, *also* ráybid) *adj.* **1.** Of or afflicted with rabies. **2.** Fanatical; extreme. **3.** Raging; uncontrollable: *rabid thirst.* [Latin *rabidus,* raving, from *rabere,* to rave.] **—ra·bid·i·ty** (rə-bíddəti, ra-, ráy-), **rab·id·ness** *n.* **—rab·id·ly** *adv.*
ra·bies (ráy-beez, -biz, -bi-eez) *n.* An acute, infectious, often fatal viral disease of most warm-blooded animals, especially wolves, cats, and dogs, that is transmitted to humans by the bite of infected animals. It affects the central nervous system and is characterised by convulsions and aversion to water. Also called "hydrophobia". [New Latin, from Latin *rabiēs,* rage, from *rabere,* to rave.] **—ra·bi·et·ic** (ráybi-éttik) *adj.*
Ra·bin (rə-béén, rábin), **Yitzhak** or **Itzhak** (1922–95). Israeli statesman and Labour prime minister (1974–77, 1992–95). An army officer who headed the armed forces during the Six Day War (1967), he signed the 1993 agreement with the PLO granting limited self-rule to Palestinians and in 1994 a peace agreement with Jordan. He was awarded the 1994 Nobel peace prize jointly with Shimon Peres and Yasser Arafat. In 1995 a second peace agreement was signed with the Palestinians and in that year he was assassinated by an Israeli extremist while attending a peace rally.
R.A.C. 1. Royal Armoured Corps. **2.** Royal Automobile Club.
rac·coon, ra·coon (ra-kŏon, rə-) *n., pl.* **-coons** or collectively **raccoon. 1.** A carnivorous North American mammal, *Procyon lotor,* having greyish-brown fur, black, masklike facial markings, and a bushy, black-ringed tail. Also *U.S.* "coon". **2.** The fur of this animal. **3.** Any of various similar or related animals. [Algonquian (Virginia) *aroughcoune, arathkone.*]
raccoon dog *n.* A wild dog, *Nyctereutes procyonoides,* of east Asia, having golden-brown hair and black eye patches like a raccoon.
race¹ (rayss) *n.* **1. a.** A local geographic or global human population distinguished by a more or less distinct group by genetically transmitted physical characteristics. **b.** The division of mankind according to such characteristics: *discrimination on the grounds of race.* **2.** Loosely, any species, especially mankind as a whole: *the human race.* **3.** Any group of people united or classified together on the basis of common history, nationality, or geographical distribution. **4.** A genealogical line; a lineage; a family. **5.** Any group of people having a particular characteristic or profession in common. **6.** *Biology.* **a.** A plant or animal population that differs from others of the same species in one or more hereditary traits; a subspecies. **b.** A breed or strain, as of domestic animals. —See Usage Note at **nation.** [French, group of people, generation, from Italian *razza†.*]
race² *n.* **1. a.** A competition of speed. **b.** *Plural.* A series of such competitions, especially in horse riding, held at a specific time: *winning money at the races.* **2.** Any contest or pursuit of supremacy: *the race for top position.* **3. a.** Steady or rapid onward movement. **b.** *Archaic.* A steady onward movement, course, or span: *the sun's race.* **c.** *Archaic.* A human lifetime. **4. a.** A strong or swift current of water. **b.** The channel of such a current. **c.** An artificial channel built to transport water and utilise its energy. **5.** A groovelike part of a machine in which a moving part slides or rolls; especially, any of the rings holding the balls or rollers in a bearing. Also called "raceway". **6.** *Australian.* A fenced track for sheep or other livestock, especially one leading to a dip. **7.** *Aeronautics.* A **slipstream** *(see).*
~*v.* **raced, racing, races.** *—intr.* **1.** To compete in a contest of speed. **2.** To move rapidly or at top speed. **3.** To run too rapidly because of decreased resistance or a lighter load. Used of engines. *—tr.* **1.** To compete against in a contest of speed. **2.** To cause (an animal or vehicle) to compete in such a contest, especially habitually or professionally. **3.** To cause to move rapidly or at top speed. **4.** To cause (an engine with the gears disengaged, for example) to run too fast. [Middle English *ra(a)s,* from Old Norse *rās.*]
race³ *n.* A root, especially of ginger. [Old French *rais, raiz,* root, from Latin *rādix* (stem *rādīc-*).]
race·card, race card (ráyss-kaard) *n.* A printed list or programme of the races, their times, and their runners, at a race meeting. Also called "card".
race·course (ráyss-kawrss ǁ -kórss) *n.* A course or track laid out for horseracing.
race·horse (ráyss-hawrss) *n.* A horse bred and trained to race.

ra·ceme (rə-seém, ra-, ray-) *n. Botany.* An inflorescence in which stalked flowers are arranged singly along a common main axis with the youngest at the top, as in the lily of the valley. [Latin *racēmus†*, stalk of a cluster of grapes, bunch of berries.]

race meeting *n.* A series of races, usually horse races, held at a particular time or place.

ra·ce·mic (rə-seémik, ra-, ray-, -sémmik) *adj.* Of or designating a chemical mixture containing equal quantities of dextrorotatory and laevorotatory isomers so that it does not have a net optical activity. [French *racémique*, from Latin *racēmus*, RACEME.]

racemic acid *n.* An optically inactive form of tartaric acid, $C_4H_6O_6$· H_2O, that can be separated into dextrorotatory and laevorotatory components and is sometimes found in grape juice during wine-making.

ra·ce·mi·form (rə-seémi-fawrm, ra-, ray-) *adj. Botany.* Resembling a raceme in form. [RACEM(E) + -I- + -FORM.]

ra·ce·mise, ra·ce·mize (rássi-mīz) *v.* -mised, -mising, -mises. —*tr.* To convert (an optically active compound) into an optically inactive racemic mixture. —*intr.* To become racemic; change into a racemic mixture. —**rac·e·mi·sa·tion** (-mī-záysh'n ‖ *U.S.* -mi-) *n.*

rac·e·mism (rə-seém-iz'm, rássim-) *n. Chemistry.* The condition or state of being racemic.

rac·e·mose (rássim-ōz, -ōss) *adj.* 1. *Botany.* Designating any inflorescence in which the main axis continues to grow at the tip so that the oldest flowers are at the bottom and the youngest towards the tip. 2. *Anatomy.* Having a structure of clustered parts. Said of glands. [Latin *racēmōsus*, full of clusters, from *racēmus*, RACEME.] —**rac·e·mose·ly** *adv.*

rac·er (ráyssər) *n.* 1. One that takes part in races or is capable of great speed. 2. Any of various fast-moving North American snakes of the genus *Coluber.*

race relations *pl.n.* Interaction and relationships between people of different races, especially with reference to their quality in a given social environment.

race riot *n.* A riot inspired by racial hatred or resentment, especially one resulting in a violent confrontation between groups of people of different races.

race suicide *n.* The gradual extinction of a people or race caused by the birth rate falling below the death rate as a result of an intentional limitation on the number of children.

race·track (ráyss-trak) *n.* 1. A track, circuit, or course laid out for motor racing, greyhound racing, or the like. 2. *U.S.* A racecourse.

race·way (ráyss-way) *n.* 1. An artificial channel for transporting water. 2. A racetrack. 3. A machine race *(see).*

Ra·chel (ráychəl). The second wife of Jacob and mother of his sons Joseph and Benjamin. Genesis 29–35. [Hebrew *rāḥēl*, "ewe".]

ra·chis (ráy-kiss) *n., pl.* -**chises** or -**chides** (-ki-deez). *Biology.* A main axis or shaft, such as the main stem of an inflorescence, the shaft of a contour feather, or the spinal column. [New Latin, from Greek *rhakhis*, spine, backbone.] —**ra·chi·al** *adj.*

ra·chi·tis (ra-kítiss, rə-) *n.* A childhood and infant disease, **rickets** *(see).* [New Latin, from Greek *rhakhitis*, disease of the spine : RACHIS + -ITIS.] —**ra·chit·ic** (-kíttik) *adj.*

Rach·man·i·nov (rak-mánni-nof ‖ rakh-, *U.S.* raak-maáni-; *Russian* -nəf), **Sergei (Vasilyevich)** (1873–1943). Russian composer. A virtuoso pianist, he excelled at the interpretation of the late Romantic composers; his own work is essentially a continuation of the genre. He left Russia (1917) to live in Switzerland and latterly in the United States.

Rach·man·ism (rák-mən-iz'm) *n.* The severe exploitation and intimidation, often violent, of slum tenants by a landlord or landlords. [After Peter (Perec) *Rachman* (1920–1962), Polish-born British landlord who practised such intimidation.]

ra·cial (ráysh'l) *adj.* 1. Pertaining to or typical of a race or races, or an ethnic group or groups. 2. Arising from or based upon differences between races, especially physically distinguished human races, or ethnic groups. —**ra·cial·ly** *adv.*

Ra·cine (ra-seén), **Jean** (1639–99). French playwright. The greatest of the French classical period, he wrote plays based on classical Greek and Roman themes, which include *Andromaque* (1667), *Britannicus* (1669), and *Phèdre* (1677). —**Ra·cin·i·an** *adj.*

ra·cism (ráyssiz'm) *n.* Also **ra·cial·ism** (ráysh'l-izm). 1. The belief that certain races, especially one's own, are inherently superior to others. 2. Discriminatory behaviour or practices based on this view. —**rac·ist, ra·cial·ist** *n. & adj.*

rack¹ (rak) *n.* 1. A framework or stand for holding or displaying various articles, especially: **a.** A small frame or ridged structure on which washed crockery or cutlery is placed to drain: *a plate rack.* **b.** A receptacle for livestock feed: *a hay rack.* **c.** A secure ledge for luggage. **d.** A series of hooks in a frame: *a hat rack.* **e.** A frame for holding bombs in an aeroplane. **f.** *Printing.* An upright framework for holding cases of type or galley proof. **g.** *U.S.* In billiards, snooker, and the like, a **frame** *(see).* 2. A toothed bar that meshes with another toothed structure, such as a pinion or gearwheel. 3. An instrument of torture, consisting of a frame on which the victim's body is stretched. Often preceded by *the.* —**on the rack**. Under great strain or in anguish.

~*tr.v.* **racked, racking, racks**. 1. To place in or upon a rack. 2. To torture by means of a rack. 3. To torment; make suffer: *racked with pain.* 4. To subject to stress or violent shaking. 5. To strain with great effort; make heavy or taxing demands on. 6. To rack-rent. 7. To move (a machine part) by use of a toothed rack. —**rack up**. *U.S. Slang.* To accumulate: *rack up points.* [Middle English

rekke, rakke, probably from Middle Dutch *rec,* framework, *recken,* to stretch, from Germanic.] —**rack·er** *n.*

rack² *n.* A rapid, showy gait of a horse, in which each foot strikes the ground separately. Also called "single-foot".

~*intr.v.* **racked, racking, racks**. To go or move with this gait. [Perhaps of Arabic origin and akin to *rikwa,* easy-paced.]

rack³, wrack (rak) *n.* A thin mass of wind-driven clouds.

~*intr.v.* **racked** or **wracked, racking** or **wracking, racks** or **wracks**. To be driven by the wind. Used of clouds. [Middle English *rak,* probably from Scandinavian, akin to Swedish *rak.*]

rack⁴, wrack *n.* Destruction; decay. Now used only in the phrase *rack and ruin.* [Variant of WRACK (ruin).]

rack⁵ *tr.v.* **racked, racking, racks**. To drain or draw off (wine or cider) from the dregs. [Middle English *rakken,* from Provençal *arracar,* from *raca†,* dregs, stems and husks of grapes.]

rack⁶ *n.* 1. A rib cut of lamb between the shoulder and the loin. 2. A crown roast of lamb. [Perhaps from RACK (framework).]

rack-and-pin·ion (rák-ən-pín-yən) *n.* A device for the conversion of rotary to linear motion, consisting of a pinion and a mated rack.

rack·et¹, rac·quet (rackit) *n.* 1. A light bat with a long handle attached to a head consisting of a nearly elliptical hoop strung with a network of catgut, nylon, or silk, used in various ball games. 2. A snowshoe resembling the head of a racket. [French *rachette, raquette,* from Italian *racchetta,* from dialectal Arabic *râḥet,* palm of the hand.]

racket² *n. Informal.* 1. A clamour; an uproar; a din. 2. **a.** A business that obtains money through fraud or extortion. **b.** An illegal or dishonest practice. 3. *Informal.* Any business or job. 4. A lively and often dissipated social life. —See Synonyms at **noise**.

~*intr.v.* **racketed, -eting, -ets**. To lead a lively and often dissipated social life. Often used with *about.* [16th century (clamour) : probably imitative.]

rack·et·eer (rácki-teér) *n.* One engaged in an illegal business.

~*intr.v.* **racketeered, -eering, -eers**. To engage in a dishonest racket.

rack·et·press (rákit-press) *n.* A frame usually consisting of two rigid pieces kept pressed together by a spring or screws and nuts, used to keep the head of a racket in shape.

rack·ets, rac·quets (rackits) *n. Used with a singular verb.* A game resembling squash, played on a four-walled court.

rack·et·tail (rackit-tayl) *n.* Any of various birds having a racket-shaped tail, especially certain hummingbirds and kingfishers.

rack·et·y (rackiti) *adj.* Noisy; raucous; rowdy.

Rack·ham (rackəm), **Arthur** (1867–1939). British book illustrator. His graceful, ethereal style was best suited to fairy stories, such as *Peter Pan* (1906); among his other works is an edition of *A Christmas Carol* (1915).

rack railway *n.* A cog railway *(see).*

rack-rent (rák-rent) *n.* An exorbitant rent.

~*tr.v.* **rack-rented, -renting, -rents**. To exact exorbitant rent for or from. [From RACK (to torture).]

ra·con (ráy-kon) *n.* A radar beacon. [*Ra*dar bea*con.*]

rac·on·teur (rák-on-túr, -ON-) *n.* One who recounts stories and anecdotes with skill and wit. [French, from Old French, from *ra-conter,* to tell : *re-,* again + *aconter,* tell : *a-,* from Latin *ad-,* to + *co(u)nter,* to COUNT.]

racoon. Variant of **raccoon.**

racquet. Variant of **racket.**

rac·y (ráyssi) *adj.* -**ier, -iest**. 1. Full-flavoured; piquant or pungent: *a racy wine.* 2. Vigorous; lively: *a racy manner.* 3. Humorous and slightly sexually improper; risqué. [From RACE (lineage, in the sense of a distinctive kind).] —**rac·i·ly** *adv.* —**rac·i·ness** *n.*

rad (rad) *n. Physics.* A unit of energy absorbed from ionising radiation, equal to 0.01 joule per kilogram of irradiated material. [Short for RADIATION.]

rad 1. radian. 2. radiator.

rad. 1. radical. 2. radio. 3. radius. 4. radix.

RADA, R.A.D.A. (ráadə). In Britain, the Royal Academy of Dramatic Art.

ra·dar (ráydaar) *n.* 1. A method of detecting distant objects and determining their position, velocity, or other characteristics by analysis of very high frequency radio waves reflected from their surfaces. 2. The equipment used in such detection. [*Ra*dio *det*ection *and* ranging.]

radar astronomy *n.* The technique of investigating celestial objects in the solar system by reflecting radio waves off them and detecting and analysing the reflected waves.

radar beacon *n.* A fixed device that sends or receives, amplifies, alters, and returns a radar signal, permitting a distant receiver to determine its bearing and sometimes its range. Also called "racon".

radar picket *n.* A ship or aircraft posted, usually during hostilities, to keep a radar watch for approaching aircraft.

ra·dar·scope (ráydaar-skōp) *n. Electronics.* The oscilloscope viewing screen of a radar receiver. [RADAR + (OSCILLO)SCOPE.]

Rad·cliffe (rád-klif), **Ann**, born Ann Ward (1764–1823). British novelist. She pioneered the "Gothic" novel. Although her books, including *The Mysteries of Udolpho* (1794), were popular thrillers, they also had a notable influence on the Romantic movement.

Rad·cliffe-Brown (rád-klif-brówn), **Alfred Reginald** (1881–1955). British anthropologist. His work on kinship, based on field work among the Andaman islanders and Australian Aborigines, laid the foundations of British anthropology.

rad·dle¹ (rádd'l) *tr.v.* -**dled, -dling, -dles**. To twist together or interweave. [Old French *rudelle, redelle,* rod twisted between upright stakes, perhaps from Middle High German *reidel.*]

raddle². Variant of **ruddle.**

rad·dled (rádd'ld) *adj.* Worn-out, as by debauchery or general deterioration. Usually said of a person. [Probably alluding to the heavily rouged face of an old or debauched person. See **ruddle.**]

ra·di·al (ráydi-əl) *adj.* **1. a.** Of, pertaining to, or arranged like rays or the radii of a circle. **b.** Radiating from or converging to a common centre. **2.** Having or characterised by parts so arranged or so radiating. **3.** Moving or directed along a radius. **4.** *Anatomy.* Of, pertaining to, or near the radius or forearm: *the radial nerve.* **5.** Developing symmetrically about a central point. **6.** Radial-ply. *~n.* **1.** A radial part, such as a ray, spoke, or radius. **2.** Any basal fin ray in a bony fish. **3.** A radial-ply tyre. [Medieval Latin *radiālis,* from Latin *radius,* rod, ray. See **radius.**] **—ra·di·al·ly** *adv.*

radial engine *n.* An internal-combustion engine, as formerly used in propeller-driven aircraft, with radially arrayed cylinders.

ra·di·al-ply (ráydi-əl-plī) *adj.* Designating a vehicle tyre in which the cords in the fabric casing run radially, giving flexibility to the walls of the tyre. Compare **cross-ply.**

radial symmetry *n.* **1.** Symmetrical arrangement of constituents, especially of radiating parts, about a central point. **2.** *Biology.* The arrangement of the parts of an organism around a central axis such that a vertical cut through the axis in any plane produces two halves that are mirror images of each other. Compare **bilateral symmetry.**

ra·di·an (ráydi-ən) *n. Abbr.* **rad** *Mathematics.* A unit of angular measure equal to the angle subtended at the centre of a circle by an arc of length equal to the radius of the circle. It is equal to $^{360}/_{2\pi}$°, or approximately 57°17′44.6″. [RADI(US) + -AN.]

ra·di·ance (ráydi-ənss) *n.* Also **ra·di·an·cy** (-ən-si). **1.** The quality or state of being radiant. **2.** *Physics.* The radiant energy emitted per unit time in a given direction by a projected unit area of an emitting surface. Compare **irradiance.**

ra·di·ant (ráydi-ənt) *adj.* **1.** Emitting heat or light. **2.** Consisting of or emitted as radiation: *radiant heat.* **3. a.** Filled with light; bright. **b.** Glowing or beaming, as with health or happiness. **4.** *Physics.* Designating photometric quantities that depend on energy measurements rather than on measurements of visible light: *radiant exitance.* In this sense, compare **luminous.** —See Synonyms at **bright.** *~n.* **1.** An object or point from which light or heat rays are emitted. **2.** *Astronomy.* The apparent celestial origin of a meteoric shower. **3.** The part of a gas fire or other heater that gives out heat. [Latin *radiāns* (stem *radiant-*), present participle of *radiāre,* to RADIATE.] **—ra·di·ant·ly** *adv.*

radiant efficiency *n. Symbol* η_e *Physics.* A measure of the efficiency of a source of radiation, equal to the power it emits divided by the power consumed by the source.

radiant energy *n. Physics.* Energy transferred by radiation, especially by an electromagnetic wave.

radiant exitance *n. Symbol* M_e *Physics.* The radiant flux emitted from a surface per unit area at a given point.

radiant flux *n. Symbol* ϕ_e *Physics.* The rate of flow of energy as electromagnetic radiation.

radiant heat *n.* Heat transferred as radiation, especially as infrared radiation.

radiant intensity *n. Symbol* I_e *Physics.* The radiant flux per unit solid angle emitted from a given point.

ra·di·ate (ráydi-ayt) *v.* **-ated, -ating, -ates.** *—intr.* **1.** To emit radiation. **2.** To issue or emerge in rays. **3.** To spread out or converge radially, in the manner of the spokes of a wheel. *—tr.* **1.** To emit (heat or light, for example). **2.** To diffuse or cause to go out from or as if from a centre. **3.** To manifest in a glowing manner: *He radiated confidence.* **4.** To illuminate; light up. *~adj.* (*also* -ət, -it). **1.** *Botany.* Having rays, raylike parts, or ray flowers: *a radiate inflorescence.* **2.** *Biology.* Characterised by **radial symmetry** *(see).* **3.** Surrounded with rays. Said of a representation of a head, especially on a coin. [Latin *radiāre,* to emit beams, furnish with spokes, from *radius,* ray. See **radius.**]

ra·di·a·tion (ráydi-áysh'n) *n.* **1.** The act or process of radiating. **2.** *Physics.* **a.** The emission and propagation of waves or particles. **b.** The propagating waves or particles, such as light, sound, radiant heat, or particles emitted by radioactivity. **3.** *Anatomy.* Radial arrangement of parts, as of a group of nerve fibres connecting different areas of the brain. **4.** *Biology.* A form of evolution, **adaptive radiation** *(see).*

radiation pattern *n. Electronics.* A diagram representing the strength of emission of electromagnetic radiation and its direction around a transmitting aerial.

radiation sickness *n.* Illness induced by ionising radiation, ranging in severity from nausea, vomiting, headache, and diarrhoea to loss of hair and teeth, reduction in red and white blood cell count, extensive haemorrhaging, sterility, and death.

ra·di·a·tive (ráydi-ətiv, -aytiv) *adj. Physics.* Of or involving the emission of radiation, especially electromagnetic radiation.

ra·di·a·tor (ráydi-aytər) *n.* **1. a.** A heating device consisting of a series of connected pipes or a flat structure containing ducts, through which hot water or steam can be circulated in a central-heating system. **b.** A similar portable device containing oil, which is heated electrically. **2. a.** A cooling device, as in automotive engines, through which water or other fluids circulate as a coolant. **b.** The grille at the front of such a device on a motor vehicle. **3.** *Physics.* A body that emits radiation. **4.** A transmitting aerial.

rad·i·cal (ráddik'l) *adj.* **1.** Arising from or going to a root or source. **2. a.** Affecting the basis of something; fundamental in its effect: *a radical revision of the procedure.* **b.** Broadly, having a profound or far-reaching effect: *radical reductions in staff levels.* **3.** Advocating or intended to effect fundamental or thoroughgoing changes, especially of economic and political structures. **4.** *Linguistics.* Of or designating a word root. **5.** *Botany.* Of, pertaining to, or growing from the root. **6.** *Medicine.* Designating treatment directed to the complete cure of a disease rather than simply to the relief of symptoms. *~n.* **1.** One who advocates profound political, social, or other change. **2.** *Mathematics. Abbr.* **rad.** The root of a quantity as indicated by the radical sign. **3.** *Chemistry. Abbr.* **R.** An atom or group of atoms with at least one unpaired electron. **4.** *Linguistics. Abbr.* **rad.** A word element, a **root** *(see).* [Middle English, of the root, fundamental, from Late Latin *rādīcālis,* having roots, from Latin *rādix* (stem *rādīc-*), root.] **—rad·i·cal·ly** *adv.* **—rad·i·cal·ness** *n.*

radical chic *n.* **1.** The adoption or affectation by people in fashionable society of radical left-wing policies and opinions and the styles and tastes associated with these views. **2.** Such people collectively. [Coined by Tom WOLFE.]

radical expression *n.* A mathematical expression or form in which radical signs appear.

rad·i·cal·ise, rad·i·cal·ize (ráddik'l-īz) *tr.v.* **-ised, -ising, -ises.** To make radical or more radical, especially in political affairs. **—rad·i·cal·i·sa·tion** (-ī-záysh'n || *U.S.* -i-) *n.*

rad·i·cal·ism (ráddik'l-iz'm) *n.* **1.** The doctrines or practices of political or other radicals. **2.** The state or quality of being radical.

radical sign *n.* **1.** The sign $\sqrt{}$ placed before a quantity, indicating extraction of the root designated by a raised integral index. When extracting a square root, the index is customarily omitted. **2.** This sign together with a horizontal bar extending from its top to the end of the expression from which a root is to be extracted.

rad·i·cand (ráddi-kand, -kánd) *n.* The quantity under a radical sign: *3 is the radicand of* $\sqrt{3}$. [Latin *rādīcandum,* neuter gerundive of *rādīcāre,* to take root, from *rādix,* root. See **radical.**]

rad·i·ces. Alternative plural of **radix.**

rad·i·cle (ráddik'l) *n.* **1.** *Botany.* The part of the plant embryo that develops into the primary root. **2.** *Anatomy.* A small structure resembling a root, such as a fibril of a nerve. [Latin *rādīcula,* diminutive of *rādix* (stem *rādīc-*), root.]

ra·di·i. Alternative plural of **radius.**

ra·di·o (ráydi-ō) *n., pl.* **-os.** *Abbr.* **rad. 1.** The use of electromagnetic waves in the approximate frequency range from 10 kilohertz to 300 000 megahertz to transmit or receive electric signals without wires connecting the points of transmission and reception. **2.** Communication of audible signals, such as music, encoded in electromagnetic waves so transmitted and received. **3. a.** Transmission of programmes for the public by this means; radio broadcasting as an industry or medium. **b.** Programmes transmitted by radio: *The radio was interesting last night.* **c.** Used in the title of certain broadcasting stations: *Radio 3.* **4. a.** The equipment used to transmit radio signals; a transmitter. **b.** The equipment used to receive radio signals; a receiver. **c.** A complex of equipment capable of both transmitting and receiving radio signals. **5.** A message sent by radio.
~adj. **1.** Of, pertaining to, or sent by radio. **2.** Of, pertaining to, or designating oscillations of **radio frequency** *(see).*
~v. **radioed, -oing, -os.** *—tr.* **1.** To transmit a message to, or communicate with, by radio. **2.** To broadcast by radio. *—intr.* To transmit a message by radio. [Short for RADIOTELEGRAPHY.]

radio- *comb. form.* Indicates emission and propagation of radiation; for example, **radioactive.** [From RADIATION.]

ra·di·o·ac·tive (ráydi-ō-áktiv) *adj. Physics.* Of or exhibiting radioactivity. **—ra·di·o·ac·tive·ly** *adv.*

radioactive dating *n.* Any method of determining the age of organic material, such as wood or fossils, using the decay rates of naturally occurring radioactive isotopes. See **radiocarbon dating.**

radioactive decay *n.* A progressive decrease in the number of radioactive atoms in a substance by spontaneous nuclear disintegration or transformation. Also called "decay".

radioactive series *n.* A group of nuclides related by a sequence of radioactive decay processes in which the heavier members of the group are transformed into successively lighter ones, the lightest being stable. Also called "decay chain".

ra·di·o·ac·tiv·i·ty (ráydi-ō-ak-tívvəti) *n.* **1.** The spontaneous emission of radiation, either directly from unstable atomic nuclei or as a consequence of a nuclear reaction. **2.** The radiation so emitted, including alpha particles, nucleons, electrons, and gamma rays.

radio astronomy *n.* The study of celestial objects and phenomena by observation and analysis of emitted or reflected radio waves.

ra·di·o·au·tog·ra·phy (ráydi-ō-aw-tóggrəfi) *n.* **Autoradiography** *(see).*

radio beacon *n.* A fixed radio transmitter that broadcasts distinctive signals as a navigational aid.

radio beam *n.* A focused beam of radio signals transmitted by a radio beacon to guide aircraft or ships. Also called "beam".

ra·di·o·bi·ol·o·gy (ráydi-ō-bī-óllə-ji) *n.* **1.** The study of the effects of radiation on living organisms. **2.** The use of radioactive tracers to study biological processes. **—ra·di·o·bi·o·log·i·cal** (-bī-ə-lójik'l) *adj.* **—ra·di·o·bi·o·log·i·cal·ly** *adv.* **—ra·di·o·bi·ol·o·gist** (-ollə-jist) *n.*

radio cab *n.* A licensed taxi operating from a central unit to which customers can telephone to hire cabs. Also called "radio taxi".

radio car *n.* A car equipped with a mobile radio transmitter, used for example in outside-broadcast radio programmes.

ra·di·o·car·bon (ráydi-ō-kárbən) *n.* Radioactive carbon, especially **carbon 14** *(see).*

radiocarbon dating *n.* A technique of radioactive dating in which the age of a specimen can be calculated by measuring its content of carbon-14, absorbed from the atmosphere during its lifetime, which decays at a known rate. Also called "carbon dating".

ra·di·o·chem·is·try (ráydi-ō-kémmistri) *n.* The chemistry of radioactive materials. **—ra·di·o·chem·i·cal** *adj.*

radio compass *n.* A navigational aid consisting of an automatic radio receiver that determines the transmission direction of incoming radio waves.

ra·di·o·el·e·ment (ráydi-ō-éllimənt) *n.* Any naturally occurring or artificially produced radioactive element.

radio frequency *n. Abbr.* **RF** 1. The frequency of the waves transmitted by a specific radio station. 2. Any frequency in the range within which radio waves may be transmitted, from about 10 kilohertz to about 300 000 megahertz. Radio frequency groups are: *very low frequency* (vlf), 10 to 30 kilohertz; *low frequency* (lf), 30 to 300 kilohertz; *medium frequency* (mf), 300 to 3 000 kilohertz; *high frequency* (hf), 3 000 to 30 000 kilohertz; *very high frequency* (vhf), 30 to 300 megahertz; *ultrahigh frequency* (uhf), 300 to 3 000 megahertz; *superhigh frequency* (shf), 3 000 to 30 000 megahertz; *extremely high frequency* (ehf), 30 000 to 300 000 megahertz.

ra·di·o·gen·ic (ráydi-ō-jénnik) *adj.* Caused by radioactivity. [RADIO- + -GENIC.]

ra·di·o·gram (ráydi-ō-gram) *n.* 1. *British.* A unit resembling a small cabinet and containing a radio and record-player. 2. A message transmitted by wireless telegraphy. 3. A radiograph.

ra·di·o·graph (ráydi-ō-graaf, -graf) *n.* An image produced on a radiosensitive surface, such as a photographic film, by radiation other than visible light, especially X-rays passed through an object, or by photographing a fluoroscopic image. Also called "radiogram". *—tr.v.* **radiographed, -graphing, -graphs.** To make a radiograph of. [RADIO- + -GRAPH.]

ra·di·og·ra·phy (ráydi-óggrəfi) *n.* Examination of the internal structure of a solid object by passing X-rays or gamma rays through it to produce a radiograph. The technique is used in industry and medicine. See **radiology**. **—ra·di·og·ra·pher** (-óggrəfər) *n.* **—ra·di·o·graph·ic** (-ə-gráffik, -ō-) *adj.* **—ra·di·o·graph·i·cal·ly** *adv.*

radio ham *n.* A licensed amateur radio operator who broadcasts and receives radio messages on his own equipment, as a hobby. Also informally called "ham".

ra·di·o·im·mu·no·as·say (ráydi-ō-i-méwnō-ə-sáy, -ássay) *n.* The technique of using radioactively labelled substances, particularly hormones, to measure the amounts of particular antibodies or hormones in the blood. [RADIO- + IMMUNE + ASSAY.]

radio interferometer *n.* A form of radio telescope in which two or more separate receiving antennae are connected to a single detector, information being obtained by analysis of the interference patterns produced by detected radio waves.

ra·di·o·i·so·tope (ráydi-ō-í-sə-tōp) *n.* A naturally or artificially produced radioactive isotope of an element.

ra·di·o·lar·i·an (ráydi-ō-laír-i-ən) *n.* Any of various marine protozoans of the order Radiolaria, having rigid siliceous skeletons and radiating spicules. [New Latin *Radiolaria*, from Late Latin *radiolus*, small sunbeam, diminutive of Latin *radius*, ray. See **radius**.]

ra·di·o·lo·ca·tion (ráydi-ō-lə-káysh'n, -lō-) *n.* The detection of distant objects by radar.

ra·di·ol·o·gy (ráydi-óllə-ji) *n.* 1. The use of ionising radiation for radiotherapy and medical diagnosis; especially, the use of X-rays in medical radiography or fluoroscopy. 2. Radioscopy. [RADIO- + -LOGY.] **—ra·di·o·log·i·cal** (-ə-lójik'l) *adj.* **—ra·di·ol·o·gist** (-óllə-jist) *n.*

ra·di·o·lu·cent (ráydi-ō-lóoss'nt, -léwss'nt) *adj.* Allowing the passage of radiation, especially X-rays. [RADIO- + (TRANS)LUCENT.]

ra·di·om·e·ter (ráydi-ómmitər) *n.* Any of various devices for detecting or measuring radiation. See **Crookes radiometer**. [RADIO- + -METER.] **—ra·di·o·met·ric** (-ə-méttrik, -ō-) *adj.* **—ra·di·om·e·try** (-ómmətri) *n.*

ra·di·o·nu·clide (ráydi-ō-néw-klīd || -nóo-) *n.* A radioactive nuclide.

ra·di·o·paque (ráydi-ō-páyk) *adj.* Also **ra·di·o·o·paque** (-ō-ō-). Absorbing, and therefore being opaque to, radiation, especially X-rays. Radiopaque substances are used, for example, in medical radiography as contrast media. [RADIO- + OPAQUE.]

ra·di·o·phone (ráydi-ō-fōn) *n.* A radiotelephone. **—ra·di·o·phon·ic** (-fónnik) *adj.*

ra·di·o·pho·to·graph (ráydi-ō-fṓtə-graaf, -graf) *n.* Also **ra·di·o·pho·to** (-fṓtō). A photograph transmitted by radio waves, each image point being reproduced by a received electric impulse. **—ra·di·o·pho·tog·ra·phy** (-fə-tóggrəfi) *n.*

ra·di·o·scope (ráydi-ō-skōp) *n.* A fluoroscope *(see).* [RADIO- + -SCOPE.]

ra·di·os·co·py (ráydi-óskəpi) *n.* The examination of the inner structure of opaque objects by X-rays or other penetrating radiation. Also called "radiology". [RADIO- + -SCOPY.] **—ra·di·o·scop·ic** (-ə-skóppik, -ō-), **ra·di·o·scop·i·cal** *adj.*

ra·di·o·sen·si·tive (ráydi-ō-sén-si-tiv) *adj.* Sensitive to radiation. Said especially of certain forms of cancer.

ra·di·o·sonde (ráydi-ō-sond) *n.* An instrument carried aloft, chiefly by balloon, to gather and transmit meteorological data.

radio source *n.* A celestial source of radio waves, such as a quasar or supernova remnant.

radio spectrum *n.* The entire range of electromagnetic communica-

tions frequencies, including those used for radio, radar, and television; the radio-frequency spectrum.

radio taxi *n.* A **radio cab** *(see).*

ra·di·o·tel·e·graph (ráydi-ō-télli-graaf, -graf) *n.* 1. The sending of messages by radiotelegraphy. 2. A message sent by this means. **—ra·di·o·tel·e·graph** *v.* **—ra·di·o·tel·e·graph·ic** (-graffik) *adj.*

ra·di·o·te·leg·ra·phy (ráydi-ō-ti-léggrəfi, -te-, -tə-) *n.* **Wireless telegraphy** *(see).*

ra·di·o·tel·e·phone (ráydi-ō-télli-fōn) *n.* A telephone in which audible communication is established by radio. Also called "radiophone", "wireless telephone". **—ra·di·o·tel·e·phon·ic** (-fónnik) *adj.* **—ra·di·o·te·leph·o·ny** (-ti-léffəni, -te-, -tə-) *n.*

radio telescope *n.* A sensitive, directional radio-antenna system used to detect and analyse radio waves from space.

ra·di·o·ther·a·py (ráydi-ō-thérrəpi) *n.* The treatment of disease, particularly cancer, with radiation, especially by selective irradiation with X-rays or other ionising radiation and by ingestion of radioisotopes.

radio wave *n.* A radio-frequency electromagnetic wave. Formerly called "Hertzian wave".

radio window *n.* A region in the radio spectrum (10 000 to 40 000 megahertz) in which radio waves are not absorbed by the atmosphere or reflected by the ionosphere and can pass between Earth and space.

rad·ish (ráddish || réddish) *n.* 1. Any of various plants of the genus *Raphanus;* especially, *R. sativus,* having a thickened, edible root. 2. The pungent root of this plant, eaten raw as an appetiser and in salads. [Middle English *radiche,* Old English *rædic,* from Latin *rādix* (stem *rādīc-*), root.]

ra·di·um (ráydi-əm) *n. Symbol* **Ra** A rare brilliant-white, luminescent, highly radioactive metallic element having 16 isotopes of which radium 226 with a half-life of 1,622 years is the most common. It is used in cancer radiotherapy, as a neutron source for some research purposes, and as a constituent of luminescent paints. Atomic number 88, melting point 700°C, boiling point 1,737°C, valency 2. [New Latin, from Latin *radius,* ray (radium emits rays that penetrate opaque matter). See **radius**.]

radium therapy *n.* The use of radium in radiotherapy, especially in treating cancer.

ra·di·us (ráydi-əss) *n., pl.* **-dii** (-ī) or **-uses.** 1. *Abbr.* **R, r, rad. a.** A line segment that joins the centre of a circle with any point on its circumference. **b.** A line segment that joins the centre of a sphere with any point on its surface. **c.** A line segment that joins the centre of a closed figure, such as a polygon or ellipse, to a point on the circumference. 2. The length of any such line segment. 3. A measure of circular area or extent: *every family within a radius of 25 miles.* 4. A measure of range of activity or influence. 5. A radial part or structure, such as a mechanically pivoted arm or the spoke of a wheel. 6. *Anatomy.* **a.** A long, prismatic, slightly curved bone, the shorter and thicker of the two forearm bones, located on the outer side of the ulna. **b.** A similar bone in many vertebrates. [Latin *radius†,* spoke of a wheel, ray.]

radius of curvature *n.* In geometry, the reciprocal of the curvature of a given curve at a given point.

radius vector *n. Mathematics.* 1. A line segment that joins any variable point to the origin of polar or spherical coordinates. 2. The length of such a line segment.

ra·dix (ráydiks) *n., pl.* **-dices** (ráydi-seez, ráddi-) or **-dixes.** 1. *Biology.* A root or point of origin. 2. *Abbr.* **rad.** *Mathematics.* The base of a system of numbers, as 2 is of the binary system and 10 is of the decimal system. [Latin *rādix,* root.]

radix point *n.* A decimal point *(see).*

Rad·nor·shire (rád-nər-shər, -sheer, *also* -nawr- || -shīr) *n. Welsh.* **Sir Fae·sy·fed** (sheer vī-súvved). Former county of east central Wales. A mountainous region, known for its sheep rearing, it became part of the new county of Powys (1974).

ra·dome (ráy-dōm) *n.* A domelike protective housing for a radar antenna used especially in certain aircraft. [*radar* + *dome.*]

ra·don (ráy-don) *n. Symbol* **Rn** A colourless, radioactive, inert gaseous element formed by disintegration of radium. It is used as a radiation source in radiotherapy and to produce neutrons for research. Atomic number 86, atomic weight 222, melting point –71°C, boiling point –61.8°C, relative density (solid) 4, valency 0, half-life 3.823 days. [New Latin : RAD(IUM) + *-on,* suffix indicating inert gases.]

rad·u·la (ráddew-lə) *n., pl.* **-lae** (-lee). *Zoology.* In molluscs, a ribbon-like strip on the tongue, bearing rows of horny teeth used for scraping food. [New Latin, from Latin *rādula,* scraper, from *rādere,* to scrape.] **—rad·u·lar** *adj.*

RAF, R.A.F. *(often* raf) *n.* In Britain, the Royal Air Force.

raf·fi·a, raph·i·a (ráffi-ə) *n.* 1. An African palm tree, *Raphia ruffia,* having large leaves that yield a useful fibre. Also called "raffia palm". 2. The fibre of these leaves, used for mats, baskets, and other products. [Malagasy.]

raf·fi·nose (ráffin-ōz, -ōss) *n.* A white crystalline sugar, $C_{18}H_{32}O_{16}$, obtained from cottonseed meal and sugar beets. [French, from *raffiner,* to refine : *re-,* again + *affiner,* to refine : *a-,* to, from Latin *ad-* + *fin,* refined, from Old French, FINE.]

raff·ish (ráffish) *adj.* 1. Vulgar; showy. 2. Slightly disreputable; rakish. [Probably from dialectal *raff,* trash, from Middle English *raf.* See **raft** (amount).] **—raff·ish·ly** *adv.* **—raff·ish·ness** *n.*

raf·fle¹ (ráff'l) *n.* 1. The disposing of an item as a prize in a competition by a lottery, in which the winning ticket is chosen at random. **2.** The competition itself.

~v. **raffled, -fling, -fles.** *—tr.* To dispose of in a raffle. Often used with *off.* *—intr.* To conduct or take part in a raffle. [Middle English *rafle,* a type of dice game, from Old French *rafflet,* act of snatching.] **—raf·fler** *n.*

raffle² *n.* Rubbish; debris. [Middle English, perhaps from Old French *ne rafle,* nothing at all.]

Raf·fles (ráff'lz), **Sir (Thomas) Stamford (Bingley)** (1781–1826). British colonial administrator. He is best known for his acquisition (1819) of Singapore for the East India Company, and his founding of the city there. He was also a founder and the first president of London Zoo.

raf·fle·si·a (ra-fléez-i-ə ‖ -fléezh-ə) *n.* Any of various parasitic leafless plants of the tropical Asian genus *Rafflesia;* especially, *R. arnoldi,* having large flowers smelling of rotten meat and pollinated by carrion flies. [New Latin, after Sir Stamford RAFFLES.]

raft¹ (raaft ‖ raft) *n.* **1.** A flat structure, typically made of planks, logs, or barrels, that floats on water and is used for transport or as a platform for swimmers. **2.** A life raft *(see).* **3.** A collection of floating ice, logs, or debris. **4.** In building, a layer of reinforced concrete used as a foundation to distribute the weight of a building, especially on subsiding ground.

~v. **rafted, rafting, rafts.** *—tr.* **1.** To convey on a raft. **2.** To make a raft from. *—intr.* To travel by raft. [Middle English *rafte,* from Old Norse *raptr,* beam, rafter.]

raft² *n. U.S. Informal.* A great number, amount, or collection; a lot. [Variant of Scottish *raff,* trash, from Middle English *raf,* perhaps from Scandinavian, akin to Old Norse *hreppa,* to catch, from Germanic *hrap-* (unattested).]

raft·er (raáf-tər ‖ ráf-) *n.* Any of the sloping beams that support a pitched roof. [Middle English *rafter,* Old English *ræfter,* from Germanic.]

rag¹ (rag) *n.* **1.** A scrap of cloth. **2.** Such scraps collectively, used, for example, as stuffing material or for pulp in papermaking. Also used adjectively: *the rag content of a sheet of paper.* **3.** A scrap or fragment. **4.** *Slang.* A newspaper, especially one regarded as sensational or contemptible. **5.** *Plural.* **a.** Threadbare or tattered clothing. **b.** *Informal.* Clothes. **6.** *British Informal.* A flag. **7.** A jagged piece; a rough projection. **—chew the rag.** *Informal.* To complain. [Middle English *ragge,* probably back-formation from RAGGED.]

rag² *tr.v.* **ragged, ragging, rags.** *Slang.* **1.** To tease; taunt. **2.** To scold. **3.** *British.* To play a practical joke on.

~n. British. **1.** A practical joke; a prank. **2.** A period during a college term when students hold comic parades and other activities to raise money for charity. Also used adjectively: *rag week.* [18th century : origin obscure.]

rag³ *n.* **1.** A roofing slate with one rough surface. **2.** Any coarsely textured rock. [Middle English *ragghet,* later associated with RAG (cloth).]

rag⁴ *tr.v.* **ragged, ragging, rags.** To compose or play (a piece of music) in ragtime.

~n. A piece of music written in ragtime. [Short for RAGTIME.]

ra·ga (raága, raag) *n.* A traditional form in Hindu music, consisting of a theme that expresses some aspect of religious feeling and sets forth a tonal system on which variations are improvised within a prescribed framework of typical progressions, melodic formulas, and rhythmic patterns. [Sanskrit *rāga,* colour, musical colour.]

rag·a·muf·fin (rággə-muffin) *n.* A dirty or unkempt child. [After *Ragamoffyn,* demon in *Piers Plowman* (c. 1393), probably based on RAG (cloth).]

rag-and-bone man (rág-ən-bón) *n.* A person who buys or gathers old clothes, furniture, and other junk, and sells it. Also *U.S.* "junk man".

rag·bag (rág-bag) *n.* A jumbled collection; a mixture.

rag bolt *n.* A bolt having a jagged projection on the shank keeping it in place when driven in.

rag doll *n.* A doll made from or stuffed with scraps of cloth.

rage (rayj) *n.* **1. a.** Extreme, vehement anger; fury. **b.** A fit of anger. **2.** Furious intensity, as of a storm or disease. **3.** Burning desire or passion. **4.** *Informal.* A fad; a craze. **—See Synonyms at anger. —all the rage.** *Informal.* Very fashionable.

~intr.v. **raged, raging, rages.** **1.** To speak or act furiously. **2.** To move with great violence or intensity. **3.** To spread, prevail, or continue unchecked. [Middle English, from Old French, from Vulgar Latin *rabia* (unattested), from Latin *rabiēs,* madness, from *rabere,* to rave.]

rag·ged (rággid) *adj.* **1.** Tattered. **2.** Dressed in tattered or threadbare clothes. **3.** Unkempt or shaggy. **4.** Having a rough surface or edges; jagged. **5.** Uneven; sloppy; lacking smoothness or polish: *a ragged performance.* **6.** Harsh; rasping: *a ragged cry.* [Middle English, from Old Norse *roggvathr,* tufted, from *roggt,* tuft of fur.] **—rag·ged·ly** *adv.* **—rag·ged·ness** *n.*

ragged robin *n.* A plant, *Lychnis flos-cuculi,* native to Eurasia, having reddish or white flowers with deeply lobed petals. Also called "cuckooflower". [From the ragged appearance of the petals.]

ragged school *n.* Formerly, a free school for poor children.

ra·gi (raági, rággi) *n.* A grass, *Eleusine coracana,* of Africa and Asia, where it is cultivated for its edible grain. [Hindi *rāgī,* from Sanskrit, from Dravidian *rāki* (unattested).]

rag·lan (rágglən) *n.* A loose coat, jacket, or sweater with slanted shoulder seams and with the sleeves extending in one piece to the neckline.

~adj. Having the shoulder seams extending diagonally from armhole to neckline: *a raglan sleeve.* [After Lord RAGLAN.]

Rag·lan (rágglən), **Fitzroy James Henry Somerset, 1st Baron** (1788–1855). British field marshal. He lost an arm at Waterloo and rose to become military secretary to Wellington (1827–52) and commander of the British forces in the Crimean War.

ra·gout (rággōō, ra-gōō) *n.* A rich stew of meat and vegetables. [French *ragoût,* from *ragoûter,* to renew the taste : *re-,* again + *a-,* from Latin *ad,* to + *goût,* taste, from Latin *gustus.*]

rag·tag (rág-tag) *n.* Rabble; riffraff. Also called "ragtag and bobtail".

~adj. Also **rag·gle-tag·gle** (rágg'l-tagg'l). Low, coarse, and unkempt; ragged. [RAG (scrap) + TAG.]

rag·time (rág-tīm) *n.* A style of jazz characterised by elaborately syncopated rhythm in the melody and a steadily accented accompaniment. [Perhaps from *ragged time,* referring to the syncopation.]

rag trade *n. Informal.* The clothing trade. Preceded by *the.*

Ragusa. See **Dubrovnik.**

rag·weed (rág-weed) *n.* **1.** Any American plant of the genus *Ambrosia;* especially, *A. artemisiifolia* or *A. trifida,* whose profuse pollen is a chief cause of hay fever. Also called "bitterweed". **2.** The ragwort. [From the raggedness of the leaves.]

rag·worm (rág-wurm) *n.* Any of various marine polychaete worms of the genus *Nereis;* especially, *N. cultrifera,* swimming by means of paired, paddle-like appendages. Also *U.S.* "clamworm". [Referring to the raglike appearance of its appendages.]

rag·wort (rág-wurt ‖ -wawrt) *n.* Any of several plants of the genus *Senecio,* having yellow daisy-like flowers; especially, *S. jacobaea,* of Europe. Also called "ragweed". [From the raggedness of the leaves.]

raid (rayd) *n.* **1. a.** A sudden attack, such as one made by thieves for seizing something. **b.** A swift incursion, especially into hostile territory, in order to accomplish a specific task, such as the destruction of enemy installations. **c.** A sudden and forcible invasion by the police. **2.** An act of depleting resources, as if by carrying them off in an attack. Often used humorously: *made a raid on our savings.* **3.** An attempt by speculators to drive stock prices down by selling.

~v. **raided, raiding, raids.** *—tr.* To make a raid on. *—intr.* To conduct or participate in a raid. [Middle English, Scottish dialect form of Old English *rād,* ROAD.] **—raid·er** *n.*

rail¹ (rayl) *n.* **1.** A bar or series of bars placed, usually horizontally, some distance above the ground and supported by vertical posts or a solid structure, as in a railing, balustrade, fence, or the like. **2. a.** A bar or rod attached to a wall and used to hang objects from: *a picture rail.* **b.** A bar or rod on the side of a staircase used to hold on to for support or balance: *a hand rail.* **3.** A steel bar used, usually in pairs, as a track for a railway, tramway, or the like. **4.** The railway as a means of transport: *We went by rail.* **5.** A horizontal piece of wood in a door or in panelling. **—off the rails.** *Chiefly British.* **1.** Haywire; out of control. **2.** Behaving oddly or erratically.

~tr.v. **railed, railing, rails.** **1.** To supply with a rail or rails. **2.** To enclose or separate with a rail or rails. Usually used with *off* or *in.* [Middle English *raile,* from Old French *reille,* bar, from Latin *rēgula,* rod, straight piece of wood.]

rail² *n., pl.* **rails** or collectively **rail.** Any of various marsh birds of the family Rallidae, characteristically having brownish plumage and short wings adapted for only short flights. [Middle English *ra(i)le,* from Old French *raale,* from Old Northern French *raille,* Vulgar Latin *rasc(u)la* (unattested), perhaps imitative.]

rail³ *intr.v.* **railed, railing, rails.** To use bitter, harsh, or abusive language. Used with *at* or *against.* [Middle English *railen,* from Old French *railler,* to mock, from Old Provençal *ralhar,* to scold, from Vulgar Latin *ragulāre* (unattested), to bray, from Late Latin *rageret,* to neigh, roar.] **—rail·er** *n.*

rail·head (ráyl-hed) *n.* **1.** The farthest point on a railway to which rails have been laid. **2.** *Military.* The section of a railway where supplies are unloaded.

rail·ing (ráyling) *n.* **1. a.** *Often plural.* A banister, balustrade, or fence made of rails. **b.** The upper, longitudinal part of a balustrade. **2.** Rails collectively. **3.** Material for making rails.

rail·ler·y (ráylori) *n., pl.* **-ies.** **1.** Good-natured teasing or ridicule; banter. **2.** An instance of this. [French *raillerie,* from Old French *railler,* to RAIL (use harsh language).]

rail·road (ráyl-rōd) *n. U.S.* A **railway** (senses 1, 2, 4).

~tr.v. **railroaded, -roading, -roads.** *Informal.* **1.** To pressure or coerce. Often used with *into: railroaded us into signing the contract.* **2.** To push or force hurriedly by exerting unfair pressure. Usually used with *through: They railroaded the bill through Parliament.*

rail·way (ráyl-way) *n. Abbr.* **r., R., Rwy., Ry.** **1.** A road composed of parallel steel rails providing a track for locomotive-drawn trains and other rolling stock. **2.** The entire system of such track, together with the land, stations, rolling stock, and other property used in rail transport. **3.** Any similar transport system using a fixed track: *a cable railway.* **4.** Any track on which something can move.

rai·ment (ráymənt) *n. Archaic.* Clothing; garments. [Middle English *rayment,* short for obsolete *arrayment,* from Old French *araiement, araie,* an array, from *arayer,* to ARRAY.]

rain (rayn) *n.* **1. a.** Water condensed from atmospheric vapour, falling to earth in drops. **b.** The descent of such water. **c.** A fall of such water; a rainstorm or shower. **d.** Rainy weather. **2.** The rapid falling of anything in large numbers or quantities. **3.** *Plural.* The rainy season or seasonal rainfalls, as in certain tropical areas. **—as**

right as rain. *British.* Quite all right; fine; healthy. **—rain or shine.** 1. Regardless of the weather. 2. Under all circumstances. ~*v.* **rained, raining, rains.** —*intr.* 1. To fall in drops of water from the clouds: *It rained every day.* 2. To fall like rain. 3. To release rain. —*tr.* 1. To send or pour down. 2. To offer, give, or deal out abundantly or forcefully: *His opponent rained down on him.* **—rain off.** *British.* To cause the postponement or cancellation of (a picnic or sports event, for example) because of rain. Often used in the passive. [Middle English *reyn, rain*, Old English *regn, rēn, regnian*, from Germanic.]

rain·bird (ráyn-burd) *n.* Any of various birds, such as the green woodpecker, whose cry is supposed to presage rain.

rain·bow (ráyn-bō) *n.* 1. a. An arc of colours appearing in the sky opposite the sun as a result of the refractive dispersion of sunlight in drops of rain or mist. b. Any similar arc, as in a waterfall mist or graded display of colours. 2. An illusory objective or hope: *chasing the rainbow of a quick fortune.* [Middle English *reinbowe*, Old English *rēnboga* : RAIN + BOW.]

rainbow bird *n.* A brightly coloured Australian bee-eater, *Merops ornatus.*

rainbow trout *n.* A North American food fish, *Salmo gairdneri*, having a reddish longitudinal band and black spots.

rain check *n.* *U.S.* A ticket stub for an outdoor sports event entitling the holder to admission at a future date if the original event is rained off. **—take a rain check.** To postpone acceptance of an offer on the understanding that the offer may be taken up later.

rain·coat (ráyn-kōt) *n.* A waterproof or water-resistant coat.

rain·drop (ráyn-drop) *n.* A drop of rain.

Raine (rayn), **Kathleen (Jessie)** (1908–). British poet and critic. Her poetic work, as in the collection *Stone and Flower* (1943), is both visionary and lyrical.

rain·fall (ráyn-fawl) *n.* 1. A shower or fall of rain. 2. *Meteorology.* The total quantity of water, as measured by a rain gauge, condensed or precipitated as rain, snow, hail, dew, hoar frost, rime, or sleet in a given area and time interval.

rain forest *n.* A dense evergreen forest occupying a tropical region with a large annual rainfall (over 250 centimetres or 100 inches).

rain gauge *n.* A device for measuring rainfall. Also called "pluviometer", "udometer".

Rai·ni·er III (ráyni-ay), **Prince de Monaco** (1923–). Ruling Prince of Monaco (1949–). He succeeded his grandfather Louis II, and relinquished many of his absolutist powers in 1962. He married the U.S. film star Grace Kelly in 1956.

Rai·ni·er, Mount (ráyni-ər, ray-néer) Mountain in Mount Rainier National Park, Washington State, United States. At 4 392 metres (14,408 feet), it is the highest peak in the Cascade Range.

rain·mak·er (ráyn-maykər) *n.* A person supposedly capable of producing rain by artificial or supernatural means, especially among American Indians.

rain·mak·ing (ráyn-mayking) *n.* 1. The ceremony and rituals observed by a rainmaker. 2. *Informal.* **Cloud seeding** (*see*).

rain·out (ráyn-owt) *n.* Radioactive fallout carried down by rain.

rain·proof (ráyn-prōōf ‖ -prōōf) *adj.* Impenetrable by rain. Said of coverings such as clothes or roofs. **—rain·proof** *tr.v.*

rain shadow *n.* A region with a relatively low rainfall, sheltered by adjacent high ground from prevailing, rain-bearing winds.

rain·spout (ráyn-spowt) *n.* A spout draining a roof gutter.

rain·storm (ráyn-stawrm) *n.* A storm accompanied by rain.

rain tree *n.* A Central American tree, *Samarea saman*, widely planted as an ornamental in the tropics, having red-and-yellow flowers and leaflets that close when it starts to rain.

rain·wash (ráyn-wosh) *n.* *Geology.* Decomposed rock and similar matter washed away by rain.

rain·wat·er (ráyn-wawtər ‖ *U.S. also* -wottər) *n.* Water precipitated as rain, as opposed to well water or tapwater, with little dissolved mineral matter.

rain·wear (ráyn-wair) *n.* Waterproof clothing.

rain·y (ráyni) *adj.* **-ier, -iest.** Characterised by, full of, or bringing rain. **—rain·i·ly** *adv.* **—rain·i·ness** *n.*

rainy day *n.* A time of need or trouble.

Rais or **Retz** (ray), **Gilles de (Baron de Laval)** (1404–40). French marshal. A commander in the victorious campaigns of 1428–31 against the English, he later resorted to alchemy and witchcraft to finance his excessive lifestyle. He was tried and executed for murdering about 140 children, and entered folklore as Bluebeard.

raise (rayz) *v.* **raised, raising, raises.** —*tr.* 1. To move or cause to move upwards or to a higher position; elevate; lift. 2. a. To place or set upright; make erect. b. To cause to project or stand up or out. c. To cause (a blister, for example) to form. 3. To erect or build. 4. a. To cause to arise, appear, or exist. b. To awaken from or as if from death. 5. To increase in size, quantity, or worth: *raise prices.* 6. To increase in intensity, degree, strength, or pitch: *raise one's expectations.* 7. To elevate in rank or dignity; promote. 8. a. To grow or breed. b. To bring up; rear. 9. To put forward for consideration. 10. *Law.* To begin or set (a lawsuit) in operation. 11. To express or utter (a cry or shout, for example). 12. To bring about; cause; provoke: *raise a cheer.* 13. To arouse or stir up: *raise a revolt.* 14. To gather together; collect: *raise money.* 15. To cause (dough) to puff up. 16. To end or abandon (a siege, blockade, or the like). 17. To remove or withdraw (an order). 18. a. To increase (a poker bet). b. To bet more than (a preceding bettor in poker). c. To increase the bid of (one's bridge partner). 19. *Nautical.* To bring (a shoreline or another ship, for example) into sight by ap-

proaching nearer. 20. To establish radio contact with. 21. To bring up the nap on the surface of (fabric). 22. *Scottish.* To make angry; enrage. 23. *Mathematics.* To multiply (a number) by a certain power or by itself a certain number of times: *4 raised to the power 3 (4^3) equals 64.* —*intr.* To increase the stakes in poker or gambling. —See Synonyms at **lift.**
~*n.* 1. An act of raising or increasing. 2. *Chiefly U.S.* An increase in salary; a rise. [Middle English *reisen, raisen*, from Old Norse *reisa.*] **—rais·er** *n.*

raised (rayzd) *adj.* 1. Represented in relief, as a design might be; embossed. 2. *U.S.* Leavened by yeast.

raised pie *n.* A tall, straight-sided, usually savoury, pie made from hot-water crust pastry that has been moulded over a base, such as a large jam jar, or set in a pie mould.

rai·sin (ráyz'n) *n.* A sweet grape of several varieties, dried either in the sun or artificially. [Middle English *raisin*, from Old French, grape, from Latin *racēmus*, RACEME.]

rai·son d'ê·tre (ráy-ZON-déttr, -dáytrə) *n., pl.* **raisons d'être** (*pronounced as singular*). Reason for being; point or justification for existing. [French.]

raj (raaj; *also* raazh) *n.* In India, dominion or sovereignty. **—the (British) Raj.** British rule in India. [Hindi *rāj*, reign, from Sanskrit *rājā*, from *rājati*, he rules.]

Raj·ab (rújəb, rə-jáb) *n.* The seventh month of the Muslim calendar. [Arabic.]

ra·jah, ra·ja (ráajə) *n.* A prince, chief, or ruler in India and certain other eastern countries such as Malaysia. [Hindi *rājā*, from Sanskrit *rājan*, king.]

Ra·ja·sthan (ráajə-stáan). State in northwest India formed (1848) from a number of former principalities of Rajputana. It is divided into the Thar desert in the west and the more fertile Deccan plateau in the east. The two regions are separated by the Aravalli Mountains, which yield salt, sandstone, marble, coal, mica, and gypsum. The state capital is Jaipur.

Raj·put, Raj·poot (ráaj-pōōt ‖ -pōōt) *n.* A member of a Hindu people claiming descent from the warlike and powerful rulers of north India from the 8th to the 13th century.

rake[1] (rayk) *n.* 1. A long-handled implement with a row of projecting teeth at its head, used to gather leaves or mown grass, or to loosen or smooth earth. 2. Any similarly shaped implement, as for removing ashes from an oven or drawing betting chips across a table. 3. Any of various toothed and often wheeled mechanical implements used for gathering hay, straw, or the like. ~*v.* **raked, raking, rakes.** —*tr.* 1. To gather or move with or as if with a rake. 2. To smooth, scrape, or loosen with a rake or similar implement. 3. To search or examine thoroughly. 4. To scrape; scratch; graze. 5. To aim heavy gunfire along the length of. 6. To direct one's gaze along the length of: *rake the horizon.* —*intr.* 1. To use a rake. 2. To conduct a search. **—rake in.** To gain (money) in abundance. **—rake up.** To revive or bring to light: *rake up a scandal.* [Middle English *rake*, Old English *raca, racu.*] **—rak·er** *n.*

rake[2] *n.* A profligate, sexually promiscuous man. [Short for RAKE-HELL.]

rake[3] *v.* **raked, raking, rakes.** —*intr.* To slant or incline from the vertical, as a ship's funnel does. —*tr.* To cause to lean or slant. ~*n.* 1. Inclination from the vertical or from the horizontal. 2. A slope or slant; especially the slope from the back of a theatre stage down to the front. 3. The angle between the cutting edge of a tool and a plane perpendicular to the working surface to which the tool is applied. 4. *Aeronautics.* The angle of inclination of an aircraft's wings. [17th century : probably akin to German *ragen†*, to project.]

rake·hell (ráyk-hel) *n. Archaic.* A rake; a roué. ~*adj. Archaic.* Dissolute; profligate. [Probably from the phrase, *to rake hell.*]

rake·off (ráyk-off, -awf) *n. Slang.* A percentage or share of the profits of an enterprise, especially one given or accepted as a bribe. [From the rake used by a croupier in a gambling house.]

rake's progress *n.* A continuous and dissolute decline; a descent into vice. [From William Hogarth's series of engravings, *A Rake's Progress* (1735).]

rak·i, rak·ee (ráaki, raa-kée ‖ rácki) *n.* A brandy of Turkey and the Balkan Peninsula, distilled from grapes or plums and flavoured with anise. [Turkish *rāqī.*]

rak·ish[1] (ráykish) *adj.* 1. *Nautical.* Having a trim, streamlined appearance: *"We were schooner-rigged and rakish, with a long and lissom hull"* (John Masefield). 2. Dashing; jaunty; smart. [From RAKE (to incline), from the raked masts on some fast pirate ships.] **—rak·ish·ly** *adv.* **—rak·ish·ness** *n.*

rakish[2] *adj.* Characteristic of a roué or rake; debauched; dissolute. **—rak·ish·ly** *adv.* **—rak·ish·ness** *n.*

rale, râle (raal) *n.* An abnormal crackling sound heard through a stethoscope over the lungs. [French *râle*, from *râler*, to make a rattling sound in the throat, from Old French, probably from Vulgar Latin *rasclāre* (unattested), to scrape.]

Ra·leigh (ráw-li, ráa-). Capital of North Carolina, United States, in the central part of the state.

Ra·leigh (ráwli, ráali, rál-i), **Sir Walter** (c. 1552–1618). British explorer, admiral, and writer. A favourite of Elizabeth I, he campaigned in Ireland and Cadiz, explored Guiana, colonised Virginia, and introduced tobacco and the potato to Europe. Found guilty of treason by James I, he was released for yet another expedition to Guiana, and was executed on its failure. His literary output includes memoirs, poetry, and a history of the world.

ral·len·tan·do (rál-ən-tán-dō, -en- ‖ *U.S.* ra′al-, -ta′an-) *adv. Abbr.* **rall.** *Music.* So as to slacken gradually in tempo; ritardando. Used as a direction.
—*n., pl.* **rallentandos.** *Music.* A passage or movement performed with a gradual reduction in tempo. [Italian, slowing down, from *rallentare*, to relax : *re-* (intensifier) + *allentare*, to slow down, from Late Latin *allentāre* : Latin *ad-*, to + *lentus*, slow.] —**ral·len·tan·do** *adj.*

ral·line (rál-īn ‖ -in) *adj.* Of, pertaining to, or belonging to the Rallidae, a family of birds containing the rails, crakes, and coots.

ral·ly¹ (rál-i) *v.* **-lied, -lying, -lies.** —*tr.* **1.** To call together for a common purpose; assemble. **2.** To reassemble and restore to order. **3.** To rouse or revive (one's strength, for example) from inactivity or decline. —*intr.* **1.** To meet for a common purpose. **2.** To join in a common effort or for a common purpose: *The workers rallied round to help.* **3.** To reassemble for a renewed effort, especially after being dispersed: *The brigade rallied for a final attack.* **4.** To recover abruptly from a setback or disadvantage. **5.** To show sudden improvement in health or spirits. **6.** *Finance.* To improve or rise after a fall. Said of stock market prices. **7.** In tennis and similar games, to exchange several strokes. —See Synonyms at **gather.**
—*n., pl.* **rallies. 1.** An assembly, especially one intended to inspire enthusiasm for a cause. **2. a.** A reassembling, as of dispersed troops. **b.** The signal ordering this. **3.** A sharp improvement in health, vigour, or spirits. **4.** *Finance.* A notable rise in market prices and active trading after a decline. **5.** In tennis and similar games, an exchange of several strokes. **6.** A race in which cars are driven over a fixed course with specific rules. [French *rallier*, from Old French *ralier* : *re-*, again + *alier*, to unite, ALLY.] —**ral·li·er** *n.*

rally² *tr.v.* **-lied, -lying, -lies.** To tease good-humouredly; banter. [French *railler*, from Old French, to RAIL (abuse).] —**ral·li·er** *n.*

ram (ram) *n.* **1.** A male sheep. **2.** *Capital* **R.** A constellation and sign of the zodiac, **Aries** (*see*). **3.** Any of several devices used to drive, batter, or crush by forceful impact: **a.** A weapon, the **battering-ram** (*see*). **b.** The weight that drops in a pile driver or steam hammer. **c.** The plunger or piston of a force pump or hydraulic press. **4. a.** A projection on the prow of a warship, used to batter or cut into an enemy vessel. **b.** A ship having such a projection. **5.** A pump, a **hydraulic ram** (*see*).
—*v.* **rammed, ramming, rams.** —*tr.* **1.** To strike or drive against with a heavy impact; butt. **2.** To force, press, or drive down or into place. **3.** To cram; stuff. —*intr.* **1.** To crash; collide. [Middle English *ram*, Old English *ramm*, from Germanic *ramma-* (unattested).] —**ram·mer** *n.*

RAM (ram) *n.* Random-access memory.

R.A.M. Royal Academy of Music (in Britain).

Ra·ma (ra′amə, raam) *n. Hinduism.* Any of three of the incarnations of Vishnu, regarded as heroes: Balarama, Parashurama, and especially Ramachandra. [Sanskrit *Rāma†*, dark-coloured, black.]

Ra·ma·chan·dra (ra′amə-chúndrə) *n. Hinduism.* The seventh of Vishnu's incarnations and hero of the Hindu epic poem *Ramayana.* Also called "Rama".

Ram·a·dan, Ram·a·dhan (rámmə-da′an, ra′amə-, -dán) *n.* Also **Ram·a·zan** (-za′an, -zán). **1.** The ninth month of the Muslim year, spent in fasting from sunrise to sunset. **2.** The fasting itself. [Arabic *Ramaḍān*, the hot month, from *ramaḍ*, dryness.]

Ra·man (ra′amən), **Sir Chandrasekhara (Venkata)** (1888–1970). Indian physicist. A specialist in spectroscopy, he discovered the Raman effect, for which he was awarded the Nobel prize (1930).

Raman effect *n. Physics.* The alteration in frequency and random alteration in phase of light scattered in a material medium, used for investigating the structure of molecules. [After Sir C.V. RAMAN.]

Raman spectroscopy *n. Physics.* A form of spectroscopy for investigating the structure of molecules by analysing the spectrum (*Raman spectrum*) of light scattered from a sample. [After Sir C.V. RAMAN.]

Ra·ma·nu·ja (ra′amə-nōō′jə) (11th century A.D.). Indian theologian. Rejecting the impersonal tradition of Hindu deities, he founded the *bhakti¹* movement, advocating devotion to the personalised deity Vishnu and a greater involvement with the temporal world.

ra·mate (ráymayt) *adj.* Having branches. [Latin *rāmus*, branch.]

Ra·ma·ya·na (raa-mí-ənə, -maa-yənə) *n.* A Sanskrit epic poem of ancient India, regarded as sacred by Hindus. It relates the adventures of Ramachandra. Compare **Mahabharata.** [Sanskrit *Rāmā-yama* : *Rāma*, RAMA + *-ayana*, suffix meaning "pertaining to".]

Ram·bam (rám-bam). See **Maimonides.**

Ram·bert (róm-bair), **Dame Marie,** born Cyvia Rabbam; also known as Miriam Rambach (1888–1982). Polish-born British ballet dancer and producer. She joined Diaghilev in 1913, became a British citizen in 1918, and, with her husband, founded the Carmargo Society (later the Ballet Rambert) in 1920. A teacher of many outstanding dancers, she greatly influenced ballet in Britain.

ram·ble (rámb'l) *intr.v.* **-bled, -bling, -bles. 1.** To walk or wander aimlessly and for pleasure; stroll or roam. **2.** To follow an irregularly winding course of motion or growth. **3.** To speak or write with many digressions. —See Synonyms at **wander.**
—*n.* A leisurely stroll. [Probably from Middle Dutch *rammelen*, (of animals) to wander about in sexual heat, from *rammen*, to copulate with; akin to RAM.]

ram·bler (rámblər) *n.* **1.** One who rambles. **2.** A person who takes long country walks, especially as a regular leisure pursuit. **3.** A variety of cultivated rose having weak stems that trail over the ground, other vegetation, and the like. In this sense, also called "rambler rose".

ram·bling (rámbling) *adj.* **1.** Extended over an irregular area; sprawling: *a large, rambling Elizabethan house.* **2.** Lengthy and desultory; long-winded. —**ram·bling·ly** *adv.*

Ram·bouil·let¹ (rón-bōō-yáy). Town in the département of Yvelines, north France, set in the forest of Rambouillet. Its famous chateau is the official summer residence of French presidents.

Ram·bouil·let² (róm-bōō-yay, rám-, -lay) *n.* Any of a breed of merino sheep of French origin, raised for wool and meat. [After RAMBOUILLET.]

ram·bunc·tious (ram-búngkshəss) *adj. U.S. Informal.* Boisterous; disorderly. [Probably variant of RUMBUSTIOUS.]

ram·bu·tan (ram-bōōt'n) *n.* **1.** A tree, *Nephelium lappaceum*, of Southeast Asia, bearing edible, oval red fruit with soft spines. **2.** The fruit of this tree. [Malay *rambutan*, from *rambut*, hair, from the hairy covering of the fruit.]

R.A.M.C. Royal Army Medical Corps (in Britain).

Ra·meau (ra′amō, raa-mō, ra-), **Jean Philippe** (1683–1764). French composer and critic. Although he was an organist, it is his orchestral works which display the greatest innovations. His opera-ballets include *Les Indes galantes* (1735).

ram·e·kin, ram·e·quin (rámmi-kin, rám-) *n.* **1.** A cheese preparation made with eggs, breadcrumbs, or pastry, baked and served in individual dishes. **2.** A small individual dish used for both baking and serving this. [French *ramequin*, from Middle Dutch *rameken*, diminutive of *ram*, cream, from Middle Low German *rōm(e)*.]

ra·men·tum (rə-mén-təm) *n., pl.* **-ta** (-tə). Any of the brown scaly structures on the stems of fern fronds. [New Latin, from Latin *rādere*, to scrape + *-mentum*, -MENT.]

ra·mi. Plural of **ramus.**

ram·ie (rámmi, ra′ami) *n.* **1.** A woody Asian plant, *Boehmeria nivea*, having broad leaves. **2.** The flaxlike fibre from the stem of this plant, used in making fabrics and cordage. [Malay *rami*.]

ram·i·fi·ca·tion (rámmifi-káysh'n) *n.* **1.** The act or process of branching out or dividing into branches. **2.** A branch or other subordinate part extending from a main body. **3.** An arrangement of branches or branching parts. **4.** A development or consequence growing out of and often complicating a problem, plan, or statement.

ram·i·form (rámmi-fawrm) *adj.* Branchlike or branching. [RAM(US) + -I- + -FORM.]

ram·i·fy (rámmi-fī) *v.* **-fied, -fying, -fies.** —*tr.* To divide into, or cause to extend in, branches or branchlike parts. —*intr.* To branch out or become divided into branches. [French *ramifier*, from Medieval Latin *rāmificāre*, from Latin *rāmus*, branch.]

ra·min (ra-mín) *n.* **1.** Any of various trees of the genus *Gonystylus*, native to Southeast Asia; especially *G. bancanus*, valued for its pale hardwood. **2.** The wood of any such tree. [Malay.]

ram·jet (rám-jet) *n.* **1.** A jet engine that compresses and heats its air intake for the fuel mixture by means of a specially shaped intake duct. It has no revolving parts and operates only at speed, requiring take-off assistance. **2.** An aircraft propelled by such an engine. Also called "athodyd".

ra·mose (ráy-mōz, -mōss, ra-mōss) *adj.* Having many branches. [Latin *rāmōsus*, from *rāmus*, branch.]

ra·mous (ráyməss) *adj.* **1.** Of or resembling branches. **2.** Branching; ramose. [Latin *rāmōsus*, RAMOSE.]

ramp¹ (ramp) *n.* **1.** A sloping passage or roadway connecting different levels, as of a building or road. **2.** *Architecture.* A concave bend of a handrail where a sharp change in level or direction occurs, such as at a stair landing. **3.** A mobile staircase for entering and leaving an aeroplane. **4.** A sudden bump or change in level in a road surface, sometimes introduced deliberately to keep traffic to a low speed. **5.** A small platform straddling a cable, hosepipe, or the like and enabling vehicles to pass over it without touching it. **6.** A short upward projection from which a person or vehicle may be launched, as on a ski-jump or aircraft-carrier. [French *rampe*, from *ramper*, to slope, creep, from Old French, to RAMP.]

ramp² *intr.v.* **ramped, ramping, ramps. 1.** To act threateningly or violently; rage. **2.** To assume a threatening stance. **3.** To stand in the rampant position.
—*n.* The act of ramping. [Middle English *rampen*, from Old French *ramper*, to climb, rear up, from Frankish *rampōn* (unattested).]

ramp³ *n. British.* A fraudulent act; a swindle. [19th century : origin obscure.]

ram·page (rámpayj, ram-páyj) *n.* A course of violent, frenzied, and destructive action or behaviour. —**on the rampage.** Behaving violently and destructively.
—*intr.v.* (ram-páyj). **rampaged, -paging, -pages.** To rush about wildly or violently; rage. [18th century (Scottish) : perhaps from RAMP (to rear up).]

ram·pa·geous (ram-páyjəss) *adj.* Raging; frenzied: *"The hot rampageous horses of my will"* (W.H. Auden). —**ram·pa·geous·ly** *adv.* —**ram·pa·geous·ness** *n.*

ram·pant (rámpənt) *adj.* **1.** Extending unchecked; unrestrained; widespread. **2.** Characterised by ungoverned vehemence and extravagance. **3.** Rearing or ramping on the hind legs. **4.** *Heraldry.* Rearing on the left hind leg with the forelegs raised, the right above the left, and usually with the head in profile. **5.** *Architecture.* Springing from a support or abutment higher at one side than at the other. Said of an arch or vault. [Middle English *rampaunt*, from

Old French *rampant*, present participle of *ramper*, to climb, RAMP.]
—**ram·pan·cy** *n.* —**ram·pant·ly** *adv.*

ram·part (rám-paart, -port) *n.* **1.** A fortification consisting of an elevation or embankment, often provided with a parapet. **2.** Anything that serves to protect or defend: *The cliff was a rampart against the ocean.* —See Synonyms at **bulwark**.
~*tr.v.* **ramparted, -parting, -parts.** To protect or defend with or as if with a rampart. [French *rempart,* from *remparer,* to fortify : *re-* (intensifier) + *emparer,* to defend, fortify, from Provençal *antparar, amparar,* from Vulgar Latin *anteparāre* (unattested), to prepare for defence : Latin *ante-,* before + *parāre,* to prepare.]

ram·pi·on (rámp-yən, -i-ən) *n.* **1.** A Eurasian plant, *Campanula rapunculus,* having clusters of bluish flowers and an edible root used in salads. **2.** Any of various similar plants of the genus *Phyteuma.* [Probably from Old French *raiponce,* from Medieval Latin *rapontium,* probably from Latin *rāpa, rāpum,* turnip, RAPE.]

ram·rod (rám-rod) *n.* **1.** A metal rod used to force the charge into a muzzleloading firearm. **2.** A rod used to clean the barrel of a firearm. **3.** A person who resembles a ramrod in inflexibility.

Ram·say (rámzi), **Allan** (1713–84). British portrait painter. He was court painter to George III. His portraits include George's wife, Queen Charlotte (National Portrait Gallery, London), and Jean-Jacques Rousseau (National Gallery, Edinburgh).

Ramsay, Sir William (1852–1916). British chemist. Investigating his colleague Rayleigh's observation that atmospheric nitrogen seemed heavier than laboratory-prepared nitrogen, he discovered the inert gases argon (1894), helium (1895), neon, xenon, and krypton (1898). He got the Nobel prize for chemistry (1904).

Ram·ses, Rameses (II) (rám-seez), also known as Ramses the Great (*c.*1300–1224 B.C.). Egyptian king. He is best known for his prodigious building activities: most famous archaeological sites in Egypt bear some evidence of his patronage. Known to the Greeks as Sesostris, he was probably the king connected with the Jewish exodus from Egypt.

Ram·sey (rámzi), **Sir Alf(red Ernest)** (1922–). English football manager and player. He was appointed England manager in 1963 and masterminded England's victory in the 1966 World Cup, but resigned in 1974.

Rams·gate (rámz-git, -gayt). Port and resort in Kent, southeast England. It is a major yachting centre and has a busy commercial harbour as well. It became a popular resort in the 19th century. There is a car ferry service to Dunkirk, France.

ram·shack·le (rám-shack'l) *adj.* Likely to fall apart because of shoddy construction or lack of maintenance; rickety. [Back-formation from *ramshackled, ransackled,* from *ransackle,* frequentative of Middle English *ransaken,* to RANSACK.]

ram's horn *n. Judaism.* A shofar *(see).*

Ram Singh (rám síng, raám) (1816–85). Indian religious leader. As chief of the Kuka sect of Sikhs, he organised an early civil disobedience campaign against the British, but was imprisoned when his more fanatical followers attacked Muslims. He later died in exile.

ram·son (rám-z'n, -s'n) *n. Usually plural.* **1.** A broad-leaved Eurasian garlic, *Allium ursinum,* having a bulbous root used in salads and relishes. **2.** The root of this plant. [Middle English *ramsyn,* Old English *hramsan* (plural of *hramsa*), mistaken as singular.]

ram·til (rám-til) *n.* An African plant, *Guizotia abyssinica,* grown for its oil-rich seeds. The seed is called "Niger seed". [Hindi *rāmtil* : Sanskrit *rāma,* dark (see **Rama**) + *tila†,* sesame.]

ra·mu·lose (rámmew-lōz, -lòss) *adj.* Also **ram·u·lous** (-ləss). *Biology.* Having numerous small branches. [Latin *rāmulōsus,* from *rāmulus,* diminutive of *rāmus,* branch, RAMUS.]

ra·mus (ráy-məss) *n., pl.* **-mi** (-mī). *Biology & Anatomy.* A branchlike part of a structure, such as a branch of a nerve fibre or a thin process projecting from a bone. [New Latin, from Latin, branch.]

ran. Past tense of **run.**

Ran (ran). *Norse Mythology.* The goddess of the sea who caught drowning persons in her net.

R.A.N. Royal Australian Navy.

Rance (raanss, RONSS). River in northwest France. 100 kilometres (62 miles) long, it flows from Landes du Mene northeastwards across Brittany to enter the English Channel through the Golfe de St. Malo. The world's first marine power station using the energy of the tides was opened on its estuary in 1966.

ranch (raanch ‖ ranch) *n.* **1.** An extensive farm, especially one in North America, on which large herds of cattle, sheep, or horses are raised. **2.** Any large farm on which a particular crop or kind of animal is raised. **3.** A fish farm in the open sea for breeding migratory fish such as salmon.
~*intr.v.* **ranched, ranching, ranches.** To work on or manage a ranch. [Mexican Spanish *rancho,* from Spanish, mess room, from Old Spanish *rancher, ranchar,* be billeted, from Old French *ranger,* to put in a line, from *renc,* line, row, from Frankish *hring* (unattested), ring.]

ranch·er (raán-chər ‖ rán-) *n.* One who owns, manages, or works on a ranch.

ran·che·ro (raan-chaír-ō ‖ ran-) *n., pl.* **-ros.** *Southwestern U.S.* A rancher. [Mexican Spanish, from *rancho,* RANCH.]

ranch house *n.* **1.** The building on a ranch occupied by its owner or manager. **2.** A rectangular, one-storey house with a low-pitched roof, a style common on Western U.S. ranches.

ranch·man (raánch-mən ‖ ránch-) *n., pl.* **-men** (-mən). *U.S.* A rancher.

ranch mink *n.* An American mink bred in captivity from Alaskan and Labrador strains for special pelt colours and qualities.

ran·cho (raán-chō ‖ rán-) *n., pl.* **-chos.** *Southwestern U.S.* **1.** A hut or group of huts in which ranch workers live. **2.** A ranch. [Mexican Spanish, RANCH.]

ran·cid (rán-sid) *adj.* **1.** Stale or decomposed. Said of fats or oils. **2.** Having the disagreeable odour or taste of decomposed oils or fats; sour; rank. **3.** Disagreeable; mean-spirited; nasty: *a scowling, rancid old man.* [Latin *rancidus,* from *rancēre†* (unattested), to stink.] —**ran·cid·i·ty** (ran-síddəti), **ran·cid·ness** *n.*

ran·cour, *U.S.* **ran·cor** (rángkər) *n.* Bitter resentment; deep-seated ill will. [Middle English *rancour,* from Old French, from Late Latin *rancour* (stem *rancōr-*), rancidity, from *rancēre,* to stink. See **rancid.**] —**ran·cor·ous** *adj.* —**ran·cor·ous·ly** *adv.* —**ran·cor·ous·ness** *n.*

rand¹ (rand, raant, ront) *n., pl.* **rand** or **rands. 1.** The basic monetary unit of the Republic of South Africa, equal to 100 cents. **2.** A note or coin worth one rand. [After *the* Rand, WITWATERSRAND.]

rand² (rand, raant, ront) *n., pl.* **rands** or **rande** (-ə). *South African.* A ridge of hills or an extended area of high ground. [Afrikaans, from Dutch, strip, ridge, from Germanic *randa* (unattested), rim, edge.]

rand³ (rand) *n.* **1.** A strip of leather inserted between the heel and sole of a shoe or boot. **2.** *British Regional.* A border or space around something, such as the unploughed area around a field. [Middle English, Old English, rim, margin, border, from Germanic.]

Rand, the. See **Witwatersrand.**

ran·dan (rán-dan) *n.* **1.** A type of boat designed to be rowed by three persons. **2.** The way of rowing this boat, in which the persons fore and aft use one oar each, and the person in the middle uses two. [19th century : origin obscure.]

R & B rhythm and blues.

R & D research and development.

ran·dom (rándəm) *adj.* **1.** Having no specific pattern or objective; lacking causal relationships; haphazard. **2.** *Statistics.* **a.** Of or designating a phenomenon that does not produce the same outcome or consequences every time it occurs under identical circumstances. **b.** Of or designating an event having a relative frequency of occurrence that approaches a stable limit as the number of observations of the event increases to infinity. **c.** Of or designating a sample drawn from a population so that each member of the population has an equal chance to be drawn. **d.** Of or pertaining to a member of such a sample: *a random number.* —See Synonyms at **chance.** —**at random.** Without definite method or purpose; unsystematically: *chose one man at random from the volunteers.* [Middle English *randoun,* from Old French *randon,* haphazard, from *randir,* to run, from Frankish *rant†* (unattested), a running.] —**ran·dom·ly** *adv.*

ran·dom-ac·cess (rándəm-ák-sess) *adj. Computing.* Giving access directly to any required part of a computer store: *a random-access memory.* Also called "direct access". Compare **sequential access.** See **read-write.**

ran·dom·ise, ran·dom·ize (rándəm-īz) *tr.v.* **-ised, -ising, -ises.** To make random, especially for scientific experimentation. —**ran·dom·i·sa·tion** (-ī-záysh'n ‖ *U.S.* -i-) *n.*

random variable *n. Statistics.* A variable having numerical values determined by the results of a chance experiment. Also called "stochastic variable".

ran·dy (rándi) *adj.* **-dier, -diest. 1.** *Chiefly British Slang.* Sexually aroused; lustful. **2.** Coarse and shrewish. Said of a woman.
~*n., pl.* **randies.** *Chiefly Scottish.* A shrewish woman. [Scottish, from *rand,* variant of RANT.] —**rand·i·ly** *adv.* —**rand·i·ness** *n.*

ranee. Variant of **rani.**

rang. Past tense of **ring.**

ran·ga·ti·ra (rúng-gə-téer-ə, ráng-) *n. N.Z.* A Maori chief or noble person. [Maori.]

range (raynj) *n. Abbr.* **r. 1. a.** The extent of perception, knowledge, experience, or ability of someone or something. **b.** The area or sphere covered by or included in something; the scope: *Personal relations lie outside the range of sociology.* **c.** The limits within which something is valid or applicable; effective scope: *a long-range weather forecast; within the range of possibilities.* **2. a.** An amount or extent of variation: *a wide price range.* **b.** *Music.* The extent of pitch variation within the capacity of a voice or instrument. **c.** The limits between which a meter or other measuring instrument can be operated. **3. a.** The maximum or effective distance that can be traversed, as by bullets or by radiation. **b.** The distance to a target. **4.** The maximum distance that a ship or other vehicle can travel before exhausting its fuel supply. **5.** A place for shooting at targets. **6.** A testing area in which rockets and missiles are fired and flown. **7.** *U.S.* An extensive area of open land on which livestock wander and graze. **8.** The geographical region in which a particular kind of plant or animal normally lives or grows. **9.** The act of or opportunity for wandering or roaming over a large area: *gave free range to her imagination.* **10.** *Mathematics.* The totality of points in a set established by a **mapping** *(see).* Also called "codomain". Compare **domain. b.** The order of the highest nonzero determinant contained in a given matrix. **11.** *Statistics.* A measure of dispersion equal to the difference or interval between the smallest and largest of a set of quantities. **12.** A class, rank, or order. **13.** An extended group or series, especially of mountains. **14.** Any of a series of double-faced bookcases in a library stack room. **15.** A set of products or services of the same general type; a line: *a new range of sportswear.* **16.** A large cooking stove of a type usually heated by solid fuel and having one or more ovens, on which several foods may be cooked at the same time. **17.** The action or an act of ranging. **18.** *Geology.* A mineral belt.

~*v.* **ranged, ranging, ranges.** —*tr.* **1.** To arrange or dispose in a particular order, especially in rows or lines. **2.** To assign to a particular category; classify. **3.** To align (a gun or telescope, for example) with a target; train; sight. Usually used with *on.* **4.** To determine the distance of (a target). **5.** To move or travel over or through (a region), as in exploration. **6.** *Printing.* To set (lines of type) so that they are flush with the margin. **7.** *Nautical.* To uncoil (an anchor cable) on deck so that the anchor may descend easily. **8.** *U.S.* To turn (livestock) out onto a range to graze. —*intr.* **1.** To vary within specified limits: *Her humour ranged from subtle irony to practical jokes.* **2.** To extend in a particular direction: *a river ranging to the east.* **3.** To extend in the same direction. **4.** To move over or through a given area as in exploration: *"his eye . . . ranged with delight over the treasures"* (Washington Irving). **5.** To roam or wander; rove. Used with *over.* **6.** To live or grow within a particular region. Used with *over.* **7.** To be capable of reaching a specified distance: *Our missiles range farther than theirs.* **8.** *Printing.* To lie flush at the margin. Said of lines of type. —See Synonyms at **wander.** [Middle English, series, line, from Old French *range, renge,* range, rank, from *renc, reng,* line, row, from Frankish *hring* (unattested), circle, ring.]

range finder *n.* Any of various optical, electronic, or acoustical instruments used to determine the distance of an object.

range light *n. Nautical.* **1.** Any of two or more lights used to guide a ship through a narrow channel at night. **2.** *Plural.* Two or more lights in a pattern on a powered vessel, used at night to indicate its course or size.

rang·er (ráynjər) *n.* **1.** *British.* The keeper of a royal forest or park. **2.** A person employed to patrol and guard a forest. **3.** *Usually capital* **R.** A senior member of the Girl Guides. **4.** *Capital* **R.** A member of a group of U.S. soldiers specially trained for making raids. Compare **commando. 5.** A wanderer or rover.

rang·ing rod (ráynjing) *n.* A patterned pole used as a marker in surveying. Also called "ranging pole".

Ran·goon (ráng-gōōn, rang-). Also **Yan·gon.** Capital city and chief port of Burma (Myanmar). Lying on the river Rangoon near its entrance into the Gulf of Martaban, it is the natural focus of Burma's transport network, and its commercial and industrial centre. The major exports are rice, cotton, timber, rubber, and petroleum products. Rangoon is dominated by the golden-spired Shwe Dagon Pagoda. It was severely damaged by an earthquake and tidal wave in 1930.

2. *Chiefly U.S.* Providing ample range; roomy.

ra·ni (raá-nee, raa-neé) *n., pl.* **-nis.** Also **ra·nee. 1.** The wife of a rajah. **2.** A reigning Hindu princess or queen. [Hindi *rānī,* from Sanskrit *rājñī,* feminine of *rājan,* king.]

Ran·jit Singh (rún-jit síng), **Maharaja** (1780–1839). Sikh prince of the Punjab. After capturing Lahore (1799), he proclaimed himself maharajah, and wrested control of the Punjab from the Afghans and Pathans, thus earning himself the title "Lion of the Punjab".

Ran·jit·singh·ji Vi·bha·ji (rúnjit-síng-jee vee-baá-jee), **Kumar Shri, Maharajah Jam Sahib of Nawanagar** (1872–1933). Indian prince, cricketer, and politician. He was an enlightened prince and chancellor of the Chamber of Princes (1932). As a cricketer, he was a spectacular batsman who played for Sussex and England, and the first player to score 3,000 runs in a single season (1899).

rank[1] (rangk) *n.* **1. a.** A relative position in society. **b.** An official position or grade: *the rank of sergeant.* **c.** A relative position or degree of value in any graded scale: *"The critical power is of lower rank than the creative."* (Matthew Arnold). **d.** High or eminent station or position: *persons of rank.* **2.** A row, line, series, or range of people or things. **3.** *Military.* **a.** A line of soldiers, vehicles, or other military equipment standing side by side in close order. Compare **file. b.** *Plural.* The armed forces. **c.** *Plural.* Members of the armed forces excluding officers. Preceded by *the* or *other.* **4.** Any of the horizontal lines of squares on a chessboard. **5.** *Mathematics.* The number of rows of the greatest order determinant extracted from a given matrix. **6.** *Music.* A row or set of pipes in an organ that are controlled by the same stop. **7.** A place where taxis park while waiting to be hired. **—break ranks. 1.** *Military.* To fail to remain in line, especially during battle. **2.** To fail to support one's colleagues in a joint enterprise. **—close ranks.** To consolidate strength, as when under threat or attack. **—pull rank.** To use one's superior position to get one's way or gain an advantage.

~*v.* **ranked, ranking, ranks.** —*tr.* **1.** To place in a row or rows. **2.** To give a particular order or position to; classify. **3.** *U.S.* To outrank or take precedence over. —*intr.* **1.** To hold a particular rank or place: *rank first.* **2.** *Chiefly U.S.* To hold a senior position or have authority or precedence. [Old French *ranc, renc,* rank, RANGE.]

rank[2] *adj.* **ranker, rankest. 1.** Growing profusely or with excessive vigour: *rank weeds.* **2.** Yielding a profuse, often excessive, crop; highly fertile: *rank earth.* **3.** Strong and offensive in odour or taste. **4.** Indecent; disgusting. **5.** Absolute; complete: *a rank amateur.* —See Synonyms at **flagrant.** [Middle English *rank,* Old English *ranc,* haughty, full-grown, overbearing, from Germanic.] **—rank·ly** *adv.* **—rank·ness** *n.*

Rank (rangk), **J(oseph) Arthur, 1st Baron** (1888–1972). British film producer and entrepreneur. A Methodist evangelist, he saw in films a means of spreading Christianity. He soon became aware of the commercial possibilities, and made his first secular film in 1935. In 1946 he founded the Rank Organisation and virtually controlled the British film industry, with a wide network of concerns covering every aspect of production and distribution.

Rank, Otto (1884–1939). Austrian psychologist. A protégé of Freud, though later disowned by him, he studied the psychiatric aspects of myth and creativity, and also suggested that emotional disorders could be caused at the time of birth.

rank and file *pl. n.* **1.** The common soldiers of an army excluding officers. **2.** Those who form the major portion of any group or organisation, excluding the leaders and officers.

Ran·ke (rángkə), **Leopold von** (1795–1886). German historian. He is best known for pioneering the modern methods of exhaustively analysing source documents; his *History of the Latin and Teutonic Nations 1494–1535* (1824) and subsequent works on Prussian, French, English, Spanish, Italian, and Serbian history are regarded as the first examples of modern historical criticism.

rank·er (rángkər) *n. British.* **1.** A soldier in the ranks. **2.** A commissioned officer who has risen from the ranks.

Ran·kine scale (ráng-kin) *n.* A scale of absolute temperature using Fahrenheit degrees, in which the freezing point of water is 491.69° and the boiling point of water is 671.69°. [After William J.M. *Rankine* (1820–72). British physicist.]

rank·ing (rángking) *adj. Chiefly U.S.* High-ranking; preeminent.

~*n.* A place or position on a usually specified scale: *has a high ranking on the squash ladder.*

ran·kle (rángk'l) *intr.v.* **-kled, -kling, -kles. 1.** To cause persistent irritation or resentment. **2.** *Archaic.* To become sore or inflamed; fester. [Middle English *ranclen,* from Old French *rancler, draoncler,* from *rancle, draoncle,* ulcer, festering sore, from Late Latin *dracunculus,* something twisted like a serpent, from Latin, diminutive of *dracō* (stem *dracōn-*), serpent.]

ran·sack (rán-sak) *tr.v.* **-sacked, -sacking, -sacks. 1.** To search or examine (a room or box, for example) thoroughly, usually disordering the contents in the process. **2.** To search (a house or town, for example) for plunder; pillage. —See Synonyms at **rob.** [Middle English *ransaken,* from Old Norse *rannsaka,* search a house : *rann,* house, from Common Germanic *razn-* (unattested) + *-saka,* search.] **—ran·sack·er** *n.*

ran·som (rán-səm) *n.* **1.** The release of a person or property in return for payment of a stipulated price. **2.** The price or payment demanded or paid. **3.** *Theology.* A redemption from sin and its consequences. **—hold to ransom. 1.** To confine or retain possession of, until a stipulated price is paid. **2.** To try to force concessions from: *The unions are holding the country to ransom.*

~*tr.v.* **ransomed, -soming, -soms. 1.** To obtain the release of (a person or property) by paying a certain price. **2. a.** To hold captive or keep possession of while demanding such a payment. **b.** To release after receiving a ransom. **3.** *Theology.* To deliver from sin and its consequences. [Middle English *ransoun,* from Old French *rançon,* from Latin *redemptiō,* REDEMPTION.] **—ran·som·er** *n.*

Ran·som (rán-səm), **John Crowe** (1888–1974). U.S. poet and critic. Best known for his critical work *The New Criticism* (1941). His collections of poetry include *Chills and Fever* (1924).

Ran·some (rán-səm), **Arthur (Mitchell)** (1884–1967). British writer. He was a prominent journalist, recording travels through such places as the U.S.S.R. and the Far East, but is best known as the author of several children's books, including *Swallows and Amazons* (1931).

rant (rant) *v.* **ranted, ranting, rants.** —*intr.* To speak or declaim in a violent, loud, or vehement manner. Often used in the phrase *rant and rave.* —*tr.* To exclaim with violence or extravagance.

~*n.* **1.** Violent, loud, or extravagant speech. **2.** *Chiefly Scottish.* Wild or uproarious merriment. [Probably from Dutch *ranten*†.] **—rant·er** *n.* **—rant·ing·ly** *adv.*

ran·u·la (ránnew-lə) *n., pl.* **-lae** (-lee). A cyst on the underside of the tongue caused by obstruction of a duct or a salivary gland. [New Latin, from Latin, swelling in tongues of cattle, diminutive of *rāna*†, frog.]

ra·nun·cu·lus (rə-núngkew-ləss) *n., pl.* **-luses** or **-li** (-lī). Any plant of the genus *Ranunculus,* including the buttercups, typically having yellow flowers. [New Latin, from Latin *rānunculus,* diminutive of *rāna*†, frog.]

rap[1] (rap) *v.* **rapped, rapping, raps.** —*tr.* **1.** To hit sharply and swiftly; strike. **2.** To utter sharply and abruptly. Used with *out.* —*intr.* **1.** To strike a quick, light blow or blows; knock. **2.** *Chiefly U.S. Informal.* To talk freely; chat. **3.** To improvise words and vocal sounds to an instrumental accompaniment. Compare **scat**[2].

~*n.* **1.** A quick, light blow or knock. **2.** A knocking or tapping sound. **3. a.** *Chiefly U.S.* A talk, conversation, or discussion. **b.** The improvisation of words and vocal sounds to an instrumental accompaniment. Also used adjectivally: *rap music.* Compare **scat**[2]. **c.** A piece of rap music. **4.** *Informal.* **a.** A reprimand or censure. **b.** Unpleasant consequences of wrongdoing, especially when one is not personally to blame. Used in the phrase *take the rap.* **5.** *Slang.* A prison sentence. **—beat the rap.** *U.S. Slang.* To escape punishment or be acquitted of a charge. [Middle English *rappen,* akin to Norwegian *rappe,* Swedish *rappa,* (imitative).] **—rap·per** *n.*

rap[2] *n.* **1.** A counterfeit halfpenny passed in Ireland during the 18th century. **2.** *Informal.* The least bit: *I don't care a rap.* [Short for Irish Gaelic *ropaire*†, counterfeit halfpenny.]

ra·pa·cious (rə-páyshəss) *adj.* **1.** Taking by force; plundering. **2.** Greedy; avaricious. **3.** Subsisting on live prey. Said especially of birds. [Latin *rapax* (stem *rapāc-*), from *rapere,* to seize.] **—ra·pa-**

cious·ly *adv.* —**ra·pa·cious·ness, ra·pac·i·ty** (-pássəti) *n.*

rape¹ (rayp) *n.* **1. a.** The crime of forcing a female to submit to sexual intercourse without her consent. **b.** Such a crime committed against a male. **2.** The fact of having been raped. **3.** *Archaic.* The act of seizing and carrying off by force; abduction. **4.** Abusive or improper treatment; violation; profanation: *a rape of justice.* **5.** The act of plundering or despoiling a country or city, especially in war. ~ *v.* **raped, raping, rapes.** —*tr.* **1.** To force to submit to sexual intercourse. **2.** *Archaic.* To seize and carry off by force. **3.** To plunder or pillage. —*intr.* To commit rape. [Middle English, from Old French *raper,* from Latin *rapere,* to seize.] —**rap·ist** *n.*

rape² *n.* A Eurasian plant, *Brassica napus,* cultivated for its seed, which yields a useful oil, and as fodder. Also called "colza". See **cole.** [Middle English, from Latin *rāpa, rāpum,* turnip.]

rape³ *n. Often plural.* The refuse of grapes left after the extraction of the juice in wine making. [French *râpe,* grape stalk, from Old French, from *rasper,* to scrape off, RASP.]

rape oil *n.* The edible oil extracted from rapeseed, also used as a lubricant and in the manufacture of various products.

rape·seed (ráyp-seed) *n.* The seed of the rape plant.

Raph·a·el¹ (ráf-ə-əl, -ayl, -i-əl), born Raffaello Sanzio or Santi (1483–1520). Italian painter, one of the towering figures of the High Renaissance. He came to early prominence in Florence, but his most famous paintings were done in Rome, especially the great frescoes for the Stanza della Segnatura in the Vatican. Completed in 1511, they include *The School of Athens* and the *Triumph of Religion,* also called *Disputà.* In Rome, too, he painted what is considered his greatest altarpiece, the *Sistine Madonna* (1512), and many portraits. —**Raph·a·el·esque** (-ésk) *adj.*

Raph·a·el² (ráf-ə-əl, ráyf-, -i-, -ī-, -el, ráffayl ‖ ráyf-). One of the archangels. [Hebrew *Rəphā'ēl,* "God has healed".]

ra·phe, rha·phe (ráy-fi) *n., pl.* **-phae** (-fee). *Biology.* A seamlike line or ridge between two similar parts, as in the scrotum, the coat of certain seeds, or the valves of a diatom. [New Latin, from Greek *rhaphē,* seam, from *rhaptein,* to sew.]

raphia. Variant of **raffia.**

ra·phide (ráy-fīd, rá-) *n., pl.* **-phides** (-z, ráffi-deez). Also **ra·phis** (-fiss) *pl.* **-phides.** *Botany.* Any of a bundle of needle-shaped crystals, composed chiefly of calcium oxalate, occurring in many plant cells. [Back-formation from *raphides,* plural, from New Latin, from Greek *rhaphis* (stem *rhaphid-*), needle, from *rhaptein,* to sew.]

rap·id (ráppid) *adj.* **1.** Moving, acting, or occurring with great speed; swift. **2.** Happening in a very short time: *a rapid change.* —See Synonyms at **fast.** ~ *n. Usually plural.* A fast-flowing section of a river usually caused by a sudden steepening of the riverbed. [Latin *rapidus,* hurrying, seizing, from *rapere,* to seize.] —**rap·id·ly** *adv.* —**ra·pid·i·ty** (rə-píd-dəti, ra-), **rap·id·ness** *n.*

rapid eye movement *n. Abbr.* **REM** Constant movement of the eyeballs behind the closed eyelids during **paradoxical sleep** *(see),* occurring when dreaming takes place.

rap·id-fire (ráppid-fír) *adj.* **1.** Designed to fire shots in rapid succession. **2.** Marked by continual, rapid occurrence: *rapid-fire questions.*

rapid transit *n. Chiefly U.S.* An urban passenger-transport system using elevated or underground trains or a combination of both.

ra·pi·er (ráyp-yər, -i-ər) *n.* **1.** A long, slender, two-edged sword with a cuplike hilt, used in the 16th and 17th centuries. **2.** An 18th-century, lighter, sharp-pointed sword lacking a cutting edge and used only for thrusting. [French *rapière,* originally *(espée) rapière†,* rapier (sword).]

rap·ine (ráp-īn, -in) *n. Law.* Forcible seizure of another's property; plunder. [Middle English *rapyne,* from Old French *rapine,* from Latin *rapīna,* from *rapere,* to RAPE (seize).]

rap·pa·ree (ráppə-rée) *n.* **1.** A freebooting soldier of 17th-century Ireland. **2.** *Archaic.* A bandit or robber. [Irish Gaelic *rapaire,* short pike, either from English RAPIER or French *rapière,* RAPIER.]

rap·pee (ra-pée) *n.* A strong snuff made from a dark, coarse tobacco. [French *râpé,* "grated" (as tobacco), from *râper,* to grate, from Old French *rasper,* to RASP.]

rap·pel (ra-pél) *n.* The act or method of descending from a mountainside or cliff by means of a double rope passed under one thigh and over the opposite shoulder, or through karabiners attached to a harness. ~ *intr.v.* **rappelled, -pelling, -pels.** To descend from a steep height by rappel. [French, "recall", from Old French *rapel,* from *rapeler,* to summon : *re-,* again + *apeler,* to summon, APPEAL.]

rap·port (ra-pór, rə- ‖ -pôr) *n.* A relationship; especially, one of mutual trust or emotional affinity. [French, from *rapporter,* to bring back, yield, from Old French *raporter* : *re-,* back, again + *aporter,* to bring, from Latin *apportāre* : *ad-,* to + *portāre,* to carry.]

rap·por·teur (ráp-awr-tér ‖ -ôr-) *n.* A person appointed by a committee who prepares reports for it or records its proceedings. [French. See **rapport.**]

rap·proche·ment (ra-prósh-moN ‖ *U.S.* -prósh-, -món) *n.* A re-establishing of cordial relations, as between two countries. [French, from *rapprocher,* to bring together : *re-,* again + *approcher,* to approach, from Late Latin *appropriāre* : Latin *ad-,* to + *prope,* near.]

rap·scal·li·on (rap-skál-i-ən) *n.* A rascal; a scamp. [Variant of obsolete *rascallion,* perhaps from RASCAL.]

rapt (rapt) *adj.* **1.** Transported with powerful emotion; enraptured. **2.** Deeply absorbed; engrossed. **3.** Expressing rapture: *a rapt expression on her face.* [Middle English, from Latin *raptus,* "seized",

from the past participle of *rapere,* to seize.]

rap·tor (ráp-tər, -tawr) *n.* **1.** A bird of prey. **2.** A carnivorous birdlike dinosaur. [From Latin *raptor,* "one who seizes", from *raptus,* RAPT.]

rap·to·ri·al (rap-táwri-əl ‖ -tóri-) *adj.* **1.** Subsisting by seizing prey, predatory. **2.** Adapted for the seizing of prey. Said of the feet of birds of prey. **3.** Of, or pertaining to, or characteristic of raptors.

rap·ture (rápchər) *n.* **1.** The state of being transported by a powerful emotion; great joy; ecstasy. **2.** *Often plural.* An expression or utterance of great delight. **3.** *Archaic.* The transporting of a person from one place to another, especially to heaven. —See Synonyms at **ecstasy.** ~ *tr.v.* **raptured, -turing, -tures.** *Archaic.* To enrapture. [Medieval Latin *raptūra,* "ecstasy", from *raptus,* RAPT.]

rap·tur·ous (rápchərəss) *adj.* Expressing great joy or delight; ecstatic. —**rap·tur·ous·ly** *adv.* —**rap·tur·ous·ness** *n.*

ra·ra a·vis (ráarə ávviss, ráir-ə áyviss) *n., pl.* **rara avises** or **rarae aves** (ráarī ávvayz, ráir-ee áyveez). A rare or unique person or thing. [Latin, "rare bird".]

rare¹ (rair) *adj.* **rarer, rarest. 1.** *Abbr.* **r.** Infrequently occurring; uncommon; unusual. **2.** Highly valued owing to unusualness; special. **3.** Thin in density; rarefied. Said of gases. **4.** Of unusual excellence; exceptional: *a rare novel.* [Middle English, from Latin *rārus,* loose, thin, scarce, remarkable.] —**rare·ness** *n.*

rare² *adj.* **rarer, rarest.** Underdone so as to retain redness. Said of meat. [Variant of obsolete *rear,* half-cooked (originally of eggs) Middle English *rere,* Old English *hrēr.*] —**rare·ness** *n.*

rare·bit (ráirbit) *n.* A cheese dish, **Welsh rabbit** *(see).* [Folk-etymological variant of (WELSH) RABBIT.]

rare earth *n.* **1.** Any of various oxides of the rare-earth elements. **2.** Loosely, a rare-earth element.

rare-earth element (ráir-érth) *n.* Any of a group of metallic elements with atomic numbers from 57 to 71. Also called "rare earth", "lanthanide", "lanthanon". [Originally contrasted with the socalled "common-earth elements" (calcium, magnesium, and aluminium).]

rar·ee show (ráir-ee) *n.* **1.** A peepshow *(see).* **2.** A street show. [From RARE (excellent).]

rar·e·fac·tion (ráir-i-fáksh'n) *n.* Also **rar·e·fi·ca·tion** (-fi-káysh'n). **1.** The act or process of rarefying. **2.** The state of being rarefied. —**rar·e·fac·tive** *adj.*

rar·e·fied (ráir-i-fīd) *adj.* **1.** Belonging or restricted to a small and select group; esoteric. **2.** Marked by a lofty or exalted style or quality: *a rarefied academic atmosphere.*

rar·e·fy (ráir-i-fī) *v.* **-fied, -fying, -fies.** —*tr.* **1.** To make thin, less compact, or less dense. **2.** To purify or refine. —*intr.* To become thin, less dense, or purer. [Middle English *rarefien,* from Old French *rarefier,* from Latin *rārēfacere* : *rārus,* RARE + *facere,* to make.] —**rar·e·fi·a·ble** (-fī-əb'l ‖ -fī-) *adj.*

rare gas *n. Chemistry.* An **inert gas** *(see).*

rare·ly (ráirli) *adv.* **1.** Not often; seldom; infrequently: *"The truth is rarely pure and never simple."* (Oscar Wilde). **2.** In an unusual degree; exceptionally. **3.** *Regional.* With uncommon excellence.

Usage: The use of *ever* following *rarely* is commonly used for emphasis in informal speech (*I rarely ever go there*), but in formal contexts it is criticised as redundant. Generally acceptable are such combinations as *rarely if ever* and *rarely or never.*

rare-ripe (ráir-rīp) *adj. U.S.* Ripening early. ~ *n. U.S.* A fruit or vegetable that ripens early. [*Rare-,* variant (perhaps influenced by RARE, underdone) of RATHE.]

rar·ing (ráir-ing) *adj. Informal.* Full of eagerness; enthusiastic. Followed by an infinitive: *We're raring to go.* [From dialectal *rare,* variant of REAR (to arouse, raise up).]

rar·i·ty (ráir-əti) *n., pl.* **-ties. 1.** Something that is especially valued because it is rare. **2.** The quality or state of being rare; infrequency of occurrence.

Ra·ro·ton·ga (ráir-ə-tóng-gə). A volcanic island in the South Pacific Ocean, site of Avarua, capital of the Cook Islands.

R.A.S. **1.** Royal Agricultural Society **2.** Royal Astronomical Society.

ras·bo·ra (raz-báw-rə ‖ -bô-) *n.* Any of various tropical fishes of the genus *Rasbora,* of which several brightly coloured species are kept in home aquariums. [From a native East Indian name.]

ras·cal (ráask'l ‖ rásk'l) *n.* **1.** An unscrupulous or dishonest person; a scoundrel. **2.** One who is playfully mischievous; a scamp. Often used affectionately or humorously, especially of children. **3.** *Archaic.* One belonging to the rabble. ~ *adj. Archaic.* Of or suited to the rabble; base. [Middle English, from Old French *rascaille,* rabble, perhaps from Old Northern French *rasque* (unattested), dregs, mud, filth, from Vulgar Latin *rasica* (unattested), from Latin *rādere,* to scrape. Compare **rash** (eruption).] —**ras·cal·ly** *adj.*

ras·cal·i·ty (raa-skál-əti ‖ ra-) *n., pl.* **-ties. 1.** The behaviour or character of a rascal. **2.** A base or mischievous act.

rase. Variant of **raze.**

rash¹ (rash) *adj.* **rasher, rashest. 1.** Acting without forethought or due caution; impetuous. **2.** Characterised by or resulting from illconsidered haste or boldness: *a rash decision.* —See Synonyms at **reckless.** [Middle English *rasch,* nimble, quick, eager, perhaps from Middle Dutch *rasch;* probably cognate with RATHE.] —**rash·ly** *adv.* —**rash·ness** *n.*

rash² *n.* **1.** Any eruption of the skin in spots or blotches. **2.** An outbreak of many instances within a brief period: *a rash of defections to the other party.* [Possibly from obsolete French *rache,* from

Old French *rasche,* scurf, from *raschier,* to scratch, from Vulgar Latin *rasciāre* (unattested), to scrape, from Latin *rādere* (past participle *rāsus*).]

rash·er (ráshər) *n.* A thin slice of bacon or ham to be fried or grilled. [16th century : origin obscure.]

Ras·mus·sen (ráss-mə-sən || *U.S.* ra͡ass-), **Knud Johan Victor** (1879–1933). Danish explorer and ethnologist. Of Eskimo descent, he spent much of his time in Arctic America studying the inhabitants, and argued that the Eskimo and the American Indian were descended from common ancestors.

ra·so·ri·al (rə-sáw-ri-əl, -záw- || -sō-, -zō-) *adj.* Characteristically scratching the ground for food. Said of poultry. [Late Latin *rāsor,* "scraper", from Latin *rādere* (past participle *rāsus*), to scrape.]

rasp (raasp || rasp) *v.* **rasped, rasping, rasps.** *—tr.* **1.** To file or scrape with a rasp. **2.** To utter in a rough, grating tone. **3.** To irritate; grate upon (nerves or feelings). *—intr.* **1.** To grate; scrape harshly. **2.** To make a harsh, grating sound.
~n. **1.** A coarse file having abrasive, pointed projections. **2.** The act of filing with a rasp. **3.** A harsh, grating sound. [Middle English *raspen,* from Old French *rasper,* from Old High German *raspōn,* from Germanic *hrap-* (unattested), to snatch. See **raffle.**] **—rasp·er** *n.* **—rasp·ing·ly** *adv.* **—rasp·y** *adj.*

ras·pa·to·ry (ra͡aspə-tri, -təri || ráspə-) *n., pl.* **-ies.** A surgical instrument used for scraping the surface of a bone. [Medieval Latin *raspatorium* (unattested), or French *raspatoire,* from Old French *rasper, raspe,* RASP.]

rasp·ber·ry (ra͡az-bri, ra͡ass-, -bəri || ráz-, ráss-, -berri) *n., pl.* **-ries.** **1.** Any of various shrubby, usually prickly plants of the genus *Rubus,* bearing edible berries, such as *R. idaeus,* of Europe. **2.** The fruit of any of these plants, consisting of a mass of small, fleshy, usually red drupelets. **3.** Moderate to dark or purplish red. **4.** *Slang.* A derisive or contemptuous sound made by vibrating the extended tongue and the lips while exhaling. [From obsolete *raspis*† + BERRY.] **—rasp·ber·ry** *adj.*

Ras·pu·tin (rass-péw-tin, -po͞o-), **(Grigory Yefimovich),** born G. Y. Novykh (1872–1916). Russian monk and faith healer. A Siberian peasant, he preached and lived a peculiar religious life of "sinning in order to be forgiven" (Rasputin can mean debauchee). His relative success in treating the Tsarevich's haemophilia and his magnetic personality gained him great influence at the Imperial court. He was murdered by nobles anxious to uphold the monarchy.

Ras·ta (rástə, *also* rústə) *n., pl.* **-tas.** *Informal.* A Rastafarian. Also called "Rastaman".

Ras·ta·fa·ri·an, Ras Ta·fa·ri·an (rástə-fáir-i-ən) *n.* A member of a cult of black nationalists, originating in Jamaica, that regard Ras Tafari, the title and surname of the former Ethiopian emperor **Haile Selassie** *(see),* as God. They typically have dreadlocks and wear beret-like hats called toms. **—Ras·ta·fa·ri·an·ism** *n.* **—Ras·ta·fa·ri·an** *adj.*

ras·ter (rástər) *n. Electronics.* A pattern of lines produced by scanning an electron beam, as on a television screen. [German *Raster,* screen, from Latin *rastrum,* rake, from *rādere* (past participial stem *rās-*), to scrape.]

rat (rat) *n.* **1.** Any of various long-tailed rodents resembling, but larger than, mice; especially, any of the genus *Rattus,* such as the common black rat, *R. rattus.* See **brown rat. 2.** Any of various similar animals. **3.** *Slang.* A despicable, sneaky person, especially one who abandons his associates in time of trouble. **4.** *Slang.* A blackleg; a scab. **5.** *Chiefly U.S. Slang.* One who informs on or betrays his associates. **—smell a rat.** *Slang.* To suspect that something underhand or treacherous is going on.
~intr.v. **ratted, ratting, rats. 1.** To hunt for or catch rats, especially with the aid of dogs. **2.** *Slang.* To desert or betray one's associates or friends. Used with *on.* [Middle English *rat,* Old English *ræt,* from Germanic *ratt-* (unattested).]

ra·ta *n.* Either of two New Zealand trees of the genus *Metrosideros, M. robusta* or *M. lucida,* having crimson flowers and hard wood.

rat·a·ble, rate·a·ble (ráyt-əb'l) *adj.* **1.** Capable of being rated, estimated, or appraised. **2.** *British.* Liable to assessment or rates. **—rat·a·bil·i·ty** (-ə-bílləti), **rat·a·ble·ness** *n.* **—rat·a·bly** *adv.*

ratable value *n. British.* The value at which property is assessed by a local authority for the payment of rates. Also called "ratal".

rat·a·fi·a (ráttə-féer, -fée-ə) *n.* Also **rat·a·fee** (-fee). **1.** A liqueur flavoured with fruit kernels or almonds. **2.** A small macaroon flavoured with almonds. [French, from West Indian French Creole.]

rat·al (ráyt'l) *n. British.* Ratable value.
~adj. British. Of or pertaining to rates or their payment or assessment. [RAT(E) + -AL.]

ratan. Variant of **rattan.**

rat·a·plan (ráttə-plan) *n.* A tattoo, as of a drum, the hooves of a galloping horse, or machine-gun fire. [French (imitative).]

rat-arsed (rát-árssst, -a͡asst) *adj. British Vulgar Slang.* Drunk.

rat-a-tat-tat (ráttə-tát-tát) *n.* A series of short, sharp sounds, such as those made by knocking on a door. [Imitative.]

ra·ta·touille (ráttə-to͞o-i, -twée) *n.* A vegetable stew made from tomatoes, peppers, courgettes, and aubergines. [French (dialect), from *touiller,* to stir.]

rat·bag (rát-bag) *n.* **1.** *Chiefly Australian & N.Z. Slang.* A scoundrel or rascal. Sometimes used affectionately or humorously. **2.** *British Informal.* An obnoxious person. **—rat·bag·ger·y** (-əri) *n.*

rat-bite fever (rát-bīt) *n.* Either of two infectious diseases contractible from the bite of a rat: **1.** That arising from *Streptobacillus moniliformis* and characterised by skin inflammation, back and joint pains, headache, and vomiting. **2.** That arising from *Spirillum minus,* with ulceration at the site of the bite, a purplish rash, and recurrent fever. Also called "rat-bite disease".

rat-catch·er (rát-kachər) *n.* A person who rids houses of rats or other vermin.

ratch·et (ráchit) *n.* **1.** A mechanism consisting of a pawl, or hinged catch, that engages the sloping teeth of a bar, permitting motion in one direction only. **2.** The pawl, wheel, or bar of such a mechanism. **3.** The toothed wheel in such a mechanism. Also called "ratchet wheel". [French *rochet,* from Old French *rocquet,* head of a lance, from Frankish *rokko* (unattested), a distaff.]

rate[1] (rayt) *n.* **1. a.** A measured quantity, as of speed, cost, or value, calculated by its relation to some other quantity: *at the rate of 60 miles per hour; the birth rate.* **b.** A ratio that is fixed as a standard between two sums, quantities, or the like: *the rate of exchange.* **2.** The speed at which something moves, changes, or progresses: *driving at a very dangerous rate.* **3.** The cost per unit of a commodity or service. **4.** A charge or payment calculated in relation to any particular sum or quantity. **5.** A specified level of relative quality. Used in combination: *first-rate; tenth-rate.* **6.** *Plural.* In Britain, a tax on property assessed and levied by a local authority to pay for local services. **—at any rate.** Whatever the case may be; anyway.
~v. **rated, rating, rates.** *—tr.* **1.** To calculate the value of; appraise. **2.** To place in a particular rank or grade. **3.** To regard or account: *The play was rated a great success.* **4.** To value for purposes of taxation. **5.** To specify the performance limits of (a machine or firearm, for example). **6.** *Informal.* To think highly of: *I don't really rate this job.* **7.** *Informal.* To merit or deserve: *rate special treatment.* *—intr.* **1.** To be ranked in a particular class or grade. **2.** *Chiefly U.S. Informal.* To have status, importance, or influence. —See Synonyms at **estimate.** [Middle English, from Old French, from Medieval Latin *rata,* calculated, fixed, from the feminine past participle of Latin *rērī,* to calculate.] **—rat·er** *n.*

rate[2] *tr.v.* **rated, rating, rates.** To berate angrily. [Middle English *raten,* perhaps from Old Norse *hrata.*]

rate-cap·ping (ráyt-kápping) *n.* In Britain, the imposing by central government of a ceiling on the rates a local authority could levy.

ra·tel (ráy-t'l, -tel || *South African* ra͡at'l) *n.* An animal, the **honey badger** *(see).* [Afrikaans *ratel*†.]

rate of exchange *n.* The ratio at which the unit of currency of one country may be, or is, exchanged for the unit of currency of another country. Also called "exchange rate".

rate·pay·er (ráyt-payər) *n. British.* One who is liable to pay rates.

rat·fink (rát-fingk) *n. U.S. Slang.* A contemptible, obnoxious, or otherwise undesirable person. [RAT (to betray) + FINK.]

rat·fish (rát-fish) *n., pl.* **-fishes** or collectively **ratfish. 1.** A fish, *Hydrolagus affinis,* of Pacific waters, having a long, narrow tail. **2.** The **rabbitfish** *(see).*

Rat·haus (rát-howss; *German* ra͡at-) *n. German.* In Germany, a government or municipal building; a town hall.

rathe (rayth, raath || rath) *adj. Archaic & Poetic.* **1.** Appearing or ripening early in the year. **2.** Prompt; eager. [Middle English *rathe,* early, rapid, Old English *hræd, hræth,* from Germanic.]

Ra·the·nau (ra͡atə-now), **Walter** (1867–1922). German industrialist and politician, one of the leading figures in the period of German reconstruction after World War I. As foreign minister (1922), he negotiated the Treaty of Rapallo with the U.S.S.R. He was assassinated by anti-Semites shortly afterwards.

rath·er (ra͡a-thər || rá-; -thér *for sense 7*) *adv.* **1.** More readily; preferably: *I'd rather stay at home.* **2.** With more reason, logic, wisdom, or other justification. **3.** With more accuracy: *He's my friend, or rather he was my friend.* **4.** To a certain extent; somewhat: *rather nice.* **5.** On the contrary: *Locks are not for opening doors; rather, they are for keeping them firmly shut.* **6.** *West & South African.* Instead or in preference: *I don't feel like swimming—let's go for a walk rather.* **7.** *Chiefly British.* Most certainly. Used as an emphatic affirmative reply. **8.** *Obsolete.* More quickly; earlier. [Middle English *rather,* Old English *hrathor,* comparative of *hrathe, hræth,* early, RATHE.]

Usage: In constructions expressing preference, *rather* is generally preceded by *would,* either in full or abbreviated form *('d),* when followed by a bare infinitive: *I would rather leave now than stay until midnight. Should* is also possible in this construction. When followed by a clause, *rather* may also be preceded by *had: I had rather you left now,* and this is especially common in American English, where there is also a preference for *had* in statements using the infinitive construction. Of course, in informal speech, the distinction between *would* and *had* in statements disappears, as both are reduced to *'d.* Nor is there a usage issue in relation to question forms, where *would* is the only possible construction: *Would you rather stay? Would you rather I stayed?*

When pronouns follow *rather than,* they may occur either in subject or object form, depending on their role in relation to the rest of the sentence. For example, in the sentence *I asked you rather than him, him* is the object because it is governed by the verb *ask,* whereas in *You, rather than he, caused the trouble,* the pronoun *he* is used because it is part of the subject of the verb *cause.* In informal speech, however, there is a tendency for object forms to be used universally.

rat·i·fy (rátti-fī) *tr.v.* **-fied, -fying, -fies.** To give formal sanction to; approve and so make valid. See Synonyms at **approve, confirm.** [Middle English *ratifien,* from Old French *ratifier,* from Medieval Latin *ratificāre* : Latin *ratus,* "fixed" (see **rate**) + *facere,* to make.]

—**rat·i·fi·ca·tion** (-káysh'n) *n.* —**rat·i·fi·er** *n.*
rat·i·ne (ra-teén) *n.* Also **rat·i·né** (rátti-nay || *U.S.* -náy). A loosely woven fabric with a coarse, knotted texture. [French, past participle of *ratiner*†, to adorn.]
rat·ing[1] (ráyting) *n.* **1.** A place assigned on a scale; a standing. **2.** In the Royal Navy and certain other navies, a seaman. **3.** An evaluation of the financial status of a business or an individual: *has a very good credit rating.* **4.** A specified performance limit, as of capacity, range, or operational capability: *power rating.* **5.** *Plural.* An estimate of the number of listeners or viewers of a particular radio or television programme, used as an index of its popularity. **6.** Any of the classes into which racing yachts are divided according to tonnage, dimensions, or the like.
rating[2] *n.* A scolding.
ra·ti·o (ráy-shi-ō || *U.S. also* -shō) *n., pl.* **-tios.** **1.** The relation in number between two similar magnitudes, determined by the number of times an object exists in one quantity as compared with the other: *the ratio of managerial staff to all employees.* **2.** *Mathematics.* The relative size of two quantities expressed as the quotient of one divided by the other: *The ratio of 7 to 4 is written 7:4 or 7/4.* [Latin *ratiō*, computation, from *rērī* (past participle *ratus*), to consider.]
ra·ti·oc·i·nate (rátti-óssi-nayt || *U.S. also* ráshi-, -ō-si-) *intr.v.* **-nated, -nating, -nates.** To reason methodically and logically. [Latin *ratiōcinārе*, from *ratiō*, RATIO.] —**ra·ti·oc·i·na·tion** (-náysh'n) *n.* —**ra·ti·oc·i·na·tive** (-nətiv, -naytiv) *adj.* —**ra·ti·oc·i·na·tor** (-náytər) *n.*
ra·tion (rásh'n || *U.S. also* ráysh'n) *n.* **1.** *Often plural.* A fixed portion; especially, an amount of food, clothing, fuel, or the like, allotted to persons in military service or to civilians in times of scarcity. Also used adjectivally: *a ration book.* **2.** *Plural.* Provisions. **3.** An allotted or deserved amount: *He's used up his ration of goodwill.*
—*tr.v.* **rationed, -tioning, -tions.** **1.** To supply with rations. **2. a.** To distribute in restricted allocations, as during wartime. **b.** To give sparingly, as if in rations. Often used with *out*: *The stern father rationed even his love out to his sons.* —See Synonyms at **distribute.** [French, from Latin *ratiō* (stem *ratiōn-*), RATIO.]
ra·tion·al (rásh'n'l) *adj.* **1.** Having or exercising the ability to reason. **2.** Of sound mind; sane. **3.** Manifesting or based upon reason; logical. **4.** *Mathematics.* Designating an algebraic expression or equation in which no variable appears in an irreducible radical or with a fractional exponent. [Latin *ratiōnālis*, from *ratiō*, reason, RATIO.] —**ra·tion·al·ly** *adv.* —**ra·tion·al·ness** *n.*
ra·tion·ale (ráshə-naál, *rarely* -i) *n.* **1.** The fundamental reasons for something; a logical basis. **2.** An exposition of principles or reasons. [Latin *ratiōnāle*, neuter of *ratiōnālis*, RATIONAL.]
ra·tion·al·ise, ra·tion·al·ize (rásh'n'l-īz) *v.* **-ised, -ising, -ises.** —*tr.* **1.** To make conformable to reason; make rational. **2.** To interpret from a rational standpoint. **3.** *Psychology.* To devise self-satisfying but inadequate reasons for (one's behaviour), especially while being unaware of unconscious motivation. **4.** *Mathematics.* To remove radicals without changing the value of (an expression) or roots of (an equation). **5.** *Chiefly British.* To bring modern, efficient methods to (an industry, for example). —*intr.* **1.** To think in a rational or logical way. **2.** *Psychology.* To rationalise one's behaviour. —**ra·tion·al·i·sa·tion** (-ī-záysh'n || *U.S.* -i-) *n.* —**ra·tion·al·is·er** *n.*
ra·tion·al·ism (rásh'n'l-iz'm) *n.* **1.** *Theology.* **a.** The theory that the exercise of reason, rather than the acceptance of authority or spiritual revelation, provides the only valid basis for belief, and that reason is the prime source of spiritual truth. **b.** The rejection of religion on the grounds that it can have no logical or rational basis. **2.** In ethics, the theory that the exercise of reason provides the only valid basis for moral beliefs and rules of conduct. **3.** *Philosophy.* The theory, as exemplified in the philosophy of Descartes and Spinoza, that the exercise of reason, rather than empiricism, provides the only valid basis for and source of knowledge. Compare **empiricism.** —**ra·tion·al·ist** *n. & adj.* —**ra·tion·al·is·tic** (-ístik) *adj.* —**ra·tion·al·is·ti·cal·ly** *adv.*
ra·tion·al·i·ty (ráshə-nál-əti) *n., pl.* **-ties.** **1.** The quality or condition of being rational. **2.** A rational belief or practice.
rational number *n.* Any number capable of being expressed as an integer or quotient of integers.
rat·ite (rát-īt) *adj.* Designating any of a group of flightless birds having a flat breastbone without the keel characteristic of most flying birds and feathers lacking barbs.
—*n.* A ratite bird, such as the ostrich, emu, or kiwi. [New Latin *Ratitae* (group), from Latin *ratis*, raft (so named in allusion to the "keelless" sternum).]
rat kangaroo *n.* Any of various Australian marsupials of the subfamily Potoroinae, like kangaroos but with a long, ratlike face.
rat·line, rat·lin (rát-lin) *n. Nautical.* **1.** Any of the small ropes fastened horizontally to the shrouds of a ship and forming a ladder for going aloft. **2.** The rope used for this purpose.
RATO rocket assisted takeoff.
ra·toon, rat·toon (ra-tóōn) *n.* A basal shoot sprouting from a plant such as the banana, pineapple, or sugar cane.
—*v.* **ratooned** or **rattooned, -tooning, -toons.** —*intr.* To produce or grow as a ratoon or ratoons. —*tr.* To propagate (a crop) from ratoons. [Spanish *retoño*, sprout, from *retoñar*, to sprout : *re-*, again + *otoñar*, to grow in the autumn, from *otoño*, autumn, from Latin *autumnus*, AUTUMN.]
rat race *n. Informal.* Ceaseless, hectic, and fiercely competitive activity, especially when involving a struggle for power or promotion: *As a merchant banker you can't avoid the rat race.*
rats (rats) *interj. Informal.* Used to express contemptuous disbelief or irritation.
rats·bane (ráts-bayn) *n.* **1.** *Literary.* Rat poison. **2.** Arsenic trioxide.
rat snake *n.* Any of several nonvenomous, rodent-eating snakes such as those of the genera *Elaphe* and *Ptyas.*
rat-tail (rát-tayl) *adj.* Also **rat·tailed** (-tayld). **1.** Shaped like a rat's tail: *a rat-tail file.* **2.** Designating a spoon whose handle is prolonged like a tail along the back of the bowl.
—*n.* **1.** A fish, the **grenadier** *(see).* **2. a.** A horse's tail that is hairless. **b.** A horse with such a tail. **3.** A round file shaped like a rat's tail, used especially to widen holes in metal. Also "rat's tail".
rat·tan, ra·tan (rə-tán, ra-) *n.* **1.** Any of various climbing palms of the genera *Calamus, Daemonorops,* or *Plectomia,* of tropical Asia, having long, tough, slender stems. **2.** The stems of any of these palms, used to make wickerwork. **3.** A switch, stick, or cane made from such a stem. [Malay *rotan*, probably from *raut*, trim.]
rat·ter (ráttər) *n.* **1.** A cat, dog, or person who catches and kills rats. **2.** *Slang.* A deserter, betrayer, or traitor.
Rat·ti·gan (ráttigən), **Sir Terence (Mervyn)** (1911–77). British playwright. He first made his name with two farces, *French Without Tears* (1936) and *While the Sun Shines* (1943). Perhaps his best-known play is *The Winslow Boy* (1946), which won a New York Critics' Award. He was knighted in 1971.
rat·tle[1] (rátt'l) *v.* **-tled, -tling, -tles.** —*intr.* **1.** To make or emit a quick succession of short, sharp sounds, as of pebbles being shaken in a container. **2.** To move with such sounds: *a train rattling along the track.* **3.** To talk rapidly and at length, usually without much serious content. Used with *on.* —*tr.* **1.** To cause to rattle. **2.** To utter or perform rapidly or effortlessly: *rattle off a list of names.* **3.** *Informal.* To disconcert; unnerve; fluster.
—*n.* **1.** A rapid succession of short, percussive sounds. **2.** A device for producing these sounds, such as a baby's toy. **3.** A rattling sound in the throat caused by obstructed breathing. **4.** The series of horny structures at the end of a rattlesnake's tail. **5.** Loud or rapid talk; babble. **6.** Idle or trivial chatter. **7.** An incessant talker. **8.** Any of several related European plants having a seed capsule that rattles, such as the red rattle, *Pedicularis palustris,* or the yellow rattle, *Rhinanthus minor.* [Middle English *ratelen*, from Middle Low German *rattelen*, akin to Middle High German *razzeln*†.]
rattle[2] *tr.v.* **-tled, -tling, -tles.** *Nautical.* To secure ratlines to (a rigging). Used with *down.* [Back-formation from *rattling*, variant of RATLINE.]
Rattle, Sir Simon (1955–). British conductor. He won an international conducting competition at the age of seventeen and made his debut at the Royal Albert Hall in 1976. He was principal conductor of the City of Birmingham Symphony Orchestra (1980–91) and its music director (1991–98).
rat·tle·box (rátt'l-boks) *n.* Any of various plants or shrubs of the genus *Crotalaria,* having inflated pods in which the seeds rattle.
rat·tle·brain (rátt'l-brayn) *n. Informal.* A talkative, foolish person. Also called "rattlehead", "rattlepate". —**rat·tle·brained** (-braynd) *adj.*
rat·tler (ráttlər) *n.* **1.** One who or that which rattles. **2.** *Informal.* An outstanding example of something. **3.** *Chiefly U.S.* A rattlesnake. **4.** *U.S. Informal.* A goods train.
rat·tle·snake (rátt'l-snayk) *n.* Any of various venomous New World snakes of the genera *Crotalus* and *Sistrurus,* having at the end of the tail a series of loosely attached, horny segments that can be vibrated to produce a rattling or buzzing sound.
rattlesnake plantain *n.* Any of various small orchids of the genus *Goodyera,* having mottled or striped leaves and spikes of whitish flowers. [From its leaves, which resemble a rattlesnake's skin.]
rat·tle·trap (rátt'l-trap) *n. Informal.* A rickety, worn-out vehicle.
rat·tling (rátt'l-ing, ráttling) *adj. Informal.* **1.** Animated; brisk: *rattling conversation.* **2.** Very good.
—*adv. Informal.* Very; especially: *a rattling good yarn.*
rat·tly (rátt'l-i, rátli) *adj.* Rattling or apt to rattle; clattering.
rattoon. Variant of **ratoon.**
rat·trap, rat-trap (rát-trap) *n.* **1.** Any of various traps used for catching rats. **2.** A bicycle pedal of a type having metal teeth, and often a toe clip, to provide a firm grip for the foot.
rat·ty (rátti) *adj.* **-tier, -tiest.** **1.** Of or characteristic of rats. **2.** Infested by rats. **3.** *Chiefly British Slang.* Peevish; irritable. **4.** *Slang.* Unkempt and dirty. Said of hair. **5.** *U.S. Slang.* Dilapidated and shabby. —**rat·ti·ly** *adv.* —**rat·ti·ness** *n.*
rau·cous (ráwkəss) *adj.* Rough-sounding and harsh. [Latin *raucus*, hoarse, harsh.] —**rau·cous·ly** *adv.* —**rau·cous·ness** *n.*
raun·chy (ráwnchi) *adj.* **-chier, -chiest.** **1.** *Chiefly U.S. Slang.* **a.** Earthy; coarse; vulgar. **b.** Smutty; indecent. **2.** *Informal.* Marked by loud, driving rhythms. Said especially of rock music. [20th century : origin obscure.] —**raunch·i·ly** *adv.* —**raunch·i·ness** *n.*
Rausch·en·berg (rówsh'n-berg), **Robert** (1925–). U.S. painter and sculptor. He developed an individual, somewhat pop-art style out of the collage and *objet trouvé* methods. One of his most notable works is *The Bed* (1955), which consists of his own bed, daubed with paint and hung vertically.
rau·wol·fi·a (raw-wóolfi-ə, row-) *n.* Any of various tropical trees and shrubs of the genus *Rauwolfia;* especially, *R. serpentina,* of southeast Asia. The root of this species is the source of alkaloid drugs such as reserpine, formerly used as tranquillisers but now used chiefly to treat high blood pressure. [New Latin, after Leonhard *Rauwolf* (died 1596), German botanist.]

rav·age (rávvij) *v.* **-aged, -aging, -ages.** —*tr.* To destroy or despoil; devastate: *Invaders ravaged the countryside; a face ravaged by grief.* —*intr.* To wreak destruction.
—*n.* **1.** The act or practice of ravaging. **2.** *Usually plural.* Damage; destructive effects: *the ravages of disease.* [French, from Old French, from *ravir,* to RAVISH.] —**rav·ag·er** *n.*

rave (rayv) *v.* **raved, raving, raves.** —*intr.* **1.** To speak wildly, irrationally, or incoherently: *raving like a madman.* **2.** To roar; rage. **3.** *Informal.* To speak with wild enthusiasm: *He raved about her looks.* **4.** To speak in an angry and vehement manner. **5.** *British Slang.* To engage in wild, festive activities. Often used in the phrase *rave it up.* —*tr.* To utter in a wild and unrestrained manner.
—*n.* **1.** The state or act of raving. **2.** *British Slang.* **a.** A wild party. **b.** A large overnight gathering of young people, often in a warehouse, barn or open field, for the enjoyment of loud, electronic music. **3.** *British Slang.* A current fashion or trend.
—*adj. Informal.* Wildly enthusiastic: *rave reviews.* [Middle English *raven,* to be delirious, wander, from Old Northern French *raver*†.]

rav·el (rávv'l) *v.* **-elled** or *U.S.* **-eled, -elling** or *U.S.* **-eling, -els.** —*tr.* **1.** To separate the fibres or threads of (cloth, for example); unravel. Often used with *out.* **2.** To clarify by separating the aspects of. Often used with *out: "Must I ravel out my weaved-up folly"* (Shakespeare). **3.** To entangle or knot. **4.** To complicate or confuse. —*intr.* **1.** To become separated into component threads; unravel; fray. Used of cloth. **2.** To become entangled, knotted, or confused.
—*n.* **1.** A broken or frayed thread. **2.** A tangle or knot. [Dutch *rafelen,* to unravel, from obsolete Dutch *ravelen*†, to entangle.] —**rav·ell·er** *n.*

Ra·vel (ra-vél), **Maurice** (1875–1937). French composer, with Debussy the leading figure of the so-called Impressionist school. He is perhaps best known for his piano compositions, especially *Pavane pour une infante défunte* (1899) and *Le Tombeau de Couperin* (1917). He wrote two piano concertos, one for the left hand only (1931). His other major orchestral scores include the song cycle, *Schéhérazade* (1903), and the ballet, *Daphnis et Chloé* (1912).

rave·lin (ráv-lin, rávvə-) *n.* A triangular, embanked salient outside the main ditch of a fortress. [French, from obsolete Italian *ravellino, rivellino,* perhaps from diminutive of *riva,* bank, from Latin *rīpa.*]

rav·ell·ing (rávv'l-ing) *n.* A thread or fibre that has become separated from a woven material.

rav·el·ment (rávv'l-mənt) *n. Archaic.* Confusion or entanglement.

ra·ven¹ (ráyv'n) *n.* **1.** A large bird, *Corvus corax,* related to the crow, having black plumage and a croaking cry. **2.** Shiny black. [Middle English *raven,* Old English *hræfn,* from Germanic.] —**ra·ven** *adj.*

rav·en² (rávv'n) *v.* **-ened, -ening, -ens.** —*tr.* **1.** To consume greedily; devour. **2.** To seek or seize (prey or plunder). —*intr.* **1.** To seek or seize prey or plunder. **2.** To eat ravenously; be voracious.
—*n.* Variant of **ravin.** [Old French *raviner,* ravage, seize by force, from Vulgar Latin *rapīnāre* (unattested), from Latin *rapīna,* rapine, from *rapere,* to seize.] —**rav·en·er** *n.*

rav·en·ing (rávv'n-ing) *adj.* **1.** Predatory; voracious. **2.** *Archaic.* Rabid. —**rav·en·ing·ly** *adv.*

Ra·ven·na (rə-vénnə). Capital of Ravenna province in Emilia-Romagna, north central Italy. It is an agricultural market and industrial centre, connected to the Adriatic coast by canal. Ravenna rose to importance under the Romans and is famous for its colourful mosaics and for its Roman and Byzantine buildings.

rav·en·ous (rávv'n-əss, rávvin-) *adj.* **1.** Extremely hungry; famished. **2.** Greedy; rapacious; voracious: *ravenous for power.* [Middle English, rapacious, from Old French *ravineux,* from *raviner,* to RAVEN.] —**rav·en·ous·ly** *adv.* —**rav·en·ous·ness** *n.*

rav·er (ráyvər) *n. British Slang.* A person who appears to lead a very exciting and uninhibited social life.

rave-up (ráyv-up) *n. British Slang.* A wild party; a rave.

ra·vi·gote (rávvi-gōt, -gŏt) *n.* A vinegar sauce spiced with minced onion, capers, and herbs, served with boiled meats or fish. [French, from *ravigoter,* to add new vigour : *re-,* again + *a-,* to, from Latin *ad-* + *vigueur,* vigour, from Latin *vigor,* VIGOUR.]

rav·in, rav·en (rávvin) *n. Poetic.* **1.** Plundering or pillage. **2.** Something taken as prey. **3.** The act or practice of preying. [Middle English *ravine,* from Old French, rapine, from Latin *rapīna,* from *rapere,* to seize.]

ra·vine (rə-veén) *n.* A deep, narrow cleft or gorge in the earth's surface, especially one worn by the flow of water. [French, mountain torrent, from Old French, rapine. See **ravin.**]

rav·ing (ráyving) *adj.* **1.** Talking or behaving irrationally; wild: *a raving maniac.* **2.** *Informal.* Exciting admiration or notice: *a raving beauty.*
—*adv.* Used as an intensive: *raving mad.*
—*n. Often plural.* Delirious, irrational speech. —**rav·ing·ly** *adv.*

ra·vi·o·li (rávvi-ōli || *U.S. also* raávi-) *pl.n.* **1.** Small casings of pasta filled with chopped meat, cheese, or other ingredients and usually served with a sauce. **2.** *Used with a singular verb.* A dish consisting of ravioli. [Italian, plural of dialectal *raviolo,* diminutive of *rava,* turnip, from Latin *rāpa,* turnip.]

rav·ish (rávvish) *tr.v.* **-ished, -ishing, -ishes.** **1.** *Literary.* To seize and carry away by force. **2.** *Literary.* To rape; deflower; violate. **3.** To enrapture. Usually used in the passive: *ravished by his charm.* [Middle English *ravisshen,* from Old French *ravir* (present stem *raviss-*), from Vulgar Latin *rapīre* (unattested), from Latin *rapere,* seize.] —**rav·ish·er** *n.* —**rav·ish·ment** *n.*

rav·ish·ing (rávvishing) *adj.* **1.** Entrancing; delightful. **2.** *Informal.* Extremely beautiful; gorgeous. —**rav·ish·ing·ly** *adv.*

raw (raw) *adj.* **1.** Uncooked: *raw meat.* **2.** Being in a natural condition; not subjected to manufacturing, refining, or finishing processes: *raw wool.* **3.** Untrained and inexperienced: *a raw recruit.* **4.** *Chiefly U.S.* Recently finished; fresh: *raw plaster.* **5.** Having subcutaneous tissue exposed: *a raw wound.* **6.** Penetratingly damp and cold. **7.** *Informal.* Cruel and unfair. **8.** Outspoken; crude. **9.** Undiluted; neat. Said of spirits. **10.** Not analysed or modified. Said of statistics. **11.** Unhemmed or unfinished. Said of the edge of cloth. —**in the raw. 1.** In a crude or unrefined state. **2.** *Informal.* Nude; naked. —**on the raw.** On a sensitive area or topic: *Her comment about small men touched him on the raw.* [Middle English *raw,* Old English *hrēaw.*] —**raw·ly** *adv.* —**raw·ness** *n.*

Ra·wal·pin·di (ráwl-píndi, raá-wəl-). City in the Punjab, north Pakistan, lying in the foothills of the Himalayas. It is an important industrial and commercial centre, its industries including oil refining, railway engineering, chemicals, furniture, and textiles. After the British occupied the Punjab (1849), it became a major British military outpost. It was the temporary capital of Pakistan (1959–70), during the building of the new capital, Islamabad.

raw·boned (ráw-bōnd) *adj.* Having a lean, gaunt frame with prominent bones.

raw·hide (ráw-hīd) *n.* **1.** The untanned hide of cattle or other animals. **2.** A whip or rope made of such hide.

ra·win·sonde (ráy-win-sond) *n.* A meteorological balloon carrying instruments and a radar target, used for measuring wind speed in the upper atmosphere. [*Radar* + *wind* + radio *sonde.*]

Rawl·plug (ráwl-plug) *n.* A trademark for a small hollow plug of plastic or wool fibre, inserted into holes to secure nails and screws.

raw material *n.* **1.** *Often plural.* The natural products or basic materials on which manufacturing processes are carried out to give finished products. **2.** Somebody or something regarded as having the basic attributes or potential for a particular purpose.

raw sienna *n.* **1.** A brownish-yellow pigment made from untreated sienna. **2.** Brownish orange to light brown. Also called "sienna".

raw silk *n.* **1.** Untreated silk as reeled from the cocoon. **2.** Fabric woven from such silk.

Raws·thorne (ráwss-thawrn), **Alan** (1905–71). British composer. His works include *Theme and Variations* for two violins (1938) and the *Symphonic Studies* (1939), as well as three symphonies, various concertos, and vocal and chamber music.

ray¹ (ray) *n.* **1.** A thin line or narrow beam of radiation, especially of light. **2.** Any graphic or other representation of such a line. **3.** A slight trace or hint; a gleam. **4.** In geometry, a straight line extending indefinitely from a point. **5.** Any structure having the form of lines extending from a point. **6.** *Botany.* A ray flower. **7.** *Zoology.* **a.** Any of the bony spines supporting the membrane of a fish's fin. **b.** Any of the arms of a starfish or related animal.
—*v.* **rayed, raying, rays.** —*tr.* **1.** To send out as rays; emit. **2.** To decorate with rays or radiating lines. **3.** To cast rays upon; irradiate. —*intr.* To extend or issue forth in rays. Used of lines or light, for example. [Middle English, from Old French *rai,* from Latin *radius.* See **radius.**]

ray² *n.* Any of various marine cartilaginous fishes of the order Rajiformes (or Batoidei), having large, winglike, pectoral fins horizontally flattened bodies, and narrow tails. See **electric ray.** [Middle English *raye,* from Old French *raie,* from Latin *raia*†.]

ray³, re (ray) *n. Music.* In tonic sol-fa, a syllable representing the second note of a diatonic scale. [Middle English, from Medieval Latin. See **gamut.**]

Ray¹ (ray), **Man,** born Emanuel Rabinovitch (1890–1976). U.S. artist. A founder of the Dadaist movement, he moved to Paris (1921) and experimented with surrealism. He later became a fashion photographer and film-maker.

Ray² (rī, ray), **Satyajit** (1921–92). Indian film director, the most acclaimed of his generation. His films, such as *Pather Panchali* (1955) and *Distant Thunder* (1973), are notable for their realistic portrayal of everyday life, and the artistic composition of their camera-work.

ray flower *n.* Any of the flat, strap-shaped marginal flowers in the flower head of certain composite plants, such as the daisy. Also called "ray floret". Compare **disc flower.**

ray gun *n.* In science fiction, a weapon that emits rays that can paralyse, stun, kill, or vaporise.

Ray·leigh scattering (ráyli) *n.* The scattering of light waves by particles with dimensions much smaller than their wavelengths, resulting in angular separation of colours, and responsible for the reddish colour of sunset and the blue of the sky. [Explained by Lord Rayleigh (1842–1919) in 1871.]

ray·less (ráy-ləss, -liss) *adj.* **1.** Lacking rays: *a rayless flower.* **2.** Lacking light; gloomy: *a rayless dungeon.*

ray·on (ráy-on, *rarely* -ən) *n.* **1.** Any of several similar synthetic textile fibres produced by forcing a cellulose solution through fine spinnerets and solidifying the resulting filaments. **2.** Any fabric made from such fibres. [From RAY¹ (light).] —**ray·on** *adj.*

raze, rase (rayz) *tr.v.* **razed** or **rased, razing** or **rasing, razes** or **rases.** **1.** To tear down or demolish; level to the ground. **2.** To erase. **3.** *Archaic.* To scrape; graze. —See Synonyms at **ruin.** [Middle English *rasen,* from Old French *raser,* from Vulgar Latin *rasāre* (unattested), from Latin *rādere* (past participle *rāsus*), to scrape.]

ra·zee (ray-zeé, *also* rázzee) *n., pl.* **-ees.** Formerly, a sailing ship made smaller by the removal of its upper deck or decks.
—*tr.v.* **razeed, -eeing, -ees.** To remove the upper deck or decks

from (a sailing ship). [French *rasée*, from *raser*, to shave close.]

ra·zor (ráyzər) *n.* **1.** A sharp-edged cutting instrument, used especially for shaving the face. **2.** An instrument with electrically driven blades, used for shaving.

~*tr.v.* **razored, -oring, -ors.** To use a razor on; shave or cut with a razor. [Middle English *raso(u)r*, from Old French *rasor*, from *raser*, to scrape, RAZE.]

ra·zor·back (ráyzər-bak) *n.* **1.** A whale, the **rorqual** *(see).* **2.** A semi-wild pig of the southeastern United States, having a narrow body with a ridged back. **3.** *U.S.* A sharp, ridged hill.

ra·zor·bill (ráyzər-bil) *n.* A sea bird, *Alca torda*, of the northern Atlantic, having black-and-white plumage and a flattened, white-ringed bill. Also called "razorbilled auk".

razor cut *n.* A hairstyle produced by trimming the hair fairly short with a razor in layers so that it tapers towards the nape of the neck.

ra·zor-edge (ráyzər-ej, -éj) *n.* **1.** A keen, sharp edge, as of a knife or mountain ridge. **2.** A thin dividing line: *the razor-edge of legality.* **3.** A critical or dangerous state of affairs. Used especially in the phrase *on a razor-edge*. Also called "razor's edge".

razor shell *n.* Any of various long, narrow burrowing bivalve molluscs of the family Solenidae. Also *U.S.* "razor clam".

razz (raz) *n. U.S. Slang.* A derisive sound, a **raspberry** *(see).*
~*tr.v.* **razzed, razzing, razzes.** *Chiefly U.S. Slang.* To deride, heckle, or tease. [Short for *razzberry*, variant of RASPBERRY.]

raz·zi·a (rázzi-ə) *n., pl.* **-zias.** A raid carried out for plunder or slaves, especially as formerly practised by Muslims in North Africa. [French, from Arabic (Algerian) *gazīa*, from Arabic *gazwa*.]

raz·zle (rázz'l) *n. Slang.* **1.** A wild spree, especially a drinking spree. Used chiefly in the phrase *on the razzle*. **2.** A razzle-dazzle. [Shortened from RAZZLE-DAZZLE.]

razzle-dazzle (rázz'l-dazz'l, -dázz'l) *n.* **1.** An exciting, glittering display, especially one intended to dazzle or impress, as in advertising. **2.** Ebullient energy; vigour. **3.** A razzle. [Reduplication of DAZZLE.]

razz·ma·tazz (ráz-mə-táz, -taz) *n.* Also **razz·a·ma·tazz** (rázzə-). Noisy excitement and show, especially when designed to impress or attract. [Variant of RAZZLE-DAZZLE.]

Rb The symbol for the element rubidium.

RBC red blood cell.

RBE *Physics.* relative biological effectiveness.

R.C. **1.** Red Cross. **2.** reinforced concrete. **3.** Reserve Corps. **4.** Roman Catholic.

R.C.A. **1.** Royal College of Art. **2.** Royal Canadian Academy. **3.** Radio Corporation of America.

R.C.A.F. Royal Canadian Air Force.

R.C.M. Royal College of Music.

R.C.M.P. Royal Canadian Mounted Police.

R.C.N. **1.** Royal Canadian Navy. **2.** Royal College of Nursing.

R.C.O. Royal College of Organists.

R.C.P. Royal College of Physicians.

rcpt. receipt.

R.C.S. **1.** Royal College of Science. **2.** Royal College of Surgeons. **3.** Royal Corps of Signals.

rct. recruit.

R.C.T. Royal Corps of Transport.

R.C.V.S. Royal College of Veterinary Surgeons.

rd rod (unit of length).

rd. **1.** road. **2.** round.

Rd. road.

R.D. *Finance.* refer to drawer.

re¹. *Music.* Variant of **ray.**

re² (ree, ray) *prep.* Concerning; in reference to; in the case of. Used in commercial or legal contexts. [Latin *rē*, from *rēs*, thing.]

Re The symbol for the element rhenium.

Re. Variant of **Ra.**

re– *prefix.* Indicates: **1.** Restoration to a previous or improved condition or position; for example, **repay, rehouse, redecorate. 2.** Repetition of a previous action; for example, **reactivate.** *Note:* Many compounds other than those entered here may be formed with *re-*. In forming compounds *re-* is normally, in this dictionary, joined with the following element without space or hyphen: *reopen.* If the second element begins with *e*, it is preferable to separate it with a hyphen: *re-entry.* However, such compounds may often be found written solid and are indicated here as fully acceptable variants. If a compound that resembles a familiar word is intended in a special sense, the hyphen is necessary to make the distinction: *re-creation*, meaning "creation anew". The hyphen may also be necessary to clarify an unusual nonce formation: *re-realignment*, or a compound that produces a series of three or more vowels: *re-aerify.* [Middle English *re-*, from Old French, from Latin *re-, red-*, in the following senses: **1.** Back, as in **rebuke.** **2.** Back to an earlier state or condition, as in **repair.** **3.** Back in place, as in **remain.** **4.** Backward, away, as in **refract.** **5.** Again, repeatedly, in return for, as in **respond.** **6.** Behind, as in **relinquish.** **7.** Contrary, in the sense of negating, as in **repeal.** **8.** Against, as in **reluctant.** **9.** In response to, as in **requiem.** **10.** As an intensive, as in **revere.**]

Re. rupee.

R.E. **1.** Religious Education. **2.** Right Excellent. **3.** Royal Engineers. **4.** Royal Exchange.

're (ər). Contraction of *are.*

reach (reech) *v.* **reached, reaching, reaches.** —*tr.* **1.** To stretch out or put forth (a bodily part); extend. Often used with *out: reached her hand out to touch the ceiling.* **2.** To touch or take hold of by extending some bodily part, especially the hand or something held

therein: *Can you reach the table?* **3.** To get to, go as far as, or arrive at: *reach maturity; reach the end of a journey.* **4.** To communicate with; contact: *You can reach me at the office.* **5. a.** To extend as far as: *His property reached the edge of the forest.* **b.** To carry as far as: *His cry reached our ears.* **6.** To aggregate or amount to. **7.** *Informal.* To give or hand over to someone: *Reach me the sugar.* **8.** To hit or strike, especially in fencing or boxing. **9.** To make an impression on; affect: *reached the hearts of thousands.* —*intr.* **1.** To extend or thrust out something. **2.** To try to grasp, touch, or attain something: *reach for a gun; reach for the stars.* **3. a.** To extend in time or space: *His land reaches to the bottom of the hill.* **b.** To extend in influence or effect: *The effects of their policies reach throughout the land.* **4.** *Nautical.* To sail with the wind abeam.
~*n.* **1.** The act or an instance of reaching out. **2.** Power of or capacity for reaching, as: **a.** The extent or distance something can reach. **b.** The range or scope of influence or effect: *beyond the reach of the law.* **c.** The extent of one's ability to attain or achieve: *The larger model is beyond our reach.* **3.** An unbroken expanse of water, especially on a river or canal. **4.** *Plural.* A level, position, or grouping: *the upper reaches of the civil service.* **5.** A pole connecting the rear axle of a vehicle, such as a wagon, with the front. **6.** *Nautical.* The tack of a sailing vessel with the wind abeam. [Middle English *rechen*, Old English *ræcan*, from West Germanic *raikjan* (unattested). —**reach·er** *n.*

Synonyms: *reach, achieve, attain, gain, compass, accomplish.*

reach-me-down (réech-mi-down) *n.* Something of inferior quality through being secondhand or imitative. Also used adjectivally: *churned out plodding, reach-me-down verse.*

re·act (ri-ákt, ree-) *v.* **-acted, -acting, -acts.** —*intr.* **1.** To act in response or opposition to some former act or state. Used with *against, on,* or *upon.* **2. a.** To be affected or influenced by circumstances or events. **b.** *Medicine.* To be affected, especially adversely by a drug, allergen, or the like. **3.** *Chemistry.* To undergo chemical change. —*tr. Chemistry.* To cause (substances) to undergo chemical change. [RE- + ACT, influenced by Medieval Latin *reagere* (past participle *reactus*), to react.]

re·ac·tance (ri-áktənss, ree-) *n. Symbol* **X** Opposition to the flow of alternating electric current caused by the inductance and capacitance in a circuit. See **impedance.**

re·ac·tant (ri-áktənt, ree-) *n.* A substance participating in a chemical reaction; especially, a directly reacting substance present at the initiation of the reaction.

re·ac·tion (ri-áksh'n, ree-) *n.* **1. a.** A response to a stimulus or former action; especially, a response indicating a person's feelings or views about something. **b.** Reciprocal action between two things. **2.** A reverse or opposing action. **3. a.** A tendency to revert to a former state. **b.** A tendency, as in art and especially politics, towards conservatism and opposition to progressive trends. **4.** A chemical change or transformation in which a substance decomposes, combines with other substances, or interchanges constituents with other substances. **5.** A nuclear reaction *(see).* **6.** A force produced in a system by an applied force, equal in magnitude to the applied force and acting in the opposite direction. **7. a.** The effect of a drug; especially, an adverse effect. **b.** The effect of a substance upon a person who is allergic to that substance. **c.** An adverse response by a person to such drugs or allergens. **8.** A period of depression, exhaustion, mental disorder, or the like, as occurs following shock or excessive exertion.

re·ac·tion·ar·y (ri-áksh'n-əri, ree-, -ri ‖ -erri) *adj.* Also **re·ac·ticn·ist** (-ist). Characterised by reaction; especially, opposing progressive trends or wishing to return to a former, outmoded state.
~*n., pl.* **reactionaries.** A person who is reactionary.

reaction engine *n.* An engine that develops thrust by the expulsion of matter, especially ignited fuel gases. Also "reaction motor".

reaction time *n. Biology.* The time interval between the application of a stimulus and the detection of a response.

reaction turbine *n.* A type of turbine in which part of the torque is produced by pressure from fluid moving out of the rotating part.

re·ac·ti·vate (ri-ákti-vayt, ree-) *tr.v.* **-vated, -vating, -vates.** **1.** To make active again. **2.** To restore the effectiveness or ability to function of. —**re·ac·ti·va·tion** (-váysh'n) *n.*

re·ac·tive (ri-áktiv, ree-) *adj.* **1.** Tending to be responsive or to react to a stimulus. **2.** Characterised by reaction. **3.** *Chemistry & Physics.* Tending to participate in reactions. **4.** *Electricity.* Having electrical reactance.

reactive depression *n.* Mental depression that arises in response to unfavourable external circumstances without necessarily reflecting, as does endogenous depression, deep-seated personality or physiological problems.

re·ac·tor (ri-áktər, ree-) *n.* **1.** A person or thing that reacts. **2.** *Electricity.* A circuit element, such as a coil, used to introduce reactance into a circuit. **3.** *Physics.* A nuclear reactor *(see).*

read (reed) *v.* **read** (red), **reading, reads.** —*tr.* **1.** To comprehend, take in the meaning of, or be able to convert into the intended sound (something written or printed) by looking at or, in the case of blind people, touching the characters or words and interpreting them. **2.** To utter or render aloud (something written or printed). **3.** To have the knowledge of (a language) necessary to understand printed or written material: *I can read Russian but I can't speak it.* **4. a.** To seek to interpret the true nature or meaning of (someone or something) through close scrutiny: *read the sky for signs of snow.* **b.** To ascertain the true thoughts, intent, or mood of: *He read her mind.* **5.** To interpret the signs or arrangement of: *read a map.*

6. To ascribe a special meaning or interpretation, often mistakenly, to (something read, heard, experienced, or observed): *He read her tears as sadness, not joy: Don't read too much into what he says.* **7. a.** To foretell or predict (the future). **b.** To foretell the future by interpreting the arrangement of (lines on a hand or tea leaves, for example). **8.** To perceive, receive, or comprehend (a signal, message, or its sender): *I read you loud and clear.* **9.** To be engaged in the study of: *read law at university.* **10.** To learn or get knowledge from (something written or printed): *He read that crime was rife.* **11.** To have or adopt as a reading in a particular passage: *For "color" read "colour".* **12.** To indicate, register, or show: *The dial reads 0°.* **13.** To be interpreted as; mean: *The law reads that he is guilty.* **14.** To obtain or detect and transfer (information) from a computer storage device. **15.** To cause to be in a specified state by reading: *read me to sleep.* **16.** To interpret or be able to interpret (musical notation) and reproduce the appropriate notes. **17.** In various sports to anticipate correctly (the moves or tactics of one's teammates or opponents). *—intr.* **1.** To read printed or written characters, as of words or music. **2.** To utter or render aloud the words that one is reading. **3.** To learn by reading. Used with *about* or *of*: *I read about it in the paper.* **4.** To have a particular wording: *The line reads thus.* **5.** To have a specified character or quality for the reader: *His poems read well.* **6.** To study: *reading for the bar.* **—read (oneself) in.** In the Anglican Church, to enter into a benefice by a public reading of the Thirty-nine Articles. **—read up.** To acquire information or improve one's skill by reading or studying. Often used with *on.*

~n. **1.** The act or an instance of reading. **2.** Material suitable for reading or something to be read: *a good read.*

~adj. (red). Informed by reading; learned. Used in combination: *well-read.* [Read (infinitive), read (past tense and past participle); Middle English *reden, redde, red,* Old English *rǣdan,* to advise, explain, read, *rædde, ræden,* from Germanic *rǣdhan* (unattested).]

Read (reed), **Sir Herbert (Edward)** (1893–1968). British poet and literary and art critic. His first volume of poetry, *Naked Warriors,* appeared in 1919, the *Collected Poems* in 1966. He is more famous as a critic, for books such as *Art and Industry* (1934), *Art and Society* (1937), *Art and Alienation* (1967), *Form in Modern Poetry* (1932), and *Phases of English Poetry* (1950).

read·a·ble (ree͞d-əb'l) *adj.* **1.** Capable of being read easily; legible. **2.** Pleasurable or interesting to read. **—read·a·bil·i·ty** (-ə-bílləti), **read·a·ble·ness** *n.* **—read·a·bly** *adv.*

Reade (reed), **Charles** (1814–84). British novelist and playwright. His best-known novel was *The Cloister and the Hearth* (1861).

read·er (réedər) *n.* **1.** One who reads, especially, a person who enjoys reading very much. **2.** A professional reciter of literary works. **3. a.** In the Roman Catholic Church, a **lector. b.** In the Anglican Church, a **lay reader** *(see).* **4.** A person employed by a publisher to read and evaluate manuscripts. **5.** A corrector of printers' proofs; a proofreader. **6.** *Chiefly British.* A senior university lecturer. **7.** *U.S.* A teaching assistant who reads and grades examination papers. **8.** A textbook of reading exercises designed as part of a course for people learning to read, especially for children. **9.** A computer device for converting data from one form into another.

read·er·ship (réedər-ship) *n.* **1.** The readers collectively or the total number of readers of a publication or publications. **2.** *Chiefly British.* The office or rank of a reader in a university.

read·i·ly (réddili, rédd'l-i) *adv.* **1.** Promptly; quickly. **2.** Willingly. **3.** Easily; without difficulty or hindrance.

read·i·ness (réddi-nəss, -niss) *n.* The quality or state of being ready or willing.

read·ing (réeding) *n.* **1.** The skill of being able to read. Also used adjectivally: *reading age.* **2.** Written or printed material. **3.** The act of rendering aloud written or printed matter. **4.** An official or public recitation of written material: *the reading of a will.* **5. a.** A personal interpretation or perception: *What's your reading of the situation?* **b.** A personal interpretation or appraisal of a text or passage. **6.** The precise form of a particular passage in a text. **7.** The information indicated by a gauge or graduated instrument. **8.** In parliamentary procedure, the formal presentation of a bill to a legislative body at any of the stages of its passage; the *first reading* is for the introduction of the bill; the *second reading* is for approving the general principles of the bill; the *third reading* is for the accepting of details of the bill as debated in committee.

~adj. Designed or used for reading: *a reading lamp.*

Read·ing (rédding). City in southern England, situated at the confluence of the rivers Thames and Kennet. It is an important railway junction, and its industries include electronics, printing, brewing, and engineering.

Reading, Rufus Daniel Isaacs, 1st Marquess of. (1860–1935). British politician, lawyer, and businessman, who became the first commoner to achieve a marquisate in over a century. He was in turn a Liberal M.P. (1904–13), Attorney-General (1910–13), Lord Chief Justice (1913–18, 1919–21), ambassador to the United States (1918–19), Viceroy of India (1921–26), and Foreign Secretary (1931).

re·ad·just (rée-ə-júst) *v.* **-justed, -justing, -justs.** *—tr.* To adjust or arrange again *—intr.* To adjust or adapt oneself, as to a new environment or changed circumstances. **—re·ad·just·er** *n.* **—re·ad·just·ment** *n.*

read-on·ly (réed-ṓnli) *adj. Computing.* Designating or pertaining to devices in which the information held cannot be changed: *a read-only memory.* Compare **random-access.**

read out *tr.v.* **1.** To read (a text, passage, or the like) aloud. **2.** *U.S.* To expel by proclamation from a social, political or other group.

read-out (réed-owt) *n.* Presentation of computer data, usually in digital form, from calculations or storage, often displayed on a V.D.U. Compare **print-out.**

read-write (réed-rīt) *adj. Computing.* **1.** Of, pertaining to, or designating hardware or software enabling the transfer of information to and from magnetic tape or disk: *a read-write head.* **2.** Designating a memory in which the information held may be altered or read at will. See **random-access.**

read·y (réddi) *adj.* **-ier, -iest. 1.** Prepared or available for service or action. **2.** Mentally disposed; willing: *He was ready to believe them.* **3.** Liable or about to do something. Used with an infinitive: *ready to leave.* **4.** Prompt in understanding or reacting: *a ready intelligence; a ready response.* **5.** Available: *ready money.* **—at the ready. 1.** In position for aiming and firing. Said of a rifle. **2.** In a position for immediate use or action.

~tr.v. **readied, readying, readies.** To cause to be ready. [Middle English *redy,* Old English *rǣde,* from Germanic *raidh-* (unattested), prepare.]

read·y-made (réddi-máyd) *adj.* **1.** Made to a set pattern rather than to individual specifications. Compare **made-to-order. 2.** Already existing and available for use: *a ready-made answer.* **3.** Unoriginal and commonplace: *ready-made prose.*

~n. **1.** Something that is ready-made. **2.** In art, especially in Dada, an ordinary object, or group of objects, such as a rubbish bin or pile of bricks, that is removed from its original surroundings and viewed as a work of art.

read·y-mix (réddi-miks) *n.* Liquid concrete mixed before delivery to the site at which it is used.

read·y reckoner *n.* A table of conversions, percentages, discounts, or the like, used as an aid in calculation.

read·y-to-wear (réddi-tə-wáir, -tōō-) *adj.* Made to a set pattern; off-the-peg; ready-made. Said of clothes.

re·af·firm (rée-ə-fúrm) *tr.v.* **-firmed, -firming, -firms.** To affirm or assert again. **—re·af·fir·ma·tion** (rée-affər-máysh'n) *n.*

re·af·for·est (rée-ə-fórrist) *tr.v.* **-ested, -esting, -ests.** Also **re·for·est** (rée-fórrist). To replace or plant trees in (an area that was formerly a forest). **—re·af·for·est·a·tion** (-áysh'n), **re·for·est·a·tion** *n.*

Rea·gan (ráygən), **Ronald (Wilson)** (1911–). U.S. actor and politician. After a moderately successful career in Hollywood, he was elected governor of California (1966), a post he held for the Republicans for eight years. In 1980, he was elected 40th president of the United States, and was re-elected by a record margin (1984–88).

re·a·gent (ree-áyjənt, ri-) *n.* Any substance used in a chemical reaction to detect, measure, examine, or produce other substances. [RE- + AGENT, after REACT.]

re·a·gin (ri-áyjin, ree-) *n.* An antibody present in the blood of individuals allergic to a particular substance (allergen). Subsequent contact with the allergen provokes a reaction with the antibody that is responsible for the allergic response. [*Reagent* + -IN.]

re·al[1] (reerl, rée-əl, reel) *adj.* **1.** Being or occurring in fact or actuality; having verifiable existence: *a real fortune.* **2.** True and actual; not illusory or fictitious: *the real explanation.* **3.** Emphatically having all the attributes normally associated with the specified person or thing: *a real man.* **4.** Genuine and authentic; not artificial or spurious. **5.** *Philosophy.* Existing actually and objectively; not contingent. **6.** *Physics & Chemistry.* Designating a gas in which deviations from ideal gas behaviour occur because of interactions between the constituent gas molecules. **7.** Of, pertaining to, or designating an image formed by light rays that converge in space. **8.** *Mathematics.* Of, pertaining to, or designating the non-imaginary part of a complex quantity. **9.** *Law.* Consisting of or pertaining to stationary or fixed property, such as buildings or land. Compare **personal. 10.** *Economics.* Valued according to current purchasing power rather than the nominal amount: *real incomes.* **11.** *Informal.* Used as an intensive: *a real idiot.* **—for real.** *Slang.* Not illusory or experimental; genuine and serious. **—the real.** The totality of actual, existing things, as opposed to imaginary things.

~adv. Chiefly U.S. Informal. Very: *real sorry.* [Middle English, of real property or things, from Anglo-French, from Late Latin *reālis,* actual, real, from Latin *rēs,* thing.] **—real·ness** *n.*

Synonyms: *real, actual, true, authentic, concrete, existent, genuine, tangible, veritable.*

re·al[2] (ray-áal) *n., pl.* **reals** or **-ales** (-ayz, *Spanish* -ess). A former Spanish silver monetary unit. [Spanish, from *real,* "royal", from Latin *rēgālis,* regal, from *rēx* (stem *rēg-*), king.]

re·al[3] (ray-áal) *n., pl.* **reals** or **reis** (rayss, *Portuguese* raysh). Either of two former monetary units of Portugal and Brazil. [Portuguese, from *real,* "royal". See **real** (Spanish coin).]

real ale *n.* Beer that is put in cask while the yeast is still alive and thus matures in the cask. It is usually rich and strong. Compare **keg beer.**

real estate *n. Chiefly U.S. Law.* **Real property** *(see).*

real image *n. Optics.* An optical image that is formed by converging rays.

re·al·gar (ri-ál-gər, ree-, -gaar) *n.* A soft orange or red arsenic ore, As_2S_2, used in fireworks, tanning, and as a pigment. [Middle English, from Medieval Latin, from Arabic *rajh al-ghār,* powder (of) the mine or cave.]

re·al·i·sa·tion (réer-lī-záysh'n, rée-ə- || *U.S.* -li-) *n.* **1.** The act or fact of realising, or the condition of being realised. **2.** The result of realising.

re·al·ise, re·al·ize (réer-līz, rée-ə- || rée-līz) *v.* **-ised, -ising, -ises.**

—*tr.* **1. a.** To comprehend completely or correctly. **b.** To become aware of; notice. **2.** To make real or actualise (a plan or ambition, for example): *realise a dream.* **3.** To make or cause to appear realistic. **4.** To obtain or achieve, as gain or profit: *realise a return on an investment.* **5.** To bring in (a sum) as profit by sale. **6.** To convert (property) into money. **7.** *Music.* To complete or reconstruct in full (a part or harmonies, especially for a piece of baroque music) from the figured base. **8.** *Phonetics.* To produce the sound of (a phoneme) in speech; articulate. —*intr.* To become conscious or aware of something. [French *réaliser,* from Old French *realiser,* from *real,* real, from Late Latin *reālis,* REAL.] **—re·al·is·a·ble** *adj.* **—re·al·is·er** *n.*

re·al·ism (réer-liz'm, rée-ə-) *n.* **1.** Inclination towards literal truth rather than towards the abstract, romantic, or ideal. **2.** Inclination towards a pragmatic, practical, and material way of life rather than an idealistic or morally absolute one. **3.** *Often capital* **R.** In art and literature, a style favouring the representation of life or objects as they actually exist rather than romanticising or idealising them or presenting them in an abstract form. **4.** *Philosophy.* **a.** The doctrine that universal or general ideas and principles have an objective existence. Compare **nominalism. b.** The doctrine that the objects of perception exist independently of the perceiver. Compare **idealism. c.** Broadly, the view that theories, especially scientific or other explanatory theories, are objectively true or false.

re·al·ist (réer-list, rée-ə-) *n.* **1.** One inclined to literal truth and pragmatism. **2.** A person who practises or believes in artistic or philosophical realism. Also used adjectivally: *a realist doctrine.*

re·al·is·tic (réer-lístik, reer-, rée-ə- || rée-listik) *adj.* **1.** Inclined towards the literal truth, as opposed to the abstract, romantic, or ideal. **2. a.** Closely resembling the object, scene, or person being represented; lifelike: *a realistic landscape.* **b.** Concerned with or seeking to represent what is objectively real, as in art or literature. **3.** Of or pertaining to philosophical realism. **4.** Practical-minded as opposed to idealistic; pragmatic: *Let's be realistic now and agree to at least a few of their demands.*

re·al·i·ty (ri-ál-əti, ree-) *n., pl.* **-ties. 1.** The quality or state of being actual or true. **2.** A person, entity, or event that is actual. **3.** The totality of all things possessing actuality, existence, or essence. **4.** That which exists objectively and in fact. **5.** *Philosophy.* The sum of all that is real, absolute, and unchangeable. **—in reality.** In actual fact.

re·al·ly (réerli, rée-ə-li || réeli) *adv.* **1.** In reality or fact. **2.** Truly; thoroughly. **3.** Used as an intensive: *You really shouldn't have done it.*

~*interj.* Used to express mild surprise, incredulity, or boredom.

realm (relm) *n.* **1.** A kingdom. **2.** Any field, sphere, or province: *the realm of science.* [Middle English *realme, reaume,* from Old French, from Latin *regimen,* system of government, from *regere,* to rule.]

real number *n.* Any rational or irrational number. See **number.**

re·al·po·li·tik (ray-ál-polli-teek) *n. Often capital* **R.** A harshly realistic national policy having as its sole principle the advancement of the national interest. [German, "realistic politics".]

real presence *n. Theology.* The doctrine that Christ's actual body and blood are present in the Eucharist.

real property *n. Law.* Fixed property, such as buildings and land. Also *chiefly U.S.* "real estate", "realty".

real tennis (reel, *rearely* rayl) *n.* An early form of tennis, from which lawn tennis developed. It is played in a large indoor court having a specially marked-out floor, high cement walls on three sides, and a buttress on the fourth side, off which the ball may be played. Also called "royal tennis", *U.S.* "court tennis".

real time *n. Computing.* A computer response which occurs almost at the same rate as the data that has been input. **—real-time** *adj.*

re·al·tor (réerl-tər, rée-əl-, réel-, -tawr, *also* ri-ál-, ree-) *n. Often Capital* **R.** *U.S.* An estate agent. [From REALTY.]

re·al·ty (réerl-ti, rée-əl-, réel-) *n., pl.* **-ties.** *Law. Chiefly U.S.* Real property. [REAL + -TY.]

ream¹ (reem) *n.* **1.** *Abbr.* **rm.** A quantity of paper, formerly 480 sheets, now 500 sheets or, in a printer's ream, 516 sheets. **2.** *Usually plural.* An extensive amount, as of paper or written or printed material: *wrote reams of verse.* [Middle English *rem(e),* from Old French *remme,* from Arabic *rizmah,* bundle.]

ream² *tr.v.* **reamed, reaming, reams. 1.** To form, shape, taper, or enlarge (a hole) with or as if with a reamer. **2.** To remove (material) by reaming. **3.** *U.S.* To squeeze the juice out of (fruit) with a squeezer. [19th century : perhaps from Middle English *remen,* to make room, Old English *rȳman,* to widen.]

ream·er (réemər) *n.* **1.** Any of various tools used to shape or enlarge holes. **2.** *U.S.* A lemon or orange squeezer. **3.** One that reams.

reap (reep) *v.* **reaped, reaping, reaps.** —*tr.* **1.** To cut (a crop) for harvest with a scythe, sickle, or reaper. **2.** To harvest (a crop so cut). **3.** To harvest a crop from. **4.** To obtain as a result of effort. —*intr.* **1.** To cut or harvest a crop. **2.** To obtain a return or reward. [Middle English *repen,* Old English *rīpan*†.]

reap·er (réepər) *n.* **1.** One who reaps. **2.** A machine for harvesting grain or pulse crops.

re·ap·por·tion (rée-ə-pórsh'n || -pōrsh'n) *tr.v.* **-tioned, -tioning, -tions.** To distribute anew. **—re·ap·por·tion·ment** *n.*

re·ap·prais·al (rée-ə-práyz'l) *n.* A new or fresh appraisal or evaluation. **—re·ap·praise** *v.*

rear¹ (reer) *n.* **1.** The hind part of something. **2.** The point or area farthest from the front of something. **3.** The part of a military deployment usually farthest from the fighting front. **4.** *Informal.* The buttocks. **—bring up the rear.** To be last, as in in a line or race.

~*adj.* Of, at, or located in the rear. [Short for ARREAR.]

rear² *v.* **reared, rearing, rears.** —*tr.* **1.** To care for (a child or children) during the early stages of life; bring up. **2.** To lift upright; raise. **3.** To build; erect. **4.** To tend (growing plants or animals). —*intr.* **1.** To rise on the hind legs, as a horse does. Often used with *up.* **2.** To rise high in the air; tower. Often used with *up* or *over.* [Middle English *reren,* to lift up, raise, Old English *rǣran;* akin to RAISE.] **—rear·er** *n.*

rear·ad·mi·ral (réer-ádmərəl) *n. Abbr.* **Rear Adm., R.A.** An officer of the Royal Navy and various other navies ranking between a vice admiral and a commodore, equivalent in rank to a major general in the Army and an air vice marshal in the Air Force.

rear·guard (réer-gaard) *n.* A detachment of troops that protects the rear of a military force.

~*adj.* Designating policies or actions designed to ward off attack while retreating or to resist almost inevitable change or certain defeat. [Middle English *reregarde,* from Old French : *rere,* backward, behind, from Latin *retrō* + *garde,* AGUARD.]

rear light *n.* Either of a pair of red lights on the back of a motor vehicle. Also called "rear lamp", *chiefly U.S.* "taillight".

re·arm (rée-árm, ree-) *v.* **-armed, -arming, -arms.** —*tr.* **1.** To arm again. **2.** To equip with better weapons. —*intr.* To arm oneself again. **—re·ar·ma·ment** (-əmənt) *n.*

rear·most (réer-mōst) *adj.* Farthest in the rear; last.

re·ar·range (rée-ə-ráynj, reer-) *tr.v.* **-ranged, -ranging, -ranges.** To change or restore the arrangement of. **—re·ar·range·ment** *n.*

rear·view mirror (réer-véw) *n.* **1.** A small adjustable mirror centrally attached at the top or bottom of the windscreen in a motor vehicle to allow the driver a view of what is directly behind. **2.** A similar mirror attached to the handlebar of a motorcycle or bicycle.

rear·ward¹ (réer-wərd) *adj.* Directed towards or situated at the rear.

~*adv. Chiefly U.S.* Rearwards.

rear·ward² (réer-wawrd) *n.* A position at rear; especially the rearguard of an armed force. [Middle English *rerewarde,* from Anglo-French : *rere,* behind, from Latin *retrō* + *warde,* guard, from Germanic.]

rear·wards (réer-wərdz) *adv.* Also *chiefly U.S.* **rearward.** Towards, to, or at the rear.

rea·son (réez'n) *n.* **1.** The basis or motive for an action, decision, or conviction. **2.** A declaration or argument advanced to explain or justify an action, decision, or conviction. **3.** An underlying fact or cause that provides a logical justification for a premise or occurrence. **4. a.** The power to think, judge, and draw logical conclusions. **b.** The intellect as opposed to emotions, feelings, instincts, or intuitions. **5.** Good judgment; sound sense; intelligence. **6.** A sound mental state; sanity. **7.** *Logic.* A premise, usually the minor premise, of an argument. —See Synonyms below and at **mind.** —See Usage note at **because, cause. —by reason of.** Because of. **—in** or **within reason.** Within the bounds of good sense or practicality. **—listen to reason.** To allow oneself to be persuaded by logical or sensible arguments. **—reasons of State.** A political justification for an action or measure. **—stand to reason.** To be logical or likely. Usually used impersonally: *It stands to reason that he will win.* **—with reason.** With good cause; justifiably.

~*v.* **reasoned, -soning, -sons.** —*intr.* **1.** To use the faculty of reason; think logically. **2.** To talk or argue logically and persuasively. **3.** To seek to persuade someone with reasons. Used with *with.* **4.** *Archaic.* To engage in conversation or discussion: *"Come . . . let us reason together"* (Isaiah 1:18). —*tr.* **1.** To determine, solve, or conclude by logical thinking. Often used with *out.* **2.** To seek to persuade (someone) with reasons. Used with *out of* or *into.* **3.** To discuss; debate. [Middle English *reisun,* from Old French, from Vulgar Latin *ratiōne* (unattested), from Latin *ratiō* (stem *ratiōn-*), calculation, judgment, reasoning, from *ratus,* past participle of *rērī,* to think, reason.] **—rea·son·er** *n.*

Synonyms: *reason, intuition, understanding, discernment, judgment.*

rea·son·a·ble (réez'n-əb'l) *adj.* **1.** Capable of reasoning; rational. **2.** Governed by or in accordance with reason or sound thinking. **3.** Within the bounds of common sense or normal expectations. **4.** Not excessive or extreme; fair; moderate. **—rea·son·a·bil·i·ty** (-ə-bílləti), **rea·son·a·ble·ness** *n.* **—rea·son·a·bly** *adv.*

rea·soned (réez'nd) *adj.* Having been well thought out; reasonable: *a reasoned argument.*

rea·son·ing (réez'n-ing) *n.* **1.** The mental processes of one who reasons; especially, the drawing of conclusions or inferences from observation, facts, or hypotheses. **2.** The particular evidence or arguments used in this procedure.

re·as·sure (rée-ə-shóor, réer-, -shór || -shéwr) *tr.v.* **-sured, -suring, -sures. 1.** To restore confidence to. **2.** To assure again. **3.** To reinsure. **—re·as·sur·ance** *n.* **—re·as·sur·ing·ly** *adv.*

reast. Variant of **reest.**

reata. Variant of **riata.**

Ré·au·mur, Re·au·mur (ráy-ə-mewr, -ō-, -mər) *adj. Abbr.* **R, R., Réaum.** Designating or indicated on a temperature scale that registers the freezing point of water as 0° and the boiling point as 80°. [Introduced by René de RÉAUMUR.]

Ré·au·mur (ráy-ə-mewr, -ō-, -mər, *French* -mŭr), **René Antoine Ferchault de** (1683–1757). French physicist and natural scientist, one of the leading figures of 18th-century science. He is best known for his invention of the alcohol thermometer (*c.* 1730) and the temperature scale named after him, but he also developed opaque glass and wrote a six-volume study of insects (1734–42).

reave[1] (reev) *v.* **reft** (reft) or **reaved, reaving, reaves.** *Archaic. —tr.* **1.** To seize and carry off forcibly. **2.** To deprive of; bereave. Used with *of. —intr.* To rob, plunder, or pillage. [Middle English *reven,* to plunder, Old English *rēafian.*]

reave[2] *tr.v.* **reft** (reft) or **reaved, reaving, reaves.** *Archaic.* To break or tear apart. [Middle English *reven,* variant (influenced by *riven,* RIVE) of REAVE (seize).]

Reb[1] (reb) *n. Sometimes small* **r.** *U.S. Informal.* A Confederate soldier in the American Civil War. [Short for REBEL.]

Reb[2] *n.* A Jewish title of respect, approximately equivalent to "Mr." or "Sir", but used with the first name rather than the surname. [Yiddish, from Hebrew *rabbī,* my teacher, RABBI.]

re·bar·ba·tive (ri-bárbətiv, rə-) *adj.* Extremely unattractive; repellent. [French *rébarbatif,* from Old French *rebarber,* "to face beard to beard", face an enemy, hence, to be repellent : *re-,* back, against + *barbe,* beard, from Latin *barba.*]

re·bate[1] (reébayt, ri-báyt, rə-) *n.* A deduction from an amount to be paid or a return of part of an amount already paid.
~tr.v. **rebated, -bating, -bates. 1.** To deduct or return (an amount) from a payment or bill. **2.** *Archaic.* To dull or blunt (a weapon, for example). **3.** *Archaic.* To lessen; diminish. [Middle English *rebaten,* to deduct, subtract, from Old French *rabattre,* to beat down again, reduce : *re-,* again + *abattre,* to beat down : *a-,* to, from Latin *ad-* + *battre,* to beat, from Latin *battuere.*] **—re·bat·er** *n.*

rebate[2]. Variant of **rabbet.**

re·ba·to (ri-baátō) *n., pl.* **-tos.** Also **ra·ba·to** (rə-). A stiff, flaring collar of lace or other fabric, worn by both men and women in the early part of the 17th century. [Old French *rabat,* turndown collar, from *rabattre,* to turn down again, REBATE.]

re·bec, re·beck (reébek, rébbek) *n.* A pear-shaped, two- or three-stringed musical instrument of medieval times, played with a bow. [Old French *rebec,* variant (influenced by *bec,* beak, because of the shape of the instrument) of *rebebe,* from Old Provençal *rebab,* from Arabic (dialectal) *rebāb.*]

Re·bec·ca, Re·bek·ah (ri-béckə, rə-). The wife of Isaac and the mother of Jacob and Esau. Genesis 24:1–67.

re·bel (ri-bél, rə-) *intr.v.* **-belled, -belling, -bels. 1.** To refuse allegiance to and oppose by force an established government or ruling authority. Often used with *against.* **2.** To resist or defy any authority or generally accepted convention. **3.** To feel or express strong unwillingness or distaste: *rebelled at the unwelcome suggestion.*
~n. **reb·el** (rébb'l). **1.** A person who rebels or is in rebellion. **2.** A person who refuses to comply with accepted conventions.
~adj. **reb·el** (rebb'l). **1.** Of, pertaining to, or consisting of rebels. **2.** Rebellious; defiant. [Middle English *rebellen,* from Old French *rebeller,* from Latin *rebellāre,* to make war again : *re-,* again + *bellāre,* to make war, from *bellum,* war.]

re·bel·li·on (ri-bél-i-ən, rə-) *n.* **1.** An uprising or organised opposition intended to change or overthrow an existing government or ruling authority. **2.** An act or show of defiance towards any authority or established convention. [Middle English, from Old French, from Latin *rebelliō* (stem *rebelliōn-*), from *rebellāre,* to REBEL.]
Synonyms: *rebellion, revolt, insurrection, uprising, coup d'état, revolution, mutiny.*

re·bel·li·ous (ri-bél-i-əss, rə-) *adj.* **1.** Participating in or inclined towards rebellion. **2.** Of or characteristic of a rebel. **3.** Resisting management or control; unruly. —See Synonyms at **insubordinate.** **—re·bel·li·ous·ly** *adv.* **—re·bel·li·ous·ness** *n.*

Re·ber (ráybər), **Grote** (1911–). U.S. astronomer. He built the world's first radio telescope in 1937, and has continued to play an active part in the development of subsequent telescopes.

re·bind (reé-bīnd) *tr.v.* **-bound** (-bownd || *West Indies also* -búngd), **-binding, -binds.** To bind again; especially, to put a new binding on (a book).

re·birth (reé-búrth, ree- || -burth) *n.* **1.** A second or new birth; a reincarnation. **2.** A spiritual regeneration. **3.** A renaissance or revival.

re·bore (reé-bawr || -bōr) *n.* The process of drilling out the cylinder of an engine and fitting a slightly larger piston.
~tr.v. (-bór || -bőr) **rebored, -boring, -bores.** To give (an engine) a rebore.

re·born (reé-bórn, ree-) *adj.* Born again; emotionally or spiritually revived or regenerated.

re·bound (ri-bównd, reé- || *West Indies also* -búngd) *v.* **-bounded, -bounding, -bounds.** *—intr.* **1.** To spring or bounce back after hitting or colliding with something. **2.** To harm the person responsible for an act, especially an act of malice: *Their efforts to discredit me rebounded on them.* **3.** To re-echo; resound. *—tr.* To cause to rebound.
~n. (reé-bownd, -bównd, ri- || *West Indies also* -búngd). **1.** A springing or bounding back; a recoil. **2.** In soccer, hockey, and other ball games, a ball that has rebounded, as off a goal post. **3.** *Informal.* One whose affections are sought by someone on the rebound: *Does she really love him or is he just a rebound?* **—on the rebound. 1.** In the act of springing or bounding back. **2.** In reaction to disappointment, rejection, or depression: *marriage on the rebound.* [Middle English *rebounden,* from Old French *rebondir* : *re-,* again, back + *bondir,* to resound, BOUND (leap).]

re·bo·zo (ri-bṓ-zō, -sō; *Spanish* -thō, -sō) *n., pl.* **-zos.** A long scarf worn over the head and shoulders, especially by Mexican women. [Spanish *rebozo*†.]

re·broad·cast (reé-bráwd-kaast || -kast) *tr.v.* **-cast** or **-casted, -casting, -casts. 1.** To repeat the broadcast of (a programme). **2.** To receive and send out (a broadcast) again. **—re·broad·cast** *n.*

re·buff (ri-búf) *n.* **1.** A blunt or abrupt repulsing or refusal, as to an offer of help or sympathy or to a person making unwelcome advances; a snub. **2.** Any check or abrupt setback to progress or action.
~tr.v. **rebuffed, -buffing, -buffs. 1.** To refuse or reject bluntly or contemptuously; snub. **2.** To repel or drive back. —See Synonyms at **refuse.** [Old French *rebuffer,* from Italian *ribuffare,* to scold, rebuff, from *ribuffo,* reprimand : *re-,* back, again, from Latin + *buffo,* puff, gust (imitative).]

re·build (reé-bíld, ree-) *tr.v.* **-built** (-bílt), **-building, -builds. 1.** To build again. **2.** To make extensive structural repairs to. **3.** To restore, as from a condition of ruin: *plans to rebuild the economy.*

re·buke (ri-béwk, rə-) *tr.v.* **-buked, -buking, -bukes.** To criticise or reprove sharply; reprimand. —See Synonyms at **admonish.**
~n. A sharp reproof. [Middle English *rebuken,* from Old Northern French *rebuke;* akin to Old French *buchier,* to beat, chop down wood, from *busche,* log.]

re·bus (reébəss) *n., pl.* **-buses.** A riddle whose answer, composed of words or syllables, is depicted by symbols or pictures that suggest the sounds or give clues to the meanings of the words or syllables they represent. [Latin *rēbus,* by things, from *rēs,* thing.]

re·but (ri-bút) *v.* **-butted, -butting, -buts.** *—tr.* **1.** To refute, especially by offering opposing evidence or arguments, as in a legal case. **2.** *Archaic.* To repel. *—intr.* To present opposing evidence or arguments. [Middle English *rebuten,* from Old French *rebuter* : *re-,* again, back + *buter,* to BUTT.]

re·but·tal (ri-bútt'l) *n.* The act of rebutting.

re·but·ter (ri-búttər) *n.* **1.** One that refutes or rebuts. **2.** *Law.* The defendant's answer to the plaintiff's surrejoinder.

rec (rek) *n. Informal.* A recreation ground.

rec. 1. receipt. **2.** recipe. **3.** record; recorder; recording. **4.** recreation.

re·cal·ci·trant (ri-kál-si-trənt, rə-) *adj.* Stubbornly resistant to authority, domination, or guidance. See Synonyms at **unruly.**
~n. A recalcitrant person. [Latin *recalcitrāns* (stem *recalcitrant-*), present participle of *recalcitrāre,* to kick back : *re-,* back, again + *calcitrāre,* to kick, from *calx* (stem *calc-*), heel.] **—re·cal·ci·trance, re·cal·ci·tran·cy** *n.*

re·cal·esce (reé-kə-léss) *intr.v.* **-esced, -escing, -esces.** To undergo recalescence. Used of a cooling metal.

re·ca·les·cence (reé-kə-léss'nss) *n. Metallurgy.* A sudden increase of heat in a cooling metal caused by an exothermic structural change. [Latin *recalescens* (stem *recalescent-*), present participle of *recalescere,* to grow warm again : *re-,* back, again + *calescere,* become warm, from *calēre,* to be warm.] **—re·ca·les·cent** *adj.*

re·call (ri-káwl, rə-) *tr.v.* **-called, -calling, -calls. 1.** To call back; ask or order to return. **2.** To summon back, as from a daydream or digression, to awareness of or concern with the subject or situation at hand. **3. a.** To remember or recollect. **b.** To cause to remember. **4.** To cancel, take back, or revoke. **5.** To request purchasers to return (defective goods, for example). **6.** To bring back; restore.
~n. (*also* reé-kawl). **1.** The act of recalling or summoning back; especially, an official order to return. **2.** A signal, such as a bugle call, used to summon servicemen back to their posts. **3.** The ability to remember information or experiences. **4.** The act of revoking or cancelling. **5.** *Computing.* A measure of the efficiency of an information retrieval system. **—re·call·a·ble** *adj.*

Ré·ca·mier (ray-kámmi-ay), **Jeanne Françoise Julie Adélaïde,** born Julie Bernard (1777–1849). French society hostess. Through her beauty and wit she attracted many influential figures to her *salon,* and she was painted by David and Gérard.

re·cant (ri-kánt) *v.* **-canted, -canting, -cants.** *—tr.* To make a formal retraction or disavowal of (a statement or belief to which one has previously committed oneself). *—intr.* To make a formal retraction or disavowal of a previous statement or previously held belief. [Latin *recantāre* : *re-,* back + *cantāre,* sing, chant, frequentative of *canere,* sing.] **—re·can·ta·tion** (reé-kan-táysh'n) *n.* **—re·cant·er** *n.*

re·cap[1] (reé-káp, ree-) *tr.v.* **-capped, -capping, -caps. 1.** To replace a cap or caplike covering on. **2.** *U.S.* To bond new rubber onto the tread and lateral surface of (a worn car tyre).
~n. (reé-kap). *U.S.* A tyre thus reconditioned.

re·cap[2] (reé-kap, -káp) *tr.v.* **-capped, -capping, -caps.** *Informal.* To recapitulate.
~n. Informal. A recapitulation. [Short for RECAPITULATE.]

re·ca·pit·u·late (reé-kə-píttew-layt) *v.* **-lated, -lating, -lates.** *—tr.* **1.** To repeat in concise form the main points of (a speech, discussion, or the like); sum up. **2.** *Biology.* To appear to repeat (the evolutionary stages of the species) during the embryonic development of the individual organism. *—intr.* To summarise the main points. [Late Latin *recapitulāre* : *re-,* back, again + *capitulāre,* to put under headings, from Latin *capitulum,* heading, small head, diminutive of *caput,* head.] **—re·ca·pit·u·la·tive** (-lətiv, -laytiv), **re·ca·pit·u·la·to·ry** (-lə-tri, -təri, -laytəri || -láytəri) *adj.*

re·ca·pit·u·la·tion (reé-kə-píttew-láysh'n) *n.* **1.** The act or process of recapitulating. **2.** A summary or concise review. **3.** *Biology.* The apparent repetition of some evolutionary stages of the species during embryonic development. Also called "palingenesis". **4.** *Music.* The restatement of the exposition of a theme after its development, forming the final section of a movement in sonata form.

re·cap·tion (ri-kápsh'n, reé-) *n. Law.* The act of claiming and retaking that which has been wrongfully taken or detained, such as goods or a child. It is legal so long as there is no breach of the peace. [RE- + CAPTION ("seizure").]

re·cap·ture (rée-kápchər) *tr.v.* **-tured, -turing, -tures.** **1.** To capture again; retake or recover. **2.** To recall or revive the feeling or quality of: *an attempt to recapture that wonderful moment.* **3.** *U.S.* To acquire by the government procedure of recapture.
—n. **1. a.** The act of recapturing. **b.** The condition of being recaptured. **2.** Anything recaptured. **3.** *U.S.* The lawful taking by a government of a fixed amount of the profits of a public utility company in excess of a stipulated rate of return.

re·cast (rée-kaast || -kást) *tr.v.* **-cast, -casting, -casts.** **1.** To mould again: *recast a bell.* **2.** To set down or present (ideas, for example) in a new or different arrangement. **3.** To change the cast of (a theatrical production, film, or the like).
—n. (rée-kaast || -kast). **1.** The act or process of recasting. **2.** Something produced by recasting.

rec·ce (récki) *v.* **-ced** or **-ceed, -ceing, -ces.** *Slang.* To reconnoitre.
—n. Slang. A reconnaissance. [Shortening.]

recd., rec'd. received.

re-cede (rée-seéd) *tr.v.* **-ceded, -ceding, -cedes.** To cede back; yield or grant to one formerly in possession.

re·cede (ri-seéd, rée-) *intr.v.* **-ceded, -ceding, -cedes.** **1.** To move back or away from a limit, point, or mark. **2.** To slope backwards. **3.** To become or seem to become more distant. **4.** To become less; diminish. **5.** To withdraw or retreat from an agreement, stated position, or the like. **6. a.** To gradually cease to grow above the forehead or on the temples. Used of a man's hair. **b.** To move backwards from the forehead. Used of a man's hairline. [Latin *recēdere,* to go back : *re-,* back, again + *cēdere,* to go.]

re·ceipt (ri-seét, rə-) *n. Abbr.* **rec., rcpt., rept., rec't, rect.** **1.** A written acknowledgment that a stipulated article, sum of money, or delivery of merchandise has been received. **2. a.** The act of receiving something. **b.** The fact of being received. **3.** *Usually plural.* The quantity or amount of something received: *cash receipts.* **4.** *Archaic & Regional.* A recipe.
—tr.v. **receipted, -ceipting, -ceipts.** **1.** To mark (a bill) as having been paid. **2.** *Chiefly U.S.* To give or write a receipt for (money paid or goods delivered). [Middle English *receite,* from Old Northern French, from Medieval Latin *recepta,* from Latin *recipere* (past participle *receptus*), to take, RECEIVE.]

re·ceiv·a·ble (ri-seévəb'l, rə-) *adj.* **1.** Suitable for being received or accepted, especially as payment. **2.** Awaiting or requiring payment; due or collectable: *accounts receivable.*
—n. Plural. Business assets represented by the total amount of accounts due for payment.

re·ceive (ri-seév, rə-) *v.* **-ceived, -ceiving, -ceives.** *—tr.* **1. a.** To take or acquire (something given or offered). **b.** To take or accept (something delivered or transmitted, such as a letter or telephone call). **2.** To acquire knowledge of or information about: *receive bad news.* **3.** To have (a blessing or title, for example) bestowed on one. **4.** To meet with; experience: *receive sympathetic treatment.* **5.** To have inflicted or imposed on oneself: *receive a penalty.* **6.** To bear the weight or force of; support. **7.** To take or intercept the impact of (a blow, for example). **8.** To take in, hold, or contain. **9.** To admit as to a state or society: *receive new members.* **10.** To greet or welcome, especially in a formal manner. **11.** To perceive or acquire mentally: *receive a bad impression.* **12.** To accept as valid or regard with approval: *theories that are widely received.* **13.** To respond or react to in the specified way: *His suggestion was received with howls of derision.* **14.** To listen to and formally and authoritatively acknowledge: *receive an oath of allegiance.* **15.** To take (the sacraments). **16.** *Chiefly British.* To accept and pay for (goods known to be stolen), especially in order to resell them. **17.** To face (the service), as in tennis. *—intr.* **1.** To acquire or get something; be a recipient. **2.** To admit or welcome guests or visitors. **3.** To partake of the Eucharist. **4.** *Electronics.* To convert incoming electrical or electromagnetic waves into visible or audible signals. **5.** *Chiefly British.* To accept and pay for goods known to be stolen, especially in order to resell them. **6.** To be required to face and return the service, as in tennis. [Middle English *receiven,* from Old Northern French *receivre,* from Latin *recipere,* to take back, regain : *re-,* back, again + *capere,* to take.]

re·ceived (ri-seévd, rə-) *adj.* **1.** Generally accepted or believed. **2.** Conventional; clichéd: *received wisdom.* Often used derogatorily.

Received Pronunciation *n. Abbr.* **R.P.** The form of English pronunciation based typically on that of the upper and upper-middle classes in England, having no characteristics peculiar to any region within England and being generally accepted within England as a de facto standard accent.

re·ceiv·er (ri-seévər, rə-) *n.* **1.** One who receives something; a recipient. **2.** An official appointed to receive and account for money due. **3.** *Law.* A person appointed by a court administrator to take into custody property or funds of others that are pending litigation, such as the property or funds of a person declared bankrupt or of unsound mind. **4.** One who knowingly buys or receives stolen goods. **5.** A receptacle intended for a specific purpose, as for collecting the products of distillation. **6.** *Electronics.* A device, such as a part of a radio, television set, or telephone, that receives incoming electrical or electromagnetic signals and converts them to perceptible forms.

re·ceiv·er·ship (ri-seévər-ship, rə-) *n. Law.* **1.** The office or functions of a receiver. **2.** The state of being held in the custody of a receiver.

re·ceiv·ing end (ri-seéving, rə-) *n. Informal.* A position in which one is subjected directly to an unpleasant experience, especially criticism or abuse. Used chiefly in the phrase *on the receiving end.*

receiving order *n. Law.* A court order appointing a receiver to take custody of the property or funds of a debtor when an act of bankruptcy has been established.

re·cen·sion (ri-sénsh'n, rə-) *n.* **1.** A critical revision of a text incorporating the most plausible elements found in varying sources. **2.** A text so revised. [Latin *recēnsiō* (stem *recēnsiōn-*), a reviewing, an enumeration, from *recēnsēre,* to survey again, review : *re-,* again, back + *cēnsēre,* to estimate, assess.]

re·cent (reéss'nt) *adj.* **1.** Of, belonging to, or occurring at a time immediately prior to the present. **2.** Modern; new. **3.** *Capital* **R.** *Geology.* Of, belonging to, or designating the Holocene epoch.
—n. Capital **R.** *Geology.* The **Holocene epoch** *(see).* Preceded by *the.* [Latin *recēns* (stem *recent-*), fresh, new.] **—re·cen·cy, re·cent·ness** *n.* **—re·cent·ly** *adv.*

re·cept (reé-sept) *n.* A mental image formed from what is common to successive perceptions. [RE- + (CON)CEPT.]

re·cep·ta·cle (ri-séptək'l, rə-) *n.* **1.** Something that holds or contains; a container. **2.** *Botany.* **a.** The tip of a flower stalk, that bears and supports the floral organs. **b.** In certain seaweeds, the part of the blade that bears the reproductive structures. [Latin *receptāculum,* from *receptāre,* to take again, frequentative of *recipere* (past participle *receptus*), to RECEIVE.]

re·cep·tion (ri-sépsh'n, rə-) *n.* **1.** The act or process of receiving or accepting or of being received or accepted. **2. a.** A welcome, greeting, or acceptance: *a friendly reception.* **b.** A response or reaction: *Her speech got a very hostile reception.* **3.** A formal social function held to meet guests, as after a wedding, or entertain visitors, such as foreign dignitaries. **4.** *Electronics.* **a.** The action of receiving electrical or electromagnetic signals. **b.** The condition or quality of received signals. **6. a.** The place, as in an office or hospital, where clients or visitors are received and appointments made. **b.** The place in a hotel where guests register or make reservations. [Latin *receptiō* (stem *receptiōn-*), from *recipere* (past participle *receptus*), to RECEIVE.]

re·cep·tion·ist (ri-sépsh'n-ist, rə-) *n.* A person employed, as in an office, hotel, or hospital, to receive callers or clients, answer the telephone, and deal with enquiries.

re·cep·tive (ri-séptiv, rə-) *adj.* **1.** Capable of or qualified for receiving. **2.** Ready or willing to receive favourably. **3.** Quick to apprehend new ideas, impressions, or the like. **—re·cep·tive·ly** *adv.* **—re·cep·tiv·i·ty** (reé-sep-tivvəti, ré-), **re·cep·tive·ness** *n.*

re·cep·tor (ri-séptər) *n. Anatomy.* A cell or group of cells specialised to sense or to receive stimuli.

re·cess (ri-séss, rə-, reé-sess) *n.* **1.** A temporary cessation of customary activities or proceedings, such as at the end of a Parliamentary session: *the Easter recess.* **2.** The period of such cessation. **3.** *Usually plural.* A remote, secret, or secluded place. **4.** *Anatomy.* An indentation or small hollow in an organ. **5.** An alcove.
—v. **recessed, -cessing, -cesses.** *—tr.* **1.** To place in a recess. **2.** To create or fashion a recess in. **3.** *U.S.* To suspend for a recess. *—intr.* *U.S.* To take a recess. [Latin *recessus,* from the past participle of *recēdere,* to RECEDE.]

re-ces·sion (reé-sésh'n) *n.* The act of restoring possession to a former owner.

re·ces·sion (ri-sésh'n, rə-) *n.* **1.** A decline in economic activity that occurs during a period of otherwise increasing prosperity, but is not as severe as a depression. **2.** The act of withdrawing or receding back. **3.** The filing out of clergy and choir members after a church service. [Latin *recessiō* (stem *recessiōn-*), from *recessus,* RECESS.]

re·ces·sion·al (ri-sésh'n'l, rə-) *adj.* Of or pertaining to recession.
—n. A hymn that accompanies the exit of the clergy and choir after a service.

re·ces·sive (ri-séssiv, rə-) *adj.* **1.** Tending to go backwards or recede. **2.** *Genetics.* Of, pertaining to, or designating an allele that does not produce a phenotypic effect when paired with a dominant allele. Compare **dominant. 3.** *Phonetics.* Designating a stress that falls near the beginning of a polysyllabic word.
—n. Genetics. **1.** A recessive allele or trait. **2.** An organism having a recessive trait. **—re·ces·sive·ly** *adv.*

Re·cha·bite (ré-kə-bīt) *n.* **1.** One who abstains from alcohol. **2.** A member of the Independent Order of Rechabites, a temperance society founded in 1835. [After Jonadab, son of *Rechab,* who founded an order of abstainers from wine. Jeremiah 35:6–7.]

ré·chauf·fé (ray-shṓ-fay || *U.S.* ráy-shō-fáy) *n.* **1.** Leftover food that is warmed up. **2.** Old material reworked or rehashed. [French, "warmed up", from *réchauffer,* to heat again, from Old French : *re-,* again, back + *chauffer,* to warm (see **chafe**).]

re·cher·ché (rə-shaír-shay || *U.S.* -sháy) *adj.* **1.** Highly sought after; rare. **2.** Exquisite; refined. **3.** Familiar or known only to experts or connoisseurs. **4.** Overrefined; affected and forced. [French, past participle of *rechercher,* to search for, RESEARCH.]

re·chris·ten (reé-kriss'n) *tr.v.* **-ened, ening, ens.** **1.** To christen again. **2.** To rename.

re·cid·i·vism (ri-síddi-viz'm) *n.* A tendency to relapse into a former pattern of behaviour; especially, a tendency to return to criminal habits. [From *recidivist,* from French *récidiviste,* relapser, from *récidiver,* to relapse, from Medieval Latin *recidīvāre,* from Latin *recidīvus,* a falling back, from *recidere,* fall back : *re-,* back, again + *cadere,* fall.] **—re·cid·i·vist** *n.* **—re·cid·i·vis·tic** (-vístik), **re·cid·i·vous** *adj.*

Re·ci·fe (re-séefi) Formerly **Pernambuco.** Capital of the state of Pernambuco in eastern Brazil. It is a port and industrial centre.

rec·i·pe (réssi-pi, réssə-, -pee) *n.* **1.** *Abbr.* **rec.** A formula for preparing a mixture or compound, especially in cooking or pharmacology, with a list of measured ingredients and often a set of directions for their use or application. **2.** *Symbol* ℞ A medical prescription. Not in current technical usage. **3.** A procedure or set of circumstances likely to lead to a specified end: *a recipe for disaster.* [Latin, "take", imperative of *recipere,* to take, RECEIVE.]

re·cip·i·ent (ri-síppi-ənt, rə-) *adj.* Functioning as a receiver.
~*n.* **1.** One that receives or is receptive. **2.** *Medicine.* A person who receives blood or transplanted tissue from a donor. [Latin *recipiēns* (stem *recipient-*), present participle of *recipere,* to RECEIVE.]

re·cip·ro·cal (ri-sípprə-k'l, rə-) *adj.* **1.** Performed or given in return: *a reciprocal present.* **2.** Interchanged, given, or owed by each of two parties to the other: *reciprocal funds.* **3.** Performed, experienced, or felt by both sides: *reciprocal hatred.* **4.** Equivalent or corresponding. **5.** *Grammar.* Expressing mutual action or relationship. Said of some verbs and compound pronouns. **6.** *Mathematics.* Of or pertaining to a quantity divided into 1.
~*n.* **1.** Anything that is reciprocal to something else; a converse or complement. **2.** *Mathematics.* The quotient of a specific quantity divided into 1. For example, the reciprocal of 7 is $^1/_7$; the reciprocal of $^2/_3$ is $^3/_2$. [Latin *reciprocus,* alternating, returning.] **—re·cip·ro·cal·i·ty** (-kál-əti), **re·cip·ro·cal·ness** *n.* **—re·cip·ro·cal·ly** *adv.*

reciprocal ohm *n. Physics.* A **siemens** (*see*).

reciprocal pronoun *n. Grammar.* A pronoun or pronominal phrase expressing mutual action or relationship, such as *each other.*

re·cip·ro·cate (ri-síprrə-kayt, rə-) *v.* **-cated, -cating, -cates.** *—tr.* **1.** To give or take mutually; interchange. **2.** To show or feel in response or return. **3.** To cause to move back and forth alternately. *—intr.* **1.** To move back and forth alternately. **2.** To give and take something mutually. **3.** To make a return for something given or done. **4.** To be complementary or equivalent. [Latin *reciprocāre,* to move back and forth, from *reciprocus,* RECIPROCAL.] **—re·cip·ro·ca·tive** (-kətiv, -kaytiv) *adj.* **—re·cip·ro·ca·tor** (-kaytər) *n.*

re·cip·ro·cat·ing engine (ri-sípprə-káyting, rə-) *n.* An engine having a crankshaft turned by linearly reciprocating pistons.

re·cip·ro·ca·tion (ri-sípprə-káysh'n, rə-) *n.* **1.** An alternating back-and-forth movement. **2.** The act or fact of reciprocating; a mutual giving or receiving; an interchange.

rec·i·proc·i·ty (réssi-próssəti) *n., pl.* **-ties.** *Abbr.* **recip. 1.** A reciprocal condition or relationship. **2.** A mutual or cooperative interchange of favours or privileges; especially, one constituting a commercial policy or trade agreement between two or more parties.

re·ci·sion (ri-sízh'n, rə-) *n.* The act or an instance of rescinding; an annulment or cancellation. [Latin *recīsiō* (stem *recīsiōn-*), a cutting off, from *recīsus,* past participle of *recīdere,* to cut down : *re-,* back, back down, again + *caedere,* to cut.]

recit. *Music.* recitative.

re·cit·al (ri-sī́t'l, rə-) *n.* **1.** A public reciting of poetry or prose. **2.** A retelling in detail; a narration. **3.** Something thus told. **4.** A performance of music or dance, especially by a soloist or small ensemble. **5.** *Law.* A preliminary part of a document setting out relevant facts. **—re·cit·al·ist** *n.*

rec·i·ta·tion (réssi-táysh'n) *n.* **1.** The act of reciting poetry or prose from memory, especially in a public performance. **2.** The material so recited.

rec·i·ta·tive¹ (ri-sī́tətiv, réssi-taytiv) *adj.* Pertaining to or having the character of a recital or recitative.

rec·i·ta·tive² (réssitə-téev) *n.* Also **re·ci·ta·ti·vo** (-téevō; *Italian* ré-chee-ta-) *pl.* **-vi** (-vee) or **-vos** (-vōz). *Abbr.* **recit. 1.** A musical style used in opera and oratorio, in which the text is declaimed in the rhythm of natural speech with slight melodic variation. **2.** A passage rendered in this form. [Italian *recitativo,* from *recitare,* to recite, from Latin *recitāre,* to RECITE.]

re·cite (ri-sī́t, rə-) *v.* **-cited, -citing, -cites.** *—tr.* **1.** To repeat aloud or declaim (a poem or passage) that has been rehearsed or memorised, especially before an audience or teacher. **2.** To relate in detail. **3.** To list or enumerate. *—intr.* To deliver a recitation. [Middle English *reciten,* from Old French *reciter,* from Latin *recitāre,* to read out, cite again : *re-,* back, again + *citāre,* to CITE.] **—re·cit·er** *n.*

reck (rek) *v.* **recked, recking, recks.** *Archaic & Regional. —tr.* To take heed of; be concerned about: *He does not reck death. —intr.* To take heed; have caution. [Middle English *recken, recchen,* to be careful, to take care, Old English *reccan*†, *recan* (unattested).]

reck·less (rék-ləss, -liss) *adj.* **1. a.** Heedless or careless. **b.** Headstrong; rash: *a reckless lover.* **2.** Having no regard for consequences; uncontrolled; wild: *a reckless driver.* [Middle English *recheles, reckeles,* Old English *rēcelēas.*] **—reck·less·ly** *adv.* **—reck·less·ness** *n.*

Synonyms: *reckless, adventurous, rash, precipitate, foolhardy, audacious, daring.*

reck·on (réckən) *v.* **-oned, -oning, -ons.** *—tr.* **1.** To count or compute. **2.** To consider as being; regard as. **3.** *Informal.* To think or assume. **4.** *Slang.* To think well of; regard highly: *I don't reckon him as captain. —intr.* **1.** To make a calculation; figure. Often used with *up.* **2.** To make assumptions about something; place reliance. Used with *on* or *upon*: *reckon on financial aid.* **3.** To make allowance for a possibility; anticipate something. Used with *on* or *upon*: *I didn't reckon on your being here.* —See Synonyms at **calculate, consider. —reckon with. 1.** To come to terms or settle accounts with. **2.** To recognise as significant: *a force to be reckoned with.* **—reckon without.** To fail to take into account. [Middle English *reknen,* Old English *gerecenian,* to enumerate, from Germanic.]

reck·on·er (réckənər) *n.* **1.** One that reckons. **2.** A handbook of mathematical tables to facilitate computation; a ready reckoner.

reck·on·ing (réckəning) *n.* **1.** Computation. **2.** An itemised bill or statement of a sum due. **3.** The settlement of a bill or account. **4.** Calculation of the position of a ship, aircraft, or the like. **5.** Judgment of or retribution for past misdeeds. Used chiefly in the phrase *day of reckoning.*

re·claim (ri-kláym, rée-) *tr.v.* **-claimed, -claiming, -claims. 1.** To make (marshland or desert, for example) suitable for cultivation or habitation, as by stabilising, irrigating, or fertilising. **2.** To procure (usable substances) from refuse or waste products. **3.** To turn (a person) from error, evil, or barbarism; reform. **4.** To demand or effect the return of. **5.** *Archaic.* To tame (a falcon, for example). **6.** To produce (land) by filling in an area previously submerged by the sea. —See Synonyms at **recover, save.**
~*n.* The act of reclaiming or condition of being reclaimed. [Middle English *reclamen,* to call back, from Old French *reclamer,* from Latin *reclāmāre,* to exclaim against : *re-,* back, against + *clāmāre,* to call out.] **—re·claim·a·ble** *adj.* **—re·claim·ant, re·claim·er** *n.*

rec·la·ma·tion (récklə-máysh'n) *n.* **1.** The act or process of reclaiming or condition of being reclaimed. **2.** A restoration, as to usefulness, or morality. [Old French, a protest, from Latin *reclāmātiō* (stem *reclamātiōn-*), cry of opposition, from *reclāmāre,* to RECLAIM.]

ré·clame (ray-kláam, re-) *n.* **1.** Public acclaim. **2.** A taste or flair for publicity. [French, publicity, from *réclamer,* to reclaim, from Old French *reclamer,* to RECLAIM.]

rec·li·nate (récklin-ayt) *adj. Botany.* Bent or turned downwards towards the base. Said especially of leaves and stems. [Latin *reclīnātus,* past participle of *reclīnāre,* to RECLINE.]

re·cline (ri-klī́n, rə-) *v.* **-clined, -clining, -clines.** *—tr.* To cause to assume a leaning or supine position. *—intr.* To lie back or down. [Middle English *reclinen,* from Old French *recliner,* from Latin *reclīnāre* : *re-,* back, again + *-clīnāre,* to bend.] **—rec·li·na·tion** (réckli-náysh'n) *n.* **—re·clin·er** *n.*

re·cluse (ri-kló͞oss || -kléwss, *U.S. also* rék-lo͞oss, -lo͞oz) *n.* One who withdraws to live in solitude and seclusion; a hermit.
~*adj.* Withdrawn from the world; solitary. [Middle English *reclus(e),* from Old French, past participle of *reclure,* to shut up, from Latin *reclūdere,* to close off, unclose, open : *re-* (intensifive), again + *claudere,* to close. **—re·clu·sion** (-kló͞ozh'n || -kléwzh'n) *n.*]

re·clu·sive (ri-kló͞o-siv || -kléw-, -ziv) *adj.* **1.** Seeking or preferring seclusion or isolation. **2.** Providing seclusion: *a reclusive hut.*

re·cog·ni·sance, re·cog·ni·zance (ri-kóg-ni-z'nss, rə-, -kónni-) *n.* **1.** *Law.* **a.** An obligation of record entered into before a court or magistrate by which a person binds himself to perform a particular act, such as to appear in court or pay a sum of money. **b.** A sum of money pledged to assure the performance of such an act. **2.** *Archaic.* A recognition. [Middle English *recognizance, reconissaunce,* recognition, from Old French *reconoissance,* from *reconoistre,* to RECOGNISE.] **—re·cog·ni·sant** *adj.*

rec·og·nise, rec·og·nize (réckəg-nīz, *also* réckə-. *Note: the pronunciation* réckə-nīz, *although used by many educated speakers, is widely condemned*). *tr.v.* **-nised, -nising, -nises. 1.** To know or be aware that (something perceived) has been perceived by oneself before: *recognise a face.* **2.** To know or identify from past experience or knowledge: *recognise a red-winged blackbird.* **3. a.** To realise; comprehend and appreciate fully: *recognised the value of the discovery.* **b.** To perceive or acknowledge the validity or reality of: *recognise a demand.* **4.** To acknowledge the presence of; greet: *refused to recognise me in the street.* **5.** To give permission to (a person) to speak in a debate. Used especially of a chairman. **6.** To acknowledge or accept the national status of (a new government). **7.** To show approval or appreciation of: *recognise services rendered.* [Old French *reconoistre* (stem *reco(g)noiss-*), from Latin *recognōscere,* to know again : *re-,* again + *cognōscere,* to know : *co-,* with + *gnōscere,* become acquainted.] **—rec·og·nis·a·ble** (-nīzəb'l, *also* -nī́zəb'l) *adj.* **—rec·og·nis·a·bly** *adv.* **—rec·og·nis·er** *n.*

rec·og·nised (réckəg-nīzd, *also* réckə-. *See note at* **recognise**). *adj.* Generally approved or acknowledged as meeting appropriate requirements: *a recognised brand or paint.*

rec·og·ni·tion (réckəg-nísh'n, *also* réckə- *See note at* **recognise.**) *n.* **1.** The act of recognising or state of being recognised, especially: **a.** An awareness that something perceived has previously been perceived by oneself. **b.** An acknowledgment, as of a claim or fact. **2.** Attention or favourable notice: *Her achievements won her general recognition.* **3.** An acknowledgment of the national status of a new government by another nation. [Latin *recognitiō* (stem *recognitiōn-*), from *recognōscere* (past participle *recognitus*), to RECOGNISE.] **—re·cog·ni·to·ry** (ri-kóg-ni-tri, -təri), **re·cog·ni·tive** *adj.*

re·coil (ri-kóyl, rə-) *intr.v.* **-coiled, -coiling, -coils. 1.** To spring back, as a shotgun does when fired. **2.** To shrink back, as in fear or repugnance. **3.** To harm the person responsible for an act, especially an act of malice. Used with *on* or *upon: Vice recoils upon the guilty men.*
~*n.* (rée-koyl, ri-kóyl). **1.** The amount of space used by a firearm as it recoils upon firing. **2.** The act or state of recoiling. [Middle English *recoilen, reculen,* from Old French *reculer* : *re-,* back, again + *cul,* backside, from Latin *cūlus.*] **—re·coil·er** *n.*

Synonyms: *recoil, blench, cower, quail, cringe, flinch, shrink.*

re·col·lect (rée-kə-lékt) *tr.v.* **-lected, -lecting, -lects. 1.** To collect again. **2.** To calm or control (oneself).

rec·ol·lect (récкə-lékt) *v.* **-lected, -lecting, -lects.** —*tr.* To recall to mind; remember. —*intr.* To have a recollection; remember. [Medieval Latin *recolligere* (past participle *recollectus*), to recall, from Latin, to gather again : *re-*, again + *colligere,* to gather, COLLECT.] **—rec·ol·lec·tive** *adj.* **—rec·ol·lec·tive·ly** *adv.*

rec·ol·lec·tion (récкə-léksh'n) *n.* **1.** The act or power of recollecting. **2.** Something recollected. —See Synonyms at **memory.**

re·com·bi·nant (rée-kómbinənt, ree-) *n.* An individual in which genetic recombination has occurred.
~*adj.* Of, pertaining to, or characterised by genetic recombination. [RECOMBIN(E) + -ANT.]

recombinant DNA *n.* DNA prepared by laboratory manipulation in which genes from one species are combined with those of another species.

re·com·bi·na·tion (rée-kómbi-náysh'n) *n.* The formation in an offspring of gene combinations not present in either of its parents.

re·com·mence (rée-kə-ménss) *v.* **-menced, -mencing, -mences.** To begin or commence again.

rec·om·mend (récкə-ménd) *tr.v.* **-mended, -mending, -mends.** **1.** To commend to the attention of another as reputable, worthy, or desirable. **2.** To make attractive or acceptable: *He has little to recommend him.* **3.** To counsel or advise (a particular course of action). **4.** *Archaic.* To commit to the charge of another: *recommended his soul to God.* [Middle English *recommenden,* from Medieval Latin *recommendāre* : Latin *re-*, again + *commendāre,* to COMMEND.] **—rec·om·mend·a·ble** *adj.* **—rec·om·mend·er** *n.*

rec·om·men·da·tion (récкə-men-dáysh'n, -mən-) *n.* **1.** The act of recommending. **2.** Something that recommends; specifically, a favourable statement concerning a person's character or qualifications. **3.** Someone or something that is recommended. **—rec·om·men·da·to·ry** (-mén-də-tri, -təri, -dáytəri) *adj.*

re·com·mit (rée-kə-mít) *tr.v.* **-mitted, -mitting, -mits.** **1.** To commit again. **2.** To refer (a bill) to a committee again, for further consideration. **—re·com·mit·ment, re·com·mit·tal** *n.*

rec·om·pense (récкəm-penss) *tr.v.* **-pensed, -pensing, -penses.** **1.** To reward or pay for services. **2. a.** To award compensation for (loss or damage, for example); make a return for. **b.** To award compensation to.
~*n.* **1.** Amends for something, such as damage or loss. **2.** Payment for something given or done, such as services. [Middle English *recompensen,* from Old French *recompenser,* from Late Latin *recompensāre* : Latin *re-*, back, again + *compensāre,* to COMPENSATE.]

re·com·pose (rée-kəm-pṓz || -kom-) *tr.v.* **-posed, -posing, -poses.** **1.** To compose again. **2.** To restore to composure; calm. **—re·com·po·si·tion** (rée-kompə-zísh'n) *n.*

re·con (rée-kon) *n.* The smallest genetic unit that is capable of recombination. [*Re*combination + *-on,* as in *codon.*]

rec·on·cil·a·ble (récкən-sīl-əb'l, -sīl-) *adj.* Capable of reconciliation or able to be reconciled. **—rec·on·cil·a·bil·i·ty** (-ə-bílləti), **rec·on·cil·a·ble·ness** *n.* **—rec·on·cil·a·bly** *adv.*

rec·on·cile (récкən-sīl) *tr.v.* **-ciled, -ciling, -ciles.** **1.** To re-establish friendship between. **2.** To settle or resolve (a dispute, for example). **3.** To bring to acceptance or acquiescence: *reconcile oneself to defeat.* **4.** To make compatible or consistent. Often used with *to* or *with*: *reconcile my way of thinking with yours.* **5.** To purify (a consecrated place) in a special ceremony, after an act of desecration. [Middle English *reconcilen,* from Old French *reconcilier,* from Latin *reconciliāre* : *re-*, again + *conciliāre,* to CONCILIATE.] **—rec·on·cile·ment, rec·on·cil·i·a·tion** (-sílli-áysh'n) *n.* **—rec·on·cil·er** *n.* **—rec·on·cil·i·a·to·ry** (-sílli-ətri, -ətəri) *adj.*

rec·on·dite (récкən-dīt, ri-kóndīt, rə-) *adj.* **1.** Not easily understood; abstruse: *life's recondite origin.* **2.** Concerning abstruse or obscure subjects: *recondite scholarship.* [Latin *reconditus,* past participle of *recondere,* to hide, put up again : *re-*, again + *condere,* bring together.] **—rec·on·dite·ly** *adv.* **—rec·on·dite·ness** *n.*

re·con·di·tion (rée-kən-dísh'n || -kon-) *tr.v.* **-tioned, -tioning, -tions.** **1.** To restore by repairing, renovating, or rebuilding. **2.** To overhaul and restore to good working order.

re·con·nais·sance (ri-kónni-s'nss, rə-, -kónnə- || -z'nss) *n.* **1.** The process or activity of investigating or surveying. **2. a.** A preliminary survey made of a region to examine its terrain or to determine the disposition of enemy forces. **b.** A party making such a survey. [French, from Old French *reconoissance,* RECOGNISANCE.]

re·con·noi·tre, *U.S.* **re·con·noi·ter** (récкə-nóytər || réekə-) *v.* **-tred** or *U.S.* **-tered, -tring** or *U.S.* **-tering, -tres** or *U.S.* **-ters.** —*tr.* To make a preliminary inspection of (an area or enemy positions, for example). —*intr.* To make a reconnaissance.
~*n.* An act of reconnoitring. [Obsolete French *reconnoître,* from Old French *reconoistre,* RECOGNISE.] **—re·con·noi·tr·er** *n.*

re·con·sid·er (rée-kən-síddər || -kon-) *v.* **-ered, -ering, -ers.** —*tr.* To consider (a decision, for example) again, with a view to possible revision. —*intr.* To consider a matter again and, especially, to come to a different decision. **—re·con·sid·er·a·tion** (-áysh'n) *n.*

re·con·sti·tute (rée-kón-sti-tewt || -tōōt) *tr.v.* **-tuted, -tuting, -tutes.** **1.** To restore the constitution of (a concentrate or dried food, for example), as by the addition of water. **2.** To restore to existence or to an original condition; reconstruct. **—re·con·sti·tu·tion** (-téwsh'n || -tṓōsh'n) *n.*

re·con·struct (rée-kən-strúkt || -kon-) *tr.v.* **-structed, -structing, -structs.** **1.** To construct again; rebuild. **2. a.** To remake (something that is incomplete or damaged) guided by the available evidence: *reconstruct the orchestral score from the piano version.* **b.** To represent (an occurrence, such as a crime or historical event) in dramatic form on the basis of available evidence.

re·con·struc·tion (rée-kən-strúksh'n || -kon-) *n.* **1.** The act or result of reconstructing. **2.** *Capital* **R.** The period (1865–77) in the United States after the Civil War during which the states of the Southern Confederacy were reorganised prior to their full readmission to the Union. **3.** *Finance.* **Reorganisation** *(see).* **—re·con·struc·tive** *adj.*

re·con·vey (rée-kən-váy || -kon-) *tr.v.* **-veyed, -veying, -veys.** To convey back to a former owner or place. **—re·con·vey·ance** *n.*

rec·ord (récкawrd || *chiefly U.S.* récкərd) *n. Abbr.* **rec.** **1. a.** An account made in an enduring form, especially in writing, that preserves the knowledge or memory of events or facts. **b.** The fact or condition of serving as such an account for future reference: *a newspaper of record.* **2.** Something on which such an account is made. **3.** *Often plural.* Information or data on a particular subject collected and preserved: *look up parish records.* **4.** The known history of performance or achievement: *a fine war record.* **5.** The best performance known officially, as in a sport: *broke the world record.* **6.** *Law.* **a.** An account officially written and preserved as evidence or testimony. **b.** An account of judicial or legislative proceedings written and preserved as evidence. **c.** The documents or volumes containing such evidence. **7.** A disc structurally coded to reproduce sound when played on a record player; a gramophone record. Also used adjectivally: *a record company.* **8.** Anything that provides a source of information about the past or preserves facts for reference: *Pop music is a record of contemporary youth culture.* **9.** An official report kept by the police of an individual's previous convictions. **10.** *Computing.* A small amount of data that is stored, processed, and retrieved as a single convenient unit. **—for the record.** For the sake of accuracy; as an official fact. **—off the record.** Confidentially or unofficially; not for publication. **—on record.** **1.** Noted in official recordings of past facts or events: *the warmest summer on record.* **2.** Officially recorded or noted for public disclosure: *He is on record as having stated his acceptance of the new regime.*
~*v.* **re·cord** (ri-kórd, rə-), **-corded, -cording, -cords.** —*tr.* **1.** To set down for preservation in writing or other permanent form. **2.** To serve as a source of information about or as evidence of: *Her novel records a past way of life.* **3.** To register or indicate: *A thermometer records temperatures.* **4. a.** To register (a voice or piece of music, for example) in permanent form by mechanical or electrical means for reproduction. **b.** To perform (a piece of music, for example) that is to be registered in this way. —*intr.* To record something.
~*adj.* **rec·ord** (récкawrd || *chiefly U.S.* récкərd). *Abbr.* **rec.** Establishing a record: *a record crowd.* [Middle English *recorde,* from Old French *record,* from *recorder,* to record, from Latin *recordārī,* to remember, think over : *re-*, again + *cor* (stem *cord-*), mind, heart.]

rec·ord-break·ing (récкawrd-brayking || récкərd-) *adj.* That establishes a new record: *a record-breaking time.*

re·cord·ed delivery (ri-kórdid, rə-) *n.* **1.** A service provided by the Post Office that makes an official record of the posting and delivery of mail. **2.** A delivery of post provided by this service.
~*adv.* By or using this service.

re·cord·er (ri-kórdər, rə-) *n.* **1.** One that records, such as: **a.** An instrument for recording measurements. **b.** An official who records proceedings. **c.** A **tape recorder** *(see).* **2.** A fipple flute with eight fingerholes existing in various ranges. **3.** *Law.* In England and Wales, a barrister or solicitor of at least ten years' standing who acts as a part-time judge in the crown court and can also sit as a judge for a county court. **4.** *Capital* **R.** Used as part of the title of certain newspapers: *The Halifax Recorder.*

re·cord·ing (ri-kórding, rə-) *n. Abbr.* **rec.** **1.** A gramophone record or magnetic tape or wire upon which sound has been recorded. **2.** The sounds so recorded. **3.** The process of registering sound in a permanent form on a record or tape. **4.** A radio or television programme that has been prerecorded.

Recording Angel *n.* An angel who supposedly registers the good and evil acts of every person.

record-player *n.* A device for playing gramophone records, consisting of a single unit having a turntable, a pickup for converting vibrations of the needle into electrical signals, an amplifier, and one or more loudspeakers.

re-count (rée-kównt || *West Indies also* -kúngt) *tr.v.* **-counted, -counting, -counts.** To count again.
~*n.* (rée-kownt, *rarely* -kównt). An additional count; especially, a second count of votes cast in an election.

re·count (ri-kównt || *West Indies also* -kúngt) *tr.v.* **-counted, -counting, -counts.** **1.** To narrate the facts or details of. **2.** To enumerate. [Middle English *recounten,* from Old French *reconter* : *re-*, again, back + *conter, compter,* to relate, COUNT.] **—re·count·al** *n.*

re·coup (ri-kṓōp) *v.* **-couped, -couping, -coups.** —*tr.* **1.** To receive or get back an equivalent for; make up for: *recoup the loss.* **2.** To return as an equivalent for; reimburse. **3.** *Law.* To deduct or withhold (part of something due) for a legally recognised reason. —*intr.* To regain a former favourable position. —See Synonyms at **recover.** [Middle English *recoupen,* from Old French *recouper,* to cut back, retrench : *re-*, back + *couper,* to cut, strike, from *coup,* blow, COUP.] **—re·coup·a·ble** *adj.* **—re·coup·ment** *n.*

re·course (ri-kórss, rə- || -kōrss, *also* rée-kawrss, -kōrss) *n.* **1.** A turning or applying to a person or thing for aid or security: *have recourse to the courts.* **2.** One that is turned or applied to for aid or security: *His only recourse was the police.* See Usage note at **resort.** **3.** *Law.* The right to demand payment from the endorser of a bill of exchange or other commercial paper when the first party liable fails to pay. **—without recourse.** Disclaiming liability for nonpayment.

Used as a formula by an endorser of a bill of exchange to avoid liability. [Middle English *recours,* from Old French, from Latin *recursus,* a running back, from *recurrere,* to run back : *re-,* again, back + *currere,* to run.]

re·cov·er (rée-kúvvər) *tr.v.* **-ered, -ering, -ers.** To cover again.

re·cov·er (ri-kúvvər, rə-) *v.* **-ered, -ering, -ers.** —*tr.* **1. a.** To get back or regain possession or control of: *recovered property; recovered memories.* **b.** To retrieve; make up for: *recovered the time lost in the strike.* **2.** To restore (oneself) to a normal state, as after an illness or setback. **3.** To regain the use or enjoyment of: *recovered his health; land recovered from the sea.* **4.** *Law.* To gain as compensation by means of a favourable judgment in a civil lawsuit: *recover damages.* **5.** To derive (useful substances) from waste material. —*intr.* **1.** To regain a normal or usual condition or state, as of health or economic development. Often used with *from.* **2.** To receive a favourable judgment in a civil lawsuit. **3.** In swimming or rowing, to stretch the arm or oar forwards ready to take another stroke. [Middle English *recoveren,* from Old French *recoverer,* from Latin *recuperāre,* to RECUPERATE.] —**re·cov·er·a·ble** *adj.* —**re·cov·er·er** *n.*

Synonyms: *recover, reclaim, regain, recoup, retrieve.*

re·cov·er·y (ri-kúvvəri, rə-) *n., pl.* **-ies.** **1.** An act, instance, process, or duration of recovering; recuperation. **2.** A return to a normal condition. **3.** Something gained or restored in recovering. **4.** The obtaining of usable substances from unusable sources, such as waste material. **5.** *Law.* The process of recovering compensation, damages, or the like by a lawsuit. **6.** In fencing, the returning to an on guard position. **7.** In swimming or rowing, the action of recovering. **8.** In golf, a stroke to bring a ball out of a bunker or away from the rough.

recovery room *n.* A hospital room used for the care and observation of patients immediately after surgery.

rec·re·ant (réckri-ənt) *adj. Literary.* **1.** Unfaithful or disloyal to a belief, promise, or cause. **2.** Craven or cowardly.
—*n. Literary.* **1.** A faithless or disloyal person; an apostate. **2.** A coward. [Middle English *recreant,* from Old French, present participle of *recroire,* to yield, surrender, from Medieval Latin *recrēdere* : Latin *re-,* back, contrarily + *crēdere,* entrust, believe.] —**rec·re·ance, rec·re·an·cy** *n.* —**rec·re·ant·ly** *adv.*

re-cre·ate (rée-kri-áyt, -kree-) *tr.v.* **-ated, -ating, -ates.** To reproduce (something that formerly existed); create anew. —**re-cre·a·tion** *n.*

rec·re·ate (réckri-ayt) *v.* **-ated, -ating, -ates.** —*tr.* To impart fresh life to; refresh mentally or physically. —*intr.* To take recreation; amuse oneself. [Latin *recreāre,* to create anew : *re-,* back, again + *creāre,* to CREATE.] —**rec·re·a·tive** (-ətiv, -aytiv) *adj.*

rec·re·a·tion (réckri-áysh'n) *n. Abbr.* **rec.** **1.** Refreshment of one's mind or body through diverting activity. **2.** A form of relaxation or pleasurable exercise that fosters this.

rec·re·a·tion·al (réckri-áyshənəl) *adj.* Of or for recreation: *recreational vehicles; recreational drugs like Ecstasy.* —**rec·re·a·tion·al·ly** *adv.*

recreation ground *n.* A piece of public land used for recreational activities, often equipped with swings, slides, and the like.

rec·re·ment (réckri-mənt) *n.* Waste matter; refuse; dross. [Latin *recrēmentum* : *re-,* back, again + *cernere,* to separate, sift.] —**rec·re·men·tal** (-mént'l) *adj.*

re·crim·i·nate (ri-krímmi-nayt, rə-) *v.* **-nated, -nating, -nates.** —*tr.* To accuse in return. —*intr.* To counter one accusation with another. [Medieval Latin *recrīmināre* : Latin *re-,* again, back + *crīmināre,* to accuse, from *crīmen,* accusation.] —**re·crim·i·na·tive** (-nətiv, -naytiv), **re·crim·i·na·to·ry** (-nətri, -nətəri, -náytəri) *adj.* —**re·crim·i·na·tor** (-naytər) *n.*

re·crim·i·na·tion (ri-krímmi-náysh'n, rə-) *n.* **1.** The act of recriminating, especially in a bitter way; mutual accusation. **2.** A countercharge.

re·cru·desce (rée-kroo͞-déss, réckroo͞-) *intr.v.* **-desced, -descing, -desces.** To break out anew after a dormant or inactive period. Used especially of something undesirable, such as a disease or state of discontent. [Latin *recrūdēscere* : *re-,* again + *crūdēscere,* to get worse, from *crūdus,* harsh, raw.] —**re·cru·des·cence** *n.* —**re·cru·des·cent** *adj.*

re·cruit (ri-kroo͞t, rə- || -kréwt) *v.* **-cruited, -cruiting, -cruits.** —*tr.* **1.** To enlist for military service. **2.** To strengthen or raise (an armed force) by enlistment. **3. a.** To obtain (new members or employees, for example). **b.** To supply with new members or employees. **4.** To enrol (another) in support of oneself or one's ideas. **5.** To replenish. **6.** To renew or restore (health or vitality). —*intr.* **1.** To seek or enlist new members or recruits. **2.** To regain lost health or strength; recover.
—*n.* **1.** *Abbr.* **rct.** A newly enlisted member of a military force; especially, one of the lowest rank or grade. **2.** A new member of any organisation or body. [Obsolete French dialect *recrute,* new growth, from *recrue,* past participle of *recroître,* to grow again, from Latin *recrēscere* : *re-,* again + *crēscere,* to grow.] —**re·cruit·er** *n.* —**re·cruit·ment** *n.*

re-crys·tal·lise, re-crys·tal·lize (rée-kríst'l-īz) *v.* **-lised, -lising, -lises.** —*tr.* To dissolve (a substance) and then crystallise, especially so as to purify. —*intr.* **1.** To be recrystallised. **2.** To form new crystals or crystal structure. Used of a deformed metal. —**re-crys·tal·li·sa·tion** (-ī-záysh'n || *U.S.* -i-) *n.*

rec't receipt.

rect. **1.** receipt. **2.** rectangle; rectangular. **3.** rectified. **4.** rector; rectory.

rec·tal (rékt'l) *adj.* Pertaining to, near, or administered via the rectum. —**rec·tal·ly** *adv.*

rec·tan·gle (rék-tang-g'l) *n. Abbr.* **rect.** *Geometry.* A parallelogram with a right angle. [Medieval Latin *rēctangulum* : Latin *rēctus,* right + *angulus,* ANGLE.]

rec·tan·gu·lar (rek-táng-gew-lər) *adj. Abbr.* **rect.** **1.** Having the shape of a rectangle. **2.** Having right angles. Said of a geometric figure, such as a spherical triangle. **3.** Having or pertaining to lines or planes that are mutually perpendicular: *a rectangular coordinate system.* **4.** Having a base that is a rectangle. Said of geometric solids. —**rec·tan·gu·lar·i·ty** (-lárrəti) *n.* —**rec·tan·gu·lar·ly** *adv.*

rectangular coordinate *n. Geometry.* A coordinate in a **Cartesian coordinate system** *(see)* that has the coordinate axes at right angles.

rectangular hyperbola *n. Geometry.* A hyperbola for which the two asymptotes are at right angles. It has an equation of the form $xy = e$ in Cartesian coordinates.

rec·ti·fi·er (rékti-fī-ər) *n.* **1.** A person or thing that rectifies. **2.** *Electricity.* A device, such as a diode, that converts alternating current to direct current. **3.** A worker who blends or dilutes whisky or other alcoholic beverages. **4.** *Chemistry.* A condenser used to separate or purify.

rec·ti·fy (rékti-fī) *tr.v.* **-fied, -fying, -fies.** **1.** To set right; correct. **2.** To correct by calculation or adjustment. **3.** *Chemistry.* To refine or purify, especially by distillation. **4.** *Electricity.* To convert (alternating current) into direct current. **5.** To adjust (the proof of alcoholic spirit) by adding water or other liquids. —See Synonyms at **correct.** [Middle English *rectifien,* from Old French *rectifier,* from Medieval Latin *rēctificāre* : Latin *rēctus,* straight + *facere,* to make.] —**rec·ti·fi·a·ble** *adj.* —**rec·ti·fi·ca·tion** (-fi-káysh'n) *n.*

rec·ti·lin·e·ar (rékti-línni-ər) *adj.* Moving in, consisting of, bounded by, or characterised by a straight line or lines. [Late Latin *rēctilīneus* : *rēctus,* straight + *līnea,* LINE.] —**rec·ti·lin·e·ar·ly** *adv.*

rec·ti·tude (rékti-tewd || -to͞od) *n.* **1.** Moral uprightness. **2.** Rightness, as of intellectual judgment. **3.** Straightness. [Middle English, from Old French, from Late Latin *rēctitudō,* from Latin *rēctus,* straight.]

rec·to (réktō) *n., pl.* **-tos.** The right-hand page of a book or front side of a leaf, as opposed to the **verso** *(see).* [Latin *rēctō (foliō),* on the right side of (a page), ablative of *rēctus,* right, straight.]

rec·tor (réktər) *n. Abbr.* **R., rect.** **1. a.** In the Church of England, a clergyman who has charge of a parish and formerly owned the tithes from it. **b.** In other Episcopalian churches, a clergyman in charge of a parish. **2.** *Roman Catholic Church.* A priest appointed to be the administrative as well as spiritual head of a church or other institution such as a seminary or university. **3. a.** The principal of certain schools, colleges, and universities. **b.** In Scottish universities, a representative, often a prominent public figure, elected by the students to the governing body. [Latin *rēctor,* governor, from *rēctus,* past participle of *regere,* to rule.] —**rec·tor·ate** (-ət, -it) *n.* —**rec·to·ri·al** (rek-táwri-əl || -tōri-) *adj.*

rec·to·ry (réktri, réktəri) *n., pl.* **-ries.** *Abbr.* **rect.** **1.** The house in which a rector lives. **2.** A rector's office.

rec·trix (rék-triks) *n., pl.* **rectrices** (-tri-seez, *also* -trī-seez). Any of the stiff main feathers of a bird's tail. [Latin, feminine of *rēctor,* governor (the feathers help regulate flight). See **rector.**]

rec·tum (rék-təm) *n., pl.* **-tums** or **-ta** (-tə). The portion of the large intestine extending from the sigmoid flexure of the colon to the anal canal. Also called "back passage". [New Latin *rectum (intestinum),* straight (intestine), from Latin *rēctus,* straight.]

rec·tus (rék-təss) *n., pl.* **-ti** (-tī). Any of various straight muscles, as of the abdomen, eye, neck, and thigh. [New Latin, from Latin *rēctus,* straight.]

re·cum·bent (ri-kúmbənt, rə-) *adj.* **1.** Lying down; reclining. **2.** Resting; idle. **3.** *Biology.* Resting upon the surface from which it arises: *a recumbent organ.* **4.** *Geology.* Designating or pertaining to a fold in a rock formation in which the strata in the fold lie almost parallel to those in the rest of the formation. [Latin *recumbēns* (stem *recumbent-*), present participle of *recumbere,* to lie down : *re-,* back, again + *-cumbere,* to lie.] —**re·cum·bence, re·cum·ben·cy** *n.* —**re·cum·bent·ly** *adv.*

re·cu·per·ate (ri-kéwpə-rayt, rə-, -ko͞opə-) *v.* **-ated, -ating, -ates.** —*intr.* **1.** To return to health or strength; recover. **2.** To recover from financial loss. —*tr.* **1.** To restore to health or strength. **2.** To regain. [Latin *recuperāre* : RE- + *cup-,* from *capere,* to take.] —**re·cu·per·a·tion** (-ráysh'n) *n.* —**re·cu·per·a·tive** (-rətiv, -raytiv), **re·cu·per·a·to·ry** (-rətri, -rətəri, -ráytəri) *adj.*

re·cu·per·a·tor (ri-kéwpə-raytər, -rə-) *n.* A heat exchanger using the waste heat from the flue gases of a furnace to heat the incoming air.

re·cur (ri-kúr, rə-) *intr.v.* **-curred, -curring** (-kúr-ing, *rarely* -kúrring), **-curs.** **1.** To happen or come up again or repeatedly. **2.** To return to one's thoughts or attention: *a recurring nightmare.* **3.** To go back, as in thought, memory, or discourse. Used with *to.* **4.** *Mathematics.* To occur or be repeated an infinite number of times. Used of digits or groups of digits in a repeating decimal fraction. —See Synonyms at **return.** [Latin *recurrere,* to run back : *re-,* back + *currere,* to run.] —**re·cur·rence** (-kúrrənss) *n.*

re·cur·rent (ri-kúrrənt, rə-) *adj.* **1.** Occurring or appearing again or repeatedly; returning regularly. **2.** *Anatomy.* Running in a reverse direction. Said of arteries and nerves that turn back on themselves. —**re·cur·rent·ly** *adv.*

recurring decimal *n. Mathematics.* A **repeating decimal** *(see).*

recurrent fever *n.* **Relapsing fever** *(see).*

re·cur·sion (ri-kúrsh'n, rə- || -kúrzh'n) *adj. Mathematics & Logic.*

1. A repeated process or formula for generating or defining a series of terms, such as successive terms in a polynomial expression. Used adjectivally. 2. An expression generated in this way. [Late Latin *recursiō* (stem *recursiōn-*), a return, from Latin *recurrere* (past participle *recursus*), to RECUR.] —**re·cur·sive** (-kúr-siv) *adj.*

re·cur·vate (ri-kúrv-ət, -it, -ayt) *adj.* Bent or curved backwards. [Latin *recurvātus*, past participle of *recurvāre*, to RECURVE.]

re·curve (rée-kúrv) *v.* **-curved, -curving, -curves.** —*tr.* To bend or curve backwards or downwards. —*intr.* To become recurved. [Latin *recurvāre* : *re-*, back, backward + *curvāre*, to curve, from *curvus*, CURVE.] —**re·cur·va·tion** (rée-kur-váysh'n) *n.*

rec·u·sant (réckewz'nt, ri-kéwz'nt, rə-) *n.* 1. A Roman Catholic who refused to attend the services of the Church of England between the reigns of Henry VIII and George II. 2. A dissenter; a nonconformist. [Latin *recusāns* (stem *recusant-*), present participle of *recusāre*, to refuse : *re-*, contrary to, back + *causa*, CAUSE.] —**rec·u·san·cy** (réckewz'nssi, ri-kéwz'nssi, rə-) *n.* —**rec·u·sant** *adj.*

re·cuse (ri-kéwz, rə-) *tr.v.* **-cused, -cusing, -cuses.** To challenge or object to (a judge or juror) on such grounds as his prejudice or lack of qualification. [Latin *recusāre*, to refuse. See **recusant**.]

re·cy·cle (rée-sík'l) *tr.v.* **-cled, -cling, -cles.** 1. To put or pass through a cycle again, as for further treatment. 2. To start a different cycle in. 3. **a.** To make new use of or to process for re-use (used and discarded objects and material). **b.** To extract useful materials from (rubbish, waste, or the like). **c.** To extract and reuse (useful substances found in waste). —**re·cy·cla·ble** *adj.*

red¹ (red) *n.* 1. Any of a group of colours that may vary in lightness and saturation, whose hue resembles that of fresh blood; the hue of the long-wavelength end of the spectrum; one of the additive or light primaries; one of the psychological primary hues, evoked in the normal observer by the long-wavelength end of the spectrum. See **primary colour.** 2. A pigment or dye having or giving this hue. 3. Something that has this hue such as: **a.** Clothing or material: *She wore red.* **b.** A red ball used in some games, such as billiards, snooker, or croquet. **c.** One of the two colours on which bets may be placed in roulette and rouge-et-noir. **d.** A **red light** *(see).* 4. *Often capital* **R.** *Informal.* **a.** A Communist or radical revolutionary activist. **b.** A supporter or member of a Communist or left-wing socialist party. **c.** *Slang.* A citizen of a Communist country. *Often used derogatorily.* —**in the red.** Having a debit rather than a credit balance; in debt. —**see red.** To become suddenly furious.
~*adj.* **redder, reddest.** 1. Having a colour resembling that of blood. 2. Reddish in colour, or having parts that are reddish in colour. Used in animal and plant names: *red fox; red oak.* 3. **a.** Designating hair or an animal's coat having a colour ranging from orange and copper-coloured, to reddish brown. **b.** Having a coppery skin tone. 4. Having a ruddy or flushed complexion, as from exertion or embarrassment. 5. Bloodshot or red-rimmed. Said of eyes. 6. Coloured by the skins of the black grapes from which it is made. Said of wine. 7. Involving or concerned with bloodshed or violence. 8. *Often capital* **R.** **a.** Radical or revolutionary in nature: *red political theories.* **b.** Of, pertaining to, or caused by revolution or revolutionary: *red scare.* **c.** Communist or having a Communist government: *Red China.* 9. Designating one of the three quark colours. The other two are blue and green. [Middle English *red, read,* Old English *rēad.*] —**red·ly** *adv.* —**red·ness** *n.*

red². Variant of **redd.**

red. reduced; reduction.

re·dact (ri-dákt) *tr.v.* **-dacted, -dacting, -dacts.** 1. To draw up or draft (a proclamation or edict, for example). 2. To make ready for publication; edit or revise. [Latin *redigere* (past participle *redactus*), to collect, drive back : *re-*, back + *agere*, to drive, do.] —**re·dac·tor** (ri-dák-tər ‖ -tawr) *n.* —**re·dac·tion** (ri-dáksh'n) *n.*

red admiral *n.* A Eurasian butterfly, *Vanessa atalanta,* the wings of which are black with red and white markings.

red alert *n.* A state of readiness for an imminent danger, such as a natural disaster or enemy attack.

red algae *pl.n.* Algae of the division Rhodophyta, characteristically red or reddish in colour and including dulse and similar seaweeds.

re·dan (ri-dán) *n.* A fortification consisting of two walls that form a salient angle. [French, from earlier *redent,* a notching : RE- + *dent,* tooth.]

red·back spider (réd-bak) *n.* A poisonous long-legged Australian spider, *Latrodectus hasseltii,* the female of which has a round black abdomen with a red marking on the back.

red bark *n.* A form of cinchona that is reddish in colour and has a high alkaloid content.

red beds *pl.n.* *Geology.* Sequences of red sedimentary rocks, especially sandstones or shales, formed in a highly oxidising environment, the iron present being oxidised to red ferric oxide.

red biddy *n.* *Slang.* Cheap red wine with added methylated spirits.

red blood cell *n. Abbr.* **RBC.** An **erythrocyte** *(see).* Also called "red blood corpuscle".

red-blood·ed (réd-blúddid) *adj. Informal.* Strong, brave, or virile.

red·breast (réd-brest) *n.* Any of various birds with a red breast; especially the **robin** *(see).*

red·brick (réd-brík, -brik) *adj.* Of or designating a British university dating from the late 19th century, especially as distinguished from Oxford or Cambridge, and from those founded since World War II.

Red·bridge (réd-brij). Borough in northeastern London, England. It was created (1965) by the merger of the boroughs of Ilford, Wanstead, and Woodford, and parts of Dagenham and Chigwell.

Red Brigade *n.* A terrorist group formed in Italy in 1969 and com-

mitted to the abolition of capitalist society.

red·bud (réd-bud) *n.* Any of several American shrubs or small trees of the genus *Cercis.* See **Judas tree.**

red·cap (réd-kap) *n.* 1. *British Informal.* A member of the military police. 2. A European bird, the **goldfinch** *(see).*

red carpet *n.* 1. A carpet laid down for important visitors, as outside the door of a public building. 2. Deferential or ceremoniously hospitable treatment. Used chiefly in the phrase *roll out the red carpet.* Also used adjectivally: *red-carpet treatment.*

red cedar *n.* 1. A tall evergreen coniferous tree, *Thuya plicata,* of western North America. Also called "savin". 2. The reddish, aromatic, durable wood of this or of similar trees.

red cell *n.* An **erythrocyte** *(see).* Also called "red corpuscle".

Red China. An informal name for the People's Republic of **China.**

red clover *n.* A Eurasian plant, *Trifolium pratense,* widely naturalised and planted as a forage or cover crop. It has leaflets in groups of three and globular heads of fragrant, rose-purple flowers.

red·coat (réd-kōt) *n.* Formerly, a British soldier.

red coral *n.* Any of various corals of the genus *Corallium,* having pinkish-red skeletons used to make jewellery and ornaments.

Red Crescent *n.* 1. A branch of the Red Cross Society in a Muslim country. 2. The emblem of such a branch.

Red Cross *n.* 1. *Abbr.* **R.C.** An international organisation, formed according to the terms of the Geneva Convention of 1864, for the care of the wounded, sick, and homeless in wartime and now also during and following natural disasters. Also officially called "Red Cross Society". 2. Any national branch of this organisation. 3. The emblem of the organisation, a Geneva cross or red Greek cross on a white background.

red·cur·rant (réd-kúrrənt) *n.* 1. Any of several shrubs of the genus *Ribes* that are cultivated for their small, acid-tasting, red fruits. 2. The fruit of such a shrub, used to make jams and other preserves. Also used adjectivally: *redcurrant jelly.*

redd, red (red) *tr.v.* **redd** or **redded, redding, redds.** *Chiefly Scottish.* To put in order; arrange. Used with *up.* [Middle English *redden,* probably variant of *ridden,* to RID.]

red deer *n.* A common Eurasian deer, *Cervus elaphus,* having a reddish-brown coat and many-branched antlers.

red·den (rédd'n) *v.* **-dened, -dening, -dens.** —*tr.* To make red or redder. —*intr.* To become red; to become flushed or to blush.

red·dish (réddish) *adj.* Mixed or tinged with red; somewhat red. —**red·dish·ness** *n.*

reddle. Variant of **ruddle.**

red duster *n. British Informal.* The **Red Ensign** *(see).*

red dwarf *n. Astronomy.* Any of a small class of mostly main-sequence stars that are generally cool and small.

rede (reed) *tr.v.* **reded, reding, redes.** *Archaic.* 1. To give advice to; counsel. 2. To interpret; explain or tell.
~*n. Archaic.* 1. Advice or counsel. 2. An interpretation or narration. [Middle English *reden,* to guide, direct, Old English *rǣdan.*]

re·dec·o·rate (rée-déckə-rayt) *v.* **-rated, -rating, -rates.** —*tr.* To change the décor of, as by painting and renewing furnishings. —*intr.* To change the décor of a room, building, or the like. —**re·dec·o·ra·tion** (-ráysh'n) *n.*

re·deem (ri-déem, rə-) *tr.v.* **-deemed, -deeming, -deems.** 1. **a.** To recover ownership of by paying a stipulated sum. **b.** To recover (pawned goods or mortaged land, for example) by payment. 2. To pay off (a promissory note or loan, for example). 3. To turn in (coupons or trading stamps, for example) and receive something in exchange. 4. To fulfil (an oath, pledge, or promise). 5. **a.** To convert (tokens or shares, for example) into cash. **b.** To convert (banknotes) into specie. Used of a bank. 6. To rescue or set free by paying a ransom. 7. *Theology.* To save from a state of sinfulness and its consequences. 8. To make up for; amends for. 9. To put (oneself) back in favour. —See Synonyms at **save.** [Middle English *redemen,* from Latin *redimere,* to buy back : *red-, re-,* back, again + *emere,* to take, buy.]

re·deem·a·ble (ri-déeməb'l, rə-) *adj.* 1. Capable of being converted into cash. Said, for example, of tokens or shares. 2. Able to be repaid and thereby cancelled either at a fixed date or subject to notice. Said, for example, of bonds or debentures. 3. Capable of being saved or redeemed.

re·deem·er (ri-déemər, rə-) *n.* 1. One who redeems; a saviour. 2. *Capital* **R.** Jesus Christ, who, in Christian belief, redeemed mankind from sinfulness by his death on the Cross.

re·deem·ing (ri-déeming, rə-) *adj.* Making up for or compensating for other faults or inadequacies: *He has one redeeming feature.*

re·de·fine (rée-di-fín, -də-) *tr.v.* **-fined, -fining, -fines.** To define again, especially in a different way.

re·demp·tion (ri-démp-sh'n, rə-, -dém-) *n.* 1. The act or an instance of redeeming or the condition of being redeemed. 2. A recovery of something pawned or mortgaged; a repurchase. 3. **a.** The payment of an obligation, such as a government's payment of the value of its bonds. **b.** The conversion of banknotes into specie by a bank. 4. *Theology.* Salvation from sin through Christ's death on the Cross. 5. Release from a danger or evil. —**beyond** or **past redemption.** No longer able to be saved, made good, or restored. [Middle English *redempcioun,* from Old French *redemption,* from Latin *redemptiō* (stem *redemptiōn-*), from *redimere* (past participle *redemptus*), to REDEEM.] —**re·demp·tion·al, re·demp·tive, re·demp·to·ry** (-tri, -təri) *adj.*

re·demp·tion·er (ri-démpsh'n-ər, rə-) *n.* In Colonial America, an emigrant from Europe who paid for his voyage by serving as a bondservant for a stipulated period.

Re·demp·tor·ist (ri-démptərist) *n.* A member of a Roman Catholic order, the Congregation of the Most Holy Redeemer, founded by St. Alphonsus de Liguori in 1732 to do missionary work. [Latin *redemptor,* redeemer.]

Red Ensign *n.* A red flag with the Union Jack in the inner top corner; the ensign of the British Merchant Navy.

re·de·ploy (rée-di-plóy, -də-) *tr.v.* **-ployed, -ploying, -ploys.** 1. To move (military forces) from one combat zone to another. 2. To assign new tasks to (workers). **—re·de·ploy·ment** *n.*

re·de·sign (rée-di-zín, -də-) *tr.v.* **-signed, -signing, -signs.** To produce a new design for. **—re·de·sign** *n.*

re·de·vel·op (rée-di-vélləp, -də-) *v.* **-oped, -oping, -opes.** —*tr.* 1. To develop (something) again. 2. *Photography.* To tone or intensify (a developed negative) by a second developing process. 3. To rebuild (an area, for example) according to new plans. —*intr.* To develop again. **—re·de·vel·op·er** *n.* **—re·de·vel·op·ment** *n.*

redevelopment area *n.* An urban area that is replanned and almost completely rebuilt.

red-eye (réd-ī) *n.* 1. *U.S. Slang.* Whiskey of an inferior grade. 2. Any of several red-eyed fishes; especially, the **rudd** (see).

red-faced (réd-fáyst) *adj.* Having a flushed face owing to embarrassment, anger, intoxication, or the like. **—red-faced·ly** *adv.*

red·fin (réd-fin) *n.* Any of several small, freshwater fishes of the genus *Notropis,* such as *N. cornutus,* that have reddish fins and are often kept in aquariums.

red fir *n.* 1. An evergreen coniferous tree, *Abies magnifica,* of California and Oregon, having reddish wood valued as timber. 2. The wood of this tree, or of similar trees, such as the **Douglas fir** *(see).*

red fire *n.* Any of various combustible compounds, especially containing salts of lithium or strontium, that burn with a bright red flame and are used in flares and fireworks.

red·fish (réd-fish) *n., pl.* **-fishes** or collectively **redfish.** 1. A male salmon that has just spawned. Compare **blackfish.** 2. Any of several fishes that are reddish in colour; especially, a bright-red, European food fish, *Sebastes marinus* of North Atlantic waters.

red fox *n.* Any of several foxes of the genus *Vulpes,* having reddish fur; especially, *V. vulpes,* of the Northern Hemisphere.

Red·ford (réd-fərd), **Robert** (1937–). U.S. actor and film director. His reputation as one of the biggest box-office stars was established in films such as *Butch Cassidy and the Sundance Kid* (1969), *The Candidate* (1972), *The Way We Were* (1973), *The Sting* (1973), and *All the President's Men* (1976). For the first film he directed, *Ordinary People,* he won an Academy Award as best director (1981).

red giant *n. Astronomy.* Any of a class of stars that are usually cool, very large, and are believed to be formed in the final stages of the evolution of certain stars.

Red·grave (réd-grayv), **Sir Michael (Scudamore)** (1908–85). British actor. Beginning his stage career with the Liverpool Repertory Theatre in 1934, he went on to become one of the leading actors of his generation, especially in the plays of Shakespeare. His films include *The Lady Vanishes* (1938), the *Dam Busters* (1954), and *Goodbye Mr. Chips* (1969). His daughters Lynn Redgrave (1943–) and Vanessa Redgrave (1937–), and his son Corin Redgrave (1939–), are all experienced stage and screen actors.

Redgrave, Vanessa (1937–). British actress, daughter of Sir Michael. She won the *Evening Standard* award as best actress (1961) for her performances in *The Taming of the Shrew* and *As You Like It* with the Royal Shakespeare company. Her films include *Morgan, a Suitable Case for Treatment* (1966), *Isadora* (1969), *Julia* (1977), for which she won an Academy Award as best supporting actress, *Howard's End* (1992), and *Mrs. Dalloway* (1997).

red grouse *n.* A reddish-brown grouse, *Lagopus lagopus* occurring on the moorlands of Great Britain and Ireland. Formerly called "moorcock".

Red Guard *n.* A member of a militant Chinese youth organisation that denounced opposition to the **Cultural Revolution** *(see).*

red gum[1] *n.* 1. Any of several Australian trees of the genus *Eucalyptus,* especially, *E. camaldulensis.* 2. The hard, reddish wood of any of these trees.

red gum[2] *n.* A disease, **strophulus** *(see).*

red-hand·ed (réd-hándid) *adj.* In the act of committing, or having just committed, a crime; in flagrante delicto: *caught red-handed.* **—red-hand·ed** *adv.* **—red-hand·ed·ly** *adv.*

red hat *n.* 1. A large, red, tasselled hat presented to a newly created cardinal. It is never worn. 2. This hat as a symbol of a cardinal's office.

red·head (réd-hed) *n.* 1. A person with red hair. 2. A North American duck, *Aythya americana,* of which the male has black and grey plumage and a reddish head.

red heat *n.* 1. The temperature of a red-hot substance. 2. The physical condition of a red-hot substance.

red herring *n.* 1. Something that draws attention away from the matter or issue at hand. 2. A smoked herring having a reddish colour. [Sense 2 from the use of red herring to give the scent in exercising hunting dogs.]

red-hot (réd-hót) *adj.* 1. Heated so as to emit red light (a temperature of about 500°C). 2. Very hot. 3. Heated, as with excitement, anger, or enthusiasm. 4. New; very recent: *red-hot information.*

red-hot poker *n.* Any of several plants of the African genus *Kniphofia,* cultivated as garden plants for their cylindrical heads of red or yellow flowers.

re·di·a (réedi-ə) *n., pl.* **-diae** (-ee). A larva of parasitic flukes that gives rise to other rediae or to cercaria larvae. [New Latin, after Francesco *Redi* (1629–97), Italian naturalist.]

Re·dif·fu·sion (rée-di-féwzh'n) *n.* A trademark for a system of cable television *(see).*

Red Indian *n.* A North American Indian.

red·in·gote (rédding-gōt) *n.* 1. A man's long double-breasted overcoat with a full skirt. 2. A woman's full-length unlined coat or dress open down the front to show a dress or underskirt. [French, from English *riding coat.*]

red·in·te·grate (red-ínti-grayt, rid-) *v.* **-grated, -grating, -grates.** —*tr.* To restore to a complete, whole, or harmonious state. —*intr. Psychology.* To undergo redintegration. [Middle English, from Latin *redintegrāre* : *red-,* RE- + *integrāre,* to INTEGRATE.]

red·in·te·gra·tion (red-ínti-gráysh'n, rid-) *n.* 1. *Psychology.* The revival of a complete previous mental state due to recurrence of part of the complex of stimuli that gave rise to that previous mental state. 2. The act or process or redintegrating.

re·dis·trib·ute (rée-diss-tríbbewt || -distri-bewt) *tr.v.* **-uted, -uting, -utes.** To distribute again in a different way; reallocate. **—re·dis·tri·bu·tion** (rée-distri-béwsh'n) *n.* **—re·dis·trib·u·tive** (rée-diss-tríb-bewtiv || -distri-bewtiv) *adj.*

red lead *n.* A bright-red powder, Pb_3O_4, used in paints, glass, pottery, and pipe-joint packing. Also called "minium".

red-let·ter (réd-léttər) *adj.* Memorable: *a red-letter day.* [From the rubrication of feasts in church calendars.]

red light *n.* 1. A red traffic light or other signal to stop. Also called "red". 2. A danger signal.

red-light district (réd-lít) *n.* A district containing many brothels.

red man *n. Informal.* A North American Indian. Often considered offensive.

red meat *n.* Dark-coloured meat, such as beef or lamb. Compare **white meat.**

Red·mond (réd-mənd), **John Edward** (1856–1918). Irish politician. Succeeding Parnell as the leader of the Parliamentary Home Rule movement, he achieved many of the movement's objectives. His support for Britain during World War I and the rise of Sinn Fein undermined his influence.

red mullet *n. British.* Any marine fish of the family Mullidae, several species of which are used as food. Also *U.S.* "goatfish".

red·neck (réd-nek) *n. Informal.* 1. Any of the white rural labouring class in the southern United States. 2. *Chiefly U.S.* A manual worker having bigoted views. Used derogatorily. [Referring to the sunburnt necks of labourers.]

re·do (rée-dōō) *tr.v.* **-did** (-díd), **-done** (-dún), **-doing, -does** (-dúz). 1. To do again. 2. To redecorate thoroughly; refurbish.

red ochre *n.* 1. A natural red mixture of clay and iron oxide; an **ochre** *(see).* 2. A refined form of this mixture used as pigment.

red·o·lent (réddələnt) *adj.* 1. Having or emitting fragrance; pleasantly odorous. 2. Smelling. Used with *of: boatyards redolent of tar.* 3. Evocative or reminiscent. Used with *of* or *with: music redolent of Mozart.* [Middle English, from Old French, from Latin *redolēns* (stem *redolent-*), present participle of *redolēre,* to emit an odour : *red-, re-,* in response, back + *olēre,* to smell.] **—red·o·lence, red·o·len·cy** *n.* **—red·o·lent·ly** *adv.*

Re·don (rə-dón), **Odilon** (1840–1916). French painter, lithographer, and etcher, regarded by the surrealists as one of their forerunners. He first gained notice by his eerie, dreamlike lithographs, and was especially famous for his paintings of flowers.

re·dou·ble (rée-dúbb'l, ri-) *v.* **-bled, -bling, -bles.** —*tr.* 1. To increase or intensify greatly: *redouble one's efforts.* 2. To double. 3. *Archaic.* To echo or re-echo. 4. To double (a double) in bridge. —*intr.* 1. To increase or intensify greatly: *Our efforts redoubled.* 2. To be doubled; become twice as much or as great. 3. *Archaic.* To echo; reverberate. 4. To double a double in bridge.

re·doubt (ri-dówt, rə-) *n.* 1. A small, often temporary defensive fortification, usually standing alone. 2. Any defensive stronghold. 3. Any place of refuge. [French *redoute,* from obsolete Italian *ridotta,* from Medieval Latin *reductus,* concealed place, from Latin, withdrawn, from the past participle of *redúcere,* withdraw : *re-,* back + *dúcere,* to lead.]

re·doubt·a·ble (ri-dówtəb'l, rə-) *adj.* 1. a. Awesome; fearsome. b. Formidable. 2. Worthy of respect or honour. [Middle English, from Old French *redoutable,* from *redouter,* to dread : *re-* (intensive) + *douter,* to fear, DOUBT.] **—re·doubt·a·bly** *adv.*

re·dound (ri-dównd, rə- || *West Indies also* -dúngd) *intr.v.* **-dounded, -dounding, -dounds.** 1. To have an effect or consequence. 2. To return, rebound, or recoil. Used with *on* on *upon.* 3. *Archaic.* To contribute; accrue. [Middle English *redounen,* to abound, from Old French *redonder,* from Latin *redundāre,* to overflow : *red-, re-* (intensive) + *undāre,* to overflow, surge, from *unda,* wave.]

re·dox (rée-doks) *n. Chemistry.* **Oxidation-reduction** *(see).* Also used adjectively: *a redox reaction.* [*Red*uction of *ox*idation.]

red pepper *n.* 1. **pimiento** *(see).* 2. **Cayenne pepper** *(see).*

red pine *n.* A New Zealand coniferous tree, *Dacrydium cupressinum.* Also called "rimu".

Red Planet *n. Informal.* The planet **Mars** *(see).* Preceded by *the.*

red-poll (réd-pōl, -pol) *n.* Any of several finches of the genus *Acanthis;* especially *A. flammea,* having brownish plumage and a red crown.

Red Poll *n.* Also **Red Polled.** Any of a breed of reddish, hornless cattle developed in England and raised for dairy and meat products.

re·draft (rée-draáft || -dráft) *tr.v.* **-drafted, -drafting, -drafts.** To make a new or revised version of (a written document, for example). ~*n.* **1.** A second draft; a revision. **2.** A second bill of exchange on a drawee for the amount of a dishonoured bill plus costs.

re·dress (ri-dréss, rə-) *tr.v.* **-dressed, -dressing, -dresses. 1.** To set right; remedy or rectify. **2.** To make amends for. **3.** To adjust (a balance, for example) so as to produce a condition of equality. —See Synonyms at **correct.**
~*n.* (ri-dréss, rə- || rée-dress). **1.** Satisfaction or amends for wrong done; compensation. **2. a.** Correction or setting right. **b.** A means of rectification: *We had no redress.* —See Synonyms at **reparation.** [Middle English *redressen,* from Old French *redresser* : *re-,* back + *dresser,* to make straight, DRESS.] **—re·dress·able, re·dress·i·ble** *adj.* **—re·dress·al** *n.* **—re·dress·er, re·dres·sor** *n.*

red salmon *n.* The **sockeye salmon** *(see).*

Red Sea. Sea running northwest from the Gulf of Aden to the Sinai Peninsula in Egypt, where it branches into the Gulf of Aqaba to the east and the Gulf of Suez to the west. It has been joined to the Mediterranean Sea by the Suez Canal since 1869 and is one of the world's major shipping routes, connecting Europe with the Far East and Australia. It is coloured red at certain times of the year owing to the reddish algae that appear in it.

red setter *n.* An **Irish setter** *(see).*

red·shank (réd-shangk) *n.* **1.** An Old World wading bird, *Tringa totanus,* having long red legs. **2.** A plant, **persicaria** *(see).*

red shift, red·shift (réd-shíft, -shift) *n.* **1.** An increase apparent in the wavelength of radiation emitted by a receding celestial body as a consequence of the **Doppler effect** *(see)* as seen by a stationary observer. Compare **blue shift. 2.** A similar increase in wavelength resulting from the presence of a high gravitational field. In this sense, also called "Einstein shift", "gravitational red shift".

red·shift (réd-shíft) *v.* **-shifted, -shifting, -shifts.** —*tr.* To cause (radiation or spectral lines) to change to a longer wavelength. —*intr.* To move or change to a longer wavelength.

red-short (réd-shórt) *adj.* Brittle when red-hot. Said of iron or steel. **—red-short·ness** *n.*

red·skin (réd-skin) *n. Informal.* A North American Indian. Usually considered offensive.

red snapper *n.* Any of several tropical and semitropical marine food fishes of the genus *Lutjanus,* having red or reddish bodies.

red spider *n.* Also **red spider mite.** See **spider mite.**

Red Spot *n. Astronomy.* A very large, reddish, variable oval patch (about 1 400 kilometres by up to 48 000 kilometres) occurring south of the equator in the atmosphere of the planet Jupiter. Also called "Great Red Spot".

red squirrel *n.* **1.** A Eurasian squirrel, *Sciurus vulgaris* having reddish or tawny fur. **2.** Any of several reddish North American squirrels. See **chickadee.**

red·start (réd-staart) *n.* **1.** Any bird of the Eurasian genus *Phoenicurus;* especially, *P. phoenicurus,* of Europe, which has a greyish plumage with a black throat and a red tail. **2.** A North American bird, *Setophaga ruticilla,* the male of which is black with orange markings on wings and tail. [RED + obsolete *start,* tail, from Middle English *stert,* Old English *steort.*]

red tape *n.* Official requirements and procedures, such as the filling in of forms, considered as an obstructive bureaucratic device. [From the tape used to tie English governmental documents.]

red tide *n.* Ocean waters coloured by the proliferation of red, one-celled, plantlike animals occurring in sufficient numbers to kill fish.

re·duce (ri-déwss, rə- || -dóoss) *v.* **-duced, -ducing, -duces.** —*tr.* **1. a.** To lessen in extent, amount, number, degree, price, or other quality; diminish. **b.** To degrade or lower in rank, position, social circumstances, or the like. **2.** To gain control of, especially by conquest. **3.** To put in order or arrange systematically. **4.** To separate into components by analysis. **5.** To bring to a specified state or condition, as by simplification or transformation: *reduced him to tears.* **6.** To powder or pulverise. **7.** To cause (meat juices, for example) to thicken by evaporating excess water. **8.** *Chemistry.* **a.** To remove oxygen from (a compound), as in the smelting of metal ores. **b.** To add hydrogen to (a compound), as in hydrogenation reactions. **c.** To add electrons to (a compound, ion, or group), as in the change of ferric ions (Fe^{3+}) to ferrous ions (Fe^{2+}). **9.** *Mathematics.* To simplify the form of (an expression) without changing the value. **10.** To remove some of the silver from (an emulsion) forming a photographic image. **11.** To restore (a fracture or dislocation, or a fractured or displaced body part) to normal. —*intr.* **1. a.** To become diminished. **b.** To lose weight, as by dieting. **2.** To amount to or be viewable as something specified. Used with *to*: *the problem reduces to a question of time and money.* **3.** To thicken, especially by evaporation. Used of sauces and other liquids. **4.** *Chemistry.* To undergo reduction; lose oxygen or gain hydrogen or electrons. Used of chemical compounds. —See Synonyms at **decrease.** [Middle English *reducen,* to bring back, from Latin *redūcere* : *re-,* back, again + *dūcere,* to lead.] **—re·duc·i·bil·i·ty** (-ə-bílləti) *n.* **—re·duc·i·ble** *adj.* **—re·duc·i·bly** *adv.*

re·duced (ri-déwst, rə- || -dóost) *adj.* **1.** Less in extent, amount, number, degree, price, or other quality: *at a reduced rate.* **2.** Less prosperous than formerly: *in reduced circumstances.*

re·duc·er (ri-déwssər, rə- || -dóossər) *n.* **1.** One that reduces. **2.** A chemical solution for reducing the density of photographic negatives or prints. **3.** A threaded cylinder for connecting pipes of different diameter.

re·duc·ing agent (ri-déwssing || -dóossing) *n.* A substance that chemically reduces other substances.

re·duc·tase (ri-dúkt-ayz, rə-, -ayss) *n.* Any enzyme that catalyses biochemical reduction reactions. [REDUCT(ION) + -ASE.]

re·duc·ti·o ad ab·sur·dum (ri-dúk-ti-ō ad əb-súrdəm, -shi-, ab-) *n.* **1.** Disproof of a proposition by showing the absurdity of its inevitable conclusion. **2.** Proof of a proposition by disproving its negation by means of reductio ad absurdum. **3.** The following through of a principle or idea to absurdity. [Latin, "reduction to absurdity"].

re·duc·tion (ri-dúksh'n, rə-) *n. Abbr.* **red. 1. a.** The act or process of reducing. **b.** The process or state of being reduced. **2. a.** The result of reducing. **b.** A reprographic copy of a picture, text, or the like, that is smaller than the original. **3.** The amount by which anything is lessened or diminished. **4.** The process of reducing or a chemical reaction in which something is reduced. Compare **oxidation. 5. a.** The cancelling of common factors in the numerator and denominator of a fraction. **b.** The converting of a fraction to its decimal equivalent. [Middle English *reduccion,* from Old French *reduction,* from Late Latin *reductiō* (stem *reductiōn-*), from Latin, from *redūcere,* to REDUCE.] **—re·duc·tion·al, re·duc·tive** *adj.*

reduction division *n. Biology.* **1.** The first meiotic division, in which the chromosome number is halved. **2. Meiosis** *(see).*

re·duc·tion·ism (ri-dúksh'n-iz'm, rə-) *n.* **1.** The systematic reduction of complicated information or objects to simple components. **2.** The theory or belief that a complex system can be understood completely on the basis of its simple constituents. **—re·duc·tion·ist** *n. & adj.*

re·dun·dan·cy (ri-dún-dən-si) *n., pl.* **-cies.** Also **re·dun·dance** (-dənss). **1.** The state, condition, or quality of being redundant, especially: **a.** Superfluity or excess. **b.** Unnecessary repetition. **c.** *Chiefly British.* The losing of a position that has been eliminated within an organisation; dismissal from a position that then ceases to exist: *the threat of redundancy.* **2.** *Chiefly British.* **a.** An instance of the loss of a position which has been eliminated: *They made 13 redundancies.* **b.** Loosely, compensation for being made redundant; redundancy payment. **3.** Duplication or repetition of elements in electronic or mechanical equipment to provide alternative functional channels in case of failure. **4.** Repetition of parts or all of a message to circumvent transmission errors.

re·dun·dant (ri-dúndənt) *adj.* **1.** Exceeding what is necessary or natural; superfluous. **2.** Needlessly repetitive; verbose. **3.** Copious or profuse. **4.** *Chiefly British.* Unemployed or about to be unemployed because of the elimination of one's job. [Latin *redundāns* (stem *redundant-*), present participle of *redundāre,* to overflow, run back : *red-, re-,* back + *undāre,* to overflow, from *unda,* wave.] **—re·dun·dant·ly** *adv.*

re·du·pli·cate (ri-déwpli-kayt, rə- || -dóopli-) *v.* **-cated, -cating, -cates.** —*tr.* **1.** To repeat or redouble. **2.** *Linguistics.* **a.** To double (the initial syllable or all of a root word) to produce an inflectional or derivational form. **b.** To form (a new word) by doubling all or part of a word. —*intr.* To be doubled.
~*adj.* (-ət, -it). **1.** Doubled. **2.** *Botany.* Having outward-curved margins: *reduplicate petals.* [Late Latin *reduplicāre* : Latin *re-,* again + *duplicāre,* to DUPLICATE.]

re·du·pli·ca·tion (ri-déwpli-káysh'n, rə- || -dóopli-) *n.* **1.** Reduplicating or the state of being reduplicated; duplication; redoubling. **2.** A product or result of reduplicating. **3.** A word formed by or containing a reduplicated element. **4.** The added element in a word form that is reduplicated. **—re·du·pli·ca·tive** (-kətiv, -kaytiv) *adj.* **—re·du·pli·ca·tive·ly** *adv.*

re·du·vi·id (ri-déwvi-id, rə- || -dóovi-) *n.* Any bloodsucking insect of the family Reduviidae. [New Latin *Reduviidae,* from Latin *reduvia, redivia,* hangnail, exuviae : *red-,* RE- + *-uvia,* from *-uere,* to put on.] **—re·du·vi·id** *adj.*

red·wa·ter (réd-wawtər || *U.S. also* -wottər) *n.* A disease of cattle caused by infestation with the protozoan *Babesia bovis* and characterised by the passage of red urine due to the destruction of red blood cells.

red whortleberry *n.* A shrub, the **cowberry** *(see).*

red·wing (réd-wing) *n.* A European thrush, *Turdus illacus,* having reddish feathers under the wings and a white eyestripe.

red·wood (réd-wood) *n.* **1.** A very tall evergreen coniferous tree, *Sequoia sempervirens,* of coastal and northern California. Compare **giant sequoia. 2.** The soft, reddish wood of this tree. **3.** Any of various woods of reddish colour or yielding red dye.

reebok. Variant of **rhebok.**

re·ech·o, re·echo (ree-éckō, ri-) *v.* **-oed, -oing, -oes.** —*intr.* **1.** To be repeated again and again by or as if by an echo. **2.** To resound or reverberate with or as if with repeated echoes. —*tr.* To echo back repeatedly.

reed (reed) *n.* **1. a.** Any of various tall aquatic grasses having jointed, hollow stalks; especially, any of the genus *Phragmites,* such as *P. communis.* **b.** The stalk of any of these plants. **c.** A mass of reeds. **d.** Reeds collectively, especially for use as thatching material. **2.** A primitive wind instrument made of such a hollow stalk. **3.** *Music.* **a.** A flexible strip of cane or metal set into the mouthpiece of certain musical instruments to produce tone by vibrating in response to a stream of air. **b.** An instrument, such as an oboe or clarinet, fitted with a reed. **4.** A narrow, movable frame on a loom, fitted with reed or metal strips that separate the warp threads. **5.** *Architecture.* A reeding. **6.** An ancient Hebrew unit of length, equivalent to six cubits.

~*tr.v.* **reeded, reeding, reeds.** **1.** To thatch with reed. **2.** *Architecture.* To decorate with reeding. [Middle English *rede, reod,* Old English *hrēod.*]

Reed (reed), **Sir Carol** (1906–76). British film director, one of the most acclaimed of the post-World War II era. His most notable films since the war were *The Third Man* (1949), *Our Man in Havana* (1959), *The Agony and the Ecstasy* (1965), and *Oliver!* (1968), the last of which won him an Academy Award.

Reed, John (1887–1920). U.S. journalist and Communist leader. As a reporter in World War I he was in Petrograd during the October Revolution (1917), and recorded the experience in his famous book, *Ten Days That Shook the World* (1919), the best eye-witness account of the Bolshevik seizure of power. Expelled from the U.S. Socialist Convention in 1919, he organised the left-wing splinter group of the movement into the Communist Labor party. In 1919 he returned to the U.S.S.R., where he worked in the department of propaganda. He died of typhus and was buried in the Kremlin.

reed·buck (réed-buk) *n.* Any of several African antelopes of the genus *Redunca,* having incurved horns. Also called "nagor". [Translation of Afrikaans *rietbok.*]

reed bunting *n.* A common European bunting, *Emberiza schoeniclus,* that frequents reed beds and has a brownish plumage. The head of the male is black in summer. Also called "reed sparrow".

reed grass *n.* A perennial Eurasian grass, *Glyceria maxima,* having tall erect stems and growing in rivers and ponds.

reed·ing (réeding) *n.* **1.** *Architecture.* A convex decorative moulding having parallel strips resembling thin reeds. **2.** The indentations on the edge of a coin; milling.

reed·ling (réedling) *n.* A bird, the **bearded reedling** *(see).*

reed mace *n.* Any of various reedlike marsh plants of the genus *Typha;* especially, *T. latifolia,* having dense, cylindrical heads of small brown flowers. Also called "bulrush", "cat's tail".

reed organ *n.* Any of various keyboard instruments in which vibrating reeds produce notes when acted upon by currents of air.

reed pipe *n.* An organ pipe with a reed that vibrates and produces a note when air is forced through it. Compare **flue pipe.**

reed stop *n.* A stop on an organ made up of reed pipes. Compare **flue stop.**

re-ed·u·cate (rée-éddew-kayt, ree-) *tr.v.* **-cated, -cating, -cates.** **1.** To educate again or anew; especially, to indoctrinate (criminals and political dissidents, for example) for purposes of rehabilitation. **2.** To retrain to function effectively, especially in a new working capacity. **—re-ed·u·ca·tion** (-káysh'n) *n.*

reed warbler *n.* An Old World warbler of the genus *Acrocephalus;* especially, *A. scirpaceus,* which frequents reed beds and has red-dish-brown plumage.

reed·y (réedi) *adj.* **-ier, -iest.** **1.** Full of reeds. **2.** Made of reeds. **3.** Resembling a reed especially in being slender or fragile. **4.** Having or designating a tone like that of a reed instrument; shrill or high-pitched. **—reed·i·ness** *n.*

reef¹ (reef) *n.* **1.** *Geology.* A strip or ridge of rocks, sand, or soil that rises to or near the surface of a body of water. **2.** A **coral reef** *(see).* **3.** In mining, a vein of ore. **4.** In Africa, the Precambrian gold-bearing conglomerates. —See Usage note at **shoal.** [Earlier *riff,* from Middle Dutch *rif,* ridge, perhaps from Old Norse, rib, ridge.] **—reef·y** *adj.*

reef² *n. Nautical.* A portion of a sail rolled and tied down to lessen the area exposed to the wind.

~*v.* **reefed, reefing, reefs.** *—tr.* **1.** To reduce the size of (a sail) by tucking in a part and tying it to or rolling it around a yard. **2.** To shorten (a topmast or bowsprit) by taking part in. *—intr.* To reduce the size of a sail by taking in reefs. [Middle English *riff,* from Old Norse *rif,* ridge, rib.]

Reef, the. See **Witwatersrand.**

reef·er¹ (réefər) *n.* **1.** One who reefs, such as a midshipman. **2.** A short, heavy, close-fitting, double-breasted jacket. In this sense also called "reefing jacket".

reefer² *n. Slang.* A marijuana cigarette. Not in current usage. [Perhaps from REEF (to roll up and shorten a sail).]

reef knot *n.* A common knot composed of two overhand knots with ends lying parallel. Also called "flat knot", *U.S.* "square knot".

reek (reek) *v.* **reeked, reeking, reeks.** *—intr.* **1. a.** To give off or become permeated with a strong and unpleasant odour. **b.** *Regional.* To give off smoke, steam, or fumes. **2.** To be pervaded by something, especially of an unpleasant nature: *The whole business reeks of corruption.* *—tr.* **1.** To emit or exude (smoke or odours, for example). **2.** To process or treat by exposing to the action of smoke.

~*n.* **1.** A strong and offensive odour; a stench. **2.** *Regional.* Vapour; smoke; steam. [Middle English *reken,* Old English *rēocan,* from Germanic.] **—reek·er** *n.* **—reek·y** *adj.*

reel¹ (reel) *n.* **1.** A cylinder, spool, or frame that turns on an axis and is used for winding rope, tape, or other flexible materials. **2.** Such a device attached to a fishing rod to let out or wind up the line. **3.** *British.* A small spool with wide ends round which sewing thread is wound. **4. a.** The wire, film, or other material wound on a reel. **b.** The quantity of such material wound on one reel.

~*tr.v.* **reeled, reeling, reels.** **1.** To wind upon a reel. **2.** To wind or draw on a reel. Used with *in, out,* or *up*: *reel in a fish.* **3.** To recite rapidly and effortlessly. Used with *off.* [Middle English *reel,* Old English *hrēol*†.] **—reel·a·ble** *adj.*

reel² *v.* **reeled, reeling, reels.** *—intr.* **1.** To be thrown off balance or fall back: *He reeled under the blow.* **2.** To stagger, lurch, or sway, as from drunkenness. **3.** To go round and round in a whirling motion. **4.** To feel dizzy. *—tr.* To cause to reel.

~*n.* A staggering, swaying, or whirling movement. [Middle English *relen,* probably from REEL (spool).] **—reel·er** *n.*

reel³ *n.* **1.** Any of various fast dances in 4/4 time, of Scottish origin. **2.** The music for a reel. [From REEL (whirl).]

reel-to-reel (réel-tə-réel, -tōō-) *adj.* Of, using, or designating magnetic tape that is wound onto one typically exposed reel from another: *reel-to-reel tape recorder.* Compare **cassette.**

re-en·act, re·enact (rée-i-nákt, -e-) *tr.v.* **-acted, -acting, -acts.** **1.** To act out again (an earlier incident, for example). **2.** To enact (a law, for example) again or anew. **—re-en·act·ment** *n.*

re-en·trant, re·en·trant (ree-éntrənt, ri-) *adj.* Pointing inwards.

~*n.* **1.** A re-entrant angle or part. **2.** A marked indentation into a landform.

re-entrant angle *n.* An interior angle of a polygon greater than 180°.

re-en·try, re·en·try (ree-éntri) *n., pl.* **-tries.** **1.** The act of entering again or anew; a second or subsequent entry. **2.** *Law.* The recovery of possession of premises by the lessor under a right reserved in the lease or contract. **3.** In bridge and whist: **a.** The act of regaining the lead by taking a trick. **b.** The card that will take a trick and thus regain the lead. **4.** *Aerospace.* The return of a missile or spacecraft into the earth's atmosphere.

reest (reest) *intr.v.* **reested, reesting, reests.** *Chiefly Scottish.* To stop suddenly and refuse to budge; baulk. Used of a horse. [Probably variant of Scottish *arreest,* to ARREST.] **—reest·y** *adj.*

reeve¹ (reev) *n.* **1.** A high officer of local administration appointed by the Anglo-Saxon kings. **2.** In the later medieval period, a bailiff or steward of a manor. **3.** Any of various minor local officers. **4.** The elected president of a local council in some parts of Canada. [Middle English *reve, reeve,* Old English *(ge)rēfa,* from *rōf* (unattested), assembly.]

reeve² *tr.v.* **rove** (rōv) or **reeved, reeving, reeves.** *Nautical.* **1.** To pass (a rope or rod) through a hole, ring, pulley, or block. **2.** To fasten (a block, for example) by such a procedure. [Probably from Dutch *rēven,* to REEF (sail).]

reeve³ *n.* A bird, the female **ruff** *(see).* [17th century.]

Reeves (reevz), **William Pember** (1857–1932). New Zealand politician. He entered the New Zealand parliament as a Liberal in 1887 and as Minister of Labour (1891–96) was chiefly responsible for introducing the most progressive welfare and labour legislation then known in the world. He resigned his seat in 1896 to write a history of New Zealand, *The Long White Cloud* (1898), and other books. From 1905 to 1908 he was high commissioner to London and from 1908 to 1919 director of the London School of Economics.

re-ex·am·ine, re·ex·am·ine (rée-ig-zámmin, -eg-, -ik-) *tr.v.* **-ined, -ining, -ines.** **1.** To examine again or anew; review. **2.** *Law.* To question (one's own witness) again after cross-examination. Used of a lawyer. **—re-ex·am·i·na·tion** (-áysh'n) *n.*

re-ex·port, re·ex·port (rée-ek-spórt, -ik-, *also* -ékspawrt ‖ -spōrt) *tr.v.* **-ported, -porting, -ports.** To export (imported goods), often after processing.

~*n.* (rée-ék-spawrt ‖ -spōrt). **1.** The act of re-exporting. **2.** Something re-exported. **—re-ex·por·ta·tion** (-spawr-táysh'n ‖ -spōr-) *n.*

ref (ref) *n. Informal.* A referee at a sports event.

ref. **1.** referee. **2.** reference; referred. **3.** refining. **4.** reformation; reformed. **5.** refunding.

re·face (rée-fáyss) *tr.v.* **-faced, -facing, -faces.** **1.** To renew or repair the surface of (a building, for example). **2.** To give a new facing to (a garment, for example).

re·fect (ri-fékt, rə-) *tr.v.* **-fected, -fecting, -fects.** *Archaic.* To supply with food and drink. [Latin *reficere* (past participle *refectus*), to refresh : *re-,* again + *facere,* to make.]

re·fec·tion (ri-féksh'n, rə-) *n. Archaic.* **1.** Refreshment with food and drink. **2.** A light meal or repast. [Middle English *refeccioun,* from Old French *refection,* from Latin *refectiō* (stem *refectiōn-*), a restoring, from *reficere,* to refresh. See **refect.**]

re·fec·to·ry (ri-féktəri, rə-; *also, chiefly in monasteries,* réffik-tri, réffi-, -təri) *n., pl.* **-ries.** A room where meals are served, as in an institution such as a monastery or college. [Late Latin *refectōrium,* from Latin *reficere,* to REFECT.]

re·fer (ri-fér, rə-) *v.* **-ferred, -ferring, -fers.** *—tr.* **1.** To direct to a source for help or information: *refer a patient to a specialist.* **2.** *Formal.* To assign or attribute (an effect, for example) to some cause; ascribe responsibility for: *referred the cure to prayer.* **3.** To assign to or regard as belonging to a specified category, place, or time: *referred sharks to the fishes; referred dinosaurs to prehistoric times.* **4.** To submit (a matter in dispute) to an authority for arbitration, decision, or examination. **5.** To direct a person's attention to: *referred the article to me.* **6.** *British.* To fail (a student, for example) in an examination. **7.** To return (a text, for example) to its originator for improvement. **8.** To cause or experience. In most senses, with *to,* or sometimes *back to.* *—intr.* **1.** To pertain; concern; apply: *a provision referring only to officers.* **2.** To allude or direct notice or attention; make reference. **3.** To have recourse, as for information or authority. Used with *to* in all senses. [Middle English *refer(r)en,* from Old French *referer,* from Latin *referre,* refer to, carry back : *re-,* back again + *ferre,* to carry.] **—ref·er·a·ble** (réffrəb'l), **re·fer·ra·ble** (ri-fér-əb'l, rə-) *adj.* **—re·fer·ral** (ri-fér-əl) *n.* **—re·fer·rer** *n.*

Usage: In the general sense of "directing to a source", formal usage avoids the use of *refer back,* unless the implication is that a second act of reference is involved *(I referred him back to the passage he had mentioned earlier). Let me refer you to a good book on the subject* is the standard form, *back* being unnecessary.

ref·e·ree (réffə-rée) *n. Abbr.* **ref. 1.** One to whom something is referred, as for settlement or decision; an arbitrator. **2.** *Sports.* An official supervising and judging play, as in boxing and football. **3. a.** One willing to testify to the ability or character of an applicant, especially for employment. **b.** One who carefully reads a new scientific or scholarly work to decide whether it should be published. **4.** *Law.* A judicial official to whom certain cases are referred for adjudication, especially in civil cases in which both parties agree to this procedure or in which complex documents must be analysed. See **Official Referee.** —See Synonyms at **judge.**
~*v.* **refereed, -reeing, -rees.** —*tr.* To judge or supervise as referee. —*intr.* To act as referee.

ref·er·ence (réffrənss, réffərənss) *n. Abbr.* **ref. 1.** The act of referring or the state of being referred. **2.** That to which something refers. **3.** Relation, connection, or correspondence: *with reference to your complaint.* **4. a.** A direction or attention: *many references to learned journals.* **b.** An allusion, as to a person, event, or situation. **5. a.** A note in a publication referring the reader to another passage or source. **b.** The passage or source so referred to. **c.** A mark directing the reader to a footnote or other information. Also called "reference mark". **6.** *Law.* The submission of a case to a referee. **7. a.** A statement by one person attesting to another's ability, experience, character, or creditworthiness. **b.** Someone willing to provide such a testimonial. **8. a.** A source of information and facts: *works of reference.* Also used adjectivally: *a reference library.* **b.** The act of searching for information: *for quick reference.* **9.** An object or activity taken as a norm; a standard: *using the dollar as a reference.* Also called "point of reference". —*tr.v.* **referenced, -encing, -ences. 1.** To furnish (a text or publication, for example) with references. **2.** To refer to or quote as a reference. **—ref·er·enc·er** *n.* **—ref·er·en·tial** (réffə-rénsh'l) *adj.*

reference book *n.* **1.** A book, such as a dictionary or an encyclopedia, that is consulted for specific points of information, rather than read continuously. **2.** In South Africa formerly, an identity document, recording domicile and employment record and other personal information, that all black adults were required to carry in white areas. In this sense, also called "pass", "passbook".

reference group *n. Sociology.* A group of people whose standards and behaviour affect and are admired by a person not necessarily in the group. Compare **membership group, peer group.**

ref·er·en·dum (réffə-réndəm) *n., pl.* **-dums** or **-da** (-də). **1. a.** The submission of a proposed public measure or actual statute to a direct popular vote. **b.** Such a vote. Compare **plebiscite. 2.** The submission of any matter concerning a group to the direct vote of its members. **3.** A note from a diplomat to his government requesting instructions. [Latin, neuter gerundive of *referre,* to REFER.]

ref·er·ent (réffrənt, réffərənt) *n.* **1.** One that is referred to; specifically, the object, event, or idea that a word, phrase, or sign represents. **2.** One that refers. **3.** *Logic.* The first term in a proposition, from which the relation proceeds; for example, in the sentence *Dogs like bones, dogs* is the referent. [Latin *referēns* (stem *referent-*), present participle of *referre,* REFER.] **—ref·er·ent** *adj.*

re·ferred pain (ri-férd, rə-) *n.* Pain felt in a part of the body other than the site of the disease or injury.

ref·fo, re·fo (réffō) *n., pl.* **-fos.** *Australian Slang.* A refugee, usually from Europe.

re·fill (rée-fíl) *v.* **-filled, -filling, -fills.** —*tr.* To fill again. —*intr.* To become full again.
~*n.* (rée-fil, *rarely* -fíl). **1.** A product, such as an ink cartridge, intended to replace the used contents of a container. **2. a.** A second or subsequent filling. **b.** *British Informal.* A further measure of a drink, especially an alcoholic drink, poured into a person's glass or cup when it is empty.

re·fine (ri-fīn, rə-) *v.* **-fined, -fining, -fines.** —*tr.* **1.** To remove unwanted substances from; purify. **2.** To separate (crude oil, for example) into distinct substances. **3.** To remove by purifying. Used with *out* or *away.* **4.** To free from coarse characteristics; make more elegant, polished, or subtle. **5.** To improve, as by making more precise: *refine a theory.* —*intr.* **1.** To become free of impurities. **2.** To acquire polish or elegance. **3.** To use subtlety and precise distinctions in thought or speech. **4.** To make improvements, as by making something clearer or more precise. Used with *on* or *upon.* [RE- + FINE (verb).] **—re·fin·a·ble** *adj.* **—re·fin·er** *n.*

re·fined (ri-fīnd, rə-) *adj.* **1.** Free from coarseness or vulgarity; polite; genteel. **2.** Free of impurities; purified. **3.** Precise to a fine degree; subtle; exact.

re·fine·ment (ri-fīn-mənt, rə-) *n.* **1. a.** An act or process of refining. **b.** The state or quality of being refined. **2.** The result of refining; an improvement or elaboration. **3.** Fineness of thought, manners, or expression; polish; cultivation. **4.** A precise phrasing; a subtlety or subtle distinction. —See Synonyms at **culture.**

re·fin·er·y (ri-fīnəri, rə-) *n., pl.* **-ies.** An industrial plant for purifying a crude substance, such as petroleum, sugar, fat, or ore.

re·fit (rée-fít) *v.* **-fitted, -fitting, -fits.** —*tr.* To prepare and equip for further or additional use; especially, to modernise and re-equip (a ship, for example). —*intr.* To be made ready for further use.
~*n.* (rée-fit, -fít). **1.** An act or process of refitting, especially of a ship. **2.** A secondary or subsequent preparation of supplies and equipment. **—re·fit·ment** *n.*

refl. 1. reflection; reflective. **2.** reflex; reflexive.

re·flate (rée-fláyt) *v.* **-flated, -flating, -flates.** —*tr. Economics.* To cause reflation in (a country's economy, for example). —*intr. Economics.* To cause reflation. Used of a government authority. Compare **deflate.**

re·fla·tion (rée-fláysh'n) *n. Economics.* An increase of the money in circulation, effected by a government in order to increase consumer demand and thereby to stimulate the economy. **—re·fla·tion·a·ry** (-ri, -əri || -erri) *adj.*

re·flect (ri-flékt, rə-) *v.* **-flected, -flecting, -flects.** —*tr.* **1.** To throw or bend back (heat, light, or sound, for example) from a surface. **2.** To form an image of; mirror. **3.** To manifest or express: *His work reflects intelligence.* **4.** *Mathematics.* To transform by reversing the sign of one coordinate. **5.** To consider, think, or realise: *He reflected that all was well.* **6.** To throw or bring (credit or discredit, for example) onto someone or something. **7.** *Archaic.* To bend back. —*intr.* **1.** To be thrown or bent back. Used especially of heat, light, or sound. **2. a.** To give back a likeness: *This surface reflects.* **b.** To become mirrored: *The statue reflected in the water.* **3.** To think, meditate, or consider seriously. Often used with *on* or *upon.* **4. a.** To bring blame or reproach. Used with *on* or *upon.* **b.** To cause the character of a person or thing to appear in a specified light. Used with *on* or *upon*: *The argument reflects badly on you.* [Middle English *reflecten,* from Old French *reflecter,* from Latin *reflectere,* to bend back : *re-,* back + *flectere,* to FLEX.]

re·flec·tance (ri-fléktənss, rə-) *n.* The ratio of the total radiant flux (as of light) reflected by a surface to the total falling on the surface. Compare **absorptance, transmittance.**

reflecting telescope *n.* An optical telescope in which the principal image-forming element is a parabolic or spherical mirror. Also called "reflector". Compare **refracting telescope.**

re·flec·tion (ri-fléksh'n, rə-) *n.* Also *chiefly British* **re·flex·ion.** *Abbr.* **refl. 1.** The act of reflecting or state of being reflected. **2.** Something reflected, such as light, radiant heat, sound, or an image. **3. a.** Concentration of the mind; careful consideration. **b.** A result of such consideration, communicated or not; a thought. **4. a.** An imputation of censure or discredit; reproach. Used chiefly in the phrase *cast reflections on* or *upon.* **b.** An expression, often discreditable, of the character of a person or thing. Used with *on* or *upon*: *a reflection on your honesty.* **5. a.** The act or an instance of bending back. **b.** *Anatomy.* A structure or part bent back upon itself. **6.** *Mathematics.* **a.** A transformation in which the sign of one coordinate is reversed. **b.** A symmetry relationship involving such a transformation. **—re·flec·tion·al** *adj.* **—re·flec·tion·less** *adj.*

reflection nebula *n.* See **nebula.**

re·flec·tive (ri-fléktiv, rə-) *adj. Abbr.* **refl. 1. a.** Of, pertaining to, produced by, or resulting from reflection. **b.** Capable of or producing reflection. **2.** Meditative; pensive. —See Synonyms at **pensive. —re·flec·tive·ly** *adv.* **—re·flec·tive·ness** *n.*

re·flec·tiv·i·ty (rée-flek-tívvəti) *n., pl.* **-ties. 1.** The quality of being reflective. **2.** The ability to reflect. **3.** *Physics.* The ratio of the intensity of the total radiation, as of light, reflected from a surface to the total falling on the surface.

re·flec·tor (ri-fléktər, rə-) *n.* **1.** That which reflects. **2.** A surface that reflects radiation. **3.** A small red reflective disc or strip, usually attached to the rear of a vehicle to increase its visibility. **4.** A reflecting telescope. **5.** *Physics.* A layer of material placed around the core of a nuclear reactor to reflect neutrons back into the core.

re·flet (rə-fláy) *n.* A lustrous or iridescent effect, as on pottery. [French, from Italian *riflesso,* reflection.]

re·flex (rée-fleks) *adj. Abbr.* **refl. 1.** *Physiology.* Of or designating an action or response performed without conscious control, such as a sneeze, blink, or hiccup. **2.** Broadly, of or designating any action or response performed unintentionally, automatically, or without deliberation: *a reflex response to danger.* **3.** Reflected or directed back upon the source: *reflex thoughts; reflex effort.* **4.** Designating light that is reflected. **5.** Turned, thrown, or bent backwards.
~*n. Abbr.* **refl. 1.** *Physiology.* A response to a stimulus performed without conscious control. **2.** *Psychology.* An automatic, instinctive, or mechanical response to a situation or other stimulus. **3.** *Plural.* The ability to respond to outside influences, usually considered in terms of speed: *For karate you need fast reflexes.* **4.** Reflection or an image produced by reflection. **5.** See **reflex camera. 6.** A linguistic form when viewed as descended from a usually specified earlier form; for example, *mother* and *fire* are reflexes of the Indo-European *māter* and *pūr* respectively.
~*tr.v.* (ri-fléks, rə-) **reflexed, -flexing, -flexes. 1.** To bend, turn back, or reflect. **2.** To cause to undergo a reflex process. [Latin *reflexus,* past participle of *reflectere,* to REFLECT.]

reflex angle *n.* An angle greater than 180° and less than 360°.

reflex arc *n.* The neural path of a physiological reflex, the simplest form of which consists of a sensory neurone and a motor neurone linked in the brain or spinal cord by a synapse.

reflex camera *n.* A camera fitted with a mirror to reflect the exact focused image onto a coupled viewing screen.

re·flex·ive (ri-fléksiv, rə-) *adj.* **1.** *Abbr.* **refl.** *Grammar.* Pertaining to, involved in, or expressing an action or relationship affecting the agent, subject, or source of the action; for example, in *She dressed herself,* the verb *dressed* and the pronoun *herself* are reflexive. **2.** *Logic.* Designating such a relationship. **3.** Designating or pertaining to a relation that is independent of the order of the terms. For example, equality is reflexive, for if $a = b$ then $b = a$. **4.** Of or pertaining to a reflex.
~*n.* A reflexive verb or pronoun. **—re·flex·ive·ly** *adv.* **—re·flex·**

ive·ness, re·flex·iv·i·ty (rée-flek-sívvəti) *n.*
re·flex·ol·o·gy (rée-flek-sólləji) *n.* **1.** The study of reflexes. **2.** The practice of foot massage to treat ailments in all parts of the body.
ref·lu·ent (réffloo-ənt) *adj. Rare.* Flowing back; ebbing. [Latin *refluēns* (stem *refluent-*), present participle of *refluere,* flow back : *re-,* back + *fluere,* flow.] **—ref·lu·ence** *n.*
re·flux (rée-fluks) *n.* **1.** The process or an act of flowing back; ebb. **2.** The pathological flow of liquid against its normal direction of movement, such as the flow of stomach contents into the oesophagus. **3.** *Chemistry.* The process of refluxing. Also used adjectivally: *reflux extraction.*
~tr.v. **refluxed, -fluxing, -fluxes.** *Chemistry.* To boil (a liquid) in a vessel attached to a condenser so that the liquid continuously condenses and runs back into the vessel. This process is used for extracting substances or carrying out reactions. [Middle English : RE- + FLUX.]
refo. Variant of **reffo.**
reforest. Variant of **reaforrest.**
re·form (rée-fórm) *v.* **-formed, -forming, -forms.** *—tr.* To form again. *—intr.* To become formed again.
re·form (ri-fórm, rə-) *v.* **-formed, -forming, -forms.** *—tr.* **1.** To improve, as by alteration, correction of error, or abolition of abuses and malpractices. **2.** To abolish (abuses or malpractices). **3.** To cause (a person) to abandon irresponsible or immoral practices. **4.** *Chemistry.* To change the structure of (hydrocarbons in petroleum) by heat and pressure, usually using catalysts, so as to produce hydrocarbons suitable for petrol. *—intr.* To abandon irresponsible or immoral practices. —See Synonyms at **correct.**
~n. **1.** The correction of abuses or evils. **2.** A change for the better; an improvement.
~adj. Pertaining to or favouring reform. [Middle English *reformen,* from Old French *reformer,* from Latin *refōrmāre* : *re-,* again, back + *fōrmāre,* to form, from *fōrma,* FORM.] **—re·form·a·ble** *adj.* **—re·form·a·bil·i·ty** (-ə-bílləti) *n.* **—re·form·a·tive** *adj.* **—re·form·er** *n.*
ref·or·ma·tion (réffər-máysh'n, *rarely* réffawr-) *n. Abbr.* **ref. 1.** The act of reforming or the state of being reformed. **2.** *Capital* **R.** The 16th-century movement that aimed at reforming Western Christianity, resulting in the separation of the Protestant churches from the Roman Catholic Church. **—ref·or·ma·tion·al** *adj.*
re·for·ma·to·ry (ri-fórmə-tri, -tər-i) *adj.* Serving or tending to reform.
~n., pl. **reformatories.** In many countries but no longer in Britain, a penal institution for the discipline, reformation, and training of juvenile and first offenders. Also called "reform school". [REFORMAT(ION) + -ORY.]
re·formed (ri-fórmd, rə-) *adj. Abbr.* **ref. 1.** Improved in conduct or character. **2.** *Capital* **R.** Of, pertaining to, or denoting the Protestant churches that follow the teachings of Calvin and Zwingli. **3.** *Capital* **R.** Of, pertaining to, or designating Reform Judaism.
re·form·ism (ri-fórm-iz'm, rə-) *n.* The advocacy of social or economic reform, especially in contrast to revolution. **—re·form·ist** *n.*
Reform Judaism *n.* A branch of Judaism introduced in the 19th century that endeavours to reconcile historical Judaism with modern life without requiring strict observance of traditional law. Compare **Conservative Judaism, Orthodox Judaism.**
re·fract (ri-frákt, rə-) *tr.v.* **-fracted, -fracting, -fracts. 1.** To deflect (light, for example) by refraction. **2.** To measure the refractive power of (a lens, for example). [Latin *refringere* (past participle *refractus*), to break off : *re-,* away, backwards + *frangere,* to break.]
refract·ing telescope (ri-frákting) *n.* A telescope in which the final image is produced entirely by lenses. Also called "refractor". Compare **reflecting telescope.**
re·frac·tion (ri-fráksh'n, rə-) *n. Abbr.* **refr. 1.** *Physics.* The deflection of a propagating wave, as of light or sound, at the boundary between two mediums, or in a passage through a medium of nonuniform density, occurring when the speed of the wave is different in the different mediums or regions. **2.** *Astronomy.* The apparent positional elevation of celestial objects caused by deflection of light entering the Earth's atmosphere. **3. a.** The capacity of the eye to refract light. **b.** The measurement of the angle through which an eye refracts light. **—re·frac·tion·al** *adj.*
re·frac·tive (ri-fráktiv, rə-) *adj.* **1.** Of or pertaining to refraction. **2.** Causing refraction. Said especially of such materials as diamond, with a high refractive index. **—re·frac·tive·ly** *adj.* **—re·frac·tive·ness, re·frac·tiv·i·ty** (rée-frak-tívvəti) *n.*
refractive index *n. Physics.* The ratio of the speed of light in a vacuum to the speed of light in the medium under consideration. Also called "index of refract".
re·frac·tom·e·ter (rée-frak-tómmitər) *n.* Any of several optical instruments that measure indices of refraction. **—re·frac·to·met·ric** (ri-fráktə-méttrik, rə-) *adj.* **—re·frac·tom·e·try** (-tómmətri) *n.*
re·frac·tor (ri-fráktər, rə-) *n.* **1.** One that refracts. **2.** A refracting telescope.
re·frac·to·ry (ri-fráktəri, rə-) *adj.* **1.** Obstinate; unmanageable. **2.** Difficult to melt or work; resistant to heat. **3.** Not responsive to treatment. **4.** *Physiology.* Designating the period following transmission of a nerve impulse during which a neurone will not respond to further stimulation. —See Synonyms at **unruly.**
~n., pl. **refractories. 1.** Any of various materials such as alumina, silica, and magnesite that do not significantly deform or change chemically at high temperatures. **2.** *Plural.* Bricks of such materials and of various shapes used to line furnaces. [Earlier *refractary,* from Latin *refractārius,* from *refringere* (past participle *refractus*), to break off, REFRACT.] **—re·frac·to·ri·ly** *adv.* **—re·frac·to·ri·ness** *n.*
re·frain[1] (ri-fráyn, rə-) *v.* **-frained, -fraining, -frains.** *—intr.* To hold oneself back; abstain. Used with *from.* *—tr. Archaic.* To restrain or hold back; curb. [Middle English *refreynen,* from Old French *refrener,* from Latin *refrēnāre,* hold back, bridle : *re-,* back + *frēnum,* bridle.] **—re·frain·er** *n.* **—re·frain·ment** *n.*
refrain[2] *n.* **1. a.** A phrase or verse repeated at intervals throughout a song or poem, especially at the end of each stanza. **b.** Music for the refrain of a poem. **2.** Loosely, a tune. **3.** A repetitious utterance or theme. [Middle English *refreyn,* from Old French *refrain,* from *refraindre,* to echo, break off (a refrain "breaks off" to recur at intervals), from Vulgar Latin *refrangere* (unattested), from Latin *refringere,* to break off, REFRACT.]
re·fran·gi·ble (ri-fránj-ib'l, rə-) *adj.* Capable of being refracted. [New Latin *refrangibilis,* from *refrangere,* variant of Latin *refringere,* to REFRACT.] **—re·fran·gi·bil·i·ty** (-ibílləti), **re·fran·gi·ble·ness** *n.*
re·fresh (ri-frésh, rə-) *v.* **-freshed, -freshing, -freshes.** *—tr.* **1.** To revive (a person) with or as if with rest, food, or drink. **2.** To make cool, clean, or damp; freshen. **3.** To restore by some treatment: *refresh the paintwork.* **4.** To renew by stimulation: *refresh one's memory.* *—intr.* **1.** To take refreshment. **2.** To become revived; reinvigorate. [Middle English *refresshen,* from Old French *refreschir, refreschier* : *re-,* again + *freis, fresche,* FRESH.]
re·fresh·er (ri-fréshər, rə-) *n.* **1.** One that refreshes. **2.** *British.* An extra payment made to a barrister during a prolonged legal case.
~adj. Serving to reacquaint one with material previously studied: *a refresher course.*
re·fresh·ing (ri-fréshing, rə-) *adj.* **1.** Serving to refresh. **2.** Pleasantly new and different; unusual. **—re·fresh·ing·ly** *adv.*
re·fresh·ment (ri-fréshmənt, rə-) *n.* **1.** The act of refreshing or state of being refreshed; reinvigoration; revival. **2.** Something that refreshes, such as food or drink. **3.** *Plural.* A light meal or snack and drinks.
re·frig·er·ant (ri-fríjərənt, rə-) *adj.* **1.** Cooling or freezing; refrigerating. **2.** *Medicine.* Reducing fever.
~n. **1.** A substance, such as air, ammonia, water, or carbon dioxide, used to produce refrigeration, either as the working substance of a refrigerator or by direct absorption of heat. **2.** *Medicine.* Any agent used to produce cooling or reduce fever.
re·frig·er·ate (ri-fríjə-rayt, rə-) *tr.v.* **-ated, -ating, -ates. 1.** To cool or chill (a substance). **2.** To preserve (food) by chilling. [Latin *refrigerāre* : *re-,* repeatedly, again + *frigerāre,* to make cool, from *frigus* (stem *frigor-*), cool.] **—re·frig·er·a·tion** (-ráysh'n) *n.* **—re·frig·er·a·tive** (-rətiv ‖ -raytiv) *adj. & n.* **—re·frig·er·a·to·ry** (-rə-təri, -tri, -raytəri) *adj.*
re·frig·er·a·tor (ri-fríjə-raytər, rə-) *n.* An apparatus for reducing and maintaining the temperature of a chamber below the temperature of the external environment; for example, a household appliance for keeping food and drink. Also informally called "fridge".
re·frin·gent (ri-frínjənt, rə-) *adj.* Of, pertaining to, or producing refraction; refractive. [Latin *refringēns* (stem *refringent-*), present participle of *refringere,* to REFRACT.]
reft. Alternative past tense and past participle of **reave.**
re·fu·el (rée-féw-əl, -féwl) *v.* **-elled** or *U.S.* **-eled, -elling** or *U.S.* **-eling, -els.** *—tr.* To supply again with fuel. *—intr.* To take on a fresh supply of fuel.
ref·uge (réffewj) *n.* **1.** Protection or shelter, as from danger or hardship. **2.** A place providing protection or shelter; a haven or sanctuary; specifically, a place providing shelter for victims of domestic violence. **3.** Anything to which one may turn for help, relief, or escape: *Silence was his only refuge.* **4.** *British.* A **traffic island** *(see).* —See Synonyms at **shelter.**
~v. **refuged, -uging, -uges.** *Archaic.* *—tr.* To give refuge to. *—intr.* To take refuge. [Middle English, from Old French, from Latin *refugium,* from *refugere,* flee back : *re-,* away, back + *fugere,* to flee.]
ref·u·gee (réffew-jée) *n.* A person who flees to find refuge; especially, one who escapes from invasion, oppression, or persecution, often to another country. [French *réfugié,* from the past participle of *réfugier,* to put in a refuge, from *refuge,* REFUGE.]
re·ful·gent (ri-fúljənt, rə-) *adj.* Shining radiantly; brilliant; resplendent. [Latin *refulgēns* (stem *refulgent-*), present participle of *refulgēre,* to flash back : *re-,* back + *fulgēre,* to flash.] **—re·ful·gence, re·ful·gen·cy** *n.* **—re·ful·gent·ly** *adv.*
re·fund[1] (ri-fúnd, rə-, rée-) *v.* **-funded, -funding, -funds.** *—tr.* **1.** To return or repay; give back. **2.** To repay (a person); reimburse. *—intr.* To make repayment.
~n. (rée-fund). **1.** A repayment of funds. **2.** The amount repaid. [Middle English *refunden,* to pour back, from Old French *refunder,* from Latin *refundere* : *re-,* back + *fundere,* to pour.] **—re·fund·er** (-fúndər) *n.* **—re·fund·ment** *n.*
re·fund[2] (rée-fúnd) *tr.v.* **-funded, -funding, -funds. 1.** To fund anew. **2.** *Finance.* To pay back (a debt) with new borrowing; especially, to replace (a bond issue) with a new bond issue.
re·fur·bish (rée-fúrbish, ri-, rə-) *tr.v.* **-bished, -bishing, -bishes.** To make clean or fresh again; renovate. **—re·fur·bish·ment** *n.*
re·fus·al (ri-féwz'l, rə-) *n.* **1.** The act of refusing. **2.** The opportunity to accept or reject; option: *He gave me first refusal.*
re·fuse[1] (ri-féwz, rə-) *v.* **-fused, -fusing, -fuses.** *—tr.* **1.** To make known or declare that one is unwilling to, or will not, do, accept, give, or allow. **2.** To be unwilling and fail to jump (an obstacle).

Used of a horse. —*intr.* To decline to do, accept, allow, or give something. [Middle English *refusen,* from Old French *refuser,* from Vulgar Latin *refūsāre* (unattested), from Latin *refundere* (past participle *refūsus*), to pour back. See **refund.**] —**re·fus·er** *n.*

Synonyms: *refuse, decline, reject, spurn, rebuff, ignore.*

ref·use² (réffewss) *n.* Anything discarded or rejected as useless or worthless; rubbish; waste matter.

~*adj.* Discarded or rejected as useless or worthless. [Middle English, something rejected, from Old French *refus,* refusal, from *refuser,* to REFUSE.]

re·fuse·nik (ri-féwznik, rə-) *n.* Formerly, a Soviet citizen whose application for a visa to emigrate was refused. [REFUSE + -NIK.]

ref·u·ta·tion (réffew-táysh'n) *n.* Also **re·fu·tal** (ri-féwt'l, rə-). **1.** The act of refuting. **2.** Something that refutes.

re·fute (ri-féwt, rə-) *tr.v.* **-futed, -futing, -futes. 1.** To prove (a statement or argument) to be false or erroneous; disprove. **2.** To prove (a person) to be wrong. [Latin *refutāre,* rebut, drive back.] —**ref·ut·a·bil·i·ty** (réff-ewtə-bílləti, ri-féwtə-) *n.* —**ref·ut·a·ble** *adj.* —**ref·ut·a·bly** *adv.* —**re·fut·er** *n.*

Usage: There is a widespread misuse of *refute* with the meaning "to deny"; it attracts criticism as it lacks the strong sense of "proof" that is inherent in the word.

reg (reg) *n.* A flat, stony desert, especially in the Sahara, where sheets of gravel and pebbles cover the surface. [Arabic.]

reg. 1. regent. **2.** regiment. **3.** region. **4.** register; registered. **5.** registrar. **6.** registry. **7.** regular; regularly. **8.** regulation. **9.** regulator.

Reg. 1. Regent. **2.** Regina.

re·gain (ri-gáyn, rée-) *tr.v.* **-gained, -gaining, -gains. 1.** To recover possession of; get back again. **2.** To manage to reach again. —See Synonyms at **recover.** —**re·gain·er** *n.*

re·gal¹ (réeg'l) *adj.* **1.** Pertaining to a king or queen; royal. **2.** Belonging to or befitting a king or queen: *regal attire.* **3.** Dignified; stately. [Middle English, from Old French, from Latin *rēgālis,* royal, from *rēx* (stem *rēg-*), king.] —**re·gal·ly** *adv.*

regal² *n.* A small, portable reed organ often used in dramatic works in the 16th and 17th centuries. [French *régale,* perhaps feminine of *régal,* REGAL.]

re·gale (ri-gáyl, rə-) *v.* **-galed, -galing, -gales.** —*tr.* **1.** To delight or entertain; give pleasure to: *regaled us with folk songs.* **2.** To entertain sumptuously with food and drink; provide a feast for. —*intr.* To feast. —See Synonyms at **amuse.**

~*n. Obsolete.* **1.** A great feast; a sumptuous repast. **2.** A choice food or drink; a delicacy. **3.** Refreshment. [French *régaler,* from Old French *regaler,* from *regal,* REGAL.] —**re·gale·ment** *n.*

re·ga·li·a (ri-gáyli-ə, rə-) *pl.n. Often used with a singular verb.* **1.** The emblems and symbols of royalty, such as the crown and sceptre. **2.** The distinguishing symbols of any rank, office, order, or society. **3.** Magnificent attire; finery. [Medieval Latin *rēgālia,* plural of *rēgāle,* royal prerogative, from Latin, neuter of *rēgālis,* REGAL.]

re·gal·i·ty (ri-gál-əti, ree-) *n., pl.* **-ties. 1.** Royalty or sovereignty; kingship or queenship. **2.** A country or area under a monarch; a kingdom. **3.** The rights or privileges of a king or queen.

re·gard (ri-gárd, rə-) *v.* **-garded, -garding, -gards.** —*tr.* **1.** To look upon or consider in a specified way: *I regard him as a fool.* **2.** To look at attentively; observe closely. **3.** To have great affection or admiration for: *She regards her father highly.* **4.** To relate to, concern, or refer to: *This item regards your question.* **5.** To consider or take account of. **6.** *Obsolete.* To take care of. —*intr.* **1.** To look; gaze. **2.** To give heed; pay attention. —**as regards.** Relating to; concerning. —See Synonyms at **consider.**

~*n.* **1.** Careful thought or attention; concern; heed: *He gives little regard to his appearance.* **2.** Respect, affection, or esteem: *He has won the regard of all.* **3.** A look or gaze. **4.** *Plural.* Sentiments of respect or affection; good wishes: *send one's regards.* **5.** Reference or relation: *with regard to this case.* **6.** A particular point or respect: *I agree in this regard.* **7.** *Obsolete.* Appearance or aspect. [Middle English *regarden,* from Old French *regarder, reguarder,* to look at, regard : *re-,* back, back at + *guarder, garder,* to GUARD.]

Synonyms: *regard, esteem, admiration, approbation.*

Usage: *Regard* occurs in a range of constructions, some of which require an additional *-s* in standard English. Thus one has: *to have regard to* ("to take into account"), *to have regard for* ("to show consideration for"), *with regard to* ("concerning"), and *without regard to* ("without taking into account"), alongside *as regards* ("concerning"), *give one's regards to* ("greet"), and *kind regards* (as a letter ending). In informal English, there is a tendency to use the *-s* form more widely, as in *with regards to,* but this attracts criticism. The use of *regarding* and *respecting* as prepositions *(Regarding your visit . . .)* is also sometimes criticised. When the sense of "a particular" is required, formal usage prefers *respects* to *regards*: *In some respects, she is a good choice.* As a verb with the sense of "consider", *regard* is normally used with *as (I regard it as a good thing).*

re·gar·dant (ri-gárd'nt, rə-) *adj. Heraldry.* With the face turned backwards in profile: *a lion regardant.* [Middle English, from Old French, from *regarder,* to REGARD.]

re·gard·ful (ri-gárdf'l, rə-) *adj.* **1.** Showing regard; observant; heedful. Often used with *of.* **2.** Showing deference; respectful; considerate. —**re·gard·ful·ly** *adv.* —**re·gard·ful·ness** *n.*

re·gard·ing (ri-gárding, rə-) *prep.* In reference to; with respect to; concerning. See Usage note at **regard.**

re·gard·less (ri-gárd-ləss, rə-, -liss) *adj.* Heedless; unmindful. Often used with *of.*

~*adv.* In spite of everything; anyway. —**re·gard·less·ly** *adv.* —**re·gard·less·ness** *n.*

re·gat·ta (ri-gáttə, rə- || -gáatə) *n.* A boat race or series of boat races. [Italian (Venetian dialect) *regatta, regata*†, gondola race.]

regd. registered.

re·ge·late (réeji-layt) *intr.v.* **-lated, -lating, -lates.** To undergo regelation. [RE- + Latin *gelāre,* to freeze.]

re·ge·la·tion (réeji-láysh'n) *n.* **1.** Successive melting and freezing of ice when pressure is applied and relaxed at the interface of two blocks of ice. **2.** The fusion of two blocks of ice by regelation.

re·gen·cy (réejən-si) *n., pl.* **-cies. 1.** The office, area of jurisdiction, or government of a regent or regents. **2.** A person or group selected to govern in place of a king or other ruler in the case of minority, absence, incompetence, or sickness. **3.** The period during which a regent governs, especially: **a.** *Capital* **R.** In British history, the period 1811–20 during which George, Prince of Wales (later George IV) was regent for his father George III. **b.** *Capital* **R.** In French history, the period 1715–23 during which Philippe, Duke of Orléans, was regent for the young Louis XV.

~*adj. Usually capital* **R.** Of, pertaining to, or characteristic of the style, especially in furniture, prevalent during the Regency periods in Britain and France.

re·gen·er·a·cy (ri-jénnərə-si, rə-, rée-) *n.* The state of being regenerated.

re·gen·er·ate (ri-jénnə-rayt, rə-, -rée) *v.* **-ated, -ating, -ates.** —*tr.* **1.** To reform or revitalise spiritually or morally. **2.** To form, construct, or create anew. **3.** *Biology.* To replace (a lost or damaged organ or part) by formation of new tissue. **4.** *Electronics.* To amplify (a signal in a radio receiver, for example) by positive feedback. —*intr.* **1.** To become formed or constructed again. **2.** To undergo spiritual conversion or rebirth. **3.** To effect regeneration.

~*adj.* (ri-jénnə-rət, -rit, rə-). **1.** Spiritually or morally revitalised. **2.** Restored; refreshed; renewed. [Latin *regenerāre,* to reproduce : *re-,* again + *generāre,* to beget, GENERATE.] —**re·gen·er·a·ble** *adj.* —**re·gen·er·a·tive** (-rətiv || -raytiv) *adj.* —**re·gen·er·a·tive·ly** *adv.*

re·gen·er·a·tion (ri-jénnə-ráysh'n, rə-, rée-) *n.* **1.** The act or process of regenerating or the state of being regenerated. **2.** Spiritual or moral revival or rebirth. **3.** *Biology.* The regrowth of lost or destroyed parts or organs.

re·gen·er·a·tor (ri-jénnə-raytər, rə-, rée-) *n.* One that regenerates.

Re·gens·burg (*German* ráygənss-boork). Formerly **Rat·is·bon** (rát-tiz-bon). Town in the state of Bavaria, Germany. It is a commercial, industrial, and transport centre. Dating from Roman times, it was the permanent seat of the Imperial Diet (1663–1806), and passed to Bavaria in 1810.

re·gent (réejənt) *n. Abbr.* **reg., regt., Regt. 1.** One who rules during the minority, absence, or disability of a sovereign. **2.** *Archaic.* One acting as a ruler or governor. **3.** In the United States, a person serving on a board that governs a university or other educational institution or system. [Middle English, from Old French, ruling, from Medieval Latin *regēns* (stem *regent-*), from Latin, present participle of *regere,* to rule.] —**re·gent** *adj.*

regent bird *n.* An Australian bowerbird, *Sericulus chrysocephalus.*

reg·gae (réggay, réggi) *n.* A type of popular music originating in the West Indies with an insistent rhythm heavily accentuating the third beat of the bar. [20th century : of West Indian origin.]

Reg·gio di Calabria (réj-ō). Also **Reggio** or **Reggio Calabrio.** Seaport and industrial centre in Calabria, southwest Italy. Originally a Greek colony, it was taken by the Romans in 270 B.C.

Reggio nell'E·mi·lia (nel e-méel-yə). Also **Reggio** or **Reggio Emilia.** Capital city of the province of Reggio nell'Emilia in north Italy on the river Crostolo. It lies on the ancient Via Emilia and is a commercial centre for the surrounding rich agricultural area.

reg·i·cide (réji-sīd) *n.* **1.** The killing of a king. **2.** One who kills or helps to kill a king. [Latin *rēx* (stem *rēg-*), king + -CIDE.] —**reg·i·ci·dal** (-sīd'l) *adj.*

re·gime, ré·gime (ray-zhéem, re-, ri-) *n.* **1. a.** A system of management or government. **b.** A government holding power, especially a totalitarian one. **2.** A social system or pattern. **3.** A regimen. **4.** The pattern of seasonal fluctuation in a climate or in the volume of a river. **5.** *Informal.* The accepted way of doing or running things: *the new office regime.* [French *régime,* from Latin *regimen,* from *regere,* to rule.]

reg·i·men (réji-mən, -men) *n.* **1.** A system of therapy: *a dietetic regimen.* **2.** A set of rules or prescribed procedure for regulating life or achieving some end. [Middle English, from Latin, REGIME.]

reg·i·ment (réjimənt) *n.* **1.** *Abbr.* **reg., regt., Regt.** A permanent military unit consisting of at least two battalions and sometimes other units and usually commanded by a colonel. **2.** A large, organised group. **3.** *Archaic.* Rule: *"the monstrous regiment of women"* (John Knox).

~*tr.v.* (réji-mént) **regimented, -menting, -ments. 1.** To organise or form into a regiment or regiments. **2.** To appoint to a regiment. **3.** To put into order; systematise. **4.** To force uniformity and discipline upon. [Middle English, from Old French, from Late Latin *regimentum,* from Latin *regere,* to rule.] —**reg·i·men·tal** *adj.* —**reg·i·men·tal·ly** *adv.* —**reg·i·men·ta·tion** (-men-táysh'n) *n.*

reg·i·men·tals (réji-mént'lz) *pl.n.* **1.** The uniform and insignia characteristic of a particular regiment. **2.** Military dress.

Re·gi·na¹ (ri-jīnə, rə-) *n. Abbr.* **R., Reg. 1.** The reigning queen. Used as a title and signature on documents. **2.** *Law.* The Crown. Used in lawsuits when the monarch is a queen: *Regina v. Jones.* [Latin.]

Regina². Capital of Saskatchewan province, Canada, built on the

Indian settlement of Wascana. It is a major agricultural centre.

re·gion (réejən) *n. Abbr.* **reg.** **1.** Any large, usually continuous segment of a surface or space; an area. **2.** A large and indefinite portion of the Earth's surface. **3.** A specific district or territory. **4.** A field of interest or activity; a sphere. **5.** A part of the Earth characterised by distinctive animal or plant life. **6.** An area of the body having natural or arbitrarily assigned boundaries: *the abdominal region.* **7.** *Usually plural.* The different areas of a country excluding the capital: *Politics in the regions differs from politics in Westminster.* **8.** Range; vicinity: *a price in the region of £5,000.* **9.** *Mathematics.* A **domain** *(see).* —See Synonyms at **area.** [Middle English *regioun,* kingdom, from Old French *region,* from Latin *regiō* (stem *regiōn-),* direction, boundary, from *regere,* to direct.]

re·gion·al (réejən'l) *adj.* **1.** Of, pertaining to, or characteristic of a large geographical region. **2.** Of, pertaining to, or characteristic of a particular region or district; localised. **3.** Of, belonging to, or characteristic of a form of a language that is distributed in identifiable geographical areas and has identifiable phonetic, structural, and other differences from the standard form of the language; dialectal. **—re·gion·al·ly** *adv.*

regional ileitis *n. Medicine.* Inflammation, thickening, and ulceration of any part of the digestive tract, particularly the ileum. Also called "Crohn's disease".

re·gion·al·ise, re·gion·al·ize (réejən'l-īz) *tr.v.* **-ised, -ising, -ises.** To divide into regions for administrative purposes; especially, to divide into partially autonomous administrative units. **—re·gion·al·i·sa·tion** (-ī-záysh'n || *U.S* -i-) *n.*

re·gion·al·ism (réejən'l-iz'm) *n.* **1.** The political division of territory into partially autonomous regions. **2.** The theory or advocacy of such a political system. **3.** Attachment to one's native region. **4.** A feature, as of language, associated with a particular region.

ré·gis·seur (réji-súr; *French* rayzhee-sőr) *n., pl.* **-seurs** (-súrz, -sőr). *French.* The director of a ballet.

reg·is·ter (réjistər) *n. Abbr.* **reg.** **1.** A formal or official recording of items, names, or actions. **2.** A book for such entries. **3.** An entry in a register. **4.** A device that automatically indicates a quantity or number. **5.** An adjustable, grille-like device through which heated or cooled air is released into a room. **6.** *Music.* **a.** The range of an instrument or voice. **b.** A part of such a range that has similar quality. **c.** A group of matched organ pipes; a stop. **7.** The style or form of language typically used in particular social situations: *scientific register; colloquial register.* **8.** *Printing.* **a.** The exact alignment of printed lines for columns on both sides of a page. **b.** The exact alignment of different colour plates in the printing of a picture. **9.** *Computing.* A specific location in a storage device, especially one assigned to a particular operation.
~*v.* **registered, -tering, -ters.** —*tr.* **1.** To enter in a register; record officially; enrol. **2.** To indicate, as on an instrument or scale. **3.** To show (emotion). **4.** To cause (post) to be officially recorded by payment of a fee. **5.** To cause to align or correspond. —*intr.* **1.** To place or cause placement of one's name in a register or on an official list: *We registered to vote.* **2.** To be indicated, as on an instrument or scale. **3.** To be shown. **4.** To create an impression on someone's mind. **5.** To be aligned; correspond. [Middle English *registre,* from Old French, from Medieval Latin *registrum, regest(r)um,* from Late Latin *regesta,* list, neuter plural past participle of Latin *regerere,* to bring back : *re-,* back + *gerere,* to bring, carry.] **—reg·is·ter·er** *n.* **—reg·is·tra·ble** (réjistrəb'l) *adj.*

registered post *n.* **1.** Mail that is recorded by the post office when sent and is insured by payment of a fee against loss or damage. **2.** The Post Office service by which such mail is sent.

registered nurse *n. Abbr.* **R.N.** *U.S.* A trained nurse who has passed a state registration examination.

reg·is·trant (réjistrənt) *n.* One who registers or is registered.

reg·is·trar (réji-strár, -straar) *n. Abbr.* **reg., regr.** **1.** One who is in charge of registers or official records. **2.** *British.* An official in charge of a registry office, who is licensed to perform marriages. **3.** An officer in a college or university who keeps records of the enrolment and academic standing of students. **4.** *British.* A specialist physician or surgeon in a hospital, subordinate to a consultant, but senior to a house officer or senior house officer.

reg·is·tra·tion (réji-stráysh'n) *n.* **1.** A registering, as of voters or students. **2.** The number of persons registered; an enrolment. **3.** An entry in a register. **4. a.** A selected combination of organ stops. **b.** The technique of selecting and adjusting organ stops.

registration number *n.* The official set of numerals and letters on the number plates of a motor vehicle indicating when and where it was registered.

registration plate *n.* A **number plate** *(see).*

reg·is·try (réjistri) *n., pl.* **-tries.** *Abbr.* **reg.** **1.** Registration. **2.** A ship's registered nationality. **3.** A place where registers are kept.

registry office *n. British.* **1.** An office where official records of births, marriages, and deaths are kept and where civil marriages are performed by a registrar. Also formally called "register office". **2.** Formerly, an employment agency for domestic servants.

Re·gi·us professor (réeji-əss, réej-) *n.* One holding a professorship established by royal bounty at any of certain older British universities. [Latin *rēgius,* royal, from *rēx* (stem *rēg-*), king + PROFESSOR.]

reg·let (rég-lit, -lət) *n.* **1.** *Architecture.* A narrow, flat moulding. **2.** *Printing.* A flat piece of wood used to separate lines of type. [French *réglet,* from Old French *reglet,* from *regle,* rule, straight edge, from Latin *rēgula,* rule.]

reg·nal (régnəl) *adj.* Designating a specified year of a sovereign's reign calculated from the date of accession: *in her thirtieth regnal year.* [Medieval Latin *regnālis,* from Latin *rēgnum,* REIGN.]

reg·nant (régnənt) *adj.* **1. a.** Reigning; ruling. **b.** Ruling in one's own right and not merely as a consort: *Queen regnant.* **2.** Predominant. **3.** Widespread; prevalent. [Latin *regnāns* (stem *regnant-*), present participle of *regnāre,* to reign, from *rēgnum,* REIGN.]

reg·o·lith (réggə-lith) *n.* Loose material, including soils, broken rock, volcanic ash, and glacial material, overlying the bedrock. Also called "mantle rock". [Greek *rhēgos,* blanket + -LITH.]

re·gorge (ri-górj) *v.* **-gorged, -gorging, -gorges.** —*tr.* To disgorge. —*intr.* To flow back again. [French *regorger,* from Old French : *re-,* back + *gorger,* to gorge, from *gorge,* throat, GORGE.]

reg·o·sol (rég-ə-sol, -ō- || -sōl) *n.* An unconsolidated azonal soil formed from alluvium or sands. [Greek *rhēgos,* blanket + Latin *solum,* soil.]

regr. registrar.

re·grate (ri-gráyt) *tr.v.* **-grated, -grating, -grates.** **1.** Formerly, to purchase (goods, especially foodstuffs) in order to resell at a profit at or near the same marketplace. **2.** To retail or sell again (goods so purchased). [Middle English *regraten,* from Old French *regrater,* from *regratier* : perhaps *re-,* against + *grater,* to scratch, from Germanic.]

re·gress (ri-gréss, rə-) *intr.v.* **-gressed, -gressing, -gresses.** To go back; return to a previous condition, state, or behaviour pattern.
~*n.* (rée-gress). **1.** Return or withdrawal. **2.** The act of reasoning from an effect to a cause. [Latin *regressus,* past participle of *regredī,* to go back : *re-,* back + *gradī,* to step, go.]

re·gres·sion (ri-grésh'n, rə-) *n.* **1.** Reversion; retrogression. **2.** Relapse to a less perfect or developed state. **3.** *Psychology.* Reversion to a more primitive or less mature behaviour pattern. **4.** *Statistics.* The tendency for the expected value of a random variable to approach more closely the mean value of its set than does the independent variable by means of which it was predicted.

re·gres·sive (ri-gréssiv, rə-) *adj.* **1.** Tending to return or revert. **2.** Characterised by regression or a tendency to regress. **3.** Designating taxation in which the rate lessens as the amount taxed increases. **—re·gres·sive·ly** *adv.* **—re·gres·sive·ness** *n.*

re·gret (ri-grét, rə-) *tr.v.* **-gretted, -gretting, -grets.** **1.** To feel disappointed, distressed, or repentant about. **2.** To feel sorrow or grief over; mourn.
~*n.* **1.** Distress, repentance, sorrow, or disappointment over a desire unfulfilled or an action performed or not performed. **2.** A sense of loss and longing for someone or something gone. **3.** *Often plural.* An expression of grief or disappointment; especially, a courteous declining to accept an invitation. [Middle English *regretten,* from Old French *regreter,* to lament : perhaps *re-* (intensive), again + Old Norse *grata,* to moan, sob.]

Synonyms: *regret, sorrow, grief, anguish, woe, heartache.*

re·gret·ful (ri-grét-f'l, rə-) *adj.* Full of regret or sorrow. **—re·gret·ful·ly** *adv.* **—re·gret·ful·ness** *n.*

re·gret·ta·ble (ri-gréttəb'l, rə-) *adj.* Eliciting or deserving regret. See Synonyms at **pathetic.**

regret·ta·bly (ri-gréttəbli, rə-) *adv.* **1.** In a regrettable manner. **2.** It is regrettable that: *Regrettably, the book won't be finished on time.*

re·group (rée-gro͞op), *v.* **-grouped, -grouping, -groups.** —*intr.* To become an ordered group or formation again after dispersal or disordering: *We regrouped after the attack.* —*tr.* To cause to regroup.

regt., Regt. **1.** regent. **2.** regiment.

reg·u·lar (réggewlər) *adj. Abbr.* **reg.** **1.** Customary, usual, or normal. **2.** Orderly, even, or symmetrical. **3.** Conforming to set procedure, principle, or discipline. **4.** Methodical; well-ordered. **5.** Occurring at fixed intervals; periodic. **6.** Constant; not varying. **7.** Formally correct; proper. **8.** Having the required qualifications for an occupation. **9.** Perfect; complete; thorough: *a regular villain.* **10.** *U.S. Informal.* Good; nice: *a regular guy.* **11.** *Botany.* Having similar and symmetrically arranged parts. **12.** *Grammar.* Belonging to a standard mode of inflection or conjugation. **13.** Belonging to a religious order and bound by its rules: *the regular clergy.* Compare **secular.** **14.** In geometry: **a.** Having equal sides and equal angles. Said of polygons. **b.** Having faces that are congruent regular polygons with congruent polyhedral angles. Said of polyhedra. **15.** Belonging to or constituting the permanent army of a nation. **16.** Menstruating or defecating at normal intervals. **17.** In crystallography, having radial symmetry. —See Synonyms at **normal.**
~*n. Abbr.* **reg.** **1.** A soldier belonging to a regular army. **2.** *Informal.* A habitual customer or patron. **3.** A clergyman or other member of a religious order. [Middle English *reguler,* under religious rule, from Old French, from Latin *rēgulāris,* containing rules, from *rēgula,* rule, ruler.] **—reg·u·lar·i·ty** (-lárriti) *n.* **—reg·u·lar·ly** *adv.*

reg·u·lar·ise, reg·u·lar·ize (réggewlə-rīz) *tr.v.* **-ised, -ising, -ises.** To make regular; cause to conform. **—reg·u·lar·i·sa·tion** (-rī-záysh'n || *U.S.* -ri-) *n.*

reg·u·late (réggewlayt) *tr.v.* **-lated, -lating, -lates.** **1.** To control or direct according to a rule or procedure. **2.** To adjust in conformity to a specification or requirement. **3.** To adjust (a mechanism) for accurate and proper functioning. [Late Latin *rēgulāre,* from Latin *rēgula,* a rule.] **—reg·u·la·tive** (-lətiv, -laytiv), **reg·u·la·to·ry** (-laytəri, -láy-, -lə-, -tri) *adj.*

reg·u·la·tion (réggewláysh'n) *n. Abbr.* **reg.** **1.** The act of regulating. **2.** A principle, rule, or law designed to control or govern behaviour. **3.** A governmental order having the force of law. **4.** The ability of an embryo to continue normal development following injury to or alteration of a structure.

~*adj. Abbr.* **reg.** Prescribed in accordance with a rule or standard procedure: *a regulation uniform.*
reg·u·la·tor (réggewlaytər) *n. Abbr.* **reg.** **1.** One that regulates. **2. a.** The mechanism in a watch by which its speed is governed. **b.** An accurate clock used as a standard for timing other clocks. **3. a.** A device to maintain uniform speed in a machine; a governor. **b.** A device to control the flow of gases, liquids, or electric current.
regulator gene *n.* A gene that controls the expression of an **operon** *(see).*
reg·u·lus (réggew-ləss) *n., pl.* **-li** (-lī) or **-luses.** *Metallurgy.* **1.** The metallic part of a charge that sinks under the slag to the bottom of a furnace or crucible. **2.** A relatively impure product of various ores in smelting, **matte** *(see).* [Medieval Latin *rēgulus,* from Latin, a petty king (this metallic antimony combines readily with gold, the king of metals), diminutive of *rēx,* king.] **—reg·u·line** (-līn, -lin) *adj.*
Regulus *n.* A bright triple star in the constellation Leo. Also called "Alpha Leonis".
Regulus, Marcus Atilius (died *c.* 250 B.C.). Roman general, hero of the First Punic War. Appointed consul in 267 B.C. and again in 256 B.C., he was captured by the Carthaginians in 255, and sent to sue for peace with the Roman senate; instead Regulus pleaded with the senate to reject the enemy's proposals. He returned to Carthage rather than break his parole, and died there.
re·gur (rég-ər, ráyg-) *n.* A dark coloured tropical soil, notably in the cotton-growing area of the northwest Deccan, India. Also called "tropical black earth". [Hindi *regar.*]
re·gur·gi·tate (ri-gúrji-tayt, rée-) *v.* **-tated, -tating, -tates.** *—intr.* **1.** To rush or surge back. **2.** To bring partially digested food back into the mouth to feed the young. Used especially of certain birds. *—tr.* **1.** To cause to pour back; especially, to vomit up (partially digested food). **2.** To bring (partially digested food) back into the mouth. Used especially of certain birds. **3.** To reproduce (facts, for example) in an unthinking fashion. [Medieval Latin *regurgitāre* : *re-,* back + Late Latin *gurgitāre,* to engulf, flood, from Latin *gurges,* a whirlpool.] **—re·gur·gi·ta·tion** (-táysh'n) *n.*
re·ha·bil·i·tate (rée-ə-bílli-tayt, -hə-) *tr.v.* **-tated, -tating, -tates.** **1.** To restore (a handicapped or delinquent person, for example) to useful life through education and therapy. **2.** To reinstate the good name of. **3.** To restore the former rank, privileges, or rights of. [Medieval Latin *rehabilitāre* : Late Latin *re-,* again + *habilitāre,* HABILITATE.] **—re·ha·bil·i·ta·tion** (-táysh'n) *n.* **—re·ha·bil·i·ta·tive** (-tətiv -taytiv) *adj.*
re·hash (rée-hásh) *tr.v.* **-hashed, -hashing, -hashes.** To repeat, rework, or rewrite (old material) without significant alteration.
~*n.* (rée-hash). A repeated or unoriginal account; a rehashing. [RE- + HASH (to chop over).]
re·hear (rée-héer) *tr.v.* **-heard** (-hérd), **-hearing, -hears.** **1.** To hear again. **2.** *Law.* To give a second consideration to (a case).
re·hears·al (ri-hérss'l, rə-) *n.* **1.** The act or an instance of practising for a performance, especially for a public performance. **2.** A verbal repetition; a detailed enumeration: *a rehearsal of his woes.*
re·hearse (ri-hérss, rə-) *v.* **-hearsed, -hearsing, -hearses.** *—tr.* **1. a.** To practise (all or part of a play, concert, entertainment, or the like) in preparation for a public performance. **b.** To make rehearse; direct in rehearsal. **2.** To perfect or cause to perfect (an action) by repetition. **3.** To retell or recite. **4.** To list or enumerate. *—intr.* To rehearse a concert, entertainment, play, or the like. [Middle English *rehercen,* from Old French *rehercer,* to repeat, originally "to harrow again" : *re-,* again + *hercer,* to harrow, from *herce,* a harrow, from Latin *hirpex* (see **hearse**).] **—re·hears·er** *n.*
re·heat (rée-héet) *tr.v.* **-heated, -heating, -heats.** **1.** To add fuel to (exhaust gas in a jet engine) in order to give further combustion and improve the power. **2.** To heat again.
~*n.* The process of reheating exhaust gases in a jet engine.
Re·ho·bo·am (rée-ə-bṓ-əm, -hə-) *n. Often small* **r.** A large wine bottle often used for champagne, holding the equivalent of six standard bottles. [After *Rehoboam,* son of King Solomon (by analogy with JEROBOAM).]
re·house (rée-hówz) *tr.v.* **-housed, -housing, -houses.** To put or re-establish in a new, usually improved, dwelling or shelter.
Reich (rīk; *German* rīkh) *n.* The territory or government of a German empire or republic; specifically: the *First Reich,* the Holy Roman Empire (ninth century to 1806); the *Second Reich,* the German Empire (1871–1919); the Weimar Republic (1919–33); and the *Third Reich* (1933–45). [German, from Old High German *rīhhi,* realm.]
Reich, Wilhelm (1897–1957). Austrian psychologist. He was Freud's assistant in Vienna (1922–28), but rejected his ideas. In 1939 he settled in the U.S.A., where he claimed to discover a kind of energy called *orgone,* discharged through sexual release. In 1954 the Food and Drug Administration ordered the destruction of all *orgone accumulators,* boxes in which Reich advised patients to sit to restore this energy. For defying a ban and continuing to publish, Reich was convicted of contempt of court in 1956, and died in prison.
Reichs·mark (rīks-maark; *German* rīkhs-) *n., pl.* **reichsmark** or **-marks.** *Abbr.* **RM.** A former monetary unit of Germany, until 1948, having a value of 100 Reichspfennigs. See **Deutschmark.** [German : *Reichs,* genitive of REICH + MARK (money).]
Reichs·pfen·nig (rīks-fennig; *German* rīkhs-pfennikh) *n.* A former bronze German coin, worth 1/100 of a Reichsmark. See **pfennig.** [German : *Reichs,* genitive of REICH + PFENNIG.]
Reichs·tag (rīks-taag; *German* rīkhs-taak) *n.* **1.** The representative and legislative assembly of the German Empire (1871–1919) and of the Weimar Republic (1919–33). **2.** The building in Berlin in which the assembly met. [German : *Reichs,* genitive of REICH + *Tag,* council, diet, from *tagen,* to deliberate.]
Reid (reed), **Sir George Houston** (1845–1918). Australian politician, born in Scotland. He was premier of New South Wales (1894–99) and prime minister of Australia (1904–05). He was knighted in 1909, served as high commissioner to London (1910–15), and sat in the British parliament (1916–18).
re·i·fy (rée-i-fī, ráy-) *tr.v.* **-fied, -fying, -fies.** To regard or treat (an abstraction or ideal) as if concretely or materially existing. [Latin *rēs,* a thing + -FY.] **—re·i·fi·ca·tion** (-fi-káysh'n) *n.* **—re·i·fi·er** *n.*
reign (rayn) *n.* **1.** The exercise of sovereign power, as by a monarch. **2.** A period during which sovereignty is held. **3.** Dominance or widespread influence: *the reign of reason.*
~*intr.v.* **reigned, reigning, reigns.** **1.** To exercise sovereign power. **2.** To hold the title of sovereign, but with limited authority. **3.** To be predominant or prevalent. [Middle English *rei(n)gne,* from Old French *reigne,* from Latin *rēgnum,* from *rēx* (stem *rēg-*), a king.]
reign·ing (ráyning) *adj.* Designating the current holder of a championship or other competitive title: *the reigning Miss World.*
Reign of Terror *n.* **1.** The period (1793–94) of the French Revolution during which thousands of persons were executed. **2.** *Small* **r,** *small* **t.** Any period of widespread violence or intimidation.
Reik (rīk), **Theodor** (1888–1969). U.S. psychologist, born in Vienna. He was one of Freud's students and worked with him (1910–38), after which he settled in the United States. His numerous books included *The Secret Self* (1952), and *Myth and Guilt* (1957).
re·im·burse (rée-im-búrss) *tr.v.* **-bursed, -bursing, -burses.** **1.** To repay: *He reimbursed his creditors.* **2.** To pay back or compensate (a person) for money spent, or losses or damages incurred. [RE- + obsolete *imburse,* to pay, to pocket money, from Old French *embourser* : EN- + *borser,* to obtain money, from *borse,* a purse, from Late Latin *bursa,* "oxhide", from Greek, hide, skin.] **—re·im·burs·a·ble** *adj.* **—re·im·burse·ment** *n.*
re·im·port (rée-im-pórt || -pōrt) *tr.v.* **-ported, -porting, -ports.** To bring back into a country (goods made from raw materials originally exported from that country).
~*n.* (-ím-pawrt || -pōrt) **1.** The act of reimporting. **2.** Goods reimported. **—re·im·por·ta·tion** (-táysh'n) *n.*
re·im·pres·sion (rée-im-présh'n) *n.* **1.** A second or subsequent impression. **2.** A reprinting of a book.
Reims (RANSS). *English* **Rheims** (reemz). City in the département of Marne in northeast France on the river Vesle. It is a major marketing centre for champagne wines. The site of the coronation of most French kings after Louis VII (1137), it has a fine Gothic cathedral. The German surrender was signed at Allied headquarters in Reims at the end of World War II (May 1945).
rein (rayn) *n.* **1. a.** *Plural.* A pair of long, narrow leather straps attached to the bit of a bridle and used by a rider or driver to control a horse or other animal. **b.** Any strap forming part of a harness, such as a bearing rein. **2.** *Plural.* A harness used to control a young child. **3.** *Often plural.* Any means of restraint, check, or guidance. **4.** *Often plural.* Any means of control: *the reins of government.* **—draw rein. 1.** To exert pressure on the reins. **2.** To slow or stop. **—give (free) rein to.** To release from restraints. **—keep a tight rein on.** To exercise close control over.
~*v.* **reined, reining, reins.** *—tr.* **1.** To check or hold back (a horse or other animal). Often used with *in, back,* or *up.* **2.** To guide or control. **3.** *Archaic.* To equip with reins. *—intr.* To control a horse or other animal with reins. Often used with *in, back,* or *up.* [Middle English *re(i)ne,* from Old French *re(s)ne,* from Vulgar Latin *retina* (unattested), from Latin *retinēre,* to RETAIN.]
re·in·car·nate (ree-íng-kaar-nayt, rée-in-kár-) *tr.v.* **-nated, -nating, -nates.** To furnish with another body; incarnate again. Usually used in the passive: *believed he'd be reincarnated as a snake.*
~*adj.* (rée-in-kár-nət, -nit, -nayt). Reborn in another body; reincarnated. **—re·in·car·na·tion** (rée-in-kaar-náysh'n) *n.*
rein·deer (ráyn-deer) *n., pl.* **-deers** or collectively **reindeer.** A large deer, *Rangifer tarandus,* of arctic regions of the Old World and Greenland, having branched antlers in both sexes. It is identical to the caribou, but can be domesticated. [Middle English *reyndere,* from Old Norse *hreindyri* : *hreinn,* reindeer + *dyr,* deer.]
reindeer moss *n.* An erect, greyish, branching lichen, *Cladonia rangiferina,* of arctic regions, used as food for reindeer.
re·in·fec·tion (rée-in-féksh'n) *n.* A second infection that follows recovery from a previous infection by the same causative agent.
re·in·force (rée-in-fórss || -fōrss) *tr.v.* **-forced, -forcing, -forces.** **1.** To give more force or effectiveness to; strengthen; support. **2.** *Military.* To strengthen with additional manpower or equipment. **3.** To strengthen, as by adding extra support or padding. **4.** To increase in number. **5.** *Psychology.* To encourage by means of reinforcement. [RE- + *inforce,* variant of ENFORCE.]
reinforced concrete *n. Abbr.* **R.C.** Poured concrete containing steel bars or metal netting to increase its tensile strength. Also called "ferroconcrete".
re·in·force·ment (rée-in-fórss-mənt || -fōrss-) *n.* **1.** The act or process of reinforcing, or the condition of being reinforced. **2.** Something that reinforces. **3.** *Often plural.* Additional troops, vessels, or equipment sent to support a military action. **4.** *Psychology.* **a.** The occurrence or experimental introduction of an unconditioned stimulus along with a conditioned stimulus. **b.** The strengthening of a conditioned response by such means. **c.** The strengthening of

an instrumental or operant conditioned response leading to satisfaction; reward. **d.** Loosely, any condition strengthening learning.
Rein·hardt (rīn-haart), **Django** (1910–53). Belgian Gypsy jazz guitarist. He began his professional career in 1922. His left hand was mutilated in a fire in 1928, but he devised a fingering technique to overcome the disability. In 1934, with Stephane Grappelli and others, he founded the Quintette du Hot Club de France.
Reinhardt, Max (1873–1943). Austrian stage actor, producer, and director. He managed his own theatre in Berlin (1902–05); in 1919 he founded the *Grosse Schauspielhaus,* and in 1920 the Salzburg Festival. In 1933 he fled Germany and settled in the United States. He was famous for his ambitious stage-setting and crowd scenes.
reins (raynz) *pl.n. Archaic.* **1.** The kidneys, loins, or lower back region. **2.** The seat of the affections and passions, which were formerly regarded as having their source in the kidneys and loins. [Middle English, from Old French, from Latin *rēnēs.* See **renal.**]
re·in·state (rée-in-stáyt) *tr.v.* **-stated, -stating, -states.** To restore to a previous condition or position. **—re·in·state·ment** *n.*
re·in·sure (rée-in-shóor, -shór || -shéwr) *tr.v.* **-sured, -suring, -sures.** **1.** To insure again. **2.** To insure by transferring in whole or in part a risk or contingent liability already covered under an existing contract. **—re·in·sur·ance** *n.* **—re·in·sur·er** *n.*
re·in·vest (rée-in-vést) *tr.v.* **-vested, -vesting, -vests.** To invest (capital or earnings) again. Used especially of receipts derived from a securities portfolio. **—re·in·vest·ment** *n.*
reis. Alternative plural of **real** (Portuguese monetary unit).
re·is·sue (rée-ishoo, -issew) *tr.v.* **-sued, -suing, -sues.** To issue again; make available again.
~n. **1.** A second or subsequent issue, as of a book altered in format or price. **2.** A reprinting of postage stamps from unchanged plates.
re·it·er·ate (ree-ítta-rayt) *tr.v.* **-ated, -ating, -ates.** To say or do over again; repeat. [Latin *reiterāre* : *re-,* again + *iterāre,* ITERATE.] **—re·it·er·a·tion** (-ráysh'n) *n.* **—re·it·er·a·tive** (-rətiv, -raytiv) *adj.* **—re·it·er·a·tive·ly** *adv.*
Reith of Stonehaven (reeth), **John (Charles Walsham), 1st Baron** (1889–1971). British radio, television, and airline manager. As director-general (1927–38) of the BBC, he helped to establish its framework and ensure its independence of government control. In 1938 he became chairman of Imperial Airways, which he merged with British Airways to form the new British Overseas Airways Corporation in 1939. He was director of Combined Operations Material at the Admiralty (1943–45) and chairman of the Commonwealth Telecommunications Board (1946–50).
reive (reev) *intr.v.* **reived, reiving, reives.** *Northern British.* To raid, rob, or plunder. [Variant of REAVE.] **—reiv·er** *n.*
re·ject (ri-jékt, rə-) *tr.v.* **-jected, -jecting, -jects.** **1.** To refuse to accept, recognise, or make use of; repudiate. **2.** To refuse to consider or grant; deny. **3.** To refuse affection or recognition to (a person). **4.** To discard as defective or useless; throw away. **5.** To spit out or vomit. **6.** To fail to accept (transplanted tissues or organs) owing to immunological incompatibility. —See Synonyms at **refuse.**
~n. (rée-jekt). Something or someone that has been rejected as unsatisfactory or below standard. [Middle English *rejecten,* from Latin *rejicere* (past participle *rejectus*), to throw back : *re-,* back, away + *jacere,* to throw.] **—re·ject·er** (ri-jéktər, rə-) *n.*
re·jec·tion (ri-jéksh'n, rə-) *n.* **1.** The act or process of rejecting. **2.** The condition of being rejected. **3.** Something rejected.
re·jec·tor (ri-jéktər, rə-) *n.* One that rejects; specifically, an electronic circuit that cuts out signals of a designated frequency range. Compare **acceptor.**
re·jig (rée-jíg) *tr.v.* **-jigged, -jigging, -jigs.** **1.** To re-equip (a factory, workshop, or the like) with different machines or equipment. **2.** *Informal.* To revise, rework, or rearrange. **—re·jig·ger** *n.*
re·joice (ri-jóyss, rə-) *v.* **-joiced, -joicing, -joices.** *—intr.* **1.** To feel or be joyful. **2.** To possess or be lucky in possessing something. Used with *in*: *He rejoiced in the name of Herbert Sidebottom.* *—tr.* To fill with joy; gladden. [Middle English *rejoicen,* from Old French *rejoir* (stem *rejoiss-*) : *re-* (intensive) + *joir,* to be joyful, from Latin *gaudēre.*] **—re·joic·er** *n.*
re·joic·ing (ri-jóyssing, rə-) *n.* The feeling or expressing of joy or an instance of this; joyful celebration.
re·join[1] (rée-jóyn, ri-) *v.* **-joined, -joining, -joins.** *—tr.* **1.** To come again into the company of: *rejoined his regiment.* **2.** To join or put together again; reunite. *—intr.* To be or become joined again.
re·join[2] (ri-jóyn, rə-) *v.* **-joined, -joining, -joins.** *—tr.* To say as a reply. *—intr.* **1.** To respond; answer. **2.** *Law.* To answer a plaintiff's replication. [Middle English *rejoinen,* from Old French *rejoindre* : *re-,* back, again + *joindre,* to JOIN.]
re·join·der (ri-jóyndər, rə-) *n.* **1.** An answer, especially in response to a reply. **2.** *Law.* A second pleading by a defendant, in answer to a plaintiff's replication. [Middle English *rejoyner,* from Old French *rejoindre* (substantive infinitive), to REJOIN (answer).]
re·ju·ve·nate (ri-jóov-ə-nayt, rə-, -i-) *tr.v.* **-nated, -nating, -nates.** **1.** To restore the youthful vigour or appearance of. **2.** To stimulate (a stream) to renewed erosive activity, as by a local uplift of land or an increase in precipitation. [RE- + Latin *juvenis,* a youth.] **—re·ju·ve·na·tion** (-náysh'n) *n.* **—re·ju·ve·na·tor** (-náytər) *n.*
re·ju·ve·nes·cence (ri-jóov-ə-néss'nss, rée-, -i-) *n.* The act of making youthful again; rejuvenation. **—re·ju·ve·nes·cent** *adj.*
re·kin·dle (rée-kínd'l) *v.* **-kindled, kindling, -kindles.** *—tr.* **1.** To relight. **2.** To revive or renew: *rekindle one's interest in books.* *—intr.* To be relit or revived.
rel. **1.** relating. **2.** relative; relatively. **3.** released. **4.** religion; religious.
re·lapse (ri-láps, rə-) *intr.v.* **-lapsed, -lapsing, -lapses.** **1.** To fall back into or revert to a former habit or state. **2.** To regress after partial recovery from illness. **3.** To slip back into bad ways; backslide.
~n. (*also* rée-laps). The act or an instance of relapsing. [Latin *relapsus,* past participle of *relābī,* to slide back : *re-,* back + *lābī,* to slide.] **—re·laps·er** *n.*
relapsing fever *n.* Any of several infectious diseases characterised by chills and fever, and caused by spirochaetes of the genus *Borrelia* transmitted by lice and ticks. Also called "recurrent fever".
re·late (ri-láyt, rə-) *v.* **-lated, -lating, -lates.** *—tr.* **1.** To narrate or tell. **2.** To bring into logical or natural association. *—intr.* **1.** To have connection, relation, or reference. Used with *to.* **2.** To form mutually responsive relationships; interact with others in an effective manner. Sometimes used with *to.* —See Synonyms at **join.** [Latin *relātus* (past participle of *referre,* to carry back, REFER) : *re-,* back + *-lātus,* "carried".] **—re·lat·er** *n.*
re·lat·ed (ri-láytid, rə-) *adj.* **1.** Connected; associated. **2.** Connected by kinship, marriage, or common origin. **3.** *Music.* Having a specified harmonic connection. **—re·lat·ed·ness** *n.*
re·la·tion (ri-láysh'n, rə-) *n.* **1.** A logical or natural association between two or more things; relevance of one to another; a connection. **2.** The connection of people by blood or marriage; kinship. **3.** A person related to another by blood or marriage; a relative. **4.** The mode or way in which a person or thing is connected with another. **5.** *Plural.* The connections or associations drawing together persons, groups, or nations in personal, business, or diplomatic affairs: *public relations.* **6.** Reference; regard: *in relation to your query.* **7. a.** The act of telling or narrating. **b.** A narrative; an account. **8.** *Plural.* Sexual intercourse.
re·la·tion·al (ri-láysh'n'l, rə-) *adj.* **1.** Of or arising from kinship. **2.** Indicating or constituting relations. **3.** *Grammar.* Expressing a syntactic relation.
re·la·tion·ship (ri-láysh'n-ship, rə-) *n.* **1.** The condition or fact of being related. **2.** Connection by blood or marriage; kinship. **3. a.** A particular kind of connection existing between people having dealings with one another: *I have a good working relationship with my boss.* **b.** A close emotional, sexual, or romantic connection between two people.
rel·a·tive (réllətiv) *adj. Abbr.* **rel.** **1.** Having pertinence or relevance; connected; related. **2.** Considered in comparison with something else. **3.** Dependent upon or interconnected with something else for intelligibility or significance; not absolute. **4.** Referring to or qualifying an antecedent. **5.** *Grammar.* Designating a pronoun that introduces a relative clause and has reference to an antecedent. In the sentence *He who hesitates is lost,* the relative pronoun is *who.* Compare **demonstrative, interrogative.** **6.** *Music.* Having the same key signature. Said of major and minor scales and keys. **7.** *Physics & Chemistry.* Pertaining to or designating a physical quantity that is expressed as a ratio of the measured value to the value for some standard system: *relative density; relative humidity.*
~n. **1. a.** One related by kinship; a relation. **b.** One related by a common origin. **2.** One that is relative. **3.** *Grammar.* A relative term. [Middle English *relatif,* from Old French, from Late Latin *relātīvus,* from Latin *relātus.* See **relate.**] **—rel·a·tive·ly** *adv.* **—rel·a·tive·ness** *n.*
relative atomic mass *n. Symbol* A_r *Chemistry.* **Atomic weight** *(see).*
relative biological effectiveness *n. Abbr.* **RBE** *Physics.* A measure of the capacity of a specific ionising radiation to produce a specific biological effect, usually expressed as the dose of a standard type of radiation relative to the dose of the ionisation in question required to produce the effect.
relative clause *n. Grammar.* A dependent clause introduced by a relative pronoun. In the sentence *He who hesitates is lost,* the relative clause is *who hesitates.*
relative density *n. Symbol* **d** The density of a substance relative to the density of some standard substance; specifically: **1.** The ratio of the density of a liquid or solid substance to the density of water. Unless otherwise specified, it is assumed that the substance is at room temperature (20° C) and the water is at its temperature of maximum density (4° C). Also called "specific gravity". **2.** The ratio of the density of a gas to the density of hydrogen, usually under conditions of standard temperature and pressure.
relative humidity *n. Abbr.* **r.h.** The ratio of the amount of water vapour in the air at a specific temperature to the maximum capacity of the air at that temperature. Compare **absolute humidity.**
relative majority *n.* The number of votes cast for the winning candidate that exceed those cast for the runner-up, when no one candidate receives more than 50 per cent of all votes cast. Also *U.S.* "plurality". Compare **absolute majority.**
relative molecular mass *n. Symbol* M_r *Chemistry.* **Molecular weight** *(see).*
relative permeability *n. Symbol* μ_r *Physics.* The ratio of the magnetic permeability of a given medium to that of free space (that is, to the magnetic constant).
relative permittivity *n. Symbol* ϵ_r *Physics.* The ratio of the electric permittivity of a given medium to that of free space (that is, to the electric constant). Also called "dielectric constant".
relative pitch *n.* **1.** The pitch of a note as determined by its position in a scale. **2.** The ability to recognise or produce a note by mentally establishing a relationship between its pitch and that of a recently heard note. Compare **absolute pitch.**

rel·a·tiv·ism (réllətiv-iz'm) *n.* Any of various philosophical attitudes holding that moral value, knowledge, or truth is not absolute but relative, for example to an individual, a culture, historical circumstances, or a theoretical framework.
rel·a·tiv·ist (réllətivist) *n.* **1.** A proponent of relativism. **2.** A physicist specialising in the theories of relativity.
rel·a·tiv·is·tic (rélləti-vístik) *adj.* **1.** Of or pertaining to relativism. **2.** *Physics.* **a.** Of, pertaining to, or resulting from speeds that are approaching the speed of light: *relativistic increase in mass.* **b.** Of or pertaining to phenomena explicable by Special or General relativity: *relativistic mechanics.*
rel·a·tiv·i·ty (réllə-tívvəti) *n.* **1.** The quality or state of being relative. **2.** A state of dependence in which the existence, quality, or significance of one entity is determined by that of another. **3.** A theory of relative motion, space, and time developed by Albert Einstein in two parts. *Special relativity* (1905) deals with uniform motion at constant relative velocity, and is based on the principles that the speed of light is a constant, irrespective of the motion of the observer, and that physical laws are the same for all observers. *General relativity* (published 1916) extends this to non-uniform (accelerated) motion and is applied particularly to gravitation.
re·la·tor (ri-láytər, rə-) *n.* One who relates or narrates.
re·lax (ri-láks, rə-) *v.* **-laxed, -laxing, -laxes.** —*tr.* **1.** To make lax or loose: *relax one's grip.* **2.** To make less severe, formal, or strict. **3.** To reduce in intensity; slacken. **4.** To relieve from effort or strain. —*intr.* **1.** To take one's ease; rest. **2.** To become lax or loose. **3.** To become less severe. **4.** To become less formal or tense. [Middle English *relaxen,* from Latin *relaxāre* : *re-,* back + *laxāre,* to loosen, from *laxus,* lax, loose.] **—re·lax·a·ble** *adj.* **—re·lax·er** *n.*
re·lax·ant (ri-láksənt, rə-) *n.* A drug or therapeutic treatment that relaxes or relieves muscular or nervous tension.
~adj. Tending to relax or to relieve tension.
re·lax·a·tion (réelak-sáysh'n, rélləks-) *n.* **1. a.** The act of relaxing. **b.** The state of being relaxed. **2.** Refreshment of body or mind; recreation: *play golf for relaxation.* **3.** A loosening or slackening. **4.** A reduction in strictness or severity. **5.** *Physiology.* The return to normal length of inactive muscle or muscle fibres following contraction. **6.** *Physics.* The return or adjustment of a system to equilibrium following a small displacement or abrupt change. **7.** *Mathematics.* A numerical method in which the errors, or residuals, resulting from an initial approximation are reduced by succeeding approximations until all errors are within specific limits. —See Synonyms at **rest. —re·lax·a·tive** (ri-láksətiv, rə-) *adj.* & *n.*
relaxation time *n.* *Physics.* The time required for an exponential variable to decrease to $1/e$ (0.368) of its initial value.
re·laxed (ri-lákst, rə-) *adj.* **1.** Free from strain or tension. **2.** Informal or easy-going in manner. **—re·laxed·ly** (re-láksidli) *adv.* **—re·laxed·ness** *n.*
re·lax·in (rī-láksin, rə-) *n.* A female hormone secreted by the corpus luteum in the final stages of pregnancy that causes the cervix to dilate and relaxes the pelvic ligaments in childbirth. [RELAX + -IN.]
re·lay (rée-láy) *tr.v.* **-laid** (-láyd), **-laying, -lays.** To lay again.
re·lay (rée-lay, ri-láy) *n.* **1.** A crew of labourers who relieve another crew at work; a shift. **2.** A fresh team, as of horses or dogs, to relieve weary animals in a hunt, task, or journey. **3.** An act of passing something along from one person, group, or station to another. **4.** A relay race, or any one of its lengths or laps. **5.** An automatic electromagnetic or electromechanical device that responds to a small current or voltage change by activating switches or other devices in an electric circuit.
~tr.v. (ri-láy, rə-, rée-lay), **relayed, -laying, -lays. 1.** To pass or send along by or as if by relay: *relay a message.* **2.** To supply with fresh relays. **3.** *Electronics.* To control or retransmit by means of a relay. **4.** *British.* To broadcast from a theatre, concert hall, or the like via a transmitter. [Middle English *relai,* from Old French, from *relaier,* to relay, leave behind : *re-,* back + *laier,* to leave, variant of *laissier,* from Latin *laxāre,* to loosen, from *laxus,* lax, loose.]
relay race *n.* A race between two or more teams, in which each team member runs only a set part of the race, and then is relieved by another member of his team.
relay station *n.* An installation for receiving telecommunications signals and amplifying and retransmitting them.
re·lease (rée-léess) *tr.v.* **-leased, -leasing, -leases.** To lease again.
re·lease (ri-léess, rə-) *tr.v.* **-leased, -leasing, -leases. 1.** To set free from confinement, restraint, or bondage; liberate. **2.** To free, unfasten, or let go of. **3.** To relieve from debt or obligation. **4. a.** To allow performance, sale, publication, distribution, or circulation of. **b.** To make known or available. **5.** To relinquish (a right or claim, for example). **6.** *Chemistry.* To free from chemical combination.
~n. **1.** A deliverance; liberation. **2.** An authoritative discharge from an obligation or from prison. **3.** An unfastening or letting go of something caught or held fast. **4.** A device or catch for locking or releasing a mechanism. **5. a.** A freeing or issuing of something for general publication, use, or circulation: *a film on general release.* **b.** Something thus issued or released: *a press release; a record release.* **6.** *Law.* **a.** The relinquishment of a right, title, or claim to another. **b.** The document authorising such a relinquishment. [Middle English *relesen,* from Old French *relessier, relaissier,* from Latin *relaxāre,* to RELAX.]
re·leas·er (ri-léessər, rə-) *n.* **1.** One that releases. **2.** *Zoology.* Any stimulus or combination of stimuli that elicits an instinctive behavioural pattern.
rel·e·gate (rél-i-gayt, -ə-) *tr.v.* **-gated, -gating, -gates. 1.** To send or consign, especially to an obscure or inferior place, position, or condition. **2.** To move to a lower division. Used of a sports team, especially one in a Football League. **3.** To refer or assign (a matter or task, for example) for decision or execution. **4.** To cast out; banish; exile. [Latin *relēgāre,* to send away : *re-,* back, away + *lēgāre,* to send.] **—rel·e·ga·tion** (-gáysh'n) *n.*
re·lent (ri-lént, rə-) *intr.v.* **-lented, -lenting, -lents.** To become softened or gentler in attitude, temper, or determination; go back on a harsh decision. —See Synonyms at **yield.** [Middle English *relenten,* from Medieval Latin *relentāre* (unattested) : *re-* (intensive), again + *lentāre,* soften, from Latin, bend, from *lentus,* pliable.]
re·lent·less (ri-lént-ləss, rə-, -liss) *adj.* **1.** Unyielding; pitiless: *relentless persecution.* **2.** Steady and persistent; unremitting: *the relentless advance of the tide.* **—re·lent·less·ly** *adv.* **—re·lent·less·ness** *n.*
rel·e·vant (rél-i-vənt, -ə-) *adj.* **1.** Related to the matter at hand; to the point; pertinent. **2.** *Linguistics.* Serving to distinguish one phoneme from others; distinctive. [Medieval Latin *relevāns* (stem *relevant-*), from Latin, present participle of *relevāre,* to lift up, RELIEVE.] **—rel·e·vance, rel·e·van·cy** *n.* **—rel·e·vant·ly** *adv.*
***Synonyms:** relevant, pertinent, germane, material, apt, apposite, apropos.*
re·li·a·ble (ri-lī́-əb'l, rə-) *adj.* Capable of being relied upon; trustworthy; dependable. **—re·li·a·bil·i·ty** (-ə-bílləti), **re·li·a·ble·ness** *n.* **—re·li·a·bly** *adv.*
re·li·ance (ri-lī́-ənss, rə-) *n.* **1.** The act of relying. **2.** Confidence; dependence; trust. **3.** Something or someone depended on; a mainstay. —See Synonyms at **trust.**
re·li·ant (ri-lī́-ənt, rə-) *adj.* Dependent; relying or trusting. Used with *on.* **—re·li·ant·ly** *adv.*
rel·ic (réllik) *n.* Also *archaic* **rel·ique** (réllik, ri-léek). **1.** Something that has survived the passage of time; especially, an object or custom whose original cultural environment has disappeared. **2.** *Biology.* A relict. **3.** Something cherished for its age or associations with a person, place, or event; a keepsake. **4.** An object of religious veneration; especially, an article reputed to be associated with a saint or martyr. **5.** Anything old, leftover, or remaining; a remnant. **6.** *Plural.* A corpse; the remains of a dead person. [Middle English *relik(e),* from Old French *relique,* from Late Latin *reliquiae,* remains (especially of a martyr), from Latin, from *relinquere,* to leave behind, RELINQUISH.]
rel·ict (réllikt) *n.* **1.** *Biology.* An organism or species of an earlier time surviving in an environment that has undergone considerable change. **2.** *Rare.* A widow.
~adj. Geology. Pertaining to something that has survived, such as structures or minerals after destructive processes. [Latin *relictus,* past participle of *relinquere,* to leave behind, RELINQUISH.]
re·lief (ri-léef, rə-) *n.* **1. a.** Ease from or lessening of pain or discomfort. **b.** Ease or lessening of a burden or something imposed, such as a levy: *tax relief.* **2. a.** Anything that lessens pain, discomfort, fear, anxiety, or the like. **b.** The feeling of buoyancy or well-being that immediately follows the removal or lessening of anxiety, pain, discomfort, or the like. **3.** Assistance, in the form of money or food, given to the needy, aged, or to the inhabitants of any disaster-stricken region. **4. a.** A release from a job, post, or duty, as of a sentinel. **b.** The person or group of persons taking over the duties of another. **5. a.** The projection of figures or forms from a flat background, or such a projection that is apparent only, as in painting. **b.** Any work of art featuring such projection. Also called "relievo." **6.** *Geography.* The variations in elevation of any area of the earth's surface. **7.** Distinction or prominence resulting from contrast: *Her dark hat brought her pallor into relief.* **8.** A diversion; a pleasant or amusing change: *light relief.* **9.** A bus, aircraft, ferry, or train that supplements or replaces an existing service. **10.** The act of raising a siege or blockade. **11.** *Law.* The obtaining of reparation or redress. **12.** In feudal law, a payment made by the heir of a deceased tenant to a lord for the privilege of succeeding to the tenant's estate. **—on relief.** *U.S.* Receiving government funds because of need or poverty. [Middle English, from Old French, from *relever,* to RELIEVE.]
relief map *n.* A map that depicts land configuration, as with contour lines, shading, or colours.
relief model *n.* A three-dimensional model of land configuration.
relief road *n.* A road, such as a bypass, that takes traffic away from another overcongested road or roads or a town.
re·lieve (ri-léev, rə-) *tr.v.* **-lieved, -lieving, -lieves. 1.** To lessen or alleviate (something painful, oppressive, or distressing); ease: *hypnotic suggestion may relieve pain.* **2.** To free from pain, anxiety, fear, or the like. **3. a.** To furnish assistance or aid to. **b.** To raise a siege or blockade of. **4.** To release (a person) from obligation or oppression, as by law or legislation. **5.** To free from a particular duty by providing or acting as a substitute. **6.** To make less oppressive, monotonous, or uniform: *a laugh relieved the tension.* **7.** To make distinct or effective through contrast; set off: *A black sash relieves a white gown.* **8.** *Informal.* To rob; take from: *I was relieved of my handbag.* **—relieve (oneself).** To empty one's bowels or bladder. [Middle English *releven,* from Old French *relever,* relieve, raise again, from Latin *relevāre* : *re-,* again + *levāre,* to raise.] **—re·liev·a·ble** *adj.* **—re·liev·er** *n.*
***Synonyms:** relieve, allay, alleviate, assuage, comfort, lighten, soothe, mitigate.*
re·liev·ing arch *n.* An arch built for reinforcement, or to distribute weight more evenly.

re·lie·vo (ri-léevō, rə-) n., pl. -vos. Relief in art and architecture. [Italian rilievo, from rilievare, to emphasise, raise, from Latin relevāre, to RELIEVE.]

re·lig·ion (ri-líjən, rə-) n. Abbr. rel., relig. 1. The expression of man's belief in and reverence for a superhuman power or powers regarded as creating or governing the universe. 2. Any personal or institutionalised system of beliefs or practices embodying this belief or reverence: the Hindu religion. 3. The spiritual or emotional attitude of one who recognises the existence of a superhuman power or powers. 4. Any objective pursued with zeal or conscientious devotion: A collector might make a religion of his hobby. 5. The monastic way of life. 6. Archaic. Sacred rites or practices. [Middle English religioun, from Old French religion, from Latin religiō (stem religiōn-), bond between man and the gods, perhaps from religāre, to bind back : re-, back + ligāre, to bind, fasten.]

re·lig·ion·ism (ri-líjə-niz'm, rə-) n. Excessive or affected religious zeal. —re·lig·ion·ist n.

re·li·gi·ose (ri-líji-ōss, rə-, -ōz) adj. Excessively religious, particularly in an affected or sentimental manner. [From RELIGIOUS.]

re·lig·i·os·i·ty (ri-líji-óssəti, rə-) n., pl. -ties. 1. The state of being religious. 2. Excessive or affected piety.

re·lig·ious (ri-líjəss, rə-) adj. Abbr. rel. 1. Of, pertaining to, or teaching religion. 2. Adhering to or manifesting religion; pious; godly. 3. Extremely scrupulous or conscientious. 4. Pertaining to or belonging to an order taking vows of poverty, chastity, and obedience. ~n., pl. religious. Abbr. rel. A person belonging to a religious order, especially a monk or nun. [Middle English, from Old French, from Latin religiōsus, from religiō, RELIGION.] —re·li·gious·ly adv. —re·li·gious·ness n.

Religious Society of Friends n. A Christian sect founded in about 1650 in England by George Fox; it has no ritual, formal creed, or priesthood, and rejects violence. Preceded by the. Also known as the "Society of Friends", "Quakers".

re·line (rée-lĭn) tr.v. -lined, -lining, -lines. 1. To make new lines on. 2. To put a new lining in (a garment, for example).

re·lin·quish (ri-língkwish, rə-) tr.v. -quished, -quishing, -quishes. 1. To retire from; give up; abandon. 2. To put aside or desist from (something practised, professed, or intended). 3. To surrender; renounce. 4. To let go or release (a grasp, for example). [Middle English relinquysshen, from Old French relinquir (stem relinquiss-), from Latin relinquere, to leave behind : re-, behind + linquere, to leave.] —re·lin·quish·er n. —re·lin·quish·ment n.

Synonyms: relinquish, yield, resign, abdicate, abandon, surrender, cede, waive, forgo, renounce.

rel·i·quar·y (rélli-kwəri ‖ U.S. -kwerri) n., pl. -ies. A receptacle, such as a coffer or shrine, for keeping or displaying religious relics. [French relinquaire, from Medieval Latin reliquiārium, from reliquia, singular of Late Latin reliquiae, remains. See relic.]

re·liq·ui·ae (ri-líkwi-ee, rə-) pl.n. Remains, especially of fossil organisms. [Latin.]

rel·ish (réllish) n. 1. An appetite for something; an appreciation or liking: a relish for luxury. 2. a. Pleasure; zest. b. Anything that lends pleasure or zest. 3. A spicy or savoury condiment, such as pickles or chutney. 4. The flavour of a food, especially when appetising. 5. A trace or suggestion of some pleasurable quality. ~v. relished, -ishing, -ishes. —tr. 1. To enjoy; take pleasure in. 2. To look forward to with eagerness: I don't relish the prospect of working this weekend. 3. To like the flavour of. 4. To give flavour to; spice. —intr. To have a pleasing or distinctive taste. —See Synonyms at like. [Alteration (through influence of -ISH) of obsolete reles, a taste, from Old French reles, variant of relais, something remaining, from relaissier, to leave behind, release, from Latin relaxāre, to loosen, RELAX.] —rel·ish·a·ble adj.

re·live (rée-lív) v. -lived, -living, -lives. —tr. To undergo again (an experience, for example), especially in the imagination.

re·lo·cate (rée-lō-káyt ‖ U.S. also -lṓ-kayt) v. -cated, -cating, -cates. —tr. To establish (one's home, a factory, or the like) in a new place. —intr. To become established in a new home, area, or place of business: The company relocated in the suburbs. —re·lo·ca·tion n.

re·lu·cent (ri-lóō-sənt, -léw-) adj. Literary. Reflecting light; shining. [Latin relūcēns (stem relūcent-), present participle of relūcēre, to shine back : re-, back + lūcēre, to shine.]

re·luct (ri-lúkt, rə-) intr.v. -lucted, -lucting, -lucts. Archaic. To show reluctance. [Latin reluctārī, to struggle against : re-, against + luctārī, to struggle.]

re·luc·tance (ri-lúktənss, rə-) n. Also rare re·luc·tan·cy (-tən-si). 1. The state of being reluctant; unwillingness. 2. Physics. A magnetic quantity analogous to electric resistance and equal in a closed magnetic circuit to the ratio of magnetomotive force (analogous to voltage) to magnetic flux (analogous to current).

re·luc·tant (ri-lúktənt, rə-) adj. 1. Unwilling; averse: reluctant to help. 2. Marked by unwillingness. 3. Archaic. Offering resistance; opposing. [Latin reluctāns (stem reluctant-), present participle of reluctārī, to struggle against, RELUCT.] —re·luc·tant·ly adv.

rel·uc·tiv·i·ty (rélluk-tívvəti, rée-luk-, ri-lúk-) n., pl. -ties. Physics. A measure of the resistance of a material to the establishment of a magnetic field within it, equal to the reciprocal of magnetic permeability (see). [Reluctance + conductivity.]

re·lume (ri-lóōm, -léwm) tr.v. -lumed, -luming, -lumes. Poetic. To make bright or clear again; illuminate again. [RE- + (IL)LUME.]

re·ly (ri-lĭ, rə-) intr.v. -lied, -lying, -lies. 1. To use unquestioningly for support, assistance, or the like; to have as one's main recourse; depend. Used with on or upon. 2. To trust; have confidence. Used with on or upon: rely on the children to behave. [Middle English relien, to gather, rally, from Old French relier, from Latin religāre, to bind back : re-, back + ligāre, to fasten, to tie.]

Synonyms: rely, trust, depend, bank, count.

REM[1] n. See rapid eye movement.

REM[2], rem n. See roentgen equivalent man.

rem. remittance.

re·main (ri-máyn, rə-) intr.v. -mained, -maining, -mains. 1. To continue in a specified condition, quality, or place. 2. To stay or be left over after the removal, departure, loss, or destruction of others. 3. To be left as still to be dealt with: A cure remains to be found. 4. To endure or persist: Despite therapy his fears remained. —See Synonyms at stay. [Middle English remaynen, from Old French remanoir, remaindre, from Latin remanēre, to stay behind : re-, back in place + manēre, to stay.]

re·main·der (ri-máyndər, rə-) n. 1. Something that is left over after other parts have been taken away; the rest. 2. Mathematics. a. In division, the dividend minus the product of the divisor and quotient. b. In subtraction, the difference (see). 3. Law. An estate effective and enjoyable only after the termination of another estate created at the same time. 4. A copy of a book remaining with a publisher after sales have fallen off, usually sold at a reduced price. ~adj. Remaining; leftover. ~tr.v. remaindered, -dering, -ders. To sell (books) as remainders. [Middle English remaynder, from Old French remainder, from remaindre, to REMAIN.]

Synonyms: remainder, rest, residue, residuum, residuals, balance, remnant, leavings, remains, relic.

re·mains (ri-máynz, rə-) pl.n. 1. All that is left after other parts have been taken away, used up, or destroyed. 2. A corpse. 3. The unpublished writings of a deceased author. 4. Ancient ruins or fossils. —See Synonyms at remainder.

re·make (rée-máyk) tr.v. -made (-máyd), -making, -makes. To make anew; reconstruct. ~n. (rée-mayk). 1. An instance of making anew. 2. Something made again; a new version of something: a remake of an old film.

re·mand (ri-máand, rə- ‖ -mánd) tr.v. -manded, -manding, -mands. 1. To send or order back. 2. Law. To hold on bail or send back (a defendant in criminal proceedings) to prison, to another court, or to another agency for further proceedings. —on remand. Remanded on bail or in custody. ~n. 1. The state of being remanded. 2. The act of remanding. 3. A person remanded. [Middle English remaunden, from Old French remander, from Late Latin remandāre, to send back word : Latin re-, back + mandāre, to send word.] —re·mand·ment n.

remand home n. Formerly, an institution for juvenile offenders due to appear before a court. Also called "remand centre".

rem·a·nence (rémmənənss) n. 1. Rare. The state of remaining or enduring. 2. Physics. The magnetic induction that remains in a material after removal of the magnetising field. [Middle English remanent, remaining, from Latin remanēns (stem remanent-), present participle of remanēre, to REMAIN.] —rem·a·nent adj.

re·mark (ri-márk, rə-) v. -marked, -marking, -marks. —tr. 1. To say or write briefly and casually as a comment. 2. To take notice of; observe. —intr. To make a comment or observation. Used with on or upon. —See Synonyms at see. ~n. 1. The act of noticing or observing; observation; mention: a place worthy of remark. 2. A casual or brief expression of opinion; a comment. 3. Variant of remarque. [French remarquer, RE- (intensive) + MARK.] —re·mark·er n.

re·mark·a·ble (ri-márkəb'l, rə-) adj. 1. Worthy of notice. 2. Extraordinary; striking; uncommon. —re·mark·a·ble·ness n. —re·mark·a·bly adv.

re·marque, re·mark (ri-márk, rə-) n. 1. A mark made in the margin of a plate in engraving to indicate its stage of development prior to completion. 2. A print or proof from a plate carrying such a mark. [French, from remarquer, to REMARK.]

Re·marque (rə-márk), Erich Maria (1898–1970). German-born U.S. novelist. From his experience in the trenches in World War I he drew the material for his first, and most famous, novel, All Quiet on the Western Front (1929).

re·match (rée-mach) n. Sports. A contest between opponents who have previously met each other in competition.

Rem·brandt (rém-brant, -brənt), born Rembrandt Harmenszoon van Rijn (1606–69). Dutch painter, generally regarded as the greatest master of the Dutch school. He worked in his native town of Leiden until c. 1632, thereafter chiefly in Amsterdam. Most of his early paintings were on religious and allegorical themes and display, in their mastery of light and shade, the influence of Caravaggio. In Amsterdam, he established himself as the city's leading portrait painter. Among his most famous paintings are the group portraits, The Shooting Company of Captain Frans Banning Cocq (1642; known also as The Night Watch) and The Syndics of the Cloth Guild (1662). His series of self-portraits (1629–69) records the progress of his life with great perception. —Rem·brandt·esque adj.

R.E.M.E., RE·ME (often réemi) n. Royal Electrical and Mechanical Engineers.

re·me·di·a·ble (ri-méedi-əb'l, rə-) adj. Capable of being remedied. —re·me·di·a·ble·ness n. —re·me·di·a·bly adv.

re·me·di·al (ri-méedi-əl, rə-) adj. 1. Supplying a remedy. 2. Intended to correct something, such as a physical defect. 3. Designating or pertaining to teaching methods intended to cater for backward or slow pupils: remedial classes. —re·me·di·al·ly adv.

rem·e·dy (rémmidi, rémmədi) n., pl. **-dies. 1.** Something, such as medicine or therapy, that relieves pain, cures disease, or corrects a disorder. **2.** Something that corrects any evil, fault, or error. **3.** Law. A legal means of preventing or correcting a wrong or enforcing a right. **4.** The allowance by a mint for deviation from the standard weight or quality of coins.
~tr.v. **remedied, -dying, -dies. 1.** To relieve or cure (a disease or disorder). **2.** To counteract or rectify (an error, wrong, or defect); set right. —See Synonyms at **correct.** [Middle English remedie, from Anglo-French, from Latin remedium, medicine : re-, again + medērī, to heal.] —**rem·e·di·less** adj.

re·mem·ber (ri-mémbər, rə-) v. **-bered, -bering, -bers.** —tr. **1. a.** To bring back to the mind through an act of memory. **b.** To become aware of or think of again. **2.** To recall to the mind with effort or determination. **3.** To retain in the mind; keep carefully in memory: remember a poem. **4.** To keep (someone) in mind as worthy of affection, reward, or recognition: He remembered her in his will. **5.** To reward with a gift or tip. **6.** To mention (someone, usually oneself) to another as sending greetings: Remember me to your mother. **7.** Archaic. To remind. —intr. To have or use the faculty of memory. [Middle English remembren, from Old French remembrer, from Late Latin rememorārī, to remember again : re-, again + memorārī, to remind, from Latin memor, mindful.] —**re·mem·ber·a·ble** adj. —**re·mem·ber·er** n.

re·mem·brance (ri-mémbrənss, rə-) n. **1.** The act of remembering. **2.** The state of being remembered. **3.** Something serving to celebrate or honour the memory of a person or event; a memorial. **4.** The length of time over which one's memory extends. **5.** Something remembered; a reminiscence. **6.** A memento or souvenir. **7.** Plural. Greetings. —See Synonyms at **memory.** [Middle English, from Old French, from remembrer, to REMEMBER.]

re·mem·branc·er (ri-mémbrən-sər, rə-) n. **1.** One that causes another to remember; a reminder. **2.** Capital R. **a.** An officer of the British judiciary responsible for collecting debts due to the Crown. In this sense, also called "King's (or Queen's) Remembrancer". **b.** An official who represents the City of London on ceremonial occasions, before parliamentary committees, and the like.

Remembrance Sunday n. In Britain, the Sunday nearest November 11, when those who died in both World Wars are remembered and honoured. Also called "Poppy Day", "Remembrance Day".

re·mex (rée-meks) n., pl. **remiges** (rémmi-jeez). A quill or flight feather of a bird's wing. [New Latin, from Latin rēmex (stem rēmig-), oarsman : rēmus, oar + agere, to drive.] —**re·mig·i·al** (ri-míji-əl, rə-) adj.

re·mind (ri-mínd, rə-) tr.v. **-minded, -minding, -minds.** To cause (someone) to remember or think of. Used with of, an infinitive, or a clause: The song reminded me of summer; Remind me to give you the address. —**re·mind·er** n.

Rem·ing·ton (rémmington), **Eliphalet** (1793–1861). U.S. arms manufacturer. In 1816 he began making flintlock rifles and in 1847 he manufactured the U.S. navy's first breech-loading rifle, the Jenks carbine. His Remington Arms Company became a major arms supplier to the U.S. government, and, under his son Philo (1816–89), a major manufacturer of sewing machines and typewriters.

rem·i·nisce (rémmi-níss) intr.v. **-nisced, -niscing, -nisces.** To recollect and tell of past experiences or events. [Back-formation from REMINISCENT.]

rem·i·nis·cence (rémmi-níss'nss) n. **1.** The act or process of recalling the past. **2.** A thing remembered; a memory. **3.** Often plural. A narration or account of past experiences. **4.** An event that brings to mind a similar, former event. —See Synonyms at **memory.** [Late Latin reminiscentia. See reminiscent.]

rem·i·nis·cent (rémmi-níss'nt) adj. **1.** Having the quality of or containing reminiscence or reminiscences. **2.** Tending to recall or suggest: an evening reminiscent of happier times. [Late Latin reminiscens (stem reminiscent-), present participle of reminiscī, to recollect : RE- + min-, from mēns (stem ment-), mind.] —**rem·i·nis·cent·ly** adv.

re·mise[1] (ri-míz, rə-) tr.v. **-mised, -mising, -mises.** Law. To relinquish a claim to; surrender by deed. [Middle English, from Old French, from the feminine past participle of remettre, to remit, from Latin remittere, to REMIT.]

re·mise[2] (rə-méez, ri-) n. In fencing, a second thrust made after the first has failed.
~intr.v. **remised, -mising, -mises.** To make a remise. [French, from past participle of remettre, to put back. See remit.]

re·miss (ri-míss, rə-) adj. **1.** Lax in attending to duty; negligent. **2.** Inclined to idleness; slack. [Middle English, from Latin remissus, slack, past participle of remittere, to REMIT.] —**re·miss·ness** n.

re·mis·si·ble (ri-míssə-b'l, rə-) adj. Capable of being remitted or forgiven. —**re·mis·si·bil·i·ty** (-bílləti) n.

re·mis·sion (ri-mísh'n, rə-) n. **1. a.** The act of remitting. **b.** The condition of being remitted. **2. a.** Release, as from a debt, penalty, or obligation. **b.** Forgiveness; pardon. **3.** A lessening of intensity or degree; an abatement; especially, a temporary abatement of the symptoms of a disease. **4.** A reduction in a prison sentence, for good behaviour.

re·mit (ri-mít, rə-) v. **-mitted, -mitting, -mits.** —tr. **1.** To send (money), as by post. **2. a.** To cancel (a penalty or punishment). **b.** To pardon; forgive. **3.** To restore to an original condition; put back. **4. a.** Law. To refer (a case) back to a lower court for further consideration. **b.** To refer (a matter) back for further consideration to a committee, authority, or the like. **5.** To relax; slacken. **6.** To

defer; postpone. —intr. **1.** To send money. **2.** To diminish; abate.
~n. (rée'mit). **1.** A case remitted to a lower court. **2. a.** A matter for further consideration by a committee or authority. **b.** An area of study or enquiry for a committee or authority. **3.** British. Brief; authority: go beyond one's remit. [Middle English remitten, from Latin remittere, to send back, release : re-, back + mittere, to send.] —**re·mit·ta·ble** (ri-míttəb'l, rə-) adj.

re·mit·tal (ri-mítt'l, rə-) n. Remission.

re·mit·tance (ri-mítt'nss, rə-) n. Abbr. **rem. 1.** Money or credit sent to someone. **2.** The act of sending money or credit.

remittance man n. A person living abroad on funds sent from home, especially in former times.

re·mit·tent (ri-mítt'nt, rə-) adj. Characterised by temporary abatements in severity. Said especially of diseases.
~n. A remittent fever. —**re·mit·tence, re·mit·ten·cy** n. —**re·mit·tent·ly** adv.

re·mit·ter (ri-míttər, rə-). Also **re·mit·tor** (for sense 3). **1.** Law. The principle or act by which an individual holds property by a valid title dated prior to a defective title under which he at first held ownership. **2.** Law. The act of transferring a case for decision to another court, generally a lower one. **3.** One that remits.

rem·nant (rémnənt) n. **1.** Something left over; a remainder. **2.** A leftover piece of fabric remaining after the rest has been used or sold. **3.** A surviving trace or vestige, as of a former condition. **4.** Often plural. A small, remaining group of people. —See Synonyms at **remainder.**
~adj. Remaining; leftover. [Middle English remenant, from Old French, present participle of remanoir, remaindre, to REMAIN.]

re·mod·el (rée-módd'l) tr.v. **-elled** or U.S. **-eled, -elling** or U.S. **-eling, -els. 1.** To model again. **2.** To remake with a new structure or in a new style; reconstruct; renovate. —**re·mod·el·ler** n.

re·mon·e·tise, re·mon·e·tize (rée-múnni-tīz ‖ -mónni-) tr.v. **-tised, -tising, -tises.** To restore (silver, for example) to use as legal tender. —**re·mon·e·ti·sa·tion** (-tī-záysh'n ‖ U.S. -ti-) n.

re·mon·strance (ri-mónstrənss, rə-) n. **1.** The act of remonstrating. **2.** A speech or gesture of protest, opposition, or reproof; especially, a formal statement of public grievances.

re·mon·strant (ri-mónstrənt, rə-) adj. Characterised by remonstrance; expostulatory.
~n. **1.** One who remonstrates or signs a remonstrance. **2.** Capital R. **a.** Any of the Dutch Arminians who, in 1610, formally stated the grounds of their dissent from strict Calvinism. **b.** A member of the Protestant denomination founded by these dissenters.

re·mon·strate (rémmən-strayt, ri-món-, rə-) v. **-strated, -strating, -strates.** —tr. To say or plead in protest, objection, or reproof. —intr. To make objections; argue or plead against some action: remonstrate with one's superiors. —See Synonyms at **object.** [Medieval Latin remōnstrāre, to demonstrate : Latin re-, completely + monstrāre, to show, from monstrum, an omen, a portent, from monēre, to warn.] —**re·mon·stra·tion** (-stráysh'n) n. —**re·mon·stra·tive** (ri-mónstrətiv ‖ rémmən-straytiv) adj. —**re·mon·stra·tor** n.

re·mon·tant (ri-móntənt, rə-) adj. Blooming more than once during a season, as certain roses do.
~n. A remontant rose. [French, "rising again", from the present participle of remonter, to rise again, REMOUNT.]

rem·o·ra (rémmərə, ri-máw-rə ‖ -mō-) n. Any of several marine fishes of the family Echeneidae, having on the head a sucking disc with which they attach themselves to larger animals, ships, or other moving objects. Also called "suckerfish", "shark sucker". [Latin, "delay" (they were believed to be able to delay ships by sticking to them) : re-, back + mora, a delay.]

re·morse (ri-mórss, rə-) n. **1.** Moral anguish arising from repentance for past misdeeds; bitter regret. **2.** Obsolete. Compassion. [Middle English, from Old French remors, from Medieval Latin remorsus, from Latin, a biting back, from the past participle of remordēre, to bite again : re-, again + mordēre, to bite.] —**re·morse·ful** adj. —**re·morse·ful·ly** adv. —**re·morse·ful·ness** n.

re·morse·less (ri-mórss-ləss, rə-, -liss) adj. **1.** Having no pity or compassion; merciless. **2.** Relentless, very persistent. —**re·morse·less·ly** adv. —**re·morse·less·ness** n.

re·mote (ri-mōt, rə-) adj. **-moter, -motest. 1. a.** Located far away; relatively distant in space: Our hotel was remote from the city centre. **b.** Outlying; isolated; out-of-the-way: a remote hamlet. **2.** Distant in time: the remote past. **3. a.** Very slight or faint: hadn't the remotest interest in what I was saying. **b.** Having only a vague connection: a cause very remote from everyday concerns. **4.** Being distantly related by blood or marriage: a remote descendant. **5.** Distant in manner; aloof. **6.** Of, pertaining to, or designating computing devices or systems situated at some distance from the central computer that communicate with it usually by means of cables. —See Synonyms at **distant.** [Latin remōtus, past participle of removēre, to move back or away : re-, back, away + movēre, to move.] —**re·mote·ly** adv. —**re·mote·ness** n.

remote control n. The direction of an activity, process, or machine from a distant point, as by radioed instructions or coded signals.

ré·mou·lade (rémmə-láyd, rémmōō-, -la'ad) n. A piquant cold sauce for cold poultry, meat, and shellfish, made of mayonnaise with chopped pickles, capers, anchovies, and herbs. [French rémoulade, variant of Picard dialect ramolas, horseradish, variant of Latin armoracea, of Italic origin.]

re·mould (rée-mōld) tr.v. **-moulded, -moulding, -moulds.** To mould again; especially, to mould new rubber walls and tread on (a tyre).
~n. (rée'mōld). Anything remoulded; especially, a remoulded tyre.

re·mount (rée-mównt) *tr.v.* **-mounted, -mounting, -mounts. 1.** To mount again. **2.** To supply with fresh horses.
~n. (*also* rée-mownt). A fresh horse. [Middle English *remounten,* from Old French *remonter* : *re-,* again + *monter, munter,* to MOUNT.]
re·mov·a·ble (ri-mŏŏvə-b'l, rə-) *adj.* That can be removed. **—re·mov·a·bil·i·ty** (-bílləti), **re·mov·a·ble·ness** *n.* **—re·mov·a·bly** *adv.*
re·mov·al (ri-mŏŏv'l, rə-) *n.* **1. a.** The act of removing. **b.** The fact of being removed. **2.** Relocation, as of a home or business. Also used adjectivally: *a removal van.* **3.** Dismissal, as from office.
re·mov·a·list (rə-mŏŏv'l-ist) *n. Australian.* A person or business engaged in moving household or office furniture to a new location.
re·move (ri-mŏŏv, rə-) *v.* **-moved, -moving, -moves.** *—tr.* **1.** To move from a position occupied: *remove the dishes from the table.* **2.** To convey from one place to another: *removed the family to safety.* **3.** To take from one's person; doff: *remove one's hat.* **4.** To do away with; eliminate: *remove stains; removed his anxieties.* **5.** To dismiss from office. *—intr.* **1.** To change one's place of residence or business; move. **2.** *Poetic.* To depart; go away.
~n. **1.** The act of removing; a removal. **2.** The distance or degree of space, time, or status that separates persons or things: *at one remove from poverty.* **3.** *British.* An intermediate class or form in certain schools, especially private schools. **4.** A dish that succeeds another at a meal. [Middle English *removen,* from Old French *removoir,* from Latin *removēre,* to move back : *re-,* back + *movēre,* to move.] **—re·mov·er** *n.*
re·moved (ri-mŏŏvd, rə-) *adj.* **1.** Distant in space, time, or nature; remote. **2.** Separated in relationship by a specified degree of descent: *My first cousin's child is my first cousin once removed.* **3.** *Archaic.* Succeeded by another dish at a meal: *fish removed by beef.* —See Synonyms at **distant. —re·mov·ed·ly** (-mŏŏvidli) *adj.* **—re·mov·ed·ness** *n.*
re·mu·ner·ate (ri-méwnə-rayt, rə-) *tr.v.* **-ated, -ating, -ates. 1.** To pay (a person) for goods provided, services rendered, or losses incurred. **2.** To compensate for; make up for: *remunerate his efforts.* [Latin *remūnerāre* : *re-,* intensive + *mūnerāre,* to give, from *mūnus,* a gift.] **—re·mu·ner·a·bil·i·ty** (-rə-bílləti) *n.* **—re·mu·ner·a·ble** *adj.* **—re·mu·ner·a·tor** *n.*
re·mu·ner·a·tion (ri-méwnə-ráysh'n, rə-) *n.* **1.** An act of remunerating. **2.** That which remunerates; recompense; payment.
re·mu·ner·a·tive (ri-méwnə-rətiv, rə- || -raytiv) *adj.* **1.** Likely to be well remunerated; profitable. **2.** Serving to remunerate. **—re·mu·ner·a·tive·ly** *adv.* **—re·mu·ner·a·tive·ness** *n.*
Re·mus (réeməss). *Roman Mythology.* The twin brother of **Romulus** *(see).*
ren·ais·sance (ri-náyss'nss, rə-, rén-ay-SONSS, -e-, -SÓNSS || *U.S. also* -ZÓNSS) *n.* **1.** A rebirth; a revival. **2.** *Capital* **R. a.** The humanistic revival of classical art, literature, and learning that originated in Italy in the 14th century and later spread throughout Europe. **b.** The period of this revival (roughly 14th–16th century). **3.** *Sometimes capital* **R.** Any similar period of revived intellectual or artistic achievement or enthusiasm: *the Celtic Renaissance.*
~adj. Capital **R. 1.** Of, pertaining to, or characteristic of the Renaissance or its artistic and intellectual works and styles. **2.** Of or designating the style of architecture and decoration prevalent during the Renaissance. [French, a rebirth, from Old French, from *renaistre* (present stem *renais-*), to be born again, from Latin *renascī* : *re-,* again + *nascī,* to be born.]
Renaissance man or **woman** *n.* A man or woman whose intellectual interests and achievements are wide-ranging; especially, one whose talents encompass both the arts and the sciences.
re·nal (réen'l) *adj.* Of, pertaining to, resembling, or in the region of the kidneys. [French *rénal,* from Late Latin *rēnālis,* from Latin *rēnēs*†, kidneys.]
renal pelvis *n.* A small funnel-shaped cavity in the kidney in which urine collects before being discharged into the ureter. Also called "pelvis".
re·nas·cence (ri-náss'nss, rə-, -náyss'nss) *n.* **1.** A new birth or life; a rebirth. **2.** A cultural revival; a renaissance.
re·nas·cent (ri-náss'nt, rə, -náyss'nt) *adj.* Coming into being again; showing renewed growth or vigour. [Latin *renascēns* (stem *renascent-*), present participle of *renascī,* to be born again. See **renaissance.**]
ren·coun·ter (ren-kówntər) *n. Archaic.* **1.** An unplanned meeting. **2.** A sudden encounter with an enemy.
~v. **rencountered, -tering, -ters.** *Archaic. —tr.* To meet unexpectedly. *—intr.* To have an unexpected meeting. [French *rencontre,* from *rencontrer,* to have a (hostile) meeting : *re-,* again, against + *encontrer,* to ENCOUNTER.]
rend (rend) *v.* **rent** (rent) **rending, rends.** *—tr.* **1. a.** To tear or pull; wrench. **b.** To rip apart or into pieces; split. **2.** To remove forcibly; wrest. **3.** To penetrate and disturb as if by tearing: *Screams rent the silence.* **4.** To cause pain or distress to (the heart, for example). *—intr.* To burst; come apart. —See Synonyms at **tear.** [Middle English *renden,* Old English *rendan.*] **—rend·er** *n.*
ren·der (réndər) *tr.v.* **-dered, -dering, -ders. 1.** To submit or present for consideration, payment, or approval: *render a bill.* **2.** To give or make available: *render assistance.* **3.** To give what is due or proper: *asked much and rendered little.* **4.** To give in return or retribution: *render an apology for his rudeness.* **5.** To surrender or relinquish; yield. **6.** To represent in, as in painting, writing, or music; depict in artistic form: *This poem renders precisely the pains of love.* **7.** To perform an interpretation of (a musical piece, for example). **8.** To express in another language or form; translate. **9.** To pronounce formally; hand down (a verdict, for example). **10.** To cause to become; make: *"This study renders men acute, inquisitive"* (Edmund Burke). **11.** To reduce, convert, or melt down (fat) by heating. **12.** To coat (brick, for example) with plaster or cement.
~n. A payment in kind, services, or cash from a tenant to a feudal lord. [Middle English *rendren,* to give in return, relinquish, from Old French *rendre,* to give back, from Vulgar Latin *rendere* (unattested), variant of Latin *reddere* : *re-,* back + *dare,* to give.] **—ren·der·a·ble** *adj.* **—ren·der·er** *n.*
ren·der·ing (réndəring) *n.* A coat of plaster, cement, or the like covering a surface.
ren·dez·vous (rón-di-vōō, RÓN-, -day-) *n., pl.* **-vous** (-vōōz). **1. a.** An arrangement or appointment to meet. **b.** A prearranged meeting place; especially, an assembly point for troops, ships, or spacecraft. **2.** The meeting itself. **3.** A popular gathering place.
~v. **rendezvoused** (-vōōd), **-vousing** (-vōō-ing), **-vous** (-vōōz). *—tr.* To bring together (persons or military units) at a prearranged time and place. *—intr.* To meet together at a prearranged time and place. [Old French, from *rendez vous,* "present yourselves" : *rendez,* imperative of *rendre,* to RENDER + *vous,* you.]
ren·di·tion (ren-dísh'n) *n.* **1.** The act of rendering. **2.** An interpretation of a musical score or dramatic piece. **3.** A performance of a musical or dramatic work. **4.** A translation, often interpretive. [Obsolete French, from Old French *rendre,* to give back, RENDER.]
ren·dzi·na (ren-dzéenə, -jéenə) *n.* A dark soil which develops under grass on limestone and chalk. [Russian, from Polish *redzina.*]
ren·e·gade (rénni-gayd) *n.* **1.** One who rejects a religion, cause, allegiance, or group for another; a deserter. **2.** An outlaw; a rebel.
~adj. Of or like a renegade; treacherous. [Spanish *renegado,* from Medieval Latin *renegātus,* one who denies, from the past participle of *renegāre,* to deny : Latin *re-,* intensive + *negāre,* to deny.]
re·nege, re·negue (ri-néeg, rə-, -nayg, -neg) *v.* **-neged** or **-negued, -neging** or **-neguing, -neges** or **-negues.** *—intr.* **1.** To fail to carry out a promise or commitment: *renege on a contract.* **2.** In card games, to fail to follow suit when able and required by the rules to do so. *—tr. Obsolete.* To renounce; disown.
~n. The act of reneging in card games. [Medieval Latin *renegāre,* to deny. See **renegade.**] **—re·neg·er** *n.*
re·ne·go·ti·ate (réeni-gōshi-ayt) *tr.v.* **-ated, -ating, -ates.** To negotiate anew; especially, to revise the terms of (a contract) so as to limit or get back excess profits gained by the contractor. **—re·ne·go·ti·a·ble** *adj.* **—re·ne·go·ti·a·tion** (-áysh'n) *n.*
re·new (ri-néw, rə- || -nōō) *v.* **-newed, -newing, -news.** *—tr.* **1.** To make new or as if new again; restore. **2.** To take up again; resume. **3.** To repeat so as to reaffirm: *renewed her promise of support.* **4.** To regain (spiritual or physical vigour); revive. **5. a.** To arrange for the extension of: *renew a contract.* **b.** To extend the period of loan of: *renew a library book.* **6.** To replenish. **7.** To bring into being again; re-establish. *—intr.* **1.** To become new again. **2.** To start again. **3.** To renew a contract, lease, or other agreement.
re·new·a·ble (ri-néw-ə-b'l, rə- || -nōō-) *adj.* **1.** Able to be renewed. **2.** Designating an energy source, such as the sun or wave power, that may be considered for practical purposes as inexhaustible. **—re·new·a·bil·ity** (-bílləti) *n.*
re·new·al (ri-néw-əl, rə- || -nōō-) *n.* **1. a.** The act or an instance of renewing. **b.** The state of being renewed. **2.** Something renewed.
re·new·ed·ly (ri-néw-idli, rə- || -nōō-) *adv.* Over again; anew.
Ren·frew (rén-frōō). Royal burgh on the river Clyde in western Scotland. It is mainly an industrial centre and it is the site of Glasgow airport.
Ren·frew·shire (rén-frōō-shər, -sheer, -shír). County of west central Scotland. In 1975 it became part of Strathclyde Region; in 1996 a Unitary Authority area.
Re·ni (rénni), **Guido** (1575–1642). Italian painter and engraver, forerunner of late 17th-century Roman classicism. He worked in Rome and his native Bologna. His best-known works are the *Crucifixion of St. Peter* (1605) and the *Aurora* fresco (1613–14).
reni–, reno– *comb. form.* Indicates kidney or kidneys; for example, **reniform** [Latin *rēnēs,* kidneys.]
ren·i·form (rénni-fawrm, réeni-) *adj.* Shaped like a kidney: *a reniform leaf.* [RENI- + -FORM.]
ren·in (réenin || rénnin) *n.* A protein-digesting enzyme, released by the kidneys in response to stress, which acts to raise blood pressure. [RENI- + -IN.]
re·ni·tent (ri-nīt'nt, rə-, rénni-) *adj. Rare.* **1.** Resisting pressure; not pliant. **2.** Reluctant to yield or be swayed; recalcitrant. [Latin *renītens* (stem *renītent-*), present participle of *renītī,* to struggle against, resist : *re-,* back, against + *nītī,* to press forward, push.] **—ren·i·tence, ren·i·ten·cy** *n.*
Ren·ner (rénnər), **Karl** (1870–1950). Austrian politician, president of the Austrian republic (1945–50). After the abdication of the Emperor Charles I (1918), he became the first chancellor (1919–20) of the Austrian republic. In 1945 he became prime minister, foreign minister, and later president of the liberated republic.
Rennes (ren). Capital of the Ille-et-Vilaine département, northwest France. It is a railway junction and agricultural market centre.
ren·net (rénnit) *n.* **1.** The inner lining of the fourth stomach of calves and other young mammals. **2.** A dried extract of this lining especially from young calves, used to curdle milk. [Middle English *rennet,* Old English *rynet* (unattested).]
ren·nin (rénnin) *n.* A milk-coagulating enzyme produced by the stomach. It is an active constituent of rennet and is used in making cheeses and junkets. Also called "chymosin". [RENN(ET) + -IN.]

Re·no (réenō). City in western Nevada, United States, lying on the river Truckee. Tourism is the major industry and the city is noted for the ease with which a divorce may by obtained owing to the state's short-term residence requirements.

Re·noir (rə-nwáar), **Jean** (1894–1979). French film director. The son of the painter Auguste Renoir, he made artistic films like *La Grande Illusion* (1937), *La Bête humaine* (1938), and *La Règle du jeu* (1939). In Hollywood after 1941, he made *The Southerner* (1945) and others.

Renoir, (Pierre) Auguste (1841–1919). French impressionist painter. In the 1870s he began to exhibit at the Impressionist salons. He developed the so-called "rainbow palette", from which black was eliminated. Among his best-known paintings are *Le Moulin de la Galette* (1876) and *Les Parapluies* (1883). In the mid-1880s he developed a more classical manner, as in *Le Jugement de Paris* (*c.* 1914).

re·nounce (ri-nównss, rə-) *v.* **-nounced, -nouncing, -nounces.** —*tr.* **1.** To give up (a title or activity, for example), especially by formal announcement. **2.** To reject; disown. —*intr.* **1.** In card games, to fail to follow suit because one does not hold a card of the required suit. **2.** *Law.* To give up a right. —See Synonyms at **relinquish.**
~*n.* In card games: **1.** An act of renouncing. **2.** An opportunity to renounce. [Middle English *renouncen,* from Old French *renoncer,* from Latin *renūntiāre,* to bring back word, protest against, report : *re-*, back, against + *nūntiāre,* inform, from *nūntium,* message.] —**re·nounce·ment** *n.* —**re·nounc·er** *n.*

ren·o·vate (rén-ə-vayt, -ō-) *tr.v.* **-vated, -vating, -vates. 1.** To restore to an earlier, good condition; improve by repairing or remodelling. **2.** To impart new vigour to; revive. [Latin *renovāre* : *re-*, again + *novāre,* to make new, from *novus,* new.] —**ren·o·va·tion** (-váysh'n) *n.* —**ren·o·va·tor** (-vaytər) *n.*

re·nown (ri-nówn, rə-) *n.* **1.** The quality of being honoured and acclaimed; celebrity. **2.** *Archaic.* Report; rumour. —See Synonyms at **fame.** [Middle English *renoun(e),* from Old French *renon, renom,* from *renomer,* to name again, make famous : *re-*, again, from Latin + *nomer,* to name, from Latin *nōmināre,* from *nōmen,* a name.]

re·nowned (ri-nównd, rə-) *adj.* Having renown; famous.

rent[1] (rent) *n.* **1. a.** Payment, usually of an amount fixed by contract, made by one person or agency at stated regular intervals in return for the right to occupy or use the land or property of another. **b.** A similar payment made for the use of a facility or service provided by another, such as a telephone. **2.** *Economics.* **a.** The return derived from cultivated or improved land after deduction of all production costs. **b.** The revenue yielded by a piece of land in excess of that yielded by the poorest or least favourably located land, under equal market conditions.
~*v.* **rented, renting, rents.** —*tr.* **1.** To obtain occupancy or use of (another's property, or a facility or service provided by another) in return for regular payments. **2.** To grant temporary occupancy or use of (one's own property or a service) in return for regular payments. Often used with *out.* —*intr.* To be rented or be available for renting: *The cottage rents at £200 a week.* [Middle English *rente,* income from property, from Old French, from Vulgar Latin *rendita* (unattested), from the feminine past participle of *rendere* (unattested), to RENDER.] —**rent·a·ble** *adj.*

rent[2]. Past tense and past participle of **rend.**
~*n.* **1.** An opening made by or as if by rending; a rip or gap. **2.** A breach of relations between people or groups; a rift.

rent-a- *comb. form.* Indicates: **1.** For hire; for example, **rent-a-car. 2.** *Informal.* Hired, paid, or induced to act as the thing or persons specified; for example, **rent-a-crowd, rent-a-mob.** In this sense, used derogatorily or humorously.

rent·al (rént'l) *n.* **1.** An amount charged as rent. **2.** A list of tenants and rents. **3.** *Chiefly U.S.* Property available for renting. **4.** The act of renting.
~*adj.* Of, concerning, or available for rent.

rent boy *n.* A boy who is a male prostitute. [Perhaps from the notion that such boys are "for rent".]

rente (ʀᴏɴᴛ) *n., pl.* **rentes** *(pronounced as singular). French.* **1.** Annual income, especially from government bonds; annuity. **2. a.** *Usually plural.* The government bonds of various European countries, especially of France. **b.** The interest paid on these bonds.

rent·er (réntər) *n.* **1.** One who receives payment in exchange for the use of his property by another. **2.** One who pays rent for the use of another's property; a tenant. **3.** *British.* One who distributes films, in return for payment, to commercial cinemas.

rent-free (rént-frée) *adj.* Not subject to rent.
~*adv.* Without having to pay, or without paying, rent.

ren·ti·er (rónti-ay, *French* ʀᴏɴᴛ-yáy) *n. French.* One who derives an unearned income from rents or investments.

rent-roll (rént-rōl) *n.* **1.** A list of property owned by an individual, together with the rent due and received from it. **2.** The income accruing to an individual from such property.

rent strike *n.* A collective refusal, for example by all the tenants in one building or area, to pay rent, usually as a form of protest or in order to bring rents down.

re·num·ber (rée-númbər) *tr.v.* **-bered, -bering, -bers.** To number again or in a different order.

re·nun·ci·a·tion (ri-nún-si-áysh'n, rə-) *n.* **1.** The act or an instance of renouncing: *the renunciation of pleasures.* **2.** A declaration in which something is renounced. [Middle English, from Latin *renūntiātiō* (stem *renūntiātiōn-*) from *renūnitiāre,* to RENOUNCE.] —**re·nun·ci·a·tive** (-ətiv || -aytiv), **re·nun·ci·a·to·ry** (-ə-təri, -tri) *adj.*

re·o·pen (rée-ṓpən, ri-) *v.* **-pened, -pening, -pens.** —*tr.* To open or take up again. —*intr.* To start again; resume.

re·or·der (rée-áwrdər, ri-) *v.* **-dered, -dering, -ders.** —*tr.* **1.** To order again. **2.** To straighten out or put in order again. **3.** To rearrange. —*intr.* To order the same goods again.
~*n.* A further order of goods previously supplied.

re·or·gan·i·sa·tion (rée-áwrgə-nī-záysh'n, ri- || *U.S.* -ni-) *n.* **1.** The act or process of organising again or differently. **2.** *Finance.* A thorough alteration of the structure of a business enterprise, especially after a bankruptcy. In this sense, also called "reconstruction".

re·or·gan·ise, re·or·gan·ize (rée-áwrgə-nīz, ri-) *v.* **-ised, -ising, -ises.** —*tr.* To organise again or anew. —*intr.* To undergo or effect changes in organisation. —**re·or·gan·is·er** *n.*

re·or·i·ent·ate (rée-áwri-en-tayt, -órri-, -ən- || -ṓri-) *tr.v.* **-ated, -ating, -ates. 1.** To change the direction of; give a new orientation to. **2.** To change the general views or way of thinking of. —**re·or·ien·ta·tion** (-táysh'n) *n.*

re·o·vi·rus (rée-ō-vīr-əss) *n.* Any of a group of spherical, RNA-containing viruses that are widely distributed in humans. They are found in the respiratory and digestive tracts but do not appear to cause disease. [*R*espiratory *e*nteric *o*rphan *virus.*]

rep[1], **repp** (rep) *n.* A ribbed or corded fabric of various materials, such as cotton, wool, or silk. [French *reps*†.]

rep[2] *n. Informal.* A representative; a travelling salesman.

rep[3] *n. Physics.* A unit of absorbed radiation dose, equal to the absorbed dose in water that has been exposed to one roentgen. The rep has been largely replaced by the **rad** *(see).* [*R*oentgen + *e*quivalent + *p*hysical.]

rep[4] *n. Informal.* **1.** A **repertory company** *(see).* **2. Repertory** *(see).*

Rep. 1. *U.S.* representative. **2.** republic. **3.** *U.S.* Republican (Party).

re·pack·age (rée-páckij) *tr.v.* **-aged, -aging, -ages.** To package again or anew; especially, to put in a new kind of package.

re·pair[1] (ri-páir, rə-) *tr.v.* **-paired, -pairing, -pairs. 1.** To restore to sound condition after damage or injury; mend. **2.** To set right; remedy: *repair an oversight.* **3.** To renew or revitalise. **4.** To make up for or compensate for (a loss or wrong, for example).
~*n. Abbr.* **rep. 1.** The work, act, or process of repairing: *beyond repair.* **2.** General condition after use or maintenance: *in good repair.* **3. a.** An instance of repairing. **b.** Something that has been repaired. [Middle English *repairen,* from Old French *reparer,* from Latin *reparāre* : *re-*, back (to an earlier state) + *parāre,* to put in order, prepare.] —**re·pair·a·ble** *adj.* —**re·pair·er** *n.*

repair[2] *intr.v.* **-paired, -pairing, -pairs.** *Formal.* **1.** To betake oneself; go: *We all repaired to the restaurant.* **2.** To resort; go for help.
~*n. Archaic.* **1.** An act of going or sojourning. **2.** A place to which one goes frequently or habitually; a haunt. [Middle English *reparen,* to return, from Old French *repairer,* from Late Latin *repatriāre,* to REPATRIATE.]

re·pair·man (ri-páir-mən, rə-) *n., pl.* **-men** (-mən, -men). A man whose occupation is making repairs: *a bicycle repairman.*

re·pand (ri-pánd, rə-) *adj. Botany.* Having a wavy margin: *a repand leaf.* [Latin *repandus,* bent back : *re-*, back, backwards + *pandus,* bent, turned, past participle of *pandere,* to spread.]

rep·a·ra·ble (répprə-b'l, réppərə-b'l) *adj.* Also **re·pair·a·ble** (re-páirəb'l, rə-). Able to be repaired or made good. —**rep·a·ra·bil·i·ty** (-bílləti) *n.* —**rep·a·ra·bly** *adv.*

rep·a·ra·tion (réppə-ráysh'n) *n.* **1. a.** The act or process of repairing. **b.** The condition of being repaired. **2.** The act or process of making amends; expiation. **3.** Something done or paid to make amends; compensation. **4.** *Plural.* Compensation or remuneration required of a defeated nation for damage or injury during a war. [Middle English *reparacioun,* from Old French *reparation,* from Late Latin *reparātiō* (stem *reparatiōn-*), from Latin *reparāre,* to REPAIR.]
Synonyms: *reparation, redress, amends, restitution, indemnity.*

re·par·a·tive (ri-párrətiv, rə-) *adj.* Also **re·par·a·to·ry** (ri-párrə-təri, rə-, -tri). **1.** Tending to repair. **2.** Of, pertaining to, or of the nature of reparations.

rep·ar·tee (rép-aar-tée || -ər-, *U.S. also* -táy) *n.* **1.** A swift, witty reply; a ready or spirited retort. **2.** Witty and spirited conversation characterised by such replies. **3.** Skill in making such replies or conversation. —See Synonyms at **wit.** [French *repartie,* from *repartir,* to reply readily, from Old French, to depart again : *re-*, again + *partir,* to part, from Latin *partīre,* from *pars,* a part.]

re·par·ti·tion (réepaar-tísh'n) *n.* **1.** Distribution; apportionment. **2.** A partitioning again or in a different way.
~*tr.v.* **repartitioned, -tioning, -tions.** To partition again; redivide.

re·past (ri-páast, rə- || -pást) *n.* **1.** *Formal.* A meal, or the food eaten or provided at a meal. **2.** *Obsolete.* Food; nourishment. [Middle English, from Old French, from *repaistre,* to feed, from Late Latin *repascere,* to feed again : Latin *re-*, again + *pascere,* to feed.]

re·pa·tri·ate (rée-páttri-ayt, ri- || *chiefly U.S.* -páytri-) *tr.v.* **-ated, -ating, -ates.** To return to the country of birth, citizenship, or ownership: *repatriate war refugees; repatriate the stolen statue.*
~*n.* (-ət, -it, -ayt). Someone who has been repatriated. [Late Latin *repatriāre* : Latin *re-*, back + *patria,* native country.] —**re·pa·tri·a·tion** (-áysh'n) *n.*

re·pay (ri-páy, rée-) *v.* **-paid** (-páyd), **-paying, -pays.** —*tr.* **1.** To pay back (money); refund. **2.** To pay (someone) back, either in return or in compensation. **3.** To make compensation for; make a return for. **4.** To make or do in return: *repay a call.* —*intr.* To make repayment or recompense. —**re·pay·a·ble** *adj.* —**re·pay·ment** *n.*

re·peal (ri-péel, rə-) *tr.v.* **-pealed, -pealing, -peals.** To revoke or rescind; withdraw or annul officially or formally: *Parliament re-*

pealed the law. —See Synonyms at **nullify.**
~*n.* The act or process of repealing. [Middle English *repelen,* from Anglo-French *repeler,* from Old French *rapeler* : *re-,* back, contrary + *apeler,* to APPEAL.] —**re·peal·a·ble** *adj.* —**re·peal·er** *n.*

re·peat (ri-pe͞et, rə-) *v.* **-peated, -peating, -peats.** —*tr.* **1.** To utter or state again. **2.** To utter in duplication of another's utterance. **3.** To recite from memory. **4.** To pass on (something told in confidence) to another. **5.** To do, experience, or produce again. **6.** To manifest or express (oneself) in the same way or words: *History repeats itself.* —*intr.* **1.** To do or say something again. **2.** To occur more than once; recur. **3.** To strike the hour, half-hour, or quarter-hour, when a spring is pressed. Used of a watch or clock. **4.** To fire, or be capable of firing, several shots without being reloaded. Used of a gun. **5.** *Informal.* To be tasted again, often as a result of belching, after having been swallowed. Used of food: *Onions repeat on me.*
~*n.* **1.** The act of repeating. Also used adjectivally: *a repeat performance.* **2.** Something repeated; especially, a television or radio programme that has been broadcast before. **3.** *Music.* **a.** A passage or section that is repeated. **b.** A sign usually consisting of a vertical pair of dots, indicating a passage to be repeated. **4. a.** A repeated or duplicate order for goods. **b.** The goods so ordered. [Middle English *repeten,* from Old French *repeter,* from Latin *repetere,* to go back to, seek again : *re-,* again + *petere,* to go to, seek.]

re·peat·ed (ri-pe͞etid, rə-) *adj.* Said, done, or occurring again and again. —**re·peat·ed·ly** *adv.*

re·peat·er (ri-pe͞etər, rə-) *n.* **1.** Someone or something that repeats. **2.** A watch or clock with a pressure-activated mechanism that strikes the hour and, often the half-hour and quarter-hour. **3.** A firearm capable of firing repeatedly without reloading. **4.** An electrical circuit in a transmission line for amplifying and retransmitting signals, to compensate for power losses.

repeating decimal *n.* A decimal in which, after a certain digit, a pattern of one or more digits is repeated indefinitely, as in 1.5461616161. . . . Also called "circulating decimal", "recurring decimal".

re·pel (ri-pél, rə-) *v.* **-pelled, -pelling, -pels.** —*tr.* **1.** To drive back; ward off or keep away: *repel insects.* **2.** To offer successful resistance to; fight off: *repel an invasion.* **3.** To refuse to accept; reject: *repel an offer.* **4.** To turn away from; spurn. **5.** To cause aversion or distaste in: *His rudeness repels everyone.* **6.** To be resistant to; be incapable of absorbing or mixing with. **7.** To present an opposing force to; push back or away by a force: *Electric charges of the same sign repel each other.* —*intr.* **1.** To offer a resistant force to something. **2.** To cause aversion or distaste. [Middle English *repellen,* from Latin *repellere* : *re-,* back + *pellere,* to drive.] —**re·pel·er** *n.*

Usage: *Repel* and *repulse* both have the physical sense of driving back or off: an invasion, for example, may be repelled or repulsed. *Repulse* may also apply to rebuffing or rejecting someone in a hostile or impolite manner *(I repulsed every attempt he made to get to know me)*; but only *repel* is used in the sense of causing distaste or aversion to someone *(The picture repelled me).*

re·pel·lent (ri-péllənt, rə-) *adj.* Also *rare* **re·pel·lant.** **1.** Serving or tending to repel; capable of repelling something. **2.** Inspiring aversion or distaste; repulsive. **3.** Resistant or impervious to an often specified substance. Often used in combination: *a water-repellent fabric.* —See Synonyms at **hateful.**
~*n.* Also *rare* **re·pel·lant.** Something that repels; especially: **1.** A substance used to repel insects. **2.** A substance or treatment for making a fabric or surface impervious or resistant to something. —**re·pel·lence, re·pel·len·cy** *n.*

re·pent[1] (ri-pént, rə-) *v.* **-pented, -penting, -pents.** —*intr.* **1.** To feel remorse or self-reproach for what one has done or failed to do; be contrite. **2.** To feel such remorse or regret for past conduct as to change one's mind regarding it. Used with *of: He repented of his severity.* **3.** To feel remorse or contrition for one's sins and to renounce sinful ways. —*tr.* **1.** To feel regret or self-reproach for. **2.** To change one's mind regarding (past conduct). [Middle English *repenten,* from Old French *repentir* : *re-,* in response to + *pentir,* to be sorry, from Vulgar Latin *penitīre* (unattested), to cause to repent, from Latin *paenitēre* (see **penitent**).] —**re·pent·er** *n.*

re·pent[2] (re͞epənt) *adj. Botany.* Creeping along the ground; prostrate. [Latin *rēpēns,* present participle of *rēpere,* to creep.]

re·pen·tance (ri-péntənss, rə-) *n.* **1.** Remorse or contrition for past conduct or sin. **2.** The act or process of repenting.

re·pen·tant (ri-péntənt, rə-) *adj.* Characterised by or demonstrating repentance; penitent. —**re·pen·tant·ly** *adv.*

re·per·cus·sion (re͞epər-kúsh'n) *n.* **1.** An effect, influence, or result, often indirect, produced by an event or action. **2.** A recoil, rebounding, or reciprocal motion after impact. **3.** A reflection, especially of sound; an echo. [Latin *repercussiō* (stem *repercussiōn-*), from *repercussus,* past participle of *repercutere,* to cause to rebound : *re-,* back + *percutere,* to PERCUSS.] —**re·per·cus·sive** *adj.*

rep·er·toire (réppər-twaar) *n.* Also **rep·er·to·ry** (-təri, -tri). **1.** The stock of songs, plays, operas, or other pieces that a player or company is able to perform. **2.** The range or number of skills or special accomplishments of a particular person or group. [French *répertoire,* from Late Latin *repertōrium,* REPERTORY.]

rep·er·to·ry (réppər-təri, -tri) *n., pl.* **-ries.** **1.** A repertoire. **2. a.** The performance of plays by a theatrical company, from a specific repertoire, usually in alternation. Also informally called "rep". **b.** A repertory company. **3.** A storehouse or other place where a stock of things is kept. **4.** Something stored in or as if in such a place; a stock or collection: *a repertory of photographic techniques.* [Late Latin *repertōrium,* from Latin *repertus,* past participle of *reperīre,* to find out, find again : *re-,* again + *parīre,* to produce, invent.] —**rep·er·to·rial** (-táwri-əl || -tōri-əl) *adj.*

repertory company *n.* **1.** A theatrical company that presents and performs plays from a specific repertoire. **2.** A theatrical company presenting a number of plays for a limited period during a season. Also called "repertory", informally "rep".

rep·e·tend (réppi-tend, -ténd) *n.* **1.** A word, sound, or phrase that is repeated; a refrain. **2.** *Mathematics.* The digit or group of digits that repeats infinitely in a repeating decimal; for example, 61 in 1.54616161. . . . [Latin *repetendum,* neuter gerundive of *repetere,* to REPEAT.]

ré·pé·ti·teur (ray-pétti-tér, ri-, -tőr) *n.* A coach for opera singers, ballet dancers, or other artists. [French.]

rep·e·ti·tion (réppi-tísh'n, réppə-) *n.* **1.** The act or process of repeating; the saying, doing, or producing of something again. **2.** A recitation or recital, especially of prepared or memorised material. **3.** Something repeated; a copy or reproduction. [Latin *repetītiō* (stem *repetītiōn-*), from *repetere,* to REPEAT.]

rep·e·ti·tious (réppi-tíshəss, réppə-) *adj.* Characterised by or filled with repetition, especially needless or tedious repetition. —**rep·e·ti·tious·ly** *adv.* —**rep·e·ti·tious·ness** *n.*

re·pet·i·tive (ri-péttitiv, rə-, -péttətiv) *adj.* Characterised by repetition; tending to repeat. —**re·pet·i·tive·ly** *adv.* —**re·pet·i·tive·ness** *n.*

repetitive strain injury *n. Abbr.* **RSI.** Injury (such as tenosynovitis) said to be due to repeated strain, as from the repetitive movements required by some activities, such as using a word processor. Tennis elbow and writer's cramp might be types of repetitive strain injury.

re·phrase (re͞e-fráyz, ri-) *tr.v.* **-phrased, -phrasing, -phrases.** To phrase again; especially, to state in a new, clearer, or different way.

re·pine (ri-pīn, rə-) *intr.v.* **-pined, -pining, -pines.** To be discontented or low in spirits; complain or fret. [RE- + PINE (pain).]

re·place (ri-pláyss, re͞e-) *tr.v.* **-placed, -placing, -places.** **1. a.** To place again. **b.** To put back in place. **2.** To take or fill the place of; supplant or supersede. **3.** To be or provide a substitute for. **4.** To provide a new version of, especially by purchase: *replaced the broken lamp.* —**re·place·a·ble** *adj.* —**re·plac·er** *n.*

re·place·ment (ri-pláyssmənt, re͞e-) *n. Abbr.* **repl.** **1.** The act or process of replacing or of being replaced. **2.** One that replaces, such as a player who takes the place of an injured colleague in a team. **3.** *Chemistry.* A type of reaction in which one atom or group in a compound is replaced by another. See **substitution.** **4.** *Geology.* A process in which one mineral is gradually replaced by another through deposition and removal.

re·plant (re͞e-plaánt || -plánt) *tr.v.* **-planted, -planting, -plants.** **1.** To plant something again, or in a new place. **2.** To supply with new plants: *replant a window box.*
~*n.* (re͞e-plaant || -plant). **1.** Something that has been replanted. **2.** *Chemistry.* A type of reaction in which one atom or group in a compound is replaced by another. See **substitution.**

re·play (re͞e-pláy) *tr.v.* **-played, -playing, -plays.** To play over again: *replay a match; replay a tape.*
~*n.* (re͞e-play). **1.** The act or process of replaying something. **2.** Something replayed; especially: **a.** A football match between two teams whose previous meeting has ended in a draw. **b.** A part of a television broadcast showing a particular sequence or piece of action, sometimes in slow motion. See **action replay.**

re·plen·ish (ri-plénnish, rə-) *tr.v.* **-ished, -ishing, -ishes.** **1.** To fill or make complete again; add a new stock or supply to: *replenish the larder.* **2.** To renew a supply of. [Middle English *replenisshen,* from Old French *replenir* (present stem *repleniss-*) : *re-,* again + *plenir,* to fill, from *plein,* full.] —**re·plen·ish·er** *n.* —**re·plen·ish·ment** *n.*

re·plete (ri-ple͞et, rə-) *adj.* **1.** Plentifully supplied; abounding. Used with *with.* **2.** Filled to satiation; gorged. [Middle English *replet,* from Old French, from Latin *replētus,* past participle of *replēre,* to refill : *re-,* again + *plēre,* to fill.] —**re·plete·ness** *n.*

re·ple·tion (ri-ple͞esh'n, rə-) *n.* **1.** The condition of being fully supplied or completely filled. **2.** A state of excessive fullness.

re·plev·i·a·ble (ri-plévvi-əb'l, rə-) *adj.* Also **re·plev·is·a·ble** (-səb'l). *Law.* Capable of being recovered by replevin.

re·plev·in (ri-plévvin, rə-) *n.* Also **re·plev·y** (-plévvi). *Law.* **1.** An action to recover personal property unlawfully taken. **2.** The recovery of property by this action subject to the recoverer's willingness to have the matter settled finally in court. **3.** The writ or procedure by which the property is recovered.
~*tr.v.* **replevined, -ining, -ins.** *Law.* To replevy. [Middle English *replevyn,* from Anglo-French *replevine,* a pledge, from Old French *replevir,* to recover, "to pledge back" : *re-,* back + *plevir,* pledge, from Frankish *plegan* (unattested).]

re·plev·y (ri-plévvi, rə-) *tr.v.* **-ied, -ying, -ies.** *Law.* To regain possession of (goods) by a writ of replevin.
~*n. Law.* Replevin. [Anglo-French *replevir,* from Old French. See **replevin.**]

rep·li·ca (répplikə) *n.* **1.** A copy or reproduction of a work of art, especially one made by the original artist. **2.** Any copy or close reproduction, especially one on a smaller scale. [Italian, from *replicare,* to repeat, from Latin *replicāre,* to REPLICATE.]

rep·li·cate (réppli-kayt) *tr.v.* **-cated, -cating, -cates.** **1.** To duplicate, copy, reproduce, or repeat. **2.** To fold over; bend (something) back upon itself.
~*adj.* (-kət, -kit, -kayt). Also **rep·li·cat·ed** (-kaytid). Folded over or

bent back upon itself: *a replicate leaf.* [Late Latin *replicāre,* to repeat, from Latin, to fold back : *re-,* back + *plicāre,* to fold.]

rep·li·ca·tion (réppli-káysh'n) *n.* **1.** A fold or a folding back. **2.** A reply; a response, especially to an answer. **3.** *Law.* The plaintiff's response to the defendant's answer or plea. **4.** An echo or reverberation. **5.** A copy or reproduction. **6.** The act or process of duplicating or reproducing something. **7.** The process by which exact copies of genetic material, such as DNA molecules, are produced.

re·ply (ri-plí, rə-) *v.* **-plied, -plying, -plies.** *—intr.* **1.** To give an answer in speech or writing. **2.** To respond by some action or gesture: *He replied by shrugging his shoulders.* **3.** To echo. **4.** *Law.* To answer a defendant's plea. *—tr.* To say or give as an answer: *He replied that he was ill.* —See Synonyms at **answer.**
~n., pl. **replies. 1.** An answer in speech or writing. **2.** A response by action or gesture. **3.** *Law.* A plaintiff's speech or argument in answer to that of a defendant. [Middle English *replien,* from Old French *replier,* to fold back, reply, from Latin *replicāre,* to REPLICATE.] **—re·pli·er** *n.*

reply-paid (ri-plí-páyd, rə-) *adj.* **1.** With the reply prepaid by the sender. Said especially of a telegram. **2.** With the postage paid by the addressee. Said of a postcard, envelope, or the like.

re·point (rée-póynt) *tr.v.* **-pointed, -pointing, -points.** To reset (bricks) in new mortar or cement; point (brickwork) again.

re·port (ri-pórt, rə- || -pōrt) *n. Abbr.* **rep., rept., rpt. 1.** An account, a result of an investigation, an announcement, or the like that is prepared, presented, or delivered, usually in formal or organised form. **2.** A formal, detailed account of the proceedings or transactions of a group. **3.** *Usually plural. Law.* A published collection of authoritative accounts of court cases or of judicial decisions. **4.** Rumour or gossip; common talk: *According to report, they eloped.* **5.** Reputation; repute: *a man of bad report.* **6.** An explosive noise: *the sharp report of a rifle.* **7.** *British.* An account and summary of a pupil's work, achievement, progress, and behaviour at school.
~v. **reported, -porting, -ports.** *—tr.* **1.** To make or present an account of (an inquiry, for example), often officially, formally, or regularly. **2.** To relate or tell about: *reported the discovery in a learned journal.* **3.** To write or provide an account or summary of for publication or broadcast. **4.** To submit or relate the results of considerations concerning: *The committee reported the bill.* **5.** To carry back and repeat to another. **6.** To complain about or denounce: *Report him to the police.* *—intr.* **1.** To make a report. **2.** To serve as a reporter for a newspaper, broadcasting company, or other news medium. **3.** To present oneself: *report for duty.* **4.** To be accountable: *He reports directly to the chairman.* [Middle English, from Old French, from *reporter,* to carry back, from Latin *reportāre,* "to carry back" : *re-,* back + *portāre,* to carry.] **—re·port·a·ble** *adj.*

re·port·age (ri-pórt-ij, réppawr-taázh || -pōrt-, réppōr-, réppər-) *n.* **1.** The reporting of news or information of general interest. **2.** The style of such reporting.

re·port·ed·ly (ri-pórt-idli, rə- || -pōrt-) *adv.* By report; supposedly.

reported speech *n.* **Indirect speech** *(see).*

re·port·er (ri-pórt-ər, rə- || -pōrt-) *n. Abbr.* **rep. 1.** A person who reports. **2.** A writer, investigator, or (especially on radio and television) presenter of news stories. **3.** A person authorised to write and issue official accounts of judicial or legislative proceedings. **—rep·or·to·ri·al** (réppawr-táwri-əl, réppər-, rée-pawr- || -pōr-, -tōri-) *adj.*

report stage *n.* The stage in the passage of a bill through the British Parliament when the committee examining it has completed its work and resubmits the bill to the House of Commons.

re·pose[1] (ri-pōz, rə-) *n.* **1. a.** The act of resting; a rest. **b.** The state of being at rest; relaxation. **2.** Peace of mind; freedom from anxiety; composure. **3.** Calm; tranquillity. —See Synonyms at **rest.**
~v. **reposed, -posing, -poses.** *—tr.* **1.** To lay (oneself or part of one's body) down. **2.** To rest or relax (oneself). *—intr.* **1.** To lie at rest; relax. **2.** To lie or be supported by something. **3.** To lie dead: *repose in the grave.* [Middle English *reposen,* from Old French *reposer, repauser,* from Late Latin *repausāre* : *re-* (intensifier), again + *pausāre,* to rest, from Latin *pausa,* a stop, pause, from Greek *pausis,* from *pauein,* to stop.] **—re·pos·al** *n.* **—re·pos·er** *n.*

repose[2] *tr.v.* **-posed, -posing, -poses.** To place (faith or trust, for example) in. [Middle English *reposen* : RE- + POSE (formed by analogy with Latin *repōnere,* to put back).]

re·pose·ful (ri-pōzf'l, rə-) *adj.* Expressing repose; calm. **—re·pose·ful·ly** *adv.* **—re·pose·ful·ness** *n.*

re·pos·it (ri-pózzit, rə-) *tr.v.* **-ited, -iting, -its.** To put away; store. [Latin *repōnere* (past participle *repositus*), to put back, replace : *re-,* back + *pōnere,* to place.] **—re·po·si·tion** (rée-pə-zísh'n, réppə-) *n.*

reposition (réepə-zísh'n) *tr.v.* **-tioned, -tioning, -tions.** To change or restore the position of [RE + POSITION.]

re·pos·i·to·ry (ri-pózzi-təri, rə-, -tri) *n., pl.* **-ries. 1.** A place where things may be put for safekeeping. **2.** A warehouse. **3.** A museum. **4.** A burial vault; a tomb. **5.** One that contains or is a store for something specified: *She was a repository of ancient herbal lore.* **6.** One who is entrusted with secrets or confidential information.

re·pos·sess (rée-pə-zéss || -pō-) *tr.v.* **-sessed, -sessing, -sesses. 1.** To take back possession of (property), as from someone who has not kept up hire-purchase repayments; regain possession of. **2.** To give back possession to. **—re·pos·ses·sion** *n.*

re·pous·sé (rə-pōō-say, ri- || -pōō-sáy) *adj.* **1.** Raised in relief. Said of a design worked in metal. **2.** Decorated with raised designs.
~n. **1.** A design hammered in relief. **2.** The technique of hammering such a design. [French, past participle of *repousser,* to push back, from Old French : *re-,* back + *pousser,* to PUSH.]

repp. Variant of **rep** (fabric).

repr. representing.

rep·re·hend (réppri-hénd, réppra-) *tr.v.* **-hended, -hending, -hends.** To reprove; censure. See Synonyms at **criticise.** [Middle English *reprehenden,* from Latin *reprehendere,* rebuke, hold back : *re-,* back + *prehendere,* to seize.]

rep·re·hen·si·ble (réppri-hén-si-b'l, réppra-, -sə-) *adj.* Deserving of rebuke or censure; blameworthy. [Late Latin *reprehēnsibilis,* from Latin *reprehendere* (past participle *reprehēnsus*), to REPREHEND.] **—rep·re·hen·si·bil·i·ty** (-bílləti), **rep·re·hen·si·ble·ness** *n.* **—rep·re·hen·si·bly** *adv.*

rep·re·hen·sion (réppri-hénsh'n, réppra-) *n.* Rebuke; censure.

rep·re·sent (réppri-zént, réppra-) *tr.v.* **-sented, -senting, -sents. 1. a.** To stand for; symbolise. **b.** To indicate or communicate by signs or signals. **2.** To depict; portray. **3.** To present clearly to the mind. **4.** To point out forcefully: *represented the need for caution.* **5.** To describe or put forward (a person or thing) as an embodiment of some specified quality. **6. a.** To serve as the official and authorised delegate or agent for; act as a spokesman for. **b.** To be present in the name of. **7.** To serve as an example of: *The class of mammals is represented by seven species in this museum.* **8.** To be the equivalent of. **9. a.** To stage (a play, for example); present; produce. **b.** To act the part or role of. —See Synonyms at **mean.** [Middle English *representen,* from Latin *repraesentāre,* show, bring back : *re-,* back, again + *praesentāre,* to PRESENT.] **—rep·re·sent·a·ble** *adj.* **—rep·re·sent·a·bil·i·ty** (-ə-bílləti) *n.*

rep·re·sen·ta·tion (réppri-zen-táysh'n, réppra-, -zən-) *n.* **1.** The act of representing or the state of being represented. **2.** That which represents. **3.** *Often plural.* **a.** An account or statement, as of facts, allegations, or arguments. **b.** An expostulation; a protest: *make representations to a higher authority.* **4.** A presentation or production, as of a play. **5.** The state or condition of serving as an official delegate, agent, or spokesman. **6.** The right or privilege of being represented by delegates having a voice in a legislative body. **7.** *Law.* A statement of fact made by one party in order to induce another party to enter into a contract.

rep·re·sen·ta·tion·al (réppri-zen-táysh'n'l, réppra-, -zən-) *adj.* Of or pertaining to representation, especially to realistic and naturalistic graphic representation in art, as opposed to abstraction.

rep·re·sen·ta·tion·al·ism (réppri-zen-táysh'n'l-iz'm, réppra-, -zən-) *n.* Also **rep·re·sen·ta·tion·ism** (-táysh'n-iz'm) (for sense 1). **1.** *Philosophy.* A theory of perception that holds that since external objects are perceived through the mediation of the human mind, they can never be perceived directly as they really are, but only as representations of the "real" object. **2.** The practice and active support of representational art.

rep·re·sen·ta·tive (réppri-zéntətiv, réppra-) *n. Abbr.* **rep., Rep. 1.** A person or thing serving as an example or type for others of the same classification; a typical instance. **2. a.** One qualified to serve as an authorised official delegate or agent. **b.** One present in the name of another person or body. **c.** One who travels around on behalf of a company, trying to obtain orders or custom. **3. a.** A member of a governmental body, usually legislative, chosen by popular vote. **b.** In the United States, a member of the House of Representatives, the lower house of Congress, or of a state legislature.
~adj. **1.** Representing, depicting, portraying, or able to do so. **2.** Authorised to act as an official delegate or agent. **3.** Of, pertaining to, or characteristic of government by representation. **4.** Exemplary of others in the same class; typical. **—rep·re·sen·ta·tive·ly** *adv.* **—rep·re·sen·ta·tive·ness** *n.*

re·press (ri-préss, rə-) *tr.v.* **-pressed, -pressing, -presses. 1.** To hold back; restrain: *repress a laugh.* **2.** To suppress; quell: *repress a rebellion.* **3.** To control forcibly and oppresively; subjugate: *His parents repressed him in childhood.* **4.** *Psychology.* To force (memories, ideas, or fears, for example) into the subconscious mind. [Middle English *repressen,* from Latin *reprimere* (past participle *repressus*) : *re-,* back + *premere,* to press.] **—re·press·i·ble** *adj.* **—re·pres·sive** *adj.* **—re·pres·sive·ly** *adv.* **—re·pres·sive·ness** *n.*

re·pres·sion (ri-présh'n, rə-) *n.* **1. a.** The action of repressing. **b.** The state of being repressed. **2.** The unconscious exclusion of painful memories, desires, or fears from the conscious mind.

re·pres·sor, re·press·er (ri-préssər, rə-) *n.* **1.** One that represses. **2.** *Biology.* A protein that prevents the synthesis of other proteins by interfering with the action of DNA.

re·prieve (ri-préev, rə-) *tr.v.* **-prieved, -prieving, -prieves. 1.** To postpone or cancel the punishment of. **2.** To bring relief to.
~n. **1. a.** The postponement or cancellation of a punishment. **b.** A warrant for such a postponement or cancellation. **2.** Temporary relief, as from danger or pain. [Variant of earlier *reprive, repry,* from Middle English *repryen,* from Old French *reprendre* (past participle *repris*), to take back, from Latin *reprehendere,* to hold back, REPREHEND.] **—re·priev·a·ble** *adj.*

rep·ri·mand (réppri-maand, -maánd || -mánd, -mand) *tr.v.* **-manded, -manding, -mands.** To rebuke or censure severely. See Synonyms at **admonish.**
~n. (-maand || -mand). A severe or formal rebuke or censure. [French *reprimender,* from *reprimende,* a reprimand, ultimately from Latin *reprimenda,* neuter plural gerundive of *reprimere,* to REPRESS.]

re·print (rée-print) *n. Abbr.* **rep. 1.** Something that has been printed again; especially: **a.** A new or additional edition; a facsimile impression of an original. **b.** An offprint; a separately printed excerpt. **2.** A facsimile of a stamp printed after the original issue of the stamp has ceased.

~*tr.v.* (rée-prínt) **reprinted, -printing, -prints.** To print again; make a new copy or edition of. **—re·print·er** *n.*

re·pri·sal (ri-príz'l, rə-) *n.* **1.** *Often plural.* Retaliation for an injury with the intent of inflicting at least as much injury in return. **2.** The forcible seizure of an enemy's goods or subjects in retaliation for inflicted injuries. **3.** An act or instance of any kind of retaliation. [Middle English *reprisail,* from Anglo-French *reprisaille,* from Medieval Latin *repraesālia,* contraction of *repraehensālia,* from Latin *reprehensus,* past participle of *reprehendere,* to REPREHEND.]

re·prise (ri-préez, rə-) *n.* **1.** *Music.* A repetition of a phrase or verse; a return to an original theme. **2.** A repetition; a repeat.
~*tr.v.* **reprised, -prising, -prises.** —*tr.* To repeat; make a reprise of. [Middle English, from Old French, "a taking back", from the feminine past participle of *reprendre,* to take back, from Latin *reprehendere,* to REPREHEND.]

re·pro (rée'prō) *n. Informal.* Reproduction furniture.
~*adj. Informal.* Made to resemble an antique: *a repro chair.*

re·proach (ri-próch, rə-) *tr.v.* **-proached, -proaching, -proaches. 1.** To blame for something; rebuke; censure. **2.** *Archaic.* To bring shame upon; disgrace. —See Synonyms at **admonish.**
~*n.* **1.** Censure; rebuke; blame. **2.** That which causes rebuke or blame. **3.** Disgrace; shame. **—beyond reproach.** So good as to preclude any possibility of criticism. [Middle English *reprochen,* from Old French *reprochier,* from Vulgar Latin *repropiāre* (unattested), bring back near : Latin *re-,* back + *prope,* near.] **—re·proach·a·ble** *adj.* **—re·proach·a·ble·ness** *n.* **—re·proach·a·bly** *adv.* **—re·proach·er** *n.*

re·proach·ful (ri-próch-f'l, rə-) *adj.* Expressing reproach or blame. **—re·proach·ful·ly** *adv.* **—re·proach·ful·ness** *n.*

rep·ro·bate (rép-rə-bayt, -rō-, -bət, -bit) *n.* **1.** A morally unprincipled person; a rogue; a scoundrel. Often used humorously or affectionately. **2.** *Theology.* One who is predestined to damnation.
~*adj.* **1.** Morally unprincipled; shameless. **2.** *Theology.* Rejected by God and without hope of salvation.
~*tr.v.* (-bayt) **reprobated, -bating, -bates. 1.** To disapprove of; condemn. **2.** *Theology.* To abandon to eternal damnation. [Late Latin *reprobātus,* past participle of *reprobāre,* to reprove : Latin *re-,* back, against + *probāre,* to test, PROVE.] **—rep·ro·ba·tion** (-báysh'n) *n.*

re·pro·duce (rée-prə-déwss ‖ -prō-, -dóoss) *v.* **-duced, -ducing, -duces.** —*tr.* **1.** To produce a counterpart, image, or copy of. **2.** *Biology.* To generate (offspring) by sexual or asexual means. **3.** To produce again or anew; re-create. **4.** To bring to mind again (a memory, for example). —*intr.* **1.** To generate offspring. **2.** To undergo copying. **—re·pro·duc·er** *n.* **—re·pro·duc·i·ble** *adj.*

re·pro·duc·tion (rée-prə-dúksh'n ‖ -prō-) *n.* **1.** The act of reproducing or being reproduced. **2.** That which is reproduced, especially with reference to its faithfulness to an original: *disappointed by the poor quality of the sound reproduction.* **3.** A copy of a work of art, antique, or the like. Also used adjectively: *reproduction furniture.* **4.** *Biology.* The sexual or asexual process by which organisms generate others of the same kind.

reproduction proof *n. Printing.* A proof of metal type made for reproduction through a photographic process such as photo-offset lithography.

re·pro·duc·tive (rée-prə-dúktiv ‖ -prō-) *adj.* **1.** Of or pertaining to reproduction. **2.** Tending to reproduce. **—re·pro·duc·tive·ly** *adv.* **—re·pro·duc·tive·ness** *n.*

rep·ro·graph·ics (répprə-gráffiks, rée'prō-) *n. Usually used with a singular verb.* **1.** The technique of reprography. **2.** The materials, equipment, and processes used in reprography.

re·prog·ra·phy (ri-próggrəfi, rée-) *n.* The process of reproducing, reprinting, or copying graphic material by mechanical, especially electronic, means. [REPRO(DUCE) + -GRAPHY.] **—rep·ro·graph·ic** (répprə-gráffik, rée'prə-) *adj.* **—rep·ro·graph·i·cal·ly** *adv.*

re·proof¹ (ri-próof, rə- ‖ -próof) *n.* An act or expression of reproving; a rebuke.

re·proof² (rée-próof ‖ -próof) *tr.v.* **-proofed, -proofing, -proofs. 1.** To make a new proof of (printed matter). **2.** To make resistant again, as by making heatproof or waterproof.

re·prove (ri-próov, rə-) *tr.v.* **-proved, -proving, -proves.** To rebuke for a fault or misdeed; scold. See Synonyms at **admonish.** [Middle English *reproven,* from Old French *reprover,* from Late Latin *reprobāre,* REPROBATE.] **—re·prov·a·ble** *adj.* **—re·prov·er** *n.* **—re·prov·ing·ly** *adv.*

rept. 1. receipt. **2.** report.

rep·tant (réptənt) *adj. Biology.* Creeping or crawling. [Latin *reptāns* (stem *reptant-*), present participle of *reptāre,* to crawl, frequentative of *repere,* to crawl.]

rep·tile (rép-tīl ‖ *U.S. also* -t'l, -til) *n.* **1.** Any of various coldblooded, usually egg-laying vertebrates of the class Reptilia, such as a snake, lizard, crocodile, turtle, or dinosaur, having an external covering of scales or horny plates, and breathing by means of lungs. **2.** A despicable or repulsive person.
~*adj.* **1.** Of, pertaining to, or characteristic of reptiles. **2.** Despicable; repulsive. **3.** *Archaic.* Creeping. [Middle English *reptil,* from Old French *reptile,* from Late Latin *reptile,* neuter of *reptilis,* creeping, from Latin *repere,* to creep.]

rep·til·i·an (rep-tílli-ən) *adj.* **1.** Of or pertaining to reptiles. **2.** Re-

sembling or characteristic of a reptile. **3.** Repulsive, contemptible, or devious.
~*n.* A reptile.

Rep·ton (réptən), **Humphry** (1752–1818). English landscape gardener. Like Capability Brown, he planned carefully informal gardens, though with more classical elements in them. His work is best seen at Cobham Hall, Kent, and at Sheringham Hall, Norfolk.

re·pub·lic (ri-públik, rə-) *n. Abbr.* **rep., Rep., Repub. 1.** Any political order that is not a monarchy. **2. a.** A constitutional form of government, especially a democratic and representative one, in which the head of state is not a monarch, and supreme power is vested in the people or their elected representatives. **b.** A country having such a form of government. **3.** A particular republican administration constituting a stage in a country's political history: *the third republic.* **4.** Any group of people working freely and equally for the same cause: *the republic of letters.* **5.** An autonomous or partially autonomous political and territorial unit belonging to a sovereign federation; specifically, such a unit in the U.S.S.R. or Yugoslavia. [French *république,* from Latin *rēspūblica* : *rēs,* a thing, matter, affair + *pūblica,* feminine of *pūblicus,* PUBLIC.]

re·pub·li·can (ri-públikən, rə-) *adj.* **1.** Of, pertaining to, or characteristic of a republic. **2.** In favour of a republican form of government. **3.** *Capital* **R. a.** *Abbr.* **R., Rep., Repub.** Of, belonging to, or supporting the Republican Party of the United States. **b.** Of, belonging to, or supporting the nationalist cause in Ireland, opposed to the partition of Ireland and seeking reunification. **c.** Of, belonging to, or supporting the government side in the Spanish Civil War.
~*n.* **1.** A person who favours a republican form of government. **2.** *Capital* **R. a.** A member of the Republican Party of the United States. **b.** A supporter of the Republican cause in Ireland. **c.** A supporter of the Republican side in the Spanish Civil War. **—re·pub·li·can·ism** *n.*

Republican calendar *n.* The **Revolutionary calendar** (see).

re·pub·li·can·ise, re·pub·li·can·ize (ri-públikə-nīz, rə-) *tr.v.* **-ised, -ising, -ises.** To make republican. **—re·pub·li·can·i·sa·tion** (-nī-záysh'n ‖ *U.S.* -ni-) *n.*

Republican Party *n.* **1.** One of the two major political parties of the United States, organised in 1854 to oppose slavery. **2.** The Democratic-Republican Party, a former political party of the United States, organised in 1792 by Thomas Jefferson. See **Democratic Party.**

re·pub·li·ca·tion (rée-públi-káysh'n) *n.* **1.** The act of republishing. **2.** That which is republished.

re·pub·lish (rée-públish) *tr.v.* **-lished, -lishing, -lishes. 1.** To publish anew or again. **2.** *Law.* To revive (a cancelled will, for example). **—re·pub·lish·er** *n.*

re·pu·di·ate (ri-péwdi-ayt, rə-) *tr.v.* **-ated, -ating, -ates. 1.** To reject emphatically as unfounded or unjust. **2. a.** To refuse to recognise the validity or authority of. **b.** To refuse to pay. **3. a.** To disown (a son or a wife, for example). **b.** To refuse to have any dealings with. [Latin *repudiāre,* to reject, cast off, from *repudium,* a casting off.] **—re·pu·di·a·tive** (-ətiv ‖ , -aytiv) *adj.* **—re·pu·di·a·tor** *n.*

re·pu·di·a·tion (ri-péwdi-áysh'n, rə-) *n.* **1.** The act of repudiating or the state of being repudiated. **2.** The act of refusing to acknowledge a contract or debt.

re·pugn (ri-péwn, rə-) *v.* **-pugned, -pugning, -pugns.** *Archaic.* —*tr.* To oppose or resist. —*intr.* To be opposed; conflict. [Middle English *repugnen,* from Old French *repugner,* from Latin *repugnāre,* to fight against : *re-,* against + *pugnāre,* to fight.]

re·pug·nance (ri-púg-nənss, rə-) *n.* Also **re·pug·nan·cy** (-nən-si). **1.** Extreme dislike or aversion. **2.** Contradiction; inconsistency.

re·pug·nant (ri-púg-nənt, rə-) *adj.* **1.** Offensive; distasteful; repulsive. **2.** Contradictory; inconsistent. [Middle English, from Old French, from Latin *repugnāns* (stem *repugnant-*), present participle of *repugnāre,* REPUGN.] **—re·pug·nant·ly** *adv.*

re·pulse (ri-púlss, rə-) *tr.v.* **-pulsed, -pulsing, -pulses. 1.** To drive back; repel. **2.** To spurn or reject with rudeness, coldness, or denial. —See Usage note at **repel.**
~*n.* **1.** The act of repulsing or the fact of being repulsed. **2.** Rejection; refusal. [Latin *repulsus,* past participle of *repellere,* to REPEL.] **—re·puls·er** *n.*

re·pul·sion (ri-púlsh'n, rə-) *n.* **1.** The act of repulsing, or the condition of being repulsed. **2.** Extreme aversion or dislike. **3.** *Physics.* A force that tends to increase the distance between two bodies having like magnetic poles or like electric charges.

re·pul·sive (ri-púl-siv, rə-) *adj.* **1.** Causing repugnance, extreme dislike, or aversion; disgusting. **2.** Tending to repel or drive off. **3.** *Physics.* Opposing in direction: *a repulsive force.* **—re·pul·sive·ly** *adv.* **—re·pul·sive·ness** *n.*

rep·u·ta·ble (réppewtə-b'l) *adj.* Having a good reputation; honourable; trustworthy: *buy from a reputable dealer.* **—rep·u·ta·bil·i·ty** (-billəti) *n.* **—rep·u·ta·bly** *adv.*

rep·u·ta·tion (réppew-táysh'n) *n.* **1.** The general estimation in which a person or thing is held by the public; what is known, said, or thought about a person. **2.** The state or fact of being highly thought of or having a good reputation. **3.** A specified character or trait ascribed to a person or thing: *a reputation for courtesy.* [Middle English *reputacion,* from Latin *reputātiō* (stem *reputātiōn-*), a reckoning, from *reputāre,* to consider, REPUTE.]

re·pute (ri-péwt, rə-) *tr.v.* **-puted, -puting, -putes.** To consider, suppose, or regard. Usually used in the passive.
~*n.* **1.** Reputation. **2.** Good reputation. —See Synonyms at **fame.** [Middle English *reputen,* from Old French *reputer,* from Latin *repu-*

tāre, to count over, consider : *re-,* over, again + *putāre,* to compute, consider.]

re·put·ed (ri-péwtid, rə-) *adj.* Generally considered or supposed.

re·put·ed·ly (ri-péwtidli, rə-) *adv.* According to what is generally believed or supposed.

re·quest (ri-kwést, rə-) *tr.v.* **-quested, -questing, -quests. 1.** To ask for; express a desire for. **2.** To ask (a person) to do something.
~*n.* **1.** An expressed desire; an act of asking. **2.** That which is asked for. **—by request.** In response to an expressed desire. **—in request.** In great demand. **—on request.** When asked for.
~*adj.* Having been desired or demanded: *a request performance.* [Middle English, from Old French *requester,* from *requeste,* a request, from Vulgar Latin *requaesita* (unattested), from Latin *requīrere,* to seek again, REQUIRE.]

Usage: As a noun, *request* is generally followed by *for*: *He made a request for an increase in salary.* For the verb, however, formal English prefers alternative constructions: *He requested an increase from his boss* is preferred to *He requested his boss for an increase* or *He requested his boss to give him an increase.*

request stop *n.* A stop on a bus or coach route at which one must signal to the vehicle's driver if one wishes to be picked up.

re·qui·em (réckwi-əm, -em || *U.S. also* ráykwi-, réekwi-) *n.* **1.** *Capital* **R.** *Roman Catholic Church.* **a.** A mass for a deceased person or persons. **b.** A musical composition for such a mass. **2.** Any hymn, composition, or service for the dead. [Middle English, from Latin (first word of the introit of the mass for the dead), accusative of *requiēs,* rest : *re-,* again + *quiēs,* rest.]

req·ui·es·cat (réckwi-éss-kat || -kaat) *n.* A prayer for the repose of the souls of the dead. [Latin, "may he (or she) rest", from *requiescere,* to rest : *re-,* again + *quiescere,* to be quiet, rest, from *quiēs,* quiet, rest.]

re·quire (ri-kwír, rə-) *tr.v.* **-quired, -quiring, -quires. 1.** To have use for as a necessity; need. **2.** To ask or demand formally or authoritatively: *His presence was required in court.* **3.** To compel or oblige. **4.** To call for; demand as necessary or appropriate: *matters requiring our attention.* [Middle English *requiren,* from Old French *requere,* from Vulgar Latin *requaerere* (unattested), from Latin *requīrere,* to seek again, search for, inquire : *re-,* again + *quaerere,* to seek, to ask.] **—re·quir·a·ble** *adj.* **—re·quir·er** *n.*

re·quired (ri-kwírd, rə-) *adj. Abbr.* **req.** Needed; essential: *required reading.* See Synonyms at **necessary.**

re·quire·ment (ri-kwír-mənt, rə-) *n.* **1.** That which is required; something needed or wanted. **2.** Something obligatory; a prerequisite.

req·ui·site (réckwizit) *adj.* Required; necessary; essential.
~*n.* A necessity; something needed, especially for a particular purpose: *toilet requisities.* See Synonyms at **need.** [Middle English, from Latin *requīsītus,* past participle of *requīrere,* to REQUIRE.] **—req·ui·site·ly** *adv.* **—req·ui·site·ness** *n.*

req·ui·si·tion (réckwi-zísh'n) *n. Abbr.* **req. 1. a.** A formal written request for something that is needed. **b.** An order claiming something for official, especially military, use. **c.** The act of making any such request or claim. **2.** A formal request made by one government to another, demanding the return of a criminal.
~*tr.v.* **requisitioned, -tioning, -tions. 1.** To demand, as for military needs or in a time of emergency. **2.** To make demands of.

re·quit·al (ri-kwít'l, rə-) *n.* **1.** The act of requiting. **2.** Return, as for an injury or for some friendly act.

re·quite (ri-kwít, rə-) *tr.v.* **-quited, -quiting, -quites. 1.** To make repayment or return for: *requite another's love.* **2.** To repay (a person): *requited the stranger for his help.* **3.** To avenge. [RE- + obsolete *quite,* variant of QUIT.] **—re·quit·a·ble** *adj.* **—re·quit·er** *n.*

re·read (rée-réed) *tr.v.* **-read** (-réd), **-reading, -reads.** To read again; especially, to read (a work) with a fresh critical approach.

rere·dos (réer-doss) *n.* **1.** A decorative screen or facing on the wall at the back of an altar. **2.** The back of an open hearth of a fireplace. [Middle English, from Old French *areredos* : *arere,* back, behind, from Vulgar Latin *ad retrō* (unattested) : Latin *ad,* to + *retrō,* backwards + *dos,* back, from Latin *dorsum.*]

re·run (rée-run) *n.* A repeat broadcast, production, or showing of a television series, play, or the like.
~*tr.v.* (-rún) **reran** (-rán), **-running, -runs.** To present a second production, broadcast, or showing of.

res. 1. research. **2.** reserve. **3.** residence; resident; resides. **4.** resolution.

re·sale (rée-sayl, -sáyl) *n.* The selling again of a purchase. Also used adjectivally: *resale value.*

resale price maintenance *n. Abbr.* **R.P.M.** An agreement among manufacturers or between wholesalers and retailers not to sell goods below a fixed price, usually imposed by the manufacturer. Such an agreement in Britain is only legal when shown to be in the public interest.

re·sched·ule (rée-shéddewell *U.S.* -skéj-əl, ōōl, *Canadian* -shéj-) *tr.v.* **1.** To schedule again or differently: *reschedule a programme later in the week.* **2.** To adjust the repayment timetable of, typically so as to be lenient to a borrower: *reschedule a debt.*

re·scind (ri-sínd, rə-) *tr.v.* **-scinded, -scinding, -scinds.** To void; repeal. See Synonyms at **nullify.** [Latin *rēscindere,* to cut off, abolish : *re-* (intensive) + *scindere,* to cut.] **—re·scind·a·ble** *adj.* **—re·scind·er** *n.* **—re·scind·ment** *n.*

re·scis·sion (ri-sízh'n, rə-) *n.* The act of rescinding. [Late Latin *rescissiō* (stem *rescissiōn-*), from Latin *rēscissus,* past participle of *rēscindere,* RESCIND.]

re·scis·so·ry (ri-síss-əri, rə-, -síz-) *adj.* Pertaining to rescission or having the effect or power of rescinding. [Late Latin *rescissōrius,* from Latin *rescissus,* past participle of *rescindere,* RESCIND.]

re·script (rée-skript) *n.* **1.** A formal decree or edict. **2.** An act of rewriting or something that is rewritten. **3.** In ancient Rome, a reply from the Roman emperor to a magistrate's query on a point of law. **4.** *Roman Catholic Church.* A response from the Pope to a question regarding discipline or doctrine. [Latin *rēscriptum,* from the neuter past participle of *rēscrībere,* to write back or in reply : *re-,* back + *scrībere,* to write.]

res·cue (réskew) *tr.v.* **-cued, -cuing, -cues. 1.** To save, as from danger or imprisonment. **2.** *Law.* To take from legal custody by force. —See Synonyms at **save.**
~*n.* **1.** An act of freeing or saving. Also used adjectivally: *a rescue team.* **2.** *Law.* Removal from legal custody by force. [Middle English *rescuen,* from Old French *rescourre,* from Vulgar Latin *reexcutere* (unattested), to drive away, shake off : Latin *re-* (intensive) + *excutere,* to shake out or off : *ex,* out + *quatere,* to shake.] **—res·cu·a·ble** *adj.* **—res·cu·er** *n.*

re·search (ri-sérch, rə-, -zérch, rée-serch) *n. Abbr.* **res. 1.** Investigation or inquiry in order to gather new information or to collate what is already known about a subject, especially as an academic pursuit. Also used adjectivally: *a research grant.* **2.** Information gathered during such a course of investigation or inquiry.
~*v.* **researched, -searching, -searches.** —*intr.* To engage in or perform research. —*tr.* **1.** To study or investigate thoroughly. **2.** To carry out research for. [From obsolete French *recerche, recercher,* to seek out, to search again : *re-,* again + *cerch(i)er,* to SEARCH.] **—re·search·er** *n.*

re·seat (rée-séet) *tr.v.* **-seated, -seating, -seats. 1.** To fit (a valve, for example) in a new seating. **2.** To provide with a different or new seat or seats.

ré·seau, re·seau (rézzō, ray-zō || ree-, ri-) *n., pl.* **-seaus** (-z, *or pronounced as singular)* or **-seaux** (-z, *or pronounced as singular).* **1.** A net or mesh foundation for lace. **2.** *Astronomy.* A reference grid of fine lines forming uniform squares on a photographic plate or print, used in measuring stars, for example. **3.** In colour photography, a mosaic screen of fine lines of three colours. [French, from Old French *reseuil,* diminutive of *raiz, roiz,* a net, from Latin *rētis, rēte.*]

re·sect (ri-sékt, ree-) *tr.v.* **-sected, -secting, -sects.** To perform a resection of; cut off or pare down. [Latin *resectus,* past participle of *resecāre,* to cut off : *re-,* back, off + *secāre,* to cut.]

re·sec·tion (ri-séksh'n, ree-) *n.* The surgical removal of part of an organ or structure.

re·se·da (réssidə, rézzidə, ri-séedə || *for sense 2, U.S. also* ráyzi-daa) *n.* **1.** Any plant of the genus *Reseda,* which includes the mignonette. **2.** Greyish or dark green to yellow green or light olive. [New Latin, from Latin *resēda*†.] **—re·se·da** *adj.*

re·sem·blance (ri-zémblənss, rə-) *n.* **1.** The condition or quality of resembling something; similarity in nature, form, or appearance; likeness. **2.** The extent to or manner in which something resembles something else. **3.** A point in which one thing or person resembles another; a likeness. —See Synonyms at **likeness.**

re·sem·ble (ri-zémb'l, rə-) *tr.v.* **-bled, -bling, -bles.** To have a similarity to; be like. [Middle English *resemblen,* from Old French *resembler* : *re-* (intensifier) + *sembler,* to be like, from Latin *simulāre, similāre,* to imitate, from *similis,* like.] **—re·sem·bler** *n.*

re·sent (ri-zént) *tr.v.* **-sented, -senting, -sents.** To feel indignantly aggrieved at (an act, situation, or person). [From obsolete French *resentir,* to feel strongly : *re-* (intensive) + *sentir,* to feel, from Latin *sentīre.*]

re·sent·ful (ri-zent-f'l) *adj.* Full of, characterised by, or inclined to feel resentment. **—re·sent·ful·ly** *adv.* **—re·sent·ful·ness** *n.*

re·sent·ment (ri-zéntmənt) *n.* Indignation, bitterness, or ill will felt towards an act, situation, or person. See Synonyms at **anger.**

re·ser·pine (réssərpin, ri-sér-pin, -peen) *n.* A white to yellowish powder, $C_{33}H_{40}N_2O_9$, isolated from the roots of certain species of rauwolfia, especially *Rauwolfia serpentina.* See **rauwolfia.** [German *Reserpin,* from New Latin *Rauwolfia serpentina,* a species of snakeroot.]

res·er·va·tion (rézzər-váysh'n) *n.* **1.** The act of reserving; a keeping back or withholding. **2.** Something that is kept back or withheld. **3. a.** A limiting qualification, condition, or exception. **b.** A misgiving or doubt: *has reservations about his reliability.* See Synonyms at **qualm. 4.** A tract of land set apart, especially in the United States, for a special purpose, as one for the use of a North American Indian people. **5. a.** An arrangement by which something, such as a ticket or hotel accommodation, is secured in advance. **b.** That which is so secured. **c.** The record or promise of such an arrangement. **6.** *British.* A strip of land between two carriageways of a road. Also called "reserve". **7.** *Law.* **a.** A clause in a conveyance retaining for the grantor a right or interest in the estate conveyed. **b.** The right or interest so retained. **8.** In the Christian Church, the practice of keeping consecrated hosts in a church after the celebration of the Eucharist.

re·serve (ri-zérv, rə-) *tr.v.* **-served, -serving, -serves. 1.** To keep back or save for future use or treatment, or for a special purpose. **2. a.** To set apart for a particular person or use. **b.** To secure (a ticket or hotel room, for example) in advance; book. **3.** To keep or secure for oneself; retain: *I reserve the right to disagree.* **4.** To refrain from giving or expressing (judgment) immediately, especially in order to obtain further evidence. —See Synonyms at **keep.**
~*n. Abbr.* **res. 1.** Something kept back or saved for future use or a

special purpose. **2.** The state of being kept back, set aside, or saved: *funds held in reserve.* **3.** A reservation, condition, or qualification: *accepted her story without reserve.* **4.** The keeping of one's feelings, thoughts, or affairs to oneself. **5.** Self-restraint in action or expression; reticence. **6.** Lack of enthusiasm; sceptical caution. **7.** An amount of capital held back from investment by a bank or a portion of profits not distributed by a company in order to meet probable or possible demands. **8.** An area of public land kept for a particular purpose: *a game reserve.* **9.** A central reservation, especially on a motorway. **10.** *Often plural.* **a.** A fighting force kept uncommitted until strategic need arises. **b.** The part of a country's armed forces not on active duty but subject to call in an emergency. **11.** *Sports.* **a.** An extra member of a team kept in readiness in case any of the playing members should be injured or unable to play. **b.** *Plural.* The second or substitute team of a club. **12.** A reserve price. **13.** *Canadian.* A **reservation** (sense 4).
~*adj.* Held in or forming a reserve: *a reserve supply of food.* [Middle English *reserven,* from Old French *reserver,* from Latin *reservāre,* to keep back : *re-,* back + *servāre,* to save, keep.] **—re·serv·a·ble** *adj.* **—re·serv·er** *n.*

reserve bank *n.* Any of the 12 main banks of the U.S. Federal Reserve System.

reserve currency *n.* Foreign currency that is kept in reserve by a government for the paying of international debts.

re·served (ri-zérvd, rə-) *adj.* **1.** Held in reserve; kept back or set aside. **2.** Not outgoing in manner or speech; undemonstrative; reticent. —See Synonyms at **humble.** **—re·serv·ed·ly** (-zérvidli) *adv.* **—re·serv·ed·ness** (-zérvid-nəss, -niss) *n.*

reserved occupation *n. British.* An occupation that exempts one from conscription into the armed forces.

reserve price *n.* The minimum fixed price at which property will be sold at an auction.

re·serv·ist (ri-zérvist, rə-) *n.* A member of a military reserve.

res·er·voir (rézzər-vwaar || rézzə-) *n.* **1.** A body of water collected and stored in a natural or artificial lake. **2.** A receptacle or chamber for storing a fluid. **3.** *Anatomy.* A **cisterna** *(see).* **4.** A large supply of something; a reserve: *a reservoir of gratitude.* [French *réservoir,* from *réserver,* to RESERVE.]

re·set (rée-sét) *tr.v.* **-set, -setting, -sets.** **1.** To set (a broken bone or printing type, for example) again. **2.** To change the setting of (a dial, for example); especially, in computing, to set (a counting device) back to zero or some other given value.
~*n.* (rée-set). **1.** An act of resetting. **2.** Something that is reset. **—re·set·ter** *n.*

res ges·tae (ráyss géss-tī, ráyz, jéss-, -tee) *pl.n.* **1.** Things done; deeds. **2.** *Law.* The facts of a case that are admissible in evidence. [Latin.]

resh (resh, raysh) *n.* The 20th letter of the Hebrew alphabet, corresponding to the letter *r* in English. [Hebrew *rēsh,* from *rōsh,* "head".]

re·shuf·fle (rée-shúff'l) *tr.v.* **-fled, -fling, -fles.** **1.** To shuffle again. **2.** To reorganise the allocation of positions or jobs within (a cabinet or board of directors, for example).
~*n.* (rée-shuff'l). An act of reshuffling; especially, a reshuffling of positions or jobs.

re·side (ri-zīd, rə-) *intr.v.* **-sided, -siding, -sides.** **1.** *Formal.* To live in a place for an extended or permanent period of time. **2.** To be inherently present; exist. Used with *in.* **3.** To be vested. Used with *in.* [Middle English *residen,* from Old French *resider,* from Latin *residēre,* "to sit back", "remain sitting" : *re-,* back, back in place + *sedēre,* to sit.] **—re·sid·er** *n.*

res·i·dence (rézzidənss) *n. Abbr.* **res.** **1.** The place in which one lives; a dwelling; an abode. **2.** The act or a period of residing somewhere. **3. a.** A large house or mansion. **b.** A residency. **—in residence.** Living in or appointed to a particular place or institution in order to carry out a specified job or set of duties: *writer in residence.*

res·i·den·cy (rézzi-dən-si || -den-) *n., pl.* **-cies.** **1. a.** A protected state in which the powers of the protecting state are exercised by a resident representative; specifically, such a territory in India during the British Raj. **b.** The official residence of such a representative. **2.** Residence. **3.** A long-term engagement for a musical group to appear and play at a particular venue. **4.** *U.S.* The period during which a doctor receives specialised clinical training.

res·i·dent (rézzi-d'nt || -dent) *n. Abbr.* **res.** **1.** One who resides in a particular place; a long-term or permanent inhabitant as opposed to a visitor. **2. a.** Formerly, the British representative of a governor general at an Indian native court. **b.** Formerly, a representative of the British government in a protected state. **3.** A nonmigratory bird or other animal. **4.** *U.S.* A doctor serving his period of residency.
~*adj.* **1.** Dwelling in a particular place; residing. **2.** Living somewhere in connection with duty or work. **3.** Inherently present. **4.** Nonmigratory. Said of birds and other animals. **5.** *Informal.* Acting in a specified capacity as a member of a group: *our resident expert on football.*

res·i·den·tial (rézzi-dénsh'l) *adj.* **1.** Of, pertaining to, or involving residence: *a residential course.* **2.** Having residence; especially, residing in a place for occupational reasons: *a residential social worker.* **3.** Of, suitable for, or limited to private residences.

res·i·den·ti·ar·y (rézzi-dén-shəri || -shi-erri) *adj.* **1.** Having a residence, especially an official one. **2.** Involving or required to live in an official residence.
~*n., pl.* **residentiaries.** **1.** A resident. **2.** A member of the clergy required to live in an official residence.

re·sid·u·al (ri-zíddew-əl, rə-) *adj.* **1.** Pertaining to or characteristic of a residue. **2.** Remaining as a residue. **3.** Persisting: *residual resentment.*
~*n.* **1.** The quantity left over at the end of a process; a remainder. **2.** *Statistics.* **a.** The difference between a given single value and the mean value of a number of observations. **b.** The difference between an observed value and the theoretical value. **3.** *Usually plural. U.S.* Payment made to a performer on a recorded television programme for repeat showings. —See Synonyms at **remainder.**

re·sid·u·ar·y (ri-zíddew-əri, rə- || -erri) *adj.* **1.** Of, pertaining to, or constituting a residue. **2.** *Law.* Entitled to the residue of an estate.

res·i·due (rézzi-dew || -dōō) *n.* **1.** The remainder of something after removal of a part. **2.** Matter remaining after completion of any abstractive chemical or physical process, such as evaporation, combustion, distillation, or filtration; a residuum. **3.** *Law.* The remainder of a testator's estate after all claims, debts, and bequests are satisfied. Also called "residuum". **4.** *Geology.* Rock, soil, or the like produced by weathering of other rocks with associated removal of material. —See Synonyms at **remainder.** [Middle English, from Old French *residu,* from Latin *residuum,* from *residuus,* remaining, from *residēre,* RESIDE.]

re·sid·u·um (ri-zíddew-əm, rə-) *n.* **1.** Something remaining after removal of a part; a residue. **2.** *Law.* Residue. —See Synonyms at **remainder.** [Latin, RESIDUE.]

re-sign (rée-sīn) *tr.v.* **-signed, -signing, -signs.** To sign anew.

re·sign (ri-zīn, rə-) *v.* **-signed, -signing, -signs.** —*tr.* **1.** To give over or submit (oneself); force (oneself) to acquiesce. **2.** To give up (a job or position). **3.** To relinquish (a privilege, right, or claim). —*intr.* To give up one's job or office, especially by giving formal notice: *resign from the company.* —See Synonyms at **relinquish.** [Middle English *resignen,* from Old French *resigner,* from Latin *resignāre,* to unseal, resign : *re-,* back + *signāre,* to seal, sign, from *signum,* a mark, sign.] **—re·sign·er** *n.*

res·ig·na·tion (rézzig-náysh'n) *n.* **1.** The act of resigning. **2.** An oral or written statement that one is resigning a position or office. **3.** Unresisting acceptance; passive submission. —See Synonyms at **patience.**

re·signed (ri-zīnd, rə-) *adj.* Feeling or marked by resignation; acquiescent. **—re·sign·ed·ly** (-zīnidli) *adv.*

re·sile (ri-zīl, rə-) *intr.v.* **-siled, -siling, -siles.** **1.** To draw back; recoil. **2.** To spring back; especially, to resume a prior position or form after being stretched or pressed. [Latin *resilīre,* to leap back, recoil : *re-,* back + *salīre,* to leap.]

re·sil·i·ence (ri-zílli-ənss, rə-) *n.* Also **re·sil·ien·cy** (-ən-si). **1.** The ability to recover quickly from illness, change, or misfortune; buoyancy. **2.** The property of a material that enables it to resume its original shape or position after being bent, stretched, or compressed; elasticity. **—re·sil·i·ent** *adj.* **—re·sil·i·ent·ly** *adv.*

res·in (rézzin) *n.* **1.** Any of numerous clear to translucent, yellow or brown, solid or semisolid substances of plant origin, such as copal, rosin, and amber, obtained as exudations and used principally in lacquers, varnishes, synthetic plastics, and pharmaceuticals. **2.** Any of numerous similar polymerised synthetic materials or chemically modified natural resins including thermoplastic materials, such as polyvinyl, polystyrene, and polyethylene, and thermosetting materials, such as polyesters, epoxies, and silicones, that are used with fillers, stabilisers, pigments, and other components to form plastics.
~*tr.v.* **resined, -ining, -ins.** To treat or rub with a resin; apply resin to. [Middle English *resyn,* from Old French *resine,* from Latin *rēsīna,* from Greek *rhētinē*†.] **—res·in·ous** *adj.*

res·in·ate (rézzi-nayt) *tr.v.* **-ated, -ating, -ates.** To impregnate, permeate, or flavour with a resin.

resin canal *n.* A long intercellular channel found in certain conifers, such as pine, which is lined with glandular cells that secrete resin into the cavity. Also called "resin duct".

res·in·if·er·ous (rézzi-niffərəss) *adj.* Yielding resin.

res·in·oid (rézzi-noyd) *adj.* Characteristic of, pertaining to, or containing resin.
~*n.* A resinoid synthetic, especially a thermosetting resin.

re·sist (ri-zíst, rə-) *v.* **-sisted, -sisting, -sists.** —*tr.* **1.** To strive or work against; fight off; oppose actively. **2.** To remain firm against the action or effect of; withstand: *resist rust.* **3.** To keep from giving in to or enjoying; abstain from: *could not resist a cake.* —*intr.* To offer resistance; act in opposition. —See Synonyms at **oppose.**
~*n.* A substance that can cover and protect a surface, as from corrosion. [Middle English *resisten,* from Latin *resistere,* to stand back, resist : *re-,* back, against + *sistere,* to place.] **—re·sist·er** *n.*

re·sis·tance (ri-zístənss, rə-) *n.* **1.** The act or an instance of resisting, or the capacity to resist. **2.** Any force that tends to oppose or retard motion. **3.** The natural ability of the body to ward off disease. **4.** *Symbol* **r, R** *Electricity.* **a.** The opposition to the flow of electric current characteristic of a medium, substance, or circuit element. Also used adjectivally: *resistance loss.* **b.** A resistor. **5.** *Physics.* Any of various physical quantities analogous to electrical resistance, measuring such properties as opposition to sound. **6.** In psychoanalysis, a process in which the ego opposes the conscious recall of unpleasant experiences. **7.** *Often capital* **R.** An underground organisation engaged in a struggle for the national liberation of a country under military occupation. Also used adjectivally: *a resistance movement.*

resistance thermometer *n. Physics.* An accurate type of thermometer in which temperature is measured by determining the electrical resistance of a coil of thin wire, usually platinum.

resistance welding *n.* A method of welding by forcing two pieces of metal together and passing a high electric current across the junction, so as to heat the metals by the contact resistance at the junction.
re·sis·tant (ri-zístənt, rə-) *adj.* **1.** Showing or marked by resistance. **2.** Able to withstand the effects of heat, corrosion, or the like. Often used in combination: *rust-resistant.*
re·sist·i·ble (ri-zístə-b'l, rə-) *adj.* Capable of being resisted. **—re·sist·i·bil·i·ty** (-bílləti) *n.* **—re·sist·i·bly** *adv.*
re·sis·tive (ri-zístiv, rə-) *adj.* Capable of or tending towards resistance; resisting. **—re·sis·tive·ly** *adv.*
re·sis·tiv·i·ty (reéziss-tívviti, ri-ziss-, rə-, rézziss-) *n.* **1.** The capacity for or tendency towards resistance. **2.** *Electricity.* The resistance per unit length of a substance with uniform unit cross-sectional area; the reciprocal of conductivity. Formerly called "specific resistance".
re·sist·less (ri-zíst-ləss, rə-, -liss) *adj. Archaic.* **1.** Incapable of being resisted. **2.** Powerless to resist. **—re·sist·less·ly** *adv.*
re·sis·tor (ri-zístər, rə-) *n.* An electric circuit element used to provide resistance. Also called "resistance".
re·sit (reé-sít) *tr.v.* **-sat, -sitting, -sits.** To take (an examination) again. **—re·sit** (reé-sit) *n.*
res ju·di·ca·ta (ráyss jo͞odi-kaátə, ráyz, reéz) *n.* Also **res ad·ju·di·ca·ta** (a-jo͞odi-). An adjudicated precedent in law that cannot be altered. [Latin, "thing decided".]
Res·nais (re-náy), **Alain** (1922–). French New Wave film director. His two most famous films are *Hiroshima, Mon Amour* (1959) and *Last Year in Marienbad* (1961). Other films include *Providence* (1977), *Smoking*, and *No Smoking* (both 1993).
re·sol·u·ble (ri-zóllew-b'l, rə-) *adj.* Capable of being resolved; resolvable. [Late Latin *resolūbilis*, from Latin *resolvere*, RESOLVE.] **—re·sol·u·bil·i·ty** (-bílləti), **re·sol·u·ble·ness** *n.*
res·o·lute (rézzə-lo͞ot, -lewt) *adj.* **1.** Characterised by firmness or determination. **2.** Pursuing a fixed purpose; unwavering. [Latin *resolūtus*, past participle of *resolvere*, to RESOLVE.] **—res·o·lute·ly** *adv.* **—res·o·lute·ness** *n.*
res·o·lu·tion (rézzə-lo͞o-sh'n, -léw-) *n. Abbr.* **res. 1.** The state or quality of being resolute; firm determination. See Synonyms at **courage. 2.** The act of resolving to do something. **3.** A course of action determined or decided upon. **4.** A formal statement of a decision or expression of opinion put before or adopted by an assembly. **5.** The action or process of separating or reducing something into its constituent parts: *the prismatic resolution of sunlight into its spectral colours.* **6.** *Medicine.* The subsiding or termination of an abnormal condition, as of a fever or inflammation. **7.** The act or process of finding a solution, as of a problem or puzzle. **8.** *Music.* **a.** The progression of a dissonant note or chord to a consonant note or chord. **b.** The note or chord to which such a progression is made. **9.** *Physics.* The efficiency with which an instrument or technique can separate or distinguish the component parts of something; resolving power.
re·sol·u·tive (ri-zóllewtiv, rə-, rézzə-lo͞otiv, -lewtiv) *adj.* Having the power to disintegrate or dissolve something.
re·solv·a·ble (ri-zólv-əb'l, rə- || *Southern England also* -zōlv-) *adj.* Capable of being resolved; solvable. **—re·solv·a·bil·i·ty** (-ə-bílləti), **re·solv·a·ble·ness** *n.*
re·solve (ri-zólv, rə- || *Southern England also* -zōlv) *v.* **-solved, -solving, -solves.** *—tr.* **1. a.** To make a firm decision about (a matter of controversy, for example); settle: *resolve a question.* **b.** To decide upon (a course of action); determine: *resolved to tell the truth.* **2.** To cause (a person) to reach a decision. **3.** To decide or express by formal vote. **4.** To separate (something) into constituent parts. **5.** To change or convert. Usually used reflexively: *His resentment resolved itself into resignation.* **6.** To find a solution to; solve. **7.** To remove or dispel (doubts or misunderstandings); clear up. **8.** To bring to a conclusion: *resolve a conflict.* **9.** *Medicine.* To reduce (an inflammation). **10.** *Music.* To cause (a note or chord) to progress from dissonance to consonance. **11.** *Chemistry.* To separate (a racemic compound or mixture) into its optically active constituents. **12.** *Optics.* **a.** To render visible and distinguish parts of (an image). **b.** To separate or distinguish (different lines) in a spectrum. **13.** *Mathematics.* To separate (a vector, for example) into coordinate components. **14.** *Obsolete.* To melt or dissolve (something). *~intr.* **1.** To reach a decision. With *on* or *upon*: *resolve on a proposal.* **2.** To become separated or reduced to constituents. With *into.* **3.** *Music.* To undergo resolution. —See Synonyms at **decide.**
~n. **1.** Firmness of purpose; determination. **2.** A decision; a fixed purpose. **3.** *U.S.* A formal resolution made by a deliberative body. [Middle English *resolven*, to analyse, untie, solve, from Latin *resolvere*, to release, unbind, annul, resolve : *re-* (intensive), again + *solvere*, untie, release.] **—re·solv·er** *n.*
re·solved (ri-zólvd, rə- || -zōlvd) *adj.* Fixed in purpose; firmly determined; resolute. **—re·solv·ed·ly** (-idli) *adv.*
re·sol·vent (ri-zól-vənt, rə- || -zōlv-) *adj.* **1.** Causing or capable of causing separation into constituents; solvent. **2.** Causing reduction in inflammation or swelling.
~n. A resolvent substance, especially: **1.** A solvent. **2.** A medicine that reduces inflammation or swelling.
re·solv·ing power (ri-zólv-ing, rə- || -zōlv-) *n. Physics.* A measure of the ability of an instrument to resolve optical images or spectra.
res·o·nance (rézzənənss) *n.* **1.** The quality or condition of being resonant. **2.** *Physics.* **a.** The enhancement of the response of an electrical or mechanical system to a periodic driving force when the driving frequency is equal to the natural undamped frequency of the system. **b.** The condition of a system of subatomic particles in which the probability of a particular reaction, as for example nuclear capture of a neutron, is a maximum; the occurrence of a cross-section maximum. **c.** The event corresponding to such a maximum, especially the particle state so formed, having only a few possible modes of decay and characterised by a lifetime considerably longer than neighbouring states. **3.** The intensification and prolongation of sound, especially of a musical note, produced by sympathetic vibration. **4.** *Medicine.* The sound produced by diagnostic percussion of the chest, abdomen, or other hollow organ. **5.** *Chemistry.* The phenomenon occurring in a chemical compound whereby its molecular structure can be represented by two or more conventional structures, the actual structure being regarded as a hybrid form of the representations. Used adjectivally: *a resonance hybrid.* **6.** *Phonetics.* The intensification of vocal tones during articulation, as by the air cavities of the mouth and nasal passages.
res·o·nant (rézzənənt) *adj.* **1.** Producing resonance: *resonant frequency excitation.* **2.** Having a prolonged, subtle, stimulating effect beyond the initial impact: *resonant Shakespearian verse.* [Latin *resonāns* (stem *resonant-*), present participle of *resonāre*, to RESOUND.] **—res·o·nant·ly** *adv.*
resonant circuit *n.* An electrical circuit with inductance and capacitance chosen to produce a specific value of the natural frequency of the circuit. Also called "resonator".
res·o·nate (rézzə-nayt) *intr.v.* **-nated, -nating, -nates. 1.** To exhibit resonance or resonant effects. **2.** To resound. [Latin *resonāre*, to RESOUND.] **—res·o·na·tion** (-náysh'n) *n.*
res·o·na·tor (rézzə-naytər) *n.* **1.** A resonating system. **2.** A hollow chamber or cavity with dimensions chosen to permit internal resonant oscillation of electromagnetic or acoustical waves of specific frequencies. **3.** *Electronics.* **a.** Any of various microwave-generating tubes or devices containing such resonant chambers or cavities. **b.** A resonant circuit.
re·sorb (ree-sórb, ri-, -zórb) *v.* **-sorbed, -sorbing, -sorbs.** *—tr.* **1.** To absorb again. **2.** *Biology.* To dissolve and assimilate (bone tissue, for example). *—intr.* To be resorbed. [Latin *resorbēre* : *re-*, back + *sorbēre*, to suck.] **—re·sorp·tion** (-sórp-sh'n, -zórp-) *n.*
res·or·cin·ol (ri-zór-si-nol, rə- || -nōl) *n.* Also **res·or·cin** (-sin). A white crystalline compound, $C_6H_4(OH)_2$, used to treat certain skin diseases and in dyes, resin adhesives, and pharmaceuticals. [RES(IN) + ORC(HIL) + -IN + -OL.]
re·sort (reé-sórt) *tr.v.* **-sorted, -sorting, -sorts.** To sort again.
re·sort (ri-zórt, rə-) *intr.v.* **-sorted, -sorting, -sorts. 1.** To seek assistance, relief, or an expedient; have recourse. Used with *to*: *The government resorted to censorship of the press.* **2.** To go customarily or frequently; repair. Used with *to.*
~n. **1.** A place frequented by people for holidays or recreation: *a winter resort.* **2.** A customary or frequent going or gathering: *a popular place of resort.* **3.** A person or thing turned to for aid or relief: *a last resort.* **4.** The act of turning to a person or thing for aid or relief; recourse. [Middle English *resorten*, return, revert, from Old French *resortir*, to come out again, to resort : *re-*, again + *sortir*, to go out (see **sortie**).]
Usage: *Resort* and *recourse* are used in slightly different constructions in standard English: for example, *He resorted to force, He had recourse to force.* To *have resort to* is often heard, but the usage attracts criticism. Similarly, standard usage requires *as a last resort*, not *as a last recourse.*
re·sound (ri-zównd, rə-) *v.* **-sounded, -sounding, -sounds.** *—intr.* **1.** To be filled with sound; reverberate. **2.** To make a loud, long, or reverberating sound. **3.** To become famous, celebrated, or extolled. *—tr.* **1.** To send back (sound); re-echo. **2.** To extol; celebrate. [Middle English *resounen*, from Old French *resoner*, from Latin *resonāre*, to sound again, echo : *re-*, again + *sonāre*, to sound.]
re·sound·ing (ri-zównding, rə-) *adj.* **1.** Resonating or reverberating; loud: *resounding applause.* **2.** Emphatic; decisive: *a resounding victory.* **—re·sound·ing·ly** *adv.*
re·source (ri-zórss, -sórss, rə- || -zōrss, -sōrss, *or with initial stress* reé-sawrss) *n.* **1.** Something that can be used for support or help: *financial and human resources.* **2.** An available supply that can be drawn upon when needed. **3.** The ability to deal effectively with a difficult or troublesome situation; initiative; capability. **4.** Any means of coping with a difficult situation. **5. a.** *Plural.* The total means available to a country for its economic and political development, including such elements as mineral wealth, manpower, and armaments. **b.** *Plural. Now sometimes singular.* The total means available to a company for increasing production or profit, including such elements as plant, labour, and raw materials. **c.** Any such element considered individually. [French *ressource*, from Old French *ressourse*, relief, recovery, from *resourdre*, to rise again, from Latin *resurgere* : *re-*, again + *surgere*, to rise, SURGE.]
re·source·ful (ri-zórss-f'l, rə-, -sórss-, || -sōrss-, -zōrss-) *adj.* Readily able to act effectively, especially in a difficult situation or emergency; capable. **—re·source·ful·ly** *adv.* **—re·source·ful·ness** *n.*
resp. 1. respective; respectively. **2.** respiration.
re·spect (ri-spékt, rə-) *tr.v.* **-spected, -specting, -spects. 1.** To feel or show esteem for; honour. **2.** To show consideration for; avoid violation of; treat with deference. **3.** *Archaic.* To relate or refer to.
~n. **1.** A feeling of deferential regard; honour; esteem. **2.** The state of being regarded with honour or esteem. **3.** Willingness to show consideration or regard: *Have some respect for her feelings.* **4.** *Plural.* Polite expressions of consideration or deference: *pay one's respects.* **5.** A particular aspect, feature, or detail: *is identical in*

many respects. **6.** Relation; reference. Used chiefly in the phrases *in respect of* and *with respect to.* **—pay (one's) last respects.** To show signs of respect to a dead person before or at a funeral. **—with respect.** Used by a speaker to introduce a statement that disagrees with or rejects a remark just made by a previous speaker. [Latin *respectus,* past participle of *respicere,* to regard, look back : *re-,* back + *specere,* to look.] **—re·spect·ful** *adj.* **—re·spect·ful·ly** *adv.* **—re·spect·ful·ness** *n.*

re·spect·a·bil·i·ty (ri-spéktə-bílləti, rə-) *n., pl.* **-ties. 1.** The quality, state, or characteristic of being respectable. **2.** Respectable members of a community.

re·spect·a·ble (ri-spéktəb'l, rə-) *adj.* **1.** Meriting respect or esteem; worthy. **2.** Conforming or tending to conform to conventionally accepted moral standards and behaviour. **3.** Of moderately good quality: *a respectable day's work.* **4.** Considerable in amount, number, or size: *a respectable sum of money.* **5.** Of reasonable social standing; honest and decent. **6.** Having an acceptable appearance; presentable: *a respectable hat.* **—re·spect·a·ble·ness** *n.* **—re·spect·a·bly** *adv.*

re·spec·ter (ri-spéktər, rə-). *n.* One who respects. **—no respecter of persons.** One not biased towards the rich or powerful.

re·spect·ing (ri-spékting, rə-) *prep.* In relation to; concerning.

re·spec·tive (ri-spéktiv, rə-) *adj. Abbr.* **resp.** Belonging or pertaining to two or more persons or things regarded individually; particular: *"The two women stood by their respective telephones"* (Doris Lessing). **—re·spec·tive·ness** *n.*

re·spec·tive·ly (ri-spéktivli, rə-) *adv. Abbr.* **resp.** Singly in the order designated or mentioned: *gave Paul and Anne a book and a record respectively.*

re·spell (rée-spél) *tr.v.* **-spelled** or **-spelt** (-spélt), **-spelling, -spells.** To spell again or in a new way, as with a phonetic alphabet.

Re·spi·ghi (re-spéegi), **Ottorino** (1879–1936). Italian composer. He wrote prolifically in almost every form, but little of his music is now performed, except for the symphonic poems *The Fountains of Rome* (1917) and *The Pines of Rome* (1924).

res·pi·ra·ble (réspir-əb'l, ri-spír-, rə-) *adj.* **1.** Suitable for breathing. **2.** Capable of or adapted for breathing. **—res·pi·ra·bil·i·ty** (-ə-bílləti) *n.*

res·pi·ra·tion (réspə-ráysh'n, réspi-) *n. Abbr.* **resp. 1. a.** The act or process of inhaling and exhaling; breathing. **b.** The act or process whereby an organism without lungs, such as a fish or plant, exchanges gases with its environment. **2.** The metabolic process by which an organism assimilates oxygen, oxidises organic substances in the cells, with the release of energy, and releases carbon dioxide and other products of oxidation.

res·pi·ra·tor (réspə-raytər, réspi-) *n.* **1.** An apparatus used in administering artificial respiration, such as an **iron lung** *(see).* **2.** A screenlike device worn over the mouth or nose, or both, to protect the respiratory tract.

res·pi·ra·to·ry (ri-spír-ə-tri, re-, rə-, réspirə-, -təri, réspi-raytəri) *adj.* Of, pertaining to, affecting, or used in respiration.

respiratory distress syndrome *n.* A condition in newborn, especially premature, infants, in which the lungs are imperfectly expanded, leading to extreme difficulty in breathing. Also called "hyaline membrane disease".

re·spire (ri-spír, rə-) *v.* **-spired, -spiring, -spires.** *—intr.* **1.** To breathe in and out; inhale and exhale. **2.** To undergo the metabolic process of respiration. **3.** *Archaic.* To breathe easily again, as after a period of exertion or trouble. *—tr.* To inhale and exhale (air); breathe. [Middle English *respyren,* to breathe again, from Latin *respīrāre* : *re-,* again + *spīrāre,* to breathe.]

res·pite (réss-pit, -pīt || ri-spīt, rə-) *n.* **1. a.** A temporary cessation or postponement, usually of something disagreeable. **b.** An interval of rest or relief. **2.** The temporary suspension of a death sentence; a reprieve.

~tr.v. **respited, -piting, -pites. 1.** To provide with a period of temporary rest or relief. **2. a.** To grant (someone) a reprieve. **b.** To grant a reprieve from (a punishment or sentence). [Middle English *respit,* from Old French, from Latin *respectus,* looking back, refuge, from past part. of *respicere* : *re-,* back + *specere,* to look.]

re·splen·dent (ri-spléndənt, rə-) *adj.* Splendid or dazzling in appearance; brilliant. [Middle English, from Latin *resplendēns* (stem *resplendent-*), present participle of *resplendēre,* to shine brightly : *re-* (intensive) + *splendēre,* to shine.] **—re·splen·dence, re·splen·den·cy** *n.* **—re·splen·dent·ly** *adv.*

re·spond (ri-spónd, rə-) *v.* **-sponded, -sponding, -sponds.** *—intr.* **1.** To make a reply; answer. **2.** To act in return or in answer. **3.** To react; especially, to react positively or cooperatively: *The patient responded well to the treatment.* *—tr.* To say in reply; answer. —See Synonyms at **answer.**

~n. **1.** *Architecture.* A pilaster supporting an arch. **2.** A chanted or sung response in a liturgy. [Latin *respondēre,* "to promise in return" : *re-,* back, in return + *spondēre,* to promise.] **—re·spon·der** *n.*

re·spon·dent (ri-spóndənt, rə-) *adj.* **1.** Giving or given as a responsive. **2.** *Law.* Being a defendant.

~n. **1.** A person who responds. **2.** *Law.* A defendant, especially in a divorce suit. **—re·spon·dence, re·spon·den·cy** *n.*

re·sponse (ri-spónss, rə-) *n.* **1.** A reply or answer. **2.** Any act of responding; a reaction: *Public response has been overwhelming.* **3. a.** A reaction, such as that of an organism or mechanism, to a specific stimulus. **b.** A measure of this; for example, the ratio of the output signal of an electronic device to the input signal. **4.** *Abbr.* **R. a.** That which is spoken or sung by a congregation or choir in answer to the officiating minister or priest. **b.** A responsory. **5.** In the game of bridge, a bid made in reply to a partner's bid. [Middle English *respons,* from Old French, from Latin *responsum,* from past participle of *respondēre,* "to promise in return", RESPOND.]

re·spon·si·bil·i·ty (ri-spón-sə-bílləti, rə-) *n., pl.* **-ties. 1.** The state or fact of being responsible. **2.** A thing or person that one is answerable for; a duty, obligation, or burden. **3.** The power or ability to act without superior authority or guidance; the quality of being responsible.

re·spon·si·ble (ri-spón-səb'l, rə-) *adj.* **1. a.** Legally or ethically accountable for the care or welfare of another. **b.** Having control or authority over something; in charge: *She is responsible for sales.* **2.** Involving personal accountability or ability to act without guidance or superior authority. **3.** Being the source, explanation, or cause of something. Used with *for: He was responsible for the accident.* **4. a.** Capable of making moral, practical, or rational decisions on one's own, and therefore answerable for one's behaviour. **b.** Able to be trusted or depended upon; reliable. **5.** Based upon or characterised by good judgment or sound thinking. **6.** Having the means to pay debts or fulfil obligations. **7.** Required to render account; answerable. Used with *to: The cabinet is responsible to Parliament.* [From obsolete French, correspondent to, from Latin *respondēre,* to RESPOND.] **—re·spon·si·bly** *adv.*

Synonyms: *responsible, answerable, liable, accountable, amenable.*

re·spon·sive (ri-spón-siv, rə-) *adj.* **1.** Answering or replying; responding. **2.** Readily reacting, as to suggestions, influences, stimuli, or efforts. **3.** Containing or using responses: *responsive liturgy.* **—re·spon·sive·ly** *adv.* **—re·spon·sive·ness** *n.*

re·spon·so·ry (ri-spón-səri, rə-) *n., pl.* **-ries.** A chant or anthem recited or sung after a reading in a church service. Also called "response". [Middle English, from Late Latin *responsōria,* from Latin *respondēre* (past participle *responsus*), RESPOND.]

re·spon·sum (ri-spón-səm, rə-) *n., pl.* **-sa** (-sə). An answer by a rabbi to a question concerning Jewish law or its observance. [Latin, response.]

re·spray (rée-spráy) *tr.v.* **-sprayed, -spraying, -sprays.** To spray (a car, for example) again, as to renew or change the colour of the paintwork. **—re·spray** (rée-spray) *n.*

res pu·bli·ca (ráyss pŏŏblikə, ráyz) *n.* The state; the republic. [Latin. See **republic.**]

rest¹ (rest) *n.* **1. a.** The act or state of ceasing from work, activity, or motion; quiet. **b.** A period during which someone is not required to work or something is not used: *gave the engine a rest.* **2.** Peace, ease, or refreshment resulting from sleep or the cessation of an activity. **3.** Sleep or quiet relaxation. **4.** The repose of death: *laid to rest.* **5.** Relief or freedom from disquiet or disturbance. **6.** Mental or emotional tranquillity. **7.** Termination or absence of motion. **8.** *Music.* **a.** An interval of silence corresponding to any of the possible time values within the measure. **b.** A mark or symbol indicating such a pause and its length. **9.** In prosody, a short pause in a line of verse; a caesura. **10.** A device used as a support or prop. Often used in combination: *a footrest.* **11.** In billiards, snooker, and similar games, a **bridge** *(see).* **12.** A place for lodging or shelter, especially for sailors or travellers. Often used in the name of a hotel, inn, or the like. **—at rest. 1.** In a state of rest or repose, especially: **a.** Asleep. **b.** Dead. **c.** Motionless. **2.** Free from anxiety or distress.

~v. **rested, resting, rests.** *—intr.* **1.** To refresh oneself by ceasing work or activity or by lying down, sleeping, or relaxing in some other manner. **2.** To cease temporarily from work, motion, or activity. **3.** To sleep. **4. a.** To be at peace or ease; be tranquil. **b.** To have peace in death: *resting in Highgate cemetery.* **5.** To remain in a particular state; receive no further attention: *let the issue rest here; rest assured of the outcome.* **6.** To be supported; lie, lean, or sit. Used with *in, on, upon,* or *against.* **7.** To be imposed or vested as a responsibility or burden. Used with *on, upon,* or *with: The final decision rests with the chairman.* **8.** To depend or rely. Used with *on, upon,* or *with: His argument rests on a false assumption.* **9.** To be located or be in a specified place: *now rests in the British Museum.* **10.** To settle, fall, or be fixed: *his eyes rested on her.* **11.** To remain; linger. Used with *on* or *upon.* **12.** *Law.* To cease voluntarily the presentation of evidence in a case. *—tr.* **1. a.** To give rest or repose to; refresh by rest. **b.** To stop using, cultivating, or working. **2.** To place, lay, or lean for ease, support, or repose. **3.** To base or ground: *rested his conclusion on that fact.* **4.** To fix or direct (the eyes or gaze, for example). **5.** *Law.* To cease voluntarily the introduction of evidence in (a case). [Middle English *reste,* Old English *reste, ræst,* rest, resting place, from Common Germanic *rast-* (unattested).] **—rest·er** *n.*

Synonyms: *rest, relaxation, repose, leisure, ease, comfort.*

rest² *n.* **1.** That part which is left over after something has been removed; the remainder. **2.** *Used with a plural verb.* The ones remaining: *The rest are coming later.* —See Synonyms at **remainder.**

~intr.v. **rested, resting, rests. 1.** To be or continue to be; remain: *rest easy.* **2.** *Obsolete.* To remain or be left over. [Middle English, from Old French *reste,* from *rester,* to remain, from Latin *restāre,* to keep back, stand firm : *re-,* back + *stāre,* to stand.]

rest³ *n.* On medieval armour, a support for the butt of a lance on the side of the breastplate, used when charging. [Middle English *(a)rest,* an arresting, from Old French, from *arester,* to ARREST.]

re·state (rée-stáyt) *tr.v.* **-stated, -stating, -states.** To state again or in a new form. **—re·state·ment** *n.*

res·tau·rant (réstə-RON, rést-, -ront, -rənt) *n.* A place where meals are served, usually for payment, to the public. [French, "restorative", from *restaurer,* to restore, from Old French *restorer,* to RESTORE.]

restaurant car *n. British.* A dining car *(see).*

res·tau·ra·teur (rĕss-tərə-túr, -torrə-, -tawrə- ‖ -tóor) *n.* Also *nonstandard* **res·taur·ant·eur** (-tə-ron-, -tə-RON-). The manager or owner of a restaurant or restaurants. [French, from *restaurer,* to restore. See **restaurant.**]

rest cure *n.* A complete rest from one's usual activities taken as part of a course of treatment, especially treatment for nervous disorders.

rest energy *n. Physics.* The energy equivalent of the rest mass of a body, equal to the rest mass multiplied by the speed of light squared.

rest·ful (rĕst-f'l) *adj.* 1. Giving tranquillity. 2. At rest; quiet. —See Synonyms at **comfortable.** —**rest·ful·ly** *adv.* —**rest·ful·ness** *n.*

rest·har·row (rĕst-harrō) *n.* Any of several Old World plants of the genus *Ononis,* having tough, woody stems and roots, and pink, purplish, or yellow pealike flowers. [Middle English *(a)resten,* ARREST + HARROW (because its roots obstruct or "arrest" the harrow).]

rest home *n.* A place for the care of the elderly or frail.

rest·ing (rĕsting) *adj.* 1. a. In a state of inactivity or rest. b. Out of work. Said euphemistically of an actor. 2. *Biology.* Dormant. Said especially of spores that germinate after a prolonged period.

resting cell *n. Biology.* A cell that is not actively in the process of dividing.

resting place *n.* The grave. Used euphemistically, chiefly in the phrase *last resting place.*

resting potential *n. Physiology.* The difference in charge that exists between the inside and outside of the cell membrane of a nonconducting nerve or muscle cell.

res·ti·tu·tion (rĕsti-tĕw-sh'n ‖ -tóo-) *n.* 1. The act of restoring to the rightful owner something that has been taken away, lost, or surrendered. 2. The act of making good or compensating for loss, damage, or injury; indemnification; reparation. 3. A return to or restoration of a previous state or position; for example, the return of a system to its original state after deformation. —See Synonyms at **reparation.**

res·tive (rĕstiv) *adj.* 1. Impatient or nervous under restriction, delay, or pressure; uneasy; restless. 2. Difficult to control; refractory; unruly. [Middle English *restyffe,* unwilling to move, stationary, from Old French *restif,* from Vulgar Latin *restīvus* (unattested), remaining stationary, from Latin *restāre,* to keep back : *re-,* back + *stāre,* to stand.] —**res·tive·ly** *adv.* —**res·tive·ness** *n.*

rest·less (rĕst-ləss, -liss) *adj.* 1. Without quiet, repose, or rest: *a restless night.* 2. Unable or unwilling to rest or relax: *a restless child.* 3. Never still or motionless: *the restless sea.* 4. Agitated or uneasy. —**rest·less·ly** *adv.* —**rest·less·ness** *n.*

rest mass *n.* The physical mass of a body that is at rest relative to the observer.

re·stock (rée-stók) *tr.v.* **-stocked, -stocking, -stocks.** To stock again; furnish new stock for.

res·to·ra·tion (rĕss-tə-ráysh'n, -taw-) *n.* 1. The act of restoring or reinstating someone or something, or the state of being restored: *the restoration of the death penalty.* 2. The repairing and refurbishing of furniture, buildings, or works of art to return them to something close to their original condition. 3. That which has been restored, such as a renovated building. —**the Restoration.** 1. The return of Charles II to the British throne in 1660. 2. a. The period between the return of Charles II and the Revolution of 1688. b. Loosely, the period from 1660 until the end of the 17th century. Also used adjectivally: *Restoration prose.*

Restoration comedy *n.* A genre of dramatic comedy characterised by social satire and wit that flourished especially during the period of the Restoration in England, from about 1660 until the end of the 17th century.

re·stor·a·tive (ri-stórrə-tiv, rə-, re-, -stáwrə- ‖ -stǒrə-) *adj.* Tending to renew or restore something, such as health or strength.
~*n.* Something that restores or revives, such as a drug.

re·store (ri-stór, rə- ‖ -stǒr) *tr.v.* **-stored, -storing, -stores.** 1. To bring back into existence or use; re-establish: *restore law and order.* 2. To bring back to a previous, normal, or original condition, as by repair, cleaning, or reconstruction: *restore a work of art.* 3. To put (a person) back in a prior position: *restore the emperor to the throne.* 4. To give or bring back; make restitution of: *restore the stolen funds.* [Middle English *restoren,* from Old French *restorer,* from Latin *restaurāre* : *re-,* back + *instaurāre,* to renew.] —**re·stor·er** *n.*

re·strain (ri-stráyn, rə-) *tr.v.* **-strained, -straining, -strains.** 1. a. To control; check; repress. b. To hold (a person) back; prevent. Used with *from: restrained them from going.* 2. To deprive of freedom or liberty. 3. To limit or restrict. [Middle English *restreynen,* from Old French *restraindre* (present stem *restrain-*), from Latin *restringere,* to RESTRICT.] —**re·strain·a·ble** *adj.*

Synonyms: *restrain, restrict, curb, check, inhibit.*

re·strained (ri-stráynd, rə-) *adj.* Showing or exercising restraint or self-restraint. —**re·strain·ed·ly** (-stráynidli) *adv.*

re·strain·er (ri-stráynər, rə-) *n.* A substance, often potassium bromide, added to photographic developer to reduce the fog on the film.

re·straint (ri-stráynt, rə-) *n.* 1. The act of holding back or restraining. 2. Loss or abridgment of freedom. 3. Any influence that inhibits or restrains; a limitation. 4. An instrument or means of controlling or restraining. 5. a. Control or repression of feelings.

b. Avoidance of excess or outlandishness. [Middle English *restreinte,* from Old French *restrainte,* from the past participle of *restraindre,* RESTRAIN.]

restraint of trade *n.* Any action or condition that tends to prevent free competition in business, such as the creation of a monopoly or the limiting of a market.

re·strict (ri-strĭkt, rə-) *tr.v.* **-stricted, -stricting, -stricts.** To hold down or keep within limits. See Synonyms at **limit, restrain.** [Latin *restringere* (past participle *restrictus*), to bind back tight : *re-,* back + *stringere,* to bind.]

re·strict·ed (ri-strĭktid, rə-) *adj.* 1. Subject to limits or restrictions. 2. Not for general circulation. Said of documents. 3. *British.* Designating a zone or area in which speed limits or parking restrictions for vehicles apply. 4. *Chiefly U.S.* Excluding or unavailable to certain groups. —**re·strict·ed·ly** *adv.*

re·stric·tion (ri-strĭksh'n, rə-) *n.* 1. The act of limiting or restricting. 2. The state of being limited or restricted. 3. Something that restricts; a limiting or restraining factor, condition, or regulation.

re·stric·tive (ri-strĭktiv, rə-) *adj.* 1. Tending or serving to restrict. 2. *Grammar.* Designating a subordinate clause, phrase, or term considered to limit the application or reference of the word or word group that it modifies, thus being essential to the meaning of the sentence and usually not marked off by commas. In the sentence *People who read a great deal have large vocabularies,* the restrictive clause is *who read a great deal.* Compare **nonrestrictive.** —**re·stric·tive·ly** *adv.*

restrictive practice *n. British.* 1. An agreement between buyers and sellers that interferes with or prevents free competition and is viewed as being against the public interest, for example fixing the prices, quantities, or quality of goods traded. Also called "restrictive trade practice". 2. An agreement or activity by a trade union or its members that affects another union, other employees, or employers, as in reserving certain jobs for particular unions.

rest room *n. Chiefly U.S.* A public lavatory.

re·sult (ri-zúlt, rə-) *intr.v.* **-sulted, -sulting, -sults.** 1. To occur or exist as a consequence. Often used with *from.* 2. To end in a particular way. Used with *in.* 3. *Law.* To revert to a former owner owing to having been partially or ineffectually disposed of. Used of property. —See Synonyms at **follow.**
~*n.* 1. The consequence of a particular action, operation, or course; an outcome. 2. A particular consequence. 3. *Often plural.* A positive or useful effect: *He may be stern but he certainly gets results.* 4. *Often plural.* An answer or finding arrived at through research or calculation: *published the results of the survey.* 5. *Often plural.* The final score, mark, or outcome of any encounter or endeavour involving competition: *football results; the election result.* 6. *British Informal.* A win, especially in a team sport: *England need a result to square the cricket series.* —See Synonyms at **effect.** [Middle English *resulten,* from Medieval Latin *resultāre,* from Latin, to leap back, rebound : *re-,* back + *saltāre,* to leap, frequentative of *salīre,* to leap.]

re·sul·tant (ri-zúltənt, rə-) *adj.* Issuing or following as a consequence or result.
~*n.* 1. That which results; an outcome. 2. *Mathematics & Physics.* A vector or vector quantity that results from the addition or two or more vectors, for example, a net force resulting from the simultaneous application of other component forces. Also used adjectivally: *resultant force; resultant velocity.*

re·sume (ri-zéwm, rə-, -zóom ‖ -zhóom) *v.* **-sumed, -suming, -sumes.** —*tr.* 1. To continue after interruption or adjournment. 2. To occupy or take again: *resume your seats.* 3. To take on or take back again: *resume a gift.* —*intr.* To continue after interruption or adjournment. [Middle English *resumen,* from Old French *resumer,* from Latin *resūmere,* to take up again : *re-,* again + *sūmere,* to take up.] —**re·sum·a·ble** *adj.*

rés·u·mé (rĕz-yoo-may, ráyz-, -oo- ‖ -ə-, -máy) *n.* 1. A summing up; a summary. 2. *U.S.* A curriculum vitae. [French, from the past participle of *résumer,* to RESUME.]

re·sump·tion (ri-zúmpsh'n, rə-) *n.* The act or an instance of resuming. [Middle English, from Old French, from Late Latin *resūmptiō* (stem *resūmptiōn-*), from Latin *resūmere,* RESUME.]

re·su·pi·nate (ri-séw-pi-nət, rə-, -sóo-, -nit, -nayt) *adj. Biology.* Inverted or seemingly turned upside-down. [Latin *resupīnatus,* bent back, past participle of *resupīnāre,* to bend back : *re-,* back + *supīnus,* SUPINE.] —**re·su·pi·na·tion** (-náysh'n) *n.*

re·su·pine (ri-séw-pīn, -sóo- ‖ rée-sə-, rĕssə-, -pīn) *adj.* Lying on the back; supine. [Latin *resupīnus,* from *resupīnāre.* See **resupinate.**]

re·surge (ri-súrj, rə-) *intr.v.* **-surged, -surging, -surges.** 1. To rise again; re-emerge to prominence or vitality. 2. To sweep or surge back again. [Latin *resurgere* : *re-,* again + *surgere,* SURGE.]

re·sur·gent (ri-súrjənt, rə-) *adj.* Rising or tending to rise or emerge again; resurging. —**re·sur·gence** *n.*

res·ur·rect (rézzə-rĕkt) *v.* **-rected, -recting, -rects.** —*tr.* 1. To bring back to life; raise from the dead. 2. To bring back into practice, notice, or use. —*intr.* To rise from the dead; return to life. [Backformation from RESURRECTION.]

res·ur·rec·tion (rézzə-rĕksh'n) *n.* 1. A rising from the dead or returning to life. 2. The state of those who have returned to life. 3. A returning or bringing back to practice, notice, or use; a revival. —**the Resurrection.** 1. The rising again of Christ on the third day after the Crucifixion. 2. The rising again of the dead at the Last Judgment. [Middle English *resurreccion,* from Old French *resurrection,* from Late Latin *resurrēctiō* (stem *resurrēctiōn-*), from Latin *resurgere* (past participle *resurrēctus*), to RESURGE.] —**res·ur·rec·tion·al** *adj.*

res·ur·rec·tion·ist (rézzə-réksh'n-ist) *n.* Formerly, one who stole bodies from the grave in order to sell them for dissection.

resurrection plant *n.* Any of several plants that appear dead during dry periods and expand and continue to grow under moist conditions; especially, the **rose of Jericho** (*see*).

re·sus·ci·tate (ri-sússi-tayt, rə-) *v.* **-tated, -tating, -tates.** —*tr.* To restore consciousness, vigour, or life to. —*intr.* To return to life or consciousness; revive. [Latin *resuscitāre*, to revive : *re-*, again + *suscitāre*, to raise, stir up : *sub-*, below, up from below + *citāre*, to set moving, from *citus*, quick, past participle of *ciēre*, *cīre*, to stir.] —**re·sus·ci·ta·ble** (-təb'l) *adj.* —**re·sus·ci·ta·tion** (-táysh'n) *n.* —**re·sus·ci·ta·tive** (-tətiv, -taytiv) *adj.* —**re·sus·ci·ta·tor** (-taytər) *n.*

ret (ret) *tr.v.* **retted, retting, rets.** To moisten or soak (flax or hemp, for example) to soften and separate the fibres by partial rotting. [Middle English *reten*, perhaps from Old Norse *reyta* (unattested), from Germanic *rutjan* (unattested), to ROT.]

ret. 1. retain. 2. retired. 3. return; returned.

re·ta·ble (ri-táyb'l ‖ rée-tayb'l, réttəb'l) *n.* A structure forming the back of an altar, especially: 1. An overhanging shelf for lights and ornaments. 2. A frame enclosing carved or painted panels. [French, from Spanish *retablo*, from Medieval Latin *retabulum* (unattested), shortening of *retrōtabulum*, structure at the back of an altar : *retrō-*, back + *tabulum*, table, from Latin *tabula*, board, tablet (see **table**).]

re·tail (rée-tayl, *rarely* ree-táyl) *n.* The sale of commodities in small quantities direct to the consumer. —*adj.* Of, pertaining to, or engaged in the sale of goods in this way. —*adv.* At retail; from a retailer. —*v.* (ree-táyl, ri-, rée-tayl) **retailed, -tailing, -tails.** —*tr.* 1. To sell in small quantities. 2. To tell and retell (a story, especially gossip or scandal) in detail. —*intr.* To be sold at retail: *retails at about five pounds.* [Middle English *retaile*, "division", from Old French *retaille*, from *retaillier*, to cut up : *re-* (intensive) + *taillier*, to cut (see **tailor**).] —**re·tail·er** (*usually* rée-taylər) *n.*

retail price index *n.* In Britain, an official monthly price index showing the changes in the retail prices of those goods and services typically bought by the average consumer.

re·tain (ri-táyn, rə-) *tr.v.* **-tained, -taining, -tains.** 1. **a.** To keep or hold in one's possession. **b.** To continue to have: *he retained their support.* 2. To continue to adopt (a practice or name, for example); maintain: *The American edition retains the British spelling.* 3. To keep or hold in a particular place, condition, or position. 4. To keep in mind; remember. 5. To hire (a barrister) by the payment of a preliminary fee. 6. To keep in one's service or pay. —See Synonyms at **keep**. [Middle English *reteinen*, from Old French *retenir*, from Latin *retinēre* : *re-*, back + *tenēre*, to hold.] —**re·tain·a·ble** *adj.* —**re·tain·ment** *n.*

re·tained object (ri-táynd, rə-) *n.* An object in a passive construction that is identical to the object in the corresponding active construction, such as *story* in *Susan was told the story by John.*

re·tain·er[1] (ri-táynər, rə-) *n.* 1. A person or thing that keeps or retains. 2. **a.** One who served in a noble household, as in the feudal period, but who ranked higher than a servant; an attendant. **b.** A domestic servant, especially one who has been with the same family for a long period of time. 3. Any device, frame, or groove that restrains or guides something.

retainer[2] *n.* 1. The act of retaining a barrister or other adviser, or the fact of being so retained. 2. **a.** A preliminary fee paid to engage the services of a barrister, consultant, or other professional. **b.** A regular fee paid to an outside consultant so that one may call upon his services when required. 3. A fee paid to reserve rented accommodation or retain it during one's absence.

re·take (rée-táyk, ree-) *tr.v.* **-took** (-tŏŏk ‖ -tŏŏk), **-taken** (-táykən) **-taking, -takes.** 1. To take back or again. 2. To photograph or film again. —*n.* (rée-tayk). 1. A taking again. 2. A scene or shot that has been or is to be filmed or photographed again. —**re·tak·er** *n.*

re·tal·i·ate (ri-tál-i-ayt, rə-) *v.* **-ated, -ating, -ates.** —*intr.* 1. To return like for like; especially, to return evil for evil in kind. 2. To respond to aggression with another attack. —*tr.* To pay back (an injury) in kind. [Latin *retaliāre*, repay in kind : *re-*, back + *tāliō*, repayment in kind.] —**re·tal·i·a·tion** (-áysh'n) *n.* —**re·tal·i·a·to·ry** (-ə-təri, -tri) *adj.*

re·tard (ri-tárd, rə-) *v.* **-tarded, -tarding, -tards.** —*tr.* To impede or delay; cause to proceed slowly. —*intr.* To become delayed. —See Synonyms at **delay, hinder.** —*n. Rare.* Retardation. [Middle English *retarden*, from Old French *retarder*, from Latin *retardāre* : *re-*, back, back in place + *tardāre*, to delay, from *tardus*, slow (see **tardy**).] —**re·tard·er** *n.*

re·tar·dant (ri-tárdənt, rə-) *n.* Something that retards; specifically, a substance that slows down chemical reaction. —*adj.* Causing retardation.

re·tar·date (ri-tárd-ayt, rə-, -ət, -it) *n.* A mentally retarded person.

re·tar·da·tion (réetaar-dáysh'n) *n.* Also **re·tard·ment** (re-tárdmənt). 1. The act of retarding. 2. The condition of being retarded. 3. The extent to which, or amount by which, something is retarded. 4. *Psychology.* **Mental deficiency** (*see*).

re·tard·ed (ri-tárdid, rə-) *adj.* Relatively slow or backward in mental or emotional development or in academic achievement.

retch (rech, reech) *intr.v.* **retched, retching, retches.** To try to vomit or make the motion of vomiting.

—*n.* The act or sound of this, usually involuntary. [Ultimately from Old English *hrǣcan*, to cough up phlegm, from Germanic (imitative).]

retd retired.

re·te (réeti) *n., pl.* **retia** (rée-ti-ə, -shə). An anatomical mesh or network, as of veins or nerves. [New Latin, from Latin *rēte*, a net.]

re·tell (rée-tél) *tr.v.* **-told** (-tŏld), **-telling, -tells.** To relate or tell again.

re·ten·tion (ri-ténsh'n, rə-) *n.* 1. The act of retaining. 2. The condition of being retained. 3. The capacity to remember; memory; remembrance. 4. The ability to retain. 5. *Pathology.* Involuntary withholding of normally eliminated bodily wastes or secretions. [Middle English *retencion*, from Old French, from Latin *retentiō* (stem *retentiōn-*), from *retinēre*, RETAIN.]

re·ten·tion·ist (ri-ténsh'n-ist, rə-) *n.* One who favours the retention of something; especially, one who favours the retention of capital punishment.

re·ten·tive (ri-téntiv, rə-) *adj.* Having the ability, tendency, or capacity to retain: *a retentive memory.* —**re·ten·tive·ness, re·ten·tiv·i·ty** (-tívvəti) *n.*

re·think (rée-thíngk) *v.* **-thought** (-tháwt), **-thinking, -thinks.** —*tr.* To consider or think through again, especially in order to resolve difficulties or with a view to changing one's opinion. —*intr.* To rethink something; think again. —*n.* (rée-thingk). An act of rethinking.

re·ti·ar·y (rée-ti-əri, -shi- ‖ *U.S.* -erri) *adj.* Of, resembling, or forming a net or web. [From Latin *rēte*, net.]

ret·i·cent (rétti-sənt) *adj.* 1. Characteristically silent or taciturn in temperament; reserved in speech. 2. Unwilling to make disclosures or give information. 3. Restrained or reserved in style. [Latin *reticēns* (stem *reticent-*), present participle of *reticēre*, to keep silent : *re-* (intensive), again + *tacēre*, to be silent.] —**ret·i·cence** *n.* —**ret·i·cent·ly** *adv.*

ret·i·cle (réttik'l) *n.* A **graticule** (*see*). [Latin *rēticulum*, diminutive of *rēte*, net.]

re·tic·u·lar (ri-tíckewlər, re-, rə-) *adj.* 1. Netlike. 2. Intricate; entangled. [New Latin *reticularis*, from Latin *rēticulum*, RETICLE.]

re·tic·u·late (ri-tíckewləte, re-, rə-, -lit, -layt) *adj.* Resembling or forming a network: *reticulate veins of a leaf.* —*v.* (-layt) **reticulated, -lating, -lates.** —*tr.* 1. To make a net or network of. 2. To mark with lines resembling a network. —*intr.* To form a net or network. [Latin *rēticulātus*, from *rēticulum*, RETICLE.]

re·tic·u·la·tion (ri-tíckewláysh'n, re-, rə-) *n.* A network.

ret·i·cule (rétti-kewl) *n.* 1. A woman's handbag of a former type, often in the form of a pouch with a drawstring and originally made of a netted fabric. 2. A **graticule** (*see*). [French *réticule*, from Latin *rēticulum*, RETICLE.]

re·tic·u·lo·cyte (ri-tíckew-lō-sīt, re-, rə-) *n.* An immature red blood cell containing a network of filaments. [RETICUL(UM) + -CYTE.]

re·tic·u·lo·en·do·the·li·al system (ri-tíckew-lō-éndō-théeli-əl, re-, rə-) *n.* The widely diffused bodily system comprising all phagocytic cells except the leucocytes. [From RETICUL(UM) + ENDOTHELIAL.]

re·tic·u·lum (ri-tíckew-ləm, re-, rə-) *n., pl.* **-la** (-lə). 1. A netlike formation or structure; a network. 2. *Zoology.* The second compartment of the stomach of ruminant mammals, lined with a membrane having honeycombed ridges. [Latin *rēticulum*, RETICLE.]

Re·tic·u·lum (ri-tíck-yŏŏləm, re-, ri-) *n.* A constellation in the Southern Hemisphere near Dorado and Horologium. [Latin *rēticulum*, RETICLE.]

Re·tief (rə-téef), **Piet(er)** (1780–1838). One of the leaders of the Great Trek, he was killed by the Zulu chief Dingane.

re·ti·form (rée·ti-fawrm, rétti-) *adj.* Arranged like a net; reticulate. [Latin *rēte*, net + -FORM.]

ret·i·na (réttina ‖ *U.S. also* rétnə) *n., pl.* **-nas** or **-nae** (rétti-nee ‖ *U.S. also* rétnee). A delicate, multilayer, light-sensitive membrane lining the inner eyeball and connected by the optic nerve to the brain. [Middle English *rethina*, from Medieval Latin *retina*, from Latin *rēte*, net.] —**ret·i·nal** *adj.*

ret·i·nal (réttin'l) *n.* A crystalline retinal pigment, $C_{19}H_{27}CHO$, a component of **rhodopsin** (*see*). Also called "retinene". [Greek *rhētínē*, resin + -AL.]

ret·i·ni·tis (rétti-nítiss) *n. Pathology.* Inflammation of the retina. [RETIN(O)- + -ITIS.]

retino-, retin- *comb. form.* Indicates the retina; for example, **retinitis.**

ret·i·nol (rétti-nol ‖ -nōl) *n.* 1. **Rosin oil** (*see*). 2. A derivative of **vitamin A** (*see*). [Greek *rhētínē*, resin + -OL.]

ret·i·no·scope (rétti-nə-skōp, -nō) *n.* An optical instrument for examining refraction of light in the eye. Also called "skiascope". [RETINO- + -SCOPE.]

ret·i·nos·co·py (rétti-nóskəpi) *n.* Medical examination and analysis of the refractive properties of the eye. Also called "skiascopy". [RETINO- + -SCOPY.] —**ret·i·no·scop·ic** (-nə-skóppik, -nō-) *adj.*

ret·i·nue (rétti-new ‖ -nōō) *n.* The attendants, aides, or retainers accompanying a person of importance or rank. [Middle English *retenue*, from Old French, from the feminine past participle of *retenir*, to RETAIN.]

re·ti·ral (ri-tīr-əl, rə-) *n. Chiefly Scottish.* Retirement from work or office.

re·tire (ri-tír, rə-) *v.* **-tired, -tiring, -tires.** —*intr.* 1. To go away; depart, as for rest, seclusion, or shelter. 2. To go to bed. 3. To give up one's occupation, office, or the like, so as to live at leisure on one's income, savings, or pension. **4.** To fall back; retreat. **5.** To withdraw from a competition or contest, as through injury. **6.** In cricket, to voluntarily suspend or terminate one's innings, as through injury. —*tr.* **1.** To remove from office or active service. **2.** To lead back or away (troops, for example) from action; withdraw. **3.** To take out of circulation: *retire bonds.* **4.** In baseball, to put out (a batter or side); dismiss. [French *retirer* : *re-*, back + *tirer,* to draw (see **tier**).]

re·tired (ri-tī́rd, rə-) *adj. Abbr.* **ret., retd** **1.** Withdrawn; secluded. **2.** Having given up business or office, usually because of age.

re·tire·ment (ri-tī́r-mənt, rə-) *n.* **1.** The act of retiring. **2.** The condition of being retired, as from one's former occupation or office. **3.** Seclusion or privacy. **4.** A retreat; a place of seclusion. —See Synonyms at **solitude.**

retirement age *n.* The age at which workers generally retire; especially, the age at which a retirement pension is payable.

retirement pension *n. British.* The pension paid by the government to a retired man over 65 or a woman over 60. Formerly called "old age pension".

re·tir·ing (ri-tī́r-ing, rə-) *adj.* **1.** Shy and modest; reticent. See Synonyms at **humble, shy.** **2.** At which one retires: *retiring age.* —**re·tir·ing·ly** *adv.*

retiring collection *n.* A collection taken as people leave after a church service, performance, or other gathering.

re·tool (rée-tóol) *tr.v.* **-tooled, -tooling, -tools.** To fit out anew with tools; especially, to re-equip (a factory or workshop).

re·tort[1] (ri-tórt, rə-) *v.* **-torted, -torting, -torts.** —*tr.* **1.** To return in kind; pay back. **2. a.** To reply; especially, to answer in a quick, sharp manner. **b.** To present a counterargument to. —*intr.* To make a retort. —See Synonyms at **answer.**

~*n.* **1.** A quick, incisive reply; especially, one that turns the first speaker's words to his own disadvantage. **2.** A counterargument. [Latin *retorquēre* (past participle *retortus*), to bend back : *re-*, back + *torquēre,* to bend, twist.] —**re·tort·er** *n.*

re·tort[2] (ri-tórt, rə- || *U.S. also* rée-tawrt) *n.* A closed laboratory vessel with an outlet tube, used for distillation, sublimation, or decomposition by heat. [French *retorte,* from Medieval Latin *retorta,* feminine of Latin *retortus,* "bent back" (the neck of the vessel is bent over), from *retorquēre,* to bend back, RETORT.]

re·tor·tion, re·tor·sion (ri-tórsh'n, rə-) *n.* Retaliation in kind by a state upon the citizens of another state. [RETORT + -ION, perhaps by analogy with CONTORTION.]

re·touch (rée-túch) *tr.v.* **-touched, -touching, -touches.** **1.** To add new details or touches to (make-up or a painting, for example), for correction or improvement. **2.** *Photography.* To improve or change (a negative or print) by adding details or removing flaws.

~*n.* (rée-tuch). **1.** A detail changed or improved in a painting, photograph, or the like. **2.** A painting, photograph, or the like, that has been retouched. **3.** The act or art of altering or retouching.

re·trace (rée-tráyss, ri-) *tr.v.* **-traced, -tracing, -traces.** **1.** To trace back to the source or origin. **2.** To go back over (a route): *retrace one's steps.* **3.** To go back over in one's mind. —**re·trace·a·ble** *adj.*

re·tract (ri-trákt, rə-) *v.* **-tracted, -tracting, -tracts.** —*tr.* **1.** To take back or disavow (a statement, accusation, offer, or verbal contract); recant. **2.** To draw back or in: *The turtle retracted its head.* **3.** To withdraw or pull back (machinery, especially the undercarriage of an aircraft). **4.** *Phonetics.* **a.** To utter (a sound) with the tongue drawn back. **b.** To draw back (the tongue). —*intr.* **1.** To take back or disavow a statement, accusation, or the like. **2.** To be withdrawn or pulled back. **3.** To shrink or draw back. [Middle English *retracten,* from Old French *retracter,* from Latin *retractāre,* to handle again, frequentative of *retrahere* (past participle *retractus*), to draw back : *re-*, back, again + *trahere,* to draw.] —**re·tract·a·bil·i·ty** (-ə-bílləti) *n.* —**re·tract·a·ble, re·tract·i·ble** *adj.* —**re·trac·ta·tion** (rée-trak-táysh'n) *n.* —**re·trac·tive** *adj.*

re·trac·tile (ri-trák-tīl, rə- || *U.S. also* -t'l) *adj.* Capable of being drawn back or in: *Cats have retractile claws.* —**re·trac·til·i·ty** (rée-trak-tílləti) *n.*

re·trac·tion (ri-tráksh'n, rə-) *n.* **1.** The act of recanting or disavowing a statement, accusation, or the like. **2.** The act or power of drawing back or of being drawn back.

re·trac·tor (ri-tráktər, rə-) *n.* **1.** One that retracts. **2.** *Anatomy.* A muscle, such as a flexor, that retracts an organ or part. **3.** *Medicine.* An instrument that holds back the edges of a wound or surgical incision.

re·tral (réetrəl, réttrəl) *adj.* **1.** *Biology.* At, close to, or towards the back. **2.** Backward; reverse. [Latin *retrō,* backward, behind.] —**re·tral·ly** *adv.*

re·tread (rée-tréd) *tr.v.* **-trod** (-tród), **-trodden** (-trodd'n), **-treading, -treads.** To tread (one's steps or route, for example) again.

re·tread (rée-tréd) *tr.v.* **-treaded, -treading, -treads.** To fit (a rubber tyre) with a new tread.

~*n.* (rée-tred). A retreaded tyre.

re·treat (ri-tréet, rə-) *n.* **1.** The act of retiring or withdrawing. **2.** A quiet, private, or secure place; a refuge. **3.** A period of seclusion, retirement, or solitude. **4. a.** The withdrawal of a military force from a dangerous position or from an enemy attack. **b.** The signal for such a withdrawal, made on a drum or trumpet. **5.** *Military.* A bugle call signalling the lowering of the flag at sunset. **6. a.** A period spent in spiritual renewal, as through prayer, meditation, contemplation, or spiritual reading. **b.** A place, such as a monastery, where such a period can be spent. **7.** An institution, often private, for the treatment of alcoholics, the mentally ill, or others in need of care. —See Synonyms at **shelter.** —**beat a retreat. 1.** *Military.* To give a signal for withdrawal of forces. **2.** To withdraw; flee.

~*v.* **retreated, -treating, -treats.** —*intr.* **1. a.** To withdraw or retire. **b.** To withdraw from a battle. Used of troops. **2.** To slope backwards; recede. —*tr.* In chess, to move (a piece) back. [Middle English *retret,* from Old French *retrait,* from the past participle of *retraire,* to draw back, from Latin *retrahere,* to RETRACT.]

re·trench (ri-trénch, rə-) *v.* **-trenched, -trenching, -trenches.** —*tr.* **1.** To cut down or curtail (expenditure or costs). **2. a.** To delete (parts of a literary work). **b.** To shorten or abridge (a literary work). **3.** To deduct or remove. **4.** *Military.* To provide with a retrenchment. —*intr.* To curtail expenses; economise. [Obsolete French *retrencher,* from Old French *retrenchier*: *re-* (intensive), again + *trenchier,* to cut off (see **trench**).]

re·trench·ment (ri-trénchmənt, rə-) *n.* **1.** The act or result of retrenching; especially, the cutting down of expenditure. **2.** *Military.* An inner line of defence, usually consisting of a trench and parapet.

re·tri·al (rée-trī́-əl) *n.* A second trial, as of a legal case.

ret·ri·bu·tion (réttri-béwsh'n) *n.* **1.** Something given or demanded in repayment; especially, punishment or vengeance for a wrong or injury. **2.** *Theology.* Punishment or reward distributed in a future life according to performance in this one. [Middle English *retribucion,* from Old French *retribution,* from Late Latin *retribūtiō* (stem *retribūtiōn-*), from Latin *retribuere,* to pay back : *re-*, back + *tribuere,* to grant, pay (see **tribute**).]

re·trib·u·tive (ri-tríbbew-tiv, rə- || réttri-béw-) *adj.* Also **re·trib·u·to·ry** (-təri, -tri). Of, involving, or characterised by retribution.

re·trib·u·ti·vism (ri-tríbbewti-viz'm, rə-) *n.* The belief that criminals ought to be punished for the sake of vengeance rather than in order to prevent crime or rehabilitate the criminal. —**re·trib·u·ti·vist** *n.*

re·triev·al (ri-tréev'l, rə-) *n.* **1.** An act or the process of retrieving. **2.** The possibility of repossession or restoration: *beyond retrieval.*

re·trieve (ri-tréev, rə-) *v.* **-trieved, -trieving, -trieves.** —*tr.* **1.** To get back; regain. **2.** To revive; restore. **3. a.** To put right; rectify. **b.** To rescue, as from trouble or danger. **4.** To recall to mind; remember. **5.** To find and carry back; fetch. **6.** To manage to return (a difficult shot), as in tennis. **7.** *Computing.* To obtain (stored data) from a disk, tape, or other storage device. —*intr.* To find and bring back game. Used of a dog. —See Synonyms at **recover.**

~*n.* An act of retrieving. [Middle English *retreven,* to find again, from Old French *retrover*: *re-*, again + *trover,* to find, perhaps from Vulgar Latin *tropāre* (unattested), to write, compose, from Latin *tropus,* trope, a manner of singing, a song, from Greek *tropos,* "a turning".] —**re·triev·a·bil·i·ty** (-ə-bílləti) *n.* —**re·triev·a·ble** *adj.* —**re·triev·a·bly** *adv.*

re·triev·er (ri-tréevər, rə-) *n.* **1.** One that retrieves. **2.** A dog of any of several breeds developed and trained to retrieve game; especially, a golden retriever.

ret·ro (réttrō) *n.* **1.** A **retrorocket** *(see).* **2.** Retro fashions, chic, or the like.

~*adj.* Retrospective; specifically, nostalgically retrospective: *adopt a retro look.*

retro– *prefix.* Indicates: **1.** Backwards or back; for example, **retrorocket.** **2.** Situated behind; for example, **retrolental.** [Latin *retrō,* backwards, behind.]

ret·ro·act (réttrō-ákt) *intr.v.* **-acted, -acting, -acts.** **1.** To act in opposition or reciprocally. **2.** To be retroactive in application. Used of a law or pay rise, for example.

ret·ro·ac·tion (réttrō-áksh'n) *n.* **1.** A retroactive action. **2.** An opposing or reciprocal action; a reaction.

ret·ro·ac·tive (réttrō-áktiv) *adj.* **1.** Influencing or applying to a period prior to enactment. **2.** Effective from a date in the past: *a retroactive pay increase.* [French *rétroactif,* from Latin *retroactus,* past participle of *retroagere,* to drive back : RETRO- + *agere,* to drive.] —**ret·ro·ac·tive·ly** *adv.* —**ret·ro·ac·tiv·i·ty** (-ak-tívvəti) *n.*

ret·ro·cede (réttrō-séed, réttra-, réetrə-) *v.* **-ceded, -ceding, -cedes.** —*intr.* To go back; recede. —*tr.* To cede or give back; return. [Latin *retrōcēdere,* to go back : RETRO- + *cēdere,* to go.] —**ret·ro·ces·sion** (-sésh'n) *n.*

ret·ro·choir (réttrō-kwīr, réttra-, réetrə-) *n.* The area behind the high altar in a cathedral or large church. [Medieval Latin *retrochorus* : RETRO- + CHOIR.]

ret·ro·flex (réttrō-fleks, réttra-, réetrə-) *adj.* Also **ret·ro·flexed** (-flekst). **1.** Bent, curved, or turned backwards. **2.** *Phonetics.* Pronounced with the tip of the tongue turned back against the roof of the mouth.

~*n.* A retroflex consonant. [New Latin *retroflexus,* from Late Latin *retrōflectere,* to bend back : RETRO- + Latin *flectere,* to bend, FLEX.] —**ret·ro·flex·ion, ret·ro·flec·tion** (-fléksh'n) *n.*

ret·ro·grade (réttrō-grayd, réttra-, réetrə-) *adj.* **1.** Moving or tending backwards; retiring; retreating. **2.** Inverted or reversed, especially in order. **3. a.** Reverting to an earlier or inferior condition; declining or degenerating. **b.** Reversing or obstructing progress: *a retrograde decision.* **4.** *Astronomy.* **a.** Having or pertaining to orbital motion in an opposite direction to that of the Earth about the Sun. **b.** Having or pertaining to motion about a given planet in an opposite direction to the planet's orbital motion around the Sun. **c.** Having an apparent clockwise rotation, resulting from the fact that the rotational period is greater than the orbital period. Said of a planet such as Venus. **d.** Having or designating an apparent backward motion on the celestial sphere, resulting from the fact that the orbital velocity about the Sun is lower that that of the Earth.

~*intr.v.* **retrograded, -grading, -grades.** **1.** To move or seem to move backwards. **2.** To decline; degenerate; deteriorate. [Middle English, from Latin *retrōgradus* : RETRO- + *gradus,* a step, grade.] **—ret·ro·gra·da·tion** (-gray-dáysh'n, -grə-) *n.*

ret·ro·gress (réttrō-gréss, -gress, réttra-, réetrə-) *intr.v.* **-gressed, -gressing, -gresses. 1.** To return to an earlier, inferior, or less complex condition. **2.** To go or move backwards. [Latin *retrōgradī* (past participle *retrōgressus*), to go backwards : RETRO- + *gradī,* to step.] **—re·tro·gres·sive** *adj.* **—re·tro·gres·sive·ly** *adv.*

ret·ro·gres·sion (réttrō-grésh'n, réttra-, réetrə-) *n.* **1.** The act or process of deteriorating or declining. **2.** *Biology.* A return to a less complex or more primitive state or stage.

ret·ro·ject (réttrō-jékt, réttra-, réetrə-) *tr.v.* **-jected, -jecting, -jects.** To throw backwards. Compare **project.** [RETRO- + *-ject,* as in PROJECT (verb).]

ret·ro·len·tal (réttrō-lént'l, réttra-, réetrə-) *adj.* Behind a lens, especially the lens of the eye. [RETRO- + New Latin *lens* (stem *lent-*), LENS + -AL.]

ret·ro·rock·et (réttrō-rockit, réttra-, réetrə-) *n.* A rocket engine used to retard, arrest, or reverse the motion of an aircraft, missile, spacecraft, or other vehicle. Also called "braking rocket", "retro".

re·trorse (ri-trórss, rə-, rée-trawrss) *adj.* Directed or turned backwards or downwards. Said especially of plant parts. [Latin *retrōrsus,* contraction of *retrōversus* : RETRO- + *versus,* "turned", past participle of *vertere,* to turn.] **—re·trorse·ly** *adv.*

ret·ro·spect (réttrō-spekt, réttra-, réetrə-) *n.* A review, survey, or contemplation of things in the past. Used chiefly in the phrase *in retrospect.*

ret·ro·spec·tive (réttrō-spéktiv, réttra-, réetrə-) *adj.* **1.** Looking back on, contemplating, or directed towards the past. **2.** Looking or directed backwards. **3.** Applying to or influencing the past; retroactive. **4.** Of, pertaining to, or designating an exhibition showing the entire work of an artist or school over a period of years or a representative selection of an artist's entire work.
~n. A retrospective art exhibition. **—ret·ro·spec·tive·ly** *adv.*

re·trous·sé (rə-trōō-say, ri-) *adj.* Turned up at the end. Said of a nose. [French, past participle of *retrousser,* to turn back, from Old French : *re-,* back + *trousser,* to TRUSS.]

ret·ro·ver·sion (réttrō-vérsh'n, -vérzh'n, réttra-, réetrə-) *n.* **1.** A turning or tilting backwards. **2.** The state of being turned or tilted backwards. [Latin *retrōversus,* RETRORSE.]

re·try (rée-trī) *tr.v.* **-tried, -trying, -tries.** To try (a law case) again.

ret·ro·vi·rus (réttrōvīr-əss) *n.* A virus of a type that has its genetic information coded in RNA rather than DNA, can make DNA from RNA, and is implicated in the causation of some cancers and perhaps other diseases and conditions such as AIDS. [RETRO-, backwards, reverse + VIRUS: from the reversal in such viruses of the typical direction of genetic information, from DNA to RNA.] **—ret·ro·vi·ral** *adj.*

ret·si·na (ret-séenə, rétsinə) *n.* A resinated Greek wine. [Modern Greek, from Italian *resina,* resin, from Latin *rēsīna,* RESIN.]

re·turn (ri-túrn, rə-) *v.* **-turned, -turning, -turns.** *—intr.* **1.** To go or come back, as to an earlier condition or place. **2.** To revert in speech, thought, or practice. **3.** To recur; appear again: *Her cold has returned.* **4.** To answer; retort; respond. *—tr.* **1.** To send, put, give, or carry back: *return surplus supplies to the store.* **2.** To give or send back in reciprocation: *return a compliment.* **3.** To produce or yield (profit or interest) as a result of labour, investment, or expenditure. **4.** To reflect or send back (light or sound). **5. a.** To submit (a writ, report, or statement) to a judge or other person in authority. **b.** To render or deliver (a verdict). **c.** To declare to be as specified: *was returned not guilty.* **6.** To say in reply. **7.** To elect or re-elect, as to a legislative body. **8.** In card games, to respond to (a partner's lead) by leading the same suit. **9.** *Architecture.* To place (a wall moulding or the like) at an angle to or turned away from the previous line of direction. **10.** In racket games and certain other sports, to hit, throw, or play (a ball) back: *tried to return his opponent's serve.*
~n. Abbr. **ret. 1.** The act or state of going, coming, bringing, or sending back. **2. a.** Something that is brought or sent back, such as a defective or unsold article. **b.** Something that goes or comes back. **3.** A recurrence, as of a periodic occasion or event. **4. a.** Something exchanged for that received; a repayment. **b.** The repaying or reciprocating of something received. **5.** A reply; a response; an answer. **6. a.** The profit made on an exchange of goods or other commercial transaction. **b.** *Often plural.* A profit or yield, as from labour or investments. **c.** The profit per unit, as in the manufacturing of a particular product. **7.** A statement, report, or compilation of data, typically one of a formal or official character that is submitted to an appropriate authority, especially: **a.** A statement of a person's income for tax purposes, or the form on which such a statement is made. **b.** *Usually plural.* A report on the vote in an election. **8.** In card games, a lead that responds to the lead of one's partner. **9.** In racket games and certain other sports: **a.** The act of returning the ball to one's opponent. **b.** The ball so returned. **10.** *Architecture.* **a.** The extension of a moulding, projection, or other part at an angle (usually 90°) to the main part. **b.** A part of a building set at an angle to the façade. **11.** A channel, such as a pipe, carrying something back to its source. **12.** A return ticket. **13.** *Law.* **a.** A report by a sheriff or other officer of the court showing how he has discharged a duty laid upon him. **b.** The bringing or sending back of a writ, subpoena, or other document, with a short written report on it, by a sheriff or other officer, to the court from which it was issued. **—by return of post.** *British.* By the following post. **—many happy returns (of the day).** Used as an expression of greetings or congratulations to a person on his or her birthday.
~adj. **1.** Of or for coming back: *the return voyage.* **2.** Given, sent, or done in reciprocation or exchange: *a return visit.* **3.** Played or staged a second time, offering the original loser a chance to win: *a return boxing match.* **4. a.** Reversing or changing direction. **b.** Formed by a reversal or change in direction, as a bend in a road. **5.** *Chiefly British.* Of or designating a ticket for travel to a destination and back, usually within a stated period. [Middle English *reto(u)rnen,* from Old French *retorner,* from Vulgar Latin *retornāre* (unattested), to turn back : Latin *re-,* back + *tornāre,* to turn in a lathe, from *tornus,* lathe, from Greek *tornos.*] **—re·turn·er** *n.*

re·turn·a·ble (ri-túrnəb'l, rə-) *adj.* **1. a.** Capable of being returned or brought back. **b.** Designating a bottle or other container that is returned when empty to the vendor, who refunds a deposit paid at the time of purchase. **2.** Legally required to be returned.
~n. A returnable bottle or container.

return crease *n.* In cricket, either of two lines at right angles to the bowling creases, from a line inside of which the bowler must bowl the ball.

re·turn·ing officer (ri-túrning, rə-) *n.* An official in charge of an election who announces the number of votes cast for each candidate.

re·tuse (ri-téwss, rə- || -tōōss) *adj.* Having a rounded or blunt apex with a shallow notch. Said chiefly of leaves. [Latin *retūsus,* past participle of *retundere,* to beat back : *re-,* back + *tundere,* to strike, beat.]

Retz. See **Rais, Gilles de.**

Reu·ben¹ (rōō-bin, -bən || réw-). Jacob's eldest son, the ancestor of one of the tribes of Israel. Genesis 29:32. [Hebrew *Re'ū-bēn,* "behold, a son" (from Genesis 29:32) *ra'u,* imperative plural of *ra'ah,* to behold, see + *ben,* son.]

Reuben² *n.* The tribe of Israel descended from Reuben.

re·u·ni·fy (ree-yōōni-fī, rée-) *tr.v.* **-fied, -fying, -fies.** To make whole again; restore (especially a divided country) to a united state. **—re·u·ni·fi·ca·tion** (rée-yōōni-fi-káysh'n, ree-yōōni-) *n.*

re·un·ion (rée-yōōn-yən, ree-, ri-, -i-ən) *n.* **1.** The act of reuniting. **2.** The state of being reunited. **3.** A gathering of the members of a group, such as a family, who have been separated.

Ré·u·nion (ráy-ōōn-yón; *French* -ün-). One of the Mascarene Islands, east of Madagascar in the Indian Ocean. It is an overseas département of France. It consists mainly of one active and several extinct volcanoes, with settlement and cultivation in the coastal lowlands. Sugar, molasses, and rum are the main exports. St. Denis is the capital and chief port. See map at **Indian Ocean.**

re·u·nite (rée-yōō-nīt, -yōō-) *v.* **-nited, -niting, -nites.** *—tr.* To bring together again. *—intr.* To come together again. [Medieval Latin *reūnīre* : *re-,* again + *ūnīre,* from Late Latin, to UNITE.]

Reu·ter (róytər), **Paul Julius, Baron von,** born Israel Beer Josaphat (1816–99). German industrialist, the founder of Reuter's Telegraph Company. In 1849 he began his own small pigeon post service in Germany. Two years later he settled in London and opened a news office. By 1858 he had succeeded in having his foreign telegrams published by the English press. He eventually built up worldwide cable connections.

rev (rev) *n. Informal.* **1.** A revolution, as of an engine. **2.** A revolution per minute.
~v. **revved, revving, revs.** *Informal. —tr.* To increase the speed of (an engine). Often used with *up.* *—intr.* To operate at an increased speed. Often used with *up.*

Rev. 1. Revelation (New Testament). **2.** Reverend (title).

re·val·o·rise, re·val·o·rize (rée-vál-ə-rīz) *tr.v.* **-rised, -rising, -rises.** To establish a new value for (currency, assets, or the like). [Back-formation from *revalorisation,* from French : RE- + VALORISATION.] **—re·val·o·ri·sa·tion** (rée-vál-ə-rī-zaysh'n || *U.S.* -ri-) *n.*

re·val·ue (rée-vál-yōō) *tr.v.* **-ued, -uing, -ues.** Also *U.S.* **re·val·u·ate, -ated, -ating, -ates.** To give a new value to (currency), especially an increased value. Compare **devalue. —re·val·u·ation** (rée-val-yoo-áysh'n) *n.*

re·vamp (rée-vámp) *tr.v.* **-vamped, -vamping, -vamps. 1.** To patch up or restore; renovate. **2.** To revise or reconstruct (a manuscript, for example). **3.** To vamp (a shoe or boot) anew.
~n. The act, process, or result of revamping.

re·vanch·ism (ri-vánch-iz'm, rə-, -vóɴsh-) *n.* A foreign policy motivated by a desire to regain territory that was lost to an enemy. [French *revanche,* revenge, from *revancher,* to revenge, from Old French *revencher,* to REVENGE.] **—re·vanch·ist** *n. & adj.*

rev counter *n. Informal.* An instrument for counting the rate at which an engine is revolving; a tachometer.

Revd Reverend.

re·veal¹ (ri-véel, rə-) *tr.v.* **-vealed, -vealing, -veals. 1.** To divulge or disclose; make known. **2.** To bring to view; expose; show. **3.** To make known by divine or supernatural means, as through revelation. Used of God. [Middle English *revelen,* from Old French *reveller,* from Latin *revēlāre,* to unveil, reveal : *re-,* back, back to a prior condition + *vēlāre,* to veil, from *vēlum,* a veil.] **—re·veal·a·ble** *adj.* **—re·veal·er** *n.* **—re·veal·ment** *n.*
Synonyms: *reveal, expose, disclose, divulge, impart, betray.*

reveal² *n. Architecture.* The internal, vertical side of a recess or opening, as of a doorway or window. [From obsolete *revale,* to lower, from Old French *revaler* : RE- + *avaler,* to lower (see **vail**).]

re·vealed religion (ri-véeld, rə-) *n.* Religion that is based on ideas or beliefs gained through revelation by God rather than through natural reasoning.

re·veal·ing (ri-véeling, rə-) *adj.* **1.** Significant; telling. **2.** Showing parts of the body considered to be sexually inviting: *a revealing dress.* **—re·veal·ing·ly** *adv.*

re·veil·le (ri-váli, rə-, -vélli) || *U.S.* révvəli) *n.* **1.** The sounding of a bugle early in the morning to awaken and summon persons in a military camp or garrison. **2.** The first military formation of the day. [French *réveillez,* imperative of *réveiller,* to rouse, awaken, from Old French *reveiller* : *re-,* again + *veiller,* to rouse, from Latin *vigilāre,* to watch, from *vigil,* awake.]

rev·el (révv'l) *intr.v.* **-elled** or *U.S.* **-eled, -elling** or *U.S.* **-eling, -els.** **1.** To take great pleasure or delight. Used with *in*: *revels in scandal.* **2.** To engage in uproarious festivities; make merry. ~*n. Often plural.* A noisy, festive occasion. [Middle English *revelen,* from Old French *reveller,* to make noise, "to rebel", from Latin *rebellāre,* to REBEL.] **—rev·el·ler** *n.*

rev·e·la·tion (révvə-láysh'n) *n.* **1.** An act of revealing or something revealed; especially, a dramatic disclosure of something not previously known or realised. **2.** Something that reveals unexpected qualities or provides fresh understanding. **3.** *Theology.* A manifestation of divine will or truth. [Middle English, from Old French, from Late Latin *revēlātiō* (stem *revēlātiōn-*), from Latin *revēlāre,* REVEAL.] **—rev·e·la·tion·al** *adj.*

Rev·e·la·tion *n. Abbr.* **Rev.** Also **Revelations.** The last book in the New Testament, attributed to St. John. Also called the "Apocalypse", the "Revelation of St. John the Divine".

rev·e·la·tion·ist (révvə-láysh'n-ist) *n.* One who believes in divine revelation.

rev·el·ry (révv'l-ri) *n., pl.* **-ries.** Boisterous merrymaking. **—rev·el·rous** *adj.*

rev·e·nant (révvənənt) *n.* **1.** One that returns after an absence. **2.** One who returns after death; a ghost. [French, from the present participle of *revenir,* to return, from Latin *revenīre* : *re-,* again, back + *venīre,* to come.]

re·venge (ri-vénj, rə-) *tr.v.* **-venged, -venging, -venges.** **1.** To inflict punishment in return for (injury or insult); retaliate. **2.** To seek or take vengeance for (oneself or another person). ~*n.* **1.** Vengeance; retaliation. **2.** The act of taking vengeance. **3.** A desire for revenge; vindictiveness. **4.** An opportunity for, or instance of, getting one's own back for an earlier reversal or defeat. [Middle English *revengen,* from Old French *revenger, revencher,* from Late Latin *revindicāre,* to avenge : Latin *re-* (intensive), again + *vindicāre,* to VINDICATE.]

re·venge·ful (ri-vénj-f'l, rə-) *adj.* Desiring revenge. See Synonyms at **vindictive.** **—re·venge·ful·ly** *adv.* **—re·venge·ful·ness** *n.*

rev·e·nue (révvə-new, révvi-; *in senses 1 and 4 sometimes* ri-vénnew, rə- || -noo) *n. Abbr.* **rev.** **1.** The income of a government from all sources appropriated for the payment of public expenses. **2.** Yield from property or investment; income. **3.** A single source of income. **4.** A government department set up to collect public funds. Also used adjectivally: *a revenue officer.* [Middle English, return, return to place, from Old French, from the fem. past part. of *revenir,* to return, from Latin *revenīre* : *re-,* back, again + *venīre,* to come.]

revenue cutter *n.* A small, armed coastguard boat formerly used in patrols to catch smugglers.

revenue tariff *n.* A tariff imposed to raise public funds rather than to affect trade.

re·ver·ber·ate (ri-vérbə-rayt, rə-) *v.* **-ated, -ating, -ates.** —*intr.* **1.** To re-echo; resound. **2.** To be repeatedly reflected. **3.** To rebound or recoil; redound. —*tr.* **1.** To re-echo (a sound). **2.** To reflect (heat or light) repeatedly. [Latin *reverberāre,* to cause to rebound : *re-,* back + *verberāre,* to whip, lash, from *verbera,* whips, rods.] **—re·ver·ber·a·tion** (-ráysh'n) *n.* **—re·ver·ber·ant, re·ver·ber·a·tive** (-rətiv || -raytiv) *adj.* **—re·verb·e·ra·tor** *n.*

reverberation pedal *n.* On a piano, the "loud pedal" or **sustaining pedal** *(see).*

reverberation time *n.* The time taken for a sound in a room to diminish in intensity by 60 decibels, used as a measure of the acoustic properties of the room.

re·ver·ber·a·to·ry (ri-vérbə-rə-tri, -təri, -ráytəri) *adj.* Of, pertaining to, or causing reverberation. ~*n.* A reverberatory furnace.

reverberatory furnace *n.* A furnace for smelting metals in which the fuel and the ore are separated and the heat is reflected onto the ore by a curved roof. Also called "reverberatory".

re·vere (ri-véer, rə-) *tr.v.* **-vered, -vering, -veres.** To regard with awe, great respect, or devotion; venerate. [Latin *reverērī* : *re-* (intensive), again + *verērī,* to respect, feel awe of.] **—re·ver·er** *n.*

Synonyms: *revere, worship, venerate, adore, idolise.*

Re·vere (ri-véer, rə-), **Paul** (1735–1818). U.S. revolutionary hero. On April 18, 1775, he went on his famous ride to Lexington, celebrated in a poem by Longfellow, to warn the people of Massachusetts that a British expedition was advancing towards Lexington.

rev·er·ence (révvərənss, révvrənss) *n.* **1.** A feeling of profound awe and respect and often of love; veneration. **2.** An act of showing respect; especially, an obeisance. **3.** The state of being revered. **4.** *Archaic & Irish. Capital* **R.** A title of respect for a clergyman. Preceded by *His* or *Your.* —See Synonyms at **honour.** ~*tr.v.* **reverenced, -encing, -ences.** To regard with reverence.

rev·er·end (révvərənd, révvrənd) *adj.* **1.** Deserving of reverence. **2.** Pertaining to or characteristic of the clergy; clerical. **3.** *Often capital* **R.** *Abbr.* **Rev., Revd** Designating a member of the clergy. ~*n. Informal.* A clergyman. [Middle English, from Old French, from Latin *reverendus,* gerundive of *reverērī,* REVERE.]

Reverend Mother *n.* A title of or form of address for the superior of a convent.

rev·er·ent (révvərənt, révvrənt) *adj.* Feeling or expressing reverence. [Middle English, from Latin *reverēns* (stem *reverent-*), present participle of *reverērī,* REVERE.] **—rev·er·ent·ly** *adv.*

rev·er·en·tial (révvə-rénsh'l) *adj.* Showing reverence: *a reverential tone of voice.* **—rev·er·en·tial·ly** *adv.*

rev·er·ie (révvəri) *n.* **1. a.** Absent-minded musing; daydreaming. **b.** A daydream: *a reverie of years long past.* **2.** *Music.* A piece of music evoking a dreamy state. **3.** *Archaic.* A fantastic or deluded notion. [Middle English, from Old French, from *rever*†, to dream.]

re·vers (ri-véer, rə-, -váir) *n., pl.* **revers** (-z). A part of a garment turned back to show the reverse side, such as a lapel. [French, from Old French, REVERSE.]

re·ver·sal (ri-vérss'l, rə-) *n.* **1.** An act or instance of reversing. **2.** The state of being reversed. **3.** An unfavourable change: *a reversal of fortune.* **4.** *Law.* A changing or setting aside, as of a lower court's decision by an appellate court.

re·verse (ri-vérss, rə-) *adj. Abbr.* **rev.** **1. a.** Turned backwards in position, direction, or order; opposite; contrary. **b.** Upside-down, back to front, or inverted. **2.** Moving or acting in a manner contrary to the usual. **3.** Causing backward movement: *reverse gear.* **4.** *Printing.* Having the black and white areas reversed. ~*n. Abbr.* **rev.** **1.** The opposite or contrary of something. **2. a.** The back or rear of something. **b.** The side of a coin not carrying the principal design. Compare **obverse.** **3.** A change to an opposite position, condition, or direction. **4.** A change in fortune from better to worse; a setback. **5. a.** A mechanism for reversing movement, as a gear in a motor vehicle. **b.** The reverse position or operating condition of such a mechanism. **—in reverse.** In the contrary direction, order, or position. **—the reverse of.** Far from; not at all. ~*v.* **reversed, -versing, -verses.** —*tr.* **1. a.** To turn to the opposite direction or tendency. **b.** To cause to move in a direction opposite to the normal one: *reverse a car.* **2.** To turn inside out or upside down. **3.** To exchange the positions of; transpose. **4.** To cause to be completely different or opposite in character or effect: *reversed their policy on wage restraint.* **5.** *Law.* To revoke or annul (a decision or decree). **6.** To cause (the charge for a telephone call) to be paid by the recipient. —*intr.* **1. a.** To turn or move in the opposite direction. **b.** To move backwards. **2.** To reverse the action of an engine. [Middle English *revers,* from Old French, from Latin *reversus,* past participle of *revertere,* REVERT.] **—re·verse·ly** *adv.* **—re·vers·er** *n.*

reverse-charge call *n. Chiefly British.* A telephone call that is paid for by the recipient. Also called "transfer charge call", *U.S., Australian, & N.Z.* "collect call".

reversed fault *n. Geology.* A fault in which older beds on one side of the fault plane are thrust over younger beds on the other side as a result of compression. Also called "reverse fault".

reverse forecast *n.* A bet in which any of two, three,or more horses are backed to finish in any of the first two, three, or more places. Compare **forecast bet.**

reverse tran·scrip·tase (tran-skríp-tayz, traan-, -tayss) *n.* An enzyme that allows synthesis of DNA.

re·ver·si (ri-vérsi, rə-) *n.* A game played on a draughts board with counters that are coloured differently on each side. These are turned over when captured and become the captor's pieces. [French. See **reverse.**]

re·vers·i·ble (ri-vérsəb'l, rə-, -si-) *adj.* **1.** Capable of being reversed or revoked, or of returning to a former state. **2.** *Chemistry & Physics.* Capable of successively assuming or producing either of two states: *a reversible reaction.* **3.** In thermodynamics, pertaining to or occurring by processes that are at thermodynamic equilibrium: *a reversible electric cell.* **4.** Patterned, woven, or finished so that either side may be worn or used as the outer side: *a reversible coat.* ~*n.* A reversible item of clothing. **—re·vers·i·bil·i·ty** (-bílləti), **re·vers·i·ble·ness** *n.* **—re·vers·i·bly** *adv.*

re·vers·ing light (ri-vérssing, rə-) *n.* A light on the back of a motor vehicle that is automatically illuminated when reverse gear is engaged.

re·ver·sion (ri-vérsh'n, rə-, -vérzh'n) *n.* **1.** A return to a former condition, belief, or practice. **2.** A turning away or in the opposite direction. **3.** *Genetics.* Loosely, **atavism** *(see).* **4.** *Law.* **a.** The return of an estate or an interest in it to the grantor or his heirs after the grant has expired. **b.** The estate thus returned. **c.** The right to succeed to such an estate. **5.** The right or expectation of obtaining or succeeding to something at a future time. **6.** The sum payable by an insurance company on an insured person's death.

re·ver·sion·ar·y (ri-vérsh'n-əri, rə-, -vérzh'n- || *U.S.* -erri) *adj. Law.* Also **re·ver·sion·al** (-vérsh'n'l, -vérzh'n'l). Of or connected with the reversion of an estate.

re·ver·sion·er (ri-vér-sh'n-ər, -zhn-) *n. Law.* A person entitled to receive an estate in reversion.

re·vert (ri-vért, rə-) *intr.v.* **-verted, -verting, -verts.** **1.** To return to a former, often less desirable, condition, practice, subject, or belief. **2.** *Law.* To return to the former owner or his heirs. Used of money or property. **3.** *Biology.* To return to a simpler or more primitive form or condition. Used of organisms, organs, and the like. [Middle English *reverten,* from Old French *revertir,* from Latin *revertere,* to turn back : *re-,* back + *vertere,* to turn.] **—re·vert·er** *n.* **—re·vert·i·ble** *adj.* **—re·ver·tive** *adj.*

re·vest (rée-vést) *tr.v.* **-vested, -vesting, -vests.** To vest (power or possession, for example) once again in a person or agency. [Middle

English *revesten,* to dress (in ecclesiastical garments), from Old French *revestir,* from Late Latin *revestīre,* to clothe again : Latin *re-,* again + *vestīre,* to clothe, from *vestis,* clothes.]
re·vet (ri-vét, rə-) *v.* **-vetted, -vetting, -vets.** *—tr.* To face (a wall of earth) with a layer of stone or other suitable material. *—intr.* To construct a revetment. [French *revêtir,* from Old French *revestir,* to clothe again. See **revest.**]
re·vet·ment (ri-vétmənt, rə-) *n.* **1.** A facing, as of masonry, used to support an embankment, wall, or the like. **2.** A barricade against explosives.
re·view (ri-véw, rə-) *v.* **-viewed, -viewing, -views.** *—tr.* **1.** To look over, study, or examine again. **2.** To consider retrospectively; look back on. **3.** To examine with an eye to criticism or correction. **4.** To write or give a critical report on (a book or artistic production). **5.** *Law.* To examine (an action or verdict), especially in a higher court, in order to correct possible errors. **6.** To subject to a formal inspection, especially a military inspection. *—intr.* **1.** To go over or re-examine material. **2.** To act as a reviewer, especially for a newspaper or magazine. **3.** *U.S.* To revise, as for an examination.
—n. Abbr. **rev. 1.** A re-examination or reconsideration. **2.** A retrospective view or survey. **3.** An inspection or examination for the purpose of evaluating something. **4.** A published report or essay giving a critical estimate of an artistic work or performance, for example. **5.** A periodical publication devoted primarily to such reports. **6.** A formal military inspection. **7.** *Law.* An examination of an action or verdict, especially by a higher court, in order to correct possible errors. **8.** An entertainment, a **revue** *(see).* [From obsolete French *revoir* (past participle *reveu*), to see again, look over : *re-,* again, over + *voir,* to see, from Latin *vidēre.*] **—re·view·a·ble** *adj.*
re·view·al (ri-véw-əl, rə-) *n.* The act or an instance of reviewing.
re·view·er (ri-véw-ər, rə-) *n.* One who reviews; specifically, a critic writing for a newspaper or magazine.
re·vile (ri-vīl, rə-) *v.* **-viled, -viling, -viles.** *—tr.* To denounce with abusive language; rail against. *—intr.* To use abusive language. —See Synonyms at **malign, scold.** [Middle English *revilen,* from Old French *reviler* : *re-* (intensive), again + *vil,* VILE.] **—re·vile·ment** *n.* **—re·vil·er** *n.* **—re·vil·ing·ly** *adv.*
re·vis·al (ri-vīz'l, rə-) *n.* The act of revising; revision.
re·vise (ri-vīz, rə-) *v.* **-vised, -vising, -vises.** *—tr.* **1.** To change or modify: *revise an earlier opinion.* **2.** *British.* To restudy or go over (academic work), especially in preparation for an examination. *—intr.* To restudy work for an examination. **3.** To prepare a newly edited version of (a text). —See Synonyms at **correct.**
—n. Abbr. **rev.** (|| *U.S. also* rée-vīz) *Printing.* A proof made from an earlier proof on which corrections have been made. [Latin *revīsere,* to look back : *re-,* again, back + *vīsere,* look at, from *vidēre* (past participle *vīsus*), to see.] **—re·vis·a·ble** *adj.* **—re·vis·er** *n.*
Re·vised Standard Version (ri-vīzd, rə-) *n. Abbr.* **R.S.V.** A modern American revision (1946–57) of the American Standard edition of the English Bible, in the King James tradition.
Revised Version *n. Abbr.* **R.V., Rev. Ver.** A revision of the King James Version of the Bible, prepared by a committee of scholars from Britain and the United States (1870–84).
re·vi·sion (ri-vízh'n, rə-) *n. Abbr.* **rev. 1.** The act or procedure of revising. **2.** The result of revising; a corrected or new version. **3.** *British.* The process or activity of revising for an examination. **—re·vi·sion·al, re·vi·sion·ar·y** (-əri || *U.S.* -erri) *adj.*
re·vi·sion·ism (ri-vízh'n-iz'm, rə-) *n.* **1.** A policy of modification or change, especially of a political or religious doctrine. **2.** *Often capital* **R.** A recurrent tendency within the Communist movement to revise Marxist theory in such a way as to provide justification for a retreat from the original doctrine. Often used derogatorily. **—re·vi·sion·ist** *n. & adj.*
re·vis·it (rée-vízzit) *tr. v.* **-ited, -iting, -its.** To visit again: *Brideshead Revisited* (Evelyn Waugh).
—n. A second or repeated visit. **—re·vis·i·ta·tion** (-áysh'n) *n.*
re·vi·so·ry (ri-vīzəri, rə-) *adj.* Of, pertaining to, effecting, or having the power of revision.
re·vi·tal·ise, re·vi·tal·ize (rée-vīt'l-īz) *tr.v.* **-ised, -ising, -ises.** To impart new life or vigour to; restore the vitality of. **—re·vi·tal·i·sa·tion** (-ī-záysh'n || *U.S.* -i-) *n.*
re·viv·al (ri-vīv'l, rə-) *n.* **1.** The act of reviving, or the condition of being revived. **2. a.** A restoration to use, acceptance, activity, or vigour after a period of obscurity or quiescence. **b.** A return to use or fashion, as of former styles, manners, or activities: *the Gothic Revival.* **3.** A new presentation of a play, film, or the like. **4.** A reawakening of faith or interest in religion. **5.** An evangelistic meeting or series of meetings for the purpose of reawakening religious faith, often characterised by impassioned preaching and public declarations of faith.
re·viv·al·ism (ri-vīv'l-iz'm, rə-) *n.* The spirit or activities characteristic of religious revivals.
re·viv·al·ist (ri-vīv'l-ist, rə-) *n.* **1.** A person who promotes or leads religious revivals. **2.** A person who revives practices or ideas of an earlier time. **—re·viv·al·ist, re·viv·al·is·tic** (-istik) *adj.*
re·vive (ri-vīv, rə-) *v.* **-vived, -viving, -vives.** *—tr.* **1.** To bring back to life or consciousness; resuscitate. **2.** To impart new health, vigour, or spirit to. **3.** To restore to use, currency, activity, or notice. **4.** To restore the validity or effectiveness of. **5.** To renew in the mind; recall. **6. a.** To put on a new production of (a stage work). **b.** To bring back (a former artistic style, for example) into popularity or fashion. *—intr.* **1.** To return to life or consciousness. **2.** To regain health, vigour, or good spirits. **3.** To return to use, currency, or notice; flourish again. **4.** To return to validity, effectiveness, or operative condition. [Middle English *reviven,* from Old French *revivre,* from Late Latin *revīvere* : Latin *re-,* again + *vīvere,* to live.] **—re·viv·er** *n.*
re·viv·i·fy (ree-vívvi-fī, ri-, rée-) *tr.v.* **-fied, -fying, -fies.** To impart new life to. [French *revivifier,* from Late Latin *revīvificāre* : *re-,* again + *vīvificāre,* to VIVIFY.] **—re·viv·i·fi·ca·tion** (-fi-káysh'n) *n.*
rev·i·vis·cence (révvi-víss'nss, rée-vī-, ri-vívviss'nss, rə-) *n.* A return to life or vigour; a revival. [Late Latin *reviviscentia,* from Latin *reviviscere,* "to start to live again", ultimately from *vivere,* to live.] **—rev·i·vis·cent** *adj.*
rev·o·ca·ble, re·vok·a·ble (révvəkə-b'l, ri-vōkə-, rə-) *adj.* Capable of being revoked. **—rev·o·ca·bil·i·ty** (-bílləti), **rev·o·ca·ble·ness** *n.* **—rev·o·ca·bly** *adv.*
rev·o·ca·tion (révvə-káysh'n) *n.* The act of revoking, or the condition of being revoked; cancellation; repeal. **—rev·o·ca·to·ry** (révvəkə-tri, ri-vōkə-, rə-, -təri) *adj.*
re·voke (ri-vōk, rə-) *v.* **-voked, -voking, -vokes.** *—tr.* To void or annul by recalling, withdrawing, or reversing; cancel; rescind: *revoke a decree.* *—intr.* In card games, to fail to follow suit when one is required and able to do so. —See Synonyms at **nullify.**
—n. In card games, an act of revoking; a failure to follow suit. [Middle English *revoken,* from Old French *revoquer,* from Latin *revocāre,* to call back : *re-,* back + *vocāre,* to call.] **—re·vok·er** *n.*
re·volt (ri-vōlt || -vólt) *v.* **-volted, -volting, -volts.** *—intr.* **1.** To institute or take part in a rebellion against authority, especially that of the state; rebel or mutiny. **2.** To be affected by or turn away in disgust or revulsion. Used with *against, at,* or *from.* *—tr.* To fill with disgust or abhorrence; repel.
—n. **1.** An uprising against state authority; a rebellion. **2.** Any act of protest or rejection. **3.** The state of a person or persons in rebellion: *be in revolt.* —See Synonyms at **rebellion.** [French *révolter,* from Italian *rivoltare,* from Vulgar Latin *revolvitāre* (unattested), from Latin *revolvere,* to roll back, REVOLVE.] **—re·volt·er** *n.*
re·volt·ing (ri-vōlt-ing || -vólt-) *adj.* **1.** Causing disgust; repulsive; abhorrent. **2.** *Informal.* Nasty; disagreeable. **—re·volt·ing·ly** *adv.*
rev·o·lute (révvə-lōōt, -lewt) *adj. Botany.* Rolled back on the undersurface from the tip or margins, as some leaves are. [Latin *revolūtus,* past participle of *revolvere,* to roll back, REVOLVE.]
rev·o·lu·tion (révvə-lōōsh'n, -léwsh'n) *n. Abbr.* **rev. 1.** A sudden political overthrow brought about from within a given system, especially: **a.** A forcible substitution of rulers or of ruling cliques: *a palace revolution.* **b.** Seizure of state power by the militant vanguard of a subject class or nation. —See Synonyms at **rebellion. 2.** A recognisably momentous change in any situation, field, or sphere or activity: *the revolution in physics.* **3. a.** Orbital motion about a point, especially as distinguished from axial rotation: *the planetary revolution about the Sun.* **b.** A turning or rotational motion about an axis. **c.** A single complete cycle of such orbital or axial motion. [Middle English *revolucioun,* from Old French *revolution,* from Late Latin *revolūtiō* (stem *revolūtiōn-*), from Latin *revolvere* (past participle *revolūtus*), REVOLVE.]
rev·o·lu·tion·ar·y (révvə-lōōsh'n-əri, -léwsh'n- || *U.S.* -erri) *adj.* **1.** Of, pertaining to, or bringing about a political or social revolution. **2.** Characterised by or resulting in radical change: *a revolutionary discovery.* **3.** Completely original or new: *a revolutionary approach to public relations.* **4.** Moving in circles; revolving. **5.** *Capital* **R. a.** Of or pertaining to any of various other revolutions, especially the French Revolution. **b.** Of or pertaining to the activities or period of the War of American Independence.
—n., pl. **revolutionaries.** Also *chiefly U.S.* **rev·o·lu·tion·ist.** One who advocates or fights in a revolution.
Revolutionary calendar *n.* The calendar introduced in France on November 24, 1793, by the National Convention and abolished under Napoleon on December 31, 1805, reckoning time from September 22, 1792, the date of the founding of the First Republic. Also called "Republican calendar".
rev·o·lu·tion·ise, rev·o·lu·tion·ize (révvə-lōōsh'n-īz, -léwsh'n-) *tr.v.* **-ised, -ising, -ises. 1.** To bring about a radical change in; alter extensively or drastically. **2.** To cause (a country) to undergo a political, industrial, or social revolution. **3.** To imbue with revolutionary principles. **—rev·o·lu·tion·is·er** *n.*
re·volve (ri-vólv, rə- || *Southern England also* -vōlv) *v.* **-volved, -volving, -volves.** *—intr.* **1.** To orbit a central point. **2.** To turn on an axis; rotate. **3.** To recur in cycles or at periodic intervals. *—tr.* **1.** To cause to revolve. **2.** *Literary.* To think over (a problem); ponder or reflect on. **3.** To have as a central theme or concern. Used with *about* or *around*: *The family seems to revolve around the dog.* —See Synonyms at **turn.** [Middle English *revolven,* from Latin *revolvere,* to roll back : *re-,* back + *volvere,* to roll.] **—re·volv·a·ble** *adj.*
re·volv·er (ri-vólv-ər, rə- || *Southern England also* -vōlv-) *n.* **1.** A pistol having a revolving cylinder with several cartridge chambers. **2.** One that revolves.
re·volv·ing credit (ri-vólv-ing, rə- || -vōlv-) *n.* **1.** *Finance.* A bank credit that can be drawn on for: **a.** A limited total amount that is renewable as soon as it is paid back. **b.** A limited amount at any one time, with no limit on the number of times. **2.** A form of credit made available to customers of a retail shop, whereby they are allowed a constant stipulated amount of credit in return for regular payment to the shop.
revolving door *n.* A door having several partitions attached to a central axis on which it turns, thus keeping out draughts.

revolving fund *n. Finance.* A fund of money from which loans or investments are made, which is kept at a constant level by repayment of the loans with interest or by the returns from the investments that it finances.

re·vue, re·view (ri-véw, rə-) *n.* An entertainment consisting of sketches, songs, and dances, often satirising current events, trends, and personalities. [French, from Old French, past participle of *revoir,* to REVIEW.]

re·vul·sion (ri-vúlsh'n, rə-) *n.* **1.** A sudden and strong change or reaction in feeling; especially, a feeling of violent disgust or loathing. **2.** A withdrawing or turning away from something. **3.** *Medicine.* Treatment of a diseased part or organ by diverting the blood to another part of the body, as by counterirritation. [Latin *revulsiō* (stem *revulsiōn-*), from *revellere* (past participle *revulsus*), to pull back or away : *re-,* back + *vellere,* to pull, tear.]

re·vul·sive (ri-vúl-siv, rə-) *n. Medicine.* A substance that produces revulsion. [REVULS(ION) + -IVE.] —**re·vul·sive** *adj.*

Rev. Ver. Revised Version (of the Bible).

re·ward (ri-wáwrd, rə-) *n.* **1. a.** Something given or received in recompense for worthy behaviour or a service rendered. **b.** Requital or retribution for harm done. **2.** Money offered for some special service, such as the return of a lost article or the capture of a criminal. **3.** A satisfying return or result; a profit. —See Synonyms at **bonus.** ~*tr.v.* **rewarded, -warding, -wards. 1.** To bestow a reward on. **2.** To give a reward because of or in return for: *They rewarded his bravery with a medal.* **3.** To satisfy or gratify: *Her patience was rewarded.* [Middle English *rewarden,* to heed, regard, reward, from Anglo-French *rewarder,* "to look at" : *re-* (intensive) + *warder,* to watch over, from Germanic.] —**re·ward·er** *n.*

re·ward·ing (ri-wáwrding, rə-) *adj.* Worthwhile or gratifying: *a rewarding experience.* —**re·ward·ing·ly** *adv.*

re·wa·re·wa (rée-wə-rée-wə, ráy-, -ráy-, -ré-) *n.* A New Zealand tree, *Knightia excelsa,* the red, figured timber of which is used in cabinetmaking. Also called "honeysuckle". [Maori.]

re·wind (rée-wínd) *tr.v.* **-wound** (-wównd), **-winding, -winds.** To wind again or anew. ~*n.* (rée-wīnd). The act or process of rewinding something, such as film or tape. —**re·wind·er** *n.*

re·wire (rée-wír) *tr.v.* **-wired, -wiring, -wires.** To provide with new wiring.

re·word (rée-wúrd) *tr.v.* **-worded, -wording, -words.** To state, express, or compose again using different words.

re·work (rée-wúrk) *tr.v.* **-worked, -working, -works. 1.** To work over again; revise or rewrite. **2.** To use (a theme or metaphor, for example) in a new or different context, often in an altered form. **3.** To subject to a repeated or new process.

re·write (rée-rít) *tr.v.* **-wrote** (-rōt), **-written** (-rítt'n), **-writing, -writes.** To write again, especially in a different form. ~*n.* (rée-rīt). Something that has been rewritten. —**re·writ·er** *n.*

Rex (reks) *n. Abbr.* **R. 1.** The reigning king. Used as a title and signature on documents. **2.** *Law.* The Crown. Used in lawsuits when the monarch is a king: *Rex v. Overton.* [Latin *rēx,* king.]

Rey·kja·vik or **Rey·kja·vík** (ráyk-yə-vik, -veek). Capital city and chief port of Iceland, lying on Faxaflói bay in the southwest of the country. The centre of the cod-fishing industry, it is the commercial and industrial hub of Iceland.

Rey·nard (rén-ərd, -aard, ráynaard). The fox, as personified in folklore and fable.

Rey·naud (re-nō), **Paul** (1878-1966). French politician. He held several cabinet posts in the 1930s before becoming prime minister in March, 1940. In October, he was arrested by the Vichy regime of Pétain, tried in 1942, and imprisoned in Germany (1942-45). After the war he served as finance minister (1948), and later helped to draw up the constitution for the Fifth Republic (1958).

Reyn·olds (rénn'ldz), **Sir Joshua** (1723-92). British painter, the first president of the Royal Academy. He was the leading painter of his day and one of the most important in the history of English painting. In the course of his lifetime he painted more than 2,000 historical subjects and portraits.

Reynolds number *n. Physics.* A dimensionless number characterising the type of flow in a fluid, used especially in the study of the effects of viscosity and velocity control in fluid systems. [After Osborne *Reynolds* (1842–1912), British physicist.]

Re·za Shah Pah·la·vi (ráyzə, re-záá; páələ-vée), born Reza Khan (1877–1944). Iranian soldier, shah of Iran from 1925 to 1941. In 1935 he officially changed the name of Persia to its older name, Iran. He did much to modernise Iranian life, but in 1941 Soviet and British forces occupied Iran and forced him to abdicate in favour of his son, Muhammad Reza Shah (1919–80), overthrown 1979. See **Iran.**

RF radio frequency.

R factor *n.* A genetic element in bacteria that gives them immunity or resistance to antibiotics and is transmitted from one bacterium to another by conjugation. [*Resistance factor.*]

R.F.C. Rugby Football Club.

R.G.S. Royal Geographical Society.

Rh 1. The symbol for the element rhodium. **2.** rhesus. See **Rh factor.**

R.H. Royal Highness.

R.H.A. Royal Horse Artillery.

rhab·do·man·cy (ráb-də-man-si, -dō-) *n.* Divination by means of a wand or a rod, especially in searching for underground water or ores. [Late Greek *rhabdomanteia* : *rhabdos,* rod + -MANCY.] —**rhab·do·man·cer** *n.*

rhab·do·my·o·ma (ráb-dō-mī-ṓ-mə, -də-) *n., pl.* **-mas** or **-mata** (-mətə). *Pathology.* A benign tumour in striated muscular fibres. [New Latin, from Greek *rhabdos,* rod + MYOMA.]

Rhad·a·man·thine (ráddə-mán-thīn, -thin) *adj.* Of or characteristic of Rhadamanthus; especially, rigorously and uncompromisingly adhering to the letter of the law.

Rhad·a·man·thus (ráddə-mánthəss). *Greek Mythology.* The judge of the dead in the underworld.

Rhae·ti·a (rée-shiə, -sh-ə). An ancient Alpine Roman province that included portions of modern Switzerland and Austria. —**Rhae·ti·an** *adj. & n.*

Rhae·to-Ro·man·ic (réetō-rō-mánnik, -rə-) *adj.* Also **Rhae·to-Ro·mance** (-mánss). Of or belonging to a group of closely related Romance dialects spoken in southern Switzerland, northern Italy, and the Tyrol. ~*n.* Also **Rhae·to-Ro·mance.** These dialects considered as a distinct Romance language.

rhaphe. Variant of **raphe.**

rhap·sod·ic (rap-sóddik) *adj.* Also **rhap·sod·i·cal** (-'l). **1.** Of, resembling, or characteristic of a rhapsody. **2.** Impassioned or enthusiastic; ecstatic. —**rhap·sod·i·cal·ly** *adv.*

rhap·so·dise, rhap·so·dize (rápsə-dīz) *v.* **-dised, -dising, -dises.** —*intr.* To express oneself in an immoderately enthusiastic manner. —*tr.* To recite in the manner of a rhapsody.

rhap·so·dist (ráp-sədist) *n.* Also **rhap·sode** (-sōd). **1.** In ancient Greece, a reciter of epic poetry, especially of the works of Homer. **2.** A person who uses extravagantly enthusiastic or impassioned language.

rhap·so·dy (rápsədi) *n., pl.* **-dies. 1. a.** Exalted or excessively enthusiastic expression of feeling in speech or writing. **b.** *Often plural.* An extravagant expression of enthusiasm. **2.** In ancient Greece, an epic poem, or a portion of one, suitable for uninterrupted recitation. **3.** A literary work written in an impassioned or exalted style. **4.** *Music.* A composition that is free or irregular in form, often improvisatory in character, and typically has a melodic content based on folk tunes. [Latin *rhapsōdia,* from Greek *rhapsōidia,* from *rhapsōidos,* "weaver of songs", rhapsodist : *rhaptein,* to sew together + *ōidē,* ode, song.]

rhat·a·ny (rátt'n-i) *n., pl.* **-nies. 1.** Either of two South American shrubs, *Krameria triandra* or *K. argentea,* having thick, fleshy roots. **2.** The dried root of either of these plants, formerly used as an astringent. Also called "krameria". [Spanish *ratania,* from Quechua *ratánya.*]

rhbdr. rhombohedron.

rhe·a (reer, rée-ə) *n.* Any of several flightless South American birds of the genus *Rhea,* resembling the ostrich but somewhat smaller and having three toes instead of two. [New Latin *Rhea,* arbitrarily named after RHEA.]

Rhe·a (reer, rée-ə). *Greek Mythology.* One of the Titans, the wife of Cronos and mother of Zeus.

rhe·bok, ree·bok (rée-buk, -bok) *n.* An antelope, *Pelea capreolus,* that is found in southern Africa and has brownish-grey hair. [From Dutch *reebok,* ROEBUCK.]

Rhee (ree), **Syngman** (1875–1965). Korean politician, president of South Korea (1948–60). After World War II he was a key figure in the administration of American-occupied South Korea and in 1948 he became the first president of the Republic of Korea. He was re-elected in 1952, 1956, and 1960, but in May, 1960, he was forced from office by public demonstrations and went into exile in Hawaii.

Rheims. See **Reims.**

Rhein. See **Rhine.**

rhe·mat·ic (ri-máttik, ree-) *adj.* **1.** Of or pertaining to word formation. **2.** Derived from or pertaining to a verb. [Greek *rhēmatikos,* from *rhēma,* word, verb.]

Rhen·ish (rénnish, réenish) *adj.* Of or pertaining to the river Rhine or the lands bordering on it. ~*n. Archaic.* Rhine wine.

rhe·ni·um (rééni-əm) *n. Symbol* **Re** A rare dense silvery-white metallic element with a very high melting point. It is used for electrical contacts and with tungsten for high-temperature thermocouples. Atomic number 75, atomic weight 186.2, melting point 3,180°C, boiling point 5,627°C, relative density 21.02, valencies 1, 2, 3, 4, 5, 6, 7. [New Latin, from Latin *Rhēnus,* the RHINE.]

rheo- *comb. form.* Indicates a flow or current; for example, **rheology.** [Greek *rheos,* current, stream, from *rhein,* to flow.]

rhe·o·base (rée-ō-bayss) *n.* The weakest nerve impulse that is needed to produce a response in a tissue.

rhe·ol·o·gy (ree-ólləji) *n.* The study of the deformation and flow of matter. [RHEO- + -LOGY.] —**rhe·o·log·i·cal** (rée-ə-lójik'l) *adj.* —**rhe·ol·o·gist** (-ólləjist) *n.*

rhe·om·e·ter (ree-ómmitər) *n.* An instrument for measuring the flow of viscous liquids, as of blood. [RHEO- + -METER.]

rhe·o·stat (rée-ə-stat, -ō-) *n.* A continuously variable electrical resistor used to regulate current, typically having a coil of wire with a sliding contact. [RHEO- + -STAT.] —**rhe·o·stat·ic** (-státtik) *adj.*

rhe·o·tax·is (rée-ə-táksiss, -ō-) *n.* The movement of an organism in response to a current, usually of water. [RHEO- + -TAXIS.] —**rhe·o·tac·tic** (-ták-tik) *adj.*

rhe·sus baby (rée-səss) *n.* A baby affected by **haemolytic disease** (see).

rhesus factor *n.* Rh factor (see).

rhesus monkey *n.* A brownish macaque monkey, *Macaca mulatta,* of India, used extensively in biological experimentation. [New

Latin *rhesus*, arbitrarily from Latin *Rhēsus*, name of a mythological king of Thrace.]

rhe·tor (rée-tər ‖ -tawr) *n.* **1.** A teacher of rhetoric in ancient Greece or Rome. **2.** An orator. In this sense, often used disparagingly. [Middle English, from Medieval Latin *rēthor*, from Greek *rhētōr*.]

rhet·o·ric (rétˈtərik) *n.* *Abbr.* **rhet.** **1.** The study of the elements used in literature and public speaking, such as content, structure, cadence, and style. **2.** The art of oratory, especially the persuasive use of language to influence the thoughts and actions of listeners. **3. a.** Affectation, grandiloquence, or insincerity in speech or writing. **b.** Speech or writing that is impressive or persuasive, but often insincere or empty. [Middle English *rethorik*, from Old French *rethorique*, from Latin *rhētorica*, from Greek *rhētorikē (tekhnē)*, "rhetorical (art)", from *rhētorikos*, rhetorical, from *rhētōr*, RHETOR.]

rhe·tor·i·cal (ri-tórrik'l, rə-) *adj.* **1.** Concerned primarily with style or effect; showy, inflated, or insincere. **2.** Of or pertaining to rhetoric; oratorical. **—rhe·tor·i·cal·ly** *adv.*

rhetorical question *n.* A question to which no answer is required or expected, or to which only one answer may be made.

rhet·o·ri·cian (rétˈtə-ríshˈn) *n.* **1.** An expert in or teacher of rhetoric. **2.** An eloquent speaker or writer. **3.** One given to verbal extravagance.

rheum (rōōm ‖ rewm) *n.* A watery or thin mucous discharge from the eyes or nose. [Middle English *reume*, from Old French, from Latin *rheuma*, from Greek, stream, humour of the body, rheum.] **—rheum·y** *adj.*

rheu·mat·ic (rōō-máttik, rōō- ‖ rew-) *adj.* Of, pertaining to, or afflicted with rheumatism.
~*n.* **1.** A person suffering from rheumatism. **2.** *Plural. Informal.* Pains due to rheumatism. [Middle English *rewmatyk*, from Latin *rheumaticus*, troubled with rheum, from Greek *rheumatikos*, subject to rheum, from *rheuma*, stream, body humour, RHEUM.]

rheumatic fever *n.* A severe disease occurring chiefly in children as a complication of streptococcal infection of the throat, characterised by fever and painful inflammation of the joints, and frequently resulting in permanent damage to the valves of the heart.

rheu·mat·ick·y (rōō-máttiki, rōō- ‖ rew-) *adj. Informal.* Suffering from stiffness or pain in the joints, such as that caused by rheumatism.

rheu·ma·tism (rōōmə-tizz'm ‖ rewmə-) *n.* Any of several disorders, such as fibrositis and rheumatoid arthritis, that affect the muscles, tendons, joints, or bones, and are characterised by discomfort and disability. [Latin *rheumatismus*, rheum, catarrh, from Greek *rheumatismos*, from *rheumatizesthai*, to suffer from a flux, from *rheuma*, stream, flux, RHEUM.]

rheu·ma·toid (rōōmə-toyd ‖ rewmə-) *adj.* Of, resembling, or afflicted with rheumatism. **—rheu·ma·toi·dal·ly** *adv.*

rheumatoid arthritis *n.* A chronic disease marked by stiffness and inflammation of the membranes of the joints, weakness, loss of mobility, and deformity.

rheumatoid factor *n.* An antibody present in the blood serum of many patients with rheumatoid arthritis that can be a means of diagnosing the disease.

rheu·ma·tol·o·gy (rōōmə-tólləji ‖ rewmə-) *n.* The branch of medicine concerned with the diagnosis and treatment of rheumatic diseases. [RHEUMAT(ISM) + -LOGY.] **—rheu·ma·tol·o·gist** *n.*

Rh factor *n.* Any of several antigens on the surface of red blood cells of Rh positive blood that induce adverse reactions with blood cells that lack these antigens (Rh negative cells). Also called "rhesus factor". [First discovered in the blood of RHESUS MONKEYS.]

R.H.G. Royal Horse Guards.

rhi·nal (rin'l) *adj.* Of or pertaining to the nose; nasal. [RHIN(O)- + -AL.]

Rhine (rin). *German* **Rhein**; *French* **Rhin** (raN); *Dutch* **Rijn.** Longest river in western Europe, about 1 320 kilometres (820 miles) long. Its two principal headwaters, the Vorder Rhine and Hinter Rhine, rise in the Swiss Alps, and join near Chur to form the Rhine proper. The Rhine carries more traffic than any other waterway in the world. The chief commodities that are transported are iron ore, coal, petroleum, sand, gravel, and steel products. Canals link the river with the Maas, Rhône-Saône, Marne, and Danube valleys, thus forming a comprehensive waterway network.

Rhine·land (rin-land, -lənd). A historical region in modern western Germany, consisting of those areas adjoining the Rhine.

Rhine·land-Pa·lat·i·nate (rin-land-pə-látti-nət, -lənd-, -nit, -nayt). *German* **Rhein·land-Pfalz** (rin-lant-pfálts). State (land) in western Germany. It consists of forested uplands intersected by fertile river valleys, the chief rivers being the Rhine and Mosel. The cultivation of vines is widespread and some of Germany's best-known wines are produced there. The state is nevertheless heavily industrialised. Mainz is the capital.

rhi·nen·ceph·a·lon (rinen-séffə-lon, -kéffə-, -lən) *n., pl.* **-la** (-lə). The olfactory region of the brain, in the cerebrum. [RHIN(O)- + ENCEPHALON.] **—rhi·nen·ce·phal·ic** (-si-fál-ik) *adj.*

rhine·stone (rin-stōn) *n.* A colourless, artificial gem of paste or glass, often with facets that sparkle in imitation of diamond. [Translation of French *caillou du Rhin;* originally made at Strasbourg.]

Rhine wine *n.* **1.** Any of several typically white wines produced in the Rhine valley. **2.** Any similar light, dry wine produced elsewhere.

rhi·ni·tis (ri-nítiss) *n.* Inflammation of the nasal mucous membranes, as occurs in the common cold. [New Latin : RHIN(O)- + -ITIS.]

rhi·no¹ (rino) *n., pl.* **-nos.** *Informal.* A rhinoceros.

rhino² *n. British Slang.* Money; cash. Not in current usage. [17th century : origin obscure.]

rhino-, rhin- *comb. form.* Indicates nose or nasal; for example, **rhinoscopy, rhinitis.** [Greek *rhis†* (stem *rhin-*), nose.]

rhi·noc·er·os (ri-nóssərəss) *n., pl.* **-oses** or collectively **rhinoceros.** Any of several large, thick-skinned, herbivorous mammals of the family Rhinocerotidae, of Africa and Asia, having one or two upright horns on the snout. An example is the one-horned Indian rhinoceros, *Rhinoceros unicornis.* [Middle English *rinoceros*, from Latin *rhinocerōs*, from Greek *rhinokerōs*, "nose-horned" : RHINO- + *keras*, horn.] **—rhi·noc·e·rot·ic** (-nóss-ə-róttik, -i-) *adj.*

rhinoceros beetle *n.* Any of several scarabaeid beetles having one or more rhinoceros-like horns on the head, such as *Oryctes rhinoceros*, a pest of oriental coconut palms.

rhinoceros bird *n.* The oxpecker (see).

rhi·nol·o·gy (ri-nólləji) *n.* The anatomy, physiology, and pathology of the nose. [RHINO- + -LOGY.] **—rhi·nol·o·gist** *n.*

rhi·no·plas·ty (rino-plasti) *n.* Plastic surgery of the nose. [RHINO- + -PLASTY.] **—rhi·no·plas·tic** (-plástik) *adj.*

rhi·nos·co·py (ri-nóskəpi) *n.* Examination of the nasal passages. [RHINO- + -SCOPY.]

rhi·no·vi·rus (rino-vir-əss) *n* Any of a group of RNA-containing viruses that cause the common cold and other infections of the respiratory tract.

rhizo-, rhiz– *comb. form.* Indicates a root; for example, **rhizomorphous, rhizoid.** [Greek *rhiza*, root.]

rhi·zo·bi·um (ri-zō-bi-əm) *n., pl.* **-bia** (-bi-ə). Any of various nitrogen-fixing bacteria of the genus *Rhizobium* that form nodules on the roots of leguminous plants such as clover and beans. [New Latin *Rhizobium* : RHIZO- + Greek *bios*, life.]

rhi·zo·carp (rizo-kaarp) *n.* **1.** A plant having persistent roots but stems and leaves that die down at the end of each growing season. **2.** A plant that produces subterranean flowers and fruit. [RHIZO- + -CARP.] **—rhi·zo·car·pous** (-kárpəss) *adj.*

rhi·zo·ceph·a·lan (rizo-séffl-ən) *n.* Any of various small aquatic crustaceans of the order Rhizocephala that are parasitic on other crustaceans. [New Latin *Rhizocephala*, "root-headed ones" (from the rootlike processes extending from the limbless body) : RHIZO- + -cephala, from -cephalus, -CEPHALOUS.] **—rhi·zo·ceph·a·lous** *adj.*

rhi·zo·gen·ic (rizo-jénnik) *adj.* Also **rhi·zo·ge·net·ic** (-jə-néttik), **rhi·zog·e·nous** (ri-zójənəss). *Botany.* Giving rise to roots: *rhizogenic tissue.* [RHIZO- + -GENIC.]

rhi·zoid (ri-zoyd) *adj.* Rootlike.
~*n.* **1.** A slender, rootlike filament by which mosses, liverworts, and ferns attach to the substratum and absorb nourishment. **2.** A rootlike extension of the thallus of a fungus. [RHIZ(O)- + -OID.] **—rhi·zoi·dal** (ri-zóyd'l) *adj.*

rhi·zome (ri-zōm) *n. Botany.* A rootlike, usually horizontal stem growing under or along the ground, and sending out roots from its lower surface, and leaves or shoots from its upper surface. Also called "rootstock", "rootstalk". [New Latin *rhizoma*, from Greek *rhizōma*, mass of roots of a tree, from *rhizousthai*, to take root, from *rhiza*, root.] **—rhi·zom·a·tous** (ri-zómmə-təss, -zōmə-) *adj.*

rhi·zo·morph (rizo-mawrf) *n.* A rootlike part, such as the threadlike structure in certain fungi, consisting of strands of hyphae. [RHIZO- + -MORPH.]

rhi·zo·mor·phous (rizo-mórfəss) *adj. Botany.* Having the form of a root. [RHIZO- + -MORPHOUS.]

rhi·zoph·a·gous (ri-zóffəgəss) *adj.* Feeding on roots. [RHIZO- + -PHAGOUS.]

rhi·zo·pod (rizo-pod) *n.* Any protozoan of the class Rhizopoda, such as an amoeba, characteristically moving and taking in food by means of pseudopodia. [New Latin *Rhizopoda*, "root-footed" (from its rootlike pseudopodia) : RHIZO- + -POD.] **—rhi·zop·o·dan** (ri-zóppədən) *adj. & n.* **—rhi·zop·o·dous** *adj.*

rhi·zo·pus (riz-ə-pəss, -ō-) *n.* Any of various often destructive fungi of the genus *Rhizopus*, such as *R. nigricans*, the common bread mould. [New Latin, "one having rootlike feet" (from its rhizoids) : RHIZO- + Greek *pous*, foot (see **-pod**).]

rhi·zo·sphere (ri-zō-sfeer, -zə-) *n.* The soil immediately surrounding the root system of a plant.

rhi·zot·o·my (ri-zóttəmi) *n., pl.* **-mies.** Surgical severance of spinal nerve roots to relieve severe pain or muscle spasm. [RHIZO- + -TOMY.]

Rh negative *adj.* Lacking an **Rh factor** (see).

rho (rō) *n.* The 17th letter in the Greek alphabet written P, ρ. Transliterated in English as *rh* or *r.* [Greek *rhō*, perhaps shortened from *rhōs*, head, of Semitic origin, akin to Hebrew *rēsh, rōsh,* "head", RESH.]

rho·da·mine (rōdə-meen, -min) *n.* Any of several synthetic red to pink dyes. [RHOD(O)- + AMINE (the dyes are prepared from aminophenol).]

Rhode Island (rōd iland, iland ‖ *U.S.* rō-diland). State in New England, northeast United States. It is the smallest state in the Union but one of the most densely populated. Manufacturing is the chief employer, metalwares, textiles, and plastics being the main products. Fishing and tourism are important, and the state's resorts include Newport. Providence is the capital.

Rhode Island Red *n.* A domestic fowl of an American breed having dark reddish-brown feathers and producing brown eggs.

Rhodes (rōdz). *Greek* **Ró·dhos** (róthoss). Largest island in the Greek Dodecanese group, lying off the southwest coast of Turkey. The interior is mountainous but the island has fertile coastal strips and valleys where wheat, tobacco, cotton, olives, vines, oranges, and vegetables are grown. Tourism is also economically important. Rhodes, the capital, was founded in 408 B.C. and was the site of the Colossus of Rhodes, one of the Seven Wonders of the World, which was destroyed (*c.* 244 B.C.) by an earthquake.

Rhodes (rōdz), **Cecil (John)** (1853–1902). British industrialist and imperialist. In 1870 he went to South Africa and a year later staked a claim in the Kimberley diamond fields. In 1880 he founded the De Beers Mining Company, and he organised the British South Africa Company in 1889, thus gaining a virtual monopoly over mining in South Africa. In 1890 he became prime minister of the Cape Colony, but was forced to resign (1896) after being implicated in the Jameson Raid of 1895. He spent the rest of his life developing Rhodesia. He left a large fortune, most of which he willed to public causes such as the Rhodes scholarships.

Rhodes, Wilfred (1877–1973). British cricketer. He played for Yorkshire from 1898 to 1930 and in his career took 4,187 first-class wickets (an all-time record) and made nearly 40,000 runs. On 16 occasions he did the double of 100 wickets and 1,000 runs in a season, and he had a long and distinguished Test record as one of the greatest all-rounders in the history of the game.

Rhodesia. See **Zimbabwe.** —**Rho·de·sian** *adj. & n.*

Rho·de·sia and Ny·as·a·land, Federation of (rō-dée-shə, -zhə, -si-ə, -zi-ə; nī-ássə-land, ni–, *properly* nyássə–). From 1953 to 1963, a federation in central Africa consisting of the self-governing colony of Southern Rhodesia (now Zimbabwe) and the British protectorates of Northern Rhodesia (now Zambia) and Nyasaland (now Malawi).

Rhodesian man *n.* An extinct species of man, with a low forehead and massive brow ridges, whose fossil remains were found in central Zambia (formerly Northern Rhodesia), now classified as *Homo sapiens rhodesiensis.*

Rhodesian ridgeback *n.* A large dog of a breed developed in Africa, having short, yellowish-tan hair that forms a ridge along the back. Also called "ridgeback".

Rhodes Scholarship *n.* A scholarship available to students from the United States and the Commonwealth to study at Oxford University. —**Rhodes scholar** *n.*

rho·di·um (rōdi-əm) *n. Symbol* **Rh** A hard, durable, silvery-white metallic element that is used to form high-temperature alloys with platinum and is plated on other metals to produce a durable corrosion-resistant coating. Atomic number 45, atomic weight 102.905, melting point 1,966°C, boiling point 3,727°C, relative density 12.41, valencies 2, 3, 4, 5, 6. [New Latin, "rose red" (from the colour of its compounds), from Greek *rhodon,* rose.]

rhodo–, rhod– *comb. form.* Indicates rose or rose-red; for example, **rhodolite.** [Greek *rhodon,* rose.]

rho·do·chro·site (rōdo-krō-sīt) *n.* A naturally occurring impure form of manganese carbonate, $MnCO_3$, light-pink to rose-red in colour with a pearly or vitreous lustre, used as a manganese ore. [German *Rhodochrosit* : RHODO- + Greek *khrōsis,* colouring, from *khrōs, khroos,* colour, skin + -ITE.]

rho·do·den·dron (rō-də-déndrən, -di-) *n.* Any of various evergreen shrubs of the widely cultivated genus *Rhododendron,* of the North Temperate Zone, having clusters of variously coloured flowers. See **azalea.** [New Latin, from Latin, from Greek, "rose tree" : RHODO- + Greek *dendron,* tree.]

rho·do·lite (rōdə-līt, róddə-) *n.* A rose-red or pink variety of garnet, used as a gem. [RHODO- + -LITE.]

rho·do·nite (rōdə-nīt, róddə-) *n.* A pink to rose-red mineral, essentially $MnSiO_3$, used as an ornamental stone. Also called "manganese spar". [German *Rhodonit* : Greek *rhodon,* rose + -ITE.]

rho·dop·sin (rō-dóp-sin, rə-, ro-) *n.* The light-sensitive pigment in the retinal rods of the eyes, consisting of opsin and retinal. Also called "visual purple". [RHODO- + Greek *opsis,* sight + -IN.]

rhomb. Variant of **rhombus.**

rhom·ben·ceph·a·lon (rómben-séffl-on, -kéffl-, -ən) *n.* The portion of the embryonic brain from which the metencephalon, myelencephalon, and subsequently the cerebellum, pons, and medulla oblongata develop. Also called "hindbrain". [New Latin : RHOMB(US) + ENCEPHALON.]

rhom·bic (rómbik) *adj.* 1. Having the shape of a rhombus. 2. *Crystallography.* **Orthorhombic** *(see).*

rhom·bo·he·dron (rómbō-hée-drən) *n., pl.* **-drons** or **-dra** (-drə). *Abbr.* **rhbdr.** A prism with six faces, each a rhombus. [New Latin : RHOMBUS + -HEDRON.] —**rhom·bo·he·dral** *adj.*

rhom·boid (róm-boyd) *n.* 1. A parallelogram with unequal adjacent sides. 2. Either of two muscles in the upper part of the back.
—*adj.* Having a shape like a rhomboid. [Greek *rhomboeidēs* : RHOMBUS + -OID.] —**rhom·boi·dal** (-bóyd'l) *adj.*

rhom·bus (róm-bəss) *n., pl.* **-buses** or **-bi** (-bī). Also **rhomb** (rom). An equilateral parallelogram. [Latin, from Greek *rhombos,* bull-roarer, magic wheel, rhombus.]

rhon·chus (róng-kəss) *n., pl.* **-chi** (-kī). A coarse sound somewhat like snoring, usually caused by secretion in the bronchial tube. [Late Latin, snoring, from Greek *rhonkhos, rhonkos.*] —**rhon·chal, rhon·chi·al** (-ki-əl) *adj.*

Rhon·dda (rónthə). District in south Wales, extending along the valleys of the rivers Rhondda Fawr and Rhondda Fach. The chief industry, coalmining, has declined in importance since

the 1920s and 1930s and there has been a steady decrease in population in recent decades.

Rhône (rōn). Major European river, about 800 kilometres (500 miles) long. It issues from the Rhône Glacier in the Swiss Alps and flows through Lake Geneva, then southwards through France to the Mediterranean. The river is important for hydroelectric power, and its valley south of Lyon is noteworthy for its excellent vineyards. The Rhône-Saône valley is a main north-south communications route. South of Lyon the river is navigable and an extensive canal system links it with other major rivers.

rho·tic (rōtik) *adj. Phonetics.* 1. Pertaining to, designating, or speaking a variety of English in which the consonant sound (r) has not been lost before a consonant sound or pause. Thus Scottish English is rhotic; Southern English is not. 2. Designating a consonant sound which is a variety of (r). [From the Greek letter RHO.]

r.h.p. rated horsepower.

Rh positive *adj.* Containing an Rh factor *(see).*

rhu·barb (rōō-baarb ‖ réw-) *n.* 1. Any of several plants of the genus *Rheum,* characterised by large, long-stalked leaves; especially, *R. rhaponticum,* the common garden rhubarb, having long, green or reddish, acid leafstalks that are edible when cooked and sweetened. 2. The dried, bitter-tasting rhizome and roots of *R. palmatum* or *R. officinale,* of central Asia, used as a laxative. 3. *U.S. Slang.* A heated discussion, quarrel, or fight.
~*interj.* Used to convey an indistinct mumbling sound, as for background talk in a play. [Middle English *rubarbe,* from Old French *r(e)ubarbe,* probably from Medieval Latin *reubarb(ar)um,* probably alteration of *rha barbarum,* barbarian rhubarb : Late Latin *rha,* rhubarb, from Greek *rha, rhēon,* probably from *Rha,* former name of the Volga, on whose banks rhubarb was grown, + Latin *barbarus,* BARBAROUS.]

rhumb (rum ‖ rumb) *n.* 1. A rhumb line. 2. Any of the points of the mariner's compass. [Earlier *rumb,* from Old Spanish *rumbo* and Old French *rumb,* modifications (influenced by Latin *rhombus,* RHOMBUS) of Middle Dutch *ruum, rume,* room, space.]

rhumba. Variant of **rumba.**

rhum·ba·tron (rúmbə-tron) *n. Electronics.* A cavity resonator *(see).* [RHUMBA (rumba) + -TRON (alluding to the rhythmical variations of the waves).]

rhumb line *n.* 1. An imaginary line that cuts all the Earth's meridians at a given constant angle. Also called "loxodrome", "loxodromic curve". 2. The course of a ship following such a line; a course sailed using a constant compass bearing.

rhyme (rīm) *n.* Also *archaic* **rime.** 1. Correspondence of terminal sounds of words or of lines of verse. See **assonance, consonance, feminine rhyme, masculine rhyme.** 2. A poem or verse having a regular correspondence of sounds, especially at the ends of lines: *a nursery rhyme.* 3. Poetry or verse of this kind. 4. A word that corresponds with another in terminal sound, such as *night* and *fight,* and *baboon* and *harpoon.*
~*v.* **rhymed, rhyming, rhymes.** Also *archaic* **rime.** —*intr.* 1. To form a rhyme; correspond in sound: *Death rhymes with breath.* 2. To compose rhymes or verse. 3. To make use of rhymes in composing verse. —*tr.* 1. To put into rhyme or compose with rhymes. 2. a. To use (a word or words) as a rhyme or rhymes. b. To pronounce as a rhyme. [Middle English *rime, ryme,* from Medieval Latin *rithmus,* variant of Latin *rhythmus,* RHYTHM.]

rhym·er (rīmər) *n.* One who composes verse, especially of low quality. See Synonyms at **poet.**

rhyme royal *n.* A stanza form consisting of seven lines in iambic pentameter with the first line rhyming with the third, the second with the fourth and fifth, and the last two with each other.

rhyme·ster (rím-stər) *n.* One who makes up light verse that rhymes. See Synonyms at **poet.**

rhym·ing slang (rīming) *n. British.* A type of humorous slang in which a word is replaced by a word or words that rhyme with it; for example, *brown bread* meaning *dead,* and *mince pies* meaning *eyes,* are instances of rhyming slang. Often only the first element is used, as *plates* (meaning *feet*) from *plates of meat.*

rhyn·cho·ce·phal·i·an (ríngkō-si-fál-i-ən, -fáyl-) *adj.* Of or belonging to the Rhynchocephalia, an order of lizard-like reptiles of which only one species, the tuatara, is extant.
~*n.* A rhynchocephalian reptile. [New Latin *Rhynchocephalia* : Greek *rhunkhos,* snout, bill, beak + CEPHAL(O)- + -IA.]

rhy·o·lite (rí-ə-līt, -ō-) *n.* A fine-grained extrusive, acid igneous rock, the mineralogical equivalent of granite, consisting largely of quartz and feldspar, and often mica. [German *Rhyolit* : irregularly from Greek *rhuax,* stream (of lava), from *rhein,* to flow + -ITE.] —**rhy·o·lit·ic** (-líttik) *adj.*

Rhys (reess), **Jean** (1894–1979). British novelist and short-story writer, born in Dominica. She went to Paris, where she published the collection of stories *The Left Bank* (1927). Her other works include *Voyage in the Dark* (1934), *Wide Sargasso Sea* (1966).

rhythm (rith'm) *n.* 1. a. Any kind of movement characterised by the regular recurrence of strong and weak elements: *the rhythm of the tides.* b. Action characterised by a smooth, regular, settled movement: *The crowd put the tennis player off his rhythm.* 2. Nonrandom variation, especially uniform or regular variation, of any quantity or condition characterising a process, as in the body. 3. *Music.* a. The part of music concerned with patterns of sound based on such elements as accent and tempo. b. A specified kind of this rhythm: *a waltz rhythm.* 4. a. The metrical flow of sound with a regulated pattern of long and short, or accented and unaccented syllables,

best exemplified in poetry or verse. **b.** A specified kind of such a metrical flow: *sprung rhythm*. **5.** In painting, sculpture, and other visual arts, a regular or harmonious pattern created by lines, forms, and colours. [French *rhythme*, from Latin *rhythmus*, from Greek *rhuthmos*, recurring motion, rhythm, akin to *rhein*, to flow.]
    Synonyms: *rhythm, metre, cadence, beat.*

rhythm and blues *n. Abbr.* **R & B.** An urban form of blues using electrically amplified instruments, developed in the United States in the 1940s.

rhyth·mi·cal (ríthmik'l) *adj.* Also **rhyth·mic** (ríthmik). Pertaining to or characterised by rhythm; especially, recurring with measured regularity. **—rhyth·mi·cal·ly** *adv.*

rhyth·mics (ríthmiks) *n. Used with a singular verb.* The study of rhythm.

rhyth·mist (ríthmist) *n.* One who is expert in, or has a keen sense of, rhythm.

rhythm method *n.* A birth-control method dependent on avoidance of sexual intercourse during the ovulatory phase of the menstrual cycle.

rhythm section *n.* The members of a musical band or group, such as the drummer and bass guitarist, that supply the rhythm.

rhy·ton (rí-t'n, -ton) *n.* In ancient Greece, a drinking vessel or horn tapering to a hole in the bottom through which the wine could run. [Greek *rhuton*, from *rhutos*, flowing, from *rhein*, to flow.]

R.I. **1.** Rhode Island. **2.** Royal Institution. **3.** King and Emperor [Latin *Rex et Imperator*]. **4.** Queen and Empress [Latin *Regina et Imperatrix*].

ri·a (reer, ree-ə) *n.* A long narrow sea inlet, caused by flooding of a narrow valley , which unlike a fiord deepens towards the sea, and is typically found in southwest Ireland and northwest Spain. [Spanish, "river mouth".]

Riad. See **Riyadh.**

ri·al (rí-əl, ree-áal) *n.* **1. a.** The basic monetary unit of Iran, equal to 100 dinars. **b.** A coin worth one rial. **2.** The basic monetary unit of Yemen, equal to 100 fils; riyal. [Persian, from Arabic *riyāl*, from Spanish *real*, REAL (coin).]

ri·al·to (ri-ál-tō, ree-) *n., pl.* **-tos.** An exchange or trading centre. [After the *Rialto,* Venice, an island forming the centre of the city.]

ri·a·ta, re·a·ta (ree-áata, -átta) *n. U.S.* A lariat; a lasso. [Spanish *(la) reata,* (the) lasso, LARIAT.]

rib (rib) *n.* **1. a.** Any of the long, curved bones occurring, in humans, in 12 pairs and extending from the spine to or towards the breastbone and enclosing the heart and lungs. **b.** A similar bone in most other vertebrates. **2.** Any part or piece considered similar to a rib and serving to shape or support: *the rib of an umbrella.* **3.** A cut of meat enclosing one or more ribs. **4.** Any of the curved members attached to the keel of a boat and extending upwards and outwards to form the framework of the hull. **5.** Any of the formed transverse pieces along the length of an aeroplane wing used to establish shape. **6.** *Architecture.* **a.** An arch or a projecting arched member of a vault. **b.** Any of the curved pieces of an arch. **7. a.** A knitting stitch formed by working alternate plain and purl on one row, reversing this order on the next, and so on. **b.** The evenly ridged pattern formed by this. **c.** Material knitted in rib, usually found at the collar, waist, and neck of a woollen garment. **8.** *Botany.* Any of the main veins of a leaf or similar organ. **9.** A ridge of a mountain. **10.** *Mining.* A vein of ore.
    ~*tr.v.* **ribbed, ribbing, ribs. 1.** To shape, support, or provide with a rib or ribs. **2.** To work in rib: *Rib 30 rows, then cast off.* **3.** To make with ridges or raised markings. **4.** *Informal.* To tease or make fun of. [Middle English *rib(be),* Old English *rib(b),* from Germanic.]

R.I.B.A. Royal Institute of British Architects.

rib·ald (ríbb'ld || ríbawld) *adj.* Characterised by or indulging in vulgar, lewd, coarse humour. See Synonyms at **coarse.**
    ~*n.* A ribald person. [Middle English *ribaud,* retainer of low rank, lewd person, rascal, blasphemer, from Old French *ribauld, ribaut,* from *riber,* to be wanton, from Old High German *rīban,* to be in heat, copulate, "to rub".]

rib·ald·ry (ríbb'ldri) *n., pl.* **-ries.** Ribald language or joking.

rib·and (ríbbənd) *n. Archaic.* A ribbon, especially one used as a decoration. [Middle English, from Old French *riban,* probably from a Germanic compound of BAND.]

rib·band (ríbbənd) *n.* A length of flexible wood or metal used to hold the ribs of a ship in place while the exterior planking or plating is being applied. [RIB + BAND (strip).]

Rib·ben·trop (ríbbən-trop), **Joachim von** (1893–1946). German politician. In 1938 Hitler made him foreign minister, and he played a major role in the negotiation of the German-Soviet non-aggression pact of 1939. He remained foreign minister until Hitler's death in 1945. He was convicted of war crimes at Nuremberg and hanged.

rib·bing (ríbbing) *n.* **1.** Ribs collectively. **2.** An arrangement of ribs, as in a boat. **3.** Knitted rib. **4.** *Informal.* An instance of teasing.

rib·bon (ríbbən) *n.* **1.** A narrow strip or band of fine fabric, such as satin or velvet, finished at the edges and used for trimming or tying. **2.** Anything resembling a ribbon, such as a measuring tape. **3.** *Plural.* Tattered or ragged strips: *a dress torn to ribbons.* **4.** An inked strip of cloth used for making the impression of typed characters, as in a typewriter. **5.** A band of coloured cloth signifying an award, as of a military decoration or membership in an order. **6.** *Plural. Informal.* Reins for driving horses.
    ~*tr.v.* **ribboned, -boning, -bons. 1.** To decorate or tie with ribbons. **2.** To tear into ribbons or shreds. [Middle English *riban,* variant of RIBAND.]

ribbon development *n.* Land development marked by continuous building along a road leading away from a town and not having a natural social centre.

rib·bon·fish (ríbbən-fish) *n., pl.* **-fishes** or collectively **ribbonfish.** Any of several marine fishes, chiefly of the genus *Trachipterus,* having long, narrow, compressed bodies. See **oarfish.**

rib·bon·wood (ríbbən-wŏŏd) *n.* A New Zealand evergreen tree, *Hoheria populnea,* the timber of which is used in cabinetmaking and the bark for making cord.

ribbon worm *n.* A **nemertean** *(see).*

rib cage *n.* The enclosing structure formed by the ribs and the bones to which they are attached.

Ri·be·ra (ree-baír-ə), **José de,** also known as Lo Spagnoletto (1591–1652). Spanish painter. He studied in Rome (*c.* 1613–14) where he came under the influence of Caravaggio. In 1616 he settled in Naples. He painted chiefly religious subjects but also secular subjects such as *The Laughing Girl with Tambourine.*

ri·bo·fla·vin (ríbō-fláyvin) *n.* A crystalline orange-yellow pigment, $C_{17}H_{20}O_6N_4$, that is part of the vitamin B complex, being essential for carbohydrate metabolism. It is found in milk, leafy vegetables, fresh meat, and egg yolks, and produced synthetically. Also called "lactoflavin", "vitamin B₂", "vitamin G". [RIBO(SE) + FLAVIN.]

ri·bo·nu·cle·ase (ríbō-néw-kli-ayz, -ayss || -nŏŏ-) *n. Abbr.* **RNAase.** Any of various enzymes that promote the hydrolysis of RNA.

ri·bo·nu·cle·ic acid (ríbō-new-kléé-ik, -kláy- || -nŏŏ-) *n.* See RNA. [RIBO(SE) + NUCLEIC ACID.]

ri·bose (rí-bōz, -bōss) *n.* A pentose sugar, $C_5H_{10}O_5$, occurring as a component of RNA and certain coenzymes. [German *Ribon(säure),* a tetrahydroxyl acid from which ribose is obtained : *Ribon-,* arbitrary alteration of English *arabinose,* ribose : (GUM) ARAB(IC) + -IN + -OSE + *Säure,* acid.]

ribosomal RNA *n. Abbr.* **rRNA.** The RNA that forms a constituent of ribosomes.

ri·bo·some (ríbə-sōm) *n.* Any of numerous spherical cytoplasmic particles, consisting of RNA and protein, that are the sites of protein synthesis in the cell. [RIBO(SE) + -SOME (body).] **—ri·bo·so·mal** (-sŏm'l) *adj.*

rib·wort (ríb-wurt || *U.S.* also -wawrt) *n.* A weedy plant, *Plantago lanceolata,* having lancelike, ribbed leaves and a dense spike of small whitish flowers.

Ri·car·do (ri-kárdō), **David** (1772–1823). English political economist, one of the chief founders of the so-called classical school of economists. His most important work, *Principles of Political Economy and Taxation* (1817), supported the law of supply and demand in a free market. He also enunciated the "labour theory of value" which was taken up by Marx.

Ric·ci (réechi), **Matteo** (1552–1610). Italian Jesuit. He was sent as a missionary to China in 1582. His reports of life in China were the first knowledgeable accounts of Chinese life received by the West.

rice (ríss) *n.* **1.** A cereal grass, *Oryza sativa,* that is cultivated extensively in warm climates, and is a staple food throughout the world. **2.** The starchy edible seed of this grass.
    ~*tr.v.* **riced, ricing, rices.** *U.S.* To sieve (food) to the consistency of rice. [Middle English *rys, ryce,* from Old French *ris,* from Italian *riso,* from Latin *oryza,* from Greek *oruzon, oruza,* from East Iranian *vrīz-* (unattested), akin to Sanskrit *vrīhi†.*]

rice·bird (ríss-burd) *n.* Any of various birds that frequent rice fields, such as the Java sparrow.

rice bowl *n.* An area where rice is grown in abundance.

rice paper *n.* A thin, edible paper made chiefly from the pith of the rice-paper tree.

rice-pa·per tree (ríss-paypər) *n.* A shrub or small tree, *Tetrapanax papyriferum,* of eastern Asia, grown as a source of fibre for rice paper.

rice pudding *n.* A dessert made from rice baked in sweetened milk.

ri·cer·car (ree-chər-kár, -cher-, -chair-) *n. Music.* Also **ri·cer·ca·re** (-ay). A composition developing a basic theme, similar to a fugue.

rice weevil *n.* A small, destructive insect, *Sitophilus oryzae,* that infests stored grain and cereal products.

rich (rich) *adj.* **richer, richest. 1.** Possessing great wealth; owning much money, goods, or land. **2.** Composed of rare or valuable materials; made with fine or elaborate craftsmanship; costly: *a rich brocade.* **3.** Of great worth; valuable. **4.** Elaborate or sumptuous: *a rich feast.* **5.** Plentiful; abundant; ample. **6.** Abundantly or copiously supplied. Used with *in* or *with*: *rich in tradition.* **7.** Abounding in natural resources: *a rich land.* **8.** Producing or yielding much; abundant: *a rich harvest.* **9.** Of or designating food that contains a large or excessive proportion of tasty, fatty ingredients, such as eggs, butter, or cream: *a rich sauce.* **10.** Pleasing and satisfying to the senses, owing to a quality such as fullness, mellowness, or intensity: *a rich tenor voice; a rich blue.* **11.** Containing a large proportion of fuel to air. Said of a fuel mixture. **12.** *Informal.* Full of amusement; satisfyingly funny: sometimes used ironically: *That's rich!* [Middle English *riche,* originally powerful, great, partly from Old French *riche,* from Frankish *rīki* (unattested), and partly from Old English *rīce.*] **—rich·ly** *adv.* **—rich·ness** *n.*

Rich·ard I (ríchərd), also known as Richard Coeur de Lion (Richard the Lionheart) (1157–99). King of England (1189–99), third son and successor of Henry II. He set out on the Third Crusade in 1190 and gained, by a treaty with Saladin, access for Christians to Jerusalem. He was captured by Leopold V of Austria in 1192, handed over to the Emperor Henry VI, and ransomed in 1194. He was in

England in 1194, before returning to France where he was slain in a minor engagement.

Richard II (1367–1400). King of England (1377–99), son of the Black Prince and successor to his grandfather, Edward III. At the age of 14 he made a heroic appearance before the rebels taking part in the Peasants' Revolt (1381), placating them with promises of concessions which were immediately revoked. From 1386 until the end of his reign he was at odds with the baronial opposition in Parliament and his rule became increasingly authoritarian. In 1399 Richard took over the estates of his uncle John of Gaunt. John's heir, Henry Bolingbroke, compelled him to abdicate. Richard was imprisoned in Pontefract Castle where he died.

Richard III (1452–85). King of England (1483–85), younger brother of Edward IV and last of the Yorkist kings. When Edward IV died in 1483, Richard seized his two sons, including the rightful heir, Edward V, and imprisoned them in the Tower of London. Richard was then crowned king. The two princes were murdered in the Tower, possibly on Richard's orders. In 1485 Richard was slain at the Battle of Bosworth Field.

Richard, Sir Cliff, born Harry Roger Webb (1940–). British pop singer and actor. His first hit song was *Move It* (1958). He has made several films, and appears frequently on television.

Rich·ards (ríchərdz), **Sir Gordon** (1902–86). British jockey. He won the jockey's championship every year from 1925 to 1953; except 1926, 1930, and 1941. He set the record of 269 victories in one season in 1947 and over his career rode 4,870 winners.

Richards, (Isaac) Vivian (Alexander), known as Viv (1952–). West Indian cricketer, who was the first man to score more than 6000 runs in one-day internationals. West Indies captain 1985–91.

Richards, I(vor) A(rmstrong) (1893–1979). British literary critic and grammarian. In the 1920s he collaborated with Charles Ogden in the formulation of Basic English, publishing with him *The Foundations of Aesthetics* (1921) and *The Meaning of Meaning* (1923).

Rich·ard·son (ríchərd-sən), **Henry Handel,** pen name of Ethel Richardson Robertson (1870–1946). Australian novelist. She lived in England after 1903 and published her first novel, *Maurice Guest,* in 1908. Her best work is usually considered to be the trilogy of Australian life, *The Fortunes of Richard Mahony* (1930).

Richardson, Sir Ralph (David) (1902–83). British stage and film actor. He made his great reputation chiefly as a character actor. He was noted for his strong characterisation in his performances of classic roles as well as in contemporary works, such as Pinter's *No Man's Land* (1975). He was knighted in 1947.

Richardson, Samuel (1689–1761). English novelist. He worked as a printer until the age of 50, when he began to write his first work, *Pamela* (1740). It was written in the form of a series of letters as were its successors, *Clarissa* (1747–48) and *The History of Sir Charles Grandison* (1753–54).

Richardson, Tony (1928–91). British film director. He established his reputation in the 1950s with a series of films in the then prevailing mood of social realism, *Look Back in Anger* (1958), *A Taste of Honey* (1961), and *The Loneliness of the Long Distance Runner* (1962). He also directed *Tom Jones* (1962).

Rich·bo·rough (rích-brə, -bərə ‖ -burrə). Site of the Roman port of Rutupiae, situated on the river Stour just north of Sandwich, Kent.

Riche·lieu (réesh-lyer, -lew; *French* -əl-yo̅), **Armand Jean du Plessis, Duc de** (1585–1642). French prelate and statesman, chief minister of Louis XIII, generally known as Cardinal Richelieu. He worked devotedly to strengthen the authority of the monarchy, suppressing numerous conspiracies by the nobles and directing France during the Thirty Years' War (1618–48). He founded the French Academy in 1635.

rich·es (ríchiz) *pl.n.* **1.** Abundant wealth. **2.** Valuable or precious possessions. [Middle English *riches, richesse,* wealth (taken as a plural), from Old French *riche,* powerful, RICH.]

Rich·ler (ríchlər), **Mordecai** (1931–). Canadian writer. His comic novels, mainly about Jewish themes, include *The Apprenticeship of Duddy Kravitz* (1959), *The Incomparable Atuk* (1963), and *Cocksure* (1968). Autobiography: *The Street* (1972).

rich·ly (ríchli) *adv.* **1.** In a rich way or manner. **2.** In full measure; thoroughly: *richly rewarded.*

Rich·mond¹ (ríchmənd). Market town and tourist centre in North Yorkshire, England, situated on the river Swale.

Richmond². Capital of Virginia, eastern United States. Situated on the James river, it is a port exporting coal and tobacco, and it manufactures tobacco products and chemicals. Settled in 1637, it was capital of the Confederacy during the American Civil War.

Richmond-upon-Thames. Borough of southwest Greater London, England. Largely residential, it has within its boundaries Richmond Park, Kew Gardens, and Hampton Court Palace.

Rich·ter (ríkhtər), **Hans** (1843–1916). Hungarian conductor. He was especially famous for his performances of Wagner, and he helped Wagner to prepare the final scores of *Die Meistersinger* and the *Ring* cycle. He was conductor of the Hallé Orchestra in Manchester (1900–1911).

Richter, Svyatoslav Toefilovich (1915–). Russian pianist, much admired for his interpretation of Schubert and Beethoven. He was not heard in the West until 1960, when he performed in Finland and the United States.

Richter scale (*also* ríktər) *n.* A logarithmic scale ranging from 1 to 10, used to express the magnitude of an earthquake. [After Charles F. Richter (1900–85), U.S. seismologist.]

Richt·ho·fen (ríkht-hōf'n), **Manfred, Baron von,** also known as the Red Baron (1892–1918). German pilot. During World War I he was credited with shooting down 80 enemy aircraft, making him the leading ace of the war. He was killed in action in 1918.

ri·cin (rí-sin, ríssin) *n.* A highly poisonous protein extracted from castor-oil beans and used as a biochemical reagent. [Latin *ricinus†,* castor-oil plant.]

ri·cin·o·le·ic acid (ríssin-ō-lée-ik, rí-sin-, -ólí-ik) *n.* An unsaturated fatty acid, $C_{18}H_{34}O_3$, prepared from castor oil and used in making soaps and in textile finishing. [Latin *ricinus,* castor-oil plant (see **ricin**) + OLEIC.]

rick¹ (rik) *n.* A stack of hay, straw, or similar material, especially when covered or thatched for protection from the weather. —*tr.v.* **ricked, ricking, ricks.** To pile in ricks. [Middle English *reke,* Old English *hrēac,* akin to Old Norse *hraukr†.*]

rick² *tr.v.* **ricked, ricking, ricks.** *British.* To sprain, strain, or pull (one's back, for example). —*n.* A sprain or similar injury. [Middle English *wricken,* from Middle Low German *wricken†,* to sprain.]

rick·ets (ríkkits) *n. Used with a singular verb.* A deficiency disease resulting from a lack of vitamin D, characterised by defective bone growth, and occurring chiefly in children. Also called "rachitis". [Variant of RACHITIS.]

rick·ett·si·a (ri-két-si-ə) *n., pl.* **-siae** (-si-ee). Any of various microorganisms, mostly of the genus *Rickettsia,* carried as parasites by ticks, fleas, and lice. Transmitted to humans, they cause diseases such as typhus, Q fever, and trench fever. [After Howard T. *Ricketts* (1871–1910), U.S. pathologist.] —**rick·ett·si·al** *adj.*

rick·et·y (ríck-əti, -i-ti) *adj.* **-ier, -iest. 1.** Likely to break or fall apart; shaky. **2.** Feeble with age; infirm: *a rickety old man.* **3.** Of, having, or resembling rickets. [From RICKETS.] —**rick·et·i·ness** *n.*

rick·ey (rícki) *n., pl.* **-eys.** A drink of soda water, lime juice, and usually gin. [20th century : origin obscure.]

rick·rack, ric·rac (rík-rak) *n.* A flat, narrow braid in zigzag form, used as a trimming. [Reduplication of RACK (to torture).]

rick·shaw (rík-shaw) *n.* A small two-wheeled oriental carriage drawn by one or two men. Also called "jinricksha". [Short for JINRICKSHA.]

ric·o·chet (ríckə-shay, -shet, -sháy, -shét) *intr.v.* **-cheted** (-shayd) or **-chetted** (-shettid), **-cheting** (-shay-ing) or **-chetting** (-shetting), **-chets.** To rebound at least once from a surface or surfaces. Used of a projectile, such as a bullet. —*n.* An instance of such deflection. [French *ricochet†.*]

ri·cot·ta (ri-kóttə) *n.* An Italian cottage cheese made from the whey drained from other cheeses made with sheep's milk. [Italian, from Latin *recocta,* feminine past participle of *recoquere,* to cook again : *re-,* again + *coquere,* to cook.]

ric·tus (ríktəss) *n.* The expanse of an open mouth, a bird's beak, or similar structure. [Latin *rictus,* from the past participle of *ringī†,* to gape.] —**ric·tal** *adj.*

rid (rid) *tr.v.* **rid** or **ridded, ridding, rids.** To free from something objectionable or undesirable: *Let me rid your mind of fear.* —**get rid of.** To dispose of. [Middle English *rud(d)en, rid(d)en,* from Old Norse *rythja* (past participle *ruddr*), from Germanic *rudjan* (unattested).] —**rid·der** *n.*

rid·dance (rídd'nss) *n.* A welcome removal of or deliverance from something. —**good riddance.** Used to express relief at the removal or prospect of the removal of an unwanted person or thing. [RID + -ANCE.]

rid·den (rídd'n). Past participle of **ride.** —*adj.* Dominated; oppressed. Usually used in combination: *disease-ridden; cliché-ridden.*

rid·dle¹ (rídd'l) *tr.v.* **-dled, -dling, -dles. 1.** To pierce with numerous holes; perforate. **2.** To put through a coarse sieve. **3.** To permeate and thereby weaken or damage: *riddled with errors.* —*n.* A coarse sieve for separating and grading materials such as gravel: *a potato riddle.* [Middle English *rid(d)len,* to sift, from *riddil,* sieve, Old English *hriddel, hridder.*] —**rid·dler** *n.*

riddle² *n.* **1.** A question or statement requiring one to puzzle over it to answer or understand; a conundrum. **2.** Something perplexing; an enigma. —*v.* **riddled, -dling, -dles.** —*tr.* To solve or explain (a riddle). —*intr.* **1.** To solve or propound riddles. **2.** To speak in riddles. [Middle English *redel(es), ridil,* Old English *rædelse,* from *rædan* (unattested), to READ.] —**rid·dler** *n.*

ride (rīd) *v.* **rode** (rōd), **ridden** (rídd'n), **riding, rides.** —*intr.* **1.** To sit on, control, and be conveyed by an animal or a machine: *riding sidesaddle on the horse.* **2.** To be conveyed or transported, as in a vehicle, boat, or aircraft: *ride in a bus.* **3.** To travel over a surface: *This car rides well.* **4.** To lie at anchor. Used of a ship. **5.** *Literary.* To seem to be floating in space: *a star riding in the sky.* **6.** To progress effortlessly; be swept along as if by some relentless force: *rode to power on a surge of patriotism.* **7.** *Archaic.* To carry a rider or support something in a particular manner. **8.** To lie over something; overlap. Used especially of bones. **9.** To work or move from the proper place. Used with *up: Her tight skirt kept riding up.* **10.** To continue undisturbed by any action: *We let the problem ride.* —*tr.* **1.** To sit on, control, and be transported by: *ride a bike.* **2.** To be supported or carried upon. **3.** To travel over, along, or through: *ride the roads.* **4.** To rest upon by overlapping; overlie. **5.** To take part in or do by riding: *He rode his last race.* **6.** To control or dominate. **7.** To cause to ride, as by taking on one's shoulders: *riding his son on his back.* **8.** To keep (a vessel) at anchor. **9.** *U.S. Informal.* To tease or ridicule. **10.** To mount so as to copulate with.

—ride down. 1. To catch up and overtake on horseback. 2. To trample under horses' hooves. **—ride high.** To be elated, as from success. **—ride out.** To withstand or survive successfully. **—ride roughshod over.** To take a course of action without regard for the feelings, opinions, or welfare of.

~*n.* 1. An excursion or journey by any means of conveyance, as on horseback, in a car, or on a boat. 2. A path made for riding on horseback, especially through woodlands. 3. At funfairs or similar places, any of various entertainments in which persons ride for pleasure or excitement. 4. An experience of a specified type to which one is subjected: *The committee gave the minister a rough ride.* **—take for a ride.** *Informal.* To deceive or swindle. [Ride, rode, ridden; Middle English *riden, rad* (or *rod*), *riden,* Old English *rīdan, rād, riden* (unattested), from Germanic.]

rid·er (rīdər) *n.* 1. One who or that which rides; especially, one who rides horses. 2. *Plural.* Material, such as iron plates, added to a ship's frame to strengthen it. 3. A clause, usually having little relevance to the main issue, added to a document, such as a parliamentary bill. 4. An amendment or addition, as to a document or statement: *The jury added a rider to the verdict.* 5. A small weight that can slide along an arm of a chemical balance, used to make small changes to the balancing weight. 6. *Mathematics.* A problem that can be posed arising from a theorem, especially in geometry. 7. *Mining & Geology.* A thin seam lying over a thicker seam.

ridge (rij) *n.* 1. The long, narrow upper section or crest of something: *ridge of a wave.* 2. A long, narrow land elevation; a long hill or chain of mountains. 3. A long, narrow, or crested part of the body: *the ridge of the nose.* 4. The horizontal line formed by the juncture of two sloping planes; especially, the line formed by the surfaces of a roof. 5. Any narrow raised strip, as in cloth or on ploughed land. 6. *Meteorology.* An area of high pressure extending from the centre of an anticyclone and separating two low-pressure regions.

~*v.* **ridged, ridging, ridges.** *—tr.* To mark with, form into, or provide with ridges. *—intr.* To form ridges. [Middle English *rigge,* back, ridge, Old English *hrycg,* from Germanic.] **—ridg·y** *adj.*

ridge·back (ríj-bak) *n.* A dog, a **Rhodesian ridgeback** *(see).*

ridge·ling, ridg·ling (ríjling) *n.* In veterinary medicine, a male animal, such as a horse, with one or two undescended testicles. Also called "rig". [Obsolete *ridgel,* probably "(animal) with testes near the back", from RIDGE.]

ridge·pole (ríj-pōl) *n.* 1. A horizontal beam at the ridge of a roof, to which the rafters are attached. 2. The horizontal pole at the top of a tent. Also called "ridge beam", "ridge piece".

ridge·way (ríj-way) *n. British.* A road, track, or other path along the top of a hill or range of hills.

rid·i·cule (ríddi-kewl) *n.* 1. Words or actions intended to evoke contemptuous laughter at or feelings towards a person or thing. 2. Subjection to such a contemptuous attitude.

~*tr.v.* **ridiculed, -culing, -cules.** To deride, mock, or make fun of. [French *ridicule,* from Latin *rīdiculum,* joke, jest, from *rīdiculus,* laughable, RIDICULOUS.] **—rid·i·cul·er** *n.*

Synonyms: *ridicule, mock, taunt, twit, deride, gibe.*

ri·dic·u·lous (ri-díckewləss, rə-) *adj.* Deserving or inspiring ridicule; absurd or preposterous; silly or laughable. See Synonyms at **foolish.** [Latin *rīdiculōsus, rīdiculus,* laughable, from *rīdēre*†, to laugh.] **—ri·dic·u·lous·ly** *adv.* **—ri·dic·u·lous·ness** *n.*

rid·ing¹ (rīding) *n.* The action or skill of one who rides a horse.

~*adj.* Pertaining to, used in, or worn for riding: *a riding school; riding boots.*

riding² *n.* 1. Formerly, one of the three administrative divisions of Yorkshire, England: North Riding, East Riding, and West Riding. 2. Any similar administrative division; specifically, in Canada, a parliamentary constituency. [Middle English *riding, rithing* (with loss of the initial *th-* due to preceding *-t* in *east, west),* Old English *thrithing* (unattested), "thirding", from Old Norse *thrithjungr,* third part, from *thrithi,* third.]

riding habit *n.* A horsewoman's costume, especially formerly.

riding lamp. *n.* A lamp or light hung on a vessel at anchor.

Rid·ley (rídli), **Nicholas** (*c.* 1500–55). English Protestant churchman and martyr. He was appointed Bishop of London in 1550 and helped to prepare the Edwardian prayer books. Under the Catholic Mary I he was tried as a heretic and burnt at Oxford with Latimer.

Ri·dol·fi (ri-dólfi), **Roberto** (1531–1612). Florentine banker who settled in London (1555) and conspired against Elizabeth I. A Catholic and supporter of Mary Queen of Scots, he helped to plan a rebellion (1570–71) backed by Spain. The plot was discovered while Ridolfi was organising support abroad, but his fellow-conspirator, the Duke of Norfolk, was exposed and executed.

Rie·beeck (rée-bayk), **Jan van** (1619–77). Dutch administrator. Trained as a doctor, he joined the Dutch East India Company and in 1652 headed an expedition which founded Cape Town.

Rie·fen·stahl (réef'n-shtaal), **Leni** (1902–). German film director and photographer. In her youth she made pro-Nazi films, including *Triumph of the Will* (1934) and *The Olympic Games* (1936), covering the Berlin Olympics. Her later works include photographic studies of Sudanese peoples, among them *Last of the Nuba* (1973). She worked as a photojournalist in the 1970s, under the name Helen Jacobs. Her autobiography, *The Sieve of Time,* was published in 1993.

ri·el (ree-él) *n.* The basic monetary unit of Cambodia, divided into 100 sen.

Rie·mann (rée-man), **Georg Friedrich Bernhard** (1826–66). German mathematician, a pioneer of non-Euclidean geometry. From 1851 he developed an approach, now known as Riemannian geometry, by which a generalised space was studied without a prior framework for calculating distances between points. His work influenced Einstein's theory of relativity.

Rie·mann·i·an geometry (ree-mánni-ən) *n.* A non-Euclidean geometry based on the postulate that there are no parallel lines. Also called "elliptic geometry". [After G. F. B. RIEMANN.]

Ries·ling (réess-ling, réez-) *n.* 1. A sweet or dry white wine with a light, flowery bouquet produced especially in Germany and Alsace. 2. The type of grape used in the making of this wine. [German, earlier *Rüssling*†.]

rif·amp·i·cin (ríf-ámpi-sin) *n.* An antibiotic active against various infections, used chiefly to treat tuberculosis. [From *rifamycin,* earlier *rifomycin* (*r*eplication *i*nhibiting *f*ungus + -MYCIN), its source + *ampicillin* (to which it is comparable in efficacy).]

rife (rīf) *adj.* **rifer, rifest.** 1. Frequently or commonly happening or appearing; widespread; prevalent. 2. Abundant; numerous. 3. Abounding; full. Used with *with: That department is rife with incompetents.* —See Synonyms at **prevailing.** [Middle English *rif, ryfe,* Old English *rȳfe,* probably from Old Norse *rífr,* acceptable.]

riff (rif) *n.* In jazz and rock music, a short rhythmic phrase repeated so as to provide a rhythmic impulse. [20th century : origin obscure.]

Riff (rif) *n.* A member of a Berber people of the Rif country in northern Morocco, Africa.

rif·fle (riff'l) *n.* 1. The act of shuffling cards. 2. *Mining.* **a.** The sectional stone or wood bottom lining of a sluice, arranged to trap mineral, especially gold, particles. **b.** A groove or block in such a lining. 3. *U.S.* **a.** A rocky shoal or sandbar lying just below the surface of a waterway. **b.** A stretch of choppy water caused by such such a shoal or sandbar; a rapid.

~*v.* **riffled, -fling, -fles.** *—tr.* 1. To shuffle (playing cards) by holding part of a pack in each hand and raising up the edges before releasing them to fall alternately in one stack. 2. To thumb through (the pages of a book, for example). *—intr.* 1. To shuffle cards. 2. To thumb through pages. 3. To become choppy. [Perhaps blend of RUFFLE (disturb) and RIPPLE.]

rif·fler (rífflər) *n.* A file with curved ends suitable for scraping. [Old French *rifloir,* from *rifler*†, to scratch, file.]

riff·raff (ríf-raf) *n.* Worthless, uncultured, or disreputable persons. Used derogatorily. [Middle English *riffe raffe, rif and raf,* one and all, from Old French *rif et raf* : *rifler,* to file (see **riffler**) + *raffe,* a sweeping, from Middle High German *raffen,* to snatch (see **raffle**).]

ri·fle¹ (rīf'l) *n.* 1. A firearm with a rifled bore designed to be fired from the shoulder. 2. An artillery piece or naval gun that has been rifled. 3. *Plural.* Troops armed with rifles.

~*tr.v.* **rifled, -fling, -fles.** To cut spiral grooves within (a gun barrel, for example) to improve the accuracy of the projectile's flight. [Originally "spiral groove", from *rifle,* to cut spiral grooves, from Old French *rifler,* to file. See **riffler.**]

rifle² *tr.v.* **-fled, -fling, -fles.** 1. **a.** To ransack with intent to steal. **b.** To plunder; pillage. 2. To rob; strip bare: *rifle a safe.* [Middle English *riflen,* from Old French *rifler,* to scratch, file, plunder. See **riffler.**] **—ri·fler** *n.*

ri·fle·bird (rīf'l-burd) *n.* Any of several birds of paradise of the genus *Ptiloris,* of Australia and New Guinea. [From its cry.]

ri·fle·man (rīf'l-mən, -man) *n., pl.* **-men** (-mən, -men). 1. One trained or expert in firing a rifle; especially a private in a rifle regiment of the British Army. 2. A New Zealand wren, *Acanthisitta chloris.*

rifle range *n.* An area set aside for shooting practice at targets, using rifles.

ri·fle·ry (rīf'l-ri) *n.* 1. The art and practice of marksmanship.

ri·fling (rīfling) *n.* Spiral grooves cut inside a gun barrel.

rift¹ (rift) *n.* 1. A narrow fissure, cleft, or chink, as in rock. 2. A break in friendly relations.

~*v.* **rifted, rifting, rifts.** *—intr.* To split open; burst; break. *—tr.* To cause to split open or break. [Middle English *rift, ryft,* from Scandinavian, akin to Danish *rift,* breach.]

rift² *n. U.S.* 1. A shallow area in a waterway. 2. The backwash of a wave that has broken upon a beach. [Probably variant of *riff,* dialectal variant of REEF.]

rift valley *n.* A long, narrow depression in the earth's surface formed when the land sinks between two fairly parallel faults.

rig¹ (rig) *tr.v.* **rigged, rigging, rigs.** 1. To fit out or provide (an aircraft, for example) with equipment. 2. **a.** To equip (a ship) with sails, shrouds, and yards. **b.** To fit (sails, shrouds, and the like) to masts and yards. 3. *Informal.* To dress, clothe, or adorn: *rigged out in her best dress.* 4. To make, construct, or erect, often in haste or in a makeshift manner. Often used with *up.* 5. To manipulate dishonestly for personal gain: *rig a competition.*

~*n.* 1. The arrangement of masts, spars, and sails on a sailing vessel: *a square rig.* 2. **a.** Any special equipment or gear for a particular purpose. **b.** A citizens' band receiver and transmitter. 3. The installation and apparatus used for drilling oil and gas wells. 4. *Slang.* A lorry. 5. *U.S.* A vehicle with one or more horses harnessed to it. [Middle English *riggen,* probably from Scandinavian, akin to Norwegian *rigga.*]

rig² *n.* A **ridgeling** *(see).*

Ri·ga (réegə, *formerly also* rīgə). Capital of Latvia. It is a port city, situated on the Baltic coast on the Gulf of Riga. A member of the Hanseatic League from 1282, it passed to Poland (1581), Sweden (1621), and Russia (1710), and was capital of the earlier independent state of Latvia (1919–40).

rig·a·doon (ríggə-dŏŏn) *n.* **1.** A lively jumping quickstep for one couple. **2.** Music for this dance, usually in rapid duple time. [French *rigaudon, rigodon,* said to have been invented by a famous dancing master of Marseille named *Rigaud.*]

rigamarole. Variant of **rigmarole.**

rig·a·to·ni (ríggə-tṓni) *n.* Large, ribbed, macaroni tubes, slightly curved and cut into short lengths. [Italian, plural of *rigato,* past participle of *rigare,* to draw a line, corrugate, from *riga,* line, from Germanic.]

Ri·gel (rī́-jəl, -g'l) *n.* A bright double star in the constellation Orion. [Arabic *rijl,* (Orion's) foot.]

rig·ger[1] (ríggər) *n.* **1.** One who rigs, specifically: **a.** One who fits rigging to sailing ships. **b.** One who assembles or aligns aircraft parts or parachutes. **c.** One who works with hoisting tackle, cranes, pulleys, and scaffolds. **d.** One who works on an oil rig.

rigger[2] *n.* A metal bracket attached to the side of a racing or rowing boat that supports a rowlock. Also called "outrigger".

rig·ging (rígging) *n.* **1.** The system of ropes, chains, and tackle used to support and control the masts, sails, and yards of a sailing vessel. **2.** Any system of gear for a specific task.

right (rīt) *adj.* **righter, rightest.** *Abbr.* **R., r., rt. 1.** In accordance with or conformable to justice, law, morality, or similar principle: *right action.* **2.** In accordance with fact, reason, or truth; correct: *the right answer.* **3.** Fitting, proper, or appropriate: *the right one for the job.* **4.** Most favourable, desirable, or convenient: *the right time to act.* **5.** In a satisfactory state or condition; in good order: *I'll put it right in a moment.* **6.** Mentally sound or normal; sane: *in one's right mind.* **7.** Physically normal or healthy; well: *Are you feeling quite right?* **8.** Intended to be worn facing outwards or towards an observer: *the right side of cloth.* **9. a.** *Archaic.* Genuine; not spurious. **b.** *Informal.* Real; thorough: *I felt a right fool.* **10. a.** Designating, belonging to, or located on the side of the body to the east when the subject is facing north. **b.** Designating or located on the corresponding side of anything that can be considered to have a front: *the bird's right wing.* **c.** Designating or located on that side of anything which an observer directly facing it perceives to be on or towards his right side. **11.** *Often capital* **R.** Of or tending towards the political Right. **12.** In geometry: **a.** Formed by or in reference to a line or plane that is perpendicular to another line or plane. **b.** Having the axis perpendicular to the base. Said of solids: *right cone.* **13.** *Archaic.* Straight; uncurved; direct: *a right line.*
—*n.* **1.** That which is just, morally good, legal, proper, or fitting: *Two wrongs don't make a right.* **2. a.** The right side or direction: *My house is on the right.* **b.** That which is on or towards the right side or direction. **3.** *Often capital* **R. a.** The individuals and groups pursuing generally conservative or reactionary political policies, in opposition to broadly egalitarian or socialist policies. **b.** Support for such policies measured in terms of an imaginary political continuum: *moving further to the right.* **4.** In boxing, the right hand or a blow given by the right hand. **5.** That which is due to anyone by law, tradition, or nature: *She was given her rights.* **6.** A just or legal claim or title. **7.** *Finance.* **a.** A shareholder's privilege of buying additional shares in a company at a special price, usually at par or at a price below the current market value. **b.** *Often plural.* A privilege of subscribing for a particular stock or bond. **—by right** or **rights.** Justly; properly. **—in (one's) own right.** By virtue of one's own position, efforts, or achievements. **—to rights.** In a satisfactory or orderly condition: *set the place to rights.*
—*adv.* **1.** In a straight line; directly; straight. Often used with *to, into,* or *through: He went right to the heart of the matter.* **2.** Properly; suitably; conveniently; well: *The suit doesn't fit right.* **3.** Exactly; just: *It happened right over there.* **4.** Immediately: *She will be right down.* **5.** Completely; thoroughly; quite: *The wind blew right through him.* **6.** According to law, morality, or justice. **7.** Accurately; correctly. **8.** On or towards the right side or direction. **9. a.** *Archaic.* Extremely: *He answered right well.* **b.** *Regional.* Very; thoroughly: *had a right good time.* **10.** Very. Used in certain titles: *the Right Reverend; Right Honourable.* **—right, left, and centre.** From or on every side.
—*v.* **righted, righting, rights.** —*tr.* **1.** To put in or restore to an upright or proper position: *They righted their boat.* **2.** To put in order or set right; correct. **3.** To make reparation or amends for; redress: *right a wrong.* —*intr.* To regain an upright position.
—*interj.* Used to indicate assent, agreement, or comprehension. **—right on.** *Chiefly U.S. Slang.* Used to express enthusiastic approval or agreement. [Middle English *riht, right,* Old English *riht.*] **—right·er** *n.* **—right·ness** *n.*

Synonyms: *right, privilege, prerogative, perk, franchise, birthright, title.*

right about turn *n.* See **about-turn.**

right angle *n.* An angle formed by the perpendicular intersection of two straight lines; an angle of 90 degrees. **—at right angles.** Forming such an angle.

right-an·gled (rīt-ang-gl'd, -áng-) *adj.* Forming or containing one or more right angles: *a right-angled triangle.*

right ascension *n. Abbr.* **R.A.** The angular distance of a celestial body or point on the celestial sphere, measured eastwards from the vernal equinox along the celestial equator to the hour circle of the body or point, and expressed in degrees or in hours.

right away *adv.* Without hesitation; immediately.

right·eous (rī́t-yəss, rī́chəss) *adj.* **1.** Meeting accepted standards of what is right and just; morally right; virtuous. **2.** Having justification or good reason: *righteous anger.* See Synonyms at **moral.** [Middle English *rightwise, ryghtuous,* Old English *rihtwīs* : *riht,* RIGHT + *wīs,* WISE (way).] **—right·eous·ly** *adv.* **—right·eous·ness** *n.*

right·ful (rī́t-f'l) *adj.* **1.** Right or proper; just. **2.** Having a just or proper claim: *Return this dog to its rightful owner.* **3.** Held or owned by just or proper claim: *This dog is my rightful property.* **—right·ful·ly** *adv.* **—right·ful·ness** *n.*

right-hand (rīt-hánd) *adj.* **1.** Of or located on the right: *a right-hand drive car.* **2.** Directed towards the right side: *a right-hand turn.* **3.** Of, for, or done by the right hand. **—righthand·er** *n.*

right-hand·ed (rīt-hándid) *adj.* **1.** Using the right hand more easily or skilfully than the left. **2.** Done with the right hand. **3.** Made to be used by the right hand. **4.** Turning or spiralling from left to right; clockwise. **—right-hand·ed·ness** *n.*

right-hand man *n.* A subordinate who is a close associate of his superior.

right·ism (rī́tiz'm) *n. Sometimes capital* **R.** Reactionary or conservative political activities or ideas. **—right·ist** *adj.* & *n.*

right·ly (rī́tli) *adv.* **1.** With correctness or certainty: *I can't rightly say when I'll come.* **2. a.** Uprightly; with honesty. **b.** Justifiably: *She was rightly angered.* **3.** Properly; suitably.

right-mind·ed (rīt-míndid) *adj.* Having principles and views based on what is considered to be right. **—right-mind·ed·ness** *n.*

right·o (rī-tṓ) *interj. British Informal.* Used to express assent. [RIGHT + O.]

right of asylum *n.* The right of receiving **asylum** *(see).*

right of search *n. Law.* The right of a warring nation to stop any neutral vessel on the high seas and search it for contraband.

right of way *n.* **1.** *Law.* **a.** The right to pass over property owned by another party. **b.** The path or thoroughfare on which such passage is made. **2.** *U.S.* The strip of land over which facilities such as motorways, railways, or power lines are built. **3.** The customary or legal right of a person, vessel, or vehicle to pass in front of another.

rights issue *n.* An offer of new shares by a company to its shareholders at a preferential price.

right whale *n.* Any of several whalebone whales of the Balaenidae family, characterised by a large head and absence of a dorsal fin.

right wing *n.* **1.** The political right. **2.** A division holding relatively conservative views within a larger political group. **—right-wing** (rīt-wíng) *adj.* **—right-wing·er** *n.*

rig·id (ríjid) *adj.* **1.** Not bending; stiff; inflexible. **2.** Not moving; fixed. **3.** Rigorous; harsh; severe. **4.** Scrupulously strict; undeviating: *a rigid point of view.* —See Synonyms at **stiff.** [French *rigide,* from Latin *rigidus,* from *rigēre,* to be stiff.] **—rig·id·ly** *adv.* **—rig·id·ness** *n.*

ri·gid·i·ty (ri-jíddəti) *n., pl.* **-ties. 1.** The state or quality of being rigid; stiffness; inflexibility. **2.** An instance of being rigid.

rigidity modulus *n. Symbol* ζ *Physics & Engineering.* A modulus of elasticity measuring the response of a material to torsion or other shear, given by the ratio of the shear stress to the shear strain. Also called "shear modulus".

rig·ma·role (ríg-mə-rōl) *n.* Also **rig·a·ma·role** (ríggə-). **1.** Confused, rambling, or incoherent speech or writing; nonsense. **2.** A complicated and petty set of procedures. [Alteration of obsolete *ragman roll,* list, catalogue (in Middle English referring to a written roll used in a game of chance), of obscure origin.]

rig·or (ríggər, rī́-gawr, -gər) *n.* **1.** *Medicine.* An attack of shivering or trembling with a sensation of coldness, which marks the start of a fever. **2.** *Physiology.* A state of rigidity in living tissues or organs, as caused by shock, that prevents response to stimuli. **3.** *U.S.* Variant of **rigour.** [Middle English, from Latin *rigor,* stiffness, severity, from *rigēre,* to be stiff.]

rig·or·ism (ríggə-riz'm) *n.* Severity or strictness in conduct, judgment, or practice; especially, in Roman Catholic theology, the stance that the rigorous or strict course is to be preferred in doubtful matters of conscience. **—rig·or·ist** *n.* **—rig·or·is·tic** (-rístik) *adj.*

rigor mor·tis (mórtiss) *n.* Muscular stiffening following death, due to chemical change in the tissues. [Latin, "the stiffness of death".]

rig·or·ous (ríggərəss) *adj.* **1.** Characterised by or acting with rigour; rigid and severe. **2.** Full of rigours; trying; harsh: *a rigorous climate.* **3.** Demanding or characterised by strict accuracy or observance of standards: *rigorous tests.* —See Synonyms at **burdensome. —rig·or·ous·ly** *adv.* **—rig·or·ous·ness** *n.*

rig·our, *U.S.* **rig·or** (ríggər) *n.* **1.** Strictness or severity, as in temperament, action, or judgment. **2.** A harsh or trying circumstance; a hardship: *the rigours of winter.* **3.** Harshness or austerity in living, especially as part of religious observance. [Middle English, from Old French, from Latin *rigor,* from *rigēre,* to be stiff.]

Rig-Ve·da (ríg-váydə || -veédə) *n.* The most ancient collection of Hindu sacred verses. [Sanskrit *ṛgveda* : *ṛc* (stem *ṛg-*), "praise", hymn + *veda,* "knowledge", sacred writing, Veda.]

Ri·je·ka (ree-yéckə). *Italian.* **Fiu·me** (féw-may). Largest port of Croatia, and formerly of Yugoslavia, situated in the northwest of the country. An Italian force under Gabriele D'Annunzio seized it from the Hungarians in 1919, and it was formally awarded to Italy by a treaty of 1924. In 1947 it was transferred to Yugoslavia.

rijs·ta·fel (rī́ss-taaf'l) *n.* A Dutch-Indonesian meal of rice served with piquant side dishes of meat and vegetables.

Riks·mål (réeks-mawl) *n.* **Bokmål** *(see).*

rile (rīl) *tr.v.* **riled, riling, riles. 1.** To vex; anger; irritate. **2.** *U.S.* To stir up (liquid). [Variant of ROIL.]

Ri·ley (rī́li). **—lead** or **live the life of Riley.** *Informal.* To lead a life of pleasure and easy enjoyment. [20th century : the reason for the choice of the name is unknown.]

Riley, Bridget (Louise) (1931–). British painter, a leading exponent of op art. Working from predetermined mathematical grids, she produced undulating optical patterns of lines and squares, usually in black and white.

Ril·ke (rílkə), **Rainer Maria** (1875–1926). Austrian poet, born in Prague. His verse is marked by a strain of mystic lyricism, his collections including *The Book of Hours* (1905), *Sonnets to Orpheus,* (1923), and *The Duino Elegies* (1923).

rill (ril) *n.* Also **rille** (for sense 2). **1.** A small brook; a rivulet. **2.** Any of various long, narrow, straight depressions on the Moon's surface. [Dutch *ril* or Low German *rille.*]

rill·et (ríllit) *n.* A small rill.

rim (rim) *n.* **1.** The border, edge, or margin of an object, especially one that is circular. **2.** The circular outer part of a wheel farthest from the axle; specifically, the circular metal structure around which a tyre is fitted. —See Synonyms at **border.**

~tr.v. **rimmed, rimming, rims. 1.** To furnish with a rim; put a rim around; border. **2.** *Sports.* To roll round the rim of (a hole, basket, or cup) without falling in. Used of a ball. [Middle English *rime, rym,* Old English *rima,* from Germanic *rimō* (unattested).]

Rim·baud (rámbō, *French* raɴ-bṓ), **(Jean) Arthur** (1854–91). French poet. His stormy relationship with Verlaine is alluded to in the prose poem *Une Saison en Enfer* (1873). Rimbaud gave up writing at 19 and lived an adventurous life in Europe, the Near East, and North Africa, dying in Marseille at the age of 37. A collection of his poems, *Les Illuminations* (1886), was published by Verlaine and strongly influenced the Symbolist movement.

rime¹ (rīm) *n.* Granular ice formed from supercooled fog droplets accumulating on the windward side of trees and other objects.

~tr.v. **rimed, riming, rimes.** To cover with or as if with rime. [Middle English *rim,* Old English *hrīma,* from Germanic *hrīmaz* (unattested), hoarfrost.] **—rim·y** *adj.*

rime². Variant of **rhyme.**

rime riche (réem réesh) *n., pl.* **rimes riches** (*pronounced as singular*). Rhyme using words or parts of words that are pronounced identically but have different meanings, for example, *write-right* or *port-deport.* [French, "rich rhyme".]

Ri·mi·ni (rímmini, réemini). Popular Adriatic resort in Emilia-Romagna, Italy. It has many Roman and medieval remains.

ri·mose (rí-mōss, -mōz) *adj.* Full of chinks, cracks, or crevices. [Latin *rīmōsus,* from *rīma,* cleft, crevice, fissure.] **—ri·mose·ly** *adv.* **—ri·mos·i·ty** (rī-móssəti) *n.*

Rim·sky-Kor·sa·kov (rímski kór-sə-kof, *Russian* -sə-kəf), **Nikolai Andreyevich** (1844–1908). Russian composer. His music often incorporates Russian folk themes; he wrote the opera *The Snow Maiden* (1881), and the orchestral piece *Scheherezade* (1888).

ri·mu (réemōō) *n.* A tree, the **red pine** *(see).* [Maori.]

rind (rīnd) *n.* A tough outer covering, such as bark, the skin of some fruits, or the surface layer on cheese or bacon. [Middle English *rinde,* Old English *rind(e).*]

rin·der·pest (ríndər-pest) *n.* An acute, contagious virus disease, chiefly of cattle, characterised by ulceration of the intestinal tract. Also called "cattle plague". [German *Rinderpest* : *Rinder,* plural of *Rind,* ox, cow, from Old High German *(h)rind* + *Pest,* pestilence, plague, from Latin *pestis,* PEST.]

rin·for·zan·do (rín-fawrt-sán-dō, réen- ‖ *U.S.* -saán-) *adv. Music.* With a sudden increase of emphasis. Used as a direction. [Italian, present participle of *rinforzare,* to reinforce : *ri-,* from Latin *re-,* again + *inforzare,* from Old French *enforcier,* to ENFORCE.]

ring¹ (ring) *n.* **1.** Any circular object, form, or arrangement with an empty circular centre: *blew smoke rings; a ring of bystanders.* **2.** A small circular band, generally made of precious metal, often set with jewels, and worn on a finger: *a wedding ring.* **3.** Any circular band used for carrying, holding, or containing something: *a napkin ring.* **4.** An electric element, gas burner, or the like, used as a source of heat, especially for cooking. **5.** A circular movement or course, as in dancing. **6.** An enclosed, usually circular area in which exhibitions, sports, or contests take place: *a circus ring.* **7. a.** A rectangular arena set off by stakes and ropes, in which boxing or wrestling contests are held. **b.** The sport of boxing. Preceded by *the.* **8. a.** An enclosed area in which bets are placed at a racecourse. **b.** Bookmakers collectively. **9. a.** An exclusive group of persons acting privately or illegally to advance their own interests, as in business or politics. **b.** A group of dealers illegally agreeing not to bid against each other at an auction, so as to achieve a lower sale price for a lot which is then reauctioned amongst themselves. **10. a.** A circular strip of bark removed from a tree trunk or branch to inhibit or stop growth. **b.** *Botany.* An **annual ring** *(see).* **11.** A field of contenders in a contest: *an unknown candidate entering the ring.* **12.** In geometry, the planar area between two concentric circles; an annulus. **13.** Any of the turns comprising a spiral or helix. **14.** *Chemistry.* A group of atoms chemically bound in a manner graphically representable as a circular form. Also called "closed chain". **—run rings round.** *Informal.* To show far greater skill than.

~v. **ringed, ringing, rings.** *—tr.* **1.** To surround with a ring; encircle. **2.** To form into a ring or rings, as by cutting. **3.** To ornament or supply with a ring or rings. **4.** To remove a circular strip of bark around the circumference of (a tree trunk or branch) in order to kill it or retard its growth; ring-bark. **5.** To put a ring in the nose of (a pig, bull, or other animal). **6.** To hem in (cattle or other animals) by riding in a circle around them. **7.** To toss a ring over (a peg) in a game. **8.** To put a ring round the leg of (a bird) for subsequent identification. *—intr.* **1.** To form a ring or rings. **2.** To move, run, or fly in a spiral or circular course. [Middle English *ring,* Old English *hring,* from Germanic.]

ring² *v.* **rang** (rang) or *nonstandard* **rung** (rung), **rung, ringing, rings.** *—intr.* **1.** To give forth a clear, resonant sound when caused to vibrate. **2.** To cause a bell or bells to sound. **3. a.** To sound a bell in order to summon someone. **b.** To make a telephone call: *I'll ring later.* **4.** To have a sound or character suggestive of a specified quality: *a perception that rings true.* **5.** To be filled with sound; resound. **6.** To persist vividly in the mind: *his plea still ringing in my ear.* **7.** To hear a persistent humming or buzzing: *ears ringing from the blast.* *—tr.* **1.** To cause (a bell, chimes, or the like) to ring. **2.** To produce (a sound) by or as if by ringing. **3. a.** To announce, proclaim, or signal by or as if by ringing. **b.** To summon or usher in in this way. Used with *in* or *out*: *ring in the new year.* **4.** To telephone (someone). Often used with *up.* **5.** To test (a coin, for example) for quality by the sound it produces when struck against something. **—ring back.** To return a telephone call or make another call later on. **—ring off.** To end a telephone call. **—ring up. 1.** To make a telephone call. **2.** To record (a price) on a cash register.

~n. **1.** The sound created by a bell or other sonorous, vibrating object. **2.** Any loud sound, especially one that is repeated or continued. **3.** A telephone call. **4.** A suggestion of a particular quality: *Her offer has a suspicious ring.* **5.** A set of bells. **6.** An act or instance of sounding a bell. [Middle English *ringen,* Old English *hringan.* Rang, rung; Middle English *rang, rungen,* analogous formations to verbs such as SING.]

ring-bark (ríng-baark) *tr.v.* **-barked, -barking, -barks.** To ring (a tree trunk or branch).

ring binder *n.* A booklike file with two or more circular clasps inside the spine that can be opened to allow loose leaves to be inserted.

ring·bolt (ríng-bōlt ‖ -bolt) *n.* A bolt having a ring fitted through an eye at its head.

ring·bone (ríng-bōn) *n.* A bony growth on the fetlock, pastern, or coffin bone of a horse's foot, usually causing lameness. [It tends to spread around a horse's foot like a ring.]

ring·dove (ríng-duv) *n.* **1.** An Old World pigeon, *Streptopelia risoria,* having black markings forming a half circle on the neck. Also called "Barbary dove". **2.** The **wood pigeon** *(see).*

ringed (ríngd) *adj.* **1.** Wearing a ring or rings. **2.** Encircled or surrounded by bands or rings. **3.** Having ringlike markings.

rin·gent (rínjənt) *adj. Biology.* Having gaping liplike parts, as the corolla of some flowers or the shells of certain bivalves do. [Latin *ringēns* (stem *ringent-*), present participle of *ringī,* to open wide the mouth, gape. See **rictus.**]

ring·er¹ (ríng-ər) *n.* **1.** One that rings. **2.** A horseshoe or quoit thrown so that it encircles the peg.

ringer² *n.* **1.** One that sounds a bell or chime. **2.** *Informal.* A person or thing bearing a striking resemblance to another. **3.** *U.S. Slang.* A contestant entered dishonestly into a competition.

Ring·er's solution (ríngərz) *n.* A solution of the chlorides of sodium, potassium, and calcium, used to maintain living tissues and organs *in vitro* and to treat dehydration. [After Sydney *Ringer* (1835–1910), British physician.]

ring fence *n.* A fence that completely surrounds a property.

ring-fence (ríng-féns) *tr. v.* **-fenced, -fencing, -fences.** To protect or seal off with or as if with a ring fence: *ring-fenced pension funds kept safe for retiring employees.*

ring finger *n.* The fourth finger of the hand, especially the left hand, as counted from the thumb.

ring·git (ríng-git) *n.* The basic monetary unit of Malaysia, divided into 100 sen.

ring·hals (ríng-halss, ríngk-, -alss) *n., pl.* **ringhals.** Also **rink·hals** (ríngk-). An African snake, *Haemachates haemachatus,* that spits venom. Also called "spitting cobra", "spitting snake". [Afrikaans *ringhals, rinkals,* "ring-necked" : *ring,* ring, circle, from Middle Dutch *rinc* + *hals,* neck, from Middle Dutch.]

ring·lead·er (ríng-leedər) *n.* A person who leads others, especially in unlawful or improper activities.

ring·let (ríng-lət, -lit) *n.* **1.** A spirally curled lock of hair. **2.** A small circle or ring. **3.** Any of various butterflies of the family Satyridae having brownish wings marked with white rings. **—ring·let·ed** *adj.*

ring main *n.* A mains electrical circuit in a building in which the sockets are connected in a single closed ring to the mains supply.

ring·mas·ter (ríng-maastər ‖ -mastər) *n.* A person in charge of the performances in a circus ring.

Ring Nebula *n.* A planetary nebula in the constellation Lyra. [From its resemblance to a smoke ring.]

ring-necked pheasant (ríng-nekt) *n.* A widely distributed bird, *Phasianus colchicus,* native to the Old World, the male of which has brightly coloured plumage and a white ring around the neck.

ring ousel *n.* A European thrush, *Turdus torquatus,* of mountainous regions, the male of which is black with a white neck band.

ring-pull (ríng-pōōl) *n.* A **tab** *(see),* especially on a canned drink.

ring road *n.* A road that encircles a town or city, used as a bypass for motorists. Also called "orbital".

ring·side (ríng-sīd) *n.* **1.** The area or seats immediately outside an arena or ring, as at a boxing match. **2.** Any place providing a close view of a spectacle. Also used adjectivally: *ringside seats.*

ring·tail (ríng-tayl) *n.* **1.** An animal with ringlike markings on its tail; especially, the **cacomistle** *(see).* Also called "ring-tailed cat". **2.** Any of various Australian phalangers with prehensile tails.

ring-tailed (ríng-tayld) *adj.* **1.** Having a tail with ringlike markings. **2.** Having a tail that curls to form a ring.
ring·worm (ríng-wurm) *n.* Any of a number of contagious skin diseases caused by several related fungi, and characterised by ring-shaped, scaly, itching patches on the skin. Also called "tinea".
rink (ringk) *n.* **1.** An area surfaced with smooth ice for skating, hockey, or curling. **2.** A smooth floor suited for roller-skating. **3.** A building that houses a surface prepared for skating. **4.** A section of a bowling green large enough for play. **5.** A team of players in quoits, bowling, or curling. [Middle English (Scottish) *rinc,* jousting area, perhaps from Old French *renc, ranc,* row, range, RANK.]
rinkhals. Variant of **ringhals.**
rinse (rinss) *tr.v.* **rinsed, rinsing, rinses. 1.** To wash lightly with water. **2.** To remove (soap, dirt, or impurities) from clothing or hair, for example, by rinsing in clean water.
~n. **1.** The act or an instance of rinsing. **2.** The water or other solution used in this process. **3. a.** A cosmetic solution used in conditioning or tinting the hair. **b.** A hairstyle treated with such a solution. [Middle English *ryncen,* from Old French *rincer, raincier*†.] **—rins·er** *n.*
Ri·o de Ja·nei·ro (rée-ō də jə-néer-ō, day; *Portuguese* rée-ōō di zhə-náy-rōō). Also **Rio.** Chief seaport and former capital of Brazil, lying on Guanabara Bay in the southeast of the country. Brazil's second largest city, it is backed by towering mountains, the most spectacular of which are Sugar Loaf Mountain and Corvocado peak, which is surmounted by a colossal statue of Christ. A tourist centre, it has magnificent beaches, including the famous Copacabana. It is also a cultural, financial, commercial, manufacturing, and transport centre.
Ri·o Gran·de (rée-ō grándi, rī-ō gránd). Also **Río Bravo (del Norte).** River in the southern United States. Rising in the San Juan Mountains of southwestern Colorado, it flows 3 035 kilometres (1,885 miles) south, then southeast, to the Gulf of Mexico. For much of its length it forms the border between United States and Mexico.
ri·ot (rī-ət) *n.* **1.** A wild or turbulent disturbance created by a large number of people. **2.** *Law.* A violent disturbance of the public peace by three or more persons assembled for a common private purpose. Also used adjectivally: *riot police.* **3.** An unrestrained outbreak, as of laughter or passions. **4.** A wild profusion, as of colours. **5. a.** Unrestrained merrymaking; revelry. **b.** *Archaic.* Debauchery. **6.** *Slang.* An irresistibly funny person or thing. **7.** In hunting, the following by a hound of the scent of the wrong prey. **—run riot. 1.** To move or act with wild abandon. **2.** To grow luxuriantly or abundantly.
~v. **rioted, -oting, -ots.** *—intr.* **1.** To take part in a riot. **2.** To live wildly or engage in uncontrolled revelry. *—tr. Literary.* To waste (money or time) in wild or wanton living. Used with *away* or *out.* [Middle English *riot(e),* debauchery, revel, riot, from Old French *ri(h)ot(e),* from *r(u)ihoter*†, to quarrel.] **—ri·ot·er** *n.*
Riot Act *n.* **1.** A law, enacted in England in 1715, providing that if 12 or more persons unlawfully assemble and disturb the public peace, they must disperse upon proclamation or be considered guilty of felony. **2.** *Small* **r**, *small* **a.** Any severe or forceful warning or reproach. Used chiefly in the phrase *read the riot act.*
Rí·o·tin·to, Mi·ñas de (méen-yass day rée-ō tíntō). Also **Río Tinto.** Town in Huelva province, Andalucia, Spain. It is famous for its mineral deposits, first worked by the Phoenicians.
ri·ot·ous (rī-ətəss) *adj.* **1.** Of, pertaining to, or resembling a riot. **2.** Taking part in or inciting to riot or uproar. **3.** Uproarious; boisterous. **4.** Dissolute; profligate. **5.** Abundant or luxuriant: *a riotous growth.* **—ri·ot·ous·ly** *adv.* **—ri·ot·ous·ness** *n.*
rip[1] (rip) *v.* **ripped, ripping, rips.** *—tr.* **1.** To cut or tear apart roughly or energetically; slash: *ripped open the parcel.* **2.** To remove by cutting or tearing roughly: *ripped the plaster off her leg.* **3.** To split or saw (wood) along the grain. **4.** *Informal.* To produce, display, or exclaim suddenly. Used with *out: ripped out a gun; ripped out a vicious oath.* *—intr.* **1.** To become torn or split apart. **2.** *Informal.* To move quickly or violently. **3.** *Informal.* To make a vehement verbal attack. Used with *into: ripped into her opponent's record.* **—let rip.** To give full vent to one's feelings: *let rip and told him what she thought of him.* —See Synonyms at **tear.**
~n. **1.** A torn or split place, especially along a seam; a tear. **2.** The act of ripping. [Middle English *rippen*†.] **—rip·per** *n.*
rip[2] *n.* **1.** An area of turbulence in the sea caused by the meeting of tidal streams, or by a tidal stream suddenly entering shallow water. **2.** An area of turbulence in the sea caused when water carried up a shore by strong waves returns down the shore. Also called "rip current", "rip tide". [Perhaps from RIP (the act of tearing).]
rip[3] *n. Archaic.* **1.** A dissolute person. **2.** An old or worthless horse. [Perhaps shortened variant of REPROBATE.]
R.I.P. rest in peace. [Latin *requiescat in pace.*]
ri·par·i·an (rī-páiri-ən, ri-) *adj.* **1.** Of, on, or pertaining to the bank of a river. **2.** Designating a right due to an owner of riparian land, for example a right to fish.
~n. One who owns riparian land. [Latin *rīpārius,* from *rīpa,* bank, shore.]
rip·cord (ríp-kawrd) *n.* **1.** A cord pulled to release the pack of a parachute. **2.** A cord pulled to release gas from a balloon.
rip current *n.* A rip (in the sea).
ripe (rīp) *adj.* **1.** Fully developed or mature; especially, ready for harvesting or consumption: *ripe pears.* **2.** Resembling matured fruit, as in fullness: *a ripe figure.* **3.** Sufficiently advanced in preparation or ageing to be used: *ripe cheese.* **4.** Thoroughly matured, as by study or experience; seasoned: *ripe judgment.* **5.** Advanced in years: *the ripe old age of 85.* **6.** Fully developed; prepared to do or undergo something; ready: *ripe for picking.* **7.** Sufficiently advanced; opportune. Said of time. [Middle English *ripe,* Old English *rīpe.*] **—ripe·ly** *adv.* **—ripe·ness** *n.*
rip·en (rīpən) *v.* **-ened, -ening, -ens.** *—tr.* To make ripe; cause to mature. *—intr.* To become ripe; mature. **—rip·en·er** *n.*
ri·pi·e·no (ríppi-áynō, rip-yénnō) *n. Music.* A passage in which the whole orchestra plays. [Italian, "full".]
rip off *tr.v. Slang.* **1.** To exploit, swindle, cheat, or defraud. **2.** To steal: *ripped off a case of whisky.* **3.** To steal from; rob: *Shoplifters ripped off the store.*
rip-off (ríp-off, -awff) *n. Slang.* **1. a.** An act of exploitation or overcharging. **b.** Something that is overpriced. **2.** A theft.
Rip·on (rīppən). Market town of North Yorkshire, England, famous for its cathedral (12th–16th century).
ri·poste, ri·post (ri-póst, -pŏst) *n.* **1.** A quick, retaliatory action or retort. **2.** In fencing, a quick thrust given after parrying an opponent's lunge.
~intr.v. **riposted, -posting, -postes.** To make a riposte. [French, from Italian *risposta,* answer, feminine past participle of *rispondere,* to answer, from Latin *respondēre,* to RESPOND.]
rip·ping (rípping) *adj. British Informal.* Wonderful; splendid. Not in current usage.
rip·ple[1] (rípp'l) *v.* **-pled, -pling, -ples.** *—intr.* **1.** To form or display little undulations or waves on the surface, as on disturbed water. **2. a.** To flow with such undulations or waves on the surface. **b.** To have a movement resembling rippling water: *rippling muscles.* **3.** To rise and fall gently in tone or volume: *Laughter rippled.* *—tr.* To cause to form small waves or undulations.
~n. **1.** A slight wave or undulation. **2.** Anything resembling such undulations in appearance: *ripples in the fabric.* **3.** A sound that gently rises and falls. **4.** *Electronics.* A small alternating, usually undesirable, signal superimposed on an otherwise constant signal. **5.** *U.S.* A small rapid. [17th century (verb): origin obscure.] **—rip·pler** *n.* **—rip·pling·ly** *adv.* **—rip·ply** *adj.*
ripple[2] *n.* A comblike, toothed instrument for removing seeds from flax and other fibres.
~tr.v. **rippled, -pling, -ples.** To remove seeds from (flax or other fibres) with a ripple. [Middle English *rip(e)len,* to remove seeds, from Germanic, akin to Middle Low German *repelen.*]
rip·plet (rípplit) *n.* A little wave or ripple.
rip·rap (ríp-rap) *n. U.S.* **1.** A loose assemblage of broken stones erected in water or on soft ground as a foundation. **2.** The broken stones used for this.
~tr.v. **riprapped, -rapping, -raps.** *U.S.* **1.** To construct a riprap in or upon. **2.** To strengthen with a riprap. [Reduplication of RAP (to strike).]
rip-roar·ing (ríp-rawring || -rōring) *adj. Informal.* Noisy, lively, and exciting. [RIP + (UP)ROAR(IOUS).]
rip·saw (ríp-saw) *n.* A coarse-toothed handsaw for cutting wood along the grain.
rip·snort·er (ríp-snawrtər) *n. Slang.* A person or thing remarkable for strength, intensity, or excellence. **—rip·snort·ing** *adj.*
rip tide *n.* A rip (*see*) (in the sea).
Rip·u·ar·i·an (rippew-áir-i-ən) *adj.* Of or designating a group of Franks who lived along the Rhine, near Cologne, in the fourth century. **—Rip·u·ar·i·an** *n.* [Medieval Latin *Ripuārius*†.]
Rip Van Winkle (rip van wíngk'l) *n.* One who is completely unaware of current trends and conditions. [After a character who slept for 20 years in a tale (1819) by Washington Irving.]
rise (rīz) *v.* **rose** (rōz), **risen** (rízz'n), **rising, rises.** *—intr.* **1.** To assume a standing position after lying, sitting, or kneeling. **2.** To get out of bed, especially after a night's rest. **3.** To move from a lower to a higher position; ascend. **4.** To increase in height or level: *The lake rose after the rain.* **5.** To appear above the horizon: *The Sun rises in the East.* **6.** To extend upwards; be prominent: *The tower rose above the hill; a cliff rising to 200 metres.* **7.** To slant or slope upwards: *Fields rose above the river.* **8.** To originate; come into existence: *a storm rising in the north.* **9.** To be built or erected. **10.** To appear at the surface of the water. Used of fish. **11.** To puff up or become larger during cooking or as a result of leavening: *Bread dough rises.* **12.** To become stiff and erect: *Hackles rose.* **13.** To increase in quantity, value, or price: *rising prices.* **14. a.** To increase in intensity, force, pitch, or prominence: *The temperature rises in summer.* **b.** To register an increase: *The index rose sharply.* **15.** To attain a higher status: *rose in her esteem.* **16. a.** To become apparent to the mind or senses: *Fears rose to haunt him.* **b.** To become elated: *Her spirits rose.* **17.** To uplift oneself to meet a demand: *rose to the challenge.* **18.** To return to life. **19.** To rebel. Often used with *up.* **20.** To close a session of an official assembly; adjourn. *—tr.* **1.** To cause to rise. **2.** *Nautical.* To cause (a distant object at sea) to become visible above the horizon by advancing closer.
~n. **1.** The act of rising; an ascent. **2.** The degree of elevation or ascent; an upward slope. **3.** The appearance of the Sun or other heavenly body above the horizon. **4.** An increase in height, as of the level of water. **5.** A gently sloping hill or elevation. **6.** An origin, beginning, or source: *the rise of a river.* **7.** *British.* An increase in salary or wages. **8.** The emergence of a fish seeking food or bait at the water's surface. **9.** An increase in price, worth, quantity, or degree. **10.** An increase in intensity, volume, or pitch. **11.** Elevation in social status, prosperity, or importance. **12.** The height of a

flight of stairs or of a single step. **—get** or **take a rise out of.** *Slang.* To provoke or tease (someone) successfully. **—give rise to.** Give occasion or opportunity to: *give rise to doubt.* [Rise, rose, risen; Middle English *risen, ros, risen,* Old English *rīsan, rās, risen.* (*Rās* and *risen* are attested only in compounds.)]

Synonyms: *rise, ascend, climb, soar, mount.*

ris·er (rīzər) *n.* **1.** A person who rises, especially from sleep: *a late riser.* **2.** The vertical part of a stair step.

ris·i·bil·i·ty (ríz-i-bílləti, rīz-, -ə-) *n., pl.* **-ties.** **1.** The ability or tendency to laugh. **2.** Laughter; hilarity.

ris·i·ble (ríz-ib'l, rīz-, -ə-) *adj.* **1.** Capable of laughing or inclined to laugh. **2.** Pertaining to or used in laughter. **3.** Apt to excite laughter; ludicrous; laughable. [Late Latin *rīsibilis,* from Latin *rīdēre* (past participle *rīsus*), to laugh. See **ridiculous.**] **—ris·i·bly** *adv.*

ris·ing (rīzing) *adj.* **1.** Ascending, sloping upwards, or advancing: *rising ground.* **2.** Approaching maturity or prominence; emerging: *the rising generation; a rising young actress.*

~n. **1.** An uprising; a revolt. **2.** A prominence or projection. **3.** The leaven or yeast used to make dough rise in baking.

~adv. Almost or approaching a specified age.

rising damp *n.* Damp that enters a building through the foundations, rising up the walls by capillary action.

risk (risk) *n.* **1.** The possibility of suffering harm or loss; danger: *There is the risk we won't return.* **2.** A factor, element, or course involving uncertain danger; a hazard: *The stormy weather is a risk we shall have to take.* **3.** *Insurance.* **a.** The danger or probability of loss to the insurer. **b.** The amount that the insurance company stands to lose. **c.** A person or thing considered with respect to the possibility of loss to an insurer: *a poor risk.* —See Synonyms at **danger.**

~tr.v. **risked, risking, risks.** **1.** To expose to a chance of loss or damage; hazard. **2.** To incur the risk of: *risking death.* **3.** To take the risk arising from: *I'll risk staying another hour.* [French *risque(r),* from Italian *risco†,* danger, *riscare†,* to run into danger.] **—risk·er** *n.*

risk capital *n. British.* Money invested in an enterprise subject to risk, such as a new business venture.

risk·y (ríski) *adj.* **-ier, -iest.** **1.** Accompanied by or involving risk or danger; hazardous. **2.** Risqué. **—risk·i·ness** *n.*

Ri·sor·gi·men·to (ri-sórji-méntō, -zórji-) *n.* The period of or the movement for the liberation and political unification of Italy, beginning about 1750 and lasting until 1870. [Italian, "resurrection", from *risorgere,* to resurrect, from Latin *resurgere,* to rise again : *re-,* again + *surgere,* to rise. See **surge.**]

ri·sot·to (ri-zóttō, -sóttō) *n.* An Italian dish of rice cooked in stock with grated cheese or vegetables and seasonings, often served with chopped meat or seafood. [Italian, from *riso,* rice.]

ris·qué (ríss-kay, reéss- || riss-káy) *adj.* Suggestive of or bordering on indelicacy or impropriety: *a risqué joke.* [French, from the past participle of *risquer,* to RISK.]

ris·sole (ríssōl) *n.* A small ball or cake made with a minced meat or fish mixture coated with breadcrumbs and egg, and usually fried. [French, from Old French *roissole,* from (unattested) Vulgar Latin *russeola (pasta),* "reddish (pastry)", from the feminine of Late Latin *russeolus,* diminutive of Latin *russeus,* reddish, from *russus,* red.]

ris·so·lé (ríssō-lay, reé-sō-, -láy) *adj.* Browned by frying. [French, past participle of *rissoler,* to brown by deep frying, from *rissole,* RISSOLE.]

ri·sus sar·do·ni·cus (reé-səss saar-dónnikəss, rī-) *n.* A fixed, abnormal grin seen, for example, in cases of tetanus. [(New) Latin, sardonic laugh.]

ri·tar·dan·do (ríttaar-dán-dō || *U.S.* -daán-) *adv. Abbr.* **rit., ritard.** *Music.* Gradually slowing in tempo. Used as a direction. [Italian, from Latin *retardandum,* gerund of *retardāre,* to RETARD.]

rite (rīt) *n.* **1.** The prescribed or customary form for conducting a religious or other solemn ceremony: *the rite of baptism.* **2.** A ceremonial act or series of acts: *fertility rites.* **3.** *Often capital* **R.** The liturgy of a Christian church, especially one of the historical forms of the Eucharistic service: *the Anglican Rite.* **4.** *Often capital* **R.** A branch or division of the Christian church as determined by specific liturgy and law: *Catholics of the Latin Rite.* **5.** Any formal practice, custom, or procedure. [Middle English *ryte,* from Latin *rītus.*]

rite of passage *n.* A ceremony, as in a primitive society, that marks a person's change of status, for example at puberty or on marriage.

ri·tor·nel·lo (ríttər-néllō, ríttawr-) *n., pl.* **-nelli** (-néllee) or **-los.** *Music.* **1.** An instrumental interlude recurring between verses in a vocal work. **2.** A passage for full orchestra in a baroque concerto grosso. **3.** An instrumental interlude in early 17th-century opera. [Italian, a refrain, diminutive of *ritorno,* return, from *ritornare,* to return, from Vulgar Latin *retornāre* (unattested), to RETURN.]

rit·u·al (ríchōō-əl, ríttew-, ríchōōl) *n.* **1.** The prescribed form or order of conducting a religious or solemn ceremony. **2.** A body of ceremonies or rites. **3.** A book of rites or ceremonial forms. **4. a.** A ceremonial act or a series of such acts. **b.** The performance of such acts. **5.** Any habitual detailed method of procedure: *Her household chores have become a ritual with her.*

~adj. **1.** Of or characterised by a rite or rites. **2.** Performed as a rite or ritual: *a ritual fire dance.* [Latin *rītuālis,* from *rītus,* RITE.] **—rit·u·al·ly** *adv.*

rit·u·al·ise, rit·u·al·ize (ríchōō-ə-līz, ríttew-) *v.* **-ised, -ising, -ises.** *—intr.* To engage in or practise ritualism. *—tr.* To make into or convert to ritual. **—rit·u·al·i·sa·tion** (-ī-záysh'n || *U.S.* -i-) *n.*

rit·u·al·ism (ríchōō-ə-liz'm, ríttew-) *n.* **1.** The study, practice, or observance of ritual. **2.** Insistence upon or adherence to ritual.

rit·u·al·ist (ríchōō-ə-list, ríttew-) *n.* **1.** An authority on or student of ritual. **2.** A person who practises or advocates the observance of ritual. **—rit·u·al·ist** *adj.*

rit·u·al·is·tic (ríchōō-ə-lístik, ríttew-) *adj.* Pertaining to, characterised by, or devoted to ritual or ritualism. **—rit·u·al·is·ti·cal·ly** *adv.*

ritz·y (rítsi) *adj.* **-ier, -iest.** *Informal.* Elegant; luxurious and fashionable. [From the *Ritz* hotels founded by César *Ritz* (1850–1918), Swiss hotelier.]

riv·age (rívvij) *n. Archaic.* A coast, shore, or bank. [Middle English, from Old French, from *rive,* bank, shore, from Latin *rīpa.*]

ri·val (rīv'l) *n.* **1.** A person who attempts to equal or surpass another, or who pursues the same object as another; a competitor: *They were rivals for the same job.* **2.** One that equals or almost equals another in some respect. —See Synonyms at **opponent.**

~adj. Acting as or being a rival; competing.

~v. **rivalled** or *U.S.* **rivaled, -valling** or *U.S.* **-valing, -vals.** *—tr.* **1.** To attempt to equal or surpass. **2.** To be the equal of; be a match for: *"rivalled the beauties of the best Grecian architecture"* (Henry Fielding). *—intr. Archaic.* To be a competitor or rival; compete. Used with *with.* [Latin *rīvālis,* "one using the same brook as another", rival, from *rīvālis,* of a brook, from *rīvus,* brook.]

Synonyms: *compete, rival, vie, emulate.*

ri·val·ry (rīv'lri) *n., pl.* **-ries.** **1.** The act or an instance of competing or emulating. **2.** The state or condition of being a rival.

rive (rīv) *v.* **rived, rived** or **riven** (rívv'n), **riving, rives.** *Archaic.* *—tr.* **1.** To rend or tear apart. **2.** To break into pieces, as by a blow; cleave or split asunder. **3.** To break or distress (the heart or spirit, for example). *—intr.* To be or become broken or split. [Middle English *riven,* from Old Norse *rifa.*]

riv·er (rívvər) *n.* **1.** *Abbr.* **R., r., riv.** A large natural stream of water flowing towards an ocean, lake, or other body of water. **2.** Any stream or abundant flow resembling this: *rivers of blood.* **—sell down the river.** To betray or deceive. **—up the river.** *U.S. Slang.* In or to prison. [Middle English, from Anglo-French *rivere,* river bank, river, from Vulgar Latin *rīpāria* (unattested), feminine of Latin *rīpārius,* on a bank, from *rīpa,* bank.]

Ri·ver·a (ri-vérrə), **Diego** (1886–1957). Mexican artist. His murals celebrate the struggle for independence and draw inspiration from his socialist beliefs, exalting the Indian peasantry at the expense of the ruling classes. He married artist Frida Kahlo (1907–54).

river basin *n.* A **basin** (sense 5) *(see).*

riv·er·bed (rívvər-bed) *n.* The area covered or once covered by water, between the banks of a river.

river horse *n. Informal.* The **hippopotamus** *(see).*

Riv·e·ri·na (rívvə-reénə). Region of New South Wales, Australia. Situated between the rivers Murray, Lachlan, and Murrumbidgee, it consists mainly of a fertile plain, producing wheat, rice, and fruit.

riv·er·ine (rívvə-rīn || -rin) *adj.* **1.** Pertaining to or resembling a river. **2.** Located on or inhabiting the banks of a river; riparian.

riv·er·side (rívvər-sīd) *n.* The bank of a river.

~adj. On or close to a bank of a river.

riv·et (rívvit, rívvət) *n.* A metal bolt or pin, having a head on one end, used to fasten metal plates or other objects together by inserting the shank through a hole in each piece and hammering down the plain end so as to form a new head.

~tr.v. **riveted, -eting, -ets.** **1.** To fasten or secure with, or as if with, a rivet. **2.** To hammer the headless end of (a bolt, pin, or similar device) so as to form a head and fasten something. **3.** To fasten or secure firmly; fix. **4.** To engross; grip: *riveted by the scene.* [Middle English *ryvette,* from Old French *river†,* to fix.] **—riv·et·er** *n.*

riv·et·ing (rívvit-ing, rívvət-) *adj.* Completely absorbing the attention; fascinating.

Riv·i·er·a (rívvi-áir-ə) *n.* **1.** The coastal region stretching along the Mediterranean Sea from Hyères in southeast France to La Spezia, Italy, that includes the fashionable resorts of Cannes, Monte Carlo, Nice, and St. Tropez. Preceded by *the.* **2.** *Small* **r. 2.** Any resort area extending along a coastline. [Italian, "shore", from Vulgar Latin *rīpāria* (unattested). See **river.**]

ri·vi·ère (rívvi-áir) *n.* A necklace of diamonds or other precious stones, generally in one strand. [French, short for *rivière de diamants,* "stream of diamonds", from Old French *rivere,* RIVER.]

riv·u·let (rívvew-lət, -lit) *n.* A small brook or stream; a streamlet. [Earlier *rivelet,* probably from Italian *rivoletto,* diminutive of *rivolo,* small stream, from Latin *rīvulus,* diminutive of *rīvus,* brook, stream.]

Ri·yadh or **Ri·ad** (reé-ad, ri-yaád). Capital of Saudi Arabia. Situated in an oasis in Nejd province, of which it is capital, it was once a walled town.The impact of the country's oil wealth has made it a commercial centre with much modern architecture.

ri·yal (ri-yaál, reé-al) *n.* Also **ri·al** (for sense 2). **1.** The basic monetary unit of Saudi Arabia, equal to 100 halalas. **2.** The basic monetary unit of Yemen, equal to 100 fils; rial. [Arabic *riyāl,* from Spanish *real,* REAL (coin).]

R.L. Rugby league.

RM reichsmark.

rm. **1.** ream. **2.** room.

R.M. **1.** Royal Mail. **2.** Royal Marines.

R.M.A. Royal Military Academy.

rms root mean square.

R.M.S. **1.** Royal Mail Service. **2.** Royal Mail Steamer.

Rn The symbol for the element radon.

R.N. Royal Navy.

RNA *n.* Ribonucleic *a*cid: a nucleic acid occurring in all living cells, consisting of a single-stranded chain of alternating phosphate and ribose units with the bases adenine, guanine, cytosine, and uracil bonded to the ribose. RNA occurs in several forms, mostly in the cytoplasm, and has an essential role in protein syntheses. See **messenger RNA, ribosomal RNA, transfer RNA.**

RNAase *n.* **Ribonuclease** *(see).*

R.N.A.S. 1. Royal Navy Air Service. 2. Royal Navy Air Station.

R.N.L.I. Royal National Lifeboat Institution.

R.N.R. Royal Naval Reserve.

R.N.V.R. Royal Naval Volunteer Reserve.

ro. rood (measure).

roach¹ (rōch) *n., pl.* **roaches** or collectively **roach.** 1. A freshwater game fish, *Rutilus rutilus,* of northern Europe, having reddish fins. 2. Any of various similar or related fishes. [Middle English *roche,* from Old French *roche*†.]

roach² *n.* 1. *U.S.* An insect, the **cockroach** *(see).* 2. *Slang.* The butt or filter, usually homemade, of a marijuana cigarette.

roach³ *n. Nautical.* The upward curvature of the bottom edge of a square sail intended to prevent chafing. [18th century : origin obscure.]

Roach, Hal (1892–1992). U.S. film director. His film company produced comedies featuring Harold Lloyd, Laurel and Hardy, and others, and he directed films such as *Fraternally Yours* (1933) and *Of Mice and Men* (1940).

road (rōd) *n. Abbr.* **Rd., rd., R., r.** 1. **a.** An open way, generally public and usually having a hard tarmac or other surface, for the passage of vehicles, persons, and animals. **b.** *Capital* **R.** Used as part of certain street names: *the Old Kent Road.* 2. A course or path: *the road to success.* 3. A passage or tunnel in a mine. 4. *U.S.* A railway. 5. *Usually plural. Nautical.* A roadstead *(see).* **—hit the road.** *Informal.* To begin a journey. **—on the road.** 1. On tour. Said especially of a theatrical company. 2. Travelling or moving around, especially as a salesman or vagrant. **—one for the road.** A last drink before setting out. [Middle English *rood, rode,* riding, journey, Old English *rād*.]

road·bed (rōd-bed) *n.* 1. **a.** The foundation upon which the sleepers, rails, and ballast of a railway are laid. **b.** A layer of ballast directly under the sleepers. 2. The foundation and surface of a road.

road·block (rōd-blok) *n.* An obstruction across a road set up, as by the police or army, for purposes of detection, security, or defence.

road hog *n. Informal.* A driver who drives inconsiderately and selfishly, often keeping his vehicle near the middle of the road.

road·hold·ing (rōd-hōlding) *n.* The ability of a motor vehicle to retain its grip or hold on a surface without skidding.

road·house (rōd-howss) *n.* An inn, restaurant, or nightclub situated on a road, especially in the countryside.

road·ie (rōdi) *n., pl.* **-ies.** A person who is responsible for the travelling arrangements of a pop group on tour, and who supervises their instruments and equipment. Also called "road manager".

road metal *n.* Crushed or broken stone, cinders, or similar material used in the construction and repair of roads and roadbeds.

road rage *n.* Rage on the road; specifically, the stress-induced rage of motorists against other motorists, cyclists, or pedestrians.

road·run·ner (rōd-runnər) *n.* A swift-running, crested bird, *Geococcyx californianus,* of southwestern North America, having streaked, brownish plumage and a long tail.

road sense *n.* The ability to use public roads and negotiate traffic safely.

road show *n.* A touring entertainment, especially one given by pop groups or similar artists.

road·side (rōd-sīd) *n.* The area bordering on a road.

road·stead (rōd-sted) *n. Nautical.* A sheltered, offshore anchorage area for ships. Also called "roads".

road·ster (rōd-stər) *n.* 1. An open car having no back seats. 2. A horse for riding on a road.

road test *n.* A test designed to assess the performance and roadworthiness of a vehicle by driving it on a road. **—road-test** *tr.v.*

road·way (rōd-way) *n.* A road, especially the part over which vehicles travel.

road·work (rōd-wurk) *n.* Outdoor long-distance running, especially as part of a sportsman's training.

road·works (rōd-wurks) *pl.n.* Construction or repair works on a road, often causing a delay for motorists.

road·worth·y (rōd-wurthi) *adj.* Fit to be driven on a public road. Said of a motor vehicle. **—road·worth·i·ness** *n.*

roam (rōm) *v.* **roamed, roaming, roams.** *—intr.* To move or travel without purpose or plan; rove; wander. *—tr.* To wander over or through. **—See Synonyms at wander.**

~n. The act of roaming. [Middle English *roment*†.] **—roam·er** *n.*

roan (rōn) *adj.* 1. Having a chestnut *(strawberry roan),* bay *(red roan),* or black *(blue roan)* coat thickly sprinkled with white or grey hairs. Said chiefly of horses. 2. Made or prepared from roan leather.

~n. 1. The characteristic colouring of a roan horse. 2. A roan horse or other animal. 3. A soft, flexible sheepskin leather, often treated to resemble morocco, and used in bookbinding. In this sense, also called "roan leather". [Old French *roan*†.]

Ro·a·noke Island (rō-ə-nōk, rō-nōk). Island off the coast of North Carolina, United States, and the site of the first English colonies in North America. They were founded at the instigation of Sir Walter Raleigh (1585, 1587), but by 1591 all the colonists had disappeared, perhaps killed by Indians or by disease.

roar (ror ‖ rōr) *v.* **roared, roaring, roars.** *—intr.* 1. To utter a loud, deep, prolonged sound, especially in distress, rage, or excitement. 2. To utter a loud, harsh, growling sound, like that characteristic of a lion. 3. To laugh loudly or excitedly. 4. To make or produce a harsh, loud noise or din: *the wind roaring in the trees.* 5. To move or operate with a loud noise: *roared through the town on motorbikes.* 6. To breathe with a rasping sound. Used of a horse. *—tr.* 1. To utter or express with a deep, loud, and prolonged sound. 2. To bring (oneself) into a specified state by roaring: *The crowd roared itself hoarse.*

~n. 1. A loud, deep sound or cry, as of a person in distress or rage. 2. The loud, deep cry characteristic of a lion. 3. A loud, prolonged noise, such as that produced by waves, motorbikes, or gunfire. 4. A loud burst of laughter. [Middle English *roren, raren,* Old English *rārian* (imitative).] **—roar·er** *n.*

roar·ing (ráwring ‖ rōring) *adj. Informal.* Very lively or successful; thriving: *a roaring trade.*

~adv. Informal. Extremely; very: *roaring drunk.*

Roaring Forties. The area of the southern oceans south of latitude 40°S, characterised by constant, strong northwest to west winds, gales, and damp, raw weather.

roast (rōst) *v.* **roasted, roasting, roasts.** *—tr.* 1. To cook (meat, for example), as: **a.** With dry heat, especially with fat in an oven. **b.** By direct exposure to dry heat, as over an open fire or in hot ashes. 2. To prepare (coffee beans, for example) for use by heating. 3. To dry, brown, or parch by exposing to heat. 4. To expose to great or excessive heat. 5. *Metallurgy.* To heat (ores) in a furnace in order to dehydrate, purify, or oxidise. 6. *Informal.* To criticise or ridicule harshly. *—intr.* 1. To cook meat or other food in an oven. 2. To undergo roasting. 3. *Informal.* To feel extremely hot.

~n. 1. Something roasted. 2. A cut of meat suitable or prepared for roasting. 3. The act or process of roasting.

~adj. Roasted: *roast chicken.* [Middle English *rosten,* from Old French *rostir,* probably from Old High German *rōsten,* from *rōst,* grate, gridiron, from Germanic *raust* (unattested).]

roast·er (rōstər) *n.* 1. One that roasts. 2. A special dish or apparatus for roasting. 3. Something fit for roasting, such as a chicken.

rob (rob) *v.* **robbed, robbing, robs.** *—tr.* 1. To take property from (a place, person, or persons) illegally, by using or threatening to use violence or force; commit robbery against: *robbed by muggers; robbed a bank.* 2. To deprive (a person) of something belonging, desired, or legally due by any unjust procedure: *rob a person of his reputation.* 3. To deprive of something important, essential, or desirable: *robbed the joke of its point.* *—intr.* To commit or engage in robbery. [Middle English *robben,* from Old French *rober,* from Germanic.] **—rob·ber** *n.*

Synonyms: *rob, steal, burgle, filch, pilfer, thieve, plunder, loot, ransack.*

rob·a·lo (róbbə-lō, róbə-) *n., pl.* **-los** or collectively **robalo.** Any of various chiefly tropical marine food and aquarium fishes of the family Centropomidae, such as the **snook** *(see).* [Spanish *róbalo, robálo,* probably modification of *lobaro* (unattested), from *lobo,* wolf, "wolflike fish", from Latin *lupus.*]

Robbe-Gril·let (rob-gree-yáy), **Alain** (1922–). French novelist. He is an exponent of the French new novel, on which he has written in *Vers un nouveau roman* (1964). His novels include *Jealousy* (1957), presented through the clinically detached prose of an observer who neither speaks nor appears in person. He has directed his own films, *L'Immortelle* (1963) and *Trans-Europe Express* (1967). 1994 saw *Les Derniers Jours de Corinthe.*

Rob·ben Island (rób-in, -ən). Small island in Table Bay, South Africa, 10 kilometres (6 miles) from Cape Town. A penal settlement, the island has housed many South African political prisoners, including Nelson Mandela.

robber baron *n.* A feudal lord who robbed travellers passing through his domain.

robber crab *n.* A large Indo-Pacific crab, *Birgo latus,* that feeds on coconuts broken open with its pincers. Also called "coconut crab".

robber fly *n.* Any of various predatory flies of the family Asilidae, characteristically having long, bristly legs.

rob·ber·y (róbbəri) *n., pl.* **-ies.** 1. The act of unlawfully taking the property of another by the use of force or intimidation. 2. An instance of this.

Robbia, della. See **della Robbia.**

Rob·bins (róbbinz), **Jerome** (1918–98). U.S. choreographer. Trained as a dancer, he staged his first ballet in 1944 and later won fame for creating the dance sequences in hit musicals such as *West Side Story* (1957: Oscar) and *Fiddler on the Roof* (1964).

robe (rōb) *n.* 1. A long, loose, flowing outer garment, especially: **a.** An official garment worn on formal occasions to show office or rank, as by a judge or high church official. **b.** *U.S.* A dressing gown or bathrobe. 2. *Plural.* Clothes in general; dress. 3. *U.S.* A blanket or covering made of fur, cloth, or other material: *a lap robe.*

~v. **robed, robing, robes.** *—tr.* To clothe or dress in or as if in a robe or robes. *—intr.* To put on a robe or robes. [Middle English, from Old French, from Vulgar Latin *rauba* (unattested), "clothes taken away as booty", robe, from Germanic; akin to ROB.]

Rob·ert I (róbbərt), known as Robert the Bruce (1274–1329). King of Scotland (1306–29). He seized the crown in 1306 and gradually extended his control over Scotland. In 1314 he won effective independence from England by his victory at Bannockburn, formally acknowledged by England at the treaty of Northampton (1328). He is buried in Dunfermline Abbey, Scotland.

Robert II¹ (1316–90). The first Stuart King of Scotland (1371–90). The son of Walter, the Steward of Scotland, by a daughter of Robert the Bruce, he several times acted as regent during the exile and captivity of David II. Known as the Steward, he succeeded David and initiated the Stuart dynasty.

Robert II², known as Robert Curthose (c.1054–1134). Duke of Normandy (1087–1106), the eldest son of William the Conqueror. He acquired Normandy on the Conqueror's death, but the English crown went to Robert's younger brother, William Rufus. He planned to contest the English crown with the new king, his youngest brother, Henry I, but was defeated by Henry at Tinchebrai (1106) in Normandy. He was held captive in England for the rest of his life.

Rob·erts (róbbərts), **Frederick Sleigh, 1st Earl** (1832–1914). British soldier, commander in chief of the British army during the second Boer War (1899–1902). He won the Victoria Cross during the Indian Mutiny (1857–8) and in the Boer War he led the victorious advance on Pretoria.

Roberts, Tom, born Thomas William Roberts (1856–1931). Australian painter, born in England. He studied in Europe (1881–85) and later brought impressionism to Australia.

Robe·son (rōb-sən), **Paul** (1898–1976). U.S. actor and singer. He won fame playing the title role in Eugene O'Neill's *Emperor Jones* (1925), further establishing his reputation in *Showboat* (1928) in which he sang "Ol' Man River", a song with which he is especially associated. A campaigner for civil rights, Robeson was attracted to Communism in the late 1940s.

Robes·pierre (rōbz-pyair; *French* rōbz-pyaíe), **Maximilien François Marie Isidore** (1758–94). French revolutionary leader. The chief architect of the Reign of Terror, Robespierre was famous for his austere and incorruptible character. He introduced laws permitting the confiscation of property and arrest of suspected traitors. A reaction to these measures led to his arrest and execution.

rob·in (róbbin) *n.* **1.** A small Eurasian songbird, *Erithacus rubecula,* having an orange breast and a brown back. **2.** A similar North American songbird, *Turdus migratorius.* Also called "American robin". **3.** Any of various birds resembling a robin. [Middle English, from Old French, from the name *Robin.*]

Robin Goodfellow. See **Puck.**

Rob·in Hood (róbbin hood). Legendary English outlaw. He is first mentioned in *Piers Plowman* (c. 1377), and ballads concerning his exploits became popular in the following centuries. Though he may have been an entirely mythical folk hero, various historical prototypes have been suggested, including a 12th-century Earl of Huntingdon and a disinherited follower of Simon de Montfort.

ro·bin·i·a (rə-bínni-ə, rō-, rō-) *n.* Any tree of the genus *Robinia;* especially, the **false acacia** (*see*). [New Latin, after Jean *Robin* (died 1629), French botanist.]

Rob·in·son (róbbin-sən), **Edward G,** born Emmanuel Goldenberg (1893–1973). U.S. film actor, born in Romania. He made his reputation in gangster films, such as *Little Caesar* (1930) and *Kid Galahad* (1937), and later played character parts, as in *Double Indemnity* (1944) and *The Cincinatti Kid* (1965).

Robinson, John (Arthur Thomas) (1919–83). British churchman. As Bishop Suffragan of Woolwich (1959–69) he published *Honest to God* (1963), a controversial appraisal of New Testament teaching in the context of the modern world.

Robinson, Mary Therese Winifred (1944–). President of Ireland (1990–97). A lawyer known for her work in the areas of human rights and civil liberties, she was a member of the Irish Senate 1969–89. Supported in her candidacy by the Labour Party and the Workers' Party, she became in 1990 the first woman to be elected Irish President, and in 1997 U.N. High Commissioner for Human Rights.

Robinson, W(illiam) Heath (1872–1944). British cartoonist and book illustrator. He is especially remembered for his humorous drawings of fantastic inventions collected in *Absurdities* (1934), among other volumes.

Robinson Cru·soe (krōosō). The hero of Daniel Defoe's novel *Robinson Crusoe* (1719), based on the castaway Alexander Selkirk, a shipwrecked sailor who lived for years on a small tropical island.

ro·bo·rant (rōbə-rənt, róbbə-) *adj.* Restoring vigour or strength. —*n.* A roborant drug; a tonic. [Latin *rōborāns* (stem *rōborant-*), present participle of *rōborāre,* to strengthen, from *rōbur,* strength.]

ro·bot (rō-bot, -bət) *n.* **1.** An externally manlike mechanical device capable of performing human tasks or behaving in a human manner. **2.** Any machine or device that works automatically or by remote control; especially, a machine in a factory that can be programmed to perform a variety of different tasks normally done by humans. Also called "automaton". **3.** A person who works mechanically without original thought. **4.** *South African.* A set of traffic lights. [Czech (in Karel Čapek's (1890–1938) play *R.U.R.* (*Rossum's Universal Robots),* 1920), from *robota,* compulsory labour, drudgery.] —**ro·bot·ism** *n.* —**ro·bot·is·tic** (-ísstik) *adj.*

ro·bot·ics (rō-bóttiks, rə-) *n.* The science of the designing, building, and application of robots. [ROBOT + -ICS.]

robot pilot *n.* An **automatic pilot** (*see*).

Rob Roy (rób róy), born Robert Macgregor (1671–1734). Scottish clan chief and cattle dealer. He was outlawed (1712) for failing to pay his debts and began a career of banditry which lasted until his arrest in 1722. He was pardoned in 1727. Sir Walter Scott's novel *Rob Roy* (1818) was based on his career.

Rob·son (rób-sən), **Dame Flora** (1902–84). British actress. She made her stage debut in 1921 and won acclaim for her roles in

classical drama; after 1931 she also appeared in many films.

ro·bust (rō-búst, rə- ‖ rō-bust) *adj.* **1.** Full of health and strength; vigorous; hardy. **2.** Powerfully built; hefty. **3.** Sturdy in construction. **4.** Requiring or suited to physical strength or endurance: *robust work.* **5.** Boisterous; rough. **6.** Marked by richness and fullness; full-bodied: *a robust wine.* **7.** Down-to-earth; straightforward: *a robust intellect.* —Synonyms at **healthy.** [Latin *rōbustus,* oaken, from *rōbur, rōbus,* oak, strength.] —**ro·bust·ly** *adv.* —**ro·bust·ness** *n.*

roc (rok) *n.* A legendary bird of prey of enormous size and strength. [From Spanish *rocho,* from Arabic *rukhkh,* from Persian *rukh†.*]

ro·caille (ro-kí, rō-) *n.* The light, shell-like, curving decoration used in rococo architecture. [French, "rockwork", from Old French *roche,* ROCK.]

roc·am·bole (róckəm-bōl) *n.* **1.** A European plant, *Allium scorodoprasum,* having a garlic-like bulb. **2.** The bulb of this plant, used as a seasoning. [French, from German *Rockenbolle,* "distaff bulb" : *Rocken,* distaff, from Old High German *rocko* + *Bolle,* bulb, from Old High German *bolla,* ball.]

Roch·dale (róch-dayl). Industrial town near Manchester, northwest England. The birthplace of the cooperative movement (1844), its industries include textiles, engineering, and asbestos.

Roche (rosh), **Mazo de la** (1885–1961). Canadian novelist. She wrote 15 novels about the Whiteoak family of Jalna, the first of which was *Jalna* (1927).

Rochelle, La. See **La Rochelle.**

Ro·chelle powder (ro-shél) *n.* A cathartic, **Seidlitz powder** (*see*).

Rochelle salt *n.* A colourless efflorescent crystalline compound, $KNaC_4H_4O_6\cdot4H_2O$, used in making mirrors, in electronics, and as a laxative. [After LA ROCHELLE.]

roche mou·ton·née (rōsh mōo-tə-náy, rósh, -to-) *n., pl.* **roches moutonnées** (*pronounced as singular, or* -z). A glacially moulded mass of rock, worn smooth on the upstream side by abrasion, the downstream side being rough as a result of the plucking action of the ice. Also called "sheepback". [French, "fleecy rock".]

Roch·es·ter¹ (róchistar). Port in southeast England. Situated on the estuary of the river Medway just west of Chatham, it was held by the Romans, and has a Norman castle and a cathedral.

Rochester². Port of New York State, United States, situated on the river Genesee on the south side of Lake Ontario.

Rochester, John Wilmot, 2nd Earl of (1647–80). British poet. A wit and libertine at the court of Charles II, he is especially remembered for his satirical writings, which include *A Satire Against Mankind* (1675), and for his amorous poems.

roch·et (róchit) *n.* A ceremonial vestment made of linen or lawn, worn by bishops and other church dignitaries. [Middle English, from Old French, from Frankish *rok* (unattested), coat.]

rock¹ (rok) *n.* **1.** A relatively hard naturally formed mass of mineral or petrified matter; stone. **2. a.** A relatively large body of such material, as a cliff or peak. **b.** *Chiefly U.S.* A relatively small piece or fragment of such material; a stone. **3.** *Geology.* Any naturally formed mineral mass or aggregate that constitutes a significant part of the earth's crust. **4.** A person or thing suggestive of a mass of stone in stability, solidity, or strength: *St. Peter was the rock upon which the church was built.* **5.** *Usually plural. U.S. Slang.* Money. **6.** *Slang.* A large gem, especially a diamond. **7.** *Chiefly British.* A kind of hard sweet, usually peppermint-flavoured, and produced as a brightly coloured stick. —**on the rocks.** **1.** *Informal.* In a state of destruction or ruin: *Their marriage is on the rocks.* **2.** Without money; bankrupt. **3.** Served over ice cubes without water or a mixer. —**The Rock.** *Informal.* The Rock of **Gibraltar** (*see*). [Middle English *rokke,* from Old Northern French *roque,* variant of Old French *roche,* from Medieval Latin *rocca†.*]

rock² *v.* **rocked, rocking, rocks.** —*intr.* **1.** To move back and forth or from side to side, especially gently or rhythmically: *The boat rocked on the waves.* **2.** To sway violently, as from a blow or shock; shake. **3.** To be washed and panned in a cradle or rocker. Used of ores. **4.** To dance to rock'n'roll music. —*tr.* **1.** To sway back and forth or from side to side; especially, to soothe or lull to sleep: *rocked the baby in his arms.* **2.** To cause to shake or sway violently. **3.** To disturb or distress deeply; shock: *The scandal rocked the town.* **4.** To wash or pan (ore) in a cradle or rocker. **5.** In mezzotint engraving, to roughen (a copper plate) with various rockers and roulettes. —See Synonyms at **swing.** —*n.* **1.** The act of rocking. **2.** A rocking motion. **3. Rock 'n' roll** (*see*). **4. Rock music** (*see*). [Middle English *rokken,* Old English *roccian,* perhaps from Germanic *rukk-* (unattested).] —**rock·ing·ly** *adv.*

rock·a·bil·ly (rócka-billi) *n.* A form of rock music combining elements of country music and rhythm and blues. [*Rock* music + hill*billy.*]

Rock·all (rók-awl). Uninhabited islet, situated in the Atlantic Ocean 350 kilometres (220 miles) off the Hebrides.

rock-and-roll. Variant of **rock 'n' roll.**

rock bass *n.* **1.** A freshwater food fish, *Amblopites rupestris,* of eastern and central North America. **2.** Any of various similar or related fishes.

rock bottom *n.* The lowest level; the absolute bottom: *Prices have reached rock bottom.* —**rock-bot·tom** (rók-bóttəm) *adj.*

rock-bound (rók-bownd) *adj.* Hemmed in by or bordered with rocks: *a rock-bound lake.*

rock cake *n.* A small, sweet, relatively hard cake containing dried fruit and usually having a rough surface. Also called "rock bun".

rock crystal n. Transparent colourless quartz.

rock dove n. A bird, *Columba livia,* native to Europe but widely distributed elsewhere, having grey plumage with iridescent neck markings. It is the ancestor of the common domestic pigeon. Also called "rock pigeon".

Rock·e·fel·ler (rócke-fellər), **John D(avison)** (1839–1937). U.S. business magnate. He made his wealth through founding the Standard Oil Company (1870), the first major oil monopoly in the United States. From 1890 he established a number of institutions to promote medical research and education. His philanthropy was continued by his son, John D. Rockefeller Jr. (1874–1960).

Rockefeller, Nelson A(ldrich) (1908–79). U.S. Republican politician, the grandson of John D. Rockefeller. He was governor of New York (1958–73), and vice-president (1974–77).

rock·er (róckər) n. **1.** Any of various mechanical devices or parts that operate with a rocking motion. **2.** A rocking chair. **3.** A rocking horse. **4.** Either of the two curved pieces upon which a cradle, rocking chair, or similar device rocks. **5.** *Mining.* A cradle for washing or panning ores. **6.** A small steel plate with a curved, toothed edge, used to roughen a copper plate for a mezzotint. **7.** An ice skate with a curved blade. **8.** *Sometimes capital* **R.** In Britain, especially in the 1960s, a youth belonging to a gang of motorcyclists, typically having slicked-back hair and wearing a leather jacket, and often in conflict with **mods** *(see).* **—off (one's) rocker.** *Slang.* Out of (one's) mind; crazy.

rocker arm n. A pivoted lever, as in an internal-combustion engine, used to transfer cam or pushrod motion to a valve stem.

rock·er·y (róckəri) n., pl. **-ies.** A small-scale rock garden, usually forming part of a larger garden.

rock·et¹ (róckit) n. **1. a.** Any device propelled by ejection of matter, especially by the high-velocity ejection of the gaseous combustion products produced by internal ignition of solid or liquid fuels, used for launching a spacecraft or as a signal, for example. **b.** A rocket engine. **2. a.** A weapon carrying an explosive or other warhead, and using rocket power. **b.** An incendiary weapon with a rounded hollow warhead filled with explosives and formerly fired from a ship. **3.** A firework for aerial display that rises vertically then explodes and sprays a shower of coloured stars. Also called "skyrocket". **4.** *British Slang.* A strong reproof or reprimand.
~v. **rocketed, -eting, -ets.** —*intr.* **1.** To move or fly directly and swiftly, as a rocket does. **2.** To rise rapidly or unexpectedly: *prices rocketed.* —*tr.* **1.** To assault with rockets. **2.** To carry by means of a rocket. [French *roquette,* from Italian *rocchetto,* diminutive of *rocca,* ROCK (referring to cylindrical shape of firework).]

rocket² n. **1.** A plant, *Eruca sativa,* native to Eurasia, having yellowish-white flowers and leaves that are sometimes used in salads. **2.** Any of several related plants, especially one of the genera *Sisymbrium,* such as *S. irio* (London rocket), *Cakile* (sea rocket), or *Diplotaxis* (wall rocket). [French *roquette,* from Italian *ruchetta,* diminutive of *ruca,* from Latin *ērūca,* "caterpillar," plant with downy stems, perhaps from *er,* hedgehog.]

rock·et·eer (rócki-téer) n. A person who designs, launches, studies, or pilots rockets.

rocket engine n. An engine that propels, especially one that propels spacecraft or aircraft, by means of rockets.

rocket motor n. A rocket engine, especially one using solid fuel.

rock·et·ry (róckitri) n. The science and technology of rocket design, construction, and flight.

rock·et·sonde (róckit-sond) n. Recording equipment adapted for use on a rocket, and used for observation in the upper atmosphere.

rock·fish (rók-fish) n., pl. **-fishes** or collectively **rockfish. 1.** Any of various fishes living among rocks. **2.** Any of various fishes, chiefly of the genus *Sebastodes,* of Pacific waters.

rock flour n. Pulverised rock produced, for example, along the faces of a moving fault or during movement of a glacier.

rock garden n. A rocky area in which plants especially adapted to such terrain are cultivated.

rock hopper n. A New Zealand penguin, *Eudyptes crestatus,* with a yellow head crest.

Rock·ies (róckiz). The **Rocky Mountains** *(see).*

rock·ing chair (rócking) n. A chair mounted on rockers or springs, so that the sitter may rock on it.

rocking horse n. A toy horse large enough for a child to ride, mounted upon rockers or springs.

rock·ling (róckling) n., pl. **-lings** or collectively **rockling.** Any of various small marine fishes of the family Gadidae, of North Atlantic coastal waters, having barbels around the mouth. [ROCK (stone) + LING (fish).]

rock lobster n. The **spiny lobster** *(see).*

rock music n. A form of western popular music that became established in the late 1950s, growing out of various types of U.S. folk music, such as blues and gospel, and is characterised by strong repetitive rhythms. Also called "rock".

rock'n'roll, rock-and-roll (rók-ən-ról) n. **1.** Popular music combining elements of rhythm and blues with country and western music, and having a heavily accented beat. Also called "rock". **2.** A form of jive which developed from jitterbug in response to rock music, originating in the 1950s among U.S. blacks. [In 1950s black American slang, *rock and roll* refers to sexual intercourse.] **—rock'n'roll** *adj. & intr.v.* **—rock'n'rol·ler** n.

rock oil n. *Chiefly British.* **Petroleum** *(see).*

rock·oon (ro-kōōn) n. A rocket carrying scientific instruments to study the upper atmosphere that is carried to a certain height by balloon, then fired. [*Rocket* + ball*oon.*]

rock pigeon n. The **rock dove** *(see).*

rock plant n. Any plant adapted for growing among rocks or in rocky ground.

rock python n. The **amethystine python** *(see).*

rock-ribbed (rók-ríbd) adj. **1.** Having rocks or rock outcroppings. **2.** Stern and unyielding.

rock-rose (rók-róz) n. Any of various plants or shrubs of the genus *Helianthemum* and related genera, having roselike yellow, white, or reddish flowers, and often cultivated as garden ornamentals.

rock salmon n. *British.* Any of various coarse fish, such as the dogfish, that are used as food.

rock salt n. A mineral form of common salt (sodium chloride). Also called "halite".

rock samphire n. A plant, **samphire** *(see).*

rock-shaft (rók-shaaft ‖ -shaft) n. A shaft that oscillates or rocks upon its bearings, but does not revolve.

rock-work (rók-wurk) n. Ornamental stonework, as in a rock garden or rockery.

rock·y¹ (rócki) adj. **-ier, -iest. 1.** Consisting of, containing, or abounding in rock or rocks. **2.** Resembling or suggesting rock; firm or hard; tough; unyielding. **3.** Marked by obstructions or difficulties: *the rocky road to success.* **—rock·i·ness** n.

rock·y² adj. **-ier, -iest. 1.** Unsteady; unstable; shaky. **2.** *Informal.* Weak, dizzy, or nauseous. **—rock·i·ness** n.

Rocky Mountains. Also **Rockies.** Mountain system of west North America, forming the Continental Divide. It extends 4 800 kilometres (3,000 miles) from the north Mexican border to the Yukon but is sometimes taken to include its continuation through the Yukon to Alaska. It rises to 4 399 metres (14,431 feet) at Mount Elbert and in its extended form to 6 050 metres (19,850 feet) at Mount Logan.

ro·co·co (rə-kṓkō, rō- ‖ *U.S. also* rṓkə-kṓ) n. **1.** A style of art, developed from the baroque, that originated in France (about 1720) and soon spread throughout Europe; especially, this style used in architecture and decoration, characterised by elaborate, profuse designs of scrolls and curves intended to produce a delicate effect. **2.** *Music.* The style immediately following the baroque in Europe (about 1726 to 1775).
~*adj.* **1.** Of or in rococo style. **2.** Profuse or elaborate; overdone; florid: *rococo writing.* [French, fanciful alteration of ROCAILLE.]

rod (rod) n. **1.** A straight, thin piece or bar of metal, wood, or other material: *a curtain rod.* **2.** A shoot or stem cut from, or growing as part of, a woody plant. **3.** A stick, or a bundle of sticks, used for beating, as for punishment. **4.** A **fishing rod** *(see).* **5.** A wand or staff symbolising power or authority. **6.** Power or dominion, especially of a tyrannical nature: *"under the rod of a cruel slavery."* (John Henry Newman). **7.** A metal bar in a machine: *a piston rod.* **8.** A measuring stick. **9.** See **levelling rod. 10.** A **lightning conductor** *(see).* **11.** A **divining rod** *(see).* **12.** *Abbr.* **rd, r. a.** A linear measure equal to 5.5 yards, 16.5 feet, or 5.03 metres. Also called "pole", "perch". **b.** A square rod, equal to 30.25 square yards. **13.** *Chiefly U.S. Vulgar.* A penis. **14.** *Anatomy.* Any of various rod-shaped cells in the retina that contain the pigment rhodopsin and are sensitive to dim light. Compare **cone. 15.** Any elongated microorganism; especially, a bacterium. **16.** *U.S. Slang.* A pistol or revolver. [Middle English *rodd,* Old English *rodd.*]

rode. Past tense of **ride.**

ro·dent (rṓd'nt) n. Any of various mammals of the order Rodentia, such as a mouse, rat, squirrel, or beaver, characterised by large, continuously growing incisors adapted for gnawing or nibbling.
~*adj.* **1.** Gnawing. **2.** Of or pertaining to rodents. [New Latin *Rodentia,* from Latin *rōdēns* (stem *rōdent-*), present participle of *rōdere,* to gnaw.]

ro·dent·i·cide (rō-dénti-sīd) n. An agent used to kill rodent pests. [RODENT + -CIDE.]

rodent ulcer n. A malignant tumour of the face, especially the lips and nostrils, that destroys the underlying muscle and bone.

ro·de·o (rō-dáy-ō, rə-; *also* rṓdi-ō) n., pl. **-os.** In North America: **1.** A public entertainment including riding broncos, lassoing, and similar displays. **2.** A cattle roundup. **3.** An enclosure for keeping cattle that have been rounded up. [Spanish, from *rodear,* to surround, from Latin *rotāre,* to ROTATE.]

Rodg·ers (rójərz), **Richard (Charles)** (1902–79). U.S. composer. He collaborated with the librettist Lorenz Hart (1895–1943) on *Pal Joey* (1940) and other musicals, but is especially remembered for those he produced with Oscar Hammerstein II, including *Oklahoma!* (1943), *South Pacific* (1949), *The King and I* (1951), and *The Sound of Music* (1959).

Ro·din (rṓ-daN, *French* rō-dáN), **(François) Auguste (René)** (1840–1917). French sculptor. He first exhibited at the Paris Salon in 1877, and later won an immense reputation for the originality of his compositions, which recall Michelangelo in their sense of tragic grandeur. His controversial public commissions included *The Burghers of Calais* (1894) and an effigy of Balzac in his dressing gown. His most ambitious work was the *Gates of Hell* on which he worked from the 1880s until his death.

rod·o·mon·tade (róddə-mon-táyd, -moN-, -táad) n. **1.** *Often plural.* Pretentious boasting or bragging; bluster. **2.** A pretentious boast.
~*adj.* Pretentiously boastful or bragging.
~*intr.v.* **rodomontaded, -tading, -tades.** To boast or brag; bluster; rant. [French, from obsolete Italian *rodomontada,* from *rodomonte,* braggart, after *Rodomonte,* a boastful Moorish king in the epics

Orlando Innamorato (1487) and *Orlando Furioso* (1516).]

Rod·ri·go (rod-réegō), **Joaquin** (1902–). Spanish composer. Blind from the age of three, he has written many works, especially for guitar, including the *Concierto de Aranjuez* (1940), often blending the classsical tradition with picturesque folk elements.

roe¹ (rō) *n.* **1.** The egg-laden ovary of a fish. Also called "hard roe". **2.** The egg mass of certain crustaceans, such as the lobster. **3. Soft roe** *(see).* [Middle English *roof, roughe, row,* from Middle Low German or Middle Dutch *roge.*]

roe² *n., pl.* **roes** or collectively **roe.** A **roe deer** *(see).*

roe·buck (rō-buk) *n.* A male roe deer.

roe deer *n.* A small Eurasian deer, *Capreolus capreolus,* having a brownish coat and short, branched antlers in the male. Also called "roe." [*Roe,* Middle English *ro, ra(a),* Old English *rā, rāha,* from Germanic.]

roent·gen, rönt·gen (rónt-gən, rúnt-, rúrnt-, rőnt-, jən || rént-) *n.* *Symbol* **R** A unit of radiation dosage, for X-rays or gamma rays, the dose that will produce ions of one sign having a total charge of 0.258 x 10^{-3} coulomb when totally absorbed in one kilogram of dry air under standard conditions. See **rad.** [After Wilhelm Konrad ROENTGEN.]

Roent·gen or **Rönt·gen** (*German* rőntgən), **Wilhelm Konrad** (1845–1923). German physicist. He discovered X-rays and developed X-ray photography, revolutionising medical diagnosis, and was awarded the first Nobel prize for physics (1901).

roentgen equivalent man *n. Abbr.* **REM** A unit of radiation dose that would produce the same effect in a person as one roentgen of X-rays or gamma rays.

roent·gen·ise, roent·gen·ize (rónt-gə-nīz, rúnt-, rúrnt-, rőnt-, -jə- || rént-) *tr.v.* **-ised, -ising, -ises.** To subject to the action of X-rays. **—roent·gen·i·sa·tion** (-nī-záysh'n || *U.S.* -ni-) *n.*

Roentgen ray *n.* An **X-ray** *(see).*

ro·ga·tion (rō-gáysh'n, rə-) *n.* **1.** *Usually plural.* A solemn prayer or supplication, especially as chanted during the rites of the Rogation Days. **2.** A law proposed by a tribune or consul to the people of ancient Rome for acceptance or rejection. [Middle English *rogacioun,* from Latin *rogātiō* (stem *rogātiōn-*), from *rogāre,* to ask, supplicate.] **—ro·ga·tion·al** *adj.*

Rogation Days *pl.n. Ecclesiastical.* The three days preceding Ascension Day, designated as days of special prayer.

rog·a·to·ry (róggə-təri, -tri, rō-gáytəri, rə-) *adj. Law.* **1.** Requesting information, especially with proper authorisation: *rogatory letters.* **2.** Empowered to carry out investigations: *a rogatory commission.* [French *rogatoire,* from Medieval Latin *rogātōrius,* from Latin *rogāre,* to ask, supplicate.]

rog·er¹ (rójər) *interj. Often capital* **R. 1.** Used in telecommunications to indicate that a message has been received and understood. **2.** *Slang.* Used to express agreement or understanding.
~n. Often capital **R.** The **Jolly Roger** *(see).* [From the name *Roger,* in signalling code representing *R* and (message) *received.*]

roger² *v.* **-ered, -ering, -ers.** *British Vulgar.* *—tr.* To have sexual intercourse with. *—intr.* To have sexual intercourse. [From obsolete *roger,* penis, humorous use of *Roger,* man's name.]

Rog·ers (rójerz), **Ginger,** born Virginia McMath (1911–95). U.S. actress and entertainer. She is best remembered for her partnership with Fred Astaire in a number of 1930s film musicals, including *Top Hat* (1935), *Follow the Fleet* (1936), and *Shall We Dance* (1937).

Rogers, Richard (George), Baron (1933–). British architect. His work includes the Centre Georges Pompidou in Paris (1977), the Lloyd's Building in the City of London (1986), and the European Court of Human Rights, Strasbourg (1995).

Rog·et (rózhay, rő-zhay), **Peter Mark** (1779–1869). British philologist and polymath. A physician and secretary of the Royal Society, he was the author of the *Thesaurus of English Words and Phrases* (1852), which has appeared in many subsequent editions.

ro·gon (rōgon) *n.* Tomato. Used in Indian cuisine. [Indic.]

rogue (rōg) *n.* **1.** An unprincipled and dishonest person; a scoundrel. **2.** A person who is playfully mischievous; a rascal or scamp. Used humorously. **3.** *Archaic.* A wandering beggar; a vagrant or vagabond. **4.** A vicious and solitary animal; especially, an elephant separated from its herd. **5.** An organism, especially a cultivated plant, that shows an undesirable variation from a standard.
~v. **rogued, roguing, rogues.** *—tr.* **1.** To defraud. **2. a.** To remove (diseased or abnormal specimens) from a group, as of plants of the same variety. **b.** To remove such specimens from (a field, for example). *—intr.* To remove undesired plant specimens.
~adj. **1.** Vicious and solitary. Said of an animal. **2.** Taking an independent and often rebellious stance; maverick: *a rogue trade union.* **3.** Defective. Said expecially of a new motor vehicle. [16th century (cant) : origin obscure.]

ro·guer·y (rōgəri) *n., pl.* **-ies. 1.** Behaviour characteristic of a rogue; trickery. **2.** An unprincipled or dishonest act. **3.** A mischievous act.

rogues' gallery *n.* **1.** A collection of photographs of criminals maintained in police files and used for making identifications. **2.** Broadly, any collection of people of some particular, usually disreputable, type, such as criminals.

ro·guish (rōgish) *adj.* **1.** Dishonest or unprincipled. **2.** Playfully mischievous. **—ro·guish·ly** *adv.* **—ro·guish·ness** *n.*

Röhm (röm), **Ernst** (1887–1934). German soldier and politician. He took part in the Munich putsch (1923) and in 1930 was appointed chief of staff of the *Sturmabteilung,* or Brownshirts, a uniformed branch of the Nazi party. Under Röhm the S.A. became a paramilitary force which threatened to rival the authority of the regular army. In 1934, Hitler had Röhm and other leaders executed.

roil (royl) *v.* **roiled, roiling, roils.** *—tr.* **1.** To make (a liquid) muddy or cloudy by stirring up sediment. **2.** To displease or disturb; irritate; vex. *—intr.* To be in a state of turbulence or agitation. [Perhaps from Old French *ruiler,* to mix mortar, from Late Latin *regulāre,* to REGULATE.]

roil·y (róyli) *adj.* **-ier, -iest.** *U.S.* **1.** Muddy; cloudy. **2.** Agitated.

roist·er (róystər) *intr.v.* **-ered, -ering, -ers. 1.** To engage in boisterous merrymaking; revel noisily. **2.** To behave in a blustering manner; swagger. [Probably from Old French *rustre,* churl, boor, alteration of *ruste,* rude, rough, churlish, from Latin *rūsticus,* RUSTIC.] **—roist·er·er** *n.* **—roist·er·ous** *adj.* **—roist·er·ous·ly** *adv.*

Ro·ki·tan·sky (rócki-tán-ski), **Karl, Freiherr von** (1804–78). Austrian pathologist, a pioneer of pathological anatomy. He helped to establish the study of disease autopsy as a medical science.

Ro·land (rōlənd, ro-lóN). A legendary hero, nephew of Charlemagne killed in battle at Roncesvalles (A.D. 778).

role, rôle (rōl) *n.* **1.** A character or part to be played by an actor in a dramatic production. **2.** The behaviour expected of or associated with an individual or group in society, as determined by social position, sex, or other factors. **3.** A function or position: *your role as a journalist.* [French *rôle,* from Old French *rol(l)e,* roll (on which a part is written), from Medieval Latin *ro(tu)lus, ro(tu)la,* roll of parchment, from Latin *rotulus,* small wheel. See **roll.**]

Usage: The use of the circumflex accent is still common in formal English, but the unaccented form is more common nowadays, and is particularly widespread in American English.

role-play·ing (rōl-play-ing) *n.* **1.** The usually subconscious adoption of behaviour or attitudes felt to be characteristic of a given position in society. **2.** The taking on of another's position and psychological perspective, usually in order to evaluate responses to likely situations or problems, especially as a training method for social workers and others or as a technique in psychotherapy. **—role-play** *n.*

role reversal *n.* The adoption of a social role opposite to that normally taken by the subject.

rolf¹ (rolf) *intr.v.* **rolfed, rolfing, rolfs.** *Chiefly U.S. Slang.* To vomit.

rolf² (rolf, rōf) *tr.v.* **rolfed, rolfing, rolfs.** To administer rolfing to. **—rolf·er** *n.*

Rolfe (rōf, *also* rolf), **Frederick William,** also known by his pen name of Baron Corvo (1860–1913). British novelist. A convert to Roman Catholicism he was an unsuccessful candidate for the priesthood and vented his frustration in his most famous work *Hadrian the Seventh* (1904), the story of a convert who becomes Pope.

rolf·ing (rólf-ing, rōf-) *n.* Deep massage designed to relieve muscular and emotional tension and to reorientate the body to the force of gravity. [After Ida *Rolf* (1897–1979), U.S. physiotherapist.]

roll (rōl) *v.* **rolled, rolling, rolls.** *—intr.* **1.** To move forward along a surface by revolving on an axis or by repeatedly turning over. **2.** To travel or be moved on wheels or rollers. **3.** To travel or be carried in a vehicle: *rolled past the cornfields in the car.* **4. a.** To move or flow with an undulating rhythm: *The waves rolled towards the shore.* **b.** To be carried on a stream. **5. a.** To operate: *The presses began to roll.* **b.** *Informal.* To get underway; proceed: *The political campaign began to roll.* **6.** To go by; elapse. Used with *on, away,* or *by*: *The hours rolled on.* **7.** To recur periodically; progress as in cycles. Sometimes used with *round* or *around*: *Summer has rolled round again.* **8.** To move in a periodic revolution, as does a planet in its orbit. **9.** To turn and twist from side to side: *The puppy rolled in the mud.* **10.** To rotate: *His eyes rolled with fright.* **11.** To turn round or revolve on or as on an axis. **12.** To extend or appear to extend in gentle rises and falls: *rolling hills.* **13.** To move or rock from side to side. Used of a ship. Compare **pitch. 14.** To walk with a swaying, unsteady motion. **15.** To form the shape of a ball or cylinder. Often used with *up*: *The caterpillar rolled up.* **16.** To become flattened by or as if by pressure applied by a roller. **17.** To make a deep, prolonged, surging sound. Said especially of thunder. **18.** To make a sustained, trilling sound, as do certain birds. **19.** *U.S.* To wander; travel round: *rolling from town to town.* *—tr.* **1.** To cause to move forward along a surface by revolving on an axis, or by repeatedly turning over. **2.** To move or push along on or as if on wheels or rollers: *roll the plane out of the hangar.* **3.** To impel or send onwards in a steady, undulating motion: *The sea rolls its waves onto the sand.* **4.** To impart a swaying, rocking motion to: *Heavy seas rolled the ship.* **5.** To cause to turn round or rotate: *roll one's eyes.* **6.** To pronounce or utter with a trill: *You must roll your "r's" when speaking Spanish.* **7.** To utter or emit in full, sonorous tones. **8.** To beat (a drum) with a continuous series of short blows. **9. a.** To wrap (something) round and round upon itself or around something else. Often used with *up*: *roll up a scroll.* **b.** To form (oneself) into a ball, as a hedgehog does. **10. a.** To envelop or enfold in a covering: *roll laundry in a sheet.* **b.** To shape into a ball or cylinder, as by rubbing between the hands or turning over and over: *rolled a cigarette; rolled snow into a ball.* **11.** To spread, compress, or flatten by applying pressure with a roller: *roll out dough.* **12.** *Printing.* To apply ink to (type) with a roller or rollers. **13.** To cause (a film camera, for example) to operate. **14.** *U.S.* To throw (dice) in craps or other games. **15.** *U.S. Slang.* To rob (a drunken, sleeping, or otherwise helpless person). —See Synonyms at **turn. —roll about.** *Informal.* To be overcome with laughter. **—roll in. 1.** To arrive in large numbers; pour in. **2.** *Informal.* To arrive at one's destination: *rolled in late again.* **3.** *Informal.* To abound in; be plentifully supplied with: *rolling in money.* **—roll (one's) own.** *Slang.* To make one's own cigarettes.

~*n.* **1.** The act or an instance of rolling. **2. a.** Anything rolled up in the form of a cylinder: *a roll of carpet.* **b.** A length of leather or other material that may be wound up, with pockets for storing toiletries, tools, or other useful objects. **3.** A quantity of something, such as cloth or wallpaper, rolled into a cylinder, often considered as a unit of measure. **4.** A piece of parchment or paper bearing an inscription that may be or is rolled up; a scroll. **5.** A register or catalogue. **6.** A list of names of persons belonging to a given group: *call the roll.* **7.** A mass of something in cylindrical or rounded form: *a roll of tobacco.* **8. a.** A small rounded portion of bread, that may be cut in half, buttered, and filled: *a cheese roll.* **b.** A cake or pudding made by rolling up dough on which a filling has been spread: *a jam roll.* **c.** Any food that is prepared by rolling up, especially by wrapping pastry round a filling: *a sausage roll.* **9.** A rolling, swaying, or rocking motion or gait. **10.** A gentle swell or undulation of a surface: *the roll of the plains.* **11.** A deep reverberation or rumble. **12.** A rapid succession of short sounds: *the roll of a drum.* **13.** A trill: *the roll of her "r's."* **14.** A resonant, rhythmical flow of words. **15.** A roller; especially, a cylinder on which to roll something up or with which to flatten something. **16.** *Architecture.* A volute on a Corinthian or Ionic capital. **17.** A gymnastic movement in which the body performs a complete turn on itself, normally head over heels. **18.** A manoeuvre in which an aeroplane makes a single, complete rotation about its longitudinal axis without changing direction or losing altitude. **19.** *U.S. Slang.* Money; especially, a wad of paper money. **—strike off the rolls.** To **strike off** (sense 1). [Middle English *rol(l)en,* from Old French *rol(l)er,* from Vulgar Latin *rotulāre* (unattested), from Latin *rotulus, rotula,* small wheel, from *rota,* wheel.]

Rol·land (ro-lóN), **Romain** (1866–1944). French novelist, biographer, dramatist, and man of letters. His varied works include *Jean Christophe* (1904–12), a ten-volume novel about a German musical genius. His essentially pacifist philosophy was much influenced by Tolstoy and Gandhi. He was awarded the Nobel prize for literature in 1915.

roll bar, roll-bar (ról-baar) *n.* A strong steel frame reinforcing the roof of a car for protection in case the car should roll over, found especially in cars used for race events.

roll call *n.* **1.** The reading aloud of a list of names of people, as in a classroom or barracks, to determine who is absent. **2.** The time fixed for such a reading.

roll-call vote (ról-kawl) *n. U.S.* **1.** A procedure of voting in a legislative assembly or other body, in which each member votes when his name is called from the roll. **2.** An instance of such a voting procedure.

rolled gold (róld) *n.* Metal with a thin decorative layer of gold, used especially in jewellery, pens, and the like. Also *U.S.* "filled gold".

rolled oats *n. Used with a singular or plural verb.* **1.** Flakes produced by simultaneously heating and flattening hulled oat grains between rollers. **2.** A breakfast cereal made by simmering such flakes in water or milk.

rolled-steel joist (róld-stéel) *n.* An **RSJ** (see).

roll·er (ról-ər) *n.* **1.** One that rolls. **2.** Any of various cylindrical devices, specifically: **a.** A small, spokeless wheel, such as that of a roller skate or caster. **b.** An elongated cylinder upon which something is wound, such as a window blind or roll of foil. **c.** A heavy cylinder used to perform levelling or crushing operations. **d.** *Printing.* A cylinder, usually of hard rubber, used to ink the type before the paper is impressed. **e.** A cylinder of wire mesh, foam rubber, or other material around which a strand of hair is wound to produce a soft curl or wave. **f.** A device for spreading paint, consisting of a revolving cylinder of foam rubber or fibre fitted to a bracket and handle. **g.** A small steel cylinder in a roller bearing. **h.** Any of a set of revolving cylinders along which heavy objects may be rolled. **3.** A roller bandage. **4.** A heavy, swelling wave that breaks on the coast. **5.** Any of various birds of the family Coraciidae, mostly of warm regions of the Old World, having bright-blue wings, stocky bodies, and hooked bills, and noted for their aggressiveness. **6.** A tumbler pigeon of a breed that somersaults during flight. **7.** *Australian.* A wool-shed hand who trims and rolls fleeces after shearing. **8.** A **steamroller** (see).

roller bandage *n.* A long strip of bandage in the form of a roll.

roller bearing *n.* A bearing using rollers to reduce friction between machine parts.

Roll·er·blades (ról-ər-blaydz) *pl., n.* Trademark for roller skates with the wheels of each skate set in one straight line so as to resemble the blade of an ice skate.

roller coaster *n.* **1.** A steep, sharply banked, elevated railway with small open passenger cars, operated as a fairground attraction. Also called "big dipper", "switchback". **2.** Something like a roller coaster in having lots of ups and downs or highs and lows. Also used adjectivally: *a roller-coaster love affair.*

roller derby *n.* A relay race on roller skates; especially, a type of race run mainly in the United States on an oval track with two teams of skaters often involving aggressive tactics.

roller disco *n.* **1.** Dancing on roller skates to disco music. **2.** A discotheque designed for this type of dancing.

roller skate *n.* A skate having four small wheels instead of a runner, for skating on pavements and hard, smooth surfaces.

roll·er·skate (ról-ər-skayt) *intr.v.* **-skated, -skating, -skates.** To skate on roller skates. **—roller skater** *n.*

roller towel *n.* A long towel with its ends sewn together that is hung from a roller.

roll film *n.* Photographic film rolled on a spool.

rol·lick (róllik) *intr.v.* **-licked, -licking, -licks.** To behave or move in a carefree, frolicsome manner; romp. ~*n.* A carefree escapade; a lark. [Probably a blend of ROMP or ROLL and FROLIC.] **—rol·lick·some, rol·lick·y** *adj.*

rol·lick·ing (rólliking) *adj.* Carefree and high-spirited; boisterous. **—rol·lick·ing·ly** *adv.*

roll·ie (ról-i) *n. British Slang.* A **roll-up** (see).

roll·ing (ról-ing) *adj.* Progressive; developing or increasing with time: *rolling devolution; a 24-hour rolling news service.*

rolling hitch *n. Nautical.* A hitch for tying the end of one rope to a spar or the middle of another rope. The knot jams when tension is applied.

rolling mill *n.* **1.** A factory in which metal is rolled into sheets, bars, or other forms. **2.** A machine used for rolling metal.

rolling pin *n.* A smooth cylinder usually of wood and with a handle at each end, used for rolling out pastry or dough.

rolling stock *n.* The locomotives, carriages, wagons, and other wheeled vehicles used on a railway.

rolling stone *n.* A wanderer or other person of restless or unsettled habits.

Rolling Stones, The. British rock group, in the vanguard of the 1960s revolution in popular music. It consisted originally of Mick Jagger (1943–), Brian Jones (1942–69), Keith Richard (1943–), Charlie Watts (1941–), and Bill Wyman (1936–). Its many hit records include the singles *Satisfaction,* and *Honky Tonk Women.*

rolling strike *n.* An industrial strike in which groups within one work force strike in sequence, usually one group each day.

roll·mop (ról-mop) *n.* Also **roll·mops** *pl.* **rollmops.** A marinated fillet of herring sometimes wrapped around a gherkin or onion, and served as an hors d'oeuvre. [German *Rollmops : rollen,* to ROLL + *Mops,* pug dog.]

roll·neck (ról-nek) *n. Chiefly British.* **1.** A high neck on a garment, especially a sweater, that may be folded over. Also used adjectivally: *a rollneck sweater.* **2.** A sweater or other garment with such a neck.

roll on *tr.v.* To apply or put on by means of a rolling action. ~*interj. British Informal.* Used to express eager impatience for some specified event or time: *roll on Christmas!*

roll-on (ról-on) *n.* **1.** A liquid deodorant applied by a revolving ball in the mouth of a container. Also used adjectivally: *a roll-on deodorant.* **2.** A woman's corset made of light elastic material.

roll-on roll-off *adj.* **1.** Designating a ferry or other ship designed so that large or heavy vehicles can drive on and drive off. **2.** Of, pertaining to, or designating systems of transport operating in this way: *roll-on roll-off cargo.*

roll·o·ver (rólōvər) *adj.* Carried over: *a rollover jackpot.*

roll-top desk (ról-top) *n.* A desk fitted with a flexible, sliding lid made of parallel slats. Also called "roll top".

roll up *intr.v.* **1.** *Informal.* To arrive, especially in a vehicle. **2.** *Informal.* To come along; gather round. **3.** To pile up or increase; become progressively larger. **—tr.v. Military.** To drive (the enemy's flank or line) round and back on itself.

roll-up (ról-up) *n.* **1.** *British Informal.* A cigarette put together by the smoker with a cigarette paper and tobacco. **2.** *Australian.* A gathering or assembly of people.

ro·ly-po·ly (róli-póli) *adj.* Short and plump; pudgy. ~*n., pl.* **roly-polies. 1.** A roly-poly person. **2.** *Chiefly British.* A pudding made by rolling up jam or fruit in pastry dough and cooking it. Also called "roly-poly pudding". [Perhaps from ROLL + POLL (head).]

ROM (rom) *n. Computing.* A read-only memory.

rom. roman (type).

Rom. 1. Roman. **2.** Romance (language). **3.** Romans (New Testament).

Roma. See **Rome.**

Ro·ma·ic (rō-máy-ik) *n. Rare.* Modern vernacular Greek. [Modern Greek *Rhōmaikos,* from Greek, Roman (especially, of the eastern Roman Empire at Byzantium), from *Rhōmē, Rhōma,* Rome, from Latin *Rōma,* ROME.] **—Ro·ma·ic** *adj.*

ro·maine (rō-máyn) *n. Chiefly U.S.* A lettuce, the **cos** (see). [French, from the feminine of *Romain,* Roman, from Old French, ROMAN.]

ro·ma·ji (rómaa-jee) *n.* The Roman alphabet as used to transliterate Japanese. [Japanese, from *Roman.*]

ro·man (rómən) *n. Sometimes capital* R *Abbr.* **rom.** The most common style of type, characterised by upright letters having serifs and vertical lines thicker than horizontal lines. This definition is printed in roman. Compare **italic.** ~*adj. Sometimes capital* R *Abbr.* **rom.** Of, set in, or printed in roman. [It represents the style used in ancient Roman inscriptions and manuscripts.]

Ro·man (rómən) *adj. Abbr.* **Rom. 1.** Of, pertaining to, derived from, or characteristic of Rome and its people, especially ancient Rome. **2.** Of, in, pertaining to, or characteristic of the Latin language. **3.** Of or pertaining to the Roman Catholic Church. **4.** Of or designating an architectural style developed by the ancient Romans, characterised by great, round arches and barrel vaults, masonry construction, and classical orders as decorative features. ~*n. Abbr.* **Rom. 1.** A native, resident, or citizen of Rome, especially ancient Rome. **2.** The Italian language as spoken in Rome. **3.** A member of the Roman Catholic Church. [Middle English *Roman* and *Romain,* respectively from Old English *Rōmān,* a Roman, and

Old French *Romain*, Roman, a Roman, both from Latin *Rōmānus*, from *Rōma*, ROME.]

ro·man à clef (rŏ-món a kláy, -món aa) *n., pl.* **romans à clef** (-mónz, *or pronounced as singular*). *French.* A novel in which actual persons, events, or places are depicted in fictional guise. ["Novel with key".]

Roman alphabet *n.* **1.** The alphabet evolved by the ancient Romans from that of the Greeks by way of the Etruscan alphabet, consisting of 23 letters upon which are founded the modern western European alphabets. Also called "Latin alphabet". **2.** Any of the modern alphabets derived from this.

Roman calendar *n.* A lunar calendar used by the ancient Romans until it was superseded by the **Julian calendar** *(see)* in 46 B.C. It consisted of ten months and in each month designated the day of the new moon as the **calends** *(see),* the day of the full moon as the **ides** *(see),* and the ninth day before the ides as the **nones** *(see).* Dates were calculated backwards from these three points.

Roman candle *n.* A firework consisting of a tube from which streams of sparks are ejected. [Originated in Italy.]

Roman Catholic *adj. Abbr.* **R.C., Rom. Cath.** Of, designating, belonging to, or pertaining to the Roman Catholic Church.
~*n.* A member of the Roman Catholic Church.

Roman Catholic Church *n. Abbr.* **R.C.Ch.** The Christian church recognising the primacy of the see of Rome and the authority of the Pope, characterised by a hierarchical structure of bishops and priests in which doctrinal and disciplinary authority are dependent upon apostolic succession. Also called "Catholic Church", "Church of Rome".

Roman Catholicism *n.* The doctrines, practices, and institutions of the Roman Catholic Church. Also called "Catholicism".

ro·mance (rə-mánss, rŏ- ‖ rŏ-manss) *n.* **1.** A novel, story, or film dealing with a love affair, especially in a sentimental fashion. **2.** The class or style of fictional works about idealised love. **3. a.** A love affair; especially, a short-lived but passionately idealistic attachment of two young people. **b.** Love or romantic involvement, especially when idealised. **c.** A strong, usually short-lived attachment or enthusiasm. **4.** Inclination towards love, adventure, or mystery; romantic spirit. **5.** A fictitiously embellished account or explanation. **6.** A long, medieval narrative in prose or verse, telling of the adventures of chivalric heroes. **7. a.** Any long, fictitious tale of heroes and extraordinary or mysterious events, usually set in a distant time and place. **b.** Any sequence of real events resembling such a tale in excitement, nobility, or idealised love. **8.** The class of literature of such tales. **9.** A quality suggestive of the adventure, mystery, and idealised exploits found in such tales. **10.** A short, lyrical song or instrumental piece.
~*v.* **romanced, -mancing, -mances.** —*intr.* **1.** To invent, write, or recount tales or adventure, nobility, or love. **2.** To tell extravagant and exaggerated lies. **3.** To think or behave in a romantic manner. —*tr. Informal.* To behave romantically towards; woo. [Middle English *roma(u)ns, roma(u)nce,* French, work written in French, from Old French *romanz, romant,* from Vulgar Latin *Rōmānicē* (unattested), in the vernacular (as opposed to *Latinē,* in Latin), from Latin *Rōmānicus,* Roman, made in Rome, from *Rōmānus,* ROMAN.] —**ro·manc·er** *n.*

Ro·mance (rə-mánss, rŏ-, rŏ´-manss) *adj. Abbr.* **Rom.** Of, designating, or belonging to any of the languages that developed from Latin, the principal ones being French, Italian, Portuguese, Romanian, and Castilian Spanish and Catalan.
~*n.* The Romance languages. [From ROMANCE (French, "the Roman tongue").]

Roman Empire *n.* **1.** The lands governed by the ancient Romans. In A.D. 395 it was divided into the East Roman Empire or **Byzantine Empire** *(see)* and the **Western Roman Empire** *(see).* **2.** The government of Rome and its lands from 27 B.C by Augustus and the later emperors. **3.** Any empire held to be the successor of the Roman Empire, such as the Byzantine Empire or Holy Roman Empire.

Rom·a·nes (rómmə-niss, -ness) *n.* The Gypsy language; Romany. [Romany.]

Ro·man·esque (rŏmən-ésk) *adj.* **1.** Of, pertaining to, or designating a transitional style of European architecture prevalent from the 9th to the 12th century, and characterised by rounded arches, massive vaulting, and thick walls. See **Norman. 2.** Of, pertaining to, or designating the styles in art prevalent in this period.
~*n.* The Romanesque style. [From ROMAN.]

ro·man-fleuve (rŏ-món flérv, flöv) *n., pl.* **romans-fleuves** (*pronounced as singular*). *French.* A long novel, often in many volumes, chronicling the history of an individual, family, or community. Also called "saga novel". See **novel sequence.** [French, "river-novel" (because the development of its plot is now rapid, now slow, like the flow of a river), coined by Romain Rolland.]

Roman holiday *n.* **1.** A time of enjoyment derived from the suffering of others. **2.** Any savage and spectacular entertainment reminiscent of the staged public battles of Roman gladiators. [So called from the gladiatorial contests of the ancient Romans.]

Ro·ma·ni·a or **Ru·ma·ni·a** or **Rou·ma·ni·a,** (rŏŏ-máyni-ə, rŏŏ-, rŏ-). Republic of southeast Europe. It is dominated by the Carpathians, with the Transylvanian uplands to the northwest, and lower Danubian plains in the southeast. Romania achieved rapid industrial expansion during the 1960s and 1970s, and machinery, chemicals, and consumer goods, as well as agricultural produce, oil, and gas became major exports; but from 1984 there was economic recession. The country was formed by the union of Walachia and Moldavia (1861), and achieved independence in 1878. After World War II it became a Soviet satellite, but under President Ceauçescu pursued an increasingly independent course. In 1989 Ceauçescu was overthrown and executed during a violent revolution. Area, 238 391 square kilometres (92,043 square miles). Population, 22,610,000. Capital, Bucharest.

Ro·ma·ni·an, Ru·ma·ni·an (rŏŏ-máyni-ən, rŏŏ-, rŏ-) *adj. Abbr.* **Rom.** Of or pertaining to Romania, its people, or their language.
~*n.* **1.** An inhabitant, native, or citizen of Romania. **2.** The Romance language of the Romanian people.

Ro·man·ic (rŏ-mánnik, rə-) *adj.* **1.** Of or derived from the ancient Romans or their language. **2.** Of or pertaining to the Romance languages.
~*n.* Romance. [Latin *Rōmānicus,* from *Rōmānus,* ROMAN.]

Ro·man·ise, Ro·man·ize (rŏmən-īz) *v.* **-ised, -ising, -ises.** —*tr.* **1.** To convert (a person) to Roman Catholicism. **2.** To make (a ritual, for example) Roman Catholic in character. **3.** To make Roman in character: *Our laws were Romanised.* **4.** To write or translit-

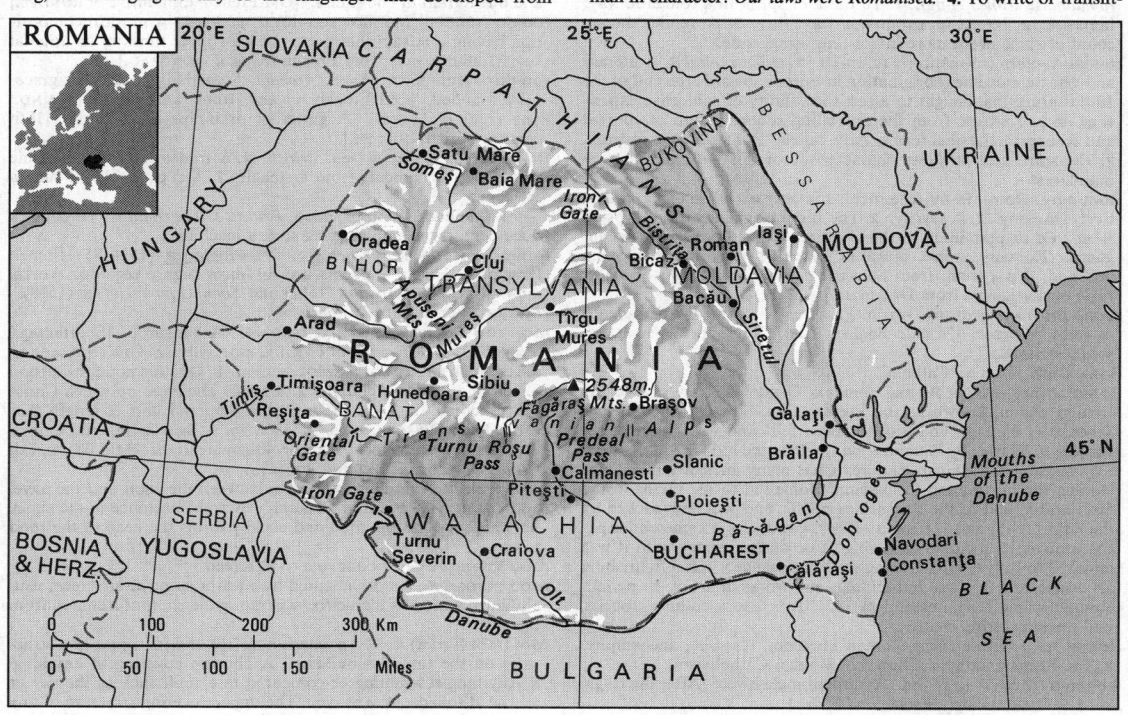

ROMANIA

erate (a language, for example) into the Roman alphabet. —*intr.*
1. To be converted to Roman Catholicism. **2.** To adopt Roman
Catholic practices. —**Ro·man·i·sa·tion** (-ī-záysh'n || *U.S.* -i-) *n.*

Ro·man·ism (rṓmən-iz'm) *n.* **1.** Roman Catholicism. Usually used
derogatorily. **2.** Admiration for the spirit of ancient Rome.

Ro·man·ist (rṓmən-ist) *n.* **1. a.** A Roman Catholic. Usually used
derogatorily. **b.** A member of the Church of England who favours
Catholic ritual. **2.** A student of or authority on Roman law, culture,
and institutions.
~*adj.* **1.** Of, belonging to, or designating the Roman Catholic
Church. Usually used derogatorily. **2.** Favouring Catholic ritual.

Roman law *n.* The system of laws of ancient Rome, upon which the
legal systems of many countries are based. See **civil law**.

Roman nose *n.* A nose with a high, prominent bridge.

Roman numerals *pl.n.* Certain letters of the Roman alphabet used
as numerical symbols by the ancient Romans and still used today in
certain formal contexts. In this system I stands for 1, V for 5, X for
10, L for 50, C for 100, D for 500, and M for 1000. Compare **Arabic
numerals**.

Romano- *comb. form.* Indicates Roman; for example, *Romano-
Celtic.*

Ro·ma·nov (rṓmən-off; *Russian* ra-maánəf). The imperial dynasty
(1613–1917) in Russia. The line began with the accession of Tsar
Michael and ended with the abdication of Nicholas II during the
Russian Revolution.

Ro·mans (rṓmənz) *n. Used with a singular verb. Abbr.* **Rom.** A
book of the New Testament, an epistle of Saint Paul to the Christians of Rome.

Ro·mansch, Ro·mansh (rō-mánsh, rə- || *U.S. also* -maánsch) *n.*
The Rhaeto-Romanic dialects spoken in eastern Switzerland and in
neighbouring parts of Italy. [Romansch *Ruman(t)sch, Roman(t)sch,*
"Roman", "Romance language", from Vulgar Latin *Rōmānicē* (unattested), in the Roman manner, in the Roman tongue. See **romance.**]

Roman snail *n.* A large snail, *Helix pomatia,* that is the more commonly used edible species.

ro·man·tic (rō-mántik, rə-) *adj.* **1. a.** Of, pertaining to, designating, characterised by, or evoking feelings of love, especially of a
passionate or sentimental nature: *romantic lighting.* **b.** Given
or inclined to such feelings or thoughts: *a romantic young girl.*
2. Of or pertaining to a sexual relationship. **3. a.** Of or pertaining
to a literary romance. **b.** Characteristic of the atmosphere or mood
of such romances; idealistic, heroic, exciting, and noble.
4. Imaginative but impractical: *romantic notions.* **5.** Not based on
fact; fictitious. **6.** *Often capital* **R.** Of or characteristic of romanticism in the arts.
~*n.* **1.** A person who is orientated towards love, adventure, or
high ideals; a romantic person. **2.** A person who enjoys the artistic
products of Romanticism; a romanticist. **3.** *Often capital* **R.** A
writer or other artist creating works of art in the style or spirit of
Romanticism; especially, one who lived in the romantic era; a
romanticist. [French *romantique,* from Old French *romant, romanz,* ROMANCE.] —**ro·man·ti·cal·ly** *adv.*

ro·man·ti·cise, ro·man·ti·cize (rō-mánti-sīz, rə-) *v.* **-cised, -cising,
-cises.** —*tr.* **1.** To make romantic in style or character. **2.** To consider or portray in an often inappropriately romantic way: *Don't
romanticise crime.* —*intr.* **1.** To think or speak in a romantic way;
fantasise. **2.** To act in a romantic way; flirt. **3.** To render the account of some event more interesting; exaggerate.

ro·man·ti·cism (rō-mánti-siz'm, rə-) *n. Often capital* **R.** A literary
and artistic movement originating in Europe towards the end of the
18th century that sought to assert the validity of subjective experience and to escape from the prevailing subordination of content
and feeling to classical forms. Also called "Romantic Movement".
2. The spirit and attitudes characteristic of this movement. —**ro·
man·ti·cist** *n.*

Rom·a·ny, Rom·ma·ny (rómməni, rṓməni) *n., pl.* **-nies** or collectively **Romany. 1.** A Gypsy. **2.** The Indic language of the Gypsies.
~*adj.* Of or pertaining to the Gypsies, their culture, or their language. [Romany *romani,* plural of *romano,* gypsy, from *rom,* man,
husband, gypsy man, from Sanskrit *ḍomba, ḍoma,* man of a low
caste of musicians, from Dravidian.]

ro·maunt (rō-máwnt, rə-, -maánt) *n. Archaic.* A medieval romance
in verse or prose. [Middle English, from Old French *romant, romanz,* ROMANCE.]

Rom. Cath. Roman Catholic.

Rome¹ (rōm), *Italian* **Ro·ma** (rṓmaa). Capital of Italy and of the
Latium region, known as the Eternal City. Situated on the river
Tiber, it is built on and around seven hills and was founded, according to legend, by Romulus, on the Palatine hill (753 B.C.). Once
the centre of the Roman Empire, it has many ancient remains, including the Forum and Colosseum. Rome fell to the Goths in the
5th century, and to the Byzantines in 552, and was later sacked by
the Arabs (846) and Normans (1084). Gradually it came under papal control, its fortunes following those of the papacy until it was
annexed to Italy (1870). During the Renaissance it was a flourishing
art centre, and it is rich in buildings and works of art of the period.
Rome became Italy's capital in 1871. It is also a cultural, tourist,
and manufacturing centre.

Rome² *n.* **1.** The ancient Roman kingdom, republic, and empire.
2. The Roman Catholic Church or Roman Catholicism.

Ro·me·o (rṓmi-ō) *n., pl.* **-os.** An ardent male lover. [After the tragic
hero of Shakespeare's *Romeo and Juliet.*]

Rom·ish (rṓmish) *adj.* Of or pertaining to the Roman Catholic
Church. Often used derogatorily.

Rom·mel (rómm'l), **Erwin** (1891–1944). German general, nicknamed the Desert Fox, famous for his desert campaigns of World
War II. In 1941 he was made commander in chief of the newly
formed Afrika Korps. Following victories at Tobruk and Benghazi
(1942), he invaded Egypt, but was forced to withdraw after the
battle of El Alamein (1942) and recalled to Europe in 1943. He was
implicated in the July Plot (1944) to assassinate Hitler, and committed suicide when his complicity was discovered.

Rom·ney (róm-ni, rúm-), **George** (1734–1802). British portrait
painter. A Lancashire cabinetmaker's son, he trained under an itinerant artist and later set up as a commercial portrait painter. In
1762 he moved to London, where he acquired a fashionable clientele to rival that of Reynolds.

romp (romp) *intr.v.* **romped, romping, romps. 1.** To play or frolic
boisterously. **2.** *British Informal.* To succeed in some venture without effort. Used with *through: He romped through his exams.* **3.** To
proceed easily or effortlessly. Often used with *about* or *along.*
—**romp home** or **in.** To win a race or other competition with ease.
~*n.* **1.** An occasion of lively, merry play; a frolic. **2.** *Archaic.* One
who sports and frolics, especially a girl. **3.** An easy win. [Variant of
RAMP (to rage).]

romp·ers (rómpərz) *pl.n.* **1.** A one-piece baby's playsuit, usually
with short legs. **2.** *N.Z.* Baggy gym shorts worn by schoolgirls.

Rom·u·lus (rómmewləss). *Roman Mythology.* The son of Mars and
a vestal virgin, who, with his twin brother Remus, was abandoned
as an infant to die but was suckled by a she-wolf. He later killed
Remus and founded Rome in 753 B.C.

Romulus Au·gus·tu·lus (aw-gústewləss) (born *c.* A.D. 460). The last
Roman emperor in the West (A.D. 475–6). As a youth he was deposed by the German ruler Odoacer who spared his life. He died in
retirement at an unknown date.

Ron·ces·valles (rón-sə-válz; *Spanish* -thess-vál-yess). *French*
Ronce·vaux (roNss-vṓ). Mountain pass and village of Navarra,
northern Spain. It was the site of the defeat and massacre of the
rearguard of Charlemagne's army, under Roland, by the Basques
(778).

ron·da·vel (rón-daáv'l) *n. South African.* A round house, hut, or
outbuilding with a conical roof. Originally a one-roomed native hut
with a thatched roof, it now often has several rooms and can be
made of modern materials. [Afrikaans *rondawel†.*]

rond de jambe (róN də zhóNb) *n., pl.* **ronds de jambe.** In ballet, a
circular movement of the leg from below the knee, executed either
in the air or on the ground.

ron·deau (róndō || *U.S. also* ron-dṓ) *n., pl.* **-deaux** (-z). **1.** A lyrical
poem of French origin having 13, or sometimes 10, lines with two
rhymes throughout and with the opening phrase repeated twice as a
refrain. Also called "roundel". **2.** *Music.* **a.** An originally monophonic medieval song of the trouvères or troubadours. **b.** An early
rondo. [French, variant of RONDEL.]

ron·del (rónd'l || *U.S. also* ron-dél) *n.* A rondeau that usually has 14
lines. Also called "roundel". [Middle English, from Old French,
"small circle" (from the repetition of the first lines at the end of the
poem), from *ronde, rounde,* ROUND.]

ron·de·let (róndə-let) *n.* A short rondeau having five or seven lines
and one refrain in one stanza. [Old French, diminutive of RONDEL.]

ron·do (róndō || *U.S. also* ron-dṓ) *n., pl.* **-dos.** A musical composi-
tion having a refrain that occurs at least three times in its original
key. [Italian *rondò,* from French *rondeau,* RONDEAU.]

ron·dure (rón-dewr, -jər) *n. Archaic.* Something circular or gracefully rounded. [Old French *rondeur,* from *rond, rounde,* ROUND.]

rone (rōn) *n. Scottish.* A gutter or drainpipe on a house. [19th
century : origin obscure.]

Ro·ne·o (rṓni-ō) *n., pl.* **-os.** *British.* **1.** A trademark for a machine
that copies documents from a stencil. **2.** A copy made on such a
machine.
~*tr.v.* **Roneod, -neoing, -neos.** *British. Often small* **r.** To copy (a
document, for example) using such a machine.

Ron·sard (róN-saar, *French* roN-sár), **Pierre de** (1524–85). French
lyric poet. His love poems are his most highly regarded works,
among them *Les Amours* (1552) and *Sonnets pour Hélène* (1578).

röntgen. Variant of **roentgen.**

roo, 'roo (rōō) *n. Australian Informal.* A kangaroo. [Shortening.]

rood (rōōd) *n.* **1.** A cross or crucifix, especially: **a.** One representing
the cross on which Christ was crucified. **b.** One surmounting a rood
screen in a medieval church. **2.** *Archaic.* The cross on which Christ
was crucified. **3.** *Abbr.* **ro.** A British Imperial unit of length that
varies from 5½ to 8 yards. **4.** *Abbr.* **ro.** A British Imperial unit of
area usually equal to ¼ acre or 40 square rods. [Middle English
ro(o)d, Old English *rōd,* rod, cross.]

rood arch *n.* An arch in a church, between the choir and the nave.

rood beam *n.* A beam in a church across the entrance to the choir,
where it supports the rood and usually forms the head of the rood
screen.

rood loft *n.* A gallery above a rood screen.

rood screen *n.* An ornamented wooden or stone altar screen, usually surmounted by a crucifix, separating the choir of a church from
the nave.

roof (rōōf || rŏŏf) *n.* **1.** An exterior surface and its supporting struc-
tures on the top of a building. **2.** The top covering of anything.
3. Anything resembling or compared to a roof, such as the sky or
overhead foliage. **4.** *Anatomy.* The upper covering structure of any

part of the body: *roof of the mouth.* **5.** The highest point; the summit: *the roof of the world.* **—a roof over (one's) head.** Somewhere to live. **—go through** or **hit the roof.** *Slang.* To lose one's temper suddenly. **—raise the roof.** *Informal.* **1.** To be extremely noisy and boisterous. **2.** To complain loudly and bitterly.

~tr.v. **roofed, roofing, roofs.** To furnish or cover with a roof. Often used with *in* or *over.* [Middle English *ro(o)f,* Old English *hrōf.*]

roof·er (rōōf-ər || rŏŏf-) *n.* One who makes or repairs roofs.

roof garden *n.* A garden on a flat roof of a building.

roof·ing (rōōf-ing || rŏŏf) *n.* **1.** The act of constructing a roof. **2.** A roof of a building. **3.** Materials used in building a roof.

roof·less (rōōf-ləss, -liss || rŏŏf-) *adj.* **1.** Lacking a roof. **2.** Having no home or shelter; homeless.

roof rack *n. Chiefly British.* A metal rack fixed to the top of a motor vehicle for carrying luggage or other objects.

roof·top (rōōf-top || rŏŏf-) *n.* The upper part of a roof of a building.

roof·tree (rōōf-tree || rŏŏf-) *n.* A long horizontal beam extending along the ridge of a roof; a ridgepole.

rooi·nek (róy-nek) *n. South African.* An Englishman or English South African. Formerly used derogatorily. [Afrikaans, "red neck".]

rook[1] (rŏŏk || rōōk) *n.* **1.** A crowlike Old World bird, *Corvus frugilegus,* with white patches at the base of its bill, that nests in colonies near the tops of trees. **2.** *Slang.* A swindler; especially, one who cheats when gambling.

~tr.v. **rooked, rooking, rooks.** *Slang.* To swindle, especially by overcharging or by cheating when gambling. [Middle English *rok, ruke,* Old English *hrōc.*]

rook[2] *n. Abbr.* **R** A chess piece that may move in a straight line over any number of empty squares in a rank or file. Also called "castle". [Middle English *rok(e),* from Old French *roc(k),* from Arabic *rukh,* from Persian *rukh*†.]

rook·er·y (rŏŏk-əri || rōōk-) *n., pl.* **-ies. 1. a.** A place where rooks nest and breed. **b.** A colony of rooks or their nests. **2. a.** The breeding ground of certain other birds and animals, such as seals. **b.** A colony of such birds or animals. **3.** *Informal.* A crowded tenement.

rook·ie (rŏŏki) *n. Slang.* **1.** An untrained recruit, especially in an army. **2.** Any inexperienced person. [Alteration of RECRUIT (influenced by the bird ROOK).]

room (rōōm, rŏŏm) *n. Abbr.* **rm. 1.** Space that is or may be occupied by something; open space: *a desk that takes up too much room.* Sometimes used in combination: *Shelf-room.* **2.** An area or part inside a building enclosed by a floor, a ceiling, and walls. **3.** The people present in such an area: *The whole room was amazed.* **4.** *Plural.* Living quarters; lodgings. **5.** Scope; opportunity. Used with *for* or *to*: *room for error.* **—make room.** To make more space available, usually by giving way or removing something.

~intr.v. **roomed, rooming, rooms.** *U.S.* To occupy a room; lodge. [Middle English *roum,* Old English *rūm.*]

room divider *n.* A partition dividing up a room.

room·ful (rōōm-fŏŏl, rŏŏm-) *n., pl.* **-fuls. 1.** As much or as many as a room will hold. **2.** The number of people in a room.

room·ing house (rōōm-ing, rŏŏm-) *n. U.S.* A lodging house.

room-mate (rōōm-mayt, rŏŏm-) *n.* **1.** A person with whom one shares a room. **2.** *U.S.* A flatmate.

room service *n.* **1.** A service in a hotel attending to guests' requirements, especially for refreshments, in their rooms. **2.** The staff providing this service.

room temperature *n.* A temperature of about 20° C; a comfortable living temperature inside a room.

room·y (rōōmi, rŏŏmi) *adj.* **-ier, -iest.** Having plenty of room; spacious; large. **—room·i·ly** *adv.* **—room·i·ness** *n.*

Roo·se·velt (rōzə-vəlt, -velt, *also* rōōss-), **Franklin D(elano)** (1882–1945). U.S. statesman, Democratic president, the 32nd (1933–45). His career was interrupted in 1921 when he was crippled by polio, but he went on to become governor of New York (1928–32). As president he fulfilled his promise of a New Deal for the American people by initiating relief programmes, measures to aid employment, and assist industrial and agricultural recovery from the Depression. He was the only U.S. president to be re-elected three times (1936, 1940, 1944). His wife, Eleanor Roosevelt (1884–1962), was an active crusader for human rights and a delegate to the United Nations.

Roosevelt, Theodore (1858–1919). U.S. statesman, Republican president, the 26th (1901–09). As president, he won, through forceful diplomacy, the United States' concession to build the Panama Canal (1903). His foreign policy exemplified his principle "speak softly and carry a big stick", and in 1906 he won the Nobel peace prize for his mediation in the Russo-Japanese War (1904–5).

roost (rōōst) *n.* **1.** A perch on which domestic fowls or other birds rest or sleep. **2.** A place with perches for fowls or other birds. **3.** A place for temporary rest or sleep. **—come home to roost.** To recoil unpleasantly upon the doer: *His corrupt practices came home to roost.* **—rule the roost.** To be in charge; be in a dominant position.

~v. **roosted, roosting, roosts.** *—intr.* **1.** To rest or sleep on a perch or roost. **2.** To settle down for the night. *—tr.* To supply with a sleeping place for the night. [Middle English *rooste,* Old English *hrōst.*]

roost·er (rōōstər) *n. Chiefly U.S.* **1.** The adult male of the common domestic fowl; a cock. **2.** A pugnacious and cocky person.

root[1] (rōōt || rŏŏt) *n.* **1. a.** The usually underground portion of a plant that serves as support, draws water and mineral ions from the surrounding soil, and in some plants stores food. **b.** Any similar underground plant part, such as a rhizome, corm, or tuber. **c.** Any of numerous small, hairlike growths that serve to attach and support plants such as the ivy and other vines. **2.** *Anatomy.* **a.** The embedded part of an organ or structure such as a hair or tooth. **b.** The point of emergence of a nerve from the spinal cord, consisting of a bundle of nerve fibres. **3. a.** Any base or support. **b.** A part of an object by which it is attached to a base or larger object: *the root of a propeller.* **4.** Any base or support. **5.** An essential part or element; a basic core or fundamental nature: *strikes at the roots of our democracy.* **6.** A primary source or cause; an origin: *money is the root of all evil.* Also used adjectivally: *the root cause.* **7.** An antecedent or ancestor. **8.** An emotional or psychological attachment or historical association with a particular place or society: *Her roots lie in Antrim.* **9.** *Linguistics.* **a.** In etymology, a word or word element from which other words are formed. **b.** In morphology, a base to which prefixes and suffixes may be added. Also called "radical". **10.** *Mathematics.* **a.** A number that when multiplied by itself a specified number of times forms a product equal to a given number: *a fourth root of 16 is 2.* Also called "numerical root". **b.** A number or quantity that when substituted for the variable, satisfies the polynomial equation $f(x)=0$. See **function. c.** A **multiple root** *(see).* **11.** *Music.* **a.** The note from which a chord is built. **b.** The first or lowest note of a triad or chord. **12.** *Australian Vulgar Slang.* An act of sexual intercourse. —See Synonyms at **origin. —put down roots.** To settle; become established, as by taking up permanent residence in a place. **—take root. 1.** To put out roots and grow. **2.** To become fixed, established, or recognised. **—root and branch.** Entirely; utterly; radically: *overhauled the vetting procedures root and branch.*

~v. **rooted, rooting, roots.** *—intr.* **1.** To grow a root or roots. **2.** To become firmly established, settled, or entrenched. *—tr.* **1.** To cause to put out roots and grow. **2.** To implant by or as if by the roots; fix: *stood rooted to the spot.* **3.** To pull or dig up by or as if by the roots. Used with *up* or *out.* **4.** To eliminate; remove totally. Used with *out*: *root out abuses.* **5.** *Australian Vulgar Slang.* To have sexual intercourse with. [Middle English *rot(e),* Old English *rōt,* from Old Norse.] **—root·er** *n.*

root[2] *v.* **rooted, rooting, roots.** *—tr.* **1.** To dig (the ground, for example) with or as with the snout or nose. **2.** To bring to light or turn up by searching. Often used with *out*: *rooted out dark secrets from his past.* *—intr.* **1.** To dig in the ground with or as with the snout or nose. Used chiefly of pigs. **2.** To search about or rummage for something. Often used with *about* or *around.* [Alteration (influenced by ROOT of a plant) of earlier *wroot,* Middle English *wroten,* Old English *wrōtan.*] **—root·er** *n.*

root[3] *intr.v.* **rooted, rooting, roots.** *Chiefly U.S.* To give encouragement or support, especially to a team or contestant. Used with *for.* [Perhaps from ROOT (to dig with the snout).] **—root·er** *n.*

root·age (rōōt-ij || rŏŏt-) *n.* **1.** A system or growth of roots. **2.** Establishment or fixing by or as if by roots.

root·ball (rōōt-bawl || rŏŏt-) *n.* The tightly packed mass of roots and soil produced by a plant grown in a container.

root beer *n. U.S.* A carbonated soft drink made from extracts of the roots of several plants.

root canal *n.* The pulp-filled cavity in a root of a tooth.

root cap *n. Botany.* A thimble-shaped mass of cells that covers and protects the tip of a growing root.

root·ed (rōōt-id || rŏŏt-) *adj.* **1.** Deep-seated or deeply felt. **2.** *Australian Slang.* Exhausted. **—get rooted!** *Australian Vulgar Slang.* Go away!

root hair *n. Botany.* A thin, hairlike outgrowth of a plant root that absorbs water and minerals from the soil.

root·less (rōōt-ləss, -liss || rŏŏt-) *adj.* **1.** Having no roots: *a rootless tooth.* **2.** Not belonging to any particular place or society: *the rootless refugees in a strange country.* **—root·less·ness** *n.*

root·let (rōōt-lət, -lit || rŏŏt-) *n.* A small root or division of a root.

root mean square *n. Abbr.* **rms** The square root of the arithmetic mean of the squares of a set of numbers.

root mean square deviation *n. Statistics.* **Standard deviation** *(see).*

root·stock (rōōt-stok || rŏŏt-) *n.* **1.** A rootlike underground stem, such as a **rhizome** *(see).* **2.** A root or part of a root used as a stock for grafting. **3.** A source of origin.

root vegetable *n.* A vegetable, such as a carrot or beetroot, that is grown for its edible root.

root·y (rōōti || rŏŏti) *adj.* **-ier, -iest. 1.** Full of roots. **2.** Consisting of or resembling roots. **—root·i·ness** *n.*

rop·a·ble, rope·a·ble (rōpəb'l) *adj.* **1.** Able to be roped. **2.** *Australian.* Wild and untamable. Said of an animal. **3.** *Australian Informal.* Angry and often violent. Said of a person.

rope (rōp) *n.* **1. a.** Flexible, heavy cord of twisted hemp, flex, nylon, wire or other material. **b.** A section of such cord. **c.** Any strand or other object resembling a rope, especially one consisting of braided or wound material. **2.** A cord with a noose at one end for hanging a person. **3.** Death by hanging. Preceded by *the.* **4.** *Plural.* Several cords strung between poles to enclose a boxing ring. Preceded by *the.* **5.** Any string of items attached in one line by twisting or braiding: *a rope of onions.* **6.** *Plural.* The special procedures, details, or conditions of a field of activity: *Please show me the ropes.* **—give (someone) enough rope to (hang himself).** To deliberately allow (someone) sufficient freedom of action to cause his own downfall. **—on the ropes.** *Informal.* Nearing total collapse, defeat, or ruin.

~v. **roped, roping, ropes.** *—tr.* **1.** To tie or fasten with or as with rope. **2.** To enclose, mark off, or divide with a rope. Usually used

with *off*. **3.** *British Informal*. To persuade or force (a person) to help or become involved in an activity. Used with *in*: *roped them in to paint the house*. **4.** To join or connect (mountaineers) securely with a rope. Used with *up*: *The guide roped the party up*. **5.** *Chiefly U.S.* To catch with a rope. **6.** *U.S. Informal*. To trick or deceive. Usually used with *in*. —*intr*. In mountaineering, to tie oneself to the other climbers. Used with *up*. [Middle English *rop(e)*, Old English *rāp*.]

rope ladder *n*. A flexible ladder made from two ropes linked by rungs.

rope's end *n*. A short length of usually thick rope formerly used on ships for flogging sailors.

rope·walk (rōp-wawk) *n*. A long, narrow path or building where ropes are manufactured by twisting fibres together.

rope·way (rōp-way) *n*. A system of overhead cables and supporting towers used to transport goods or passengers in containers or cabins suspended from the cables, as at a ski resort.

rope yarn *n*. The fibres of hemp, nylon, or other material from which rope is made.

rop·y (rōpi) *adj*. **-ier, -iest. 1.** Resembling a rope or ropes. **2.** *British Informal*. Of poor or inferior quality. **3.** Forming sticky glutinous strings or threads. —**rop·i·ly** *adv*. —**rop·i·ness** *n*.

roque (rōk) *n*. A form of croquet played in the United States on a hard court. [Alteration of CROQUET.]

Roque·fort (rók-fawr ‖ *U.S.* rōk-fərt) *n*. A French cheese made from ewes' and goats' milk, and containing a blue mould, *Penicillium roqueforti*. [After *Roquefort*-sur-Soulzon, village in southeast France.]

roqu·e·laure (róckə-lawr, rōkə-) *n*. A man's knee-length cloak popular during the 18th and early 19th centuries. [After the Duc de *Roquelaure* (1656–1738), French marshal.]

ro·quet (rō-ki, -kay) *v*. **-queted, -queting, -quets.** —*tr*. In croquet: **1.** To cause one's ball to strike (another player's ball). **2.** To strike (another ball). Used of a ball. —*intr*. In croquet, to strike another player's ball with one's own.
—*n*. The act of roqueting. [Arbitrarily formed from CROQUET.]

ror·qual (rórkwəl) *n*. Any of several whalebone whales of the genus *Balaenoptera*, having longitudinal grooves on the throat, and a small, pointed dorsal fin. Also called "finback","razorback". [French, from Norwegian *rørhval*, from Old Norse *reytharhvalr* : *reythr*, rorqual, "red whale" (from its red streaks), from *rauthr*, red + *hvalr*, whale.]

Ror·schach test (rór-shaak, -shak, -shaakh; *German* -shakh) *n*. *Psychology*. A type of projective test of personality in which a subject's interpretations of ten abstract inkblot designs are analysed as a measure of emotional and intellectual functioning and integration. [Devised by Hermann *Rorschach* (1884–1922), Swiss psychiatrist.]

Ro·ry O'Con·nor (ráw-ri ō-kónnər, ə- ‖ rō-), also known as Roderic O'Connor. (c. 1116–98). King of Connaught (1156–98) and the last High King of Ireland (1166–98). In 1175 Rory was forced to accept vassalage under Henry II of England, though he remained overlord within Ireland. He retired to a monastery in 1191.

Ro·sa (rōzə), **Salvator** (1615–73). Italian painter, born near Naples. He developed a distinctive preoccupation with wild landscapes and battle scenes. He was also a poet, actor, and musician.

ro·sa·ceous (rōz-áyshəss) *adj*. *Botany*. **1.** Of or belonging to the Rosaceae, the plant family that includes the roses. **2.** Resembling the flower of a rose. [New Latin *Rosaceae*, from Latin *rosāceus*, made of roses : ROSE + -ACEOUS.]

ros·an·i·line (rōz-ánni-leen, -lin) *n*. Also **ros·an·i·lin** (-lin). A brownish-red crystalline organic compound, $C_{20}H_{19}N_3$, derived from aniline and used in the manufacture of dyes. [ROSE (flower) + ANILINE.]

Ro·sa·ri·o (rō-záari-ō, -sáari-). Chief port of east central Argentina, situated on the river Paraná.

ro·sa·ry (rōzəri) *n., pl.* **-ries. 1.** *Roman Catholic Church.* **a.** A form of devotion to the Virgin Mary, consisting of a recitation of any of three sets of five decades each of the Ave Maria, each decade preceded by a Lord's Prayer, ending with a Gloria Patri, and commemorating an event in the life of Christ or Our Lady. See **mystery. b.** A string of beads on which these prayers are counted. **2.** Similar beads used by other religious groups. [Middle English, from Medieval Latin *rosārium*, from Latin, rose garden, from *rosa*, ROSE.]

rosary pea *n*. A woody vine, **Indian liquorice** (see).

Rosce·lin (ross-lán) (c. 1050–c. 1120). Also called Roscellinus. French philosopher and theologian, a pioneer of nominalism. He taught that universal concepts are mere expressions of speech; each component is in reality an independent entity, and a "whole" cannot thus be divided into "parts". He was ordered to recant at the synod of Soissons (1092). His notion of the Trinity challenged orthodox teaching.

Ros·ci·us (róssi-əss, róshi-), born Quintus Roscius Gallus (c. 126–62B.C.). The most celebrated Roman comic actor. A friend of Cicero, he wrote a treatise on the relative merits of acting and oratory as means of expression.

Ros·com·mon (ross-kómmən). County of Connacht province, north central Republic of Ireland. Bounded by the river Shannon in the east, it is largely boggy and has several lakes. Its county town is Roscommon.

rose¹ (rōz) *n*. **1.** Any of numerous shrubs or vines of the genus *Rosa*, usually having prickly stems, compound leaves, and variously coloured, often fragrant flowers. **2.** The flower of any of these plants, occurring in a wide variety of colours, such as pink, red, yellow, and white. **3.** Any of various plants related to or resembling the rose.

4. A dark pink to purplish pink, to moderate red or purplish red. **5.** *Usually plural*. A rosy colour of the cheeks. **6.** An ornament resembling a rose in form; a rosette. **7.** A perforated nozzle for spraying water from a hose or watering can. **8. a.** A form of gem cut, marked by a flat base and a faceted, hemispheric upper surface. **b.** A diamond so cut. **9.** A **rose window** (see). **10.** A **compass card** (see).
—*adj*. Rose-coloured. [Middle English *rose*, Old English *rose*, *rōse*, from Latin *rosa*.]

rose². Past tense of **rise**.

ro·sé (rōzay, rō-záy) *n*. A pink, light wine, traditionally made from red grapes from which the skins are removed during fermentation. [French "pink", from Old French *rose*, rosy, a rose, from Latin *rosa*, ROSE.]

rose apple *n*. An East Indian tree, *Eugenia jambos*, cultivated in the tropics for its edible fruit and ornamental flowers.

ro·se·ate (rōzi-ət, -it, -ayt) *adj*. **1.** Rose-coloured. **2.** Cheerful; optimistic; rosy. [Latin *roseus*, from *rosa*, ROSE.] —**ro·se·ate·ly** *adv*.

rose·bay (rōz-bay) *n*. **1.** Any of several American rhododendrons. **2.** A shrub, the **oleander** (see). **3.** See **willowherb**.

Rose·be·ry (rōz-bri, -bəri ‖ -berri), **Archibald Philip Primrose, 5th Earl of** (1847–1929). British statesman, Liberal prime minister (1894–95). A strong imperialist, he was also popular as a witty speaker and successful racehorse owner, his horses winning the Derby on three occasions (1894, 1895, 1905).

rose·bud (rōz-bud) *n*. The bud of a rose.

rose·bush (rōz-bōōsh) *n*. A shrub that bears roses.

rose campion *n*. A widely naturalised European plant, *Lychnis coronaria*, that is covered with white, woolly down and has rose-red flowers. Also called "dusty miller".

rose chafer *n*. A golden-green beetle, *Catonia aurata*, that causes damage to garden plants, especially roses. Also called "rose beetle".

rose geranium *n*. A woody plant, *Pelargonium graveolens*, having rose-pink flowers and fragrant leaves used for flavouring and in perfumery.

rose·hip (rōz-hip) *n*. The fruit of the rose, a **hip** (see).

ro·sel·la (rō-zéllə) *n*. Any of various brightly coloured, Australian parrots of the genus *Platycercus*. [Alteration of *Rosehiller*, after *Rosehill*, New South Wales, where the parrots were first found.]

ro·selle (rō-zél) *n*. A tropical Old World plant, *Hibiscus sabdariffa*, with yellow flowers. Its immature floral bracts are used to make jelly and beverages. [Origin uncertain.]

rose·mar·y (rōz-məri, -mri ‖ -mair-i) *n., pl.* **-ies.** An aromatic evergreen shrub, *Rosmarinus officinalis*, native to southern Europe but widely cultivated, having light-blue flowers and greyish-green leaves that are used in cooking and perfume manufacture. [Middle English, alteration (influenced by ROSE and MARY) of *rosmarine*, from Latin *rōs marīnus*, "sea dew" : *rōs*, dew + *marīnus*, of the sea, from *mare*, sea.]

rose moss *n*. **1.** Any moss of the genus *Rhodobryum;* especially, *R. roseum*, characterised by conspicuous terminal leaf rosettes. **2.** A garden plant, **portulaca** (see).

Ro·sen·berg (rōz'n-berg), **Julius** (1918–53). U.S. government weapons inspector who helped to transmit nuclear secrets to the Russian vice-consul in New York. He was executed with his wife, Ethel Rosenberg, in 1953. Their deaths caused much controversy, as they were the first U.S. civilians to be executed for espionage.

rose of Jericho *n*. A fernlike desert plant, *Anastatica hierochuntica*, that forms a tight ball when dry, and unfolds and blooms under moist conditions. Also called "resurrection plant".

rose of Sharon *n*. **1.** A tall shrub, *Hibiscus syriacus*, having large reddish, purple, or white flowers. Also called "althaea". **2.** A shrubby plant, *Hypericum calycinum*, native to Eurasia, having evergreen leaves and yellow flowers. Also called "St. John's wort".

ro·se·o·la (rō-zée-ələ, rə-) *n*. Any red skin rash, such as that associated with measles. [New Latin, diminutive of Latin *roseus*, rosy, from *rosa*, ROSE.]

rose pink *n*. A light purplish pink to moderate or strong pink. —**rose-pink** (rōz-píngk) *adj*.

rose quartz *n*. A pinkish quartz used as a gemstone.

rose·root (rōz-rōōt ‖ -rŏŏt) *n*. A plant, *Sedum roseum*, of the Northern Hemisphere, having fleshy leaves and greenish-yellow or purple flowers.

Roses, Wars of the *pl.n*. A sporadic dynastic war (1455–85) in England between the supporters of the House of York (white rose) and of the House of Lancaster (red rose) for possession of the English Crown.

Ro·set·ta stone (rō-zéttə, rə-) *n*. A basalt tablet now in the British museum, inscribed with a decree of Ptolemy V of 196 B.C. in Greek, Egyptian hieroglyphics, and demotic characters, that was discovered in 1799 near the town of Rosetta (*Arabic* Rashid), Egypt, and provided the key to the decipherment of hieroglyphics.

ro·sette (rō-zét, rə-) *n*. **1.** An ornament made of ribbons gathered into a shape resembling a rose, especially: **a.** One worn as a badge showing the wearer's support for a particular political party or football club, for example. **b.** One given as a prize in a competition, as at a showjumping or agricultural event. **2.** Any roselike marking or formation, such as one of the clusters of spots on a leopard's fur. **3.** *Architecture*. A painted, carved, or sculptured ornament in a stylised circular pattern resembling a rose. **4.** *Botany*. A circular cluster of leaves or other plant parts. [French, "small rose", from Old French, from *rose*, rose, from Latin *rosa*, ROSE.]

Rose·wall (rōz-wawl), **Ken(neth Ronald)** (1934–). Australian tennis player. In an outstanding career, he took most major titles, but as a professional from 1956 he was barred at Wimbledon until 1968, and never took the Wimbledon singles title.

rose·wa·ter (rōz-wawtər ‖ *U.S. also* -wottər) *n.* A fragrant preparation made by steeping or distilling rose petals in water, used in cosmetics and in cookery.

rose window *n.* A circular window, usually of stained glass, with radiating tracery in the form of a rose.

rose·wood (rōz-wŏŏd) *n.* 1. Any of various tropical or semitropical trees, chiefly of the genus *Dalbergia,* having hard reddish or dark wood with a strongly marked grain. 2. The wood of any of these trees, used in cabinetmaking.

Rosh Ha·sha·nah (rōsh hə-shaánə, rōsh; *Hebrew* hasha-naá) *n.* The Jewish New Year, a solemn occasion celebrated on the first or first and second of Tishri (usually late September or early October). [Hebrew *rōsh hashshānāh,* beginning of the year : *rōsh,* head + *hash-shānāh,* the year.]

Ro·si·cru·cian (rōzi-krŏŏsh-'n, rōzzi-, -iən) *n.* 1. A member of a secret religious organisation active in the 17th and 18th centuries and claiming to have esoteric and magical knowledge. 2. A member of a modern international fraternity, the Rosicrucian Order, supposedly descended from the Rosicrucians and devoted to the application of esoteric religious doctrine to modern life. [Medieval Latin *(Frater) Rosae Crucis,* translation of the German name (Friar) Christian *Rosenkreutz,* supposed founder of the society in the 15th century.] —**Ro·si·cru·cian** *adj.* —**Ro·si·cru·cian·ism** *n.*

ros·in (rózzin) *n.* A translucent yellowish to dark-brown resin derived from the sap of various pine trees, and used to increase sliding friction on the bows of certain stringed instruments and in a wide variety of manufactured products including varnishes, inks, linoleum, and soldering fluxes. Also called "colophony".
~*tr.v.* **rosined, -ining, -ins.** To coat or rub with rosin. [Middle English *rosyn, rosine,* variants of RESIN.] —**ros·in·y** *adj.*

rosin oil *n.* A white to brown viscous liquid obtained by fractional distillation of rosin and used in lubricants, electrical insulation, and printing inks. Also called "retinol", "rosinol".

ros·in·weed (rózzin-weed) *n.* Any of several North American plants of the genus *Silphium* and related genera, having a resinous juice; especially, the compass plant of central North America, which has yellow flowers and lower leaves that tend to align in a north-south plane.

Ros·kil·de (*Danish* róskilə). Town of east Zealand, Denmark. Situated on the Roskilde Fjord, it was the Danish capital until 1443, and its cathedral (begun in the 12th century) has many royal tombs.

RoS·PA (róspə). Royal Society for the Prevention of Accidents (in Britain).

Ross (ross ‖ rawss), **Sir James Clark** (1800–62). British polar explorer. Having entered the navy he explored the Arctic with his uncle, Sir John Ross (1777–1856), discovering the north magnetic pole in 1831. On a voyage to the Antarctic (1839–43) he discovered the sea later named after him.

Ross and Crom·ar·ty (krómmərti). Former county of northern Scotland. It included Lewis in the outer Hebrides, which became part of the Western Isles (1975), and a part of the mainland which was absorbed into the Highland Region (1975), which became the Highland Unitary Authority area (1996).

Rosse (ross ‖ rawss), **William Parsons, 3rd Earl of** (1800–67). Irish astronomer. He developed one of the first large-scale reflecting telescopes. Its 183-centimetre (72-inch) reflector was in operation by 1845, and with it he pioneered the study of nebulae.

Ros·sel·li·ni (róss-i-léeni, -e-), **Roberto** (1906–77). Italian film director. With de Sica he pioneered the neorealist school of cinema, characterised by informal camera technique and concern with the underprivileged. His films include *Rome, Open City* (1945), describing conditions in Rome under the German occupation.

Ros·set·ti (rə-zétti, rō-, -sétti), **Christina (Georgina)** (1830–94). British poet, the sister of Dante Gabriel Rossetti. Her first publication, *Goblin Market and Other Poems,* appeared in 1862 and a posthumous volume, *New Poems,* in 1896.

Rossetti, Dante Gabriel (1828-82). British painter and poet. He was a leading member of the Pre-Raphaelite Brotherhood which he helped to found (1848) with Millais and Holman Hunt. His paintings include many portraits of Elizabeth Siddal, whom he married in 1860 and who died two years later of an overdose of laudanum. He buried the manuscripts of many early poems in his wife's coffin, but later disinterred them, and published them as *Poems* (1870).

Ross Ice Shelf. A mass of floating ice, the largest in the world, situated at the head of the Ross Sea on the Pacific coastline of Antarctica. Its estimated size ranges from 496 000-540 000 square kilometres (192,000-208,000 square miles).

Ros·si·ni (ro-séeni, rə-), **Gioacchino Antonio** (1792–1868). Italian composer. He established his reputation with a series of 36 operas, all written in the space of 19 years. They include *Tancredi* (1813), *The Barber of Seville* (1816), and *William Tell* (1829).

Ross Island. Island in the Ross Sea, Antarctica. It is the site of Mount Terror, and the active volcano Mount Erebus.

Ross Sea. Area of the South Pacific Ocean lying east of Victoria Land, Antarctica.

Ros·tand (ro-stón), **Edmond** (1868–1918). French playwright. He is chiefly remembered for the verse drama *Cyrano de Bergerac* (1897), a chivalric comedy based loosely on the 17th-century French writer and adventurer of that name.

ros·tel·late (róstə-layt, ross-téllayt) *adj.* Having a rostellum. [New Latin *rostellatus,* from ROSTELLUM.]

ros·tel·lum (ross-télləm) *n., pl.* **-tella** (-téllə). *Biology.* A small, beaklike part, such as a projection on the stigma of an orchid, a tubular mouth part on some insects, or the hooked projection on the head of a tapeworm. [New Latin, from Latin, diminutive of *rostrum,* beak, ROSTRUM.] —**ros·tel·lar** *adj.*

ros·ter (róstər) *n.* A plan or list showing the order in which each member of an organisation, military unit, or other group becomes liable for a particular duty.
~*tr.v.* **rostered, -tering, -ters.** To place on a roster. [Dutch *rooster,* gridiron, list (on a ruled sheet), from Middle Dutch, gridiron, from *roosten,* to roast, from *roost,* gridiron, from Germanic *raust* (unattested). See roast.]

Ros·tock (róss-tok). Baltic industrial port of Germany. Situated on the estuary of the river Warnow 18 kilometres (11 miles) from the Baltic Sea, it was an important member of the Hanseatic League (14th century) and has many medieval remains.

Ros·tov-na-Do·nu (rəstóf-nə-dənŏŏ). *English* **Rostov-on-Don.** Industrial port in southeast Russia. It lies on the river Don near the Sea of Azov, and is also a cultural and scientific centre.

Ros·tro·po·vich (róstrə-pŏvish; *Russian* rəstra-), **Mstislav (Leopoldovich)** (1927–). Russian cellist, noted for his outstanding range of tone. He travelled widely in the West from 1947 and had works written for him by Khachaturian, Prokofiev, Shostakovich, and Britten. In 1975 he left the U.S.S.R. He was musical director of the National Symphony Orchestra in Washington, D.C. (1977–94).

ros·trum (róss-trəm) *n., pl.* **-trums** or **-tra** (-trə) (the only form for sense 2). 1. A dais, platform, or similar raised place used, for example, by public speakers or conductors. 2. *Often plural.* In ancient Rome, the speakers' platform in the Forum, which was decorated with the prows of captured enemy ships. 3. A stable but adjustable structure supporting a cinecamera or television camera and the object it is trained on, so that the relative positions of camera and object can be controlled. Also used adjectivally: *rostrum camera.* 4. *Biology.* A beaklike or snoutlike projection. [Latin, beak, ship's prow.] —**ros·tral** (-trəl) *adj.* —**ros·trate** (-trayt) *adj.*

ros·y (rózi) *adj.* **-ier, -iest.** 1. Having the characteristic pink or red colour of a rose. 2. Flushed with a healthy glow. 3. Optimistic or giving cause for optimism. —**ros·i·ly** *adv.* —**ros·i·ness** *n.*

rosy pastor *n.* A bird, the **pastor** *(see).*

rot¹ (rot) *v.* **rotted, rotting, rots.** —*intr.* 1. To undergo decomposition, especially organic decomposition; decay. 2. To disappear or fall by decaying. Used with *off* or *away.* 3. To undergo moral or intellectual decay; become decadent or degenerate. 4. To waste away, as from neglect or inactivity. —*tr.* To cause to decompose, deteriorate, or decay. —See Synonyms at **decay.**
~*n.* 1. The process of rotting or the condition of being rotten. 2. A condition of degeneration or decline: *brought in a new director in an attempt to stop the rot.* 3. **Foot rot** *(see).* 4. Any of several plant diseases characterised by the breakdown of tissue, and caused by various bacteria, fungi, or other microorganisms. See **dry rot, wet rot.** 5. *Medicine. Archaic.* Any disease causing the decay of flesh. 6. *Informal.* Foolish talk; nonsense.
~*interj.* Used to express contempt or impatience, especially in reaction to foolish talk. [Middle English *roten, rotyen,* Old English *rotian,* from Germanic *rutjan* (unattested).]

rot². Variant of **ret.**

rot. rotating; rotation.

ro·ta (rótə) *n., pl.* **-tas.** 1. *Chiefly British.* A roster, especially one regulating unofficial activities: *a rota for driving the children to school.* 2. *Capital R.* The supreme court of the Roman Catholic Church, called in full the Sacred Roman Rota and functioning as a court of final appeal, especially in cases regarding the dissolution of marriages. [Latin, wheel.]

Ro·tar·i·an (rō-taír-i-ən) *n.* A member of a Rotary Club.

ro·ta·ry (rótəri) *adj.* 1. Of, pertaining to, causing, or characterised by rotation, especially rotation round an axis. 2. Operating by means of a rotary part or parts: *a rotary mower.*
~*n., pl.* **rotaries.** 1. A part or device that rotates round an axis. 2. *U.S.* A traffic roundabout. [Medieval Latin *rotārius,* from Latin *rota,* wheel.]

Rotary Club *n.* Any club belonging to *Rotary International,* an organisation pledged to give service to the community.

rotary engine *n.* An engine, such as a turbine, in which power is supplied directly to vanes or other rotary parts.

rotary harrow *n.* A harrow, consisting of a series of freely turning wheels rimmed with spikes. Also called "rotary hoe".

rotary plough *n.* A plough having a series of hoes arranged on a revolving power-driven shaft. Also called "rotary tiller".

rotary press *n.* A printing press having a cylinder to which curved plates are attached so that, when revolving, they will print onto a continuous roll of paper.

ro·tate (rō-tayt, rə- ‖ *chiefly U.S.* rṓ-tayt) *v.* **-tated, -tating, -tates.** —*intr.* 1. To turn or spin on an axis. 2. To proceed in sequence; alternate. —*tr.* 1. To cause to rotate. 2. To plant or grow (crops) in a fixed order of succession. 3. To perform in a fixed order of succession; alternate. —See Synonyms at **turn.**
~*adj. Botany.* Having radiating parts; wheel-shaped. [Latin *rotāre,* to revolve, from *rota,* wheel.] —**ro·tat·a·ble** *adj.*

ro·ta·tion (rō-táysh'n, rə-) *n. Abbr.* **rot.** 1. Motion in which the path of every point in the moving object is a circle or circular arc centred on a specific axis, especially on an internal axis: *the axial rotation of the earth.* 2. A single complete cycle of such motion; a revolution.

3. *Geometry.* A coordinate transformation consisting of an angular displacement, or successive angular displacements, of coordinate axes with the origin remaining fixed. **4. a.** A regularly recurring sequence: *The chairmanship goes to each member in strict rotation.* **b.** The use or application of a planned sequence, as in the growing of crops. —**ro·ta·tion·al** *adj.*

ro·ta·tive (rṓtətiv, rō-táytiv) *adj.* **1.** Of, pertaining to, causing, or characterised by rotation. **2.** Characterised by or occurring in alternation or succession. —**ro·ta·tive·ly** *adv.*

ro·ta·tor (rṓtətər) *n.* **1.** One that rotates. **2.** Any of several muscles that effect rotation of a part of the body.

ro·ta·to·ry (rṓtə-tri, -təri, rō-táytəri) *adj.* **1.** Of, pertaining to, causing, or characterised by rotation. **2.** Occurring or proceeding in alternation or succession.

Ro·ta·va·tor (rṓtə-vaytər) *n. British.* A trademark for a motor-driven machine with rotating blades, used for breaking up and turning over soil in preparation for cultivation. —**ro·ta·vate** (-vayt) *tr.v.*

rote¹ (rōt) *n.* **1.** Memorisation by means of repetition and with little or no comprehension: *learn by rote.* **2.** Mechanical routine; unthinking repetition. [Middle English *rote†.*]

rote² *n.* A medieval stringed instrument. [Middle English, from Old French, from Germanic.]

ro·te·none (rṓti-nōn) *n.* A white crystalline compound, $C_{23}H_{22}O_6$, extracted from the roots of derris and cubé, and used as an insecticide. [Japanese *rōten*, derris plant + -ONE.]

rot·gut (rót-gut) *n. Slang.* Alcoholic drink of a very inferior kind.

Roth·er·ham (rṓthərəm). Town near Sheffield, northern England. Situated on the river Don in a coalmining area, its industries include iron and steel, brass, glassware, pottery, and machinery.

Roth·er·mere (rṓthər-meer), **Harold Sydney Harmsworth, 1st Viscount** (1868–1940). British newspaper magnate and politician. The younger brother of Lord Northcliffe, he assisted in the founding and purchase of several papers, and was Air Minister (1917–18). He acquired the *Daily Mirror* (1914) from his brother, and bought the *Daily Mail* (1922) on Northcliffe's death.

Rothe·say (rṓth-si, -say). Port and capital of the Isle of Bute, west Scotland. It is a tourist centre and fishing town.

Roth·ko (rṓth-kō), **Mark**, born Marcus Rothkovitch (1903–1970). In the late 1940s and early 1950s he produced a series of large, abstract canvasses employing horizontal bands of colour with blurred edges. *Number 10* (1950) is characteristic of his style.

Roth·schild (rṓth-chīld, róss-, rṓths-). A banking family of German Jewish origin. The Rothschild bank was founded at Frankfurt by Mayer Amschel Rothschild (1743–1812). His eldest son took over the Frankfurt business, and four younger sons set up branches in Vienna, London, Naples and Paris. All of the founding members were created Austrian barons, and the family won international fame by negotiating major loans to European governments.

ro·ti (rṓti) *n.* A flat, usually circular, piece of unleavened bread, similar to a chapatti. [Hindi, bread.]

ro·ti·fer (rṓtifər) *n.* Any of various minute, multicellular aquatic organisms of the phylum Rotifera, having at the anterior end a wheel-like ring of cilia used for feeding and locomotion. Also called "wheel animalcule". [New Latin *Rotifera* : Latin *rota*, wheel (see **rotate**) + -FER.] —**ro·tif·er·al** (rō-tíffərəl), **ro·tif·er·ous** (rō-tíffərəss) *adj.*

ro·tis·se·rie (rō-tíssəri) *n.* **1.** A cooking device equipped with a rotating spit on which meat or other food is roasted. **2.** A shop or restaurant specialising in meats roasted in this way. [French *rôtisserie*, from Old French *rostisserie*, from *rostir* (present stem *rostiss-*), to ROAST.]

rot·l (rótt'l) *n.* Any of various units of weight used in countries bordering on the eastern Mediterranean, varying in amount from about half a kilogram to two and a half kilograms (one to five pounds). [Arabic *raṭl, riṭl*, perhaps altered by metathesis from Greek *litra.* See **litre**.]

ro·to·gra·vure (rṓt-ō-grə-véwr, -ə-) *n.* **1.** An intaglio printing process in which letters and pictures are transferred from an etched copper cylinder to a web of paper, plastic, or similar material in a rotary press. **2.** Printed material, such as a newspaper section, produced by this process. [Latin *rota*, wheel + GRAVURE.]

ro·tor (rṓtər) *n.* **1.** A rotating part of a mechanical device; especially, the moving part of an electric motor or generator. Compare **stator.** **2.** An assembly of rotating horizontal aerofoils, such as that of a helicopter. **3.** The rotating part of the distributor in an internal-combustion engine. In this sense, also called "rotor arm". [Short for ROTATOR.]

rotor ship *n.* A ship propelled by one or more tall cylindrical rotors operated by wind power.

Ro·to·ru·a (rṓtə-rṓo-ə). City of central North Island, New Zealand. It is a spa resort situated on a picturesque volcanic plateau in a region of mudpools, hot springs, lakes, and active volcanoes.

rot·ten (rótt'n) *adj.* **-tener, -tenest. 1.** In a state of putrefaction or decay; decomposed. **2.** Having a foul odour resulting from or suggestive of decay; putrid. **3.** Made weak or unsound by rot. **4.** Morally corrupt or despicable. **5.** *Informal.* Very bad; wretched, as by being: **a.** Disagreeable; unpleasant: *had a rotten time.* **b.** Unkind: *a rotten thing to do.* **c.** Unwell. **d.** Ashamed: *felt a bit rotten about letting them down.* **e.** Inferior; of a poor standard: *a rotten actor.* [Middle English *roten, rotin,* from Old Norse *rotinn,* from Germanic *ruteno-* (unattested), akin to *rutjan* (unattested), to ROT.] —**rot·ten·ly** *adv.* —**rot·ten·ness** *n.*

rotten borough *n.* In England prior to the Parliamentary reform of

1832, a constituency entitled to send a representative to Parliament despite having hardly any voters. Compare **pocket borough.**

rot·ten·stone (rótt'n-stōn) *n.* A friable variety of tripoli, the product of decomposed siliceous limestone, used for polishing.

rot·ter (róttər) *n. Chiefly British Informal.* An objectionable or despicable person. [ROT + -ER.]

Rot·ter·dam (róttər-dam, -dám). Seaport and industrial city of South Holland province, Netherlands. It lies on the Nieuwe Maas river near its mouth on the North Sea, and is a major world port, and the heart of the largest conurbation in the Netherlands. The city's inner port is connected to the Hook of Holland, its outer port, by the New Waterway (constructed 1866–90). Adjoining Europoort, built in the 1960s, handles mostly petroleum. Rotterdam is also the main seaport for the heavily industrialised Ruhr district of West Germany. The city's industries include shipbuilding, petrochemicals, engineering, paper, and foodstuffs.

Rott·wei·ler (rót-wīlər, -vīlər) *n.* A dog of an ancient German breed, having a stocky body, a short black coat, and tan face markings, and able to serve as a watchdog. [Originally bred in *Rottweil*, town in southwestern Germany.]

ro·tund (rō-túnd, rə- ‖ rṓ-tund) *adj.* **1.** Rounded; plump. **2.** Sonorous in delivery or grandiloquent in style. —See Synonyms at **fat.** [Latin *rotundus*, round.] —**ro·tund·ly** *adv.* —**ro·tund·i·ty** (rō-túndəti, rə-), **ro·tund·ness** *n.*

ro·tun·da (rō-túndə, rə-) *n.* A circular building, hall, or room, especially one with a dome. [Italian *rotonda*, from Latin *rotunda*, feminine of *rotundus*, round.]

ro·tu·ri·er (rō-téwr-i-ay ‖ -tóor-) *n.* A person of low rank; a commoner. [French, from Old French, from *roture*, newly broken land, obligation to a lord for land, hence, a commoner, from Vulgar Latin *ruptūra*, from Latin, a RUPTURE.]

Rou·ault (rṓo-ō), **Georges (Henri)** (1871–1958). French artist. Apprenticed to a glazier in his youth, he worked on stained glass windows and retained as an artist a fondness for flat areas of luminous colour enclosed by strong, dark outlines. His works include *The Clown* (1905) and a series of 60 prints *Miserere* (1916–27).

Rou·bil·lac (rṓo-bee-yak, -yák), **Louis François** (1695–1762). French sculptor who worked chiefly in England. His works include several statues in Westminster Abbey. His statue of Handel stands in Poets' Corner.

rou·ble, ru·ble (rṓob'l) *n. Abbr.* **r., R. 1.** The basic monetary unit of the former U.S.S.R., equal to 100 kopecks. **2.** A coin or note worth one rouble. [Russian *rubl'*, "silver bar", from Old Russian, "bar", "block", from *rubiti*, to cut up, build, from Balto-Slavic *romb-* (unattested).]

rouche. Variant of **ruche.**

rou·é (rṓo-ay ‖ U.S. rṓo-áy) *n.* A debauched and dissipated man; a profligate. [French, "broken on the wheel", completely tired, from the past participle of *rouer*, to break on the wheel, from Medieval Latin *rotāre*, to turn, from Latin, to ROTATE.]

Rou·en (rṓo-oN; *French* rwoN). Capital of the Seine-Maritime département, northern France. Situated on the river Seine, it is a port handling trade for Paris. It is also a cultural and industrial centre, and a centre for the wine trade. Once the capital of Normandy, it was held by England between 1419 and 1449. It has fine Gothic architecture, including a cathedral (12th-15th century).

rouge (rṓozh) *n.* **1.** A red or pink cosmetic for colouring the cheeks. **2.** A form of iron oxide, **jeweller's rouge** (*see*). ~*v.* **rouged, rouging, rouges.** —*tr.* To put rouge on; colour with rouge. —*intr.* To use rouge as a cosmetic. [French, from Old French, red, from Latin *rubeus*.]

rouge et noir (rṓozh ay nwár) *n.* A gambling card game played at a table marked with two red and two black diamond-shaped spots, on which bets are placed. Also called "trente et quarante". [French, "red and black".]

rough (ruf) *adj.* **rougher, roughest. 1.** Having an uneven surface; full of bumps, ridges, or other irregularities; not smooth. **2.** Rugged, uneven, or uncultivated. Said of land. **3.** Coarse, shaggy, or uneven in texture: *a rough bearskin.* **4.** Characterised by violent motion; turbulent; agitated: *rough waters.* **5.** Severely inclement; stormy; tempestuous: *rough weather.* **6.** Characterised by rowdy, unruly, or boisterous behaviour: *a rough neighbourhood.* **7. a.** Marked by lack of care, gentleness, or consideration; harsh or brutal: *rough treatment.* **b.** Lacking amenities or comforts: *a rough hotel.* **8.** Lacking refinement; uncouth; unmannerly. **9. a.** Produced, performed, or dispensed without attention to precision, elaboration, or completeness: *a rough translation; rough justice.* **b.** Tentative or approximate: *a rough idea of the cost.* **c.** Used in doing work of a preliminary kind: *rough paper.* **d.** *Informal.* Of low quality; substandard. **10.** Harsh to the ear. **11.** Harsh or sharp to the taste: *a rough wine.* **12.** In a natural state: *rough diamonds.* **13.** Requiring physical strength rather than intelligence; unskilled: *rough work.* **14.** *Informal.* Difficult, unpleasant, or unfair. **15.** *Informal.* Unwell: *feeling a bit rough.*

~*n.* **1.** Uneven or overgrown ground. **2.** The part of a golf course left unmown and uncultivated, as distinguished from the fairway and the greens. **3.** A rough, disagreeable, or difficult aspect or condition: *take the rough with the smooth.* **4.** Something in an unfinished or hastily worked-out state. **5.** A rough, unruly, or violent person; a hooligan. —**in the rough.** In a crude or unfinished state.

~*tr.v.* **roughed, roughing, roughs. 1.** To make rough; roughen. **2.** To subject to rough treatment or physical violence. Used with *up.* **3.** To prepare or indicate in a rough or unfinished form: *rough in the*

illustrations for a book. **—rough it.** To get along without the usual comforts: *rough it on a camping trip.*
~adv. In a rough manner; roughly: *slept rough.* [Middle English *ruch, r(o)wgh,* Old English *rūh.*] **—rough·er** *n.* **—rough·ly** *adv.* **—rough·ness** *n.*
Synonyms: *rough, jagged, rugged, scabrous, uneven.*
rough·age (rúffij) *n.* **1.** Any rough or coarse material. **2.** The relatively coarse, indigestible parts of certain foods and fodder that contain cellulose and stimulate peristalsis; dietary fibre.
rough-and-read·y (rúf-ən-réddi, -ənd-) *adj.* Rough or crude but effective or usable.
rough-and-tum·ble (rúf-ən-túmb'l, -ənd-) *adj.* Characterised by roughness and disregard for order or rules.
~n. **1.** A disorderly scuffle. **2.** A rough-and-tumble quality: *enjoyed the rough-and-tumble of a game of rugger.*
rough breathing *n.* **1.** An aspirate sound in ancient Greek like that of the letter *h* in English. **2. a.** The mark (ʽ) placed over initial sounds in Greek to indicate a preceding aspirate. **b.** This mark in Modern Greek as an orthographic feature.
rough·cast (rúf-kaast || -kast) *n.* **1.** A coarse plaster used for outside wall surfaces. Also called "slapdash". **2.** A rough, preliminary model or form.
~tr.v. **roughcast, -casting, -casts. 1.** To plaster (a wall, for example) with roughcast. **2.** To shape or work into a rough or preliminary form. **—rough·cast·er** *n.*
rough diamond *n.* A coarse-mannered but basically decent and likable person.
rough·dry (rúf-drī) *tr.v.* **-dried, -drying, -dries.** To dry (something laundered) without ironing or smoothing out.
~adj. Laundered but not ironed.
rough·en (rúff'n) *v.* **-ened, -ening, -ens.** *—tr.* To make rough. *—intr.* To become rough.
rough·hew (rúf-héw) *tr.v.* **-hewed** or **-hewn** (-héwn), **-hewing, -hews. 1.** To hew or shape (timber or stone, for example) roughly, without finishing. **2.** To make in rough form; roughcast.
rough·house (rúf-howss) *n.* Rowdy, uproarious play or behaviour.
~v. **roughhoused, -housing, -houses.** *—intr.* To engage in boisterous or rowdy activity. *—tr.* To handle or treat roughly, usually in fun.
rough-leg·ged buzzard (rúf-leggid, -legd) *n.* A buzzard, *Buteo lagopus,* having dark plumage and whitish feathers covering the legs.
rough·neck (rúf-nek) *n.* **1.** A rough, pugnacious man. **2.** *Chiefly U.S.* A worker on an oil rig.
rough·shod (rúf-shod) *adj.* Shod with horseshoes having projecting nails or points to prevent slipping.
rough trade *n. Slang.* Men of aggressively masculine but unpolished appearance considered as potential sexual partners.
roul. *Philately.* roulette.
rou·lade (rōō-laád) *n.* **1.** A musical embellishment consisting of a rapid run of several notes sung to one syllable. **2.** A slice of meat rolled around a filling and cooked. [French, "a rolling", from *rouler,* to roll, from Old French *roller,* to ROLL.]
rou·leau (rōō-lō, rōō-lō) *n., pl.* **-leaux** (-z) or **-leaus. 1.** A small roll, especially of coins wrapped in paper. **2.** A roll or fold of ribbon used for piping. [French, from Old French *rolel,* diminutive of *rol(l)e,* a roll, from Latin *rotulus,* small wheel. See **roll.**]
rou·lette (rōō-lét, rōō-) *n.* **1.** A gambling game played with a shallow bowl enclosing a rotating disc, that has numbered slots alternately coloured red and black, the players betting on which slot, or which colour, a small ball will come to rest in. **2.** A small, toothed disc of tempered steel attached to a handle and used to make rows of dots, slits, or perforations, as in engraving or on a sheet of postage stamps. **3.** *Abbr.* **roul.** In stamp-collecting, any of the short consecutive incisions made between individual stamps in a sheet for easy separation. Compare **perforation. 4.** *Geometry.* A curve, such as a cycloid or epicycloid, that is generated by the motion of a point on one curve as it rolls along another.
~tr.v. **rouletted, -letting, -lettes.** To mark or divide with a roulette. [French, from Old French, from *rouelle,* from Late Latin *rotella,* diminutive of Latin *rota,* a wheel.]
Roumania. See **Romania.**
Roumelia. See **Rumelia.**
round[1] (rownd || *West Indies also* rungd) *adj. Abbr.* **rd. 1.** Spherical; globular; ball-shaped. **2.** Circular, or circular in cross-section. **3. a.** Having a curved edge or surface; not flat or angular: *a round arch.* **b.** Full; plump: *round cheeks.* **4.** Formed or articulated with the lips assuming an oval shape: *a round vowel.* **5.** Whole or complete; full; entire: *a round dozen.* **6. a.** Expressed or designated as a whole number or integer; not fractional; integral. **b.** Adjusted so as to express an exact number in an approximate, more convenient form: *That's a thousand pounds in round figures.* **c.** Approximate; rough; not exact: *a round estimate.* **7.** Large; ample; considerable: *a round sum.* **8. a.** Fully characterised or drawn; substantial; developed: *the novel lacks round characters.* **b.** Brought to a satisfying perfection; finished: *a round, polished writing style.* **9. a.** Sonorous; full in tone. **b.** Full-bodied; satisfying: *a round taste.* **10.** Brisk; rapid; smart: *a round pace.* **11.** Outspoken; candid; blunt. **12.** Made with full force; unrestrained: *a round thrashing.*
~n. **1.** The state of being round. **2.** Something round, as a circle, disc, globe, or ring; a curved or rounded form or part. **3.** A rung or crossbar, as on a ladder or chair. **4.** The part of the thigh on a beef animal between the rump and shank, considered as a joint of meat. **5.** A distinct set, group, or session: *a round of negotiations.* **6.** Movement around a circle, or about an axis. **7.** A round dance. **8.** A complete course, succession, or series, often ending at the starting point: *a round of parties.* **9.** *Often plural.* **a.** A course of customary or prescribed actions, duties, or places: *the daily round; a sentry's rounds.* **b.** A set of calls or visits for a particular purpose: *a doctor's round; delivery rounds.* **10.** A complete range or extent. **11. a.** Drinks for a group of people, bought at one time: *I'll buy a round.* **b.** One's turn to buy these drinks: *It's my round.* **12.** A single outburst of applause or cheering. **13. a.** A single shot or volley from a gun or guns. **b.** Ammunition for a single shot. **14. a.** A whole slice of bread. **b.** A sandwich made with two whole slices of bread. **15.** *Archery.* A specified number of arrows shot from a specified distance to a target. **16. a.** An interval of play in various games and sports that occupies a specific time, comprises a certain number of plays, or allows each player a turn. **b.** A stage or set of games, as in a knockout competition. **c.** A playing of all the holes in golf. **17.** *Music.* A short, rhythmical canon in which each part enters in unison at equal time intervals. **—go the rounds.** To be widely circulated. Used of news. **—in the round. 1.** With the stage in the centre of the audience: *theatre in the round.* **2.** Not attached to a background; freestanding. Said of sculpture.
~v. **rounded, rounding, rounds.** *—tr.* **1.** To make round. **2.** To pronounce with rounded lips; labialise. **3.** To lessen in angularity; fill out; make plump. **4.** To bring to completion or perfection; finish. **5.** To make a complete circuit of; go or pass around. **6.** To make a turn about or to the other side of: *rounded a bend in the road.* **7.** To encompass; surround. **8.** To move or cause to proceed in a circular course. **9.** To bring (a number) to the nearest whole or round number. Used with *up* or *down*: *Round it up to the nearest £100.* *—intr.* **1.** To become round. **2.** To take a circular course; complete or partially complete a circuit. **3.** To turn about, as on an axis; reverse. **4.** To become curved, filled out, or plump. Often used with *out.* **—round off. 1.** To express (a number) approximately, or only to a specified number of decimals. **2.** To bring or come to completion or perfection: *round off the meal.* **—round on.** To attack suddenly; turn on angrily.
~adv. **1.** On or to all sides or in all directions: *pass the word round.* **2.** In a circle or circular motion: *spinning round.* **3.** In a cycle or cyclic motion: *Payday comes round soon.* **4.** Taking a particular, often circuitous, route: *Go round by the pond and see the ducks.* **5.** In or towards the opposite direction, position, or attitude: *switch them round; turn round.* **6.** Measuring in circumference: *one metre round.* **7.** From one place to another; here and there: *wander round.* **8.** To each member of a group; to every one of a set: *enough to go round.* **9.** To a specific place or area, such as one's home: *when you come round again.* **10.** To a normal or desired state: *He'll come round eventually.* **—get round to.** To find time or occasion to give one's attention to. See Usage note at **around.**
~prep. **1.** On all sides of. **2.** So as to enclose, surround, or envelop. **3.** About the circumference or periphery of; encircling. **4.** About the central point of: *the Earth's motion round the Sun.* **5.** In or to various places within, from, or near: *drive round the town; the countryside round Brighton.* **6.** On or to the farther side of: *the house round the corner.* **7.** In the area of; near: *Do you live round here?* **8.** From the beginning to the end of; throughout: *a plant that grows round the year.* **—round about.** Approximately at or equal to: *round about 5.30; round about £5.* See Usage note at **about.** [Middle English, from Old French *ronde,* from Latin *rotundus.*] **—round·ness** *n.*
round[2] *tr.v.* **rounded, rounding, rounds.** *Archaic.* To say in a whisper. [Middle English *r(o)unen,* Old English *rūnian.*]
round·a·bout (równd-ə-bowt) *n.* **1.** *British.* A circular one-way road round a central island at the junction of three or more roads, around which traffic flows to move from one road to another. Also *U.S.* "traffic circle", "rotary". **2.** A **merry-go-round** *(see).*
~adj. Indirect; oblique; circuitous: *in a roundabout way.*
round angle *n.* An angle of 360°.
round-arm (równd-aarm) *adj.* **1.** In cricket, designating a now illegal form of bowling, with the arm swung horizontally or not going much higher than the shoulder. **2.** Performed with a circular, horizontal swing of the arm: *a round-arm blow.* **—round-arm** *adv.*
round bracket *n. British.* A **parenthesis** *(see).*
round dance *n.* **1.** A folk dance performed with the dancers arranged in a circle. **2.** A ballroom dance performed with circular movements around the room. Also called "round".
round·ed (równdid) *adj.* **1.** Made round; shaped in a circle or sphere. **2.** Pronounced with the lips shaped ovally; labialised. **3.** Complete; balanced.
roun·del (równd'l) *n.* **1.** A curved form; especially: **a.** A semicircular panel, window, or recess. **b.** *Heraldry.* A circular design or symbol. **2.** In poetry: **a.** A **rondel** *(see).* **b.** A **rondeau** *(see).* **c.** An English variation of the rondeau, consisting of three triplets with a refrain after the first and third. [Middle English, from Old French *rondel,* "small circle", RONDEL.]
roun·de·lay (równdə-lay) *n.* **1.** A poem or song with a regularly recurring refrain. **2.** A dance in a circle; a round dance. [Old French *rondelet,* diminutive of *rondel,* ROUNDEL.]
round·er (równdər) *n.* **1.** One that rounds; specifically, a tool for rounding corners and edges. **2.** One who makes rounds, such as a watchman. **3.** A complete circuit, made without stopping, of all the bases in rounders.
round·ers (równdərz) *n.* *Used with a singular verb.* A ball game

played with a rounded bat or stick between two teams, usually of nine players, in which members of the batting side successively attempt to hit the ball and run round all the bases without stopping before the ball is retrieved, thus scoring rounders.

round game n. Any game in which players play individually, as opposed to in teams or with partners.

round hand n. A style of handwriting in which the letters are rounded and full, rather than angular.

Round-head (równd-hed) n. A member or supporter of the Parliamentary or Puritan party during the English Civil War (1642–49). Used as a term of derision by the Royalists in reference to the Puritans' close-cropped hair. Compare **Cavalier.**

round-house (równd-howss) n. 1. A circular building for housing and repairing locomotives, having radial tracks converging on a large turntable. 2. A cabin on the after part of the quarter-deck of a ship.

round-ish (równdish) adj. Rather round. —**round-ish-ness** n.

round-let (równd-lət, -lit) n. A little circle or a small circular object. [Middle English *roundelet,* from Old French *rondelet,* diminutive of *rondel,* small circle, RONDEL.]

round-ly (równdli) adv. 1. In the form of a circle or sphere. 2. In a forceful manner; bluntly; candidly. 3. Fully; thoroughly.

round robin n. 1. A petition or protest on which the signatures are arranged in the form of a circle in order to conceal the order of signing. 2. A letter sent among members of a group, often with comments added by each person in turn. 3. A tournament in which each contestant is matched against every other contestant.

round-shoul-dered (równd-shōldərd, -shōldərd) adj. Having the shoulders bent forward and drooping and the upper back rounded.

rounds-man (równdz-mən) n., pl. **-men** (-mən). One who makes rounds, such as a deliveryman.

Round Table n. 1. The table of King Arthur, made circular in order to avoid disputes about precedence among his knights. 2. King Arthur and his knights as a group. 3. An organisation of local associations of business and professional men who meet as a club and do charitable work. 4. *Small* **r,** *small* **t.** A conference or discussion with several participants all on an equal footing.

round-the-clock (równd-thə-klók, równ-) adj. Throughout the entire day and night; continuous. —**round the clock** adv.

round trip n. A trip from one place to another, and back again, often by a different route.

round up tr.v. 1. To seek out and bring together; gather. 2. To herd together for inspection, branding, or shipping.

round-up (równd-up) n. 1. **a.** The herding together of cattle for inspection, branding, or shipping. **b.** The cattle that are herded together. **c.** The cowboys and horses employed in such herding. 2. Any similar gathering up, as of persons under suspicion by the police. 3. A summing up; a summation; a résumé.

round-worm (równd-wurm) n. A **nematode** *(see).*

roup¹ (rōōp) n. An infectious disease of poultry and pigeons characterised by inflammation and discharge from the mouth and eyes. [16th century : origin obscure.]

roup² (rowp) n. *Chiefly Scottish.* A sale by auction. —*tr.v.* **rouped, rouping, roups.** To sell by auction. [Middle English *roupen,* to shout, from Scandinavian.]

rouse (rowz) v. **roused, rousing, rouses.** —*tr.* 1. To cause to come out of a state of slumber, complacency, apathy, or depression. 2. **a.** To excite, as to anger or action; spur. **b.** To provoke (an emotion): *roused her fury.* 3. To startle (game) from a covert or lair. —*intr.* 1. To awaken, as from sleep, repose, or unconsciousness. 2. To stir; become active. 3. To rise or start from cover, as game birds do. —See Synonyms at **provoke.** [Originally "to startle (game) from cover", Middle English *rowsen†,* to shake feathers or body.] —**rous-er** n.

Usage: **Rouse** and *arouse* are usually distinguishable. *Arouse* generally refers to an immediate and often brief response *(arouse interest, fear, criticism...);* *rouse* implies a deeper, stronger response *(rouse to anger, action...).*

rouse-a-bout (rówss-ə-bowt) n. *Australian & N.Z.* A person who works on a sheep station, especially during the shearing season; a farmhand. Also called "roustabout", informally "rousie", "rouser". [Variant of ROUSTABOUT.]

rous-ing (rówzing) adj. 1. Inducing enthusiasm or excitement; stirring: *a rousing sermon.* 2. Active; lively; vigorous: *a rousing march tune.* —**rous-ing-ly** adv.

Rous sarcoma (rowss) n. A malignant tumour that can be produced on chickens by inoculation with the specific viral causative agent *(Rous sarcoma virus).* [After Francis Peyton *Rous* (1879–1970), U.S. pathologist.]

Rous-seau (rōō-sō; *French* rōō-sô), **Henri,** also known as Le Douanier (the customs official) (1844–1910). French primitive painter. A collector of tolls, he retired at 41 to take up painting full time. His early work was mocked for its naive style and apparently inept draughtsmanship. However a few artists, including Picasso, were impressed by his work. His paintings include the apocalyptic *War* (1894), jungle scenes such as *The Snake Charmer* (1907), and group portraits such as *The Cart of Père Juniet* (1908).

Rousseau, Jean-Jacques (1712–78). French philosopher, born in Geneva. Rousseau held that mankind is essentially good but corrupted by society, and his novel *The New Héloïse* (1761) proposed spiritual refreshment through a return to nature. In his major political work *On the Social Contract* (1762) he argued that individuals surrendered their natural rights to society and that these should

find expression through the general will.

Rousseau, Théodore (1812–67). French painter, a leading member of the Barbizon group. He sketched direct from nature, but usually reworked his canvasses before submitting them for exhibition. His many rural scenes, often muted in tone, include *Sortie de la Forêt de Fontainebleau* (1848).

roust (rowst) tr.v. **rousted, rousting, rousts.** To force or drive out, especially out of bed. [Alteration of ROUSE.]

roust-a-bout (równst-ə-bowt) n. 1. A general labourer on an oil installation. 2. *U.S.* An unskilled labourer. 3. *Australian & N.Z.* A rouseabout. [ROUST + ABOUT.]

rout¹ (rowt) n. 1. A disorderly retreat or flight following defeat. 2. An overwhelming defeat. 3. A disorderly crowd of persons; a boisterous mob; a rabble. 4. A public disturbance; a riot. 5. *Archaic.* A company of people or animals, especially of knights or wolves. 6. *Archaic.* A large evening party. —*tr.v.* **routed, routing, routs.** 1. To put to disorderly flight or retreat. 2. To defeat overwhelmingly. —See Synonyms at **defeat.** [Middle English *route,* troop, disorderly crowd (influenced by French *deroute,* defeat), from Old French, dispersed group, troop, from Vulgar Latin *rupta* (unattested), from Latin *rumpere* (past participle *ruptus),* to break.]

rout² v. **routed, routing, routs.** —*intr.* 1. To dig for food with the snout; root. 2. To search; poke around; rummage. —*tr.* 1. To dig up with the snout. 2. To expose to view or uncover. 3. To hollow, scoop, or gouge out. 4. To fetch, force, or drive out after searching. Often used with *out.* 5. To cut grooves or shapes in (wood, metal, or the like). Often used with *out.* [Variant of ROOT (to dig up).]

route (rōōt; *militarily also* rowt ‖ rowt) n. *Abbr.* **rte.** 1. A road, course, or way for travel from one place to another. 2. A regular way taken from one place to another; a customary line of travel. 3. *Medicine.* The means by which a drug is introduced into the body: *the intravenous route.* —See Synonyms at **way.** —*tr.v.* **routed, routing, routes.** 1. To send along; forward. 2. To schedule or dispatch on a particular route: *The travel agency routed them to Paris by way of Luxembourg.* [Middle English, from Old French, from unattested Vulgar Latin *rupta (via),* "broken or beaten (way)". See rout (retreat).]

route-march, route march (rōōt-march) n. A long and hard march by soldiers in training. —**route-march** intr.v.

rout-er¹ (rōōtər ‖ rówtər) n. One that routes.

rout-er² (rówtər) n. One that routs; specifically, a machine tool for cutting grooves or shapes.

rou-tine (rōō-téen, rōō-) n. 1. A prescribed and detailed course of action to be followed regularly; a standard procedure. 2. A set of customary and often mechanically performed procedures or activities. 3. **a.** A particular sequence of dance steps. **b.** A set piece of entertainment, especially in a nightclub or theatre. 4. A computer program, or part of a program, for performing a particular task. —See Synonyms at **method.** —*adj.* 1. In accordance with established procedure. 2. Habitual; regular. 3. Lacking in interest or originality. [French, from Old French, from ROUTE (beaten path).] —**rou-tine-ly** adv. —**rou-tin-ism** n. —**rou-tin-ist** n.

rou-tin-ise, rou-tin-ize (rōō-téen-īz) tr.v. **-ised, -ising, -ises.** 1. To establish a routine for. 2. To reduce to a routine. —See Synonyms at **wander.** —**rou-tin-is-a-tion** (-ī-záysh'n ‖ *U.S.* -i-) n.

roux (rōō) n., pl. **roux** (rōōz, rōō). A mixture of flour and butter or other fat, heated together and used as a basis for many sauces. [French *(beurre) roux,* browned (butter), from *roux,* reddish brown, from Old French *rous,* from Latin *russus,* red.]

Roux (rōō), **(Paul) Emile** (1853–1933). French bacteriologist. He worked closely with Pasteur, helped produce a vaccine against anthrax and developed an antitoxin for diphtheria.

rove¹ (rōv) v. **roved, roving, roves.** —*intr.* 1. To wander about at random, especially over a wide area; roam. 2. To move or look around without settling: *his gaze roved around the room.* —*tr.* To roam or wander over or through. —See Synonyms at **wander.** —*n.* An act of roaming; a ramble. [Middle English *roven,* (in archery) to shoot at a random mark (sense influenced by ROVER, a pirate), probably from Scandinavian, akin to Icelandic *râfa,* to wander, loiter.]

rove² tr.v. **roved, roving, roves.** 1. To card (wool). 2. To stretch and twist (fibres), before spinning; ravel out. —*n.* A slightly twisted and extended fibre or sliver. [18th century : origin obscure.]

rove³. Alternative past tense and past participle of **reeve.**

rove⁴ n. A metal ring or small plate over which the end of a rivet is flattened. [Old Norse *ró.*]

rove beetle n. Any of numerous beetles of the family Staphylinidae, often found in decaying matter and having slender bodies and short wing covers. [Perhaps from ROVE (to wander about).]

rov-er¹ (rōvər) n. 1. One who roves; a wanderer; a nomad. 2. **a.** In croquet, a ball that has gone through all the hoops but has not hit the winning peg. **b.** A player of such a ball. 3. *Archery.* A mark selected by chance. 4. In Australian Rules football, a player who takes and clears the ball after a ruck. [Middle English, from *roven,* to shoot at a random mark. See rove (to wander about).]

rover² n. 1. A pirate. 2. A pirate vessel. [Middle English, from Middle Dutch *rôver,* robber, from *rôven,* to rob.]

rov-ing (rōving) adj. 1. Wandering or having a tendency to wander or roam. 2. Not limited to a specific area or sphere of activity: *a roving commission; a roving ambassador.*

row[1] (rō) *n.* **1. a.** A horizontal linear arrangement or array. **b.** A line of things or people placed or occurring side by side. **2.** A line of adjacent seats, as in a theatre, auditorium, or classroom. **3.** A street flanked by a continuous line of buildings on one or both sides. **4.** *Mathematics.* A horizontal line of quantities in a determinant or matrix. **—in a row.** In succession: *That's the third bill in a row.* [Middle English *raw, row,* Old English *rāw, rǣw.*]

row[2] (rō) *v.* **rowed, rowing, rows.** *—intr.* **1.** To propel a boat with or as if with oars. **2.** To race in rowing boats as a sport. *—tr.* **1.** To propel (a boat) with or as if with oars. **2.** To carry in or on a boat propelled by oars. **3.** To propel or convey in a manner resembling rowing. **4.** To employ (a specified number of oars or oarsmen). **5.** To pull (an oar) as part of a racing crew. **6.** To race against by rowing.
—n. **1.** An act of rowing. **2.** A trip or excursion in a rowing boat. [Middle English *rowen,* Old English *rōwan.*] **—row·er** *n.*

row[3] (row) *n.* **1.** A boisterous disturbance or quarrel; a brawl. **2.** Noise; clamour; uproar. **3.** A loud or strong protest; trouble. Used chiefly in the phrases *make a row* or *kick up a row.*
—intr.v. **rowed, rowing, rows.** To take part in a row. [18th century (slang) : origin obscure.]

R.O.W. **1.** right of way. **2.** Rights of Women.

row·an (rō-ən, row-) *n.* See **mountain ash.** [Of Scandinavian origin, akin to Old Norse *reynir.*]

row·dy (rowdi) *n., pl.* **-dies.** A rough, disorderly person.
—adj. **rowdier, -diest.** Disorderly; rough and noisy. [Probably from ROW (quarrel).] **—row·di·ly** *adv.* **—row·di·ness, row·dy·ism** *n.*

row·el (row-əl) *n.* **1.** A sharp-toothed wheel inserted into the end of the shank of a spur. **2.** A disc of leather or other material with a central hole, which is inserted beneath the skin of a horse in order to drain an abscess, for example.
—tr.v. **rowelled** or *U.S.* **roweled, -elling** or *U.S.* **-eling, -els.** To spur; urge with a rowel. [Middle English *rowelle,* from Old French *roele,* from Late Latin *rotella,* diminutive of Latin *rota,* a wheel.]

row·en (row-ən) *n.* A second crop of hay in a season; an aftermath. [Middle English *rewayn,* from Old Northern French, Old French *regain* : *re-,* again + *gain,* rowen, from *gaaignier,* to till, "to obtain food", "gain".]

row·ing boat (rō-ing) *n.* A small boat propelled by oars. Also *U.S.* "rowboat".

rowing machine *n.* An exercise apparatus resembling the bottom and sides of a rowing boat with oars and a sliding seat.

Row·land·son (rōlənd-s'n), **Thomas** (1756–1827). British caricaturist. He delighted particularly in satirising grossness and sensuality in crowded social scenes. His *Tour of Dr. Syntax* (1812–21) was especially popular, and he also illustrated works by Sterne, Smollett, Swift, and Goldsmith.

Row·ley (rōli), **William** (*c.* 1585–*c.* 1642). British playwright. Much of his best work was produced in collaboration with other dramatists, notably *The Changeling* (1622), written with Middleton.

row·lock (róllək, *also* rúllək *or as a spelling pronunciation* rō-lok) *n.* A device used as a fulcrum to hold an oar in place while rowing, usually a U-shaped metal hoop on a swivel fixed to the side of the boat. Also *U.S.* "oarlock".

Rowse (rowss), **A(lfred) L(eslie)** (1903–97). British historian and man of letters. He was especially known as a scholar of the Tudor period, which he has described in *The Elizabethan Renaissance* (1971–72) and other works.

Rox·burgh·shire (róks-brə-shər, -bərə-, -sheer ‖ -shīr). Former county of southern Scotland. Put into the Borders Region (1975), now Borders Unitary Authority area, it is largely hilly sheep pastureland.

Roy (roy) *n. Australian.* A young, trendy, middle-class man, typically portrayed as a middlebrow, sports-car-owning executive. Compare **Alf, ocker.** [From the name *Roy.*]

roy·al (róy-əl, royl) *adj. Abbr.* **R. 1.** Of or pertaining to a king, queen, or other monarch. **2.** Of the rank of a king or queen. **3.** Of, pertaining to, or designating the family of a monarch. **4.** Issued or performed by a monarch. **5.** Founded, chartered, or authorised by a monarch. **6.** Befitting a king; stately; majestic. **7.** Superior in size or quality. **8.** Magnificent; first-rate: *a royal welcome.*
—n. **1.** A sail set on the royal mast. **2.** A paper size, 20 by 25 inches for printing, 19 by 24 inches for writing. **3.** *Informal.* A member of a royal family. **4.** A stag having antlers with at least 12 branches. Also called "royal stag". [Middle English *roial,* from Old French, from Latin *rēgālis,* from *rēx* (stem *rēg-*), king.] **—roy·al·ly** *adv.*

Royal Academy (of Arts) *n. Abbr.* **R.A.** An art society founded in 1768 by George III to support and encourage the visual arts in Britain by instruction and the holding of exhibitions. The number of academicians is limited to 40.

Royal Air Force *n. Abbr.* **R.A.F.** The air force of the United Kingdom.

royal assent *n.* The consent given by a monarch to a parliamentary bill, after which it becomes an act.

royal blue *n.* Deep to strong blue. **—roy·al-blue** *adj.*

Royal British Legion. The official name for the British Legion (*see*).

Royal Canadian Mounted Police *n. Abbr.* **R.C.M.P..** The Canadian federal police force. Also called "Mounties".

Royal Commission *n.* A group of people formally commissioned by the monarch on the recommendation of the government to inquire into and report on issues, laws, institutions, and the like.

Royal Engineers *n.* The branch of the British army in charge of

military engineering works such as the building of fortifications and bridges.

royal fern *n.* A deep-rooted fern, *Osmunda regalis,* of worldwide distribution, having tall, upright fronds.

royal flush *n.* The highest hand attainable in poker, consisting of the five highest cards of one suit.

Royal Highness *n.* A title of or form of address for a member of a royal family. Used with *His, Her,* or *Your.*

royal icing *n.* A type of hard icing made from icing sugar and egg whites and used to decorate rich fruit cakes, such as wedding cakes.

Royal Institution (of Great Britain) *n. Abbr.* **R.I.** A British scientific society, founded in London in 1799 as a research centre.

roy·al·ist (róy-əl-ist) *n.* **1.** A supporter of a monarch or of the principle of monarchy. **2.** *Capital* **R.** An Englishman loyal to Charles I; a Cavalier. **3.** *Capital* **R.** A supporter of the House of Bourbon's claims to the French throne since the French Revolution. **4.** *Capital* **R.** A Colonial American loyal to British rule. **—roy·al·ist, roy·al·is·tic** (-ístik) *adj.* **—roy·al·ism** *n.*

royal jelly *n.* A nutritious substance secreted in the pharyngeal glands of worker bees, serving as food for the young larvae, and as the only food for those that develop into queen bees.

Royal Leamington Spa. See **Leamington Spa.**

Royal Marines *n.* A corps of troops serving on land, sea, or in the air, administered by the Royal Navy but having ranks corresponding to those of the army.

royal mast *n.* The small mast immediately above the topgallant mast.

Royal Navy *n. Abbr.* **R.N.** The navy of the United Kingdom.

royal palm *n.* Any of several palm trees of the genus *Roystonea,* mostly from the West Indies; especially, *R. regia,* having a tall, naked trunk surmounted by a large tuft of pinnate leaves.

royal penguin *n.* A crested penguin, *Eudyptes schlegeli,* having white cheeks and throat, found on Macquarie Island, off Tasmania.

royal poinciana *n.* A tropical and semitropical tree, *Delonix regia,* native to Madagascar, having clusters of large scarlet and yellow flowers and long pods. Also called "flamboyant".

Royal prerogative *n.* The special powers and rights belonging to a monarch. They include personal prerogatives, such as immunity from legal action, and political prerogatives (now exercised on the advice of the government), such as the dissolution of Parliament or the appointment of ministers.

royal purple *n.* A moderate or strong violet to deep purple or dark reddish purple. **—roy·al-pur·ple** *adj.*

Royal Society *n. Abbr.* **R.S.** The oldest and most prestigious British scientific society, incorporated by royal charter in 1662 by Charles II.

royal tennis *n.* **Real tennis** (*see*).

roy·al·ty (róy-əlti, róylti) *n., pl.* **-ties. 1. a.** A king, queen, or other person of royal lineage. **b.** Monarchs and their families collectively. **2.** The lineage or rank of a king or queen. **3.** The power, status, or authority of monarchs. **4.** Royal quality or bearing. **5.** A right or prerogative of the crown, as that of receiving a percentage of the proceeds from mines in the royal domain. **6. a.** The granting of a right by a sovereign to a business enterprise or individual to exploit natural resources. **b.** The payment for such a right. **7. a.** A share paid to an author or composer out of the proceeds resulting from the sale or performance of his work. **b.** A share in the proceeds paid to an inventor or proprietor for the right to use his invention or services.

Royce (royss), **Sir (Frederick) Henry** (1863–1933). British car designer and manufacturer. Working in Manchester, he founded the engineering firm of Royce Ltd (1884), later merging it with the company of Charles Rolls (1877–1910) to form Rolls-Royce Ltd (1906). Royce designed the first of the famous Silver Ghost cars in the same year. During World War I he designed aeroengines. The first transatlantic flight (1919) by Alcock and Brown was made in a plane with Rolls-Royce engines.

roz·zer (rózzər) *n. British Slang.* A policeman. [19th century : origin obscure.]

R.P., RP **1.** Received Pronunciation. **2.** Reformed Presbyterian. **3.** Regius Professor.

r.p.m. revolutions per minute.

R.P.M resale price maintenance.

r.p.s. revolutions per second.

rpt. report.

R.Q. respiratory quotient.

R.R. Right Reverend (title).

–rrhagia *n. comb. form. Pathology.* Indicates an abnormal or excessive flow or discharge; for example, **menorrhagia.** [New Latin, from Greek, from *rhēgnunai,* to burst forth.]

–rrhoea *n. comb. form.* Also *chiefly U.S.* **-rrhea.** *Pathology.* Indicates a flow or discharge; for example, **seborrhoea, amenorrhoea.** [Middle English *-ria,* from Late Latin *-rrhoea,* from Greek *-rrhoia,* from *rhoia,* a flowing, flux, from *rhein,* to flow.]

RR Lyrae variable *n. Astronomy.* A type of pulsating variable star characterised by periods that range from several hours to about one day and having absolute magnitudes close to 0.6.

rRNA *n.* **Ribosomal RNA** (*see*).

RRP retailers' recommended price.

R.S. Royal Society.

RSI repetitive strain injury.

R.S.F.S.R. Formerly, Russian Soviet Federative Socialist Republic.

RSJ *n.* A rolled-steel joist: a steel beam, usually an H- or I-beam, used in building construction.

R.S.M. 1. Regimental Sergeant-Major. 2. Royal Society of Medicine.

R.S.P.B. Royal Society for the Protection of Birds.

R.S.P.C.A. Royal Society for the Prevention of Cruelty to Animals.

R.S.V. Revised Standard Version (of the Bible).

R.S.V.P. répondez s'il vous plaît (English *please reply*).

rt. right.

rte. route.

Rt. Hon. Right Honourable (title).

Rt. Rev. Right Reverend (title).

Ru The symbol for the element ruthenium.

Ruanda-Urundi. See Rwanda, Burundi.

Ru·a·pe·hu, Mount (rōō-ə-páy-hōō). Intermittently active volcano and highest peak of North Island, New Zealand. Situated in Tongariro National Park, it is 2 797 metres (9,175 feet) high.

rub (rub) *v.* **rubbed, rubbing, rubs.** —*tr.* 1. To apply pressure and friction to (a surface), manually or mechanically. 2. To clean, polish, or manipulate by applying pressure and friction. 3. To apply firmly and with friction upon a surface. 4. To move (an object or objects) against another or each other repeatedly and with friction. 5. To cause to become worn, chafed, or irritated. 6. To remove or erase. Used with *out, off,* or *away.* —*intr.* 1. To exert pressure and friction on something. 2. To move along in contact with a surface; graze or scrape. 3. To become worn or chafed from friction. 4. To be removed by pressure and friction. Used with *off* or *out.* 5. In bowls, to be diverted or slowed down by unevenness on the green. Used of a bowl. —**rub along.** *Informal.* 1. To manage or proceed despite difficulties. 2. To maintain a reasonably friendly relationship. —**rub it in.** To remind someone repeatedly of some mistake, shortcoming, or failure. —**rub off.** To be communicated or transferred; be infectious: *Her enthusiasm rubbed off on me.* —**rub out.** *Slang.* To murder. —**rub up.** To refresh one's memory of. —**rub (someone) up the wrong way.** *Informal.* To arouse hostility or irritation in; antagonise.

—*n.* 1. An act of rubbing. 2. An unevenness on a surface. 3. Difficulty: "*Aye, there's the rub*" (Shakespeare). [Middle English *rubben*, perhaps from Middle Low German *rubben*†.]

Rub'al Kha·li (rōōb-al-kha'ali). Vast desert area in southern Saudi Arabia. The name is Arabic for "Empty Quarter".

ru·basse (rōō-báss, -bà'ass) *n.* A dark red variety of quartz containing iron oxide. [French *rubace*, from Old French *rubi, rubis,* RUBY.]

ru·ba·to (rōō-bà'atō, rōō-) *n., pl.* **-tos.** *Music.* Variation of tempo within a phrase or measure without altering its length.

—*adj.* Characterised by rubato. [Italian, *(tempo) rubato*, "stolen (time)", from the past participle of *rubare,* to rob, from Germanic.]

rub·ber[1] (rúbbər) *n.* 1. A light cream to dark amber, amorphous, elastic, solid polymer of isoprene, $(C_5H_8)_n$, generally prepared by coagulation and drying of the milky sap, or latex, of various tropical plants, especially the **rubber tree** *(see).* Also called "caoutchouc", "India rubber". 2. Any of various materials made from natural rubber by curing, vulcanising, adding pigment, and otherwise modifying for use in a wide variety of manufactured products including electric insulation, elastic bands and belts, tyres, and containers. 3. Any of numerous synthetic elastic materials of varying chemical composition, with properties similar to those of natural rubber. 4. *Chiefly U.S. Slang.* A condom. 5. **a.** One who rubs. **b.** One who gives a massage; a masseur or masseuse. 6. Something used for rubbing or erasing; specifically, an eraser made of rubber.

—*adj.* Made of or pertaining to rubber. [RUB + -ER (sense 1, from its original use in erasing pencil marks).]

rubber[2] *n. Abbr.* **r.** 1. In bridge, whist, and other games and sports, a series of games of which two out of three or three out of five must be won to terminate the play. 2. The game that breaks a tie and ends such a series. [17th century (in bowls) : origin obscure.]

rubber band *n.* An elastic loop of natural or synthetic rubber, used to hold papers or objects together. Also called "elastic band".

rub·ber-base paint (rúbbər-bayss) *n.* **Latex paint** *(see).*

rubber bullet *n.* A projectile, considered less dangerous than a conventional bullet, that is fired to wound or deter, as in riot control. Compare **plastic bullet.**

rubber cement *n.* A solution of rubber in a volatile solvent, used as an adhesive.

rubber cheque *n.* A cheque returned by a bank because of insufficient funds in the account on which it is drawn. Used humorously.

rub·ber·ise, rub·ber·ize (rúbbər-īz) *tr.v.* **-ised, -ising, -ises.** To coat, treat, or impregnate with rubber.

rub·ber·neck (rúbbər-nek) *n. U.S. Slang.* A gawking tourist or sightseer.

rubber plant *n.* 1. Any of several tropical plants yielding sap that can be coagulated to form crude rubber. 2. A plant, *Ficus elastica,* that has large, glossy, leathery leaves, and is popular as a house plant. It grows as a tall tree in its native India and Malaysia.

rubber stamp *n.* 1. A piece of rubber affixed to a handle and bearing raised characters, used to make ink impressions of names, dates, and the like. 2. A person or body that gives perfunctory approval or endorsement of a policy without assessing its merit. 3. A perfunctory authorisation or endorsement.

rub·ber-stamp (rúbbər-stámp) *tr.v.* **-stamped, -stamping, -stamps.** 1. To mark with the imprint of a rubber stamp. 2. To endorse, vote for, or approve without question or deliberation.

rubber tree *n.* A tree, *Hevea braziliensis,* native to tropical America

but widely cultivated throughout the tropics, yielding a milky juice, or latex, that is a major source of commercial rubber.

rub·ber·y (rúbbəri) *adj.* Of or like rubber; elastic; resilient.

rub·bing (rúbbing) *n.* A representation of a raised or indented surface made by placing paper over the surface and rubbing the paper gently with a marking agent such as charcoal or chalk.

rub·bish (rúbbish) *n.* 1. Something discarded as refuse; debris; litter. 2. Worthless material. 3. Foolish talk or writing; nonsense.

—*tr.v.* **rubbished, -bishing, -bishes.** *Informal.* To dismiss or reject (something or somebody) as being worthless, foolish, or hopeless. [Middle English *robishe, robys, robous,* from Anglo-French *robbous,* plural of *robel* (unattested), RUBBLE.] —**rub·bish·y** *adj.*

rub·ble (rúbb'l) *n.* 1. Fragments of rock or masonry crumbled by natural or manmade forces. 2. **a.** Irregular fragments or pieces of rock used in masonry. **b.** The masonry made with such rocks. In this sense, also called "rubblework". [Middle English *robyl,* from Anglo-French *robel* (unattested), from Old French *robe,* booty; see **robe.**] —**rub·bly** *adj.*

Rub·bra (rúbbrə), **Edmund** (1901–86). British composer. He made his reputation as a symphonic composer and was also noted for his chamber music, which often employs polyphonic effects.

rub down *tr.v.* 1. To clean and dry (oneself, or a horse, for example) by rubbing vigorously. 2. To massage.

rub·down (rúb-down) *n.* 1. An energetic massage of the body. 2. An act or instance of cleaning or drying by rubbing.

ru·be·fa·cient (rōōbi-fáy-shənt, -si-ənt ‖ réwbi-) *adj.* Producing redness and warmth of the skin.

—*n.* A substance that irritates the skin, causing redness, and often used as a counterirritant. [Latin *rubefaciēns* (stem *rubefacient-*), present participle of *rubefacere,* to redden : *rubeus,* red, reddish + *facere,* to make.] —**ru·be·fac·tion** (-fáksh'n) *n.*

ru·bel·la (rōō-béllə, rōō- ‖ rew-) *n.* A disease, **German measles** *(see).* [New Latin, from Latin, feminine of *rubellus,* reddish, from *rubeus,* red, reddish.]

ru·bel·lite (rōō-béllīt, rōōbi-līt ‖ rew-) *n.* A pink or red variety of tourmaline used as a gemstone. [Latin *rubellus,* reddish (see **rubella**) + -ITE.]

Ru·bens (rōō-binz, -bənz, -benz; *Dutch* rú-bənss), **Peter Paul** (1577–1640). Flemish baroque painter. Appointed court painter (1609) to the Archduke Albert, he set up a studio in Antwerp and, aided by assistants, produced many paintings often with religious, historical, or allegorical themes. *An Allegory of War and Peace* (1629) is among examples of his grand style, while *The Straw Hat* (1622–5) shows his more tender and intimate portraiture. He was knighted by Charles I of England (1629), who commissioned from him the ceiling of the Banqueting House in Whitehall.

ru·be·o·la (rōō-bée-ə-lə, rōō-, -ō- ‖ rew-) *n.* A disease, **measles** *(see).* [New Latin, neuter plural diminutive of Latin *rubeus,* red.] —**ru·be·o·lar** *adj.*

ru·bes·cent (rōō-béss'nt, rōō- ‖ rew-) *adj.* Reddening. [Latin *rubescēns* (stem *rubescent-*), present participle of *rubescere,* to grow red, inchoative of *rubēre,* to be red.] —**ru·bes·cence** *n.*

Ru·bi·con (rōō-bi-kən ‖ réw-, -kon). A small river in northern Italy rising just north of San Marino and flowing northeast to the Adriatic Sea. Caesar's crossing it with his army in 49 B.C. constituted an illegal entry into Italy and thereby initiated civil war. —**cross** or **pass the Rubicon.** To embark on an undertaking from which one cannot turn back.

ru·bi·cund (rōō-bi-kənd ‖ réw-, -kund) *adj.* Having or showing a healthy rosiness; ruddy. [Latin *rubicundus,* from *rubēre,* to be red.] —**ru·bi·cun·di·ty** (-kúndəti) *n.*

ru·bid·i·um (rōō-bíddi-əm, rōō- ‖ rew-) *n. Symbol* **Rb** A soft, silvery-white alkali-metal element that ignites spontaneously in air and reacts violently with water. It is used in photocells and in the manufacture of vacuum tubes. Atomic number 37, atomic weight 85.47, melting point 38.89°C, boiling point 688°C, relative density (solid) 1.532, valency 1. [New Latin, from Latin *rubidus,* red (from the red lines in its spectrum).]

ru·bid·i·um–stron·ti·um dating (rōō-bíddi-əm-strónti-əm ‖ rew-, -strónsh-) *n.* A method of dating rocks and minerals by measuring the amount of the isotope strontium-87 present as a result of the radioactive decay of rubidium-87. It is used for ages up to 10^9 (a thousand million) years.

ru·big·i·nous (rōō-bíjinəss, rōō- ‖ rew-) *adj.* Rust-coloured; reddish-brown. [Latin *rūbīginōsus,* from *rūbīgo, rōbīgo,* rust.]

Ru·bik's cube (rōō-biks ‖ réw-) *n.* Also **Rubik cube.** A puzzle consisting of a cube with each face made up of nine smaller coloured cubes joined by internal connections so that the faces can be rotated. The test of skill is to rearrange the puzzle so that each face has a different single colour, starting from a position in which each face is randomly made up of different colours. [After Ernö *Rubik,* its inventor, 20th-century Hungarian teacher of architecture.]

Ru·bin·stein (rōōbin-stīn), **Anton Grigoryevich** (1829–94). Russian composer and pianist. Of German-Jewish extraction, he was, in his time, considered a rival to Liszt. He helped to found (1862) the St. Petersburg Conservatoire.

Rubinstein, Artur (1887–1982). Polish-born U.S. pianist. Performing in public by the time he was 11 years old, he went on to acquire an international reputation for his interpretations of the works of Chopin. He became a U.S. citizen in 1946.

ru·bi·ous (rōō-bi-əss ‖ réw-) *adj.* Having the colour of a ruby; red.

ruble. Variant of **rouble.**

Ru·blyov (rōō-blyóff), **Andrey,** also known as Rublev (*c.* 1370–*c.*

1430). Russian artist. He trained as an iconographer in the Byzantine tradition before retiring to the monastic life.

ru·bric (rōō-brik ‖ rēw-) *n.* **1.** A part of a manuscript or book, such as a title, heading, or initial letter, that appears in decorative red lettering, or is in some other way distinguished from the rest of the text. **2.** A title or heading of a statute or chapter in a code of law, originally written or printed in red. **3.** A name for a class or category; a title. **4.** *Ecclesiastical.* A direction in a missal, hymnal, or other liturgical book. **5.** Any brief, authoritative rule or direction. **6.** A short commentary or explanation covering a broad subject. **7.** The instructions to the candidate in an examination paper. **8.** *Archaic.* Red ochre. [Middle English *rubrike,* from Old French *rubriche,* from Latin *rubrīca (terra),* "red earth", "red ochre", from *ruber,* red.] —**ru·bri·cal** *adj.*

ru·bri·cate (rōō-bri-kayt ‖ rēw-) *tr.v.* **-cated, -cating, -cates. 1.** To arrange, write, or print as a rubric. **2.** To provide with rubrics. **3.** To establish rules for. [Late Latin *rubrīcāre,* from *rubrica,* RUBRIC.] —**ru·bri·ca·tor, ru·bri·ca·tion** (-káysh'n) *n.*

ru·bri·cian (rōō-brísh'n ‖ rew-) *n.* A person learned in the rubrics of ecclesiastical ritual.

ru·by (rōōbi ‖ rēwbi) *n., pl.* **-bies. 1.** A deep red, transparent form of corundum, highly valued as a precious stone. Also called "Oriental ruby", "true ruby". **2.** Something made from a ruby, as a watch bearing. **3.** A dark or deep red to deep purplish red.
~*adj.* **1.** Of or having the colour of rubies. **2.** Designating a fortieth anniversary: *a ruby wedding.* [Middle English, from Old French *rubi,* from Medieval Latin *rubīnus (lapis),* "red stone", from Latin *rubeus,* red.]

ruby silver *n.* A mineral, **pyrargyrite** *(see).*

ruby spinel *n.* A red form of **spinel** *(see)* used as a gemstone.

R.U.C. Royal Ulster Constabulary.

ruche, rouche (rōōsh) *n.* A ruffle, gather, or pleat of lace, muslin, or other fine fabric used for trimming women's garments.
~*tr.v.* **ruched, ruching, ruches.** To decorate with ruches. [French, beehive, frill (pleated like a straw beehive), from Old French *ruche,* bark of a tree, beehive made of barks, from Medieval Latin *rūsca,* from Gaulish *rūska* (unattested), akin to Old Irish *rūsc†,* bark.]

ruch·ing (rōōshing) *n.* **1.** Ruches collectively. **2.** Fabric for ruches.

ruck¹ (ruk) *n.* **1.** A large number mixed together; a jumble. **2.** The multitude of ordinary people. **3.** In Rugby football, a loose scrum occurring when the ball is on the ground. **4.** In Australian Rules football, players who play all over the field, following the ball.
~*v.* **rucked, rucking, rucks.** —*tr.* In Rugby football, to extract (the ball) from a ruck by clawing backwards using the foot. —*intr.* To ruck a ball. [Middle English *ruket†,* heap, stack.]

ruck² *v.* **rucked, rucking, rucks.** Also **ruck·le** (rúck'l). —*tr.* To make a fold in; crease. Often used with *up.* —*intr.* To become creased. Often used with *up.*
~*n.* Also **ruckle.** A crease or pucker, as in cloth. [Ultimately from Old Norse *hrukka,* wrinkle, crease.]

ruck·sack (rúk-sak, rōōk-) *n.* A bag with straps fitting round the shoulders, worn on the back and often supported by a light frame, used by hikers or travellers for carrying equipment, supplies, or the like. [German *Rucksack* : *Rücken,* back, from Old High German *hrukki* + *Sack,* sack, from Old High German *sac,* from Latin *saccus,* SACK.]

ruck·us (rúckəss) *n. Informal.* A noisy disturbance; a commotion. [Probably RUC(TION) + (RUMP)US.]

ruc·tion (rúcksh'n) *n. Informal.* A riotous disturbance; a noisy quarrel. [19th century : origin obscure.]

ru·da·ce·ous rock (rōō-dáyshəss) *n.* A sedimentary rock composed of fragments of disintegrated rock material 2 millimetres (0.08 inch) or more in diameter. [New Latin, from Latin *rūdus,* rubble + -ACE-OUS.]

rud·beck·i·a (rud-bécki-ə) *n.* Any plant of the genus *Rudbeckia,* native to North America but widely cultivated for their showy, yellow, daisy-like flowers. See **black-eyed Susan.** [New Latin, after Olaus *Rudbeck* (1630–1702), Swedish botanist.]

rudd (rud) *n.* A European freshwater fish, *Scardinius erythrophthalmus,* having a brownish body and red fins. [Probably from obsolete *rud,* a ruddy colour. See **ruddle.**]

rud·der (rúddər) *n.* **1.** A vertically hinged plate mounted at the stern of a vessel for directing its course. **2.** A similar structure at the tail of an aircraft, used for effecting horizontal changes in course. **3.** Anything that controls direction; a guide. [Middle English *rother, rodyr,* Old English *rōther,* steering oar.]

rud·der·post (rúddər-pōst) *n.* The vertical shaft of a rudder, allowing it to pivot when the tiller or steering gear is operated. Also called "rudderstock".

rud·dle (rúdd'l) *n.* Also **red·dle** (rédd'l), **rad·dle** (rádd'l). Red ochreous iron ore, an earthy variety of haematite, used in dyeing and marking.
~*tr.v.* **ruddled, -dling, -dles.** Also **red·dle, rad·dle.** To dye or mark with red ochre. [Diminutive of obsolete *rud,* a ruddy colour, Middle English *rud(d)e,* Old English *rudu.*]

rud·dle·man (rúdd'l-mən, -man) *n., pl.* **-men** (-mən, -men). A man who sells ruddle, or red ochre.

rud·dock (rúddək) *n. British Regional.* The robin. [Middle English *ruddok,* Old English *rudduc : rudu* (see **ruddle**) + *-uc,* -OCK.]

rud·dy (rúddi) *adj.* **-dier, -diest. 1.** Having a healthy, reddish colour. **2.** Reddish; rosy. **3.** *Informal.* Damned; bloody. Used euphemistically.
~*adv. Informal.* Used as an intensive: *ruddy awful play.* [Middle

English *rudie,* Old English *rudig,* from *rudu,* red colour.] —**rud·di·ly** *adv.* —**rud·di·ness** *n.*

rude (rōōd ‖ rewd) *adj.* **ruder, rudest. 1.** Ill-mannered; uncivil; discourteous. **2.** Lacking the graces of civilised life; unrefined; uncouth. **3.** Lowly; humble: *a rude thatched hut.* **4.** Primitive; uncivilised. **5.** Formed without skill or precision; makeshift; crude: *made a rude shelter.* **6.** Approximate; rough: *"the height of the cliffs thus affording a rude measure of the age of the streams"* (Charles Darwin). **7.** Vigorous; robust. **8. a.** Harsh; severe: *rude winters.* **b.** Violent and upsetting: *a rude shock.* **9.** Discordant: *"rude harsh-sounding rhymes"* (Shakespeare). **10.** Sexually titillating or obscene. Used euphemistically or humorously. [Middle English, from Old French, from Latin *rudis,* rough, raw, akin to *rūdus†,* broken stone.] —**rude·ly** *adv.* —**rude·ness** *n.*

ru·der·al (rōō-dərəl ‖ rēw-) *adj. Botany.* Growing in rubbish, poor land, or waste places.
~*n. Botany.* A ruderal plant. [New Latin *rūderālis,* from Latin *rūdera,* ruins, rubbish, plural of *rūdus†,* broken stone.]

ru·di·ment (rōō-di-mənt ‖ rēw-) *n.* **1.** *Often plural.* A fundamental element, principle, or skill, as of a field of learning. **2.** *Often plural.* Something in an incipient or undeveloped form; beginnings: *the rudiments of social behaviour in children.* **3.** *Biology.* An initial group of cells which gives rise to a structure; a vestige. [French, from Latin *rudīmentum,* beginning (formed after *elementum,* ELEMENT), from *rudis,* RUDE.]

ru·di·men·ta·ry (rōō-di-méntri, -méntəri ‖ rēw-) *adj.* Also **ru·di·men·tal** (-mént'l). **1.** Of, pertaining to, or involving basic facts or principles that must be learned first; elementary. **2.** In the earliest stages of development; incipient. **3.** *Biology.* Imperfectly or incompletely developed; vestigial: *a rudimentary organ.* —**ru·di·men·ta·ri·ly** (-méntrəli ‖ -men-térrəli) *adv.* —**ru·di·men·ta·ri·ness** *n.*

Ru·dolf I (rōō-dolf), also known as Rudolph of Habsburg (1218–91). German king. In 1273 he became the first Habsburg to be elected Holy Roman Emperor. His conquest of Austria and the surrounding territories formed the power base for his descendants until 1918.

Rudolf. See **Turkana, Lake.**

rue¹ (rōō ‖ rew) *v.* **rued, ruing, rues.** —*tr.* To feel remorse or sorrow because of; regret; repent. —*intr.* To feel remorse or sorrow; be penitent or regretful.
~*n. Archaic.* Sorrow; regret. [Middle English *ruen,* Old English *hrēowan,* to make penitent, distress.] —**ru·er** *n.*

rue² *n.* An aromatic Eurasian plant of the genus *Ruta;* especially, *R. graveolens,* having evergreen leaves that yield an acrid, volatile oil formerly used in medicine. Formerly called "herb-of-grace". [Middle English, from Old French, from Latin *rūta,* from Greek *rhutē.*]

Rue-il-Mal-mai-son (rṓ-i-mal-me-zón). Western suburb of Paris, in the Hauts-de-Seine département, France. Its Château de Malmaison was a favourite residence of Napoleon.

rue·ful (rōō-f'l ‖ rēw-) *adj.* **1.** Inspiring pity or compassion. **2.** Causing, feeling, or expressing sorrow or regret. **3.** Expressive of a faintly sardonic regret; wry. —**rue·ful·ly** *adv.* —**rue·ful·ness** *n.*

ru·fes·cent (rōō-féss'nt ‖ rēw-) *adj. Botany.* Tinged with red. [Latin *rūfēscēns* (stem *rūfēscent-),* present participle of *rūfēscere,* to become reddish, from *rūfus,* reddish.] —**ru·fes·cence** *n.*

ruff¹ (ruf) *n.* **1.** A stiffly starched, frilled or pleated circular collar of lace, muslin, or other fine fabric, worn by men and women especially in Europe in the 16th and 17th centuries. **2.** A distinctive collar-like projection around the neck, as of feathers on a bird or of fur on a mammal. **3. a.** A Eurasian sandpiper, *Philomachus pugnax,* the male of which has collar-like, erectile feathers around the neck during the breeding season. **b.** The male of this bird. The female is called a "reeve". [Short for RUFFLE (frill).] —**ruffed** *adj.*

ruff² *n.* In card games: **1.** The playing of a trump card when one cannot follow suit. **2.** An old game resembling whist.
~*v.* **ruffed, ruffing, ruffs.** In card games: —*tr.* To trump. —*intr.* To play a trump. [Old French *roffle,* name of a card game, earlier *ronfle,* probably from Italian *ronfa,* perhaps alteration of *trionfa,* "triumph", trump card, from Latin *triumphus,* TRIUMPH.]

ruffe, ruff (ruf) *n.* A European freshwater fish, *Acerina cernua,* related to the perches. Also called "pope". [Middle English *ruf, ruffe,* sea bream, perhaps from *ruch, r(o)wgh,* ROUGH (from its rough scales).]

ruf·fi·an (rúf-yən, -i-ən) *n.* **1.** A tough, violent man. **2.** A thug or gangster. [French *rufien, ruf(f)ian,* from Italian *ruffiano,* pander, "filthy or scabby person", from *roffia, ruffia,* scab, filth, probably from Germanic.] —**ruf·fi·an·ism** *n.* —**ruf·fi·an, ruf·fi·an·ly** *adj.*

ruf·fle¹ (rúff'l) *n.* **1.** A strip of frilled or closely pleated fabric used for trimming or decoration. **2.** Something resembling such trimming, such as a bird's ruff. **3.** A slight discomposure; an agitation. **4.** An irregularity in smoothness; a slight disturbance. **5.** A low continuous beating of a drum that is not as loud as a roll.
~*v.* **ruffled, -fling, -fles.** —*tr.* **1.** To disturb the smoothness or regularity of; ripple: *wind ruffled the surface of the water.* **2.** To pleat or gather (fabric) into a ruffle. **3.** To erect (the feathers). Often used with *up.* **4.** To discompose; fluster. **5.** To flip through (the pages of a book). **6.** To beat a ruffle on (a drum). **7.** To shuffle (cards). —*intr.* **1.** To become irregular or rough. **2.** To flutter. **3.** To become flustered. [Middle English *ruffelen†.*]

ruffle² *intr.v.* **-fled, -fling, -fles.** To behave arrogantly or roughly; swagger. [Middle English *ruffelen†.*] —**ruf·fler** *n.*

ru·fous (rōō-fəss ‖ rēw-) *adj. Zoology.* Reddish brown. [Latin *rūfus,* red, reddish.]

rug (rug) *n.* **1.** A piece of heavy, usually woollen, fabric, used to cover a portion of a floor and typically smaller than a carpet. **2.** An animal skin used as a floor covering. **3.** *Chiefly British.* A blanket or piece of thick, warm fabric or fur used as a coverlet or wrap. [Probably from Scandinavian; akin to Swedish *rugg*, ruffled hair, and to Old Norse *rogg*, tuft. See **rugged**.]

ru·ga (rōō-gə ‖ réw-) *n., pl.* **-gae** (-jee, -gī). *Biology & Anatomy.* A fold, crease, or wrinkle, as in the lining of the stomach. [Latin *rūga*, fold.]

Rug·by (rúg-bi). Town of Warwickshire, central England, an important railway junction and manufacturing centre.

Rugby fives *n.* See **fives.**

Rugby football *n.* Either of two types of football played with an oval ball which players are allowed to handle. *Rugby Union* is a strictly amateur game, played between two teams of 15 players. Also called "rugger". *Rugby League* is both amateur and professional and is played between two teams of 13 players. [After *Rugby School,* in RUGBY, where it originated.]

rug·ged (rúggid) *adj.* **1.** Having a rough, irregular surface. **2.** Having strong features marked with furrows or wrinkles. **3.** Austere; stern. **4.** Demanding great effort, ability, or endurance. **5.** Lacking culture or polish. **6.** Vigorous; sturdy; hardy. —See Synonyms at **rough.** [Middle English, shaggy, probably from Scandinavian; akin to Old Norse *rögg,* tuft, from Germanic *rawwō* (unattested).] —**rug·ged·ly** *adv.* —**rug·ged·ness** *n.*

rug·ger (rúggər) *n. British.* Rugby Union. See **Rugby football.**

ru·gose (rōō-gōz, -gōss ‖ réw-) *adj.* Also **ru·gous** (-gəss), **ru·gate** (-gayt). **1.** Having many wrinkles or creases. **2.** *Botany.* Having a rough and ridged surface, as certain prominently veined leaves do. [Latin *rūgōsus,* creased, from *rūga,* fold.] —**ru·gose·ly** *adv.* —**ru·gos·i·ty** (-góssəti) *n.*

Ruhr (roor). A major industrial region of the world, lying in western Germany. It comprises the valley of the river Ruhr, which rises in Sauerland and flows west to the Rhine at Duisburg, and the Lippe valley to the north. The Ruhr provides much of Germany's coal and electricity supply. Raw materials are imported via Rotterdam and the Rhine, and the region's products include iron, steel, chemicals, and glass.

ru·in (rōō-in ‖ réw-) *n.* **1.** Total destruction or disintegration, rendering something formless, useless, or valueless. **2.** The cause of such destruction: *A single flaw is the ruin of a diamond.* **3.** *Often plural.* A condition of total destruction or collapse. **4.** *Often plural.* The remains of something destroyed, disintegrated, or decayed. **5.** A person whose physical or mental capacities have been destroyed. **6. a.** The loss or severe impairment of one's health, position, or honour. **b.** *Archaic.* Loss of virginity in an unmarried woman. **7.** The cause of such loss. ~*v.* **ruined, -ining, -ins.** —*tr.* **1.** To destroy or demolish; reduce to ruin or disintegrate. **2.** To harm, damage, or spoil irreparably. **3.** To reduce to poverty or bankruptcy. **4.** *Archaic.* **a.** To deprive of chastity. **b.** To seduce and abandon (a woman). —*intr. Archaic.* To fall into ruin. [Middle English *ruine,* from Old French, from Latin *ruīna,* "fall", from *ruere,* to fall, crumble.] —**ru·in·a·ble** *adj.* —**ru·in·er** *n.*

Synonyms: ruin, raze, demolish, destroy, devastate, damage, wreck.

ru·in·a·tion (rōō-i-náysh'n ‖ réw-) *n.* **1. a.** The act of ruining. **b.** The condition of being ruined. **2.** The cause of ruin.

ru·in·ous (rōō-inəss ‖ réw-) *adj.* **1.** Causing or apt to cause ruin; destructive. **2.** Falling to ruin; dilapidated or decayed. **3.** *Informal.* Very expensive. —**ru·in·ous·ly** *adv.* —**ru·in·ous·ness** *n.*

Ruis·dael (réez-daal, ríz-, -dayl; *Dutch* rō-iz-daal), **Jacob van** (*c.* 1628–82). Dutch artist. Possibly the greatest Dutch landscape painter, he composed baroque, tranquil works which proved profoundly influential on Western European landscape painting.

rule (rōōl ‖ rewl) *n.* **1. a.** Governing power, or its possession or use; authority; control: *under the rule of Henry VIII.* **b.** The period of time that such authority lasts: *the nineteen-year rule of Henry VIII.* **2.** An authoritative direction for conduct or procedure, specifically: **a.** Any of the regulations governing procedure in a legislative body. **b.** A principle of conduct observed by the members of a group. **c.** A regulation observed by the players in a game, sport, or contest. **3.** A code of principles for the conduct of religious services or activities. **4.** An established standard or habit of behaviour. **5.** Something that generally prevails or obtains. **6.** A standard method or procedure for solving a class of mathematical problems. **7.** *Law.* **a.** A court order limited in application to a specific case. **b.** A subordinate regulation governing a particular matter. **8.** A straight-edged measuring or drawing device; a ruler. **9.** *Printing.* **a.** A thin, straight line used to make a border or to separate columns. **b.** A dash used as a punctuation mark: *an em rule; an en rule.* **c.** A thin metal strip of various widths and designs, used to print rules. **10.** The discipline and regulations under which a religious order lives: *the Benedictine rule.* —**as a rule.** Usually; normally. ~*v.* **ruled, ruling, rules.** —*tr.* **1.** To exercise control over; govern. **2.** To dominate by powerful influence; hold sway over. **3.** To keep within proper limits; restrain. **4.** To decide or declare as a judgment; decree. **5. a.** To mark with straight parallel lines: *ruled notepaper.* **b.** To mark (a straight line), as with a ruler. —*intr.* **1.** To exercise authority; be in control or command. **2.** To formulate and issue a decree or decision. —**rule out. 1.** To make impossible. **2.** To exclude as a possibility; dismiss. —See Synonyms at **decide.** [Middle English *riule, reule,* from Old French, from Latin *rēgula,*

straight stick, ruler, rule, pattern.] —**rul·a·ble** *adj.*

ruled surface (rōōld ‖ rewld) *n.* A surface, such as a cone or a cylinder, generated by the motion of a straight line.

rule of thumb *n.* A useful principle with wide application, not intended to be strictly accurate. [From the use of the thumb in measuring.]

rul·er (rōōl-ər ‖ réwl-) *n.* **1.** One that rules or governs; especially, a sovereign. **2.** A straight-edged strip, as of wood or metal, for drawing straight lines and measuring lengths.

rules (rōōlz ‖ rewlz) *n. Used with a singular verb.* **1.** Formerly, areas around the King's Bench, Marshalsea, and Fleet prisons in London in which some prisoners, mainly debtors, were allowed to live subject to certain regulations and restrictions. **2.** *Capital* R. Australian **Rules** (see).

rul·ing (rōōl-ing ‖ rewl-) *adj.* Exercising control or dominion; predominant. ~*n.* **1.** An authoritative or official decision. **2.** A ruled line or ruled lines.

rum¹ (rum) *n.* **1.** An alcoholic drink distilled from fermented molasses or sugar cane. **2.** Intoxicating beverages. [17th century : perhaps shortened from *rumbullion†.*]

rum² *adj.* Also **rum·my** (rúmmi). *British Informal.* Odd; strange. [16th century (cant) : originally "fine", "lively", perhaps from Romany *rom,* man.]

Rum. See **Byzantine Empire.**

Rùm or **Rhum** (rum). Mountainous island of the Inner Hebrides, in Highland Region, northwest Scotland.

Rumania. See **Romania.**

Rumanian. Variant of **Romanian.**

rum·ba, rhum·ba (rúm-bə ‖ rōōm-) *n.* **1.** A complex syncopated dance that originated among black Cubans. **2.** A modern ballroom adaptation of this dance. **3.** A piece of music composed in the rhythm of this dance. [American Spanish, from *rumbo,* carousel, from Spanish, pomp, perhaps extended use of *rumbo,* bearing, rhumb line, from Middle Dutch *rume.*]

rum baba *n.* A baba (see).

rum·ble (rúmb'l) *v.* **-bled, -bling, -bles.** —*intr.* **1.** To make a continuous, deep, heavy, reverberating sound, as thunder does. **2.** To move or proceed with such a sound. —*tr.* **1.** To utter with a rumbling sound. **2.** To polish or mix (metal parts) in a tumbling box. **3.** *Informal.* To bring to light; uncover; find out: *rumbled our plot.* ~*n.* **1.** A continuous, deep, heavy, rolling sound. **2.** A tumbling **box** (see). **3.** *U.S.* A luggage compartment or servant's seat in the rear of a carriage. **4.** *Chiefly U.S. slang.* A gang fight. [Middle English *romblen,* probably from Middle Dutch *rommelen* (imitative).] —**rum·bler** *n.* —**rum·bling·ly** *adv.* —**rum·bly** *adj.*

rum·bus·tious (rum-búss-chəss, -bústi-əss) *adj.* Lively and noisy; boisterous. [Probably alteration of ROBUSTIOUS.]

Ru·me·li·a or **Rou·me·li·a** (rōō-méel-i-ə, rōō-). The possessions of the former Ottoman Empire in the Balkan Peninsula, including Macedonia, Albania, and Thrace.

ru·men (rōō-men ‖ réw-) *n., pl.* **-mina** (-minə) or **-mens.** The first division of the stomach of a ruminant animal, in which food is partly digested before being regurgitated for further chewing. [Latin *rūmen†,* throat, gullet.]

Rum·ford (rúmfərd), **Benjamin Thompson, Count** (1753–1814). American born British scientist and diplomat. After serving as a spy and administrator in America, Britain, and France, he became a minister of the Elector of Bavaria. His observations of the Elector's artillery growing hot with sustained firing helped him to establish, on his return to England, the motive theory of heat.

ru·mi·nant (rōō-minənt ‖ réw-) *n.* Any of various hoofed, even-toed, usually horned mammals of the suborder Ruminantia, such as cattle, sheep, goats, deer, and giraffes, characteristically having a stomach divided into four compartments, and chewing a cud consisting of regurgitated, partially digested food. ~*adj.* **1.** Characterised by the chewing of cud. **2.** Of or belonging to the Ruminantia. **3.** Meditative; contemplative. [Latin *rūmināns* (stem *rūminant-*), present participle of *rūmināri,* to chew cud, RUMINATE.]

ru·mi·nate (rōō-mi-nayt ‖ réw-) *v.* **-nated, -nating, -nates.** —*intr.* **1.** To chew cud. **2.** To meditate at length; muse. Often used with *on* or *upon.* —*tr.* To meditate or reflect on. [Latin *rūmināri,* from *rūmen,* RUMEN.] —**ru·mi·nat·ing·ly, ru·mi·na·tive·ly** *adv.* —**ru·mi·na·tive** (-nətiv, -naytiv) *adj.* —**ru·mi·na·tor** (-naytər) *n.* —**ru·mi·na·tion** (-náysh'n) *n.*

rum·mage (rúmmij) *v.* **-maged, -maging, -mages.** —*tr.* **1.** To search thoroughly by handling, turning over, or disarranging the contents of. **2.** To discover by searching thoroughly. Used with *up* or *out.* —*intr.* To make a thorough, energetic search. ~*n.* **1.** An act of rummaging; a thorough search among a number of things. **2.** A confusion of miscellaneous articles. [Originally "arrangement of cargo in a ship's hold", odds and ends, from Anglo-French *rumage* (unattested), variant of Old French *arrumage,* from *arrumer,* to put in a ship's hold : *a-,* from Latin *ad-,* to, at + *run,* ship's hold, from Middle Dutch *ruim,* ROOM.] —**rum·mag·er** *n.*

rummage sale *n.* **1.** A sale of unclaimed or excess goods, as at a warehouse or docks. **2.** *U.S.* A jumble sale. (see).

rum·mer (rúmmər) *n.* A large drinking glass. [Perhaps from German *Römer,* from Dutch *roemer,* "glass for drinking toasts", from *roemen,* to praise, extol.]

rum·my¹ (rúmmi) *n.* A card game, played in many variations, in which the object is to obtain sets of three or more cards of the same denomination or suit. [20th century : origin obscure.]

rummy[2]. *British Slang.* Variant of **rum** (odd).

ru·mour, *U.S.* **ru·mor** (ro͞o-mər || réw-) *n.* **1.** Unverified information of uncertain origin usually spread by word of mouth; gossip; hearsay. **2.** An instance of this; a current but unverified report or assertion.

~tr.v. **rumoured** or *U.S.* **rumored, -mouring** or *U.S.* **-moring, -mours** or *U.S.* **-mors.** To spread or tell by rumour. [Middle English *rumo(u)r,* from Old French, from Latin *rūmor.*]

ru·mour·mon·ger (ro͞o-mər-mung-gər || réw-, -mong-) *n.* One who spreads rumours.

rump (rump) *n.* **1.** The fleshy hindquarters of an animal. **2.** A cut of beef or veal from this part. **3.** The human buttocks. **4.** The part of a bird's back nearest the tail. **5.** The part that remains after the removal or departure of a larger, more valuable, or more important part; a worthless, insignificant, or unrepresentative remnant. **6.** A legislature having only a small part of its original membership and so unrepresentative or lacking authority. **—the Rump.** The Rump Parliament. [Middle English *rumpe,* from Scandinavian, akin to Danish *rumpe*†, buttocks.]

rum·ple (rúmp'l) *v.* **-pled, -pling, -ples.** *—tr.* To wrinkle, tousle, or form into folds or creases. *—intr.* To become rumpled.

~n. An uneven fold; an irregular or untidy crease. [Obsolete *rumple (*noun), from Middle Dutch *rompelen, rumpelen,* from *rompe,* wrinkle.] **—rum·ply** *adj.*

Rump Parliament *n.* The part of the **Long Parliament** *(see)* that remained after Pride's Purge (1648) until dismissed by Cromwell (1653). It was recalled (1659), but again disbanded at the restoration of Charles II (1660). Also called the "Rump".

rum·pus (rúmpəss) *n.* A noisy clamour. [18th century : probably fanciful coinage.]

rumpus room *n. U.S.* A room for play and parties.

run (run) *v.* **ran** (răn), **run, running, runs.** *—intr.* **1. a.** To move on foot at a pace faster than the walk and in such a manner that both feet leave the ground during each stride. **b.** To move at a gait faster than the canter; gallop. Used of a horse. **2.** To retreat rapidly; flee: *turn and run.* **3.** To move freely and without restraint: *children running about in the park.* **4.** To move or roll forward, as if out of control: *The car ran down the hill and into a wall.* **5.** To make a short, quick trip or visit: *run down to the shops.* **6. a.** To swim rapidly: *A trout took the fly and ran upstream.* **b.** To shoal or migrate inshore or upstream, especially prior to spawning. **7.** To move or act quickly or hurriedly: *Her eye ran down the list.* **8.** To have frequent recourse: *always running to the doctor.* **9.** To take part in a race. **10.** To compete for elected office; stand: *running for parliament.* **11.** To finish a race in a specified position: *He ran second.* **12. a.** To be in operation: *The car's engine is running.* **b.** To be powered in the specified way: *runs on 2-star petrol.* **13.** To provide regular transport from one place to another; ply: *The ferry runs every hour.* **14.** *Nautical.* To sail or steer before the wind or on a specified course: *run before the storm; run into port.* **15.** To operate or progress in the specified way in relation to a schedule: *Tonight's programmes are running an hour late; made the trains run on time.* **16.** To flow in a steady stream, as fluids or loose particles do. **17.** To melt and flow: *Tin must be hot for the solder to run.* **18.** To flow and spread, as dyes in a fabric sometimes do: *The colours ran.* **19.** To be wet; flow with liquid; stream: *The street ran with blood.* **20.** To discharge liquid or reach a specified state by discharging liquid: *left the hot tap running; The well has run dry.* **21.** To discharge pus or mucus: *a running sore; a running nose.* **22.** To surge, as waves or the tides do: *A heavy surf was running.* **23.** To extend in space; stretch or reach: *a line running down the middle of the road; The pipes run under the floorboards.* **24.** To spread or climb. Used of a creeping plant. **25.** To spread rapidly: *A rumour ran through the crowd.* **26.** To impress itself persistently on one's consciousness: *a tune running through my head all day.* **27.** *Chiefly U.S.* To unravel; ladder: *Her stocking ran.* **28.** To continue to have legal force; remain valid: *The lease has two years to run.* **29.** To continue to be performed or shown. Used of a play or film. **30.** To pass: *Days ran into weeks.* **31.** To persist or recur: *Gout runs in the family.* **32.** *Law.* To be concurrent: *Fishing rights run with ownership of the land.* **33. a.** To accumulate or accrue. **b.** To become payable: *Your note runs, with interest, to June 1st.* **34.** To be or have enough: *I don't think our budget will run to a new car.* **35.** To be expressed in a given way: *His reasoning ran thus.* **36.** To tend or incline: *His tastes run to the macabre.* **37.** To vary or range in quality, price, size, proportion, or the like: *House prices were running high.* **38.** To come into or out of a specified condition: *We ran into debt.* *—tr.* **1. a.** To traverse on foot at a pace faster than the walk: *run the entire distance.* **b.** To cause (a horse) to move at a gait faster than the canter. **2.** To allow to move without restraint: *He runs his sheep on hill pasture.* **3.** To do or accomplish by or as if by running: *run errands.* **4.** To hunt or pursue: *Wolves ran the sheep in the night.* **5.** To bring to a specified condition by or as if by running: *ran himself into the ground.* **6.** To cause to pass, move, or go lightly or quickly: *ran his fingers over the keyboard; ran a comb through her hair.* **7.** To compel to leave: *They ran him out of town.* **8. a.** To compete in (a race). **b.** To cause to compete in or as if in a race: *He ran two horses in the Derby.* **c.** To cause (a race) to take place: *the last Grand National to be run at Aintree.* **9.** *Chiefly U.S.* To present or nominate for elective office: *They ran him for mayor.* **10.** To compete in a given manner against: *He ran them a close second.* **11.** To cause to move or progress freely: *run up the jib.* **12.** To cause to function; operate: *He ran his engine.* **13.** To convey or transport: *Run me into town.* **14.** To cause to ply: *They don't run the ferries here in winter.* **15.** To cause (a boat or car, for example) to move on a specified course: *ran our boat into a cove; ran the car into a tree.* **16. a.** To smuggle: *run rifles.* **b.** To evade and pass through (a blockade, for example). **17.** To move swiftly down or through: *run the rapids.* **18. a.** To cause to flow: *run water into a bath.* **b.** To fill (a bath) with water. **19.** To emit or flow with: *The fountains ran wine.* **20. a.** To melt, fuse, or smelt (metal). **b.** To mould or cast (molten metal): *run gold into ingots.* **21.** To cause to extend in a specified way: *run a road into the hills.* **22.** To mark or trace on a surface: *run a pencil line between two points.* **23.** To sew with a continuous line of stitches: *run a seam.* **24.** *Chiefly U.S.* To cause to unravel; ladder. **25.** To cause to penetrate: *She ran a pin into her thumb.* **26.** To cause to continue being shown or performed: *They ran the film for a month.* **27.** To publish in a periodical: *They're running a special feature on European cookery.* **28.** To cause or allow (an account, for example) to accumulate. **29.** To expose oneself or be subjected to (risk, for example). **30.** To have (a fever) as a symptom. **31.** In cricket, to score (one or more runs). **32.** To score (balls or points) consecutively in billiard games: *run 15 balls.* **33.** To carry out or perform (a test or experiment, for example). **34. a.** To be the manager or proprietor of: *runs a greengrocer's.* **b.** To be in charge of; conduct, control, or direct: *What a way to run a business!* **35.** To own and drive (a vehicle). **36.** To unite or combine: *We ran two companies into one.* **—run across.** To meet or find by chance. **—run after. 1.** To pursue; chase. **2.** *Informal.* To seek the company or attentions of. **—run away with. 1. a.** To make off with. **b.** To elope with. **2.** To cause to lose control; get the better of: *His ambition ran away with him.* **3.** To win (an election or competition) by a large margin. **4.** To form (an impression or opinion) too hastily: *Don't run away with the idea that it'll be easy.* **—run for it.** To attempt to escape. **—run into. 1.** To meet by chance. **2.** To encounter; be faced with: *ran into difficulties.* **3.** To collide with. **4.** To reach as far as; add up to: *The cost could run into millions.* **—run over. 1.** To knock down or drive over, as in a car. **2.** To overflow. **3.** To examine, review, or rehearse. **4.** To extend beyond.

~n. **1. a.** A pace faster than the walk. **b.** A gait faster than the canter. **2. a.** An act of running. **b.** A running race: *a cross-country run.* **c.** An act of running away; a bolt: *made a run for it.* **3. a.** A distance covered by or as if by running. **b.** The time taken to cover it: *a two minute run from the station.* **4.** A quick trip or visit, especially by car: *a run into town.* **5.** In cricket: **a.** A successful act of running from one popping crease to the other by both batsmen. **b.** The point so scored. **6.** In baseball, an act of successfully completing a circuit of the bases and returning to home plate. **7.** The distance a golf ball rolls after hitting the ground. **8.** A migration of fish inshore or upstream, especially prior to spawning: *the shad run.* **9.** Unrestricted freedom or use: *I had the run of their library.* **10.** A stretch or period of riding, as in a race or to hounds. **11.** A track or slope along or down which something can travel: *a ski run.* **12. a.** A journey between points on a scheduled or regular route. **b.** The distance so covered. **c.** The time taken to cover this distance. **13. a.** A continuous period of operation, as by a machine or factory. **b.** The production achieved during such a period. **14.** The final approach of a military aircraft to its target: *a bombing run.* **15.** A transit of smuggled goods. **16. a.** A movement or flow, as of fluid or sand. **b.** The duration of such a flow. **c.** The amount of such a flow. **17.** A pipe or channel through which something flows: *a mill run.* **18.** *U.S.* A small, fast-flowing stream or brook. **19.** *Mining.* A fall or slide, as of sand or mud. **20.** A continuous length or extent of something: *a ten-foot run of tubing.* **21.** *Mining.* A vein or seam, as of ore or rock. **22.** The direction, configuration, or lie of something: *the run of the grain in leather.* **23.** A trail or burrow made or frequented by animals: *a rabbit run.* **24. a.** An outdoor enclosure for domestic animals or poultry. **b.** *Australian.* A large stretch of grazing land; a station. **25.** *Chiefly U.S.* A length of unravelled stitches; a ladder. **26.** An unbroken series or sequence: *a run of dry summers.* **27.** An unbroken sequence of theatrical performances. **28.** *Music.* A rapid sequence of notes; a roulade. **29. a.** Urgent and heavy demand for a product. **b.** Urgent and heavy demand by depositors, creditors, or the like: *a run on the bank.* **c.** Pressure on a currency caused by widespread selling. **30. a.** In certain games, a continuous set or sequence, as of playing cards in one suit. **b.** A successful sequence of shots or points. **31.** A sustained state or condition: *a run of good luck.* **32.** A trend or tendency: *the run of events.* **33.** The average type, group, or category; majority: *The broad run of voters want him to win.* **—a run for (one's) money. 1.** Strong competition. **2.** A degree of satisfaction or enjoyment derived from an expenditure of money or effort. **—in the long run.** In the final analysis or outcome. **—on the run. 1. a.** In rapid retreat. **b.** In hiding, as a fugitive might be. **2.** Hurrying busily from place to place. **—the runs.** *Slang.* Diarrhoea.

~adj. **1.** In a liquid state; melted. **2.** Poured into a mould while liquid: *run metal.* **3.** Drained; extracted: *run honey.* [Run, ran, run; Middle English *runnen, ran, runnen,* Old English *rinnan* (but influenced by the past participle), *ran(n), gerunnen,* reinforced by Old Norse cognate verb *rinna.*]

run·a·bout (rún-ə-bowt) *n.* **1. a.** A usually small car used for short journeys. **b.** A light aircraft. **c.** *Chiefly U.S.* A small motorboat. **2.** A vagabond or wanderer.

run·a·gate (rúnnə-gayt) *n. Archaic.* **1.** A renegade or deserter. **2.** A vagabond. [Variant of RENEGADE (influenced by RUN).]

run·a·round (rún-ə-rownd) n. **1.** *Informal.* Deception, evasion, or delaying tactics. Used chiefly in the phrase *give someone the run-around.* **2.** *Printing.* Type set in a column narrower than the body of the text, as on either side of a picture.

run·a·way (rún-ə-way) n. **1.** One that runs away, such as a fugitive or a horse that has bolted. **2.** An act of running away. ~*adj.* **1.** Escaping or having escaped. **2.** Of or done by running away. **3.** Easily won, as a victory in a race. **4.** Completely out of control: *a runaway train; runaway inflation.*

run·ci·ble spoon (rúnssib'l) n. A three-pronged fork, such as a pickle fork, curved like a spoon and having a cutting edge. [*Runcible,* a nonsense word coined by Edward Lear.]

run·ci·nate (rún-si-nət, -nit, -nayt) adj. *Botany.* Having saw-toothed divisions directed backwards: *runcinate leaves.* [Latin *runcinātus,* past participle of *runcināre,* to plane, from *runcina,* carpenter's plane (formerly taken also to mean a saw), from Greek *rhukanē†.*]

Run·corn (rúng-kawrn). Industrial port and new town in northwest England, situated on the river Mersey.

run down *intr.v.* **1.** To lose power and stop working: *The battery has run down.* **2.** To grow gradually weaker; suffer a loss of health or vigour. —*tr.v.* **1. a.** To pursue and capture. **b.** To find by diligent searching; track down: *ran down the source of the trouble.* **2.** To hit with a moving vehicle. **3.** To disparage; denigrate. **4.** To cause to decline in numbers, size, output, or the like: *running down the firm's South African operations.*

run-down (rún-down) n. A summary or résumé. ~*adj.* (rún-dówn) **1. a.** In poor physical condition; weak or exhausted. **b.** In a poor state of repair; dilapidated. **2.** Unwound and not running.

rune (roōn ‖ rewn) n. **1.** Any of the letters of an alphabet used by ancient Germanic peoples, especially by the Scandinavians and Anglo-Saxons. **2.** Any poem, riddle, or the like written in runic characters. **3.** Any character or symbol supposed to have magical powers or significance. **4.** A Finnish poem or canto. [In sense 4, from Finnish *runo.* In other senses, Middle English *roun, rune,* secret writing, rune, from Old Norse *rūn* (unattested).]

rung¹ (rung) n. **1. a.** A rod or bar forming a step of a ladder. **b.** Anything resembling this. **2.** A crosspiece supporting the legs or back of a chair. **3.** A point or level in a hierarchy or similar series of ascending stages. **4.** *Nautical.* Any of the spokes or handles on a ship's steering wheel. [Middle English *rung, rong,* Old English *hrung,* akin to Old High German *runga,* Gothic *hrugga†.*]

rung². Past tense and past participle of **ring**.

ru·nic (roō-nik ‖ réw-) adj. **1.** Consisting of, inscribed with, or written in runes. **2.** Made in the ornate interlacing style characteristic of rune-bearing monuments. **3.** Having a cryptic or magical significance.

run in *tr.v.* **1.** To insert or include as something extra. **2.** *Printing.* To make (a body of text) solid without a paragraph or other break. **3.** *Slang.* To take into legal custody. **4.** To run (an engine or car) for a certain period at low speed when new so that engine parts in contact become smooth.

run-in (rún-in) n. **1.** *Chiefly U.S.* A quarrel; an argument; a fight. **2.** *Printing.* Matter added to a text.

run·let (rún-lət, -lit) n. A rivulet. [Diminutive of RUN (stream).]

run·nel (rúnn'l) n. **1.** A rivulet; a brook. **2.** A narrow channel or course, as for water. **3.** On a beach, a long narrow hollow between two shingle ridges running parallel to the coastline. [Middle English *rynel,* Old English *rynel,* from *rinnan,* to run, flow.]

run·ner (rúnnər) n. **1.** One that runs, as: **a.** One that competes in a race. **b.** A messenger or errand boy. **c.** In cricket, a player who takes runs on behalf of a batsman who is unable to run himself. **2.** An agent or collector, as for a bank or brokerage house. **3.** One who solicits business for others. **4.** A smuggler or a vessel engaged in smuggling. Often used in combination: *a gun-runner.* **5.** An antique dealer who has no retail outlet but acts as a go-between for other dealers. **6.** A device in or on which a mechanism slides or moves, as: **a.** The blade of a skate. **b.** Either of the pieces of wood or metal on which a sledge runs. **c.** The supports on which a drawer slides. **7.** A long narrow carpet. **8.** A long narrow tablecloth. **9.** A channel along which molten metal is poured into a mould; a gate. **10. a.** A slender, creeping stem that puts forth roots and shoots either from nodes along its length or at the tip. **b.** A plant, such as the strawberry, having such a stem. **c.** A twining vine.

runner bean n. **1.** A widely cultivated tropical American climbing bean plant, *Phaseolus coccineus,* with typically scarlet flowers and long, slender, edible pods. **2.** A pod of this plant, eaten as a vegetable. Also called "scarlet runner".

run·ner-up (rúnnər-úp) n. One that takes second place in a race, competition, or election.

run·ning (rúnning) n. **1.** The act or sport of one that runs. **2. a.** The act or skill of managing something. **b.** The act or process of operating something. Also used adjectivally: *high running costs.* —**in (or out of) the running**. Still in (or no longer in) serious contention, as in a race or other competitive situation. —**make the running**. To determine the speed at which something progresses or develops; set the pace. ~*adj.* **1.** Performed while running: *a running jump.* **2.** Intended for the use of runners: *a running track; running shoes.* **3.** Piped and supplied by taps: *running water.* **4.** Continuous: *A running battle.* **5.** Describing events as they happen: *a running commentary.* ~*adv.* Consecutively: *four years running.*

running board n. A narrow footboard extending under and beside the doors of some cars and other vehicles.

running gear n. **1.** The working parts of a car, locomotive, or other vehicle. **2.** Running rigging.

running hand n. A type of handwriting done rapidly without lifting the pen from the paper.

running head n. *Printing.* A title printed at the top of every page or every other page. Also called "running headline", "running title".

running knot n. A slipknot (see).

running light n. **1.** Any of several lights on a boat or ship kept lighted between dusk and dawn. **2.** Any of several similar lights on an aircraft; a navigation light.

running mate n. *Chiefly U.S.* **1.** A horse used as a pacemaker for another horse of the same stable. **2.** The candidate or nominee for the lesser of two closely associated political offices, such as the vice-presidency.

running rigging n. The part of a ship's rigging that comprises the ropes with which sails are raised, lowered, or trimmed, and booms and gaffs are operated. Also called "running gear".

running stitch n. Any of a series of small, even stitches.

run·ny (rúnni) adj. **-nier, -niest. 1.** Inclined to run or flow. **2.** Discharging mucus. Said of the nose.

Run·ny·mede (rúnni-meed). A meadow on the south bank of the river Thames, near Egham, Surrey, where King John sealed the Magna Carta in 1215. [Middle English *Runimede,* "meadow on the council island" : Old English *Rūnīeg,* council island : *rūn,* secret, secret council + *īeg, īg,* ISLAND + *mede,* MEAD (meadow).]

run off *intr.v.* **1.** To run away, abscond, or elope. **2.** To flow off or drain away. —*tr.v.* **1.** To cause to flow off or drain away. **2.** To decide (a contest or competition) by a run-off. **3.** To produce (a copy), as with a printing or duplicating machine.

run-off (rún-off, -awf) n. **1. a.** The overflow of a fluid from a container. **b.** The amount of precipitation that reaches streams and rivers, and flows away to the sea. **2.** Eliminated waste products from manufacturing processes. **3.** A final round or contest to decide the winner in a race or in the event of a tie.

run-of-the-mill (rún-əv-thə-míl) adj. Ordinary; not special; average. See Synonyms at **average**. [From *run of (the) mill,* products of a mill that are not graded for quality.]

run on *intr.v.* **1.** To continue on and on. **2.** To talk at length and without a break. —*tr.v. Printing.* To continue (a text) without a formal break.

run-on (rún-on ‖ -awn) n. *Printing.* Matter that is appended or added without a formal break.

run out *intr.v.* **1.** To become completely used up. Used of a supply or allocation of something. **2.** To exhaust one's supply of something. Often used with *of.* —*tr.v.* In cricket, to dismiss (a batsman who is taking a run) by hitting the wicket with the ball before he has completed his run.

run-out (rún-owt) n. An instance of running a batsman out in cricket.

runt (runt) n. **1.** An undersized animal; especially, the smallest animal of a litter. **2.** A person of small stature. Used derogatorily. [16th century : origin obscure.] —**runt·i·ness** n. —**runt·ish, runt·y** adj.

run through *tr.v.* **1.** To pierce: *ran him through with my sword.* **2.** To use up (money, for example) wastefully; fritter away. **3.** To examine, review, or rehearse quickly.

run-through (rún-throō) n. A complete but rapid review or rehearsal of something, such as a theatrical work.

run up *tr.v.* **1.** *Informal.* To make quickly by sewing. **2.** To raise (a flag) on a flagpole. **3.** *Informal.* To allow (a debt, for example) to accumulate.

run-up (rún-up) n. **1.** *Informal.* The time leading up to a particular event; a preliminary period. **2.** *Sports.* A player's running approach, such as that of a fast bowler gaining speed prior to delivering a cricket ball.

run·way (rún-way) n. **1.** A strip of level ground, usually paved, on which aircraft take off and land. **2.** A path, channel, or track over which something runs. **3.** *Chiefly U.S.* A chute down which logs are skidded. **4.** A narrow walkway from a stage into an auditorium.

Run·yon (rún-yən), **(Alfred) Damon** (1884-1946). U.S. writer. From his experiences as a journalist of New York low-life, he wrote many popular stories in collections such as *Guys and Dolls* (1931), later the subject for a hit musical of the same name.

ru·pee (roō-pée, roō- ‖ rew-, *U.S. also* roōpi) n. *Abbr.* Re., r., R. **1. a.** The basic monetary unit of India, equal to 100 paise. **b.** The basic monetary unit of Nepal, equal to 100 paisa or pice. **c.** The basic monetary unit of Pakistan, equal to 100 paisa. **d.** The basic monetary unit of Sri Lanka, the Seychelles, and Mauritius, equal to 100 cents. **e.** The basic monetary unit of the Maldives, equal to 100 laris. **2.** A coin or note worth one rupee. [Hindi *rupaīyā,* from Sanskrit *rūpya,* wrought silver, from *rūpa†,* shape, image.]

Ru·pert (roō-pərt ‖ réw-), **Prince, Duke of Cumberland.** (1619-82). German-born British general. A maternal grandson of James I, he was the senior Royalist cavalry commander in the Civil War. Following the Restoration, he served as an admiral in the Dutch Wars. He was also a patron of the art and sciences.

Rupert's Land n. The Canadian territory granted the Hudson's Bay Company in 1670, most of which was incorporated in the Northwest Territories after its purchase by Canada in 1869. Also known as Prince Rupert's Land.

ru·pi·ah (roō-pée-ə, -aa) n., *pl.* **rupiah** or **-ahs. 1.** The basic monetary unit of Indonesia, equal to 100 sen. **2.** A note worth one rupiah. [Hindi *rupaīyā,* RUPEE.]

rup·ture (rúpchər) *n.* **1. a.** The act of breaking open or bursting. **b.** The state of being broken open or burst. **2.** A break in friendly relations between individuals or nations. **3.** *Pathology.* **a.** A **hernia** *(see),* especially of the groin or intestines. **b.** A tear in bodily tissue.
—*v.* **ruptured, -turing, -tures.** —*tr.* **1.** To break open; burst. **2.** To cause a break in (friendly relations). **3.** To cause to suffer a hernia. —*intr.* To undergo or suffer a rupture. [Middle English *ruptur,* from Old French *rupture,* from Latin *ruptūra,* from *rumpere* (past participle *ruptus*), to break.] —**rup·tur·a·ble** *adj.*

ru·ral (ro͝or-əl || réwr-) *adj.* **1.** Of, pertaining to, or characteristic of the country as opposed to the city; rustic. **2.** Of or pertaining to people who live in the country. **3.** Of or pertaining to farming; agricultural. [Middle English, from Old French, from Latin *rūrālis,* from *rūs* (stem *rūr-*), country.] —**ru·ral·ism** *n.* —**ru·ral·ist** *n.* —**ru·ral·i·ty** (roor-rál-əti || ro͞o-, rew-) *n.* —**ru·ral·ly** *adv.*

rural dean *n.* In the Church of England, a clergy member who supervises the running of a number of parishes.

Ru·ri·ta·ni·a (ro͝or-i-táyn-i-ə || réwr-) *n.* An imaginary central European kingdom used as a setting for tales of romance, adventure, and suspense. [After the setting of Anthony Hope's novels *The Prisoner of Zenda* (1894) and *Rupert of Hentzau* (1898).] —**Ru·ri·ta·ni·an** *adj.*

ruse (ro͞oz || rewz) *n.* An action meant to confuse or mislead; a clever trick. See Synonyms at **artifice.** [Middle English, detour of a hunted animal, from Old French, from *ruser,* to repulse, detour. See **rush** (to dash off).]

rush¹ (rush) *v.* **rushed, rushing, rushes.** —*intr.* **1.** To move, act, or proceed with great speed and vigour. **2.** To act or proceed with impetuous haste: *rushed into marriage.* **3.** To make a sudden or swift attack or charge. Used with *on* or *upon.* —*tr.* **1.** To cause to move, act or proceed with unusual haste or vigour: *Medical supplies were rushed to the scene.* **2.** To pressurise into hasty action. **3.** To perform with great haste. **4.** To attack swiftly and suddenly. **5.** *British Informal.* To charge (a customer) excessively: *rushed us £5 for two coffees.* **6.** *U.S.* To attempt to impress or seek the favour of.
—*n.* **1.** The act of rushing; a sudden forward motion or turbulent movement. **2.** An eager, often competitive movement of people in pursuit of some object: *a rush for the best seats; a gold rush.* **3.** Urgency; need for haste: *There's no rush.* **4.** A sudden attack; an onslaught. **5.** A great flurry of activity or press of business: *the usual last-minute rush.* **6.** *Slang.* A sudden, pleasurable rushing sensation induced by taking certain drugs. **7.** *Often plural.* The first, unedited print of a scene in a cinema film.
—*adj.* Requiring or marked by haste or urgency: *a rush job.* [Middle English *russhen,* from Anglo-French *russher,* variant of Old French *ruser,* to repulse, from Latin *recusāre,* to object to (in Vulgar Latin, "to repel") : *re-,* back + *causārī,* to plead, give as a reason, from *causa,* CAUSE.] —**rush·er** *n.*

rush² *n.* **1.** Any of various grasslike marsh plants of the genus *Juncus,* having pliant, hollow, or pithy stems and clusters of small, brownish flowers. **2.** Any of similar, usually aquatic plants, such as the woodrush. **3.** The stem of a rush, used in making baskets, mats, and chair seats. [Middle English *rush, rish,* Old English *rysc.*]

Rush·die (rúsh-di), **(Ahmed) Salman** (1947–). Indian-born British novelist. *Midnight's Children* (1981), about the period following Indian independence, won the Booker prize and brought him international recognition. His later achievements as a writer have been overshadowed by the death sentence invoked by the Ayatollah Khomeini of Iran in 1989 because parts of his novel *The Satanic Verses* (1988) were interpreted by some Muslims as being blasphemous. He has since lived under police protection. His most recent work includes *The Moor's Last Sigh* (1995).

rush hour *n.* Either of the two periods in the working day when most people are travelling to or from work. —**rush-hour** *adj.*

rush·light (rúsh-līt) *n.* A candle consisting of a rush wick in tallow. Also called "rush candle".

rush·y (rúshi) *adj.* **-ier, -iest. 1.** Resembling or characteristic of rushes; rushlike. **2.** Abounding in rushes: *a rushy marsh.*

rusk (rusk) *n.* A piece of sweet or plain bread that has been dried and browned in an oven, often given to babies. [Spanish and Portuguese *rosca*†, a coil, twisted roll.]

Rus·kin (rúskin), **John** (1819–1900). British art critic. He developed a philosophy in which art, morality, economics, and religion are interrelated, and which is expressed in works such as *The Stones of Venice* (1851–53) and *Sesame and Lilies* (1865).

Rus·sell (rúss'l), **Bertrand (Arthur William), 3rd Earl** (1872–1970). British philosopher. In his *Principia Mathematica* (1910–1913) he attempted to show that mathematics was an extension of logic. He later developed interests in social morality, epistemology, languages, and education. He was a prominent pacifist in both World Wars and, as the doyen of British philosophy, he was an important figure in the CND movement. In 1950 he was awarded the Nobel prize for literature.

Russell, John, 1st Earl (1792–1878). British politician. A champion of Parliamentary reform throughout his career, he was elected to parliament in 1813, and held cabinet posts in Whig governments from 1835. He served two terms as Prime Minister (1846–52, 1865–66). He was also a writer and a biographer.

Russell, Ken, born Henry Kenneth Alfred Russell (1927–). British film and television director. His films, such as *Women in Love* (1969), *The Music Lovers* (1970), *Mahler* (1974), and *Valentino* (1977), are notable for their use of spectacular visual effects. Later work includes *The Rainbow* (1989) and, on TV, *Lady Chatterley* (1993).

Russell diagram *n. Astronomy.* A **Hertzsprung-Russell diagram** *(see).*

rus·set (rússit) *n.* **1.** Moderate to deep reddish brown. **2.** A coarse rough reddish-brown skin. [Middle English, from Old French *rousset,* from *rous,* red, from Latin *russus.*] —**rus·set** *adj.*

Rus·sia (rúshə). **1.** See **Russian Federation. 2.** See **Union of Soviet Socialist Republics.**

reddish-brown to brown homespun cloth. **3.** An eating apple with a

Rus·sian (rúsh'n) *n. Abbr.* **Rus., Russ. 1. a.** Formerly, a native or inhabitant of the U.S.S.R. **b.** A native or inhabitant of the Russian Federation. **c.** A native or inhabitant of the former Russian Empire. **2.** One who is of Russian descent. **3.** The Slavonic language of the Russian people, the official language of the Russian Federation.
—*adj.* **1.** Of or pertaining to the Russian Federation, its people, or their language. **2.** Loosely, of or pertaining to the former U.S.S.R., especially when considered as a political power.

Russian Federation. Also **Russia.** Largest country in the world, formerly, as the Russian Soviet Federative Socialist Republic, the largest constituent republic of the U.S.S.R. It stretches from the Baltic Sea to the Pacific Ocean, and from the Arctic Ocean to the Black Sea. More than 80 per cent of the republic's inhabitants are Russian. With the disintegration of the U.S.S.R. in 1991, it emerged as a new country, embracing some 76 per cent of the Soviet Union's land and 52 per cent of its people. A decline in Russian power and influence after the break-up aroused nationalism on left and right, and economic liberalisation measures led to widespread hardship. Attempts in 1991 and 1993 failed to reverse political and economic reform and to check the increasing powers of Boris Yeltsin's presidency, but after elections in 1993 right-wing nationalists appeared as the strongest single party. However, Yeltsin himself was re-elected (1996). Area, 17 075 400 square kilometres (6,592,821 square miles). Population, 147,740,000. Capital, Moscow. See **Union of Soviet Socialist Republics,** and map at **Commonwealth of Independent States.**

Russian Orthodox Church *n.* **1.** An independent branch of the Eastern Orthodox Church in Russia headed by the Patriarch of Moscow. **2.** A branch of this church outside Russia.

Russian roulette *n.* **1.** An act of bravado, traditionally done as a wager, in which a person spins the cylinder of a revolver loaded with one bullet, aims the muzzle at his head, and pulls the trigger. **2.** Any exceptionally hazardous or foolhardy venture.

Russian salad *n.* A salad of diced cooked vegetables mixed with a piquant mayonnaise dressing *(Russian dressing).*

Russian wolfhound *n.* A dog, the **borzoi** *(see).*

Russian wedding ring *n.* A ring consisting of three interlaced loops, each made of a different type of gold.

Russo– *comb. form.* Indicates Russia; for example, **Russophilia.** [From RUSSIA.]

Rus·so-Jap·a·nese War (rússō-jáppə-néez || -néess) *n.* A war (1904–05) between Russia and Japan arising out of their conflicting interests in Manchuria and resulting in defeat for Russia.

Rus·so·phil·i·a (rúss-ō-filli-ə, -ə-) *n.* Interest in or enthusiasm for Russia, its culture, people, government, or language. [RUSSO- + -PHILIA.] —**Rus·so·phile** (-fīl || -fil) *n.*

Rus·so·pho·bi·a (rúss-ō-fōbi-ə, -ə-) *n.* Dislike or fear of Russia or its policies. [RUSSO- + -PHOBIA.] —**Rus·so·phobe** (-fōb) *n.*

rust (rust) *n.* **1.** Any of various powdery or scaly reddish-brown or reddish-yellow hydrated ferric oxides formed on iron and steel by low-temperature oxidation in the presence of water. **2.** Any of various metallic coatings, especially oxides, formed by corrosion. **3.** A stain or coating resembling iron rust. **4.** Any deterioration of ability or character resulting from inactivity or neglect. **5.** *Botany.* **a.** Any of various parasitic fungi of the order Uredinales, that are injurious to a wide variety of plants, including cereals. **b.** A plant disease caused by such fungi, characterised by reddish or brownish spots on leaves, stems, and other parts. **6.** Strong reddish brown.
—*v.* **rusted, rusting, rusts.** —*intr.* **1.** To become corroded; form rust. **2.** To deteriorate or degenerate through inactivity or neglect. **3.** To become the colour of rust. **4.** To develop a disease caused by a rust fungus. —*tr.* **1.** To corrode or subject (a metal) to rust formation. **2.** To impair or spoil by misuse, inactivity, and the like.
—*adj.* Rust-coloured. [Middle English *rust,* Old English *rūst.*] —**rust·a·ble** *adj.* —**rust·less** *adj.*

rus·tic (rústik) *adj.* **1.** Of, pertaining to, or characteristic of country life. **2. a.** Charmingly simple and unsophisticated. **b.** Lacking refinement or polish; uncouth. **3.** Made of rough tree branches: *rustic furniture.* **4.** Having a rough surface with deep or chamfered joints. Said of masonry. —See Synonyms at **rural.**
—*n.* **1.** A rural person. **2.** An awkward or unpolished simpleton. [Middle English *rustyk,* from Old French *rustique,* from Latin *rūsticus,* from *rūs,* country.] —**rus·ti·cal·ly** *adv.* —**rus·tic·i·ty** (russ-tíssəti) *n.*

rus·ti·cate (rústi-kayt) *v.* **-cated, -cating, -cates.** —*intr.* **1.** To go to or live in the country. **2.** To lead a simple, rustic life. —*tr.* **1.** To send to the country. **2.** To impart a rustic character to. **3.** *British.* To suspend (a student) from a university or school. **4.** To construct (masonry) in the rustic style. [Latin *rūsticārī,* from *rūsticus,* RUSTIC.] —**rus·ti·ca·tion** (-káysh'n) *n.* —**rus·ti·ca·tor** (-kaytər) *n.*

rus·tle¹ (rúss'l) *v.* **-tled, -tling, -tles.** —*intr.* To move with soft whispering sounds. —*tr.* To cause to make such sounds.
—*n.* A soft whispering sound: *The gentle rustle of a silken gown.* [Middle English *rustlen, rustelen,* akin to Frisian *russelje,* Dutch *ridselen* (imitative).] —**rus·tler** *n.* —**rus·tling·ly** *adv.*

rustle² v. **-tled, -tling, -tles.** —tr. Chiefly U.S. To steal (cattle or other livestock). —intr. Chiefly U.S. **1.** To steal livestock. **2.** Informal. To act or proceed energetically; hustle. **—rustle up.** To prepare or produce, especially hastily or in an improvised fashion. [Probably from RUSTLE (to move with soft sounds).] **—rus·tler** (rússlər) n.

rust·proof (rúst-proof ‖ -proof) adj. Specially treated so as to be incapable of rusting. **—rust·proof** tr.v.

rust·y (rústi) adj. **-ier, -iest. 1.** Covered with or affected by rust; corroded. **2.** Consisting of or produced by rust. **3.** Rust-coloured. **4.** Working or operating stiffly or incorrectly because of or as if because of rust. **5.** Weakened or impaired by neglect, disuse, or lack of practice. **—rust·i·ly** adv. **—rust·i·ness** n.

rut¹ (rut) n. **1.** A sunken track or groove made by the passage of vehicles. **2.** A fixed, monotonous routine of thought or action. ~tr.v. **rutted, rutting, ruts.** To furrow. [Old French rote, route, way, ROUTE.]

rut² n. **1.** A cyclically recurring condition of sexual excitement and reproductive activity in male mammals, such as deer. **2.** The comparable condition of female mammalian sexual activity; oestrus. ~intr.v. **rutted, rutting, ruts.** To be in rut. [Middle English rutte, from Old French rut, ruit, "bellowing (of stags in rut)", from Late Latin rūgitus, from Latin rūgīre, to roar.]

ru·ta·ba·ga (roota-báygə, roota-, -béggə) n. U.S. A vegetable, the **swede** (see). [Swedish (dialectal) rotabagge, "baggy root" : rot, root, from Old Norse rōt + bagge, from Old Norse baggi, BAG.]

ruth (rooth ‖ rewth) n. Archaic. **1.** Compassion or pity. **2.** Sorrow; misery; grief. [Middle English ruthe, rewthe, from rewen, to rue, from Old English hrēowan.]

Ruth¹ (rooth ‖ rewth). In the Old Testament, a Moabite widow who went to Bethlehem where she later married Boaz.

Ruth² n. A book of the Old Testament in which the story of Ruth is told.

Ru·the·ni·a (roo-theeni-ə, roo- ‖ rew-). Region of eastern Europe, in western Ukraine, west of the Carpathian Mountains. Part of it constituted a province of Czechoslovakia (1918–39) and all of it was annexed by the U.S.S.R. in 1945, becoming the Zakarpatskaya Oblast, also known as Transcarpathian Ukraine. [Medieval Latin, Russia, from Rut(h)enī, Russians, from Russian Rusin, from Old Russian Rus', "Norsemen".]

Ru·the·ni·an (roo-theeni-ən, roo- ‖ rew-) n. **1.** A member of a group of Ukrainians living in Ruthenia. **2.** A Ukrainian dialect spoken by these people. **—Ru·the·ni·an** adj.

ru·then·ic (roo-thénnik, roo-, -théenik ‖ rew-) adj. Chemistry. Of or pertaining to ruthenium. Said especially of a compound that contains ruthenium with a high valency.

ru·the·ni·um (roo-theeni-əm, roo- ‖ rew-) n. Symbol **Ru** A hard white acid-resistant metallic element found in platinum ores. It is used to harden platinum and palladium for jewellery and in alloys for nonmagnetic wear-resistant instrument pivots and electrical contacts. Atomic number 44, atomic weight 101.07, melting point 2,250°C, boiling point 3,900°C, relative density 12.41, valencies 1, 2, 3, 4, 5, 6, 7, 8. [New Latin; discovered in the Ural Mountains in Russia, from Medieval Latin Ruthenia, Russia. See **Ruthenia**.]

ru·then·i·ous (roo-theeni-əss, roo- ‖ rew-) adj. Chemistry. Of or pertaining to ruthenium. Said especially of a compound that contains ruthenium with a low valency.

ruth·er·ford (rúthər-fərd) n. A unit of radioactivity equal to the quantity of radioactive material that undergoes one million disintegrations per second. [After Ernest RUTHERFORD.]

Rutherford, Ernest, 1st Baron (rúthər-fərd) (1871–1937). New Zealand-born British scientist. He classified radiation into alpha, beta, and gamma types; his discovery that alpha radiation consists of positive charged helium atoms led to his discovery (1906) of the atomic nucleus. He won the Nobel prize for chemistry (1908).

Rutherford, Dame Margaret (1892–1972). British actress. Starting her film career in 1936, she appeared in more than 40 films, mostly comedies, in parts characterised by a uniquely British eccentricity. In Murder She Said (1962) and its sequels, she played Agatha Christie's detective, Miss Marple.

ruth·er·for·di·um (rúthər-fórdi-əm ‖ -fórdi-) n. The element **unnilquadium** (see). Not in current technical usage. [After Ernest RUTHERFORD.]

ruth·ful (rooth-f'l ‖ rewth-) adj. Archaic. **1.** Full of or causing sorrow. **2.** Compassionate. **—ruth·ful·ly** adv. **—ruth·ful·ness** n.

ruth·less (rooth-ləss, -liss ‖ rewth-) adj. Having or showing no compassion, pity, or leniency; merciless. See Synonyms at **cruel**. **—ruth·less·ly** adv. **—ruth·less·ness** n.

ru·ti·lant (rooti-lənt ‖ rewti-) adj. Archaic. Having a reddish glow or gleam. [Middle English rutilaunt, from Latin rutilāns (stem rutilant-), from rutilāre, to make reddish, from rutilus, reddish.]

ru·tile (roo-tīl ‖ rew-, -teel) n. The lustrous red, reddish-brown, yellowish, or black natural mineral form of titanium dioxide, TiO_2, used as a gemstone, as a source of titanium, and in paints and fillers. [German Rutil, from Latin rutilus, reddish. See **rutilant**.]

Rut·land (rút-lənd). County of central England. Absorbed into Leicestershire (1974) despite local opposition, it regained its administrative status in 1997. It is the smallest county of England. Its county town is Oakham.

rut·tish (rúttish) adj. Lustful; libidinous.

rut·ty (rútti) adj. **-tier, -tiest.** Full of ruts. **—rut·ti·ness** n.

Ru·wen·zo·ri Mountains (roo-en-záw-ri, -ən- ‖ -zō-). Mountain range between Uganda and Zaire, central Africa. Extending from Lake Albert to Lake Edward, the range rises to 5 120 metres (16,798 feet) at Mount Ngaliema (Mount Stanley). The peaks are snow-capped, and are thought to be Ptolemy's Mountains of the Moon.

R.V. Revised Version (of the Bible).

Rwan·da (roo-ándə), **Republic of.** Small republic of central Africa. It is chiefly mountainous with part of Lake Kivu to the west, and the volcanic Virunga mountains in the northwest. Densely populated, it was a refuge in the days of the slave trade and was administered with Burundi by Belgium as Ruanda-Urundi from 1919 until independence (1962). There was sporadic violence between the two main ethnic groups, the Hutu and Tutsi, from 1959, culminating in civil war in 1994. A poor, predominantly agricultural country, Rwanda relies on exports of coffee and tea, but its considerable mineral resources are now being developed. Area, 26 338 square kilometres (10,169 square miles). Population, 5,400,000. Capital, Kigali. See map at **Tanzania**.

-ry. Variant of **-ery.**

ryd·berg (rid-berg) n. A unit of energy, the **hartree** (see). [After Johannes Robert Rydberg (1854–1919), Swedish physicist.]

Rydberg constant n. Physics. Symbol **R.** A constant used in formulae for series of lines in atomic spectra, equal to 1.09737 x 10^7m⁻¹.

Ry·der, Sue, Baroness (rídər) (1923–). British philanthropist. The wife of Group Captain Leonard Cheshire, she founded the Sue Ryder Foundation for the Sick and Disabled of All Age Groups, which grew from her work with refugees after World War II.

rye¹ (rī) n. **1.** A widely cultivated cereal grass of the genus Secale, the seeds of which are valued as grain. **2.** The grain of this plant, used in making flour and whiskey and for livestock feed. **3.** Rye bread. **4.** Rye whisky. [Middle English rye, ruge, Old English ryge.]

rye² n. A gentleman among Gypsies. [Romany rai, from Sanskrit rājan, king.]

Rye (rī). Market town and resort of East Sussex, southeast England. It is one of the Cinque Ports but silt deposits have moved the coast-line 3 kilometres (2 miles) from the town.

rye bread n. Bread made partially or entirely from rye flour.

rye brome n. A Eurasian grass, Bromus secalinus, widely introduced, having rough leaves and wheatlike ears. Also U.S. "chess".

rye grass n. Any of several pasture or meadow grasses of the genus Lolium, native to Eurasia, some species of which are cultivated for forage.

rye whisky n. Whisky distilled from rye.

Ry·kov (rée-kof; Russian -kəf), **Aleksei Ivanovich** (1881–1938). Soviet politician. He succeeded Lenin as chairman of the Council of Peoples' Commissars, but was obliged to resign (1930) for his opposition to Stalin's disastrous collectivisation of agriculture. He was eventually executed after a public trial for treason.

Ryle, Sir Martin (rīl) (1918–85). British astronomer. He was best known for pioneering the technique of setting up a line of two or more radio telescopes and using the Earth's rotation to multiply their effective aperture. In 1974 he shared with Antony Hewish (1924–) the Nobel prize for physics.

ry·ot (rī-ət) n. A peasant or tenant farmer in India. [Hindi ra'īyat, from Arabic ra'īyah, herd, peasants, from ra'ā, pasture.]

Ryu·kyu Islands (ri-oo-kew; Japanese réw-). Island group of the west Pacific Ocean. Forming an arc between Kyushu Island (Japan) and Taiwan, they were seized from China by Japan (1879) and were occupied by the United States from 1945, returning to Japan in 1953 and 1972. Okinawa is the main island. See map at **Japan**.

S

s, S (ess) *n., pl.* **s's, S's** or **Ss.** **1.** The 19th letter of the modern English alphabet. **2.** Any of the speech sounds represented by this letter. **3.** Anything shaped like the letter **S**.

s, S, s., S. *Note:* As an abbreviation or symbol, *s* may be a small or a capital letter, with or without a full stop. Established forms or those generally preferred precede the definition. When no form is given, all four forms are in general use in that sense. **1. S.** Sabbath. **2. S.** saint. **3. S.** Saturday. **4. S.** Saxon. **5. s., S.** school. **6. s., S.** sea. **7. s** second (unit of time). **8. s** second of arc. **9. s.** see. **10. s.** semi-. **11. S.** September. **12. s.** shilling. **13. S.** *Medicine.* signature. **14. S.** signor; signore. **15. s.** singular. **16. s.** sire. **17. s.** sister. **18. s.** small. **19. s., S.** society. **20. s.** son. **21.** south; southern. **22. s** stere. **23. S** *Physics.* strangeness. **24. s.** substantive. **25. S** The symbol for the element sulphur. **26. S.** Sunday.

–s[1] *n. suffix.* Indicates the plural form, for which it is used: **a.** In most nouns not ending in a sibilant (such as *s* or *sh*), an affricate (such as *ch*), or a postconsonantal *y;* for example, *charms, toys.* **b.** In abbreviations, numbers, or symbols used as nouns; for example, *MAs, D.T.s, 1960s, As.* Compare **-es** (in nouns). [Middle English *-es, -s,* Old English *-as,* nominative and accusative plural ending of some nouns.]

–s[2] *v. suffix.* Indicates the third person singular form of the present indicative, for which it is used in most verbs not ending in a sibilant, an affricate, or a postconsonantal *y;* for example, she *sleeps,* one *stays.* Compare **-es** (in verbs). [Middle English *-es,* Old English *-es, -as.*]

–s[3] *adv. suffix.* **1.** Used in the formation of certain adverbs; for example, **unawares.** **2.** Used, especially in American English, to form adverbs indicating regular repetition of action; for example, *mornings,* (in *Mornings he takes the train*), *nights* (in *She works nights*). [Middle and Old English *-es,* genitive singular ending used to form adverbs from some nouns and adjectives.]

–'s[1] *n. & pron. suffix.* Indicates the possessive case, for which it is used in singular nouns, in some pronouns, and in irregularly formed plural nouns; for example, **nation's, somebody's, men's.** [Middle and Old English *-es,* genitive singular ending.]

–'s[2] *n. suffix.* Indicates the plural form in abbreviations, numbers, or symbols used as nouns; for example, *MA's, D.T.'s, 1960's, A's.* [From -s (plural suffix).]

–'s[3]. **1.** Contraction of *is: She's here.* **2.** Contraction of *has: He's been eating.* **3.** Contraction of *us: Let's go.* **4.** *Nonstandard.* Contraction of *does: What's it mean?*

s.a. without date [Latin *sine anno.*]

S.A. **1.** Salvation Army. **2.** South Africa. **3.** South America. **4.** South Australia. **5.** Sturmabteilung.

Saa·nen (sáanən) *n.* A dairy goat of a breed developed in Switzerland, having a white, short-haired coat and no horns. [After *Saanen,* a town in southwest Switzerland.]

Saar·brück·en (sár-bröockən; *German* zaar-brückən). *French* **Sarrebruck** (saar-brük). Capital of Saarland, southwestern Germany. Situated on the river Saar near the French border, it is the industrial centre of the Saar coalfield.

Saa·ri·nen (sáari-nən; *Finnish* -nen), **Eero** (1910–61). Finnish-born U.S. architect. His innovative designs include the General Motors Technical Center at Warren, Michigan, and the Trans World Airlines terminal at New York's John F. Kennedy Airport.

Saar·land (sár-land; *German* zár-lant) Formerly **Saar·ge·biet** (-gə-beet) or **Saar (Territory)** *French* **Sarre** (sar). State of southwestern Germany, bordered by Luxembourg and France. With rich coal deposits, it has heavy industries including iron and steel and metal goods, and also glass and textiles. A German-speaking border territory, Saarland became the Saar Territory, administered by France under the League of Nations (1919). After a plebiscite, the territory was constituted the German province of Saarland (1935). It became part of the French zone of occupied Germany in 1945, and joined a customs union with France (1948). A referendum (1955) rejected plans for an autonomous, neutral state and the area gained its present status (1957). Saarbrücken is the capital.

Sab. Sabbath.

sab·a·dil·la (sábbə-díllə) *n.* **1.** A tropical American plant, *Schoenocaulon officinale,* having poisonous seeds used in insecticides. **2.** The dry, ripe seeds of this plant. [Spanish *cebadilla,* diminutive of *cebada,* barley, from *cebo,* feed, from Latin *cibus,* food, probably of non-Indo-European origin.]

Sa·bah (sáa-baa, -bə). State of East Malaysia, on the island of Borneo. It was the British protectorate of North Borneo from 1882 and joined the Federation of Malaysia (1963). It has been claimed by the Philippines. Sabah produces rubber, copra, cocoa, rice, and wood, and has oil and copper resources. Its capital is Kota Kinabalu.

Sab·a·oth (sábbay-oth, sa-báy-, sə-, -əth) *pl.n.* Hosts; armies: *the Lord of Sabaoth.* Romans 9:29; James 5:4. [Latin *Sabaōth,* from Greek, from Hebrew *ṣəbhā'oth,* from *sābhā',* host, army.]

sa·ba·yon (sábbī-ón) *n.* A dessert sauce made with beaten egg yolks. [French, from Italian *zabaione,* ZABAGLIONE.]

sab·bat (sábbət, sa-báa) *n.* The **witches' Sabbath** *(see).* [French, "Sabbath", from Latin *sabbatum,* SABBATH.]

Sab·ba·tar·i·an (sábbə-taír-i-ən) *n.* **1.** A person who observes Saturday as the Sabbath, as in Judaism and some sects of Christianity. **2.** A person who believes in strict observance of the Sabbath. *~adj.* Of the Sabbath or Sabbatarians. [Late Latin *sabbatārius,* from Latin *sabbatum,* SABBATH.] **—Sab·ba·tar·i·an·ism** *n.*

Sab·bath (sábbəth) *n. Abbr.* **S., Sab. 1.** Saturday, taken as the seventh day of the week, named in the Ten Commandments as the day of rest and worship and observed as such by the Jews and some Christian sects. **2.** Sunday, taken as the first day of the week, observed as the day of rest by most Christian churches. [Middle English *sabat(h),* from Old English *sabat* and Old French *sab(b)at,* both from Latin *sabbatum,* from Greek *sabbaton,* from Hebrew *shabbāth,* from *shābhath,* to rest.]

sab·bat·i·cal (sə-báttik'l) *adj.* Also **sab·bat·ic** (sə-báttik). **1.** *Sometimes capital* **S.** Pertaining or appropriate to the Sabbath as the day of rest. **2.** Designating a period of paid leave granted, as to a university lecturer, for travel, research, or rest: *sabbatical leave.* *~n.* A sabbatical year. [Late Latin *sabbaticus,* from Greek *sabbatikos,* from *sabbaton,* SABBATH.]

sabbatical year *n.* **1.** A year's sabbatical leave, usually granted every seventh year. **2.** *Often capital* **S.** A year during which land remained fallow, observed every seven years by the ancient Jews.

S.A.B.C. South African Broadcasting Corporation.

Sa·be·an, Sa·bae·an (sa-bée-ən, sa-) *n.* **1.** An inhabitant of ancient Sheba. **2.** The Semitic language of ancient Sheba. [Latin *Sabaeus,* from Greek *Sabaios,* from *Saba,* SHEBA.] **—Sa·be·an** *adj.*

Sa·bel·li·an (sə-bélli-ən) *n.* **1.** An extinct division of the subfamily of Italic Indo-European languages, including ancient Aequian, Sabine, and Volscian. **2.** A member of any of the Sabellian-speaking peoples of ancient Italy, who included the Sabines and the Samnites. [Latin *Sabellus†,* Sabine.] **—Sa·bel·li·an** *adj.*

saber. *Chiefly U.S.* Variant of **sabre.**

sa·bin (sáybin, sábbin) *n.* A unit of acoustic absorption, equivalent to the absorption by one square foot of a surface that absorbs all incident sound. [After W.C.W. *Sabine* (1868–1919), U.S. physicist.]

Sab·ine (sáb-īn ‖ *chiefly U.S.* sáy-bīn) *n.* **1.** A member of an ancient tribe of central Italy, conquered and assimilated by the Romans in 290 B.C. **2.** The Sabellian language of this people. [Middle English *Sabyn,* from Latin *Sabīnus†.*] **—Sab·ine** *adj.*

Sa·bin vaccine (sáybin) *n.* A live but nonvirulent form of the polio virus taken orally to immunise against poliomyelitis. [After A.B. *Sabin* (1906–93), U.S. microbiologist.]

sa·ble (sáyb'l) *n.* **1. a.** A carnivorous mammal, *Martes zibellina,* of northern Europe and Asia, having soft, dark fur. **b.** The highly valued pelt or fur of this animal. **2.** The similar fur of other species of martens; especially, the fur of the American marten, *Martes americana.* In this sense, also called "American sable". **3. a.** The colour black, especially in heraldry. **b.** *Usually plural. Literary.* Black clothing worn in mourning. **4.** Greyish yellowish brown. *~adj.* **1.** Made of or trimmed with sable fur. **2.** Having the colour of sable fur. **3. a.** Of the colour black, as in heraldry or mourning. **b.** *Literary.* Dark; sombre. [Middle English, from Old French, from Medieval Latin *sabelum,* from Slavic, akin to Russian *sobol†.*]

sable antelope *n.* A large African antelope, *Hippotragus niger,* having a usually dark coat and backward-curving horns.

sab·ot (sáb-ō ‖ -ət) *n.* **1.** A shoe carved from a single piece of wood, worn in several European countries. **2.** A wooden-soled sandal or shoe having a leather upper. [French, from Old French, perhaps blend of *savate,* shoe, akin to Spanish *zapáto,* shoe, perhaps of Oriental origin, + *bote,* BOOT.]

sab·o·tage (sábbə-taazh, -taaj) *n.* **1.** The deliberate damaging of property or disruption of procedure carried out, as by enemy agents or dissatisfied workers, with the intention of obstructing productivity or normal functioning. **2.** Any underhand action intended to defeat or frustrate an endeavour; deliberate subversion. *~tr.v.* **sabotaged, -taging, -tages.** To deliberately and maliciously damage or frustrate. [French, from *saboter,* "to clatter shoes", work clumsily, deliberately wreck, from SABOT.]

sab·o·teur (sábbə-tér, -ter, -tôr) *n.* A person who commits sabotage. [French, from *saboter,* to work clumsily, SABOTAGE.]

sa·bra (sáabrə) *n.* A native-born Israeli. [Modern Hebrew *sābrāh,* "prickly pear", a plant widespread in the Negev.]

sa·bre, *U.S.* **sa·ber** (sáybər) *n.* **1.** A heavy cavalry sword with a one-edged, slightly curved blade. **2. a.** A fencing sword having a tapering two-edged blade and a guard that covers the back of the hand. **b.** The art of fencing with the sabre. *~tr.v.* **sabred** or *U.S.* **sabered, -bring** or *U.S.* **-bering, -bres** or *U.S.* **-bers.** To strike, wound, or kill with a sabre. [French, earlier *sable,* from German *Sabel, Säbel,* from Hungarian *szablya* or Polish *szabla.*]

sabre-rattling *n.* An ostentatious display of military power or the threatening of war.

sa·bre-toothed tiger (sáybər-tōōtht) *n.* Any of various extinct cats of the Oligocene to the Pleistocene epoch, characterised by long upper canine teeth; especially, one of the larger members of the genus *Smilodon.* Also called "sabre-toothed cat".

sab·u·lous (sábbew-lass) *adj.* Gritty; sandy. [Latin *sabulōsus,* from *sabulum,* coarse sand.] —**sab·u·los·i·ty** (-lóssəti) *n.*

sac (sak) *n.* A pouchlike part in a plant or animal, sometimes filled with fluid. [French, a bag, from Latin *saccus,* a SACK.]

S.A.C. senior aircraftman.

sac·cate (sák-ayt, -ət, -it) *adj.* Shaped like or having a pouch or sac. [New Latin *saccatus,* from Latin *saccus,* a bag, SACK.]

sac·cha·rase (sáckər-ayz, -ayss) *n.* An enzyme, **invertase** *(see).* [SACCHAR(O)- + -ASE.]

sac·cha·rate (sáckə-rayt) *n.* A salt or ester of saccharic acid. [SACCHAR(IC ACID) + -ATE.]

sac·char·ic acid (sə-kárrik) *n.* A white crystalline acid, COOH(CHOH)$_4$COOH, formed by the oxidation of glucose. [SACCHAR(O)- + -IC.]

sac·cha·ride (sáckə-rīd ‖ -rid) *n.* Any of a series of compounds of carbon, hydrogen, and oxygen in which the atoms of the latter two elements are in the ratio of 2:1, especially sugars and other carbohydrates containing the group C$_6$H$_{10}$O$_5$. [SACCHAR(O)- + -IDE.]

sac·char·i·fy (sə-kárri-fī, sa-) *tr.v.* **-fied, -fying, -fies.** Also **sac·cha·rise** (sáckə-rīz), **-rised, -rising, -rises.** To convert (starch, for example) into sugar. [SACCHAR(O)- + -FY.] —**sac·char·i·fi·ca·tion** (-fi-káysh'n) *n.*

sac·cha·rim·e·ter (sáckə-rímmitər) *n.* **1.** A polarimeter that indicates the concentration of sugar in a solution. **2.** An instrument that determines the sugar content of a fermenting sample from carbon dioxide measurements. [SACCHAR(O)- + -METER.]

sac·cha·rin (sáckə-rin, -reen) *n.* A white crystalline powder, C$_7$H$_5$NO$_3$S, having a taste about 500 times sweeter than cane sugar, used as a calorie-free sweetener. [SACCHAR(O)- + -IN.]

sac·cha·rine (sáckə-rin, -reen, -rīn) *adj.* **1.** Pertaining to, or of the nature of sugar or saccharin; sweet. **2.** Ingratiatingly or cloyingly sweet: *a saccharine smile.* [SACCHAR(O)- + -INE.] —**sac·cha·rine·ly** *adv.* —**sac·cha·rin·i·ty** (-rínnəti) *n.*

saccharo-, sacchar- *comb. form.* Indicates sugar; for example, **saccharometer, saccharide, saccharin.** [Latin *saccharum,* sugar, from Greek *sakkharon,* from Pali *sakkharā,* from Sanskrit *śarkarā,* gravel, SUGAR.]

sac·cha·roid (sáckə-royd) *adj.* Also **sac·cha·roi·dal** (-róyd'l). Designating rocks and minerals having a granular structure similar to that of loaf sugar. [SACCHAR(O)- + -OID.]

sac·cha·rom·e·ter (sáckə-rómmitər) *n.* A hydrometer that determines the amount of sugar in a solution from relative density measurements. [SACCHARO- + -METER.]

sac·cha·ro·my·cete (sáckərō-mī-seet) *n.* Any of the yeast fungi, many of which ferment sugar. [SACCHARO- + -MYCETE.] —**sac·cha·ro·my·ce·tic** (-séttik), **sac·cha·ro·my·ce·tous** (-séetəss) *adj.*

sac·cha·rose (sáckə-rōz, -rōss) *n.* A sugar, **sucrose** *(see).* [SACCHAR(O)- + -OSE.]

sac·cu·late (sáckew-layt, -lət, -lit) *adj.* Also **sac·cu·lat·ed** (-laytid), **sac·cu·lar** (-lər). **1.** Formed of or divided into a series of saclike dilations or pouches. **2.** Possessing a saccule or saccules. [New Latin *sacculus,* SACCULE + -ATE.]

sac·cule (sáckewl) *n.* Also **sac·cu·lus** (sáckew-ləss) *pl.* **-li** (-lī). **1.** A small sac. **2.** The smaller of two membranous sacs in the vestibule of the labyrinth of the ear. [New Latin *sacculus,* from Latin, diminutive of *saccus,* bag, SACK.]

sac·er·do·tal (sássər-dōt'l, sáckər-) *adj.* **1.** Of or pertaining to priests or the priesthood; priestly. **2.** Of or pertaining to sacerdotalism. [Middle English, from Old French, from Latin *sacerdōtālis,* from *sacerdōs* (stem *sacerdōt-*), a priest.] —**sac·er·do·tal·ly** *adv.*

sac·er·do·tal·ism (sássər-dōt'l-iz'm, sáckər-) *n.* **1.** The belief that ordained priests are invested with supernatural powers and are the indispensable mediators between God and man. **2.** The assumption of excessive authority by the priesthood over the laity, based on such a belief.

sa·chem (sáychəm) *n.* **1.** The chief of a tribe or confederation among some North American Indian peoples. Also called "sagamore". **2.** *U.S.* Any of the high officials of the Tammany Society. [Narraganset *sâchim,* "chief", from Proto-Algonquian *saakimaawa* (unattested). See also **sagamore.**]

sa·cher·tor·te (zákhər-tawrtə) *n.* A rich chocolate cake filled with jam and chocolate and coated in chocolate icing. [German *Sachertorte : Sacher,* 19th- and 20th-century family of Viennese hotel owners + TORTE.]

sa·chet (sáshay ‖ *U.S.* sa-sháy) *n.* **1.** A small bag or packet containing perfumed powder and used to scent clothes, as in trunks or wardrobes. **2.** A small sealed packet containing a quantity of a product, such as shampoo or dried yeast, that is enough for use on a single occasion. [French, from Old French, a small bag, diminutive of *sac,* a bag, from Latin *saccus,* SACK.]

Sachs (zaks), **Hans** (1494–1576). German poet and dramatist. A cobbler by trade, he became a Meistersinger of Nuremberg. Though much of his vast output of songs seems dull by modern standards, his shorter plays and verse anecdotes still amuse. His life inspired Wagner's opera, *Die Meistersinger von Nürnberg.*

Sachsen. See **Saxony.**

sack[1] (sak) *n.* Also **sacque** (for sense 2). **1.** *Abbr.* **sk. a.** A large bag of strong, coarse material for holding foodstuffs or other objects in bulk. **b.** The contents of such a bag. **c.** The amount a sack will hold, used as a unit of measure for various commodities. **2. a.** A short, loose-fitting coat for women and children. **b.** A woman's loose-fitting dress. **3.** *Informal.* Dismissal from employment: *His boss finally gave him the sack.* **4.** *Chiefly U.S. Slang.* A bed, mattress, or sleeping bag. —**hit the sack.** *Informal.* To go to bed. ~*tr.v.* **sacked, sacking, sacks. 1.** To place in a sack or sacks. **2.** *Informal.* To discharge from employment. [Middle English *sack, sak,* Old English *sæcc, sacc,* from Latin *saccus,* from Greek *sakkos,* from Semitic; akin to Hebrew *śaq,* sack, sackcloth.]

sack[2] *tr.v.* **sacked, sacking, sacks.** To loot or pillage (a captured city, for example). ~*n.* **1.** The looting or pillaging of a captured town. **2.** Plunder; loot. [French *(mettre à) sac,* (to put in) a sack, to plunder, from Italian *sacco,* bag, from Latin *saccus,* SACK.]

sack[3] *n.* Any of various strong white wines from Spain and the Canary Islands, imported to England in the 16th and 17th centuries. [16th-century *wyne seck,* from Old French *(vin) sec,* dry (wine), from Latin *siccus,* dry.]

sack·but (sák-but, -bət) *n.* A medieval musical instrument resembling the trombone. [French *saquebute, saqueboute,* "hooked lance": *saquer, sachier†,* to pull, draw + *bouter,* to push, thrust against, from Common Romance *bottāre* (unattested), from Germanic.]

sack·cloth (sák-kloth ‖ -klawth) *n.* **1.** Sacking. **2. a.** A rough cloth of camel's hair, goat hair, hemp, cotton, or flax. **b.** Garments made of this cloth, worn as a symbol of mourning or penitence.

sackcloth and ashes *n.* An outward show of repentance. [From the traditional symbols of mourning or penitence, of Biblical origin (in numerous passages, for example Matthew 11:21).]

sack·ful (sák-fŏŏl) *n., pl.* **-fuls.** The amount a sack will hold; a sack.

sack·ing (sácking) *n.* A coarse, stout woven cloth, made of jute, hemp, or the like, used for making sacks.

sack race *n.* A race in which the competitors, whose legs are enclosed in sacks, proceed by short jumps.

Sack·ville-West (sák-vil-wést), **Vita.** See Sir Harold **Nicolson.**

sa·cral[1] (sáykrəl ‖ *U.S. also* sáckrəl) *adj.* Of, near, or pertaining to the sacrum. [New Latin *sacralis,* from SACRUM.]

sacral[2] *adj.* Pertaining to sacred rites or observances. [Latin *sacer* (stem *sacr-*), SACRED.]

sac·ra·ment (sáckrəmənt) *n.* **1.** Any of various religious rites considered to have been instituted or observed by Jesus as a visible sign of inner grace or a means of achieving grace, specifically: **a.** In the Roman Catholic and Eastern Churches, the rites of baptism, confirmation, the Eucharist, matrimony, holy orders, penance, and the Sacrament of the Sick. **b.** In the Protestant Churches, baptism and the Eucharist. **2.** *Often capital* **S. a.** The Eucharist. **b.** The consecrated elements of the Eucharist; especially, the bread or Host. **3.** Something considered to have sacred or mystical significance; a spiritual symbol or bond. [Middle English, from Old French *sacrement,* from Latin *sacrāmentum,* from Latin, oath, solemn obligation, from *sacrāre,* to consecrate, from *sacer* (stem *sacr-*), SACRED.]

sac·ra·men·tal (sáckrə-mént'l) *adj.* **1.** Pertaining to, of, the nature of, or used in a sacrament. **2.** Having the force and sacred character of a sacrament: *a sacramental obligation.* ~*n.* Any rite, action, or sacred object instituted by some Christian churches for use in worship. —**sac·ra·men·tal·ly** *adv.*

sac·ra·men·tal·ism (sáckrə-mént'l-iz'm) *n.* **1.** The doctrine that observance of the sacraments is necessary for salvation and that such participation can confer grace. **2.** Emphasis upon the efficacy of a sacramental. —**sac·ra·men·tal·ist** *n.*

sac·ra·men·tar·i·an (sáckrə-men-taír-i-ən) *n. Often capital* **S.** A person who regards the sacraments, especially the Eucharist, as merely visible symbols, not inherently efficacious nor corporeally manifesting Christ. ~*adj.* **1.** *Often capital* **S.** Of or pertaining to sacramentarians. **2.** Of or pertaining to sacramentalism. [Translation of German *Sakramenter, Sakramentierer.*] —**sac·ra·men·tar·i·an·ism** *n.*

Sac·ra·men·to (sáckrə-méntō). Capital of California, western United States. Situated on the Sacramento river, it was founded as Fort Sutter (1839) and expanded with the gold rush of 1848. It became the state capital (1854) and terminus of the Pony Express postal system (1860). It has a deep-water port connected to the Pacific.

Sacrament of the Sick *n. Roman Catholic Church.* A sacrament in which a priest anoints and prays for a sick person, especially one in danger of death. Also called "extreme unction".

sa·crar·i·um (sa-kráir-i-əm, sə-) *n., pl.* **-ia** (-i-ə). **1.** The sanctuary of a church. **2.** In the Roman Catholic Church, a **piscina** *(see).* [Medieval Latin *sacrārium,* from Latin, a place for keeping holy things, from *sacer,* SACRED.]

sa·cred (sáykrid) *adj.* **1.** Dedicated, consecrated, or set apart for the worship of a deity. **2.** Dedicated or devoted exclusively to a single use, purpose, or person. **3.** Worthy of reverence or respect; venerable: *the sacred teachings of Buddha.* **4.** Entitled, because of religious or quasi-religious feeling, to immunity from violation; sacrosanct: *a football match at Lord's —is nothing sacred?* **5.** Of or pertaining to religious objects, rites, or practices. [Middle English, from the past participle of *sacren,* to consecrate, from Old French *sacrer,* from Latin *sacrāre,* from *sacer* (stem *sacr-*), dedicated, holy, sacred.] —**sa·cred·ly** *adv.* —**sa·cred·ness** *n.*

Sacred College *n.* The **College of Cardinals** *(see).*

sacred cow *n.* A person, idea, institution, or object regarded as immune from reasonable criticism. [Referring to the veneration of cows as sacred by Hindus.]

Sacred Heart *n. Roman Catholic Church.* **1. a.** The heart of Christ, regarded as a symbol of his sacrifice and an object of devotion. **b.** Christ himself symbolised in this way. **2.** A picture of the Sacred Heart.

sacred mushroom *n.* Any of various mushrooms, such as species of *Psilocybe* and *Amanita,* that are ritually eaten for their hallucinogenic effects in various parts of the world.

sac·ri·fice (sáckri-fīss) *n.* **1. a.** The act of offering something to a deity in propitiation or homage; especially, the ritual slaughter of an animal or person for this purpose. **b.** That which is so offered. **2. a.** The forfeiture of something highly valued, as an idea, object, or friendship, for the sake of someone or something considered to have a greater value or claim. **b.** Something so forfeited. **3. a.** A relinquishing of something at less than its presumed value. **b.** Something so relinquished. **c.** A loss so sustained. ~*v.* **sacrificed, -ficing, -fices.** —*tr.* **1.** To offer as a sacrifice to a deity. **2.** To forfeit (something of value) for something considered to have a greater value or claim. **3.** To sell at a loss. **4.** In chess, to allow one's opponent to capture (a piece) without the loss of an equivalent piece, as for tactical reasons. —*intr.* To make or offer a sacrifice. [Middle English, from Old French, from Latin *sacrificium*: *sacer,* holy, SACRED + *facere,* to do, make.] —**sac·ri·fic·er** *n.*

sac·ri·fi·cial (sáckri-físh'l) *adj.* Pertaining to, intended as, or concerned with a sacrifice: *a sacrificial lamb.* —**sac·ri·fi·cial·ly** *adv.*

sacrificial anode *n. Metallurgy.* A piece of electropositive metal, such as magnesium or zinc, connected by a wire to a steel structure and buried in the ground, used to inhibit corrosion of the steel. [The magnesium corrodes instead (sacrifices itself for the steel).]

sac·ri·lege (sáckri-lij) *n.* **1.** The misuse, theft, desecration, or profanation of anything consecrated to a deity. **2.** An act of gross disrespect towards something regarded as sacred: *thought it sacrilege to put milk in China tea.* [Middle English, from Old French, from Latin *sacrilegium,* from *sacrilegus,* one who steals sacred things: *sacer,* SACRED + *legere,* to gather, pluck, steal.] —**sac·ri·le·gist** (-lij-ist ‖ chiefly U.S. -léej-) *n.*

sac·ri·le·gious (sáckri-líj-əss, *rarely* -líji- ‖ *chiefly U.S.* -léej-) *adj.* **1.** Disrespectful or irreverent towards anything regarded as sacred; impious; profane. **2.** Guilty of sacrilege. —See Synonyms at **profane.** —**sac·ri·le·gious·ly** *adv.* —**sac·ri·le·gious·ness** *n.*

sa·cring bell (sáykring) *n.* A bell rung at the elevation of the Host in the Mass. [Middle English *sacringe belle*: *sacringe,* gerund of *sacren,* to consecrate (see **sacred**) + BELL.]

sac·ris·tan (sáckristən) *n.* Also **sa·crist** (sáckrist, sáykrist) **1.** A person in charge of a sacristy. **2.** *Archaic.* A sexton. [Middle English, from Medieval Latin *sacristānus,* from *sacrista,* "one in charge of sacred vessels", from Latin *sacer* (stem *sacr-*), SACRED.]

sac·ris·ty (sáckristi) *n., pl.* **-ties.** A room in a church housing the sacred vessels and vestments; a vestry. [French *sacristie,* from Medieval Latin *sacristia,* from *sacrista,* SACRISTAN.]

sac·ro·il·i·ac (sáykrō-ílli-ak, sáckrō-) *adj. Anatomy.* Of, pertaining to, or affecting the sacrum and ilium, their articulation, or associated ligaments. ~*n.* The sacroiliac joint or region. [SACR(UM) + ILI(UM) + -AC.]

sac·ro·sanct (sáck-rə-sangkt, -rō-) *adj.* Regarded as sacred and inviolable. Often used to imply undeserved immunity to questioning, change, or attack. [Latin *sacrōsanctus,* consecrated with religious ceremonies: *sacrō,* by a sacred rite, ablative of *sacrum,* a holy thing, religious rite, from *sacer,* SACRED + *sanctus,* past participle of *sancīre,* to consecrate.] —**sac·ro·sanc·ti·ty** (-sángktəti) *n.*

sa·crum (sáy-krəm ‖ *U.S. also* sá-) *n., pl.* **-cra** (-krə). **1.** A triangular bone consisting, in humans, of five fused vertebrae and forming the posterior section of the pelvis. **2.** The corresponding bone in other vertebrates. [New Latin, from Late Latin *(os) sacrum* (translation of Greek *hieron osteron,* "sacred bone", because it was used in sacrifice), from Latin, a sacred thing, from *sacer,* SACRED.]

sad (sad) *adj.* **sadder, saddest. 1.** Low in spirits; dejected; sorrowful. **2.** Expressive of or characterised by sorrow or gloom. **3.** Causing sorrow or gloom; depressing. **4.** Deplorable; sorry. **5.** Dark-hued; sombre. [Middle English *sad,* grave, sad, full (of something), Old English *sæd,* sated, weary, from Germanic.] —**sad·ly** *adv.* —**sad·ness** *n.*

Synonyms: sad, melancholy, depressed, dejected, downcast, sorrowful, doleful, desolate, miserable, wretched.

SAD seasonal affective disorder.

Sadat (sə-dát, -dáat), **Muhammad Anwar El** (1918–81). Egyptian politician, who succeeded to the presidency on Nasser's death (1970). For his dramatic visit to Israel and his attempts to initiate a lasting settlement between the two countries, he was awarded the Nobel peace prize jointly with Menachem Begin (1978). He was assassinated by Muslim fundamentalists.

sad·den (sádd'n) *v.* **-dened, -dening, -dens.** —*tr.* To make sad. —*intr.* To grow sad.

saddhu. Variant of **sadhu.**

sad·dle (sádd'l) *n.* **1.** A leather seat for a rider, secured on an animal's back by a girth. **2.** The padded part of a driving harness fitting over a horse's back. **3.** The part of an animal's back upon which a saddle is placed. **4.** Something resembling or suggestive of a saddle in position, function, or shape, as: **a.** The seat of a bicycle, motorcycle, or similar vehicle. **b.** A cut of meat, especially lamb or mutton, consisting of part of the backbone and both loins. **c.** The lower part of a male fowl's back. **d.** A saddle-shaped depression in the ridge of a hill; a col. **e.** A ridge between two peaks. **f.** The **clitellum** *(see)* of an earthworm. **5.** *Geometry.* A saddle-shaped surface. —**in the saddle.** In a position of control or dominance. ~*v.* **saddled, -dling, -dles.** —*tr.* **1.** To put a saddle on (a horse, for example). **2.** *Informal.* To load or burden; encumber: *saddled with ten children.* **3.** *Informal.* To impose (a burdensome responsibility) upon another: *She saddled her debts on him.* —*intr.* To saddle a horse or get into a saddle. Often used with *up.* [Middle English *sadel,* Old English *sadol,* from Germanic.]

sad·dle·back (sádd'l-bak) *n.* **1.** A roof having a gable at each end connected by a ridge. Also called "saddle roof". **2.** A rare New Zealand songbird, *Philesturnus carunculatus,* having black plumage with a brown back patch and orange wattles.

sad·dle·bag (sádd'l-bag) *n.* A bag or pouch, usually one of a pair, hung across the saddle of an animal or behind the saddle of a bicycle or motorcycle.

sad·dle·bill (sádd'l-bil) *n.* A tropical African stork, *Ephippiorhynchus senegalensis,* having a black and white plumage and a large red bill with a black band round the middle.

sad·dle·bow (sádd'l-bō) *n.* The arched upper front part of a saddle; a pommel. [Middle English *sadelbowe,* Old English *sadulboga*: SADDLE + BOW (arch.).]

sad·dle·cloth (sádd'l-kloth ‖ -klawth) *n.* A cloth placed between a saddle and a horse's back to prevent rubbing.

saddle horse *n.* A horse bred or schooled for riding.

sad·dler (sáddlər) *n.* One who makes, repairs, or sells saddles and other riding equipment.

sad·dler·y (sáddləri) *n., pl.* **-ies. 1.** Saddles, harnesses, and other equipment for horses; tack. **2.** A shop selling such equipment. **3.** The craft or business of a saddler.

saddle soap *n.* A preparation containing mild soap and neat's-foot oil, used for cleaning and softening leather.

sad·dle·sore (sádd'l-sôr) *adj.* **1.** Having sores caused by an improperly fitted saddle. **2.** Sore as a result of riding.

saddle stitch *n.* **1.** A simple running stitch used primarily as ornament on the edges of clothing and accessories, and usually done in a thread contrasting in colour with the fabric of the garment. **2.** *Bookbinding.* A stitch used in sewing together the leaves of a book at the fold lines. —**sad·dle·stitch** *tr.v.*

sad·dle·tree (sádd'l-tree) *n.* The frame of a saddle.

Sad·du·cee (sáddew-see) *n.* A member of a Jewish sect flourishing from the second century B.C. to the first century A.D., that retained the older interpretation of the written Mosaic law against the oral tradition and denied the resurrection of the dead. Compare **Pharisee.** [Middle English *Saducee,* Old English *Sadducēas* (plural), from Late Latin *Saddūcaeus,* from Late Greek *Saddoukaios,* from Hebrew *Ṣəddūqī,* probably "descendant of *Ṣādōq*", Zadok, "righteous", high priest of Israel in King David's time (II Samuel 8:17).] —**Sad·du·ce·an** (-see-ən) *adj.* —**Sad·du·cee·ism** *n.*

sa·de, sa·dhe, tsa·de (sáa-di, tsáa-, -də) *n.* The 18th letter of the Hebrew alphabet. [Hebrew *ṣadhe.*]

Sade (saad), **Donatien Alphonse François, Comte de,** known as the Marquis de Sade (1740–1814). French novelist. While imprisoned during the 1780s and 1790s for prohibited sexual practices, he wrote several pornographic fantasies, whose preoccupation with sexual violence led to the term sadism.

sad·hu, sad·dhu (sáadōō) *n.* A Hindu ascetic holy man. [Sanskrit *sādhu,* from adjective, "straight", right, holy, from Indo-Iranian *sādh* (unattested).]

sad·i·ron (sád-īrn, -ī-ərn) *n.* A heavy flatiron, having points at both ends and a removable handle. [SAD (in the dialectal sense of "heavy") + IRON.]

sa·dism (sáyd-iz'm, *rarely* sád-) *n.* **1.** *Psychology.* An abnormal condition in which a person derives sexual gratification from inflicting pain and humiliation on others. **2.** Broadly, delight in mental or physical cruelty. [After Comte Donatien de SADE.] —**sa·dist** *n.* —**sa·dis·tic** (sə-dístik, sa-) *adj.* —**sa·dis·ti·cal·ly** *adv.*

sa·do·mas·och·ism (sáydō-mássə-kiz'm) *n.* The combination of sadism and masochism in one person, marked by the gaining of pleasure from both inflicting and submitting to pain. [SAD(ISM) + MASOCHISM.] —**sa·do·mas·och·ist** *n.* —**sa·do·mas·o·chis·tic** (-kístik) *adj.*

sad sack *n. U.S. Informal.* An extremely inept or clumsy person.

s.a.e. stamped addressed envelope.

Sa·far, Sa·phar (sə-fár) *n.* The second month of the Muslim calendar. [Arabic.]

sa·fa·ri (sə-fáari) *n., pl.* **-ris. 1.** An overland expedition, especially for hunting or observing wild animals in Africa. **2.** The people, animals, and equipment of such an expedition. [Arabic *safarīy,* a journey, from *safara,* to travel, set out.]

safari park *n.* A type of zoo in which wild animals are allowed to roam over an extensive area and can be viewed by the public from cars or buses.

safari suit *n.* A lightweight outfit consisting of a loose, shirtlike jacket and matching trousers or skirt.

safe (sayf) *adj.* **safer, safest. 1.** Free from harm or injury; unhurt: *safe and sound after their ordeal.* **2. a.** Free from the threat of harm or danger. **b.** Affording protection against harm or danger: *a safe place; a safe haven.* **c.** Unable or unlikely to cause harm or danger: *a safe drug; safe sex.* **3.** Free from the risk of loss or failure: *a safe parliamentary seat; a safe investment.* **4. a.** Cautious; disinclined to

1345

provoke controversy or take risks: *a safe speech; better safe than sorry.* **b.** Reliable; dependable: *a safe pair of hands.*
~n. **1.** A metal container usually having a lock, used for storing valuables; a strongbox or safe-deposit box. **2.** Any repository for protecting stored items, such as a **meat safe** *(see).* **3.** *U.S. Slang.* A condom. [Middle English *sauf,* from Old French, from Latin *salvus,* healthy, uninjured, safe.] **—safe·ly** *adv.* **—safe·ness** *n.*
safe-blow·er (sáyf-blō-ər) *n.* A safe-breaker who uses explosives.
safe-break·er (sáyf-braykər) *n.* A criminal skilled in breaking open safes. **—safe-break·ing** *n.*
safe-con·duct (sáyf-kón-dukt) *n.* **1.** An official document assuring unmolested passage, as through enemy territory. **2.** The protection thus afforded.
~tr.v. (*also* -kən-dúkt || -kon-) **safe-conducted, -ducting, -ducts.** **1.** To grant a safe-conduct to. **2.** To escort with a safe-conduct.
safe-de·pos·it (sáyf-di-pozzit, -də-, -pózzit) *n.* A vault or strongroom usually containing rows of small safes *(safe-deposit boxes)* for individual use for storing papers, jewellery, or other valuables.
safe·guard (sáyf-gaard) *n.* **1.** One that serves as a protection or precaution, as: **a.** A mechanical device or technical improvement designed to prevent accidents. **b.** A protective stipulation, as in a contract. **2.** A safe-conduct.
~tr.v. **safeguarded, -guarding, -guards.** To keep safe or secure, as from danger, attack, or violation; protect. See Synonyms at **defend.**
safe house *n.* A house or flat offering safe conditions for clandestine activities, such as: **1.** One used by intelligence officers, as for the debriefing of a person seeking political asylum. **2.** One in which an escaped prisoner, especially a prisoner of war, may seek refuge.
safe·keep·ing (sáyf-kéeping) *n.* The act of keeping in safety or the state of being kept safe; protection; care.
safe·light (sáyf-līt) *n.* A lamp having one or more colour filters capable of permitting moderate darkroom illumination without exposure of photosensitive film or paper.
safe period *n.* The days of a woman's menstrual cycle during which sexual intercourse is considered least likely to result in pregnancy. See **rhythm method.**
safe·ty (sáyfti) *n., pl.* **-ties.** **1.** Freedom from or prevention of danger, risk, or injury. **2.** Any of various devices designed to prevent accident; specifically, a lock on a firearm preventing accidental firing. Also called "safety catch". **3.** In American football: **a.** A touchdown behind one's own goal line. **b.** Either of two defensive backs, usually positioned closest to the goal line they defend.
~adj. Contributing to or insuring safety; protective.
safety belt *n.* A **seat belt** *(see).*
safety curtain *n.* A fireproof curtain or screen lowered between the stage and auditorium in a theatre when no performance is taking place to contain any possible outbreak of fire.
safety factor *n.* A **factor of safety** *(see).*
safety film *n.* Nonflammable photographic film.
safety fuse *n.* **1.** A slow-burning fuse used for detonating an explosive from a safe distance. **2.** An electrical **fuse** *(see).*
safety glass *n.* Glass that has been toughened, reinforced, or otherwise modified so as to diminish the risk of breakage or to reduce the risk of injury should breakage occur. The main types either have a laminated structure including wire or plastic sheet (*laminated glass*), or are strained so that they can break into small pieces without sharp edges (*toughened glass*).
safety helmet *n.* A reinforced hat made of plastic or metal worn especially by workers on building sites.
safety lamp *n.* **1.** A miner's lamp with a protective wire gauze surrounding the flame to prevent ignition of flammable gases. **2.** Any specially protected lamp.
safety match *n.* A match that can be lighted only by being struck against a chemically prepared friction surface. See **match.**
safety net *n.* **1.** A net held above the ground to break a person's fall, especially one for acrobats and similar performers. **2.** Any arrangement or measure providing for an emergency.
safety pin *n.* **1.** A pin in the form of a clasp, having a sheath to enclose the point, thus giving protection to the user. **2.** A pin that prevents the premature or accidental detonation of a bomb, grenade, or other explosive.
safety razor *n.* A razor in which the blade is fitted into a holder with guards to prevent cutting of the skin.
safety valve *n.* **1.** A valve in a pressure container, as in a steam boiler, that automatically opens when pressure reaches a dangerous level. **2.** Any outlet for the release of an excess, as of emotion.
saf·flow·er (sáf-lowr, -low-ər) *n.* **1.** A plant, *Carthamus tinctorius,* native to Asia, having orange flowers that yield a dyestuff and seeds that are the source of an oil used in cooking, cosmetics, paints, and medicine. **2.** The dried flowers of this plant. **3.** Any of the products of this plant. [Earlier *safflore,* from Dutch *saffloer* or German *Safflor,* from Old French *saffleur,* from obsolete Italian *saffiore*†.]
saf·fron (sáffrən) *n.* **1.** A plant, *Crocus sativus,* native to the Old World, having purple or white flowers with orange stigmas. **2.** The dried stigmas of this plant, used to colour foods and as a cooking spice and a dyestuff. **3.** Any of various similar or related plants, such as the meadow saffron. See **autumn crocus.** **4.** Moderate orange-yellow to moderate orange. Also called "saffron yellow". [Middle English *saffran,* from Old French *safran,* from Medieval Latin *safranum,* from Arabic *za'farān.*] **—saf·fron** *adj.*
S.Afr. South Africa.
saf·ra·nine (sáffrən-een, -in) *n.* Also **saf·ra·nin** (-in). Any of a family of dyes based on phenazine, used in the textile industry and as a biological stain. [French *safran,* SAFFRON + -INE.]
saf·role (sáffrōl) *n.* A colourless or pale yellow oily liquid, $C_{10}H_{10}O_2$, derived from oil of sassafras and other essential oils and used in making flavourings, perfume, and soap. [French *safran,* SAFFRON + -OLE.]
sag[1] (sag) *v.* **sagged, sagging, sags.** *—intr.* **1.** To sink, curve, or bulge downwards, as from pressure, weight, or slackness. **2.** To hang loosely or unevenly; droop. **3.** To diminish in firmness, strength, or vigour; weaken: *Morale is sagging.* **4.** To decline in value or price. **5.** *Nautical.* To drift to leeward. *—tr.* To cause to sag or curve in the middle.
~n. **1.** The act, degree, or extent of sagging. **2.** A sunken place or area; a depression. **3.** A decline, as in price or value. **4.** *Nautical.* A drift to leeward. [Middle English *saggen,* from Middle Low German *sacken,* to settle, ultimately of Scandinavian origin.]
sag[2] (sag || saag) *n.* Spinach. Used in Indian cuisine. [Indic.]
sa·ga (saágə || *U.S. also* sággə) *n.* **1.** An Icelandic prose narrative of the 12th and 13th centuries recounting historical and legendary events and exploits. **2.** Broadly, any long, heroic narrative. **3.** A novel or series of novels relating the history of a family. **4.** A series of events occurring over a relatively long time, such as one concerning an involved domestic drama: *the saga of our washing machine.* [Old Norse, a story, legend; akin to SAW (saying).]
sa·ga·cious (sə-gáyshəss) *adj.* Possessing or showing sound judgment and keen perception; wise. See Synonyms at **shrewd.** [Latin *sagāx* (stem *sagāc-*).] **—sa·ga·cious·ly** *adv.* **—sa·ga·cious·ness** *n.*
sa·gac·i·ty (sə-gássəti) *n.* Keen intelligence; shrewdness.
sag·a·more (sággə-mawr || -mōr) *n.* **1.** A subordinate chief among the Algonquian Indians of North America. **2.** A North American Indian chief, a **sachem** *(see).* [Eastern Abnaki *sàkama,* from Proto-Algonquian *saakimaawa* (unattested). See also **sachem.**]
Sa·gan (sa-góɴ), **Françoise,** pen name of Françoise Quoirez (1935–). French novelist and playwright. Her work generally deals with sexual ennui amongst prosperous, middle-class characters. Her works include the popular success, *Bonjour Tristesse* (1954).
saga novel *n.* A **roman-fleuve** *(see).*
sage[1] (sayj) *n.* A person, usually an elderly man, who is venerated for his experience, judgment, and wisdom.
~adj. **sager, sagest.** **1.** Having, proceeding from, or showing wisdom and calm judgment; judicious; wise. **2.** *Obsolete.* Serious; solemn: *"a sage Requiem"* (Shakespeare). [Middle English, from Old French, from Vulgar Latin *sapius* (unattested), from Latin *sapere,* to be sensible, be wise.] **—sage·ly** *adv.* **—sage·ness** *n.*
sage[2] *n.* **1.** Any of various plants and shrubs of the genus *Salvia*; especially, *S. officinalis,* having aromatic greyish-green leaves used as a cooking herb. See **salvia.** **2.** The leaves of this plant. **3.** Sage green. [Middle English *sauge,* from Old French *sauge,* from Latin *salvia,* "the healing plant", from *salvus,* healthy, safe.]
sage·brush (sáyj-brush) *n.* Any of several aromatic American plants of the genus *Artemisia*; especially, *A. tridentata,* a shrub of arid regions of western North America, having silver-green leaves and large clusters of small white flowers.
sage Derby *n.* A hard yellow cheese, flavoured with sage and streaked with green colouring, originally made in Derby.
sage green *n.* Greyish green. **—sage-green** *adj.*
sage grouse *n.* A bird *Centrocercus urophasianus,* of western North America, the male of which has long, pointed tail feathers that can be spread in a fan during courtship displays.
sag·gar, sag·ger (sággər) *n.* **1.** A protective casing of fire clay in which delicate ceramic articles are fired. **2.** Clay used to make such casings.
~tr.v. **saggared, -garing, -gars.** To place or bake in a saggar. [Perhaps a contraction of SAFEGUARD.]
Sa·git·ta (sə-jíttə) *n.* A constellation in the Northern Hemisphere near Aquila and Cygnus. [Latin *sagitta*†, Sagitta, arrow.]
sag·it·tal (sájit'l) *adj.* **1.** Of or like an arrow or arrowhead. **2.** *Anatomy.* Of or designating the suture uniting the two parietal bones of the skull. **3.** *Zoology & Anatomy.* Of or designating the vertical plane that divides the body of a symmetrical animal into right and left halves. [Latin *sagitta*†, arrow.] **—sag·it·tal·ly** *adv.*
Sag·it·ta·ri·an (sáji-táir-i-ən, *rarely* sággi-, -taár-) *n.* One born under the sign of Sagittarius. **—Sag·it·ta·ri·an** *adj.*
Sag·it·ta·ri·us (sáji-táir-i-əss, *rarely* sággi-, -taár-) *n.* **1.** A constellation in the Southern Hemisphere near Scorpius and Capricornus. **2. a.** The ninth sign of the **zodiac** *(see).* Also called the "Archer". **b.** A Sagittarian. [Middle English, from Latin *sagittārius,* an archer, Sagittarius, from *sagitta*†, arrow.]
sag·it·tate (sáji-tayt) *adj.* Also **sa·git·ti·form** (sa-jítti-fawrm, sə-). *Botany.* Having the shape of an arrowhead: *sagittate leaves.* [Latin *sagitta*†, arrow.]
sa·go (sáygō) *n.* **1.** A powdery starch obtained from the trunks of the sago palm and used in puddings and as a thickener in sauces. **2.** A milk pudding made from this. [Malay *sāgū.*]
sago palm *n.* **1.** Any of various tropical Asian palm trees, especially of the genus *Metroxylon,* yielding starch from their trunks. **2.** A palmlike cycad, *Cycas revoluta,* which yields starch from its stem.
sa·gua·ro (sə-gwaárō, -waárō) *n., pl.* **-ros.** **1.** A very large cactus, *Carnegiea gigantea,* of the southwestern United States and northern Mexico, having upward-curving branches, white flowers, and edible red fruit. **2.** The fruit of this cactus. [Mexican Spanish, probably of Piman origin.]
Sa·gun·to (sa-gŏŏntō). Formerly **Mur·vie·dro** (moorv-yáydrō). Latin name **Sa·gun·tum** (sə-gúntəm). Town in the Spanish prov-

ince of Valencia, situated in a major orange-producing region. Its industries include iron and steel founding and oil refining. The siege and capture of Sagunto by Hannibal (219–218 B.C.) signalled the start of the Second Punic War, and it later fell to the Romans (214 B.C.). The city was taken by the Moors (A.D. 713), and reconquered by Aragon (1238). The city is noted for Roman remains.

Sa·hap·tin (sə-háp-tin, saa-) *n., pl.* **-tins** or collectively **Sahaptin**. Also **Sha·hap·tin** (shə-, shaa-). **1.** A member of a North American Indian people of Idaho, Washington, and Oregon. **2.** The language of this people.

Sa·ha·ra (sə-háarə ‖ U.S. -háarrə). The largest desert in the world, covering some 9 065 000 square kilometres (c.3,500,000 square miles) of North Africa. It extends from the Atlantic Ocean to the Red Sea, and merges with the Sahel to the south. With one of the harshest climates in the world, much of it averages less than 125 millimetre (c. 5 inches) of rain a year, has a daily temperature range of up to 30°C (86°F), and is swept by sandstorms. Stone deserts, tracts of bare rock (hamada), and of gravel (reg) cover some 70 per cent of the Sahara, and sand dunes (erg) another 15 per cent. Desert peoples include the Tuareg of the central mountains, those of largely Negroid descent in the Tibesti Massif, and people of mixed Berber and Arab origin. Of the Sahara's traditional inhabitants, some 60 per cent farm in the oases, both natural and those irrigated by water pumped from great depths. The rest rely on the herding of goats, camels, and sheep. The desert is rich in minerals, including deposits of oil, gas, phosphates, manganese, zinc, iron ore, and salt. —**Sa·ha·ran** *adv.*

Saharan Arabic Republic. See **Western Sahara.**

Sa·hel (saá-hel, -hél). Semidesert and dry grassland region fringing the south of the Sahara. It stretches across eight countries from Senegal eastwards into Sudan. In the late 1960s and throughout the 1970s it suffered drought, with 12 consecutive years when the rainfall was below normal.

sa·hib (saáb, saá-ib, -hib) *n.* In India, a title of respect or form of address equivalent to *master* or *sir*. Used especially for European colonials. [Hindi *ṣāḥib,* master, lord, from Arabic, friend, companion, master.]

said (sed ‖ sayd). Past tense and past participle of **say.**
~*adj.* Named or mentioned before; aforementioned. Used especially in legal proceedings or documents.

sai·ga (sígə) *n.* A Eurasian antelope, *Saiga tatarica,* having a stubby, proboscis-like nose. [Russian *saíga,* from Chagatai *saigak.*]

Saigon. See **Ho Chi Minh City.**

Sai·go Ta·ka·mo·ri (sígō táckə-máwri, taáka-) (1828–77). Japanese soldier and statesman. A samurai, he was instrumental in the overthrow of the Shogunate and the establishment of the Meiji restoration (1867), but he left the government (1873) in protest at the reform of the feudal system. He committed ritual suicide.

sail (sayl) *n.* **1.** A length of shaped canvas or other strong material attached to a ship, boat, or other vessel to catch the wind and propel it through the water. **2.** A sailing vessel. **3. a.** Sails collectively. **b.** Sailing vessels collectively. **4.** A trip or voyage in a sailing vessel. **5.** Something resembling a sail in form or function; especially, the blade of a windmill, turned by the wind. —**in sail.** Having the sails set. —**make sail. 1.** To unfurl a ship's sail or sails. **2.** To begin a voyage. —**set sail. 1.** To hoist the sails preparatory to a voyage. **2.** To begin a trip or voyage. —**take in sail. 1.** To reduce the area of sail exposed to the wind; reef. **2.** To modify one's ambitions or aims. —**under sail** or **sails.** With sails set and catching the wind; sailing.
~*v.* **sailed, sailing, sails.** —*intr.* **1.** To move across the surface of water, especially by means of a sail. **2.** To travel by water in a vessel. **3.** To start out on a voyage; set sail. **4.** To operate a sailing craft, especially for sport. **5.** To glide smoothly and easily: *skiers sailing down the slopes.* **6.** To move in a stately, self-confident manner, like a ship in full sail. —*tr.* **1.** To navigate or manage (a vessel). **2.** To voyage upon or across (a body of water): *sail the Pacific.* —**sail through.** To accomplish (a task, for example) with great ease: *sailed through his finals.* [Middle English *sail(le),* Old English *segl,* from Germanic *seglam* (unattested).]

sail·cloth (sáyl-kloth ‖ -klawth) *n.* **1.** Cotton canvas or other strong fabric suitable for making sails, tents, or the like. **2.** A light canvas fabric used for making clothing.

sailed (sayld) *adj.* Having sails, especially of a specified type or number. Used chiefly in combination: *white-sailed.*

sail·fish (sáyl-fish) *n., pl.* **-fishes** or collectively **sailfish. 1.** Any of various large marine fishes of the genus *Istiophorus,* having the upper jaw prolonged into a spearlike bone and a large, sail-like dorsal fin. **2.** A basking shark *(see).*

sail·ing (sáyling) *n.* **1.** The act, skill, or sport of sailing a vessel, especially a sailing boat. **2.** The skill required to operate and navigate a sailing vessel; navigation. **3.** The departure or time of departure of a vessel: *The sailing is at 2:00 p.m.*

sailing boat *n.* A boat propelled by wind in her sails rather than by oars or an engine. Also U.S. "sailboat".

sailing ship *n.* A large vessel powered by the wind.

sail·or (sáylər) *n.* **1.** One who serves in a navy or who earns his living by working on a ship; especially, an ordinary seaman. **2.** One travelling by water, especially with reference to his susceptibility to seasickness: *a poor sailor.* **3.** A sailor hat. [Variant of earlier *sailer,* from SAIL (verb).] —**sail·or·ly** *adj.*

sailor hat *n.* A low-crowned straw hat with a flat top and a flat brim.

sailor suit *n.* A suit imitating the uniform of a sailor, worn especially by a child.

sain·foin (sán-foyn ‖ chiefly U.S. sáyn-) *n.* A plant, *Onobrychis viciifolia,* native to Eurasia, that has compound leaves and pink flowers and is often used as fodder. [French, from Old French, from Medieval Latin *sānum faenum,* "wholesome hay" (formerly used as a medicinal herb) : Latin *sānum, sānus,* healthy, whole + *faenum, fēnum,* hay.]

saint (saynt, *weak forms* sənt, sən) *n.* **1.** *Abbr.* **S., St.** Theology. **a.** A person, whose life on earth was exceptionally holy, officially recognised by the Roman Catholic Church and certain other Christian churches as being entitled to public veneration and as being capable of interceding for people on earth; one who has been canonised. **b.** Any person who has died and gone to heaven. **c.** Any baptised believer in Christ, according to the New Testament. **d.** *Capital* **S.** A member of any of various religious groups; especially, a **Latter-Day Saint** *(see).* **2.** A very holy person. **3.** A charitable, unselfish, or patient person.
~*tr.v.* **sainted, sainting, saints.** To name, recognise, or venerate as a saint; canonise. [Middle English, from Old French, from Latin *sanctus,* sacred, from the past participle of *sancīre,* to sanctify.]

Saint. Entries not found under **Saint** may appear at **St.** Biographies of Saints appear at the name of the individual Saint; for **Saint Paul,** see **Paul.**

Saint Agnes' Eve *n.* The night of January 20th, when, according to legend, a woman will dream of her future husband. [After St. *Agnes* (died A.D. 304), Christian child martyr, who was beheaded for refusing to marry.]

Saint Andrew's cross *n.* A cross shaped like the letter X.

Saint Anthony's cross *n.* A cross in the shape of a T. Also called "tau cross".

Saint Bernard *n.* A large, strong dog of a breed developed in Switzerland, having a thick brown and white coat, and originally used by monks of the hospice of St. Bernard in the Swiss Alps to help patrol the snow-covered region for travellers in distress.

saint·dom (sáynt-dəm) *n.* The condition or quality of being a saint.

Sainte-Beuve (saNt-bérv, -bŏv), **Charles-Augustin** (1804–69). French writer. He is best known for his criticism, wide-ranging in interest, which encouraged the Romantic movement.

Saint Chris·to·pher (krístəfər) *n.* A medallion, or sometimes a small statuette, representing Christ as a child being carried on the shoulders of St. Christopher, worn by travellers as a supposed protection against danger. [After *St. Christopher,* the patron saint of travellers.]

saint·ed (sáyntid) *adj.* **1.** Enrolled among the saints; canonised. **2.** Of saintly character; holy.

Saint-Ex·u·péry (sáN-teg-zōōpəri; *French* -zü-pay-rée), **Antoine de** (1900–44). French writer. His novels, and his famous children's book, *Le Petit Prince* (1943), were inspired by his career as an pilot, particularly on the mail routes of North Africa and South America. He died on an air force mission in World War II.

Saint George's cross *n.* A red cross on a white background, as used in the Union Jack.

Saint George's Day *n.* April 23, observed in honour of St. George, the patron saint of England.

Saint He·le·na (sénti-léenə, *also* saynt hi-). Volcanic island in the South Atlantic Ocean, 122 square kilometres (47 square miles) in area. Jamestown is the main port and seat of government. Napoleon died there in exile (1821). See map at **Atlantic Ocean.**

saint·hood (sáynt-hōōd) *n.* **1.** The status, character, or condition of being a saint. **2.** Saints collectively.

Saint John (jon). City and port in New Brunswick, eastern Canada, situated at the mouth of the Saint John river. Founded by the French as a trading post (1635), it became the eastern terminus of the Canadian Pacific Railway. It has an ice-free port.

Saint John's wort *n.* Any of various plants of the genus *Hypericum,* having yellow, five-petalled flowers with many stamens. See **rose of Sharon, tutsan.** [After *St. John the Baptist;* the plants were formerly gathered on St. John's Eve for magical and medicinal use.]

Saint-Just (saN-zhǔst), **Louis (Antoine Léon) de** (1767–94). French politician and soldier. He was the Committee of Public Safety's military supervisor, and led the French at Fleurus (1794), but was executed with Robespierre that same year.

Saint-Laurent (sáN-law-róN), **Yves** (1936-). French fashion designer. Becoming Dior's assistant at the age of 17, he eventually succeeded him, but lost control of the fashion house in 1960. He subsequently founded (1962) his own house, and (from 1966) his much-imitated chain of Rive Gauche ready-to-wear boutiques.

saint·ly (sáyntli) *adj.* **-lier, -liest.** Resembling, pertaining to, or befitting a saint. —**saint·li·ness** *n.*

Saint Nicholas. See **Santa Claus.**

Saint Patrick's Day *n.* March 17, observed in honour of St. Patrick, the patron saint of Ireland.

saint·pau·li·a (sənt-páwli-ə ‖ saynt-) *n.* A plant, **African violet** *(see).* [New Latin, after W. von *Saint Paul-Illaire* (died 1910), German soldier who discovered it.]

Saint-Saëns (sáN-sónss), **(Charles) Camille** (1835–1921). French composer and critic. The light-hearted orchestral suite *Carnival of the Animals* (1886) is still his most popular work. As a critic, he championed Liszt, Wagner, and Berlioz. He wrote 12 operas, of which the most famous is *Samson and Delilah* (1877), 5 symphonies, and 5 piano concertos.

saint's day *n.* A day nominated by the church for the commemoration of a particular saint.

Saint-Si·mon (sán-see-món), **Claude Henri de Rouvroy, Comte de** (1760–1825). French political philosopher. He envisaged an industrial state run by technocrats, in which poverty would be abolished and religion replaced by rationalism. His ideas greatly influenced the development of socialism, particularly in France.

Saint-Simon, Louis de Rouvroy, Duc de (1675–1755). French courtier and writer. His *Mémoires* for the years 1694 to 1723 provide a personal and prejudiced picture of the court of Louis XIV, whom he particularly disliked.

Saint Valentine's Day *n.* February 14, on which valentines are traditionally exchanged. [Birds were believed to pair on this day.]

Sa·is (sáy-iss). Ancient Egyptian city on the Nile delta; a capital of Lower Egypt in the seventh and sixth centuries B.C.. —**Sa·ite** (-īt) *n.* —**Sa·it·ic** (-ittik) *adj.*

saith (seth ‖ sayth, say-ith). *Archaic.* Third person singular present indicative of **say.**

saithe (sayth, *also* sayth) *n.* The **coalfish** (see). [Old Norse *seithr.*]

Sai·va (sī´-və, shī´-) *n.* In Hinduism, a member of the cult of the god Siva. —**Sai·vism** *n.* —**Sai·vite** *n. & adj.*

sake¹ (sayk) *n.* **1.** The purpose, motive, or end: *a quarrel only for the sake of argument.* **2.** Advantage; good: *for the sake of her health.* **3.** Personal benefit or interest; welfare: *for his own sake.* **4.** Used in combination in various expressions of anger, irritation, impatience, or the like: *for Pete's sake; for God's sake.* [Middle English *sake,* contention, lawsuit, guilt (the phrase "for the sake of" probably originated in legal usage), Old English *sacu,* lawsuit, from Germanic *sakō,* (unattested), charge, accusation.]

sa·ke², sa·ki (sáaki) *n.* A Japanese alcoholic drink made from fermented rice. [Japanese, "alcohol".]

sa·ker (sáykər) *n.* A southern Eurasian falcon, *Falco cherrug,* having brown plumage and often trained for falconry. [Middle English *sagre,* from Old French *sacre,* from Arabic *saqr.*]

Sakh·a·rov (sácka-rov, -roff; *Russian* sákhərəf), **Andrei Dimitrievich** (1921–89). Soviet physicist. After working on nuclear power in the 1940s and 1950s, he became an outspoken critic of his government's part in the arms race. He was exiled, but released in 1987. In 1975 he was awarded the Nobel peace prize.

sa·ki (sáaki) *n.* Any small South American monkey belonging to either of two genera, *Pithecia* or *Chiroptes,* and having curly hair and a long, bushy tail. [French, from Tupi *saqi.*]

Saki. See H.H. **Munro.**

Sakkara. See **Saqqara.**

Sakta. Variant of **Shakta.**

Sakti. Variant of **Shakti.**

sal (sal) *n.* Salt. Used chiefly in compounds: *sal volatile.* [Latin *sal.*]

sa·laam (sə-láam) *n.* **1.** A Muslim salutation or ceremonial greeting performed by bowing low while placing the right palm on the forehead. **2.** In the East, a respectful or ceremonial greeting.
~*v.* **salaamed, -laaming, -laams.** —*tr.* To greet with a salaam. —*intr.* To perform a salaam. [Arabic *salām,* "peace" (part of *assalām 'alaikum,* "peace to you").]

salable. Variant of **saleable.**

sa·la·cious (sə-láyshəss) *adj.* **1.** Stimulating to the sexual imagination; especially, morbidly appealing to lust: *salacious writing.* **2.** Lustful; lecherous. [Latin *salāx* (stem *salāc-*), fond of leaping (said of male animals), lustful, from *salīre,* to leap.] —**sa·la·cious·ly** *adv.* —**sa·la·cious·ness, sa·lac·i·ty** (sə-lássəti) *n.*

sal·ad (sál-əd) *n.* **1.** A cold dish typically consisting of green, leafy raw vegetables, such as lettuce, often with radish, cucumber, or tomato, often tossed with a dressing. **2.** A dish consisting of this as an accompaniment to a main food such as meat or fish. **3.** A cold dish of chopped fruit, vegetables, meat, fish, eggs, or other food, usually prepared with mayonnaise or other dressing. **4.** Any green vegetable or herb eaten raw or used in salad. [Middle English *salade,* from Old French, from Provençal *salada,* from Vulgar Latin *salāta* (unattested), from the feminine past participle of *salāre* (unattested), to salt, from Latin *sāl,* salt.]

salad burnet *n.* A short perennial plant, *Sanguisorba minor,* with compound leaves sometimes used in salads, and petal-less flowers borne in round heads.

salad cream *n.* A sauce resembling mayonnaise in consistency, but having a more pungent taste, used especially in Britain to accompany salad.

salad days *pl.n.* The time of youth, innocence, and inexperience. [From Shakespeare: "my salad days when I was green in judgment, cold in blood" (*Antony and Cleopatra,* Act 1, scene 5).]

salad dressing *n.* A sauce, as of mayonnaise or oil and vinegar, served on salad.

Sal·a·din (sál-ə-din), Arabic name Salah ad-Din Yusuf ibn-Aiyub (*c.* 1137–93). Kurdish general and Sultan of Egypt. As a vizir he conquered Egypt (1169), founded a dynasty (1175), conquered Syria, and took Jerusalem (1187), thereby precipitating the Third Crusade. He became renowned throughout Islam and Christendom for his chivalry and generosity to the poor of all faiths.

Sa·lam (sa laám), **Abdus** (1926–96). Pakistani physicist. The director of the International Centre for Theoretical Physics in Trieste, he won a Nobel prize (1979) for work done at Imperial College London, on weak interaction and electromagnetic interaction.

Sal·a·man·ca (sál-ə-mángkə). Capital of Salamanca province in central Spain, situated on the river Tormes. Conquered by Hannibal (220 B.C.), it prospered as a cultural centre following the found-

ing of its university (1230), which is the oldest in Spain. The city's many historic sites include the old university buildings, a 12th-century cathedral, and a fine 18th-century plaza.

sal·a·man·der (sál-ə-mandər, *rarely* -maandər) *n.* **1.** Any of various small, lizard-like amphibians of the order Caudata, having porous, scaleless skin and four legs that are often weak or rudimentary. **2. a.** A mythical creature, generally resembling a lizard, once thought capable of living in or withstanding fire. **b.** One who is capable of enduring fire, heat, or the like. **c.** According to Paracelsus, an elemental spirit supposed to live in fire. **3.** An object used in fire or capable of withstanding heat, such as a poker. **4.** *Metallurgy.* A mass of solidified material, largely metallic, left in a blast-furnace hearth. **5.** A portable stove used to heat or dry buildings under construction. [Middle English *salamandre,* from Old French, from Latin *salamandra,* from Greek *salamandra†.*]

sa·la·mi (sə-láami) *n.* A highly spiced and salted sausage, flavoured with garlic, that originated in Italy. [Italian, plural of *salame,* "salted pork", from *salare,* to salt, from Vulgar Latin *salāre* (unattested). See **salad.**]

Sal·a·mis (sál-ə-miss). Greek island in the Saronic Gulf west of Athens. The Battle of Salamis (480 B.C.) was a major Greek naval victory over the Persians. It was fought in the narrow straits which separate the island from the coast of Attica, allowing the Greeks' smaller ships to overcome the Persians' superior numbers.

sal ammoniac *n.* A chemical, **ammonium chloride** (see). [Middle English *sal ammoniak,* from Medieval Latin *sāl armōniacus,* from Latin *sāl ammōniacus* : SAL + AMMONIAC.]

sal·a·ried (sál-ə-rid ‖ -reed) *adj.* Earning or yielding a regular salary: *a salaried job; a salaried worker.*

sal·a·ry (sál-əri ‖ -ri) *n., pl.* **-ries.** A fixed amount of money, usually for nonmanual services, paid to a person on a regular, often monthly or quarterly, basis. Compare **wage.** [Middle English *salarie,* from Anglo-French, Old French *salaire,* from Latin *salārium,* originally "money given to Roman soldiers to buy salt", from *salārius,* of salt, from *sal,* salt.]

Sa·la·zar (sál-ə-zár; *Portuguese* səl-), **Antonio de Oliveira** (1889–1970). Portuguese politician. Following a military coup, he twice served as finance minister (1926, 1928), and in 1932 became prime minister. His corporatist policies stabilised the country but repressed opposition, and his attempts to retain Portugal's colonies led to numerous wars and much international criticism. His dictatorship lasted until 1968.

sal·chow (sál-kō) *n.* A jump in ice-skating performed by taking off from the back inside edge of one skate, making a complete turn, and landing on the back outside edge of the other skate. [After Ulrich Salchow (1877–1949), Swedish skater who introduced it.]

Sal·da·nha Bay (sal-dáanə). Large bay on the southwestern coast of South Africa, roughly 90 kilometres (56 miles) north of Cape Town, offering a fine natural harbour.

sale (sayl) *n.* **1. a.** The exchange of property or services for a given amount of money or its equivalent; the act or an instance of selling. **b.** An amount or quantity sold. **2.** An opportunity for selling; a market; a demand. **3.** Availability for purchase. Often preceded by *for* or *on: a flat for sale.* **4.** A selling of goods to the highest bidder; an auction. **5. a.** A special disposal of goods (such as excess stock, or secondhand items) at lowered prices. **b.** Such a sale conducted in or from a specified place: *a garage sale, a (car-)boot sale.* **6.** *Plural.* The branch of a business enterprise that deals with the selling and marketing of goods or services: *She's head of sales.* Also used adjectivally: *a sales conference.* [Middle English *sale,* Old English *sala,* from Old Norse.]

Sa·lé (sál-i, sə-láy). *Arabic* **Sla** (slaa). Port on the Atlantic coast of Morocco. A Muslim trading centre in medieval times, it became an independent republic in the 17th century and won notoriety as a haunt of the Barbary pirates known as the Sallee Rovers.

sale·a·ble, sal·a·ble (sáylə-b'l) *adj.* **1.** Offered or suitable for sale. **2.** Easily sold. —**sale·a·bil·i·ty** (-billəti) *n.*

sale or return *n.* A business agreement in which a retailer has the right to return to the wholesaler those goods which he has been unable to sell, without having to pay for them.

sal·ep (sál-ep, sə-lép) *n.* A starchy meal ground from the dried roots of various Old World orchids of the genus *Orchis* and used for food and formerly as a medicine. [French or Spanish, from Turkish *sālep,* from Arabic *sahleb,* variant of *khasyu aththa'lab,* "the fox's testicles", a kind of orchid.]

sal·e·ra·tus (sál-ə-ráytəss) *n.* Sodium or potassium bicarbonate used as a leavening agent; baking soda. [New Latin *sal aeratus,* "aerated salt".]

Sa·ler·no (sə-lér-nō, -laír-). Latin name **Sa·ler·num** (-nəm). Port in Campania, southwestern Italy, capital of Salerno province. Originally a Roman colony, the town came under Norman rule from 1076. During the Norman period a magnificent cathedral was founded, and Salerno won fame for its medical school around which one of Europe's earliest universities developed.

sale·room (sáyl-rōom, -rŏŏm) *n.* A room in which articles to be auctioned are put on show. Also *U.S.* "salesroom".

sales·clerk (*U.S.* sáylz-klerk ‖ -klark) *n. U.S.* A shop assistant.

Sa·le·si·an (sə-léez-i-ən, -léezh- ‖ saa-) *n.* A member of the Society of St. Francis de Sales, a Roman Catholic order founded in Turin in 1845 and dedicated chiefly to education and missionary work. —**Sa·le·sian** *adj.*

sales·man (sáylz-mən) *n., pl.* **-men** (-mən, -men). A man employed to sell merchandise, either in a shop or direct to domestic or business customers in a designated area.

sales·man·ship (sáylz-mən-ship) *n.* **1.** The work or occupation of a salesman. **2.** Skill or ability in selling, as by persuasive speaking.

sales·per·son (sáylz-perss'n) *n.* A salesman or saleswoman.

sales resistance *n.* A lack of interest in or willingness to buy a product, on the part of a person or the public.

sales talk *n.* Argument or other persuasion intended to induce a person to purchase a product or service or accept an idea or suggestion. Also called "sales pitch".

sales tax *n.* A tax levied on the retail price of goods and services.

sales·wom·an (sáylz-wŏŏmən) *n., pl.* **-women** (-wimmin). A woman or girl employed to sell goods, especially in a department store. Also called "salesgirl", "saleslady".

Sal·ford (sáwl-fərd ‖ sól-, sál-; *locally* sól-). City near Manchester, northwestern England, on the river Irwell. A cotton town, it expanded from 1894 after the opening of the Manchester Ship Canal. Salford today is Manchester's docking centre, with industries which include textiles, chemicals, electrics, and engineering.

sali– *comb. form.* Indicates salt; for example, **salimeter**. [Latin *sāl* (stem *sali*-), salt.]

Sa·li·an (sáyli-ən) *n.* A member of a tribe of Franks, the Salii, who settled in the Rhine region of the Netherlands in the fourth century A.D. [Late Latin *Saliī†*, the Salian Franks.] —**Sa·li·an** *adj.*

sal·ic (sál-ik) *adj.* Pertaining to or designating minerals, such as quartz and the feldspars, containing large amounts of silica and alumina. [S(ILICA) + AL(UMINA) + -IC.]

Sal·ic (sál-ik ‖ sáyl-) *adj.* Also **Sal·ique** (*also* sə-léek). **1.** Pertaining to the Salian Franks. **2.** Pertaining to the Salic law or to the legal code of the Salian Franks. [Old French *salique*, from Medieval Latin *Salicus*, from Late Latin *Saliī†*, the Salian Franks.]

sal·i·cin (sál-i-sin) *n.* A bitter glucoside, $C_{13}H_{18}O_7$, obtained mainly from the bark of poplar and willow trees and formerly used as an analgesic and antipyretic. [French *salicine* : Latin *salix* (stem *salic*-), willow + -IN.]

Salic law *n.* A law, thought to derive from the code of the Salic Franks, prohibiting a woman from succession to the throne and later used to exclude women from the thrones of France and Spain.

sal·i·cyl·ate (sə-líssi-layt, -lət, -lit) *n.* A salt or ester of salicylic acid. [SALICYL(IC ACID) + -ATE.]

sal·i·cyl·ic acid (sál-i-síllik) *n.* A white crystalline acid, $C_7H_6O_3$, used in making aspirin, as a preservative, and in the external treatment of certain skin conditions such as eczema. [French *salicyle*, the radical of salicylic acid : SALIC(IN) + -YL.]

sal·i·cyl·ism (sál-i-síl-iz'm, sə-líssil-) *n.* Poisoning caused by an overdose of aspirin or other drug containing salicylic acid, characterised by headache, dizziness, vomiting, collapse, and, in many cases, kidney failure. [SALICYL(IC ACID) + -ISM.]

sa·li·ence (sáyli-ənss) *n.* Also **sa·li·en·cy** (-ən-si). **1.** The quality or condition of being salient. **2.** A pronounced feature or part.

sa·li·ent (sáyli-ənt) *adj.* **1.** Projecting or jutting beyond a line or surface; protruding up or out: *a salient angle.* **2.** Striking; outstanding; conspicuous: *the salient point in her lecture.* **3.** *Zoology.* Springing; jumping: *salient tree toads.*
~*n.* **1.** The part of a battle line, trench, fortification, or other military defence that projects out towards the enemy. **2.** A salient angle or part. [Latin *saliēns* (stem *salient*-), present participle of *salīre*, to leap, jump.] —**sa·li·ent·ly** *adv.* —**sa·li·ent·ness** *n.*

sa·li·en·ti·an (sáyli-énshi-ən) *n.* A type of amphibian, an **anuran** *(see).* [New Latin *Salientia*, from Latin, neuter plural of *saliēns*, leaping, SALIENT.]

Sa·lie·ri (sal-yaír-i, sál-i-aír-i), **Antonio** (1750–1825). Italian composer. Teacher to Beethoven, Schubert, and Liszt, he became (1788) composer to the Imperial Court of Australia. He was more popular (but less talented) than his rival, Mozart, who accused him of trying to poison him. This allegation inspired Rimsky-Korsakov's Pushkin-based opera *Mozart and Salieri* (1898) and Peter Shaffer's play *Amadeus* (1979).

sa·lif·er·ous (sa-liffərəss, sə-) *adj.* Containing or yielding salt. [SALI– + -FEROUS.]

sa·li·fy (sál-i-fī) *tr.v.* **-fied, -fying, -fies.** **1.** To form or convert into a salt, as by chemical combination. **2.** To mix or impregnate with a salt. [French *salifier* : SALI– + -FY.] —**sal·i·fi·a·ble** *adj.* —**sal·i·fi·ca·tion** (-fi-káysh'n) *n.*

sa·lim·e·ter (sa-límmitər, sə-) *n.* *Chemistry.* A specially graduated hydrometer that indicates directly the percentage of a salt in a salt solution. [SALI– + -METER.] —**sal·i·met·ric** (sál-i-méttrik) *adj.* —**sal·im·e·try** (-límmətri) *n.*

sa·li·na (sə-línə) *n.* A salt marsh, spring, pond, or lake. [Spanish, from Latin *salīnae*, salt pits, feminine plural of *salīnus*, SALINE.]

sa·line (sáy-līn, *rarely* sál-īn, sə-lín ‖ *U.S. also* -leen) *adj.* **1.** Of, pertaining to, or containing salt; salty. **2.** Of or pertaining to mineral salts having the characteristics of common salt.
~*n.* **1.** Any salt of the alkali or alkaline-earth metals, used in medicine as a cathartic. **2.** A saline solution, especially one that is isotonic with blood and is used in medicine. In this sense, also called "physiological saline". [Middle English *salyne*, from Latin *salīnus*, from *sāl*, salt.] —**sa·lin·i·ty** (sə-línnəti, sa-) *n.*

Sal·in·ger (sál-in-jər), **J(erome) D(avid)** (1919–). U.S. author. He achieved recognition for his novel about adolescence, *The Catcher in the Rye* (1951). His other works concentrate mainly on the lives and times of the Jewish Glass family; these stories include *Raise High the Roofbeam, Carpenters* and *Seymour: an Introduction*

(1963). The novella *Hapworth 16, 1924* (1997) was his first work to be published since 1965.

sal·i·nom·e·ter (sál-i-nómmitər) *n.* Any of various instruments, especially a salimeter, used to measure the amount of salt in a solution. [SALIN(E) + -METER.] —**sal·i·no·met·ric** (-nə-méttrik) *adj.* —**sal·i·nom·e·try** (-nómmətri) *n.*

Salique. Variant of **Salic.**

Salis·bur·y¹ (sáwlz-bri, -bəri ‖ sólz-, -berri). Also **New Sarum** (saír-əm). City in Wiltshire, southeast England, situated at the confluence of the rivers Avon and Wylye. Old Sarum nearby is the site of an Iron Age fort whose earthworks survive. Salisbury cathedral (1220–58) is a magnificent example of Early English architecture, with the tallest spire in England (123 metres; 404 feet). The town, a market centre, attracts many tourists, and has some light industry. It is the Melchester of the Wessex novels of Thomas Hardy.

Salisbury². See Harare.

Salisbury, Robert Arthur Talbot Gascoyne-Cecil, 3rd Marquess of (1830–1903). British politician. Before becoming a peer he was a Conservative M.P. (1853–1868). His isolationist diplomacy favouring non-alignment dominated British foreign policy from 1878 until his death. He served three terms as prime minister: 1885–86, 1886–92, and 1895–1902.

Salisbury Plain. Chalk plateau in Wiltshire, situated to the north of Salisbury in southern England. The area is rich in prehistoric remains which include the megalithic monument of Stonehenge.

Sa·lish (sáy-lish) *n.* **1.** A family of languages spoken by North American Indian tribes, including the Flathead, in the northwestern United States and British Columbia. **2.** *Used with a plural verb.* The Indians speaking languages of this family. —**Sa·lish·an** (-'n, sál-ish'n) *adj.*

sa·li·va (sə-lívə) *n.* The watery, tasteless liquid mixture of salivary and oral mucous gland secretions that lubricates chewed food, moistens the oral walls, and contains the enzyme ptyalin, which functions in the predigestion of starches. [Latin *salīva†*.] —**sal·i·var·y** (sál-i-vəri, sə-lī- ‖ -verri) *adj.*

salivary gland *n.* A gland that secretes saliva; especially, any of three pairs of large glands, the parotid, submandibular, and sublingual, the secretions of which enter the mouth and mingle in saliva.

sal·i·vate (sál-i-vayt) *v.* **-vated, -vating, -vates.** —*intr.* **1.** To secrete or produce saliva. **2.** To be excited or eager for something. —*tr.* To produce an excessive salivation in (a person or animal). [Latin *salīvāre*, to spit out, from *salīva*, SALIVA.]

sal·i·va·tion (sál-i-váysh'n) *n.* **1.** The act or process of secreting saliva. **2.** An abnormally abundant flow of saliva.

Salk vaccine (sawlk) *n.* A vaccine made from a deactivated (or killed) virus, formerly used to immunise actively against poliomyelitis. [After Jonas *Salk* (1914–95), U.S. microbiologist.]

sal·lee, sal·ly (sál-i) *n. Australian.* Any of various species of acacia or eucalyptus. [From a native Australian language.]

sal·let (sál-it) *n.* A light medieval helmet, sometimes fitted with a visor and with a piece at the back to protect the neck. [Middle English *sal(l)et*, from Old French *salade*, from Old Italian *celata*, perhaps from Vulgar Latin *caelāta* (unattested), from Latin, feminine past participle of *caelāre*, to engrave (as on the metal of a helmet), from *caelum*, chisel.]

sal·low¹ (sál-ō) *adj.* **-lower, -lowest.** Of a pale, sickly yellowish hue or complexion.
~*tr.v.* **sallowed, -lowing, -lows.** To make sallow. [Middle English *salowe*, Old English *salo*, dusky, from Germanic.] —**sal·low·ish** *adj.* —**sal·low·ness** *n.*

sal·low² *n.* Any of several of the broader-leaved European willows, especially the three common species *Salix caprea, S. cinerea,* and *S. aurita.* [Middle English *salwe*, Old English *sealh*, from Germanic.]

Sal·lust (sál-əst). Latin name Gaius Sallustius Crispus (c. 86–c. 34 B.C.). Roman politician and historian. He became governor of Numidia, but resigned after being implicated in corruption. He then turned to historical writing, producing his well-known accounts of the Catilinarian conspiracy and the Jugurthine war.

sal·ly¹ (sál-i) *intr.v.* **-lied, -lying, -lies.** **1.** To rush or leap forth suddenly; especially, to issue suddenly from a defensive or besieged position to make an attack upon an enemy. **2.** To set out on a trip or excursion. Often used with *forth.*
~*n., pl.* **sallies.** **1.** A sudden rush forward; a leap. **2.** An assault from a defensive position; a sortie. **3.** A sudden emergence, as from rest to action or from silence to comment; an outburst. **4.** A quick witticism or bantering remark; a quip. **5.** A venturing forth; an excursion; a jaunt. —See Synonyms at **joke.** [Old French *saillie*, a sally, from the feminine past participle of *salir, saillir* to leap or rush forward, from Latin *salīre*, to leap.]

sally² *n.* The woollen covering of the end of a bellrope. [Perhaps from SALLY; referring to the sudden movement of the bell.]

Sal·ly Army (sál-i) *n. Informal.* The **Salvation Army** *(see).*

Sally Lunn (lun) *n.* A round, light tea cake, like a muffin. [Perhaps from the name of a girl who sold them in Bath about 1800.]

sal·ma·gun·di (sál-mə-gúndi) *n.* **1.** A salad of chopped meat, anchovies, eggs, and onions, often arranged in rows on lettuce, and served with vinegar and oil. **2.** Any mixture or assortment; a potpourri. [French *salmigondis, salmigondin†*.]

sal·mi, sal·mis (sál-mi, sal-mée) *n.* A highly spiced dish consisting of a roasted game bird, minced and stewed in wine. [French *salmis*, short for *salmigondis*, SALMAGUNDI.]

salm·on (sámmən ‖ *Scottish also* saámən) *n., pl.* **-mons** or collectively **salmon.** **1.** Any of various large food and game fishes of the genera *Salmo* and *Oncorhynchus,* of northern waters, characteristically swimming from salt to fresh water to spawn, and having a delicate pinkish flesh. **2.** *Australian.* Any of various similar unrelated fishes, such as the barramundi. **3.** Salmon pink. [Middle English *samoun, salmon,* from Anglo-French, Old French *saumon,* from Latin *salmo* (stem *salmon-*), probably akin to *salīre,* to leap.] **—salm•on** *adj.*

sal•mo•nel•la (sál-mə-néllə) *n., pl.* **salmonella** or **-nellas** or **-nellae** (-néllee). **1.** Any of various rod-shaped bacteria of the genus *Salmonella,* many of which are pathogenic. **2.** Salmonellosis. In this sense, not in technical usage. [New Latin, after Daniel E. *Salmon* (1850–1914), U.S. pathologist.]

sal•mo•nel•lo•sis (sál-mə-nel-ṓ-siss) *n.* Food poisoning caused by salmonella. [SALMONELL(A) + -osis.]

sal•mo•noid (sámmən-oyd) *adj.* **1.** Resembling or characteristic of a salmon. **2.** Of or belonging to the family Salmonidae, which includes the salmon, trout, and whitefishes. **—sal•mo•noid** *n.*

salmon pink *n.* Yellowish pink. **—salmon-pink** *adj.*

salmon trout *n.* Any of various salmon-like fish, especially the sea trout.

Sa•lò, Republic of (sə-lṓ, sa-). Puppet regime in northern Italy (1943–45), set up by Mussolini after Italy's surrender in World War II. The regime was named after the town of Salò, on Lake Garda, and ended with the German withdrawal and Mussolini's death at the hands of Italian partisans.

sal•ol (sál-ol || -ōl) *n.* A white crystalline powder, $C_{13}H_{10}O_3$, derived from salicylic acid, and used in the manufacture of plastics and sun-tan oils and medicinally as an analgesic and antipyretic. [Originally a trademark : SAL(ICYLIC ACID) + -OL.]

Sa•lo•me (sə-lṓmi). Daughter of Herodias and niece of Herod Antipas, who granted her the head of John the Baptist in return for her dancing. Matthew 14:6-11.

sa•lon (sál-ON, -on || *U.S.* sə-lón; *French* sa-lÓN) *n.* **1.** A drawing room or other large room or hall for receiving and entertaining guests, especially one in a French mansion. **2.** A reception held in such a room for a group of people, especially of social, artistic, or intellectual distinction, as in France in the 18th century. **3.** A hall or gallery for the exhibition of works of art. **4.** *Often capital* **S.** Any of various exhibitions of works by living artists held annually in France. **5.** A commercial establishment offering some product or service related to fashion or beauty. [French, from Italian *salone,* augmentative of *sala,* a hall, room, from Germanic.]

Salonika. See **Thessaloniki.**

sa•loon (sə-lōōn) *n.* **1.** A large room or hall for receptions, public entertainment, or exhibitions, or for a particular use, such as dancing. **2.** A large, comfortable social lounge for passengers on a ship. **3.** An enclosed car having two or four doors and front and rear seats. Also *U.S.* "sedan". **4. a.** *British.* A saloon bar. **b.** *U.S.* Any place where alcoholic drinks are sold and drunk. [French *salon,* SALON.]

saloon bar *n. British.* A bar in a public house or hotel that is usually more luxuriously furnished and where drinks are more expensive than in the public bar. Also called "lounge bar", "saloon".

sa•loop (sə-lōōp) *n.* A hot drink, formerly used medicinally, made from salep, sassafras, or similar aromatic herbs. [Variant of SALEP.]

Salop. See **Shropshire.**

salp (salp) *n.* Any of various free-swimming primitive chordates of the genus *Salpa,* of warm seas, having a translucent, somewhat flattened, keglike body. Also called "salpa". [New Latin *salpa,* from Latin, a kind of stockfish, from Greek *salpē*†.] **—sal•pi•form** (sálpi-fawrm) *adj.*

sal•pi•glos•sis (sál-pi-glóssiss) *n.* Any of various plants of the Chilean genus *Salpiglossis,* especially those grown as garden ornamentals for their showy tubular flowers. [New Latin, "trumpet-tongue", irregularly from Greek *salpinx* (stem *salping-*), trumpet + *glōssa,* tongue.]

sal•pin•gec•to•my (sál-pin-jéktəmi) *n., pl.* **-mies.** The surgical removal of a Fallopian tube. [New Latin *salpinx* (stem *salping-*), SALPINX + -ECTOMY.]

sal•pin•gi•tis (sál-pin-jītiss) *n. Pathology.* Inflammation of a Fallopian or Eustachian tube. [New Latin : *salpinx* (stem *salping-*), SALPINX + -ITIS.]

sal•pinx (sál-pingks) *n., pl.* **salpinges** (sal-pín-jeez). **1.** The Fallopian tube. **2.** The Eustachian tube. [New Latin, from Greek *salpinx*†, trumpet.] **—sal•pin•gi•an** (sal-pínji-ən) *adj.*

sal•sa (sál-sə) *n.* **1.** A type of music of Latin-American origin, combining elements of rock and jazz. **2.** A dance performed to this music. [Spanish, SAUCE (alluding to the blending of styles).]

sal•si•fy (sál-si-fi, sáwl- || sól-, *U.S. also* -fī) *n.* **1.** A plant, *Tragopogon porrifolius,* native to Europe, having grasslike leaves, purple flowers, and an edible taproot. **2.** The oyster-flavoured root of this plant, eaten as a vegetable. Also called "vegetable oyster", "oyster plant". [French *salsifis,* from (obsolete) Italian *salsifica*†.]

sal soda *n.* A cleansing agent, **washing soda** *(see).*

salt (sawlt || solt) *n.* **1.** A colourless or white crystalline solid, chiefly **sodium chloride** *(see),* used as a food seasoning and preservative. **2.** A chemical compound formed by replacing all or part of the hydrogen atoms of an acid with one or more metal ions or other positive ions from a base. **3.** *Often plural.* Any of various mineral salts used medicinally, such as **Epsom salts** or **Glauber's salts** *(both of which see).* **4.** *Plural.* **Smelling salts** *(see).* **5.** An element that gives flavour, piquancy, or zest. **6.** Sharp, lively wit; pungency of expression. **7.** *Informal.* A sailor, especially when old or experienced. **8.** A saltcellar. **—rub salt in the wound.** To make a painful situation worse, as by a further act of humiliation or mockery. **—salt of the earth.** A person or group regarded as worthy and admirable. [Matthew 5:13.] **—take with a grain** or **pinch of salt.** To treat with sceptical reserve. **—worth (one's) salt.** Of some merit or competence: *Any plumber worth his salt could do it.* [From the former custom of paying for some jobs in salt rather than money.] *~adj.* **1.** Tasting of, containing, or filled with salt; salty. **2.** Preserved in salt or a salt solution. **3. a.** Flooded with sea water. **b.** Found in or near such a flooded area: *salt grasses.* **4.** Sharp or pungent.
~tr.v. **salted, salting, salts.** **1. a.** To add salt to; season with salt. **b.** To sprinkle salt on (snow) to melt it. **2.** To cure or preserve by treating with salt or a salt solution. **3.** *Informal.* To stock up or store away (money, for example); hoard. Often used with *away* or *down.* **4.** *U.S.* To provide salt for (livestock). **5.** To add zest or liveliness to; season: *salt a lecture with anecdotes.* **6.** To give an appearance of value to by fraudulent means; especially, to place valuable minerals in (a mine, for example) for the purpose of deceiving. **—salt out.** To separate (a dissolved substance) by adding a salt to the solution so as to increase the number of ions. [Middle English *salt,* Old English *sealt.*] **—salt•ish** *adj.* **—salt•ness** *n.*

SALT (sawlt || solt) *n.* Strategic Arms Limitation Talks.

salt-and-pepper *n.* See **pepper-and-salt.**

sal•tant (sál-tənt, sáwl- || sól-) *adj. Biology.* Differing from other organisms of the same species because of saltation. [Latin *saltāns* (stem *saltant-*), present participle of *saltāre,* to leap, frequentative of *salīre* (past participle *saltus*), to jump.]

sal•ta•rel•lo (sál-tə-réllō) *n., pl.* **-relli** (-réllee). **1.** A lively Italian dance with a skipping step at the beginning of each measure. **2.** Music for this dance, generally in triple or sextuple time. [Italian, from *saltare,* to leap, from Latin *saltāre.* See **saltant.**]

sal•ta•tion (sal-táysh'n, sawl- || sol-) *n.* **1.** The act of leaping, jumping, or dancing. **2.** An abrupt, discontinuous movement, transition, or development. **3.** *Biology.* Abrupt variation within a species, usually caused by mutation. [Latin *saltātiō* (stem *saltātiōn-*), from *saltātus,* past participle of *saltāre,* to leap. See **saltant.**]

sal•ta•to•ri•al (sál-tə-táwri-əl, sáwl- || sól-, -tṓri-) *adj.* **1.** Of or relating to leaping or dancing. **2.** *Zoology.* Adapted for or characterised by leaping.

sal•ta•to•ry (sál-tə-tri, sáwl-, -təri; sal-táytəri, sawl- || sól-) *adj.* **1.** Of, pertaining to, or adapted for leaping or dancing. **2.** Proceeding by leaps, hops, or abrupt movements. [Latin *saltātōrius,* from *saltātus,* past participle of *saltāre,* to leap. See **saltant.**]

salt cake *n.* Impure sodium sulphate, used in making paper pulp, soaps and detergents, glass, ceramic glazes, and dyes.

salt•cel•lar (sáwlt-sellər || sólt-) *n.* **1.** A small container or shaker for holding and dispensing salt. **2.** *Informal.* Either of the two hollows above the collarbones, especially noticeable in very thin people. [Variant (influenced by CELLAR) of Middle English *salt saler* : SALT + *saler,* saltcellar, from Old French *saliere,* from Latin *salārius,* of salt, from *sāl,* salt.]

salt dome *n. Geology.* A dome-shaped formation in stratified rock with a core of salt. Oil and gas are often found in association with salt domes. Also called "salt plug".

salt•ed weapon (sáwltid || sóltid) *n.* A type of nuclear weapon designed to capture neutrons on exploding, so as to produce higher levels of radiation.

salt•er (sáwltər || sóltər) *n.* **1.** A person who manufactures or sells salt. **2.** A person who treats meat, fish, or other foods with salt.

salt•ern (sáwl-tərn || sól-) *n.* **1.** A building or place of salt manufacture; a saltworks. **2.** A series of salt-water pools producing salt by natural evaporation. [Ultimately from Old English *sealtærn, sealtern* : *sealt,* SALT + *ærn, ern,* house.]

salt flat *n.* A wide, flat, stretch of country that has very salty soil, owing to the former presence of water.

salt glaze *n.* A glaze given to stoneware by burning salt in the kiln when the ware is fired. **—salt-glaze** (sáwlt-glayz || sólt-) *tr.v.*

salt grass *n.* Any of various grasses, such as those of the genus *Distichlis,* that grow in salt marshes and alkaline regions.

sal•ti•grade (sál-ti-grayd, sáwl- || sól-) *adj.* Adapted for or proceeding by leaping. Said of certain insects and spiders. [New Latin *Saltigradae,* former designation for saltigrade spiders : Latin *saltus,* a leap, from the past participle of *salīre,* to leap + *gradī,* to step.]

sal•tim•boc•ca (sál-tim-bóckə) *n.* An Italian dish consisting of thin slices of veal, each rolled round a slice of ham and a sage leaf and cooked in Marsala or white wine.

sal•tire (sáwl-tīr, sál- || sól-) *n. Heraldry.* An ordinary in the shape of a St. Andrew's cross, formed by the crossing of a bend and a bend sinister. [Middle English *sawturoure, sawtire,* from Old French *sau(l)toir,* originally a cross-shaped stile to keep cattle from straying, but which people could jump over, from *sau(l)ter,* to jump, from Latin *saltāre.* See **saltant.**]

Salt Lake City. Capital of Utah in the central western United States, situated near the Great Salt Lake. Founded by a party of Mormons led by Brigham Young, it is today the headquarters of the Mormon Church.

salt lick *n.* **1.** A natural deposit of exposed salt that animals lick. **2.** A block of salt or an artificial medicated saline preparation set out for cattle, sheep, or deer to lick.

salt marsh *n.* Low coastal grassland frequently inundated by the tide. Also called "salt meadow", "marsh".

Salto Angel. See **Angel Fall.**

salt pan *n.* **1.** A depression in the ground from which sea water evaporates to leave a salt deposit. **2.** A shallow vessel used for the same process.

salt·pe·tre, *U.S.* **salt·pe·ter** (sáwlt-péetər, -peetər || sólt-) *n.* **1. Potassium nitrate** *(see).* **2. Sodium nitrate** *(see).* [Variant of earlier *salpetre,* from Middle English, from Old French, from Medieval Latin *salpetra,* probably "salt rock" (so called because it appears as a saltlike crust on rocks) : Latin *sāl,* salt + *petra,* rock, from Greek.]

sal·tus (sál-təss) *n., pl.* **-tuses.** A sudden break in a sequence, as in the logical steps in an argument. [Latin, leap.]

salt·water (sáwlt-wawtər || sólt-, *U.S. also* -wottər) *adj.* Pertaining to, consisting of, or inhabiting salt water.

salt·works (sáwlt-wurks || sólt-) *n., pl.* **saltworks.** A place or building where salt is manufactured commercially.

salt·wort (sáwlt-wurt || sólt-, -wawrt) *n.* **1.** Any of several plants of the genus *Salsola;* especially, *S. kali,* native to the Old World, having stiff, prickly leaves, and growing on sandy seashores. Also called "glasswort". **2.** A plant, the **sea milkwort** *(see).*

salt·y (sáwlti || sólti) *adj.* **-ier, -iest. 1.** Pertaining to, containing, or tasting of salt. **2.** Suggesting of the sea or sailing life. **3. a.** Piquant; witty. **b.** Racy; risqué. **—salt·i·ly** *adv.* **—salt·i·ness** *n.*

sa·lu·bri·ous (sə-lōō-bri-əss, -léw-) *adj.* Conducive or favourable to health or well-being; wholesome: *a salubrious climate.* [Latin *salūbris,* from *salūs,* health.] **—sa·lu·bri·ous·ly** *adv.* **—sa·lu·bri·ous·ness, sa·lu·bri·ty** (-brəti) *n.*

sa·lu·ki (sə-lōō-ki, -léw-) *n., pl.* **-kis.** *Often capital* **S.** A tall, slender dog of an ancient breed developed in Arabia and Egypt, having a smooth, silky, variously coloured coat. [Arabic *salūqīy,* (dog) of *Salūq,* ancient southern Arabian city.]

sal·u·tar·y (sál-yoo-tri, -təri || -terri) *adj.* **1.** Effecting or intended to effect an improvement; beneficially corrective: *salutary advice.* **2.** Favourable or conducive to health or recovery; wholesome or curative. [Middle English, Old French *salutaire,* from Latin *salūtāris,* of health, from *salūs* (stem *salūt-*), health.] **—sal·u·tar·i·ly** *adv.* **—sal·u·tar·i·ness** *n.*

sal·u·ta·tion (sál-yoo-táysh'n) *n.* **1. a.** A polite expression of greeting or good will. **b.** A gesture of greeting, such as a bow or kiss. **2.** Words of greeting, such as *Dear Sir* in a letter or *Ladies and Gentlemen* in a speech. [Middle English *salutacioun,* from Latin *salūtātiō* (stem *salūtātiōn-*), from *salūtātus,* past participle of *salūtāre,* to SALUTE.] **—sa·lu·ta·to·ry** (-táytəri, sə-lōōt-ə-tri) *adj.*

sa·lute (sə-lōōt, -léwt) *v.* **-luted, -luting, -lutes.** *—tr.* **1.** To greet or address with an expression of welcome, goodwill, or respect. **2. a.** To recognise (a military superior) with a gesture prescribed by regulations, as by raising the hand to the cap. **b.** To honour formally and ceremoniously. **3.** To express appreciative acknowledgment of; commend. *—intr.* To perform a salute.

~n. **1.** An act, gesture, or expression of welcome, honour, respect, or courteous recognition: *They stood in silence as a salute to his courage.* **2. a.** An act of respect towards a military superior, normally performed by raising the outstretched hand, palm forwards, to the cap. **b.** A similar act made by a superior officer to return another's salute. **c.** Any formal military display of honour or greeting, as firing cannon or presenting arms. [Middle English *saluten,* from Latin *salūtāre,* to preserve, salute, wish health to, from *salūs* (stem *salūt-*), health, safety.] **—sa·lut·er** *n.*

sal·va·ble (sál-vəb'l) *adj.* **1.** Capable of being saved. **2.** Able to be salvaged. [Late Latin *salvāre,* to save, SALVAGE.]

Sal·va·dor (sál-və-dawr, *Brazilian Portuguese* sów-). Formerly **São Salvador** or **Bahia.** Seaport and capital of Bahia State, northeastern Brazil. It is also a major industrial centre. Founded by the Portuguese in 1549, it was the capital of Portuguese America until this was transferred to Rio de Janeiro (1763).

Sal·va·do·ri·an (sál-və-dáwri-ən || -dōri-) *n.* Also **Sal·va·do·ran** (-dáwr- || -dōr-). A native or inhabitant of Salvador or El Salvador. **—Sal·va·do·ri·an** *adj.*

sal·vage (sál-vij) *tr.v.* **-vaged, -vaging, -vages. 1.** To save (a ship or its cargo, for example) from loss or destruction. **2.** To save (discarded or damaged material) for further use. **3.** To save as if from disaster or loss: *salvage the project.* **4.** To retrieve (something liable to be included in a loss or disaster): *Most of the orders were cancelled but we salvaged a few.*

~n. **1. a.** The rescue of a ship or its crew or cargo from fire, shipwreck, or the like. **b.** That which has been thus rescued. **2.** Compensation given to those who voluntarily aid in such a rescue. **3. a.** The act of saving anything in danger. **b.** That which is saved. [French, the act of saving, from Old French, from *salver,* to save, from Late Latin *salvāre,* from Latin *salvus,* unharmed, safe.] **—sal·vage·a·ble** *adj.* **—sal·vag·er** *n.*

Sal·var·san (sál-vər-s'n, -san) *n.* A trademark for an arsenic compound, **arsphenamine** *(see),* used to treat syphilis.

sal·va·tion (sal-váysh'n) *n.* **1.** Preservation or deliverance from evil or difficulty. **2.** A source, means, or cause of such deliverance or preservation. **3.** The deliverance, through Christ, of man or his soul from the power of sin and consequent penalties; redemption. [Middle English, from Old French, from Late Latin *salvātiō* (stem *salvātiōn-*), from *salvāre,* to save, to SALVAGE.] **—sal·va·tion·al** *adj.*

Salvation Army *n. Abbr.* **S.A.** An international evangelical and charitable organisation founded (1865) by William Booth and organised on military lines.

sal·va·tion·ist (sal-váysh'n-ist) *n.* **1.** *Usually capital* **S.** A member of the Salvation Army. **2.** An evangelist, especially one emphasising salvation. **—sal·va·tion·ism** *n.*

salve¹ (salv, saav || *U.S. also* sav) *n.* **1.** An analgesic or medicinal ointment. **2.** Anything that soothes or heals; a balm: *Bach was her salve for depression.*

~tr.v. **salved, salving, salves. 1.** To soothe as if with salve; quiet; appease. **2.** To dress (a wound or sore) with salve. [Middle English *salf, salve,* Old English *salf, sealf,* from Germanic.]

salve² (salv) *tr.v.* **salved, salving, salves.** To save (a ship, for example) from danger or loss. [Back-formation from SALVAGE.]

sal·ver (sál-vər) *n.* A tray or platter, usually made of or plated with silver or gold, and used to present food or visiting cards, for example. [French *salve* (influenced by *platter*), a tray for presenting food (to the king), from Spanish *salva,* originally "foretasting of food to detect poison", from *salvar,* to foretaste food or drink, "to save", from Late Latin *salvāre,* to save, to SALVAGE.]

sal·vi·a (sál-vi-ə) *n.* Any of various plants and shrubs of the genus *Salvia;* especially, *S. splendens,* native to South America and widely cultivated for its showy scarlet flowers. [New Latin, from Latin, "the healing plant", SAGE.]

sal·vo¹ (sál-vō) *n., pl.* **-vos** or **-voes. 1.** A simultaneous discharge of firearms. **2. a.** The simultaneous release of a rack of bombs or rockets, as from an aircraft. **b.** The projectiles thus released. **3.** A sudden outburst of cheers, applause, or the like. [Earlier *salve, salva,* from Italian *salva,* salute, volley, from Latin *salvē,* hail, imperative of *salvēre,* to be in good health, from *salvus,* safe, well.]

salvo² *n., pl.* **-vos. 1.** A reservation or saving clause, as in a document; a proviso. **2.** An excuse, evasion, or other means of saving face or allaying a guilty conscience. Sometimes used derogatorily. [(Medieval) Latin, ablative of *salvus,* SAFE, in such phrases as *salvō iurē,* with (someone's) right kept safe.]

sal vol·a·ti·le (və-láttəli, vō-) *n.* **1.** A preparation used for smelling salts, a solution of ammonium carbonate and aromatic oils in alcohol and aqueous ammonia. Also called "spirits of ammonia". **2. Ammonium carbonate** *(see).* [New Latin, volatile salt.]

sal·vor (sál-vər) *n.* A person or ship involved in salvaging a ship or cargo at sea. [From SALVE (to salvage).]

Salz·burg (sálts-burg, sáalts-; *German* zálts-boork). Capital of Salzburg state, Austria, situated on the river Salzach near the German border. It is one of Austria's main tourist centres, and its many historic buildings include the 11th-century fortress of Hohensalzburg and a fine 17th-century cathedral. Mozart was born in the city, and a Salzburg Festival of music is held annually. Salzburg University (1623) was refounded in 1963. Originally a Celtic settlement and then a Roman trading post, Salzburg developed in the eighth century around a Benedictine monastery. For nearly a thousand years from *c.*800, it was governed by its autocratic archbishops, princes of the Holy Roman Empire from 1278.

SAM (sam) *n.* A *s*urface-to-*a*ir *m*issile.

sam·a·ra (sə-máarə || -márrə, sámmərə) *n. Botany.* A winged, one-seeded fruit that does not split open, such as that of the ash or sycamore. Also called "key fruit". [New Latin, from Latin *samara*†, seed of the elm.]

Sa·ma·ra (sə-maarə). Formerly **Kuy·by·shev** (kōō-i-bí-sheff, *Russian* -shəff). Industrial city and river port on the Volga, in Russia. As Kuybyshev, it was the capital of the U.S.S.R. (1941–42) when Moscow was under German attack.

Sa·ma·ri·a¹ (sə-máir-i-ə). Region of the Middle East, now in Israel and Jordan. In ancient times it was the centre of Palestine, between Galilee in the north and Judah in the south.

Samaria² Modern **Sabastiya.** Hill city in ancient Palestine, now a village in Jordan (occupied by the Israelis in 1967). It was built by King Omri as the capital of the Northern Kingdom (Israel) in the early ninth century B.C., but later fell to Sargon of Assyria (721 B.C.). Its people were deported to Babylon, and foreign settlers, many from Syria and Mesopotamia, were brought in. Most of these non-Jewish settlers adopted Judaism, but recognised only the Pentateuch, causing hostility with the Jews. Samaria was destroyed by John Hyrcanus (one of the Maccabees) in 120 B.C. and restored by Herod the Great as **Sebaste.** It has Roman remains, and excavations in the 20th century have revealed remnants of Omri's palace.

Sa·mar·i·tan (sə-márrit'n) *n.* **1. a.** A native or inhabitant of ancient Samaria. **b.** A member of a people descended from the ancient non-Jewish inhabitants of Samaria, now inhabiting the area around Tel Aviv in Israel and in Jordan. **c.** The Semitic language of this people, a variety of Aramaic. **2.** A member of an organisation, *the Samaritans,* for helping those in a state of emotional distress and suicidal despair. **3.** A **Good Samaritan** *(see).* **—Sa·mar·i·tan** *adj.*

sa·mar·i·um (sə-máir-i-əm) *n.* Symbol **Sm** A silvery or pale-grey metallic rare-earth element found in monazite and bastnaesite and used as a dopant for laser materials, in infrared absorbing glass, and as a neutron absorber in certain nuclear reactors. Atomic number 62, atomic weight 150.35, melting point 1,072°C, boiling point 1,900°C, relative density (approximately) 7.50, valencies 2, 3. [New Latin : SAMAR(SKITE) + -IUM.]

Sam·ar·kand or **Sam·ar·qand** (sám-aar-kánd, -ər-). City in Uzbekistan. A key station on the ancient Silk Road, it was taken by the Arabs (A.D. 712) and became a great centre of Islamic culture. Pillaged by Genghis Khan (1220), it became prominent again from 1365 as the royal city of the Mongol ruler, Timur. The Russians conquered the city in 1868.

Sa·mar·ra (sə-máarə). City in central Iraq, situated on the river Tigris. From 836 to 892 it replaced Baghdad as the capital of the Abbassid caliphs, and it is today an important centre of pilgrimage for Shiite Muslims.

sa·mar·skite (sə-mär-skīt) *n.* A black mineral oxide with red-brown streaks that is a source of several rare-earth elements. [After Colonel von *Samarski*, 19th-century Russian mine official.]

sam·ba (sámbə ‖ *U.S. also* saámbə) *n.* **1.** A dance, originating in Africa, that was modified in Brazil as a ballroom dance. **2.** Music in 4/4 time for dancing the samba. [Portuguese, of African origin.] —**sam·ba** *intr.v.*

sam·bal (sám-bal, -bəl) *n.* A sharp, spicy, and vinegary sauce or chutney of raw vegetables or fruit, used as a relish or in cookery. [Malay, condiment.]

sam·bar (saám-bər, sám-, -baar) *n.* Also **sam·bur** (-bər). A large deer, *Cervus* (or *Rusa*) *unicolor*, of southeastern Asia, having a reddish-brown coat and three-pronged antlers. [Hindi *sābar, sāmbar*, from Sanskrit *śambaraṭ*.]

Sam Browne belt (sám brówn) *n.* A belt worn as part of a military officer's uniform, supported by a shoulder strap that runs diagonally across the chest. [Modelled after the sword belt invented by Sir *Samuel James Browne* (1824–1901), British general who having lost his left arm could not support his sword with his left hand.]

same (saym) *adj.* **1.** Being the very one; not different; identical: *went to the same school.* **2.** Exhibiting close similarity with another; being alike in every or almost every respect: *We were both wearing the same dress.* **3.** Conforming absolutely; unaltered; unchanged. Often used with *as: playing according to the same rules as before.* **4.** Being the one previously mentioned or indicated; aforesaid: *This same man turned out to be my old school friend.*
~*pron.* **1.** The person, thing, or event identical with or similar to another: *Let's do the same as we did last week.* **2.** The person or thing previously mentioned or described. See Usage note. —**all the same. 1.** Nevertheless. **2.** Of no importance; of little significance: *It's all the same to me what we do.* —**just the same.** Nevertheless. —**not the same without.** Less pleasant without the presence of: *It's just not the same without Faye and Sarah.*
~*adv.* In like manner; in the identical way: *He walks the same as his father.* [Middle English, from Old Norse *samr.*]
Synonyms: same, selfsame, identical, equal, equivalent.
Usage: The use of *same,* with or without the article, to replace another pronoun in the sense of "aforesaid thing or person" is most common in formal legal or commercial contexts *(We hope to receive same next week),* and even there it is increasingly less commonly used. It is usually considered inappropriate outside such contexts, unless used humorously. The elliptical omission of *the,* in such sentences as *He goes by train, same as I do,* is a feature of informal British English.

sa·mekh (saá-mek, -mekh) *n.* The 15th letter of the Hebrew alphabet. [Hebrew *sāmekh.*]

same·ness (sáym-nəss, -niss) *n.* **1.** The condition of being the same; identity. **2.** A lack of variety or change; monotony.

same·y (sáymi) *adj. Informal.* Monotonously alike. [SAME + -Y (adjective suffix).]

sam·foo, sam·fu (sám-foó) *n.* A type of loose suit consisting of an jacket and trousers, worn by Chinese women, especially in Southeast Asia. [Cantonese *saam foo,* "shirt and trousers".]

Sa·mi·an (sáymi-ən) *adj.* Of or pertaining to the island of Samos or its inhabitants.
~*n.* A native or inhabitant of Samos.

Samian ware *n.* A type of pottery produced in southern Gaul in the first three centuries A.D., and commonly found in Roman sites in Britain. [From the type of earth, similar to that found in SAMOS.]

sam·iel (sám-yel) *n.* A wind, simoom *(see).* [Turkish *samyeli : sam,* poisonous + *yel,* wind.]

sam·i·sen (sámmi-sen) *n.* A Japanese musical instrument resembling a banjo, having a very long neck and three strings played with a plectrum. [Japanese, "three-stringed" : *sam,* three + *-mi,* taste, touch + *sen,* string, chord, from Chinese *sān, wèi, xiàn.*]

sam·ite (sám-īt, sáym-) *n.* A heavy silk fabric, often interwoven with gold or silver, worn in the Middle Ages. [Middle English *samit,* from Old French, from Medieval Latin *examitum,* from Medieval Greek *hexamiton,* from Greek *hexamitos,* of six threads : HEXA- (six) + *mitos,* thread of the warp.]

sam·iz·dat (sámmiz-dát) *n.* Formerly in the U.S.S.R., the printing and distributing of literature that had been officially banned by the government. [Russian, from *sam,* self + *izdatel'stvo,* publisher, from *izdat',* to publish (*iz,* out + *dat',* to give).]

Sam·nite (sám-nīt) *n.* **1.** In ancient Italy, a member of a people, related to the Sabines, who inhabited Samnium. **2.** The Oscan language spoken by this people. —**Sam·nite** *adj.*

Sam·ni·um (sám-ni-əm) An ancient region of southern central Italy that was eventually absorbed into the Roman commonwealth in the third century B.C., after a series of wars against Rome.

Sa·mo·a¹ (sə-mṓ-ə, saa-). Mainly volcanic archipelago in the South Pacific. Discovered by the Dutch in 1722, the tropical islands were disputed by the United States, Britain, and Germany in the 19th century, and there were rivalries among native chiefs. Finally a treaty of 1899 assigned the smaller eastern group of islands to the United States and the western group to Germany.

Samoa² Independent state, formerly Western Samoa, part of the archipelago of Samoa. It was controlled by Germany (1900–19) and then by New Zealand until 1962, when it became the first independent Polynesian state. It formally joined the Commonwealth in 1970 and in 1976 became a member of the United Nations. The largest island is Savaii. The second largest, Upolu, has about two-thirds of the population. Exports include copra,

taro, and timber, and tourism is increasingly important. Area, 2831 square kilometres (1,093 square miles). Population, 170,000. Capital, Apia, on Upolu. See map at **Pacific Ocean.**

Samoa, American. Territory of the United States, comprising eight islands of the archipelago of **Samoa.** It has a land area of 197 square kilometres (76 square miles). Tutuila is the largest island, with the capital and port of Pago Pago.

Sa·mo·an (sə-mṓ-ən, saa-) *adj.* Of or pertaining to Samoa, its Polynesian inhabitants, or their language.
~*n.* **1.** A native or inhabitant of Samoa. **2.** The Polynesian language of the Samoans.

Sa·mos (sáy-moss; *Greek* saá-). *Turkish* **Susam Adası.** Greek island in the Aegean Sea, lying close to mainland Turkey. In the seventh century B.C. it became an important Greek commercial centre, reaching its cultural zenith under the sixth-century tyrant, Polycrates. Pythagoras was born here. Held by Persia (522–479 B.C.), Athens, Sparta, Rome, Byzantium, and Genoa, Samos fell to the Ottoman Turks in 1475. It was restored to Greece in 1912. The island is fertile and produces citrus fruit, grapes, olives, and tobacco.

sa·mo·sa (sə-mṓ-sə) *n.* Also **sa·moo·sa, sa·mou·sa, sa·mu·sa** (sə-moó-sə). A snack or savoury food of Indian origin, consisting of a triangular envelope of crisp pastry with a spicy meat or vegetable filling.

Sam·o·thrace (sám-ə-thrayss, -ō-). *Modern Greek* **Samothraki;** *Turkish* **Semadrek.** Mountainous Greek island in the northern Aegean Sea. It was a centre of worship in ancient times. The statue of *Winged Victory* (now in the Louvre, Paris) dating back to the fourth century B.C., was found here in 1863.

sam·o·var (sám-ə-vaar, -ō-, -vár) *n.* A metal urn originating in Russia, having a heating device inside to boil water for tea. [Russian, "self-boiler" : *samo,* self + *varit',* to boil, cook, probably from Old Church Slavonic *variti.*]

Sam·o·yed (sám-oy-éd, -ə-yed; *for sense 3 also* sə-móy-ed) *n.* **1.** A member of a Ural-Altaic people inhabiting the tundra lands of the northeastern part of Russia and northwestern Siberia. **2.** A branch of the Uralic family of languages represented by four living languages spoken by the Samoyed tribes inhabiting this region. **3.** A dog of a breed originally developed by the Samoyed people, having a thick, long white coat. [Russian *samoed,* from Lapp *Sāme-Äednàma,* "of Lapland".] —**sam·o·yed·ic** (sám-oy-éddik, -ə-yéddik) *adj.*

samp *n. U.S. and Canadian.* **1.** Crushed maize kernels, a staple food among poor indigenous peoples. **2.** A boiled porridge made from samp. [Narraganset *nasaump,* "softened by water", samp, soup.]

sam·pan (sám-pan) *n.* Any of various flat-bottomed skiffs, usually propelled by oars, used on the waterways of the Orient. [Chinese, *sān bān,* "three board".]

sam·phire (sám-fīr) *n.* Any of several Old World plants of coastal areas; especially: **1.** *Crithmum maritimum,* having fleshy divided leaves and small yellow flowers. Also called "rock samphire". **2.** *Inula crithmoides,* having linear fleshy leaves and yellow daisy-like flowers. Also called "golden samphire". **3.** The marsh samphire or **glasswort** *(see).* [Variant (perhaps influenced by earlier *camphire,* camphor) of earlier *sampere,* from Old French *(herbe de) Saint Pierre,* "Saint Peter's herb".]

sam·ple (saám'pl ‖ sámp'l) *n.* **1.** A portion, piece, entity, or segment regarded as representative of a whole or of a group; a specimen. Also used adjectivally: *a sample copy; a sample question.* **2.** *Statistics.* A set of elements drawn from and analysed to estimate the characteristics of a population. In this sense also called "sampling". —See Synonyms at **example.**
~*tr.v.* **sampled, -pling, -ples.** To take a sample of; especially, to evaluate or examine by a sample. [Middle English, short for Old French *essample,* EXAMPLE.]

sam·pler (saám-plər ‖ sám-) *n.* **1.** One that takes, appraises, or analyses a sample, such as a machine for testing food products. **2.** A piece of cloth embroidered with various designs or mottoes so as to show the skill of the sewer.

sam·pling (saám-pling ‖ sám-) *n.* **1.** *Statistics.* A sample. **2.** The process of selecting a sample.

sam·sa·ra (səm-saárə) *n.* **1.** In Hinduism, the eternal cycle of birth, suffering, death, and rebirth. **2.** In Buddhism, the world and existence as experienced by unenlightened beings, characterised by insubstantiality, impermanence, and the endless round of birth, old age, disease, and death. [Sanskrit *saṃsāra,* "a passing through" : *sam,* together, completely + *sarati,* it runs, it flows.]

Sam·son¹ (sám-s'n, sámps'n). An Israelite judge of extraordinary strength, betrayed to the Philistines by Delilah. Judges 14–16. [Hebrew *Shimshōn,* "like the sun", from *shemesh,* sun.]

Samson² *n.* A man of great physical strength. [After SAMSON.]

Sam·u·el¹ (sámmew-əl ‖ sámmewl). Hebrew judge and prophet of the 11th century B.C.

Samuel² *n. Abbr.* **Sam.** Either of two books, I and II Samuel, of the Old Testament.

sam·u·rai (sámmoo-rī, sámmew-) *n., pl.* **samurai.** *Often capital* **S. 1.** A warrior belonging to the military aristocracy of feudal Japan. **2.** A modern descendant of a samurai. [Japanese, "warrior".]

Sa·n'a or **Sa·naa** (san-aá, saan-). Capital of Yemen. It lies in the centre of the country on a high plain (2,210 metres; 7,250 feet). A walled city celebrated in the early Islamic period, it has many fine buildings, the most important of which is the Jami' Masjid (Great Mosque).

San An·dre·as Fault (sán-an-dráy-əss). Fracture in the Earth's crust running through California, western United States. More than 960 kilometres (600 miles) long, it is a strike-slip fault where two of the Earth's tectonic plates are moving slowly past each other in the horizontal plane. At irregular intervals, the immense strain is released in tremors and earthquakes which have included the major earthquake that devastated San Francisco in 1906.

San An·to·ni·o (sán-an-tō-ni-ō, -tōn-yō). City in Texas, southern United States, situated on the San Antonio river. A Catholic mission was founded here in 1718 and its chapel, the Alamo, was the site of a famous Mexican attack (1836) during the struggle for Texan independence. Its ruins are a major tourist attraction, and there are also military and air force establishments, the city being one of the largest U.S. military centres.

san·a·tive (sánnətiv) adj. Able to cure or heal; curative. [Middle English, from Old French sanatif or Late Latin sānātīvus, from sānāre, to cure, from sānus, sound, SANE.]

san·a·to·ri·um (sánnə-táwri-əm ‖ -tôri-). n., pl. **-ums** or **-toria** (-táwri-ə). Also U.S. **san·i·ta·ri·um** (-taír-i-əm ‖ -tôri-). 1. An institution for the treatment of chronic diseases, such as tuberculosis, or for medically supervised convalescence. 2. British. A building or part of a building at a college or boarding school reserved for those who are sick. [New Latin, from Late Latin sānātōrius, neuter of sānātōrius, from Latin sānātus, past participle of sānāre, to heal, from sānus, healthy, SANE.]

san·be·ni·to (sán-bə-néetō, -be-) n., pl. **-tos.** 1. A yellow garment with Saint Anthony's cross on its front and back, worn by a penitent under the Spanish Inquisition. 2. A similar but black garment with painted flames and devils on it, for impenitents at an auto-da-fé. [Spanish sambenito, after San Benito, Saint BENEDICT (from its resemblance to the Benedictine scapular).]

San·cho Pan·za (sánchō pánzo) n. A companion who is simple and down-to-earth. [After the squire in Cervantes' Don Quixote.]

sanc·ti·fied (sángkti-fīd) adj. 1. Made holy; dedicated to sacred use; consecrated. 2. Archaic. Sanctimonious.

sanc·ti·fy (sángkti-fī) tr.v. **-fied, -fying, -fies.** 1. To reserve for sacred use; consecrate. 2. To make holy; purify. 3. To give religious sanction or legitimacy to: sanctify a marriage. 4. To make productive of holiness or blessing. [Middle English sanctifien, from Old French sanctifier, from Late Latin sanctificāre : Latin sanctus, holy, sacred, from the past participle of sancīre, to consecrate + facere, to make.] **—sanc·ti·fi·ca·tion** (-fi-káysh'n) n. **—sanc·ti·fi·er** n.

sanc·ti·mo·ni·ous (sángkti-mōni-əss) adj. Making a pretence of sanctity, piety, or righteousness. [Latin sanctimōnia, sanctity, from sanctus, sacred (see **sanctify**) + mōnia, -MONY + -OUS.] **—sanc·ti·mo·ni·ous·ly** adv. **—sanc·ti·mo·ni·ous·ness, sanc·ti·mo·ny** (-mən-i ‖ U.S. -mōni) n.

sanc·tion (sángksh'n) n. 1. **a.** Authoritative permission or approval that makes a course of action valid. **b.** The ratification or confirmation of a law or other measure. 2. Support or encouragement, as from public opinion or established custom. 3. The penalty for noncompliance or the reward for compliance with a law or decree. 4. Any consideration or principle that influences ethical choices or otherwise acts to ensure compliance or conformity. 5. A coercive measure adopted usually by several nations acting together against a nation violating international law: Trade sanctions were implemented against the Boggato Republic. 6. Archaic. A law or decree, especially an ecclesiastical decree.
~tr.v. **sanctioned, -tioning, -tions.** 1. To authorise; legitimise; ratify. 2. To approve, support, or encourage: sanctioned by the frequency of its occurrence. —See Synonyms at **approve.** [French, from Latin sanctiō (stem sanctiōn-), an ordaining, a sanction, from sanctus, sacred. See **sanctify.**]

sanc·ti·ty (sángktəti) n., pl. **-ties.** 1. Saintliness, holiness, or godliness. 2. The quality or condition of being considered hallowed or sacred; inviolability. 3. Anything considered sacred. [Middle English saunctite, from Old French sainctite, from Latin sanctitās (stem sanctitāt-), from sanctus, sacred. See **sanctify.**]

sanc·tu·ar·y (sángk-tew-əri, -chəri ‖ U.S. -choo-erri) n., pl. **-ies.** 1. A sacred place, such as a church, temple, or mosque. 2. The most holy part of a sacred place, such as the area around the altar in a church. 3. A church or other sacred place in which fugitives formerly were safe from arrest or punishment. 4. Immunity from arrest or punishment, by taking refuge in or as if in a sacred place: sought sanctuary at the French embassy in Prague. 5. Any place of refuge or asylum. 6. A reserved area in which wildlife is protected from hunting or other molestation. —See Synonyms at **shelter.** [Middle English sanctuarie, from Old French sainctuarie, from Late Latin sanctuārium, from Latin sanctus, sacred. See **sanctify.**]

sanc·tum (sángk-təm) n., pl. **-tums** or **-ta** (-tə). 1. A sacred or holy place. 2. A private room or study where one is not to be disturbed. [Latin, neuter of sanctus, sacred. See **sanctify.**]

sanctum sanc·to·rum (sángk-táwrəm ‖ -tôrəm) n. 1. The **holy of holies** (see). 2. An inviolably private place. Often used humorously. [Late Latin, "the holy of holies" (translation of Greek to hagion tōn hagiōn, translation of Hebrew qōdesh ha-qqodāshīm).]

Sanc·tus (sángktəss) n. 1. The hymn of praise that follows on from the Preface in many eucharistic liturgies. 2. A musical setting of this. [Middle English, from Medieval Latin, first word of the hymn, from Late Latin, "holy" (first word of the hymn sung by the angels in Isaiah 6:3), from Latin. See **sanctify.**]

sand (sand) n. 1. Loose, granular, gritty particles of worn or disintegrated rock, especially quartz, finer than gravel and coarser than

dust. 2. Usually plural. A tract or stretch of land covered with this material, as a beach or desert. 3. **a.** This material in an hourglass. **b.** Plural. Moments of allotted time or duration: "The sands are number'd that make up my life" (Shakespeare). 4. U.S. Slang. Grit; courage. 5. Light greyish brown to yellowish grey. **—build on sand.** To base on a foundation that is insecure or uncertain.
~tr.v. **sanded, sanding, sands.** 1. To sprinkle or cover with sand or similar particles: sanded the icy road. 2. To polish or scrape with sand or sandpaper. 3. To mix or adulterate with sand. [Middle English sand, Old English sand, from Germanic sandam, sandaz (unattested).]

Sand (sɒND), George, pen name of Amandine Aurore Lucie Dupin; also known as Baronne Dudevant (1804–76). French writer. She married Casimir Dudevant in 1822 and her first novel, Indiana, which was a plea for feminine independence, was published in 1832, a year after she had left her husband and gone to live with Jules Sandeau. She wrote many successful novels, including La Mare au diable (1846), and could count Alfred de Musset and Frédéric Chopin among her lovers.

san·dal[1] (sánd'l) n. 1. A light shoe consisting of a sole fastened to the foot by thongs or straps, and worn especially in warm weather. 2. A lightweight shoe, typically having a perforated design in the upper and a flat, spongy sole, worn especially by children. 3. A strap or band for fastening a low shoe or slipper on the foot. [Middle English sandalie, from Latin sandalium, from Greek sandalion, diminutive of sandalon, sandal, probably of Asiatic origin.]

sandal[2] n. Sandalwood. [Middle English, from Old French, from Medieval Latin sandalum, santalum, from Greek santalon, sandanon, probably from Sanskrit candanaḥ.]

san·dal·wood (sánd'l-wŏod) n. 1. Any of several south Asian or Australasian evergreen trees of the genus Santalum; especially, S. album, having aromatic yellowish heartwood that is used in cabinet-making and wood carving, and that yields an oil used in perfumery. Also called "sandal". 2. The wood of this tree or of similar trees. 3. Any of various similar trees; especially, red sandalwood, Pterocarpus santalinus, the dark-red wood of which yields a dye. 4. Light to moderate or greyish brown.

san·da·rac, san·da·rach (sándə-rak) n. 1. A tree, Tetraclinis articulata (or Callitris quadrivalvis), of northern Africa, having wood yielding a brittle, translucent resin used in varnishes. 2. The resin of this tree. [Latin sandaraca, red pigment, beebread, from Greek sandarak(h)ē, (red pigment derived from) realgar.]

sand·bag (sánd-bag) n. 1. A bag filled with sand, used, especially: **a.** In piles to form protective walls, as against flooding or gunfire. **b.** As a ballast in a balloon or boat. 2. A small, narrow bag partially filled with sand, used as a weapon to hit someone.
~tr.v. **sandbagged, -bagging, -bags.** 1. To put sandbags in, on, or around as a means of protection. 2. **a.** To hit with a sandbag. **b.** U.S. To force by crude means.

sand·bank (sánd-bangk) n. A bank of sand in a sea or river formed by currents and often exposed at low tide.

sand·bar (sánd-baar) n. An offshore shoal of sand built up by the action of waves or currents.

sand·blast (sánd-blaast ‖ -blast) n. 1. A blast of air or steam carrying sand at high speed to etch glass or to clean stone or metal surfaces. 2. A machine used to apply such a blast.
~tr.v. **sandblasted, -blasting, -blasts.** To apply a sandblast to for the purpose of cleaning or engraving. **—sand·blast·er** n.

sand·blind (sánd-blīnd) adj. Archaic. Partially blind; dim-sighted. [Middle English sand-blind, Old English sāmblind (unattested) : sām-, half + BLIND.] **—sand-blind·ness** n.

sand·box (sánd-boks) n. A box or receptacle for sand, especially: 1. A small vessel formerly used to sprinkle sand on wet ink. 2. A container on a locomotive for sprinkling sand on icy rails. 3. U.S. A **sandpit** (see) a boxlike enclosure.

sandbox tree n. A tropical American tree, Hura crepitans, having a spiny trunk and woody seed capsules that split explosively when ripe. [So called because the capsules were formerly used to hold sand for drying ink.]

sand·cast (sánd-kaast ‖ -kast) tr.v. **-cast, -casting, -casts.** To make (a casting) by pouring molten metal into a sand mould.

sand·cas·tle (sánd-kaass'l ‖ -kass'l) n. A mound of sand built up to resemble a castle, especially by children at the seaside.

sand crack n. A fissure in the side of a horse's hoof, often causing lameness.

sand dollar n. Any of various thin, circular echinoderms; especially, Echinarachnius parma, of sandy ocean bottoms of the northern Atlantic and Pacific.

sand dune n. A dune (see).

sand eel n. Any of several small marine fishes of the genus Ammodytes, having a slender body with a forked tail fin, and often burrowing in coastal sand or shingle. Also called "launce", "sand launce".

sand·er (sándər) n. 1. One that spreads sand. 2. One that sands surfaces; especially, a machine with an abrasive-covered disc or belt, used for smoothing or polishing.

san·der·ling (sándər-ling) n. A small shore bird, Crocethia (or Calidris) alba, having predominantly grey and white plumage. [Perhaps from SAND + -LING.]

sand flea n. Any of various small crustaceans living on sandy beaches, such as the sand hopper.

sand fly n. 1. Any of various small biting flies of the genus Phleboto-

mus, of tropical areas, some of which transmit diseases. **2.** Any of various similar or related flies.

sand glass *n.* An instrument, such as an hourglass, consisting of two glass chambers with a narrow connecting channel, and containing sand that takes a definite time to trickle from one chamber to the other.

sand-grouse (sánd-growss) *n.* Any of various sandy-coloured pigeon-like birds of the genera *Pterocles* and *Syrrhaptes,* of arid and semiarid regions of the Old World.

san-dhi (sánd-i, súnd-, -ee, -hee) *n. Linguistics.* The modification of the sound or form of a word because of its position in certain contexts; for example, the difference between the pronunciation of *the* in *the house* and in *the other house* is an instance of sandhi. [Sanskrit *saṁdhi,* "a placing together" : *sam,* together + *dadhāti,* to place.]

sand-hog (sánd-hog ‖ -hawg) *n. U.S.* A labourer who works in a pressure chamber, as in the construction of underwater tunnels.

sand hopper *n.* Any small, jumping crustacean of the genera *Orchestia* and *Talitrus,* common in intertidal zones.

Sand-hurst (sánd-hurst). Village near Aldershot in south central England. It is famous as the site of the Royal Military Academy where many British and Commonwealth army officers are trained.

San Di-e-go (sándi-áygō). City and seaport in southern California, western United States, situated on San Diego Bay. The city has an oceanographic institute, a major naval and marine base, and shipbuilding, aviation, and aerospace industries.

San-di-nis-ta (san-di-neés-tə, -nís-) *n., pl.* **-tas.** A supporter of the government of Nicaragua that came to power in 1979 after the overthrow of President Somoza. Compare **Contra.** [Spanish, from A.C. *Sandino* (killed 1933), Nicaraguan rebel leader + *-ista, -ist.*]

sand launce *n.* The **sand eel** *(see).*

sand lizard *n.* A light brown to greyish European lizard, *Lacerta agilis,* which has, in the male, bright green underparts.

sand-man (sánd-man) *n.* A character in fairy tales and folklore who puts children to sleep by sprinkling sand in their eyes.

sand martin *n.* A small European martin, *Riparia riparia,* which has white underparts with a brown breast band and nests in sand and gravel banks.

sand mould *n.* A mould used in a foundry, made from sand in which a design has been impressed.

sand painting *n.* **1.** A ceremonial design of the Navaho Indians of North America made by trickling fine coloured sand onto a base of neutral sand. **2.** The art of making such designs.

sand-pa-per (sánd-paypər) *n.* Paper coated on one side with sand or other abrasive material, used for smoothing.
~*tr.v.* **sandpapered, -pering, -pers.** To rub with sandpaper for the purpose of smoothing, polishing, or finishing.

sand-pi-per (sánd-pīpər) *n.* Any of various small wading birds of the family Scolopacidae, usually having a long, straight bill, and characteristically frequenting the seashore in flocks.

sand-pit (sánd-pit) *n.* **1.** A pit from which sand can be excavated. **2.** *British.* A pit or low container filled with sand, used by children for play and by athletes in the high and long jump.

San-dring-ham (sándring-əm). Village in Norfolk, in eastern England. Sandringham House, its estate, has been a country residence of English royalty since 1863.

sand-shoe (sánd-shōō) *n. British.* A light summer or sports shoe, often made of canvas with a rubber sole.

sand smelt A widely distributed fish of the genus *Atherina,* closely related to the grey mullet and found in inshore waters, especially estuaries.

sand-stone (sánd-stōn) *n.* Variously coloured sedimentary rock composed predominantly of sandlike quartz grains cemented by lime, silica, or other materials.

sand-storm (sánd-stawrm) *n.* A strong wind carrying clouds of sand through the air near the ground, especially in a desert.

sand table *n.* A table on which a relief model of a town or terrain is built out of sand and used for the study of military tactics and manoeuvres.

sand trap *n. Chiefly U.S.* In golf, a **bunker** *(see).*

sand viper *n.* Any of various snakes of sandy areas, such as *Vipera ammodytes,* a venomous species of southern Europe and Asia Minor, or the **horned viper** *(see).*

sand-wich (sán-wij, sánd-, -wich) *n.* **1.** Two or more slices of bread with meat, cheese, jam, or other filling placed between them. **2.** Any arrangement resembling a sandwich.
~*tr.v.* **sandwiched, -wiching, -wiches. 1.** To insert between two things of another type. **2.** To fit with difficulty between two other things; make room or time for: *sandwich a meeting between lunch and leaving the office.* [After the 4th Earl of SANDWICH.]

Sand-wich (sán-wich, sánd-, -wij, sánnij). Market town in Kent, southeastern England. It was one of the original Cinque Ports.

Sandwich, John Montagu, 4th Earl of (1718–92). He is said to have sustained long periods at the gaming table by eating cold beef placed between slices of bread, so giving rise to the word sandwich.

sandwich board *n.* Either of two large boards bearing advertising placards, hinged at the top by straps for hanging on a carrier's shoulders.

sandwich cake *n. British.* A layer cake consisting of a filling, such as jam and cream, between two round thick slices of sponge.

sandwich compound *n.* A type of chemical compound, such as ferrocene, in which a metal atom or ion is sandwiched between two parallel organic rings.

sandwich course *n. British.* An educational course, especially a vocational one, in which periods of academic study alternate with periods of practical experience.

sandwich man *n.* A man hired to carry sandwich boards.

sand-worm (sánd-wurm) *n.* Any of various segmented worms, especially of the genera *Nereis* and *Arenicola,* generally inhabiting coastal mud or sand, and often used as fishing bait.

sand-wort (sánd-wurt ‖ -wawrt) *n.* Any of numerous low-growing plants of the genera *Arenaria, Minuartia,* and *Moehringia,* having small, usually white flowers.

sand-y (sándi) *adj.* **-ier, -iest. 1.** Covered with, consisting of, or containing a high proportion of sand: *sandy soil.* **2.** Like sand, as in being unstable. **3. a.** Having the colour of sand; yellowish red. **b.** Having hair of this colour. —**sand-i-ness** *n.*

sand yacht *n.* A vehicle with wheels and sails, designed to be propelled across flat stretches of sand, as on a beach, by the wind. —**sand-yacht-ing** *n.*

sane (sayn) *adj.* **saner, sanest. 1.** Mentally healthy; of sound mind. **2.** Having or showing sound judgment; reasonable; rational. [Latin *sānus,* sound, whole, healthy.] —**sane-ly** *adv.* —**sane-ness** *n.*

San-for-ized (sán-fər-īzd) *adj.* A trademark designating fabrics preshrunk by a patented mechanical process before being made into clothing so as to minimise later shrinkage.

San Fran-cis-co (sán-frən-sískō, -fran-). Major city and seaport in California, western United States, situated on a peninsula between San Francisco Bay and the Pacific Ocean, which are linked by the strait known as the Golden Gate. Founded as a Spanish mission in 1776, it boomed during the Californian gold rush of 1848 and further expanded after the opening of the transcontinental railway (1869). Lying on the **San Andreas Fault,** it was partially destroyed in an earthquake and fire in 1906, and has been subject to lesser tremors at irregular intervals. In 1989, an earthquake killed 63 people. The city is the financial centre of the West Coast, and also serves a prosperous agricultural and mining region. Among its famous sights are the Golden Gate Bridge, the municipal cable car system, Chinatown, and the island of **Alcatraz,** which lies in the Bay. The Haight-Ashbury district of San Francisco won fame in the 1960s as the centre of hippy counterculture. —**San Fran-cis-can** *adj. & n.*

sang. Past tense of **sing.**

san-ga-ree (sáng-gə-reé) *n.* A cold drink usually made of wine, often Madeira, and grated nutmeg. [Spanish *sangría,* "a bleeding", from *sangre,* blood, from Latin *sanguis.* See **sanguine.**]

Sang-er (sáng-ər), Frederick (1918–). British biochemist. He determined the order of amino acids in the insulin molecule and was awarded the Nobel prize for chemistry in 1958 and 1980.

sang-froid (són-frwáa, sáng-) *n.* Composure; coolness; imperturbability. See Synonyms at **equanimity.** [French, "cold blood".]

sangh (sungg) *n.* An association in India that promotes the consolidation of the different groups in Hinduism. [Hindi *sāg,* from Sanskrit *saṅga,* association, from *sajati,* he adheres.]

san-gha (sáng-gə, súng-, -g-hə) *n.* The monastic community in Buddhism, considered collectively. [Sanskrit. See **sangh.**]

San-graal (sang-gráyl) *n.* The **grail** *(see).* [Old French, "holy grail".]

san-gri-a (sang-greé-ə) *n.* A cold drink made of red or white wine mixed with fruit juice or lemonade, and sometimes brandy, and garnished with fruit. [Spanish *sangría,* "bleeding", from *sangre,* blood, from Latin *sanguis.* See **sanguine.**]

san-gui-na-ri-a (sáng-gwi-naír-i-ə) *n.* A North American plant of the genus *Sanguinaria;* especially, *S. candensis,* the bloodroot, the dried rhizome of which is used as an emetic. [New Latin, from Latin *sanguinarius,* bloody, from *sanguis* (stem *sanguin-*), blood.]

san-gui-nar-y (sáng-gwin-əri ‖ -erri) *adj.* **1.** Accompanied by bloodshed and carnage. **2.** Bloodthirsty. **3.** Consisting of or stained with blood. [Latin *sanguinārius,* of blood, from *sanguis* (stem *sanguin-*), blood.] —**san-gui-nar-i-ly** *adv.* —**san-gui-nar-i-ness** *n.*

san-guine (sáng-gwin) *adj.* **1. a.** *Archaic.* Of the colour of blood; red. **b.** Ruddy; florid. Said of the complexion. **2.** Dominated by the humour of blood in terms of medieval physiology. See **humour.** **3.** Having the courageous or passionate temperament and ruddy complexion formerly thought to be characteristic of one dominated by this humour. **4.** Eagerly optimistic; cheerful; hopeful. [Middle English *sanguin,* from Old French, from Latin *sanguineus,* of blood, bloody, from *sanguis†* (stem *sanguin-*), blood.] —**san-guine-ly** *adv.* —**san-guine-ness, san-guin-i-ty** (sang-gwínnəti) *n.*

san-guin-e-ous (sang-gwínni-əss) *adj.* **1. a.** Pertaining to or involving blood or bloodshed. **b.** Bloodthirsty; sanguinary. **2.** Blood-red. **3.** Cheerful; optimistic; sanguine. [Latin *sanguineus,* SANGUINE.]

san-guin-o-lent (sang-gwínnələnt) *adj.* Of, mixed with, or tinged with blood. [Latin *sanguinolentus,* full of blood, from *sanguis* (stem *sanguin-*), blood. See **sanguine.**]

San-he-drin (sán-i-drin, -ə-, -e-, *also* san-hé-) *n.* Also **San-he-drim** (-drim). **1.** The highest judicial and ecclesiastical council of the ancient Jewish nation, composed of from 70 to 72 members. Also called "Great Sanhedrin". **2.** A similar but less important assembly with 23 members. [Hebrew *sanhedhrīn,* from Greek *sunedrion,* a council, from *sunedros,* sitting within council : SYN- (together) + *hedra,* a seat, a sitting.]

san-i-cle (sánnik'l) *n.* Any of various plants of the genus *Sanicula,* having clusters of small, greenish-white or pale pink flowers and reputedly having medicinal value as an astringent. [Middle English, from Old French, from Medieval Latin *sanicula,* probably from Latin *sānus,* healthy, SANE (because the plant was once thought to have healing powers).]

sa·ni·es (sáyni-eez) *n.* A thin, fetid, greenish fluid consisting of serum and pus discharged from a wound, ulcer, or fistula. [Latin *saniēs†.*] —**sa·ni·ous** (-əss) *adj.*

sanitarium. Variant of **sanatorium.**

san·i·tar·y (sánni-tri, -təri ‖ -terri) *adj.* **1. a.** Pertaining to or used for the preservation of health. **b.** Pertaining to or concerned with sanitation: *sanitary ware; the sanitary department.* **2.** Free from dirt and infection; clean; hygienic. [French *sanitaire,* from Latin *sānitās,* health, SANITY.] —**san·i·tar·i·ly** *adv.*

sanitary belt *n.* A band, usually of elastic, for holding a sanitary towel in place.

sanitary engineer *n.* An engineer specialising in the maintenance of services and conditions conducive to the preservation of public health, such as the disposal of sewage and provision of pure water. —**sanitary engineering** *n.*

sanitary towel *n.* A usually disposable pad of absorbent material worn to absorb menstrual flow. Also *chiefly U.S.* "sanitary napkin".

san·i·ta·tion (sánni-táysh'n) *n.* **1.** The formulation and application of measures designed to protect public health. **2.** The disposal of sewage and refuse. [From SANITARY.]

san·i·tise, san·i·tize (sánni-tīz) *tr.v.* **-tised, -tising, -tises.** **1.** To make sanitary. **2.** To make innocuous or inoffensive.

san·i·ty (sánnəti) *n.* **1.** The condition of having sound mental health; saneness. **2.** Soundness of judgment or reason. [Middle English *sanite,* from Old French, from Latin *sānitās* (stem *sānitāt-*), health, sanity, from *sānus,* healthy, SANE.]

san·jak (sán-jak) *n.* In the Ottoman Empire, an administrative district that was a subdivision of a vilayet. [Turkish *sancak,* "banner".]

San Jo·se (sán-hō-záy, -ə-). City in California, western United States. It is an important centre for fruit canning and drying, and wine production, along with some light industry.

San José (sán hō-záy, ə-, *Spanish* -sáy). Capital of Costa Rica, situated in the centre of the country. Founded in 1738, it became the capital in 1823. The city lies on a temperate upland plateau and is a centre for coffee processing and distribution.

San Jose scale *n.* A destructive scale insect, *Quadraspidiotus perniciosus,* that does considerable damage to fruit trees and fruit-bearing plants. [First seen in the United States in SAN JOSE.]

San Juan (sán waán, hwaán). Capital and chief port of Puerto Rico, situated on the northeastern coast of the island. Developed by the Spaniards from 1533, the city was taken by U.S. troops in 1898. San Juan is a tourist centre, with industries which include food processing and machinery.

sank. Past tense of **sink.**

San·khya (saángk-yə) *n.* A system of Hindu philosophy based on the distinction between spirit and matter. [Sanskrit *sāmkhya-,* "based on calculation", from *samkhyā-,* calculation, from *samkhyāti†,* he counts up.]

San Ma·ri·no, Republic of (sán mə-réenō). Small republic situated in the Apennine mountains of central Italy. Traditionally founded in the fourth century, it became a city-state whose independence was recognised by the Pope in 1631. In 1862 it joined a customs union with Italy, and a treaty of mutual friendship was signed in 1897. The main agricultural products are wine, cereals, and cattle. Tourism and ceramics are among the chief industries. Area, 61 square kilometres (24 square miles). Population, 30,000. Capital, San Marino. See map at **Italy.** —**San Mar·i·nese** (marri-neéz) *n. & adj.*

San Mart·ín (sán maar-teén), **José de.** (1778–1850) South American soldier and statesman, born in Argentina. He devoted himself to the struggle of South American countries to throw off the authority of Spain and played a major part in freeing Chile (1817–18) and Peru (1821).

san·nup (sánnəp) *n.* A married male North American Indian. [From a Massachusetts word akin to Eastern Abnaki *sénape,* "man".]

san·nya·si (sun-yaá-si) *n.* Also **san·nya·sin** (-sin). An ascetic Hindu holy man or mendicant. [Hindi and Urdu, from Sanskrit *samnyā-sin,* setting aside : *sam,* together + *ni,* down + *as,* throw.]

sans (sanz; *French* SON) *prep. Archaic.* Without. [Middle English *saunz, san(s),* from Old French *san(s), sen(s),* from Vulgar Latin *sene* (unattested), from Latin *sine* (influenced by Latin *absentiā,* in the absence of).]

San Sal·va·dor (san sálvə-dawr; *Spanish* -dór). Capital of El Salvador, situated in the interior of the country. Founded in 1528 on high volcanic slopes, it has been repeatedly damaged by severe earthquakes. The city witnessed frequent shootings by left-wing guerrillas and right-wing death squads after the military coup in El Salvador (1979). Products include textiles, cigars, and processed food.

San Salvador Island. Formerly **Watling Island.** Island in the Bahamas group of the West Indies. It was Columbus's first landfall (1492) during his first voyage to the Americas.

sans-cu·lotte (sánz-kew-lót, són-, -kü-) *n., pl.* **sans-culottes.** **1.** An extreme republican during the French Revolution. **2.** Broadly, any revolutionary extremist. [French *sans-culotte,* "without breeches" (the revolutionaries wore pantaloons instead of the kneebreeches worn by members of the upper classes) : SANS + CULOTTES.] —**sans-cu·lot·tic** *adj.* —**sans-cu·lot·tism** *n.*

San Se·bas·tián (sán si-bást-yən; *Spanish* se-bast -yaán). Coastal resort and capital of Guipúzcoa province, northern Spain, situated on the Bay of Biscay. Overlooked by the fortress of Castillo de la Mota, the city was the summer residence of the Spanish court. The

city also has fishing, paper, and steel industries.

san·se·vie·ri·a (sán-sə-veér-i-ə) *n.* Any of various tropical Old World plants of the genus *Sansevieria,* having thick, lance-shaped leaves and often cultivated as a house plant. Also called "mother-in-law's tongue". [New Latin, after Raimondo di Sangro (1710–71), Prince of *San Severo,* Italy.]

San·skrit, San·scrit (sán-skrit) *n. Abbr.* **Skt., Skr. 1.** An ancient language of India, belonging to the Indic branch of the Indo-Iranian subfamily of Indo-European languages, of which it is the oldest known member. It is the language of the Vedas and of Hinduism. **2.** The literary language of ancient and medieval India, classical Sanskrit, the grammar of which was fixed by Indian grammarians before the fourth century B.C., now used only for sacred or scholarly writings. [Sanskrit *samskrta,* put together, well-formed, refined : *sam,* together + *kr,* to make.] —**San·skrit·ist** *n.*

San·skrit·ic (san-skríttik) *adj.* **1.** Designating or belonging to a large group of Indian languages and dialects, both ancient and modern, such as Hindi, Pali, Bengali, and Punjabi. **2.** Of, relating to, or written in Sanskrit.
~*n.* The Sanskritic group of languages.

sans serif, san·ser·if (sán-sérrif) *n.* Any of a number of typefaces without serifs.

San·ta An·na (sántə ánnə), **Antonio López de** (1794–1876). Mexican general and statesman. He led revolts against Iturbide (1823), Guerrero (1828), and Bustamante (1832) before becoming president of Mexico (1833–36). He tried to crush the Texan revolt at the Alamo (1836) but was defeated and captured at San Jacinto (1836). He was made dictator in 1841, deposed in 1845, and recalled in 1846, only to be driven from Mexico City by the U.S. army before being exiled in 1848. He was recalled once more to be president (1853–55) before being exiled again, returning at last to Mexico City in 1874 to die in poverty.

San·ta Claus (sántə kláwz, klawz) *n.* A mythological person or personification of the spirit of Christmas, based originally on Saint **Nicholas** and represented as a jolly, fat old man with a white beard and a red suit, who is supposed to come down chimneys on Christmas Eve to bring presents for children. Also called "Father Christmas". [Variant (U.S.) of Dutch (dialectal) *Sante Klaas,* unexplained shortening of *Sint Nicolaes,* Saint Nicholas.]

San·ta Fe (sántə fáy). Capital of New Mexico, in the southwestern United States, on the Santa Fe river. It was founded at the terminus of the Santa Fe Trail, which led from Missouri. Surviving examples of Spanish colonial architecture include the original governor's palace (1610). Santa Fe is a market centre, and a major tourist resort noted for its Indian and Mexican crafts.

San·ta Fé (sántə fáy). River port on the Salado river in northeastern Argentina, and capital of Santa Fé province. Founded in 1573, it is the centre of a grain-growing and stock-rearing area. Its port was opened to oceangoing ships in 1911, and is linked to the Parana river by canal.

San·tan·der (sán-tan-daír ‖ *U.S. also* saán-taan-). Port and capital of Santander province in northern Spain, situated on the Bay of Biscay. A major port for the Americas in colonial days, it is now an important tourist centre, and its industries include fishing and fish processing, shipbuilding, and iron working. Nearby are the famous caves of Altamira, with prehistoric paintings.

San·ta·ya·na (sántə-yaánə ‖ -yánnə), **George** (1863–1952). Spanish-born philosopher. He moved to the U.S. in 1872 and gained a degree at Harvard, where he lectured for a while before going to live in Europe. He wrote volumes of verse and novels as well as many works of philosophy, of which the keystone was the largely materialist series *Realms of Being* (1927–40).

San·ti·a·go (sánti-aágō; *Spanish* sant-ya'agō). Also **Santiago de Chile.** Capital city of Chile and of Santiago province. It lies on the river Mapocho, and was founded by the Spanish conquistador Pedro de Valdivia in 1541. Greater Santiago contains nearly a third of Chile's population and produces half the nation's total industrial output.

Santiago de Com·po·ste·la (kóm-poss-téllə, -pəss-). City in Galicia, northwest Spain. Its Romanesque cathedral is reputedly sited over the tomb of Saint James (*Santiago* in Spanish), patron saint of Spain. Santiago has been one of the most important centres of pilgrimage in Europe since the ninth century.

Santiago de Cuba. Seaport and capital of Oriente province in southern Cuba. It is Cuba's second largest city, and has the largest cathedral in Cuba and a university. On July 26, 1953 Fidel Castro began his revolt here by leading a guerrilla attack on the Moncada army barracks.

San·to Do·min·go (sántō də-míng-gō, do-). Formerly (1936–1961) **Ciudad Trujillo.** Capital city and chief port of the Dominican Republic, situated on its south coast at the mouth of the river Ozama. It is the oldest continuously inhabited settlement established by Europeans in the Western Hemisphere, having been founded by Bartholomew Columbus, brother of Christopher, in 1496. Its cathedral (1514) is the oldest in the New World. The city has been the country's capital since 1844, and is a major manufacturing and tourist centre.

san·ton·i·ca (san-tónnikə) *n.* **1.** A wormwood, *Artemisia maritima* (or *A. cina*), of the Old World, having flowers that yield santonin. **2.** The dried unopened flowers of this plant. Also called "wormseed". [New Latin, from Latin (*herba*) *santonica,* from the feminine of *santonicus,* of the *Santoni,* a people of Aquitania.]

san·to·nin (sántə-nin) *n.* A colourless crystalline compound,

$C_{15}H_{18}O_3$, obtained from species of wormwood, especially santonica, and used as a vermifuge. [SANTON(ICA) + -IN.]

Santorini. See **Thira.**

San·tos (sán-toss, *Portuguese* -tōosh). Seaport of São Paulo state, southeast Brazil. It is the world's largest coffee-exporting port, and also a fashionable residential and resort area.

São Pau·lo (sown pów-lō, -lōo). Largest city in Brazil and capital of São Paulo state. It was founded on the river Tiete by Portuguese Jesuits in 1554. Brazilian independence from Portugal was proclaimed here in 1822. The spread of coffee growing in the state stimulated rapid growth of the city from the 1880s. Today the ultra-modern metropolis is the biggest financial, commercial, and industrial centre in South America.

São To·mé and Prín·ci·pe, Democratic Republic of (sówn tōo-máy; prín-si-pə). Small country consisting of four islands off the coast of West Africa in the Gulf of Guinea. The two main islands (São Tomé and Principe) and the islets of Pedras Tinhosas and Rôlas make up the group. The archipelago was discovered by the Portuguese in 1471 and proclaimed a colony of Portugal (1522). The Dutch held the islands from 1641 until 1740, when they were recovered by the Portuguese who ruled them until their independence (1975). The economy is almost entirely agricultural, and cocoa, coffee, palm oil, and bananas are exported. Area, 1001 square kilometres (386.5 square miles). Population, 140,000. Capital, São Tomé. See map at **Cameroon.**

sap¹ (sap) *n.* **1. a.** The watery fluid that circulates through a plant, carrying food and other substances to the tissues. **b.** Any plant juice or fluid. **2.** Any essential bodily fluid. **3.** Health and energy; vitality. **4.** *Informal.* A weak, foolish, or gullible person. **5.** *Chiefly U.S. Slang.* A small club or bludgeon; a cosh.
~*tr.v.* **sapped, sapping, saps.** *Chiefly U.S. Slang.* To hit with a sap; cosh. [Middle English *sap,* Old English *sæp.*] —**sap·less** *adj.*

sap² *n.* **1.** The process of making a covered trench or tunnel to a point near to, inside, or underneath an enemy position that is under siege. **2.** A narrow trench dug for protection against enemy fire while approaching enemy positions.
~*v.* **sapped, sapping, saps.** —*tr.* **1.** To undermine the foundations of (a fortification). **2.** To deplete or weaken gradually or insidiously: *Strength and energy were sapped by the hot sun.* —*intr.* To dig a sap. [Earlier *sappe,* trench, from French *sappe,* "an undermining", or Italian *zappa,* probably from Arabic.]

sap·a·jou (sáppə-jōo) *n.* A monkey, the **capuchin** (*see*). [French, from Tupi.]

sapanwood. Variant of **sappanwood.**

sa·pe·le (sə-péeli, sa-) *n.* **1.** Any of several West African trees of the genus *Entandrophragma,* yielding a hard, dark wood resembling mahogany. **2.** The wood of such a tree used in furniture making. [West African name.]

Saphar. Variant of **Safar.**

sap·head (sáp-hed) *n. Chiefly U.S. Slang.* A fool. [SAP¹ (sense 4) (dupe) + HEAD.] —**sap·head·ed** *adj.*

sa·phe·na (sə-fée-nə) *n., pl.* **-nae** (-nee). Either of two large superficial veins on the inner and outer sides of the leg and foot. [Middle English, from Medieval Latin, from Arabic *sāfīn.*] —**sa·phe·nous** *adj.*

sap·id (sáppid) *adj. Rare.* **1.** Having a distinctive, usually pleasant flavour; savoury. **2.** Pleasing to the mind; engaging. [Latin *sapidus,* tasty, from *sapere,* to taste, savour.] —**sa·pid·i·ty** *n.*

sa·pi·ent (sáypi-ənt) *adj.* Having wisdom; wise; discerning. Sometimes used ironically. [Middle English, from Old French, from Latin *sapiēns* (stem *sapient-*), present participle of *sapere,* to have good taste, to be sensible or wise.] —**sa·pi·ence** *n.* —**sa·pi·ent·ly** *adv.*

Sa·pir (sə-péer), Edward (1884–1939). U.S. anthropologist and linguist, born in Germany. He was a professor at Chicago (1925–31) and then Yale. He is renowned for his studies of the ethnology and languages of the American Indians of the northwest and for his interest in the ways that language shapes thought.

sap·ling (sáp-ling) *n.* **1.** A young tree. **2.** A youth. **3.** A greyhound less than one year old. [SAP (juice) + -LING.]

sap·o·dil·la (sáppə-dílla) *n.* **1.** An evergreen tree, *Achras zapota,* of tropical America, having latex that yields chicle. **2.** The edible russet fruit of this tree. Also called "sapodilla plum". Also called "naseberry", "sapota". [Spanish *zapotillo,* diminutive of *zapote,* sapodilla fruit, from Nahuatl *tzapotl.*]

sap·o·na·ceous (sáp-ə-náyshəss, -ō-) *adj.* Having the qualities of soap. [New Latin *saponaceus* : Latin *sāpō* (stem *sāpōn-*), soap + -ACEOUS.] —**sap·o·na·ceous·ness** *n.*

sa·po·na·ted (sáp-ə-naytid, -ō-) *adj.* Combined or treated with a soap. [Latin *sāpō* (stem *sāpōn-*), soap.]

sa·pon·i·fi·ca·tion (sə-pónnifi-káysh'n, sa-) *n. Chemistry.* The hydrolysis of an ester by an alkali, producing a free alcohol and an acid salt; especially, alkaline hydrolysis of fats to make soap.

sa·pon·i·fy (sə-pónni-fī, sa-) *v.* **-fied, -fying, -fies.** *Chemistry.* —*tr.* **1.** To convert (an ester) by saponification. **2.** To convert (fats) into soap. —*intr.* To undergo saponification. [French *saponifier* : Latin *sāpō* (stem *sāpōn-*), soap.] —**sa·pon·i·fi·a·ble** (-fī-əb'l, -fī-) *adj.* —**sa·pon·i·fi·er** *n.*

sap·o·nin (sáppənin) *n.* Any of various plant glucosides that form soapy colloidal solutions when mixed and agitated with water, used in detergents, synthetic sex hormones, foaming agents, and emulsifiers. [French *saponine* : Latin *sāpō* (stem *sāpōn-*), soap + -IN.]

sap·o·nite (sáppə-nīt) *n.* An amorphous, hydrous silicate of alumin-

ium and magnesium, occurring as a soaplike mass in the cavities of certain rocks, such as diabase. [Swedish *saponit* : Latin *sāpō* (stem *sāpōn-*), soap + -ITE.]

sa·por (sáy-pər, -pawr) *n.* A quality perceptible to the sense of taste; flavour. [Middle English, from Latin *sapor,* taste, from *sapere,* to taste.] —**sap·o·rif·ic** (-pə-riffik), **sap·o·rous** *adj.*

sap·pan·wood, sa·pan·wood (sáppan-wōod, sə-pán-) *n.* **1.** A tree, *Caesalpinia sappan,* of tropical Asia, having wood that yields a red dye. **2.** The wood of this tree. [Malay *sapang* + WOOD.]

sap·per (sáppər) *n.* **1.** A soldier skilled in sapping. **2.** In the British army, a member, especially a private, of the Royal Engineers.

Sap·per (sáppər), pen name of Herman Cyril McNeile (1888–1937). British author. He achieved popular success with his novel *Bulldog Drummond* (1920) and its numerous sequels.

Sap·phic (sáffik) *adj.* **1.** Of or pertaining to the Greek poet Sappho. **2. a.** Designating a verse meter of 11 syllables with a dactyl at the third foot; for example, the line *Trumpet, cello, timpani join together* exhibits Sapphic meter. **b.** Designating a stanza of three lines in such meter followed by a shorter line of a dactyl and spondee. **3.** *Usually small* **s.** Of, pertaining to, or designating homosexuality among women; lesbian.
~*n.* A Sapphic meter, line, stanza, or poem.

sap·phire (sáffīr) *n.* **1.** Any of several relatively pure forms of corundum, especially a blue form used as a gemstone. **2.** A corundum gem. **3.** The deep blue colour of a gem sapphire.
~*adj.* Having the colour of a blue sapphire. [Middle English *saphir, safir,* from Old French *safir,* from Latin *sapphīrus,* from Greek *sappheiros*; perhaps akin to Sanskrit *śanipriya,* "precious to the planet Saturn" : *Sani†,* the planet Saturn + *priya-,* precious.]

sap·phi·rine (sáffə-reen, -rin) *adj.* Of or resembling sapphire.
~*n. Mineralogy.* A rare light blue or green aluminium-magnesium silicate mineral.

sap·phism (sáffiz'm) *n.* Lesbianism. [After SAPPHO, referring to her supposed homosexuality.]

Sap·pho (sáffō) (*c.* 612–*c.* 580 B.C.). Greek lyric poet. She lived on Lesbos and her passionate poetry appears to have been directed at her coterie of female admirers. Only fragments of her work have survived, but it was ranked very highly by the ancients.

Sap·po·ro (sə-páw-rō, saa- ‖ -pó-). City in Japan, capital of the island of Hokkaido. It is a popular winter resort with an annual festival in which giant figures of carved ice are displayed.

sap·py (sáppi) *adj.* **-pier, -piest.** **1.** Full of sap; juicy. **2.** Vital; vigorous. **3.** *Chiefly U.S. Informal.* Silly or foolish. —**sap·pi·ly** *adv.* —**sap·pi·ness** *n.*

sa·prae·mi·a (sa-préemi-ə, sə-) *n.* A form of toxaemia, caused by saprophytic bacteria, in which the bacterial toxins poison the bloodstream but the bacteria themselves do not invade the blood. [New Latin : SAPR(O)- + -AEMIA.] —**sa·prae·mic** *adj.*

sapro-, sapr- *comb. form.* Indicates dead or decaying material; for example, saprophyte, sapraemia. [Greek, from *sapros,* rotten, putrid, akin to *sēpein,* to rot. See septic.]

sap·robe (sápprób) *n.* An organism that derives its nourishment from nonliving or decaying organic matter. [SAPRO- + Greek *bios,* life.] —**sa·pro·bic** (sə-próbik), **sa·pro·bi·cal·ly** *adv.*

sap·ro·gen·ic (sáppró-jénnik, sápprə-) *adj.* Also **sa·prog·e·nous** (sa-prójənəss, sə-). **1.** Producing decay or putrefaction: *saprogenic bacteria.* **2.** Resulting from decay or putrefaction. [SAPRO- + -GENIC.] —**sap·ro·ge·nic·i·ty** (-jə-níssəti, -je-) *n.*

sap·ro·lite (sáppró-līt, sápprə-) *n.* Clay, silt, or other remnants remaining in the site of a disintegrated rock. [SAPRO- + -LITE.]

sap·ro·pel (sáppró-pel, sápprə-) *n.* An organic sludge that accumulates on the beds of lakes or seas. It consists of the decomposed remains of aquatic organisms, mainly algae. [SAPRO- + Greek *pēlos,* clay, mud.] —**sa·pro·pel·ic** (-péllik) *adj.*

sa·proph·a·gous (sa-próffəgəss, sə-) *adj.* Feeding on decaying matter. [SAPRO- + -PHAGOUS.]

sap·ro·phyte (sápprə-fīt, sáppró-) *n. Biology.* A living organism, such as a fungus or bacterium, that lives on and derives its nourishment from dead or decaying organic matter. [SAPRO- + -PHYTE.] —**sap·ro·phyt·ic** (-fíttik) *adj.*

sap·ro·zo·ic (sáppra-zō-ik, sáppró-) *adj.* **1.** Pertaining to or designating nutrition by absorption of dissolved organic materials, as in protozoans and some fungi. **2.** Feeding on dead or decaying organic matter. [SAPRO- + -ZOIC.]

sap·wood (sáp-wōod) *n.* Newly formed living wood that lies just inside the bark of a tree or woody plant, is actively involved in food and water transport, and is lighter in colour than the heartwood. Also called "alburnum".

Saq·qa·ra or **Sak·ka·ra** (sáckərə). Historical site near the village of Saqqara in lower Egypt. It lies close to the site of the ancient city of Memphis, and its most prominent monument is the stone-built stepped pyramid of King Zoser (or Djoser).

sar·a·bande, sar·a·band (sárrə-band) *n.* **1.** A stately court dance, originally from Spain, of the 17th and 18th centuries, in slow triple time. **2.** The music for this dance, usually forming one of the movements of the classical suite. [French, from Spanish *zarabanda†.*]

Sar·a·cen (sárrə-s'n, *rarely* -sen, -sin) *n.* **1.** A member of a pre-Islamic nomadic people of the Syrian-Arabian deserts. **2.** An Arab. **3.** Any Muslim of the time of the Crusades. [Middle English, from Old French *Saracin,* from Late Latin *Saracēnus,* from Late Greek *Sarakēnos,* probably from Arabic *sharqīyīn,* "Easterners", from *sharq,* sunrise, east, from *shāraqa,* to rise.] —**Sar·a·cen, Sar·a·cen·ic** (-sénnik) *adj.*

Saragossa. See **Zaragoza.**

Sa·rah (saír-ə). The wife of Abraham and mother of Isaac. Genesis 17:15. [Hebrew *Sārāh,* "princess".]

Sa·ra·je·vo (sárrə-yáyvō, saárə-). Also **Se·ra·je·vo** (sérrə-). Capital and chief industrial city of the republic of Bosnia and Herzegovina. In 1914 the Archduke Francis Ferdinand, heir apparent to the throne of Austria-Hungary, was assassinated here by Gavrilo Princip, a Serbian nationalist, an event which precipitated World War I. In 1992–93 it suffered a long siege by ethnic Serbs.

sa·ran (sə-rán) *n.* Any of various thermoplastic resins derived from vinyl compounds and used to make packaging films, corrosion-resistant pipes, fittings, and bristles, and as a fibre in screens, carpets, curtain materials, and other heavy textiles. [From the trademark *Saran,* coined by Dow Chemical Co., its developers.]

sarape. Variant of **serape.**

Sa·ra·wak (sə-ráa-wak, -wək, -wə, *also* sárrə-wák). State of Malaysia on the northwest coast of the island of Borneo. It has a mountainous interior, and a swampy coastal plain where rubber, pepper, and rice are grown. It is rich in oil, its main export. Sarawak was given to the English adventurer Sir James (Rajah) Brooke (1803–68) by the Sultan of Brunei in 1841 and ruled by the Brooke family, under British protection, until the Japanese occupation of 1941–45. In 1946 it was ceded to the British Crown but joined Malaysia in 1963. Kuching is the capital.

sar·casm (sár-kaz'm) *n.* **1.** Sharply mocking or contemptuous language, typically using statements or implications pointedly opposite or irrelevant to the meaning that the speaker wishes to convey; for example, to say "congratulations" to someone who has dropped a plate would be an instance of sarcasm. **2.** The use of such language. —See Synonyms at **wit.** [French *sarcasme,* from Greek *sarkasmos,* from *sarkazein,* "to tear flesh", bite the lips in rage, speak bitterly, from *sarx* (stem *sark-*), flesh.]

sar·cas·tic (saar-kástik) *adj.* **1.** Characterised by or full of sarcasm. **2.** Given to using sarcasm. [French *sarcastique,* from *sarcasme,* SARCASM.] —**sar·cas·ti·cal·ly** *adv.*

Usage: sarcastic, ironic, caustic, satirical, sardonic. These adjectives apply to language or remarks that are bitter, cutting, or derisive. *Sarcastic* and *ironic* both pertain to a form of expression in which meanings are conveyed obliquely. *Sarcastic* suggests taunting and ridicule; *ironic* suggests a milder and subtler form of mockery. *Caustic* can apply to any expression that is mocking or ironic in a harsh or cutting way. *Satirical* refers to expression that seeks to expose wrong or folly to ridicule, often by means of sarcasm or irony. *Sardonic* can describe both the content and manner of expression and implies scorn or mockery overlaid with cynicism and amusement.

sarce·net, sarse·net (sárss-nit) *n.* A fine, soft silk cloth. [Middle English *sarsenet,* from Anglo-French *sarzinett,* perhaps diminutive of *(drap) Sarzin,* Saracen (cloth), from Latin *Saracēnus,* SARACEN.]

sarco-, sarc– *comb. form.* Indicates flesh; for example, **sarcoma, sarcophagus.** [Greek *sarx* (stem *sark-*), flesh.]

sar·co·carp (sár-kō-kaarp, -kə-) *n. Botany.* The fleshy pulp surrounding the seed of a drupaceous fruit such as a peach or plum. [French *sarcocarpe* : SARCO- + -CARP.]

sar·coid (sár-koid) *adj.* Pertaining to or resembling flesh. ~*n.* A fleshy tumour. [Greek *sarkoeidēs* : SARC(O)- + -OID.]

sar·co·ma (saar-kṓmə) *n., pl.* **-mas** or **-mata** (-tə). A malignant tumour arising from non-epithelial connective tissues, such as bone, blood, fat, or the like. [New Latin, from Greek *sarkōma,* fleshy excrescence : *sarkoun,* to make fleshy, from *sarx* (stem *sark-*), flesh + -OMA.] —**sar·co·ma·toid,** or **sar·co·ma·tous** *adj.*

sar·co·ma·to·sis (saar-kṓmə-tṓ-siss) *n. Pathology.* A condition characterised by the formation of numerous sarcomas in the body. [New Latin : *sarcoma* (stem *sarcomat-*), SARCOMA + -OSIS.]

sar·co·mere (sár-kō-meer, -kə-) *n.* A contractile unit in a striated muscle fibril. [SARCO- + -MERE.]

sar·coph·a·gus (saar-kóffə-gəss) *n., pl.* **-gi** (-gī, -jī). A stone coffin, often inscribed or decorated with sculpture. [Latin *sarcophagus (lapis),* "flesh-eating (stone)", from Greek *(lithos) sarkophagos* : SARCO- + -PHAGOUS.]

sar·co·plasm (sár-kō-plaz'm, -kə-) *n.* The cytoplasm of striated muscle fibres occurring between the muscle fibrils. [SARCO- + -PLASM.] —**sar·co·plas·mic** (-plázmik) *adj.*

sar·cous (sárkəss) *adj.* Of, pertaining to, or consisting of flesh or muscle. [Greek *sarx* (stem *sark-*), flesh.]

sard (sard) *n.* A clear or translucent deep orange-red to brownish red chalcedony *(see).* Also called "sardius". [French *sarde,* from Latin *sarda,* perhaps variant of Greek *sardion,* "the Sardian stone", from *Sardeis,* SARDIS.]

sardar. Variant of **sirdar.**

sar·dine (sár-déen) *n.* **1.** Any of various small or half-grown edible herrings or related fishes of the family Clupeidae, especially a young pilchard, frequently canned in oil. **2.** Any of numerous unrelated small, silvery freshwater or marine fishes that are similarly processed. **3.** *Plural.* A game, similar to hide-and-seek, in which one person hides and others seek him. If a seeker discovers the hider, he must join him until all the seekers but one have gathered at the hiding-place, at which point the game is over. —**like sardines.** Closely packed together. [Middle English *sardeyn,* from Old French *sardine,* from Latin *sardīna,* from Greek *sardinos,* possibly from *Sardō,* SARDINIA.]

Sar·din·i·a (saar-dínni-ə). *Italian* **Sar·de·gna** (-dáyn-ya). Island in the Mediterranean, which with some small neighbouring islands constitutes the Italian autonomous region of Sardinia. It is largely mountainous, its chief agricultural area being the fertile Campidano plain in the southwest. Cereals, olives, and vines are grown, and sheep and goats are raised. Sardinia is rich in minerals, including zinc, lead, coal, and copper. The island was ceded to Savoy (1720) and became part of the kingdom of Piedmont, which was the basis of a united Italy. Cagliari is the capital.

Sar·din·i·an (saar-dínni-ən) *n.* **1.** A native or inhabitant of Sardinia. **2.** A Romance language spoken in Sardinia. —**Sar·din·i·an** *adj.*

Sar·dis (sár-diss). Also **Sar·des** (-deez). Capital city of ancient Lydia, now a small village in west Turkey. When Lydia was absorbed into the Persian empire following the defeat of Croesus (*c.* 550 B.C.), Sardis remained the provincial capital of Asia Minor. It later became an early centre of Christianity–one of the Seven Churches of Asia (Minor). Extensive excavations of the site have yielded the earliest known coins, dating from *c.* 700 B.C.

sar·don·ic (saar-dónnik) *adj.* Scornful or mocking, especially in a cynical way. See Usage note at **sarcastic.** [French *sardonique,* from Latin *Sardonius (rīsus),* bitter (laugh), from Late Greek *Sardonios,* Sardinian, alteration (influenced by Latin *herba Sardonia,* "Sardinian herb", a poisonous plant supposed to distort the face of the eater) of *sardanios,* bitter, scornful.] —**sar·don·i·cal·ly** *adv.* —**sar·don·i·cism** (saar-dónni-siz'm) *n.*

sar·do·nyx (sárd-əniks, -onniks, -ónniks) *n.* A variety of chalcedony with alternating brown and white bands. [Middle English *sardonix,* from Latin *sardonyx,* from Greek *sardonux* : probably *sardion,* SARD + *onux,* ONYX.]

sar·gas·so (saar-gássō) *n.* A seaweed, **gulfweed** *(see).* [Portuguese *sargaço*†.]

Sar·gas·so Sea (saar-gássō). Large area of the North Atlantic between latitudes 20° and 35°N and longitudes 30° and 70°W. Ocean currents sweep clockwise round it, leaving its centre relatively still. The sea is named after the floating seaweed, *Sargassum bacciferum,* found there in abundance.

sarge (sarj) *n. Informal.* A sergeant. Often used as a term of address.

Sar·gent (sárjənt), **John Singer** (1856–1925). U.S. portrait painter. He is famous for his portraits and watercolours, including his celebrated World War I landscape *Gassed* (1918), done as a War artist.

Sargent, Sir Malcolm born Harold Malcolm Watts-Sargent (1895–1967). British conductor. He was the chief conductor of the BBC Symphony Orchestra (1950–57) and a popular conductor-in-chief of the London Promenade Concerts (1957-67).

Sar·gon (sár-gon), also known as Sargon II (erroneously) (722–705 B.C.). King of Assyria, founder of the last major Assyrian dynasty. He continued his predecessor's war against the northern Jewish kingdom of Israel (later known as Samaria) and destroyed it utterly (721), taking many Israelite captives. Sargon also conquered Carchemish, Babylon, and part of Kurdistan.

Sargon of Akkad, also known as Sargon I (erroneously) (*c.* 2335–*c.*2280 B.C.). Semi-legendary king in Mesopotamia. He usurped royal power and founded the Semitic dynasty of Akkad, building an empire that stretched from the Persian Gulf to the Mediterranean.

sa·ri (saári) *n., pl.* **-ris.** An outer garment, worn as traditional dress chiefly by Hindu women, consisting of a length of lightweight cloth with one end wrapped about the waist to form a skirt and the other draped over the shoulder or covering the head. [Hindi *sārī,* from Sanskrit *śāṭī*†, "cloth", sari.]

sark (sark) *n. Chiefly Scottish.* A shirt. [Middle English *serk,* from Old Norse *serkr,* from Germanic.]

Sark (sark). One of the Channel Islands in the English Channel, and part of the bailiwick of Guernsey. Sark comprises Great Sark and Little Sark, connected by a narrow isthmus called the Coupée. Created a seigneury by Elizabeth I, the island is still ruled in a semi-feudal manner by a seigneur or dame. No motor cars are allowed.

sark·y (sárki) *adj.* **-ier, -iest.** *British Informal.* Sarcastic or sardonic. [SARC(ASTIC) + -Y.] —**sark·i·ly** *adv.*

Sar·ma·ti·a (saar-máyshə, -máyshi-ə). An ancient region in eastern Europe between the Vistula and the Volga in present-day Poland and the U.S.S.R.

sar·men·tose (saar-mént-ōss) *adj.* Also **sar·men·tous** (-əss). *Botany.* Having slender, prostrate stems or runners that root at intervals, as the strawberry does. [Latin *sarmentōsus,* full of twigs, from *sarmentum,* twigs, from *sarpere,* to cut off, prune.]

Sar·nath (sarnát). Archaeological site near Varanasi (Benares) in Uttar Pradesh, north India. It was in the deer park here that, according to tradition, Gautama Buddha first taught.

sar·nie (sárni) *n. British Informal.* A sandwich.

sarod (sarṓd) *n.* An Indian musical instrument having two sets of strings, one of which provides a drone while the strings of the other are plucked. [Hindi.]

sa·rong (sə-róng ‖ *U.S. also* sə-ráwng) *n.* A length of brightly coloured cloth wrapped about the body and hanging as a skirt, worn by both men and women of the Malay Archipelago and the Pacific islands. [Malay, sheath, covering, sarong.]

sa·ros (saír-oss) *n.* A cycle of 6585.32 days during which solar and lunar eclipses occur at regular intervals in the same sequence. [Greek, from Babylonian *šāru,* 3600 (years); the modern use is apparently based on a misinterpretation of the original cycle as one of 18.5 years.]

Sa·roy·an (sə-róy-ən), **William** (1908–81). U.S. writer. He achieved success as a short-story writer with *The Daring Young Man on the Flying Trapeze* (1934). He also produced novels and plays.

Sar·raute (sə-rōt, sa-), **Nathalie** (1900–). French novelist. Her work, which includes *Tropismes* (1939) and *Les Fruits d'Or* (1963), is less concerned with style, plot, and characterisation than with the impersonal psychological analysis of human reactions.

sar·rus·o·phone (sə-rōō-sə-fōn, -zə- ‖ -rēw-) *n.* A wind instrument made of brass with a double reed, played like a bassoon. [After *Sarrus*, 19th-century French bandmaster who invented it (1856).]

sar·sa·pa·ril·la (särspə-rílla, sär-səpə- ‖ sáspə-) *n.* **1.** The dried roots of any of several tropical American plants of the genus *Smilax*, especially *S. aristolochiaefolia*, of Mexico, used as a flavouring and, formerly, as an emetic and to treat psoriasis. Also the plants from which sarsaparilla is obtained. **2.** Either of two North American plants, *Aralia hispida* or *A. nudicaulis*. [Spanish *zarzaparrilla* : *zarza*, bramble, from Arabic *sharaṣ*, thorny plant + *parrilla*, diminutive of *parra*†, vine.]

sar·sen (särss'n) *n.* A sandstone boulder of Tertiary age, found mainly on the chalk lands of southern England. [17th century : from earlier *Sardens, Saracen's stones*, probably from SARACEN.]

sarsenet. Variant of **sarcenet.**

Sarto, Andrea del. See **Andrea del Sarto.**

sar·to·ri·al (saar-táw-ri-əl ‖ -tō-) *adj.* **1.** Of or pertaining to a tailor or tailoring. **2.** Of or pertaining to clothing or fashion, especially men's. **3.** *Anatomy.* Of or pertaining to the sartorius. [Latin *sartor*, a tailor. See **sartorius.**] —**sar·to·ri·al·ly** *adv.*

sar·to·ri·us (saar-táw-ri-əss ‖ -tō-) *n.* A flat, narrow thigh muscle, the longest of the human body, crossing the front of the thigh obliquely from the hip to the inner side of the tibia. [New Latin *sartorius (musculus)*, "tailor's (muscle)" (because it enables one to sit in a cross-legged position like a tailor at work), from Latin *sartor*, a tailor, from *sartus*, past participle of *sarcīre*, to mend.]

Sar·tre (sártrə, sartr), **Jean-Paul** (1905–80). French philosopher and writer. A friend of Simone de Beauvoir and a Marxist sympathiser, he was a founder and leading exponent of the existentialist school. He worked for the French Resistance in World War II. His work includes novels such as the *Roads to Freedom* trilogy (1945–49), philosophical essays such as *Being and Nothingness* (1943), and many plays, including *In Camera* (1944). In 1964 he refused the Nobel prize for literature, for "personal reasons".

Sarum. See **Salisbury.**

SAS *n.* *Special Air Service*: a British army regiment of highly trained troops used on special assignments.

sash[1] (sash) *n.* A band or ribbon worn about the waist of a dress, as for ornament, or over the shoulder, as a symbol of military or other rank. [Earlier *shash*, from Arabic *shāsh*, muslin.]

sash[2] *n.* A frame in which the panes of a window or door are set; especially, either of the two movable frames in a sash window.
~*tr.v.* **sashed, sashing, sashes.** To furnish with a sash. [Variant of earlier *shashes* (plural), from French *châssis*, a frame, CHASSIS.]

sash·ay (sásh-ay, sa-sháy) *intr.v.* **-shayed, -shaying, -shays.** *Chiefly U.S. Informal.* **1. a.** To flounce and sway. **b.** To glide. **2.** To perform the chassé in dancing.
~*n.* *Chiefly U.S. Informal.* An excursion; a sally. [Variant of CHASSÉ.]

sash window *n.* A window consisting of a fixed frame enclosing two movable frames (sashes) set in grooves one above the other, which can slide up and down; they are held in position by a *sash cord* running over a pulley attached to the outer frame, and a counterbalancing weight (a *sash weight*).

sas·in (sássin) *n.* The black buck (*see*).

Sas·katch·e·wan[1] (sass-kácha-wən, səss-, -won). Province of south central Canada. Its southern prairies provide two-thirds of Canada's wheat, and the province is also rich in minerals, including uranium, copper, zinc, coal, potash, oil, and natural gas. The area was under the control of the Hudson's Bay Company (1670–1869), and became a province in 1905. Regina is the capital.

Saskatchewan[2]. River in central Canada. It is formed by the confluence of the North and South Saskatchewan rivers just east of Prince Albert, and flows east to Lake Winnipeg. The Qu'Appelle and Gardiner dams are major elements in the South Saskatchewan river project for hydroelectric power and irrigation.

Sas·ka·toon (sáska-tōōn). City in central Saskatchewan, Canada. Founded in 1883 on the South Saskatchewan river, it is a major rail junction and distribution centre for a large agricultural area.

sass (sass) *n.* *Chiefly U.S. Informal.* Impertinence; backchat.
~*tr.v.* **sassed, sassing, sasses.** *U.S. Informal.* To argue impudently with; answer back. [Back-formation from SASSY (impudent).]

sas·sa·by (sássəbi) *n., pl.* **-bies** or collectively **sassaby.** Also **tses·se·be** (tséssəbi) *pl.* **-bes** or collectively **tsessebe.** An African antelope, *Damaliscus lunatus*, having curved, ridged horns. [Bantu (Tswana) *tshêsêbê*.]

sas·sa·fras (sássə-frass) *n.* **1.** A North American tree, *Sassafras albidum*, having irregularly lobed leaves and aromatic bark. **2.** The dried root bark of this tree, used as flavouring and as a source of a volatile antiseptic oil containing camphor, safrole, and pinene. **3.** Any of various other trees with aromatic bark, such as the Australian species *Doryphora sassafras* and *Atherosperma moschatum*. [New Latin, from Spanish *sasafrás*†.]

Sas·sa·nid (sássənid) *n., pl.* **-nids** or **-nidae** (sə-sánni-dee). Also **Sas·sa·ni·an** (sə-sáyni-ən). A member of the dynasty of Persian kings ruling from the third to the middle of the seventh century A.D. [Medieval Latin *Sassanidae* (plural), from *Sassan*, grandfather of

Ardashir I, founder of the dynasty.] —**Sas·sa·nid** *adj.*

Sas·se·nach (sássə-nak, -nakh) *n.* *Chiefly Scottish.* An English person. Used derogatorily. [Irish *Sasanach*, from *Sasan-*, Saxon, from Late Latin *Saxonēs*, SAXON(s).] —**Sas·se·nach** *adj.*

Sas·soon (sa-sōōn), **Siegfried** (1886–1967). British poet and writer. He served in the army with distinction in Palestine and France until 1917, when disgust at the course of World War I led him to make a public refusal to serve further. His work includes *War Poems* (1919) and several largely autobiographical novels.

sas·sy[1] (sássi) *adj.* **-sier, -siest.** *U.S. Informal.* **1.** Impudent. **2.** Jaunty. [Variant of SAUCY.] —**sas·si·ly** *adv.* —**sas·si·ness** *n.*

sassy[2] *n.* A tree, *Erythrophloeum guineense*, of west Africa, having bark that yields a poison. Also called "sasswood", "sassy bark". [Probably of African origin.]

sas·tru·ga (sə-strōō-gə, sa-) *n., pl.* **-gi** (-gee, -jee). Also **zas·tru·ga** (zə-, za-). A long, wavelike ridge of snow formed by the wind and found on the polar plains. [Russian *zastruga*, groove.]

sat. Past tense and past participle of **sit.**

Sat. Saturday.

Sa·tan (sáyt'n) *n.* In Judaism and Christianity, the chief adversary of God and mankind; the Devil. [Middle English, Old English, from Late Latin *Satān*, from Greek *Satan*, from Hebrew *śāṭān*, devil, adversary, from *śāṭan*, to accuse.]

sa·tang (sa-táng, sə- ‖ *U.S.* -táang) *n., pl.* **satang.** A coin equal to 1/100 of the baht of Thailand. [Thai *satāñ*.]

sa·tan·ic (sə-tánnik, say-) *adj.* Also **sa·tan·i·cal** (-'l). **1.** Pertaining to or suggestive of Satan or Satanism. **2.** Profoundly cruel or evil; fiendish. —**sa·tan·i·cal·ly** *adv.*

Sa·tan·ism (sáyt'n-iz'm) *n.* **1.** Worship of Satan, especially in the form of a travesty of Christian ritual. **2.** Evil or satanic practices or tendencies. —**Sa·tan·ist** *n.*

sat·ay (sát-ay, sáat-) *n.* A Malaysian and Indonesian dish consisting of pieces of meat barbecued on skewers and usually eaten with a spicy peanut sauce. [Malay.]

S.A.T.B. soprano, alto, tenor, bass. Used in choral music.

satch·el (sáchəl) *n.* A small bag, often having a shoulder strap, and used especially by schoolchildren for carrying books. [Middle English *sachel*, from Old French, from Latin *saccelus*, diminutive of *saccus*, a bag, SACK.]

sate[1] (sayt) *tr.v.* **sated, sating, sates. 1.** To indulge (a person or his appetite or desire) fully. **2.** To indulge to excess; glut. —*See* Synonyms at **satiate.** [Probably variant (influenced by SATIATE) of obsolete *sade*, Middle English *sad(d)en*, Old English *sadian*.]

sate[2]. *Archaic.* Past tense of **sit.**

sa·teen (sa-téen, sə-) *n.* A cotton fabric with a satin weave and a glossy sheen. [Variant of SATIN (influenced by VELVETEEN).]

sat·el·lite (sátt'l-īt) *n.* **1.** *Astronomy.* A relatively small body orbiting a planet; a moon. **2.** *Aerospace.* A man-made object that orbits the Earth, Moon, or another planet. Also called "artificial satellite". **3.** One who attends a powerful dignitary. **4.** One that is dependent on another, as: **a.** A subservient follower. **b.** A nation that is dominated politically by another. **c.** A small town, such as a dormitory town, that is economically dependent on a larger neighbouring town or city. [French, from Latin *satelles* (stem *satellit-*), an attendant, escort, probably from Etruscan *satnal.*]

sa·tem (sáttəm, sáatəm) *adj.* Of, pertaining to, or constituting the group of those Indo-European languages in which the velar *k* of primitive Indo-European became *s* and the labiovelar *kw* became *k*. Compare **centum.** [Avestan *satəm*, hundred (an arbitrarily chosen word in which initial *s* represents initial Indo-European *k*).]

Sati *n.* *Hinduism.* The goddess Devi as a self-sacrificing mother.

sa·ti·a·ble (sáyshi-əb'l, sáysh-) *adj.* Capable of being satiated. [Latin *satiābilis*, from Latin *satiāre*, SATIATE.] —**sa·ti·a·bil·i·ty** (-ə-bílləti), **sa·ti·a·ble·ness** *n.* —**sa·ti·a·bly** *adv.*

sa·ti·ate (sáyshi-ayt) *tr.v.* **-ated, -ating, -ates. 1.** To gratify to excess; surfeit. **2.** To satisfy (an appetite or desire) fully; sate.
~*adj.* *Archaic.* Filled to satisfaction; satiated. [From Latin *satiāre*, from *satis*, sufficient, enough.] —**sa·ti·a·tion** (-áysh'n) *n.*

Synonyms: satiate, sate, glut, gorge, surfeit.

Sa·tie (sa-tée), **Erik,** born Alfred Erik Leslie-Satie (1866–1925). French composer, chiefly of piano works and ballets, noted for his eccentricity and humour. He used simplicity of technique to achieve surreal effects, as in the *Gymnopédies* (1888), which have had some influence on younger composers.

sa·ti·e·ty (sə-tī-əti, sáyshi-əti) *n.* **1.** The condition of being full to satisfaction, as with food. **2.** The condition of being gratified beyond the point of satisfaction; surfeit. [Obsolete French *sacieté*, from Latin *satietās* (stem *satietāt-*), sufficiency, from *satis*, sufficient, enough.]

sat·in (sáttin ‖ sátt'n) *n.* A smooth silk, cotton, rayon, or nylon fabric woven with a glossy face and a dull back.
~*adj.* **1.** Made of satin. **2.** Resembling satin, as in texture or appearance. [Middle English, from Old French, from Arabic possibly ultimately from Chinese.] —**sat·in·y** *adj.*

sat·i·net, sat·i·nette (sátti-nét) *n.* A thin satin or an imitation satin, such as a blend of cotton and silk or cotton and wool. [French, from Old French, diminutive of SATIN.]

sa·tin-flow·er (sáttin-flowr) *n.* A European plant, *Stellaria holostea*, with white flowers.

satin stitch *n.* An embroidery stitch worked in close parallel lines to give a smooth finish.

satin weave *n.* A basic weave construction with the interlacing of the threads so arranged that the face of the cloth is covered with warp yarn or filling yarn and no twill line is distinguishable.

sat·in·wood (sáttin-wŏŏd) *n.* **1. a.** A tree, *Chloroxylon swietenia,* of southern Asia, having hard, yellowish, close-grained wood. **b.** The wood of this tree, used in cabinetwork. **2. a.** Any of several other trees having similar wood. **b.** The wood of any of these trees.

sat·ire (sáttīr) *n.* **1.** A dramatic or literary work or entertainment in which irony, derision, caricature or wit in any form is used to expose folly or wickedness, especially by ridiculing aspects of and personalities in contemporary society. **2.** The branch of entertainment or art, especially literature, comprising such works. **3.** The use of derisive wit in any context to attack or ridicule folly or wickedness. —See Synonyms at **caricature.** [French, from Latin *satira, satura,* satire, medley, mixture, mixed fruits, from the feminine of *satur,* full of food, sated.]

sa·tir·i·cal (sə-tírrik'l) *adj.* Also **sa·tir·ic** (-tírrik). Constituting, characteristic of, or inclined to the use of satire. See Usage note at **sarcastic.** —**sa·tir·i·cal·ly** *adv.* —**sa·tir·i·cal·ness** *n.*

sat·i·rise, sat·i·rize (sáttə-rīz, sátti-) *tr.v.* **-rised, -rising, -rises.** To ridicule or attack by means of satire.

sat·i·rist (sáttə-rist, sátti-) *n.* **1.** A writer of satirical works. **2.** One who uses or tends to use satire.

sat·is·fac·tion (sáttiss-fáksh'n) *n.* **1.** The fulfilment or gratification of a desire, need, or appetite. **2.** Pleasure or contentment, as derived from the gratification of a desire or from a personal achievement or attainment: *gets a lot of satisfaction from her work.* **3.** Reparation in the form of penance for sin; atonement. **4.** Compensation for injury or loss, as to one's honour or reputation; amends. **5.** A source of gratification. **6.** Assurance; certainty.

sat·is·fac·to·ry (sáttiss-fáktri, -fáktəri) *adj.* **1.** Giving satisfaction; sufficient to meet a demand or requirement; adequate: *a satisfactory reason.* **2.** Warranting some pleasure; gratifying. **3.** Serving to atone for sin. —**sat·is·fac·to·ri·ly** *adv.* —**sat·is·fac·to·ri·ness** *n.*

sat·is·fy (sáttiss-fī) *v.* **-fied, -fying, -fies.** —*tr.* **1.** To gratify the need, desire, or expectation of. **2.** To fulfil (a need or desire). **3.** To relieve of doubt or question; assure. **4.** To suffice to dispel (a doubt or question). **5.** To fulfil or discharge (an obligation, contract, or debt). **6.** To discharge an obligation to (a creditor). **7.** To conform to the requirements of (a standard or rule, for example). **8.** To make reparation to (a wronged party). **9.** *Mathematics.* To fulfil the conditions of (a theorem, equation, or the like). —*intr.* To give satisfaction. [Middle English *satisfien,* from Old French *satisfier,* from Latin *satisfacere* : *satis,* sufficient, enough + *facere,* to do, make.] —**sat·is·fi·er** *n.* —**sat·is·fy·ing·ly** *adv.*

Sa·to (saá-tō), **Eisaku** (1901–75). Japanese Conservative politician. He was prime minister from 1964 to 1972, presiding over Japan's economic expansion and pursuing an independent foreign policy. In 1974 he shared the Nobel prize for peace for his opposition to nuclear weapons.

sa·to·ri (sə-táwri, saa- || -tōri) *n.* A state of spiritual enlightenment sought in Zen Buddhism. [Japanese, "insight".]

sa·trap (sáttrap, sáttrəp || *U.S. also* sáy-trap) *n.* **1.** A governor of a province in ancient Persia. **2.** Any colonial governor or subordinate ruler. [Middle English *satrape,* from Old French, from Latin *satrapēs,* from Greek, from Old Persian *khshathrapāvan,* "protector of the country" : *khshathra-,* province, country + *-pāvan,* protector.]

sa·trap·y (sáttrəpi || sáytrəpi) *n., pl.* **-ies.** **1.** The territory or sphere under the rule of a satrap. **2.** The office of satrap. **3.** The period of rule of a satrap. [French *satrapie,* from Latin *satrapia,* from Greek *satrapeia,* from *satrapēs,* SATRAP.]

sat·su·ma (sat-sŏŏmə, sátsŏŏmə) *n.* **1.** A variety of the small citrus tree, *Citrus reticulata,* native to Japan, grown widely for its sweet mandarin-like fruit. **2.** The fruit of this tree, having a loose orange rind and segmented pulp. [After *Satsuma,* former province of Kyushu, Japan, where it was originally grown.]

Sa·tsu·ma ware (sat-sŏŏmə) *n.* A yellow porcelain ware originally made at Satsuma, a former province of Kyushu, Japan.

sat·u·rant (sáchər-ənt, sáttewr-) *n.* A substance used to saturate a solution. [Latin *saturāns* (stem *saturānt-*), present participle of *saturāre,* SATURATE.] —**sat·u·rant** *adj.*

sat·u·rate (sáchər-ayt, sáttewr-) *tr.v.* **-rated, -rating, -rates.** **1.** To wet thoroughly; fill with moisture. **2.** To steep, imbue, or impregnate thoroughly. **3.** To fill to capacity or beyond; surfeit; sate. **4.** *Chemistry.* **a.** To cause (a solution) to be saturated. **b.** To cause (a compound) to be saturated. **5.** *Military.* To subject (a target) to heavy bombardment with the aim of totally destroying enemy defences. [Latin *saturāre,* to fill, satiate, from *satur,* full of food, sated.] —**sat·u·ra·bil·i·ty** (-ə-bíllәti) *n.* —**sat·u·ra·ble** (-əb'l) *adj.* —**sat·u·ra·tor** (-aytər) *n.*

sat·u·rat·ed (sáchər-aytid, sáttewr-) *adj.* **1.** Unable to hold or contain more of a substance; full. **2.** *Chemistry.* **a.** Containing all the solute that can normally be dissolved at a given temperature. Said of a solution. **b.** Containing all the water vapour or other vapour that can normally be present at a given temperature. Said of a gas. **c.** Having all available valency bonds filled. Said especially of organic compounds. **3.** *Geology.* Of or designating minerals that can crystallise from magmas even in the presence of excess silica. **4.** In a state of saturation. Said of a colour.

sat·u·ra·tion (sáchər-áysh'n, sáttewr-) *n.* **1. a.** The act or process of saturating. **b.** The condition of being saturated. **2.** *Physics.* A state of a ferromagnetic substance in which an increase in applied magnetic field strength does not produce an increase in magnetic field strength. **3.** *Chemistry.* The state of a compound or solution that is fully saturated. **4.** *Meteorology.* A condition in which air at a specific temperature contains all the moisture vapour possible without precipitating; 100 per cent relative humidity. **5.** Vividness of hue; degree of difference of a colour from a grey of the same lightness or brightness. **6.** *Military.* The striking of a target with so many missiles that it is totally destroyed. Also used adjectivally: *saturation bombing.* **7.** The flooding of a market with all of a commodity that its consumers can possibly purchase.

saturation point *n.* **1.** *Chemistry.* The point at which a substance will receive no more of another substance in solution. **2.** The point at which no more can be absorbed, assimilated, or incorporated.

saturation zone *n.* The layers of rock below the water table which are saturated with water.

Sat·ur·day (sáttər-di, -day || sát-) *n. Abbr.* **Sat.** The day of the week following Friday; the first day of the weekend. [Middle English *Saterday,* Old English *Sæterdæg,* short for *sæternesdæg,* "Saturn's day" : *Sæterṇ, Saturnus,* SATURN + *dæg,* DAY.]

Sat·urn[1] (sáttum, sátt'n) An Italic and Roman deity identified with the Greek god Cronos. [Middle English *Saturnus, Satourn,* Old English *Saturnus,* from Latin *Sāturnus,* Saturn (the god), Saturn (the planet), probably of Etruscan origin.]

Saturn[2] *n.* **1.** The sixth planet from the Sun and the second-largest in the Solar System, having an equatorial diameter of about 120 000 kilometres (75,000 miles), a mass 95 times that of Earth, and an orbital period of 29.5 years at a mean distance from the Sun of about 1 427 million kilometres (886 million miles). It has 18 known moons and is encircled by a system of rings composed of many small, solid, icy bodies. **2.** In alchemy, the element lead.

sat·ur·na·li·a (sáttər-náyli-ə) *n., pl.* **-lias** or **saturnalia.** An occasion or period of unrestrained or orgiastic revelry and licentiousness. [Latin *sāturnālia,* festival of SATURN (celebrated in December in ancient Rome and marked by wild revelry.] —**sat·ur·na·li·an** *adj.*

Sa·tur·ni·an (sə-túrni-ən) *adj.* **1.** Of or pertaining to the planet Saturn or to its supposed astrological influence. **2.** Of or pertaining to the god Saturn or to the golden age of his reign.

sa·tur·ni·id (sə-túrni-id) *n.* Any of various often large and colourful moths of the mainly tropical family Saturniidae. [New Latin *Saturniidae,* from *Saturnia* (type genus), from Latin *Sāturnia,* daughter of SATURN.] —**sa·tur·ni·id** *adj.*

sat·ur·nine (sáttər-nīn) *adj.* **1.** Having a gloomy, taciturn, and somewhat sinister character; having or showing the temperament of one born under the supposed astrological influence of the planet Saturn. **2.** *Archaic.* Pertaining to or resembling lead or produced by the absorption of lead.

sat·urn·ism (sáttər-niz'm) *n. Pathology.* **Lead poisoning** *(see).* [Middle English *saturne,* from Medieval Latin *sāturnus,* lead, from Latin *Sāturnus,* SATURN + -ISM.]

sat·ya·gra·ha (sət-yaágrə-hə) *n. Often capital* **S.** The policy of nonviolent resistance initiated in India by Mahatma Gandhi as a means of pressing for political reform. [Sanskrit *satyāgraha,* "insistence on truth" : *satya,* truth, reality, from *sat, sant,* existing, true + *āgraha,* the act of holding firmly to, insistence : *ā,* to + *gṛbhṇāti,* he seizes.]

sat·yr (sáttər || *U.S. also* sáytər) *n.* **1.** *Greek Mythology.* Any of a class of manlike woodland gods or demons often having the pointed ears, legs, and short horns of a goat. **2.** A lecher. **3.** A man afflicted with satyriasis. **4.** Any of various butterflies of the subfamily Satyridae, having brown wings marked with eyelike spots. In this sense, they are also called "brown", "satyrid". [Middle English, from Latin *satyrus,* from Greek *saturos*†.] —**sa·tyr·ic** (sə-tírrik), **sa·tyr·i·cal** *adj.*

sat·y·ri·a·sis (sátti-rī́-ə-siss, sáttə-) *n.* Abnormally strong sexual drive in the heterosexual male. Also called "satyromania". Compare **nymphomania.** [Late Latin, from Greek. See **satyr, -iasis.**]

satyr play *n.* A comic drama in a burlesque style, having a chorus of satyrs, traditionally staged following a series of tragic plays at ancient Greek dramatic festivals. See **tetralogy.**

sauce (sawss) *n.* **1.** Any soft or liquid dressing or relish, usually cooked, served as an accompaniment to food. **2.** *U.S.* Stewed or puréed sweetened fruit, eaten as a dessert. **3.** *U.S. Regional.* Vegetables; greens. **4.** Anything that adds zest, flavour, or piquancy to something. **5.** *Informal.* Impudence; sauciness.
~*tr.v.* **sauced, saucing, sauces.** **1.** To season or flavour with sauce. **2.** To add piquancy or zest to. **3.** *Informal.* To be impertinent or impudent to. [Middle English, from Old French, from Latin *salsa,* feminine of *salsus,* salted, from the past participle of *sallere,* to salt, from *sāl,* salt.]

sauce béarnaise. See **béarnaise sauce.**

sauce béchamel. See **béchamel sauce.**

sauce·boat (sáwss-bōt) *n.* A low, boat-shaped vessel with a wide lip at one end and a handle at the other end, used chiefly for serving gravies and sauces.

sauce bordelaise *n.* See **bordelaise sauce.**

sauce·box (sáwss-boks) *n. Informal.* An impertinent person.

sauce·pan (sáwss-pən || sóss-, -pan) *n.* A long-handled cooking pan of medium depth, usually having a lid.

sau·cer (sáwssər) *n.* **1.** A small, round, shallow dish having a slight circular depression in the centre for holding a cup. **2.** Any dish or other object having a similar shape: *a flying saucer.* **3.** As much as a saucer can hold: *a saucer of milk.* In this sense, also called "saucerful". [Middle English, sauce dish, from Old French *saussier,* from *sausse, sauce,* SAUCE.]

sau·cy (sáwssi) *adj.* **-cier, -ciest.** **1.** Impertinent or disrespectful; impudent. **2.** Piquant; pert. **3.** Risqué; racy. —**sau·ci·ly** *adv.* —**sau·ci·ness** *n.*

Saud (sowd; *Arabic* sa-ōod), born Saud ibn Abd al-Aziz (1902–69). King of Saudi Arabia (1953–64). He was deposed by his brother Faisal following his failure to deal with the difficulty of using his country's wealth from oil to modernise a conservative nation.

Sau·di Arabia, Kingdom of (sówdi, *also* sáwdi). *Arabic* **Al-Mamlakah al-'Arabiyah as-Sa'udiyah.** Also *informal* **Saudi.** Country in southwest Asia. The kingdom, which covers most of the Arabian peninsula, was founded in 1932 by Ibn Saud, a descendant of the puritanical Wahhabi Muslim rulers of the 18th century. The rulers of the country are the guardians of the holiest shrines of Islam at Mecca and Medina, and these attract many hundreds of thousands of pilgrims annually. Saudi Arabia is mostly desert and includes the world's largest continuous sand area—the Rub al-Khali, or Empty Quarter. Only Asir in the southwest and the various oases are cultivated. Food and consumer goods are imported on a lavish scale made possible by the country's enormous wealth in oil. The country is the world's greatest exporter of oil and possesses a significant proportion of the world's proven reserves. Area, 2 240 000 square kilometres (864,869 square miles). Population, 18,840,000. Capital, Riyadh. —**Saudi, Saudi Arabian** *adj., n.*

sauer·kraut (sówr-krowt) *n.* Chopped or shredded cabbage that is salted and fermented in its own juice. [German *Sauerkraut* : *sauer,* sour + *Kraut,* cabbage.]

sau·ger (sáwgər) *n.* A small North American freshwater fish, *Stizostedion canadense,* having a spotted, spiny dorsal fin.

Saul (sawl). First king of Israel (11th century B.C.); proclaimed by Samuel; succeeded by David. [Hebrew *Shā-ul,* "asked for".]

Saul of Tarsus. See **Saint Paul.**

sau·na (sáwnə, sównə) *n.* **1.** A steam-bath treatment or recreation originating in Finland, in which the bather is first subjected to steam produced originally by running water over heated rocks, and then to a cold bath and sometimes a light beating with twigs. **2.** A room or building in which this bath is taken. [Finnish.]

saun·ter (sáwntər) *intr.v.* **-tered, -tering, -ters.** To walk at a leisurely pace; stroll.
~*n.* A leisurely pace; a stroll. [Probably Middle English *santeren†,* to muse.]

saur-, sauro- *comb. form.* Indicates lizard-like; for example, **sauropod.** [New Latin *saurus,* lizard, from Latin, from Greek, *savros†.*]

-saur, -saurus *n. comb. form.* Indicates a lizard-like creature; for example, **brontosaur.** [New Latin *saurus,* lizard. See **saur-.**]

sau·ri·an (sáwri-ən) *n.* Any of various reptiles of the former order Sauria (now the Lacertilia), which includes the true lizards.
~*adj.* Of, belonging to, or characteristic of the Sauria; lizard-like. [New Latin *Sauria,* from *saurus,* lizard. See **saur-.**]

sau·ro·pod (sáwr-ə-pod, -ō-) *n.* Any of various large, semiaquatic, herbivorous dinosaurs of the suborder Sauropoda, of the Jurassic

and Cretaceous periods. [New Latin *Sauropoda* : SAUR- + -POD.]
—**sau·ro·pod, sau·rop·o·dous** (saw-róppədoss) *adj.*

sau·ry (sáwri) *n., pl.* **-ries.** Any of several offshore marine fishes of the family Belonidae, found in tropical and temperate waters and related to the needlefishes. Also called "skipper". [New Latin *saurus,* saury, lizard. See **saur-.**]

sau·sage (sóssij || *U.S.* sáwssij) *n.* **1.** An item of food, consisting of seasoned minced meat and other filling that has been stuffed into a prepared animal intestine or similar cylindrical casing, and usually cooked before serving. **2. a.** A similar item of food, usually larger, in which the meat is cured or precooked, slices of which are eaten, usually cold, and an hors d'oeuvre or in sandwiches, for example. **b.** A piece, or pieces collectively, cut off from such a sausage: *Do you want cheese or sausage on your roll?* **3.** *Informal.* Any sausage-shaped object, such as an observation balloon. —**not a sausage.** *Informal.* Nothing. [Middle English *sausige,* from Old North French *saussiche,* from Late Latin *salsīcia,* from *salsīcius,* prepared by salting, from Latin *salsus,* salted. See **sauce.**]

sausage dog *n. British Informal.* A **dachshund** *(see).* [Referring to its elongated body.]

sausage meat *n.* Finely minced meat with bread, cereal, or other filling, seasoned and used in sausages or as a stuffing.

sausage roll *n.* A cylindrical piece of sausage meat covered in flaky or puff pastry.

Saus·sure (sō-séwr, *French* -sür), **Ferdinand de** (1857–1913). Swiss linguist. He was professor of Sanskrit at Geneva from 1901, but his greatest contribution to modern linguistics was made in his *Cours de linguistique générale* (1916), which was posthumously assembled from his students' lecture notes. Saussure developed a number of concepts that have been highly influential, notably the distinction between **langue** and **parole** *(both of which see).* —**saus·sur·e·an, saus·sur·i·an** (sō-séwr-i-ən) *adj. & n.*

sau·té (sō-tay || sáw-, -ti, sō-táy) *tr.v.* **-téed, -téing, -tés.** To fry lightly in fat in a shallow, open pan.
~*n.* Sautéed food.
~*adj.* Sautéed. [French, "tossed (in a pan)", from the past participle of *sauter,* to leap, from Old French, from Latin *saltāre,* frequentative of *salīre* (past participle *saltus*), to leap.]

Sau·ternes, Sau·terne (sō-térn, -táírn) *n. Sometimes small* **s.** A delicate, sweet white dessert wine. [French, made in *Sauternes,* commune in southwest France.]

sau·vi·gnon (sōveen-yón) *n.* A variety of white grape used widely in western France for making white wine. Compare **cabernet sauvignon.** [French, of obscure origin.]

sav·age (sávvij) *adj.* **1.** Not domesticated; wild; untamed. **2.** Not civilised; in a primitive state. **3.** Ferocious; fierce. **4.** Vicious or merciless; brutal: *savage cuts in spending.* **5.** Lacking polish or man-

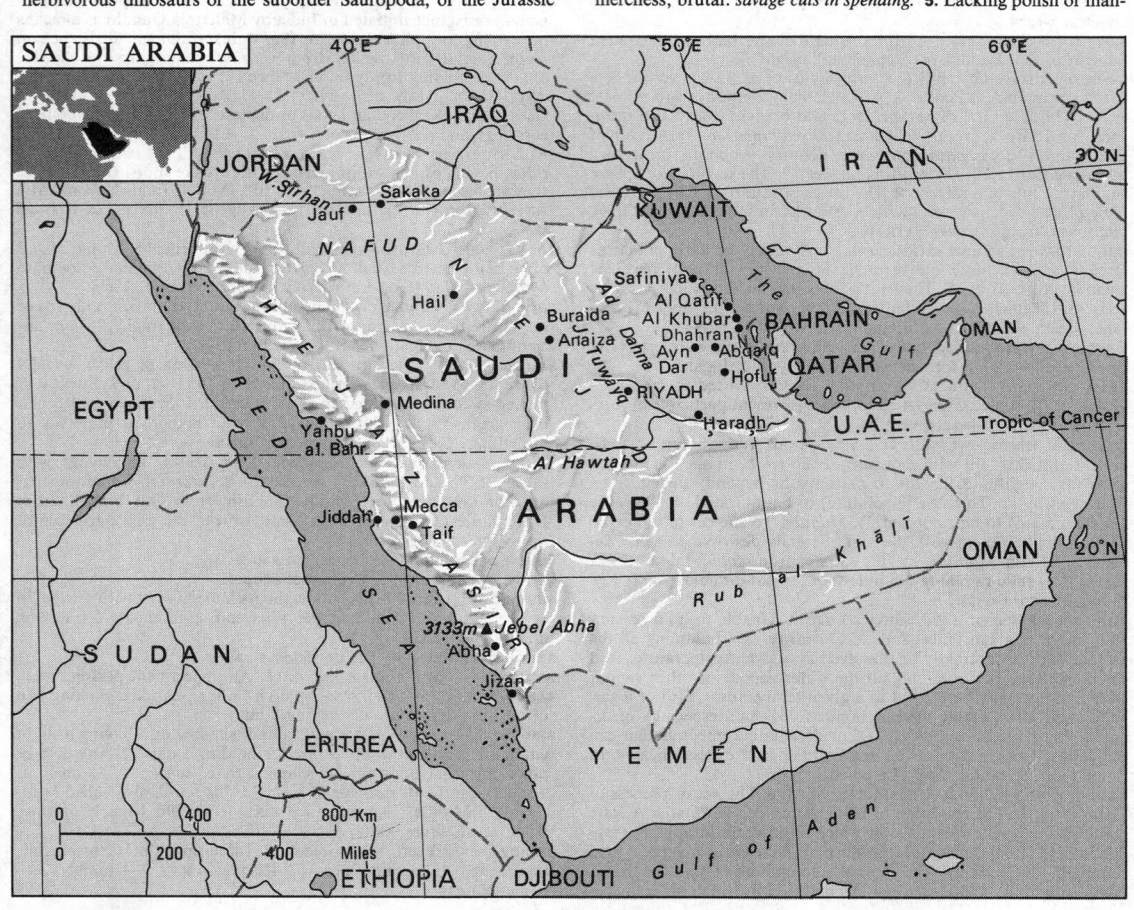

ners; rude. **6.** Rugged; desolate: *savage terrain.*
~n. **1.** A primitive or uncivilised person. **2.** A brutal, fierce, or vicious person. **3.** A rude person; a boor.
~tr.v. **savaged, -aging, -ages.** **1.** To attack violently. **2.** To bite or maul ferociously. [Middle English *sauvage,* from Old French, from Vulgar Latin *salvāticus* (unattested), from Latin *silvāticus,* of the woods, wild, from *silva,* woods, forest. See **sylvan.**] **—sav·age·ly** *adv.* **—sav·age·ness** *n.*

Sav·age (sávvij), **Michael Joseph** (1872–1940). New Zealand politician. Born in Australia, he went to New Zealand in 1907 and worked as a miner. He entered Parliament in 1919 and led his country's first Labour government in 1935 when he became prime minister.

sav·age·ry (sávvij-ri, -əri) *n., pl.* **-ries.** **1.** The condition or quality of being savage. **2.** A cruel or barbarous action.

sa·van·nah, sa·van·na, sa·van·a (sə-vánnə) *n.* Open grassland with tall grasses, scattered trees, and bushes, of drier tropical or subtropical regions. [Earlier *zavana,* from Spanish, from Taino *zabana.*]

sa·vant (sávv'nt, *French* sa-vóɴ) *n. Feminine* **sa·vante** (*French* -vóɴt). A learned, scholarly person. [French, from the present participle of *savoir,* to know, from Vulgar Latin *sapēre* (unattested), from Latin *sapere,* to be sensible, be wise.]

sav·a·rin (sávvə-rin, -ráɴ) *n.* A yeast-leavened cake baked in a ring-shaped mould and served moistened with liqueur or fruit syrup and with fruit or other filling in the centre. [After Anthelme Brillat-*Savarin* (1755–1826), French writer and gourmet.]

save[1] (sayv) *v.* **saved, saving, saves.** *—tr.* **1.** To deliver or preserve from disaster, harm, danger, or loss. **2.** To keep in a safe, intact condition; safeguard. **3.** To prevent or reduce the waste, loss, or expenditure of: *Save energy—insulate your home.* **4.** To keep for future use or enjoyment; store. Often used with *up.* **5.** To treat with care in order to avoid fatigue, wear, or damage; spare: *Save your legs and travel by bus.* **6.** To make unnecessary; obviate: *This will save you an extra trip.* **7.** *Theology.* To deliver from sin its consequences; redeem. **8.** In sports such as football and hockey: **a.** To stop (a ball, puck, or the like) going into the goal. **b.** To prevent (a goal). *—intr.* **1.** To avoid wasting, losing, or spending something, especially habitually; be economical: *drove slowly to save on petrol.* **2.** To accumulate money for future use. **3.** To preserve a person or thing from harm or loss.
~n. An act or instance of saving a goal. [Middle English *saven, salven,* from Old French *sauver,* from Late Latin *salvāre,* from Latin *salvus,* safe.] **—sav·a·ble, save·a·ble** *adj.* **—sav·a·ble·ness** *n.*
Synonyms: *save, rescue, reclaim, redeem, deliver.*

save[2] *prep.* With the exception of; except; but: *all save one.*
~conj. Archaic. **1.** Were it not; except; but. Usually used with *that.* **2.** Unless. [Middle English *save, sa(u)f,* from Old French *sa(u)f, salf,* from Latin *salvō,* without injury or prejudice to, except, ablative singular of *salvus,* safe, sound, healthy.]

save-all (sáyv-awl) *n.* Any device or contrivance that prevents the waste, damage, or loss of something, or that catches the waste products of a process for further use in manufacture.

sav·e·loy (sávvə-loy, -lóy) *n.* A highly seasoned smoked pork sausage. [Variant of obsolete French *cervelat,* from Italian *cervellato,* from *cervello,* brain (the sausage is sometimes made from the brain of pigs), from Latin *cerebellum,* diminutive of *cerebrum,* brain.]

sav·er (sáyvər) *n.* **1.** One that saves; especially, a person who saves money regularly. **2.** Something that prevents loss, waste, or expenditure. Usually used in combination: *money-saver; time-saver.*

sav·in, sav·ine (sávvin) *n.* **1.** An evergreen Eurasian shrub, *Juniperus sabina,* the young shoots of which yield an oil formerly used medicinally. **2.** *U.S.* Any of several similar or related shrubs or trees; especially, the **red cedar** *(see).* [Middle English *savin,* from Old English *safīne* and Old French *savine,* both from Latin *(herba) Sabīna,* "Sabine (plant)", from *Sabīnus,* SABINE.]

sav·ing (sáyving) *adj.* **1.** Redeeming; compensating: *saving graces.* **2.** Making or containing a reservation; qualifying: *a saving clause.*
~n. **1.** Preservation or rescue from harm, danger, or loss. **2.** Avoidance of wastage; economy. **3.** A reduction in expenditure or cost: *a saving of £20.* **4.** *Plural.* A sum of money saved. **5.** Anything that is saved. **6.** *Law.* An exception or reservation.
~prep. With the exception of.
~conj. Archaic. Except; save.

sav·ings account (sáyvingz) *n.* An account, held in a savings bank, into which individual depositors pay their savings and usually receive a higher rate of interest than on deposit accounts.

savings bank *n.* A bank that receives and invests the savings of private depositors and pays interest on the deposits.

sav·iour, *U.S.* **sav·ior** (sáyv-yər) *n.* **1.** One that rescues someone or something from dire circumstances. **2.** *Capital* **S.** Christ. Usually preceded by *the.* [Middle English *saviour, sauveur,* from Old French *sauveour,* from Late Latin *salvātor,* from *salvāre,* to SAVE.]

sa·voir-faire (sávwaar-fáir) *n.* The ability to say and do the right thing in any situation; social adroitness; tact. See Synonyms at **tact.** [French, "knowing how to do".]

sa·voir-vivre (sávwaar-véevrə, -véevr) *n.* Worldly knowledge and sophistication. [French, "knowing how to live".]

Sav·o·na·ro·la (sávvənə-rṓlə), **Girolamo** (1452–98). Italian religious reformer. A Dominican friar, he gained a vast popular following with his fervent preaching, which enabled him to lead a revolt that turned the Medici family out of Florence in 1494. He became the virtual ruler of Florence, but after criticising Pope Alexander VI he was excommunicated in 1497 and later executed.

sa·vor·y (sáyvəri) *n., pl.* **-ies.** **1.** Either of two aromatic herbs, *Satureja hortensis* or *S. montana,* native to the Old World. The former species is also called "summer savory" and the latter "winter savory". **2.** The leaves of either of these plants, used as seasoning. [Middle English *saverey,* variant (perhaps influenced by SAVOURY) OF OLD ENGLISH *sœtherie,* from Latin *saturēia*†.]

sa·vour, *U.S.* **sa·vor** (sáyvər) *n.* **1.** The quality of a thing which affects the sense of taste or smell; taste or aroma. **2.** A specific taste or smell. **3.** A distinctive or typical quality. **4.** Power or the quality of exciting interest; zestfulness. —See Synonyms at **smell.**
~v. **savoured** or *U.S.* **savored, -vouring** or *U.S.* **-voring, -vours** or *U.S.* **-vors.** *—intr.* **1.** To have a specified savour. Used with *of*: *The kitchen savoured of fresh bread.* **2.** To have an implication or suggestion; smack. Used with *of*: *savours of corruption.* *—tr.* **1.** To impart a flavour or scent to. **2.** To taste, smell, or experience with appreciation and enjoyment; relish. [Middle English *savour,* from Old French, from Latin *sapor,* taste, savour, from *sapere,* to taste, savour.] **—sa·vour·er** *n.* **—sa·vour·less** *adj.* **—sa·vor·ous** *adj.*

sa·vour·y, *U.S.* **sa·vor·y** (sáyvəri) *adj.* **1.** Appetising to the taste or smell. **2.** Piquant, pungent, or salty to the taste; not sweet. **3.** Pleasant or inoffensive. **4.** Morally respectable.
~n., pl. **savouries.** A savoury dish, such as Welsh rabbit or anchovies on toast, sometimes served in Britain as an hors d'oeuvre or at the end of a meal instead of a dessert. [Middle English *savory, savure,* from Old French *savoure,* from the past participle of *savourer,* to savour, from Late Latin *sapōrāre,* from Latin *sapor,* SAVOUR.] **—sa·vour·i·ly** *adv.* **—sa·vour·i·ness** *n.*

sa·voy (sə-vóy) *n.* A variety of cabbage with crinkled leaves and a compact head. [After SAVOY, where it was cultivated.]

Sa·voy (sə-vóy). *French* **Sa·voie** (sa-vwáa); *Italian* **Sa·voi·a** (sa-vóy-ə). Region on the French-Italian border in the western Alps, ruled by the House of Savoy from the 11th century. Savoy grew to include Nice in France and Piedmont in Italy, and became a duchy in 1416. The House of Savoy gained control of Sardinia in 1713, and Savoy, with Piedmont and the island of Sardinia, formed the kingdom of Sardinia. Genoa was added in 1815. On the unification of Italy in 1860, French Savoy was ceded to France. Today, Savoy comprises mainly the French départements of Haute-Savoie and Savoie. Chambéry is the chief city.

Sa·voy·ard (sə-vóy-aard, sávvoy-árd) *n.* **1.** A native or inhabitant of Savoy. **2.** A dialect of French spoken in Savoy. **3.** Any performer in or enthusiastic admirer of Gilbert and Sullivan operas, most of which were first staged at London's Savoy Theatre.
~adj. Of or pertaining to Savoy, its inhabitants, or their dialect.

sav·vy (sávvi) *intr.v.* **-vied, -vying, -vies.** *Slang.* To understand or know; comprehend. **—no savvy.** *Slang.* To fail to understand. Often used without the relevant pronoun.
~n. Slang. Practical understanding or knowledge; common sense. [Probably from West African pidgin or Atlantic creole, from phonetic approximation to Spanish *sabe (usted),* (you) know, from *saber,* to know, from Latin *sapere,* to be sensible, be wise.]

saw[1] (saw) *n.* **1.** A tool, usually portable and either hand-operated or power-operated, having a thin metal blade or disc with a sharp-toothed edge, used for cutting wood, metal, or other hard materials. **2.** A powered disc tool lacking teeth, used for cutting metal. **3.** A fixed machine for the operation of a saw or series of saws.
~v. **sawed, sawn** (sawn) or **sawed, sawing, saws.** *—tr.* **1.** To cut or divide with or as if with a saw. **2.** To produce or shape with or as if with a saw. *—intr.* **1.** To use a saw. **2.** To cut. Used of a saw. **3.** To admit of cutting with a saw: *This board saws evenly.* [Middle English *sawe,* Old English *sagu* (unattested), *saga.*] **—saw·er** *n.*

saw[2] *n.* A familiar, proverbial saying, especially when trite. See Synonyms at **saying.** [Middle English *sawe,* Old English *sagu,* speech, talk, from Germanic *sagō* (unattested); akin to SAGA.]

saw[3]**.** Past tense of **see.**

saw·bill (sáw-bil) *n.* A duck, the **merganser** *(see).* [Referring to the serrated edges of its bill.]

saw·bones (sáw-bōnz) *n. Slang.* A surgeon. Used humorously.

saw·dust (sáw-dust) *n.* The small particles of wood that fall from a wooden object as a result of sawing.

saw-edged (sáw-ejd, *often* sáwr-) *adj.* Having jagged, serrated edges.

saw·fish (sáw-fish) *n., pl.* **-fishes** or collectively **sawfish.** Any of various marine fishes of the genus *Pristis,* related to the rays and skates, and having a bladelike snout with teeth along both sides.

saw·fly (sáw-flī) *n., pl.* **-flies.** Any of various destructive insects, chiefly of the family Tenthredinidae, the females of which have sawlike ovipositors used for cutting into plant tissue to deposit eggs.

saw·horse (sáw-hawrss) *n.* A rack or trestle used to support a piece of wood being sawn.

saw·mill (sáw-mil) *n.* **1.** A plant where timber is machine-cut into boards. **2.** A large machine for sawing timber.

sawn. Past participle of **saw.**

sawn-off (sáwn-óff, -áwf) *adj.* Also *U.S.* **sawed-off** (sáwd-). **1.** Designating a shotgun that has the barrels shortened by sawing to make it less conspicuous and increase the spread of shot over short ranges. **2.** *Informal.* Shorter than average. Said of a person.

saw set *n.* An instrument used to deflect the teeth of a saw by bending each tooth slightly, alternate teeth being bent in the same direction.

saw-toothed (sáw-tōōtht || -tōōtht) *adj.* Having teeth resembling the teeth of a saw; serrate.

saw-wort (sáw-wurt || -wawrt) *n.* Either of two thistle-like plants, *Serratula tinctoria* of moist meadows and *Saussurea alpina* of mountain grassland. [Referring to its serrated leaves.]

saw-yer (sáw-yər) *n.* **1.** One employed at sawing wood, as in a sawmill. **2.** *U.S.* Any of several longicorn beetles having larvae that bore holes in wood. [Middle English *sawier*, from *sawen*, to SAW.]

sax¹ (saks) *n.* Also **zax** (zaks). A hatchet-like tool used for trimming roofing slates. [Middle English, Old English *seax*, knife, from Germanic *sahsam* (unattested).]

sax² *n. Informal.* A saxophone.

Sax. Saxon; Saxony.

saxe blue (saks) *n.* A light greyish blue. [French *Saxe*, SAXONY, origin of a dye of this colour.] **—saxe-blue** *adj.*

sax-horn (sáks-hawrn) *n.* Any of a family of valved brass wind instruments, resembling the bugle and having a full, even tone and wide range. [Invented (1845) by Adolphe *Sax* (1814-94), Belgian musical instrument maker.]

sax-ic-o-lous (sak-sickə-ləss) *adj.* Also **sax-ic-o-line** (-līn). Growing on or living among rocks. [Latin *saxum*, rock + -COLOUS.]

sax-i-frage (sáksi-frij, -frayj, -frayzh) *n.* Any of numerous plants of the genus *Saxifraga*, of temperate regions, having small flowers and leaves often forming a basal rosette. [Middle English, from Old French, from Late Latin *saxifraga (herba)*, "rock-breaking (herb)" (because it grows in rock crevices), from Latin *saxifragus* : *saxum*, rock + *frangere* (stem *frag-*), to break.]

Sax-on (sáks'n) *n. Abbr.* **S., Sax. 1.** A member of a West Germanic people that inhabited north Germany and invaded England in the fifth and sixth centuries with the Angles and Jutes. See **Anglo-Saxon. 2.** A native or inhabitant of Saxony. **3.** The West Germanic language or dialect of any Saxon people. **4.** The Germanic elements in Modern English rather than the French or Latin elements. *~adj.* **1.** Of or pertaining to the Saxons or their language. **2.** Of Anglo-Saxon origin. **3.** Of or pertaining to Saxony, the German Saxons, or their language. [Middle English, from Old French, from Late Latin *Saxō* (stem *Saxon-*), from Greek *Saxones* (plural), from West Germanic *Saxon-* (unattested), probably from Germanic *sahsam* (unattested), knife (perhaps their typical weapon); compare Old English *Seaxan*, Saxon, and *seax*, knife, SAX (tool).]

Saxon blue *n.* A dye made from indigo dissolved in a sulphuric acid solution. [After SAXONY, where it originated.]

sax-o-ny (sáksəni) *n. Often capital* **s. 1.** A high-grade wool, of a type originally from sheep raised in Saxony. **2.** A fine soft woollen fabric made from this wool.

Sax-o-ny¹ (sáksəni). *German* **Sach-sen** (záks'n). Area of north Germany, the original home of the Saxons. Conquered by Charlemagne in the eighth century, it became a duchy after his death. This was frequently divided after 1180, and re-formed in various ways, moving generally southeastwards. The dukes became electors of the Holy Roman Empire (1356), and made Dresden their capital. Raised to kingship (1806), the elector lost half his territory to Prussia (1815). This province of Prussia later became part of East Germany (1949). The kingdom of Saxony was part of the German Empire (1871–1918), and, as the state of Saxony, part of pre-war Germany, and then part of East Germany (1949).

Saxony². State of Germany, created from former East German regions.

Sax-o-ny-An-halt (sáksəni án-halt). State of Germany, created from former East German regions.

sax-o-phone (sáksə-fōn) *n.* A wind instrument having a single-reed mouthpiece, a conical usually metal bore, and finger keys, and made in a variety of sizes. [Invented (1846) by Adolphe *Sax*. See **saxhorn**.] **—sax-o-phon-ist** (sak-sóffənist, sáksə-fōnist) *n.*

sax-tu-ba (sáks-téwbə || -tōōbə) *n.* A large bass saxhorn. [SAX-(HORN) + TUBA.]

say (say) *v.* **said** (sed || sayd), **saying, says** (sez || sayz). *—tr.* **1.** To utter aloud; pronounce; speak. **2.** To express in words; state; declare. **3.** To state (an opinion, for example) with positive assurance or conviction. **4.** To repeat or recite: *say grace.* **5.** To report or maintain; allege: *They say she's won.* **6.** To estimate or suppose; assume: *Let's say that you're right.* **7.** To classify or describe. Usually used in the passive: *The player is then said to be offside.* **8.** To mean to express or convey; signify: *What is Picasso saying in this painting?* **9.** To indicate; show: *When I woke, the clock said midnight.* **10.** To adduce in favour or defence of something: *There's a lot to be said for the system.* **11.** To state by way of instruction. Used with an infinitive: *He said to start without him if he was late.* *—intr.* To make a statement or express an opinion. **—go without saying.** To be so self-evident as to need no justification or explanation. **—I say.** Used to express surprise or dismay, or to call for attention. **—not to say.** Indeed; perhaps in fact: *seemed unwelcoming, not to say hostile.* **—that is to say.** In other words; meaning. *~n.* **1.** One's turn or chance to speak. **2.** What one has to say; one's opinion. **3.** The right or power to influence a decision; voice; authority: *have a say in the matter.* *~adv.* **1.** Approximately: *There were, say, 500 people present.* **2.** For instance: *a woodwind, say an oboe.* *~interj. U.S.* Used to gain the attention of someone. [Say, said (past tense and past participle); Middle English *seggen* (later *sayen*), *saide*, Old English *secgan, sægde* (past tense), *(ge)sægd* (past participle).] **—say-er** *n.*

S.A.Y.E. *n.* Save as you earn: a government saving scheme in Britain in which monthly deposits earn tax-free interest.

Say-ers (sáy-ərz, sairz), **Dorothy L(eigh)** (1893–1957). British novelist and translator. She is best known for her detective stories, usually featuring Lord Peter Wimsey, the gentlemanly, amateur investigator, who made his first appearance in *Whose Body?* (1923). Later in life she concentrated on religious books and drama, particularly her cycle of radio plays, *The Man Born To Be King.*

say-ing (sáy-ing) *n.* **1.** An adage; a maxim. **2.** A word of wit or wisdom. **Synonyms:** *saying, maxim, adage, saw, motto, epigram, proverb, aphorism.*

say-so (sáy-sō) *n., pl.* **-sos.** *Informal.* **1.** An unsupported statement or assurance. **2.** An authoritative assertion; a dictum. **3.** The right of final decision; authority.

say-yid, say-id (sí-id) *n.* A Muslim claiming descent from Muhammad. Used as a title of respect. [Arabic, "lord".]

Sb The symbol for the element antimony [Latin *stibium*].

S-bend (éss-bend) *n.* An S-shaped bend, as in a road or pipe.

'sblood (zblud) *interj. Archaic.* Used as an oath. [Contraction of *God's blood.*]

Sc The symbol for the element scandium.

sc. 1. scene. **2.** scilicet. **3.** scruple (weight). **4.** sculpsit.

Sc. Scotch; Scots; Scottish.

s.c. *Printing.* small capitals.

S.C. Signal Corps.

scab (skab) *n.* **1. a.** The crustlike material that covers a healing wound. **b.** A small patch of such material. **2.** Scabies or mange in domestic animals or livestock. **3. a.** Any of various plant diseases caused by fungi or bacteria and resulting in crustlike spots on fruit, leaves, or roots. **b.** A spot or the spots caused by such a disease. **4.** *Informal.* **a.** A worker who refuses to join a trade union. **b.** An employee who works while others are on strike; a strikebreaker; a blackleg. Also used adjectivally: *scab labour.* **5.** *Informal.* A low or contemptible person. Not in current use. *~intr.v.* **scabbed, scabbing, scabs. 1.** To form a scab. **b.** To become covered with a scab. **2.** *Chiefly U.S. Informal.* To take a job held by a worker on strike; act as a scab. [Middle English *scabbe*, from Old Norse *skabb.*]

scab-bard (skábbərd) *n.* A sheath or container for a dagger, sword, or other similar weapon. [Middle English *scauberc*, from Anglo-French *escaubers* (plural) : probably Old High German *scār*, scissors, sword + *-berc*, protection, from *bergan*, to protect.]

scabbard fish *n.* Any of several narrow-bodied marine fishes of the family Trichiuridae; especially, *Lepidopus caudatus*, of Mediterranean waters. [From its narrow, sheathlike body.]

scab-ble (skább'l) *tr.v.* **-bled, -bling, -bles.** To work or dress (stone) roughly. [Earlier *scapple*, Middle English *scaplen*, from Old French *eschaler*, "to cut off", dress timber : *es-*, from Latin *ex-*, off + *chapler*, to cut, from Late Latin *capulāre.*]

scab-by (skábbi) *adj.* **-bier, -biest. 1.** Having, consisting of, or covered with scabs or something resembling scabs. **2.** Suffering from scabies. **3.** *Informal.* Low; mean; vile: *a scabby trick.* **—scab-bi-ly** *adv.* **—scab-bi-ness** *n.*

sca-bi-es (skáy-bi-eez, -beez) *n. Used with a singular verb.* **1.** A contagious skin disease caused by a mite, *Sarcoptes scabiei*, and characterised by intense itching. **2.** A similar disease in animals, especially sheep. [Latin *scabiēs*, roughness, scurf, itch, from *scabere*, to scratch.] **—sca-bi-et-ic** (-bi-éttik) *adj.*

sca-bi-ous¹ (skáybi-əss || skábbi-) *adj.* **1.** Of or pertaining to scabies. **2.** Having scabs. [Latin *scabiōsus*, scabby, from SCABIES.]

scabious² *n.* **1.** Any of various plants of the genera *Knautia, Succisa*, or *Scabiosa*; especially, *K. arvensis* and *Scabiosa columbaria*, having opposite leaves and blue compound flower heads. See **devil's bit scabious. 2.** Sheep's bit scabious *(see).* [Middle English *scabiose*, from Medieval Latin *scabiōsa (herba)*, "(herb) for scabies", from Latin, feminine of *scabiōsus*, SCABIOUS.]

scab-rous (skáyb-rəss || *chiefly U.S.* skáb-) *adj.* **1.** Roughened with small projections; rough to the touch; scaly. **2.** Difficult to handle tactfully; thorny. **3.** Indelicate or salacious; indecent: *a scabrous novel.* —See Synonyms at **rough.** [Latin *scabrōsus*, rough, from *scaber*, rough, scurfy.] **—scab-rous-ly** *adv.* **—scab-rous-ness** *n.*

scad (skad) *n., pl.* **scads** or collectively **scad.** Any of several marine fishes of the family Carangidae; especially, the **horse mackerel** *(see).* [17th century : origin obscure.]

scads (skadz) *pl.n. Chiefly U.S. Informal.* A large number or amount: *scads of people.* [19th century : origin obscure.]

Sca-fell Pike (skáw-fél). Highest point in England, situated in Cumbria's Lake District. Its height is 977 metres (3,205 feet).

scaf-fold (skáff'ld, skáffōld) *n.* **1.** A raised wooden framework or platform. **2.** A platform for the execution of condemned prisoners. Usually preceded by *the.* **3.** Scaffolding. *~tr.v.* **scaffolded, -folding, -folds.** To provide or support with scaffolding. [Middle English, from Old North French *escafaut*, variant of Old French *eschafaud*, from *chafaud*, scaffold, from Vulgar Latin *catafalicum* (unattested), CATAFALQUE.] **—scaf-fold-er** *n.*

scaf-fold-ing (skáff'ld-ing || skáffōld-) *n.* **1.** A temporary platform or system of platforms, usually made of planks and tubular metal poles, used by workmen when constructing, repairing, or cleaning a building. **2.** The materials for scaffolding.

sca-glio-la (skal-yóla) *n.* Plasterwork in imitation of ornamental marble, consisting of ground gypsum and glue coloured with marble or granite dust. [Italian, diminutive of *scaglia*, scale, chip, small piece of marble, from Germanic.]

sca-lar (skáy-lər, *also* -laar) *n.* A quantity, such as mass, length, or time, completely described by a number on an appropriate scale. Scalars have magnitude but not direction. Compare **vector.** [Latin *scālāris,* of a staircase, from *scālae,* stairs, SCALE.] —**sca·lar** *adj.*

sca·la·re (skə-laír-i, -laár-) *n.* The **angelfish** *(see).* [New Latin, "ladder-like" (from its parallel stripes), from Latin, neuter of *scālāris,* of a staircase, from *scālae,* stairs, SCALE.]

sca·lar·i·form (skə-lárri-fawrm) *adj. Biology.* Ladder-like; having rungs: *scalariform xylem vessels.* [New Latin *scalariformis :* Latin *scālāris,* of a ladder (see **scaler**) + -I- + FORM.]

scalar product *n.* The numerical product of the lengths of two vectors and the cosine of the angle between them. Also called "dot product", "inner product". Compare **vector product.**

scalawag. *Chiefly U.S.* Variant of **scallywag.**

scald¹ (skawld ‖ skold) *v.* **scalded, scalding, scalds.** —*tr.* **1.** To burn with or as if with hot liquid or steam. **2.** To subject to or treat with boiling water; especially: **a.** To blanch or partly cook vegetables in boiling water. **b.** To sterilise (instruments, for example). **3.** To heat a (liquid) almost to the boiling point. —*intr.* To be or become scalded.
~*n.* **1.** A burn or injury caused by scalding. **2. a.** A superficial discoloration on fruit, vegetables, leaves, or tree trunks caused by sudden exposure to intense sunlight or the action of gases. **b.** A disease of some cereal grasses, caused by a fungus of the genus *Rhynchosporium.* [Middle English *scalden,* from Old North French *escalder,* from Late Latin *excaldāre,* to wash in hot water : Latin *ex-,* to bring into a certain condition + *cal(i)da,* hot water, from the feminine of *calidus,* warm.]

scald². **1.** Variant of **skald. 2.** Variant of **scall.**

scald head *n.* Any of various scaly disorders of the scalp. Not in current technical usage. [From SCALD.]

scald·ing (skáwld-ing ‖ skóld-) *adj.* **1.** Burning hot to the touch or taste. **2.** Cutting; biting: *a scalding review.*

scale¹ (skayl) *n.* **1. a.** Any of the small, flattened, hard plates characteristically forming the external covering of fishes, reptiles, and certain mammals. **b.** A similar part, such as any of the minute structures overlapping to form the covering on the wings of butterflies and moths. **2.** *Pathology.* A dry, thin flake of epidermis shed from the skin. **3.** A small, thin, platelike piece of anything that flakes off from a surface. **4.** *Botany.* Any of various thin, often overlapping parts, such as any of the protective rudimentary leaves covering the buds of certain trees, or a membranous bract. **5. a.** A scale insect. **b.** A plant disease or infestation caused by scale insects. **6. a.** A flaky oxide film formed on a metal, as on iron, heated to high temperatures. **b.** A flake of rust. **7.** A coating of calcium carbonate formed inside boilers, kettles, and similar hot-water devices in hard-water regions; fur.
~*v.* **scaled, scaling, scales.** —*tr.* **1.** To clear or strip of scale or scales. **2.** To remove in layers or scales. **3.** To cover with scales; cause incrustation to form on. —*intr.* **1.** To come off in layers or scales; flake. **2.** To become covered with incrustation. [Middle English, from Old French *escale,* "shell", "husk", from Germanic.]

scale² *n.* **1.** A system of ordered marks at fixed intervals used as a reference standard in measurement. **2.** An instrument or device bearing such marks. **3. a.** The proportion used in determining the relationship of a representation to that which it represents. Also used adjectivally: *a scale drawing.* **b.** A calibrated line, as on a map or architectural plan, to indicate such a proportion. **4.** A progressive classification, as of size, amount, importance, or rank: *a salary scale; the social scale.* **5.** A relative level or degree: *entertain on a lavish scale.* Also used adjectivally in combination: *a small-scale exporter.* **6.** *Mathematics.* A system of notation in which the value of numbers is determined by their place relative to the fixed constant of the system: *decimal scale.* **7.** *Music.* An ascending or descending series of notes proceeding by a particular scheme of intervals and varying in pitch arrangement and interval size. In this sense, see **chromatic, diatonic.** —**to scale.** According to or in a uniform proportion or ratio.
~*v.* **scaled, scaling, scales.** —*tr.* **1.** To climb up to the top of or over, with or as if with a ladder, rope, or other device. **2.** To draw or reproduce in accordance with a particular proportion or scale. **3.** To adjust according to a proportion; regulate. **4.** To increase or decrease the size or importance of in fixed proportions. Used with *up* or *down.* —*intr.* **1.** To go up; climb; ascend. **2.** To ascend in steps or stages. [Middle English *scalen,* ladder, graduation, from Late Latin *scāla,* ladder, from Latin *scālae,* stairs.]

scale³ *n.* **1.** *Often plural.* Any instrument or machine for weighing: *bathroom scales.* **2.** Either of the pans, trays, or dishes of a balance. —**turn** or **tip the scales. 1.** To exercise a decisive effect. **2.** To amount in weight to; weigh. Used with *at.*
~*tr.v.* **scaled, scaling, scales. 1.** To weigh with scales. **2.** To have a weight of. [Middle English, from Old Norse *skāl,* bowl, scale of a balance.]

scale armour *n.* Armour made of small overlapping plates of metal or other hard material sewn or riveted to a strong backing of fabric or leather.

scale-board (skáyl-bawrd ‖ -bōrd) *n.* **1.** Thin sheets of wood used as a veneer or a backing for pictures, mirrors, and the like. **2.** A wooden strip used for aligning hand-set type.

scale insect *n.* Any of various destructive sucking insects of the family Coccidae, the females of which secrete and remain under waxy scales on plant tissue.

scale leaf *n.* A membranous, often small, modified leaf, such as one that protects flower buds.

scale moss *n. Botany.* Any of various leafy liverworts of the order Jungermanniales.

sca·lene (skáy-leen, skay-léen, ska-) *adj.* **1.** Having unequal sides. Said of geometrical figures, especially triangles. **2.** *Anatomy.* Designating or pertaining to the scalenus. [Late Latin *scalēnus,* from Greek *skalēnos,* uneven.]

sca·le·nus (skə-lée-nəss, skay-) *n., pl.* -**ni** (-nī). Any one of four paired muscles in the neck, responsible for bending the neck and for raising the top two ribs when breathing in. Also called "scalene muscle". [New Latin. See **scalene.**]

scal·er (skáylər) *n.* **1.** An electronic circuit that records the aggregate of a specific number of signals that occur too rapidly to be recorded individually. **2.** A dental instrument used for removing tartar from teeth.

Scales (skaylz) *pl.n.* The constellation and sign of the zodiac, **Libra** *(see).* Preceded by *the.*

Scal·i·ger (skál-ijər), **Julius Caesar** (1484–1558). Italian scholar. He wrote commentaries on classical texts, the most famous being *Poetice* (1561). This analysis of Aristotelian theories of tragedy inspired later generations of French dramatists.

scall (skawl) *n.* Also **scald** (skawld ‖ skold). A scaly eruption of the skin or scalp. Not in current technical usage. [Middle English *scalle,* from Old Norse *skalli,* baldhead.]

scal·li·on (skál-i-ən) *n. Chiefly U.S.* **1.** A young onion before the enlargement of the bulb, such as a spring onion. **2.** A **shallot** *(see).* [Middle English *scalo(u)n,* from Anglo-French, from Vulgar Latin *escalōnia* (unattested), from Latin *Ascalōnia (caepa),* "Ascalonian (onion)", from *Ascalō,* Ascalon, ancient port in southern Palestine.]

scal·lop (skól-əp, *also* skál-) *n.* Also **scol·lop** (skól-). **1.** Any of various marine bivalve molluscs of the family Pectinidae, having fan-shaped shells with a radiating fluted pattern. **2.** The edible adductor muscle of a scallop. **3.** A scallop shell, or a similarly shaped dish, used for baking and serving seafood. **4.** Any of a series of variously curved projections forming an ornamental border, as on fabrics or lace.
~*tr.v.* **scalloped, -loping, -lops.** Also **scol·lop. 1.** To design or border (material or part of a garment, for example) with scallops. **2.** To bake in a scallop shell or in a casserole with milk or a sauce and often with breadcrumbs. [Middle English *scalop,* from Old French *escalope,* shell, probably from Germanic.] —**scal·lop·er** *n.*

scal·ly (skál-i) *n. Northern English Informal.* A **scallywag** (sense 1).

scal·ly·wag (skál-i-wag) *n.* Also *chiefly U.S.* **scal·ca·wag, scal·la·wag** (-ə-). **1.** A rascal; a reprobate; a good-for-nothing. **2.** *U.S.* A white Southerner supporting the policies of the Republican party, especially the abolition of slavery, after the American Civil War. Used derogatorily by U.S. Southern Democrats. [19th century (U.S. slang) : origin obscure.]

sca·lop·pi·ne, sca·lop·pi·ni (skál-ə-péeni ‖ *U.S. also* skaál-) *pl.n.* **1.** Small, thin slices of veal or other meat, especially when cooked in a sauce of wine or tomatoes and seasonings. **2.** *Used with a singular verb.* A dish of scaloppine. [Italian *scaloppine,* plural of *scaloppina,* diminutive of *scaloppa,* fillet of meat, from Old French *escalope,* shell (the fillets are served curled like shells). See **scallop.**]

scalp (skalp) *n.* **1.** *Anatomy.* The skin covering the top of the human head. **2.** This skin with attached hair formerly cut or torn from an enemy as a battle trophy by certain North American Indians. **3.** Any trophy of victory.
~*tr.v.* **scalped, scalping, scalps. 1.** To cut or tear the scalp from. **2.** *Informal.* To defeat, especially in a humiliating or spectacular manner. **3.** *U.S.* **a.** To buy and resell (securities and commodities) to make a small but quick profit. **b.** To buy and resell (tickets) at inflated prices. **c.** To take advantage of or cheat (a customer, for example) by selling at inflated prices. [Middle English, probably from Scandinavian; akin to Old Norse *skalpr,* sheath, "shell".] —**scalp·er** *n.*

scal·pel (skál-p'l ‖ *U.S. also* skal-pél) *n.* A small straight knife with a very thin, sharp, sometimes removable blade, used especially in surgery and dissection. [Latin *scalpellum,* diminutive of *scalper,* knife, from *scalpere,* to cut, scratch.]

scalp lock *n.* A long lock of hair left on the shaven head by certain North American Indians as a challenge to an enemy.

scal·y (skáyli) *adj.* **-ier, -iest. 1.** Covered or partially covered with scales or scale. **2.** Shedding scales; flaking. —**scal·i·ness** *n.*

scaly anteater *n.* A mammal, the **pangolin** *(see).*

scam (skam) *n. Chiefly U.S. Informal.* A fraudulent business operation; a swindle. [20th century : origin obscure.]

scam·mo·ny (skámməni) *n., pl.* -**nies. 1.** A plant, *Convolvulus scammonia,* of the eastern Mediterranean region, having large roots formerly used as a purgative. **2.** A resinous preparation made from the roots of this plant. [Middle English *scamonie,* from Latin *scammōnea,* from Greek *skammōnia*†.]

scamp¹ (skamp) *n.* **1.** A rogue; a rascal. **2.** A mischievous or prankish child or youth. [Originally "highwayman", "robber", from obsolete *scamp,* to skip away, bolt, probably from Middle Dutch *schampen,* from Old French *escamper,* to SCAMPER.]

scamp² *tr.v.* **scamped, scamping, scamps.** To perform in a careless or perfunctory way. [Probably a blend of SCANT and SKIMP.] —**scamp·er** *n.*

scam·per (skámpər) *intr.v.* -**pered, -pering, -pers.** To run or go hurriedly or playfully.
~*n.* A hasty or playful run or departure. [Flemish *scamperen,* to decamp, from Old French *escamper,* from Vulgar Latin *excampāre* (unattested) : Latin *ex-,* out of, away + *campus,* field (see **camp**).] —**scam·per·er** *n.*

scam·pi (skámpi) *n., pl.* **scampi**. Large prawns, especially when fried in batter. [Italian *scampi†*.]

scan (skan) *v.* **scanned, scanning, scans.** —*tr.* **1.** To examine or consider in close detail; scrutinise. **2.** To look over (a wide area) quickly but thoroughly, as from one end to another. **3.** To analyse (verse) into metrical feet and rhythm patterns. **4.** *Electronics.* **a.** To move a finely focused beam of light or electrons in a systematic pattern over (a surface) in order to reproduce, or sense and subsequently transmit, an image. **b.** To move a radar beam over (a sector of sky) in search of a target. **c.** *Computing.* To search (a series of punched cards or a magnetic tape) automatically for specific data. **d.** *Medicine.* To examine (a part of the body) using a scanner. **5.** To look over or leaf through hastily. —*intr.* **1.** To analyse verse into metrical feet. **2.** To conform to a metrical pattern. Used of verse. **3.** *Electronics.* To undergo electronic scanning. **4.** To use a scanner to examine a part of the body. —See Synonyms at **see**. ~*n.* An act or instance of scanning. [Middle English *scannen*, from Late Latin *scandere*, "to analyse the rising and falling rhythm in verses", from Latin, to climb.] —**scan·na·ble** *adj.*

Usage: The transitive use of *scan* is noteable in that it expresses two meanings which are opposites. On the one hand, it may mean "to examine closely" (*He scanned the examination paper for misprints*); on the other hand, it may mean "to make a quick inspection of" (*He scanned the newspaper for news of the battle*). The latter sense is somewhat more informal. Ambiguity is often possible.

Scand. Scandinavia; Scandinavian.

scan·dal (skánd'l) *n.* **1.** Any act or set of circumstances that brings about disgrace or offends accepted standards of morality or propriety; a public disgrace. **2.** The reaction caused by such an act or set of circumstances; outrage; shame. **3.** Any talk damaging to the character; malicious gossip. **4.** Damage to reputation or character caused by offensive or grossly improper behaviour; disgrace. **5.** One whose conduct brings about disgrace or defamation. —See Synonyms at **disgrace**. ~*tr.v.* **scandalled** or *U.S.* **scandaled, -dalling** or *U.S.* **-daling, -dals.** *Archaic.* To spread scandal about; defame. [French *scandale*, from Late Latin *scandalum*, from Greek *skandalon*, trap, snare, stumbling block.]

scan·dal·ise, scan·dal·ize (skánda-līz) *tr.v.* **-ised, -ising, -ises.** To shock the moral sensibilities of. —**scan·dal·is·er** *n.*

scan·dal·mong·er (skánd'l-mung-gər ‖ -mong-) *n.* A person who spreads scandal or gossip.

scan·dal·ous (skándələss) *adj.* **1.** Causing scandal; shocking; offensive. **2.** Containing defamatory or libellous material. —**scan·dal·ous·ly** *adv.* —**scan·dal·ous·ness** *n.*

scandal sheet *n.* A newspaper or other periodical that habitually prints stories of a sensational or defamatory nature.

scan·dent (skándənt) *adj. Botany.* Climbing: *a scandent vine.* [Latin *scandēns* (stem *scandent-*), present participle of *scandere,* to climb.]

scan·di·a (skándi-ə) *n.* Scandium oxide. [From SCANDIUM.]

Scan·di·an (skándi-ən) *adj.* Scandinavian. [Latin *Scandia,* variant of *Scandinavia,* SCANDINAVIA.] —**Scan·di·an** *n.*

scan·dic (skándik) *adj.* Of, pertaining to, or containing scandium.

Scan·di·na·vi·a (skándi-náyvi-ə) *n. Abbr.* **Scand.** Region of north Europe. Strictly it is the peninsula comprising the kingdoms of Norway and Sweden, but culturally it also takes in Denmark, Finland, Iceland, and the Faeroe Islands are often included.

Scan·di·na·vi·an (skándi-náyvi-ən) *n. Abbr.* **Scand.** **1.** A native or inhabitant of Scandinavia. **2.** The North Germanic languages; the languages spoken in Scandinavia. —**Scan·di·na·vi·an** *adj.*

Scandinavian Peninsula. The peninsula in northwest Europe comprising Norway and Sweden. See **Scandinavia**.

scan·di·um (skándi-əm) *n. Symbol* **Sc** A silvery-white, very lightweight metallic element found in various rare minerals. An artificially radioactive isotope of it is used as a tracer in oil-well and pipeline studies. Atomic number 21, atomic weight 44.956, melting point 1,539°C, boiling point 2,727°C, relative density 2.992, valency 3. [New Latin, from Latin *Scandia,* ancient name for Scandinavia, where it was discovered.]

scandium oxide *n.* A white amorphous powder, Sc_2O_3, used as a source of scandium and in the manufacture of ceramics. Also called "scandia".

scan·ner (skánnər) *n.* One that scans; specifically: **1.** An electronic device that provides a visual representation on a cathode-ray screen of the distribution of a radioactive compound in a particular system, such as the human body. **2.** A device that transmits or receives a radar signal within a predetermined solid angle. See **optical scanner**.

scan·ning (skánning) *n.* Any of various electronic or optical techniques by which images or recorded information are sensed for subsequent modification, integration, or transmission. Also used adjectivally: *a scanning device.*

scanning electron microscope *n.* An electron microscope capable of forming a three-dimensional image on a cathode-ray screen by means of a focused beam of electrons that is scanned across the object to be viewed; the image is formed both by the electrons the object scatters and by the secondary electrons produced.

scan·sion (skánsh'n) *n.* **1.** The analysis of verse into metrical feet and rhythm patterns. **2.** The way a line or verse scans. [Late Latin *scansiō* (stem *scansiōn-*), from Latin, a climbing, from *scandere* (past participle *scansus*), to climb.]

scan·so·ri·al (skan-sáw-ri-əl ‖ -sṓ-) *adj. Zoology.* Adapted to or specialised for climbing. [Latin *scansōrius,* from *scandere* (past par-

ticiple *scansus*), to climb.]

scant (skant) *adj.* **scanter, scantest.** **1.** Deficient in quantity or amount; meagre; inadequate. **2.** Being only just, or just short of, a specified measure: *a scant three miles.* **3.** Inadequately supplied. Used with *of: scant of breath.* —See Synonyms at **meagre**. ~*tr.v.* **scanted, scanting, scants.** **1.** To provide with an inadequate portion or allowance; skimp. **2.** To limit, as in amount or share; stint. **3.** To reduce the size or amount of; cut down. **4.** To deal with or treat inadequately or neglectfully. [Middle English, from Old Norse *skamt,* neuter of *skammr,* short.] —**scant·ly** *adv.* —**scant·ness** *n.*

scant·ling (skánt-ling ‖ -lin) *n.* **1.** A small piece of timber, usually one having a cross-section no more than five inches square. **2.** Such pieces of timber collectively. **3.** The dimensions of building materials such as stone or timber, especially in breadth and thickness. **4.** *Usually plural. Nautical.* The dimensions of the structural parts of a vessel, such as its frames, plates, and girders. **5.** A very small amount. [Alteration of obsolete *scantlon,* Middle English *scantilon,* carpenter's gauge, dimension, from Old French *escantillon, eschandillon,* probably from Vulgar Latin *scandilia* (unattested), measure, scale, from Latin *scandere,* to climb.]

scant·y (skánti) *adj.* **-ier, -iest.** **1.** Barely sufficient or adequate. **2.** Deficient in extent or degree; small; insufficient. —See Synonyms at **meagre**. —**scant·i·ly** *adv.* —**scant·i·ness** *n.*

Scap·a Flow (skáppə, skáapə). Sheltered stretch of sea in the Orkney Islands, north Scotland. It was the base of the British home fleet in both World Wars. In June 1919, 71 surrendered German warships were scuttled here. Following the sinking of the *Royal Oak* by a German submarine within Scapa Flow (1939), a barrier was built to seal off the eastern entrances.

scape¹ (skayp) *n.* **1.** *Botany.* A leafless flower stalk growing from a basal rosette of leaves. **2.** A similar stalklike part, such as a feather shaft or a segment of an insect's antenna. **3.** *Architecture.* The shaft of a column. [Latin *scāpus†,* stalk.]

scape² *Archaic.* Variant of **escape**.

–scape *n. comb. form.* Indicates scene or view; for example, **seascape, moonscape, cityscape.** [Back-formation from LANDSCAPE.]

scape·goat (skáyp-gōt) *n.* **1.** A person or group made to bear the blame for others, or unjustly regarded as being responsible for hardship or disaster, and often persecuted as a result. **2.** A live goat over whose head Aaron confessed all the sins of the children of Israel and which was sent into the wilderness symbolically bearing their sin on the Day of Atonement. Leviticus 16. [(E)SCAPE + GOAT (improper translation of Hebrew *azāzel,* probably "goat for Azazel" (desert demon), misconstrued as *ēz-ōzēl,* "goat that escapes".]

scape·grace (skáyp-grayss) *n.* An unprincipled or incorrigible person; a rascal. [(E)SCAPE + GRACE.]

scaph·oid (skáf-oyd) *adj.* Boat-shaped. ~*n. Anatomy.* The **navicular** *(see).* [New Latin *scaphoides,* from Greek *skaphoeidēs : skaphē,* tub, boat + -OID.]

sca·pho·pod (skáf-pod, -ō-) *n. Zoology.* A **tusk shell** *(see).* [New Latin *scaphopoda :* Greek *skaphos,* boat + -POD.]

scap·o·lite (skáppə-līt) *n.* Any of a series of variously coloured mineral silicates of aluminium, calcium, and sodium. Also called "wernerite". [French : Latin *scāpus,* stalk, SCAPE (from its prismatic crystals) + -ITE.]

sca·pose (skáyp-ōz, -ōss) *adj. Botany.* Resembling or consisting of a scape.

scap·u·la (skáppew-lə) *n., pl.* **-las** or **-lae** (-lee). **1.** *Anatomy.* Either of two large, flat, triangular bones forming the back part of the shoulder. Also called "shoulder blade". **2.** The corresponding bone in other vertebrates. [Latin, shoulder blade, shoulder.]

scap·u·lar (skáppew-lər) *n.* Also **scap·u·lar·y** (-lɔri ‖ -lerri) *pl.* **-ies.** **1.** A monk's sleeveless outer garment hanging from the shoulders and sometimes having a cowl. **2.** Two pieces of cloth joined by strings and worn under the clothing about the shoulders as a badge or token of affiliation to certain religious orders. **3.** Any of the feathers covering the shoulder of a bird. ~*adj. Anatomy.* Of or pertaining to the shoulder or scapula. [Middle English *scapulare,* from Medieval Latin *scapulāre, scapulārium,* "shoulder cloak", from Latin *scapula,* shoulder, SCAPULA.]

scar¹ (skar) *n.* **1.** A mark left on the skin or other tissue following the healing of a surface injury or wound. **2.** Any impression or sign of damage caused by or remaining as evidence of mental or physical injury. **3.** *Botany.* A mark indicating a former attachment, as of a leaf to a stem. **4.** A mark, dent, or other blemish made by use, motion, or contact. ~*v.* **scarred, scarring, scars.** —*tr.* To mark with or as if with a scar. —*intr.* To form a scar. [Middle English *(e)scare,* from Old French *esc(h)are,* scab, from Late Latin *eschara,* from Greek *eskhara†,* hearth, scab caused by burning.]

scar² *n.* Also *Scottish* **scaur** (skawr). *Geology.* A bare rock-face, especially in northern England, where it indicates a limestone cliff. [Middle English *skerre,* from Old Norse *sker,* low reef.]

scar·ab (skárrəb) *n.* Also **scar·a·bae·us** (skárrə-bée-əss) *pl.* **-uses** or **-baei** (-bée-ī). **1.** Any scarabaeid beetle; especially, *Scarabaeus sacer,* regarded as sacred by the ancient Egyptians. **2.** A representation of a scarab beetle, especially one cut from a stone or gem, used in ancient Egypt as a talisman and a symbol of the soul. [Latin *scarabaeus†.*]

scar·a·bae·id (skárrə-bée-id) *n.* Any of the numerous beetles of the family Scarabaeidae, which includes the chafers and dung beetles. [New Latin *Scarabaeidae,* from Latin *scarabaeus,* SCARAB.] —**scar·**

a·bae·id, scar·a·bae·oid (-bée-oyd), **scar·a·boid** (-boyd) *adj.*

Scar·a·mouch, Scar·a·mouche (skárrə-mōōsh, -mōōch, -mowch) *n.* A stock character in old Italian comedy and pantomime, depicted as a boastful, cowardly braggart or buffoon. [French *Scaramouche*, from Italian *Scaramuccia*, jocular use of *scaramuccia*, SKIRMISH.]

Scar·bo·rough (skár-brə, -bərə ‖ -burrə). Seaside resort of North Yorkshire. There are remains of a fourth-century Roman signalling station above the town.

scarce (skairss) *adj.* **scarcer, scarcest. 1.** Uncommonly or infrequently seen or found. **2.** Insufficient to meet a demand or requirement; not plentiful or abundant. **—make (oneself) scarce.** *Informal.* To leave hurriedly or surreptitiously. *—adv. Literary.* Scarcely. [Middle English *scars*, from Anglo-French *escars*, from Vulgar Latin *excarpsus* (unattested), "picked", "choice", hence "rare", variant of Latin *excerptus*, past participle of *excerpere*, to pick out, select : *ex-*, out + *carpere*, to pick, pluck.] **—scarce·ness** *n.*

scarce·ly (skáirssli) *adv.* **1.** By a small margin; just; barely. **2.** Almost not; hardly. **3.** Certainly not. **—See Synonyms at hardly.**

Usage: Because *scarcely* has a negative meaning, formal English disapproves of its use with another negative word in the same clause: *He could scarcely hear her* is preferable to *He couldn't scarcely hear her*, or *She departed with scarcely a word* is preferable to *She departed without scarcely a word.* Standard English also prefers the use of *when* rather than *than* with a following clause: *Scarcely had he entered when the telephone rang.*

scar·ci·ty (skáirssəti) *n., pl.* **-ties. 1.** An insufficient amount or supply; a shortage. **2.** Infrequency of appearance or occurrence; rarity.

scare (skair) *v.* **scared, scaring, scares.** *—tr.* **1.** To startle with fear; frighten; alarm; terrify. **2.** To force or drive by frightening. Used with *away, off, out,* or other adverbs. **3.** *Informal.* To cause to be in a specified state by frightening: *It scared him silly. —intr.* To become frightened. **—See Synonyms at frighten. —scare up.** *Chiefly U.S. Informal.* To gather or prepare hurriedly; improvise. *—n.* **1.** A condition or sensation of sudden fear. **2.** A general state of alarm, especially when exaggerated or groundless; a panic. **3.** Something that causes unreasonable or exaggerated alarm. Also used adjectivally: *scare stories.* [Middle English *skerren*, from Old Norse *skirra*, from *skjarr*, shy, timid, from North Germanic *skerza-* (unattested).] **—scar·er** *n.* **—scar·ing·ly** *adv.*

scare·crow (skáir-krō) *n.* **1.** An object, usually a crude figure of a man, set up in a field to scare birds away from crops. **2.** Something frightening but not inherently dangerous. **3.** A person resembling a scarecrow, especially in being shabbily dressed or very thin.

scared (skaird) *adj.* Frightened or alarmed.

scared·y-cat (skáirdi-kat) *n. Informal.* One timid or easily scared.

scare·mon·ger (skáir-mung-gər ‖ -mong-) *n.* A person who spreads frightening rumours; an alarmist.

scarf[1] (skarf) *n., pl.* **scarves** (skarvz) or **scarfs.** A rectangular or triangular piece of cloth, worn about the neck, shoulders, or head for protection, warmth, or decoration. [Probably from Old North French *escarpe*, variant of Old French *escherpe*, originally "pilgrim's wallet suspended from the neck", from Frankish *skirpja* (unattested), from Latin *scirpea*, basket made of rushes, from *scirpeus*, of rushes, from *scirpus†*, rush, bulrush. See also **scrip** (wallet).]

scarf[2] *n., pl.* **scarfs. 1.** A joint made by cutting and notching the ends of two timbers and strapping or bolting them together to make a continuous piece. Also called "scarf joint". **2.** The end of a timber notched in this fashion. **3.** A cut made into the body of a whale in order to remove the blubber. *—tr.v.* **scarfed, scarfing, scarfs. 1.** To join by means of a scarf joint. **2.** To cut a scarf in. [Middle English *skarf†.*]

Scarfe (skarf), **Gerald** (1936–). British cartoonist. His caricatures are noted for their violent but recognisable distortions.

scarf·skin (skárf-skin) *n.* The epidermis or outermost layer of skin.

Scar·gill (skár-gil), **Arthur** (1938–). British miners' leader. Elected president of the National Union of Mineworkers in 1981, he led a year-long strike in 1984–85. In 1996 he founded a Socialist Labour Party.

scar·i·fi·ca·tor (skárri-fi-kaytər, skáir-i-) *n.* A surgical instrument with several spring-operated lancets, used for skin scarification.

scar·i·fy (skárri-fī, skáir-i-) *tr.v.* **-fied, -fying, -fies. 1.** To make superficial incisions in (the skin), as when vaccinating. **2.** To break up the surface of (topsoil, for example). **3.** To wound with severe criticism. **4.** *Botany.* To slit or soften the outer coat of (seeds) to speed germination. [Middle English *scarifien*, to make incisions on the bark of a tree, from Old French *scarifier*, from Late Latin *scarīfīcāre*, variant of Latin *scarīfāre*, from Greek *skariphasthai*, to scratch an outline, sketch, from *skariphos*, stylus.] **—scar·i·fi·ca·tion** (-fi-káysh'n) *n.* **—scar·i·fi·er** (-fīər) *n.*

scar·i·ous (skáir-i-əss) *adj.* Also **scar·i·ose** (-ōz, -ōss). *Botany.* Thin, membranous, and dry: *scarious bracts.* [New Latin *scariosus†.*]

scar·la·ti·na (skárlə-téenə) *n.* Scarlet fever. [New Latin, from Italian *(febbre) scarlattina*, scarlet (fever), diminutive of *scarlatto*, SCARLET.] **—scar·la·ti·noid** (skárlə-téen-oyd) *adj.*

Scar·lat·ti (skaar-látti ‖ *U.S.* -láati), **Domenico** (1685–1757). Italian composer, son of the prolific composer Alessandro Scarlatti (1660–1725). In Portugal and Spain after 1720, he was a virtuoso harpsichordist, and his numerous works for the instrument were influential in the development of keyboard music generally, and of the sonata form.

scar·let (skár-lət, -lit) *n.* **1.** Strong to vivid red or reddish orange.

2. Clothing or cloth having this colour. [Middle English, from Old French *escarlate†.*] **—scar·let** *adj.*

scarlet fever *n.* An acute contagious disease caused by a haemolytic streptococcus, occurring mainly in children and characterised by a scarlet skin rash and high fever. Also called "scarlatina".

scarlet pimpernel *n.* See **pimpernel.**

scarlet runner *n.* The **runner bean** *(see).*

scarlet woman *n.* **1.** A sexually promiscuous woman. **2.** *Capital* **S,** *capital* **W.** The Roman Catholic Church. Used derogatorily by some Protestants. [Biblical allusion (Revelation 17).]

scarp (skarp) *n.* An escarpment. Not in current technical usage. *—tr.v.* **scarped, scarping, scarps.** To cut or make into a steep slope. [Italian *scarpa*, probably from Gothic *skarpō* (unattested), pointed object.]

scar·per (skárpər) *intr.v.* **-pered, -pering, -pers.** *British Slang.* To run away; leave hastily. [Perhaps from Italian *scappare*, to ESCAPE, associated with SCAPA FLOW, rhyming slang for *go.*]

Scar·ron (ska-rón, skaa-), **Paul** (1610–60). French writer. Though a noted dramatist, his best-known work is the burlesque epic and novel, *Le Roman comique* (1651–57).

scar tissue *n.* A dense, often hard layer of connective tissue formed over a healing wound or cut.

scarves. Alternative plural of **scarf.**

scar·y (skáir-i) *adj.* **-ier, -iest.** *Informal.* Frightening; alarming.

scat[1] (skat) *intr.v.* **scatted, scatting, scats.** *Informal.* To go away hastily; leave at once. Usually used in the imperative. [Perhaps short for SCATTER.]

scat[2] *n.* A type of jazz singing consisting of the improvisation and repetition of meaningless syllables sung to a melody. Also used adjectivally: *a scat singer.* *—intr.v.* **scatted, scatting, scats.** To sing scat. [Perhaps imitative.]

scat[3] *n.* Any of several fishes of the genus *Scatophagus*, of tropical Asia and adjacent areas; especially, *S. argus*, having a flat, rounded, spotted or striped body, and popular as an aquarium fish. [Shortened from New Latin *Scatophagus*, from Greek *skatophagos*, SCATOPHAGOUS.]

scat[4] *n.* Often *plural.* The faeces of animals, especially animals being hunted; droppings. [Greek *skōr* (stem *skat-*).]

scathe (skay<u>th</u>) *tr.v.* **scathed, scathing, scathes. 1.** To criticise severely. **2.** To harm or injure severely especially by fire or heat; wither; sear. *—n. Archaic.* Harm; injury. [Middle English *skathen*, from Old Norse *skadha.*]

scath·ing (skáy<u>th</u>ing) *adj.* **1.** Extremely severe or harsh; bitterly denunciatory: *scathing criticism.* **2.** Harmful or painful; injurious. **—scath·ing·ly** *adv.*

scato- *comb. form.* Indicates faeces or excrement; for example, **scatology.** [Greek *skato-*, from *skōr* (stem *skat-*), dung, ordure.]

sca·tol·o·gy (ska-tólləji, skə-) *n.* **1.** The study of faecal excrement, as in medicine or palaeontology. **2.** An obsession with excrement or excretory functions. **3.** Preoccupation with obscenity, as in literature. [SCATO- + -LOGY.] **—scat·o·log·ic** (skáttə-lójik), **scat·o·log·i·cal** (-'l) *adj.* **—sca·tol·o·gist** (-tólləjist) *n.*

sca·toph·a·gous (ska-tóffəgəss, skə-) *adj.* Feeding on dung, as a beetle or fly might. [Greek *skatophagos* : SCATO + -PHAGOUS.]

scat·ter (skáttər) *v.* **-tered, -tering, -ters.** *—tr.* **1.** To cause to separate and go in various directions; disperse. **2. a.** To distribute widely or loosely by or as if sprinkling or throwing or dropping randomly. **b.** To cover or strew (a surface) by scattering. **3.** *Physics.* To deflect (radiation or particles). *—intr.* **1.** To separate and go in several directions; disperse. **2.** To appear, occur, or fall over a wide area and at widely spaced intervals. *—n.* **1.** The act of scattering. **2.** The condition or extent of being scattered. **3.** That which is scattered. [Middle English *scateren*, probably variant of *schateren*, SHATTER.] **—scat·ter·er** *n.*

scat·ter·brained (skáttər-braynd) *n. Informal.* Lacking in power of concentration or attention; forgetful, disorganised, or thoughtless. **—scat·ter·brain** *n.*

scatter cushion *n.* A small cushion, typically any one of several that are strewn here and there on the furniture in a room. Also *U.S.* "throw pillow".

scat·ter·ing (skáttəring) *n.* **1.** A sparse distribution or irregular occurrence of something: *a scattering of applause.* **2.** *Physics.* The dispersal of a beam of particles or of radiation into a range of directions resulting from physical interactions. *—adj. Chiefly U.S.* Placed at intervals or occurring irregularly.

scat·ty (skátti) *adj.* **-tier, -tiest.** *British Informal.* **1.** Slightly crazy. **2.** Scatterbrained. [From SCATTERBRAINED.] **—scat·ti·ly** *adv.* **—scat·ti·ness** *n.*

scaup (skawp) *n.* Either of two diving ducks, *Aythya marila* or *A. affinis*, having predominantly black and white plumage. Also called "scaup duck". [Perhaps from Scottish *scaup*, variant of SCALP (rare sense "bed of mussels"), because these ducks feed on shellfish.]

scaur. *Scottish.* Variant of **scar** (rock).

scav·enge (skávvinj) *v.* **-enged, -enging, -enges.** *—tr.* **1.** To collect and remove refuse from; clean up. **2.** To search through (rubbish, discarded matter, or the like) for reusable material, such as food. **3.** To collect (reusable material) by searching. **4.** To expel (exhaust gases) from a cylinder of an internal-combustion engine. **5.** *Metallurgy.* To clean (molten metal) by chemically removing impurities. *—intr.* To act as a scavenger; especially, to search through discarded material for edible or useful things. [Back-formation from SCAVENGER.]

scav·en·ger (skávvinjər) *n.* **1.** Any organism that feeds on dead animal flesh or other decaying organic matter. **2.** One who scavenges. **3.** *Chemistry.* A substance added to a mixture to remove impurities or to counteract the undesirable effects of other constituents. **4.** *Metallurgy.* A metal added to a molten metal or alloy that acts, by combining with oxygen or nitrogen, to remove impurities, which then remain behind the slag. [Middle English *scavager,* collector of tolls (later, street cleaner), from Anglo-French *scawager,* from *scawage,* a toll levied on foreign merchants, variant of Old North French *escauwage,* inspection, from *escauwer,* to inspect, from Flemish *scawuen,* to look at, SHOW.]

S.C.E. Scottish Certificate of Education.

sce·nar·i·o (si-naár-i-ō, se-, sə- || -naír-) *n., pl.* **-os. 1.** An outline of the plot of a dramatic or literary work. **2.** A **screenplay** *(see).* **3.** An outline of an imagined chain of events; a possible state of affairs or course of action: *worst-case scenarios.* [Italian, "scenery", from Late Latin *scaenārius,* of the stage, from Latin *scaena,* stage, SCENE.]

sce·nar·ist (seénər-ist, si-naár- || -naír-) *n.* A writer of scenarios.

scend, send (send) *intr.v.* **scended** or **sended, scending** or **sending, scends** or **sends.** *Nautical.* To rise upwards or plunge downwards on a wave or swell.

~*n.* The rising and falling movement of a ship on a wave or swell. [Perhaps from earlier *'scend,* short for DESCEND or ASCEND.]

scene (seen) *n.* **1.** A locality as seen by a viewer; a view. **2. a.** The surroundings and place where an action or event occurs: *The police arrived at the scene of the accident.* **b.** Such a place or setting marked by a specified feature or characteristic: *The road was a scene of carnage following the accident.* **3.** *Abbr.* **sc.** The place in which the action of a play, film, novel, or other narrative occurs; a setting; a locale. **4.** *Abbr.* **sc.** A subdivision of an act in a dramatic presentation in which the setting is fixed and the time continuous. **5.** *Abbr.* **sc.** A shot or series of shots in a film constituting a unit of continuous related action. **6.** The scenery and properties for a dramatic presentation. **7.** *Archaic.* A theatre stage. **8.** A real or fictitious episode, especially when described. **9.** A public display of passion or temper. **10.** *Informal.* A place or realm of a particular activity or interest: *The battle for promotion has livened up the football scene.* **11.** *Informal.* What one likes or is interested in: *Opera is more your scene than mine.* **—behind the scenes. 1.** Backstage. **2.** In private. **—set the scene.** To describe the events leading up to, or the surrounding location of, a particular scene or event. **—steal the scene.** To draw favourable attention on to oneself and away from others. [French *scène,* from Old French *scene,* stage, from Latin *scaena,* stage, theatre, from Greek *skēnē*†, "tent".]

scen·er·y (seénəri) *n.* **1.** The overall appearance of the natural surroundings of an area, especially when considered aesthetically; the landscape. **2.** Painted backdrops and similar properties on a theatrical stage. [Italian *scenario,* SCENARIO.]

scene-shift·er (seén-shiftər) *n.* A stagehand who moves scenery.

sce·nic (seénik) *adj.* **1.** Of, pertaining to, or having picturesque natural landscapes: *a scenic route.* **2.** Of or pertaining to theatrical scenery. **3.** Representing an event, piece of action, or the like. Said of a work of art. **—sce·ni·cal·ly** *adv.*

scenic railway *n.* **1.** A miniature railway as at a fairground. **2.** A railway that extends through picturesque natural scenery.

scent (sent) *n.* **1.** A distinctive odour or smell, especially a pleasant one. **2.** A perfume. **3.** An odour left by the passing of an animal. **4. a.** The trail of a hunted animal or fugitive. **b.** Any trail, set of clues, or the like that may be followed. **5. a.** The sense of smell. **b.** The power of following a trail, set of clues, or the like. **6.** A hint of something imminent; a suggestion. —See Synonyms at **smell.**

~*v.* **scented, scenting, scents.** —*tr.* **1.** To perceive or identify by the sense of smell. **2.** To suspect or detect as if by smelling: *scent danger.* **3.** To perfume. —*intr.* To hunt by means of the sense of smell. Used of hounds. [Middle English *sent,* from *senten,* to smell, scent, from Old French *sentir,* from Latin *sentīre,* to feel.]

scent gland *n.* A specialised exocrine gland in many mammals that secretes a strong-smelling substance.

scep·tic, *U.S.* **skep·tic** (sképtik) *n.* **1.** One who instinctively or habitually doubts, questions, or disagrees with assertions or generally accepted conclusions. **2.** One inclined to scepticism in religious matters. **3. a.** *Often capital* **S.** An adherent of any philosophical school of scepticism. **b.** *Capital* **S.** A member of an ancient Greek school of philosophical scepticism, especially that of Pyrrho of Elis. [Latin *Scepticus,* singular of *Scepticī,* followers of Pyrrho of Elis, from Greek *Skeptikoi,* from *skeptesthai,* to examine, consider.]

scep·ti·cal (sképtik'l) *adj.* **1.** Doubting; disbelieving. **2.** Pertaining to or characteristic of sceptics or scepticism. **—scep·ti·cal·ly** *adv.*

scep·ti·cism (sképti-siz'm) *n.* **1.** A doubting or questioning attitude or disposition; a critical, often reasoned, uncertainty. **2.** The philosophical doctrine that absolute knowledge is impossible and that inquiry must be a process of doubting in order to acquire approximate or relative certainty. **3.** Doubt or disbelief about religion, especially Christianity. —See Synonyms at **uncertianty.**

scep·tre, *U.S.* **scep·ter** (séptər) *n.* **1.** A staff held by a sovereign on ceremonial occasions as an emblem of authority. **2.** Sovereign office or power.

~*tr.v.* **sceptred** or *U.S.* **sceptered, -tring** or *U.S.* **-tering, -tres** or *U.S.* **-ters.** To invest with royal authority. [Middle English *(s)ceptre,* from Old French, from Latin *scēptrum,* from Greek *skēptron*†, "staff", "stick".]

sch. school.

Scha·den·freu·de (shaád'n-froydə) *n.* A feeling of pleasure caused by another's unhappiness or misfortune; malicious delight. [German : *Schade,* harm + *Freude,* joy.]

sched·ule (shéddewl || *U.S.* skéj-əl, -ōōl, *Canadian* shéj-) *n.* **1.** A written list or statement, usually in tabular form, such as: **a.** A listing of rates or prices. **b.** An agenda. **c.** *U.S.* A timetable, as for buses or trains. **2.** A programme of forthcoming events or appointments. **3.** A production plan allotting work to be done and specifying deadlines. **4.** A supplementary statement of details appended to a document.

~*tr.v.* **scheduled, -uling, -ules. 1.** To enter on a schedule. **2.** To make up a schedule for. **3.** To plan or appoint for a certain time or date. [Middle English *cedule, sedule,* slip of parchment or paper, short note, from Old French *cedule,* from Late Latin *schedula,* diminutive of Latin *scheda, scida,* papyrus leaf, from Greek *skhedē.*]

sched·uled castes (shéddewld || skéj-əld, shéj-, -ōōld) *pl.n.* The **harijans** *(see).*

scheduled territories *pl.n.* Those territories using sterling or currencies linked to sterling and subject to United Kingdom exchange controls. They are the United Kingdom, the Channel Islands, the Isle of Man, Gibraltar, and formerly the Republic of Ireland. Also called "sterling area", "sterling bloc".

Scheel (shayl), **Walter** (1919–). West German politician. He entered the Bundestag (1953), and became minister for economic cooperation (1961), vice-president (1967), and vice-chancellor and foreign minister (1969). He was federal president from 1974 to 1979.

schee·lite (sheé-līt, sháy-) *n.* A variously coloured natural form of calcium tungstate, $CaWO_4$, found in igneous rocks and used as a source of tungsten. [After K. *Scheele* (1742–86), Swedish chemist.]

She·her·a·za·de (shə-hérrə-zaádə, -heér-ə-, -zaád). The fictional narrator of the tales in *The Arabian Nights.*

Scheldt (shelt, skelt). *French* **Escaut** (ess-kṓ); *Dutch* **Schelde** (s<u>kh</u>éldə). River in northwestern Europe. Rising in Aisne département, France, it flows 435 kilometres (270 miles) through Belgium and the port of Antwerp to join the North Sea in the Netherlands via the West Scheldt estuary (Westerschelde). The river was cut off from its East Scheldt outlet (Oosterschelde) by dykes built in the 19th century. The Scheldt is navigable for most of its length, and connects with the Belgian and Dutch canal systems.

sche·ma (skeé-mə) *n., pl.* **-mata** (-mətə, *also* skee-maátə). **1.** A summarised or diagrammatic representation of something; an outline. **2.** A pattern or structure, especially of a logical proof or argument. [German *Schema,* from Greek *skhēma,* form. See **scheme.**]

sche·mat·ic (skee-máttik, ski-) *adj.* Pertaining to or in the form of a scheme or schema; diagrammatic.

~*n.* A structural or procedural diagram, especially of an electrical or mechanical system.

sche·ma·tise, sche·ma·tize (skeémə-tīz) *tr.v.* **-tised, -tising, -tises.** To form into, or express by means of, a scheme or schema. [Greek *skhēmatizein,* to give a form to, from *skhēma,* form, manner. See **scheme.**] **—sche·ma·ti·sa·tion** (-tī-záysh'n || *U.S.* -ti-) *n.*

sche·ma·tism (skeémə-tiz'm) *n.* The patterned disposition or arrangement of constituents within a given system.

scheme (skeem) *n.* **1.** A systematic plan of action. **2.** An orderly combination of related or successive parts or things; a system. **3.** An underhand or secret plan; a plot; an intrigue. **4.** An official or commercial plan, policy, or project: *an insurance scheme.* **5.** A chart, diagram, or outline of a system or object. **6.** *Scottish.* A housing estate, especially a council estate.

~*v.* **schemed, scheming, schemes.** —*tr.* **1.** To contrive a plan or scheme for. **2.** To plot. —*intr.* To make devious plans. [Latin *schēma,* form, figure, manner, from Greek *skhēma.*] **—schem·er** *n.*

schem·ing (skeéming) *adj.* Given to plotting or intrigue.

schemozzle. Variant of **shemozzle.**

scher·zan·do (skairt-sándō, skert- || *U.S.* -saándō) *adv. Music.* In a playful or sportive manner. Used as a direction to the performer.

~*n., pl.* **scherzandos.** *Music.* A scherzando passage or movement. [Italian, gerund of *scherzare,* to joke, from *scherzo,* joke, SCHERZO.] **—scher·zan·do** *adj.*

scher·zo (skaírt-sō, skért-) *n., pl.* **-zos** or **-zi** (-see). *Music.* A lively movement commonly in ¾ time. [Italian, joke, from Middle High German *scherz,* from *scherzen,* to joke, leap with joy.]

Schia·pa·rel·li (skyáppə-rélli), **Elsa** (1896–1973). Italian-born French fashion designer noted for her bold use of colour. She helped to make Paris the world centre of fashion design.

Schiaparelli, Giovanni Virginio (1835–1910). Italian astronomer. He is best known for his discovery of linear markings on the surface of Mars, which he thought were water channels. His theory that Mercury and Venus always have the same side facing the sun was not refuted until the 1960s.

Schick test (shik) *n.* A test of susceptibility to diphtheria in which diphtheria toxin is injected into the skin. A red patch indicates the absence of antibodies and therefore the need for immunisation. [After Bela *Schick* (1877–1967), U.S. paediatrician.]

Schiele (sheélə), **Egon** (1890–1918). Austrian painter, a leader of the Austrian expressionist movement. His paintings, erotic and disturbing, were influenced by Freudian psychology.

Schiff's reagent (shifs) *n.* An aqueous solution of rosaniline and sulphurous acid used to test for the presence of aldehydes, which oxidise the reduced form of the dye rosaniline back to its original magenta colour. [After Hugo *Schiff* (1834–1915), German chemist.]

schil·ler (shíllər) *n.* A lustrous, almost metallic sheen on certain minerals caused by internal reflections from microscopic inclusions.

[German *Schiller,* iridescence, from Middle High German *schilher,* iridescent taffeta, from *schilhen,* to wink, blink, from Old High German *scilihen.*]

Schil·ler (shíllər), **(Johann Christoph) Friedrich (von)** (1759–1805). German poet and dramatist. His historical plays include *Wallenstein* (1798–99), *Mária Stuart* (1800), and *Wilhelm Tell* (1804), and he also wrote a study of aesthetics. He is an important figure in the Romantic movement.

schil·ling (shílling) *n.* **1.** The basic monetary unit of Austria, equal to 100 gröschen. **2.** A coin worth one schilling. [German *Schilling,* from Middle High German *schillinc,* from Old High German *skilling,* from Germanic *skillingaz* (unattested), SHILLING.]

schip·per·ke (shíppər-ki, skíppər- || -kə) *n.* A small dog of a breed developed in Belgium, having a dense, long, black coat. [Flemish, "little skipper" (it is often trained as a watchdog on a boat), from *schipper,* skipper, from Middle Dutch, from *schip,* ship.]

schism (síz'm, *also* skíz'm) *n.* **1.** A separation or division into hostile, opposing groups or factions; especially, a formal breach of union within a Christian church. **2.** The offence of attempting to promote or perpetuate such a split within a church or religious group. **3.** A body or sect that has brought about, or is the result of, a separation or division. [Middle English *(s)cisme,* from Old French, from Late Latin *schisma,* from Greek *skhisma,* a split, division, from *skhizein,* to split.] —**schis·mat·ic** (siz-máttik, skiz-) *n. & adj.* —**schis·mat·i·cal·ly** *adv.*

schist (shist) *n.* Any of various medium- to coarse-grained metamorphic rocks composed of parallel layers, which are often wavy and flaky. [French *schiste,* from Latin *(lapis) schistos,* "fissile (stone)", from Greek *skhistos (lithos),* talc, from *skhizein,* to split.] —**schis·tose** (-ōz, -ōss), **schis·tous** (-əss) *adj.* —**schis·tos·i·ty** (shi-stóssəti) *n.*

schis·to·some (shíst-ə-sōm, -ō-) *n.* Any of several chiefly tropical trematode worms of the genus *Schistosoma,* many of which are parasitic in the blood of humans and other mammals. Also called "bilharzia", "blood fluke". [New Latin *Schistosoma,* "cleft body" : Greek *skhistos,* cleft, from *skhizein,* to split + -SOME (body).]

schis·to·so·mi·a·sis (shíst-ə-sō-mí-ə-siss, -ō-) *n.* Any of various generally tropical diseases caused by infestation with schistosomes. Also called "bilharziasis". [New Latin : *Schistosoma,* SCHISTOSOME + -IASIS.]

schiz·o (skítsō) *adj. Informal.* Schizophrenic.
—*n., pl.* **schizos.** *Informal.* A schizophrenic. [Shortening.]

schizo–, schiz– *comb. form.* Indicates division, split, or cleavage; for example, **schizophrenia, schizont.** [New Latin, from Greek *skhizo-,* from *skhizein,* to split.]

schiz·o·carp (skíz-ə-kaarp, skíts-, -ō-) *n.* A dry fruit that splits at maturity into two or more closed carpels, each usually containing one seed, as in the mallow. [SCHIZO- + -CARP.] —**schiz·o·car·pic** (-kárpik), **schiz·o·car·pous** (-kárpəss) *adj.*

schiz·o·gen·e·sis (skíts-ō-jénnə-siss, skíz-, -ə-) *n. Biology.* Reproduction by fission. [New Latin : SCHIZO- + -GENESIS.] —**schiz·o·ge·net·ic** (-jə-néttik, -je-) *adj.*

schi·zog·o·ny (skit-sóggəni, ski-zóggəni) *n. Biology.* Reproduction by multiple asexual fission, characteristic of many protozoans. [New Latin *schizogonia* : SCHIZO- + -GONY.] —**schi·zog·o·nous,** **schiz·o·gon·ic** (skítsə-gónnik, skízzə-) *adj.*

schiz·oid (skítsoyd) *adj.* **1.** Characteristic of, tending to, or resembling schizophrenia. **2.** Loosely, marked by extremes of mood or temperament.
—*n.* A schizoid person. [SCHIZ(O)- + -OID.]

schiz·o·my·cete (skíts-ō-mi-séet, skíz-, -ə-, -mí-seet) *n.* Any of numerous single-celled microorganisms of the class Schizomycetes, which includes the bacteria. [New Latin *Schizomycetes,* "fission fungi" (from their multiplying by fission) : SCHIZO- + -MYCETE.] —**schiz·o·my·ce·tous** (-séetəss) *adj.*

schiz·ont (skíts-ont, skíz-) *n.* A protozoan cell produced by schizogony in the life cycle of a sporozoan. [SCHIZO- + -ont, being, from Greek *ōn* (stem *ont-),* present participle of *einai,* to be.]

schiz·o·phre·ni·a (skíts-ə-fréeni-ə, skidz-, -ō-) *n.* Any of a group of psychotic conditions characterised by withdrawal from reality and accompanied by highly variable affective, behavioural, and intellectual disturbances. Formerly called "dementia praecox". [New Latin, "split mind" : SCHIZO- + -PHRENIA.] —**schiz·o·phren·ic** (-frénnik) *adj. & n.*

schiz·o·phyte (skíts-ə-fīt, skíz-, -ō-) *n.* Any of various single-celled or simple colonial organisms of the division Schizophyta, including bacteria and the blue-green algae, reproducing asexually, usually by fission. [New Latin *Schizophyta* : SCHIZO- + -PHYTE.] —**schiz·o·phyt·ic** (-fíttik) *adj.*

schiz·o·pod (skíts-ə-pod, skíz-, -ō-) *n.* Any of various shrimplike crustaceans of the orders Euphausiacea and Mysidacea (formerly included in the single order Schizopoda). [New Latin *Schizopoda,* "split-footed ones" (from the splitting of the thoracic limbs) : SCHIZO- + -POD.] —**schiz·op·o·dous** (skit-sóp-ədəss, ski-zóp-) *adj.*

schiz·o·thy·mi·a (skíts-ə-thími-ə, -ō-) *n.* Schizoid behaviour that resembles schizophrenia in the tendency to withdraw and introversion but remains within the limits of normality. [New Latin, "split spirit" : SCHIZO- + -THYMIA.] —**schiz·o·thy·mic** (-thímik) *adj.*

Schle·gel (shláyg'l), **August Wilhelm von** (1767–1845). German critic and translator. Best known for his translations of the works of Shakespeare, he also translated other foreign authors, and contributed critical work to the Romantic movement.

Schlegel, (Carl Wilhelm) Friedrich von (1772–1829). German

writer and critic. A Sanskrit scholar, he was a leader of the Romantic movement, formulating its aims and publishing his poetry and philosophy in the magazine *Das Athenäum.*

schle·miel (shlə-méel) *n. Chiefly U.S. Slang.* An unlucky and habitual bungler; a dolt. [Yiddish, perhaps from Hebrew *Shelûmîel,* character in the Bible.]

schlen·ter (shlén-tər, slén-) *n. South African.* A counterfeit diamond.
—*adj.* Fake or counterfeit. [Dutch *slenter,* a trick.]

schlep (shlep) *v.* **schlepped, schlepping, schleps.** *Chiefly U.S. Slang.* —*tr.* To carry clumsily or with difficulty; lug. —*intr.* **1.** To carry something clumsily. **2.** To go or travel.
—*n. Chiefly U.S. Slang.* **1.** An arduous journey. **2.** A clumsy or stupid person. **3.** A boring event or period of time. [Yiddish *shleppen,* to drag, trail, from Middle Low German *slêpen.*]

Schles·in·ger (shléssinjər, sléssinjər), **John (Richard)** (1926–). British theatre, opera, film, and television director. His films, often dourly naturalistic, include *Billy Liar* (1963), *Midnight Cowboy* (1969: Oscar), and *Sunday Bloody Sunday* (1970).

Schles·wig (shléz-wig, -vig; *German* shláyss-vikh). Former duchy on the Jutland peninsula, north Europe, to the north of the river Eider. The greater part of it is now incorporated in the German state of **Schleswig-Holstein.**

Schles·wig-Hol·stein (shléz-wig-hól-shtīn, -vig-, -hól-, -stīn; *German* shláyss-vikh-hól-shtīn). State of Germany. It comprises most of the two former duchies of **Schleswig** and **Holstein.** These were inherited by the Danish royal house in 1460. Centuries of conflict ensued as the Danes periodically sought to make them part of Denmark, while their predominantly German populations resisted or sought union with German states, later the German Confederation. Eventually (1866) Prussia annexed both duchies. The northern part of Schleswig was awarded to Denmark after a plebiscite (1920), and it now forms the Danish county of Sønderjylland (South Jutland). Schleswig-Holstein is a low-lying, largely fertile area. There are good harbours along the coast, and tourist resorts on offshore islands. The port of Kiel is the state capital.

Schlick (shlik), **Moritz** (1882–1936). German-born Austrian philosopher. He organised (1928) a group of philosophers, the Vienna circle, which developed the theories of logical positivism. He held that the meaning of a statement lies in its experimental verification.

Schlie·mann (shlée-man, -mən), **Heinrich** (1822–90). German archaeologist. Retiring from business (1863), he began to excavate for Homer's Troy at Hissarlik in Turkey. His carelessness and determination to prove the existence of the city somewhat devalued the veracity of his results. From Troy, he went on to excavate most of the sites of Mycenaean Greece.

schlie·ren (shlée·rən) *pl.n.* **1.** *Geology.* Irregular tabular bodies occurring as essential components of plutonic rock but differing in structure or composition from the principal mass. **2.** *Physics.* Regions of a transparent medium, as of a flowing gas, that exhibit densities different from that of the bulk of the medium. [German *Schlieren,* plural of *Schliere,* streak, from dialectal German *Schlier,* "slimy mass", from Middle High German *slier,* mud, slime.]

schli·ma·zel (shli-maáz'l) *n. U.S. Slang.* An extremely unlucky or inept person, a habitual failure. [Yiddish, "bad luck".]

schlock (shlok) *n. Chiefly U.S. Slang.* Goods, creative artefacts, entertainments, or the like, that are of meretricious or obviously inferior quality. [Yiddish, "broken merchandise", perhaps from German *Schlag,* a blow, from Middle High German *slac,* from Old High German *slag.*] —**schlock** *adj.*

schm–, shm– (shm-) *prefix & infix. Slang.* Inserted before the dismissive repetition of all or part of a word: *Oedipus-Schmoedipus, who cares? Graffiti-graschmiti, it's vandalism.* [Abstracted from Yiddish words in *schm-,* such as SCHMUK.]

schmaltz, shmalz (shmawlts, shmolts) *n.* **1.** *Informal.* Excessive sentimentality, especially in art or music. **2.** *Informal.* Excessively profuse flattery or praise. **3.** Animal fat used as food, especially chicken fat. [German, "melted fat", from Middle High German *smalz,* from Old High German.] —**schmaltz·y** *adj.*

Schmidt (shmit), **Helmut** (1918–). German politician. A member of the Social Democrat party, he was minister of defence (1969–72) in West Germany, and minister of finance (1972–74). From 1974 to 1982 he was federal chancellor. He retired from federal politics in 1983.

Schmidt telescope *n.* A reflecting telescope consisting of a concave spherical mirror and a transparent plate of glass at its centre of curvature, used to offset spherical aberration, coma, and astigmatism. [After Bernhard *Schmidt* (1879–1935), Swedish-born German astronomer, who invented it.]

schmo, schmoe (shmō) *n., pl.* **schmoes.** *Chiefly U.S. Slang.* A dull or stupid person. [Yiddish *shmok,* from Slovene *šmok.*]

schmuck (shmuk) *n. Chiefly U.S. Slang.* A clumsy or stupid person; an oaf. [Yiddish *schmuck,* "penis", from German *Schmuck,* ornament, from Middle Low German *smuck.*]

Schna·bel (shnaáb'l), **Artur** (1882–1951). Austrian pianist. Performing mostly in the United States, he was regarded as the leading interpreter of Beethoven's piano sonatas.

schnap·per (snáppər) *n. Australian.* A fish, the **snapper** (see). [Pseudo-German spelling of SNAPPER (fish).]

schnapps (shnaps || *U.S. also* shnaaps) *n.* Any of various strong alcoholic spirits; especially, a kind of Dutch gin. [German *Schnaps,* from Low German *snaps,* mouthful, dram, from *snappen,* to snap, from Middle Low German, SNAP.]

schnau·zer (shnówtsər || *U.S.* shnówzər) *n.* A dog of a breed developed in Germany, having a wiry grey or black coat and a blunt muzzle. [German *Schnauzer,* from *Schnauze,* snout.]

schnit·zel (shníts'l) *n.* A thin cutlet of veal. [German *Schnitzel,* diminutive of *Schnitz,* slice, from Middle High German *sniz.*] See also **Wiener schnitzel.**

Schnitz·ler (shnítslər), **Arthur** (1862–1931). Austrian playwright and novelist. His work portrays Viennese cafe society. His best-known work, *Reigen* (1900), also known as *La Ronde,* met with such controversy for its sexual explicitness that he forbade it to be performed until 50 years after his death.

schnook (shnŏŏk) *n. U.S. Slang.* A stupid or easily victimised person; a dupe. [Yiddish *shmok,* variant of *shmok,* SCHMO.]

schnor·rer (shnáw-rər || shnŏ-) *n. Chiefly U.S. Slang.* One who takes advantage of the generosity of friends; a parasite; a sponger. [Yiddish, from *schnorren,* to beg (while playing a pipe or harp), from Middle High German *snurren,* to hum, whirr.]

schnoz·zle (shnózz'l) *n. Chiefly U.S. Slang.* The nose. [Probably alteration (influenced by NOZZLE) of Yiddish *shnoitsl,* diminutive of *shnoits,* snout, from German *Schnauze.*]

Schoen·berg (shúrn-berg; *German* shŏn-bairk), **Arnold,** born Arnold Schönberg (1874–1951). Austrian composer and teacher. His style is usually called "atonal", a term he disliked. An example is *Pierrot Lunaire* (1912), a set of recitations with chamber accompaniment which also makes use of **Sprechgesang** (*see*). He emigrated to the United States in 1933 to escape Nazi persecution.

schol·ar (skóllər) *n.* **1. a.** A learned or erudite person. **b.** A specialist in some given branch of the humanities. **2. a.** One who studies; especially, a school pupil. **b.** One considered in the light of his ability to learn: *a poor scholar.* **3.** A student who holds a scholarship. [Middle English *scoler,* from Old French *escoler,* from Late Latin *scholāris,* of a school, from Latin *schola,* SCHOOL.]

schol·ar·ly (skóllərli) *adj.* Pertaining to, characteristic of, or befitting scholars or scholarship. **—schol·ar·li·ness** *n.*

schol·ar·ship (skóllər-ship) *n.* **1.** The methods, qualities, and attainments of a scholar; learning; erudition. **2.** Existing knowledge resulting from scholarly research in a particular field. **3. a.** An award of financial aid to a student or pupil, usually gained through competitive examination, that is given by a fund or endowment set up for such a purpose. **b.** The position of a student or pupil who has won such an award. **—See Synonyms at knowledge.**

scho·las·tic (skə-lástik, sko-) *adj.* **1.** Of or pertaining to schools, scholars, or education. **2.** *Usually capital* **S.** Pertaining to or characteristic of the medieval Schoolmen or Scholasticism: *Scholastic theology.* **3.** Pedantic; dogmatic.
—*n.* **1.** *Usually capital* **S.** A Schoolman. **2.** A dogmatist; a pedant. **3.** A formalist in art. **4.** A Jesuit student at a scholasticate, between the novitiate and the priesthood. [Latin *scholasticus,* from Greek *skholastikos,* academic, from *skholazein,* to study, attend lectures, from *skholē,* school.] **—scho·las·ti·cal·ly** *adv.*

scho·las·ti·cate (skə-lásti-kayt, sko-, -kət, -kit) *n.* In the Roman Catholic Church: **1.** An institution where Jesuit scholastics undergo a period of general study before beginning their theological studies and entering the priesthood. **2. a.** A scholastic. **b.** The status or period of being a scholastic. [New Latin *scholasticātus,* from Latin *scholasticus,* SCHOLASTIC.]

scho·las·ti·cism (skə-lásti-siz'm, sko-) *n.* **1.** *Usually capital* **S.** The dominant theological and philosophical school of medieval western Europe, based on the authority of the Latin Fathers and of Aristotle and his commentators. **2. a.** Close adherence to the traditional doctrines of a school or religious order. **b.** Pedantry.

scho·li·ast (skóli-ast) *n.* Any of the ancient commentators who annotated the classical authors. [Late Greek *skholiastēs,* from *skholiazein,* to comment on, from *skholion,* SCHOLIUM.]

scho·li·um (skŏ-li-əm) *n., pl.* **-ums** or **-lia** (-li-ə). **1.** An explanatory note or commentary, as on a Greek or Latin text. **2.** A note amplifying a proof or process, as in mathematics. [New Latin, from Greek *skholion,* diminutive of *skholē,* lecture, SCHOOL.]

school¹ (skŏŏl) *n. Abbr.* **s., S., sch. 1.** An institution for the instruction or education of children or young people. Often used adjectivally or in combination: *school fees; schoolboy.* **2.** An institution within a college or university for instruction in a specialised field: *medical school.* **3.** Any institution that provides instruction, especially of a practical or technical nature: *a driving school; drama school.* **4.** The pupils and sometimes the teachers of a school. **5.** The building or group of buildings housing a school, in which instruction is given or in which pupils work and live. **6.** *U.S.* A college or university. **7.** The process of being educated; especially, formal education comprising a planned series of courses over a number of years. **8.** A session or period of instruction at a school: *went swimming before school.* **9.** A group of persons, especially intellectuals or artists, whose thought, work, or style demonstrates some common influence or unifying belief. **10.** A class of people distinguished by shared values, opinions, or principles: *a politician of the old school.* **11.** The education provided by a set of circumstances or experiences. **12.** *Plural. Often capital* **S.** The medieval universities and Schoolmen. **13.** *Plural. British.* At Oxford University, the final examinations of an honours course for the degree of Bachelor of Arts. **14.** *British Slang.* A group of people playing cards, usually for money: *a poker school.*
—*tr.v.* **schooled, schooling, schools. 1.** To instruct; educate. **2.** To train; discipline. **—See Synonyms at teach.** [Middle English *scole,* Old English *scōl,* from Medieval Latin *scōla,* from Latin

schola, leisure, school, from Greek *skholē,* leisure (devoted to learning), lecture, school.]

school² *n.* A large group of aquatic animals, especially fish, swimming together; a shoal. See Synonyms at **flock.**
—*intr.v.* **schooled, schooling, schools.** To swim in, or form into, a school. [Middle English *scole,* from Middle Dutch *schōle,* troop, group.]

school board *n.* **1.** In Britain, a local education authority formerly empowered to establish and maintain elementary schools. **2.** *U.S.* A local education authority.

school·boy (skŏŏl-boy) *n.* A boy attending school.

school·child (skŏŏl-chīld) *n., pl.* **-children** (-children). A child attending school.

school·girl (skŏŏl-gurl) *n.* A girl attending school.

school·house (skŏŏl-howss) *n.* **1.** A building used as a school, especially in a rural area. **2.** A house provided for a head teacher, usually attached to a school.

school·ing (skŏŏling) *n.* **1.** Instruction or training given at school; especially, a programme of formal education. **2.** The training of a horse or of a horse and rider in dressage.

school·man (skŏŏl-mən, -man) *n., pl.* **-men** (-mən, -men) **1.** *Often capital* **S.** A philosopher or theologian of a medieval university; an adherent of Scholasticism. **2.** *Chiefly U.S.* A professional teacher or scholar.

school·marm (skŏŏl-maarm) *n. Informal.* **1.** A woman schoolteacher, especially one who is pedantic, old-fashioned, or a priggish disciplinarian. **2.** A woman who resembles a schoolmarm in being prim, old-fashioned, and priggish. [Dialectal *marm,* variant of *ma'am,* MADAM.] **—school·marm·ish** *adj.*

school·mas·ter (skŏŏl-maastər || -mastər) *n.* **1.** A male teacher or headmaster. **2.** A reddish-brown food fish, the snapper *Lutjanus apodus,* of the tropical Atlantic and the Gulf of Mexico.

school·mate (skŏŏl-mayt) *n.* A school companion or associate. Also called "schoolfellow".

school·mis·tress (skŏŏl-miss-triss, -trəss) *n.* **1.** A woman teacher. **2.** A headmistress of a school.

school of thought *n.* A number of people who share an opinion or view.

school·room (skŏŏl-rŏŏm, -rŏŏm) *n.* A classroom.

school ship *n.* **1.** A ship on which training in seamanship is given, especially for persons entering the navy. **2.** A ship that is made available for educational cruises.

school·teach·er (skŏŏl-teechər) *n.* One who teaches in a school.

school year *n.* The period of a year that constitutes a complete annual session of school.

schoo·ner (skŏŏnər) *n.* **1.** A ship with two or more masts, all of which are fore-and-aft-rigged, the mainmast being abaft of and taller than the foremast. **2.** *British.* A measure of or large glass for sherry. **3.** *U.S. & Australian.* A large beer glass, generally holding a pint or more. [18th century : origin obscure.]

Scho·pen·hau·er (shŏpən-how-ər, shóppən-), **Arthur** (1788–1860). German philosopher. Rejecting the theories of Hegel, he held that primordial reality—the will to live—is irrational, and that attempts to understand the world rationally are doomed to failure. His major work was the *The World as Will and Idea* (1819).

schorl (shorl) *n.* A black, opaque variety of tourmaline. [German *Schörl†.*] **—schor·la·ceous** (shawr-láyshəss) *adj.*

schot·tische (sho-teesh || shóttish) *n.* **1.** A German round dance in 2/4 time, resembling a slow polka. **2.** A piece of music for this dance. [German *Schottische,* short for *(der) schottische (Tanz),* (the) Scottish (dance).]

Schrei·ner (shrínər), **Olive (Emilie Albertina)** (1855–1920). South African novelist. She is best known for *The Story of An African Farm* (1883), a thinly-veiled autobiographical work.

Schrö·ding·er (shrúr-ding-ər, shrŏ-; *German* shrŏ-), **Erwin** (1887–1961). Austrian physicist. He won the Nobel prize (1933) for his development of quantum theory. He left Austria, for Ireland, after the Nazi Anschluss, returning in the 1950s.

Schrödinger wave equation *n. Physics.* A partial differential equation, fundamental to wave mechanics, describing the behaviour of a particle in a potential, based on the de Broglie hypothesis of wave-particle duality: $(h/2\pi)(\partial\psi/\partial t) = H\psi$, where h is Planck's constant, H is the Hamiltonian, ψ is the wave function of the particle, and ∂t is the partical differential operator. Also called "wave equation".

Schu·bert (shŏŏbərt), **Franz (Peter)** (1797–1828). Austrian composer. In addition to his 600 songs, which established the tradition of the German *lied,* his genius for the lyrical is evident in his nine surviving symphonies, and his many other choral, chamber, piano and orchestral works. **—Schu·bert·i·an** (shŏŏ-bérti-ən) *adj.*

Schu·man (shŏŏ-mən, -man), **Robert** (1886–1963). French statesman. He was prime minister (1947–48), and president of the Assembly of the European Economic Community (1958–60). While foreign minister (1948–53), he prepared the Schuman Plan which led to the establishment of the European Coal and Steel Community.

Schu·mann (shŏŏ-man, -mən), **Clara (Josephine),** born Clara Wieck (1819–96). German pianist. The daughter of Friedrich Wieck (1788–1873), she married his pupil Robert Schumann in 1840, and became the foremost interpreter and editor of his works.

Schumann, Elisabeth (1885–1952). German-born U.S. singer. From 1938 she won great popularity in the United States for her interpretation of the works of Mozart and Richard Strauss.

Schumann, Robert (Alexander) (1810–56). German composer. One of the earliest composers of the Romantic movement, he started by writing for the piano only, but later moved to emotional and inventive works for full orchestra.

Schusch·nigg (shōosh-nig; *German* -nik), **Kurt von** (1897–1977). Austrian politician. He became chancellor (1934) after the assassination of Dollfuss. After Austria was annexed by Germany in the Anschluss of 1938, Schuschnigg resigned and was later imprisoned by the Germans.

schuss (shŏoss) *intr.v.* **schussed, schussing, schusses**. To make a fast straight run in skiing.
~*n.* **1.** A straight, steep course for skiing. **2.** The act of skiing such a course. [German *Schuss*, shot, from Middle High German *schuz*, from Old High German *scuz*.]

Schutz·staf·fel (*German* shŏots-shtaff'l) *n., pl.* **-feln** (-shtaff'ln). *German*. The **SS** (*see*).

schwa (shwaa; *German* shvaa) *n.* **1.** A mid-central vowel sound. In English it occurs in many unstressed syllables, as in those of the words *mother* and *about*. **2.** The symbol (ə) used to represent this sound. [German *Schwa*, from Hebrew *shəwā'*, probably from *shaw'*, emptiness.]

Schwaben. See **Swabia.**

Schwann (shvan), **Theodor** (1810–82). German physiologist. He developed cell theory, showing that animals are formed of cells and coining the term "metabolism".

Schwann cell (shwon, shvan) *n.* A cell responsible for the formation of a myelin sheath around certain nerve fibres. [After Theodor SCHWANN.]

Schwarz·kopf (shvárts-kopf), **Dame Elizabeth** (1915–). German-born British soprano. She is noted for her interpretation of lieder and of operas by Mozart and Richard Strauss.

Schwarz·wald (shvárts-valt). Also **Black Forest**. Highland region of southwestern Germany, extensively forested. It stretches from the Swiss border northwards to the river Main.

Schweit·zer (shwĭt-sər, shvĭt-), **Albert** (1875–1965). German-born French missionary from Alsace. From 1913 he ran a hospital in the Gabon village of Lambaréné, financed by his organ recitals of the music of Bach. His books include *The Quest for the Historical Jesus* (1906). His own theology was based on "reverence for life". He was awarded the Nobel prize for peace (1952).

Schweiz. See **Switzerland.**

Schwit·ters (shvíttərz), **Kurt** (1887–1948). German artist and poet. He founded his own version of the Dada movement in Hanover. His work, for which he coined the nonsense word "Merz", consists mainly of collages of random words and objects.

sci. science; scientific.

sci·a·gram, ski·a·gram (sĭ-ə-gram, skĭ-) *n.* Also **sci·a·graph** (-graaf || -graff). A picture or photograph made up of shadows or outlines. [Greek *skia*, shadow + -GRAM.]

sci·ag·ra·phy, ski·ag·ra·phy (sĭ-ággrəfi, skĭ-) *n.* The art or technique of making sciagrams. [SCIA(GRAM) + -GRAPHY.]

sci·am·a·chy, ski·am·a·chy (sĭ-ámməki, skĭ-) *n.* Fighting with shadows or imaginary enemies. [Greek *skiamakhia* : *skia*, shadow + *-makhia*, -fighting.]

sci·at·ic (sĭ-áttik) *adj.* **1.** *Anatomy.* Of or pertaining to the **ischium** (*see*). **2.** Of or pertaining to sciatica. [French *sciatique*, from Late Latin *(i)sc(h)iaticus*, variant of Latin *ischiadicus*, from Greek *iskhiadikos*, from *iskhion*, hip joint, ISCHIUM.]

sci·at·i·ca (sĭ-áttikə) *n.* Neuralgia of the sciatic nerve, characterised by pain down the back of the leg, often caused by pressure from a slipped disc. [Middle English, from Medieval Latin *sciatica (passiō)*, "(suffering) in the hip", from Late Latin *sciaticus*, SCIATIC.]

sciatic nerve *n. Anatomy.* A sensory and motor nerve originating in the sacral plexus and running through the pelvis and down the leg.

sci·ence (sĭ-ənss) *n. Abbr.* **sci. 1.** Learning or study concerned with demonstrable truths or observable phenomena, and characterised by the systematic application of scientific method. **2.** Such learning or study concerned with the phenomena of the physical universe; any or all of the natural sciences: *the biological sciences.* **3.** Any branch of knowledge conducted according to scientific method: *forensic science.* **4.** Any methodological activity, discipline, or study. **5.** Any skill or technique that may be developed through systematic learning: *the science of drawing.* **6.** *Archaic.* Knowledge; especially, knowledge gained through experience. —**blind with science.** To confuse or overawe with a display of specialist knowledge. [Middle English, knowledge, learning, from Old French, from Latin *scientia*, from *sciēns* (stem *scient-*), present participle of *scīre*, to know.]

science fiction *n. Abbr.* **SF** A literary or cinematic genre in which fantasy, typically based on speculative scientific discoveries and developments, forms an element of plot or background; especially, imaginative work based on prediction of future scientific discoveries, environmental changes, space travel, and life on other planets. —**sci·ence-fic·tion** (sĭ-ənss-fíksh'n) *adj.*

sci·en·ter (sĭ-éntər) *adv. Law.* Deliberately or knowingly. [Latin, from *scīre*, to know.]

sci·en·tial (sĭ-énsh'l) *adj.* **1.** Of or producing knowledge or science. **2.** Having knowledge or skill.

sci·en·tif·ic (sĭ-ən-tiffik) *adj. Abbr.* **sci. 1.** Of, pertaining to, or used in science. **2.** Broadly, having or appearing to have an exact, objective, factual, systematic, or methodological basis. [Medieval Latin *scientificus*, "producing knowledge" : Latin *scientia*, knowledge, SCIENCE + -FIC.] —**sci·en·tif·i·cal·ly** *adv.*

scientific method *n.* The totality of principles and processes regarded as characteristic of or necessary for scientific investigation, generally taken to include rules for concept formation, conduct of observations and experiments, and validation of hypotheses by observations or experiments.

sci·en·tism (sĭ-ən-tiz'm) *n.* **1.** The theory that investigational methods used in the natural sciences should be applied in all fields of inquiry. **2.** The application of quasi-scientific techniques or justifications to unsuitable subjects or topics. —**sci·en·tis·tic** (-tístik) *adj.*

sci·en·tist (sĭ-əntist) *n.* **1.** A student of or expert in a science, especially one or more of the natural sciences. **2.** *Capital* S. A Christian Scientist.

sci·en·tol·o·gy (sĭ-ən-tóllǝji) *n. Often capital* **S.** The church and religious system founded by L. Ron Hubbard and based on his system of **dianetics** (*see*). [Latin *scientia*, knowledge, SCIENCE + -LOGY.] —**sci·en·tol·o·gist** *n.*

sci–fi (sĭ-fí) *n. Informal.* Science fiction.

scil·i·cet (sĭli-set, sílli-, skéeli-ket) *adv. Abbr.* **sc., scil., ss** That is to say; namely. Used when introducing an explanation of an obscure or ambiguous part of a text or when supplying a missing word. [Latin, short for *scīre licet*, "it is permitted to know", it is evident, of course, namely : *scīre*, to know + *licet*, third person singular present of *licēre*, to be allowed (see **leisure**).]

scil·la (sílla) *n.* Any bulbous plant of the genus *Scilla;* a **squill** (*see*). [New Latin, from Greek *skilla*, SQUILL.]

Scil·ly, Isles of (sílli). Also **Scil·lies** (sílliz). Archipelago in the northeast Atlantic, lying approximately 40 kilometres (25 miles) off the southwest tip of mainland England and forming part of the county of Cornwall. Five of the 140 islands are inhabited. Hugh Town, on St. Mary's, is the chief town and administrative centre.

scim·i·tar (símmi-tər, -taar) *n.* A curved Oriental sword with an edge on the convex side. [French *cimeterre*, from Italian *scimitarra*, from Persian *šimšīr†*.]

scin·tig·ra·phy (sin-tíggrəfi) *n.* A technique used in medical diagnosis, in which the distribution of a radioactive tracer in a part of the body is measured by a scintillation counter and recorded on a *scintigram*. See **scintiscan**. [SCINTI(LLATION) + -GRAPHY.]

scin·til·la (sin-tíllə) *n.* A minute amount; a trace. [Latin, spark.]

scin·til·late (sínti-layt) *v.* **-lated, -lating, -lates.** —*intr.* **1.** To throw off sparks; flash. **2.** To sparkle or shine. **3.** To be animated and witty. —*tr.* To give off (sparks or flashes). —See Synonyms at **flash.** [Latin *scintillāre*, from *scintilla*, spark.] —**scin·til·lant** *adj.* —**scin·til·lat·ing·ly** *adv.*

scin·til·la·tion (sínti-láysh'n) *n.* **1.** The action of scintillating. **2.** A spark; a flash. **3.** *Astronomy.* Rapid variation in the light of a celestial body caused by turbulence in the Earth's atmosphere; a twinkling. **4.** *Physics.* A flash of light produced in certain media by absorption of an ionising particle or photon.

scintillation counter *n.* A device for detecting and counting scintillations produced by ionising radiation.

scin·til·la·tor (sínti-laytər) *n. Physics.* A substance that scintillates when hit by high-energy particles or photons.

scin·ti·scan (sínti-skan) *n.* A diagram of the distribution of radiation produced when the body is scanned using the technique of scintigraphy. [SCINTI(GRAPHY) + SCAN.]

sci·o·lism (sĭ-ə-liz'm) *n.* A pretentious attitude of scholarship; superficial knowledgeability. [Late Latin *sciolus*, smatterer, diminutive of *scius*, knowing, from *scīre*, to know + -ISM.] —**sci·o·list** *n.* —**sci·o·lis·tic** (-lístik) *adj.*

sci·o·man·cy (sĭ-ə-man-si) *n.* Divination by the apparent consulting of ghosts. [Late Latin *sciomantia*, from Greek *skia*, shade, ghost + -MANCY.] —**sci·o·man·cer** *n.* —**sci·o·man·tic** (-mántik) *adj.*

sci·on (sĭ-ən) *n.* **1.** A descendant, heir, or young member of a family. **2.** A detached shoot or twig containing buds from a woody plant and used in grafting. [Middle English, from Old French *ciun, cion,* twia, sprout, from Germanic.]

Scip·i·o[1] (skíppi-ō || síppi-ō), full name Publius Cornelius Scipio Aemilianus Africanus Minor (*c.* 185–129 B.C.). Roman general. In the Third Punic War he was responsible for the final destruction of Carthage (146 B.C.).

Scipio[2], full name Publius Cornelius Scipio Africanus Major (234–183 B.C.). Roman general. In 204 he invaded North Africa, and ended the Second Punic War by defeating Hannibal in 202.

sci·re fa·ci·as (sír-i fáyshi-əss, -ass) *n. Law.* **1.** Formerly, a writ requiring the party against whom it is issued to appear and show cause why a judicial record should not be enforced, repealed, or annulled. **2.** A judicial proceeding under such a writ. [Latin *scīre facias*, "you are to cause (him) to know" (phrase commonly used in the writ) : *scīre*, to know + *facias*, second person singular present subjunctive of *facere*, to make, do.]

scirocco. Variant of **sirocco.**

scir·rhus (sírrəss, skírrəss) *n., pl.* **-rhi** (sírrī, skírrī) or **-rhuses.** A hard cancerous growth. [New Latin, from Greek *skirros, skiros†*, hard.] —**scir·rhous, scir·rhoid** (sírroyd, skírroyd) *adj.*

scis·sel (síss'l, skíss'l) *n.* The scrap metal left when discs are punched out of a sheet of metal. [French *cisaille*, "clippings", from *cisailler*, to clip.]

scis·sile (síssīl || *U.S. also* síss'l) *adj.* Capable of being cut or split easily. [French, from Latin *scissilis*, from *scindere* (past participle *scissus*), to cut. See **scission**.]

scis·sion (sízh'n, sísh'n) *n.* The act of cutting or severing; division; fission. [French, from Late Latin *scissiō* (stem *scissiōn-*), from Latin *scindere* (past participle *scissus*), to cut.]

scis·sor (sízzər) *tr.v.* **-sored, -soring, -sors.** To cut or clip with scissors or shears.

scis·sors (sízzərz) *n., pl.* **scissors.** 1. *Used with a plural verb.* A cutting implement consisting of two blades, each with a loop handle, joined by a swivel pin that allows the cutting edges to be opened and closed. Also called "pair of scissors". 2. *Used with a singular verb.* A movement in certain sports, as: **a.** In wrestling, a hold in which the legs are locked about the head or body of the opponent. **b.** A movement of the legs, as in swimming, jumping, or gymnastics, that suggests the opening and closing of scissors. [Middle English *sisoures*, from Old French *cisoires*, from Medieval Latin *cīsōria*, plural of Late Latin *cīsōrium*, cutting instrument, from Latin *caedere* (past participle *caesus*, in compounds *-cīsus*), to cut.]

scis·sor·tail (sízzər-tayl) *n.* A bird, *Muscivora forficata*, of the southwestern United States, Mexico, and Central and South America, with a long, forked tail. Also "scissor-tailed fly-catcher".

sci·u·rine (sī-yoor-īn, -in) *adj.* 1. Of pertaining to, or belonging to the rodent family Sciuridae, which includes the squirrels and marmots. 2. Resembling a squirrel. [Latin *sciūrus*, squirrel, from Greek *skiouros*, "shadow tail", squirrel, (*skia*, shadow + *oura*, tail) + -INE.] **—sci·u·rine** *n.*

sci·u·roid (sī-yoor-oyd, sī-yoor-oyd) *adj.* 1. Resembling or characteristic of a squirrel; sciurine. 2. *Botany.* Similar in shape to a squirrel's tail; bushy and curved. [Latin *sciūrus*, SQUIRREL + -OID.]

sclaff (sklaf) *v.* **sclaffed, sclaffing, sclaffs.** *—intr.* In golf, to scrape or strike the ground with the club behind the ball before hitting it. *—tr.* 1. To strike (the ground) with the club before hitting the ball. 2. To hit (a ball) in this way.
—n. A golf stroke made in this manner. [Scottish, to strike with a flat surface (imitative).] **—sclaff·er** *n.*

scle·ra (skleer-ə) *n.* Also **scle·rot·ic** (sklə-róttik, skleer-, skle-), **scle·rot·i·ca** (-ə). The tough, white, fibrous outer envelope of tissue covering all of the eyeball except the cornea. [New Latin, from Greek *sklēros*, hard.] **—scle·ral** (skleer-əl) *adj.*

scle·re·id (skleer-i-id) *n.* Any of various cells (except fibres) that make up sclerenchyma. [Greek *sklēros*, hard.]

scle·ren·chy·ma (skleer-éng-kimə, sklə-réng-) *n.* Supportive or protective plant tissue consisting of thick-walled, usually lignified cells. [New Latin : SCLER(O)- + -ENCHYMA.] **—scle·ren·chym·a·tous** (skleer-eng-kímmətəss) *adj.*

scle·rite (skleer-īt) *n.* Any of the hard outer plates forming part of the exoskeleton of an arthropod, especially an insect. [SCLER(O)- + -ITE.] **—scle·rit·ic** (sklə-ríttik, skleer-, skle-) *adj.*

scle·ri·tis (skleer-ítiss, sklə-rítiss) *n.* Also **scle·ro·ti·tis** (skleer-ō-títiss). Inflammation of the sclera. [New Latin : SCLER(O)- + -ITIS.]

sclero-, scler- *comb. form.* Indicates: 1. Hardness; for example, **scleroderma, sclerite.** 2. Of or affecting the sclera; for example, **sclerotomy, scleritis.** [New Latin, from Greek *sklēros*, hard.]

scle·ro·der·ma (skleer-ō-dérmə) *n.* Pathological thickening and hardening of the skin or other connective tissue. [New Latin : SCLERO- + -DERMA.]

scle·ro·der·ma·tous (skleer-ō-dérmətəss) *adj.* 1. Characterising or afflicted with scleroderma. 2. *Zoology.* Having an outer covering of hard plates or bony scales.

scle·roid (skleer-oyd) *adj. Biology.* Hard or hardened; indurated. [SCLER(O)- + -OID.]

scle·ro·ma (skleer-rōmə, sklə-) *n., pl.* **-mata** (-mətə). An abnormally hard patch of skin or mucous membrane. [New Latin, from Greek *sklērōma*, hardening, from *sklēroun*, to harden, from *sklēros*, hard.]

scle·rom·e·ter (skleer-rómmitər, sklə-) *n.* An instrument used to determine relative hardness of solids, especially minerals and metals, by measurement of the pressure required on a standard diamond stylus to achieve penetration. [SCLERO- + -METER.]

scle·ro·phyll (sklérrə-fil) *n.* Any woody plant with leathery, evergreen leaves that are specialised to reduce water loss. [SCLERO- + -PHYLL.]

scle·ro·pro·tein (skleer-ō-prō-teen, -tee-in) *n.* Any of a large class of proteins, such as keratin, elastin, and collagen, found in skeletal and connective tissue. Also called "albuminoid".

scle·rosed (skleer-ōst, -ōzd) *adj.* 1. Affected with sclerosis; hardened. 2. Lignified. [From SCLEROSIS.]

scle·ro·sis (skleer-rō-siss, sklə-, skle-) *n., pl.* **-ses** (-seez). 1. **a.** *Pathology.* A thickening or hardening of a body part, as of an artery or the spinal cord, especially from tissue overgrowth or disease. **b.** A disease characterised by sclerosis. See **arteriosclerosis, atherosclerosis, multiple sclerosis.** 2. *Botany.* The hardening of an outer cell wall by formation or deposit of lignin. [Middle English *sclirosis*, from Medieval Latin *sclīrōsis*, from Greek *sklērōsis*, hardening, from *sklēroun*, to harden, from *sklēros*, hard.] **—scle·ro·sal** (-róss'l) *adj.*

scle·rot·ic (skleer-róttik, sklə-, skle-) *adj.* 1. Affected or characterised by sclerosis. 2. *Anatomy.* Of or pertaining to the sclera.
—n. Variant of **sclera.** [New Latin *scleroticus*, from SCLEROSIS and SCLERA.]

sclerotica. Variant of **sclera.**

sclerotitis. Variant of **scleritis.**

scle·ro·ti·um (skleer-rō-shi-əm, sklə-) *n., pl.* **-tia** (-shi-ə). A dense mass of branching filaments, or hyphae, in certain fungi, containing stored food and capable of remaining dormant for long periods. [New Latin, from Greek *sklērotēs*, hardness, from *sklēros*, hard.] **—scle·ro·ti·al** *adj.*

scle·rot·o·my (skleer-róttə-mi, sklə, skle-) *n., pl.* **-mies.** Surgical incision into the sclera. [SCLERO- + -TOMY.]

scle·rous (skleer-əss) *adj.* Hardened; toughened; bony. [Greek *sklēros*, hard.]

S.C.M. 1. State Certified Midwife (in Britain). 2. Student Christian Movement.

scoff¹ (skof ‖ skawf) *intr.v.* **scoffed, scoffing, scoffs.** To jeer or mock; speak derisively. Often used with *at.*
—n. An expression of derision or scorn; a jeer. [Middle English *scoffen*, from *scof*, mockery, probably from Scandinavian, akin to Danish *skof*, jest.] **—scoff·er** *n.* **—scoff·ing·ly** *adv.*

scoff² *v.* **scoffed, scoffing, scoffs.** *British Informal.* *—tr.* To eat (food) quickly and greedily *—intr.* To eat greedily.
—n. British Informal. 1. A meal. 2. Food. [Variant of dialect *scaff*, associated with Afrikaans *schoff*, Dutch *schoft*, a quarter of a day, hence, a meal.]

Sco·field (skó-feeld), **(David) Paul** (1922–). British actor. A member of the National Theatre, and sometime associate director (1970–72), he has played many Shakespearean roles. His performance as Sir Thomas More in the film version of *A Man For All Seasons* (1966) won him an Academy Award. Recent stage performances include *Heartbreak House* (1992) and *John Gabriel Borkman* (1996).

scold (skōld) *v.* **scolded, scolding, scolds.** *—tr.* To reprimand harshly or noisily. *—intr.* To find fault angrily or persistently.
—n. A person, especially a woman, who persistently nags or criticises. [Middle English *scalden, scolden*, from *scald, scold*, ribald or abusive person, perhaps from Old Norse *skáld*, poet.] **—scold·er** *n.* **—scold·ing·ly** *adv.*
Synonyms: *scold, upbraid, berate, revile, nag.*

scold·ing (skōlding) *n.* A sharp or rude reprimand.

scol·e·cite (skólli-sīt, skóli-) *n.* A white zeolite mineral, Ca Al$_2$ Si$_3$ O$_{10}$ .3H$_2$ O, consisting of monoclinic crystals. [Greek *skōlēx* (stem *skōlek-*), worm (from its appearance).]

sco·lex (skó-leks) *n., pl.* **-leces** or **-lices** (-li-seez). The knoblike anterior end of a tapeworm, having suckers or hooklike parts that serve as organs of attachment to the host. [New Latin, from Greek *skōlēx*, worm, grub.]

sco·li·o·sis (skólli-ō-siss ‖ skóli-) *n.* Also **sco·li·o·ma** (-ōmə). Abnormal lateral curvature of the spine. [New Latin, from Greek *skiliōsis*, crookedness, from *skolios*, crooked.] **—sco·li·ot·ic** (-óttik) *adj.*

scollop. Variant of **scallop.**

scol·o·pen·drid (skólla-pén-drid) *n.* Any of various centipedes of the family Scolopendridae, which includes some large, poisonous, tropical species. [New Latin *Scolopendridae*, from Latin *scolopendra*, millipede, from Greek *skolopendra*†.] **—scol·o·pen·drid, scol·o·pen·drine** (-drīn, -drin) *adj.*

scom·broid (skóm-broyd) *adj.* Of or belonging to the suborder Scombroidei, which includes marine fishes such as the mackerel.
—n. A scombroid fish. [New Latin *Scombroidei*, from Latin *scomber*, mackerel, from Greek *skombros*†.]

sconce¹ (skonss) *n.* A small earthwork or fort for defence. [Dutch *schans*, from Middle High German *Schanze*, fortification originally made of latticework, from Italian *scanso*, defence, from *scansare*, to turn off, ward off, from Vulgar Latin *excampsāre* (unattested) : Latin *ex-*, out + *campsāre*, to turn around, sail by, from Greek *kamptein* (aorist stem *kamps-*), to bend, curve, turn.]

sconce² *n.* 1. A decorative wall bracket for candles or lights. 2. A flattened candlestick that has a handle. [Middle English, from Old French *esconse*, lantern, hiding place, from Medieval Latin *(a)sconsa*, from Latin *absconsus*, past participle of *abscondere*, to hide away : *(abs*), away + *condere*, to hide.]

sconce³ *n. Archaic.* 1. The head or skull. 2. Sense or wit. [Jocular use of SCONCE (wall bracket).]

sconce⁴ *tr.v.* **sconced, sconcing, sconces.** At Oxford and Cambridge Universities, to challenge (a fellow student) to drink a large amount of beer for having committed an offence against table etiquette. 2. Broadly, to subject to exaction or extortion.
—n. An act or instance of sconcing. [Perhaps from SCONCE (head), jocular reference to a head tax.]

scone (skon, skōn) *n.* 1. A round, soft, plain, doughy cake made with very little fat. 2. See **drop scone.** [Short for Dutch *schoonbrood*, fine white bread, from Middle Dutch *schoonbroot*, from *schoon*, beautiful, bright, white + *broot*, bread.]

Scone (skōn). Village in Perthshire and Kinross, central Scotland. Pictish and Scottish kings were crowned in Old Scone until 1651. Early kings sat on the Stone of Scone (or Stone of Destiny), but this was captured by the English (1296), and is now incorporated in the coronation chair in Westminster Abbey, London.

scoop (skōop) *n.* 1. A shovel-like utensil, usually having a deep, curved dish and short handle, used for taking up and transferring loose material such as grain or sugar. 2. A long-handled utensil with a round bowl, especially one for liquids; a ladle. 3. An implement for bailing water from a boat. 4. A narrow, spoon-shaped instrument for surgical extraction in cavities or cysts. 5. **a.** A thick-handled kitchen utensil for dispensing balls of ice cream, mashed potatoes, or the like, usually having a sweeping band in the dish which is levered by the thumb to free the contents. **b.** A portion gathered in such a scoop. 6. The bucket or shovel of a steam shovel or dredge. 7. A scooping movement or action; a sweep. 8. A wide hole or bowl-shaped cavity. 9. *Informal.* A large, sudden profit, especially one gained through speculation. 10. *Informal.* A usually sensational story acquired by luck or initiative and reported by a paper in advance of its competitors.

~*tr.v.* **scooped, scooping, scoops.** **1.** To take up or dip into with or as if with a scoop; spoon. **2.** To hollow out or excavate; form by digging. Used with *out.* **3.** To gather or collect swiftly and unceremoniously; grab. Used with *up.* **4.** *Informal.* To forestall or outmanoeuvre (a competitor), especially in acquiring and publishing an important news story. **5.** To make (a large profit) suddenly or by luck. **6.** In hockey, golf, or the like, to hit (the ball) from underneath so that it rises steeply. [Middle English, from Middle Low German and Middle Dutch *schōpe.*] **—scoop·er** *n.*

scoot (skōōt) *intr.v.* **scooted, scooting, scoots.** To go speedily; dart or scurry off; hurry.

~*n.* A darting or scurrying off; a hurried departure. [19th century (U.S.) : earlier *scout,* origin obscure.]

scoot·er (skōōtər) *n.* **1.** A child's vehicle consisting of a long footboard between two small end wheels, the front wheel being controlled by an upright steering handle. **2.** A **motor scooter** *(see).* [From SCOOT.]

scop (skop) *n.* A bard or minstrel of Anglo-Saxon England. [Middle English *scop(e),* Old English *scop,* from Germanic.]

scope (skōp) *n.* **1.** Range of perceptions or mental activity. **2.** Breadth or opportunity to function or extend; outlet. **3. a.** The area covered by a given activity or subject. **b.** Agreed or stipulated limits of application or treatment. **4.** The length or sweep of a mooring cable. **5.** *Informal.* A microscope, periscope, telescope, or the like. [Originally "something aimed at", "purpose", from Italian *scopo,* from Greek *skopos,* watcher, goal, aim.]

-scope *n. comb. form.* Indicates an instrument for observing or detecting; for example, **oscilloscope, telescope, microscope.** [Latin *-scopium,* from Greek *-skopion,* from *skopein,* to see.]

sco·pol·a·mine (skə-póllə-meen, -min || skō-, skṓpə-lámmin) *n.* A thick, syrupy, colourless alkaloid, $C_{17}H_{21}NO_4$, extracted from such plants as henbane and used as a mydriatic, smooth-muscle relaxant, sedative, and truth serum. Also called "hyoscine". [German *Scopolamin* : New Latin *Scopolia,* genus of plants from which the alkaloid is extracted, named after Giovanni *Scopoli* (1723–88), Italian naturalist + -AMINE.]

sco·po·phil·i·a (skṓpə-fílli-ə) *n.* Also **scop·to·phil·i·a** (skóptə-). The derivation of sexual pleasure from viewing sexual organs or erotic scenes; voyeurism. [New Latin : Greek *skopein,* to see + -PHILIA.]

scop·u·la (skóppew-lə) *n., pl.* **-lae** (-lee). A dense, brushlike tuft of hairs, as on the legs of certain spiders. [Late Latin *scōpula,* diminutive of Latin *scopa*†, twigs, broom.] **—scop·u·late** (-layt) *adj.*

-scopy *n. comb. form.* Indicates viewing, examining, or observing; for example, **microscopy, telescopy.** [Greek *-skopia,* from *skopein,* to look into, behold.]

scor·bu·tic (skawr-béwtik) *adj.* Related to, resembling, or suffering from scurvy. [New Latin *scorbuticus,* from Late Latin *scorbūtus,* scurvy, from Russian *skrobota,* "scratch", from *skrest',* to scratch, scrape.] **—scor·bu·ti·cal·ly** *adv.*

scorch (skorch) *v.* **scorched, scorching, scorches.** *—tr.* **1.** To burn slightly so as to alter the colour or taste. **2.** To wither or parch with intense heat; char. **3.** To subject to severe censure or anger; excoriate. *—intr.* **1.** To become scorched or singed. **2.** *British Informal.* To move at a very fast pace. —See Synonyms at **burn.**

~*n.* **1.** A slight or surface burn. **2.** A discoloration caused by heat. Also used adjectivally: *a scorch mark.* **3.** Brown spotting on plant leaves caused especially by fungi, heat, or lack of water. [Middle English *scorchen, scorcnen,* perhaps from Old Norse *skorpna,* to shrivel.] **—scorch·ing·ly** *adv.*

scorched-earth policy (skórcht-érth) *n.* A military policy of devastating all land and buildings in the course of an advance or retreat, so as to leave nothing of use to the enemy.

scorch·er (skórchər) *n.* **1.** One that scorches. **2.** *Informal.* An extremely hot day. **3.** *British Informal.* Something that is outstanding or remarkable, especially in terms of speed, excitement, or severity.

scorch·ing (skórching) *adj. Informal.* **1.** Very hot. Said of the weather. **2.** Biting; scathing: *scorching criticism.*

~*adv. Informal.* Used as an intensive: *scorching hot.* **—scorch·ing·ly** *adv.*

score (skor || skōr) *n., pl.* **scores** or (for sense 7) **score. 1.** A notch or incision, made by or as if by a sharp instrument. **2.** An evaluative record, usually numerical, of any competitive event: *keeping score.* **3. a.** The total number of points, goals, or the like made by each competitor or side in a contest, either finally or at a given stage. **b.** The number of points, goals, or the like attributed to any one competitor or team. **c.** The act of scoring a point, goal, or the like. **4.** *Chiefly U.S.* A result, usually expressed numerically, of a test or examination. **5. a.** An amount due, as on a customer's account. **b.** A harboured grievance; a grudge: *I have a score to settle with him.* **6.** A ground; a reason: *I've no grudge against her on that score.* **7.** A group of 20 items. Sometimes used in combination: *threescore years and ten.* **8.** *Plural.* A large number. **9.** The written form of a musical composition for orchestral or vocal parts, either complete or for a particular instrument or voice. **10.** The music composed for a musical or film. **—know the score.** *Informal.* To be aware of the true facts of a situation.

~*v.* **scored, scoring, scores.** *—tr.* **1. a.** To mark with lines, notches, or incisions. **b.** To make (lines, notches, or incisions) on a surface. **2.** To cancel or eliminate by or as if by superimposing lines. Used with *out.* **3.** In cooking, to mark the surface of (meat, for example) with cuts that are usually parallel. **4. a.** To gain (a point or points) in a game or contest: *scored a goal in the last minute.* **b.** To achieve or win in total: *had scored 300 by close of play.* **5. a.** To award (a certain number of points) in a competition: *The judge scored 19 to the English skaters.* **b.** To award a number of points to: *scored him 19.* **6.** To count as or be worth: *A try scores four points.* **7.** To keep a record of (a debt or offence, for example). Used with *against* or *to.* **8.** To achieve or gain (a success or advantage, for example). **9.** *U.S.* To evaluate and assign a mark to. **10.** *Music.* **a.** To orchestrate or arrange (music) for a particular instrument or voice. **b.** To compose music for (a film, for example). **11.** *U.S.* To criticise cuttingly; berate. **12.** *Slang.* To be successful in obtaining (something, especially an illicit drug): *score heroin.* *—intr.* **1.** To gain points in a game or contest. **2.** To keep the score of a game or contest. **3.** To achieve a purpose or advantage, often at another's expense. **4.** To succeed in obtaining illicit drugs. **5.** *Slang.* To seduce a woman. Used of a man. [Middle English *scor,* Old English *scoru* (attested only in plural *scora*), twenty, from Old Norse *skor,* notch, twenty.] **—score·less** *adj.*

score·board (skór-bawrd || skṓr-bōrd) *n.* A large board, used especially in sports, that records and displays a score.

score·card (skór-kaard || skṓr-) *n.* **1.** A printed card enabling a spectator to identify players and record the progress of a game. **2.** A small card used by an individual player, as in golf, to record his own performance.

score draw *n.* A soccer match in which each side has scored the same number of goals, distinguished from a goalless draw and scoring more points on a football-pools coupon.

scor·er (skáwrər || skṓrər) *n.* **1.** One who keeps score in a game. **2.** A player who scores a point, goal, or the like.

sco·ri·a (skáwri-ə || skṓri-ə) *n., pl.* **-riae** (-ee). **1.** *Geology.* Rough fragments of burnt, basic lava, darker and more cindery than pumice. Also called "cinders", "slag". **2.** *Metallurgy.* The refuse of a smelted metal or ore; slag. [Middle English, slag, dross, from Latin *scōria,* from Greek *skōria,* from *skōr,* excrement.] **—sco·ri·a·ceous** (-áyshəss) *adj.*

sco·ri·fy (skáwri-fī || skṓri-) *tr.v.* **-fied, -fying, -fies.** To separate (an ore) into scoria and a precious metal. [SCORI(A) + -FY.] **—sco·ri·fi·ca·tion** (-fi-káysh'n) *n.* **—sco·ri·fi·er** *n.*

scorn (skorn) *n.* **1.** Contempt or disdain, as felt towards a person or thing considered despicable or inferior. **2.** An object of scorn or contempt. **3.** *Archaic.* An expression of scorn; a taunt.

~*v.* **scorned, scorning, scorns.** *—tr.* **1.** To consider or treat as contemptible or unworthy. **2.** To reject with derision. *—intr. Archaic.* To express contempt. [Middle English *scornen, schornen,* to despise, from Old French *escharnir,* from Vulgar Latin *escarnīre* (unattested), from Germanic *skarnjan* (unattested).] **—scorn·er** *n.* **—scorn·ful** *adj.* **—scorn·ful·ly** *adv.* **—scorn·ful·ness** *n.*

scor·pae·noid (skawr-péenoyd) *adj.* Of or belonging to the suborder Scorpaenoidei, which includes the scorpion fishes and gurnards.

~*n.* A scorpaenoid fish. [New Latin *Scorpaenoidei* : *Scorpaena* (genus), from Latin, a fish, from Greek *skorpaina,* feminine of *skorpios,* a sea fish, SCORPION + *-oidei,* plural of Latin *-oidēs,* -OID (likeness).]

Scor·pi·o (skórpi-ō) *n.* **1.** The eighth sign of the **zodiac** *(see).* Also called the "Scorpion". **2.** One born under this sign. **3.** Variant of **Scorpius.** [Latin, scorpion.]

scor·pi·oid (skórpi-oyd) *adj.* **1.** Pertaining to or resembling a scorpion. **2.** *Botany.* Curved or curled like the tail of a scorpion: *a scorpioid inflorescence.* [Greek *skorpioeidēs,* scorpion-like : *skorpios,* SCORPION + -OID.]

scor·pi·on (skórpi-ən) *n.* **1.** Any of various arachnids of the order Scorpionida, of warm, dry regions, having a segmented body and an erectile tail tipped with a venomous sting. **2.** Any of various similar arachnids, such as the **whip scorpion** *(see).* **3.** *Capital* **S. a.** The constellation Scorpius. **b.** A sign of the zodiac, Scorpio. **4.** A type of whip usually thought to have been armed with knotted cords or steel spikes. I Kings 12:11. [Middle English *scorpioun,* from Old French *scorpion,* from Latin *scorpiō* (stem *scorpiōn-*), from Greek *skorpios*†.]

scorpion fish *n.* Any of numerous small, often brilliantly coloured marine fishes of the family Scorpaenidae, having poisonous spines in the dorsal fin in most species.

scorpion fly *n.* Any insect of the order Mecoptera, having in the male of most species a curved genital structure that resembles the sting of a scorpion.

scorpion grass *n.* The **forget-me-not** *(see).*

Scor·pi·us (skórpi-əss) *n.* Also **Scor·pi·o** (-ō), **Scor·pi·on** (-ən). A constellation in the Southern Hemisphere near Libra and Sagittarius. It contains the star Antares. Also called "Scorpion". [New Latin, from Latin *scorpius, scorpiō,* SCORPION.]

scor·zo·ner·a (skórzə-néer-ə) *n.* Any of several Eurasian plants of the genus *Scorzonera,* similar and related to the salsify; especially, the Mediterranean species *S. hispanica,* the roots of which are eaten as a vegetable. [Italian, from *scorzone,* a poisonous snake, alteration of Medieval Latin *curtio*† (stem *curtiōn-*), poisonous snake; the plant was perhaps used as an antidote.]

Scot (skot) *n.* **1.** A native or inhabitant of Scotland. **2.** A member of the ancient Gaelic tribe that migrated to the northern part of Britain from Ireland in about the sixth century A.D. [Middle English, from Old English (attested in plural, *Scottas*), from Late Latin *Scottus*†.]

Scot. Scotch; Scotland; Scottish.

scot and lot (skot) *n.* A municipal tax formerly levied in Great Britain on the members of a community proportionate to their ability to pay. **—pay scot and lot.** To pay in full; settle all obligations.

[Middle English *scot*, tax, contribution, partly from Old Norse *skot* and partly from Old French *escot*, from Frankish *skot* (unattested).]

scotch¹ (skoch) *tr.v.* **scotched, scotching, scotches.** 1. To put an abrupt and decisive end to; crush; stifle: *scotch a rumour.* 2. *Archaic.* To cut or score; scratch. 3. *Archaic.* To injure so as to render harmless; cripple.
~*n.* 1. A surface cut or abrasion; a gash or scratch. 2. A line drawn on the ground, such as one used in playing hopscotch. [Middle English *scocchen*, from Anglo-French *escocher*, to cut a notch : *es*-, from Latin *ex*- (intensifier) + Old French *coche*, notch, from Vulgar Latin *cocca†* (unattested).]

scotch² *tr.v.* **scotched, scotching, scotches.** To hold (a wheel or log, for example) with a wedge to prevent rolling or slipping.
~*n.* A block or wedge used as a prop behind or under a wheel or other object likely to roll. [Perhaps variant of *scatch*, stilt, from Old French *escache*, "wooden leg", from Frankish *skakkja* (unattested), from *skakan* (unattested), to run fast, from Germanic *skakan* (unattested), to SHAKE.]

Scotch (skoch) *n. Abbr.* **Sc., Scot.** 1. *Used with a plural verb.* The people of Scotland; the Scots. Preceded by *the.* 2. Their language; Scots. 3. Scotch whisky. [Contraction of SCOTTISH.] —**Scotch** *adj.*
   Usage: The people of Scotland are variously referred to as *Scotsmen* and *Scotswomen*, with *Scots* being used as a more informal and neutral term. *Scotchman/woman* are forms sometimes heard outside of Scotland, but many people find them mildly offensive. *The Scottish* is a generally acceptable collective term. Of the corresponding adjectives, *Scotch*, though fairly common, is now used chiefly of products originating in or associated with Scotland (*Scotch whisky, Scotch broth, Scotch wool). Scottish* is used most frequently when the sense of "located in or pertaining to Scotland" is referred to *(Scottish universities, Scottish newspapers)*; and *Scots* is most commonly used of people.

Scotch broth *n.* A nourishing soup made from vegetables, pearl barley, and stock.

Scotch catch *n. Music.* A short note on the beat followed by a longer one, found, for example, in Scottish dance music. Also called "Scotch snap".

Scotch egg *n.* A cold snack or savoury consisting of a hard-boiled egg wrapped in sausage meat that is coated with breadcrumbs and deep-fried.

Scotch·man (skóch-mən) *n., pl.* **-men** (-mən). A male Scot.

Scotch mist *n.* 1. A dense, wet mist. 2. A *mizzle* (see).

Scotch pancake *n.* A drop scone *(see).*

Scotch tape *n. U.S.* A trademark for a cellulose adhesive tape of a type similar to **Sellotape** *(see).*

Scotch terrier *n.* A **Scottish terrier** *(see).*

Scotch whisky *n.* Whisky distilled in Scotland from malted barley, and often blended with grain spirit.

Scotch·wom·an (skóch-wŏomən) *n. pl.* **-women** (-wimmin). A female Scot.

Scotch woodcock *n.* A savory dish consisting of scrambled eggs on toast with anchovies or anchovy paste. [By humorous analogy with WELSH RABBIT.]

sco·ter (skōtər) *n.* Any of several dark-coloured marine diving ducks of the genera *Oidemia* and *Melanitta*, of northern coastal areas. [Perhaps related to Old Norse *skoti*, shooter, and *skjóta*, to shoot (from its swiftness).]

scot-free (skót-frée) *adv.* 1. Without having to pay; free from obligation. 2. Without incurring any penalty; unpunished. [Middle English *scot*, tax. See scot and lot.] —**scot-free** *adj.*

sco·tia (skōshə) *n.* A hollow concave moulding at or near the base of a column. [Latin, from Greek *skotia*, from *skotos*, darkness (referring to the shadow produced by the cavity).]

Sco·tia (skōshə) *n. Poetic.* Scotland. [Medieval Latin, from Late Latin *Scottus*, Scotsman, Irishman. See **Scot**.]

Sco·tism (skót-iz'm) *n.* The scholastic philosophy of John **Duns Scotus** *(see).* —**Sco·tist** *n.*

Scot·land (skótlənd). Country in northwest Europe. It is part of the United Kingdom and occupies the northern part of the island of Great Britain. The population is concentrated in the heavily industrialised Central Lowlands, which occupy the valleys of the Clyde and Forth between the Southern Uplands and the Highlands of the north. The Scots themselves were immigrants from Ireland, who together with the native Picts and with immigrants from Scandinavia formed a kingdom by the ninth century. Frequent wars with England ended when the two crowns were united (1603) under James I of England (James VI of Scotland). In a referendum (1997) the Scots approved devolution : a Scottish parliament with some tax-varying powers. Tourism is a major industry and the discovery of North Sea oil brought new prosperity to some parts of the country. Area, 78 749 square kilometres (30,405 square miles). Capital, Edinburgh.

Scotland Yard *n.* 1. The headquarters of the London Metropolitan Police, formerly housed at New Scotland Yard on the Thames embankment, now at Broadway, Victoria. 2. The London Metropolitan Police, especially the Criminal Investigation Department (C.I.D.). Also officially called "New Scotland Yard" and informally the "Yard".

sco·to·ma (sko-tŏmə, skə-) *n., pl.* **-mas.** An area of pathologically diminished vision within the visual field. [New Latin, from Medieval Latin, dim sight, from Greek *skotōma*, dizziness, vertigo, from *skotoun*, to darken, from *skotos*, darkness.]

sco·to·pi·a (sko-tŏpi-ə, skə-, skō-) *n.* The ability of the eyes to adapt to dim light. [New Latin : Greek *skotos*, darkness (see **scotoma**) + -OPIA.] —**sco·to·pic** (-tŏpik, -tŏppik) *adj.*

Scots (skots) *adj. Abbr.* **Sc.** Scottish. See Usage note at **Scotch.**
~*n.* Any of the dialects of English spoken in Scotland.

Scots·man (skóts-mən) *n., pl.* **-men** (-mən). A male Scot.

Scots pine *n.* 1. A Eurasian pine tree, *Pinus sylvestris,* having prickly cones and needle-like leaves, and valued for its timber. 2. The wood of this tree.

Scots·wom·an (skóts-wŏomən) *n., pl.* **-women** (wimmin). A female Scot.

Scott (skot), **Sir (George) Gilbert** (1811 – 78). British architect. He was a leading figure of the Gothic Revival. Among the public buildings he designed are the Foreign Offices at Whitehall (1861), the Albert Memorial (1864), and St. Pancras station (1865).

Scott, Sir Robert Falcon (1868 – 1912). British Antarctic explorer. On his second expedition to Antarctica (1910 – 12) he attempted to be the first to reach the South Pole, but discovered that Amundsen had beaten him to it by a month. On the return journey, he and his four companions died of exposure. He was knighted posthumously.

Scott, Sir Walter (1771–1832). Scottish novelist and poet. His romantic ballads did much to popularise the history and folklore of Scotland, especially of the Borders. His historical novels, beginning with *Waverley* (1814), influenced the development of the form.

Scot·ti·cism (skótti-siz'm) *n.* An idiom or other expression characteristic of Scottish English.

Scot·tie, Scot·ty (skótti) *n., pl.* **-ties.** 1. *Informal.* A Scotsman. 2. A Scottish terrier.

Scot·tish (skóttish) *adj. Abbr.* **Sc., Scot.** Of, pertaining to, or characteristic of Scotland, its people, or its dialects. See Usage note at **Scotch.**
~*n.* 1. Any of the dialects of English spoken in Scotland. 2. *Used with a plural verb.* The people of Scotland. Preceded by *the.*

Scottish Certificate of Education *n. Abbr.* **S.C.E.** An examination in Scotland, equivalent in level to the English G.C.E.

Scottish Gaelic *n.* The Gaelic language of the Scottish Highlanders. Also called "Erse".

Scottish terrier *n.* A terrier of a breed originating in Scotland, having a heavy-set body, short legs, blunt muzzle, and a dark, wiry coat. Also called "Scotch terrier", and formerly "Aberdeen terrier".

scoun·drel (skówn-drəl) ‖ *West Indies also* skúng-) *n.* A villain; a rogue. [16th century : origin obscure.] —**scoun·drel·ly** *adj.*

scour¹ (skowr) *v.* **scoured, scouring, scours.** —*tr.* 1. a. To clean, polish, or wash by scrubbing vigorously, usually with an abrasive. b. To remove by scrubbing. 2. To remove dirt or grease from (cloth or fibres) by means of a detergent. 3. *Archaic.* To clear (an area) of someone or something undesirable. 4. To clear (a channel or pipe) by removing obstructions or flushing with water. 5. To cause (livestock) to purge their bowels. 6. *Geology.* To erode by the action of a strong current. —*intr.* 1. To scrub something in order to clean or polish it. 2. To have diarrhoea. Used of livestock.
~*n.* 1. A scouring action or effect. 2. A place that has been scoured, as by flushing with water. 3. A cleansing agent for wool or other cloth or fibres. 4. *Usually plural.* Diarrhoea in livestock. [Middle English *scouren*, from Middle Dutch *scūren*, from Old French *escurer*, from Late Latin *excūrāre*, to clean out : Latin *ex*-, out + Late Latin *cūrāre*, to clean, from Latin, to take care of, from *cūra*, care, cure.] —**scour·er** *n.*

scour² *v.* **scoured, scouring, scours.** —*tr.* 1. To range over (an area) quickly and energetically. 2. To search through or over thoroughly. —*intr.* 1. To range over or about an area, especially in a search. 2. To move swiftly; scurry; run. [Middle English *scouren*, perhaps from Old Norse *skȳra*, to rush in.]

scourge (skurj) *n.* 1. A whip used to inflict punishment. 2. Any means of inflicting severe suffering, vengeance, or punishment. 3. A cause of widespread affliction, as pestilence or war might be.
~*tr.v.* **scourged, scourging, scourges.** 1. To flog. 2. To chastise severely; excoriate. 3. To afflict with severe or widespread suffering; devastate. [Middle English, from Old French *escorge*, from *escorgier*, to whip, from Vulgar Latin *excorrigiāre* (unattested) : Latin *ex*- (intensive) + *corrigia*, thong, shoelace, "whip", from Celtic.] —**scourg·er** *n.*

scour·ing rush (skówr-ing) *n.* Any of several species of horsetail; especially, *Equisetum hyemale,* having rough-ridged stems formerly used for scouring utensils.

scour·ings (skówr-ingz) *pl.n.* 1. Refuse matter removed by scouring. 2. Dregs; scum.

scouse (skowss) *n.* Also **scous·er** (-ər) (for sense 1). *British Informal.* 1. A native of Liverpool. 2. *Often capital* **S.** The dialect of English spoken in Liverpool. [Shortened from LOBSCOUSE (dish particularly associated with Liverpool).] —**scouse** *adj.*

scout¹ (skowt) *n.* 1. a. A person, aircraft, or ship dispatched from a main body to gather information, as about the terrain or enemy ahead. b. The action so performed; a reconnoitring. 2. A person employed to discover and recruit persons with talent, as in sports or entertainment: *a talent scout.* 3. *Usually capital* **S.** A member of the Scout Association. 4. *British.* A person employed by a college, especially one at Oxford University, to clean students' rooms. Compare **bedder.** 5. A companion; a fellow: *He's a good scout.*
~*v.* **scouted, scouting, scouts.** —*tr.* To observe or explore carefully in order to obtain information. —*intr.* 1. To act as a scout, especially as a scout for talent. 2. To search or look. Often used with *about* or *around.* [Middle English *scoute*, from Old French

escoute, "listener", spy, from *escouter,* to listen, from Vulgar Latin *ascultāre* (unattested), variant of Latin *auscultāre.*] —**scout·er** *n.*

scout² *v.* **scouted, scouting, scouts.** —*tr.* To reject contemptuously; dismiss with disdain or derision. —*intr.* To scoff. Used with *at.* [Probably from Scandinavian; akin to Old Norse *skúta, skúti,* mockery, taunt.]

Scout Association *n.* A worldwide organisation of young men and boys, founded in England in 1908, for developing character, practical skills, and self-reliance.

scout car *n. Military.* A fast, armoured reconnaissance vehicle.

scout·ing (skówting) *n.* The activities of the Scout Association.

scout·mas·ter (skówt-maastər ‖ -mastər) *n.* The adult leader in charge of a troop in the Scout Association.

scow (skow) *n. Chiefly U.S.* A large flat-bottomed boat with square ends, used chiefly for transporting cargo. [Dutch *schouw,* ferryboat, from Middle Dutch *scoude, scouwe,* akin to Old Saxon *skaldan†,* to push a boat from the shore.]

scowl (skowl) *n.* A look of anger, sullenness, or strong disapproval. ~*intr.v.* **scowled, scowling, scowls.** To lower or contract the brows in an expression of anger, disapproval, or bitterness; frown angrily. [Middle English *scoulen,* probably from Scandinavian; akin to Danish *skule†,* to scowl.] —**scowl·er** *n.* —**scowl·ing·ly** *adv.*

SCP single-cell protein.

SCR silicon-controlled rectifier.

scr. scruple (unit of weight).

S.C.R. Senior Common Room.

scrab·ble (skrább'l) *v.* **-bled, -bling, -bles.** —*intr.* **1.** To scrape or grope about frenetically with or as if with the hands or claws. Often used with *about* or *around.* **2.** To struggle, especially in a frantic or confused manner. **3.** To make hasty, disordered markings; scribble. —*tr.* **1.** To make or obtain by scraping or scratching. **2.** To scribble on. **3.** To make scrabbling movements on or with. ~*n.* **1.** The act or an instance of scrabbling. **2.** A scribble; a doodle. **3.** A confused fight or struggle. [Middle Dutch *schrabbelen,* frequentative of *schrabben,* to scrape.]

Scrab·ble (skrább'l) *n.* A trademark for a board game in which players build words with small lettered blocks.

scrag (skrag) *n.* **1.** A bony or scrawny person or animal. **2.** A piece of inferior bony meat, especially from a neck of lamb. **3.** *Informal.* The human neck. ~*tr.v.* **scragged, scragging, scrags.** *Informal.* **1.** To wring the neck of; kill by strangling. **2.** To seize and manhandle roughly. [Variant of obsolete *crag(ge),* neck, throat, Middle English *crag, crage,* from Middle Dutch *crāghe.*]

scrag·gly (skrággli) *adj.* **-glier, -gliest.** Ragged; irregular; untended or unkempt. [From SCRAG.]

scrag·gy (skrággi) *adj.* **-gier, -giest. 1.** Bony and lean; scrawny. **2.** Jagged; ragged; rough. —**scrag·gi·ly** *adv.* —**scrag·gi·ness** *n.*

scram¹ (skram) *intr.v.* **scrammed, scramming, scrams.** *Slang.* To leave a scene at once; go abruptly. Usually used in the imperative. [Short for SCRAMBLE.]

scram² *n.* A rapid shutting down of a nuclear reactor, especially in an emergency. [From SCRAM (to leave hastily).]

scram·ble (skrámb'l) *v.* **-bled, -bling, -bles.** —*intr.* **1.** To move or climb hurriedly, especially on the hands and knees. **2.** To struggle urgently, as with competitors, in order to get something: *all scrambled for the best seat.* **3.** *Military.* To take off with all possible haste, as to intercept enemy aircraft. **4.** To ride a motorcycle across rough terrain, especially in a race. —*tr.* **1.** To mix or throw together confusedly. **2.** To gather together in a hurried or disorderly fashion. Often used with *up.* **3.** To cook (beaten eggs) until of a firm but soft consistency. **4.** *Electronics.* To distort or garble (a signal) so as to render it unintelligible without a special receiver. **5.** *Military.* To cause (aircraft) to scramble. ~*n.* **1.** The act or an instance of scrambling. **2.** An arduous hike over rough terrain. **3.** An unceremonious scuffle for something. **4.** A motorcycle race across rough terrain. [Imitative; compare dialect *scamble†,* to struggle for, and *cramble†,* to crawl.]

scram·bled eggs (skrámb'ld) *n.* Also **scrambled egg. 1.** Eggs or an egg beaten and cooked until of a firm but soft consistency. **2.** *Informal.* The gold braid worn on the peak of the cap of a high-ranking officer in the armed forces.

scram·bler (skrámblər) *n.* **1.** One that scrambles. **2.** An electronic device that scrambles telecommunication signals to make them unintelligible to an eavesdropper. **3.** A **trail bike** *(see).*

scran (skran) *n. Regional Slang.* Provisions; food. [18th century : origin obscure.]

scrap¹ (skrap) *n.* **1. a.** A small detached piece or bit; a fragment. **b.** A shred; a particle. **2.** An unincorporated fragment of writing. **3.** *Plural.* Leftover and unwanted bits of food. **4.** Material left over or discarded as refuse; especially, metal suitable for reprocessing. Also used adjectivally and in combination: *scrapyard.* ~*tr.v.* **scrapped, scrapping, scraps. 1.** To break down into parts for disposal or salvage. **2.** *Informal.* To discard as useless or worthless. [Middle English, from Old Norse *skrap,* trifles, remains.]

scrap² *n. Informal.* A fight; a scuffle. [Perhaps variant of SCRAPE.] —**scrap** *intr.v.* —**scrap·per** *n.*

scrap·book (skráp-bŏŏk ‖ -bŏŏk) *n.* A book with blank pages for the mounting and preserving of pictures, cuttings, or the like.

scrape (skrayp) *v.* **scraped, scraping, scrapes.** —*tr.* **1.** To rub, scratch, or grate roughly over or against (a surface). **2.** To draw (a sharp or abrasive object) forcefully over a surface. **3.** To clean, abrade, or smooth by drawing a sharp edge or rough instrument over, especially repeatedly. **4.** To remove (an outer layer or adherent matter) by scraping. **5.** To injure the skin of by rubbing against something rough or sharp. **6.** To amass or produce with difficulty. Used with *together* or *up: scrape up a few pennies.* —*intr.* **1.** To come into sliding, abrasive contact. **2.** To rub or move with a harsh grating noise. **3.** To draw the foot backwards along the floor when bowing. **4.** To scrimp; be very thrifty. **5.** To proceed or manage precariously or with difficulty; succeed narrowly. Usually used with *along* or *through: She scraped through the test.* ~*n.* **1.** The act or a result of scraping. **2.** The sound of scraping. **3.** An abrasion on the skin. **4.** *Informal.* **a.** An embarrassing predicament. **b.** A fight; a scuffle. **5.** A **dilatation and curettage** *(see).* [Middle English *scrapen,* from Old Norse *skrapa* or Middle Dutch *schrapen.*]

scrap·er (skráypər) *n.* **1.** One that scrapes. **2.** A tool for scraping off paint or other adherent matter.

scrap·er·board (skráypər-bawrd ‖ -bōrd) *n.* A board covered with white clay and a black surface layer which is scraped away to produce white-line drawings.

scrap·heap (skráp-heep) *n.* **1.** A pile or heap of waste material. **2.** *Informal.* The state of being discarded, old, useless, or unemployable: *an executive on the scrapheap at 50.*

scra·pie (skráypi) *n.* A spongiform encephalopathy of sheep, with progressive degeneration of the central nervous system. [From SCRAPE (extreme itching causes the sheep to rub against trees, and so on).]

scrap·ing (skráyping) *n.* **1.** *Often plural.* Something that is scraped, or left to be scraped. **2.** The sound made by something being scraped.

scrap·py¹ (skráppi) *adj.* **-pier, -piest.** Composed of scraps; fragmentary or disjointed. —**scrap·pi·ly** *adv.* —**scrap·pi·ness** *n.*

scrap·py² *adj.* **-pier, -piest.** *Informal.* Quarrelsome; contentious. —**scrap·pi·ly** *adv.* —**scrap·pi·ness** *n.*

scratch (skrach) *v.* **scratched, scratching, scratches.** —*tr.* **1.** To make a thin, shallow cut or mark on (a surface) with a sharp instrument. **2.** To draw something abrasive, especially the nails, across (the skin) to relieve itching. **3. a.** To scrape or graze on an abrasive surface: *scratched my hand on the brambles.* **b.** To scrape or abrade (a surface). **4. a.** To form (words or pictures, for example) by scratching. **b.** To write or draw hurriedly or haphazardly. **5.** To strike out or cancel (a word, name, or passage) by or as if by drawing lines through. Often used with *out.* **6.** To withdraw (an entry) from a contest. —*intr.* **1.** To use the nails or claws to dig, scrape, or wound. **2. a.** To draw something abrasive, especially the nails, across the skin to relieve itching. **b.** To produce a chafing or itching sensation. **3.** To make a harsh, scraping sound. **4.** To claw and scrape the ground searching for food, as hens do. **5.** To withdraw from a contest. **6.** In billiards, to make a scratch. **7.** To get along or manage with difficulty, especially in making a living. Often used with *along.* —**scratch together** or **up.** To assemble or put together haphazardly or with difficulty. ~*n.* **1. a.** An act of scratching, as to relieve irritation. **b.** A linelike mark produced by scratching. **c.** A slight wound resembling a line or series of lines. **2.** A mark or scribble hastily made. **3.** A sound made by scratching, as on a gramophone record. **4.** *Sports.* **a.** A starting line for a race. **b.** A line formerly drawn across a prize ring at which the boxers began each round. **c.** The starting time or position or initial score of a competitor who has no handicap or allowance. **5.** A contestant who has been withdrawn or who has withdrawn from a contest. **6.** In billiards: **a.** A shot that results in a penalty, as when the cue ball falls into a pocket or jumps the cushion. **b.** A fluke or chance shot. **7.** Poultry feed. **8.** *Slang.* Money. —**from scratch.** From the very beginning. —**up to scratch.** *Informal.* **1.** Meeting the requirements or standards. **2.** In a fit condition. ~*adj.* **1.** Done haphazardly or by chance. **2.** Assembled hastily or at random. **3.** *Sports.* Without handicap or allowance. [Middle English, probably blend of *scrat, scratten†,* and *cratch, cracchen†,* both meaning "to scratch".] —**scratch·er** *n.*

scratch card *n.* A card you scratch off part of the surface of in the hope that beneath it there is a symbol, number, or word that will entitle you to a prize.

scratch test *n.* A test for allergy performed by scratching the skin and applying an allergen to the wound.

scratch·y (skráchi) *adj.* **-ier, -iest. 1.** Characterised by or consisting of scratches. **2.** Making a harsh, scratching noise: *a scratchy record; a scratchy pen.* **3.** Irregular; uneven: *played a scratchy stroke.* **4.** Harsh and irritating: *a scratchy fabric.* —**scratch·i·ly** *adv.* —**scratch·i·ness** *n.*

scrawl (skrawl) *v.* **scrawled, scrawling, scrawls.** —*tr.* To write hastily or illegibly. —*intr.* To write in a sprawling, irregular manner. ~*n.* **1.** Irregular, often illegible handwriting. **2.** Something, such as a note, written hastily or illegibly. [Perhaps blend of SPRAWL and CRAWL.] —**scrawl·er** *n.* —**scrawl·y** *adj.*

scraw·ny (skráwni) *adj.* **-nier, -niest.** Unattractively thin and bony; skinny. See Synonyms at **lean.** [Variant of dialect *scranny,* probably from Scandinavian; compare Norwegian *scran,* shrivelled.] —**scraw·ni·ness** *n.*

scream (skreem) *v.* **screamed, screaming, screams.** —*intr.* **1.** To utter a long, loud, piercing cry, as of pain. **2.** To make or move with a loud, piercing sound. Used of machinery, for example. **3.** To speak or write in a heated, hysterical manner. **4.** To be conspicuous

or obvious; cry out. **5.** To laugh wildly or uncontrollably. *—tr.* **1.** To utter or say in or as if in a screaming voice. **2.** To cause to be in a specified state by screaming: *screamed herself sick.*
~n. **1.** A long, loud, piercing cry or sound. **2.** *Informal.* Someone or something hilariously or ridiculously funny. [Middle English *scremen,* from Old Norse *skræma.*]
Synonyms: *scream, shriek, screech.*
scream·er (skréemər) *n.* **1.** One that screams. **2.** *Slang.* An exclamation mark. **3.** *Slang.* Something that evokes screams or laughter. **4.** *Chiefly U.S. Slang.* A sensational headline. **5.** Any of several large aquatic birds of the family Anhimidae, of South America, having a harsh, resonant call.
scream·ing·ly (skréeming-li) *adv.* So as to produce uproarious, uncontrolled laughter: *screamingly funny.*
scree (skree) *n.* **1.** Loose rock debris, usually comprising coarse, angular fragments. Also called "talus". **2.** A slope of this at the base of a steep incline or cliff. [Back-formation from *screes* (plural), contraction of *screethes* (unattested), from Old Norse *skrīdha,* landslide, from Germanic *skrīth-* (unattested).]
screech (skreech) *n.* **1.** A high-pitched, harsh, piercing cry; a shriek. **2.** A sound resembling this.
~v. **screeched, screeching, screeches.** *—tr.* To say or utter in or as if in a screeching voice. *—intr.* **1.** To utter a high-pitched, strident sound, as in pain or fright. **2.** To make a prolonged, shrill, grating noise. **—**See Synonyms at **scream.** [Earlier *scritch,* Middle English *scrichen,* from Old Norse *skraekja* (imitative).] **—screech·er** *n.* **—screech·y** *adj.*
screech owl *n.* **1.** Any of various small owls of the genus *Otus;* especially, *O. asio,* of North America, having a whistle-like call. Compare **hoot owl. 2.** Any owl having a screeching call.
screed (skreed) *n.* **1. a.** A long, monotonous harangue or piece of writing. **b.** *Often plural.* Any lengthy piece of writing, such as a letter. **2. a.** A strip of wood, plaster, or metal placed on a wall or horizontal surface as a guide for the even application of plaster or concrete. **b.** A layer or strip of material used to level off a horizontal surface, such as a floor. **c.** A smooth, final surface, as of concrete, applied to a floor. **3.** *Scottish.* A rent; a tear. [Middle English, probably variant of SHRED.]
screen (skreen) *n.* **1. a.** A movable device, especially a framed construction such as a hinged or sliding room divider, designed to divide, conceal, or protect. **b.** A decorative partition, as one in a church. **2.** Anything that serves to divide, conceal, or protect. **3. a.** A coarse sieve used for sifting out fine particles, as of sand, gravel, or coal. **b.** A system for appraising and selecting personnel. **4.** An insertion of framed wire or plastic mesh used in windows and doors to keep out insects. **5.** The white or silver surface upon which a picture is projected for viewing. **6.** The film industry. Preceded by *the.* **7.** *Electronics.* **a.** The electrode placed between the anode and the control grid in a tetrode valve. Also called "screen grid". **b.** The phosphorescent surface upon which the image is formed in a cathode-ray tube. **8.** *Printing.* A glass plate marked off with crossing lines, placed before the lens of a camera when photographing for halftone reproduction. **9.** A body of troops or ships sent in advance of or surrounding a larger body, in order to warn of attack or protect. **10. a.** A **windscreen** *(see).* **b.** A **sightscreen** *(see).* **11.** *Meteorology.* A wooden, white-painted box with louvred sides which stands 1.25 metres (4 feet) above the ground, and in which meteorological instruments are kept so that readings unaffected by strong winds and direct sunshine may by taken.
~tr.v. **screened, screening, screens. 1. a.** To provide with a screen. **b.** To divide or separate with a screen. Often used with *off: screen off the porch.* **2. a.** To conceal from view. **b.** To protect, guard, or shield. **3. a.** To sift or sift out by means of a sieve or screen. **b.** To vet or examine (applicants or candidates, for example) systematically in order to determine suitability. **4.** To show (a film, for example) on a screen. **5.** To test or examine for the presence of disease, for example. **—**See Synonyms at **hide.** [Middle English *screne,* from Old Northern French *escren, escran,* from Frankish *skrank* (unattested), barrier.] **—screen·er** *n.*
screen·ing (skréening) *n.* **1.** *Plural.* Refuse, such as waste coal, separated out by a screen; siftings. **2.** The mesh material used to make door or window screens. **3.** A presentation of a film.
screening test *n.* A programme of diagnostic tests, such as mass X-rays or cervical smears, carried out as a routine on a large section of the population.
screen memory *n. Psychology.* A memory of something that is unconsciously used to repress recollection of an associated but distressing event.
screen·play (skréen-play) *n.* The script for a film, including camera directions and descriptions of scenes. Also called "scenario".
screen-print (skréen-print) *tr.v.* **-printed, -printing, -prints.** To print using the silk-screen process. **—screen-print·er** *n.*
screen-print·ing (skréen-printing) *n.* The **silk-screen process** *(see).*
screen test *n.* A brief filmed sequence made to test the ability of an aspiring actor or actress. **—screen-test** (skréen-test) *tr.v.*
screen·writer (skréen-rītər) *n.* A writer of screenplays.
screw (skrōō ‖ skrew) *n.* **1. a.** A cylindrical rod incised with one or more helical or advancing spiral threads, such as a lead screw or worm screw. **b.** The tapped collar or socket that receives this. **2.** A metal pin with incised thread or threads, having a broad slotted head so that it can be driven as a fastener by turning it with a screwdriver, especially: **a.** A tapered and pointed wood screw. **b.** A cylindrical and flat-tipped machine screw. **3.** A device having helical form, such as a corkscrew. **4.** A **propeller** *(see).* **5.** A twist or turn of or as if of a screw. **6.** *Vulgar Slang.* **a.** An act of sexual intercourse. **b.** A person considered as a partner in sexual intercourse. **7.** *British Slang.* Salary; wages. **8.** *British.* A small twisted paper packet, as of tobacco. **9.** *British Slang.* An old broken-down horse. **10.** *Chiefly British Slang.* A stingy or crafty bargainer. **11.** *Slang.* A prison warder. **12.** *Usually plural.* **a.** A former instrument of torture, a **thumbscrew** *(see).* **b.** Any means of coercion or intimidation. Used chiefly in the phrase *put the screws on.* **13.** In billiards, snooker, or the like: **a.** The curving or backward motion of the cue ball hit just below and to one side of the centre. **b.** A stroke imparting such motion to the cue ball. **—have a screw loose.** *Slang.* **1.** To behave in an eccentric or whimsical manner. **2.** To be insane.
~v. **screwed, screwing, screws.** *—tr.* **1.** To drive or tighten (a screw). **2. a.** To fasten, tighten, or attach by or as if by means of a screw. **b.** To attach (a tapped or threaded fitting or cap) by twisting into place. Used with *on* or *in.* **c.** To rotate (a part) on a threaded axis. **3. a.** To contort (one's face). Often used with *up.* **b.** To twist or crumple (paper, for example). Often used with *up.* **4.** *Slang.* To take unfair advantage of; cheat or exploit. **5.** To use force or pressure to obtain. **6.** *Vulgar Slang.* To have sexual intercourse with. **7.** *Slang.* To burgle. **8.** To give (a ball) a curving or backward motion, as in billiards or snooker. *—intr.* **1.** To turn or twist. Used with *around.* **2. a.** To become attached by means of screw threads. Used with *into, on,* or *to.* **b.** To be capable of such attachment. **3.** *Vulgar Slang.* To engage in sexual intercourse. **—screw up. 1.** *Informal.* To muster or summon up. **2.** *Slang.* **a.** To make a mess of; bungle. **b.** To fail in an undertaking as a result of bungling. **3.** *Slang.* To make neurotic and anxious. [Middle English *skrewe,* from Old French *escroue,* originally "screw socket", from West Germanic *scrūva* (unattested), from Latin *scrōfa,* sow (probably because screw threads coil like a sow's tail, and perhaps influenced in sense by Latin *scrobis,* ditch, pudenda, hence, in Vulgar Latin, screw socket).] **—screw·er** *n.* **—screw·like** *adj.*
screw·ball (skrōō-bawl ‖ skréw-) *n. U.S. Slang.* An eccentric, impulsively whimsical, or irrational person.
~adj. U.S. Slang. Odd; eccentric; zany.
screw cap *n.* A cap that screws onto the threaded mouth of a container, such as a bottle, jar, or the like.
screw·driv·er (skrōō-drīvər ‖ skréw-) *n.* **1.** A tool used for turning screws. **2.** A cocktail of vodka and orange juice.
screwed (skrōōd ‖ skrewd) *adj. British Slang.* **1.** Drunk. **2.** In trouble or danger. [Past participle of SCREW, perhaps humorous allusion to *tight* (drunk) and *in a tight corner* (in trouble).]
screw eye *n.* A wood screw with an eyelet in place of a head.
screw jack *n.* A lifting device having a screw thread; especially, one used to raise a motor vehicle to change a wheel. Also called "jack".
screw log *n. Nautical.* A **patent log** *(see).*
screw pine *n.* A plant, the **pandanus** *(see).*
screw propeller *n.* A **propeller** *(see).*
screw thread *n.* **1.** The continuous helical groove on a screw or on the inner surface of a nut. **2.** One complete turn of a screw thread.
screw-worm (skrōō-wurm ‖ skréw-) *n.* The parasitic larva of the screwworm fly which can cause injury or death to livestock.
screw·y (skrōō-i ‖ skréw-i) *adj.* **-ier, -iest.** *Slang.* Eccentric; crack-brained or ludicrously odd.
Scria·bin (skréer-bin, skri-ábbin ‖ *U.S.* -áabin), **Alexandr** (1872–1915). Russian composer. He is noted for works for the keyboard that include chords on the interval of the fourth.
scrib·ble¹ (skríbb'l) *v.* **-bled, -bling, -bles.** *—tr.* **1.** To write hurriedly without heed to legibility or grammatical form. **2.** To cover with such writing or with meaningless marks. **3.** To draw hurriedly or carelessly. *—intr.* **1.** To write or draw in a hurried, careless way. **2.** To be a writer, as of novels or poetry. Used humorously or derogatorily.
~n. **1.** Careless, hurried writing or drawing. **2.** Meaningless marks and lines. [Middle English *scriblen,* from Medieval Latin *scrībillāre,* frequentative of Latin *scrībere,* to write.]
scrib·ble² *tr.v.* **-bled, -bling, -bles.** To card (wool or cotton) coarsely. [Probably from Low German and akin to SCRUB (rub hard).]
scrib·bler (skríbblər) *n.* **1.** One who scribbles. **2.** A very minor or untalented author.
scribe (skrīb) *n.* **1.** A public clerk or secretary, especially in ancient times. **2.** A professional copyist of manuscripts and documents, as in ancient or medieval times. **3.** A writer or journalist. Usually used humorously. **4.** A scriber. **5.** In ancient times, a scholar or teacher of the Jewish Law.
~v. **scribed, scribing, scribes.** *—tr.* To mark or produce with a scriber. *—intr. Archaic.* To work as a scribe. [Middle English, from Latin *scrība,* official writer, clerk, scribe, from *scrībere,* to write.] **—scrib·al** *adj.*
scrib·er (skrībər) *n.* A sharply pointed tool used for marking lines on wood, metal, ceramic, or the like.
scrim (skrim) *n.* **1.** A durable, loosely woven cotton or linen fabric used for curtains, upholstery lining, or in industry. **2.** *Chiefly U.S.* A similar fabric used in the theatre for creating special effects of light or atmosphere. [18th century : origin obscure.]
scrim·mage (skrímmij) *n.* **1.** A rough and confused struggle; a tussle. **2.** In American football: **a.** The contest between two teams from the time the ball is snapped back until it becomes out of play. **b.** A team's practice session. **3.** In Rugby football, a scrum. Not in

current usage.

~*intr.v.* **scrimmaged, -maging, -mages.** In American football, to engage in a scrimmage. [Alteration of *scrimish*, obsolete variant of SKIRMISH.]

scrimp (skrimp) *v.* **scrimped, scrimping, scrimps.** —*intr.* To economise severely. Often used with *on* or the phrase *scrimp and save.* ~*tr.* **1.** To be excessively sparing with or of. **2.** To cut or make too small or scanty. [18th century (Scottish) : origin obscure.] —**scrimp·y** *adj.* —**scrimp·i·ness** *n.*

scrim·shank (skrím-shangk) *intr.v.* **-shanked, -shanking, -shanks.** *British Slang.* To avoid work or duty. [19th century : origin obscure.]

scrim·shaw (skrím-shaw) *v.* **-shawed, -shawing, -shaws.** —*tr.* To decorate (whale ivory, bone, or shells) with intricate carvings or designs. —*intr.* To produce such work. ~*n., pl.* **scrimshaws** or collectively **scrimshaw. 1.** A bone or ivory article so fashioned. **2.** The art of producing such articles. [19th century (nautical use) : perhaps from the surname *Scrimshaw.*]

scrip[1] (skrip) *n.* A small scrap of paper, especially one with writing, such as a list or a schedule. [Variant of SCRIPT (influenced by SCRAP).]

scrip[2] *n. Finance.* **1.** A provisional certificate entitling the holder to a fractional share of stock or of other jointly owned property. **2.** Such certificates collectively. [Short for *subscription (receipt)*, receipt for portion of a loan.]

scrip[3] *n. Archaic.* A wallet, small satchel, or bag. [Middle English *scrippe*, from Old French *escreppe*, variant of Old Northern French *escarpe*, "pilgrim's knapsack". See **scarf.**]

scrip issue *n. Finance.* An issue of shares made by a company free of charge to existing shareholders. Also called "bonus issue".

scrip·sit (skrípsit) *Latin.* He (or she) wrote (it). Placed after the author's name on a manuscript.

script (skript) *n.* **1. a.** Handwriting as distinguished from print. **b.** A style of writing with cursive characters. **c.** A particular system of writing: *cuneiform script.* **2. a.** A type that imitates handwriting. **b.** Matter printed with this type. **3.** *Law.* An original document, as distinguished from a copy. **4.** The text of a play, broadcast, or film; especially, a copy of a text used by a director or performer. **5.** *British.* An examinee's written paper. ~*tr.v.* **scripted, scripting, scripts.** To write a script for (a film or broadcast): *Perelman scripted several Marx Brothers movies.* [Middle English *skript*, from Old French *escript*, from Latin *scrīptum*, from *scrīptus*, past participle of *scrībere*, to write.]

Script. Scriptural; Scriptures.

scrip·to·ri·um (skrip-táw-ri-əm ‖ -tṓ-) *n., pl.* **-riums** or **-ia** (-ri-ə). A room in a monastery set aside for the copying, writing, or illuminating of manuscripts and records. [Medieval Latin, from Latin *scrībere* (past participle *scrīptus*), to write.]

scrip·tur·al (skrípchərəl) *adj. Abbr.* **Script.** Often capital **S.** Of, pertaining to, based upon, or contained in the Scriptures. —**scrip·tur·al·ly** *adv.*

Scrip·ture (skrípchər) *n.* **1.** Often plural. *Abbr.* **Script. a.** A sacred writing or book; especially, the **Holy Scripture** *(see).* **b.** A passage from such a writing or book. **2.** *Small* **s.** A statement regarded as authoritative and definitive, such as a code of regulations. [Middle English, from Late Latin *scrīptūra*, from Latin, act of writing, from *scrībere* (past participle *scrīptus*), to write.]

script·writ·er (skrípt-rītər) *n.* A person who writes copy to be used by an announcer, performer, or director in a film or broadcast.

scriv·en·er (skrívnər, skrívv'n-ər) *n. Archaic.* **1.** A professional copyist; a scribe. **2.** A notary. [Middle English *scriveiner*, from *scrivein*, scribe, from Old French *escrevein*, from Vulgar Latin *scrībānem* (unattested), accusative of Latin *scrība*, SCRIBE.]

scro·bic·u·late (skrō-bíckew-lət, -lit, -layt) *adj. Biology.* Marked with many shallow depressions, grooves, or pits. [Latin *scrobiculus*, diminutive of *scrobis*, trench.]

scrod (skrod) *n. U.S.* A young cod or haddock, especially one split and boned for cooking. [19th century : origin obscure.]

scrof·u·la (skróffewla) *n.* Tuberculosis of the lymph nodes, a now rare condition chiefly affecting children and characterised by running sores in the neck region. Also called the "King's evil". [Middle English *scrophulas* (plural), from Medieval Latin *scrófulae*, swelling of the glands, "small sows", from Latin *scrófa*, sow (probably after Greek *khoirades*, scrofula, from *khoiras*, like a pig's back).]

scrof·u·lous (skróffewləss) *adj.* **1.** Pertaining to, affected with, or resembling scrofula. **2.** Morally degenerate; corrupt. —**scrof·u·lous·ly** *adv.* —**scrof·u·lous·ness** *n.*

scroll (skrōl) *n.* **1. a.** A roll of parchment, papyrus, or the like. **b.** An ancient book or volume written on a scroll. **2.** A list of names. **3.** Ornamentation resembling a partially rolled scroll of paper; especially: **a.** The volute in Ionic and Corinthian capitals. **b.** The curved head on an instrument of the violin family. **c.** *Heraldry.* A ribbon inscribed with a motto. ~ *v.* **scrolled, scrolling, scrolls.** —*tr.v.* **1.** To inscribe on a scroll. **2.** To roll up into a scroll. **3.** To ornament with a scroll or scrolls. **4.** To move (material) up, down, or across a VDU as if rolling up or unrolling a scroll. —*intr.v.* **1.** To scroll material in a VDU. **2.** To be scrolled on a VDU: *The text scrolled past quickly.* [Middle English *scrowle*, variant (influenced by *rowle*, a roll) of *scrow*, from Old French *escro(u)e*, strip of parchment, from Frankish *skrōda* (unattested), piece, shred.]

scroll saw *n.* A hand or power saw with a narrow ribbon-like blade for cutting curved or irregular shapes. See **fretsaw, jigsaw.**

scroll·work (skrṓl-wurk) *n.* Embellishment with a scroll motif; especially, ornamentation executed in wood with a scroll saw.

Scrooge (skrōoj) *n.* A mean-spirited, miserly person; a skinflint. [After Ebenezer *Scrooge* in Charles Dickens's *Christmas Carol.*]

scroop (skrōop) *intr.v.* **scrooped, scrooping, scroops.** *Archaic.* To make a squeaking or grating sound. [Imitative.] —**scroop** *n.*

scro·tum (skrṓ-təm) *n., pl.* **-ta** (-tə) or **-tums.** The external sac of skin enclosing the testes in most mammals. [Latin *scrōtum.*] —**scro·tal** (skrṓt'l) *adj.*

scrounge (skrownj) *v.* **scrounged, scrounging, scrounges.** *Informal.* —*tr.* **1.** To sponge; cadge. **2.** To obtain by salvaging or foraging; round up. —*intr.* **1.** To obtain something by cadging or sponging. **2.** To forage about in an effort to acquire something at no cost. [Variant of dialectal *scrunge†*, to steal.] —**scroung·er** *n.*

scrub[1] (skrub) *v.* **scrubbed, scrubbing, scrubs.** —*tr.* **1.** To rub hard, as with a brush, soap, and water, in order to clean. **2.** To remove (dirt or stains) by such rubbing. **3.** To cleanse (a gas) in a scrubber. **4.** *Informal.* To cancel or abandon. —*intr.* To clean or wash something by hard rubbing. —**scrub up.** To wash the hands and arms thoroughly before an operation. Used of a surgeon. ~*n.* An act of scrubbing. [Middle English *scrobben*, from Middle Low German or Middle Dutch *schrobben, schrubben.*]

scrub[2] *n.* **1.** Vegetation characterised by straggly, stunted trees, shrubs, or brushwood. **2.** A growth or tract of stunted vegetation. Sometimes used in combination: *scrubland.* **3.** A domestic animal of inferior breeding or poor appearance. **4.** An undersized or insignificant person. **5.** *Australian.* Remote rural areas. Preceded by *the.* **6.** *Sports. U.S.* A player not in the first team. ~*adj.* **1.** Undersized, stunted, or inferior. **2.** *U.S.* Made up of or participated in by scrubs: *a scrub team.* [Middle English, variant of *schrubbe,* SHRUB.]

scrub·ber (skrúbber) *n.* **1.** One that scrubs. **2.** An apparatus for removing impurities from a gas. **a.** *Chiefly British Slang.* **a.** A sexually promiscuous woman. **4.** A prostitute. Used derogatorily.

scrub·bing brush (skrúbbing) *n.* A brush with strong, stiff bristles used for doing dirty cleaning jobs.

scrub bird *n.* Either of two rare Australian birds of the genus *Atrichornis,* having a brown plumage and long, pointed tails.

scrub·by (skrúbbi) *adj.* **-bier, -biest. 1.** Covered with or consisting of scrub or underbrush. **2.** Small; straggly; stunted. **3.** Shabby or paltry; wretched. —**scrub·bi·ness** *n.*

scrub fowl *n.* A megapode *(see).*

scrub oak *n.* Any of several shrubby or small oaks, such as *Quercus ilicifolia,* of eastern North America.

scrub pine *n.* Any of several small, straggling pine trees, such as *Pinus virginiana,* of the eastern United States.

scrub typhus *n.* An acute infectious disease common in southeast Asia and the western Pacific, caused by a parasitic microorganism, *Rickettsia tsutsugamushi,* and transmitted by a mite. Also called "tsutsugamushi disease", "Japanese river fever".

scrub wallaby *n.* A small wallaby, the **pademelon** *(see).*

scruff (skruf) *n.* The back of the neck; the nape. [Variant of obsolete *scuff,* perhaps from Old Norse *skoft,* hair on the head.]

scruf·fy (skrúffi) *adj.* **-fier, -fiest.** Shabby; untidy. [From *scruff,* variant of SCURF.]

scrum (skrum) *n.* A formation in Rugby football: **1.** A *set scrum,* in which the two sets of forwards must interlock together against each other, the ball is thrown in, and the opposing hookers try to kick the ball backwards out to their own team. **2.** A *loose scrum,* in which the players join together in the struggle to win the ball during play. Also called "scrummage" and formerly "scrimmage". ~*intr.v.* **scrummed, scrumming, scrums.** To engage in or form a scrum. Often used with *down.* [Shortened from SCRUMMAGE.]

scrum half *n.* **1.** In Rugby football, the player who throws the ball into a set scrum. **2.** The position of this player in a team.

scrum·mage (skrúmmij) *v.* In Rugby football, a scrum. ~*intr.v.* **scrummaged, -maging, -mages.** To engage in a scrum. [Variant of SCRIMMAGE.] —**scrum·mag·er** *n.*

scrump (skrump) *intr.v.* **scrumped, scrumping, scrumps.** *British Regional.* To steal fruit, especially apples. [From dialect *scrump†,* small apple. See **scrumpy.**]

scrump·tious (skrúmpshəss) *adj. Informal.* **1.** Delicious. **2.** Splendid; delightful. [19th century : origin obscure.]

scrump·y (skrúmpi) *n.* A rough, strong, cider brewed in southwest England. [From dialect *scrump†,* small apple.]

scrunch (skrunch ‖ skrōonch) *v.* **scrunched, scrunching, scrunches.** —*tr.* **1.** To crush or crunch. **2.** To crumple or squeeze. Often used with *up.* —*intr.* To move with or make a crunching sound: *scrunching along the gravel path.* ~*n.* A crunching sound. [Variant of CRUNCH.]

scru·ple (skrōop'l ‖ skréw'p'l) *n.* **1.** *Often plural.* A feeling of doubt or uncertainty as to whether a course of action is ethically right or justifiable; a dictate of conscience. **2.** *Abbr.* **sc., scr.** A unit of apothecary weight equal to 20 grains. **3.** *Archaic.* A minute part or amount. —See Synonyms at **qualm.** ~*intr.v.* **scrupled, -pling, -ples.** To hesitate through the demands of conscience or principle. [French *scrupule,* from Latin *scrūpulus,* small sharp stone, small weight, scruple, from *scrūpus†,* rough stone.]

scru·pu·lous (skrōo-pew-ləss ‖ skréw-) *adj.* **1.** Having scruples; principled. **2.** Very conscientious and exacting; punctilious. —See Synonyms at **meticulous.** [Middle English, from Latin *scrūpulōsus,* from *scrūpulus*, SCRUPLE.] —**scru·pu·los·i·ty** (-lóssəti), **scru·pu·lous·ness** *n.* —**scru·pu·lous·ly** *adv.*

scru·ta·ble (skrŏŏt-əb'l ‖ skréwt-) *adj. Rare.* Comprehensible through scrutiny. [Medieval Latin *scrūtabilis,* searchable, from Latin *scrūtāri,* to search. See **scrutiny.**]

scru·ta·tor (skrŏŏ-táytər ‖ skrew-) *n.* A person who scrutinises; a scrutineer. [Latin, from *scrūtāri,* to search. See **scrutiny.**]

scru·ti·neer (skrŏŏ-ti-néer, -t'n-éer ‖ skrew-) *n.* A person who examines or checks; especially, a person who checks and counts votes. [SCRUTIN(Y) + -EER.]

scru·ti·nise, scru·ti·nize (skrŏŏ-ti-nīz, -t'n-īz ‖ skrew-) *tr.v.* **-nised, -nising, -nises.** To examine or observe with great care; inspect minutely or critically. —**scru·ti·nis·er** *n.* —**scru·ti·nis·ing·ly** *adv.*

scru·ti·ny (skrŏŏ-ti-ni, -t'n-i ‖ skrew-) *n., pl.* **-nies.** 1. A close, careful examination or study; a critical, sustained look. 2. Close observation; surveillance. 3. An official examination of the votes cast in an election. [Middle English, from Latin *scrūtinium,* from *scrūtāri,* to search, examine (originally said of ragpickers), "to rummage in a heap of rubbish", from *scrūta,* rubbish.]

scry (skrī) *intr.v.* **scried, scrying, scries.** To see or predict the future by means of a crystal ball. [Apheptic variant of DESCRY.]

scu·ba (skŏŏbə) *n.* An apparatus containing compressed air used for underwater breathing. Also used adjectivally: *scuba diver.* [*S*elf-*c*ontained *u*nderwater *b*reathing *a*pparatus.]

scud (skud) *intr.v.* **scudded, scudding, scuds.** 1. To run or skim along swiftly and easily. 2. *Nautical.* To run before a gale with little or no sail set.
~*n.* 1. The act of scudding. 2. *Sometimes plural.* **a.** A ragged mass of cloud, driven along by the wind at a lower level than the main cloud layer. **b.** Loosely, a sudden light shower or gust of wind. [Perhaps variant of SCUT (rabbit's tail, hence "run like a rabbit").]

Scud (skud) *n.* The NATO code name for a Russian-made, long-range, ground-to-ground missile.

scu·do (skŏŏ-dō) *n., pl.* **-di** (-dee). A former monetary unit and coin of Italy and Sicily. [Italian, "shield", from Latin *scūtum.*]

scuff (skuf) *v.* **scuffed, scuffing, scuffs.** —*intr.* 1. To scrape or drag the feet while walking; shuffle. 2. To become scratched or scraped with wear: *These shoes scuff easily.* —*tr.* To scrape or scratch the surface of (shoes, for example) with use.
~*n.* 1. The sound or act of scuffing. 2. A worn or rough spot resulting from scuffing. 3. *Chiefly U.S.* A flat, backless slipper. [Imitative.]

scuf·fle¹ (skúff'l) *intr.v.* **-fled, -fling, -fles.** 1. To fight or struggle confusedly at close quarters. 2. **a.** To shuffle. **b.** To go or move about in a hurried and confused manner.
~*n.* 1. A rough, disorderly struggle at close quarters. 2. The action or sound of scuffling. —See Synonyms at **conflict.** [Probably from Scandinavian; akin to Old Norse *skúfa,* to push.] —**scuf·fler** *n.*

scuffle² *n. U.S.* A type of hoe manipulated by pushing rather than pulling. Also called "scuffle hoe". [Dutch *schoffel,* from Middle Dutch *schoffel, schuffel,* shovel.]

scull (skul) *n.* 1. A long oar twisted from side to side over the stern of a boat to propel it. 2. Either of a pair of short-handled oars used by a single rower. 3. A small, light boat used for sculling, especially a racing boat. 4. *Plural.* A race between such boats.
~*v.* **sculled, sculling, sculls.** —*tr.* To propel (a boat) with a scull or sculls. —*intr.* To use a scull or sculls to propel a boat. [Middle English *scullet*†.] —**scull·er** *n.*

scul·ler·y (skúl-ri, skúlləri) *n., pl.* **-ies.** A small room adjoining a kitchen in which dishwashing and dirty kitchen chores are done. [Middle English, from Anglo-French *squillerie,* Old French *escuelerie,* from *escuelier,* keeper of dishes, from *escuele,* dish, from Vulgar Latin *scūtella* (unattested), variant (influenced by Latin *scūtum,* SCUTUM) of Latin *scutella,* salver, diminutive of *scutra*†, platter.]

Scul·lin (skúllin), **James Henry** (1876–1953). Australian politician. He was leader of the Labor Party (1928–35) and prime minister (1929–31).

scul·li·on (skúlli-ən, skúl-yən) *n. Archaic.* 1. A servant employed to do menial tasks in a kitchen. 2. A despicable or contemptible person. [Middle English *scalyon,* probably from Old French *escovillon,* dishcloth, diminutive of *escouve,* broom, from Latin *scopa.* See **scopula.**]

scul·pin (skúlpin) *n., pl.* **-pins** or collectively **sculpin.** Any of various marine and freshwater fishes of the family Cottidae, of northern waters, having a large, flattened head and prominent spines. Also called "bullhead". [Perhaps variant of obsolete *scorpene,* from Latin *scorpaena,* sea scorpion. See **scorpaenoid.**]

sculp·sit (skúlpsit). *Latin. Abbr.* **sc., sculp., sculpt.** He (or she) sculptured (it). Placed after the artist's name.

sculpt (skulpt) *v.* **sculpted, sculpting, sculpts.** —*tr.* To sculpture. —*intr.* To be a sculptor. [French *sculpter, sculper,* from Latin *sculpere,* to carve. See **sculpture.**]

sculp·tor (skúlptər) *n.* 1. One who sculptures; especially, an artist who works in stone, metal, or other hard or plastic material. 2. *Capital* S. A constellation in the Southern Hemisphere near Cetus and Phoenix. Also called "Sculptor's Workshop". [Latin, from *sculpere* (past participle *sculptus*), to carve. See **sculpture.**]

sculp·tress (skúlp-triss, -trəss) *n.* A woman who sculptures.

sculp·ture (skúlpchər) *n. Abbr.* **sculp.** 1. The art or practice of shaping figures or designs, as by carving wood, chiselling marble, modelling clay, or casting in metal. 2. **a.** A work of art created in this manner. **b.** Such works collectively. 3. Ridges, indentations, or other markings, as on a shell, formed by natural processes.
—*v.* **sculptured, -turing, -tures.** —*tr.* 1. To fashion (stone, bronze, wood, or the like) into a three-dimensional figure. 2. To represent in sculpture. 3. To ornament with sculpture. 4. To give sculptural shape or contour to, as by erosion. —*intr.* To make sculptures. [Middle English, from Latin *sculptūra,* from *sculpere* (past participle *sculptus*), to carve.] —**sculp·tur·al·ly** *adv.*

sculp·tur·esque (skúlpchər-ésk) *adj.* Suggestive of sculpture; having the qualities of sculpture. —**sculp·tur·esque·ly** *adv.* —**sculp·tur·esque·ness** *n.*

scum (skum) *n.* 1. A filmy layer of extraneous or impure matter that forms on or rises to the surface of a liquid or body of water. 2. The refuse or dross of molten metals. 3. Any refuse or worthless matter. 4. *Informal.* An element of society or an individual regarded as being vile or worthless.
~*v.* **scummed, scumming, scums.** —*tr.* To remove the scum from; skim. —*intr.* To become covered with scum. [Middle English *scume, scome,* from Middle Dutch *schūm,* from Germanic *skūma-* (unattested), cover.] —**scum·mer** *n.* —**scum·my** *adj.*

scum·ble (skúmb'l) *tr.v.* **-bled, -bling, -bles.** In painting and drawing, to soften the colours or outlines of by covering with a film of opaque or semiopaque colour or by rubbing.
~*n.* 1. The effect produced by scumbling. 2. Material used for scumbling. [Probably frequentative of SCUM.]

scun·cheon (skúnchən) *n. Architecture.* The inside, vertical face of a door or window frame. [Middle English, from Old French *escoinson* (French *écoinçon*), a bevelled inside edge : *es-,* EX- + *coin,* corner, COIGN + *-son,* from Latin *-siōn-,* -TION.]

scun·gy (skúnji) *adj.* **-gier, -giest.** *Australian & N.Z. Informal.* Sordid or dingy. [Probably blend of SCUM + DINGY.]

scun·ner (skúnnər) *n. Chiefly Scottish.* 1. A strong dislike; an aversion. 2. A cause of vexation; a nuisance.
~*v.* **scunnered, -nering, -ners.** *Chiefly Scottish.* —*intr.* To feel aversion or dislike. —*tr.* To cause to feel aversion or dislike. [Middle English *skunner*†.]

Scun·thorpe (skún-thawrp). Town in North Lincolnshire in east England. It is an iron and steel manufacturing centre.

scup (skup) *n., pl.* **scups** or collectively **scup.** A food fish, *Stenotomus chrysops,* of western Atlantic waters, related to and resembling the porgies. [Short for Narraganset *mishcúp.*]

scup·per¹ (skúppər) *n.* 1. *Nautical.* An opening in the side of a ship at deck level to allow water to run off. 2. Any opening for draining off water, as on a building. [Middle English *skopper,* perhaps from Old French *escopir,* to spit (imitative).]

scupper² *tr.v.* **-pered, -pering, -pers.** *Chiefly British Slang.* 1. To overwhelm or massacre. 2. To ruin or destroy. [19th century (military use) : origin obscure.]

scup·per·nong (skúppər-nong ‖ *U.S. also* -nawng) *n.* 1. A grape, the **muscadine** *(see)*; especially, a cultivated American variety having sweet, yellowish fruit. 2. A sweet American wine made from such grapes. [Short for *Scuppernong grape,* grown in the *Scuppernong* River basin, North Carolina.]

scurf (skurf) *n.* 1. Scaly or shredded dry skin, as in dandruff. 2. Any loose, scaly crust coating a surface, especially of a plant. [Middle English *scurf, scorf,* Old English *scurf,* variant (probably influenced by Old Norse *skurföttr,* scurfy) of *sceorf, sceorfan,* to gnaw.] —**scurf·y** *adj.* —**scurf·i·ness** *n.*

scur·ril·i·ty (sku-ríllǝti, skǝ-) *n., pl.* **-ties.** 1. The quality of being scurrilous. 2. A scurrilous remark or piece of writing.

scur·ri·lous (skúrrilǝss) *adj.* 1. Given to the use of vulgar, obscene, or abusive language. 2. Coarse, obscene, or abusive. [Latin *scurrilis,* buffoon-like, jeering, from *scurra,* buffoon, perhaps from Etruscan.] —**scur·ri·lous·ly** *adv.* —**scur·ri·lous·ness** *n.*

scur·ry (skúrri) *intr.v.* **-ried, -rying, -ries.** 1. To go with light running steps; hurry; scamper. 2. To flurry or swirl about.
~*n., pl.* **scurries.** 1. The act or noise of scurrying. 2. A light whirling movement; a flurry. 3. A short run or race on horseback. [Probably short for HURRY-SCURRY.]

scur·vy (skúrvi) *n.* A disease caused by deficiency of vitamin C, characterised by spongy and bleeding gums, bleeding under the skin, and extreme weakness.
—*adj.* **scurvier, -viest.** Mean; worthless; contemptible. [From SCURF (but used later to render like-sounding French *scorbut,* the skin disease, from Medieval Latin *scorbūtus.* See **scorbutic**).] —**scur·vi·ly** *adv.* —**scur·vi·ness** *n.*

scurvy grass *n.* A plant, *Cochlearia officinalis,* of northern regions, having bitter foliage, formerly used to cure scurvy.

scut (skut) *n.* A stubby erect tail, such as that of a hare, rabbit, or deer. [Middle English *scut*†, hare.]

scu·tage (skéwtij) *n.* In feudal times, a tax paid in lieu of military service. [Middle English, from Medieval Latin *scūtāgium,* "shield money", from *scūtum,* shield, SCUTUM.]

Scutari. See **Shkodër** (Albania), **Üsküdar** (Turkey).

scu·tate (skéwt-ayt) *adj.* 1. *Zoology.* Covered with bony plates or scales. 2. *Botany.* Round in shape like a buckler or shield. [New Latin *scutatus,* from Latin *scūtātus,* equipped with a shield, from *scūtum,* shield, SCUTUM.]

scutch (skuch) *tr.v.* **scutched, scutching, scutches.** To separate the valuable fibres of (flax or other textile material) from the woody parts by beating.
~*n.* An implement for scutching. [Obsolete French *escoucher,* from Old French *escousser,* from Vulgar Latin *excussāre* (unattested), frequentative of Latin *excutere* (past participle *excussus*), to shake out : *ex-,* out + *quatere,* to shake.] —**scutch·er** *n.*

scutch·eon (skúchən) *n.* **1.** Variant of **escutcheon.** **2.** A shield-shaped object, such as a scute.
scutch grass *n.* **1.** Bermuda grass *(see).* **2.** Couch grass *(see).*
scute (skewt) *n. Zoology.* A horny, chitinous, or bony external plate or scale, as on the shell of a turtle. [New Latin, SCUTUM.]
scu·tel·late (skew-tél-ayt, skéwtil-, -ət, -it) *adj.* Also **scu·tel·lat·ed** (skéwti-laytid) (for sense 1). **1.** *Zoology.* **a.** Covered with bony plates or scales. **b.** Having a scutellum. **2.** *Botany.* Shaped like a shield or platter. [From SCUTELLUM.]
scu·tel·la·tion (skéwti-láysh'n) *n.* An arrangement or covering of scales, as on a bird's leg.
scu·tel·lum (skew-téllom) *n., pl.* **-tella** (-téllə). **1.** *Zoology.* A shield-like bony plate or scale, as on the thorax of some insects. **2.** *Botany.* Any of several shield-shaped structures, such as the cotyledon of a grass. [New Latin, diminutive of SCUTUM.]
scu·ti·form (skéwti-fawrm) *adj.* Shield-shaped: *scutiform leaves.* [New Latin scutiformis : Latin scūtum, SCUTUM + -FORM.]
scut·ter (skúttər) *intr.v.* **-tered, -tering, -ters.** *British Informal.* To scurry. [Variant (influenced by SCATTER) of SCUTTLE (to run).]
scut·tle¹ (skútt'l) *n.* **1.** A small opening or hatch with a movable lid in the deck, side, wall, or roof of a ship or in the roof, wall, or floor of a building. **2.** The lid or hatch for this.
~*tr.v.* **scuttled, -tling, -tles.** **1.** To cut or open a hole or holes in (a ship's hull). **2. a.** To sink (a ship) by this means. **b.** To sink (a ship) by opening the seacocks. **3.** *Informal.* **a.** To scrap; discard. **b.** To undermine; sabotage. [Middle English skottell, from obsolete French escoutille, from Spanish escotilla, diminutive of escota, opening in a garment, "seam", probably from Gothic skaut, seam, hem.]
scuttle² *n.* **1.** See **coal scuttle.** **2.** *Archaic.* A shallow open basket for carrying vegetables, flowers, grain, or the like. **3.** The part of a motor car connecting the bonnet with the rest of the body. [Middle English scutel, Old English scutel, ultimately from Latin scutella, salver. See **scullery.**]
scuttle³ *intr.v.* **-tled, -tling, -tles.** To run with short hurried movements; scurry. [Variant of dialectal scuddle, frequentative of SCUD.] —**scut·tle** *n.*
scut·tle·butt (skútt'l-but) *n.* **1.** A drinking fountain on a ship. **2.** Formerly, a cask on a ship used to hold the day's supply of drinking water. **3.** *Slang.* Gossip; rumour. [SCUTTLE (hatch) + BUTT (cask).]
scu·tum (skéw-təm) *n., pl.* **-ta** (-tə). **1.** *Zoology.* A bony, calcareous, chitinous, or horny scale or plate, as on certain barnacles and on the thorax of an insect. **2.** *Capital S. Astronomy.* A constellation in the equatorial region of the southern sky near Sagittarius and Serpens Cauda. [Latin scūtum, shield.]
Scyl·la (síllə) *n.* A headland on the Italian side of the Strait of Messina, opposite the whirlpool Charybdis, personified by Homer as a female sea monster who devoured sailors. —**between Scylla and Charybdis.** In a position where avoidance of one danger exposes one to destruction by another.
scy·phis·to·ma (sī-fístə-mə) *n., pl.* **-mae** (-mee) or **-mas.** A sedentary polyp-like form in the life cycle of scyphozoans, which gives rise to free-swimming medusoid forms. [New Latin, from Greek skuphos, cup + stoma, mouth.]
scy·pho·zo·an (sīf-ə-zō-ən, -ō-) *n.* Any of various marine coelenterates of the class Scyphozoa, including the jellyfishes. [New Latin Scyphozoa, "cuplike creatures" : Greek skuphos, cup + -ZOA.] —**scy·pho·zo·an** *adj.*
scythe (sīth) *n.* An implement consisting of a long, curved single-edged blade with a long, bent handle, used for mowing or reaping. ~*tr.v.* **scythed, scything, scythes.** To cut with or as if with a scythe. [Middle English sithe, sythe, Old English sīthe, from Germanic.]
Scyth·i·a (síthi-ə, síthi-ə). An ancient region of Asia and southeast Europe, north of the Black Sea.
Scyth·i·an (síthi-ən, síthi-) *n.* **1.** A member of the ancient nomadic people inhabiting Scythia. **2.** The extinct Iranian language of these people. —**scyth·i·an** *adj.*
s.d. **1.** sine die. **2.** *Statistics.* standard deviation.
S.D. *Statistics.* standard deviation.
SDP Social Democratic Party.
S.D.R., S.D.Rs special drawing rights (from the International Monetary Fund).
Se The symbol for the element selenium.
SE southeast; southeastern.
sea (see) *n.* **1.** *Abbr.* **s., S. a.** The continuous body of salt water covering most of the earth's surface; especially, this body regarded as a geophysical entity distinct from earth and sky. Usually preceded by *the.* **b.** A tract of water in an ocean, such as the North Sea. **c.** A relatively large body of salt water completely or partly landlocked, such as the Caspian Sea. **d.** A body of fresh water, such as the Sea of Galilee. **2.** *Sometimes plural.* The condition of the ocean's surface with regard to its course, flow, swell, or turbulence: *a high sea.* **3.** Something that suggests the sea in extent or quantity. **4.** Seafaring as a way of life. **5.** A lunar *mare (see).* —**at sea. 1.** On the open waters of the ocean. **2.** At a loss; perplexed. —**go to sea. 1.** To become a sailor. **2.** To set out on an ocean voyage. —**put (out) to sea.** To leave port. [Middle English se(e), Old English sǣ, from Common Germanic saiwa- (unattested).]
sea anchor *n. Nautical.* A drag, usually in the form of a canvas-covered conical frame, floating behind a vessel to prevent drifting or to maintain a heading into the wind. Also called "drag anchor", "drift anchor", "drogue".

sea anemone *n.* Any of numerous flower-like marine coelenterates of the order Actiniaria.
sea bag *n.* A strong canvas bag, usually with a drawstring at the top, in which a sailor carries his belongings.
sea bass *n.* Any of various marine food fishes of the genus *Centropristes* and related genera; especially, *C. striatus,* of coastal Atlantic waters of the United States. Also called "sea perch".
sea·bed (sée-bed) *n.* The floor of the sea or the ocean.
Sea·bee (sée-bee) *n.* A member of one of the U.S. Navy's construction battalions, established to build naval aviation bases. [Variant of *cee bee,* from the initials of *Construction Battalion.*]
sea bird *n.* A bird, such as a petrel or albatross, that frequents the sea, especially far from shore.
sea biscuit *n.* Hardtack.
sea·board (sée-bawrd || -bōrd) *n.* **1.** The seacoast. **2.** Land near the sea. [SEA + BOARD (obsolete sense "border").] —**sea·board** *adj.*
sea·borne (sée-bawrn || -bōrn) *adj.* **1.** Conveyed by sea; transported by ship. **2.** Carried on or over the sea.
sea bream *n.* Any of various marine food fishes of the family Sparidae; especially, *Pagellus centrodontus,* of European waters.
sea breeze *n.* A cool breeze blowing inland from the sea during the afternoon, especially in equatorial regions.
sea buckthorn *n.* A Eurasian coastal shrub, *Hippophae rhamnoides,* having narrow leaves, greenish flowers, and orange fruits.
sea butterfly *n.* A marine organism, a **pteropod** *(see).*
sea·coast (sée-kōst) *n.* Land bordering the sea.
sea·cock (sée-kok) *n.* A valve through which water can be let into or pumped out of the interior of a ship.
sea cow *n.* **1.** Any of several marine mammals of the order Sirenia, such as a manatee or dugong. **2.** *Archaic.* Any of several other aquatic animals, such as a walrus.
sea cucumber *n.* Any of various cucumber-shaped echinoderms of the class Holothuroidea. See **trepang.**
sea dog *n.* A sailor with long experience of the sea.
sea·dog (sée-dog || -dawg) *n.* A **fogbow** *(see).*
sea duck *n.* Any of various diving ducks, such as the eider or scoter, of coastal areas.
sea eagle *n.* Any of various fish-eating eagles or similar birds, especially any of the genus *Haliaetus.*
sea ear *n.* A mollusc, the **ormer** *(see).*
sea elephant *n.* The **elephant seal** *(see).*
sea fan *n.* Any of various yellowish to reddish fan-shaped corals of the genus *Gorgonia.*
sea·far·er (sée-fairər || *U.S.* -farrər, -ferrər) *n.* A sailor or mariner.
sea·far·ing (sée-fairing) *n.* **1.** Travel by sea. **2.** The calling of a sailor. ~*adj.* **1.** Following a life at sea. **2.** Travelling by sea.
sea feather *n.* Any of several anthozoans of the family Pennatulidae, having a feather-like shape.
sea·food, sea food (sée-fōod) *n.* Edible fish, shellfish, and the like, from the sea.
sea·fowl (sée-fowl) *n.* **1.** A sea bird. **2.** Sea birds collectively.
sea·front (sée-front) *n.* A strip of land at the very edge of the sea, especially when part of a town.
sea·girt (sée-gurt) *adj. Literary.* Surrounded by the sea.
sea·go·ing (sée-gō-ing) *adj.* **1.** Designed or used for ocean voyages. **2.** Seafaring.
sea gooseberry *n.* A marine organism of the genus *Pleurobrachia.* See **ctenophore.** [From its round, berry-like shape.]
sea green *n.* Moderate bluish green. —**sea-green** *adj.*
sea·gull (sée-gul) *n.* A gull, especially any appearing near coastal areas.
sea hare *n.* Any of various marine gastropod molluscs of the family Aplysiidae, having a soft body and two earlike tentacles.
sea holly *n.* An Old World plant, *Eryngium maritimum,* growing on seashores and having prickly leaves and blue or purplish flowers.
sea horse *n.* **1.** Any small marine fish of the genus *Hippocampus,* characteristically swimming in an upright position, and having a prehensile tail, a horselike head, and a body covered with bony plates. **2.** Loosely, a walrus. **3.** A mythical animal, half fish and half horse, ridden by Neptune and other sea gods.
Sea Island cotton *n.* **1.** A species of cotton, *Gossypium barbadense,* native to tropical America and widely cultivated for its fine, long-staple fibres. **2.** The fibres or cloth derived from this plant. [After the *Sea Islands* off South Carolina and Georgia, United States, where it was originally cultivated.]
sea kale *n.* A European plant, *Crambe maritima,* having cabbage-like leaves and young shoots that are edible.
sea king *n. Literary.* A piratical Scandinavian chief of the early Middle Ages.
seal¹ (seel) *n.* **1. a.** A die or signet having a raised or incised emblem, used to stamp an impression upon a receptive substance such as wax or lead. **b.** The impression made. **c.** The design or emblem itself, belonging exclusively to the user: *the king's seal.* **d.** A small disc or wafer of wax, lead, or paper bearing such an imprint and affixed to a document to prove authenticity or to seal it. **2.** Any act, event, or sign that is regarded as a confirmation or guarantee. **3.** An adhesive agent such as wax, paraffin, or putty used to close or secure something or to prevent seepage of moisture or air. **4.** A device or fluid in a drainpipe preventing the upward passage of gas. **5.** An airtight closure. **6.** A small decorative paper sticker: *a Christmas seal.* —**set (one's) seal on. 1.** To impart something of one's personal character to: *set his seal on the magazine.* **2.** To approve;

endorse. —**set the seal on. 1.** To sanction in a formal or authorative way. **2.** To bring to an end, especially in an appropriate manner. —**under seal of.** In confidence or secrecy on specified grounds: *under seal of confession.*

~*tr.v.* **sealed, sealing, seals. 1.** To affix a seal to so as to prove authenticity or attest to accuracy, quality, or conformity to an appropriate standard. **2. a.** To close with or as if with a seal: *seal an envelope; seal one's lips.* **b.** To close hermetically. **c.** To make fast or fill up as with plaster or cement. **d.** To give a protective coating to (a porous surface, for example). **3.** To grant, certify, or designate under seal or authority. **4.** To establish or determine irrevocably. **5.** To settle or agree upon; confirm: *sealed the bargain.* **6.** To provide (a road) with a hard surface. —**seal off.** To close off or enclose (a road or area) so as to prevent entry or exit. [Middle English, from Anglo-French, Old French, from Latin *sigillum,* seal, diminutive of *signum,* sign.] —**seal·a·ble** *adj.*

seal² (seel) *n.* **1.** Any of various aquatic, fish-eating mammals of the families Phocidae *(earless seals)* and Otariidae *(eared seals),* having a sleek, torpedo-shaped body and limbs that are modified into paddle-like flippers. **2.** The pelt or fur of a seal, especially a fur seal. **3.** Leather made from the hide of a seal.

~*intr.v.* **sealed, sealing, seals.** To hunt seals. [Middle English *selch, seel,* Old English *seolh,* from Germanic.]

sea lamprey *n.* A common marine lamprey, *Petromyzon marinus.*

sea lane *n.* An established course along which sea traffic moves, as when leaving or entering port.

seal·ant (se'elənt) *n.* A sealing agent.

sea lavender *n.* Any of several salt-marsh plants of the genus *Limonium,* having clusters of small lavender or pinkish flowers.

sea lawyer *n. Nautical Slang.* An argumentative or fault-finding sailor.

sealed-beam (seeld-beem) *adj.* Designating a motor vehicle headlamp in which the lens is sealed to the prefocused reflector in order to maintain a vacuum in the lamp cavity.

sealed move (seeld) *n.* In chess, the last move by a player before an adjournment, written down and kept secret from the other player until the game is resumed.

sealed orders *pl.n.* Written orders that are not to be read or opened until a stipulated time.

sea legs *pl.n. Informal.* The ability to walk on board ship with steadiness, especially in rough seas. —**get (one's) sea legs.** To become accustomed to the motion of a ship at sea; especially, to be unaffected by seasickness.

seal·er¹ (se'elər) *n.* **1.** One that seals. **2.** An undercoat of paint or varnish used to size a surface. **3.** An officer who inspects, tests, and certifies weights and measures.

sealer² *n.* A person or ship engaged in seal hunting.

seal·er·y (se'eləri) *n., pl.* **-ies.** A place where seals are hunted.

sea lettuce *n.* Any of several green seaweeds of the genus *Ulva,* having thin, irregularly shaped fronds sometimes used as food.

sea level *n.* The level of the ocean's surface; especially, the **mean sea level** *(see).*

sea lily *n.* Any of various marine crinoids having a flower-like body supported by a long stalk.

seal·ing wax (se'eling) *n.* A resinous preparation of shellac, turpentine, a filler, and a dye that is soft and fluid when heated but solidifies upon cooling, used to seal letters, jars, or other objects.

sea lion *n.* Any of several seals of the family Otariidae, having distinct external ears, especially *Zalophus californianus,* of the northern Pacific.

sea loch *n.* An arm of the sea extending inland.

Sea Lord *n. British.* A naval officer who is a member of the Admiralty Board of the Ministry of Defence.

seal point *n.* A type of Siamese cat having dark brown ears, muzzle, paws, and tail.

seal ring *n.* A finger ring bearing a seal.

seal·skin (se'el-skin) *n.* **1.** The pelt or fur of a fur seal, especially the underfur. **2.** A garment made of this skin. —**seal·skin** *adj.*

Sea·ly·ham terrier (se'eli-əm ‖ -ham) *n.* A terrier of a breed developed in Wales, having a wiry white coat, a long head, and short legs. [Originally bred at *Sealyham,* Pembrokeshire, Wales.]

seam (seem) *n.* **1. a.** A line of junction formed by sewing together two pieces of material along their edges. **b.** A similar line, ridge, or groove made by fitting, joining, or lapping together two sections along their edges. **c.** A suture or scar, as left on the skin after surgery. **2.** Any line across a surface, such as a crack, fissure, or wrinkle. **3.** A thin layer or stratum, as of coal or rock. —**bursting at the seams.** Overcrowded or too full.

~*v.* **seamed, seaming, seams.** —*tr.* **1.** To fasten or join with or as if with a seam. **2.** To mark with a groove, wrinkle, scar, or other seamlike line. **3.** In cricket, to bowl (the ball) so that it changes direction as it pitches on the stitched seam. —*intr.* To crack open; become fissured or furrowed. [Middle English *se(e)m,* Old English *seam,* from Germanic.] —**seam·er** *n.*

sea-maid·en (se'e-mayd'n) *n.* Also **sea-maid** (-mayd). A mermaid or sea nymph.

sea·man (se'e-mən) *n., pl.* **-men** (-mən, -men). **1.** A mariner or sailor. **2.** In the British Navy and certain other navies, a sailor ranking below a petty officer.

sea·man·ship (se'emən-ship) *n.* Skill in managing or navigating a boat or ship.

sea·mark (se'e-maark) *n.* **1.** A landmark visible from the sea, as used

a guide in navigation. **2.** The mark along a coastline indicating the upper tidal limits.

seam bowler *n.* In cricket, a bowler, usually of fast or medium pace, who uses the stitched seam of the ball to make it change direction as it pitches. Also called "seamer".

sea mew *n.* Any of various gulls frequenting coastal areas, especially *Larus canus,* of Europe.

sea mile *n.* A former unit of length equal to 6,000 feet or 1,000 fathoms. Compare **nautical mile.**

sea milkwort *n.* A fleshy plant, *Glaux maritima,* of shores and brackish marshes, having pink flowers. Also called "saltwort".

seam·less (se'em-ləss, -liss) *adj.* **1.** Without seams; woven without a seam: *seamless stockings.* **2.** Having a steady or rhythmic flow; harmonious: *seamless prose.* —**seam·less·ness** *n.*

sea·mount (se'e-mownt) *n.* A submerged submarine mountain rising at least 1 000 metres (3,300 feet) above the ocean floor.

sea mouse *n.* Any of various segmented marine worms of the genus *Aphrodite;* especially, *A. aculeata,* having a flattened elliptical body with overlapping scales covered by long hairs.

seam·ster (sem'-stər, semp'- ‖ se'em-) *n. Archaic.* A tailor. [Middle English *semester,* Old English *seamestre : seam,* SEAM + -STER.]

seam·stress (sem'-striss, semp'-, -strəss ‖ se'em-) *n.* A woman who sews, especially for a living.

seam·y (se'emi) *adj.* **-ier, -iest. 1.** Having, marked with, or showing a seam or seams. **2.** Unattractively or unpleasantly rough and raw; sordid: *the seamy side of life.* —**seam·i·ness** *n.*

Sean·ad Éir·eann (sán'naad áirən; *Irish* shán'naad) *n.* The Senate, or upper house of parliament, in the Republic of Ireland. [Irish *seanad,* senate, from Latin *senātus,* SENATE + *Éireann,* of Ireland.]

sé·ance (sáy-onss) *n.* **1.** A meeting of persons to receive messages from or communicate with the spirits of the dead. **2.** A meeting, session, or sitting. [French, "a sitting", from Old French, from *seoir,* to sit, from Latin *sedēre,* to sit.]

sea onion *n.* A plant, *Urginea maritima,* of the Mediterranean area, cultivated for its bulb that yields a powder used medicinally and as a rat poison. Also called "sea squill", "red squill".

sea otter *n.* A large marine otter, *Enhydra lutris,* of northern Pacific coasts, formerly hunted for its soft dark-brown coat.

sea parrot *n.* A bird, the **puffin** *(see).*

sea pen *n.* Any of various marine anthozoans of the families Stylatulidae and Funiculinidae. [From its resemblance to a quill pen.]

sea perch *n.* A fish, the **sea bass** *(see).*

sea pink *n.* A plant, the **thrift** *(see).*

sea·plane (se'e-playn) *n.* An aircraft equipped with floats for landing on or taking off from a body of water.

sea·port (se'e-port ‖ -pōrt) *n.* A harbour or town having facilities for seagoing ships.

sea power *n.* **1.** A nation having naval strength. **2.** Naval strength.

sea purse *n.* A **mermaid's purse** *(see).*

sea purslane *n.* A small Eurasian shrub, *Halimione portulacoides,* that grows on salt marshes and has small, greenish flowers.

sea·quake (se'e-kwayk) *n.* An earthquake under the sea floor.

sear¹ (seer) *v.* **seared, searing, sears.** —*tr.* **1.** To make withered; dry up or shrivel. **2.** To char, scorch, or burn the surface of with or as if with a hot instrument. —*intr.* To become withered or dried up; shrivel. —See Synonyms at **burn.**

~*n.* Any condition, such as a scar, produced by searing. [Middle English *seren,* Old English *sēarian,* from *sēar,* withered.]

sear² *n.* The catch in a gunlock that keeps the hammer halfcocked or fully cocked. [Probably from Old French *serre,* grasp, lock, from *serrer,* to grasp. See **serried.**]

sea raven *n.* A large sculpin, *Hemitripterus americanus,* of the western Atlantic.

search (serch) *v.* **searched, searching, searches.** —*tr.* **1.** To make a thorough examination of (a place, building, or receptacle, for example) in order to find something; look over; explore. **2.** To make a careful examination or investigation of; probe: *search one's conscience.* **3.** To make a thorough check of (a legal document or records, for example); scrutinise: *search a title.* **4.** To examine the person or personal effects of in order to find something concealed, especially as part of a police procedure. **5.** To come to know by investigation; learn. Used with *out.* **6.** To probe (a wound) so as to remove a foreign body. **7.** *Military.* To penetrate every part of (an area), as with gunfire. —*intr.* To conduct a thorough investigation; seek. Often used with *for.* —**search me.** *Informal.* Used to indicate that one is perplexed or unable to answer a question.

~*n.* **1.** An act of searching; an investigation, examination, or probe. **2.** The exercise of **right of search** *(see).* [Middle English *serchen,* from Anglo-French *sercher,* Old French *cerchier,* "to go round", from Late Latin *circāre,* from Latin *circus,* circle.] —**search·a·ble** *adj.* —**search·er** *n.*

search·ing (sérching) *adj.* Penetrating; keen: *a searching gaze.* —**search·ing·ly** *adv.*

search·light (sérch-līt) *n.* **1.** An apparatus containing a light source and a reflector for projecting a bright beam of approximately parallel rays of light. **2.** The beam of light so projected.

search party *n.* A group of persons who make a search, as for a missing person or a fugitive.

search warrant *n.* A warrant, issued in Britain by a Justice of the Peace, giving legal authorisation to a policeman or other officer to make a search.

sear·ing (se'er-ing) *adj.* **1.** Scorching. **2.** Intense; withering.

Searle (serl), **Ronald (William Fordham)** (1920–). British cartoonist. His grotesque draughtsmanship, popular in both the United Kingdom and France, combines wickedness with humour.

sea robin n. Any of various American marine fishes of the family Triglidae, having extremely long pectoral fins with finger-like rays.

sea room n. Space at sea adequate for manoeuvring a ship.

sea·scape (seé-skayp) n. A view or picture of the sea. [SEA + -SCAPE.]

sea scorpion n. Any of various marine fishes of the family Cottidae, having a tapering body and a large bony or spiny head.

Sea Scout n. A member of a Scout unit that gives training in seamanship.

sea serpent n. A large snakelike or dragon-like legendary marine animal.

sea·shell (seé-shel) n. The calcareous shell of a marine mollusc or similar marine organism.

sea·shore (seé-shawr ‖ -shōr) n. 1. Land immediately adjoining the sea. 2. Law. Ground between high-water and low-water marks.

sea·sick·ness (seé-sik-nəss, -niss) n. Nausea and vomiting provoked by the motion of a vessel at sea. **—sea·sick** adj.

sea·side (seé-sīd) n. 1. The seashore. 2. Any coastal area as a place of resort or recreation. Also used adjectivally: a seaside hotel.

sea slug n. Any of various shell-less marine gastropods of the suborder Nudibranchia. Also called "nudibranch".

sea snail n. Any of various small marine fishes of the family Liparidae, especially Liparis liparis, having a soft, tadpole-shaped body with a ventral sucker.

sea snake n. Any of various venomous tropical marine snakes of the family Hydrophidae, chiefly of the Pacific and Indian oceans.

sea·son (seé'z'n) n. 1. a. Any of the four equal divisions of the year, spring, summer, autumn, and winter, indicated by the passage of the sun through an equinox or solstice and derived from the apparent north-south movement of the sun caused by the fixed direction of the earth's axis in solar orbit. b. Any division of the year, rainy or dry, in tropical climates. 2. A recurrent period that is characterised by certain occupations, events, festivities, or crops: the Christmas season. 3. a. The time of year during which a tourist resort is at its busiest; the holiday season: It's quieter out of season. b. The time of year, especially formerly, when fashionable society assembled in a place for a period of intense social activity: the London season. 4. A suitable, natural, or convenient time. 5. Any period of time. 6. The period of year during which a certain activity may legally take place, such as the hunting of a certain species of animal. 7. A sequence of showings or performances having a common theme or feature: a season of Polish films. **—in season.** 1. Available or ready for eating or other use. 2. Legally permitted to being hunted or fished during a stipulated time. 3. At the right moment; opportunely. 4. On heat. Said of animals. **—out of season.** 1. Not available or ready for eating or hunting. 2. Not at the right or proper moment; inopportunely. ~v. **seasoned, -soning, -sons. —tr.** 1. To improve or enhance the flavour of (food) by adding salt, spices, or other flavourings. 2. To add zest, piquancy, or interest to. 3. To dry (timber) until it is usable; cure. 4. To render competent through trial and experience. 5. To accustom; inure. 6. To moderate; temper. **—intr.** To become seasoned. [Middle English sesoun, from Old French seson, from Latin satiō (stem satiōn-), act of sowing (in Vulgar Latin, "sowing time"), from serere (past participle satus), to sow, plant.]

sea·son·a·ble (seé'z'n-əb'l) adj. 1. In keeping with the time or the season: very seasonable weather. 2. Occurring or performed at the proper time; timely. **—sea·son·a·bly** adv.

sea·son·al (seé'z'n'l) adj. Of or dependent upon a particular season: seasonal variations in employment. **—sea·son·al·ly** adv.

seasonal affective disorder n. Abbr. **SAD.** Seasonal mood-swings; specifically, recurrent autumn or winter depression believed due to lack of light.

sea·son·ing (seé'z'n-ing) n. 1. Anything used to flavour food, especially salt and pepper. 2. The act or process by which something, such as timber, is seasoned.

season ticket n. A ticket entitling the holder to some service, such as travel or admission, over a stipulated period of time.

Sea·speak (seé-speek) n. An international maritime language, based on simplified English, enabling communication of essential messages between mariners of different nations.

sea spider n. Any of various marine arachnids of the class Pycnogonida, having long legs and a relatively small body.

sea squill n. A plant, the **sea onion** (see).

sea squirt n. Any of various sedentary marine animals of the class Ascidiacea. [It squirts water when disturbed.]

seat (seet) n. 1. Something that may be sat upon, such as a chair, bench, or the like. 2. A place in which one may sit; especially, a place in which one is entitled to sit, as by the purchase of a ticket. 3. The part of something on which one rests in sitting. 4. a. The buttocks. b. That part of a garment covering the buttocks. 5. a. A part serving as the base of something. b. The surface or part upon which another part sits or rests. 6. a. The place where anything is or is held to be located or based: the seat of the emotions. b. A centre of authority; a capital: the seat of government. 7. A place of abode or residence; especially, a large house that is part of an estate. 8. a. Membership of an official or controlling body, as of a board of directors. b. Membership or the right of membership in a legislative body, obtained by election, appointment, or inheritance. c. Chiefly British. A constituency for parliament. 9. The manner in which one sits and grips the saddle on a horse: She has a good seat.

~tr.v. **seated, seating, seats.** 1. a. To place in or on a seat. b. To cause or assist to sit down. 2. To have or provide seats for: We can seat 300. 3. To repair or replace the seat of (a chair or pair of trousers, for example). 4. To install in a position of authority or eminence. 5. To fix firmly in place. [Middle English sete, from Old Norse sæti, from Germanic.]

sea tangle n. Any of various brown seaweeds, especially of the genus Laminaria.

seat belt n. A safety strap to secure the occupant of a seat in a vehicle or aircraft. Also called "safety belt".

seat·ing (seéting) n. 1. The arrangement or provision of seats in a room, auditorium, or the like. 2. The member or part upon or within which another part is seated. 3. Material for upholstering seats.

SEA·TO (seétō) n. Southeast Asia Treaty Organisation.

seat-of-the-pants adj. Informal. Using practical experience rather than theoretical knowledge: seat-of-the-pants methods for solving real-life problems. [From the notion that experienced pilots fly "by the seat of their pants"; that is, use the experience accumulated while sitting in the cockpit rather than from studying textbooks.]

sea trout n. 1. Any of several trouts or similar fishes that live in the sea but migrate to fresh water to spawn. 2. Any of several marine fishes of the genus Cynoscion, especially the **weakfish** (see).

Se·at·tle (si-átt'l). Port in the northwest of the United States. It is the major port of Washington State.

sea urchin n. Any of various echinoderms of the class Echinoidea, having a soft body enclosed in a round, spiny casing.

sea wall n. An embankment to prevent erosion of a shoreline.

sea walnut n. Any of several ctenophores of the genus Mnemiopsis and related genera, having a translucent, ovoid body with lengthways ridges and rows of hairlike cilia.

sea·wards (seé-wərdz) adv. Also Chiefly U.S. **sea·ward** (-wərd). Towards the sea. **—sea·ward** (seé-wərd) adj.

sea·ware (seé-wair) n. Seaweed that has been cast ashore and is collected for use as fertiliser. [SEA + ware, seaweed, Middle English ware, Old English wār.]

sea·way (seé-way) n. 1. A sea route. 2. An inland waterway for ocean shipping. 3. A ship's progress through the water; headway. 4. A rough sea.

sea·weed (seé-weed) n. 1. Any of numerous marine algae, such as a kelp, rockweed, or gulfweed. 2. Any of various other marine plants.

sea wormwood n. A wormwood, Artemisia maritima, of the Old World, having flowers that yield **santonin** (see).

sea·wor·thy (seé-wurthi) adj. Designating a vessel that is fit to sail or make a sea voyage. **—sea·wor·thi·ness** n.

sea wrack n. Any material cast ashore, especially seaweed.

se·ba·ceous (si-báyshəss) adj. Physiology. 1. Of, pertaining to, or resembling fat or sebum; fatty. 2. Secreting fat or sebum. [Latin sēbāceus : sēbum, tallow (see sebum) + -ACEOUS.]

sebaceous gland n. Any of various glands in the dermis of the skin that open into a hair follicle and produce and secrete sebum.

se·bac·ic acid (si-bássik, -báy-sik) n. A white crystalline acid, $C_{10}H_{18}O_4$, used in the manufacture of certain synthetic resins and fibres, various plasticisers, and polyester rubbers. Also called "decanedioic acid". [Sebacic, from SEBACEOUS (because originally obtained from melted suet).]

Se·bas·ti·an (si-básti-ən, se-, sə-), Saint (third century A.D.). Roman martyr. Believed to have been an officer of the Praetorian Guard, he was executed by a squad of archers. Other legends allege that he survived to be beaten to death by Diocletian.

Se·bas·ti·a·no del Pi·om·bo (si-básti-áanō del pi-ómbō), born Sebastiano Luciano (c. 1485–1547). Venetian painter. Securing the patronage of Pope Clement VII, he was appointed Keeper of the Papal Seals (Piombi), hence his adopted name.

Sebastopol. See Sevastopol.

sebi-, sebo– comb. form. Indicates fat or fatty material; for example, **sebiferous, seborrhoea.** [New Latin, from Latin sēbum, tallow. See **sebum.**]

se·bif·er·ous (si-bíffərəss, se-) adj. Producing or secreting fatty, oily, or waxy matter; sebaceous. [SEBI- + -FEROUS.]

seb·or·rhoe·a (sébbə-reé-ə) n. A disease of the sebaceous glands characterised by excessive secretion of sebum or an alteration in its quality, resulting in an oily coating, crusts, or scales on the skin. [SEBO- + -RRHOEA.] **—seb·or·rhoe·al, seb·or·rhoe·ic** adj.

se·bum (seébəm) n. The oily secretion of the sebaceous glands, which protects the skin from desiccation. Also called "smegma". [Latin sēbum†, tallow.]

sec¹ (sek) adj. 1. Dry. Said of wines. 2. Somewhat sweet. Said of champagne. Compare brut. [French.]

sec² n. Informal. A second or moment: Just a sec!

sec³ 1. secant. 2. second (unit of time). 3. second (unit of angular measure).

SEC Securities and Exchange Commission (in the United States).

sec. 1. secondary. 2. secretary. 3. sector.

SE·CAM (seé-kam) n. Système électronique couleur avec mémoire: a system of colour-television broadcasting used in France.

se·cant (seé-kənt ‖ U.S. also -kant) n. Abbr. **sec** 1. In geometry. a. A straight line intersecting a curve at two or more points. b. The straight line drawn from the centre through one end of a circular arc and intersecting the tangent to the other end of the arc. 2. In trigonometry. a. The reciprocal of the cosine of an angle. b. For an acute angle, the ratio of the hypotenuse to the side of a right-angled triangle adjacent to the acute angle. [French (ligne) secante, "cutting line", from Latin *secāns* (stem *secant-*), present participle of *secāre*, to cut.]

sec·a·teurs (séckə-térz, -tərz) *pl.n. Chiefly British.* Pruning shears made to be used with one hand, often spring-assisted.

sec·co (séckō) *n., pl.* **-cos.** The art or an example of painting on dry plaster. Compare **fresco.** [Italian, "dry", from Latin *siccus.*]

se·cede (si-séed) *intr.v.* **-ceded, -ceding, -cedes.** To withdraw formally from membership in an organisation, association, or alliance. [Latin *sēcēdere,* to go away : *sē-,* apart + *cēdere,* to go.]

se·cern (si-sérn) *tr.v.* **-cerned, -cerning, -cerns. 1.** To discern as separate; distinguish. **2.** *Physiology.* To secrete. Used of a gland or follicle. [Latin *sēcernere,* to separate : *sē,* apart + *cernere,* to separate, discern.] **—se·cern·ment** *n.*

se·ces·sion (si-sésh'n) *n.* **1.** The act or an instance of seceding. **2.** *Usually capital* **S.** *U.S.* The withdrawal of 11 Southern states from the Federal Union in 1860–61, precipitating the American Civil War. [Latin *sēcessiō* (stem *sēcessiōn-*), from *sēcēdere* (past participle *secessus*), SECEDE.] **—se·ces·sion·al** *adj.*

se·ces·sion·ism (si-sésh'n-iz'm) *n.* The policy of those maintaining the right of secession. **—se·ces·sion·ist** *adj. & n.*

se·clude (si-klōōd ‖ -klewd) *tr.v.* **-cluded, -cluding, -cludes. 1.** To remove or set apart from others; place in solitude. **2.** To screen from view; make private. [Middle English *secluden,* to shut off, keep away, from Latin *sēclūdere* : *sē,* apart + *claudere,* to shut.]

se·clud·ed (si-klōōd-id ‖ -klewd-) *adj.* **1.** Removed or remote from others; solitary. **2.** Screened from view; hidden or private. **—se·clud·ed·ly** *adv.* **—se·clud·ed·ness** *n.*

se·clu·sion (si-klōō-zh'n ‖ -klew-) *n.* **1. a.** The act of secluding. **b.** The state of being secluded. **2.** A secluded place or abode. **—See** Synonyms at **solitude.** [Medieval Latin *sēclūsiō* (stem *sēclūsiōn-*), from Latin *sēclūdere* (past participle *sēclūsus*), SECLUDE.]

se·clu·sive (si-klōō-siv ‖ -klew-, -ziv) *adj.* Fond of, seeking, or tending to seclusion. **—se·clu·sive·ly** *adv.* **—se·clu·sive·ness** *n.*

sec·ond[1] (séckənd ‖ séckənt) *n.* **1.** *Abbr.* **s, sec** *Symbol* ″ **a.** A unit of time equal to ¹/₆₀ of a minute. **b.** The SI unit of time equal to the duration of 9,192,631,770 periods of the radiation produced by the transition between two hyperfine levels in the ground state of caesium-133. **2.** *Informal.* A brief lapse of time; a moment. **3.** *Abbr.* **s, sec** *Symbol* ″ In geometry, a unit of angular measure equal to ¹/₆₀ of a minute of arc. **—See** Synonyms at **moment.** [Middle English *seconde,* unit in geometry, from Old French, from Medieval Latin *(pars minūta) secunda,* "second (small part)" (after the second sexagesimal division), from Latin, feminine of *secundus,* SECOND (in number).]

sec·ond[2] (séckənd) *adj.* **1. a.** Coming next after the first in order, place, rank, time, or quality. **b.** Graded or judged to be between the first and third grades or levels. **2. a.** Repeating an initial instance; another: *a second chance.* **b.** Alternate: *every second year.* **c.** Similar to or evoking the memory of a specified person or event from the past: *a second Hitler.* **3.** Inferior to another; subordinate: *second to none.* **4.** *Music.* **a.** Having a lower pitch. **b.** Singing or playing a part having a lower range. **c.** Singing or playing a part subordinate to the principal one. **5.** Designating the next-to-lowest forward gear, as in a motor vehicle or bicycle.

~*n.* **1.** The ordinal number two in a series. **2.** One that is next in order, place, time, or quality after the first. **3.** An article of merchandise that is imperfect in some way. **4.** The official attendant of a contestant in a duel or boxing match. **5.** *Music.* **a.** The interval between consecutive notes on the diatonic scale. **b.** A note separated by this interval from another note. **c.** A combination of two such notes in notation or in harmony. **d.** The second part, instrument, or voice in a harmonised composition. **6.** An utterance of endorsement of a proposal or nomination, as in debating procedure. **7.** The next-to-lowest forward gear, as in a motor vehicle or bicycle, having the second-highest ratio. **8.** *Plural. Informal.* A second helping of a dish or a second or pudding course of a meal. **9.** *British.* A second-class honours degree.

~*tr.v.* **seconded, -onding, -onds. 1.** To attend (a duellist, for example) as an aide or assistant. **2.** To promote or encourage; reinforce. **3.** To endorse (a motion or nomination) as a required preliminary to discussion or vote.

~*adv.* **1.** In the second order, place, or rank. **2.** But for one other; save one. Sometimes used in combination: *the second-highest peak.* [Middle English, from Old French, from Latin *secundus,* following, coming next.]

se·cond[3] (si-kónd, sə-) *tr.v.* **-conded, -conding, -conds.** *British.* **1.** To transfer (an employee) temporarily to another department, branch, or task. **2.** *Military.* To remove (an officer) from service with a view to transferral to another post, such as a staff or nonregimental post. [French *en second,* in second rank (or position).]

Second Advent *n.* The **Second Coming** (see).

sec·on·dar·y (séckən-dəri, -dri ‖ -derri) *adj. Abbr.* **sec. 1. a.** One step removed from the first; of the second rank; not primary. **b.** Inferior; lesser. **2.** Derived from what is primary or original: *a secondary source.* **3.** Of, pertaining to, or designating the shorter flight feathers projecting along the inner part of the edge of a bird's wing. **4.** *Electricity.* Having an induced current that is generated by an inductively coupled primary. Said of a circuit or coil. **5.** *Chemistry.* **a.** Designating a compound in which two hydrogen atoms have been replaced by a metal, radical, or alkyl group. **b.** Designating an organic compound having a functional group attached to a carbon that is attached to one hydrogen and two other groups. **6.** *Geology.* Resulting from changes in the pre-existing minerals. **7.** Of, pertain-

ing to, or designating education received at secondary school. **8.** Designating an industry that uses the raw materials gathered by a primary industry and processes or manufactures products from them. **9.** *Linguistics.* Having been patterned on a word that was itself derived from another word, such as *hauntingly,* from *haunting,* from *haunt.* **10.** *Botany.* Designating plant growth of a type caused by activity of the cambium and resulting in an increase in the width of stems and branches.

~*n., pl.* **secondaries. 1.** One that acts in an auxiliary, subordinate, or inferior capacity. **2.** Any of the shorter flight feathers projecting along the inner part of the edge of a bird's wing. **3.** *Electricity.* A coil or circuit having an induced current. **4.** *Astronomy.* A body that orbits a primary; a satellite. **5.** A secondary colour. [Middle English, from Latin *secundārius,* from *secundus,* SECOND.] **—sec·on·dar·i·ly** *adv.* **—sec·on·dar·i·ness** *n.*

secondary accent *n.* An accent weaker than a primary accent, but stronger than a tertiary or weak stress. Also called "secondary stress". Compare **primary accent, tertiary accent.**

secondary battery *n. Electricity.* A **storage battery** (see).

secondary cell *n.* A rechargeable electric cell that converts chemical energy into electrical energy by a reversible chemical reaction. Also called "storage cell". Compare **primary cell.**

secondary colour *n.* A colour produced by mixing two primary colours in approximately equal proportions.

secondary depression *n.* A small, concentrated area of low atmospheric pressure on the margin of a main depression.

secondary electron *n.* An electron produced in secondary emission.

secondary emission *n. Physics.* The emission of electrons from the surface of a substance that has been bombarded by electrons or ions.

secondary group *n. Sociology.* An association of people on the basis of some shared formal characteristic, often a large group involving little contact between members, such as a professional or sporting body. Compare **primary group.**

secondary modern school *n.* Formerly in Britain, a secondary school for students who failed their eleven-plus, specialising in more technical or practical subjects than a grammar school. Compare **comprehensive, grammar school, public school.**

secondary picketing *n.* Action taken in support of a picket by persons other than those directly involved in the dispute in question. **—secondary picket** *n.*

secondary school *n.* Any school providing education for young people, usually between the ages of 11 and 18, after primary school but preceding university or an occupation.

secondary sexual characteristic *n.* Any of various anatomical, physiological, or behavioural characteristics, such as voice quality, abundance of facial hair, or breast development, that first appear in humans at puberty and differentiate between the sexes without having a direct reproductive function.

second best *n.* One that is slightly or just below the best, as in quality, value, or importance. **—sec·ond-best** (séckənd-bést) *adj.*

second chamber *n.* The upper house in a bicameral legislative body.

second childhood *n.* Senility; dotage.

second class *n.* **1.** The group or class that is next below the first or highest, as in quality, rank, or value. **2.** The class on a train or other means of transport ranking next below first class.

sec·ond-class, second class (séckənd-klaáss ‖ séckənt-, -klass) *adj.* **1. a.** In the rank or class that is next below the first or best. **b.** Inferior; second-rate. **c.** Socially, economically, or politically disadvantaged: *a second-class citizen.* **2.** Of, pertaining to, or designating travel accommodation ranking below the highest or first class. **3.** Of, pertaining to, or designating a class of mail in the United Kingdom that is handled and delivered more slowly than first-class mail. **4.** *British.* Pertaining to or designating an honours degree or examination result in the class below one of first class. **—sec·ond·class** *adv.*

Second Coming *n.* The return of Christ as judge upon the last day. Also called "Second Advent", "parousia".

second cousin *n.* See **cousin.**

sec·ond-de·gree burn (séckənd-di-grée) *n.* A burn that damages underlying skin tissue. Not in current technical usage.

Second Empire *n.* **1.** The empire and government of the Emperor Napoleon III of France. **2.** The period of the reign of Napoleon III (1852–70).

~*adj.* Of, resembling, or pertaining to the ornate style of furniture and architecture developed in the Second Empire.

sec·ond-gen·e·ra·tion (séckənd-jénnə-ráysh'n) *adj.* Pertaining or belonging to a generation whose grandparents were original migrants: *second-generation Australians.*

second growth *n.* Trees that cover an area after the removal of the original forest growth as by cutting or fire.

sec·ond-guess (séckənd-géss) *v.* **-guessed, -guessing, -guesses.** *Chiefly U.S.* —*tr.* **1.** To criticise (a decision) after the outcome is known. **2.** To anticipate the moves of; outwit. —*intr.* To criticise a decision in retrospect. **—sec·ond-guess·er** *n.*

second hand[1] *n.* The hand of a timepiece that marks the seconds.

second hand[2] *n.* An intermediary person or source. Usually preceded by *at: heard at second hand.*

sec·ond·hand, sec·ond-hand (séckənd-hánd ‖ séckənt-) *adj.* **1.** Previously used or owned by another; not new. **2.** Dealing in

previously used goods. **3.** Obtained or derived from another; not original. **—sec·ond·hand, sec·ond-hand** *adv.*
sec·ond-in-com·mand (séckənd-in-kə-ma̋and || -mánd) *n., pl.* **sec-onds-in-command.** The person next in authority to someone in charge; especially, a military officer ranking second to a commanding officer.
second lieutenant *n.* An officer of the British Army of the lowest commissioned grade, ranking below a lieutenant, equivalent in rank to a sublieutenant in the Navy and a pilot officer in the Air Force.
sec·ond·ly (séckəndli) *adv.* In the second place; second. Used chiefly to introduce a second enumerated point.
second mate *n.* The officer on a merchant ship ranking below the first mate. Also called "second officer".
se·cond·ment (si-kóndmənt, sə-) *n. British.* A transfer, as of an officer or employee, to a different position or department, where his expertise is needed temporarily, or where he may gain experience.
second mortgage *n.* A mortgage on property that is already mortgaged and that has a claim secondary to the first mortgage.
second nature *n.* An acquired personal disposition, tendency, or habit so long practised as to seem innate.
se·con·do (se-kón-dō, si-) *n., pl.* **-di** (-dee). *Music.* **1.** The second part in a concert piece; especially, the lower part in a piano duet. **2.** One who performs such a part. [Italian, "second", from Latin *secundus,* SECOND (next).]
second person *n. Grammar.* The form of a pronoun, verb, or verb inflection used in referring to the person or persons addressed; for example, *you* and *shall* in *you shall not enter.*
sec·ond-rate (séckənd-ráyt) *adj.* Not of the best quality; mediocre; inferior. **—sec·ond-rat·er** *n.*
second reading *n.* The intermediate stage in the enactment of a law in a legislative body, especially: **1.** In Britain, the debate and vote on a bill's general features. **2.** In the United States, the debate and vote on a bill, sometimes with amendments, after a committee has reported on it.
Second Republic *n.* **1.** The French republic and government from 1848 to 1852. **2.** The period of this republic's existence.
second sex *n.* Women collectively; the female sex. Preceded by *the.* Usually considered offensive.
second sight *n.* The ability to perceive future or remote events or things; clairvoyance.
sec·ond-strike (séckənd-strīk) *adj.* Designating, based on, or employing nuclear weapons capable of retaliating after an initial enemy attack: *a second-strike force; second-strike capability.*
second string *n. British.* A person or thing held in reserve.
~*adj.* Also **sec·ond-string** (séckənd-stríng). *Chiefly U.S.* **1.** Designating or pertaining to a reserve player or team. **2.** Second-rate; inferior.
second thought *n. Usually plural.* A revised opinion on a matter, especially when it has previously been considered too quickly. **—on second thoughts.** Used to introduce a revised opinion.
second wind *n.* Renewed energy or ability to function, as after fatigue or breathlessness through exertion.
Second World *n.* The countries of the Soviet bloc. See **First World.**
Second World War *n.* **World War II** *(see).*
se·cre·cy (seékrə-si) *n.* **1.** The fact or condition of being secret or hidden. **2.** The ability to keep secrets. **3.** A tendency to be secretive or to conceal things. [Middle English, variant of *secretee,* from *secre(t),* SECRET.]
se·cret (seé-krit, -krət) *adj.* **1.** Kept from general knowledge or view; kept hidden. **2.** Tending not to disclose information; discreet. **3.** Operating in a clandestine or confidential manner. **4.** Not visibly expressed or acknowledged. **5.** Not frequented; secluded. **6.** Known or shared only by the initiated: *secret rites.* **7.** Beyond ordinary understanding; mysterious. **8.** Of, pertaining to, or containing information whose secrecy is important to national security.
~*n.* **1.** Something kept hidden from others or known only to oneself or to a few. **2.** Something that remains beyond understanding or explanation; a mystery. **3.** A factor or element needed to achieve a particular end or state: *the secret of her success.* **4.** *Capital* **S.** A variable prayer said after the Offertory and before the Preface in the Tridentine Mass. **—in secret.** In a manner or place not known to others; in secrecy. [Middle English *secre(t),* from Old French, from Latin *sēcrētus,* separate, out of the way, secret, from the past participle of *sēcernere,* to put apart, separate : *sē,* apart + *cernere,* to separate.] **—se·cret·ly** *adv.*
Synonyms: *secret, stealthy, covert, clandestine, furtive, surreptitious, underhand.*
secret agent *n.* A spy.
se·cret·a·gogue (si-kreétə-gog || -gōg) *n. Physiology.* An agent that stimulates glandular secretion. [SECRET(E) + -AGOGUE.]
sec·re·taire (séckrə-táir) *n.* Also *U.S.* **secretary.** A writing desk with a compartment that can be closed. [French, secretary.]
sec·re·tar·i·at (séckrə-táir-i-ət, -at) *n.* **1. a.** A department of an international or public organisation that administers and executes the organisation's decisions and programmes under the direction of a secretary-general or secretary. **b.** The premises or staff of such a department. **2.** The position of a secretary. **3.** A group of secretaries in a company or other organisation.
sec·re·tar·y (séckrə-tri || -terri) *n., pl.* **-ies.** *Abbr.* **sec., secy. 1. a.** A person employed to handle correspondence, keep files, and do clerical work for an individual or company. **b.** An officer who keeps records of meetings and legal transactions and is responsible for the day-to-day business of a club, society, or similar organisation. **c.** A company secretary *(see).* **2.** *Often capital* **S. a.** In Britain, a secretary of state. **b.** In the United States, Australia, and certain other countries, a minister who is the head of a government department: *Secretary Shultz.* **3.** A diplomatic officer assisting an ambassador or minister. **4.** Variant of **secretaire.** [Middle English *secretarie,* from Medieval Latin *sēcrētārius,* confidential officer, secretary, from Latin *sēcrētus,* SECRET.] **—sec·re·tar·i·al** (-táir-i-əl) *adj.*
secretary bird *n.* A large southern African bird of prey, *Sagittarius serpentarius.* [The quills on its crest resemble quill pens.]
sec·re·tar·y-gen·er·al (séckrə-tri-jén-rəl, -jénnə- || -terri-) *n., pl.* **secretaries-general.** *Sometimes capital* **S,** *capital* **G.** A principal administrative officer, as in certain political parties or international bodies: *the secretary-general of NATO.*
secretary of state *n., pl.* **secretaries of state.** *Often capital* **S,** *capital* **S. 1.** A British minister who heads any of several government departments. **2.** The foreign minister of the United States.
se·crete[1] (si-kreét) *tr.v.* **-creted, -creting, -cretes.** To generate and separate out (a substance) from cells or bodily fluids. [Back-formation from SECRETION.] **—se·cre·tor** *n.*
se·crete[2] *tr.v.* **-creted, -creting, -cretes. 1.** To conceal. **2.** To appropriate (money, for example) secretly. —See Synonyms at **hide.** [From obsolete *secret,* to conceal, keep secret, from SECRET.]
se·cre·tin (si-kreétin) *n.* A hormone secreted in the duodenum to stimulate the flow of pancreatic juice. [SECRET(ION) + -IN.]
se·cre·tion (si-kreésh'n) *n.* **1.** The process of secreting a substance, especially one that is not a waste, from blood or cells. **2.** A substance so secreted. [Latin *sēcrētiō* (stem *sēcrētiōn-*), separation, from *sēcernere,* to separate. See **secret.**]
se·cre·tive (seékrətiv, si-kreétiv) *adj.* **1.** Tending not to disclose information; uncommunicative. **2.** Secretory. **—se·cre·tive·ly** *adv.* **—se·cre·tive·ness** *n.*
se·cre·tor (si-kreétər) *n.* A person in whose saliva and other body fluids the A or B antigens determining blood group can be detected.
se·cre·to·ry (si-kreétəri) *adj.* Pertaining to or performing the function of secretion.
secret police *n.* A police force, operating largely in secrecy and often with illegal methods, serving to control dissidents and ensure the security of the state.
secret service *n.* **1.** A government agency pursuing intelligence and counterintelligence activities. **2.** The activities of such an agency. **3.** *Capital* **S,** *capital* **S.** The branch of the U.S. Treasury Department concerned with the protection of the President, other leading public figures, and their families, and with the suppression of counterfeiting. In this sense, preceded by *the.*
sect (sekt) *n.* **1.** A group of people forming a distinct unit within a larger group by virtue of certain refinements or distinctions of belief or practice. **2. a.** A breakaway religious body; especially, one regarded as extreme, intolerant, or exclusive by the larger group from which it has separated. **b.** Any religious denomination, especially one regarded as exclusive or outlandish. **3.** Any small faction united by common interests or beliefs: *a Maoist sect.* [Middle English *secte,* from Old French, from Latin *secta,* "following", from *sectus,* archaic past participle of *sequī,* to follow.]
sect. sector.
-sect *v. comb. form.* Indicates cut or divide; for example, **trisect, bisect.** [Latin *sectus,* past participle of *secāre,* to cut.]
sec·tar·i·an (sek-táir-i-ən) *adj.* **1.** Pertaining to, characteristic of, or involving a sect or faction or its members. **2.** Adhering or confined to the dogmatic views of a sect.
~*n.* **1.** A member of a sect. **2.** One characterised by bigoted adherence to a factional viewpoint. **—sec·tar·i·an·ise** *v.* **—sec·tar·i·an·ism** *n.*
sec·ta·ry (séktəri) *n., pl.* **-ries. 1.** A sectarian. **2.** A dissenter from an established church; specifically, a Protestant nonconformist in the 17th and 18th centuries. [Medieval Latin *sectārius,* from Latin *secta,* SECT.]
sec·tile (sék-tīl || *U.S. also* -t'l) *adj.* Capable of being cut or severed smoothly by a knife. [Latin *sectilis,* from *secāre,* to cut.] **—sec·til·i·ty** (sek-tilləti) *n.*
sec·tion (séksh'n) *n.* **1. a.** Any of several component or constituent parts or groups; a portion. **b.** A part separated from a main body by or as if by cutting. **2.** Any division or grouping within an organised whole: *the accounts section.* **3.** A subdivision of a written work. **4.** A division of a statute or legal code. **5.** A grouping in an orchestra or band, consisting of members who play the same type of instrument. **6.** In printing, a **signature** *(see).* **7.** The act or process of separating or cutting; especially, the surgical separation of tissue. **8.** A thin slice, as of tissue, suitable for microscopic examination. **9.** A segment of a fruit, especially a citrus fruit. **10.** The representation of a solid object as it would appear if cut by an intersecting plane, so that the internal structure is displayed. **11.** In geometry, the planar configuration formed by the intersection of a solid by a plane. Also called "plane section". **12.** *U.S.* A district or area with some particular characteristic. **13. a.** *N.Z.* A plot of land. **b.** *U.S.* A land unit of one square mile. **14. a.** *Military.* An army tactical unit smaller than a platoon and larger than a squad. **b.** A unit of vessels or aircraft within a division. **15. a.** A character (§) used in printing to mark the beginning of a section. **b.** This character used as the fourth in a series of reference marks for footnotes. In both senses, also called "section mark". **—in section.** In the view revealed by taking a section.
~*tr.v.* **sectioned, -tioning, -tions. 1.** To separate or divide into parts. **2.** To separate (tissue) surgically. **3.** To cut so as to reveal a

section. **4.** *British.* To get (a person) committed to a mental hospital under the relevant section of the mental health legislation. [French, from Latin *sectiō* (stem *sectiōn-*), a cutting, from *sect-*, past participial stem of *secāre*, to cut.]

-section *n. comb. form.* Indicates the act or process of dividing or cutting; for example, **vivisection.** [From SECTION.]

sec·tion·al (séksh'n'l) *adj.* **1.** Pertaining to or characteristic of a particular section: *sectional prejudice in society.* **2.** Composed of or divided into component sections. **—sec·tion·al·ly** *adv.*

sec·tion·al·ise, sec·tion·al·ize (séksh'n'l-īz) *tr.v.* **-ised, -ising, -ises.** **1.** To divide into sections, especially into geographical sections. **2.** To make sectional in nature or outlook. **—sec·tion·al·i·sa·tion** (-ī-záysh'n || *U.S.* -i-) *n.* **—sec·tion·al·ism** *n.* **—sec·tion·al·ist** *n. & adj.*

sec·tor (sék-tər || -tawr) *n. Abbr.* **sec., sect.** **1.** In geometry, the portion of a circle bounded by two radii and one of the intercepted arcs. **2.** A measuring instrument consisting of two graduated arms hinged together at one end. **3.** *Military.* **a.** A division of a defensive position for which one unit is responsible. **b.** A division of an offensive position; a zone of action. **4.** A part or division of something, such as a specialised field of activity or interest: *the public sector of the economy.* [Late Latin, from Latin, cutter, from *secāre,* to cut.] **—sec·tor·al, sec·tor·i·al** (sek-táwr-i-əl || -tṓr-) *adj.*

sec·u·lar (séckewlər) *adj.* **1.** Of or pertaining to temporal rather than to spiritual matters; worldly. **2.** Not pertaining to or concerned with religion or a religious body: *secular schools.* **3.** Advocating or characterised by secularism: *a secular outlook.* **4.** Not following monastic vows or living in a religious community. Said of the clergy. Compare **regular. 5.** Occurring or observed once in an age or century. **6.** Lasting for centuries.

~n. **1.** A secular clergyman. **2.** A layman. [Middle English *seculer,* from Old French, from Latin *saeculāris,* from *saeculum*†, generation, age.] **—sec·u·lar·ly** *adv.*

sec·u·la·rise, sec·u·la·rize (séckewlə-rīz) *tr.v.* **-rised, -rising, -rises.** **1.** To transfer from ecclesiastical or religious to civil or lay use or ownership. **2.** To draw away from religious influences or orientation; make worldly. **3.** To lift the monastic rules from (a cleric); make secular. **—sec·u·lar·i·sa·tion** (-rī-záysh'n || *U.S.* -ri-) *n.* **—sec·u·la·ris·er** *n.*

sec·u·lar·ism (séckewlə-riz'm) *n.* **1.** Religious scepticism or indifference. **2.** The view that religious considerations should be excluded from civil affairs or public education. **—sec·u·lar·ist** *n.* **—sec·u·lar·is·tic** (-rístik) *adj.*

sec·u·lar·i·ty (séckew-lárrəti) *n., pl.* **-ties.** **1.** The condition or quality of being secular. **2.** Something secular.

secular parallax *n. Astronomy.* The continuously increasing angular displacement in the position of stars resulting from the motion of the sun through space. See **parallax.**

se·cund (si-kúnd, sée-kund, sé-) *adj. Botany.* Arranged on or turned to one side of an axis. [Latin *secundus,* following, second.]

sec·un·dines (séckən-dīnz, -dinz, si-kúndinz) *pl.n. Physiology.* The **afterbirth** *(see).* [Late Latin *secundīnae,* from Latin *secundus,* second, following. See **second.**]

se·cure (si-kéwr, sə-) *adj.* **-curer, -curest.** **1.** Free from danger or risk of loss or escape; safe. **2.** Free from fear or doubt; not anxious or unsure. **3. a.** Not likely to fail or give way; stable; strong. **b.** Well-fastened. **4.** Assured; certain; guaranteed. **5.** *Archaic.* Careless or overconfident.

~v. **secured, -curing, -cures.** *—tr.* **1.** To guard from danger or risk of loss; specifically, to fortify or consolidate (a military position). **2.** To make firm or tight; fasten. **3.** To make certain; guarantee; ensure. **4. a.** To guarantee payment to (a creditor). **b.** To guarantee payment of (a loan, for example) with a pledge. **5.** To confine or lock up. **6.** To get possession of; acquire; procure. **7.** To bring about; effect. *—intr.* To become or make oneself safe. Used with *against.* [Latin *sēcūrus,* "without care" : *sē,* without + *cūra,* care.] **—se·cur·a·ble** *adj.* **—se·cure·ly** *adv.* **—se·cure·ment** *n.* **—se·cure·ness** *n.* **—se·cur·er** *n.*

Securities and Exchange Commission *n. Abbr.* **SEC** A U.S. governmental agency that supervises the issue and exchange of securities so as to protect investors against malpractice.

se·cu·ri·ty (si-kéwr-əti-, sə-) *n., pl.* **-ties.** **1.** The state of being secure; especially: **a.** Freedom from risk or danger. **b.** Freedom from doubt, anxiety, or fear. **2.** Anything that gives or assures safety. **3.** Something deposited or given as assurance of the fulfilment of an obligation; a pledge. **4.** One who undertakes to guarantee the obligation of another; a surety. **5. a.** A document that guarantees the right of the holder to repayment, as of a debt or claim. **b.** *Plural.* Broadly, investments in the form of stocks, shares, and bonds. **6. a.** Measures adopted to thwart theft, espionage, escape, or attack. **b.** An organisation or department entrusted with such operations. [Middle English *securite,* from Latin *sēcūritās* (stem *sēcūritāt-*), from *sēcūrus,* SECURE.]

security blanket *n. Chiefly U.S.* A blanket or other familiar object carried about by a child to give a feeling of security.

security clearance *n.* **1.** The investigation of persons or groups to ensure that they are not a security risk, before allowing them access to confidential information or to people or places requiring protection. **2.** The permission or clearance subsequently granted.

Security Council *n. Abbr.* **SC** The permanent peace-keeping organ of the United Nations, composed of five permanent members and ten elected members.

security risk *n.* **1.** A government servant or candidate for government service thought to be a danger to national security because of dissident political beliefs, liability to blackmail, or unreliability of character. **2.** Any person thought likely to be disloyal.

secy. secretary.

se·dan (si-dán, sə-) *n.* **1.** A sedan chair. **2.** *U.S.* A saloon car. [Perhaps obscurely from Vulgar Latin *sedda* (unattested), variant of Latin *sella,* seat, chair.]

sedan chair *n.* A portable enclosed chair for one person, fashionable in Britain in the 17th and 18th centuries, having poles front and rear and carried by two men. Also called "sedan".

se·date[1] (si-dáyt) *adj.* Serenely deliberate in character or manner; composed; collected. See Synonyms at **serious.** [Latin *sēdātus,* past participle of *sēdāre,* to settle, calm, compose, from *sedēre,* to sit.] **—se·date·ly** *adv.* **—se·date·ness** *n.*

se·date[2] *tr.v.* **-dated, -dating, -dates.** To administer a sedative to (a patient). [Back-formation from SEDATIVE.]

se·da·tion (si-dáysh'n) *n.* **1.** The reduction of stress or excitement by administration of a sedative. **2.** The calm relaxed condition induced by a sedative.

sed·a·tive (séddətiv) *adj.* Having a soothing, calming, or tranquillising effect.

~n. A sedative agent or drug. [Middle English, from Medieval Latin *sēdātīvus,* from *sēdāre,* to calm, settle; see **sedate** (adjective).]

Sed·don (sédd'n), **Richard (John),** also known as King Dick (1845–1906). British-born New Zealand politician. He became a Liberal cabinet minister in 1891 and was prime minister (1893–1906).

sed·en·tar·y (sédd'n-təri, -tri || *U.S.* -terri) *adj.* **1.** Characterised by or requiring much sitting: *a sedentary job.* **2.** Accustomed to sitting or to taking little exercise. **3.** Remaining in one area; not migratory: *sedentary birds.* **4.** Seated or in a sitting posture: *a sedentary statue.* **5.** *Zoology.* Attached to a surface and not free-moving. Said of a barnacle, for example. [French *sédentaire,* from Latin *sedentārius,* from *sedēns* (stem *sedent-*), present participle of *sedēre,* to sit.] **—sed·en·tar·i·ly** *adv.* **—sed·en·tar·i·ness** *n.*

Se·der (sáydər) *n., pl.* **-ders** or **Sedarim** (si-daárim, sáydər-éem). *Sometimes small* **s.** *Judaism.* The feast commemorating the exodus of the Israelites from Egypt, celebrated on the first evening or first two evenings of Passover. [Hebrew *sēdher,* "order", "arrangement".]

se·de·runt (si-déer-ənt, say-, -dáir-, -ōōnt) *n. Scottish.* **1.** A session or sitting, especially of an ecclesiastical assembly. **2.** The people present at such a session. **3.** Any session of talking or drinking. [Latin, they (the persons named below) sat, from *sedēre,* to sit.]

sedge (sej) *n.* Any of numerous plants of the family Cyperaceae, especially of the genus *Carex,* resembling grasses but having solid rather than hollow stems and often found near water. [Middle English *segge,* Old English *secg,* from Germanic.] **—sedg·y** *adj.*

sedge warbler *n.* A small bird, *Acrocephalus schoenobaenus,* commonly found near water, having a brown streaked plumage.

se·dil·i·a (si-dí-li-ə, se-, dée-, -dí-) *pl.n. Singular* **sedile** (-li). *Usually used with a plural verb.* The seats or set of seats, generally three, in the sanctuary of a church for the use of the celebrant and his ministers. [Latin *sedīlia,* plural of *sedīle,* seat, from *sedēre,* to sit.]

sed·i·ment (séddi-mənt) *n.* **1.** Material that settles to the bottom of a liquid; dregs; lees. **2.** Material comprising weathered particles of pre-existing rock, or particles of chemical or organic origin, deposited by wind, water, or glacial ice. [French, from Latin *sedimentum,* a settling, from *sedēre,* to sit, settle.]

sed·i·men·ta·ry (séddi-mén-təri, -tri) *adj.* **1.** Of, containing, resembling, or derived from sediment. **2.** *Geology.* Of, designating, or pertaining to rocks formed from sediment.

sed·i·men·ta·tion (séddi-men-táysh'n, -mən-) *n.* The act or process of depositing sediment; especially, the process of forming sedimentary rocks.

sed·i·men·tol·o·gy (séddi-men-tólləji, -mən-) *n.* The study of the classification and origin of sedimentary rocks and associated geological deposits. [SEDIMENT + -LOGY.] **—sed·i·men·tol·o·gic·al** (-méntə-lójik'l) *adj.* **—sed·i·men·tol·o·gist** (-tólləjist) *n.*

se·di·tion (si-dísh'n, sə-) *n.* **1.** Conduct or language inciting to rebellion against the authority of the state. **2.** *Archaic.* An insurrection; a rebellion. [Middle English *sedicioun,* from Old French *sedition,* from Latin *sēditiō* (stem *sēditiōn-*), "a going apart", separation : *sē, sēd,* apart + *itiō,* act of going, from *īre* (past participle *itus*), to go.]

se·di·tious (si-díshəss, sə-) *adj.* **1.** Of, resembling, or characterised by sedition. **2.** Engaged in or inclined to sedition. —See Synonyms at **insubordinate. —se·di·tious·ly** *adv.* **—se·di·tious·ness** *n.*

se·duce (si-déwss || -dōōss) *tr.v.* **-duced, -ducing, -duces.** **1.** To induce to have sexual intercourse with one. **2. a.** To persuade or beguile. Often used with *into.* **b.** To win over; attract. **3. a.** To lead (a person) away from duty or proper conduct. **b.** Broadly, to entice into wrongful behaviour; corrupt. —See Synonyms at **lure.** [Middle English *seduisen,* from Old French *seduire* (present stem *seduis-*), from Latin *sēdūcere,* to lead away : *sē,* apart + *dūcere,* to lead.] **—se·duc·er** *n.* **—se·duce·a·ble, se·duc·i·ble** *adj.*

se·duc·tion (si-dúksh'n) *n.* Also *archaic* **se·duce·ment** (si-déwss-mənt || -dōōss-). **1.** The act of seducing or the condition of being seduced. **2.** Something that seduces or has the qualities to seduce to wrongdoing; a temptation. **3.** *Often plural.* Something that attracts; an enticement. [French *séduction,* from Latin *sēductiō* (stem *sēductiōn-*), from *sēdūcere* (past participle *sēductus*), SEDUCE.]

se·duc·tive (si-dúktiv) *adj.* Tending to seduce; alluring; beguiling. **—se·duc·tive·ly** *adv.* **—se·duc·tive·ness** *n.*

se·duc·tress (si-dúk-triss, -trəss) *n.* A female seducer.

sed·u·lous (séddewləss) *adj.* **1.** Diligent; assiduous. **2.** Deliberate and industrious; painstaking: *sedulous flattery.* —See Synonyms at **busy.** [Latin *sēdulus,* diligent, zealous, from *sē dolō,* "without guile", hence with zeal : *sē,* without + *dolus,* guile.] **—se·du·li·ty** (si-déw-ləti ‖ -dóo-), **sed·u·lous·ness** *n.* **—sed·u·lous·ly** *adv.*

se·dum (séedəm) *n.* Any of numerous rock plants of the genus *Sedum,* having thick, fleshy leaves and clusters of starlike flowers. See **orpine, stonecrop.** [Latin *sedum*†, houseleek.]

see[1] (see) *v.* **saw** (saw), **seen** (seen), **seeing, sees.** *—tr.* **1.** To perceive with the eye. **2.** To realise or come to know by seeing: *saw that the driver was in difficulties.* **3.** To have a mental image of; visualise. **4.** To understand; comprehend. **5.** To regard in a particular way; view: *Sees things differently now.* **6. a.** To imagine; believe possible: *I don't see him as a teacher.* **b.** To consider as likely: *I can see her getting angry when she finds out.* **7.** To foresee. **8.** To know through first-hand experience; undergo: *He saw some service in North Africa.* **9.** To be characterised by, be the occasion of, or bring forth: *Her long reign saw the heyday of colonialism.* **10.** To find out; ascertain: *See if he's ready.* **11.** *Abbr.* **s.** To refer to; read: *See page xi of the Introduction.* **12.** To discern; recognise: *saw the snags straight away.* **13. a.** To meet socially, especially often or regularly. **b.** To visit socially or for consultation: *see a doctor.* **c.** To receive, as for consultation. **14.** To cause to undergo something unpleasant. Used only in expressions of defiant anger: *I'll see him in hell before I agree.* **15.** To find attractive: *What do you see in him?* **16.** To watch without taking action: *How can you see a dog being kicked?* **17.** To watch or view as a spectator or tourist: *seeing the sights of London.* **18.** To escort; attend: *saw them home.* **19.** To make sure; take care: *See that it gets done right away.* **20.** To learn, as by reading or hearing on the radio: *I see that the railway strike has been called off.* **21.** In card games: **a.** To match (a bet). **b.** To match the bet of (another player). *—intr.* **1. a.** To have the power to see objects. **b.** To exercise that power. **c.** To perceive things with any of the senses, as if by the power of sight: *see with one's fingers.* **2.** To understand; comprehend. **3.** To consider; think a matter over: *Let's see, which should we take?* **4.** To have foresight: *We can see only to the end of the year.* **—see about. 1.** To attend to. **2.** To investigate. **—see here.** Used to demand a more reasonable attitude. **—see off. 1.** To be present to wish goodbye to (a person leaving on a journey). **2.** To be rid of, as by outlasting, ousting, or defeating. **—see out.** To last until the end, departure, or death of. **—see over.** To inspect by visiting. **—see (someone) right.** *Informal.* To make sure that (someone) is well looked after or properly rewarded. **—see to.** To attend to. **—See you.** *Informal.* Used as a farewell. [See, saw, seen; Middle English *se(e)n, sauh, seyen,* Old English *sēon, seah* (plural *sāwon*), *gesewen.*]

Synonyms: *see, behold, note, notice, espy, descry, observe, contemplate, survey, view, perceive, discern, remark, scan.*

see[2] *n.* **1.** The official seat, centre of authority, jurisdiction, or office of a bishop. **2.** A diocese. [Middle English, from Anglo-French *se, sed,* from Vulgar Latin *sedem* (unattested), from Latin *sēdem,* accusative of *sēdes,* "seat", "residence".]

See·beck effect (sée-bek; *German* záy-) *n.* The production of an electric current in a circuit consisting of two wires of different metals joined at their ends, when the junctions so formed are maintained at different temperatures. Compare **Peltier effect.** [After Thomas *Seebeck* (1770–1831), German physicist.]

seed (seed) *n.* **1.** A fertilised and ripened plant ovule containing an embryo and its food source. **2.** The hard, seedlike fruit of certain plants, such as grasses. **3.** Broadly, any propagative part of a plant, such as a tuber or spore. **4.** Seeds collectively. **5.** Anything resembling a seed in size or shape. **6.** A source or beginning; a germ. **7.** *Formal.* Offspring; progeny. **8.** *Archaic.* Sperm; semen. **9.** A **seed oyster** *(see).* **10.** A small crystal added to a supersaturated solution or a supercooled liquid to cause crystallisation. **11.** *Sports.* A seeded player. **—go** or **run to seed. 1.** To pass into the seed-bearing stage. **2.** To become weak or devitalised; deteriorate. **—in seed.** Bearing seeds. Said of a plant.

~v. **seeded, seeding, seeds.** *—tr.* **1.** To plant seeds in (land); sow. **2.** To plant in soil. **3.** To remove the seeds from (fruit). **4. a.** To add a small crystal to (a supersaturated solution or a supercooled liquid) to cause crystallisation. **b.** To sprinkle (a supercooled cloud) with particles, as of silver iodide, in order to produce rain by condensation and precipitation. **5.** *Sports.* **a.** To arrange (the drawing for positions in a tournament) so that the more skilled contestants meet only in the later rounds. **b.** To rank (a contestant) in this way. *—intr.* **1.** To sow seed. **2.** To produce or shed seed. [Middle English *seed, seid,* Old English *sǣd.*] **—seed·less** *adj.* **—seed·like** *adj.*

seed bank *n.* A place where plant seeds are stored at low temperatures.

seed·bed (séed-bed) *n.* **1.** A piece of land prepared for seeding. **2.** A place favourable to the development of something.

seed cake *n.* A sweet cake containing aromatic seeds, usually caraway seeds.

seed capsule *n.* The part of a fruit surrounding the seeds; the pericarp. Also called "seed case".

seed coat *n.* The outer protective covering of a seed; the testa.

seed corn *n.* **1.** Cereal grain that is kept or sold for sowing. **2.** Someone or something that forms a basis for future development.

seed·er (séedər) *n.* **1.** A machine or implement used for planting seeds. **2.** A machine used to remove the seeds from fruit.

seed fern *n.* Any seed-bearing fernlike plant of the extinct group Pteridospermae. Also called "pteridosperm".

seed leaf *n. Botany.* A **cotyledon** *(see).*

seed·ling (séedling) *n.* A young plant that develops by germination of a seed.

seed money *n.* Money needed or provided to start a new project.

seed oyster *n.* A young oyster; especially, one suitable for transplanting to another bed. Also called "seed".

seed pearl *n.* A very small, often imperfect, pearl.

seed plant *n.* A seed-bearing plant; a spermatophyte.

seed·pod (séed-pod) *n.* A **pod** *(see).*

seed potato *n.* A small potato tuber used for planting.

seeds·man (séedz-mən) *n., pl.* **-men** (-mən, -men). A dealer in seed.

seed·y (séedi) *adj.* **-ier, -iest. 1.** Having many seeds. **2.** Shabby-looking; disreputable in appearance. **3.** Tired or sick; out of sorts. **—seed·i·ly** *adv.* **—seed·i·ness** *n.*

see·ing (sée-ing) *conj.* Also **seeing that,** *informal* **seeing as.** Inasmuch as; in view of the fact that.

~n. Astronomy. The state of the atmosphere with respect to observation through telescopes.

seeing eye dog *n. U.S.* A **guide-dog** *(see).*

seek (seek) *v.* **sought** (sawt), **seeking, seeks.** *—tr.* **1.** To try to locate or discover; search for. **2.** To endeavour to obtain or reach. **3.** To move to; go to or towards: *Water seeks its own level.* **4.** To ask for; request: *seek professional advice.* **5.** To try; endeavour. Used with an infinitive: *sought to persuade them.* **6.** *Archaic.* To explore. *—intr.* To make a search or investigation. Often used with *after* or *for.* **—seek out.** To search determinedly for and find. [Seek, sought, sought; Middle English *seken, so(u)hte, soht,* Old English *sēcan, sōhte, sōht.*] **—seek·er** *n.*

seel (seel) *tr.v.* **seeled, seeling, seels.** To stitch closed the eyes of (a falcon, for example). [Middle English *silen,* from Old French *ciller,* from Medieval Latin *ciliāre,* from Latin *cilium,* eyelid.]

seem (seem) *intr.v.* **seemed, seeming, seems. 1.** To give the impression of being; appear. **2.** To appear, according to one's perception of the situation: *I can't seem to get the story straight.* **3.** To appear to be so; be evident: *It seems you object to the plan.* **4.** To appear to exist: *There seems no reason to postpone it.* [Middle English *semen,* to beseem, seem, from Old Norse *sœma,* to conform to, honour, from *sœmr,* fitting.]

Usage: Constructions like *can't seem* and *won't seem,* followed by an infinitive, are common in speech and informal writing: *I can't seem to find the key; He won't seem to learn.* They have sometimes attracted criticism, however, usually on the grounds that auxiliary verbs such as *can't/won't* apply to the main verb, and should not be made to apply to *seem.* Formal English would prefer alternative constructions, such as *do not seem able, seems that he won't.*

seem·ing (séeming) *adj.* Apparent, but usually not real; ostensible.

~n. Outward appearance; semblance. **—seem·ing·ly** *adv.* **—seem·ing·ness** *n.*

seem·ly (séemli) *adj.* **-lier, -liest. 1.** Conforming to accepted standards of conduct and good taste; proper; suitable. **2.** *Archaic.* Of pleasing appearance; handsome.

~adv. In a seemly manner. [Middle English *semely, semeliche,* from Old Norse *sœmiligr,* from *sœmr,* fitting.] **—seem·li·ness** *n.*

seen. Past participle of **see.**

seep (seep) *intr.v.* **seeped, seeping, seeps. 1.** To pass slowly through small openings or pores; ooze. **2.** To become gradually diffused: *The news seeped out.*

~n. **1.** A spot where water or petroleum oozes out of the ground. **2.** A seepage. [Perhaps variant of dialectal *sipe,* from Middle English *sipen,* Old English *sipian.*.]

seep·age (séepij) *n.* **1.** The act or process of seeping or oozing; a leakage. **2.** A quantity of something that has seeped.

seer[1] (seer, sée-ər) *n.* **1.** One that sees; specifically, someone able to see into the future; a clairvoyant. **2.** Someone possessing spiritual insight; a sage. [Middle English, from *seen,* to SEE.]

seer[2] (seer) *n.* Any of several varying Indian units of weight; especially, a unit of weight equivalent to one kilogram (2.2 pounds). [Hindi *ser.*]

seer·ess (séer-iss, sée-ər-, -ess) *n.* A female seer.

seer·suck·er (séer-suckər) *n.* A light, thin fabric, generally cotton or rayon, with a crinkled surface and often a striped pattern. [Hindi *sirsakar,* from Persian *shīr-o-shakar,* "milk and sugar" : *shīr,* milk, from Avestan *khshīra,* perhaps from Dravidian + *shakar,* sugar, akin to Sanskrit *śarkāra,* SUGAR.]

see·saw, see-saw (sée-saw, -sáw) *n.* **1.** A long plank balanced on a central fulcrum so that, sitting with a person on either end, one end goes up as the other goes down. Also *U.S.* "teeter", "teeter-totter". **2.** The act or game of riding a seesaw. **3.** A back-and-forth or up-and-down movement. Also used adjectivally: *a seesaw motion.* **4.** An alternation between two situations or positions.

~intr.v. **seesawed** or **see-sawed, -sawing, -saws. 1.** To play on a seesaw. **2.** To move back and forth or up and down. **3.** To alternate or oscillate. [Reduplication of SAW (to cut), from the up-and-down movement of sawing.]

seethe (seeth) *v.* **seethed, seething, seethes.** *—intr.* **1.** To churn and foam as if boiling. Used of a liquid. **2.** To move in agitated confusion. **3.** To be violently excited or agitated. Often used with *with: seething with fury.* **4.** *Archaic.* To come to a boil. *—tr. Archaic.* **1.** To boil. **2.** To soak; steep. [Middle English *sethen,* Old English *sēothan.*] **—seethe** *n.*

see through *tr.v.* **1.** To understand the true character or nature of.

2. *British.* To help or provide for in time of trouble or need. **3.** To stay with (something) until completion: *see the job through.*

see-through, see·through (sée-thrōō) *adj.* Partially or completely transparent.

Se·fer·is (sə-fáir-iss, se-), **George,** pen name of Georgios Seferiadis (1900–71). Greek poet. A diplomat by profession, he was hailed as the poet of the future on the publication of such works as *Strophé* (1931). He won the Nobel prize for literature (1963).

seg·ment (ségmənt) *n.* **1.** Any of the parts into which something is or can be divided. **2.** In geometry, a portion of a figure cut off by a line or plane; especially: **a.** The area bounded by a chord and the arc of a curve subtended by the chord. **b.** The portion of a curve between any two points on the curve. **c.** The portion of a sphere bounded by two parallel planes intersecting or tangent to the sphere. **3.** *Biology.* A clearly differentiated, repeated subdivision of an organism or part, such as a metamere. ~*v.* (seg-mént, səg-) **segmented, -menting, -ments.** —*tr.* To divide into segments. —*intr.* To become divided into segments. [Latin *segmentum,* from *secāre,* to cut.] —**seg·men·tal** (seg-mént'l, səg-), **seg·men·tar·y** (ségmən-təri, -tri ‖ *U.S.* -terri) *adj.* —**seg·men·tal·ly** *adv.*

seg·men·ta·tion (ség-men-táysh'n, -mən-) *n.* **1.** Division into segments. **2.** *Biology.* **Cleavage** (see). **3.** *Zoology.* **Metameric segmentation** (see).

segmentation cavity *n. Biology.* A **blastocoel** (see).

se·gno (sénn-yō, sáyn-) *n., pl.* **-gni** (-yee). *Music.* A notational sign; especially, the sign marking the beginning or end of a repeat. [Italian, sign, from Latin *signum.*]

se·go lily (sée-gō) *n.* A plant, *Calochortus nuttallii,* of western North America, having showy flowers. [*Sego,* from Paiute.]

Se·go·vi·a (si-gōvi-ə, se-). Capital of Segovia province, central Spain. Built on a hill above the river Eresma, it is still supplied from the river by a Roman aqueduct.

Segovia, Andrés (1893-1987). Spanish guitarist. Segovia stimulated new interest in the guitar as an instrument for serious music through his arrangements of Bach, Handel, and others.

Se·grè (sə-gráy, say-), **Emilio Gino** (1905–89). Italian-born U.S. physicist. In 1937 he produced the first artificial element, technetium. He discovered antiprotons with Owen Chamberlain (1955), and they were jointly awarded the 1959 Nobel prize for physics.

seg·re·gate (séggri-gayt) *v.* **-gated, -gating, -gates.** —*tr.* **1.** To separate or isolate from others or from a main body or group. **2.** To enforce the separation of (a race, class, or minority) from the rest of society. **3.** To divide (a society or community) along racial lines. —*intr.* **1.** To become separated from a main body or mass. **2.** To practise a policy of racial segregation. **3.** *Genetics.* To undergo segregation. [Latin *sēgregāre,* "to separate from the flock" : *sē,* apart + *grex* (stem *greg*-), flock.] —**seg·re·gate** (-gət, -git, -gayt) *adj.* —**seg·re·ga·tive** (-gaytiv), *adj.* —**seg·re·ga·tor** *n.*

seg·re·gat·ed (séggri-gaytid) *adj.* **1.** Practising or characterised by segregation, especially along racial lines. **2.** Restricted to the members of one race or other group: *a segregated school.* **3.** Providing separate facilities or divided for members of different races or other groups: *segregated buses.*

seg·re·ga·tion (séggri-gáysh'n) *n.* **1.** The act or process of segregating or the condition of being segregated. **2.** The policy and practice of imposing separation of races, as in schools, housing, and industry; especially, discriminatory practices against nonwhites in a society dominated by whites. **3.** *Genetics.* The separation into different gametes of paired alleles in meiosis.

seg·re·ga·tion·ist (séggri-gáysh'n-ist) *n.* One who advocates or practices a policy of racial segregation. —**seg·re·ga·tion·ist** *adj.*

seg·ue (ség-way, sáyg-) *n.* **1.** *Music.* An uninterrupted transition from one movement or piece of music to another. Also used as a direction to proceed to the next movement without a pause. **2.** A smooth transition. ~ *intr.v.* **segued, -gueing, -gues.** To make a segue. [Italian, "it follows", from *sequire,* to follow, from Latin *sequī.*]

se·gui·di·lla (séggi-déel-yə, -dée-) *n.* **1.** A Spanish stanza form of four to seven short verses. **2.** A lively Spanish dance. **3.** The music for this dance, in triple time. [Spanish, from *seguida,* "sequence", from the feminine past participle of *seguir,* to follow, from Vulgar Latin *sequere* (unattested), from Latin *sequī,* to follow.]

sei·cen·to (say-chéntō) *n.* The 17th century, especially with regard to the Italian literature and art of the period. [Italian *(mil) seicento,* (one thousand) six hundred : *sei,* six, from Latin *sex* + *cento,* hundred, from Latin *centum.*]

seiche (saysh) *n.* A vibration of the surface of lakes, bays, channels, or inland seas as a result of seismic or atmospheric disturbances. [Swiss French *seiche*†.]

Seid·litz powder (séddlits) *n. Sometimes plural.* A cathartic consisting of Rochelle salts, sodium bicarbonate, and tartaric acid. Also called "Rochelle powder". [So called because it has laxative properties similar to those of the spring water of *Seidlitz,* the German name of Sedlice, village in Bohemia.]

seif·dune *n.* A ridge of sand, often many miles long, crossing the desert parallel to the direction of the prevailing wind. [*Seif,* Arabic, sword.]

sei·gneur (sen-yúr, seen-; *French* se-nyŏr *n.* **1.** Formerly, a feudal lord or landowner, especially in France. **2.** Formerly in Canada, the landlord of a large estate subdivided into smallholdings. **3.** The hereditary civil head of government of the island of Sark. [French, from Old French, from Vulgar Latin *senior.* See **seignior.**] —**sei·gneur·i·al** *adj.*

sei·gneur·y, sei·gneur·ie (sáyn-yəri, sén-, séen-) *n., pl.* **-ies. 1.** The power, status, estate, or house or a seigneur. **2.** The official designation of the island of Sark.

seign·ior (sáyn-yər ‖ -yawr) *n.* A man of rank; specifically, a feudal lord. [Middle English *seignour,* from Old French *seigneur,* from Medieval Latin *senior,* from Latin, older, comparative of *senex,* old.] —**sei·gnio·ri·al** (sayn-yáwr-i-əl ‖ -yŏr-) *adj.*

seign·ior·age (sáyn-yərij) *n.* A profit or revenue raised by the Crown from the minting of coins, usually by means of the difference between the value of the bullion used and the face value of the coin. [Middle English *seigneurage,* duty imposed by a lord as his prerogative, from Old French, from *seigneur,* SEIGNIOR.]

seign·ior·y (sáyn-yəri) *n., pl.* **-ies. 1.** The estate of a feudal lord; a manor. **2.** The authority and power of a feudal lord.

seine (sayn) *n.* A large fishing net made to hang vertically in the water by weights at the lower edge and floats at the top. ~*v.* **seined, seining, seines.** —*intr.* To fish with a seine. —*tr.* To fish for or catch with a seine. [Middle English *seine,* Old English *segne,* from West Germanic *sagina* (unattested), from Latin *sagēna,* from Greek *sagēnē*†.]

Seine (sayn; *French* sen). River of north France rising in the Langres Plateau. It flows approximately 770 kilometres (480 miles), passing through Paris and reaching the English Channel at Le Havre. The Seine channel is dredged to allow ocean-going vessels to reach Rouen.

seise. *Law.* Variant of **seize.**

sei·sin (séezin) *n. Law.* Also *chiefly U.S.* **sei·zin.** Legal possession of a freehold estate. [Middle English, from Anglo-French *sesine,* Old French *seisine,* from *seisir,* to SEIZE.]

seism (síz'm) *n.* An **earthquake** (see). [Greek *seismos,* from *seiein,* to shake.]

seis·mic (sízmik) *adj.* Of, subject to, or caused by an earthquake or a natural or man-made earth vibration. [SEISM(O)- + -IC.] —**seis·mi·cal·ly** *adv.* —**seis·mic·i·ty** (síz-míssəti) *n.*

seismic wave *n.* A vibration emitted by an earthquake or a man-made explosion.

seis·mism (síz-miz'm) *n.* The collective phenomena involved in earthquakes. [SEISM(O)- + -ISM.]

seismo-, seism- *comb. form.* Indicates earthquake; for example, seismograph, seismism. [Greek *seismos,* SEISM.]

seis·mo·gram (síz-mə-gram, -mō-) *n.* The record of an earth tremor made by a seismograph. [SEISMO- + -GRAM.]

seis·mo·graph (síz-mə-graf, -mō-, -graaf) *n.* An instrument for automatically detecting and recording the intensity, direction, and duration of any movement of the ground, especially that caused by an earthquake or man-made explosion. [SEISMO- + -GRAPH.] —**seis·mo·graph·ic** (-gráffik) *adj.* —**seis·mog·ra·pher** (síz-móggrəfər) *n.* —**seis·mog·ra·phy** *n.*

seis·mol·o·gy (síz-móllə ji) *n.* The geophysical science of earthquakes and of the mechanical properties of the earth's interior. [SEISMO- + -LOGY.] —**seis·mo·log·ic** (-mə-lójik), **seis·mo·log·i·cal** *adj.* —**seis·mo·log·i·cal·ly** *adv.* —**seis·mol·o·gist** (-móllə jist) *n.*

seis·mom·e·ter (síz-mómmitər) *n.* A detecting device that receives seismic waves. [SEISMO- + -METER.] —**seis·mo·metric** (sízmə-méttrik), **seis·mo·met·ri·cal** *adj.*

seis·mo·scope (sízmə-skōp) *n.* An instrument that indicates the occurrence or time of occurrence of a seismic wave. [SEISMO- + -SCOPE.] —**seis·mo·scop·ic** (-skóppik) *adj.*

sei whale (say) *n.* A widely distributed, dark blue rorqual, *Balaenoptera borealis,* valued for its whalebone. [Partial translation of Norwegian *sei-val* : *sei,* coalfish + *whale,* whale.]

seize (seez) *v.* **seized, seizing, seizes.** Also **seise** (for sense 5c). —*tr.* **1.** To grasp suddenly and forcibly; lay hold of; clutch or grab. **2.** To grasp with the mind; comprehend. **3.** To have a sudden and overpowering effect upon; possess or overwhelm. **4.** To take into custody; make a prisoner of; arrest. **5. a.** To take quick and forcible possession of; capture. **b.** To take possession of by legal authority or process; confiscate. **c.** *Law.* To put in legal possession, as of an estate or other property. Used chiefly in the passive with *of.* **6.** To avail oneself eagerly and immediately of (an opportunity). **7.** *Nautical.* To bind with turns of small line. —*intr.* **1.** To take up or lay hold eagerly or forcibly. Used with *on* or *upon.* **2. a.** To cohere or fuse with another part as a result of high pressure or temperature, restricting or preventing further motion. Often used with *up.* **b.** To come to a halt. Used with *up: The talks seized up.* [Middle English *saisen, seisen,* from Old French *seisir, saisir,* from Gallo-Latin *sacīre* (unattested), to claim, from Germanic.] —**seiz·a·ble** *adj.*

seizin. Variant of **seisin.**

seiz·ing (séezing) *n. Nautical.* A binding of larger lines made with multiple turns of smaller line.

sei·zure (séezhər) *n.* **1.** The act or an action of seizing or the state of being seized. **2.** A sudden paroxysm, such as an epileptic convulsion or heart attack.

se·jant (séejənt) *adj. Heraldry.* In a sitting position with forepaws extended to the ground: *a lion sejant.* [Variant of *seant,* from Old French, present participle of *seoir,* to sit, from Latin *sedere.*]

Sejm (saym) *n.* The unicameral legislative body of Poland. [Polish, assembly.]

se·la·chi·an (si-láyki-ən) *adj.* Of or belonging to the order Selachii, which includes the sharks and rays.

~*n.* A member of the Selachii. [New Latin *Selachii,* from Greek *selakhē,* plural of *selakhos†,* cartilaginous fish.]

sel·a·gi·nel·la (sélləji-nélla) *n.* Any of numerous fernlike, usually prostrate plants of the genus *Selaginella,* having small scalelike leaves and bearing spores in cones. [New Latin, from Latin *selāgō†* (stem *selāgin-*), plant resembling the savin.]

se·lah (séela) *n.* A Hebrew word of unknown meaning often marking the end of a verse in the Psalms and Habakkuk and thought to be a term indicating a pause or rest. [Hebrew *selāh.*]

Se·lan·gor (si-láng-ər, sə-, -awr). State in the west of Peninsular Malaysia. Lying on the Strait of Malacca, it was a sultanate before becoming a British protectorate (1874). It has chemical, rubber, tin, and coal industries. Shah Alum is the capital.

sel·dom (séldəm) *adv.* Not often; infrequently; rarely.
~*adj.* Archaic. Infrequent; rare. [Middle English *selden, seldom,* Old English *seldan,* from Common Germanic *seldo-* (unattested).] —**sel·dom·ness** *n.*

> *Usage:* Acceptable idioms include *seldom if ever* and *seldom or never,* but not *seldom or ever* or *seldom ever,* though the latter pair are sometimes encountered in informal speech. See also **rarely.**

se·lect (si-lekt, sə-) *v.* **-lected, -lecting, -lects.** —*tr.* To choose from among several; take in preference; pick out. —*intr.* To make a choice or selection; choose. —See Synonyms at **choose.**
~*adj.* **1.** Singled out in preference; chosen; picked out. **2.** Of special value or quality; choice. **3.** Open to or made up of a limited number of people, especially those of high social or economic status: *select company.* [Latin *sēligere* (past participle *sēlectus*), to choose out : *sē,* apart + *legere,* to choose.] —**se·lect·ness** *n.*

select committee *n.* In the British Parliament, a committee appointed by either of the two Houses to investigate a matter.

se·lec·tion (si-léksh'n, sə-) *n.* **1. a.** The act of selecting or the fact of being selected; choosing; choice. **b.** That which is selected. **2.** A carefully chosen or representative collection of persons or things. **3.** *Sports.* A contestant or runner singled out, as by a sports writer, as being likely to win or gain a place in a contest or race. **4.** A range of items of the same kind, as of goods for sale: *a good selection of wines.* **5.** *Biology.* A process that favours or induces the survival and perpetuation of one kind of organism in competition with others. See **natural selection. 6.** In Australia, a piece of farmland provided under a government scheme (*free selection*) that offered favourable terms of purchase to early settlers. —See Synonyms at **choice.** [Latin *sēlectiō* (stem *sēlectiōn-*). See **select.**]

se·lec·tive (si-léktiv, sə-) *adj.* **1.** Of or characterised by selection or discrimination; tending to select or empowered to select: *selective import controls.* **2.** Careful in selecting; fastidious; particular. **3.** *Electronics.* Capable of rejecting frequencies other than those selected or tuned. —**se·lec·tive·ly** *adv.* —**se·lec·tive·ness** *n.*

se·lec·tiv·i·ty (si-lék-tívvəti, sillek-, séelek-) *n.* **1.** The state or quality of being selective. **2.** *Electronics.* The degree to which an electronic receiver or other circuit is selective.

se·lect·man (si-lékt-mən, sə-, -mán) *n., pl.* **-men** (-mən, -men). A member of a board of town officers chosen annually in New England communities to manage local affairs.

se·lec·tor (si-léktər, sə-) *n.* **1.** One that selects; specifically, a member of a committee that selects a sports team. **2.** A device forming part of an automatic telephone switching system that connects one circuit to one or more other circuits.

sel·e·nate (sélli-nayt) *n.* A salt or ester of selenic acid. [From SELENIUM.]

Se·len·e (si-léeni, sə-). The Greek goddess of the Moon. [Greek *selēnē,* Moon.]

se·le·nic acid (si-léenik, -lénnik) *n.* A highly corrosive, hygroscopic, white solid acid with composition H_2SeO_4. [From SELENIUM.]

sel·e·nite (sélli-nīt) *n.* Gypsum in the form of colourless clear crystals. [Latin *selēnītēs,* from Greek *selēnītēs* (lithos), "moon (stone)" (because its brightness supposedly waxed and waned with the Moon), from *selēnē,* Moon.]

se·le·ni·um (si-léeni-əm) *n. Symbol* **Se** A nonmetallic element, red in powder form, black in vitreous form, and metallic grey in crystalline form, resembling sulphur and obtained primarily as a by-product of electrolytic copper refining. It is widely used in rectifiers, as a semiconductor, and in xerography, and certain forms exhibit photovoltaic and photoconductive action, making it useful in photocells, photographic exposure meters, and solar cells. Atomic number 34, atomic weight 78.96, melting point (of grey selenium) 217°C, boiling point (grey) 684.9°C, relative density (grey) 4.79, (vitreous) 4.28, valency 2, 4, or 6. [New Latin, from Greek *selēnē,* Moon (named by analogy to a related element, tellurium, which is from Latin *tellus,* Earth).]

selenium cell *n.* A photoconductive cell consisting of an insulated selenium strip between two suitable electrodes.

sel·e·nod·e·sy (sélli-nóddəsi) *n.* The study or mapping of the physical characteristics of the Moon, such as its exact shape, size, and gravity; lunar geodesy. [Greek *selēnē,* Moon + (GEO)DESY] —**sel·e·nod·e·sist** *n.* **sel·e·no·det·ic** (-nə-déttik) *adj.*

se·le·no·dont (si-léenə-dont, sə-) *adj.* Having crescent-shaped ridges on the crowns of the teeth, as deer do.
~*n.* A selenodont mammal. [Greek *selēnē,* moon + -ODONT.]

sel·e·nog·ra·phy (sélli-nóggrəfi, séeli-) *n.* The study of the physical features of the moon. [New Latin *selenographia* : Greek *selēnē,* Moon + -GRAPHY.] —**sel·e·nog·ra·pher, sel·e·nog·ra·phist** *n.* —**sel·e·no·graph·ic** (-nə-gráffik, si-lée-), **sel·e·no·graph·i·cal** *adj.* —**sel·e·no·graph·i·cal·ly** *adv.*

sel·e·nol·o·gy (sélli-nólləji, séeli-) *n.* The astronomical study of the moon. [Greek *selēnē,* Moon + -LOGY.] —**se·le·no·log·i·cal** (-nə-lójik'l, si-lée-) *adj.* —**sel·e·nol·o·gist** (-nólləjist) *n.*

se·le·no·mor·phol·o·gy (si-léenō-mawr-fólləji, sə-) *n.* The study of the surface and landscape of the moon. [Greek *selēnē,* Moon + MORPHOLOGY.]

se·le·nous acid (si-léenəss, séllinəss) *n.* Also **se·le·ni·ous acid** (si-léeni-əss). A transparent, colourless crystalline acid, H_2SeO_3, used as a chemical reagent. [From SELENIUM.]

Se·leu·ci·a¹ (si-lŏo-shi-ə, -léw-, -si-) Ancient city of Mesopotamia, on the Tigris southeast of modern Baghdad. It was the eastern capital of the Seleucid empire.

Seleucia² or **Seleucia Pi·e·ri·a** (pī-írriə). Ancient city on the Orontes river, Syria. It was founded by Seleucus I as the seaport for Antioch, and was visited by St. Paul (Acts 13:4).

Se·leu·cid (si-lŏo-sid, -léw-) *n., pl.* **Seleucids** or **-cidae** (-si-dee). A member of a Hellenistic dynasty founded by Seleucus I after the death of Alexander, and ruling in Babylonia from 312 B.C. and in Syria from 301 B.C. to 64 B.C. —**Se·leu·cid, Se·leu·ci·dan** *adj.*

self (self) *n., pl.* **selves** (selvz). **1.** The total, essential, or particular being of one person; the individual. **2.** The qualities of one person distinguishing him from another; a person's typical personality or character: *not his usual cheerful self.* **3.** An individual's consciousness of his own being or identity; subjectivity; ego. **4.** One's own interests, welfare, or advantage; selfish concerns.
~*pron.* Myself, yourself, himself, or herself: *a living wage for self.*
~*adj.* **1.** *Obsolete.* Same or identical. **2. a.** Uniform throughout. Said of a colour. **b.** Self-coloured. **3.** Homogeneous, as in colour, design, or material; matching. Said especially of clothes: *a self scarf.* [Middle English *se(o)lf, silf,* noun, pronoun, and adjective, Old English *self, silf.*]

> *Usage:* The use of a reflexive pronoun as a means of emphasising a previously stated pronoun is often criticised, though it is very common in spoken English: *I myself believe him.* The use of *self* alone, as a pronoun, is found only in commercial English (*sold to self three boxes*), especially in certain fixed phrases (*your good self/selves*) which business usage these days tends to avoid.

self- *comb. form.* Indicates: **1.** Oneself or itself; for example, **self-correcting, self-perpetuating. 2.** Of the self, oneself, or itself; for example, **self-control, self-government, self-knowledge. 3.** With regard to oneself; for example, **self-assurance, self-interest. 4.** By, by means of, or relying solely upon, oneself; for example, **self-appointed, self-educated, self-help. 5.** Acting on or directed towards oneself or itself; for example, **self-addressed, self-pity. 6.** In oneself or itself; inherently; for example, **self-contradictory, self-evident. 7.** Autonomous, automatic, or automatically; for example, **self-propelled, self-winding.** *Note:* Many compounds other than those entered here may be formed with *self-.* When *self-* is joined with a word that can stand alone, it is joined by a hyphen: *self-deception.* In the rare cases when *self-* is joined with a form that cannot stand alone as a word, it is joined without space or hyphen: *selfhood.* [Middle English, Old English, from SELF.]

self-a·base·ment (self-ə-báyssmənt) *n.* Degradation or humiliation of oneself, especially because of feelings of guilt or inferiority.

self-ab·ne·ga·tion (self-ábni-gáysh'n) *n.* The setting aside of self-interest for the sake of others or for a belief or principle. —**self-ab·ne·gat·ing** (-gayting) *adj.*

self-a·buse (self-ə-béwss) *n.* **1.** Criticism of oneself or one's abilities. **2.** Masturbation. Not in current usage.

self-act·ing (self-ákting) *adj.* Capable of acting or working automatically.

self-ad·dressed (self-ə-drést) *adj.* Addressed to oneself.

self-ag·gran·dise·ment (self-ə-grándizmənt) *n.* The act or practice of enhancing one's own importance, power, or reputation. —**self-ag·gran·dis·ing** (-grándīzing) *adj.*

self-an·neal·ing (self-ə-néeling) *adj.* Designating those metals, such as lead and tin, that do not harden as a result of cold-working.

self-an·ni·hi·la·tion (self-ə-nī-ə-láysh'n, -i-, -hi-) *n.* **1.** Self-destruction. **2.** Complete loss of the ego or consciousness of self, as in a mystical state.

self-ap·point·ed (self-ə-póyntid) *adj.* Designated or chosen by oneself rather than by due authority; unsanctioned and usually ill-qualified: *a self-appointed authority on English grammar.*

self-as·ser·tion (self-ə-sérsh'n) *n.* Forceful assertion of one's own personality, wishes, claims, or views. —**self-as·ser·tive** *adj.* —**self-as·ser·tive·ly** *adv.*

self-as·sured (self-ə-shóord ‖ -shéwrd) *adj.* Having or showing confidence and sureness. —**self-as·sur·ance** *n.*

self-a·ware (self-ə-waír) *adj.* Aware of one's own personality or individual qualities. —**self-a·ware·ness** *n.*

self-cen·tred (self-séntərd) *adj.* Engrossed in oneself and one's affairs. —**self-cen·tred·ly** *adv.* —**self-cen·tred·ness** *n.*

self-cer·ti·fi·ca·tion (self-sértifi-káysh'n, -sər-tíffi-) *n.* In Britain, a procedure whereby a sick person personally gives notice of absences from work, rather than producing a doctor's certificate.

self-col·oured (self-kúllərd) *adj.* **1.** In the natural or original colour. **2.** Of only one colour.

self-com·mand (self-kə-maánd ‖ -mánd) *n.* Full presence of mind; self-control.

self-con·fessed (self-kən-fést ‖ -kon-) *adj.* According to one's own admission; avowed.

self-con·fi·dence (self-kónfidənss) *n.* Confidence in oneself or one's abilities. —**self-con·fi·dent** *adj.* —**self-con·fi·dent·ly** *adv.*

self·con·scious (sélf-kónshəss) *adj.* **1.** Conscious to the point of discomfort or embarrassment of one's appearance or manner; socially ill at ease. **2.** Having or showing an excessive concern for one's impact upon others; unnatural or contrived: *a very self-conscious style of poetry*. **3.** Aware of oneself or one's own being, actions, or thoughts. —See Synonyms at **humble**. —**self·con·scious·ly** *adv.* —**self·con·scious·ness** *n.*

self·con·tained (sélf-kən-táynd ‖ -kon-) *adj.* **1.** Constituting a complete and independent unit: *a self-contained flat*. **2. a.** Not dependent on others; self-sufficient. **b.** Keeping to oneself; reserved.

self·con·tent (sélf-kən-tént ‖ -kon-) *n.* Also **self·con·tent·ment** (-mənt). Satisfaction, especially complacent satisfaction, with oneself and one's condition. —**self·con·tent·ed** *adj.* —**self·con·tent·ed·ly** *adv.*

self·con·tra·dic·tion (sélf-kóntrə-díksh'n) *n.* **1.** The act, state, or fact of contradicting oneself or itself. **2.** An idea or statement containing contradictory elements. —**self·con·tra·dic·to·ry** (-dík-təri, -tri) *adj.*

self·con·trol (sélf-kən-tról ‖ -kon-) *n.* Control of one's emotions, desires, or actions by one's own will. —**self·con·trolled** *adj.*

self·cor·rec·ting (sélf-kə-rékting) *adj.* Correcting its or one's own mistakes; especially, designating a typewriter with a mechanism facilitating correction of typing errors.

self·crit·i·cal (sélf-krítik'l) *adj.* Critical of oneself; watchful for one's own faults and weaknesses. —**self·crit·i·cal·ly** *adv.* —**self·crit·i·cism** *n.*

self·de·ceived (sélf-di-séevd, -də-) *adj.* Deceived by one's own illusion or error.

self·de·cep·tion (sélf-di-sépsh'n, -də-) *n.* Also **self·de·ceit** (-séet). The act of deceiving oneself or the state of being deceived by oneself. —**self·de·cep·tive** *adj.*

self·de·feat·ing (sélf-di-féeting, -də-) *adj.* Conflicting with or going against one's or its own purposes or welfare.

self·de·fence (sélf-di-fénss, -də-) *n.* **1.** The act or skill of defending oneself against physical attack. **2.** Defence of what belongs to oneself, as of one's rights or beliefs. **3.** *Law.* The right to protect oneself against violence or threatened violence with whatever force or means are reasonably necessary. —**self·de·fen·sive** *adj.*

self·de·ni·al (sélf-di-ní-əl, -də-) *n.* Sacrifice of one's own comfort or gratification; restraint of one's natural desires. See Synonyms at **abstinence**. —**self·de·ny·ing** *adj.* —**self·de·ny·ing·ly** *adv.*

self·dep·re·cat·ing (sélf-déppri-kayting) *adj.* Tending to undervalue oneself and one's abilities. —**self·dep·re·cat·ing·ly** *adv.* —**self·dep·re·ca·tion** (-káysh'n) *n.*

self·de·struct (sélf-di-strúkt, -də-) *n.* A mechanism forming part of a missile or other device that enables it to destroy itself under predetermined circumstances or on command. Also used adjectivally: *a self-destruct mechanism.*
~ *intr. v.* **self-destructed, -structing, -structs.** To destroy itself or itself, especially automatically.

self·de·struc·tive (sélf-di-strúktiv, -də-) *adj.* Marked by an impulse or tendency to harm or kill oneself. —**self·de·struc·tion** *n.* —**self·de·struc·tive·ly** *adv.* —**self·de·struc·tive·ness** *n.*

self·de·ter·mi·na·tion (sélf-di-térmi-náysh'n, -də-) *n.* **1.** Determination of one's own fate or course of action without compulsion; free will. **2.** Freedom of a people or area to determine its own political status and alignment; independence.

self·dis·ci·pline (sélf-díssiplin) *n.* Training and control of one's impulses and conduct, usually for personal improvement.

self·dis·cov·e·ry (sélf-di-skúvvəri) *n.* The act or process of achieving understanding or knowledge of oneself.

self·doubt (sélf-dówt) *n.* Lack of self-esteem. —**self·doubt·ing** *adj.*

self·drive (sélf-drív) *adj.* Designating a hired car to be driven by the hirer.

self·ed·u·cat·ed (sélf-éddew-kaytid) *adj.* Educated by one's own efforts, not by formal instruction. —**self·ed·u·ca·tion** (-káysh'n) *n.*

self·ef·fac·ing (sélf-i-fáy-sing, -ə-) *adj.* Not drawing attention to oneself; modest or shy. —**self·ef·face·ment** *n.*

self·em·ployed (sélf-im-plóyd, -em-) *adj.* Earning one's livelihood directly from one's own trade or business, not as an employee.

self·es·teem (sélf-i-stéem, -ə-) *n.* Pride in oneself; self-respect.

self·ev·i·dent (sélf-évvi-dənt ‖ -dent) *adj.* Requiring no proof or explanation. —**self·ev·i·dence** *n.* —**self·ev·i·dent·ly** *adv.*

self·ex·am·i·na·tion (sélf-ig-zámi-náysh'n ‖ -eg-, -ik-) *n.* **1.** Careful, introspective consideration of one's own thoughts, feelings, or motives. **2.** Examination of one's own body for medical reasons; especially, examination by a woman of her breasts as a precaution against cancer.

self·ex·cit·ed (sélf-ik-sítid, -ek-) *adj. Electricity.* **1.** Designating an oscillator that provides its own energy source. **2.** Designating an electrical machine in which the current that excites the magnetic field is generated by the machine itself.

self·ex·plan·a·to·ry (sélf-ik-splánnə-tri, -ek-, -təri) *adj.* Needing no explanation; obvious in meaning.

self·ex·pres·sion (sélf-ik-sprésh'n, -ek-) *n.* Expression of one's own personality, feelings, or ideas, as through speech or art.

self·fer·til·i·sa·tion (sélf-fértilī-záysh'n ‖ *U.S.* -fért'l-i-) *n.* Fertilisation by sperm from the same animal, as in some hermaphrodites, or by pollen from the same flower. See **autogamy**. —**self·fer·ti·lised, self·fer·ti·lis·ing, self·fer·tile** (-fértīl ‖ *U.S.* -fért'l) *adj.*

self·ful·fill·ing (sélf-fŏŏl-fílling) *adj.* Achieving fulfilment as a result of having been predicted or expected: *a self-fulfilling prophecy.*

self·gov·ern·ment (sélf-gúvvərnmənt) *n.* **1.** Political independence;

autonomy. **2.** *Archaic.* Self-control. —**self·gov·erned, self·gov·ern·ing** *adj.*

self·hard·en·ing (sélf-hárd'n-ing) *adj.* Of, designating, or pertaining to materials, such as certain steels, that harden without special treatment.

self·heal (sélf-héel) *n.* Any of several plants reputed to have healing powers; especially, *Prunella vulgaris,* a plant native to Europe, having violet-blue flowers. Also called "heal-all", "all-heal".

self·help (sélf-hélp) *n.* The act or an instance of helping or providing for oneself without assistance from others. Also used adjectivally: *a self-help project; a self-help group.*

self·hood (sélf-hŏŏd) *n.* **1.** The state of having a distinct identity; individuality. **2.** The fully developed self; achieved personality. **3.** Self-centredness. [Translation of German *Selbheit.*]

self·im·age (sélf-ímmij) *n.* One's mental concept of oneself or one's position in relation to others; how one sees oneself.

self·im·por·tance (sélf-im-pórtəns) *n.* Excessively high opinion of one's own importance or station; pomposity; conceit. —**self·im·por·tant** *adj.* —**self·im·por·tant·ly** *adv.*

self·im·posed (sélf-im-pózd) *adj.* Imposed by oneself on oneself; voluntarily assumed or endured.

self·im·prove·ment (sélf-im-prŏŏvmənt) *n.* Improvement of one's condition through one's own efforts.

self·in·duced (sélf-in-déwst ‖ -dŏŏst) *adj.* **1.** Induced by oneself or itself; wilfully acquired or brought on. **2.** *Electricity.* Produced by self-induction.

self·in·duct·ance (sélf-in-dúktənss) *n. Electricity.* The ratio of the electromotive force produced in a circuit by self-induction to the rate of change of current producing it. It is expressed in henries. Also called "coefficient of self-induction".

self·in·duc·tion (sélf-in-dúksh'n) *n.* The generation by a changing current of an electromotive force in the same circuit that tends to counteract such change. —**self·in·duc·tive** *adj.*

self·in·dul·gence (sélf-in-dúljənss) *n.* Excessive indulgence of one's own appetites, desires, or attitudes. —**self·in·dul·gent** *adj.* —**self·in·dul·gent·ly** *adv.*

self·in·flict·ed (sélf-in-flíktid) *adj.* Inflicted or imposed upon oneself: *a self-inflicted punishment.* —**self·in·flic·tion** *n.*

self·in·ter·est (sélf-íntərəst, -trist, -tə-rest) *n.* **1.** Personal advantage or interest; selfish motive or gain. **2.** Pursuit of or excessive regard for such advantage or interest. —**self·in·ter·est·ed** *adj.*

self·ish (sélfish) *adj.* **1.** Concerned chiefly or only with one's own welfare, pleasure, or advantage, without regard for the well-being of others; egoistic. **2.** Arising from, characterised by, or showing such concern: *a selfish whim.* —**self·ish·ly** *adv.* —**self·ish·ness** *n.*

self·jus·ti·fy·ing (sélf-jústi-fī-ing) *adj.* **1.** Making excuses for one's behaviour. **2.** Automatically arranging type to fill a full line.

self·knowl·edge (sélf-nóllij) *n.* Knowledge of one's own nature, abilities, and limitations; insight into oneself.

self·less (sélf-ləss, -liss) *adj.* Without concern for oneself; unselfish. —**self·less·ly** *adv.* —**self·less·ness** *n.*

self·liq·ui·dat·ing (sélf-líkwi-dayting) *adj.* **1.** Designating a loan advanced to finance the purchase or production of goods that can be quickly converted into cash. **2.** Producing a return equal to the sum invested to create or maintain it: *a self-liquidating toll-bridge project.*

self·load·ing (sélf-lóding) *adj.* Automatically ejecting the shell and chambering the next round from the magazine; automatic or semiautomatic. Said of a firearm.

self·loc·king (sélf-lócking) *adj.* Locking automatically when shut.

self·love (sélf-lúv) *n.* The instinct or desire to promote one's own well-being; regard for or love of self. —**self·lov·ing** *adj.*

self·made (sélf-máyd) *adj.* **1.** Having achieved success purely by one's own efforts: *a self-made man.* **2.** Made by oneself or itself.

self·man·age·ment (sélf-mánnijmənt) *n.* Management, as of a factory or other enterprise, by those employed in it.

self·o·pin·ion·at·ed (sélf-ə-pín-yənaytid) *adj.* Given to forceful, sometimes obstinate, assertion of one's own opinions.

self·per·pet·u·at·ing (sélf-pər-péttew-ayting) *adj.* Having the power to renew or perpetuate itself indefinitely.

self·pit·y (sélf-pítti) *n.* Pity for oneself, especially of an exaggerated or self-indulgent kind. —**self·pit·y·ing** *adj.* —**self·pit·y·ing·ly** *adv.*

self·pol·li·na·tion (sélf-pólli-náysh'n) *n.* The transfer of pollen from an anther to a stigma of the same flower. —**self·pol·li·nat·ed, self·pol·li·nat·ing** *adj.*

self·por·trait (sélf-pór-trit, -trət, -trayt ‖ -pór-) *n.* A portrait, pictorial or literary, of oneself created by oneself.

self·pos·ses·sion (sélf-pə-zésh'n ‖ -pō-) *n.* Full command of one's faculties, feelings, and behaviour, especially in difficult circumstances; presence of mind; poise. —**self·pos·sessed** *adj.*

self·pres·er·va·tion (sélf-prézzər-váysh'n) *n.* **1.** Protection of oneself from harm or destruction. **2.** The instinct for such individual preservation; the innate desire to stay alive.

self·pro·claimed (sélf-prə-kláymd, -prō-) *adj.* So called by oneself; self-styled.

self·pro·pelled (sélf-prə-péld ‖ -prō-) *adj.* Containing its own means of propulsion. Said of a vehicle, for example.

self·rais·ing flour (sélf-ráyzing) *n.* A commercially produced mixture of flour and a leavening agent, usually baking powder. Also *U.S.* "self-rising flour".

self·re·al·i·sa·tion (sélf-réer-lī-záysh'n, -rée-ə- ‖ *U.S.* -li-) *n.* The complete development or fulfilment of the self's potential.

self·re·cord·ing (sélf-ri-kórding, -rə-) *adj.* Automatically recording its own functions or operations. Said of a machine or instrument.

self·re·gard (sélf-ri-gárd, -rə-) n. 1. Consideration of oneself or one's interests. 2. Self-respect.

self·reg·u·lat·ing (sélf-réggew-layting) adj. Regulating itself automatically.

self·re·li·ance (sélf-ri-lí-ənss, -rə-) n. Reliance upon one's own capabilities, judgment, or resources. —**self-re·li·ant** adj. —**self-re·li·ant·ly** adv.

self·re·proach (sélf-ri-próch, -rə-) n. The act or habit of blaming or finding fault with oneself. —**self-re·proach·ful** adj. —**self-re·proach·ful·ly** adv.

self·re·spect (sélf-ri-spékt, -rə-) n. Due respect for oneself and one's personal worth. —**self-re·spect·ing** adj.

self·re·straint (sélf-ri-stráynt, -rə-) n. Restraint of one's emotions, desires, or inclinations; self-control.

self·right·eous (sélf-ríchəss, -rī't-yəss) adj. Piously sure of one's righteousness. —**self-right·eous·ly** adv. —**self-right·eous·ness** n.

self·right·ing (sélf-ríting) adj. Able to right itself when overturned.

self·rule (sélf-róol ‖ -réwl) n. Self-government.

self·sac·ri·fice (sélf-sáckri-fīss) n. Sacrifice of one's personal interests or well-being for the sake of others or for a cause. —**self-sac·ri·fic·ing** adj.

self·same (sélf-saym, sáym) adj. Exactly identical; the very same. See Synonyms at **same**. [Middle English *selve same* : *self*, SELF (obsolete sense "same") + SAME.] —**self·same·ness** n.

self·sat·is·fac·tion (sélf-sáttiss-fáksh'n) n. Satisfaction, especially complacent satisfaction, with oneself or one's own accomplishments. —**self-sat·is·fied** adj.

self·seal·ing (sélf-séeling) adj. Able to be sealed without the application of moisture: *a self-sealing envelope.*

self·seed·ed (sélf-séedid) adj. Self-sown.

self·seek·ing (sélf-séeking) n. The determined pursuit of one's own ends or interests. —**self-seek·er** n. —**self-seek·ing** adj.

self·serv·ice (sélf-sérviss) adj. Designating a retail commercial enterprise in which the customers serve themselves and pay a cashier.

self·serv·ing (sélf-sérving) adj. Serving one's own interests, especially without consideration for the needs or interests of others.

self·sown (sélf-sôn) adj. Growing from seed disperal by natural means rather than sown by man; self-seeded. Said of plants.

self·start·er (sélf-stártər) n. 1. A device for starting an engine, a **starter** (see). 2. A person with initiative.

self·stud·y (sélf-stúddi) n. A form of study in which the student is to a large extent responsible for his own instruction. Also used adjectivally: *a self-study course.*

self·styled (sélf-stīld) adj. As characterised by oneself, often without right or justification: *the self-styled "Voice of Britain".*

self·suf·fi·cient (sélf-sə-físh'nt) adj. 1. Able to provide for oneself without the help of others; not dependent on others for food, energy, or the like. 2. *Archaic.* Having undue confidence; smug or overbearing. —**self-suf·fi·cien·cy** n.

self·sup·port (sélf-sə-pórt ‖ -pórt) n. The act of or capacity for supporting oneself, especially financially, without the help of others. —**self-sup·port·ed, self-sup·port·ing** adj.

self·taught (sélf-táwt) adj. Having taught oneself without formal instruction or the help of others.

self·will (sélf-wíl) n. Wilfulness, especially in satisfying one's own desires or adhering to one's own opinions. —**self-willed** adj.

self·wind·ing (sélf-wínding) adj. Having a mechanism that does not need winding. Said of watches in which the spring is wound by a weight activated by the movement of the wearer's hand.

Sel·juk (sel-jōōk, sél-jōōk) n. A member of any of several Turkish dynasties ruling over central and western Asia from the 11th to the 13th century. [Turkish, after *Seljūk*, the reputed eponymous ancestor.] —**Sel·juk** adj.

Sel·kirk (sél-kurk). Also **Sel·kirk·shire** (-shər, -sheer). A former county of southern Scotland, now part of Borders. Its administrative centre was Selkirk, a royal burgh on Ettrick Water.

Selkirk, Alexander (1676–1721). Scottish sailor whose experiences inspired Defoe's *Robinson Crusoe.* In 1704 he was marooned on the uninhabited island of Juan Fernández. He was discovered there in 1709.

Selkirk bannock n. A sweet Scottish bread containing dried fruit. [After SELKIRK, Scottish county, where it originated.]

sell (sel) v. **sold** (sōld), **selling, sells.** —*tr.* 1. To exchange or deliver for money or its equivalent, as goods, services, or property; dispose of for a price. 2. To deal in; offer for sale as one's business: *sells computers for an American company.* 3. To give up or surrender, often treacherously or dishonourably, in exchange for a price or reward: *witches who had sold themselves to Satan.* 4. To promote the sale of; cause to be sold: *Publicity sold that product.* 5. **a.** To convince of the worth or desirability of something. Used with *on: He's completely sold on the idea.* **b.** To convince someone of the worth or desirability of (an idea or product, for example): *made efforts to sell their policy to the electorate.* 6. To achieve sales of: *has already sold half a million copies in hardback.* 7. *Informal.* To cheat or dupe. —*intr.* 1. To exchange ownership for money or its equivalent; engage in selling goods or services. 2. To be sold or be on sale. 3. To attract prospective buyers; be popular on the market: *an item that sells well.* 4. To be approved of; gain acceptance. —**sell off.** To get rid of by selling, often at reduced prices; deplete. —**sell short.** 1. *Finance.* To contract for the sale of securities or commodities one expects to own at a later date and on more advantageous terms. 2. To undervalue (oneself or another); fail to appreciate the worth of. —**sell up.** *Chiefly British.* 1. To sell (one's business, for exam-

ple). 2. To dispose of the assets of (a bankrupt or insolvent person) in order to pay creditors.
~ n. 1. The act of selling. 2. A sales presentation of a specified type. See **hard sell, soft sell.** 3. *Slang.* A hoax or swindle. [Sell, sold, sold; Middle English *sellen, sold, sold,* Old English *sellan, sealde, seald,* to give, betray, sell.] —**se·lla·ble** adj.

sell-by date (sél-bī) n. 1. The date by which a perishable commodity should have been sold. 2. *Informal.* The limit of relevance, appeal, novelty, or fitness: *Are Gilbert and Sullivan past their sell-by date?*

sell·er (séllər) n. 1. A person who sells; a salesman or vendor. 2. An item that sells in a particular manner: *a best seller.*

Sel·lers (séllərz), **Peter** (1925–80). British comic actor, noted for the brilliance and variety of his characterisations. He won fame in the 1950s radio series *The Goon Show* and established an international reputation in films such as *Dr. Strangelove* (1963) and the *Pink Panther* series (1963–77).

sellers' market n. *Economics.* A market condition characterised by relatively high prices, occurring when the supply of commodities falls short of market demand. Compare **buyers' market.**

sell·ing point (sélling) n. A particularly attractive aspect, as of a product or idea, that is stressed in order to promote its sale.

Sel·lo·tape (sél-ə-tayp, -ō-) n. A trademark for a type of transparent adhesive tape. —**Sel·lo·tape** *tr.v.*

sell out *tr.v.* 1. To sell the whole of (one's stock). 2. To sell (one's share in a business). 3. To betray (a cause, a principle, or a colleague), especially for the sake of gain: *sold out his artistic principles.* —*intr.v.* 1. To sell the whole of one's stock: *We've sold out of bread.* 2. To sell one's share in a business. 3. To betray one's principles, colleagues, or other loyalties.

sell·out (sél-owt) n. 1. A betrayal. 2. An event for which all the tickets are sold. 3. One who has betrayed principles or a cause.

sel·syn (sél-sin) n. A device for the instantaneous transmission and reception, from a generator to a motor, of the angular movement of rotating parts. Also called "synchro". [Short for *self-synchronous*.]

selt·zer (séltsər) n. 1. A natural effervescent spring water of high mineral content. 2. Such water artificially prepared and containing carbon dioxide. Also called "seltzer water". [German *Selterser (Wasser),* "(water) of Nieder Selters", a district near Wiesbaden, West Germany, locality of the springs.]

sel·va (sélvə) n. 1. Dense tropical rain forest occurring in the Amazon basin. 2. Any area of such forest. [Portuguese, from Latin *silva,* forest.]

sel·vage, sel·vedge (sélvij) n. 1. The edge of a fabric woven so that it will not unravel; especially, an ornamental fringe at either end of an oriental carpet. 2. Any edge similar to this, usually a tapelike one. 3. The edge plate of a lock with a slot for a bolt. [Middle English : *selve, self,* SELF + *egge,* EDGE (after obsolete Dutch *selfegghe*).]

selves. Plural of **self.**

Sel·wyn-Lloyd (sélwin-lóyd), **John, Baron** (1904–78). British Conservative politician. He was foreign secretary (1955–60) in the Suez crisis and Chancellor of the Exchequer (1960–62) under Macmillan.

Selz·nick (sélznik), **David O(liver)** (1902–65). U.S. film producer. He established his reputation with films such as *David Copperfield* (1935), *A Star is Born* (1937), and *Gone with the Wind* (1939).

sem. seminary.

se·man·tic (si-mántik, sə-) adj. 1. Pertaining to meaning in language. 2. Of, pertaining to, or according to the science of semantics. [Greek *sēmantikos,* significant, from *sēmainein,* to signify, show by a sign, from *sēma,* sign.]

se·man·ti·cist (si-mánti-sist, sə-) n. A specialist in semantics.

se·man·tics (si-mántiks, sə-) n. *Used with a singular verb.* 1. *Linguistics.* The study or science of meaning in language forms, particularly with regard to its historical change. 2. *Logic.* The study of relationships between signs and symbols and what they represent. 3. Subtleties in meaning. Often used derogatorily.

sem·a·phore (sémmə-fawr ‖ -fōr) n. 1. Any visual signalling apparatus with flags, lights, or mechanically moving arms, as on a railway. 2. A visual system of sending information by means of two flags, one in each hand, using an alphabetic code based on the positions of the signaller's arms.
~v. **semaphored, -phoring, -phores.** —*tr.* To send (a message) by semaphore. —*intr.* To signal with a semaphore. [Greek *sēma,* sign + -PHORE.]

se·ma·si·ol·o·gy (si-máy-si-óllə ji, -zi-) n. Semantics, especially the study of semantic development. [Greek *sēmasia,* meaning, from *sēmainein,* to signify, mean (see **semantic**) + -LOGY.] —**se·ma·si·o·log·i·cal** (-ə-lójik'l) adj. —**se·ma·si·ol·o·gist** (-óllə jist) n.

se·mat·ic (si-máttik) adj. Serving as a warning or signal of danger, particularly to predators. Said especially of the colouring of certain animals. [Greek *sēma* (stem *sēmat-*), sign.]

sem·bla·ble (sémbləb'l) adj. *Archaic.* Appearing real; apparent. [Middle English, from Old French, from *sembler,* to resemble, seem, from Latin *similāre, simulāre,* to SIMULATE.] —**sem·bla·bly** adv.

sem·blance (sémblənss) n. 1. An outward or token appearance. 2. A representation or resemblance. 3. The barest trace; a modicum. [Middle English, from Old French, from *semblant,* present participle of *sembler,* to resemble, seem. See **semblable**.]

se·mé (sémmay, sémmi ‖ se-máy) adj. *Heraldry.* Having a design embellished with small, delicate figures, as a lacing of stars or flowers. [French, past participle of *semer,* to sow, scatter, from Latin *sēminare,* from *sēmen,* seed.]

semeiology. Variant of **semiology.**

semeiotic. Variant of **semiotic.**

se·meme (sée-meem) *n.* The meaning expressed by a morpheme. [SEM(ANTIC) + -EME.]

se·men (sée-men, -mən) *n.* **1.** The viscous whitish fluid that is ejaculated from the male reproductive organs of animals and transports the spermatozoa. **2.** Sperm. [Middle English, from Latin *sēmen,* "seed".]

se·mes·ter (si-méstər, sə-) *n.* Either of the two 15 to 18 week sessions into which an academic year is divided, especially in U.S. universities. [German *Semester,* from Latin *(cursus) sēmēstris,* "(period) of six months" : *sex,* six + *mēnsis,* month.]

sem·i (sémmi ‖ *U.S. also* sémmī) *n., pl.* **semis.** *Informal.* **1.** British. A semidetached house. **2.** A semifinal. **3.** *U.S. & Australian.* A semitrailer.

semi– *prefix. Abbr.* **s.** Indicates: **1.** Partly, partially, or incompletely; for example, **semiaquatic, semiliterate. 2.** Half of; for example, **semicircle. 3.** Occurring twice within a particular period of time; for example, **semimonthly.** *Note:* Many compounds other than those entered here may be formed with *semi-.* In this dictionary, in forming compounds, *semi-* is normally joined with the following element without space or hyphen: *semiannual.* However, many users prefer the hyphenated form, especially if the second element begins with a capital letter or with *i*: *semi-Americanised, semi-idle.* The prefix is often pronounced (sémmī-) in the United States; this variant is not shown in entries below. [Latin *sēmi-.*]

sem·i·an·nu·al (sémmi-ánnew-əl) *adj.* Happening or issued twice a year. —**sem·i·an·nu·al·ly** *adv.*

sem·i·a·quat·ic (sémmi-ə-kwáttik ‖ -kwóttik) *adj.* Adapted for living or growing in or near water; not entirely aquatic.

sem·i·ar·id (sémmi-árrid) *adj.* Designating regions often found in continental interiors, that are transitional between Savannah grassland and the desert, having relatively low rainfall and scrubby vegetation with coarse grasses; partly arid.

sem·i·au·to·mat·ic (sémmi-áwtə-máttik) *adj.* **1.** Partially automatic. **2.** Having an automatic reloading mechanism but requiring a pull of the trigger for each shot; autoloading. Said of a firearm. Compare **automatic.** —**sem·i·au·to·mat·ic** *adj.*

sem·i·au·ton·o·mous (sémmi-aw-tónnəməss) *adj.* Partially self-governing; especially, having powers of self-government within a larger organisation or structure.

sem·i·breve (sémmi-breev ‖ *U.S. also* -brev) *n. Music.* The longest note in ordinary use, having a time value equal to two minims. Also *U.S.* "whole note".

sem·i·cir·cle (sémmi-surk'l) *n.* **1.** A half of a circle as divided by a diameter. **2.** An object or arrangement of objects or people in the shape of a half-circle. —**sem·i·cir·cu·lar** (-súrkewlər) *adj.*

semicircular canal *n.* One of the three tubular and looped structures in the labyrinth of the inner ear, together functioning in the maintenance of a sense of balance and orientation.

sem·i·civ·i·lised (sémmi-sívvilīzd) *adj.* Partly civilised.

sem·i·co·lon (sémmi-kṓ-lən, -kō-, -lon) *n.* A mark of punctuation (;) indicating a degree of separation intermediate in value between the comma and the full stop.

sem·i·con·duc·tor (sémmi-kən-dúktər ‖ -kon-) *n.* Any of various solid crystalline substances, such as germanium or silicon, having electrical conductivity greater than insulators but less than good conductors.

sem·i·con·scious (sémmi-kónshəss) *adj.* Half-conscious; not fully conscious or aware. —**sem·i·con·scious·ly** *adv.* —**sem·i·con·scious·ness** *n.*

sem·i·des·ert (sémmi-dézzərt) *n.* A semiarid area. —**sem·i·des·ert** *adj.*

sem·i·de·tached (sémmi-di-tácht) *adj.* Attached to another building on one side only. Said of either of a pair of houses joined by a common wall. —**sem·i·de·tached** *adj.*

sem·i·di·am·e·ter (sémmi-dī-ámmitər) *n.* The apparent angular radius of a celestial body when seen as a disc from the Earth.

sem·i·di·ur·nal (sémmi-dī-úrn'l) *adj.* **1.** Of, pertaining to, occurring, or performed during a half-day. **2.** Occurring or coming approximately once every 12 hours, as the tides do. **3.** Designating the arc described by a celestial body between its meridian passage and its points of rising or setting.

sem·i·dome (sémmi-dōm) *n.* A roof covering a semicircular space; half a dome.

sem·i·el·lip·ti·cal (sémmi-i-líptik'l) *adj.* Having the form or shape of half of an ellipse, especially when divided along the major axis.

sem·i·fi·nal (sémmi-fín'l) *n.* **1.** One of the two competitions of the next to the last round in an elimination tournament. **2.** A match, competition, or other event that precedes the final event. —**sem·i·fi·nal** *adj.* —**sem·i·fi·nal·ist** *n.*

sem·i·flu·id (sémmi-flṓo-id ‖ -fléw-) *adj.* Also **sem·i·flu·id·ic** (-floo-íddik). Intermediate in flow properties between solids and liquids; highly viscous. —**sem·i·flu·id** *n.* —**sem·i·flu·id·i·ty** (-íddəti) *n.*

sem·i·for·mal (sémmi-fórm'l) *adj.* Somewhat formal.

sem·i·group (sémmi-grṓop) *n. Algebra.* A non-empty set with an associative binary multiplication.

sem·i·liq·uid (sémmi-líkwid) *adj.* Intermediate in properties, especially flow properties, between liquids and solids.

~*n.* A semiliquid substance.

sem·i·lit·er·ate (sémmi-líttər-ət, -it) *adj.* **1.** Having achieved an ele-

mentary level of literacy. **2.** Having limited knowledge or understanding, as of a technical subject.

sé·mil·lon (sémmi-yón, sáymi-) *n.* A variety of white grape used in making sauternes. [French, diminutive of Old French *seme,* seed, from Latin *semen* (stem *semin-*), seed.]

sem·i·log·a·rith·mic (sémmi-lóggə-ríth-mik ‖ -ríth-) *adj.* **1.** Having one logarithmic and one arithmetic scale: *semilogarithmic graph paper.* **2.** Characteristic of a relationship expressed using such scales.

sem·i·lu·nar (sémmi-lṓo-nər, -léw-) *adj.* Also **sem·i·lu·nate** (-nayt-). Shaped like a half-moon; crescent.

semilunar bone *n. Anatomy.* The **lunate bone** *(see).*

semilunar valve *n.* Either of two crescent-shaped valves, each having three cusps, located in the aorta and in the pulmonary artery and preventing blood from flowing back into the heart.

sem·i·month·ly (sémmi-múnthli) *adj.* Occurring or issued twice a month.

~*n., pl.* **semimonthlies.** A semimonthly publication.

~*adv.* Twice monthly; at half-monthly intervals. See Usage note at **bimonthly.**

sem·i·nal (sémmin'l, séemin'l) *adj.* **1.** Of, relating to, or containing semen or seed. **2.** Highly influential in an original way; constituting or providing a basis for further development. [Middle English, from Old French, from Latin *sēminālis,* from *sēmen* (stem *sēmin-*), seed, SEMEN.] —**sem·i·nal·ly** *adv.*

sem·i·nar (sémmi-naar) *n.* **1. a.** A small group, usually of advanced students, engaged in original research and meeting regularly, under the guidance of a tutor, to exchange and discuss their views and findings. **b.** A course of study so pursued. **c.** A scheduled meeting of such a group. **2.** A meeting for an exchange of ideas on a particular topic; a conference. [German *Seminar,* from Latin *sēminārium,* seed plot, nursery. See **seminary.**]

sem·i·nar·i·an (sémmi-naír-i-ən) *n.* Also **sem·i·nar·ist** (-nərist). A seminary student.

sem·i·nar·y (sémmi-nəri ‖ *U.S.* -nerri) *n., pl.* **-ies.** *Abbr.* **sem. 1.** A place of education, especially: **a.** A theological school for the training of priests, ministers, or rabbis. **b.** *Archaic.* A private secondary school for girls. **2.** A place or environment in which something is developed or nurtured. [Middle English, seed plot, place for cultivation, nursery garden, from Latin *sēminārium,* garden, seed plot, nursery, from *sēminārius,* of seeds, from *sēmen* (stem *sēmin-*), seed.]

sem·i·na·tion (sémmi-náysh'n) *n. Rare.* The dispersal or production of seed. [Latin *sēminātiō* (stem *sēminātiōn-*), propagation, from *sēminātus,* past participle of *sēmināre,* to sow, from *sēmen* (stem *sēmin-*), seed.]

sem·i·nif·er·ous (sémmi-níffərəss) *adj. Biology.* **1.** Conveying or producing sperms: *the seminiferous tubules of the testis.* **2.** Bearing seed. [Latin *sēmen* (stem *sēmin-*), SEMEN + -FEROUS.]

Sem·i·nole (sémmi-nōl) *n., pl.* **-noles** or collectively **Seminole. 1.** A member of a Muskhogean-speaking North American Indian people, now living chiefly in Oklahoma. **2.** The language of this people. [Creek *simanóli, simalóni,* from American Spanish *cimarrón,* wild, runaway. See **maroon** (to abandon).] —**Sem·i·nole** *adj.*

sem·i·no·mad (sémmi-nṓ-mad) *n.* One of a people whose living habits are largely nomadic but who plant some crops. —**sem·i·no·mad·ic** (-nō-máddik) *adj.*

sem·i·of·fi·cial (sémmi-ə-físh'l ‖ -ṓ-) *adj.* Having some official authority or sanction. —**sem·i·of·fi·cial·ly** *adv.*

se·mi·ol·o·gy, se·mei·ol·o·gy (sémmi-ólləji, séemi- ‖ *U.S. also* séemī-, sémmī-) *n.* **1.** The science dealing with signs, sign language, or systems of signalling. **2.** *Medicine.* **Symptomatology** *(see).* [New Latin *semaeologia* : Greek *sēmeion,* mark, sign, from *sēma,* sign, signal + -LOGY.]

se·mi·ot·ic, se·mei·ot·ic (sémmi-óttik, séemi- ‖ *U.S. also* séemī-, sémmī-) *adj.* **1.** Of or relating to semiotics. **2.** *Medicine.* Relating to symptomatology. [Greek *sēmeiōtikos,* observant of signs, from *sēmeioun,* to mark, give signals, note, from *sēmeion,* sign. See **semiology.**]

se·mi·ot·ics, se·mei·ot·ics (sémmi-óttiks, séemi- ‖ *U.S. also* séemī-, sémmī-) *n. Used with a singular verb.* **1.** The study of all forms of human communicative behaviour, especially of signs and symbols. **2.** *Medicine.* **Symptomatology** *(see).* —**se·mi·o·ti·cian** (-ə-tísh'n) *n.*

sem·i·pal·mate (sémmi-pál-mət, -páal-, -mit, -mayt) *adj.* Also **sem·i·pal·mat·ed** (-máytid, -maytid). Having partial or reduced webbing between the toes, as some wading birds do.

sem·i·par·a·site (sémmi-párrə-sīt) *n. Biology.* A **hemiparasite** *(see).* —**sem·i·par·a·sit·ic** (-síttik) *adj.* —**sem·i·par·a·sit·ism** (-sit-iz'm) *n.*

sem·i·per·me·a·ble (sémmi-pérmi-əb'l ‖ *U.S. also* -pér-) *adj.* **1.** Partially permeable. **2.** Of or relating to a natural or artificial membrane that is permeable to some molecules in a mixture or solution but not to all. See **osmosis.**

sem·i·po·lar bond (sémmi-pṓlər) *n. Chemistry.* A **coordinate** *(see).*

sem·i·por·ce·lain (sémmi-pór-səlin, -slin ‖ -pṓr-) *n.* Any of several glazed ceramic wares resembling porcelain but having little or no translucency.

sem·i·pre·cious (sémmi-préshəss) *adj.* Designating stones of less value than precious stones, such as the topaz.

sem·i·pro (sémmi-prṓ) *adj. Informal.* Semiprofessional. —**sem·i·pro** *n.*

sem·i·pro·fes·sion·al (sémmi-prə-fésh'n'l ‖ -prō-) *adj.* **1.** Taking part in a sport or other activity for pay, but not full-time. **2.** Composed of or engaged in by semiprofessional players.

~*n.* A semiprofessional person.

sem·i·qua·ver (sémmi-kwayvər) *n. Music.* A note having a time value equal to half a quaver. Also *U.S.* "sixteenth note".

Se·mir·a·mis (se-mírrəmiss). The legendary founder of Babylon and wife of Ninus.

sem·i·rig·id (sémmi-ríjid) *adj.* **1.** Moderately rigid. **2.** Having some rigid components.

sem·i·round (sémmi-równd) *adj.* Having a round side and a flat side. —**sem·i·round** *n.*

sem·i·skilled (sémmi-skíld) *adj.* Possessing or requiring some skills or training, but less than those required for specialised work.

sem·i·skimmed milk (sémmi-skímd) *n.* Milk from which some but not all cream has been skimmed. —**sem·i·skimmed** *adj., n.*

sem·i·sol·id (sémmi-sóllid) *adj.* Intermediate in properties, especially in rigidity, between solids and liquids.

~*n.* A semisolid substance, such as a stiff dough or firm gelatine.

Sem·ite (sée-mīt, sémmīt) *n.* Also **Shem·ite** (shémmīt). A member of a people of Caucasian stock comprising chiefly Jews and Arabs but in ancient times also including Babylonians, Assyrians, Phoenicians, and others of the eastern Mediterranean area. [New Latin *semita*, from Late Latin *Sēm*, Shem (traditional ancestor of the Semites), from Greek, from Hebrew *Shem.*]

Se·mit·ic (si-míttik, sə-, se-) *adj.* **1.** Of, pertaining to, or designating a subfamily of the Afro-Asiatic family of languages including Arabic, Hebrew, Ethiopic, Akkadian, and Aramaic. **2.** Of, pertaining to, or designating any of the people who speak a Semitic language; especially, the Jewish people.

~*n.* **1.** The Semitic subfamily of languages. **2.** Any one of these languages.

Se·mit·ics (si-míttiks, sə-, se-) *n. Used with a singular verb.* The study of the history, languages, and cultures of the Semitic peoples.

Sem·i·tism (sémmitiz'm) *n.* **1.** A Semitic word, idiom, or characteristic. **2.** A policy of favouring Jewish interests.

Sem·i·to-Ha·mit·ic (sémmitō-ha-míttik) *n.* A family of languages, **Afro-Asiatic** (*see*). —**Sem·i·to-Ha·mit·ic** *adj.*

sem·i·tone (sémmi-tōn) *n. Music.* The smallest interval normally used in Western music, equal to half a tone in the standard diatonic scale. Also *U.S.* "half tone". —**sem·i·ton·ic** (-tónnik) *adj.*

sem·i·trail·er (sémmi-traylər) *n.* A trailer with wheels at the rear only, the forward end being supported by the towing vehicle.

sem·i·trans·par·ent (sémmi-transs-párrənt, -tranz-, -páir-ənt) *adj.* Not completely transparent.

sem·i·trop·i·cal (sémmi-tróppik'l) *adj.* Partly tropical; subtropical.

sem·i·vow·el (sémmi-vow-əl, -vów-) *n. Phonetics.* A speech sound that from the articulatory viewpoint is a vowel but that functions as a consonant in the sound system of a particular language; for example, (w) and (y) in English are semivowels. Also called "glide".

sem·i·week·ly (sémmi-wéekli) *adj.* Issued or happening twice a week.

~*n., pl.* **semiweeklies.** A semiweekly publication.

~*adv.* Twice weekly. See Usage note at **bimonthly.**

Semmelweis (zémmel-vīs), **Ignaz Philipp** (1818–65). Hungarian physician. He discovered that puerperal fever was an infectious disease transmitted by medical staff after carrying out post-mortems. His theory was not heeded and it was left to Joseph Lister to pioneer antiseptic techniques.

sem·mit (sémmit) *n. Scottish.* A vest. [Middle English *semmit*†.]

sem·o·li·na (sémmə-léenə) *n.* **1.** The gritty, coarse particles of wheat left after flour has been sifted. **2.** A milk pudding prepared from this. [Variant of Italian *semolino*, diminutive of *semola*, bran, from Latin *simila*, fine flour. See **simnel.**]

sem·pi·ter·nal (sémpi-térn'l) *adj.* Eternal; perpetual. [Middle English, from Old French *sempiternel*, from Late Latin *sempiternālis*, from Latin *sempiternus* : *semper*, always + *aeternus*, eternal.] —**sem·pi·ter·ni·ty** (-térnəti) *n.*

sem·pli·ce (sémplichi) *adv. Music.* Simply; plainly. Used as a direction. [Italian, from Latin *simplex* (stem *simplic-*), simple.] —**sem·pli·ce** *adj.*

sem·pre (sémpri, sémpray) *adv. Music.* In the same manner throughout. Used as a direction. [Italian, "always", from Latin *semper.*]

semp·stress (sémp-striss, -strəss) *n.* A seamstress. [Variant of SEAMSTRESS.]

sen (sen) *n., pl.* **sen.** **1. a.** A former monetary unit equal to ¹/₁₀₀ of the yen of Japan. **b.** A monetary unit equal to ¹/₁₀₀ of the dollar of Brunei. **c.** A monetary unit equal to ¹/₁₀₀ of the rupiah of Indonesia. **d.** A monetary unit equal to ¹/₁₀₀ of the riel of Kampuchea. **e.** A monetary unit equal to ¹/₁₀₀ of the dollar or ringgit of Malaysia. **2.** A coin worth one sen. [Japanese, from Chinese (Mandarin) *qián*, money, coin.]

SEN, S.E.N. State Enrolled Nurse (in Britain).

sen., Sen. **1.** senate; senator. **2.** senior.

Sen·a·nay·a·ke (sénnə-nī́-əkə), **D(on) S(tephen)** (1884–1952). Ceylonese statesman, prime minister (1947–52). He headed the movement for constitutional reform which led to independence and was the first prime minister of Ceylon (now Sri Lanka). His son Dudley (1911–73) succeeded him as premier.

se·nar·i·us (se-náar-i-əss, -náir-) *n., pl.* **-narii** (-náir-i-ī). A Greek or Latin verse consisting of six feet. [Latin *sēnārius*, from adjective, SENARY.]

sen·ar·mon·tite (sénnaar-món-tīt) *n.* A white or greyish mineral, Sb₂O₃, that occurs in cubic crystalline form. [After Henri de *Sénarmont* (died 1862), French mineralogist.]

sen·a·ry (séenəri, sénnəri) *adj.* Of or pertaining to the number six;

having six things or parts. [Latin *sēnārius*, from *sēnī*, six each, from *sex*, six.]

sen·ate (sénnit, sénnət) *n. Abbr.* **sen., Sen.** **1.** An assembly or council of citizens having the highest deliberative and legislative functions in a government, especially: **a.** *Capital* **S.** The upper house of Congress in the United States, to which two members are elected from each state. **b.** *Capital* **S.** The upper legislative house in Australia, Canada, France, and other countries. **c.** The supreme council of state of the ancient Roman republic and, nominally, of the empire. **2.** The building or hall in which a senate meets. **3.** The governing body of some universities, composed of faculty members and sometimes student representatives. [Middle English *senat*, from Old French, from Latin *senātus*, from *senex*, old, an old man, an elder.]

sen·a·tor (sénnətər) *n. Often capital* **S.** *Abbr.* **Sen., sen.** A member of a senate. —**sen·a·tor·ship** *n.*

sen·a·to·ri·al (sénnə-táwr-i-əl ‖ -tór-) *adj.* **1.** Of, concerning, or befitting a senator or a senate. **2.** Composed of senators. **3.** *U.S.* Designating a district from which a senator is elected. —**sen·a·to·ri·al·ly** *adv.*

se·na·tus con·sul·tum (se-náa-təss kon-súl-tōōm, si-, -náy-, -sóōl-, -təm ‖ *U.S. also* kōn-) *n., pl.* **senatus consulta** (-súltə). *Latin.* A decree of the ancient Roman senate.

send¹ (send) *v.* **sent**, **sending, sends.** —*tr.* **1. a.** To cause to be conveyed to a destination by an intermediary or means of communication: *sent his reply by telegram.* **b.** To express for conveyance: *She sends her love.* **2.** To cause or order to go, especially: **a.** To direct to go on a mission or errand. **b.** To enable or arrange for (someone) to go: *sent all their children to private schools.* **c.** To command or request to depart; dismiss: *Send the guard away.* **d.** To direct or require to go or be taken; consign: *sent them to the gallows.* **e.** To cause to go or move in a specified way or direction: *The rain sent them hurrying indoors.* **f.** To direct (a person) to a source of information; refer. **3. a.** To give off; emit (heat or smoke, for example). Often used with *forth* or *out.* **b.** To produce; cause to grow: *sending forth new roots.* **4.** To direct or propel with force: *an explosion that sent glass flying everywhere.* **5.** To cause to take place or befall; bestow or inflict: *a punishment sent by the gods.* **6. a.** To put or drive into some state or condition: *His lecture sent me to sleep.* **b.** *Slang.* To transport with delight; carry away. —*intr.* To dispatch a messenger or message. —**send away for.** To order by mail. —**send down.** *British.* **1.** To suspend or dismiss from a university. **2.** *Informal.* To send to prison. —**send for.** **1.** To order. **2.** To summon —**send packing.** *Informal.* To dismiss summarily or abruptly. [Send, sent, sent; Middle English *senden, sente, sent,* Old English *sendan, sende, sended.*] —**send·er** *n.*

send². Variant of *scend.*

sen·dal (sénd'l) *n.* A light, thin silk used in the Middle Ages. [Middle English *cendal*, from Old French, obscurely akin to Greek *sindōn*†, a fine linen cloth.]

send off *tr.v.* **1.** *Sports.* To order (a player) to leave the field because of a serious violation of the rules. **2.** To give a send-off to.

send-off (sénd-off, -awff) *n.* **1.** A demonstration of affection and good wishes for one about to leave on a journey or to begin a new undertaking. **2.** A start given to someone or something.

send up *tr.v.* **1.** *Chiefly British.* To satirise or make fun of, especially by mimicry or parody. **2.** *U.S. Informal.* To send to prison.

send-up (sénd-up) *n.* An amusing imitation or parody.

Sen·e·ca¹ (sénnikə) *n., pl.* **Seneca** or **-cas.** **1.** A member of an Iroquoian-speaking North American Indian people formerly inhabiting western New York. **2.** The language of this people.

Seneca². Latin name Marcus Annaeus Seneca; known as Seneca the Elder (*c.* 55 B.C.–*c.* A.D. 39). Roman writer on rhetoric. His works include the *Controversiae,* a series of imaginary legal cases which illustrate various approved methods of oratorical presentation.

Seneca³. Latin name Lucius Annaeus Seneca; known as Seneca the Younger (*c.* 4 B.C.–A.D. 65). Roman writer, philosopher, and politician. The son of Seneca the Elder, he was tutor to the young Nero and became one of the emperor's chief advisors on his accession. He produced several works of moral philosophy, advocating Stoicism, and also wrote nine tragedies. Seneca was forced to commit suicide for alleged conspiracy against Nero.

se·nec·ti·tude (si-nékti-tewd, sə- ‖ -tōod) *n.* Old age. [Medieval Latin *senectitūdō*, from Latin *senectūs*, from *senex*, old.]

sen·e·ga (sénnigə) *n.* The dried root of a North American plant, *Polygala senega*, used as an expectorant. [Variant of SENECA.]

Sé·né·gal (sénni-gáwl; *French* -gál). A river of west Africa. Formed by the confluence of the Bafing and Bakoy rivers, both of which rise in the Fouta Djallon in northern Guinea, it flows 1 690 kilometres (1,050 miles) to the Atlantic at St. Louis in Senegal.

Sen·e·gal, Republic of (sénni-gáwl). *French* **Sé·né·gal** (-gál). A state of West Africa, which takes its name from the Sénégal river. Consisting mainly of lowland plains it has important phosphate and iron ore deposits. Following the Sahel droughts of the 1970s, groundnuts, which accounted for over three-quarters of the country's total exports, now accounts for only a quarter. Fishing and tourism are increasingly also important. Senegal is one of West Africa's most industrialised countries, producing textiles, beer, foodstuffs, tobaccos, and cement. By 1887, the French had conquered all of Senegal. It gained independence in 1960, but maintains close ties with France. It joined with Gambia to form the Confederation of Senegambia (1982–89). Area, 196 722 square kilometres (75,934 square miles). Population 8,570,000. Capital, Dakar. See map at **West African States**.

Sen·e·gam·bi·a, Confederation of (sénni-gámbi-ə). Union formed from December 1981 to 1989 by the states of Senegal and Gambia. It was not a political union, but did involve some economic integration and close ties in foreign policy matters.

se·nes·cence (si-néss'nss, sə-) n. The state associated with advancing age of an organism or part, usually characterised by a reduced capacity to repair and maintain tissues. **—se·nes·cent** adj.

sen·e·schal (sénnish'l) n. An official in a royal or noble medieval household in charge of domestic arrangements and the administration of servants; a steward. [Middle English, from Old French, from Medieval Latin siniscalcus, from Germanic.]

Sen·ghor (seng-gór, saN-), **Léopold Sédar** (1906–). Senegalese writer and statesman, president (1960–80). A noted poet whose collections include *Chants d'Ombre* (1945), he led his country to independence in 1960 as head of line of the Senegalese Progressive Union. He became Senegal's first president.

se·nile (séenīl ‖ U.S. also sénnīl) adj. 1. Pertaining to, characteristic of, or proceeding from old age. 2. Exhibiting senility. 3. *Geology.* Worn away nearly to the base level, as at the end of an erosion cycle. [French sénile, from Latin senīlis, from senex (stem sen-), old.] **—se·nile·ly** adv.

senile dementia n. Progressive deterioration of mental faculties in old age. See **presenile dementia**.

se·nil·i·ty (si-nílləti, se-) n. 1. The state of being senile. 2. Mental and physical deterioration with old age.

sen·ior (séen-yər, séeni-ər) adj. Abbr. **Sr.**, **sr.**, **Sen.**, **sen.**, **Snr.** 1. More advanced in age. Used especially after a name to denote the older of two persons who share the same name, such as a father and son: *Douglas Fairbanks Senior.* 2. **a.** Pertaining to or having a high or higher rank: *senior levels of management.* **b.** Above others in terms of length of service or appointment. 3. Of, designating, or intended for older or more advanced students or pupils.
~ n. 1. A senior person, especially: **a.** One who is older: *He is three years my senior.* **b.** U.S. A senior citizen. 2. U.S. A final-year student at university or high school. [Latin, comparative of senex, old.]

senior citizen n. A person of or over the age of retirement; O.A.P.

Usage: The phrase *senior citizen* is now widely used as a euphemism for "elderly person", especially in the fields of politics and advertising. While many people find it unobjectionable, the phrase has attracted criticism on the grounds that it lacks any real meaning, and that it distracts people's attention from the problems involved in society's care (or lack of care) of the aged.

senior common room n. Abbr. **S.C.R.** A common room for faculty members, especially at a British university.

Senior Executive Officer n. Abbr. **S.E.O.** An administrative officer in the British Government service in the grade between a Principal and a Higher Executive Officer.

se·ni·or·i·ty (sée-ni-órrəti) n., pl. **-ties.** 1. The state of being older or higher in rank. 2. Precedence of position; especially, precedence over others of the same rank by reason of a longer span of service.

senior nursing officer n. In Britain, a senior nurse in charge of all the nurses and ancillary staff (but not the doctors) in a hospital, or in one department of a hospital. Formerly called "matron".

senior service n. British. The Royal Navy. Preceded by *the.*

sen·na (sénnə) n. 1. Any of various plants of the genus *Cassia,* having compound leaves and usually yellow flowers. 2. The dried leaves or pods of *C. angustifolia* or *C. acutifolia,* used medicinally as a cathartic. [New Latin, from Arabic sanā'.]

Sen·nach·er·ib (se-náckərib, si-, sə-) (died 681 B.C.). King of Assyria (704–681). The son of Sargon II, he is especially remembered for his building works which included the restoration of Nineveh.

sen·net (sénnit) n. A call on a trumpet or cornet signalling the ceremonial exits and entrances of actors in Elizabethan drama. [Perhaps variant of SIGNET.]

Sen·nett (sén-it, -ət), **Mack** born Michael Sinnott (1884–1960). U.S. film producer and director, born in Canada. His many slapstick films included the Keystone comedies (1912–16).

sen·night, se'n·night (sénnīt) n. Archaic. A week. [Middle English seoveniht, sennet, Old English seofon nihta : seofon, SEVEN + nihta, plural of niht, NIGHT.]

sen·nit (sénnit) n. Also **sin·net** (sínnit). Nautical. Braided cordage formed by plaiting several strands of rope fibre or similar material. [17th century : origin obscure.]

sen·o·pi·a (sen-ṓpi-ə) n. Improvement of near vision sometimes occurring in the aged because of swelling of the crystalline lens in incipient cataract. [Latin senex, old + -OPIA.]

se·ñor (sen-yór) n., pl. **señores** (-ayz; Spanish -ayss). Abbr. **Sr.** 1. The Spanish title of courtesy for a man, equivalent to the English *Mr.* or *sir.* It may be used alone or prefixed to a name. 2. A Spanish or Spanish-speaking man.

se·ño·ra (sen-yáw-rə; Spanish -ra) n., pl. **señoras** (-z; Spanish -ss). Abbr. **Sra.** 1. The Spanish title of courtesy for a married woman, equivalent to the English *Mrs.* or *madam.* It may be used alone or prefixed to a name. 2. A Spanish or Spanish-speaking woman.

se·ño·ri·ta (sényaw-rée-tə; Spanish -ta) n., pl. **-tas** (-z; Spanish -ss). Abbr. **Srta.** 1. The Spanish title of courtesy for an unmarried young woman or a girl, equivalent to the English *Miss.* It may be used alone or prefixed to a name. 2. A Spanish or Spanish-speaking unmarried woman or girl.

sen·sate (sén-sayt) adj. Perceived by the senses. [Late Latin sēnsātus, gifted with sense, from Latin sēnsus, SENSE.] **—sen·sate·ly** adv.

sen·sa·tion (sen-sáysh'n, sən-) n. 1. **a.** A perception associated with stimulation of a sense organ or with a specific bodily condition: *the sensation of heat.* **b.** The faculty to feel or perceive; physical sensibility: *He had little sensation left in his leg.* 2. An emotional state that is hard to define but is associated with particular conditions or circumstances: *a strange sensation of relief.* 3. **a.** A condition of intense public interest and excitement. **b.** An event, person, or object causing such public excitement. [Medieval Latin sēnsātiō (stem sēnsātiōn-), from Late Latin sēnsātus, SENSATE.]

sen·sa·tion·al (sen-sáysh'n'l, sən-) adj. 1. Of or pertaining to sensation. 2. Arousing or intended to arouse strong curiosity, interest, or reaction, especially by exaggerated or lurid details. 3. Outstanding; wonderful. **—sen·sa·tion·al·ise, sen·sa·tion·al·ize** v. **—sen·sa·tion·al·ly** adv.

sen·sa·tion·al·ism (sen-sáysh'n'l-iz'm, sən-) n. 1. **a.** The use of sensational matter or methods, as in writing, art or politics. **b.** Sensational subject matter. **c.** Interest in or the effect of such subject matter. 2. *Philosophy.* The theory that sensation is the only source of knowledge. Also called "sensualism". 3. The ethical doctrine that feeling is the only criterion of good. **—sen·sa·tion·al·ist** n. **—sen·sa·tion·al·is·tic** (-ístik) adj.

sense (senss) n. 1. Any of the animal functions of hearing, sight, smell, touch, and taste. 2. The faculty of external perception exemplified by these functions. 3. *Plural.* The faculties of sensation as means of providing physical gratification and pleasure. 4. **a.** Intuitive or acquired perception or ability to make appropriate judgments: *good dress sense.* **b.** A capacity to appreciate or understand: *a sense of humour.* **c.** A vague feeling, impression, or presentiment: *a sense of impending trouble.* **d.** Recognition or awareness of moral issues and their relevance to one's own conduct: *a sense of duty.* 5. **a.** Usually plural. One's normal conscious or rational state: *Come to your senses.* **b.** A capacity for sound practical judgments; common sense: *hasn't got an ounce of sense.* **c.** The quality of being consistent with good judgment: *There's no sense in waiting.* 6. **a.** Import; point; intended meaning. **b.** Lexical meaning. **c.** The meaning of a word in a particular context. 7. The prevailing view; the consensus. **—make sense. 1.** To be coherent or intelligible. 2. *Informal.* To be practical or advisable. **—See Synonyms at meaning, mind.** ~ tr.v. **sensed, sensing, senses.** 1. To become aware of, often on the basis of intuition rather than explicit information; perceive. 2. To detect something automatically: *sense radioactivity.* 3. *Chiefly U.S. Informal.* To grasp; understand. [Latin sēnsus, the faculty of perceiving, from the past participle of sentīre, to perceive by senses, to feel.]

sense datum n. A basic unanalysable experience resulting from the stimulation of a sense organ.

sense·less (sénss-ləss, -liss) adj. 1. Without sense or meaning; meaningless. 2. Foolish; lacking sense: *a senseless boy.* 3. Insensate; unconscious. **—sense·less·ly** adv. **—sense·less·ness** n.

sense organ n. A specialised organ or structure, such as the eye, the stimulation of which initiates a process of sensory perception.

sense perception n. Perception by the bodily senses.

sen·si·bil·i·ty (sén-si-bílləti, -ə-) n., pl. **-ties.** 1. The ability to feel or perceive. 2. **a.** Keen intellectual or aesthetic perception: *the sensibility of a painter to colour.* **b.** The capacity for sensitive emotional response, as to the feelings of another; sensitiveness. 3. Often plural. **a.** Receptiveness to impression, whether pleasant or unpleasant; acuteness of feeling. **b.** Acute susceptibility to emotional influences; oversensitiveness. 4. *Botany.* The susceptibility of plants to environmental influences.

sen·si·ble (sén-sib'l, -səb'l) adj. 1. Acting with or showing good sense: *a sensible choice.* 2. Practical and unpretentious: *sensible shoes.* 3. Having a perception of something; cognisant; aware. 4. Perceptible by the senses or by the mind. 5. Readily perceived; appreciable. 6. Having the faculty of sensation; able to feel or perceive. **—See Usage note at sensitive.** [Middle English, from Old French, from Latin sēnsibilis, from sēnsus, SENSE.] **—sen·si·ble·ness** n. **—sen·si·bly** adv.

sen·si·tise, sen·si·tize (sén-si-tīz, -sə-) v. **-tised, -tising, -tises.** —tr. 1. To make sensitive. 2. *Photography.* To make (a film or plate) sensitive to light, especially to light of a specific wavelength. —intr. To become sensitive. **—sen·si·ti·sa·tion** (-tī-záysh'n ‖ U.S. -ti-) n. **—sen·si·tis·er** n.

sen·si·tive (sén-si-tiv, -sə-) adj. 1. Capable of perceiving with a sense or senses. 2. Responsive to and readily affected by external conditions or emotional stimulation: *a sensitive part of the body; a sensitive child.* 3. Susceptible to the attitudes, feelings, or circumstances of others; acutely or sympathetically aware. 4. **a.** Easily upset. **b.** Quick to take offence; touchy. 5. Easily irritated: *sensitive skin.* 6. Readily altered by the action of some agent: *sensitive to light.* 7. Registering very slight differences or changes of condition. Said of an instrument. 8. Unusually susceptible to external conditions and tending to fluctuate. Said of stock market prices. 9. **a.** Dealing with classified information, usually involving national security: *a sensitive post in the Foreign Office.* **b.** Liable to arouse controversy or strong feelings: *a sensitive issue.* [Middle English, from Old French sensitif, from Medieval Latin sēnsitīvus, from Latin sēnsus, SENSE.] **—sen·si·tive·ly** adv. **—sen·si·tive·ness** n.

Usage: Sensitivity can be used as the noun relating to any of the senses of *sensitive,* but *sensitiveness* is the form usually employed for the personal tendency to be offended easily or to react readily to criticism. *Sensitive* should also be clearly distinguished from *sensible, sensual,* and *sensuous. Sensitive* refers primarily to the delicate nature of someone's feelings (*he's very sensitive about that issue*); *sensible* emphasises one's conscious awareness of something (*he was sensible that a lot remained to be done*); *sensual* applies specifically to gratification of the physical senses, especially those associated with sexual activity (*sensual pleasures*); *sensuous* refers to satisfaction of any of the senses, especially through the aesthetic enjoyment of nature, art, and so on (*sensuous colours/music*).

sensitive plant *n.* **1.** A woody tropical American plant, *Mimosa pudica,* having leaflets and stems that fold and droop when touched. **2.** Any of various similar plants.

sen·si·tiv·i·ty (sén-si-tívvəti, -sə-) *n., pl.* **-ties. 1.** The quality or condition of being sensitive. **2.** *Electronics.* The minimum input signal required to produce a specific output signal. **3.** *Photography.* The degree of response of a plate or film to light, especially to light of a particular wavelength.

sen·si·tom·e·ter (sén-si-tómmitər) *n.* A device used for measuring the sensitivity of photographic film to light. [SENSIT(IVE) + -METER.] **—sen·si·tom·e·try** *n.*

sen·sor (sén-sər, -sawr) *n.* A device, such as a photoelectric cell, that receives and responds to a signal or stimulus. [Latin *sēnsus,* SENSE.]

sen·so·ri·mo·tor (sén-səri-mṓtər) *adj.* Of, pertaining to, or combining the functions of the sensing and motor activities. Said of nerves. [*sensory* + *motor.*]

sen·so·ri·um (sen-sáwr-i-əm || -sṓr-) *n., pl.* **-ums** or **-soria** (sáwr-i-ə). **1.** The part of the brain that receives and correlates the impressions conveyed from various sensory areas. **2.** The entire sensory system. [Late Latin *sēnsōrium,* organ of sensation, from Latin *sēnsus,* SENSE.]

sen·so·ry (sén-səri) *adj.* Also **sen·sor·i·al** (sen-sáwr-i-əl || -sṓr-). **1.** Of or pertaining to the senses or sensation. **2.** Transmitting impulses from sense organs to nerve centres; afferent.

sensory deprivation *n.* A situation in which a subject undergoes complete deprivation of sensory stimulation, so that his physical and psychological reactions may be observed.

sen·su·al (sénssew-əl, -shoo-əl) *adj.* **1.** Pertaining to or affecting any of the senses or a sense organ; sensory. **2. a.** Pertaining to, consisting in, or excessively fond of the gratification of the physical appetites, especially sexual appetites. **b.** Suggesting sexuality or a sensual disposition; voluptuous. **c.** Carnal rather than spiritual or intellectual; worldly. —See Synonyms at **sensuous.** —See Usage note at **sensitive.** [Middle English, from Latin *sēnsuālis,* from *sēnsus,* SENSE.] **—sen·su·al·ly** *adv.* **—sen·su·al·ness** *n.*

sen·su·a·lise, sen·su·al·ize (sénssew-ə-līz, -shoo-) *v.* **-ised, -ising, -ises.** To make sensual. **—sen·su·al·i·sa·tion** (-lī-záysh'n || *U.S.* -li-) *n.*

sen·su·al·ism (sénssew-ə-liz'm, -shoo-) *n.* **1.** Sensuality. **2.** The ethical doctrine that the pleasures of the senses are the highest good. **3.** *Philosophy.* **Sensationalism** *(see).* **—sen·su·al·ist** *n.* **—sen·su·al·is·tic** (-lístik) *adj.*

sen·su·al·i·ty (sénssew-ál-əti, -shoo-) *n., pl.* **-ties. 1.** The quality or state of being sensual. **2.** Excessive devotion to sensual pleasures.

sen·su·ous (sén-əss, -shoo-) *adj.* **1.** Pertaining to or derived from the senses. **2.** Having qualities that appeal to the senses, especially on an aesthetic level. **3.** Readily susceptible to influences perceived by the senses; highly appreciative of the pleasures of sensation. —See Usage note at **sensitive.** [Latin *sēnsus,* SENSE + -OUS.] **—sen·su·ous·ly** *adv.* **—sen·su·ous·ness** *n.*

Synonyms: *sensuous, sensual, luxurious, sybaritic, epicurean.*

sent. Past tense and past participle of **send.**

sen·tence (séntənss) *n.* **1.** A complete and independent grammatical unit comprising a word or a group of words, and usually consisting of at least one subject with its predicate, containing a finite verb or verb phrase; for example, *The door is open* and *Go!* are sentences. **2. a.** A judicial decision of what punishment is to be inflicted on a convicted person. **b.** The punishment so meted out. **3.** *Archaic.* An opinion; especially, one given formally after deliberation. **4.** *Archaic.* An aphorism.
∼*tr.v.* **sentenced, -tencing, -tences. 1.** To pass sentence upon (a convicted person). **2.** To cause to undergo something undesirable; condemn. [Middle English, opinion, judgment, thought, from Old French, from Latin *sententia,* a way of thinking, opinion, from *sentīre,* to feel.] **—sen·tenc·er** (sentən-sər) *n.* **—sen·ten·tial** (sen-ténsh'l) *adj.* **—sen·ten·tial·ly** *adv.*

sen·ten·tious (sen-ténshəss) *adj.* **1.** Fond of using maxims. **2.** Given to pompous moralising. **3.** Terse, pithy, and aphoristic in expression. [Latin *sententiōsus,* full of meaning, from *sententia,* opinion, SENTENCE.] **—sen·ten·tious·ly** *adv.* **—sen·ten·tious·ness** *n.*

sen·ti·ence (sén-sh'nss, -shi-ənss || -ti-ənss) *n.* Also **sen·ti·en·cy** (-ən-si). **1.** The quality or state of being sentient; consciousness. **2.** Feeling as distinguished from perception or thought.

sen·ti·ent (sén-sh'nt, -shi-ənt || -ti-ənt) *adj.* Having the power of sensation; conscious.
∼*n.* A sentient being. [Latin *sentiēns* (stem *sentient-*), present participle of *sentīre,* to feel.] **—sen·ti·ent·ly** *adv.*

sen·ti·ment (séntimənt) *n.* **1. a.** A thought, attitude, or general mental disposition modified or coloured by emotion: *a certain amount of anti-American sentiment.* **b.** *Often plural.* An opinion about a specific matter; a view. **2.** The emotional import of a passage, work of art, or the like, as distinguished from the form of expression. **3. a.** Susceptibility to delicate or refined feeling. **b.** An expression of this, especially in art or literature. **4.** Excessive susceptibility to such feeling; emotion that borders on mawkishness. —See Synonyms at **opinion.** [Middle English *sentement,* from Old French, from Medieval Latin *sentīmentum,* from Latin *sentīre,* to feel.]

sen·ti·men·tal (sénti-mént'l) *adj.* **1. a.** Characterised by, influenced by, or exhibiting delicate or refined feeling. **b.** Affectedly or extravagantly emotional; mawkish. **2.** Based on or influenced by emotional considerations rather than reason: *kept the watch for sentimental reasons.* **3.** Appealing to the sentiments, especially to romantic feelings: *sentimental music.* **—sen·ti·men·tal·ly** *adv.*

sen·ti·men·tal·ise, sen·ti·men·tal·ize (sénti-mént'l-īz) *v.* **-ised, -ising, -ises.** —*tr.* To be sentimental about or impart a sentimental quality to. —*intr.* To behave in a sentimental manner. **—sen·ti·men·tal·i·sa·tion** (-lī-záysh'n || *U.S.* -li-) *n.*

sen·ti·men·tal·ism (sénti-mént'l-iz'm) *n.* **1.** A predilection for the sentimental. **2.** An idea or expression marked by excessive sentiment. **—sen·ti·men·tal·ist** *n.*

sen·ti·men·tal·i·ty (sénti-men-tál-əti, -mən-) *n., pl.* **-ties. 1.** The condition or quality of being excessively or affectedly sentimental. **2.** Any expression of this.

sen·ti·nel (séntin'l) *n.* One that keeps guard; a sentry.
∼*tr.v.* **sentinelled** or *U.S.* **sentineled, -nelling** or *U.S.* **-neling, -nels. 1.** To watch over as a sentinel. **2.** To provide with a sentinel. **3.** To post as a sentinel. [French *sentinelle,* from Italian *sentinella,* perhaps from *sentire,* to perceive, watch, from Latin *sentīre,* to perceive, feel.]

sen·try (séntri) *n., pl.* **-tries. 1.** A guard, especially a soldier posted at some spot to prevent the passage of unauthorised persons. **2.** The duty of a sentry; a watch. [Perhaps short for obsolete *centrinell,* variant of SENTINEL.]

sentry box *n.* A small shelter for a sentry at his post.

sentry palm *n.* The **Kentia palm** *(see).*

S.E.O. Senior Executive Officer.

Se·oul (sōl). *Japanese* **Keijo.** Also **Kyongsong.** The capital of the Republic of Korea, and also of Kyonggi province. The capital of Korea since 1392, it became the capital of South Korea on partition of the country in 1948. It suffered severe damage during the Korean War. Its industries include cotton, flour, paper, chemicals, and engineering. Inchon serves as the city's port.

se·pal (sépp'l, séep'l) *n.* One of the usually green segments forming the calyx of a flower. Compare **petal.** [French *sépale,* from New Latin *sepalum* : *sepa,* sepal, variant of Greek *skepē*†, covering + (PET)AL, misnamed by N.J. de Necker (died 1790), who combined the terms petal and sepal, not distinguishing between the corolla and calyx.] **—se·palled, se·paled, sep·a·lous** (sépp'l-əss) *adj.*

se·pal·oid (sépp'l-oyd, séep'l-) *adj.* Also **se·pal·ine** (-īn, -in). Resembling or characteristic of a sepal.

-sepalous *adj. comb. form.* Indicates sepals of a certain type or number; for example, **polysepalous.**

sep·a·ra·ble (séppərə-b'l, séppərə-) *adj.* Capable of being separated. [French *séparable* or Latin *sēparābilis,* from *sēparāre,* to SEPARATE.] **—sep·a·ra·bil·i·ty** (-bílləti) *n.* **—sep·a·ra·bly** *adv.*

sep·a·rate (séppə-rayt) *v.* **-rated, -rating, -rates.** —*tr.* **1. a.** To set apart; disunite or disjoin. **b.** To occupy the space or time between; keep or cause to be apart: *separates the ancient and modern parts of the city.* **c.** To space apart. **2.** To differentiate or discriminate between; distinguish. **3.** To remove from a compound or complex whole; isolate, extract, or sort into constituent elements. **4.** To part (a married couple) by decree. **5.** *U.S.* To terminate a contractual relationship with; discharge. —*intr.* **1.** To become disconnected or severed; come apart; part. **2.** To withdraw or secede. **3.** To part company; disperse. **4.** To cease living together in a conjugal relationship. **5.** To become divided into components or parts.
∼*adj.* (-rət, -rit, sépprət, sépprit). **1.** Set apart from the rest; not connected; disjoined; detached. **2.** Existing as a distinct and independent entity: *on three separate occasions.* **3.** Dissimilar; peculiar to oneself or itself: *went their separate ways.* **4.** Not shared; individual. **5.** *Archaic.* Withdrawn from others; solitary; isolated.
∼*n.* (-rət, -rit, sépprət, sépprit). A garment, such as a skirt, jacket, or pair of slacks, that may be purchased separately and worn in various combinations with other garments. Usually used in the plural. [Middle English *separaten,* from Latin *sēparāre* (past participle *sēparātus*) : *sē,* apart + *parāre,* to make ready, prepare.] **—sep·a·rate·ly** *adv.* **—sep·a·rate·ness** *n.*

Synonyms: *separate, divide, part, sever, sunder, divorce, diverge.*

separate development *n.* The South African policy of apartheid, especially as it envisaged the establishment of black homelands.

sep·a·ra·tion (séppə-ráysh'n) *n.* **1. a.** The act or process of separating. **b.** The state of being separated. **2.** The place where a division or parting occurs. **3.** An interval or space that separates; a gap. **4.** *Law.* An agreement or court decree terminating the conjugal relationship of a husband and wife. See **judicial separation.**

sep·a·ra·tist (séppə-rət-ist, sép- || -rayt-) *n.* Also **sep·a·ra·tion·ist** (séppə-ráysh'n-ist). One who secedes or advocates separation, as from an established church or political unit; a secessionist. **—sep·a·ra·tism** *n.* **—sep·a·ra·tist, sep·a·ra·tis·tic** (-ístik) *adj.*

sep·a·ra·tive (séppə-rət-iv, sép- || -rayt-) *adj.* Tending to separate or causing separation.

sep·a·ra·tor (séppə-raytər) *n.* **1.** One that separates. **2.** A device for separating cream from milk.

Se·phar·di (se-fár-di, si-) *n., pl.* **-dim** (-dim). A member of one of the two main divisions of Jews; a Spanish or Portuguese Jew or a descendant from one of these. Compare **Ashkenazi.** [Modern Hebrew *Səphāradhī,* Spaniard, from *Səphāradh,* Spain.] **—Se·phar·dic** *adj.*

se·pi·a (séepi-ə) *n.* **1.** A dark-brown ink or pigment originally prepared from the secretion of the cuttlefish. **2. a.** A drawing or picture done in this pigment. **b.** A photograph in a brown tint. **3.** Dark greyish yellowish brown to dark or moderate olive brown. ~*adj.* **1.** Of the colour sepia. **2.** Done in sepia. [Italian *seppia,* from Latin *sēpia,* cuttlefish, dark-brown pigment prepared from its secretion, from Greek, akin to *sēpein,* to rot. See **septic.**]

se·pi·o·lite (séepi-ə-līt) *n. Mineralogy.* **Meerschaum** *(see).* [German *Sepiolith* : Greek *sēpion,* cuttlebone, from *sēpia,* cuttlefish (see **se-pia**) + -LITE.]

se·poy (sée-poy) *n.* Formerly, a native of India serving as a soldier under European, especially British, command. [Perhaps from Portuguese *sipae,* from Urdu *sipāhī,* from Persian, from *sipāh,* army, from Old Persian *spādat.*]

sep·pu·ku (sep-pōōkōō) *n. Japanese.* **Hara-kiri** *(see).* [Japanese, "to cut open the stomach".]

sep·sis (sépsiss) *n.* **1.** The presence of pus-forming microorganisms in the blood or tissues. **2.** *Archaic.* A putrefactive process in the body. [New Latin, from Greek *sēpsis,* putrefaction, from *sēpein,* to make rotten. See **septic.**]

sept (sept) *n.* A division of a tribe or clan, especially in medieval Ireland or Scotland. [Perhaps variant of SECT.]

Sept. September.

sep·ta. Plural of **septum.**

sep·tal (séptəl) *adj.* Of or pertaining to a septum.

sep·tar·i·um (sep-taír-i-əm) *n., pl.* **-ia** (-i-ə). An irregular polygonal system of calcite-filled cracks occurring in certain rock concretions. [New Latin : SEPT(I)- (partition) + -ARIUM.] —**sep·tar·i·an** *adj.*

sep·tate (séptayt) *adj.* Having a septum or septa. [New Latin *septatus,* from SEPTUM.]

Sep·tem·ber (sep-témbər, səp-, sip-) *n. Abbr.* **Sept.** The ninth month of the year, according to the Gregorian calendar. September has 30 days. [Middle English *Septembre,* from Old French, from Latin *September,* the seventh month (of the Roman calendar), from *septem,* seven.]

sep·te·nar·i·us (séptə-naír-i-əss) *n., pl.* **-narii** (-naír-i-ee). A Greek or Latin verse consisting of seven feet. [Latin *septēnārius,* SEPTENARY.]

sep·te·nar·y (sep-téenəri, séptə-nəri || *U.S.* -nerri) *adj.* Of, pertaining to, or based on the number seven. ~*n., pl.* **septenaries.** A set or group of seven. [Latin *septēnārius,* from *septēnī,* seven each, from *septem,* seven.]

sep·ten·ni·al (sep-ténni-əl) *adj.* **1.** Occurring every seven years. **2.** Lasting for or containing seven years. [Latin *septennium,* period of seven years, from *septennis,* of seven years : *septem,* seven + *annus,* year.] —**sep·ten·ni·al·ly** *adv.*

sep·ten·tri·on (sep-téntri-ən || -on) *n. Archaic.* The north; northern regions. [Middle English *septemtrioun,* from Old French *septentrion,* from Latin *septentriōnēs,* "seven plough-oxen", northern constellation : *septem,* seven + *triōnēs,* plough-oxen.] —**sep·ten·tri·o·nal** (-ən'l) *adj.*

sep·tet, sep·tette (sep-tét, sép-) *n.* **1.** A group of seven. **2.** *Music.* **a.** A composition for seven voices or instruments. **b.** The musicians performing such a composition. [German *Septet,* from Latin *septem,* seven.]

septi-¹ *comb. form.* Indicates seven; for example, **septilateral.** [Latin, from *septem,* seven.]

septi-², sept- *comb. form.* Indicates partition or septum; for example, **septarium, septifragal.** [From SEPTUM.]

sep·tic (séptik) *adj.* **1.** Of, pertaining to, characterised by or of the nature of sepsis. **2.** Causing sepsis; putrefactive. [Latin *sēpticus,* putrefying, septic, from Greek *sēptikos,* from *sēptos,* rotten, from *sēpein†,* to make rotten.] —**sep·tic·i·ty** (sep-tíssiti) *n.*

sep·ti·cae·mi·a (sépti-séemi-ə) *n.* A systemic disease caused by pathogenic organisms or their toxins in the bloodstream. Also called "blood poisoning". [New Latin : Latin *sēpticus,* SEPTIC + -AEMIA.] —**sep·ti·cae·mic** (-séemik) *adj.*

sep·ti·ci·dal (sépti-sīd'l) *adj. Botany.* Splitting along the junctions of the carpels. Said of a seed capsule. [SEPTI- (partition) + -cidal, from -CIDE.] —**sep·ti·ci·dal·ly** *adv.*

septic tank *n.* A sewage disposal tank in which a continuous flow of waste material is decomposed by anaerobic bacteria.

sep·tif·ra·gal (sep-tíffrəg'l) *adj. Botany.* Characterised by the breaking apart of fruits along natural dividing walls. [From SEPTI- (partition) + Latin *frangere,* to break.]

sep·ti·lat·er·al (sépti-láttrəl, -láttərəl) *adj.* Seven-sided. [SEPTI- (seven) + LATERAL.]

sep·til·li·on (sep-tíllian, -tíl-yən) *n.* **1.** In British usage, the cardinal number represented by 1 followed by 42 zeros, usually written 10^{42}. **2.** The cardinal number represented by 1 followed by 24 zeros, usually written 10^{24}. Called in British usage "quadrillion". [French : SEPTI- (seven) + (MI)LLION.] —**sep·til·li·onth** *n. & adj.*

Septimius. See **Severus.**

sep·tu·a·ge·nar·i·an (sép-tew-əji-naír-i-ən || -too-) *adj.* **1.** Being seventy years old or between seventy and eighty years old. **2.** Of or like someone of this age. ~*n.* A person of seventy or between seventy and eighty years of age. [Latin *septuāgēnārius,* noun and adjective, from *septuāgēnī,* seventy each, from *septuāgintā,* seventy. See **Septuagint.**]

Sep·tu·a·ges·i·ma (sép-tew-ə-jéssimə || -too-) *n.* The third Sunday before Lent. Also called "Septuagesima Sunday". [Middle English *Septuagesime,* Septuagesima, the seventy days following it, from Old French, from Late Latin *septuāgēsima,* feminine of *septuāgēsimus,* seventieth, from *septuāgintā,* seventy. See **Septuagint.**]

Sep·tu·a·gint (sép-tew-ə-jint || -too-) *n. Abbr.* **LXX.** A Greek translation of the Old Testament made in the third century B.C. [Latin

septuāgintā, seventy, "the Seventy", designation of the 70 or 72 Jewish scholars who, according to an unhistorical tradition, completed the translation in 72 days on the island of Pharos : *septem,* seven + -gintā, decimal suffix, ten times.]

sep·tum (sép-təm) *n., pl.* **-ta** (-tə). **1.** A thin partition or membrane between two cavities or soft masses of tissue in a plant or animal. **2.** In filamentous organisms, a cell wall at right angles to the length of the filament. [Latin *sēptum, saeptum,* partition, from *sēpīre, saepīre,* to surround with a hedge, from *sēpes, saepes†,* hedge.]

sep·tu·ple (sép-tyōō-p'l || sep-tyōō-p'l, -tōō-) *adj.* **1.** Consisting of or having seven parts, members, or copies. **2.** Multiplied by seven; seven times as such, as many, or as large. ~*n.* A sevenfold amount or number. ~*v.* **septupled, -pling, -ples.** —*tr.* To multiply or increase by seven. —*intr.* To be multiplied sevenfold. [Late Latin *septuplus,* sevenfold : Latin *septem,* seven + -*plex,* -fold.]

se·pul·chral (si-púlkrəl, sə-, sō-) *adj.* **1.** Of or pertaining to a sepulchre. **2.** Suggestive of the grave; gloomy. —**se·pul·chral·ly** *adv.*

se·pul·chre, *U.S.* **sep·ul·cher** (sépp'lkər) *n.* A burial vault. ~*tr.v.* **sepulchred,** or *U.S.* **sepulchered, -chring** or *U.S.* **-chering, -chres** or *U.S.* **-chers.** To place in a sepulchre; inter. [Middle English *sepulcre,* from Old French, from Latin *sepulcrum,* from *sepultus,* past participle of *sepelīre,* to bury.]

seq. **1.** sequel. **2.** the following (Latin *sequens*).

seqq. the following (ones) (Latin *sequentes, sequentia*).

se·qua·cious (si-kwáyshəss, se-, sə-) *adj.* **1.** *Archaic.* Disposed to follow others in a slavish unquestioning way. **2.** Following in logical sequence and regularity. [Latin *sequāx* (stem *sequāc-*), pursuing, sequacious, from *sequī,* to follow.] —**se·qua·cious·ly** *adv.* —**se·quac·i·ty** (-kwássəti) *n.*

se·quel (séekwəl) *n. Abbr.* **seq.** **1.** Anything that follows; a continuation. **2.** A film, play, or literary work complete in itself but continuing the narrative of an earlier work. **3.** A result or consequence. —See Synonyms at **effect.** [Middle English *sequele,* from Old French *sequelle,* from Latin *sequēla,* from *sequī,* to follow.]

se·que·la (si-kwée-lə, -kwé-) *n., pl.* **-lae** (-lee). Something that follows; especially, a pathological condition or the various complications resulting from a disease. [Latin *sequēla,* SEQUEL.]

se·quence (séekwənss) *n.* **1.** A following of one thing after another; succession. **2.** An order of succession. **3.** A related or continuous series. **4.** Three or more playing cards in consecutive order; a run. **5.** A series of single shots in a film, so edited as to constitute an aesthetic or dramatic unit; an episode. **6.** *Music.* A melodic or harmonic pattern successively repeated at different pitches, with or without a key change. **7.** *Roman Catholic Church.* In the Tridentine Mass, a hymn read or sung between the gradual and the gospel. **8.** *Mathematics.* An ordered set of quantities, as $x, 2x^2, 3x^3, 4x^4$. **9.** A subsequent or consequent event or development. —See Synonyms at **series.** [Middle English, from Late Latin *sequentia,* from Latin *sequēns* (stem *sequent-*), present participle of *sequī,* to follow.]

se·quenc·er (séekwənssər) *n.* **1.** A device for sorting information into a predetermined order for data processing. **2.** An electronic device that sets into a predetermined order a sequence of operations. [SEQUENC(E) + -ER.]

se·quent (séekwənt) *adj.* **1.** Following in order or time; subsequent. **2.** Following as a result; consequent. ~*n.* That which follows, in sequence or in consequence. [Latin *sequēns.* See **sequence.**]

se·quen·tial (si-kwén-sh'l, sə-) *adj.* **1.** Forming a sequence or characterised by ordered sequence, as of notes or units. **2.** Sequent. —**se·quen·ti·al·i·ty** (-shi-ál-əti) *n.* —**se·quen·tial·ly** *adv.*

sequential access *n.* A method of obtaining information from a computer file by reading through it from the start. Compare **random access.**

se·ques·ter (si-kwéstər, sə-) *v.* **-tered, -tering, -ters.** —*tr.* **1.** To remove or set apart; segregate. **2.** *Law.* To take temporary possession of (property) as security against legal claims. **3.** To requisition or confiscate, especially by legal authority. **4.** To isolate or withdraw into seclusion. Usually used reflexively or in the passive: *to sequester oneself; a sequestered spot.* —*intr. Chemistry.* To undergo sequestration. [Middle English, from Late Latin *sequestrāre,* to separate, give up for safekeeping, from Latin *sequester,* depository.]

se·ques·trant (si-kwéstrənt, sə-) *n.* A chemical that promotes sequestration.

se·ques·trate (sée-kwiss-trayt, -kwess-, si-kwéss-) *tr.v.* **-trated, -trating, -trates.** **1.** *Law.* To seize. **2.** *Archaic.* To set apart. [Late Latin *sequestrāre,* to SEQUESTER.] —**se·ques·tra·tor** (-traytər) *n.*

se·ques·tra·tion (sée-kwiss-tráysh'n, -kwess-) *n.* **1.** The act of sequestering or state of being sequestered; segregation or separation. **2.** *Law.* **a.** Seizure of property. **b.** A writ authorising seizure of property. **3.** *Chemistry.* The inhibition or prevention of normal ion behaviour by combination with added materials; especially, the prevention of metallic ion precipitation from solution by formation of a coordination complex with a phosphate.

se·ques·trum (si-kwéss-trəm) *n., pl.* **-tra** (-trə). A dead bone fragment that has separated from healthy bone. [New Latin, from Latin, deposit, "something separated", from *sequester,* depository.]

se·quin (séekwin) *n.* **1.** A small shiny ornamental disc, often sewn on cloth; a spangle. **2.** A gold coin of the Venetian Republic. In this sense, also called "zecchino". [French, from Italian *zecchino,* from *zecca,* the mint, from Arabic *sikkah,* coin die.] —**se·quinned, se·quined** *adj.*

se·quoi·a (si-kwóy-ə, se-) *n.* Any very large evergreen tree of the genus *Sequoia*, which includes the **redwood** and the **giant sequoia** (*both of which see*). [New Latin, after *Sequoiah*, a Cherokee Indian who wrote a syllabary for Cherokee.]

sé·rac (sérrak) *n.* An ice pinnacle between intersecting crevasses in an icefall in a glacier. [Swiss French, piece of white cheese (which the ice resembles), perhaps from Latin *serum*, whey.]

se·ra·gli·o (si-ráali-ō, se-, sə-, -ráal-yō ‖ -rál-yō) *n., pl.* **-glios.** 1. A large harem. 2. A sultan's palace. [Italian *serraglio*, probably from Turkish *serai*†, a palace, lodging, from Persian.]

se·ra·pe, sa·ra·pe (sə-ráppi, -ráapi) *n.* A woollen cloak or poncho worn by Latin-American men. [Mexican Spanish *sarape*†.]

ser·aph (sérrəf) *n., pl.* **-aphs** or **seraphim** (sérrəfim). 1. A celestial being having three pairs of wings. Isaiah 6:2. 2. One of the nine orders of angels. See **angel**. [Back-formation from plural *seraphim*, from Middle English *seraphin*, Old English *seraphin*, from Late Latin *seraphim, seraphin*, from Hebrew *Sərāphīm*, plural of *sārāph*.] **—se·raph·ic** (si-ráffik, se-, sə-) *adj.* **—se·raph·i·cal·ly** *adv.*

Se·ra·pis (sérrəpiss ‖ *U.S.* sə-ráypiss). A god combining features of Egyptian and Greek deities, whose worship became widespread in the ancient world from the Hellenistic period onwards.

Serb (serb) *n.* A Serbian. [Serbo-Croatian *Srb*†.] **—Serb** *adj.*

Ser·bi·a (sérbi-ə). *Serbo-Croat* **Sr·bi·ja**; *English (before 1918)* **Ser·vi·a** (sérvi-ə). Largest constituent republic of Yugoslavia, lying in the northeast of the country. Largely mountainous in the west and south, it descends to the fertile Danubian plain in the north. It has large mineral deposits, and is also the country's main agricultural producer. Settled by the Serbs in the seventh century A.D., it was established as an independent kingdom in the 12th century, but was subsequently held by the Turks (1389–1829). After World War I, the Kingdom of the Serbs, Croats, and Slovenes under Peter I of Serbia was proclaimed (1918), but was later renamed Yugoslavia (1929). In 1946 Serbia became a constituent republic of Yugoslavia under the new constitution. It opposed and refused to recognise the secession of other Yugoslav republics in 1991–2.

Ser·bi·an (sérbi-ən) *n.* 1. A member of a southern Slavic people that is the dominant ethnic group of Serbia. 2. Serbo-Croat. **—Ser·bi·an** *adj.*

Ser·bo-Cro·at (sérbō-krō-at) *n.* Also **Ser·bo-Cro·a·tian** (-krō-áysh'n). The Slavonic language of the Serbs and Croats, usually written in Cyrillic letters in Serbia and in Roman letters in Croatia. Also called "Croatian", "Serbian". *~adj.* Of or pertaining to this language or those who speak it.

sere¹ (seer) *adj. Literary.* Withered; dry. [Middle English *sere*, Old English *sēar*.]

sere² *n.* The entire sequence of ecological communities successively occupying an area. [From SERIES.]

ser·e·nade (sérrə-náyd, sérri-) *n.* 1. **a.** A musical performance given outdoors in the evening, especially, one given by a lover for his sweetheart. **b.** A piece of music so performed. 2. An instrumental form comprising characteristics of the suite and the sonata. *~v.* **serenaded, -nading, -nades.** *—tr.* To perform a serenade for. *—intr.* To perform a serenade. [French *sérénade*, from Italian *serenata*, evening serenade, from *sereno*, serene (influenced in meaning by *sera*, evening), from Latin *serēnus*, SERENE.] **—ser·e·nad·er** *n.*

ser·en·dip·i·ty (sérrən-díppəti, sérren-) *n.* The faculty of making fortunate and unexpected discoveries by accident. [Coined (1754) by Horace Walpole after the characters in the fairy tale *The Three Princes of Serendip* (that is, Sri Lanka), who made such discoveries.] **—ser·en·dip·i·tous** *adj.*

se·rene (si-réen, sə-) *adj.* 1. Unruffled; tranquil; dignified. 2. Unclouded; fair; bright. 3. *Often capital* **S.** August. Used as part of a title of respect for certain royal personages: *His Serene Highness.* —See Synonyms at **calm.** [Latin *serēnus*, serene, bright, clear.] **—se·rene·ly** *adv.* **—se·rene·ness** *n.*

se·ren·i·ty (si-rénnəti, sə-) *n., pl.* **-ties.** 1. The state or quality of being serene; dignified calm; quiet. 2. Clearness, brightness, and stillness, as of the air and sky. —See Synonyms at **equanimity.**

serf (serf) *n.* 1. A person in a condition bordering on slavery, especially a member of the lowest feudal class in medieval Europe, bound to the land and subject to the control of a lord. 2. Anyone in a state of servitude or oppression. [Old French, from Latin *servus*, slave.] **—serf·dom** *n.*

serge (serj) *n.* A twilled cloth of worsted or worsted and wool, often used for suits. [Middle English *sarge, serge*, from Old French, from Vulgar Latin *sārica* (unattested), from Latin *sērica (lāna)*, (wool) of the Seres (a people), that is, silk, from Greek *sērikos*, of silk, originally "pertaining to the Seres". See **silk.**]

ser·geant (sárjənt) *n.* 1. **a.** A noncommissioned officer in the British Army, the Royal Air Force, and the Royal Marines, ranking above a corporal. **b.** A noncommissioned officer of equivalent rank in certain similar forces elsewhere. 2. A police officer of middle rank, especially: **a.** An officer in a British force ranking above a constable and below an inspector. **b.** An officer in a U.S. force ranking below a captain, or sometimes a lieutenant. —See **serjeant at arms, serjeant at law.** [Middle English *sergeaunte, sergant*, from Old French *sergent*, from Latin *serviēns* (stem *servient-*), present participle of *servīre*, to serve, from *servus*, slave, servant.] **—ser·gean·cy, ser·geant·ship** *n.*

sergeant at arms *n.* Variant of **serjeant at arms.**

sergeant major *n. Abbr.* **Sgt. Maj., S.M.** 1. A warrant officer in the British Army and the Royal Marines. 2. A noncommissioned officer of the highest rank in the U.S. and other armed forces. 3. A fish, *Abudefduf saxatilis*, of warm seas, having a flattened body with

dark vertical stripes.

se·ri·al (séer-i-əl) *adj.* 1. **a.** Of, forming, or arranged in a series. **b.** Used to indicate a series of acts of the type suggested: *serial killers; serial killing; a serial killing; serial adulterers; serial adultery; "a serial seducer" (Radio Times).* 2. Published or produced in instalments, as a novel might be. 3. Pertaining to such publication or production. 4. *Music.* Designating or pertaining to music based on a series of intervals chosen by the composer, especially on a 12-note row, rather than on the diatonic scale. 5. *Computing.* Designating or pertaining to a system of computer operation in which processing is carried out sequentially. In this sense compare **parallel.** *~n.* A literary or dramatic work published or produced in instalments. [From SERIES.] **—se·ri·al·ly** *adv.*

se·ri·al·ise, se·ri·al·ize (séer-i-ə-līz) *tr.v.* **-ised, -ising, -ises.** To write, publish, or produce in serial form. **—se·ri·al·i·sa·tion** *n.*

se·ri·al·ism (séer-i-ə-liz'm) *n.* 1. Serial music. 2. The theory or composition of serial music.

serial number *n.* A number that is one of a series, used for identification, as of a machine or banknote, for example.

se·ri·ate (séer-i-ət, -it, -ayt) *adj.* Arranged or occurring in a series or in rows. [From SERIES.] **—se·ri·ate·ly** *adv.*

se·ri·a·tim (séer-i-áytim, sérri-, -áatim) *adv.* One after another; in a series. [Medieval Latin, from Latin *seriēs*, SERIES.]

se·ri·ceous (si-ríshəss, se-) *adj. Biology.* Covered with soft, silky hairs. [Late Latin *sēriceus*, from *sēricus*, of Seres. See **serge.**]

ser·i·cin (sérri-sin) *n.* A viscous, gelatinous protein that forms on the surface of raw-silk fibres. [Latin *sēricus*, silken, of Seres (see **serge**) + -IN.]

ser·i·cul·ture (sérri-kulchər) *n.* The production of raw silk and the breeding of silkworms for this purpose. [French *sériculture* : Latin *sēricus*, silken, of Seres (see **serge**) + CULTURE.] **—ser·i·cul·tur·al** (-kúlchərəl) *adj.* **—ser·i·cul·tur·ist** *n.*

se·ri·e·ma (sérri-éemə) *n.* Either of two cranelike South American birds, *Cariama cristata* or *Chunga burmeisteri*, having a tuftlike crest at the base of the bill. [Tupi *seriema, çariama,* "crested".]

se·ries (séer-iz, -eez, *rarely* -i-eez) *n., pl.* **series.** 1. A number of things, events, or people having some common characteristic and following one another in order of their occurrence in space or time. 2. A set of publications, typically in a uniform format, having some common theme or feature: *a series of phrase books.* 3. A set of sporting games played between two teams, especially at international level. 4. A group of thematically connected performances; especially, a set of radio or television programmes featuring the same fictional characters in a succession of self-contained episodes. 5. A group of objects related in terms of their composition, structure, or properties: *the paraffin series.* 6. *Mathematics.* A finite or sequentially ordered infinite set of terms expressed in the form $x_1 + x_2 + x_3 + \ldots$ where x_i is a real or complex number. 7. *Grammar.* A succession of coordinate elements in a sentence. 8. An arrangement of electrical components such that the current flows through each in turn. Compare **parallel.** 9. *Geology.* A subdivision of a system that represents the rocks formed during an epoch. [Latin *seriēs*, from *serere*, to join.]

Synonyms: *series, succession, progression, sequence, chain, train, string.*

series circuit *n.* An electrical circuit connected so that current passes through each circuit element in turn without branching. See **parallel** (sense 6).

se·ries-wound (séer-iz-wownd, -eez-) *adj.* Designating an electric motor or dynamo with its armature circuit and field circuit connected in series with the external circuit. Compare **shunt-wound.**

ser·if (sérrif) *n. Printing.* A fine line finishing off the main strokes, as at the top and bottom of *M* or ending the cross stroke of *T.* [Perhaps from Dutch *schreef*, line, from Middle Dutch *scrēve.*]

ser·i·graph (sérri-graaf, -graf) *n.* A print made by the silk-screen process. [Latin *sēri(cum)*, SILK + -GRAPH.] **—se·rig·ra·phy** (sə-ríggrəfi) *n.*

ser·in (sérrin) *n.* Any of several Old World finches of the genus *Serinus*, having yellowish streaked plumage. See **canary.** [French, from Old French, perhaps from Old Provençal *serena*, bee-eater, from Latin *sīrēn*, a kind of bird, from *Sīrēn*, SIREN.]

ser·ine (sérrin, séer-in, -een) *n.* An amino acid, $C_3H_7NO_3$, that is a common constituent of many proteins. [SER(ICIN) + -INE.]

se·rin·ga (sə-ríng-gə, si-) *n.* 1. **Syringa** (see). 2. Any of several rubber trees of the Brazilian genus *Hevea.*

se·ri·o·com·ic (séer-i-ō-kómmik) *adj.* Combining serious and comic characteristics. [SERIO(US) + COMIC.]

se·ri·ous (séer-i-əss) *adj.* 1. Grave in character or manner; responsible. 2. Said, done, or acting in earnest; marked by sincerity or commitment. 3. Concerned with important rather than trivial matters. 4. Requiring or employing considerable thought, effort, or concentration: *serious music.* 5. Causing anxiety; critical; dangerous. 6. Not to be taken lightly; of considerable significance, amount, gravity, or effect: *serious damage; serious money.* —See Synonyms at **critical.** [Middle English *seryous*, from Old French *serieux*, from Late Latin *sēriōsus*, from Latin *sērius.*] **—se·ri·ous·ly** *adv.* **—se·ri·ous·ness** *n.*

Synonyms: *serious, sober, grave, solemn, earnest, sedate, staid.*

ser·jeant at arms, sergeant at arms (sárjənt) *n.* An officer responsible for the maintenance of order in a legislative body, court of law, or other organisation.

serjeant at law, sergeant at law *n.* Formerly in Britain, a member of a class of barristers of the highest rank.
ser·mon (sérmən) *n.* **1.** A religious discourse delivered as part of a church service. **2.** Any discourse or speech; especially, a lengthy and tedious reproof or exhortation. [Middle English *sermun,* from Anglo-French, from Latin *sermō* (stem *sermōn-*), a speaking, a discourse.] **—ser·mon·ic** (ser-mónnik) *adj.*
ser·mon·ise, ser·mon·ize (sérmən-īz) *v.* **-ised, -ising, -ises.** *—tr.* To preach to. *—intr.* To deliver, or speak as though delivering, a sermon. **—ser·mon·is·er** *n.*
Sermon on the Mount *n.* A discourse of Jesus, traditionally delivered on the Mountain of the Beatitudes. Matthew 5–7.
sero– *comb. form.* Indicates serum, as **serology.** [From SERUM.]
se·rol·o·gy (si-rólləji, seer-) *n.* The medical study of serum. [SERO- + -LOGY.] **—se·ro·log·ic** (seér-ə-lójik || *U.S.* sírr-), **ser·o·log·i·cal** *adj.* **—se·rol·o·gist** *n.*
se·ro·sa (si-rṓ-sə, seer- || -zə) *n., pl.* **-sas** or **-sae** (-see || -zee). A serous membrane. [New Latin, feminine of *serosus,* SEROUS.]
se·ro·ther·a·py (seér-ō-thérrəpi) *n.* Treatment of disease by administration of a serum or antitoxin. [SERO- + THERAPY.]
ser·o·tine (sérrə-tīn) *adj.* Also **se·rot·i·nous** (si-róttinəss), **se·rot·i·nal** (-róttin'l). *Biology.* Late in developing or blooming.
∼n. A European insectivorous bat, *Eptesicus Serotinus.* [Latin *sērōtinus,* late, from *sērō,* late, from *sērus,* late.]
se·ro·to·nin (seér-ə-tṓnin, -ō-, sérrə-) *n.* A neurotransmitter $C_{10}H_{12}N_2O$ or 5-HT, found in animal and human tissue, especially the brain, blood serum, and gastric mucosa, and capable of raising the body temperature, contracting smooth muscle, and changing behaviour. Also called "hydroxytryptamine". [SERO- + TON(IC) + -IN.]
se·ro·type (seér-ə-tīp, -ō-, sérrə-) *n.* A subspecific category of microorganisms, distinguished by having the same serological activity. Also called "serological type". [*Sero*logical *type.*]
se·rous (seér-əss) *adj.* Containing, secreting, or resembling serum. [New Latin *serosus,* from SERUM.]
serous cavity *n.* A body cavity lined with serous membrane.
serous membrane *n.* A thin membrane lining a closed bodily cavity. Also called "serosa".
se·row (sérrō, sə-rṓ) *n.* Any of several goatlike antelopes of the genus *Capricornis,* of mountainous regions of eastern Asia, having short horns and a dark coat. [Lepcha *să-ro,* Tibetan goat.]
Ser·pens (sér-penz, -pənz) *n.* A constellation in the equatorial region of the northern sky, made up of two parts: *Serpens Cauda,* the "tail", and *Serpens Caput,* the "head", both near Hercules and Ophiuchus. Also called the "Serpent." [Latin *serpēns,* SERPENT.]
ser·pent (sérpənt) *n.* **1.** A snake, especially a large one. **2.** *Often capital* **S.** The creature that tempted Eve; Satan. Genesis 3. **3.** A sly or treacherous person. **4.** A kind of firework that writhes while burning. **5.** *Music.* A deep-toned wind instrument of serpentine shape, used principally in the 18th century. [Middle English, from Old French, from Latin *serpēns* (stem *serpent-*), "crawling thing", from the present participle of *serpere,* to crawl, creep.]
ser·pen·tine (sérpən-tīn || -teen) *adj.* **1.** Of or resembling a serpent, as in form or movement; sinuous. **2.** Subtle, sly, and treacherous.
∼n. A greenish, brownish, or spotted mineral, $Mg_6(Si_4O_{10})\,(OH)_8$, used as a source of magnesium and in architecture as a decorative stone. [Middle English, from Old French *serpentin,* from Late Latin *serpentīnus,* from Latin *serpēns,* SERPENT.]
ser·pi·go (ser-pīgō, sər-) *n.* A spreading skin eruption or lesion, such as ringworm. [Middle English, from Medieval Latin *serpīgo,* from Latin *serpere,* to creep.] **—ser·pig·i·nous** (-píjinəss) *adj.*
ser·pu·la (sérpew-lə) *n.* Any of various polychaete worms of the family Serpulidae, especially of the genus *Serpula,* that live in specially secreted calcareous tubes attached to stone. [New Latin, from Late Latin, small serpent, from Latin *serpere,* to creep.]
ser·ra·nid (sə-ránnid, se-, sérrənid) *n.* Also **ser·ra·noid** (sérrə-noyd), **ser·ran** (sérrən). Any of various fishes belonging to the family Serranidae, which includes the sea basses and groupers. [New Latin *Serranidae,* from *Serranus* (genus), from Latin *serra,* saw (perhaps from its serrated dorsal fin). See **serrate.**] **—ser·ra·nid, ser·ra·noid** *adj.*
ser·rate (sérr-ət, -it, -ayt) *adj.* **1.** Having notched, toothlike projections. **2.** Having the edge or margin notched with toothlike projections: *serrate leaves.*
∼tr.v. (se-ráyt, si-, sə- || sérrayt) **serrated, -rating, -rates.** To provide or mark with notched, toothlike projections. [Latin *serrātus,* saw-shaped, from Latin *serra*†, saw.]
ser·ra·tion (se-ráysh'n, si-, sə-) *n.* **1.** The state of being serrate. **2.** A series or set of teeth or notches. **3.** A single such tooth or notch.
ser·ried (sérrid) *adj.* Pressed together in rows; in close order: *"Troops in serried ranks assembled"* (W.S. Gilbert). [From past participle of obsolete *serry,* to press together, from Old French *serré,* past participle of *serrer,* to close, from Vulgar Latin *serrāre* (unattested), from Latin *sērāre,* to fasten with a bolt, from *sera,* lock.]
ser·ru·late (sérrŏŏlət, sérrew-, -lit, -layt) *adj.* Also **ser·ru·lat·ed** (-lay-tid). Having small, toothlike notches along the edge; minutely serrate. [New Latin *serrulatus,* from Latin *serrula,* diminutive of *serra,* saw. See **serrate.**]
ser·tu·lar·i·an (sértew-laír-i-ən) *n.* Any of various colonial hydroids of the genus *Sertularia,* having stalkless polyps arranged in pairs along a long, branching stem. [New Latin *Sertularia,* from Latin *sertula,* diminutive of *serta,* melilot, garland, from the feminine past participle of *serere,* to join, entwine.]
se·rum (seér-əm) *n., pl.* **-rums** or **sera** (seér-ə). **1.** The clear yellowish fluid obtained upon separating blood into its solid and liquid components. Also called "blood serum". **2.** The fluid from the tissues of immunised animals, used especially as an antitoxin. **3.** Any watery fluid from animal tissue, as is found in oedema. **4. Whey** *(see).* [Latin, whey, serum.]
serum albumin *n.* The main protein fraction of blood serum that is involved in maintaining osmotic pressure, and that is used in the treatment of shock.
serum globulin *n.* A protein fraction of blood serum chiefly containing antibodies.
serum hepatitis *n.* See **hepatitis.**
serum sickness *n.* An allergic reaction, such as a skin eruption, vomiting, or fever, that may follow injection of serum.
serv. 1. servant. **2.** service.
serum therapy *n.* **Serotherapy** *(see).*
ser·val (sérv'l || sər-vál) *n.* A long-legged wild cat, *Felis serval,* of Africa, having a yellowish coat with black spots. [French, from Portuguese *(lobo) cerval,* deerlike (wolf), from *cervo,* deer, from Latin *cervus.*]
ser·vant (sérvənt) *n. Abbr.* **serv. 1.** One that serves another or others. **2.** Someone privately employed to perform domestic services. **3.** Someone publicly employed to perform services, as for a government. **—your humble** or **obedient servant.** Used chiefly in letters as a conventional expression of politeness. [Middle English, from Old French, from the present participle of *servir,* to SERVE.]
serve (serv) *v.* **served, serving, serves.** *—tr.* **1.** To be a servant to or of; work for (an employer or company, for example): *served the firm for 30 years.* **2. a.** To prepare and offer (food or drink): *serve tea.* **b.** To place food or drink before (someone); wait on. **c.** To attend to (a customer in a shop): *Are you being served?* **d.** To assist the celebrant during (Communion or Mass). **3.** To meet the requirements of; provide with something useful or needed: *a bus serving the rural areas; served the public for 100 years.* **4.** To be useful or adequate for fulfilling (a need or purpose); suffice for: *not quite big enough, but it will serve the purpose.* **5.** To be of assistance to; promote the interests of; aid: *serving the national interest.* **6.** To perform or complete (a stipulated term), as in prison, elective office, or an apprenticeship. **7.** To fight or undergo military service for: *served his country in two World Wars.* **8.** To give homage and obedience to. **9. a.** To treat in a specified, usually unpleasant way; requite: *It will serve her right.* **b.** To perform a function for in a specified way; avail: *if my memory serves me well.* **10.** To copulate with. Used of male animals: *The buck served the doe.* **11.** To be used in common by: *One phone serves the whole office.* **12.** To enable (a cannon, for example) to keep firing: *serve the guns.* **13.** *Law.* **a.** To deliver or present (a legal writ or summons). **b.** To present such a writ to. **14.** To put (the ball or shuttlecock) in play in games such as tennis or badminton. **15.** To bind (a rope) with fine cord or wire. *—intr.* **1.** To be employed as a servant. **2. a.** To do military service: *served under Montgomery.* **b.** To perform or discharge an official duty; hold office: *served under four prime ministers.* **3. a.** To be of service or use; function: *serve as a reminder.* **b.** To be reliable or safe: *if memory serves.* **c.** To function so as to produce a specified effect: *a repressive measure that merely served to increase opposition to the government.* **4. a.** To meet requirements or needs; satisfy; suffice: *"'Tis not so deep as a well . . . but 'twill serve"* (Shakespeare). **b.** To be suitable or favourable. Used of a tide, weather conditions, and the like. **5.** To wait at table; provide people with food or drink: *Shall I serve?* **6.** To put a ball or shuttlecock into play in games such as tennis or badminton. **7.** To assist the celebrant during Mass or a Communion service.
∼n. In many games played on a court: **1.** The manner or act of serving. **2.** One's turn or right to serve which, in tennis, lasts throughout a game. **3.** In tennis, the game in which a particular player serves: *lost her serve.* [Middle English *serven,* from Old French *servir,* from Latin *servīre,* from *servus,* slave.]
serv·er (sérvər) *n.* **1.** One that serves. **2.** Something used in serving food or drink, such as a tray or utensil: *salad servers.* **3.** An attendant to the celebrant at a Communion service or Mass. **4.** The player who serves, as in tennis or badminton.
serv·ice (sérviss) *n. Abbr.* **serv. 1.** The occupation, condition, or duties of a servant. **2.** Employment in duties or work for another; especially, such employment for a government: *in the service of the Crown.* **3.** A branch or department of an organisation or government, together with its employees: *the diplomatic service.* **4.** Any branch of the armed forces of a nation. **5. a.** Useful work or duty performed by a person or thing: *has done good service.* **b.** The performance of work or duty, as of an official or military nature: *jury service; killed on active service.* **c.** The condition of being used for the performance of work: *Some of the old planes are still in service.* **6. a.** The action of helping others; assistance: *if I may be of service.* **b.** An act of helping others; a favour: *did us all a great service.* **7.** Power to control or make use of some resource; disposal: *My staff is at your service.* **8. a.** Installation, maintenance, or repairs provided or guaranteed by a dealer or manufacturer: *after-sales service.* **b.** A regularly-performed inspection and carrying out of repairs, as of a car or other machine, for the purpose of routine maintenance. **9.** *Often plural.* Work done for others as an occupation or business: *needed the services of a good accountant.* **10.** An organisation or system providing the public with something useful or necessary: *a bus service; the BBC World Service.* **11.** A nonmaterial commodity produced by human labour, especially as distinguished from a manufactured product. **12. a.** A meeting for public

worship. **b.** A particular religious rite: *the burial service.* **13.** The act or manner of serving food, attending to customers, or the like: *fast, friendly service.* **14.** A set of dishes or utensils: *a silver tea service.* **15.** The act, manner, turn, or right of serving in racket games; a serve. **16.** Copulation by a male animal with a female. **17.** *Law.* The serving of a writ or summons. **18.** Any material, such as cord, used in binding or wrapping rope.

~*adj.* **1.** Concerned with the provision of services rather than the production of goods: *service industries.* **2.** Not for use by the general public; reserved for employees, deliveries, or the like: *a service lift.* **3.** Of or pertaining to the armed forces.

~*tr.v.* **serviced, -vicing, -vices. 1.** To perform routine maintenance on so as to ensure effective operation: *service a car.* **2.** To provide with services. **3.** To copulate with. Used of a male animal. **4.** To meet the interest payments on (a loan). [Middle English *servis(e),* from Old French *service,* from Latin *servitium,* servitude, slavery, from *servus,* slave.]

serv·ice·a·ble (sérvi-sə-b'l) *adj.* **1.** Ready or suitable for service; useful or usable. **2.** Able to give good service; long-wearing. **—serv·ice·a·bil·i·ty** (-bílləti), **serv·ice·a·ble·ness** *n.* **—serv·ice·a·bly** *adv.*

service area *n.* An area adjoining a motorway in which garage facilities, restaurants, and lavatories are provided.

serv·ice·ber·ry (sér-viss-berri || *U.S. also* sár-) *n., pl.* **-ries. 1.** The fruit of the service tree. **2.** The **shadbush** *(see),* or one of its fruit. [SERVICE (TREE) + BERRY.]

service break *n.* A game won during an opponent's serve, as in tennis.

service car *n.* **1.** *Australian.* A minibus or large car providing public transport in rural areas, and sometimes also carrying mail. **2.** *N.Z.* A coach.

service charge *n.* **1.** A charge added to a customer's bill, as at a restaurant, to pay for service. **2.** An additional charge for a service for which there is often already a basic fee.

service flat *n. British.* A flat for which certain services, such as cleaning and porterage, are automatically provided for a charge.

serv·ice·man (sériss-man, -mən) *n., pl.* **-men** (-mən, -men). A male member of the armed forces.

service module *n.* The part of the third stage of an Apollo spacecraft containing the rocket motor, fuel supply, and various service facilities, which is jettisoned prior to reentry into the earth's atmosphere.

service road *n.* A narrow road running parallel to a main road to provide access to houses, shops, and the like, along its length.

service station *n.* A place that supplies petrol, oil, and similar products for motor vehicles, often also having facilities for carrying out repairs and services.

service tree *n.* Either of two Old World trees, *Sorbus domestica* or *S. torminalis,* having clusters of white flowers and brownish, edible fruit. [Middle English *serves,* plural of *serve,* Old English *syrfe,* from Vulgar Latin *sorbea* (unattested), from Latin *sorbus*†.]

ser·vice·wom·an (sériss-wŏŏmən) *n., pl.* **-women** (-wimmin). A female member of the armed forces.

ser·vi·ette (sérvi-ét) *n.* A table napkin. [French, from Old French, towel, napkin, from *servir,* to SERVE.]

ser·vile (sér-vīl || *U.S. also* -v'l) *adj.* **1.** Slavish in character or attitude; obsequious; submissive. **2.** Of or suitable to a slave or servant: *"freed from servile bands"* (John Bunyan). —See Synonyms at **obedient.** [Middle English, from Latin *servīlis,* from *servus,* slave.] **—ser·vile·ly** *adv.* **—ser·vile·ness, ser·vil·i·ty** (ser-vílləti) *n.*

serv·ing (sérving) *n.* An individual portion or helping of food or drink.

~*adj.* Pertaining to or used for serving.

ser·vi·tor (sérvi-tər || -tawr) *n. Archaic.* A servant; an attendant. [Middle English, from Old French, from Latin *servītor,* from Latin *servīre,* to SERVE.] **—ser·vi·tor·ship** *n.*

ser·vi·tude (sérvi-tewd || -tŏŏd) *n.* **1.** Submission to the control, will, or political domination of another; slavery. **2.** Forced labour imposed as a punishment for crime: *penal servitude.* **3.** *Law.* A right that grants use of another's property for certain purposes. [Middle English, from Old French, from Latin *servitūdō,* from *servus,* slave.]

Synonyms: *servitude, bondage, slavery.*

ser·vo·mech·a·nism (sérvō-meckə-niz'm, -méckə-) *n.* A feedback system that consists of a sensing element, an amplifier, and a servomotor, and is used in the automatic control of a mechanical device. Also called "servo". [SERVO(MOTOR) + MECHANISM.]

ser·vo·motor (sérvō-mōtər) *n.* An electric motor or hydraulic piston that supplies power to a servomechanism. Also called "servo". [French *servo-moteur* : *servo-,* from Latin *servus,* slave + French *moteur,* MOTOR.]

ses·a·me (séssəmi) *n.* **1.** A plant, *Sesamum indicum,* of tropical Asia, bearing small, flat seeds used as food and as a source of oil. **2.** The seeds of this plant. Also called "benne". [Latin *sēsamum, sīsamum,* from Greek *sēsamon, sēsamē,* of Semitic origin; akin to Arabic *simsim,* Akkadian *shamashshamu.*]

ses·a·moid (séssə-moyd) *adj.* Of or designating a small bone, such as the kneecap, that develops in a tendon. [Greek *sēsamoeidēs,* shaped like a sesame seed : SESAME + -OID.] **—ses·a·moid** *n.*

Se·so·tho (si-sŏŏtŏŏ) *n.* The dialect of **Sotho** *(see)* spoken in Lesotho. Formerly called "Basuto".

sesqui- *comb. form.* Indicates one and a half; for example, **sesquicentennial.** [Latin, from *semisque* (unattested), one-half more : *sēmis,* half + *-que* (enclitic), and.]

ses·qui·car·bon·ate (séskwi-kárbə-nayt, -nət, -nit) *n.* A mixed salt consisting of a carbonate and a hydrogen carbonate, such as sodium sesquicarbonate, $NaCO_3NaHCO_3$.

ses·qui·cen·ten·ni·al (séskwi-sen-ténni-əl) *adj.* Of or pertaining to a period of 150 years.

~*n.* A 150th anniversary or its celebration. [SESQUI- + CENTENNIAL.]

ses·qui·ox·ide (séskwi-ók-sīd) *n.* An oxide that contains three oxygen atoms for every two atoms of the element, such as Cr_2O_3.

ses·qui·pe·da·li·an (séskwi-pi-dáyli-ən, -pe-) *adj.* **1.** Long and ponderous; polysyllabic. **2.** Given to using long words.

~*n.* A long word. [Latin *sesquipedalis,* of a foot and a half in length : SESQUI- + *pes* (stem *ped-*), foot.]

Ses·shu (sésh-shŏŏ), also called Sesshu Toyo (1420–1506). Japanese painter, known for his landscapes and Zen Buddhist pictures. His work combines Chinese with Japanese influences.

ses·sile (séssīl || *U.S. also* séss'l) *adj.* **1.** *Botany.* Stalkless and attached directly at the base: *sessile leaves.* **2.** *Zoology.* Permanently attached or fixed; not free-moving. [Latin *sessilis,* of sitting, low (said of plants), from *sessus,* past participle of *sedēre,* to sit.]

sessile oak *n.* An oak, the **durmast** *(see).*

ses·sion (sésh'n) *n.* **1.** A meeting of a legislative or judicial body for the purpose of transacting business. **2.** The term or period during which such meetings are held. **3.** *Chiefly U.S. & Scottish.* The part of a year during which teaching is given at a university or college; an academic year. **4.** *Plural.* A sitting or sittings of justices of the peace. See **petty sessions, quarter sessions. 5. a.** Any period of time devoted to a specific activity. **b.** A period of time spent singing or playing and recording music in a studio; a recording session. **6.** The ruling body of a Presbyterian church.

~*adj.* Designating a professional musician who provides instrumental or vocal accompaniment during recording sessions for other people's records: *a session guitarist.* [Middle English *sessioun,* a session, a sitting, from Old French *session,* from Latin *sessiō* (stem *sessiōn-*), from *sessus,* past participle of *sedēre,* to sit.] **—ses·sion·al** *adj.* **—ses·sion·al·ly** *adv.*

Ses·sions (sésh'nz), **Roger (Huntington)** (1896–1985). U.S. composer. His early works show the influence of Stravinsky, but with his *Violin Sonata* (1953) he began to introduce serialism into his work.

ses·terce (séss-tərss, -terss) *n.* A silver or bronze coin of ancient Rome, equivalent to 1/4 denarius. [Latin *sestertius,* (coin) worth two and a half (asses) (i.e., two plus a half of a third ass) : *sēmis,* a half + *tertius,* a third.]

ses·ter·ti·um (sess-tér-shi-əm, -ti-) *n., pl.* **-tia** (-shi-ə, -ti-ə). A money of account in ancient Rome, equivalent to 1,000 sesterces. [Latin *(mille) sestertium,* (a thousand) sesterces, from the genitive plural of *sestertius,* SESTERCE.]

ses·tet (sess-tét) *n.* A stanza constituting the last six lines of a sonnet. Compare **octet.** [Italian *sestetto,* from *sesto,* sixth, from Latin *sextus.*]

ses·ti·na (sess-téenə) *n.* An originally Provençal verse form consisting of six six-line stanzas and a three-line envoi, repeating the end words of the first stanza in the other five stanzas according to an elaborate pattern. [Italian, from *sesto,* sixth, from Latin *sextus.*]

set[1] (set) *v.* **set, setting, sets.** —*tr.* **1.** To put or cause to be situated in a specified place or position: *Set the box on the table.* **2.** To put (a broken or dislocated bone) into a position that will restore a proper and normal state. **3. a.** To adjust according to a standard: *set one's watch by the station clock.* **b.** To adjust to a specified point or calibration: *set the alarm for six o'clock.* **4.** To fix (the hair) in position while wet so as to achieve a particular style. **5.** To arrange scenery upon (a theatre stage) or in (a television or film studio). **6. a.** To put (a precious stone, for example) in a setting; mount. **b.** To apply jewels to; stud. **7. a.** To arrange (type or filmset characters) preparatory to printing; compose. **b.** To transpose (text) into filmset characters or type. **8.** To place in a sitting position; seat: *set the child on his knee.* **9. a.** To put (a hen) on eggs for the purpose of hatching them. **b.** To put (eggs) beneath a hen or in an incubator. **10.** To bring into or cause to be in a specified condition or relation: *sets her apart from others.* **11.** To cause to be taken into account so as to offset or compensate for something else; balance: *set these losses against tax.* **12.** To cause to take up a hostile position or attitude; pit (one person) against another. **13.** To focus (one's hopes or attention, for example) towards a particular purpose. **14.** To put into a rigid position showing defiance or determination: *set one's jaw.* **15. a.** To put an edge or point on (a cutting instrument). **b.** To adjust (a saw) by deflecting the teeth. **16.** To prepare for effective use or action, as: **a.** To make (a table) ready for a meal. **b.** To make (a trap) ready to operate. **17.** To detail or assign to a particular duty, task, or station: *set them to work cleaning up.* **18.** To allot or prescribe (a task): *set some homework.* **19.** To determine, fix, or assign: *set a date.* **20.** To establish (a record). **21.** To present as a model for emulation: *set an example.* **22.** To consider as having a particular value or worth; rate: *set great store by punctuality.* **23.** To provide (a scene or story) with a specified background in space and time: *a novel set in 18th-century England.* **24.** To compose music to fit (a given text). **25.** To cause (a liquid or a soft substance) to become firm or solid. **26.** To incite to make an attack: *set his dogs on us.* **27.** To point to the location of (game) by holding a fixed attitude. Used of a hunting dog. **28.** *Horticulture.* To produce, as after pollination: *set seed.* **29.** To sink (a nail) so that its head lies below the surrounding surface. —*intr.* **1.** To go

down towards and below the horizon. Used of the sun or any other heavenly body. **2.** To diminish or decline; wane. **3.** To sit on eggs. Used of a hen. **4.** To solidify, harden, or congeal. **5.** To embark upon a journey. Used with *out, forth,* or *off.* **6.** To become restored to a normal state; knit. Used of a broken bone. **7.** To have or follow a specified course or direction. Used of a wind, current, or the like. **8.** *Horticulture.* To mature or develop, as after pollination. **9.** To point to the position of game by holding a fixed attitude. Used of a hunting dog. **10.** *Regional.* To sit. **—set about.** To start or begin doing. **—set down. 1.** To put into written or printed form; record. **2.** To regard or consider. **3.** To attribute. **4.** To allow (a passenger) to alight. **5.** To land (an aircraft), especially in abnormal circumstances. **—set forth.** To make known or propound (plans or ideas, for example). **—set in.** To begin to happen and become established. **—set out. 1.** To display for exhibition or sale. **2.** To describe or expound; put forward in detail. **3.** To lay out (a room, town, or garden, for example); plan. **4.** To plant out (seedlings, for example).
~adj. **1.** Fixed or prescribed by authority, agreement, or convention: *set mealtimes.* **2.** Consisting of or offering a fixed number and combination of dishes for one price: *a set menu.* **3.** Fixed, rigid, or unmoving: *a set smile.* **4.** Clichéd or stereotyped: *set phrases.* **5.** Rigid and unchanging in disposition: *set in one's ways.* **6.** Holding resolutely to a particular attitude or intention: *set on going; dead set against it.* **7.** Ready for action: *get set.*
~n. **1. a.** The act or process of setting. **b.** The condition resulting from setting. **2.** A permanent firming or hardening of a substance, as by cooling. **3.** The manner in which something is positioned. **4.** The carriage or bearing of a part of the body. **5.** An inclination or tendency, as of the mind or character, in a particular direction. **6.** The direction or course of wind or water. **7.** An act of styling the hair by setting it: *a shampoo and set.* **8.** A seedling, slip, or cutting that is ready for planting. **9.** Variant of **sett.** [Set (infinitive, past tense, past participle); Middle English *setten, sette,* to cause to sit, place, Old English *settan, sette, sett.*]

set[2] *n.* **1.** A group of persons, things, or circumstances that belong together by virtue of similarities, as in appearance, character, or function, especially: **a.** A group of persons who associate with each other and share a common lifestyle and common interests: *the jet set.* **b.** A group of related objects having the same or a similar function and often used together in a particular activity: *a chess set; a set of wine glasses.* **c.** A group of situations, events, or the like considered collectively or as forming a whole: *a set of lectures.* **2.** A part of a programme or a session of music, typically popular music or jazz, performed at one time: *played a relaxed set.* **3. a.** A basic configuration of dancers, as in a country dance or a square dance. **b.** The series of movements constituting such a dance. **4. a.** The scenery constructed for a dramatic performance. **b.** The area, as in a studio or on location, in which a film is shot. **5.** An apparatus that receives radio or television signals; a receiver. **6.** *Mathematics & Logic.* A collection or group specified in such a way that, given any object, it can be determined whether that object does or does not belong to that collection or group: *the empty set; the set of positive integers.* **7.** In tennis and other games, a group of games constituting one division or unit of a match. **8.** *British.* A grouping of pupils whose ability in a particular subject is similar, and who are taught that subject as a group. —See Synonyms at **circle.**
~v. **set, setting, sets.** *—tr.* **1.** To group (pupils) into sets. **2.** To teach (a subject) in sets. *—intr.* To do a series of country-dance or square-dance steps facing one's partner. Used with *to.* [Middle English *sette,* sect, set, from Old French, from Latin *secta,* SECT (later confused with *set,* to place, taken as "a group or number set together").]

se·ta (séetə) *n., pl.* **setae** (séetee). *Biology.* **1.** A stiff hair, bristle, or bristle-like growth or organ. **2.** *Botany.* The stalk that bears the capsule in mosses. [New Latin, from Latin *sēta, saeta*†, bristle.] **—se·tal** *adj.*

se·ta·ceous (si-táyshəss, se-) *adj.* **1.** Having or consisting of bristles; bristly. **2.** Resembling a bristle or bristles; bristle-like. [New Latin *setaceus* : SET(A) + -ACEOUS.]

set aside. *tr.v.* **1. a.** To separate and reserve for a special purpose or later consideration. **b.** To withdraw from a previous use. **2.** To dismiss or discard. **3.** To declare invalid or void; annul.

set-a·side (séttəsīd) *n.* Something set aside; specifically, land withdrawn from agricultural production in order to reduce surpluses. **—set-aside** *adj.*

set back *tr.v.* **1.** To impede the progress or advance of. **2.** *Informal.* To cost (a person) a specified amount.

set·back (sét-bak) *n.* **1.** An unanticipated or sudden check in progress; a reverse. **2. a.** A steplike recession in a wall. **b.** Any of a series of such recessions in the rise of a tall building.

set book *n.* A text prescribed for study as part of an examination syllabus.

set chisel *n.* A chisel with a cutting edge on a tapered shaft; a cold chisel.

Seth (seth). The third son of Adam. Genesis 4:25.

se·tif·er·ous (si-tíffərəss, se-) *adj.* Also **se·tig·er·ous** (-tíjərəss). Setose. [From Latin *seta,* bristle + -FEROUS.]

se·ti·form (séeti-fawrm) *adj.* Having the shape of a seta or bristle. [SET(A) + -FORM.]

set·line (sét-līn) *n.* A long fishing line towed by a boat and supporting many smaller lines bearing baited hooks. Also *U.S.* "trawl", "trawl line".

set off *tr.v.* **1.** To show to best advantage; enhance by contrast. **2.** To cause to explode. **3. a.** To cause (sudden or hurried activity); spark off: *set off a wave of selling.* **b.** To cause (a person) to start some activity: *set him off on one of his boring stories.*

set·off (sét-off, -awff) *n.* **1.** Anything that has the effect of enhancing something else, especially by contrast. **2.** Anything that offsets or compensates for something else. **3.** A counterbalancing debt. **4.** An **offset** *(see).*

se·tose (sée-tōss || -tōz) *adj.* Bristly or bristle-like; setaceous. [Latin *sētōsus,* from *sēta,* bristle, SETA.]

set piece *n.* **1.** An often brilliantly executed artistic or literary work, or part of a work, characterised by a formal pattern. **2.** A realistic piece of stage scenery constructed to stand by itself. **3.** An elaborate firework display that forms a pattern. **4.** A carefully planned and executed operation, especially a military operation. **5.** In soccer, hockey, and similar games, a specially rehearsed plan of action put into effect by a team in a situation, such as a free kick or corner, outside the run of normal play.

set point *n.* A point that, if won, wins a set, as in tennis.

set·screw (sét-skrōō || -skrew) *n.* **1.** A screw, often without a head, used to hold two parts in a position relative to each other without motion. **2.** A screw used to regulate the tension of a spring.

set square *n.* A device used in technical drawing consisting of a flat sheet, usually of plastic or wood, in the shape of a right-angle triangle, used to draw vertical lines in conjunction with a T-square and also to construct angles of 30°, 45°, and 60°.

sett, set (set) *n.* **1.** A badger's burrow. **2.** A small square or rectangular block, usually made of granite, used especially formerly as a paving stone. **3. a.** A square section in a tartan pattern. **b.** The pattern itself. **4.** An adjustment made to the reeds in a loom so as to weave a particular pattern.

set·tee (se-tée, sə-) *n.* A long seat with a back and usually arms; a sofa. [Perhaps variant of SETTLE (bench).]

set·ter (séttər) *n.* **1.** One that sets. **2.** A dog of any of several long-haired breeds, originally trained to show the presence of game by crouching in a set position. See **English setter, Irish setter, red setter.**

set theory *n.* The study of the mathematical properties of sets.

set·ting (sétting) *n.* **1.** The context or surroundings in which an event, story, or the like is set. **2.** A mounting, as for a jewel. **3.** The scenery constructed for a theatrical, film, or television performance. **4.** Music composed or arranged to fit a text. **5.** Any of the positions in which a machine or instrument can be set. **6.** The cutlery, glassware, and the like for one person at table.

set·tle (sétt'l) *v.* **-tled, -tling, -tles.** *—tr.* **1.** To place, dispose, or establish in a desired position; especially, to place (oneself) in a comfortable position. **2.** To put in order; arrange in a final or satisfactory form. **3.** To reach decisive agreement regarding (a course of action, for example); decide on: *settled the details.* **4.** To conclude or resolve (a dispute, for example). **5.** To decide (a lawsuit) by mutual agreement of the involved parties, usually without court action: *settled the affair out of court.* **6. a.** To cause to take up residence in a place. **b.** To colonise or otherwise provide (a place) with inhabitants or settlers. **7.** To fix or establish in a more or less permanent and unvarying form: *a settled life.* **8.** To cause to become less disturbed or agitated; restore calmness or quiet to: *settle one's stomach.* **9.** To pay or pay back (what is owing): *settle an account; a few old scores to settle.* **10. a.** To cause to come to rest, sink, or become compact. **b.** To cause (a liquid) to become clear by forming a sediment. **11.** *Law.* To secure or assign (property or title, for example) to another by a legal settlement. Used with *on* or *upon.* *—intr.* **1.** To discontinue moving and come to rest in one place. **2.** To subside gradually; shift to a lower level. **3.** To sink and become more compact: *The dust settled.* **4. a.** To become clear. Used of liquids. **b.** To be separated from a solution or mixture as a sediment. **5.** To become less agitated or restless; regain calmness or composure. Often used with *down.* **6.** To take up permanent residence. **7.** To reach a decision; determine. Used with *on, upon,* or *with.* **8.** To decide a lawsuit by mutual agreement: *settled out of court.* **9.** To pay what is owing. Often used with *up.* —See Synonyms at **decide. —settle down. 1.** To begin living a more ordered life, as by marrying or taking a permanent job. **2.** To apply one's attention purposefully and diligently. **—settle for.** To accept in spite of incomplete satisfaction. **—settle in. 1.** To become comfortably adapted to a new environment or situation. **2.** To help (someone) to settle in.
~n. A long wooden bench with a high back, often including storage space beneath the seat. [Middle English *setlen,* to place in order, seat, Old English *setlan,* from *setl,* seat.]

set·tle·ment (sétt'lmənt) *n.* **1.** The act or process of settling. **2. a.** The establishment of a new population in a place. **b.** A newly colonised region. **3.** A small community, especially in a thinly-populated or newly-settled area. **4.** An understanding or agreement by which differences are resolved. **5. a.** An arrangement or legal instrument by which property is settled on a person. **b.** Property thus transferred. **6.** A welfare centre providing community services in a deprived inner-city area. Also called "settlement house". **7.** Slow sinking, as of a wall or building, due to subsidence.

set·tler (sétt'l-ər, séttlər) *n.* One that settles; especially, a person who settles in a new and previously uncolonised region.

set·tlings (sétt'l-ingz, séttlingz) *pl.n.* Sediment; dregs.

set to *intr.v.* **1.** To begin working actively or eagerly. **2.** To begin fighting.

set-to (sét-tōō, -tōō) *n., pl.* **-tos.** A brief but usually heated fight or contest.

set up *tr.v.* **1.** To place in a raised or upright position; erect or elevate. **2.** To establish in a position of power: *set up a dictator.* **3.** To cause or produce: *set up a din.* **4.** To restore or improve the health and well-being of. **5.** To establish; found. **6.** To establish (a person) in business by providing capital, equipment, and the like. **7.** To put forward or propose. **8.** To put (especially oneself) forward, often without justification, as having some quality: *sets himself up as an expert on wine.* **9.** To create conditions favourable for the scoring of (a goal, try, or the like). **10.** *Informal.* To provide (drinks) for a person or group. **11.** *Informal.* To arrange for (someone) to be discovered in incriminating or embarrassing circumstances. *—intr.v.* To start in business: *has set up as a decorator.*

set-up (sét-up) *n. Informal.* **1.** The way in which anything operates or is constituted or arranged. **2.** A situation prearranged to place someone in an incriminating or embarrassing position. **3.** *Chiefly U.S.* A task, undertaking, or contest prearranged so that it is accomplished or won without any real difficulty.

~*adj.* Of or having a physically developed body or bearing: *a well set-up man.*

Seu·rat (súr-raa; *French* sö-raá), **Georges (Pierre)** (1859–91). French painter, the founder of pointillism. Developing the impressionist concerns with light and atmosphere, he evolved a distinctive technique for rendering appearances through innumerable dots of pure colour, which produced a number of masterpieces, including *Une Baignade* (1884) and *La Grande Jatte* (1886).

Se·vas·to·pol (*Russian* si-vuss-tóppəl). *English* **Se·bas·to·pol** (si-bástə-p'l, se-, sə-, -pol). Seaport in the Crimea, in southern Ukraine. It became the main base of the Russian Black Sea fleet (1804). It was twice captured after prolonged sieges: 322 days (1854–55) by the Allies in the Crimean War, and 250 days (1941–42) by the Germans in World War II.

sev·en (sévv'n) *n.* **1. a.** The cardinal number that is one more than six. **b.** A symbol representing this, such as 7, VII, or vii. **2.** A set made up of seven persons or things. **3. a.** The seventh in a series. **b.** A playing card marked with seven pips. **4.** Seven parts: *cut in seven.* **5.** A size, as in clothing, designated as seven. **6.** Seven hours after midnight or midday. [Middle English *seven,* Old English *seofon.*] **—sev·en** *adj.* **—sev·en·fold** (-fōld) *adj. & adv.*

seven deadly sins *pl.n.* The sins of pride, lust, envy, anger, covetousness, gluttony, and sloth. Also called "cardinal sins".

seven seas *pl.n.* All the oceans of the world.

Seven Sisters *pl.n. Astronomy.* The **Pleiades** *(see).*

sev·en·teen (sévv'n-teén), *n.* **1. a.** The cardinal number that is one more than 16. **b.** A symbol representing this, such as XVII. **2.** A set made up of 17 persons or things. **3.** The seventeenth in a series. **4.** A size, as in clothing, designated 17. [Middle English *seventene,* Old English *seofontīne* : SEVEN + -TEEN.] **—sev·en·teen** *adj.*

sev·en·teenth (sévv'n-teénth) *n.* **1.** The ordinal number 17 in a series. Also written 17th. **2.** One of 17 equal parts. **—sev·en·teenth** *adj. & adv.*

sev·en·teen-year locust (sévv'n-teen-yeér, -yér) *n.* A cicada of the genus *Magicicada,* of the eastern United States, which as a nymph remains underground for 17 or sometimes 13 years.

sev·enth (sévv'nth) *n.* **1.** The ordinal number seven in a series. Also written 7th. **2.** One of seven equal parts. **3.** *Music.* **a.** A note that is on the seventh diatonic degree with respect to another given note. **b.** The interval encompassing two such notes. **c.** A chord consisting of a note together with its third, fifth, and seventh. In this sense, also called "seventh chord". **—sev·enth** *adj. & adv.*

Sev·enth-Day Adventist (sévv'nth-day) *n.* A member of a sect of Adventism distinguished chiefly for its observance of the Sabbath on Saturday. See **Adventist.**

seventh heaven *n.* **1.** A state of great joy and satisfaction. **2.** The furthest of the concentric spheres containing the stars and comprising the dwelling place of God and the angels in the Muslim and cabbalist systems.

sev·en·ty (sévv'nti) *n., pl.* **-ties 1. a.** The cardinal number that is 10 more than 60. **b.** A symbol representing this, such as 70 or LXX. **2.** A set made up of 70 persons or things. **3.** The seventieth in a series. **4.** A size, as in clothing, designated as 70. **5.** *Plural.* **a.** The range of numbers from 70 to 79 considered as a range of age, price, temperature, or the like. **b.** *Often capital* **S.** The years numbered 70 to 79 in a century. In this sense, also used adjectivally: *a well-known seventies group.* **—sev·en·ti·eth** *adj. & adv. & n.* **—sev·en·ty** *adj.*

seventy-eight *n.* An old-time gramophone record.

sev·en-up (sévv'n-úp) *n. U.S.* A card game, **all fours** *(see).*

Seven Wonders of the World *pl.n.* Seven monuments of the ancient world that appeared on various lists of late antiquity. Most commonly, they are: the Colossus of Rhodes, the Pharos at Alexandria, the Hanging Gardens (and Walls) of Babylon, the temple of Artemis at Ephesus, the pyramids of Giza, the tomb of Mausolus at Halicarnassus, and the statue of Zeus at Olympia. Preceded by *the.*

sev·en-year itch (sévv'n-yeer, -yer) *n.* A tendency towards infidelity that is supposed to develop after seven years of marriage.

sev·er (sévvər) *v.* **-ered, -ering, -ers.** *—tr.* **1.** To divide or separate into parts; keep apart or make distinct. **2.** To cut or break off forcibly; remove by cutting. **3.** To break off (a relationship, for example); dissolve. *—intr.* **1.** To become cut or broken apart. **2.** To divide; separate or go apart. —See Synonyms at **separate, tear.** [Middle English *severen,* from Anglo-French *severer,* from Vulgar Latin *sēperāre* (unattested), from Latin *sēparāre,* to SEPARATE.] **—sev·er·a·ble** (sévvərəb'l) *adj.*

sev·er·al (sévvrəl, sévvərəl) *adj.* **1.** More than two but not many; of an indefinitely small number. **2.** Single; distinct. **3.** Respectively different; diverse; various. **4.** *Law.* Pertaining separately to each party involved.

~*pron.* Several persons or things; a few. [Middle English *severall,* separate, distinct, from Anglo-French *several,* from Medieval Latin *sēparālis,* from Latin *sēpār,* separate, from *sēparāre,* to SEPARATE.] **—sev·er·al·ly** *adv.*

sev·er·ance (sévvərənss) *n.* **1.** The act or process of severing, division, or separation. **2.** The condition of being severed.

severance pay *n.* Money paid by an employer to an employee who has lost his job through no fault of his own.

se·vere (si-veér, sə-) *adj.* **-verer, -verest. 1.** Having or showing a harsh, unsparing, and inflexible disposition in one's treatment of or attitude towards others; stern; strict. **2.** Adhering to or based on stringent and exacting rules or standards: *severe discipline.* **3.** Grave and austere in appearance, manner, or temperament; forbidding. **4.** Extremely plain and unadorned, as in dress or style; sober and restrained. **5.** Causing intense pain or distress; hard; grievous: *a severe winter; severe depression.* **6.** Extremely difficult to perform or accomplish; arduous. [French *severe,* from Latin *sevērus.*] **—se·vere·ly** *adv.* **—se·vere·ness, se·ver·i·ty** (si-vérrəti, sə-) *n.*

***Synonyms:** severe, stern, austere, ascetic, strict, exacting.*

Sev·ern (sévvərn). *Welsh* **Haf·ren** (háv-ren). Britain's longest river. It rises on the northeastern slopes of Plynlimon and flows for 352 kilometres (220 miles) through the Vale of Powys, and to the Bristol Channel via an exceptionally long estuary; the tidal bore can reverse the flow of the river as far up as Gloucester. It is crossed by a rail tunnel and a suspension bridge. A second bridge was completed in 1996 which, at a length of 5 kilometres (3.2 miles), is the UK's longest.

Se·ve·rus (se-vaírəss), full name Lucius Septimius Severus (A.D. 146–211). Roman emperor (193–211) born in Roman North Africa. He restored order to the empire after a turbulent period, and consolidated the eastern frontier. He died at York while planning a major campaign into Scotland.

Se·ve·so (sáyv-sō; *Italian* sévve-zō). A town near Milan, northern Italy. Between July 1976 and September 1977, it was evacuated after an escape of poisonous dioxin gas from a factory.

Sé·vi·gné (sáyveen-yáy), **Marie de Rabutin-Chantal, Marquise de** (1626–96). French writer. A widow from the age of 25, she is remembered for her prolific correspondence. Her *Letters* (1725), including many to her daughter, radiate lively wit and understanding and vividly depict aristocratic life in the age of Louis XIV.

Se·ville (sə-víl, se-, si-, *also* sévvil). *Spanish* **Se·vi·lla** (se-veél-ya). A port of southwest Spain, the capital of Sevilla province. It was an important Moorish stronghold and centre of culture and learning (712–1248), and prospered as the main port for the Spanish colonies in the New World from 1492 until eclipsed by Cádiz in the late 17th century. Seville is also noted for its school of painting, whose artists included Velásquez and Murillo.

Seville orange *n.* **1.** A citrus tree, *Citrus aurantium,* that bears bitter oranges, used to make marmalade. **2.** The fruit of this tree. Also called "bitter orange". [After SEVILLE where it is cultivated.]

Sè·vres (sáyvrə, sayvr; *French* sévvrə) *n.* A fine porcelain made in Sèvres, northern France. Also called "Sèvres ware".

sew (sō) *v.* **sewed, sewn** (sōn) or **sewed, sewing, sews.** *—tr.* **1.** To make, repair, or fasten using a needle and thread. **2.** To close, enclose, or attach by means of stitches. *—intr.* To work with a needle and thread or with a sewing machine. **—sew up.** *Informal.* **1.** To bring (a business deal) to a successful close. **2.** *Chiefly U.S.* To gain control of. [Middle English *sewen,* Old English *seowian.*]

sew·age (séw-ij, sóo-) *n.* Liquid and solid waste carried off with ground water in sewers or drains. [SEW(ER) + -AGE.]

sewage farm *n.* A place where sewage is treated so that the solid constituents may be used as fertiliser, or so as to render it nontoxic.

Sew·all Wright effect (sóo-əl) *n.* **Genetic drift** *(see).* [After *Sewall Wright* (1889–1988), U.S. geneticist and statistician.]

Sew·ell (séw-əl, sóo-), **Anna** (1820–78). British author of the children's classic, *Black Beauty* (1877). Partially crippled from childhood, she wrote her one novel, set in the form of the autobiography of a horse, to expose the maltreatment of animals in her day.

se·wel·lel (si-wéllel) *n.* A **mountain beaver** *(see).*

sew·er[1] (séw-ər, sóo-) *n.* An artificial, usually underground conduit for carrying off sewage or rainwater. [Middle English *sewer,* from Anglo-French *sever(e),* from Vulgar Latin *exaquāria* (unattested) : Latin *ex-,* out of + *aqua,* water.]

sew·er[2] (séw-ər, sóo-) *n.* A medieval servant who supervised the serving of meals. [Middle English *sewer,* from Anglo-French *asseour,* from Old French *asseoir,* to cause to sit (seating of guests was a sewer's responsibility), from Latin *assidēre,* to sit down.]

sew·er[3] (só-ər) *n.* One that sews.

sew·er·age (séw-ərij, sóo-) *n.* **1.** A system of sewers. **2.** The removal of waste materials by means of a sewer system. **3.** Sewage.

sew·in, sew·en (séw-in, sóo-) *n.* A salmon trout found along the west coast of Britain and in Ireland. [16th century : origin obscure.]

sew·ing (só-ing) *n.* **1.** The act, skill, or hobby of one who sews. **2.** An article that is or is to be worked on with needle and thread; needlework.

sewing machine *n.* A machine that sews, often having additional attachments for special stitching.

sewn. Past participle of **sew.**

sex (seks) *n.* **1. a.** The sum of properties by which organisms are classified according to their reproductive functions. **b.** Either of

two divisions, designated *male* and *female*, of this classification. **2.** Males or females collectively. **3.** The condition or character of being male or female; the physiological, functional, and psychological differences that distinguish the male and the female. **4.** The sexual urge or instinct or sexual desire as it manifests itself in behaviour. **5.** Sexual intercourse.
~*adj.* Of, based on, or concerned with sex or sexual intercourse.
~*tr.v.* **sexed, sexing, sexes.** To determine the sex of. [Middle English, from Old French *sexe*, from Latin *sexus*†.]

sex– *comb. form.* Indicates six; for example, **sexpartite.** [Latin *sex*, six.]

sex·a·ge·nar·i·an (sĕksə-ji-naír-i-ən, -jə-) *adj.* **1.** Being sixty years old or between sixty and seventy years old. **2.** Of or like someone of this age.
~ *n.* A sexagenarian person. [Latin *sexāgēnārius*, from *sexāgēnī*, sixty each, from *sexāgintā*, sixty : SEX + *-ginta*, ten times.]

Sex·a·ges·i·ma (sĕksə-jéssimə) *n.* The second Sunday before Lent. Also called "Sexagesima Sunday". [Late Latin *sexāgēsima*, sixtieth (day before Easter), from Latin, feminine of *sexāgēsimus*, sixtieth, from *sexāgintā*, sixty. See **sexagenarian.**]

sex·a·ges·i·mal (sĕksə-jéssim'l) *adj.* Relating to or based upon the number 60. [From Latin *sexāgēsimus*, sixtieth, from *sexāgintā*, sixty. See **sexagenarian.**]

sex appeal *n.* Attractiveness that arouses sexual desire; the possession of qualities that are sexually attractive.

sex·cen·te·nar·y (sĕk-sen-téenəri, -sin-, -ténnəri, -sénti-nəri ‖ -nerri) *adj.* Pertaining to 600 or to a 600-year period.
~*n., pl.* **sexcentenaries.** A 600th anniversary or its commemoration. [From Latin *sexcentēnī*, six hundred each : SEX- + *centēnī*, a hundred each, from *centum*, hundred.]

sex chromosome *n.* Either of a pair of chromosomes, usually designated X or Y, that combine to determine the sex of an individual. In humans, XX results in a female and XY in a male. See **X chromosome, Y chromosome.**

sex·en·ni·al (sek-sénni-əl) *adj.* **1.** Occurring every six years. **2.** Of or for six years. [Latin *sexennium*, (period of) six years : SEX- + *annus*, year.] —**sex·en·ni·al·ly** *adv.*

sex hormone *n.* Any of various animal hormones, such as oestrogen and androgen, affecting the growth or function of the reproductive organs and the development of secondary sex characteristics.

sex·ism (séksiz'm) *n.* **1.** Discrimination based on sex; especially, prejudice against the female sex. **2.** Any arbitrary stereotyping of males and females on the basis of their gender. [SEX + -ISM, after RACISM.] —**sex·ist** *adj. & n.*

sex·less (séks-ləss, -liss) *adj.* **1.** Lacking sexual characteristics; asexual; neuter. **2.** Arousing or exhibiting no sexual interest or desire. —**sex·less·ly** *adv.* —**sex·less·ness** *n.*

sex linkage *n.* The condition in which a gene responsible for a specific phenotypic trait is located on a sex chromosome, usually on the X chromosome but not on the Y chromosome, resulting in sexually dependent inheritance of the trait.

sex-linked (séks-língkt) *adj.* **1.** Carried by a sex chromosome, especially an X chromosome. Said of genes. **2.** Broadly, sexually determined. Said especially of inherited traits.

sex object *n.* One who is valued, or is portrayed as having value, purely for her or his sexual attributes.

sex·ol·o·gy (sĕk-sólləji) *n.* The study of human sexual behaviour. [SEX + -LOGY.] —**sex·o·log·ic** (-sə-lójik), **sex·o·log·i·cal** *adj.* —**sex·ol·o·gist** (-sólləjist) *n.*

sex·par·tite (séks-pártīt) *adj.* Composed of or divided into six parts. [SEX- + PARTITE.]

sex·pot (séks-pot) *n. Informal.* A woman who is sexually attractive in an uninhibited way.

sext (sekst) *n.* **1.** The fourth of the seven **canonical hours** (see). **2.** The time of day set aside for this prayer, usually the sixth hour, or noon. [Middle English *sexte*, from Latin *sexta (hora)*, sixth (hour), from the feminine of *sextus*, sixth.]

Sex·tans (séks-tanz, -tənz) *n.* A constellation in the equatorial region of the sky near Leo and Hydra. Also called the "Sextant". [New Latin, SEXTANT.]

sex·tant (sékstənt) *n.* **1.** An instrument used in navigation for measuring the altitudes of celestial bodies and hence determining the position of the observer. **2.** *Capital S.* The constellation Sextans. [New Latin *sextans* (stem *sextant-*), from Latin, a sixth part (the instrument has an arc graduated in sixths of a circle).]

sex·tet (séks-tét) *n.* **1. a.** A group of six vocalists or musicians. **b.** A musical composition written for six performers. **2.** Any group of six persons or things. [Respelling of SESTET, after Latin *sex*, six.]

sex·tile (sékstīl) *adj.* Designating the position of two celestial bodies when they are 60 degrees apart. [Latin *sextīlis*, one sixth (of a circle), from *sextus*, sixth.]

sex·til·li·on (séks-tillien, -til·yən) *n.* **1.** In British usage, the cardinal number represented by 1 followed by 36 zeros, usually written 10^{36}. **2.** The cardinal number that is represented by 1 followed by 21 zeros, usually written 10^{21}. [French : SEX- + (M)ILLION.] —**sex·til·li·onth** *n. & adj.*

sex·to·dec·i·mo (sékstō-déssimō) *n., pl.* **-mos.** **1.** The page size of a book composed of printer's sheets folded into 16 leaves or 32 pages. **2.** A book composed of pages of this size. Also called "sixteenmo". Also written *16 mo, 16°.* [Latin *sextōdecimō*, ablative of *sextusdecimus*, a sixteenth : *sextus*, sixth + *decimus*, tenth, from *decem*, ten.] —**sex·to·dec·i·mo** *adj.*

sex·ton (sékstən) *n.* A church officer responsible for the care and upkeep of the church, its furnishings and vestments, the churchyard, and sometimes for bell-ringing or gravedigging. [Middle English *segerstone, sexton,* from Anglo-French *segerstaine,* from Medieval Latin *sacristānus,* SACRISTAN.]

sexton beetle *n.* The **burying beetle** *(see).*

sex·tu·ple (séks-tewp'l ‖ -téwp'l, -too͞op'l, -tupp'l, -túpp'l) *adj.* **1.** Consisting of or having six parts, members, or copies. **2.** Multiplied by six; six times as much, as many, or as large.
~*n.* A sixfold amount or number.
~*v.* **sextupled, -pling, -ples.** —*tr.* To multiply or increase by six. —*intr.* To be multiplied sixfold. [Medieval Latin *sextuplus,* irregularly (influenced by *quintuplus,* QUINTUPLE) from Latin *sex,* six.] —**sex·tu·ply** *adv.*

sex·tu·plet (séks-tew-plət, -téw-, -plit ‖ -too͞o-, -tú-) *n.* **1.** One of six offspring delivered at one birth. **2.** A collection or set of six similar persons or things; a sextet. **3.** *Music.* A set of six equal notes to be performed in the time normally given for four notes of the same value. [SEXTU(PLE + TRI)PLET.]

sex·tu·pli·cate (séks-téw-pli-kət, -kit ‖ -too͞o-, -túppli-) *adj.* **1.** Six times as many or as much; sixfold. **2.** Sixth in a group or set.
~*n.* One of six similar things. [SEXTU(PLE + DU)PLICATE.] —**sex·tu·pli·cate·ly** *adv.* —**sex·tu·pli·ca·tion** (-káysh'n) *n.*

sex·u·al (sék-sew-əl, -sewl, -shoo-əl, -shool) *adj.* **1.** Pertaining to, affecting, or associated with sex, the sexes, or the sex organs and their functions. **2.** Of or pertaining to the desire or urge for physical contact and stimulation with another person that, typically, is satisfied by sexual intercourse. **3.** Having a sex or sexual organs. [From Late Latin *sexuālis,* from Latin *sexus,* SEX.] —**sex·u·al·ly** *adv.*

sexual harassment *n.* Harassment involving unwelcome sexual advances (as at work).

sexual intercourse *n.* **1.** Copulation between a man and a woman, involving the insertion of the erect penis into the vagina. **2.** Intercourse between two or more individuals involving genital stimulation. Also called "intercourse".

sexual reproduction *n.* Reproduction involving the union of male and female gametes.

sex·u·al·i·ty (sék-sew-al-əti, -shoo-) *n.* **1.** The condition of being characterised and distinguished by sex. **2.** Concern or preoccupation with sex. **3.** The quality of possessing a sexual character or potency. **4.** The condition of having sexual feelings and desires of a certain kind; a particular sexual nature.

sexual selection *n.* A Darwinian adjunct of natural selection hypothesising the selection by females of characteristics involved in male courtship displays and combat and hence the retention of such characteristics in future generations.

sex·y (séksi) *adj.* **-ier, -iest.** *Informal.* Arousing or intended to arouse sexual desire or interest.

Sey·chelles, Republic of (sáy-shélz, say-). A state of the northwestern Indian Ocean, comprising an archipelago of some 85 coral or granite islands, northeast of Madagascar. It was discovered by Vasco da Gama (1502), settled by the French (1770s), and seized by the British (1794). The Seychelles became an independent republic within the Commonwealth in 1976. Its economy rests on tropical produce, particularly copra and cinnamon, and, increasingly, on tourism and fishing. Mahé is the largest island, with more than 60 per cent of the population. Area, 454 square kilometres (175.3 square miles). Capital, Victoria (on Mahé). Population, 80,000. See map at **Indian Ocean.** —**Sey·chel·lois** (sáy-shel-wáa) *n. & adj.*

Sey·fert galaxy (sí-fərt, sée-) *n.* Any of a number of spiral galaxies with an exceptionally bright nucleus. [After Carl K. *Seyfert* (1911–60), U.S. astronomer.]

Sey·mour (sée-mawr ‖ -mōr), **Jane** (c. 1509–37). English noblewoman, the third wife of Henry VIII and the mother of Edward VI. A lady-in-waiting to Anne Boleyn, she married Henry in 1536 soon after Anne's execution. She died shortly after providing the king with his only male heir.

sez (sez). *Nonstandard.* Variant of **says.**

SF science fiction.

sferics. *U.S.* Variant of **spherics.**

sfor·zan·do (sfawrt-sán-dō ‖ -saán-) *adv.* Also **for·zan·do** (fawrt-). *Abbr.* **sf., sfz.** Suddenly and strongly accented. Used as a musical direction.
~*n.* Also **forzando.** A sforzando note or chord. [Italian, gerund of *sforzare,* to use force : *s-,* from Latin *ex-,* out of + *forzare,* to force, from Vulgar Latin *fortiāre* (unattested), from *fortia* (unattested), FORCE.] —**sfor·zan·do** *adj.*

S.G. solicitor general.

sgd. signed.

Sgt. sergeant.

Sgt. Maj. sergeant major.

sgraf·fi·to (sgrə-féetō, sgra-; *Italian* zgra-) *n., pl.* **-fiti** (-féetee). **1.** Decoration, as on a wall or piece of pottery, produced by scratching through a surface of plaster or glazing to reveal a different colour beneath. **2.** Something decorated in this way. [Italian, from the past participle of *sgraffire,* to scratch, from *sgraffio,* a scratch, from *sgraffiare,* to produce sgraffito : *s-,* from Latin *ex-,* out of + *graffiare,* to scratch (see **graffito**).]

's Gravenhage. See **Hague, The.**

sh (sh) *interj.* Used to urge silence.

sh. **1.** share. **2.** sheet. **3.** shilling.

Shaan·xi or **Shan·si** or **Shen·si** (shaán-shée, shón-, -sée). Province in north central China, lying to the south of the Huang He. It is crossed by the Wei river valley, one of the earliest cultural and political centres of northern China, and today a rich agricultural region and the most densely populated part of the province. Since the 1960s Shaanxi has developed industrially. Following the "long march", the province was the headquarters of the Chinese Communist Party (1935–49). Xi'an is the capital.

Sha·ba (shaábə). Formerly **Ka·tan·ga** (kə-táng-gə, ka-) Province of southeast Congo (Dem. Rep.). Its extensive mineral deposits, particularly copper, have made it the country's richest province. Shortly after Congo's independence (1960), Katanga seceded and was not reconstituted a province until 1967. Lubumbashi is the capital.

Sha·ban, shaa·ban (shə-baán, shaa-) *n.* The eighth month of the year on the Muslim calendar. [Arabic *sha'bān.*]

Shab·bat (shaa-baát, shə-, shaábəss) *n., pl.* **-batim** (-baátim, -báwsim). The Jewish Sabbath. [Hebrew *shabbāth,* SABBATH.]

shab·by (shábbi) *adj.* **-bier, -biest.** **1.** Threadbare; worn-out. **2.** Wearing worn-out clothes; seedy. **3.** Dilapidated; in poor repair. **4.** Despicable; mean. **5.** Unfair. [Obsolete *shab,* a scab, from Middle English *schab(be),* Old English *sceabb,* from Old Norse *skabbr* (unattested). See **scab.**] **—shab·bi·ly** *adv.* **—shab·bi·ness** *n.*

Shabuoth. Variant of **Shavuot.**

shack (shak) *n.* A small, crudely built cabin; a shanty. **—shack up.** *Informal.* To live together or with another in a sexual relationship while unmarried. Usually used with *with.* [Short for Mexican Spanish *jacal,* from Aztec *xacatti,* thatched cabin.]

shack·le (sháck'l) *n.* **1.** A metal fastening, usually one of a pair, for encircling and confining the ankle or wrist of a prisoner or captive; a fetter; a manacle. **2.** Any of several devices, such as a clevis, used to fasten or couple. **3.** Anything that confines or restrains.
~tr.v. **shackled, -ling, -les.** **1.** To put shackles on; fetter. **2.** To fasten or connect with a shackle. **3.** To restrict; confine; hamper. [Middle English *schackle,* Old English *sceacel,* fetter, from Germanic *skakulo-* (unattested).] **—shack·ler** *n.*

Shack·le·ton (sháck'ltən), **Sir Ernest Henry** (1874–1922). British Antarctic explorer. In 1907–9 he led an expedition which came within 161 kilometres (100 miles) of the South Pole. On a second expedition, Shackleton's ship *Endurance* became ice-bound and he made a gruelling journey to South Georgia to get help. He died on South Georgia, leading his third expedition (1921–22).

shad (shad) *n., pl.* **shads** or collectively **shad.** **1.** Any of several food fishes of the genus *Alosa,* related to the herrings but atypical in swimming to estuaries or up streams from marine waters to spawn. **2.** Broadly, any of various unrelated silvery fishes. [Middle English *shad,* Old English *sceadd*†.]

shad·ber·ry (shád-berri) *n., pl.* **-ries.** **1.** The fruit of the shadbush. **2.** The fruit of the service tree.

shad·bush (shád-bo͝osh) *n.* Any of various North American shrubs or trees of the genus *Amelanchier,* having white flowers and edible blue-black or purplish fruit. Also called "shadblow", "serviceberry", "Juneberry". [So called because the flowers bloom at about the same time shad appear in U.S. rivers.]

shad·dock (sháddək) *n.* **1.** A tropical tree, *Citrus maxima* (or *C. grandis*), closely related to the grapefruit. **2.** The edible yellow, pear-shaped fruit of this tree. Also *chiefly U.S.* "pomelo". [After Captain *Shaddock,* commander of an East India Company ship, who took the seed to Jamaica in 1696.]

shade (shayd) *n.* **1.** Light diminished in intensity as a result of the interception of the rays; comparative darkness. **2.** Cover or shelter from the sun provided by an object's interception of its rays. **3.** A place or area sheltered from the sun. **4.** Any of various devices, such as a lampshade, used to reduce or screen light or heat. **5.** *Plural. Slang.* Sunglasses. **6.** Relative obscurity or inconspicuousness. **7.** *Plural.* Dark shadows occurring at dusk: *shades of evening.* **8.** The part of a picture or photograph depicting darkness or shadow. **9.** The degree to which a colour is mixed with black or is decreasingly illuminated; gradation of darkness. **10.** A colour that resembles a standard colour but is slightly different in saturation, hue, or luminosity: *a shade of red.* **11.** A slight difference or variation; a nuance. **12.** A small amount; a trace; a jot. **13.** A disembodied spirit; a ghost. **—shades of.** Used humorously to suggest some association with or evocation of the person or thing specified.
~v. **shaded, shading, shades.** *—tr.* **1.** To screen from light or heat. **2.** To obscure or darken. **3. a.** To represent the effect of shade in (a picture). **b.** To produce gradations of light or colour in (a picture). **c.** To cover in (part of a picture) with fine pencil lines, brushstrokes, or the like. **4.** To change or vary by slight degrees: *shade the meaning.* *—intr.* To change gradually or imperceptibly, as from one state or colour into another. Often used with *off.*
~adj. Providing or intended to provide shade: *a shade tree.* [Middle English *schade,* Old English *sceadu, scead.*]

shad·ing (sháyding) *n.* **1.** Screening against light or heat. **2.** The lines or other marks used in a sketch, engraving, or painting to represent gradations of light or colour. **3.** Any small variation, gradation, or difference.

shad·ow (sháddō) *n.* **1.** An area that is not, or is only partially, irradiated or illuminated because of the interception of radiation by an opaque object between the area and the source of radiation. **2.** The rough image of the intervening object, especially the umbral image, that delimits the shaded area. **3.** An imperfect, insubstantial, or delusive imitation; a semblance. **4.** *Plural.* The darkness following sunset. **5.** Gloom or unhappiness or an influence that causes such feeling. **6.** A shaded area in a picture or photograph. **7.** A mirrored image or reflection. **8.** A phantom; a ghost. **9.** One who constantly follows another around, such as: **a.** A constant companion. **b.** A detective. **10.** A faint indication; a premonition. **11.** A vestige; a remnant. **12.** An insignificant portion or amount; a slight trace. **13.** Shelter; protection. **14.** An influence that dominates or overshadows: *grew up in his brother's shadow.*
~adj. Belonging to a shadow cabinet and acting as the counterpart in opposition of a particular member of the government.
~tr.v. **shadowed, -owing, -ows.** **1.** To cast a shadow upon; shade. **2.** To make gloomy or dark; to cloud. **3.** To represent vaguely, mysteriously, or prophetically. **4.** To follow after, especially in secret; trail. [Middle English *schadow,* Old English *sceaduwe,* oblique case of *sceadu,* SHADE.] **—shad·ow·er** *n.*

shad·ow·box (sháddō-boks) *intr.v.* **-boxed, -boxing, -boxes.** To spar with an imaginary opponent, as in training.

shadow cabinet *n.* The members of the main opposition party in Parliament who act as spokesmen for their party on the issues dealt with by their ministerial counterparts in government, and who are expected to hold positions in the cabinet when their party is returned to power.

shad·ow·graph (sháddō-graaf, -graf) *n.* An image produced by casting a shadow on a screen.

shadow play *n.* A play presented by casting shadows of puppets or actors on a screen.

shad·ow·y (sháddō-i) *adj.* **-ier, -iest.** **1.** Resembling a shadow; insubstantial; unreal. **2.** Full of shadows; dark; shady. **3.** Barely perceptible; indistinct; dim. —See Synonyms at **dark.** **—shad·ow·i·ness** *n.*

Sha·drach (sháy-drak, shá-). A Hebrew captive who miraculously escaped death in Nebuchadnezzar's fiery furnace. Daniel 3.

shad·y (sháydi) *adj.* **-ier, -iest.** **1.** Full of shade; shaded. **2.** Providing shade. **3. a.** Of dubious character or honesty. **b.** Legally or morally questionable. —See Synonyms at **dishonest, dark.** **—shad·i·ly** *adv.* **—shad·i·ness** *n.*

Shaf·fer (sháffər), **Peter (Levin)** (1926–). British playwright. His works include *Equus* (1973), the historical dramas *The Royal Hunt of the Sun* (1964) and *Amadeus* (1979), the comedy *Lettice and Lovage* (1987), and *Gift of the Gorgon* (1992).

shaft[1] (shaaft || shaft) *n.* **1.** The long, narrow stem or body of a spear or arrow. **2.** A spear, arrow, or the like. **3.** Something suggestive of an arrow in appearance or effect: *shafts of satire.* **4.** A ray or beam of light. **5.** The handle of any of various tools or implements. **6.** The rib of a feather. **7.** *Anatomy.* **a.** The midsection of a long bone; the diaphysis. **b.** The section of a hair projecting from the surface of the body. **c.** Any elongated cylindrical body part. **8.** The section of a column or pillar between the capital and base. **9.** One of two parallel poles between which an animal is harnessed. **10.** *Machinery.* A long, generally cylindrical bar, especially one that rotates and transmits power: *a drive shaft.* [Middle English *shaft,* Old English *sceaft,* from Germanic *skaftaz* (unattested).]

shaft[2] *n.* **1.** A long, narrow passage sunk into the earth; a tunnel. **2.** A vertical passage housing a lift. **3.** A duct or conduit for the passage of air, as for ventilation or heating.

Shaftes·bur·y (shaáfts-bri, -bəri || sháfts-, -berri), **Anthony Ashley Cooper, 1st Earl of** (1621–83). English politician, the father of the Whig party. Shaftesbury came over to the Parliamentarians in early 1644, during the English Civil War, and was appointed to official posts in 1648–49 by Cromwell's government. In 1654 he withdrew his support from Cromwell and took part in the restoration of Charles II in 1660. In 1667 he became one of the five ministers in the so-called **cabal** (after the initials of the five leaders) administration, rising to be Lord Chancellor as the Earl of Shaftesbury in 1672. Dismissed from office in the following year, he organised an opposition faction, which was the origin of the Whig party.

Shaftesbury, Anthony Ashley Cooper, 7th Earl of (1801–85). British politician. An M.P. from 1826, he pioneered social and industrial reform. He helped to introduce laws that banned sweeps from using climbing boys (1840), excluded women and children from the mines (1842), and established the 10-hour day for factory workers (1847).

shaft·ing (shaáft-ing || sháft-) *n.* **1.** A system of shafts, as in a mechanical device, for transmitting motion or power. **2.** Material from which shafts are made.

shag[1] (shag) *n.* **1.** A tangle or mass, especially of rough, matted hair. **2. a.** A coarse long nap, as on some woollen cloth. **b.** Cloth having such a nap. **3.** Coarse shredded tobacco.
~tr.v. **shagged, shagging, shags.** To make shaggy; roughen. [Middle English *shagge* (unattested), Old English *sceacga,* beard, from Germanic *skag-* (unattested).] **—shag** *adj.*

shag[2] *n.* A dance step of the 1930s consisting of a hop on each foot in alternation. [20th century : origin obscure.] **—shag** *intr.v.*

shag[3] *n.* A marine bird, of the genus *Phalacrocorax (P.aristotelis)* which also includes the cormorants. The mature bird is black and has a short crest and yellow beak. [Perhaps from its shaggy crest.]

shag[4] *tr.v.* **shagged, shagging, shags.** *Slang.* **1.** *Vulgar.* To have sexual intercourse with. **2.** To tire; exhaust. Usually used with *out.*

shag·bark (shág-baark) *n.* A North American hickory tree, *Carya ovata,* having shaggy bark, compound leaves, and edible nuts with a hard shell. Also called "shellbark".

shag·gy (shággi) *adj.* **-gier, -giest.** **1.** Having, covered with, or resembling long, rough hair or wool. **2.** Bushy and matted. **3.** Poorly groomed; unkempt. **—shag·gi·ly** *adv.* **—shag·gi·ness** *n.*

shaggy cap *n.* An edible ink cap fungus, *Coprinus comatus,* having a long white stalk and a greyish-white flaking cap.

shag·gy-dog story (shággi-dóg || -dáwg) *n.* A long, drawn-out anecdote depending for humour upon an absurd or anticlimactic punch line.

shaggy parasol *n.* A basidiomycete fungus, *Lepiota rhacodes,* having a broad, pale brown cap covered in brown scales.

sha·green (sha-greén, shə-) *n.* **1.** The rough hide of a shark or ray, covered with numerous bony denticles, and used as an abrasive and as leather. **2.** Leather with a granular surface, prepared from the skins of various animals. [From French *chagrin,* "rough hide". See **chagrin.**] **—sha·green** *adj.*

shag·pile (shágg-pīl) *n.* A long shaglike or soft pile on a carpet.

shah (shaa) *n.* The monarch of certain lands of the Middle East, especially, formerly, Iran. [Persian *shāh,* from Old Persian *khshāyathiya.*]

Shah Ja·han (jə-haán) (1592–1666). Mogul emperor of India (1628–58), who brought the Mogul Empire to its golden age. A noted patron of the arts, he was also a great builder and had the Taj Mahal erected (1638–48). He was deposed by his son, Aurangzeb.

shai·tan, shei·tan (shī-taán) *n.* **1.** *Often capital* **S.** *Islam.* Satan; the Devil. **2.** An evil spirit; a fiend. [Arabic *shaiṭān,* from Hebrew *śāṭān,* SATAN.]

Shak. Shakespeare.

Sha·ka (shaá-gə, -kə) (*c.* 1787–1828). Chief of the Zulu (1816–28) who made the Zulu state the strongest in southern Africa. An outstanding war leader, he built a disciplined, mobile, and highly successful army.

shake (shayk) *v.* **shook** (shŏŏk || shōōk), **shaken** (sháykən), **shaking, shakes.** *—tr.* **1.** To cause to move to and fro with short jerky movements. **2.** To cause to quiver or tremble; vibrate or rock: *A severe tremor shook the ground.* **3.** To cause to stagger or waver; upset; unsettle. **4.** To remove or dislodge by jerky movements: *shake the dust out.* **5.** To bring to a specified condition by or as if by jerky movements: *shook her out of her complacency.* **6.** To disturb or agitate; unnerve. Often used with *up.* **7.** To brandish or wave: *shake one's fist.* **8.** To clasp (hands or another's hand) in greeting or leave-taking or as a sign of agreement. **9.** To free oneself from; get rid of. Usually used with *off.* **10.** *Music.* To trill (a note). **11.** To rattle and mix (dice) before casting. **12.** To make unstable; weaken: *His convictions were shaken.* **13.** *Australian Slang.* To rob; steal. *—intr.* **1.** To move to and fro in short jerky movements. **2.** To tremble, as from cold or in anger. **3.** To totter or waver; become unsteady. **4. a.** *Music.* To trill. **b.** To change pitch rapidly or tremulously because of emotion. Used of the voice. **5.** To shake hands. *~n.* **1.** An act of shaking. **2.** A trembling or quivering movement. **3.** *Informal.* An earthquake. **4.** A fissure in rock. **5.** A crack in timber caused by wind or frost. **6.** *Music.* A trill. **7.** A drink in which the ingredients are mixed by shaking: *a milk shake.* **8.** *Informal.* An instant; a moment: *She'll be here in two shakes.* **—no great shakes.** *Informal.* Unexceptional; ordinary; mediocre. **—the shakes.** *Informal.* **1.** The chill accompanying intermittent fever. **2.** Uncontrollable trembling, especially as a symptom of alcoholism or metal poisoning. [Shake, shook, shaken; Middle English *schaken, schook, schaken,* Old English *sceacan, sceōc, sceacen,* from Germanic *skakan* (unattested).] **—shak·a·ble, shake·a·ble** *adj.*

Synonyms: *shake, tremble, quake, quiver, shiver, shudder.*

shake down *intr.v.* **1.** To put together hurriedly, or settle down on, a makeshift bed. **2.** To settle down or settle in comfortably. *—tr.v. U.S. Informal.* **1.** To extort money from. **2.** To make a thorough search of. **3.** To subject to a shakedown cruise.

shake·down (sháyk-down) *n.* **1.** A hastily made up resting place; a makeshift bed. **2.** *U.S. Informal.* An extortion of money by blackmail or other means. **3.** *U.S. Informal.* A thorough search of a place or person. **4.** *U.S. Informal.* A test run for appraising operating performance, as of a new ship or plane, followed by adjustments to improve efficiency or functioning. Also used adjectivally.

shak·er (sháykər) *n.* **1.** One that shakes. **2.** A container used for shaking something out: *a salt shaker.* **3.** A container used to mix or blend by shaking: *a cocktail shaker.*

Shaker *n.* A member of a millenarian religious sect originating in England in 1747, practising communal living and observing celibacy. [From the former custom of dancing with shaking movements during ceremonies.]

Shake·speare (sháyk-speer), **William** (1564–1616). English dramatist and poet, the greatest writer in English literature. He was born at Stratford-on-Avon, the son of a tradesman, was educated at the free grammar school, and in 1582 married Anne Hathaway. By 1592 he had established a reputation in London both as an actor and playwright. His first play, *Henry VI* (in three parts) dates from 1590–91, while his first major poem, *Venus and Adonis,* appeared in 1593 and was dedicated to his patron, the Earl of Southampton. Shakespeare's prolific dramatic output for the open-air Globe Theatre includes such historical plays as *Julius Caesar* and *Henry V* (1598–1600), and such comedies as *As You Like It* and *Twelfth Night* (1598–1600). His tragedies begin with *Romeo and Juliet* (1594–5) and include *Hamlet* (1600–01), *Othello* (1604–05), *King Lear* (1605), and *Macbeth* (1605–06). Shakespeare's later fantasy plays *The Winter's Tale* (*c.* 1610) and *The Tempest* (*c.* 1611) were written for an indoor theatre at Blackfriars. The first collected edition of his works, known as the First Folio, contained 36 plays and was published posthumously in 1623.

Shake·spear·e·an, Shake·spear·i·an (shayk-speér-i-ən) *adj.* Of, pertaining to, or like Shakespeare, his works, or his style. *~n.* A scholar of Shakespeare or his works.

Shakespearean sonnet *n.* The sonnet form used by Shakespeare, composed of three quatrains and a final couplet with the rhyme pattern *abab cdcd efef gg,* and retaining the break or pause in theme that falls between the octave and sestet in earlier sonnet forms. Also called "Elizabethan sonnet", "English sonnet".

shake up *tr.v. Informal.* To reorganise or rearrange drastically.

shake-up (sháyk-up) *n.* A thorough or drastic reorganisation, as in the personnel of a business or government.

shak·ing palsy (sháyking) *n.* **Parkinson's disease** *(see).*

shak·o (sháckō || shaá-kō, sháy-) *n., pl.* **-os** or **-oes.** A stiff, cylindrical military dress hat with a metal plate in front, a short visor, and a plume. [French *schako,* from Hungarian *csákó,* from *csákó (süveg),* pointed (cap), from *csák,* peak, from German *Zacken,* point, from Middle High German *zacke.*]

Shak·ta (shaák-tə, shúk-) *n.* Also **Sak·ta** (saák-, súk-). A member of a Hindu sect that worships Shakti. [Sanskrit *śākta,* from *śakti,* SHAKTI.] **—Shak·tism** *n.* **—Shak·tist** *n.*

Shak·ti (shaák-ti, shúk-). Also **Sak·ti** (saák-, súk-). *Hinduism.* **1.** The female principle, especially as personified by the wife of the god Shiva. **2.** The personification of nature and generative power. [Sanskrit *śakti,* from *śaknōti,* is strong.]

shak·y (sháyki) *adj.* **-ier, -iest. 1.** Trembling or quivering; tremulous; shaking. **2.** Unsteady or unsound; weak: *a shaky table.* **3.** Not to be depended upon; insecure. **—shak·i·ly** *adv.* **—shak·i·ness** *n.*

shale (shayl) *n.* A sedimentary rock produced from clay, which has a fine-grained structure in well-defined narrow strata 0.1. to 0.4 millimetre (0.004 to 0.016 inch) thick. [Probably from German *Schale,* from Old English *sc(e)alu.* See **scale.**]

shale oil *n.* A fuel oil obtained from oil shales.

shall (shal, *weak forms* sh'l, shə, sh) *v.* past **should** (shŏŏd, *weak forms* shəd, shd) or *archaic* **shouldst** (shŏŏdst) or **shouldest** (shŏŏdist) for second person singular, present **shall** or *archaic* **shalt** (shalt, *weak form* sh'lt) for second person singular. Used as an auxiliary followed by a simple infinitive or, in reply to a question or suggestion, with the infinitive understood. It can indicate: **1.** In the first person singular or plural, simple futurity: *I shall be twenty-eight tomorrow.* **2.** In the second and third persons: **a.** Determination or promise: *Your services shall be rewarded.* **b.** Inevitability: *That day shall come.* **c.** Command: *Thou shalt not kill.* **d.** Compulsion, with the force of *must,* in statutes, deeds, and other legal documents: *The penalty shall not exceed two years in prison.* **3.** *Formal.* In all persons, indefinite futurity, in conditional clauses and in clauses expressing doubt, anxiety, or desire: *If you shall ever change your opinion, come to me again.* [Shall, shalt, should; Middle English *schal, schalt, scholde,* Old English *sceal, scealt, sceolde.*]

Usage: Traditional grammars and manuals of usage have insisted on a systematic distinction between the use of *shall* and *will* since the 18th century. It is recommended that *shall* be used in the first person to express simple futurity *(I shall visit you next week),* and in the second and third persons to express such meanings as obligation or determination *(You shall go to the ball). Will,* by contrast, is supposed to be used to express simple futurity in the second and third persons *(He will see you next week),* and such meanings as obligation or determination in the first person. The two verbs are thus thought to complement each other nicely, and many people try to speak and write according to these rules, especially in British English. However, these distinctions are not closely observed in speech, and often not in writing, and it is questionable whether the language ever maintained such a systematic distinction. In modern English speech, contracted forms are in such common use that it is impossible to say which verb is involved *(I'll, You'll,* etc.); extra emphasis is hence largely a matter of extra stress (*I* SHALL *go* and *I* WILL *go* seem to be semantically indistinguishable). American English has largely dropped the distinction, and uses *will* in all except the most formal styles; similarly, *won't* is standard usage for all persons, *shan't* being extremely rare. The distinction is more often maintained in British English, especially in formal styles. In England it is in standard use in most first-person question forms *(Shall I answer? Shall we go? I'll answer, shall I?),* though here American English prefers *should. Shall* is also avoided in Scottish and Irish English, *will* being used instead *(Will I drop you here or at your house?).* In standard English, *will* is used rather than *shall* in first-person question forms if a prediction or specific information about the future is required *(Will I look awful if I cut my hair?).*

shal·loon (sha-lŏŏn) *n.* A lightweight wool or worsted twill fabric, used chiefly for coat linings. [French *chalon,* after *Châlons*-sur-Marne, France.]

shal·lop (shál-əp) *n.* An open boat fitted with oars, sails, or both. [French *chaloupe,* from Dutch *sloep,* SLOOP.]

shal·lot (shə-lót) *n.* **1.** A plant, *Allium ascalonicum,* closely related to the onion, cultivated for its edible bulb that divides into smaller sections. Also called "scallion". **2.** The mildly flavoured bulb of this plant, used in cookery. [Obsolete *eschalot,* from obsolete French *eschalotte,* from Old French *eschaloigne,* from Vulgar Latin *iscalōnia* (unattested), from Latin *Ascalōnia (caepa),* (onion) of Ascalon. See **scallion.**]

shal·low (shál-ō) *adj.* **-lower, -lowest. 1. a.** Measuring little from bottom to top or surface; not deep. **b.** Gently sloping or curved; not steep. **2.** Lacking depth, as in intellect, character, or significance: *shallow criticism.* —See Synonyms at **superficial.** *~n. Usually plural.* A shallow part of a body of water; a shoal. *~v.* **shallowed, -lowing, -lows.** *—tr.* To make shallow. *—intr.* To become shallow. [Middle English *schalowe,* akin to Old English *sceald,* shallows. See **shoal.**] **—shal·low·ly** *adv.* **—shal·low·ness** *n.*

shal·low-fry (shál-ō-frí) *tr.v.* **-fried, -frying, -fries.** To cook in a small amount of fat or oil, so that only part of the food being fried is in contact with the fat or oil at one time.

sha·lom (shə-lóm, sha- ‖ -lóm) *interj. Hebrew.* Used as a greeting or farewell. [Hebrew "peace".]

shalom a·lei·chem (ə-láy-kəm, a-, -khəm) *interj. Hebrew.* Used as a greeting or farewell. [Hebrew, "peace be with you".]

shalt. *Archaic.* Second person singular present tense of **shall.** Used with *thou.*

sham (sham) *n.* **1.** Something false or empty purporting to be genuine; a spurious imitation. **2.** The quality of deceitfulness; empty pretence. **3.** A person who assumes a false character; an impostor. **4.** *Archaic.* A decorative cover made to simulate an article of household linen and used over or in place of it: *a pillow sham.* —*adj.* Not genuine; fake, pretended, or counterfeit. —*v.* **shammed, shamming, shams.** —*tr.* To simulate; feign. —*intr.* To assume a false appearance or character; dissemble. [Perhaps northern dialect of SHAME.] —**sham·mer** *n.*

sham·an (shámmən ‖ sháy-mən, sháa-) *n.* **1.** A priest of shamanism. **2.** A medicine man among certain North American Indians. [German *Schamane,* from Russian *shaman,* from Tungus *šaman,* from Tocharian *ṣamāne,* from Prakrit *samaṇa,* from Sanskrit *śramaṇāṣt,* "ascetic".]

sham·an·ism (shámmə-niz'm ‖ sháymə-, sháamə-) *n.* **1.** The religious practices of certain peoples of northern Asia who believe that good and evil spirits pervade the world and can be summoned or heard through inspired priests acting as mediums. **2.** Any similar form of spiritualism, such as that practised among certain North American Indian tribes. —**sha·man·ist** *n.* —**sha·man·is·tic** (-nístik) *adj.*

Sha·mash (sháamash). The sun-god of Assyro-Babylonian religion, worshipped as the author of justice and compassion. [Akkadian, "sun", akin to Hebrew *shémesh.*]

sham·a·teur (shámmə-tər, -ter, -tewr, -chər ‖ -toor) *n.* A sports player who professes to be, and plays as, an amateur but who receives large financial rewards from participating in the sport. [SHAM + (AM)ATEUR.]

sham·ble (shámb'l) *intr.v.* **-bled, -bling, -bles.** To walk in an awkward, lazy, or unsteady manner, shuffling the feet. —*n.* A shambling walk; a shuffling gait. [From earlier *shamble,* ungainly, perhaps from *shamble legs,* probably referring to legs which were ungainly like those of a meat table. See **shambles.**]

sham·bles (shámb'lz) *n. Used with a singular verb.* **1.** A scene or condition of complete disorder or ruin: *left the room in a shambles.* **2.** A place or scene of bloodshed or carnage. **3.** *Archaic.* A meat market or slaughterhouse. **4.** *British. Archaic.* A row of covered market tables or stalls. [From plural of earlier *shamble,* table for display or sale of meat, Middle English *shamel,* Old English *sc(e)amul,* table, from West Germanic *skamel* (unattested), from Latin *scamellum,* diminutive of *scamnum,* bench.]

sham·bo·lic (shamm-bóllik) *adj.* Hopelessly disorganised or inept.

shame (shaym) *n.* **1.** A painful emotion caused by a strong sense of guilt, embarrassment, unworthiness, or disgrace. **2.** Capacity for such a feeling: *Have you no shame?* **3.** A person or thing that brings dishonour, disgrace, or condemnation. **4.** A condition of disgrace or dishonour; ignominy. **5.** A great disappointment or an occasion for pity or regret. —See Synonyms at **disgrace.** —**put to shame. 1.** To fill with shame; disgrace. **2.** To outdo thoroughly; surpass. —*tr.v.* **shamed, shaming, shames. 1.** To cause to feel shame. **2.** To bring dishonour or disgrace upon. **3.** To force by making ashamed. Used with *into* or *out of: He was shamed into an apology.* —*interj.* **1.** Used to express strong disapproval. **2.** *South African.* Used to express sympathy or tender admiration. [Middle English *s(c)hame,* Old English *sc(e)amu,* from Germanic *skamô.*]

shame·faced (sháym-fayst, -fáyst) *adj.* **1.** Indicative of shame; ashamed: *a shamefaced explanation.* **2.** Extremely modest or shy; bashful. [Variant (influenced by FACE) of earlier *shamefast,* from Middle English *sham(e)fast,* Old English *sceamfæst* = *sceamu,* SHAME + *fæst,* FAST (firm), as if held firm by shame.] —**shame·fac·ed·ly** (*also* -fáyssid-li) *adv.* —**shame·fac·ed·ness** *n.*

shame·ful (sháymf'l) *adj.* **1.** Bringing or deserving shame; disgraceful; indecent. **2.** *Archaic.* Full of shame; shamefaced; ashamed. —**shame·ful·ly** *adv.* —**shame·ful·ness** *n.*

shame·less (sháym-ləss, -liss) *adj.* **1.** Not subject to the restraint of shame; impudent or immodest; brazen. **2.** Done without shame: *a shameless lie.* —**shame·less·ly** *adv.* —**shame·less·ness** *n.*

Synonyms: shameless, brazen, barefaced, brash, bold, impudent, unblushing, forward.

sham·mes (sháaməss) *n., pl.* **shammosim** (shaa-máw-sim). *Judaism.* **1.** A sexton in a synagogue. Also called "beadle". **2.** The candle used to light the other eight candles of the Chanukah Menorah. [Yiddish *shames,* from Hebrew *shammāsh,* from Aramaic *shəmmāsh,* to serve.]

shammy. Variant of **chamois.**

sham·poo (sham-póō, shán-) *n., pl.* **-poos. 1.** Any of various liquid or cream preparations of soap or detergent used to wash the hair and scalp. **2.** Any of various cleaning agents, as for rugs, upholstery, or cars. **3.** An act of washing or cleaning with shampoo. —*v.* **shampooed, -pooing, -poos.** —*tr.* To wash or clean with shampoo. —*intr.* To wash the hair with shampoo. [From Hindi *chāmpo,* from *chāmpnā,* massage, press, mark.]

sham·rock (shám-rok) *n.* Any of several plants, such as a trefoil, medick, clover, or wood sorrel, having compound leaves with three small leaflets, considered the national emblem of Ireland. [From Irish *seamrog,* diminutive of *seamar,* clover, from Old Irish *semart.*]

sha·mus (sháa-məss, sháy-) *n. U.S. Slang.* A policeman or private detective. [Perhaps variant of SHAMMES.]

Shan (shaan ‖ shan) *n.* **1.** A member of a group of Mongoloid tribes living in Burma, Thailand, and southern China. **2.** The northern Tai language spoken by these tribes. —**Shan** *adj.*

Shan·dong *or* **Shan·tung** *or* **Shan-tung** (shán-dóng ‖ -túng). Densely populated maritime province of northeast China. It is crossed by the lower Huang-He and the Grand Canal, and has mountains in the east, and centre, where the sacred Tai Shan mountains reach 1 500 metres (5,000 feet). The lowlands are highly fertile, but with low, unreliable rainfall, famines used to occur. Settled by Chinese farmers since earliest times, Shandong became a province under the Ming dynasty.

shan·dy (shándi) *n.* A drink of beer and lemonade or ginger beer. Also *chiefly U.S.* "shandygaff". [19th century : origin obscure.]

Shang (shang) *n.* A Chinese dynasty (*c.*1525–*c.*1027 B.C.). Its capital was Yin, present-day **Anyang** (*see*).

shang·hai (sháng-hí) *tr.v.* **-haied, -haiing, -hais.** *Informal.* **1.** To kidnap (a man) for compulsory service aboard a ship, especially after rendering him insensible. **2.** To trick or coerce (a person) into some action. [After SHANGHAI, from the former custom of kidnapping sailors to man ships going to that city.]

Shang·hai *or* **Shang-hai** (sháng-hí). Largest city in China, lying within, but independent of, the eastern province of Jiangsu, on the river Huangpu at its confluence with the Chang Jiang (Yangtze) estuary. One of the world's leading seaports, it is also the most important industrial centre in China. Its commercial and industrial importance dates from 1842, when the Treaty of Nanking opened the port to western trade. In the 19th century much of the city was ceded to Britain (1843) and the United States (1862), the two cessions being merged into the International Settlement in 1863. The French maintained a separate cession (1849). Great Britain and the United States gave up their claims during World War II and France withdrew in 1946. Shanghai is surpassed only by Beijing as a leading educational and cultural centre of China.

Shan·gri-la (sháng-gri-láa) *n.* An imaginary, remote paradise on earth; utopia. [After *Shangri-La,* the imaginary land in *Lost Horizon* (1933) by James Hilton (1900–54).]

shank (shangk) *n.* **1.** *Anatomy.* The part of the human leg between the knee and ankle or the corresponding part in other vertebrates. **2.** The whole leg of a human being. **3.** A cut of meat from the leg of an animal. **4.** The long, narrow part of a nail or pin. **5.** A stem, stalk, or similar part. **6.** The stem of an anchor. **7.** The long shaft of a fishhook. **8.** That part of a tobacco pipe between the bowl and stem. **9.** The shaft of a key. **10.** The narrower part of a spoon's handle. **11. a.** The narrow part of a shoe's sole under the instep. **b.** A piece of metal or other material used to reinforce or shape this part. **12.** The ring or other projection on the back of some buttons by which they are sewn to the cloth. **13. a.** The part of a drill or other tool that connects the functioning head to the handle. **b.** A tang (*see*). **14.** Any of various long-legged wading birds of the genus *Tringa;* especially, the redshank and greenshank. [Middle English *shanke,* Old English *sc(e)anca.*]

Shan·kar (sháng-kər, -kaar). **Ravi** (1920–). Indian sitar player who has stimulated appreciation of Indian classical music throughout the Western world, and founded the National Orchestra of India.

shank·piece (shángk-peess) *n.* An arch support inserted into the shank of a shoe.

shanks's pony (shangks, shángksiz). *n. Informal.* One's own legs as a means of transport. Also *U.S.* "shank's mare".

Shan·non (shánnən). Chief river of the Republic of Ireland, and the longest river in the British Isles. About 390 kilometres (240 miles) long, it rises in northwest Cavan, and flows south to Limerick, where it broadens into a long, wide estuary, which empties into the Atlantic. Shannon International Airport lies on the north bank of the estuary, some 24 kilometres (15 miles) west of Limerick.

shan·ny (shánni) *n., pl.* **-nies.** A goby-like marine fish, the common blenny, *Blennius pholis.* See **blenny.** [19th century : origin obscure.]

Shansi. See **Shanxi.**

shan't (shaant ‖ shant). Contraction of *shall not.*

shan·tung (shán-túng) *n.* **1.** A heavy silk fabric with a rough, nubby surface, made of spun wild silk. **2.** An imitation of this fabric, made of rayon or cotton. [Manufactured in SHANDONG.]

Shantung. See **Shandong.**

shan·ty[1] (shánti) *n., pl.* **-ties. 1.** A roughly built or ramshackle cabin; a shack. **2.** *Australian.* A rough or shabby, usually unlicensed, hotel. [19th century (originally American, often used of houses of Irish immigrants) : perhaps from Irish *sean tig,* "old house" : *sean,* old + *tig,* house, from Old Irish *tech.*]

shan·ty[2] (shánti) *n., pl.* **-ties.** Also **chan·ty** (chaánti ‖ chánti), *chiefly U.S.* **chan·tey** (chánti), **chan·tey** (shántí) *pl.* **-teys.** A song sung, especially formerly, by sailors to the rhythm of their work movements. [Probably from French *chantez,* imperative plural of *chanter,* to sing.]

shan·ty·town (shánti-town) *n.* A town or district of a town consisting of ramshackle huts or shanties.

Shan·xi *or* **Shansi·xi** *or* **Shan·si** (shán-sée). Strategic province of northeast China. Much of it is a high plateau cut by the Fen He, a tributary of the Huang He. With fertile loess soils, Shansi was part of the Chinese "heartland". Taiyuan is the capital.

shape (shayp) *n.* **1.** The outline or characteristic surface configuration of a thing; a contour; a form. **2.** The contour of a person's body; a figure. **3.** Developed, definite, or proper form. **4.** Any form or condition in which something may exist or appear; an embodiment. **5.** Assumed or false appearance; guise. **6.** An imaginary or ghostly form; a phantom. **7. a.** Something used to give or determine form, such as a mould or pattern. **b.** Something formed by a pattern or set in a mould. **8.** *Informal.* Condition as regards health, efficiency, state of repair, or the like: *in good shape.* **—lick into shape.** To put right or in a better state or condition. **—See Synonyms at form.**
~*v.* **shaped, shaped** or *archaic* **shapen** (sháypən), **shaping, shapes.** *—tr.* **1.** To give a particular form to. **2.** To cause to conform to a particular form or pattern; modify; adapt to fit. **3.** To plan and supervise. *—intr.* **1.** *Informal.* To take a definite form; develop. Often used with *into* or *up.* **2.** *Informal.* To proceed or develop in a satisfactory or desirable manner. Used with *up.* [Middle English *schap, shape,* Old English *(ge)sceap.*]
SHAPE (shayp). Supreme Headquarters Allied Powers, Europe.
shaped (shaypt) *adj.* **1.** Formed by shaping: *shaped clay.* **2.** Having the shape of or possessing a similar shape to something specified. Often used in combination: *egg-shaped.*
shape·less (sháyp-ləss) *adj.* **1.** Having no distinct shape. **2.** Lacking symmetrical or attractive form; not shapely. **—shape·less·ly** *adv.* **—shape·less·ness** *n.*
shape·ly (sháypli) *adj.* **-lier, -liest.** Having a pleasing or attractive shape; well-proportioned. **—shape·li·ness** *n.*
shard (shard) *n.* Also **sherd** (sherd). **1.** A piece of broken pottery; a potsherd *(see).* **2.** A fragment of a brittle substance, as of glass or metal. **3.** *Zoology.* A tough sheath; especially, the outer wing covering of a beetle. [Middle English *sherd,* Old English *sceard.*]
share¹ (shair) *n.* **1.** A part or portion belonging to, distributed to, contributed by, or owed by a person or group. **2.** An equitable, reasonable, or full amount. **3.** *Abbr.* **sh., shr.** Any of the equal parts into which the capital stock of a company is divided. **—go shares.** To be involved equally or jointly, as in a business venture.
~*v.* **shared, sharing, shares.** *—tr.* **1.** To divide and parcel out in shares; apportion. **2.** To participate in, use, or experience in common with others. **3.** To communicate in a caring and heartfelt way: *I'd like to share that this weekend has meant a lot to me. —intr.* To have or take a part or share. **—share and share alike.** To share equally; have equal shares. [Middle English *share,* division, share, Old English *scearu,* division or fork of the body, tonsure.] **—shar·er** *n.*
Synonyms: share, participate, partake.
share² *n.* A ploughshare. [Middle English *shaar,* Old English *scēar.*]
share certificate *n.* A legal document, issued to a shareholder by a company, declaring ownership of shares and specifying their class, quality, and serial numbers.
share·crop·per (sháir-kroppər) *n.* A tenant farmer, especially in the United States, who gives a share of his crop to the landlord in lieu of rent. **—share·crop** *v.*
share·hold·er (sháir-hōldər) *n.* A person or institution that owns or holds a share or shares in a company.
share out *tr.v.* To distribute; give out in shares. **—share·out** (sháir-owt) *n.*
share-push·er (sháir-pŏŏshər) *n.* A broker who deals dishonestly in worthless stocks and shares. Also called "share-hawker".
sharif. Variant of **sherif.**
shark¹ (shark) *n.* Any of numerous chiefly marine, sometimes ferocious, fishes of the order Pleurotremata, having a cartilaginous skeleton and tough skin covered with small, toothlike scales. [16th century : origin obscure.]
shark² *n.* **1.** A ruthless, greedy, or dishonest person; a swindler. **2.** *U.S. Slang.* A person with unusually great skill in some field of activity. [Perhaps from SHARK (fish).]
shark·skin (shárk-skin) *n.* **1.** A shark's skin *.* **2.** Leather made from a shark's skin. **3.** A rayon and acetate fabric having a smooth, somewhat shiny surface.
shark sucker *n.* A remora *(see).*
sharp (sharp) *adj.* **sharper, sharpest. 1.** Having a thin, keen edge or a fine, acute point; suitable for or capable of cutting or piercing: *a sharp knife.* **2.** Having an acute edge or point; not rounded or blunt; peaked: *a sharp nose.* **3.** Abrupt or acute; not gradual; sudden. **4.** Clear or marked; distinct. **5.** Shrewd; astute. **6.** Artful; underhand. **7.** Vigilant; alert. **8.** Brisk; vigorous. **9. a.** Harsh; biting; acrimonious. **b.** Stinging; bitter; pungent: *a sharp taste.* **c.** Bitterly cold. **10.** Fierce or impetuous; violent. **11. a.** Intense; severe. **b.** Painful. **12.** Sudden and shrill. **13.** Composed of hard, angular particles: *sharp sand.* **14.** *Music.* **a.** Raised in pitch by a semitone. **b.** Above the proper pitch. **c.** Having the key signature in sharps. Compare **flat. 15.** *Phonetics.* Voiceless. Said of a consonant. **16.** Attractively stylish; snappy: *a sharp dresser.*
~*adv.* **1.** In a sharp manner. **2.** Punctually; exactly. **3.** *Music.* Above the true or proper pitch.
~*n.* **1. a.** A musical note raised one semitone above its normal pitch. **b.** A sign (#) indicating this. Compare **flat. 2.** A slender sewing needle with a very fine point. **3.** *Informal.* A sharper.
~*v.* **sharped, sharping, sharps.** *U.S. Music. —tr.* To raise by a semitone. *—intr.* To sound above the proper pitch. [Middle English *s(c)harp,* Old English *scearp.*] **—sharp·ly** *adv.* **—sharp·ness** *n.*
Synonyms: sharp, keen, acute.
Sharp (sharp), **Cecil (James)** (1859–1924). British musician and

collector of folk music. He founded the English Folk Dance and Song Society (1911) and is chiefly remembered for his collections and arrangements of English folk songs and dances.
sharp·en (shárpən) *v.* **-ened, -ening, -ens.** *—tr.* To make sharp or sharper. *—intr.* To become sharp or sharper. **—sharp·en·er** *n.*
sharp end *n.* *Informal.* The point of direct action, confrontation, or decision-making.
sharp·er (shárpər) *n.* One who deals dishonestly with others; especially, a gambler who cheats.
sharp-eyed (shárp-īd) *adj.* **1.** Having keen eyesight. **2.** Keenly perceptive or observant; alert.
sharp-shoot·er (shárp-shōōtər) *n.* An expert marksman.
sharp-tongued (shárp-túngd ‖ -tóngd) *adj.* Harsh, critical, or sarcastic.
shash·lik, shash·lick (shásh-lik, shaásh-, -lík) *n.* A kind of kebab of Russian origin. [Russian *shashlyk,* of Turkic origin.]
Shas·ta daisy (shásta) *n.* A cultivated variety of *Chrysanthemum* (or *Leucanthemum*) *maximum,* of the Pyrenees, having large, white, daisy-like flowers. [After Mt. *Shasta,* California; named by Luther Burbank, who lived in California.]
Shas·tri (sháss-tri, shaáss-), **Shri Lal Bahadur** (1904–66). Indian statesman. He succeeded Nehru as prime minister (1964–66), and his major achievement was to negotiate, with Ayub Khan, a cease-fire in the war between India and Pakistan.
shat. *Vulgar.* Past tense and past participle of **shit.**
Shatt al Ar·ab (shát al árrəb). Tidal river flowing for about 195 kilometres (121 miles) into the northern end of the Gulf, and formed by the confluence of the rivers Tigris and Euphrates. It is navigable as far up as Basra, the chief port of Iraq. Across from Basra are the Iranian ports of Khorramshahr and Abadan. Control of the river has been in dispute between Iran and Iraq since 1935, when an international commission awarded it to Iraq.
shat·ter (sháttər) *v.* **-tered, -tering, -ters.** *—tr.* **1.** To cause to break or burst suddenly into pieces, as with a violent blow. **2.** To damage seriously; disable; ruin. **3.** To disturb or severely upset. **4.** *Informal.* To tire completely; exhaust. *—intr.* **1.** To break into pieces; smash or burst. **—See Synonyms at break.**
~*n.* *Usually plural. Rare.* A splintered or fragmented condition. [Middle English *schateren,* akin to SKATTER.]
shat·ter·proof (sháttər-prōōf ‖ -prŏŏf) *adj.* **1.** Designed to resist shattering. **2.** Designed to break into small, round granules rather than sharp, jagged pieces.
shave (shayv) *v.* **shaved, shaved** or **shaven** (shayv'n), **shaving, shaves.** *—tr.* **1.** To remove the beard or other body hair from. **2.** To cut (the beard, for example) at the surface of the skin with a razor. Often used with *off.* **3.** To crop, trim, or mow closely. **4.** To remove thin slices from. **5.** To cut into thin slices; shred. **6.** To come close to or graze in passing. **7.** *Informal.* To take off or away. *—intr.* To remove one's own beard or hair with a razor.
~*n.* **1.** The act, process, or result of shaving. **2.** A thin slice or scraping; a shaving. **3.** Any of various tools used for shaving. [Middle English *shaven,* to scrape, shave, Old English *sceafan.*]
shav·er (sháyvər) *n.* **1. a.** A person who shaves. **b.** An electric or mechanical device used to shave, especially an electric razor. **2.** *Informal.* A young person, especially a boy.
Sha·vi·an (sháyvi-ən) *adj.* Of or characteristic of George Bernard Shaw or his works: *Shavian wit.*
~*n.* An admirer or disciple of George Bernard Shaw. [From *Shavius,* pseudo-Latin form of the name *Shaw.*]
shav·ing (sháyving) *n.* A thin slice; a sliver: *wood shavings.*
~*adj.* Used in or for shaving the face: *a shaving mirror.*
Sha·vu·ot, Sha·bu·oth (shə-vōō-əss, -ot,-oth) *n.* A Jewish holiday commemorating the revelation of the Law on Mount Sinai and the celebration of the wheat festival in ancient times, observed on the sixth and seventh of Sivan. Also called "Feast of Weeks". [Hebrew *shābhū'ōth,* from *shābhūa',* week.]
Shaw (shaw), **Artie,** born Arthur Arshawsky (1910–). U.S. jazz clarinettist, composer, and band leader, who headed various bands (1935–55, 1980s) organised around his clarinet virtuosity.
Shaw, George Bernard (1856–1950). Irish dramatist and writer. He established a reputation in London as a controversial music and theatre critic and an idiosyncratic spokesman for socialism. Shaw was a founder member of the Fabian Society (1884) and an early enthusiast of Wagner and Ibsen. He won further recognition through his many plays, often satirical in theme, which include *Man and Superman* (1905), *Pygmalion* (1912), and *St. Joan* (1924). His prolific writings on social, political, and religious issues include *The Intelligent Woman's Guide to Socialism and Capitalism* (1928). He was awarded the Nobel prize for literature in 1925.
shawl (shawl) *n.* A square or oblong piece of cloth, knitted fabric, or the like worn especially by women as a covering for the head, neck, and shoulders.
~*tr.v.* **shawled, shawling, shawls.** To cover with a shawl. [Earlier *shal, shaul,* from Urdu, from Persian *shāl†.*]
shawm (shawm) *n.* Any of various early double-reed wind instruments, forerunners of the modern oboe. [Middle English *schallemele, schalme,* from Old French *chalemel,* from Vulgar Latin *calamellus* (unattested), diminutive of Latin *calamus,* reed, from Greek *kalamos.*]
Shaw·nee (shaw-née) *n., pl.* **Shawnee** or **-nees. 1.** A member of an Algonquian-speaking North American Indian people, formerly living in the Tennessee Valley and adjacent areas, now surviving in Oklahoma. **2.** The language of this people.

Shaw·wal (shə-waal) *n.* The tenth month of the year in the Muslim calendar. [Arabic *Shawwāl.*]

she (shee, *weak form* shi) *pron.* The third person singular pronoun in the nominative case, feminine gender. **1.** Used to represent the female person, animal, or other being last mentioned or implied. **2.** Used traditionally of certain objects and institutions such as ships, cars, and nations. **3.** *Australian.* Applied to the circumstances or events in question; it: *She'll be right!*
~*n.* A female animal or person. Often used in combination: *a she-cat.* [Middle English *s(c)ho, s(c)he,* Old English *sēo,* she (Old English *hēo,* she, remained in Middle English dialects but only appears in Modern English HER). See Usage note at **me.**]

s/he. She or he.

she·a (shee-ə, sheer, shee) *n.* The **shea tree** (*see*).

shea butter *n.* A whitish or yellowish fat obtained from the nut of the **shea tree** (*see*), used as food and for making soap and candles.

shead·ing (shee-ding) *n.* Any of the six administrative divisions of the Isle of Man.

sheaf (sheef) *n., pl.* **sheaves** (sheevz). **1.** A bundle of cut stalks of grain or similar plants, usually laid lengthways, bound with straw or twine. **2.** Any gathering or collection of articles, especially papers, held or bound together. **3.** An archer's quiver of arrows.
~*tr.v.* **sheafed, sheafing, sheafs.** To bind into a sheaf. [Middle English *sheef, shefe,* Old English *scēaf.*]

shear (sheer) *v.* **sheared** or *archaic* **shore** (shor), **shorn** (shorn), or **sheared, shearing, shears.** —*tr.* **1.** To remove (fleece, hair, or the like) by cutting or clipping with a sharp instrument. **2.** To remove the hair or fleece from. **3.** To cut with or as if with shears. **4.** To strip, divest, or deprive of something. **5.** To cause to break or fracture, especially as a result of shearing strain. —*intr.* **1.** To use shears or a similar cutting tool. **2.** To move or proceed by or as if by cutting. Used with *through.* **3.** *Physics.* To become deformed by forces tending to produce a shearing strain. **4.** To break or fracture, especially as a result of shearing strain.
~*n.* **1.** The act, process, or result of shearing. **2.** Something cut off by shearing. **3.** A shearing. Used to indicate a sheep's age: *a two-shear ram.* **4.** *Physics.* **a.** An applied force or system of forces that tends to produce a shearing strain. Also called "shear stress", "shearing stress". **b.** Shearing strain. **5.** Any device for cutting material by means of a knife blade. [Shear, shore, shorn; Middle English *sc(h)eren, share, shorn,* Old English *sceran, scǣron* (third person plural), *scoren.*] —**shear·er** *n.*

shear·ing strain (sheering) *n.* A condition in or deformation of an elastic body caused by forces that tend to produce an opposite but parallel sliding motion of the body's planes.

shear legs *n.* Also **sheer·legs** (sheer-legz). An apparatus used to lift heavy weights, consisting of two or more spars joined at the top and spread at the base, the tackle being suspended from the top. Also called "shears", "sheers".

shear·ling (sheerling) *n.* **1.** A year-old sheep that has been shorn once. **2.** The skin of such a sheep, or of any newly shorn sheep, tanned and with the wool on. [Middle English *scherling : scheren,* to SHEAR + -LING.]

shear modulus *n.* A **rigidity modulus** (*see*).

shear pin *n.* A replaceable pin placed in a machine in such a position that it will shear and arrest the movement of the machine if the stress exceeds a predetermined value.

shears (sheerz) *pl.n.* **1.** Large-sized scissors. **2.** Any of various other implements or machines that cut with scissor-like action. **3.** *Used with a singular verb.* A lifting crane, a shear legs. [Middle English *s(c)here* (singular), scissors, Old English *scēara* (plural).]

shear·wa·ter (sheer-wawtər || *U.S. also* -wottər) *n.* Any of various oceanic birds of the family Procellariidae, especially of the genus *Puffinus,* having long wings and a hooked bill. See **Manx shearwater.** [From its habit of skimming close to the water.]

sheat·fish (sheet-fish) *n., pl.* **-fishes** or collectively **sheatfish.** A large freshwater catfish, *Silurus glanis,* of Eurasia. [Variant of obsolete *sheath-fish* : SHEATH (probably from its shell-like covering or its sheathlike shape) + FISH.]

sheath (sheeth) *n., pl.* **sheaths** (sheethz || sheeths). **1.** A case for the blade of a knife, sword, or similar instrument. **2.** Any of various coverings applied like or resembling a sheath. **3.** *Biology.* An enveloping structure or part, such as the tubular base of a leaf surrounding a stem. **4.** A close-fitting dress, usually having a straight skirt and no belt. **5.** A protective covering for an electric cable. **6.** A **condom** (*see*). [Middle English *s(c)hethe,* Old English *scēath, scǣth.*]

sheath·bill (sheeth-bil) *n.* Either of two shore birds, *Chionia alba* or *C. minor,* of Antarctic regions, having white plumage and a horny covering on the base of the bill.

sheathe (sheeth) *tr.v.* **sheathed, sheathing, sheathes. 1.** To insert into or provide with a sheath. **2.** To retract into a sheath or sheaths: *sheathed its claws.* **3.** To encase in sheathing. —**sheath·er** *n.*

sheath·ing (sheething) *n.* **1.** A layer of boards or of other wood or fibre materials applied to the outer studs, joists, and rafters of a building to strengthen the structure and serve as a base for an exterior weatherproof cladding. **2.** An exterior covering, usually metal, on the underwater part of a ship's hull, to protect against marine growths. **3.** The action of providing sheathing for something.

sheath knife *n.* A knife having a fixed blade and fitting into a sheath.

shea tree *n.* An African tree, *Butyrospermum parkii,* having fruit containing oily seeds that yield an edible fat called shea butter. Also called "shea". [From Bambara *si.*]

sheave¹ (sheev) *tr.v.* **sheaved, sheaving, sheaves.** To bind into a sheaf or sheaves; gather; collect.

sheave² *n.* A wheel with a grooved rim, especially one used as a pulley. [Middle English *shive, sheve,* Old English *scife* (unattested).]

sheaves (sheevz) **1.** Plural of **sheaf.** **2.** Plural of **sheave.**

She·ba (sheebə). *Arabic* **Sa·ba** (saabaa). Biblical name for an ancient region of southern Arabia in present-day Yemen. On the trade route between India and Africa, it became a region of great wealth at its height in the sixth and fifth centuries B.C.

Sheba, Queen of. A queen who came from southern Arabia to test the wisdom of King Solomon. I Kings 10:1.

she·bang (shi-báng, shə-) *n. Chiefly U.S. Informal.* A situation, organisation, contrivance, or set of facts or things. Used chiefly in the phrase *the whole shebang.* [19th century : origin obscure.]

Shebat. Variant of **Shevat.**

she·been (shi-béen) *n. Chiefly Irish & South African.* A place where alcohol is sold and drunk illegally. [Anglo-Irish *sibín;* akin to *séibe,* mugful.]

shed¹ (shed) *v.* **shed, shedding, sheds.** —*tr.* **1.** To pour forth or cause to pour forth: *shed a tear.* **2.** To send forth; diffuse or radiate: *shed light; shed confidence.* **3.** To repel without allowing penetration: *A duck's feathers shed water.* **4.** To lose by natural process: *shedding leaves in winter.* **5.** To drop; cause to fall or fall off: *A lorry has shed its load on the A23.* **6.** To get rid of (jobs or workers): *Multinational to Shed 3,000 Jobs.* —*intr.* **1.** To lose a natural growth or covering by natural process: *Trees shed in winter.* **2.** To pour forth, fall off, or drop out: *All the leaves have shed.*
~*n.* An elevation in the earth's surface from which water flows in two directions; a watershed. [Shed, shed (past tense and past participle); Middle English *sheden, schede, scheden,* shed, divide, Old English *scēadan, scēad, scēaden,* to divide.]

shed² *n.* **1.** A small, usually low, structure, either freestanding or attached to a larger structure, serving for storage or shelter. **2.** A large structure, often open on all sides, for storage, locomotive repair, sheepshearing, shelter, or the like. [Earlier *shadde,* perhaps specialised use of SHADE.]

she'd (sheed, shid). **1.** Contraction of *she had.* **2.** Contraction of *she would.*

shed·der (shéddər) *n.* One that sheds by a natural process, such as a long-haired animal, a crab, or a lobster.

she-dev·il (shee-devv'l) *n.* A malicious or cruel woman.

shed·hand (shéd-hand) *n. Australian.* An unskilled worker who moves the shorn wool in a sheepshearing shed.

sheen (sheen) *n.* **1.** A smooth, glossy shine on a surface. **2.** Glistening brightness; radiance. **2.** *Poetic.* Splendid attire. [From obsolete *sheen,* beautiful, bright, Old English *scīene, scēne.*]

Sheene (sheen), **Barry** born Stephen Frank Sheene (1950–). British racing motorcyclist. He was 500 cc world champion (1976–77).

sheep (sheep) *n., pl.* **sheep. 1.** Any of various usually horned, ruminant mammals of the genus *Ovis;* especially, the domesticated species *O. aries,* raised in many breeds for its wool, edible flesh, or skin. **2.** The skin of a sheep or leather made from it. **3.** One who is meek, submissive, or easily led. —**separate the sheep from the goats.** To distinguish or discriminate between the worthy and the unworthy. [Middle English *she(e)p,* Old English *scē(a)p,* from West Germanic *skǣpa* (unattested).]

sheep·back (sheep-bak) *n. Geology.* **Roche moutonnée** (*see*).

sheep·cote (sheep-kōt) *n.* A sheepfold. [Middle English *shepcote* : SHEEP + COTE.]

sheep dip *n.* **1.** Any of various liquid disinfectants used to destroy parasites in the wool of sheep prior to shearing. **2.** A deep trough containing a disinfectant in which sheep are dipped.

sheep·dog (sheep-dog || -dawg) *n.* A dog trained to guard and herd sheep. See **Old English sheepdog, Shetland sheepdog.**

sheep·fold (sheep-fōld) *n.* A pen for sheep.

sheep·herd·er (sheep-herdər) *n. U.S.* A shepherd.

sheep·ish (sheepish) *adj.* **1.** Embarrassed or bashful, as by consciousness of a fault: *a sheepish grin.* **2.** Resembling a sheep in meekness or stupidity. —**sheep·ish·ly** *adv.* —**sheep·ish·ness** *n.*

sheep ked *n.* See **ked.**

sheep's-bit scabious (sheeps-bit) *n.* A plant, *Jasione montana,* with blue flowers in a globular head that superficially resemble those of a scabious. Also called "sheepsbit".

sheep's eyes *pl.n.* Bashful, amorous glances.

sheep's fescue *n.* A forage grass, *Festuca ovina,* with narrow leaves that roll inwards.

sheep·shank (sheep-shangk) *n.* A knot used to shorten a line.

sheep·shear·ing (sheep-sheer-ing) *n.* **1.** The act of shearing sheep. **2. a.** The time or season when sheep are sheared. **b.** The festivities held at this time. —**sheep·shear·er** *n.*

sheep·skin (sheep-skin) *n.* The skin of a sheep either tanned with the fleece left on or in the form of leather or parchment.

sheep's sorrel *n.* A sorrel, *Rumex acetosella,* common on dry heaths and acid soils.

sheep station *n. Australian.* A large sheep farm.

sheep tick *n.* A tick, *Ixodes ricinus,* parasitic on many mammals and birds, which bears the virus of louping ill in sheep and cattle.

sheep·walk (sheep-wawk) *n. British.* A piece of pastureland where sheep are grazed.

sheep·wash (sheep-wosh || -wawsh) *n.* A **sheep dip** (*see*).

sheer¹ (sheer) *v.* **sheered, sheering, sheers.** —*intr.* To swerve or deviate from a course. Usually used with *away* or *off.* —*tr.* To cause to swerve or deviate. Usually used with *away* or *off.*

~n. **1.** A swerving or deviating course. **2.** *Nautical.* **a.** The upward curve, or the amount of upward curve, of the longitudinal lines of a ship's hull as viewed from the side. **b.** The position in which a ship is placed to enable it to keep clear of a single bow anchor. [Perhaps a variant of SHEAR.]

sheer² *adj.* **sheerer, sheerest.** **1.** Thin, fine, and transparent; diaphanous. Said of a fabric. **2.** Not mixed or blended with anything; undiluted; pure: *sheer luck.* **3.** Perpendicular or nearly perpendicular; steep: *sheer rocks; a sheer drop.*
~adv. **1.** Perpendicularly or nearly perpendicularly. **2.** Absolutely; outright. [Perhaps Middle English *schir,* bright, shining, Old English *scīr.*] **—sheer·ly** *adv.* **—sheer·ness** *n.*

sheerlegs, sheers. Variants of **shear legs.**

sheet¹ (sheet) *n. Abbr.* **sh.** **1.** A rectangular piece of linen, cotton, or similar material serving as a basic article of bedding, commonly used in pairs, one above and one below the body of the sleeper. **2.** A broad, thin, usually rectangular mass or piece of any material, such as paper, metal, glass, or plywood. **3.** A broad, flat, continuous surface or expanse: *a sheet of rain.* **4.** A newspaper; especially, a tabloid: *a scandal sheet.* **5.** *Geology.* A broad, relatively thin deposit or layer of igneous or sedimentary rock. **6.** The large block of stamps printed by a single impression of a plate before the individual stamps have been separated. **7. a.** A piece of paper. **b.** A piece of paper printed and folded ready to be bound as pages in a book.
~v. **sheeted, sheeting, sheets.** *—tr.* To cover with, wrap in, or provide with a sheet or sheets. *—intr.* To fall in sheets, as heavy rain does. [Middle English *s(c)hete,* cloth, sheet, towel, Old English *scēte.*]

sheet² (sheet) *n. Nautical.* A rope or chain attached to one or both of the lower corners of a sail, serving to move or extend it. **—three sheets to the wind.** *Informal.* Drunk.
~intr.v. **sheeted, sheeting, sheets.** *Nautical.* To extend in a certain direction. Used of the sheets of a sail. [Middle English *s(c)hete,* Old English *scēata,* corner of a sail.]

sheet anchor *n.* **1.** A large extra anchor intended for use in emergency. **2.** A person or thing that can be turned to in time of emergency, especially one that can be relied on if all else fails.

sheet bend *n.* A knot in which one rope or piece of string is made fast to the bight of another.

sheet glass *n.* Molten glass drawn into a wide sheet which, after annealing and hardening, is cut into required lengths.

sheet·ing (shéeting) *n.* Any material, such as metal or cloth, in the form of or used to make a sheet.

sheet lightning *n.* Lightning that appears as a broad, sheetlike illumination, caused by diffusion of a lightning flash by a thunder cloud.

sheet metal *n.* Metal that has been rolled into a sheet thinner than plate but thicker than foil.

sheet music *n.* Music printed on unbound sheets of paper.

sheets (sheets) *pl.n. Nautical.* The spaces at the bow and stern of an open rowing boat that are not occupied by oarsmen.

Shef·field (shéffeeld). Industrial city in south Yorkshire, northern England, lying at the counfluence of the river Don and four tributaries. Since the 14th century it has been the most important centre for cutlery manufacture in the country. It is also a leading centre for silver and for heavy steel manufacture.

Sheffield plate *n.* An article or articles of tableware made of copper and coated with a thin layer of silver by a former process now replaced by electroplating. [After SHEFFIELD where it was made.]

sheik, sheikh (sháyk || sheek) *n.* **1.** A Muslim religious official. **2.** The leader of an Arab family, village, or tribe. [Arabic *shaikh,* old man, from *shākha,* to be old.] **—sheik·dom** *n.*

shei·la (shéelə) *n. Australian & N.Z. Informal.* A woman. [Earlier *shaler*†, assimilated to the name *Sheila.*]

shek·el (shéck'l) *n.* **1.** The basic monetary unit of Israel, equal to 100 new agora. **2. a.** Any of several ancient units of weight; especially, an ancient Hebrew unit equal to about half an ounce. **b.** A gold or silver coin equal in weight to one of these units; especially, the chief silver coin of the Hebrews. **3.** *Plural. Slang.* Cash; money. [Hebrew *sheqel,* from *shāqal,* to weigh.]

She·ki·nah (she-kīnə, shi-; *Hebrew* -khee-naá) *n.* A visible manifestation of the divine presence as described in Jewish theology. [Hebrew *shəkhīnāh,* from *shākhan,* to dwell.]

shel·duck (shél-duk) *n., pl.* **-ducks** or collectively **shelduck.** **1.** Any of various large Old World ducks of the genus *Tadorna;* especially, *T. tadorna,* having predominantly black and white plumage. **2.** Any of several other ducks. [Middle English : *sheld-,* variegated, perhaps of Low German origin, akin to Middle Dutch *schillede* + DUCK.]

shel·drake (shél-drayk) *n., pl.* **-drakes** or collectively **sheldrake.** The shelduck, especially the male shelduck.

shelf (shelf) *n., pl.* **shelves** (shelvz). **1.** A flat, usually rectangular structure of a rigid material, such as wood, glass, or metal, fixed at right angles to a wall or other vertical surface and used to hold or store objects. **2.** The contents or capacity of such a structure. **3.** Anything resembling such an object, such as a balcony or a ledge of rock. **4.** A **continental shelf** *(see).* **5.** *Mining.* Bedrock. **—on the shelf.** **1.** In a state of disuse; put aside. **2.** *Informal.* Unmarried and likely to remain so. [Middle English *shelf(e),* perhaps from Middle Low German *schelf.*]

shelf ice *n.* An extension of glacial ice floating on coastal waters. Also called "barrier ice".

shelf life *n.* The amount of time that something, such as a drug or packaged food, may be stored without deteriorating.

shell (shel) *n.* **1. a.** The usually hard outer covering that encases certain organisms such as molluscs, certain insects, or tortoises. **b.** A similar outer covering on an egg, fruit, or nut. **2.** The material composing such a covering. **3.** Anything resembling such a covering, especially: **a.** A framework, case, or exterior, as of a building, motor vehicle, or machine. **b.** A thin layer of pastry. **c.** The hull of a ship. **d.** The external part of the ear. **e.** A long, narrow racing boat propelled by oarsmen. **4. a.** A projectile or piece of ammunition; especially, the hollow tube containing explosives used to propel such a projectile. **b.** A metal or cardboard case, containing the charge, primer, and shot, fired from a shotgun; a cartridge. **5. a.** An attitude or manner adopted to mask one's true feelings. **b.** *Informal.* A state of shyness or reserve: *brought her out of her shell.* **6.** *Physics.* **a.** Any of the set of hypothetical spherical surfaces centred on the nucleus of an atom that contain the orbits of electrons having the same principal quantum number; hence, all the electrons in an atom that have the same principal quantum number. **b.** Any of a set of groupings of nucleon energy states in a nucleus, or of nucleons occupying such states, in which the binding energies of states differ from one another by much less than from the binding energies of states in another grouping.
~v. **shelled, shelling, shells.** *—tr.* **1. a.** To remove the shell of. **b.** To remove from a shell, pod, or the like. **2.** To separate (grains, kernels of maize, or the like) from the ear, husk, or cob. **3.** To fire artillery shells at; bombard. *—intr.* To shed or become free of a shell. **—shell out.** *Informal.* To pay or hand out (money). [Middle English *shell,* Old English *scell, scill.*] **—shell·er** *n.* **—shell·y** *adj.*

she'll (sheel, shil). **1.** Contraction of *she will.* **2.** Contraction of *she shall.*

shel·lac (shə-lák, she-, shéllak) *n.* **1.** A purified resin formed into thin yellow or orange flakes or buttons and widely used in varnishes, paints, stains, inks, and sealing wax. **2.** A thin varnish made by dissolving shellac in denatured alcohol, used as a wood coating. **3.** *Informal.* Seventy-eights contrasted with forty-fives, LPs, or CDs. Compare **vinyl.**
~tr.v. **shellacked, -lacking, -lacs.** To apply shellac to. [SHEL(L) + LAC (lacquer), translation of French *laque en écailles,* lac (melted) in thin plates.]

shell·back (shél-bak) *n.* A veteran sailor; especially, one who has crossed the equator. [Referring to a sailor hardened by experience.]

shell·bark (shél-baark) *n.* A tree, the **shagbark** *(see).*

Shel·ley (shélli), **Mary Wollstonecraft,** born Mary Godwin. (1797–1851). British novelist, the daughter of the feminist writer Mary Wollstonecraft and the philosopher William Godwin, and the wife of Percy Bysshe Shelley. She eloped with Shelley in 1814 and married him two years later. She is famous as the author of *Frankenstein, or the Modern Prometheus* (1818).

Shelley, Percy Bysshe (1792–1822). British Romantic poet. In 1811 he was sent down from Oxford University for circulating an atheist pamphlet; in 1813, *Queen Mab,* a poem that virulently attacked the monarchy, church, and other established institutions, was privately printed. His works include the verse dramas *The Cenci* (1819) and *Prometheus Unbound* (1820), and several odes, among them *To the West Wind* and *To a Skylark.*

shell·fire (shél-fīr) *n.* The firing of artillery projectiles at, or their reception in, a target area.

shell·fish (shél-fish) *n., pl.* **-fishes** or collectively **shellfish.** Any aquatic animal having a shell or shell-like exoskeleton, as a mollusc or crustacean, especially those having edible flesh.

shell pink *n.* Pinkish white to strong yellowish pink, including greyish and light yellowish pinks. **—shell-pink** (shél-píngk) *adj.*

shell shock *n.* Any of various usually acute, often hysterical neuroses originating in trauma suffered under fire in modern warfare. **—shell-shocked** (shél-shokt) *adj.*

shell suit *n.* A track suit with a waterproof outer layer likened to a protective "shell".

Shel·ta (shéltə) *n.* An ancient secret language based on Gaelic and used by itinerant tinkers and Gypsies in Ireland and some parts of Britain. [19th century : origin obscure.]

shel·ter (shéltər) *n.* **1. a.** Something that provides cover or protection, as from the weather or bombardment. **b.** The cover or protection so provided. **2.** A refuge; a haven. **3.** The state of being covered or protected.
~v. **sheltered, -tering, -ters.** *—tr.* To provide cover or protection for. *—intr.* To take cover; find refuge. **—shel·ter·er** *n.*
Synonyms: *cover, retreat, refuge, asylum, sanctuary, haven.*

shel·tered (shéltərd) *adj.* **1.** Protected or overprotected from harm or harsh realities: *a sheltered life.* **2.** Designating accommodation for the elderly or disabled where they may live alone, or as independently as possible, in separate autonomous units, but under the care of a supervisor: *sheltered housing.* **3.** Designating a workplace that has special facilities and provides work for the disabled.

shel·tie, shel·ty (shélti) *n. pl.* **-ties.** **1.** A **Shetland pony** *(see).* **2.** A **Shetland sheepdog** *(see).* [Norse *sjalti,* Shetland pony, Shetlander, from Old Norse *Hjalti,* Shetlander, from *Hjaltland,* Shetland, probably from *hjalt,* hilt, from Germanic *heltaz* (unattested), HILT.]

shelve (shelv) *v.* **shelved, shelving, shelves.** *—tr.* **1.** To place or arrange on a shelf or shelves. **2.** To put away as though on a shelf; put aside; postpone: *"as usual, Dixon shelved this question"* (Kingsley Amis). **3.** To cause to retire from service; dismiss. **4.** To furnish with shelves. *—intr.* To slope gradually; incline. [From SHELVES.]

shelves. Plural of **shelf.**

shelv·ing (shélving) n. 1. Shelves collectively. 2. Material for shelves.

Shem (shem). The eldest son of Noah. Genesis 5:32.

Shemite. Variant of **Semite.**

she·moz·zle, sche·moz·zle (shi-mózz'l) n. 1. A muddle; a state of chaos. 2. An uproar; a noisy row. [Yiddish.]

Shen·an·do·ah Valley (shénnən-dō-ə ‖ shánnə-). Part of the Great Appalachian Valley in Virginia, eastern United States, lying between the Allegheny Mountains to the west and the Blue Ridge Mountains to the east. In the American Civil War (1861–65) the valley was the scene of several of Thomas J. "Stonewall" Jackson's Valley Campaigns.

she·nan·i·gans (shi-nánnigənz) pl.n. Informal. 1. Prankishness; mischief. 2. Treachery; deceit. [19th century : origin obscure.]

Shensi. See **Shaanxi.**

Shen·yang or **Shen-yang** (shŏn-yáng), formerly **Muk·den** (moŏk-dən). City in northeastern China, the capital of Liaoning province. The fourth-largest city in China, it is the centre of a highly developed industrial region and a major strategic centre. It was there that the Mukden, or Manchurian, Incident took place (1931), when the Japanese used an explosion on the railway as an excuse to occupy the city and begin the occupation of Manchuria.

Shen·zhen (shén-jén). Area of 2020 square kilometres (780 square miles) in southern China, just north of Hong Kong, designated as a Special Economic Zone in which capitalism is encouraged. A stock exchange began to operate there in 1988.

she-oak (shée-ōk) n. Any of various Australian trees of the genus Casuarina, such as the beefwood. See **Casuarina.** [SHE (used in the obsolete sense of a lesser plant) + OAK.]

she-ol (shée-ol, -ōl) n. 1. Hell. 2. Capital S. A place described in the Old Testament as the abode of the dead. [Hebrew shə̄ōl.]

Shep·ard (shéppərd), **Alan Bartlett, Jr.** (1923–98). U.S. astronaut. On 5 May 1961, he became the first American in space, and commanded the Apollo 14 mission to the Moon in 1971.

Shepard, E(rnest) H(oward) (1879–1976). British cartoonist and illustrator. He worked for Punch, and is remembered for his illustrations to A.A. Milne's Winnie the Pooh books.

shep·herd (shéppərd) n. 1. One who herds, guards, and cares for sheep. 2. One who cares for a group of people, such as a priest or teacher. 3. Australian. One who owns the rights to a mine or mining claim but does not work it.
~tr.v. **shepherded, -herding, -herds.** 1. To herd, guard, or care for as or in the manner of a shepherd. 2. Australian. To own the right to, but not to work, (a mine or mining claim). [Middle English sheepherde, Old English scēaphirde : scēap, SHEEP + hirde, HERD (herdsman).]

shepherd dog n. A sheepdog.

shep·herd·ess (shéppər-diss, -dess, -déss) n. A woman shepherd.

shepherd's needle n. A European plant, Scandix pecten-veneris, with finely divided leaves and conspicuous needle-like fruit.

shepherd's pie n. A dish of minced beef or lamb with gravy, topped by a layer of mashed potatoes. Also called "cottage pie".

shep·herd's-purse (shéppərdz-púrss) n. A common weed, Capsella bursa-pastoris, having small white flowers and flat, heart-shaped fruit. [From its pouchlike pods.]

shepherd's weatherglass n. A plant, the **pimpernel** (see).

sher·ard·ise, sher·ard·ize (shérrər-dīz) tr.v. **-ised, -ising, -ises.** To form a layer of zinc on (iron or steel) by heating with zinc dust. [After Sherard Cowper-Coles (died 1936), British inventor.] —**sher·ard·i·sa·tion** (-dī-záysh'n ‖ U.S. -di-) n.

Sher·a·ton (shérrətən) adj. Of or designating a style of English furniture originated by Thomas Sheraton, and characterised by straight lines and graceful proportions.

Sheraton, Thomas (1751–1806). British furniture designer. His four-volume Cabinet-Maker and Upholsterer's Drawing Book (1791–94) provides an elegant and influential survey of contemporary taste.

sher·bet (shérbət) n. 1. An effervescent powder eaten as a sweet, or used to make fizzy drinks. 2. Chiefly U.S. **sorbet** (see). [Turkish sherbet and Persian sharbat, from Arabic sharbah, drink, from shariba, to drink. See also **syrup, shrub.**]

sherd. Variant of **shard.**

Sher·i·dan (shérrid'n), **Richard Brinsley (Butler)** (1751–1816). British dramatist and politician, born in Ireland. He is known for his comedies of manners, especially The Rivals (1775) and The School for Scandal (1777). Elected an M.P. in 1780, he became an outstanding Whig orator, and was treasurer of the Navy (1806–07).

she·rif (she-reéf, shə-) n. Also **sha·rif** (sha-, shə-). 1. a. A descendant of the prophet Muhammad through his daughter Fatima. b. The title of certain Arab princes claiming such descent. 2. The chief magistrate of Mecca. Also called "grand sherif". 3. A Moroccan ruler. [Arabic sharīf, "noble", from sharafa, to be highborn.]

sher·iff (shérrif) n. 1. In England and Wales, the chief officer of the Crown in every county, whose powers are now mainly ceremonial, but include some legal powers such as the summoning of juries in some courts, and acting as returning officer in parliamentary elections. Also officially called "high sheriff". 2. In Scotland, a judge presiding over a sheriff court (roughly equivalent to an English county court and the middle tier of a Crown court). 3. The chief executive of the courts of superior jurisdiction in a U.S. county; the chief law-enforcement officer in a county. [Middle English shir(r)eve, shirrif, Old English scīrgerēfa : scīr, SHIRE + gerēfa, officer, REEVE.]

sher·iff-dep·ute (shérrif-déppewt) n., pl. **sheriffs-depute.** In Scotland, a judge carrying out various administrative duties and hearing both civil and criminal cases. Also called "sheriff principal".

Sher·lock Holmes (shérlok hōmz). English detective with superb powers of observation and deduction, a central character in stories and novels by Sir Arthur Conan Doyle.

Sher·man (shérmən), **William Tecumseh** (1820–91). U.S. soldier, a Union general in the Civil War. As commander of all Federal forces in the west from 1864, he helped secure Union victory through his capture of Atlanta and march through the Carolinas (1864–65).

Sher·pa (shérpə) n., pl. **-pas** or collectively **Sherpa.** A member of a Tibetan people living in northern Nepal.

Sher·ring·ton (shérrington), **Sir Charles Scott** (1857–1952). British physiologist, known for his pioneering work on the nervous system. For his research into the function of the neuron, he shared the Nobel prize for physiology or medicine in 1932.

sher·ry (shérri) n., pl. **-ries.** 1. A fortified Spanish wine ranging from very dry to sweet, and usually drunk as an aperitif. 2. A similar wine made outside Spain. [Earlier sherris, "wine of Jerez", from Xeres, older form of JEREZ.]

sher·wa·ni (shair-waáni) n. A tight-fitting, knee-length formal coat with a high collar, worn by men in India. [Hindi shērwāni.]

Sher·wood Forest (shér-woŏd). Ancient royal forest, mainly in Nottinghamshire, central England, famous as the scene of Robin Hood's exploits. Today only parts of it remain, near Mansfield.

she's (sheez, shiz). 1. Contraction of she is. 2. Contraction of she has.

Shet·land (shéttlənd) adj. Of or from the Shetland Islands.
~n. 1. A fine, loosely twisted yarn made from the wool of Shetland sheep and used for knitting and weaving. Also called "Shetland wool". 2. A garment, especially a sweater, made of this wool.

Shetland Islands. Also **Shetlands.** The most northerly part of Britain, comprising about 100 islands off northern Scotland. They lie northeast of the Orkney Islands, and constitute the Shetland Island Authority area. The largest of them are Mainland, Yell, Unst, Fetlar, and Whalsey, and 19 are inhabited. The poor soil supports some crops, chiefly oats and barley, but the main economic activities are the raising of sheep, cattle, and Shetland ponies, fishing and tourism, and the islands are noted for their wool, knitwear, and knitted lace. Under Norse rule from the late 9th century, the Shetland Islands were annexed to the Scottish crown in 1472. Lerwick on Mainland is the administrative centre. —**Shet·land·er** n.

Shetland pony n. A small, compactly built pony of a breed originating in the Shetland Islands. Also called "sheltie".

Shetland sheepdog n. A dog of a breed developed in the Shetland Islands, having a rough coat and resembling a small collie. Also called "sheltie".

She·vat (shə-vaát) n. Also **She·bat** (-baát, -vaát). The fifth month of the Hebrew calendar. [Hebrew shəbhāt.]

shew (shō) v. **shewed, shewing, shews,** Archaic. To show.

shew·bread, show·bread (shō-bred) n. The 12 loaves of blessed, unleavened bread placed every Sabbath in the sanctuary of the Tabernacle by the ancient Hebrew priests. Exodus 25:20. Leviticus 24:5-9. [16th century (Tindale) : translating German Schaubrot, from Hebrew lēchem pānim, "bread of presence" (that is, the bread left in the presence of God in the temple).]

Shi·ah, Shi·a (shée-ə) n. 1. The principal minority sect of Islam, composed of the followers of Ali, the cousin and son-in-law of Muhammad, who regard the heirs of Ali as the legitimate successors to the Prophet and reject the other caliphs and the Sunnite legal and political institutions. Compare **Sunni.** 2. A Shiite (see).
~adj. Shiite. [Arabic shī'ah, following (of Ali), from shā'a, to follow, accompany.]

shi·at·su (shee-aát-soō, -át-) n. A form of therapeutic massage intended to affect bodily sites such as the points into which acupuncture needles are inserted. [Japanese, "finger pressure", from shi, finger + atsu, pressure.]

shib·bo·leth (shíbbə-leth, shíbbō- ‖ -ləth, -lith) n. 1. A password, phrase, custom, or usage that reliably distinguishes the members of one group or class from another. 2. A slogan, catchword, or saying, especially one distinctive of a particular group. 3. An outmoded custom, doctrine, slogan or the like that was once thought to be important or even fashionable but no longer has any importance for those who adhered to or used it. [Hebrew shibbōleth, an ear of corn, stream (password used by the Gileadites in the Bible, Judges 12:6).]

shield (sheeld) n. 1. An article of protective armour made of metal or other rigid material carried on the forearm to ward off blows or missiles. 2. A means of defence; protection. 3. Something resembling a shield in shape, such as a trophy or badge. 4. a. Something such as a protective plate that screens off potentially dangerous machinery or equipment. b. Military. A steel sheet attached to a gun to protect the gunners from small-arms fire. 5. Zoology. A protective plate or similar hard outer covering. 6. Heraldry. A design or drawing of a shield on which a coat of arms is displayed. 7. Physics. A mass of material, such as lead or cement, that encloses a nuclear reactor in order to reduce the amount of radiation that escapes into the surrounding area. 8. Geology. A craton (see). —v. **shielded, shielding, shields.** —tr. 1. To protect or defend with or as if with a shield; guard. 2. To cover up; conceal. —intr. 1. To act or serve as a shield or safeguard. —See Synonyms at **defend.** [Middle English shild, sheld, Old English scild, sceld.] —**shield·er** n.

shield·bug (shéeld-bug) n. Any of numerous flattened,

shield-shaped, plant-eating insects.

shield-fern (shéeld-fern) n. Either of two large tufted ferns, *Polystichum aculeatum* of *P. setiferum*, having round, shield-shaped indusia (spore-protecting coverings).

Shield of David n. A six-pointed star, the **Star of David** (see).

shiel-ing (shéeling) n. *Scottish.* A shepherd's hut. [Scottish *shiel*, shed, hut, Middle English *schele, shale*, probably from Scandinavian; akin to Old Norse *skjol*, shelter, hut.]

shift (shift) v. **shifted, shifting, shifts.** —*tr.* 1. To move or transfer from one place or position to another. 2. To exchange for or replace with something similar in quality or kind; switch. 3. *U.S.* To change (gear) in a car. 4. *Linguistics.* To alter phonetically or as part of a systematic change. 5. *Informal.* To remove: *I can't shift this dirty mark.* —*intr.* 1. To change position, direction, place, form, or the like. 2. **a.** To provide for one's needs; get along; manage: *I can shift for myself.* **b.** To get along by resourceful or evasive means. 3. *U.S.* To change gear, as when driving a car. 4. *Informal.* To be removed: *That mark won't shift.*
~*n.* 1. A change, transference, or displacement from one individual, position, or configuration to another. 2. A change of direction or form. 3. **a.** A group of workers who work for a particular period, and are replaced by the next group. **b.** The working period or time of such a group: *The night shift ends at six.* 4. *Music.* A change of the position of the hand in playing the violin or a similar instrument. 5. *Linguistics.* **a.** A systematic change of the phonetic or phonemic structure of a language. **b.** **Functional shift** (see). 6. **a.** A woman's dress hanging straight from the shoulders. Also called "chemise". **b.** A woman's undergarment; a slip; a chemise. 7. An ingenious, evasive, or fraudulent expedient; a trick. [Middle English *shiften*, to arrange, apportion, change, Old English *sciftan*, to arrange, from Germanic *skip-* (unattested).] —**shift-er** n.

shift-less (shift-lass, -liss) adj. 1. Showing a lack of ambition or purpose; lazy. 2. Showing a lack of resourcefulness or efficiency; not capable. [From SHIFT (archaic sense "resourcefulness").] —**shift-less-ly** adv. —**shift-less-ness** n.

shift-y (shifti) adj. **-ier, -iest.** 1. Tricky; crafty. 2. Suggesting craft, guile, or deceitfulness; furtive. —**shift-i-ly** adv. —**shift-i-ness** n.

shi-gel-la (shi-géllə) n. Any bacterium of the genus *Shigella*, some species of which cause dysentery in humans. [New Latin, after K. *Shiga* (1870–1957), Japanese bacteriologist who discovered it.]

shih-tzu (shée-tsōō) n. A small long-haired dog of a breed originating in Tibet, resembling a terrier or pekingese. [Chinese, "Lion".]

Shi-ism, Shi'-ism (shée-iz'm) n. The religion or doctrines of the **Shiah** (see).

Shi-ite, Shi'-ite (shée-īt) n. A member of the **Shiah** (see) branch of Islam. Also called "Shiah". —**Shi-ite, Shi-it-ic** (shee-ittik) adj.

shi-ka-ree, shi-ka-ri (shi-kaári) n. *Anglo-Indian.* A big-game hunting guide. [Hindi, from Persian *shikārī*, from *shikār*, hunting, from Middle Persian *shkār†.]

Shi-ko-ku (shi-kō-kōō). Smallest of the four main islands of Japan. It covers 18 770 square kilometres (7,247 square miles) and lies across the Inland Sea from Kyushu and Honshu.

shik-sa, shik-se, shick-sa (shíksə) n. 1. A non-Jewish girl or young woman. Usually used derogatorily. 2. A Jewish girl or young woman who fails to live up to traditional Jewish teachings or practices. Usually used derogatorily. [Yiddish *shikse*, feminine of *sheygets*, from Hebrew *sheques*.]

shil-le-lagh, shil-la-lah (shi-láy-li, -lə) n. In Ireland, a club or cudgel, especially one of oak or blackthorn. [Such clubs were originally made in *Shillelagh*, town in County Wicklow, Ireland.]

shil-ling (shilling) n. *Abbr.* **s., sh.** 1. Formerly, a coin equal to 1/20 of the pound of the United Kingdom, the Republic of Ireland, and a number of former British dominions. 2. The basic monetary unit of Kenya, Somalia, Tanzania, and Uganda, equal to 100 cents. [Middle English *shilling*, Old English *scilling*, from Germanic *skillingaz* (unattested).]

shil-ly-shal-ly (shilli-shal-i) intr.v. **-lied, -lying, -lies.** 1. To put off acting; hesitate or waver. 2. To idle or dawdle.
~*adj.* Hesitant; vacillating.
~*n., pl.* **shilly-shallies.** Procrastination; hesitation.
~*adv.* In a hesitant manner; irresolutely. [Originally in phrases such as *stand* (or *go*), *shill I? shall I?* reduplication of *shall I?*] —**shil-ly-shal-li-er** n.

shim (shim) n. A thin washer or tapered piece of metal, wood, stone, or other material, used to adjust a space or as a filler between materials or to make parts of it.
~*tr.v.* **shimmed, shimming, shims.** To make (parts) fit by inserting a shim or shims. [18th Century : origin obscure.]

shim-mer (shímmər) intr.v. **-mered, -mering, -mers.** To shine with a soft tremulous or flickering light. See Synonyms at **flash.**
~*n.* A flickering or tremulous light; a glimmer. [Middle English *schimeren*, Old English *scimerian, scimrian*, from Germanic; akin to SHINE.] —**shim-mer-y** adj.

shim-my (shímmi) n., pl. **-mies.** *Chiefly U.S.* 1. A dance popular in the 1920s, characterised by rapid shaking of the body. Also called "shimmy shake". 2. Abnormal vibration or wobbling, as in the chassis of a car. 3. *Regional.* A chemise.
~*intr.v.* **shimmied, -mying, -mies.** 1. To vibrate or wobble. 2. To shake the body in or as if in dancing the shimmy. [Short for *shimmy-shake*, perhaps "to shake one's chemise", from *shimmy*, incorrect form of CHEMISE.]

shin¹ (shin) n. 1. *Anatomy.* **a.** The front part of the leg below the knee and above the ankle. **b.** The front of the tibia. 2. A cut of

meat from the lower part of the foreleg in beef cattle, as opposed to the upper foreleg or shank.
~*v.* **shinned, shinning, shins.** —*tr.* 1. To climb (a rope or pole, for example) by gripping and pulling alternately with the hands and legs. Usually used with *up.* 2. To kick or hit in the shins. —*intr.* To climb something by shinning. Usually used with *up.* [Middle English *shine*, Old English *sinu.*]

shin² (shin, sheen) n. The 22nd letter in the Hebrew alphabet. [Hebrew *shīn*, variant of *shēn*, tooth (from the shape of the letter).]

shin-bone (shín-bōn) n. *Anatomy.* The **tibia** (see).

shin-dig (shín-dig) n. *Slang.* 1. A noisy party or celebration. Also called "shindy". 2. A shindy. [Probably an alteration of SHINDY.]

shin-dy (shíndi) n., pl. **-dies.** *Slang.* 1. A commotion; a row; an uproar. Also called "shindig". 2. A shindig. [Alteration of SHINTY.]

shine (shīn) v. **shone** (shon ‖ *U.S.* shōn) or **shined** (for transitive sense 2), **shining, shines.** —*intr.* 1. To emit light; be radiant; beam. 2. To reflect light; glint or glisten. 3. To distinguish oneself in some sphere; excel: *shine at tennis.* 4. To become clearly apparent. —*tr.* 1. To aim or cast the beam or glow of: *Shine the torch over here.* 2. To make glossy or bright by polishing.
~*n.* 1. Brightness; radiance; lustre. 2. An act of shining something: *gave her shoes a shine.* 3. Fair weather. Used in the phrase *rain or shine.* —**take a shine to.** *Informal.* To like spontaneously. [Shine, shone (past tense); Middle English *shinen, schon*, Old English *scīnan, scān* (past singular). The past participle *shone* is formed in Modern English from the past tense *shone.*]

shin-er (shínər) n. 1. One that shines. 2. *Slang.* A black eye. 3. **a.** Any of numerous small, often silvery North American freshwater fishes of the family Cyprinidae, especially one of the genus *Notropis.* **b.** Any of various other small silvery fishes, especially the mackerel.

shin-gle¹ (shíng-g'l) n. 1. A thin oblong piece of wood, asbestos, or other material, laid in overlapping rows to cover the roofs and sides of houses. 2. A woman's close-cropped layered haircut.
~*tr.v.* **shingled, -gling, -gles.** 1. To cover (a roof or building) with shingles. 2. To cut (a woman's hair) short and in layers so that the hair is full out at the back of the head and tapers in to the nape of the neck. [Middle English *scincle, scingle*, from Latin *scindula*, variant of *scandula*, a roofing shingle, from *scandere*, to ascend.] —**shin-gler** n.

shingle² A mass of rounded, water-worn stones of various sizes, often found on beaches. [16th century : origin obscure.] —**shin-gly** adj.

shingle³ *tr.v.* **-gled, -gling, -gles.** To hammer the slag out of (puddled iron) during the manufacture of wrought iron. [French *cingler*, from German *zängeln*, from *Zange*, TONG(s).]

shin-gles (shíng-g'lz) n. *Usually used with a singular verb. Pathology.* A viral infection caused by chickenpox viruses and characterised by skin eruptions along the routes of cutaneous nerves on one side of the body, often accompanied or followed by severe neuralgia. The virus may remain latent within the body between outbreaks. Also called "herpes zoster", "zoster". [Middle English, from Medieval Latin *cingulus*, from Latin *cingulum*, girdle, from *cingere*, to gird.]

shin-ny (shínni) v. **-nied, -nying, -nies.** *Informal.* —*intr.* To climb by shinning. —*tr.* To climb (a rope, for example) by shinning.

shin-plas-ter (shín-plaastər ‖ -plastər) n. 1. *U.S.* A note of paper currency issued privately; especially, such a note devalued by lack of backing or by inflation. 2. *Australian.* A promissory note used in the outback as currency. [From the comparison of such notes to small squares of brown paper soaked with vinegar or tobacco juice and used by poor people to treat sore legs.]

Shin-to (shíntō) n. Also **Shin-to-ism** (-iz'm). The indigenous religion of Japan, marked by the veneration of nature spirits and of ancestors. [Japanese *shintō*, "the way of the gods" : *shin*, from Chinese *shén*, god(s), + *tō*, for do, way, from Chinese (Mandarin) *dào*, way.] —**Shin-to-ist** n. & adj.

shin-ty (shínti) n. Also *U.S.* **shinny.** 1. A vigorous game similar to hockey. 2. The curved stick used in this game. [Perhaps from the cry of *shin ye* used in the game.]

shin-y (shíni) adj. **-ier, -iest.** Having a surface that reflects light, as: 1. Glossy; glistening: *shiny satin.* 2. Bright; polished: *shiny shoes.* 3. Clear; shining: *shiny-eyed.* 4. Worn away so as to appear smooth and glossy. Said of fabric. —**shin-i-ness** n.

ship (ship) n. 1. Any vessel of considerable size adapted for deep-water navigation and powered by wind or engines. 2. A three-masted sailing vessel with square mainsails on all masts. 3. *Maritime Law.* A vessel intended for marine transport without regard to form, rig, or means of propulsion. 4. A ship's company. 5. A spaceship or airship. —**dress ship.** To display the ensign, signal flags, and bunting on a ship.
~*v.* **shipped, shipping, ships.** —*tr.* 1. To place or take on board a ship. 2. **a.** To send or transport. **b.** *Informal.* To dispatch to a specified destination. 3. To bring into a vessel; especially, to lift (oars) from the water and place inside the boat without removing them from the rowlocks. 4. To take in (water) over the side. 5. To set (a mast or rudder, for example) in place for use. —*intr.* 1. To go or travel by means of a ship. 2. To hire oneself out or enlist for service on a ship. [Middle English *s(c)hip*, Old English *scip.*]

-ship n. *suffix.* Indicates: 1. The quality or condition of; for example, **friendship, scholarship.** 2. The status, rank, or office of; for example, **professorship, authorship.** 3. The art or skill of; for example, **penmanship, leadership.** [Middle English *-s(c)hip(e)*, Old English *-scipe.*]

ship·board (shíp-bawrd || -bõrd) n. Obsolete. The side of a ship. **—on shipboard.** On board a ship.
~adj. Occurring on board a ship: a shipboard romance.

ship·build·ing (shíp-bilding) n. The industry or occupation of constructing ships. **—ship·build·er** n.

ship canal n. A canal deep enough for ships. Also "shipway".

ship chandler n. A person who deals in equipment for ships.

ship fever n. **Typhus** (see), especially as it formerly occurred on overcrowded ships.

ship·load (shíp-lõd) n. **1.** The cargo or passengers carried by a ship. **2.** A capacity cargo for a ship.

ship·man (shíp-mən) n., pl. **-men** (-mən, -men). Archaic. **1.** A sailor. **2.** A shipmaster.

ship·mas·ter (shíp-maastər || -mastər) n. The master or captain of a ship.

ship·mate (shíp-mayt) n. A sailor serving on the same ship as another; a fellow sailor.

ship·ment (shípmənt) n. Abbr. **shpt. 1.** The act of sending or transporting goods. **2.** A quantity of goods or cargo transported.

ship money n. A former tax on English maritime towns and shires to provide revenue for the construction of warships.

ship of state n. A country or its affairs symbolised as a ship bound on a course.

ship of the line n. Formerly, a warship large enough to take a position in the line of battle.

ship·per (shíppər) n. A person or company that consigns or receives goods for shipping; a shipping agent.

ship·ping (shípping) n. **1.** The act or business of transporting goods, especially by ship. **2.** The body of ships belonging to one port, industry, or country, often referred to in aggregate tonnage. **3.** Ships collectively.

shipping clerk n. A person employed to manage the shipment or receipt of goods.

shipping lane n. A regular or prescribed route for ships.

ship·rigged (shíp-rigd) adj. Nautical. Rigged as a ship, with three or more masts and square sails.

ship's biscuit n. A type of bread, **hardtack** (see).

ship·shape (shíp-shayp) adj. Neatly arranged; orderly; tidy. [Originally, "arranged in a manner befitting a ship" (said of rigging).] **—ship·shape** adv.

ship's papers pl.n. The documents giving details of ownership, nationality, destination, or the like that international law requires a ship to carry and be able to provide on demand for inspection.

ship-to-shore (shíp-tə-shór || -shõr) adj. In operation between a ship and the shore. Said of a radio system. **—ship-to-shore** adv.

ship·way (shíp-way) n. **1.** The structure supporting a ship during construction or in dry dock. **2.** A **ship canal** (see).

ship·worm (shíp-wurm) n. Any of various wormlike marine molluscs of the genera Teredo and Bankia, having rudimentary shells with which they bore into wood, often doing extensive damage.

ship·wreck (shíp-rek) n. **1.** The destruction of a ship, as by storm or collision. **2.** The remains of a wrecked ship. **3.** Complete failure or ruin.
~tr.v. **shipwrecked, -wrecking, -wrecks. 1.** To cause (a ship or its passengers) to suffer shipwreck. **2.** To ruin utterly. [Earlier shipwrack, Middle English shipwrak, Old English scipwræc, cargo thrown overboard to lighten a ship in danger : SHIP + wræc, thing driven by the sea, WRACK.]

ship·wright (shíp-rīt) n. A skilled worker, such as a carpenter, employed in the construction or maintenance of ships.

ship·yard (shíp-yaard) n. A place where ships are built or repaired.

shi·ra·lee (shírrə-lée, -lee) n. Australian. A bag or bundle of personal belongings carried by a traveller or swagman; a swag. [20th century : origin obscure.]

Shi·raz (shéer-raáz). City in southwestern Iran, the capital of Fars province. It has been a leading commercial and administrative town since the eighth century. It is noted especially for its metalwork, wines, and carpets.

shire (shīr) n. **1.** Any of the counties of the United Kingdom. Used chiefly in combination: Lancashire. **2.** Australian. A division of a state, often rural, having its own elected administration. **—the Shires.** The counties of the Midlands, especially those renowned for foxhunting, such as Leicestershire. [Old English scīr†.]

shire horse n. A large, powerful draught horse of a breed originating in the shires of Lincoln, Cambridge, or Huntingdon.

shirk (shurk) v. **shirked, shirking, shirks.** —tr. To put off or avoid discharging (work or duties). —intr. To avoid work or duty.
~n. A person who avoids work or duty. Also called "shirker". [From obsolete shirk, parasite, rogue, probably from German Schurke, scoundrel, perhaps from Old High German (fiur)-scurgo, "fire stirrer", stoker, hence devil (as an infernal stoker), from scurigen, to poke.]

Shir·ley poppy (shúrli) n. A variety of the field poppy having scarlet, pink, or salmon single or double flowers. [After Shirley Vicarage, Croydon, Surrey, where it was first grown.]

shirr (shur) tr.v. **shirred, shirring, shirrs. 1.** To gather (cloth) with decorative parallel rows using fine elastic thread. **2.** U.S. To cook (eggs) by baking unshelled in moulds.
~n. A decorative gathering of cloth into parallel rows. Also called "shirring". [19th century : origin obscure.]

shirt (shurt) n. A garment for the upper part of the body, especially a man's, typically made of light fabric and having a collar, long or short sleeves, and a buttoned front opening. **—keep (one's) shirt on.** Informal. To remain calm or patient. **—lose (one's) shirt.** Informal. To lose everything one has or owns. **—put (one's) shirt on.** To bet or gamble everything one has on. [Middle English sherte, scurte, Old English scyrte; akin to Old Norse skyrta (whence SKIRT), from Germanic skurt- (unattested), SHORT.]

shirt·ing (shúrting) n. Fabric suitable for making shirts.

shirt·sleeve (shúrt-sleev) n. A sleeve of a shirt. **—in (one's) shirtsleeves.** Informally dressed. **—shirt·sleeved** adj.

shirt·waist·er (shúrt-waystər) n. A woman's dress with the bodice styled like a tailored shirt. Also U.S. "shirtwaist".

shirt·y (shúrti) adj. **-tier, -tiest.** Chiefly British Informal. Annoyed and rude; bad-tempered. [See idioms at **shirt.**]

shish ke·bab (shísh ki-báb, -bab) n. Also U.S. **shish ke·bob, shish ka·bob** (-bob). A dish consisting of pieces of seasoned marinated meat cooked on skewers, often over charcoal. Also called "kebab". [Turkish şiş kebabıu : şiş, skewer + kebap, roast meat.]

shit (shit) v. **shat** or **shitted, shitting, shits.** Vulgar. —intr. To excrete faeces; defecate. —tr. **1.** To excrete (faeces). **2.** To soil by defecating on.
~n. **1.** Vulgar. Faeces. **2.** Vulgar. An act of defecating. **3.** Vulgar. Slang. Nonsense; rubbish. **4.** Vulgar Slang. A thoroughly unpleasant person. **5.** Vulgar Slang. An unpleasant situation; trouble. Used in the phrase in the shit. **6.** Vulgar Slang. Business: She's really got her shit together.
~interj. Vulgar Slang. Used as an expression of annoyance, anger, or amazement.
~adv. Vulgar Slang. Used as an intensive: shit-scared. [Old English scite, scītan (unattested), from Germanic skit-, skīt- (unattested); compare Middle Dutch schitte, dung, Old Norse skíta, to defecate.] **—shit·ti·ly** adv. **—shit·ty** adj.

shit-hot (shít-hót shít-hot) adj. Vulgar Slang. Excellent.

shit·less (shít-ləss, -liss) adj. Vulgar Slang. Terrified. Used especially in the phrases scare someone shitless, scared shitless.

shit·tim·wood (shíttim-wóod) n. **1.** A tree, probably a species of acacia, that was a source of a wood mentioned frequently in the Bible. Also called "shittah tree". **2.** The wood of this tree, used to make the ark of the Tabernacle. Exodus 25:10. [Hebrew shittīm, plural of shiṭṭāh, related to Egyptian sont, acacia.]

shiv (shiv) n. Slang. A knife or razor, especially when considered as a weapon. [Romany chiv†, "blade".]

shi·va, shi·vah (shívvə) n. Judaism. A seven-day period of formal mourning observed after the funeral of a close relative. [Yiddish, from Hebrew shiv'āh, seven.]

Shiva. Variant of **Siva.**

shivaree. U.S. Variant of **charivari.**

shive (shīv) n. **1.** A thin, flat cork used to stop wide-mouthed bottles. **2.** Archaic. A slice. [Middle English, slice, probably from Middle Dutch or Middle Low German schīve.]

shiv·er¹ (shívvər) v. **-ered, -ering, -ers.** —intr. **1.** To shudder or shake, as from cold or excitement; tremble. **2.** To quiver or vibrate, as by the force of wind. —tr. Nautical. To cause (a sail) to flutter in the wind. **—See Synonyms at shake.**
~n. **1.** An act of shivering; a tremble. **2.** Often plural. A tingling sensation caused by fear, excitement, or the like: It sent shivers up my spine. [Middle English shiveren, earlier chiveren, perhaps alteration of chevelen, to shiver, originally "to chatter" (used of teeth), from Old English ceafl, the jaw.]

shiv·er² v. **-ered, -ering, -ers.** —intr. To break into fragments or splinters; shatter. —tr. To cause to break into fragments. **—See Synonyms at break.** [Middle English, from scivre, fragment, perhaps of Low German origin, akin to Middle Low German schever.]

shiv·er·y¹ (shívvəri) adj. **1.** Trembling, as from cold or fear. **2.** Making one shiver with cold or fear; chilling.

shivery² adj. Archaic. Easily broken; brittle.

Shko·dër (shkõ-dər) or **Shko·dra** (-draa). Italian **Scu·ta·ri** (skõõ-taʹari; Italian skõõtəri). City in Albania, capital of Shkodër province. It is the manufacturing and cultural centre of northern Albania.

shm-. Variant of **schm-.**

S.H.M. simple harmonic motion.

shmo. Variant of **schmo.**

shoal¹ (shõl) n. **1.** A shallow area in any body of water. **2.** An elevation of the bottom of a body of water, constituting a hazard to navigation; a sandbank, mudbank, or pebble bank.
~ v. **shoaled, shoaling, shoals.** —intr. To become shallow. —tr. **1.** To make shallow. **2.** To come or sail into a shallower area of (water): The ship shoaled water.
~adj. Having little depth; shallow. [Middle English schald, sholde, originally "shallow", Old English sc(e)ald, from Germanic skaldaz (unattested).] **—shoal·y** adj.

Usage: shoal, reef, bar, bank. These nouns have reference to elevations of ground under water. A shoal is an elevation coming close to but not above the surface of the water. The term is also applied to the shallow area thus formed. A reef is a ridge, usually of rock or coral, or slightly above the low-tide mark. A bar is a ridge, usually of sand, near the surface and often exposed at low water. A bank in this comparison is a large, totally submerged plateau of mud or sand that is not a danger to shipping.

shoal² n. **1.** A large group; a crowd. **2.** A school of fish or other marine animals.
~intr.v. **shoaled, shoaling, shoals.** To come together in a shoal. [Probably from Middle Dutch or Middle Low German schōle. See **school** (of fish).]

shoat, shote (shōt) *n.* A young pig just after weaning. [Middle English *shote*, probably Low German origin, akin to West Flemish *schote*.]

shock¹ (shok) *n.* **1.** A violent collision or impact; a heavy blow. **2.** Something that jars the mind or emotions as if with a violent, unexpected blow. **3.** The disturbance of function, equilibrium, or emotional and mental state caused by such a blow. **4.** *Pathology.* A generally temporary state of massive physiological reaction to bodily damage or emotional trauma, usually characterised by a cold sweat, marked loss of blood pressure, and the depression of vital processes such as respiration. **5.** The sensation and muscular spasm caused by an electric current passing through the body or through a bodily part. Also called "electric shock". **6.** Shock therapy *(see).* ~*v.* **shocked, shocking, shocks.** —*tr.* **1.** To fill with a powerful feeling of disgust, incredulity, horror, or the like. **2.** To outrage; scandalise. **3.** To induce a state of shock in (a person). **4.** To subject (an animal or person) to an electric shock. —*intr.* **1.** To be susceptible to shock. **2.** *Archaic.* To come into contact violently, as in battle; collide. [French *choc*, from *choquer†*, to strike (with fear).] —**shock·a·ble** *adj.*

shock² *n.* A number of sheaves of corn stacked upright in a field for drying. ~*tr.v.* **shocked, shocking, shocks.** To gather (sheaves of corn) into shocks. [Middle English *shokke*, probably from Middle Dutch or Middle Low German *schok*, shock, group of sixty, akin to Old Saxon *scok†*.]

shock³ *n.* A thick, shaggy, heavy mass: *a shock of hair.* ~*adj.* Thick and shaggy. [Perhaps from SHOCK (stack).]

shock absorber *n.* Any of various devices used to absorb mechanical shocks; especially, a hydraulically damped coupling used to absorb impulsive forces generated by the contact of the wheels of a motor vehicle with irregular road surfaces.

shock·er (shóckər) *n.* **1.** One that startles, shocks, or horrifies; especially, a sensational story or novel. **2.** *Informal.* A thoroughly unpleasant person.

shock-head·ed (shók-héddid) *adj.* Having thick, shaggy hair.

shock·ing (shócking) *adj.* **1.** Highly disturbing emotionally. **2.** Highly offensive; indecent or distasteful. **3.** Very vivid or intense in tone: *shocking pink.* **4.** *Informal.* Nasty; very bad. —**shock·ing·ly** *adv.*

Shock·ley (shóckli), **William Bradford** (1910–89). U.S. physicist, born in England. He directed U.S. naval research into anti-submarine warfare during World War II, and in 1948 developed the transistor jointly with Bardeen and Brattain. The three were awarded the 1956 Nobel physics prize for their work. Latterly he expressed controversial views on the inheritance of intelligence.

shock·proof (shók-proof) *adj.* Able to withstand the effects of collisions or blows.

shock stall *n. Aeronautics.* Air resistance on an aircraft when it is close to the speed of sound that may lead to stalling.

shock therapy *n.* The inducing of shock by electric current or drugs, sometimes causing convulsions, as a therapy for mental illness. Also called "shock treatment".

shock treatment *n.* **1.** Shock therapy. **2.** Any brutally direct approach to a problem.

shock troops *pl.n. Military.* Highly experienced and capable soldiers specially trained to lead attacks.

shock tube *n. Physics.* A long tube in which a shock wave can be produced for spectrosopic investigation of radicals and excited molecules formed by the high temperature of the wave.

shock wave *n.* A large-amplitude compression wave, such as that produced by an explosion or by supersonic motion of a body in a medium.

shock workers *pl.n.* Labourers and skilled workers in Communist countries such as the U.S.S.R. and Poland who performed extremely arduous tasks, such as constructing buildings and roads in record time, particularly in the 1950s.

shod·dy (shóddi) *n., pl.* **-dies.** **1.** Wool fibres obtained by shredding unfelted woollen or worsted rags or worn garments. **2.** Yarn, fabric, or garments made from or containing such recycled wool fibres. **3.** Inferior or imitation goods; cheap, derivative material. ~*adj.* **shoddier, -iest.** **1.** Transparently imitative or inferior. **2.** Of poor quality or workmanship; trashy. **3.** Made of or containing shoddy or other inferior material. [19th century : of obscure (dialectal) origin.] —**shod·di·ly** *adv.* —**shod·di·ness** *n.*

shoe (shoo) *n., pl.* **shoes** or *archaic* **shoon** (shoon). **1. a.** A durable covering for the human foot; especially, either of a matched pair made of leather or similar material and having a rigid sole and a heel of variable height. **b.** *British.* Such a foot covering reaching to just below the ankle. **c.** *U.S.* Such a foot covering reaching to just below or just above the ankle. **2.** A horseshoe. **3.** A part or device placed at an end, foot, or bottom, especially: **a.** A strip of metal fitted onto the bottom of a sledge runner. **b.** A skid placed under the wheel of a vehicle to retard its motion. **c.** A metal or rubber rim or casing protecting the bottom end of a walking stick, cane, or the like. **4.** The part of a brake that presses against the wheel or drum to retard its motion. **5. a.** The sliding contact plate on an electric train or tram that conducts electricity from the third rail. **b.** An oblong box used for holding and dealing cards in some gambling card games in which several packs of cards are used. —**fill (someone's) shoes.** To take the place of; succeed (another). —**in (someone's) shoes.** In someone else's position or predicament. ~*tr.v.* **shod** (shod), **shod** or **shodden** (shódd'n), **shoeing, shoes.**

1. To furnish or fit with shoes. **2.** To cover with a wooden or metal guard to protect against wear. [Middle English *sho(o)*, Old English *scōh*, from Germanic *skōhaz* (unattested).]

shoe·bill (shoo-bil) *n.* A tall wading bird, *Balaeniceps rex*, native to swampy regions of eastern tropical Africa, and having slaty plumage, long black legs, a stubby neck, and a large shoelike bill with a hook on the upper mandible.

shoe·black (shoo-blak) *n.* A **bootblack** *(see).*

shoe·horn (shoo-hawrn) *n.* A curved implement, often of horn or smooth metal, inserted at the heel to help slip on a shoe.

shoe·lace (shoo-layss) *n.* A string or cord used for lacing and fastening a shoe.

shoe·mak·er (shoo-maykər) *n.* A person who makes or repairs shoes and boots as an occupation. —**shoe·mak·ing** *n.*

sho·er (shoo-ər) *n.* A person who shoes horses; a blacksmith.

shoe·string (shoo-string) *n.* **1. a.** A shoelace. **2.** A small sum of money; barely adequate funds: *living on a shoestring.* ~*adj.* **1.** Having or using a barely adequate amount, especially of money. **2.** *Chiefly U.S.* Cut to or in the shape of a shoestring; long and slender: *shoestring potatoes.*

shoe·tree (shoo-tree) *n.* A foot-shaped form inserted into a shoe when it is not being worn to preserve its shape.

sho·far, sho·phar (shō-faar) *n., pl.* **-fars** or **sho·froth** (shō-frówt). *Judaism.* A trumpet made of a ram's horn, blown for warning, summoning, and ritual purposes by the ancient Hebrews, and now sounded in the synagogue at Rosh Hashanah and Yom Kippur. [Hebrew *shōphār*, "ram's horn".]

sho·gun (shō-goon, -gun) *n.* Any of a line of military leaders of Japan who, until 1867, exercised absolute rule under the nominal leadership of the emperor. [Japanese *shōgun*, "general", from Chinese *jiāng jūn* : *jiāng*, to lead, command + *jūn*, army.]

sho·gun·ate (shōgə-nət, -nit, -nayt) *n. Sometimes capital* **S.** The government of a shogun.

sho·ji (shōji) *n., pl.* **shoji** or **-jis.** A translucent paper screen forming a sliding door or partition in a Japanese house. [Japanese *shōji*, from Chinese *zhàngzi*.]

Sho·lem A·lei·chem (shól-əm ə-láykhəm, sháwl-), pen name of Sholem Yakov Rabinowitz (1859–1916). Russian writer, known for his Yiddish tales, which are celebrated for their homespun wisdom. He settled in the United States at the outbreak of World War I.

Sho·lo·khov (shō-lə-kov; *Russian* -khəf), **Mikhail Alexandrovich** (1905–84). Russian novelist. The four-part novel by which he is best known is published in English as *And Quiet Flows the Don* (1934) and *The Don Flows Home to the Sea* (1940); the work spans the pre- and post-revolutionary periods and was acclaimed in the U.S.S.R. as an outstanding example of socialist realism. Sholokhov was awarded the 1965 Nobel prize for literature.

Sho·na (shōnə) *n., pl.* **nas** or collectively **Shona.** Also **Ma·sho·na** (mə-shónnə). **1.** A member of any of various closely related groups of southern African people, living chiefly in Zimbabwe. **2.** The Bantu language of this people. —**Sho·na** *adj.*

shone. Past tense and past participle of **shine.**

shoo (shoo) *interj.* Used to scare away animals or birds. ~*v.* **shooed, shooing, shoos.** —*tr.* To drive or scare away, as by crying "shoo". —*intr.* To cry "shoo". [Middle English *schowe* (imitative).]

shoo-in (shoo-in) *n. U.S. Informal.* A contestant or candidate who seems certain of winning.

shook¹ (shook) *n.* A set of parts for assembling a barrel or packing case. [18th century : origin obscure.]

shook². Past tense of **shake.**

shook-up (shook-úp ‖ shook-) *adj. U.S. Slang.* Emotionally upset.

shoot (shoot) *v.* **shot** (shot), **shooting, shoots.** —*tr.* **1.** To hit, wound, or kill with a missile fired from a weapon; especially, to kill with a bullet. **2.** To fire or let fly (a missile) from a weapon. **3.** To discharge or fire (a weapon). **4.** To cause to move directly and swiftly by or as if by a sudden release of tension. **5.** To send forth swiftly or dartingly: *She shot a look of contempt at him.* **6.** To pass over or through swiftly: *shoot the rapids.* **7.** To cover (country) in hunting for game. **8.** To record in photographs or on on film. **9.** To record (a film sequence). **10.** To put forth; begin to grow or produce; generate. Used especially of a plant. **11.** To pour, empty out, or discharge down or as if down a chute. **12.** In golf, to make (a specified number of strokes). **13.** *Sports.* **a.** To move or propel (a ball), as by hitting or kicking, towards a goal. **b.** To score (a goal). **c.** *U.S.* To play (golf, craps, or pool). **14.** To slide into or out of a fastening: *shoot a door bolt.* **15.** To measure the altitude of with a sextant or other instrument: *shoot a star.* **16.** *Slang.* To inject (a narcotic drug) directly into a vein. —*intr.* **1.** To discharge a missile from a weapon. **2.** To discharge fire; go off. **3.** To move swiftly, as if discharged from a weapon; dart: *shot past in a car; pain shot through his leg.* **4.** To protrude; extend; project. **5.** To hunt game, for example, with a weapon: *shoot in the marshes.* **6.** To put forth new growth; germinate; sprout. **7. a.** To take pictures; film. **b.** To start filming. **8.** To propel a ball, as by kicking or hitting, towards the goal. **9.** To move fast and low after pitching. Used of a ball. **10.** To begin questioning someone. Used in the imperative. —**shoot down.** **1.** To bring down (an aircraft, for example) by hitting and damaging with a missile. **2.** *Informal.* **a.** To ruin the plans, hopes, aspirations of, as by penetrating argument. **b.** To show (a plan or idea, for example) to be impractical or invalid. —**shoot through.** *Australian Informal.* To go away; depart. —**shoot up.** **1.** *Informal.* **a.** To grow or get taller rapidly. **b.** To rise or increase

rapidly. **2.** *Informal.* To hit many times with shot or other projectiles. **3.** *Informal.* To terrorise (an area) by lawless, wild shooting. **4.** *Slang.* To inject a narcotic drug directly into a vein.
~*n.* **1.** The motion or movement of something that is shot; a forward or upward advance. **2. a.** The young growth arising from a germinating seed; a sprout. **b.** A bud or young leaf on a plant. **3.** Any new growing part. **4.** A narrow and swift or turbulent section of a stream; a rapid. **5.** See **chute. 6. a.** A party or expedition engaged in shooting game. **b.** Land where game may be shot. **7.** *Informal.* The launching of a rocket or similar missile. **8.** An act of or occasion for filming. **9.** In rowing, the interval between strokes. **—the whole shoot.** *Slang.* Everything. [Middle English *shoten,* past *shote,* past participle *shote(n),* Old English *scēotan, scēat* (past singular), *scoten.*]

shoot·er (shóōtər) *n.* **1.** One that shoots. **2.** *Slang.* A firearm.

shoot·ing box (shóōting) *n. British.* A small house for the use of those engaged in shooting game. Also called "shooting lodge".

shooting brake *n. British.* An **estate car** *(see).*

shooting gallery *n.* An enclosed target range for shooting practice or competition.

shooting iron *n. U.S. Informal.* A firearm, such as a pistol.

shooting star *n.* A briefly visible **meteor** *(see).*

shooting script *n.* A script giving details of camerawork, including the order in which sequences are to be shot.

shooting stick *n.* A type of walking stick opening into a seat at one end, typically used by spectators at a shoot.

shooting war *n.* A war in which hostilities have reached the point of open military aggression as opposed to the use of diplomatic or economic sanctions, for example.

shoot-out (shóōt-owt) *n.* A confrontation in which armed opponents fire guns at one another.

shop (shop) *n.* **1.** A place, such as a building or room, where retail goods or certain services may be obtained. **2.** A workshop for the manufacture or repair of machinery, for example: *a machine shop.* **3.** *Informal.* **a.** Any commercial or industrial establishment. **b.** A business or other similar activity: *set up shop; close up shop.* **—all over the shop.** *British Informal.* **1.** In a state of confusion or disarray. **2.** In every place; everywhere. **—talk shop.** To talk about one's business or occupation, especially to the exclusion of other topics. —See Usage note at **store.**
~*v.* **shopped, shopping, shops.** —*intr.* To visit shops for the purpose of looking for and buying goods. Often used with *for.* —*tr. British Slang.* To betray to the police. **—shop around. 1.** To investigate the different prices and quality of certain goods before deciding on a purchase. **2.** To investigate a number of possibilities before deciding on a course of action. [Middle English *shoppe,* Old English *sceoppa,* booth, stall, from Germanic *skupp-* (unattested).]

shop floor *n.* **1.** The area, in a factory for example, where manual workers, as opposed to management, operate. **2.** These workers, especially when organised as a union. **—shop-floor** (shóp-flór) *adj.*

shop·keep·er (shóp-keepər) *n.* An owner or manager of a shop.

shop·lift·er (shóp-liftər) *n.* One who steals goods on display in a shop. **—shop·lift** *v.* **—shop·lift·ing** *n.*

shop·per (shóppər) *n.* One who buys goods at shops; a customer.

shop·ping (shópping) *n.* Items purchased from shops.

shopping centre *n.* The part of a town or suburban area providing a group of shops situated close together.

shop·soiled (shóp-soyld) *adj. British.* **1.** Faded, worn, or in some other state of deterioration as a result of being on display in a shop. **2.** Unfavourably marked by experience.

shop steward *n.* A union member chosen by fellow workers to represent them in their dealings with the management.

shop·talk (shóp-tawk) *n. Chiefly U.S.* Talk or conversation concerning one's business or occupation.

shop·walker (shóp-wawkər) *n. British.* An employee of a department store who supervises sales personnel and assists customers. Also *U.S.* "floor walker".

shop·worn (shóp-wawrn) *adj. U.S.* **1.** Shopsoiled; faded or worn. **2.** Trite; hackneyed: *shopworn anecdotes.*

sho·ran (sháwr-an || shōr-) *n.* A relatively short-range radar navigation system by which a ship or aircraft can determine its position with high precision by measuring the times required for a radio signal to reach each of two ground stations of known position and to return. [*Sho*rt *ra*nge *n*avigation.]

shore[1] (shor || shōr) *n.* **1.** The land along the edge of an ocean, sea, lake, or river. **2.** Land: *set foot on shore.* **3.** *Often plural.* A country: *When will you see these shores again?* **4.** *Law.* See **foreshore.**
~*tr.v.* **shored, shoring, shores.** To put or set on shore. [Middle English, from Middle Dutch and Middle Low German *schore*†.]

shore[2] *tr.v.* **shored, shoring, shores.** To prop up or support with or as if with an inclined timber. Usually used with *up.*
~*n.* A beam or timber propped against a ship, wall, or other structure as a temporary support. [Middle English, *shoren,* from Middle Dutch *schōren*†.]

shore bird *n.* Any of various birds, such as the sandpiper, plover, or snipe, that frequent the shores of coastal or inland waters. Also called "wader".

shore leave *n.* **1.** Permission granted to a sailor to spend time ashore. **2.** The amount of time so allowed.

shore·line (shór-līn || *U.S. also* shōr-) *n.* The line marking the edge of a body of water.

shor·ing (shór-ing || shōr-) *n.* A system of shores or props used for supporting something.

shorn. Alternative past participle of **shear.**

short (short) *adj.* **shorter, shortest. 1.** Having little length; not long: *a short corridor; short arms.* **2.** Having little height; not tall; low: *Jockeys must be short.* **3.** Having a small extent in time; brief. **4.** Not attaining that which is required; inadequate; insufficient: *in short supply.* **5.** Lacking the required length, extent, or amount: *a plank two inches short.* **6.** Lacking; inadequately supplied with something: *I'm short of cash.* **7.** Not lengthy; concise; succinct: *short and to the point.* **8.** *Finance.* **a.** Not owning the stocks or commodities one is selling. **b.** Pertaining to or designating a sale of stocks or goods not yet owned by the seller, but which he must produce to meet the terms of a contract. **9.** Lacking in retentiveness: *a short memory.* **10.** Rudely brief; abrupt; curt. **11.** Containing shortening; crisp; friable: *short pastry.* **12.** In prosody, designating a syllable that is of relatively brief duration in classical verse and unstressed in English verse. **13.** *Phonetics.* **a.** Designating a particular pronunciation of the letters for the vowel sounds, such as the sound of (a) in *pan,* of (e) in *pen,* of (i) in *pin,* of (o) in *pond,* of (ōō) in *put,* and of (u) in *putt,* as distinguished from the sound of (ay) in *pane,* of (ee) in *penal,* of (ī) in *pine,* of (ō) in *post,* and of (ōō) in *poop.* **b.** Designating a speech sound of relatively brief duration, as opposed to the same or similar sound of relatively long duration. **14.** In cricket: **a.** Designating a fielder or fielding position close to the batsman. **b.** Designating a bowled ball that lands some distance from the batsman. —See Usage note at **brief. —for short.** As an abbreviated form: *My name is Robert, but call me Rob for short.* **—in short.** To sum up concisely. **—short and sweet.** Brief and to the point, especially when contrary to expectation: *Fortunately, the negotiations were short and sweet.* **—short for.** In shortened form: *"Jim" is short for "James".* **—short of. 1.** Not equivalent to; less than: *something short of a mile.* **2.** Lacking a sufficient amount of: *short of breath.* **3.** Without reaching an extreme of; almost including: *took every step short of mining his back garden.* **4.** Except for; apart from: *Short of buying a car, I don't know how I'll get in to work.* **—short on.** Lacking in: *short on ideas.*
~*adv.* **1.** Abruptly; suddenly: *stop short.* **2.** Rudely; crossly. **3.** Concisely. **4.** Without owning what one is selling: *sell short.* **—caught** or **taken short. 1.** Unexpectedly lacking what is necessary. **2.** Having a sudden need to urinate or defecate. **—fall short.** To fail to meet expectations or requirements.
~*n.* **1.** Anything that is short, especially: **a.** A briefly articulated or unaccented syllable. **b.** A short vowel. **c.** A short sale, or a person who sells short. **d.** *Plural.* Short trousers extending to the knee or above. **e.** *Plural. U.S.* Men's underpants. **f.** A short film shown before the main feature film. **2.** *Plural.* A by-product of wheat processing, consisting of bran mixed with coarse meal or flour. **3.** A strong drink of an alcoholic spirit, especially one that is undiluted. **4. a.** A short circuit. **b.** A malfunction caused by a short circuit.
~*v.* **shorted, shorting, shorts.** —*tr.* To cause a short circuit in. ~*intr.* To short-circuit. [Old English *sceort,* from Germanic *skurtaz* (unattested).] **—short·ish** *adj.* **—short·ness** *n.*

Short, Nigel (David) (1965–). British Grandmaster chess player who unsuccessfully challenged Garry Kasparov for the world title in 1993, having won the qualifying competition in 1992.

short account *n.* The account of a person who sells short.

short·age (shórtij) *n.* A deficiency in amount; a deficit.

short-arm (shórt-aarm) *adj.* Designating a blow in which the arm is kept in a bent position rather than punched out straight.

short·bread (shórt-bred) *n.* A type of rich, crumbly biscuit made with flour, sugar, and butter.

short·cake (shórt-kayk) *n.* **1.** A type of rich semisweet biscuit, similar to shortbread. **2.** A dessert consisting of a cake made with rich biscuit dough, split and filled with strawberries or other fruit, and topped with cream.

short-change (shórt-cháynj) *tr.v.* **-changed, -changing, -changes. 1.** To give less change than is due. **2.** *Informal.* To swindle, cheat, or trick. **—short-chang·er** *n.*

short circuit *n.* An accidentally established low-resistance connection between two points in an electric circuit that bypasses the load and causes an excessive current to flow. Also called "short".

short-cir·cuit (shórt-súrkit || -surkit) *v.* **-cuited, -cuiting, -cuits.** —*tr.* **1.** To cause to have a short circuit. **2.** To avoid; bypass. —*intr.* To become affected with a short circuit.

short·com·ing (shórt-kumming, -kúmming) *n.* A deficiency or flaw.

short covering *n.* The buying of securities, stocks, or commodities to make provision for a short sale.

short·crust pastry (shórt-krust) *n.* Pastry made from flour and a shortening, such as fat or butter, which, when cooked, has a brittle, dense texture, as opposed to flaky or puff pastry.

short cut *n.* **1.** A quicker, more direct route than the customary one. **2.** Any means of speeding up a process: *Becoming famous is a short cut to getting your book published.*

short-dat·ed (shórt-dáytid) *adj. Finance.* Designating gilt-edged securities redeemable after a time less than five years away. Compare **long-dated, medium-dated.**

short-day (shórt-dáy) *adj.* Designating or producing plants that will flower only when exposed to periods of daylight of less than 12 hours: *short-day seeds.* Compare **long-day.**

short division *n.* A division of one number by another, usually no more than two digits, without writing out the remainders.

short·en (shórt'n) *v.* **-ened, -ening, -ens.** —*tr.* **1.** To make short or shorter. **2.** To take in (a sail) so that less canvas is exposed to the wind. **3.** To cause to come down or decrease: *shortened the odds.*

4. To add shortening to (dough) so as to produce a crumbly texture. —*intr.* **1.** To become short or shorter. **2.** To decrease; lessen.

short·en·ing (shórt'n-ing) *n.* A fat, such as butter, lard, or vegetable oil, used to make cake or pastry light or flaky.

short·fall (shórt-fawl) *n.* **1.** A failure to attain a required amount or level; a shortage; a deficiency. **2.** The amount by which a supply falls short of expectation, need, or demand.

short·hand (shórt-hand) *n.* **1. a.** A system of rapid handwriting employing symbols to represent words, phrases, and letters; stenography. **b.** The handwriting itself. **2.** Any system, form, or instance of abbreviated or formulaic reference: *"The classical error is to regard a scientific law as only a shorthand for its instances."* (Jacob Bronowski). **—short·hand** *adj.*

short·hand·ed (shórt-hándid) *adj.* Lacking the usual or necessary number of workmen, employees, or assistants.

shorthand typist *n.* A typist who records speech in shorthand and then transcribes it on a typewriter. Also *U.S.* "stenographer".

short-haul (shórt-háwl) *adj.* Involving or designating the transport of goods or passengers over short distances.

short·horn (shórt-hawrn) *n.* Any of a breed of beef or dairy cattle originating in northern England and having short, curved horns. Also called "Durham".

short hundredweight *n.* A **hundredweight** *(see).*

shor·tie, shor·ty (shórti) *n. Informal.* A short person or thing. ∼*adj. Informal.* Short in length: *a shortie jacket.*

short list *n. British.* A list of names of the most likely candidates, as for a job or position, who have been selected from the larger number of original applicants.

short-list (shórt-líst-, -list) *tr.v.* **-listed, -listing, -lists.** *British.* To put (a person) on a short list.

short-lived (shórt-lívd || *U.S. also* -lívd) *adj.* Living or lasting only a short time; ephemeral.

short·ly (shórtli) *adv.* **1.** In a short time; soon; presently. **2.** In a few words; concisely. **3.** Abruptly or curtly.

short-range (shórt-ráynj) *adj.* Of or having a limited range in distance or time: *a short-range forecast.*

short shrift *n.* **1.** Summary and unsympathetic treatment or dismissal. **2.** *Archaic.* The short space of time granted a condemned prisoner for his confession before execution. **—make short shrift of** or **give short shrift to. 1.** To dispose of summarily or without consideration. **2.** To make quick work of; dispatch.

short·sight·ed (shórt-sítid) *adj.* **1.** Suffering from myopia; nearsighted. **2.** Lacking foresight. **3.** Resulting from a lack of foresight. **—short·sight·ed·ly** *adv.* **—short·sight·ed·ness** *n.*

short-spo·ken (shórt-spókən) *adj.* Given to shortness or abruptness in manner or speech; curt.

short story *n.* A piece of fictional prose much shorter than a novel and typically concentrating on a single event, situation, or character.

short-tem·pered (shórt-témpərd) *adj.* Easily moved to anger.

short-term (shórt-térm) *adj.* **1.** Lasting or extending for a relatively short period of time: *short-term measures.* **2.** Payable or reaching maturity within a relatively short time: *a short-term loan.* **—short·term·ism** *n.*

short ton *n.* A unit of weight, a **ton** *(see).*

short-waisted (shórt-wáystid) *adj.* Having or being of less than average length from shoulders to waist: *a short-waisted dress.*

short wave *n. Abbr.* **sw** An electromagnetic wave with wavelength in the short-wave region.

short-wave (shórt-wáyv) *adj. Abbr.* **sw 1.** Having a wavelength in the range 10 to 100 metres. **2.** Capable of receiving or transmitting at such wavelengths.

short-wind·ed (shórt-wíndid) *adj.* **1.** Having shortness of breath; easily winded. **2.** Not discursive; brief: *a short-winded speech.*

shorty. Variant of **shortie.**

Sho·sho·ne (shō-shóni, shə-) *n., pl.* **-nes** or collectively **Shoshone.** Also **Sho·sho·ni. 1.** A member of a Uto-Aztecan-speaking North American Indian people, formerly occupying parts of the American West. **2.** The language of this people.

Sho·sho·ne·an (shō-shóni-ən, shə-, shōshə-née-ən) *n.* An Indian linguistic group in western North America, comprising most of the Uto-Aztecan languages in the United States. **—Sho·sho·ne·an** *adj.*

Shos·ta·ko·vitch (shóstə-kóvich), **Dmitri Dmitrievich** (1906–75). Russian composer, one of the most prolific and most widely acclaimed of the 20th century. He wrote in all forms, but is perhaps best known for his 15 symphonies and his chamber music.

shot¹ (shot) *n., pl.* **shots** or **shot** (for sense 2). **1.** A firing or discharge of a weapon, such as a gun or bow. **2. a.** Tiny pellets, especially made of lead, discharged from a shotgun in one charge. **b.** Any of these pellets. **c.** A projectile, such as an iron ball, fired from a cannon, for example. **3.** In certain games, such as soccer, snooker, golf, or tennis, a hit or kick of the ball. **4.** One who shoots, considered with regard to the accuracy of his aim: *a good shot.* **5.** The distance over which something is shot; range. **6.** An attempt to hit or land on something with a missile or rocket: *a moon shot.* **7.** *Informal.* An attempt, guess, or opportunity: *had a shot at playing bridge.* **8.** The heavy metal ball that an athlete throws in the shot-put. **9.** *Mining.* A charge of explosives used in blasting. **10. a.** A photograph or one in a series of photographs. **b.** A single cinematic view or take. **11.** *Informal.* A hypodermic injection. **12.** *Informal.* A drink of spirits, especially a jigger. **13.** *Nautical.* A unit designating chain length, in the United Kingdom equal to 12½ fathoms and in the United States equal to 15 fathoms. **—by a long shot.** By a considerable extent or margin. **—get shot of.** *Informal.* To lose, shake off, or get rid of. **—like a shot.** Quickly; in an instant. **—shot in the arm.** That which revives or stimulates: *a shot in the arm for the industry.* **—shot in the dark.** A completely wild guess. ∼*tr.v.* **shotted, shotting, shots.** To load or weight with shot. [Middle English *shot,* Old English *sceot.*]

shot² *adj.* **1.** Of changeable, variegated, or iridescent colour. Said of fabric having different-coloured warp and weft. **2.** *Informal.* Worn-out; ruined; exhausted. **—shot through with.** Filled or riddled with: *a poem shot through with vivid imagery.*

shot³. Past tense and past participle of **shoot.**

shote. Variant of **shoat.**

shot·gun (shót-gun) *n.* A shoulder-held firearm that fires multiple pellets through a smooth bore.

shotgun wedding *n.* A wedding which one or both of the partners are forced to enter into, especially as a consequence of the woman becoming pregnant. Also called "shotgun marriage". [Alluding to the bride's father or relatives armed to force the groom to marry.]

shot hole *n.* A hole drilled into rock or other material into which an explosive charge is inserted for blasting purposes.

shot-put (shót-pŏŏt) *n.* **1.** An athletic event in which the contestants attempt to throw or put a shot or heavy ball as far as possible. **2.** One such throw. **—shot-put·ter** *n.*

shott (shot) *n.* Also **chott** (chott). **1.** A shallow intermittent salt lake or salt marsh in a hot desert. **2.** The depression or hollow occupied by such a salt lake or salt marsh.

shot·ten (shótt'n) *adj.* **1.** Having recently spawned and being thus less desirable as food. Said of fish, especially herring. **2.** *Archaic.* Of no value; worthless. [Archaic past participle of SHOOT (specialised sense "to spawn").]

shot tower *n.* A tower formerly used for making lead shot by dropping molten lead from the top into water at the bottom.

should (shŏŏd; *weak forms* shəd, shd, sht). Past tense of **shall,** but more often used as an auxiliary verb expressing various shades of attendant meaning indicating: **1.** Obligation; duty; necessity: *They should tell him the bad news.* **2.** Anticipation of a probable occurrence; expectation: *They should arrive at noon.* **3.** Condition; contingency of one condition upon another: *Should he so much as move, shoot him dead.* **4.** Moderation of the directness or bluntness of a request or statement: *I should like to query that figure.* **5.** An implication of the unusual or surprising: *Who should I bump into in the street but my ex-husband!* **6.** A piece of advice: *I should apologise if I were you.* **7.** *Informal.* An ironic negative, asserting the negative in a positive way: *With his talent, he should worry* (meaning *should not worry*) *about winning!*

Usage: Traditional grammars argue that a distinction needs to be maintained between *would* and *should* parallel to that recommended for *will* and *shall*: *should* is to be used in first person forms for the expression of simple conditionality, *would* in second and third person forms; and the opposite situation obtains when other meanings (such as determination or compulsion) are to be expressed. In practice, this distinction is hardly ever maintained. American English uses *would* with all three persons for expressing conditionality, and prefers this form to *should.* British English usage is mixed: older people and more formal styles still maintain *should,* especially in the first person; younger people generally use *would.* Thus we find *If I had the money, I would go* or *I would like to go* (American English and some British English) and *If I had the money, I should go* or *I should like to go* (more formal British English). In referring to past time, both the following constructions occur without any difference in meaning: *I would/should like to have gone, I would/should have liked to go.* The double use of *have,* as in *I would/should have liked to have gone,* is not standard though it will sometimes be heard in casual speech. *If I would have found it . . .* is a possible construction in informal American English, but in British English a construction with *had* is standard *(If I had found it . . .).* See also Usage notes at **shall, ought.**

shoul·der (shóldər) *n.* **1.** *Anatomy.* **a.** The part of the human body between the neck and upper arm. **b.** The joint connecting the arm with the trunk. **2.** The corresponding part of an animal. **3.** *Plural.* **a.** The two shoulders and the area of the back between them. **b.** This area of the back considered as the part to bear burdens. **4.** The forequarter of some animals. **5.** The part of a garment that covers the shoulder. **6.** The angle between the face and the flank of a bastion in fortifications. **7.** *Printing.* The extended flat surface on the body of type beyond the letter or character. **8.** A cut of meat, as lamb, consisting of the top part of the foreleg. **9. a.** The edge or ridge running on either side of a main road. **b.** Any projection or slope that resembles a shoulder in shape. **—rub shoulders with.** *Informal.* To meet or associate with. **—shoulder to shoulder.** United in a common cause or effort. **—straight from the shoulder.** With utter frankness.

∼*v.* **shouldered, -dering, -ders.** —*tr.* **1.** To carry (a burden, for example) on or as on the shoulders; bear or support; assume. **2.** To push (one's way) through with or as if with the shoulder. **3.** To apply force to with or as if with the shoulder. —*intr.* To push with the shoulder or shoulders. [Middle English *shulder,* Old English *sculdor,* from Germanic *skuldra-* (unattested).]

shoulder bag *n.* A handbag or travelling bag that is supported by means of a long strap passing over the shoulder.

shoulder blade *n.* The **scapula** *(see).*

shoulder girdle *n.* The **pectoral girdle** *(see).*

shoulder patch *n.* A military identification patch worn on the upper portion of the sleeve to designate one's regiment, for example.

shoulder strap *n.* **1.** A strap attached to the shoulder of a military uniform to show rank. **2.** A strap that fits over the shoulder, such as one that supports a garment.

should·n't (shŏŏd'nt). Contraction of *should not*.

shouldst (shŏŏdst). Also **should·est** (shŏŏdist). *Archaic.* Second person singular past tense of **shall.** Used with *thou.*

shout (shout) *n.* **1.** A loud, vigorous, cry, often expressing strong emotion or a command. **2.** *Chiefly Australian Informal.* A person's turn to buy drinks; a round.

~*v.* **shouted, shouting, shouts.** —*tr.* **1.** To utter with a shout. **2.** *Chiefly Australian Informal.* **a.** To treat (a person) to a round of drinks, for example. **b.** To treat a person to a (a round of drinks). —*intr.* **1.** To utter a loud cry; yell. **2.** To speak or laugh loudly. —**shout down.** To overwhelm or silence by shouting loudly. [Middle English *shouten†*.] —**shout·er** *n.*

shove (shuv) *v.* **shoved, shoving, shoves.** —*tr.* **1.** To cause to move with a sudden push or thrust. **2.** To push roughly or rudely; jostle. **3.** *Informal.* To put or place somewhere. —*intr.* To push rudely or roughly or with sudden force. —**shove off. 1.** To set a beached boat afloat. **2.** *Informal.* To leave. Often used in the imperative. **~***n.* The act of shoving; especially, a rude push. [Middle English *sho(u)ven,* Old English *scūfan,* from Germanic.] —**shov·er** *n.*

shove-half·pen·ny (shŏv-háyp-əni) *n. British.* A game in which players try to propel old halfpennies along a marked wooden board so that they land between any two parallel lines.

shov·el (shŭvv'l) *n.* **1.** A tool with a handle and a somewhat flattened scoop for picking up earth, coal, or other materials. **2.** A large mechanical device for heavy digging or excavation, usually a jawed scoop suspended from a boom or crane. **3.** *Informal.* A shovel hat.

~*v.* **shovelled** or *U.S.* **shoveled, -elling** or *U.S.* **-eling, -els.** —*tr.* **1.** To dig into or move with a shovel. **2.** To clear or make (a path, for example) with a shovel. **3.** To convey roughly or in large quantities, as with a shovel: *shovelled cake into her mouth.* —*intr.* To dig or work with a shovel. [Middle English *shovel,* Old English *scofl,* from Germanic.] —**shov·el·ler** *n.*

shovelboard. Variant of **shuffleboard.**

shov·el·er (shŭvv'l-ər, shŭvv'lər) *n.* A widely distributed duck, *Anas clypeata,* having a long, broad bill.

shov·el·ful (shŭvv'l-fŏŏl) *n., pl.* **-fuls.** The amount a shovel will hold.

shovel hat *n.* A stiff, broad-brimmed, low-crowned hat, turned up at the sides and projecting in front, formerly worn by some clergymen. Also informally called "shovel".

shov·el·head (shŭvv'l-hed) *n.* A shark, *Sphyrna tiburo,* of Atlantic and Pacific waters.

shov·el·nosed (shŭvv'l-nŏzd) *adj.* Having a broad, flattened snout, bill, or head.

show (shŏ) *v.* **showed, shown** (shōn ‖ shŏ-ən) or **showed, showing, shows.** —*tr.* **1. a.** To cause or allow to be seen; make visible: *a white carpet shows the dirt; showed her talent.* **b.** To present to the view of: *She showed me her operation scar.* **c.** To exhibit or present to the public: *Which film is being shown at the Plaza?* **d.** To present (an animal of a recognised breed) for judging in a competitive exhibition. **2.** To conduct; guide: *Show me round your garden.* **3. a.** To point out; demonstrate. **b.** To make clear; prove. **c.** To teach by practical demonstration: *Show me how to knit.* **4. a.** To manifest; reveal. **b.** To indicate; register. **5.** To grant; confer; bestow: *showed great devotion to the cause.* **6.** *Law.* To plead; allege: *show cause.* —*intr.* **1.** To be or become visible or evident: *If you're nervous, it certainly doesn't show.* **2.** To appear: *His face showed red.* **3.** To be exhibited; run: *The film will show for three days.* **4.** *Informal.* To make an appearance; show up. **5.** *Sports. U.S.* To finish third for betting purposes. —**show for.** As evidence of gain, as from a course of action: *nothing to show for my efforts.* —**show up. 1.** To expose or reveal (faults, flaws, or the like). **2.** To be clearly or ultimately visible: *The white shows up well against the dark background.* **3.** *Informal.* To put in an appearance; arrive. **4.** *Informal.* To cause to feel shame or inferiority.

~*n.* **1.** The act of showing or revealing. **2. a.** A display; a manifestation; a demonstration: *a show of force.* **b.** An outward appearance; a semblance: *A show of kindness concealed her diabolical motives.* **4.** A striking appearance or display; a spectacle. **5.** A pompous or ostentatious display: *It's all done for show.* **6. a.** A public exhibition or competition: *a flower show.* **b.** An entertainment such as a play or film: *a television show.* **7. a.** A trace; an indication. **b.** In obstetrics, a discharge of blood occurring at the start of labour. **8.** *Informal.* Any affair or undertaking: *Who is supposed to be running this show?* **9.** *Informal.* An attempt or try; an effort: *put up a bad show.* **10.** *Sports. U.S.* Third place for betting purposes. —**good** (or **bad**) **show.** Used to express approval (or disapproval). —**show of hands.** A raising of hands among the members of a group so that a vote may be taken. —**steal the show.** *Informal.* To gain the greatest amount of adulation or applause.

~*adj.* Of, in, or used for a show or shows. [Middle English *shewen, showen,* to look at, cause to look at, show, Old English *scēawian,* to look at, see, from Germanic.] —**show·er** (shŏ-ər) *n.*

Synonyms: show, display, expose, parade, exhibit, flaunt.

show bill *n.* An advertising poster.

show biz *n. Slang.* Show business.

show·boat (shŏ-bōt) *n.* Especially in the United States, a river steamboat having a troupe of actors and a theatre on board giving performances on the river.

showbread. Variant of **shewbread.**

show business *n.* The entertainment business, especially that part of it concerned with theatre and films.

show·case (shŏ-kayss) *n.* **1.** A display case or cabinet, as in a shop or museum. **2.** A setting in which something may be displayed to advantage: *The Great War was a showcase for the effectiveness of tanks.*

show·down (shŏ-down) *n.* **1.** *Informal.* A confrontation that forces a disputed issue to a conclusion. **2.** In card games such as poker, the laying down of the players' hands of cards for the purpose of determining the winner.

show·er (showr, shŏ-ər) *n.* **1.** A brief fall of rain, hail, snow, or sleet. **2.** Any brief or sudden fall resembling a spray or shower: *a meteor shower.* **3.** An abundant flow; an outpouring: *a shower of abuse.* **4.** A stream of elementary particles resulting from the impact of a high-energy particle, especially a cosmic-ray particle, on a target particle **5.** *British Slang.* A group of untidy, ill-assorted people. **6.** *U.S.* A party held to honour and present gifts to someone, especially a bride-to-be. **7. a.** A bath in which water is sprayed onto the bather by means of a device, usually situated overhead. **b.** A device so used to spray water, usually having a nozzle through which fine jets of water may pass. **c.** A room or cubicle equipped for such baths. Also called "shower bath".

~*v.* **showered, -ering, -ers.** —*tr.* **1.** To sprinkle; spray. **2. a.** To bestow on abundantly: *showered her with gifts.* **b.** To present in abundance: *showered gifts on her.* —*intr.* **1.** To fall or pour down in a shower. **2.** To have a shower bath. [Middle English *shour,* Old English *scūr,* from Germanic.] —**show·er·y** *adj.*

show·er·proof (shŏ-ər-prŏŏf) *adj. British.* Able to repel water, though not fully waterproof. —**show·er·proof** *tr.v.*

show·girl (shŏ-gurl) *n.* A chorus girl or similar entertainer as opposed to a serious actress.

show·ing (shŏ-ing) *n.* **1.** A performance, as in a competition or test of skill: *a poor showing.* **2.** A presentation of evidence, facts, or figures: *On the present showing he will pass easily.*

show·jump·ing (shŏ-jumping) *n.* A horseriding competition in which competitors must complete a course of fences and obstacles and are judged on the number of errors committed and sometimes on time taken. —**show·jump·er** *n.*

show·man (shŏ-mən) *n., pl.* **-men** (-mən, -men). **1.** A theatrical producer. **2.** A person whose behaviour displays a flair for showiness or the dramatic. —**show·man·ship** *n.*

shown. Past participle of **show.**

show off *tr.v.* To display in such a way as to invite admiration. —*intr.v. Informal.* To behave like a show-off.

show·off (shŏ-off, -awf) *n. Informal.* One who self-confidently displays his talent or ability, especially to an excessive degree.

show·piece (shŏ-peess) *n.* **1.** An exhibition piece. **2.** That which is exemplary of its kind.

show·place (shŏ-playss) *n.* A place that is visited for its beauty, historical interest, or the like.

show·room (shŏ-rŏŏm, -rŏŏm) *n.* A room in which goods are on display.

show stopper *n. Informal.* **1.** A person or event, such as a theatrical act, that receives enthusiastic applause and so causes a short interruption in the proceedings. **2.** Broadly, anything that receives instant and enthusiastic admiration or approval.

show trial *n.* A public judicial trial that is primarily designed to serve the propaganda needs of a regime.

show·y (shŏ-i) *adj.* **-ier, -iest. 1.** Making a conspicuous display; striking: *showy flowers.* **2.** Displaying brilliance and virtuosity of ability or performance. **3.** Ostentatious; gaudy; flashy. —See Synonyms at **ornate.** —**show·i·ly** *adv.* —**show·i·ness** *n.*

shpt. shipment.

Shqiperi. See Albania, Socialist People's Republic of.

shr *Finance.* share.

shrank. Past tense of **shrink.**

shrap·nel (shrápnəl) *n. Military.* **1. a.** An antipersonnel projectile containing metal balls, fused to explode in the air above enemy troops. **b.** These projectiles collectively. **2.** Shell fragments from any high-explosive shell. [After Henry *Shrapnel* (1761-1842), British artillery officer who invented it.]

shred (shred) *n.* **1.** A long, thin, irregular strip cut or torn off. **2.** A small amount; a particle; a scrap: *not a shred of evidence.*

~*tr.v.* **shredded** or **shred, shredding, shreds.** To cut or tear into shreds. [Middle English *shrede,* Old English *scrēade.*] —**shred·der** *n.*

shrew (shrŏŏ ‖ shrew) *n.* **1.** Any of various small, chiefly insectivorous mammals of the family Soricidae, having a long, pointed nose and small, often poorly developed eyes. Sometimes called "shrewmouse". **2.** A woman with a violent, scolding, or nagging temperament; a scold. [Middle English *shrewe* (unattested), Old English *scrēawa.*]

shrewd (shrŏŏd ‖ shrewd) *adj.* **shrewder, shrewdest. 1.** Having or showing keen insight; sharp; astute: *a shrewd political commentator.* **2.** Having experience, cleverness, and cunning, especially in practical affairs: *a shrewd businessman.* —See Synonyms at **clever.** [Middle English *shrewed,* wicked, dangerous, serious, from SHREW (evil person).] —**shrewd·ly** *adv.* —**shrewd·ness** *n.*

Synonyms: shrewd, sagacious, astute, quick-witted.

shrew·ish (shrŏŏ-ish ‖ shrĕw-) *adj.* Like a shrew in temperament;

ill-tempered; nagging. —**shrew·ish·ly** *adv.* —**shrew·ish·ness** *n.*

shrew mole *n.* Any of several shrewlike moles of the family Talpidae; especially, *Neurotrichus gibbsi*, of western North America, or *Uropsilus soricipes*, of eastern Asia.

Shrews·bur·y (shrŏz-bri, -bəri ‖ shrŏ̄o-, shréwz-). County town of Shropshire in western England, lying on the river Severn.

shriek (shreek) *n.* **1.** A shrill outcry; a high-pitched scream; a screech. **2.** Any sound suggestive of a shriek.

~*v.* **shrieked, shrieking, shrieks.** —*intr.* **1.** To utter a shriek. **2.** To make a shrill sound similar to a shriek: *"the winds shriek through the clouds"* (Ezra Pound). —*tr.* To utter with a shriek. —See Synonyms at **scream.** [Middle English *shriken* (imitative), probably from Old Norse *skrækja*.] —**shriek·er** *n.*

shriev·al·ty (shréev'lti) *n.* The office, tenure, or jurisdiction of a sheriff. —**shrie·val** *adj.*

shrift (shrift) *n. Archaic.* **1.** The act of shriving. **2.** Confession or absolution given by a priest. **3.** See **short shrift.** [Middle English *shrift(e)*, Old English *scrift*, from *scrīfan*, to SHRIVE.]

shrike (shrīk) *n.* **1.** Any of various carnivorous birds of the genus *Lanis*, having a hooked bill, and often impaling its prey on sharp-pointed thorns or barbs of wire fencing. Some species are also called "butcherbird". **2.** Any of various similar but unrelated birds. [Probably from Middle English *shrik* (unattested), from Old English *scrīc*, thrush (imitative).]

shrill (shril) *adj.* **shriller, shrillest. 1.** High-pitched and piercing. **2.** Producing a sharp, high-pitched tone or sound. **3.** Insistently nagging or sharp in tone: *shrill attacks on the government.*

~*v.* **shrilled, shrilling, shrills.** —*tr.* To utter in a shrill manner; scream; shriek. —*intr.* To produce a shrill cry or sound. [Middle English *shrille*, from *shrillen*, to shriek, perhaps from Scandinavian; akin to Norwegian *skrylla*.] —**shrill·ness** *n.* —**shril·ly** *adv.*

shrimp (shrimp) *n., pl.* **shrimps** or collectively **shrimp. 1. a.** Any of various small, slender-bodied, chiefly marine decapod crustaceans of the order Crangon, many species of which are edible. **b.** Any of various similar unrelated crustaceans. **2.** *Informal.* A diminutive or unimportant person.

~*intr.v.* **shrimped, shrimping, shrimps.** To fish for shrimps. [Middle English *shrimpe*, pigmy, shrimp, perhaps of Low German origin; akin to Middle Low German *schrempen*, to shrink, wrinkle.]

shrimp plant *n.* A shrubby plant, *Beloperone guttata*, having inconspicuous flowers borne between shrimp-like reddish bracts.

shrine (shrīn) *n.* **1.** A container or receptacle for sacred relics; a reliquary. **2.** The tomb of a saint or other venerated person. **3.** A site, as a church, or an object, as an altar, devoted to a holy person. **4.** Any place hallowed by a venerated person or object, or their associations.

~*tr.v.* **shrined, shrining, shrines.** To enshrine. [Middle English *shrin(e)*, box, chest, reliquary, Old English *scrīn*, from Latin *scrīnium†*, box, bookcase.]

shrink (shringk) *v.* **shrank** (shrangk) or **shrunk** (shrungk), **shrunk** or **shrunken** (shrúngkən), **shrinking, shrinks.** —*intr.* **1.** To draw together or constrict from heat, moisture, or cold; contract. Used especially of fabrics. **2.** To become reduced in amount or value; dwindle. **3.** To draw back; recoil, as through shyness: *shrank into the corner.* **4.** To be reluctant; flinch: *Shrank from the task of leading the charge.* —*tr.* To cause to shrink. —See Synonyms at **contract, decrease.**

~*n.* **1.** A shrinking or shrinkage. **2.** *Slang.* A psychiatrist or psychoanalyst. [Shrink, shrank, shrunk; Middle English *shrinken, shrank* (also *shrunk*), *shrunken*, Old English *scrincan, scranc* (plural *scruncon*), *(ge)scruncen*.] —**shrink·a·ble** *adj.* —**shrink·er** *n.*

Usage: This verb has two past tenses, *shrank* and *shrunk*, the former being more common. The past participle form is *shrunk. Shrunken* is occasionally used in this way, but generally this form is restricted to adjectival use (*a shrunken figure*).

shrink·age (shríngkij) *n.* **1.** The act or process of shrinking. **2.** A reduction or depreciation, as in value. **3.** Loss of stock through shoplifting. **4.** The amount of weight lost by livestock, as during shipment, before being marketed.

shrinking violet (shríngking) *n. Informal.* A shy or retiring person.

shrink wrapping *n.* A transparent form-fitting plastic wrapping, especially of polythene or polyvinyl chloride, used to protect a commodity from dust, moisture, and abrasion.

shrink-wrap (shríngk-ráp, -rap) *tr.v.* **-wrapped, -wrapping, -wraps.** To enclose (an article) in shrink wrapping.

shrive (shrīv) *v.* **shrove** (shrōv) or **shrived, shriven** (shrívv'n) or **shrived, shriving, shrives.** *Archaic.* —*tr.* **1.** To hear the confession of and give absolution to (a penitent). **2.** To obtain absolution for (oneself) by confessing and doing penance. —*intr.* **1.** To make or go to confession. **2.** To hear confessions. [Shrive, shrove, shriven; Middle English *shriven, shrove, shriven*, Old English *scrīfan, scrāf* (past singular), *scrifen(e)*, from West Germanic *skrīban* (unattested), to write, "prescribe (penance)", from Latin *scrībere*, to write.] —**shriv·er** *n.*

shriv·el (shrívv'l) *v.* **-elled** or *U.S.* **-eled, -elling** or *U.S.* **-eling, -els.** —*intr.* **1.** To shrink and wrinkle, often in drying. Often used with *up.* **2.** To lose vitality; become wasted and useless. —*tr.* To cause to become shrivelled. [Perhaps from Old Norse *skrifla*, to wrinkle.]

Shrop·shire (shróp-shər, -sheer ‖ -shīr). Formerly **Sal·op** (sáləp). County of western England, lying on the Welsh border. It is predominantly agricultural, with plains to the north and east of the river Severn, and hills to the southwest. Shrewsbury is the county town.

shroud (shrowd) *n.* **1.** A cloth used to wrap a body for burial; a winding sheet. **2.** Something that conceals, protects, or screens: *a shroud of darkness.* **3.** *Plural.* A set of ropes or wire cables stretched from the masthead to a vessel's sides to support the mast. **4.** A similar support for a chimney or comparable structure. **5.** The ropes connecting the harness and canopy of a parachute.

~*v.* **shrouded, shrouding, shrouds.** —*tr.* **1.** To wrap (a corpse) in burial clothing. **2.** To envelop; screen; hide. **3.** *Archaic.* To shelter; protect. —*intr. Archaic.* To take cover; find shelter. [Middle English *sc(h)rud*, garment, clothing, Old English *scrūd*, from Germanic.]

shroud-laid (shrówd-layd) *adj.* Designating a rope made from four strands twisted to the right, usually round a core.

Shrove·tide (shrōv-tid) *n.* The three days, Shrove Sunday, Shrove Monday, and Shrove Tuesday, preceding Ash Wednesday. [Middle English *schroftyde* : *schrof-*, "shriving", irregularly from *schrov-*, past stem of *shriven*, SHRIVE + *tyde, tid(e)*, TIDE (time).]

Shrove Tuesday (shrōv) *n.* The day before Ash Wednesday, on which, in Britain, pancakes are traditionally eaten.

shrub[1] (shrub) *n.* A woody plant of relatively low height, distinguished from a tree by having several stems rather than a single trunk; a bush. [Middle English *schrubbe*, Old English *scrybb.*]

shrub[2] *n.* A drink made from fruit juice, sugar, and a spirit such as rum or brandy. [Arabic *shurb*, a drink, from *shariba*, to drink. See also **sherbet, syrup.**]

shrub·ber·y (shrúbbəri) *n., pl.* **-ies. 1.** A group or plantation of shrubs. **2.** Shrubs collectively.

shrub·by (shrúbbi) *adj.* **-bier, -biest. 1.** Consisting of, planted with, or covered with shrubs. **2.** Of or resembling a shrub; shrublike. —**shrub·bi·ness** *n.*

shrug (shrug) *v.* **shrugged, shrugging, shrugs.** —*tr.* To raise (the shoulders) as a gesture of doubt, disdain, or indifference. —*intr.* To make this gesture. —**shrug off. 1.** To minimise the importance of. **2.** To get rid of without trouble: *shrug off a cold.*

~*n.* **1.** An act of shrugging. **2.** *U.S.* A short jacket or sweater, open down the front. [Middle English *shruggen†.*]

shrunk. Past participle and alternative past tense of **shrink.**

shrunken. Alternative past participle of **shrink.**

shtum (shtŏo̅m) *adj.* Also **stumm.** *British slang.* Mum. Used chiefly in the phrase *keep shtum: "Not something to brag about in the banking world. Just keep shtum." (London Regional Transport advertisement.)* [German or Yiddish *stumm* mute, silent.]

shuck (shuk) *n. U.S.* The outer covering of something, such as a pea pod, maize husk, or oyster shell.

~*tr.v.* **shucked, shucking, shucks.** *U.S.* **1.** To remove the husk or shell from. **2.** *Informal.* To cast off (clothing, for example). [17th century : origin obscure.] —**shuck·er** *n.*

shucks (shuks) *interj. U.S.* Used to express disappointment, disgust, or annoyance. [From SHUCK (in U.S. sense "thing of no value").]

shud·der (shúddər) *intr.v.* **-dered, -dering, -ders. 1.** To tremble or shiver convulsively, as from fear, cold, or aversion. **2.** To vibrate; quiver: *The engine shuddered to a halt.* —See Synonyms at **shake.**

~*n.* A convulsive shiver, as from fear or cold. [Middle English *shoddren, shudren*, from Middle Low German *schöderen.*] —**shud·der·ing·ly** *adv.*

shuf·fle (shúff'l) *v.* **-fled, -fling, -fles.** —*tr.* **1.** To move (the feet) in short dragging movements along the floor or ground while walking or dancing. **2.** To move back and forth or from one place to another. **3.** To mix together or otherwise handle (papers, for example) in a disordered, haphazard fashion. **4.** To put aside or conceal hastily; cover up: *Important issues were quickly shuffled off.* **5.** To mix together (playing cards, for example) to change the order of arrangement. —*intr.* **1.** To move by shuffling one's feet. **2.** To dance the shuffle. **3.** To shift about from side to side. **4.** To act in a shifty or deceitful manner; equivocate. **5.** To shuffle playing cards.

~*n.* **1.** The act or an instance of shuffling. **2.** A dance in which the feet scrape along the floor at each step. **3.** An evasive or deceitful action; a dodge. **4. a.** The act of mixing cards. **b.** A player's turn to do this. [Probably from Low German *schüffeln*, to walk clumsily, shuffle cards.] —**shuf·fler** *n.*

shuf·fle·board (shúff'l-bawrd ‖ -bōrd) *n.* Also **shov·el·board** (shúvv'l-). **1.** A game, played especially on a ship, in which discs are pushed or slid along a smooth, level surface towards numbered squares with a pronged cue. **2.** The surface on which this game is played. [Alteration (influenced by SHUFFLE) of earlier *shove-board* : SHOVE + BOARD.]

shuf·ti (shŏofti) *n., pl.* **-tis.** *British Slang.* A look: *took a quick shufti at the paper.* [Arabic.]

shun (shun) *tr.v.* **shunned, shunning, shuns.** To avoid (a person, group, or thing) deliberately and consistently; keep away from. See Synonyms at **escape.** [Middle English *shun(n)en*, Old English *scunian†*, to avoid, be afraid, abhor.] —**shun·ner** *n.*

shunt (shunt) *n.* **1.** The act or an instance of shunting. **2.** A railway point. **3.** A low-resistance connection between two points in an electric circuit that forms an alternative path for a portion of the current. Also called "bypass". **4.** *Slang.* A collision between two cars, especially racing cars. **5.** *Medicine.* A passage through which blood passes from one part or organ to another. It may be created by surgery or occur as a congenital abnormality.

~*v.* **shunted, shunting, shunts.** —*tr.* **1.** To turn or move (something) aside or onto another course. **2.** To move or switch (a train or carriage) from one track to another. **3.** *Electricity.* To provide or divert (current) by means of a shunt. **4.** To evade or avoid (a task, for example) by refusing or putting aside. **5.** *Informal.* To transfer to a different position or task, usually a less demanding or important one. —*intr.* **1.** To move or turn aside. **2.** To move from one track to another. Used of a train. **3.** *Electricity.* To become diverted by means of a shunt. Used of a circuit. [Middle English *shunten,* to flinch, shy, run away, perhaps from *shun(n)en,* SHUN.]

shunt·er (shúntər) *n.* A railway locomotive used in shunting rather than in pulling trains on journeys.

shunt-wound (shúnt-wownd) *adj.* Of or designating a direct-current motor or generator in which the field coil is connected in parallel with the armature so that the same voltage appears across each. Compare **series-wound.**

shush (shŏŏsh, shush) *interj.* Used to express a demand for silence. —*tr.v.* **shushed, shushing, shushes.** To demand silence from by saying "shush": *"Simon shushed him quickly as though he had spoken too loudly in church."* (William Golding). [Imitative.]

shut (shut) *v.* **shut, shutting, shuts.** —*tr.* **1. a.** To move (a door, lid, or valve, for example) into closed position over or within an opening. **b.** To bring (something that extends or opens out) into a folded or compact state: *shut the book.* **c.** To bring the two edges of together: *shut your eyes.* **2.** To block passage or access to; close: *shut the garage.* **3.** To fasten or secure with a lock, catch, or latch. Often used with *up.* **4.** To deny (someone) access to a place; bar: *She was shut out of her house.* **5.** To keep from leaving a place; confine: *I was shut in the cellar.* **6.** To cause to reject or ignore: *shut his mind to criticism.* **7.** To catch something as it is being shut: *shut my sleeve in the door.* **8.** To close (a business establishment). Often used with *up.* —*get shut of. Informal.* To dispose of (an unwanted person or thing); rid oneself of. —*intr.* **1.** To become shut; close. **2.** To admit of being shut: *The door shuts easily now you've oiled the hinges.* —*shut up.* **1.** *Informal.* To silence (a person). **2.** *Informal.* To be or become silent: *I'll have my say and then I'll shut up.* ~*n.* **1.** The line of connection between welded pieces of metal. **2.** *Archaic.* The act or time of closing or shutting. ~*adj.* Closed. [Middle English *shutten,* originally a West Midland form of *shitten, shetten,* Old English *scyttan.*]

shut down *tr.v.* **1. a.** To cause (an industrial plant, for example) to close. **b.** To stop the operation of (a machine, for example). **2.** To put a check on or stop to. —*intr.v.* To stop working; close. Used of a factory, machine, or the like.

shut·down (shút-down) *n.* **1.** A temporary or permanent closing of an industrial plant. **2.** The failure or intentional cessation of operation of any apparatus or enterprise.

Shute (shŏŏt), **Nevil,** born Nevil Shute Norway (1899–1960). British novelist, who lived in Australia after 1950. His many internationally popular novels include *A Town Like Alice* (1950) and *On The Beach* (1957).

shut·eye (shút-ī) *n. Slang.* Sleep.

shut-in (shút-in) *n. U.S.* An invalid. ~*adj.* (-ín). *U.S.* Confined to a house or hospital, as by illness.

shut off *tr.v.* **1.** To stop or prevent from flowing or working: *shut off the water supply.* **2.** To separate or isolate.

shut-off (shút-off, -awf) *n. Chiefly U.S.* **1.** A device that shuts something off. **2.** A stoppage or interruption.

shut out *tr.v.* **1.** To forbid access to; bar; exclude. **2.** To keep from being seen: *shut out the view of the gasworks.*

shut-out (shút-owt) *n.* **1.** A **lockout** (see). **2.** *Sports. U.S.* A game in which one side does not score.

shut·ter (shúttər) *n.* **1.** One that shuts. **2.** A hinged window cover, usually made of wood and fitted with louvres, and used to exclude light but not necessarily air. **3.** Any of the movable louvres on a pipe organ, controlled by pedals, that open and close the swell box. **4.** A mechanical device that opens and shuts the lens aperture of a camera to expose a plate or film. **5.** A similar device in a film projector that enables an image to be thrown onto the screen only when the film is momentarily stationary. ~*tr.v.* **shuttered, -tering, -ters.** To furnish or close with a shutter or shutters.

shut·tle (shútt'l) *n.* **1.** A device used in weaving to carry the woof thread back and forth between the warp threads. **2.** A device for holding the thread in tatting, in netting, and in a sewing machine. **3. a.** A train, bus, or aircraft making short, frequent trips to and fro between two points. Also used adjectivally: *a shuttle service.* **b.** A space shuttle. **4.** The act of shuttling. ~*v.* **shuttled, -tling, -tles.** —*intr.* To go, move, or travel back and forth by or as if by a shuttle. —*tr.* To move or transport by or as if by a shuttle. [Middle English *schutyle,* Old English *scytel,* dart.]

shut·tle·cock (shútt'l-kok) *n.* **1.** A small rounded piece of cork or similar material with a crown of feathers, used in the games of badminton and battledore. **2.** The game of battledore. ~*tr.v.* **shuttlecocked, -cocking, -cocks.** To send or bandy back and forth like a shuttlecock. [SHUTTLE + COCK (bird).]

shuttle diplomacy *n.* A type of diplomacy in which a statesman of a country neutral to two others in dispute travels back and forth between them as mediator.

shy¹ (shī) *adj.* **shier** or **shyer, shiest** or **shyest. 1.** Easily startled; timid. Said especially of an animal. **2.** Nervous in company; unsure of oneself; reserved. **3.** Distrustful; wary; cautious. **4.** *Informal.* Not having paid an amount due, as one's ante in poker. **5.** *Informal.* Short; lacking: *We're still £5 shy.* **6.** Reluctant to engage in or associate with a specified thing, activity, or group. Usually used in combination: *work-shy.* ~*intr.v.* **shied, shying, shies. 1.** To move suddenly, as if startled:

The horse shied at the noise. **2.** To draw back, as through fear or caution: *He shied away from responsibility.* ~*n., pl.* **shies.** A sudden movement, as from fright; a start. [Middle English *schey,* timid, Old English *scēoh,* from Germanic *skiuhwaz* (unattested).] —**shy·er** *n.* —**shy·ly** *adv.* —**shy·ness** *n.*

Synonyms: *shy, bashful, timid, self-conscious, diffident, retiring, modest, coy, demure.*

shy² *v.* **shied, shying, shies.** —*tr.* To throw with a swift sideways motion. —*intr.* To throw something in this manner. ~*n., pl.* **shies. 1.** A quick throw; a fling. **2.** *Informal.* A gibe; a sneer. **3.** *Informal.* An attempt; a try. [Earliest senses, "to take sudden fright", "shrink", "flinch", probably from SHY (timid).]

Shy·lock (shī-lok) *n.* A heartless, exacting creditor. [After *Shylock,* the ruthless usurer in Shakespeare's *Merchant of Venice* (1596).]

shy·ster (shīstər) *n. Chiefly U.S. Slang.* A person given to unethical or unscrupulous practices, especially in business, law, or politics. [Perhaps after *Scheuster,* an unscrupulous 19th-century New York lawyer, or blend of German *Scheis(ser),* shitter + English -STER.]

si (see) *n. Music.* The former name for **ti** *(see).*

Si The symbol for the element silicon.

SI International System of measurement. See **SI unit.** [French *Système international.*]

si·al (sī-al) *n.* The silicon and aluminium-rich rocks which form the earth's continental upper crust. Compare **sima.** [*Si*lica + *al*umina.] —**si·al·ic** *adj.*

si·al·a·gogue, si·al·o·gogue (sī-əl-ə-gog, sī-ál-) *n. Medicine.* Any drug or agent that stimulates the flow of saliva. [New Latin *sialagōgus,* from Greek *sialon,* saliva + -AGOGUE.] —**si·al·a·gog·ic** (-gójik), **si·al·o·gog·ic** *adj.*

Siam. See **Thailand.**

si·a·mang (see-ə-mang, sī-) *n.* A large black gibbon, *Symphalangus syndactylus* (or *Hylobates syndactylus*), of Sumatra and the Malay Peninsula, having an inflatable throat sac and webbing joining the second and third toes. [Malay.]

Si·a·mese (sī-ə-meéz ‖ -meéss) *adj.* Thai. ~*n., pl.* **Siamese. 1.** A **Thai** *(see).* **2.** The language, **Thai** *(see).*

Siamese cat *n.* A short-haired cat of a breed developed in the Orient, having blue eyes and a pale fawn or grey coat with often darker ears, face, tail, and feet.

Siamese fighting fish *n.* A small, often brightly coloured freshwater fish, *Betta splendens,* native to tropical Asia and popular in home aquariums.

Siamese twin *n.* Either of a pair of twins born with their bodies joined together in any manner. [After Chang and Eng (1811–74), joined twins born in *Siam.*]

Sian. See **Xi'an.**

sib (sib) *n.* **1. a.** A blood relation; a kinsman. **b.** Relatives collectively. **2.** A brother or sister; a sibling. **3.** A plant that is the product of a self-pollination, especially one in a group of plants that are mainly the products of cross-pollinations. Also called "sibling". ~*adj.* Related by blood; akin. Used with *to.* [Middle English *sib(be),* Old English *sibb.*]

Sib·bald's rorqual (síbb'ldz) *n.* The **blue whale** *(see).* [After Sir R. Sibbald (1644–1722), Scottish scientist and physician.]

Si·be·li·us (si-báyli-əss), **Jean (Julius Christian)** (1865–1957). Finnish composer, the most famous of his country. Often looked upon as a nationalist composer, he is best known popularly for the symphonic tone poem, *Finlandia* (1900). He also wrote seven symphonies and a violin concerto (1903–05).

Si·be·ri·a (sī-beér-i-ə). Vast geographical region of Russia comprising the northern third of Asia, stretching from the Urals in the west to the Pacific Ocean in the east, and south from the Arctic Ocean to the Mongolian border. About two fifths of the region is covered in forest. Most of the population lives in the southwest, which is now one of the most densely industrialised parts of Russia owing largely to the Kuznetsk Basin, rich in coal and iron deposits. Large petroleum and natural gas fields are also exploited in the western lowlands, and huge hydroelectric stations are located on the river Angara at Irkutsk and Bratsk. The chief city of western Siberia is Novosibirsk. —**Si·be·ri·an** *adj. & n.*

Siberian husky *n.* A husky of a breed from northeast Asia.

sib·i·lant (síbbilənt) *adj.* **1.** Producing a hissing sound. **2.** *Phonetics.* Characterised by the sound of (s) or (sh). ~*n. Phonetics.* A speech sound that suggests hissing, such as (s), (sh), (z), or (zh). **2.** A sibilant consonant. [Latin *sībilāns* (stem *sībilant-*), present participle of *sībilāre,* to hiss, whistle, SIBILATE.] —**sib·i·lance, sib·i·lan·cy** *n.* —**sib·i·lant·ly** *adv.*

sib·i·late (síbbi-layt) *v.* **-lated, -lating, -lates.** —*intr.* To utter a hissing sound; hiss. —*tr.* To pronounce with a hissing sound. [Latin *sībilāre,* to hiss, whistle.] —**sib·i·la·tion** (-láysh'n) *n.*

Si·biu (si-beé-ŏŏ, -béw). German **Her·mann·stadt** (haír-man-shtat); Hungarian **Nagy·sze·ben** (nóch-sebben). City in central Romania, lying at the foot of the Transylvanian Alps.

sib·ling (síbbling) *n.* **1.** One of two or more persons having one or normally both parents in common; a brother or sister. **2.** A plant, a sib. [Middle English *siblyng,* Old English *sibling* : SIB + -LING.]

sib·yl (síbbil, sibb'l) *n.* **1.** Any of various women regarded as oracles or prophetesses in the ancient world. **2. a.** A prophetess. **b.** A witch; a sorceress. [Middle English *Sibile, Sybylle,* from Old French *Sibile, Sebile,* from Latin *Sibylla,* from Greek *Sibulla*†.] —**sib·yl·line** (-īn), **si·byl·ic** (si-bíllik) *adj.*

sic¹ (sik ‖ seek) *adv. Latin.* Thus; so. Used in written texts to indicate that a surprising or dubious word, phrase, or fact is not a mistake and is to be read as it stands. [Latin *sīc.*]

sic², sick (sik) *tr.v.* **sicked, sicking, sics** or **sicks. 1.** To urge to attack or chase. **2.** To set upon or chase. Used only in the imperative, as a command to a dog. [Dialectal variant of SEEK.]

Si·ca·ni·an (si-káyni-ən) *adj.* Sicilian.

sic·ca·tive (síckətiv) *n.* A substance added to paints and some medicines to promote drying; a drier. [Latin *siccātīvus,* drying, from *siccāre,* to dry, from *siccus,* dry.] **—sic·ca·tive** *adj.*

sice. Variant of **syce.**

Si·chuan (sích-wáan). Also **Sze·chwan** (séch-). Province in southwestern China, lying to the east of Tibet. The capital is Chengdu. It forms a natural geographical region, being entirely ringed by mountains. It is China's leading producer of rice, and is also important for its sugar cane, cotton, and cattle-farming.

Sic·i·ly (síssili, siss'l-i). *Italian* **Si·ci·lia** (see-chéel-ya). Region of southern Italy, consisting mainly of the island of Sicily, separated from the extreme southwestern tip of the mainland by the narrow Strait of Messina. The region also includes the Egadi, Lipari, and Pelagie island groups, and the islands of Pantelleria and Ustica. The main island is the largest in the Mediterranean. It is almost entirely hilly and mountainous, the highest point being Mount Etna, an active volcano, which rises to 3 323 metres (10,902 feet). Palermo is the capital. **—Si·cil·i·an** (si-síl-i-ən) *adj. & n.*

sick¹ (sik) *adj.* **sicker, sickest. 1. a.** Not in normal health physically or psychologically; ill; unwell. **b.** Wishing to vomit or in the act of vomiting: *She was sick in the sink.* **2.** Of or for sick persons: *sick leave.* **3. a.** Producing or characterised by black humour; unwholesome; in deliberately bad taste: *a sick joke.* **b.** Culturally ailing or unsound; rotten; decadent: *a sick society.* **4.** *Informal.* **a.** Deeply distressed; chagrined; upset: *felt sick at losing the game.* **b.** Disgusted; revolted. **c.** Weary; tired. Usually used with *of*: *sick of it all.* **d.** Pining; longing. Used with *for.* **5.** In need of repairs. Said of a ship. **6.** Unable to produce a profitable yield of crops, especially as a result of excessive cultivation of a single crop. Often used in combination: *rose-sick soil.* **7.** *Informal.* In a position of obvious embarrassment, humiliation, or inferiority: *Now that she's walked out on him, he looks pretty sick.* **—sick up.** *Informal.* To vomit.
~*n. Informal.* Vomit. [Middle English *sēk, sīk,* Old English *sēoc,* from Germanic *siukaz* (unattested).] **—sick·ish** *adj.*
Synonyms: *sick, ill, indisposed, poorly, unwell.*

sick². Variant of **sic** (to urge to attack).

sick·bay (sík-bay) *n.* An area, as on a ship, used as a hospital or infirmary.

sick·bed (sík-bed) *n.* A sick person's bed.

sick call *n. Military.* **1. a.** The daily line-up of personnel requiring medical attention. **b.** The signal announcing this. **2.** A call made by a doctor to a sick person.

sick·en (síckən) *v.* **-ened, -ening, -ens.** —*tr.* To make sick; fill with nausea or revulsion. —*intr.* To become sick or show signs of sickness. **—sick·en·er** *n.*

sick·en·ing (síckəning) *adj.* **1.** Causing sickness or nausea. **2.** Revolting or disgusting; loathsome. **3.** *Informal.* Very annoying or disagreeable. **—sick·en·ing·ly** *adv.*

Sick·ert (síckərt), **Walter (Richard)** (1860–1942). British painter, born in Munich. He studied with Whistler, then with Degas in Paris in 1883, and did not live permanently in England until after 1905. His studio in Bloomsbury became a centre for the transmission to England of influences from the impressionist movement. Sickert was at his best in painting figures from the world of the theatre.

sick headache *n.* **1.** A headache accompanied by nausea. **2.** An attack of migraine.

sick·le (síck'l) *n.* An implement having a semicircular blade attached to a short handle, for cutting grain or tall grass.
~*tr.v.* **sickled, -ling, -les.** *Chiefly U.S.* To cut with a sickle. [Middle English *sikel,* Old English *sicol, sicel,* from West Germanic, from Vulgar Latin *sicila* (unattested), variant of Latin *sēcula.*]

sick leave *n.* Leave of absence given because of sickness.

sick·le·bill (síck'l-bil) *n.* Any of several birds having sharply curved bills; especially, *Falculea palliata,* of Madagascar.

sickle cell *n.* An abnormal crescent-shaped red blood cell.

sickle cell anaemia *n.* A hereditary anaemia mainly affecting black people, characterised by the presence of oxygen-deficient sickle-shaped red blood cells.

sickle feather *n.* Any of the long, curving feathers of a cock's tail.

sick list *n.* A list of sick personnel, as in the army.

sick·ly (síckli) *adj.* **-lier, -liest. 1.** Prone to sickness; ailing. **2.** Of, caused by, or associated with sickness: *a sickly pallor; a sickly shade of green.* **3.** Conducive to ill health; unhealthy. **4.** Inducing vomit; nauseating; sickening: *sickly, rich food.* **5.** Mawkish; weak.
~*adv. U.S.* In a sick manner.
~*tr.v.* **sicklied, -lying, -lies.** *Archaic.* To make sickly, as in colour. **—sick·li·ness** *n.*

sick·ness (sík-nəss, -niss) *n.* **1.** The condition of being sick; illness. **2.** A disease; a malady. **3.** Nausea.

sickness benefit *n.* Money paid by the state, in weekly instalments, to one who is unable to work through being ill.

sick·room (sík-rōōm, -rŏŏm) *n.* A room occupied by a sick person.

sic pas·sim (sík pássim || séek). *Latin.* Thus everywhere. Used in textual annotation to indicate that a term or idea is to be found throughout the work cited.

Sid·dons (sídd'nz), **Sarah (Kemble)** (1755–1831). British actress, the most illustrious member of the theatrical Kemble family. From 1785, when she first played Lady Macbeth, to 1812, when she gave her last performance in the same role, she was acknowledged as the finest Shakespearean actress of her day.

Sid·dhar·tha (si-dártə). See **Buddha.**

sid·dur (síddər, síddoor) *n., pl.* **siddurim** (síddoo-réem) or **-durs.** A Jewish prayer book containing prayers for the various days of the year. Compare **machzor.** [Hebrew *siddūr,* "order", "arrangement (of prayers)", from *siddēr,* to arrange.]

side (sīd) *n.* **1.** *Geometry.* **a.** A line bounding a plane figure. **b.** A surface bounding a solid figure. **2.** A surface of an object; especially, a surface joining a top and bottom: *Hold the box by its sides.* **3.** A surface of an object that extends more or less perpendicularly from an observer standing in front of it: *the side of the mountain.* **4. a.** Either of the two surfaces of a flat object, such as a piece of paper. **b.** The amount of writing it takes to fill a side of paper: *wrote four sides in the exam.* **5. a.** The area to the left or right of the observer, or of an axis: *played on the left side of the field.* **b.** The left or right half of the trunk of a human or the corresponding part of an animal body: *a side of mutton.* **6.** The space immediately next to someone or something: *stood at her side.* Often used in combination: *roadside.* **7.** One of two or more contrasted parts or places within an area, identified by its location with respect to a centre: *the north side of the park.* **8. a.** An area separated from another area by some intervening line, barrier, or other feature: *on this side of the Atlantic.* **b.** That which comes before some dividing line: *this side of madness.* **9. a.** One of two or more opposing groups, teams, or sets of opinions. **b.** A sports team: *one of the best sides in Europe.* **c.** Any of the positions maintained as in a dispute or debate: *He always takes her side in arguments.* **10.** A distinct aspect or quality: *the cruel side of her nature.* **11.** A line of descent: *my aunt on my mother's side.* **12.** *British Slang.* Arrogance or affected superiority: *has got too much side.* **13.** *Informal.* A television channel: *What's on the other side?* **14.** In certain games, such as snooker, tennis, or table tennis, a spin imparted to the ball by a sideways motion of the bat or cue, usually causing a variation in the ball's movement. **—let the side down.** To fail or disappoint one's comrades. **—on the side.** *Informal.* **1.** In addition to a main activity, occupation, or arrangement, often with a suggestion of illegality: *was making a bit of money on the side.* **2.** *U.S.* Served as a side dish. **—on the (specified) side.** Tending towards a specified condition, quality, or amount: *she's a bit on the slow side.* **—put to** or **on one side.** To set apart from the main subject under consideration. **—side by side.** Next to each other; close together. **—split (one's) sides.** To be convulsed with laughter. **—take sides.** To associate oneself with a faction, contested opinion, or cause. **—the other side.** The realm of the dead; the spirit world.
~*adj.* **1.** Located on a side: *a side chapel.* **2.** From or to one side; oblique: *a side view.* **3.** Minor; incidental: *a side interest.* **4.** In addition to the main part; supplementary: *a side benefit.*
~*intr.v.* **sided, siding, sides.** To align oneself. Used with *with* or *against*: *sided with Peter against Paul.* [Middle English *side,* Old English *sīde,* from Germanic.]

-side *n. comb. form.* Indicates a region bordering a river or estuary, especially when heavily industrialised; for example, *Clydeside, Humberside.*

side arms *pl.n.* Weapons carried at the side or waist, such as swords or pistols.

side·band (sīd-band) *n.* Either of the two bands of frequencies, one just above and one just below a carrier frequency, that result from modulation of a carrier wave.

side·board (sīd-bawrd || -bōrd) *n.* A piece of dining-room furniture originally for holding dishes of food and usually having drawers and shelves for storing tableware.

side·boards (sīd-bawrdz || -bōrdz) *pl.n.* Growths of hair or whiskers down the sides of a man's face in front of the ears. Also *chiefly U.S.* "sideburns".

side·car (sīd-kaar) *n.* **1.** A one-wheeled car for a single passenger, attached to the side of a motorcycle. **2.** A cocktail combining brandy, an orange-flavoured liqueur, and lemon juice.

side chain *n. Chemistry.* A radical, group, or chain of atoms attached to a carbon atom in the main chain of an organic molecule or to the cyclic nucleus of such a molecule.

sid·ed (sīdid) *adj.* Having sides usually of a specified number or kind. Used in combination: *straight-sided.*

side dish *n.* A small dish, as of salad, served with a main course.

side-dress (sīd-dress) *tr.v.* **-dressed, -dressing, -dresses.** To treat (plants) by placing fertiliser near their roots, on or in the soil.

side drum *n.* A small double-headed snare drum, traditionally worn at the side by soldiers.

side effect *n.* A peripheral or secondary effect; especially, an undesirable secondary effect of a drug or therapy.

side issue *n.* An issue that is not directly relevant to the main point under consideration.

side·kick (sīd-kik) *n. Informal.* A close friend or associate. [Earlier *sidekicker,* perhaps from *kicker* (in draw poker), an unmatched card held with a pair or three of a kind for purposes of bluffing or improving the hand.]

side·light (sīd-līt) *n.* **1.** A light coming from the side. **2.** Either of two small lights on the front of a motor vehicle used to indicate its presence when parked or when moving on well-lit streets at night. **3.** *Nautical.* Either of two lights, red to port, green to starboard, shown by ships at night. **4.** Incidental information.

side·line (sīd-līn) *n.* **1. a.** A line along either of the two sides of a playing court or field, marking its limits. **b.** *Plural.* The space out-

side such limits, occupied by spectators. **c.** *Plural.* The position or point of view of those who observe and do not participate in some activity. **2.** A subsidiary line of merchandise. **3.** An activity pursued in addition to one's regular occupation.
~ *tr.v.* **sidelined, -lining, -lines.** *Chiefly U.S.* To remove or keep from active participation, as or as if in athletic contests.

side·ling (sīdling) *adj.* **1.** Directed to one side; oblique. **2.** Sloping. ~ *adv.* Obliquely; sideways. [Middle English *sideling* : SIDE + -LING (adverbial suffix).]

side·long (sīd-long ‖ -lawng) *adj.* Directed to one side; sideways. ~ *adv.* On, from, or towards the side; obliquely; sideways. [Alteration of SIDELING.]

side·man (sīd-man) *n., pl.* **-men** (-men). *U.S.* Any player in a jazz band who is not the leader of it.

si·de·re·al (sī-dēer-i-əl, si-) *adj.* **1.** Of, pertaining to, or concerned with the stars or constellations; stellar. **2.** Measured or determined in relation to the stars: *sidereal time.* [Latin *sīdereus*, from *sīdus* (stem *sīder-*), constellation.]

sidereal day *n.* The time required for a complete rotation of the Earth, measured as the interval between two successive transits of a star over the same meridian, or 23 hours, 56 minutes, 4.09 seconds of solar time.

sidereal hour *n.* A 24th part of a sidereal day.

sidereal month *n.* See **month.**

sidereal time *n.* Time based upon the axial and orbital rotation of the Earth with reference to the background of stars.

sidereal year *n.* The time required for one complete revolution of the Earth about the Sun, relative to the fixed stars, or 365.256 mean solar days.

sid·er·ite (sīdə-rīt ‖ sīddə-) *n.* **1.** An impure yellowish-brown iron carbonate mineral. **2.** An iron meteorite. [SIDER(O)- + -ITE.] —**sid·er·it·ic** (-rīttik) *adj.*

sidero-, sider– *comb. form.* Indicates iron; for example, **siderolite, siderosis.** [Greek *sidēros†*, iron.]

side road *n.* A road that joins and is subsidiary to a main road.

si·der·o·lite (sīdərə-līt ‖ sīddərə-) *n.* A meteorite that contains iron, nickel, silicon, magnesium, and small amounts of other elements. [SIDERO- + -LITE.]

si·der·o·sil·i·co·sis (sīdərə-silli-kō-siss) *n.* A lung disease caused by excessive inhalation of dust containing silica and iron oxide.

si·der·o·sis (sīdə-rō-siss ‖ sīddə-) *n.* A chronic disease of the lungs caused by excessive inhalation of dust containing iron oxide or iron particles. [SIDER(O)- + -OSIS.] —**sid·er·ot·ic** (sīdə-róttik) *adj.*

si·der·o·stat (sīdər-ō-stat, -ə- ‖ sīddər-) *n.* An optical system consisting of a rotating clock-driven mirror that reflects light from a celestial body in a relatively fixed direction to a fixed telescope or other bulky instrument. [Latin *sīdus* (stem *sīder-*), constellation (see **sidereal**) + -STAT.] —**sid·er·o·stat·ic** (-ə-státtik) *adj.*

side·sad·dle (sīd-sadd'l) *n.* A saddle designed so that a woman may sit with both legs on one side of the horse. ~ *adv.* On or as if on a sidesaddle.

side show *n.* **1.** A small show offered in addition to the main attraction, as at a circus. **2.** A diverting incident or spectacle.

side·slip (sīd-slip) *intr.v.* **-slipped, -slipping, -slips.** To slip or skid to one side. ~ *n.* **1.** A sideways skid, as of a motor vehicle. **2.** *Aeronautics.* Movement sideways and downwards along the lateral axis as the result of banking too steeply, or caused deliberately in order to reduce altitude steeply without gaining speed.

sides·man (sīdz-mən) *n., pl.* **-men** (-mən, -men). In the Church of England, one whose task is to help the parish churchwarden.

side·split·ting (sīd-splitting) *adj.* Causing convulsions of laughter. —**side·split·ting·ly** *adv.*

side step *n.* A step to one side, as in dancing or to avoid something.

side-step (sīd-step) *v.* **-stepped, -stepping, -steps.** —*intr.* **1.** To step aside. **2.** To dodge an issue or responsibility. —*tr.* **1.** To step out of the way of (an opponent in a sports match, for example). **2.** To evade (an issue, for example); skirt. —**side-step·per** *n.*

side street *n.* A relatively minor and quiet street, usually providing access to residential areas rather than serving as a main thoroughfare.

side stroke *n.* A swimming stroke in which a person swims on one side and thrusts the arms backwards and downwards while performing a scissors kick with the legs.

side·swipe (sīd-swīp) *tr.v.* **-swiped, -swiping, -swipes.** To deal a sideswipe to (a person). ~ *n.* **1.** A glancing blow on or along the side. **2.** A caustic remark made in the course of other comments.

side·track (sīd-trak) *tr.v.* **-tracked, -tracking, -tracks.** To divert from a main issue or course. ~ *n.* **1.** An instance of sidetracking. **2.** *U.S.* A railway siding.

side·valve (sīd-valv) *adj.* Designating an internal-combustion engine with the inlet and outlet valves located within the cylinder block rather than the cylinder head. Compare **overhead valve.**

side·walk (sīd-wawk) *n. U.S.* A **pavement** (see).

side wall *n.* A side surface of a pneumatic tyre.

side·ward (sīd-wərd) *adj.* Moving or directed towards one side. ~ *adv. Chiefly U.S.* Variant of **sidewards.**

side·wards (sīd-wərdz) *adv.* Also *chiefly U.S.* **side·ward.** Towards or from one side.

side·ways (sīd-wayz) *adv.* Also **side·wise** (-wīz). **1.** Towards one side; leaning or moving in a sideward direction. **2.** From one side. **3.** Presenting the side instead of the front or back.

~ *adj.* Also **side·wise.** Towards or from one side.

side wheel *n.* A paddle wheel on the side of a steamboat. —**side·wheel** (sīd-weel, -hweel) *adj.* —**side-wheel·er** *n.*

side-whis·kers (sīd-wiskərz, -hwiskərz) *pl.n.* Whiskers growing on the sides of the face.

side·wind·er (sīd-wīndər) *n.* **1.** A small rattlesnake, *Crotalus cerastes,* of the southwestern United States and Mexico, that moves by a distinctive sideways looping motion of its body. **2.** *U.S.* A powerful blow by the fist delivered from the side. **3.** *Military.* A short-range supersonic air-to-air missile.

Si·di-bel-Ab·bès (sīddi-bel-ábbess, -a-béss). City in northwest Algeria, the headquarters of the French Foreign Legion until Algeria gained its independence in 1962.

sid·ing (sīding) *n.* **1.** A short section of railway line connected to a main line either to provide access, as to a factory or mine, or to provide storage space for rolling stock. **2.** *U.S.* Material, such as planks or shingles, used for surfacing the outside of a building.

Siding Spring Mountain. Mountain peak in the Warrumbungle range of New South Wales, Australia, the site of the Siding Spring Observatory. This technically sophisticated observatory has a 3.9-metre (153-inch) reflecting telescope, one of the world's largest.

si·dle (sīd'l) *intr.v.* **-dled, -dling, -dles.** To move sideways; edge along. **2.** To move in a nervous, furtive manner: *sidled into the office late.* ~ *n.* A sidling movement. [Back-formation from SIDELING and SIDELONG.] —**si·dling·ly** *adv.*

Sid·ney or **Syd·ney** (sīd-ni), **Sir Philip** (1554–86). English poet, critic, soldier, and courtier. His most important works are a collection of pastoral idylls, *Arcadia,* a sonnet sequence, *Astrophel and Stella,* and two essays of criticism, *The Defence of Poesie* and *An Apology for Poetry* (all published posthumously).

Si·don (sīd'n, *rarely* sī-don). Ancient Phoenician seaport, on the Mediterranean coast, occupying the site of present-day Saida, in Lebanon. It was one of the oldest Phoenician trading centres, famous for its glass and purple dyes.

siege (seej, *also* seezh) *n.* **1.** The surrounding and blockading of a town or fortress by an army intent on capturing it. **2.** A prolonged attempt to break the resistance of a person or group, as by force or psychological pressure: *The siege began when the police surrounded the terrorist hideout.* **3.** *Obsolete.* **a.** A seat. **b.** A seat of rule. —**lay siege to.** To begin a siege against.
~ *tr.v.* **sieged, sieging, sieges.** To lay siege to; besiege. [Middle English *sege,* from Old French, "seat", from Vulgar Latin *sedicum* (unattested), from *sedicāre* (unattested), "to seat oneself", from Latin *sedēre,* to be seated.]

Sieg·fried (seeg-freed; *German* zéek-freet). The hero of the first part of the **Nibelungenlied** *(see)* and other medieval epics. [German, from Old High German *Sigifrith* : *sigu, sigo,* victory + *fridu,* peace.]

sie·mens (seemənz) *n.* The SI unit of electrical conductance equal to the conductance of a device that has a resistance of one ohm. Formerly called "mho", "reciprocal ohm". [After Ernst Werner von SIEMENS.]

Siemens (seemənz), **Ernst Werner von** (1816–92). German electrical engineer. He installed the first telegraph line between Frankfurt and Berlin in 1848–49 and the first lines in Russia in 1850. With his brothers Wilhelm and Karl he went on to install lines between India and Europe, as well as across the Atlantic. The Siemens unit of electrical conductance is named after him.

Siemens, Sir William, born Karl Wilhelm Siemens (1823–83). British electrical engineer, born in Germany. After developing an electroplating method with his brother, Ernst, he settled in England in 1844 and for the rest of his life managed the English division of their joint telegraphic and electrical firm.

Si·en·a (si-énnə). City in north central Italy, the capital of Siena province. In the 13th and 14th centuries it boasted the finest painters in Italy, known as the Sienese School. The city is rich in fine architecture. The Palio festival, with its horse race through the streets of the town centre, is held twice each summer. —**Si·en·ese** (-ənéez) *n. & adj.*

Sien·kie·wicz (shenk-yáy-vich), **Henryk** (1846–1916). Polish novelist. Although he is most widely known for his historical novel, *Quo Vadis?* (1895), his critical reputation rests on his trilogy dealing with Poland's struggle for national liberation, *With Fire and Sword* (1883), *The Deluge* (1886), and *Pan Michael* (1888). He was awarded the Nobel prize for literature in 1905.

si·en·na (si-énnə) *n.* **1.** A special clay containing iron and manganese oxides, used as a pigment for oil and water-colour painting. **2. Raw sienna** *(see).* **3. Burnt sienna** *(see).* [From *terra-sienna,* from Italian *terra di Sienna,* "earth of SIENA".]

si·er·ra (si-érrə, séer-ə) *n.* **1.** A rugged range of mountains having an irregular or serrated profile. **2.** Any of several mackerel-like fishes of the genus *Scomberomorus,* of tropical seas. [Spanish, "a saw", from Latin *serra.* See **serrate.**] —**si·er·ran** *adj.*

Sierra Le·o·ne (li-ōn, -ōni). Republic on the west coast of Africa. Although the economy is predominantly agricultural, the country has an important mining industry, with diamonds, bauxite, and titanium accounting for some 70 per cent of the country's exports by value. Freetown was founded as a British colony for ex-slaves in 1787 and thereafter British control gradually extended into the interior, over which a protectorate was proclaimed in 1896. The country gained its independence within the Commonwealth in 1961. Area, 71 740 square kilometres (27,699 square miles). Population, 4,300,000. Capital, Freetown. See map at **West African States.**

Sierra Ma·dre (maáa-dray, -dri). Chief mountain system of Mexico, comprising three principal ranges: the Sierra Madre Oriental, running roughly parallel to the coast of the Gulf of Mexico, the Sierra Madre Occidental, running parallel to the Pacific coast, and the Sierra Madre del Sur, a continuation of the latter range, running south from Guadalajara. The two highest peaks, Orizaba and Popocatépetl, are both above 5 000 metres.

Sierra Nevada¹. Chief mountain range in southern Spain, in the Granada region, extending for about 100 kilometres (60 miles) parallel to the Mediterranean coast. It contains the highest peak in Spain, Mulhacen, which rises to 3 487 metres (11,440 feet).

Sierra Nevada². Range in eastern California containing the highest peak in the United States (excluding Alaska), Mount Whitney, which rises to 4 418 metres (14,495 feet).

si·es·ta (si-éstə) *n.* A short sleep or rest, usually taken after the midday meal, especially in hot countries. [Spanish, from Latin *sexta (hora),* sixth (hour after sunrise), noon, from *sextus,* sixth.]

sieve (siv) *n.* **1.** Any meshwork, especially a utensil of wire mesh or closely perforated metal, used for straining, sifting, or separating. **2.** *Informal.* One who is prone to give away secrets.
~*tr.v.* **sieved, sieving, sieves.** To pass through a sieve; sift. [Middle English *sive,* Old English *sife.*]

sieve tube *n.* A series of cells joined end to end, with pores in their connecting walls, forming a tube through which nutrients are conducted in vascular plants.

Sie·yès (si-ay-yéss), **Emmanuel Joseph** (1748–1836). French clergyman and revolutionary leader, usually known as Abbé Sieyès. His pamphlet, *What is the Third Estate* (1789), was one of the most influential attacks on the ancien régime. After helping to bring Napoleon to power, he served for a few months as one of the consular triumvirate with Napoleon and Ducos (1799), but thereafter his political influence waned.

si·fa·ka (si-faákə) *n.* Either of two Madagascan primates, *Propithecus diadema* or *P. verreauxi,* that are related to lemurs and have long, often brightly coloured fur. [From Malagasy.]

sift (sift) *v.* **sifted, sifting, sifts.** —*tr.* **1.** To put through a sieve or other straining device in order to separate the fine from the coarse particles. **2.** To apply by scattering with a sieve: *Sift icing sugar on the cake.* **3.** To separate by or as if by using with a sieve; screen. **4.** To examine closely and carefully: *sift the evidence.* —*intr.* **1.** To sift something. **2.** To fall through or as if through a sieve: *White light sifted through the spreading cedar tree.* **3.** To make a careful and critical examination. Used with *through.* [Middle English *siften,* Old English *siftan.*] —**sift·er** *n.*

sift·ings (síftingz) *pl.n.* Material removed or separated with or as if with a sieve.

sig. 1. signal. **2.** signature. **3.** signor; signore.

Sig. 1. signor; signore. **2.** *Medicine.* signature.

sigh (sī) *v.* **sighed, sighing, sighs.** —*intr.* **1.** To exhale audibly in a long, deep breath, as from sorrow, weariness, or relief. **2.** To produce a similar sound: *willows sighing in the wind.* **3.** *Literary.* To feel yearning, longing, or grief; mourn. —*tr.* **1.** To express with or as if with an audible exhalation. **2.** *Archaic.* To lament; mourn.
~*n.* An act or a sound of sighing. [Middle English *sighen,* probably altered from *siken* (weak past tense *sighte*), Old English *sīcan,* from West Germanic *sīk-* (unattested).]

sight (sīt) *n.* **1.** The ability to see; the faculty of vision: *Surgeons saved her sight.* **2.** The act or fact of seeing. **3.** The field or range of one's vision: *Get out of my sight!* **4.** The way in which one sees and evaluates experience; a point of view; an estimation: *In his sight she was perfect.* **5.** Something that is seen; an object of vision; a view: *The garden is a lovely sight.* **6.** Something worth seeing; an attraction or spectacle: *the sights of London.* **7.** *Informal.* Something unsightly: *Her hair was a sight.* **8. a.** A device used to assist aim by guiding the eye, as on a firearm or surveying instrument. **b.** *Often plural.* An aim or observation taken with such a device: *A rabbit came into his sights.* **c.** *Plural.* An aim; a goal; an ambition: *set his sights on promotion.* **9.** *Informal.* A considerable amount; a lot: *a sight more than what he's earning.* —**sight for sore eyes.** Something pleasurable to behold; a welcome sight. —**at first sight. 1.** Immediately; at once: *love at first sight.* **2.** Without a close examination; according to initial impressions. —**at** or **on sight.** As soon as seen: *shoot on sight.* —**catch sight of.** To manage to see; glimpse. —**in sight. 1.** Able to be seen. **2.** Coming closer; approaching: *The end is in sight.* —**know by sight.** To recognise (a person) by his appearance rather than by his name or any other personal detail. —**lose sight of.** To allow to be neglected or remain unconsidered: *mustn't lose sight of our objectives.* —**out of sight. 1.** Not able to be seen; concealed; hidden. **2.** *Informal.* To a very great extent; with much severity: *They were beaten out of sight by a superior team.* **3.** *Chiefly U.S. Slang.* Incredible; marvellous.
~*tr.v.* **sighted, sighting, sights. 1.** To see or observe within one's field of vision: *sight land.* **2.** To observe or take a sight of with an instrument: *sight a target.* **3.** To adjust the sights of (a rifle, for example). **4.** To provide with sights. **5.** To take aim with (a firearm). [Middle English *si(g)ht,* Old English *sihth, gesiht,* eyesight, vision, thing seen.]

sight bill *n.* A bill payable upon demand or presentation. Also *chiefly U.S.* "sight draft".

sight·ed (sītid) *adj.* **1.** Having sight; not blind. **2.** Having eyesight of a specified kind. Used in combination: *short-sighted.*

sight·less (sīt-ləss, -liss) *adj.* **1.** Blind. **2.** Invisible. —**sight·less·ly** *adv.* —**sight·less·ness** *n.*

sight·ly (sītli) *adj.* **-lier, -liest.** Pleasing to see; handsome.

sight-read (sīt-reed) *v.* **-read** (-red), **-reading, -reads.** —*tr.* To read or perform (music) at first sight without preparation. —*intr.* To sight-read music. —**sight-read·er** *n.*

sight rule *n.* An **alidade** *(see).*

sight screen *n.* In cricket, a large, white screen placed on the boundary behind the bowler to facilitate the batsman's view of the bowled ball. Also called "screen", *Australian* "sightboard".

sight·see·ing (sīt-see-ing) *n.* The act or pastime of touring places of interest. —**sight·see** *intr.v.* —**sight·se·er** *n.*

sig·il (síjil, síggil) *n.* **1.** A seal; a signet. **2.** A supposedly magical sign or image. [Latin *sigillum,* diminutive of *signum,* SIGN.]

sigill. seal. [Latin *sigillum.*]

Sig·int (síg-int) *n.* **1.** A department in Britain monitoring and gathering intelligence from broadcasts and other communications from foreign countries. **2.** The intelligence gathered by this department. [*Sig*nal + *int*elligence.]

sig·lum (síg-ləm) *n., pl.* **-gla** (-lə). A letter, especially an initial, used for identification. [From Late Latin *sigla* (plural), perhaps from *singula,* neuter plural of *singulus,* single.]

sig·ma (síg-mə) *n.* **1.** The 18th letter in the Greek alphabet, written Σ,σ. Transliterated in English as *S, s.* **2.** *Physics.* *Symbol* Σ. Any of three elementary particles in the baryon family. [Greek, from Semitic, akin to Hebrew *sāmekh,* SAMEK.] —**sig·mate** (-mayt) *adj.*

sig·moid (síg-moyd) *adj.* Also **sig·moi·dal** (sig-móyd'l). **1.** Having the shape of the letter S. **2.** Of or pertaining to the sigmoid colon. [Greek *sigmoeidēs* : SIGMA + -OID.]

sigmoid colon *n. Anatomy.* An S-shaped bend in the final part of the colon between the descending section and the rectum. Also called "sigmoid flexure".

sig·moid·o·scope (sig-móydə-skōp) *n.* An instrument equipped with a light that is inserted into the anus in order to inspect the rectum and sigmoid colon. [SIGMOID + -SCOPE.] —**sig·moid·os·co·py** (síg-moyd-óskəpi) *n.*

sign (sīn) *n., pl.* **signs** or **sign** (for sense 8 only). **1.** Something that points to the presence or existence of a fact, condition, or quality not immediately evident; an indication: *showed no sign of life.* **2.** An action or gesture used to convey an idea, command, or the like: *blew a kiss as a sign of her affection.* **3.** A board, poster, or placard displayed in a public place to advertise or to convey information or a direction: *a road sign; a stop sign.* **4.** A conventional figure or device that stands for a word, phrase, or operation; especially, a symbol, as in mathematics or musical notation: *the plus and minus signs.* **5.** *Medicine.* Any bodily manifestation that indicates the presence of a malfunction or disease to an observer but need not be apparent to the patient. Compare **symptom. 6.** A portentous incident or event; especially, something that indicates a supernatural existence. **7.** *U.S.* An indicator, such as a spoor or scent, of the presence or trail of an animal: *deer sign.* **8.** *Astrology.* Any of the 12 divisions of the zodiac, each named after a constellation and represented by a symbol. Also called "sign of the zodiac".
~*v.* **signed, signing, signs.** —*tr.* **1.** To affix one's signature to: *signed the letter.* **2.** To write (one's signature). **3.** To approve, authorise, or ratify by affixing a signature, seal, or other mark: *signed the petition.* **4.** To engage by means of obtaining a signature on a contract: *sign a new player.* **5.** To relinquish or transfer (title or ownership, for example) to by signature. Used with *away, off,* or *over.* **6.** To express or signify with a sign; signal. **7.** To make a mark with a sign; especially, to consecrate with the sign of the cross. —*intr.* **1.** To make a sign or signs; signal. **2.** To write one's signature. —**sign in.** To sign one's signature in a book upon arriving at a destination. —**sign off. 1.** In broadcasting, to announce the end of transmission, as at the end of the day. **2.** To end a letter, as with a signature or a message of affection. **3.** *Informal.* In Britain, to cease drawing unemployment benefit. —**sign on. 1.** In broadcasting, to announce the beginning of transmission, as at the start of the day. **2.** To join or enlist; sign up: *signed on as a midshipman.* **3.** *Informal.* In Britain, to register so as to draw unemployment benefit. **4.** To engage the services of; employ. —**sign out.** To sign one's signature in a book before leaving to go elsewhere. —**sign up. 1.** To join or enlist; sign on. **2.** To engage the services of; employ: *signed up two players.* [Middle English *signe,* from Old French, from Latin *signum,* distinctive mark or figure, seal, signal.]
Synonyms: *sign, badge, mark, token, indication, symptom.*

Si·gnac (seenyáck), **Paul** (1863–1935). French neoimpressionist painter and theoretician, a disciple of Georges Seurat. He painted mainly landscapes and marines, like the *Port of St. Tropez* (1916). He was an exponent of pointillism.

sig·nal (síg-n'l) *n. Abbr.* **sig. 1. a.** A sign, gesture, mechanical device, or other indicator serving as a means of communication: *Tears are a signal of grief; The railway signal was green.* **b.** A message communicated by such means. **2.** That which is the occasion for or incites action: *The execution was the signal for mass protests.* **3.** *Electronics.* An impulse or fluctuating electric quantity, such as voltage, current, or electric field strength, the variations of which represent coded information. **4.** The sound, image, or message transmitted or received in telegraphy, telephony, radio, television, or radar.
~*adj.* **1.** Out of the ordinary; remarkable; conspicuous: *a signal feat.* **2.** Used or acting as a signal: *a signal flare.*
~*v.* **signalled** or *U.S.* **-naled, -nalling** or *U.S.* **-naling, -nals.** —*tr.* **1.** To make a signal or signals to (a person or thing); communicate with by signals: *signalled her to stop her car.* **2.** To relate or make

known, as by signals; herald: *Gunfire signalled the start of the battle.* —*intr.* To make a signal or signals. [French, from Old French *s(e)ignal,* from Medieval Latin *signāle,* from Latin *signālis,* of a sign, from *signum,* SIGN.] —**sig·nal·ler** *n.*

signal box *n.* A building containing manually operated levers or the automatic control system operating the signals on a railway network in a particular area.

sig·nal·ise, sig·nal·ize (sígnə-līz) *tr.v.* **-ised, -ising, -ises. 1.** To make remarkable or conspicuous. **2.** To point out particularly.

sig·nal·ly (síg-nəli) *adv.* Conspicuously; noticeably; especially.

sig·nal·man (síg-n'l-mən, -man) *n., pl.* **-men** (-mən, -men). **1.** One whose job it is to operate railway signals. **2.** A soldier trained to communicate by signals. In this sense, also called "signaller".

sig·nal·ment (síg-n'l-mənt) *n. U.S.* A detailed description of the appearance of a person, as for police files. [French *signalement,* from *signaler,* to mark out, describe, from *signal,* SIGNAL.]

signal-to-noise ratio (síg-n'l-tə-nóyz, -tōō-) *n.* The ratio of the amplitude of the signal in an electronic device to the amplitude of the noise in that device.

sig·na·to·ry (sig-nə-tri, -təri) *adj.* Bound by signed agreement.
~*n., pl.* **signatories.** A person or nation that has signed a treaty or other document. [Latin *signātōrius,* from *signāre,* to mark, affix one's seal to, from *signum,* SIGN.]

sig·na·ture (síg-ni-chər, -nə- || *chiefly U.S.* -choor) *n. Abbr.* **sig. 1. a.** The name of a person as written by himself, especially to approve a document. **b.** The act of signing one's name. **2.** Any sign that indicates the presence or activity of a person, group, or thing: *The robbery bore the signature of a professional.* **3.** *Music.* **a.** A **key signature** *(see).* **b.** A **time signature** *(see).* **4.** In printing: **a.** A group of printed pages, most commonly 16 or 32, folded from a single sheet, that is bound together with others to make up a book. Also called "gather", "section". **b.** A letter, number, or symbol placed at the bottom of the first page of such a group of printed pages of a book as a guide to the proper sequence of the sheets in binding. **5.** *Abbr.* **S., Sig.** That part of a medical prescription giving the doctor's instructions to the patient. [Medieval Latin *signātura,* from Latin *signāre,* to mark with a sign, from *signum,* SIGN.]

signature tune *n.* A short, distinctive tune that is used to signify the beginning or end of a particular television or radio programme or to accompany the appearance of an individual performer.

sign·board (sīn-bawrd || -bōrd) *n.* A board that bears a sign giving information.

sign·er (sīnər) *n.* **1.** One that signs. **2.** A person skilled in sign language, especially as an interpreter for the deaf.

sig·net (síg-nit) *n.* **1.** A small seal; especially, an official seal used on a document. **2.** The impression made with such a seal.
~*tr.v.* **signeted, -neting, -nets.** To mark or endorse with a signet. [Middle English, from Old French, diminutive of *signe,* SIGN.]

signet ring *n.* A finger ring bearing a signet or set of initials.

sig·nif·i·cance (sig-níffi-kənss, -nívvi-) *n.* Also **sig·nif·i·can·cy** (-kən-si). **1.** The state or quality of being significant; meaning. **2.** Importance; consequence: *an event of great significance.* **3.** Implied or underlying meaning: *I understand the words, but not their significance.* —See Synonyms at **importance, meaning.**

sig·nif·i·cant (sig-níffikənt, -nívvikənt) *adj.* **1.** Having or expressing a meaning; meaningful. **2.** Having or expressing a covert meaning: *She darted me a significant glance.* **3.** Important; notable; valuable. [Latin *significāns* (stem *significant-*), present participle of *significāre,* to SIGNIFY.] —**sig·nif·i·cant·ly** *adv.*

significant figures *pl.n. Mathematics.* The digits of the decimal form of a number beginning with the digit farthest to the left and higher than zero and extending to the right to include all digits warranted by the accuracy of measuring devices used to obtain the numbers or to include a specific number of digits after rounding up or down. Also called "significant digits".

sig·ni·fi·ca·tion (síg-nifi-káysh'n) *n.* **1.** Intended meaning; sense. **2.** The act or process of signifying. —See Synonyms at **meaning.**

sig·nif·i·ca·tive (sig-níffi-kətiv, -nívvi-, -kaytiv) *adj.* **1.** Indicative; significant. **2.** Signifying; symbolic.

sig·ni·fy (sígni-fī) *v.* **-fied, -fying, -fies.** —*tr.* **1.** To serve as a sign or symbol of; betoken; denote. **2.** To make known; intimate: *signified her approval with a gesture.* —*intr.* To have meaning or importance. —See Synonyms at **mean** (convey sense). [Middle English *signifien,* from Old French *signifier,* from Latin *significāre* : *signum,* SIGN + *facere,* to make.] —**sig·ni·fi·er** *n.*

sign language *n.* A system of communication by means of hand gestures, as used by deaf and dumb people.

sign manual *n., pl.* **signs manual.** A person's signature; especially, the signature of a monarch at the top of a royal decree.

sign of the cross *n.* A gesture in the form of a cross, made in token of faith in Christ or as an invocation of blessing or divine protection; especially, such a gesture of the right hand from the forehead to the breast and then from the shoulder to shoulder.

sign of the zodiac *n. Astrology.* A **sign** *(see).*

si·gnor (séen-yawr || -yōr, *chiefly U.S.* seen-yór, -yōr) *n., pl.* **signori** (seen-yáwr-ee || -yōr-) or **-gnors.** Also **si·gnior.** *Abbr.* **S., sig., Sig. 1.** The Italian title of courtesy for a man used before a surname and equivalent to the English *Mr.* **2.** In an Italian-speaking country, a gentleman. [See **signore.**]

si·gno·ra (seen-yór-ə || -yōr-) *n., pl.* **signore** (-ay) or **-ras.** The Italian title of courtesy for or form of address to a married woman, equivalent to the English *Mrs.* or *madam.* [See **signore.**]

si·gno·re (seen-yór-ay || -yōr-) *n., pl.* **signori** (-ee). *Abbr.* **S., sig., Sig. 1.** The Italian form of address to a man, equivalent to the English *sir.* **2.** In an Italian-speaking country, a gentleman. [Italian, from Latin *senior,* older, SENIOR.]

Si·gno·rel·li (séen-yaw-rélli), **Luca** (*c.*1441–1523). Italian painter of the Umbrian school. His masterpiece is the fresco cycle at Orvieto cathedral depicting the end of the world and the last judgment.

si·gno·ri·na (séen-yaw-rée-nə) *n., pl.* **-ne** (-nay) or **-nas.** The Italian title of courtesy for or form of address to an unmarried woman, equivalent to the English *Miss.* [Italian, diminutive of SIGNORA.]

sign·post (sīn-pōst) *n.* **1.** A post supporting a sign. **2.** Anything that serves as an indication, sign, or guide.
~*tr.v.* **signposted, -posting, -posts.** *Chiefly British.* **1.** To equip with signposts. **2.** To make obvious; indicate; show: *She signposted her intentions.*

Sig·urd (sig-oord, -urd). *Norse Mythology.* The hero who slew the dragon Fafnir. He corresponds to Siegfried of the *Nibelungenlied.*

Si·ha·nouk (sée-ə-no͝ok, -no͝ok), **King (Samdech Preah) Norodom** (1922–). Ruler of Cambodia, son of King Norodom Suramarit. He was elected king in 1941 and abdicated in March, 1955 to become prime minister and minister of foreign affairs in the following October. In 1960 he was elected head of state, a position which he held until he was deposed by a right-wing faction. He was restored in 1975 when the Khmer Republic was overthrown, but resigned in 1976. In 1982 he became leader in exile of a coalition fighting the Vietnam-backed government, and returned as president (1991–93) and king again (1993–).

si·ka (séekə) *n.* A deer, *Cervus nippon,* of southern Asia and Japan, having a white-spotted brown coat in summer and, in the male, slender antlers. [Japanese *shika.*]

Sikh (seek) *n.* An adherent of Sikhism.
~*adj.* Of or pertaining to the Sikhs or Sikhism. [Hindi, from Sanskrit *śiṣya,* "disciple", from *śikṣati,* he helps, pays homage, learns, serves, desiderative of *śaknōti,* he can, is able to do.]

Sikh·ism (séek-iz'm) *n.* The doctrines and practices of a monotheistic religious sect that broke away from orthodox Hinduism in the 16th century.

Si Kiang. See **Xi Jiang.**

Sik·kim (síckim, sickím). State of northern India. It was formerly a constitutional monarchy (controlled by India), but was incorporated into India in 1975. Almost the entire state lies within the eastern Himalayas. Most of the people are subsistence farmers, but spices and tea are grown for sale. The capital is Gangtok. —**Sik·kim·ese** (síckim-éez) *adj. & n.*

Si·kor·ski (si-kórski; *Polish* shi-), **Władysław** (1881–1943). Polish general and politician. He served in several Cabinet posts in the 1920s before his dismissal following Piłsudski's coup (1926). After 1939 he was prime minister of the Polish government-in-exile and commander in chief of the Free Polish forces in World War II. He was killed in an air crash. His body was returned to Poland for a state funeral in 1993.

si·lage (sīlij) *n.* Fodder prepared by storing and fermenting green forage plants in a silo or pit. [Alteration (influenced by SILO) of ENSILAGE.]

si·lane (sī-layn) *n.* Any of a class of silicon hydrides with the general formula Si_nH_{2n+2}. They are similar to the alkanes and are named by the number of silicon atoms in the molecule (as disilane, Si_2H_6). [*Sil*icon + -ANE.]

sild (sild) *n.* Any of various small Norwegian herrings, especially when tinned or otherwise prepared for eating. [Norwegian.]

sil·den·a·fil (sil-dénəfil) *n.* An anti-impotence drug, **Viagra** *(see).*

si·lence (sīlənss) *n.* **1.** The condition or quality of being or keeping silent; avoidance of speech or noise. **2.** The absence of sound; stillness. **3.** A period of time without communication by word or noise: *two minutes' silence.* **4.** Refusal or failure to speak out.
~*tr.v.* **silenced, -lencing, -lences. 1.** To make silent or bring to silence. **2.** To curtail the expression of; suppress. [Middle English, from Old French, from Latin *silentium,* from *silēre,* to be silent.]

si·lenc·er (sīlən-sər) *n.* **1.** One that silences. **2.** A device in the exhaust system of an internal-combustion engine, especially one fitted to a motor vehicle, in which the sound is deadened by making the exhaust gases pass through a system of baffle plates. **3.** A device attached to the muzzle of a firearm to muffle the report.

si·lent (sīlənt) *adj.* **1. a.** Making no sound or noise; quiet. **b.** Free of all sound. **2.** Not disposed to speak; taciturn. **3.** *Chiefly U.S.* Unable to speak; mute. **4.** Refusing or failing to give information or an opinion: *remained silent on the matter.* **5.** Not voiced or expressed; tacit: *silent declarations of love.* **6.** Inactive or undisturbed; quiescent: *a silent volcano.* **7.** Having no phonetic value; unpronounced; for example, the letter *b* in *subtle* is silent. **8.** Having no sound track: *a silent film.* —See Synonyms at **still.**
~*n.* A silent film. [Latin *silēns* (stem *silent-*), present participle of *silēre,* to be silent.] —**si·lent·ly** *adv.* —**si·lent·ness** *n.*

silent majority *n.* A group, held to represent the majority of a population or membership, that does not normally express its views but may be taken to favour the status quo.

silent partner *n. Chiefly U.S.* A **sleeping partner** *(see).*

si·le·nus (sī-lée-nəss) *n., pl.* **-ni** (-nī). *Greek Mythology. Sometimes capital* **S.** Any of various minor woodland deities or spirits and companions of Dionysus.

Si·le·nus (sī-léenəss). *Greek Mythology.* A satyr, the foster father of Bacchus.

si·le·si·a (sī-léezi-ə, -léezhə, -lée-si-ə, -lée-shə) *n.* A thin, light, twilled cotton fabric used for linings. [After SILESIA, where it was first produced.]

Si·le·si·a (sī-léezi-ə, -léezhə, -lée-si-ə, -leeshə). *Polish* **Śląsk** (shlONSk); *Czech* **Slez·sko** (sléskō); *German* **Schle·si·en** (shláyzi-ən). Region of east central Europe, extending along the foot of the Sudeten mountains and the west Carpathians, and into the Oder valley. Most of it now lies in Poland, with the rest in the Czech Republic and eastern Germany. The area is mostly agricultural land and forest, but the south forms one of Europe's main coalmining and manufacturing regions. —**Si·le·si·an** *n. & adj.*

sil·hou·ette (sílloo-ét, -et) *n.* **1.** A representation of the outline of something, especially a person's profile, usually filled in with black or another solid colour. **2.** The shadow image or outline of something, such as one produced on a white, illuminated screen by an object interposed between the screen and the source of light. ~*tr.v.* **silhouetted, -etting, -ettes.** To represent or cause to be seen as a silhouette. [French, short for *portrait à la silhouette*, from *silhouette*, object intentionally marred or incomplete, after Étienne de *Silhouette* (1709–67), French controller-general.]

sil·i·ca (síllikə) *n.* A white or colourless crystalline compound, SiO₂, occurring abundantly as quartz, sand, flint, agate, and many other minerals, and used to manufacture a wide variety of materials, notably glass and concrete. Also called "silicon dioxide". [New Latin, from Latin *silex* (stem *silic-*), flint.]

silica gel *n.* Amorphous silica that resembles white sand and is used as a drying and dehumidifying agent, a catalyst and catalyst carrier, an anticaking agent in cosmetics, and in chromatography.

sil·i·cate (sílli-kət, -kit, -kayt) *n.* Any of numerous compounds containing silicon, oxygen, and a metallic or organic radical, occurring in many rocks, and with silicon dioxide (quartz) forming at least 95 per cent of the earth's crust. [SILIC(A) + -ATE.]

si·li·ceous (si-líshəss) *adj.* Containing, resembling, pertaining to, or consisting of silica. [Latin *siliceus*, of flint, from *silex*, flint.]

silici-, silic- *comb. form.* Indicates silica or silicon; for example, **siliciferous, silicide.** [From SILICA.]

si·lic·ic (si-líssik) *adj.* Pertaining to, resembling, or derived from silica or silicon. [SILIC- + -IC.]

silicic acid *n.* A jelly-like substance, SiO₂.nH₂O, produced when sodium silicate solution is acidified and used for the same purposes as silica gel.

sil·i·cide (sílli-sīd) *n.* A compound of silicon with another element or radical. [SILIC(I)- + -IDE.]

sil·i·cif·er·ous (sílli-síffərəss) *adj.* Bearing, producing, or in partial combination with silica. [SILICI- + -FEROUS.]

si·lic·i·fy (si-líssi-fī) *v.* **-fied, -fying, -fies.** —*tr.* To convert into silica. —*intr.* To be converted into silica. [SILICI- + -FY.] —**si·lic·i·fi·ca·tion** (-fi-káysh'n) *n.*

sil·i·cle (síllik'l) *n.* Also **si·lic·u·la** (si-líckew-lə). *Botany.* A short, flat siliqua, such as the fruit of the plant honesty. [Latin *silicula*, diminutive of *siliqua*, seed pod, SILIQUA.]

sil·i·con (sílli-kən ‖ -kon) *n.* Symbol **Si** A nonmetallic element occurring extensively in the earth's crust in silica and silicates, having both an amorphous and a crystalline allotrope, and used in combination with other materials in glass, semiconducting devices, concrete, brick, refractories, pottery, and silicones. Atomic number 14, atomic weight 28.086, melting point 1 410°C, boiling point 2 355°C, relative density 2.33, valency 4. [From SILICA.]

silicon carbide *n.* A bluish-black crystalline compound, SiC, one of the hardest known substances, used as an abrasive and heat-refractory material, and in single crystals as a semiconductor, especially in high-temperature applications.

silicon chip *n.* A **chip** based on a silicon wafer, used in microprocessors.

sil·i·con-con·trolled rectifier (síllikən-kən-trōld ‖ -kon-) *n. Abbr.* **SCR.** An electronic device consisting of a four-layer chip of semiconducting material in which the anode-cathode current is controlled by the signal applied to a third electrode, called the gate.

silicon dioxide *n. Chemistry.* **Silica** (see).

sil·i·cone (sílli-kōn) *n.* Any of a group of semi-inorganic polymers based on the structural unit R₂SiO, where R is an organic group, characterised by thermal stability, water repellence, and physiochemical inertness. They are used in adhesives, lubricants, protective coatings, paints, electrical insulation, synthetic rubber, and prosthetic replacements for bodily parts. Compare **siloxane.** [SILIC(I)- + -ONE.]

sil·i·co·sis (sílli-kó-siss) *n.* Fibrosis of the lungs caused by long-term inhalation of silica dust and resulting in a chronic shortness of breath. [New Latin : SILIC(I)- + -OSIS.]

si·li·qua (síllikwə, si-léekwə) *n.* Also **si·lique** (si-léek). A long pod that is divided by a membranous partition and splits at both seams, characteristic of the fruit of the mustards and related plants. [French, from Latin *siliqua*†, pod.] —**sil·i·quous** (sílli-kwəss), **sil·i·quose** (-kwōz, -kwōss) *adj.*

silk (silk) *n.* **1.** The fine, lustrous fibre produced by certain insect larvae and spiders; especially, fibre produced by a silkworm to form its cocoon. **2.** Thread or fabric made from this fibre. **3. a.** A garment made from this fabric, such as a gown. **b.** *Plural.* Brightly coloured silk garments used to identify a jockey. **4.** Any silky, filamentous material, such as the styles forming a tuft on an ear of maize. **5.** *British Informal.* A Queen's or King's Counsel. —**take silk.** *British.* To become a Queen's or King's Counsel. ~*adj.* Of, resembling, or pertaining to silk. [Middle English *silk, selk,* Old English *sioloc, seoloc,* from Late Latin *sericum* (noun),

Latin *sericus* (adjective), from *seres,* from Greek *Sēres,* an oriental people (probably originally meaning "the silk people"), from Chinese *sī,* silk. See also **serge, sericeous.**]

silk cotton *n.* Any of several silky fibres of plant origin; especially, **kapok** (see).

silk-cot·ton tree (silk-kótt'n) *n.* Any of several trees of the family Bombacaceae; especially, *Ceiba pentandra,* native to tropical America, cultivated for its leathery fruit containing the fibre **kapok** (see). Also called "cotton tree".

silk·en (sílkən) *adj.* **1.** Made of silk. **2.** Resembling silk; smooth and lustrous: *silken hair.* **3.** Delicately pleasing or caressing in effect: *a silken voice.* **4.** Dressed in or wearing silk.

silk hat *n.* A man's silk-covered top hat.

Silk Road. Ancient trade route between China and the Mediterranean, linking China to the Roman Empire. Its length was about 6 400 kilometres (4,000 miles). It was the route followed by Marco Polo on his historic trip to Cathay.

silk-screen process (sílk-skreen) *n.* A method of producing a stencil for printing in which a design is imposed upon a screen of silk or other fine fabric, coated on areas to be left blank with an impermeable substance. Ink is forced through the cloth onto the printing surface. Also called "screen printing".

silk·worm (sílk-wurm) *n.* Any of various caterpillars that produce silk cocoons; especially, the larva of a Chinese moth, *Bombyx mori,* that spins a cocoon of fine, lustrous fibre that is the source of commercial silk.

silk·y (sílki) *adj.* **-ier, -iest. 1.** Resembling silk; soft and smooth; lustrous. **2.** *U.S.* Made of silk; silken. **3.** Having long, silklike hairs or a silky covering: *a silky leaf.* **4.** Ingratiatingly smooth; seductive. —**silk·i·ly** *adv.* —**silk·i·ness** *n.*

silky oak *n.* A tree, *Grevillea robusta,* native to Australia, having divided leaves and showy clusters of orange flowers.

sill (sil) *n.* **1.** The horizontal member, often of wood or stone, that bears the upright portion of a frame; especially, the base of a window or door frame. **2.** The horizontal member at the base of a window protruding beyond the frame. **3.** *Geology.* A relatively thin sheet of igneous rock intruded between beds of other rock. [Middle English *sille, selle,* Old English *syll(e),* threshold, sill.]

sillabub. Variant of **syllabub.**

sil·li·ma·nite (síllimə-nīt) *n.* A grey, brown, or green mineral, Al₂SiO₅, that occurs in metamorphic rocks. [After Benjamin *Silliman* (1779–1864), U.S. chemist.]

Sil·li·toe (sílli-tō), **Alan** (1928–). British novelist, one of the leading figures in the kitchen-sink movement of the 1950s and 1960s. His two most famous novels of working-class life, *Saturday Night and Sunday Morning* (1958) and *The Loneliness of the Long Distance Runner* (1959), were both made into successful films.

Sills (silz), **Beverly**, born Belle Silverman (1929–). U.S. coloratura soprano. She made her debut with the New York City Opera in 1955 and became its general director (1979–89) and chairwoman of Lincoln Center (1994).

sil·ly (sílli) *adj.* **-lier, -liest. 1.** Showing a lack of good sense; unreasoning; foolish. **2.** Showing a lack of or disregard for intelligence; fatuous. **3.** *Informal.* Semiconscious; dazed: *knocked me silly.* **4.** Extremely close to the facing batsman. Said of a fielder in cricket: *silly point.* **5.** *Archaic.* Innocent; harmless; helpless. ~*n., pl.* **sillies.** *Informal.* A silly person. —See Synonyms at **foolish.** [Middle English, "pitiable", originally variant of *seely,* happy, blessed, Old English *gesǽlig.*] —**sil·li·ly** *adv.* —**sil·li·ness** *n.*

sil·ly-bil·ly (sílli-bílli) *n., pl.* **-billies.** *Informal.* A silly person. Used affectionately or humorously.

silly season *n.* A period during the summer months when an absence of serious news is supposed to lead newspapers to publish frivolous articles. Preceded by *the.*

si·lo (sílō) *n., pl.* **-los. 1. a.** A tall, cylindrical, airtight structure in which fodder is stored. **b.** A pit dug for the same purpose. **2.** *Military.* A sunken missile shelter with facilities either for lifting the missile to a launch position or for launching from underground. ~*tr.v.* **siloed, -loing, -los.** To store in a silo. [Spanish, from Latin *sirus,* from Greek *siros*†, pit for the storage of grain.]

si·lox·ane (si-lóks-ayn) *n.* Any of a class of organic or inorganic chemical compounds of silicon, oxygen, and usually carbon and hydrogen, based on the structural unit R₂SiO, where R is CH₃, H, C₂H₅, or a more complex group. Compare **silicone.** [*Sil*icon + *ox*ygen + -ANE.]

silt (silt) *n.* A sedimentary material consisting of fine mineral particles intermediate in size between sand and clay. ~*v.* **silted, silting, silts.** —*intr.* To become filled with silt. Usually used with *up.* —*tr.* To fill with silt. Usually used with *up.* [Middle English *cylte,* probably from Scandinavian, akin to Danish and Norwegian *sylt,* salt marsh.] —**sil·ta·tion** (sil-táysh'n) *n.*

silt·stone (sílt-stōn) *n.* A sandstone formed from consolidated silt.

Si·lu·res (sī-lóor-eez, -léwr-, -ayz ‖ *U.S.* síllewr-) *pl.n.* A people described by the Roman historian Tacitus as occupying southwestern Britain at the time of the Roman invasion.

Si·lu·ri·an (sī-lóor-i-ən, si-, -léwr-) *adj.* **1.** Of, belonging to, or designating the geological time or system of rocks of the third period of the Palaeozoic era, characterised by the appearance of land plants. **2.** Of or pertaining to the Silures or their culture. ~*n. Geology.* The Silurian period or system of rocks. Preceded by *the.* [After the SILURES, the rocks having been first identified in the part of Wales supposed to have been inhabited by them.]

si·lu·rid (sī-lóor-id, si-, -léwr-) *adj.* Of or belonging to the family

Siluridae, which includes various freshwater catfishes of Europe and Asia.

~*n.* A silurid fish. [New Latin *Siluridae,* from Latin *silurus,* a large freshwater fish, probably the sheatfish, from Greek *silouros.*]

sil·va, syl·va (sílvə) *n.* The trees or forests of a region. [Latin, forest. See **sylvan.**]

silvan. Variant of **sylvan.**

sil·ver (sílvər) *n.* **1.** *Symbol* **Ag** A lustrous white, ductile, malleable metallic element, occurring both uncombined and in ores such as argentite, having the highest thermal and electrical conductivity of the metals. It is highly valued for jewellery, tableware, and other ornamental use, and is widely used in coinage, photography, dental and soldering alloys, electrical contacts, and printed circuits. Atomic number 47, atomic weight 107.870, melting point 960.8°C, boiling point 2 212°C, relative density 10.50, valencies 1, 2. See **sterling silver. 2.** This metal as a commodity or medium of exchange. **3.** Coins made of this metal or a metal similar in colour. **4. a.** Tableware, especially cutlery, and other domestic articles made of or plated with this metal. **b.** Any tableware. **5.** Lustrous light grey to white. **6.** *Photography.* A silver salt, especially silver nitrate, used to sensitise paper. **7.** A silver medal.

~*adj.* **1.** Made of, containing, or coated with silver. **2.** Of, pertaining to, or based on silver: *the silver standard.* **3.** Having a lustrous medium-grey colour: *silver hair.* **4.** Having a sonorous, ringing sound. **5.** Eloquent; persuasive: *a silver tongue.* **6.** Of or designating a 25th anniversary: *a silver jubilee.*

~*v.* **silvered, -vering, -vers.** —*tr.* **1.** To cover, plate, or adorn with silver or a similar lustrous substance, usually by chemical reduction of silver nitrate solution or by deposition of an evaporated metal film in vacuum. **2.** To cause to resemble silver: *Moonlight silvered the waves.* **3.** To coat (photographic paper) with a film of silver nitrate or other silver salt. —*intr.* To become silvery. [Old English *siolfor, seolfor,* Common Germanic *silubhra-†* (unattested).]

silver age *n. Classical Mythology.* The second of the great periods of the world's history characterised by the diminishing awareness and practice of morality and religion. Compare **golden age, iron age.**

silver band *n.* A group of musicians, a brass band, whose instruments are silver plated.

silver birch *n.* A Eurasian birch tree, *Betula pendula,* having silvery-white, peeling bark.

silver bromide *n.* A pale-yellow powder, AgBr, that darkens on exposure to light, and is used as the light-sensitive component in ordinary photographic films and plates.

silver chloride *n.* A white granular powder, AgCl, that darkens on exposure to light and is used in photography and glass.

silver-eye (sílvər-ī) *n.* An Australian songbird, the **white-eye** *(see).*

silver fir *n.* Any of various coniferous trees of the genus *Abies,* the leaves of which have a silvery undersurface. See **fir.**

sil·ver·fish (sílvər-fish) *n., pl.* **-fishes** or collectively **silverfish. 1.** A silvery, wingless insect, *Lepisma saccharina,* that often causes extensive damage to bookbindings, starched clothing, and similar material. **2.** Any of various fishes having silvery scales, such as a variety of the goldfish *Carassius auratus.*

silver fox *n.* **1.** A variety of the red fox in a colour phase in which it has black fur tipped with white. **2.** The fur of this animal.

silver frost *n.* **Glaze ice** *(see).*

silver iodide *n.* A pale yellow powder, AgI, that darkens on exposure to light and is used in artificial rainmaking, in photography, and as an antiseptic.

silver medal *n.* A medal awarded for achieving second place in a race or similar competition.

sil·vern (sílvərn) *adj. Poetic.* Like silver; silvery.

silver nitrate *n.* A poisonous, colourless crystalline compound, AgNO₃, that darkens when exposed to light in the presence of organic matter and is used in photography, mirror manufacturing, hair dyeing, silver plating, and as an external medicine.

silver paper *n.* Thin paper backed with silver-coloured foil, used especially for wrapping confectionery.

silver plate *n.* **1.** Tableware or other household articles made of metal plated with silver. **2.** The thin layer of silver used to plate such articles.

sil·ver-plate (sílvər-pláyt) *tr.v.* **-plated, -plating, -plates.** To cover (a base metal or article) with a thin layer of silver.

sil·ver-point (sílvər-poynt) *n.* **1.** A sketching process using a silver-tipped stylus and specially prepared paper. **2.** The stylus used in this process.

silver salmon *n.* The **coho salmon** *(see).*

silver screen *n.* **1.** *Informal.* Cinematic films collectively. Preceded by *the.* **2.** A screen used for showing a film.

sil·ver·side (sílvər-sīd) *n.* Also **sil·ver·sides** (-sīdz) (for sense 2). **1.** *British.* A boned joint of beef cut from the outer side of the round (the top part of the leg), and often salted and boiled, or roasted. **2.** Any of various marine and freshwater fishes of the family Atherinidae, having a silvery band along each side.

sil·ver·smith (sílvər-smith) *n.* A person who makes, repairs, or replates articles of silver or silver plate. —**sil·ver·smith·ing** *n.*

silver standard *n.* A monetary standard under which a fixed quantity of silver constitutes the basic unit of currency.

silver thaw *n.* **Glaze ice** *(see).*

sil·ver-tongued (sílvər-túngd) *adj.* Fluent and persuasive in speech; eloquent.

sil·ver·ware (sílvər-wair) *n.* Articles, especially cutlery, made of or plated with silver.

sil·ver·weed (sílvər-weed) *n.* **1.** A plant, *Potentilla anserina,* having yellow flowers and leaves that often have silvery hairs. **2.** Any of various twining shrubs of the genus *Argyreia* of southeastern Asia, having purple flowers and silvery leaves.

sil·ver·y (sílvəri) *adj.* **1.** Like silver in colour or lustre. **2.** Having a clear, ringing sound. **3.** Containing or coated with silver. —**sil·ver·i·ness** *n.*

sil·vi·cul·ture (sílvi-kulchər) *n.* The care and cultivation of forest trees; forestry. [French : Latin *silva, sylva,* forest, SILVA + CULTURE.] —**sil·vi·cul·tur·al** (-kúlchərəl) *adj.* —**sil·vi·cul·tur·ist** *n.*

si·ma (símə) *n.* The lower layer of the earth's outer crust, rich in silica and magnesium, that underlies the **sial** *(see).* [German *Sima* : New Latin *silica* + *magnesium.*]

sim·ba (símbə) *n. East African.* A name for a lion, especially as used in folktales.

Sim·chath To·rah (sím-kaass tãwrə, -kass ‖ tôrə, *Hebrew* -khass) *n.* A Jewish holiday celebrated on the 23rd day of Tishri, marking the end of the cycle of reading the Torah, and coinciding with the last day of Succoth. [Hebrew *shimḥath tōrāh,* "rejoicing over the Law" : *śimḥath,* inflectional form of *śimḥāh,* joy, merriment, from *śāmaḥ,* he rejoiced + TORAH.]

Si·me·non (séemə-noN; *French* -nón), **Georges (Joseph Christian)** (1903–89). Belgian novelist and short-story writer. He began to publish in 1922 and during the next 14 years produced more than 1500 short stories, writing under more than a dozen pseudonyms. The first novel introducing his famous detective, Inspector Maigret, was published in 1931. He published 212 novels, including 80 in the Maigret series.

Sim·e·on (símmi-ən). **1.** In the Old Testament, the second son of Jacob and Leah and the name of the tribe of Israel descended from him. Genesis 29:33. **2.** The man who, upon seeing the infant Jesus, spoke the **Nunc Dimittis** *(see).* Luke 2:25–35.

Simeon Sty·li·tes (stī-lĭt-eez ‖ *U.S. also* sti-), **Saint** (c. 390–459). Syrian monk. He entered a monastery near Aleppo, but was forced to leave it and became a hermit. He then spent 40 years on a high column, from c. 420, and thus became the first-known Christian stylite, or "column-dweller".

sim·i·an (símmi-ən) *adj.* Also **sim·i·ous** (-əss). Pertaining to, characteristic of, or resembling an ape or monkey.

~*n.* An ape or monkey. [Latin *sīmia,* ape, perhaps from *sīmus,* snub-nosed, from Greek *simos†,* bent upwards, snub-nosed.]

sim·i·lar (sím-i-lər, -ə-) *adj.* **1.** Showing some resemblance; related in appearance or nature; alike though not identical. **2.** *Geometry.* Designating figures having corresponding angles equal and corresponding line segments proportional. [French *similaire,* from Latin *similis,* like.] —**sim·i·lar·ly** *adv.*

Usage: Similar is an adjective only, and is not used adverbially in standard English. *X is similar to Y* is acceptable, but *X works similar to Y* is nonstandard.

sim·i·lar·i·ty (sím-i-lárrəti, -ə-) *n., pl.* **-ties. 1.** The condition or quality of being similar; resemblance. **2.** A respect in which persons or things are similar. —See Synonyms at **likeness.**

sim·i·le (sím-i-li, -ə- ‖ -lee) *n.* A figure of speech in which two different things are compared, the comparison usually being made explicit by being introduced with *like* or *as;* for example, *"saw the crowd race away like scattered sheep"* (Saki). Compare **metaphor.** [Latin, neuter of *similis,* SIMILAR.]

si·mil·i·tude (si-mílli-tewd ‖ -tōod) *n.* **1.** Similarity. **2.** Something closely resembling another; a counterpart; a double. **3.** A simile, allegory, or parable. —See Synonyms at **likeness.** [Middle English, from Old French, from Latin *similitūdo,* from *similis,* SIMILAR.]

Sim·la (símmlə). City in northwest India, capital of Himachal Pradesh state. Situated in the foothills of the Himalayas, its pleasant climate made it a popular holiday and health resort, and it was India's summer capital from 1865 to 1939.

Sim·men·tal (símmən-taal; *German* zímmən-) *n.* Any of a breed of European cattle reared for milk, meat, and as draught animals, having a reddish or yellowish coat. —**Sim·men·tal** *adj.*

sim·mer (símmər) *v.* **-mered, -mering, -mers.** —*intr.* **1.** To cook gently just below or at the boiling point. **2.** To be filled with barely controlled anger or resentment; seethe. —*tr.* To cook just below or at the boiling point. —**simmer down. 1.** To reduce the liquid volume of by boiling slowly. **2.** To become calm after excitement or anger.

~*n.* The state or process of simmering. [Earlier *simper,* Middle English *simperen* (imitative).]

sim·nel (sím-n'l) *n. British.* A rich fruit cake, often covered with marzipan, traditionally eaten at Eastertide. Also called "simnel cake". [Middle English *simenel,* from Old French, from Latin *simila,* fine flour, or Greek *semidalis,* perhaps from Semitic, akin to Akkadian *samīdu.* See also **semolina.**]

Sim·nel (sím-n'l), **Lambert** (c. 1475–1525). Fraudulent pretender to the English throne. He was trained to impersonate Edward, Earl of Warwick. In 1487, supported by some Yorkists, he made his bid for the throne, but was defeated by Henry VII's forces at Stoke. He was pardoned and sank into obscurity.

si·mo·ni·ac (sī-mōni-ak, si-) *n.* One who practises simony. —**sim·o·ni·a·cal** (síma-ní-ək'l ‖ símmə-) *adj.* —**sim·o·ni·a·cal·ly** *adv.*

Simon Peter. See **Saint Peter.**

si·mon-pure (símən-péwr) *adj. Literary.* Genuine; thoroughgoing; real. [From the *real Simon Pure,* after *Simon Pure,* a character who is impersonated by a rival in Susanna Centlivre's play *A Bold Stroke for a Wife* (1717).]

Si·mons·town (sī́mənz-town). Town in South Africa, lying on False Bay, just south of Cape Town. It was the headquarters of the British Atlantic fleet from 1814 to 1957.

sim·o·ny (sī́məni ‖ *U.S. also* síḿməni) *n.* The buying or selling of ecclesiastical pardons, offices, or emoluments. [Middle English *simonie,* from Old French, from Late Latin *sīmōnia,* after *Simon Magus,* a Samaritan who offered money to the Apostles Peter and John for the power of conferring the Holy Ghost on whomsoever he wished. Acts 8:18–19.] —**sim·o·nist** *n. & adj.*

Simon Ze·lo·tes (zi-lṓ-teez). Christian leader of the first century A.D.; one of the Twelve Apostles. He was a former Zealot.

si·moom (si-mōōm) *n.* Also **si·moon** (-mōōn). A strong hot sand-laden wind of the Sahara and Arabian deserts. Also called "samiel". [Arabic *samūm,* "poisonous", from *samma,* "he poisoned", from *sam,* poison, from Aramaic *sammā,* drug, poison.]

simp (simp) *n. U.S. Slang.* A simpleton; a fool. [From SIMPLE.]

sim·pa·ti·co (sim-pátti-kō, -páati-) *adj. Informal.* **1.** Of like mind or temperament; compatible. **2.** Having attractive qualities; likeable. [Italian, from *simpatia,* sympathy, from Latin *sympathīa,* SYMPATHY.]

sim·per (síḿpər) *v.* **-pered, -pering, -pers.** —*intr.* To smile in a silly, coy, self-conscious manner. —*tr.* To utter or express with a simper.

~*n.* A silly or self-conscious smile. [Scandinavian, akin to Danish dialectal *simper†,* affected.] —**sim·per·er** *n.* —**sim·per·ing·ly** *adv.*

sim·ple (síḿp'l) *adj.* **-pler, -plest.** **1.** Having or composed of one thing or part only; not combined or compound: *a simple device.* **2.** Not involved or complicated; easy. **3.** Without additions or modifications; bare; mere: *the simple facts.* **4.** Without embellishment; not ornate or adorned: *a simple black dress.* **5.** Not elaborate, elegant, or luxurious: *a simple dwelling.* **6.** Not affected; unassuming or unpretentious. **7.** Not guileful or deceitful; sincere. **8.** Humble or lowly in condition or rank: *a simple peasant.* **9.** Ordinary or common: *not migraine, just a simple headache.* **10.** Not important or significant; trivial. **11. a.** Having or manifesting little sense or intellect; stupid. **b.** Mentally subnormal: *a bit simple in the head.* **12.** *Biology.* Having no divisions or subdivisions; not compound: *a simple leaf.* **13.** *Chemistry.* Consisting of only one compound; not complex or mixed: *a simple salt.* **14.** *Music.* Without figuration or ornamentation: *simple harmony.* —See Synonyms at **naive.**

~*n. Archaic.* **1.** A fool; a simpleton. **2.** A person of humble birth or condition. **3.** A medicinal plant or the medicine obtained from it. [Middle English, from Old French, from Latin *simplus.*]

simple fraction *n.* A fraction in which both the numerator and the denominator are integers. Also called "common fraction", "vulgar fraction".

simple fracture *n.* See **fracture.**

simple fruit *n. Botany.* A fruit developed from a single pistil that may consist of one carpel or several united carpels.

simple harmonic motion *n. Abbr.* **S.H.M.** *Physics.* A periodic motion that may be described as a sinusoidal function of time; specifically, the motion of a particle that obeys the equation $x = A\cos(kt + \phi)$, where x is the displacement of the particle from the origin at any time t, A is the maximum displacement, ϕ is the initial phase or angular displacement at $t = 0$, and k is a constant equal to 2π times the frequency of the oscillation.

simple interest *n.* Interest paid only on the original principal, not on the interest accrued. Compare **compound interest.**

simple machine *n.* A device for changing the magnitude or direction of a force, a **machine** *(see).*

simple microscope *n.* A microscope having one lens or lens system, such as a magnifying glass or hand lens.

sim·ple-mind·ed (simp'l-mīndid) *adj.* **1.** Not sophisticated; artless. **2.** Stupid or silly. **3.** Mentally subnormal. —**sim·ple-mind·ed·ly** *adv.* —**sim·ple-mind·ed·ness** *n.*

simple pendulum *n.* A **pendulum** *(see).*

simple sentence *n.* A sentence having no coordinate or subordinate clauses; for example, *The cat purred.* Compare **complex sentence.**

Simple Simon *n. Informal.* A foolish fellow; a simpleton. [After the title character of a nursery rhyme.]

simple sugar *n.* A **monosaccharide** *(see).*

simple tense *n. Grammar.* A tense in which the verb is expressed without an auxiliary; for example, the simple past tense of "go", *I went,* as opposed to the perfect (or present perfect) tense, *I have gone.* Compare **compound tense.**

simple time *n. Music.* A time in which each beat in the bar is divisible into two. Compare **compound time.**

sim·ple·ton (símp'l-tən) *n.* A silly or feeble-minded person; a fool. [SIMPLE + *-ton,* "town" (as in surnames derived from place names).]

sim·plex (síḿpleks) *adj.* Designating a system of telegraphy in which only one message may be sent in either direction at one time. Compare **duplex, multiplex.**

~*n.* A simplex system. [Latin *simplex,* simple, single.]

sim·plic·i·ty (sim-plíssəti) *n., pl.* **-ties.** The state or quality of being simple, especially: **1.** Absence of complexity, adornment, or artificiality. **2.** Lack of good sense or intelligence; foolishness. [Middle English *symplicite,* from Old French, from Latin *simplicitās,* from *simplex,* simple.]

sim·pli·fy (síḿpli-fī) *tr.v.* **-fied, -fying, -fies.** To make simple or simpler; render less complex or intricate. [French *simplifier,* from Medieval Latin *simplificāre* : Latin *simplus,* SIMPLE + *facere,* to make.] —**sim·pli·fi·ca·tion** (-fi-káysh'n) *n.* —**sim·pli·fi·er** *n.*

sim·plis·tic (sim-plístik) *adj.* **1.** Showing a tendency to oversimplify an issue or problem by ignoring complexities or complications. **2.** *Informal.* Extremely simple or uncomplicated. —**sim·plism** (sím-pliz'm) *n.* —**sim·plis·ti·cal·ly** (sim-plístik'l-i, -plístikli) *adv.*

Sim·plon Pass (sán-plon; *French* saN-plón). Pass in the Lepontine Alps, southern Switzerland, at an altitude of 2 010 metres (6,590 feet). It is crossed by a railway connecting Brig in Switzerland with Iselle in Italy through the Simplon Tunnel, which runs for 19.8 kilometres (12.3 miles) and is the longest in the world.

sim·ply (síḿpli) *adv.* **1.** In a simple manner; plainly. **2.** Merely; only: *I left simply to avoid her.* **3.** Absolutely; altogether: *a simply marvellous film.* **4.** Speaking frankly; candidly: *You are, quite simply, inadequate for this job.*

Simp·son Desert (símps'n). Uninhabited, arid wilderness in central Australia, lying mainly in Northern Territory, but extending slightly into Queensland and South Australia. It occupies about 145 000 square kilometres (56,000 square miles).

sim·u·la·crum (simmew-láy-krəm, -lá-) *n., pl.* **-cra** (-krə). Also *archaic* **sim·u·la·cre** (-kər) *pl.* **-cres.** **1.** An image or representation of something. **2.** An unreal or false semblance of something. [Latin, from *simulāre,* to SIMULATE.]

sim·u·lar (símmew-lər ‖ -laar) *n. Archaic.* One that simulates.

~*adj. Archaic.* Simulated; sham.

sim·u·late (símmew-layt) *tr.v.* **-lated, -lating, -lates.** **1. a.** To have or take on the appearance, form, or sound of; imitate. **b.** To make so as to resemble the real or genuine thing: *simulated diamonds.* **2.** To make a pretence of; feign: *simulate an interest.* **3.** To imitate or create the conditions of, as for an experiment or for training. —See Synonyms at **imitate, pretend.**

~*adj.* (-lət, -lit, -layt). *Archaic.* Simulated; assumed; pretended. [Latin *simulāre,* from *similis,* SIMILAR.] —**sim·u·la·tive** (-lətiv, -laytiv) *adj.* —**sim·u·lant** (-lənt) *adj. & n.*

sim·u·la·tion (simmew-láysh'n) *n.* **1.** The act or process of simulating. **2.** An imitation. **3.** The assumption of a false appearance; a feigning or pretending. **4.** A process for studying or finding a solution to a problem or for calculating the effects of a course of action, by representing it in mathematical terms, especially using a computer.

sim·u·la·tor (símmew-laytər) *n.* One that simulates; especially, an apparatus that generates test conditions approximating actual or operational conditions.

sim·ul·cast (símm'l-kaast ‖ -kast, *U.S.* sím'l-) *tr.v.* **-casted, -casting, -casts.** To broadcast simultaneously by radio and television.

~*n.* A broadcast so transmitted. [*Simul*taneous + broad*cast.*]

sim·ul·ta·ne·ous (simm'l-táyni-əss ‖ *chiefly U.S.* sím'l-) *adj.* **1.** Happening, existing, or done at the same time. **2.** *Mathematics.* Collectively restricting the values of a set of variables: *simultaneous equations.* —See Synonyms at **contemporary.** [Formed by analogy with INSTANTANEOUS from Latin *simul,* at the same time.] —**sim·ul·ta·ne·i·ty** (-tə-née-əti, -náy-), **sim·ul·ta·ne·ous·ness** *n.* —**sim·ul·ta·ne·ous·ly** *adv.*

sin¹ (sin) *n.* **1.** A transgression of a religious or moral law, especially when deliberate. **2.** *Theology.* A condition of estrangement from God resulting from a transgression of His known will. **3.** Any course of action regarded as shameful or deplorable: *It's a sin the way they treat that dog.* —**live in sin.** To cohabit as wife and husband without being married.

~*intr.v.* **sinned, sinning, sins.** **1.** To commit a sinful act; violate a religious or moral law. **2.** To commit an offence or violation; do wrong. Usually used with *against.* [Middle English *sinne, sunne,* Old English *syn(n).*]

sin² (seen) *n.* The 21st letter of the Hebrew alphabet. [Hebrew *sin,* variant of *shīn,* "tooth", SHIN (letter).]

sin³ (sīn) *Trigonometry.* sine.

Si·na·i (sī́-ni-ī, -nay-, -nī). Triangular peninsula forming the northeastern part of Egypt and providing a land bridge between Africa and Asia. It lies between the Suez Canal and the Gulf of Suez on the west and Israel and the Gulf of Aqaba on the east. Mount Sinai, of sacred importance in the Jewish, Christian, and Islamic traditions, has usually been identified with Mount Musa in the southern mountainous region of the peninsula. Sinai has rich deposits of manganese and petroleum and has been of central strategic significance in the Arab-Israeli hostilities since 1956.

sin·an·thro·pus (sī́-nánthrə-pəss, si-, sín-an-thrō-, sín-an-) *n.* An extinct humanlike primate, *Sinanthropus pekinensis,* known as Peking man. It is now designated as *Homo erectus.* [New Latin *Sinanthropus,* "Chinese human" : SIN(O)- + -ANTHROPUS.]

sin·a·pism (síńə-piz'm) *n.* A mustard plaster. [French *sinapisme,* from Late Latin *sināpismus,* from Greek *sinapismos,* use of a mustard plaster, from *sinapizein,* to apply a mustard plaster, from *sinapi,* mustard, from earlier *napu,* probably from Egyptian.]

Si·na·tra (si-náatrə), **Frank,** born Francis Albert Sinatra (1915–98). U.S. popular singer since the late 1930s and 1940s and screen actor. After World War II he began a long and successful film career, appearing in such films as *On The Town* (1949) and *Guys and Dolls* (1955). He won an Academy Award as best supporting actor for his performance in *From Here to Eternity* (1953).

sin bin *n.* **1.** In sports such as ice hockey, a place for players to wait at the side of a playing area when they have been sent off temporarily for rule infringements. **2.** *Informal.* A place of temporary detention or punishment.

since (sinss) *adv.* **1.** From a time in the past up to the present; from then until now. Often preceded by *ever*: *She arrived last week and* *has been here ever since.* **2.** At a time between a past time or event and the present; between then and now. **3.** At some past time; before now; ago: *long since forgotten.*

~prep. 1. During the time following: *She has not been home since Easter.* **2.** Continuously throughout the time following: *up since seven.*

~conj. 1. During the time after which: *She hasn't been home since she graduated.* **2.** Continuously from the time when: *She hasn't spoken since she sat down.* **3.** As a result of the fact that; inasmuch as. [Middle English *sin(ne)s,* contraction of *sithen(es),* Old English *siththan,* "after that".]

sin·cere (sin-séer) *adj.* **-cerer, -cerest. 1.** Not feigned or affected; true: *sincere indignation.* **2.** Presenting no false appearance; not hypocritical; honest: *a sincere believer.* **3.** *Archaic.* Pure; unadulterated. [Latin *sincērus,* clean, pure, genuine, honest.] **—sin·cere·ly** *adv.* **—sin·cere·ness** *n.*

Synonyms: *sincere, natural, unaffected, unfeigned, wholehearted, heartfelt.*

sin·cer·i·ty (sin-sérrəti || *U.S. also* -séer-əti) *n., pl.* **-ties. 1.** The quality or condition of being sincere; sincereness. **2.** A sincere feeling or expression.

sin·ci·put (sín-si-put, -pət) *n., pl.* **-puts** or **sincipita** (sin-síppitə). *Anatomy.* **1.** The upper half of the cranium, especially the anterior portion above and including the forehead. **2.** The forehead. [Latin, from earlier *sēmicaput* (unattested) : SEMI + *caput,* head.] **—sin·cip·i·tal** (sin-síppit'l) *adj.*

Sin·clair (sing-kláir, sin-, sin-klair || *chiefly Scottish* -klər), **Sir Clive Marles** (1940–). British inventor and manufacturer. He pioneered the pocket calculator in the early 1970s and the cheap home computer in the early 1980s.

Sinclair, Upton (1878–1968). U.S. novelist. His first novel, *The Jungle* (1906), exposed the insanitary conditions in the Chicago stockyards and helped to form the wave of public protest which led to reform legislation. He won a Pulitzer prize for *Dragon's Teeth* in 1942.

Sind (sind). Province of southeastern Pakistan, bordering on the Arabian Sea and on India to the south and east. It occupies the lower Indus valley. The capital is Karachi. The leading industrial centre in this chiefly agricultural province is Hyderabad.

Sin·dhi (síndi, sínd-hi) *n., pl.* **-dhis** or collectively **Sindhi. 1.** A member of the predominantly Muslim people of Sind. **2.** The Indic language of Sind. **—Sin·dhi** *adj.*

sine (sīn) *n. Abbr.* **sin 1.** The ordinate of the endpoint of an arc of a unit circle centred at the origin of a Cartesian coordinate system, the arc being of length x and measured anticlockwise from the point $(1, 0)$ if x is positive, or clockwise if x is negative. **2.** In a right-angled triangle, the function of an acute angle that is the ratio of the opposite side to the hypotenuse. [Medieval Latin *sinus,* "fold of a garment" (mistranslation of Arabic *jayb,* chord of an arc, sine, through confusion with Arabic *jayb,* fold of a garment), from Latin, curve, fold, hollow. See **sinus.**]

si·ne·cure (síni-kewr, sínni-) *n.* **1.** An office, position, or charge that is remunerated but requires little or no work. **2.** An ecclesiastical benefice not involving any of the spiritual duties of a parish. [Medieval Latin *(beneficium) sine cūrā,* (benefice) without care (of souls) : *sine,* without + *cūrā,* ablative of *cūra,* cure, care.] **—si·ne·cur·ism** *n.* **—si·ne·cur·ist** *n.*

sine curve (sīn) *n.* The graph of the equation $y = \sin x$. Also called "sinusoid".

si·ne di·e (síni dí-ee, sínni dée-ay) *adv. Abbr.* **s.d.** Indefinitely: *Parliament was dismissed sine die.* [Latin, "without a day (fixed)".]

si·ne qua non (síni kway nón, sínni kwaa, nōn) *n.* An essential element or condition. [Latin, "without which not".]

sin·ew (sínnew) *n.* **1.** A tendon. **2.** Vigorous strength; muscular power. **3.** *Often plural.* The source or mainstay, as of vitality or strength. [Middle English *sin(e)we, sen(e)ue,* Old English *sinu, seonu,* from Germanic.]

sine wave (sīn) *n. Physics.* A waveform that has an amplitude variation which can be expressed as the sine or cosine of a linear function of time or space or both.

sin·ew·y (sínnew-i) *adj.* **1.** Like or consisting of sinews. **2.** Lean and muscular. **3.** Strong; vigorous.

sin·fo·ni·a (sin-fə-néer, -née-ə, sin-fón-i-ə) *n., pl.* **-nias** or **-nie** (-née-ay). *Music.* **1.** A symphonic work. Sometimes used as part of the name of an orchestra. **2.** An overture, especially to an early Italian opera. [Italian, symphony.]

sin·fo·ni·et·ta (sín-fən-yéttə, -fōn-i-éttə) *n., pl.* **-tas.** *Music.* A small-scale symphony, either one that is short in length or one that uses a small orchestra. Sometimes used as part of the name of a small orchestra. [Italian, diminutive of SINFONIA.]

sin·ful (sín-f'l) *adj.* Marked by or full of sin; wicked. **—sin·ful·ly** *adv.* **—sin·ful·ness** *n.*

sing (sing) *v.* **sang** (sang) or *rare* **sung** (sung), **sung, singing, sings.** **—intr. 1.** To utter a series of words or sounds in musical tones. **2. a.** To perform songs for an audience, especially as a profession. **b.** To render a song or songs to an accompaniment. Used with *to*: *sing to the guitar.* **3. a.** To make noises that are melodious or sound like music. Used chiefly of birds. **b.** To give or have the effect of melody; lilt. **4.** To produce musical sounds when played. **5.** To make a high whine or hum. **6.** To be filled with a buzzing sound. Used chiefly of the ears or head. **7. a.** To proclaim or extol something in verse. **b.** To relate a tale in a song. Used with *of: sang of ancient heroes.* **8.** *Chiefly U.S. Slang.* **a.** To give information or evi-

dence against someone. **b.** To confess to a crime. **—tr. 1.** To utter (a song or lyrics, for example) with musical inflections of the voice. **2.** To intone; chant. **3.** To proclaim or extol, often in verse: *sings your praises.* **4.** To bring to a specified state by singing: *Sing me to sleep.* **—sing out. 1.** To sing loudly. **2.** To shout out.

~n. 1. *Informal.* An act of singing. **2.** *U.S.* A gathering of people for group singing. [Middle English *singen, sang, sungen,* Old English *singan, sang* (past singular), *sungen.*] **—sing·a·ble** *adj.*

sing. singular.

Sin·ga·pore (síng-ə-pór, -gə- || -pōr, *chiefly U.S.* -pawr, -pōr). Independent republic lying off the southern tip of the Malay peninsula. In addition to the main island of Singapore it includes about 60 smaller islands. A major commercial centre with a large shipping and shipbuilding industry, Singapore has one of the highest standards of living in southeast Asia. It is highly industrialised, petroleum products, electronics, and rubber accounting for half its exports, and tourism is also important. Three-quarters of the population is Chinese. In 1963 Singapore joined the Federation of Malaysia, but withdrew two years later to become an independent republic. Area, 646 square kilometres (249.5 square miles). Population, 3,040,000. Capital, Singapore. **—Sin·ga·por·e·an** *adj. & n.*

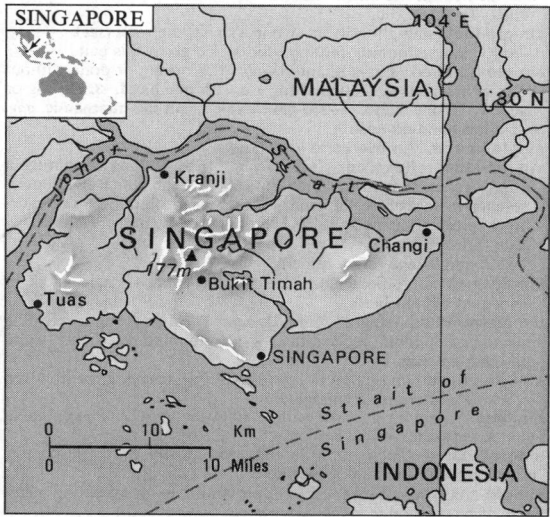

singe (sinj) *tr.v.* **singed, singeing, singes. 1.** To burn superficially; scorch. **2.** To burn the ends of. **3.** To burn off the feathers or bristles of by subjecting briefly to flame. **—See Synonyms at burn.** **~n.** A burn that is superficial. [Middle English *sengen,* Old English *sencgan,* from Germanic.] **—sing·er** (sínjər) *n.*

sing·er (síng-ər) *n.* **1.** A person who sings, especially a trained or professional vocalist. **2.** A poet, especially in ancient or medieval times. **3.** A songbird.

Sing·er (síng-ər), **Isaac Bashevis** (1904–91). Polish-born U.S. novelist and short-story writer in Yiddish, writing mostly about Polish Jews. He published such collections as *Gimpel the Fool and Other Stories* (1957) and *A Crown of Feathers* (1973). He was awarded the Nobel prize for literature in 1978.

Singhalese. Variant of **Sinhalese.**

sin·gle (síng-g'l) *adj.* **1. a.** Not accompanied by another or others; solitary. **b.** Even one, not to mention others. Used with a negative: *Not a single person offered to help.* **2.** Consisting of one form or part; not double or multiple. **3.** One throughout; undiversified; uniform. **4.** Separate from others; distinct; individual: *every single day.* **5.** Designed to accommodate or be sufficient for one person: *a single bed.* **6.** *Chiefly British.* Of or designating a ticket entitling the holder to travel to a destination but not back again. Compare **return. 7. a.** Unmarried. **b.** Of or associated with the state of being unmarried: *living in single bliss.* **8.** Without a partner: *a single parent.* **9.** *Botany.* Having only one rank or row of petals: *a single flower.* **10.** One-against-one: *single combat.*

~n. 1. A separate unit; an individual. **2.** Something, such as a room or bed, intended for use by one person. **3.** An unmarried person. **4.** A one-pound note or a one-dollar bill. **5.** A single ticket. **6.** In cricket, a single run. **7. a.** A small record, often with only one piece of music or track on each side, usually to be played at 45 revolutions per minute. Also called "forty-five". **b.** A piece of music or track on one side of such a record. **8.** See **singles.**

~tr.v. singled, -gling, -gles. To choose or distinguish from among others. Used with *out.* [Middle English *sengle,* from Old French, from Latin *singulus.*] **—sin·gle·ness** *n.*

Synonyms: *single, sole, unique, solitary, individual.*

sin·gle-act·ing (síng-g'l-ákting) *adj.* Designating a steam engine or pump in which the pistons are pressurised on one side only. Compare **double-acting.**

sin·gle-ac·tion (sing-g'l-áksh'n) *adj.* Having a hammer that must be cocked by hand after each shot. Said of a firearm.

single-blind (síng-g'l-blínd) *adj.* Pertaining to or designating an experimental procedure, such as one to test reactions to medicinal drugs, in which the experimenters know the composition of the test items and control substances but the subjects do not. Compare **double-blind.**

single bond n. Chemistry. A type of chemical bond formed by one pair of shared electrons.

sin·gle-breast·ed (síng-g'l-bréstid) adj. Closing with a narrow overlap and a single row of fasteners. Said of a coat or jacket.

single-cell protein (síng-g'l-sel) n. Any protein produced by a mass of cells that have been cultured from a single cell.

single crochet n. A stitch or method of stitching in crochet. See **slip stitch.**

single cross n. Genetics. A first-generation hybrid produced by a cross between two inbred lines.

sin·gle-deck·er (síng-g'l-déckər) n. A bus with only one floor to accommodate passengers. **—sin·gle-deck·er** adj.

single entry n. A system of bookkeeping in which a business keeps only a single account showing amounts due and amounts owed. Compare **double entry. —sin·gle-en·try** adj.

single eye n. Sole devotion: has a single eye for her work.

single file n. A line of people, animals, or things standing or moving one behind the other. Also called "Indian file".
~adv. In single file.

sin·gle-foot (síng-g'l-fŏŏt) n. A horse's gait, the **rack** (see).
~intr.v. **single-footed, -footing, -foots.** To go at this gait.

sin·gle-hand·ed (síng-g'l-hándid) adj. 1. Working or done without help; unassisted. 2. Designed for use with one hand. 3. Having or using only one hand. **—sin·gle-hand·ed, sin·gle-hand·ed·ly** adv. **—sin·gle-hand·ed·ness** n.

single knot n. An overhand knot (see).

sin·gle-lens reflex (síng-g'l-lénz) adj. Abbr. **SLR** Designating a form of reflex camera in which the lens through which light enters the camera to expose the film also serves to illuminate the viewfinder screen after the light has been reflected by a retractable viewfinder mirror.
~n. A single-lens reflex camera.

single malt n. A Scotch whisky distilled from a single batch of fermented malted barley.

sin·gle-mind·ed (síng-g'l-míndid) adj. 1. Having one overriding purpose or opinion. 2. Steadfast. **—sin·gle-mind·ed·ly** adv. **—sin·gle-mind·ed·ness** n.

sin·gle-phase (síng-g'l-fáyz) adj. Producing, carrying, or powered by a single alternating voltage.

sin·gles (síng-g'lz) n. Used with a singular verb. A match, as in tennis, between two players only.

singles bar n. Chiefly U.S. A bar used mostly by single people, especially with the aim of pairing off.

sin·gle-sex (síng-g'l-séks) adj. Of, pertaining to, or accepting members of one sex only: single-sex schools.

sin·gle-space (síng-g'l-spáyss) v. **-spaced, -spacing, -spaces.** —tr. To type (copy) without leaving a blank line between the lines of print. —intr. To type copy without line spaces.

sin·gle-stick (síng-g'l-stik) n. 1. A one-handed fencing stick fitted with a hand guard. Also called "backsword". 2. The art, sport, or exercise of fencing with such a stick.

sin·glet (síng-glit, -glət) n. 1. Chiefly British. **a.** A man's sleeveless vest. **b.** Australian & N.Z. Any, usually sleeveless, undershirt. **c.** Chiefly British. A sleeveless vest worn for running or other sports. 2. Physics. A multiplet with a single member. 3. Chemistry. A single, shared electron in a chemical bond. [From single (in sense 1, referring to an unlined garment), after DOUBLET.]

single tax n. Economics. A system by which all public revenue is derived from a tax on one object, especially on the value of land.

sin·gle·ton (síng-g'l-tən) n. 1. A playing card that is the only one of its suit in a player's hand. 2. An individual as distinguished from a pair or group. [From single (by analogy with SIMPLETON).]

sin·gle-tongu·ing (síng-g'l-túng-ing ‖ Northern English -tóng-) n. The playing of a wind instrument, interrupting the wind stream by moving the tongue as if to pronounce a t sound repeatedly. Compare **double-tonguing, triple-tonguing. —single-tongue** v.

sin·gle-tree (síng-g'l-tree) n. Chiefly U.S. A swingletree (see).

sin·gly (síng-gli) adv. 1. Without company or help; alone. 2. One by one; individually.

Sing Sing. Prison in Ossining, New York State.

sing·song (síng-song ‖ U.S. also -sawng) n. 1. Verse characterised by mechanical regularity of rhythm and rhyme. 2. Enunciation marked by a repetitive rise and fall in pitch. 3. Chiefly British. An impromptu or informal session of singing or a meeting to sing.
~adj. Characterised by repetitive rise-and-fall tone.

Sing·spiel (zing-shpeel) n. German. A type of opera consisting of spoken dialogue with songs interspersed, popular in the 18th century, especially in Germany. ["Singing play".]

sin·gu·lar (síng-gew-lər) adj. 1. Being only one; separate; individual. 2. **a.** Remarkable; extraordinary; rare. **b.** Deviating strongly from a norm; peculiar; odd. 3. Abbr. **s., sing.** Grammar. Of, pertaining to, or being the grammatical number denoting a single person or thing or several considered as a single unit. Compare **plural.** 4. Logic. Of or pertaining to the specific as distinguished from the general; individual. **—See Synonyms at strange.**
~n. Abbr. **s., sing.** Grammar. The singular number, a form denoting it, or a word having a singular number. [Middle English singuler, solitary, single, from Old French, from Latin singulāris, from

singulus, SINGLE.] **—sin·gu·lar·ly** adv. **—sin·gu·lar·ness** n.

sin·gu·lar·ise, sin·gu·lar·ize (sing-gewlər-īz) tr.v. **-ised, -ising, -ises.** To make conspicuous; distinguish from others. **—sin·gu·lar·i·sa·tion** (-ī-záysh'n ‖ U.S. -i-) n.

sin·gu·lar·i·ty (síng-gew-lárrəti) n., pl. **-ties.** 1. The condition or quality of being singular. 2. A trait marking out a person or thing as distinct from others; a peculiarity. 3. Something uncommon or unusual. 4. Physics. A point in space-time at which there is an infinite density of matter, theoretically the ultimate fate of matter within the event horizon of a black hole. A singularity without an event horizon is a **naked singularity** (see).

sin·gul·tus (sing-gúl-təss) n. A hiccup (see). [Latin, sob.]

sinh (shīn, also sinsh) hyperbolic sine.

Sin·ha·lese (sing-hə-léez, -gə-, also sín-hə-, sínnə- ‖ -leess) n., pl. **Sinhalese.** Also **Sin·gha·lese.** 1. A member of a people constituting the major portion of the population of Sri Lanka. 2. The Indic language of this people.
~adj. Also **Sin·gha·lese.** Of or pertaining to the Sinhalese or their language. [Sanskrit sinhalam, Sri Lanka.]

Sin·i·cism (síni-siz'm, sínni-) n. A custom or trait peculiar to the Chinese. [Medieval Latin Sinicus, Chinese, from Late Latin Sinae, the Chinese. See **Sino-.**]

sin·is·ter (sínnistər) adj. 1. **a.** Suggesting an evil force or motive: a sinister smile. **b.** Evil or base. 2. Presaging trouble; ominous. 3. Archaic. On the left side; left. 4. Heraldry. On the left of the bearer and hence on the right of the observer. Compare **dexter.** [Middle English sinistre, from Old French, from Latin sinister†, left, on the left, hence evil, unlucky (in augury the left side being regarded as inauspicious).] **—sin·is·ter·ly** adv. **—sin·is·ter·ness** n.

sin·is·tral (sínnistrəl) adj. 1. Of, facing, or situated on the left side. 2. Left-handed. Compare **dextral.** 3. Zoology. Designating or pertaining to a gastropod shell that has its aperture to the left when facing the observer with the apex upwards. **—sin·is·tral·ly** adv.

sin·is·tro·dex·tral (sínniss-trō-dékstrəl, -trə-) adj. Moving or directed from left to right: a sinistrodextral text. [Sinistro-, from Latin sinister, left + DEXTRAL.]

sin·is·trorse (sínniss-trawrss, -trórss) adj. Growing upwards in a spiral that turns from right to left: a sinistrorse vine. Compare **dextrorse.** [New Latin sinistrorsus, turned towards the left : SINISTER (left) + versus, past participle of vertere, to turn.] **—sin·is·trorse·ly** adv.

sin·is·trous (sínnistrəss) adj. Archaic. Sinister; ill-omened: "The arrival of a beggar on an island is accounted a sinistrous event." (Samuel Johnson). **—sin·is·trous·ly** adv.

Si·nit·ic (sī-níttik, si-) n. One of the two branches of the Sino-Tibetan linguistic group, comprising all the various Chinese languages and dialects, including Mandarin, Cantonese, and Fukien. **—Si·nit·ic** adj.

sink (singk) v. **sank** (sangk) or **sunk** (sungk), **sunk** or **sunken** (súngkən), **sinking, sinks.** —intr. 1. To descend beneath the surface or to the bottom of a liquid or soft substance; especially, to cease to float through lack of buoyancy: The ship sank. 2. To move to a lower level; go down slowly or in stages. 3. To appear to move downwards or below the horizon. 4. To slope downwards; incline. 5. To pass into a worsened physical condition; approach death. 6. **a.** To become weaker, quieter, or less forceful: Her voice sank and died away. **b.** To fall down or give way, as through weakness or fatigue: sank into a chair. 7. To diminish, as in value or amount. 8. **a.** To suffer a loss of morale, spirit, or vitality. Used with in or into: sank into a deep depression. **b.** To be depressed or dismayed: My heart sank. **c.** To decline, as in morality or reputation. Used with in or into: sank into anonymity. 9. To penetrate or cut through something. Used with in or into: The blade sank in. 10. Informal. To penetrate or be absorbed by the mind; approach death. Used with in or into: The message finally sank in. 11. To seep or be soaked up. Used with in or into. 12. To become hollowed or shrunken. Used of the cheeks. —tr. 1. To cause to descend beneath the surface; especially, to cause (a vessel) to lose buoyancy and cease to float. 2. To cause or allow to fall; drop or lower. 3. **a.** To force into the ground: sink piles into a river bed. **b.** To cause to cut through or penetrate: sank her fork into the steak. 4. To dig or drill (a mine or well) in the earth. 5. To degrade; debase the character or reputation of. 6. To cause to diminish, as in value or price. 7. To suppress; hide; conceal: sink our differences for the sake of appearances. 8. To cause to fail or suffer a reverse; defeat: could sink the whole project. 9. To invest (money). Used with in or into. 10. To lose (part or all of an investment). 11. To pay off (a debt). 12. To cause (a ball) to enter a target in games such as golf, snooker, or basketball. 13. Informal. To drink. **—sink or swim.** To succeed through one's own efforts, or else fail completely.
~n. 1. A water basin fixed to a wall or floor and having a drainpipe and generally a piped supply of water. 2. A cesspool. 3. A **sinkhole** (see). 4. In thermodynamics, the part of a system from which heat or, more generally, energy is removed from the system. 5. Any place regarded as an abode of wickedness and corruption. [Middle English sinken, sank, sunken, Old English sincan, sanc (past singular), suncen.] **—sink·a·ble** adj. **—sink·age** n.
Usage: The past tense of this verb is most commonly sank, though sunk is often heard, especially informally. The past participle is sunk; sunken is usually only adjectival (sunken treasure).

sink·er (síngkər) n. 1. One that sinks. 2. A weight used for sinking fishing lines, nets, or the like. 3. U.S. Slang. A doughnut.

sink estate n. British. A dilapidated, squalid council housing estate, inhabited by those unable to be housed elsewhere, usually belonging to the poorest, most disadvantaged group of society.

sink·hole (síngk-hōl) n. **1.** A natural depression in a land surface communicating with a subterranean passage, generally occurring in limestone regions and formed by solution or by collapse of a cavern roof. **2.** A natural hole or hollow in limestone or chalk into which surface water disappears. In this sense, also called "swallow hole".

Sinkiang Uighur Autonomous Region. See **Xinjiang Uigur Zizhiqu.**

sink·ing feeling n. A sensation in the pit of the stomach caused, for example, by hunger, fear, or anxiety.

sinking fund n. A fund accumulated over a period and invested for the paying off of a public or corporate debt.

sin·less (sín-ləss, -liss) adj. Free from or without sin or guilt. —**sin·less·ly** adv. —**sin·less·ness** n.

sin·ner (sínnər) n. Especially in Christianity, one who sins.

sinnet. Variant of **sennit.**

Sinn Fein (shín fáyn) n. An Irish nationalist organisation founded in about 1905, that constitutes the political branch of the **I.R.A.** (see), and is dedicated to the political and economic independence of a united Ireland. It split into the **Official** and **Provisional** wings (both of which see), after a similar split in the I.R.A. in 1969. [Irish sinn féin, "we ourselves".] —**Sinn Fein·er** n. —**Sinn Fein·ism** n.

Sino– comb. form. Indicates Chinese; for example, **Sinophile.** [French, from Late Latin Sinae, the Chinese, from Greek Sinai, from Arabic Sīn, China, from Chinese (Mandarin) Qín, dynastic name of the country. See also **China.**]

si·no·a·tri·al node (sínō-áytri-əl) n. A group of specialised cells in the wall of the right atrium of the heart that initiates the heartbeat. Also called "pacemaker". [Sino-, from Latin sinus, cavity + ATRIAL.]

Sin·o·logue (sína-log, sínnə- ‖ U.S. also -lawg) n. A student of Sinology. [French sinologue : SINO- + -LOGUE.]

Si·nol·o·gy (sī-nólləji, si-) n. The study of Chinese language, literature, or civilisation. [French sinologie : SINO- + -LOGY.] —**Sin·o·log·i·cal** (sínə-lójik'l, sínnə-) adj. —**Si·nol·o·gist** n.

Sin·o·phile (sín-ə-fīl, sín-, -ō-) n. One friendly to the Chinese and their interests. [SINO- + -PHILE.] —**Sin·o·phile** adj.

Sin·o·Ti·bet·an (sínō-ti-bétt'n, sínnō-) n. A linguistic group that includes the Sinitic and Tibeto-Burman families. —**Sin·o·Ti·bet·an** adj.

sin·ter (síntər) n. **1.** Geology. A crust of porous silica, deposited by a hot spring or geyser. **2.** A mass formed by sintering. ~v. **sintered, -tering, -ters.** —tr. To weld together (metallic powder, for example) partially and without melting. —intr. To form a homogeneous mass by heating without melting. [German Sinter, iron dross, from Old High German sintar.]

Sin·tra (sín-trə, seén-). Formerly **Cin·tra.** Town in the Estremadura region of western Portugal, lying near the Atlantic coast just west of Lisbon. It was a Moorish centre until 1147.

sin·u·ate (sínnew-ət, -it, -ayt) adj. Also **sin·u·at·ed** (-aytid). Having a wavy indented margin. Said of a leaf. [Latin sinuātus, past participle of sinuāre, to bend, wind, from sinus, a bend, curve, fold. See **sinus.**] —**sin·u·ate·ly** adv. —**sin·u·a·tion** (-áysh'n) n.

sin·u·os·i·ty (sínnew-óssəti) n., pl. -**ties. 1.** The quality of being sinuous. **2.** A bending or curving shape or movement.

sin·u·ous (sínnew-əss) adj. **1.** Supple and lithe in movement. **2.** Characterised by many curves or turns; winding. **3.** Devious and intricate. [Latin sinuōsus, from sinus, a bend, curve, fold. See **sinus.**] —**sin·u·ous·ly** adv. —**sin·u·ous·ness** n.

si·nus (sínəss) n. **1.** A depression or cavity formed by a bending or curving. **2.** Anatomy. **a.** Any of various air-filled cavities in the cranial bones, especially one communicating with the nostrils. **b.** A wide channel for the passage of blood, especially venous blood. **3.** Pathology. A fistula or channel to a suppurating cavity. **4.** Botany. A notch or indentation between lobes of a leaf or corolla. [Latin sinus†, a bend, curve, fold, hollow.]

si·nus·i·tis (sínə-sítiss ‖ sínew-) n. Inflammation of a sinus membrane, especially in the nasal region.

si·nus·oid (sínə-soyd ‖ sínew-) n. **1.** Mathematics. A sine curve (see). **2.** Anatomy. A minute blood vessel occurring in such organs as the liver and adrenal gland. [Medieval Latin sinus, sine, from Latin, a curve + -OID.] —**si·nus·oi·dal** (-sóyd'l) adj.

sinusoidal projection n. A map projection in which the standard parallel is the equator, the other parallels of latitude are drawn as horizontal lines spaced at true intervals, and the meridians of longitude, apart from the standard meridian, are drawn as sine curves. It is an equal-area projection, but can be used for the whole globe. Also called "Sanson-Flamsteed Projection".

Sion. Variant of **Zion.**

Siou·an (sōō-ən) n. A large North American Indian language family spoken from Lake Michigan to the Rocky Mountains and southwards to Arkansas by many peoples, including the Omaha, Iowa, Winnebago, Sioux, and Crow groups. —**Siou·an** adj.

Sioux (sōō) n., pl. **Sioux** (-z, or as singular). **1.** A member of any of the various groups of Siouan-speaking North American Indian peoples, formerly occupying parts of the Great Plains in the Dakotas, Minnesota, and Nebraska. **2.** Any Siouan language. See **Dakota.** —**Sioux** adj.

sip (sip) v. **sipped, sipping, sips.** —tr. To drink delicately and in small quantities: She sipped the hot tea. —intr. To drink in sips. ~n. **1.** The act of sipping. **2.** A small quantity of liquid sipped.

[Middle English sippen, probably of Low German origin; akin to Low German sippen, to sip.]

si·phon, sy·phon (síf'n) n. **1.** A pipe or tube fashioned or deployed in an inverted U shape and filled until atmospheric pressure is sufficient to force a liquid from a reservoir in one end of the tube over a barrier higher than the reservoir and out of the other end. **2.** A bottle from which soda water may be dispensed under pressure. **3.** Zoology. A tubular organ, especially of aquatic invertebrates such as squids, by which water is taken in or expelled. ~v. **siphoned, -phoning, -phons.** —tr. **1.** To draw off or convey through a siphon. **2.** To divert (money, for example) for another purpose. Used with off. —intr. To pass through a siphon. [French, from Latin sīphō, sīphōn, from Greek siphōn†, pipe, tube.] —**si·phon·al, si·phon·ic** (sī-fónnik) adj.

si·pho·no·phore (sífənə-fawr, sī-fónnə- ‖ -fōr) n. Any of various colonial marine coelenterates of the order Siphonophora, which includes the Portuguese man-of-war. [New Latin Siphonophora, "tube-bearers" (from their feeding tube) : Latin sīphō(n), tube, SIPHON + New Latin -phora, neuter plural of -phorus, -PHOROUS.]

si·pho·no·stele (sífənə-steel, sī-fónnə-) n. A vascular tube surrounding the pith in the stems of certain plants. [SIPHON + STELE (vascular tissue).] —**si·pho·no·ste·lic** adj.

si·phun·cle (sí-fungk'l) n. Zoology. **1.** A tubelike structure in the body of a shelled cephalopod, such as a chambered nautilus, extending through each chamber of the shell. **2.** A dorsal tube in an aphid, secreting a waxy fluid. Formerly called "nectary". [Latin sīphunculus, diminutive of sīphō, sīphōn, tube, SIPHON.]

sip·pet (síppit) n. A small piece of toast or fried bread soaked in gravy or other juice or served as a garnish on soups or stews. [Sip, alteration of SOP + -ET.]

sir (sur, weak form sər) n. **1. a.** A respectful or polite form of address for a man. **b.** Capital **S.** A conventional form of address used instead of a man's name at the opening of a letter. **2.** Capital **S.** A title of honour used before the first name or the full name of baronets and knights. **3.** Obsolete. A form of address used with a noun indicating a man's profession, rank, or the like. Sometimes used humorously or derogatorily. **4.** Archaic. A gentleman of rank. [Middle English, unstressed variant of SIRE.]

Siracusa. See **Syracuse.**

sir·dar (súr-daar) n. Also **sar·dar** (sər-dár). **1.** A person of rank in India or Pakistan. **2.** A military chief or leader in India or Pakistan. **3.** Formerly, the British commander of the Egyptian army. [Hindi sardār, from Persian : sar, head + dār, possession, from Old Persian, from dar-, to hold, possess.]

Sir Ddinbych. See **Denbighshire.**

sire (sīr) n. **1.** Poetic. A father or forefather. **2.** Abbr. **s.** The male parent of an animal, especially a domesticated mammal, such as a horse. **3.** Archaic. Capital **S.** A title or form of address for a nobleman, especially for a king. ~tr.v. **sired, siring, sires. 1.** To be the father of. Used especially of a stallion. **2.** Poetic. To give rise to; beget. [Middle English, from Old French, from Vulgar Latin seior (unattested), variant of Latin senior, older, from senex, old.]

si·ren (sír-ən, -in) n. **1.** Greek Mythology. Often capital **S.** Any of a group of sea nymphs who, by their sweet singing, lured sailors to destruction on the rocks surrounding their island. **2.** A dangerously seductive woman; a temptress. **3.** A device in which compressed air or steam is driven against a rotating perforated disc to create a loud, penetrating whistle, wailing, or other sound as a signal or warning. **4.** Any instrument producing a similar sound as a signal or warning. **5.** Any of several North American amphibians of the family Sirenidae, having an eel-like body and no hind limbs. ~adj. Suggesting the effect of the mythological sirens; bewitching. [Middle English ser(e)yne, siren, from Old French sereine, from Late Latin sīrēna, from Latin Sīrēn, from Greek Seirēn.]

si·re·ni·an (sīr-réeni-ən, sī-, si-) n. Any herbivorous aquatic mammal of the order Sirenia, including the manatee and the dugong. ~adj. Of or belonging to the Sirenia. [New Latin Sīrēnia (order), from Latin Sīrēn, SIREN.]

Sir·i·us (sírri-əss, rarely sīr-i-) n. A star in the constellation Canis Major. It appears as the brightest star in the sky, and is approximately 8.7 light years distant from Earth. Also called "Canicula", "Dog Star". [Latin, from Greek Seirios, from seirios†, burning, glowing.]

sir·loin (súr-loyn) n. A cut of beef from the upper part of the loin between the rump and the porterhouse. [Earlier surloyn(e), from Old French surlonge : sur, above, from Latin super + longe, loigne, loin, from Latin lumbus.]

si·roc·co (si-róckō) n., pl. -**cos.** Also **sci·roc·co** (shi-). A hot, humid south or southeast wind of southern Italy, Sicily, and the Mediterranean islands, originating in the Sahara as a dry, dusty wind but becoming moist as it passes over the Mediterranean. [Italian, from Arabic sharuq, "east (wind)", from sharaqa, (the sun) rose.]

sir·rah (sírrə) n. Archaic. Fellow. Used as a contemptuous form of address. [Probably alteration of Middle English SIRE (sir).]

sir·ree, sir·ee (sə-rée) n. U.S. Informal. Sir. Used with yes or no for emphasis.

Sir Rog·er de Cov·er·ley (sər rójər də kúvvərli) n. An English country dance performed by an unspecified number of couples initially facing each other in a long line. [After the fictitious character in a series of essays by Addison and Steele in the Spectator.]

sirup. U.S. Variant of **syrup.**

sir·vente (sər-vént, seer-, -vónt) n., pl. -**ventes** (-s, or pronounced as *singular*). Also **sir·ventes.** A form of lyric verse used by the Provençal troubadours to satirise political, social, or moral themes. [French, from Provençal *sirventes,* "a servant's song", from *sirvent, servent,* servant, from Latin *serviēns* (stem *servient-*), present participle of *servīre,* to serve, from *servus,* servant.]

sis¹ (siss) *n. Informal.* Sister.

sis² *interj. South African.* Used to express disgust, revulsion, or strong disapproval. [Afrikaans *sies,* possibly from Hottentot *si, tsi.*]

si·sal (sī́-s'l ‖ -z'l) *n.* **1.** A fleshy plant, *Agave sisalana,* native to Mexico, widely cultivated for its large leaves that yield a stiff fibre used for cordage and rope. **2. a.** The fibre of this plant. **b.** The fibre of certain similar or related plants. [Mexican Spanish, after *Sisal,* town in Yucatán, Mexico.]

sis·kin (sískin) *n.* Any of several small birds of the family Fringillidae; especially, *Carduelis spinus,* of Eurasia, having a yellow and black plumage. [Middle Dutch *sīseken,* formed as diminutive of Middle Low German *sīsek,* from Slavonic; akin to Czech *čiž,* Russian *chizh* (imitative).]

sis·si·fied (síssi-fīd) *adj. Informal.* Womanish; effeminate. Said of a male.

sis·sy, cis·sy (síssi) *n., pl.* **-sies. 1.** An effeminate or weak boy or man; a milksop. **2.** A timid or cowardly person. [From *sis,* short for SISTER.] **—sis·sy** *adj.*

sis·ter (sístər) *n.* **1.** *Abbr.* **s.** A female having the same mother and father as another person *(full sister),* having one parent in common with another person *(half sister),* having one parent in common with another person by marriage rather than by blood *(stepsister),* or having a shared mother and father after adoption *(adoptive sister).* **2.** A female who shares a common ancestry, allegiance, character, or purpose with another or others, especially: **a.** A kinswoman. **b.** A female fellow member, as of a trade union. **c.** A female who shares feminist beliefs, principles, and aspirations. **d.** A fellow woman, friend, or companion. **3.** *U.S. Informal.* A girl or woman. Used as a form of direct address. **4.** *Capital* **S. a.** *Abbr.* **Sr.** A member of a religious order of women; a nun. **b.** A title or form of address for such a person. **5.** *British.* **a.** The nurse in charge of a hospital ward. **b.** A title or form of address for such a person. **6.** One identified as female and closely related to another.
~*adj.* Standing in the relationship of a sister; related by or as if by sisterhood: *sister souls.* [Middle English *suster, sister,* Old English *sweostor, swuster.*]

sis·ter·hood (sístər-hood) *n.* **1.** The state or relationship of being a sister or sisters. **2.** The quality of being sisterly. **3.** A society of women; especially, a religious society of women. **4. a.** The feminist movement. **b.** Feminists collectively. Preceded by *the.*

sis·ter-in-law (sístər-in-law) *n., pl.* **sisters-in-law. 1.** The sister of one's wife or husband. **2.** The wife of one's brother. **3.** The wife of the brother of one's spouse.

sis·ter·ly (sístərli) *adj.* Characteristic of or befitting a sister or sisters.
~*adv.* As a sister. **—sis·ter·li·ness** *n.*

Sis·tine (sís-teen) *adj.* Also **Six·tine** (síks-). **1.** Of or concerning any of the popes named Sixtus. **2.** Of or pertaining to the Sistine Chapel, built for pope Sixtus IV. [Italian *sistino,* from New Latin *sixtinus,* from the name *Sixtus.*]

sis·troid (síss-troyd) *adj.* Lying between the convex sides of two curves. Compare **cissoid.** [SISTR(UM) + -OID.]

sis·trum (síss-trəm) *n., pl.* **-trums** or **-tra** (-trə). An ancient Egyptian musical instrument consisting of a thin metal frame with rods or loops that rattle. [Middle English, from Latin, from Greek *seistron,* from *seiein,* to shake.]

si·Swa·ti (si-swáa-ti) *n.* The Bantu language, **Swazi** *(see).* **—si·Swa·ti** *adj.*

Sis·y·phe·an (síssi-feé-ən) *adj.* **1.** Of or pertaining to Sisyphus. **2.** *Often small* **s.** Endless and to no avail.

Sis·y·phus (síssifəss) *n. Greek Mythology.* A cruel king of Corinth who because of disrespect to Zeus was condemned forever to roll a huge stone up a hill in Hades, only to find it roll down again on nearing the top.

sit (sit) *v.* **sat** (sat) or *archaic* **sate** (sayt, sat), **sat, sitting, sits.** *—intr.* **1.** To rest with the body supported upon the buttocks and the torso vertical. **2.** To rest with the hindquarters lowered onto a supporting surface. Used of animals. **3.** To perch. Used of birds. **4.** To cover eggs for hatching; brood. **5.** To be situated; lie. **6.** To take and maintain a position for an artist or photographer; pose. **7. a.** To occupy a seat in an official capacity, as a judge, or as a member of a deliberative body: *sits on the transport committee.* **b.** To be in session. Used of a deliberative or judicial body. **8.** To remain inactive or unused. **9.** To lie or rest in a specified manner: *sat uneasily on the edge of the chair.* **10.** To affect one with or as if with a burden; weigh. Used with *on* or *upon*: *Official duties sat heavily on her.* **11. a.** To fit, fall, or hang in a specified manner. Used of clothing: *That dress sits well on her.* **b.** To be suitable or appropriate: *Arrogance does not sit well on them.* **12.** To lie, rest, or belong in a specified place: *Those sit on the top shelf.* **13.** To blow from a particular direction. Used of the wind. **14.** To baby-sit or keep watch over an invalid. **15.** To take an examination: *sitting for her A levels.* *—tr.* **1.** To cause to sit; to seat. Often used reflexively: *Sit yourself over there.* **2.** To keep one's seat upon (a horse or other animal). **3.** *Chiefly British.* To take (an examination), as for a degree. **—sit back.** To relax; not concern or worry oneself: *sit back and enjoy the film.* **—sit on** or **upon.** *Informal.* **1.** To suppress or delay publication of (information, news, or a decision, for example). **2.** To rebuke sharply; reprimand. **—sit out. 1.** To stay until the end of: *sit out a speech.* **2.** To remain seated throughout; take no part in (a dance or game, for example). **3.** To lean out over the side of a small sailing vessel with the back towards the water when sailing close to the wind, so as to keep the boat level. **—sit tight.** *Informal.* To be patient and await the next move. **—sitting pretty.** *Informal.* In an advantageous or favourable position. **—sit up. 1.** To sit straight or erect. **2.** To stay up later than one's customary bedtime. **3.** To become suddenly alert or attentive.
~*n.* An act, instance, or period of sitting. [Sit, sat (past); Middle English *sitten, sat(e),* Old English *sittan, sæt* (plural *sǣton*). Sat (past participle); Middle English *sat,* adopted from the past tense *sat(e)* and replacing the regular *seten,* Old English *(ge)seten.*]

si·tar (si-tár, sít-aar) *n.* A Hindu stringed instrument made of seasoned gourds and teak and having a track of 20 metal frets with 3 to 7 main playing strings above and 13 sympathetic resonating strings below. [Hindi *sitār,* "three-stringed" : Persian *si,* three + *tār,* string, from Avestan *tąthra-* (unattested).] **—si·tar·ist** *n.*

sit·com (sít-kom) *n. Informal.* A **situation comedy** *(see).* **—sit·com** *adj.*

sit down *intr.v.* To seat oneself; take a seat.
~*tr.v.* To seat (oneself or another).

sit-down (sít-down ‖ *West Indies also* -dung) *adj.* Served to and eaten by people seated at a table. Said of a meal: *a sit-down dinner.*
~*n.* A sit-in.

sit-down strike *n.* A sit-in.

site (sīt) *n.* **1.** The place or plot of land where something was, is, or is to be situated, especially a place where construction work is taking place. **2.** The place or setting of an event.
~*tr.v.* **sited, siting, sites.** To situate or locate on a site: *siting a power plant.* [Middle English, from Old French, from Latin *situs,* place, locality, from *situs,* past participle of *sinere*†, to allow (to remain in a place), hence lay, put.]

site of special scientific interest *n. Abbr.* **SSSI** In Britain, a site defined, listed, and protected to some degree by the Nature Conservancy Council because of its interesting flora, fauna, or geology. There are also larger areas of special scientific interest.

sith (sith) *conj. Archaic.* Since. [Middle English *sith(th)e,* Old English *siththa, siththan,* SINCE.] **—sith** *adv. & prep.*

sit in *intr.v.* **1.** To participate in a sit-in. **2.** To take the place of an absent person: *sat in for me at the meeting.* **3.** To be present as an observer or guest: *sat in on the meeting.*

sit-in (sít-in) *n.* A form of industrial action in which workers strike while occupying their place of work. Also called "sit-down", "sit-down strike". **2.** A form of protest, as against racial discrimination or the policies of a government or company, in which demonstrators occupy appropriate premises to call attention to their views. Also called "sit-down". Compare **work-in.**

Sit·ka (sít-kə). Town on Baranof Island, in the Alexander archipelago of Alaska. From 1867 to 1900 it was the capital of Alaska.

Sitka spruce *n.* A North American spruce tree, *Picea sitchensis,* that is an important source of softwood.

si·tol·o·gy (sī-tólləji) *n. Rare.* The science of foods, nutrition, and diet. [Greek *sitos*†, food, grain + -LOGY.]

si·tos·ter·ol (sī-tóstə-rol ‖ -rōl) *n.* Any of various sterols extracted from soya beans for the preparation of medicines, such as synthetic steroid hormones, and cosmetics. [Greek *sitos,* food + STEROL.]

sit·tel·la (si-téllə) *n.* Any of various Australian birds of the genus *Neositta,* some species of which use small twigs to draw out of concealment the grubs on which they feed. Also called "tree-runner". [New Latin, diminutive of Latin *sitta,* nuthatch.]

sit·ter (síttər) *n.* **1.** One that sits; especially, one who sits for an artist or photographer. **2.** A brooding hen. **3.** *Informal.* Something that is easy to do, such as an easy catch at cricket.

sit·ting (sítting) *n.* **1.** The act or position of one that sits. **2.** A period during which one is seated and occupied with a single activity, such as posing for a portrait or reading a book. **3.** A term or session, as of a legislature or court. **4.** A time at which a meal is served, typically one of several such periods allocated in order to make full use of limited facilities. **5. a.** An act or period of incubation of eggs by a bird. **b.** The number of eggs under a brooding bird.

Sitting Bull, *Sioux* Tatanka Iyotake (*c.* 1831–90). Dakota Sioux chief. He led the Indian forces during the Sioux war against the U.S. army (1876–77), defeating General Custer's cavalry at the Battle of the Little Big Horn (1876).

sitting duck *n. Informal.* An easy target or victim. Also called "sitting target".

sitting room *n.* A living room in a private house.

sitting tenant *n.* A tenant who is actually in occupation of rented premises.

sitting trot *n.* A slow trot during which the rider of the horse stays seated in the saddle.

sit·u·ate (síttew-ayt, síchoo- ‖ *Welsh also* síttoo-) *tr.v.* **-ated, -ating, -ates. 1.** To place in a certain spot or position; locate. **2.** To place under particular circumstances or in a given condition.
~*adj.* (-ayt, -ət, -it). *Archaic & Law.* Situated. [Medieval Latin *situāre,* to put, place, from *situs,* place, SITE.]

sit·u·a·tion (síttew-áysh'n, síchoo- ‖ *Welsh also* síttoo-) *n.* **1.** A place or position in which something is situated; a location. **2.** A position or status with regard to conditions and attendant circumstances; especially, a person's financial position or status. **3.** A combination of circumstances at a given moment; a state of affairs. **4.** A critical

or problematic combination of circumstances. **5.** A position of employment; a post. —See Synonyms at **state.** [Middle English, from Medieval Latin *situātiō* (stem *situātiōn-*), from *situāre,* to SITUATE.] **—sit·u·a·tion·al** *adj.*
situation comedy *n.* **1.** A genre of comedy in which the humour is derived from the reactions of a regular cast of characters to unusual situations, such as misunderstandings or embarrassing coincidences. **2.** A radio or television programme or series using this type of comedy. In this sense, also called "sitcom".
si·tus (sítəss) *n., pl.* **situs.** Position; especially, the normal position of a bodily organ. [Latin *situs,* place, SITE.]
Sit·well (sít-wəl, -wel), **Dame Edith (Louisa)** (1887–1964). British poet, biographer, and critic. One of the most famous literary eccentrics of the 20th century, she wrote *English Eccentrics* (1933), by which time she had already established a reputation by her poetry, written in the obscure manner of the French symbolists. *Façade,* near-nonsense verse to be read against music composed by William Walton, was first performed by her in 1922. Her brother, Sir Osbert Sitwell (1892–1969), was a poet, novelist, and short-story writer.
sitz bath (sits) *n.* A type of bath in which one bathes in a sitting position. [Partial translation of German *Sitzbad* : *Sitz,* a sitting, from Old High German *siz,* from *sizzen,* to sit + *Bad,* bath.]
sitz·krieg (síts-kreeg, zíts-) *n.* A war in which very little actual fighting takes place; a nonaggressive war. [German, "sitting-war".]
SI unit (éss-ī) *n.* Any of the units that form part of the Système international d'unités, used for all scientific purposes. The seven base units are the metre, kilogram, second, ampere, kelvin, candela, and mole; the radian and the steradian are treated as supplementary units. All other units are derived from these units.
Si·va (shée-və, sée-). Also **Shi·va** (shée-). *Hinduism.* The god of destruction and reproduction, a member of the Hindu triad along with Brahma and Vishnu. [Sanskrit *Śíva,* "the auspicious (one)", from *siva,* auspicious, dear.] **—Si·va·ism** *n.* **—Si·va·ist** *n. & adj.*
Si·van (sívv'n, see-vaán) *n.* The ninth month of the Hebrew year. [Hebrew *Sīwān,* from Assyro-Babylonian *Simānu,* possibly related to Persian *Sefend,* an Iranian deity.]
six (siks) *n.* **1. a.** The cardinal number that is one more than five. **b.** A symbol representing this, such as 6, VI, or vi. **2.** A set made up of six persons or things. **3. a.** The sixth in a series. **b.** A playing card marked with six pips. **4.** Six parts: *cut into six.* **5.** A size, as in clothing, designated as six. **6.** Six hours after midnight or midday. **7. a.** In cricket, a ball hit beyond the boundary line that does not touch the ground and thus scores six runs. **b.** The six runs scored. **8.** A group of six Brownies or Cub Scouts constituting a division of a pack. **—at sixes and sevens.** *Informal.* In a state of confusion or disorder. **—knock (someone) for six.** *Informal.* To surprise or stun (someone) completely. **—six of one and half a dozen of the other.** A merely nominal difference; a situation in which neither choice is clearly preferable. **—six of the best.** Six strokes of the cane as a punishment. [Middle English *six, sex,* Old English *s(i)ex, six.*] **—six** *adj.* **—six·fold** *adj. & adv.*
six·ain (síks-ayn) *n.* A stanza consisting of six lines. [French, from *six,* SIX.]
Six Counties *pl.n.* The six counties of Northern Ireland: Antrim, Armagh, Down, Fermanagh, Londonderry, and Tyrone.
six·er (síksər) *n.* The leader of a six of Brownies or Cub Scouts.
six-foot·er (síks-fŏŏtər) *n.* A person who is six feet tall or more.
Six Nations. See **Iroquois.**
six-pack (síks-pak) *n.* A pack of six cans of a drink, especially beer.
six·pence (síks-pənss; *for sense 2, also* -pénss) *n. British.* **1.** A coin worth six old pennies or half a shilling (2.5 new pence), no longer in circulation. **2.** The sum of six pennies.
six·pen·ny (síks-pəni || *U.S. also* -penni) *adj.* **1.** Valued at, selling for, or worth sixpence (2.5 new pence). **2.** Of little worth; cheap; paltry. **3.** Designating a nail of a certain size, generally two inches.
six-shoot·er (síks-shŏŏtər) *n. Informal.* A six-chambered revolver. Also called "six-gun".
six·teen (síks-téen) *n.* **1. a.** The cardinal number that is one more than 15. **b.** A symbol representing this, such as 16 or XVI. **2.** A set made up of 16 persons or things. **3.** The sixteenth in a series. **4.** A size, as in clothing, designated as 16. [Middle English *sixtene,* Old English *sixtȳne* : SIX + -TEEN.] **—six·teen** *adj.*
six·teen·mo (siks-téen-mō) *n., pl.* **-mos. Sextodecimo** *(see).*
six·teenth (síks-téenth) *n.* **1.** The ordinal number 16 in a series. **2.** Any of 16 equal parts. **—six·teenth** *adj. & adv.*
sixteenth note *n. Music. U.S.* A **semiquaver** *(see).*
sixth (siksth) *n.* **1.** The ordinal number six in a series. **2.** One of six equal parts. **3.** *Music.* **a.** An interval of six degrees in a diatonic scale. **b.** A note separated by this interval from a given note. **c.** The chord consisting of two notes separated by this interval. **d.** The sixth note of a scale; the submediant. **—sixth** *adj. & adv.*
sixth form *n.* In the British secondary school system, the form containing the oldest pupils, normally preparing for A levels over two or more years. **—sixth-form·er** (síksth-fawrmər) *n.*
sixth-form college (síksth-fawrm) *n.* A college where students of 16 or over can follow A-level or, sometimes, vocational courses.
sixth sense *n.* A power of perception seemingly independent of and additional to the five senses.
six·ti·eth (síksti-əth, -ith) *n.* **1.** The ordinal number 60 in a series. **2.** Any of 60 equal parts. **—six·ti·eth** *adj. & adv.*
Sixtine. Variant of **Sistine.**
six·ty (síksti) *n., pl.* **-ties. 1. a.** The cardinal number that is ten more than fifty. **b.** A symbol representing this, such as 60 or LX. **2.** A set made up of sixty persons or things. **3.** The sixtieth in a series. **4.** A size, as in clothing, designated as sixty. **5.** *Plural.* **a.** The range of numbers from 60 to 69, considered as a range of age, price, temperature, or the like. **b.** *Sometimes capital* **S.** The years numbered 60 to 69 in a century. Also used adjectivally: *sixties music.* **—six·ty** *adj.*
six·ty-fourth note (síksti-fórth || -fōrth) *n. U.S. Music.* A **hemidemisemiquaver** *(see).*
sixty-four thousand dollar question (síksti-fór || -fōr) *n.* A question that is crucial or very difficult to answer. Also called "sixty-four dollar question". [Referring to the highest prize given in a U.S. television quiz.]
siz·a·ble (sízəb'l) *adj.* Also **size·a·ble.** Of considerable size; fairly large. **—siz·a·ble·ness** *n.* **—siz·a·bly** *adv.*
size[1] (sīz) *n.* **1.** The physical dimensions, proportions, magnitude, or extent of something. **2.** Any of a series of graduated categories of dimension whereby articles for sale are classified. **3.** Considerable extent, amount, or dimensions: *grown to quite a size.* **4.** Qualities or status with reference to relative importance or the capacity to meet certain requirements: *of no great size in her field.* **5.** The actual state of affairs or truth of the matter: *That's about the size of it.* **—cut down to size.** *Informal.* **1.** To reduce the self-importance of. **2.** To reduce to manageable proportions. **—try (out) for size.** *Informal.* To test out.
~*tr.v.* **sized, sizing, sizes. 1.** To arrange, classify, or distribute according to size. **2.** To make, cut, or shape to a required size. **—size up. 1.** *Informal.* To make an estimate or form a judgment of. **2.** To meet certain specifications or requirements. [Middle English *syse,* fixed amount, assize, from Old French *sise,* short for *assise,* ASSIZE.]
size[2] *n.* Any of several gelatinous or glutinous substances usually made from glue, wax, or clay and used as a glaze or filler for porous materials such as paper, cloth, or wall surfaces. Also called "sizing".
~*tr.v.* **sized, sizing, sizes.** To treat or coat with size or a similar substance. [Middle English *cyse, syse,* probably a specialised use of SIZE (dimension).] **—siz·y** *adj.*
sized (sīzd) *adj.* Having a particular or specified size. Often used in combination: *medium-sized.* Also "-size": *medium-size.*
siz·ing (sízing) *n.* A glaze or filler; size.
siz·zle (sízz'l) *intr.v.* **-zled, -zling, -zles. 1.** To make the hissing sound characteristic of frying fat. **2.** *Informal.* To seethe with anger or indignation. **3.** *Informal.* To be extremely hot.
~*n.* A hissing sound. [Imitative.]
siz·zler (sízzlər) *n. Informal.* A very hot day.
S.J. Society of Jesus.
Sjæl·land (*Danish* syéllan). *English* **Zea·land** (zée-lənd). Denmark's largest island, lying off the extreme southwestern coast of Sweden. Low-lying and fertile, the island is the site of Copenhagen.
sjam·bok (shám-bok, *rarely* -buk) *n. South African.* A stiff whip made from the hide of a rhinoceros or hippopotamus.
~*tr.v.* **sjambokked, -bokking, -boks.** *South African.* To flog with such a whip. [Afrikaans, from Malay *chambok,* from Urdu *chābuk.*]
sk. sack.
ska (skaa || *Jamaican* skya) *n.* A type of West Indian popular music similar to reggae but lighter and with a more fluid rhythm. [20th century : origin obscure.] **—ska** *adj.*
Skag·er·rak (skággə-rak). Strait separating Norway and Denmark, linking the North Sea and the Baltic Sea by way of the Kattegat and extending for about 240 kilometres (150 miles). Here the British and German fleets engaged in the Battle of Jutland (1916).
skald, scald (skaald, skawld) *n.* An ancient Scandinavian poet; a bard. [Old Norse *skāld.*] **—skald·ic** *adj.*
Skar·a Brae (skárrə bráy). Stone-age village on the west coast of Mainland, Orkney, Scotland, dating from *c.* 2000 B.C.–1500 B.C. It is perhaps the most completely preserved in Europe.
skat (skat) *n.* **1.** A card game for three persons played with 32 cards, the sevens up to and including the aces. **2.** One of the combinations of cards occurring in this game. [German *Skat,* from Italian *scarto,* a discarded card, from *scartare,* to reject, discard : *s-,* negative prefix, from Latin *ex-,* out of + *carta,* card, from Latin *charta,* leaf of papyrus (see **card**).]
skate[1] (skayt) *n.* **1. a.** An **ice skate** *(see).* **b.** The bladelike metal runner of an ice skate. **2.** A **roller skate** *(see).* **—get (one's) skates on.** *Informal.* To make haste; hurry.
~*intr.v.* **skated, skating, skates.** To glide or move along on or as if on skates. **—skate over.** To deal with (an important or complicated subject or matter) in a deliberately superficial manner. [Mistaken as singular of earlier *scates,* from Dutch *schaats,* a skate, from Old North French *escace,* stilt, from Frankish *skakkja* (unattested), from *skakan* (unattested), to run fast. See **scotch** (block).]
skate[2] *n.* Any of various marine cartilaginous fishes of the family Rajidae, having a flattened body with the pectoral fins forming winglike lateral extensions; a large ray. [Middle English *scate,* from Old Norse *skata*†.]
skate·board (skáyt-bawrd || -bōrd) *n.* An elongated oval or oblong board on wheels, designed to be ridden standing up.
~*intr.v.* **skateboarded, -boarding, -boards.** To ride on a skateboard, using one's feet and weight to propel oneself and change direction. **—skate·board·er** *n.* **—skate·board·ing** *n.*
skat·er (skáytər) *n.* **1.** One who skates. **2.** A **pond skater** *(see).*
skating rink *n.* An **ice rink** *(see).*
skat·ole, ska·tol (skát-ōl) *n.* A white crystalline organic compound, C_9H_9N, having a strong faecal odour, found naturally in faeces, beets, and coal tar, and used as a fixative in the manufacture of perfume. [Greek *skōr* (stem *skat-*), dung + -OLE.]

ske·an (skḗe-ən, shkḗe- ‖ skeen, shkeen) *n.* A type of double-edged dagger formerly used in Ireland and Scotland. [Gaelic *sgian,* knife.]

skean dhu (dōō) *n.* A small dagger worn in a man's stocking with Highland dress. [Gaelic, black knife.]

ske·dad·dle (ski-dádd'l) *intr.v.* **-dled, -dling, -dles.** *Informal.* To run off or leave hastily.

~*n.* *Informal.* A hurried retreat. [19th century : origin obscure.]

skeet (skeet) *n.* A variety of clay-pigeon shooting in which clay targets are thrown from traps to simulate birds in flight and are fired at from eight different stations by the shooter. [Ultimately from Old Norse *skjōta,* to shoot.]

skeg (skeg) *n.* **1.** A timber that connects the keel and the sternpost of a ship. **2.** An arm extending to the rear of the keel to support the rudder and protect the propeller. **3.** A series of timbers attached to the stern of a small boat, serving as a keel to keep the boat on course. [Dutch *scheg(ge),* from Old Norse *skegg,* beard, projection.]

skein (skayn, skeen) *n.* **1.** A length of thread or yarn wound in a loose, elongated coil. **2.** Something like or suggestive of this; a tangle. **3.** A flock of geese or similar birds in flight. [Middle English *skeyne,* from Old French *escaigne†.*]

skel·e·tal (skéllit'l) *adj.* Pertaining to, forming, or resembling a skeleton. **—skel·e·tal·ly** *adv.*

skeletal muscle *n.* A striated muscle (*see*).

skel·e·ton (skéllit'n) *n.* **1. a.** The internal vertebrate structure composed of bone and cartilage that protects and supports the soft organs, tissues, and parts. **b.** Such a structure when the flesh has been removed after death. **c.** The hard external supporting and protecting structure in many invertebrates and certain vertebrates, such as turtles; the exoskeleton. **2.** Any supporting structure or essential framework, as of a building. **3.** A bare outline or sketch. **4.** *Informal.* A very thin or emaciated person or animal. **5.** A scandalous or humiliating fact that is kept secret from others. Used chiefly in the phrases *skeleton in the cupboard, family skeleton.*

~*adj.* **1.** Of or resembling a skeleton. **2.** Having or consisting only of an outline, essential parts, or the smallest practicable number: *a skeleton staff.* [New Latin, from Greek, neuter of *skeletos,* dried up, withered.]

Skeleton Coast. Remote and desolate stretch of the Namib desert that runs along the coast of Namibia (South West Africa). In former days anyone shipwrecked on this arid coast was virtually doomed to die of thirst.

skel·e·ton·ise, skel·e·ton·ize (skéllit'n-īz) *tr.v.* **-ised, -ising, -ises. 1.** To create an outline of or framework for. **2.** To reduce to a minimum.

skeleton key *n.* A key with a large portion of the bit filed away so that it can open different locks. Also called "passkey".

skel·lum (skéllǝm) *n.* *Archaic.* A villain; a rogue. [Dutch; akin to Old High German *skelmo,* devil.]

skelm (skéllǝm, skelm) *n.* *South African Informal.* A mischievous or criminal person. [Afrikaans, from Dutch. See **skellum.**]

Skel·mers·dale (skélmǝrz-dayl). New town in northwestern England. It was designated as Lancashire's first new town in 1961 to alleviate overcrowding in Liverpool.

skelp¹ (skelp) *tr.v.* **skelped, skelping, skelps.** *Scottish.* To smack or hit.

~*n.* A slap or slapping noise. [Probably imitative.]

skelp² *n.* A sheet of metal used to make a pipe or tube. [Perhaps from Scottish Gaelic *sgealbh,* thin wooden strip.]

skep (skep) *n.* **1.** A beehive, especially one of straw. **2.** *Regional.* A large straw or wickerwork basket. [Middle English *skep(pe),* Old English *sceppe,* the quantity held by a skep, from Old Norse *skeppa†,* basket.]

skeptic. *U.S.* Variant of **sceptic.** **—skeptical** *adj.* **—skepticism** *n.*

sker·rick (skérrik) *n.* *Australian & U.S.* A tiny amount or small bit. Used chiefly in the phrase *not a skerrick.* [From northern English dialect, probably from Scandinavian.]

sker·ry (skérri) *n., pl.* **-ries.** *Chiefly Scottish.* A small, sometimes rocky isle. [Orkney dialect, from Old Norse *sker,* SCAR (crag).]

sketch (skech) *n.* **1.** A hasty or undetailed drawing or painting, often done as a preliminary study. **2.** A brief, general account or presentation; an outline. **3. a.** A brief, light, or informal short story, essay, or other literary composition. **b.** A short, usually humorous, scene or play in a revue or variety show. **c.** *Music.* A brief composition, especially for the piano.

~*v.* **sketched, sketching, sketches.** *—tr.* **1.** To make a rough drawing or sketch of. **2.** To outline; describe briefly. Often used with *out* or *in.* *—intr.* To make a sketch or sketches. [Dutch *schets* or German *Skizze,* from Italian *schizzo,* from *schizzare,* to sketch, from Vulgar Latin *schediāre,* from Latin *schedius,* hastily put together, from Greek *skhedios,* impromptu.] **—sketch·er** *n.*

sketch·book (skéch-bŏŏk ‖ -bŏŏk) *n.* **1.** A pad consisting of sheets of paper used for sketching. **2.** A book of literary sketches.

sketch·y (skéchi) *adj.* **-ier, -iest. 1.** Resembling a sketch; giving only an outline. **2.** Incomplete; slight; vague. **—sketch·i·ly** *adv.* **—sketch·i·ness** *n.*

skew (skew) *v.* **skewed, skewing, skews.** *—intr.* **1.** To take an oblique course or direction. **2.** To look obliquely or sideways. *—tr.* **1.** To turn or place at an angle. **2.** To give a bias to; distort.

~*adj.* **1.** Placed or turned to one side; asymmetrical. **2.** Distorted or biased in meaning or effect. **3.** Having a part that diverges, as from a straight line or a right angle, as in gearing. **4. a.** *Geometry.* Neither parallel nor intersecting. Said of straight lines in space.

Compare **parallel. b.** *Statistics.* Not symmetrical about the mean. Said of distributions.

~*n.* An oblique or slanting movement, position, or direction. [Middle English *skewen,* to skew, escape, from Old North French *eskuer,* from Germanic *skiuhwan* (unattested). See **eschew.**] **—skew·ness** *n.*

skew arch *n.* *Architecture.* An arch whose line is not at right angles to the abutments.

skew·back (skéw-bak) *n.* *Architecture.* Either of two inset abutments sloped to support a segmental arch.

skew·bald (skéw-bawld) *adj.* Having spots or patches of white and a colour other than black on its coat: *a skewbald horse.* Compare **piebald, pinto.**

~*n.* A horse with this colouring. [From earlier *skued† +* BALD.]

skew·er (skéw-ǝr) *n.* **1.** A long metal or wooden pin used to secure meat during cooking or to hold pieces of meat and vegetables during grilling. **2.** Any of various picks or rods having a similar function or shape.

~*tr.v.* **skewered, -ering, -ers.** To hold together or pierce with or as if with a skewer. [Variant of dialectal *skiver†.*]

skew·whiff, skew·iff (skéw-wif) *adj. Chiefly British Informal.* Lopsided; askew. [18th century (dialectal) : based on ASKEW.] **—skew·whiff, skew·iff** *adv.*

ski (skee, *rarely* shee) *n., pl.* **skis** or **ski. 1.** Either of a pair of long, flat runners of wood, metal, or other material that curve upwards in front and may be attached to a boot for gliding or travelling over snow. **2.** A water-ski (*see*).

~*adj.* Of, pertaining to, or associated with skiing: *a ski resort.*

~*v.* **skied, skiing, skis.** *—intr.* To travel on skis, especially as a sport. *—tr.* To travel over on skis. [Norwegian *ski(d),* from Old Norse *skīth,* ski, snowshoe.] **—ski·er** *n.* **—ski·ing** *adj.*

skiagram. Variant of **sciagram.**

skiagraphy. Variant of **sciagraphy.**

skiamachy. Variant of **sciamachy.**

ski·a·scope (skī́-ǝ-skōp) *n. Optometry.* A retinoscope (*see*). [Greek *skia,* shadow + -SCOPE.]

ski·as·co·py (skī-áskǝpi) *n. Optometry.* Retinoscopy (*see*).

ski binding *n.* An attachment on a ski used to secure the ski to the skier's boot.

ski·bob (skée-bob) *n.* A kind of bicycle with two small skis instead of wheels, used for travelling downhill over snow by a rider wearing miniature skis for balance. [SKI + BOB(SLEIGH).] **—ski·bob·ber** *n.* **—ski·bob·bing** *n.*

skid (skid) *n.* **1.** An act or state of sliding or slipping over a surface, often uncontrollably and sideways. **2. a.** A plank, log, or timber, usually one of a pair, used as a support or as a track for sliding or rolling heavy objects. **b.** A small platform for stacking merchandise to be moved or temporarily stored. **c.** *U.S.* One of several logs or timbers forming a skid road. **3.** *Plural. Nautical.* A wooden framework attached to the side of a ship to prevent damage, as when unloading. **4.** A shoe or drag applying pressure to a wheel to brake a vehicle. **5.** A runner in the landing gear of certain aircraft. **—on the skids.** *Slang.* On a downward path to ruin, failure, or depravity. **—put the skids under.** *Slang.* To hasten the failure of.

~*v.* **skidded, skidding, skids.** *—intr.* **1.** To slip or slide sideways, usually out of control, while moving because of loss of traction. Used chiefly of a vehicle. **2.** To slide without revolving. Said of a wheel that does not turn while the vehicle is in motion. **3.** *Aviation.* To move sideways in a turn because of insufficient banking. *—tr.* **1.** To brake (a wheel) with a skid. **2.** *Chiefly U.S.* To haul on a skid or skids. [17th century : origin obscure.]

skid·lid (skíd-lid) *n. Chiefly British Slang.* A crash helmet.

skid pan *n. British.* A road or track that has been treated to make it slippery to enable road vehicle drivers to practise controlling skids.

skid road *n. U.S.* **1.** A track made of logs laid transversely, spaced about five feet apart, and used to haul logs to a loading platform or a mill. **2.** *Slang.* Skid row.

skid row *n. Chiefly U.S. Slang.* A squalid area of a town, where down-and-outs gather. [Variant (influenced by ROW) of SKID ROAD.]

skiff (skif) *n. Nautical.* An open boat with a flat or rounded bottom having a pointed bow and a square stern and propelled by oars, sail, or motor. [French *esquif,* from Italian *schifo.*]

skif·fle (skiff'l) *n. Chiefly British.* A type of music, popular especially in the 1950s, that rendered folk songs or simple melodies to a fast, rhythmic beat, using improvised instruments, especially percussion instruments such as bottles or washboards. Also used adjectivally: *a skiffle band.* [Probably imitative.]

ski·jor·ing (skée-jáwr-ing, -jawr- ‖ -jōr-, -jōr-) *n.* A sport in which a skier is drawn over ice or snow by a horse or vehicle. [Norwegian *skikjøring* : SKI + *kjøring,* driving, from *kjøre,* to drive, from Old Norse *keyra.*] **—ski·jor·er** *n.*

ski jump *n.* **1.** A jump or leap made by a skier. **2.** A steep slope ending in a high ramp overhanging a slope, used for such a jump. **3.** A ramp used to assist the takeoff of a jump jet. **—ski-jump** (skée-jump) *intr.v.* **—ski-jump·er** *n.*

skil·ful, *U.S.* **skill·ful** (skilf'l) *adj.* **1.** Possessing or exercising skill; able; expert. **2.** Characterised by, showing, or requiring skill. **—See** Synonyms at **proficient. —skil·ful·ly** *adv.* **—skil·ful·ness** *n.*

ski lift *n.* Any of various power-driven conveyors, usually with attached towing bars, suspended chairs, or gondolas, used to carry skiers to the top of a trail or slope.

skill (skil) *n.* **1.** The capacity to accomplish successfully something requiring special knowledge or ability; proficiency. **2.** An art, trade, or technique acquired through training or experience, particularly one requiring use of the hands or body. **3.** *Obsolete.* Understanding. —See Synonyms at **ability.** [Middle English *skil(e),* reason, skill, from Old Norse *skil.*]

skilled (skild) *adj.* **1.** Having or showing skill; expert. **2.** Having or requiring specialised ability or training, especially in a trade or craft: *a skilled occupation.* —See Synonyms at **proficient.**

skil·let (skíllit) *n.* **1.** *Chiefly British.* A long-handled stewing pan or saucepan sometimes having legs. **2.** *Chiefly U.S.* A frying pan. [Middle English *skelet,* probably from *skele,* pail, from Scandinavian, akin to Old Norse *skjóla.*]

skil·li·on (skílli-ən) *n. Chiefly Australian.* An outhouse or lean-to with a roof that does not have a peak and slopes in one direction away from the main building. Also used adjectivally: *a skillion roof.* [From English dialect *skilling†,* outhouse.]

skil·ly (skílli) *n. British.* A thin broth or gruel, usually made with oatmeal. [Shortened from *skilligalee†.*]

skim (skim) *v.* **skimmed, skimming, skims.** —*tr.* **1.** To remove floating matter from (a liquid). **2.** To remove (floating matter, especially scum or cream) from a liquid. **3.** To coat or cover with or as if with a thin layer, as of scum or ice. **4. a.** To hurl across and close to the surface of water, ice, or the like, so as to bounce: *skimming stones.* **b.** To glide or pass quickly and lightly over. **5.** To read or glance through quickly or superficially; peruse hastily. —*intr.* **1.** To move or pass swiftly and lightly over or near a surface; glide; graze. **2.** To give a quick and superficial reading, scrutiny, or consideration. Used with *over* or *through.* **3.** To become coated with a thin layer. Used with *over.*
~*n.* **1.** The act of skimming. **2.** Something that has been skimmed, such as skim milk. **3.** A thin layer or film. [Middle English *skymen,* from Old French *escumer,* from *escume,* foam, from Old High German *scūm.*]

skim·mer (skímmər) *n.* **1.** One that skims. **2.** A flat utensil, usually perforated and resembling a ladle, used in skimming liquids. **3.** A wide-brimmed hat with a flat shallow crown. **4.** Any of several chiefly tropical coastal birds of the genus *Rynchops,* having long narrow wings and a long bill with a longer lower mandible for skimming the water's surface for food.

skim·mi·a (skímmi-ə) *n.* Any shrub of the genus *Skimmia,* native to south and southeast Asia but grown elsewhere for its ornamental foliage and red berries. [New Latin, from Japanese *mijama-skimmi.*]

skim milk *n.* Also **skimmed milk** (skimd). Milk from which the cream has been removed.

skim·ming (skímming) *n. Usually plural.* That which is skimmed off a liquid.

skimp (skimp) *v.* **skimped, skimping, skimps.** —*tr.* **1.** To do hastily, carelessly, or with poor material. **2.** To be extremely sparing with; scrimp. —*intr.* To be very or unduly thrifty. Usually used with *on: skimp on the budget.*
~*adj.* Scanty; skimpy. [Perhaps a variant of SCRIMP.]

skimp·y (skímpi) *adj.* **-ier, -iest. 1.** Inadequate in size, fullness, or amount; scanty. **2.** Unduly thrifty; stingy; niggardly. —See Synonyms at **meagre.** —**skimp·i·ly** *adv.* —**skimp·i·ness** *n.*

skin (skin) *n.* **1.** The tissue forming the external, protective covering of the body of a vertebrate. It consists of an outer **epidermis** and an inner **dermis** (both of which see). Also used adjectivally: *a skin graft.* **2.** An animal pelt, especially the comparatively pliable pelt of a small or young animal. Often used in combination: *pigskin; sheepskin.* **3.** Anything resembling skin in function or appearance; any outer layer, accretion, or protection, such as the rind of fruit, the surface film on boiled milk, or the plating on a ship or rocket. **4.** A container for liquid made of animal skin. **5.** *Often plural. Slang.* A drum. **6.** *Slang.* A cigarette paper used for rolling a cigarette, especially one containing cannabis. **7.** *Slang.* A skinhead *(see).* —**by the skin of (one's) teeth.** By the smallest margin; very closely; scarcely or barely. —**get under (someone's) skin. 1.** To anger or irritate. **2.** To be or become an obsession to. —**have a thick** (or **thin**) **skin.** To be unperturbed (or easily hurt) by criticism or insults. —**jump out of (one's) skin.** To be suddenly very startled or frightened. —**no skin off (someone's) nose.** *Informal.* Being a matter that does not adversely affect one. —**save (one's) skin.** To escape harm or avoid death.
~*v.* **skinned, skinning, skins.** —*tr.* **1.** To remove skin from; flay or peel. **2.** To cover with or as if with skin. Often used with *over.* **3.** To remove or peel off (skin or any outer covering). **4.** *Slang.* To fleece; swindle. **5.** To bruise, cut, or scrape the skin or surface of: *a skinned knee.* —*intr.* To become covered with or as if with skin. Often used with *over.* —**skin up.** *Slang.* To roll a cigarette containing cannabis. [Middle English, from Old Norse *skinn.*]

skin-deep (skín-déep) *adj.* Superficial or shallow.
~*adv.* Shallowly; to a superficial degree.

skin-dive (skín-dīv) *intr.v.* **-dived, -diving, -dives.** To engage in skin diving.

skin diving *n.* Underwater swimming, exploration, or fishing in which the diver is equipped with goggles, flippers, and a snorkel or other breathing device. —**skin diver** *n.*

skin effect *n.* The tendency of electric current density in a conductor carrying alternating current to be greater at the surface than at the centre, producing an increase in resistance.

skin flick *n. Slang.* A cinematic film containing pornographic nudity. Also called "nudie".

skin-flint (skín-flint) *n.* A miser; a niggard. [From the notion that one would go so far as to try to skin a flint for money.]

skin friction *n.* Friction caused by a fluid crossing the surface of bodies, such as rockets, moving at high speeds. Also called "skin drag".

skin·ful (skín-fōōl) *n., pl.* **-fuls.** *Slang.* An amount of alcoholic drink that can make a person drunk: *I've had a skinful.*

skin graft *n.* A surgical graft of skin from one part of the body to another or from one individual to another. —**skin grafting** *n.*

skin·head (skín-hed) *n.* In Britain, a member of a gang of youths with shaven heads and usually wearing heavy, black, lace-up boots, drainpipe trousers worn off the ankle and with braces, and typically having rough and aggressive behaviour. Also called "skin".

skink (skingk) *n.* Any of numerous, mainly tropical, smooth, shiny lizards of the family Scincidae, having a cylindrical body and short or rudimentary legs. [Latin *scincus,* from Greek *skinkos†.*]

skinned (skind) *adj.* Having skin, especially of a specified kind. Used in combination: *fair-skinned.*

skin·ner (skínnər) *n.* A person who flays, dresses, or sells animal skins.

Skin·ner (skínnər), **B(urrhus) F(rederic)** (1904–90). U.S. psychologist, the foremost representative of the Behaviourist school. His first important publication was *The Behaviour of Organisms* (1938). His most influential has been *Beyond Freedom and Dignity* (1971).

Skinner box *n.* A box used to study learning behaviour in animals. It is fitted with levers that the animal (usually a rat) can press to obtain a reward or punishment. [After B.F. SKINNER.]

skin·ny (skínni) *adj.* **-nier, -niest.** Very thin or slender; especially, unattractively thin. —See Synonyms at **lean.** —**skin·ni·ness** *n.*

skin·ny-dip (skínni-dip) *intr.v.* **-dipped, -dipping, -dips.** *Informal.* To swim in the nude. —**skin·ny-dip·per** *n.*

skin·ny-rib (skínni-rib) *n.* A tight-fitting ribbed sweater.

skint (skint) *adj. British Slang.* Having or carrying no money. [Variant of *skinned,* past participle of SKIN.]

skin test *n.* A test for an allergy or infectious disease, performed by means of a **patch test, scratch test** (both of which see), or an injection beneath the skin of an allergen or extract of the disease-causing organism.

skin·tight (skín-tît, -tīt) *adj.* Fitting or clinging closely to the skin. Said of clothes.

skip¹ (skip) *v.* **skipped, skipping, skips.** —*intr.* **1. a.** To bound or trip lightly, especially by taking two steps at a time with each foot; hop and step; caper. **b.** To use a skipping rope. **2.** To bounce over or be deflected from a surface; skim or ricochet. **3.** To pass from point to point omitting or disregarding what intervenes. Often used with *through.* **4.** *Informal.* To leave hastily; abscond: *She skipped off somewhere.* —*tr.* **1.** To leap or jump lightly over. **2.** To pass over, omit, or disregard: *skipped the first page.* **3.** To cause to ricochet or skim. **4.** To deliberately avoid or not attend in: *skip classes.* **5.** *Chiefly U.S. Informal.* To leave hastily or secretly: *has skipped the country.* —**skip it.** *Informal.* To abandon or forget a subject, topic, or the like. Used in the imperative.
~*n.* **1.** A leaping or jumping movement; especially, a gait in which hops and steps alternate. **2.** A passing over or omission. [Middle English *skippen†.*]

skip² *n. Informal.* Used as a form of address for: **1.** A skipper, as of a boat or sports team. **2.** The leader of a Scout group.

skip³ *n.* **1.** A large container for rubbish, as on a building site, that can be hoisted onto and taken away by a specially designed lorry. **2.** A large cage or bucket for lowering and raising people or material into or out of a mine. [Variant of SKEP.]

skip⁴ *n. British.* A person employed at a college to clean students' rooms, especially at Trinity College Dublin. [Probably from obsolete *skip-kennel,* from SKIP (jump, skip) + KENNEL (gutter).]

skip distance *n.* The smallest separation between a transmitter and a receiver that permits radio signals of a specific frequency to travel from one to the other by reflection from the ionosphere.

skip·jack (skíp-jak) *n., pl.* **-jacks** or collectively **skipjack. 1.** Any of several tropical or subtropical marine food fishes of the genus *Euthynnus;* especially, *E. pelamis,* related to and resembling the tuna. **2.** Any of various other fishes, as certain herrings. **3.** The **click beetle** *(see).* [Originally "a fop" : SKIP + JACK (fellow).]

skip·per¹ (skíppər) *n.* **1.** The master of a ship, especially of a small one. **2.** The captain of an aeroplane or other aircraft. **3.** *Informal.* The captain of a side in sports. **4.** The leader of a Scout group.
~*tr.v.* **skippered, -pering, -pers.** To act as the skipper of. [Middle English *skypper,* from Middle Dutch *schipper,* from *schip,* ship.]

skip·per² *n.* **1.** One that skips. **2.** Any of numerous butterflies of the family Hesperiidae, having a hairy, mothlike body and a darting flight pattern. **3.** Any of several related marine fishes; especially, a **saury** *(see).*

skip·pet (skíppit) *n.* A small box used, especially formerly, to enclose a seal attached to a document. [Middle English *skippet†.*]

skip·ping-rope (skípping-rōp) *n. Chiefly British.* A rope that has handles at either end and is swung over and over so that the person holding it or another person can jump over it.

skirl (skurl) *v.* **skirled, skirling, skirls.** —*intr.* To produce a shrill, piercing tone. Used of bagpipes. —*tr.* To play (music) on the bagpipes.
~*n.* **1.** The shrill sound made by the bagpipes. **2.** Any shrill, piercing sound. [Middle English *skirlen, skrillen,* probably of Scandinavian origin; akin to Norwegian dialectal *skrylla..*]

skir·mish (skúrmish) *n.* **1.** A minor encounter in war between small bodies of troops, often unconnected with or at a distance from the main operations. **2.** Any minor or preliminary conflict or dispute. ~*intr.v.* **skirmished, -mishing, -mishes.** To engage in a skirmish. [Middle English *skirmisshe, skarmuch,* from Old French *eskermir* (present stem *eskirmiss-*), to fight with the sword, from Germanic.]

skirr (skur) *intr.v.* **skirred, skirring, skirrs.** To move or fly rapidly, especially with a whirring sound. Used with *away, off,* or other adverbs. [Perhaps variant of SCOUR (search).]

skir·ret (skírrit) *n.* An Old World plant, *Sium sisarum,* having a sweetish, edible root. [Middle English *skirwhite,* variant (influenced by *skir,* bright, and *whit,* white) of Old French *eschervi,* probably a variant of *carvi,* caraway, from Arabic *alkarawyā,* CARAWAY.]

skirt (skurt) *n.* **1.** That part of a garment, such as a dress or coat, that hangs from the waist down. **2.** A separate garment hanging from the waist, as worn by women and girls. **3. a.** One of the leather flaps hanging from the side of a saddle. **b.** The lower outer section of a rocket vehicle. **c.** A hanging part around the base of a hovercraft or certain racing cars. **4.** A border, margin, or outer edge. **5.** *Plural.* The edge or outskirts, as of a town. **6.** *Slang.* **a.** A woman or girl. **b.** Women collectively, considered as sexual objects. Used chiefly in the phrase *a bit of skirt.* Considered offensive. **7.** *British.* A cut of beef from the lower flank. ~*v.* **skirted, skirting, skirts.** —*tr.* **1.** To lie along, form the border of, or surround; bound. **2.** To move or pass around rather than across or through. **3.** To evade or elude (a topic of conversation, for example) by circumlocution. —*intr.* To be near or move along the edge or border of something. [Middle English, from Old Norse *skyrta,* SHIRT.]

skirt·ing (skúrting) *n.* Boarding that runs around the base of an interior wall next to the floor, to protect it from dirt, knocks, or damage.

skirting board *n.* A piece of skirting. Also *U.S.* "baseboard", "mopboard".

ski run *n.* A slope or course, usually marked, down which skiers ski.

ski-scoot·er (skée-skōotər) *n. British.* A motorised sledge with small skis at the front and moving on endless tracks at the back.

ski stick *n.* Either of a pair of sticks usually made of metal, with pointed ends, used by skiers to assist in turning and to gain momentum. Also called "ski pole".

skit (skit) *n.* **1.** A short, usually comic theatrical sketch. **2.** A short humorous or satirical piece of writing. [Perhaps from Old Norse; akin to *skjóta,* to SHOOT.]

skite[1] *intr.v.* **skited, skiting, skites.** *Scottish.* To slide or lose balance, as on a slippery surface. [Scottish and northern English dialect; akin to Old Norse *skjóta,* to shoot about, SHOOT.]

skite[2] (skīt) *intr.v.* **skited, skiting, skites.** *Australian & N.Z. Informal.* To boast or show off. ~*n. Australian & N.Z. Informal.* A person who boasts or shows off. [Scottish and northern English dialect *skite*† (noun).]

ski tow *n.* A type of ski lift in which skiers cling to a continuous rope as they are hauled up a slope.

skit·ter (skíttər) *v.* **-tered, -tering, -ters.** —*intr.* **1.** To skip, scamper, or move lightly or rapidly along a surface; dart; flit. **2.** To fish by drawing a lure or baited hook over the surface of the water with a skipping movement. —*tr.* To cause to skitter. [Frequentative of dialectal *skite,* to run rapidly, shoot about, SKITE (slide).]

skit·tish (skíttish) *adj.* **1.** Excitable or nervous. **2. a.** Extremely lively or frivolous in action or character. **b.** Undependable or fickle. **3.** Shy, coy, or timid. [Middle English, perhaps ultimately from Old Norse *skjóta,* to shoot, shoot about.] —**skit·tish·ly** *adv.* —**skit·tish·ness** *n.*

skit·tle (skítt'l) *n. Chiefly British.* A wooden or plastic pin, wide at the base and tapering at the top, used in the game of skittles. Also called "ninepin". ~*tr.v.* **skittled, skittling, skittles.** In cricket, to get (batsmen) out in rapid succession and for very few runs. Usually used with *out.* [17th century : origin obscure.]

skit·tles (skítt'lz) *n. Used with a singular verb.* A game in which a wooden ball is bowled with the aim of knocking down nine pins. Also called "ninepins". —**all beer and skittles.** Nothing but pleasure and enjoyment.

skive[1] (skīv) *tr.v.* **skived, skiving, skives.** To shave or cut off the surface of (leather or rubber); pare. [Ultimately from Old Norse *skifa,* to slice.]

skive[2] *v.* **skived, skiving, skives.** *British Slang.* —*intr.* To shirk or avoid work or duty. Sometimes used with *off.* —*tr.* To shirk or avoid (work or duty). [20th century : origin obscure.]

skiv·er[1] (skívər) *n.* **1.** A soft, thin leather split off the outside of skin and used especially for bookbinding. **2.** A person who skives leather. **3.** A knife or other cutting device used in skiving.

skiver[2] *n. British Slang.* One who avoids work or duty.

skiv·vy (skívvi) *n., pl.* **-vies.** *British Slang.* A menial, usually female, servant, especially one who does washing and cleaning. Sometimes used derogatorily. ~*intr.v.* **skivvied, -vying, -vies.** *British Slang.* To work as a skivvy. [20th century : origin obscure.]

skoal, skol (skōl) *interj.* Used as a drinking toast. [Norwegian and Danish *skaal* and Swedish *skål,* from Old Norse *skál,* drinking cup.]

skok·i·aan (skócki-aan, skáwki-) *n. South African.* A strong homebrew made with yeast, usually illicitly. [Afrikaans : origin obscure.]

Skop·je (skóp-yi; *Macedonian* -ye). Capital of the Former Yugoslav Republic of Macedonia, lying on the river Vardar. From its capture by the Turks in 1392 until the fall of Constantinople in 1453, it was

the most important Turkish city in Europe. Much of the city was destroyed by an earthquake in 1963.

Skr., Skt. Sanskrit.

sku·a (skéw-ə) *n.* Any of various predatory gull-like sea birds of the family Stercorariidae, of polar regions, having brownish plumage. [New Latin, from Faroese *skúvur,* Old Norse *skúfr*†, tassel.]

skul·dug·ger·y, skull·dug·ger·y (skul-dúggəri) *n. Informal.* Crafty deception or trickery. [From earlier (Scottish) *sculduddery*†, wantonness.]

skulk (skulk) *intr.v.* **skulked, skulking, skulks.** **1.** To lurk; lie in hiding. **2.** To move about stealthily or furtively. **3.** To evade work or obligations. ~*n.* One who skulks. [Middle English *skulken,* from Scandinavian; akin to Danish *skulke*†.] —**skulk·er** *n.*

skull (skul) *n.* **1.** The framework of the head of vertebrates, made up of the bones of the **cranium** (*see*) and face. **2.** This as a symbol of death. **3.** The head, especially regarded as the seat of thought or intelligence. Usually used derogatorily: *can't get it into your thick skull.* **3.** *Plural. Music.* A set of percussion instruments, consisting of inverted, fish-head-shaped, wooden objects that are hit with a stick to produce a clunking sound that varies in pitch according to size. [Middle English *schulle, skullet*†.]

skull and crossbones *n. Used with a singular or plural verb.* A representation of a human skull above two long crossed bones, a symbol of death once used by pirates, especially on their flag, and now often used as a warning label on poisons.

skull·cap (skúl-kap) *n.* **1. a.** A light, close-fitting, brimless cap sometimes worn indoors. **b.** A similar cap worn by Roman Catholic prelates and by male Jews. **2.** Any of various plants of the genus *Scutellaria,* having clusters of two-lipped, helmet-shaped flowers. **3.** *Anatomy.* The **calvaria** (*see*).

skunk (skungk) *n.* **1.** Any of several small, carnivorous New World mammals of the genus *Mephitis* and related genera; especially, *M. mephitis,* having a bushy tail and black fur with white markings and ejecting an unpleasant-smelling secretion from glands near the anus. **2.** *Slang.* A mean or despicable person. ~*tr.v.* **skunked, skunking, skunks.** *U.S. Slang.* **1.** To defeat overwhelmingly, especially by keeping from scoring in a game. **2.** To cheat, as by failing to pay. [Massachuset *squnck,* from Proto-Algonquian *shekäkwa* (unattested) : *shek-* (unattested), to urinate + *-ākw-* (unattested), small mammal.]

skunk cabbage *n.* An ill-smelling swamp plant, *Symplocarpus foetidus,* of eastern North America, having minute flowers enclosed in a mottled greenish or purplish spathe.

sky (skī) *n., pl.* **skies.** **1. a.** The upper atmosphere, appearing as a hemisphere above the earth. **b.** The apparent hemispherical dome, as seen from the Earth's surface, upon which the celestial bodies seem to move; it appears blue in the daytime and almost black at night. **2.** The highest level or degree of something; the ultimate: *reaching for the sky.* **3.** The celestial or heavenly regions. **4.** *Often plural.* **a.** The appearance of the upper air: *blue skies.* **b.** The climate or weather, as indicated by the sky. —**praise to the skies.** To praise in an extravagantly enthusiastic way. ~*tr.v.* **skied, skying, skies.** **1.** To hit or throw (a ball, for example) high in the air. **2.** To hang (a painting, for example) above the line of vision. [Middle English, from Old Norse *skȳ,* cloud, from Common Germanic *skewja-* (unattested).]

sky blue *n.* Light to pale blue. —**sky-blue** (skī-blóo) *adj.*

sky·borne (skī-bawrn ‖ -bōrn) *adj.* Airborne.

sky·dive (skī-dīv) *intr.v.* **-dived, -diving, -dives.** *Sports.* To jump from an aircraft, performing various manoeuvres before pulling the ripcord of one's parachute. —**sky·div·er** *n.* —**sky·div·ing** *n.*

Skye (skī). Largest and most northerly island of the Inner Hebrides, off west Scotland. It is part of the Highland Authority Area and since 1995 connected by a new bridge to the mainland. Bonnie Prince Charlie took refuge there in 1746 after his defeat at Culloden Moor.

Skye terrier *n.* A small terrier of a breed native to the Isle of Skye, having a long, low body, short legs, and shaggy hair.

sky·ey (skī-i) *adj. Literary.* **1.** Of or from the skies: *skyey influences.* **2.** Blue like the sky. **3.** Lofty.

sky-high (skī-hī) *adv.* **1.** At or to an exceptionally high level: *the price of property has gone sky-high.* **2.** In a lavish or enthusiastic manner. **3.** In pieces or to pieces; apart: *blew it sky-high.* ~*adj.* **1.** High up in the air. **2.** Exorbitantly high.

sky·jack (skī-jak) *tr.v.* **-jacked, -jacking, -jacks.** To hijack (an aircraft, especially one in flight) through the use or threat of force. [SKY + (HI)JACK.] —**sky·jack·er** *n.*

Sky·lab (skī-lab) *n.* Any of several space stations launched into Earth orbit from the United States in the 1970s.

sky·lark (skī-laark) *n.* An Old World bird, *Alauda arvensis,* having brownish plumage and noted for its singing while in flight. ~*intr.v.* **skylarked, -larking, -larks.** To frolic or have fun.

sky·light (skī-līt) *n.* An overhead window admitting daylight.

sky·line (skī-līn) *n.* **1.** The line along which the surface of the earth and sky appear to meet; the horizon. **2.** An outline, as of a group of buildings or a mountain range, seen against the sky.

sky pilot *n. Slang.* A clergyman, especially a service chaplain.

sky·rock·et (skī-rockit) *n.* A firework, a **rocket** (*see*). ~*intr.v.* **skyrocketed, -eting, -ets.** To rise rapidly or suddenly, as in amount, position, or reputation.

sky·sail (skī-sayl, -s'l) *n.* A small square sail above the royal in a square-rigged vessel.

sky·scrap·er (skī-skraypər) *n.* A very tall building, especially a multistorey office block.

sky·ward (skī-wərd) *adj.* Moving or going towards the sky.

sky·wards (skī-wərdz) *adv.* Also **skyward.** Towards the sky.

sky wave *n.* A radio wave transmitted from one point on the earth's surface and received at another point after reflection by the ionosphere. Also called "ionospheric wave". Compare **ground wave.**

sky·writ·ing (skī-rīting) *n.* 1. The process of writing in the sky by releasing a visible vapour from a flying aircraft. 2. The letters or words thus formed. —**sky·writ·er** *n.*

s.l. without place. Used in book cataloguing. [Latin *sine loco.*]

slab[1] (slab) *n.* 1. A broad, flat, somewhat thick piece, as of cake, stone, or cheese. 2. An outside piece cut from a log when squaring it to make planks. 3. *British Informal.* The table on which a corpse is put in a mortuary. ~*tr.v.* **slabbed, slabbing, slabs.** 1. To make or shape into a slab or slabs. 2. To cover or pave with slabs. 3. To dress (a log) by cutting slabs. [Middle English *s(c)labbe*†.]

slab[2] *adj. Archaic.* Viscous. Used in the phrase *thick and slab.* [Probably of Scandinavian origin; akin to Danish *slab,* mud.]

Slab·bert (slábbərt), **Frederik van Zyl** (1940–). South African sociologist and politician. He was leader of South Africa's Progressive Federal Party 1979–86, and as such was leader of the opposition in the South African Parliament.

slab-sid·ed (sláb-sīdid) *adj. U.S. Informal.* 1. Having flat sides. 2. Tall and slim; lanky; lean.

slack[1] (slak) *adj.* 1. Not lively or moving; slow; dull; sluggish. 2. Not active or busy; lacking in work. 3. Not tense or taut; loose. 4. Lacking firmness; weak; relaxed: *a slack grip.* 5. *Informal.* Lacking in diligence; idle or negligent. 6. Flowing or blowing with little speed. Said of the wind or tide. 7. *Phonetics.* Lax. ~*v.* **slacked, slacking, slacks.** —*tr.* To slacken. —*intr.* To be or become slack; especially, to be or become idle or inactive. —**slack off.** To decrease in activity or intensity; fall off; abate. ~*n.* 1. A loose or slack part or portion of something, such as a rope or sail. 2. A period of little activity; a lull. 3. **a.** A cessation of movement in a current of air or water. **b.** An area of still water. 4. *Plural.* A pair of trousers for casual wear. ~*adv.* In a slack manner. [Middle English *slak,* Old English *slæc.*] —**slack·ly** *adv.* —**slack·ness** *n.*

slack[2] *n.* A mixture of coal fragments, coal dust, and dirt that remains after screening coal. [Middle English *sleck,* probably from Middle Dutch *slacke.*]

slack[3] *n.* 1. A small dell or hollow. 2. A bog; a morass. 3. A depression between lines of sand dunes along a coast or in a desert. [Middle English *slak,* from Old Norse *slakki*†.]

slack·en (sláckən) *v.* **-ened, -ening, -ens.** —*tr.* 1. To make slower; slow down. 2. To lessen, as in vigour, intensity, firmness, or severity. 3. To reduce the tension or tautness of; loosen. —*intr.* 1. To slow down. 2. To become slacker in some way, as by growing less energetic, active, firm, or strict. 3. To become less tense or taut; loosen. In all senses, often used with *off.*

slack·er (sláckər) *n.* A person who shirks work or responsibility.

slack water *n.* 1. The period at high or low tide when there is no visible flow of water. 2. An area in a sea or river unaffected by currents; still water.

SLADE Society of Lithographic Artists, Designers, Engravers and Process Workers (a trade union in Britain).

slag (slag) *n.* 1. The vitreous mass left as a residue by the smelting of metallic ore. Also called "cinder". 2. Volcanic refuse, **scoria** *(see).* 3. A mixture of coal dust, shale, and other waste mineral matter produced during coalmining. 4. *British Slang.* A vulgar, coarse, or sexually promiscuous woman or girl. Used derogatorily. ~*v.* **slagged, slagging, slag.** —*tr.* To change into slag. —*intr.* To form slag; become slaglike. —**slag (someone) off.** *British Slang.* To criticise or abuse (someone) verbally, in an extremely offensive or vulgar manner. [Middle Low German *slagge,* perhaps from *slagen,* to strike (alluding to fragments of rock).] —**slag·gy** *adj.*

slag heap *n.* A large mound consisting of slag deposited as a waste product from coalmining operations.

slain. Past participle of **slay.**

slàin·te (slaanjə) *interj. Scottish & Irish.* Used as a drinking toast, especially when drinking whisky. [Gaelic, health.]

slais·ter (sláystər) *n. Scottish.* A wet or slobbery mess. [18th century : origin obscure.]

slake (slayk) *v.* **slaked, slaking, slakes.** —*tr.* 1. To quench; allay; satisfy. 2. *Poetic.* To lessen the force or activity of; moderate. 3. To cool or refresh by moistening. 4. To combine (lime) chemically with water or moist air. —*intr.* To undergo a slaking process; crumble or disintegrate. Used of lime. [Middle English *slaken,* to lessen, Old English *slacian,* from *slæc,* SLACK (loose).]

slaked lime *n. Chemistry.* **Calcium hydroxide** *(see).*

sla·lom (slaáləm) *n.* 1. Skiing in a zigzag course. 2. A race, especially a skiing race, along a zigzag course, usually marked with poles. [Norwegian, "sloping path" : *sla(d)†,* sloping + *lom, låm,* path, from Northwest Germanic *lanu-* (unattested).]

slam[1] (slam) *v.* **slammed, slamming, slams.** —*tr.* 1. To shut (a door or window, for example) with force and loud noise. 2. To put, throw, or otherwise forcefully move so as to produce a loud noise. 3. To hit or strike with great force. 4. *Slang.* To criticise harshly; attack verbally. 5. *Informal.* To beat easily and by a wide margin. 6. To operate (brakes) suddenly and harshly. Used with *on.* —*intr.* 1. To close or swing into place with force so as to produce a loud

noise. 2. To hit something with force; crash. 3. To enter or leave a place violently or angrily: *slammed out of the house.* ~*n.* 1. A forceful closing or other movement that produces a loud noise. 2. The noise so produced. [Perhaps from Scandinavian, akin to Old Norse *slam(b)ra,* to strike at.]

slam[2] *n.* In bridge, whist, or other card games derived from these, the winning of all the tricks *(grand slam)* or all but one *(little slam)* during the play of one hand. [Probably from SLAM (a stroke).]

slam-bang (slám-báng) *adv.* 1. Loudly and violently. 2. *U.S.* Recklessly.

s.l.a.n. without place, year, or name. Used in book cataloguing. [Latin *sine loco, anno vel nomine.*]

slan·der (slaándər ‖ slándər) *n.* 1. *Law.* The utterance of defamatory statements that are injurious to the reputation or well-being of a person. Compare **libel.** 2. A malicious statement or report. ~*tr.v.* **slandered, -dering, -ders.** To utter damaging or defamatory reports about. —See Synonyms at **malign.** [Middle English *s(c)laundre,* from Old French *esclandre,* variant of *escandle,* from Latin *scandalum,* SCANDAL.] —**slan·der·er** *n.* —**slan·der·ous** *adj.* —**slan·der·ous·ly** *adv.*

slang (slang) *n.* 1. Language, typically of an ephemeral nature, whose use is usually restricted to informal contexts and among people familiar with or similar to one another. 2. Language peculiar to a group; argot or jargon. ~*v.* **slanged, slanging, slangs.** —*tr.* To direct abusive language at (somebody); insult. —*intr.* To use abusive or insulting language. [18th-century (cant) : origin obscure.] —**slang·i·ly** *adv.* —**slang·i·ness** *n.* —**slang·y** *adj.*

slang·ing match (sláng-ing) *n. British.* A quarrel or dispute in which abusive insults are exchanged.

Slán·ský (slaán-ski), **Rudolf** (1901–52). Czech Communist leader. In 1948 he became deputy premier in the new Communist government. In 1951, during Stalinist purges, he was convicted of spying and Zionist activities, along with 13 others, and executed. In 1963 he was cleared of the charges.

slant (slaant ‖ slant) *v.* **slanted, slanting, slants.** —*tr.* 1. To give an oblique direction to. 2. To present (information) so as to give it a particular bias, as by emphasising certain facts. —*intr.* 1. To incline or move obliquely. 2. To have a bias. Used with *towards.* ~*n.* 1. **a.** A sloping direction, plane, or course; an incline. **b.** Slope; obliquity. 2. A particular bias, emphasis, or point of view. ~*adj.* Slanting or sloping. [Earlier *slent,* from Middle English *slenten*†, from Old Norse *sletta,* to throw.] —**slant·ing·ly** *adv.*

slant·wise (slaánt-wīz ‖ slánt-) *adv.* Also **slant·ways** (-wayz). At a slant or slope; obliquely. ~*adj.* Slanting; oblique.

slap (slap) *n.* 1. **a.** A smacking blow, as made with the open hand. **b.** The sound so made. 2. An injury, as to one's pride; a rebuff or rebuke. Used chiefly in the phrase *a slap in the face.* ~*v.* **slapped, slapping, slaps.** —*tr.* 1. To strike with a flat object, especially the palm of the hand. 2. To put or place with a slapping sound: *slapped a fiver on the bar.* 3. To set or apply in an emphatic manner: *slapped a tax on eggs.* 4. To put or place carelessly or in a hurried manner: *slap a few pictures on the wall.* —*intr.* To strike or beat with the force and sound of a slap. —**slap down.** To put (a person) down; rebuff or reprimand. ~*adv. Informal.* Directly and with force. [Low German *slapp* (imitative).] —**slap·per** *n.*

slap and tickle *n. Used with a singular verb. Informal.* Light-hearted sexual play.

slap-bang (sláp-báng) *adv. Chiefly British Informal.* 1. Exactly or directly. 2. In a careless, hasty, or violent manner.

slap·dash (sláp-dash) *adj.* Acting or done hastily or carelessly. ~*adv.* In a reckless, haphazard manner. ~*n.* 1. Careless or hasty work. 2. Roughcast *(see).*

slap·hap·py (sláp-happi) *adj. Informal.* **-pier, -piest.** 1. Dazed, silly, or incoherent from or as if from blows to the head. 2. Reckless or casual in a jolly, cheerful manner.

slap·jack (sláp-jak) *n. U.S.* A pancake. [SLAP + (FLAP)JACK.]

slap·stick (sláp-stik) *n.* 1. Comedy characterised by boisterous knockabout farce and broad visual humour. Also used adjectivally. 2. A paddle designed to produce a loud whacking sound, formerly used in farces to simulate the sound of a heavy blow.

slap-up (sláp-up) *adj. British Informal.* Excellent and extravagant. Said especially of a meal.

slash (slash) *v.* **slashed, slashing, slashes.** —*tr.* 1. To cut or form by violent sweeping strokes. 2. To lash violently with sweeping strokes. 3. To make a gash or gashes in. 4. To cut a slit or slits in (a garment) to reveal the lining: *a slashed sleeve.* 5. To criticise sharply: *a slashing attack.* 6. To reduce or curtail drastically: *Profits were slashed.* —*intr.* To make violent and sweeping strokes with or as with a sharp instrument. —See Synonyms at **tear.** ~*n.* 1. A sweeping stroke made with a sharp instrument. 2. A cut or other injury made by such a stroke; a gash; a slit. 3. An ornamental slit in a fabric or article of clothing. 4. *U.S.* **a.** Branches and other residue left on a forest floor after the cutting of timber. **b.** Wet or swampy ground overgrown with bushes and trees. 5. *Printing.* A **solidus** *(see).* 6. *British Slang.* An act of urinating. [Middle English *slaschen,* perhaps from Old French *esclaschier, esclachier,* to break (imitative).] —**slash·er** *n.*

Śląsk. See **Silesia.**

slat[1] (slat) *n.* 1. A narrow strip of metal or wood, as in a Venetian

blind. 2. A movable auxiliary aerofoil running along the leading edge of the wing of an aircraft.
~*tr.v.* **slatted, slatting, slats.** To provide or make with slats. [Middle English *s(c)lat,* from Old French *esclat,* splinter, fragment, from *esclater*†, to splinter.]
slat² *tr.v.* **slatted, slatting, slats.** *Archaic & Regional.* To throw or knock violently or carelessly.
~*n. Archaic & Regional.* A blow or slap. [Middle English, from Scandinavian; akin to Old Norse *sletta,* to slap.]
slate¹ (slayt) *n.* **1.** A fine-grained metamorphic rock that splits into thin, smooth-surfaced layers. **2. a.** A piece of this rock cut for use as a roofing tile. **b.** A piece of slate or similar material, used, especially formerly, as a writing tablet. **3.** *U.S.* A list of the candidates of a political party running for various offices. **4.** Dark grey to purplish grey. **5.** An actual or imaginary record of money owed: *£5 on the slate.* **—start with a clean slate** or **wipe the slate clean.** To overlook past failures and make a fresh start.
~*tr.v.* **slated, slating, slates. 1.** To cover (a roof, for example) with slates. **2.** *U.S.* To put on a list of candidates. **3.** *U.S.* To designate or destine: *"I was slated to amass wealth beyond the dreams of avarice"* (S.J. Perelman). [Middle English *s(c)late,* from Old French *esclate,* feminine of *esclat,* fragment, splinter. See **slat.**] **—slat·y** *adj.*
slate² *tr.v.* **slated, slating, slates.** *British Informal.* **1.** To criticise unfairly or harshly. **2.** To reprimand or scold. [Perhaps from SLATE (cover with slates).]
slate blue *n.* Greyish blue to dark bluish grey. **—slate-blue** (sláyt-blo͞o) *adj.*
slat·er (sláytər) *n.* **1.** One employed to lay slate roofs. **2.** Any of several small isopod crustaceans; especially, a woodlouse.
slath·er (sláthər) *tr.v.* **-ered, -ering, -ers.** *U.S. Informal.* **1.** To use great amounts of; lavish. **2. a.** To spread thickly with. **b.** To spread thickly.
~*n. Plural. Slang.* A great amount; a lot: *slathers of money.* [19th century : origin obscure.]
slat·ing¹ (sláyting) *n.* **1.** The act, process, or occupation of laying slates. **2.** Slates collectively, used as a building material.
slating² *n. British Informal.* A harsh attack or reprimand.
slat·tern (sláttərn) *n.* A woman who is untidy or slovenly in person or habits; a slut. [Perhaps variant of dialectal *slattering,* present participle of *slatter*†, to spill awkwardly.]
slat·tern·ly (sláttərnli) *adj.* **1.** Slovenly; untidy. **2.** Characteristic of a slattern. —See Synonyms at **sloppy. —slat·tern·li·ness** *n.*
slaugh·ter (sláwtər) *n.* **1.** The killing of animals for food. **2.** The killing of a large number of persons; carnage; massacre.
~*tr.v.* **slaughtered, -tering, -ters. 1.** To kill (animals) for food; butcher. **2. a.** To kill in large numbers; massacre. **b.** To kill in a violent or brutal manner. **3.** *Informal.* To defeat easily. [Middle English *slau(g)hter,* probably from Old Norse *slātr,* butchered meat.] **—slaugh·ter·er** *n.* **—slaugh·ter·ous** *adj.*
slaugh·ter·house (sláwtər-howss) *n.* **1.** A place where animals are butchered; an abattoir. **2.** A scene of massacre or carnage.
Slav (slaav || *U.S. also* slav) *n.* A member of any of the Slavonic-speaking peoples of eastern Europe. [Middle English *Sclave,* from Medieval Latin *S(c)lavus,* from Late Greek *Sklabos*†.]
Slav. Slavonic.
slave (slayv) *n.* **1.** One who is legally bound in absolute obedience and servitude to a person or household to perform labour. **2.** One who is submissive to or hopelessly in the power of a particular person or influence: *a slave to her eating habits.* **3.** One whose condition is likened to that of slavery, as through having to work extremely hard or under duress. **4.** A machine or component that is controlled, powered, or fed information by another machine or component. Also used adjectivally: *a slave cylinder.*
~*intr.v.* **slaved, slaving, slaves.** To work like a slave; drudge. Often used with *away.* [Middle English *sclave,* from Old French *esclave,* slave, from Medieval Latin *sclavus,* from *Sclavus,* SLAV (the Slavs were reduced to slavery by conquest).]
slave-driv·er (sláyv-drīvər) *n.* **1.** A severely exacting employer or supervisor. **2.** An overseer of slaves at work, especially formerly.
slav·er¹ (slávvər, *rarely* sláyvər) *intr.v.* **-ered, -ering, -ers. 1.** To slobber. **2.** To fawn; drivel. Often used with *over.*
~*n.* **1.** Saliva drooling from the mouth. **2.** Slobbering flattery or drivel. [Middle English *slaveren,* probably from Old Norse *slafra.*]
slav·er² (sláyvər) *n.* **1.** A ship engaged in slave traffic. **2.** One trading in slaves. **—slav·ing** *n.*
slav·er·y (sláyvəri) *n., pl.* **-ies. 1.** Bondage to a master or household as a slave. **2.** A mode of production in which slaves constitute the principal work force. **3.** The condition of being subject or addicted to a particular influence. **4.** A condition of subjection likened to that of a slave: *wage slavery.* —See Synonyms at **servitude.**
Slave State *n.* In the United States, any of the 15 southerly states in which slavery was legal before the Civil War.
slave trade *n.* Traffic in slaves; specifically, that of black Africans to America. **—slave-trad·er** *n.* **—slave-trad·ing** *n.*
slav·ey (sláyvi) *n., pl.* **-eys.** *British Informal.* A maidservant, especially one who is overworked.
Slavic. *Chiefly U.S.* Variant of **Slavonic.**
slav·ish (sláyvish) *adj.* **1.** Pertaining to or characteristic of a slave; servile. **2.** Pertaining to or characteristic of the institution of slavery; oppressive. **3.** Blindly dependent on or imitative of something: *a slavish copy of the original.* **4.** Extremely laborious or difficult. **—slav·ish·ly** *adv.* **—slav·ish·ness** *n.*
Slav·ism (slaáv-iz'm || *U.S. also* sláv-) *n.* Anything peculiar to or characteristic of the Slavs or the Slavonic languages.
Sla·von·ic (slə-vónnik, sla-, slaa-) *adj. Abbr.* **Slav.** Also *chiefly U.S.* **Slav·ic** (slaávik, slávvik). Of or pertaining to the Slavs or their languages or cultures.
~*n. Abbr.* **Slav.** Also *chiefly U.S.* **Slavic.** A branch of the Indo-European language family, divided into East Slavonic, South Slavonic, and West Slavonic.
Slav·o·phile (slaáv-ə-fīl, sláv-, -ō-) *n.* Also **Slav·o·phil** (-fil). **1.** A person who admires the Slavs. **2.** *Sometimes small* **s.** In 19th-century Russia, one who advocated the supremacy of Slavonic, especially Russian, culture. [SLAV + -PHILE.] **—Slav·o·phile, Slav·o·phil** *adj.* **—Sla·voph·i·lism** (-iz'm, slə-vóffil-) *n.*
slay (slay) *tr.v.* **slew** (slo͞o || slew) or (for sense 2) **slayed, slain** (slayn) or (for sense 2) **slayed, slaying, slays. 1.** To kill violently, as in battle. **2.** *Slang.* To overwhelm, as with admiration, laughter, or love: *He slays all the girls.* [Slay, slew, slain; Middle English *slen(en), slew, slayn,* Old English *slēan, slōh, slægen.*] **—slay·er** *n.*
Usage: The usual past tense form of this verb is *slew,* past participle *slain.* But regular variants have emerged in informal speech, with *slayed* being used for both past tense and participle, in the sense "overwhelm" *(I slayed them at the Empire last week).*
S.L.B.M. submarine-launched ballistic missile.
SLD Social and Liberal Democrats: former name of the Liberal Democratic Party.
sleave (sleev) *tr.v.* **sleaved, sleaving, sleaves.** *Archaic.* To separate or disentangle (a twisted mass of threads, for example).
~*n. Archaic.* Any tangled or knotted thread. [Middle English *sleven* (unattested), Old English *slǣfan,* to cut, cut up, akin to *-slīfan,* to splice. See **sliver.**]
sleave silk *n.* Raw untwisted silk; floss, as for embroidery.
sleaze (sleez) *n. Informal.* **1.** Squalidness or disreputableness; sleaziness. **2.** A sleazy person. [From SLEAZY.]
slea·zy (sleézi) *adj.* **-zier, -ziest. 1. a.** Having a sordid, squalid, or disreputable character: *a sleazy restaurant.* **b.** Corrupt: *sleazy deals; sleazy politicians.* **2.** Flimsy or thin. Said of fabric. **3.** Made of low-quality materials; shoddy. [17th century : origin obscure]. **—slea·zi·ly** *adv.* **—slea·zi·ness** *n.*
sledge (slej) *n.* Also **sled** (sled). **1.** A vehicle mounted on low runners, drawn by horses, dogs, or other work animals, and used for transport or travel across ice and snow. **2.** A **toboggan** *(see).*
~*v.* **sledged, sledging, sledges.** *—tr.* To carry or convey on a sledge. *—intr.* **1.** To travel on a sledge. **2.** *Chiefly British.* To ride down slopes on a sledge; toboggan. [Dutch (dialectal) *sleeds,* from Middle Dutch *sleedse.*]
sledge·ham·mer (sléj-hammər) *n.* A long, heavy hammer, often wielded with both hands, used for driving wedges and posts and for other heavy work.
~*tr.v.* **sledgehammered, -mering, -mers.** To strike with or as if with such a hammer.
~*adj.* Ruthlessly severe; crushing. [Middle English *sleg(g)e,* Old English *slecg* + HAMMER.]
sledg·ing (sléj-ing) *n. Slang.* In cricket, a form of gamesmanship whereby a fielding side attempts to unsettle a batsman as by chatting to him. [Perhaps from SLEDGEHAMMER.]
sleek (sleek) *adj.* **sleeker, sleekest. 1. a.** Smooth and lustrous as if polished; glossy. **b.** Smooth, shiny, and healthy-looking. Said of the coat or fur of an animal. **2.** Appearing well-fed or well-groomed; prosperous-looking; thriving. **3.** Polished or smooth in behaviour, especially in an unctuous way; slick.
~*tr.v.* **sleeked, sleeking, sleeks. 1.** To make sleek; smooth or polish. **2. a.** To make calm or free from agitation. **b.** To cause to appear in a favourable light; gloss over. Used with *over.* [Variant of SLICK.] **—sleek·ly** *adv.* **—sleek·ness** *n.*
sleek·it (sleékit) *adj. Scottish.* **1.** Crafty; sly. **2.** Sleek. [From past participle of SLEEK.]
sleep (sleep) *n.* **1.** A natural, periodically recurring physiological state of rest, characterised by relative physical and nervous inactivity, unconsciousness, and lessened responsiveness to external stimuli. See **paradoxical sleep, orthodox sleep. 2.** A period of this form of rest. **3.** Any similar condition of inactivity, such as unconsciousness, dormancy, or hibernation. **4.** *Botany.* **Nyctinasty** *(see).* **5.** *Poetic.* Death. Often used euphemistically. **6.** *Informal.* The matter that collects in the corners of the eyes after a period of sleeping: *wipe the sleep from one's eyes.* **—go to sleep 1.** To fall asleep. **2.** To become numb because of pressure on a blood vessel. Used chiefly of limbs. **—put to sleep.** To kill (an animal) humanely.
~*v.* **slept** (slept || slep), **sleeping, sleeps.** *—intr.* **1.** To be in the state of sleep or to fall asleep. **2.** To be in a condition resembling sleep, such as hibernation, dormancy, or inattentiveness. **3.** To have sexual intercourse. Used with *with* or *together.* **4.** *Poetic.* To be dead. Often used euphemistically. *—tr.* **1. a.** To pass (time) by sleeping. **b.** To get rid of by sleeping: *went home to sleep it off.* **2.** To provide (a certain number of people) with accommodation for sleeping. **—sleep around.** *Informal.* To be sexually promiscuous. **—sleep in. 1.** To sleep at one's place of employment. **2.** *Chiefly British.* To sleep past one's usual hour of waking. **—sleep on.** To give (a matter) long consideration, especially by delaying one's decision until the next day. **—sleep out. 1.** To sleep at one's own home rather than at one's place of work. **2.** To sleep outdoors. **—sleep rough.** To sleep outdoors through homelessness rather than choice. [Middle English *slep(e), sleep,* Old English *slǣp, slǣpan.*]
sleep·er (sleépər) *n.* **1.** A person or animal that sleeps. **2.** A sleeping car or compartment on a railway train. **3.** Any of various usu-

ally small marine and freshwater fishes of the tropical family Eleotridae, related to the gobies. **4.** *British.* A heavy beam used as a support for rails on a railway. Also *U.S.* "tie". **5.** *British.* A thin ring, usually of gold, worn in a pierced ear in order to keep the hole open when earrings are not being worn. **6.** A person who is planted as a spy for future use. **7.** *Slang.* A sleeping pill. **8.** *Chiefly U.S. Informal.* One that achieves unexpected recognition or success, such as a racehorse, book, or marketed product.

sleep·ing-bag (sléeping-bag) *n.* A large, warmly lined bag, often having a zip, in which a person may sleep outdoors.

sleeping car *n.* A railway carriage providing bunks or beds.

sleeping draught *n.* A drink containing a sedative or hypnotic drug to induce sleep.

sleeping partner *n.* A person who makes a financial investment in a business enterprise but does not participate in its management. Also *U.S.* "silent partner".

sleeping pill *n.* A sedative or hypnotic drug in the form of a pill or capsule used to relieve insomnia.

sleeping policeman *n.* A small hump built across a road to restrict the speed of motorists, especially in built-up areas.

sleeping sickness *n.* **1.** An often fatal, endemic infectious disease of man and animals in tropical Africa, caused by either of two protozoans of the genus *Trypanosoma,* transmitted by the tsetse fly, and characterised by fever and lethargy. Also called "African trypanosomiasis". **2.** *Pathology.* **Encephalitis lethargica** *(see).*

sleep-learn·ing (sléep-lerning) *n.* A method of learning by listening to a tape recording while asleep, the information supposedly being absorbed by the unconscious. Also called "sleep-teaching".

sleep·less (sléep-ləss, -liss) *adj.* **1.** Without sleep; wakeful; restless; unquiet. **2.** Never sleeping or resting; always alert or active. **—sleep·less·ly** *adv.* **—sleep·less·ness** *n.*

sleep·walk·ing (sléep-wawking) *n.* Walking while asleep or in a sleep-like condition. Also called "noctambulation", "noctambulism", "somnambulance", "somnambulation", "somnambulism". **—sleep·walk** *intr.v.* **—sleep·walk·er** *n.*

sleep·y (sléepi) *adj.* **-ier, -iest.** **1.** Ready for or needing sleep; drowsy. **2.** Sluggish, inattentive, or lethargic; dull. **3.** Inducing sleep; soporific. **4.** Quiet and without activity: *a sleepy little town.* **—sleep·i·ness** *n.* **—sleep·i·ly** *adv.*

sleep·y·head (sléepi-hed) *n. Informal.* **1.** A drowsy or sleepy person. **2.** A slow or dull person.

sleet (sleet) *n.* A mixture of rain and snow or melting snow.
~*intr.v.* **sleeted, sleeting, sleets.** To shower sleet. [Middle English *slete,* Old English *slēte* (unattested).] **—sleet·y** *adj.*

sleeve (sleev) *n.* **1.** The part of a garment that covers all or a part of the arm. **2.** Any encasement or shell into which a piece of equipment fits. **3.** A sleeve coupling. **4.** A paper or cardboard envelope for storing a gramophone record in. **—laugh up (one's) sleeve.** To be secretly amused, especially over the discomfiture of another. **—up (one's) sleeve.** Hidden but ready to be used when needed; in reserve. [Middle English *slefe, sleve,* Old English *slīf, slēf.*] **—sleeve·less** *adj.*

sleeve board *n.* A small ironing board used for ironing sleeves.

sleeve coupling *n.* A thin steel cylinder uniting two lengths of shafting or pipe. Also called "sleeve".

sleeved (sleevd) *adj.* Having a sleeve or sleeves, especially of a specified kind. Often in combination: *short-sleeved.*

sleeve notes *pl.n.* Notes printed on a record sleeve, giving details of its contents and the performers, and other information.

sleev·ing (sléeving) *n.* Flexible plastic tubing into which bare wires are inserted for insulation in electrical and electronic equipment.

sleigh (slay) *n.* A light vehicle mounted on runners for use on snow or ice, having one or more seats and usually drawn by a horse.
~*intr.v.* **sleighed, sleighing, sleighs.** To ride in or drive a sleigh. [Dutch *slee,* from *slede,* from Middle Dutch *slēde.*] **—sleigh·er** *n.*

sleight (slīt) *n. Archaic.* **1.** Deftness; dexterity; skill. **2. a.** Cunning; trickery. **b.** A skilful trick or deception; a stratagem. [Middle English *sle(i)ght,* from Old Norse *slœgdh,* from *slœgr,* sly.]

sleight of hand *n.* **1.** The skill, as in conjuring, of performing tricks or feats so quickly that their manner of execution cannot be observed; legerdemain. **2.** Any trick or feat so performed. **3.** Cunning deception or sophistry, or any act in which such skills are employed. **—sleight-of-hand** (slīt-əv-hánd) *adj.*

slen·der (sléndər) *adj.* **1.** Having little width in proportion to the height or length; elongated. **2.** Gracefully slim; willowy. **3.** Spare or small in amount or extent; meagre; inadequate: *slender wages.* **4.** Having little force, justification, or foundation; limited; feeble: *only a slender chance of success.* [Middle English *s(c)lendre*†.] **—slen·der·ly** *adv.* **—slen·der·ness** *n.*

slen·der·ise (sléndər-īz) *v.* **-ised, -ising, -ises.** *—intr.* To become slender or more slender. *—tr.* **1.** To make slender or more slender. **2.** To cause to appear slender. Used especially of a garment.

slept. Past tense and past participle of **sleep.**

sleuth (slōōth, slewth) *n.* **1.** A detective. **2.** A sleuth-hound.
~*v.* **sleuthed, sleuthing, sleuths.** *—tr.* To track or follow. *—intr.* To act as a detective. [Short for SLEUTHHOUND.]

sleuth·hound (slōōth-hownd, sléwth-) *n.* **1.** Formerly, a dog used for tracking or pursuing, such as a bloodhound. Also called "sleuth". **2.** A detective. [Middle English : *sleuth,* track of an animal, from Old Norse *slōdh*† + HOUND.]

slew[1], slue (slōō || slew) *n. U.S. Informal.* A large amount or number; a lot: *a whole slew of her friends.* [Irish Gaelic *sluagh,* from Old Irish *slúag, slóg.*]

slew[2]. Past tense of **slay.**

slew[3], *U.S.* **slue** *v.* **slewed** or *U.S.* **slued, slewing** or *U.S.* **sluing, slews** or *U.S.* **slues.** *—tr.* **1.** To turn or twist (something) off course or sideways. **2.** To twist (a mast or boom) around on its axis. *—intr.* To turn, twist, veer, or skid off course or to the side.
~*n.* Also *U.S.* **slue. 1.** The act of slewing. **2.** The position or angle to which something has slewed. [18th century (verb sense 2) : origin obscure.]

slewed (slōōd, slewd) *adj. Chiefly British Slang.* Drunk. [From SLEW (turn off course).]

slice (slīss) *n.* **1.** A thin, flat, or wedge-shaped piece cut from a larger object. **2.** A portion or share. **3. a.** A knife with a broad, thin, flexible blade, used for cutting and serving food. **b.** A similar implement for spreading printing ink. **c.** A wide serving spatula, often perforated to drain cooking liquid. **4.** *Sports.* **a.** A stroke that causes a ball to curve off course to the right or, if the player is left-handed, to the left. **b.** The course followed by such a ball.
~*v.* **sliced, slicing, slices.** *—tr.* **1.** To cut or divide into slices. **2.** To cut or remove from a larger piece. Often used with *off* or *away.* **3.** To cut through or across with or as if with a knife. **4.** To spread, work at, or clear away with a bladed tool such as a slice bar. **5.** *Sports.* To hit (a ball) with a slice. *—intr.* **1.** To cut with or as if with a knife; pass cleanly or effortlessly: *The wind sliced through us.* **2.** To slice a ball. [Middle English *s(c)lice,* slice, splinter, from Old French *esclice,* from *esclicer,* to reduce to splinters, from West Germanic *slītjan* (unattested), from Germanic *slītan* (unattested), to SLIT.] **—slice·a·ble** *adj.* **—slic·er** *n.*

slice bar *n.* An iron tool with a flat, broad end, used to loosen and clear out clinker from furnace grates.

slice of life *n.* A vividly realistic portrayal, as in drama or literature, of a segment of real life. **—slice-of-life** (slīss-əv-līf) *adj.*

slick (slik) *adj.* **1.** Deftly executed; neat. **2.** Superficially attractive or skilful but without real quality; glib. **3.** Shrewd; wily. **4.** Smooth and slippery, as if covered with oil or ice.
~*n.* **1.** A smooth or slippery surface or area. **2.** An **oil slick** *(see).* **3.** Any of various implements, especially a chisel, used for smoothing and polishing. Also called "slick chisel". **4.** A racing-car tyre with a smooth tread. **5.** *U.S.* A glossy magazine.
~*tr.v.* **slicked, slicking, slicks.** To make (hair, for example) sleek, smooth, or glossy. [Middle English *slike,* perhaps from Old English *slice* (unattested).]

slick·en·side (slíckən-sīd) *n.* A polished and striated rock surface caused by one rock mass sliding over another in a fault plane. [Dialectal *slicken,* glossy, variant of SLICK + SIDE.]

slick·er (slíckər) *n. Informal.* **1.** A stylish, sophisticated city-dweller: *a city slicker.* **2.** *Chiefly U.S.* A cheat; a swindler. **3.** *U.S.* A glossy raincoat, especially one made of oilskin.

slide (slīd) *v.* **slid** (slid), **sliding, slides.** *—intr.* **1.** To move in smooth, continuous contact with a surface. **2.** To move or pass smoothly and quietly; glide. **3.** To pass gradually into a new, often less desirable, state; drift: *slid into a life of crime.* **4.** To go unattended or unacted upon: *Let it slide.* **5.** To lose one's balance or intended direction on a slippery surface. **6.** To undergo a gradual decline. *—tr.* **1.** To cause to slide. **2.** To place quietly and unobtrusively: *slid his hand into the drawer.*
~*n.* **1.** A sliding movement, action, or progression: *a further slide in share prices.* **2.** A smooth surface or track for sliding. **3.** A playground apparatus for children to slide down, typically consisting of a smooth metal chute mounted by means of a ladder. **4.** A part or mechanism that operates by sliding, such as a sliding seat in a rowing boat, or the U-shaped section of tube on a trombone that is moved to produce different notes. **5.** An image on a transparent celluloid plate for use with a viewer or projector. **6.** A small glass plate for mounting specimens to be examined under a microscope. **7.** An avalanche of rock or soil. **8.** *Music.* **a.** A **portamento** *(see).* **b.** An ornament of two grace notes approaching the main note. **9.** A **hair-slide** *(see).* [Slide, slid, slid; Middle English *sliden, slydde, slide,* Old English *slīdan, -slād, -sliden.*] **—slid·er** *n.*

slide guitar *n.* **1.** A style of guitar playing, **bottleneck** *(see).* **2.** A guitar played in the bottleneck style.

slid·er (slīdər) *n. Scottish.* An ice cream between wafers.

slide rule *n.* A device consisting essentially of two logarithmically scaled rules mounted to slide along each other so that multiplication, division, and sometimes more complex calculations may be reduced to the mechanical equivalent of addition or subtraction.

slide valve *n.* A valve that slides back and forth over ports in the cylinder wall of a steam engine, permitting the intake and outflow of steam to move the piston.

sliding scale *n.* A scale in which indicated prices, taxes, or wages vary in accordance with some other factor, such as wages with the cost-of-living index or prices with a customer's income.

slight (slīt) *adj.* **slighter, slightest.** **1.** Small in size, degree, or amount; meagre. **2.** Of small importance; inconsiderable; trifling. **3.** Slender or frail; delicate: *a slight figure.*
~*tr.v.* **slighted, slighting, slights.** **1.** To treat with disdain or discourteous indifference; snub. **2.** To fail to give sufficient consideration or attention to; treat as unimportant.
~*n.* An act of pointed disrespect or discourtesy. [Middle English *sl(e)ight,* smooth, slight, from Old Norse *slēttr,* smooth, sleek.] **—slight·ness** *n.*

slight·ing (slīting) *adj.* Constituting or conveying a slight; disparaging; disrespectful. **—slight·ing·ly** *adv.*

slight·ly (slīt-li) *adv.* **1.** To a small degree or extent; somewhat.

2. In a slight or delicate way: *She is slightly built.*
Sli·go (slīgō). County in the northwest of the Republic of Ireland. The county town is also called Sligo. The Atlantic coastline is indented and much of the interior is mountainous. Beef and dairy farming are the chief occupations of the people.
slily. Variant of **slyly.**
slim (slim) *adj.* **slimmer, slimmest. 1.** Small in girth or thickness in proportion to height or length: *a slim volume.* **2.** Pleasantly thin; slender: *a slim build.* **3.** Small in quality or amount; scant; meagre.
~*v.* **slimmed, slimming, slims.** —*tr.* To reduce in volume or amount. Often used with *down: slim down the work force.* —*intr.* **1.** To become slim. **2.** To diet for the purpose of losing weight. [Dutch, small, inferior, from Middle Dutch *slim,* slanting, bad.] **—slim·ly** *adv.* **—slim·ness** *n.*
Slim (slim), **William Joseph, 1st Viscount** (1891–1970). British field marshal. He commanded the army in Burma (1943–45). He served as Governor-General of Australia from 1953 to 1960.
slime (slīm) *n.* **1. a.** Viscous mud. **b.** Any substance having a runny or glutinous consistency, especially when considered unpleasant or offensive. **2.** A mucous substance secreted by certain animals, such as fish or slugs.
~*v.* **slimed, sliming, slimes.** —*tr.* **1.** To smear with slime. **2.** To remove slime from (fish, for example). —*intr. Informal.* To ingratiate oneself. Often used with *up to: slimed up to the boss.* [Middle English *slim(e),* Old English *slīm,* akin to Latin *limus,* mud.]
slime mould *n.* Any of various fungi of the class Myxomycetes, having both plant and animal characteristics, with a body consisting of a naked creeping mass of protoplasm. Also called "slime fungus", "myxomycete".
slim·line (slím-līn) *adj.* Slim or compact, especially by comparison with larger or more bulky objects of the same class: *a slimline diary for the handbag.* [SLIM + LINE, by analogy with STREAMLINE.]
slim·y (slīmi) *adj.* **-ier, -iest. 1.** Consisting of or resembling slime; viscous. **2.** Covered with or exuding slime. **3.** Vile; disgusting; foul. **4.** Sycophantic; ingratiating. **—slim·i·ly** *adv.* **—slim·i·ness** *n.*
sling[1] (sling) *n.* **1. a.** A weapon consisting of a looped strap with which a stone is whirled and then let fly. **b.** A catapult. **2.** A looped rope, strap, or chain for supporting, cradling, or hoisting something; especially: **a.** A strap used to carry a rifle over the shoulder. **b.** *Nautical.* A rope or chain for supporting a yard. **c.** *Nautical.* An arrangement, as of looped ropes or nets, for supporting cargo that is being transferred. **d.** A band suspended from the neck to support an injured arm or hand. **e.** A baglike device made of soft material, equipped with straps and worn over the back or chest and used for carrying a baby. **3.** An act of slinging.
~*tr.v.* **slung** (slung), **slinging, slings. 1.** To hurl from or as if from a sling; fling. **2.** To carry or support by means of a sling: *with his rifle slung over his shoulder.* **3.** To move by means of a sling; raise or lower in a sling. **4.** To cause to hang loosely or freely; let swing. —See Synonyms at **throw.** [Middle English, perhaps from Middle Low German *slinge.*] **—sling·er** (slíng-ər) *n.*
sling[2] *n.* A drink of brandy, whisky, or gin, sweetened and usually lemon-flavoured. See **gin sling.** [18th century : origin obscure.]
sling·back (slīng-bak) *n.* An open-backed shoe held in place by a strap above the heel.
sling·shot (slíng-shot) *n. U.S.* A catapult.
slink (slingk) *v.* **slunk** (slungk), **slinking, slinks.** —*intr.* To move in a quiet, furtive manner; sneak. —*tr.* To give birth to prematurely. Used especially of a cow.
~*n.* **1.** An animal, especially a calf, born prematurely. **2.** The flesh or skin of a slink.
~*adj.* Born prematurely. [Middle English *slynken,* Old English *slincan.*] **—slink·ing·ly** *adv.*
slink·y (slíngki) *adj.* **-ier, -iest. 1.** Of feline sleekness and grace. **2.** Soft, close-fitting, and usually glamorous. Said of women's clothing. **3.** *Informal.* Stealthy; furtive. **—slink·i·ness** *n.*
slip[1] (slip) *v.* **slipped, slipping, slips.** —*intr.* **1.** To move lightly and smoothly; glide. **2.** To move or pass swiftly, stealthily, or imperceptibly: *The years slipped by.* **3. a.** To slide unexpectedly and by accident; lose one's balance. **b.** To slide out of place; shift position. **c.** To escape, as from a fastening or grip. **4.** To get away completely; escape; be lost: *let chances slip by.* **5.** To be said unintentionally, as through lack of discretion: *let slip that he'd had a rise.* **6.** To put on or take off clothing quickly or smoothly. Used with *into* or *out of.* **7.** To fall below a usual or prescribed standard; decline or deteriorate. **8. a.** To make a mistake. **b.** To fall into error; lapse. **9.** To slide sideways; sideslip. Used of an aircraft. **10.** To fail to engage. Used of the clutch of a motor or vehicle. —*tr.* **1.** To cause to move in a smooth, easy, or sliding motion. **2.** To place, insert, or introduce smoothly. **3.** To put on or remove (clothing) quickly or smoothly. Used with *on* or *off.* **4.** To free oneself or itself from; get loose from: *slipped its moorings.* **5.** To pass out of (one's memory or attention) so as to be forgotten or unnoticed: *It slipped my mind.* **6.** To bring forth (young) prematurely. Used of an animal. **7.** To unleash or free (a dog or hawk, for example). **8.** To undo or unfasten: *slip the knot.* **9.** To dislocate (a bone), or suffer displacement of (an intervertebral disc). **10.** *Informal.* To give surreptitiously: *slipped me a fiver.* **11.** In knitting, to pass (a stitch) from one needle to the other without working it. **—slip one over on.** *Informal.* To hoodwink; trick.
~*n.* **1.** An act of slipping, sliding, or falling. **2. a.** An error in judgment or procedure; a fault or deviation. **b.** A slight mistake or oversight in speech or writing: *a slip of the pen.* **3. a.** A **slipway** *(see).* **b.** *U.S.* A space for a ship between two docks or wharves. **4.** A woman's loose, sleeveless undergarment serving as a lining for a dress or skirt. **5.** A pillowcase. **6.** A leash allowing quick release of the dog. **7.** In cricket: **a.** A fielder positioned closely behind and to the offside of the batsman, typically any of three or four. **b.** *Often plural.* The position of such a fielder: *fielding in the slips; caught at slip.* **8.** The difference between a vessel's actual speed through water and the speed at which the vessel would move if the screw were propelling against a solid. **9.** The difference between optimal and actual output in a mechanical device. **10.** *Geology.* A smooth crack at which rock strata have moved relative to each other. **11.** Movement between two parts where none should exist, as between the clutch plates of a motor vehicle. **12.** *Aeronautics.* The sliding movement of an aircraft in certain attitudes of the plane. See **sideslip. 13.** *Geology.* The relative movement along a fault plane. —See Synonyms at **error. —give (someone) the slip.** *Informal.* To escape or elude. [Middle English *slippen,* to slip, slip away, probably from Middle Low German.]
slip[2] *n.* **1.** A part of a plant cut or broken off for grafting or planting; a scion or cutting. **2.** Any long, narrow piece; a strip. **3.** A youthful, slender person: *a slip of a girl.* **4.** A small piece of paper; especially, a small form or list: *a sales slip.* **5. a.** *Plural. Chiefly British.* The area along the sides of the gallery in a theatre. **b.** *U.S.* A narrow pew in a church. **6.** *British.* A galley proof.
~*tr.v.* **slipped, slipping, slips.** To make a slip from (a plant or plant part). [Middle English *slippe*†, a strip.]
slip[3] *n.* Thinned potter's clay used for decorating or coating ceramics. [Middle English *slyppe,* a soft mass, curds, mud, Old English *slypa,* slime.]
slip·case (slíp-kayss) *n.* An open-ended protective box for a book.
slip·cov·er (slíp-kuvvər) *n. U.S.* A **loose cover** *(see).*
slip·knot (slíp-not) *n.* **1.** A knot made with a loop so that it slips easily along the rope or cord around which it is tied. Also called "running knot". **2.** A knot made so that it can readily be untied by pulling one free end.
slip-on (slíp-on || -awn) *adj.* Designed to be easily put on or taken off: *slip-on shoes.*
~*n.* A slip-on garment or shoe.
slip·o·ver (slíp-ōvər) *adj.* Designed to be put on or taken off over the head.
~*n.* A slipover garment, such as a sweater.
slip·page (slíppij) *n.* **1.** A slipping. **2.** The amount or extent of slipping. **3.** Loss of motion or power due to slipping.
slipped disc (slipt) *n.* Protrusion of the inner pulp of an intervertebral disc through its fibrous wall, causing pressure on adjacent nerves and hence sciatica or back pain.
slip·per (slíppər) *n.* **1.** A light, low, slip-on shoe for indoor wear, having an upper made of soft material. **2.** A woman's light slip-on shoe for dancing or evening wear.
slipper bath *n. Chiefly British.* A bath in the shape of a slipper.
slipper orchid *n.* Any of various tropical orchids of the genus *Paphiopedilum* and related genera, having slipper-shaped flowers.
slip·per·wort (slíppər-wurt || -wawrt) *n.* A plant, the **calceolaria** *(see).*
slip·per·y (slíppəri) *adj.* **-ier, -iest. 1.** Causing or tending to cause sliding or slipping, as a waxed, greasy, or wet surface may. **2.** Tending to slip or slide, as from one's grasp or from a position of being secured. **3.** Elusive; evasive; untrustworthy: *a slippery customer.* [Perhaps coined by Miles Coverdale (1535) to translate German *schlipfferig,* based on dialect *slipper,* from Middle English *sli(p)per,* Old English *slipor.*] **—slip·per·i·ly** *adv.* **—slip·per·i·ness** *n.*
slippery elm *n.* A tree, *Ulmus rubra,* of eastern North America, having twigs and leaves with a mucilaginous, aromatic juice formerly used medicinally.
slip·py (slíppi) *adj.* **-pier, -piest.** *Informal.* **1.** Slippery. **2.** *British.* Quick; nimble; alert. Often used in the phrase *look slippy.*
slip ring *n.* A metal ring mounted on a rotating part of a machine to provide a continuous electrical connection through brushes on stationary contacts.
slip road *n. British.* A narrow road, usually having a one-way traffic flow, that gives access to a motorway or other main road.
slip-sheet (slíp-sheet) *n. Printing.* A blank sheet of paper slipped between newly printed sheets to prevent offsetting.
~*tr.v.* **slip-sheeted, -sheeting, -sheets.** *Printing.* To insert blank sheets between (printed sheets).
slip·shod (slíp-shod) *adj.* **1.** Made or done carelessly and unsystematically. **2.** Slovenly in appearance; shabby; seedy. [Originally "wearing slippers or loose shoes" : SLIP + SHOD.]
slip·slop (slíp-slop) *n.* **1.** *Archaic.* Sloppy, unappetising food; slops. **2.** Trivial or sentimental talk or writing; twaddle. **3.** *South African.* A simple, backless rubber sandle; a flip-flop. [Reduplication of SLOP.]
slip·stitch (slíp-stich) *n.* **1.** A stitch used wherever stitching must be invisible, as on hems and facings, made by picking up one or two threads of fabric and then passing the needle diagonally through the hem edge. **2.** The basic chain stitch used for edgings in crochet. In this sense also called "single crochet". **—slip·stitch** *v.*
slip-stream (slíp-streem) *n.* **1.** The turbulent flow of air driven backwards by the propeller or propellers of an aircraft. Also called "race". **2.** The stream of air behind any fast moving object.
~*intr.v.* **slip-streamed, -streaming, -streams.** In cycling or motor racing, to drive in the slip-stream of another vehicle as a way of maintaining a high speed while conserving energy or fuel.

slip up *intr.v. Informal.* To make a mistake; blunder.
slip-up (slíp-up) *n. Informal.* An error or oversight; a mistake.
slip·way (slíp-way) *n.* A sloping incline leading down to the water, on which ships are built or repaired. Also called "slip".
slit (slit) *n.* A long, narrow, usually straight cut, tear, or opening. ~*tr.v.* **slit, slitting, slits. 1.** To make a long, narrow incision in. **2.** To cut lengthways into strips; split. See Synonyms at **tear**.
~*adj.* Having or resembling a slit: *slit eyes; a slit skirt.* [Middle English *slitte,* perhaps Old English *geslit,* a tearing, akin to *slītan,*to slit, from Germanic *slītan* (unattested).]
slith·er (slíthər) *v.* **-ered, -ering, -ers.** —*intr.* **1.** To slip and slide, as on a loose or uneven surface. **2.** To move along by gliding, as a snake does. —*tr.* To cause to slither.
~*n.* A slithering movement or gait. [Middle English *slideren,* Old English *slid(o)rian,* frequentative of *slīdan,* to SLIDE.] **—slith·er·y** *adj.*
slit trench *n.* A narrow, shallow trench dug during combat for the protection of a single soldier or a small group.
sliv·er (slívvər; *also* slīvər *for sense 2*) *n.* **1.** A sharp, slender piece cut, split, or broken off; a splinter. **2.** A continuous strand of loose wool, flax, or cotton, ready for drawing and twisting.
~*v.* **slivered, -ering, -ers.** —*tr.* To split, cut, or form into slivers. —*intr.* To become split into slivers. [Middle English *slivere,* from *slyven,* to split, Old English *-slīfan*† (unattested). See **sleave.**]
sli·vo·vitz (slívvə-vits) *n.* A dry, colourless plum brandy common in southeastern Europe. [Serbo-Croat *šljivovica,* from *šljiva,* plum.]
Sloane (slōn), **Sir Hans** (1660–1753). English physician and botanist, secretary (1693–1712) and president (1727–41) of the Royal Society and president of the Royal College of Physicians (1719–35); founder of the Botanic Garden at Chelsea Manor.
Sloane Ranger *n.* In Britain, any of a group of young upper-middle-class people readily identified by characteristic styles of dress. [After *Sloane* Square (in an affluent area of southwest London), by analogy with the *Lone Ranger,* character in old westerns.]
slob (slob) *n. Informal.* An obnoxious, uncouth, or slovenly person. [Irish *slab,* mud, probably from Scandinavian; akin to Old Danish *slab,* mud.]
slob·ber (slóbbər) *v.* **-bered, -bering, -bers.** —*intr.* **1.** To let saliva dribble from the mouth; slaver; drool. **2.** To indulge in mawkish sentimentality in speech or writing. —*tr.* To wet or smear with or as if with saliva or food dribbled from the mouth.
~*n.* **1.** Saliva or liquid running from the mouth; drivel; slaver. **2.** Drivelling, oversentimental speech or writing. [Middle English *sloberen,* perhaps of Low German origin, akin to Low German *slubberen* (imitative).] **—slob·ber·er** *n.* **—slob·ber·y** *adj.*
sloe (slō) *n.* **1.** A shrub, the **blackthorn** *(see).* **2.** The tart, blue-black, plumlike fruit of this shrub. [Middle English *slo(o),* Old English *slā(h).*]
sloe-eyed (slō-īd) *adj.* **1.** Having dark, blue-black eyes. **2.** Having slanted eyes.
sloe gin *n.* A liqueur made by steeping sloes in gin.
slog (slog) *v.* **slogged, slogging, slogs.** —*tr.* To strike powerfully, or wildly or unskilfully, as in cricket or boxing. —*intr.* **1.** To walk with a slow, plodding gait. **2.** To work doggedly; toil. Often used with *at* or *away.* **3.** To slog the ball in cricket.
~*n.* **1.** Hard, unremitting work, or a spell of this. **2.** A long, exhausting march or hike. **3.** A powerful swipe, as in cricket. [19th century : origin obscure.] **—slog·ger** *n.*
slo·gan (slōgən) *n.* **1.** A catch phrase or motto expressing some characteristic quality, stance, or purpose, and typically used in political campaigning or advertising. **2.** A battle cry, as formerly used by a Scottish clan. [Earlier (Scottish) *slog(g)orne,* from Gaelic *sluagh-ghairm* : *sluagh,* host, army + *gairm,* shout, cry.]
sloop (sloōp) *n. Nautical.* A single-masted, fore-and-aft-rigged sailing boat with a single headsail set from the forestay. Compare **cutter.** [Dutch *sloep(e)*†.]
sloot (sloōt, sloō-ət) *n. South African.* **1.** A furrow or channel dug for the conveyance of water. **2.** A natural ditch, as caused by rain. [Afrikaans, ditch, from Dutch.]
slop¹ (slop) *n.* **1.** Liquid spilled or splashed. **2.** Soft mud or slush. **3.** Unappetising, watery food or soup. **4.** *Usually plural.* Waste food used to feed pigs or other animals; swill. **5.** *Usually plural.* Liquid or semiliquid waste, such as: **a.** Liquid household refuse. **b.** Human excreta. **c.** Beer spilt while being drawn from a barrel. **6.** Repulsively effusive writing or speech.
~*v.* **slopped, slopping, slops.** —*intr.* **1.** To spill, splash, or overflow. **2.** To heave to and fro within a container. Usually used with *about.* **3.** To move in an awkward or slovenly manner as if plodding through mud. —*tr.* **1.** To spill (liquid). **2.** To spill liquid upon. **3.** To dish out or serve unappetisingly or clumsily. **4.** To feed slops to (animals). **—slop out.** To empty one's chamber pot, usually as part of a daily routine. Used of a prisoner. [Middle English *sloppe,* a muddy place, probably Old English *sloppe* (unattested).]
slop² *n.* **1.** *Plural.* Articles of clothing and bedding issued to sailors from a ship's stores. **2.** *Plural.* Short, full trousers or breeches as worn by men in the 16th century. **3.** A loose outer garment, such as a smock or overalls. **4.** *Plural. Chiefly British.* Cheap, ready-made garments. [Middle English *sloppe,* a kind of garment, perhaps Old English *(ofer)slop,* surplice.]
slop basin *n. British.* A small bowl used as a receptacle for tea leaves or coffee grounds from the bottoms of cups. Also called "slop bowl".
slope (slōp) *v.* **sloped, sloping, slopes.** —*intr.* **1.** To incline upwards or downwards; lie on a slant. **2.** To follow a sloping course; ascend or descend at an angle. **3.** *Informal.* To go surreptitiously. Usually used with *off.* —*tr.* **1.** To cause to slope. **2.** *Military.* To bring (a rifle) into a sloping position resting on the shoulder. Used chiefly in the command *slope arms.*
~*n.* **1.** Any inclined line, surface, plane, position, or direction. **2.** A stretch of ground forming a natural or artificial incline: *ski slopes.* **3.** Any deviation from the horizontal. **4.** The amount or degree of such deviation. **5.** *Mathematics.* The rate at which an ordinate of a point on a line on a plane containing the line changes with respect to a change in its abscissa. [Middle English *slope,* sloping, short for *aslope,* perhaps Old English *āslopen* (unattested), past participle of *āslūpan,* to slip away : *ā-,* away + *slūpan,* to slip.] **—slop·er** *n.* **—slop·ing·ly** *adv.*
slop·py (slóppi) *adj.* **-pier, -piest. 1.** Wet, slushy, or muddy. **2.** Watery and unappetising: *a sloppy stew.* **3.** Spotted or splashed with liquid or slop. **4.** *Informal.* Careless; untidy or unsystematic. **5.** *Informal.* Loose or ill-fitting; baggy. **6.** *Informal.* Oversentimental; slushy. **—slop·pi·ly** *adv.* **—slop·pi·ness** *n.*
Synonyms: *sloppy, slovenly, slatternly, blowzy, frowzy, unkempt.*
sloppy joe *n.* A long, baggy sweater.
slop·work (slóp-wurk) *n.* **1.** The manufacture of cheap, ready-made clothes. **2.** Such clothes. **3.** Any work of inferior quality.
slosh (slosh) *v.* **sloshed, sloshing, sloshes.** —*tr.* **1.** To pour or splash (a liquid). **2.** To stir or agitate in a liquid: *slosh clothes in water.* **3.** *British Informal.* To hit or punch heavily. —*intr.* **1.** To splash or flounder in water or another liquid. **2.** To splash about or move through being agitated: *Water sloshed about the basin.*
~*n.* **1.** Slush. **2.** The sound of splashing liquid. **3.** *British Informal.* A punch or blow. [Variant of SLUSH.] **—slosh·y** *adj.*
sloshed (slosht) *adj. Chiefly British Informal.* Drunk.
slot¹ (slot) *n.* **1.** A long, narrow groove, opening, or notch, as for receiving coins in a vending machine. **2.** A gap between a main and an auxiliary aerofoil to provide space for airflow and facilitate the smooth passage of air over the wing. **3.** *Informal.* A place in a programme or schedule.
~*v.* **slotted, slotting, slots.** —*tr.* **1.** To cut or make a slot or slots in. **2.** To place or fit in or as if in a slot. —*intr.* To fit into a slot. Often used with *in: This board slots in easily.* [Middle English, hollow between the breasts, from Old French *esclot*†.]
slot² *n.* The track or trail of an animal, especially a deer. [Old French *esclot,* horse's hoofprint, probably from Old Norse *slōdh,* animal's track. See **sleuthhound.**]
sloth (slōth || sloth, slawth) *n.* **1.** Aversion to work or exertion; laziness; indolence. **2.** Any of various shaggy, slow-moving, arboreal mammals of the family Bradypodidae, of tropical America, including: **a.** Any member of the genus *Bradypus.* Also called "ai". **b.** Any member of the genus *Choloepus.* Also called "unau". [Middle English *slowthe,* from *slow,* SLOW.]
sloth bear *n.* A bear, *Melursus ursinus,* of south-central Asia, having a long snout and dark, shaggy hair.
sloth·ful (slōth-f'l || slóth-, sláwth-) *adj.* Lazy; indolent; sluggish. **—sloth·ful·ly** *adv.* **—sloth·ful·ness** *n.*
slot machine *n.* **1.** A vending machine having a slot or slots through which coins are inserted in order to operate it. **2.** *Chiefly U.S.* A **fruit machine** *(see).*
slouch (slowch) *v.* **slouched, slouching, slouches.** —*intr.* **1.** To sit, stand, or walk with an awkward, drooping posture; assume an excessively relaxed position. **2.** To droop or hang down.
~*n.* **1.** A slouching movement, posture, or position. **2.** *Informal.* An ungainly, lazy, or incompetent person. [16th century : origin obscure.] **—slouch·i·ly** *adv.* **—slouch·i·ness** *n.* **—slouch·y** *adj.*
slouch hat *n.* A soft hat with a broad, flexible brim.
slough¹ (slow || *chiefly U.S.* sloō) *n.* Also **slue** (sloō) (for sense 2). **1. a.** A depression or hollow, usually filled with mud. **b.** *U.S.* A stagnant inlet or backwater. **2.** A state of despair or degradation. [Middle English *slo(g)h,* Old English *slōh, slō(g).*] **—slough·y** *adj.*
slough² (sluf) *n.* **1.** The dead outer skin shed by a snake or amphibian. **2.** *Medicine.* Dead tissue separated from a living structure. **3.** Broadly, anything that can be shed, such as an outer layer.
~*v.* **sloughed, sloughing, sloughs.** —*intr.* **1.** To be cast off or shed; come off. **2.** To shed a slough. **3.** *Medicine.* To separate from surrounding tissue. Used of dead tissue. —*tr.* **1.** To shed; throw off. **2.** To get rid of; discard as undesirable or unfavourable. Often used with *off.* [Middle English *slugh(e), slouh,* perhaps of Low German origin, akin to Low German *slu(we),* husk, shell, from Common Germanic *slūhwō* (unattested).]
slough of despond (slow || sloō) *n.* A state of depression or despair. [After the place in Bunyan's *Pilgrim's Progress* (1678).]
Slo·vak (slō-vak || *chiefly U.S.* -vaak) *n.* Also **Slo·vak·i·an** (slə-vácki-ən, slō-, -vaáki-). **1.** A member of a Slavonic people living in Slovakia. **2.** The West Slavonic language of these people, closely related to Czech. **—Slo·vak, Slo·vak·i·an** *adj.*
Slo·vak·i·a (slō-vácki-ə, slə-, -vaáki-). Country in central Europe formed in 1993 from the Slovak Republic, a constituent republic of former Czechoslovakia. It is mountainous, covered largely by the Carpathian mountains, which are a popular tourist area. Mining, shipbuilding and metal processing are highly developed. The main products are wine, timber, potatoes, sugar beet, cereals, livestock and salt. The people are mainly Slovaks, but there is a substantial Hungarian ethnic minority. Area, 49 023 square kilometres (18,928 square miles). Population, 5,370,000. Capital, Bratislava. See map at **Czech Republic and Slovakia.**

slov·en (slúvv'n) *n.* One who is careless and untidy in his behaviour, personal appearance, or work. [Middle English *sloveyn,* perhaps from Middle Dutch *sloft,* negligent.]

Slo·vene (slō-véen, *rarely* slō-véen) *n.* **1.** A native or inhabitant of Slovenia. **2.** The South Slavonic language spoken in Slovenia.
~*adj.* Of or pertaining to Slovenia, the Slovenes, or their language.

Slo·ve·ni·a, Republic of (slō-véeni-ə, slə-). Country in central Europe, formerly the northernmost constituent republic of Yugoslavia, lying mainly in the Julian Alps and the Karst plateau. It was the richest and most industrialised part of Yugoslavia. Area, 20 251 square kilometres (7,818 square miles). Population, 1,990,000. Capital, Ljubljana. —**Slo·ve·ni·an** *n. & adj.*

slov·en·ly (slúvv'nli) *adj.* **-lier, -liest. 1.** Having the habits or appearance of a sloven. **2.** Showing qualities associated with a sloven; specifically, **a.** Untidy; messy. **b.** Careless; marked by negligence; slipshod: *a slovenly piece of work.* —See Synonyms at **sloppy.**
—**slov·en·li·ness** *n.* —**slov·en·ly** *adv.*

slow (slō) *adj.* **slower, slowest. 1. a.** Not moving or able to move quickly; proceeding at a low speed: *a slow boat.* **b.** Marked by a low speed or tempo: *a slow waltz.* **2. a.** Taking or requiring a long time: *the slow job of making bread.* **b.** Taking more time than is necessary: *a slow worker.* **c.** Made or achieved over a long period of time; gradual: *a slow recovery.* **3.** Registering a time or rate behind or below the correct one: *a slow clock.* **4. a.** Lacking in promptness or willingness: *slow to accept; a slow response.* **b.** Not easily aroused; not precipitate: *slow to anger.* **5.** Sluggish; inactive: *Business was slow.* **6.** *Informal.* Lacking in interest; boring: *a slow film.* **7.** Mentally dull; obtuse: *a slow student.* **8. a.** Only moderately warm; low: *a slow oven.* **b.** Burning without strength: *a slow flame.* **9.** Not conducive to fast movement. Said of a sports surface: *a slow wicket.* —See Synonyms at **stupid.**
~*adv.* Slowly.
~*v.* **slowed, slowing, slows.** —*tr.* To make slow or slower. Often used with *up* or *down.* —*intr.* To become slow or slower; go or act slowly or more slowly. Often used with *up* or *down: The doctor told him to slow up for the sake of his health.* —See Synonyms at **delay.** [Middle English *slow, slaw,* Old English *slāw,* from Germanic *slǣwaz* (unattested).] —**slow·ly** *adv.* —**slow·ness** *n.*

Usage: Slow has an adverbial use, alongside *slowly,* but the two words are often not interchangeable. *Slowly* is the preferred form in written usage, and in formal speech; but spoken commands and exhortations generally use *slow (Go slow!),* and it is the expected form in certain idiomatic phrases *(my watch is running slow, the trains are running slow today),* with *how (How slow!),* and in some compound words *(slow-moving traffic).*

slow·coach (slō-kōch) *n. British Informal.* One who is excessively slow in action or movement. Also *U.S.* "slowpoke".

slow·down (slō-down) *n.* **1.** A slackening of pace. **2.** *U.S.* A **go-slow** *(see).*

slow handclap *n. British.* Slow and regular clapping used to express boredom or impatience, as by spectators at a sports match.

slow match *n.* A fuse that burns slowly, used to set off explosives.

slow motion *n.* **1.** In films, the technique whereby the action shown appears to be slower than the original action, achieved by projecting the sequence at a slower speed than that at which it was filmed. **2.** Broadly, a rate of action that is below normal. —**slow-mo·tion** (slō-mōsh'n) *adj.*

slow neutron *n.* A **thermal neutron** *(see).*

slow virus *n.* Any infectious virus that has a long incubation period in the body before symptoms of disease appear.

slow·wit·ted (slō-wittid) *adj.* Slow to comprehend; dull; stupid.
—**slow·wit·ted·ly** *adv.* —**slow·wit·ted·ness** *n.*

slow·worm (slō-wurm) *n.* A limbless European lizard, *Anguis fragilis,* having a smooth, snakelike body. Also called "blindworm". [Middle English *slowurm,* Old English *slāwyrm : slā,* perhaps "slime" + *wyrm,* WORM.]

SLR single-lens reflex (camera).

slub (slub) *tr.v.* **slubbed, slubbing, slubs.** To draw out and twist (a sliver of silk or other textile fibre) in preparation for spinning.
~*n.* **1.** A soft, thick nub in yarn that is either an imperfection or purposely set for a desired effect. **2.** A slightly twisted roll of fibre, as of silk or cotton.
~*adj.* Having an uneven, irregular appearance. Said of material. [18th century : origin obscure.]

sludge (sluj) *n.* **1.** Mud, mire, or ooze covering the ground or forming a deposit, as on a river bed. **2.** Slushy matter or sediment such as that precipitated by the treatment of sewage or collected in a boiler. **3.** Finely broken or half-formed ice on a body of water. [17th century : origin obscure (probably akin to SLUSH).] —**sludg·y** *adj.*

slue¹. Variant of **slew** (a large number).

slue². Variant of **slough** (backwater).

slug¹ (slug) *n.* **1.** A round bullet or pellet, as used in an airgun. **2.** *Informal.* A swig or measure of a drink, especially a spirit. **3.** A lump of metal or glass ready to be processed. **4.** *Printing.* **a.** A strip of type metal, less than type-high used for spacing. **b.** A line of cast type in a single strip of metal. **c.** A compositor's type line of identifying marks or instructions. **5.** *Physics.* A unit of mass equal to the mass accelerated at the rate of one foot per second per second when acted upon by a force of one pound weight. Also called "geepound". **6.** *U.S.* A small metal disc for use in a slot machine, especially one used illegally. [Probably from the animal SLUG (from its shape); sense 2, perhaps from Irish Gaelic *slog,* swallow.]

slug² *n.* **1.** Any of various terrestrial gastropod molluscs of the family Limacidae and other genera, having an elongated body with no shell. **2.** The smooth, soft larva of certain insects, especially the sawfly. Also called "slugworm". **3.** *Informal.* A lazy person; a sluggard. [Middle English *slugge,* slow person or animal, probably from Scandinavian; akin to Norwegian (dialectal) *slugg.*]

slug³ *tr.v.* **slugged, slugging, slugs.** *Chiefly U.S.* To strike heavily, especially with the fist.
~*n. Chiefly U.S.* A hard, heavy blow, as with the fist or a baseball bat; a slog. —**slug·ger** *n.* [19th century : origin obscure.]

slug·a·bed (slúggə-bed) *n.* One inclined to stay in bed out of laziness. [SLUG (sluggard) + ABED.]

slug·gard (slúggərd) *n.* A slothful, lazy person; an idler. [Middle English *sluggart,* probably from *sluggen,* to be lazy, from Scandinavian; akin to Swedish (dialectal) *slugga.*] —**slug·gard·ly** *adj.*
—**slug·gard·ness** *n.*

slug·gish (slúggish) *adj.* **1.** Displaying little movement or activity; slow; inactive. **2.** Lacking in alertness, vigour, or energy; dull or lazy. **3.** Slow to perform or respond to treatment or stimulation. [Middle English, perhaps from *sluggen,* to be lazy. See **sluggard.**] —**slug·gish·ly** *adv.* —**slug·gish·ness** *n.*

sluice (slōoss ‖ slewss) *n.* **1.** An artificial structure equipped with a valve or gate and used for holding back or regulating the flow of a body of water. **2.** The body of water so regulated or held back. **3.** The valve or gate used in a sluice. Also called "sluice gate", "sluice valve". **4.** A channel or drain, especially one for carrying off excess water. Also called "sluiceway". **5.** A long inclined trough, as for carrying logs or for washing gold ore.
~*v.* **sluiced, sluicing, sluices.** —*tr.* **1. a.** To flood or drench by means of a sluice. **b.** To pour or splash water over or upon. **c.** To wash with a sudden flow of water; flush. Often used with *out* or *away.* **2.** To draw off or let out by a sluice. **3.** To send (logs) down a sluice. **4.** To wash (gold ore) in a sluice. —*intr.* To flow out from or as if from a sluice. [Middle English *scluse,* from Old French *excluse,* from Gallo-Roman *exclūsa* (unattested), from the feminine past participle of Latin *exclūdere,* to shut out, EXCLUDE.]

slum (slum) *n.* **1.** *Often plural.* A heavily populated urban area characterised by poor housing and squalor: *the slums of Glasgow.* **2.** *Informal.* Any place that is uncared for, untidy, or squalid.
~*intr.v.* **slummed, slumming, slums.** To visit a slum or any place considered inferior to one's usual environment, as from curiosity. Usually used in the phrase *go slumming.* —**slum it.** *Informal.* To live below the standards to which one is accustomed. [19th century (cant) : origin obscure.]

slum·ber (slúmbər) *v.* **-bered, -bering, -bers.** —*intr.* **1.** To sleep or doze. **2.** To be dormant or quiescent. —*tr.* To pass (time) in sleep. Often used with *away.*
~*n.* **1.** *Often plural.* Sleep: *was woken from her slumbers.* **2.** A state of inactivity or dormancy. [Middle English *slum(b)eren,* perhaps frequentative of *slumen,* to doze, probably from *slume,* sleep, Old English *slūma.*] —**slum·ber·er** *n.* —**slum·ber·ing·ly** *adv.*

slum·ber·ous (slúmbərəss) *adj.* **1.** Sleepy; drowsy. **2. a.** Suggestive of or like sleep. **b.** Peaceful; tranquil. **3.** Causing or inducing sleep; soporific. —**slum·ber·ous·ly** *adv.* —**slum·ber·ous·ness** *n.*

slump (slump) *intr.v.* **slumped, slumping, slumps. 1.** To fall or sink suddenly and heavily; plump; collapse. **2.** To decline suddenly; suffer a slump. **3.** To droop, as in sitting or standing; slouch.
~*n.* A sudden falling off or decline, as in interest, prices, or business. [17th century ("to sink in a bog") : perhaps from Scandinavian; akin to Norwegian *slumpa,* to fall, Low German *slump,* bog.]

slung. Past tense and past participle of **sling.**

slunk. Past tense and past participle of **slink.**

slur (slur) *tr.v.* **slurred, slurring, slurs. 1.** To pass over lightly or carelessly; treat without due consideration. Often used with *over.* **2.** To pronounce (words or sounds) indistinctly. **3.** To speak slightingly of; disparage; slander. **4.** *Music.* **a.** To glide over (a series of notes) smoothly without a break. **b.** To mark with a slur. **5.** *Printing.* To blur or smudge.
~*n.* **1. a.** A disparaging remark; an aspersion. **b.** A blot or stain, as on one's reputation. **2.** A slurred utterance or manner of speech. **3.** *Music.* **a.** A curved line connecting notes on a score to indicate that they are to be played or sung legato. **b.** A group of notes so connected. **4.** Slurred written or printed matter. [Middle English *sloor, slore,* mud, perhaps from Middle Dutch; compare Low German *slüren,* Middle Dutch *sloren,* to drag, trail]

slurp (slurp) *v.* **slurped, slurping, slurps.** —*tr.* To eat or drink in a noisy manner. —*intr.* To eat or drink something noisily. [Dutch

slurpen, to slurp, lap, from Middle Dutch *slorpen.*]

slur·ry (slúrri) *n., pl.* **-ries.** A thin mixture of a liquid, especially water, and a finely divided substance, such as cement, plaster of Paris, or clay particles. [Middle English *slory,* probably akin to *sloor,* mud. See **slur.**]

slush (slush) *n.* **1.** Partially melted snow or ice. **2.** Soft mud; mire. **3.** Refuse grease or fat from a ship's galley. **4.** Maudlin speech or writing; sentimental drivel.

~*v.* **slushed, slushing, slushes.** —*tr.* **1.** To splash or soak with slush. **2.** To fill (joints in masonry) with mortar. Usually used with *up.* —*intr.* **1.** To walk or proceed through slush. **2.** To make a splashing or slushy sound. [17th century : origin obscure.] **—slush·i·ness** *n.* **—slush·y** *adv.*

slush fund *n. Chiefly U.S.* A contingency fund kept, as by a political group, to finance corrupt practices such as bribing public officials. [From SLUSH (sense 3), alluding to greasing as bribery.]

slut (slut) *n.* **1.** A slovenly, dirty woman; a slattern. **2. a.** A woman of loose morals. **b.** A prostitute. [Middle English *slutte*†.] **—slut·tish** *adj.* **—slut·tish·ly** *adv.* **—slut·tish·ness** *n.*

sly (slī) *adj.* **slier** or **slyer, sliest** or **slyest. 1.** Stealthily clever; crafty; cunning: *He was a sly old dog.* **2.** Secretive rather than open; underhand; deceitful. **3.** Playfully mischievous; roguish; arch. **—on the sly.** Secretively or surreptitiously. [Middle English *sli, sleih,* from Old Norse *slœgr,* cunning, clever, "able to strike", from *slōg-,* past stem of *slā,* to strike.] **—sly·ly, sli·ly** *adv.* **—sly·ness** *n.*

Synonyms: *sly, cunning, tricky, crafty, wily, foxy, artful.*

sly·boots (slī-bōōts) *n. Informal.* A sly person.

slype (slīp) *n. Architecture.* A covered passage, especially one between the transept and chapter house of a cathedral. [Probably from Middle Flemish *slijpen,* to slip.]

smack[1] (smak) *v.* **smacked, smacking, smacks.** —*tr.* **1.** To strike, as with the flat of the hand, heartily and noisily. **2.** To make a sound by pressing together (the lips) and opening them again quickly. **3.** To move or place with force, causing a smacking sound: *smacked the money on the bar.* —*intr.* To make or give a smack.

~*n.* **1.** A sharp blow or slap. **2.** The loud, sharp sound of smacking. **3.** A noisy kiss. **4.** *Informal.* An attempt; a go. Used in the phrase *have a smack at.* **—smack in the eye** or **face.** *Informal.* A setback or rebuff.

~*adv.* **1.** With a smack: *fell smack on her head.* **2.** Directly; right: *went smack against the rules.* [Middle Low German or Middle Dutch *smacken* (imitative).]

smack[2] *n.* **1. a.** A distinctive flavour or taste. **b.** A suggestion or trace. **2.** A small amount; a smattering. **3.** *Slang.* Heroin.

~*intr.v.* **smacked, smacking, smacks. 1.** To have a distinctive taste. Used with *of.* **2.** To give an indication; suggest. Used with *of*: *smacks of foul play.* [Middle English, Old English *smæc.*]

smack[3] *n.* A single-masted boat, such as a sloop, used chiefly in fishing. [Dutch *smak,* from Middle Dutch *smacke*†.]

smack·er (smáckər) *n. Slang.* **1.** A loud kiss. **2.** A resounding blow. **3.** A pound or, in the United States, a dollar.

smack·ing (smácking) *adj.* **1.** Given with a smacking sound: *a smacking kiss.* **2.** Brisk; vigorous; spanking: *a smacking breeze.*

small (smawl) *adj.* **smaller, smallest.** *Abbr.* **s. 1.** Little or relatively little; of less than usual or average size, number, quantity, magnitude, or extent: *a small house; a small portion of pie.* **2.** Limited in importance or significance; trivial. **3.** Limited in degree, scope, or intensity: *paid small attention; had small hope.* **4.** Lacking position, influence, or status; minor. **5.** Engaged in commercial or other activity on a relatively limited scale: *small businesses.* **6.** Unpretentious; modest. **7.** Not fully grown; very young. **8.** Showing littleness of mind or character; petty: *very small of him to object.* **9.** Belittled; humiliated: *made him feel small.* **10. a.** Designating a letter written or printed in lower case. **b.** Lower-case in order to distinguish a specified word from the same word when capitalised: *catholic with a small c.* **11.** Soft; low: *a small voice.*

~*adv.* **1.** In small pieces: *Cut it up small.* **2.** In a small manner.

~*n.* **1.** A small, slender part: *the small of the back.* **2.** *Plural. British Informal.* Small items of laundry, such as underclothes. [Middle English *smal(l),* Old English *smæl.*] **—small·ness** *n.*

Synonyms: *small, little, diminutive, minute, tiny, minuscule, infinitesimal.*

small ad *n.* A **classified advertisement** *(see).*

small arms *n.* Firearms small enough to be carried in the hand.

small beer *n.* Someone or something of little consequence. [Popularised by its use in Shakespeare's *Othello* ("To suckle fools and chronicle small beer", Act II, scene 1).]

small capital *n. Abbr.* **s.c.** A letter having the form of a capital letter but lower in height; for example, the words SMALL CAPITALS are printed in small capitals.

small change *n.* **1.** Coins of low denomination. **2.** Something of little value or significance.

small chop *n. West African.* Party snacks, such as olives and nuts.

small circle *n.* In geometry, a circle on the surface of a sphere with a radius that is not a radius of the sphere. Compare **great circle.**

small·clothes (smáwl-klōthz, -klōz) *pl.n. Archaic.* Men's close-fitting knee breeches worn in the 18th century.

small fry *pl.n.* **1.** Young or small fish. **2.** Young, unimportant, or insignificant persons or things.

small·hold·er (smáwl-hōldər) *n. Chiefly British.* One who owns or rents a smallholding.

small·hold·ing (smáwl-hōlding) *n. Chiefly British.* An area of agricultural land smaller than an average farm.

small hours *pl.n.* The early hours of the morning before dawn.

small intestine *n.* The part of the intestine in which digestion is completed, extending from the pylorus to the caecum and consisting of the duodenum, the jejunum, and the ileum.

small-mind·ed (smáwl-mīndid) *adj.* Having or characterised by a narrow, petty, or selfish attitude; lacking breadth of sympathy or interest. **—small-mind·ed·ly** *adv.* **—small-mind·ed·ness** *n.*

small·pox (smáwl-poks) *n.* An infectious disease, now eradicated, caused by a virus and characterised by widespread pimples which blister and form pockmarks. Also called "variola".

small print *n.* Small printed matter; especially, sections, as of contracts or guarantees, printed in small type and often containing important provisions or conditions that might easily be overlooked.

small-scale (smáwl-skáyl) *adj.* **1.** Small or limited in scope, range, or extent. **2.** Having a small scale. Said of a map.

small screen *n. Informal.* Television. Compare **big screen.**

small·sword (smáwl-sawrd || -sōrd) *n.* A lightweight, tapering sword used, especially in former times, for fencing.

small talk *n.* Casual, light, or trivial conversation.

small-time (smáwl-tīm) *adj. Informal.* Insignificant or unimportant; minor: *a small-time comedian.* **—small-tim·er** *n.*

smalt (smawlt || smolt) *n.* A deep-blue paint and ceramic pigment made by pulverising a glass made of silica, potash, and cobalt oxide. [French, from Italian *smalto,* from Germanic; akin to SMELT.]

smarm (smarm) *v.* **smarmed, smarming, smarms.** *Informal.* —*tr.* To flatten (hair) by smoothing with grease. Often used with *down.* —*intr.v.* To act or behave in an unctuous, obsequious manner. Often used with *up to.* [19th century (dialect) : origin obscure.]

smarm·y (smármi) *adj.* **-ier, -iest.** *Informal.* Having or characterised by an unpleasantly smooth, obsequious manner.

smart (smart) *intr.v.* **smarted, smarting, smarts. 1. a.** To cause a sharp, usually superficial, stinging pain, as an acrid liquid or a slap may. **b.** To be the source of such a pain, as a wound may. **c.** To feel such a pain. **2.** To suffer acutely, as from mental distress, wounded feelings, or remorse: *smarting from wounded pride.* **3.** To suffer or pay a heavy penalty. Usually used with *for.*

~*n.* Sharp mental or physical pain.

~*adj.* **smarter, smartest. 1. a.** Characterised by sharp, quick thought; bright. **b.** Amusingly or impertinently clever; witty: *a smart answer.* **2.** Characterised by sharp, quick movement; specifically: **a.** Forceful; stinging: *a smart slap.* **b.** Brisk; energetic: *a smart pace.* **3 a.** Characterised by or involving astuteness or shrewdness. **b.** Able to vary in operation or effect in response to variations in data or signals: *a smart bomb that can change direction; a smart credit card that can foil fraud.* **4.** Neat, fresh, and spruce, as in dress or appearance. **5.** Associated with or consisting of persons of fashion and sophistication; fashionable. —See Synonyms at **intelligent.**

~*adv.* In a smart manner: *play it smart.* [Middle English *smarten, smerten,* Old English *smeortan.*] **—smart·ly** *adv.* **—smart·ness** *n.*

smart al·eck (ál-ik, -ek). *Informal.* One who shows off his cleverness in a self-assertive and arrogant way. [SMART + *Aleck,* pet form of the name *Alexander.*] **—smart-al·eck·y** *adj.*

smart·en (smárt'n) *v.* **-ened, -ening, -ens.** —*tr.* **1.** To improve in appearance or stylishness; spruce up. Usually used with *up.* **2.** To make brighter or quicker: *smarten the pace.* —*intr.* To make oneself smart or smarter. Usually used with *up.*

smart money *n.* **1.** Compensation made for injury or disablement, especially when sustained on military service. **2.** Money paid to obtain discharge from the army. **3.** *Chiefly U.S.* Money gambled or invested by experienced gamblers or those having privileged information.

smash (smash) *v.* **smashed, smashing, smashes.** —*tr.* **1.** To break into pieces suddenly, noisily, and violently; shatter: *smashed the glass.* **2. a.** To throw or dash (something) violently so as to shatter or crush: *smashed the vase against the wall.* **b.** To strike with a heavy blow; batter: *smashed the door in.* **3.** To hit (a ball or shuttlecock) with an aggressive overhead stroke. **4.** To crush or destroy completely; ruin. **5.** To break up; put an end to: *smash a drugs ring.* —*intr.* **1.** To move or be moved suddenly into violent contact with another object: *smashed into a wall.* **2.** To break into pieces, as from a violent blow or collision. **3.** To smash a ball or shuttlecock. **4.** To become wrecked or destroyed. **5.** To go bankrupt. Often used with *up.* —See Synonyms at **break.**

~*n.* **1. a.** The act or sound of smashing. **b.** The condition of having been smashed. **2. a.** Total defeat, destruction, or ruin. **b.** Financial failure; bankruptcy. **3.** A collision or crash. **4.** An aggressive overhead stroke in tennis, badminton, or the like. **5.** *Informal.* A resounding success. **6.** *U.S.* A drink made of mint, sugar, soda water, and alcoholic spirit, usually brandy.

~*adj. Informal.* Of, pertaining to, or being a resounding success: *a smash hit.*

~*adv.* With a sudden, violent crash. [Imitative; perhaps blend of SMACK and CRASH.] **—smash·er** *n.*

smash-and-grab (smásh'n-gráb) *adj.* Designating a robbery in which a shop window is smashed, as with a brick, and goods taken from the window display. **—smash-and-grab** *n.*

smashed (smasht) *adj. British Informal.* Intoxicated; drunk.

smash·er (smáshər) *n. British Informal.* One that is outstandingly fine or attractive.

smash·ing (smáshing) *adj. Informal.* Extraordinarily or unusually impressive, fine, or attractive; wonderful; admirable.

smash·up (smásh-up) *n.* **1.** A total collapse or defeat. **2.** A serious collision between vehicles; a crash.

smat·ter (smáttər) *v.* **-tered, -tering, -ters.** *Archaic.* *—tr.* **1.** To speak (a language) without fluency. **2.** To study or approach superficially; dabble in. *—intr.* To have a superficial knowledge; dabble.
~*n.* A smattering. [Middle English *smat(e)ren* (probably imitative).] **—smat·ter·er** *n.*

smat·ter·ing (smáttəring) *n.* **1.** A fragmented or superficial knowledge. **2.** A small amount or number; a scattering. [From SMATTER.]

smear (smeer) *v.* **smeared, smearing, smears.** *—tr.* **1. a.** To spread or daub with a sticky, greasy, or dirty substance. **b.** To spread or daub (a sticky, greasy, or dirty substance) on a surface. **2.** To stain or blur by or as if by smearing. **3.** To stain or attempt to destroy the reputation of; vilify. *—intr.* To be or become smeared.
~*n.* **1.** A mark made by smearing; a spot; a blot. **2.** A substance to be spread on a surface; especially, a substance or preparation placed on a slide for microscopic examination. **3.** A malicious, unsubstantiated charge made in an attempt to destroy someone's reputation; a slander. Also used adjectivally: *a smear campaign.* [Middle English *smeren,* to anoint, cover, daub, Old English *smierwan, smerian.*] **—smear·y** *adj.*

smear test *n.* A **Pap test** *(see).*

smec·tic (sméktik) *adj. Chemistry.* Of, pertaining to, or designating one of the two types of anisotropic melts characteristic of a liquid crystal, in which the molecules are linearly orientated in a planar arrangement. Compare **nematic.** [Greek *smēktikos,* cleansing, detergent, from *smēkhein,* to cleanse (referring to the soapy consistency of such substances).]

smeg·ma (smég-mə) *n.* **1. Sebum** *(see).* **2.** The sebaceous substance secreted under the foreskin. [Greek *smēgma* (stem *smēgmat-*), detergent, from *smēkhein,* to cleanse (referring to the soaplike consistency).] **—smeg·ma·tic** (smeg-máttik) *adj.*

smell (smel) *v.* **smelled** or **smelt** (smelt), **smelling, smells.** *—tr.* **1.** To perceive the scent of (something) by means of the olfactory nerves. **2. a.** To sense the presence of by or as if by the olfactory nerves; detect: *to smell danger.* **b.** To find or discover by smelling. Used with *out.* *—intr.* **1.** To use the sense of smell; perceive the scent of something. **2.** To have or emit an odour of a specified kind: *doesn't smell fresh; smells of old socks.* **3.** To be suggestive; smack of something. Used with *of*: *smells of dishonesty.* **4.** To have or emit an unpleasant odour; stink. **5.** *Chiefly U.S.* To appear to be dishonest; suggest evil or corruption.
~*n.* **1.** The sense by which odours are perceived; the olfactory sense. **2. a.** That quality of something that may be perceived by the olfactory sense; odour; scent. **b.** An unpleasant odour. **3.** The act or an instance of smelling. **4.** A distinctive or pervasive quality; an aura: *the smell of corruption.* [Middle English *smellen, smullen*†.]
Synonyms: *smell, odour, scent, aroma, fragrance, perfume, bouquet, savour, stink, stench.*
Usage: The past tense and participle forms of this verb may be *smelled* (preferred in American English) or *smelt* (preferred in British English). The verb may be followed either by an adjective or by an adverb, but different senses are involved. With an adjective, the sense is "emit an odour": *The flowers smell beautiful today.* The adverb is used only in the context of "emit an unpleasant odour": *They smell terribly.*

smelling salts *pl.n.* Any of several preparations based on spirits of ammonia, sniffed as a restorative after dizziness and fainting.

smell·y (smélli) *adj.* **-ier, -iest.** *Informal.* Having an unpleasant or offensive odour. **—smell·i·ness** *n.*

smelt[1] (smelt) *v.* **smelted, smelting, smelts.** *—tr.* **1.** To extract the metallic constituents from (ore) by melting. **2.** To extract (metal) from ore in this way. *—intr.* To melt or fuse. Used of ores. [Dutch or Low German *smelten,* from Middle Dutch or Middle Low German.]

smelt[2] *n., pl.* **smelts** or **smelt.** **1.** Any of various small marine and freshwater food fishes of the family Osmeridae; especially, *Osmerus eperlanus,* of Europe. Also called "sparling". **2.** The sand smelt, *Atherina presbyter.* [Middle English, Old English *smelt, smylt.*]

smelt[3]. Alternative past tense and past participle of **smell.**

smelt·er (sméltər) *n.* Also **smelt·er·y** (-i) (for sense 1b). **1. a.** Any apparatus for smelting, usually a furnace. **b.** An establishment for smelting. **2.** A person engaged in the smelting industry.

Sme·ta·na (sméttənə), **Bedřich** (1824–84). Czech composer. He played a leading part in the founding of the Czech national opera (1862), and was its principal conductor until 1874. His most famous works are the opera *The Bartered Bride* (1866), the tone poem *Ma Vlast* "My Country" (1879), and two string quartets both called *From My Life* (1876, 1882).

smew (smew) *n.* A small, crested Old World duck, *Mergellus albellus,* having a narrow bill and white and black plumage in the male. [17th century : origin obscure.]

smid·gen, smid·gin (smíjin, smíjən) *n. Chiefly U.S. Informal.* A very small quantity or portion; a bit. [Probably variant of dialectal *smitch,* probably variant of SMUTCH.]

smi·lax (smī́-laks) *n.* **1.** Any plant of the genus *Smilax,* which mainly comprises climbing vines. The dried roots of certain species are also called "sarsaparilla". **2.** A vine, *Asparagus asparagoides,* that is popular as a floral decoration. [New Latin, from Latin *smīlax,* a kind of oak, smilax, bindweed, from Greek *smilax*†.]

smile (smīl) *n.* **1.** A facial expression characterised by an upward curving of the corners of the mouth, typically expressing pleasant feelings such as amusement, affection, or approval, but sometimes arising from bitterness, cynicism, or derision. **2.** A pleasant or favourable disposition or aspect.
~*v.* **smiled, smiling, smiles.** *—intr.* **1.** To have or form a smile. **2. a.** To express approval or beneficence. Often used with *upon* or *on.* **b.** To regard with detached amusement or patient resignation. Often used with *at: smiled at misfortune.* *—tr.* **1.** To express with a smile. **2.** To act upon or change with or as if with a smile: *She smiled away her cares.* [Middle English *smilen,* perhaps from Scandinavian, akin to Swedish *smila.*] **—smil·er** *n.* **—smil·ing·ly** *adv.*

Smiles (smīlz), **Samuel** (1812–1904). British writer, the most famous populariser of the Victorian ethic of self-improvement and hard work, especially in *Self-Help* (1859) and *Thrift* (1875).

smirch (smurch) *tr.v.* **smirched, smirching, smirches.** **1.** To soil, stain, or dirty, as with grime. **2.** To dishonour or defame.
~*n.* Something that smirches; a blot, smear, or stain. [Middle English *smorchen*†.]

smirk (smurk) *intr.v.* **smirked, smirking, smirks.** To smile in a self-conscious, knowing, or self-satisfied manner.
~*n.* A knowing, self-satisfied smile. [Middle English *smirken,* Old English *smearcian,* to smile.] **—smirk·er** *n.* **—smirk·ing·ly** *adv.*

Smirke (smurk), **Sir Robert** (1781–1867). British architect, a supporter of the early 19th-century Neoclassical movement. His best-known building is the British Museum, which was begun in 1823 and completed in 1855 by his brother, Sydney (1798–1877).

smite (smīt) *v.* **smote** (smōt) or *archaic* **smit** (smit), **smitten** (smítt'n) or **smit** or **smote, smiting, smites.** *Archaic & Literary.* *—tr.* **1.** To strike heavily with or as if with the hand, a tool, a weapon, or the like. **2.** To attack, damage, or destroy by or as if by blows. **3. a.** To affect, as with disease; afflict: *smitten with plague.* **b.** To strike down in retribution; chasten or chastise. Used of God. **c.** To affect sharply with deep feeling: *smitten with love.* *—intr.* To strike or beat: *smote upon the oaken door.* [Smite, smote or smit, smitten; Middle English *smiten, smot* or *smite, smitten,* Old English *smītan, smiton* (plural) or *smāt* (singular), *smiten.*] **—smit·er** *n.*

smith (smith) *n.* **1.** A metalworker; especially, one who works metal when it is hot and malleable. Often used in combination: *silversmith, goldsmith.* **2.** A **blacksmith** *(see).* **3.** A person who makes or creates something specified. Used in combination: *a wordsmith; a songsmith.* [Middle English, Old English.]

Smith (smith), **Adam** (1723–90). Scottish economist and moral philosopher. He came to prominence with his *Theory of Moral Sentiments* (1759), but is best known for his great work of political economy *An Inquiry into the Nature and Causes of the Wealth of Nations* (1776) which laid the foundations of classical "free-market" economic theory.

Smith, Bessie (*c.* 1894–1937). American jazz singer. She was known as the "Empress of the Blues", thanks to her recordings in the 1920s with leading jazz musicians such as Louis Armstrong.

Smith, F(rederick) E(dwin). See **Birkenhead, 1st Earl of.**

Smith, Ian (Douglas) (1919–). Rhodesian politician. He formed the Rhodesian Front party in 1961 to campaign for Southern Rhodesia's independence from Great Britain. In 1964 he became prime minister of Rhodesia and in 1965 he unilaterally declared its independence. In 1970 his rebel regime proclaimed Rhodesia a republic. For the next decade his white supremacist party fought a losing battle against Black guerrilla forces. He led the white minority in the new parliament of Zimbabwe (1980–87).

Smith, Joseph (1805–44). U.S. religious leader, founder of the Mormon church, known as the Church of Jesus Christ of Latter-day Saints. He alleged that a vision had shown him the hiding place of sacred tablets, which he unearthed in 1827 and transcribed in the publication the *Book of Mormon* (1830). The following year he founded his new church at Fayette, New York. In 1844 he was arrested with his brother on charges of treason and conspiracy, and was murdered by a mob at the prison in Carthage, Illinois.

Smith, Sir Keith Macpherson (1890–1955) and **Sir Ross Macpherson** (1892–1922). Australian aviators, brothers, who made the first flight from England to Australia (1919).

Smith, Dame Maggie, born Margaret Natalie Smith (1934–). British actress. She joined the Old Vic company in 1959 and the National Theatre in 1963, establishing a reputation in both Shakespearean and modern roles. Among her many awards is an Academy Award as best actress in 1969 for *The Prime of Miss Jean Brodie.*

Smith, Stevie, pen name of Florence Margaret Smith (1902–1971). British poet, novelist, and artist. Her best-known collection of verse is *Not Waving but Drowning* (1957). Her novels include *Novel on Yellow Paper* (1936) and *The Holiday* (1949).

Smith, Wilbur (Addison) (1933–). South African novelist, born in Northern Rhodesia (now Zambia). Among his best-known works are *When the Lion Feeds* (1964) and *Shout at the Devil* (1968).

smith·er·eens (smíthə-reénz) *pl.n. Informal.* Fragments or splintered pieces; bits: *The dish broke into smithereens.* [Perhaps from Irish *smidirīn,* diminutive of *smiodar*†, small fragment.]

smith·er·y (smíthəri) *n., pl.* **-ies.** **1.** The occupation or craft of a smith. **2.** A smithy.

Smith·field (smíth-feeld). District in the northern part of the City of London, famous for its meat market. There has been a market on the site since the late 12th century. Smithfield is also the site of one of London's oldest hospitals, St. Bartholomew's, founded in 1123.

Smith·son (smíth-s'n), **James** (1765–1829). British chemist and mineralogist. He was elected to the Royal Society at the age of 22. He endowed the U.S. Smithsonian Institution in his will.

smith·son·ite (smíths'n-īt) *n.* A white or yellow-to-brown mineral, chiefly zinc carbonate (ZnCO₃), used as a source of zinc. Also called "dry-bone ore", "hemimorphite"; formerly called "calamine". [After James SMITHSON.]

smith·y (smíthi ‖ *U.S. also* smíthi) *n., pl.* **-ies.** A blacksmith's workshop; a forge. [Middle English *smythy,* from Old Norse *smidhja.*]

smock (smok) *n.* **1.** A loose shirtlike outer garment worn, as by artists, to protect the clothes while working. **2.** A similar garment, usually knee-length and often decorated with smocking, as worn formerly by farm labourers. Also called "smock frock". **3.** A loose dress gathered in below the bust rather than at the waist, worn especially by pregnant women.
~*tr.v.* **smocked, smocking, smocks.** To decorate (fabric) with smocking. [Middle English *smok,* women's undergarment, smock, Old English *smoc.*]

smock·ing (smócking) *n.* Needlework decoration accomplished by stitching small regularly spaced gathers into a honeycomb or diamond-shaped pattern. [From SMOCK (verb).]

smock mill *n.* A type of windmill in which the top part only, rather than the entire body, turns in the wind.

smog (smog ‖ *U.S. also* smawg) *n.* A thick, yellow fog over a built-up area, where soot dust promotes condensation, and sulphur dioxide acridity. [Blend of SMOKE and FOG.] —**smog·gy** *adj.*

smoke (smōk) *n.* **1.** Small particles of carbonaceous matter in the air from the incomplete combustion of wood, coal, or the like. **2.** A suspension of particles in a gaseous medium. **3.** Anything insubstantial, unreal, or transitory. **4. a.** An act of smoking any form of tobacco. **b.** *Informal.* Tobacco in any form that can be smoked; especially, a cigarette. **5.** Greyish blue to dark grey. —**the Smoke.** *British Slang.* London. Compare **big smoke.**
~*v.* **smoked, smoking, smokes.** —*intr.* **1. a.** To emit smoke or a smokelike substance. **b.** To emit smoke excessively. **2. a.** To draw in and exhale smoke from a cigarette, cigar, pipe, or the like. **b.** To do this habitually. —*tr.* **1.** To draw in and exhale the smoke of (burning tobacco, for example). **2.** To preserve or cure (meat or fish) by exposure to the smoke of burning wood. **3.** To fumigate. **4.** To expose (glass) to smoke in order to darken or change its colour. —**smoke out. 1.** To force out of a place of hiding or concealment by the use of smoke. **2.** To detect and bring to public view; expose; reveal. [Middle English, Old English *smoca.*]

smoke bomb *n.* A bomb that is designed to give out thick smoke upon exploding, used especially to provide cover or concealment.

smoke-dried (smók-drīd) *adj.* Cured in smoke. Said of fish or meat.

smoked rubber (smōkt) *n.* A crude, raw form of natural rubber made by coagulating latex with acid and drying sheets of it over wood fires.

smokeho. Variant of **smoko.**

smoke·house (smók-howss) *n.* A structure in which meat or fish is cured with smoke.

smoke·jack (smók-jak) *n.* A device for turning a roasting spit in a chimney, activated by the current of rising gases.

smoke·less (smók-ləss, -liss) *adj.* **1.** Emitting little or no smoke: *smokeless fuel.* **2.** Designating an area in which emission of smoke is prohibited by law.

smokeless powder *n.* A propellant charge composed mainly of nitrocellulose, which produces little or no smoke, used in projectiles and small artillery rockets.

smok·er (smókər) *n.* **1.** One that smokes. **2.** A section of a train carriage in which smoking is permitted. Also called "smoking compartment". **3.** An informal social gathering or entertainment.

smoker's cough *n.* A cough to which those who smoke are prone, characterised by a harsh, rasping sound and short convulsive movements of the body.

smoke screen *n.* **1.** A mass of dense artificial smoke used to conceal military areas or operations from an enemy. **2.** Any action or statement used to conceal plans or intentions.

smoke·stack (smók-stak) *n.* A large chimney through which combustion vapours, gases, and smoke are discharged.

smoke tree *n.* Either of two trees, *Cotinus coggygria,* of Eurasia or *C. obovatus,* of the southern United States, having plumelike clusters of small yellowish flowers. The latter species is also called "chittamwood". [The flower clusters resemble puffs of smoke.]

smok·ing jacket (smóking) *n.* A man's evening jacket, often made of a fine fabric, elaborately trimmed, and usually worn at home.

smoking room *n.* A room, as in a hotel, reserved for those who wish to smoke.

smo·ko, smoke·ho (smókō) *n.* *Australian and N.Z. Informal.* A tea or coffee break. [From SMOKE (noun).]

smok·y (smóki) *adj.* **-ier, -iest. 1.** Emitting smoke profusely. **2.** Full of smoke. **3.** Resembling or suggestive of smoke, especially in taste or colour. **4.** Darkened, stained, or discoloured by smoke. —**smok·i·ly** *adv.* —**smok·i·ness** *n.*

smoky quartz *n.* A mineral, **Cairngorm** *(see).*

smolder. *U.S.* Variant of **smoulder.**

Smo·lensk (smo-lénsk, smə-; *Russian* smul-yénsk). City in western Russia, on the river Dnepr. An important trade centre from the ninth century, it was held briefly by Poland (1611–54), France (1812), and Germany (1941–43). It is today a major railway junction with engineering and textile industries.

Smol·lett (smóllit), **Tobias (George)** (1721–71). Scottish novelist, one of the founders of the English novel. Among his works are *Peregrine Pickle* (1751) and *Humphry Clinker* (1771).

smolt (smōlt) *n.* A young salmon at the stage at which it turns silvery and migrates from fresh water to the sea. [Middle English,

obscurely related to Old English *smelt,* SMELT (fish).]

smooch (smōōch) *n. Slang.* A long, intimate kiss.
~*intr.v.* **smooched, smooching, smooches.** *Slang.* To kiss with a smooch. [From dialect *smouch* (imitative).]

smooth (smōōth) *adj.* **smoother, smoothest. 1. a.** Having a surface free from irregularities, roughness, or projections; even: *a smooth lawn.* **b.** Free from hair or bristles; soft. **2.** Having a surface whose roughness or projections have been worn level by use: *smooth tyres.* **3. a.** Having a fine, uniform consistency or texture; not lumpy: *smooth custard.* **b.** Free from harshness or acidity: *a smooth white wine.* **4. a.** Having an even or gentle motion: *a smooth drive.* **b.** Having flowing regularity: *smooth rhythm.* **5.** Having no obstructions or difficulties: *a smooth operation.* **6.** Having or showing an unruffled temperament; serene. **7.** Not harsh or coarse in sound; mellifluous. **8. a.** Polite and affable; polished. **b.** Excessively or suspiciously suave; plausible; persuasive: *a smooth talker.* **9.** *Phonetics.* Not aspirated. —See Synonyms at **level, suave.**
~ *v.* **smoothed, smoothing, smooths.** —*tr.* **1.** to make (something) even, level unwrinkled, or the like. Sometimes used with *out* or *down: smoothed down his hair.* **2. a.** To rid of obstructions, hindrances, difficulties, or the like: *smooth the way for a settlement.* **b.** To remove (obstructions or difficulties): *smooth away a problem.* **3.** To soothe or alleviate; make calm. Sometimes used with *over: smoothed over hurt feelings.* **4.** *Archaic.* To make less harsh or crude; refine. —*intr.* To become smooth.
~*n.* **1.** A smooth part or surface. **2.** The act of smoothing. [Middle English *smoth(e),* Old English *smóth;* akin to Old Saxon *smóthi†.*] —**smoothe** *v.* —**smooth·er** *n.* —**smooth·ly** *adv.* —**smooth·ness** *n.*

smooth·bore (smōōth-bawr ‖ -bōr) *adj.* Having an unrifled barrel. Said of a firearm.
~*n.* Also **smooth bore.** A firearm having no rifling.

smooth breathing *n.* **1.** The symbol (') written over some initial vowels in Greek, that in classical Greek indicated that they were not aspirated. **2.** The absence of aspiration so indicated.

smooth·en (smōōth'n) *v.* **-ened, -ening, -ens.** —*tr.* To smooth. —*intr.* To become smooth.

smooth-hound (smōōth-hownd) *n.* A **hound shark** *(see).*

smooth·ie (smōōthi) *n. Informal.* One who is smooth and charming, sometimes excessively so, as when socialising with members of the opposite sex.

smooth muscle *n.* The unstriated involuntary muscle of the internal organs, as of the intestine, bladder, and blood vessels, excluding the heart.

smooth snake *n.* A common, small, European snake, *Coronella austriaca,* whose young hatch immediately from newly laid eggs.

smooth-talk (smōōth-tawk) *tr.v.* **-talked, -talking, -talks.** *Informal.* To make or persuade by means of plausible, persuasive talk.

smor·gas·bord (smór-gəss-bawrd, smúr- ‖ bōrd) *n.* Also *Swedish* **smör·gås·bord** (smörgawss-boord). A meal consisting of a varied number of dishes, such as salads, cheeses, and pâté, served buffet-style. [Swedish *smörgåsbord* : *smörgås,* (open-faced) sandwich, bread and butter : *smör,* butter, from Old Norse *smör, smjör,* fat + *gås,* goose, piece of butter, from Old Norse *gās* + *bord,* table, from Old Norse *bordh.*]

smote. Past tense and alternative past participle of **smite.**

smoth·er (smúthər ‖ smóthər) *v.* **-ered, -ering, -ers.** —*tr.* **1. a.** To suffocate (a person or animal) by depriving of air. **b.** To deprive (a fire) of the oxygen necessary for it to burn. **2.** To conceal, suppress, or hide: *smothered a yawn; smothered the report.* **3.** To cover (a foodstuff) thickly with another foodstuff: *smothered the chips with vinegar.* **4.** To overwhelm, as with kisses or affection. —*intr.* **1.** To suffocate. **2.** To be concealed, stifled, or suppressed.
~*n.* **1.** Anything that smothers, such as a dense cloud of smoke or dust or a spray of spume. **2.** A disordered mass or confusion. **3.** *Archaic.* A state of smouldering, as in coals or ashes. [Middle English *smotheren, smortheren,* from *smorther,* a smother, from Old English *smorian†,* to suffocate, smother.] —**smoth·er·y** *adj.*

smoul·der, *U.S.* **smol·der** (smóldər) *intr.v.* **-dered, -dering, -ders. 1.** To burn or smoke slowly without flame. **2.** To exist in a hidden or suppressed state. **3.** To manifest repressed anger, hatred, or the like: *eyes smouldering with revenge.*
~*n.* A fire burning slowly with smoke but without flame.

smudge (smuj) *v.* **smudged, smudging, smudges.** —*tr.* **1.** To make a small, dirty mark on. **2.** To smear or blur (writing, for example). **3.** *U.S.* To fill (an orchard or other planted area) with dense smoke from a smudge pot in order to prevent damage from insects or frost. —*intr.* **1.** To make a smudge, as with dirt, soot, or ink. **2.** To become smudged.
~*n.* **1.** A dirty mark, blotch or smear. **2.** *U.S.* A smoky fire used as a protection against insects or frost. [Middle English *smogen†.*] —**smudg·i·ly** *adv.* —**smudg·i·ness** *n.* —**smudg·y** *adj.*

smudge pot *n. U.S.* A receptacle in which oil or other smoky fuel is burned, as to protect an orchard from insects or frost or to indicate wind direction.

smug (smug) *adj.* **smugger, smuggest.** Pleased with oneself; complacent; self-satisfied. [Probably from Low German *smuck,* neat, smooth, sleek, from Middle Low German, from *smucken,* to adorn.] —**smug·ly** *adv.* —**smug·ness** *n.*

smug·gle (smúgg'l) *v.* **-gled, -gling, -gles.** —*tr.* **1.** To import or export without paying lawful customs charges or duties. **2.** To bring in or take out illicitly or by stealth. **3.** To place in concealment; hide. Often used with *away.* —*intr.* To engage in smuggling.

[Earlier *smuckle,* from Low German *smukkelen, smuggeln* and Dutch *smokkelen.*] —**smug·gler** *n.*

smut (smut) *n.* **1. a.** A particle or flake of soot or dirt. **b.** A dirty mark or smudge made by soot, smoke, or dirt. **2.** Obscenity, or obscene matter for reading or viewing. **3. a.** Any of various plant diseases, particularly affecting cereals, caused by fungi of the order Ustilaginales and producing black, powdery masses of spores on the affected parts. **b.** A fungus causing such a disease.
~*v.* **smutted, smutting, smuts.** —*tr.* **1.** To blacken or smudge, as with smoke or grime. **2.** To affect (a plant) with smut. **3.** To free (grain, for example) from smut. —*intr.* To become affected with smut, as a plant may. [Perhaps from Low German *smutt†.*] —**smut·ti·ly** *adv.* —**smut·ti·ness** *n.* —**smut·ty** *adj.*

smutch (smuch) *tr.v.* **smutched, smutching, smutches.** *Archaic.* To soil, stain, or besmirch.
~*n. Archaic.* A stain or spot of dirt. [Variant of SMUDGE.] —**smutch·y** *adj.*

Smuts (smuts, smŏts), **Jan (Christiaan)** (1870–1950). South African statesman. He was a lawyer and political journalist before becoming a general in the Second Anglo-Boer War (1899–1902). He later became prime minister of the Union of South Africa (1919–24, 1939–48). He was an early proponent of a British Commonwealth, and a prime mover in the formation of the League of Nations; and he later drafted the preamble to the declaration of human rights that was included in the Charter for the United Nations Organisation.

Smyrna. See **Izmir.**

Sn The symbol for the element tin. [Latin *stannum.*]

snack (snak) *n.* **1.** A hurried or light meal. **2.** A small amount of food eaten between meals.
~*intr.v.* **snacked, snacking, snacks.** *U.S.* To eat a hurried or light meal. [Middle English *snake,* a snatch with the teeth, bite (especially of a dog), from Middle Dutch *snac(k);* akin to SNAP.]

snack bar *n.* A café or counter where light meals are served.

snaf·fle (snáff'l) *n.* A bit for a horse, consisting of two bars jointed at the centre. Also called "snafflebit".
~*tr.v.* **snaffled, -fling, -fles. 1.** *British Informal.* To take, seize, or steal. **2.** To put a snaffle on or control with a snaffle. [Probably from Low Dutch; compare Middle Dutch *snavel,* beak, nose.]

sna·fu (sna-fōō) *adj. U.S. Slang.* In a state of complete confusion.
~*tr.v.* **snafued, -fuing, -fus.** *U.S. Slang.* To make chaotic or confused.
~*n., pl.* **snafus.** *U.S. Slang.* Any chaotic or confused situation. [Situation normal: *all fucked up.*]

snag (snag) *n.* **1.** Any rough, sharp, or jagged protuberance, such as: **a.** A tree or a part of a tree that protrudes above the surface in a body of water, and is hazardous to shipping. **b.** The stump of a broken off branch. **c.** An unaligned or broken tooth; a snaggletooth. **2.** A break, pull, or tear in a fabric that has been caught on a snag. **3.** An obstacle or difficulty, especially one that is unforeseen or hidden. —See Synonyms at **obstacle.**
~*tr.v.* **snagged, snagging, snags. 1. a.** To hinder, obstruct, or impede by or as if by a snag. **b.** To tear or catch on a snag. **2.** To free or clear of snags. **3.** *U.S. Informal.* To catch unexpectedly and quickly. [Probably from Scandinavian, akin to Old Norse *snagi†,* peg.] —**snag·gy** *adj.*

snag·gle·tooth (snágg'l-tōōth ‖ -tŏŏth) *n., pl.* **-teeth** (-teeth). A tooth that is broken or out of alignment. [From dialectal *snaggled,* snaggletoothed, from SNAG.] —**snag·gle·toothed** (-t) *adj.*

snail (snayl) *n.* **1.** Any of numerous aquatic or terrestrial molluscs of the class Gastropoda, characteristically having a spirally coiled shell, a broad retractile foot, and a distinct head. **2.** A slow-moving or lazy person. [Middle English, Old English *snæg(e)l, sneg(e)l.*]

snail mail *n.* Ordinary mail held to be as slow as a snail compared to e-mail or faxes.

snail's pace *n.* A very slow pace or rate of progress.

snake (snayk) *n.* **1.** Any of various scaly, legless, sometimes venomous reptiles of the suborder Serpentes, having a long, tapering, cylindrical body. **2.** *Capital* **S.** The constellation **Hydra** (see). **3.** A treacherous person. **4.** A long, highly flexible metal wire used for cleaning drains. —**the Snake.** An agreement between member countries of the European Economic Community whereby the exchange rates of their respective currencies are allowed to fluctuate against each other only within relatively narrow limits.
~*v.* **snaked, snaking, snakes.** —*tr.* To follow (a course) in the manner of a snake. —*intr.* To move with a sinuous, snakelike motion. [Middle English, Old English *snaca.*]

Snake (snayk). River in northwest United States. It rises in Yellowstone National Park, Wyoming, and flows 1 670 kilometres (1,038 miles) westwards to join the Columbia river near Pasco.

snake·bird (snáyk-burd) *n.* Any of several long-necked, long-billed birds of the genus *Anhinga.* [From its elongated, snakelike neck.]

snake·bite (snáyk-bīt) *n.* **1.** The bite of a snake. **2.** Poisoning resulting from the bite of a venomous snake.

snake charmer *n.* An entertainer who, through music and bodily movements, causes a snake to dance or perform simple tricks.

snake dance *n.* **1.** A dance performed as part of a biennial religious ceremony of the Hopi Indians, in which the dancers carry live rattlesnakes in their mouths. **2.** *U.S.* An informal procession of persons who join hands and move forward in a zigzag line.

snake fly *n.* Any of various predatory insects of the family Raphidiidae having an elongated, snakelike neck.

snake in the grass *n.* A false friend or lurking danger.

snake mackerel *n.* A fish, the **escolar** *(see).*

snake plant *n.* Any of several tropical Old World plants of the genus *Sansevieria,* having narrow, rigid, often mottled leaves and widely cultivated as a house plant.

snake-root (snáyk-rōōt ‖ -rŏŏt) *n.* Any of various plants having roots or rhizomes reputed to cure snakebite.

snakes and ladders *n. Used with a singular verb.* A board game in which each player throws dice to advance a counter to the finish. Landing on the foot or head of any of the pictured ladders and snakes speeds up or retards progress respectively.

snakes·head (snáyks-hed) *n.* A plant, the **fritillary** *(see).*

snake·skin (snáyk-skin) *n.* The skin of a snake, especially when prepared as leather.

snake·weed (snáyk-weed) *n.* Any of various plants reputed to cure snakebite; especially, **bistort** *(see).*

snak·y (snáyki) *adj.* **-ier, -iest. 1.** Pertaining to or characteristic of snakes. **2.** Having the form or movement of a snake; serpentine. **3.** Overrun with snakes. **4.** Treacherous; sly. **5.** *Australian Informal.* Annoyed; tetchy. —**snak·i·ly** *adv.* —**snak·i·ness** *n.*

snap (snap) *v.* **snapped, snapping, snaps.** —*intr.* **1.** To make a brisk, sharp, cracking sound. **2.** To break suddenly with such a sound. **3.** To give way abruptly under pressure or tension: *The weight of responsibility made her nerves snap.* **4.** To bring the jaws briskly together, often with a clicking sound; bite or attempt to bite. Often used with *at.* **5.** To snatch or grasp eagerly. Often used with *up* or *at.* **6.** To speak abruptly or irritably. Often used with *at.* **7.** To move swiftly and smartly: *snap to attention.* **8.** To open or close with a click: *The lock snapped shut.* —*tr.* **1.** To snatch at with or as if with the teeth; bite. **2.** To cause to come apart or break with a snapping sound. **3.** To utter abruptly or irritably: *snapped out an order* **4. a.** To cause to emit a snapping sound: *snap a whip.* **b.** To cause to move into place or close with a snapping sound. **5.** To pick up or get hold of quickly and smartly. Often used with *up: snapped up a bargain.* **6. a.** To take (a photograph). **b.** To take a photograph of. **7.** In American football, to move (the ball) backwards to put it into play. —**snap out of it.** *Informal.* To recover quickly from a state of depression or a bad mood.
~*n.* **1.** A sudden, sharp, cracking sound or the action producing such a sound. **2.** A sudden breaking of something brittle, such as a twig. **3.** A clasp, catch, or other fastening device that operates with a snapping sound. **4.** A sudden attempt to bite, snatch, or grasp. **5. a.** The sound produced by rapid movement of the second finger pressed down from the tip of the thumb to its base. **b.** The act of producing this sound. **6.** A curt or irritable retort or manner of speech: *answered me with a snap.* **7.** A thin, crisp biscuit: *a ginger snap.* **8.** *Informal.* Briskness, liveliness, or energy. **9.** A brief spell of cold weather. **10.** A snapshot. **11.** *British.* A card game in which the player who first notices that two cards, which have been turned up from two packs, have an equal value says "snap", and thus wins all the cards turned up. **12.** *U.S. Informal.* An effortless task; a snip.
~*adj.* **1.** Made, done, or brought about on the spur of the moment, with little warning or consideration: *a snap decision; a snap election.* **2.** Fastening with a snap. Said of a locking device.
~*interj. British.* **1.** Used by a player in the game of snap. **2.** Used to express one's realisation of the similarity of two things.
~*adv.* With a snap. [Partly from Middle Low German or Middle Dutch *snappen,* to seize, speak hastily; partly imitative.]

snap bean *n. Chiefly U.S.* A bean, such as the **string bean** *(see),* cultivated for its unripe, crisp pods.

snap-brim (snáp-brim) *n.* A hat having a flexible brim, usually turned down in front and up at the back.

snap·drag·on (snáp-draggan) *n.* Any of several plants of the genera *Antirrhinum* or *Misopates;* especially, *A. majus,* of the Mediterranean region, having clusters of two-lipped, variously coloured flowers. [From a fanciful likening of the flower to a dragon's mouth.]

snap fastener *n. Chiefly U.S.* A **press stud** *(see).*

snap·per (snáppər) *n., pl.* **snappers** or collectively **snapper** (for senses 2, 3, and 4). **1.** One that snaps. **2.** Any of numerous widely distributed marine fishes of the family Lutjanidae. **3.** A large, red carnivorous Australian fish of the genus Pagrosomus. **4.** A New World freshwater turtle of the family Chelydridae whose jaws snap shut on its prey. Also called "snapping turtle".

snapping beetle *n.* The **click beetle** *(see).*

snap·pish (snáppish) *adj.* **1.** Liable to snap or bite, as a dog might be. **2.** Liable to speak sharply or curtly; irritable; curt. —**snap·pish·ly** *adv.* —**snap·pish·ness** *n.*

snap·py (snáppi) *adj.* **-pier, -piest. 1.** *Informal.* Lively or energetic; brisk. **2.** *Informal.* Smart or chic in appearance. **3.** Snappish. —**make it snappy.** *Informal.* Be quick; hurry up. —**snap·pi·ly** *adv.* —**snap·pi·ness** *n.*

snap ring *n.* In mountaineering, an oval-shaped or pear-shaped steel ring which is snapped to the eye of a piton and through which a rope is run.

snap roll *n.* An aerial manoeuvre in which an aircraft is put through a sharp roll of 360 degrees about its longitudinal axis.

snap·shot (snáp-shot) *n.* An informal photograph taken with a small hand-held camera.

snare¹ (snair) *n.* **1.** A trapping device, often consisting of a noose, used for capturing birds and small animals. **2.** Anything that serves to entangle, trap, or catch out the unwary. **3.** A surgical instrument with a wire loop controlled by a mechanism in the handle, used to remove growths, such as tumours and polyps.

~*tr.v.* **snared, snaring, snares. 1.** To trap (an animal) with a snare. **2.** To entrap or ensare. [Middle English, Old English *sneare,* from Old Norse *snara.*] **—snar·er** *n.*

snare² *n.* **1.** Any of the wires or cords stretched across the lower skin of a snare drum to increase reverberation. **2.** A snare drum. [Probably from Middle Dutch, string.]

snare drum *n.* A small double-headed drum having a snare or snares stretched across the lower head to increase reverberation.

snarl¹ (snarl) *v.* **snarled, snarling, snarls.** *—intr.* **1.** To growl viciously while baring the teeth. **2.** To speak angrily or threateningly. *—tr.* To utter with anger or hostility.

~*n.* **1.** A vicious growl. **2.** Any vicious or hostile utterance or expression. [From obsolete *snar,* to snarl, from Middle Low German *snarren.*] **—snarl·er** *n.* **—snarl·ing·ly** *adv.* **—snarl·y** *adj.*

snarl² *n.* **1.** A tangled mass, as of hair or yarn. **2.** Any confused, complicated, or tangled situation.

~*v.* **snarled, snarling, snarls.** *—intr.* To become tangled or confused. *—tr.* **1.** To tangle or knot (hair or yarn, for example). **2.** To bring into a confused or tangled condition. Often used with *up: Traffic was snarled up at the lights.* [Middle English *snarle*; perhaps akin to SNARE (trap).] **—snarl·er** *n.* **—snarl·y** *adj.*

snarl-up (snárl-up) *n. British Informal.* A situation in which there is confusion, obstruction, or entanglement: *a traffic snarl-up.*

snatch (snach) *v.* **snatched, snatching, snatches.** *—tr.* **1.** To grasp or seize abruptly or violently: *snatched her handbag.* **2.** To take, get, or obtain hurriedly, unexpectedly, or improperly: *snatch a bite to eat; snatched a goal in the closing minutes.* **3.** To rescue or save opportunely: *snatched from death.* *—intr.* To seize or grasp, or attempt to seize or grasp. Used with *at: snatched at the chance.*

~*n.* **1.** The act or an action of snatching; a quick grasp or grab. **2.** A brief period of time: *slept in snatches.* **3.** A small amount; a bit or fragment: *a snatch of dialogue.* **4.** In weightlifting, a lift in which one raises the weight from the floor to above one's head in one movement. **5.** *British Informal.* A robbery: *a wages snatch.* **6.** *U.S. Slang.* A kidnapping. [Middle English *snacchen, snecchen*†, to make a sudden gesture.] **—snatch·er** *n.*

snatch block *n. Nautical.* A block that can be opened on one side to receive the looped part of a rope.

snatch·y (snáchi) *adj.* **-ier, -iest.** Occurring in snatches; intermittent; spasmodic.

snaz·zy (snázzi) *adj. Informal.* **-zier, -ziest.** Smooth, fashionable, or flashy. [Perhaps a blend of SNAPPY and JAZZY.]

sneak (sneek) *v.* **sneaked** or *U.S. nonstandard* **snuck** (snuk), **sneaking, sneaks.** *—intr.* **1.** To go or move in a quiet, stealthy way; slink: *sneaked out of the meeting.* **2.** To behave in a furtive or cowardly manner. **3.** *British Slang.* To tell tales or inform on others. *—tr.* **1.** To move, give, take, or put in a quiet, stealthy manner: *sneak a chocolate into one's mouth.* **2.** *Informal.* To steal.

~*n.* **1.** One who sneaks; a stealthy, cowardly, or underhand person. **2.** *Chiefly U.S.* An instance of sneaking, such as a stealthy movement. **3.** *British Slang.* One who tells tales or sneaks.

~*adj.* Acting with or involving secrecy, stealth, or surprise: *a sneak attack.* [Of dialectal origin, perhaps ultimately akin to Old English *snīcan,* to crawl, Old Norse *snīkja*†.]

sneak·er (snéekər) *n.* **1.** One who sneaks. **2.** *Chiefly U.S.* A canvas shoe with a soft rubber sole.

sneak·ing (snéeking) *adj.* **1.** Acting in a stealthy, furtive way. **2.** Unavowed; secret: *a sneaking affection.* **3.** Gradually growing or persistent: *a sneaking suspicion.* **—sneak·ing·ly** *adv.*

sneak preview *n.* **1.** *Informal.* A chance or opportunity to see something before it is on public view: *was given a sneak preview of her new dress.* **2.** *U.S.* A single showing of a film prior to its general release, usually as an addition to an announced programme.

sneak thief *n.* A burglar who enters without breaking in.

sneak·y (snéeki) *adj.* **-ier, -iest.** Furtive, underhand, or deceitful. **—sneak·i·ly** *adv.* **—sneak·i·ness** *n.*

sneer (sneer) *n.* **1.** A scornful facial expression characterised by a slight raising of one corner of the upper lip. **2.** Any contemptuous facial expression, sound, or statement.

~*v.* **sneered, sneering, sneers.** *—tr.* To utter with a sneer or in a sneering manner. *—intr.* **1.** To assume a sneer to express a scornful, contemptuous, or derisive attitude: *sneered at his amateur efforts.* **2.** To speak or write in a scornful, contemptuous, or derisive manner. [16th century : perhaps from Low Dutch *sneere*†.] **—sneer·er** *n.* **—sneer·ful** *adj.* **—sneer·ing·ly** *adv.*

sneeze (sneez) *intr.v.* **sneezed, sneezing, sneezes.** To expel air forcibly from the mouth and nose in an explosive, spasmodic, involuntary action resulting from irritation, as from dust, in the nose. **—sneeze at.** *Informal.* To dismiss lightly; consider as of little worth. Used in negative statements: *an offer not to be sneezed at.*

~*n.* An instance of sneezing. [Middle English *snesen,* misreading of obsolete *fnesen,* Old English *fnēosan* (unattested), from Old Norse *fnȳsa* (imitative).] **—sneez·er** *n.* **—sneez·y** *adj.*

sneeze·wort (snéez-wurt || -wawrt) *n.* A plant, *Achillea ptarmica,* native to Europe, having loosely clustered, daisy-like white flowers. [The dried leaves were used to induce sneezing.]

Snell's Law (snelz) *n. Physics.* The principle that in refraction of a light ray at a boundary between two mediums, the sine of the angle of incidence divided by the sine of the angle of refraction at the boundary is a constant for the given mediums. [After Willebrord *Snell* van Royen (1591–1626), Dutch physicist.]

snib (snib) *tr.v.* **snibbed, snibbing, snibs.** *Chiefly Scottish.* To bolt (a door).

~*n.* A latch or bolt. [Origin obscure.]

snick (snik) *tr.v.* **snicked, snicking, snicks. 1.** To make a cut or notch in. **2.** In cricket, to hit (a ball) off the edge of the bat.

~*n.* **1.** A small cut, notch or incision. **2.** In cricket, a hit in which the ball is snicked. [Perhaps from SNICKERSNEE, or perhaps from Scandinavian; compare Old Norse *snikka,* to whittle.]

snick·er (sníckər) *n.* **1.** A whinny. **2.** *Chiefly U.S.* A snigger.

~*intr.v.* **snickered, -ering, -ers.** To make a snicker. [Imitative.] **—snick·er·ing·ly** *adv.*

snick·er·snee (sníckər-snée || *chiefly U.S.* -snee) *n.* A large knife resembling a sword. Used humorously. [Earlier *stick or snee,* a fight with knives : Dutch *steken,* to stick, stab, from Middle Dutch + *snijden,* to cut, from Middle Dutch *snīden.*]

snide (snīd) *adj.* **1.** Derogatory in a malicious, superior way; sarcastic. **2.** Fake; counterfeit. [19th century (cant) : origin obscure.]

sniff (snif) *v.* **sniffed, sniffing, sniffs.** *—intr.* **1.** To inhale a short, audible breath through the nose, as in smelling something or stopping one's nose from running. **2.** To indicate ridicule, contempt, or doubt by or as if by sniffing. Often used with *at.* *—tr.* **1.** To inhale (a powdered drug, for example) forcibly through the nose. **2.** To smell or try to smell by sniffing. **3.** To perceive or detect by or as if by sniffing. **4.** To utter contemptuously, with or as if with a sniff.

~*n.* **1.** An instance or the sound of sniffing. **2.** Anything that is sniffed or perceived by sniffing; an odour; a whiff. [Middle English *sniffen* (imitative).]

snif·fle (sníff'l) *intr.v.* **-fled, -fling, -fles.** To breathe audibly through a congested nose, as when crying or suffering from a cold.

~*n.* **1.** An act or sound of sniffling. **2.** *Plural. Informal.* A condition, such as a head cold, accompanied by sniffles. Preceded by *the.* [Frequentative of SNIFF.]

snif·fy (sníffi) *adj.* **-fier, -fiest.** *Informal.* Disposed to showing arrogance or contempt; haughty; disdainful.

snif·ter (sníftər) *n.* **1.** *Slang.* A small amount of an alcoholic drink. **2.** *U.S.* A pear-shaped glass with a narrow top, as used in serving brandy. [From dialectal *snifter,* to sniff, perhaps from Scandinavian; compare Middle Swedish *snypta,* Middle Danish *snyfte.*]

snig·ger (sníggər) *n.* A snide, slightly stifled laugh.

~*v.* **sniggered, -gering, -gers.** *—intr.* To utter a snigger. *—tr.* To express by means of a snigger. [Variant of SNICKER.]

snip (snip) *v.* **snipped, snipping, snips.** *—tr.* To cut, clip, or separate in a short, quick stroke or strokes with scissors or shears. *—intr.* To cut or clip with short, quick strokes.

~*n.* **1.** An act of snipping or the sound produced by snipping. **2. a.** A small cut made with scissors or shears. **b.** A small piece cut or clipped off. **3.** *Informal.* **a.** Something accomplished without difficulty. **b.** *British.* A bargain. **4.** *Plural.* Small shears used in cutting sheet metal. Also called "tinsnips". **5.** *U.S. Informal.* A small, insignificant person or thing, especially one that is irritating. [Low German or Dutch *snippen,* to snap (imitative).]

snipe (snīp) *n., pl.* **snipe** or **snipes. 1.** Any of various long-billed wading birds of the genus *Gallinago;* especially, the common, widely distributed species *G. gallinago.* **2.** Any of various similar or related birds. **3.** A shot or gunshot from a concealed place.

~*intr.v.* **sniped, sniping, snipes. 1.** To shoot at individuals from a concealed place. Often used with *at.* **2.** To direct snide, carping criticism, especially from a safe position. Often used with *at.* [Middle English, perhaps from Old Norse *(mýri)snīpa*†, (moor) snipe.]

snipe fish *n.* Any fish of the family Macrorhamphosidae, having a long snout.

snipe fly *n.* Any of various two-winged predatory flies of the family Rhagionidae.

snip·er (snīpər) *n.* One who shoots at people from a concealed place, especially a marksman detailed to pick off enemy soldiers.

snip·pet (Snippit) *n.* A small piece; a fragment. [Diminutive of SNIP.]

snitch (snich) *v.* **snitched, snitching, snitches.** *Slang.* *—tr.* To steal (especially something of little value). *—intr.* To turn informer. Usually used with *on.*

~*n. Slang.* **1.** An informer; a sneak. **2.** The nose. [17th century (in the sense, nose, to strike the nose) : origin obscure.]

sniv·el (snívv'l) *intr.v.* **-elled** or *U.S.* **-eled, -elling** or *U.S.* **-eling, -els. 1.** To cry or weep with sniffling. **2.** To speak or whine tearfully. **3.** To run at the nose. **4.** To sniffle.

~*n.* **1.** The act or an instance of sniffling or snivelling. **2.** Nasal mucus. [Middle English *snevelen,* Old English *snyflan* (unattested), akin to *snyflung, snofl,* mucus.] **—sniv·el·er, sniv·el·ler** *n.*

snob (snob) *n.* **1.** One who overvalues rank and status, and despises his supposed inferiors. **2.** An arrogant or affected person who strives to flatter, imitate, or associate with people of higher status or prestige. **3.** One who has or affects refined or esoteric tastes in cultural matters, and who despises anything that does not match these standards. [18th century (meaning "shoemaker", now dialect) : origin obscure.] **—snob·ber·y, snob·bism** *n.* **—snob·bish** *adj.* **—snob·bish·ly** *adv.* **—snob·bish·ness** *n.*

Sno-cat (snṓ-kat) *n.* A trademark for a type of snowmobile.

snoek (snŏŏk) *n. South African.* An edible fish, the **barracuda** *(see),* often dried and salted and eaten cold. [Afrikaans. See **snook¹**.]

snog (snog) *intr.v.* **snogged, snogging, snogs.** *British Informal.* To kiss and cuddle.

~*n.* An act of snogging. [20th century : origin obscure.]

snood (snŏŏd) *n.* **1.** A small netlike cap worn by women to keep the hair in place. **2.** A headband or fillet.

~*tr.v.* **snooded, snooding, snoods.** To hold (the hair) in place with a snood. [Middle English (unattested), Old English *snōd*†.]

snook¹ (snŏŏk ‖ snŏŏk) *n., pl.* **snook** or **snooks.** Any of several chiefly marine fishes of the family Centropomidae; especially, *Centropomus undecimalis,* of warm Atlantic waters. Also called "robalo". [Dutch *snoek,* pike, from Middle Dutch *snoec*†.]

snook² (snŏŏk, snŏŏk) *n. British.* A deliberately offensive gesture signifying contempt or disrespect, made by putting the thumb to the nose, with the fingers stretched out; an act of thumbing the nose. **—cock a snook. 1.** To make such a gesture. **2.** To show contempt or disrespect. [19th century : origin obscure.]

snoo·ker (snŏŏkər ‖ *chiefly U.S.* snŏŏkər) *n.* **1.** A game played on a billiard table with 15 red balls and 6 others of different colours, each becoming, in a fixed order, the object ball which must be hit into one of the side pockets by the cue ball, which is white. **2.** A position in this game in which the cue ball is so placed that a player cannot hit the object ball directly.

~tr.v. **snookered, -kering, -kers. 1.** To make (one's opponent) play from the position of a snooker. **2.** To put in a difficult or impossible position; prevent from succeeding; thwart. [Perhaps from British army slang *snooker,* new cadet, the game being invented by British Army officers in India in 1875.]

snoop (snŏŏp) *intr.v.* **snooped, snooping, snoops.** *Informal.* To pry into the private affairs of others, especially by prowling about.

~n. Informal. One who snoops. [Dutch *snoepen,* to eat on the sly.] **—snoop·er** *n.*

snoop·y (snŏŏpi) *adj.* **-ier, -iest.** *Informal.* Tending to snoop; prying.

snoot (snŏŏt) *n. Slang.* The nose. [Variant of SNOUT.]

snoot·y (snŏŏti) *adj.* **-ier, -iest.** *Informal.* Snobbish or aloof; haughty. [20th century : origin obscure.]

snooze (snŏŏz) *intr.v.* **snoozed, snoozing, snoozes.** *Informal.* To take a light nap; doze.

~n. Informal. A brief light sleep. [18th century (cant) : origin obscure.]

snore (snor ‖ snôr) *intr.v.* **snored, snoring, snores.** To make snorting noises caused by the vibration of the soft palate, by breathing through both nose and mouth while sleeping.

~n. An instance of snoring or the noise produced by snoring. [Middle English *snoren,* to snort (probably imitative).] **—snor·er** *n.*

snor·kel (snôrk'l, *also* shnôrk'l) *n.* **1.** A retractable vertical tube in a submarine, containing air-intake and exhaust pipes for the engines and for ventilation and which permits extended periods of submergence at periscope depth. **2.** A breathing apparatus used by skin divers, consisting of a long tube held in the mouth which projects above the surface of the water.

~intr.v. **snorkelled** or *U.S.* **-keled, -kelling** or *U.S.* **-keling, -kels.** To swim under water using a snorkel. [German *Schnorchel,* from (dialectal) German, snout, from *schnarchen,* to snore, from Middle High German *snarche(l)n.*]

Snor·ri Stur·lu·son (snórri stúrləss'n) (1178–1241). Icelandic chieftain and historian. His works include *Heimskringla,* a series of sagas, and the Younger or Prose *Edda.*

snort (snort) *v.* **snorted, snorting, snorts.** *—intr.* **1. a.** To exhale forcibly and noisily through the nostrils, as a horse does. **b.** To inhale forcibly through the nose or mouth and so produce from the soft palate a vibratory snoring noise. **2.** To express scorn, ridicule, or contempt with or as if with a snort. **3.** *Informal.* To emit a loud outburst of laughter. *—tr.* **1.** To express with a snort. **2.** To eject from the nostrils with or as with a snort. **3.** *Slang.* To inhale (a powdered drug, such as cocaine) through the nose.

~n. **1.** The act or sound of snorting. **2.** *Slang.* A small alcoholic drink, especially when swallowed in one gulp. [Middle English *snorten* (imitative).]

snort·er (snórtər) *n.* **1.** One that snorts. **2.** *Informal.* Anything that is outstanding, as in size, appearance, or severity.

snot (snot) *n.* **1.** Nasal mucus; phlegm. Often considered vulgar. **2.** *Slang.* A nasty or contemptible person. [Middle English *snot(te),* from Low German *snotte,* or from Old English *gesnot;* akin to SNOUT.]

snot·rag (snót-rag) *n. British Slang.* A handkerchief.

snot·ty (snótti) *adj.* **-tier, -tiest.** *Slang.* **1.** Dirtied with nasal mucus. **2. a.** Nasty; unpleasant. **b.** Snooty; self-important.

snout (snowt) *n.* **1.** The projecting nose, jaws, or front part of an animal's muzzle. **2.** A similar extended front part of the head in certain insects, such as weevils. **3.** A spout, nozzle, or similar projection likened to a snout. **4.** *Slang.* The human nose. [Middle English *sn(o)ute,* probably from Middle Dutch *snūt(e).*]

snout beetle *n.* A weevil (*see*).

snow (snō) *n.* **1. a.** Solid precipitation in the form of small white or translucent ice crystals of various shapes originating in the atmosphere as frozen particles of water vapour. **b.** A mass of fallen snow lying on the ground: *children playing in the snow.* **2. a.** Anything resembling snow, such as frozen carbon dioxide. **b.** The white specks on a television screen resulting from weak reception. **3.** A fall of snow. **4.** *Slang.* Cocaine or heroin in powdered form.

~v. **snowed, snowing, snows.** *—intr.* To fall as snow. *—tr.* **1.** To cover, shut off, or close in with snow. Used with *in, over, under,* or *up.* **2.** *Chiefly U.S. Slang.* To overwhelm with insincere talk, especially with flattery. **—snow under.** To overwhelm, especially with work. [Middle English *snawe, snow,* Old English *snāw.*]

Snow (snō), **C(harles) P(ercy), Baron** (1905–80). British novelist, noted for his interest in the "two cultures" of science and the humanities. His long, semi-autobiographical novel sequence *Strangers and Brothers* includes such works as *The Masters* (1951) and *The*

Corridors of Power (1964). He became a senior civil servant and parliamentary secretary in the ministry of technology (1964–66).

snow·ball (snō-bawl) *n.* **1.** A mass of soft, wet snow packed into a ball that can be thrown, as in play. **2.** A drink consisting of advocaat and lemonade.

~v. **snowballed, -balling, -balls.** *—intr.* **1.** To throw snowballs. **2.** To grow rapidly and uncontrollably, as in size or significance, like a snowball rolling over snow. *—tr.* To throw snowballs at.

snowball tree *n.* The cultivated variety of the guelder rose, having ball-like clusters of sterile flowers.

snow·ber·ry (snō-bri, -bəri, -berri) *n., pl.* **-ries.** Any of various shrubs of the genus *Symphoricarpos;* especially, *S. rivularis,* having small pinkish flowers and white berries.

snow·bird (snō-burd) *n.* **1.** Any of several birds, such as the junco, seen mainly in winter conditions. **2.** Any white or partly white bird, such as the snow bunting.

snow blindness *n.* Usually temporary conjunctivitis and deteriorated vision caused by sunlight reflected from snow or ice. **—snow·blind** (snō-blīnd) *adj.*

snow·blink (snō-blingk) *n.* A white glow in the sky reflected from snowfields.

snow·bound (snō-bownd) *adj.* Confined in one place by heavy snow; snowed-in.

snow·broth (snō-broth ‖ -brawth) *n.* Melted snow; slush.

snow bunting *n.* A bird, *Plectrophenax nivalis,* of northern regions, having black and white plumage in the male.

snow·cap (snō-kap) *n.* A cap of snow, as on a mountaintop. **—snow·capped** *adj.*

snow chain *n.* A linked metal covering for a tyre, used for improved grip on snowy or icy surfaces. Also called "tyre chain".

Snow·don (snōd'n). *Welsh* **Yr Wydd·fa** (ər ŏŏ-ithvə). Highest peak in Wales, situated in northwestern Wales, in the Snowdon range. The summit rises to 1 085 metres (3,560 feet) and can be reached by a rack and pinion railway. The scenic surrounding area has been a part of the Snowdonia National Park since 1951.

Snowdon, Anthony (Charles Robert) Armstrong-Jones, Earl of (1930–). British photographer. He married Princess Margaret in 1960. They were divorced in 1978.

snow·drift (snō-drift) *n.* A bank of snow heaped up by the wind.

snow·drop (snō-drop) *n.* Any of several bulbous plants of the genus *Galanthus,* native to Eurasia; especially *G. nivalis,* having solitary, nodding white flowers that bloom early in spring.

snow·fall (snō-fawl) *n.* **1.** The amount of snow that falls during a given period or in a given area. **2.** A fall of snow.

snow·field (snō-feeld) *n.* A large, permanently snow-covered area.

snow·flake (snō-flayk) *n.* **1.** An aggregation of ice crystals which fall as snow. **2.** Any of several bulbous plants of the genus *Leucojum,* native to Europe, having white or whitish flowers.

snow goose *n.* A goose, *Chen caerulescens,* that breeds in northern regions, having white plumage with black wing tips.

snow job *n. U.S. Slang.* An effort to overwhelm or deceive with insincere talk, especially flattery.

snow leopard *n.* A large feline mammal, *Uncia uncia,* of the highlands of central Asia, having long, thick, whitish fur with dark markings. Also called "ounce".

snow line *n.* The lower altitudinal boundary of a permanently snow-covered area, such as the snowcap of a mountain, higher in summer than in winter.

snow·man (snō-man) *n., pl.* **-men** (-men). A figure, usually intended to resemble a man, made of a packed mass of snow.

snow·mo·bile (snō-mō-beel, -mə-) *n.* A small vehicle with ski-like runners in front and tanklike treads, used for moving on snow. [SNOW + (AUTO)MOBILE.]

snow mould *n.* A plant disease affecting turf, forage grasses, and cereals caused by the fungus *Fusarium nivale* and occurring after snow or during prolonged cold weather.

snow peas *n. Chiefly U.S.* **Mangetout** (*see*).

snow·plough (snō-plow) *n.* **1.** Any ploughlike device or vehicle used to remove snow, as from roads and railway tracks. **2.** A skiing action in which the toes are turned inwards so that the skis meet in a V-shape, enabling the skier to slow down or stop.

snow·shoe (snō-shŏŏ) *n.* A racket-shaped frame containing interlaced leather strips that can be attached to the foot to facilitate walking on deep snow.

~intr.v. **snowshoed, -shoeing, -shoes.** To go or walk on snowshoes. **—snow·sho·er** *n.*

snow·storm (snō-stawrm) *n.* A storm marked by heavy snowfall and high winds; a blizzard.

snow-white (snō-wīt, -hwīt) *adj.* White as snow.

snow·y (snō-i) *adj.* **-ier, -iest. 1.** Abounding in snow; covered with or characterised by snow. **2.** Resembling or suggestive of snow; white; pure. **—snow·i·ly** *adv.* **—snow·i·ness** *n.*

Snowy Mountains. Mountain range in the Australian Alps of New South Wales, southeast Australia. Mount Kosciusko, Australia's highest mountain, is among its peaks. The Snowy Mountains Hydroelectric Scheme provides water for irrigation and hydroelectricity for Victoria and New South Wales.

snowy owl *n.* A large owl, *Nyctea scandiaca,* of tundra and high northern moorland regions, having predominantly white plumage with black or brownish markings on the upper parts.

S.N.P. Scottish National Party.

snr., Snr. senior.

snub (snub) *tr.v.* **snubbed, snubbing, snubs. 1.** To treat with scorn

or contempt; slight by ignoring or behaving coldly towards. **2.** To reprove or stop short in a sharp, cutting manner; rebuke. **3. a.** To check suddenly the movement of (a rope or cable running out) by turning it about a post. **b.** To secure (a vessel or animal, for example) in this manner.
~*n.* **1.** A deliberate slight or affront. **2.** A sudden checking, as of a rope or cable running out.
~*adj.* Short and slightly flattened at the tip. Said of a nose. [Middle English *snubben,* to rebuke, from Old Norse *snubba.*] —**snub·ber** *n.*

snub-nosed (snúb-nōzd) *adj.* Having a short nose with a slightly flattened tip.

snuck. *U.S. Nonstandard.* Past tense and past participle of **sneak.**

snuff¹ (snuf) *v.* **snuffed, snuffing, snuffs.** —*tr.* **1.** To inhale through the nose; sniff. **2.** To sense, perceive, or examine by or as if by smelling. —*intr.* To snort or sniff.
~*n.* An act of snuffing or the sound produced in snuffing; a sniff. [Probably from Middle Dutch *snuffen.*]

snuff² *n.* The charred portion of a candlewick.
~*tr.v.* **snuffed, snuffing, snuffs. 1.** To cut off the charred portion of (a candlewick). **2.** To extinguish (a candle or lamp, for example), especially by smothering the flame. Often used with *out.* **3.** To put a sudden end to; destroy. Usually used with *out.* **4.** *Slang.* To kill. —**snuff it.** *Slang.* To die. [Middle English *snoffe†* (noun).]

snuff³ *n.* **1.** A preparation of finely pulverised tobacco that can be drawn up into the nostrils by inhaling. **2.** The quantity of this inhaled at a single time; a pinch of snuff. **3.** Any powdery substance, such as a medicine, taken by inhaling. —**up to snuff.** *Informal.* **1.** *Chiefly British.* Not easily deceived. **2.** *Chiefly U.S.* As good as usual or as expected; up to scratch.
~*intr.v.* **snuffed, snuffing, snuffs.** To take snuff. [Dutch *snuf,* short for *snuf(tabak),* (tobacco) for snuffing, from Middle Dutch *snuffen,* to SNUFF.]

snuff-box (snúf-boks) *n.* A small, often highly decorative box with a hinged lid that is used for carrying snuff in the pocket.

snuff-er¹ (snúffər) *n.* One who uses snuff.

snuffer² *n.* **1.** A small hollow cone with a handle, used to snuff out candles. **2.** *Plural.* An instrument resembling a pair of shears that is used for cutting the snuff from or for extinguishing candles.

snuf-fle (snúf'l) *v.* **-fled, -fling, -fles.** —*intr.* **1.** To breathe noisily, as through a congested nose or when crying; to sniffle. **2.** To talk whiningly or nasally; snivel. —*tr.* To utter in a snuffling tone or express by means of a snuffle.
~*n.* **1.** An act or the sound of snuffling. **2.** *Plural. Informal.* A condition, such as a head cold, accompanied by snuffles. Preceded by *the.* [Probably from Low German or Dutch *snuffelen.*] —**snuf·fler** *n.*

snug (snug) *adj.* **snugger, snuggest. 1.** Comfortably sheltered from the cold and the weather; cosy. **2.** Small but well-arranged; compact: *a snug little flat.* **3. a.** Closely secured and well-built; especially, adequately protected against bad weather. Said of a ship. **b.** Seaworthy. **4.** Close-fitting. Said of a garment. **5.** Providing adequate means for a relatively comfortable life: *a snug income.* —See Synonyms at **comfortable.**
~*tr.v.* **snugged, snugging, snugs. 1.** To make snug or secure. **2.** *Nautical.* To prepare (a vessel) to weather a storm, as by taking in sail or securing movable gear. Often used with *down.*
~*n. British.* A small, enclosed or private bar in a public house or inn. [16th century (a nautical term meaning neat, trim) : perhaps from Scandinavian; akin to Old Norse *snöggr,* "close-cropped".] —**snug, snug·ly** *adv.* —**snug·ness** *n.*

snug-ger·y (snúggəri) *n., pl.* **-ies. 1.** A snug position or place. **2.** A snug.

snug-gle (snúg'l) *v.* **-gled, -gling, -gles.** —*intr.* To lie or press close together; nestle or cuddle. Often used with *together, with,* or *up.* —*tr.* To draw close or hold closely, as for comfort or in affection; hug. [Frequentative of SNUG (verb).]

so¹ (sō; *occasional weak form* sə) *adv.* **1. a.** In the manner described, shown, expressed, implied, or indicated; thus: *"She became his loyal friend and remained so to the end"* (Constantine Fitzgibbon). **b.** In such a manner: *The table was so arranged that I sat next to him.* **2. a.** To the amount or degree expressed or understood; in such quantity or to such an extent: *He was so weary that he fell.* **b.** To a certain degree or limit: *so far, so good; I can only do so much.* **c.** To the same degree or extent: *not quite so hot as yesterday.* **3.** To ε great extent or degree; very or very much: *so kind of you to come; loved her so.* **4.** Because of the reason given; consequently; as a result: *He was weary and so he fell.* **5.** In the same way; also; likewise: *You were on time and so was I.* **6.** Then; apparently. Used in expressing astonishment, disapproval, or sarcasm: *So you think you've got troubles?* **7.** In truth; indeed: *"Your button's undone". "So it is!"* —**so as to.** In order to: *started early so as to avoid the rush.* —**so there.** My decision is final. Used to add force to expressions of defiance or refusal: *Well I'm going to do it anyway, so there* —**so what?** Also **so?** What relevance or importance does that have?
~*adj.* **1.** True; factual: *Is it so.* **2.** Perfectly ordered or arranged. Usually used in the phrase *just so.*
~*conj.* **1.** With the purpose or reason that; in order that. Usually used with *that: I stopped so that you could catch up.* **2.** With the result or consequence that: *He agreed, so they went ahead.*
~*pron.* **1.** That; this; the same as has already been implied or specified: *I don't think so; Did he say so?* **2.** Approximately that

quantity, amount, or number: *another ten minutes or so.*
~*interj.* Used to express surprise or comprehension. [Middle English *so, s(w)a,* Old English *swā.*]
Usage: *So,* used as a conjunction, is generally followed by *that* when it introduces a clause stating purpose or reason *(He stayed a day longer so that he could avoid the traffic),* but the *that* is often dropped in informal contexts. In the expression of result or consequence, the use of *so* without *that* is more widely acceptable *(The traffic was very heavy, so he stayed a day longer),* though some stylists prefer alternative constructions (such as *and therefore he stayed a day longer).* See also Usage note at **as.**

so². *Music.* Variant of **soh.**

So. *Chiefly U.S.* south; southern.

s.o. seller's option.

soak (sōk) *v.* **soaked, soaking, soaks.** —*tr.* **1.** To make thoroughly wet or saturated; drench; wet through. **2. a.** To immerse in liquid, often for a prolonged period; steep. **b.** To remove or draw out by immersion. Usually used with *out: soak out blood stains.* **3.** To absorb (liquid) through pores or interstices. Usually used with *up.* **4.** *Informal.* To take in eagerly or effortlessly, as if by absorption; absorb or assimilate. Used with *up: soaking up the sun; to soak up facts.* **5.** *Informal.* **a.** To drink (alcohol), especially to excess. **b.** To make (a person) drunk. **6.** *Informal.* To charge or tax excessively; force to pay too much. —*intr.* **1.** To be immersed until thoroughly saturated. **2.** To penetrate or permeate; seep. Often used with *in, into, through,* or *away.* **3.** *Slang.* To drink to excess.
~*n.* **1.** The act or process of soaking or the condition of being soaked. **2.** *Informal.* A drunkard. [Middle English *soken,* Old English *socian,* akin to *sūcan,* to SUCK.] —**soak·er** *n.*

soak·age (sōkij) *n.* **1.** The process of soaking or the condition of being soaked. **2.** The amount of liquid that soaks into or through an object or seeps out of it.

soak·a·way (sōk-ə-way) *n. Chiefly British.* A place, such as a pit or depression in the ground filled with broken bricks and covered with soil, through which water (usually rainwater conducted by a pipe) drains away.

Soames (sōmz), **(Arthur) Christopher (John), Baron** (1920–87). British politician and diplomat. He was British ambassador to Paris (1968–72) and from December 1979 to April 1980 governor of Southern Rhodesia, before its independence as Zimbabwe.

so-and-so (sō-ən-sō) *n., pl.* **-sos. 1.** A person or thing left unspecified. **2.** *Informal.* A very unpleasant person. Used euphemistically in place of various unsavoury epithets: *He's a real so-and-so.* Also used adjectively: *her so-and-so father.*

soap (sōp) *n.* **1.** A cleansing agent, manufactured in bars, granules, flakes, or liquid form, consisting of a mixture of the sodium salts of various fatty acids made from natural oils and fats. Compare **detergent. 2.** *Chemistry.* A mixture of metallic salts of long chain fatty acids, especially: **a.** One containing sodium salts (*a hard soap*). **b.** One containing potassium salts (*a soft soap.*) **3.** *Slang.* Flattery. **4.** *Informal.* A soap opera. —**no soap.** *U.S. Slang.* Impossible or without success; nothing doing: *tried to talk him out of it, but no soap.*
~*tr.v.* **soaped, soaping, soaps.** To treat or cover with soap. [Middle English *sope, saip,* Old English *sāpe.*]

soap-bark (sōp-baark) *n.* **1.** A tree, *Quillaja saponaria,* of western South America, having bark used as soap and as a source of saponin. **2.** The bark of this tree. **3.** Any of several other trees or shrubs having similar bark.

soap-ber·ry (sōp-berri) *n., pl.* **-ries. 1.** Any of various chiefly tropical New World trees of the genus *Sapindus,* having pulpy fruit that lathers like soap. **2.** The fruit of any of these trees.

soap-box (sōp-boks) *n.* Also **soap box. 1.** A box or crate used as a temporary platform for making an impromptu or nonofficial public speech. **2.** A child's crude vehicle made of a wooden box mounted on a wheeled frame.
~*adj.* Designating speech-making or a public speaker characterised by ranting, fanaticism, or eccentricity. —**soap·box·er** *n.*

soap bubble *n.* **1.** A bubble formed from soapy water. **2.** Anything beautiful but transient, insubstantial, or illusory.

soap opera *n.* A broadcast serial, typically having a domestic theme and characterised by sentimentality and melodrama. [Many were originally sponsored in the United States by soap companies.]

soap plant *n.* **1.** A plant, *Chlorogalum pomeridianum,* of California, having small white flowers and a bulbous root formerly used as soap. **2.** Any of several other plants having parts used as soap.

soap-stone (sōp-stōn) *n.* **Steatite** (see). [From its soapy texture.]

soap-suds (sōp-sudz) *pl.n.* Lather or foam from soapy water.

soap-wort (sōp-wurt ‖ -wawrt) *n.* A Eurasian plant, *Saponaria officinalis,* with pale pink flowers, the leaves and stems of which make a lather when rubbed together. Also called "bouncing Bet".

soap-y (sōpi) *adj.* **-ier, -iest. 1.** Containing or consisting of soap; covered or filled with soap. **2.** Pertaining to or resembling soap. **3.** *Slang.* Unctuous; flattering in an oily way. —**soap·i·ly** *adv.* —**soap·i·ness** *n.*

soar (sor ‖ sôr) *intr.v.* **soared, soaring, soars. 1. a.** To fly upwards or rise high into the air; climb swiftly or powerfully. **b.** To rise steeply; be at a great height. **2.** To fly or glide high in the air without visibly moving the wings. **3.** *Aviation.* To glide while maintaining altitude. **4.** To rise suddenly above a normal or usual level; increase greatly. **5.** To rise to an exalted level; be inspired: *My heart soared.* —See Synonyms at **rise.**
~*n.* **1.** The act of soaring. **2.** The altitude or scope attained in

soaring. [Middle English *soren,* from Old French *esorer,* from Vulgar Latin *exaurāre* (unattested) : Latin *ex-,* out of + *aura,* the air, a breeze, from Greek, a breeze.] **—soar·er** *n.* **—soar·ing·ly** *adv.*
Soa·res (swáar-ess, *Portuguese* -ish), **Mário Alberto Nobre Lopes** (1924-). Portuguese politician. Frequently imprisoned for his political views, he was eventually exiled (1970), but returned after a coup (1974) and as leader of the Socialist party became Prime Minister (1976–78, 1983–85). He was president of Portugal (1986–96).
so·a·ve (sō-áavay) *n.* A dry white Italian table wine. [Italian, "sweet", from Latin *suāvis,* pleasing.]
sob (sob) *v.* **sobbed, sobbing, sobs.** *—intr.* **1.** To weep aloud with convulsive gasping and sniffling; cry uncontrollably. **2.** To make a sound resembling that of sobbing. *—tr.* **1.** To utter with sobs. **2.** To put or bring (oneself) into a specified condition by sobbing: *sob oneself to sleep.* —See Synonyms at **cry.**
∼n. An act of sobbing or the sound produced in sobbing; a short, audible catch of the breath. [Middle English *sobben,* to catch breath, probably imitative and of Low German origin; akin to Dutch dialectal *sabben*†, to suck.] **—sob·bing·ly** *adv.*
so·ber (sṓbər) *adj.* **-berer, -berest. 1.** Habitually abstemious in the use of alcohol; temperate. **2.** Not intoxicated. **3.** Having or showing an earnest, dignified disposition; serious or grave. **4.** Plain or subdued; not garish or gay. Said of clothes or colours. **5.** Without frivolity, excess, exaggeration, or speculative imagination: *sober facts.* **6.** Characterised by self-control or sanity; reasonable; rational. —See Synonyms at **serious.**
∼v. **sobered, -bering, -bers.** *—tr.* To make sober, make less intoxicated or more serious and thoughtful. Often used with *up: a sobering experience.* *—intr.* To become sober. Often used with *up.* [Middle English *sobre,* from Old French, from Latin *sōbrius.*] **—so·ber·ly** *adv.* **—so·ber·ness** *n.*
So·bers (sṓbərz), **Sir Garfield (St Auburn),** known as Gary Sobers (1936-). West Indian cricketer. He played for Barbados, Nottinghamshire, and the West Indies captaining the national side from 1965 to 1974.
sober·sides (sṓbər-sīdz) *n., pl.* **sobersides.** *Informal.* A serious, sedate person lacking a sense of humour.
So·bran·je (sō-bráan-yi, sə-) *n.* The Bulgarian national assembly. [Bulgarian, "assembly".]
so·bri·e·ty (sō-brī́-əti, sə-) *n.* **1.** Seriousness or gravity, as in manner or approach. **2.** Absence of drunkenness. [Middle English, from Old French *sobrieté* or Latin *sōbrietās,* from *sōbrius,* SOBER.]
so·bri·quet (sṓbri-kay ‖ -káy, -ket, -két) *n.* Also **sou·bri·quet** (sṓbri-, sóobri-). **1.** An affectionate or humorous nickname. **2.** An assumed name. [French *sobriquet,* earlier *soubriquet*†, (originally "a tap under the chin").]
sob sister *n.* A journalist, especially a woman, employed as a writer or editor of sob stories.
sob story *n.* A tale of personal hardship or misfortune intended to arouse pity or given as an excuse or rationalisation.
So·bu·kwe (sō-bóo-kway), **Robert Mangaliso** (1924–78). Black South African leader. He was leader of the African National Congress, and subsequently the more violence-orientated Pan-Africanist Congress. He was imprisoned by the South African government (1960–69) and kept under house arrest (1969–78).
soc·age (sóckij) *n.* Feudal tenure of land by a tenant not a knight, in return for agricultural or other nonmilitary services or for payment. [Middle English *sokage,* from *soke,* SOKE.] **—soc·ag·er** *n.*
so-called (sō-káwld) *adj.* Designated thus or known by this term. Often used to imply that the thing or person so designated does not merit the term: *a so-called teetotaller.*
Usage: The hyphen is used when the words are used before a noun *(these so-called friends),* and in these circumstances it is not usually felt to be necessary to add quotation marks as well. After a noun, the hyphen is not used: *his friends, so called.*
soc·cer (sóckər) *n.* The most common type of football, in which two teams of 11 players each play on a rectangular field with net goals at either end, manoeuvring a round ball mainly by kicking, heading, or by using any part of the body except the arms and hands in attempts to score points by getting the ball into the opposing team's goal. Also called "association football", "football". [From (AS)SOC., abbr. of *Association (Football)* + -ER[1] (sense 2).]
so·cia·bil·i·ty (sṓshə-bílləti) *n., pl.* **-ties. 1.** The disposition or quality of being sociable. **2.** An instance of being sociable.
so·cia·ble (sṓshəb'l) *adj.* **1.** Pleasant, friendly, and enjoying good company. **2.** Providing occasion for conversation and conviviality. [French, from Latin *sociābilis,* from *sociāre,* to join, to share, from *socius,* partner.] **—so·cia·ble·ness** *n.* **—so·cia·bly** *adv.*
so·cial (sṓsh'l) *adj.* **1. a.** Living or tending to live together in communities. **b.** Of, pertaining to, or characteristic of the activities of and the relations between human beings living in a community. **c.** Of or pertaining to human society and its modes of organisation: *social classes.* **2.** Living in an organised group or similar close aggregate: *social insects.* **3.** In Greek and Roman history, involving allies or members of a confederacy. **4.** Of or pertaining to fashionable or polite society: *social graces.* **5.** Sociable; fond of the company of others. **6. a.** Intended for convivial activities. **b.** Done or acting thus only in convivial circumstances rather than habitually: *social drinking.* **7.** Pertaining to or occupied with matters affecting human welfare: *social policy.* **8.** Growing thickly in clumps, often covering a large area. Said of plant species.
∼n. An informal social gathering, as of the members of a club or church congregation. [From French or Latin *sociālis,* of companionship, from *socius,* companion, partner.]
social anthropology *n.* The branch of anthropology dealing with communal relationships and social customs and beliefs (such as kinship systems) in human societies, especially primitive societies.
social chapter *n.* The EU's official social policy, especially with respect to workers rights. Formerly called "social charter".
social class. See **class** (sense 3).
social climber *n.* One striving to become a member of a higher social class.
social contract *n.* **1.** A theory of the ideal basis of political rule, advanced by political philosophers such as Hobbes, Locke, and especially Rousseau, which holds that government must rest on the consent of the governed, who freely give up certain individual rights and liberties in exchange for the advantages of having an organised government. **2.** Any reciprocal system whereby individuals or organisations give up certain freedoms in exchange for the benefits a government can bestow; specifically, an agreement by trade unions to limit wage demands in return for other favourable government measures. Also called "social compact".
social credit *n.* **1.** An economic and political theory, formulated by the British engineer C.H. Douglas, holding that every person in a society should be paid dividends from the profits of industry and commerce. **2.** *Capital* **S,** *capital* **C.** A Canadian political party advocating this theory. **—Social Crediter** *n.*
Social Darwinism *n.* The application of some aspects of the Darwinian theory of evolution to the history and development of human society.
social democracy *n.* **1.** A political theory advocating a gradual advance towards socialism through democratic means. **2.** *Often capital* **S,** *capital* **D.** The aims or principles of the Social Democratic Party. **—social democrat** *n.* **—social democratic** *adj.*
Social Democratic Party *n. Abbr.* **SDP** A British centre party (1981–90), founded chiefly by ex-members of the Labour Party, believing in a mixed economy and the European Community.
social disease *n.* **1.** Venereal disease. Used euphemistically. **2.** A disease occurring especially among particular social classes predisposed to it by a given set of living or working conditions.
social engineering *n.* The attempt to adjust or manage institutional arrangements or patterns of behaviour in a society by applying principles of a social science. **—social engineer** *n.*
social insurance *n.* A national system of insurance, as against sickness, unemployment, or disability, usually financed jointly by employers, employees, and the government.
so·cial·ise, so·cial·ize (sṓsh'l-īz) *v.* **-ised, -ising, -ises.** *—tr.* **1.** To fit for companionship with others; train or bring up so as to be well adapted, as in attitude or manners, for life in society. **2.** To place under government or group ownership or control; establish on a socialistic basis. **3.** To convert or adapt to the needs of society. *—intr.* To enter into social relationships or social activities. **—so·cial·i·sa·tion** (-ī-záysh'n ‖ *U.S.* -i-) *n.* **—so·cial·is·er** *n.*
socialised medicine *n. U.S.* The provision of medical and hospital care for all at a nominal cost, by means of government regulation of health services and subsidies derived from taxation.
so·cial·ism (sṓsh'l-iz'm) *n.* **1.** A social system in which the means of producing and distributing goods are owned collectively and political power is exercised by the whole community. **2.** The theory or practice of those who support such a social system. **3.** In Marxist-Leninist theory, the building, under the dictatorship of the proletariat, of the material base for communism, a transitional stage between capitalism and communism.
so·cial·ist (sṓsh'l-ist) *n.* **1.** An advocate of socialism. **2.** *Abbr.* **soc.** *Often capital* **S.** A member of a socialist party.
∼adj. **1.** Of, promoting, or practising socialism. **2.** *Capital* **S.** Of, belonging to, or constituting a socialist party.
so·cial·is·tic (sṓsh'l-ístik) *adj.* Of, advocating, or tending towards socialism. **—so·cial·is·ti·cal·ly** *adv.*
socialist realism *n.* An official Marxist theory of art, strongly held and propagated in the Soviet Union and other Communist countries, holding that the purpose of any art is to promote socialism.
so·cial·ite (sṓsh'l-īt) *n.* One prominent in fashionable society.
so·ci·al·i·ty (sṓshi-ál-əti) *n., pl.* **-ties. 1. a.** The state or quality of being sociable; sociability. **b.** An instance of sociableness. **2.** The tendency to form communities and societies.
so·cial·ly (sṓsh'l-i) *adv.* **1.** In a social manner; with regard to social relations: *socially inept.* **2.** With regard to society: *socially important.* **3.** By society.
social market *n.* A market economy that does not neglect social justice.
social mobility *n.* The movement of individuals from one social class to another, especially from a lower class to a higher one.
social psychology *n.* The branch of psychology concerned with the relationships between individuals and groups.
social realism *n.* *Sometimes capital* **S,** *capital* **R.** A movement in painting, literature, and other arts rejecting romanticism and concentrating on the realistic portrayal of contemporary political, economic, and social conditions.
social register *n.* In the United States, a directory listing persons of social prominence in the community.
social science *n.* **1.** The study of society and of individual relationships in and to society, generally regarded as including sociology, psychology, anthropology, economics, political science, and history. **2.** Any of these disciplines.
social security *n.* **1.** The provision by the state of financial and

other assistance to those in need, such as the unemployed, the elderly, the disabled, and those with low incomes. **2.** *Often capital* **SS.** The government system providing such assistance; this may be a single scheme or, as in Britain, a combination of social insurance schemes (such as unemployment benefit) and noncontributory schemes, both means-tested (such as payments to low-income families) and non-means-tested (such as child benefit).

social service *n.* **1.** *Usually plural.* **a.** Services and facilities that are government-funded and usually controlled by national or local government, such as health care, education, and social work. **b.** The staff running these services and facilities. **2.** Social work.

social studies *pl.n.* A course of study, often taught in schools, that includes sociology, geography, history, and politics.

social wage *n.* Benefits, especially government-provided ones such as health care and unemployment insurance, to which members of a society may be entitled in addition to their individual wages, and which should be considered in assessing their overall standard of living. Typically preceded by *the.*

social work *n.* The provision of welfare work, assistance, and advice to those in need such as the poor, the aged, and those with domestic and emotional problems. **—social worker** *n.*

so·ci·e·tal (sə-sī́-ət'l || sō-) *adj.* Of or pertaining to the structure, organisation, or functioning of society. **—so·ci·e·tal·ly** *adv.*

so·ci·e·ty (sə-sī́-əti || sō-) *n., pl.* **-ties.** *Abbr.* **S., s., Soc., soc. 1. a.** The totality of social relationships among human beings. **b.** A group of human beings broadly distinguished from other groups by mutual interests, participation in characteristic relationships, shared institutions, and a common culture. **c.** The institutions and culture of a distinct self-perpetuating group. **2. a.** The rich, privileged, and fashionable social class. **b.** A particular section of a community or population, and its customs: *polite society; middle-class society.* **3. a.** Companionship; company. **b.** Participation in social or communal activity: *He's not much of a one for society.* **4.** *Biology.* A colony or community of organisms, usually of the same species. **5.** An organisation of people associated on the basis of common aims, beliefs, interests, or occupations. —See Synonyms at **circle.** [From Old French *societe,* from Latin *societās* (stem *societāt-*), fellowship, union, society, from *socius,* companion.]

Society Islands. Group of volcanic and coral islands in the central South Pacific, forming part of French Polynesia. They comprise the Windward Islands which include Tahiti, and the Leeward Islands.

Society of Friends *n.* The **Religious Society of Friends** *(see).*

Society of Jesus *n. Abbr.* **S.J.** The **Jesuits** *(see).*

So·cin·i·an (sō-sínni-ən, sə-) *n.* An adherent of a sect holding unitarian views, including denial of the divinity of Jesus, founded by Laelius and Faustus Socinus, Italian theologians of the 16th century. **—So·cin·i·an** *adj.* **—So·cin·i·an·ism** *n.*

socio– *comb. form.* Indicates: **1.** Society; for example, **sociometry. 2.** Social; for example, **socioeconomic.** [From French, from Latin *socius,* companion.]

so·ci·o·bi·ol·o·gy (sō-si-ō-bī-óllə-ji, -shi-) *n.* The study of the social behaviour and organisation of animal species and their relationship to human social evolution. **—so·ci·o·bi·o·log·i·cal** (-bī-ə-lójik'l) *adj.* **—so·ci·o·bi·o·log·i·cal·ly** *adv.* **—so·ci·o·bi·o·log·ist** (-jist) *n.*

so·ci·o·ec·o·nom·ic (sō-si-ō-éekə-nómmik, -shi-, -éckə-) *adj.* Of, based on, or influenced by a combination of social and economic considerations.

so·ci·o·lin·guis·tics (sō-si-ō-ling-gwístiks, -shi-) *n. Used with a singular verb.* The study of language in the context of its use in a particular society, and of the social and cultural factors that influence its acquisition and development. **—so·ci·o·lin·guis·tic** *adj.*

so·ci·ol·o·gy (sō-si-óllǝji, -shi-) *n.* The study of human social behaviour; especially, the study of the origins, organisation, institutions, and development of human society. [French *sociologie* : SOCIO- + -LOGY.] **—so·ci·o·log·ic** (-ə-lójik), **so·ci·o·log·i·cal** *adj.* **—so·ci·o·log·i·cal·ly** *adv.* **—so·ci·ol·o·gist** (-óllǝjist) *n.*

so·ci·om·e·try (sō-si-ómmətri, -shi-) *n.* The quantitative study of relationships between individuals in groups and populations, especially the study and measurement of preferences.

so·ci·o·po·li·ti·cal (sō-si-ō-pə-líttik'l, -shi-) *adj.* Of, based on, or influenced by a combination of social and political considerations.

sock[1] (sok) *n., pl.* **socks** (for all senses) or *U.S.* **sox** (for sense 1). **1.** A soft covering for the foot or foot and leg, reaching a point between the ankle and the knee and usually worn inside a shoe; a short stocking. **2. a.** A light shoe worn by comic actors in ancient Greek and Roman plays. Compare **buskin. b.** *Archaic.* Comic drama; comedy. **3.** A **windsock** *(see).* **—pull (one's) socks up.** *British Informal.* To make an effort to do better; sort oneself out; try harder. **—put a sock in it.** *British Informal.* To be quiet; shut up. **—socked in.** *U.S.* Closed because of bad weather. Said of an airport. [Middle English *socke,* Old English *socc,* a kind of light shoe, from Latin *soccus,* probably from Greek *sukkhos*†.]

sock[2] *v.* **socked, socking, socks.** *Slang.* —*tr.* To hit or strike forcefully; punch. —*intr.* To deliver a blow. **—sock it to (someone).** *Slang.* **1.** To impress (someone) forcefully. **2.** To attack vigorously. ~*n. Slang.* A hard blow or punch. [18th century : origin obscure.]

sock·et (sóckit) *n.* **1.** An opening or cavity that acts as the receptacle for an inserted part. **2.** Any of various devices or fitments into which something is inserted, especially: **a.** An electrical power point in which a plug or light bulb fits. **b.** A recessed piece of metal used, in conjunction with a bar or wrench, to turn bolts or nuts. **3. a.** The hollow part of a joint that receives the end of a bone. **b.** A hollow or concavity into which a part, such as the eye, fits.

~*tr.v.* **socketed, -eting, -ets.** To furnish with or insert into a socket. [Middle English *soket,* spearhead shaped like a ploughshare, socket, from Anglo-French *soket,* diminutive of Old French *soc,* ploughshare, probably from Celtic origin.]

sock·eye salmon (sók-ī) *n.* A salmon, *Oncorhynchus nerka,* of northern Pacific coastal waters. Also called "red salmon". [By folk etymology from Salish (dialectal) *suk-kegh.*]

so·cle (sōk'l, sóck'l) *n.* A plain low block or plinth, serving as a pedestal, as for a vase or a column, or supporting a wall. [French *socle,* from Italian *zoccolo,* "wooden shoe", from Latin *socculus,* diminutive of *soccus,* a light shoe. See **sock** (stocking).]

soc·man (sók-mən, sōk-) *n., pl.* **-men** (-men, -mən). Also **soke·man** (sōk-). A tenant holding land under the system of socage. [Medieval Latin *sokemannus* : Old English *sōcn,* SOKE + *mann,* MAN.]

Soc·ra·tes (sóckrə-teez) (*c.* 469–399 B.C.). Greek philosopher. He initiated a method of teaching through question and answer whereby man could get to know himself. He argued that virtue is knowledge, vice is ignorance, and no one wittingly does wrong. His stance led to his being charged with atheism and corrupting the minds of the youth. He was sentenced to death and drank hemlock and died in the presence of his pupils. His theories have survived only through the writings of Plato, his most important pupil, and to a lesser extent of Xenophon.

So·crat·ic (so-kráttik, sə-, sō-) *adj.* Also **So·crat·i·cal** (-'l). Of, pertaining to, or characteristic of Socrates or his philosophical methods of instruction and argument.

~*n.* An adherent of the teachings of Socrates. **—So·crat·i·cal·ly** *adv.* **—So·crat·i·cism** (-krátti-siz'm) *n.*

Socratic irony *n.* Pretended ignorance, as used by Socrates as a method of instruction or to reveal inconsistencies in the arguments of an opponent. Also called "irony".

Socratic method *n.* A philosophical procedure used by Socrates as a form of instruction, using repeated and pointed questioning to elicit truths assumed to be innate in all rational beings.

sod[1] (sod) *n.* **1.** A section of grass-covered surface soil held together by matted roots; turf. **2.** The ground, especially when covered with grass. **3.** See **old sod.**

~*tr.v.* **sodded, sodding, sods.** To cover with sod. [Middle English *sod(de),* from Middle Low German or Middle Dutch *sode,* akin to Old Frisian *sāda*†.]

sod[2] *n. Vulgar Slang* **1.** An obnoxious or contemptible person. **2.** A person; fellow. Used humorously. **3.** Something that is troublesome or infuriating.

~*tr.v.* **sodded, sodding, sods.** *Vulgar Slang.* To damn; curse. Used chiefly in an interjection: *Sod you! Sod it!* **—sod off.** *Vulgar Slang.* To go away or cease being annoying. Used in the imperative. [Shortened from SODOMITE.]

so·da (sōdə) *n.* **1. a.** Any of various forms of sodium carbonate, especially **washing soda** *(see).* **b.** Loosely, chemically combined sodium. **2. a.** Soda water. **b.** *U.S.* Any carbonated soft drink; pop. **3.** A beverage made from soda water, ice cream, and sometimes flavouring. **4.** In faro, the card turned face up at the beginning of the game. [Medieval Latin *soda*†, perhaps from *sodānum,* glasswort (a plant used to treat headaches), from Arabic *sudā,* headache, from *sada'a,* to split.]

soda ash *n.* Crude anhydrous **sodium carbonate** *(see),* used especially as an industrial chemical.

soda bread *n.* Bread made with bicarbonate of soda, cream of tartar, and soured milk.

soda fountain *n. U.S.* **1.** An apparatus with taps for dispensing soda water and other soft drinks. **2.** A counter or café serving soft drinks, ice-cream dishes, and other snacks.

soda lime *n.* A mixture of calcium oxide and sodium or potassium hydroxide, used as a drying agent and carbon dioxide absorbent.

so·dal·ist (sōd'l-ist) *n.* A member of a sodality.

so·da·lite (sōdə-līt) *n.* A blue-white vitreous mineral, essentially $3(NaAlSiO_4)\cdot NaCl$, found in igneous rocks.

so·dal·i·ty (sō-dál-əti, sə-) *n., pl.* **-ties. 1.** A society or association; especially, in the Roman Catholic Church, a devotional or charitable society. **2.** Brotherhood; fellowship. [From Latin *sodālitās,* fellowship, brotherhood, from *sodālis,* fellow, intimate.]

soda nitre *n. Chemistry.* **Sodium nitrate** *(see).*

soda pop *U.S. Informal.* A carbonated soft drink; pop.

soda water *n.* Effervescent water charged under pressure with purified carbon dioxide gas, used as a beverage or mixer. Also called "carbonated water", "soda".

sod·den (sódd'n) *adj.* **1.** Thoroughly soaked; saturated. **2.** Soggy and heavy from improper cooking; doughy. **3.** Bloated and dulled, especially from overindulgence in drink. **4.** *Archaic.* Boiled.

~*v.* **soddened, -dening, -dens.** —*tr.* To make sodden; saturate. —*intr.* To become sodden. [Middle English, Old English *soden,* from the past participle of *sethen, sēothan,* to SEETHE.] **—sod·den·ly** *adv.* **—sod·den·ness** *n.*

sod·ding (sódding) *adj. Slang.* Damned. Used as an intensive and often considered vulgar: *a sodding nuisance.* **—sod·ding** *adv.*

Sod·dy (sóddi), **Frederick** (1877–1956). British chemist and physicist. With Lord Rutherford he put forward the theory of atomic disintegration. His discovery that certain elements which possessed the same chemical properties differed in their nuclear mass *(Soddy's law),* laid the foundation of the isotope theory. He was awarded the Nobel prize for his work on radioactivity in 1921.

so·di·um (sōdi-əm) *n. Symbol* **Na** A soft, light, extremely malleable silver-white metallic element that reacts explosively with water. It is naturally abundant in combined forms, especially in common salt, and is present in a wide variety of industrially important compounds. Atomic number 11, atomic weight 22.99, melting point 97.8°C, boiling point 892°C, relative density 0.968, valency 1. [New Latin : SOD(A) + -IUM.]

sodium ammonium phosphate *n.* A colourless, odourless crystalline compound, $NaNH_4HPO_4 \cdot 4H_2O$, used as an analytical reagent.

sodium benzoate *n.* The sodium salt of benzoic acid, C_6H_5COONa, used as a food preservative, antiseptic, and intermediate in dye manufacture, and in the production of pharmaceuticals. Also called "benzoate of soda".

sodium bicarbonate *n.* A white crystalline compound, $NaHCO_3$, with a slightly alkaline taste, used in making effervescent salts and beverages, artificial mineral water, baking soda, pharmaceuticals, and in fire extinguishers. Also called "baking soda", "bicarbonate of soda", "sodium hydrogencarbonate", and informally "bicarb".

sodium borate *n.* A crystalline compound, $Na_2B_4O_7 \cdot 10H_2O$, used in the manufacture of glass, detergents, and pharmaceuticals. Also called "borax".

sodium carbonate *n.* A compound used in the manufacture of sodium bicarbonate, sodium nitrate, glass, ceramics, detergents, and soap, chiefly used as a white powder (Na_2CO_3, sal soda) or a white crystalline decahydrate ($Na_2CO_3 \cdot IOH_2O$, washing soda).

sodium chlorate *n.* A colourless crystalline compound, $NaClO_3$, used as a bleaching and oxidising agent and in explosives.

sodium chloride *n.* A colourless crystalline compound, $NaCl$, used in the manufacture of chemicals and as a food preservative and seasoning. Also called "common salt", "table salt".

sodium cyanide *n.* A poisonous white crystalline compound, $NaCN$, used in extracting gold and silver from ores and in dye manufacture.

sodium cyclamate *n.* A soluble white crystalline powder, $C_6H_{11}NHSO_3Na$, 30 times as sweet as sugar (sucrose) and formerly a major constituent of low-calorie sweetening agents.

sodium dichromate *n.* A red-orange crystalline compound, $Na_2Cr_2O_7 \cdot 2H_2O$, used as an oxidising agent.

sodium glutamate *n.* Monosodium glutamate (see).

sodium hydrogencarbonate *n.* Sodium bicarbonate.

sodium hydrosulphite *n.* A yellowish powder, $(NAO)_2S_2O_4 \cdot 2H_2O$, used as a bleaching and reducing agent. Also called "sodium hyposulphite", "sodium dithionite".

sodium hydroxide *n.* A strongly alkaline compound, $NaOH$, used in the manufacture of chemicals and soaps and in petroleum refining. Also called "caustic soda", "lye".

sodium hypochlorite *n.* An unstable salt, $NaOCl$, usually stored in solution and used as a fungicide and an oxidising bleach.

sodium hyposulphite *n.* Sodium thiosulphate (see).

sodium nitrate *n.* A white crystalline compound, $NaNO_3$, used in solid rocket propellants and in the manufacture of explosives and tobacco. Also called "nitre", "saltpetre", "soda nitre", "Chile saltpetre", "caliche".

sodium pentobarbital *n.* Pentobarbitone sodium (see).

sodium pentothal *n.* *Chemistry.* Thiopental sodium (see).

sodium perborate *n.* A white odourless crystalline compound, $NaBO_2 \cdot H_2O_2 \cdot 3H_2O$, used as a mild alkaline oxidising agent in dentifrices, as a deodorant, and as an industrial reagent.

sodium peroxide *n.* A yellowish-white powder, Na_2O_2, employed industrially as an oxidising and bleaching agent and medically as a germicide, antiseptic, and disinfectant.

sodium phosphate *n.* Any of the three sodium salts of phosphoric acid, NaH_2PO_4, Na_2HPO_4, and Na_3PO_4, widely used in industry, pharmaceutical manufacturing, medicine, and chemistry.

sodium propionate *n.* A clear crystalline compound, C_2H_5COONa, capable of retarding the growth of moulds and bacteria and used to prevent food spoilage.

sodium silicate *n.* Any of various water-soluble silicate glass compounds used as a preservative for eggs, in plaster and cement, and in various purification and refining processes. Also called "liquid glass", "soluble glass", "water glass".

sodium sulphate *n.* A white crystalline compound, Na_2SO_4, used to manufacture paper, glass, dyes, and pharmaceuticals.

sodium sulphide *n.* A hygroscopic yellow compound, Na_2S, used as a metal ore reagent in photography, engraving, and printing.

sodium sulphite *n.* A white crystalline or powdered compound, Na_2SO_3, used in preserving foods, silvering mirrors, developing photographs, and making dyes.

sodium thiosulphate *n.* A white crystalline compound, $Na_2S_2O_3 \cdot 5H_2O$, used as a photographic fixing agent and as a bleach. Also called "hypo", "hyposulphite", "sodium hyposulphite".

so·di·um-va·pour lamp (sṓdi-əm-váypər) *n.* An electric lamp containing a small amount of sodium and neon gas, used in generating yellow light for street lighting.

Sod·om[1] (sódдəm). City of ancient Palestine, possibly located south of the Dead Sea, which, with nearby Gomorrah, was destroyed by "brimstone and fire from the Lord" (Genesis 19:24).

Sodom[2] *n.* Any place of exceptional wickedness or depravity.

sod·o·mise, sod·o·mize (sódдə-mīz) *tr.v.* **-ised, -ising, -ises.** To practise sodomy on.

sod·om·ite (sódд-mīt) *n.* A person who indulges in sodomy. [Middle English, from Old French, from Late Latin, from Greek *Sodomitēs*, inhabitant of Sodom.]

sod·o·my (sódдəmi) *n.* **1.** *Law.* Anal sexual intercourse. **2.** Broadly, sexual intercourse between men, or any of various unnatural sexual

acts, especially between humans and animals. [Middle English, from Medieval Latin *sodomia*, from Late Latin *peccatum sodomiticum*, the sin of Sodom.]

Sod's Law (sódz) *n.* Any of various satirically pessimistic observations propounded as quasi-scientific laws, such as: "The degree of failure is directly proportional to the effort made and to the need for success." [Personification of SOD (contemptible person, etc.).]

so·ev·er (sō-évvər) *adv.* At all; in any way. Used to generalise or emphasise a word or phrase, usually in combination, as with *how, what, when,* or *where*: "Space to breathe, how short soever" (Ben Jonson). [SO + EVER.]

so·fa (sṓfə) *n.* A long upholstered seat with a back and arms. [Originally a raised dais with carpets and cushions, ultimately from Arabic *suffah*; perhaps akin to Hebrew *sapāh*, carpet, divan.]

sofa bed *n.* A sofa, the seat of which unfolds to form a bed.

so·far (sṓ-faar) *n.* A system for determining a position at sea, especially that of lost survivors, by the sound ranging of the explosion of an underwater charge by three widely separated shore stations. [Sound fixing and ranging.]

sof·fi·o·ne (sóffi-ŏni ‖ U.S. also sṓfi-) *n., pl.* **sof·fi·o·ni** (-ŏ-nee). A jet of steam, and other vapours, that issues from the ground in volcanic regions. [Italian, augmentative form of *soffio*, a puff, from *soffiare*, to blow, from Latin *sufflare*, to blow upon.]

sof·fit (sóffit) *n.* The underside of a structural component, such as a beam, arch, staircase, or cornice. [French *soffite*, from Italian *soffito, soffita*, from Vulgar Latin *suffictus* (unattested), from Latin *suffixus*, "something fastened beneath". See **suffix**.]

Sofia, Sophia (sṓfi-ə). *Bulgarian* **Sofiya.** Capital of Bulgaria, situated in the country's western mountains, and the chief industrial, communications, cultural and commercial centre. Its monuments include the ruined seventh-century church of St. Sofia.

S. of Sol. Song of Solomon (Old Testament).

soft (soft ‖ sawft) *adj.* **softer, softest. 1. a.** Offering little resistance; easily moulded, cut, or worked; malleable; not hard. **b.** Yielding readily to pressure or weight; not firm. **c.** Marked by wet or sodden ground: *The going was soft.* **2.** Marked by or done with relatively little force; light: *a soft tap with a hammer.* **3. a.** Smooth or fine to the touch; not harsh or coarse. **b.** Lacking sharpness or acidity; bland; mellow. **4.** Not loud or strident; low-toned. **5.** Not brilliant or glaring; subdued: *soft lights.* **6.** Not sharply drawn or delineated: *soft contours.* **7.** Gentle; agreeable; mild; balmy: *soft weather; a soft breeze.* **8.** Having or showing a mild, gentle, or sympathetic disposition, as: **a.** Not stern or rigorous; lenient: *too soft on offenders.* **b.** Adopting a moderate rather than an aggressive approach or position: *the soft Left.* **c.** Easily moved; compassionate. **d.** Easily swayed; yielding; compliant. **9. a.** Tender; affectionate: *soft glances.* **b.** Amorously inclined; infatuated. Used with *on.* **10. a.** Lacking powers of endurance or exertion, especially as a result of prolonged ease or self-indulgence; weak; not robust. **b.** Out of condition; flabby. **11.** *Informal.* Simple; feeble-minded: *soft in the head.* **12.** *Military.* Lacking protection against bombs, missiles, or rockets: *a soft target.* **13.** Soft-core: *soft porn.* **14.** *Finance.* **a.** Designating a loan issued on very favourable terms. **b.** Fluctuating and tending to decline; not firm. Said of prices on a stock market. **15.** Having low dissolved mineral content. Said of water. **16. a.** Sibilant rather than guttural, as *c* in *certain* and *g* in *gem.* **b.** Voiced and weakly articulated: *a soft consonant.* **c.** Palatalised, as certain consonants in Slavonic languages are. **17.** *Physics.* **a.** Of low penetrating power. Said of radiation. **b.** Having a relatively high pressure. Said of a vacuum.
~*n.* A soft object or part.
~*adv.* Softly; soft. [Middle English *soft(e)*, agreeable, pleasant, Old English *sōfte, sēfte*, from Germanic *samfti-* (unattested).] —**soft·ly** *adv.* —**soft·ness** *n.*

sof·ta (sóftə ‖ sáwftə) *n.* A Muslim student of theology and religious law. [Turkish, from Persian *sōkhta*, "aflame, burning" (devoted to learning).]

soft·ball (sóft-bawl ‖ sáwft-) *n.* **1.** A variation of baseball played on a smaller diamond with a larger, softer ball that is pitched underhand. **2.** The ball used.

soft-boiled (sóft-bóyld ‖ sáwft-) *adj.* **1.** Boiled to a soft consistency. Said of an egg. **2.** *Informal.* Soft-hearted; lenient.

soft coal *n.* Bituminous coal (see).

soft-core (sóft-kór ‖ sáwft-, -kŏr) *adj.* Intended to be sexually titillating but not explicit; not hard-core: *soft-core pornography.*

soft-cov·er (sóft-kúvvər ‖ sáwft-) *n.* **1.** A paperback. **2.** A paperback format. Also used adjectivally: *a soft-cover edition.*

soft currency *n.* A currency that is not backed by government credit and so is not readily exchangeable for other currencies. Compare **hard currency**.

soft drink *n.* A nonalcoholic, usually fizzy, drink.

soft drug *n.* A drug, such as marijuana, that is considered not to be physically addictive, and hence to be less damaging to the health than a hard drug.

sof·ten (sóff'n ‖ sáwf'n, *also* sóftən, sáwftən) *v.* **-tened, -tening, -tens.** —*tr.* To make less severe or softer. —*intr.* To become soft or softer. —**soften up.** To weaken the defences and reduce the morale of (an enemy), as by bombardment prior to full-scale attack. **2.** To cajole, flatter, or otherwise reduce the resistance of (a potential customer, for example). —**sof·ten·er** *n.*

soft-finned (sóft-find ‖ sáwft-) *adj.* *Zoology.* Having fins supported by flexible cartilaginous rays. Compare **spiny-finned**.

soft focus *n.* A slightly blurred photographic effect, usually obtained by setting a lens slightly out of focus. —**soft-focus** *adj.*

soft fruit *n.* Soft, stoneless fruit such as raspberries, blackberries, and strawberries.

soft furnishings *pl.n. British.* Curtains, rugs, furniture covers, and similar textile items.

soft goods *pl.n.* Textiles, clothing, and similar items of trade. Also *U.S.* "dry goods".

soft grass *n.* A downy grass, *Holcus mollis,* found on acid soils.

soft hail *n.* A form of hail, **graupel** *(see).*

soft-head (sóft-hed || sáwft-) *n.* A foolish or feeble-minded person; a simpleton.

soft-head·ed (sóft-héddid || sáwft-) *adj.* Lacking judgment, realism, or firmness: *a soft-headed concession.* —**soft-head·ed·ly** *adv.*

soft-heart·ed (sóft-hártid || sáwft-) *adj.* Easily moved; tender; merciful. —**soft-heart·ed·ly** *adv.* —**soft-heart·ed·ness** *n.*

soft landing *n.* The landing of a space vehicle on a celestial body in such a way as to prevent damage or destruction.

soft·ly-soft·ly (sóft-li-sóft-li || sáwft-) *adj. Informal.* Cautious, tentative, and deliberate: *a softly-softly approach.*

soft-mouthed shark *n.* A **hound shark** *(see).*

soft option *n.* A course of action open to one which is undemanding: *regarded History as a soft option.*

soft palate *n.* The movable fold, consisting of muscular fibres enclosed in mucous membrane, that is suspended from the rear of the hard palate and closes off the nasal cavity from the oral cavity during swallowing or sucking.

soft paste, soft-paste (sóft-payst || sáwft-) *n.* Any of various ceramics containing frit and refined clay.

soft pedal *n.* A pedal on a piano operating a mechanism that softens or mutes the sound.

soft-ped·al (sóft-péddl || sáwft-) *tr.v.* **-alled** or *U.S.* **-aled, -alling** or *U.S.* **-aling, -als.** 1. To soften or mute the tone of (a piano) by depressing the soft pedal. 2. *Informal.* To make less emphatic or obvious; moderate; play down.

soft roe *n.* The spermatozoa or testes of a fish; milt. The soft roe of certain fish, such as cod and herring, is tinned and eaten.

soft rot *n.* Any of various bacterial plant diseases characterised by watery disintegration of the tissues. Compare **dry rot.**

soft sciences *pl.n. Informal.* The social sciences as opposed to the physical sciences.

soft sell *n. Informal.* A subtly persuasive, unaggressive method of selling or advertising. Compare **hard sell.**

soft-shell (sóft-shel || sáwft-) *adj.* Also **soft-shelled** (-shéld). Having a soft, brittle, or unhardened shell.

soft-shell clam *n. U.S.* A **gaper** *(see).*

soft-shell crab *n.* A marine crab before its shell has hardened after moulting.

soft-shoe (sóft-shoō || sáwft-) *adj.* Of or pertaining to a type of tap dancing performed without metal taps on the shoes.

soft soap *n* 1. A fluid or semifluid soap, usually consisting of potassium salts of fatty acids. 2. **Green soap** *(see).* 3. *Informal.* Cajolery.

soft-soap (sóft-sṓp || sáwft-) *tr.v.* **-soaped, -soaping, -soaps.** *Informal.* To cajole or flatter. —**soft-soap·er** *n.*

soft sore *n.* A **chancroid** *(see).*

soft-spo·ken (sóft-spṓkən, -spṓkən || sáwft-) *adj.* 1. Speaking with a soft or gentle voice. 2. Smooth; suave; ingratiating.

soft spot *n.* 1. A place in one's heart or affections; a tender or sentimental feeling. 2. In the skull of an infant, either of the points of juncture of the sagittal and lambdoid or the sagittal, coronal, and frontal sutures; the **fontanelle** *(see).*

soft top *n.* 1. A car with a roof that folds back; a convertible. 2. The folding top of such cars, normally made of leather, canvas, or similar material.

soft touch *n. Informal.* A person who is easily persuaded to donate or lend money.

soft verge *n.* A border of soft earth or grass running along the edge of a road. Also called "soft shoulder".

soft·ware (sóft-wair || sáwft-) *n.* 1. Written or printed data, such as programs, routines, and symbolic languages, essential to the operation of computers. 2. Documents containing information on the operation and maintenance of computers, such as manuals, circuit diagrams, and flow charts. Compare **hardware, firmware.** [Coined after HARDWARE ("the machines").]

soft water *n.* Water containing little or no dissolved salts of calcium or magnesium, especially water containing less than 85.5 parts per million of calcium carbonate. Compare **hard water.**

soft·wood (sóft-wōod || sáwft-) *n.* 1. The wood of a coniferous tree. 2. A coniferous tree. Compare **hardwood.**

soft·y (sófti || sáwfti) *n., pl.* **-ies.** *Informal.* A weak, effeminate, or sentimental person.

SOGAT (sṓ-gat) Society of Graphical and Allied Trades.

Sog·di·an (sógdi-ən) *n.* 1. A member of an ancient Iranian people of Sogdiana. 2. Their extinct Iranian language. —**Sog·di·an** *adj.*

Sog·di·a·na (sógdi-áynə, -áənə || *U.S. also* -ánnə). Modern name **Trans·ox·i·a·na** (tránz-óksi-, traánz-). An ancient region of central Asia and a province of the Persian Empire.

sog·gy (sóggi) *adj.* **-gier, -giest.** 1. Saturated or sodden with moisture; soaked. 2. Lacking spirit; dull. 3. Humid; sultry. [From dialectal *sog†,* a marsh.] —**sog·gi·ly** *adv.* —**sog·gi·ness** *n.*

soh, so (sō) *n.* Also **sol** (sol || sōl). *Music.* In tonic sol-fa, a syllable representing the fifth note of a diatonic scale. [Middle English *sol,* from Latin *solve.* See **gamut.**]

So·ho (sō-hō, -hṓ). District of central London, situated in the City of Westminster. A haunt of foreign emigrés from the 17th century, Soho is known today for its restaurants, theatres, cinemas, nightclubs, and sex shops.

soi-di·sant (swáa-dee-zóN, -déezoN) *adj. French.* Self-styled; so-called.

soi·gné (swáan-yay || *U.S.* swaan-yáy) *adj. Feminine* **soi·gnée.** *French.* 1. Showing sophisticated care in performance, detail, or design. 2. Well-groomed; polished; elegant.

soil[1] (soyl) *n.* 1. The top layer of the earth's surface, suitable for the growth of plant life. 2. A particular kind of earth or ground: *sandy soil.* 3. Country; territory; region: *native soil.* 4. Land, usually with agricultural or rural connotations: *a man of the soil.* [Middle English, from Anglo-French, from Latin *solium,* seat (influenced in meaning by *solum,* base, ground).]

soil[2] *v.* **soiled, soiling, soils.** —*tr.* 1. To make dirty, particularly on the surface; begrime; smudge. 2. To disgrace; tarnish: *It soiled his reputation.* 3. To pollute with sin; defile. —*intr.* To become dirty, stained, or tarnished.

~*n.* 1. **a.** The state of being soiled. **b.** A stain or discoloration caused by dirt and grime. 2. Moral stain. 3. Filth, sewage, or refuse matter. 4. Manure, especially human faeces, used as fertiliser. [Middle English *soilen,* from Old French *souiller, suill(i)er,* from Vulgar Latin *suculāre* (unattested), from Latin *suculus, sucula,* diminutives of *sūs,* pig.]

soil[3] *tr.v.* **soiled, soiling, soils.** 1. To feed (livestock) with soilage. 2. To purge (livestock) by feeding with green food. [Perhaps from obsolete *soil,* to manure, from SOIL (manure).]

soil·age (sóylij) *n.* Green crops cut for feeding penned livestock.

soil erosion *n.* The removal of soil by wind, water, ice or gravity faster than the natural soil-forming process can replace it.

soil pipe *n.* A drain pipe that carries off waste from a lavatory.

soil·ure (sóyl-yər) *n. Archaic.* 1. Soiling or the condition of being soiled. 2. A blot, stain, or smudge.

soi·ree, soi·rée (swáa-ray, swó- || *U.S.* swaa-ráy) *n.* A party or other social gathering held in the evening, often one featuring a musical or literary recital. [French *soirée,* from *soir,* evening, from Latin *sērum,* late hour, neuter of *sērus,* late.]

so·journ (sój-ərn, súj-, -urn || *U.S.* sṓ-, sō-júrn) *intr.v.* **-journed, -journing, -journs.** To stay for a time; reside temporarily.

~*n.* A temporary stay; a brief residence. [Middle English *sojournen,* from Old French *sojorner,* from Vulgar Latin *subdiurnāre* (unattested) : Latin *sub-,* during, under + Late Latin *diurnum,* day, from Latin *diurnus,* daily, from *diēs,* day.] —**so·journ·er** *n.*

soke (sōk) *n.* 1. In early English law, the right of local jurisdiction, generally one of the feudal rights of lordship. 2. The district over which such jurisdiction was exercised. [Middle English, from Medieval Latin *sōca,* from Old English *sōcn,* inquiry, right of local jurisdiction, from Germanic *sōkniz* (unattested), akin to SEEK.]

sokeman. Variant of **socman.**

sol[1]. Variant of **soh.**

sol[2] (sol) *n.* 1. A former monetary unit of France, equal to 12 deniers. 2. An old French coin of this value. [Middle English, from Old French, from Latin *solidus,* SOLIDUS.]

sol[3] (sōl, sol) *n., pl.* **soles** (-ayss). 1. The basic monetary unit of Peru, equal to 100 centavos. 2. A coin or note worth one sol. [Spanish, "sun" (depicted on the coin), from Latin *sōl.*]

sol[4] (sol || sōl) *n. Chemistry.* A colloidal dispersion of a solid in a liquid medium. [Short for HYDROSOL.]

Sol (sol || sōl) *n.* The sun personified. [Middle English, from Latin *sōl.*]

so·la. 1. Feminine of **solus.** 2. A plural of **solum.**

sol·ace (sól-əss, -iss) *n.* Also **sol·ace·ment** (-mənt). 1. Comfort in sorrow, misfortune, or distress; consolation. 2. That which furnishes comfort or consolation.

~*tr.v.* **solaced, -acing, -aces.** 1. To comfort, cheer, or console, as in trouble or sorrow. 2. To allay or assuage. [Middle English *solas,* from Old French, from Latin *sōlācium, sōlātium,* from *sōlārī,* to comfort, console.] —**sol·ac·er** *n.*

so·la·num (sə-láynəm, sō-, -láanəm) *n.* Any plant of the genus *Solanum,* which includes the potato, aubergine, and certain nightshades. [New Latin, from Latin, nightshade.]

so·lar (sṓlər) *adj.* 1. Of, pertaining to, or proceeding from the sun: *solar rays.* 2. Utilising or operated by energy derived from the sun: *solar heating.* 3. Determined or measured with respect to the sun.

~*n.* Solar power. [Middle English, from Latin *sōlāris,* from *sōl,* sun.]

solar battery *n.* A system consisting of a large number of connected solar cells.

solar cell *n.* A semiconductor device that converts the energy of sunlight into electric energy.

solar constant *n.* The amount of solar radiation perpendicularly impinging on a surface of unit area at a distance of one astronomical unit from the sun in a unit interval of time, having an average value of 1388 watts per square metre.

solar day *n.* The interval between two successive meridian passages of the sun.

solar eclipse *n.* An **eclipse** *(see)* of the sun.

solar flare *n.* A temporary outburst of solar gases from a small area of the sun's surface, a source of intense radiation.

solar furnace *n.* A parabolic reflector that focuses solar radiation at a point to obtain high temperatures (up to 4 000°C.)

solar house *n.* A house having large quantities of heat-absorbing material behind large glass areas, designed to supplement or replace conventional heating methods.

so·lar·im·e·ter (sōlə-rímmitər) *n.* An instrument used to measure the flux of solar radiation through a surface. Also called "pyranometer". [SOLAR + -METER.]

so·lar·ise, so·lar·ize (sōlə-rīz) *v.* **-ised, -ising, -ises.** —*tr.* To expose (photographic film) briefly to the sun after developing and re-develop, so as to reverse some tones and increase highlights. —*intr. Photography.* To be overexposed. **—so·lar·i·sa·tion** (-rī-záysh'n ‖ *U.S.* -ri-) *n.*

so·lar·i·um (sə-láir-i-əm, sō-) *n., pl.* **-laria** or **-iums. 1.** A room, gallery, or glassed-in porch exposed to the sun, as in a sanitarium. **2.** A room or establishment with apparatus for artificial suntanning. [Latin *sōlārium,* sundial, terrace, balcony, from *sōl,* sun.]

solar month *n.* One-twelfth of a tropical year.

solar plexus *n.* The large network of sympathetic nerves and ganglia located in the peritoneal cavity behind the stomach and having branching tracts that supply nerves to the abdominal viscera. [From the branching ganglia resembling the sun's rays.]

solar power *n.* Power or energy obtained by direct conversion of radiation from the sun, either by its heating effect or by use of photoelectric cells to generate electricity. Also "solar".

solar system *n. Often capital* **S,** *capital* **S.** The sun together with the nine planets, asteroids, comets, and all other celestial bodies that orbit the sun.

solar wind *n.* The flow of charged particles from the sun, affecting the earth's magnetic field and causing the aurora.

solar year *n.* A **tropical year** *(see).*

so·la·ti·um (sō-láyshi-əm, sə-) *n., pl.* **-tia** (-ə). *Law.* Compensation for damage to the feelings as distinct from financial loss or physical suffering. [Late Latin *sōlātium,* SOLACE.]

sola topi *n.* A sun hat made from the pith of the sola, an East Indian reed; a pith helmet.

sold. Past tense and past participle of **sell.**

sol·dan (sól-dən ‖ sōl-) *n. Archaic.* A sultan. [Middle English *soldan, soudan,* from Old French, from Arabic *sulṭān,* SULTAN.]

sol·der (sól-dər ‖ sōl-, *chiefly U.S.* sóddər, sáwdər) *n.* **1.** Any of various fusible alloys used to join metallic parts when applied in the melted state to the solid metal. The two types are *soft solder,* which contains tin and lead and often flux and is used for electrical connections, and *hard solder,* which is an alloy of copper and zinc used for brazing. **2.** Anything that joins or cements.
~*v.* **soldered, -dering, -ders.** —*tr.* **1.** To unite or repair with solder. **2.** To serve as a bond between; join closely. —*intr.* To be capable of being soldered. Used of metals. [Middle English *souldour, soudur,* from Old French *soudure, soldure,* from *souder, solder,* to solder, from Latin *solidāre,* to make solid, from *solidus,* SOLID.] **—sol·der·er** *n.*

soldering iron *n.* A copper tip held in a handle, usually heated electrically, and used for applying soft solder.

sol·dier (sōljər, *rarely* sōld-yər) *n.* **1.** One who serves in an army. **2.** A private or a noncommissioned officer as distinguished from a commissioned officer. **3.** One who possesses military skill and experience to a specified degree: *a fine soldier.* **4.** An active and loyal follower or worker.
~*intr.v.* **soldiered, -diering, -diers. 1.** To be or serve as a soldier. **2.** To make a show of working or to feign illness in order to avoid work; shirk or malinger. **—soldier on.** To persevere in face of adverse conditions; carry on doggedly. [Middle English *souldeour,* mercenary, from Old French *soud(i)er, soldier,* from *soulde,* pay, from Latin *solidus,* SOLIDUS.]

soldier ant *n.* A form of worker ant with a large head and large mandibles, usually performing particular functions such as guarding the nest and fighting off predators.

soldier beetle *n.* Any of various carnivorous beetles of the family Cantharidae commonly seen on flowers; especially, species of the genera *Cantharis* and *Rhagonycha.*

sol·dier·ly (sōljərli) *adj.* Befitting a good soldier.

soldier of fortune *n.* One who serves in a military capacity wherever there may be profit or adventure; a mercenary.

soldier orchid *n.* The **military orchid** *(see).*

sol·dier·y (sōljəri) *n., pl.* **-ies. 1.** Soldiers collectively. **2.** A body of soldiers. **3.** The military profession.

sole[1] (sōl) *n.* **1.** The undersurface of the foot. **2.** The under-surface of a shoe, sock, or boot. **3.** The part on which something rests while standing, especially: **a.** The bottom surface of a plough. **b.** The bottom surface of the head of a golf club.
~*tr.v.* **soled, soling, soles. 1.** To furnish (a shoe or boot) with a sole. **2.** *Golf.* To put the sole of (a club) on the ground, as in preparing to make a stroke. [Middle English, from Old French *sole,* from Vulgar Latin *sola* (unattested), from Latin *solea,* sandal, from *solum,* bottom, ground, sole of the foot.]

sole[2] *adj.* **1.** Being the only one; existing or functioning without another or others; only. **2.** Of or pertaining to only one individual or group; exclusive: *The court has the sole right to decide.* **3.** *Archaic & Law.* Single or unmarried. **4.** *Archaic.* Solitary. —See Synonyms at **single.** [Middle English *soul(e), sole,* unmarried, alone, from Old French, from Latin *sōlus,* alone, single.]

sole[3] *n., pl.* **sole** or **soles. 1.** Any of various chiefly marine flatfishes of the family Soleidae, related to and resembling the flounders; especially, the European species, *Solea solea,* the Dover sole, valued as a food fish. **2.** Any of various other flatfishes, such as the lemon sole. [Middle English, from Old French, sole (fish), SOLE (of the foot), from the shape of the fish.]

sol·e·cism (sól-i-siz'm, -e-, -ə- ‖ sōl-) *n.* **1.** A nonstandard usage or grammatical construction. **2.** A violation of etiquette; an instance of bad manners or incorrect behaviour. **3.** Any impropriety, mistake, or incongruity. [From Latin *soloecismus,* from Greek *soloikismos,* from *soloikos,* speaking incorrectly, referring to the corrupt Attic dialect spoken by Athenian colonists at *Soloi,* in Cilicia.] **—sol·e·cist** *n.* **—sol·e·cis·tic** (-sístik) *adj.*

sole·ly (sōl-li ‖ sōli) *adv.* **1.** Alone; singly. **2.** Entirely; exclusively.

sol·emn (sólləm) *adj.* **1.** Deeply earnest; serious; grave: *a solemn voice.* **2.** Of impressive and serious nature: *a solemn occasion.* **3.** Performed with full ceremony: *a solemn high Mass.* **4.** Invoking the force of religion; sacred: *a solemn vow.* **5.** Gloomy; sombre. —See Synonyms at **serious.** [Middle English *solem(p)ne,* from Old French, from Latin *sollemnis,* stated, established, appointed.] **—sol·emn·ness** *n.* **—sol·emn·ly** *adv.*

sol·em·nise, sol·em·nize (sólləm-nīz) *tr.v.* **-nised, -nising, -nises. 1.** To celebrate or observe (a religious occasion, for example) with formal ceremonies or rites. **2.** To perform with formal ceremony: *solemnise a marriage.* **3.** To make serious or grave. —See Synonyms at **observe. —sol·em·ni·sa·tion** (-nī-záysh'n ‖ *U.S.* -ni-) *n.*

so·lem·ni·ty (sə-lém-nəti, so-) *n., pl.* **-ties. 1.** The condition or quality of being solemn; gravity; seriousness. **2.** A solemn proceeding or observance, as of a religious feast.

so·len·o·don (sə-lénnə-don, so-, sō-) *n.* Either of two small insectivorous mammals, *Solenodon cubana,* of Cuba, or *Solenodon paradoxus,* of Haiti, which resemble shrews.

so·le·noid (sōl-ə-noyd, sól-, -i-) *n.* **1.** A cylindrical coil of wire used to produce an axial magnetic field by a flow of electric current. **2.** An assembly consisting essentially of such a coil and a metal core free to slide along the coil axis under the influence of the magnetic field, often used as a switch as in connecting the battery to the starter motor in a motor vehicle. [From French *solénoïde,* from Greek *sōlēnoeidēs,* pipe-shaped, grooved, tubular : *sōlēn*†, channel, pipe + -OID.] **—so·le·noi·dal** (-nóyd'l) *adj.* **—so·le·noi·dal·ly** *adv.*

So·lent, The (sōlənt). Sea channel separating the Isle of Wight from the coast of Hampshire, Portsmouth and Southampton.

sole·plate (sōl-playt) *n.* The undersurface of a clothes iron.

sol-fa (sól-faá ‖ sōl-) *n. Music.* **Tonic sol-fa** *(see).* [SOL (note) + FA.]

sol·fa·ta·ra (sól-fə-taárə ‖ sōl-) *n.* A volcanic fissure that gently emits sulphurous vapours and water vapour. [Italian *Solfatara,* name of a sulphurous volcano near Naples, from *solfo,* SULPHUR.] **—sol·fa·ta·ric** *adj.*

sol·feg·gio (sol-féji-ō ‖ sōl-, -féj-) *n., pl.* **-feggi** (-féjee) or **-gios.** Also **sol·fège** (-fáyzh, -fézh). *Music.* **1.** The study and use of the tonic sol-fa syllables based on solmisation to train the ear and voice, using a fixed system in which the lowest note is always C. **2.** A singing exercise using the tonic sol-fa syllables. [Italian, from *solfeggiare,* "to sol-fa", from *solfa,* sol-fa : SOL (note) + *fa,* FA.]

sol·fe·ri·no (sól-fə-reénō ‖ sōl-) *n.* Moderate purplish red. [From a dye discovered in the year of the Battle of *Solferino* (1859). Compare **magenta.**] **—sol·fe·ri·no** *adj.*

so·lic·it (sə-líssit ‖ sō-) *v.* **-ited, -iting, -its.** —*tr.* **1.** To seek to obtain by persuasion, entreaty, or formal application: *solicit votes.* **2.** To petition (a person) persistently; importune. **3.** To entice or incite (a person) to action, particularly to an immoral or illegal action. **4.** To approach or accost (a person) with an offer of sexual services. —*intr.* **1.** To make an earnest or urgent request or petition for something desired. **2.** To approach someone with an offer of sexual services. [Middle English *soliciten,* to disturb, fill with concern, from Old French *solliciter,* from Latin *sollicitāre,* to disturb, agitate, from *sollicitus,* SOLICITOUS.] **—so·lic·i·ta·tion** (-áysh'n) *n.*

so·lic·i·tor (sə-líssitər ‖ sō-) *n. Abbr.* **sol. 1.** A lawyer who advises clients on legal matters, provides legal services such as the drawing up of conveyances or wills, and prepares a client's case for a barrister to represent the client in court. A solicitor may represent a client as an advocate, but only in certain lower courts. Compare **barrister. 2.** *Chiefly U.S.* One who solicits, as for a business or charity. **3.** The chief law officer of some U.S. cities, towns, or government departments. —See Usage note at **lawyer.**

Solicitor General *n., pl.* **Solicitors General.** *Abbr.* **S.G. 1.** In the United Kingdom, a Crown law officer ranking below the Attorney-General (in England, Wales, and Northern Ireland) or below the Lord Advocate (in Scotland). **2.** *Small* **s.,** *small* **g.** In the United States: **a.** A law officer assisting an attorney general. **b.** The chief law officer in a state not having an attorney general.

so·lic·i·tous (sə-líssitəss ‖ sō-) *adj.* **1.** Anxious and concerned; apprehensive. **2.** Taking or showing great care; meticulous or attentive. **3.** Full of desire; eager. —See Synonyms at **thoughtful.** [From Latin *sollicitus,* thoroughly moved, agitated : *sollus,* whole, entire + *citus,* past participle of *ciēre,* to put in motion, move.] **—so·lic·i·tous·ly** *adv.* **—so·lic·i·tous·ness** *n.*

so·lic·i·tude (sə-líssi-tewd ‖ sō-, -tōōd) *n.* **1.** The state of being solicitous or concerned. **2. a.** Anxiety; concern. **b.** *Usually plural.* That which causes anxiety or concern. —See Synonyms at **anxiety.**

sol·id (sóllid) *adj.* **1.** Of definite shape and volume; not liquid or gaseous. **2.** Not hollowed out or having internal spaces; consisting of solid matter throughout: *a solid block of wood.* **3.** Being the same substance throughout: *solid gold.* **4. a.** Of or pertaining to three-dimensional geometric figures: *solid geometry.* **b.** Having three dimensions: *a solid angle.* **5. a.** Without gaps or openings; continuous: *a solid line of people.* **b.** Without breaks or interruptions: *three*

solid weeks. **6.** Of good quality and substance; well-made: *solid foundations.* **7.** Having a close rather than loose consistency; hard and firm: *solid rock.* **8.** Substantial; satisfying: *a solid meal.* **9.** Sound; well-grounded; concrete: *solid facts.* **10.** Financially sound. **11.** Reputable and dependable: *a solid citizen.* **12.** Sensible, reliable, and consistent, but without brilliance or excellence; steady: *a solid worker.* **13.** Written or printed without a hyphen or space. Said of words. **14.** *Printing.* Without leads between the lines. **15. a.** Acting together; unanimous: *a solid voting bloc.* **b.** Firmly united: *a solid marriage.* **16.** *Geology.* Not superficial.
~n. **1.** A substance that is neither liquid nor gaseous, the atoms being packed more closely than in a liquid or gas; a solid substance. **2.** A geometric figure having three dimensions. **3.** *Plural.* Solid, rather than liquid, food. [Middle English *solide,* whole, solid, from Old French, from Latin *solidus.*] **—sol·id·ly** *adv.* **—sol·id·ness** *n.*

solid angle *n.* An angle subtended at a point by a surface, measured in steradians with respect to the area delimited on the unit sphere centred on that point by the locus of points of intersection of the sphere with the lines joining the point to the perimeter of the surface. Compare **polyhedral angle.**

sol·i·dar·i·ty (sólli-dárrəti) *n., pl.* **-ties. 1.** A feeling or quality of fellowship, arising from a union of interests, aspirations, or sympathies among members of a group: *A feeling of solidarity within the Women's Movement.* **2.** The firm holding together of such interests and fellow-feeling: *The solidarity of the campaign led to its success.*

Solidarity *n.* An independent trade union seeking to represent all working people in Poland, organised both by work-place and by region. Granted official recognition from November 1980 to December 1981, it was then banned until 1989. See **Walesa, Lech.** [Polish *Solidarność,* from *solidar*(ny), solidarity + *-ność,* cognate with Russian *-nost'* (as in GLASNOST) and English *-ness.*]

solid fuel *n.* **1.** Fuel such as wood, coal, or coke, that is solid rather than liquid or gas. Also used adjectivally: *a solid-fuel heating system.* **2.** A solid propellant in a rocket.

so·lid·i·fy (sə-líddi-fī, so-) *v.* **-fied, -fying, -fies.** *—tr.* **1.** To make solid, compact or hard. **2.** To make strong or united. *—intr.* To become solidified. **—so·lid·i·fi·ca·tion** (-fi-káysh'n) *n.*

so·lid·i·ty (sə-líddəti, so-) *n., pl.* **-ties. 1.** The condition or property of being solid. **2.** Soundness, as of judgment, moral character, or finances; stability.

solid of revolution *n.* A volume generated by the rotation of a plane figure about an axis in its plane.

solid propellant *n.* A rocket propellant in solid form, combining both fuel and oxidiser in the form of a compact, cohesive grain.

solid solution *n. Chemistry.* A homogeneous crystalline structure in which one or more types of atoms or molecules may be partly substituted for the original atoms and molecules without changing the crystal structure.

sol·id-state (sóllid-stáyt) *adj.* **1.** Characteristic of or pertaining to the physical properties of solid materials, especially to the electromagnetic, thermodynamic, and structural properties of crystalline solids. **2.** Based on or consisting chiefly or exclusively of semiconducting materials, components, and related devices: *solid-state audio equipment, solid-state watches.*

sol·i·dus (sólli-dəss) *n., pl.* **-di** (-dī). **1.** A diagonal mark (/) used especially: **a.** To separate alternatives, as in *and/or.* **b.** To represent the word *per,* as in *kilometres/hour.* **c.** To separate the numerator from the denominator in writing fractions, as in *3/4.* **d.** To indicate the end of verse lines printed continuously, as in *"Let us honour if we can/The vertical man."* **e.** Formerly, to denote shillings, as in *5/–.* Also called "oblique", "shilling mark", "slash", "virgule". **2.** An ancient Roman coin used until the fall of the Byzantine Empire. [Middle English, from Latin, from adjective, SOLID.]

sol·i·fid·i·an (sólli-fíddi-ən || sṓli-) *n.* A person who believes that faith alone is sufficient to ensure salvation. [From New Latin *solifidius* : Latin *sōlus,* alone + *fidēs,* faith.] **—sol·i·fid·i·an·ism** *n.*

so·li·fluc·tion (sōli-flúksh'n) *n.* The downhill flow of surface deposits, such as soil or clay, saturated with thaw water, over a slope that is still frozen.

so·lil·o·quise, so·lil·o·quize (sə-lílla-kwīz, so- || sō-) *v.* **-quised, -quising, -quises.** *—intr.* To utter or deliver a soliloquy. *—tr.* To put into the form of a soliloquy. **—so·lil·o·quist, so·lil·o·quis·er** *n.*

so·lil·o·quy (sə-lílləkwi, so- || sō-) *n., pl.* **-quies. 1.** A literary or dramatic form of discourse in which a character talks to himself or reveals his thoughts in the form of a monologue without addressing a listener. **2.** The act of speaking to oneself in or as if in solitude. [From Late Latin *sōliloquium* : Latin *sōlus,* alone + *loquī,* to speak.]

sol·ip·sism (sól-ipsiz'm, sṓl-) *n. Philosophy.* **1.** The theory that the self is the only thing that can be known and verified. **2.** The theory or view that the self is the only reality. Compare **objectivism.** [Latin *sōlus,* alone + *ipse*†, self + -ISM.] **—sol·ip·sist** *n.* **—sol·ip·sis·tic** (-ip-sístik) *adj.*

sol·i·taire (sólli-taír, -tair) *n.* **1.** A diamond or other gemstone set alone, as in a ring. **2.** A game for one person played on a special board in which marbles or pegs are arranged in slots in a pattern, the object being to remove each marble or peg, save one, by jumping others over them. **3.** *U.S.* Any of a number of card games played by one person, **patience** *(see).* [French, from Old French, solitary, from Latin *sōlitārius,* SOLITARY.]

sol·i·tar·y (sólli-tri, -təri || -terri) *adj.* **1. a.** Existing, living, or going without others; alone. **b.** Avoiding the company of others; not gregarious. **2.** Happening, done, or made alone. **3.** Remote; secluded; unfrequented: *a solitary retreat.* **4.** Having no companions; lonely. **5.** Single; sole. **6.** *Zoology.* Not living in groups or organised colonies: *solitary wasps.* —See Synonyms at **single.**
~n., pl. **solitaries. 1.** A person who lives alone; a recluse. **2.** *Informal.* Solitary confinement. [Middle English, from Latin *sōlitārius,* from *sōlus,* alone.] **—sol·i·tar·i·ly** *adv.* **—sol·i·tar·i·ness** *n.*

solitary confinement *n.* The confinement of a prisoner in a cell in which he is isolated from all others.

sol·i·tude (sólli-tewd || -tōōd) *n.* **1.** The state of being alone or remote from others; isolation. **2.** A lonely or secluded place. [Middle English, from Old French, from Latin *sōlitūdo,* from *sōlus,* alone.]
Synonyms: *solitude, isolation, seclusion, retirement.*

sol·ler·et (sóllə-ret, -rét) *n.* A steel shoe made of overlapping plates, forming a part of a suit of armour. [Old French, diminutive of *soller,* shoe, from Medieval Latin *subtēlāris,* from Late Latin *subtēl,* hollow of the foot : Latin *sub-,* under + *tālus,* ankle (see **talus**).]

sol·mi·sa·tion (sólmi-záysh'n) *n. Music.* A system of using syllables to name the notes of a scale, as in **tonic sol-fa** *(see).* [French *solmisation,* from *solmiser,* to sol-fa : SOL (note) + MI.]

so·lo (sṓlō) *n., pl.* **-los. 1.** A musical composition or passage for an individual voice or instrument, with or without accompaniment. **2.** Any performance or endeavour accomplished by a single individual, such as an aeroplane flight in which the pilot is unaccompanied. **3.** Any of various card games in which one player singly opposes others, such as *solo whist* in which each player plays independently, rather than as one of a pair.
~adj. **1.** Composed, arranged for, or performed by a single voice or instrument. **2.** Made or done by a single individual.
~adv. Unaccompanied; alone.
~intr.v. **soloed, -loing, -los.** To perform alone; especially, to fly an aeroplane without a companion or instructor. [Italian, from Latin *sōlus,* alone.]

so·lo·ist (sṓ-lō-ist) *n.* One who performs a solo or solos.

Solomon Islands. Also **Solomons.** Country comprising part of the Solomon Islands group in the southwestern Pacific. There are six main islands: Choiseul, New Georgia, Santa Isabel, Guadalcanal, Malaita, and San Cristobal, and many smaller islands and groups. Most of the islands are mountainous and wooded, and the chief products are timber, copra, and coconuts. A British protectorate was established over most of them by 1899. They witnessed fierce fighting in World War II, notably on Guadalcanal (1942–3). The Solomons became an independent state within the Commonwealth in 1978. Area, 27 556 square kilometres (10,639 square miles). Population, 390,000. Capital, Honiara. See map at **Pacific Ocean.**

Solomon, King (*c.* 973–*c.* 933 B.C.). King of Israel. Succeeding his father, David, he built the Temple of Jerusalem. The Bible attributes great wisdom to him.

Solomon's seal *n.* **1.** A six-pointed star or hexagram, like a Star of David, supposed to possess mystical powers and sometimes used as a charm or amulet. **2.** Any of several plants of the genus *Polygonatum,* having paired, drooping, greenish white flowers. [The plant is probably so called from the seal-like markings on the root stocks.]

So·lon (sṓ-lon, -lən), (*c.* 638–*c.* 559 B.C.). Athenian lawgiver and poet. His reforms preserved a class system based on wealth, but ended privilege by birth. The political franchise was extended, and serfdom effectively abolished by outlawing the use of an individual's freedom as security for debt. The reforms were controversial but became the basis of Greek law.

so long *interj. Chiefly U.S. Informal.* Goodbye.

sol·stice (sól-stiss || sṓl-) *n.* **1.** *Astronomy.* Either of two times of the year when the sun has no apparent northward or southward motion, at the most northern or most southern point of the ecliptic. In the Northern hemisphere, the summer solstice, the longest day of the year, when the sun is in the zenith at the tropic of Cancer, occurs about June 21 or 22, and the winter solstice, the shortest day, when it is over the tropic of Capricorn, occurs about December 21 or 22. The solstices are reversed in the Southern hemisphere. **2.** A turning point or culmination; a limit. [Middle English, from Old French, from Latin *sōlstitium* : *sōl,* sun + *sistere* (past participial stem *stit-*), to make stand.] **—sol·sti·tial** (-stísh'l) *adj.*

Sol·ti (shólti), **Sir Georg** (1912–97). Hungarian-born British conductor. He was musical director, Royal Opera, Covent Garden (1961–71) and conductor of the Chicago Symphony Orchestra (1969–91).

sol·u·bil·ise, sol·u·bil·ize (sóllewb'l-īz) *tr.v.* **-ised, -ising, -ises.** To make (such substances as fats and lipids, which are not appreciably soluble under standard conditions) soluble in water by the action of a detergent or similar agent.

sol·u·bil·i·ty (sóllew-bílləti) *n., pl.* **-ties. 1.** The quality or condition of being soluble. **2.** The maximum amount of a substance that can be dissolved in a given amount of solvent, usually expressed as the mass or volume of solute in a unit mass or volume of solvent at a given temperature.

sol·u·ble (sóllewb'l) *adj.* **1.** Capable of being dissolved; especially, having a high solubility. **2.** Capable of being solved or explained. [Middle English, from Old French, from Late Latin *solūbilis,* from *solvere,* to loosen.] **—sol·u·ble·ness** *n.* **—sol·u·bly** *adv.*

soluble RNA *n. Abbr.* **sRNA** *Genetics.* **Transfer RNA** *(see).*

so·lum (sṓ-ləm) *n., pl.* **-la** (-lə) or **-lums.** The surface layers of a soil profile in which topsoil formation occurs. [New Latin, from Latin, base, foundation. See **sole** (of a shoe).]

so·lus (sṓ-ləss) *adj. Feminine* **so·la** (-lə). *Latin.* Alone; by oneself. Used especially in stage directions.

sol·ute (sóllewt, so-léwt, -lōōt || sṓ-lōōt) *n. Chemistry.* A substance dissolved in another substance, usually the component of a solution present in the lesser amount. Compare **solvent**. [From Latin *solūtus*, past participle of *solvere*, to loosen.] —**sol·ute** *adj*.

so·lu·tion (sə-lōōsh'n, -léwsh'n) *n*. **1.** *Abbr*. **soln** A homogeneous mixture of two or more substances, retaining its constitution in subdivision to molecular volumes, displaying no settling, and having various possible proportions of the constituents, which may be solids, liquids, gases, or intercombinations. **2.** The process of forming such a mixture. **3.** The state of being dissolved. **4.** The method or process of solving a problem. **5.** The answer to or explanation of a problem. **6.** *Law*. The payment of a claim or debt or the discharging of an obligation. **7.** The action of separating or breaking up; a dissolution. **8.** *Mathematics*. A number, function, or set of numbers or functions, that yields a true statement when substituted in a given equation. [Middle English, from Old French, from Latin *solūtiō* (stem *solūtiōn-*), from *solūtus*. See **solute**.]

So·lu·tre·an, So·lu·tri·an (sə-lōō-tri-ən, -léw-) *adj*. *Anthropology*. Of or relating to an Upper Palaeolithic culture in Europe that succeeded the Aurignacian and was characterised by improved flint implements and stylised symbolic forms of art. [Classified from finds made at *Solutré*, Saône-et-Loire département France.]

solv·a·ble (sólv-əb'l ‖ *South of England also* sólv-) *adj*. Capable of being solved. —**solv·a·bil·i·ty** (-ə-bílləti), **solv·a·ble·ness** *n*.

sol·va·tion (sol-váysh'n ‖ sōl-) *n*. Any of a class of chemical reactions, such as the formation of hydrated copper sulphate in aqueous solution, in which solvent molecules combine with ions of the solvent. Compare **solvolysis**. [SOLV(ENT) + -ATION.]

Solvay process (sól-vay) *n*. A process used to manufacture sodium carbonate from salt, ammonia, carbon dioxide, and limestone. [Invented by Ernest *Solvay* (1838–1922), Belgian chemist.]

solve (solv ‖ *South of England also* sōlv) *tr.v*. **solved, solving, solves**. **1.** To find a solution to; answer; explain. **2.** To work out a correct solution to (a mathematical problem). [Middle English *solven*, to loosen, unbind, from Latin *solvere*.] —**solv·er** *n*.

sol·vent (sól-vənt ‖ sōl-) *adj*. **1.** Able to meet financial obligations. **2. a.** Capable of dissolving another substance. **b.** Causing or promoting dissolution or disintegration.
~*n*. **1.** *Chemistry*. **a.** The component of a solution that is present in excess or that undergoes no change of state. **b.** A liquid capable of dissolving another substance. Compare **solute**. **2.** Something that weakens, loosens, or dissipates. [Latin *solvēns* (stem *solvent-*), present participle of *solvere*, loosen. See **solve**.] —**sol·ven·cy** *n*.

solvent abuse *n*. **Glue-sniffing** (*see*).

sol·vol·y·sis (sol-vóllə-siss ‖ sōl-) *n*. Any of a class of ionic chemical reactions, such as hydrolysis, in which solute and solvent react to form other products. Compare **solvation**. [SOLV(ENT) + -LYSIS.]

Sol·way Firth (sól-way). Inlet of the Irish Sea, lying between the coast of Cumbria in England and Dumfries and Galloway in Scotland. There is a tidal bore.

Sol·zhe·nit·syn (sól-zhə-nítsin ‖ sól-, -jə-), **Alexandr (Isayevich)** (1918–). Russian writer. He was sentenced for criticising Stalin to labour camps and exile in Siberia (1945–56), and works like *One Day in the Life of Ivan Denisovich* (1962) describe the experience. *The Gulag Archipelago*, originally published only outside the U.S.S.R., is a history of the labour camp system. He was awarded the Nobel prize for literature in 1970 and forcibly expelled from the U.S.S.R. in 1974. He returned to Russia in 1994.

so·ma¹ (sómə) *n*., *pl*. **-mata** (-tə) or **-mas**. *Biology*. The body of an organism, exclusive of the germ cells. [New Latin, from Greek.]

soma² *n*. **1.** An intoxicating drink prepared from the juice of an unidentified plant, used in Vedic rituals in ancient India. **2.** The plant from which this drink is prepared. [Sanskrit *sóma*.]

So·ma·li (sə-maáli, sō-) *n*., *pl*. **-lis** or collectively **Somali**. **1.** A member of one of a group of Hamitic tribes of Somaliland. **2.** Their Hamitic language. **3.** A native or inhabitant of Somalia. —**So·ma·li** *adj*.

So·ma·li·a (sə-maáli-ə, sō-). Official name **Somali Democratic Republic**. Country in East Africa. It is hot and arid, and one of the world's poorest states. The population is chiefly Muslim and largely nomadic. Livestock, bananas, and plantains are exported. The state was created (1960) from former British and Italian possessions in Somaliland. The armed forces seized power (1969) establishing a Revolutionary Council under Siad Barre. In 1977–8 there was conflict with Ethiopia over Ethiopia's Ogaden border region. Many Somali Ethiopians fled to Somalia, where more than 1,000,000 people became refugees. Civil war broke out in 1988, and three years later Barre was expelled. In 1992 United Nations forces landed to impose order, but violence continued. The former British Somaliland has declared its independence, but not got international recognition. Area, 637 657 square kilometres (264,201 square miles). Population, 9,820,000. Capital, Mogadishu.

So·ma·li·land (sə-maáli-land, sō-). Region of northeast Africa, also known as the Horn of Africa. It is now divided between Djibouti, Ethiopia, Eritrea, and Somalia. The area is peopled mainly by Somali nomads, converted to Islam in the seventh to tenth centuries. Its strategic value after the opening of the Suez Canal (1869) led to European colonisation in the 19th century. French Somaliland became the French Territory of the Afars and Issas (1967), and gained independence as Djibouti (1977). Italian Somaliland with the Somali-speaking part of Ethiopia (the Ogaden) became a province of Italian East Africa (1936). This was taken by British forces in World War II. Italian Somaliland was made the U.N. Trust Territory of Somalia under Italian control (1950). The British returned the Ogaden to Ethiopia and Italy granted the trust territory internal

self-government as Somalia (1956). British Somaliland and Somalia combined as the independent state of Somalia (1960).

so·mat·ic (sō-máttik, sə-) *adj*. **1.** Of or pertaining to the body, especially as distinguished from a bodily part, the mind, or the environment; physical. **2.** Of or pertaining to the wall of the body cavity, especially as distinguished from the head, limbs, or viscera. **3.** Of or pertaining to the soma or somatoplasm. [From Greek *sōmatikos*, from *sōma*, body, SOMA.]

somatic cell *n*. Any cell other than a germ cell.

somato– *comb. form*. Indicates body; for example, **somatology**. [From Greek *sōma* (stem *sōmat-*), body.]

so·ma·to·gen·ic (sōmə-tə-jénnik, -tō-, sō-máttə-) *adj*. Arising within the body in response to environmental stimuli on somatic cells. [SOMATO- + -GENIC.]

so·ma·tol·o·gy (sōmə-tólləji) *n*. **1.** The physiological and anatomical study of the body. **2. Physical anthropology** (*see*). [SOMATO- + -LOGY.] —**so·ma·to·log·i·cal** (-tə-lójik'l) *adj*.

so·ma·to·plasm (sōmə-tə-plaz'm, -tō-, sō-máttə-) *n*. **1.** The entirety of specialised protoplasm, other than germ plasm, constituting the body. **2.** The protoplasm of a somatic cell. [SOMATO- + -PLASM.]

so·ma·to·pleure (sōmə-tə-ploor, -tō-, sō-máttə-, -plur ‖ -plewr) *n*. A complex sheet of embryonic cells in certain vertebrates, formed by association of part of the mesoderm with the ectoderm and developing as the internal body wall. [SOMATO- + PLEURA.]

so·ma·to·tro·phin (sōmə-tə-trófin, -tō-, sō-máttə-) *n*. **Growth hormone** (*see*). [SOMATO- + Greek *trophē*, nourishment (from *trephein*, to feed) + -IN.]

so·ma·to·type (sōmə-tə-tīp, -tō-, sō-máttə-) *n*. The morphological type of a human body; physique. See **endomorph**, **mesomorph**, **ectomorph**. —**so·ma·to·typ·ic** (-típpik) *adj*.

som·bre, *U.S.* **som·ber** (sómbər) *adj*. Also *archaic* **som·brous** (sómbrəss). **1. a.** Gloomy or shadowy; dim. **b.** Dark in colour; dull; sober. **2.** Melancholy; dismal. [French from Old French, shade, from Vulgar Latin *subombrāre* (unattested), to shade : Latin *sub-*, under + *umbra*, shade.]

som·bre·ro (som-bráir-ō, -bréer-) *n*., *pl*. **-ros**. A broad-brimmed Spanish or Mexican hat of felt or straw. [Spanish, hat, from *sombra*, shade, from Vulgar Latin *subombrāre*. See **sombre**.]

some (sum; *weak form* səm) *adj*. **1.** Being an unspecified or unknown thing or things: *some people from the office; Some fool laughed*. **2.** Being an unspecified quantity; a certain part or number but not all: *I'll have some cake*. **3.** Being an appreciable amount; considerable: *some way to go yet*. **4.** At least a little of; a small amount of: *You might give me some idea*. **5.** Remarkable or impressive: *That was some (kind of a) party!* **6.** No sort of; no person or thing of the specified kind at all. Used ironically: *Some hope!*
~*pron*. **1.** An unspecified amount or part but not all: *Can I have some?* **2.** Certain, unspecified people or things: *Some like it hot*.
~*adv*. **1.** Approximately; about: *some 30 years ago*. **2.** *U.S. Informal*. To a certain degree: *She thought about him some*.

–some¹ (-səm) *adj. suffix*. Indicates: **1.** Being or tending to be; for example, **burdensome**. **2.** Likely or inclined to; for example, **quarrelsome, tiresome**. **3.** Tending or likely to produce; for example, **awesome**. [Middle English *-som*, Old English *-sum*.]

–some² *n. comb. form*. Indicates body; for example, **chromosome**. [New Latin *-soma*, from Greek *sōma*, body.]

–some³ (-səm) *n. suffix*. Indicates a group of. Used with numerals; for example, **threesome**. [Middle English *-sum*, from *sum, som*, SOME.]

some·bod·y (súm-bədi, -boddi) *pron.* An unspecified or unknown person; someone.
~*n., pl.* **somebodies.** *Informal.* A person of importance.
Usage: Somebody and someone are regarded as singulars, in formal usage: *Someone has left his coat.* Informally, especially in speech, plural pronouns are used, but the verb always remains in the singular: *Someone has left their coat.* There is a stress contrast between *someone* and *some one* (where a person or thing has been singled out of a group): *Some one of us will have to do it.*

some·day (súm-day) *adv.* At some time in the future.
Usage: Someday and sometime express indefinite future time: *I'll do it someday.* When a particular day or time is implied (but not made explicit), two word forms are used: *I want you to choose some day that won't be too busy.* Sometime also has an informal use in the sense of "occasional", but is criticised as it allows confusion with the meaning "former": *He's a musician and sometime composer.*

some·how (súm-how, *occasionally* -ow) *adv.* In a way not specified, understood, or known.

some·one (súm-wun ‖ -wən, *North of England also* -won) *pron.* Some person; somebody. See Usage note at **somebody.**

some·place (súm-playss) *adv.* *U.S. Informal.* Somewhere.

som·er·sault, sum·mer·sault (súmmər-sawlt ‖ -solt) *n.* Also *archaic* **som·er·set, sum·mer·set** (-set). **1.** An acrobatic feat in which the body rolls in a complete circle, heels over head, either along the ground or in midair. **2.** Loosely, any complete reversal, as of sympathies or opinions.
~*intr.v.* **somersaulted, -saulting, -saults.** Also **sum·mer·sault,** *archaic* **som·er·set, sum·mer·set, -setted, -setting, -sets.** To execute a somersault. [From Old French *sombresau(l)t,* variant of *sobresault,* from Old Provençal *sobresaut* (unattested) : *sobre-,* over, above, from Latin *suprā* + *saut,* leap, from Latin *saltus,* leap.]

Som·er·set (súmmər-set, -sit). Also **Som·er·set·shire** (-shər,- sheer). County in southwestern England. It borders the Bristol Channel and comprises a lowland plain flanked by the uplands of Exmoor, the Quantocks, the Blackdown Hills and the Mendips. Dairy and fruit farming are important and the county is famous for its cider. Cheddar Gorge and the ancient Arthurian site of Glastonbury are among its tourist attractions. Taunton is the county town.

Somerset, Edward Seymour, Duke of (1506–1552). Lord Protector of England during the early part of the reign of Edward VI. He defeated a Scottish force at Pinkie (1547), but was later indicted by the Earl of Warwick. He was tried for felony and executed.

some·thing (súm-thing) *pron.* **1.** An undetermined or unspecified thing. **2.** A certain quantity, part, number, or quality: *There's something of her mother about her; something more than three weeks hence; I know something of French literature.* **3.** Used as a substitute for a name, word, or thing that has been forgotten or is not known: *She's something in publishing; Jane Something.* **4.** A thing, amount, or achievement of at least some value; a little more or better than nothing: *managed to salvage a few bits of furniture, which was something.* **5.** A person, thing, event, or achievement that is impressive or important: *That's really something!* —**make something of. 1.** To cause trouble over. **2.** To do well with; make effective or profitable use of. —**see something of.** To see occasionally. —**something of.** In someway; to some extent: *It's something of a mystery.*
~*adv.* **1.** Rather; to some extent: *She sounds something like me.* **2.** *British Nonstandard.* To a great degree. Used with an adjective to form an adverbial phrase: *messed it up something rotten.*

something else *pron.* *Chiefly U.S. Slang.* Something spectacular or impressive.

some·time (súm-tīm) *adv.* **1.** At an indefinite or unstated time. **2.** At an indefinite time in the future. **3.** *Archaic.* Sometimes. **4.** *Archaic.* Formerly.
~ *adj.* **1.** Having been at some prior time; former: *a sometime secretary.* **2.** *Informal.* Occasional. See Usage note at **someday.**

some·times (súm-tīmz) *adv.* **1.** On some occasions; at times; now and then. **2.** *Obsolete.* At some prior time; once; formerly.

some·what (súm-wot, -hwot ‖ *U.S. also* -wut, -hwut, *or with final stress*) *adv.* To some extent or degree; rather.
~*pron.* Some amount, part, or degree; something. Usually used with *of: He is somewhat of a fool.*

some·where (súm-wair, -hwair) *adv.* **1.** At, in, or to a place not specified or known; some place. **2.** At or to some unspecified point in time, amount, or degree. Usually used with *in* or *about.* —**get** or **go somewhere.** To achieve something or make progress.
~*pron.* An unknown or unspecified place.

so·mite (sóm-īt) *n.* **1.** *Zoology.* A body segment, a **metamere** *(see).* **2.** *Embryology.* One of the segmental masses of mesoderm in the vertebrate embryo, occurring in pairs along the notochord. [SOM(A) + -ITE.] —**so·mit·ic** (sōmíttik) *adj.*

Somme (som). River in northern France. It rises in the Aisne département and flows west through Amiens and Abbeville to the English Channel. It is 243 kilometres (152 miles) long. The Battle of the Somme (1916) was one of the bloodiest engagements in history, in which tanks were used for the first time.

som·nam·bu·late (som-námbew-layt) *intr.v.* **-lated, -lating, -lates.** To walk while asleep. [SOMN(I)- + AMBULATE.]

som·nam·bu·lism (som-námbew-liz'm) *n.* Also **som·nam·bu·lance, som·nam·bu·la·tion** (-láysh'n). The condition or practice of **sleep-walking** *(see).* —**som·nam·bu·list, som·nam·bu·la·tor** *n.* —**som·nam·bu·lis·tic** (-lístik), **som·nam·bu·lar** *adj.*

somni–, somn– *comb. form.* Indicates sleep; for example, **somnifacient, somnambulate.** [From Latin *somnus,* sleep.]

som·ni·fa·cient (sóm-ni-fáy-si-ənt, -shi- ‖ -fáysh'nt) *adj.* Tending to produce sleep; hypnotic. [SOMNI- + -FACIENT.]

som·nif·er·ous (som-níffərəss) *adj.* Also **som·nif·ic** (-níffik). Inducing sleep. [From Latin *somnifer:* SOMNI- + -FEROUS.]

som·no·lence (sóm-nələnss) *n.* Drowsiness; sleepiness.

som·no·lent (sóm-nələnt) *adj.* **1.** Drowsy; sleepy. **2.** Inducing or tending to induce sleep; soporific. [Middle English *sompnolent,* from Old French, from Latin *somnolentus,* from *somnus,* sleep.] —**som·no·lent·ly** *adv.*

son (sun) *n. Abbr.* **s. 1.** A male offspring. **2.** Any male descendant. **3. a.** An adopted male child. **b.** A son-in-law. **4.** A male person associated with or considered as a product of something such as a place, activity, or cause: *sons of toil.* **5.** A young man. Used as a familiar term of address. —**the Son.** The second person of the Trinity, Christ. [Middle English *son(e),* Old English *sunu.*]

so·nant (sónənt, *also* sónnənt) *adj.* Phonetics. Voiced.
~*n. Phonetics.* **1.** A voiced speech sound. **2.** A syllabic consonant; a sonorant. [Latin *sonāns* (stem *sonānt-*), present participle of Latin *sonāre,* to sound.]

so·nar (só-naar) *n.* **1.** A system using transmitted and reflected acoustic waves to detect and locate submerged objects. **2.** An apparatus using such a system, as in a submarine. [*So*und *na*vigation *r*anging.]

so·na·ta (sə-naátə ‖ sō-) *n.* A musical composition, as for the piano, violin, or other instrument, consisting of three or four independent movements varying in key, mood, and tempo. [Italian, from the feminine past participle of *sonare,* to sound, from Latin *sonāre.*]

sonata form *n.* A musical form consisting of three sections, the exposition, development, and recapitulation, often followed by a coda.

so·na·ti·na (sónnə-tée-nə ‖ sónə-) *n., pl.* **-nas** or **-ne** (-nay). A short sonata. [Italian, diminutive of SONATA.]

sonde (sond) *n.* A device, such as a **radiosonde** *(see),* launched into the atmosphere, used for making meteorological or other observations. [French. See **sound** (to measure water).]

sone (sōn) *n.* A subjective unit of loudness, equal to the loudness of a pure note having a frequency of 1,000 hertz at 40 decibels above the listener's threshold of hearing. [From Latin *sonus,* a sound.]

son et lu·mi·ère (són ay lóomi-air, *-áir; French* soN-nay-lüm-yaír) *n.* A theatrical entertainment given at night in a historic, usually outdoor setting, using recorded sound, lighting, and other effects to present the history of the place. [French, sound and light.]

song (song ‖ *U.S. also* sawng *(and in compounds)*) *n.* **1.** A usually brief musical composition consisting of words set to music, written or adapted for singing. **2.** The act or art of singing. **3.** A melodious utterance, such as a bird call. **4. a.** *Poetic.* Poetry; verse. **b.** A lyric poem or ballad. **5.** *Informal.* A small amount of money; a very low price: *picked it up for a song.* [Middle English *song, sang,* Old English *sang.*]

Song. See Sung.

Song (song, sŏong), **Mei-ling** (1897 –). Wife of Nationalist Chinese president Jiang Jieshi (Chiang Kai-shek) and sister of T.V. Song. Educated in the United States, she introduced her husband to western culture and publicised his cause in the West.

Song Qing-Ling, also known as Soong, or Sung Ch'ing-Ling. (1892–1981). Chinese politician. The sister of T.V. Song, she married the Nationalist leader Sun Zhong-shan (Sun Yat-sen), and became an active member of the movement. In modern China she has been honoured as a link between the original revolutionary movement and the present Communist regime.

Song, T.V. born Sung Tzu-Wen (1894–1971). Chinese financier and politician. He financed the Guomindang (Nationalist) Party of Sun Zhong-shan and established (1924) the Central Bank of China at Canton. He held various offices in the Guomindang governments and as foreign affairs minister negotiated (1945) the Sino-Soviet treaty of friendship. In 1949, he left China for the United States.

song and dance *n. Informal.* **1.** A great fuss, commotion, display of anger, or rigmarole. **2.** *Chiefly U.S.* An overelaborate effort to explain or justify.

song·bird (sóng-burd) *n.* A bird, especially one of the order Passeriformes, having a melodious song or call.

song form *n.* Ternary form *(see).*

song·ful (sóng-f'l) *adj.* Melodious; tuneful.

Song of Solomon *n. Abbr.* **S. of Sol.** A book of the Old Testament consisting of a dramatic love poem traditionally attributed to Solomon. Also called "Canticle of Canticles", "Song of Songs".

song·ster (sóng-stər) *n.* **1.** One that sings. **2.** A writer of songs or verses.

song thrush *n.* An Old World songbird, *Turdus philomelos,* having brown upper plumage and a spotted breast. Formerly also called "mavis", "throstle".

song·writ·er (sóng-rītər) *n.* One who writes lyrics or composes tunes, or both, for songs, especially popular songs.

son·ic (sónnik) *adj.* **1.** Of or relating to audible sound: *a sonic wave.* **2.** Having a speed approaching or being that of sound in air, approximately 332 metres per second (738 miles per hour) at sea level. [From Latin *son(us),* sound + -IC.]

sonic barrier *n.* The large increase in aerodynamic drag that acts on an aircraft as it approaches the speed of sound. Also called "sound barrier".

sonic boom *n.* A loud transient explosive sound caused by the shock wave preceding an aircraft travelling at supersonic speeds.

son-in-law (sún-in-law) *n., pl.* **sons-in-law** (súnz-). The husband of one's daughter.

son·net (sónnit) *n.* A 14-line poem usually in iambic pentameter and often made up either of a stanza of eight lines (an octet) followed by one of six lines (a sestet), or, in the Shakespearean form, three sets of four lines followed by a couplet, embodying the statement and the resolution of a single theme. [French, from Italian *sonetto,* from Old Provençal *sonet,* diminutive of *son,* song, from Latin *sonus,* sound.]

son·net·eer (sónni-téer) *n.* 1. A composer of sonnets. 2. An inferior poet.

son·ny (súnni) *n., pl.* **-nies.** Little boy; young man. Used as a familiar and sometimes contemptuous form of address. [Diminutive of SON.]

son of a bitch *n., pl.* **sons of bitches.** *Chiefly U.S. Slang.* A person for whom one feels intense dislike or contempt. Often considered vulgar.

son of a gun *n. pl.* **sons of guns.** *Chiefly U.S. Slang.* A man regarded with the admiring approval of his fellows, usually because of his macho qualities; a rogue. Often used in address.

so·no·rant (sónnə-rənt, sónə- ‖ sə-nór-, -nór-) *n. Phonetics.* 1. Any of a class of phonemes, such as (1), (r), (n), and (m), articulated without friction, being vocalic or consonantal in function according to context. 2. Either of the semivowels (w) and (y). [SONOR(OUS) + -ANT.]

so·nor·i·ty (sə-nórrəti, sō- ‖ -náwrəti) *n.* The quality or state of being sonorous; resonance. [SONOR(OUS) + -ITY.]

so·no·rous (sónnə-rəss, sónə-, sə-náw- ‖ sə-nó-) *adj.* 1. Having or producing sound. 2. Having or producing a full, deep, or rich sound. 3. Rich and impressive, as in style or delivery; grandiloquent. [Latin *sonōrus,* from *sonor,* sound, from *sonāre,* to sound.] —**so·no·rous·ly** *adv.*

son·sy, son·sie (són-si) *adj. Chiefly Scottish.* 1. Plump. Used appreciatively. 2. Cheerful. 3. Bringing good luck. [Gaelic *sonas,* good luck, from *sona,* lucky.]

Soochow. See Suzhou.

soon (sōon ‖ sōon) *adv.* **sooner, soonest.** 1. Within a short time; not long after the present time or the time in question. 2. Without delay or hesitation; quickly; promptly: *came as soon as he got our message; the sooner the better.* 3. Before the usual or appointed time; early. 4. *Obsolete.* Immediately. —**as soon.** Willingly; by preference: *I'd as soon stay at home.* —**no sooner.** Immediately or immediately after. Used with *than.* —**sooner or later.** Inevitably. —**would sooner.** Would prefer to; would rather: *would sooner die than marry him.* [Middle English *sone, soon(e),* Old English *sōna,* from Germanic *sænō* (unattested).]

Usage: No sooner is generally followed by *than* in constructions such as *No sooner had she come in than the phone rang,* though *when* is a common alternative in informal speech.

soot (sōot ‖ sōot, sut) *n.* A fine dispersion of black particles, chiefly carbon, produced by the incomplete combustion of coal, oil, wood, or other fuels.
~*tr.v.* **sooted, sooting, soots.** To cover or smudge with soot. [Middle English *so(o)t,* Old English *sōt.*]

sooth (sōoth) *adj. Archaic.* 1. True; truthful. 2. Soft; soothing.
~*n. Archaic.* Truth; reality. [Middle English *so(o)th,* Old English *sōth.*] —**sooth·ly** *adv.*

soothe (sōoth) *v.* **soothed, soothing, soothes.** —*tr.* 1. To calm; mollify; placate. 2. To reduce the intensity of (pain or emotions, for example); assuage; alleviate. —*intr.* To bring comfort, composure, or relief. —See Synonyms at **relieve.** [Middle English *sothen,* to show to be true, Old English *sōthian,* from *sōth,* truth, SOOTH.] —**sooth·er** *n.* —**sooth·ing·ly** *adv.* —**sooth·ing·ness** *n.*

sooth·fast (sōoth-faast ‖ -fast) *adj. Archaic.* 1. Truthful; honest. 2. True; real. [Middle English *sothfast,* Old English *sōthfæst : sōth,* SOOTH + *fæst,* FAST (firm).]

sooth·say (sōoth-say) *intr.v.* **-said** (-sed), **-saying, -says** (-sez ‖ -sayz). To foretell future events; predict; prophesy. [Back-formation from SOOTHSAYER.]

sooth·say·er (sōoth-say-ər) *n.* One who claims to predict future events; a prophet; a seer. [Middle English *sothsayer : soth,* SOOTH + *sayer,* one who says, from *sayen,* to SAY.]

soot·y (sōotti ‖ sōoti, sútti) *adj.* **-ier, -iest.** 1. Covered with soot. 2. Of or producing soot. 3. Black or dark like soot.

sooty mould *n.* 1. A fungal growth of mycelium and sooty spores on the surface of a leaf. 2. Any various epiphytic fungi, such as species of *Cladosporium,* producing such growths.

sooty tern *n.* An oceanic bird, *Sterna fuscata,* mainly from tropical Atlantic regions, having dark upper plumage.

sop (sop) *v.* **sopped, sopping, sops.** —*tr.* 1. To dip, soak, or drench in a liquid; saturate. 2. To take up by absorption. Usually used with *up.* —*intr.* To be or become thoroughly soaked or saturated.
~*n.* 1. A bit of bread or other food soaked in a liquid. 2. Something of little value offered in order to gain the favour or mollify the feelings of the recipient. [From Middle English *soppe,* dipped bread, Old English *sopp.*]

SOP standard operating procedure.

sop. soprano.

soph·ism (sóffiz'm) *n.* 1. A plausible but fallacious argument. 2. Any deceptive or fallacious form of argument; sophistry. [Middle English *sophime,* from Old French *sophi(s)me,* from Latin *sophisma,* from Greek, acquired skill, clever device, from *sophizesthai,* to play subtle tricks. See **sophist.**]

soph·ist (sóffist) *n.* 1. *Capital* **S.** Any of a class of ancient Greek philosophers active during the second half of the fifth century B.C., who specialised in providing instruction in ethics and the art of public speaking, and came to be disparaged for their oversubtle, self-serving reasoning. 2. A scholar or thinker, especially one skilful in devious argumentation. [From Latin *sophistēs,* from Greek, expert, deviser, from *sophizesthai,* to play subtle tricks, from *sophos†,* skilled, clever.]

so·phis·tic (sə-fístik, so-) *adj.* Also **so·phis·ti·cal** (-'l). 1. Of, pertaining to, or characteristic of sophists, especially the ancient Sophists. 2. Fond of sophistry; specious. —**so·phis·ti·cal·ly** *adv.*

so·phis·ti·cate (sə-físti-kayt) *v.* **-cated, -cating, -cates.** —*tr.* 1. To cause to become less natural or simple; especially, to make less naive and more worldly-wise. 2. To make less true, genuine, or honest; corrupt, pervert, or adulterate. 3. To make more complex; refine. —*intr.* To use sophistry.
~*n.* (-kət, -kit, -kayt). A sophisticated person. [From Medieval Latin *sophisticāre,* from Latin *sophisticus,* sophistic, from Greek *sophistikos,* from *sophistēs,* SOPHIST.] —**so·phis·ti·ca·tor** *n.* —**so·phis·ti·ca·tion** (-káysh'n) *n.*

so·phis·ti·cat·ed (sə-físti-kaytid) *adj.* 1. **a.** Having acquired worldly knowledge; lacking natural simplicity or naiveté. **b.** Having acquired worldly refinement; urbane; cultured. 2. Complex or complicated; elaborate. 3. Suitable for or appealing to the tastes of sophisticated people. —**so·phis·ti·cat·ed·ly** *adv.*

soph·is·try (sóffistri) *n., pl.* **-tries.** 1. A plausible but misleading or fallacious argument. 2. Plausible but faulty reasoning.

Soph·o·cles (sóffə-kleez). (c. 495–406 B.C.). Greek dramatist. Together with **Euripides** and **Aeschylus,** he was one of the three greatest dramatists of ancient Greece. Of more than 100 plays written by him only seven survive. These include *Ajax,* probably the earliest, *Oedipus Rex,* considered his masterpiece, *Antigone,* and *Oedipus at Colonus.* —**Soph·o·cle·an** (-klée-ən) *adj.*

soph·o·more (sóffə-mawr ‖ -mōr, *U.S. also* sóff-) *n.* A second-year student in a four-year course at a U.S. university or high school. Also used adjectively: *a sophomore year.* [Probably from earlier *sophumer,* "arguer", from obsolete *sophum,* variant of SOPHISM.]

So·phy, so·phi (sófi) *n., pl.* **-phies.** A title formerly given to kings of Persia. [Persian *Safi,* surname of ruling Persian dynasty (1500–1736), from Arabic *Safi-ud-din,* "purity of religion".]

-sophy *n. comb. form.* Indicates knowledge or a system of thought; for example, **theosophy.** [From Greek *sophia,* wisdom, and *sophos,* wise. See **sophist.**]

so·por (só-pər, -pawr) *n.* An abnormally deep sleep; stupor. [Latin *sopor,* sleep.]

so·po·rif·er·ous (sóppə-ríffərəss, sópə-) *adj.* Inducing sleep; soporific. [From Latin *soporifer : SOPOR + -FEROUS.*] —**so·po·rif·er·ous·ly** *adv.* —**so·po·rif·er·ous·ness** *n.*

so·po·rif·ic (sóppə-ríffik, sópə-) *adj.* 1. Inducing or tending to induce sleep. 2. Drowsy.
~*n.* A sleep-inducing drug. [SOPOR + -FIC.]

sop·ping (sópping) *adj.* Soaked thoroughly; drenched.
~*adv.* Used as an intensive in the phrase *sopping wet.*

sop·py (sóppi) *adj.* **-pier, -piest.** 1. Soaked; sopping. 2. *Informal.* Oversentimental in a silly way. —**sop·pi·ness** *n.*

sop·ra·ni·no (sópprə-néenō ‖ sóprə-) *adj.* Having a pitch higher than a soprano. Said of a musical instrument.
~*n., pl.* **sopraninos.** A sopranino instrument. [Italian, diminutive of SOPRANO.]

so·pran·o (sə-práa-nō ‖ *U.S. also* -prá-) *n., pl.* **-os** *or* **-prani** (-nee). *Abbr.* **sop.** *Music.* 1. The highest natural human voice, found in some women and in young boys. 2. A singer having such a voice. 3. A part for such a voice in four-part harmony. 4. The tonal range characteristic of a soprano. 5. The highest-pitched musical instrument in certain families of instrument.
~*adj.* Of, pertaining to, for, or in the range of a soprano: *a soprano saxophone.* [Italian, from *sopra,* above, from Latin *suprā.*]

sorb[1] (sorb) *tr.v.* **sorbed, sorbing, sorbs.** To take up and hold, as by absorption. [Back-formation from ABSORB.]

sorb[2] *n.* 1. Any of several Old World trees of the genus *Sorbus* or related genera, such as the white beam or the rowan. 2. The fruit of such a tree. In this sense, also called "sorb apple". [French *sorbe,* from Latin *sorbus,* SERVICE (tree).] —**sorp·tion** *n.*

Sorb (sorb) *n.* A Wend *(see).* [German *Sorbe,* perhaps variant of *Serbe,* Serb, from Serbian *Srb,* SERB.]

sor·be·fa·cient (sórbi-fáy-shənt, -si-ənt, -shi-) *adj.* Bringing about absorption.
~*n.* A drug that either causes or facilitates absorption. [From Latin *sorbēre,* to absorb + -FACIENT.]

sor·bet (sórb-ət, -it) *n.* A water ice made with fruit juice or fruit purée. Also *chiefly U.S.* "sherbet". [French, from Italian *sorbetto,* from Turkish *sherbet,* SHERBET.]

Sor·bi·an (sórbi-ən) *n.* 1. A Wend *(see).* 2. Wendish *(see).* [From SORB.] —**Sor·bi·an** *adj.*

sor·bic acid (sórbik) *n.* A white crystalline solid, $C_6H_8O_2$, found in the berries of the mountain ash and also synthesised, and used as a food preservative and fungicide. [From SORB (tree).]

sor·bi·tol (sórbi-tol ‖ -tōl) *n.* A white sweet crystalline alcohol, $C_6H_8(OH)_6$, found in certain fruits and manufactured from sucrose for use as an artificial sweetener and raw material for making ascorbic acid and some plastics.

sor·bo rubber (sórbō) *n.* A form of spongy rubber. [*Sorbo,* from ABSORB.]

sor·bose (sórb-ōz, -ōss) *n.* A white crystalline sugar, $C_6H_{12}O_6$, used in the manufacture of ascorbic acid. [SORB (tree) + -OSE.]

sor·cer·er (sór-sərər) *n.* One who practices sorcery; a wizard or magician. [Middle English *sorser*, from Old French *sorcier*, from Vulgar Latin *sortiārius* (unattested), caster of lots, from *sors* (stem *sort-*), lot.]

sor·cer·ess (sór-sə-riss, -ress) *n.* A female sorcerer.

sor·cer·y (sór-səri) *n., pl.* **-ies.** The use of supernatural powers in order to produce supernatural effects, especially through the assistance of evil spirits; witchcraft; black magic. See Synonyms at **magic.** [Middle English *sorcerie*, from Old French, from *sorcier*, SORCERER.] **—sor·cer·ous** *adj.* **—sor·cer·ous·ly** *adv.*

sor·did (sórdid) *adj.* **1.** Filthy or dirty; foul: *a sordid sewer.* **2.** Depressingly squalid; wretched: *sordid shantytowns.* **3.** Morally degraded; vile; despicable: *sordid betrayal.* **4.** Exceedingly mercenary; grasping; selfish. [French *sordide*, from Latin *sordidus*, from *sordēre*, to be dirty.] **—sor·did·ly** *adv.* **—sor·did·ness** *n.*

sor·di·no (sawr-dée-nō) *n., pl.* **-ni** (-nee). Also **sor·dine** (sór-deen). A mute for a musical instrument. [Italian, from *sordo*, deaf, mute, from Latin *surdus.*]

sore (sor ‖ sōr) *adj.* **sorer, sorest. 1.** Causing physical pain, as from injury or disease; aching or tender: *a sore foot.* **2.** Feeling physical pain; hurting: *I'm still sore today.* **3.** Causing or involving hardship misery, or distress; grievous: *sore need.* **4.** Causing embarrassment, irritation, or the like: *a sore subject.* **5.** Full of distress; grieved; sorrowful. **6.** *Chiefly U.S. Informal.* Angered; annoyed. *~adv. Archaic.* Sorely. *~n.* **1.** An open wound or ulcer on the skin or a mucous membrane. **2.** Any source of pain, distress, or irritation. [Middle English *sar, sor,* Old English *sār.*] **—sore·ness** *n.*

so·re·di·um (sə-réedi-əm, so-) *n.* A type of asexual spore produced by some lichens, consisting of a few algal cells enclosed in fungal hyphae. [New Latin, irregularly from Greek *sōros,* heap.]

sore·head (sór-hed ‖ sōr-) *n. U.S. Informal.* A person who is easily offended, annoyed, or angered.

sore·ly (sór-li ‖ sōr-) *adv.* **1.** Severely; painfully; grievously. **2.** Extremely; greatly: *His skill was sorely needed.*

sore throat *n.* Any of various inflammations of the tonsils, pharynx, or larynx characterised by pain in swallowing.

sor·ghum (sórgəm) *n.* **1.** An Old World grass of the genus *Sorghum;* especially, *S. vulgare,* several varieties of which are widely cultivated as grain and forage or as a source of syrup. **2.** Syrup made from the juice of this plant. [New Latin, from Italian *sorgo,* perhaps from Vulgar Latin *syricum (grāmen)* (unattested), Syrian (grass), from Latin *Syricum,* SYRIAN.]

sor·go, sor·gho (sórgō) *n., pl.* **-gos.** Any of various sorghums cultivated as a source of syrup. [Italian *sorgo,* SORGHUM.]

so·ri. Plural of **sorus.**

sor·i·cine (sórri-sīn ‖ sáwri-, sōri-, -seen) *adj.* Of or belonging to the family Soricidae, which includes the shrews. [From Latin *sōricīnus,* from *sōrex* (stem *sōric-*), shrew, akin to Greek *hurax,* HYRAX.]

so·ri·tes (so-ríteez, sə-) *n., pl.* **sorites.** *Logic.* A form of argument in which a series of incomplete syllogisms is so arranged that the predicate of each premise forms the subject of the next. [Latin *sōrītēs,* from Greek *sōreitēs,* from *sōros,* heap, pile.]

So·rop·ti·mist (sə-rópti-mist, so-) *n.* A member of a Soroptimist Club.

Soroptimist Club *n.* Any club belonging to *Soroptimist International,* an organisation of professional women dedicated to community service both locally and abroad. [*sorority* + *optimist.*]

so·ro·ral (sə-ráw-rəl, so- ‖ -rō-) *adj.* Pertaining to or like a sister; sisterly. [Latin *soror,* sister.]

so·ror·ate (sə-ráw-rət, so-, -rit ‖ -rō-) *n.* The custom of marriage of a man to his wife's sister or sisters, usually after the first wife has died or proved sterile. [From Latin *soror,* sister.]

so·ror·i·cide (sə-rórri-sīd, so- ‖ -ráwri-) *n.* **1.** The killing of one's sister. **2.** One who kills his own sister. [Medieval Latin *sororicidium* : Latin *soror,* sister + -CIDE.] **—so·ror·i·cid·al** (-síd'l) *adj.*

so·ror·i·ty (sə-rórrəti, so- ‖ -ráwrəti) *n., pl.* **-ties. 1.** A sisterhood. **2.** *U.S.* A social club for female students, as at a university. Compare **fraternity.** [From Medieval Latin *sororitās,* from Latin *soror,* sister.]

so·ro·sis (sə-rṓ-siss, so-) *n., pl.* **-ses** (-seez). *Botany.* A fleshy composite fruit, such as a pineapple, formed from an enlarged spike or perianth. [From Greek *sōros,* heap.]

sorp·tion (sórpsh'n) *n. Chemistry.* **1.** The process of sorbing. **2.** The state of being sorbed. [Back-formation from ABSORPTION and ADSORPTION.]

sor·rel¹ (sórrəl ‖ sáwrəl) *n.* **1.** Any of several plants of the genus *Rumex,* having acid-flavoured leaves sometimes used as salad greens; especially, *R. acetosella,* a widely naturalised species native to Eurasia. **2.** Any of various plants of the genus *Oxalis.* See **wood sorrel.** [Middle English *sorel,* from Old French *surele,* from *sur,* sour, from Germanic.]

sorrel² *n.* **1.** Brownish orange to light brown. **2.** A horse of this colour. [Middle English *sorelle,* sorrel-coloured, from Old French *sorel,* from *sor,* red-brown, from Germanic.]

sor·row (sórrō ‖ sáwrō) *n.* **1.** Mental anguish or suffering, especially because of injury or loss; sadness. **2.** Something that causes such suffering; misfortune. **3.** The expression of such suffering; grieving. —See Synonyms at **regret.** *~intr.v.* **sorrowed, -rowing, -rows.** To feel or display sorrow;

grieve. [Middle English *sorge, sorow,* Old English *sorh, sorg,* anxiety, sorrow.] **—sor·row·er** *n.*

sor·row·ful (sórrō-f'l, sórrə- ‖ sáwrō-, sáwrə-) *adj.* Causing, feeling, or expressing sorrow; mournful. See Synonyms at **sad. —sor·row·ful·ly** *adv.* **—sor·row·ful·ness** *n.*

sor·ry (sórri ‖ *U.S. also* sáwri) *adj.* **-rier, -riest. 1. a.** Feeling sympathy, pity, or distress; sorrowful. **b.** Feeling regret or penitence. Often used to express apology: *I am sorry to be late.* **2.** Inspiring a mixture of pity and scorn; pitiful; deplorable: *a sorry sight.* **3.** Worthless or inferior; contemptible; paltry: *a sorry attempt at apology.* **4.** Causing sorrow or grief; sad; distressing. *~interj.* Used to express apology or to ask someone to repeat what he has just said. [Middle English *sary, sory,* Old English *sārig,* painful, sad.] **—sor·ri·ly** *adv.* **—sor·ri·ness** *n.*

sort (sort) *n.* **1.** A particular class or kind of persons or things grouped together on the basis of some common characteristic. **2.** The character or nature of something; type; quality. **3.** Something that approximates to a certain, often inadequate, degree to the specific thing: *a job of a sort; lives in a sort of a penthouse.* **4.** *Informal.* **a.** A person: *a good sort.* **b.** *Australian.* A woman or girl. **5.** *Archaic.* Manner; way. **6.** *Usually plural. Printing.* One of the characters in a font of type. —See Synonyms at **type. —of sorts. 1.** Of a mediocre or inferior kind. **2.** Of one kind or another. **—out of sorts.** *Informal.* **1.** Somewhat ill; slightly sick. **2.** In a bad mood; irritable; cross. **—sort of.** *Informal.* Somewhat; rather. *~v.* **sorted, sorting, sorts.** *—tr.* **1.** To classify, separate, or arrange according to quality, size, or some other criterion. **2.** *Scottish Informal.* To repair; restore to working order. **3.** *British.* To sort out. *—intr. Formal.* To be in harmony; fit in; agree. Used with *with.* [Middle English, from Old French *sorte,* probably from Common Romance *sorta* (unattested), "kind", from Latin *sors* (stem *sort-*), lot, of fortune.] **—sort·a·ble** *adj.* **—sort·er** *n.*

Usage: The numerical status of *sort of* and *kind of,* when used with a plural noun, has long been a source of controversy. The informal usage shown in *These sort of problems need to be solved* attracts criticism, on the grounds that the singular noun requires a singular modifier. In defence of the construction (which has literary precedent going back to Shakespeare), it is argued that the modifier *these/those* is used because of the collective plural sense of the whole noun phrase (*These (sort of) problems need to be solved*). However, many people prefer not to use the problematic construction, and use some other phrasing, such as *Problems of this sort . . .*

sor·tie (sór-ti, -tee) *n. Military.* **1.** A sally by besieged forces upon the besiegers. **2.** A single flight of an aircraft on a combat mission. [French, "a going out", from past participle of *sortir†,* go out.]

sor·ti·lege (sórtilij) *n.* The act or practice of foretelling the future by drawing lots. [Middle English, from Old French, from Medieval Latin *sortilegium,* from *sortilegus,* diviner : Latin *sors* (stem *sort-*), lot + *legere,* to read.]

sor·ti·tion (sawr-tísh'n) *n.* The drawing of lots, as in the selection of candidates for office. [Latin *sortitiō* (stem *sortitiōn-*), from *sortīrī,* to cast lots, from *sors,* lot.]

sort out *tr.v.* **1.** To separate or abstract (one kind, for example) from others. **2.** To resolve, deal with, or put to rights. **3.** *British Informal.* To punish or physically attack.

sort-out (sórt-owt) *n. British Informal.* An act of putting things in order.

so·rus (sáw-rəss ‖ sṓ-) *n., pl.* **sori** (-rī). *Botany.* **1.** A cluster of spore cases borne by ferns on the undersides of the fronds. **2.** A similar structure in certain fungi and lichens. [New Latin, from Greek *sōros,* heap.]

S O S *n.* **1.** The letters represented by the radiotelegraphic signal ···— ——···, used internationally as a distress signal, particularly by ships and aircraft. **2.** Any call or signal for help.

so-so (sṓ-sō ‖ -sṓ) *adj. Informal.* Neither very good nor very bad; mediocre; passable. See Synonyms at **average.** *~adv. Informal.* Indifferently; tolerably; passably.

sos·te·nu·to (sósta-nōō-tō, sósti-, -néw-) *adv. Abbr.* **sost.** *Music.* In a sustained or prolonged manner. Used as a direction. *~n., pl.* **sostenutos** or **-ti** (-tee). *Abbr.* **sost.** *Music.* A passage played or sung in this manner. [Italian, past participle of *sostenere,* to SUSTAIN.] **—sos·te·nu·to** *adj.*

sot (sot) *n.* A chronic drunkard. [Middle English *sot,* a fool, Old English *sott,* from Medieval Latin *sotius†.*]

so·te·ri·ol·o·gy (sō-téer-i-óllaji) *n.* The theological doctrine of salvation as effected by Christ. [Greek *sōtērion,* deliverance, from *sōtēr,* saviour, from *sōzein,* to save, from *saos,* safe + -LOGY.] **—so·te·ri·o·log·i·cal** (-ə-lójik'l) *adj.*

So·thic (sṓthik, sóthik) *adj.* **1.** Designating the ancient Egyptian year, consisting of 365¹/₄ days. **2.** Designating a cycle consisting of 1,461 years of 365 days in the ancient Egyptian calendar. [Greek *Sōthis,* the star Sirius, which appeared on the eastern horizon at sunrise when the year commenced.]

So·this (sṓthiss) *n.* Sirius, the Dog Star. [Greek *Sōthis,* the Egyptian, the star Sirius. See **Sothic.**]

So·tho (sṓō-tōō, -tōō, sṓtō) *n., pl.* **-thos** or collectively **Sotho. 1.** A group of Bantu languages spoken in Lesotho, Botswana, and South Africa. **2.** A member of a Sotho-speaking people. **3.** The dialect of Sotho spoken in Lesotho. In this sense also called "Sesotho".

sot·tish (sóttish) *adj.* **1.** Stupefied from or as if from drink. **2.** Tending to drink excessively; drunken. **—sot·tish·ly** *adv.*

sot·to vo·ce (sóttō vṓchi) *adv.* Very softly; especially, so as not to be overheard; in an undertone. [Italian, "under the voice".]

sou (sōō) *n.* **1.** A former French coin of very low value. **2.** A very small amount of money. [French, back-formation from Old French *sous,* plural of *sout,* from Latin *solidus,* SOLIDUS.]

sou·brette (sōō-brét) *n.* **1. a.** A saucy, coquettish, and intriguing lady's maid in comedies or comic opera. **b.** An actress or singer taking such a part. **2.** Any flirtatious or frivolous young woman. [French, from Provençal *soubreto,* feminine of *soubret,* coy, from *sobrar.* to be above, from Latin *superāre,* from *super,* above.]

soubriquet. Variant of **sobriquet.**

sou·chong (sōō-chóng, -shóng, -chong, -shong) *n.* One of several varieties of black tea native to China and adjacent regions. [Chinese *xiǎo zhǒng,* small kind.]

souf·flé (sōō-fláy || *U.S.* sōō-fláy) *n.* A light, fluffy baked dish made with egg yolks and beaten egg whites combined with various other ingredients and served as a main dish or sweetened as a dessert. ~*adj.* Also **souf·fléed** (flayd || -fláyd). Made light and puffy by beating or cooking. [French, from the past participle of *souffler,* to blow, puff up.]

sough (sow, suf) *intr.v.* **soughed, soughing, soughs.** To make a soft murmuring or rustling sound: *a gentle soughing wind.* ~*n.* A deep, soft murmuring sound, as of the wind or a gentle surf. [Middle English *swoghen,* Old English *swōgan.*]

sought. Past tense and past participle of **seek.**

sought-af·ter (sáwt-aaftər, -aáftər || -aftər, -áftər) *adj.* In great demand; highly-regarded.

souk, soukh (sōōk) *n.* A marketplace in an Arabic-speaking region. [Arabic *sōōq,* market]

soul (sōl) *n.* **1.** The animating and vital principle in humankind credited with the faculties of thought, action, and emotion and conceived as forming an immaterial entity distinguished from but temporally coexistent with the body. **2.** *Theology.* The spiritual nature of man considered in relation to God, regarded as immortal, separable from the body at death, and susceptible to happiness or misery in a future state. **3.** The disembodied spirit of a dead human being. **4.** The vital, central part or feature of something. **5.** A human being: *a village of 200 souls.* **6.** A person considered as the perfect embodiment of some quality; a personification. **7.** A person considered as an inspiring force; a prime mover. **8.** The emotional nature in humankind as distinguished from the mind or intellect. **9.** Depth and sincerity of feeling, or the ability to convey this effectively. **10. a.** A capacity for intense and uninhibited emotional feeling, especially considered as a characteristic quality of black American culture. **b.** Soul music. [Middle English *soul,* Old English *sāwol,* from Common Germanic *saiwalō* (unattested).]

soul brother *n. U.S. Slang.* A fellow black of the male sex.

soul-de·stroy·ing (sōl-di-stróy-ing, -də-) *adj.* Monotonous and totally unstimulating; stultifying.

soul·food (sōl-fōōd) *n. U.S.* Food that belongs to the traditional diet of blacks in the southern United States.

soul·ful (sōl-f'l) *adj.* Full of or expressing deep feeling; profoundly emotional. —**soul·ful·ly** *adv.* —**soul·ful·ness** *n.*

soul·less (sōl-ləss, -liss) *adj.* **1.** Devoid of sensitivity or the capacity for deep feeling. **2.** Devoid of human qualities; depressingly impersonal: *a big soulless office.* —**soul·less·ly** *adv.* —**soul·less·ness** *n.*

soul mate *n.* A person with whom one shares a deep empathy in terms of disposition, point of view, or sensitivity.

soul music *n.* Music derived from black American gospel music with elements of rhythm and blues, characterised by emotional fervour and earthiness.

soul-search·ing (sōl-serching) *n.* The penetrating examination of oneself, one's motives, convictions, and feelings.

soul sister *n. U.S. Slang.* A fellow black of the female sex.

sound[1] (sownd || *West Indies also* sungd) *n.* **1. a.** A vibratory disturbance characterised by longitudinal waves in the pressure and density of a fluid, or in the elastic strain in a solid, with frequency in the approximate range between 20 and 20,000 hertz, and capable of being detected by the organs of hearing. **b.** Loosely, such a disturbance of any frequency. **2. a.** The sensation stimulated in the organs of hearing by such a disturbance. **b.** Such sensations collectively. **3.** A distinctive auditory effect produced by a particular cause: *the sound of the whistle.* **4.** The distance over which something can be heard; earshot: *within sound of cannon fire.* **5. a.** An articulation made by the vocal apparatus. **b.** The distinctive character of such an articulation. For example, *bear* and *bare* have the same sound. **6.** A mental impression conveyed; import; implication: *I don't like the sound of that.* **7.** Auditory material that is recorded, as for a film or television programme. **8.** A style of popular music associated with a particular place, person, or the like: *the Tamla-Motown sound.* **9.** *Archaic.* Rumour; report. ~*v.* **sounded, sounding, sounds.** —*intr.* **1.** To make or give forth a sound. **2. a.** To produce a particular effect when heard: *Your exhaust sounds very noisy.* **b.** To present a particular impression; seem to be: *That argument sounds reasonable; sounds as if we've lost.* —*tr.* **1.** To cause to give forth or produce a sound. **2.** To summon, announce, or signal by a sound: *sound a warning.* **3.** To articulate (a speech sound); pronounce. **4.** To make known; celebrate. **5.** To examine (a bodily organ or part) by causing to emit sound; auscultate. —**sound off.** *Informal.* To express one's opinions, complaints, or prejudices in a loud, vigorous tone. [Middle English *sun, soun,* from Old French *son,* from Latin *sonus.*]

sound[2] *adj.* **sounder, soundest.** **1.** Free from defect, decay, or damage; in good condition. **2.** Free from disease or injury; healthy: *sound in body and mind.* **3.** Having a firm basis; solid; substantial: *a* **sound foundation. 4.** Financially secure or stable; reliable: *a sound economy.* **5. a.** Founded on valid reasoning; free from misapprehension or logical flaws; sensible and cogent: *a sound observation.* **b.** Marked by or showing common sense and good judgment; level-headed: *Sound advice.* **c.** Marked by or showing impressive breadth of learning; well-versed. **6.** Thorough; severe: *a sound flogging.* **7.** Deep and unbroken; undisturbed: *a sound sleep.* **8.** Free from moral defect; upright; honourable. **9.** Worthy of confidence; trustworthy. **10.** Compatible with an accepted point of view; orthodox, especially in a theological sense. **11.** *Law.* Legally valid. —See Synonyms at **healthy, valid.** ~*adv.* Deeply: *sound asleep.* [Middle English *sund,* Old English *gesund.*] —**sound·ly** *adv.* —**sound·ness** *n.*

sound[3] *n.* **1.** A long, relatively wide body of water wider than a strait or a channel, connecting larger bodies of water. **2.** A long, wide ocean inlet. **3.** The air bladder of a fish. [Middle English *sound,* sound, swimming, Old English *sund,* swimming.]

sound[4] *v.* **sounded, sounding, sounds.** —*tr.* **1.** To measure the depth of (water), especially by means of a weighted line; fathom. **2.** To try to find out the attitudes or intentions of (a person), especially by indirect questioning. Usually used with *out.* **3.** *Surgery.* To probe (a bodily cavity) with a sound. —*intr.* **1.** To measure depth. **2.** To dive swiftly downwards. Used of a whale or fish. ~*n. Surgery.* An instrument used to examine body cavities. [Middle English *sounden,* from Old French *sonder,* from *sonde,* a sounding line, probably from Old English *sund-,* from *sund,* sea.] —**sound·a·ble** *adj.*

Usage: Sound out, in the sense of 'search for an opinion', is now well-established as a transitive verb (*I'll sound them out and see what they think*), but it occasionally attracts criticism from purists who feel that the *out* is an unnecessary recent addition.

sound barrier *n.* The **sonic barrier** (*see*).

sound bite *n.* A short excerpt from a longer stretch of sound (such as a soundtrack or a speech), recorded and typically played to suggest the whole of which it is a part: *"Politicians no longer address us in speeches, but in 30-second sound bites and photo opportunities."* (Michael Ignatieff, *The Independent.*) [From the notion that it is a chunk "bitten out" of the whole.]

sound box *n.* A hollow chamber in the body of a musical instrument, such as a violin, that intensifies the resonance of the tone.

sound camera *n.* A cine camera equipped to record sound and image synchronously.

sound effects *pl.n.* Imitative sounds, as of thunder or an explosion, produced artificially for use in a film, play, or other performance.

sound·er (sówndər || *West Indies also* súngdər) *n.* One that sounds; specifically, a device for making soundings of the sea.

sound·ing[1] (sównding || *West Indies also* súngding) *n.* **1.** Measurement or examination by sounding. **2.** An environmental probe for scientific observation. **3.** *Often plural.* **a.** The measurement of depth by a hand line or by sonic or ultrasonic means. **b.** A measured depth of water. **c.** Water shallow enough for depth measurements to be taken by a hand line. **4.** An investigation of opinions or attitudes; a probe.

sounding[2] *adj.* **1.** Emitting a full sound; resonant. **2.** Having a rich or impressive sound but little significance; high-sounding.

sounding board *n.* **1.** A thin board forming the upper portion of the resonant chamber in a musical instrument, such as a violin or piano, and serving to increase resonance. Also called "sound board". **2.** A dome or other structure suspended behind or over a pulpit or platform to reflect the speaker's voice to the audience. **3.** Any person or group whose reactions to an idea, opinion, or point of view will serve as a measure of its effectiveness or acceptability.

sounding lead *n.* The metal weight at the end of a sounding line.

sounding line *n.* A line marked at intervals of fathoms and weighted at one end, used to determine the depth of water.

sounding rocket *n.* A rocket used to make observations anywhere within the earth's atmosphere.

sound·less (sównd-ləss, -liss || *West Indies also* súngd-) *adj.* Having or making no sound; silent. —**sound·less·ly** *adv.* —**sound·less·ness** *n.*

sound·proof (sównd-prōōf || -prōōf, *West Indies also* súngd-) *adj.* Not penetrable by audible sound. ~*tr.v.* **soundproofed, -proofing, -proofs.** To make soundproof.

sound ranging *n.* The electronic location of a sound source, as of enemy weapons, by checking time intervals indicated by microphones of known position.

sound stage *n.* A room or studio, usually soundproof, used for the production of cinematic films.

sound system *n.* A set of equipment for playing back recorded sound usually consisting of a record deck, amplifier, speakers and often a cassette player and radio.

sound·track (sównd-trak || *West Indies also* súngd-) *n.* **1.** The narrow strip at one side of a cine film that carries the sound recording. **2.** A recording of the music featured in a film.

sound wave *n.* A wave of **sound** (*see*).

soup (sōōp) *n.* **1.** A liquid food prepared from meat, fish, or vegetable stock with various other ingredients added, served either hot or cold. **2.** *Slang.* Anything suggestive of the consistency of soup, especially: **a.** Dense fog. **b.** Nitroglycerine. See **primordial soup.** —**in the soup.** *Informal.* In trouble; having difficulties. —**soup up.** *Informal.* **1.** To increase the power or speed potential of (an engine). **2.** To improve; make more effective. [French *soupe,* from

Old French, broth, sop, from Late Latin; from Germanic.]

soup·çon (sōōp-son ‖ *U.S.* sōōp-són) *n.* A very small amount; a trace; a touch. [French, SUSPICION.]

Sou·phan·ou·vong (sōō-fannoo-vóng), **Prince** (1902–). Laotian politician. He became first president of the republic of Laos in 1975.

soup kitchen *n.* A place where food is offered freely or at very low cost to the needy.

soup·spoon (sōōp-spōōn) *n.* A spoon used for eating soup, about the same size as a dessertspoon but with a more rounded bowl.

soup·y (sōōpi) *adj.* **-ier, -iest. 1.** Having the consistency or appearance of soup. **2.** Foggy. **3.** *Informal.* Inordinately sentimental.

soup·strain·er (sōōp-straynər) *n. Informal.* A bushy moustache that completely covers the upper lip.

sour (sowr) *adj. Rare* **sourer, sourest. 1.** Having a taste characteristic of that produced by acids; sharp, tart, or tangy, as lemons or vinegar are. **2.** Made acid or rancid by fermentation; spoiled. Said of milk for example. **3.** Having the characteristics of fermentation or rancidity; tasting or smelling of decay. **4.** Bad-tempered and morose; cross; peevish: *a sour temper.* **5. a.** Disagreeable; unpleasant. **b.** Turning out wrong; failing to fulfil expectations. **6.** Designating soil that is excessively acid and damaging to crops. **7.** Containing excessive amounts of sulphur compounds. Said of petrol.
~*n.* **1.** The sensation of sour taste, one of the four primary tastes. **2.** Anything that is sour. **3.** *Chiefly U.S.* A cocktail of spirits, such as whisky, with lime or lemon juice and sugar.
~*v.* **soured, souring, sours.** —*tr.* To make sour: "*Continued adversity had soured Johnson's temper*" (T.B. Macaulay). —*intr.* To become sour. [Middle English *so(u)r*, Old English *sūr*, from Germanic.] —**sour·ly** *adv.* —**sour·ness** *n.*

source (sorss ‖ sōrss) *n.* **1.** A spring, lake, or other body of water at which a stream or river originates. **2. a.** The place or thing from which something originates; the starting point: *the source of their quarrel.* **b.** That from which someting comes or is derived: *a source of income; alternative sources of energy.* **c.** One that causes, creates, or initiates something: *a source of continual annoyance.* **3.** A person or place that supplies information. Also used adjectivally: *a source book.* **4.** A book, document, or other record supplying primary or firsthand information. **5.** The electrode in a field-effect transistor from which the majority carriers flow into the interelectrode region. **6.** In thermodynamics, the part of a system at which heat, or more generally energy, is added to the system. In this sense, compare **sink.** —See Synonyms at **origin.**
~*tr.v.* **sourced, sourcing, sources.** To obtain (materials) from a producer: *sourcing steel from Germany.* [Middle English *sours, source,* from Old French *sourse,* from the feminine past participle of *sourdre,* to rise, from Latin *surgere,* to SURGE.]

source language *n.* A language out of which a translation is made. Compare **target language.**

source program *n.* A computer program as written in the original programming language for conversion into machine language by the computer.

sour cherry *n.* **1.** A tree, *Prunus cerasus,* native to Eurasia, having white flowers and tart red fruit. **2.** The edible fruit of this tree.

sour cream *n.* Also **soured cream.** A smooth, thick, cream, artificially soured by the use of lactic acid bacteria, widely used as an ingredient in soups, salads, and various meat dishes.

sour·dough (sówr-dō) *n.* **1.** *Regional.* Sour fermented dough used as leaven in making bread. **2.** *U.S. & Canadian Slang.* An old-time settler or prospector, especially in Alaska and northwest Canada.

sour grapes *n.* The adoption of a disparaging attitude towards something that one secretly wants or admires but cannot attain. [From Aesop's fable of the fox that, unable to reach the grapes it wants, decides that they are unripe.]

sour mash *n. U.S.* **1.** A mixture of new mash and mash from a preceding run used to distil certain malt whiskeys. **2.** The whiskey distilled from this mash.

sour·puss (sówr-pōōss) *n. Informal.* A person with a habitually gloomy or sullen expression or attitude. [SOUR + PUSS (face).]

sour·sop (sówr-sop) *n.* **1.** A tropical American tree, *Annona muricata,* bearing spiny fruit with tart, edible pulp. **2.** The fruit of this tree.

Sou·sa (sōō-zə, *also* -sə), **John Philip** (1854–1932). American bandmaster and composer. He wrote comic operas, as well as marches such as *Liberty Bell* and *Washington Post March.*

sou·sa·phone (sōō-zə-fōn, -sə-) *n.* A large brass wind instrument similar to the tuba, having a flaring bell. [After John Philip SOUSA.]

souse[1] (sowss) *v.* **soused, sousing, souses.** —*tr.* **1.** To plunge in a liquid. **2.** To make soaking wet; drench. **3.** To steep in a mixture, as in pickling. **4.** *Slang.* To make intoxicated. —*intr.* To become immersed or soaking wet.
~*n.* **1.** The act or process of sousing. **2. a.** *Chiefly U.S.* Food steeped in pickle; especially, the feet, ears, and head of a pig. **b.** The liquid used in pickling; brine. **3.** *Slang.* A drunkard. [Middle English *sousen,* to souse, to pickle, from *souse,* pickled meat, from Old French *sous, souz,* from Old Saxon *sultia,* Old High German *sulza,* brine.]

souse[2] *v.* **soused, sousing, souses.** *Archaic.* —*tr.* To pounce upon; attack. —*intr.* To swoop down, as an attacking hawk does. Used with *on* or *upon.* [Middle English *souce,* swooping motion, perhaps variant of *sours,* SOURCE.]

sou·tache (sōō-tásh) *n.* A narrow flat braid in a herringbone effect,

used for trimming. [French, from Hungarian *sujtás.*]

sou·tane (sōō-tán, -taan) *n.* A cassock worn by Roman Catholic priests. [French, from Italian *sottana,* garment worn under (religious vestments), from *sotto,* under, from Latin *subtus,* beneath, from *sub,* under.]

south (sowth) *n. Abbr.* **s, S, s., S., So., Sth. 1. a.** The direction along a meridian to the right of an observer facing in the direction of the earth's rotation; the direction to the right as one faces the rising sun. **b.** The cardinal point on the mariner's compass, 180° clockwise from north. **2.** Any area or region lying in this direction. **3.** *Often capital* **S. a.** One of the four positions at 90° intervals that lies in the south, points north, and stands at right angles to west and east. **b.** In games such as bridge and mah-jong, a player who occupies or is said to occupy this position. —**the South. 1.** The southern or Antarctic part of the Earth. **2.** The southern part of any country or region, as: **a.** The southern part of England, as distinguished from the Midlands and the North. **b.** In the United States, the states lying south of Pennsylvania and east of the Mississippi. **3.** The developing countries of the world, considered as chiefly occupying the southern regions of the earth; the Third World. **4.** The Republic of Ireland as distinguished from Northern Ireland.
~*adj.* **1.** To, towards, of, facing, or in the south. **2.** Coming from or originating in the south. Said of a wind. **3.** *Capital* **S.** Officially or conventionally designating the southern part of a country, continent, or other geographical area: *South America.*
~*adv.* In, from, or towards the south. [Middle English *south,* Old English *sūth.*]

South Africa, Republic of. *Afrikaans* **Republiek van Suid-Afrika.** Formerly **Union of South Africa.** *Afrikaans* **Unie van Suid-Afrika.** Southernmost, richest, most industrialised country of Africa. Its narrow coastal plains rise sharply to interior plateaus, flanked by the Drakensberg Mountains in the east. Desert areas in the north-west include part of the Kalahari. The population is chiefly Bantu-speaking Africans (67 per cent), with a white minority (19) and Asians (3) and Coloureds (of mixed race) (11). The country has immense mineral resources, including gold, diamonds, chrome, platinum, phosphates, copper, iron, and coal. Mining accounts for some 13 per cent of the country's home production, manufacturing 24 per cent, and agriculture 8 per cent. Manufactures include steel and other metals, machinery, chemicals, and textiles. Only about 12 per cent of the land is cultivable, but 74 per cent is suited to grazing, and South Africa is noted for citrus fruits, apples, grapes, wines, cereals, cotton, beef, and wool. Forestry, fishing, and fish processing are also important. With no oil deposits, and following Middle Eastern conflicts and embargoes, South Africa now produces 47 per cent of its oil from coal. Johannesburg is the main industrial centre and Durban the chief port. The Portuguese were the first Europeans to reach South Africa (1488). Dutch settlers arrived in the 17th century and Britain eventually gained formal possession of the Cape (1814). Europeans from the Cape met the first African peoples at the Great Fish river, and the first major conflict between them occurred in 1781. Hostility between British and Dutch settlers (known as Boers or Afrikaners) led to the Great Trek (from 1835), a migration of Boers from the Cape who founded Natal, Orange Free State, and Transvaal. After the Anglo-Boer Wars (1880-81, 1899-1902), the British and former Boer territories were combined as the Union of South Africa (1910). In 1961, this became an independent republic and withdrew from the Commonwealth. Its ruling National Party's policy of apartheid, which provided for separate development of ethnic groups, led to internal opposition and the hostility of many nations. A new constitution approved by referendum (1983) gave limited political rights to Asians and Coloureds. With the release from jail in 1990 of the leading figure in the African National Congress, Nelson Mandela, far-reaching reforms were initiated, and were endorsed by a referendum of the white electorate in 1992. All apartheid legislation was repealed, and a draft constitution paving the way for a multi-racial, democratic government was agreed in 1993. After elections in 1994 the A.N.C. was the largest party in Parliament, and Nelson Mandela became the nation's first black President. Area, 1 219 080 square kilometres (470,689 square miles). Capitals: Pretoria (seat of government); Cape Town (seat of the legislature); Bloemfontein (seat of the judiciary). Population, 39,270,000. See map, next page.

South African *n.* A native or inhabitant of the Republic of South Africa. —**South African** *adj.*

South America. See **Americas, the.**

Southampton (sowth-ámp-tən, -hámp-, -ám-, -hám). City and major port in Hampshire, southern England, at the head of Southampton Water. Britain's largest passenger port, Southampton also has considerable freight trade and industries which include ship and yacht building, marine engineering, electronics, and aircraft.

Southampton, Henry Wriothesley, 3rd Earl of (1573–1624). English soldier and statesman. He was a patron of the Elizabethan poets, especially Shakespeare, who dedicated *Venus and Adonis* (1593), and *Rape of Lucrece* (1594) to him.

South Australia. State in central southern Australia, much of which is inhospitable terrain, with deserts, mountains, salt lakes, and swampland. The Murray, in the extreme southeast, is the only important river. Some two thirds of the state's population are in the Adelaide metropolitan area. Agriculture, which produces cereals, vines, sheep, and livestock, is confined mostly to the Murray river area. There are valuable mineral deposits in the state; iron ore, salt, and gypsum are mined, and coal and natural gas are exploited.

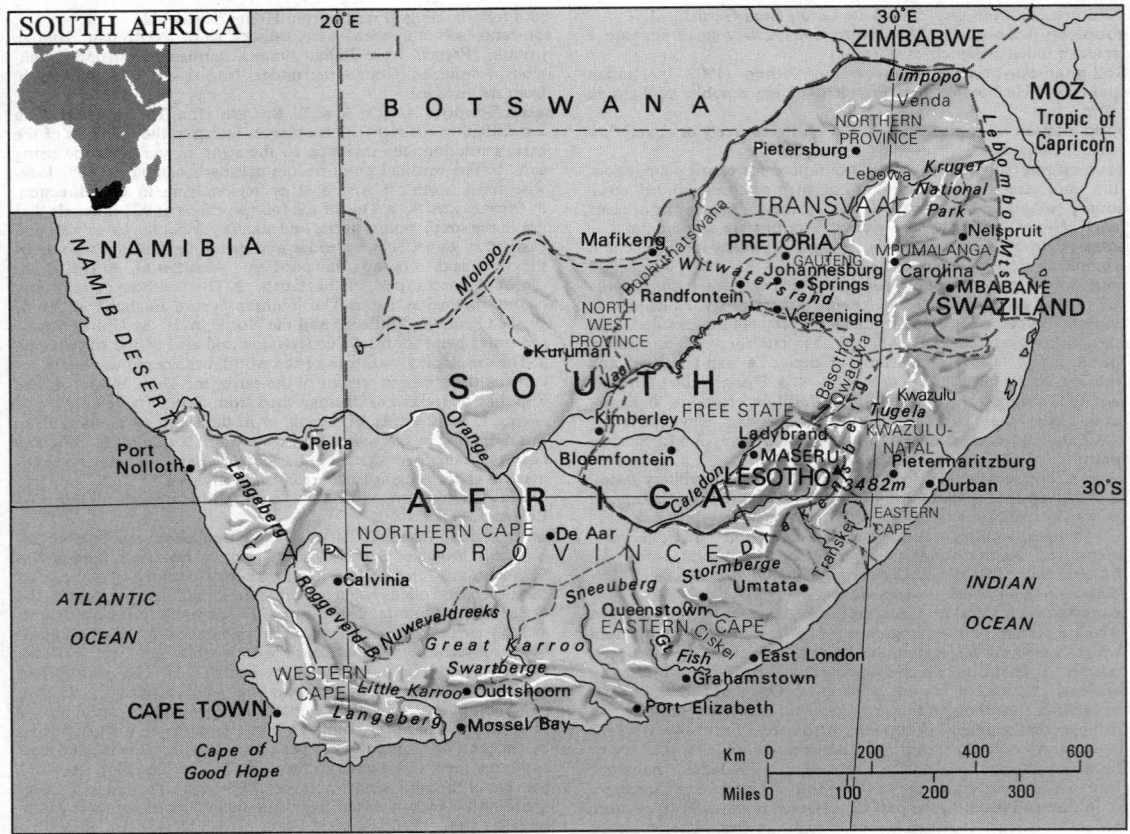

SOUTH AFRICA

Adelaide, the capital, is the chief industrial centre, and Whyalla has steelworks and the largest shipyards in Australia.

south-bound (sówth-bownd) *adj.* Going towards the south.

south by east *n. Abbr.* **SbE** The direction, or point on the mariner's compass, halfway between due south and south-southeast. It is 168° 45′ east of due north. —**south by east** *adj. & adv.*

south by west *n. Abbr.* **SbW** The direction, or point on the mariner's compass, halfway between due south and south-southwest. It is 168° 45′ west of due north. —**south by west** *adj. & adv.*

South Carolina. State in the southeastern United States. Extensive coastal lowlands rise to inland plateaus, which flank the Appalachian Mountains. Traditionally known for its cotton and tobacco plantations, the state is also extensively forested and manufactures furniture, wood pulp, and paper. Other important industries include textiles and chemicals. Columbia is the capital.

south celestial pole *n. Astronomy.* The **South Pole** (see).

South China Sea. Arm of the western Pacific Ocean, lying off Southeast Asia and partially enclosed by Taiwan, the Philippines, and Borneo. It is subject to violent typhoons.

South Dakota. State in north central United States. It is bisected by the Missouri river, with fertile prairies to the east. The Great Plains to the west include the Black Hills and also the Badlands in the south. Gold and other minerals are mined, but the state's main products are cereals, soya beans, flax, and livestock. The Mount Rushmore National Memorial is a noted tourist attraction. Sioux Falls and Rapid City are the main urban areas. Pierre is the capital.

South Devon *n.* Any of a breed of red English cattle reared for milk and meat.

South-down (sówth-down) *n.* Any of a breed of small, hornless sheep of English origin, having dense, short, fine-textured wool. [From the *South Downs* in southern England.]

south-east (sówth-éest; *nautical* sow-éest) *n. Abbr.* **SE 1.** The direction, or point on the mariner's compass, halfway between south and east. It is 135° east of due north. **2.** *Sometimes capital* **S.** The part of any country or region lying in this direction.

~*adj.* **1.** Situated, towards, facing, or in the southeast. **2.** Coming from the southeast. Said of a wind.

~*adv.* In, from, or towards the southeast. —**south·east·ern** *adj.*

Southeast Asia. Subcontinent comprising the ten modern states of Burma (Myanmar), Thailand, Laos, Cambodia, Vietnam, Malaysia, Singapore, Brunei, Indonesia, and the Philippines. It covers 3 per cent of the world's land area and has 8 per cent of its people. The mainland is traversed by part of the Alpine-Himalayan mountain belt, which continues in the island arcs of the East Indies. Several major fertile valleys cross the area, including those of the Irrawaddy and Mekong. The region is the wettest of the major land areas, its equatorial lowlands having some 3 000 millimetres (about 120 inches) of rain a year, and also temperatures averaging 27°C (81°F).

Elsewhere there is a pronounced dry season. Rain forest with rich wild-life covered much of the region, and it still provides 18 per cent of the world's hardwoods. Soils are generally poor, but farming is important except in Singapore, and Southeast Asia produces more than 19 per cent of the world's rice and 27 per cent of its cassava. Commercial products include rice, palm oil, cane sugar, coffee, natural rubber (more than 85 per cent), and copra (over 70 per cent). The region is rich in minerals. It accounts for more than 50 per cent of the world's tin, and Singapore has a thriving import-export trade. Southeast Asia has some of the world's poorest countries, including Cambodia and Laos.

Southeast Asia Treaty Organisation *n. Abbr.* **SEATO** The signatories to the Southeast Asian Collective Defence Treaty of 1954: Australia, France, New Zealand, Pakistan, the Philippines, Thailand, the United Kingdom, and the United States. The organisation was abolished in June 1977.

southeast by east *n. Abbr.* **SEbE** The direction, or point on the mariner's compass, halfway between southeast and east-southeast. It is 123° 45′ east of due north. —**southeast by east** *adj. & adv.*

southeast by south *n. Abbr.* **SEbS** The direction, or point on the mariner's compass, halfway between southeast and south-southeast. It is 146° 15′ east of due north. —**southeast by south** *adj. & adv.*

south·east·er (sówth-éestər; *nautical* sow-) *n.* A storm or wind blowing from the southeast.

south·east·er·ly (sówth-éestərli; *nautical* sow-) *adj.* **1.** Towards or in the southeast. **2.** Coming from the southeast. Said of a wind. ~*n., pl.* **south·east·er·lies.** A storm or wind blowing from the southeast. —**south·east·er·ly** *adv.*

south·east·ward (sówth-éest-wərd; *nautical* sow-) *adj.* Situated towards or facing the southeast.

~*n.* **1.** A direction or point towards the southeast. **2.** A region or part situated in or towards the southeast.

~*adv. Chiefly U.S.* Variant of **southeastwards.** —**south·east·ward·ly** *adj. & adv.*

south·east·wards (sówth-éest-wərdz) *adv.* Also *chiefly U.S.* **south·eastward.** Towards the southeast.

south·er (sówthər) *n.* A strong wind coming from the south.

south·er·ly (súthərli) *adj.* **1.** Situated in or towards the south. **2.** Coming from the south. Said of a wind.

~*n., pl.* **southerlies.** A storm or wind blowing from the south. —**south·er·ly** *adv.*

southerly burster *n.* A strong dry wind bringing exceptionally low temperatures to New South Wales, Australia, when a mass of polar air pulled northwards behind a low "bursts" into warmer areas.

south·ern (súthərn) *adj. Abbr.* **s, S, s., S., So., Sou. 1.** Situated towards, in, or facing the south. **2.** Coming from the south. Said of a wind. **3.** Native to or growing in the south. **4.** *Often capital* **S.** Of, pertaining to, or characteristic of southern regions or the South.

[Middle English *southerne,* Old English *sūtherne.*]

Southern Alps. Mountain range in New Zealand, forming the backbone of South Island. It contains Mount Cook, at 3 763 metres (12,346 feet), the country's highest peak.

Southern Confederacy *n.* The **Confederate States of America** *(see).*

Southern Cross *n.* A constellation, **Crux** *(see).*

Southern Crown *n.* A constellation, **Corona Australis** *(see).*

south·ern·er (sŭ́thərnər) *n. Sometimes small* **s.** A native or inhabitant of the southern part of a country, especially of England or the United States.

south·ern-fried (sŭ́thərn-frīd) *adj.* Cooked in a style characteristic of the Southern states of the United States: **southern-fried chicken.**

Southern Hemisphere *n.* The half of the earth lying south of the equator.

south·ern·ism (sŭ́thərn-iz'm) *n.* A word, phrase, or mannerism that is peculiar to the southern part of a country, especially of England or the United States.

southern lights *pl.n.* The **aurora australis** *(see).*

south·ern·most (sŭ́thərn-mōst) *adj.* Farthest south.

Southern Rhodesia. See **Zimbabwe, State of.**

south·ern·wood (sŭ́thərn-wŏŏd) *n.* A woody plant, *Artemisia abrotanum,* native to south Europe, having finely divided greyish, aromatic foliage. Also called "old man".

Sou·they (sŏ́wthi, *also* sŭ́thi), **Robert** (1774–1843). English poet and historian. He was one of the Lake poets and a pioneer of the Romantic movement, a friend of Coleridge and Wordsworth. In 1813 he became Poet Laureate.

South Georgia. See **Falkland Islands.**

South Glamorgan. From 1974 to 1996, county in southern Wales, formed from southern Glamorgan and parts of Monmouthshire. The east of the county is dominated by the industrial centres of Cardiff and Barry, while the west consists of arable lowlands. It is now subdivided into Unitary Authority areas.

South Holland. Also **Zuid-Holland** or **Zuidholland.** Province of southwestern Netherlands, bordering the North Sea. It is fragmented in the south by a network of rivers, canals, and channels. The province is densely populated, being both heavily industrialised and intensively farmed. It includes Rotterdam, Leiden, Delft, and Gouda. Its capital, The Hague, is also the nation's seat of government.

south·ing (sŏ́wthing) *n.* In navigation: **1.** The difference in latitude between two positions as a result of a movement to the south. **2.** Progress towards the south. **3.** *Astronomy.* A south declination.

South Island. Also **Middle Island.** The larger, but the less populous, of the two main islands of New Zealand. The principal cities are Christchurch and Dunedin. Much of the southwestern part of the island is taken up by the Fiordland National Park.

South Korea. See **Korea, South.**

South Orkney Islands. See **British Antarctic Territory.**

south·paw (sŏ́wth-paw) *n. Informal.* **1.** A boxer who leads with his right hand rather than with his left. **2.** A left-handed person.
~*adj. Informal.* Left-handed.

South Pole *n.* **1.** The southern end of the earth's axis of rotation. **2.** The celestial zenith of the heavens as viewed from the south terrestrial pole. Also called "south celestial pole". **3.** *Small* **s,** *small* **p.** The south-seeking **magnetic pole** *(see)* of a magnet.

south·ron (sŭ́thrən) *n. Chiefly Scottish. Often capital* **S.** A person who lives in the south, especially an Englishman.
~*adj. Chiefly Scottish.* Southern; English. [Middle English (Scottish), variant of *southren, southerne,* SOUTHERN.]

South Sandwich Islands. See **Falkland Islands.**

South Sea Bubble *n.* A scheme launched in 1720 by which the South Sea Company took partial responsibility for the national debt in exchange for a monopoly of trade with the South Sea Islands. The subsequent wild speculation was followed by a massive collapse in the same year.

South Shetland Islands. See **British Antarctic Territory.**

south-south·east (sŏ́wth-sowth-ḗest; *nautical* sŏ́w-sow-) *n. Abbr.* **SSE** The direction, or point on the mariner's compass, halfway between due south and southeast. It is 157° 30′ east of due north.
~*adj.* Situated towards, facing, or in this direction.
~*adv.* In, from, or towards this direction.

south-south·west (sŏ́wth-sowth-wḗst; *nautical* sŏ́w-sow-) *n. Abbr.* **SSW** The direction, or point on the mariner's compass, halfway between due south and southwest. It is 157° 30′ west of due north.
~*adj.* Situated towards, facing, or in this direction.
~*adv.* In, from, or towards this direction.

South Suffolk *n.* Any of a New Zealand breed of sheep, producing lean meat and short, fine-textured wool, originally bred by crossing Southdown and Suffolk sheep.

South·um·bri·an (sow-thŭ́mbri-ən) *n.* A native or inhabitant of the northern part of the Anglo-Saxon kingdom of Mercia. —**South·um·bri·an** *adj.*

south·ward (sŏ́wth-wərd; *nautical* sŭ́thərd) *adj.* Situated towards, facing, or in the south.
~*n.* **1.** A direction towards the south. **2.** A region situated in or towards the south.
~*adv. Chiefly U.S.* Variant of **southwards.** —**south·ward·ly** *adj. & adv.*

south·wards (sŏ́wth-wərdz) *adv.* Also *chiefly U.S.* **southward.** Towards the south.

South·wark (sŭ́thərk). Borough of Greater London, England, lying across the river Thames from the City.

south·west (sŏ́wth-wḗst; *nautical* sow-) *n. Abbr.* **SW** **1.** The direction, or point on the mariner's compass, halfway between south and west. It is 135° west of due north. **2.** *Sometimes capital* **S.** The part of any country or region lying in this direction.
~*adj.* **1.** To, towards, of, facing, or in the southwest. **2.** Coming from the southwest. Said of a wind.
~*adv.* In, from, or towards the southwest. —**south·west·ern** *adj.*

Southwest Africa. See **Namibia.**

southwest by south *n. Abbr.* **SWbS** The direction, or point on the mariner's compass, halfway between southwest and south-southwest. It is 146° 15′ west of due north. —**southwest by south** *adj. & adv.*

southwest by west *n. Abbr.* **SWbW** The direction, or point on the mariner's compass, halfway between southwest and west-southwest. It is 123° 45′ west of due north. —**southwest by west** *adj. & adv.*

south·west·er (sŏ́wth-wḗstər, sow-) *n.* A storm or wind from the southwest.

south·west·er·ly (sŏ́wth-wḗstərli; *nautical* sow-) *adj.* **1.** Towards or in the southwest. **2.** Comping from the southwest. Said of a wind.
~*n., pl.* **southwesterlies.** A storm or wind blowing from the southwest. —**south·west·er·ly** *adv.*

south·west·ward (sŏ́wth-wḗstwərd; *nautical* sow-) *adj.* Situated towards, facing, or in the southwest.
~*n.* **1.** A direction towards the southwest. **2.** A region or part situated in or towards the southwest.
~*adv. Chiefly U.S.* Variant of **southwestwards.** —**south·west·ward·ly** *adj. & adv.*

south·west·wards (sŏ́wth-wḗst-wərdz) *adv.* Also *chiefly U.S.* **southwestward.** Towards the southwest.

South Yemen. Former republic in southwest Asia. See **Yemen, Republic of.**

South Yorkshire. Former metropolitan county in northern England (1974–96). It was created from parts of the former West Riding of Yorkshire and Nottinghamshire and Barnsley, Doncaster, Rotherham, and Sheffield. Now subdivided into Unitary Authority areas.

Sou·tine (sŏŏ-tḗen), **Chaim** (1894–1943). French artist, born in Lithuania. His style is a vivid and turbulent expressionism; he is noted for his portraits. His works include *Choirboys* (1927) and *The Old Actress* (1924).

sou·ve·nir (sŏŏvə-nḗer) *n.* Something serving as a token of remembrance, as of a place, occasion, or experience; a memento. Also used adjectivally: *a souvenir stall.* [French, "memory", from *souvenir,* come to mind, recall, from Latin *subvenīre,* come to aid, come to mind : *sub-,* up to + *venīre,* to come.]

sou·vla·ki (sŏŏ-vla̋a-ki) *n., pl.* **-kia.** A Greek dish of skewered chunks of meat, typically grilled over a charcoal fire; kebabs. Also used adjectivally: *a souvlaki stall.* [Modern Greek, from *souvla,* a skewer.]

sou'west·er (sow-wḗstər) *n.* A waterproof hat worn especially by sailors, with a broad brim at the back to protect the neck. Also called "nor'wester." [From SOUTHWESTER.]

sov. sovereign.

sove·reign (sŏ́v-rin, -rən ‖ sŏ́vvə-) *n.* Also *literary* **sov·ran** (-rən) (for sense 1). **1.** The head of state in a monarchy; a king or queen; a monarch. **2.** *Abbr.* **sov.** A former British gold coin having a nominal value of one pound.
~*adj.* Also *literary* **sov·ran.** **1.** Self-governing; independent: *a sovereign state.* **2.** Having supreme rank or power. **3.** Paramount; supreme. **4. a.** Of superlative quality or efficacy: *a sovereign remedy.* **b.** Unmitigated: *sovereign contempt.* [Middle English *souverein,* from Old French, from Vulgar Latin *superānus* (unattested), from Latin *super,* above.] —**sove·reign·ly** *adv.*

sove·reign·ty (sŏ́v-rin-ti, -rən- ‖ sŏ́vvə-) *n., pl.* **-ties.** **1. a.** Supremacy of authority or rule, especially as exercised by the sovereign body in a state: *the sovereignty of Parliament.* **b.** The right to exercise such authority. **2.** Royal rank, authority, or power. **3.** The condition of political independence and self-government. **4.** A sovereign territory.

So·vetsk (səv-yḗtsk). *German* **Til·sit** (tĭlzĭt). Town in western Russia, lying on the river Neman. Formerly in East Prussia, it is a marketing, cultural, and manufacturing centre.

so·vi·et (sŏ́v-i-ət, sŏ́v-, -yət, -yet) *n.* Formerly in the U.S.S.R., any of the popularly elected legislative assemblies at local, regional, and national levels, organised on the basis of the workers', soldiers', and peasants' councils of the revolutionary period. See **Supreme Soviet.** [Russian *sovet,* "council", from Old Russian *suvětu.*]

Soviet *adj.* Pertaining to the Union of Soviet Socialist Republics.
~*n. Plural.* The Russians, especially the Russian government.

so·vi·et·ise, so·vi·et·ize (sŏ́v-i-ət-īz, sŏ́v-, -yət-, -yet-) *tr.v.* **-ised, -ising, -ises.** *Sometimes capital* **S.** **1.** To cause to come under Soviet control. **2.** Formerly, to bring into line with the cultural, economic, or political norms of the U.S.S.R. —**so·vi·et·i·sa·tion** (-ī-záysh'n ‖ *U.S.* -i-) *n.*

So·vi·et·ol·o·gy (sŏ́v-i-ət-ólləji, sŏ́v-, -yət, -yet) *n.* Formerly, the study and analysis of Soviet politics, economics, and everyday life; kremlinology. —**So·vi·et·ol·o·gist** *n.*

Soviet Union. See **Union of Soviet Socialist Republics.**

sov·khoz (sŏ́v-kóz, -koz; *Russian* saaf-kháwss) *n., pl.* **-khozy** (kózi). Formerly in the U.S.S.R., a large state-owned farm that paid wages to its workers. [Russian, shortened from *sovetskoe khozyaistvo,* soviet economy.]

sow¹ (sō) *v.* **sowed, sown** (sōn) or **sowed, sowing, sows.** —*tr.*

1. To scatter or plant (seed) over or in the ground for growing. **2.** To plant seed in (land). **3. a.** To implant and cause to arise; introduce: *sow doubts.* **b.** To disseminate; cause to spread: *sow rebellion.* **4.** To strew or cover with anything; spread thickly. —*intr.* To scatter seed for growing. [Middle English *sowen, sawan,* Old English *sāwan.*] —**sow·er** n.

sow² (sow) n. **1.** An adult female pig. **2. a.** A channel that conducts molten iron to the moulds in a pig bed. **b.** The mass of metal solidified in such a channel or mould. [Middle English *sow(e),* Old English *sugu.*]

So·we·to (sə-wéttō, sō-). Group of black African townships situated to the southwest of Johannesburg, South Africa. In June 1976, following the introduction of the compulsory use of Afrikaans for instruction in schools, students rioted in Soweto. Some 200 people were killed, and more than 1,000 were wounded. [*South Western Townships.*]

sow thistle n. The **milk thistle** *(see).*

sox. *U.S.* Alternative plural of **sock.**

soy·a bean (sóy-ə) n. Also chiefly U.S. **soy·bean** (sóy-been). **1.** A leguminous Asiatic plant, *Glycine max,* widely cultivated for forage and for its nutritious, edible seeds. **2.** The seed of this plant, used as a food and as a source of oil and flour.

soya sauce n. A salty brown liquid condiment made by fermenting soya beans in brine, and used in Chinese and Japanese cooking. Also called "soy sauce". [Japanese *shō-yu,* from Chinese *shi-yu* : *shi,* salted beans + *yu,* oil]

So·yin·ka (soy-íngkə, saw-yíngkə), **Wole (Akinwande Oluwole Soyinka)** (1934–). Nigerian dramatist and poet. His works, which portray the experience of modern Africa, but often use Yoruiba themes and techniques, include plays (*Kongi's Harvest,* 1965), novels (*The Interpreters,* 1964), and memoirs (*The Man Died,* 1972). He won the Nobel prize for literature in 1986, but his play *The Beautification of Area Boy* (1995) was banned by the Nigerian government.

soz·zled (sózz'ld) adj. *Informal.* Completely drunk. [Perhaps from dialect *sozzle,* to mix in a sloppy manner; akin to SOUSE (drench, make or become drunk).]

sp. 1. special. **2.** specialist. **3.** species. **4.** specific. **5.** spelling.

Sp. Spain; Spanish.

s.p. *Genealogy.* without issue. [Latin *sine prole.*]

S.P. starting price.

spa (spaa) n. **1.** A mineral spring. **2.** A resort area where such springs exist; a watering place. [After Spa (Belgium).]

Spaak (spaak), **Paul Henri** (1899–1972). Belgian statesman. He was the first president of the United Nations Assembly (1946), and of the Assembly of the Council of Europe (1949). He was also Secretary General of N.A.T.O. (1957–61).

space (spayss) n. **1. a.** A set of elements or points satisfying given geometric postulates: *a non-Euclidean space.* **b.** The infinite three-dimensional extent in which all matter exists. **c.** The expanse beyond the earth's atmosphere in which the Solar System, stars, and galaxies exist; the universe. **3. a.** A measurable interval or extent existing between two or more points or bounded by limits in three dimensions: distance, area, or volume. **b.** Such an interval or extent considered as being unoccupied; unfilled space: *clear a space in the cupboard; wide open spaces.* **c.** An amount of room available or designated for a particular purpose: *a parking space; used a smaller size of type to save space.* **4.** A period or interval of time. **5.** *Music.* Any of the intervals between the lines of a staff. **6.** *Printing.* Any of the blank pieces of type or other means used for separating words or characters. **7.** Any of the intervals during the telegraphic transmission of a message when the key is open or not in contact. ~*tr.v.* **spaced, spacing, spaces. 1.** To place or arrange with spaces between. Often used with *out.* **2.** To separate or keep apart. [Middle English, time interval, from Old French *espace,* from Latin *spatium†,* space, distance.] —**spac·er** n.

space age n. The period, starting in the middle of the twentieth century, when humans have been able to travel in space. ~*adj.* Also **space-age** (spáyss-ayj). Extremely modern in design; based on or suggestive of the technology used in spacecraft.

space biology n. **Exobiology** *(see).*

space capsule n. A **capsule** *(see)* used in space flights.

space·craft (spáyss-kraaft ‖ -kraft) n., pl. **spacecraft.** A vehicle designed to be launched into space. Also called "space vehicle", "spaceship".

spaced-out (spáyst-ówt) adj. *Slang.* **1.** Elated or stupefied as a result of taking a narcotic or hallucinogenic drug; high. **2.** Dazed or lacking concentration.

space flight n. A flight of a vehicle into space.

space heater n. A heater, especially a portable free-standing one, used to heat an enclosed area.

space lab n. A large manned satellite specially equipped for carrying out experimental work in space.

space lattice n. Any of the 14 possible geometric arrangements of points in three-dimensional space at which the components of a crystal may occur. Also called "Bravais lattice".

space-less (spáyss-ləss, -liss) adj. Having no spatial limits.

space·man (spáyss-man) n., pl. **-men** (-men). **1.** Someone who travels in outer space; an astronaut. **2.** In science fiction, one who comes to Earth from outer space.

space medicine n. The medical science of the biological, physiological, and psychological effects of space flight upon humans.

space·port (spáyss-pawrt ‖ -pōrt) n. An installation for testing and launching spacecraft.

space probe n. A spacecraft carrying instruments designed to explore the physical properties of outer space or of celestial bodies other than Earth. Also called "probe".

space science n. **1.** Any of several scientific disciplines, such as exobiology, that study phenomena occurring in the upper atmosphere, in space, or on celestial bodies other than Earth. **2.** Disciplines related to or dealing with the problems of space flight.

space shuttle n. A space vehicle capable of making repeated journeys to and from space.

space sickness n. Any of various ailments affecting humans during or as a result of space flight.

space station n. A large manned satellite designed for permanent orbit around Earth and used for scientific research, military reconnaissance, or as an assembly point for long-range spacecraft.

space suit n. A protective pressure suit having an independent air supply and other devices designed to permit the wearer relatively free movement in space.

space-time (spáyss-tīm) n. The four-dimensional continuum of one temporal and three spatial coordinates, in which any event or physical object is located. Also called the "space-time continuum".

space walk n. An excursion by an astronaut outside a spacecraft in space; extravehicular activity. —**space walker** n.

space writer n. A writer, especially a journalist, paid according to the amount of space his material occupies in print.

spacial. Variant of **spatial.**

spac·ing (spáyssing) n. **1.** The action or result of arranging with intervening spaces. **2.** A temporal or spatial interval, typically one forming part of a regular arrangement; a space.

spa·cious (spáyshəss) adj. **1.** Providing or having much space or room; roomy; extensive. **2.** Expansive in range or scope; all-inclusive. [Middle English, from Old French *spacios* or Latin *spatiōsus;* see **space, -ous.**] —**spa·cious·ly** adv. —**spa·cious·ness** n.

spade¹ (spayd) n. **1.** A sturdy digging tool having a long thick handle and a heavy, flat iron blade that can be pressed into the ground with the foot. **2.** Any of various digging or cutting tools resembling the spade. **3.** *Military.* A sharp metal piece at the back of a gun-carriage trail that embeds into the ground to retard the backward motion of the carriage during recoil. —**call a spade a spade.** To call a thing by its proper name; speak frankly and directly. ~*tr.v.* **spaded, spading, spades.** To dig or cut with a spade. [Middle English *spade,* Old English *spadu.*] —**spad·er** n.

spade² n. **1.** The black symbol appearing on one of the four suits of playing cards, in the shape of an inverted heart with a short stalk at the fissure of the two lobes. **2.** A card bearing this symbol. [Italian *spada,* "broad sword" (from its flat, broad shape), from Latin *spatha,* spatula, from Greek *spathē,* broad blade.]

spade·fish (spáyd-fish) n., pl. **-fishes** or collectively **spadefish.** Any of several marine food fishes of the family Ephippidae, especially of the genus *Chaetodipterus.* [From their flat, spade-shaped bodies.]

spades n. *Used with a singular or plural verb.* One of the four suits of playing cards, identified by the symbol of a spade.

spade·work (spáyd-wurk) n. The usually dull and arduous preparatory work necessary to a project or activity.

spa·dix (spáy-diks) n., pl. **spadices** (-di-seez). *Botany.* A clublike spike bearing minute flowers, usually enclosed within a sheathlike spathe, as in the calla and the cuckoopint. [Latin *spādīx,* broken-off palm branch, from Greek *spadix;* akin to Greek *spasmos,* SPASM.] —**spa·di·ceous** (spay-díshəss) adj.

spae·wife (spáy-wīf) n. *Scottish.* A woman thought to have clairvoyant powers; a fortuneteller. [Scottish *spae,* foretell, from Middle English, from Old Norse *spā.*]

spa·ghet·ti (spə-gétti) n. **1.** An Italian pasta consisting of long, solid strings of flour paste, cooked by boiling. **2.** *Electricity.* A slender tube of insulating material into which bare wire is inserted, especially in radio circuits. [Italian, plural diminutive of *spago†,* string.]

spa·ghet·ti·ni (spág-e-téeni, -i-) n. An Italian pasta, thinner than spaghetti. [Italian, diminutive of SPAGHETTI.]

spaghetti western n. A western made by the Italian film industry and filmed in Europe.

spa·gyr·ic (spə-jírrik) adj. Of or pertaining to alchemy; alchemical. [New Latin *spagiricus†,* coined by Paracelsus.]

Spain (spayn). Spanish **E·spa·ña** (ess-pánya). Country occupying most of the Iberian peninsula, southwest Europe. Most of it is a high plateau, the Meseta, which is broken by mountain ranges and great river valleys. Spain is industrialising, and 25 per cent of its workers are in manufacturing, and 17 per cent in agriculture and fishing. With few fossil fuel resources, the country has an ambitious nuclear programme, and is a major uranium producer. The chief exports are fruit and vegetables, chemicals, engineering goods, footwear and leather goods, textiles, wine, olive oil, fish, and cork. Tourism is very important, with more than 35 million visitors a year. Spain, the ancient Roman province of Hispania, eventually emerged as a nation with the joining of the kingdoms of Aragon and Castile (1497), and the expulsion of its last Moorish conquerors (1492). The next two centuries were a golden age, in which a vast empire was built. However, most of this was lost in the 19th century, when the New World colonies gained independence. Spain remained neutral in both World Wars. After elections (1931) a republic was declared, but a bitter civil war (1936–39) brought the dictator General Franco to power. Following his death (1975), Juan Carlos, grandson of the last king, became head of state, and the

SPAIN

Spaniards endorsed a parliamentary monarchy in a referendum (1978). The new government joined the European Economic Community in 1986, and sought the return of Gibraltar, ceded to Britain in 1713. Seventeen autonomous regions were created (1978), including the Catalan and Basque provinces, but separatist activity persists. Area, 504 782 square kilometres (194,846 square miles). Population, 39,270,000. Capital, Madrid.

spake. *Archaic.* Past tense of **speak.**

spall (spawl) *n.* A chip or fragment from a piece of stone or ore. ~*v.* **spalled, spalling, spalls.** —*tr.* To break up into chips or fragments. —*intr.* To chip or crumble. [Middle English *spalle†*.]

spal·la·tion (spə-láysh'n, spaw-) *n.* A nuclear reaction in which many particles are ejected from an atomic nucleus by an incident particle of sufficiently high energy. [SPALL + -ATION.]

Spam (spam) *n.* A trademark for a type of tinned processed meat made mainly from ham.

span¹ (span) *n.* **1.** The full extent of space or time between two extremities: *the span of a bridge; a short life span.* **2.** The distance between the tips of an aircraft's wings. **3.** The section between two intermediate supports of a bridge. **4.** The length of time during or over which something functions effectively: *a child's attention span.* **5.** A former unit of measure equal to the length of the fully extended hand from the tip of the thumb to the tip of the little finger, generally considered as nine inches. ~*tr.v.* **spanned, spanning, spans.** **1.** To measure by, or as if by, the fully extended hand. **2.** To encircle with the hand or hands, in or as if in measuring. **3.** To reach or extend over or across (an extent in space or time): *a life that spanned three reigns.* **4.** To provide with something that extends over; bridge. [Middle English *span(ne),* short interval, distance, Old English *span(n).*]

span² *n.* **1.** *Nautical.* A stretch of rope made fast at either end. **2.** *Chiefly U.S.* A pair of animals, especially horses or oxen matched in size, strength, or colour and driven together. **3.** *Plural. South African Slang.* A large amount or number: *spans of teenagers.* [Middle Dutch *span,* from *spannen,* unite.]

span³. *Archaic.* Past tense and past participle of **spin.**

Span. Spanish.

Span·dau (shpán-dow, spán-). Industrial district of Berlin, Germany, surrounding the canal port at the confluence of the rivers Havel and Spree. Its old fortress, demolished in 1987, was a prison where the Nazi war criminal Rudolf Hess was detained.

span·drel, span·dril (spándrəl) *n. Architecture.* **1.** The triangular space between the left or right exterior curve of an arch and the rectangular framework surrounding it. **2.** The space between two adjacent arches and the horizontal moulding or cornice above them. [Middle English *spaundrell,* perhaps diminutive of Anglo-French *spaund(e)re,* from Old French *espandre,* to spread out, expand, from Latin *expandere,* EXPAND.]

spang (spang) *adv.* Precisely; squarely; firmly: *spang in the middle of the table.* [20th century : origin obscure.]

span·gle (spáng-g'l) *n.* **1.** A small, often circular piece of sparkling metal or plastic that may be sewn on clothing for decoration; a sequin. **2.** Any small sparkling object, drop, or spot. ~*v.* **spangled, -gling, -gles.** —*tr.* To adorn or cause to sparkle by covering with or as with spangles: *"the network of lights spangled the long, straight streets"* (Alec Waugh). —*intr.* To sparkle in the manner of spangles. [Middle English *spangele,* diminutive of *spange,* from Middle Dutch, ornament, clasp, buckle.] —**span·gly** *adv.*

Span·iard (spán-yərd) *n.* A native or inhabitant of Spain.

span·iel (spán-yəl, *also* spánn'l) *n.* **1.** Any of several breeds of small to medium-sized dogs, originally bred as sporting dogs and usually having drooping ears, short legs, and a silky, wavy coat. **2.** An obsequious or servile person. [Middle English *spaynel,* from Old French *espaignol,* "Spanish", from Vulgar Latin *spāniōlus* (unattested), from Latin *Hispāniōlus,* from *Hispānia,* SPAIN.]

Span·ish (spánnish) *adj. Abbr.* **Sp., Span.** Of or pertaining to Spain, its inhabitants, or their language or culture. ~*n.* **1.** The Romance language of Spain and Spanish America. **2.** *Used with a plural verb.* The people of Spain. Preceded by *the.*

Spanish America *n.* The parts of America inhabited mostly by Spanish-speaking people and including: **1.** South America, except ing Brazil, Guyana, Surinam, and French Guiana. **2.** Central America, excepting Belize. **3.** Mexico, Cuba, Puerto Rico, and the Dominican Republic.

Span·ish-A·mer·i·can (spánnish-ə-mérrikən) *adj.* **1.** Of or pertaining to the countries or people of Spanish America. **2.** Of or pertaining to people of Spanish descent residing in the United States. ~*n.* **1.** A native or inhabitant of a Spanish-American country. **2.** A person of Spanish descent who lives in the United States.

Spanish Armada *n.* A fleet sent against England by Philip II of Spain in 1588, considered invincible but defeated and subsequently devastated by storms. Also called the "Armada".

Spanish bayonet *n.* Any of several New World plants of the genus *Yucca;* especially, *Y. aloifolia,* having a tall, woody stem, stiff, pointed leaves, and a large cluster of white flowers, or the similar species *Y. filamentosa,* which is also called "Adam's needle".

Spanish cedar *n.* **1.** Any of several tropical American trees of the genus *Cedrela*; especially, *C. odorata,* having reddish, aromatic wood. **2.** The wood of this tree.

Spanish chestnut *n.* See **chestnut** (sense 1).

Spanish Civil War *n.* The civil war (1936–39) in Spain in which nationalist forces under General Franco overthrew the legitimate republican government. The nationalists were aided by the fascist regimes of Italy and Germany, while the republicans attracted support from socialists all over Europe.

Spanish flu *n.* A form of influenza that broke out in pandemic proportions in 1918 and caused millions of deaths. [Perhaps so called after a great epidemic in 1557, which appears to have begun in Spain.]

Spanish fly *n.* **1.** A European blister beetle, *Lytta vesicatoria.* **2.** A preparation, **cantharides** *(see),* produced from these beetles.

Spanish Guinea. See **Equatorial Guinea.**

Spanish Inquisition. The state tribunal of the Roman Catholic Church, instituted in Spain in 1480 to suppress heresy and infamous for its ruthless methods. It was abolished in 1834.

Spanish mackerel *n.* Any of various marine food fishes of the family Scombridae; especially, a commercially important species, *Scomber colias,* of European and east North American coastal water.

Spanish Main *n.* **1.** In the 16th and 17th centuries, the Spanish possessions in the coastal regions of northern South America between Panama and the Orinoco. **2.** Those parts of the Caribbean traversed by Spanish ships in colonial times.

Spanish Morocco *n.* A former Spanish colony on the northern coast of Morocco, part of Morocco since 1956.

Spanish moss *n.* An epiphytic plant, *Tillandsia usneoides,* growing on trees of the southeastern United States and tropical America, having grey, threadlike stems drooping in long, matted clusters.

Spanish Netherlands. The southern part of the Netherlands which remained under Spanish Habsburg rule when the Dutch Netherlands won independence in 1648. In 1714 it passed to the Austrian Habsburgs, and as the Austrian Netherlands declared its independence as Belgium in 1789.

Spanish omelette *n.* An omelette made by frying chopped vegetables, such as onions, tomatoes, green peppers, and potatoes, before adding the beaten eggs.

Spanish onion *n.* A mild-flavoured, yellow-skinned onion, probably derived from *Allium fistulosum.*

Spanish paprika *n.* A mild seasoning made from pimientos.

Spanish rice *n.* A dish consisting of rice, tomatoes, spices, chopped onions, and green peppers.

Spanish Sahara. See **Western Sahara.**

spank (spangk) *v.* **spanked, spanking, spanks.** —*tr.* To slap on the buttocks with a flat object or with the open hand, especially as punishment. —*intr.* To move briskly or spiritedly. —*n.* Also **spanking.** A smart slap or series of slaps on the buttocks. [Perhaps imitative.]

spank·er (spángkər) *n.* **1.** *Nautical.* A quadrilateral gaff sail set abaft the after mast of a square-rigged sailing ship. Also called "driver". **2.** *Informal.* Something of exceptional quality or remarkable appearance.

spank·ing (spángking) *adj.* **1.** *Informal.* Exceptional of its kind in size, strength, quality, or, especially, smartness. **2.** Moving quickly and smartly; brisk; lively: *set off at a spanking pace.* —*adv.* Splendidly: *spanking new.* —*n.* A spank.

span·ner (spánnər) *n.* A hand tool with jaws or a ring at one end or both ends for tightening or slackening nuts and bolts. —**a spanner in the works.** *British Informal.* A source of trouble, confusion, or delay. [German *Spanner,* from *spannen,* to stretch, tighten, from Old High German *spannan.*]

span roof *n.* A roof which has two equal sloping sides.

span spek (spán-spek, spón-) *South African.* A sweet muskmelon, the cantaloupe, having a rough, ridged rind and orange flesh. [Afrikaans, from Dutch *spaenspek.*]

spar¹ (spar) *n.* **1.** *Nautical.* A wooden or metal pole, used as a mast, boom, yard, or bowsprit, or in any other way to support rigging. **2.** A similar pole, used as part of a crane or derrick. **3.** *Aeronautics.* A principal structural member in an aircraft wing that runs from tip to tip or from root to tip. —*tr.v.* **sparred, sparring, spars.** **1.** To supply with spars. **2.** *Archaic.* To fasten with a bolt. [Middle English *sparre,* rafter, pole, from Old French *esparre* or from Old Norse *sperra,* beam, both from Germanic.]

spar² *intr.v.* **sparred, sparring, spars.** **1. a.** To box without exerting oneself to the full, as in a training session. **b.** To fight in any matched and generally indecisive contest. **2.** To bandy words about in argument; dispute. **3.** To fight by striking with the feet and spurs. Used of cocks. —*n.* **1.** The act of sparring. **2.** A boxing match. **3.** A cock-fight. [Middle English *sparren,* to thrust or strike rapidly, Old English *sperran*†, to strike.]

spar³ *n.* **1.** Any of various bright, nonmetallic, readily cleavable minerals with a vitreous lustre, such as feldspar. **2.** A fragment of such a mineral. **3.** An ornament made of spar. [Low German, from Middle Low German; akin to Old English *spær*†, gypsum.]

sparable. Variant of **sparrowbill.**

spa·rax·is (spə-ráksiss, spa-) *n.* Any plant of the South African genus *Sparaxis,* related to the iris and having colourful flowers.

spar deck *n.* A light upper deck of a ship. —**spar-decked** *adj.*

spare (spair) *v.* **spared, sparing, spares.** —*tr.* **1. a.** To treat mercifully; deal with leniently. **b.** To refrain from harming or destroying. **2.** To save or relieve (a person) from enduring (something unpleasant): *Spare us the gory details.* **3.** To refrain from using or applying; use with restraint. **4.** To give or grant out of one's resources; afford: *Can you spare ten minutes?* —*intr.* **1.** To be frugal. Usually used in the negative: *Don't spare on the cream.* **2.** *Literary.* **a.** To be merciful or lenient. **b.** To refrain or forbear. —**and to spare.** (And) In abundance. —**with (something) to spare.** Leaving (something) left over unused or as a margin.

—*adj.* **sparer, sparest.** **1. a.** Not in immediate or regular use but ready when needed. **b.** In excess of what is needed; extra: *spare cash.* **c.** Unoccupied; leisure: *spare time.* **2. a.** Economical; meagre. **b.** Thin or lean. —**go spare.** *Informal.* To become frantic; panic: *The boss is going spare over the schedule again.* —See Synonyms at **lean, meagre.**

—*n.* **1.** A replacement, such as a spare tyre, reserved for future use. **2.** A spare part. In tenpin bowling: **a.** The act of knocking down all ten pins with two successive rolls of the ball by a single player. **b.** The score so made. [Middle English *sparen,* to leave unharmed, show mercy, Old English *sparian,* from Germanic *sparōjan* (unattested).] —**spare·ly** *adv.* —**spare·ness** *n.* —**spar·er** *n.*

spare part *n. Chiefly British.* An exact duplicate, as of a machine part, used to replace a worn or faulty part. Also called "spare".

spare part surgery *n. Informal.* Surgery involving the transplantation of body organs.

spare rib *n.* Also **spare ribs** (for sense 1). **1.** A cut of pork consisting of the ribs with most of the meat trimmed off. **2.** Any of these ribs. [Probably transposed variant of Low German *ribbespēr,* from Middle Low German : *ribbe,* rib + *spēr,* spit (influenced by SPARE).]

spare tyre *n.* **1.** An extra tyre carried for emergencies with a motor vehicle. **2.** *Informal.* A roll of flab around the middle of the body.

sparge (sparj) *tr.v.* **sparged, sparging, sparges.** To spray or sprinkle with moisture. [Probably from Latin *spargere,* to sprinkle.] —**sparg·er** *n.*

spar·id (spárrid) *adj.* Also **spar·oid** (spárroyd). Of or belonging to the family Sparidae, which includes the bream and similar fishes. —*n.* Also **sparoid.** A member of the Sparidae. [New Latin *sparidae* : *Sparus* (genus), from Latin, gilthead, from Greek *sparos*† + -ID.]

spar·ing (spáir-ing) *adj.* **1.** Economical; frugal: *Sparing in her use of words.* **2.** Scanty; not profuse: *a sparing application.* **3.** Forbearing; lenient. —**spar·ing·ly** *adv.* —**spar·ing·ness** *n.*
Synonyms: sparing, frugal, thrifty, economical.

spark¹ (spark) *n.* **1.** An incandescent particle, especially: **a.** One thrown off from a burning substance. **b.** One resulting from friction. **c.** One remaining in an otherwise extinguished fire; an ember. **2.** A glistening particle of something, such as metal. **3. a.** A flash of light; especially, a flash produced by electric discharge. **b.** A short pulse or discharge of electric current. **4.** A trace or suggestion, as: **a.** A quality or feeling with latent potential; a seed: *the spark of genius.* **b.** An animating or activating factor: *the spark of revolt.* **5.** *Electricity.* **a.** The luminous phenomenon resulting from a disruptive discharge through an insulating material. **b.** The discharge itself, especially as occurring in an internal-combustion engine. **6.** A small diamond or other gem.

—*v.* **sparked, sparking, sparks.** —*intr.* **1.** To give off sparks. **2.** To operate correctly by producing a spark. Used of the ignition system of an internal-combustion engine. —*tr.* **1.** To set in motion; activate; provoke. Usually used with *off: sparked off a strike.* **2.** *U.S.* To rouse to action. —See Synonyms at **flash.** [Middle English *sparke,* Old English *spearca, spærca;* akin to Middle Dutch *sparke*†.] —**spark·er** *n.*

spark² *n.* **1.** A clever person. Used ironically in the phrase *bright spark.* **2.** *Rare.* A lover; a suitor. —*v.* **sparked, sparking, sparks.** *Rare.* —*tr.* To court or woo. —*intr.* To play the suitor. [Perhaps figurative use of SPARK (burning particle).]

Spark, Dame Muriel (Sarah) (1918–). British novelist, poet, and critic. Among her works, noted for their black humour, are *The Ballad of Peckham Rye* (1960), *The Prime of Miss Jean Brodie* (1961), and *A Far Cry from Kensington* (1988). Autobiography: *Curriculum Vitae* (1992).

spark arrester *n.* **1.** A device to keep sparks from escaping, as at a chimney opening. **2.** A device to control electric sparking at a point where a circuit is made or broken.

spark chamber *n.* A device consisting of electrically charged parallel metal plates in a chamber filled with inert gas, used to detect and measure charged elementary particles as they pass from one plate to another, leaving a trail of sparks.

spark coil *n.* An induction coil used to produce a spark, as in an internal-combustion engine.

spark gap *n.* A gap in an otherwise complete electric circuit across which a discharge occurs at some prescribed voltage.

spar·kle (spárk'l) *intr.v.* **-kled, -kling, -kles.** **1.** To give off sparks. **2.** To give off or reflect flashes of light; glitter. **3.** To be witty and animated. **4.** To perform brilliantly; shine. **5.** To effervesce. —See Synonyms at **flash.** —*n.* **1.** A small spark or gleaming particle. **2.** A glittering appearance. **3.** Animation; vivacity. **4.** Effervescence. [Middle English *sparklen,* frequentative of *sparken,* to SPARK.]

spar·kler (spárklər) *n.* **1.** One that sparkles. **2.** A firework on a piece of wire held in the hand that burns down gradually and gives off a shower of sparks. **3.** *Informal.* A diamond.

spar·kling wine *n.* Any of various effervescent, usually white wines, made by a process that involves fermentation in the bottle.

spark-plug (spárk-plug) *n.* Also *British* **spark·ing plug.** A device inserted in the head of an internal-combustion-engine cylinder that ignites the fuel mixture by means of an electric spark.

sparks (sparks) *n., pl. sparks. Informal.* **1.** A ship's radio operator. **2.** An electrician, especially in the building trade. [From SPARK (electrical discharge).]

spark transmitter *n. Electronics.* A now obsolete radio transmitter using a discharge across a spark gap to create a signal.

spar·ling (spárling) *n.* **1.** A fish, the European **smelt** *(see).* **2.** *U.S.* A young herring. [Middle English *sperlinge,* from Old French *esperlinge,* from Germanic.]

sparoid. Variant of **sparid.**

spar·ring partner (spaáring) *n.* **1.** A boxer who fights with another in training bouts. **2.** Any partner in a friendly contest or dispute.

spar·row (spárrō) *n.* **1.** Any of various small Old World birds of the genus *Passer,* especially the **house sparrow** *(see),* having greyish or brownish plumage. **2.** Any of various American finches resembling Old World sparrows. [Middle English *sparowe,* Old English *spearwa,* from Germanic.]

spar·row-bill (spárrō-bil, spárrə-) *n.* Also **spar·a·ble** (spárrə-bil). A small headless wedge-shaped iron nail used in fixing shoe soles.

spar·row·grass (spárrō-graass || spárrə-, -grass) *n.* Also **spar·ry·grass** (spárri-). *Regional.* Asparagus. [By folk etymology from ASPARAGUS.]

spar·row·hawk (spárrō-hawk) *n.* **1.** Any of various small hawks of the genus *Accipiter,* which prey on small birds and mammals; especially, *A. nisus,* of Europe and Asia. **2.** A small North American falcon, *Falco sparverius,* that hunts small birds and mammals.

sparse (sparss) *adj.* **sparser, sparsest.** Growing or distributed at widely spaced intervals; not dense: *a sparse crop.* See Synonyms at **meagre.** [Latin *sparsus,* past participle of *spargere,* to strew, scatter.] **—sparse·ly** *adv.* **—sparse·ness, spar·si·ty** (-əti) *n.*

Spar·ta (spártə). City-state of ancient Greece. Founded in *c.*1000 B.C., it became one of the most powerful city-states, renowned for its dedication to military discipline. The Spartans defeated the Athenians in the Peloponnesian Wars (431–404 B.C.), but finally fell to the Macedonians in the fourth century B.C. The modern settlement of Sparta was founded close by in the mid-19th century.

Spar·ta·cus (spártəkəss) (died 71 B.C.). Thracian gladiator. He raised an army of slaves that terrorised Roman Italy for two years (73-71 B.C.). He was finally defeated and killed by Crassus.

spar·tan (spárt'n) *adj.* **1.** *Capital* **S.** Of or pertaining to Sparta or its people. **2.** Resembling the Spartans in fortitude or self-discipline; rigorous; austere. **3.** Frugal: *a spartan existence.*
~*n.* **1.** *Capital* **S.** A citizen of Sparta. **2.** Someone of spartan character. **—Spar·tan·ism** *n.*

spasm (spáz'm) *n.* **1.** A sudden, involuntary contraction of a muscle or group of muscles. **2.** Any sudden burst of energy, activity, or emotion. [Middle English *spasme,* from Old French, from Latin *spasmus,* from Greek *spasmos,* from *span*†, to draw, pull.]

spas·mod·ic (spaz-móddik) *adj.* **1.** Pertaining to, affected by, or having the character of a spasm; convulsive. **2.** Happening intermittently; fitful: *spasmodic rifle fire.* **3.** Jerky; disjointed: *spasmodic prose.* **4.** Occurring suddenly and violently: *spasmodic fury.* [New Latin *spasmodicus,* from Greek *spasmodikos,* from *spasmos,* SPASM.] **—spas·mod·i·cal·ly** *adv.*

Spass·ky (spáski || spaáski), **Boris (Vasilievich)** (1937–). Russian chess player. He was U.S.S.R. Grand Master, International Grand Master, and World Chess Student champion, and U.S.S.R. and World Chess Champion (1969–72). He now works in Paris as a journalist. See **Fischer, Bobby.**

spas·tic (spástik) *adj.* **1.** Pertaining to or characterised by spasms; continuously convulsing or contracting. **2.** Caused by spasms or spastic paralysis. **3.** *Slang.* **a.** Awkward or ungainly. **b.** Poor in quality: *a spastic football match.* Usually considered offensive.
~*n.* **1.** A person suffering from muscular spasms. **2.** A person suffering from spastic paralysis. [Latin *spasticus,* from Greek *spastikos,* from *span,* to pull, draw. See **spasm.**] **—spas·ti·cal·ly** *adv.* **—spas·tic·i·ty** (spass-tíssəti) *n.*

spastic paralysis *n.* A chronic pathological condition involving weakness of the limbs with exaggerated tendon reflexes and muscular spasms. It is a common result of cerebral palsy.

spat[1]. Past tense and past participle of **spit** (eject saliva).

spat[2] (spat) *n., pl.* **spat** or **spats.** An oyster or similar bivalve mollusc in the larval stage, especially when it settles to the bottom and begins to develop a shell.
~*intr.v.* **spatted, spatting, spats.** To spawn. Used of oysters and similar molluscs. [Anglo-French *spat*†.]

spat[3] *n.* A cloth or leather gaiter covering the shoe upper and the ankle and fastening under the shoe with a strap. [Short for earlier SPATTERDASH.]

spat[4] *n.* **1.** A brief, petty quarrel. **2.** *Informal.* A slap or smack. **3.** A spattering sound, as of raindrops.
~*v.* **spatted, spatting, spats.** *—intr.* **1.** To engage in a brief, petty quarrel. **2.** To strike with a light spattering sound; slap. *—tr. Informal.* To slap. [Probably imitative.]

spatch·cock (spách-kok) *n.* A freshly killed fowl, split and cooked immediately.
~*tr.v.* **1.** To cook like a spatchcock. **2.** *British Informal.* To interpolate or sandwich, especially in an inappropriate context. [18th century (Irish) : said to be shortened from *dispatch-cock,* but perhaps variant of earlier SPITCHCOCK.]

spate (spayt) *n.* **1.** A flash flood resulting from a downpour of rain or melting of snow: *The river was in full spate.* **2.** A sudden flood, rush, or outbreak. [Middle English *spate*†.]

spathe (spayth) *n. Botany.* A leaflike organ that encloses or spreads from the base of the spadix of certain plants, such as the cuckoopint or the calla. [Latin *spatha,* broad flat instrument, from Greek *spathē,* broad blade.] **—spa·tha·ceous** (spə-tháyshəss), **spa·those** (spáyth-ōz, spáth-, -ōss) *adj.*

spath·ic (spáthik) *adj.* Having good cleavage. Said of minerals. [From obsolete *spath,* spar, from German *Spat(h),* from Middle High German *spat.*]

spa·tial, spa·cial (spáysh'l) *adj.* Of, pertaining to, involving, or having the nature of space. [Latin *spatium,* SPACE.] **—spa·ti·al·i·ty** (spáyshi-ál-əti) *n.* **—spa·tial·ly** *adv.*

spa·ti·o·tem·po·ral (spáyshi-ō-témpərəl) *adj.* **1.** Of, pertaining to, or existing in both space and time. **2.** Of or relating to space-time. [Latin *spatium,* SPACE + TEMPORAL.] **—spa·ti·o·tem·po·ral·ly** *adv.*

spat·ter (spáttər) *v.* **-tered, -tering, -ters.** *—tr.* **1.** To scatter (a liquid substance) in drops or small splashes. **2.** To spot, splash, or soil. **3.** To strike like a shower: *a handful of pebbles spattered the window.* **4.** To sully the reputation of; defame. *—intr.* **1.** To throw off drops or small splashes; splatter. **2.** To fall with a splash.
~*n.* **1.** The act of spattering. **2.** A spattering sound. **3.** A drop or splash of something spattered; a spot or stain. [Perhaps a frequentative of Dutch *spatten,* from Middle Dutch (perhaps imitative).]

spat·ter·dash (spáttər-dash) *n.* A legging worn to protect the lower leg from splashes of mud or dirt.

spat·ter·work (spáttər-wurk) *n.* The reproduction of designs by spattering colour over a stencil.

spat·u·la (spáttewlə || spáchələ) *n.* **1.** A small implement having a broad, flat, flexible blade that is used to spread or mix a semisolid substance such as icing, plaster, or paint. **2.** *Medicine.* An implement with a flat, blunt blade used to press down the tongue, to spread ointments, or to transfer powders. [Latin *spat(h)ula,* diminutive of *spatha,* blade, broad sword, from Greek *spathē.*] **—spat·u·lar, spat·u·lous** *adj.*

spat·u·late (spáttew-lət, -lit, -layt || spáchə-) *adj.* Shaped like a spatula; having a broad tip and narrow base: *spatulate leaves.*

spaud·ler (spawdlər) *n.* A piece of armour worn to protect the shoulder.

spav·in (spávvin) *n.* Either of two diseases affecting the hock joint of horses: *bog spavin,* an infusion of lymph that enlarges the joint, and *bone spavin,* a bony deposit that stiffens the joint. [Middle English *spaveyne,* from Old French *espavin*†.] **—spav·ined** *adj.*

spawn (spawn) *n.* **1.** The eggs of aquatic animals such as bivalve molluscs, fishes, and amphibians. **2.** Offspring occurring in numbers; brood. Usually used derogatorily. **3.** A person regarded as the issue of some usually undesirable parent or family: *the spawn of the devil.* **4.** The product or outcome of something. **5.** Fragments of mycelia used to start a mushroom culture.
~*v.* **spawned, spawning, spawns.** *—intr.* **1.** To deposit eggs; produce spawn. **2.** To produce offspring in numbers like spawn. *—tr.* **1.** To produce (spawn). **2.** To give birth to. Usually used derogatorily of human beings. **3.** To give rise to; engender. **4.** To plant with mycelia. [Middle English *spawne,* from *spawnen,* to spawn, from Anglo-French *espaundre,* to shed roe, from Old French *espandre,* to shed, spread, from Latin *expandere,* to spread out, EXPAND.]

spawn·er (spáwnər) *n.* A female fish, especially at spawning time.

spawn·ing bed (spáwning) *n.* A nest made on the bed of a stream by fish such as salmon or trout for depositing spawn and milt.

spay (spay) *tr.v.* **spayed, spaying, spays.** To excise the ovaries of (a female animal). [Middle English *spayen,* from Old French *espeer,* to cut with a sword, from *espee,* sword, from Latin *spatha,* broad sword, from Greek *spathē.*]

speak (speek) *v.* **spoke** (spōk) or *archaic* **spake** (spayk), **spoken** (spōkən) or *archaic* **spoke, speaking, speaks.** *—intr.* **1.** To utter words as ordinary speech; talk. **2. a.** To engage in discussion; converse; talk. Also used with an adverb to convey the speaker's attitude towards the message in such phrases as *strictly speaking, to speak frankly.* **b.** To acknowledge another; be on friendly social terms: *They are no longer speaking.* **3.** To deliver an address or lecture; make a speech. **4.** To convey a message: *Actions speak louder than words.* **5.** To be expressive. **6.** To emit a report on firing: *"Our cannons speak and the enemy's now open in full chorus"* (Ambrose Bierce). **7. a.** To make communicative sounds. **b.** To give an impression of speaking: *teach a dog to speak for a bone.* **8.** To be relevant or comprehensible: *Modern art does not always speak to modern man.* *—tr.* **1.** To articulate in a speaking voice. **2.** To converse in or be able to converse in (a language). **3. a.** To express aloud; declare; tell. **b.** To express without words: *His eyes spoke love.* **c.** To communicate in print or writing. **4.** To reveal; show to be. **5.** *Nautical.* To hail and communicate with (another vessel) at sea. **—so to speak.** That is to say; as it were. **—speak for. 1.** To speak on behalf of; represent. **2.** To claim: *This ticket is spoken for.* **—speak for itself.** To be self-evident. **—speak of.** To refer to. **—speak out** or **up. 1.** To speak more clearly or louder. **2.** To speak without hesitation or fear: *spoke up for human rights.* **—speak well for.** To express or indicate something favourable about. **—to speak of.** Worthy of mention or discussion. [Speak, spake, spoken; Middle English *speken, spake, spoken,* Old English *specan, spǣc, gespecen.* Past tense *spoke* was formed on analogy with BREAK, BROKE, BROKEN.] —**speak·a·ble** adj.

Synonyms: speak, talk, converse, discourse, chatter, gossip.

-speak n. comb. form. Indicates a jargon associated with a specified group or field of activity; for example, *teenspeak, newspeak.* [From George Orwell's novel *1984* (1949), in which faceless technocrats develop *Newspeak*, a language intended to prevent original thought.]

speak·eas·y (spéek-eezi) n., pl. **-ies.** A bar selling alcoholic drinks illegally, especially one in the United States during the period of Prohibition.

speak·er (spéekər) n. **1.** One who speaks. Often used in combination: *English-speakers.* **2.** One who delivers a public speech. **3.** *Often capital* **S.** The presiding officer of a legislative assembly, especially the British Parliament or U.S. House of Representatives. **4.** A loudspeaker (see).

Speaker's Corner. An area at the Marble Arch corner of Hyde Park, London, where, by tradition, anyone is free to make speeches to the public.

speak·ing (spéeking) adj. **1.** Of, pertaining to, or involving speech: *within speaking distance.* **2.** Inhabited largely by speakers of a specified language. Used in combination: *English-speaking countries.* **3.** Expressive or telling; eloquent. —**on speaking terms.** Sufficiently acquainted or friendly to allow conversation.

speaking clock n. *British.* A telephone service allowing callers to dial a recording giving the exact time. Formerly called "Tim".

speaking tube n. A tube or pipe formerly used for speaking from a room or building to another place.

spear (speer) n. **1.** A weapon consisting of a long shaft with a sharply pointed head. **2.** A shaft with a sharp point and barbs for spearing fish. **3.** A spearman. **4.** A slender stalk, as of asparagus. ~v. **speared, spearing, spears.** —*tr.* To pierce with or as with a spear. —*intr.* **1.** To stab with or as with a spear. **2.** To sprout like a spear. [Middle English *spere*, Old English *spere.*] —**spear·er** n.

spear·fish (spéer-fish) n., pl. **-fishes** or collectively **spearfish.** A marlin (see).

spear·head (spéer-hed) n. **1.** The sharpened head of a spear. **2. a.** The vanguard in a military thrust. **b.** A person or group seen as the driving force in a given action or endeavour. ~tr.v. **spearheaded, -heading, -heads.** To be the leader or leaders of (a drive or an attack).

spear·man (spéer-mən) n., pl. **-men** (-mən, -men). A soldier armed with a spear.

spear·mint (spéer-mint) n. An aromatic plant, *Mentha spicata*, native to Europe, having clusters of small purplish flowers and yielding an oil widely used as flavouring. [Perhaps so called from the sharpness of the leaf.]

spear side n. The male side of a family. Used humorously. Compare **distaff side.**

spear·wort (spéer-wurt ‖ -wawrt) n. Any of several plants related to the buttercup; especially, *Ranunculus flammula*, native to Eurasia, having lance-shaped leaves and yellow flowers.

spec¹ (spek) n. *Informal.* A speculative purchase or enterprise. —**on spec.** Taking a chance: in the hope of success or profit.

spec² n. *Informal.* A specification.

spec. 1. special. **2.** specification. **3.** speculation.

spe·cial (spésh'l) adj. Abbr. **sp., spec. 1.** Surpassing what is common or usual; exceptional. **2. a.** Distinct among others of a kind; singular. **b.** Primary: *their special concern.* **3.** Peculiar to a specific person or thing; particular. **4.** Having a limited or specific function, application, or scope. **5.** Esteemed; close: *special friends.* **6.** Additional; extra: *a special holiday flight.* **7.** *Informal.* Exceptionally fine: *she's pretty special.* ~n. Abbr. **sp., spec. 1.** Something arranged, issued, or made for a particular purpose or occasion, as: **a.** A dish specially featured on a menu. **b.** A television programme not forming part of a regular series and normally longer and more spectacular than an ordinary programme. **2.** A special constable. [Middle English, from Old French *especial*, from Latin *speciālis*, special, of a particular kind, from *speciēs*, kind, SPECIES.] —**spe·cial·ly** adv.

Usage: Special and *specially* have a wider application than *especial* and *especially*. *Special* and *specially* mean "particular, specific, as opposed to what is general or ordinary": *I have a special interest in such problems. People have been specially trained. Especial* and *especially* are the forms to use when the sense is that of "pre-eminence, exceptional degree": *an especial talent; Especially in Britain.*

Special Branch n. In Britain, the police department responsible for political security.

special clinic n. In Britain, a clinic, often attached to a hospital, for the detection and treatment of a particular medical condition, such as diabetes or venereal diseases.

special constable n. In Britain, an unpaid member of an auxiliary police force, assisting the regular force in such duties as traffic or crowd control. Also called "special".

special delivery n. A delivery service for important postal items, providing for delivery by a special messenger rather than by ordinary services. —**spe·cial-de·liv·er·y** adj.

special drawing rights pl.n. Abbr. **S.D.R., S.D.R.s.** Rights accorded to certain member countries of the International Monetary Fund to draw on the Fund's reserves.

special effect n. An illusory effect used in films and created by various techniques, such as animation or 3-D photography.

special hospital n. In Britain, a hospital for the care of mentally ill patients who are considered a danger to society.

spe·cial·i·sa·tion (spésh'l-ī-záysh'n ‖ U.S.-i-) n. **1.** The action of specialising or the process of becoming specialised. **2.** An area in which one specialises.

specialise, spe·cial·ize (spésh'l-īz) v. **-ised, -ising, -ises.** —*intr.* **1.** To train or employ oneself in a special study, field, or activity. **2.** *Biology.* To develop so as to become adapted to a specific environment or function. —*tr.* **1.** To make more specific or particular. **2.** To give a particular character or function to. **3.** *Biology.* To adapt by specialisation.

spe·cial·ism (spésh'l-iz'm) n. **1.** Confinement or limitation to some field of study or occupation. **2.** A field of specialisation.

spe·cial·ist (spésh'l-ist) n. Abbr. **sp. 1.** One who has devoted himself to a particular branch of study or research. **2.** A doctor specialising in a particular field of medicine. —**spe·cial·is·tic** (-ístik) adj.

spe·ci·al·i·ty (spéshi-ál-əti) n., pl. **-ties. 1.** A distinguishing mark or feature; a special characteristic; a peculiarity. **2.** *Plural.* Special points of consideration; details; particulars. **3.** *Chiefly British.* Something at which one is particularly adept or for which one makes special provision, such as a pursuit, subject, product, or service.

special licence n. In the Church of England, a licence permitting a marriage to take place without publication of banns, outside the hours prescribed for marriages, or in a church other than a parish of one of the partners.

special plea n. **1.** *Law.* A plea asserting new or special matter to offset the opposing party's allegations, as an alternative to direct denial. **2.** A presentation of an argument that emphasises only a favourable or a single aspect of the question at issue. In this sense, also called "special pleading".

special relativity n. *Physics.* The early part of the theory of **relativity** (see), dealing with uniform motion.

special session n. **1.** An extraordinary session of a court or of a legislative body. **2.** *Plural.* Sittings held by two or more British magistrates or justices for some special purpose, such as the granting of licences to sell alcoholic drinks.

special sort n. A special printing character not normally forming part of a particular font. Also called "peculiar".

spe·cial·ty (spésh'l-ti) n., pl. **-ties. 1.** *Law.* A special contract or agreement, especially a deed, kept under seal. **2.** *U.S.* A speciality (sense 3).

spe·ci·a·tion (spée-si-áysh'n, -shi-) n. *Biology.* The evolutionary process by which new species are formed. [SPECI(ES) + -ATION.]

spe·cie (spée-shee, -shi ‖ -see) n. Minted money; coin. —**in specie. 1.** In coin. **2.** *Law.* In kind; in the same kind or shape. [Latin (in) *specie*, (in) kind, from the ablative of *speciēs*, kind, SPECIES.]

specie point n. *Finance.* The **gold point** (see).

spe·cies (spée-sheez, -shiz ‖ -seez) n., pl. **species** (*Note. Some distinguish in pronunciation between singular* -shiz *and plural* -sheez.) *Abbr.* **sp. 1.** *Biology.* **a.** A fundamental category of taxonomic classification, ranking after a genus, and consisting of organisms capable of interbreeding. **b.** A group of organisms belonging to such a category, represented in taxonomic nomenclature by a Latin adjective or epithet following a genus name. **2.** The human race. Preceded by *the.* **3.** *Logic.* A class of individuals or objects grouped by virtue of their common attributes and assigned a common name; a division subordinate to a genus. **4.** A kind, variety, or type. **5.** *Roman Catholic Church.* **a.** The outward appearance or form of the Eucharistic elements that is retained after their consecration. **b.** Either of the consecrated elements of the Eucharist. [Latin *speciēs*, appearance, likeness, a particular kind, from *specere*, to look at.]

specif. specifically.

spec·i·fi·a·ble (spéssi-fī-əb'l ‖ -fī-) adj. Capable of being specified.

spe·cif·ic (spi-síffik, spə-) adj. Abbr. **sp. 1.** Explicitly designated; particular; definite. **2.** Pertaining to, characterising, or distinguishing a species. **3.** Special, distinctive, or unique, as a quality or attribute may be. **4.** Intended for, applying to, or acting upon a particular thing. **5.** Designating a disease produced by a particular microorganism or condition. **6. a.** Designating a customs charge levied upon goods by unit or weight rather than according to value. **b.** Designating a commodity rate applicable to the transport of a single commodity between named points. **7.** *Physics.* **a.** Designating an extensive physical quality per unit mass: *specific heat capacity.* **b.** Designating a property of a substance per unit mass, length, area, or volume. **c.** Designating a property of a substance divided by the same property of a standard reference substance: *specific gravity.* ~n. **1.** *Often plural.* A specific factor , such as a quality, statement, requirement, or attribute: *discussing specifics.* **2.** *Medicine.* A remedy intended for some particular ailment or disorder. [Medieval Latin *specificus*, from Latin *speciēs*, kind, SPECIES.] —**spe·cif·i·cal·ly** adv. —**spec·i·fic·i·ty** (spéssi-físəti) n.

-specific adj. comb. form. Confined in effect, relevance, or scope to the specified sphere; for example, **job-specific, sex-specific.**

spec·i·fi·ca·tion (spéssifi-káysh'n) n. Abbr. **spec. 1. a.** An act of specifying. **b.** A precisely stated requirement. **2. a.** *Usually plural.* A detailed and exact statement of particulars; especially, a statement prescribing materials, dimensions, and instructions for something to be built, installed, or manufactured. **b.** A single item or article that has been specified. **3.** An exact written description of an invention by an applicant for a patent.

specific gravity n. Abbr. **sp gr** Relative density (see).

specific heat capacity n. The amount of heat required to raise the temperature of unit mass of substance by unit interval of temperature under prescribed conditions, usually either at constant volume or constant temperature. It is measured in joules per kilogram per kelvin (SI units) or calories per gram per degree Celsius (c.g.s. units). Formerly called "specific heat".

specific impulse *n.* A performance measure for rocket propellants, equal to units of thrust per unit weight of propellant consumed per unit time. Also called "specific thrust".

specific performance *n. Law.* A remedy awarded by a court requiring the terms of a contract to be fulfilled where damages are insufficient.

specific resistance *n. Electricity.* **Resistivity** *(see).* Not in current technical usage.

specific volume *n.* The volume of unit mass of a substance; the reciprocal of density.

spec·i·fy (spéssi-fī) *tr.v.* **-fied, -fying, -fies. 1.** To state explicitly, especially as a definite requirement. **2.** To include in a specification. [Middle English *specifien,* from Old French *specifier,* from Medieval Latin *specificāre,* from *specificus,* SPECIFIC.]

spec·i·men (spéssi-min, -mən) *n.* **1.** An individual, item, or part seen as representative of a class, genus, or whole; an example. Also used adjectivally: *a specimen copy.* **2.** A sample, as of tissue, blood, or urine, used for medical or scientific analysis and diagnosis. **3.** An object or organism selected and presented as part of a collection or series: *showed me his finest specimen.* **4.** *Informal.* A person of a specified, usually unpleasant, type: *an unsavoury specimen.* —See Synonyms at **example.** [Latin *specimen,* mark, token, example, from *specere,* to look at.]

spe·ci·os·i·ty (spéeshi-óssəti) *n., pl.* **-ities. 1.** The state or quality of being specious. **2.** A specious person or thing.

spe·cious (spéeshəss) *adj.* **1.** Seemingly fair, attractive, sound, or true, but actually not so; deceptive: *a specious resemblance.* **2.** Having the ring of truth or plausibility but actually fallacious: *a specious argument.* [Middle English, attractive, fair, from Latin *speciōsus,* good-looking, from *speciēs,* outward appearance, from *specere,* to look at.] —**spe·cious·ly** *adv.* —**spe·cious·ness** *n.*

speck (spek) *n.* **1.** A small spot, mark, or discoloration. **2.** A very small bit of something; a particle.
~*tr.v.* **specked, specking, specks.** To mark with specks; spot; speckle. [Middle English *specke,* Old English *specca*†.]

speck·le (spéck'l) *n.* A speck or small spot; especially, a natural dot of colour occurring in large numbers on skin, plumage, or foliage.
~*tr.v.* **speckled, -ling, -les.** To mark with or as if with speckles. [Middle Dutch *spekkel;* akin to Old English *specca,* SPECK.]

speck·led trout (spéck'ld) *n.* The **brook trout** *(see).*

specs (speks) *pl.n. Informal.* Glasses; spectacles.

spec·ta·cle (spéktək'l) *n.* **1.** A public performance or display, especially a lavish visual entertainment. **2. a.** An object of interest; a marvel or curiosity. **b.** An object or scene considered regrettable: *made a spectacle of himself.* **3. a.** Something seen or able to be seen. **b.** The sight of something: *"We pleased ourselves with the spectacle of Dublin's commerce"* (James Joyce). **4.** *Plural.* **a.** A pair of glasses. **b.** Something resembling glasses in shape or function. —**through rose-tinted** or **rose-coloured spectacles.** Wtih naive optimism. [Middle English, from Old French, from Latin *spectāculum,* from *spectāre,* to look at, frequentative of *specere.*]

spec·ta·cled (spéktək'ld) *adj.* **1.** Wearing spectacles. **2.** Having markings suggesting spectacles. Said of animals.

spec·tac·u·lar (spek-táckew-lər) *adj.* **1.** Of the nature of a spectacle; visually impressive. **2.** Striking or remarkable; dramatic: *a spectacular resignation.*
~*n.* An entertainment, such as a film or television programme, with lavish visual presentation and usually featuring famous performers. —**spec·tac·u·lar·ly** *adv.* —**spec·tac·u·lar·i·ty** (-lárrəti) *n.*

spec·tate (spek-táyt ‖ spék-tayt) *intr.v.* **-tated, -tating, -tates.** *Informal.* To be present as a spectator.

spec·ta·tor (spek-táytər ‖ spék-taytər) *n.* **1.** One who attends and views a show, sports match, or other event. **2.** An observer of any event; an eyewitness; an onlooker. [Latin *spectātor,* from *spectāre,* look at. See **spectacle.**]

spectator sport *n.* A sport which attracts large numbers of people to come and watch it, as opposed to participate in it.

spectra. Plural of **spectrum.**

spec·tral (spéktrəl) *adj.* **1.** Of or resembling a spectre; ghostly. **2.** Of, pertaining to, or produced by a spectrum. —**spec·tral·i·ty** (spek-trál-əti), **spec·tral·ness** *n.* —**spec·tral·ly** *adv.*

spectral line *n. Physics.* A discrete peak of intensity in a spectrum; especially, one of the visible dispersed images of the slit through which light enters the collimator of a spectroscope, produced by light of a single wavelength.

spectral type *n.* Any of several methods of classifying stars according to their observed spectra. See **Harvard classification.**

spec·tre, *U.S.* **spec·ter** (spéktər) *n.* **1.** A ghost; a phantom; an apparition. **2.** Something fearful that has no reality. **3.** A mental image of something unpleasant: *the spectre of examinations.* [French, from Latin *spectrum,* appearance, image. See **spectrum.**]

spectro– *comb. form.* Indicates spectrum; for example, **spectrograph, spectroscope.** [From SPECTRUM.]

spec·tro·bo·lom·e·ter (spék-trō-bə-lómmitər, -trə-, -bō-) *n. Physics.* A bolometer combined with a spectroscope for investigating how the intensity of a source of radiant energy varies over the range of wavelengths emitted.

spec·tro·gram (spék-trə-gram, -trō-) *n. Physics.* Also **spectrograph.** A graph or photograph of a spectrum. [SPECTRO- + -GRAM.]

spec·tro·graph (spék-trə-graaf, -trō-, -graf) *n. Physics.* **1.** A spectroscope equipped to photograph spectra. **2.** Variant of **spectrogram.** [SPECTRO- + -GRAPH.] —**spec·tro·graph·ic** (-gráffik) *adj.* —**spec·tro·graph·i·cal·ly** *adv.* —**spek·tróg·ra·phy** (spek-tróggrəfi) *n.*

spec·tro·he·li·o·gram (spék-trō-héeli-ə-gram, -trə-, -ō-) *n. Physics.* A photograph of the sun taken in a narrow wavelength band centred on a selected wavelength.

spec·tro·he·li·o·graph (spék-trō-héeli-ə-graaf, -trə-, -ō-, -graf) *n. Physics.* An instrument used to make spectroheliograms. —**spec·tro·he·li·o·graph·ic** (-gráffik) *adj.*

spec·tro·he·li·o·scope (spék-trō-héeli-ə-skōp, -trə-, -ō-) *n. Physics.* An instrument used to observe solar radiation. —**spec·tro·he·li·o·scop·ic** (-skóppik) *adj.*

spec·trol·o·gy (spek-trólləji) *n.* The study of spectres.

spec·trom·e·ter (spek-trómmitər) *n. Physics.* A spectroscope equipped with calibrated scales for measuring the positions of spectral lines. [SPECTRO(SCOPE) + -METER.] —**spec·tro·met·ric** (spék-trə-méttrik, -trō-) *adj.* —**spec·trom·e·try** (spek-trómmətri) *n.*

spec·tro·pho·tom·e·ter (spék-trō-fō-tómmitər, -trə-) *n. Physics.* An instrument used to determine the distribution of energy in a spectrum of luminous radiation. —**spec·tro·pho·to·met·ric** (-fō-tō-méttrik, -tə-) *adj.* —**spec·tro·pho·tom·e·try** (-tómmətri) *n.*

spec·tro·scope (spék-trə-skōp, -trō-) *n. Physics.* Any of various instruments for resolving and observing or recording spectra. [SPECTRO- + -SCOPE.] —**spec·tro·scop·ic** (-skóppik), **spec·tro·scop·i·cal** *adj.* —**spec·tro·scop·i·cal·ly** *adv.*

spectroscopic analysis *n. Physics.* The analysis of a spectrum to determine characteristics of its source, such as the analysis of the optical spectrum of an incandescent body to determine its composition or motion.

spec·tros·co·py (spek-tróskəpi) *n. Physics.* The study of spectra, especially the experimental observation of spectra. [SPECTRO- + -SCOPY.] —**spec·tros·co·pist** *n.*

spec·trum (spék-trəm) *n., pl.* **-tra** (-trə) or **-trums. 1.** *Physics.* The distribution of a characteristic of a physical system or phenomenon, especially: **a.** The distribution of energy emitted by a radiant source, as by an incandescent body, arranged in order of wavelengths. **b.** The distribution of atomic or subatomic particles in a system, as in a magnetically resolved molecular beam, arranged in order of masses. Also called "mass spectrum". **c.** A graphic or photographic representation of any such distribution. **2. a.** The complete range of electromagnetic radiation arranged in order of frequency or wavelength. Also called "electromagnetic spectrum". **b.** The complete range of colours as dispersed from light. **3. a.** A range of values of a quantity or set of related quantities. **b.** A broad sequence or range of related qualities, ideas, or activities: *the whole spectrum of 20th-century thought.* [Latin, appearance, image, form, from *specere,* to look at.]

spec·u·lar (spéckewlər) *adj.* Of, resembling, produced, or aided by a mirror or speculum. —**spec·u·lar·ly** *adv.*

spec·u·late (spéckew-layt) *intr.v.* **-lated, -lating, -lates. 1.** To conjecture on a given subject or situation, without knowing all the facts. **2.** To engage in the buying or selling of a commodity with an element of risk on the chance of large profit. —See Synonyms at **conjecture.** [Latin *speculārī,* to spy out, watch, observe, from *specula,* watchtower, from *specere,* to look at.] —**spec·u·lat·or** *n.*

spec·u·la·tion (spéckew-láysh'n) *n. Abbr.* **spec. 1. a.** The act of speculating; consideration of or conjecture about some subject or idea. **b.** A conclusion, opinion, or theory reached by speculating. **2. a.** Engagement in risky business transactions on the chance of quick or considerable profit. **b.** An instance of commercial speculating. **3.** A card game in which players buy trumps from each other on a chance of getting the highest trump dealt.

spec·u·la·tive (spéckew-lətiv, -laytiv) *adj.* **1.** Of, characterised by, or based upon contemplative speculation; conjectural or theoretical in nature rather than pragmatic or realistic. **2. a.** Given to or spent in speculation or conjecture. **b.** Seeming to speculate: *a speculative gaze.* **3. a.** Engaging in, given to, or involving financial speculation. **b.** Involving chance; risky. —**spec·u·la·tive·ly** *adv.* —**spec·u·la·tive·ness** *n.*

speculative philosophy *n.* Philosophy that is theoretical or transcendent, rather than demonstrative or empirical.

spec·u·lum (spéckew-ləm) *n., pl.* **-la** (-lə) or **-lums. 1.** A mirror or polished metal plate, used as a reflector in optical instruments. **2.** An instrument for dilating the opening of a body cavity, especially the vagina, for medical examination. **3.** *Biology.* **a.** A bright patch of colour on the wings of certain birds, especially ducks. Also called "mirror". **b.** A transparent spot on the wings of some butterflies or moths. [Latin, mirror, from *specere,* to look at.]

speculum metal *n.* An alloy of copper, tin, and other metals that takes a high polish and is used in mirrors and reflectors.

sped. Past tense and past participle of **speed.**

speech (speech) *n.* **1. a.** The faculty or act of speaking; utterance of articulate sounds. **b.** The faculty or act of expressing or describing thoughts, feelings, or perceptions in words. **2. a.** That which is spoken; an utterance. **b.** A line or set of lines spoken by a character in a dramatic work. **3.** Conversation; vocal communication. **4. a.** A talk or public address. **b.** A printed copy of an address. **5.** A person's habitual manner or style of speaking. **6.** The language or dialect of a nation or region. **7.** The sounding of a musical instrument. **8.** The study of oral communication, speech sounds, especially for elocution or dramatic effect, and vocal physiology. **9.** *Linguistics.*

Parole (see). **10.** *Archaic.* Rumour. [Middle English *speche,* Old English *spēc, sprǣc.*]

speech community *n.* All the speakers of a particular language or dialect, whether located in one area or scattered.

speech day *n.* An annual occasion in schools in Britain and elsewhere when prizes are awarded for academic performance and speeches are made by the headmaster and others.

speech defect *n.* A defect in speaking, such as a lisp or stammer, having a physiological or psychological cause.

Speech from the Throne *n.* A speech read by the sovereign or his or her representative at the opening of Parliament in Britain and certain Commonwealth countries outlining the government's legislative programme. Also called "gracious speech", "King's speech", "Queen's speech".

speech·i·fy (spéechi-fī) *intr.v.* **-fied, -fying, -fies.** To make a speech, especially a pompous one; orate. **—speech·i·fi·ca·tion** (-fi-káysh'n) *n.* **—speech·i·fi·er** *n.*

speech·less (spéech-ləss, -liss) *adj.* **1.** Lacking the faculty of speech; dumb. **2.** Temporarily unable to speak, as through astonishment. **3.** Refraining from speech; silent. **4.** Unexpressed or inexpressible in words: *speechless admiration.* **—See Synonyms at dumb. —speech·less·ly** *adv.* **—speech·less·ness** *n.*

speech-reading *n.* **Lip-reading** (see).

speech pathology *n.* **1.** The study of speech defects and disabilities and methods of correcting them. **2.** *Chiefly U.S.* Speech therapy. **—speech pathologist** *n.*

speech therapy *n.* The practice or profession of dealing with speech defects and disabilities. Also called "logopaedics", *chiefly U.S.* "speech pathology". **—speech therapist** *n.*

speed (speed) *n.* **1.** *Mathematics & Physics.* The rate or a measure of the rate of motion, especially: **a.** *Average speed,* or the distance travelled divided by the time of travel. **b.** *Instantaneous speed,* the limit of this quotient as the time of travel becomes vanishingly small; the first derivative of distance with respect to time. **c.** The magnitude of a **velocity** (see). **2.** A rate of performance; swiftness of action. **3.** The act or state of moving rapidly; rapidity; swiftness. **4.** A transmission gear or set of gears in a motor vehicle or bicycle. **5.** A rate of rotation, especially that of a record turntable, usually expressed in revolutions per minute or other unit time. **6.** *Photography.* **a.** A numerical expression of the sensitivity of a film, plate, or paper to light. **b.** The capacity of a lens to accumulate light at an appropriate aperture. See **f-stop. c.** The length of time required for a camera shutter to open and admit light. **7.** *Slang.* Any amphetamine taken to increase energy, reduce tiredness, and produce euphoria. **8.** *Archaic.* Prosperity; success; luck. **—at speed.** Rapidly.

~v. **sped** (sped) or **speeded, speeding, speeds.** *—tr.* **1. a.** To hasten. **b.** To send or dispatch with speed or haste. **2. a.** To increase the speed or rate of; accelerate. Often used with *up.* **b.** To set the speed of (a machine). **3. a.** *Archaic.* To wish Godspeed to. **b.** *Archaic.* To help to succeed or prosper; aid. **c.** To further, promote, or expedite (a matter or legal action). Often used with *along.* *—intr.* **1. a.** To go or move rapidly. **b.** To drive fast; exceed a traffic speed limit. **2.** To pass quickly. Used of time. **3.** To move, perform, or happen at a faster rate; accelerate. Usually used with *up.* **4.** *Slang.* To take or be under the influence of amphetamines. [Middle English *sped(e),* success, prosperity, speed, Old English *spēd, spǣd.*] **—speed·er** *n.*

Synonyms: speed, hurry, hasten, quicken, accelerate, precipitate, expedite.

speed·ball (spéed-bawl) *n. Slang.* An intravenous dose of cocaine and heroin or morphine.

speed·boat (spéed-bōt) *n.* A fast motorboat.

speed limit *n.* The maximum speed legally permitted on a given stretch of road.

speed mer·chant *n.* One who habitually drives a motor vehicle excessively fast.

speed·om·e·ter (spee-dómmitər) *n.* An instrument for measuring and indicating speed. Also informally called "speedo".

speed·ster (spéed-stər) *n.* **1.** A speeder. **2.** A fast vehicle, usually a sports car.

speed trap *n.* A stretch of road on which the speed of vehicles is secretly checked by police using electronic or other devices.

speed·way (spéed-way) *n.* **1. a.** A course for motorcycle racing. **b.** The sport of motorcycle racing. **2.** *U.S.* **a.** A car racetrack. **b.** A road designed for fast-moving traffic.

speed·well (spéed-wel) *n.* Any of various plants of the genus *Veronica,* having clusters of small, usually blue flowers.

Speed·writ·ing (spéed-rīting) *n.* A trademark for a shorthand technique involving modified alphabetic symbols which represent phonetic combinations.

speed·y (spéedi) *adj.* **-ier, -iest. 1.** Characterised by rapid motion; swift. **2.** Accomplished or arrived at without delay; prompt; quick. **—See Synonyms at fast. —speed·i·ly** *adv.* **—speed·i·ness** *n.*

speer, speir (speer) *v.* **speered** or **speired, speering** or **speiring, speers** or **speirs.** *Scottish. —intr.* To ask questions. *—tr.* To ask; enquire. [Middle English, from Old English *spyrian,* to seek; akin to SPOOR.]

spe·le·ol·o·gy (speéli-ólləji, spélli-) *n.* **1.** The study of the physical, geological, and biological aspects of caves. **2.** The exploration of caves. [Latin *spēleum,* cave, from Greek *spēlaion†* + -LOGY.] **—spe·le·o·log·i·cal** (-ə-lójik'l) *adj.* **—spe·le·ol·o·gist** (-óllǝjist) *n.*

spell¹ (spel) *v.* **spelt** (spelt) or *chiefly U.S.* **spelled, spelling, spells.**

—tr. **1.** To name or write in order the letters constituting (a word or part of a word). **2.** To be the ordered letters of; form (a word). **3.** To mean; be a sign of: *that tone of voice spells trouble. —intr.* To form a word or words correctly by naming the letters. **—spell out. 1.** *Informal.* To make explicit and understandable: *He didn't need to spell out his threat.* **2.** To spell slowly, letter by letter, especially when trying to read or decipher. [Middle English *spellen,* read out, from Old French *espelir, espeller,* from Germanic.] **—spell·a·ble** *adj.*

Usage: Both *spelled* and *spelt* are used as past tenses and participles, the former being standard in American English, the latter being the usual form in British English.

spell² *n.* **1.** A word or formula used to work magic. **2.** Compelling attraction; fascination. **3.** A bewitched state; a trance. [Middle English *spell,* discourse, Old English *spel(l),* story, fable.]

spell³ *n.* **1.** A short, indefinite period of time. **2.** *Informal.* A period characterised by some specified condition, such as weather, activity, or illness: *a dry spell; a dizzy spell.* **3.** A short turn of work; a turn; a shift: *a spell at the helm.* **4.** *Australian.* A period or interval of rest. **5.** *Informal.* A short distance.

~v. **spelled, spelling, spells.** *—tr. Chiefly U.S.* **1.** To relieve (a person) from work temporarily by taking a turn. **2.** To allow to rest a while. [Perhaps from Middle English *spelen,* relieve at work, Old English *spelian†,* to substitute.]

spell·bind (spél-bīnd) *tr.v.* **-bound** (-bownd), **-binding, -binds.** To put or hold under or as if under a spell; enthral; enchant.

spell·bind·er (spél-bīndər) *n.* One that holds others spellbound.

spell·bound (spél-bownd) *adj.* Entranced; fascinated.

spell check *n.* A computer program that checks the spellings of words against those in a stored dictionary and notifies the user of any discrepancies.

spell·er (spéllər) *n.* **1.** One who spells words, usually in a specified way. **2.** An elementary textbook to teach spelling.

spellican. Variant of **spillikin.**

spell·ing (spélling) *n. Abbr.* **sp. 1. a.** The forming of words with letters in an accepted order; orthography. **b.** The art or study of orthography. **c.** A person's ability to spell. **2.** The way in which a word is spelt.

spelling bee *n.* A contest in which competitors are eliminated as they fail to spell a given word correctly. [Special (originally U.S.) use of BEE (insect, representing industrious and communal activity).]

spelling pronunciation *n.* A pronunciation of a word that is influenced by the way in which it is spelt and that often comes to replace earlier forms. The word "forehead" (fórrid), for example, is sometimes pronounced nowadays as (fór-hed).

spelt¹ (spelt) *n.* A hardy wheat, *Triticum spelta,* from which many cultivated wheats are derived. [Probably from Middle Dutch *spelte.*]

spelt². Past tense and past participle of **spell** (to form words).

spel·ter (spéltər) *n.* Impure zinc, especially in the form of ingots, slabs, or plates. [Obscurely akin to Middle Dutch *speauter†;* akin to Old French *peautre,* PEWTER.]

spe·lunk·er (spi-lúngkər, spée-lungkər) *n. U.S.* One who explores and studies caves. [From obsolete *spelunk,* cave, from Middle English, from Latin *spelunca,* from Greek *spēlunx;* akin to Greek *spēlaion.* See **speleology.**] **—spe·lunk·ing** *n.*

Spence (spenss), **Sir Basil** (1907–76). British architect. He designed the new cathedral for Coventry (finished 1962) and was consultant architect to many British universities.

spen·cer¹ (spén-sər) *n. Nautical.* A **trysail** (see). [Perhaps from the surname *Spencer.*]

spencer² *n.* **1.** A short double-breasted overcoat worn by men in the early 19th century. **2.** A close-fitting waist-length jacket formerly worn by women. **3.** A short-sleeved woman's vest. [After George *Spencer,* Earl Spencer (1758–1834).]

Spencer, Sir Stanley (1891–1959). British painter. He is best known for his religious paintings which interpret the Scriptures in terms of everyday life. He was knighted in 1959.

Spencer Gulf. Inlet of the Indian Ocean, on the southern coast of Australia between Eyre Peninsula to the west and Yorke Peninsula to the east.

Spen·ce·ri·an·ism (spen-séer-i-ən-iz'm) *n.* The system of logical positivism developed by Herbert Spencer (1820–1903), setting forth the idea that evolution is the mechanistic passage from the simple, indefinite, and incoherent to the complex, definite, and coherent. Also called "synthetic philosophy".

spend (spend) *v.* **spent** (spent), **spending, spends.** *—tr.* **1.** To pay out (money). **2.** To use, concentrate, or devote. Often used with *on: spending his energy on pleasures.* **3.** To use up, consume, or expend: *The gale spent its force.* **4.** To pass (time) in a specified manner or place. **5. a.** To throw away; waste; squander. **b.** To sacrifice. *—intr.* **1.** To pay out money. **2.** *Obsolete.* To be exhausted or consumed. [Spend, spent, spent; Middle English *spenden, spente, spent,* partly from Old English *spendan,* from Latin *expendēre,* to EXPEND, and partly from Old French *despendre,* to dispend, squander.] **—spend·a·ble** *adj.* **—spend·er** *n.*

Usage: In its main sense of "purchase", *spend* may be followed by *on* (*I've spent a fortune on a new bike*), and especially in American English by *for.* In the sense of "pass the time", it may be followed by *in: He spent the last part of his life (in) doing good.*

Spend·er (spéndər), **Sir Stephen** (1909–95). British poet and critic. He was a leading member of the group of socialist poets in the 1930s, and fought with the Republicans in the Spanish civil war. Much of his work is characterised by imagery of an industrialised society.

spend·ing money (spénding) *n.* **Pocket money** *(see).*

spend·thrift (spénd-thrift) *n.* One who squanders money; a prodigal spender.
~*adj.* Wasteful or extravagant. [SPEND + THRIFT (accumulated wealth).]

Speng·ler (spéng-glər, -lər; *German* shpéng-lər), **Oswald** (1880–1936). German philosopher. He argued that civilisations and cultures are subject to the same cycle of growth and decay as human beings. His chief work, *The Decline of the West* (1918–22), reflects the pessimistic atmosphere in Germany after World War I.

Spen·ser (spén-sər), **Edmund** (*c.*1552–99). English poet. He is known chiefly for his allegorical, epic romance *The Faerie Queen* (1590–96). His other works include the pastoral *Shepherd's Calendar* (1579) and the lyrical marriage poem, *Epithalamion* (1595).

Spen·se·ri·an sonnet (spen-séer-i-ən) *n.* A sonnet comprising three interlocking quatrains and a couplet with the rhyme pattern *abab bcbc cdcd ee.* [After Edmund SPENSER.]

Spenserian stanza *n.* A stanza consisting of eight lines of iambic pentameter and a final alexandrine, rhymed *ababbcbcc,* used by Edmund Spenser in *The Faerie Queene.*

spent (spent). Past tense and past participle of **spend.**
~*adj.* **1.** Consumed; used up; expended: *a spent bullet.* **2.** Depleted of energy, force, or strength; exhausted; worn out.

sperm[1] (sperm) *n.* **1.** A male gamete or reproductive cell, a **spermatozoon** *(see).* **2.** The male fluid of fertilisation, **semen** *(see).* [Middle English *sperme,* from Old French *esperme,* from Late Latin *sperma,* seed, sperm, from Greek *sperma.*]

sperm[2] *n.* The sperm whale or a substance associated with it, such as spermaceti or sperm oil. [Short for SPERMACETI.]

sperm-, spermi-, spermo- *comb. form.* Indicates: **1.** Sperm; for example, **spermicidal.** **2.** Seed; for example, **spermophile.** [Greek *sperma,* seed.]

-sperm *n. comb. form. Botany.* Indicates a seed; for example, **gymnosperm.** [From SPERM (semen).] —**spermous** *adj. comb. form.*

sper·ma·ce·ti (spérmə-sétti, -séeti) *n.* A white, waxy substance consisting of various esters of fatty acids, obtained from the head of the sperm whale and used for making candles, ointments, and cosmetics. [Middle English, from Medieval Latin *spermacētī,* "sperm of the whale" : Late Latin *sperma,* SPERM + Latin *cētī,* genitive of *cētus,* whale (see **cetacean**).]

sper·ma·ry (spérməri) *n., pl.* **-ries.** An organ in which male gametes are formed, especially in invertebrate animals. [New Latin *spermarium,* from Late Latin *sperma,* SPERM.]

sper·ma·the·ca (spérmə-théekə) *n.* A receptacle in certain female invertebrates, especially insects, in which spermatozoa are stored before fertilisation takes place. [New Latin : Late Latin *sperma,* SPERM + THECA.] —**sper·ma·the·cal** *adj.*

sper·mat·ic (sper-máttik) *adj.* **1. a.** Pertaining to, or resembling spermatozoa; spermous. **b.** Carrying or containing spermatozoa. **2.** Pertaining to a spermary or to a testis. [Late Latin *spermaticus,* from Greek *spermatikos,* from *sperma* (stem *spermat-*), SPERM.]

spermatic cord *n.* A cordlike structure consisting of the vas deferens and its accompanying arteries, veins, nerves, and lymphatic vessels. It passes from the abdominal cavity through the inguinal canal, and down into the scrotum to the back of the testicle, which is suspended in the scrotum by this structure.

spermatic fluid *n.* The male fluid of fertilisation, **semen** *(see).*

sper·ma·tid (spérmə-tid) *n.* Any of four haploid cells formed from a spermatocyte during meiosis in the male that develop into spermatozoa without further division. [SPERMAT(O)- + -ID.]

sper·ma·ti·um (sper-máyti-əm || *chiefly U.S.* -máyshi-, -máysh-) *n., pl.* **-tia** (-ə). *Botany.* A nonmotile, sporelike structure in red algae and certain fungi, generally acting as a male gamete. [New Latin, from Greek *spermation,* diminutive of *sperma* (stem *spermat-*), SPERM.] —**sper·ma·tial** *adj.*

spermato-, spermat– *comb. form.* Indicates: **1.** Sperm; for example, **spermatogonium, spermatid.** **2.** Seed; for example, **spermatophyte.** [Late Latin *sperma* (stem *spermat-*), SPERM.]

sper·ma·to·cyte (spérmət-ō-sīt, sper-mát-, -ə-) *n.* A diploid cell that is converted by meiotic division into four spermatids during spermatogenesis. [SPERMATO- + -CYTE.]

sper·ma·to·gen·e·sis (spérmətō-ō-jénnə-siss, sper-mát-, -ə-) *n.* The generation of spermatozoa from spermatogonia in the testis by meiosis and spermiogenesis. [New Latin : SPERMATO- + -GENESIS.] —**sper·ma·to·ge·net·ic** (-jə-néttik) *adj.*

sper·ma·to·go·ni·um (spérmət-ō-gṓni-əm, sper-mát-, -ə-) *n., pl.* **-nia** (-ə). Any of the cells of the gonads in male animals that are the progenitors of spermatocytes. [New Latin : SPERMATO- + -GONIUM.] —**sper·ma·to·go·ni·al** *adj.*

sper·ma·toid (spérmə-toyd) *adj.* Resembling sperm. [SPERMAT(O)- + -OID.]

sper·ma·to·phore (spérmət-ō-fawr, sper-mát-, -ə- || -fōr) *n.* An extruded mass or capsule of spermatozoa in certain animals, such as some molluscs, insects, and amphibians. [SPERMATO- + -PHORE.] —**sper·ma·toph·or·al** *adj.*

sper·ma·to·phyte (spérmət-ō-fīt, sper-mát-, -ə-) *n. Botany.* Any plant of the division Spermatophyta, which includes all seed-bearing plants and is divided into angiosperms and gymnosperms. [New Latin *Spermatophyta* : SPERMATO- + -PHYTE.] —**sper·mat·o·phyt·ic** (-fíttik) *adj.*

sper·ma·tor·rhoe·a (spérmət-ō-rée-ə, sper-mát-, -ə-) *n.* Involuntary seminal discharge without orgasm. [New Latin : SPERMATO- + -RRHOEA.]

sper·ma·to·zo·id (spérmət-ō-zoyd, sper-mát-, -ə-) *n. Botany.* A ciliated male gamete produced in an antheridium; an antherozoid. [SPERMATOZO(ON) + -ID.]

sper·ma·to·zo·on (spérmət-ō-zṓ-on, sper-mát-, -ə-, -ən) *n., pl.* **-zoa** (-ə). A fertilising gamete of a male animal, usually a long nucleated cell with a thin, motile tail. It is produced in the testis by spermatogenesis. Also called "sperm", "sperm cell", "zoosperm". [New Latin : SPERMATO- + -ZOON.] —**sper·ma·to·zo·al, sper·ma·to·zo·an, sper·ma·to·zo·ic** *adj.*

sperm bank *n.* A place where sperm is stored for use in artificial insemination.

sperm count *n.* An estimation of the number of spermatozoa in a specimen of semen, used as an indication of male fertility.

spermi-, spermo- Variants of **sperm-.**

sper·mi·cide (spérmi-sīd) *n.* A usually chemical agent that kills spermatozoa. [SPERMI- + -CIDE.] —**sper·mi·cid·al** (-síd'l) *adj.*

sper·mine (spér-meen) *n.* A crystalline compound, $C_{10}H_{26}N_4$, found as a phosphate in semen, yeast, and certain body tissues.

sper·mi·o·gen·e·sis (spérmi-ə-jénnə-siss, -ō-) *n.* The transformation of a spermatid into a spermatozoon. [New Latin : *spermium,* spermatozoon, probably from SPERM + -GENESIS.]

sper·mo·go·ni·um (spérm-ə-gṓni-əm, -ō-) *n., pl.* **-nia** (-ə). *Botany.* A hollow structure in which spermatia are formed, as in certain fungi. [SPERMO- + -GONIUM.]

sperm oil *n.* A yellow, waxy oil, obtained chiefly from the head of the sperm whale and used as an industrial lubricant.

sperm·o·phile (spérm-ə-fīl, -ō-) *n.* Any of various North American ground squirrels of the genus *Citellus.* [New Latin *spermophilus,* "fond of seed" : SPERMO- + -PHILE.]

sper·mous (spérməss) *adj.* Spermatic.

sperm whale *n.* A toothed whale, *Physeter catodon,* having a very large head, with cavities containing sperm oil and spermaceti, and a long, narrow, toothed lower jaw. Also called "cachalot".

sper·ry·lite (spérri-līt) *n.* A white platinum mineral, essentially $PtAs_2,$ occurring in the form of cube-shaped crystals. [After F.L. Sperry, 19th-century Canadian mineralogist.]

spes·sar·tite (spéssər-tīt) *n.* A brownish type of garnet used as a gemstone, consisting of a silicate of aluminium and manganese, usually with small amounts of iron. [French, from *Spessart,* mountain range in Germany.]

speug (spyug) *n. Scottish.* A sparrow.

spew (spew) *v.* **spewed, spewing, spews.** Also *archaic* **spue, spued, spuing, spues.** —*tr.* **1.** To vomit or spit out through the mouth. **2.** To throw out or send forth with force or vigour. Often used with *forth* or *out*: *spewing out insults.* —*intr.* **1.** To vomit. **2.** To be thrown out or sent forth with force or vigour. Often used with *forth* or *out*: *Lava spewed forth from the crater.*
~*n.* Also *archaic* **spue.** Something that is spewed; vomit. [Middle English *spewen,* Old English *spīwan* and *spīowan.*]

Spey (spay). River in northeastern Scotland, rising in the Mondhliath mountains and flowing for about 170 kilometres (105 miles) into the North Sea. Its rapid, unnavigable waters are noted for salmon, and are used in the renowned Speyside whiskies.

Spey·er (shpī-ər). *English* **Spires** (spīrz). City and port in Rhineland-Palatinate, western Germany, lying on the river Rhine south of Mannheim. Its products include ships, chemicals, paper, and textiles. The Imperial Cathedral (11th century) is one of Germany's finest Romanesque buildings.

sp gr specific gravity.

sphag·num (sfág-nəm) *n.* **1.** Any of various mosses of the genus *Sphagnum,* that decompose to form peat. **2.** A mass of these plants, used for potting plants and for surgical dressings. Also called "bog moss", "peat moss". [New Latin, from Latin *sphagnos,* a kind of moss, from Greek *sphagnos*†.] —**sphag·nous** *adj.*

sphal·er·ite (sfál-ə-rīt, sfáyl-) *n.* A yellow, brown, black, or white zinc ore, essentially ZnS with some cadmium and iron. Also called "blende", "zinc blende". [German *Sphalerit* : Greek *sphaleros,* slippery, from *sphallein*†, to trip + -ITE.]

sphene (sfeen, speen) *n.* A titanium ore, chiefly $CaTiSiO_5.$ Also called "titanite". [French *sphène,* from Greek *sphēn,* wedge.]

sphe·nic (sféenik, sfénnik) *adj.* Wedge-shaped. [SPHEN(O)- + -IC.]

spheno-, sphen– *comb. form.* Indicates wedge-shaped; for example, **sphenogram, sphenodon.** [Greek *sphēn,* wedge.]

sphe·no·don (sféenə-don, sfénnə-) *n.* A reptile, the **tuatara** *(see).* [SPHEN(O)- + -ODON.]

sphe·no·gram (sféenə-gram, sfénnə-) *n.* A cuneiform character. [SPHENO- + -GRAM.]

sphe·noid (sfée-noyd) *n.* The sphenoid bone.
~*adj.* Also **sphe·noid·al** (see-nóyd'l). **1.** Wedge-shaped. **2.** Of or pertaining to the sphenoid bone. [New· Latin *sphenoides,* from Greek *sphēnoeidēs* : SPHEN(O)- + -OID.]

sphenoid bone *n.* A compound bone with winglike projections, situated at the base of the skull. Also called "sphenoid".

spher·al (sféer-əl) *adj.* **1.** Of, pertaining to, or having the shape of a sphere; spherical. **2.** Symmetrical.

sphere (sfeer) *n.* **1.** *Geometry.* **a.** A three-dimensional surface, all points of which are equidistant from a fixed point. **b.** A figure or solid bounded by such a surface. **2.** Any object or figure resembling a sphere; a globe; a ball. **3.** *Literary.* A planet, star, or other heavenly body. **4.** *Literary.* The sky, appearing as a hemisphere to an

observer: *the sphere of the heavens.* **5.** In ancient astronomy, any of a series of concentric, transparent, revolving globes on whose transparent surfaces the Moon, Sun, planets, and stars were thought to be fixed. **6. a.** The environment in which one exists, acts, or has influence; range; domain. **b.** Any area of activity or interest; a field. **7.** One's social stratum, rank, or position.
~*tr.v.* **sphered, sphering, spheres.** *Literary.* **1.** To form into a sphere. **2.** To put in or as in a sphere. **3.** To surround or encompass. [Middle English *spere, sphere,* from Old French *espere,* from Latin *sphaera, sphēra,* ball, globe, from Greek *sphaira†.*]

-sphere *n. comb. form.* Indicates: **1.** The shape of a sphere; for example, **bathysphere. 2.** A globular surrounding mass; for example, **atmosphere.** [From SPHERE.]

sphere of influence *n.* An area of the world dominated politically or economically by one country.

spher·i·cal (sférrik'l ‖ *U.S. also* sféer-ik'l) *adj.* Also **spher·ic** (sférrik ‖ sféer-ik). **1. a.** Having the shape of a sphere; globular. **b.** Having a shape approximating to that of a sphere. **2.** Of or pertaining to a sphere or spheres. **3.** *Literary.* Of or pertaining to heavenly bodies; celestial. —**spher·i·cal·i·ty** (sférri-kál-ǝti ‖ sféer-i-), **spher·i·cal·ness** *n.* —**spher·i·cal·ly** *adv.*

spherical aberration *n.* An optical defect of refracting and reflecting spherical surfaces in which light rays from one axial point, falling on the surface at different distances from the optical axis, do not come to a common focus.

spherical angle *n.* An angle formed at the intersection of the arcs of two great circles of a sphere.

spherical astronomy *n.* The branch of astronomy dealing with positions on the celestial sphere.

spher·i·cal-co·or·di·nate system (sférrik'l-kō-órdin-ǝt, -it, -ayt ‖ sféer-ik'l-) *n.* A three-dimensional system for locating points in space by means of a radius vector and two angles measured from the centre of a sphere with respect to two arbitrary, fixed, perpendicular directions.

spherical excess *n.* The difference between the sum of the angles of a spherical triangle and the sum of the angles of a plane triangle.

spherical geometry *n.* The geometry of circles, angles, and figures on the surface of a sphere. Also called "spherics".

spherical polygon *n.* Any part of a spherical surface that is bounded by arcs of three or more great circles.

spherical triangle *n.* A triangle on the surface of a sphere, having sides which are arcs of intersecting great circles.

spherical trigonometry *n.* The modified form of trigonometry applied to spherical triangles. Also called "spherics".

sphe·ric·i·ty (sfe-ríssǝti, sfeer-) *n.* **1.** The state of being spherical. **2.** A measure of the extent to which a surface is spherical.

spher·ics (sférriks ‖ sféer-iks) *n. Used with a singular verb.* **1.** Spherical geometry or trigonometry. **2. Atmospherics** *(see).*

sphe·roid (sféer-oyd ‖ sférroyd) *n.* A spherelike body that is generated by revolving an ellipse around one of its axes. [Late Latin *sphaeroīdēs,* from Greek *sphaeroeidēs:* SPHERE + -OID.] —**sphe·roi·dal** (sfeer-róyd'l, sfe-), **sphe·roi·di·cal** *adj.* —**sphe·roi·dal·ly** *adv.* —**sphe·roi·dic·i·ty** (-íssǝti) *n.*

sphe·rom·e·ter (sfeer-rómmitǝr, sfe-) *n.* An instrument for measuring the curvature of a surface, such as that of a sphere or cylinder. [SPHER(E) + -METER.]

spher·ule (sfé-rewl, -rōōl ‖ sféer-) *n.* A miniature sphere or spherical body. [Late Latin *sphaerula,* diminutive of Latin *sphaera,* SPHERE.] —**spher·u·lar** *adj.*

spher·u·lite (sfé-rew-līt, -rōō- ‖ sféer-ǝ-) *n.* A small, usually spheroidal, crystalline body having a radiating structure and found in obsidian and certain silicic lava flows. [SPHERUL(E) + -ITE.] —**spher·u·lit·ic** (-líttik) *adj.*

sphinc·ter (sfíngktǝr) *n.* A ringlike muscle that normally maintains constriction of a bodily passage or orifice and that relaxes as required by normal physiological functioning. [Late Latin, from Greek *sphinktēr,* that which binds tight, from *sphingein†,* to bind tight.] —**sphinc·ter·al** *adj.*

sphin·go·my·e·lin (sfing-gō-mī-ǝ-lin) *n.* A compound that contains sphingosine, phosphoric acid, choline, and a fatty acid group, found in the myelin sheath of nerves. [Greek *sphingein,* to draw tight + MYELIN.]

sphin·go·sine (sfíng-gǝ-seen, -sin) *n.* A long-chain organic compound occurring as a constituent of cerebral phospholipids in the brain. [Greek *sphingos-,* from *sphingein†,* hold fast, bind, draw tight + -INE.]

sphinx (sfingks) *n., pl.* **sphinxes** *or* **sphinges** (sfin-jeez). **1.** *Greek Mythology.* Usually capital **S.** A winged monster having the head of a woman and the body of a lion that destroyed all who could not answer its riddle. **2. a.** *Usually capital* **S.** The huge stone statue having a lion's body and a man's head, at Al Giza in Egypt. **b.** Any Egyptian figure having a lion's body and the head of a man, ram, or hawk. **3.** Any enigmatic person. [Middle English *spynx,* from Latin *Sphinx,* from Greek, perhaps from *sphingein†,* to draw tight, but dialectal variants, *Phix* and *Bix,* suggest perhaps a deity from Mount *Phikion* in Boeotia.]

sphinx moth *n.* The **hawk moth** *(see).*

sphra·gis·tics (sfrǝ-jístiks) *n. Used with a singular verb.* The study of engraved seals and signets. [French *sphragistique,* from Late Greek *sphragistikos,* from Greek *sphragis†,* seal, signet.]

sphyg·mic (sfíg-mik) *adj. Physiology.* Pertaining to the pulse. [Greek *sphugmikos,* from *sphugmos,* pulsation, from *sphuzein†,* to throb.]

sphygmo-, sphygm- *comb. form.* Indicates the pulse; for example, **sphygmograph, sphygmoid.** [Greek *sphugmos,* pulsation. See **sphygmic.**]

sphyg·mo·gram (sfíg-mǝ-gram, -mō-) *n.* A record or tracing produced by a sphygmograph. [SPHYGMO- + -GRAM.]

sphyg·mo·graph (sfíg-mǝ-graaf, -mō-, -graf) *n.* An instrument for recording the character and variations of the arterial pulse. [SPHYGMO- + -GRAPH.]

sphyg·moid (sfíg-moyd) *adj. Physiology.* Resembling a pulse; pulselike. [SPHYGM(O)- + -OID.]

sphyg·mo·ma·nom·e·ter (sfíg-mō-mǝ-nómmitǝr, -ma-) *n.* Also **sphyg·mom·e·ter** (sfig-mómmitǝr). An instrument for measuring blood pressure in the arteries. [SPHYGMO- + MANOMETER.]

spi·ca (spíkǝ) *n.* A bandage applied in overlapping opposite spirals to immobilise a digit or limb. [Latin *spīca,* "point", ear of grain (from the resemblance of the V-shaped bandage to the V-shaped spikelets on an ear of grain).]

Spica *n.* The brightest star in the constellation Virgo, 210 light-years distant from Earth. [Latin *spīca,* "point", ear of grain. See **spica.**]

spi·cate (spík-ayt) *adj. Botany.* Having or forming a spike. [Latin *spīcātus,* from the past participle of *spīcāre,* provide with spikes, from *spīca,* ear of grain, SPIKE.]

spic·ca·to (spi-ka'atō) *adj. Music.* Played with, designating, or pertaining to a bowing technique in which the bow is made to bounce slightly off the string.
~*adv. Music.* Employing such a technique.
~*n., pl.* **spiccatos.** *Music.* A spiccato technique or passage. [Italian, from the past participle of *spiccare†,* to separate.]

spice (spīss) *n.* **1.** Any of various aromatic and pungent vegetable substances, such as cinnamon or nutmeg, used to flavour foods or beverages. **2.** These substances collectively. **3.** Something that adds zest, flavour, or excitement. **4.** *Rare.* A pungent aroma; a perfume.
~*tr.v.* **spiced, spicing, spices. 1.** To season with spices. **2.** To add zest or excitement to. Often used with *up.* [Middle English, from Old French *espice,* from Late Latin *speciēs,* goods, spices, from Latin, appearance, kind, SPECIES.]

spice·ber·ry (spíss-bǝri, -berri) *n., pl.* **-ries.** Any of various plants or shrubs having spicy berries, such as the wintergreen.

spice·bush (spíss-bōōsh) *n.* An aromatic shrub, *Lindera benzoin,* of eastern North America, having clusters of small, early-blooming yellow flowers. Also called "benjamin bush".

Spice Islands. See Moluccas.

spic·er·y (spí-sǝri) *n., pl.* **-ies. 1.** Spices collectively. **2.** The aromatic quality of spices. **3.** *Archaic.* A place where spices are stored.

spick-and-span, spic-and-span (spíckǝn-spán) *adj. Informal.* **1.** Neat and clean; spotless. **2.** Brand-new; fresh. [Short for obsolete *spick and spannew* : *spick,* variant of SPIKE (nail) (influenced by Dutch *spiksplinter niew* "spike-splinter-new") + *span-new.*]

spic·ule (spíckewl) *n.* Also **spic·u·la** (spíckew-lǝ) *pl.* **-lae** (-lee). **1.** A small needle-like structure or part; especially, any of the silicate or calcium carbonate growths supporting the soft tissue of certain invertebrates, especially sponges. **2.** *Astronomy.* Any of the innumerable hairlike eruptions of hot gas from the Sun's chromosphere. [Latin *spīculum,* SPICULUM.] —**spic·u·lar, spic·u·late** (-layt, -lǝt, -lit) *adj.*

spic·u·lum (spíckew-lǝm) *n., pl.* **-la** (-lǝ). A spicule or similar needle-like structure. [Latin *spīculum,* diminutive of *spīca,* point.]

spic·y (spí-si) *adj.* **-ier, -iest. 1. a.** Containing or flavoured with spice. **b.** Having the characteristics of spice, such as flavour and aroma. **2. a.** Piquant; pungent. **b.** Lively, keen, or spirited. **3.** Slightly scandalous; risqué. —**spic·i·ly** *adv.* —**spic·i·ness** *n.*

spi·der (spídǝr) *n.* **1. a.** Any of numerous arachnids of the order Araneae, having eight legs, a body divided into a cephalothorax and an abdomen, and several spinnerets that produce silk used to make nests, cocoons, or webs for trapping insects. **b.** Any of various similar arachnids. **2.** One that is similar to a spider, as in appearance, character, or movement. **3.** *Chiefly British.* A group of elastic cords radiating out from a central point and used to strap down loads, as on to a car. **4.** In snooker, a rest on high legs used when access to the cue ball is hampered by another ball. **5.** Any of various machines or devices with limbs radiating from a central point. **6.** *Australian.* An ice-cream soda. **7.** A lightly built, high cart or phaeton. [Middle English *spither, spithre,* Old English *spīthra.*]

spider crab *n.* Any of various crabs, especially of the family Majidae, having long legs and a relatively small body.

spi·der-flow·er (spídǝr-flowr, -flow-ǝr) *n.* The **cleome** *(see).*

spider-hunting wasp *n.* Any of various wasps of the family Pompilidae, which catch spiders by paralysing them with their poisonous sting.

spi·der·man (spídǝr-man, -mǝn) *n., pl.* **-men** (-men). *British.* A building worker who erects the steel framework of tall buildings.

spider mite *n.* Any of various mites of the family Tetranychidae, such as *Tetranychus urticae,* which feed on plants and are serious pests of fruit trees and other crop plants. Also called "red spider", "red spider mite".

spider monkey *n.* Any of several tropical American monkeys of the genus *Ateles,* having long legs and a long, prehensile tail.

spider orchid *n.* Any of several European orchids of the genus *Ophrys,* having broad-lipped flowers. [Referring to the velvety spider-like lip of the flowers.]

spider plant *n.* Any of several plants of the genus *Chlorophytum;* especially, the South African species *C. elatum,* which has narrow,

green and white leaves and is commonly grown as a house plant. [From the fancied resemblance of the leaves to a spider's legs.]
spi·der·wort (spídər-wurt || -wawrt) *n.* Any of various New World plants of the genus *Tradescantia*; especially, *T. virginiana*, which has blue or purple flowers and is grown as a house plant.
spi·der·y (spídəri) *adj.* **1.** Resembling or suggesting a spider. **2. a.** Resembling a spider's legs; long and slender: *spidery penstrokes.* **b.** Resembling a spider's web; especially, very fine and meshlike. **3.** Infested with spiders.
spie·gel·ei·sen (spéeg'l-īz'n) *n.* An alloy of iron with approximately 15 to 30 per cent manganese and small quantities of carbon and silicon, used in the Bessemer process. Also called "spiegel". [German *Spiegeleisen*, "mirror-iron" : *Spiegel*, mirror, from Old High German *spiagal*, from Medieval Latin *spēglum*, from Latin *speculum*, SPECULUM + *Eisen*, iron, from Old High German *īsan, īsarn.*]
spiel (speel) *n. Slang.* **1.** A voluble story or speech usually intended to persuade. **2.** Any talk that is considered glib or tedious: *gave us his usual spiel about morale.*
~*v.* **spieled, spieling, spiels.** *Slang.* —*intr.* To talk at length or extravagantly. —*tr.* To recite (a story, for example) at length or extravagantly. Often used with *off.* [German *Spiel*, "play", from Old High German *spil*, from Germanic *spillōn* (unattested), to play.] **—spiel·er** *n.*
spif·fing (spíffing) *adj. British Slang.* Excellent; very good. Not in current usage. [19th century: probably from dialect *spiff*†, smartly dressed.]
spif·li·cate, spif·fli·cate (spíffli-kayt) *tr.v.* **-cated, -cating, -cates.** *British Slang.* To overcome or destroy; annihilate. Used by schoolchildren. [18th century : jocular coinage based on *-ate* as in *castigate, annihilate*, and so on.]
spig·ot (spíggət) *n.* **1.** The vent plug of a cask. **2.** A wooden tap placed in the bunghole of a cask. **3.** A short projection on a component, such as a pipe, designed to fit into a hole or slot in a mating part. [Middle English, perhaps from Latin *spiculum*, diminutive of *spicum*, variant of *spīca*, SPICA.]
spike¹ (spīk) *n.* **1. a.** A long, thick, sharp-pointed piece of wood or metal. **b.** A heavy nail. **2. a.** A sharp point. **b.** Any object with a sharp metal point; especially, such a point set upright in a base and used to hold papers, such as bills. **3.** *Plural. Informal.* A pair of track shoes with small projections on the soles to provide a better grip. **4.** *Slang.* A hypodermic syringe. **5. a.** A peak on a graph, especially one showing a maximum, as of voltage or current usage. **b.** An occurrence producing a peak shown on a graph. **6.** An unbranched antler of a young deer. **7.** A small young mackerel.
~*tr.v.* **spiked, spiking, spikes. 1.** To secure or provide with a spike. **2.** To impale, pierce, or injure with or on a spike. **3.** To injure (another runner or player) with the spikes of one's shoes. **4.** To put an end to; thwart; block: *spike a plot.* **5.** *Slang.* To add alcohol to (a drink) without the knowledge of the drinker. **6.** *Slang.* To decide not to publish (an article or report) in a newspaper or magazine, originally by placing it on a spike. **7.** To drive (a volleyball) into the opposing court at a steep downward angle. [Middle English *spyk*, probably from Middle Dutch *spiker*; akin to SPOKE.]
spike² *n.* **1.** An ear of grain. **2.** *Botany.* A usually elongated, racemose inflorescence with stalkless or nearly stalkless flowers arranged along an axis, as in the foxglove. [Middle English *spik*, from Latin *spīca*, point, ear of grain.]
spike lavender *n.* A lavender plant, *Lavandula latifolia*, of southern Europe, yielding an oil used in perfumes and paints. [From SPIKE (inflorescence).]
spike·let (spīk-lət, -lit) *n. Botany.* A small or secondary spike; especially, one of those forming the inflorescence of grasses or similar plants.
spike·nard (spīk-naard) *n.* **1.** An aromatic plant, *Nardostachys jatamansi*, of India, having rose-purple flowers. Also called "nard". **2.** A costly ointment of the ancient world, probably prepared from this plant. Also called "nard". **3.** A North American plant, *Aralia racemosa*, having small, greenish flowers and an aromatic root. See **ploughman's spikenard.** [Middle English, from Medieval Latin *spīca nardi*, spike of a nard (translation of Greek *nardostakhus*) : Latin *spīca*, SPIKE + *nardus*, NARD.]
spik·y (spīki) *adj.* **-ier, -iest. 1.** Having a projecting sharp point or points. **2.** Resembling a spike, especially in shape. **3.** Irritable; ill-tempered. **4.** *British Informal.* Strongly favouring High Church practices and views. Used derogatorily. **—spik·i·ly** *adv.* **—spik·i·ness** *n.*
spile (spīl) *n.* **1.** A post used as a foundation; a pile. **2.** A wooden plug; a bung. **3.** *U.S.* A spout used in taking sap from a tree.
~*tr.v.* **spiled, spiling, spiles.** To support, plug, or tap with a spile. [Perhaps from Middle Dutch or Middle Low German *spile*, bar.]
spill¹ (spil) *v.* **spilt** (spilt) or **spilled, spilling, spills.** —*tr.* **1.** To cause or allow (a substance) to run or fall out of a container, especially accidentally. **2.** To shed (blood). **3. a.** To let the wind out of (a sail). **b.** To let the (wind) out of a sail. **4.** To eject or cause to fall: *The horse spilled his rider.* **5.** *Informal.* To divulge. —*intr.* **1.** To run or fall out of a container, especially accidentally. **2.** To spread out or flow as if spilt: *The audience started to spill out of the cinema.* **3.** To escape from a sail. Used of the wind.
~*n.* **1.** An act of spilling. **2.** That which is spilt. **3.** A fall, as from a horse. **4.** A spillway. [Middle English *spillen*, destroy, kill, shed (blood), spill, Old English *spillan.*] **—spill·er** *n.*
Usage: Both *spilled* and *spilt* are used as past tenses and past participles, the former being preferred in American English, the latter in British English.
spill² *n.* **1.** A piece of wood or rolled paper used to light a fire, for example. **2.** A small peg used as a plug; a spile. **3.** A spillway. [Probably from Middle Low German or Middle Dutch *spile.*]
spill·age (spíllij) *n.* **1.** An act or the process of spilling. **2.** That which is spilt; the amount spilt.
spil·li·kin, spil·i·kin (spíllikin) *n.* Also **spel·li·can** (spéllikən). A draw or stick used in the game of spillikins. Also called "jackstraw". [Diminutive of SPILL (strip of wood). See **-kin.**]
spil·li·kins, spil·i·kins (spíllikinz) *n. Used with a singular verb.* A game played with a pile of straws or thin sticks, each player in turn trying to remove one from the pile without disturbing the others. Also called "jackstraws".
spill·way (spíl-way) *n.* A channel for water overflow, as from a reservoir. Also called "spill".
spilth (spilth) *n.* Spillage. [From SPILL.]
spin (spin) *v.* **spun** (spun) or *archaic* **span** (span), **spinning, spins.** —*tr.* **1.** To draw out and twist (fibres) into thread. **2.** To form (thread or yarn) in this manner. **3. a.** To form (a thread, web, or cocoon, for example) by extruding viscous filaments. Used chiefly of spiders and caterpillars. **b.** To produce (synthetic yarn) by extruding chemical substances. **4.** To draw out and twist in a manufacturing process: *spin glass into threads.* **5.** To narrate from memory or invent from one's imagination. Used chiefly in the phrase *spin a yarn.* **6.** To cause to rotate; turn round or twirl. **7.** To turn on a lathe, usually into a round shape. **8.** To propel (a ball, especially a cricket ball) so as to revolve on an axis and change speed or direction on bouncing. **9.** To cause (an aircraft) to dive in a spin. **10.** To fish (a river, for example) using a spinner. —*intr.* **1.** To make thread or yarn by the drawing out and twisting of fibres. **2.** To form a thread, web, or cocoon, by extruding viscous filaments. **3.** To rotate rapidly; whirl. **4.** To seem to be whirling, as from dizziness; reel: *The news set my head spinning.* **5.** To ride or drive rapidly. Usually used with *along.* **6.** To fish with a spinner. **7.** To be spun by a bowler. Used of a ball, especially a cricket ball. **8.** To dive in a spin. Used of an aircraft. **—spin out. 1.** To prolong or draw out (a story or task, for example). **2.** To pass (time): *spun out the rest of the afternoon.* **3.** To cause (a sum of money) to last a long time. **4.** In cricket, to dismiss (a batsman) with spin bowling. —See Synonyms at **turn.**
~*n.* **1.** The act of spinning. **2.** A swift whirling motion. **3.** *Informal.* A state of mental confusion. **4.** *Informal.* A short excursion in or on a vehicle. **5. a.** The flight condition of an aircraft in a nose-down, spiralling, stalled descent. **b.** Any sudden, swift, or steep descending movement. **6.** A rotating motion imparted to a ball by a bowler or other sports player. **7.** *Physics.* **a.** The intrinsic angular momentum of an elementary particle. **b.** The total angular momentum of an atomic nucleus. **c.** A non-negative integral or half-integral quantum number that specifies the value of such momenta in units of Planck's constant divided by 2π. **8.** *Australian Informal.* A stroke of fortune of a specified kind: *a bad spin.* [Spin, spun, spun; Middle English *spinnen, spon* (plural), *spunne*, Old English *spinnan, spunnon* (plural), *gespunnen.*]
spi·na bi·fi·da (spīnə bíffidə) *n.* A condition, present at birth, in which part of the spinal cord protrudes through a gap in the backbone. It may result in paralysis and incontinence and be associated with **hydrocephalus** *(see).* [New Latin, bifid spine.]
spin·ach (spín-ij, -ich) *n.* **1.** A widely cultivated plant, *Spinacia oleracea*, native to Asia, having succulent, edible leaves. **2.** The leaves of this plant, eaten as a vegetable. [Probably from Middle Dutch *spinaetse*, from Old French *espinache*, from Medieval Latin *spinachia*, from Arabic *'isfānāk*, from Persian *ispānāk.*]
spi·nal (spīn'l) *adj.* **1.** Of, pertaining to, or situated near the spine or spinal cord; vertebral. **2.** Resembling a spine or spinous part.
~*n.* A spinal anaesthetic. **—spi·nal·ly** *adv.*
spinal anaesthesia *n.* **1.** Anaesthesia in part of the body produced by injecting an anaesthetic substance (*spinal anaesthetic*) into the spinal canal. **2.** *Pathology.* Loss of sensation in part of the body because of injury to or disease of the spinal cord.
spinal canal *n.* The canal formed by the successive openings in the vertebrae through which the spinal cord and its membranes pass. Also called "vertebral canal".
spinal column *n.* The series of articulated vertebrae extending from the base of the skull to the base of the trunk or the end of the tail, encasing the spinal cord and forming the supporting axis of the body; the backbone. Also called "spine", "vertebral column".
spinal cord *n.* The part of the central nervous system contained within the spinal canal and continuous at its cranial end with the medulla oblongata of the brain.
spinal meningitis *n. Pathology.* **Cerebrospinal fever** *(see).*
spin bowler *n.* In cricket, a bowler expert at spinning the ball. Also called "spinner". **—spin bowling** *n.*
spin·dle (spínd'l) *n.* **1. a.** A notched stick for spinning fibres into thread by hand. **b.** A pin or rod holding a bobbin or spool upon which thread is wound on a spinning wheel or spinning machine. **2.** Any of various slender mechanical parts that revolve or serve as axes for larger revolving parts, as in a lock or an axle. **3.** *Biology.* A group of fibres extending from one end of a cell to the other, formed during mitosis and meiosis and along which the chromosomes are distributed. **4.** Any slender, tapering rod or rodlike piece. **5.** A measure or yarn of varying length. **6.** A turned, usually decorative vertical support of a handrail.

~intr.v. **spindled, -dling, -dles.** To grow into a thin, elongated, or weakly form. Used especially of a plant. [Middle English *spindel,* rod of a spinning wheel, Old English *spinel.*]

spin·dle·legs (spínd'l-legz) *pl.n.* Also **spin·dle·shanks** (-shangks). 1. Long, thin legs. 2. *Used with a singular verb.* A tall, lanky person with long, thin legs. **—spin·dle-legged** *adj.*

spindle side *n.* The **distaff side** (see).

spindle tree *n.* Any of various shrubs or trees of the genus *Euonymus,* many species of which have pink or orange fruits. [So called because the wood is often used to make spindles.]

spin·dling (spíndling) *adj.* Spindly.
~n. A spindly plant or animal.

spin·dly (spíndli) *adj.* **-dlier, -dliest.** Slender, long, and usually weak-looking.

spin doctor *n. Informal.* A press agent or spokesperson who puts on events the interpretation most favourable to his employer or client. Humorous and mildly derogatory. [SPIN *n.* 6, 8 + DOCTOR *n.* 5.]

spin·drift (spín-drift) *n.* Wind-blown sea spray. Also called "spoondrift". [Variant of SPOONDRIFT.]

spin·dry·er, spin·dri·er (spín-drí-ər) *n.* A machine that extracts moisture from wet laundry by spinning it round rapidly. Also called "spinner". **—spin·dry** *tr.v.*

spine (spīn) *n.* 1. The spinal column of a vertebrate. 2. Any of various pointed projections or appendages of animals, such as a quill on a porcupine. 3. *Botany.* A sharp-pointed projection arising from the stem of a plant. 4. *Anatomy.* A sharp projection arising from a bone. 5. The vertical back of a book to which the pages are attached and which normally bears the title on the outside. 6. a. Strength of character. b. A main support or prop. 7. A sharp-backed hill, mountain, or ridge. [Middle English, from Old French *espine,* from Latin *spīna,* thorn, prickle, spine.] **—spined** *adj.*

spine-chill·er (spín-chillər) *n.* A book, film, or other work that arouses a pleasurably terrifying thrill. **—spine-chill·ing** *adj.*

spi·nel (spi-nél) *n.* A mineral, magnesium aluminium oxide MgAl$_2$O$_4$. Spinels show a range of colours, depending on any additional elements present, and some are used as gemstones. [Italian *spinella,* diminutive of *spina,* thorn (from its sharply pointed crystals), from Latin *spīna.*]

spine·less (spín-ləss, -liss) *adj.* 1. Lacking a vertebral column. 2. Having no spiny projections. 3. Lacking in courage, strength of character, or will-power. **—spine·less·ly** *adv.* **—spine·less·ness** *n.*

spi·nes·cent (spí-néss'nt) *adj. Biology.* 1. Having a spine or spines. 2. Having or tending towards the form of a spine. [Late Latin *spīnescēns* (stem *spīnescent-*), present participle of *spīnescere,* to grow thorny, from Latin *spīna,* thorn, SPINE.] **—spi·nes·cence** *n.*

spin·et (spín·it, -et, spi-nét) *n.* 1. A small harpsichord with a single keyboard. 2. *U.S.* A small, compact upright piano. [French *espinette,* from Italian *spinetta,* virginal, spinet, diminutive of *spina,* thorn, SPINE (referring to the plucking of the strings).]

spi·nif·er·ous (spí-nífferəss) *adj.* Also **spi·nig·er·ous** (-níjərəss). Spine-bearing; spiny. Said especially of plants. [Latin *spīnifer* : Latin *spīna,* thorn, SPINE + -FEROUS.]

spin·i·fex (spín-i-feks, -ə- ‖ *chiefly U.S.* spín-) *n.* 1. Any of various chiefly Australian grasses of the genus *Spinifex,* growing in arid regions and having spiny leaves or seeds. 2. Any of various Australian grasses of the genus *Triodia,* having spiny leaves. Also called "porcupine grass". [New Latin : SPIN(E) + Latin *-fex,* "maker".]

spin·na·ker (spínnəkər) *n. nautical* spángkər) *n.* A large triangular sail set on a spar that swings out opposite the mainsail, used on racing yachts when running before the wind. [Probably from *Sphinx,* name of the first yacht to carry a spinnaker sail, in about 1866; perhaps influenced by *spanker.*]

spin·ner (spínnər) *n.* 1. One that spins. 2. An angler's lure that spins rapidly. 3. In cricket: a. A ball bowled with a spin. b. A **spin bowler** (see). 4. A spin-dryer. 5. A fairing fitted over the hub of the propeller in some aircraft. 6. A device consisting of a dial and an arrow that is spun to indicate the next move in certain board games.

spin·ner·et (spínnə-rét, -ret) *n.* 1. A structure in spiders and certain insect larvae, containing passages through which silky filaments are secreted. 2. A device for making rayon, nylon, and other synthetic fibres, consisting of a plate pierced with holes through which plastic material is extruded in filaments. [SPINNER + -ET.]

spin·ney (spínni) *n., pl.* **-neys.** *Chiefly British.* A small grove; a thicket; a copse. [Old French *espinei,* thicket, from Vulgar Latin *spīnēta* (unattested), from Latin *spīnētum,* thorn hedge, from *spīna,* thorn.]

spin·ning (spínning) *n.* 1. The process of making fibrous or viscous material into yarn or thread. 2. The act or technique of angling with a light rod and line, drawing a rotating lure through the water to imitate the movement of a small fish or insect.

spinning frame *n.* A machine that draws and twists fibres into yarn and winds it onto spindles.

spinning jenny *n.* An early spinning machine having several spindles. [18th century : from pet form of Jane or *Janet,* applied to machines that performed some of women's traditional tasks.]

spinning mule *n.* A type of spinning machine, a **mule** (see).

spinning wheel *n.* A domestic apparatus for making yarn or thread, comprising a foot- or hand-driven wheel and single spindle.

spi·node (spínnōd) *n. Mathematics.* A **cusp** (see).

spin off *tr.v.* To throw off while rotating at speed.

spin-off (spín-off, -awf) *n.* A usually useful object or result obtained

incidentally through pursuing a different object or result.

spi·nose (spí-nōz, -nōss) *adj.* Bearing spines; spiny. Said especially of plants. [Latin *spīnōsus,* from *spīna,* thorn, SPINE.] **—spi·nose·ly** *adv.* **—spi·nos·i·ty** (spí-nóssəti) *n.*

spi·nous (spínəss) *adj.* 1. Resembling a spine or thorn. 2. Having spines or similar projections; spiny.

spinous process *n.* The rearward projection from the arch of a vertebra.

Spi·no·za (spi-nôzə), **Benedict de,** born Baruch de Spinoza (1632–77). Dutch philosopher. His controversial pantheistic doctrine advocated an intellectual love of God. His best-known work is his *Ethics* (1677). **—Spi·no·zism** (-nôz-iz'm) *n.*

spin·ster (spínstər) *n.* 1. A woman who is unmarried. 2. A woman who is traditionally regarded as fussy and prim, and as being unlikely to get married. 3. Formerly, a woman whose occupation is spinning. [Middle English *spinnester* : *spinnen,* SPIN + -STER.] **—spin·ster·hood** *n.* **—spin·ster·ish** *adj.*

spin·thar·i·scope (spin-thárri-skōp) *n.* A device for observing individual scintillations produced by ionising radiation, with the aid of a tube with a magnifying lens at one end and a phosphorescent screen and a speck of a radioactive salt at the other. [Greek *spinthariš†,* spark + -SCOPE.] **—spin·thar·i·scop·ic** (-skóppik) *adj.*

spi·nule (spínewl) *n.* A small spine or thorn. [Latin *spīnula,* diminutive of *spīna,* thorn, SPINE.]

spin·u·lose (spínnew-lōz, -lōss) *adj.* Also **spin·u·lous** (-ləss). 1. Having spinules. 2. Shaped like a spinule.

spin·y (spíni) *adj.* **-ier, -iest.** 1. Bearing or covered with spines, thorns, or similar stiff projections. 2. Shaped like a spine. 3. Difficult; troublesome. **—spin·i·ness** *n.*

spiny anteater *n.* A mammal, the **echidna** (see).

spin·y-finned (spíni-find) *adj.* Having fins supported by sharp, spiny, inflexible rays. Said of some fishes. Compare **soft-finned.**

spiny lobster *n.* Any of various edible marine decapod crustaceans of the family Palinuridae, having a spiny carapace and lacking the large pincers characteristic of true lobsters. Also called "langouste", "rock lobster", and sometimes "crayfish".

spir·a·cle (spír-ak'l ‖ spír-) *n.* 1. *Zoology.* A respiratory aperture, such as: a. Any of several tracheal openings in the exoskeleton of an insect or spider. b. A small respiratory opening behind the eye of cartilaginous fishes, such as sharks, rays, and skates. c. The blowhole of a cetacean. 2. *Geology.* A small volcanic vent formed by gases in a lava flow. 3. Any opening through which air is admitted and expelled. [Latin *spīrāculum,* a breathing hole, from *spīrāre,* to breathe.] **—spi·rac·u·lar** (spír-áckew-lər), **spi·rac·u·late** (-lət, -lit, -layt) *adj.*

spi·rae·a, *U.S.* **spi·re·a** (spír-rée-ə, spī-) *n.* Any of various plants or shrubs of the genus *Spiraea,* having clusters of small white or pink flowers, and often cultivated as garden ornamentals. [Latin *spīraea,* meadowsweet, from Greek *spieraia,* from *speira,* coil, SPIRE.]

spi·ral (spír-əl) *n.* 1. a. The locus in a plane of a point moving around a fixed centre at a monotonically increasing or decreasing distance from the centre. b. The three-dimensional locus of a point moving parallel to and about a central axis at a constant or continuously varying distance; a helix. 2. Something having the form of such a curve: *spirals of smoke.* 3. A continuously accelerating increase or decrease, often of related factors: *the wage-price spiral.* *~adj.* Of or resembling a spiral; coiled or helical: *a spiral staircase.* *~v.* **spiralled** or *U.S.* **spiraled, -ralling** or *U.S.* **-raling, -rals.** *—intr.* 1. To take a spiral form or course. 2. To rise or fall at a steady rate. *—tr.* To cause to spiral. [Medieval Latin *spīrālis,* from Latin *spīra,* coil, SPIRE (spiral).] **—spi·ral·ly** *adv.*

spiral binding *n.* A binding for notebooks and booklets in which a cylindrical spiral of wire or plastic is passed through a row of punched holes at the edge of each sheet.

spiral galaxy *n.* A galaxy having a nucleus and spiral arms consisting mainly of gas, dust, and stars. Formerly called "spiral nebula".

spiral of Archimedes *n.* The locus of a point moving towards or away from a central point at a constant speed along a line rotating around that central point at a constant speed. Its spiral has the equation $r = a\theta,$ where a is a constant.

spi·rant (spír-ənt) *n. Phonetics.* A **fricative** (see). [Latin *spīrāns* (stem *spīrant-*), present participle of Latin *spīrāre,* to breathe.] **—spi·rant** *adj.*

spire¹ (spīr) *n.* 1. A structure that tapers upwards to a point; especially a steeple. 2. The top part or point of something that tapers upwards; a pinnacle. 3. A slender, tapering shoot or stem, such as a newly sprouting blade of grass. 4. Any slender, tapering object. *~v.* **spired, spiring, spires.** *—tr.* To provide with a spire or spires. *—intr.* To rise taperingly, like a spire. [Middle English *spir(e),* slender stalk, Old English *spīr.*]

spire² *n.* 1. a. A spiral. b. A single turn of a spiral; a whorl. 2. *Zoology.* The area farthest from the aperture and nearest the apex on a coiled gastropod shell. [French, from Latin *spīra,* a coil, twist, spire, from Greek *speira.*]

spire·let (spír-lət, -lit) *n. Architecture.* A **flèche** (see).

Spires. See **Speyer.**

spi·rif·er·ous (spír-rifferəss, spī-) *adj.* Having a spire, spiral structure, or spiral parts. [SPIR(E) + -FEROUS.]

spi·ril·lum (spír-rílləm, spī-) *n., pl.* **-rilla** (-rílla). 1. Any of various flagellated aerobic bacteria of the genus *Spirillum,* having an elongated spiral form. *S. minus* causes ratbite fever. 2. Any spiral-shaped bacterium. Compare **bacillus, coccus.** [New Latin, diminutive of Latin *spīra,* SPIRE (spiral).]

spir·it (spírrit) *n.* **1.** That which is traditionally believed to be the vital principle or animating force within living beings, often contrasted with nonliving matter. **2.** *Capital* **S.** In Christian Science, God. **3.** Any supernatural being or power, such as: **a.** A ghost. **b.** One regarded as able to enter and take control of a person. **4.** That which is traditionally regarded as the nonmaterial essence or true nature of an individual, especially: **a.** The intangible, spiritual core of a person; the soul. **b.** The essential and activating principle of a person; the will. **5.** A person as characterised by a specified quality: *a free spirit.* **6.** An inclination or tendency of a specified kind: *a remark made in a spirit of friendliness.* **7. a.** *Often plural.* One's mood or emotional state: *in high spirits.* **b.** One's mood or disposition: *great in spirit.* **8.** An attitude or frame of mind: *take a remark in the spirit in which it was intended.* **9.** Liveliness; vigour; mettle. **10.** Strong loyalty or dedication: *team spirit.* **11.** The predominant mood or quality of an occasion or period: *the spirit of the age.* **12.** The real sense or significance of something: *the spirit of the law, rather than the letter.* **13.** *Often plural.* An alcohol solution of an essential or volatile substance. **14.** *Often plural.* A distilled alcoholic liquor, such as gin, whisky, or rum. **—in (the) spirit.** In the mind or the imagination. **—in (or out of) spirits.** In a cheerful (or gloomy) state of mind. **—the Spirit.** The Holy Ghost. ~*tr.v.* **spirited, -iting, -its. 1.** To carry off mysteriously or secretly. Used with *away* or *off.* **2.** To impart courage, animation, or determination to; stimulate; encourage. Usually used with *up* or *on.* [Middle English, from Anglo-French, from Latin *spīritus,* breath, breath of a god, inspiration, from *spīrāre,* to breathe.]

spir·it·ed (spírritid) *adj.* **1.** Full of or characterised by animation, vigour, or courage: *a spirited debate.* **2.** Having a specified mood or nature. Used in combination: *high-spirited.* **—spir·it·ed·ly** *adv.* **—spir·it·ed·ness** *n.*

spirit gum *n.* A glue used to attach false beards and moustaches to the face. It consists of a gum dissolved in ether or alcohol.

spir·it·ism (spírrit-iz'm) *n.* Spiritualism. **—spir·it·ist** *n.* **—spir·it·is·tic** (-ístik) *adj.*

spirit lamp *n.* A lamp burning methylated spirits or some other alcohol-based fuel.

spir·it·less (spírrit-ləss, -liss) *adj.* Lacking energy, courage, or enthusiasm. **—spir·it·less·ly** *adv.* **—spir·it·less·ness** *n.*

spirit level *n.* An instrument for ascertaining whether a surface is horizontal, consisting essentially of an encased, liquid-filled tube containing an air bubble that moves to a central window when the instrument is set on a horizontal plane. Also called "level".

spir·i·to·so (spírri-tṓ-sō) *adv. Music.* In a spirited or lively manner. Used as a direction. [Italian, spirited.] **—spir·i·to·so** *adj.*

spir·it·ous (spírritəss) *adj.* **1.** Spirituous. **2.** *Archaic.* Refined; pure.

spir·it·rap·ping (spírrit-rapping) *n.* Supposed communication from the dead through messages rapped out on a table or a similar surface. **—spir·it·rap·per** *n.*

spirits of ammonia *n. Used with a singular verb.* **Sal volatile** *(see).*

spirits of salt *n. Used with a singular verb.* **Hydrochloric acid** *(see).* No longer in technical usage.

spirits of turpentine *n. Used with a singular verb.* Refined turpentine.

spirits of wine *n. Used with a singular verb.* Also **spirit of wine.** Rectified ethanol.

spir·i·tu·al (spírri-tew-əl, -choo-) *adj.* **1.** Of, pertaining to, consisting of, or having the nature of spirit or a spirit; not tangible or material. **2.** Of, concerned with, or affecting the soul. **3.** Of, from, or pertaining to God; divine. **4.** Of or belonging to a church or religious organisation; ecclesiastical. **5.** Of, pertaining to, or having highly developed or refined qualities of mind or sensibility. **6.** Linked by or sharing a deep intellectual or emotional affinity: *his spiritual heir.* **7.** Pertaining to or having the nature of spirits; supernatural. ~*n.* **1. a.** A religious folk song of black American origin. **b.** Any work composed in imitation of a black spiritual. **2.** *Usually plural.* Religious, spiritual, or ecclesiastical matters. **3.** The realm of the spirit. [Middle English, from Old French *spirituel,* from Latin *spīrituālis.* See **spirit, -al.**] **—spir·i·tu·al·ly** *adv.* **—spir·i·tu·al·ness** *n.*

spir·i·tu·al·ise, spir·i·tu·al·ize (spírri-tew-ə-līz, -tew-līz, -choo-) *tr.v.* **-ised, -ising, -ises. 1.** To impart a spiritual nature to; refine. **2.** To invest with or treat as having a spiritual sense. **—spir·i·tu·al·i·sa·tion** (-lī-záysh'n ‖ *U.S.* -li-) *n.* **—spir·i·tu·al·is·er** *n.*

spir·i·tu·al·ism (spírri-tew-ə-liz'm, -tew-liz'm, -choo-) *n.* **1. a.** The belief that the dead communicate with the living, usually through a medium. **b.** The practices or doctrines of those holding such a belief. **2.** Any philosophy, doctrine, or religion emphasising the spiritual rather than the material; especially, any doctrine holding that spirit is the prime or only aspect of reality. Compare **materialism. —spir·i·tu·al·ist** *n.* **—spir·i·tu·al·is·tic** (-ístik) *adj.*

spir·i·tu·al·i·ty (spírri-tew-ál-əti, -choo-) *n., pl.* **-ties. 1. a.** The state, quality, or fact of being spiritual. **b.** Attachment to or involvement in religious matters. **2.** Ecclesiastics collectively; the clergy. **3.** *Often plural.* Something belonging to the church or to an ecclesiastic, such as property or revenue. [Middle English, from Old French *spiritualité,* from Late Latin *spīrituālitās.* See **spiritual, -ity.**]

spir·i·tu·al·ty (spírri-tew-əl-ti, -chool-) *n., pl.* **-ties.** Spirituality.

spir·i·tu·el (spírri-tew-él, -choo-) *adj. Feminine* **spir·i·tu·elle.** Having or showing a refined mind and wit. [French, "spiritual".]

spir·i·tu·ous (spírri-tew-əss, -choo-) *adj.* **1.** Having the nature of or containing alcohol; alcoholic. **2.** Distilled, as contrasted with fermented. **—spir·it·u·os·i·ty** (-óssəti), **spir·i·tu·ous·ness** *n.*

spirit varnish *n.* **Varnish** *(see).*

spir·ket·ting, *U.S.* **spir·ket·ing** (spúrkiting) *n. Nautical.* **1.** Deck planking near the sides of a ship. **2.** The inside planking fitted above the waterways in a wooden ship. [From obsolete *spirket*†, the space between the side or floor timbers of a ship.]

spiro-[1] *comb. form.* Indicates spiral or coiled form; for example, **spirochaete.** [Latin *spīra,* coil, SPIRE.]

spiro-[2] *comb. form.* Indicates respiration or breathing; for example, **spirograph.** [Latin *spīrāre,* to breathe.]

spi·ro·chaete, *U.S.* **spi·ro·chete** (spī́r-ə-keet, -ō-) *n.* Any of various slender, nonflagellated, twisted bacteria of the order Spirochaetales, many of which are pathogenic, causing syphilis, relapsing fever, yaws, and other diseases. [New Latin *Spirochaeta* (genus) : SPIRO- (coil) + CHAETA.] **—spi·ro·chae·tal** (-kéet'l) *adj.*

spi·ro·chae·to·sis (spī́r-ə-kee-tṓ-siss) *n.* Any of various diseases, such as syphilis, caused by a spirochaete. [New Latin : SPIRO-CHAET(E) + -OSIS.]

spi·ro·graph (spī́r-ə-graaf, -graf) *n.* An instrument for registering the depth and rapidity of respiratory movements. [SPIRO- (breathing) + -GRAPH.] **—spi·ro·graph·ic** (-gráffik) *adj.* **—spi·rog·ra·phy** (spīr-róggrəfi, spī-) *n.*

spi·ro·gy·ra (spī́r-ə-jī́r-ə) *n.* Any of various green, filamentous freshwater algae of the genus *Spirogyra,* having chloroplasts in spirally twisted bands. [New Latin : SPIRO- (coil) + Greek *guros,* ring.]

spi·roid (spī́r-oyd) *adj.* Resembling a spiral. [New Latin *spiroides,* from Greek *speiroeidēs* : *speira,* SPIRE + -OID.]

spi·rom·e·ter (spīr-rómmitər, spī-) *n.* An instrument for measuring the volume of air entering and leaving the lungs. [SPIRO- (breathing) + -METER.] **—spi·ro·met·ric** (spī́r-ə-méttrik) *adj.* **—spi·rom·e·try** (-rómmətri) *n.*

spi·ro·no·lac·tone (spī́r-ənō-láktōn) *n.* A synthetic steroid drug that inhibits the action of the hormone aldosterone and is used mainly as a diuretic. [SPIRO- + *-no-* (infix) + LACTONE.]

spirt. Variant of **spurt.**

spir·u·la (spī́r-ōō-lə, -yōō- ‖ *U.S.* spírrə-) *n., pl.* **-lae** (-lee). Any small cephalopod mollusc of the genus *Spirula;* especially, *S. peronii,* having a coiled internal shell. [Late Latin *spīrula,* small twisted cake or cracknel, diminutive of Latin *spīra,* coil, SPIRE.]

spir·y (spī́r-i) *adj.* **-ier, -iest.** Resembling a spire in shape.

spit[1] (spit) *n.* **1.** Saliva, especially when spat; spittle. **2.** The act or an instance of spitting. **3.** Something resembling saliva, such as the frothy secretion of certain insects. **4.** A brief, scattered fall of rain or snow. **5.** *Chiefly British Informal.* A spitting image. ~*v.* **spat** (spat) or **spit, spitting, spits.** —*tr.* **1.** To eject from the mouth. Often used with *out.* **2. a.** To eject as if by spitting. **b.** To utter in a violent, contemptuous, or angry manner. Often used with *out: spit out an insult.* —*intr.* **1.** To eject saliva from the mouth. **2.** To express contempt or hostility by or as if by spitting. **3.** To make a hissing or sputtering noise. **4.** To rain or snow in light, scattered drops or flakes. **—spit it out.** *Informal.* To say what one is thinking without further delay; speak up. [*Spit, spat,* Middle English *spitten,* Old English *spittan.*]

spit[2] *n.* **1. a.** A slender, pointed rod on which meat is impaled for roasting in front of or over a fire. **b.** A similar device in a gas or electric oven, a **rotisserie** *(see).* **2.** A narrow ridge of sand or shingle extending into a body of water or across a bay. ~*tr.v.* **spitted, spitting, spits.** To impale on or as if on a spit. [Middle English *spit(e),* Old English *spitu.*]

spit·al (spítt'l) *n. Archaic.* **1.** A hospital; especially, one for the poor or for those suffering from contagious diseases. **2.** A wayside shelter. [Variant of obsolete *spittle,* shortened variant of HOSPITAL.]

Spit·al·fields (spítt'l-feeldz). District in the London borough of Tower Hamlets, belonging originally to the spital or rest house of St. Mary's Priory. It was formerly a silk-weaving centre, and today has a famous wholesale market for flowers, fruit, and vegetables.

spit and polish *n. Used with a singular verb.* Close attention paid to cleanliness, smart appearance, and ceremonial, especially in the armed forces.

spitch·cock (spích-kok) *n.* An eel split, cut up, and grilled or fried. [16th century : origin obscure. Compare **spatchcock.**]

spite (spīt) *n.* **1.** Malicious ill-will prompting an urge to hurt, annoy, or humiliate another. **2.** An instance of such feeling. **—in spite of.** Regardless of; despite. ~*tr.v.* **spited, spiting, spites. 1.** To show spite towards. **2.** To thwart out of spite. [Middle English, insult, ill will, short for Old French *despit.* See **despite.**]

spite·ful (spī́tf'l) *adj.* Filled with, prompted by, or showing spite. —See Synonyms at **vindictive. —spite·ful·ly** *adv.* **—spite·ful·ness** *n.*

spit·fire (spít-fīr) *n.* A quick-tempered or highly excitable person, especially a girl or woman.

Spit·head (spít-héd). Anchorage at the entrance to Portsmouth Harbour, forming a deep channel between the Isle of Wight and the southern coast of England. It was here that the Channel fleet mutinied in 1797. Spithead is the site of periodic naval reviews.

Spitsbergen. See **Svalbard.**

spitting cobra *n.* The **ringhals** *(see).*

spitting image *n.* A perfect, usually physical, likeness or counterpart. [Perhaps from the phrase *the very spit of,* an exact likeness, as if the image has been "spat out".]

spitting snake *n.* The **ringhals** *(see).*

spit·tle (spítt'l) *n.* **1.** Spit; saliva. **2.** The frothy liquid secreted by froghoppers; cuckoo spit; frog spit. [Middle English *spetil,* Old English *spātl.*]

spit·tle·bug (spítt'l-bug) *n.* The **froghopper** *(see).* Also called "spittle insect".
spit·toon (spi-tóōn) *n.* A bowl-shaped, usually metal vessel for spitting into. Also called "cuspidor". [SPIT + *-oon,* in such words as BALLOON and DOUBLOON.]
spitz (spits) *n.* A dog of a breed originating in Germany, having a long, thick, usually white coat and a tail curled over the back. [German *Spitz,* from *spitz,* "pointed" (from its pointed muzzle), from Old High German *spizzi.*]
spiv (spiv) *n. British Slang.* **1.** A petty swindler or black marketeer. **2.** A flashily dressed and disreputable-looking man. [From dialectal *spiff†,* dandy.] **—spiv·vy** *adj.*
splanch·nic (splángk-nik) *adj.* Of or pertaining to the viscera. [Greek *splankhnikos,* of the bowels, from *splankhna,* inward parts.]
splash (splash) *v.* **splashed, splashing, splashes.** *—tr.* **1.** To dash or scatter (a liquid or semiliquid substance) about in flying masses. **2.** To dash a liquid or semiliquid substance upon; wet or soil with flying masses of such substance. **3.** To cause to dash such substance about: *He splashed his oar in the water.* **4.** To make (one's way) through such substance so as to dash or scatter it. **5.** To display (a story, poster or photograph) prominently. *—intr.* **1.** To dash or scatter a liquid or semiliquid substance about in flying masses. **2.** To fall into or move through such substance with this effect. Often used with *about* or *around.* **3.** To move, spill, or fly about in scattered masses. **—splash out.** *Chiefly British Informal.* To spend money ostentatiously or extravagantly. Often used with *on: splash out on a new car.*
~n. **1.** The act, an instance, or a sound of splashing. **2.** A flying mass of liquid or semiliquid substance. **3.** A mark or patch produced by or as if by scattered liquid or semiliquid substance: *a splash of light.* **4.** A striking though often short-lived impression; a stir. Used chiefly in the phrase *make a splash.* **5.** *British Informal.* A small amount, as of water or soda, added to a drink.
~adv. With a splash. [Variant of PLASH (splash).] **—splash·er** *n.*
splash·back (splásh-bak) *n.* A wall panel immediately above a basin, bath, sink, or cooker to protect the wall against splashes.
splash·board (splásh-bawrd || -bōrd) *n.* **1.** A structure that protects a vehicle from splashes of mud or water. **2.** A screen on a boat to keep water from splashing on the deck; a washboard.
splash down *intr.v.* To make a splashdown.
splash·down (splásh-down) *n.* The landing of a missile or spacecraft in a body of water.
splash·er (spláshər) *n.* **1.** One that splashes. **2.** Anything that protects against splashes.
splash·y (spláshi) *adj.* **-ier, -iest. 1.** Making or liable to make splashes. **2.** Covered with splashes of colour. **3.** *Informal.* Showy; ostentatious. **—splash·i·ly** *adv.* **—splash·i·ness** *n.*
splat[1] (splat) *n.* A slat of wood, such as one in the middle of a chair back. [From obsolete *splat,* to split up; akin to SPLIT.]
splat[2] *n.* A slapping noise.
~adv. With a splat. [Imitative.]
splat·ter (spláttər) *v.* **-tered, -tering, -ters.** *—tr.* To spatter or splash. *—intr.* To spatter or splash. Used especially of a liquid.
~n. A splash of liquid. [Perhaps a blend of SPLASH and SPATTER.]
splay (splay) *adj.* **1.** Spread out; broad. **2.** Turned outwards. **3.** Clumsy; awkward.
~n. **1.** An expansion; a spread. **2.** *Architecture.* Either of two side walls of a window or other opening that forms an oblique rather than right angle to the main wall.
~v. **splayed, splaying, splays.** *—tr.* **1.** To spread (the limbs, for example) out or apart, especially clumsily. Usually used with *out.* **2.** To make the edges of (a window or other aperture) slant or slope out; bevel. **3.** To dislocate (a bone). Used of an animal. *—intr.* **1.** To be spread out or apart. **2.** To slant or slope. Usually used with *out.* [Middle English *splayen,* to spread out, short for *displayen,* to DISPLAY.]
splay·foot (splay-fōōt) *n., pl.* **-feet** (-feet). **1.** A physical deformity characterised by abnormally flat and turned-out feet. **2.** A foot of this kind. **—splay·foot·ed** (-fŏŏtid) *adj.*
spleen (spleen) *n.* **1.** A large, dark red organ situated below and behind the stomach and containing lymphoid tissue. It forms lymphocytes and antibodies and helps to remove worn-out red blood cells and foreign particles from the blood stream. **2.** A homologous organ or tissue in other vertebrates. Also called "milt". **3.** *Obsolete.* **a.** This organ considered as the seat of mirth. **b.** Merriment. **c.** Caprice; whim. **4. a.** *Obsolete.* This organ considered as the seat of melancholy. **b.** Melancholy. **5.** Ill temper and malice. Used chiefly in the phrase *vent one's spleen.* [Middle English *splen(e),* from Old French *esplen,* from Latin *splēn,* from Greek.] **—spleen·y** *adj.*
spleen·ful (spleénf'l) *adj.* Ill-tempered, irritable, or spiteful. [The spleen was once thought of as the seat of negative emotions.] **—spleen·ful·ly** *adv.*
spleen·wort (spleén-wurt || -wawrt) *n.* Any of various ferns of the genus *Asplenium,* having feather-like, often evergreen fronds. [So called because it was thought to cure spleen disorders.]
splen·dent (spléndənt) *adj. Archaic.* **1.** Shining or lustrous; brilliant. **2.** Celebrated; illustrious. [Middle English, from Latin *splendēns* (stem *splendent-*) , present participle of *splendēre,* to shine.]
splen·did (spléndid) *adj.* **1.** Magnificent; grand. **2.** Imposing by reason of showiness. **3.** Glorious; illustrious. **4.** Gleaming with light or colour; radiant. **5.** Very good or satisfying: *had a splendid evening.* [French *splendide,* from Latin *splendidus,* from *splendēre,* to shine.] **—splen·did·ly** *adv.* **—splen·did·ness** *n.*
splen·dif·er·ous (splen-díffərəss) *adj.* Splendid. Usually used humorously or ironically. [Middle English, from Medieval Latin *splendiferus* : SPLENDOUR + -FEROUS.] **—splen·dif·er·ous·ly** *adv.* **—splen·dif·er·ous·ness** *n.*
splendour, *U.S.* **splen·dor** (spléndər) *n.* **1.** The state or quality of being splendid. **2.** Something splendid. **3.** *Heraldry.* The sun depicted with rays and a human face. [Middle English *splendure,* from Old French *splendeur,* from Latin *splendour,* from *splendēre,* to shine.] **—splen·dor·ous, splen·drous** (spléndrəss) *adj.*
sple·nec·to·my (spli-néktəmi) *n., pl.* **-mies.** A surgical removal of the spleen. [Latin *splēn,* SPLEEN + -ECTOMY.]
sple·net·ic (spli-néttik) *adj.* Also **sple·net·i·cal** (-'l). **1.** Of or pertaining to the spleen. **2.** Ill-tempered, irritable, or spiteful. **3.** *Archaic.* Melancholy.
~n. An ill-humoured person. [Late Latin *splēnēticus,* from Latin *splēn,* SPLEEN.] **—sple·net·i·cal·ly** *adv.*
splen·ic (splénnik, spleénik) *adj.* Of, in, near, or pertaining to the spleen. [Latin *splēnicus,* from Greek *splēnikos,* from *splēn,* SPLEEN.]
sple·ni·tis (spli-nītiss) *n.* Inflammation of the spleen. [Greek *splēnitis* : *splēn,* SPLEEN + -ITIS.]
sple·ni·us (spleéni-əss) *n., pl.* **-nii** (-ī). Either of two muscles of the back of the neck, extending from the backbone to the skull, that rotate and extend the head and neck. [New Latin, from Latin *splēnium,* patch, plaster, spleenwort, from Greek *splēnion,* from *splēn,* SPLEEN.] **—sple·ni·al** *adj.*
sple·no·meg·a·ly (spleénō-méggəli) *n.* Enlargement of the spleen. [Latin *splēn,* SPLEEN + MEGAL(O)- + -Y.]
splice (splīss) *tr.v.* **spliced, splicing, splices. 1. a.** To join (film or wire, for example) at the ends, usually with an adhesive. Often used with *to* or *together.* **b.** To join (ropes) by interweaving strands. **2.** To join (pieces of wood) by overlapping and binding or bolting. **3.** *Informal.* To unite in marriage. Usually used in the passive.
~n. **1.** A joint made by splicing. **2.** The place where parts have been spliced. [Probably from Middle Dutch *splissen.*] **—splic·er** *n.*
spline (splīn) *n.* **1. a.** Any of a series of projections on a shaft that fit into slots on a mating part, enabling one to drive the other. **b.** A slot or groove receiving such a projection. **2.** A wooden or metal strip; especially, one that fits into a groove at the edge of one board to join it to another.
~tr.v. **splined, splining, splines.** To cut splines into. [Of dialect (East Anglian) origin, perhaps akin to SPLINTER.]
splint (splint) *n.* **1.** A thin piece, as of wood, split off from a larger piece; a splinter. **2.** Any rigid device used to prevent motion of a joint or the ends of a fractured bone. **3.** A thin, flexible wooden strip, such as one used in weaving baskets and chair bottoms. **4.** A plate or strip of metal, such as one used in making armour. **5.** A bony enlargement of the cannon bone or splint bone of a horse.
~tr.v. **splinted, splinting, splints.** To support or restrict with or as if with a splint. [Middle English *splent, splint,* small strip of metal, splint, from Middle Low German or Middle Dutch *splinte.*]
splint bone *n.* Either of two small metacarpal or metatarsal bones in horses or related animals, on each side of the cannon bone.
splin·ter (splíntər) *n.* A sharp, slender piece, as of wood, bone, glass, or metal, split or broken off from a main body.
~v. **splintered, -tering, -ters.** *—intr.* **1.** To split or break into sharp, slender pieces. **2.** To split into parts; shatter. **3.** To break away from a parent group. Used with *off.* *—tr.* To cause to splinter. —See Synonyms at **break.** **—splin·ter·y** *adj.*
splinter group *n.* An independent group that has broken away from a parent group such as a church or political party.
split (split) *v.* **split, splitting, splits.** *—tr.* **1. a.** To divide sharply or cleanly, especially into lengthways sections or into two parts of approximately equal size. **b.** To separate from a whole. Often used with *off.* **2.** To break, burst, or rip apart with force; rend. **3.** To separate (persons or groups); disunite. Often used with *up.* **4.** To divide and share among people. **5.** To separate into layers, components, or parts. Often used with *up.* **6.** *Slang.* To depart from; leave. **7.** *U.S.* To mark (a vote or ballot) in favour of candidates from different parties. *—intr.* **1. a.** To become separated into parts; especially, to divide lengthways. **b.** To be separated from a whole. Often used with *off.* **2.** To become broken or ripped apart, especially as a result of internal pressure. **3. a.** To become divided or part company as a result of discord or disagreement. **b.** To end a relationship, especially to separate or divorce. Used with *up.* **4.** To divide or share something with others. **5.** *British Slang.* To betray information to the authorities; inform. Usually used with *on.* **6.** *Slang.* To depart. —See Synonyms at **break, tear.**
~n. **1.** The act or result of splitting. **2.** A gap, rift, or cleft. **3.** A piece split off from a larger whole; a splinter. **4.** A breach or rupture in a group; a schism. **5.** A split strip of flexible wood or other material used in basketmaking. **6.** *Informal.* **a.** A half-bottle of a carbonated beverage. **b.** An alcoholic drink of half the usual quantity. **7. a.** A dessert of sliced fruit, ice cream, and toppings: *banana split.* **b.** Something made up of two or more different constituents or ingredients. **8.** *Usually plural.* The act of stretching out the legs in opposite directions at right angles to the trunk while in the air or on the ground, performed in dancing, acrobatics or the like. Preceded by *the.* **9.** A single thickness of a hide split into layers. **10.** In ten-pin bowling, an arrangement of pins left standing after the first bowl with one or more intermediate pins knocked down.
~adj. **1.** Divided or separated; *split loyalties.* **2.** Fissured longitudinally; cleft. [Dutch *splitten,* from Middle Dutch.] **—split·ter** *n.*
Split (split). *Italian* **Spa·la·to** (spa-laátō). City on the Dalmatian

coast, in Croatia. It has been a major Adriatic port since the early Middle Ages, and is a cultural, market, tourist, and manufacturing centre. It was held by Venice (1420–1797), and by Austria until 1918.

split ends *pl.n.* A condition of damaged hair in which the ends of individual hairs have a tendency to split.

split infinitive *n. Grammar.* An infinitive verb form with an element, usually an adverb, interposed between *to* and the verb form.
Usage: An example of a split infinitive is *to officially propose*. Although this construction is widely used in speech, and is often found in literature, it attracts strong criticism, perhaps because the word *to* and the following verb are felt to form a unit and should therefore not be separated. However, it is often difficult to avoid this construction without either causing a highly unnatural style of speech—in *I want to really help them,* placing *really* before *to* or after *help* is undesirable—or producing a different meaning —in *I really want to help them* it is the "wanting" rather than the "helping" that is now emphasised.

split-lev·el (splít-lévv'l, -levv'l) *adj.* Of, within, or designating a building in which the floor levels of adjoining parts are separated by about half a storey.
~*n.* A split-level house.

split pea *n.* A pea dried and split, and used for cooking in soups and stews or as a vegetable.

split personality *n.* **1.** A condition in which an individual or group manifests two or more relatively distinct personalities. **2.** Such an individual or group. **3.** Loosely, **schizophrenia** *(see).*

split pin *n.* A strong, metal pin with two arms that can be bent outwards, used for holding wheels on axles and the like.

split ring *n.* A usually metal ring consisting of two spiral turns pressed flat together, between which keys or other objects may be slid on or off.

split-screen (split-skréen) *adj.* Of or designating a cinematic technique in which two or more images are projected simultaneously onto different parts of the same screen. —**split screen** *n.*

split second *n.* An instant; a flash.

split-second (split-séckənd) *adj.* **1.** Performed in a very short space of time. **2.** Requiring or showing great precision and accuracy.

split shift *n.* A working shift split into two periods by an interval considerably longer than a lunch break.

split·ting (splítting) *adj.* **1.** Acute; piercing. **2.** Extremely painful.

splodge (sploj) *n.* Also *chiefly U.S.* **splotch** (sploch). An irregularly shaped stain, spot, or discoloured area.
~*tr.v.* **splodged, sploding, splodes.** Also *chiefly U.S.* **splotch, splotched, splotching, splotches.** To mark with a splodge or splodges. [*Splodge,* variant of *splotch,* perhaps blend of SPOT + BLOTCH.] —**splodg·y** *adj.*

splosh (splosh) *n.* A splash. [Imitative.] —**splosh** *v.*

splurge (splurj) *v.* **splurged, splurging, splurges.** *Informal.* —*intr.* **1.** To indulge in extravagant expense or luxury. **2.** To be showy or ostentatious. —*tr.* To spend extravagantly or wastefully. Often used with *on: splurged £150 on a new radio.*
~*n. Informal.* **1.** An extravagant display. **2.** An extravagant spending spree. [19th century (U.S.) : probably imitative.]

splut·ter (splúttər) *v.* **-tered, -tering, -ters.** —*intr.* **1.** To make a spitting sound. **2.** To speak incoherently, as when confused or angry. —*tr.* To utter or express hastily and incoherently.
~*n.* A spluttering noise or spluttering talk. [Perhaps alteration (influenced by SPLASH) of SPUTTER.] —**splut·ter·er** *n.*

Spock (spok), **Benjamin (McLane)** (1903–98). U.S. paediatrician. He had a great influence on childcare in the West through his book *Baby and Child Care* (1946), which he drastically revised in 1979.

spode (spōd) *n. Often capital* **S.** A porcelain or chinaware of fine quality. [After Josiah Spode (1754–1827), British potter.]

spod·u·mene (spóddew-meen) *n.* A greenish to pinkish or lilac mineral, essentially $LiAlSi_2O_6$, used as a source of lithium and in transparent varieties as a gemstone. [French *spodumène,* from Greek *spodoumenos,* present participle of *spodousthai,* to be burned to ashes (because the mineral becomes ash-grey when exposed to flame), from *spodos†,* wood ashes.]

spoil (spoyl) *v.* **spoilt** (spoylt) or **spoiled, spoiling, spoils.** —*tr.* **1.** To impair the value or quality of; damage or ruin. **2. a.** To harm the character of (a child, for example) by overindulgence. **b.** To pamper; coddle. **3.** To make dissatisfied. Used with *for: spoiled him for the old life.* **4.** *Archaic.* **a.** To plunder; despoil. **b.** To take by force. —*intr.* **1.** To become tainted, rotten, or otherwise unfit for use; decay. Used especially of food. **2.** *Archaic.* To pillage. —See Synonyms at **decay, injure, pamper.** —**spoil for.** To be eager for; crave. Used chiefly in the phrase *be spoiling for a fight.*
~*n.* **1.** *Usually plural.* Goods or property seized from a victim after a conflict, especially after a military victory. **2.** *Plural.* Incidental benefits reaped by a winner. **3.** *Archaic.* The act of plundering; spoliation. **4.** Refuse material removed from an excavation. [Middle English *spoilen,* to despoil, plunder, from Old French *espoillier,* from Latin *spoliāre,* from *spolium,* hide torn from an animal, booty.]
Usage: Spoiled and *spoilt* are both used as past tense and past participle forms, the former being preferred in American English and the latter in British English.

spoil·age (spóylij) *n.* **1.** The condition or process of becoming spoiled; damage or decomposition. **2.** Material that has been spoiled. **3.** Waste caused by spoiling.

spoil·er (spóylər) *n.* **1.** One who seizes spoils or booty. **2.** One that causes spoilage; a corrupting agent. **3.** A long, narrow hinged plate on the upper surface of an aircraft wing, raised to reduce lift or speed. **4.** An air deflector on either end of a motor vehicle used to prevent the wheels from lifting off the road at high speeds.

spoil·sport (spóyl-spawrt ‖ -spōrt) *n.* One who mars the pleasures of others, often by inappropriate prudence or sobriety.

spoke[1] (spōk) *n.* **1.** Any of the rods or braces that connect the hub and the rim of a wheel. **2.** Any of the handles that project from the rim of a ship's steering wheel. **3.** A rung of a ladder. —**put a spoke in (someone's) wheel.** To thwart or foil (someone's) plans.
~*tr.v.* **spoked, spoking, spokes. 1.** To equip with spokes. **2.** To impede (a wheel) by inserting a rod. [Middle English *spake, spoke,* Old English *spāca.*]

spoke[2]. Past tense and *archaic* past participle of **speak.**

spo·ken (spókən) Past participle of **speak.**
~*adj.* **1.** Uttered; expressed orally. **2.** Speaking or using speech in a specified manner or voice. Used in combination: *soft-spoken.* —**spoken for.** Reserved or engaged.

spoke·shave (spók-shayv) *n.* A drawknife *(see).*

spokes·man (spóks-mən) *n., pl.* **-men** (-mən). A person chosen or authorised to speak on behalf of another or others. [*Spokes,* possessive case of *spoke,* "speaking", from *spoke,* archaic past participle of SPEAK + MAN.]

spokes·per·son (spóks-perss'n) *n.* A spokesman or spokeswoman. [SPOKES(MAN) + PERSON.]

spokes·wom·an (spóks-wŏŏmən) *n., pl.* **-women** (-wimmin). A female spokesman. [SPOKES(MAN) + WOMAN.]

spo·li·a·tion (spóli-áysh'n) *n. Formal.* **1.** The act of despoiling or plundering; especially, the seizure of neutral vessels at sea by a belligerent power in time of war. **2.** *Law.* The intentional alteration or destruction of a document so as to invalidate it as evidence. [Middle English *spoliacioun,* from Latin *spoliātiō* (stem *spoliātiōn-*), from *spoliāre,* to despoil. See spoil.] —**spo·li·a·tor** (-aytər) *n.*

spon·da·ic (spon-dáy-ik) *adj.* Of, pertaining to, or consisting of spondees. [French *spondaïque,* from Late Latin *spondaicus, spondiācus,* from Greek *spondeiakos,* from *spondeios,* SPONDEE.]

spon·dee (spón-dee, *rarely* -di) *n.* A metrical foot in poetry consisting of two long or stressed syllables. [Middle English *sponde,* from Old French *spondee,* from Latin *spondeum,* from Greek *spondeios (pous),* "(meter) used at a libation", from *spondē,* libation.]

spon·du·licks, spon·du·lix (spon-déw-liks ‖ -dŏŏ-) *n. Slang.* Money. [19th century : origin obscure.]

spon·dy·li·tis (spóndi-lītiss) *n.* Inflammation of the joints of the vertebrae. [New Latin : Greek *spondulos, sphondulos†,* vertebra + -ITIS.]

sponge (spunj) *n.* **1.** Any of numerous primitive, chiefly marine invertebrate animals of the phylum Porifera, characteristically having a porous body supported by a skeleton composed of fibrous material or siliceous or calcareous spicules, and often forming colonies. **2. a.** The light, fibrous, absorbent skeleton of certain of these organisms. **b.** A piece of such a skeleton, used for bathing, cleaning, and other purposes. **3.** Any of various substances having spongelike qualities, such as certain forms of plastics, rubber, or cellulose. **4.** A porous metal used to absorb gases: *a platinum sponge.* **5.** A gauze pad used to absorb blood and other fluids, as in surgery and wound dressing. **6.** Dough that is leavened or in the process of being leavened. **7. a.** Any of various light cakes, such as sponge cake. **b.** *British.* A sponge pudding. **8. a.** A wash or rub with a sponge. **b.** A sponge bath. **9.** *Informal.* A sponger. —**throw in** or **up the sponge.** *Informal.* To give up; admit defeat.
~*v.* **sponged, sponging, sponges.** —*tr.* **1.** To moisten, wipe, or clean with a sponge. Often used with *down* or *off.* **2.** To wipe out; erase. **3.** To absorb or soak up. Often used with *up.* **4.** *Informal.* To obtain free by imposing on another's generosity: *sponge a meal.* —*intr.* **1.** To fish for sponges. **2.** *Informal.* To live by imposing on the generosity of others. Often used with *off* or *on.* [Middle English *spo(u)ng(e),* Old English *sponge,* from Latin *spongia,* from Greek *sphongos,* sponge, from the same Mediterranean origin as FUNGUS.] —**spon·gi·form** *adj.* —**spon·gi·ness** *n.*

sponge bag *n.* A waterproof bag for holding toilet articles.

sponge bath *n.* A washing of the body with a sponge or cloth, without immersion.

sponge cake *n.* A very light, porous cake made of flour, sugar, beaten eggs, and flavouring, sometimes containing no shortening. Also called "sponge".

sponge cloth *n.* A loosely woven cloth, usually of cotton.

sponge finger *n.* A sponge cake resembling a finger in shape.

sponge pudding *n.* A light steamed or baked pudding of spongelike texture. Also called *British* "sponge".

spong·er (spúnjər) *n.* **1.** A person or boat that gathers sponges. **2.** *Informal.* A person who sponges on others; a parasite.

sponge rubber *n.* A soft, porous rubber used in toys, cushions, gaskets, and weather stripping, and as a vibration dampener.

spongiform encephalopathy *n.* An encephalopathy marked by increasing sponginess of the brain.

spon·gin (spúnjin) *n.* A fibrous protein that forms the skeletal structure of some sponges. [German *Spongin* : Latin *spongia,* SPONGE + -IN.]

spon·gi·o·blast (spúnji-ō-blaast, -blast) *n.* Any of the embryonic epithelial cells that give rise to the neuroglia cells. [Latin *spongia,* SPONGE + -BLAST.] —**spon·gi·o·blast·ic** (-blástik) *adj.*

spon·gy (spúnji) *adj.* **-gier, -giest. 1.** Like a sponge, especially in elasticity, absorbency, or porousness. **2.** Full of small holes. **3.** Soft and wet. **—spon·gi·ness** *n.*

spon·son (spón-s'n) *n.* **1.** Any of several structures that project from the side of a ship or tank; especially, a gun platform. **2.** An air-filled projection on the hull of a seaplane, canoe, or other vessel, giving greater stability. [19th century : origin obscure.]

spon·sor (spón-sər) *n.* **1.** A person or group that assumes responsibility for another person or group. **2.** A person or group that pledges financial support to or promotes an activity or organisation, for example. **3.** A legislator who proposes and urges the adoption of a bill. **4.** One who presents a candidate for baptism or confirmation; a godparent. **5.** A business enterprise that pays for or subsidises a broadcast, concert, sports event, or the like, usually in return for advertising time or space.
~tr.v. **sponsored, -soring, -sors.** To act as a sponsor for. [Latin, from *spondēre,* to make a solemn pledge.] **—spon·so·ri·al** (spon-sáwri-əl || -sṓri-) *adj.* **—spon·sor·ship** *n.*

spon·ta·ne·i·ty (spóntə-náy-əti, -née-) *n., pl.* **-ties. 1.** The condition or quality of being spontaneous. **2.** Spontaneous behaviour, impulses, or movements.

spon·ta·ne·ous (spon-táyni-əss) *adj.* **1.** Happening, arising, or performed without apparent external cause; self-generated. **2.** Voluntary and impulsive; unpremeditated: *spontaneous applause.* **3.** Unconstrained and unstudied in manner or characteristic behaviour. **4.** Growing without cultivation or human labour; indigenous. Said of plants. —See Synonyms below and at **voluntary.** [Late Latin *spontāneus,* from Latin *sponte,* of one's own accord, out of free will.] **—spon·ta·ne·ous·ly** *adv.* **—spon·ta·ne·ous·ness** *n.*
Synonyms: *spontaneous, impulsive, instinctive, involuntary, automatic.*

spontaneous abortion *n.* A **miscarriage** *(see).*

spontaneous combustion *n.* Ignition of a material, such as powdered coal or hay, without an external source of heat, caused by slow oxidation of the material producing a rise in temperature.

spontaneous generation *n. Biology.* The origination of live organisms from nonliving matter, once thought to explain the appearance of maggots in rotting meat. Compare **primordial soup.** See **abiogenesis.**

spon·toon (spon-tóon) *n.* A short pike carried by subordinate infantry officers in the 18th and early 19th centuries. [French *sponton,* from Italian *spuntone,* from *spuntare,* to blunt, remove the point : *s-,* from Latin *ex-* (removal) + *punto,* point, from Latin *punctum,* from *pungere,* to pierce.]

spoof (spōōf) *n.* **1.** A good-humoured hoax. **2.** A gentle satirical imitation; a light parody. **—**See Synonyms at **caricature.**
~v. **spoofed, spoofing, spoofs.** *—tr.* **1.** To deceive. **2.** To do a spoof of; satirise gently. *—intr.* To do a spoof. [Originally a card game characterised by nonsense and hoaxing, invented by Arthur Roberts (1852–1933), British comedian.] **—spoof·er** *n.*

spook (spŏŏk) *n. Informal.* **1.** A ghost; a spectre. **2.** *U.S.* A spy.
~v. **spooked, spooking, spooks.** *U.S. & South African Informal.* *—tr.* **1.** To haunt. **2.** To frighten; especially, to startle and cause sudden or violent activity among (cattle, for example). *—intr.* To become frightened. [Dutch, from Middle Dutch *spoocke,* akin to Middle Low German *spōk*†.] **—spook·ish** *adj.*

spook·y (spŏŏki) *adj.* **-ier, -iest.** *Informal.* **1.** Ghostly; eerie; unnatural. **2.** *U.S.* Easily startled; skittish; nervous. **—spook·i·ly** *adv.* **—spook·i·ness** *n.*

spool (spōōl) *n.* **1.** A small wood, metal, plastic, or cardboard cylinder upon which wire, thread, film, magnetic tape, or string is wound. It usually has raised ends and a hole through the centre. **2.** The amount of thread or other material on a particular spool. **3.** Anything similar to a spool in shape or function.
~v. **spooled, spooling, spools.** *—tr.* To wind on a spool. Often used with *up.* *—intr.* To be wound on a spool. Often used with *up.* [Middle English *spole, spule,* from Old French *espole,* from Middle Dutch *spoele,* akin to Old High German *spuolo*†.]

spoon (spōōn) *n.* **1. a.** A utensil consisting of a small, shallow bowl on a handle, used in preparing, serving, or eating food. **b.** A spoonful. **2.** Something similar to a spoon or its bowl; especially: **a.** A shiny, curved metallic fishing lure. Also called "spoon bait". **b.** A paddle or oar with a curved blade. **3.** A golf club with more loft than a brassie. **—born with a silver spoon in (one's) mouth.** Born into wealthy or privileged circumstances.
~v. **spooned, spooning, spoons.** *—tr.* **1.** To lift, scoop up, or carry (food, for example) with or as if with a spoon. Often used with *out* or *up.* **2.** To shove or scoop (a ball) feebly into the air, as in golf. *—intr.* **1.** To fish with a spoon lure. **2.** To give the ball an upward scoop, as in golf. **3.** *Informal.* To show affection by kissing, caressing, or talking amorously. In this sense, not in current usage. [Middle English *spo(o)n,* Old English *spōn,* chip of wood.]

spoon·bill (spōōn-bil) *n.* **1.** Any of several long-legged wading birds mainly of the genus *Platalea,* of tropical and subtropical regions, having a long, flat bill with a broad, spatulate tip. **2.** Any of various broad-billed ducks, such as the shoveler.

spoon·drift (spōōn-drift) *n.* **Spindrift** *(see).* [Obsolete *spoon*†, to drive back and forth (said of a boat) + DRIFT.]

spoon·er·ism (spōōnər-iz'm) *n.* A usually unintentional transposition of the initial sounds of two or more words in spoken language, as in *Let me sew you to your sheet* for *Let me show you to your seat.* [After the Rev. William A. *Spooner* (1844–1930), English scholar and Warden of New College, Oxford, noted for such slips.]

spoon·feed (spōōn-feed) *tr.v.* **-fed** (-fed), **-feeding, -feeds. 1.** To feed (a baby, for example) with a spoon. **2. a.** To present (information, lessons, or the like) in such a thoroughgoing manner as to make any independent thought or effort on the part of the recipient unnecessary. **b.** To present with information in such a manner. **3.** To mollycoddle; pamper.

spoon·ful (spōōn-fōōl) *n., pl.* **-fuls.** The amount a spoon will hold.

spoor (spoor, spor) *n.* The track, trail, or footprint of an animal, especially a wild animal. See Synonyms at **trace.**
~v. **spoored, spooring, spoors.** *—tr.* To track by following a spoor. *—intr.* To track an animal by its spoor. [Afrikaans, from Middle Dutch *spo(o)r.*]

Spor·a·des or **Sporádhes** (spórrə-deez). Two groups of Greek islands in the southeast Aegean Sea. The southern group includes the **Dodecanese** (which see).

spo·rad·ic (spə-ráddik, spo- || spō-) *adj.* **1.** Occurring at irregular intervals in time; occasional. **2.** Appearing singly or at widely scattered localities; isolated in occurrence: *a sporadic disease.* —See Synonyms at **periodic.** [Medieval Latin *sporadicus,* from Greek *sporadikos,* isolated, scattered, from *sporas,* scattered, dispersed.] **—spo·rad·i·cal·ly** *adv.* **—spo·rad·i·cal·ness** *n.*

spo·ran·gi·um (spə-ránji-əm) *n., pl.* **-gia** (-ə). An asexual spore-bearing structure in certain plants, such as fungi, mosses, and ferns. [New Latin : SPOR(O)- + Greek *angeion,* vessel, container (see **angiology**).] **—spo·ran·gi·al** *adj.*

spore (spor || spōr) *n.* **1.** An asexual, usually single-celled reproductive organ characteristic of nonflowering plants such as fungi, mosses, or ferns. **2.** A similar structure formed by or involved in sexual reproduction in some other organisms. **3.** A microorganism, such as a bacterium, in a dormant or resting state.
~intr.v. **spored, sporing, spores.** To produce or carry spores. [New Latin *spora,* from Greek, a sowing, seed.] **—spo·ra·ceous** (spə-ráyshəss, sp) *adj.*

spore case *n.* A sporangium or other structure containing spores.

spo·ri·cide (spáw-ri-sīd, spó- || spṓ-) *n.* An agent that kills spores. **—spo·ri·ci·dal** (-sīd'l) *adj.*

sporo-, spori-, spor- *comb. form.* Indicates spore; for example, **sporocarp, sporangium.** [New Latin *spora,* spore, from Greek, a sowing, seed.]

spo·ro·carp (spáw-rə-kaarp, spó-, -rō- || spṓ-) *n. Botany.* **1.** A multicellular structure in which spores are formed in aquatic ferns. **2.** An **ascocarp** *(see).* [SPORO- + -CARP.]

spo·ro·cyst (spáw-rə-sist, spó-, -rə- || spṓ-) *n. Biology.* **1.** A protective case containing the spores of sporozoan protozoans. **2.** A saclike larval stage in many trematode worms, from which redia larvae are produced. [SPORO- + -CYST.]

spo·ro·cyte (spáw-rə-sīt, spó-, -rō- || spṓ-) *n. Biology.* A cell that produces haploid spores during meiosis. [SPORO- + -CYTE.]

spo·ro·gen·e·sis (spáw-rō-jénnə-siss, spó-, -rə- || spṓ-) *n.* The production or formation of spores. [SPORO- + -GENESIS.] **—spo·rog·e·nous** (spaw-rójənəss, spo-, spə- || spō-) *adj.*

spo·ro·go·ni·um (spáw-rə-gṓni-əm, spó-, -rō- || spṓ-) *n., pl.* **-nia** (-ə). A stalked structure in mosses and liverworts that produces asexual spores. [New Latin : SPORO- + -GONIUM.]

spo·rog·o·ny (spaw-róggəni, spə-, spo- || spō-) *n.* The production of sporozoites by multiple fission of the zygote, characteristic of sporozoan protozoans. [SPORO- + -GONY.]

spo·ro·phore (spáw-rə-fawr, spó-, -rō- || spṓ-, -fōr) *n.* A spore-bearing structure, especially in fungi. [SPORO- + -PHORE.]

spo·ro·phyll (spáw-rə-fil, spó-, -rō- || spṓ-) *n.* A leaf or leaflike organ in mosses, ferns, and the like, that bears sporangia. [SPORO- + -PHYLL.]

spo·ro·phyte (spáw-rə-fīt, spó-, -rō- || spṓ-) *n.* **1.** The spore-producing phase in plants that reproduce by alternation of generations. **2.** An individual plant in this phase. Compare **gametophyte.** [SPORO- + -PHYTE.] **—spo·ro·phyt·ic** (-fíttik) *adj.*

-sporous *adj. comb. form.* Indicates having spores, especially a specified number or kind; for example, **homosporous.**

spo·ro·zo·an (spáw-rə-zṓ-ən, spó- || spṓ-) *n.* Any of numerous parasitic protozoans of the class Sporozoa, such as the malaria parasite, many of which have complex reproductive processes. [New Latin *Sporozoa* : SPORO- + -ZOA.] **—spo·ro·zo·an** *adj.*

spo·ro·zo·ite (spáw-rə-zṓ-īt, spó- || spṓ-) *n.* A sporozoan that has been formed by sporogony and is ready to penetrate a new host cell. [SPOROZO(AN) + -ITE.]

spor·ran (spórrən) *n.* A leather or fur pouch worn hanging on the belt at the front of the kilt in Highland dress. [Scottish Gaelic *sporan,* from Late Latin *bursa,* bag, from Greek, leather, hide.]

sport (sport || spōrt) *n.* **1.** A game or other activity, usually providing exercise and pleasure and involving competition. **2.** Sports collectively. **3. a.** Any pleasurable pastime; a diversion; a recreation. **b.** The pleasure provided by such a pastime. Used chiefly in the phrase *have good sport.* **4. a.** Light mockery; raillery; jest: *a remark made in sport.* **b.** An object of mockery. **5.** One at the mercy of or controlled by external forces: *a sport of fate.* **6.** *Informal.* A cheerful or good-natured person. **7.** *Informal.* A person who shows sportsmanlike qualities to a specified extent: *a bad sport.* **8.** *Informal.* A person who lives a merry, extravagant life. **9.** *Australian.* Used as an informal term of address. **10.** *Genetics.* An organism that shows a marked change from the parent stock; a mutation. **11.** *Archaic.* Amorous dalliance; flirting. **—in sport.** In jest; jokingly.
~v. **sported, sporting, sports.** *—intr.* **1.** To play happily; frolic. **2.** To joke or trifle. Often used with *with.* **3.** To mutate. *—tr.* To display or show off: *His shoes sported pink laces.*

~*adj. U.S.* Variant of **sports**. [Middle English *sporten,* to amuse, divert, short for *disporten,* DISPORT.] —**sport·ful** *adj.* —**sport·ful·ly** *adv.* —**sport·ful·ness** *n.*

sport·ing (spórt-ing ‖ spôrt-) *adj.* 1. Used in, appropriate for, or pertaining to hunting, racing, and other sports. 2. Showing sportsmanship. 3. Of or associated with gambling. —**sport·ing·ly** *adv.*

sporting chance *n. Informal.* A fair chance of success.

spor·tive (spórt-iv ‖ spôrt-) *adj.* 1. Playful; frolicsome. 2. Pertaining to or interested in sports. 3. *Archaic.* Amorous; wanton. —**spor·tive·ly** *adv.* —**spor·tive·ness** *n.*

sports (sports ‖ spôrts) *adj.* Also *U.S.* **sport.** 1. Of, pertaining to, or used in sports. 2. Suitable for casual or informal use. Said especially of clothes.

sports car *n.* A mass-produced car usually with two seats, having a low centre of gravity and, often, a folding or removable roof. Its steering and suspension are designed for precise control at high speeds on curving roads.

sports day *n. British.* A day at which athletic competitions take place in a school, college, or similar institution.

sports jacket *n.* A man's casual jacket, usually made of tweed or patterned wool fibre.

sports·man (spórts-mən ‖ spôrts-) *n., pl.* **-men** (-mən). 1. **a.** One who participates actively in sports, especially outdoor sports. **b.** One who participates in hunting, angling, or similar outdoor pursuits. 2. One who abides by the rules of a contest, plays fair, and accepts victory or defeat graciously.

sports·man·like (spórts-mən-līk ‖ spôrts-) *adj.* Also **sports·man·ly** (-li). Of, like, or befitting a good sportsman.

sports·man·ship (spórts-mən-ship ‖ spôrts-) *n.* The qualities and conduct of a good sport; fair play and abidance by the rules.

sports·wear (spórts-wair ‖ spôrts-) *n.* 1. Clothes designed to be worn for sporting activities. 2. Clothes designed for comfort and casual wear.

sports·wom·an (spórts-woomən ‖ spôrts-) *n., pl.* **-women** (-wimmin). A woman who is active in sports.

sport·y (spórti ‖ spôrti) *adj.* **-ier, -iest.** *Informal.* 1. Of or appropriate to sportsman or sports. 2. Interested or taking part in sports. 3. Smart; natty. 4. Dashing; flashy.

spor·u·late (spórrew-layt ‖ spŏr̄ə-, spáwrə-) *intr.v.* **-lated, -lating, -lates.** To produce or release spores, especially by multiple cell fission. [New Latin *sporula,* diminutive of *spora,* SPORE.] —**spor·u·la·tion** (-láysh'n) *n.*

spot (spot) *n.* 1. **a.** A particular place of relatively small and definite limits: *a holiday spot.* **b.** A place noted for a specified feature or activity: *a trouble spot; a favourite night spot.* 2. A mark on a surface differing in colour from the surroundings and usually of round or irregular shape; especially, a stain or blot. 3. A position; a location: *X marks the spot.* 4. *Informal.* A situation, especially a difficult or embarrassing one; a predicament: *in a tight spot.* 5. A brief amount of advertising time on a radio or television programme. 6. An amount of time allocated to a performer or entertainer. 7. A personal defect or blemish, often affecting one's reputation. 8. A pimple or similar blemish on the skin. 9. *Chiefly British Informal.* A small amount; a bit: *a spot of tea.* 10. *Informal.* A spotlight. 11. A coloured dot or other shape, such as a heart, on a playing card, domino, or dice used to distinguish suit, value, or the like. 12. In billiards: **a.** The white ball that is distinguished by a black spot. Also called "spot ball". **b.** The player using this ball. —**change (one's) spots.** To change (one's) character, usually for the better. Usually used in the negative. —**knock spots off.** *British Informal.* To defeat or beat with ease. —**on the spot.** 1. Without delay; at once. 2. At the scene of action. 3. In a responsible or delicate position. 4. Without moving forwards: *running on the spot.* ~*v.* **spotted, spotting, spots.** —*tr.* 1. To cause a spot or spots to appear upon; especially: **a.** To soil with spots. **b.** To decorate with spots; dot. 2. To place in a particular location; situate precisely. 3. To locate or identify; discern. —*intr.* 1. To become marked or be susceptible to marking with spots. 2. To cause a discoloration; make a stain. 3. *British.* To fall in intermittent droplets: *It's spotting with rain.* ~*adj.* 1. Paid for or delivered immediately: *spot sales.* 2. Paid immediately on delivery: *spot cash.* [Middle English *spot(te),* perhaps of Low German origin; akin to Middle Dutch *spotte,* from Common Germanic *sput-* (unattested).] —**spot·ta·ble** *adj.*

spot check *n.* A random or immediate inspection or investigation.

spot-check (spót-chék) *tr.v.* **-checked, -checking, -checks.** To subject to a spot check; inspect at random.

spot height *n.* A precise point, the height of which above sea level has been accurately measured and indicated on a map.

spot·less (spót-ləss, -liss) *adj.* 1. Perfectly clean. 2. Free from blemish; impeccable. —**spot·less·ly** *adv.* —**spot·less·ness** *n.*

spot·light (spót-līt) *n.* 1. A strong beam of light that illuminates only a small area, used especially to centre attention on a stage actor. 2. A lamp that produces such a light. Also called "spot". 3. Public notoriety or prominence. 4. Any artificial source of light with a strongly focused beam, as on a motor vehicle. ~*tr.v.* **-lighted** or **-lit** (-lit), **-lighting, -lights.** 1. To illuminate with a spotlight. 2. To focus attention on.

spot-on (spót-ón) *adj. Informal.* Exactly right or accurate.

spot·ted (spóttid) *adj.* 1. Marked or stained with spots. 2. Patterned with spots. 3. Blemished; stained.

spotted dick *n. British.* A steamed or boiled suet pudding containing currants or other dried fruit. Also called "spotted dog". [From its resemblance to a Dalmatian *(spotted dog* or *dick).*]

spotted fever *n.* An epidemic form of **cerebrospinal meningitis** *(see).*

spotted hyena *n.* An African hyena, *Crocuta crocuta,* with a spotted coat. Also called "laughing hyena".

spot·ter (spóttər) *n.* One that looks for, locates, and usually reports something; especially: 1. One that watches for enemy aircraft. 2. One that locates enemy targets, especially in order to direct artillery fire. 3. One who looks for and notes the type or number of trains, aircraft, and the like, as a hobby: *a train spotter.*

spot·ty (spótti) *adj.* **-tier, -tiest.** 1. Having or marked with spots; spotted. 2. *British Informal.* Having many pimples. 3. Lacking consistency of quality; uneven. —**spot·ti·ly** *adv.* —**spot·ti·ness** *n.*

spot-weld (spót-wéld, -weld) *tr.v.* **-welded, -welding, -welds.** To join (two metal sheets, wires, or the like) by one or more small welds created by electrically generated heat and pressure. ~*n.* A weld so formed.

spous·al (spów-z'l, -s'l) *adj. Archaic.* Of or pertaining to marriage. ~*n.* Usually plural. *Archaic.* Marriage. [Variant of ESPOUSAL.]

spouse (spowss, spowz) *n.* One's marriage partner; a husband or wife. ~*tr.v.* **spoused, spousing, spouses.** *Archaic.* To marry; wed. [Middle English *sp(o)use,* from Old French *(e)spous,* from Latin *spōnsus,* betrothed (person), betrothal, from *spondēre,* to make a solemn pledge, betroth.]

spout (spowt) *v.* **spouted, spouting, spouts.** —*intr.* 1. To gush forth in a rapid stream or in spurts. Often used with *out.* 2. To discharge a liquid or other substance continuously or in spurts. 3. *Informal.* To speak volubly and tediously. —*tr.* 1. To cause to flow or spurt out. 2. *Informal.* To utter pompously and volubly. ~*n.* 1. A tube, mouth, funnel, or pipe through which liquid or material such as grain is released or discharged, such as the mouth of a teapot or roof drainpipe. 2. A continuous stream of liquid or material such as grain. —**up the spout.** *Slang.* 1. Ruined, lost, or hopeless. 2. *British.* Pregnant. [Middle English *spouten,* perhaps from Middle Dutch *spouten, spoiten.*] —**spout·er** *n.*

spp. species (plural).

S.P.Q.R. The Senate and the People of Rome. [Latin *Senatus Populusque Romanus.*]

S.P.R. Society for Psychical Research.

Sprach·ge·fühl (shpra'akh-gə-fewl, -fül) *n. German.* A feeling for language; an ear for the idiomatically correct or appropriate. [Literally, "language feeling".]

sprag (sprag) *n.* 1. **a.** A piece of wood or metal wedged beneath a wheel or between spokes to keep a vehicle from rolling down a slope. **b.** A pointed stake lowered at an angle into the ground from a vehicle to prevent movement. 2. A prop to support a mine roof.

sprain (sprayn) *n.* 1. A painful wrenching or laceration of the ligaments of a joint. 2. The condition resulting from such an injury. ~*tr.v.* **sprained, spraining, sprains.** To cause a sprain in (a joint). [17th century : perhaps from Old French *espraindre,* to squeeze out, strain, from Vulgar Latin *expremere* (unattested), variant of Latin *exprimere,* to press out : *ex-,* out + *premere,* to press.]

spraints (spraynts) *pl.n.* Otters' dung.

sprang. Past tense of **spring**.

sprat (sprat) *n.* 1. A small marine food fish, *Clupea sprattus,* of northeastern Atlantic waters. Also called "brisling". 2. Broadly, any of various similar fish, such as a young herring. [Earlier *sprot,* Middle English *sprotte,* Old English *sprott,* akin to Middle Low German or Middle Dutch *sprot*†.]

sprawl (sprawl) *v.* **sprawled, sprawling, sprawls.** —*intr.* 1. To sit or lie with the body and limbs spread out awkwardly. Often used with *out.* 2. To spread out in a straggling or disordered fashion, as handwriting, a town, or a crowd might. —*tr.* To spread out in a straggling or disordered fashion. Usually used in the passive. ~*n.* 1. A sprawling position or posture. 2. Haphazard growth or extension outwards, especially that resulting from new housing on the outskirts of a town: *urban sprawl.* [Middle English *sprewlen, spraulen,* Old English *sprēawlian.*] —**sprawl·er** *n.*

spray[1] (spray) *n.* 1. **a.** Water or other liquid moving in a mass of dispersed droplets, as from a wave. **b.** Something resembling this, such as a cluster of small flying objects. 2. A fine jet of liquid discharged from an atomiser or a pressurised container. 3. Such a container. 4. Any of numerous commercial products, including paints, cosmetics, and insecticides, dispensed in this way. ~*v.* **sprayed, spraying, sprays.** —*tr.* 1. To disperse (a liquid) in a mass or jet of droplets. 2. To apply (a liquid) in the form of a spray. 3. To apply a spray to (a surface). 4. To shoot out small projectiles at: *sprayed them with machine-gun fire.* —*intr.* 1. To discharge sprays of liquid. 2. To move in the form of a spray. [Originally, "to sprinkle", from Middle Dutch *spraeyen*†.] —**spray·er** *n.*

spray[2] *n.* 1. A small branch bearing buds, flowers, or berries. 2. An ornament or other object resembling this in shape or design. [Middle English, Old English *sprægt* (unattested).]

spray-dry (spráy-drī) *tr.v.* **-dried, -drying, -dreis.** To dehydrate (milk, for example) into a powder form by spraying into hot air.

spray gun *n.* A gunlike device that forces liquid through a nozzle so that it emerges as a spray.

spray-on (spráy-ón) *adj.* Applied as a spray from a pressurised container: *spray-on deodorant.*

spread (spred) *v.* **spread, spreading, spreads.** —*tr.* 1. To broaden or open to a fuller extent or width; stretch. Often used with *out: He spread out the map; spread sail.* 2. To make wider the gap between;

move farther apart. **3. a.** To distribute over a surface in a layer; apply: *spread jam.* **b.** To cover with a thin layer. **4.** To extend over a considerable area or period of time; distribute widely. **5.** To cause to become widely known; disseminate. **6. a.** To prepare (a table) for eating; set. **b.** To arrange (food or a meal) on a table. *—intr.* **1.** To be extended or enlarged. **2.** To become distributed or widely dispersed; increase in range of occurrence. **3.** To become known over a wider area; be disseminated. **4.** To become distributed in a thin layer: *margarine spreads easily.* **5.** To become separated; be forced farther apart. **6.** To be displayed or revealed. Often used with *out: The valley spread out before us.* **—spread (oneself).** *British Informal.* To expend money or energy lavishly to impress others or produce an effect. Often used with *around* or *about.*

~n. **1. a.** The act of spreading; extension; dispersion. **b.** Diffusion; dissemination, as of news. **2.** *Chiefly U.S.* **a.** An open area of land; an expanse. **b.** A ranch or farm. **3.** The extent or limit to which something is or can be spread over time or space; the range. **4.** A cloth covering for a bed, table, or the like. **5.** *Informal.* An abundant meal laid out on a table. **6.** A pastelike food to be spread on bread or biscuits. **7. a.** The facing pages of a book, magazine, or newspaper with related matter extending across the fold. **b.** An article or advertisement running across two or more columns. **8.** The increase in size of the hips and waist: *middle-age spread.* **9.** A gap between two points. **10.** A difference, as between a buying and selling price. **11.** The wingspan of an aircraft.

~adj. **1.** Extended; expanded. **2.** Flat and shallow. Said of a gem. **3.** *Phonetics.* **a.** Extended to form a long, narrow opening. Said of the lips. **b.** Articulated with spread lips. Said of a vowel. [Middle English *spred(d)en,* Old English *sprǣdan* (only in compounds, such as *tō-sprǣdan*).] **—spread·a·ble** *adj.*

spread eagle *n.* **1.** A figure of an eagle with wings and legs spread, used as an emblem. **2.** A posture or design resembling this.

spread-ea·gle (spréd-éeg'l, spred- || -eeg'l) *adj.* Also **spread-eagled** (-d). With the arms and legs stretched out.

~v. **spread-eagled, -gling, -gles.** *—tr.* **1.** To place in a spread-eagle position, especially as a means of punishment. **2.** To defeat or knock out. *—intr.* To perform a spread eagle in ice skating.

spread·er (spréddər) *n.* One that spreads; specifically: **1.** An implement for scattering fertiliser or seed. **2.** A device, such as a bar, for keeping wires or stays apart.

spread-on-impact bullet *n.* A **dum-dum bullet** *(see).*

spread·sheet (spréd-sheet) *n.* **1.** A ledger-like display of data. **2.** A computer application allowing the display of data in spreadsheet format. **—spread·sheet** *adj.*

Sprech·ge·sang (shprékh-gə-zang) *n. German.* A technique of vocal production halfway between speaking and singing. [Literally, "speaking song".] **—Sprech·ge·sing·er** (-zing-ger) *n.*

spree (spree) *n.* **1.** A gay, lively outing. **2.** A period or bout of unrestrained overindulgence: *a buying spree.* [19th century : earlier *spray,* perhaps alteration of Scottish *spreath,* cattle taken as booty, raid, plunder, from Gaelic *sprèidh,* from Latin *praeda,* spoil, booty.]

sprig (sprig) *n.* **1. a.** A small shoot or twig together with its leaves and flowers. **b.** An ornament or motif resembling this. **2.** A small brad without a head. **3.** *Informal.* A young person.

~tr.v. **sprigged, sprigging, sprigs.** **1.** To decorate with a design of sprigs. **2.** To remove a sprig or sprigs from (a bush or tree). **3.** To fasten with a small headless brad. [Middle English *sprigg(e)*†.] **—sprig·ger** *n.*

sprigged (sprigd) *adj.* Designating a fabric or material decorated with a design of sprigs: *sprigged muslin.*

spright·ly (sprīt-li) *adj.* **-lier, -liest.** Buoyant or animated; full of life. See Synonyms at **nimble.**

~adv. Archaic. With briskness; gaily. [*Spright,* variant of SPRITE + -LY.] **—spright·li·ness** *n.*

spring (spring) *v.* **sprang** (sprang) or **sprung** (sprung), **sprung, springing, springs.** *—intr.* **1.** To move upwards, forwards, or in a specified manner in a single quick motion; leap: *He sprang over the fence.* **2.** To appear or emerge suddenly. Often used with *up.* **3.** To move suddenly on or as if on a spring: *The door sprang shut.* **4.** To arise from a source; develop; issue. Often used with *from.* **5.** To become warped, bent, or cracked. Used of wood. **6.** To move out of place; come loose, as a machine part may. **7.** To explode. Used of a mine. *—tr.* **1.** To cause to leap, dart, or come forth suddenly. **2.** To jump over; vault. **3.** To actuate or cause to move on or as if on a spring: *spring a bolt.* **4.** To explode (a mine). **5.** To cause to warp, bend, or crack, as by force. **6.** To develop or present unexpectedly: *spring a surprise; sprang a leak.* **7.** To provide with a spring or springs. **8.** *Slang.* To cause to escape from prison.

~n. **1.** An elastic device, such as a coil of wire, that regains its original shape after being compressed or extended. **2.** An actuating force or factor; a motive. **3. a.** The quality of elasticity; resilience. **b.** Energy; healthy bounce: *a spring in one's step.* **4.** The act or an instance of springing; especially, a jump or leap. **5.** A flock of teal. **6.** The return to normal shape after removal of stress; recoil. **7.** A natural fountain or flow of water from the earth's surface. **8.** A source, origin, or beginning. **9. a.** The season of the year, occurring between winter and summer, during which the weather becomes warmer and plants revive, extending from the vernal equinox to the summer solstice, and popularly considered to comprise March, April, and May in the Northern Hemisphere, and September, October, and November in the Southern Hemisphere. **b.** Any time of growth or youth. **10.** *Architecture.* The point where an arch or vault rises up from its support. Also called "springing". **11.** A warping, bending, or cracking, such as that caused by excessive force.

~adj. **1.** Of or acting like a spring. **2.** Having or supported by springs. **3.** Coming from a spring: *spring water.* **4.** Of, occurring in, or characteristic of the season of spring. **5.** Sown in the spring. Said of a crop. [Spring, sprang, sprung; Middle English *springen, sprang, sprungen,* Old English *springan, sprang* (past singular), *sprungen.*]

spring balance *n.* A device for weighing relatively small objects, consisting of a coiled spring, to the free end of which the object to be weighed is attached so that the spring extends. The amount of the extension is read off on a scale calibrated in units of weight.

spring·board (spríng-bawrd || -bōrd) *n.* **1.** A flexible board mounted on a fulcrum and having one end secured, used by gymnasts to gain momentum. **2.** A **diving board** *(see).* **3.** Anything that lends impetus to or helps to launch an activity, career, or the like.

spring·bok (spríng-bok) *n., pl.* **-boks** or collectively **springbok.** Also **spring·buck** (-buk) *pl.* **-bucks** or collectively **springbuck.** A small brown and white antelope, *Antidorcas marsupialis,* of southern Africa, able to leap high into the air. [Afrikaans : *spring,* to SPRING, from Middle Dutch *springen* + *bok,* male deer, BUCK.]

spring chicken *n.* **1.** A young chicken, slightly older than a poussin, weighing about 2½ pounds. **2.** *Informal.* A young or naive person. Usually used in the negative: *At her age, she's no spring chicken.*

spring-clean (spríng-kléen) *v.* **-cleaned, -cleaning, -cleans.** *—tr.* To clean (a house, for example) thoroughly and comprehensively, especially at the end of the winter. *—intr.* To spring-clean a room or house. **—spring-clean** *n.*

springe (sprinj) *n.* A device for snaring small game, made by attaching a noose to a branch under tension.

~v. **springed, springeing** or **springing, springes.** *—tr.* To trap with a springe; ensnare. *—intr.* To prepare a springe. [Middle English *sprenge, springe,* Old English *sprencg* (unattested).]

spring·er (spríng-ər) *n.* **1.** One that springs. **2.** A springer spaniel. **3.** A cow about to give birth. **4.** *Architecture.* **a.** The point where an arch is supported by a wall or column. **b.** The bottom stone of an arch resting on this point.

springer spaniel *n.* A dog of either of two breeds, the English and the Welsh springer spaniels, having drooping ears and a silky brown and white coat, and originally used for flushing game.

spring fever *n.* The feelings of languor, rejuvenation, or yearning that may affect people at the advent of spring.

Springfield rifle *n.* A magazine-fed, breech-loading, bolt-action .30-calibre rifle. Also called "Springfield". [First made at the former U.S. Armoury at *Springfield,* Massachusetts.]

spring-form mould (spríng-fawrm) *n.* A round baking tin with a high rim that can be expanded and removed from the base by releasing a clip. Also called "spring form".

spring greens *pl.n.* Young green cabbages picked before their hearts have developed.

spring·haas (spríng-haass) *n.* A nocturnal African rodent, *Pedetes capensis,* resembling a small kangaroo. [Afrikaans, "spring hare".]

spring·halt (spríng-hawlt || -holt) *n.* A **stringhalt** *(see).* [Alteration of STRINGHALT.]

spring·head (spríng-hed) *n.* A source, as of a stream.

spring·house (spríng-howss) *n. Chiefly U.S.* A small room or building constructed over a spring and used to keep food cool.

spring·ing (spríng-ing) *n. Architecture.* A **spring** *(see).*

spring·let (spríng-lət, -lit) *n.* A small spring of water; a rill.

spring-load·ed (spríng-lōdid) *adj.* Secured or returned to position by means of a spring.

spring lock *n.* A lock in which the bolt shoots automatically by means of a spring.

spring onion *n. Chiefly British.* A small, immature onion with a small bulb and long green leaves, usually eaten raw in salads.

spring roll *n. Chiefly British.* A Chinese dish consisting of a savoury filling rolled in thin egg pastry and deep fried. Also *U.S.* "egg roll".

spring·tail (spríng-tayl) *n.* Any of various small wingless insects of the order Collembola, having abdominal appendages that act as springs to catapult them through the air.

spring tide *n.* **1.** The tide generally having the greatest rise and fall, occurring at or shortly after the new moon and full moon of each month, when the Sun, Moon, and Earth are approximately aligned. Compare **neap tide.** **2.** Any flood or rush, as of emotion.

spring·time (spríng-tīm) *n.* **1.** The season of spring. Also called "springtide". **2.** The earliest or most enthusiastic period.

spring·wood (spríng-wŏŏd) *n.* Young, usually soft wood that lies directly beneath the bark and develops in early spring. Compare **summerwood.**

spring·y (spríng-i) *adj.* **-ier, -iest.** Resilient; elastic. **—spring·i·ly** *adv.* **—spring·i·ness** *n.*

sprin·kle (spríngk'l) *v.* **-kled, -kling, -kles.** *—tr.* **1.** To scatter or release (water or sand, for example) in drops or small amounts. **2.** To scatter drops or small amounts upon. **3.** To distribute or intersperse in random fashion. *—intr.* **1.** To scatter small drops or particles of something. **2.** To fall or rain in small or infrequent drops.

~n. **1.** The act or an instance of sprinkling. **2.** A light, sparse rainfall. **3.** A small amount; a sprinkling. [Middle English *sprenklen,* probably from Middle Dutch *sprenkelen.*]

sprin·kler (spríngklər) *n.* One that sprinkles; specifically: **1.** An outlet on a sprinkler system. **2.** A device, attached to a hose or watering can, for sprinkling water onto grass and other plants.

sprinkler system *n.* A fire-extinguishing system consisting of a network of water pipes equipped to release water, usually automatically, at temperatures above a predetermined limit.

sprin·kling (springkling) *n.* A small amount or quantity, especially when tossed or sparsely distributed.

sprint (sprint) *n.* **1.** A short race run, swum, or the like at top speed. **2.** A short burst of great activity.
~*v.* **sprinted, sprinting, sprints.** —*intr.* To run at top speed. —*tr.* To cover (a specified distance) by sprinting. [Of Scandinavian origin, akin to Swedish dialectal *sprinta,* to jump, akin to Old Norse *spretta,* from Germanic *sprintan* (unattested).] **—sprint·er** *n.*

sprit (sprit) *n.* **1.** A pole extending diagonally across a fore-and-aft sail from the lower part of the mast to the peak of the sail. **2.** A **bowsprit** *(see).* [Middle English *spret(te), spryt(t),* Old English *sprēot,* pole.]

sprite (sprīt) *n.* **1.** A small or elusive supernatural being; an elf or pixie. **2.** Someone resembling a sprite in smallness or delicacy. [Middle English *spr(e)it,* from Old French *esp(i)rit,* from Latin *spīritus,* SPIRIT.]

sprit·sail (sprít-s'l, -sayl) *n.* A sail extended by a sprit.

spritzer (sprít-sər, -zər) *n.* A cold sparkling drink in which soda water has been added to wine or syrup. [German *Spritzer,* splash, dash, from *spritzen* to splash, squirt.]

sprock·et (spróckit) *n.* **1.** A wheel rimmed with toothlike projections to engage the links of a chain in a drive system. Also called "sprocket wheel". **2.** Any one of these projections. **3.** A cylinder with a toothed rim that engages in the perforations in a film to pull it through a camera or projector. [16th century : origin obscure.]

sprog (sprog) *n. British Slang.* **1.** A small child. **2.** A military recruit. [20th century : origin obscure.]

sprout (sprowt) *v.* **sprouted, sprouting, sprouts.** —*intr.* **1.** To begin to grow; give off shoots or buds. **2.** To grow or develop quickly. Often used with *up.* —*tr.* To cause to grow or sprout.
~*n.* **1.** A young plant growth, such as a bud or shoot. **2.** Something resembling or suggestive of a sprout. **3.** *Plural.* A vegetable, **Brussels sprouts** *(see).* **4.** *Informal.* A young person. [Middle English *spruten,* Old English *sprūtan.*]

sprouting broccoli *n.* See **broccoli.**

spruce[1] (sproōss || sprewss) *n.* **1.** Any of various coniferous evergreen trees of the genus *Picea,* such as the **Norway spruce** *(see),* having needle-like foliage, drooping cones, and soft wood often used for paper pulp. **2.** Any of various similar or related trees. **3.** The wood of any of these trees. [Short for *Spruce fir,* "Prussian fir", from Middle English *Spruce,* alteration of *Pruce,* from Old French, from Medieval Latin *Prussia,* PRUSSIA.]

spruce[2] *adj.* **sprucer, sprucest.** Neat or dapper in appearance.
~*v.* **spruced, sprucing, spruces.** —*tr.* To make spruce; dress neatly. Usually used with *up.* —*intr.* To make oneself spruce. Used with *up.* [Perhaps from *Spruce,* Prussia, Prussian leather (from the fineness of the leather).] **—spruce·ly** *adv.* **—spruce·ness** *n.*

spruce beer *n.* A slightly fermented beverage made with an extract of spruce needles and twigs with sugar or treacle.

sprue[1] (sproō || sprew) *n.* A chronic, chiefly tropical disease characterised by diarrhoea, emaciation, and anaemia, due to deficient absorption of food from the small intestine. [Dutch *spruw,* from Middle Dutch *sprouwe,* akin to Middle Low German *sprūwe*†.]

sprue[2] *n.* **1.** A channel leading to or from a mould. **2.** Metal or plastic that solidifies in a sprue. [19th century : origin obscure.]

spruik (sprŏŏk) *intr.v. Australian Slang.* To address prospective customers, for example, fluently and enticingly. Used especially of salesmen and showmen. [20th century : perhaps akin to Dutch *spreken,* to speak.] **—spruik·er** *n.*

sprung. Past participle and alternative past tense of **spring.**
~*adj.* Supported by springs: *a sprung mattress.*

sprung rhythm *n.* A forcefully accented verse rhythm in which each foot has a stressed syllable followed by an irregular number of unstressed syllables. [Coined by Gerard Manley HOPKINS.]

spry (sprī) *adj.* **sprier** or **spryer, spriest** or **spryest.** Active, vigorous, and healthy: *a spry octogenarian.* See Synonyms at **nimble.** [18th century (dialect and U.S.) : perhaps from Scandinavian, akin to Swedish dialectal *sprygg,* active.] **—spry·ly** *adv.* **—spry·ness** *n.*

spud (spud) *n.* **1.** A sharp tool resembling a spade for rooting or digging out weeds. **2.** *Informal.* A potato.
~*tr.v.* **spudded, spudding, spuds.** **1.** To remove (weeds, for example) with a spud. **2.** To begin drilling (an oil well). [Middle English *spudde*†, short knife.]

spud-bash·ing (spúd-bashing) *n. British Military Slang.* Peeling potatoes, especially as a chore or punishment.

spume (spewm) *n.* Foam or froth, especially on the sea.
~*intr.v.* **spumed, spuming, spumes.** To froth or foam. [Middle English, from Old French *(e)spume,* from Latin *spūma.*] **—spu·mous, spum·y** *adj.*

spu·mo·ne, spu·mo·ni (spoō-mṓ-ni, spoō-) *n., pl.* **-ni** (-nee). An Italian ice cream with layers of different colours or flavours, containing candied fruit or nuts. [Italian, from *spuma,* foam, from Latin *spūma,* SPUME.]

spun. Past tense and past participle of **spin.**

spun glass *n.* **1. Glass fibre** *(see).* **2.** Fine blown glass having delicate, often spiral threading or filigree.

spunk (spungk) *n.* **1.** Touchwood or other tinder. **2.** *Informal.* Spirit; pluck. **3.** *British Vulgar Slang.* Semen. [16th century.]

spunk·y (spúngki) *adj.* **-ier, -iest.** *Informal.* Spirited. **—spunk·i·ly** *adv.* **—spunk·i·ness** *n.*

spun protein *n.* Textured vegetable protein *(see).*

spun silk *n.* A yarn made from short-fibred silk and silk waste, often mixed with cotton.

spun yarn *n.* A lightweight line made of several rope yarns loosely wound together, used for seizings on board ship.

spur (spur) *n.* **1.** Either of a pair of spikes or spiked wheels attached to a rider's heels and used to urge the horse forward. **2.** An incentive or goad; a stimulus. **3.** A spurlike attachment or projection, such as: **a.** A spinelike projection on the leg of some birds. **b.** A climbing iron; a crampon. **c.** A gaff attached to the leg of a gamecock. **d.** A short or stunted branch of a tree. **4.** A lateral ridge projecting from a mountain or mountain range. **5.** An oblique reinforcing prop or stay of timber or masonry. **6.** A branch railway line. Also called "spur track". **7.** *Botany.* A tubular extension of the corolla or calyx of a flower, as in a larkspur. **—on the spur of the moment.** On impulse or without preparation. **—win (one's) spurs.** To gain distinction, especially for the first time.
~*v.* **spurred, spurring, spurs.** —*tr.* **1.** To urge (a horse) on by the use of spurs. **2.** To incite; prompt; stimulate. Often used with *on.* **3.** To put spurs on. —*intr.* To ride quickly, as by spurring a horse. [Middle English *spore, spure,* Old English *spora, spura.*]

spurge (spurj) *n.* Any of various plants of the genus *Euphorbia,* characteristically having milky juice and small flowers that in some species are surrounded by showy bracts. [Middle English, from Old French *(e)spurge,* "purge" (certain species were formerly used as purgatives), from *espurgier,* to purge, from Latin *expurgāre* : *ex-,* away + *purgāre,* to purge, purify.]

spur gear *n.* A gear with teeth radially arrayed on the rim parallel to its axis. Also called "spur wheel".

spurge laurel *n.* A low-growing shrub, *Daphne laureola,* native to southern Europe but widely cultivated for ornament, having glossy evergreen leaves and small yellowish-green flowers.

spu·ri·ous (spéwr-i-əss) *adj.* **1.** Lacking authenticity or validity, especially in essence or origin; not genuine; counterfeit; false. **2.** *Rare.* Illegitimate; bastard. **3.** *Botany.* Similar in appearance but unlike in structure or function. Said of plant parts that superficially resemble other parts. [Late Latin *spurius,* false, from Latin, illegitimate, perhaps from Etruscan; akin to *spurcus,* dirty, impure.] **—spu·ri·ous·ly** *adv.* **—spu·ri·ous·ness** *n.*

spurn (spurn) *v.* **spurned, spurning, spurns.** —*tr.* **1.** To reject or refuse disdainfully; scorn. **2.** *Archaic.* **a.** To kick at disdainfully. **b.** To tread on; trample. —*intr. Archaic.* To refuse something contemptuously. —See Synonyms at **refuse.**
~*n.* **1.** A contemptuous rejection. **2.** *Archaic.* A kick or shove. [Middle English *spurnen, spornen,* Old English *spurnan, spornan.*] **—spurn·er** *n.*

spur-of-the-mo·ment (spúr-əv-t͟hə-mṓmənt) *adj.* Made or occurring without planning or forethought.

spurred (spurd) *adj.* **1.** Wearing spurs. **2.** *Biology.* Having a spur or spurs: *spurred flowers.*

spur·rey (spúrri) *n., pl.* **-reys.** Also **spur·ry** *pl.* **-ries.** Any of several weedy, low-growing plants of the genera *Spergula* or *Spergularia;* especially, *Spergula arvensis,* native to Europe, having whorled leaves and small white flowers. [Dutch *spurrie,* from Middle Dutch *sporie, speurie,* probably from Medieval Latin *spergula.*]

spur·ri·er (spúrri-ər) *n.* A maker of spurs. [Middle English *sporior,* from *spore,* SPUR.]

spurt (spurt) *n.* Also **spirt** (for sense 1). **1.** A sudden and forcible gush or outburst, as of water or emotion. **2.** Any sudden outbreak or short burst of energy or activity.
~*v.* **spurted, spurting, spurts.** Also **spirt, spirted, spirting, spirts** (for sense 1). —*intr.* **1.** To flow suddenly; gush. Often used with *out.* **2.** To make a short burst of effort. —*tr.* To force out in a burst; squirt. [Earlier *spirt, sprit,* to sprout, Middle English *sprutten,* Old English *sprytten.*]

sput·nik (spoŏt-nik, spút-) *n.* Any of the artificial Earth satellites launched by the U.S.S.R., especially *Sputnik 1,* the first artificial satellite to orbit the Earth, launched October 4, 1957. [Russian *sputnik (zemlyi),* "fellow traveller (of Earth)" : *s-,* for *so,* with + *put',* path, way + *-nik,* agent noun suffix.]

sput·ter (spúttər) *v.* **-tered, -tering, -ters.** —*intr.* **1.** To throw out small particles in short bursts, often with spitting sounds. **2.** To make sporadic spitting sounds. **3.** To speak in a hasty or confused fashion; stammer. **4.** *Physics.* To cause the atoms of a solid to be removed from its surface by bombardment with ions in a discharge tube. —*tr.* **1.** To throw out (food particles, for example) in short bursts, often with spitting sounds. **2.** To utter in a hasty or confused fashion. **3.** *Physics.* **a.** To coat (a solid surface) with metal atoms by sputtering. **b.** To coat a solid surface by sputtering.
~*n.* **1.** The act of sputtering. **2.** The sound of sputtering. **3.** The particles that are emitted during sputtering. **4.** Hasty or confused utterances. [Dutch *sputteren* (imitative).] **—sput·ter·er** *n.*

spu·tum (spéw-təm) *n., pl.* **-ta** (-tə). **1.** Saliva spat from the mouth. **2.** Matter, including saliva, mucus from the respiratory tract, and foreign material, coughed up and spat out. [Latin *spūtum,* from *spūtus,* past participle of *spuere,* to spit.]

spy (spī) *n., pl.* **spies.** **1. a.** An agent employed by a state to obtain secretly intelligence relating to its potential or actual enemies at home or abroad. **b.** An agent employed by a business organisation to obtain secretly information relating to its competitors. **2.** One who secretly watches another or others. **3.** The act of watching covertly or secretly.
~*v.* **spied, spying, spies.** —*tr.* **1. a.** To observe (a place or situation) carefully and secretly and gain information. Used with *out:*

spy out the land. **b.** To discover by careful and secret observation. Used with *out.* **2.** To catch sight of; see. *—intr.* **1. a.** To observe secretly and closely. Often used with *on, into,* or *upon.* **b.** To engage in espionage. **2.** To investigate; pry. Used with *into: spying into their activities.* [Middle English *spie,* from Old French *espie,* from *espier,* to spy, watch, from Frankish *spehōn* (unattested).]

spy·glass (spī-glaass || -glass) *n.* A small telescope.

spy·hole (spī-hōl) *n.* A peephole; especially, one set in a front door to permit scrutiny of any callers.

sq. 1. sequence. **2.** square. **3.** the following.

Sq. 1. Squadron. **2.** Square. Used in street names.

Sqn. Ldr. squadron leader.

squab (skwob) *n.* **1.** A young, unfledged pigeon. **2.** A short, fat person. **3.** A soft cushion. **4.** A couch; a sofa.
~adj. **1.** Newly hatched or unfledged. **2.** Short and fat; squat. [17th century : perhaps from Scandinavian, akin to Swedish dialectal *sqvabb*†, fat flesh, soft mass.] **—squab·by** *adj.*

squab·ble (skwóbb'l) *intr.v.* **-bled, -bling, -bles.** To engage in a minor but noisy quarrel; bicker. See Synonyms at **argue.**
~n. A trivial but noisy quarrel. [Imitative, probably from Scandinavian; akin to Swedish dialectal *sqvabbel,* to quarrel (imitative).] **—squab·bler** *n.*

squad (skwod) *n.* **1.** A small group of persons working or acting together. **2.** *Military.* The smallest unit of personnel, used especially as a drill formation. **3.** A group of sportsmen from whom a team is selected. [French *escouade,* variant of *escadre,* from Italian *squadra,* SQUARE.]

squad car *n. U.S.* A **patrol car** *(see).*

squad·dy, squad·die (skwóddi) *n., pl.* **-dies.** *British Slang.* A soldier of the lowest rank. [Alteration (perhaps influenced by SQUAD) of *swaddy,* diminutive of dialect *swad;* soldier, bumpkin, perhaps from Scandinavian; compare Norwegian dialect *svadde,* fellow.]

squad·ron (skwóddrən) *n. Abbr.* **Sq. 1. a.** A group of naval vessels assigned to a particular task. **b.** A basic subdivision of a fleet. **2.** An armoured or cavalry unit consisting of two to four troops, a headquarters, and certain auxiliary units. **3.** An air force unit, subordinate to a wing and consisting of two or more flights. It is the basic tactical unit. [Italian *squadrone,* "square formation (of troops)", from *squadra,* SQUAD.]

squadron leader *n. Abbr.* **Sq. Ldr.** An officer of the Royal Air Force and certain other air forces ranking below a wing commander and above a flight lieutenant.

squa·lene (skwáy-leen) *n.* A natural unsaturated aliphatic hydrocarbon, $C_{30}H_{50}$, found in human sebum and other fatty deposits, that is an intermediate in the biosynthesis of cholesterol. [New Latin *Squalus,* genus of sharks (squalene is found in the liver oil of sharks), from Latin *squalus,* a sea fish + -ENE.]

squal·id (skwóllid) *adj.* **1.** Dirty or wretched in appearance. **2.** Morally repulsive; sordid. —See Synonyms at **dirty.** [Latin *squālidus,* from *squālēre,* to be filthy, from *squālus*†, scabby, filthy.] **—squa·lid·i·ty** (skwo-líddəti), **squal·id·ness** *n.* **—squa·lid·ly** *adv.*

squall (skwawl) *n.* **1. a.** A sudden, brief burst of wind, lasting longer than a gust, and often accompanied by rain. **b.** A sudden increase in wind speed by 8 metres per second (16 knots) or more to at least 11 metres per second (22 knots) and lasting for at least one minute. **2.** *Informal.* A disturbance or commotion. **3.** A loud yell.
~intr.v. **squalled, squalling, squalls.** To scream or cry harshly and loudly. [Probably from Scandinavian, akin to Swedish and Norwegian *skval,* splash, akin to Old Norse *skvala,* SQUEAL.] **—squall·er** *n.* **—squal·ly** *adj.*

squall line *n.* A zone of squalls and other violent changes in weather, marking the replacement of a warm air current by cold air.

squal·or (skwóllər) *n.* The state or quality of being squalid. [Latin, from *squālēre,* to be filthy. See **squalid.**]

squa·ma (skwáy-mə) *n., pl.* **-mae** (-mee). **1.** *Biology.* A scale or scalelike structure. **2.** A thin plate of bone. [Latin *squāma*†, scale.] **—squa·mate** (-mayt) *adj.*

squa·ma·tion (skway-máysh'n, skwə-) *n.* **1.** The condition of being scaly or of forming scales. **2.** An arrangement of scales, as on a fish.

squa·mo·sal (skwə-mṓ-z'l, -s'l) *n.* The squamous part of the temporal bone. [Latin *squāmōsus,* SQUAMOUS.] **—squa·mo·sal** *adj.*

squa·mous (skwáy-məss) *adj.* Also **squa·mose** (-mōz, -mōss). **1.** Covered with, formed of, or resembling scales; scaly. **2.** Of or designating epithelium consisting of flat, scalelike cells. **3.** Of or designating the portion of the temporal bone that forms part of the side of the cranium. [Latin *squāmōsus,* from *squāma*†, scale.] **—squa·mous·ly** *adv.* **—squa·mous·ness** *n.*

squa·mu·lose (skwáymew-lōz, -lōss) *adj.* Having or consisting of minute scales; minutely scaly. Said especially of plants. [New Latin *squāmula,* diminutive of Latin *squāma*†, scale.]

squan·der (skwóndər) *tr.v.* **-dered, -dering, -ders. 1.** To spend wastefully or extravagantly. **2.** *Archaic.* To scatter; disperse.
~n. Rare. Extravagant expenditure; prodigality. [16th century : origin obscure.] **—squan·der·er** *n.* **—squan·der·ing·ly** *adv.*

square (skwair) *n. Abbr.* **sq. 1.** A rectangle having four equal sides and four right angles. **2.** Any object, shape, arrangement, design, or the like having this form, such as: **a.** A square scarf. **b.** Any of the small square spaces constituting the surface of a chessboard. **c.** A military drill area within a barracks. **d.** An open, usually four-sided public area in a town, often having a central garden or grass and trees, sometimes including the surrounding buildings. **e.** The central area of a cricket field, used for the pitches or wickets. **f.** A **mortarboard** *(see).* **3. a.** A T-shaped or L-shaped instrument for drawing or testing right angles. **b.** A **try square** *(see).* **4.** The product of a number or quantity multiplied by itself. **5.** *Archaic.* A standard, rule, or pattern. **6.** *Informal.* One characterised by conventional or old-fashioned attitudes, appearance, or the like. **—back to square one.** *British.* Back to the very beginning, having made no progress. **—on the square. 1.** At right angles. **2.** Honestly and openly. **—out of square.** Not at a precise right angle.
~adj. **squarer, squarest.** *Abbr.* **sq. 1.** Having four equal sides and four right angles. **2.** Forming a right angle. **3. a.** Designating an area equal to a square whose edge is of a specified length: *a square foot.* **b.** Designating a square having edges of a specified length. Used after the noun: *a foot square.* **4.** Being at right angles to something, as: **a.** In cricket, at right angles to the wicket. **b.** Set at right angles to the mast and keel. Said of the yards of a square-rigged ship. **5.** Approximately square or rectangular in cross-section: *a square house.* **6.** Characterised by blocklike solidity or sturdiness. **7.** Honest; direct: *a square answer.* **8.** Just; equitable: *a square deal.* **9.** Orderly; neat. **10.** Paid-up; settled. **11.** *Sports.* Even; tied. **12.** *Informal.* Rigidly conventional or old-fashioned.
~v. **squared, squaring, squares.** *—tr.* **1.** To make square or rectangular in shape. **2.** To test for conformity to a desired plane, straight line, or right angle. **3.** To divide into squares. Often used with *off.* **4.** To bring into conformity or agreement. **5.** To set straight or at right angles: *square one's cap.* **6.** To pay or settle: *square a debt.* **7.** *Sports.* **a.** To even the score of; tie with. **b.** To level (the score, for example). **8.** To multiply (a number or quantity) by itself. **9.** *Informal.* **a.** To bribe. **b.** To secure the assent of or otherwise come to an arrangement with, usually corruptly. **c.** To arrange, usually corruptly; fix. *—intr.* **1.** To be at right angles. **2.** To agree or conform; balance. **3.** To settle a bill or debt. Often used with *up.* **—square away.** To square the yards of a sailing vessel. **—square up** or *chiefly U.S.* **off.** To assume a fighting stance. **—square up to.** To face or confront resolutely.
~adv. **1.** At right angles. **2.** In a square shape. **3.** *Informal.* Solidly. **4.** *Informal.* Directly; straight. **5.** *Informal.* In an honest manner; straightforwardly. [Middle English, from Old French *esquare,* from Vulgar Latin *exquadra* (unattested), from *exquadrāre* (unattested), to square : Latin *ex-* (intensive) + *quadrāre,* to square, from *quadrus,* a square.] **—square·ly** *adv.* **—square·ness** *n.* **—squar·er** *n.* **—squar·ish** *adj.*

square-bash·ing (skwáir-bashing) *n. British Military Slang.* Drill on a barrack square.

square bracket *n.* Either of two symbols, [or]. See **bracket.**

square dance *n.* **1.** A dance in which sets of four couples form squares. **2.** Any of various similar group folk dances. **—square-dance** (skwáir-daanss || -danss) *intr.v.* **—square-danc·er** *n.*

square knot *n. U.S.* A **reef knot** *(see).*

square leg *n.* In cricket: **1.** A fielding position at right angles to the batsman, on the leg side. **2.** A player in this position.

square matrix *n. Mathematics.* A matrix in which there are equal numbers of rows and columns.

square meal *n.* A substantial, satisfying, and nourishing meal.

square measure *n.* A system of units used in measuring area.

square number *n.* A number that is the square of an integer: *1, 4, 9, and 16 are square numbers.*

square rig *n.* A sailing-ship rig with sails of rectangular cut set approximately at right angles to the keel line from horizontal yards. **—square-rigged** (skwáir-rígd) *adj.*

square-rig·ger (skwáir-riggər) *n.* A square-rigged vessel.

square root *n.* A number that when squared gives a specified quantity: *4 is the square root of 16.*

square sail *n.* A four-sided sail bent to a yard set athwart the mast.

square wave *n.* A rectangular-shaped wave form that alternates between two fixed values for equal periods of time.

squar·rose (skwá-rōz, skwó-, -rōss) *adj.* **1.** *Biology.* Having rough or spreading hairs or scalelike projections. **2.** *Botany.* Spreading or curved backwards at the tip: *squarrose bracts.* [Latin *squarrōsus,* alteration (influenced by Latin *squāma,* scale) of *escharōsus* (unattested), scabby, from Greek *eskhara,* hearth, scab, SCAR.]

squash[1] (skwosh || *U.S. also* skwawsh) *v.* **squashed, squashing, squashes.** *—tr.* **1. a.** To beat, squeeze, or flatten to a compressed shape or a pulp; crush. **b.** To press or squeeze in tightly. Often used with *in* or *into.* **2.** To put down or suppress; quash. **3.** To silence (a person), as with crushing words. *—intr.* **1. a.** To be crushed or flattened. **b.** To squeeze in. Used with *in* or *into.* **2.** To move with a squelching sound.
~n. **1.** An act or sound of squashing or the state of being squashed. **2.** A crush; a crowded condition; a press. **3.** *Chiefly British.* A citrus-based soft drink. **4.** A racket game played with a soft rubber ball in a closed wall court between two players. [Alteration of QUASH.] **—squash·er** *n.*

squash[2] *n. U.S.* **1.** Any of various plants of the genus *Cucurbita,* having a marrow-like, fleshy, edible fruit with a hard rind. **2.** The fruit of such a plant, used as a vegetable. [Short for *isquoutersquash,* from Massachuset *askōōtasquash* : *askōt-* (unidentified root) + Proto-Algonquian *aškw-,* plant + *-ash,* inanimate plural ending.]

squash·y (skwóshi || skwáwshi) *adj.* **-ier, -iest. 1.** Easily squashed. **2.** Marshy; boggy. **—squash·i·ly** *adv.* **—squash·i·ness** *n.*

squat (skwot) *v.* **squatted, squatting, squats.** *—intr.* **1.** To crouch close to the ground, with the weight of one's body resting on one's heels or feet, with the knees bent. **2.** To live in an unoccupied dwelling or settle on unoccupied land without legal claim. **3.** *British Informal.* To sit. *—tr.* To put (oneself) in a crouching or squatting

posture.
~*adj.* **squatter, squattest. 1.** Seated in a squatting position. **2.** Short and thick; low and broad.
~*n.* **1.** A squatting or crouching posture. **2.** The act of squatting or crouching. **3.** The place occupied by a squatter. [Middle English *squatten*, to crush, flatten, hence to squat, from Old French *esquatir* : *es-*, from Latin *ex-* (intensive) + *quatir*, to press flat, from Vulgar Latin *coactīre* (unattested), to press together, from Latin *cogere* (past participle *coāctus*), to drive together : *com-*, together + *agere*, to drive.]

squat·ter (skwóttər) *n.* **1.** One who lives in an unoccupied dwelling or settles on unoccupied land without legal claim. **2.** *Australian.* A prosperous farmer, especially a sheep farmer.

squaw (skwaw) *n.* **1.** A North American Indian woman. **2.** *U.S. Slang.* A woman or wife. Often used humorously, and considered offensive. [Massachuset *squa, eshqua*, from Proto-Algonquian *ethkwēwa* (unattested), "woman".]

squawk (skwawk) *v.* **squawked, squawking, squawks.** —*intr.* **1.** To utter a harsh scream; screech. **2.** *Informal.* To make a loud or angry protest. —*tr.* To utter with or as if with a squawk.
~*n.* **1.** A loud screech; a squall. **2.** *Informal.* A loud or insistent protest. [Imitative.] **—squawk·er** *n.*

squeak (skweek) *n.* **1.** A brief, thin, shrill cry or sound, such as that made by a mouse or an unoiled metal hinge. **2.** *Informal.* An escape. Used chiefly in the phrases *a close squeak* or *a narrow squeak.*
~*v.* **squeaked, squeaking, squeaks.** —*intr.* **1.** To utter or make a squeak. **2.** To pass or win by a slight margin. Used with *through* or *by.* **3.** *Informal.* To turn informer. —*tr.* To utter in a squeaky voice. [Middle English *squeken* (imitative); akin to Old Norse *skvakka*, to croak.] **—squeak·er** *n.*

squeak·y (skwéeki) *adj.* **-ier, -iest. 1.** Characterised by squeaking tones: *a squeaky voice.* **2.** Tending to squeak: *squeaky shoes.* **—squeak·i·ly** *adv.* **—squeak·i·ness** *n.*

squeal (skweel) *n.* **1.** A shrill, high-pitched cry, as of fear or surprise. **2.** A similar high-pitched sound, such as that made by tyres against a road surface when a car brakes suddenly.
~*v.* **squealed, squealing, squeals.** —*intr.* **1.** To utter or produce a squeal. **2.** *Slang.* To betray a friend or a secret; turn informer. **3.** *Informal.* To complain or protest shrilly. —*tr.* To utter or produce with a squeal. [Middle English *squelen* (imitative); akin to Old Norse *skvala*, to shriek.] **—squeal·er** *n.*

squeam·ish (skwéemish) *adj.* **1. a.** Easily nauseated or sickened. **b.** Nauseated: *felt squeamish at the sight of blood.* **2.** Easily shocked or disgusted. **3.** Excessively fastidious or scrupulous. [Middle English *squaymisch*, variant of *squaymous*, from Anglo-French *escoymos*†.] **—squeam·ish·ly** *adv.* **—squeam·ish·ness** *n.*

squee·gee (skwée-jée, -jee) *n.* **1.** A T-shaped implement having a crosspiece edged with rubber or leather, used to remove water from a surface such as a window. **2.** A similar implement or a rubber roller used in printing and photography.
~*tr.v.* **squeegeed, -geeing, -gees.** To wipe or smooth with a squeegee. [Probably from *squeege*, perhaps intensive variant of SQUEEZE.]

squeeze (skweez) *v.* **squeezed, squeezing, squeezes.** —*tr.* **1. a.** To press hard upon or together; compress. **b.** To press (someone's hand or arm) gently, as in affection: *squeezed her hand.* **2.** To exert pressure on, as by way of extracting liquid: *squeeze an orange.* **3. a.** To extract by applying pressure: *squeeze juice from a lemon.* **b.** To extract or produce under pressure or with difficulty. Often used with *out*: *squeezed a confession out of the suspects.* **4.** To extract by dishonest means; extort. **5.** To obtain room or passage for as by pushing or exerting pressure; cram; force: *squeezed himself into the crowded lift.* **6.** To oppress with exacting or exorbitant demands. **7.** To find time or space for; manage to fit in. Often used with *in*: *squeezed in two clients before lunch.* **8.** *Bridge.* To force (an opponent) to use a potentially winning card in a trick he cannot take. —*intr.* **1.** To give way under pressure. **2.** To exert pressure. **3.** To force one's way, as through a crowd.
~*n.* **1.** An act or instance of squeezing. **2. a.** A handclasp. **b.** A brief embrace. **c.** *Slang.* Someone's sexual partner or lover. **3.** A crowded situation; a crush: *a tight squeeze.* **4.** A small amount squeezed out of something: *a squeeze of lemon juice.* **5.** Pressure exerted to obtain some concession or goal. **6.** Financial or economic pressure, as imposed by a government, resulting in a restriction on credit, pay awards, dividends, or the like. **7.** *Informal.* An act of blackmailing: *put the squeeze on his old employer.* **8.** A forced discard of a potentially winning card in bridge. [Earlier *squease*, intensive form of *quease*, to press. Middle English *queysen*, Old English *cwȳsan*.] **—squeez·er** *n.*

squeeze·box (skwéez-boks) *n. Informal.* An accordion.

squelch (skwelch) *v.* **squelched, squelching, squelches.** —*intr.* To make or move with a splashing, squashing, or sucking sound. —*tr.* **1.** To crush by or as if by trampling; suppress; squash. **2.** *Informal.* To put down or silence, as with a crushing remark.
~*n.* **1.** An act of squelching. **2.** A sound made by squelching. **3.** An electric circuit that cuts off a radio receiver when the signal is too weak for reception of anything but noise. [Imitative.] **—squelch·er** *n.* **—squelch·y** *adj.*

squib (skwib) *n.* **1.** A small firework that hisses when lit, and eventually goes off with a bang. **2.** A brief, satirical piece of writing such as a lampoon. **3.** *Chiefly Australian Informal.* A coward.
~*v.* **squibbed, squibbing, squibs.** —*intr.* **1.** To write or publish a squib. **2.** To let off a squib. —*tr.* **1.** To attack or lampoon with squibs. **2.** *Chiefly Australian Informal.* To act like a coward. [Probably imitative.]

squid (skwid) *n., pl.* **squids** or collectively **squid.** Any of various marine cephalopod molluscs of the genera *Loligo, Rossia,* and related genera, having a usually elongated body, ten arms surrounding the mouth, a vestigial internal shell, and a pair of triangular or rounded fins. Compare **octopus.**
~*intr.v.* **squidded, squidding, squids.** To fish with squid as bait. [17th century : origin obscure.]

squif·fy (skwiffi) *adj. British Informal.* Slightly drunk or intoxicated. [19th century : origin obscure.]

squig·gle (skwígg'l) *n.* A small wiggly mark or scrawl.
~*intr.v.* **squiggled, -gling, -gles. 1.** To form a squiggle or squiggles. **2.** To squirm and wriggle. [Imitative.] **—squig·gly** *adj.*

squill (skwil) *n.* **1.** Any of several bulbous plants of the genus *Scilla*, native to Eurasia, having narrow leaves and bell-shaped blue, white, or pink flowers. Also called "scilla". Compare **sea onion. 2.** The dried inner scales of the bulbs of the sea onion, used as rat poison and formerly as a cardiac stimulant and expectorant. [Middle English, from Latin *squilla, scilla*, from Greek *skilla*†.]

squil·la (skwíl-ə) *n., pl.* **-las** or **-lae** (-ee). Any of various burrowing marine crustaceans of the order Stomatopoda, and especially of the genus *Squilla*, having a pair of jointed grasping appendages. Also called "mantis shrimp". [New Latin *Squilla*, type genus, from Latin *squilla*†, shrimp, prawn.]

squinch (skwinch) *n.* A quarter-spherical segment of masonry vaulting or corbelling thrown across the upper inside corners of a square tower as the transition to a circular or octagonal superstructure. [Variant of obsolete *scunch*, short for SCUNCHEON.]

squint (skwint) *v.* **squinted, squinting, squints.** —*intr.* **1.** To look with the eyes screwed up or almost closed, as from concentrating, close observation, or very bright light. **2.** To look or glance sideways or obliquely. Usually used with *towards* or *at.* **3.** To cross one's eyes or make them turn from looking in a parallel direction, as when attempting to look at one's nose. **4.** To suffer from **strabismus** *(see).* —*tr.* To cause (one's eyes) to squint.
~*n.* **1.** An instance of squinting. **2.** An inclination; a tendency. **3. Strabismus** *(see).* **4.** *British Informal.* A glance, view, or look: *Take a squint at it.* **5.** A **hagioscope** *(see).*
~*adj.* **1.** Not straight; oblique; askew. **2.** Affected with strabismus. [Short for ASQUINT.] **—squint·er** *n.*

squint-eyed (skwínt-īd) *adj.* **1.** Having strabismus. **2.** With squinting eyes. **3.** Looking askance.

squire (skwīr) *n.* **1.** An English country gentleman, especially one who is the chief landowner in a particular district. **2.** Formerly, a young nobleman attendant upon and ranked next below a knight in the feudal hierarchy. **3.** *U.S.* A judge or other local dignitary. **4.** A man who attends or escorts a woman. **5.** *British.* Used as an informal or familiar term of address for a man.
~*tr.v.* **squired, squiring, squires.** To attend as a squire or escort. [Middle English *squier, esquier*, from Old French *esquier, escuier*, "shield-bearer", from Late Latin *scūtārius*, from Latin *scūtum*, a shield.]

squire·ar·chy, squir·ar·chy (skwír-aarki) *n., pl.* **-chies.** Squires collectively; especially, the section of society made up of landed proprietors having considerable political power. **—squire·arch** *n.* **—squire·arch·al** (-árk'l), **squire·arch·i·cal** (-árkik'l) *adj.*

squireen (skwīréen) *n.* A minor member of the Irish landed gentry.

squirm (skwurm) *intr.v.* **squirmed, squirming, squirms. 1.** To twist about in a wriggling motion; writhe. **2.** To feel or show signs of humiliation or embarrassment.
~*n.* An act of squirming or a squirming movement; a wriggle. [Perhaps imitative (associated with WORM.] **—squirm·er** *n.* **—squirm·y** *adj.*

squir·rel (skwírrəl || *U.S.* skwúrrəl, skwurl) *n.* **1.** Any of various arboreal rodents of the genus *Sciurus* and related genera, usually with grey or reddish-brown fur and a long, flexible, bushy tail. See **grey squirrel, red squirrel. 2.** Any of various related animals of the family Sciuridae, such as the **ground squirrel** or the **flying squirrel** *(both of which see).* **3.** The fur of a squirrel. Also used adjectivally: *a squirrel coat.* **4.** A coat, jacket, or wrap made from the fur of a squirrel. [Middle English *squyrel*, from Anglo-French *esquirel*, from Vulgar Latin *scūriōlus* (unattested), diminutive of *scūrius* (unattested), variant of Latin *sciūrus*, squirrel, from Greek *skiouros*, "shadow-tail" : *skia*, shadow + *oura*, tail.]

squirrel cage *n.* **1.** A cage consisting of a number of bars fitted to the circumference of circular end plates. The cage can be mounted to enable it to rotate as a small animal inside the cage runs in a direction perpendicular to its axis. **2.** The rotor of an induction motor *(a squirrel-cage motor)* having copper bars arranged in the shape of a squirrel cage. **3.** An electric fan with long narrow blades arranged like the bars in a squirrel cage.

squir·rel·fish (skwírrəl-fish || *U.S.* skwúrrəl-, skwúrl-) *n., pl.* **-fishes** or collectively **squirrelfish.** Any of various fishes of the genus *Holocentrus* and related genera, of warm marine waters, having large eyes and a usually reddish body.

squirrel monkey *n.* Either of two tropical American monkeys, *Saimiri sciureus* or *S. örstedii*, having short, thick fur and a long, nonprehensile tail.

squir·rel-tail grass (skwírrəl-tayl || *U.S.* skwúrrəl-, skwúrl-) *n.* A European grass, *Hordeum marinum*, that grows in salt marshes and has bushy spikelets.

squirt (skwurt) *v.* **squirted, squirting, squirts.** —*intr.* **1.** To be ejected in a thin swift stream. Used of a liquid. **2.** To eject liquid in a thin swift stream. —*tr.* **1.** To eject (liquid) in a thin swift stream. **2.** To soak or wet with liquid so ejected.

~*n.* **1.** The act of squirting. **2.** A device, such as a syringe, used to squirt. **3.** A squirted stream of liquid. **4.** *Informal.* **a.** An insignificant but arrogant or bumptious person. **b.** A short or puny person. [Middle English *squirten, swirten,* of Low German origin; akin to Low German *swirtjen* (imitative).] —**squirt·er** *n.*

squirt·ing cucumber (skwúrting) *n.* A hairy vine, *Ecballium elaterium,* of the Mediterranean region, having fruit that discharges its seeds and juice explosively when ripe.

squish (skwish) *v.* **squished, squishing, squishes.** *Informal.* —*tr.* To squash or compress with a squish. —*intr.* To emit or move with a squish.

~*n.* A squashy sound, as of mud being compressed. [Variant of SQUASH.] —**squish·y** *adj.*

squit (skwit) *n. British Slang.* A small insignificant person; a squirt. —**the squits** or **squitters.** *British Slang.* Diarrhoea. [Dialectal variant of SQUIRT (noun and verb).]

Sr The symbol for the element strontium.

Sr. **1.** senior (after a surname). **2.** señor. **3.** sister (religious).

S.R.C. Science Research Council (in Britain).

Sri Lan·ka (srée lángkə, sri), **Democratic Socialist Republic of.** Formerly **Cey·lon** (si-lón, sə-). Island republic in the Indian Ocean, lying off southeastern India. Its central highlands are surrounded by coastal lowlands and swamps. With few natural resources apart from its fertile land, Sri Lanka is heavily dependent on the export of tropical products, especially tea, rubber, and coconuts. Rice is the chief import. Some 72 per cent of the inhabitants are Buddhist Sinhalese and 21 per cent Hindu Tamils of southern Indian stock, and conflict between them has recurred in recent years. In 1987 Indian army forces were called in to help defeat militant Tamil separatists, with whom a cease-fire was agreed in 1989; but violence later resumed. The island's spices attracted the Arabs (12th and 13th centuries), and Portuguese, Dutch (1658), and British, who conquered the island (1796–1815) and made it a colony (1802). Ceylon gained independence (1948) and became the Republic of Sri Lanka (1972). A new constitution was adopted in 1978. Area, 65 610 square kilometres (25,325 square miles). Population 18,300,000. Capital, Colombo.

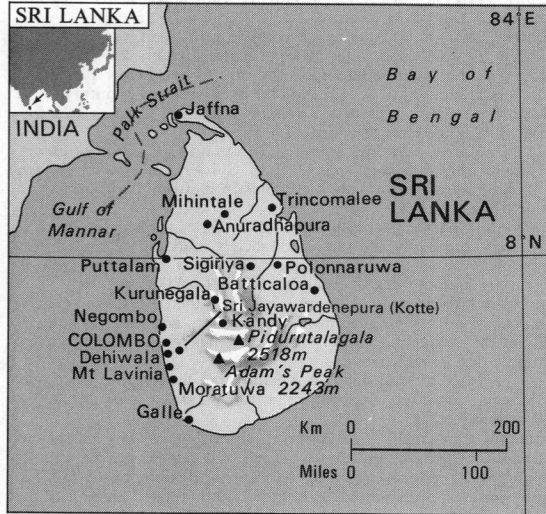

Sri·na·gar (sri-núggər, sírri-). Also **Ser·i·na·gar** (səri-). Capital of Jammu and Kashmir, northwest India. The city is noted for its mosques, gardens, palaces, fort, and its many canals.

SRN. State Registered Nurse (in Britain).

sRNA *n.* **Transfer RNA** *(see).*

S.R.O. **1.** *British.* Statutory Rules and Orders. **2.** *U.S.* standing room only.

Srta. señorita.

ss scilicet.

SS **1.** Schutzstaffel: an elite military section of the Nazi party whose functions included the policing of the rest of the German army and the protecting of Hitler's person. **2.** steamship. **3.** saints.

S.S. **1.** steamship. **2.** social security. **3.** Sunday school.

S.S.C. Solicitor to the Supreme Court (in Scotland).

SSE south-southeast.

SSM surface-to-surface missile.

ssp. subspecies.

S.S.R. Soviet Socialist Republic.

SSRI *n.* Selective Serotonin Re-Uptake Inhibitor: a type of antidepressant (such as Prozac) that is claimed to maintain brain serotonin levels by inhibiting the action of an enzyme which normally breaks serotonin down, and that is also claimed to have

few other effects on the body.

S.S.R.C. Social Science Research Council (in Britain).

SSSI Site of Special Scientific Interest.

SST supersonic transport.

SSW south-southwest.

st. **1.** stanza. **2.** statute. **3.** stet. **4.** stitch. **5.** stone. **6.** street. **7.** stumped; stumped by (in cricket).

-st. Variant of -est (verb inflection).

St. **1.** saint. **2.** statute. **3.** strait. **4.** street.

stab (stab) *v.* **stabbed, stabbing, stabs.** —*tr.* **1.** To pierce or wound with or as if with a pointed weapon. **2.** To plunge (a weapon or instrument) into something. —*intr.* **1.** To lunge with or as if with a pointed weapon. Often used with *at.* **2.** To inflict a wound in this way.

~*n.* **1.** A thrust made with a pointed instrument or weapon. **2. a.** A wound inflicted by stabbing. **b.** A sharp, localised pain; a pang. **3.** *Informal.* An attempt; a try; an effort: *had a stab at skating.* —**a stab in the back.** A treacherous attack; a betrayal. [Middle English *stabbe,* wound by stabbing, obscurely related to dialectal *stob,* to stab, perhaps from Middle English *stob,* stake, stick, variant of STUB.] —**stab·ber** *n.*

Sta·bat Ma·ter (stáa-bat máatər, -bət) *n.* **1.** A medieval Latin hymn on the sorrows of the Virgin Mary at the Crucifixion. **2.** A musical setting for this hymn. [Latin, "the mother was standing" (opening words of the hymn).]

sta·bile (stáy-bīl ‖ -b'l, -beel) *adj.* Immobile; stable; unchangeable. ~*n.* An abstract sculpture, usually of sheet metal, with no moving parts. [Latin *stabilis,* STABLE.]

sta·bi·lise, sta·bi·lize (stáy-bi-līz, stá-, -bə-) *v.* **-lised, -lising, -lises.** —*tr.* **1.** To make stable. **2.** To maintain the stability of. —*intr.* To become stable. —**sta·bi·li·sa·tion** (-lī-záysh'n ‖ *U.S.* -li-) *n.*

sta·bi·lis·er (stáy-bi-līzzər, stá-, -bə-) *n.* **1.** One that stabilises. **2.** *Nautical.* A device in a ship or boat, such as a gyroscopically controlled fin, used to prevent excessive rolling. **3.** *Aeronautics.* Any aerofoil used to stabilise an aircraft in flight. **4.** *Chemistry.* A substance that renders or maintains a solution, mixture, suspension, or state resistant to chemical change.

sta·bil·i·ty (stə-bílləti) *n., pl.* **-ties.** **1.** The condition or quality of being stable, as: **a.** Resistance to sudden change, dislodgment, or overthrow. **b.** Constancy of character, emotional state, or purpose; steadfastness. **c.** Reliability; dependability. **2.** The ability of an object, such as a ship or an aircraft, to maintain equilibrium or resume its original position after displacement by, for example, the sea or strong winds. **3.** A vow committing a Benedictine monk to one monastery for life.

stab kick *n.* In Australian Rules football, a short, low kick aimed at passing the ball to a team-mate or covering ground quickly.

sta·ble¹ (stáyb'l) *adj.* **-bler, -blest.** **1. a.** Resistant to sudden change of position or condition; not liable to change or fluctuation: *a stable personality; a stable economy.* **b.** Maintaining equilibrium; self-restoring. **2.** *Physics.* Having no known mode of decay; indefinitely long-lived. Said of certain elementary particles. **3.** Lasting or likely to last for a long time. **4.** *Chemistry.* Not easily decomposed or otherwise modified chemically. **5.** Consistently dependable or reliable. [Middle English, from Old French *estable,* from Latin *stabilis,* standing firm.] —**sta·ble·ness** *n.* —**sta·bly** *adv.*

sta·ble² *n.* **1. a.** A building for the shelter and feeding of domestic animals, especially horses and cattle. **b.** All of the racehorses belonging to a single owner or racing establishment. **2. a.** All of the racehorses belonging to a single owner or racing establishment. **b.** The personnel employed to look after and train such a collection of racehorses. **3.** Any source of common ownership, production, training, management, or the like: *boxers from the same stable.*

~*v.* **stabled, stabling, stables.** —*tr.* To put or keep (an animal) in a stable. —*intr.* To live or be kept in a stable. [Middle English, from Old French *estable,* from Latin *stabulum,* "standing place", enclosure, stable.]

sta·ble·boy (stáyb'l-boy) *n.* A man or boy who is employed in a stable to look after horses. Also called "stableman", "stablelad".

stable door *n.* A door divided in half horizontally so that either part may be left open or closed. Also *U.S.* "Dutch door".

stable fly *n.* A fly, *Stomoxys calcitrans,* that sucks the blood of humans and domestic animals.

sta·ble·mate (stáyb'l-mayt) *n.* **1.** Any of a number of horses belonging to the same stable. **2.** *Informal.* Any of a group of people who share a common experience, such as residence in a school or college.

sta·bling (stáybling) *n.* **1.** Stables collectively. **2.** Accommodation in a stable for animals.

stablish. *Archaic.* Variant of **establish.**

stac·ca·to (stə-káa-tō) *adj.* **1.** *Abbr.* **stacc.** Designating music performed with a crisp, sharp attack to simulate rests between successive notes. Often used as a direction. **2.** Composed of abrupt, distinct, emphatic parts or sounds: *staccato machine-gun fire.*

~*n., pl.* **staccatos** or **-ti** (-tee). **1.** A staccato passage or movement. **2.** An abrupt, staccato manner or sound. [Italian, past participle of *(di)staccare,* to detach, from Old French *destach(i)er.* See **detach.**] —**stac·ca·to** *adv.*

stack (stak) *n.* **1.** A large, usually conical pile of straw or fodder arranged for outdoor storage. **2.** Any orderly pile, especially one arranged in layers. **3.** A group of three or more unslung rifles, supporting each other with their butts on the ground and forming a cone. **4.** See **chimney-stack, smokestack. 5.** A vertical exhaust pipe, as on a ship or locomotive. **6.** Several rows of bookshelves

forming one structure; a bookcase. **7.** *Usually plural.* The area of a library, usually inaccessible to the public, in which books are stored on shelves. **8.** An English measure of coal or cut wood, equal to 3.06 cubic metres (108 cubic feet). **9.** An arrangement of aircraft circling an airport at prescribed levels, awaiting instructions to land. **10.** A free-standing column of rock in the sea that has been separated from the coast by erosion. **11.** *Computing.* A temporary storage area in a computer memory. **12.** *Often plural. Informal.* A large amount or quantity: *stacks of work to get through.*
~*v.* **stacked, stacking, stacks.** —*tr.* **1.** To arrange in a stack; pile. **2.** To load with stacks of some material. **3.** To cheat by prearranging the order of (playing cards); rig. **4.** To direct (two or more aircraft) to circle at different heights above an airport while waiting to land. —*intr.* To circle an airport in a stack. Used of aircraft. [Middle English *stak, sta(ke),* from Old Norse *stakkr,* haystack, from Germanic.] **—stack·er** *n.*

stac·te (sták-tee) *n.* A spice used by the ancient Jews in making incense. Exodus 30:34. [Latin *stactē,* from Greek *staktē,* from the feminine of *staktos,* oozing, distilling, from *stazein,* to ooze.]

stad·dle (stádd'l) *n.* A foundation or supporting framework; especially, a stone platform upon which hay or straw is stacked to protect it from vermin. [Middle English *stathel,* Old English *stathol.*]

stad·hold·er (stád-hōldər) *n.* Also **stadt·hold·er** (stát-). **1.** Formerly, a governor or viceroy in a province of the Netherlands. **2.** Formerly, the chief magistrate of the United Provinces of the Netherlands. [Partial translation of Dutch *stadhouder,* translation of Latin *locum tenens,* "(one) holding the place (of another)," lieutenant : *stad,* place, from Middle Dutch *stad, stat* + *houder,* holder.] **—stad·hold·er·ate** (-ət, -it, -ayt) *n.*

stad·i·a system (stáydi-ə) *n.* A method of surveying in which distances are determined at one pointing only of the telescopic instrument, this having two parallel lines, *stadia hairs,* used to intercept intervals on a calibrated rod with bold graduation marks, a *stadia rod.* Also called "stadia tacheometry". [Italian, probably from Latin, plural of STADIUM (measure of length) + SYSTEM.]

sta·di·um (stáydi-əm) *n., pl.* **-dia** (-ə) or **-diums** (for sense 3). **1.** In ancient Greece, a course on which races were held, usually semicircular and having tiers of seats for spectators. **2.** An ancient Greek measure of distance, based on the length of such a course and probably equal to about 185 metres (607 feet). **3.** A large, often unroofed structure in which sporting events are held. **4.** A stage in the progress of something, such as a disease. [Middle English, measure of distance, from Latin, from Greek *stadion,* alteration of *spadion,* racetrack (particularly the racetrack of this length at Olympia), from *span,* to draw, pull. See **spasm.**]

staff[1] (staaf || staf) *n., pl.* **staffs** (except sense 4) or **staves** (stayvz) (except sense 3). **1. a.** A stick or cane carried as an aid or support in walking or climbing. **b.** A thick stick used as a weapon; a cudgel. **c.** A pole upon which a flag is displayed. **d.** A rod, baton, or the like carried as a symbol of authority. **2.** A rule or similar graduated stick used for testing or measuring, as in surveying. **3. a.** A group of assistants responsible to a manager or other person of authority. **b.** A group of military officers who serve a commanding officer but do not participate in combat and have no authority to command. **c.** The personnel who are employed to perform a specified job or task: *the nursing staff of a hospital.* **d.** The employees of a company, institution, or the like. **4.** *Music.* The set of horizontal lines and their intermediate spaces upon which notes are written or printed. In this sense, also called "stave". **5.** Figuratively, anything that is a staple or support: *the staff of my old age.*
~*tr.v.* **staffed, staffing, staffs.** To provide with a staff of employees. [Middle English *staf,* Old English *stæf,* stick, rod.]

staff[2] *n.* A building material that resembles stucco, composed of plaster of Paris and fibre and used especially as a wall covering over the skeleton of temporary buildings. [Probably from German *staffieren,* to dress, trim, adorn, from Middle Low German *stafferen, stofferen,* from Old French *estoffer,* to STUFF.]

staff college *n.* In Britain, a college for training staff, especially one used for training military officers.

staff nurse *n.* A trained nurse in a hospital who ranks immediately below a ward sister.

staff officer *n.* A commissioned military officer who holds a position on the staff of a commander.

Staf·ford (stáffərd). County town of Staffordshire, in central England, lying on the river Sow above its confluence with the Trent. It has long been a shoemaking centre, but today electrical goods and engineering are more important industries.

Staf·ford·shire (stáffərd-shər, -sheer). County in central England. The county town is Stafford and the largest city, Stoke-on-Trent. The county has important industrial areas, with the famous Potteries district in the north.

Staffordshire bull terrier *n.* A dog of a breed developed in England, having a short, variously coloured coat, a stocky body, and widely set forelegs. Also called "Staffordshire terrier".

staff sergeant *n.* **1.** In Britain, a noncommissioned officer of the army who is the highest-ranking sergeant. **2.** In the United States, a noncommissioned officer of the rank above a sergeant and below a sergeant first class.

stag (stag) *n.* **1.** The adult male of various deer, especially the red deer. **2.** An animal, especially a pig, castrated after reaching sexual maturity. **3.** *U.S.* A man who attends a social affair without escorting a woman. **4.** *Finance.* In Britain, one who buys shares of new issue so as to make a quick profit by an immediate resale.
~*adj.* **1.** For or attended by men only: *a stag night.* **2.** *Informal.* Pornographic: *stag films.* [Middle English *stag(ge),* Old English *stagga.*]

stag beetle *n.* Any of numerous large beetles of the family Lucanidae, having long, powerful, antler-like mandibles.

stage (stayj) *n.* **1.** Any raised and level floor or platform. **2. a.** The raised platform upon which theatrical performances are presented. **b.** Any area in which actors perform. **c.** The acting profession or the world of theatre. Preceded by *the.* **3.** The scene or setting of an event or series of events: *Marston Moor was the stage for a famous Royalist defeat.* **4.** A platform on a microscope on which slides to be viewed are mounted. **5.** A workmen's scaffold. **6.** *British.* A stopping place on a bus route that marks a division of the route for which a fixed fare is charged. Also called "fare stage". **7.** The distance between stopping places on a journey; a leg of a journey: *proceeded by easy stages.* **8.** A stagecoach. **9.** *Chiefly U.S.* A level or storey of a building; a floor. **10.** *U.S.* The height of the surface of a river or other fluctuating body of water in relation to some datum: *at flood stage.* **11. a.** A level, degree, or period of time in the course of a process; a step in development: *a larval stage.* **b.** A moment or point in the course of an action or series of events: *At this early stage it is hard to see who will win.* **c.** *N.Z.* Each year of study in a particular university subject. **12.** *Aerospace.* One of two or more successive propulsion units of a rocket vehicle that fires after the preceding one has been jettisoned. See **multistage rocket.** **13.** *Geology.* A subdivision of a series representing rock formed during an age. **14.** *Electronics.* An element or group of elements in a complex arrangement of parts; especially, a single tube or transistor and its accessory components in an amplifier. **—hold the stage.** To dominate a social occasion or gathering. **—set the stage for.** To prepare or pave the way for.
~*v.* **staged, staging, stages.** —*tr.* **1. a.** To exhibit, present, or perform on or as if on a stage: *stage a boxing match.* **b.** To produce or direct (a theatrical performance). **2.** To arrange and carry out: *stage an invasion.* —*intr.* To be adaptable to or suitable for theatrical presentation. [Middle English, from Old French *estage,* from Vulgar Latin *staticum* (unattested), "standing place", position, from Latin *stāre,* to stand.]

stage business *n.* In the theatre, **business** *(see).*

stage·coach (stáyj-kōch) *n.* A four-wheeled horse-drawn vehicle formerly used to transport mail, parcels, and passengers.

stage·craft (stáyj-kraaft || -kraft) *n.* The practice of or skill in theatrical techniques such as directing, writing, or producing.

stage direction *n.* An instruction in the text of a play that prescribes how a certain part of the play should be acted or presented.

stage door *n.* A door at the back or side of a theatre admitting the actors, technicians, and other staff.

stage effect *n.* A special effect used on stage to simulate, by means of taped sounds and lighting, conditions such as thunder or wind.

stage fright *n.* Acute fear or nervousness felt by a person at the prospect of or while performing before an audience.

stage·hand (stáyj-hand) *n.* A person employed in a theatre to shift scenery, adjust lighting, or the like.

stage left *n.* The area of the stage to the left of a centrally placed actor facing the audience.

stage-man·age (stáyj-mánnij || -mannij) *tr.v.* **-aged, -aging, -ages.** **1.** To serve as overall supervisor of the stage and actors for (a theatrical production). **2.** To manipulate or contrive from behind the scenes. **—stage manager** *n.* **—stage management** *n.*

stag·er (stáyjər) *n.* One who possesses the wisdom of long experience: *an old stager.* [STAGE (of theatre) + -ER.]

stage right *n.* The area of the stage to the right of a centrally placed actor facing the audience.

stage-struck (stáyj-struk) *adj.* Enthralled with the stage or with hopes of becoming an actor.

stage whisper *n.* **1.** The conventional whisper of an actor, intended to be heard by the audience. **2.** Any whisper intended to be overheard.

stagey. Variant of **stagy.**

stag·fla·tion (stág-fláysh'n) *n. Economics.* A condition in which a high rate of price and wage inflation is coupled with stagnant consumer demand and high unemployment. [*Stag*nation + in*flation.*] **—stag·fla·tion·ar·y** (-ri, -əri || -erri) *adj.*

stag·ger (stággər) *v.* **-gered, -gering, -gers.** —*intr.* **1.** To move or stand unsteadily, as if under a great weight; totter. **2.** To lose strength or confidence; waver. —*tr.* **1.** To cause to totter, sway, or reel. **2. a.** To cause to lose confidence, have doubts, or hesitate. **b.** To overwhelm with emotion or surprise. **3.** To place regularly, in oblique lines, on or as if on alternating sides of a middle line; set in a zigzag row or rows: *theatre seats staggered for clear viewing.* **4.** To arrange in alternating or overlapping time periods: *Examinations were staggered to prevent congestion of the hall.*
~*n.* **1.** The act of staggering; a tottering, swaying, or reeling motion. **2.** A staggered pattern, arrangement, or order. [Earlier (now dialect) *stacker,* Middle English *stakeren,* from Old Norse *stakra,* frequentative of *staka,* to push, cause to stumble.] **—stag·ger·er** *n.*

stag·ger·ing (stággəring) *adj.* Astonishing; amazing: *got through a staggering amount of work.* **—stag·ger·ing·ly** *adv.*

stag·gers (stággərz) *n. Usually used with a singular verb.* **1.** Any of various diseases marked by vertigo, confusion, and weakness. **2.** Any of various diseases of the nervous system in animals; especially, a cerebrospinal disease in horses, in which the animal loses coordination, staggers, and often falls. In this sense, also called "blind staggers".

stag·horn fern (stág-hawrn) *n.* Any of several tropical epiphytic ferns of the genus *Platycerium*, having large divided fronds that resemble antlers.

stag·hound (stág-hownd) *n.* A large hound used to hunt deer.

stag·ing (stáyjing) *n.* 1. A temporary platform; a scaffold. 2. a. The business of running stagecoaches as an enterprise. b. Travel by stagecoach. 3. a. The process of producing and directing a dramatic work. b. A particular production of a dramatic work. 4. The act of jettisoning a stage of a multistage rocket.

staging area *n.* A place where troops and equipment are assembled before moving out on a mission or other military operation.

staging post *n.* A place used to rest or refuel on a long journey such as an aeroplane flight.

stag·nant (stág-nənt) *adj.* 1. Not moving or flowing; without a current; motionless. 2. Foul from standing still; polluted; stale. 3. a. Lacking liveliness or briskness; inactive; sluggish. b. Lacking growth; not developing. [Latin *stagnāns* (stem *stagnant-*), present participle of *stagnāre*, to be stagnant, from *stagnum*, pond, swamp.] —**stag·nan·cy** *n.* —**stag·nant·ly** *adv.*

stag·nate (stag-náyt || stág-nayt) *intr.v.* **-nated, -nating, -nates.** To be or become stagnant. [Latin *stagnāre*. See **stagnant.**] —**stag·na·tion** (-náysh'n) *n.*

stag party *n.* A party for men only, held especially by a prospective bridegroom a short time before his wedding. Compare **hen party.**

stag·y, stage·y (stáyji) *adj.* **-ier, -iest.** Having a theatrical character or quality; especially, artificial and affected. —**stag·i·ly** *adv.* —**stag·i·ness** *n.*

staid (stayd) *adj.* 1. Steady and reserved in style, manner, or behaviour; sober. 2. *Rare.* Fixed; permanent. —See Synonyms at **serious.** [From *staid,* obsolete past participle of STAY.] —**staid·ly** *adv.* —**staid·ness** *n.*

stain (stayn) *v.* **stained, staining, stains.** —*tr.* 1. To discolour, soil, or spot. 2. To bring into disrepute; taint; tarnish. 3. To colour (glass, for example) with a coat of penetrating liquid dye or tint. 4. To colour (specimens for the microscope) with a dye in order to heighten contrast between different structures, as of tissue. —*intr.* To produce or receive discolorations.
~*n.* 1. A stained spot or smudge, as from foreign matter like blood or gravy. 2. A blemish upon one's moral character, personality, or reputation; a blot. 3. A liquid substance applied especially to wood that penetrates the surface and imparts a rich colour. 4. A coloured solution used for staining microscopic specimens. [Middle English *steynen,* short for *disteynen,* to deprive of colour, stain, from Old French *desteindre,* from Vulgar Latin *distingere* (unattested) : Latin *dis-* (reversal) + *tingere,* to dye.] —**stain·a·bil·i·ty** (-ə-bílləti) *n.* —**stain·a·ble** *adj.* —**stain·er** *n.*

stained glass *n.* Glass coloured by mixing pigments inherently in the glass, by fusing coloured metallic oxides onto the glass, or by painting and baking transparent colours on the glass surface. It is widely used in church windows. —**stained-glass** *adj.*

stain·less (stáyn-ləss, -liss) *adj.* 1. Without stain or blemish. 2. Resistant to stain or corrosion. —**stain·less·ly** *adv.*

stainless steel *n.* Any of various steels alloyed with sufficient chromium to resist corrosion or rusting associated with exposure of ordinary steel to water and moist air. —**stain·less-steel** *adj.*

stair (stair) *n.* 1. *Usually plural.* A series or flight of steps; a staircase. 2. One of a flight of steps. —**below stairs.** *British.* In the basement of a house formerly used by the servants. [Middle English *steir(e), stair(e),* Old English *stǣger.*]

stair·case (stáir-kayss) *n.* 1. A flight or series of flights of steps connecting separate levels, and its supporting structure. 2. *British.* A virtually self-contained section of a building that is served by its own staircase.

stair rod *n.* Any of a number of thin metal bars used to keep a stair carpet in place on a flight of stairs.

stair·way (stáir-way) *n.* A flight of stairs; a staircase.

stair·well (stáir-wel) *n.* A vertical shaft around which a staircase has been built.

stake¹ (stayk) *n.* 1. A piece of wood or metal sharpened at one end for driving into the ground, or used as a marker, a fence pole, or a tent peg. 2. a. A vertical post to which an offender was formerly bound for execution by burning. b. Execution by burning at the stake. Preceded by *the.* 3. A vertical post secured at the edge of a platform, as on a lorry, to stop the load from sliding off. —**pull up stakes.** *Chiefly U.S.* To conclude one's affairs and move on.
~*tr.v.* **staked, staking, stakes.** 1. To indicate the location or limits of with or as if with stakes. Often used with *out: stake out a claim.* 2. a. To fasten or secure with a stake or stakes. b. To support with a stake or stakes. 3. To tether or tie to a stake. [Middle English *stake,* Old English *staca.*]

stake² *n.* 1. *Often plural.* a. Money or property risked in a wager or gambling game. b. The reward or prize, such as money, awarded to the winner of a contest or race, especially a horse race. c. A race offering a reward or prize to the winner; especially, a horse race in which money is contributed by the horse owners equally to make up the prize. 3. A share or interest in any enterprise, especially a financial share. 4. *U.S. Informal.* A grubstake (see). —**at stake.** In question; at risk; involved.
~*tr.v.* **staked, staking, stakes.** 1. To gamble or risk; hazard; bet. 2. *Chiefly U.S.* To provide working capital for; finance. —**stake out.** *Chiefly U.S. Slang.* To keep watch on (a place) secretly. [Per-

haps originally "something placed on a post as a wager in a game", from STAKE (post).]

stake·hold·er (stáyk-hóldər) *n.* A person who feels he has a stake in something (e.g. society) and so participates in its activities and does not feel alienated from it.

sta·lac·tite (stál-ək-tīt || *chiefly U.S.* stə-lák-) *n.* A cylindrical or conical deposit, usually of calcite or aragonite, projecting downwards from the roof of a cavern as a result of the dripping of mineral-rich water. Compare **stalagmite.** [New Latin *stalactites,* from Greek *stalaktos,* dripping, verbal adjective from *stalassein†,* to drip.] —**sta·lac·ti·form** (stə-lákti-fawrm, sta-) *adj.* —**stal·ac·tit·ic** (stál-ək-títtik), **stal·ac·tit·i·cal** *adj.*

sta·lag (stál-ag; *German* shtál-) *n.* A German prisoner-of-war camp; especially, one for noncommissioned officers and privates. [German *Stalag,* short for *Stammlager,* "base camp" : *Stamm,* a base, stem + *Lager,* a camp, sleeping place.]

sta·lag·mite (stál-əg-mīt || *chiefly U.S.* stə-lág-) *n.* A cylindrical or conical deposit, usually of calcite or aragonite, projecting upwards from the floor of a cavern as a result of the dripping of mineral-rich water. Compare **stalactite.** [New Latin *stalagmites,* from Greek *stalagmos,* a dropping, from *stalassein†,* to drip. See **stalactite.**] —**stal·ag·mit·ic** (stál-əg-míttik) **stal·ag·mit·i·cal** *adj.*

St. Al·bans (áwl-bənz || ól-). City of Hertfordshire, southeast England. The site of the Roman town of Verulamium, it has many Roman remains including an amphitheatre, a mosaic pavement, and a hypocaust. St. Alban was martyred here (c. 303).

stale¹ (stayl) *adj.* **staler, stalest.** 1. Having lost freshness, effervescence, or palatability; flat or dry. 2. Lacking in originality or spontaneity; trite: *a stale joke.* 3. Impaired in efficacy, strength, or motivation, as from constant repetition of an activity. 4. *Law.* Having lost legal efficacy or force through lack of exercise or action: *a stale claim.* —See Synonyms at **trite.**
~*v.* **staled, staling, stales.** —*tr.* To make stale. —*intr.* To become stale. [Middle English, old enough to clear, well-aged (said of alcoholic drink), from Old French *estale,* not moving, from *estaler,* to halt, from *estal,* a fixed place, from Frankish *stal* (unattested), position.] —**stale·ly** *adv.* —**stale·ness** *n.*

stale² *intr.v.* **staled, staling, stales.** To urinate. Used of horses and camels.
~*n.* Urine of horses or camels. [Middle English *stalen,* from Germanic; akin to Middle Low German *stallen.*]

stale·mate (stáyl-mayt) *n.* 1. *Chess.* A position in which a player cannot make a legal move. 2. A situation in which further action by either of two opponents is impossible; a deadlock.
~*tr.v.* **stalemated, -mating, -mates.** To bring into a stalemate. [Obsolete *stale,* stalemate, from Middle English, from Old French *estal* (see **stale**) + MATE (checkmate).]

Sta·lin (staál-in, *rarely* stál- || -een), **Joseph Vissarionovich,** born Joseph Vissarionovich Dzhugashvili (1879–1953). Soviet statesman. He was one of the main architects of the U.S.S.R., becoming leader (1927) and premier (1941). In his search for supreme power, he exiled Trotsky (1929), purged the government and army, forced the collectivisation of agriculture, and embarked on a policy of industrialisation. He triumphed as a leader during World War II, and attended the conferences at Tehran (1943), Yalta (1945), and Potsdam (1945). His rule was officially denounced in the U.S.S.R. in 1956.

Stalingrad. See **Volgograd.**

Sta·lin·ism (staá-lin-iz'm, stá-) *n.* The bureaucratic and authoritarian exercise of state power and mechanistic application of Marxist-Leninist principles associated with Stalin's leadership, especially in the U.S.S.R. and other Communist states. —**Sta·lin·ist** *n. & adj.*

stalk¹ (stawk) *n.* 1. a. The main stem of a herbaceous plant. b. A stem or similar structure that supports a plant part such as a flower, flower cluster, or leaf. 2. Any slender or elongated support or structure. [Middle English *stalk(e),* probably diminutive of *stale,* ladder rung, handle, from Old English *stalu.*] —**stalk·y** *adj.*

stalk² *v.* **stalked, stalking, stalks.** —*intr.* 1. To walk with a stiff, haughty, or angry gait: *stalked off in a huff.* 2. To move threateningly or menacingly: *Pestilence stalked through the land.* 3. To track game. —*tr.* 1. a. To pursue or track stealthily. b. To harass by stalking. 2. To traverse (a place or area) threateningly or menacingly. [Middle English *stalken,* Old English *(be)stealcian,* to walk cautiously, from Germanic; akin to STEAL.] —**stalk·er** *n.*

stalk·ing-horse (stáwking-hawrss) *n.* 1. a. A horse trained to conceal the hunter while stalking. b. A canvas screen made in the figure of a horse, used for similar concealment. 2. Anything used to cover one's true feelings, plans, or purpose; a decoy. 3. *U.S.* Any sham candidate put forward to conceal the candidature of another or to divide the opposition.

stall (stawl) *n.* 1. A compartment for one domestic animal in a barn or shed. 2. a. Any small compartment, booth, or cubicle. b. A booth from which a trader can sell his goods. 3. An enclosed seat in the chancel or choir of a church, especially one reserved for a clergyman. b. A pew in a church. 4. *Chiefly British.* a. A seat in the front part of a theatre. b. *Plural.* The area on the bottom level of a theatre towards the front. 5. Any of the compartments in which a racehorse is kept immediately preceding the start of a race. 6. A protective sheath, a **fingerstall** (see). 7. An instance of stalling by an engine. 8. The condition in which a decrease in an aircraft's speed, or increase in the angle of the aerofoil to the forward direction of the aircraft, causes a sudden fall in lift and may cause loss of

control and a sharp decrease in altitude. **9.** *U.S. Informal.* A ruse or delaying tactic.
~*v.* **stalled, stalling, stalls.** —*tr.* **1.** To put or lodge (an animal) in a stall. **2.** To maintain (an animal) in a stall for fattening. **3.** To check the motion or progress of; bring to a standstill. **4.** To evade or put off by employing delaying tactics. Often used with *off*: *stall off creditors.* **5.** Accidentally to cause (an engine) to stop running. **6.** To cause (an aircraft) to go into a stall. —*intr.* **1.** To live or be lodged in a stall. Used of an animal. **2.** To stick fast in mud or snow. **3.** To come to a standstill. **4.** To employ delaying tactics to postpone action or to evade pressing circumstances. **5.** To stop running from mechanical failure. Used of an engine. **6.** To lose forward speed causing a stall. Used of an aircraft. [Middle English *stal(l),* Old English *steall,* standing place, stable.]

stall-feed (stáwl-feed) *tr.v.* **-fed** (-fed), **-feeding, -feeds.** To lodge and feed (an animal) in a stall for the purpose of fattening.

stall·ing angle (stáwling) *n.* The angle between the chord of an aerofoil and the undisturbed air flow at which a stall occurs. Also called "critical angle", "stall angle".

stal·lion (stál-yən) *n.* An adult male horse that has not been castrated. [Middle English *stalo(u)n,* from Old French *estalon,* from Germanic.]

stal·wart (stáwl-wərt, -wurt || stól-, stál-) *adj.* **1.** Having physical strength; sturdy; robust. **2.** Resolute; uncompromisingly supportive. —See Synonyms at **strong.**
~*n.* One who is stalwart; especially, one who actively supports a cause or organisation, such as a political party. [Middle English (Scottish dialect) variant of *stalworth, stalwurth,* Old English *stælwierthe,* serviceable : *stæl,* place + *wierthe, weorth,* worth.] —**stal·wart·ly** *adv.* —**stal·wart·ness** *n.*

sta·men (stáy-men, -mən) *n., pl.* **-mens** or *rare* **stamina** (stámminə). The pollen-producing reproductive organ of a flower, usually consisting of a filament supporting an anther. [Latin *stāmen,* thread of the warp, stamen.]

stam·i·na (stámminə) *n.* **1.** The physical or mental strength required to resist or withstand disease, fatigue, or other hardship; endurance. **2.** *Rare.* Plural of stamen. [Latin, plural of *stāmen,* thread of the warp, thread of human life.]

stam·i·nal (stámmin'l) *adj.* **1.** Pertaining to, showing, or producing stamina. **2.** Pertaining to a stamen or stamens.

stam·i·nate (stámmi-nət, -nit, -nayt) *adj. Botany.* **1.** Having a stamen or stamens. **2.** Bearing stamens but lacking pistils.

stam·i·node (stámmi-nōd) *n.* Also **stam·i·no·di·um** (-nṓdi-əm) *pl.* **-dia** (-ə). *Botany.* A sterile functionless stamen. [New Latin *staminodium,* from Latin *stāmen,* STAMEN.]

stam·i·no·dy (stámmi-nōdi) *n.* The transformation of a plant part, such as a petal or sepal, into a stamen. [New Latin *stamen* (stem *stamin-*) + -ODE + -Y.]

stam·mel (stámm'l) *n.* **1.** A coarse, red woollen cloth formerly used for undergarments. **2.** *Archaic.* The red colour of this cloth.
~*adj. Obsolete.* Red. [Probably variant of *stamin,* Middle English *stamyn,* from Latin *stāminea,* feminine of *stāmineus,* made of threads, from *stāmen,* thread of the warp.]

stam·mer (stámmər) *v.* **-mered, -mering, -mers.** —*intr.* To intrude involuntary pauses or repetitions, especially of initial consonants, into one's speaking, either because of a speech disorder or through tension, fear, or the like. —*tr.* To utter with a stammer.
~*n.* An instance or habit of stammering. [Middle English *stameren,* Old English *stamerian,* from Germanic.] —**stam·mer·er** *n.* —**stam·mer·ing·ly** *adv.*

stamp (stamp) *v.* **stamped, stamping, stamps.** —*tr.* **1.** To bring down (the foot) forcibly upon a hard surface. **2.** To bring the foot down upon (an object or surface) forcibly. **3.** To bring into a specified condition by or as if by thrusting downwards forcibly with the foot: *stamped the sand smooth.* **4.** To form or cut out by application of a mould, form, or die. **5.** To imprint or impress with a mark, design, or seal. **6.** To impress forcibly or permanently: *Her face was stamped on his mind.* **7.** To affix an adhesive stamp to (an envelope, for example). **8.** To identify, characterise, or reveal: *stamps the painting as being fake.* —*intr.* **1.** To thrust the foot forcibly downwards. **2.** To walk with forcible, heavy steps. —**stamp out.** To eradicate; destroy. —See Usage note at **stomp.**
~*n.* **1.** The act of stamping. **2. a.** An implement or device used to impress, cut out, or shape something to which it is applied. **b.** The impression or shape thus formed. **3.** A mark, design, or seal, the impression of which on a piece of paper indicates payment of a fee, ownership, approval, completion, or the like. **4. a.** A small piece of gummed paper sold by a government for attachment to an article that is to be posted; a postage stamp. **b.** Any similar piece of gummed paper issued for a specified purpose, as indicating, for example, that tax has been paid by an individual. **5.** Any identifying or characterising mark or impression: *bears the stamp of originality.* **6.** Characteristic nature or quality; class; kind: *Women of her stamp are one in a hundred.* **7.** *British Informal.* A contribution for National Insurance. [Middle English *stampen,* Old English *stampian* (unattested), to pound, stamp; noun partly from verb and from Old French *estampe*; both from Germanic.]

stamp duty *n.* A tax put on certain legal documents, such as deeds or conveyances, and certified by a piece of paper that bears an authorised stamp.

stam·pede (stám-peéd, stam-) *n.* **1.** A sudden headlong rush of startled animals, especially cattle or horses. **2.** A sudden headlong rush of a crowd of people. **3.** Any precipitous mass movement.
~*v.* **stampeded, -peding, -pedes.** —*intr.* To participate in a stampede. —*tr.* To cause to stampede. [Mexican Spanish *estampida,* from Spanish, uproar, crash, "a stamping or pounding", from *estampar,* to pound, stamp, from Germanic.] —**stam·ped·er** *n.*

stamp·ing ground (stámping) *n.* One's customary resort.

stamp mill *n.* **1.** A machine that crushes ore. **2.** A building in which ore is crushed.

stance (stanss, staanss) *n.* **1.** The posture or position of a standing person or animal; especially, the position assumed by a sportsman, such as a cricketer or golfer, when preparing to make a stroke. **2.** An emotional or intellectual attitude or position. [French, from Italian *stanza,* STANZA.]

stanch (staanch || stanch) *tr.v.* **stanched, stanching, stanches.** Also **staunch** (staanch, stawnch). **1. a.** To stop or check (flow of a bodily fluid, especially blood). **b.** To stop or check the flow of (a bodily fluid, especially blood). **c.** To check the flow of blood from (a wound). **2.** To stop or check (an outflow or loss); stem: *stanched the flow of foreign investment out of the country.*
~*adj.* Variant of **staunch.** [Middle English *staunchen,* to stop from flowing, from Old French *estanch(i)er,* from Vulgar Latin *stancāre* (unattested), from *stancus*† (unattested), dried.] —**stanch·er** *n.*

stan·chion (stáan-sh'n || stán-) *n.* **1.** An upright pole, post, or support. **2.** A framework consisting usually of two vertical bars, used to secure cattle in a stall.
~*tr.v.* **stanchioned, -chioning, -chions.** **1.** To build stanchions for; equip with stanchions. **2.** To confine (cattle) by means of stanchions. [Middle English *stanchon,* from Anglo-French, from Old French *estanchon,* from *estanc(h)e,* a stay, prop, from Latin *stāre.*]

stand (stand) *v.* **stood** (stood || stood), **standing, stands.** —*intr.* **1. a.** To maintain an upright position on the feet. **b.** To be placed in or maintain an erect position upon a base, support, or bottom. **2. a.** To rise to a standing position. Often used with *up.* **b.** To assume a standing position in a manner specified: *stand straight; stand to one side.* **3.** To point or set. Used of a gun dog. **4.** To measure a specified height when in a standing position: *stands five feet tall.* **5. a.** To remain stable, upright, or intact: *hardly a house left standing after the earthquake.* **b.** To remain valid, effective, or unaltered: *The agreement still stands.* **6.** To maintain a position, attitude, or course: *stand firm.* **7. a.** To be expressed as or show a specified figure or amount. Used with *at*: *Your balance stands at £150.* **b.** To occupy a specified position or level on or as if on a scale; rank: *her reputation stands high.* **8.** To be in a position offering the likelihood or expectation of loss or gain: *stood to lose a fortune.* **9.** To be in a particular or specified state, condition, or situation: *stands corrected; stands in awe of him.* **10.** To act in the specified capacity or perform the specified function: *stand surety; stand guard.* **11.** To be situated or placed: *The castle stood in the woods.* **12. a.** To remain in a stationary position: *the train now standing at platform 9.* **b.** To remain in a state of inactivity: *machinery standing idle.* **13.** To remain without flowing or being disturbed; be stagnant. **14.** To be a candidate for public office: *will stand in the next election.* **15.** To take or hold a particular course or direction; steer: *a ship standing to windward.* —*tr.* **1.** To cause to stand; place upright. **2. a.** To resist or endure without yielding or without sustaining damage; withstand: *stand siege; can't stand the strain.* **b.** To tolerate; put up with; bear: *can't stand the sight of him.* **4. a.** To be subjected to; undergo: *stand trial.* **b.** To submit to and emerge successfully from: *an argument that will not stand close examination.* **5.** *Informal.* To pay the cost for; treat: *stand someone to a drink.* —See Synonyms at **bear.** —**stand down. 1.** *Law.* To leave the witness box, as after giving testimony. **2.** To withdraw, retire, or resign, as from a position of office or authority. **3. a.** To go off duty. Used of a member of the armed forces. **b.** To be taken off duty. —**stand for. 1. a.** To signify; indicate: *What does R.A.C. stand for?* **b.** To represent; symbolise: *the Royal Family and all it stands for.* **2.** To put oneself forward as a candidate for (a public office). **3.** To be a supporter or advocate of: *stands for freedom of the press.* **4.** *Informal.* To tolerate; endure; put up with. —**stand on. 1.** To be strict in the observance of; insist on: *Don't stand on ceremony.* **2.** In navigation, to maintain the same course or tack. —**stand over. 1.** To keep close surveillance on or watch closely, especially in a threatening manner. **2.** To hold over or be held over; postpone. —**stand to.** *British.* **1.** To take up positions in readiness for action. Used of soldiers. **2.** To cause (soldiers) to stand to.
~*n.* **1.** The act of standing. **2.** A ceasing of work or activity; a standstill; a halt. **3.** In cricket, a usually prolonged stay at the wicket by two batsmen; a partnership: *a record stand for the last wicket.* **4.** A stop on a theatrical, concert, or other performance tour: *a one-night stand.* **5.** The place or spot where a person stands. **6.** A booth, stall, or counter for the display of goods for sale. **7.** A parking space reserved for taxis. **8.** An act of or position for defence or resistance, especially when desperate or decisive in a campaign: *made a final stand at the river.* **9.** A stance or opinion one is prepared to uphold: *take a stand.* **10.** A large, raised structure for spectators at a sporting ground. **11.** A small rack, prop, or table for holding any of various articles: *a music stand.* **12.** A group or growth of tall plants or trees: *a stand of pine.* **13.** *U.S.* A **witness box** *(see).* [Stand, stood (past tense); Middle English *standen, sto(o)d,* Old English *standan, stōd* (past singular).] —**stand·er** *n.*

stan·dard (stándərd) *n. Abbr.* **std. 1.** A flag, banner, or ensign, especially: **a.** The ensign of a chief of state, nation, or city: *the Royal standard.* **b.** A pole topped with an emblem or flag of an army, especially one raised formerly in battle to indicate the rallying point for the soldiers of one side. **c.** The flag of a mounted military regiment. **2. a.** An acknowledged measure of comparison for quantitative or qualitative value; a criterion; a norm. **b.** An object that under stated conditions defines, represents, or records the magnitude of a **unit** *(see)*. **3.** The set proportion by weight of gold or silver to alloy metal prescribed for use in coinage. **4.** The commodity or commodities used to back a monetary system. **5. a.** A degree or level of requirement, excellence, or attainment. **b.** *Usually plural.* A requirement of moral conduct. **6.** *Chiefly British.* A class or level in a primary school. **7.** A pedestal, stand, or base. **8.** *Botany.* **a.** The large upper petal of the flower of a sweet pea or related plant. **b.** Any of the narrow, upright petals of an iris. **9.** A shrub or small tree that through grafting or training has a single stem of limited height with a crown of leaves and flowers at its apex. —See Synonyms at **ideal.**

~adj. 1. a. Serving as or conforming to a standard of measurement or value. **b.** Of a normal, familiar, and commonly used kind: *a standard type of plug.* **c.** Well known and widely accepted as an authority: *a standard atlas.* **d.** Of average but not exceptional quality: *The acting and production were pretty standard.* **e.** Supplied automatically as an ordinary part or feature of a product: *Its standard equipment includes a heated rear windscreen.* **2.** *Linguistics. Often capital* **S.** Conforming to usage, as in pronunciation, vocabulary, and grammatical construction, that is widely regarded as acceptable and typically associated with educated speakers of a language: *standard English.* —See Synonyms at **normal.** [Middle English, from Anglo-French *estaundart,* Old French *estendart,* flag marking a place for rallying, from *estendre,* to EXTEND.]

stan·dard-bear·er (stándərd-bair-ər) *n.* **1.** One who bears the colours of a military unit. **2.** One who is in the vanguard, as of a political or religious movement.

stan·dard-bred (stándərd-bred) *n.* One of an American breed of horses developed for harness racing.

standard candle *n.* In optics, a **candela** *(see).*

standard cell *n.* A voltaic cell that produces a constant known electromotive force, enabling it to be used as a method of calibrating electrical measuring instruments.

standard deviation *n. Abbr.* **s.d., S.D.** *Symbol* σ, s *Statistics.* **1.** The square root of the **variance** *(see).* **2.** A statistic used as a measure of dispersion in a distribution, the square root of the arithmetic average of the squares of the deviations from the mean. In this sense, also called "root mean square deviation".

standard gauge *n.* A railway track having a width of 56$^{1}/_{2}$ inches. —**stan·dard-gauge** (stándərd-gáyj) *adj.*

stan·dard·ise, stan·dard·ize (stándərd-īz) *tr.v.* **-ised, -ising, -ises.** **1.** To cause to conform to a standard. **2.** To evaluate by comparison with a standard. —**stan·dard·i·sa·tion** (-ī-záysh'n ‖ *U.S.* -i-) *n.*

standard lamp *n. British.* A lamp set on a tall polelike support resting on a base on the ground.

standard of living *n.* The quality of material comfort as enjoyed by a country, an individual, or a section of society; especially, this quality as gauged by statistical surveys of the number and type of consumer goods per household. Compare **quality of life.**

standard time *n.* The mean (solar) time of a meridian centrally located over a country or time zone and used for the whole area, that changes with longitude. Standard times are exact numbers of hours or half-hours ahead or behind Greenwich Mean Time.

stand by *intr.v.* **1.** To be available and ready for action if needed. **2.** To remain inactive; refrain from intervening: *couldn't just stand by and see him swindled.* —*tr.v.* **1.** To aid; support. **2.** To keep or maintain (one's word, policy, or promise).

stand·by (stánd-bī) *n., pl.* **-bys. 1.** One that can always be depended upon. **2.** That which is kept in readiness to fill a need: *Baked beans are a good standby to feed hungry mouths.* —**on standby.** Ready and waiting.

~adj. 1. Kept in reserve for use when needed: *a standby generator.* **2.** Issued or available only immediately prior to a journey: *a standby air ticket.* **3.** Of, pertaining to, or waiting for an aircraft on which one can travel with a standby ticket: *standby passengers.*

~adv. Using a standby ticket: *flew standby to New York.*

stand·first (stánd-furst) *n.* The sentence or paragraph of copy that prefaces an article in a newspaper or magazine, designed to catch the reader's attention and to give some idea of the contents of the text. —**stand·first** *adj.*

stand in *intr.v.* To act as a stand-in.

stand-in (stánd-in) *n.* **1.** One who substitutes for an actor during lights and camera adjustments or in hazardous stunts. **2.** Any person who acts as a substitute: *He's the stand-in for the sick teacher.*

stand·ing (stánding) *n.* **1. a.** Status with respect to credit, rank, or reputation. **b.** High reputation; esteem. **2.** Length of time; duration: *a friendship of long standing.*

~adj. 1. Remaining upright; erect. **2.** Made or performed from a standing or stationary position: *a standing jump.* **3. a.** Remaining valid or unchanged: *a standing arrangement.* **b.** Well-established and familiar: *a standing joke.* **4.** Not flowing; stagnant.

standing army *n.* A permanent army of paid soldiers.

standing crop *n. Ecology.* The total amount of living organisms in a particular area or at a particular level of a food chain at a given time, usually expressed in terms of **biomass** *(see).*

standing order *n.* **1.** An order or instruction given to a bank by a customer, requesting that a stated sum of money should be paid at regular intervals to a stated party. Also called "banker's order". **2.** Any of a series of rules stating or recommending the way in which a society or other body should conduct its business.

standing ovation *n.* An ovation in which those applauding stand.

standing room *n.* Space in which to stand, as in a public place or vehicle where all seats are filled.

standing stone *n.* A large, upright stone or slab of stone, usually found in ancient henge monuments.

standing wave *n.* A wave in which the amplitude of the resultant of a transmitted and a reflected wave is stationary in time and in which some of the energy of the transmitted wave is absorbed by the reflecting boundary. Also called "stationary wave".

stand off *intr.v.* **1.** To keep apart; remain aloof. **2.** *Nautical.* To take or maintain a course away from shore. —*tr.v. British.* To dispense with or dismiss (an employee) temporarily.

stand-off (stánd-off, -awf) *n.* **1.** *U.S.* A tie, as in a contest; a draw. **2.** *U.S.* An effect that neutralises or counterbalances. **3.** A stand-off half.

stand-off half *n.* **1.** In Rugby football, a player, especially one skilled in kicking, who provides the link between the scrum half and the rest of the backs. **2.** The position of such a player. Also called "stand-off", "fly half", *British* "outside half".

stand-off·ish (stánd-óffish, -áwfish) *adj.* Coldly reserved; aloof.

stand oil *n.* A drying oil, such as linseed, tung, or soya, heated with minimum oxidation until thickened and used in oil enamel paints.

stand out *intr.v.* **1.** To protrude; stick out. **2.** To be conspicuous, distinctive, or prominent. **3.** To hold out; maintain support or opposition. Used with *for* or *against: stand out against a verdict.* **4.** *Nautical.* To take or maintain a course away from shore.

stand-out (stánd-owt) *n. U.S.* One that is outstanding or excellent.

stand-pipe (stánd-pīp) *n.* **1.** A large vertical pipe into which water is pumped in order to produce a desired pressure. **2.** A vertical pipe with a tap erected outdoors, for use when a domestic supply is interrupted, for example.

stand-point (stánd-poynt) *n.* A position from which things are considered or judged; a point of view. [Translation of German *Standpunkt.*]

St. An·drews (ándrōoz). Coastal resort of Fife, east Scotland. It was once the ecclesiastical capital of Scotland and has the country's oldest university (1411). It is a renowned golfing centre with its Royal and Ancient Club (1754).

stand-still (stánd-stil, stán-) *n.* A condition in which activity or progress has ceased; a halt: *came to a standstill.*

stand up *intr.v.* To remain unimpaired or prove valid or satisfactory when subjected to testing conditions: *stood up to long wear.* —*tr.v. Informal.* To fail to keep an appointment with (a person). —**stand up for.** To side with; defend. —**stand up to.** To face up to; confront fearlessly.

stand-up (stánd-up) *adj.* **1.** Erect; upright: *a stand-up collar.* **2.** Taken or performed while standing: *a stand-up supper.* **3.** Designating a boxing or fist fight confined largely to heavy blows with little manoeuvring. **4.** Designating or practising a style of comic performance done solo and without stage properties.

Stan·ford-Bi·net scale (stánfərd-bi-náy) *n.* A revision of the **Binet-Simon scale** *(see)* used in one form or another since 1916. Also called "Stanford-Binet test", "Stanford Revision of the Binet scale". [Prepared at *Stanford* University, California.]

stang. *Obsolete.* Past tense of **sting.**

stan·hope (stánnəp ‖ stán-hōp) *n.* A light open horse-drawn vehicle with one seat and two wheels. [Designed by the Reverend Fitzroy *Stanhope* (1787–1864), British clergyman.]

Stan·i·slav·sky (stánni-sláv-ski), **Konstantin Sergeyevitch Alexeyev** (1863–1938). Russian actor-producer. He cofounded (1898) the Moscow Art Theatre, where he devised a method of acting in which actors develop their own conception of their roles.

stank. Past tense of **stink.**

Stan·ley (stánli). See **Port Stanley.**

Stanley, Sir Henry Morton, born John Rowlands (1841–1904). Anglo-American journalist and explorer. He found (1871) the lost explorer David Livingstone at Lake Tanganyika, and explored (1874–77) equatorial Africa. He founded (1879) the Congo Free State for Leopold II of the Belgians.

stan·na·ry (stánnəri) *n., pl.* **-ries.** A place or region where tin is mined. [Medieval Latin *stannāria,* neuter plural of Late Latin *stannum,* tin. See **stannic.**]

stan·nic (stánnik) *adj.* Of or containing tin, especially with valency 4. [Probably from French *stannique,* from Late Latin *stannum,* tin, from Latin *stannum†,* an alloy of silver and lead.]

stannic chloride *n.* A colourless caustic liquid, $Na_2SnCl_6 \cdot H_2O$, made from tin treated with chlorine and used in the manufacture of textiles, sensitised papers, and perfumes.

stan·nif·er·ous (sta-níffərəs) *adj.* Containing tin. [Late Latin *stannum,* tin + -FEROUS.]

stan·nite (stán-īt) *n.* A grey to black mineral, chiefly Cu_2FeSnS, having a metallic lustre. Also called "tin pyrites". [German *Stannit* : Late Latin *stannum,* tin (see **stannic**) + -ITE.]

stan·nous (stánnəs) *adj.* Of or containing tin, especially with valency 2. [Late Latin *stannum,* tin. See **stannic.**]

St. An·tho·ny's fire *n. Pathology.* **1.** **Erysipelas** *(see).* **2.** **Ergotism** *(see).* Not in technical usage. [From the belief that the intercession of St. Anthony helped to relieve these diseases.]

stan·za (stánzə) *n. Abbr.* **st.** Any of a number of distinct and separate units that divide up a poem, and that is composed of two or more lines usually characterised by a common pattern of metre, rhyme, and number of lines. [Italian, "a stopping or standing", from Vulgar Latin *stantia* (unattested), from Latin *stāns,* present participle of *stāre,* to stand.] **—stan·za·ic** (stan-záy-ik) *adj.*

sta·pe·li·a (stə-péeli-ə) *n.* Any plant of the African genus *Stapelia,* having fleshy stems, no leaves, and large, unpleasant-smelling flowers. Also called "carrion flower". [New Latin, after J. B. van *Stapel* (died 1636), Dutch botanist.]

sta·pes (stáy-peez) *n., pl.* **stapes** or **stapedes** (sta-pée-deez, stə-, stápi-deez). A small, sound-conducting bone of the inner ear, shaped somewhat like a stirrup. Also called "stirrup bone". Compare **anvil, malleus.** [New Latin, from Medieval Latin *stapēs,* perhaps variant of *staffa, stapha, stapeda,* stirrup : Latin *stāre,* to stand + *pēs* (stem *ped-*), foot.] **—sta·pe·di·al** (sta-péedi-əl, stə-) *adj.*

staphylo- *comb. form.* Indicates: **1.** *Anatomy.* The uvula; for example, **staphylorrhaphy. 2.** *Microbiology.* Resembling a bunch of grapes; clustered; for example, **staphylococcus.** [New Latin, from Greek *staphulē,* bunch of grapes, grapevine, uvula.]

staph·y·lo·coc·cus (stáffil-ə-kóckəss, -ō-) *n., pl.* **-cocci** (-kóksī, -kók-ī, -ee). Any of various Gram-positive, spherical bacteria of the genus *Staphylococcus,* occurring in grapelike clusters. Also called "staph". [New Latin : STAPHYLO- + -COCCUS.] **—staph·y·lo·coc·cal** (-kóck'l), **staph·y·lo·coc·cic** (-kóksik) *adj.*

staph·y·lo·plas·ty (stáffil-ō-plásti, -ə-) *n.* Corrective surgery of the uvula and the soft palate. [STAPHYLO- + -PLASTY.] **—staph·y·lo·plas·tic** *adj.*

staph·y·lor·rha·phy, staph·y·lor·a·phy (stáffil-órrəfi) *n.* The correction of a cleft palate or divided uvula by plastic surgery. [STAPHYLO- + Greek *-rrhaphia,* sewing, suture, from *rhaptein,* to sew.]

sta·ple¹ (stáyp'l) *n.* **1.** A major commodity grown or produced in a region. **2.** A commodity in steady or constant demand, such as salt, flour, or coffee. **3.** A major part, element, or feature. **4.** Raw material. **5.** The graded fibre of cotton, wool, or flax.
~adj. **1.** In constant supply and demand. **2.** Important as an article of trade, production, or consumption in a particular region: *staple exports.* **3.** Principal; main: *a staple topic of conversation.*
~tr.v. **stapled, -pling, -ples.** To grade (fibres) according to length and fineness. [Middle English *staple* market town, from Old French *estaple,* from Middle Dutch *stapel,* pillar, emporium.]

staple² *n.* **1.** A U-shaped metal loop with pointed ends, driven into a surface to hold a bolt, hook, or hasp, or to hold wiring in place. **2.** A thin piece of wire having the shape of a square bracket, used, by being forced through and flattened, as a fastening for papers, cloth, and similar materials.
~tr.v. **stapled, -pling, -ples.** To fasten by means of a staple or staples. [Middle English *stapel, stapul,* Old English *stapol,* post, pillar, from Germanic.]

sta·pler¹ (stáyplər) *n.* One who deals in staple goods or fibres.

stapler² *n.* A machine or hand-operated device used to bind material together by means of staples.

star (star) *n.* **1.** *Astronomy.* A light-emitting mass of gas in which the energy generated by nuclear reactions in the interior is balanced by the outflow of energy to the surface, and the inward-directed gravitational forces are balanced by the outward-directed gas and radiation pressures. **2.** Any of the celestial bodies visible at night from Earth as relatively stationary, usually twinkling points of light. **3.** Anything regarded as resembling such a body. **4. a.** A graphic design or emblem conventionally representing a star, having five or more radiating points, and often used as a symbol, as of rank or excellence. **b.** Any of a number of such symbols used to indicate relative position on a recognised scale of quality: *a three-star hotel.* **5. a.** An artistic performer or athlete whose superior talent or ability is acknowledged. **b.** *British Slang.* An excellent person: *Be a star, and make some coffee, will you?* **6.** An asterisk (*). **7.** A white spot on the forehead of a horse. **8.** In astrology: **a.** A heavenly body considered to influence a person's character or destiny. **b.** *Plural.* A horoscope: *Buy a magazine so I can read my stars.* **—see stars.** To experience bright, flashing sensations, as from a blow on the head. **—thank (one's) lucky stars.** To be thankful for one's good fortune.
~v. **starred, starring, stars.** *—tr.* **1.** To ornament or set with stars. **2. a.** To award or mark with or as with a star for excellence. **b.** To mark with an asterisk. **3.** To present or feature (a performer) in a leading role. *—intr.* **1.** To play the leading role in a film or theatrical production. **2.** To do an outstanding job; perform excellently.
~adj. **1.** Of or pertaining to a star: *star quality.* **2.** Pre-eminent; brilliant. [Middle English *ste(o)rre,* Old English *steorra.*]

star anise *n.* **1.** An aromatic tree, *Illicium verum,* of eastern Asia, having purple-red flowers and anise-scented fruit. **2.** The fruit of this tree, used in Oriental cooking. Also called "Chinese anise".

star apple *n.* **1.** A tropical American tree, *Chrysophyllum cainito,* bearing smooth-skinned greenish-purple fruit. **2.** The edible fruit of this tree, having a star-shaped core.

star·board (stár-bərd, *also* -bawrd || -bōrd) *n.* The right-hand side of a ship or aircraft as one faces forwards. Compare **port.**
~adj. On the right-hand side.
~tr.v. **starboarded, -boarding, -boards.** To turn or shift (the helm of a vessel) to the right. [Middle English *sterbord,* Old English *stēorbord,* "rudder side" (early Teutonic ships had rudders on the right sides) : *stēor,* rudder + *bord,* ship's side, board.]

starch (starch) *n.* **1.** A naturally abundant nutrient carbohydrate, consisting of linked units of D-glucose, found chiefly in the seeds, fruits, tubers, roots, and stem pith of plants, notably in potatoes, wheat, and rice, varying widely in appearance according to source but commonly prepared as a white, amorphous, tasteless powder. **2.** Any of various substances, including natural starch, used to stiffen fabrics after washing them. **3.** Foods having a high content of starch. **4.** Stiffness or formality in manner or behaviour.
~tr.v. **starched, starching, starches.** To stiffen with starch. [Middle English *sterche, starche,* from *sterchen,* to stiffen (with starch), Old English *stercan* (attested only by past participle *sterced-*).]

Star Chamber *n.* **1.** A former English court (abolished in 1641) consisting of judges who were appointed by the Crown and sat in closed session on cases involving the security of the state. **2.** *Small* **s,** *small* **c.** Any court or tribunal that resembles the Star Chamber, especially in the manner of its secrecy and the severity of its judgments. [So called because the ceiling of the original courtroom was decorated with gilded stars.]

starch·y (stárchi) *adj.* **-ier, -iest. 1.** Of, of the nature of, or containing starch. **2.** Stiffened with starch. **3.** *Informal.* Stiff; formal. **—starch·i·ly** *adv.* **—starch·i·ness** *n.*

star connection *n. Electricity.* A connection of three or more phase supplies that joins one end of each branch at a common point. Compare **delta connection.**

star-crossed (stár-krost || -krawst) *adj.* Beset or dogged with bad luck: *star-crossed lovers.*

star·dom (stárdəm) *n.* **1.** The status of an actor or other performer acknowledged as a star. **2.** Stars collectively, as of the cinema.

star·dust (stár-dust) *n.* **1.** Distant stars seen as a mass of tiny glittering lights. **2.** A dreamy, misty, romantic quality.

stare (stair) *v.* **stared, staring, stares.** *—intr.* **1.** To look with a steady, often wide-eyed gaze, as from interest, astonishment, or hostility. **2.** *Chiefly British.* To stand out; be conspicuous or glaring. **3.** To stand on end or bristle, as animal hair or feathers. *—tr.* To affect by staring at: *He stared the boy into submission.* —See Synonyms at **gaze. —stare down** or **out.** To cause (a person) to avert his gaze by staring fixedly.
~n. The act of staring; an intent or fixed gaze. [Middle English *staren,* Old English *starian.*] **—star·er** *n.*

star facet *n.* Any of the eight small triangular facets in the crown of a brilliant-cut gem.

star·fish (stár-fish) *n., pl.* **starfishes** or collectively **starfish.** Any of various marine echinoderms of the class Asteroidea, characteristically having five arms extending from a central disc.

star·flow·er (stár-flowr, -flow-ər) *n.* Any of several plants having starlike flowers.

star·gaze (stár-gayz) *intr.v.* **-gazed, -gazing, -gazes. 1.** To gaze at or study the stars. **2.** To daydream.

star·gaz·er (stár-gayzər) *n.* **1. a.** One who stargazes. **b.** An astronomer or astrologer. Used humorously. **2.** Any of various marine bottom-dwelling fishes of the families Uranoscopidae and Dactyloscopidae, having eyes on the top of the head.

star grass *n.* Any of various plants of the genus *Hypoxis,* having grasslike leaves and star-shaped flowers.

stark (stark) *adj.* **starker, starkest. 1.** Without elaboration; bare; blunt: *stark truth.* **2.** Complete or utter; extreme: *stark poverty.* **3.** Harsh in appearance; bleak; grim: *stark cliffs.* **4.** Clearly defined; sharp: *in stark contrast.*
~adv. Utterly; entirely; absolutely: *stark raving mad; stark naked.* [Middle English *stark(e), sterk(e),* Old English *stearc,* hard, stern, severe, cruel.] **—stark·ly** *adv.* **—stark·ness** *n.*

Stark, Dame Freya (1893–1993). British travel writer, author of *The Valley of the Assassins* (1934) and *The Lycian Shore* (1956).

stark·ers (stárkərz) *adj. British Slang.* Completely naked.

star·let (stár-lət, -lit) *n.* **1.** A small star. **2.** A young film actress publicised as a future star.

star·light (stár-līt) *n.* The light given by the stars.
~adj. Starlit.

star·ling¹ (stárling) *n.* Any of various Old World birds of the family Sturnidae, characteristically having dark, often iridescent plumage; especially, *Sturnus vulgaris.* [Middle English *sterling, starling,* Old English *stærlinc* : *stær,* starling + -LING.]

starling² *n.* A protective structure of pilings surrounding a pier of a bridge. [Probably alteration of Middle English (now dialect) *staddling,* from *stadel, stathel,* foundation, Old English *stathol.*]

star·lit (stárlit) *adj.* Illuminated by starlight.

star-nosed mole (stár-nōzd) *n.* A mole, *Condylura cristata,* of eastern North America, having 22 small fleshy tentacles encircling the end of its nose.

star-of-Beth·le·hem (staár-əv-béthli-hem, -əm) *n.* **1.** A plant, *Ornithogalum umbellatum,* native to Europe, having narrow leaves and star-shaped white flowers. **2.** Any of several similar or related plants. [Probably from a fancied resemblance to the star that guided the Magi to the infant Jesus in Bethlehem (Matthew 2:2).]

Star of David *n.* A six-pointed star, or hexagram, formed by placing two triangles together, one upon the other or interlaced. It is a symbol of Judaism and appears on the Israeli flag. Also called "Magen David", "Shield of David".

Starr (star), **Ringo,** born Richard Starkey (1940–). British rock musician. He was drummer with the rock group, the Beatles, (1962–70). When the group disbanded (1970) he pursued a separate career as a musician and actor.

star·ry (staári) *adj.* **-rier, -riest. 1.** Of or resembling a star, especially in shape or brilliance. **2.** Set or filled with stars or with, or as if with, their light: *a starry night; starry eyes.* **—star·ri·ness** *n.*

star·ry-eyed (staári-īd) *adj.* Naively enthusiastic or romantic.

Stars and Stripes *n.* The flag of the United States. Preceded by *the.*

star sapphire *n.* A sapphire with a polished convex surface exhibiting a star-shaped figure.

star shell *n.* An artillery shell that explodes in midair with a shower of lights, used for illumination and signalling.
Star-Span·gled Banner (stár-spang-g'ld) *n.* **1.** The flag of the United States. Preceded by *the.* **2.** The national anthem of the United States.
start (start) *v.* **started, starting, starts.** *—intr.* **1. a.** To begin a journey or movement; move from a position of rest; set out: *started on her travels.* **b.** To begin a process, course of action, or undertaking: *Let's start at once. The show started with a dance routine.* **2. a.** To come into being or operation: *School starts at nine. The car won't start.* **b.** To have a beginning, origin, or lower limit: *Prices start at £4,000.* **3. a.** To move involuntarily: *started with fright.* **b.** To move suddenly; spring forth. **4.** To issue suddenly and forcefully; gush. **5.** To be in the line-up at the beginning of a race. **6.** To protrude or bulge: *eyes starting out of their sockets.* **7.** To become loosened or displaced, as from shrinkage. *—tr.* **1.** To set into motion, operation, or activity: *start the show.* Sometimes used with *off* or *up*: *Start up the engine. This started him off on one of his boring explanations.* **2. a.** To bring into being; initiate: *start a rumour; start a family.* **b.** To found; establish: *start a business.* **3. a.** To indicate the beginning of (a race). **b.** *Chiefly U.S.* To enter in a race. **4.** To cause or enable to begin an activity or venture, often with encouragement or instruction: *started her on painting at an early age.* **5.** To rouse (game) from its hiding place or lair; flush. **6.** To cause to work loose. **7.** *Chiefly British.* To conceive (a child). —See Synonyms at **begin.** **—start in.** To begin work or an activity. **—start out.** To set out on a journey, a course of action, or a career. **—start something.** *British Informal.* To pick a fight. **—to start with.** First of all; as a first consideration.
~n. **1.** A beginning; a commencement. **2.** A startled reaction or movement. **3.** *Plural.* Quick, brief spurts of effort or activity. Used chiefly in the phrase *by fits and starts.* **4.** A part that has become displaced or loosened. **5. a.** A place of beginning; a starting line. **b.** A time of beginning; a starting point. **6.** A signal to begin a race. **7.** A position of advantage over others, as in a race or endeavour; a lead: *got a start over the others; She got an hour's start before he began the chase.* **8.** An opportunity granted to pursue a career or course of action: *a good start in life.* **—for a start.** To start with. [Middle English *sterten,* Old English *styrtan* (attested only in the present participle *sturtende*), to leap up.]
START Strategic Arms Reduction Talks.
start·er (stártər) *n.* **1.** One that starts. **2.** An attachment for starting an internal-combustion engine without hand cranking. Also called "starter motor". **3.** One who signals the start of a race. **4.** A person or animal that starts in a race. **5.** *Chiefly British.* The first course of a meal. **6.** A chemical agent or bacterial culture used to start a reaction, as in the formation of acid in making yogurt, cheese, or vinegar. **—for starters.** *Informal.* To start with.
star thistle *n.* Any of several plants of the genus *Centaurea*; especially, *C. calcitrapa,* native to Eurasia, having spiny purplish flower heads.
start·ing block (stárting) *n.* Either of a pair of fixed supports on an athletics track, against which a runner pushes to gain initial momentum at the start of a race. Also called "block".
starting gate *n.* Any of a set of gates that are simultaneously raised to release the competitors in a horse or dog race.
starting grid *n.* In motor racing, an area where cars are staggered according to their relative practice times, before the start of a race.
starting handle *n. Chiefly British.* A **crank** *(see).*
starting pistol *n.* A pistol that is fired to signal the start of a race.
starting price *n.* The last odds given by bookmakers before the start of a horse or dog race.
star·tle (stárt'l) *v.* **-tled, -tling, -tles.** *—tr.* **1.** To cause to make a quick involuntary movement or start; rouse suddenly. **2.** To alarm, frighten, or surprise. *—intr.* To become startled.
~n. A sudden mild shock; a start. [Middle English *stertlen,* Old English *steartlian,* to kick, struggle, frequentative of *styrtan* (unattested), to leap up, START.] **—start·ling·ly** *adv.*
star·va·tion (staar-váysh'n) *n.* **1.** The act or process of starving. **2.** The condition of being starved.
starve (starv) *v.* **starved, starving, starves.** *—intr.* **1.** To suffer or die from extreme or prolonged lack of food. **2.** To suffer from deprivation; be in need. **3.** *Informal.* To be very hungry. **4.** *Archaic or Northern English.* To suffer or die from cold. *—tr.* **1.** To cause to starve. **2.** To bring or force to a state by starving: *starved into surrender.* [Middle English *ste(o)rven,* Old English *steofan,* to die.]
starve·ling (stárv-ling) *n.* One that is starving or ill-nourished.
~adj. **1.** Hungry or ill-nourished. **2.** Poor in quality; inadequate.
Star Wars *n.* The **Strategic Defense Initiative** *(see).*
~adj. **Star-Wars.** Designating or relating to Star Wars.
star·wort (stár-wurt || -wawrt) *n.* **1.** Any of various plants having star-shaped flowers. **2.** Any of various aquatic plants of the genus *Callitriche,* having a rosette of floating leaves.
stash (stash) *tr.v.* **stashed, stashing, stashes.** *Informal.* To hide or store away in a secret place.
~n. Chiefly U.S. A secret store or cache, as of money, drugs, or valuables. [18th century : origin obscure.]
sta·sis (stáy-siss) *n., pl.* **-ses** (-seez). **1.** *Pathology.* Stagnation of a bodily fluid, especially of blood. **2.** A condition of balance among various forces. [New Latin, from Greek, a standing.]
-stasis *n. comb. form.* Indicates: **1.** Slowing or stoppage; for example, **bacteriostasis.** **2.** A stable state or a balance; for example, **homeostasis.** [New Latin, from Greek *stasis,* a standing.]

-stat *comb. form.* Indicates stationary or making stationary; for example, **rheostat, thermostat.** [New Latin *-stata,* from Greek *-statēs,* one that causes to stand.]
stat. **1.** immediately. [Latin *statim.*] **2.** stationary. **3.** statistics. **4.** statuary. **5.** statute.
stat·ant *adj. Heraldry.* In profile and having all four feet on the ground: *a lion statant.*
state (stayt) *n.* **1.** A condition or mode of being with regard to a set of circumstances; a position: *the state of play; a state of disrepair.* **2.** A condition of being in a stage or form, as of structure, growth, or development: *the foetal state.* **3.** A mental or emotional condition or disposition: *a state of shock.* **4.** *Informal.* A condition of excitement or distress: *got himself into a state.* **5.** *Physics.* The condition of a physical system as specified by a set of appropriate macroscopic or quantum variables: *the proton state of the nucleon.* **6.** A social position or rank: *lived in a way appropriate to her state.* **7.** Ceremony; pomp; formality: *robes of state.* **8.** *Sometimes capital* **S. a.** The supreme public power within a sovereign political entity. Often preceded by *the*: *has been taken over by the state.* **b.** The sphere of supreme civil power within a given polity, often contrasted with the religious authority of the church: *matters of state.* **9.** A mode of government marked by a specified characteristic: *a welfare state; a police state.* **10.** A body politic; specifically, one constituting a nation: *the member states of the European Union.* **11.** *Sometimes capital* **S.** Any of the more or less internally autonomous territorial and political units composing a federation under a sovereign government: *the United States of America.* —See Usage note at **nation.** **—lie in state.** To be placed in public view for honours prior to burial.
~tr.v. **stated, stating, states.** **1.** To set forth in words; declare. **2.** To present in speech or writing in a formal and deliberate manner: *stated the argument with cool precision.* **3.** To fix or settle; specify: *stated their conditions; at the stated time.*
~adj. Sometimes capital **S.** **1. a.** Of, pertaining to, or maintained by a national government: *a state school; state control.* **b.** Of, pertaining to, or maintained by the government of an internally autonomous state: *the state legislature of Queensland; the State University of New York.* **2. a.** Of or involving pomp and ceremony. **b.** Reserved or used for or done on ceremonial occasions: *a state banquet.* [Middle English *stat(e),* from Old French *estat,* from Latin *status,* manner of standing, condition, position, attitude.] **—state·hood** *n.*
***Synonyms:** state, condition, situation, status.*
state capitalism *n.* A form of capitalism in which state control of capital, as through ownership of industries, plays a major part in a country's economic direction.
state·craft (stáyt-kraaft || -kraft) *n.* The art of managing the affairs or business of a nation state.
State Department *n.* The foreign affairs department of the U.S. government.
State House *n.* **1.** *U.S.* A building in which a state legislature holds sessions. **2.** *Small* **s,** *small* **h.** *N.Z.* A private house built and owned by the state.
state·less (stáyt-ləss, -liss) *adj.* Having no national status. **—state·less·ness** *n.*
state·ly (stáyt-li) *adj.* **-lier, -liest.** **1.** Marked by a graceful, dignified formality: *the stately progress of the royal party.* **2.** Majestic; grand. —See Synonyms at **grand.**
~adv. In a grand, imposing manner. [Middle English *statly,* suitable to a person of rank, from *stat,* person of rank, STATE.] **—state·li·ness** *n.*
stately home *n.* In Britain, a large, imposing mansion, especially one that has historical, cultural, or architectural value and is open to public viewing.
state·ment (stáyt-mənt) *n.* **1.** The act of stating or declaring. **2.** Something stated; an assertion or formal declaration: *issued no statement.* **3.** An account showing an amount due, received, or paid, such as a bank sends regularly to one of its customers. **4.** The presentation of a phrase, tune, or theme in a musical composition.
Stat·en Island (státt'n). Island in New York Bay, southwest of Manhattan Island. It forms Staten Island borough, one of the five boroughs of New York city, and Richmond County, New York State.
state of emergency *n.* A situation, as caused by a natural disaster or political collapse, officially recognised by a ruling body as warranting special action and measures. Also called "emergency".
state of play *n. Informal.* The situation or state of affairs that obtains at a particular time: "A usage note . . . so that readers can see what the linguistic 'state of play' is, in contemporary English". *(Reader's Digest Great Illustrated Dictionary.)*
state of the art *n.* The level or stage of development reached in a particular area, such as technology or industry.
state-of-the-art (stáyt-əv-thi-árt) *adj.* Of, pertaining to, designating, or using the most advanced technology.
state of war *n.* The condition of being at war; especially, this condition as recognised by a formal declaration of war and as officially acknowledged by the two parties in conflict.
state·room (stáyt-rōōm, -rŏŏm) *n.* **1.** A large, sumptuous room used for state occasions. **2.** A private cabin or compartment on a ship or, in the United States, a train.
state's evidence *n. Sometimes capital* **S.** In the United States: **1.** Evidence for the prosecution in state or Federal trials. **2.** A person who gives evidence for the state in criminal proceedings.
States-Gen·er·al (státs-jén-rəl, -jénnə-) *n.* **1.** The legislative assem-

bly in France before the Revolution. Also called "Estates-General".
2. The two-chamber parliament of the Netherlands.

state·side (stáyt-sīd) *adj. U.S. Informal.* Of or in the United States.
∼adv. Chiefly U.S. Informal. To, towards, or in the United States.

states·man (stáyts-mən) *n., pl.* **-men** (-mən). One who takes a prominent part in national or international political affairs; especially, a political leader respected for his outstanding wisdom, ability, and integrity. **—states·man·like, states·man·ly** *adj.* **—states·man·ship** *n.*

state socialism *n.* A form of socialism in which the state has considerable control over key areas of finance and industry.

States of the Church *pl.n.* The **Papal States** (*see*).

States' rights *n.* In the United States: **1.** All rights not delegated to the Federal Government by the Constitution nor denied by it to the states. **2.** A political stance advocating strict interpretation of the Constitution with regard to the limitation of Federal powers. **—States' righter** *n.*

states·wom·an (stáyts-wŏŏmən) *n., pl.* **-women** (-wimmin). A female statesman.

stat·ic (státtik) *adj.* Also **stat·i·cal** (-'l). **1.** *Physics.* **a.** Acting but causing no motion. Said of a force. **b.** Pertaining to or involving statics. **2.** *Electricity.* Of, pertaining to, or producing stationary charges; electrostatic. **3.** Of, pertaining to, or produced by random radio noise. **4.** Not changing or developing; fixed.
∼n. Random noise produced in a receiver, such as hissing or crackling in a radio or specks on a television screen. [New Latin *staticus,* from Greek *statikos,* causing to stand, from *statos,* placed, standing.] **—stat·i·cal·ly** *adv.*

static electricity *n.* **1.** An accumulation of electric charge on an insulated body. **2.** Electric discharge resulting from this.

static line *n.* A line attached to a parachute and to an aircraft, such that the parachute is opened automatically when the wearer has jumped from the aircraft and fallen a certain distance.

stat·ics (státtiks) *n. Used with a singular verb.* A branch of mechanics dealing with the study of the forces acting on system of bodies in equilibrium. Compare **dynamics, kinetics.** [New Latin *statica,* from Greek *statikē (tekhnē),* (science) of weighing, from *statikos,* causing to stand, skilled in weighing. See **static.**]

sta·tion (stáysh'n) *n.* **1.** The place or position where a person or thing stands or is assigned to stand; a post: *a sentry station.* **2.** The place, building, or establishment from which a service is provided or operations are directed: *a police station; a petrol station; a polling station.* **3. a.** A stopping place along a route, especially one on a railway line where passengers and goods may be taken onto a train. **b.** The buildings of such a station. **4.** Social position; status; rank. **5.** An establishment equipped for observation and study: *a radar station.* **6.** An establishment equipped for radio or television transmission. **7. a.** The wavelength on which a particular television or radio programme is broadcast. **b.** The organisation broadcasting on this wavelength. **8.** In surveying, a point at which an observation may be taken. **9.** In Australia: **a.** A large farm for raising cattle or sheep. **b.** A sheep-run or cattle-run. **10.** A military post, especially one in which British officers and administrative officials formerly resided in India. **11.** Any of the stations of the cross.
∼tr.v. **stationed, -tioning, -tions.** To assign to a position or station; post. [Middle English *stacioun,* a standing still, from Latin *statiō* (stem *statiōn-*), from *stāre,* to stand.]

sta·tion·ar·y (stáysh'n-ri, -əri ‖ -əri) *adj. Abbr.* **sta., stat. 1. a.** Fixed in a position; not moving. **b.** Not able to be moved; not portable: *a stationary engine.* **2.** Remaining in a fixed condition or state, or at a fixed level: *Her temperature was stationary.* [Middle English *stationarye,* from Latin *stationārius,* from *statiō,* a standstill, STATION.]

stationary front *n.* A transition zone between two nearly stationary air masses of different density.

stationary orbit *n. Aerospace.* **Synchronous orbit** (*see*).

stationary point *n. Mathematics.* A point on a graph at which the tangent is either horizontal or vertical, indicating either a point of inflection or a maximum or minimum.

stationary satellite *n.* An artificial satellite in a synchronous orbit.

stationary wave *n.* A **standing wave** (*see*).

sta·tion·er (stáysh'n-ər) *n.* **1.** One who sells stationery. **2.** *Archaic.* A publisher or bookseller. [Middle English *staciouner,* from Medieval Latin *stationārius,* shopkeeper, from *statiō,* shop, from Latin, STATION.]

sta·tion·er·y (stáysh'n-ri, -əri ‖ -erri) *n.* **1.** Writing paper and envelopes. **2.** Writing materials such as paper, pens, and inks.

station house *n. Chiefly U.S.* A building used as a station, especially a police station.

sta·tion·mas·ter (stáysh'n-maaster ‖ -mastər) *n.* An official in charge of a railway station.

stations of the cross *pl.n. Sometimes capital* **S,** *capital* **C. 1.** A series of usually 14 crosses, often accompanied by images, set up in a church or along a path commemorating 14 events in the Passion of Jesus. **2.** The devotional meditations performed before these crosses and images.

station wagon *n. Chiefly U.S.* An **estate car** (*see*).

stat·ism (stáytiz'm) *n.* The act or policy of strengthening the economic and political power of the state, as by increasing its control over industries and the mass media. [STATE + -ISM.]

stat·ist (stáytist *for sense 1,* státtist *for sense 2) n.* **1.** An advocate of statism. **2.** A statistician. **—stat·ist** *adj.*

sta·tis·tic (stə-tístik) *n.* **1.** Any numerical datum. **2.** An estimate of a parameter, as of the population mean or variance, obtained from a sample. [Back-formation from STATISTICS.] **—sta·tis·ti·cal** (-'l) *adj.* **—sta·tis·ti·cal·ly** *adv.*

statistical mechanics *n.* The study of the theory in which the properties of a physical system are predicted by the statistical behaviour of their constituent particles.

stat·is·ti·cian (státti-stísh'n) *n.* **1.** A mathematician specialising in statistics. **2.** A compiler of statistical data.

sta·tis·tics (stə-tístiks) *n. Abbr.* **stat. 1.** *Used with a singular verb.* The mathematics of the collection, organisation, and interpretation of numerical data; especially, the analysis of population characteristics of social phenomena by inference from sampling. **2.** *Used with a plural verb.* A collection of numerical data. [German *Statistik,* originally "political science dealing with state affairs", from New Latin *statisticus,* of state affairs, from Latin *status,* state.]

sta·tive (stáytiv) *adj.* Belonging to or designating a class of verbs that express a state or condition; for example, *know, like,* and *doubt* are stative verbs.
∼n. A verb of this class.

stato– *comb. form.* Indicates: **1.** Position; for example, **statocyst. 2.** Resting, remaining, or surviving; for example, **statoblast.** [Greek *statos,* placed, standing.]

stat·o·blast (stát-ō-blast, -ə-, -blaast) *n.* An asexually produced, encapsulated bud of a freshwater bryozoan, from which new individuals develop after the parent colony has disintegrated. [STATO- + -BLAST.]

stat·o·cyst (stát-ō-sist, -ə-) *n.* A small organ of balance in many invertebrates, consisting of a fluid-filled sac containing statoliths that help indicate position when the animal moves. Also called "otocyst". [STATO- + CYST.]

stat·o·lith (stát-ō-lith, -ə-) *n.* **1.** A small, movable concretion of calcium carbonate, found in statocysts. **2.** Any of various starch grains found in some plant cells and thought to function in the plant's response to gravity. [STATO- + -LITH.]

sta·tor (stáytər) *n.* The stationary part of a motor, dynamo, turbine, or other rotary machine. [New Latin, from Latin, one that stands, from *stāre* (past participle *status*), to stand.]

stat·o·scope (státtə-skōp) *n.* A sensitive form of aneroid barometer used in aircraft to indicate small changes of height but not the absolute altitude. [Greek *statos,* stationary + -SCOPE.]

stat·u·ar·y (státtew-əri, stáchoo- ‖ -erri) *n., pl.* **-ies.** *Abbr.* **stat. 1.** Statues collectively. **2.** A sculptor. **3.** The art of making statues. *∼adj.* Of, pertaining to, or suitable for a statue or statues. [Latin *statuāria,* the art of making statues, and *statuārius,* sculptor, from *statuārius,* of a statue, from *statua,* STATUE.]

stat·ue (stáchoo, státtew) *n.* A three-dimensional figure or image, as of a famous person, sculpted, modelled, carved, or cast in material such as stone, clay, wood, or bronze. [Middle English, from Old French, from Latin *statua,* from *statuere,* to set up, erect.]

Statue of Liberty *n.* A colossal statue located in New York harbour, representing liberty as a woman with a torch raised in one hand and a book in the other arm.

stat·u·esque (státtew-ésk, stáchoo-) *adj.* Suggestive of a statue, as in proportion, grace, or dignity; stately. **—stat·u·esque·ly** *adv.*

stat·u·ette (státtew-ét, stáchoo-) *n.* A small statue.

stat·ure (stáchər) *n.* **1.** The natural height of a human or animal body in an upright position. **2. a.** A level, status, or degree, as of achievement or recognition; calibre. **b.** A high degree of worth or eminence. [Middle English *statur(e),* from Old French *(e)stature,* from Latin *statūra.*]

sta·tus (stáytəss ‖ *chiefly U.S.* státtəss) *n.* **1.** The legal character or condition of a person or thing: *What is your marital status?* **2.** A relative position; especially, relative social or professional position. **3.** High standing; prestige. **4.** A state of affairs; a situation. **—See** Synonyms at **state.** [Latin *status,* state.]

status quo (kwō) *n.* The existing condition or state of affairs. [Latin, "state in which".]

status symbol *n.* That which is desirable because of the social prestige it confers upon its possessor: *He bought a sports car purely as a status symbol.*

stat·u·ta·ble (státtew-təb'l, stáchoo-) *adj.* Enacted, regulated, recognised, or authorised by statute; statutory.

stat·ute (státtewt, stáchoot) *n. Abbr.* **st., St., stat. 1.** A law enacted by a legislative body and formally recorded in writing; often distinguished from **common law** (*see*). **2.** An established law or rule, as of a body or an institution: *club statutes.* [Middle English *statut(e),* from Old French *(e)statut,* from Late Latin *statūtum,* from the neuter of *statūtus,* past participle of *statuere,* to set up, decree.]

statute book *n.* A written record of enacted legislation: *put a law on the statute book.*

statute law *n.* A law or rule established by legislative enactment. Compare **common law.**

statute mile *n.* See **mile.**

statute of limitations *n. Law.* ·A statute setting a time limit on enforcement of a right in certain cases.

stat·u·to·ry (státtew-tri, stáchoo-, -təri ‖ stə-téwtəri) *adj.* **1.** Of or pertaining to a statute. **2.** Enacted, regulated, or authorised by statute. **3.** *Informal.* Designating an object, action, or behaviour that has become typical through its frequency: *got up and had her statutory cup of coffee.* [STATUTE + -ORY.]

statutory rape *n. U.S.* Sexual intercourse with a girl who is below the age of consent, treated as a criminal offence.

staunch (stawnch, staanch) *adj.* **stauncher, staunchest.** Also *rare*
stanch (staanch ‖ stanch). **1.** Firm and steadfast; true; loyal.

2. **a.** Having a strong or substantial construction or constitution. **b.** Watertight. —See Synonyms at **faithful.**
~*tr.v.* Variant of **stanch.** [Middle English *staunche, stanch,* watertight, firm, strong, from Old French *estanche,* feminine of *estanc,* from *estanch(i)er,* STANCH.] **—staunch·ly** *adv.* **—staunch·ness** *n.*
stau·ro·lite (stáw-rə-līt, -rō-) *n.* A brownish-black mineral, $FeAl_4Si_2O_{10}(OH)_2$, often having crossed intergrown crystals and sometimes used as a gem. [French : Greek *stauros,* cross + -LITE.] **—staur·o·lit·ic** (-líttik) *adj.*
stau·ro·scope (stáwrə-skōp) *n.* An optical instrument used to study the crystal structure of minerals with polarised light. [Greek *stauros,* cross + -SCOPE.]
Sta·vang·er (sta-váng-ər, stə-). City in southwestern Norway, lying on the Stavangerfjord. A port and market centre, its industries include shipbuilding and fish-processing.
stave (stayv) *n.* **1.** A narrow strip of wood forming part of the sides of a barrel, tub, or the like. **2. a.** A rung of a ladder. **b.** A crosspiece on a chair. **3.** A long, thick stick, especially one used as a weapon; a staff. **4.** A musical **staff** *(see).* **5.** A set of verses; a stanza.
~*v.* **staved** or **stove** (stōv), **staving, staves.** *—tr.* **1.** To break in or puncture the staves of. **2.** To break or smash a hole in: *staved in a boat.* **3.** To crush or smash inwards. *—intr.* To be or become crushed or broken in. **—stave off.** To ward off; avert. [Back-formation from *staves,* plural of STAFF.]
Usage: The normal past tense and past participle forms of this verb are *staved: I think we've staved off her visit for another month. Stove* is restricted to nautical contexts: *The ship's side was stove in.*
staves. Alternative plural of **staff.**
staves·a·cre (stáyvz-aykər) *n.* **1.** A larkspur, *Delphinium staphisagria,* of southern Europe, having deep blue flowers. **2.** The poisonous seeds of this plant, formerly used externally as a parasiticide. [Middle English *staphisagre, stafisagre,* from Latin *staphis agria,* from Greek, "wild raisin" : *staphis, astaphis*†, raisin + *agria,* feminine of *agrios,* wild, "of the field", from *agros,* field.]
stay[1] (stay) *v.* **stayed, staying, stays.** *—intr.* **1.** To remain or continue in a specified place or condition: *stayed behind; stayed in bed; stay out of trouble.* **2. a.** To remain or sojourn as a guest or lodger. **b.** *Scottish.* To reside permanently; live. **c.** To wait; pause. **3.** To hold on; endure. **4.** In poker, to meet a bet without raising it. **5.** *Archaic.* **a.** To stop moving; cease. **b.** To keep up in a race or contest: *stayed with the rest of the runners till the last lap.* *—tr.* **1.** To stop or halt; check. **2.** To postpone; delay; especially, to delay or stop the effect or course of by intervening measures: *stayed legal proceedings.* **3.** To satisfy or appease (hunger, for example) temporarily. **4.** To remain for (a specified period of time): *She stayed the week.* **5.** To endure to the end; last out: *couldn't stay the course.* **6.** *Archaic.* To wait for; await. **—stay put.** To remain in the place or position that one is occupying.
~*n.* **1.** The action of stopping or coming to a stop. **2.** A sojourn or visit. **3.** A suspension or postponement of a legal action or execution. [Middle English *steyen,* to halt, from Old French *ester* (present stem *estei-*), to stand, stop, from Latin *stāre.*] **—stay·er** *n.*
Synonyms: *stay, remain, wait, abide, tarry, linger.*
stay[2] *tr.v.* **stayed, staying, stays.** **1.** To brace, support, or prop up. Often used with *up.* **2.** To strengthen or sustain mentally or spiritually; comfort.
~*n.* **1.** A support or prop: *She was a stay during the crisis.* **2.** A strip of bone, plastic, or metal, used to stiffen a garment or part such as a corset or shirt collar. **3.** *Plural.* A corset stiffened with stays, now rarely worn. [Old French *estayer,* to support, from *estaie,* support, from Germanic; see **stay**[3] (rope).]
stay[3] *n.* **1.** A heavy rope or cable, usually of wire, used as a brace or support for a mast or spar. **2.** Any rope used for a similar purpose; a guy line. **—in stays.** In the process of coming about to the opposite tack. Said of a ship.
~*v.* **stayed, staying, stays.** *—tr.* **1.** To brace or support with a stay or stays. **2.** To put (a ship) on the opposite tack. *—intr.* To come about to the opposite tack. Used of a ship. [Middle English *stey, stay,* Old English *stæg,* from Germanic *staga-* (unattested).]
stay-at-home (stáy-ət-hōm) *n.* One who habitually stays at home; especially, one who leads a sheltered, unadventurous life. **—stay-at-home** *adj.*
stay·ing power (stáy-ing) *n.* The ability to endure or last.
stay·sail (stáy-sayl; *nautical* stáyss'l) *n.* A triangular sail hoisted on a stay.
St. Bernard Passes. Two Alpine passes. The Great St. Bernard Pass, height 2 472 metres (8,110 feet) links Piedmont, Italy, with Valais, Switzerland, and was the route by which Napoleon I crossed into Italy (1800). At its summit there is a hospice (11th century) founded by St. Bernard of Menthon, which formerly bred St. Bernard dogs to search for travellers trapped by snow. Beneath it is a road tunnel (1964). The Little St. Bernard Pass, height 2 187 metres (7,178 feet), which links Piedmont with Savoie, France, also has a hospice (11th century) founded by St. Bernard, and was the route by which Hannibal is believed to have invaded Italy.
St. Chris·to·pher. See **St. Kitts-Nevis.**
St. Cloud (saɴ klōō). Suburb of Paris, France, situated on the river Seine in the Hauts-de-Seine *département.* Formerly the site of a royal palace, it is also the site of the Sèvres porcelain factory and a racecourse.
STD sexually transmitted disease.
std. standard.
S.T.D. **1.** Doctor of Sacred Theology. **2.** Subscriber trunk dialling: a system in Britain enabling people to make long-distance telephone calls without the aid of an operator.
St. Da·vid's (dáyvidz). *Welsh* **Ty·dde·wi** (tee-thé-wi). Village of Pembrokeshire, southwest Wales. Once a major place of pilgrimage, it has a cathedral (12th to 14th centuries).
St. De·nis (saɴ də-née). Suburb of Paris, France, situated in the Seine-St. Denis *département.* Its abbey church (cathedral) (12th century) was the first in Gothic style. Several French monarchs are buried there.
stead (sted) *n.* **1.** The place, position, or function properly or customarily occupied by another. **2.** Advantage; avail. Used chiefly in the phrase *stand someone in good stead.*
~*tr.v.* **steaded, steading, steads.** *Archaic.* To be of advantage or service to; benefit; help. [Middle English, Old English *stede.*]
stead·fast, sted·fast (stéd-fəst, -faast || -fast) *adj.* **1.** Fixed or unchanging; steady: *a steadfast gaze.* **2.** Firmly loyal or constant; unswerving. —See Synonyms at **faithful.** [Middle English *stedefast,* Old English *stedefæst,* fixed in one place : *stede,* place, STEAD + *fæst,* fixed, FAST.] **—stead·fast·ly** *adv.* **—stead·fast·ness** *n.*
stead·ing (stédding) *n. Chiefly Scottish.* The outbuildings of a farmhouse.
stead·y (stéddi) *adj.* **-ier, -iest.** **1.** Firm in position or place; fixed. **2.** Direct and unfaltering; sure: *a steady aim.* **3.** Regular, even, and continuous in action, movement, quality, or pace: *slow but steady progress.* **4.** Not easily excited or upset; controlled: *steady nerves.* **5. a.** Regular; habitual: *a steady boyfriend.* **b.** Reliable; dependable. **c.** Temperate; sober.
~*v.* **steadied, -ying, -ies.** *—tr.* To make steady; stabilise. *—intr.* To become steady.
~*interj.* **1.** Used to urge care and self-control. **2.** *Nautical.* Used to direct the helmsman to keep the ship's head in the same direction.
~*n., pl.* **steadies.** *U.S. Informal.* A regular boyfriend or girlfriend.
~*adv.* In a steady manner. **—go steady.** *Informal.* To go out socially on a regular basis, as with a member of the opposite sex. [From STEAD, place (after Middle Low German *stēdig,* stable).] **—stead·i·er** *n.* **—stead·i·ly** *adv.* **—stead·i·ness** *n.*
Synonyms: *steady, even, equable, uniform, constant.*
stead·y-state theory (stéddi-stáyt) *n.* A cosmological theory that assumes that the large-scale view of the universe is independent of the position of the observer in space and time and that the expansion of the universe, required on other grounds, is compensated for by the continuous creation of matter. Compare **big-bang theory.**
steak (stayk) *n.* **1.** A slice of meat, beef unless otherwise specified, typically cut thick and usually grilled or fried. **2.** A thick slice of a large fish cut across the body. **3.** A cut of beef of any of various qualities, used for the specified purpose: *stewing steak.* [Middle English *ste(y)ke, styke,* from Old Norse *steik,* piece of meat roasted on a spit, from *steikja,* to roast on a spit.]
steak·house (stáyk-howss) *n.* A restaurant that serves steaks as a speciality.
steak tar·tare (taar-tár, tártər) *n.* Raw minced beef mixed with onion, seasoning, and raw egg. Also called "tartar steak".
steal (steel) *v.* **stole** (stōl), **stolen** (stṓlən), **stealing, steals.** *—tr.* **1. a.** To take (an object) without right or permission, often in a surreptitious way. **b.** To take or appropriate (an idea, for example) without permission or acknowledging the source. **2.** To get, take, gain, or effect secretly or artfully: *steal a kiss; steal a glance.* **3.** *Chiefly U.S.* To move, carry, or place surreptitiously: *He carefully stole the gin back into the cupboard.* *—intr.* **1.** To commit theft. **2. a.** To move stealthily or unobtrusively: *stole away from the party.* **b.** To happen, pass, or elapse gently and imperceptibly: *The days stole past.* —See Synonyms at **rob.**
~*n.* **1.** The act or an instance of stealing. **2.** *U.S. Informal.* A bargain. [Steal, stolen; Middle English *stelen, stole(n),* Old English *stelan, stolen.* Stole, Middle English *stole,* adopted from the past participle *stole(n)* and superseding the more regular form *stal,* Old English *stæl* (plural *stælon*).] **—steal·er** *n.*
stealth (stelth) *n.* **1.** The act of moving, proceeding, or acting in a covert way. **2.** Furtiveness; covertness. **3.** *Archaic.* The act of stealing. [Middle English *stalth, stelth,* probably from Old English *stǣlth* (unattested) : STEAL (move stealthily) + -TH.]
stealth·y (stélthi) *adj.* **-ier, -iest.** Characterised by stealth; cautiously unobtrusive and secretive. See Synonyms at **secret.** **—stealth·i·ly** *adv.* **—stealth·i·ness** *n.*
steam (steem) *n.* **1.** The hot gaseous phase of water formed when water boils. **2.** The white visible mist of water vapour containing small droplets of water, seen when hot water boils or evaporates. **3.** The use of steam as a source of power; especially, the use of steam-powered locomotives: *the age of steam.* Also used adjectivally: *a steam railway.* **4. a.** The power generated by the use of steam: *get up steam.* **b.** *Informal.* Energy, driving force, or means of progress: *running out of steam; got here under my own steam.* **5.** Pent-up emotions or nervous energy: *letting off steam.*
~*v.* **steamed, steaming, steams.** *—intr.* **1.** To produce or emit steam. **2.** To become or rise up as steam. **3.** To become misted or covered with steam. Used with *up.* **4.** To move by means of steam power. **5.** *Informal.* To be extremely angry or emotional. **6.** *Informal.* To move energetically and rapidly. *—tr.* **1.** To cook (food) by exposing to steam. **2.** To expose or subject to steam: *steamed a stamp off an envelope.* **3.** *Informal.* To cause to become bad tempered or irritated. Often used in the passive with *up*: *no need to get all steamed up.* [Middle English *steme,* vapour, exhalation, Old

English *steam,* from West Germanic *stauma* (unattested).]

steam bath *n.* 1. A bath in which bodily impurities are sweated out by the action and heat of steam. 2. A place where one takes such a bath.

steam·boat (steém-bōt) *n.* A small **steamship** *(see)*

steam boiler *n.* A closed tank in which water is converted into steam under pressure.

steam chest *n.* A compartment in a steam engine which encloses the slide valve and through which steam is delivered from the boiler to a cylinder.

steam engine *n.* An engine that converts the heat energy of pressurised steam into mechanical energy, especially one in which steam drives a piston in a closed cylinder.

steam·er (steémər) *n. Abbr.* **str.** 1. A steamship. 2. A container in which something, such as food, is steamed. 3. A wet suit that is especially thick. 4. A person who participates in steaming.

steamer trunk *n.* A small trunk originally designed to fit under the bunk of a steamship cabin.

steam heating *n.* A heating system by which steam is generated in a boiler and piped to radiators.

steam·ie (steémi) *n. Scottish Informal.* Especially formerly, a wash house open to the public.

steam·ing (steéming) *n.* Organised gang mugging in which some gang members keep watch and conduct diversionary activity while the victim is surrounded and robbed by the rest. [Origin obscure.]

steam iron *n.* A pressing iron that holds and heats water to be emitted as steam on the cloth being pressed.

steam organ *n.* A musical instrument fitted with steam whistles, played from a keyboard. Also *U.S.* "calliope".

steam point *n.* The temperature at which the vapour phase of water is in equilibrium with the liquid phase. At standard pressure, the steam point is 100°C. Compare **ice point**.

steam radio *n. British Informal.* Radio considered as being old-fashioned by comparison with television.

steam·rol·ler (steém-rōl-ər) *n.* 1. a. A steam-driven machine used chiefly for rolling road surfaces flat. b. Loosely, any heavy rolling machine similarly used. 2. A ruthless or irresistible force or power. ~*v.* **steamrollered, -lering, -lers.** —*tr.* 1. To work or roll (a surface) with a steamroller. 2. a. To overwhelm or suppress ruthlessly; crush. b. To bring or impel by means of an irresistible force. —*intr.* To move or proceed with overwhelming or crushing force.

steam room *n.* A room filled with steam, in which one can take a steam bath.

steam·ship (steém-ship) *n. Abbr.* **SS, S.S.** A large vessel propelled by one or more steam-driven propellers. Also called "steamer".

steam shovel *n.* A steam-driven excavating machine.

steam table *n.* 1. A table giving the properties of steam under different conditions of pressure. 2. A table equipped to hold containers of cooked food kept warm by hot water or steam.

steam turbine *n.* A turbine operated by highly pressurised steam directed against or through vanes on a rotor.

steam·y (steémi) *adj.* **-ier, -iest.** 1. Filled with, covered with, or emitting steam. 2. *Informal.* Full of sexual passion; erotic. —**steam·i·ly** *adv.* —**steam·i·ness** *n.*

ste·ap·sin (sti-ápsin) *n.* An enzyme of pancreatic juice that catalyses the hydrolysis of fats to fatty acids and glycerol. [Greek *stear,* solid fat, suet, tallow (see **stearic**) + (PE)PSIN.]

ste·a·rate (steér-ayt ‖ steé-ər-) *n.* A salt or ester of stearic acid. [STEAR(IC) + -ATE.]

ste·ar·ic (sti-árrik) *adj.* Of, pertaining to, or similar to stearin or fat. [French *stéarique,* from Greek *stear†,* solid fat, suet, tallow.]

stearic acid *n.* A colourless, odourless, waxlike fatty acid, $CH_3(CH_2)_{16}COOH$, occurring in natural animal and vegetable fats.

ste·a·rin (steér-in ‖ steé-ər-) *n.* 1. A colourless, odourless, tasteless ester of glycerol and stearic acid, $C_3H_5(C_{18}H_{35}O_2)_3$, used in the manufacture of soap and candles and for textile sizing. Also called "tristearin". 2. Stearic acid, especially as used commercially. 3. The solid form of fat. [French *stéarine* : Greek *stear,* solid fat, suet, tallow (see **stearic**) + -INE.]

ste·a·rop·tene (steér-róp-teen ‖ steé-ə-) *n.* The part of a natural essential oil that separates out as a white, crystalline solid on cooling or standing. [STEAR(IC) + Greek *ptēnos,* winged, "volatile".]

ste·a·tite (steér-tīt, steé-ə-) *n.* A massive, white-to-green talc used in paints, ceramics, and insulation. Also called "soapstone". [Latin *steatītis, steatītēs,* from Greek *steatitis, steatītēs,* "tallow stone" : STEAT(O)- + -ITE.] —**ste·a·tit·ic** (-títtik) *adj.*

steato- *comb. form.* Indicates fat; for example, **steatopygia.** [Greek, from *stear* (stem *steat-*), solid fat, tallow. See **stearic**.]

ste·a·tol·y·sis (steér-tóllə-siss, steé-ə-) *n.* The digestive emulsification of fats prior to assimilation. [New Latin : STEATO- + -LYSIS.]

ste·a·to·py·gi·a (steér-tō-píji-ə, steé-ə-) *n.* An excessive accumulation of fat on the buttocks. [New Latin : STEATO- + Greek *pugē,* rump (see **pygidium**).] —**ste·a·to·pyg·ic** (-píjik), **ste·a·to·py·gous** (-pígəss) *adj.*

ste·a·tor·rhoe·a (steér-tə-réer, steé-ə-, -tō-, -rée-ə) *n.* 1. Excessive discharge of fat in the faeces. 2. Overaction of the sebaceous glands; seborrhoea. [New Latin : STEATO- + -RRHOEA.]

steed (steed) *n. Archaic & Poetic.* A horse, especially one that is spirited. [Middle English *stede,* Old English *stēda,* stallion.]

steel (steel) *n.* 1. Any of various generally hard, strong, durable, malleable alloys of iron and carbon, usually containing between 0.02 to 1.5 per cent carbon, often with other constituents such as manganese, chromium, nickel, molybdenum, copper, tungsten, co-

balt, or silicon, depending on the desired alloy properties, and widely used as a structural material. 2. A quality suggestive of steel; especially, a hard, unflinching character. 3. Something made of steel, especially: a. A weapon such as a sword, knife, or the like. b. A knife sharpener consisting of a handled steel rod. c. A slender strip or band of steel used for stiffening corsets or dresses. 6. *Finance.* a. The steel industry. b. *Plural.* The market quotation for shares in the steel industry. 7. a. Dark grey to purplish grey. Also called "steel grey". b. Dark greyish blue. Also called "steel blue". ~*adj.* 1. Made of or with steel. 2. a. Resembling the properties of steel. b. Of the colour steel. 3. Of the production of steel. ~*tr.v.* **steeled, steeling, steels.** 1. To cover, plate, edge, or point with steel. 2. To make strong, resolute, or resistant; strengthen. [Middle English *stel(le), stiel,* Old English *stēli, stýle.*]

Steel (steel), **David (Martin Scott), Baron** (1939–). British politician. As the then leader of the Liberal Party, he created the Alliance movement with the newly formed Social Democratic Party (1981). From 1988 he was a member of the Social and Liberal Democrats (now Liberal Democrats).

steel band *n.* A musical band of a type originating in the West Indies, composed chiefly of percussion instruments fashioned from oil drums.

Steele (steel), **Sir Richard** (1672–1729). Irish-born playwright and essayist. He founded (1709) *The Tatler,* and was a leading contributor (1711–12) to the *Spectator,* for which he invented the character of the jovial English squire, Sir Roger de Coverley.

steel engraving *n.* 1. The art or process of engraving on a steel plate. 2. An impression produced with an engraved steel plate.

steel·head (steél-hed) *n.* The rainbow trout of North America, when occurring in marine waters or large inland lakes.

steel wool *n.* Fine fibres of steel woven or matted together to form an abrasive for cleaning, smoothing, or polishing.

steel·works (steél-wurk) *n., pl.* **steelworks.** A plant where steel is made. —**steel·work·er** *n.*

steel·y (steéli) *adj.* **-ier, -iest.** 1. Made of steel. 2. Like steel, as in coldness or hardness: *steely eyes.* —**steel·i·ness** *n.*

steel·yard (stíl-yərd, steél-, -yaard) *n.* A balance consisting of a scaled arm suspended off centre, a hook at the shorter end on which to hang the object being weighed, and a counterbalance at the longer end. [STEEL + YARD (rod).]

Steen (stayn), **Jan** (*c.* 1626–79). Dutch painter. He specialised in domestic and tavern scenes, among them *The Music Lesson, The Skittle Alley,* and *The Lute Player.*

steep[1] (steep) *adj.* **steeper, steepest.** 1. Having a sharp inclination; nearly perpendicular; precipitous. 2. Rising or falling rapidly or precipitously. 3. *Informal.* a. Excessive; unreasonable; exorbitant: *a steep price.* b. Difficult to believe; exaggerated. ~*n. Literary.* A precipitous slope; a steep place. [Middle English *stepe,* Old English *stēap,* lofty, deep, projecting.] —**steep·ly** *adv.* —**steep·ness** *n.*

steep[2] *v.* **steeped, steeping, steeps.** —*tr.* 1. To soak in liquid in order to cleanse, soften, or extract some property. 2. To infuse or subject thoroughly; immerse: *steeped in misery.* 3. To make thoroughly wet. —*intr.* To undergo a soaking in liquid. ~*n.* 1. a. The process of steeping. b. The state of being steeped. 2. A liquid, bath, or solution in which something is steeped. [Middle English *stepen,* from Old English *stiepan* (unattested), from Germanic.] —**steep·er** *n.*

steep·en (steépən) *v.* **-ened, -ening, -ens.** —*tr.* To make steeper. —*intr.* To become steeper.

stee·ple (steép'l) *n.* 1. A tall tower forming the superstructure of a building, especially a church, and usually surmounted by a spire. 2. A spire. [Middle English *stepel, stepyl,* Old English *stīpel, stýpel.*]

stee·ple·chase (steép'l-chayss) *n.* 1. a. A horse race over a course provided with artificial obstacles. b. A horse race across open country. 2. A long-distance running race, usually of 3000 metres, over a course provided with hurdles and other obstacles. ~*intr.v.* **steeplechased, -chasing, -chases.** To take part in a steeplechase. [Church steeples were originally used as goals in such horse races.] —**stee·ple·chas·er** *n.*

stee·ple·jack (steép'l-jak) *n.* A worker on steeples or other very high structures. [STEEPLE + JACK (labourer).]

steer[1] (steer) *v.* **steered, steering, steers.** —*tr.* 1. To guide (a vessel or vehicle) by means of a device such as a rudder, paddle, or wheel. 2. a. To direct the course of (a discussion or conversation, for example). b. To manoeuvre (a person) into a place or course of action. 3. To set and follow (a particular course): *steered a course through the straits; tried to steer a middle course.* —*intr.* 1. To guide a vessel or vehicle. 2. To follow or move in a set course. 3. To allow of being steered or guided in a specified fashion: *a boat that steers easily.* —**steer clear of.** To avoid; keep away from. [Middle English *steren,* Old English *stīeran.*] —**steer·a·ble** *adj.* —**steer·er** *n.*

steer[2] *n.* A young ox, especially one castrated and raised for beef. [Middle English *stere, steer,* Old English *stēor.*]

steer·age (steér-ij) *n.* 1. The action or practice of steering. 2. The steering apparatus of a ship. 3. The section of a passenger ship, originally near the rudder, with the cheapest accommodation.

steer·age·way (steér-ij-way) *n.* The minimum rate of motion required for the helm of a ship or boat to have effect.

steer·ing committee (steér-ing) *n.* A committee whose function it is to suggest issues to be considered and to arrange the order of business, as for a legislative body or other assembly.

steering gear *n.* The mechanism by which a vehicle, ship, or aircraft is steered.

steering wheel *n.* A wheel that is turned to control the steering gear, as on a motor vehicle or motorboat.

steers·man (steérz-mən) *n., pl.* **-men** (-mən). A helmsman.

steeve[1] (steev) *n.* A spar or derrick with a block at one end, used for stowing cargo.
~*tr.v.* **steeved, steeving, steeves.** To stow or pack (cargo) in the hold of a ship. [Middle English *steven,* to stow, from Spanish *estibar,* to cram, from Latin *stīpāre,* to stuff fully.]

steeve[2] *n. Nautical.* The angle formed by the bowsprit and the horizon or the keel.
~*v.* **steeved, steeving, steeves.** *Nautical.* —*tr.* To incline (a bowsprit) upwards at an angle with the horizon or the keel. —*intr.* To have an upward inclination. Used of a bowsprit. [17th century : origin obscure.]

Stefan-Boltzmann law (stéffən-bōlts-man; *German* shtéffan-) *n.* A physical law stating that the total energy radiated from a black body is equal to the fourth power of its absolute temperature. [After Josef *Stefan* (1835–83), Austrian physicist, and Ludwig BOLTZMANN.]

Ste·fan Du·šan (stéffan dōō-shan) (*c.* 1308–55). King of Serbia (1331–55). He created a Serbian empire by subjugating Albania, Epirus, Macedonia, and Thessaly.

steg·o·don (stéggə-don, -dən) *n.* Also **steg·o·dont** (-dont). Any of various extinct elephant-like mammals of the genus *Stegodon* and related genera, of the Pliocene to Pleistocene epoch. [New Latin *Stegodon,* "ridge-toothed" (from the distinctive ridges on its molars): Greek *stegos,* roof, "ridge", from *stegein,* to cover + -ODONT.]

steg·o·saur (stéggə-sawr) *n.* Also **steg·o·sau·rus** (-sáwrəss). Any of several herbivorous dinosaurs of the genus *Stegosaurus* and related genera, of the Triassic to the Cretaceous period, having a double row of upright bony plates along the back. [New Latin *Stegosaurus*: Greek *stegos,* roof, "ridge of plates" (see **stegodon**) + -SAUR.]

Steiermark. See **Styria.**

stein (stīn) *n.* An earthenware mug, especially one for beer, usually holding about a pint. [German *Stein,* probably short for *Steingut,* stoneware, earthenware : *Stein,* stone + *Gut,* goods, ware.]

Stein (stīn), **Gertrude** (1874–1946). U.S. author and poet. Her unique style, which experimented with syntax, was influenced by her study of psychology. Her best-known work is *The Autobiography of Alice B. Toklas* (1933).

Steinbeck (stīn-beck), **John** (1902–68). U.S. novelist. His novels deal with social and economic conditions in his native California. They include *The Grapes of Wrath* (1939) and *East of Eden* (1952). He won the Nobel prize for literature in 1962.

stein·bok (stīn-bok, -buk) *n.* Also **steen·bok** (steérn-, stáyn-). 1. An African antelope, *Raphicerus campestris neumanni,* having a brownish coat and short pointed horns in the male. 2. An **ibex** (*see*). [Afrikaans, "stone buck".]

Stei·ner (stīnər; *German* shtīnər), **Rudolf** (1861–1925). Austrian teacher and philosopher. He developed **anthroposophy** (*see*).

ste·le (stee-lee, -li) *n., pl.* **-les** or **-lae** (-lee). Also **ste·la** (-lə) (for sense 1) *pl.* **-lae.** 1. An upright stone or slab with an inscribed or sculptured surface, used, especially in ancient times, to mark a grave, as a monument, or as a commemorative tablet. 2. *Botany.* The central core of vascular tissue in a plant stem or root. [Latin *stēla,* from Greek *stēlē,* pillar.] —**ste·lar** (-lər) *adj.*

stel·lar (stéllər) *adj.* 1. Of, relating to, or consisting of stars. 2. Of, relating to, or worthy of a star performer. [Late Latin *stellāris,* from *stella,* star.]

stel·lar·a·tor (stéllə-raytər) *n.* An apparatus used in thermonuclear research to contain a plasma in a toroidal vessel by means of a magnetic field. [STELLAR + -*ator,* as in *generator*; the temperature used to heat the plasma approximates that in some stars.]

stel·late (stél-ət, -it, -ayt) *adj.* Also **stel·lat·ed** (ste-láytid ‖ stél-aytid). *Biology.* Arranged or shaped like a star; radiating from a centre. [Latin *stellātus,* from *stella,* star.] —**stel·late·ly** *adv.*

Stel·len·bosch (stéllen-boss; *Afrikaans* stéllem-bóss). City in Western Cape Province, South Africa, lying on the river Eerste. Founded in 1679 by Governor Simon Van der Stel, it is the second-oldest settlement in South Africa. It is a cultural and marketing centre.

stel·li·form (stélli-fawrm) *adj.* Star-shaped. [New Latin *stelliformis* : Latin *stella,* star (see **stellate**) + -I- + -FORM.]

stel·li·fy (stélli-fī) *tr.v.* **-fied, -fying, -fies.** To transform into a star. [Middle English *stellifien,* from Old French *stellifier,* from Medieval Latin *stellificāre* : Latin *stella,* star + *facere,* to do, make.]

stel·lu·lar (stéllewlər) *adj.* 1. Having the form of a small star or stars. 2. Adorned with small stars. [Late Latin *stellula,* diminutive of Latin *stella,* star.]

St. El·mo's fire (élmōz) *n.* A bluish electrical glow caused by corona discharge on masts and other high parts of a ship at sea before and during electrical storms. Also called "corposant". [After *St. Elmo,* patron saint of sailors.]

stem[1] (stem) *n.* 1. **a.** The main ascending axis of a plant, which bears the leaves, flowers, and axillary buds. **b.** The corresponding part in nonflowering plants. **c.** A slender stalk supporting or connecting another plant part, such as a leaf or flower; a stalk. 2. **a.** A banana stalk bearing several bunches of bananas. 3. Something analogous to a plant stem, especially: **a.** The tube of a tobacco pipe. **b.** The slender upright support of a wine glass or goblet. **c.** The small projecting shaft bearing the knob with which a watch is wound. **d.** The rounded rod in the centre of certain locks about

which the key fits and is turned. **e.** The shaft of a feather or hair. **f.** The main line of descent of a family as distinguished from a branch. **g.** The upright stroke of a typeface or letter. **h.** The vertical line extending from the head of a musical note. **i.** The main part of a word to which inflectional affixes are added. **j.** The curved upright beam at the bow of a vessel into which the hull timbers are scarfed to form the prow. **k.** In an incandescent bulb or vacuum tube, the tubular glass structure mounting the filament or electrodes. —**from stem to stern.** From one end to the other of a ship.
~*v.* **stemmed, stemming, stems.** —*tr.* 1. To remove the stem or stems of. 2. To make headway against (a tide, current, or comparable force); breast. —*intr.* To have as a point of origin; derive or develop. Usually used with *from.* [Middle English *stem,* Old English *stemn, stefn,* stem, tree trunk, (timber used to build the) prow or stern of a ship.] —**stem·less** *adj.*

stem[2] *v.* **stemmed, stemming, stems.** —*tr.* 1. To hold back (a flow, onrush, or movement) by or as if by damming. 2. To plug or stop up (a blast hole, for example). 3. To force the heel of (a ski or both skis) outwards, as in performing a stem turn. —*intr.* To force the heel of one ski or both skis outwards by shifting one's weight, in order to check one's speed, stop, or make a turn.
~*n.* In skiing, a stem turn. [Middle English *stemmen,* from Old Norse *stemma.*]

stem cell *n.* An unspecialised cell that gives rise to a certain type of specialised cell, such as a blood cell.

stem·ma (stémmə) *n., pl.* **stemmata** (-tə) or **-mas.** 1. In ancient Rome, a scroll recording the genealogy of a family. 2. Any family tree or pedigree. [Latin, garland, wreath, from Greek, from *stephein,* to encircle, crown, wreathe.]

stemmed (stemd) *adj.* 1. Having the stem or stems removed. 2. Provided with a stem or stems. Often used in combination: *thick-stemmed.*

stem·son (stém-s'n) *n. Nautical.* A piece of supporting timber bolted to the stem and keelson at their junction near the bow of a wooden vessel. [STEM[1] (sense 3j) (prow) + (KEEL)SON.]

stem turn *n.* In skiing, a turn made by stemming the downhill ski and placing one's weight upon it while bringing the other ski into a parallel position. Also called "stem christie".

stem·ware (stém-wair) *n.* Glassware mounted on a stem.

stem-wind·er (stém-wīndər) *n.* A stem-winding watch.

stem-wind·ing (stém-wīnding) *adj.* Designating a watch that is wound by turning a knob mounted on the end of the stem.

stench (stench) *n.* A strong and foul odour; a stink. See Synonyms at **smell.** [Middle English *stench,* Old English *stenc,* from Germanic *stenkw-* (unattested); akin to *stinkwan* (unattested), to STINK.]

sten·cil (stén-s'l, -sil) *n.* 1. A sheet of celluloid, cardboard, or other material in which a desired lettering or design has been cut so that when ink or paint is passed over the sheet the pattern will be reproduced on the surface placed below. 2. The lettering or design so produced. 3. A sheet of thin waxed paper that can be typed or drawn on to produce a stencil suitable for use in a duplicator.
~*tr.v.* **stencilled** or *U.S.* **-ciled, -cilling** or *U.S.* **-ciling, -cils.** 1. To mark (a surface) with a stencil. 2. To produce by stencil. [Middle English *stencel,* to adorn with brilliant colours, from Old French *estenceler,* "to cause to sparkle", from *estencele,* spark, from Latin *scintilla,* spark.] —**sten·cil·ler** *n.*

Sten·dhal (stan-dál, ston-, -dá͞al), pen name of Henri Beyle (1783–1842). French writer. His work, which shows searching psychological insight, was an important influence on the development of the French novel. His novels include *Le Rouge et le noir* (1830), and *La Chartreuse de Parme* (1839).

Sten gun (sten) *n.* A type of lightweight machine gun. [*St-* from the initials of the inventors' names, *S*hepherd and *T*urpin + -*en* as in BREN GUN.]

sten·o (sténnō) *n., pl.* **-os.** *U.S. Informal.* A stenographer.

steno– *comb. form.* Indicates narrowness; for example, **stenophagous.** [Greek *stenos,* narrow.]

sten·o·graph (sténnə-graaf, -graf) *tr.v.* **-graphed, -graphing, -graphs.** To record in shorthand. [Back-formation from STENOGRAPHY.]

ste·nog·ra·pher (stə-nóggrəfər, ste-) *n. U.S.* A **shorthand typist** (*see*).

ste·nog·ra·phy (stə-nóggrəfi, ste-) *n.* 1. The art or process of writing in shorthand. 2. Material written down in shorthand. [STENO- + -GRAPHY.] —**sten·o·graph·ic** (sténnə-gráffik) *adj.* —**sten·o·graph·i·cal·ly** *adv.*

sten·o·ha·line (sténnō-háy-līn, -há-) *adj.* Able to live only within a narrow range of salt concentration. Said of certain aquatic organisms. Compare **euryhaline.** [STENO- + Greek *hals* (stem *hal-),* salt + -INE.]

ste·noph·a·gous (sti-nóffəgəss, ste-) *adj.* Feeding on a single kind or limited range of food. [STENO- + -PHAGOUS.]

ste·no·sis (sti-nō-siss, ste-) *n., pl.* **-ses** (-seez). *Pathology.* An abnormal narrowing of a passage or canal in the body. [New Latin, from Greek *stenōsis,* from *stenoun,* to constrict, from *stenos,* narrow.] —**ste·not·ic** (-nóttik) *adj.*

sten·o·ther·mal (sténnō-thérm'l) *adj. Biology.* Of or designating organisms adapted to living only within a limited range of temperature. [German *stenotherm* : STENO- + *thermē,* heat, THERM.]

sten·o·trop·ic (sténnō-tróppik) *adj.* Also **sten·o·top·ic** (-tóppik). *Biology.* Having narrow limits of adaptation to environmental conditions. Compare **eurytropic.** [STENO- + -TROPE + -IC.]

Sten·o·type (stén-ō-tīp, -ə-) *n.* 1. A trademark for a keyboard machine used to record dictation by a phonetic system. **2.** *Small* **s.** A symbol or combination of symbols on a Stenotype representing a sound, word, or phrase. [STENO(GRAPHY) + TYPE.]

sten·o·ty·py (sténnə-tīpi) *n.* A form of shorthand using the letters of the alphabet to represent certain sounds or words. [STENOTYPE + -Y.] —**sten·o·ty·pist** *n.*

sten·tor (stén-tawr, -tər) *n.* **1.** Any of several trumpet-shaped aquatic microorganisms of the genus *Stentor,* having cilia around the oral cavity. **2.** *Often capital* **S.** A person with an extremely loud voice. [New Latin *Stentor,* from Greek *Stentōr.* See stentorian.]

sten·to·ri·an (sten-táw-ri-ən ‖ -tō-) *adj.* Extremely loud. Said of the voice. [Greek *Stentōr,* name of a loud-voiced herald in the *Iliad,* from *stenein,* to groan, moan.]

step (step) *n.* **1. a.** The single complete movement of raising one foot and putting it down in another spot in the act of walking, running, or dancing. **b.** A manner of walking; a gait. **c.** The rhythm or pace of another or others, as in a march or dance: *break step; keep step.* **d.** The sound of a tread; a footstep. **e.** A footprint. **2. a.** The distance traversed by moving one foot ahead of the other. **b.** A very short distance: *just a step away.* **c.** *Plural.* Course; path: *followed in his father's steps.* **3. a.** A rest for the foot in ascending or descending. **b.** *Plural.* Stairs. **c.** *Plural.* A stepladder. **4. a.** Any of a series of actions or measures taken towards some end: *take steps to remedy the situation.* **b.** A stage in a process. **5.** A degree in progress or a grade or rank in a scale: *a step ahead of the others.* **6.** *Nautical.* The block in which the heel of a mast is fixed. **7.** A series of foot and body movements making up part of a dance: *hasn't learnt the polka step.* **8.** Any change in the level of a surface, as on a hillside or on the sea bed, that resembles a step on a set of stairs. **9.** *Music. Chiefly U.S.* **a.** A degree in a scale. **b.** The interval between two adjacent degrees in a scale. —**in step. 1.** Moving in rhythm or time. **2.** *Informal.* In conformity or harmony. —**out of step.** Not in step. —**step by step.** By degrees; gradually. —**watch (one's) step. a.** To be careful and sensible. **b.** To behave as is demanded or required.

~*v.* **stepped, stepping, steps.** —*intr.* **1.** To put or press the foot; tread: *stepped on my toe.* **2.** To move or go, especially a short distance, by taking a step or steps: *step aside; step into my office.* **3.** To move using the feet, in a particular manner: *step lively.* **4.** To move into a new situation as if by taking a single step: *stepping into a life of ease.* —*tr.* **1.** To move by taking (a number of steps or paces): *step five paces.* **2.** To measure by pacing. Usually used with *off* or *out: step off ten yards.* **3.** To furnish with steps; make steps in. **4.** *Chiefly U.S.* To set (the foot) down: *step foot on land.* **5.** *Nautical.* To place (a mast) in its step. —**step on.** To treat harshly or with arrogant indifference. —**step on it.** *Informal.* To hurry up; speed up. —**step out.** To walk with brisk strides. [Middle English *step(pe), stap(p)e,* Old English *stæpe, stepe.*]

step– *comb. form.* Indicates relationship through the previous marriage of a spouse or through the remarriage of a parent, rather than by blood; for example, **stepbrother.** [Middle English *step-, stip-,* Old English *stēop-.*]

step·broth·er (stép-bruthər) *n.* The son of one's step-parent by a former marriage.

step·child (stép-chīld) *n., pl.* **-children** (-childrən). The child of one's spouse by a former marriage.

step·daugh·ter (stép-dawtər) *n.* The daughter of one's spouse by a former marriage.

step down *intr.v.* **1.** To take a lesser position. **2.** To abdicate; resign. —*tr.v.* To reduce (power, for example) by stages.

step-down (stép-down) *adj.* Decreasing in stages.

~*n.* A reduction in amount or size.

step-down transformer *n.* A transformer that has a greater number of turns in the primary winding than in the secondary, used to transform high voltage to low voltage.

step·father (stép-faathər) *n.* The husband of one's mother by a later marriage.

step fault *n. Geology.* A series of parallel faults along which relative displacement downwards has occurred on the same side.

steph·a·no·tis (stéffə-nōtiss) *n.* Any climbing plant of the tropical genus *Stephanotis;* especially *S. floribunda,* native to Madagascar, and widely cultivated as a house plant for its white waxy flowers. [New Latin, from Greek (adjective), fit for a wreath, from *stephanos,* wreath, crown.]

Ste·phen (stéev'n) (*c.* 1097–1154). King of England. He was elected king (1135) on the death of Henry I, despite an oath of fealty to Henry's daughter Matilda. He was a weak king and most of his reign was marked by civil war. After the death of his son (1153) he acknowledged Matilda's son (Henry II) as his heir.

Stephen, Sir Leslie (1832–1904). British man of letters. He was editor of the *Dictionary of National Biography* and his books include *Essays on Free Thinking and Plain Speaking* (1873). Father of Virginia Woolf and the artist Vanessa Bell (1879–1961).

Ste·phen·son (stéev'n-s'n), **George** (1781–1848). British engineer. He built (1814) a successful steam locomotive, and (1825) the world's first public steam railway, between Stockton and Darlington. He and his son Robert were jointly responsible for the *Rocket* locomotive, which won (1829) a prize for maintaining an average speed of 29 miles per hour.

Stephenson, Robert (1803–59). British engineer. Son of George Stephenson. He collaborated with his father in building many of the railways in Britain and abroad. He also built the Menai Strait

bridge and the high-level bridge over the Tyne at Newcastle.

step in *intr.v.* To intervene or interfere, as to provide help or take charge of a situation.

step-in (stép-in) *adj.* Put on by stepping into: *a step-in ski binding.*

~*n. Often plural.* A step-in garment, especially an undergarment.

step·lad·der (stép-laddər) *n.* A portable ladder with a hinged supporting frame and usually topped with a small platform. Also called "steps".

step·moth·er (stép-muthər) *n.* The wife of one's father by a later marriage.

step·par·ent (stép-pair-ənt) *n.* A stepfather or a stepmother.

steppe (step) *n.* A vast semiarid grass-covered plain, such as that found in southeastern Europe and Siberia. [Russian *step',* from Old Russian *step'†,* lowland.]

step·ping·stone (stépping-stōn) *n.* **1.** A stone that provides a place to stand on, as in crossing a stream. **2.** An advantageous position for advancement towards some goal.

step pyramid *n.* A pyramid with outer faces made up of stone blocks rising in steps.

step rocket *n. Aerospace.* A **multistage rocket** (see).

step·sis·ter (stép-sistər) *n.* The daughter of one's step-parent by a former marriage.

step·son (stép-sun) *n.* The son of one's spouse by a former marriage.

Step·toe (stép-tō), **Patrick Christopher** (1913–88). British obstetrician and gynaecologist. In 1978, in collaboration with Professor Robert Edwards, he produced the world's first test-tube baby.

step up *tr.v.* To increase, especially by stages: *step up production.*

step-up (stép-up) *adj.* Increasing in steps or by stages.

~*n.* An increase in size, amount, or activity.

step-up transformer *n.* A transformer that has fewer turns in the primary winding than in the secondary, used to transform low voltage to high voltage.

step·wise (stép-wīz) *adj.* **1.** Marked by a gradual progression as if step by step. **2.** *Music. U.S.* Moving one degree on a scale. —**stepwise** *adv.*

-ster *n. suffix.* Indicates: **1.** One who takes part in or is associated with; for example, **gangster, youngster. 2.** One who makes or is given to making; for example, **pollster, prankster.** [Middle English *-ster(e), -estere,* Old English *-estre, -ister,* from West Germanic *-strjōn* (unattested), agent-noun suffix (primarily feminine).]

ste·ra·di·an (stə-ráydi-ən, ste-) *n. Abbr.* **sr** A unit of measure equal to the solid angle subtended at the centre of a sphere by an area on the surface equal to the square of the radius: *The total solid angle of a sphere is 4π steradians.* [STE(REO)- + RADIAN.]

ster·co·ra·ceous (stérkə-ráyshəss) *adj.* Also **ster·co·rous** (-rəss). Consisting of or pertaining to excrement. [Latin *stercus* (stem *stercor*-), dung + -ACEOUS.]

stere (steer) *n. Abbr.* **s** A unit of volume equal to one cubic metre. [French *stère,* from Greek *stereos,* solid, hard.]

ste·re·o (stérri-ō, stéer-i-ō) *n., pl.* **-os. 1. a.** A stereophonic high-fidelity sound system. **b.** Stereophonic sound. **2.** *Printing.* A stereotype. **3.** A stereoscopic system or photograph.

~*adj.* **1.** Stereophonic. **2.** Stereoscopic.

stereo–, stere– *comb. form.* Indicates solid, firm, or three-dimensional; for example, **stereophonic, stereoscope.** [Greek *stereos,* solid, hard.]

ster·e·o·bate (stérri-ō-bayt, stéer-i-) *n. Architecture.* **1.** A stylobate. **2.** The foundation of a stone building, its top course sometimes being a stylobate. [Latin *stereobata,* from Greek *stereobatēs,* "solid base" : *stereos,* solid, STEREO- + *-batēs,* "one that is based".]

ster·e·o·chem·is·try (stérri-ō-kémmistri, stéer-i-) *n.* The chemical study of spatial arrangements of atoms in molecules and of the effects of these arrangements on the molecule's properties.

ster·e·o·chro·my (stérri-ō-krōmi, stéer-i-) *n.* The art or process of painting murals using pigments mixed with water glass. [STEREO- + -CHROME + -Y.] —**ster·e·o·chrome** *n. & tr.v.* —**ster·e·o·chro·mic** (-krōmik) *adj.* —**ster·e·o·chro·mi·cal·ly** *adv.*

ster·e·o·gram (stérri-ō-gram, stéer-i-) *n.* **1.** A stereo record player consisting of a single unit. **2.** A picture or diagram designed to give the impression of solidity. **3.** A stereograph. [STEREO- + -GRAM.]

ster·e·o·graph (stérri-ō-graaf, stéer-i-, -graf) *n.* Two stereoscopic pictures, or one picture with two superposed stereoscopic images, designed to give a three-dimensional effect when viewed through a stereoscope or special glasses.

~*tr.v.* **stereographed, -graphing, -graphs.** To make (a stereographic picture). [STEREO- + -GRAPH.]

stereographic projection *n.* An azimuthal map projection in which a point is projected onto the tangent plane from a point on the opposite end of the diameter. It is an orthomorphic projection.

ster·e·og·ra·phy (stérri-óggrəfi, stéer-i-) *n.* The art or technique of depicting solid bodies on a plane surface. [STEREO- + -GRAPHY.] —**ster·e·o·graph·ic** (-ə-gráffik), **ster·e·o·graph·i·cal** *adj.* —**ster·e·o·graph·i·cal·ly** *adv.*

ster·e·o·i·so·mer (stérri-ō-Í-səmər, stéer-i-) *n. Chemistry.* Any of the structural molecular forms of a compound that exhibits stereoisomerism. See isomer.

ster·e·o·i·som·er·ism (stérri-ō-Í-sómmə-ríz'm, stéer-i-) *n.* Isomerism created by differences in the spatial arrangement of atoms in a molecule. —**ster·e·o·i·so·mer·ic** (-sə-mérrik) *adj.*

ste·re·om·e·try (stérri-ómmətri, stéeri-) *n.* The science of measuring volume. [STEREO- + -METRY.] —**ste·re·o·me·tric** (-ō-méttrik, -ə-), **ste·re·o·me·tri·cal** *adj.*

ster·e·o·mi·cro·scope (stĕrrĭ-ō-mīkrə-skōp, stêer-ĭ-) *n.* A microscope optically equipped for stereoscopic viewing.

ster·e·o·phon·ic (stĕrrĭ-ə-fónnĭk, stêer-ĭ-, -ō-) *adj.* Of or pertaining to a high-fidelity sound system in which two channels are used to give an illusion of a more natural distribution of sources of sound. Compare **binaural, quadraphonic.** [STEREO- + PHONIC.] —**ster·e·o·phon·i·cal·ly** *adv.* —**ster·e·oph·on·y** (-óffəni) *n.*

ster·e·op·sis (stĕrrĭ-ópsis, stêer-ĭ-) *n.* Stereoscopic vision. [New Latin : STEREO- + -OPSIS.]

ster·e·op·ti·con (stĕrrĭ-ópti-kən, stêer-ĭ- ‖ -kon) *n.* A **magic lantern** (*see*), especially one consisting of two separate units arranged so as to produce dissolving views. [New Latin : STEREO- + Greek *optikon,* neuter of *optikos,* OPTIC.]

ster·e·o·scope (stĕrrĭ-ə-skōp, stêer-ĭ-) *n.* An optical instrument used to impart a three-dimensional effect to two photographs of the same scene taken at slightly different angles and viewed through two eyepieces. [STEREO- + -SCOPE.]

ster·e·o·scop·ic (stĕrrĭ-ə-skóppĭk, stêer-ĭ-) *adj.* **1.** Of or pertaining to stereoscopy; especially, three-dimensional. **2.** Of or pertaining to a stereoscope. —**ster·e·o·scop·i·cal·ly** *adv.*

ster·e·os·co·py (stĕrrĭ-óskəpi, stêer-ĭ-) *n.* **1.** The viewing of objects as three-dimensional. **2.** The technique of making or using stereoscopes. [STEREO- + -SCOPY.] —**ster·e·os·co·pist** *n.*

ste·re·o·spe·cif·ic *adj. Chemistry.* Pertaining to, involving, or producing a regular arrangement of atoms in a molecule. Said especially of polymers with a regular arrangement of atoms or of reactions or catalysts producing such compounds.

ster·e·o·tax·is (stĕrrĭ-ō-táksiss, stêer-ĭ-, -ə-) *n. Biology.* **Thigmotaxis** (*see*). —**ster·e·o·tac·tic** (-táktĭk), **ster·e·o·tac·ti·cal** *adj.* —**ster·e·o·tac·ti·cal·ly** *adv.*

ster·e·o·type (stĕrrĭ-ə-tīp, stêer-ĭ-, -ō-) *n.* **1.** A conventional, formulaic, and usually oversimplified conception, opinion, or belief. **2.** A person, group, event, or issue considered to typify or conform to an unvarying standard pattern or manner: *the stereotype of a banker.* Also used adjectivally: *a stereotype male chauvinist.* **3. a.** A metal printing plate cast from a mould made out of papier-mâché, plastic, or rubber, taken from a raised printing surface, such as type. **b.** The method or process of making such a plate. —*tr.v.* **stereotyped, -typing, -types. 1.** To make a stereotype of. **2.** To print from a stereotype. **3.** To give a fixed, unvarying form to. [French *stéréotype* : STEREO- + TYPE.] —**ster·e·o·typ·er** *n.* —**ster·e·o·typ·ic** (-típpĭk), **ster·e·o·typ·i·cal** *adj.*

ster·e·o·typed (stĕrrĭ-ə-tīpt, stêer-ĭ-, -ō-) *adj.* **1.** Not individualised; unoriginal; conventional. **2.** Printed or reproduced from stereotype plates. —See Synonyms at **trite.**

ster·e·o·typ·y (stĕrrĭ-ə-tīpi, stêer-ĭ-, -ō-) *n.* **1.** The process or art of making stereotype plates. **2.** Excessive repetition or lack of variation in movements, ideas, or patterns of speech.

ster·e·o·vi·sion (stĕrrĭ-ō-vĭzh'n, stêer-ĭ-) *n.* Visual perception of or exhibition in three dimensions.

ster·ic (stĕrrĭk, stêer-ĭk) *n.* Of or pertaining to the spatial arrangement of atoms in a molecule. [STER(EO)- + -IC.] —**ster·i·cal·ly** *adv.*

ste·rig·ma (stə-rĭg-mə, ste-) *n.* A slender spore-bearing structure formed by certain fungi. [New Latin, from Greek *stērigma,* support, from *stērizein,* to support.]

ster·i·lant (stĕrrĭ-lənt, stêrrə-) *n.* A sterilising agent.

ster·ile (stĕrrīl ‖ *U.S.* stĕrrəl) *adj.* **1. a.** Incapable of reproducing sexually; barren; infertile. **b.** Incapable of producing seed, fruit spores, or other reproductive structures. Said of plants or their parts. **2.** Capable of producing little or no vegetation: *sterile land.* **3.** Free from bacteria or other microorganisms. **4.** Lacking in imagination or vitality; not stimulating; dry. **5.** Failing to produce any useful result; fruitless: *a sterile discussion.* **6.** Containing no archaeological remains: *a sterile stratum.* [French *sterile,* from Latin *sterilis,* unfruitful.] —**ster·ile·ly** *adv.* —**ste·ril·i·ty** (ste-rĭlləti, stə-), **ster·ile·ness** *n.*

Synonyms: *sterile, infertile, barren, unfruitful, impotent.*

ster·il·i·sa·tion (stĕrrə-lī-záysh'n, stêrri- ‖ *U.S.* -lĭ-) *n.* **1.** The procedure or act of making infertile. **2.** The removal of living microorganisms from materials.

ster·i·lise, ster·il·ize (stĕrrə-līz, stêrri-) *tr.v.* **-ised, -ising, -ises.** To render sterile. —**ster·il·is·er** *n.*

ster·let (stĕrlit) *n.* A sturgeon, *Acipenser ruthenus,* of the Caspian Sea and adjacent waters. [Russian *sterlyad',* perhaps akin to Germanic *sturjōn* (unattested), STURGEON.]

ster·ling (stĕrling) *n. Abbr.* **ster., stg. 1.** British money; especially, the pound as the basic monetary unit of the United Kingdom. **2.** British coinage of silver or gold, having as a standard of fineness 0.500 for silver and 0.91666 for gold. **3. a.** Sterling silver. **b.** Articles made of sterling silver, such as tableware. —*adj. Abbr.* **ster., stg. 1.** Consisting of or relating to sterling or British money. **2.** Made of sterling silver. **3.** Of the highest quality; of genuine worth. [Middle English *sterling, starling,* "small star" (from the small star stamped on the silver pennies), probably from Old English *steorling* (unattested) : *steorra,* STAR + -LING.]

sterling area *n.* The **scheduled territories** (*see*).

sterling silver *n.* **1.** An alloy of 92.5 per cent silver with copper or another metal. **2.** Collectively, objects made of this alloy.

stern¹ (stern) *adj.* **sterner, sternest. 1.** Not inclined to leniency; strict. **2.** Expressing disapproval or displeasure: *a stern rebuke.* **3.** Grave or severe in manner or appearance; grim; austere: *a silent, stern, rather forbidding manner.* **4.** Resolute; inflexible; unyielding: *made of sterner stuff.* **5.** Inexorable; relentless: *stern necessity.*

—See Synonyms at **severe.** [Middle English *sterne, stierne,* Old English *styrne, stierne.*] —**stern·ly** *adv.* —**stern·ness** *n.*

stern² *n.* **1.** The rear part of a ship or boat. **2.** The rear part of anything. [Middle English *sterne,* probably from Old Norse *stjörn,* steering, rudder, from *stỹra,* STEER.]

ster·nal (stĕrn'l) *adj. Anatomy.* Of, near, or pertaining to the sternum. [New Latin *sternalis,* from STERNUM.]

Stern·berg (shtáirn-bairk), **Josef von** (1894–1969). Austrian film director. He is best known for his series of films starring Marlene Dietrich, which include *The Blue Angel* (1930), *Blonde Venus* (1932), *Shanghai Express* (1932), and *The Scarlet Empress* (1934).

stern chaser *n.* A gun or cannon mounted on the stern of a ship for firing at a pursuing vessel.

Sterne (stern), **Laurence** (1713–68). English novelist and clergyman. He won fame with his witty, ribald novel *The Life and Opinions of Tristram Shandy, Gentleman* (1759–67). His other works include *A Sentimental Journey* (1768).

stern·fore·most (stĕrn-fór-mōst, -məst ‖ -fŏr-) *adv. Nautical.* With the stern foremost; backwards.

stern·most (stĕrn-mōst) *adj. Nautical.* Farthest astern.

stern·post (stĕrn-pōst) *n.* The principal upright post at the stern of a vessel, usually serving to support the rudder.

stern sheets *pl.n.* The stern area of an open boat.

stern·son (stĕrn-s'n) *n.* A bar of metal or wood set between the keelson and the sternpost to fortify the joint. Also called "stern knee". [STERN + (KEEL)SON.]

ster·num (stĕr-nəm) *n., pl.* **-na** (-nə) *or* **-nums. 1.** A long flat bone articulating with the cartilages of and forming the midventral support of most of the ribs in tetrapod vertebrates, and also of the collarbone in humans and certain other vertebrates. Also called "breastbone". **2.** The chitinous plate that forms a protective covering on the ventral surface of the body segment of an arthropod. [New Latin, from Greek *sternon,* breast, breastbone.]

ster·nu·ta·tion (stĕrnew-táysh'n) *n.* **1.** The act of sneezing. **2.** A sneeze. [Latin *sternūtātiō* (stem *sternūtātiōn-*), from *sternūtāre,* frequentative of *sternuere,* to sneeze.]

ster·nu·ta·tor (stĕrnew-taytər) *n.* A substance that irritates the nasal and respiratory passages and causes sneezing.

ster·nu·ta·to·ry (ster-néwtə-tri, -təri, stĕrnew-táytəri ‖ -nŏotə-) *adj.* Causing or tending to cause sneezing.

—*n., pl.* **sternutatories.** A sternutatory substance, such as pepper.

stern·ward (stĕrn-wərd) *adj.* In or at the stern.

—*adv. Chiefly U.S.* Variant of **sternwards.**

stern·wards (stĕrn-wərdz) *adv.* Also *chiefly U.S.* **stern·ward** (-wərd). Towards the stern; astern.

stern·way (stĕrn-way) *n.* The backward movement of a vessel.

stern·wheel·er (stĕrn-wéelər, -hwéelər) *n.* A steamboat propelled by a paddle wheel at the stern.

ster·oid (stêer-oyd, stérroyd) *n.* Any of numerous naturally occurring, fat-soluble organic compounds having a 17-carbon-atom ring as a basis, and including the sterols and bile acids, many hormones, certain natural drugs such as digitalis compounds, and the precursors of certain vitamins. [STER(OL) + -OID.]

ster·ol (stêer-ol, stérrol ‖ -ōl, sterrōl) *n.* Any of a group of predominantly unsaturated solid alcohols of the steroid group, such as cholesterol and ergosterol, occurring in the fatty tissues of plants and animals. [Short for CHOLESTEROL.]

Ster·o·pe¹ (stĕrrəpi). Also **As·ter·o·pe** (a-). *Greek Mythology.* One of the **Pleiades** (*see*). [Greek *(A)steropē,* from *(a)steropē, astrapē,* lightning, "twinkling".]

Sterope² *n.* One of the stars in the constellation **Pleiades** (*see*).

ster·tor (stĕr-tər, -tawr) *n.* A heavy snoring sound in deep sleep or a coma, caused by obstruction of the air passages. [New Latin, from Latin *stertere,* to snore.] —**ster·tor·ous** (-tərəss) *adj.* —**ster·tor·ous·ly** *adv.*

stet (stet) *n. Abbr.* **st.** A printer's term directing that a letter, word, or other matter marked for omission or correction is to be retained. —*tr.v.* **stetted, stetting, stets.** To cancel a correction or omission previously made to (a letter, word, or section of printed matter) by marking with the word *stet* and with a row of dots. Compare **dele.** [Latin, let it stand, from *stāre,* to stand.]

steth·o·scope (stéthə-skōp) *n.* An instrument consisting of a hollow disc connected by a tube to an earpiece used for listening to sounds produced within the body. [French *stéthoscope* : Greek *stēthos*†, chest, breast + -SCOPE.] —**steth·o·scop·ic** (-skóppĭk) *adj.* —**steth·o·scop·i·cal·ly** *adv.* —**ste·tho·sco·py** (ste-thóskəpi) *n.*

Stet·son (stéts'n) *n.* A trademark for a hat having a high crown and wide brim, popular in the western United States. [Designed by John *Stetson* (1830–1906), U.S. hat-maker.]

Stettin. See **Szczecin.**

ste·ve·dore (stéev-ə-dawr, -ĭ- ‖ -dōr) *n.* A person employed in the loading or unloading of ships.

—*v.* **stevedored, -doring, -dores.** —*tr.* To load or unload the cargo of (a ship). —*intr.* To work as a stevedore. [Spanish *estibador,* from *estivar,* to pack, from Latin *stīpāre,* to stuff.]

stevedore's knot *n.* A knot used to prevent a line from coming out of a pulley.

ste·ven·graph (stéev'n-graaf, -graf) *n.* A colourful, usually small, picture woven in silk. [After Thomas *Stevens,* 19th-century British weaver.]

Ste·vens (stéev'nz), **Wallace** (1879–1955). U.S. poet. His poetry is distinguished by its tight construction and its intellectual but lucid content, as in the collection *The Man with the Blue Guitar and Other Poems* (1937).

Ste·ven·son (stéev'n-s'n), **Adlai (Ewing)** (1900–65). U.S. politician. He held various offices in Roosevelt's wartime administrations, and was governor (1949–53) of Illinois. He was Democratic presidential candidate (1952, 1956) for the presidency, but was beaten by Eisenhower.

Stevenson, Robert Louis (1850–94). Scottish novelist, essayist, and poet. His works include *Travels with a Donkey in the Cévennes* (1879), *Virginibus Puerisque* (1881), *Treasure Island* (1883), and *The Strange Case of Dr. Jekyll and Mr. Hyde* (1886).

stew (stew || stōō) *v.* **stewed, stewing, stews.** —*tr.* **1.** To cook (food) by simmering or boiling slowly. **2.** To leave (tea) for a long time before drinking, thus allowing the tannin to infuse and giving it an acrid taste. —*intr.* **1.** To undergo cooking by boiling slowly or simmering. **2.** *Informal.* To suffer with oppressive heat or stuffy confinement; swelter. **3.** *Informal.* To worry; fret. **4.** To become stewed. Used of tea.
∼*n.* **1.** A dish cooked by stewing; especially, a mixture of meat or fish and vegetables with stock. **2.** *Informal.* A state of mental agitation or difficulty: *in a stew over her lost keys.* **3.** *Usually plural. Archaic.* A brothel. [Middle English *stewen,* originally to bathe in hot water or steam, from Old French *estuver,* from Vulgar Latin *extūfāre* (unattested) : probably *ex-*, out of + *tufus* (unattested), hot vapour, from Greek *tuphos,* smoke, vapour, from *tuphein,* to smoke.]

stew·ard (stéw-ərd || stōō-) *n.* **1.** One who manages another's property, finances, or other affairs. **2.** One in charge of domestic arrangements, as in an institution, club, or hotel. **3.** An officer on a ship in charge of provisions and dining arrangements. **4.** Any male member of the staff of a ship or aeroplane, who waits on the passengers. **5.** An official who supervises or helps to manage an event such as a ball or race-meeting. **6.** A **shop steward** *(see).*
∼*v.* **stewarded, -arding, -ards.** —*tr.* To serve as steward of; manage; administer. —*intr.* To serve as a steward. [Middle English *stuarde, stywarde,* Old English *stigweard,* "keeper of the hall" : *stig,* hall (see **sty**) + *weard,* keeper, ward.]

stew·ard·ess (stéw-ərd-iss, -éss || stōō-) *n.* A female steward, especially one who waits on passengers on an aeroplane.

Stewart. See **Stuart.**

Stew·art (stéw-ərt || stōō-), **Jackie,** born John Young Stewart (1939–). British motor-racing driver. In his racing career (1961–73) he won a record number of 27 Grand Prix races. He was world champion in 1969, 1971, and 1973.

Stewart, James (Maitland) (1908–97). U.S. film actor, best known for his portrayals of incorruptible heroes in films such as *Destry Rides Again* (1939) and *The Philadelphia Story* (1940, Oscar).

stewed (stewd || stōōd) *adj.* **1.** Cooked by stewing: *stewed prunes.* **2.** Having an acid taste through having been left a long time before drinking. Said of tea. **3.** *Slang.* Drunk; intoxicated.

St. Ex. stock exchange.

St. George's. Capital and port of Grenada, West Indies. Situated on the southwest coast, it was founded by the French (1705) and was the capital of the British Windward Isles (1885–1958).

St. George's Channel. Strait between southeast Ireland and southwest Wales. Linking the Atlantic Ocean with the Irish Sea, it is some 160 kilometres (100 miles) long and 75–145 kilometres (46–90 miles) wide.

St. Gott·hard Pass (gót-ərd, -aard). Alpine pass, south Switzerland. Rising to a height of 2 114 metres (6,935 feet), it has long been part of a trade route linking Switzerland with Italy. Beneath the pass there is a railway tunnel (1872–80) 15 kilometres (9.25 miles) long and a road tunnel (1970–80) 16 kilometres (10 miles) long.

Sth. South.

St. Helens, Mount. Volcano in Washington state, northwest United States. It erupted in May 1980, shearing some 450 metres (about 1,500 feet) from its crest, and covering a vast area with dust. Its height before the eruption was 2 948 metres (9,671 feet).

St. Hel·i·er (hélli-ər). Capital of Jersey, the Channel Islands. A port and resort, it is a market for cattle and early vegetables.

sthenic (sthénnik) *adj.* Characterised by excessive energy; vigorous. [Greek *sthenos,* strength + -IC, by analogy with *asthenic.*]

Sthe·no (sthéenō). *Greek Mythology.* One of the three Gorgons.

stib·ine (stíb-īn, -een) *n.* **1.** A colourless, flammable, poisonous gas, SbH_3, often used as a fumigant. **2.** A derivative of this formed by replacing one or more hydrogen atoms by hydrocarbon groups. [Latin *stibium,* variant of *stibi, stimmi,* antimony, from Greek, from Egyptian *stm* + -INE.]

stib·nite (stíb-nīt) *n.* A lead-grey mineral, Sb_2S_3, that is the chief source of antimony. Also called "antimony glance". [French *stibine,* stibnite, from Latin *stibium,* antimony (see **stibine**) + -ITE.]

stich (stik) *n.* A line of verse. [Greek *stikhos,* row, line, verse.]

sti·chom·e·try (sti-kómmətri) *n.* The division of a prose piece into lines of fixed length or, occasionally, into lines whose lengths correspond to the natural divisions of sense, as in manuscripts written before the adoption of punctuation. [Greek *stikhos,* STICH + -METRY.] —**stich·o·met·ric** (stíckə-méttrik) *adj.*

stich·o·myth·i·a (stík-ə-míthi-ə, -ō-) *n.* Also **sti·chom·y·thy** (sti-kómməthi). An ancient Greek arrangement of dialogue in drama, poetry, and disputation in which single lines of verse are spoken by alternate speakers. [Greek *stikhomuthia,* from *stikhomuthein,* to speak in alternating lines : *stikhos,* STICH + *muthos,* speech, tale, MYTH.] —**stich·o·myth·ic** (-míthik) *adj.*

-stichous *adj. comb. form.* Indicates rows; for example, **polystichous.** [Greek *-stikhos,* from *stikhos,* row, line, verse.]

stick[1] (stik) *n.* **1.** A long, slender piece of wood, especially: **a.** A branch or stem cut from a tree or shrub. **b.** A tree branch or other piece of wood used for fuel, cut for timber, or shaped for a specific purpose. **c.** A wand, staff, baton, or rod. **d.** Any of various sticklike implements used in games or sports: *a hockey stick.* **e.** A cane or walking stick. **2.** Something cut into or having the shape of a stick: *a stick of dynamite; a stick of rock.* **3. a.** The **control stick** *(see)* of an aeroplane. **b.** *Informal.* The lever or rod in a motor vehicle used for changing gear. **4.** *Nautical.* A mast or a part of a mast. **5.** *Printing.* **a.** A composing stick. **b.** The type contents of a composing stick. Also called "stickful". **6. a.** *Military.* A group of bombs released to fall across a target in a straight row. **b.** A group of paratroopers jumping in succession. **7.** *Informal.* An item of furniture. **8.** *Plural. Informal.* An area far from a city or town; backwoods: *They live way out in the sticks.* **9.** *Informal.* A person, especially one who is spiritless or boring: *a dry old stick.* **10.** *Informal.* **a.** Adverse criticism: *came in for a lot of stick.* **b.** Punishment or the threat of punishment: *He'll give us stick for being so late.* **11.** A long loaf of bread. **—get the wrong end of the stick.** To completely misunderstand or misconstrue something.
∼*tr.v.* **sticked, sticking, sticks.** **1.** To prop up (a vine or other plant) with sticks or brush on which to grow. **2.** *Printing.* To set (type) in a composing stick.
∼*interj. Plural.* Used in hockey by the umpire to indicate that players have raised their sticks improperly above their shoulders. [Middle English, Old English, *sticca,* from West Germanic *stikka* (unattested).]

stick[2] *v.* **stuck** (stuk), **sticking, sticks.** —*tr.* **1.** To pierce, puncture, or penetrate with a pointed instrument, such as a knife or pin. **2.** To kill by piercing. **3.** To thrust or push (a knife, pin, or other pointed instrument) into or through another object. **4.** To fasten into place by forcing an end or point into something: *stick a hook into the wall.* **5.** To fasten or attach with or as if with pins, nails, or similar instruments. **6.** To fasten or attach with an adhesive material, glue, or tape: *stick a poster to the wall.* **7.** To cover or decorate with objects piercing the surface. **8.** To fix, impale, or transfix on a pointed object: *stick an olive on a toothpick.* **9.** To put, place, or thrust, or poke into a specified place or position: *stick your hands up; stuck a cigarette in his mouth.* **10.** *Informal.* To detain or delay. Usually used in the passive: *was stuck at the dentist all morning.* **11.** *Chiefly British Slang.* To bear; abide: *can't stick his silly jokes.* **12.** To make incapable of movement or progress; bring to a standstill or impasse. Usually used in the passive: *can't shift it—it's completely stuck; stuck on question three.* **13.** *Informal.* To confuse, baffle, or puzzle. Usually used in the passive: *never stuck for an answer.* **14.** To burden or encumber with something unpleasant or unwanted; saddle: *stuck with paying the bill.* **15.** *Informal.* To write: *Stick your address at the top of the page.* —*intr.* **1.** To be or become fixed or embedded in place by having the point thrust in. **2.** To become or remain attached or in close association by or as if by adhesion; cling: *"I'm all for us English sticking together when we're abroad"* (Somerset Maugham). **3.** To remain firm, determined, or resolute: *stick to a resolution.* **4.** To persist, endure, or persevere. Used with *at, to,* or *with*: *must stick at it in order to succeed.* **5. a.** *Informal.* To remain in the vicinity; linger. Usually used with *about* or *around*: *Stick around here until I get back.* **b.** To remain for a period of time: *Her face really stuck in my mind.* **6.** To scruple or hesitate. Used with *at* or *to*: *She sticks at nothing.* **7.** To be at or come to a standstill; become fixed, jammed, checked, or obstructed. **8.** To extend, project, or protrude. Used with *out, up, down,* or *through.* **—be stuck on.** *Informal.* To be in love with or infatuated by. **—get stuck in** or **into.** *Informal.* To begin or perform (a job) with a serious and determined attitude. **—stick by.** To remain loyal or faithful to. **—stick it out.** *Informal.* To persist or persevere to the end. **—stick out for.** To withhold consent, agreement, or compliance until something is done or granted. **—stick up for.** To defend or support. [Middle English, Old English *stician.*]

stick·er (stíckər) *n.* **1.** A person or thing that sticks. **2.** A gummed or adhesive label or patch. **3.** A tenacious, diligent, or persistent person. **4.** A thorn, prickle, or barb.

stick·ing plaster (stíking) *n.* A piece of adhesive material used to protect a wound or hold a dressing in position. Also called "plaster".

stick insect *n.* Any of several mainly tropical insects of the family Phasmidae, resembling sticks or twigs. Also *U.S.* "walking stick".

stick-in-the-mud (stíckin-thə-mud) *n. Informal.* A very staid person who lacks initiative, imagination, or enthusiasm.

stick·le (stíck'l) *intr.v.* **-led, -ling, -les.** **1.** To argue or contend stubbornly, especially about trivial or petty points. **2.** To have or raise objections; scruple. [Earlier *stightle,* to arbitrate, intervene, Middle English *stightlen,* Old English *stihtan, stihtian.*]

stick·le·back (stíck'l-bak) *n.* Any of various small freshwater and marine fishes of the family Gasterosteidae, having erectile spines along the back. [Middle English *stykylbak,* "prickly back" : *stykyl-,* from Old English *sticel,* prick, sting + *bak,* BACK.]

stick·ler (stícklər) *n.* **1.** A person who insists on something: *a stickler for neatness.* **2.** Anything puzzling or difficult.

stick·pin (stík-pin) *n. U.S.* A **tiepin** *(see).*

stick up *tr.v. Slang.* To rob, especially at gunpoint.

stick·up (stík-up) *n. Slang.* A robbery, especially at gunpoint.

stick·weed (stík-weed) *n.* Broadly, any of various plants having clinging seeds or fruit, especially ragweed.

stick·y (stícki) *adj.* **-ier, -iest.** **1.** Having the property of adhering or sticking to a surface; adhesive. **2.** Covered with an adhesive agent: *a sticky floor.* **3.** Warm and humid; muggy. **4.** *Informal.* Painful or difficult: *a sticky problem.* **5.** *Economics.* Tending to remain the same despite other changes in the economy. Said of prices or wages. —*n. Australian Informal.* An inquisitive look at something: *Let's have a sticky.* —**stick·i·ly** *adv.* —**stick·i·ness** *n.*

stick·y·beak (stícki-beek) *n. Australian & N.Z.* An interfering or inquisitive person. —*intr.v. Australian & N.Z.* **-beaked, -beaking, -beaks.** To interfere or pry.

sticky end *n. Informal.* **1.** A wretched or unhappy finish: *will come to a sticky end.* **2.** A violent or unpleasant death.

sticky tape *n.* Cellulose adhesive tape.

sticky wicket *n.* **1.** A cricket pitch drying quickly in the sun after rain thus providing highly favourable conditions for spin bowling. **2.** *Informal.* A problematical or tricky position or situation. Used especially in the phrase *on a sticky wicket.*

Stieg·litz (stéeglits), **Alfred** (1864–1946). American photographer, a pioneer of colour photography and advocate of photography as an art form.

stiff (stif) *adj.* **stiffer, stiffest.** **1.** Difficult to bend or stretch; not flexible, pliant, or limp; rigid. **2. a.** Not moving or operating easily or freely; resistant: *a stiff hinge.* **b.** Aching and lacking ease of movement, as from exertion or old age: *a stiff neck; stiff all over.* **3.** Drawn tightly; taut. **4.** Rigidly or excessively formal, awkward, or constrained; without ease or grace. **5.** Not liquid, loose, or fluid; firm; thick: *stiff batter.* **6.** Firm in purpose or resistance; stubborn; unyielding. **7.** Having a strong, swift, steady force or movement: *a stiff breeze.* **8.** Potent or strong: *a stiff drink.* **9.** Difficult to perform or deal with; demanding; arduous: *a stiff hike; a stiff examination.* **10.** Difficult to accept; harsh or severe: *a stiff penalty.* **11.** Excessively high: *stiff prices.* **12.** *Nautical.* Not heeling over much, in spite of great wind or the press of the sail. **13.** *Slang.* Well supplied; full: *The area was stiff with security men.* —*adv.* **1.** To the point of being rigid: *frozen stiff.* **2.** Completely; totally: *bored stiff.* —*n. Slang.* **1.** A corpse. **2.** An overformal, constrained, or priggish person: *a big stiff.* [Middle English *stif(fe)*, Old English *stif.*] —**stiff·ly** *adv.* —**stiff·ness** *n.*

> *Synonyms:* stiff, rigid, inflexible, inelastic, tense, taut.

stiff·en (stíf'n) *v.* **-ened, -ening, -ens.** —*tr.* To make stiff or stiffer. —*intr.* **1.** To become stiff or stiffer. **2.** To become suddenly rigid or tense, as with indignation or fear. —**stiff·en·er** *n.*

stiff-necked (stíf-nékt) *adj.* Stubborn; unyielding. See Synonyms at **obstinate.**

stiff upper lip *n.* Great restraint and composure; concealment of emotions or feelings, as of sadness or fear.

sti·fle[1] (stíf'l) *v.* **-fled, -fling, -fles.** —*tr.* **1.** To kill by preventing respiration; smother or suffocate. **2.** To interrupt or cut off (the voice or breath). **3.** To keep or hold back; suppress; repress: *stifle his opinions.* —*intr.* **1.** To die of suffocation. **2.** To feel smothered or suffocated by or as if by close confinement in a stuffy room. [Middle English *stufflen*, probably formed as a frequentative from Old French *estouffer*, to choke, smother.] —**sti·fler** *n.*

stifle[2] *n.* The joint of the hind leg corresponding to the human knee in certain quadrupeds, such as the horse. Also called "stifle joint". [Middle English *stifle†.*]

sti·fling (stífling) *adj.* Hot or stuffy almost to the point of being suffocating. —**sti·fling·ly** *adv.*

stig·ma (stíg-mə) *n., pl.* **stigmata** (-tə, *also* stig-máatə) *or* **-mas** (especially for sense 6). **1.** A mark or token of shame, disgrace, or reproach: *a certain stigma attached to being a divorcee.* **2.** *Archaic.* A mark burnt into the skin of a criminal or slave; a brand. **3.** Any small mark; a scar or birthmark. **4.** *Medicine.* **a.** A mark or rash that occurs as a symptom of hysteria. **b.** A mark indicative of a history of a disease or abnormality. **5.** *Biology.* A small mark, spot, or pore, such as the respiratory spiracle of an insect or an eyespot in certain algae. **6.** *Botany.* The apex of the pistil of a flower, upon which pollen is deposited at pollination. **7.** *Plural.* Marks or sores corresponding to and resembling the crucifixion wounds of Jesus, sometimes appearing on the bodies of certain persons in a state of religious ecstasy or hysteria. [Latin *stigma* (plural *stigmata*), from Greek, tattoo mark, from *stizein*, to prick, tattoo.]

stig·mas·ter·ol (stig-mástə-rol ‖ -ról) *n.* A sterol, $C_{29}H_{48}O$, obtained from soya beans or Calabar beans. [New Latin *(Physo)stigma*, genus of the Calabar bean (see **physostigmine**) + STEROL.]

stig·mat·ic (stig-máttik) *adj.* **1.** Pertaining to, resembling, or having a stigma or stigmata. **2. Anastigmatic** (see). —*n. Also* **stig·ma·tist** (stíg-mətist). A person marked with religious stigmata.

stig·ma·tise, stig·ma·tize (stíg-mə-tīz) *tr.v.* **-tised, -tising, -tises.** **1.** To characterise or brand as disgraceful or ignominious. **2.** To brand or mark with a stigma or stigmata. **3.** To cause stigmata to appear on. [Medieval Latin *stigmatizāre*, to brand, from Greek *stigmatizein*, to mark, tattoo, from *stigma*, tattoo mark, STIGMA.] —**stig·ma·ti·sa·tion** (-tī-záysh'n ‖ U.S. -i-) *n.* —**stig·ma·tis·er** *n.*

stig·ma·tism (stíg-mə-tiz'm) *n.* **1.** The state or condition of being affected with stigmata. **2.** *Optics.* The state of a refracting or reflecting system, especially the eye, that focuses light rays at a point, from an off-axis point. **3.** Normal eyesight.

stil·bene (stíl-been) *n.* A colourless or yellowish compound, $C_{14}H_{12}$, used in the manufacture of dyes and optical bleaches and as a phosphor. [Greek *stilbos*, shining, shimmering, from *stilbein†*, to shimmer + -ENE.]

stil·bite (stíl-bīt) *n.* A white or yellow lustrous zeolite mineral, essentially (Na₂Ca)(Al₂Si₇O₁₈)·7H₂O. [French : Greek *stilbos*, shining, shimmering (see **stilbene**) + -ITE.]

stil·boes·trol (stil-béess-trəl, -tról ‖ -tról) *n. Chemistry. Also U.S.* **stil·bes·trol** (-béss-) Diethylstilboestrol (see). [STILB(ENE) + OESTR(US) + -OL.]

stile[1] (stīl) *n.* **1.** A set or series of steps for getting over a fence or wall. **2.** A turnstile. [Middle English *stile*, Old English *stigel.*]

stile[2] *n.* A vertical member of a panel or frame, as in a door or window sash. [Probably from Dutch *stijl*, doorpost, from Middle Dutch, probably from Latin *stilus*, pole, post. See **style**.]

sti·let·to (sti-léttō) *n., pl.* **-tos** *or* **-toes.** **1.** A small dagger with a slender, tapering blade. **2.** A small, sharp-pointed instrument used for making eyelet holes in needlework. **3.** A high heel on a woman's shoe that tapers to a sharp point at the bottom. Also called "stiletto heel". **4.** *Plural.* A pair of shoes with such heels. [Italian, diminutive of *stilo*, dagger, from Latin *stilus*, sharp-pointed post, pole, stake. See **style**.]

still[1] (stil) *adj.* **stiller, stillest.** **1.** Free from sound; silent; quiet. **2.** Low in sound; hushed; subdued. **3.** Without movement; at rest. **4.** Free from disturbance, commotion, or agitation; tranquil; serene. **5.** Free from noticeable current, as water might be. **6.** Not carbonated; lacking effervescence: *still wine.* **7.** *Photography.* Of, designating, or pertaining to a single or static photograph as opposed to a cinematic film. —See Synonyms at **calm.** —*n.* **1.** Silence; quiet; calm: *the still of the night.* **2.** A still photograph, especially one taken from a scene of a cinematic film and used for promotional purposes. —*adv.* **1.** Without movement; motionlessly: *stand still.* **2.** Up to now or the time specified; now or in the future as before; yet: *still be here tomorrow; has still not finished.* **3.** In increasing amount or degree: *has become still worse.* **4.** Nevertheless; all the same: *I understand the difficulty but I still think he should go.* **5.** Even; besides: *still further complaints.* **6.** *Archaic & Regional.* Always; constantly. —See Synonyms at **but.** —*v.* **stilled, stilling, stills.** —*tr.* **1.** To make still, quiet, or tranquil. **2.** To allay; calm. —*intr.* To become still. —**still·ness** *n.* [Middle English *still(e)*, Old English *stille.*]

> *Synonyms:* still, quiet, silent, noiseless, hushed, tranquil.

still[2] *n.* **1.** An apparatus for distilling liquids, particularly alcohols, consisting of a vessel in which the substance is vaporised by heat and a cooling device in which the vapour is condensed. **2.** A distillery. [From *still*, to distil, Middle English *stillen*, short for *distillen*, DISTIL.]

stil·lage (stíllij) *n.* A bench or frame, as in a factory, used to keep objects from touching the floor, as while they are draining or drying. [Probably from Dutch *stellagie*, frame, scaffold, from *stellen*, to stand.]

still·birth (stíl-burth) *n.* **1.** The birth of a dead child, usually when gestation has continued for over 28 weeks. **2.** A child dead at birth.

still·born (stíl-bawrn) *adj.* **1.** Dead at birth. **2.** Failing right at the beginning; abortive.

still hunt *n. Chiefly U.S.* The hunting of game by stalking or ambushing. —**still·hunt** (stíl-hunt) *v.*

stil·li·cide (stílli-sīd) *n. Law.* A right or duty connected with the spilling of water from one person's roof onto another's land. [Latin *stillicidium* : *stilla*, drop (of water) + *-cidium*, from *cadere*, to fall.]

stil·li·form (stílli-fawrm) *adj.* Shaped like a drop or globule. [Latin *stillis*, a drop (see **distil**) + -i- + -FORM.]

still life *n., pl.* **still lifes.** **1.** The representation of inanimate objects, such as flowers or fruit, in painting or photography. **2.** A picture of inanimate objects. —**still-life** *adj.*

still room *n. British.* **1.** A room used for distilling. **2.** A room in a large house used for storing preserves, provisions, or the like.

Still·son wrench (stíl-s'n) *n.* A trademark for a monkey wrench with serrated jaws, one of which has slight angular movement to facilitate gripping pipes and other round objects. Compare **pipe wrench.**

still·y (stílli) *adj. Poetic.* Quiet; calm. —**still·ly** *adv.*

stilt (stilt) *n., pl.* **stilts** *or* **stilt** (for sense 3). **1.** Either of a pair of long, slender poles, each equipped with a raised footrest enabling the wearer to walk elevated above the ground. **2.** Any of various tall posts or pillars used as support, as for a dock or building. **3. a.** A long-legged wading bird, *Himantopus mexicanus* (or *H. himantopus*), having black and white plumage and a long slender bill. **b.** A related bird, *Cladorhyncus leucocephala*, of Australia. —*tr.v.* **stilted, stilting, stilts.** To place or raise on or as if on stilts. [Middle English *stilte*, stilt, crutch, perhaps of Low German origin, akin to Low German and Flemish *stilte.*]

stilt·ed (stíltid) *adj.* **1.** Stiffly or artificially dignified or formal; pompous: *a very stilted manner.* **2.** *Architecture.* Having some vertical length between the impost and the beginning of the curve. Said of an arch. —**stilt·ed·ly** *adv.* —**stilt·ed·ness** *n.*

Stil·ton (stíltən) *n.* A rich, blue-veined cheese made from whole milk with added cream and having a wrinkled rind. [Originally sold at *Stilton*, Cambridgeshire.]

stim·u·lant (stímmewlənt) *n.* **1.** Anything that temporarily arouses or accelerates physiological activity, especially of a particular organ. **2.** A stimulus or incentive: *Social unrest often provides a stimulant to literature.* **3.** A drug, food, or drink that stimulates. —*adj.* Serving as a stimulant. [Latin *stimulāns* (stem *stimulant-*),

present participle of *stimulāre*, to STIMULATE.]
stim·u·late (stímmew-layt) *v.* **-lated, -lating, -lates.** —*tr.* To rouse to activity or heightened action, as by spurring or goading; animate. —*intr.* To act or serve as a stimulant or stimulus. —See Synonyms at **provoke.** [Latin *stimulāre*, to goad on, from *stimulus*, a STIMULUS.] **—stim·u·la·tive** (-lətiv, -laytiv) *adj.* **—stim·u·la·tor** (-laytər) *n.* **—stim·u·la·tion** (-láysh'n) *n.*
stim·u·lus (stímmew-ləss) *n., pl.* **-li** (-lī, -lee). **1.** Anything causing or regarded as causing a response. **2.** An agent, action, or condition that elicits or accelerates a physiological or psychological activity. **3.** Something that incites or rouses to action: *a stimulus to the imagination.* [Latin *stimulus*†, a goad.]
sting (sting) *v.* **stung** (stung) or *obsolete* **stang** (stang), **stung, stinging, stings.** —*tr.* **1.** To pierce or wound painfully with or as if with a sharp-pointed structure or organ, such as that of certain insects. **2.** To cause to feel a sharp, smarting pain: *stinging rain; Smoke stung our eyes.* **3.** To cause to suffer keenly in the mind or feelings: *Her words stung him bitterly.* **4.** To spur on by or as if by sharp irritation. **5.** *Slang.* To cheat or overcharge. —*intr.* **1.** To have, use, or wound with a sting. **2.** To feel a sharp, smarting pain. **3.** To cause a sharp, smarting pain or keen mental distress.
∼*n.* **1.** The act of stinging. **2.** The wound or pain caused by or as if by stinging. **3.** A sharp, piercing organ or part, often ejecting a venomous secretion, such as the modified ovipositor of a bee or wasp or the spine of certain fishes. **4. a.** Something that causes a sharp pain, either physical or mental. **b.** Ability to cause pain or suffering; stinging power, quality, or capacity: *"The sting of fear is anxiety"* (Paul Tillich). **5.** A keen stimulus or incitement; a goad or spur. [Sting, stung (or stang), stung; Middle English *stingen, stang* (past plural *stungen*), *stungen*, Old English *stingan, stang* (past plural *stungon*), *stungen*.] **—sting·ing·ly** *adv.*
sting·a·ree (stíng-ə-ree; *Australian also* -rée) *n. U.S. & Australian.* A fish, the stingray. [Variant of STINGRAY.]
sting·er (stíng-ər) *n.* **1.** One that stings, as: **a.** A stinging organ or part. **b.** A sharp blow. **c.** Something that wounds mentally, such as an insult. **2.** *U.S.* A cocktail of crème de menthe and brandy.
sting·ing hair (stínging) *n.* A glandular plant hair that if touched expels an irritant fluid to deter animal predators.
stinging nettle *n.* A nettle with stinging hairs on the stem and leaves; especially, *Urtica dioica.*
sting·ray (stíng-ray) *n.* Any of various rays of the family Dasyatidae, having a whiplike tail armed with a venomous spine capable of inflicting severe injury. Also *U.S. & Australian* "stingaree".
stin·gy[1] (stínji) *adj.* **-gier, -giest.** **1.** Giving or spending reluctantly or unwillingly; mean. **2.** Scanty or meagre. [Perhaps originally "sharp", "bad-tempered", from dialectal *stinge*, act of stinging, Middle English *sting*, Old English *sting, styng*, from *stingan*, to STING.] **—stin·gi·ly** *adv.* **—stin·gi·ness** *n.*
Synonyms: *stingy, mean, close, tight-fisted, niggardly, miserly, parsimonious.*
sting·y[2] (stíng-i) *adj. Informal.* Stinging or able to sting; piercing.
stink (stingk) *v.* **stank** (stangk) or **stunk** (stungk), **stunk, stinking, stinks.** —*intr.* **1.** To emit a strong foul odour. **2. a.** To be highly offensive or abhorrent. **b.** To be in extremely bad repute. **3.** *Slang.* To have or embody something to an extreme or offensive degree. Usually used with *of* or *with*: *He stinks of success.* **4.** *Slang.* To be of an extremely low or bad quality: *This film stinks.* —*tr.* **1.** To cause to stink; fill with stink. Usually used with *out* or *up*: *The smell of garlic stank the kitchen out.* **2.** To drive or force by a strong, foul, or suffocating smell. Used with *out.*
∼*n.* **1.** A strong offensive odour; a stench. **2.** *Informal.* A great fuss or outcry: *to raise a stink.* —See Synonyms at **smell.** [Stink, stank (or stunk), stunk; Middle English *stinken, stank* (past plural *stunken*), *stunken*, Old English *stincan, stanc* (past plural *stuncon*), *stuncen*, from Germanic *stinkwan* (unattested).]
stink ball *n.* A container containing materials that emit a suffocating smoke or offensive vapours, formerly used in naval warfare. Also called "stinkpot".
stink bomb *n.* A small bomb, often in the form of a capsule, that emits a foul odour on explosion.
stink·er (stíngkər) *n.* **1.** One that stinks. **2.** *Slang.* A contemptible, disgusting, or irritating person. **3.** *Slang.* Something very difficult or very offensive: *The exam was a real stinker.*
stink·horn (stíngk-hawrn) *n.* Any of several foul-smelling fungi of the order Phallales, such as *Phallus impudicus*, having a thick, cylindrical stalk and a narrow cap.
stink·ing (stíngking) *adj.* **1.** Having a foul smell; fetid; rank. **2.** *Slang.* Very unpleasant or repulsive. **3.** *Slang.* Very drunk.
∼*adv. Slang.* To an offensive or extreme degree: *got stinking drunk; stinking rich.* **—stink·ing·ly** *adv.* **—stink·ing·ness** *n.*
stinking badger *n.* The **teledu** *(see).*
stinking iris *n.* A greyish-purple flowered iris, *Iris foetidissima*, the leaves of which emit a sickly sweet smell when crushed.
stinking mayweed A plant, the **mayweed** *(see).*
stinking smut *n.* A disease of wheat caused by the fungus *Tilletia caries* (or *T. foetida*), in which the centres of the grains are replaced by a mass of black fungal spores. Also called "bunt", "covered smut".
stink·pot (stíngk-pot) *n.* **1.** A stink ball. **2.** *Slang.* An unpleasant or comtemptible person.
stink·stone (stíngk-stōn) *n.* A variety of limestone that emits a disagreeable smell when struck or rubbed.
stink·weed (stíngk-weed) *n.* **1.** A yellow-flowered plant, *Diplotaxis muralis*, that emits an unpleasant smell if bruised. Also called "wall mustard". **2.** Any of various other plants having flowers or foliage with an unpleasant smell.
stink·wood (stingk-wŏŏd) *n.* **1. a.** A tree, *Ocotea bullata*, of southern Africa, having wood with an unpleasant smell. **b.** The hard, heavy wood of this tree, used in cabinetwork. **2.** Broadly, any of several other trees having wood with an unpleasant smell.
stint[1] (stint) *v.* **stinted, stinting, stints.** —*tr.* **1. a.** To restrict or limit, as in amount or number; be sparing with: *stinting the rations to make them last.* **b.** To restrict or limit (oneself or another): *stinted himself in order to buy a car.* **2.** *Archaic.* To stop; desist. —*intr.* **1.** To be frugal or sparing. **2.** *Archaic.* To stop or desist.
∼*n.* **1.** A fixed amount or share of work or duty to be performed within a given period of time. **2.** A limitation or restriction: *working without stint.* [Middle English *stinten*, to stop, cut short, Old English *styntan*, to blunt, dull.] **—stint·er** *n.*
stint[2] *n.* **1.** Any of several small sandpipers of the genus *Calidris*, of northern regions. **2.** *Archaic.* A **dunlin** *(see).* [Middle English *stynt*†.]
stipe (stīp) *n. Biology.* A stalk or stalklike structure, such as the stemlike support of the cap of a mushroom or the stalk of a seaweed frond. [French, from Latin *stīpes*, post, tree trunk.]
sti·pel (stīp'l) *n. Botany.* A minute or secondary stipule at the base of a leaflet. [New Latin *stipella*, diminutive of *stipula*, STIPULE.] **—sti·pel·late** (-ət, it, -ayt, *also* stī-pél-) *adj.*
sti·pend (stī-pend, -pənd) *n.* A fixed or regular payment, such as a salary for services rendered or an allowance; especially, the salary paid to a clergyman. [Middle English *stipendie*, from Old French, from Latin *stīpendium*, tax, tribute; akin to *stipulārī*, to STIPULATE.]
sti·pen·di·ar·y (stī-péndi-əri, sti- || -erri) *adj.* **1.** Receiving a stipend. **2.** Compensated by stipend: *stipendiary services.*
∼*n., pl.* **stipendiaries.** **1.** A person, such as a clergyman, who receives a stipend. **2.** A stipendiary magistrate. [Latin *stīpendiārius*, from *stīpendium*, tribute, STIPEND.]
stipendiary magistrate *n.* In England and Wales, a solicitor or barrister who is salaried and presides in a magistrates' court.
sti·pes (stī-peez) *n., pl.* **stipites** (stíppi-teez). *Zoology.* **1.** A segment of the maxilla of an insect. **2.** Any stalklike support or structure. [New Latin, from Latin *stīpes*, post, tree trunk.] **—sti·pi·form** (stíp-pi-fawrm), **stip·i·ti·form** (stī-pítti-, stíppiti-) *adj.*
stip·i·tate (stíppi-tayt) *adj.* Having or supported on a stipe. [Latin *stīpes* (stem *stīpit-*), post, tree trunk. See **stipes.**]
stip·ple (stípp'l) *tr.v.* **-pled, -pling, -ples.** **1.** To draw, engrave, or paint in dots or short strokes. **2.** To apply (paint, for example) in dots or short strokes. **3.** To dot, fleck, or speckle.
∼*n.* **1.** The method of painting, drawing, or engraving by stippling. **2.** The effect produced by stippling or a work produced in this manner. [Dutch *stippelen*, frequentative of *stippen*, to speckle, dot, from *stip*, dot, point, from Middle Dutch.] **—stip·pler** *n.*
stip·u·lar (stíppewlər) *adj. Botany.* Of, pertaining to, or resembling a stipule or stipules.
stip·u·late[1] (stíppew-layt) *v.* **-lated, -lating, -lates.** —*tr.* **1. a.** To lay down as a condition of an agreement; require by contract. **b.** To specify or arrange in an agreement: *stipulate the date and price.* **2.** To guarantee or promise in an agreement. —*intr.* **1.** To make an express demand or provision in an agreement. Used with *for.* **2.** To form an agreement. [Latin *stipulārī*†, to bargain, demand.] **—stip·u·la·tor** (-laytər) *n.*
stip·u·late[2] (stíppew-lət, -lit, -layt) *adj. Botany.* Having stipules.
stip·u·la·tion (stíppew-láysh'n) *n.* **1.** The act of stipulating. **2.** Something stipulated; a term or condition in an agreement. **—stip·u·la·to·ry** (-lə-tri, -təri, láytəri) *adj.*
stip·ule (stíppewl) *n. Botany.* Any of the usually small, paired leaflike appendages at the base of a leaf or leafstalk in certain plants. [New Latin *stipula*, from Latin, stalk, stem; akin to *stipulārī*, to STIPULATE.]
stir[1] (stur) *v.* **stirred, stirring, stirs.** —*tr.* **1. a.** To pass an implement through (a liquid) in circular motions, so as to mix or cool the contents. **b.** To introduce (an ingredient) into a liquid or mixture in this way: *stirred sugar into his tea.* **c.** To mix together the ingredients of (a cake, for example) prior to cooking or use. **2.** To cause a slight movement in or alter the placement of slightly. **3.** To move (oneself) briskly or vigorously; bestir. **4.** To rouse (a person), as from sleep or indifference. **5.** To incite, provoke, or instigate. Often used with *up*: *stir up trouble: stir up old memories.* **6.** To excite the emotions of; move or affect strongly. —*intr.* **1.** To change position slightly: *stirred in her sleep.* **2. a.** To move about actively; bestir oneself. **b.** To move away from a customary place or position; venture. **3.** To provoke trouble between others, as by spreading rumours or teasing. —See Synonyms at **provoke.**
∼*n.* **1.** An act of stirring; a mixing or poking movement. **2.** A very slight movement. **3.** A disturbance or commotion. **4.** An excited reaction; a ferment. [Middle English *stiren*, Old English *styrian*, to move, agitate, excite.] **—stir·rer** *n.*
stir[2] *n. Slang.* Prison. [19th century : origin obscure.]
stir·a·bout (stúr-ə-bowt) *n.* **1.** A kind of porridge made from boiling water or milk with oatmeal stirred into it. **2. a.** A busy, active person. **b.** A state of bustling activity or confusion.
stir crazy *adj. U.S. Slang.* Distraught or restless from long confinement in or as if in prison.
stirk (sturk) *n.* A yearling heifer or, sometimes, a bullock. [Middle English *stirk*, Old English *stirc*.]
Stir·ling (stúrling). Burgh and Unitary Authority area in central

Scotland, lying on the river Forth. It is dominated by its 11th-century castle, the birthplace of several Scottish kings. The town overlooks the battlefields of Stirling Bridge and Bannockburn, where the Scots won famous victories over the English (1297 and 1314).

Stir·ling's formula (stúrlingz) *n. Mathematics.* A formula for the approximate value of the factorial of a large number: log*n*! = *n*log*n* − *n*. [After James *Stirling* (1692–1770), Scottish mathematician.]

Stir·ling·shire (stúrling-shər, -sheer, -shír). County in central Scotland, divided (1974–96) between Central and Strathclyde Regions, now (1996–) the Stirling Unitary Authority area.

stirps (sturps, steerps) *n., pl.* **stirpes** (stúr-peez, steér-payz). **1.** A line of descendants of common ancestry; a stock. **2. a.** A group of animals, equivalent to a superfamily. **b.** A variety of plants with stable characteristics which are retained under cultivation. **3.** *Law.* One from whom a family is descended. [Latin *stirps*†, stem, root, lineage.]

stir·ring (stúr-ing) *adj.* **1.** Rousing; thrilling: *a stirring call to arms.* **2.** Active; lively. —See Synonyms at **moving.** —**stir·ring·ly** *adv.*

stir·rup (stírrəp || *also* stúr-əp) *n.* **1.** A flat-based loop or ring hung from either side of a horse's saddle to support the rider's foot in mounting and riding. Also called "stirrup iron". **2.** Any of various parts or devices shaped like an inverted U, used to support, hold, or fix something. **3.** *Nautical.* A rope on a ship hanging from a yard and having an eye at the end through which a footrope is passed for support. [Middle English *stirope,* Old English *stigrāp.*]

stirrup bone *n. Anatomy.* The **stapes** *(see).*

stir·rup-cup (stírrəp-kup || stúr-əp-) *n.* **1.** A farewell drink given to a rider who is mounted ready to depart. **2.** Any farewell drink.

stirrup leather *n.* The strap used to fasten a stirrup to a saddle. Also called "stirrup strap".

stirrup pump *n.* A type of small hand water pump that is used for fighting fires or in gardening.

stish·ov·ite (stíshəv-īt) *n.* A dense tetragonal form of silicon dioxide formed under great pressure. [After S. M. *Stishov,* 20th-century Russian mineralogist.]

stitch (stich) *n. Abbr.* **st. 1.** A single complete movement of a threaded needle in sewing or surgical suturing. **2.** A single loop of yarn around a knitting needle or similar implement. **3.** The link, loop, or knot made in this way. **4.** A particular method of arranging the threads in sewing, knitting, or crocheting: *a purl stitch.* **5.** A sudden sharp pain in one's side, often resulting from physical exertion, such as running. **6.** *Informal.* An article of clothing: *not a stitch on.* —**in stitches.** *Informal.* Laughing uncontrollably.
~*v.* **stitched, stitching, stitches.** —*tr.* **1. a.** To fasten or join with stitches. **b.** To mend or repair with stitches. Used with *up.* **2.** To decorate or ornament with stitches. **3.** To fasten together (sheets of a book, for example) with staples or thread. —*intr.* To make stitches; sew. —**stitch up.** *British Slang.* To **frame** (sense 6a). [Middle English *stiche,* Old English *stice,* a sting, prick.] —**stitch·er** *n.*

stitch·wort (stích-wurt || -wawrt) *n.* Any of several low-growing plants of the genus *Stellaria,* having small, white flowers. [Middle English *stichewort,* Old English *sticwyrt,* agrimony : STITCH + WORT (from its alleged ability to cure sharp pains in the side).]

stith·y (stíthi) *n., pl.* **-ies.** *Archaic.* **1.** An anvil. **2.** A forge or smithy. [Middle English *stethy,* from Old Norse *stedhi.*]

sti·ver (stívər) *n.* **1.** An obsolete Dutch coin worth $^1/_{20}$ of a guilder. **2.** Anything of small value; the smallest amount. [Dutch *stuiver,* from Middle Dutch *stuyver.*]

St. John's (jonz). The capital of Newfoundland, eastern Canada. An Atlantic port, it is the most easterly city in North America.

St. John's bread *n.* The long blackish, sugary, edible pod of the **carob** *(see).* [After St. JOHN the Baptist, who lived on honey and locusts while preaching (through confusion of the locusts with the carob, known also as locust bean). Matthew 3:4.]

St. Johns·wort (s'nt-jónz-wurt, s'n- || saynt-, -wawrt) *n.* Any of various plants or shrubs of the genus *Hypericum,* having yellow flowers with prominent stamens. [So called because it was gathered on *St. John's* Eve to ward off evil spirits.]

St. Kil·da (kíldə). The largest of a group of three islands in the Atlantic ocean, the most westerly of the Outer Hebrides, northwest Scotland. Its small population of Gaelic-speaking inhabitants was evacuated in 1930, and it is now a nature reserve.

St. Kitts-Ne·vis (s'nt-kíts-neéviss, s'n- || saynt-). Formerly **St. Kitts-Nevis-Anguilla** (-ang-gwíllə). Island state of the Caribbean. The two islands, St. Kitts (St. Christopher) and Nevis, five kilometres (three miles) apart, were the first Caribbean islands to be settled by the British (1623–28), but were disputed with France until 1783. In 1967 the self-governing British Associated State of St. Kitts-Nevis-Anguilla was created. However, the Anguillans resented the link, and finally became a separate United Kingdom dependency in 1980. St. Kitts-Nevis gained independence within the Commonwealth in 1983. Sugar is the mainstay of the economy, but tourism is becoming a major source of income. Area, 262 square kilometres (101 square miles). Capital, Basseterre (on St. Kitts). Population, 42,000. See map at **Latin America.**

St. Lau·rent (sáN-law-róN), **Louis Stephen** (1882–1973). Canadian prime minister from 1948–57. The St. Lawrence Seaway (opened 1959) was built during his premiership.

St. Law·rence (lórrənss || láwrənss). One of the principal rivers of North America. It issues from Lake Ontario and flows northeast to form part of the border between Canada and the United States, and enters the Gulf of St. Lawrence. Though partially icebound in winter, it remains a major artery for shipping between the Atlantic and the Great Lakes, and was improved by the opening of the St. Lawrence Seaway. From Lake Ontario to Anticosti Island, the river is some 1 200 kilometres (750 miles) long.

St. Lawrence, Gulf of. A gulf of the Atlantic Ocean, eastern Canada, into which the St. Lawrence river flows. It lies between Newfoundland and mainland Canada. Though closed to navigation by ice in the winter months, it has important fishing grounds.

St. Lawrence Seaway. A major waterway system connecting the Gulf of St. Lawrence and the Great Lakes. A joint U.S.-Canadian project, it was opened in 1959 and provides navigation channels between Montreal and Lake Ontario, and between Lake Ontario and Lake Erie. The seaway for the first time gave large ocean-going vessels access to the heart of North America.

St. Lou·is (lóo-iss). The largest city in Missouri, central United States. Founded in 1764 by the French, on the Mississippi just downstream from the confluence with the Missouri, it became an important centre for fur traders and explorers opening up the West. It was ceded to the United States in 1804, and is now a communications, commercial, industrial, and cultural centre.

St. Lu·cia (lóo-shə, *rarely* -si-ə || léw-). Volcanic island in the Windward group of the West Indies. Discovered by Columbus (1502), it changed hands repeatedly between England and France, before becoming an English colony in 1814. It won full independence within the Commonwealth (1979). The economy is primarily agricultural, but tourism is increasingly important. Area, 616 square kilometres (238 square miles). Population, 140,000. Capital, Castries. See map at **Latin America.**

St. Ma·lo (maá-lō; *French* saN ma-lō). A port and popular resort in Ille-et-Vilaine département, northwestern France. A tidal power station, one of the first in the world, opened in 1966.

St. Mo·ritz (mə-ríts, mórrits). Alpine resort in Graubünden canton, southeastern Switzerland, situated in the upper Engadine (Inn valley). A famous winter sports centre, St. Moritz is the site of the Cresta Run for bobsleighs.

sto·a (stō-ə) *n., pl.* **-as** or **stoae** (-ee). An ancient Greek covered walk or colonnade, usually having columns on one side and a wall on the other. [Greek, porch.]

stoat (stōt) *n.* A small carnivorous mammal, *Mustela erminea,* similar to but larger than the weasel and having a black-tipped tail. In northern regions the brown coat turns white in winter and is called ermine. [Middle English : origin obscure.]

sto·chas·tic (sto-kástik, stə- || stō-) *adj.* **1.** Of, designating, or characterised by conjecture; conjectural. **2.** *Statistics.* **a.** Random. **b.** Statistical. [Greek *stokhastikos,* capable of aiming, conjectural, from *stokhazesthai,* to aim at, guess at, from *stokhos,* target, aim.] —**sto·chas·tic·al·ly** *adv.*

stochastic process *n.* In statistics, a process consisting of a number of steps having a random variable, the successive values of which are not independent.

stochastic variable *n. Statistics.* A **random variable** *(see).*

stock (stok) *n. Abbr.* **stk. 1.** A supply accumulated for future use; a store or supply that may be drawn upon. **2.** The total merchandise kept on hand by a trader, commercial establishment, or manufacturer. **3.** All the animals kept or reared on a farm; livestock. **4.** *Finance.* **a.** The capital or fund that a company raises through the sale of shares entitling the holder to dividends and to other rights of ownership, such as voting rights. **b.** The number of shares that each stockholder possesses. **c.** The shares of a specified company or business enterprise. **d.** Formerly, the part of a tally or record of account given to a creditor. **e.** A debt symbolised by such a tally or tallies. **5.** The trunk or main stem of a tree or other plant as distinguished from the branches and roots. **6. a.** A plant or stem onto which a graft is made. **b.** A plant or tree from which cuttings and slips are taken. **7. a.** The original progenitor of a family line. **b.** The descendents of a common ancestor; a family line, especially one of a specified character: *comes from farming stock.* **c.** The type from which a group of animals or plants has descended. **d.** A race, family, or other related group of animals or plants. **e.** An ethnic group or other major division of mankind. **f.** A group of related languages. **g.** A group of related families of languages. **8.** The raw material out of which something is made. **9.** A broth in which meat, fish, bones, or vegetables have been simmered for a period of time, used as a base in preparing soup, gravy, or sauces. **10. a.** The chief upright part of something, particularly a supporting structure or block. **b.** *Plural.* The timber frame that supports a ship during construction. **c.** *Often plural.* A frame in which a horse or other animal is held for shoeing or for veterinary treatment. **11.** *Plural.* Formerly, an instrument of punishment, consisting of a heavy timber frame with holes for confining the ankles and, sometimes, the wrists. **12.** *Nautical.* The crosspiece at the end of an anchor's shank. **13.** The wooden block from which a bell is suspended. **14. a.** The rear wooden or metal handle or steadying support of a rifle, pistol, or automatic weapon, to which the barrel and mechanism are attached. Also called "gunstock". **b.** The long beam of field-gun carriages that trails along the ground to provide stability and support. **15.** Any handle, as of a whip, fishing rod, or various carpenter's tools. **16.** The frame of a plough, to which the share, handles, coulter, and other parts are fastened. **17.** *U.S.* The theatrical repertoire of a stock company. **18.** Any of several plants of the genus *Matthiola,* native to the Old World; especially, *M. incana,* widely cultivated for its clusters of showy, fragrant, variously coloured flowers, and *M. bicornis,* night-scented stock. **19.** That portion of a pack of cards or group of dominoes that is not dealt out but is drawn from during a game. **20.** *Geology.* An irregularly shaped intrusive body of igneous rock in the earth's crust, with an exposed surface of less than 100 square kilometres (40 square miles). **21.** Personal reputation or standing: *His stock with the students is falling.* **22.** Unexposed film. **23. a.** A stiff, long neckcloth, wound around the neck as a part of male dress in the 18th century. **b.** A long white cloth worn around the neck as a part of formal riding dress. **c.** A piece of black, or sometimes purple, silk attached to a clerical collar and worn by a clergyman over the chest. **24.** A brick of the kind most commonly used in building. **25.** See **rolling stock. 26.** See **die-stock. 27.** *Archaic.* A stocking. **—in stock.** Available for sale or use. **—on the stocks.** In the process of being constructed or prepared. **—out of stock. 1.** Not immediately available for sale or use. **2.** Not having any immediately available for sale or use. **—take stock. 1.** To take an inventory. **2.** To make an estimate or reappraisal, as of resources, prospects, or a prevailing situation. **—take stock in.** *Informal.* To be interested in or attach importance to. ~*v.* **stocked, stocking, stocks.** *—tr.* **1.** To provide or furnish with a stock of something, especially: **a.** To supply (a shop) with merchandise. **b.** To supply (a farm) with livestock. **c.** To fill (a river) with fish. **2.** To keep in stock for future sale. **3.** To provide (a rifle, for example) with a stock. **4.** *Obsolete.* To put (someone) in the stocks as a punishment. *—intr.* **1.** To gather and lay in a supply of something. Used with *up* or *up on.* **2.** To put forth or sprout new shoots. Used of a plant. ~*adj.* **1.** Kept regularly in stock. **2.** Repeated regularly without any thought or originality; trite: *a stock answer.* **3. a.** Of or pertaining to the raising of livestock: *stock farming.* **b.** Used for breeding: *a stock mare.* **4.** Designating a conventional or traditional character of a particular dramatic genre, such as farce or pantomime. [Middle English *stok(ke),* Old English *stocc,* tree trunk.]

stock·ade (sto-káyd) *n.* **1.** A defensive barrier made of strong posts or timbers driven upright into the ground, side by side. **2.** *Chiefly U.S.* Any similarly fenced or enclosed area, especially one used for protection or imprisonment. ~*tr.v.* **stockaded, -ading, -ades.** To fortify, protect, or surround with a stockade. [Obsolete French *estocade,* from Spanish *estacada,* from *estaca,* stake, from Germanic.]

stock·breed·ing (stók-breeding) *n.* The rearing of livestock **—stock·breed·er** *n.*

stock·bro·ker (stók-brōk-ər) *n.* Formerly, a person who acts, for a commission, as an agent in the buying and selling of stocks or other securities. **—stock·bro·ker·age, stock·bro·king** *n.*

stockbroker belt *n.* *British Informal.* An area just outside a city, especially just outside London, that is mainly inhabited by wealthy commuters to the city.

stock car *n.* **1.** A car of a standard make, modified for a particular type of racing *(stock car racing)* in which deliberately contrived collisions are allowed. **2.** *U.S.* A railway truck for livestock.

stock certificate *n.* *U.S.* A share certificate.

stock company *n.* *U.S.* **1.** A joint-stock company *(see).* **2.** A repertory company.

stock cube *n.* A piece of compressed, dehydrated stock for use in cooking, commercially produced in the form of a cube.

stock dove *n.* A common Old World bird, *Columba oenas,* having greyish plumage. [Probably because it lives in hollow tree trunks.]

stock exchange *n. Abbr.* **St. Ex. 1.** A place where stocks and shares or other securities are bought and sold. **2.** An association of broker-dealers who meet to buy and sell stocks and shares according to fixed regulations. **3.** The trend of prices or the business transacted at a stock exchange: *The stock exchange fell today.* Also called "stock market".

stock·fish (stók-fish) *n.* A fish, such as cod or haddock, cured by being split and air-dried without salt.

Stock·hau·sen (shtók-howz'n), **Karlheinz** (1928–). German composer, one of the leading exponents of electronic music. His works include *Gruppen* (1955–57) and *Helicopter Quartet* (1995).

stock·hold·er (stók-hōldər) *n.* **1.** One who owns a share or shares of stock in a company. **2.** *Australian & N.Z.* A farmer who raises livestock. **—stock·hold·ing** *adj. & n.*

Stock·holm (stók-hōm ‖ -hōlm). Capital city of Sweden, occupying several peninsulas and islands on the Baltic Sea at the eastern tip of Lake Mälaren. It has been the capital since 1634, and is also an important port and shipbuilding centre.

Stockholm syndrome *n.* The tendency of a hostage, under certain circumstances, to try to cooperate and occasionally even to aid his captors. [Referring to the cooperative behaviour of hostages held in a bank robbery in STOCKHOLM (1973).]

stock·i·nette, stock·i·net (stóki-nét) *n.* An elastic knitted fabric used, especially formerly, in making undergarments, bandages, or the like. [Perhaps variant of earlier *stocking-net:* STOCKING + NET.]

stock·ing (stócking) *n.* **1. a.** A close-fitting, usually knitted, covering for the foot and leg. **b.** *British Regional.* A sock. **2.** Something resembling such a covering. **—in one's stocking feet.** Wearing socks or stockings but no shoes. [From dialectal *stock,* stocking, Middle English *stokke(s),* stocking(s), probably humorous use of *stokkes,* the stocks (instrument of punishment), from *stokke,* STOCK (tree trunk).]

stocking cap *n.* A close-fitting, knitted, conical hat, often having a long tapering tassel, that resembles a stocking.

stocking filler *n. Chiefly British.* A small article, such as a toy or something to eat, for putting in a Christmas stocking.

stocking frame *n.* A knitting-machine. Also called "stocking loom", "stocking machine".

stocking stitch *n.* Alternate rows of plain and purl stitches, used in knitting. Also *U.S.* "stockinette stitch".

stock in trade *n.* **1.** All the merchandise and equipment kept on hand and used in carrying on a business. **2.** The resources available to and habitually called upon by a person in a given situation.

stock·ish (stóckish) *adj.* Slow-witted; stupid. [Apparently STOCK (trunk, stump) + -ISH.] **—stock·ish·ly** *adv.* **—stock·ish·ness** *n.*

stock·ist (stóckist) *n. British.* A person who keeps a stock of certain goods for retail sale.

stock·job·ber (stók-jobbər) *n.* **1.** *British.* Formerly, a person on the stock exchange who acts as an intermediary between brokers and does not deal with the public. **2.** *U.S.* A stockbroker. Often used derogatorily. **—stock·job·ber·y, stock·job·bing** *n.*

stock·man (stók-mən) *n., pl.* **-men** (-mən). **1.** A farmer who raises livestock. **2.** A worker employed to look after livestock. **3.** *U.S.* One employed in a stockroom or warehouse.

stock market *n.* The **stock exchange** *(see).*

stock·pile (stók-pīl) *n.* A supply of material stored for future use; especially, a carefully accrued reserve of essential or strategically important commodities. ~*v.* **stockpiled, -piling, -piles.** *—tr.* To accumulate a stockpile of. *—intr.* To accumulate a stockpile of a given material.

Stock·port (stók-pawrt ‖ -pōrt). Town near Manchester, England, lying at the head of the river Mersey. It rose to prominence during the Industrial Revolution as a cotton spinning centre.

stock·pot (stók-pot) *n.* A large pot used for simmering meat in order to make stock.

stock·room (stók-rōom, -rōōm) *n.* A room in which a store of goods or materials is kept.

stock saddle *n.* A large, heavy, often ornamented, saddle with a raised, curved pommel used especially by stockmen.

stock·still (stók-stíl) *adv.* Completely motionless.

stock·tak·ing (stók-tayking) *n.* **1.** The process of taking an inventory of goods or stocks, as in a shop or factory. **2.** A reappraisal of a situation or of one's own position or prospects.

Stock·ton, Earl of. See **Macmillan, (Maurice) Harold.**

stock whip *n.* A whip with a short handle and a long lash, used for herding cattle.

Stock·wood (stók-wŏod), **(Arthur) Mervyn, the Right Reverend** (1913–95). English church dignitary. He was Bishop of Southwark (1959–80). He was an advocate of church involvement in industrial and political issues and his publications include *Christianity and Marxism* (1949) and *The Cross and the Sickle* (1978).

stock·y (stócki) *adj.* **-ier, -iest.** Solidly built; sturdy; thickset. **—stock·i·ly** *adv.* **—stock·i·ness** *n.*

stock·yard (stók-yaard) *n.* A large enclosed yard, usually with pens or stables, in which livestock is temporarily kept until slaughtered, sold, or shipped elsewhere.

stodge (stoj) *n. Informal.* **1.** Starchy food that is heavy and filling. **2.** Someone or something that is dull and unimaginative. ~*v.* **stodged, stodging, stodges.** *—intr.* To eat greedily. *—tr.* To fill with food. [Probably blend of STUFF + *podge* (short fat person; see **podgy**), imitative.]

stodg·y (stóji) *adj.* **-ier, -iest. 1. a.** Dull, unimaginative, and commonplace. **b.** Prim or pompous; stuffy. **2.** Heavy; indigestible and starchy. [From *stodge,* thick food or mud, anything dull, from *stodge†,* to cram, gorge.] **—stodg·i·ly** *adv.* **—stodg·i·ness** *n.*

stoep (stōōp) *n. South African.* A porch, a **stoop** *(see).*

sto·gy (stógi) *n., pl.* **-gies.** *U.S.* **1.** A long, thin, inexpensive cigar. **2.** A roughly made heavy shoe or boot. [After *Conestoga,* town in Pennsylvania.]

sto·ic (stő-ik) *n.* **1.** A person seemingly indifferent to or unaffected by joy, grief, pleasure, or pain. **2.** *Capital* **S.** A member of a Greek school of philosophy, founded by Zeno about 308 B.C. and later forming an important feature of Roman culture, holding that one should be free from passion and calmly accept all occurrences in submission to divine will or the natural order. ~*adj.* Also **sto·i·cal** (-'l) (for sense 1). **1.** Indifferent to pleasure and steadfast in the endurance of pain or grief; impassive: *stoic resignation.* **2.** *Capital* **S.** Of or pertaining to the Stoics or their beliefs. [Latin *Stōicus,* a Stoic, from Greek *Stōikos,* from *stoa,* portico, the porch where Zeno taught.] **—sto·i·cal·ly** *adv.*

stoi·chi·o·met·ric, stoi·chei·o·met·ric (stóyki-ō-méttrik, -ə-) *adj.* **1.** Having exact proportions for chemical combination: *a stoichiometric reaction.* **2.** Of or pertaining to stoichiometry. [Greek *stoikheio(n),* element + -METRIC.] **—stoi·chi·o·met·ri·cal·ly** *adv.*

stoi·chi·om·e·try, stoi·chei·om·e·try (stóyki-ómmətri) *n.* The methodology and technology by which the quantities of reactants and products in chemical reactions are determined. [Greek *stoikheion,* element + -METRY.]

sto·i·cism (stő-i-siz'm) *n.* **1.** Indifference to pleasure or pain; impassivity; an attitude of endurance or bravery. **2.** *Capital* **S.** The philosophy or doctrines of the Stoics.

stoke (stōk) *v.* **stoked, stoking, stokes.** *—tr.* **1.** To stir up and feed (a fire or furnace). Often used with *up.* **2.** To tend the fire of (a furnace). *—intr.* **1.** To feed or tend a furnace fire. **2.** *Informal.* To eat steadily and in large quantities. Used with *up.*

stoke·hold (stók-hōld) *n.* The area or compartment into which a ship's furnaces or boilers open. Also called "stokehole".

stoke·hole (stók-hōl) *n.* **1.** The space about the opening in a furnace or boiler or the opening itself. **2.** A stokehold. [Translation of Dutch *stookgat.*]

Stoke-on-Trent (stōk-on-trént). City in Staffordshire, in central England. It lies on the river Trent and the Trent to Mersey canal, which was an important factor in its growth during the Industrial Revolution as a centre of the pottery industry.

stok·er (stōkər) *n.* **1.** One who is employed to feed fuel to and tend a furnace, as on a steamship or steam locomotive. **2.** A mechanical device for feeding coal to a furnace. [Dutch, from *stoken,* to poke, thrust, from Middle Dutch.]

stokes (stōks) *n. Symbol* **St** The centimetre-gram-second unit of kinematic viscosity equal to viscosity in poise divided by density in grams per cubic centimetre. [After Sir George *Stokes* (1819–1903), British physicist.]

Sto·kow·ski (stə-kóf-ski), **Leopold** (1882–1977). British-born U.S. conductor. He was associated with many U.S. orchestras and noted for his lavish orchestral arrangements.

STOL (stol ‖ stōl) short takeoff and landing. Said of aircraft.

stole[1] (stōl) *n.* **1.** A woman's long scarflike garment of fur, feathers, or other fine material, worn about the shoulders. **2.** A long scarf, usually of embroidered silk or linen, worn over the left shoulder by deacons and over both shoulders by priests and bishops while officiating. [Middle English *stole,* long robe, Old English *stol,* from Latin *stola,* from Greek *stolē,* garment, array, equipment.]

stole[2]. Past tense of **steal.**

sto·len. Past participle of **steal.**

stol·id (stóllid) *adj.* Having or showing little emotion or sensibility; impassive: *stolid patience.* [Latin *stolidus.*] —**sto·lid·i·ty** (sto-líddəti, stə-), **stol·id·ness** *n.* —**stol·id·ly** *adv.*

stol·len (stố-lən, shtố-, stú-; *German* shtố-) *n.* A rich yeast bread, originally from Germany, often containing raisins, citron, and chopped nuts. [German *Stollen,* loaf-shaped Christmas cake (symbolising the Christ child in swaddling clothes), from Middle High German *stolle,* from Old High German *stollo,* post, support.]

sto·lon (stố-lon, -lən) *n.* **1.** *Botany.* A stem growing along the ground and taking root at the nodes to form new plants. **2.** *Zoology.* A stemlike structure of certain colonial organisms, from which new individuals develop by budding. [Latin *stolō* (stem *stolōn-*), branch, shoot.]

sto·lon·i·fer·ous (stố-lə-níffərəss, -lo-) *adj.* Bearing or forming stolons. —**sto·lon·if·er·ous·ly** *adv.*

sto·ma (stốmə) *n., pl.* **-mata** (-tə, stómmətə, *also* stō-máatə) or **-mas. 1.** *Botany.* One of the minute pores in the epidermis of a leaf or stem, through which gases and water vapour pass. **2.** *Anatomy.* **a.** An opening leading into the intestine, or from one part of the intestine to another. **b.** A hypothetical opening in the surface of the peritoneum, thought to be for the passage of fluid into the lymphatic vessels. **3.** *Zoology.* A mouthlike opening, such as the oral cavity of a nematode. [New Latin, from Greek, mouth.]

stom·ach (stúm-ək ‖ -ik) *n.* **1. a.** The enlarged, saclike portion of the alimentary canal, one of the principal organs of digestion, located in vertebrates between the oesophagus and the small intestine. **b.** A similar digestive structure of many invertebrates. **2.** *Informal.* The abdomen or belly. **3.** An appetite for food. **4.** Any desire or inclination, especially for something difficult or unpleasant: *has no stomach for violence.* **5.** *Obsolete.* Courage or spirit. **6.** *Obsolete.* Pride or haughtiness.

~*tr.v.* **stomached, -aching, -achs. 1.** To bear; tolerate; endure. **2.** To take into or hold in the stomach; digest. [Middle English *stomak,* from Old French *stomaque,* from Latin *stomachus,* from Greek *stomakhos,* throat, mouth, gullet, from *stoma,* mouth.]

stom·ach·ache (stúm-ək-ayk ‖ -ik-) *n.* Pain in the abdomen.

stom·ach·er (stúm-ə-kər, *rarely* -chər, -jər ‖ -i-) *n.* A decorative, heavily embroidered or jewelled garment formerly worn, especially by women, over the chest and ending in a point over the stomach.

sto·mach·ic (stō-máckik, stə-, sto-) *adj.* Also **stom·ach·al** (stúm-ə-k'l ‖ -i-). **1.** Of or pertaining to the stomach; gastric. **2.** Beneficial to or stimulating digestion in the stomach.

~*n.* Any medicine or agent that strengthens or stimulates the stomach.

stomach pump *n.* A suction pump with a flexible tube inserted into the stomach through the mouth and oesophagus to empty the stomach in an emergency, as in a case of poisoning.

stomach worm *n.* Any of various parasitic nematode worms that infest the stomachs of animals; especially, *Haemonchus megastoma,* a parasite of sheep and other ruminants.

sto·ma·ta. Plural of **stoma.**

sto·ma·tal (stố-mə-t'l, stó-) *adj.* Also **sto·ma·tous** (-təss). Of or having a stoma or stomata.

sto·mat·ic (stō-máttik, stə-) *adj.* **1.** Of or relating to the mouth. **2.** Stomatal.

sto·ma·ti·tis (stố-mə-títiss, stómmə-) *n.* Inflammation of the mucous tissue of the mouth. [New Latin : STOMAT(O)- + -ITIS.]

stomato–, stomat– *comb. form.* Indicates the mouth or a mouthlike part; for example, **stomatopod, stomatitis.** [Greek *stoma* (stem *stomat-*), mouth.]

sto·ma·tol·o·gy (stố-mə-tólləji, stómmə-) *n.* The medical study of the physiology and pathology of the mouth. [STOMATO- + -LOGY.]

sto·ma·to·pod (stómmə-tə-pod, stố-, -tō-, stō-máttə-) *n.* Any of various marine crustaceans of the order Stomatopoda, which includes the squilla. [New Latin *stomatopoda* : STOMATO- + -POD.]

-stome *n. comb. form.* Indicates the mouth or a mouthlike opening; for example, **cyclostome.** [Greek *stoma,* opening, mouth.]

sto·mo·dae·um, sto·mo·de·um (stố·mə·dée-əm) *n., pl.* **-dea** (-dée-ə). *Embryology.* The primitive oral cavity of an embryo. [New Latin : Greek *stoma,* mouth (see **stoma**) + *hodaios,* on the way, from *hodos,* way.] —**sto·mo·dae·al** *adj.*

stomp (stomp ‖ stawmp) *intr.v.* **stomped, stomping, stomps. 1.** To tread or trample heavily or violently. **2.** To dance the stomp.

~*n.* **1.** A dance involving a rhythmical and heavy step. **2.** The jazz music for this dance. [Variant of STAMP (to pound).]

–stomy *n. comb. form.* Indicates a surgical operation in which a usually permanent opening is made into (a specified organ or part); for example, **colostomy.** [From -STOME.]

stone (stōn) *n., pl.* **stones** or **stone** (for sense 9). *Abbr.* **st. 1.** Solid and compact earthy or mineral matter; rock. **2.** Such material of a particular type. Used in combination: *sandstone; soapstone.* **3.** A small piece of rock. **4.** Rock or a piece of rock shaped or finished for a particular purpose, especially: **a.** A stone used in construction work: *a coping stone; a paving stone.* **b.** A gravestone or tombstone. **c.** A grindstone, millstone, or whetstone. **d.** A milestone or boundary. **4.** A gem or precious stone. **6.** Something like a stone in shape or hardness, such as a hailstone. **7.** *Botany.* The hard covering enclosing the kernel in certain fruits, such as the cherry or plum. **8.** *Pathology.* A mineral concretion in a hollow organ, as in the kidney. See **calculus. 9.** A unit of weight in Britain and some other English-speaking countries, 14 pounds avoirdupois, used especially to express human body weight. **10.** *Printing.* A table with a smooth surface on which page forms are composed, originally made of stone. **11.** The oblate piece of stone or iron, with a gooseneck handle, used in the game of curling. **12.** *Plural. Archaic.* The testicles. **13.** Dull light to dark grey. —**cast the first stone.** To be the first to criticise or accuse. [Biblical allusion to Jesus' saying, "He that is without sin among you, let him cast a stone at her . . ." (John 8:7)].

~*adj.* **1.** Pertaining to or made of stone: *a stone wall.* **2.** Made of stoneware or earthenware.

~*adv.* Utterly; completely: *stone cold.*

~*tr.v.* **stoned, stoning, stones. 1.** To hurl or throw stones at; pelt or kill with stones. **2.** To remove the stones from (fruit, for example). **3.** To furnish, fit, pave, or line with stones. **4.** To rub on or with a stone in order to polish or sharpen. **5.** *Obsolete.* To make hard like stone; make pitiless or indifferent. [Middle English *stane, stone,* Old English *stān.*] —**ston·er** *n.*

Stone Age *n.* The earliest known period of human culture, characterised by the use of stone tools.

stone axe *n.* An axe with two blunt edges used for hewing stone.

stone bass *n.* A large sea perch, *Polyprion americanus,* of Mediterranean and Atlantic waters. Also called "wreckfish".

stone-blind (stōn-blínd) *adj.* Completely blind.

stone boiling *n.* A primitive way of boiling water by putting heated stones into it.

stone bramble *n.* A bramble, *Rubus saxatilis,* with small white flowers and red fruit.

stone-chat (stōn-chat) *n.* A small Old World bird, *Saxicola torquata,* having dark plumage. [From the bird's cry resembling the sound of falling pebbles.]

stone-crop (stōn-krop) *n.* **1.** Any of various plants of the genus *Sedum,* having fleshy leaves and variously coloured flowers. **2.** Any of various related plants. [Middle English *stoncrop,* Old English *stāncropp* : *stān,* STONE + *cropp,* cluster, CROP.]

stone curlew *n.* A wading bird, *Burhinus oedicnemus,* with a large round head and staring yellow eyes. Also called "thick-knee", *South African* "dikkop".

stone-cut·ter (stōn-kuttər) *n.* One that cuts or carves stone; especially, a machine that dresses stone. —**stone-cut·ting** *n.*

stoned (stōnd) *adj. Slang.* **1.** Intoxicated; drunk. **2.** Under the influence of a mind-altering drug.

stone-deaf (stōn-déf) *adj.* Completely deaf.

stone-fish (stōn-fish) *n., pl.* **-fishes** or collectively **stonefish.** Any of several tropical marine fishes of the family Scorpaenidae, having spines that eject a deadly venom. [From their resemblance to encrusted stones.]

stone-fly (stōn-flī) *n., pl.* **-flies.** Any of numerous winged insects of the order Plecoptera, occurring on banks of streams and used as fishing bait. [From their aquatic larvae, found under stones.]

stone fruit *n.* A **drupe** (*see*).

Stone-henge (stōn-hénj) *n.* A megalithic circle on Salisbury Plain, Wiltshire, England. Its surrounding bank and ditch date from *c.* 2800 B.C. The stone circle itself dates from *c.* 2200–1800 B.C., and was probably used as a religious centre. The mathematical accuracy of the stones' positioning suggests that it was also an observatory, used as a calendar of the seasons and to predict eclipses.

stone lily *n.* A fossil crinoid.

stone marten *n.* **1.** A Eurasian mammal, *Martes foina,* having brown fur with lighter underfur. **2.** The fur of this animal. Also called "beech marten".

stone-ma·son (stōn-mayss'n) *n.* One who prepares and lays stones in building. —**stone-ma·son·ry** *n.*

stone parsley *n.* A hedgerow plant, *Sison amomum,* with small white flowers and a fetid smell.

stone pit *n.* A quarry.

stone's throw *n.* A short distance.

stone-wall (stōn-wáwl) *v.* **-walled, -walling, -walls.** —*intr.* **1.** In cricket, to bat defensively rather than trying to score. **2.** *Informal.* To engage in delaying or obstructionist tactics. —*tr. Informal.* To delay or obstruct; especially, to hinder (parliamentary proceedings), as by making long speeches. —**stone·wall·er** n.

stone·ware (stŏn-wair) n. A heavy, nonporous pottery, fired at a high temperature and often glazed with salt.

stone·work (stŏn-wurk) n. **1.** The technique or process of preparing, dressing, or working in stone. **2.** Work made of stone; stone masonry. —**stone·work·er** n.

stone·wort (stŏn-wurt ‖ -wawrt) n. Any of various green algae of the family Characae, that grow submerged in fresh or brackish water and are frequently encrusted with calcium carbonate deposits.

stonk (stongk) n. Heavy shelling by artillery. [Imitative.] —**stonk** tr.v.

stonk·ered (stóngkərd) adj. Australian & N.Z. Informal. **1.** Utterly exhausted or defeated. **2.** Puzzled; baffled. [20th century : from stonker†, to tire, etc.]

ston·y (stŏni) adj. **-i·er, -i·est. 1.** Covered with or full of stones. **2.** Hard as a stone. **3.** Hard and unfeeling. **4.** Impassive; showing no feeling or warmth: a stony face. **5.** Emotionally numbing or paralysing: a stony fear. —**ston·i·ly** adv. —**ston·i·ness** n.

ston·y-broke (stŏni-brŏk) adj. British Slang. Penniless; having no money at all.

stood. Past tense and past participle of **stand**.

stooge (stŏŏj) n. **1.** A person who acts as the butt or foil for a comedian's jokes, often by asking questions. **2.** Anyone who allows himself to be used for another's advantage.

~intr.v. **stooged, stooging, stooges.** To be or behave as a stooge. [20th century : origin obscure.]

stook (stŏŏk, stŏŏk) n. A shock of sheaves of corn.

~tr.v. **stooked, stooking, stooks.** To pile (sheaves of corn) into a shock. [Middle English stouk, probably from Middle Low German stuke, shock.]

stool (stŏŏl) n. **1.** A backless and armless single seat supported on legs or a pedestal. **2.** A low bench or support for the feet or knees in sitting or kneeling, such as a footrest or hassock. **3.** A seat enclosing a chamber pot; a commode. **4.** A piece of faecal matter. **5.** Horticulture. **a.** A stump or rootstock that produces shoots or suckers. **b.** A shoot or growth from such a stump or rootstock. **6.** In West Africa: **a.** The throne of a chief. **b.** The kingdom or sphere of sovereignty of a chief. —**fall between two stools.** To fail completely through being unable to reconcile or choose between two alternatives.

~intr.v. **stooled, stooling, stools. 1.** To send up shoots or suckers. **2.** Archaic. To evacuate the bowels; defecate. **3.** Slang. To act as a stool pigeon. [Middle English stol, Old English stōl.]

stool·ball (stŏŏl-bawl) n. An old English country game very similar to cricket, formerly widespread and still played, though in a modified form, by women in some areas, especially in Sussex. [STOOL (the term for the wicket) + BALL.]

stool·ie (stŏŏli) n. Chiefly U.S. Slang. A stool pigeon for the police.

stool pigeon n. **1.** A pigeon used as a decoy. **2.** Slang. A person acting as a decoy or informer; especially, a spy for the police. [Decoy pigeons were originally tied to a stool.]

stoop[1] (stŏŏp) v. **stooped, stooping, stoops.** —intr. **1.** To bend forwards and downwards from the waist or middle of the back. **2.** To walk or stand, especially habitually, with the head and upper back bent forwards. **3.** To bend or slope downwards. **4.** To lower or debase oneself. Used with to. **5.** To descend from a superior position; condescend. Used with to. **6.** To swoop down. Used especially of a bird of prey. —tr. **1.** To bend (one's head or body) forwards and downwards. **2.** Archaic. To debase or subdue; humble.

~n. **1.** The act of stooping. **2.** A forward bending of the head and upper back, especially when habitual. **3.** An act of self-abasement or condescension. **4.** A swooping down, as of a bird of prey. [Middle English stupen, Old English stūpian.]

stoop[2] n. A small porch, platform, or staircase leading to the entrance of a house or building. Also South African "stoep". [Dutch stoep, front verandah, from Middle Dutch.]

stoop[3] n. Archaic or Regional. A pillar or upright post. [Middle English, variant of dialect stulpe, probably from Old Norse stolpe.]

stoop[4]. Variant of **stoup**.

stop (stop) v. **stopped, stopping, stops.** —tr. **1.** To close (an opening) by covering, filling in, or plugging up. Often used with up. **2.** To stop the flow of something from; stanch: stop a wound. **3.** To constrict (an opening or orifice). **4.** To obstruct or block the passage of (traffic, for example). **5.** To prevent the flow or passage of: tried to stop the blood. **6. a.** To arrest the movement or progress of; cause to halt: A man stopped me and asked the time. **b.** To prevent from continuing an action; cause to cease or desist: stopped their chatter by banging on the table. **c.** To restrain or prevent from an intended action: couldn't stop him from calling the police. **7.** To desist from; cease doing. Often used with a gerund: stop running. **8.** To cause (a machine, for example) to cease operating, functioning, or moving; halt. **9.** To give instructions to one's banker to not honour (a cheque). **10.** To withold; keep back: stop his allowance. **11.** In boxing, to defeat (an opponent) by rendering him unable to continue the fight. **12.** Slang. To be given or receive (a blow, bullet, or the like). **13.** Music. **a.** To close (a hole on a wind instrument) with the finger in order to sound a desired note. **b.** To press down (a string on a stringed instrument) in order to produce a desired note. **c.** To put one's hand inside (the bell of a French horn) in order to alter the pitch or tone quality. **d.** To produce (a particular note) by any of these methods. **14.** To close (an organ pipe) at one end, in order to make it sound an octave lower. **15.** In bridge, to hold a card or cards in (a particular suit) that will prevent one's

opponents from winning all the tricks in that suit. —intr. **1.** To cease moving, progressing, acting, or operating; come to a halt or pause. **2.** To put an end to what one is doing; cease. **3.** To interrupt one's course or journey, as to make a quick visit or do an errand. Often used with in or off: stop in at the supermarket for a minute. **4.** Informal. To stay: stopped at a friend's for a few nights. —**stop at nothing.** To act with absolute determination or lack of scruples. —**stop down.** To reduce the effective aperture of (a camera lens). —**stop out.** To cover (part of an area of cloth, a printing plate, or the like) in order to prevent it being printed or etched.

~n. **1.** The act of stopping or the condition of being stopped; a cessation; a halt. **2.** A finish; an end. **3.** A stay or visit, as during a journey. **4. a.** An official stopping place: a bus stop. **b.** Any place stopped at. **5. a.** An act or instance of obstructing, blocking, or plugging up. **b.** A device or means that obstructs, blocks, or plugs up. **6. a.** See **stop payment. b.** See **stop order. 7.** A part in a machine that stops or regulates movement. **8.** A perforated screen or diaphragm that limits the effective aperture of a lens, producing an image of improved definition but lowered intensity. **9.** A punctuation mark, especially a full stop. Used in full in telegrams and cables instead of a full stop. **10.** Music. **a.** The act of stopping a string or hole on a musical instrument. **b.** A device such as a key for closing the hole on a wind instrument. **11.** Music. **a.** A tuned set of pipes, as in an organ. **b.** A knob, key, or pull that regulates such a set of pipes. **12.** Nautical. A line used for securing something temporarily: a sail stop. **13.** Phonetics. A consonant articulated with a complete obstruction of the passage of breath; specifically, (p), (b), (t), (d), (k), or (g) in English. Compare **continuant**. **14.** The depression between the muzzle and top of the skull of a dog or cat. **15.** In bridge, a **stopper** (see). **16.** Architecture. A projecting stone, often carved, at the end of a moulding. —**pull out all the stops.** To exert oneself to the utmost. [Middle English stoppen, Old English -stoppian, from West Germanic stoppōn (unattested), to plug up, from Late Latin stuppāre, to stop up with a tow, from Latin stuppa, tow, from Greek stuppē.]

Usage: In British English, one usually stops something *happening*: in American English, one usually stops something *from happening*.

stop bath n. In photography, an acid solution used to check the developing process.

stop·cock (stóp-kok) n. A valve that regulates the flow of liquid through a pipe; a tap.

stope (stōp) n. A tunnel driven parallel to the strike of a vertical or near vertical vein so that ore can be excavated from the vein.

~v. **stoped, stoping, stopes.** —tr. To remove (ore) from a stope. —intr. To mine by means of a stope. [Perhaps from Low German stope, a step, from Middle Low German stōpe.]

Stopes (stōps), **Marie (Charlotte) Carmichael** (1880–1958). British scientist and pioneer advocate of birth control. With her husband she founded Britain's first birth control clinic (1921). Her books include Married Love (1918), and Enduring Passion (1928).

stop·gap (stóp-gap) n. An improvised substitute for something lacking; a temporary expedient.

stop-go (stóp-gō) adj. British. Of, designating, or tending to produce an economic cycle in which deflation and inflation alternate.

stop·ing (stóping) n. **1.** Geology. The breaking-up of country rock by advancing intrusive magma. **2.** Mining. The mining of ore by means of stopes, often by a series of stopes.

stop·light (stóp-līt) n. U.S. **1.** A red traffic light. **2.** A brake light (see).

stop order n. An order to a broker to buy or sell a stock when it reaches a stipulated level of decline or gain.

stop over intr.v. To make a stopover on a journey.

stop·o·ver (stóp-ōvər) n. **1.** An interruption in the course of a journey for stopping at or visiting a certain place; especially, a stop made in the course of a long-distance airline flight. **2.** A place visited briefly in the course of a journey.

stop·page (stóppij) n. **1.** The act of stopping or the condition of being stopped; a halt. **2.** Something that stops, obstructs, or blocks. **3.** An amount withheld, as from a person's wages; a deduction. **4.** The act of stopping work, as during industrial action.

Stop·pard (stóppaard), **Sir Tom** (1937–). Czech-born British playwright. He first achieved success with Rosencrantz and Guildenstern are Dead (1967); later works include Jumpers (1972), The Real Thing (1982), and Indian Ink (1995). His plays are characterised by their witty dialogue and their philosophical or ethical themes.

stop payment n. An order to one's bank not to honour a cheque.

stop·per (stóppər) n. **1.** Any device, such as a cork or plug, inserted to close an opening. **2.** One that causes something to stop. **3.** In bridge, a card or cards enabling one to prevent one's opponents from winning all the tricks. Also called "stop".

~tr.v. **stoppered, -pering, -pers.** To close with a stopper.

stop·ping (stópping) n. British. A filling in a tooth.

~adj. Halting at many stations. Said of a train.

stop·ple (stópp'l) n. A stopper; a plug.

~tr.v. **stoppled, -pling, -ples.** To close with a stopple. [Middle English stoppell, from stoppen, to STOP.]

stop press n. **1.** Late news that is added to a newspaper after the printing has started. **2.** A space in a newspaper that is set aside for such news.

stop·watch (stóp-woch) n. A timepiece that can be started and stopped by a trigger to measure duration of time.

stor·age (stáw-rij ‖ stō-) n. Abbr. **stge., stor. 1. a.** The act of storing goods, as in a warehouse for safekeeping. **b.** The state of being stored. **2.** Space for storing goods. **3.** The price charged for keeping goods stored. **4.** *Computing*. A process of storing information on a storage device. Also used adjectivally: *storage capacity*.

storage battery *n.* A group of reversible or rechargeable **secondary cells** *(see)* acting as a unit. Also called "accumulator", "secondary battery".

storage cell *n.* A **secondary cell** *(see)*.

storage device *n. Computing*. A piece of equipment or medium on which computer data can be stored and from which it can be retrieved. Storage devices include magnetic tapes and tape cassettes, hard and floppy disks, and magnetic drums.

storage heater *n.* A type of electric heater that accumulates heat during off-peak electricity hours.

sto·rax (stáw-raks ‖ stŏ-) *n.* **1.** Any of various trees of the genus *Styrax*, some of which yield an aromatic resin. **2.** An aromatic resin obtained from any of these trees. **3.** A brownish, aromatic resin used in perfume and medicine and obtained from any of several trees of the genus *Liquidambar;* especially, *L. orientalis,* of Asia Minor. In this sense, also called "styrax". [Middle English, from Latin, from Greek, variant of *sturax,* probably from Semitic; akin to Hebrew *tzŏrī.*]

store (stor ‖ stōr) *n.* **1.** A stock or supply reserved for future use. **2.** *Plural.* Supplies, especially of food, clothing, or arms. **3.** A place where commodities are kept; a warehouse or storehouse. Also used in combination: *a storeman.* **4.** A great quantity or number; an abundance. **5.** *Computing.* A **memory** *(see).* **6. a.** A department store. **b.** *U.S.* Any shop. **—in store.** Set aside or reserved for the future; forthcoming. **—lay, put,** or **set store by.** To regard as important or valuable.

~*tr.v.* **stored, storing, stores. 1.** To reserve or put away for future use. **2.** To fill, supply, or stock with something. **3.** To deposit or receive in a storehouse or warehouse for safekeeping. **4.** *Computing.* To place (data) in a storage device for retention. [Middle English *stor,* from Old French *estor,* from *estorer,* to build, restore, from Latin *instaurāre.*] **—stor·a·ble** *adj.*

store·front (stór-frunt ‖ stōr-) *n.* **1.** The side of a shop facing a street. **2.** A room or set of rooms in a storefront. **—store·front** *adj.*

store·house (stór-howss ‖ stōr-) *n.* **1.** A place or building in which goods are stored; a warehouse. **2.** An abundant source or supply.

store·keep·er (stór-keepər ‖ stōr-) *n.* **1.** A person in charge of receiving or distributing stores or supplies, especially military and naval supplies. **2.** *U.S.* A shopkeeper.

store·room (stór-rōōm, -rŏŏm ‖ stōr-) *n.* A room in which things are stored.

sto·rey (stáwri ‖ stŏri) *n., pl.* **-reys.** Also *chiefly U.S.* **sto·ry** *pl.* **-ies. 1.** A complete horizontal division of a building comprising the area between two adjacent levels. **2.** The set of rooms on the same level of a building. [Middle English, from Anglo-Latin *historia,* HISTORY (perhaps originally referring to a row of painted windows or of sculptures).]

Sto·rey (stáwri ‖ stŏri), **David (Malcolm)** (1933–). British author of the novels *This Sporting Life* (1960) and *Saville* (1976), the play *In Celebration* (1969), and the poems *Storey's Lives* (1992).

storey building *n. West African.* A house that consists of more than one storey. Also called "storey house".

sto·reyed (stáw-rid ‖ stŏ-, -reed) *adj.* Also *chiefly U.S.* **sto·ried.** Having or consisting of a specified number of storeys. Used in combination: *a three-storeyed house.*

sto·ried (stáw-rid ‖ stŏ-, -reed) *adj.* **1.** *Literary.* Celebrated or famous in history or legend. **2.** Ornamented with designs representing scenes from history or legend: *storied tapestry.*

stork (stork) *n.* **1.** Any of various large wading birds of the family Ciconiidae, having long red legs, a long, red, stout bill, and black and white plumage. **2.** Such a bird conventionally considered as the bringer of babies. Preceded by *the.* [Middle English *stork,* Old English *storc.*]

stork's-bill (stórks-bil) *n.* Any of various plants of the genus *Erodium,* having fruit with a narrow, beaklike point.

storm (storm) *n.* **1.** An atmospheric disturbance manifested in strong winds accompanied by rain, snow, or other precipitation, and often by thunder and lightning. **2.** *Meteorology.* A wind whose speed is 28.5 to 32.6 metres per second (64–75 miles per hour), force 11 on the Beaufort scale. **3.** A heavy shower of objects, such as bullets or missiles. **4.** A strong or violent outburst, as of emotion or protest. **5.** A violent disturbance or upheaval, as in political, social, or domestic affairs. **6.** *Military.* A violent, sudden attack on a fortified place. **—take by storm.** To have overwhelming and captivating effect on (an audience, for example).

~*v.* **stormed, storming, storms. —intr. 1.** To blow forcefully; rain, snow, hail, or otherwise precipitate violently. Used with *it: It stormed last night.* **2.** To be extremely angry; rant and rage. **3.** To move or rush tumultuously, violently, or angrily: *She stormed into the room.* **—tr.** *Military.* To capture or try to capture by a violent, sudden attack. **—See Synonyms at attack.** [Middle English, Old English *storm.*]

storm belt *n.* A part of the earth's surface in which storms are frequent.

storm·bound (stórm-bownd) *adj.* Delayed, confined, or cut off from communication by a storm.

storm centre *n.* **1.** *Meteorology.* The central area covered by a storm; especially, the point of lowest barometric pressure within a storm. **2.** The centre or source of trouble, disturbance, or argument.

storm cloud *n.* **1.** A heavy, dark rain-cloud that threatens stormy weather. **2.** Anything that presages violence, disturbance, or war.

storm collar *n.* A high coat-collar, often one that buttons up.

storm cone *n. British.* A tarred cone, hoisted to provide a warning of high winds.

storm door *n.* An outer or additional door added for protection against inclement weather.

storm glass *n.* A glass tube containing a liquid solution that forms crystals as an indication of bad weather.

storm in a teacup *n.* Great excitement or fuss over something trivial or unimportant.

Stor·mont (stáwr-mont). The former parliament of Northern Ireland or a subsequent administrative body for the Province. [From *Stormont* Castle, where it sat.]

storm petrel *n.* A small sea bird of the family Hydrobatidae; especially, *Hydrobates pelagicus,* of the North Atlantic and the Mediterranean. Also called "stormy petrel", "Mother Carey's chicken".

storm surge *n.* A rapid rise of sea level above predicted tidal levels when water is piled up against a coast by powerful onshore winds, sometimes breaching coastal defences. Also in nontechnical usage "tidal wave".

storm trooper *n.* **1.** A member of the **Sturmabteilung** *(see).* **2.** A member of a force of shock troops.

storm warning *n.* A pattern of lights or flags displayed along a coastline or at a port, to warn of an approaching storm.

storm window *n.* A secondary window attached over the usual window to protect against the wind and cold.

storm·y (stórmi) *adj.* **-ier, -iest. 1.** Subject to, characterised by, or affected by storms; tempestuous. **2.** Characterised by violent emotions, passions, speech, or actions: *a stormy argument.* **—storm·i·ly** *adv.* **—storm·i·ness** *n.*

stormy petrel *n.* **1.** A storm petrel. **2.** A person who brings discord or appears at the onset of trouble.

Stor·no·way (stáwrnə-way). Seaport and burgh on the east coast of the Isle of Lewis in the Outer Hebrides, Scotland. It is the administrative centre of the Western Isles.

Stor·ting, Stor·thing (stór-ting ‖ stŏr-) *n.* The parliament of Norway. [Norwegian : *stor,* great + *thing,* assembly.]

sto·ry¹ (stáwri ‖ stŏri) *n., pl.* **-ries. 1.** An account or recital of an event or series of events, either true or fictitious. **2.** A prose or verse narrative, usually fictional, intended to interest or amuse the hearer or reader; a tale. **3.** A type of fictional literary composition, a **short story** *(see).* **4.** An incident or experience that would be good material for a narrative. **5.** A plot, as of a novel or play. **6.** A report, statement, or allegation of facts. **7. a.** A news article. **b.** The event, situation, or other material for such an article. **8.** An anecdote. **9.** A lie. **10.** Romantic legend or tradition. **—quite another story.** An entirely different state of affairs. **—the old** or **same old story.** The well-known or very familiar course of events.

~*tr.v.* **storied, -rying, -ries. 1.** To decorate with scenes representing historical or legendary events. **2.** *Archaic.* To tell as a story. [Middle English *storie,* from Anglo-French *estorie,* from Latin *historia,* HISTORY.]

story² *Chiefly U.S.* Variant of **storey.**

sto·ry·book (stáw-ri-bŏŏk ‖ stŏ-, -bŏŏk) *n.* A book containing a collection of stories, usually for children.

~*adj.* Of the kind that occurs in a storybook; romantic; fairytale.

story line *n.* The plot of a book, film, or a dramatic work.

sto·ry·tell·er (stáw-ri-tellər ‖ stŏ-) *n.* **1.** A person who tells or writes stories. **2.** *Informal.* A person who tells lies; a fibber. **—sto·ry·tell·ing** *n.*

stoss (stoss; *German* shtŏss) *adj.* Facing the direction from which a glacier or ice sheet moves. Said of a rock or slope in its path. [From German *stossen,* to push, thrust, from Old High German *stōzan.*]

stot (stŏt, stot) *v.* **stotted, stotting, stots.** *Scottish.* **—intr. 1.** To rebound; bounce. **2.** To lurch; stagger. **—tr.** To cause to bounce. [Middle English (Scots), of obscure origin.]

sto·tin·ka (sto-tíng-kə ‖ stŏ-) *n., pl.* **-ki** (-kee). A monetary unit equal to $1/100$ of the lev of Bulgaria. [Bulgarian : *sto-,* from *suto,* hundred + suffixes *-tin, -ka.*]

sto·tious (stŏshəss) *adj.* *Scottish & Irish Slang.* Drunk. [Probably from STOT in the sense "to lurch, stagger".]

stot·ter (stótər) *n.* *Scottish Slang.* An extremely attractive woman. [From STOT.]

stound (stownd) *n.* **1.** *Obsolete.* A short time; a while. **2.** *Chiefly Scottish.* A sudden tremor, as of pain or excitement. [Middle English *sto(u)nd,* Old English *stund.*]

stoup, stoop (stōōp) *n.* **1.** *Ecclesiastical.* A basin or font for holy water at the entrance of a church. **2.** *Northern British.* **a.** A bucket or pail. **b.** A cup, tankard, or other drinking vessel. [Middle English *stowp,* vessel, pail, from Old Norse *staup.*]

stour (stowr) *n.* *Chiefly Scottish.* **1.** Tumult; conflict. **2. a.** A driving storm. **b.** A sudden cloud of dust or spray. [Middle English, from Old French *estour,* armed combat, from Germanic; akin to Old High German *sturm,* STORM.]

stoush (stowsh) *n.* *Australian Informal.* A fight, conflict, or war. **—the big stoush.** *Australian Informal.* World War I.

~*tr.v.* **stoushed, stoushing, stoushes.** To fight or hit. [19th century : origin obscure.]

stout (stowt) *adj.* **stouter, stoutest. 1.** Determined, bold, or brave; resolute; staunch: *a stout heart.* **2.** Strong in body; sturdy. **3.** Strong in structure or substance; substantial; solid. **4.** Bulky in

figure; thickset; inclined towards fatness. **5.** Powerful; forceful. —*See Synonyms at* **strong, fat.**
~*n.* A strong, very dark beer or ale brewed with malt or barley. [Middle English, from Old French *estout,* from Germanic.] —**stout·ly** *adv.* —**stout·ness** *n.*
stout-heart·ed (stówt-hártid) *adj.* Brave; courageous; dauntless. —**stout·heart·ed·ly** *adv.* —**stout·heart·ed·ness** *n.*
stove¹ (stōv) *n.* **1.** An apparatus in which electricity or a fuel is used to provide heat, as for cooking or comfort. **2.** A heated room or box used for a particular purpose, such as a kiln or hothouse.
~*tr.v.* **stoved, stoving, stoves.** To heat, treat, or keep in a stove. [Middle English, heated chamber, from Middle Low German or Middle Dutch.]
stove². Alternative past tense and past participle of **stave.**
stove enamel *n.* A type of heat-resistant enamel paint.
stove·pipe (stōv-pīp) *n.* **1.** A pipe, usually iron, used to conduct smoke or fumes from a stove into a chimney flue. **2.** A man's tall silk hat. Also called "stovepipe hat".
sto·ver (stōvər) *n.* Any of various kinds of animal feed made from clover, stubble, or the like. [Middle English, food, provisions, short for Anglo-French *estovers,* supplies, from Old French *estovier,* to be necessary, from Latin *est opus,* it is necessary : *est* (it) is, from *esse,* to be + *opus,* need, necessity.]
stow (stō) *tr.v.* **stowed, stowing, stows. 1. a.** To place, arrange, or store away, especially in a neat, compact way. **b.** *Nautical.* To load or store (cargo, gear, or provisions) in the proper place. **2.** To fill by packing tightly. **3.** *Slang.* To cease; stop. Usually used in the imperative: *Stow it!* **4.** *Slang.* To consume (food) greedily. Often used with *away.* **5.** *Archaic.* To provide lodging for; quarter. [Middle English *stowen,* to place, put, from *stowe,* a place, Old English *stōw.*]
stow·age (stō-ij) *n.* **1. a.** The act, manner, or process of stowing. **b.** The state of being stowed. **2.** Space or room for storage. **3.** Goods in storage. **4.** A charge for storing goods.
stow away *intr.v.* To be a stowaway.
stow·a·way (stō-ə-way) *n.* One who hides aboard a ship or other form of transport in order to obtain free passage.
Stowe (stō), **Harriet Beecher** (1811–96). U.S. author. Her antislavery novel, *Uncle Tom's Cabin* (1852), had great political influence and did much to advance the cause of abolition.
St. Paul. The state capital of Minnesota, northern United States, situated at the head of navigation of the river Mississippi.
St. Peter Port. The capital of Guernsey in the Channel Islands. It is a busy port, and is also a tourist resort and yachting centre.
St. Pe·ters·burg (sənt peétərz-burg, saynt) *Russian* **Sankt·Peter·burg** (sankt peetər-bo'ork). City in northwest Russia, situated on the banks and delta islands of the river Neva, at the head of the Gulf of Finland. It is Russia's second largest city, and a leading seaport and commercial and industrial centre. It was founded in 1803 by Peter the Great, and was the capital of Russia from 1712 until 1918. From 1914 until 1924 it was called Petrograd, and from then until 1991 **Len·in·grad** (lennin-grad). The city was laid out on classical lines by French and Italian architects, and is the site of the famous Hermitage museum.
St. Pierre et Mique·lon (saN pi-aír ay meek-lóN). Two small island groups making up a French Territorial Collectivity situated in the Atlantic Ocean south of Newfoundland. Frequently contested between England and France, they finally became French in 1814, and are the last French territory in North America.
stra·bis·mus (strə-bízməss, stra-) *n.* Also **stra·bil·is·mus** (strábbi-lízməss), **stra·bism** (stráybiz'm). A visual defect in which one eye cannot focus with the other on an objective because of imbalance of the eye muscles. Also called "squint". See **walleye.** [New Latin, from Greek *strabismos,* from *strabizein,* to squint, from *strabos,* squinting.] —**stra·bis·mal, stra·bis·mic** *adj.*
stra·bot·o·my (strə-bóttəmi, stra-) *n., pl.* **-mies.** The cutting of an ocular muscle or tendon to correct strabismus. [Greek *strabos,* squinting + -TOMY.]
Stra·chey (stráychi), **(Giles) Lytton** (1880–1932). British biographer and historian. He is known chiefly for his revolutionary biographies in which he debunked the grandeur of Victorian society. His works include *Eminent Victorians* (1918), *Queen Victoria* (1921), and *Elizabeth and Essex* (1928).
strad·dle (stráddʹl) *v.* **-dled, -dling, -dles.** —*tr.* **1.** To sit, stand, or be in a position astride of; bestride. **2.** To fire shots behind and in front of (a target) in order to determine the range. **3. a.** To fall on or take in parts of (two periods or areas, for example): *Her constituency straddles two counties.* **b.** To fall or lie on either side of (a dividing line). **4.** *U.S.* To vacillate between or seem to favour both sides of (an issue). —*intr.* **1.** To sit or stand with the legs apart. **2.** To be or be spread wide apart; sprawl. **3.** *U.S.* To appear to favour both sides of an issue.
~*n.* **1.** The act or posture of sitting astride. **2.** *U.S. Finance.* The privileged option of either delivering or buying securities at a stated price within a stated period of time. Compare **call, put. 3.** *U.S.* An equivocal or noncommittal position. [Frequentative of *strad-,* obsolete past stem of STRIDE.] —**strad·dler** *n.*
Strad·i·var·i (stráddi-va'ari ‖ *U.S. also* -várri), **Antonio** (1644–1737). Italian violin maker. At his workshop in Cremona he brought violin-making to its highest point of craftsmanship. He produced over 1,000 instruments, some of which still survive.
Strad·i·var·i·us (stráddi-vaír-i-əss) *n., pl.* **-varii.** Any of the famous violins made in the workshop of Antonio Stradivari. Also informally called "Strad".

strafe (strayf, straaf) *tr.v.* **strafed, strafing, strafes.** To attack (ground troops, for example) with bombs or machine-gun fire from low-flying aircraft.
~*n.* An act of strafing. [Humorous use from German slogan (1914) *(Gott) strafe (England),* "(God) punish (England)", from *strafen,* to punish, from Middle High German *strāfen†,* to rebuke.]
Straf·ford (strátford), **Thomas Wentworth, 1st Earl of** (1593–1641). English statesman. As a chief minister of Charles I and a leading agent of his absolutist rule, he became deeply unpopular. He was impeached by the Long Parliament and executed.
strag·gle (strággʹl) *intr.v.* **-gled, -gling, -gles. 1.** To stray or fall behind. **2.** To grow, proceed, or spread out in a scattered or irregular manner or pattern. [Middle English *straglen,* perhaps frequentative of *straken,* to go, move, perhaps related to Old English *streccan,* to STRETCH.] —**strag·gler** *n.*
strag·gly (strággli) *adj.* **-glier, -gliest.** Spread out or proceeding irregularly.
straight (strayt) *adj.* **straighter, straightest. 1.** Extending continuously in the same direction. **2.** Free from curves, angles or irregularities, as: **a.** Not wavy or curly: *straight hair.* **b.** Not bent or stooping: *a straight back.* **c.** Exactly vertical or horizontal; level or upright. **3.** Characterised by honesty and fairness; scrupulous. **4. a.** Logical; reasonable: *straight thinking.* **b.** Accurate; correct; in accordance with the truth: *set the record straight.* **5.** Direct and candid; not evasive: *a straight answer.* **6.** Uninterrupted; consecutive. **7.** Unmodified; unembellished: *gave us the straight facts.* **8.** Undiluted or unmixed: *straight whisky.* **9.** Involving no additional or extraneous elements: *a straight swap; a straight fight between Labour and Conservative.* **10.** Neatly arranged; orderly. **11.** Of, designating, or involved in serious drama as opposed to comedy, musicals, or the like: *a straight actor; a straight play.* **12.** Normal or conventional; conforming to established norms, as in one's opinions, lifestyle, or sexual preferences; especially: **a.** Heterosexual. **b.** Not being a drug-user.
~*adv.* **1.** In a straight line. **2.** In an erect posture; upright. **3.** Directly; without detour or delay. **4.** Without circumlocution; candidly. Often used with *out.* **5.** Honestly or virtuously. **6.** Continuously. —**go straight.** *Informal.* To reform after having been a criminal.
~*n.* **1.** A straight line, part, piece, or condition. **2.** A straight part on a racecourse, especially between the last turn and the winning post. **3.** A poker hand containing a numerical sequence of five cards of various suits. **4.** *Slang.* A normal or conventional person, especially: **a.** A heterosexual person. **b.** A person who is not a drug-user. [Middle English *streit, streight,* from the past participle of *strecchen,* to STRETCH.] —**straight·ly** *adv.* —**straight·ness** *n.*
straight and narrow *n.* The path of honest, moral, and law-abiding behaviour.
straight·a·way, straight away (stráyt-ə-wáy) *adv.* At once; immediately.
~*adj.* Extending or proceeding in a straight line or course.
~*n.* (-way). *U.S.* A straight course, stretch, or track.
straight chain *n. Chemistry.* An open linear molecular structure with no side chains. Compare **branched chain.**
straight·edge (stráyt-ej) *n.* A rigid flat rectangular bar, as of wood or metal, with a straight edge for testing or drawing straight lines. —**straight·edged** *adj.*
straight·en (stráytʹn) *v.* **-ened, -ening, -ens.** —*tr.* **1.** To make straight. **2.** To tidy. —*intr.* To become straight. —**straighten out. 1.** To put to rights or restore order to; rectify. **2.** To reform or improve. —**straight·en·er** *n.*
straight face *n.* A face that betrays no sign of emotion, especially of amusement. —**straight·faced** (stráyt-fáyst) *adj.*
straight flush *n.* In poker, a run of five consecutive cards of the same suit.
straight·for·ward (stráyt-fór-wərd) *adj.* **1.** Proceeding in a straight course; direct. **2.** Honest; frank; candid. **3.** Simple; uncomplicated. **4.** Unambiguous; cut-and-dried. —*See Synonyms at* **fair.**
~*adv.* In a straightforward course. —**straight·for·ward·ly** *adv.* —**straight·for·ward·ness** *n.*
straight jacket *n.* Variant of **strait jacket.**
straight-line (stráyt-lín) *adj.* **1.** Of, pertaining to, or designating a type of machinery whose linkage produces or copies motion in straight lines. **2.** Designating the most usual method of amortisation of a loan or of providing for the depreciation of an asset, based on a series of equal payments or equal allowable amounts over a given period of time.
straight man *n.* One of two comedians who acts a "normal" role as a foil to his partner's obvious comedy.
straight off *adv.* Without delay or hesitation; at once.
straight ticket *n. U.S.* A vote cast for all the candidates of one party. Compare **split ticket.**
straight·way (stráyt wáy, -way) *adv. Archaic.* Immediately.
strain¹ (strayn) *v.* **strained, straining, strains.** —*tr.* **1.** To pull, draw, or stretch tight. **2.** To exert or tax to the utmost. Often used reflexively. **3.** To injure or impair by overuse or overexertion; especially, to wrench: *strain a muscle.* **4. a.** To place too great a load on: *strained the lifting mechanism.* **b.** To stretch or force beyond the proper, reasonable, or legitimate limits: *strain a point.* **5.** To alter the relations between the parts of a structure or shape by applying an external force; deform. **6.** To pass (a substance) through a strainer or other filtering agent. **7.** To draw off or remove by filtration. **8.** To embrace or clasp tightly; hug. —*intr.* **1.** To make force-

ful and continuous efforts; exert oneself physically or mentally; strive hard. **2.** To be overexerted; especially, to be wrenched or twisted. **3.** To be subjected to great stress. **4.** To pull forcibly or violently: *straining at the leash.* **5.** To hesitate, as through scruple; baulk. Used with *at.* **6.** To filter, trickle, or ooze.
~*n.* **1. a.** The act of straining. **b.** The state of being strained. **2.** A great or extreme effort, exertion, or tension. **3.** Something that makes great or excessive demands on one's mental, emotional, or physical resources. **4.** A wrench or other injury resulting from excessive effort or use. **5.** *Physics.* A deformation produced by stress, measured by the change in dimension divided by the original dimension (length, area, or volume), or by the angular shear. —See Synonyms at **effort.** [Middle English *streynen,* from Old French *estreindere,* from Latin *stringere,* to draw tight, tie.]

strain² *n.* **1.** The collective descendants of a common ancestor; a race, stock, line, or breed. **2.** Any of the various lines of ancestry united in an individual or family; ancestry; lineage. **3.** *Biology.* A group of organisms of the same species, having distinctive characteristics but not usually considered a separate breed or variety. **4.** *Archaic.* A kind; a sort. **5. a.** An inborn or inherited tendency or character. **b.** A streak; a trace. **6.** The tone or tenor of a piece of speech or writing. **7.** *Often plural.* A passage of musical expression; an air; a tune. **8.** A passage of poetic expression. [Middle English *stren(e),* Old English *strēon,* acquisition, generation, offspring.]

strained (straynd) *adj.* **1.** Forced; unnatural: *a strained smile.* **2.** Tense and uncomfortable, especially because of latent hostility: *a strained atmosphere.*

strain·er (stráynər) *n.* One that strains, especially: **1.** A filter, sieve, or the like used to separate liquids from solids. **2.** An apparatus for tightening, stretching, or strengthening.

strain gauge *n.* A device for detecting or measuring strain using the change in electrical resistance of a distorted thin wire or a piezoelectric crystal.

strain hardening *n.* The process of hardening metal by straining it so as to increase the number of internal crystal dislocations.

straining beam *n. Architecture.* A horizontal tie beam connecting two queen posts in a roof truss. Also called "straining piece".

strait (strayt) *n. Abbr.* **St., str. 1.** *Often plural.* A narrow passage of water joining two larger bodies of water. **2.** *Usually plural.* A position of difficulty, perplexity, distress, or need: *in desperate straits.*
~*adj. Archaic.* **1.** Narrow, constricting, or confined. **2.** Stringent or rigorous, as in moral conduct or religious observance. [Middle English *streit,* from Old French *estreit,* tight, narrow, from Latin *strictus,* from the past participle of *stringere,* to draw tight.]

strait·en (stráyt'n) *tr.v.* **-ened, -ening, -ens. 1.** *Archaic.* To limit, confine, or make narrow. **2.** To cause to experience difficulties or distress, particularly financial hardship. Used chiefly in the phrase *in straitened circumstances.*

strait·jack·et, straight jacket (stráyt-jackit) *n.* **1.** A long-sleeved jacket-like garment used to bind the arms tightly against the body as a means of restraining a violent patient or prisoner. Also called "strait waistcoat". **2.** Anything that restricts or restrains like a straitjacket, such as a rule or institution.
~*tr.v.* **straitjacketed, -eting, -ets.** To restrict or restrain by or as if by confining in a straitjacket.

strait-laced (stráyt-láyst) *adj.* Excessively strict in behaviour, morality, or opinions; puritanical; prudish. [Originally referring to tightly laced dress, hence, strict, exacting.]

Straits Settlements. See **Malaya, Federation of.**

strake (strayk) *n.* **1.** *Nautical.* A single continuous line of planking or metal plating extending on a vessel's hull from stem to stern. **2.** Any of the curved sections making up the metal rim of a wooden wheel. [Middle English *strake,* perhaps "thing stretched", related to Old English *streccan,* to STRETCH.]

stra·mash (strə-másh) *n. Scottish.* A state of uproar or confusion. [Probably imitative.]

stra·mo·ni·um (strə-mṓni-əm) *n.* **1.** A plant, the **thorn apple** *(see).* **2.** The dried poisonous leaves of the thorn apple, used as the source of the alkaloid, hyoscyamine. [New Latin, perhaps an alteration of Tatar *turman,* horse medicine.]

strand¹ (strand) *n.* **1.** Land bordering a body of water; especially, the area between tide marks. **2.** *Poetic.* A country or region.
~*v.* **stranded, stranding, strands.** —*tr.* **1.** To drive or force aground; beach. **2.** To bring into or leave in a difficult or helpless position: *The collapse of the airline left us stranded in New York.* —*intr.* To become stranded. [Middle English *strand,* Old English *strand,* shore, akin to Old Norse *strönd*†.]

strand² *n.* **1.** Any of the long stringlike pieces of material that are twisted together to form a rope, cable, or the like. **2.** Any single fibre, thread, or other filament: *a strand of hair.* **3. a.** A string of beads. **b.** The material on which they are strung. **4.** Anything that is plaited or twisted, such as a rope or a plait of hair. **5.** A single element forming part of an interwoven whole: *one of the strands in his complex narrative.*
~*tr.v.* **stranded, stranding, strands. 1.** To make or form (a rope or cable, for example) by twisting strands together. **2.** To break one or more of the strands in (a rope, cable, or the like). [Middle English *strond*†.]

strand line *n.* A shore line; especially, one marking an earlier and higher water level.

strange (straynj) *adj.* **stranger, strangest. 1.** Previously unknown; unfamiliar. **2.** Strikingly unusual; queer, unaccountable, or extraordinary. **3.** Not of one's own or a particular locality, environment, or kind; exotic. **4.** Inexperienced in or unacquainted with something: *still strange to the job.* **5.** Unwell or dizzy: *feeling strange.* **6.** *Literary.* Alien or foreign. **7.** *Physics.* **a.** Designating a type of quark with unit quantum number strangeness. **b.** Of or designating an elementary particle that contains one or more charmed quarks and no charmed antiquarks.
~*adv.* In a strange manner: *acting strange.* [Middle English *straunge,* from Old French *estrange,* from Latin *extrāneus,* foreign, strange, from *extrā,* outside, beyond.] **—strange·ly** *adv.*

Synonyms: *strange, peculiar, odd, queer, quaint, outlandish, singular, eccentric.*

strange·ness (stráynj-nəss, -niss) *n.* **1.** The quality of being strange. **2.** *Symbol* **S** *Physics.* A quantum number, a property of certain types of elementary particle, originally postulated to account for the long lifetime of kaons, sigma particles, and lambda particles. [Sense 2, from the original lack of understanding of the nature of the particles which it describes.]

stran·ger (stráynjər) *n.* **1.** A person whom one does not know, or does not know well. **2.** A foreigner, newcomer, or outsider. **3.** One who is unaccustomed to or unacquainted with something specified. Used with *to*: *no stranger to the bar.* **4.** A visitor or guest. **5.** A newborn baby. Used in the phrase *a little stranger.* **6.** *Law.* One who is neither privy nor party to an act, proceeding, or other form of business. [Middle English *straunger,* from Old French *estrangier,* from Vulgar Latin *extrāneārius* (unattested), from Latin *extrāneus,* STRANGE.]

stran·gle (stráng-g'l) *v.* **-gled, -gling, -gles.** —*tr.* **1. a.** To kill by choking or suffocating; throttle. **b.** To kill by cutting off the oxygen supply of. **2.** To suppress, repress, or stifle. **3.** To inhibit the growth or action of; restrict: *strangled by convention.* —*intr.* To die or suffer from suffocation or strangulation; choke. [Middle English *stranglen,* from Old French *estrangler,* from Latin *strangulāre,* to STRANGULATE.] **—stran·gler** *n.*

stran·gle·hold (stráng-g'l-hōld) *n.* **1.** Powerful control that restricts or prevents freedom of thought or action. **2.** An illegal wrestling hold used to choke an opponent.

stran·gles (stráng-g'lz) *n. Used with a singular verb.* An infectious disease of horses and related animals, caused by the bacterium *Streptococcus equi* and characterised by nasal inflammation and abscesses in the mouth. [From Middle English *strangle* (singular), strangulation, from *stranglen,* to STRANGLE.]

stran·gu·late (stráng-gew-layt) *v.* **-lated, -lating, -lates.** —*tr.* **1.** *Pathology.* To compress, constrict, or obstruct (a tube, duct, intestine, or other part) so as to cut off the flow of blood, air, or other fluid. **2.** *Rare.* To strangle. —*intr.* To be or become strangled or constricted. [Latin *strangulāre,* from Greek *strangalan,* from *strangalē,* halter.] **—stran·gu·la·tion** (-láysh'n) *n.*

stran·gu·ry (stráng-gewr-i) *n.* Also **stran·gur·i·a** (-géwr-i-ə). Slow, painful urination with spasms of the urethra and bladder. [Middle English, from Latin *strangūria,* from Greek *strangouria* : *stranx* (stem *strang-*), drop + -URIA.]

strap (strap) *n.* **1.** A flat, narrow strip of leather, canvas, or other material, usually fitted with a buckle or other adjustable fastener, and used for binding, securing, or supporting objects. **2.** A flat, thin metal band used for fastening or clamping objects together or into position. **3.** A narrow band formed into a loop for grasping with the hand. **4.** A strip of leather used for beating, especially as a punishment in schools.
~*tr.v.* **strapped, strapping, straps. 1.** To fasten or secure with a strap. **2.** To beat with a strap. **3.** To bind (a wound or injured limb, for example) with bandages. Often used with *up.* [Variant of STROP.]

strap·hang·er (stráp-hang-ər) *n.* A standing passenger, as on a bus or underground train, who grips a hanging strap for support. **—strap·hang·ing** *n.*

strap·less (stráp-ləss, -liss) *adj.* Without a strap or straps. Said especially of a dress or undergarment designed to leave the shoulders bare.

strap·pa·do (strə-paá-dō, stra-, -páy-) *n., pl.* **-does. 1.** A torture in which the victim's hands are tied behind his back and attached to a pulley by means of which he is pulled up off the ground and then dropped halfway down with a jerk. **2.** The apparatus so employed. [French *(e)strapade,* from Italian *strappata,* from *strappare,* to drag, from Old French *estraper,* variant of *estreper,* from Latin *extirpāre,* to pluck up by the stem : *ex-,* out + *stirps,* stem (see **stirps**).]

strapped (strapt) *adj. Informal.* Suffering from a shortage, especially of money: *strapped for cash.* [From STRAP (rare sense "to make penniless").]

strap·per (stráppər) *n.* A tall, sturdy person.

strap·ping (strápping) *adj. Informal.* Tall and sturdy.

Stras·bourg (stráz-burg, -boorg; *French* strass-bóor.) City in northeast France, lying close to the Franco-German border, and formerly part of Germany (1871–1919). Since 1949 it has been the seat of the Council of Europe. Its cathedral, built between the 11th and 15th centuries, is a notable example of Rhenish architecture.

strass (strass) *n.* A type of lead glass, **paste** *(see).* [German, invented by Josef *Strasser,* 18th-century German jeweller.]

stra·ta. Plural of **stratum.** See Usage note at **stratum.**

strat·a·gem (stráttə-jəm, -jim, -jem) *n.* **1. a.** A military manoeuvre designed to deceive or surprise an enemy. **b.** Any trick or scheme used to gain an advantage. **2.** Deception; trickery. —See Synonyms at **artifice.** [French *stratagème,* from Latin *stratēgēma,* from Greek, "act of a general", from *stratēgein,* to be a general, from *stratēgos,* general : *stratos,* army + *agein,* to lead.]

stra·te·gic (strə-téejik, stra-) *adj.* Also **stra·te·gi·cal** (-'l). **1.** Of or pertaining to strategy. **2. a.** Dictated by or essential for the further-ance of a military or other strategy: *a strategic withdrawal.* **b.** Es-sential to the effective conduct of war. **c.** Designed to destroy at source the military and economic potential of an enemy: *strategic nuclear weapons.* —**stra·te·gi·cal·ly** *adv.*

Strategic Defense Initiative *n.* A system of defence against ICBMs based on the belief that they can be destroyed in flight by laser beams from earth satellites. [Also "Star Wars", from the science-fiction film *Star Wars,* which depicts war in space.]

stra·te·gics (strə-téejiks, stra-) *n. Used with a singular verb.* The art of strategy.

strat·e·gist (stráttəjist) *n.* One who is skilled in strategy.

strat·e·gy (stráttəji) *n., pl.* **-gies. 1.** The science or art of military command as applied to the overall planning and conduct of large-scale combat operations. Compare **tactics. 2.** A plan of action re-sulting from the practice of this science. **3.** The use of skilful plan-ning to secure one's own advantage, as in politics, business, or personal relations. **4.** A plan or design for achieving one's aims. [French *stratégie,* from Greek *stratēgia,* office of a general, from *stratēgos,* general. See **stratagem.**]

Strat·ford-up·on-A·von (strátfərd-əp-on-áyv'n ‖ -awn-). Town in Warwickshire, central England, famous for its associations with William Shakespeare, who was born and died there. The Royal Shakespeare Theatre stages annual seasons of plays there from April to October.

strath (strath) *n. Scottish.* A steep-sided, flat-floored valley wider than a glen. [Scottish Gaelic *srath,* (mountain) valley.]

Strath·clyde Region (stráth-klíd, strath-). A former administrative region of west Scotland, formed in 1975 and comprising the former counties of Ayr, Bute, Dunbarton, Lanark, and Renfrew, with parts of Stirling and Argyll. Glasgow was the administrative centre. From 1996 Strathclyde Region has been subdivided into Unitary Authority Areas.

strath·spey (strath-spáy, strath-) *n., pl.* **-speys.** A type of Scottish reel, or the music that accompanies it. [After *Strathspey,* valley of the river SPEY.]

strati–, strato– *comb. form.* Indicates stratum or strata; for exam-ple, **stratigraphy.** [From STRATUM.]

stra·tic·u·late (strə-tíckew-lət, -lit, -layt) *adj.* Having thin strata. [New Latin *straticulus* (unattested), diminutive of STRATUM.] —**stra·tic·u·la·tion** (-láysh'n) *n.*

strat·i·fi·ca·tion (stráttifi-káysh'n) *n.* **1. a.** The act or process of stratifying. **b.** The state of being stratified. **2.** A stratified configu-ration.

strat·i·fi·ca·tion·al grammar (stráttifi-káysh'n'l) *n. Linguistics.* A theory of grammar that conceives of language in terms of a hierar-chical system of related levels, ranging from the conceptual to the phonemic, each of which has its own rules.

strat·i·form (strátti-fawrm) *adj.* Having the form of strata.

strat·i·fy (strátti-fī) *v.* **-fied, -fying, -fies.** —*tr.* **1.** To form, arrange, or deposit in strata. **2.** To arrange or divide according to different levels of caste, class, or status: *a stratified society.* **3.** To preserve (seeds) by placing them between layers of moist sand or similar material. —*intr.* To become layered; develop physical or social strata. [French *stratifier,* from New Latin *stratificare* : STRATUM + Latin *facere,* to make, do.]

stra·tig·ra·phy (strə-tíggrəfi) *n.* The study of rock strata, especially of their distribution, deposition, and chronological succession. [STRATI- + -GRAPHY.] —**strat·i·graph·i·cal** (strátti-gráffik'l), **strat·i·graph·ic** *adj.* —**strat·i·graph·i·cal·ly** *adv.*

stra·toc·ra·cy (strə-tóckrə-si) *n., pl.* **-cies.** Government by the army. [Greek *stratos,* army + -o- + -CRACY.]

stra·to·cu·mu·lus (stráytō-kéwmew-ləss, stráttō-) *n., pl.* **-li** (-lī) A low-lying heavy cloud occurring at about 450 to 1 800 metres (1,500 to 6,000 feet) as rounded grey masses, often covering the sky, but sometimes with small breaks. [STRAT(US) + -O- + CUMULUS.]

strat·o·pause (strát-ō-pawz, -ə-) *n.* The boundary between the stratosphere and the mesosphere in the Earth's atmosphere, at a height where the air becomes so thin that there are not enough oxygen molecules to form ozone.

strat·o·sphere (stráttə-sfeer) *n.* The part of the atmosphere between the troposphere and the mesosphere, extending from a height of about 15 to 50 kilometres (about 9 to 30 miles), and having a tem-perature that increases with height to a maximum of about 0°C. [French *stratosphère* : STRAT(UM) + (ATM)OSPHERE.] —**strat·o·spher·ic** (-sférrik ‖ -sfeer-ik) *adj.*

stra·tum (stráa-təm, stráy- ‖ *U.S. also* strá-) *n., pl.* **-ta** (-tə) *or rare* **-tums. 1.** *Geology.* **a.** A bed or layer of rock having the same com-position throughout. **b.** A number of beds or layers of rock of the same kind of material. **2.** A horizontal layer of any material, espe-cially one of several parallel layers arranged one on top of the other, such as: **a.** A layer of tissue or cells. **b.** Any of the layers making up the Earth's atmosphere. **c.** A layer in which the archaeological remains of a particular stage or period are deposited. **3.** A class or category regarded as occupying a level in a hierarchy: *the middle strata of society.* [New Latin, from Latin *strātum,* neuter of *strātus,* stretched out. See **status.**] —**stra·tal** *adj.*

Usage: The standard plural form is *strata: All strata of society have been affected. Stratums* and *stratas* are both occasionally heard, used by people who are unaware of the irregular status of this noun, but they have no standing in educated English. Likewise, the use of

strata as a singular is not standard, though it is often heard: *One particular strata has been affected more than others.*

stra·tus (stráy-təss, stráa- ‖ *U.S. also* strá-) *n., pl.* **-ti** (-tī). A low-altitude cloud usually occurring below 600 metres (about 2,000 feet), and typically resembling a layer of fog. [Latin *strātus,* past participle of *sternere,* to stretch out, extend.]

Strauss (strowss; *German* shtrowss), **Johann¹,** known as Johann Strauss the Elder (1804–49). Austrian violinist and composer. He composed many dances, especially waltzes, and is best known for his *Radetzky March.*

Strauss, Johann², known as Johann Strauss the Younger (1825–99). Austrian composer and conductor. He is best known for his dance music, especially the waltzes which include *The Blue Dan-ube* (1867), and his operettas, such as *Die Fledermaus* (1874).

Strauss, Richard (1864–1949). German composer and conductor. He is known chiefly for his symphonic poems which include *Till Eulenspiegel* (1895) and *Don Quixote* (1897), and his operas, among them *Salome* (1905) and *Der Rosenkavalier* (1911).

Stra·vin·sky (strə-vínski, stra-), **Igor Feodorovich** (1882–1971). Russian composer. His early ballet, *The Rite of Spring* (1913), caused a scandal at the time, but like many of his works has been recognised as one of the musical landmarks of the 20th century. His later pioneering works include the *Symphony of Psalms* (1930) and *The Rake's Progress* (1951).

straw (straw) *n.* **1. a.** Stalks of threshed grain used for thatching or as bedding for animals, or woven into hats, baskets, or other arti-cles. Also used adjectively: *a straw hat.* **b.** Any one such stalk. **2.** A slender tube used for sucking up a liquid. **3.** Something of minimal value or importance. **4.** A usually worthless expedient re-sorted to in desperation: *clutching at straws.* —**draw the short straw.** To be unluckily chosen to do something unpleasant. —**straw in the wind.** A slight hint of something to come. ~*tr.v.* **strawed, strawing, straws.** *Archaic.* To scatter; strew. [Mid-dle English *strawe,* Old English *strēaw.*]

straw·ber·ry (stráw-bri, -bəri ‖ -berri) *n., pl.* **-ries. 1.** Any of various low-growing plants of the genus *Fragaria,* having white flowers and red, fleshy, edible fruit. **2.** The fruit of any of these plants. **3.** A related plant, the barren strawberry, *Potentilla sterilis,* having straw-berry-like flowers but dry fruit. [Middle English *strawberry,* Old English *strēawberige* : STRAW (possibly from the strawlike slender runners trailing on the ground) + BERRY.]

straw·ber·ry-blonde (stráw-bri-blónd, -bəri- ‖ -berri-) *adj.* Reddish-blonde. Said of hair. ~*n.* A woman with strawberry-blonde hair.

strawberry mark *n.* A small, soft, reddish birthmark.

strawberry roan *n.* A horse having reddish hair mixed with white.

strawberry tree *n.* A tree, *Arbutus unedo,* native to southern Eu-rope, having evergreen leaves and strawberry-like fruit.

straw·board (stráw-bawrd ‖ -bōrd) *n.* A coarse yellow cardboard made of straw pulp.

straw boss *n. U.S. Informal.* A worker who acts as a boss or assist-ant foreman in addition to his regular duties.

straw man *n. U.S.* A man of straw *(see).*

straw poll *n.* An unofficial or impromptu poll to assess opinion on a candidate or issue. Also *chiefly U.S.* "straw vote."

Straw·son (stráwss'n), **Sir Peter (Frederick)** (1919–). British phi-losopher. In *Introduction to Logical Theory* (1952), he examines the general nature of formal logic. Other works include *Philosophical Logic* (1967), *Freedom and Resentment* (1974), and *Entity and Iden-tity* (1997).

straw wine *n.* A dessert wine made from grapes that have been dried on straw.

straw·worm (stráw-wurm) *n.* A caddis worm *(see).*

stray (stray) *intr.v.* **strayed, straying, strays. 1. a.** To wander from a given place or group or beyond established limits; roam. **b.** To become lost. **2.** To rove, wander about, or meander. **3.** To deviate from a course that is regarded as right or moral; go astray; err. **4.** To digress or wander from a given subject or line of thought. —See Synonyms at **wander.** ~*n.* One that has strayed; especially, a domestic animal at large or that has been lost. ~*adj.* **1.** Straying or having strayed; lost or at large. **2. a.** Scat-tered, random, or isolated: *a few stray cars.* **b.** Not in its proper place or context: *brushed back some stray hairs.* [Middle English *straien,* from Old French *estraier,* from Vulgar Latin *estragāre* (un-attested) : Latin *extrā-,* outside of + *vagārī,* to wander, roam, from *vagus,* wandering, VAGUE.] —**stray·er** *n.*

streak (streek) *n.* **1.** An irregular line, mark, or band differentiated by colour or texture from its surroundings. **2.** A trace or element of a particular quality or characteristic; a strain: *a masochistic streak.* **3.** *Informal.* A brief stretch or run: *a losing streak.* **4.** *Geology & Chemistry.* The colour of the powder of a mineral, used as a distin-guishing characteristic. **5.** A single discharge of atmospheric light-ning. Also used adjectively: *streak lightning.* **6.** An act of streaking. **7.** *Biology.* A growth of microorganisms produced by streaking. ~*v.* **streaked, streaking, streaks.** —*tr.* To mark with a streak or streaks; stripe; striate. —*intr.* **1.** To form streaks or become streaked. **2.** To move at high speed; rush. **3.** To run naked or partly naked through or across a public place as a way of attracting atten-tion or amusing the crowd. **4.** *Biology.* To inoculate a culture me-dium with microorganisms by drawing a contaminated wire along the surface. [Middle English *strick(e),* Old English *strica.*] —**streak·er** *n.*

streak·y (streéki) *adj.* **-ier, -iest. 1.** Marked with, characterised by, or occurring in streaks; streaked. **2.** Consisting of alternate streaks of meat and fat. Said of bacon. **3.** Variable or uneven in character or quality. **—streak·i·ly** *adv.* **—streak·i·ness** *n.*

stream (streém) *n.* **1.** A body of running water; especially, such a body moving over the earth's surface in a channel or bed, as a small natural watercourse. **2.** A steady current in such a body of water. **3.** A steady current of any fluid. **4. a.** A steady flow or procession, as of people or traffic, moving in the same direction. **b.** An uninterrupted succession or outpouring: *a stream of invective.* **5.** A prevailing trend or general drift, as of opinion, thought, or history. **6.** In many schools, any of the sets into which children of a given age-group are divided, usually according to ability. In this sense, compare **band. —on stream.** In or into production.
~v. **streamed, streaming, streams.** *—intr.* **1.** To flow in or as if in a stream. **2.** To pour forth or give off a stream; flow. Often used with *with*: *eyes streaming with tears.* **3.** To move or proceed in large numbers. **4.** To extend, wave, or float outwards in the air: *The banner streamed in the breeze.* **5.** To leave a continuous trail of light. *—tr.* **1.** To emit, discharge, or exude. **2.** *Chiefly British.* To group (schoolchildren) into streams. [Middle English *streme,* Old English *strēam.*] **—stream·y** *adj.*

stream·er (streémər) *n.* **1.** A long, narrow flag, banner, or pennant. **2. a.** Any long, narrow pendant strip of ribbon, coloured paper, or other material. **b.** Such a strip that is wound into a tight roll that unwinds when thrown, used for fun by children and as party decorations. **3.** A shaft or ray of light extending upwards from the horizon. **4.** A newspaper headline that runs across a full page; a banner. **5.** A long, narrow, luminous electrical discharge, as in the aurora. **6.** A cartridge or spool of magnetic tape on which is recorded a second, reserve copy of data on a magnetic disc.

stream·line (streém-līn) *n.* **1.** A line in a fluid such that the tangent at every point on the line is aligned with the fluid's local velocity. **2.** The path of any one particle in a flowing fluid. **3.** Any contour of a body constructed to offer minimum resistance to a fluid flow.
~tr.v. **streamlined, -lining, -lines.** To make streamlined.

stream·lined (streém-līnd) *adj.* **1.** Designed, constructed, or shaped so as to offer the least resistance to fluid flow. **2.** Simplified, modernised, or reorganised so as to improve efficiency. **3.** Having simple, smooth, or elegant contours.

streamline flow *n.* A flow characterised by lack of turbulence or interruption. Compare **laminar flow, turbulent flow.**

stream of consciousness *n.* **1.** *Psychology.* The conscious experience of an individual regarded as a continuous rather than a discrete series of events. **2.** A literary technique in which the thoughts and feelings of a character in a novel are recorded as they develop, by means of first-person narration. Compare **interior monologue.**

street (streét) *n. Abbr.* **st., St. 1.** A public way or thoroughfare in a city, town, or village, usually including the pavements and the buildings lining either or both sides. **2.** Such a roadway for vehicles apart from the buildings and pavements. **3.** The people living, working, or habitually gathering in or along such a roadway: *The whole street knew about it.* **—streets ahead of.** *Informal.* Far superior to. **—the Street.** *U.S.* The financial area around the Stock Exchange in Wall Street, New York. **—up (one's) street.** *Informal.* Compatible with one's interests, tastes, or abilities. **—walk the streets. 1.** To wander through the streets of a town, especially in search of work or accommodation. **2.** To seek or solicit clients in the street. Used of a prostitute.
~adj. Pertaining to, taking place in, or found on a street or the streets of a town: *street life; a street party; a street urchin.* [Middle English *strete,* Old English *strǣt,* from West Germanic *strāta* (unattested), from Late Latin *strāta,* from Latin *strātus,* past participle of *sternere,* to extend, stretch out.]
Usage: *Streets* are usually in towns, and *roads* in the country, but in British English in particular there are many exceptions, and it is not possible to state simple rules. American English often omits the term in speech: *I live at 360 Parker* (that is, Parker Street). British English also uses *in* while American English uses *on*: *I live in Parker Street.*

street Arab *n.* A homeless child who lives in the street of a city; an urchin. Also called "Arab".

street·car (streét-kaar) *n. U.S.* A **tram** *(see).*

street·light (streét-līt) *n.* Any of a series of lights that are attached to tall poles spaced at intervals along a public thoroughfare, and are illuminated automatically from dusk to dawn.

street smart. See **streetwise.**

street value *n.* The retail value of an illegal commodity, calculated on the basis of the price at which it is sold to the consumer (its *street price*): *cocaine with a street value of £200,000.*

street·walk·er (streét-wawkər) *n.* A prostitute who solicits in the streets. **—street·walk·ing** *n.*

street·wise (streét-wīz) *adj.* Experienced in the ways of rough urban areas; capable of surviving or being successful on the streets.

Strei·sand (strī́-sand), **Barbra,** born Barbara Joan Rosen (1942–). American singer and actress. Her stage and film performances include *Funny Girl* (1968), *Hello Dolly* (1969), and *A Star is Born* (1976).

stre·lit·zi·a (stre-lítsi-ə, stri-) *n.* Any plant of the South African genus *Strelitzia,* which includes the bird-of-paradise flower. [Named in honour of Charlotte of Mecklenburg-*Strelitz* (1744–1818), queen of England.]

strength (streng-th, strengk-th || strenth) *n.* **1.** The state, quality, or property of being strong; physical power. **2. a.** The power of resisting force, attack, strain, or stress; durability, solidity, or impregnability. **b.** The ability to maintain a moral or intellectual position firmly, especially in the face of opposition or temptation: *strength of character.* **3.** Capacity or potential for effective action: *a show of strength.* **4.** Military capability in terms of manpower and material resources: *the strength of the fleet.* **5.** The number of personnel constituting the normal or ideal complement of an organisation: *The police force is below strength.* **6.** The degree of intensity, force, effectiveness, or potency in terms of some particular property; for example: **a.** The degree of concentration, distillation, or saturation. **b.** Operative effectiveness or potency. **c.** Intensity, as of sound or light. **d.** The degree of ardour or vehemence, as of feelings or language: *tried to gauge the strength of support for his idea.* **7. a.** A source of power or force; that which makes strong. **b.** An attribute or quality of particular worth or utility; an asset. **8.** Effective or binding force; efficacy: *the strength of an argument.* **9.** Firmness of or a continuous rising tendency in prices, as on the stock market. **—go from strength to strength.** To become ever more powerful or successful. **—on the strength of.** Relying or depending on; based on. [Middle English *strengthe,* Old English *strengthu.*]
Synonyms: *strength, power, might, force, energy, potency.*

strength·en (stréng-thən, stréngk- || strén-) *v.* **-ened, -ening, -ens.** *—tr.* To make strong or stronger. *—intr.* To become strong or stronger. **—strength·en·er** *n.*

stren·u·ous (strénnew-əss) *adj.* **1.** Requiring or characterised by great effort or exertion: *a strenuous task.* **2.** Vigorously active; energetic, persistent, or unremitting: *strenuous opposition.* [Latin *strēnuus*†, brisk, nimble, quick.] **—stren·u·os·i·ty** (-óssəti), **stren·u·ous·ness** *n.* **—stren·u·ous·ly** *adv.*

strep (strep) *n.* **1.** Sore throat caused by infection with bacteria of the genus *Streptococcus.* **2.** A streptococcus. [Shortened form.]

strepto– *comb. form.* Indicates: **1.** A twisted chain; for example, **streptococcus. 2.** Streptococcus; for example, **streptokinase.** [Greek *streptos,* twisted, from *strephein,* to turn.]

strep·to·coc·cal (strépt-ə-kóck'l, -ō-) *adj.* Also **strep·to·coc·cic** (-kóksik). Of, pertaining to, or caused by a streptococcus.

strep·to·coc·cus (strépt-ə-kók-əss, -ō-) *n., pl.* **-cocci** (-sī, -ī, -ee). Any of various round to ovoid, often pathogenic bacteria of the genus *Streptococcus,* occurring in pairs or chains. [New Latin : STREPTO- + -COCCUS.]

strep·to·ki·nase (strépt-ə-kī́n-ayz, -ō-, -ayss) *n.* A proteolytic enzyme derived from haemolytic streptococci, capable of dissolving fibrin and used to dissolve blood clots. [STREPTO- + KINASE.]

strep·to·ly·sin (strépt-ə-lī́-sin, -ō-) *n.* An antigenic haemolysin derived from strains of *Streptococcus pyogenes.* [STREPTO- + -LYS(IS) + -IN.]

strep·to·my·cin (strépt-ə-mī́-sin, -ō-) *n.* An antibiotic, $C_{21}H_{39}N_7O_{12}$, produced from the bacterium *Streptomyces griseus* and used medicinally to combat various bacteria, especially tuberculosis. [New Latin *Streptomyces* : STREPTO- + Greek *mukēs,* fungus + -IN.]

strep·to·thri·cin (strépt-ə-thrī́-sin, -ō-, -thríssin) *n.* An antibiotic, $C_{19}H_{34}N_8O_8$, isolated from the bacterium *Streptomyces lavendulae* (or *Actinomyces lavendulae*) and active against both Gram-positive and Gram-negative bacteria. [New Latin *Streptothrix,* a genus of bacteria : STREPTO- + Greek *thrix,* hair + -IN.]

Stre·se·mann (shtráyzə-man), **Gustav** (1878–1929). German statesman. As minister of foreign affairs (1923–29), he negotiated the Locarno Pact (1925) of mutual security with France and Belgium, and secured Germany's entry (1926) into the League of Nations. He shared the Nobel peace prize with Aristide Briand (1926).

stress (stress) *n.* **1.** Importance, significance, or emphasis placed upon something: *laid great stress on the need for economy.* **2. a.** The degree of force with which a sound or syllable is spoken. **b.** The emphasis placed upon the sound or syllable spoken loudest in a given word or phrase. **3. a.** The relative emphasis given a syllable or word in verse in accordance with a metrical pattern. **b.** A syllable receiving a strong relative emphasis. **4.** *Music.* An accent. **5.** *Physics.* An applied force or system of forces that tends to strain or deform a body, measured by the force acting per unit area. **6. a.** A mentally or emotionally disruptive or disquieting influence. **b.** A state of tension or distress caused by such an influence.
~tr.v. **stressed, stressing, stresses. 1.** To place phonetic emphasis on; accent. **2.** To attribute particular importance to; emphasise. **3.** To subject to mental, physical, or mechanical stress: *felt stressed (out).* [Middle English *stresse,* hardship, distress, from Old French *estresse,* narrowness, from Vulgar Latin *strictia* (unattested), from Latin *strictus,* STRICT.] **—stress·ful** *adj.*

-stress *n. suffix.* Indicates a feminine agent; for example, **seamstress.** [-ST(ER) + -ESS.]

stretch (strech) *v.* **stretched, stretching, stretches.** *—tr.* **1.** To lengthen, widen, or distend by pulling: *stretch a woollen sweater.* **2.** To cause to extend from one place to another or across a given space. **3.** To make taut; tighten. **4.** To reach or put forth; extend. Often used with *out*: *stretched out his hand.* **5.** To extend (oneself) at full length, usually in a prone position. Often used with *out.* **6.** To straighten (oneself) by extending the limbs or flexing the muscles. **7.** To make do with or eke out: *stretch the budget by careful spending.* **8.** To extend or enlarge (the scope of a law or meaning of a word, for example) beyond the usual or proper limits. **9. a.** To make the fullest possible use of or demands upon (one's intellectual or material resources): *felt that he wasn't being stretched in the job.* **b.** To subject to unreasonable or intolerable strain: *stretch one's patience.* **10.** To wrench or strain (a muscle or ligament, for example);

sprain. **11.** To prolong: *stretch out an argument.* —*intr.* **1. a.** To become lengthened, widened, or distended. **b.** To admit of being stretched; be elastic. **2.** To extend or reach over a particular distance or area or in a particular direction: *Ahead of us stretched the plain.* **3.** To lie down at full length. Usually used with *out.* **4.** To straighten oneself out by extending the limbs or flexing the muscles. **5.** To reach, usually with one's hand. Often used with *out.* **6.** To allow for or include something specified. Used with *to: My salary won't stretch to luxuries.* **7.** To extend over a given period of time: *This story stretches over two centuries.* **—stretch (one's) legs.** To stroll about after sitting for a long time.

~*n.* **1.** The act of stretching or the state of being stretched. **2.** The extent or scope to which something can be stretched; elasticity. **3.** A continuous or unbroken length, area, or expanse: *a stretch of motorway.* **4.** A straight section of a racecourse or track, especially that section leading to the finishing line. **5. a.** A continuous period of time, especially considered as occupied by a particular activity or marked by a particular state: *would work for three days at a stretch.* **b.** *Slang.* A term of imprisonment: *a two-year stretch.* **—by no stretch of the imagination.** By no means; not at all.

~*adj.* Capable of being stretched; elastic: *a stretch sock.* [Middle English *strecchen,* Old English *streccan,* to extend, from Germanic *strakkjan* (unattested).] **—stretch·a·ble** *adj.* **—stretch·y** *adj.*

stretch·er (stréchər) *n.* **1.** A kind of portable bed, usually consisting of canvas stretched over a frame, used to transport the sick, wounded, or dead. **2.** Any of various devices used for stretching and shaping, such as the wooden framework upon which canvas is stretched for an oil painting. **3.** A usually horizontal tie beam or brace serving to support or extend a framework. **4.** A brick or stone laid parallel to the face of a wall. Compare **header. 5.** *Australian, N.Z., & South African.* A camp bed.

stretch·er-bear·er (stréchər-bair-ər) *n.* One who helps carry a stretcher or litter.

stretch marks *pl.n.* Whitish lines on the skin of the thighs, abdomen, or breasts, appearing especially as the result of stretching during pregnancy.

stret·to (strétō) *n., pl.* **-ti** (-ee) or **-tos.** *Music.* **1.** A close succession or overlapping of voices in a fugue, especially in the final section. **2.** A final section, as of an oratorio, performed with an acceleration in tempo to produce a climax. Also called "stretta".

~*adv. Music.* In a quicker time. Used as a direction. [Italian, "tight", from Latin *strictus,* STRICT.]

strew (stroo || strew) *tr.v.* **strewn** (stroon || strewn) or **strewed, strewing, strews. 1.** To spread here and there; scatter; sprinkle. **2.** To cover (a surface) with things scattered or sprinkled. **3.** To be or become dispersed over (a surface). [Middle English *strewen,* Old English *strēowian.*]

strewth. Variant of **struth.**

stri·a (strī́-ə) *n., pl.* **striae** (-ee). **1.** A thin, narrow groove or channel. **2.** *Architecture.* A thin band between the grooves on a column. **3.** A thin line or band, especially any one of several that are parallel or close together, and share some distinctive feature such as colour or composition. [Latin, furrow, channel.]

stri·ate (strī́-ət, -it, -ayt) *adj.* Also **stri·at·ed** (strī-áytid || strī́-aytid). Marked with striae; striped, grooved, or ridged.

~*tr.v.* **striated, -ating, -ates.** To mark with striae. [Latin *striātus,* past participle of *striāre,* to make furrows, from *stria,* furrow, STRIA.]

striated muscle *n.* Muscle consisting of elongated, transversely striated fibres, often operating under voluntary control. Also called "skeletal muscle", "striped muscle".

stri·a·tion (strī-áysh'n) *n.* **1.** The state of being striated or having striae. **2.** An arrangement of striae. **3.** A stria.

strick·en (strícken) *adj.* **1.** Struck or wounded, as by a projectile. **2.** Afflicted with something overwhelming, such as strong emotion, disease, or trouble. Often used in combination: *conscience-stricken; grief-stricken.* **3.** Having the contents made even with the top of a measuring device or container; level. [Past participle of STRIKE.]

strick·le (strick'l) *n.* **1.** An instrument used to level off grain or other material in a measure; a strike. **2.** A foundry tool used to shape a mould in sand or loam. **3.** A tool for sharpening scythes.

~*tr.v.* **strickled, -ling, -les.** To apply a strickle to (sand in a mould, for example). [Middle English *strikelle,* Old English *stricel.*]

strict (strikt) *adj.* **stricter, strictest. 1.** Precise; accurate; exact. **2.** Complete; absolute; maintained without exception or deviation: *strict hygiene.* **3.** Imposing an exacting discipline; allowing no indulgence or relaxation; not permissive: *strict standards.* **4.** Rigidly conforming to a particular code or norm: *a strict Muslim.* **5.** *Botany.* Stiff, narrow, and upright. —See Synonyms at **severe.** [Latin *strictus,* tight, narrow, from the past participle of *stringere,* to draw tight, tighten.] **—strict·ly** *adv.* **—strict·ness** *n.*

stric·ture (stríkchər) *n.* **1.** Something that restrains, limits, or restricts. **2.** An adverse remark or criticism; censure. **3.** *Pathology.* An abnormal narrowing of a duct or passage. [Middle English, from Latin *strictūra,* contraction, from *strictus,* STRICT.]

stride (strīd) *v.* **strode** (strōd) or *obsolete* **strid** (strid), **stridden** (stridd'n) or *obsolete* **strid, striding, strides.** —*intr.* **1.** To walk with long steps, especially in a hasty or purposeful manner. **2.** To take a single long step, as in passing over an obstruction. —*tr.* **1.** To stride over, along, or through. **2.** To straddle; bestride.

~*n.* **1.** The act of striding. **2. a.** A single long step. **b.** The distance travelled in such a step. **3. a.** A single coordinated movement of the four legs of a horse or other animal, completed when the legs are returned to their initial relative position. **b.** The distance travelled in such a cycle of movements. **4.** A progressive development; an advance: *making great strides.* **5.** *Plural. Australian Informal.* Trousers. **—take in (one's) stride.** To cope with (an unfamiliar situation, for example) without effort or difficulty. [Stride, strode (or strid), stridden; Middle English *striden, strode* (or *stride*), *stridden,* Old English *strīdan, strād* (singular, only in *bestrād*), *stridon* (plural, unattested), *striden* (unattested), from Germanic *strīdan* (unattested).] **—strid·er** *n.*

stri·dent (strī́d'nt) *adj.* **1.** Loud, harsh, and grating; shrill. **2.** Having a disagreeably assertive or insistent quality. [Latin *strīdēns* (stem *strīdent-*), present participle of *strīdēre,* to make a harsh sound.] **—stri·dence, stri·den·cy** *n.* **—stri·dent·ly** *adv.*

stri·dor (strī́d-ər, -awr) *n.* **1.** A strident sound. **2.** *Pathology.* A harsh, high-pitched sound in inhalation or exhalation. [Latin *strīdor,* from *strīdēre,* to make a harsh sound.]

strid·u·late (striddew-layt) *intr.v.* **-lated, -lating, -lates.** To produce a shrill grating or creaking sound; chirp. Used especially of insects such as crickets. [Latin *strīdulus,* creaking, STRIDULOUS.] **—strid·u·la·tion** (-láysh'n) *n.* **—strid·u·la·to·ry** (-laytəri, -lə-tri) *adj.*

strid·u·lous (striddewləss) *adj.* **1.** Making or characterised by a strident sound or chirp. **2.** Of or affected with stridor. [Latin *strīdulus,* creaking, from *strīdēre,* to make a harsh sound.]

strife (strīf) *n.* **1.** Heated, often violent dissension; a state of bitter conflict. **2.** A struggle between rivals; a dispute or conflict. **3.** *Rare.* Earnest endeavour or striving. —See Synonyms at **discord.** [Middle English *strif,* from Old French *estrif*†.]

strig·il (stríjil) *n.* **1.** An instrument used in ancient Greece and Rome for scraping the skin after a bath. **2.** A structure on the first leg of certain insects, such as bees, used for cleaning the antennae. [Latin *strigilis,* from *stringere,* to draw tight.]

stri·gose (strī́-gōz, -gōss) *adj.* **1.** *Zoology.* Marked with fine, close-set grooves or streaks. **2.** *Botany.* Having stiff, closely pressed hairs or bristles. [New Latin *strigosus,* from Latin *striga,* swath, furrow.]

Strij·dom (stráydəm), **Johannes Gerhardus** (1893–1958). National Party prime minister of South Africa (1954–58), noted for his determined maintenance of the policy of apartheid.

strike (strīk) *v.* **struck** (struk), **struck** or **stricken** (stríckən), **striking, strikes.** —*tr.* **1. a.** To hit sharply or forcefully, as with the hand or fist, or with a weapon or implement. **b.** To inflict (a blow). **c.** To send by means of a forceful blow: *struck the ball to the boundary.* **2. a.** To collide with or crash into: *struck the rocks and quickly sank.* **b.** To cause to hit sharply or forcefully; dash. **3.** To bring into a specified condition by or as if by a blow: *struck him dead.* **4. a.** To launch a military attack upon; assault. **b.** *Archaic.* To do (battle). **5.** To afflict suddenly, as with disease or impairment. **6.** To wound with the fangs. Used of a snake. **7.** To hook (a fish) that has taken the bait. **8.** To produce or impress by stamping, printing, or punching: *strike a medallion.* **9.** To play or produce by hitting a key on a musical instrument: *strike a B flat.* **10.** To indicate (the time) by a percussive sound: *The clock struck nine.* **11. a.** To produce (a flame, light, or spark) by friction. **b.** To cause to ignite by friction: *strike a match.* **12.** To delete, expunge, or remove by or as if by the stroke of a pen. Usually used with *off, out,* or *through.* **13.** To come upon, usually as the result of a search; discover: *struck gold.* **14.** To reach; fall upon: *A bright light struck her face.* **15.** To come suddenly to the mind of; occur to: *It struck me that the whole thing was a hoax.* **16. a.** To make a particular impression upon; seem to be to: *How do the new arrangements strike you? struck me as odd.* **b.** To make a powerful impression upon: *We were struck by his obvious sincerity.* **17.** To cause (an emotion) to penetrate deeply: *struck terror into their hearts.* **18. a.** To make or conclude (a bargain). **b.** To achieve or produce, as by careful calculation or contrivance: *strike a balance.* **19.** To fall into or assume (a pose, for example). **20.** *Nautical.* **a.** To haul down (a mast or sail). **b.** To lower (a flag or sail) in salute or surrender. **c.** To lower (cargo) into a hold. **21.** To remove (theatrical properties or scenery, for example) from the stage or other playing area. **22.** To take down and pack up the tents of (a camp). **23.** To level or smooth (a measure, as of grain); strickle. **24.** To put forth or send down (roots). **25.** To constitute (a jury) using a procedure whereby each party may eliminate an equal number of nominees. —*intr.* **1. a.** To deal a blow or blows with or as if with the fist or a weapon; hit. **b.** To occur or appear with devastating effect, as if dealing a blow: *All was going well when tragedy struck.* **2.** To aim a stroke or blow. **3.** To make contact suddenly or violently; collide. **4.** To begin or deliver an attack: *struck at daybreak; strikes at the roots of our democratic institutions.* **5.** To pierce; penetrate. Used chiefly of wind, cold, or damp. **6.** To jerk the line in order to hook a fish that has taken the bait. **7. a.** To make a percussive sound. **b.** To be indicated by sounds: *The hour has struck.* **8.** To become ignited. **9.** To discover something suddenly or unexpectedly. Used with *on* or *upon.* **10.** To proceed, especially in a new direction; set out; head. Often used with *off* or *out.* **11.** To engage in a strike as a form of protest or to support a demand. —See Synonyms at **affect. —strike it rich.** To gain sudden wealth. **—strike off. 1.** To remove the name of (a doctor or solicitor, for example) from a professional register, as for misconduct. **2.** To print. **—strike up. 1.** To start to play or sound vigorously: *The band struck up a waltz.* **2.** To initiate (a friendship, for example).

~*n.* **1.** An act or gesture of striking; a hit or thrust. **2.** An attack; especially, a military air attack upon a single group of targets. **3. a.** A cessation of work by employees in support of demands made upon their employer, as for higher pay or improved conditions.

b. Any cessation of normal activity undertaken as a form of protest: *a hunger strike.* **4. a.** A sudden discovery, as of a precious mineral. **b.** Any sudden or unexpected piece of good luck. **5.** A pull on a fishing line by which the fish is hooked. **6.** In cricket, the position of being the batsman who is to face the bowling: *kept the strike by scoring off the last ball of the over.* **7.** In baseball, a pitched ball that is counted against the batter, especially one swung at and missed. **8.** In tenpin bowling, the knocking down of all the pins with the first bowl of a frame. **9.** *Geology.* The direction of a horizontal line in the plane of an inclined structural feature such as a rock bed or vein. **10.** A strickle. [Strike, struck (earlier stroke), stricken (or struck); Middle English *striken, strok* (or *strak*), *striken,* Old English *strīcan,* to stroke, rub, *strāc, stricen.*]

strike·bound (strīk-bownd) *adj.* Closed, immobilised, or slowed down by a strike.

strike·break·er (strīk-braykər) *n.* One who works or provides an employer with workers during a strike. **—strike·break·ing** *n.*

strike fault *n. Geology.* A fault in the Earth's crust parallel to the strike of the rock strata.

strike out *intr.v.* **1.** To proceed or begin with vigorous effort: *struck out on his own.* **2.** In baseball, to be retired after failing to hit three pitched balls. *—tr.v.* In baseball, to retire (a batter) by the recording of three strikes.

strike·out (strīk-owt) *n.* An act of striking out in baseball.

strik·er (strīkər) *n.* **1.** An employee who is on strike against his employer. **2.** Any device for striking, such as the clapper in a bell or the firing pin in a gun. **3.** In soccer, an attacking player who remains close to his opponents' goal in order to capitalise on any scoring opportunity. **4.** In cricket, the batsman who has the strike.

strike-slip fault (strīk-slip) *n. Geology.* A fault in which the dominant movement on the fault plane is horizontal. Also called a "transcurrent fault", "tear fault".

strik·ing (strīking) *adj.* Making a powerful impression upon the mind or senses, especially because unusually attractive or prominent. **—strik·ing·ly** *adv.* **—strik·ing·ness** *n.*

striking circle *n.* In hockey, the semicircle area in front of the goal from which all scoring shots must be made. Also called "circle".

striking distance *n.* **1.** A distance over which it is possible to deliver an attack. **2.** A distance which is easily travelled over: *within striking distance of the coast.*

Strind·berg (strínd-berg), **(Johan) August** (1849–1912). Swedish dramatist and novelist. He was a leading exponent of psychological realism in drama. His plays include *The Father* (1887), *Miss Julie* (1888), and *The Dance of Death* (1901). His best known novels are *The Red Room* (1879) and *The Ghost Sonata* (1907).

Strine (strīn) *n.* English in a form used in Australia, characterised by a broad accent and picturesque vocabulary. Used humorously. *~adj. Informal.* Australian. [Exaggerated rendering of the Australian pronunciation of *Australian.*]

string (string) *n.* **1.** A cord, thicker than thread and usually made of twisted fibres, used for fastening, tying, or lacing. **2.** Anything shaped into a long, thin line. **3.** A tough plant fibre, such as one running along the side of a pod. **4.** A set of objects threaded together: *a string of beads.* **5.** A continuous series of related acts, events, or items: *a string of excuses.* **6. a.** A set of animals, especially racehorses, belonging to a single owner; a stable. **b.** A group of businesses belonging to a single owner. **7.** A player or group of players having a specified ranking according to ability: *plays in goal for the second string.* **8.** *Music.* **a.** A cord stretched across the sounding board of an instrument, that is struck, plucked, or bowed to produce notes. **b.** *Plural.* Instruments collectively that have such strings; especially, the instruments of the violin family. **c.** *Plural.* Members of an orchestra who play these instruments. **9.** Any of the cords arranged in a crisscross pattern in a sports racquet. **10.** *Architecture.* **a.** A stringboard. **b.** A stringcourse. **11.** *Informal.* A limiting or hidden condition: *a gift with no strings attached.* —See Synonyms at **series.** **—on a string.** Totally under someone's control. **—pull strings.** To use one's influence or influential connections, often in secret, to gain an advantage.

~adj. Made of string or having a string or a mesh of strings: *a string bag.*

~v. **strung** (strung), **stringing, strings.** *—tr.* **1.** To fit or furnish with a string or strings. **2.** To thread on a string. **3.** To arrange or bring together so as to form a string: *managed to string together a few clichés.* **4.** To fasten, tie, or hang with a string or strings. **5.** To extend; stretch out: *string a wire across a room.* **6.** To remove the strings from (a vegetable). **7.** *Informal.* To hang (a person). Usually used with *up.* *—intr.* **1.** To form strings or become stringlike. **2.** To extend or progress in a string, line, or succession. **3.** In billiards and similar games, to determine the order of play by hitting the cue ball to the end cushion with the aim of bringing it back as close as possible to the head rail. **—string along. 1.** To follow another's lead. **2.** To deceive, or keep waiting with deceitful promises. [Middle English *stringe,* Old English *streng.*]

string bass *n.* A **double bass** *(see).*

string bean *n.* **1.** The green pod of any bean prepared for cooking by breaking into sections that retain the beans. Also called "green bean", "snap bean". **2.** *Chiefly U.S.* A **French bean** *(see).* [From the stringy fibres on the pod.]

string·board (string-bawrd || -bōrd) *n.* A board that runs along the side of a staircase to support or cover the ends of the steps.

string·course (string-kawrss || -kōrss) *n.* A distinctive horizontal band or moulding set in the face of a building as a design element. Also called "cordon", "table".

stringed instrument *n.* A musical instrument played by plucking, striking, or bowing taut strings.

strin·gen·do (strin-jéndō) *adv. Music.* With an accelerating tempo. Used as a direction. [Italian, "tightening", from *stringere,* to press together, to tighten, from Latin.] **—strin·gen·do** *adj.*

strin·gent (strínjənt) *adj.* **1.** Imposing rigorous and exacting standards or demands; severe. **2.** Constricted; tight. **3.** Characterised by scarcity of money or by financial restrictions: *stringent market conditions.* [Latin *stringēns* (stem *stringent-*), present participle of *stringere,* to tighten.] **—strin·gen·cy** *n.* **—strin·gent·ly** *adv.*

string·er (stríng-ər) *n.* **1.** A person or thing that strings. **2.** *Architecture.* **a.** A long, horizontal structural timber used for any of several connective or supportive purposes. **b.** A stringboard. **3.** A heavy longitudinal member serving to strengthen the hull of a ship or fuselage of a plane. **4.** A part-time news correspondent who covers the news stories of his own local area.

string·halt (string-hawlt || -holt) *n.* Lameness accompanied by spasmodic movements in the hind legs of a horse. Also called "springhalt". [Perhaps STRING + HALT.]

string-pull·ing (string-pŏŏlling) *n. Informal.* The secret or unofficial use of influence to gain an advantage.

string quartet *n.* **1.** A quartet of musicians playing stringed instruments, traditionally a first and second violin, a viola, and a cello. **2.** A composition for such a quartet of performers.

string tie *n.* A narrow tie, usually tied in a bow.

string·y (string-i) *adj.* **-ier, -iest. 1.** Resembling, forming, or consisting of a string or strings. **2.** Slender and wiry. **3.** Fibrous or sinewy; tough: *stringy meat.* **—string·i·ly** *adv.* **—string·i·ness** *n.*

string·y·bark (string-i-baark) *n. Australian.* Any eucalyptus with tough, fibrous bark.

strip[1] (strip) *v.* **stripped** or *rare* **stript** (stript), **stripping, strips.** *—tr.* **1. a.** To remove the clothing or other covering from. **b.** To remove (clothing or other covering). **2. a.** To remove the furnishings from. **b.** To remove (furnishings) from. **3. a.** To deprive of honours, rank, or the like; divest. **b.** To deprive of possessions; dispossess. **4.** To reduce to essentials; remove all excess detail or extraneous matter from. **5. a.** To remove the foliage or bark from. **b.** To remove the leaves from the stalks of (tobacco). **6. a.** To remove (paint, wallpaper, or varnish, for example), as from walls or furniture, either manually or by chemical or mechanical means. **b.** To remove paint or other coverings from in this way. **7.** To dismantle (a mechanical apparatus) piece by piece. **8.** To damage or break the threads or teeth of (a nut, bolt, screw, or gear). **9.** To finish milking (a cow or other milk-giving creature). **10.** To rob; plunder; despoil. *—intr.* **1. a.** To undress completely. **b.** To perform a striptease. **2.** To fall away or be removed; peel.

~n. A striptease. Also used adjectivally: *a strip club.* [Middle English *stripen,* Old English *(be)strīepan,* to plunder, from Germanic *straupjan* (unattested).]

Synonyms: *strip, divest, denude, bare.*

strip[2] *n.* **1.** A long, narrow piece or tract, usually of uniform width. **2.** *British.* The clothes worn by a particular football team. **3.** An **airstrip** *(see).* **—tear a strip off.** *Informal.* To rebuke sharply.

~tr.v. **stripped, stripping, strips.** To cut or tear into strips. [Perhaps variant of STRIPE (line).]

strip cartoon *n. Chiefly British.* A **comic strip** *(see).*

strip-crop·ping (strip-kropping) *n.* A technique of growing cultivated and sod-forming crops in alternating strips following the contour of the land, in order to minimise erosion.

stripe[1] (strīp) *n.* **1.** A long, narrow band distinguished, as by colour or texture, from the surrounding material or surface. **2.** A fabric having such a band or bands. **3.** A strip of cloth or braid worn on a uniform to indicate rank or length of service; a chevron. **4.** *Chiefly U.S.* Sort; kind: *men of a vicious stripe.*

~tr.v. **striped, striping, stripes.** To mark with a stripe or stripes. [Middle English *strype* (unattested), from Middle Dutch *strīpe,* akin to Middle High German *strīfe*†.]

stripe[2] *n. Archaic.* A stroke or blow, as with a whip. [Middle English *strype,* perhaps from Middle Low German *strippe,* a lash, strap, from Germanic *strip-* (unattested).]

striped (strīpt || strīpid) *adj.* Having a stripe or stripes.

striped muscle *n. Anatomy.* **Striated muscle** *(see).*

strip light *n.* A long electric fluorescent light. **—strip lighting** *n.*

strip·ling (strippling) *n.* An adolescent youth. [Middle English, probably STRIP + -LING, that is "slender as a strip".]

strip mining *n. U.S.* **Open-cast mining** *(see).*

strip·per (strippər) *n.* **1.** One that strips; especially, a tool or chemical that strips wallpaper, paint, or some other coating. **2.** One who performs a striptease.

strip poker *n.* A poker game in which the player with the lowest hand forfeits an article of clothing.

strip·tease (strip-teez, -téez) *n.* A form of entertainment featuring a performer, usually a woman, who slowly removes clothing to a musical accompaniment.

strip·y (strīpi) *adj.* **-ier, -iest.** Suggestive of or marked with stripes.

strive (strīv) *intr.v.* **strove** (strōv) or *rare* **strived, striven** (strívv'n) or **strived, striving, strives. 1.** To exert much effort or energy. **2.** To struggle against another or one another; contend. Often used with *with.* [Middle English *striven,* from Old French *estriver,* perhaps from *estrif,* STRIFE. Strove, striven; Middle English *stroof, streven,* analogous formations, from *striven.*] **—striv·er** *n.*

Usage: The usual past tense and part participle forms of this verb in standard English are *strove* and *striven. Strived* is sometimes heard as an alternative to *strove,* and rather more frequently as an alternative to *striven.*

strobe (strōb) *n.* **1.** A strobe light. **2.** A stroboscope.

strobe light *n.* An electric light that produces a series of repeated intense flashes, used in stroboscopes and also in light displays. Also called "strobe". **—strobe lighting** *n.*

stro·bi·la (strə-bī́-lə) *n., pl.* **-lae** (-lee). **1.** The body of an adult tapeworm, consisting of a series of segments or proglottides. **2.** The segmented polyp stage of certain jellyfish. [New Latin, from Greek *strobilē,* plug of lint resembling a pine cone, from *strobilos,* pine cone, STROBILUS.]

stro·bi·la·ceous (strōbi-láyshəss) *adj. Botany.* Of or resembling a strobilus; conelike.

stro·bi·la·tion (strōbi-láysh'n) *n.* Segmentation of the type found in tapeworms and certain jellyfish.

stro·bi·lus (strṓ-bi-ləss) *n., pl.* **-li** (-lī). Also **stro·bile** (-bīl). *Botany.* A fruiting structure characterised by rows of overlapping scales, such as a pine cone or the fruit of the hop. [New Latin *strobilus,* from Late Latin, a pine cone, from Greek *strobilos,* "round ball", from *strobos,* a whirling around, whirlwind.]

strob·o·scope (strṓbə-skōp, stróbbə-) *n.* Any of various instruments used to view, calibrate, balance, or otherwise adjust moving, rotating, or vibrating objects by making them appear stationary, using pulsed illumination or mechanical devices that intermittently interrupt observation. [Greek *strobos,* a whirling round + -SCOPE.] **—strob·o·scop·ic** (-skóppik) *adj.* **—strob·o·scop·i·cal·ly** *adv.*

strode. Past tense of **stride.**

Stro·heim (strṓ-hīm, *German* shtrṓ-), **Erich von** (1885–1957). Austrian-born U.S. film director and actor. As a director he was noted for uncompromising realistic detail as in *Greed* (1923). As an actor he is remembered for his portrayal of Prussian officers, particularly in *La Grande Illusion* (1937).

stroke (strōk) *n.* **1. a.** The act or an action of striking; an impact; a blow. **b.** A blow, as from a cane or whip, imposed as a punishment: *sentenced to six strokes.* **2. a.** The striking of a bell, gong, or similar instrument. **b.** The sound so produced. **c.** The time so indicated: *the stroke of midnight.* **3.** An unexpected event having a powerful immediate effect for good or ill: *a stroke of luck.* **4. a.** The sudden severe onset of a malady such as apoplexy or sunstroke. **b.** An attack of apoplexy; a cerebral haemorrhage. Not in technical usage. **5.** An inspired or effective idea or act: *a stroke of genius.* **6. a.** A single completed movement of the limbs and body, as in swimming or rowing. **b.** The rate or manner of executing such a movement. **7. a.** The member of a rowing crew who sits nearest the coxswain or the stern and sets the tempo of the other oarsmen. **b.** The position he occupies. **8. a.** A movement of the upper torso and arms for the purpose of striking a ball, as in cricket or tennis. **b.** The manner of executing such a movement. **9.** In golf, a single act of striking the ball, used as a unit of scoring. **10.** Any single act or movement: *has never done a stroke of work; cut interest rates at a stroke.* **11.** Any of a series of movements of a piston from one end of the limit of its motion to the other. **12.** A single mark made by a pen, brush, or other marking implement. **13.** A single deft touch, as in literary composition. **14.** A single flash of lightning. **15.** A light caressing movement, as of the hand. **16.** In transactional analysis, a momentary sense of well-being resulting from a positive gesture, expression, or action received from another person.

~tr.v. **stroked, stroking, strokes. 1.** To give or apply a stroke to. **2.** To rub lightly, as with the hand or something held in the hand; caress. **3.** To set the pace for (a rowing crew). **4.** In transactional analysis, to hearten or reassure by means of some positive gesture, expression, or action. [Middle English *stroke,* Old English *strāc.*]

stroke play *n.* A method of scoring in golf, **medal play** *(see).*

stroll (strōl) *v.* **strolled, strolling, strolls.** *—intr.* **1.** To go for a leisurely walk. **2.** To travel from place to place giving performances: *strolling players.* *—tr.* To walk through at a leisurely pace.

~n. A leisurely walk. [Perhaps from German dialectal *strollen*†.]

stroll·er (strṓl-ər) *n.* **1.** One who strolls. **2.** A strolling player. **3.** A vagabond. **4.** A **Baby Buggy** *(see).*

stro·ma (strṓmə) *n., pl.* **-mata** (-tə). *Biology.* Any tissue that serves as a framework; especially: **1.** The colourless dense material occurring around the grana in a chloroplast. **2.** A compact mass of fungal hyphae in which fruiting bodies are produced. **3.** The fibrous connective tissue forming the framework of the ovary and testis. [New Latin, from Late Latin, from Greek *strōma,* bedspread, mattress.] **—stro·mat·ic** (strō-máttik) *adj.*

Strom·bo·li (strómbəli). One of the volcanic Lipari islands in the Tyrrhenian Sea north of Sicily. Its crater contains molten lava, and continuously emits gases, and small-scale eruptions occur frequently. Occasionally it has exploded with violence (1930, 1966).

strong (strong || strawng, *and in compounds*) *adj.* **stronger, strongest. 1.** Physically powerful; capable of exerting great physical force; muscular. **2. a.** In sound health; robust. **b.** Economically or financially sound or thriving. **3.** Characterised by power, fortitude, or resolution with regard to character, will, morality, or intelligence. **4.** Having or showing impressive ability, talent, or resources in a specified field: *a strong batting line-up.* **5.** Capable of the effective exercise of authority: *strong leadership.* **6.** Capable of enduring; solid. **7.** Capable of being defended: *a strong flank.* **8.** Having force of conviction or feeling; well-grounded: *a strong faith.* **9.** *Finance.* Marked by or showing firmness and a rising tendency in prices or value: *The pound remained strong.* **10.** Not easily upset; resistant to harmful or unpleasant influences: *strong nerves.* **11.** Having a specified number: *an army 15,000 strong.* **12.** Having force of motion or action: *a strong current.* **13. a.** Persuasive, effective, and cogent: *a strong argument.* **b.** Forceful and pointed; emphatic: *a strong statement.* **c.** Immoderate or profane: *strong language.* **14.** Extreme; drastic: *strong measures.* **15.** Intense in degree or quality: *a strong emotion.* **16.** Having an intense effect on the senses: *a strong smell.* **17.** Having a high concentration of an active or essential ingredient: *strong coffee.* **18.** Powerfully efficacious with respect to its appropriate function: *a strong painkiller.* **19.** Existing to a considerable or striking degree: *a strong resemblance; a strong possibility.* **20.** Characterised by a high degree of saturation. Said of a colour. **21.** *Linguistics.* Designating those verbs in English or other Germanic languages that form a past tense other than by means of a dental suffix such as *-ed;* for example, *fly, flew; sing, sang.* In this sense, compare **weak.**

~adv. In a strong, powerful, or vigorous manner; forcibly; forcefully. **—going strong.** Still vigorous or effective. [Middle English *strong,* Old English *strang.*] **—strong·ly** *adv.*

Synonyms: *strong, stout, sturdy, tough, stalwart, tenacious.*

strong-arm (stróng-árm) *adj. Informal.* Using physical force or coercion: *strong-arm tactics.*

strong·box (stróng-boks) *n.* A stoutly made box or safe in which valuables are deposited.

strong breeze *n.* A wind whose speed is 10.8 to 13.8 metres per second, force 6 on the Beaufort scale.

strong gale *n.* A wind whose speed is 20.8 to 24.4 metres per second, force 9 on the Beaufort scale.

strong·hold (stróng-hōld) *n.* **1.** A fortress. **2.** A place of security; a refuge. **3.** An area of predominance: *a Tory stronghold.*

strong interaction *n. Physics.* A force that acts between certain elementary particles, hadrons, and is about 100 times stronger than the electromagnetic interaction but acts over only very short distances (10^{-15} metre). Compare **electromagnetic interaction, gravitational interaction, weak interaction.**

strong man *n.* **1.** One who performs feats of strength at a circus, fair, or other show. **2.** A leader, especially a military dictator, who retains power by the use or threat of force.

strong meat *n.* Something unattractive or too difficult for the inexperienced: *Isn't Schopenhauer rather strong meat for sixth-formers?*

strong-mind·ed (stróng-mīndid) *adj.* **1.** Having a determined will. **2.** Having a vigorous mentality. **—strong-mind·ed·ly** *adv.* **—strong-mind·ed·ness** *n.*

strong point *n.* A skill or quality in which one excels.

strong room *n.* A strongly built, secure, and fireproof room designed for the safekeeping of money or valuables.

strong suit *n.* A **long suit** *(see).*

stron·gyle, stron·gyl (strón-jil, -jīl) *n.* Any of various nematode worms of the family Strongylidae, often parasitic in the gastrointestinal tract of mammals, especially horses. [New Latin *Strongylus* (genus), from Greek *strongulos*†, round, compactly formed.]

stron·gyl·o·sis (strónji-lō-siss) *n.* Infestation with strongyles.

stron·ti·a (strón-ti-ə, -shə || -chə) *n.* Strontium hydroxide. [From *strontian,* variant of STRONTIUM.]

stron·ti·an·ite (strón-ti-ə-nīt, -shi- || -chə-nīt) *n.* A grey to yellowish-green strontium ore, essentially $SrCO_3$. [*Strontian,* variant of STRONTIUM + -ITE.]

stron·ti·um (strón-ti-əm, -shəm || -chəm) *n. Symbol* **Sr** A soft, silvery, easily oxidised metallic element that ignites spontaneously in air when finely divided. It is used in pyrotechnic compounds and various alloys. Atomic number 38, atomic weight 87.62, melting point 769°C, boiling point 1,384°C, relative density 2.54, valency 2. [Earlier *strontian,* after *Strontian,* area in the Highland Region of Scotland where it was discovered.] **—stron·tic** (-tik) *adj.*

strontium hydroxide *n.* A white deliquescent powder that normally occurs as the octahydrate, $Sr(OH)_2.8\ H_2O$, and is used in sugar refining. Also called "strontia".

strontium-90 *n.* The strontium isotope with mass 90, having a half-life of 28 years, used for its high-energy beta emission in certain nuclear electric power sources and constituting a radiation hazard in fallout.

strontium unit *n. Abbr.* **SU** A measure of the concentration of strontium-90 in an organic medium, such as soil, milk, or bone, relative to the calcium concentration in the same medium; 10^{-12} curie of strontium-90 per gram of calcium.

strop (strop) *n.* A flexible strip of leather or canvas used for sharpening a razor.

~tr.v. **stropped, stropping, strops.** To sharpen (a razor) on a strop. [Middle English *stroppe,* band of leather, from Middle Low German or Middle Dutch *strop,* from West Germanic *strupa* (unattested), from Latin *stroppus,* from Greek *strophos,* twisted cord, from *strephein,* to turn.]

stro·phan·thin (strō-fánthin) *n.* A toxic glycoside or mixture of glycosides extracted from seeds of *Strophanthus Kombé* and used medicinally as a cardiac tonic. [New Latin *Strophanthus* (genus) : Greek *strophos,* twisted cord (see **strop**) + *anthos,* flower + -IN.]

stro·phe (strṓfi) *n.* **1. a.** A stanza, especially the first of a pair of stanzas of alternating form on which the structure of a given poem is based. **b.** A rhythmic system constituting a section of a poem, typically consisting of a series of asymmetric lines. **2.** The first division of the triad (strophe, antistrophe, and epode) constituting a section of a Pindaric ode. **3. a.** The movement of the chorus in classical Greek drama while turning from one side of the orchestra to the other. **b.** The part of a choral ode sung while this movement is executed. [Greek *strophē*, a turning, from *strephein*, to turn.] **—stroph·ic** (strŏffik, strōfik) *adj.*

stroph·u·lus (strŏffewləss) *n.* Formerly, any of various diseases causing a skin rash; especially a disease common among children, sometimes associated with intestinal disturbances, characterised by a papular eruption of the skin. Also called "red gum". [New Latin, from Greek *strophos*, twisted cord, from *strephein*, to turn.]

strop·py (stróppi) *adj.* **-pier, -piest.** *British Informal.* Bad-tempered, insolent, or uncooperative. [20th century : perhaps alteration of OBSTREPEROUS.]

strove. Past tense of **strive.**

struck (struk). Past tense and past participle of **strike.**

struck measure *n.* A dry measure having the contents levelled off and not heaped.

struc·tur·al (strúk-chər-əl, -choor-) *adj.* **1.** Of, pertaining to, having, or characterised by structure. **2.** Used in or necessary to construction. **3.** *Geology.* Pertaining to the structure of rocks and other aspects of the Earth's crust. **4.** *Biology.* Of or pertaining to organic structure; morphological. **5.** Pertaining to or caused by the existing economic or political structure of a community or country: *Structural unemployment.* **—struc·tur·al·ly** *adv.*

structural formula *n.* A chemical formula that represents the configuration of atoms and bonds in a molecule. Compare **empirical formula, molecular formula.**

structural gene *n.* A gene that forms part of an **operon** *(see)* and that determines a particular amino acid sequence in a protein.

struc·tur·al·ise, struc·tur·al·ize (strúk-chərə-līz) *tr.v.* **-ised, -ising, -ises.** To incorporate or arrange into a structure. **—struc·tur·al·i·sa·tion** (-lī-záysh'n || *U.S.* -li-) *n.*

struc·tur·al·ism (strúkchərəl-iz'm) *n.* **1.** An approach to linguistics characterised by the description of language in terms of irreducible structural features. **2.** An approach to the understanding of phenomena, as in the fields of anthropology, sociology, or literature, chiefly characterised by analysis or interpretation in terms of the underlying structures and principles that are felt to generate the phenomena in question. **—struc·tur·al·ist** *n. & adj.*

structural isomer. See **isomer.**

structural steel *n.* Steel shaped for use in construction.

struc·ture (strúkchər) *n.* **1.** Something constructed by the bringing together of material parts, especially a building. **2.** Any complex entity made up of mutually connected elements. **3.** The manner in which something is constructed; the configuration or organisation of constituent elements. **4.** Constitution; make-up. **5.** The interrelation of parts or the principle of organisation in a complex entity. —See Synonyms at **building.**

~tr.v. **structured, -turing, -tures.** To provide with or form into a well-defined structure. [Middle English, from Old French, from Latin *structūra*, from *struere* (past participle *structus*), to construct.]

stru·del (strōōd'l) *n.* A kind of pastry made with fruit or cheese rolled up in a thin sheet of dough and baked. [German *Strudel*, from Middle High German *strudel*, whirlpool.]

strug·gle (strúgg'l) *intr.v.* **-gled, -gling, -gles.** **1.** To make violent or strenuous physical effort, as in opposing a material force or trying to escape confinement. **2.** To contend, compete, or fight. **3.** To be strenuously engaged with a problem, task, or anything presenting a difficulty; grapple. **4. a.** To make any strenuous effort; strive: *struggling to be polite.* **b.** To strive to achieve recognition: *a struggling writer.* **5.** To progress or penetrate with difficulty.

~n. **1.** A strenuous physical effort. **2.** A determined effort to achieve a goal in spite of obstacles. **3.** Combat; strife. [Middle English *struglen*†.] **—strug·gler** *n.* **—strug·gling·ly** *adv.*

strum (strum) *v.* **strummed, strumming, strums.** *—tr.* To play (a stringed musical instrument) by running the fingers lightly over the strings. *—intr.* To play an instrument in this manner.

~n. The act or sound of strumming. **—strum·mer** *n.*

stru·ma (strōō-mə || stréw-) *n., pl.* **-mae** (-mee) or **-mas.** **1.** *Pathology.* **Goitre** *(see).* **2.** *Botany.* A cushion-like swelling, especially at the base of a moss capsule. [Latin *strūma*†, tumour.] **—stru·mat·ic** (-máttik), **stru·mose** (-mōz, -mōss), **stru·mous** (-məss) *adj.*

strum·pet (strúmpit) *n. Literary.* A prostitute. [Middle English *strompet*†.]

strung. Past tense and past participle of **string.**

strung out *adj. Slang.* **1.** Addicted to a drug. **2.** Physically debilitated or emotionally distressed, as from long-term drug addiction or because of the lack of a drug.

strut (strut) *v.* **strutted, strutting, struts.** *—intr.* To walk with pompous bearing; swagger. *—tr.* To brace with a strut or struts.

~n. **1.** A stiff, self-important gait. **2.** A bar or rod used to strengthen a framework by resisting longitudinal thrust. [Middle English *strouten*, to swell, stand out, protrude, Old English *strūtian*, to stand out stiffly.] **—strut·ter** *n.* **—strut·ting·ly** *adv.*

struth, strewth (strōōth || strewth) *interj.* Used to express surprise or annoyance. [From *God's truth.*]

stru·thi·ous (strōō-thi-əss, -thi- || stréw-) *adj.* **1.** Of, pertaining to, or resembling the ostrich or other flightless bird. **2.** Deliberately ignoring the truth. [Latin *strūthiō*, ostrich, from Greek *strouthion*, from *strouthos*†, sparrow, ostrich.]

strych·nine (strík-neen || *chiefly U.S.* -nīn, -nin) *n.* An extremely poisonous white crystalline alkaloid, $C_{21}H_{22}N_2O_2$, derived from nux vomica and related plants, and used as a poison for moles and formerly medicinally as a stimulant for the central nervous system. [French, from New Latin *Strychnos*, genus of plants including nux vomica, from Latin *strychnos*, nightshade, from Greek *strukhnos*†.]

strych·nin·ism (strík-nin-iz'm, -neen-) *n.* Poisoning from excessive or prolonged ingestion of strychnine, resulting in painful muscular spasms. [STRYCHNINE + -ISM.]

Stu·art, Stew·art (stéw-ərt || stōō-). The family name of the royal family of Scotland (1371–1707), England (1603–1707), and Great Britain (1707–14).

Stuart, Charles Edward, also known as the Young Pretender or Bonnie Prince Charlie (1720–88). Grandson of James II of England and son of James Edward Stuart. In 1745 he led the last Jacobite rising, claiming the British throne for his father. He was defeated at the battle of Culloden (1746), and escaped to France.

Stuart, James Francis Edward, also known as the Old Pretender (1688–1766). Pretender to the British throne; son of James II. He made two unsuccessful attempts (1708, 1715) to take the British throne. The Jacobite rising of 1745, led on James's behalf by his son Charles Edward Stuart, also failed.

stub (stub) *n.* **1. a.** The short blunt end remaining after something has been cut, broken off, or worn down, such as the stump of a tree, tooth, or pencil. **b.** A cigar or cigarette butt. **c.** Anything that has been shortened, blunted, or worn down. **2.** A counterfoil, such as that of a cheque or receipt.

~tr.v. **stubbed, stubbing, stubs.** **1.** To pull up by the roots. **2.** To clear (a field) of stubs. **3.** To strike (one's toe or foot) against something. **4.** To extinguish (a cigarette butt) by crushing. [Middle English *stubbe*, Old English *stybb, stubb.*]

stub axle *n.* A short axle that supports a front wheel of a motor vehicle.

stub·ble (stúbb'l) *n.* **1.** The short, stiff stalks of a grain or hay crop remaining on a field after harvesting. **2.** Anything resembling stubble, especially the short, bristly hairs on a man's unshaven face. [Middle English *stuble*, from Old French, from Latin *stup(u)la*, variant of *stipula*, straw. See **stipule.**] **—stub·bly** *adj.*

stub·born (stúbbərn) *adj.* **1.** Doggedly and unreasonably asserting one's will or refusing to comply; refractory; obstinate. **2.** Characterised by perseverance; resolute or persistent: *stubborn resistance.* **3.** Difficult to treat or deal with; resistant to treatment or effort: *stubborn stains.* —See Synonyms at **contrary, obstinate.** [Middle English *stoborne*†.] **—stub·born·ly** *adv.* **—stub·born·ness** *n.*

Stubbs (stubz), **George** (1724–1806). English painter and engraver. He published *Anatomy of the Horse* (1766), a collection of engravings made from drawings of horses he had dissected.

stub·by (stúbbi) *adj.* **-bier, -biest.** **1.** Resembling a stub; short and thick or thickset. **2.** Covered with or consisting of stubs; bristly. **—stub·bi·ly** *adv.* **—stub·bi·ness** *n.*

stub nail *n.* A short, thick nail.

stuc·co (stúckō) *n., pl.* **-coes** or **-cos.** **1.** A durable finish for exterior walls, applied wet and usually composed of cement, sand, and lime. **2.** A fine plaster for interior wall ornamentation, such as mouldings. **3.** Ornamental work done using stucco.

~tr.v. **stuccoed, -coing, -coes** or **-cos.** To finish or decorate with stucco. [Italian, from Old High German *stukki*, fragment, crust.]

stuck. Past tense and past participle of **stick.**

stuck-up (stúk-úp) *adj. Informal.* Snobbish; conceited.

stud[1] (stud) *n.* **1. a.** A boss, nail head, rivet, or the like slightly projecting from a surface, used chiefly for decorative purposes. **b.** An almost flat, usually square metal object projecting slightly from the surface of a road, usually used to mark off lanes. **c.** Any of several small cylindrical projections, as on the sole of a football boot, designed to give extra grip. **2.** An upright post in the framework of a wall for supporting sheets of lath, wallboard, or the like. **3.** A headless bolt threaded at both ends so that one end can be screwed into a metal part and the other end inserted through a hole in a mating part, the assembly being secured by a second bolt screwed onto the other end. **4.** A small ornamental button mounted on a short pin for insertion through an eyelet, as on a dress shirt. **5.** Any of various protruding pins or pegs in machinery. **6.** A metal crosspiece used as a brace in a link, as in a chain cable.

~tr.v. **studded, studding, studs.** **1.** To provide with or construct with a stud or studs. **2.** To set or adorn with studs or other prominent objects. **3.** To be dotted about on, especially ornamentally. [Middle English *stode*, post, prop, Old English *studu, stuthu.*]

stud[2] *n.* **1. a.** A group of animals, especially horses, kept for breeding. **b.** A stable or farm where they are kept. Also called a "stud farm". **2.** A stallion or other male animal kept for breeding. **3.** The condition of being available for breeding purposes: *at stud.* **4.** *Slang.* A man considered as being sexually active. **5.** Stud poker. [Middle English *stod*, Old English *stōd*, stable for breeding.]

stud·book (stúd-bŏŏk || -bŏŏk) *n.* A book registering the pedigrees of thoroughbred animals, especially of horses.

stud·ding (stúdding) *n.* **1.** The wood framework of a wall or partition. **2.** That with which a surface is studded.

stud·ding·sail (stúdding-sayl; *nautical* stún-s'l) *n. Nautical.* A narrow rectangular sail set from extensions of the yards of square-rigged ships. [Perhaps from Middle Low German and Middle Dutch *stōtinge*, a thrusting, from *stōten*, to force.]

stu·dent (stéwd'nt || stōōd'nt) *n.* **1.** A person following a course of study; especially: **a.** One studying at a university or other place of tertiary education. Also used adjectivally: *a student nurse.* **b.** *Chiefly U.S.* Any person in full-time education. **2.** One who makes a study of something. [Middle English, from Latin *studēns* (stem *student-*), present participle of *studēre*, to study, be diligent.]

stu·dent·ship (stéw-d'nt-ship || stōō-) *n.* **1.** The state of being a student. **2.** *British.* A type of scholarship, usually for postgraduate study.

students' union *n.* **1.** An organisation of the students in an establishment of higher education, providing social and recreational facilities and usually representing student interests. **2.** Its premises.

stud·ied (stúd-id || -eed) *adj.* **1.** Carefully contrived; affected or calculated: *a studied effect; a studied smile.* **2.** *Archaic.* Learned. **—stud·ied·ly** *adv.* **—stud·ied·ness** *n.*

stu·di·o (stéw-di-ō || stōō-) *n., pl.* **-os.** **1.** The workroom of an artist or photographer. **2.** An establishment where an art is taught or studied: *a dance studio.* **3.** A room or place where cinema or video films are made. **4.** A room used for the recording or live transmission of television or radio productions. **5.** A place where music is recorded for commercial distribution; a recording studio. **6.** A studio flat. [Italian, from Latin *studium,* STUDY.]

studio couch *n.* A couch that can serve as a bed.

studio flat *n.* A small flat usually consisting of a single main room together with a kitchen and bathroom. Also called "studio".

stu·di·ous (stéw-di-əss || stōō-) *adj.* **1.** Devoted to study. **2.** Earnest; diligent. **3.** Giving or suggestive of careful attention; heedful: *studious of his appearance.* **4.** *Rare.* Deliberate; studied. **5.** Conducive to study. [Middle English, from Latin *studiōsus,* from *studium,* STUDY.] **—stu·di·ous·ly** *adv.* **—stu·di·ous·ness** *n.*

stud poker *n.* Poker in which the first round of cards (and often the last) is dealt face down and the others face up. Also called "stud". [Shortened from *stud horse poker,* perhaps alluding to the cards being "at stud", that is, available to the player as long as he bets and stays in the game.]

stud·y (stúddi) *n., pl.* **-ies.** **1. a.** The act or process of studying; the pursuit of knowledge, as by reading, observation, or research. **b.** *Plural.* The work of one engaged in this act or process. **2. a.** Attentive scrutiny or careful investigation. **b.** An enquiry or examination, especially of an academic or scientific nature. **3. a.** A subject to be investigated or studied: *Human behaviour proves a fascinating study.* **b.** *Often plural.* A branch or department of learning; an academic or scientific subject: *environmental studies.* **4.** Something that deserves notice or requires careful attention: *Her attitude was a study in polite condescension.* **5.** *Formal.* An aim or endeavour: *made it my study to serve them.* **6. a.** A work resulting from academic endeavour, such as a monograph or thesis. **b.** A literary work on a particular subject. **c.** A preliminary sketch, as for a work of art. **7.** A musical composition designed as a technical exercise; an étude. **8.** A state of mental absorption, a **brown study** *(see).* **9.** A room intended or equipped for studying in. **10. a.** An actor who is memorising a part. **b.** The memorising of a part in a play.
~*v.* **studied, -ying, -ies.** *—tr.* **1. a.** To apply one's mind purposefully to the acquisition of knowledge or understanding of (any subject): *study a language.* **b.** To be engaged in the study of (a particular subject) as part of an educational course. **2.** To read, scrutinise, or investigate with close attention: *study a report; study a map.* **3.** To memorise (a part in a play). **4.** To give careful thought to; contemplate: *study the next move.* **5.** *Formal.* To endeavour; make it one's purpose. *—intr.* **1.** To apply oneself to learning, especially by reading. **2.** To pursue a course of study. **3.** To ponder; reflect; meditate. [Middle English *studie,* from Old French *estudie,* from Latin *studium,* from *studēre,* to be eager, study.]

stuff (stuf) *n.* **1.** The material out of which something is made or formed; substance. **2.** The basic substance or essential elements of anything; essence: *the stuff heroes are made of.* **3.** Any material not specifically identified. **4.** *Informal.* Household or personal articles collectively; belongings. **5.** Worthless objects; refuse or junk. **6.** Foolish or empty words or ideas. Used chiefly in the interjection *stuff and nonsense.* **7.** Woven material; especially, woollen fabric. **8.** *Informal.* A person's field of knowledge or competence: *knows her stuff.* **9.** *Slang.* **a.** Money; cash. **b.** An illegal drug, especially cannabis. **c.** Women collectively considered as sexual objects. Used chiefly in the phrase *a bit of stuff.* Considered offensive. **—do (one's) stuff.** *Informal.* To do what is expected of one; show one's particular skill.
~*v.* **stuffed, stuffing, stuffs.** *—tr.* **1. a.** To pack tightly; fill up; cram. **b.** To block (a passage or opening). **c.** To push roughly into a place: *stuffed the letter into my pocket.* **2. a.** To fill with an appropriate stuffing: *stuff a cabbage.* **b.** To fill the skin of (a dead animal) so as to restore its natural form. **3.** To fill to repletion with food. **4.** To apply a preservative and softening agent to (leather). **5.** *U.S.* To put fraudulent votes into (a ballot box). **6.** *Slang.* To take back and dispose of (something offered and rejected): *They offered me a four per cent rise, but I told them to stuff it.* **7.** *Vulgar Slang.* To have sex with (a woman). **—get stuffed.** *Vulgar Slang.* Used to express contempt for or anger with another. *—intr.* To overeat; gorge oneself. [Middle English *stuff(e),* from Old French *estoffe,* provisions, from *estoffer,* to cram, pad, from Germanic *stopfōn* (unattested), from Late Latin *stuppāre,* to plug up, from Latin *stuppa,* plug, cork, from Greek *stuppē.*] **—stuff·er** *n.*

stuffed shirt *n. Informal.* A pompous, complacently self-important person.

stuff·ing (stúffing) *n.* **1.** Material used to stuff or fill, especially: **a.** Padding put in cushions, pillows, and upholstered furniture. **b.** Food put in the cavity of meat or vegetables. **2.** *Informal.* Strength, vigour, or self-confidence: *His illness knocked the stuffing out of him.*

stuffing box *n.* An enclosure containing packing to prevent leakage around a moving machine part. Also called "packing box".

stuff·y (stúffi) *adj.* **-ier, -iest.** **1.** Lacking sufficient ventilation; airless; close. **2.** Having the respiratory passages blocked. **3.** *Informal.* Primly formal or boringly conventional; dull; stodgy: *a stuffy dinner party.* **—stuff·i·ly** *adv.* **—stuff·i·ness** *n.*

stull (stul) *n.* **1.** A timber or other prop supporting the roof of a mine opening. **2.** A platform braced against the sides of a working area in a mine.

stul·ti·fy (stúlti-fī) *tr.v.* **-fied, -fying, -fies.** **1.** To reduce to a state of uselessness, futility, or enfeeblement. **2.** To cause to appear stupid, inconsistent, or ridiculous. **3.** *Law.* To allege or prove insane and so not legally responsible. Often used reflexively. [Late Latin *stultificāre* : Latin *stultus,* foolish + *facere,* to make.] **—stul·ti·fi·ca·tion** (-fi-káysh'n) *n.* **—stul·ti·fi·er** *n.*

stum (stum) *n.* **1.** Unfermented or partly fermented grape juice; must. **2.** Vapid wine renewed by an admixture of stum.
~*tr.v.* **stummed, stumming, stums.** **1.** To revitalise (vapid wine) by adding stum so as to restart fermentation. **2.** To prevent further fermentation of (wine). [Dutch, from *stom,* unfermented, dumb, mute, translation of French *(vin) muet,* "mute (wine)".]

stum·ble (stúmb'l) *v.* **-bled, -bling, -bles.** *—intr.* **1. a.** To miss one's step in walking or running; trip and almost fall. **b.** To proceed unsteadily or falteringly; flounder. **c.** To act or speak falteringly or clumsily. **2.** To make a mistake; blunder. **3.** To fall into evil ways; err. **4.** To find accidentally or unexpectedly. Used with *on* or *upon.* *—tr.* To puzzle, embarrass, or disconcert.
~*n.* The act or an instance of stumbling. [Middle English *stumblen,* perhaps from Old Norse *stumla* (unattested).] **—stum·bler** *n.* **—stum·bling·ly** *adv.*

stum·ble·bum (stúmb'l-bum) *n. U.S. Slang.* A blundering or inept person. [STUMBLE + BUM (vagabond).]

stumbling block *n.* An obstacle or impediment.

stu·mer (stéw-mər || stōō-) *n. British Slang.* Anything worthless or fraudulent, especially a counterfeit banknote or forged cheque. [19th century : origin obscure.]

stumm (shtōōm) *adj.* Variant of **shtum.**

stump (stump) *n.* **1.** The part of a tree trunk left protruding from the ground after the tree has been felled. **2.** Any part, as of a branch, limb, or tooth, remaining after the main part has been cut away, broken off, or worn down. **3.** *Plural. Informal.* The legs. **4.** A short, thickset person. **5.** A heavy tread or footstep. **6.** A platform or other place used for making speeches in a political or other campaign. **7.** A short, pointed roll of leather or paper or a wad of rubber for rubbing on a charcoal or pencil drawing to shade or soften it. **8.** In cricket: **a.** Any one of the three upright sticks in a wicket. **b.** *Plural. Informal.* The end of the day's play: *At stumps, England were 180 behind.*
~*v.* **stumped, stumping, stumps.** *—tr.* **1.** To reduce to a stump; lop; truncate. **2.** To clear stumps from: *stump a field.* **3.** In cricket, to dismiss (a batsman who has just faced a delivery) by breaking his wicket while he is out of his crease. **4.** *Chiefly U.S.* To go through (a district) making political speeches. **5.** To shade (a drawing) with a stump. **6.** *Informal.* To baffle completely; confront with an insoluble problem. *—intr.* To walk clumsily or heavily. **—stump up.** *British Informal.* To pay (money owed or required). [Middle English *stumpe,* from Middle Low German *stump.*] **—stump·er** *n.* **—stump·i·ness** *n.* **—stump·y** *adj.*

stun (stun) *tr.v.* **stunned, stunning, stuns.** **1.** To daze or render unconscious, as by a blow. **2.** To overwhelm or daze with a loud noise. **3.** To stupefy or overwhelm with shock or astonishment; astound.
~*n.* **1.** Something that stupefies. **2.** A state of stupefaction. [Middle English *stonen,* from Old French *estoner,* from Vulgar Latin *extonāre* (unattested) : Latin *ex-* (intensive) + *tonāre,* to thunder.]

stung. Past tense and past participle of **sting.**

stun grenade *n.* A grenade designed to detonate with a loud explosion and release smoke or disabling gas but without causing physical harm, used particularly in antiterrorist operations.

stunk. Past participle and alternative past tense of **stink.**

stun·ner (stúnnər) *n.* **1.** One that stuns. **2.** *Informal.* An exceptionally attractive person or thing.

stun·ning (stúnning) *adj.* **1.** Causing or capable of causing loss of consciousness or emotional shock. **2.** *Informal.* **a.** Of a strikingly attractive appearance. **b.** Extremely impressive or well-performed. **—stun·ning·ly** *adv.*

stunt[1] (stunt) *tr.v.* **stunted, stunting, stunts.** **1.** To check the growth or development of. **2.** To check (growth or development).
~*n.* **1.** A state of retarded growth, or something causing such a state. **2.** One that is stunted. [Perhaps from Middle English *stont,* short in duration (but influenced in sense by Old Norse cognate *stuttr,* short, dwarfish), Old English *stunt,* dull, half-witted.] **—stunt·ed·ness** *n.*

stunt[2] *n.* **1.** A feat displaying unusual strength, skill, or daring. **2.** Any unusual act or display intended to attract attention.
~*intr.v.* **stunted, stunting, stunts.** To perform a stunt or stunts.

stunt man *n.* A person who substitutes for a film actor in scenes requiring physical prowess or involving physical risk.

stu·pa (stōōpə) *n.* A Buddhist shrine usually consisting of a large domed structure. Also called a "tope". [Sanskrit *stūpa,* "tuft of hair", "crown of head".]

stupe (stewp || stōōp) *n.* A hot compress, often treated with a counterirritant and applied to relieve pain. [Middle English, from Latin *stuppa,* tow, plug, from Greek *stuppē.*]

stu·pe·fa·cient (stéwpi-fáyshi-ənt || stōōpi-) *adj.* Inducing stupor.

~n. A stupefacient drug, such as a narcotic. [Latin *stupefaciēns* (stem *stupefacient-*), present participle of *stupefacere*, STUPEFY.]

stu·pe·fac·tion (stewpi-fáksh'n, styŏopi- || stŏopi-) n. 1. The act of stupefying or the state of being stupefied. 2. Great astonishment or consternation.

stu·pe·fy (stéwpi-fi, styŏopi- || stŏopi-) tr.v. **-fied, -fying, -fies.** 1. To dull the senses of; put into a stupor. 2. To stun with amazement; astonish. [French *stupéfier*, from Latin *stupefacere* : *stupēre*, to be stunned + *facere*, to make.] **—stu·pe·fi·er** n.

stu·pen·dous (stew-péndəss, styŏo- || stŏo-) adj. 1. Of awesome size, degree, force, or quality; astounding; prodigious. 2. Informal. Extremely impressive or enjoyable. **—See Synonyms at enormous.** [Latin *stupendus,* from *stupēre,* to be stunned.] **—stu·pen·dous·ly** adv. **—stu·pen·dous·ness** n.

stu·pid (stéwpid, styŏopid || stŏopid) adj. **-pider, -pidest.** 1. In a stupor; stupefied. 2. Slow to apprehend; dull; obtuse. 3. Showing a lack of sense or intelligence. 4. Uninteresting, boring, or trivial: *a stupid job.* 5. Informal. Infuriating or intractable: *couldn't get the stupid car to start.*

~n. Informal. A stupid person. [French *stupide,* from Latin *stupidus,* from *stupēre,* to be stunned.] **—stu·pid·ly** adv. **—stu·pid·ness, stu·pid·i·ty** (stew-píddəti, styŏo- || stŏo-) n.

Synonyms: stupid, slow, obtuse, dense, crass.

stu·por (stéwpər || stŏopər) n. 1. A state of near unconsciousness; lethargy; torpor. 2. A state of mental confusion; a daze. [Middle English, from Latin, from *stupēre,* to be stunned. See **stupid.**] **—stu·por·ous** adj.

stur·dy[1] (stúrdi) adj. **-dier, -diest.** 1. Substantially built; durable; strong. 2. Physically strong and healthy; robust. 3. Vigorous, lusty, or resolute: *a sturdy English sense of humour.* **—See Synonyms at strong.** [Middle English, giddy, rash, impetuous, from Old French *estourdi,* past participle of *estourir,* to stun, daze, from Vulgar Latin *exturdīre* (unattested), probably "to be stunned like a thrush drunk with grapes" : perhaps Latin *ex-,* completely + *turdus,* thrush.] **—stur·di·ly** adv. **—stur·di·ness** n.

stur·dy[2] n. A disease of sheep, gid *(see).* [From STURDY (in earlier sense "giddy").] **—stur·died** adj.

stur·geon (stúrjən) n. Any of various large, edible freshwater and marine fishes of the family Acipenseridae, of the Northern Hemisphere, valued as a source of caviar and isinglass. [Middle English, from Anglo-French, from Vulgar Latin *sturiō* (unattested), from Germanic *sturjōn* (unattested). See also **sterlet.**]

Sturluson, Snorri. See Snorri **Sturluson.**

Sturm·ab·teil·ung (shtŏorm-ap-tīloŏong) n., pl. **-teilungen** (-ən). Abbr. **S.A.** A Nazi German militia organised about 1924 and notorious for its violent and terroristic methods. Also called "Brown Shirts", "storm troopers". [German, "storm division".]

Sturm und Drang (shtŏorm ōont dráng) n. A German romantic literary movement of the late 18th century, the works of which typically depicted the impulsive man struggling against conventional society. [German, "storm and stress", originally the title of a romantic play (1776) by Friedrich Maximilian von Klinger (1752–1831), German poet and dramatist.]

stut·ter (stúttər) v. **-tered, -tering, -ters.** —intr. To speak with a spasmodic hesitation, prolongation, or repetition of sounds. —tr. To say with or as if with a stutter.

~n. The act or habit of stuttering. [Frequentative of obsolete *stut,* from Middle English *stutten,* perhaps of Low German origin, akin to Middle Low German *stōtern,* to stutter.] **—stut·ter·er** n. **—stut·ter·ing·ly** adv.

Stutt·gart (stŏot-gaart; German shtŏot-). The capital of Baden-Württemberg, on the river Neckar in southwestern Germany. It is a major industrial centre producing electrical and photographic equipment, textiles, printed materials, and motor vehicles. It is also a tourist centre, and venue for industrial fairs.

St. Vin·cent and the Gren·a·dines (vínss'nt; grénnə-déenz). Island state in the West Indies, lying in the eastern Caribbean Sea. St. Vincent, the most populous of the Windward Islands, is a major tourist area. However, its volcano, Soufrière, is still active, and erupted violently in 1979. Hundreds of small islands make up the Grenadines group. The main exports are bananas, sweet potatoes, arrowroot, and spices. Formerly a French colony, the islands finally became British in 1805, and fully independent within the Commonwealth in 1979. Area, 388 square kilometres (150 square miles). Population, 110,000. Capital, Kingstown (on St. Vincent). See map at **Latin America.**

St. Vi·tus' dance (vítəss, -ız) n. Pathology A nervous disease, cho·rea *(see).* Not in technical usage. [After St. *Vitus,* third-century Christian child martyr, invoked by sufferers of the disease.]

sty[1] (stī) n., pl. **sties.** 1. An enclosure for pigs. 2. Any filthy place. ~v. **stied, stying, sties.** —tr. To shut up in a sty. —intr. To live in a sty. [Middle English *sty,* Old English *stī, stig,* from Germanic *stijam* (unattested).]

sty[2], **stye** (stī) n., pl. **sties** or **styes.** Inflammation of one or more sebaceous glands of an eyelid. [Obsolete *styany* (taken as *sty-on-eye*), Middle English *styanye* : *styan* (unattested), sty, "swelling", from Old English *stīgend,* present participle of *stīgan,* to rise + EYE.]

styg·i·an (stíji-ən) adj. Sometimes capital S. 1. Of or pertaining to the river Styx. 2. a. Gloomy and dark. b. Infernal; hellish. [Latin *Stygius,* from Greek *Stugios,* from *Stux,* Styx.]

sty·lar (stílər) adj. 1. Of, pertaining to, or resembling a stylus. 2. Biology. Of or pertaining to a style.

sty·late (stílayt) n. Biology. Having a style or styles.

style (stīl) n. 1. The way in which something is written, said, shown, or done, as distinguished from its substance. 2. The combination of distinctive features of literary or artistic expression, execution, or performance characterising a particular person, people, school, or era. 3. A sort; a kind; a type: *a style of furniture.* 4. A quality of imagination and individuality expressed in one's actions and tastes and personal appearance: *She's got style; dresses with style.* 5. a. A comfortable and elegant way of living or behaving: *dined in style.* b. A particular mode of living: *the style of a gentleman.* 6. a. The fashion of the moment, especially of dress; a vogue. Used chiefly in the phrases *out of style* or *in style.* b. A particular fashion. 7. A particular set of conventions favoured by a publisher or publication in presenting printed material, including usage, punctuation, spelling, typography, and arrangement. 8. Formal. A name, title, or descriptive term: *has the style of Prince William of Wales.* 9. A slender, pointed instrument used to write on wax tablets in ancient times. 10. An implement used for etching or engraving. 11. The shadow-casting projection on a sundial; a gnomon. 12. Botany. The usually slender part of a pistil, rising from the ovary and tipped by the stigma. 13. Zoology. Any slender, tubular, or bristle-like process. 14. Obsolete. A pen. 15. A surgical probing instrument; a stylet. **—See Synonyms at fashion. —cramp (someone's) style.** Informal. To inhibit (someone's) freedom of action or expression: *You rather cramped my style with Sarah at the party.*

~v. **styled, styling, styles.** —tr. 1. To design; give style to: *style hair.* 2. To make consistent with the rules of style. 3. Formal. To call or name; designate: *styled themselves expert.* —intr. To admit of styling. Used of hair. [Middle English, from Old French, from Latin *stilus†,* writing instrument, style.] **—styl·er** n.

-style adv. & adj. comb. form. In or imitating the manner of the thing specified: *a thirties-style dress.*

style book n. A book giving rules and examples of usage, punctuation, and typography, used in the preparation of copy for publication. Also called "style guide".

sty·let (stílit) n. 1. A slender, pointed instrument or weapon, such as a stiletto. 2. A surgical probe; a style. 3. A wire inserted into a catheter to maintain its shape or remove an obstruction. 4. Zoology. A small, stiff, needle-like process in some invertebrates, such as the mouth parts of an aphid. [French, from Italian *stiletto,* STILETTO.]

sty·li·form (stíli-fawrm) adj. Having the shape of a style (sense 13); bristle-like. [STYLO- + -FORM.]

styl·ise, styl·ize (stíl-īz) tr.v. **-ised, -ising, -ises.** 1. To subordinate verisimilitude to principles of design in the representation of. 2. To represent conventionally; conventionalise. **—styl·i·sa·tion** (-ī-záysh'n || U.S. -i-) n. **—styl·is·er** n.

styl·ish (stílish) adj. 1. In step with current fashion. 2. Showing or having natural elegance. **—styl·ish·ly** adv. **—styl·ish·ness** n.

styl·ist (stílist) n. 1. A writer or performer who cultivates an approved or distinctive artistic style. 2. A designer of or consultant on styles in decorating, dress, cosmetics, or hairdressing.

sty·lis·tic (stī-lístik) adj. Of or pertaining to style, especially to artistic or literary style. **—sty·lis·ti·cal·ly** adv.

sty·lis·tics (stī-lístiks) n. Used with a singular verb. A branch of linguistics which studies the use of language styles in particular contexts.

sty·lite (stíl-īt) n. Any early Christian ascetic who lived unsheltered on the top of a high pillar. [Late Greek *stulitēs* : Greek *stulos,* pillar + -ITE.] **—sty·lit·ic** (stī-líttik) adj. **—sty·lit·ism** (-īt-iz'm) n.

stylo-, styl- comb. form. Indicates: 1. Biology. A style; for example, **stylopodium.** 2. A point, pillar, or styloid process; for example, **stylograph.** [Latin *stilus,* stalk, STYLE.]

sty·lo·bate (stíl-ō-bayt, -ə-) n. Architecture. The immediate foundation of a row of classical columns. See **stereobate.** [Latin *stylobata,* from Greek *stulobatēs,* column base : *stulos,* column + *-bates,* "one that is based".]

sty·lo·graph (stíl-ə-graaf, -ō-, -graf) n. A fountain pen having a tubular writing point instead of a nib. Also called "stylographic pen". [STYLO- + -GRAPH.]

sty·log·ra·phy (stī-lóggrəfi) n. The art or a method of etching, engraving, or writing with a style. [STYLO- + -GRAPHY.] **—sty·lo·graph·ic** (stílə-gráffik), **sty·lo·graph·i·cal** adj.

sty·loid (stíl-oyd) adj. Slender and pointed. [New Latin *styloides,* resembling a style (after Greek *styloeidēs,* pillar-like) : STYL(O)- + -OID.]

sty·lo·lite (stílə-līt) n. A small columnar rock development in limestone and other calcareous rocks that is usually at right angles to the bedding planes, and is of irregular cross-section with striated sides. [STYLO- + -LITE.] **—sty·lo·lit·ic** (-líttik) adj.

sty·lo·po·di·um (stílə-pŏdi-əm) n., pl. **-dia** (-ə). Botany. An enlargement at the base of the style of certain flowers. [New Latin : STYLO- + -PODIUM.]

sty·lops (stí-lops) n. Any of various minute parasitic insects of the order Strepsiptera, which live inside other insects. [New Latin, from Greek : *stulos,* pillar, column + *ōps,* eye (referring to the stalked eye of the male).]

sty·lo·stix·is (stī-lō-stíksiss, -lə-) n. Acupuncture *(see).* [New Latin, from Greek *stulos,* stylus, needle + *stixis,* spot, mark.]

sty·lus (stí-ləss) n., pl. **-luses** or **-li** (-lī). 1. A sharp, pointed instrument used for writing, marking, or engraving. 2. A needle or jewel in the cartridge of a gramophone pickup that senses the undulations in the record grooves. 3. The sharp, pointed tool used for cutting record grooves. [Latin *stilus*, STYLE.]

sty·mie, sty·my (stīmi) *n.* **1.** A situation in golf in which one ball obstructs the line of play of another on the putting green. **2.** An impasse; a quandary.
~*tr.v.* **stymied, -mieing** or **-mying, -mies.** Also **sty·my, -mied, -mying, -mies.** To block, thwart, or baffle. [19th century : origin obscure.]

styp·sis (stipsiss) *n.* The action or application of a styptic. [Late Latin *stypsis*, from Greek *stupsis*, contraction, astringency, from *stuphein*, to contract. See styptic.]

styp·tic (stiptik) *adj.* Also **styp·ti·cal** (-'l). Arresting bleeding; haemostatic; astringent.
~*n.* A styptic drug or substance. [Middle English *stiptik*, from Late Latin *stypticus*, from Greek *stuptikos*, from *stuphein*, to contract.] —**styp·tic·i·ty** (stip-tíssəti) *n.*

styptic pencil *n.* A small cosmetic applicator used to stanch shaving and similar small cuts.

sty·rax (stīr-aks) *n.* **1.** A resin, **storax** (see). **2.** Any tree of the genus *Styrax*. —**sty·ra·ca·ceous** (-ə-káyshəss) *adj.*

sty·rene (stīr-een) *n.* A colourless oily liquid, C_8H_8, the monomer for **polystyrene** (see). [Latin *styrax, storax*, STORAX (from which styrene is obtained by distillation) + -ENE.]

Styr·i·a (stéer-i-ə). German **Stei·er·mark** (shtī-ər-maark). State and ancient province in southeast Austria. It is mountainous, and is a mining area, with deposits of lignite, iron ore, and magnesite. Graz is the capital.

Styx (stiks) *n. Greek Mythology.* A river of Hades, across which Charon ferried the souls of the dead. [Latin, from Greek *stux.*]

SU Strontium unit.

su·a·ble (séw-əb'l, sōō-) *adj.* Legally subject to a court suit; capable of or liable to being sued. —**su·a·bil·i·ty** (-ə-bílləti) *n.*

sua·sion (swáyzhn) *n. Rare.* Persuasion. Used chiefly in the phrase *moral suasion.* [Middle English, from Latin *suāsiō* (stem *suāsiōn-*), from *suādēre* (past participle *suāsus*), to persuade.] —**sua·sive** (swáy-siv ‖ -ziv) *adj.*

suave (swaav, swayv) *adj.* Smoothly gracious, as in social manner; urbane. [French, from Latin *suāvis*, delightful.] —**suave·ly** *adv.* —**suav·i·ty, suave·ness** *n.*
Synonyms: *suave, smooth, urbane, diplomatic.*

sub (sub) *n. Informal.* **1.** A submarine. **2.** A substitute. **3.** A subeditor. **4.** A subscription. **5.** *British.* An advance payment of wages. **6.** A subaltern.
~*v.* **subbed, subbing, subs.** —*intr. Informal.* To act as a substitute. —*tr.* **1.** *Informal.* **a.** To give or receive (an advance payment of wages). **b.** To request a loan from. **2.** To subedit. **3.** To apply a substratum to (a photographic film or plate base).

sub– *prefix.* Indicates: **1.** Under or beneath; for example, **submarine. 2.** Inferior or secondary in rank; for example, **sublieutenant. 3.** Somewhat short of or less than; for example, **subhuman, subtropical. 4.** Forming a subordinate or constituent part of a whole; for example, **subdivision, subset.** *Note:* Many compounds other than those entered here may be formed with *sub-*. In this dictionary in forming compounds, *sub-* is normally joined with the following element without space or hyphen: *subgroup.* However, many users prefer the hyphenated form, especially in less standardised compounds: *sub-foreman.* [In borrowed Latin compounds, *sub-* indicates: 1. Under, as in **suppose.** 2. Below, beneath, as in **subaltern.** 3. Down, as in **supplicate.** 4. Up from under, from below, as in **supplant.** 5. Up, towards, as in **support.** 6. Subordinate, as in **subdeacon.** 7. Secretly, as in **suborn.** 8. In place of, as in **substitute.** Before *c, f, g, m, p,* and *r, sub-* becomes, respectively, *suc-, suf-, sug-, sum-, sup-,* and *sur-.* Sometimes it also becomes *sus-* before *c, p,* and *t.* Latin *sub-*, from *sub*, under, from below.]

sub. **1.** *Logic.* subaltern. **2.** *Music.* subito. **3.** subscription. **4.** substitute. **5.** suburb; suburban.

sub·ac·id (súb-ássid) *adj.* Moderately acid or tart. —**sub·a·cid·i·ty** (súb-ə-síddəti, -a-) *n.*

sub·a·cute (súb-ə-kéwt) *adj.* Between acute and chronic. Said of a disease. —**sub·a·cute·ly** *adv.*

sub·aer·i·al (súb-áir-i-əl) *adj.* Located or occurring on or near the surface of the earth.

sub·al·pine (súb-ál-pīn) *adj.* **1.** Of or pertaining to regions at or near the foot of the Alps. **2.** Of, designating, or growing or living in mountainous regions just below the treeline.

sub·al·tern (súbb'l-tərn ‖ *U.S.* sə-báwl-) *adj.* **1.** *Chiefly British.* Holding a military rank just below that of captain. **2.** Lower in position or rank; secondary. **3.** *Logic.* **a.** Designating a particular proposition in relation to a universal with the same subject, predicate, and quality. **b.** Designating such a relationship.
~*n.* **1.** *Chiefly British.* A subaltern officer. **2.** A subordinate. **3.** *Abbr.* **sub.** *Logic.* A subaltern proposition or relation. [Late Latin *subalternus* : Latin *sub-*, below + *alternus*, ALTERNATE.]

sub·al·ter·nate (sub-áwl-tər-nət, -nit, -nayt ‖ -ól-) *adj.* **1.** Subordinate. **2.** Arranged alternately but tending to become opposite. Said of leaves. **3.** Following in turn. —**sub·al·ter·na·tion** *n.*

sub·ant·arc·tic (súb-ant-árktik ‖ -ártik) *adj.* Of or resembling regions just north of the Antarctic Circle.

sub·ap·i·cal (súb-áypik'l, -áppik') *adj.* Located below or near an apex. —**sub·ap·i·cal·ly** *adv.*

sub·ap·o·stol·ic (súb-áppə-stóllik) *adj.* Of, pertaining to, or designating the era after that of the Apostles of Jesus.

sub·aq·ua (súb-ákwə ‖ *U.S. also* -áakwə) *adj.* Of or pertaining to underwater sport: *a subaqua club.* [SUB- + Latin *aqua*, water.]

sub·a·quat·ic (súb-ə-kwáttik, -kwóttik) *adj.* **1.** Living or growing partly on land and partly in water. **2.** Underwater.

sub·a·que·ous (súb-áykwi-əss, -ákwi-) *adj.* **1.** Formed or adapted for underwater use. **2.** Found or occurring under water.

sub·arc·tic (súb-árktik ‖ -ártik) *adj.* Of or like regions just south of the Arctic Circle.

sub·ar·id (súb-árrid) *adj.* Semiarid.

sub·a·tom·ic (súb-ə-tómmik) *adj.* **1.** Of or pertaining to the constituents of the atom. **2.** Having dimensions or participating in reactions characteristic of these constituents.

sub·au·di·tion (súb-aw-dísh'n) *n.* **1.** The act of understanding and mentally supplying a word or thought that has been implied but not expressed. **2.** A word or thought thus supplied. [Late Latin *subaudītiō*, from *subaudīre*, to supply an omitted word : *sub-*, secretly + *audīre*, to hear.]

sub·base (súb-bayss) *n. Architecture.* The lowermost front strip or moulding of a pedestal or wainscot.

sub·base·ment (súb-bayssmənt) *n.* Any storey or floor beneath the main basement of a building.

sub·bass (súb-bayss) *n. Music.* A pedal stop on an organ that produces the lowest notes, having 16 or 32 feet; a bourdon.

sub·cal·i·bre (súb-kál-ibər) *adj.* **1.** Smaller in calibre than the barrel of the gun from which it is fired. Said of projectiles. **2.** Of or pertaining to such projectiles.

sub·cat·e·go·ry (súb-kátti-gri, -gəri) *n.* A subdivision of a category.

sub·ce·les·tial (súb-si-lésti-əl ‖ -léss-chəl) *adj.* **1.** Lower than celestial; terrestrial. **2.** Mundane.
~*n.* A subcelestial object.

sub·cep·tion (súb-sépsh'n, səb-) *n. Psychology.* Subliminal perception. [*Subliminal per*ception.]

sub·chas·er (súb-chayssər) *n. Nautical.* A submarine chaser.

sub·class (súb-klaass ‖ -klass) *n.* **1.** A subdivision of a class. **2.** A taxonomic category ranking between a class and an order. **3.** *Mathematics.* A subset.
~*tr.v.* **subclassed, -classing, -classes.** To assign to a subclass.

sub·cla·vi·an (súb-kláyvi-ən) *adj. Anatomy.* **1.** Situated beneath the clavicle. **2.** Of or pertaining to a subclavian part.
~*n.* A subclavian structure, such as a vein, nerve, or muscle. [New Latin *subclavius* : SUB- + Latin *clāvis*, key (see **clavicle**).]

subclavian artery *n.* A short part of a major artery originating under the clavicle and continuous with the axillary artery extending to the upper extremities or forelimbs.

subclavian vein *n.* A part of a major vein of the upper extremities or forelimbs that is continuous with the axillary vein and is situated beneath the clavicle.

sub·cli·max (súb-klī-maks) *n.* **1.** A stage in the ecological succession of a plant or animal community immediately preceding a climax, and often persisting because of the effects of fire, flood, or other conditions. **2.** A plant or animal community at this stage. —**sub·cli·mac·tic** (-klī-máktik) *adj.*

sub·clin·i·cal (súb-klínnik'l) *adj.* Of or pertaining to a disease or the stage of a disease in which signs and symptoms are not yet apparent. —**sub·clin·i·cal·ly** *adv.*

sub·com·mit·tee (súb-kə-mitti) *n.* A subordinate committee composed of members appointed from or by the main committee, to deal with matters in more detail.

sub·con·scious (súb-kónshəss) *adj.* **1.** Not wholly conscious but capable of being made conscious. **2.** Acting or existing without being consciously recognised: *subconscious desires.*
~*n.* The subconscious mind; the unperceived source of conscious emotions, fantasies, and dreams. See Usage note at **conscious.** —**sub·con·scious·ly** *adv.* —**sub·con·scious·ness** *n.*

sub·con·ti·nent (súb-kónti-nənt) *n.* A large land mass on a continent, but in some geographical or political respect independent of it, such as India. —**sub·con·ti·nen·tal** (-nént'l) *adj.*

sub·con·tract (súb-kón-trakt) *n.* A contract that assigns some of the obligations of a prior contract to another party.
~*v.* (-kən-trákt ‖ -kon-, -kon-trakt) **subcontracted, -tracting, -tracts.** —*tr.* To make a subcontract for. Used of the original contractor. —*intr.* To make a subcontract.

sub·con·trac·tor (súb-kən-tráktər ‖ -kón-traktər) *n.* A person or company that enters into a subcontract and assumes some of the obligations of the primary contractor; specifically, one who undertakes a particular part of the work in the construction of a building.

sub·con·tra·oc·tave (súb-kóntrə-ók-tiv, -tayv) *n. Music.* The octave that begins on the fourth C below middle C.

sub·con·tra·ry (súb-kóntrəri ‖ *U.S.* -kón-trerri) —*adj. Logic.* **1.** Being or designating either or both of a pair of propositions related in such a way that they cannot both be false at once, although they may be true together.
~*n., pl.* **subcontraries.** *Logic.* Either of the two propositions of this type. —**sub·con·tra·ri·e·ty** *n.*

sub·cor·tex (súb-kór-teks) *n., pl.* **-tices** (-ti-seez). The portion of the brain immediately below the cerebral cortex. —**sub·cor·ti·cal** (-tik'l) *adj.* —**sub·cor·ti·cal·ly** *adv.*

sub·crit·i·cal (súb-kríttik'l) *n.* Not having or involving a self-sustaining chain reaction. Said of nuclear reactions and reactors.

sub·cul·ture (súb-kulchər) *n.* **1.** One culture of microorganisms derived from another. **2.** A cultural subgroup, especially of a nation, differentiated by ethnic background, religion, beliefs, lifestyle, or other factors that functionally unify the group and act collectively on each member.
~*tr.v.* **subcultured, -turing, -tures.** To transfer (bacteria from a

culture) on to a new culture medium. —**sub·cul·tur·al** *adj.*

sub·cu·ta·ne·ous (súb-kew-táyni-əss) *adj.* Located or introduced just beneath the skin. —**sub·cu·ta·ne·ous·ly** *adv.*

sub·dea·con (súb-deékən) *n.* **1. a.** Formerly in the Roman Catholic Church, a candidate ordained to the lowest of the major orders. **b.** In certain other churches, a minister with rank just below that of deacon. **2.** A minister who acts as assistant to the deacon at High Mass. [Middle English *subde(a)con,* from Late Latin *subdiaconus,* partial translation of Late Greek *hupodiakonos* : Greek *hupo-,* below, subordinate + *diakonos,* DEACON.]

sub·di·ac·o·nate (súb-dī-áckə-nət, -nit, -nayt) *n.* The office, order, or rank of subdeacon. [Late Latin *subdiaconātus,* from *subdiaconus,* SUBDEACON.] —**sub·di·ac·o·nal** *adj.*

sub·di·vide (súb-di-vīd) *v.* **-vided, -viding, -vides.** —*tr.* **1.** To divide (a part or parts resulting from earlier division) into smaller parts. **2. a.** To divide into a number of parts. **b.** *U.S.* To divide (land) into lots for sale. —*intr.* To form into subdivisions. [Middle English *subdividen,* from Late Latin *subdīvidere* : Latin *sub-,* secondary, smaller + *dīvidere,* to DIVIDE.] —**sub·di·vid·er** *n.*

sub·di·vi·sion (súb-di-vi<u>zh</u>'n, -vi<u>zh</u>'n) *n.* **1.** The act or process of subdividing. **2.** Any of the subdivided parts. **3.** *Botany.* A taxonomic category ranking between a division and a class. **4.** *U.S.* An area composed of subdivided lots. —**sub·di·vi·sion·al** *adj.*

sub·dom·i·nant (súb-dómminənt) *n. Music.* **1.** The fourth note of a diatonic scale, coming below the dominant. **2.** A key or chord based on this note.
~*adj.* **1.** Influential but not quite dominant. **2.** *Music.* Of or pertaining to a subdominant.

sub·duc·tion zone (súb-dúksh'n) *n.* A long narrow zone along which oceanic lithosphere moves down into, and is assimilated by, the Earth's interior. Also called a "Benioff zone".

sub·due (səb-déw || sub-, -dóo) *tr.v.* **-dued, -duing, -dues. 1.** To conquer and subjugate; put down; vanquish. **2.** To quieten or bring under control by physical force or persuasion; make tractable. **3.** To make less intense or prominent; suppress; tone down: *A vote of approval subdued his anger.* **4.** To bring (land) under cultivation. —See Synonyms at **defeat.** [Middle English *subduen,* from Latin *subdūcere,* to lead away, withdraw (but influenced in sense by Latin *subdere,* to put under, subdue) : *sub-,* from under, away + *dūcere,* to lead.] —**sub·du·a·ble** *adj.* —**sub·du·al** *n.* —**sub·du·er** *n.*

sub·dued (səb-déwd || sub-, -dóod) *adj.* **1.** Uncharacteristically quiet, as through tiredness or shyness. **2.** Gentle; of only moderate strength or intensity: *subdued lighting.* **3.** Expressed only in an inhibited way: *subdued laughter.*

sub·dur·al (súb-déwr-əl || -dóor-) *adj. Anatomy.* Situated or occurring below the dura mater. [SUB + *dural,* from DURA (MATER).] —**sub·dur·al·ly** *adv.*

sub·ed·it (súb-éddit) *tr.v.* **-ited, -iting, -its.** To re-edit and correct (written or printed material). —**sub·ed·i·tor** (-ər) *n.* —**sub·ed·i·to·ri·al** (-éddi-táw-ri-əl || -tō) *adj.*

sub·e·qua·to·ri·al (súb-ékwə-táwri-əl || -eékwə-, -tōri-) *adj.* Belonging to a region adjacent to the equatorial area.

su·ber·ic acid (sew-bérrik, sōō-) *n.* A colourless crystalline dibasic acid, $HOOC(CH_2)_6CO_2H$, used in drug synthesis and plastics manufacture. Also called "octanedioic acid". [French *subérique,* from Latin *sūber,* cork (from which the acid is obtained).]

su·ber·in (séwbə-rin, sóobə-) *n.* A waxy waterproof substance present in the cell walls of cork tissue in plants. [French *subérine* : Latin *sūber,* cork (see **suberic acid**) + -IN.]

su·ber·ise, su·ber·ize (séwbə-rīz, sóobə-) *tr.v.* **-ised, -ising, -ises.** To cause (plant cell walls) to become impregnated with suberin during the formation of cork. [Latin *sūber,* cork. See **suberic acid.**] —**su·ber·i·sa·tion** (-rī-záysh'n || *U.S.* -ri-) *n.*

su·ber·ose (séwbə-rōz, sóobə-, -rōss) *adj.* Also **su·ber·ous** (-rəss). Of, pertaining to, or resembling cork or cork tissue; corky. [New Latin *suberosus,* from Latin *sūber,* cork. See **suberic acid.**]

sub·fam·i·ly (súb-fám-li, -fámmili) *n., pl.* **-lies. 1.** *Biology.* A taxonomic category ranking between a family and a genus. **2.** *Linguistics.* A division of languages below a family and above a branch.

sub·fix (súb-fiks) *n.* A subscript letter or sign.

sub·fusc (súb-fusk, -fúsk) *adj.* Dusky; dull-coloured.
~*n.* **1.** Dark, usually black, clothing worn with academic dress on formal occasions at Oxford University. **2.** Loosely, formal academic dress. [Latin *subfuscus,* dusky, from *fuscus,* dark brown.]

sub·ge·nus (súb-jeénəss) *n., pl.* **-genera** (-jénnərə). *Biology.* An occasionally used taxonomic category ranking below a genus and above a species. —**sub·ge·ner·ic** (-jə-nérrik) *adj.*

sub·gla·ci·al (súb-gláy-si-əl) *adj.* Formed or deposited beneath a glacier. —**sub·gla·cial·ly** *adv.*

sub·group (súb-gróop) *n.* **1.** A distinct group within a group. **2.** In algebra, a nonempty subset of a group. **3.** A subordinate group.

sub·head (súb-hed) *n.* Also **sub·head·ing** (-ing) (for sense 1). **1.** The heading or title of a subdivision of a printed subject. **2.** A subordinate heading or title.

sub·hu·man (súb-héwmən || -yóomən) *adj.* **1.** Below the human race in evolutionary development. **2.** Not fully human.

sub·i·ma·go (sub-i-máygō, -maágō) *n.* An insect, especially the mayfly, in a stage between the pupa and the imago. —**sub·im·ag·i·nal** (-imájin'l) *adj.*

sub·in·dex (súb-ín-deks) *n., pl.* **-dices** (-di-seez) or **-dexes. 1.** *Mathematics.* A distinguishing character or symbol directly beneath or next to and slightly below a number or letter; a subscript. **2.** An index to a section of a work.

sub·in·feu·date (súb-in-féwdayt) *tr.v.* **-dated, -dating, -dates.** Also **sub·in·feud** (-féwd), **-feuded, -feuding, -feuds.** To lease (lands) by subinfeudation.

sub·in·feu·da·tion (súb-in-few-dáysh'n) *n.* **1.** The sublease of a portion of a feudal estate by a vassal to a subtenant who pays fealty to the vassal. **2.** The tenure established. **3.** The lands so leased.

sub·in·feu·da·to·ry (súb-in-féwdə-tri, -təri) *adj.* Of or pertaining to subinfeudation.
~*n., pl.* **subinfeudatories.** A person who held his fief by subinfeudation.

sub·ir·ri·gate (súb-írri-gayt) *tr.v.* **-gated, -gating, -gates.** To irrigate from beneath, as by means of underground pipes. —**sub·ir·ri·ga·tion** (-gáysh'n) *n.*

su·bi·to (sóobi-tō) *adv. Music. Abbr.* **sub.** Quickly; suddenly. Used as a direction. [Italian, from Latin *subitō,* suddenly, from *subire,* to come secretly, steal upon : *sub-,* secretly + *īre,* to go.]

subj. 1. subject. **2.** subjective. **3.** subjunctive.

sub·ja·cent (súb-jáyss'nt) *adj.* **1.** Located beneath or below; underlying. **2.** Lying at a lower level but not directly beneath. [Latin *subjacēns* (stem *subjacent-*), present participle of *subjacēre,* to lie under : *sub-,* under + *jacēre,* to lie, from *jacere,* to throw.] —**sub·ja·cen·cy** *n.* —**sub·ja·cent·ly** *adj.*

sub·ject (súb-jikt, -jekt) *adj.* **1.** Under the power or authority of another; owing obedience or allegiance to another. **2.** Prone; disposed. Used with *to.* **3.** Liable to incur or receive; exposed. Used with *to.* **4.** Contingent, conditional, or dependent. Used with *to.*
~*n. Abbr.* **subj. 1.** A person under the rule of another; especially, one who owes allegiance to a government or ruler: *a subject of the Crown.* **2. a.** A person or thing concerning which something is said or done; a topic. **b.** That which is treated or indicated in a work of art. **c.** *Music.* A **theme** *(see);* a melodic phrase which is subsequently developed. **3.** A course or area of study. **4.** A basis for action; a cause. Often used with *for: a subject for concern.* **5. a.** One that experiences or is subjected to something. **b.** One that is the object of clinical study, analysis, or treatment. **c.** A corpse intended for study and dissection. **6.** *Grammar.* A noun phrase in a sentence that denotes the doer of the action, the receiver of the action in passive constructions, or that which is described or identified. **7.** *Logic.* The term of a proposition about which something is affirmed or denied. **8.** *Philosophy.* **a.** The essential nature or substance of something as distinguished from its attributes. **b.** The mind or thinking part as distinguished from the object of thought.
~*tr.v.* (səb-jékt, súb-, *rarely* súb-jikt, -jekt) **subjected, -jecting, -jects. 1.** To submit to some discipline or authority; bring under control. **2.** To render liable to something. Often used in the passive. **3.** To cause to experience or undergo something. **4.** *Rare.* To subjugate. **5.** *Rare.* To submit for consideration. [Middle English *su(b)get, subject,* from Old French *su(b)get,* from Latin *subicere* (past participle *subjectus*), to bring under : *sub-,* under + *jacere,* to throw.] —**sub·jec·ta·ble** *adj.* —**sub·jec·tion** (səb-jéksh'n || sub-) *n.*

sub·jec·ti·fy (səb-jékti-fī, sub-) *tr.v.* **-fied, -fying, -fies.** To render subjective; interpret subjectively.

sub·jec·tive (səb-jéktiv, súb-) *adj. Abbr.* **subj. 1. a.** Proceeding from, pertaining to, or taking place within an individual's mind in a manner unrelated to external reality; unfounded: *subjective fears.* **b.** Affected by or arising from one's personality or experience rather than rational thought or observation: *a subjective view.* **c.** Particular to a given individual; personal. **2.** Pertaining to the real nature of something; essential. **3.** Moodily introspective. **4.** *Psychology.* Existing only within the mind and incapable of external verification. **5.** *Medicine.* Designating a symptom or condition perceived by the patient and not by the examiner. **6.** Expressing or bringing into prominence the individuality of the artist or author. **7.** *Grammar.* Designating or being in the nominative case. —**sub·jec·tive·ly** *adv.* —**sub·jec·tive·ness, sub·jec·tiv·i·ty** (súb-jek-tívvəti) *n.*

subjective complement *n. Grammar.* A noun, noun phrase, or adjective serving as a complement to a verb and qualifying its subject. In *He made her a good husband, husband* is a subjective complement.

subjective genitive *n. Grammar.* **1.** The genitive case as indicating the subject of a specified action. Thus in the phrase *my love for her,* meaning "the love I bear her", the subject *(I)* is transferred to the genitive case *(my).* Compare **objective genitive. 2.** A noun or pronoun in this case.

subjective idealism *n. Philosophy.* The theory that all experience is of ideas in the mind.

sub·jec·tiv·ism (səb-jéktiv-iz'm, sub-) *n.* **1. a.** The doctrine that all knowledge is restricted to the conscious self and its sensory states. **b.** Any theory or doctrine, especially theological, that emphasises the subjective elements in experience. **2.** The theory that individual conscience is the only valid standard of moral judgment. **3.** The quality of being subjective. —**sub·jec·tiv·ist** *n.* —**sub·jec·tiv·is·tic** (-ístik) *adj.*

subject matter *n.* The matter under consideration in a written work, speech, or discussion; the theme. [Translation of Latin *subjecta materia,* translation of Greek *hupokeimenē hulē,* "underlying matter".]

sub·join (súb-jóyn) *tr.v.* **-joined, -joining, -joins.** To add at the end; append; annex. [From obsolete French *subjoindre,* from Latin *subjungere* : *sub-,* in addition + *jungere,* to join.]

sub·join·der (súb-jóyndər) *n.* Something subjoined. [From SUBJOIN.]

sub ju·di·ce (súb jóodi-si, sóob yóodi-ki) *adj. Law.* **1.** Under judicial deliberation; before a judge or court of law, and thus outside the scope of public comment. **2.** Not yet decided; still subject to confidential discussion. [Latin, "under a judge".] **—sub ju·di·ce** *adv.*

sub·ju·gate (súb-jōō-gayt, -jə-) *tr.v.* **-gated, -gating, -gates. 1.** To bring under dominion; conquer; subdue. **2.** To make subservient; subdue. —See Synonyms at **defeat.** [Middle English *subjugaten,* from Latin *subjugāre,* to place under a yoke : *sub-,* under + *jugum,* yoke.] **—sub·ju·ga·tion** (-gáysh'n) *n.* **—sub·ju·ga·tor** (-gaytər) *n.*

sub·junc·tion (səb-júngksh'n, súb-) *n.* **1.** The act of subjoining or the condition of being subjoined. **2.** Something that is subjoined. [Late Latin *subjunctiō* (stem *subjunctiōn-*), from *subjungere* (past participle *subjunctus*), SUBJOIN.]

sub·junc·tive (səb-júngktiv || sub-) *adj. Abbr.* **subj.** *Grammar.* Designating a verb form or set of forms used to express a contingent or hypothetical action or state, for example one that is feared, desired, or doubted. Compare **indicative.**

~n. Abbr. **subj. 1.** The subjunctive mood. **2.** A subjunctive verb or construction. [Late Latin *(mōdus) subjunctīvus,* translation of Greek *hupotaktikē enklisis,* "mood of subordination" (originally regarded as proper to subordinate clauses), from Latin *subjungere,* SUBJOIN.] **—sub·junc·tive·ly** *adv.*

sub·king·dom (súb-king-dəm, -kíng-) *n. Biology.* A former taxonomic category constituting a major division of a kingdom.

sub·lap·sar·i·an·ism (súb-lap-sáir-i-ən-iz'm) *n. Theology.* **Infralapsarianism** *(see).* [New Latin *sublapsarius* : SUB- + LAPSE.] **—sub·lap·sar·i·an** *adj.* & *n.*

sub·lease (súb-léess) *tr.v.* **-leased, -leasing, -leases. 1.** To sublet (property). **2.** To rent (property) under a sublease.

~n. (súb-leess). A lease of property granted in turn by a lessee.

sub·les·see (súb-le-sée) *n.* One to whom a sublease is granted.

sub·les·sor (súb-le-sór) *n.* One granting a sublease.

sub·let (súb-let) *tr.v.* **-let, -letting, -lets. 1.** To rent (property one holds by lease) to another. **2.** To subcontract (work).

~n. **1.** An instance of subletting. **2.** *Chiefly U.S. Informal.* Property, especially a flat, rented by a tenant to another party.

sub·lieu·ten·ant (súb-lə-ténnənt, -le-, -lōō-, *also* -lef-) *n.* An officer in the Royal Navy and certain other navies, ranking below a lieutenant, equivalent in rank to a lieutenant in the army and a flying officer in the Royal Air Force. **—sub·lieu·ten·an·cy** *n.*

sub·li·mate (súbbli-mayt) *v.* **-mated, -mating, -mates.** *—tr.* **1.** *Psychology.* To transform (an instinctual impulse, especially a sexual urge, which cannot be immediately fulfilled) into more socially acceptable forms of expression, behaviour, or activity. **2.** To cause (a solid or a gas) to change state without becoming a liquid. *—intr.* To change directly from the solid to the gaseous state or from the gaseous to the solid state without becoming a liquid.

~n. (*also* -mət, -mit). The material formed by sublimation.

~adj. Exalted or purified. [Latin *sublīmāre,* to raise, from *sublīmis,* uplifted, SUBLIME.] **—sub·li·ma·tion** *n.*

sub·lime (sə-blīm) *adj.* **1.** Characterised by nobility; grand; majestic. **2. a.** Of high spiritual, moral, or intellectual worth. **b.** Not to be excelled; supreme. Sometimes used ironically: *sublime ignorance.* **3.** Inspiring awe; impressive; moving. **4.** *Poetic.* Of lofty appearance or bearing; proud. **5.** *Archaic.* Raised aloft; set high.

~n. **1.** That which is sublime. Preceded by *the.* **2.** *Rare.* The ultimate example of something. Preceded by *the.*

~v. **sublimed, -liming, -limes.** *—tr.* **1.** To render sublime; elevate; ennoble. **2.** *Chemistry.* To cause to sublimate. *—intr. Chemistry.* To sublimate. [Latin *sublīmis.* See **limen.**] **—sub·lime·ly** *adv.* **—sub·lim·er** *n.* **—sub·lim·i·ty** (sə-blímməti), **sub·lime·ness** *n.*

sub·lim·i·nal (súb-límmin'l, səb-) *adj. Psychology.* **1.** Being or acting below the threshold of conscious perception. Said of stimuli. **2.** Inadequate to produce conscious awareness. [SUB- + Latin *līmen* (stem *līmin-*), threshold (see **limen**).] **—sub·lim·i·nal·ly** *adv.*

subliminal advertising *n.* A now illegal advertising technique of interspersing straightforward film with persuasive, split-second images held to influence the viewer subliminally.

sub·lin·gual (súb-líng-gwəl) *adj.* Situated beneath or on the underside of the tongue: *sublingual salivary glands.*

sub·lit·to·ral (súb-líttərəl) *adj.* **1.** Near the seashore. **2.** Shallow and lying between the shoreline and the edge of the continental shelf.

sub·lu·nar·y (súb-lōō-nəri || -léw-) *adj.* Also **sub·lu·nar** (-nər). **1.** Situated beneath the moon. **2.** *Literary.* Of this world; earthly. [Late Latin *sublūnāris* : Latin *sub-,* beneath + *lūna,* moon.]

sub·lux·a·tion (súb-luk-sáysh'n) *n.* Incomplete dislocation of a joint.

sub·ma·chine gun (súb-mə-shéen) *n.* A lightweight automatic or semiautomatic gun fired from the shoulder or hip. Compare **machine gun.**

sub·man·dib·u·lar (súb-man-díbbewlər) *adj.* Submaxillary.

sub·mar·gin·al (súb-márjin'l) *adj.* **1.** Beneath a margin. **2.** Below the minimum requirements. **3.** Of low productivity; infertile.

sub·ma·rine (súb-mə-reen, -réen) *adj.* **1.** Located, occurring, or functioning beneath the surface of the water; undersea. **2.** Of or pertaining to a submarine.

~n. **1.** A vessel capable of operating submerged. **2.** *U.S. Informal.* A sandwich, a **hero** *(see).*

sub·mar·i·ner (súb-márrinər || -mə-réenər) *n.* A member of the crew of a submarine.

sub·max·il·lar·y (súb-mak-sílləri || *U.S.* -máksə-lerri) *adj.* Of or relating to the lower jaw or the region adjacent to it; submandibular.

~n., pl. **submaxillaries.** An anatomical part situated beneath the maxilla, such as the submaxillary salivary gland.

sub·me·di·ant (súb-méedi-ənt) *n. Music.* **1.** The sixth note of a diatonic scale. **2.** A key or chord based on this.

~adj. Of or pertaining to the submediant. [SUB- + MEDIANT.]

sub·merge (səb-mérj, sub-) *v.* **-merged, -merging, -merges.** *—tr.* **1.** To place or plunge under water or other liquid. **2.** To cover with water; inundate. **3.** To hide from view; obscure. **4.** To overwhelm. *—intr.* To go under or as if under water. [Latin *submergere* : *sub-,* under + *mergere,* to immerse, plunge.] **—sub·mer·gence** *n.*

sub·merged (səb-mérjd, sub-) *adj.* Also **sub·mersed** (-mérst) (for sense 1). **1.** *Botany.* Growing or remaining under water: *submerged leaves.* **2.** Growing permanently under water. Said of certain aquatic plants. **3.** Hidden.

sub·mer·gi·ble (səb-mérj-əb'l, sub-) *adj.* Submersible. **—sub·mer·gi·bil·i·ty** (-ə-bílləti) *n.*

sub·merse (səb-mérss, sub-) *tr.v.* **-mersed, -mersing, -merses.** To submerge. [Latin *submergere* (past participle *submersus*), SUBMERGE.] **—sub·mer·sion** (-mérsh'n || -mérzh'n) *n.*

sub·mers·i·ble (səb-mér-sib'l, sub-, -səb'l) *adj.* Able to be plunged into or to remain under water.

~n. **1.** A vessel capable of operating or remaining under water, such as a bathysphere. **2.** *Archaic.* A submarine.

sub·mi·cro·scop·ic (súb-mīkrə-skóppik) *adj.* Too small to be seen through an optical microscope. **—sub·mi·cro·scop·ical·ly** *adv.*

sub·min·i·a·ture (súb-mínnə-chər, -mínni-ə-, -tewr) *adj.* Smaller than miniature; exceedingly small.

sub·min·i·a·tur·ise, sub·min·i·a·tur·ize (súb-mínnə-chə-rīz, -mínni-ə-) *tr.v.* **-ised, -ising, -ises.** To make subminiature; especially, to manufacture or design (electronic equipment) in subminiature size. **—sub·min·i·a·tur·i·sa·tion** (-rī-záysh'n || *U.S.* -ri-) *n.*

sub·miss (səb-míss || sub-) *adj. Archaic.* **1.** Submissive. **2.** Soft in tone. [Latin *submissus,* past participle of *submittere,* SUBMIT.]

sub·mis·sion (səb-mísh'n || sub-) *n.* **1. a.** The act of submitting to the power of another. **b.** The state of having submitted. **2.** The state of being submissive or compliant; meekness. **3. a.** The act of submitting something, such as a document, for consideration. **b.** Something thus submitted. —See Synonyms at **surrender.**

sub·mis·sive (səb-míssiv || sub-) *adj.* **1.** Disposed to submit; docile. **2.** Indicating or marked by submission. —See Synonyms at **obedient. —sub·mis·sive·ly** *adv.* **—sub·mis·sive·ness** *n.*

sub·mit (səb-mít || sub-) *v.* **-mitted, -mitting, -mits.** *—tr.* **1.** To yield or surrender (oneself) to the will or authority of another or others. **2.** To subject to some condition or process. **3.** To refer (something) to the consideration or judgment of another. **4.** To offer as a proposition or contention: *I submit that they lied.* *—intr.* To yield or give way, especially to one considered physically, intellectually, or morally superior. —See Synonyms at **yield.** [Middle English *submitten,* from Latin *submittere,* to place under : *sub-,* under + *mittere,* to throw.] **—sub·mit·tal** *n.* **—sub·mit·ter** *n.*

sub·mon·tane (súb-móntayn || -mon-táyn) *adj.* Located under or at the base of a mountain or mountain range. [Late Latin *submontānus* : Latin *sub-,* under + *montānus,* mountainous, from *mōns,* mountain.] **—sub·mon·tane·ly** *adv.*

sub·mu·co·sa (súb-mew-kṓ-sə, -zə) *n.* The layer of connective tissue that lies beneath a mucous membrane. **—sub·mu·co·sal** *adj.*

sub·mul·ti·ple (súb-múltip'l) *n.* A number that is an exact divisor of another number: *2 is a submultiple of 10.* **—sub·mul·ti·ple** *adj.*

sub·nor·mal (súb-nórməl) *adj.* **1.** Less than normal; below the average. **2.** Mentally deficient. See **mental deficiency.**

~n. A person who is subnormal in some respect, as in intelligence or coordination. **—sub·nor·mal·ly** *adv.*

sub·nor·mal·it·y (súb-nawr-mál-əti) *n.* **1.** The state or condition of being subnormal. **2. Mental deficiency** *(see).*

sub·nu·cle·ar (sub-néw-kli-ər || -nōō-) *adj.* **1.** Of or pertaining to the constituents of the nucleus of an atom. **2.** Having dimensions or participating in reactions characteristic of such constituents.

sub·o·ce·an·ic (súb-ṓ-shi-ánnik, -si-) *adj.* Formed, situated, or occurring beneath the ocean or the ocean bed.

sub·or·der (súb-awrdər) *n.* **1.** *Biology.* A taxonomic category ranking after an order and before a family. **2.** A subdivision of any category termed an order. **—sub·or·di·nal** (-órdi-nəl) *adj.*

sub·or·di·nar·y (sub-órd'n-ri, -in-, -əri) *n.* Any of various heraldic bearings that are less important than the ordinaries.

sub·or·di·nate (sə-bórdi-nət, -bórd-, -nit || -nayt) *adj.* **1.** Belonging to a lower or inferior class or rank; minor; secondary. **2.** Occupying a secondary position; of relatively little importance. **3.** Subject to the authority or control of another.

~n. One that is subordinate.

~tr.v. (-nayt) **subordinated, -nating, -nates. 1.** To put in a lower or inferior rank or class. **2.** To treat as having little or less importance. **3.** To make subservient; subdue. [Medieval Latin *subōrdinātus,* past participle of *subōrdināre,* to put in a lower rank : Latin *sub-,* below + *ōrdināre,* to arrange in order, from *ōrdō,* order.] **—sub·or·di·nate·ly** *adv.* **—sub·or·di·nate·ness, sub·or·di·na·tion** (-náysh'n) *n.* **—sub·or·di·na·tive** (-nətiv || -naytiv) *adj.*

subordinate clause *n. Grammar.* A clause that cannot stand alone as a full sentence and that functions within a sentence as an adjectival, adverbial, or noun phrase. Also called "dependent clause".

subordinate conjunction *n. Grammar.* A conjunction that introduces a subordinate clause, such as *that, who, because,* or *if.* Compare **coordinate conjunction.**

sub·or·di·na·tion·ism (sə-bórdi-náysh'n-iz'm || su-) *n. Theology.* The doctrine, often considered heretical, that the second and third persons of the Trinity are subordinate to the first person. —**sub·or·di·na·tion·ist** *n.*

sub·orn (sə-bórn) *tr.v.* **-orned, -orning, -orns. 1. a.** To induce (a person) to commit a wrong or unlawful act. **b.** To induce (a person) to commit perjury. **2.** To procure (perjured testimony). [Latin *subōrnāre* : *sub-*, secretly + *ōrnāre,* to equip.] —**sub·or·na·tion** (súb-awr-náysh'n) *n.* —**sub·orn·er** *n.*

sub·ox·ide (súb-óksīd) *n.* An oxide containing a lower proportion of oxygen than is present in the normal or most common oxide of the element.

sub·phy·lum (súb-fī-ləm, -fī-) *n., pl.* **-la** (-lə). *Biology.* A taxonomic category ranking between a phylum and a class.

sub·plot (súb-plot) *n.* A plot, as in a novel or play, that is secondary and incidental to the main plot.

sub·poe·na (səb-péenə, súb-, sə-) *n.* A legal writ requiring appearance or production in court to give or provide evidence.
~*tr.v.* **subpoenaed, -naing, -nas.** To serve or summon with such a writ. [Latin *sub poenā,* under penalty (first words in the writ) : *sub-*, under + *poenā,* penalty, from Greek *poine.*]

sub·po·lar (súb-pōlər) *adj.* Near the polar regions.

sub-post office *n.* In Britain, a small branch post office, normally within an ordinary shop.

sub·prin·ci·pal (súb-prín-sip'l) *n.* **1.** *Chiefly U.S.* An assistant principal. **2.** An auxiliary or bracing rafter in a frame. **3.** *Music.* An open diapason sub-bass in an organ.

sub·ro·gate (súb-rə-gayt, -rō-) *tr.v.* **-gated, -gating, -gates. 1.** *Law.* To substitute (one person) for another. **2.** *Rare.* To substitute (one thing) for another. [Latin *subrogāre,* "to nominate an alternative candidate" : *sub-*, instead of + *rogāre,* to ask, propose.]

sub·ro·ga·tion (súb-rə-gáysh'n, -rō-) *n. Law.* The substitution of one person for another, especially of one creditor for another.

sub ro·sa (súb rōzə) *adv.* In secret; privately; confidentially. [Latin, "under the rose", from the practice of hanging a rose over a meeting as a symbol of secrecy, from the legend that Cupid once gave Harpocrates, the god of silence, a rose to make him keep the secrets of Venus.] —**sub rosa** *adj.*

sub·rou·tine (súb-rōō-teen) *n. Computing.* A self-contained section of a computer program that can be identified and used more than once during the running of the program.

sub·scap·u·lar (súb-skáppewlər) *adj. Anatomy.* Situated below or on the underside of the scapula.
~*n.* A subscapular part, such as an artery or nerve.

sub·scribe (səb-skrīb || sub-) *v.* **-scribed, -scribing, -scribes.** —*tr.* **1.** To sign (one's name) at the end of a document. **2.** To sign one's name to in attestation, testimony, or consent: *subscribe a will.* **3.** To pledge or contribute (a sum of money). —*intr.* **1.** To contract to receive and pay for regular receipt of a newspaper or periodical or a public service, such as a telephone. **2.** To promise to pay or contribute money. **3.** To express agreement or approval; assent. Used with *to*: *subscribe to that view.* **4.** To sign one's name. **5.** To affix one's signature to a document as a witness or to show consent. **6.** To apply for shares offered on the stock exchange in a limited company. **7.** To undertake to purchase a book prior to publication. —See Synonyms at **assent.** [Middle English *subscriben,* from Latin *subscrībere* : *sub-*, under + *scrībere,* to write.] —**sub·scrib·er** *n.*

subscriber trunk dialling *n. Abbr.* **S.T.D.** A telephone service in Britain enabling subscribers to dial long-distance calls without help from the operator.

sub·script (súb-skript) *adj.* Written beneath.
~*n.* A distinguishing character or symbol written directly beneath or next to and slightly below a letter or number. Compare **superscript.** [Latin *subscriptus,* past participle of *subscrībere,* SUBSCRIBE.]

sub·scrip·tion (səb-skrípsh'n || sub-) *n. Abbr.* **sub., subs. 1.** An order for an advance purchase, as of the issues of a periodical over a certain period of time or of tickets for a series of concerts, plays, or other cultural events. **2.** *Chiefly British.* A sum of money paid at fixed intervals for membership of a society, association, or similar body. **3.** An application for newly issued shares on the stock exchange. **4.** The act of subscribing, especially: **a.** The act of setting one's signature on a document. **b.** The acceptance of a position or belief, especially an article of faith. **c.** The act of contributing money, as to a charitable cause or to finance a future publication. **5.** That which is subscribed, especially: **a.** An inscription. **b.** A charitable donation. —**sub·scrip·tive** *adj.* —**sub·scrip·tive·ly** *adv.*

sub·sec·tion (súb-seksh'n) *n.* A division of a section.

sub·se·quence (súb-si-kwənss || -kwenss) *n.* **1.** That which is subsequent; a sequel. **2.** The fact or quality of being subsequent.

sub·se·quent (súb-si-kwənt || -kwent) *adj.* **1.** Following in time or order; succeeding. **2.** Designating a river that is a tributary to a consequent river. In this sense, compare **obsequent.** —See Usage Note at **consequent.** —**subsequent to.** Following; coming after. [Middle English, from Old French, from Latin *subsequēns,* present participle of *subsequī,* to follow close after : *sub-*, close to, after + *sequī,* to follow.] —**sub·se·quent·ly** *adv.* —**sub·se·quent·ness** *n.*

sub·serve (səb-sérv, sub-) *tr.v.* **-served, -serving, -serves.** To serve to promote (some end); be useful to; further. [Latin *subservīre,* to serve, be subject to : *sub-*, under + *servīre,* SERVE.]

sub·ser·vi·ent (səb-sérvi-ənt, sub-) *adj.* **1.** Subordinate in capacity or function. **2.** Obsequious; servile. **3.** Useful only to further some other purpose; purely instrumental. [Latin *subserviēns* (stem *subservient-*), present participle of *subservīre,* SUBSERVE.] —**sub·ser·vi·ence, sub·ser·vi·en·cy** *n.* —**sub·ser·vi·ent·ly** *adv.*

sub·set (súb-set) *n.* A set, as in mathematics, contained within a set.

sub·shrub (súb-shrub) *n.* **1.** A herbaceous plant having a woody lower stem. **2.** A low shrub; an undershrub.

sub·side (səb-sīd || sub-) *intr.v.* **-sided, -siding, -sides. 1.** To sink to a lower or normal level. **2.** To sink or settle down, as into a sofa. **3.** To sink to the bottom; settle, as sediment does. **4.** To become less agitated or active; abate. —See Synonyms at **decrease.** [Latin *subsīdere,* to sink down : *sub-*, down + *sīdere,* to settle.]

sub·sid·ence (səb-sīd'nss, súb-sidənss) *n.* The act or process of subsiding; especially, the sinking or settlement of ground or of buildings erected on it.

sub·sid·i·ar·i·ty (səb-síddi-árrəti, sub-) *n.* **1.** A principle proposed in European Economic Community discussions by which central authority within the EEC should have a subsidiary function, performing only those tasks that cannot be done better at a more immediate or local level. **2.** A Roman Catholic doctrine, formulated in 1931, by which social and political problems should always be dealt with at the lowest practicable level.

sub·sid·i·ar·y (səb-síddi-əri, -síd-yəri || sub-, -erri) *adj.* **1.** Serving to assist or supplement; auxiliary. **2.** Secondary in importance; subordinate. **3.** *U.S.* Of, pertaining to, or of the nature of a subsidy.
~*n., pl.* **subsidiaries. 1.** One that is subsidiary. **2.** A subsidiary company. **3.** *Music.* A theme subordinate to a main theme or subject. [Latin *subsīdiārius,* in reserve, supporting, from *subsidium,* support, SUBSIDY.] —**sub·sid·i·ar·i·ly** *adv.*

subsidiary company *n.* A company having more than half of its shares owned by another company. Also called "subsidiary".

sub·si·dise, sub·si·dize (súb-si-dīz, -sə-) *tr.v.* **-dised, -dising, -dises. 1.** To assist or support with a subsidy. **2.** To secure the assistance of by granting a subsidy. —**sub·si·di·sa·tion** (-dī-záysh'n || *U.S.* -di-) *n.* —**sub·si·dis·er** *n.*

sub·si·dy (súb-si-di, -sə-) *n., pl.* **-dies. 1.** A sum of money provided to assist a person, enterprise, or nation, usually one unable to be self-financing; especially, government funds for such purposes as financing research, maintaining employment, encouraging development, or stabilising price levels. **2.** Formerly, money granted to the British Crown by Parliament. —See Synonyms at **bonus.** [Middle English *subsidie,* aid, assistance, from Anglo-French, from Latin *subsidium,* reserve troops, hence support, help, from *subsidēre,* to sit down, remain, be placed in reserve : *sub-*, down + *sedēre,* to sit.]

sub·sist (səb-síst || sub-) *v.* **-sisted, -sisting, -sists.** —*intr.* **1.** To be sustained; manage to live. Used with *on* or *by*: *subsisting on a meagre pension.* **2.** To reside in or consist of something specified: *The difference subsists in the quality of their work.* **3. a.** To exist; be. **b.** To remain or continue in existence. **4.** To be logically conceivable. —*tr. Archaic.* To maintain or support with provisions. [Latin *subsistere,* to stand still, stand up, remain standing : *sub-*, from below, up + *sistere,* to cause to stand.] —**sub·sist·er** *n.*

sub·sis·tence (səb-sístənss || sub-) *n.* **1.** The act or state of subsisting, especially in a very basic state. **2.** A means of subsisting; sustenance. —See Synonyms at **livelihood.**
~*adj.* Of, involving, or designating an agricultural system in which the farmer and his family consume the produce, leaving little or nothing to sell. **2.** Of or being money paid to an employee as an advance or to cover incidental expenses. **3.** Of or designating a level of income that is barely sufficient to meet the necessities of life. —**sub·sis·tent** *adj.*

sub·soil (súb-soyl) *n.* The partially decomposed layer of rock underlying the topsoil and overlying the solid rock beneath.
~*tr.v.* **subsoiled, -soiling, -soils.** To plough or turn up the subsoil of. —**sub·soil·er** *n.*

sub·so·lar (súb-sōlər) *adj.* Situated on the Earth apparently directly beneath the Sun.

sub·son·ic (súb-sónnik) *adj.* **1.** Infrasonic. **2.** Having a speed less than that of sound in a designated medium.

sub·spe·cies (súb-spée-sheez, -shiz || -seez) *n., pl.* **subspecies.** *Abbr.* **ssp** *Biology.* A subdivision of a taxonomic species, usually based on geographical distribution. —**sub·spe·cif·ic** (-spə-síffik) *adj.*

subst. 1. substantive. **2.** substitute.

sub·stance (súb-stənss) *n.* **1.** *Philosophy.* The essential nature of anything, as considered apart from its form or attributes; the primary or basic element that receives modifications. **2.** Any kind of matter; a material of which something is composed. **3.** The essence of what is said or written; the gist. **4. a.** That which is solid or real; reality as opposed to appearance. **b.** A solid or substantial quality or character. **5.** Density; body: *Air has little substance.* **6.** Material possessions; wealth: *a man of substance.* [Middle English, essence, from Old French, from Latin *substantia,* from *substāns,* present participle of *substāre,* to be present : *sub-*, up + *stāre,* to stand.]

sub·stan·dard (súb-stándərd) *adj.* **1.** Failing to meet a standard; below standard. **2.** Considered unacceptable usage by the educated members of a speech community.

sub·stan·tial (səb-stánsh'l, -staánsh'l || sub-) *adj.* **1.** Of, pertaining to, or having substance; material. **2.** Not imaginary; true; real. **3.** Solidly built; strong. **4.** Ample; sustaining: *a substantial breakfast.* **5.** Considerable in importance, value, degree, amount, or extent: *won by a substantial margin.* **6.** Practical; virtual: *in substantial agreement.* **7.** Possessing wealth or property; well-to-do. **8.** *Informal.* Fat; stout. Used humorously: *"Running did not come easily to a middle-aged woman of her substantial proportions"* (Ivy St. David).
~*n. Plural.* **1.** The essentials. **2.** Solid things. [Middle English *substancial,* from Late Latin *substantiālis,* from Latin *substantia,* SUBSTANCE.] —**sub·stan·ti·al·i·ty** (-stánshi-ál-əti), **sub·stan·tial·ness** *n.* —**sub·stan·tial·ly** *adv.*

sub·stan·ti·ate (səb-stán-shi-ayt, -staán-, -si- || sub-) *tr.v.* **-ated, -ating, -ates.** **1.** To support with proof or evidence; verify. **2. a.** To give material form to; embody. **b.** To make firm or solid. **3.** To give substance to; make real or actual. —See Synonyms at **confirm.** [New Latin *substantiare,* from Latin *substantia,* SUBSTANCE.] —**sub·stan·ti·a·tion** (-áysh'n) *n.*

sub·stan·ti·val (súb-stən-tív'l) *adj. Grammar.* Of, pertaining to, or of the nature of a substantive. —**sub·stan·ti·val·ly** *adv.*

sub·stan·tive (súb-stən-tiv; *for sense 6, usually* səb-stán-) *adj. Abbr.* **s., sb., subst. 1.** Independent in existence or function; not subordinate. **2.** Not imaginary; genuine; real. **3.** Of or pertaining to the essence or substance of something; essential. **4.** Of substantial amount. **5.** Having a solid basis; firm. **6.** Effective and permanent. **7.** Expressing or denoting existence, as does the verb *to be.* **8.** Being or functioning as a noun or noun phrase. **9.** Pertaining to or designating that part of law concerned with legal rights and duties, rather than with procedure. Compare **adjective.**
~*n. Abbr.* **s., subst.** A word or group of words acting as a noun. [Middle English *substantif,* from Old French, from Late Latin *substantīvus,* self-existent, from Latin *substantia,* "thing that exists", SUBSTANCE.] —**sub·stan·tive·ly** *adv.* —**sub·stan·tive·ness** *n.*

sub·sta·tion (súb-staysh'n) *n.* **1.** An electrical installation in which power from the generating station is converted or transformed for distribution. **2.** A subsidiary or branch station.

sub·stit·u·ent (səb-stíttew-ənt || sub-) *n. Chemistry.* An atom, radical, or group substituted for another in a compound as a result of a chemical reaction.
~*adj.* Of such an atom or group. [Latin *substituēns* (stem *substituent-*), present participle of *substituere,* to SUBSTITUTE.]

sub·sti·tute (súb-sti-tewt || -tōōt) *n. Abbr.* **sub., subst. 1.** One that takes the place of another; a replacement, as: **a.** A substance, especially an artificial or inferior one, used in place of another. **b.** In sports such as cricket and soccer, a reserve player who may be called on to replace a member of a team for reasons of injury or tactics, for example. **2.** *Grammar.* A word or construction used in place of another word, phrase, or clause.
~*v.* **substituted, -tuting, -tutes.** —*tr.* **1.** To put or use (a person or thing) in place of another, especially: **a.** To replace (a member of a sports team) with a reserve player. **b.** To put (a reserve player) in the place of an existing member of a team. **2.** *Nonstandard.* To replace: *substitute olive oil by sunflower oil.* —*intr.* To take the place of another: *substituting for the sick player.* [Latin *substitūtus,* a replacement, from the past participle of *substituere,* to substitute : *sub-,* in place of + *statuere,* to cause to stand.] —**sub·sti·tut·a·bil·it·y** (-ə-bílləti) *n.* —**sub·sti·tut·a·ble** *adj.* —**sub·sti·tute** *adj.*

sub·sti·tu·tion (súb-sti-téwsh'n || -tōōsh'n) *n.* **1. a.** The act of substituting. **b.** The state of being substituted. **2.** That which is substituted. —**sub·sti·tu·tion·al** *adj.* —**sub·sti·tu·tion·al·ly** *adv.*

sub·sti·tu·tive (súb-sti-tew-tiv || -tōō-) *adj.* Serving or capable of serving as a substitute.

sub·strate (súb-strayt) *n.* **1.** A chemical substance or substances that undergo change as a result of being acted on by an enzyme. **2.** *Biology.* A surface on which a plant or animal grows or is attached. **3.** *Electronics.* The material upon which the elements of a semiconducting component or integrated circuit are deposited. **4.** A substratum. [From SUBSTRATUM.]

sub·stra·tum (súb-straa-təm, -stray-, -straá-, -stráy- || *U.S. also* -strá-) *n., pl.* **-ta** (-tə) or **-tums. 1.** An underlying layer. **2.** The foundation or groundwork for something. **3.** *Philosophy.* The characterless substance that supports attributes of reality. **4.** *Biology.* A substrate. **5.** A thin coating of hardened gelatine used to hold the emulsion on a photographic plate or film. **6.** *Linguistics.* An indigenous language which is replaced by that of an incoming population, but which may affect the development of the new language. In this sense, compare **superstratum.** [Medieval Latin *substrātum,* from Latin, neuter past participle of *substernere,* to lie under : *sub-,* under + *sternere,* to spread out flat.] —**sub·stra·tive** *adj.*

sub·struc·tion (sub-strúksh'n) *n.* A foundation; the substructure, as of a building. [Latin *substructiō* (stem *substructiōn-*), from *substruere* (past participle *substructus*), to build beneath : *sub-,* beneath + *struere,* to build.] —**sub·struc·tion·al** *adj.*

sub·struc·ture (súb-strukchər) *n.* **1.** The supporting part of a structure; a foundation. **2.** *U.S.* The earth bank or bed supporting railway tracks. —**sub·struc·tur·al** *adj.*

sub·sume (səb-séwm, -sōōm || sub-, -shōōm) *tr.v.* **-sumed, -suming, -sumes.** To place or include in a more comprehensive category or under a general principle. [New Latin *subsumere* : Latin *sub-,* under + *sūmere,* to take up.] —**sub·sum·a·ble** *adj.*

sub·sump·tion (səb-súmpsh'n || sub-) *n.* **1. a.** The act or an instance of subsuming. **b.** Something that is subsumed. **2.** *Logic.* The minor premise of a syllogism. [New Latin *subsumptio* (stem *subsumptiōn-*), from *subsumere,* SUBSUME.] —**sub·sump·tive** *adj.*

sub·teen (súb-teén) *n.* A child approaching teenage years. —**sub·teen** *adj.*

sub·ten·ant (súb-ténnənt) *n.* One who rents land, a house, or other property from a tenant. —**sub·ten·an·cy** *n.*

sub·tend (səb-ténd || sub-) *tr.v.* **-tended, -tending, -tends. 1.** *Geometry.* To be opposite to and delimit: *The side of a triangle subtends the opposite angle.* **2.** To underlie so as to enclose or surround. [Latin *subtendere,* to extend beneath : *sub-,* beneath + *tendere,* to extend.]

sub·ter·fuge (súb-tər-fewj) *n.* An evasive or deceitful tactic used to avoid an unwanted situation or to gain one's ends. See Synonyms at **artifice.** [French, from Late Latin *subterfugium,* from Latin *subterfugere,* to flee secretly : *subter,* secretly + *fugere,* to flee.]

sub·ter·min·al (súb-términ'l) *adj.* Coming nearly at the end.

sub·ter·ra·ne·an (súb-tə-ráyni-ən) *adj.* **1.** Situated or operating beneath the Earth's surface; underground. **2.** Hidden; existing or working in secret. [Latin *subterrāneus* : *sub-,* under + *terra,* earth.] —**sub·ter·ra·ne·an·ly** *adv.*

sub·ter·res·tri·al (súb-tə-réstri-əl, -te-) *adj.* Subterranean.
~*n.* An animal that lives underground.

sub·text (súb-tekst) *n.* A message which is not made explicit but which may be inferred from a statement or work of art or literature; an underlying meaning: *a political speech with a sinister subtext.*

sub·tile (sútt'l) *adj. Archaic.* Subtle. —**sub·tile·ly** *adv.* —**sub·til·i·ty** (-ti-, sub-tílləti), **sub·tile·ness, sub·til·ty** *n.*

sub·til·ise, sub·til·ize (sútt'l-īz) *v.* **-ised, -ising, -ises.** —*tr.* To make subtle. —*intr.* To argue or discuss with subtlety; make fine distinctions. [Medieval Latin *subtīlizāre,* from Latin *subtīlis,* SUBTLE.] —**sub·til·i·sa·tion** (-ī-záysh'n || *U.S.* -i-) *n.*

sub·ti·tle (súb-tīt'l) *n.* **1.** A secondary and usually explanatory title, as of a literary work. **2. a.** A printed narration or portion of dialogue shown on the screen between the scenes of a silent film. **b.** A printed translation of the dialogue of a foreign-language film or television broadcast, shown at the bottom of the screen.
~*tr.v.* **subtitle, subtitling, subtitles.** To provide with subtitles.

sub·tle (sútt'l) *adj.* **-tler, -tlest. 1. a.** So slight as to be difficult to detect or analyse; elusive. **b.** Not immediately obvious; abstruse. **2.** Fine or delicate: *a subtle flavour.* **3.** Able to make fine distinctions; keen. **4. a.** Characterised by skill or ingenuity; clever. **b.** Characterised by deftness or sensitivity: *the subtle approach.* **5. a.** Characterised by craft or slyness; devious. **b.** Operating in a hidden and usually injurious way; insidious. [Middle English *sutil, subtil,* thin, fine, clever, ingenious, from Old French, from Latin *subtīlis,* thin, fine.] —**sub·tle·ness** *n.* —**sub·tly** *adv.*

sub·tle·ty (sútt'lti) *n., pl.* **-ties. 1.** The quality or state of being subtle. **2.** Something subtle; especially, a nicety of thought or a fine distinction. —See Synonyms at **tact.**

sub·ton·ic (súb-tónnik) *n. Music.* The seventh tone of a diatonic scale, immediately below the tonic.

sub·top·i·a (súb-tōpi-ə) *n. British.* A suburban area, especially one that has been developed in an unattractive way. Used derogatorily. [*Sub*urban + *utopia.*] —**sub·top·i·an** *adj.*

sub·tor·rid (súb-tórrid || -táwrid) *adj.* Subtropical.

sub·to·tal (súb-tōt'l) *adj.* Less than total; incomplete.
~*n.* The total of part of a series of numbers.
~*tr.v.* **subtotalled** or *U.S.* **-taled, -talling** or *U.S.* **-taling, -tals.** To add up part of (a series of numbers).

sub·tract (səb-trákt || sub-) *v.* **-tracted, -tracting, -tracts.** —*tr.* To take away; deduct. —*intr.* To perform the arithmetical operation of subtraction. [Latin *substrahere* (past participle *substractus*), to draw away : *sub-,* away + *trahere,* to draw.] —**sub·tract·er** *n.*

sub·trac·tion (səb-tráksh'n || sub-) *n.* **1.** The act or process of subtracting; deduction. **2.** The arithmetical process or operation of finding a number or quantity that when added to one of two quantities produces the other.

sub·trac·tive (səb-tráktiv || sub-) *adj.* **1.** Producing or involving subtraction. **2.** Designating a colour produced by light passing through more than one colorant, each of which inhibits certain wavelengths, as in mixtures of pigments. Compare **additive.** See **primary colour. 3.** Designating a photographic process that produces a positive image by superposition or mixing of substances that selectively absorb coloured light.

sub·tra·hend (súb-trə-hend) *n.* A quantity or number to be subtracted from another. [Latin *subtrahendum,* gerundive of *subtrahere,* SUBTRACT.]

sub·trop·ics (súb-tróppiks) *pl.n.* The geographical areas bordering the tropics; roughly the areas 23 to 40° N and S, having no cold season. —**sub·trop·i·cal** *adj.*

su·bu·late (súbbew-lət, -lit, -layt) *adj. Biology.* Awl-shaped; tapering to a point. [New Latin *subulatus,* from Latin *sūbula,* awl.]

sub·urb (súb-urb, *rarely* -ərb) *n. Abbr.* **sub. 1.** A usually residential area or community on the edge of a city or large town. **2.** *Plural.* The perimeter of country around a major city; environs. Preceded by *the.* [Middle English, from Old French *suburbe,* from Latin *suburbium* : *sub-,* near + *urbs,* city (see **urban**).]

sub·ur·ban (sə-búrbən || su-) *adj. Abbr.* **sub. 1.** Of, pertaining to, or characteristic of a suburb or life in a suburb, especially in being unsophisticated, narrow-minded, or conventional. **2.** Located or residing in a suburb. **3.** Typical of life in the suburbs.
~*n.* A suburbanite. —**sub·ur·ban·i·ty** (súb-ur-bánnəti, -ər-) *n.*

sub·ur·ban·ite (sə-búrbən-īt || su-) *n.* One who lives in a suburb.

sub·ur·bi·a (sə-búrbi-ə || su-) *n.* **1.** Suburbs or suburbanites collectively. **2.** The typical values and lifestyle of suburbanites.

sub·ur·bi·car·i·an (sə-búrbi-káir-i-ən, su-) *adj.* Designating any of the six dioceses surrounding Rome of which the pope is the metropolitan bishop. [Late Latin *suburbicārius,* situated near Rome : *sub-,* near + *urbicārius,* of the city (especially Rome), from Latin *urbicus,* from *urbs,* city (see **urban**).]

sub·ven·tion (səb-vénsh'n, sub-) *n.* **1.** The provision of help, aid, or support. **2.** A grant of financial aid; an endowment or subsidy, as that given by a government to an institution for research. [Middle English *subvencioun,* from Old French *subvention,* from Late Latin *subventiō* (stem *subventiōn-*), from Latin *subvenīre* (past participle *subventus*), to come to help : *sub-,* from below, up + *venīre,* to come.] —**sub·ven·tion·ar·y** (-ri, -əri || -erri) *adj.*

sub·ver·sion (səb-vérsh'n, sub- || -vérzh'n) *n.* **1.** The act of subverting, especially of subverting an established government or other institution. **2.** The condition of being subverted. **3.** Anything that subverts. [Middle English *subversioun,* from Old French *subversion,* from Late Latin *subversiō* (stem *subversiōn-*), from Latin *subvertere* (past participle *subversus*), SUBVERT.] —**sub·ver·sion·ar·y** *adj.*

sub·ver·sive (səb-vér-siv, sub- || -ziv) *adj.* Intended or serving to subvert; especially, intended to overthrow or undermine an established government or other institution.
—*n.* One who advocates or is regarded as advocating subversive means or policies. —**sub·ver·sive·ly** *adv.* —**sub·ver·sive·ness** *n.*

sub·vert (səb-vért, sub-) *tr.v.* **-verted, -verting, -verts. 1.** To destroy completely; ruin: *subvert those schemes.* **2.** To undermine the character, morals, or allegiance of; corrupt. **3.** To overthrow or tend to overthrow completely: *subvert the democratic system.* [Middle English *subverten,* from Old French *subvertir,* from Latin *subvertere,* to turn upside down : *sub-,* from below, up + *vertere,* to turn.] —**sub·vert·er** *n.*

sub·way (súb-way) *n.* **1.** An underground tunnel or passage, as for pedestrians under a busy road or for a water main. **2.** *Chiefly U.S.* An underground railway.

sub·zero (súb-zéer-ō) *adj.* **1.** Less than zero, especially on a temperature scale. **2.** Of, characterised by, or for use in temperatures below zero: *subzero nights.*

suc·ce·da·ne·um (súksi-dáyni-əm) *n., pl.* **-nea** (-ə). *Formal.* A substitute. [New Latin, from Latin *succēdāneus,* substituted, "following", from *succēdere,* SUCCEED.]

suc·ceed (sək-séed || suk-) *v.* **-ceeded, -ceeding, -ceeds.** —*intr.* **1.** To come next in time, order, or sequence; follow after; especially, to replace another in an office or position. Often used with *to*: *succeed to the throne.* **2.** To accomplish something desired or intended. **3.** To do well; end favourably; prosper: *He'll succeed in New Zealand.* —*tr.* **1.** To follow in time or order; come after. **2.** To replace; follow in office: *succeeded his father as chairman.* —See Synonyms at **follow.** [Middle English *succeden,* from Old French *succeder,* from Latin *succēdere,* to follow closely, go after : *sub-,* towards, next to + *cēdere,* to go.] —**suc·ce·dent** *adj.* —**suc·ceed·er** *n.*

suc·cès de scan·dale (sŏŏk-sáy də skon-daal; *French* sük-) *n.* Acclaim or success accorded something, such as a work of art, purely on the basis of its shocking nature or the scandal surrounding it. [French, "success of scandal".]

suc·cès d'es·time (dess-téem) *n.* **1.** A critical but not popular success or achievement. **2.** A work that is admired without necessarily being read, seen, or heard. [French, "success of respect".]

suc·cess (sək-séss || suk-) *n.* **1.** The achievement of something desired, planned, or attempted. **2. a.** The gaining of fame, prosperity, or status. **b.** The extent of such gain. **3.** One that is successful. **4.** *Archaic.* Any result or outcome. [Latin *successus,* from the past participle of *succēdere,* SUCCEED.]

suc·cess·ful (sək-séssf'l || suk-) *adj.* **1.** Having a favourable outcome. **2.** Having obtained something desired or intended. **3.** Having achieved fame, prosperity, or status. —**suc·cess·ful·ly** *adv.*

suc·ces·sion (sək-sésh'n || suk-) *n.* **1.** The act or process of following in order or sequence. **2.** A group of persons or things arranged or following in order; a sequence. **3. a.** The sequence in which one person after another succeeds to a title, throne, dignity, or estate. **b.** The right of a person or line of persons to so succeed. **c.** The person or line vested with such a right. **4. a.** The act or process of succeeding to the rights or duties of another. **b.** The act or process of becoming entitled as a legal beneficiary to the property of a deceased person. **5.** *Ecology.* The series of changes that take place in a community from its initial colonisation of the habitat to formation of a stable **climax community** *(see).* —**in succession.** Following one after another, without interruption. —See Synonyms at **series.** —**suc·ces·sion·al** *adj.* —**suc·ces·sion·al·ly** *adv.*

suc·ces·sive (sək-séssiv || suk-) *adj.* **1.** Following in uninterrupted order or sequence. **2.** Of, characterised by, or involving succession. —**suc·ces·sive·ly** *adv.* —**suc·ces·sive·ness** *n.*

suc·ces·sor (sək-séssər || suk-) *n.* One that succeeds another.

success story *n.* A case involving a person or thing that proves remarkably successful: *Penicillin was a great medical success story.*

suc·cin·ate (súksi-nayt) *n.* A salt of succinic acid.

suc·cinct (sək-síngkt, suk-) *adj.* **1.** Clearly expressed in few words; concise. **2.** Characterised by brevity and clarity in speech or writing: *a succinct style.* **3.** *Archaic.* Encircled as if by a girdle; girded. —See Synonyms at **concise.** [Latin *succinctus,* girded, concise, from the past participle of *succingere,* to gird below : *sub-,* below + *cingere,* to gird.] —**suc·cinct·ly** *adv.* —**suc·cinct·ness** *n.*

suc·cin·ic (suk-sínnik, sək-) *adj.* **1.** Of or relating to amber. **2.** Containing or derived from succinic acid. [French *succinique,* from Latin *succinum,* amber.]

succinic acid *n.* A colourless crystalline compound, $CO_2H(CH_2)_2CO_2H$, occurring naturally in amber and synthesised for use in pharmaceuticals and perfumes; 1, 4-butanedioic acid.

suc·co·ry (súkəri) *n., pl.* **-ries.** A plant, **chicory** *(see).* [Alteration (influenced by Middle Dutch *sūkerie,* succory) of Middle English *cicoree,* CHICORY.]

Suc·coth, Suk·koth (sŏŏk-ōt, -ōth) *n.* A Jewish harvest festival celebrated for nine days beginning on the eve of the 15th of Tishri. [Hebrew *sukkōth,* "(feast of) booths" (commemorating the temporary shelter of the Jews in the wilderness), from *sukkāh,* booth.]

suc·cour, *U.S.* **suc·cor** (súkər) *n.* **1.** Assistance or help in time of distress; relief. **2.** One that affords assistance or relief.
—*tr.v.* **succoured** or *U.S.* **-cored, -couring** or *U.S.* **-coring -cours** or *U.S.* **-cors.** To render assistance to in time of distress. See Synonyms at **help.** [Middle English *sucurs* (taken as plural), from Old French, from Medieval Latin *succursus,* from Latin, past participle of *succurrere,* to turn to the aid of, run under : *sub-,* under + *currere,* to run.] —**suc·cour·a·ble** *adj.* —**suc·cour·er** *n.*

suc·cu·bus (súckew-bəss) *n., pl.* **-buses** or **-bi** (-bī). Also **suc·cu·ba** (-bə) *pl.* **-bae** (-bee). **1.** A female demon supposed to descend upon and have sexual intercourse with a man while he sleeps. Compare **incubus. 2.** Any evil spirit; a demon. [Medieval Latin, from Late Latin *succuba,* prostitute, from Latin *succubāre,* to lie under : Latin *sub-,* under + *cubāre,* to lie.]

suc·cu·lent (súckewlənt) *adj.* **1.** Full of juice or sap; juicy. **2.** *Botany.* Having thick, fleshy leaves or stems that conserve moisture. **3.** Desirable or attractive.
—*n.* A succulent plant, such as a sedum or a cactus. [Latin *succulentus,* from *succus,* juice.] —**suc·cu·lence, suc·cu·len·cy** *n.* —**suc·cu·lent·ly** *adv.*

suc·cumb (sə-kúm || su-) *intr.v.* **-cumbed, -cumbing, -cumbs. 1.** To yield or submit to an overpowering force or overwhelming desire; give in or give up. Often used with *to*: *succumb to temptation.* **2.** To die. Used with *to*: *succumbed to smallpox.* [Middle English *succomben,* from Old French *succomber,* from Latin *succumbere,* to lie down under : *sub-,* under + *-cumbere,* to lie.]

suc·cus·sion (sə-kúsh'n || su-) *n.* **1.** The act or process of shaking violently. **2.** The condition of being so shaken. **3.** *Medicine.* The shaking of a patient in order to detect a splashing sound, which indicates the presence of fluid in a body cavity, especially the pleural cavity. [Latin *succussiō* (stem *succussiōn-*), from *succutere* (past participle *succussus*), to shake from beneath : *sub-,* beneath + *quatere,* to shake.] —**suc·cus·sa·to·ry** (sə-kússə-tri, -təri || su-) *adj.*

such (such; *occasional weak form* səch) *adj.* **1.** Of this or that kind: *We haven't had such fun as this for years!* **2.** Being the same or the same kind as that which is specified or implied. Sometimes used as a pronoun: *The weather was such that we could not go out.* **3.** Being the same in quality or kind: *pins, needles, and other such sewing aids.* **4.** Being the same as something implied but left undefined or unsaid: *Such people are never satisfied.* **5.** Of so extreme or great a degree or quality: *He's such a fool!* —**as such. 1.** As being the person or thing implied or previously mentioned; by one's or its very nature: *A diplomat as such must negotiate.* **2.** In itself or by itself: *Money as such will seldom bring happiness.* —**such as. 1.** For example. **2.** Of the stated or implied kind or degree; like. Sometimes followed by a clause: *language such as I had never heard.*
—*pron.* **1.** Such a person or persons or thing or things. **2.** A person or persons or thing or things implied or indicated: *Such were the results of that war.* **3.** One of such kind: *papers and such.*
—*adv.* **1.** To such an extent or degree; so very: *such long hair.* **2.** Very: *has not been in such good health lately.* **3.** In such a manner or way. [Middle English *su(c)ch, swulc,* Old English *swylc, swelc.*]
Usage: Following *such as,* traditional grammars recommend the use of the subject form of personal pronouns, and this is normal in formal English: *Have you ever seen a man such as he?* Informal English usually uses the object form of the pronoun (for example, *him*) in such cases, and when the pronoun occurs at the end of a sentence this is quite common even in formal contexts.

such-and-such, such and such (súch-ənd-such) *adj.* Not yet named or known: *They agreed to meet at such and such an hour.*
—*n.* An as yet unknown or unnamed person or thing.

such·like (súch-līk) *adj.* Of a similar kind; like.
—*pron. Informal.* Persons or things of such a kind.

Su-chou. See **Suzhou.**

suck (suk) *v.* **sucked, sucking, sucks.** —*tr.* **1.** To draw (liquid) into the mouth by tensing muscles in the mouth and drawing in breath. **2. a.** To draw in by establishing a partial vacuum. **b.** To draw in by or as if by a current in a fluid. **c.** To absorb. Often used with *up* or *in.* **3.** To draw liquid or nourishment through or from. **4.** To hold, moisten, or manoeuvre (a sweet, for example) in the mouth, often by making sucking motions. —*intr.* **1.** To draw in by or as if by suction. **2.** To draw nourishment; suckle. **3.** To make a sucking sound or motion. —**suck in. 1.** *Chiefly U.S. Slang.* To take advantage of; cheat; swindle. **2.** To attract forcefully; engulf. —**suck up.** *Informal.* To flatter in order to gain favour. Used with *to.*
—*n.* **1.** The act of sucking. **2.** Suction. **3.** Something drawn in by sucking. [Middle English *s(o)uken,* Old English *sūcan.*]

suck·er (súckər) *n.* **1.** One that sucks; specifically, a young mammal before weaning. **2.** *Slang.* One who is easily deceived; a gullible person; a dupe. **3.** *Informal.* One unable to resist the appeal of something specified. Used with for: *a sucker for kittens.* **4. a.** A piston or piston valve, as in a suction pump or syringe. **b.** A tube or pipe, such as a siphon, through which anything is sucked. **5.** A flat or cup-shaped device, usually made of rubber, that can adhere to a surface by suction. **6.** *U.S.* A lollipop. **7.** Any of various fishes with sucking discs; especially, the **clingfish** *(see).* **8.** A structure or part adapted for clinging by suction, as found in certain animals. **9.** *Botany.* A secondary shoot arising from the base of a tree trunk or from the lower part of some shrubs, which gives rise to a new plant.
—*v.* **suckered, -ering, -ers.** —*tr.* **1.** To strip suckers or shoots from. **2.** *Chiefly U.S. Slang.* To take advantage of the gullibility of; fool. —*intr.* To send out suckers or shoots.

suck·er·fish (súckər-fish) *n., pl.* **-fishes** or collectively **suckerfish.** Also **suck·fish.** The **remora** *(see).*

suck·ing (súcking) *adj.* Too young to be weaned.
sucking louse *n.* Any insect of the order Anoplura. See **louse.**
suck·le (súck'l) *v.* **-led, -ling, -les.** —*tr.* **1.** To cause or allow to take milk at the breast or udder; nurse. **2.** To take in as sustenance; have as nourishment. **3.** *Literary.* To bring up; rear; nourish; foster: *suckled in poverty.* —*intr.* To suck at the breast. [Probably back-formation from SUCKLING.] **—suck·ler** *n.*
suck·ling (súckling) *n.* A young mammal or child that has not been weaned. [Middle English : SUCK + -LING.]
Suck·ling (súckling), **Sir John** (1609–42). English poet, courtier, and wit. His works included *Aglaura* (1637), *Session of the Poets* (1637), and *Brennoralt, or The Discontented Colonel* (1640).
sucks (suks) *interj.* **1.** Used to express derision or open disobedience. **2.** Used to express disappointment.
su·crase (sōō-krayz, séw-, -krayss) *n. Chemistry.* **Invertase** *(see).* [French *sucre,* SUGAR + -ASE.]
su·cre (sōō-kray) *n.* **1.** The basic monetary unit of Ecuador, equal to 100 centavos. **2.** A coin worth one sucre. [Spanish, after Antonio José de *Sucre* (1795–1830), South American revolutionary.]
Sucre (sōō-kray). City in Bolivia, situated in a mountain valley on the eastern slope of the Andes at an altitude of 2 590 metres (8,500 feet). It is the legal capital of Bolivia, though the seat of government is La Paz. Sucre has oil refineries and is an agricultural centre.
su·crose (sōō-krōz, séw-, -krōss) *n.* A crystalline disaccharide carbohydrate, $C_{12}H_{22}O_{11}$, found in many plants, mainly sugar cane, sugar beet, and maple, and used widely as a sweetener, preservative, and in the manufacture of plastics and cellulose. Also called "sugar", "saccharose". [French *sucre,* SUGAR + -OSE.]
suc·tion (súksh'n) *n.* **1.** The act or process of sucking. **2.** The force that causes a fluid or solid to be drawn into an interior space or to adhere to a surface because of the difference between the external and internal pressures.
~*adj.* Creating or operating by suction. [Late Latin *sūctiō* (stem *sūctiōn-*), from Latin *sūgere* (past participle *sūctus*), to suck.]
suction pump *n.* A pump for drawing up a liquid by means of suction produced by a piston being drawn through a cylinder.
suc·to·ri·al (suk-táw-ri-əl || -tṓ-) *adj. Biology.* **1.** Adapted for sucking or clinging by suction. **2.** Having suctorial organs or parts. [New Latin *sūctōrius,* from Latin *sūgere,* to suck. See **suction.**]
Su·dan (the) (sōō-daán, -dán). Vast region of Africa lying between the Sahara and the tropical forest lands to the south. It stretches from the Atlantic to Ethiopia and Cameroon, including the south of the Republic of the Sudan, and the Sahel region.
Sudan, Republic of the. Formerly **Anglo-Egyptian Sudan.** The largest country in Africa, lying in the northeast of the continent. The north is desert or scrubland, and south mostly savannah, a vast area suitable only for livestock herding. About 77 per cent of the labour force are in agriculture, mostly at subsistence level, and cotton, groundnuts, sesame seed, and hides and skins are the chief exports. Sudan is one of the world's poorest countries, subject to both drought and floods, and has massive foreign debts. However, its rivers have great potential for irrigation, and the Jonglei Canal will conserve water, draining much of the Sudd to provide good farmland. The country's mineral resources include extensive oil and gas reserves. The area was ruled jointly by Britain and Egypt from 1898 until independence (1956). A military coup (1969) brought to power General Nimeiry, and civil war (1955–72) between the predominantly Arab north and the black south was ended. It resumed when Nimeiry imposed strict Muslim law in 1983, and continued after he was deposed two years later. Another military coup replaced a civilian government in 1989. Area, 2 505 813 square kilometres (967,500 square miles). Population, 27,290,000. Capital, Khartoum. —**Su·dan·ese** *adj. & n.*

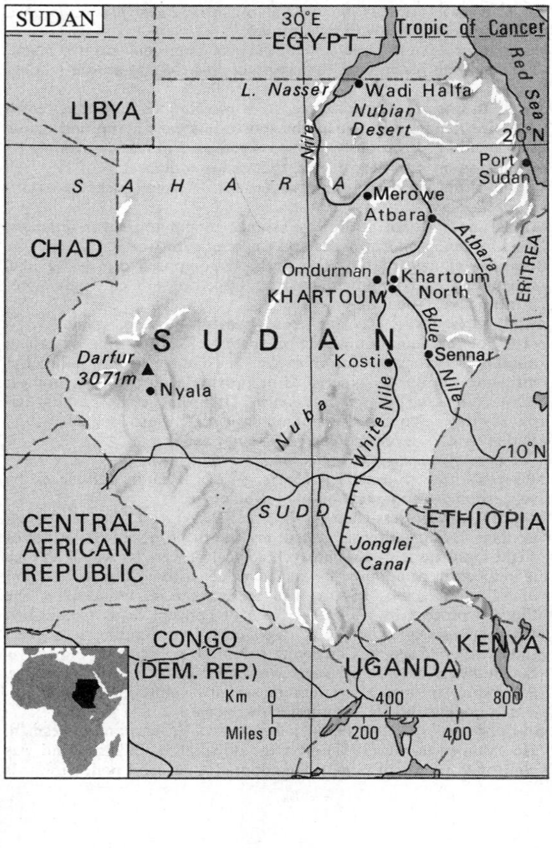
SUDAN
30°E
EGYPT
Tropic of Cancer
Red Sea
L. Nasser
Wadi Halfa
Nubian
Desert
LIBYA
Nile
20°N
Port
Sudan
S A H A R A
Merowe
Atbara
Atbara
CHAD
Omdurman
Khartoum
North
KHARTOUM
ERITREA
Blue Nile
S U D A N
Darfur
3071m
Nyala
Kosti
Sennar
Nuba
White Nile
10°N
SUDD
ETHIOPIA
CENTRAL
AFRICAN
REPUBLIC
Jonglei
Canal
CONGO
(DEM. REP.)
UGANDA
KENYA
Km 0
400
800
Miles 0
200
400

Su·dan·ic (sōō-dánnik || sew-) *adj.* **1.** Of or pertaining to the Sudan region. **2.** Of or pertaining to the languages of the region, chiefly Niger-Congo and Chari-Nile. **—Su·dan·ic** *n.*
su·da·to·ri·um (sōō-də-táw-ri-əm, séw- || -tṓ-) Also **su·da·ri·um** (-dáir-i-əm) *n., pl.* **-ia** (-ə). A hot-air room, especially in ancient Rome, for sweat baths. [Latin *sūdātōrium,* from *sūdāre,* to sweat.]
su·da·to·ry (sōō-də-tri, séw-, -təri) *adj.* Sudorific.
~*n., pl.* **sudatories. 1.** A sudatorium. **2.** A sudorific.
sudd (sud) *n.* A floating mass of vegetation that often obstructs navigation on the White Nile. [Arabic, obstruction, from *sadda,* to obstruct.]
Sudd (sud). The vast swamp in southern Sudan caused by sudd obstruction of the White Nile and its tributaries.
sud·den (súdd'n) *adj.* **1.** Happening without warning; unforeseen. **2.** Characterised by hastiness; abrupt; rash: *That decision was a bit sudden.* **3.** Characterised by rapidity; quick; swift. **—all of a sudden.** Very quickly and unexpectedly; suddenly. [Middle English *sodan(e),* from Anglo-French *sodein, sudein,* from Late Latin *subitā-nus,* variant of Latin *subitāneus,* from *subitus,* sudden, past participle of *subīre,* to approach secretly, steal upon : *sub-,* secretly + *īre,* to go.] **—sud·den·ly** *adv.* **—sud·den·ness** *n.*
sudden death *n. Sports.* **1.** An extra game point, hole, or the like played to break a tie. **2.** Extra minutes of play added to a tied game, the winning team being the first team to score. Also used adjectivally: *a sudden-death playoff.*
sudden infant death syndrome *n.* **Cot death** *(see).*
Su·de·ten·land. (sōō-dáyt'n-land; *German* zōō-, -lant). Border region of the northern Czech Republic, lying along the Sudeten Mountains. It was transferred from Austria-Hungary to Czechoslovakia (1919), and had a significant proportion of German-speaking inhabitants. The area was granted to Nazi Germany by the Munich agreement (1938), but together with similar areas of northwest and southwest Czechoslovakia (then also termed "Sudetenland"), was returned to Czechoslovakia in 1945. The area's German-speaking populations were subsequently expelled.
su·dor·if·er·ous (sōōdə-ríffərəss, séwdə-) *adj.* Producing or secreting sweat. [Late Latin *sūdōrifer* : Latin *sūdor,* sweat + -FEROUS.]
su·dor·if·ic (sōōdə-ríffik, séwdə-) *adj.* Causing or increasing sweat.
~*n.* A sudorific medicine. [New Latin *sūdōrificus* : Latin *sūdor,* sweat + -FIC.]
Su·dra (sōōdrə) *n.* **1.** The lowest of the major Hindu castes, originally composed of menials but later largely of artisans and labourers. **2.** A member of this caste. [Sanskrit *śūdra.*]
suds (sudz) *pl.n.* **1.** Soapy water containing soap bubbles. **2.** Foam; lather. [Originally, dregs, muddy water, probably from Middle Dutch *sudde, sudse,* marsh, swamp.] **—sud·sy** *adj.*
sue (sew, sōō) *v.* **sued, suing, sues.** —*tr.* **1.** To make a petition to; appeal to; beseech. **2.** To institute legal proceedings against by bringing a civil action, usually for redress of grievances. **3.** *Archaic.* To court; woo. —*intr.* **1.** To institute legal proceedings. **2.** To make an appeal or entreaty. Usually used with *for*: *sue for mercy.* **3.** *Archaic.* To woo. [Middle English *sewen,* to pursue, prosecute, from Anglo-French *suer, suire,* from Vulgar Latin *sequere* (unattested), to follow, from Latin *sequī.*] **—su·er** *n.*
suede, suède (swayd) *n.* **1.** Leather with a soft napped surface, usually produced by rubbing the flesh side. **2.** Fabric made to resemble this leather. In this sense, also called "suede cloth". [From *suède gloves,* partial translation of French *gants de suède,* "gloves of Sweden", from *Suède,* Sweden.]
su·et (sōō-it, séw-) *n.* The hard fat around the kidneys of cattle and sheep, used in cooking and making tallow. [Middle English *sewet,* from Anglo-French *sewet* (unattested), diminutive of *sue, seu,* from Latin *sēbum,* tallow, suet. See **sebum.**]
suet pudding *n.* A steamed, usually sweet, pudding containing or enclosed in a casing of suet and flour.
Su·e·to·ni·us (sōō-i-tṓni-əss, séw-, swee-), born Gaius Suetonius Tranquillus (*c.*69 – *c.*140). Roman historian and biographer. His *De Vita Caesarum,* lives of the first 12 Caesars from Julius Caesar to Domitian, survives almost complete.
Su·ez (sōō-iz, séw- || -ez, *U.S. also* sōō-éz). *Arabic* **As-Suways.** Port in northeastern Egypt, situated at the northern end of the Gulf of Suez at the entrance to the Suez Canal.
Suez, Isthmus of. The strip of land in northeastern Egypt connecting Asia and Africa and traversed by the Suez Canal.
Suez Canal. A major shipping canal in northeastern Egypt, connecting the Mediterranean Sea with the Red Sea, via the Gulf of Suez. It is 165 kilometres (103 miles) long, and extends from Port Said in the north to Suez in the south. The canal was planned by the French engineer Ferdinand de Lesseps, who also supervised its construction (1859–69). Britain became the largest shareholder in the Suez Canal Company in 1875. In 1888 an international convention proclaimed the free right of transit to all shipping, to be guaranteed

by Britain. An agreement of 1954 provided for British evacuation of the zone. In 1956 Nasser nationalised the canal company, provoking the Suez Crisis, in which Britain, France, and Israel attacked Egypt but were quickly forced to withdraw due to hostile world opinion. Restored to Egyptian control, the canal was subsequently closed (1967–75) because of Arab-Israeli hostilities.

suf. suffix.

suff. 1. sufficient. 2. suffix.

Suff. 1. Suffolk. 2. suffragan.

suf·fer (súffər) v. **-fered, -fering, -fers.** —*intr.* 1. a. To feel pain or distress, as after sustaining loss, injury, or punishment. b. To be prone to a specified medical condition: *suffers from gout.* 2. To tolerate or endure evil, injury, harm, pain, or death. 3. To appear at a disadvantage: *suffer by comparison.* —*tr.* 1. To undergo or sustain (something painful, injurious, or unpleasant): *suffer a nasty wound.* 2. To experience: *suffer a change of heart.* 3. To endure or bear; stand: *He cannot suffer boredom.* 4. Formal. To permit; allow: *Rulers suffered us to speak.* —See Synonyms at **bear**. [Middle English suff(e)ren, to undergo, endure, allow, from Anglo-French suffrir, from Vulgar Latin sufferīre (unattested), from Latin sufferre, to sustain, "to bear up" : sub-, up from under + ferre, to bear.] —**suf·fer·er** n. —**suf·fer·ing·ly** adv.

suf·fer·a·ble (súffrəb'l, súffərəb'l) adj. Capable of being suffered, endured, or permitted; tolerable. —**suf·fer·a·bly** adv.

suf·fer·ance (súffrənss, súffərənss) n. 1. The capacity to tolerate pain or distress. 2. Sanction or permission implied or given by failure to prohibit; tacit assent; tolerance. 3. Archaic. Suffering; misery. 4. Archaic. Patient endurance. —**on sufferance**. Tolerated or accepted reluctantly. [Middle English suffrance, from Old French, from Late Latin sufferentia, from Latin sufferre, SUFFER.]

suf·fer·ing (súffring, súffəring) n. 1. The condition of one who suffers. 2. The enduring of pain or distress.

suf·fice (sə-físs) v. **-ficed, -ficing, -fices.** —*intr.* 1. To meet present needs or requirements; be sufficient: *These will suffice until next week.* 2. To be capable or competent; be equal to a specified task: *No words will suffice to convey his grief.* —*tr.* To be enough or sufficient for; satisfy the needs or requirements of. —**suffice it.** Let it be enough; it is sufficient. Used chiefly in the phrase *suffice it to say.* [Middle English suffisen, from Old French suffire (present stem suffis-), from Latin sufficere, to put under, substitute, suffice : sub-, under + facere, to do, make.] —**suf·fic·er** n.

suf·fi·cien·cy (sə-físh'n-si) n. 1. The state or quality of being sufficient. 2. Adequate supplies, ability, numbers, or resources; especially, an adequate but not luxurious standard of living.

suf·fi·cient (sə-físh'nt) adj. 1. Abbr. **suff.** As much as is needed; enough; adequate: *I haven't sufficient information to make a reasonable decision.* 2. Archaic. Capable; competent; efficient.

~ n. A sufficient quantity. [Middle English, from Old French, from Latin sufficiēns (stem sufficient-), present participle of sufficere, SUFFICE.] —**suf·fi·cient·ly** adv.

sufficient condition n. Logic. A condition whose truth guarantees the truth of a proposition or state of affairs; for example, that it has just rained is a sufficient condition of the grass being wet; it is not a **necessary condition** (see), since any number of things might have made the grass wet.

suf·fix (súffiks) n. Abbr. **suf., suff.** An affix added to the end of a word or stem, serving to form a new word or to form an inflectional ending, as -ness in gentleness, -ing in walking, or -s in sits.

~ tr.v (also su·fíks, sə-) **suffixed, -fixing, -fixes.** 1. To fix or add at the end; append. 2. To add as a suffix. [New Latin suffixum, from Latin suffixus, neuter past participle of suffigere, to affix, fasten beneath : sub-, beneath + fīgere, to fix.] —**suf·fix·al** (súffiks'l, sə-fíks'l) adj. —**suf·fix·ion** (su-fíksh'n, sə-) n.

suf·fo·cate (súffə-kayt) v. **-cated, -cating, -cates.** —*tr.* 1. a. To kill by preventing access of oxygen to (a person or animal). b. To extinguish (a fire, for example) by cutting off a supply of oxygen. 2. To impair the respiration of; cause a choking sensation in. 3. To cause discomfort to by or as if by cutting off the supply of air. 4. To suppress the development, imagination, or creativity of; stifle. —*intr.* 1. To die through lack of oxygen. 2. To be stifled; smother. [Latin suffocāre : sub-, under, down + fauċēs, throat, FAUCES.] —**suf·fo·ca·tion** (-káysh'n) n. —**suf·fo·ca·tive** (-kaytiv) adj.

Suf·folk¹ (súffək). County in East Anglia, England. Low and undulating, it is primarily agricultural. Lowestoft is a fishing port, and Ipswich, the county town, is the chief industrial centre.

Suffolk² n. Any of an English breed of hornless sheep producing high-quality mutton. [Originated in SUFFOLK.]

Suffolk Punch n. Any of a breed of draught horses originating in Suffolk, having a thickset, heavy body, short legs, and a chestnut coat. [Punch, after Punch, as in Punch and Judy.]

suf·fra·gan (súffrəgən) n. Abbr. **Suff., Suffr.** 1. A bishop elected or appointed as an assistant to the bishop or ordinary of a diocese, having administrative and episcopal responsibilities but no jurisdictional functions. 2. Any bishop regarded in his position as subordinate to his archbishop or metropolitan. Also called "suffragan bishop". [Middle English, from Old French, from Medieval Latin suffrāgāneus, from suffrāgium, SUFFRAGE.] —**suf·fra·gan** adj. —**suf·fra·gan·ship** n.

suf·frage (súffrij) n. 1. The right or privilege of voting; franchise. 2. The exercise of such a right. 3. A vote cast in deciding a disputed question or in electing a person to office. 4. Usually plural. Archaic. A short intercessory prayer. [Middle English, intercessory prayer, from Old French suffrage, suffragies, from Medieval Latin suffrā-

gium, vote, support, prayer, from Latin ballot, right of voting.]

suf·fra·gette (súffrə-jét) n. In the early 20th century, a female advocate of suffrage for women; especially, a supporter of the militant Woman's Social and Political Union, led by Emmeline and Christabel Pankhurst. —**suf·fra·get·tism** n.

suf·fra·gist (súffrəjist) n. An advocate of the extension of political voting rights, especially to women.

suf·fru·tes·cent (súf-rōō-téss'nt ‖ -rew-) adj. Also **suf·fru·ti·cose** (su-frōōti-koz, sə-, -kōss ‖ -fréwti-). Botany. Having a woody stem or base and herbaceous branches; somewhat shrubby. [New Latin suffrutescens : SUB- + FRUTESCENT.]

suf·fuse (sə-féwz, su-) tr.v. **-fused, -fusing, -fuses.** To spread through or over: "The sky above the roof is suffused with deep colours" (Eugene O'Neill). [Latin suffundere (past participle suffūsus), to pour underneath or into : sub-, underneath + fundere, to pour.] —**suf·fu·sion** (-féwzh'n) n. —**suf·fu·sive** (-féw-siv ‖ -ziv) adj.

Su·fi (sōōfi) n. A member of a Muslim mystic sect that dates from the eighth century A.D. and developed chiefly in Iran. [Arabic sūfīy, "(man) of wool", from sūf, wool (probably from their woollen garments).] —**Su·fic, Su·fis·tic** (sōō-fístik) adj.

Su·fism (sōōf-iz'm) n. The beliefs and practices of the Sufis.

sug (sug) v. **sugged, sugging, sugs.** To sell under the guise of market research.

sug·ar (shŏoggər) n. 1. A sweet crystalline carbohydrate, **sucrose** (see). 2. Any of a class of water-soluble crystalline carbohydrates, including sucrose and lactose, having a characteristically sweet taste. 3. A particular amount of sugar, as a spoonful or cube: takes two sugars in her tea. 4. Chiefly U.S. A sweetheart. Used as a term of endearment.

~v. **sugared, -aring, -ars.** —*tr.* 1. To coat, cover, or sweeten with sugar. 2. To make less distasteful or more appealing. —*intr.* To form sugar; granulate. [Middle English suker, sugre, from Old French sukere, zuchre, from Italian zucchero, from Medieval Latin zuccarum, succarum, from Arabic sukkar, from Persian shakar, from Prakrit sakkara, from Sanskrit śarkarā†, pebble, gravel, sugar.] —**sug·ar·less** adj.

sugar apple n. A tree, the **sweetsop** (see), or its fruit.

sugar beet n. A form of the common beet, Beta vulgaris, having white roots from which sugar is obtained.

sugar bird n. A long-tailed South African bird, Promerops cafer, with a long curved bill used for extracting nectar from flowers.

sugar cane n. A tall grass, Saccharum officinarum, native to the East Indies, having thick, tough stems that are one of the chief commercial sources of sugar.

sug·ar-coat (shŏoggər-kōt) tr.v. **-coated, -coating, -coats.** 1. To coat with sugar. 2. To cause to seem more appealing or pleasant.

sugar daddy n. Informal. A wealthy, usually older man who gives expensive gifts to a young woman or man in return for sexual favours or companionship.

sug·ared (shŏoggərd) adj. 1. Sweetened with sugar. 2. Made more appealing or pleasant.

sugar glider n. An Australian marsupial (a phalanger), Petaurus breviceps, that glides between trees and feeds on nectar.

sugar gum n. An Australian eucalyptus tree, Eucalyptus cladocalyx, yielding heavy, yellow-brown timber.

sugar loaf n. 1. A large conical mass of pure concentrated sugar. 2. Something resembling the shape of this. —**sug·ar-loaf** (shŏoggər-lōf) adj.

sugar maple n. A maple tree, Acer saccharum, of eastern North America, having sap that is the source of maple syrup and maple sugar and hard, variously grained wood used in cabinetmaking.

sugar pea n. A variety of pea, the **mange-tout** (see).

sug·ar·plum (shŏoggər-plum) n. Archaic. A small piece of sugary confectionery.

sugar soap n. An alkaline substance resembling sugar granules, used for smoothing surfaces and cleaning paintwork.

sug·ar·y (shŏoggəri) adj. **-ier, -iest.** 1. Composed of, tasting like, resembling, or containing sugar. 2. Deceitfully or cloyingly sweet or attractive. —**sug·ar·i·ness** n.

sug·gest (sə-jést ‖ U.S. səg-) tr.v. **-gested, -gesting, -gests.** 1. To offer for consideration or action; propose. 2. To bring or call to mind by logic or association; evoke. 3. To make evident indirectly; intimate; imply. 4. To serve as or provide a motive for; prompt: Such a crime suggests apt punishment. [Latin suggerere (past participle suggestus), to carry or put underneath, furnish, suggest : sub-, underneath + gerere, to carry.] —**sug·gest·er** n.

Synonyms: suggest, imply, hint, intimate, insinuate.

sug·gest·i·ble (sə-jéstəb'l ‖ U.S. səg-) adj. Readily influenced by suggestion. —**sug·gest·i·bil·i·ty** (-ə-bíləti) n.

sug·ges·tion (sə-jéss-chən, -jésh- ‖ U.S. səg-) n. 1. The act of suggesting. 2. Something suggested; an idea or proposal. 3. A trace or slight indication. 4. a. The psychological process by which an idea is induced in or adopted by an individual without argument, command, or coercion. b. Any idea or response so induced. 5. The thought process by which one idea or concept leads to another.

sug·ges·tive (sə-jéstiv ‖ U.S. səg-) adj. 1. a. Tending to suggest thoughts or ideas. b. Conveying a hint or suggestion; indicative. Sometimes used with of: suggestive of his guilt, but not conclusive. 2. Tending to suggest something sexually improper or indecent. —**sug·ges·tive·ly** adv. —**sug·ges·tive·ness** n.

Su·har·to (sōō-hártō) (1921–). Indonesian general and statesman. He assumed power (1967) after the downfall of Sukarno and was confirmed president (1968). He adopted a peaceful policy towards

Malaysia and suppressed all opposition until demonstrations forced his resignation in 1998.

su·i·ci·dal (sōō-i-sīd'l, sew-) *adj.* **1. a.** Pertaining to, involving, or related to suicide. **b.** Feeling or showing a disposition to commit suicide. **2.** Dangerous to oneself or to one's interests; self-destructive; ruinous. **—su·i·ci·dal·ly** *adv.*

su·i·cide (sōō-i-sīd, sew-) *n.* **1.** The act or an instance of intentionally killing oneself. **2.** The destruction or ruin of one's own interests. **3.** One who commits suicide.
~*adj.* Involving suicide or extreme danger: *a suicide mission.*
~ *intr.v.* **suicided, -ciding, -cides.** To commit suicide. [New Latin *suicida* (person), *suicidium* (act) : Latin *suī*, of oneself + -CIDE.]

su·i gen·e·ris (sōō-ī jénnəriss, sew-, -ee génnəriss) *adj.* Unique; individual. [Latin, "of its own kind".]

su·i ju·ris (sōō-ī jōor-iss, sew-, -ee yŏor-) *adj. Law.* Capable of managing one's own affairs. [Latin, "of one's own right".]

su·int (sōō-int, sew-, swint) *n.* A natural grease formed from dried perspiration, found in the fleece of sheep and used as a source of potash. [French, from Old French *suer*, to sweat, from Latin *sūdāre*.]

suit (sōōt, sewt) *n.* **1. a.** A set of outer garments consisting of a coat and trousers or skirt, and sometimes a waistcoat, that match in colour or fabric or that have been designed to be worn together. **b.** A garment or set of clothes designed to be worn for a specified purpose or as a fashionable outfit. Often used in combination: *a playsuit; a flying suit.* **2.** Any group of things united into a set or series by having a common form or function. **3.** Any of the four sets of 13 playing cards, spades, hearts, diamonds, and clubs, each with similar spots or pips, that constitute a pack. **4. a.** *Law.* An act or instance of suing in court, usually to recover a right or claim; a lawsuit. **b.** An act of pleading; a request. **5.** The act or an instance of courting. **—follow suit. 1.** To play a card of the same suit as the one led. **2.** To do as another has done; follow an example.
~*v.* **suited, suiting, suits.** —*tr.* **1.** To meet the requirements of; accommodate: *This candidate does not suit our needs.* **2. a.** To make appropriate or suitable; adapt: *We can suit the building to your specifications.* **b.** To be appropriate or suitable for; go well with: *Does the climate suit you?* **3.** To please; satisfy. **4.** *Archaic.* To dress. —*intr.* To be suitable or acceptable. **—suit (oneself).** To do as one pleases in a given circumstance. [Middle English *su(i)te,* attendance at a sheriff's court, litigation, uniform, garb, from Old French *siute, suite,* from Vulgar Latin *sequita* (unattested), pursuit, from *sequere* (unattested), to follow. See **sue.**]

suit·a·ble (sōōt-əb'l, sewt-) *adj.* Appropriate to a given purpose or occasion; fitting; convenient. See Synonyms at **fit.** **—suit·a·bil·i·ty** (-ə-billəti), **suit·a·ble·ness** *n.* **—suit·a·bly** *adv.*

suit·case (sōōt-kayss, sewt-) *n.* A usually rectangular and flat or boxlike piece of luggage having a handle and used for carrying personal belongings and clothing.

suite (sweet ‖ *U.S. also* sōōt *for sense 3*) *n.* **1.** Any succession of related things intended to be used together. **2.** A series of connected rooms used as a living unit. **3.** A set of matched furniture pieces intended for use in the same room. **4.** *Music.* **a.** An instrumental composition consisting of a succession of movements, originally dances, having the same theme or in the same or (after 1750) related keys. **b.** An instrumental composition based on a selection from a larger musical work, such as a ballet or opera. **5.** A staff of attendants; a retinue. [French, from Old French *sieute,* following, retinue, from Vulgar Latin *sequita* (unattested). See **suit.**]

suit·ing (sōōt-ing, sewt-) *n.* Fabric from which suits are made.

suit·or (sōōt-ər, sewt-) *n.* **1.** A person who makes a petition or request. **2.** A person who sues in a court of law; a plaintiff; a petitioner. **3.** A man who is in the process of courting a woman. [Middle English *suitor,* from Anglo-French, follower, from Latin *secūtor,* from *sequī* (past participle *secūtus*), to follow.]

Su·kar·no (sōō-kárnō), **Achmed** (1901–70). Indonesian statesman and first president of Indonesia (1945–67). He assumed dictatorial powers (1960) but was forced to relinquish power (1967) by the army, and General Suharto took control.

Sukarno, Mount. See **Jaya Peak.**

su·ki·ya·ki (sōō-ki-yáaki, sōō-) *n.* A Japanese dish of sliced meat, vegetables, and seasoning fried together. [Japanese.]

Su·la·we·si (sōōllə-wáysi). Mountainous and forested island, lying between New Guinea and Borneo. Part of Indonesia, it was formerly called **Celebes.**

sul·cate (súl-kayt) *adj. Biology.* Having narrow longitudinal indentations; grooved. [Latin *sulcātus,* past participle of *sulcāre,* to furrow, from *sulcus,* furrow, SULCUS.]

sul·cus (súl-kəss) *n., pl.* **-ci** (-sī, -kī) **1.** A narrow, deep furrow or groove. **2.** *Anatomy.* Any of the narrow fissures separating adjacent cerebral convolutions. [Latin *sulcus,* furrow, groove.]

Su·lei·man I (sōō-lay-ma´an, -maan) (c.1494–1566). Turkish sultan, known as Suleiman the Magnificent. He brought the Ottoman empire to its peak, improved the administration of the country and encouraged the arts and sciences.

sulf– *U.S.* Variant of **sulph–.**

sulfur. *U.S.* Variant of **sulphur.**

sulk (sulk) *intr.v.* **sulked, sulking, sulks.** To be sullenly aloof, bad-tempered, or withdrawn, as in silent protest.
~*n. Usually plural.* A mood or display of sulking: *had a fit of the sulks.* [Back-formation from SULKY.]

sulk·y¹ (súlki) *adj.* **-ier, -iest. 1.** Sullenly aloof, bad tempered, or withdrawn. **2.** Characteristic of or showing sullen bad-temper: *a*

sulky face. [Perhaps from obsolete *sulke,* sluggish, perhaps ultimately from Old English *asolcen,* past participle of *āseolcan,* to be lazy, become slack.] **—sulk·i·ly** *adv.* **—sulk·i·ness** *n.*

sulky² *n., pl.* **-ies.** A light two-wheeled vehicle accommodating one person and drawn by one horse. [From SULKY (because it has only one seat for the driver).] **—sulk·y** *adj.*

Sul·la (súllə, sŏollə), **Lucius Cornelius** (138–78 B.C.). Roman general. After a successful military career, he made himself dictator (82–79 B.C.). He tried to reorganize Roman politics, but his influence did not long survive his retirement.

sul·lage (súllij) *n.* **1.** Silt deposited by a current of water. **2.** Sewage. [Probably from Old French *souiller,* to SOIL.]

sul·len (súllən) *adj.* **1.** Showing brooding ill humour or having a tendency to silent or passive gloom and resentment; glumly bad-tempered; morose. **2.** Gloomy or sombre in tone, colour, or portent: *a sullen sky.* [Middle English *solein, solain,* from Anglo-French *solein* (unattested), alone, sullen, from Old French *seul, sol,* alone, single, from Latin *sōlus.*] **—sul·len·ly** *adv.* **—sul·len·ness** *n.*

Sul·li·van (súllivən), **Sir Arthur (Seymour)** (1842–1900). British composer. He is best known for his collaboration with W.S. Gilbert in their light operas which include *H.M.S. Pinafore* (1878), *The Mikado* (1885), and *The Gondoliers* (1889).

Sullivan, John L(awrence) (1858–1918). U.S. boxer. He won (1882) the heavyweight championship by defeating Paddy Ryan at Mississippi City, fighting with bare knuckles and on the turf.

Sullivan, Louis Henri (1856–1924). U.S. architect. His experimental use of steel frames for the construction of skyscrapers earned him the title "Father of Modernism". His famous dictum, "Form follows function", influenced many architects, notably his student Frank Lloyd Wright.

sul·ly (súlli) *tr.v.* **-lied, -lying, -lies. 1.** To mar the cleanness or lustre of; soil; stain. **2.** To defile; tarnish.
~*n., pl.* **sullies.** *Archaic.* Something that sullies; a stain or spot. [Probably from Old French *souiller,* to SOIL.]

Sul·ly (súl-lee), **Maximilien de Béthune, Duc de** (1560–1641). French statesman. As finance minister (1598–1610) to Henry IV, he replenished the treasury and encouraged agriculture and industry.

Sul·ly-Pru·dhomme (súl-lee-prü-dóm), **René François Armand** (1839–1907). French poet. His early works are melancholic, while his later poems are concerned with scientific and philosophic theories. He won the Nobel prize in literature (1901).

sulph– *comb. form.* Indicates sulphur; for example, **sulphide, sulone.** [From SULPHUR.]

sul·pha·di·a·zine (súlfə-dī-ə-zeen) *n.* A sulpha drug, $C_{10}H_{10}N_4O_2S$, used in the treatment of various bacterial infections.

sul·pha drug (súlfə) *n.* Any of a group of sulphonamide compounds such as sulphathiazole and sulphadiazine, capable of inhibiting bacterial growth and activity and used to treat a wide variety of infections. [*Sulpha*nilamide + DRUG.]

sul·pha·nil·a·mide (súlfə-níllə-mīd) *n.* A white odourless crystalline sulphonamide, $H_2N.C_6H_4.SO_2NH_2$, formerly used in the treatment of various bacterial infections. [SULPH– + ANIL(INE) + AMIDE.]

sul·phate (súl-fayt) *n.* A chemical compound containing the bivalent group SO_4.
~*v.* **sulphated, -phating, -phates.** —*tr.* **1.** To treat or react with sulphuric acid or a sulphate. **2.** *Electricity.* To cause lead sulphate to form on (the plates of a lead-acid accumulator). —*intr.* To become sulphated. [French : SULPH– + -ATE.]

sul·pha·thi·a·zole (súlfə-thī-ə-zōl) *n.* A sulpha drug, $C_9H_9N_3O_2S_2$, used to treat a variety of bacterial infections.

sul·phide (súl-fīd) *n.* A compound of bivalent sulphur with an electropositive element or group, usually a metal. [SULPH– + -IDE.]

sul·phite (súl-fīt) *n.* A salt or ester of sulphurous acid. [French, variant of SULPHATE.] **—sul·phit·ic** (sul-fíttik) *adj.*

sulphon– *comb. form.* Indicates: **1.** Sulphonic; for example, **sulphonamide. 2.** Sulphonyl; for example, **sulphonmethane.** [From SULPHONE.]

sul·phon·a·mide (sul-fónnə-mīd ‖ *U.S. also* -fōnə-, -mid) *n.* Any of a group of organic sulphur compounds having the general formula RSO_2NH_2. The group includes the sulpha drugs.

sul·pho·nate (súlfə-nayt) *n.* A compound in which a hydrogen atom is replaced by the sulphonic acid group SO_2OH.
~*tr.v.* **sulphonated, -nating, -nates. 1.** To introduce one or more sulphonic-acid groups into (an organic compound), as by treating with concentrated sulphuric acid. **2.** To treat with sulphonic acid. [SULPHON– + -ATE.] **—sul·pho·na·tion** (-náysh'n) *n.*

sul·phone (súl-fōn) *n.* Any of various organic sulphur compounds having a sulphonyl group, $-SO_2$, attached to two carbon atoms; especially, such a compound used to treat leprosy or tuberculosis. [SULPH– + ONE.]

sul·phon·ic acid (sul-fónnik) *n.* Any of several organic acids containing one or more sulphonic groups, $-SO_2OH$.

sul·phon·meth·ane (súl-fon-mée-thayn, -mé-) *n.* A colourless crystalline or powdered compound, $C_7H_{16}S_2O_4$, used as a hypnotic.

sul·pho·nyl (súlfənil) *n.* The bivalent radical SO_2. Also called "sulphuryl". [SULPHON– + -YL.]

sul·phur, *U.S.* **sul·fur** (súlfər) *n.* Symbol **S 1.** A pale yellow nonmetallic element occurring widely in nature both free and combined in several allotropic forms. It is used in black gunpowder, rubber vulcanisation, the manufacture of insecticides and pharmaceuticals, and in the preparation of important sulphur compounds, such as sulphuric acid. Atomic number 16, atomic weight 32.064, melting point (rhombic) 112.8°C, (monoclinic) 119.0°C, boiling point 444.6°C, relative density, (rhombic) 2.07, (monoclinic)1.957, valencies 2,4,6. **2.** Any of various yellow or orange-yellow butterflies of the family Pieridae. [Middle English *sulphur, sulphur(e)*, from Anglo-French *sulf(e)re*, from Latin *sulphur,* sulphur†.]

sul·phu·rate (súlfə-rayt) *tr.v.* **-rated, -rating, -rates.** To treat or combine with sulphur. [Late Latin *sulfurāre*, from Latin *sulphur,* SULPHUR.] **—sul·phu·ra·tion** (-ráysh'n) *n.*

sulphur bacteria *pl.n.* Bacteria of the order Beggiatoales, which derive their energy from the oxidation of sulphides.

sul·phur-bot·tom (súlfər-bottəm) *n.* The **blue whale** (*see*).

sulphur dioxide *n.* A colourless, extremely irritating gas or liquid, SO_2, used in many industrial processes, especially the manufacture of sulphuric acid. When dissolved in water it forms sulphurous acid.

sul·phu·re·ous (sul-féwr-i-əss) *adj.* Sulphurous.

sul·phu·ret (súl-fewr-et, -fər-) *tr.v.* **-retted** or *U.S.* **-reted, -retting** or *U.S.* **-reting, -rets.** To sulphurise.
~*n.* A sulphide. [New Latin *sulfuretum*, sulphide, from Latin *sulphur,* SULPHUR.]

sul·phu·ric (sul-féwr-ik) *adj.* Of, relating to, or containing sulphur, especially with valency 6.

sulphuric acid *n.* A highly corrosive, dense oily liquid, H_2SO_4, colourless to dark brown depending on purity, used to manufacture a variety of chemicals and materials including fertilisers, dyestuffs, paints, detergents, and explosives. Also called "oil of vitriol".

sul·phu·rise, sul·phu·rize (súl-fewr-īz, -fər-) *tr.v.* **-ised, -ising, -ises. 1.** To treat or impregnate with sulphur; sulphuret. **2.** To bleach or fumigate with sulphur or sulphur dioxide. **—sul·phur·i·sa·tion** (-ī-záysh'n || *U.S.* -i-) *n.*

sul·phu·rous (súl-fər-əss, -fewr-) *adj.* **1.** Of, relating to, derived from, or containing sulphur, especially in its lower valency, 4. **2.** Characteristic of or emanating from burning sulphur. **3.** Fiery.

sulphurous acid *n.* A colourless solution of sulphur dioxide in water, H_2SO_3, characterised by a suffocating sulphurous odour, used as a bleaching agent, preservative, and disinfectant.

sulphur trioxide *n.* A corrosive compound SO_3, having three solid forms that may coexist in a given sample, used in the sulphonation of organic compounds.

sul·phur·yl (súl-fewr-il, -fər-) *n.* **Sulphonyl** (*see*).

sulphuryl chloride *n.* A colourless liquid, SO_2Cl_2, having a pungent odour, used as a chlorinating and dehydrating agent and solvent and in the manufacture of pharmaceuticals and dyestuffs.

sul·tan (súltən) *n.* The ruler of a Muslim country, especially of the former Ottoman Empire. [French, from Medieval Latin *sultānus*, from Arabic *sulṭān*, ruler, from Aramaic *shulṭānā*, "power", from *shəlēṭ*, to have power.]

sul·ta·na (sul-táanə; *for sense 3, usually* səl- || *U.S.* also -tánnə) *n.* **1.** The wife, mother, sister, or daughter of a sultan. Also called "sultaness". **2.** The mistress of a sultan, king, or prince. **3. a.** A small, sweet, seedless raisin of a kind originally produced in Asia Minor. **b.** The grape from which the sultana comes. [Italian, feminine of *sultano*, sultan, from Arabic *sulṭān,* SULTAN.]

sul·tan·ate (súltən-ət, -it, -ayt) *n.* **1.** The office, power, or reign of a sultan. **2.** The domain of a sultan.

sul·try (súltri) *adj.* **-trier, -triest. 1.** Very hot and humid. **2.** Sensual; voluptuous: *a sultry Spanish dance.* [From obsolete *sulter*, variant of SWELTER.] **—sul·tri·ly** *adv.* **—sul·tri·ness** *n.*

sum (sum) *n.* **1.** The amount obtained as a result of adding. **2.** The whole amount, quantity, or number: *the sum of our knowledge.* In both senses also called "sum total". **3.** The highest point or degree; summit. **4.** An amount of money: *They paid an enormous sum.* **5.** An arithmetical problem: *good at sums.* **6.** A summary; the gist. **—in sum.** Essentially and briefly; in short.
~*v.* **summed, summing, sums.** *—tr.* **1.** To summarise; sum up. **2.** To add. Often used with *up.* *—intr.* To add up; amount. Used with *to: The total summed to 739.* **—sum up. 1.** To summarise; recapitulate briefly. **2.** To form a judgment about; appraise: *summed up his character.* [Middle English *summe, somme*, from Old French, from Latin *(res) summa*, the highest thing, sum, total (from the Greek and Roman habit of counting upwards and writing the total at the top), from *summus*, highest, topmost.]

su·mach (shóo-mak, sóo-, séw-) *n.* Also *chiefly U.S.* **su·mac. 1.** Any of various shrubs or small trees of the genus *Rhus.* Some species, such as **poison ivy** (*see*), cause an acute itching rash on contact. **2.** The dried and powdered leaves of some *Rhus* species, especially *R. coraria*, used in tanning and dyeing. [Middle English, from Old French, from Arabic *summaq*, sumach tree, probably from Aramaic, "red".]

Su·ma·tra (soo-máatrə, sóo-, sew-). The westernmost, and second largest island of Indonesia. A volcanic range, which rises to 3 805 metres (12,483 feet), extends along the west coast, and the east is swampland, with dense rain forests in the interior. Sumatra has reserves of oil, natural gas, coal, and silver. Rubber, coffee, tea, and pepper are among the chief farm products. A Dutch colony from 1816, Sumatra was included in the new republic of Indonesia after World War II. **—Su·ma·tran** *adj. & n.*

Su·mer (sóo-mər, séw-). The southern part of ancient Mesopotamia, the site of one of the world's oldest known civilisations, dating back to the fifth millenium B.C.. The Sumerians, who spoke a non-Semitic language, are credited with the invention of the cuneiform system of writing, wheeled vehicles, and the plough. By the third millennium a number of city-states had grown up on the alluvial plains of the lower Tigris and Euphrates, among them Kish, Uruk,

and Ur. Sumer was overrun by Akkad (*c.* 2300 B.C.), and briefly revived by the third dynasty at Ur (*c.* 2100 B.C.). The civilisation declined after Amorite invasions (*c.* 2000 B.C.), and was later absorbed into the empires of Babylon and Assyria.

Su·me·ri·an (soo-méer-i-ən, sew-, sóo-) *adj.* Of or pertaining to ancient Sumer, its people, culture, or language.
~*n.* **1.** A member of an ancient Babylonian people, who established civilisation in Sumer. **2.** The unclassified language used by these people, preserved in cuneiform on clay tablets. See **Japhetic.**

sum·ma cum lau·de (sŏom-aa kŏom lów-day, súm-, -mə, kum, láw-, -di) *adv. Latin.* With the greatest praise. Used on university and college diplomas to designate the highest degree of academic distinction. Compare **cum laude, magna cum laude.** [New Latin.]

sum·ma·rise, sum·ma·rize (súmmə-rīz) *tr.v.* **-rised, -rising, -rises.** To make a summary of; abstract. **—sum·ma·ri·sa·tion** (-rī-záysh'n || *U.S.* -ri-) *n.* **—sum·ma·ri·ser** *n.*

sum·ma·ry (súmməri) *adj.* **1.** Presenting the substance in a condensed form; concise. **2.** Performed speedily and without ceremony: *summary justice.* **3.** *Law.* Of, pertaining to or designating the right of a court to try or judge a case without a jury: *summary jurisdiction.* **—See Synonyms at concise.**
~*n., pl.* **summaries.** A condensation of the substance of a larger work; an abstract or abridgment containing the main or important points. [Middle English, from Medieval Latin *summārius*, comprising the principal parts, from Latin *summa,* SUM.] **—sum·ma·ri·ly** (-li; *also, chiefly U.S.,* su-mérrəli) *adv.* **—sum·ma·ri·ness** *n.*

sum·ma·tion (su-máysh'n) *n.* **1.** The act or process of adding or totalling; addition. **2.** A sum or aggregate. **3.** A summing-up; a recapitulation. **4.** The interaction of two substances, such as drugs or hormones, with similar effects such that their combined effect is greater than their separate effects. [Medieval Latin *summātiō* (stem *summātiōn*-), from *summāre*, to sum up, from Latin *summa,* SUM.]

sum·mer¹ (súmmər) *n.* **1.** The usually warmest season of the year occurring between spring and autumn. In the Northern Hemisphere it extends from the summer solstice to the autumnal equinox and is popularly considered to comprise June, July, and August, while in the Southern Hemisphere it falls between the winter solstice and the vernal equinox or, popularly, December, January, and February. **2.** Any period regarded as a time of warmth, fruition, fulfilment, happiness, or beauty.
~*adj.* Pertaining to, characteristic of, or occurring in summer.
~*v.* **summered, -mering, -mers.** *—tr.* To lodge or keep during the summer. *—intr.* To pass the summer. [Middle English *somer, sumer,* Old English *sumor.*] **—sum·mer·ly** *adj. & adv.*

summer² *n. Architecture.* **1.** A heavy horizontal timber that serves as a supporting beam, especially for the floor above. **2.** A lintel. **3.** A large, heavy stone usually set on the top of a column or pilaster to support an arch or lintel. [Middle English *summer, somer,* from Anglo-French *sumer, somer,* "pack animal", from Vulgar Latin *saumārius* (unattested), variant of Late Latin *sagmārius,* from *sagma,* packsaddle, from Greek. See **sumpter.**]

summer cypress *n.* A plant, *Kochia scoparia*, native to Eurasia, having dense foliage that turns bright red in autumn. Also called "burning bush".

sum·mer·house (súmmər-howss) *n.* A small, roofed structure in a park or garden affording shade and rest; a gazebo.

summer pudding *n.* A pudding made from stewed soft fruits, such as raspberries and blackcurrants, enclosed in a bread casing.

summersault, summerset. Variants of **somersault.**

summer savory *n.* See **savory** (plant).

summer school *n.* An academic course held during the summer, outside university, college, or school terms.

summer solstice *n. Astronomy.* A **solstice** (*see*).

sum·mer·time (súmmər-tīm) *n.* **1.** The summer season. **2.** A daylight-saving time, such as British Summer Time.

sum·mer·wood (súmmər-wŏod) *n.* Wood that develops during the latter part of the growing season and is harder and less porous than springwood. Compare **springwood.**

sum·mer·y (súmməri) *adj.* Pertaining to or suggesting summer.

sum·ming-up (súmming-úp) *n.* A summary of the evidence in a trial by a judge, directed to a jury, together with guidance on what form the jury's decision should take in the light of their view of the evidence.

sum·mit (súmmit) *n.* **1.** The highest point or part; the top, especially of a mountain. **2.** The highest degree of achievement or status, especially of government. **3.** A conference involving heads of government and sometimes leading government ministers. Also used adjectivally: *summit talks.* [Middle English *somette,* from Old French *sommette, sumet,* diminutive of *som, sum,* top, from Latin *summum,* neuter of *summus,* highest, topmost.] **—sum·mit·al** *adj.*
   Synonyms: summit, peak, pinnacle, acme, apex, zenith, climax.

sum·mi·teer (summi-téer) *n.* One taking part in a summit conference.

sum·mon (súmmən) *tr.v.* **-moned, -moning, -mons. 1.** To call together; convene. **2.** To send for; request to appear. **3.** To order (a person) to appear in court by the issue of a summons. **4.** To order to do a specified act: *summon the captain to surrender.* **5.** To call forth; rouse; muster. Often used with *up: He summoned up a smile.* [Middle English *somo(u)nen,* from Old French *somondre,* from Vulgar Latin *summonere* (unattested), from Latin *summonēre,* to remind secretly : *sub-,* secretly + *monēre,* to remind, warn.]

sum·mon·er (súmmənər) *n.* **1.** A person who summons. **2.** Formerly, a court official who served summonses.

sum·mons (súmmənz) *n., pl.* **-monses. 1.** A call or order to appear or to do something. **2.** *Law.* An official order summoning a defendant or witness to report to a court.
~*tr.v.* **summonsed, -monsing, -monses.** To serve a court summons to. [Middle English *somo(u)ns,* from Old French *som(o)unse,* from Gallo-Roman *summonsa* (unattested), from Latin *summonita,* from the feminine past participle of *summonēre,* to remind secretly, SUMMON.]

sum·mum bo·num (soom-əm bónəm, súm-) *n. Latin.* The greatest or supreme good.

Su·mo (soo-mō, séw-) *n.* The main Japanese form of wrestling, in which the object is to make one's opponent touch the ground with his body or to force him out of the ring. [Japanese.]

sump (sump) *n.* **1.** The crankcase or oil reservoir of an internal-combustion engine. **2. a.** Any low area that receives drainage. **b.** A cesspool. **3.** A hole at the lowest point of a mine shaft into which water is drained in order to be pumped out. [Middle English *sompe,* a swamp, morass, from Middle Low German or Middle Dutch *sump.*]

sump·ter (súmptər) *n. Archaic.* A pack animal. [Middle English *sum(p)ter, sometour,* driver of a pack animal, from Old French *som(m)etier,* from Vulgar Latin *saumatārius* (unattested), from Late Latin *sagma,* packsaddle, from Greek, from *satteint,* to pack.]

sump·tu·ar·y (súmp-tew-əri, -choo- ‖ -erri) *adj.* **1.** Pertaining to expenditure; especially, regulating or limiting expenses. **2.** Regulating personal behaviour on moral or religious grounds: *sumptuary laws.* [Latin *sumptuārius,* from *sumptus,* expense, from the past participle of *sūmere,* to consume, spend, take.]

sump·tu·ous (súmp-tew-əss, -choo-) *adj.* Of a size or splendour suggesting great expense; lavish. [Middle English, from Old French *sumptueux,* from Latin *sumptuōsus,* from *sumptus,* expense. See **sumptuary.**] **—sump·tu·ous·ly** *adv.* **—sump·tu·ous·ness** *n.*

sun (sun) *n.* **1. a.** *Often capital* **S.** A star that is the basis of the Solar System and that sustains life on Earth, being the source of heat and light. It has a mean distance from Earth of about 150 million kilometres (93 million miles) and a diameter of approximately 1.39 million kilometres (865,000 miles). Also called "Sol". **b.** The sun in a particular aspect or at a particular time or place: *the midnight sun.* **2.** Any star that is the centre of a planetary system. **3.** The radiant energy, especially heat and visible light, emitted by the sun; sunshine. **4.** *Archaic.* **a.** A day. **b.** A year. **—catch the sun.** To be tanned or sunburnt.
~*v.* **sunned, sunning, suns.** **—***tr.* **1.** To expose to the sun's rays. **2.** To warm, dry, or tan in the sun. **—***intr.* To bask in the sun. [Middle English *sonne, sunne,* Old English *sunne.*]

Sun. Sunday.

sun·baked (sún-baykt) *adj.* Hardened by the heat of the sun.

sun·bathe (sún-bayth) *intr.v.* **-bathed, -bathing, -bathes.** To expose the body to the direct rays of the sun. **—sun·bath·er** *n.*

sun·beam (sún-beem) *n.* A ray of sunlight.

sun bear *n.* A small, tropical Asian bear, *Helarctos malayanus,* that feeds chiefly on honey and insects.

sun·bed (sún-bed) *n.* An apparatus consisting of a couch with an overhead sun lamp, used to acquire an artificial suntan.

sun·bird (sún-burd) *n.* Any of various small, tropical Old World birds of the family Nectariniidae, having a slender, downward-curving bill and often brightly coloured plumage in the male.

sun bittern *n.* A cranelike tropical American bird, *Eurypyga helias,* having mottled brownish plumage.

sunblind *n. British.* An awning over the outside of a window.

sun·bon·net (sún-bonnit) *n.* A child's wide-brimmed bonnet with a projecting flap at the back for protecting the neck from the sun.

sun·bow (sún-bō) *n.* A rainbow-like display of colours resulting from the refraction of sunlight through a spray of water.

sun·burn (sún-burn) *n.* **1.** Inflammation or blistering of the skin caused by overexposure to direct sunlight or a sunlamp. **2.** Suntan.
~*v.* **sunburnt** (-burnt) or **-burned, -burning, -burns.** **—***tr.* To affect with sunburn. **—***intr.* To be affected with sunburn.

sun·burst (sún-burst) *n.* **1.** A sudden burst of sunlight, as through broken clouds. **2.** A pattern or design consisting of a central disc with radiating spires projecting in the manner of sunbeams. **3.** A jewelled brooch with such a design.

sun·dae (sún-day ‖ -di) *n.* A dish of ice cream with toppings such as syrup, fruits, nuts, and whipped cream. [Perhaps from SUNDAY, for ice cream served on weekdays but left over from Sunday.]

Sun·da Islands (sún-də, soon-, soo-) *n. Dutch* **Soenda.** Group of islands lying between the Indian Ocean and South China Sea. The group comprises the Greater Sunda Islands, which include Java, Sumatra, Borneo, and Sulawesi, and the Lesser Sunda Islands, now known as Nusa Tenggara, which include Bali, Sumbawa, Sumba, and Timor. The territory is Indonesian, with the exception of Brunei, and the Malaysian states of Sabah and Sarawak.

sun dance *n.* A ritual dance performed by the North American Plains Indians at the summer solstice.

Sun·day (sún-di, -day) *n. Abbr.* **Sun., S.** The day of the week following Saturday and the second day of the weekend, observed as the Sabbath by Christians. See **Sabbath.** [Middle English *sone(n)day, sun(en)day,* Old English *sunnandæg,* "day of the sun".]

Sunday best *n. Informal.* One's best or smartest clothes. [Traditionally clothes for wearing only in church on Sundays.]

Sunday driver *n. Informal.* A slow and exaggeratedly careful motorist, such as one who drives mainly for recreation.

Sunday painter *n.* One who paints pictures purely as a hobby.

Sunday school *n. Abbr.* **S.S. 1.** A school, generally affiliated with a church, that offers religious instruction for children on Sundays. **2.** The teachers and pupils of a Sunday school.

sun deck *n.* **1.** An upper, exposed, deck on a passenger ship. **2.** *U.S.* A roof, balcony, or terrace used for sun-bathing.

sun·der (súndər) *v.* **-dered, -dering, -ders.** **—***tr.* To break apart; divide; sever. **—***intr.* To break into parts. **—See** Synonyms at **separate.**
~*n. Rare.* A division or separation. [Middle English *sund(e)ren,* Old English *syndrian, sundrian.*] **—sun·der·ance** *n.*

Sun·der·land (súndərlənd). Port and industrial town in north-eastern England, situated at the mouth of the river Wear. In Monkwearmouth, the area north of the river, there stands a seventh-century abbey, house of the Venerable Bede. Coal has been shipped from the port since 1396.

sun·dew (sún-dew ‖ -doo) *n.* Any of several insectivorous plants of the genus *Drosera* having leaves covered with sticky hairs, which trap insects. [Translation of Latin *rōs sōlis.*]

sun·di·al (sún-dī-əl, -dīl) *n.* An instrument that indicates local apparent solar time by measuring the hour angle of the sun with a style (a projecting piece) that casts a shadow on a calibrated dial.

sun disc *n.* A symbol in Egyptian art consisting of a disc set between outspread wings, representing the sun god.

sun·dog (sún-dog ‖ -dawg) *n. Meteorology.* **1.** A **parhelion** (see). **2.** A small halo or rainbow near the horizon just off the parhelic circle.

sun·down (sún-down) *n.* Sunset.

sun·down·er (sún-downər) *n.* **1.** *Informal.* In Australia, a tramp who looks for a place to sleep at sunset. **2.** An alcoholic drink taken at sunset.

sun·dress (sún-dress) *n.* A light, woman's or child's dress that exposes the back, shoulders, top of the chest, and arms to the sun.

sun·dries (sún-driz ‖ -dreez) *pl.n.* Articles too small or numerous to be itemised; miscellaneous items. [From SUNDRY.]

sun·dry (súndri) *adj.* Several; various; miscellaneous. [Middle English *sundri, sondri,* Old English *syndrig,* apart, separate.]

sun·fish (sún-fish) *n., pl.* **-fishes** or collectively **sunfish. 1.** Any of various large marine fishes of the family Molidae; especially, *Mola mola,* having a round, laterally flattened body. **2.** Any of various North American freshwater fishes of the family Centrarchidae, having a laterally flattened, often brightly coloured body. [Referring to its shape and brilliant colour.]

sun·flow·er (sún-flow-ər, -flowr) *n.* **1.** Any of several plants of the genus *Helianthus;* especially, *H. annuus,* having tall, coarse stems and large yellow-rayed flowers that produce edible seeds rich in oil. **2.** Brilliant yellow to strong or vivid orange yellow.

sung. Past participle of **sing.**

Sung, Song (soong). Chinese dynasty (960–1279). Under their rule China achieved one of its highest levels of culture and prosperity.

sun·glass (sún-glaass ‖ -glass) *n.* A **burning-glass** (see).

sun·glass·es (sún-glaassiz ‖ -glassiz) *pl.n.* Glasses with tinted or polarising lenses to protect the eyes from the sun's glare.

sun·glow (sún-glō) *n.* A rose or yellow glow in the sky preceding sunrise or following sunset.

sun·god *n.* A god that personifies the sun.

sun·grebe (sún-greeb) *n.* A bird, the **finfoot** (see).

sun·hat (sún-hat) *n.* A hat with a wide brim, worn to protect the head, face, and neck from the sun.

sunk. Past participle and alternative past tense of **sink.**

sunk·en (súngkən). Alternative past participle of **sink.**
~*adj.* **1.** Depressed, fallen in, or hollowed: *sunken cheeks.* **2.** Situated beneath the surface of the water or ground; submerged. **3.** Below the surrounding level: *a sunken meadow.*

sunk fence *n.* A **ha-ha** (see).

sun lamp *n.* **1.** A lamp that radiates over a wide range of the spectrum from ultraviolet to infrared and is used in therapeutic and cosmetic treatments. **2.** A high-intensity lamp with parabolic mirrors, used in cinema photography.

sun·less (sún-ləss, -liss) *adj.* **1.** Without sunlight; dark or overcast. **2.** Gloomy; cheerless. **—sun·less·ness** *n.*

sun·light (sún-līt) *n.* The light of the sun; sunshine.

sun·lit (sún-lit) *adj.* Illuminated by the sun.

sun lounge *n. Chiefly British.* A room with a glass roof and walls or very large windows, designed to receive maximum sunlight.

sunn (sun) *n.* **1.** A plant, *Crotalaria juncea,* of tropical Asia and Australia, having clusters of yellow flowers. **2.** A tough fibre from the stems of this plant, used for cordage. Also called "Madras hemp", "sunn hemp". [Hindi *san,* from Sanskrit *śaṇat,* hempen.]

Sun·na, Sun·nah (súnnə, soonnə) *n.* The body of traditional Muslim law, observed by the orthodox Muslims and based on the words and acts of Muhammad. [Arabic *sunnah,* form, course, rule.]

Sun·ni (súnni, soonni) *n.* The great branch of Islam following orthodox tradition and accepting the first four caliphs as rightful successors of Muhammad. Compare **Shiah.** [Arabic *sunnīy,* "adherent of the Sunna", from *sunnah,* SUNNA.]

Sun·nite (sún-īt, soon-) *n.* A Muslim of the Sunni. [From SUNNI.]

sun·ny (súnni) *adj.* **-nier, -niest. 1.** Exposed to or filled with sunshine: *a sunny room.* **2.** Cheerful; light-hearted: *a sunny smile; a sunny soul.* **—sun·ni·ly** *adv.* **—sun·ni·ness** *n.*

sunny side *n.* **1.** The sunlit side, as of a street. **2.** The positive or encouraging aspect of a situation. **—on the sunny side of.** *Informal.* Younger than the age specified.

sun·ny-side up (súnni-sīd) *adv. Chiefly U.S.* Served with the fried side down and the yolk on top. Said of eggs. —**sunny-side up** *adj.*

sun·ray (sún-ray) *n.* **1.** A sunbeam. **2.** An ultraviolet ray from a sun lamp.

sun·rise (sún-rīz) *n.* **1. a.** The event or time of the daily first appearance of the sun above the eastern horizon. **b.** The time when the centre of the rising sun is on the horizon. **2.** The atmospheric effects of sunrise. **3.** An outset or emergence, as of civilisation.

sun roof *n.* **1.** A flat roof on a building used for sunbathing. **2.** A sliding panel in the roof of a car. In this sense, also "sunshine roof".

sun screen *n.* A substance or preparation that protects the skin by blocking harmful ultraviolet rays.

sun·seek·er (sún-seekər) *n.* **1.** A holidaymaker who seeks sunny climates. **2.** A photoelectric device in spacecraft that keeps instruments constantly orientated towards the sun.

sun·set (sún-set) *n.* **1. a.** The event or time of the daily disappearance of the sun below the western horizon. **b.** The time when the centre of the setting sun is on the horizon. **2.** The atmospheric effects of sunset. **3.** The decline or final phase, as of life.

sun·shade (sún-shayd) *n.* Anything used as a protection from the sun's rays, such as an awning or a parasol.

sun·shine (sún-shīn) *n.* **1. a.** The light or warmth of the sun; the direct rays from the sun. **b.** An area lit up by the sun. **2. a.** Happiness or cheerfulness. **b.** A source of happiness or cheerfulness: *You are my sunshine.* **3.** Used as an affectionate or ironic form of address. —**sun·shin·y** *adj.*

sun·spot (sún-spot) *n.* **1.** Any of the relatively dark spots that appear briefly in groups on the surface of the Sun during an approximate 11-year cycle and are associated with strong magnetic fields. **2.** *British Informal.* A sunny place; especially, a holiday resort.

sun·star (sún-staar) *n.* Any starfish of the genus *Solaster,* having up to 13 arms.

sun·stone (sún-stōn) *n.* A type of feldspar, **aventurine** *(see).*

sun·stroke (sún-strōk) *n.* **Heat stroke** *(see)* caused by overexposure to the sun. Also "insolation". [Translation of French *coup de soleil.*]

sun·tan (sún-tan) *n.* A brownish skin colour resulting from exposure to the ultraviolet rays of the sun or a sun lamp.

~*adj.* Designating a lotion, cream, or oil used to protect the skin from damage by the sun's rays, and sometimes accelerating their tanning effects. —**sun·tanned** *adj.*

sun trap *n.* An area which is sheltered and exposed to the sun.

sun·up (sún-up) *n. Chiefly U.S.* The time of sunrise.

sun·ward (sún-wərd) *adj.* Facing or directed towards the sun.

~*adv. U.S.* Variant of **sunwards**.

sun·wards (sún-wərdz) *adv.* Also *U.S.* **sunward.** Towards the sun.

sun·wise (sún-wīz) *adv.* From left to right, like the sun's course as viewed in the Northern Hemisphere.

Sun Zhong-shan (sŏŏn-jóng-shán), also known as Sun Yat-sen (1866–1925). Chinese revolutionary politician. He played a large part in the revolution against the Manchus. He united all the revolutionary parties under the Guomindang (1911) and was appointed provisional president of the Republic after the fall of the Manchus. He resigned (1912) in favour of Yüan Shih-kay.

su·o ju·re (sŏŏ-ō jóor-i, séw-, yóor-, -ay) *adv. Law.* In one's own right. [Latin.]

su·o lo·co (sŏŏ-ō lóckō, séw-, lóko) *adv. Law.* In a person or thing's rightful place. [Latin, in its (his, her) own place.]

Suomi. See **Finland.**

sup[1] (sup) *v.* **supped, supping, sups.** —*tr.* **1.** To take (a liquid) into the mouth by sips. **2.** *Northern English Regional.* To drink. —*intr.* To take liquid into the mouth in small amounts.

~*n.* A mouthful or taste of liquid. [Middle English *s(o)upen,* Old English *sūpan.*]

sup[2] *intr.v.* **supped, supping, sups.** *Archaic.* To eat the evening meal; have supper. [Middle English *soupen, suppen,* from Old French *s(o)uper,* from *soup,* piece of bread dipped in broth, soup, from Germanic.]

sup. **1.** above [Latin *supra.*] **2.** superior. **3.** *Grammar.* superlative. **4.** supine (noun). **5.** supplement; supplementary. **6.** supply.

su·per (sŏŏ-pər, séw-) *n.* **1.** *Informal.* A police superintendent. **2.** *Informal.* An extra person, especially a **supernumerary** *(see).* **3.** An article or product of a superior size, quality, or grade. **4.** *U.S.* A porter or caretaker in a building.

~*adj. Slang.* Ideal; first-rate. Sometimes used as an interjection. [By shortening.]

super– *comb. form.* Indicates: **1.** Placement above, over, or outside; for example, **supercolumnar, superimpose. 2.** Superiority in size, quality, number, or degree; for example, **superfine, supermarket. 3. a.** A degree exceeding a specified level; for example, **supersonic. b.** An extraordinary degree; for example, **superhero. 4.** Addition; for example, **superadd. 5.** *Chemistry.* The presence of a specified ingredient in a high proportion; for example, **superphosphate.** *Note:* Many compounds other than those entered here may be formed with *super-.* In this dictionary in forming compounds, *super-* is normally joined with the following element without space or hyphen: *superrefined.* However, many users prefer the hyphenated form, especially in less standardised compounds, for example **super-tight.** [Latin *super,* above, over.]

super. **1.** superintendent. **2.** superior. **3.** supernumerary.

su·per·a·ble (sŏŏ-pərəb'l, séw-) *adj.* Capable of being overcome or surmounted. [Latin *superābilis,* from *superāre,* to go over, overcome, from *super,* above, over.] —**su·per·a·bil·i·ty** (-pərə-bílləti) *n.* **su·per·a·ble·ness** *n.* —**su·per·a·bly** *adv.*

su·per·a·bound (sŏŏ-pərə-bównd, séw-) *intr.v.* **-bounded, -bound-**

ing, **-bounds.** To be unusually or excessively abundant. [Middle English *superabounden,* from Late Latin *superabundāre* : Latin *super-,* excessively + *abundāre,* ABOUND.]

su·per·a·bun·dant (sŏŏ-pərə-búndənt, séw-) *adj.* Abundant to excess; more than ample. [Middle English, from Late Latin *superabundāns* (stem *superabundant-*), present participle of *superabundāre,* SUPERABOUND.] —**su·per·a·bun·dance** *n.* —**super·a·bun·dant·ly** *adv.*

su·per·add (sŏŏ-pər-ád, séw-) *tr.v.* **-added, -adding, -adds.** To add to something that has already been added to.

su·per·al·tern (sŏŏ-pər-áwl-tern, séw-) *n. Logic.* A universal proposition that is a ground for the immediate inference of a corresponding subalternate. [SUPER- + *altern,* as in SUBALTERN.]

su·per·an·nu·ate (sŏŏ-pər-ánnew-ayt, séw-) *tr.v.* **-ated, -ating, -ates. 1.** To allow to retire on a pension because of age or infirmity. **2.** To set aside or discard as old-fashioned or obsolete. [Back-formation from SUPERANNUATED.] —**su·per·an·nu·a·tion** (-áysh'n) *n.*

su·per·an·nu·at·ed (sŏŏ-pər-ánnew-aytid, séw-) *adj.* **1.** Retired or discharged because of age or infirmity. **2.** Too old or out of date to be worth preserving. **3.** Obsolete. —See Synonyms at **old.** [Medieval Latin *superannuātus,* past participle of *superannuāri,* to be too old : Latin *super,* above + *annus,* year, time of life.]

su·perb (sŏŏ-pérb, séw-, sŏŏ- ‖ soo-) *adj.* **1.** Of unusually high quality. **2.** Majestic; imposing. **3.** Rich; luxurious. [French *superbe,* from Latin *superbus,* superior, proud, arrogant.] —**su·perb·ly** *adv.* —**su·perb·ness** *n.*

su·per·bug (sŏŏ-pər-bug, séw-) *n. Informal.* A bacterium that has developed resistance to antibiotics.

su·per·cal·en·der (sŏŏ-pər-kál-indər, séw-, -kal-) *n.* A calender with a number of rollers for giving a high finish or gloss to paper. —**su·per·cal·en·der** *tr.v.*

su·per·car·go (sŏŏ-pər-kárgō, séw-) *n., pl.* **-goes** or **-gos.** An officer on board a merchant ship who has charge of the cargo and its sale and purchase. [Variant of earlier *supracargo,* from Spanish *sobrecargo* : *sobre-,* over, from Latin *super-* + CARGO.]

su·per·charge (sŏŏ-pər-chaarj, séw-) *tr.v.* **-charged, -charging, -charges. 1.** To increase the power of (an engine) by fitting a supercharger. **2.** To charge excessively, as with emotion or tension. **3.** To pressurise (a fluid).

~*n.* An excess or extra charge.

su·per·charg·er (sŏŏ-pər-chaarjər, séw-) *n.* A blower or compressor for supplying air under high pressure to the cylinders of an internal-combustion engine. Also called "booster".

su·per·cil·i·ar·y (sŏŏ-pər-sílli-əri, séw- ‖ -erri) *adj.* **1.** Of or pertaining to the eyebrow. **2.** Located over the eyebrow or a corresponding region in animals. [New Latin *superciliaris,* from Latin *supercilium,* eyebrow. See **supercilious.**]

su·per·cil·i·ous (sŏŏ-pər-sílli-əss, séw-, sŏŏ-) *adj.* Showing or characterised by haughty scorn or indifference; disdainful. —See Synonyms at **proud.** [Latin *superciliōsus,* from Latin *supercilium,* "upper eyelid", eyebrow, pride : *super-,* above + *cilium,* (lower) eyelid.] —**su·per·cil·i·ous·ly** *adv.* —**su·per·cil·i·ous·ness** *n.*

su·per·class (sŏŏ-pər-klaass, séw- ‖ -klass) *n. Biology.* A taxonomic category ranking below a phylum and above a class.

su·per·co·lum·nar (sŏŏ-pər-kə-lúm-nər, séw-) *adj. Architecture.* **1.** Having one order of columns above another. **2.** Situated above a colonnade or column.

su·per·con·duc·tiv·i·ty (sŏŏ-pər-kón-duk-tívvəti, séw-) *n.* A property of certain metals, alloys and ceramics whereby they exhibit virtually no electrical resistance at extremely low temperatures. —**su· per·con·duc·tive** (-kən-dúktiv ‖ -kon-) *adj.* —**su·per·con·duc·tor** (-kən-dúktər ‖ -kon-) *n.*

su·per·cool (sŏŏ-pər-kŏŏl, séw-) *v.* **-cooled, -cooling, -cools.** —*tr.* To cool (a liquid) below a transition temperature without the transition occurring; especially, to cool below the freezing point without solidification. —*intr.* To become supercooled. Used of a liquid.

su·per·crit·i·cal (sŏŏ-pər-kríttik'l, séw-) *n. Physics.* Having or involving a chain reaction that is self-sustaining and uncontrolled. Said of nuclear reactions, reactors, weapons, and the like.

su·per·dense theory (sŏŏ-pər-dénss, séw-) *n. Astronomy.* A theory of the origin of the universe, the **big-bang theory** *(see).*

su·per·dom·i·nant (sŏŏ-pər-dómminənt, séw-) *n. U.S.* The **submediant** *(see).*

su·per·du·per (sŏŏ-pər-dŏŏpər, séw-) *adj. Informal.* Great; marvellous. [Reduplication of SUPER (superior).]

su·per·e·go (sŏŏ-pər-éegō, séw-, -éggō) *n., pl.* **-egos.** *Psychology.* The division of the psyche that develops by the incorporation of the perceived moral standards of the community as they are transferred from parent to child, is mainly unconscious, and includes the conscience. See **ego, id.**

su·per·el·e·va·tion (sŏŏ-pər-élli-váysh'n, séw-) *n.* The difference in height between the outer and inner edges of a curve in a railway track or road.

su·per·em·i·nent (sŏŏ-pər-émminənt, séw-) *adj.* Pre-eminent. [Late Latin *superēminēns* (stem *superēminent-*), from Latin, present participle of *superēminēre,* to rise above : *super-,* above + *ēminēre,* to stand out (see **eminent**).] —**su·per·em·i·nence** *n.* —**su·per·em·i·nent·ly** *adv.*

su·per·e·ro·gate (sŏŏ-pər-érra-gayt, séw-, -érrō-) *intr.v.* **-gated, -gating, -gates.** *Rare.* To do more than is required, ordered, or expected. [Late Latin *superērogāre,* to spend more : Latin *super-,* excessively + *ērogāre,* to spend, pay out money from the public treasury (after asking the people's consent) : *ex-*, out of + *rogāre*, to ask.] **—su·per·er·o·ga·tor** *n.*

su·per·er·o·ga·tion (sōō-pər-érrə-gáysh'n, séw-, -érrō-) *n.* The performance of more than is required, ordered, or expected.

su·per·e·rog·a·to·ry (sōō-pər-e-róggə-tri, séw-, -i-, -təri) *adj.* Also **su·per·e·rog·a·tive** (-tiv). **1.** Performed or observed beyond the degree required or expected. **2.** Superfluous; unnecessary.

su·per·fam·i·ly (sōō-pər-fám-li, séw-, -əli) *n., pl.* **-lies.** *Biology.* A taxonomic category ranking below an order or its subdivisions and above a family.

su·per·fat·ted (sōō-pər-fáttid, séw-) *adj.* Containing extra fat. Said of soap.

su·per·fe·cun·da·tion (sōō-pər-féekən-dáysh'n, séw-, -féckən-) *n.* The fertilisation of more than one ovum within a single menstrual cycle by separate acts of coitus, especially by different males.

su·per·fe·tate (sōō-pər-fee-táyt, séw-, -fée-tayt) *intr.v.* **-tated, -tating, -tates.** To conceive when a foetus is already present in the uterus. [Latin *superfētāre* : *super-*, over, in addition to + *fētāre*, to breed, impregnate, from *fētus*, young, foetus.]

su·per·fe·ta·tion (sōō-pər-fee-táysh'n, séw-) *n.* The presence in the uterus of foetuses of different ages resulting from the fertilisation of a second ovum some time after the start of pregnancy.

su·per·fi·cial (sōō-pər-físh'l, séw-) *adj.* **1.** Of, affecting, or being on or near the surface: *a superficial wound.* **2. a.** Concerned with or comprehending only what is apparent, obvious, or insubstantial. **b.** Shallow; not thorough or searching. **3. a.** Apparent rather than actual or substantial: *a superficial likeness.* **b.** Trivial; insignificant. **4.** Involving only the surface area. Said of measurements. **5.** *Geology.* Lying on the surface; not derived from the rocks below. Said of a deposit. [Middle English, from Late Latin *superficiālis*, from Latin *superficiēs*, surface, SUPERFICIES.] **—su·per·fi·ci·al·i·ty,** (-físh-i-ál-əti), **su·per·fi·cial·ness** *n.* **—su·per·fi·cial·ly** *adv.*

Synonyms: superficial, shallow, cursory, perfunctory.

su·per·fi·ci·es (sōō-pər-físh-eez, séw-, sōō-, -i-eez) *n., pl.* **superficies.** *Rare.* **1.** The surface of an area or body. **2.** The external appearance or aspect of a thing. [Latin *superficiēs*, surface : *super-*, above, over + *faciēs*, FACE.]

su·per·fine (sōō-pər-fīn, séw-, -fīn) *adj.* **1.** Of exceptional quality or refinement. **2.** Of extra fine texture. **3.** Overdelicate or refined. **—su·per·fine·ness** *n.*

su·per·fix (sōō-pər-fiks, séw-) *n. Linguistics.* A suprasegmental feature distinguishing the meaning or grammatical function of one word or phrase from that of another.

su·per·flu·id (sōō-pər-flōō-id, séw- || -fléw-) *n.* A fluid, such as a form of helium, exhibiting frictionless flow at temperatures close to absolute zero. **—su·per·flu·id·i·ty** (-floo-íddəti) *n.*

su·per·flu·i·ty (sōō-pər-flōō-əti, séw- || -fléw-) *n., pl.* **-ties. 1.** The quality or condition of being superfluous. **2.** Something that is superfluous. **3.** Overabundance; excess.

su·per·flu·ous (sōō-pérfloo-əss, sew-, sōō- || -pérflew-) *adj.* **1.** Beyond what is required or sufficient; extra. **2.** Excessive; unnecessary or redundant. [Middle English, from Latin *superfluus*, overflowing, from *superfluere*, to overflow : *super-*, over + *fluere*, to flow.] **—su·per·flu·ous·ly** *adv.* **—su·per·flu·ous·ness** *n.*

su·per·gene (sōō-pər-jeen, séw-) *n.* A group of genes closely linked on a chromosome so that they are rarely separated by crossing over and therefore tend to function as a single gene.

su·per·gi·ant (sōō-pər-jī-ənt, séw-) *n.* Any of a class of bright low-density stars with diameters and luminosities thousands of times greater than that of the Sun.

su·per·gla·cial (sōō-pər-gláy-si-əl, séw-, -shi-, -sh'l) *adj.* Formed or originating on the surface of a glacier.

Su·per·glue (sōō-pər-glōō, séw- || -glew) *n.* The trademark for a very strong type of glue which forms a tight bond in a few seconds. **—su·per·glue** *tr.v.*

su·per·grass (sōō-pər-graass, séw- || -grass) *n. British Slang.* A criminal who gives information to the police, especially about lots of people or important offences. Compare **grass** (sense 6).

su·per·heat (sōō-pər-héet, séw-) *tr.v.* **-heated, -heating, -heats. 1.** To heat excessively; overheat. **2.** To heat (steam or other vapour not in contact with its own liquid) beyond its saturation point at a given pressure. **3.** To heat (a liquid) above its boiling point at a given pressure without causing vaporisation.

~*n.* (-heet). **1.** The amount that a vapour is superheated. **2.** The heat imparted in the process. **—su·per·heat·er** *n.*

su·per·he·ro (sōō-pər-heer-ō, séw-) *n., pl.* **-heroes.** An imaginary or mythical personage, especially a cartoon character, endowed with superhuman strength or powers. **—su·per·her·o·ine** *n.*

su·per·het·er·o·dyne (sōōpər-héttə-rə-dīn, séw-, -rō-) *adj.* Designating or pertaining to a form of radio reception in which the frequency of an incoming radio signal is converted to an intermediate frequency, by mixing with a locally generated signal, to facilitate amplification and the rejection of unwanted signals.

~*n.* A superheterodyne radio receiver. Also called "superhet". [*supersonic* + *heterodyne.*]

su·per·high frequency (sōō-pər-hī, séw-) *n. Abbr.* **shf, SHF** Any radio frequency between 3,000 and 30,000 megahertz.

su·per·high·way (sōō-pər-hī-way, séw-) *n. U.S.* A broad motorway for high-speed traffic, usually with six or more traffic lanes.

su·per·hu·man (sōō-pər-héwmən, séw- || -yōōmən) *adj.* **1.** Above or beyond the human; divine. **2.** Beyond ordinary or normal human ability, power, or experience: *a superhuman effort.* **—su·per·hu·man·i·ty** (-hew-mánnəti || -yōō-) *n.* **—su·per·hu·man·ly** *adv.*

su·per·im·pose (sōō-pər-im-pṓz, séw-) *tr.v.* **-posed, -posing, -poses.** To lay or place upon or over something else. **—su·per·im·po·si·tion** (-ímpə-zísh'n) *n.*

su·per·in·cum·bent (sōō-pər-in-kúmbənt, séw-) *adj.* Lying, resting, or suspended on or above something else. [Latin *superincumbēns* (stem *superincumbent-*), present participle of *superincumbere*, to lie down on or above : *super-*, above + *incumbere*, to lie down (see **incumbent**).] **—su·per·in·cum·bence, su·per·in·cum·ben·cy** *n.* **—su·per·in·cum·bent·ly** *adv.*

su·per·in·duce (sōō-pər-in-déwss, séw- || -dōōss) *tr.v.* **-duced, -ducing, -duces.** To introduce as an addition. [Latin *superindūcere*, to bring upon : *super-*, on, over, in addition + *indūcere*, to lead in, INDUCE.] **—su·per·in·duce·ment, su·per·in·duc·tion** (-dúksh'n) *n.*

su·per·in·fec·tion (sōō-pər-in-feksh'n, séw-, -féksh'n) *n.* An infection that develops during the course of another infection, caused by microorganisms not susceptible to the drugs used to treat the first infection.

su·per·in·tend (sōō-pər-in-ténd, séw-) *tr.v.* **-tended, -tending, -tends.** To have charge of; exercise supervision over; manage. [Late Latin *superintendere*, to oversee : *super-*, over + *intendere*, to direct one's attention to, INTEND.] **—su·per·in·ten·dence** *n.*

su·per·in·ten·dent (sōō-pər-in-téndənt, séw-) *n. Abbr.* **super., supt., Supt. 1.** A person who supervises or directs some enterprise or institution. **2. a.** In Britain, a police officer ranking between an inspector and a chief superintendent. **b.** In the United States, the head of a police department. **3.** *U.S.* A porter or caretaker in a building **—su·per·in·ten·dent** *adj.* **—su·per·in·ten·den·cy** *n.*

su·pe·ri·or (sōō-péer-i-ər, sew-, sōō-, sə-) *adj. Abbr.* **sup., super. 1.** Higher in rank, station, or authority: *a superior officer.* **2.** Of a higher nature or kind; far above average in comparison: *superior in tone to the modern instrument.* **3. a.** Of great value or excellence; extraordinary. **b.** Of high quality. **4.** Greater in number or amount. **5.** Affecting an attitude of disdain or conceit. **6.** Above being affected or influenced; indifferent or immune: *superior to envy.* **7.** Located higher; upper. **8.** *Anatomy.* Designating a part or organ situated higher in the body in relation to another part. **9.** *Astronomy.* Having an orbit further from the Sun than the orbit of the Earth. **10.** *Botany.* Located above and not in contact with the calyx and corolla. Said of an ovary. **11.** *Printing.* Set above the main line of type. **12.** *Logic.* Of wider or more comprehensive application; generic. Said of a term or proposition.

~*n. Abbr.* **sup., super. 1.** One who surpasses another in rank or quality. **2.** The head of a monastery, abbey, convent, or other ecclesiastical order or house. **3.** *Printing.* A superior character or letter. [Middle English, from Old French, from Latin, comparative of *superus*, situated above, upper, from *super*, above, over.] **—su·pe·ri·or·i·ty** (-órrəti || -áwrəti) *n.* **—su·pe·ri·or·ly** *adv.*

Superior, Lake. The largest freshwater lake in the world, and the largest of the Great Lakes of North America. The Canadian-United States border passes through it.

superior conjunction *n.* The position of a celestial body when it is on the opposite side of the Sun from Earth.

superior court *n.* **1.** In Britain, a higher court not subject to control by any other court except by way of appeal. **2.** In several U.S. states, a court of general jurisdiction, above the inferior courts and below those of final appeal.

superiority complex *n.* **1.** An unfounded conviction that one is superior to others. **2.** A psychological defence mechanism in which such a conviction counters feelings of inferiority.

superior planet *n.* Any planet of this Solar System whose mean distance from the Sun is greater than that of Earth.

su·per·ja·cent (sōō-pər-jáyss'nt, séw-) *adj.* Resting immediately above or upon something else. Used with *to.* [Latin *superjacēns* (stem *superjacent-*), present participle of *superjacēre*, to lie above or upon : *super-*, over + *jacēre*, to lie, from *jacere*, to throw, lay.]

su·per·la·tive (sōō-pérlətiv, sew-, sōō-) *adj.* **1.** Of the highest order, quality, or degree; surpassing or superior to all other or others. **2.** Excessive or exaggerated. **3.** *Grammar. Abbr.* **sup., superl.** Expressing or involving the extreme degree of comparison of adjectives and adverbs. Compare **comparative, positive.**

~*n.* **1.** Something of the highest possible excellence. **2.** The highest degree; the acme. **3.** *Grammar. Abbr.* **sup., superl. a.** The superlative degree. **b.** An adjective or adverb expressing the superlative degree; for example, *brightest* is the superlative of *bright; most slowly* is the superlative of *slowly.* [Middle English *superlatyf*, from Old French *superlative*, from Late Latin *superlātīvus*, from *superlātus* (past participle of *superferre*, to carry over) : *super-*, over + *-lātus*, "carried".] **—su·per·la·tive·ly** *adv.*

su·per·lu·nar (sōō-pər-lōō-nər, séw-, -léw-) *adj.* Also **su·per·lu·na·ry** (-nəri). **1.** Situated beyond the Moon. **2.** *Literary.* Celestial.

su·per·man (sōō-pər-man, séw-) *n., pl.* **-men** (-men). **1.** A man with more than human powers. **2.** In the philosophy of Nietzsche, an ideal superior man who, through the exercise of creative power and his ability to forgo transient pleasure, would live at a level of experience beyond standards of good and evil and would represent the goal of human evolution. [Translation of German *Übermensch.*]

Su·per·man (sōō-pər, -man, séw-). A U.S. comic-strip and film hero who fights for truth and justice with his superhuman powers.

su·per·mar·ket (sōō-pər-maarkit, séw-) *n.* A large self-service store selling food and household goods.

su·per·nal (sōō-pérn'l, sew-, sōō-) *adj.* **1.** Celestial; heavenly. **2.** Of, coming from, or being in the sky or high above. [Middle English, from Old French, from Latin *supernus.*] **—su·per·nal·ly** *adv.*

su·per·na·tant (sōō-pər-náyt'nt, séw-) *adj.* Floating on the surface. [Latin *supernatāns* (stem *supernatant-*), present participle of *super-natāre*, to swim above, float : *super-*, above + *natāre*, to swim.] —**su·per·na·tant** *n.* —**su·per·na·ta·tion** (-nay-táysh'n) *n.*

su·per·nat·u·ral (sōō-pər-nách-rəl, séw-, -náchə-) *adj.* 1. Of or pertaining to existence outside the natural world; especially, not attributable to natural forces. 2. Attributed to the immediate exercise of divine power; miraculous. 3. Of or pertaining to the miraculous. ~*n.* That which is supernatural. Usually preceded by *the*. —**su·per·nat·u·ral·ly** *adv.* —**su·per·nat·u·ral·ness** *n.*

su·per·nat·u·ral·ism (sōō-pər-nách-rəliz'm, séw-, -náchə-) *n.* 1. The quality of being supernatural. 2. Belief in a supernatural agency that intervenes in the course of natural laws. —**su·per·nat·u·ral·ist** *adj.* & *n.* —**su·per·nat·u·ral·is·tic** (-rə-lístik) *adj.*

su·per·nor·mal (sōō-pər-nórməl, séw-) *adj.* Greatly exceeding the normal or average but still obeying natural laws. —**su·per·nor·mal·i·ty** (-nawr-mál-əti) *n.* —**su·per·nor·mal·ly** *adv.*

su·per·no·va (sōō-pər-nō-və, séw-) *n., pl.* -**vae** (-vee) or -**vas**. A rare celestial phenomenon involving the explosion of most of the material in a star, resulting in an extremely bright, short-lived object that emits vast amounts of energy. Compare **nova**.

su·per·nu·mer·ar·y (sōō-pər-néwmə-rəri, séw- ‖ -nōōmə-, -rerri) *adj.* 1. Exceeding a fixed, prescribed, or standard number; extra: *a supernumerary nipple*. 2. Beyond the required or desired number. ~*n., pl.* **supernumeraries**. *Abbr.* **super**. 1. Someone or something in excess of the regular, necessary, or usual number. 2. An actor without a speaking part, such as one who appears in a crowd scene. [Late Latin *supernumerārius,* (a soldier) added to a legion in excess of its fixed number, from Latin *super numerum,* over the number : *super,* over + *numerus,* number, division of an army.]

su·per·or·der (sōō-pər-awrdər, séw-) *n. Biology*. A taxonomic category ranking above an order or one of its subdivisions and below a class.

su·per·or·di·nate (sōō-pər-órdi-nət, séw-, -nit, -nayt) *adj.* 1. Of higher status or value. 2. *Logic*. Bearing the relation of a universal proposition to a particular proposition in which the terms are the same. —**su·per·or·di·nate** *n.*

su·per·ox·ide (sōō-pər-ók-sīd, séw-) *n.* An oxide of an alkali or an alkaline-earth metal containing the ion O_2, such as NaO_2.

su·per·phos·phate (sōō-pər-fóss-fayt, séw-) *n.* 1. An acid phosphate. 2. A fertiliser made by sulphuric acid acting on phosphate rock consisting chiefly of tribasic calcium phosphate, to form a mixture of gypsum and monobasic calcium phosphate.

su·per·phys·i·cal (sōō-pər-fízzik'l, séw-) *adj.* 1. Exceeding or beyond the purely physical. 2. Not explained by known physical laws; supernatural.

su·per·pose (sōō-pər-pōz, séw-) *tr.v.* -**posed, -posing, -poses.** 1. To place (one geometric figure) over another so that all like parts coincide. 2. To set or place over or above something else. —**su·per·po·sa·ble** *adj.*

su·per·po·si·tion (sōō-pər-pə-zísh'n, séw-) *n.* 1. The act of superposing or the state of being superposed. 2. *Geology*. The principle that in a group of stratified sedimentary rocks the lowest were the earliest to be deposited.

su·per·pow·er (sōō-pər-pow-ər, -powr) *n.* A powerful and influential nation; especially, a nuclear power that dominates its satellites and allies in an international power bloc.

super rat *n.* A breed of rat which has developed an immunity, now passed on in its genes, to most rodent poisons.

su·per·sat·u·rate (sōō-pər-sáchər-ayt, séw-, -sáchoor-, -sáttewr-) *tr.v.* -**rated, -rating, -rates.** 1. To cause (a chemical solution) to be more highly concentrated than is normally possible under given conditions of temperature and pressure. 2. To cause (a vapour) to exceed the normal saturation vapour pressure at a given temperature. —**su·per·sat·u·ra·tion** (-áysh'n) *n.*

su·per·scribe (sōō-pər-skrīb, séw-) *tr.v.* -**scribed, -scribing, -scribes.** 1. To write on the outside or upper part of (a letter, for example). 2. To write (a name or address, for example) on the top or outside. [Latin *superscrībere,* to write over : *super-,* over + *scrībere,* to write.]

su·per·script (sōō-pər-skript, séw-) *adj.* Written or printed above a character or line of print. ~*n.* A character set, printed, or written above and immediately to one side of another. For example, *2* is the superscript in x^2. Compare **subscript**. [Latin *superscriptus,* past participle of *superscrībere,* SUPERSCRIBE.]

su·per·scrip·tion (sōō-pər-skrípsh'n, séw-) *n.* 1. Something written above or outside something; specifically, the address on a letter or parcel. 2. The part of a prescription that bears the Latin word *recipe* represented by the symbol ℞ in a prescription.

su·per·sede (sōō-pər-séed, séw-) *tr.v.* -**seded, -seding, -sedes.** 1. To replace or succeed. 2. To cause (something outdated or inferior) to be set aside or displaced. —See Synonyms at **replace**. [Middle English *superceden,* to postpone, from Old French *superseder,* from Latin *supersedēre,* to sit above, desist from : *super-,* above + *sedēre,* to sit.] —**su·per·sed·ence** *n.* —**su·per·sed·er** *n.* —**su·per·se·dure** (-séejər, -séedewr) *n.*

su·per·se·de·as (sōō-pər-séedi-ass, séw-, -əss) *n. Law.* A writ containing a command to stay legal proceedings, as in the halting or delaying of the execution of a sentence. [Medieval Latin, from Latin (first word in the writ), "you shall desist", from *supersedēre,* to desist from, SUPERSEDE.]

su·per·sen·si·ble (sōō-pər-sénss-əb'l, séw-, -ib'l) *adj.* Also **su·per·**

sen·so·ry (-əri). Beyond or above perception by the senses. —**su·per·sen·si·bly** *adv.*

su·per·sen·si·tive (sōō-pər-sén-sə-tiv, séw-, -si-) *adj.* Hypersensitive.

su·per·ses·sion (sōō-pər-sésh'n, séw-) *n.* The act of superseding or the state of being superseded.

su·per·son·ic (sōō-pər-sónnik, séw-) *adj.* Having, caused by, or related to a speed greater than the speed of sound in a specific medium. —**su·per·son·ic** *n.* —**su·per·son·i·cal·ly** *adv.*

su·per·son·ics (sōō-pər-sónniks, séw-) *n. Used with a singular verb.* The study of phenomena produced by the motion of a body through a medium at velocities greater than that of sound.

supersonic transport *n. Abbr.* **SST** An aircraft capable of flight at speeds exceeding the speed of sound.

su·per·star (sōō-pər-staar, séw-) *n.* A very famous figure in public entertainment, such as a film or sports star, who receives exaggerated publicity. —**su·per·star·dom** (-stárdəm) *n.*

su·per·sti·tion (sōō-pər-stísh'n, séw-) *n.* 1. **a.** An unfounded belief that some action or circumstance completely unrelated to a course of events can influence its outcome. **b.** Fear of the mysterious or unknown. 2. Any belief, practice, or rite unreasoningly upheld by faith in magic, chance, or dogma. 3. **a.** Fearful or abject dependence upon such beliefs. **b.** Idolatry. [Middle English *supersticion,* from Old French *superstition,* from Latin *superstitiō* (stem *superstitiōn-*), probably "a standing over something (in amazement and awe)", excessive fear, superstition, from *superstāre,* to stand over : *super-,* over + *stāre,* to stand.]

su·per·sti·tious (sōō-pər-stíshəss, séw-) *adj.* 1. Inclined to believe in superstitions. 2. Of, characterised by, or proceeding from superstition. —**su·per·sti·tious·ly** *adv.* —**su·per·sti·tious·ness** *n.*

su·per·store (sōō-pər-stawr, séw- ‖ -stōr) *n. Chiefly British.* A large, comprehensively stocked department store.

su·per·stra·tum (sōō-pər-stráa-təm, séw-, -stráy-, -straa-, -stray- ‖ U.S. also -stra-) *n., pl.* -**ta** (-tə) A layer superimposed upon another, especially: 1. *Geology.* A layer or stratum overlying another. 2. *Linguistics.* The language of an invading population imposed on and supplanting the indigenous tongue. Compare **substratum**.

su·per·struc·ture (sōō-pər-strukchər, séw-) *n.* 1. Any structure, whether physical or conceptual, that extends or develops from a basic form. 2. That part of a building or other structure above the foundations. 3. The parts of a ship's structure above the main deck. 4. In Marxist theory, the institutions or ideology of a society as distinct from the basic relations of economy and material production. —**su·per·struc·tur·al** (-strúkchərəl) *adj.*

su·per·sub·stan·tial (sōō-pər-səb-stánsh'l, séw-, -sub-, -stáansh'l) *adj.* Transcending material substance or all substance.

su·per·tanker (sōō-pər-tangkər, séw-) *n.* A large tanker, especially one that carries more than 75,000 tons of oil products at sea.

su·per·tax (sōō-pər-taks, séw-) *n.* In Britain, income tax paid at higher rates on incomes above a certain level.

su·per·ton·ic (sōō-pər-tónnik, séw-) *n.* 1. The second note of the diatonic scale. 2. A key or chord based on this.

su·per·vene (sōō-pər-véen, séw-) *intr.v.* -**vened, -vening, -venes.** 1. To come or occur as something extraneous, additional, or unexpected. 2. To follow immediately after; ensue. —See Synonyms at **follow, happen**. [Latin *supervenīre : super-,* in addition + *venīre,* to come.] —**su·per·ven·i·ence** *n.* —**su·per·ven·i·ent** (-i-ənt) *adj.* —**su·per·ven·tion** (-vénsh'n) *n.*

su·per·vise (sōō-pər-vīz, séw-) *tr.v.* -**vised, -vising, -vises.** 1. To direct and inspect the performance of (workers or work); oversee; superintend. 2. To watch over (pupils in an examination, for example) to maintain order. —See Synonyms at **conduct**. [Medieval Latin *supervidēre* (past participle *supervīsus*), to look over : Latin *super-,* over + *vidēre,* to see.] —**su·per·vi·sion** (-vízh'n) *n.* —**su·per·vi·so·ry** (-vīzəri, -vízəri) *adj.*

su·per·vi·sor (sōō-pər-vīzər, séw-) *n.* 1. A person who supervises. 2. A tutor in some British universities.

su·pi·nate (sōō-pi-nayt, séw-) *v.* -**nated, -nating, -nates.** —*tr.* 1. To turn or place (the hand and forearm) so that the palm is upwards. 2. To turn (the foot and lower leg) in a similar manner. —*intr.* To turn the palm and forearm upwards. [Latin *supīnāre,* to bend backwards, from *supīnus,* SUPINE.] —**su·pi·na·tion** (-náysh'n) *n.*

su·pi·na·tor (sōō-pi-naytər, séw-) *n.* A muscle in the forearm that makes supination possible.

su·pine[1] (sōō-pīn, séw-pīn) *adj.* 1. Lying on the back and facing upwards. 2. Having the palm upwards. Said of the hand. 3. Indisposed to act or object; lethargic; passive. 4. Inclined; sloping. —See Usage note at **prone**. [Latin *supīnus.*] —**su·pine·ly** *adv.* —**su·pine·ness** *n.*

su·pine[2] (sōō-pīn, séw-) *n. Abbr.* **sup**. A verbal noun found in some Indo-European languages, used usually after verbs to denote purpose; especially, the Latin supine, having an accusative in *-um* and an ablative in *-ū,* cited as the fourth of the principal parts. [Latin (*verbum*) *supīnum,* from *supīnus,* SUPINE. The reason for naming it uncertain.]

su·plex (sōō-pleks, séw-) *n.* A wrestling hold in which the victim is grasped round the waist from behind and carried backwards. [20th century : origin obscure.]

supp. supplement; supplementary.

sup·per (súppər) *n.* 1. An evening meal, especially when light. 2. A social gathering at which supper is served. 3. A snack eaten before going to bed. —**sing for (one's) supper**. To perform a service to repay a favour. [Middle English *suppere,* from Old French *so(u)per,* from *so(u)per,* SUP.]

suppl. supplement; supplementary.

sup·plant (sə-plaánt || -plánt) *tr.v.* **-planted, -planting, -plants.** To take the place of, as by force; oust. —See Synonyms at **replace.** [Middle English *supplanten,* from Old French *supplanter,* from Latin *supplantāre,* to trip up one's heel : *sub-,* up from under + *planta,* sole of the foot.] **—sup·plan·ta·tion** (sú-plaan-táysh'n, -plan-) *n.* **—sup·plant·er** *n.*

sup·ple (súpp'l) *adj.* **-pler, -plest. 1.** Readily bent; pliant. **2.** Moving and bending with agility; lithe. **3.** Mentally flexible. **4.** Yielding or changing readily; compliant. —See Synonyms at **flexible.** [Middle English *souple,* from Old French, from Latin *supplex,* beseeching, submissive.] **—sup·ple** *v.* **—sup·ple·ness** *n.*

sup·ple-jack (súpp'l-jak) *n.* A walking stick made from a strong tropical American twining plant, *Paullinia curassavica.*

sup·ple·ment (súppli-mənt || -ment) *n. Abr.* **sup., supp., suppl. 1.** Something added to complete a thing, make up for a deficiency, or extend or strengthen the whole. **2.** A section, sometimes published separately, added to a book or document to give further information or to correct errors. **3. a.** A separate section devoted to a special subject inserted into a newspaper or other periodical; especially, a colour magazine. **b.** A periodical devoted to a particular subject, associated with another publication but published separately. **4.** *Mathematics.* **a.** An angle which with an adjacent angle forms an angle of 180°. **b.** An arc which with an adjacent arc forms a semicircle. **5.** A preparation, as of iron or yeast, taken to balance a diet or remedy a dietary deficiency.
~tr.v. (-ment, -mént || -mənt) **supplemented, -menting, -ments.** To provide or form a supplement to. [Middle English, from Latin *supplēmentum,* from *supplēre,* to complete, SUPPLY.] **—sup·ple·men·tal** (-mént'l) *adj. & n.* **—sup·ple·men·ta·tion** (-men-táysh'n) *n.* **—sup·ple·men·ter** (-mentər, -méntər) *n.*

sup·ple·men·ta·ry (súppli-mént-əri, -ri) *adj.* **1.** Additional. **2.** Provided to make up a deficiency. **3.** Designating an angle that is a supplement.
~n., pl. **supplementaries.** Something that is supplementary; specifically, an additional question a member may put to a minister at question time in the British Parliament.

supplementary benefit *n. Abbr.* **S.B.** In Britain, payments formerly made weekly or fortnightly by the former Department of Health and Social Security to individuals or families without any or on a very low income, but not eligible for unemployment benefit. Replaced (1986) by *income support.*

sup·ple·tion (sə-pleésh'n) *n.* The use of an etymologically unrelated word to complete an otherwise consistent paradigm; for example, the presence of *went* in *go, went, going, goes.* [Middle English, from Old French, from Medieval Latin *supplētiō* (stem *supplētiōn-*), a completing, from Latin *supplēre,* to fill up, SUPPLY.] **—sup·ple·tive** (sə-pleétiv) *adj. & n.*

sup·pli·ant (súppli-ənt) *adj.* Asking humbly and earnestly.
~n. One who supplicates. [Middle English, from Old French, present participle of *supplier,* to entreat, from Latin *supplicāre,* to SUPPLICATE.] **—sup·pli·ance** *n.* **—sup·pli·ant·ly** *adv.*

sup·pli·cant (súpplikənt) *n.* A person who entreats or supplicates.
~adj. Supplicating.

sup·pli·cate (súppli-kayt) *v.* **-cated, -cating, -cates.** *—tr.* **1.** To ask for humbly or earnestly. **2.** To make a humble entreaty to; beseech. *—intr.* To make a humble and earnest petition, especially to a deity. [Middle English *supplicaten,* from Latin *supplicāre,* to kneel down, beg humbly : *sub-,* down, underneath + *plicāre,* to fold up.] **—sup·pli·ca·tion** (-káysh'n) *n.* **—sup·pli·ca·to·ry** (-kə-tri, -təri, -kaytəri, -káytəri) *adj.*

sup·ply[1] (sə-plī́) *v.* **-plied, -plying, -plies.** *—tr.* **1.** To make (something needed, desired, or lacking) available for use; provide. **2. a.** To furnish or equip with what is needed or lacking. **b.** *Anatomy.* To provide (a body part) with nerve impulses or a vital fluid, such as blood. **3.** To fill sufficiently; satisfy: *supply a need.* **4.** To make up for (a deficiency, for example); compensate for. **5.** To serve temporarily in (the position or office of another); occupy as a substitute. *—intr.* To fill a position as a substitute.
~n., pl. **supplies.** *Abbr.* **sup. 1.** The act of supplying. **2.** Something that is or can be supplied, especially a basic facility such as water or electricity. **3.** An amount available or sufficient for a given use; a store; a stock. **4.** *Usually plural.* Materials or provisions stored and dispensed when needed. **5.** *Plural.* The grant made the British Parliament for the cost of government. **6.** *Economics.* The amount of a commodity available for meeting a demand or for purchase at a given price. **7.** One, especially a clergyman, serving as a temporary substitute. Also used adjectivally: *a supply teacher.* [Middle English *suppl(y)en,* from Old French *so(u)pleer, soup(p)leier,* from Latin *supplēre,* to fill up, complete : *sub-,* from below, up + *plēre,* to fill.] **—sup·pli·er** *n.*

sup·ply[2] (súppli) *adv.* In a supple way.

supply and demand (sə-plī́) *n.* The availability of and willingness of consumers to purchase goods or services, considered as the economic forces governing prices in the absence of administrative control, and, through prices, output and the distribution of income.

sup·ply-side (sə-plī́-sīd) *adj.* Designating or pertaining to an economic theory that advocates reductions in taxation as encouraging investment and boosting productivity. **—sup·ply-sid·er** *n.*

sup·port (sə-pórt || -pōrt) *tr.v.* **-ported, -porting, -ports. 1.** To bear the whole or partial weight of, especially from below. **2.** To hold in position; prevent from falling, sinking, or slipping. **3.** To encourage or lend strength to, especially in difficulties. **4.** To provide for or maintain by supplying with money or other necessities. **5.** To furnish evidence for; corroborate or substantiate. **6. a.** To aid the cause of by approving, favouring, or advocating. **b.** To be an adherent of; give one's loyalty to. **7.** To bear or endure; tolerate. **8. a.** To act in a secondary or subordinate role to (a leading actor). **b.** To accompany (the main act, showing, or performance).
~n. **1. a.** The act of supporting. **b.** The state of being supported. **2.** One that supports. **3.** Maintenance or subsistence: *income support for the poor.* **4.** A medical appliance worn to support and ease an injured part. **5.** The solid material on which a painting is executed. [Middle English *supporten,* from Old French *supporter,* from Latin *supportāre,* to carry, convey : *sub-,* up, towards + *portāre,* to carry.]
Synonyms: *support, uphold, maintain, advocate, champion.*

sup·port·a·ble (sə-pórt-b'l || -pōrt-) *adj.* Bearable; endurable. **—sup·port·a·bil·i·ty** (-ə-bílləti) *n.* **—sup·port·a·bly** *adv.*

sup·port·er (sə-pórt-ər || -pōrt-) *n.* **1.** A person or thing that supports. **2.** One who promotes or advocates; a partisan; an adherent. **3.** A sports fan loyal to a particular team or player. **4.** A support or binding for some part of the body; especially, a jockstrap. **5.** *Heraldry.* An animal or figure that supports a shield in a coat of arms.

sup·por·tive (sə-pórt-iv || -pōrt-) *adj.* **1.** Furnishing support or assistance. **2.** Inclined to provide emotional or psychological support. **3.** Designating any system of medical treatment designed to maintain the patient's physiological well-being, rather than to treat a specific disorder.

support price *n.* A price level at which the European Union or other international agency will intervene and buy agricultural produce in order to maintain price stability.

support system *n.* A network of personal or professional contacts available to a person or organisation to give practical or moral support when required.

support tights *n.* Thick, strong, nylon tights designed to reduce stress on the blood vessels in the legs of dancers or people with varicose veins, for example.

sup·pose (sə-pṓz || spṓz) *v.* **-posed, -posing, -poses.** *—tr.* **1.** To assume (something) to be true or real for the sake of an argument or explanation. **2.** To believe, especially on uncertain or tentative grounds; be inclined to think. **3.** To imply as an antecedent condition; presuppose. **4.** To consider as a suggestion. Often used to introduce a proposal: *Suppose we dine together.* **5.** To expect or require. Used in the passive: *I was not supposed to be at home.* *—intr.* To make an assumption; conjecture. —See Synonyms at **presume.** [Middle English *supposen,* to believe, assume, from Old French *supposer,* from Latin *suppōnere* (past participle *suppositus*), to put under, substitute, forge : *sub-,* under + *pōnere,* to place.]
Usage: *Supposing* is generally used to express clauses of condition or reason *(Supposing nothing happens, we'll get there on time).* It may also be used to express wholly hypothetical states of affairs, although many people prefer to use *suppose* in such contexts.

sup·posed (sə-pṓzd, -pṓzid) *adj.* Presumed to be true or genuine, especially on dubious grounds. **—sup·pos·ed·ly** (sə-pṓzidli) *adv.*

sup·po·sing (sə-pṓzing, spṓzing) *conj.* In the event that. Sometimes used without a main clause to convey anxiety: *Supposing they catch us!* See Usage note at **suppose.**

sup·po·si·tion (súppə-zísh'n) *n.* **1.** The act of supposing. **2.** An unproven statement or assumption, especially one tentatively accepted. **—sup·po·si·tion·al** *adj.* **—sup·po·si·tion·al·ly** *adv.*

sup·po·si·tious (súppə-zíshəss) *adj.* **1.** Hypothetical; supposed. **2.** Fraudulent; supposititious.

sup·pos·i·ti·tious (sə-pózzi-tíshəss) *adj.* **1.** Substituted with fraudulent intent; spurious; counterfeit. **2.** Hypothetical; supposed. [Latin *suppositīcius,* substituted, from *suppōnere* (past participle *suppositus*), to place under, substitute, SUPPOSE.] **—sup·pos·i·ti·tious·ly** *adv.* **—sup·pos·i·ti·tious·ness** *n.*

sup·pos·i·tive (sə-póz-i-tiv, -ə-) *adj.* Of the nature of, including, or involving supposition.
~n. Grammar. A conjunction introducing a supposition, such as *if* or *providing.* **—sup·pos·i·tive·ly** *adv.*

sup·pos·i·to·ry (sə-pózzi-tri, -təri) *n., pl.* **-ries.** A solid medication designed to melt within a body cavity other than the mouth, especially the rectum or vagina. [Medieval Latin *suppositōrium,* "something placed underneath", from Latin *suppositōrius,* "placed under", from Latin *suppōnere,* to place under, SUPPOSE.]

sup·press (sə-préss) *tr.v.* **-pressed, -pressing, -presses. 1.** To put an end to forcibly; subdue; crush. **2.** To curtail or prohibit the activities of (a political party, for example). **3.** To keep from being revealed, published, or circulated; withhold from the public. **4.** To hold back (an impulse, for example); check: *suppress a smile.* **5.** To reduce the incidence or severity of (a haemorrhage, for example); arrest. **6.** To reduce or eliminate (noise or a specified frequency range) from an electronic signal or device. **7.** *Psychology.* To exclude (desires or thoughts) consciously from one's awareness. [Middle English *suppressen,* from Latin *supprimere* (past participle *suppressus*), to press down : *sub-,* down + *premere,* to press.] **—sup·press·ant** *adj. & n.* **—sup·press·i·ble** *adj.* **—sup·pres·sive** *adj.*

sup·pres·sion (sə-présh'n) *n.* **1.** The act of suppressing. **2.** The state of being suppressed. **3.** The act or process of suppressing an electronic frequency. **4.** *Psychology.* The conscious exclusion of painful desires or thoughts from awareness. **5.** *Botany.* The failure of an organ or part to develop.

sup·pres·sor, sup·pres·ser (sə-préssər) *n.* **1.** One that suppresses.

2. A gene that reduces the phenotypic expression of a mutant gene. **3.** A device that reduces or eliminates electrical noise from the ignition system of an internal-combustion engine to prevent interference with an electronic device, such as a radio. **4.** An electrode placed between the screen grid and anode of an electronic vacuum tube to prevent secondary electrons from the anode reaching the screen. In this sense, also called "suppressor grid".

sup·pu·rate (súppewr-ayt) *intr.v.* **-rated, -rating, -rates.** To form or discharge pus, as a wound may; fester or maturate. [Latin *suppūrāre* : *sub-*, under + *pūs* (stem *pūr-*), pus.]

sup·pu·ra·tion (súppewr-áysh'n) *n.* **1.** The formation or discharge of pus. Also called "maturation". **2.** Pus.

sup·pur·a·tive (súppewr-ətiv, -aytiv ‖ súpprətiv) *adj.* Causing suppuration. **—sup·pur·a·tive** *n.*

supr. supreme.

su·pra (sōo-prə, séw- ‖ -praa) *adv. Latin.* Above; in the text that precedes. Compare **infra.**

supra– *prefix.* Indicates above, specifically: **1.** Higher than or over; for example, **suprarenal. 2.** Greater than; for example, **supramolecular. 3.** Preceding; for example, **supralapsarian.** [Latin, from *suprā,* above, beyond, earlier.]

su·pra·glot·tal (sōo-prə-glótt'l, séw-) *adj.* **1.** *Anatomy.* Above or anterior to the glottis. **2.** *Linguistics.* Designating a phone or phoneme produced by the speech organs anterior to the glottis.

su·pra·lap·sar·i·an (sōo-prə-lap-saír-i-ən, séw-) *n.* Any of the Calvinists who believe that God's determination of the elect preceded the Fall and that the Fall itself had been predestined. [SUPRA- + Latin *lapsus,* fall, from the past participle of *lābī,* to slide.] **—su·pra·lap·sar·i·an** *adj.* **—su·pra·lap·sar·i·an·ism** *n.*

su·pra·lim·i·nal (sōo-prə-límmin'l, séw-) *adj.* Above the threshold of conscious perception. Said of stimuli.

su·pra·mo·lec·u·lar (sōo-prə-mə-léckewlər, séw-, -mō-, -mo-) *adj.* **1.** Consisting of more than one molecule. **2.** Of greater complexity than a molecule.

su·pra·na·tion·al (sōo-prə-násh'n-'l, séw-, -násh-n'l) *adj.* Going beyond national boundaries or concerns.

su·pra·or·bi·tal (sōo-prə-órbit'l, séw-) *adj.* Located above the orbit of the eye.

su·pra·re·nal (sōo-prə-réen'l, séw-) *adj.* Located on or above the kidney.
~*n.* A suprarenal gland. [New Latin *suprarenalis* : SUPRA- + Latin *rēnēs,* the kidneys (see **renal**).]

suprarenal gland *n.* An **adrenal gland** (see).

su·pra·seg·men·tal (sōo-prə-seg-mént'l, séw-, -sig-) *adj. Linguistics.* Designating those phonetic features that form the background rather than the individual segments of a word or sentence, such as stress or intonation.

su·prem·a·cist (sōo-prémmə-sist, sōo-, sew- ‖ sə-) *n.* One who believes that a certain group is or should be supreme.

su·prem·a·cy (sōo-prémmə-si, sōo-, sew- ‖ sə-) *n., pl.* **-cies. 1.** The condition or quality of being supreme. **2.** Supreme power.

su·prem·a·tism (sōo-prémmə-tiz'm, séw-, sōo- ‖ sə-) *n.* A school of geometric abstract art cultivated by Russian artists such as Malevich in the early 20th century, revived in the 1960s, and influencing constructivists. [From *suprematist,* a member of this school, from French *suprémacie,* SUPREMACY.] **—su·prem·a·tist** *n. & adj.*

su·preme (sōo-préem, sōo-, sew- ‖ sə-) *adj. Abbr.* **supr. 1.** Greatest in power, authority, or rank; paramount; dominant. **2.** Greatest in degree, significance, character, or achievement; utmost; extreme. **3.** Ultimate; final: *the supreme sacrifice.* [Latin *suprēmus,* superlative of *superus,* situated above, upper, from *super,* above.] **—su·preme·ly** *adv.* **—su·preme·ness** *n.*

su·prême (sōo-préem, sew-, sōo-, -prém ‖ sə-) *adj.* Served with a rich sauce usually made with cream and egg yolks. Used after the noun: *chicken suprême.* [French, SUPREME.]

Supreme Court *n. Abbr.* **S.C.** The highest Federal court in the United States, consisting of nine justices and having jurisdiction over all other courts in the nation.

Supreme Court of Judicature *n. Law.* In Britain, a court formed in 1873 to amalgamate most of the superior courts at the time. It now comprises the **High Court of Justice,** the **Court of Appeal,** and the **Crown Court** (*all of which see*).

Supreme Soviet *n.* Formerly, the legislature of the Soviet Union, consisting of two equal houses, the *Soviet of the Union,* whose members were elected by population, and the *Soviet of the Nationalities,* whose members were elected by the various national groups.

su·pre·mo (sōo-préemō, sew-) *n., pl.* **mos.** *British Informal.* A chief or leader having overall authority. [Spanish, SUPREME.]

supt., Supt. superintendent.

Su·qua·mish (sə-kwáamish) *n., pl.* **-mishes** or collectively **Suquamish. 1.** A member of a Salish-speaking people of North American Indians of the northwestern Pacific coast, west of Puget Sound. **2.** The language of this people.

sur– *prefix.* Indicates: **1.** Over, beyond, or above; for example, **surtax. 2.** Excessively; extremely; for example, **surbased.** [Middle English, from Old French *s(o)ur-,* from Latin *super-,* from *super,* above, over.]

su·ra (sōor-ə) *n.* Any of the 114 chapters or sections of the Koran. [Arabic *sūrah,* "a step", from Hebrew *shūrāh,* row, line.]

Su·ra·ba·ya (sōor-ə-bī-ə) *n. Dutch* **Soerabaja.** Port in Indonesia, situated in northeastern Java at the mouth of the Mas River. It is the country's second largest city and its major naval base.

su·rah (sōor-ə, séwr-ə) *n.* A soft twilled fabric of silk or of a blend of silk and rayon. [French *surat,* originally made at SURAT.]

su·ral (sōor-əl, séwr-əl) *adj.* Of or relating to the calf of the leg. [New Latin *suralis,* from Latin *sura,* calf of the leg.]

Su·rat (sōor-ət, sōo-raát, -rát). City in Gujarat state, India, situated on the river Tapti near its mouth on the Gulf of Khambat. It is an administrative and commercial centre, a small port, and a railway junction. In the 17th century British and Dutch trading posts were established here.

sur·base (súr-bayss) *n. Architecture.* A moulding or border above the base of a structure, such as a pedestal. [SUR- + BASE.]

sur·based (súr-bayst) *adj. Architecture.* **1.** Having a surbase. **2.** Pertaining to or designating an arch with a rise less than half its span. [French *surbaissé,* flattened (said of an arch), from the past participle of *surbaisser,* to depress, flatten : *sur-,* extremely + *baisser,* to lower, from *bas,* low, from Old French, low, BASE.]

sur·cease (sûr-séess ‖ *U.S. also* sûr-seess) *v.* **-ceased, -ceasing, -ceases.** *Archaic.* **—***tr.* To put an end to. **—***intr.* To cease; stop. **~***n. Archaic.* A cessation; an end. [Middle English *sursesen,* from Old French *surseoir* (past participle *sursis*), to refrain, delay, from Latin *supersedēre,* to desist from, SUPERSEDE.]

sur·charge (súr-chaarj) *n.* **1.** An additional sum added to the usual amount or cost. **2.** An overcharge, especially when unlawful. **3.** An additional or excessive burden; an overload. **4. a.** A new value or denomination overprinted on a postage or revenue stamp. **b.** The stamp to which it has been applied. **5.** *Law.* The act of surcharging. **~***tr.v.* (*also* sur-chárj) **surcharged, -charging, -charges.** **1.** To charge (a person) an additional sum. **2.** To overcharge (a person). **3. a.** To place an excessive burden upon; overload. **b.** To fill beyond usual capacity; overfill. **4.** To print a surcharge on (a postage or revenue stamp). **5.** *Law.* To show an omission of a credit in (an account). **6.** To require (a person) to reimburse funds spent without authorisation. [Middle English *surchargen,* from Old French *surcharger* : *sur-,* excessively + *charg(i)er,* CHARGE.]

sur·cin·gle (súr-sing-g'l) *n.* A girth that binds a saddle, pack, or blanket to the body of a horse. [Middle English *sursengle,* from Old French *so(u)rcengle* : *sur-,* over + *cengle,* belt, from Latin *cingula,* from *cingere,* to gird.]

sur·coat (súr-kōt) *n.* **1.** Formerly, a loose outer coat or gown. **2.** A tunic worn in the Middle Ages by a knight over his armour. [Middle English *surcote,* "overcoat", from Old French : SUR- + COAT.]

sur·cu·lose (súrkew-lōz, -lōss) *adj. Botany.* Producing suckers: *a surculose shrub.* [Latin *surculōsus,* woody, ligneous, from *surculus,* diminutive of *surus,* branch.]

surd (surd) *n.* **1.** A sum, such as $\sqrt{2} + \sqrt{3}$, containing one or more irrational roots of numbers. **2.** *Phonetics.* A voiceless consonant. No longer in technical usage.
~*adj. Phonetics.* Voiceless. No longer in technical usage. [Latin *surdus,* deaf, mute (used in mathematics to translate Arabic *jadhr aṣāmm,* "deaf root", translation of Greek *alogos,* "speechless", "irrational").]

sure (shoor, shor ‖ shewr, shur) *adj.* **surer, surest. 1.** Incapable of being doubted or disputed; completely true; certain. **2.** Not hesitating or wavering; stable; steady; firm: *sure convictions.* **3.** Confident of some established fact or future outcome; certain in one's knowledge or expectation. Used with a clause or *of* : *sure that I'm right.* **4. a.** Bound to come about or to happen; inevitable. **b.** Having one's course directed; destined; bound. **5.** Certain not to miss or err; steady. **6. a.** Worthy of being trusted or depended upon; reliable. **b.** Of which one may be confident; safe. **7.** *Obsolete.* Free from harm or danger; safe; secure. **—for sure.** Certainly; unquestionably: *We'll win for sure.* **—make sure. 1.** To establish something without doubt. **2.** To ensure something: *made sure you were told.* **—sure of (oneself).** Rather too confident of one's abilities or worth. **—to be sure.** Indeed; of course.
~*adv. Chiefly U.S. Informal.* Certainly; indeed: *sure was easy.* **—sure enough.** As was to be expected.
~*interj.* Certainly; willingly. [Middle English *s(e)ure,* from Old French *sur,* from Latin *secūrus,* "free from care", safe : *sē,* without + *cūra,* care.] **—sure·ness** *n.*
   Synonyms: sure, certain, confident, assured.

sure-fire (shóor-fír, shór- ‖ shéwr-, shúr-) *adj. Informal.* Bound to be successful or perform as expected: *a sure-fire plan.*

sure-foot·ed (shóor-fóotid, shór- ‖ shéwr-, shúr-) *adj.* Not liable to stumble or fall; agile. **—sure-foot·ed·ness** *n.*

sure·ly (shóorli, shórli ‖ shéwrli, shúrli) *adv.* **1.** Firmly and with confidence; unhesitatingly. **2.** Undoubtedly; certainly. Often used: **a.** As an intensive: *You surely can't be serious!* **b.** In incredulous questions: *Surely it's not Monday already?* **3.** Without fail: *Slowly but surely spring returns.*
~*interj.* Of course; willingly.

sure thing *n. Informal.* A guaranteed success.
~*interj. U.S.* Certainly; of course.

su·re·ty (shóor-əti, shór- *also* -ti ‖ shéwr-, shúr-) *n., pl.* **-ties. 1.** A person who has contracted to be responsible for another; especially, a person who assumes any responsibilities, debts, or obligations in the event of the default of another. **2.** A pledge or formal promise made to secure against loss, damage, or default; a guarantee or security. **3.** Something beyond doubt; a certainty. **4.** The condition of being sure, especially of oneself. **—su·re·ty·ship** *n.*

surf (surf) *n.* **1.** The foaming white spray produced by waves as they break. **2.** The sound or effect of breaking waves.
~*v.* **surfed, surfing, surfs. —***intr.v.* To engage in surfing. **—***tr.v.* To engage in the surfing of: *surf the Internet.* [Probably

variant of obsolete *suff*†.] **—surf·y** *adj.*

sur·face (súrf-iss, -əss) *n. Abbr.* **sur.** **1. a.** The outer or the topmost boundary or boundaries of an object. **b.** A material layer constituting such a boundary. **c.** Such a layer with regard to its texture. **2.** The uppermost level of the land or sea. **3.** *Geometry.* **a.** The boundary of any three-dimensional figure. **b.** The two-dimensional locus of points located in three-dimensional space. **3.** The superficial or outward appearance of anything as distinguished from inner substance or matter. **4.** *Aeronautics.* An aerofoil. **—on the surface.** To all appearances. **—scratch the surface.** To make only a slight impression; achieve no deep effect.

~*adj.* **1.** Pertaining to, on, or at a surface: *surface algae in the water.* **2.** Superficial; apparent as opposed to real.

~*v.* **surfaced, -facing, -faces.** —*tr.* **1.** To form the surface of, as by smoothing or levelling; give a surface to. **2.** To provide with a particular surface. —*intr.* **1.** To rise to the surface. **2.** To emerge after concealment. **3.** To mine at or near the ground surface. [French (formed after Latin *superficiēs,* surface) : *sur-,* above + FACE.]

sur·face-ac·tive (súr-fiss-aktiv, -fəss-) *adj.* Designating a substance capable of reducing the surface tension of a liquid in which it is dissolved. Said especially of detergents.

surface mail *n.* **1.** Mail transported over land and sea, rather than by air. **2.** Such transportation of mail.

surface noise *n.* Noise, largely of a high frequency, produced by a gramophone stylus as it follows the groove of a rotating record.

surface of revolution *n. Geometry.* A surface generated by revolving a plane curve about an axis in its plane.

surface plate *n.* A **face plate** *(see).*

surface structure *n.* In the standard theory of transformational-generative grammar, the string of words and sounds as they occur in a sentence, or a diagrammatic representation of these, which can then be analysed according to transformational rules to reveal an underlying sense or **deep structure** *(see)* not necessarily accessible to constituent analysis.

surface tension *n. Abbr.* **T** **1.** A property of liquids arising from molecular cohesive forces at or near the surface, as a result of which the surface tends to contract to a minimum area and has properties resembling those of a stretched elastic membrane. **2.** A measure of this property.

sur·face-to-air missile (súr-fiss-too-áir, -fəss- || -tə-) *n. Abbr.* **SAM** A missile launched from land or sea at an airborne target.

sur·face-to-sur·face missile (súr-fiss-tə-súr-fiss, -fəss(-), -tōō-) *n. Abbr.* **SSM.** A missile launched from land or sea at a target that is also on the earth's surface.

surface wave *n.* A wave created by an earthquake which travels along the surface of the earth.

sur·fac·tant (sur-fáktant, sər-, súr-faktənt) *n.* A surface-active agent. [*Surf*ace *act*ive + -ANT.]

surf·bird (súrf-burd) *n.* A shore bird, *Aphriza virgata,* of the Pacific coast of North and South America, having dark, spotted plumage.

surf·board (súrf-bawrd || -bōrd) *n.* A long, narrow, round-ended board used by surfers for riding on waves to the shore.

~ *intr.v.* **surfboarded, -boarding, boards.** To do surfboarding.

surf·boat (súrf-bōt) *n.* A strong seaworthy boat that can be launched or landed in heavy surf.

surf·cast·ing (súrf-kaast-ing || -kast-) *n.* The sport of fishing from shore, casting one's line into the surf. **—surf·cast·er** *n.*

sur·feit (súr-fit || -feet) *v.* **-feited, -feiting, -feits.** —*tr.* To feed or supply to fullness or excess; satiate. —*intr. Archaic.* To overindulge. —See Synonyms at **satiate.**

~*n.* **1.** The act or an instance of overindulging in food or drink. **2.** The result of such overindulgence; satiety; disgust. **3.** An excessive amount. [Middle English, from Old French, from Vulgar Latin *superfactum* (unattested), from the neuter past participle of *superficere* (unattested), to overdo : Latin *super-,* excessively + *facere,* to do.] **—sur·feit·er** *n.*

surf·er (súrfər) *n.* One who engages in surfing.

sur·fi·cial (sur-físh'l, sər-) *adj.* Of, pertaining to, or occurring on the earth's geological surface. [*surf*ace + super*ficial.*] **—sur·fi·cial·ly** *adv.*

surf·ing (súrfing) *n.* **1.** The sport of riding towards the shore on the crest or along the tunnel of a wave while lying or standing on a surfboard. Also called "surfboarding". **2.** The activity of browsing through television channels or the Internet, for example.

surf·perch (súrf-perch) *n., pl.* **-perches** or collectively **surfperch.** Any of various viviparous fishes of the family Embiotocidae, of North American Pacific coastal waters. Also called "sea perch".

surg. surgeon; surgery; surgical.

surge (surj) *v.* **surged, surging, surges.** —*intr.* **1.** To move in a billowing or swelling manner; rise and heave over violently, as waves do. **2.** *Rare.* To roll or be tossed about on waves, as a boat. **3.** To move like advancing waves: *The fans surged forward to see her.* **4.** To well or rise up suddenly and strongly: *anger surging up within us.* **5.** To increase suddenly. Used of an electric current or voltage. **6.** To slip around a windlass. Used of a rope. —*tr.* To loosen or slacken (a cable) gradually.

~*n.* **1.** A heavy, billowing, or swelling motion like that of great waves: *surge and flow.* **2. a.** A wave, ground swell, or billow. **b.** Such waves collectively. **c.** An undulating surface, such as one formed by hills. **3.** A sudden powerful onset, as of emotion. **4.** A sudden, transient increase in electric current. **5.** An instability in the power output of an engine. **6.** *Astronomy.* A short-lived, violent disturbance occurring during the eruption of a solar flare. **7.** *Nautical.* **a.** A temporary release or slackening of a cable. **b.** The part of a windlass into which the cable surges. [Old French *sourgir,* from Old Spanish *surgir,* from Latin *surgere,* "to lead straight up", rise : *sub-,* up from below + *regere,* to lead, rule.]

sur·geon (súrjən) *n. Abbr.* **surg.** **1.** A medical practitioner specialising in surgery. **2.** A medical officer in the Royal Navy. [Middle English *surg(i)en,* from Anglo-French, short for Old French *serurgien,* from *serurgie,* SURGERY.] **—sur·geon·cy** *n. Chiefly British.*

sur·geon·fish (súrjən-fish) *n., pl.* **-fishes** or **surgeonfish.** Any of various bright-coloured tropical marine fishes of the family Acanthuridae, having a sharp, erectile spine near the base of the tail. [From its lance-like spines, which resemble surgeons' instruments.]

Surgeon General *n., pl.* **Surgeons General.** *Abbr.* **Surg. Gen.** **1.** The chief general officer in the medical departments of the U.S. Army or Navy. **2.** The chief medical officer in the U.S. Public Health Service.

surgeon's knot *n.* Any of several knots used in surgery for tying ligatures or stitching incisions.

sur·ger·y (súrjəri) *n., pl.* **-ies.** *Abbr.* **surg.** **1.** The branch of medicine concerned with the treatment of injury, deformity, and disease by operations. **2.** The skill or work of a surgeon. **3.** *Chiefly British.* **a.** A place where general practitioners or dentists advise and treat patients. **b.** The period during which a doctor or other specialist is present in the surgery. **c.** *Informal.* A place where a specialist, such as an M.P. or legal expert, will give advice to members of the public. **4.** *U.S.* An operating theatre. [Middle English *surgerie,* from Old French, short for *serurgerie, cerurgerie,* from *serurgie, cerurgie,* from Latin *chirurgia,* from Greek *kheirurgia,* from *kheirurgos,* working by hand : *kheir,* hand + *ergon,* work.]

sur·gi·cal (súrjik'l) *adj. Abbr.* **surg.** **1.** Pertaining to or characteristic of surgeons or surgery. **2.** Used in surgery. **3.** Resulting from or occurring after surgery. [From SURGEON.]

surgical boot *n.* A boot or shoe designed to compensate for deformities of the leg or foot.

surgical spirit *n.* Methylated spirit with small amounts of castor oil and oil of wintergreen, used especially for sterilising the skin before surgery.

su·ri·cate (séwr-i-kayt, sŏŏr-) *n.* A small, greyish, gregarious burrowing mongoose, *Suricata suricatta,* of southern Africa, having a long tail. [French *suricate,* native name in South Africa.]

Su·ri·nam, Republic of (sŏŏr-i-nám, -naʹam). *Formerly* **Dutch Guiana** or **Netherlands Guiana.** *Dutch* **Su·ri·na·me** (sŭr-i-naʹamə). A country in northeastern South America. It has a low-lying, marshy, coastal strip, a belt of grassland, and the densely forested Guiana Highlands in the south. The major part of all cultivated land is used for rice growing. Other crops include sugar-cane, bananas, citrus fruits, and coconuts. Surinam is one of the world's largest producers of bauxite, and its products which account for most of its foreign income. The population is mixed, with Creoles, Asian Indians, and Indonesians forming the largest groups. The first Europeans to reach the area were the Spanish (1499), but it was the British who established the first colony there (1650). In 1667 the territory was ceded to the Dutch. Known as Dutch Guiana, it was renamed Surinam (1949) and became an internally autonomous part of the Netherlands (1954). It has been fully independent since 1975. Area, 163 265 square kilometres (63,037 square miles). Population, 438,000. Capital, Paramaribo. See map at **Guyana.**

Surinam toad *n.* A South American toad, the **pipa** *(see).*

sur·ly (súrli) *adj.* **-lier, -liest.** Grumpy or habitually uncivil; gruff. [Variant of obsolete *sirly,* originally "lordly", masterful, imperious, from SIR.] **—sur·li·ly** *adv.* **—sur·li·ness** *n.*

sur·mise (sur-mīz, sər-, súr-mīz) *v.* **-mised, -mising, -mises.** —*tr.* To infer reasonably, though without conclusive evidence. —*intr.* To make a guess or conjecture. —See Synonyms at **conjecture.**

~*n.* An idea or opinion based upon insufficiently conclusive evidence; a guess; a conjecture. [Middle English *surmysen,* to charge on or against, accuse, from Old French *surmettre* (past participle *surmis*), from Medieval Latin *supermittere,* from Late Latin, to throw upon : Latin *super-,* upon + *mittere,* to send off, throw.]

sur·mount (sər-mównt, sur-) *tr.v.* **-mounted, -mounting, -mounts.** **1.** To overcome (an obstacle, for example); conquer. **2.** To ascend to the top and cross to the other side of; get above and over. **3.** To place something above; top. **4.** To be above or on top of. [Middle English *surmonten,* from Old French *surmonter* : *sur-,* above + *monter,* to MOUNT.] **—sur·mount·a·ble** *adj.* **—sur·mount·a·ble·ness** *n.* **—sur·mount·er** *n.*

sur·mul·let (súr-múllit, -mullit) *n., pl.* **-lets** or collectively **surmullet.** *U.S.* The red mullet. [French *surmulet,* from Old French *sormulet* : probably *sor,* reddish brown, from Germanic + *mulet,* MULLET.]

sur·name (súr-naym) *n.* **1.** A family name as distinguished from a forename; in the West, a patrilineal name. **2.** Formerly, a nickname or epithet added to a person's name.

~*tr.v.* **surnamed, -naming, -names.** To give a surname to. [Middle English : SUR- + NAME.] **—sur·nom·i·nal** (sur-nómmin'l) *adj.*

sur·pass (sər-paʹass, sur- || -páss) *tr.v.* **-passed, -passing, -passes.** **1.** To go beyond the limit, powers, or extent of; transcend. **2.** To be or go beyond, as in quantity, degree, or amount; exceed. —See Synonyms at **excel.** [Old French *surpasser* : *sur-,* over + *passer,* PASS.]

sur·pass·ing (sər-paʹass-ing, sur- || -páss-) *adj.* Exceptional; exceeding: *monuments of surpassing splendour.*

~*adv. Archaic & Poetic.* Extremely. **—sur·pass·ing·ly** *adv.*

sur·plice (súr-pliss, -pləss) *n.* A loose-fitting white gown reaching down to the thighs or knees, having full flowing sleeves, worn over a cassock by certain clergymen and choristers. [Middle English *surplis,* from Old French *sourpeliz,* from Medieval Latin *superpellicium* (originally worn by clergymen of northern countries over their fur coats) : *super-,* over + *pellicium,* fur coat, from Latin *pellicius,* made of skin, from *pellis,* skin.] **—sur·pliced** *adj.*

sur·plus (súr-pləss || -pluss) *adj. Abbr.* **sur.** Being more than or in excess of what is needed or required: *surplus grain.*
—n. **1.** An amount or quantity in excess of what is needed; something remaining or left over. **2.** The total of assets minus the sum of all liabilities. **3.** The excess of a company's net assets over the face value of its capital stock. **4.** The excess of receipts over expenditures. [Middle English, from Old French, from Medieval Latin *superplūs* : Latin *super-,* in addition + *plūs,* more.]

sur·plus·age (súr-pləss-ij || -pluss-) *n.* **1.** A surplus. **2.** An excess of words. **3.** *Law.* Irrelevant matter in a pleading.

surplus value *n.* In the Marxian analysis of capitalism, the difference between the value of the product produced by labour and the actual price of labour as paid out in wages.

sur·print (súr-print) *tr.v.* **-printed, -printing, -prints.** In photoengraving: **1.** To overprint. **2.** To superimpose (a second negative) upon a previously printed image of the first negative.
—n. That which is surprinted.

sur·pris·al (sər-prīz'l) *n.* The act of surprising or the condition of being surprised.

sur·prise (sər-prīz, sə-) *tr.v.* **-prised, -prising, -prises.** Also *rare* **surprize. 1.** To cause to feel wonder or astonishment. **2.** To attack or capture suddenly and without warning. **3.** To take or catch (a person) unawares. **4. a.** To cause (a person) to do or say something unintended. Used with *into.* **b.** To elicit by these means. Used with *out of* or *from.*
—n. **1.** The act of surprising; an unexpected occurrence, encounter, or attack. **2.** The condition of being surprised; a feeling of amazement or wonder. **3.** Something that surprises, such as an unexpected encounter, event, or gift. **—surprised at.** Shocked by. **—take by surprise. 1.** To come upon suddenly and unexpectedly. **2.** To capture without warning. **3.** To astonish or astound. [Middle English *surprysen,* to be seized with, from Old French *surprendre* (past participle *surpris*), "to overtake" : *sur-,* over + *prendre,* to take, from Latin *prehendere,* to seize.] **—sur·pris·ed·ly** *adv.* **—sur·pris·er** *n.* **—sur·pris·ing·ly** *adv.*
Synonyms: *surprise, astonish, amaze, astound, dumbfound.*

surr. surrender.

sur·ra (sŏŏr-ə) *n.* A dangerous infectious disease of horses and other domesticated animals occurring in Asian countries. [Marathi.]

sur·re·al (sə-rée̍rl, -rée-əl, súrri-əl || -ráy-əl) *adj.* **1.** Having qualities attributed to surrealism. **2.** Dreamlike, distorted; bizarre. [Back-formation from SURREALISM.] **—sur·real·ly** *adv.*

sur·re·al·ism (sə-rée̍rl-iz'm, -rée-əl-, súrri-əl- || -ráy-əl-) *n. Often capital* **S.** A literary and artistic movement evolving from Dada and launched in 1924 by the French poet André Breton (1896–1966), proclaiming the radical transformation of social, scientific, and philosophical values through the total liberation of the unconscious. Its exponents include writers such as **Artaud** and **Beckett** and artists such as **Magritte** and **Dali** *(all of whom see),* whose work is characterised by strange juxtapositions of mundane objects and the incongruous mingling of the banal with the bizarre. [French *surréalisme* : *sur-,* beyond + *réalisme,* realism, from *réel,* real, from Old French, from Late Latin *reālis,* REAL.] **—sur·re·al·ist** *adj. & n.* **—sur·re·al·is·tic** (-ístik) *adj.* **—sur·re·al·is·ti·cal·ly** *adv.*

sur·re·but·ter (súr-ri-búttər) *n.* Also **sur·re·but·tal** (-bútt'l). *Law. Rare.* The plaintiff's reply to the defendant's rebutter.

sur·re·join·der (súr-ri-jóyndər, -rə-) *n. Law. Rare.* The plaintiff's reply to the defendant's rejoinder.

sur·ren·der (sə-réndər) *v.* **-dered, -dering, -ders.** *—tr.* **1.** To relinquish possession or control of to another because of demand or compulsion. **2.** To give up in favour of another. **3.** To give up or give back (that which has been granted): *surrender a contractual right.* **4.** To give up or abandon: *surrender all hope.* **5.** To give over or resign (oneself) to something, as to capture or to an influence or an emotion. **6.** *Law.* To restore (an estate, for example); especially, to give up (a lease) before expiration of the term. *—intr.* To give oneself up, as to an enemy. —See Synonyms at **relinquish.**
—n. Abbr. **surr. 1.** The act of surrendering. **2.** *Law.* **a.** The delivery of a prisoner, fugitive from justice, or other principal in a suit into custody. **b.** The restoring of an estate. **c.** The act of surrendering or being surrendered to bail. **3.** The voluntary discontinuation of a life insurance policy by its holder in return for a proportion of its value on maturity, its *surrender value.* [Middle English *sorendren,* from Old French *surrendre* : *sur-,* over + *rendre,* to deliver, RENDER.]
Synonyms: *surrender, submission, capitulation.*

sur·rep·ti·tious (súrrəp-tíshəss, súrrep-, súrrip-) *adj.* Performed, made, or acquired by secret or clandestine means or in a stealthy manner. See Synonyms at **secret.** [Latin *surreptīcius,* from *surripere* (past participle *surreptus*), to seize or take away secretly : *sub-,* under, secretly + *rapere,* to seize.] **—sur·rep·ti·tious·ly** *adv.* **—sur·rep·ti·tious·ness** *n.*

sur·rey (súrri) *n., pl.* **-reys.** A 19th-century American horse-drawn four-wheeled pleasure vehicle having two or four seats. [Short for *Surrey cart,* first built in SURREY.]

Sur·rey (súrri). County in southeastern England. The North Downs cross it from east to west, their course broken by the valleys of the rivers Wey and Mole. The county has many dormitory towns from which workers commute into London, including Guildford the county town, Reigate, Woking, and Weybridge.

Surrey, Henry Howard, Earl of (*c.* 1517–47). English poet. He and Sir Thomas Wyatt introduced Italian Renaissance verse forms, particularly the sonnet, into English literature. He also introduced blank verse with his translation of part of Virgil's *Aeneid.*

sur·ro·ga·cy (súrrə-gəsi) *n.* **Womb leasing** *(see).*

sur·ro·gate (súrrə-gət, -git, -gayt) *n.* **1.** A person or thing that is substituted for another; a substitute. **2.** *Psychology.* A person or thing that functions as a substitute for another individual in the life of a person or animal, such as a substitute parent. Also used adjectivally: *a surrogate mother.* **3.** In some U.S. states, a judge having jurisdiction over the probate of wills and the settlement of estates.
—tr.v. (-gayt) **surrogated, -gating, -gates. 1.** To put in the place of another, especially as a successor; replace. **2.** To appoint (another) as a replacement for oneself. [Latin *surrogāre, subrogāre,* to substitute, SUBROGATE.] **—sur·ro·gate·ship** *n.* **—sur·ro·ga·tion** (-gáysh'n) *n.*

surrogate mother *n.* **1.** A woman who bears a child on behalf of another, usually infertile, woman by receiving her fertilised ova or the sperm of her male partner. **2.** A person or animal that acts as a mother substitute.

sur·round (sə-równd || *West Indies also* -rúngd) *tr.v.* **-rounded, -rounding, -rounds. 1.** To extend on all sides of simultaneously; encircle; exist round. **2.** To enclose or confine on all sides so as to bar escape or outside communication.
—n. **1.** *Usually plural.* The grounds of a country mansion or estate. **2.** *Chiefly British.* A border; especially, the area of uncovered floor between a carpet and the walls of a room. [Middle English *sourrounden,* to submerge, overflow, from Old French *s(o)uronder,* from Late Latin *superundāre* : Latin *super-,* over + *undāre,* to rise in waves, from *unda,* wave.]

sur·round·ings (sə-równ-dingz || *West Indies also* -rúng-) *n.* The external circumstances, conditions, and objects that affect the existence and development of something; an environment.

sur·round-sound (sə-równd-sownd) *n.* High-fidelity sound reproduction which gives the impression of surrounding the listener.

sur·tax (súr-taks) *n.* **1.** An additional tax. **2.** Formerly, a graduated British income tax added to the normal income tax, levied on the amount by which a person's net income exceeded a certain sum. See **unified tax. —sur·tax** *tr.v.*

Sur·tees (súr-teez), **John** (1934–). British motorcycling and motor racing driver. He held many motorcycling championships and in 1964 was World motor racing Champion.

Surtees, Robert Smith (1803–64). British novelist. His humorous novels about Mr Jorrocks, the hunting grocer, portray the spirit of Victorian sporting life and manners. His books include *Jorrocks' Jaunts and Jollities* (1838) and *Mr Sponge's Sporting Tour* (1853).

sur·ti·tle (súr-tīt'l) *n.* Also **supertitle.** A translation displayed elsewhere than below what is presented (as above the stage during an opera sung in a foreign language). [SUR- + *title,* as in *subtitle.*]
—tr.v. **surtitled, surtitling, surtitles.** To provide with surtitles.

sur·tout (súr-tōō, -tŏŏ) *n.* Formerly, a type of single-breasted man's frock coat with diagonal front pockets. [French, "over everything".]

Surt·sey (súrtsi). Island off the south coast of Iceland. It was formed (1963) by the eruption of an underwater volcano.

sur·veil·lance (sər-váylənss, sur-) *n.* **1.** Close observation of a person or group, especially of one under suspicion. **2.** The act of observing or the condition of being observed. [French, from *surveiller,* to watch over. See **surveillant.**]

sur·veil·lant (sər-váylənt, sur-) *adj.* Exercising surveillance.
—n. One who keeps close watch. [French, present participle of *surveiller,* to watch over : *sur-,* over + *veiller,* to watch, from Latin *vigilāre,* from *vigil,* awake, watchful.]

sur·vey (sər-váy, sur- || súr-vay) *v.* **-veyed, -veying, -veys.** *—tr.* **1.** To examine or look at in a comprehensive way. **2.** To inspect carefully; scrutinise. **3.** To range one's gaze at leisure over: *From the hilltop she could survey the valley below.* **4.** To determine the boundaries, the area, or the elevations of (land or structures on the earth's surface) by means of measuring angles and distances on the ground or of aerial photography, and then using the techniques of geometry and trigonometry. **5.** *British.* To inspect and determine the structural condition of (a building). **6.** To conduct a statistical survey on. *—intr.* To make a survey. —See Synonyms at **see.**
—n. (súr-vay || sər-váy, sur-). **1.** A detailed inspection or investigation. **2.** A general or comprehensive view. **3. a.** The process of surveying. **b.** A report on or map of that which is surveyed. **c.** An area surveyed. **d.** A body of surveyors. **4. a.** A statistical enquiry, as into population characteristics or political trends, conducted through questionnaires, interviews, or general observation. **b.** A compilation of the results of such an enquiry. **c.** A random statistical sample. **5.** *British.* An inspection of a building to determine its structural condition. [Middle English *surveyen,* from Old French *survee(i)r,* from Medieval Latin *supervidēre,* to look over : Latin *super-,* over + *vidēre,* to look, see.]

sur·vey·ing (sər-váy-ing, sur- || súr-vay-) *n.* The business or occupation of a surveyor.

sur·vey·or (sər-váy-ər || súr-vay-ər) *n.* **1.** A person trained in the surveying and valuation of land or buildings. **2.** A **quantity surveyor** *(see).* **3.** A person qualified to inspect something to assess its value or to confirm that it has the qualities attributed to it.

surveyor's level *n.* A level having a telescope and attached spirit level mounted on a tripod and rotating round a vertical axis.

surveyor's measure *n.* A system of measurement used by surveyors, based on the chain as a unit.

sur·viv·al (sər-vī'l) *n.* **1.** The act of surviving or the fact of having survived. **2.** Something that survives, such as an ancient custom.

sur·viv·al·ist (sər-vī'l-ist) *n.* A person who learns survival techniques (often including armed and unarmed combat) for wild or dangerous conditions; specifically, a survivalist who expects that a future catastrophe will oblige him to use such techniques. **—sur·viv·al·ism** (-iz'm) *n.*

survival kit *n.* A compact package of necessities designed to sustain a person in an emergency, such as a natural disaster.

survival of the fittest *n.* **Natural selection** *(see),* conceived of as a struggle in which only those organisms best adapted to existing conditions survive.

survival value *n.* Usefulness in a species' struggle for survival.

sur·vive (sər-vīv') *v.* **-vived, -viving, -vives.** *—intr.* To remain alive or in existence. *—tr.* To live, exist, or remain active beyond the extent of; outlive. [Middle English *surviven,* from Old French *so(u)rvivre,* from Late Latin *supervīvere* : *super-,* over + *vīvere,* to live.] **—sur·viv·a·ble** (-vī-əb'l) *adj.* **—sur·viv·or** (-ər) *n.*

sur·vi·vor·ship (sər-vī'vər-ship) *n.* *Law.* The right of a person who survives a partner or joint owner to the entire ownership of that which was previously owned jointly.

survivor syndrome *n.* A range of symptoms any or all of which may be exhibited by the survivors of traumatic ordeals, such as earthquakes or concentration camps.

sus (suss) *n.* *Slang.* Suspicion that one has committed a crime. *~tr.v.* **sussed, sussing, susses.** *Slang.* **1.** To understand after examination or thought. Used with *out: sussed out the situation.* **2.** To suspect. Used chiefly in the phrase *sus it.*

Su·san·na[1] (sōō-zánnə, sōō-). In the Apocrypha, a captive in Babylon falsely accused of adultery and saved from death by Daniel.

Susanna[2] *n.* The book of the Apocrypha containing the story of Susanna.

sus·cep·tance (sə-séptənss) *n.* *Electricity.* The imaginary part of the complex representation of **admittance** *(see).* [*suscept*ibility + conduct*ance*.]

sus·cep·ti·bil·i·ty (sə-séptə-bílləti) *n., pl.* **-ties. 1.** The condition or quality of being susceptible. **2.** The capacity to be affected by deep emotions or strong feelings; sensitivity. **3.** *Plural.* Sensibilities; sensitive feelings. **4. Magnetic susceptibility** *(see).*

sus·cep·ti·ble (sə-séptəb'l) *adj.* **1.** Readily subject to an influence, agency, or force; unresistant; yielding. Usually used with *of* or *to.* **2.** Liable to be stricken with or by something: *susceptible to colds.* **3.** *Formal.* Capable or admitting of something. Used with *of: susceptible of misinterpretation.* **4.** Highly impressionable. [Late Latin *susceptibilis,* capable of receiving, from Latin *suscipere* (past participle *susceptus*), to take up, receive : *sub-,* up from under + *capere,* to take.] **—sus·cep·ti·ble·ness** *n.* **—sus·cep·ti·bly** *adv.*

Usage: **Susceptible** is usually followed by *to* when it means "easily affected": *very susceptible to flattery/diseases.* It is usually followed by *of,* occasionally by *to,* when it means "admitting, permitting": *a theory susceptible of several interpretations.* The use of *susceptible to,* in the sense of "often displays," has attracted purist criticism: *very susceptible to fits of pique.*

sus·cep·tive (sə-séptiv) *adj.* **1.** Receptive. **2.** Susceptible. **—sus·cep·tive·ness, sus·cep·tiv·i·ty** (sə-sép-tívvəti, sússep-) *n.*

su·shi (sōōshi) *n.* A type of cold food eaten in Japan, consisting of raw or cooked fish, served in a sweet or sour sauce with rice. [Japanese.]

sus laws *pl.n.* *Slang.* Formerly in Britain, a number of laws allowing the police to arrest a person considered to be about to commit an offence, especially a street crime, without providing formal evidence for their suspicion. [From *sus,* suspicion.]

sus·lik, souslik (sōōss-lik, súss-, sōōss-) *n.* A ground squirrel, *Citellus citellus,* of central Eurasia, with a yellowish-brown coat, large eyes, and small ears. [Russian.]

sus·pect (sə-spékt) *v.* **-pected, -pecting, -pects.** *—tr.* **1.** To surmise to be true or probable; imagine. **2.** To distrust; have doubt about. **3.** To think (a person) guilty without proof. *—intr.* To have or feel suspicion. *~n.* (sús-pekt). One who is suspected, especially of a crime. *~adj.* (sús-pekt). Open to or viewed with suspicion. [Middle English, from Latin *suspectāre,* intensive of *suspicere* (past participle *suspectus*), to look up at, watch : *sub-,* up from under + *specere,* to look at.]

sus·pend (sə-spénd) *v.* **-pended, -pending, -pends.** *—tr.* **1.** To bar for a period from a privilege, office, or position, usually as a punishment: *suspend a pupil from school.* **2.** To cause to stop for a period; interrupt. **3. a.** To maintain in an undecided state; hold in abeyance: *suspend judgment.* **b.** To render temporarily ineffective or inoperative under certain conditions: *suspend parking regulations.* **4.** To hang so as to allow free movement. **5.** To support or keep from falling without apparent attachment, as by buoyancy. *—intr.* **1.** To cease for a period; delay. **2.** To fail to make payments or meet obligations. [Middle English *suspenden,* from Old French *suspendre,* from Latin *suspendēre,* to hang up : *sub-,* up from under + *pendere,* to hang.] **—sus·pend·i·ble** *adj.*

sus·pend·ed animation (sə-spéndid) *n.* A dormant condition like death, induced by reversible cessation of the vital functions.

suspended sentence *n.* A prison sentence imposed on a convicted person but not to be served unless a further crime is committed.

sus·pend·er (sə-spéndər) *n.* **1.** *British.* An elasticated strap or garter with such a strap used to hold up a sock or stocking. **2.** *Plural. U.S.* Braces *(see).*

suspender belt *n.* An undergarment, consisting of a belt with elasticated straps attached to hold up stockings.

sus·pense (sə-spénss) *n.* **1.** The state or quality of being undecided, uncertain, or doubtful. **2. a.** Anxiety or apprehension resulting from an uncertain, undecided, or mysterious situation. **b.** Excitement arising from uncertainty over an outcome. Also used adjectivally: *a suspense novel.* [Middle English, from Old French, from the feminine of *suspens,* suspended, from Latin *suspensus,* past participle of *suspendēre,* SUSPEND.] **—sus·pense·ful** *adj.*

suspense account *n.* A temporary account for entries of credits or charges until their correct place of entry is determined.

sus·pen·sion (sə-spénsh'n) *n.* **1.** The act of suspending or the condition of being suspended, especially: **a.** A temporary abrogation or deferment. **b.** A debarment, as from office or privilege. **c.** A postponement of judgment, opinion, or decision. **2.** *Music.* **a.** The prolonging of one or more notes of a chord into a following chord to create a temporary dissonance. **b.** The note so prolonged. **3.** A device from which a part is suspended. **4.** The system of springs and other devices that insulates the body of a vehicle from shocks transmitted through the wheels. **5.** *Chemistry.* A relatively coarse, noncolloidal dispersion of solid particles in a liquid. See **colloid.** [French, or Latin *suspensio* (stem *suspensiōn-*). See **suspense.**]

suspension bridge *n.* A bridge having the roadway suspended from cables that are supported by two or more towers and are firmly anchored at both ends.

sus·pen·sive (sə-spén-siv) *adj.* **1.** Serving or tending to suspend or temporarily stop something. **2.** Characterised by or causing suspense. **—sus·pen·sive·ly** *adv.* **—sus·pen·sive·ness** *n.*

sus·pen·soid (sə-spén-soyd) *n.* A suspension of solid particles in a liquid. Also called "suspensoid sol". [SUSPENS(ION) + -OID.]

sus·pen·sor (sə-spén-sər) *n.* **1.** *Botany.* A stalklike cellular structure that forms in the zygote in flowering plants and pushes the embryo into the endosperm. **2.** Variant of **suspensory.** [New Latin, from Medieval Latin, one that suspends, from Latin *suspendēre* (past participle *suspensus*), SUSPEND.]

sus·pen·so·ry (sə-spén-səri) *adj.* **1.** Supporting or suspending: *a suspensory bandage.* **2.** Delaying the completion of something. *~n., pl.* **suspensories.** Also **sus·pen·sor** (-sər). **1.** A support or truss. **2.** *U.S.* An **athletic support.**

suspensory ligament *n.* A ligament that supports an organ or bodily part, such as the structure that supports the lens of the eye.

sus·pi·cion (sə-spish'n) *n.* **1. a.** The act or an instance of suspecting the existence of something, especially of something wrong, without sufficient evidence or proof. **b.** The state of being suspected. **2.** A minute amount; a hint; a trace. [Middle English *suspicio(u)n,* from Old French *suspicion,* from Latin *suspīciō* (stem *suspīciōn-*), from Latin *suspicere* (past participle *suspectus*), to look at secretly, SUS-PECT.] **—sus·pi·cion·al** *adj.*

sus·pi·cious (sə-spishəss) *adj.* **1.** Arousing or apt to arouse suspicion; questionable: *suspicious behaviour.* **2.** Tending to suspect; distrustful: *a suspicious nature.* **—sus·pi·cious·ly** *adv.* **—sus·pi·cious·ness** *n.*

sus·pire (sə-spīr) *intr.v.* **-pired, -piring, -pires.** *Poetic.* **1.** To breathe. **2.** To sigh. [Middle English *suspiren,* from Latin *suspīrāre,* to draw a deep breath : *sub-,* up from below + *spīrāre,* to breathe.] **—sus·pi·ra·tion** *n.*

suss (suss). Variant of **sus.**

sussed (susst) *adj. British Slang.* Streetwise.

Sus·sex (súss-iks ‖ -eks). Former English county. In 1974 it was divided into East Sussex and West Sussex.

Sussex cattle *pl.n.* Beef cattle of a reddish-brown breed developed in Sussex.

Sussex fowl *n.* A domestic fowl of a breed with white and black plumage, originally from Sussex.

Sussex spaniel *n.* A dog of a breed developed in Sussex, having long ears, short legs, and a silky golden-brown coat.

Sussex trug *n.* A **trug** *(see).*

sus·tain (sə-stáyn) *tr.v.* **-tained, -taining, -tains.** **1.** To keep in existence; maintain; prolong. **2.** To supply with necessities or nourishment; provide for. **3.** To support from below; keep from falling or sinking; prop. **4.** To support the spirits, vitality, or resolution of; encourage. **5.** To keep up (a joke or an assumed role, for example) competently. **6.** To endure or withstand; bear up under: *sustain hardships.* **7.** To experience or suffer (loss or injury). **8.** To affirm the validity or justice of. **9.** To prove or corroborate; confirm. [Middle English *suste(y)nen,* from Old French *sustenir,* from Latin *sustinēre,* to hold up : *sub-,* up from under + *tenēre,* to hold.] **—sus·tain·a·ble** *adj.* **—sus·tain·ment** *n.*

sus·tain·er (sə-stáynər) *n.* **1.** One that or that which sustains. **2.** A small rocket motor that sustains the velocity of a spacecraft after the booster has been jettisoned.

sustaining pedal *n.* The right pedal of a piano, which stops the action of the dampers, allowing the strings to vibrate freely. Also called "reverberation pedal", informally "loud pedal."

sustaining program *n.* *U.S.* A radio or television programme that has no commercial announcements.

sus·te·nance (sústinənss) *n.* **1.** The act of sustaining or the condition of being sustained. **2.** The supporting of life or health; maintenance: *"victuals for my sustenance"* (Jonathan Swift). **3.** One that or that which sustains life or health; especially, food. **4.** Means of livelihood. [Middle English *sustena(u)nce,* from Old French *so(u)s-tenance,* from *so(u)stenir, sustenir,* SUSTAIN.]

sus·ten·tac·u·lar (súss-ten-táckewlər, -tən-) *adj. Anatomy.* Supporting. Said of fibres, ligaments, and the like. [Latin *sustentāculum,* a support, from *sustentāre,* frequentative of *sustinēre,* SUSTAIN.]

sus·ten·ta·tion (súss-ten-táysh'n, -tən-) *n. Rare.* Sustenance; food. [Middle English *sustentacion,* from Old French, from Latin *sustentātiō* (stem *sustentātiōn-*), from *sustentāre,* frequentative of *sustinēre,* SUSTAIN.] —**sus·ten·ta·tive** (sə-sténtətiv, súss-ten-taytiv, -tən-) *adj.*

Su·su (soo-soo) *n., pl.* **-sus** or collectively **Susu. 1.** A member of a West African people living in Guinea, the Sudan, and along the northern border of Sierra Leone. **2.** The Mande language spoken by the Susu.

su·sur·ra·tion (séw-sə-ráysh'n, soo-). *n.* Also **su·sur·rus** (sew-súrrəss, soo-). A soft, whispering or rustling sound; a murmur; a whisper. [Middle English, from Late Latin *susurrātiō* (stem *susurrātiōn-*) from Latin *susurāre,* to whisper, from *susurrus,* whisper.] —**su·sur·rant** (sew-súrrənt, soo-), **su·sur·rous** (-súrrəss) *adj.* —**su·sur·rate** (séw-sə-rayt, soo-) *intr.v.*

Sut·cliffe (sút-klif), **Herbert** (1894–1978). British cricketer. He was an opening batsman and played for Yorkshire and England. During his career (1919–45) he totalled 50,135 runs and made 149 centuries, including 16 Test centuries.

Suth·er·land (súthərlənd). Former county of northern Scotland. In Highland Region (1975), now Highland Authority Area.

Sutherland, Graham (Vivian) (1903–80). British painter. He was an official war artist (1941–45), and is best known for his portraits and religious paintings. His works include *Somerset Maugham* (1949) and his tapestry, *Christ in Majesty.*

Sutherland, Dame Joan (1926–). Australian coloratura soprano. She did much to revive the bel canto operas of Bellini and Donizetti till her 1991 retirement.

Sut·lej (sútlej). One of the "Five Rivers" of Punjab. It flows some 1 350 kilometres (about 850 miles) from southwest Tibet, through the Himalayas to join the Panjnad.

sut·ler (súttlər) *n.* Formerly, a camp follower who sold provisions to the soldiers. [Middle Dutch *soeteler,* bad cook, camp cook, probably from Middle High German *sudelen,* to do sloppy work.]

su·tra (soo-trə ‖ séw-) *n.* Also **sut·ta** (-tə). **1.** Any of various aphoristic doctrinal summaries produced generally between 500 and 200 B.C. and later incorporated into Hindu and Buddhist literature. **2.** *Buddhism.* Any scriptural narrative; especially, any text traditionally regarded as a discourse of the Buddha. [Sanskrit *sūtra,* thread, string, collection of aphorisms or rules.]

sut·tee (súttee, su-teé) *n.* **1.** The act or practice, now forbidden by law, of a Hindu widow cremating herself on her husband's funeral pyre. **2.** A widow so cremated. [Sanskrit *satī,* good woman, faithful wife, from *sat,* "existing", virtuous.]

Sut·ton (sútt'n). Borough of Greater London, situated to the southwest of the capital. It was formed (1965) by the merger of the boroughs of Sutton and Cheam and of Beddington and Wallington, with the urban district of Carshalton.

Sutton Hoo (hoo). An archaeological site in eastern England, situated near Woodbridge in Suffolk. In 1939, a Saxon ship measuring 27 metres (89 feet) long was excavated here with a hoard of richly ornamented weapons, jewellery, and utensils. The ship may have been buried as a memorial to King Rædwald (died 624).

su·ture (soo-chər, soot-yər ‖ séw-) *n. Surgery.* **a.** The process of joining two surfaces or edges of tissue together along a line by stitching. **b.** The material used in this procedure, as thread, gut, or wire. **c.** The line so formed. **2.** Any similar join or seam. **3.** *Anatomy.* The line of junction or an immovable joint between two bones, particularly of the skull. **4.** *Biology.* A seamlike joint or line of articulation, such as the line of dehiscence in a seed or fruit or the spiral seam marking the junction of whorls of a gastropod shell. —*tr.v.* **sutured, -turing, -tures.** *Surgery.* To join by means of sutures; sew up. [French, from Latin *sūtūra,* a sewing together, seam, suture, from *suere* (past participle *sūtus*), to sew.] —**su·tur·al** *adj.* —**su·tur·al·ly** *adv.*

Su·va (soovə). The capital of Fiji, situated on the island of Viti Levu. It is a marketing centre and port for sugar, cotton, and pineapples grown on the island. Tourism is also important.

Su·wan·nee (sə-wónni) or **Swa·nee** (swónni). River in the southern United States. It rises in the Okefenokee swamp of southeast Georgia and flows south through Florida to the Gulf of Mexico. The river is about 400 kilometres (250 miles) long.

su·ze·rain (soo-zə-rayn, séw- ‖ -rən) *n.* **1.** Formerly, a feudal lord to whom fealty was due. **2.** A nation that controls another nation in international affairs but allows it domestic sovereignty. —*adj.* Characteristic of a suzerain; sovereign. [French *suzerain* : *sus,* up, above, from Latin *sūsum, sursum,* (turned) upwards, up : *sub-,* up + *versum,* neuter past participle of *vertere,* to turn + *(souv)erain,* from Old French *so(u)verein,* SOVEREIGN.]

su·ze·rain·ty (soo-zə-rayn-ti, séw-, -rən-) *n., pl.* **-ties.** The power or domain of a suzerain.

Su·zhou, Su·chou or **Soo·chow** (soo-jō). Also **Wu·xian** or **Wu·hsien** (woo-syén). City in Jiangsu province, eastern China, situated on the Grand Canal to the West of Shanghai. Founded in the fifth century B.C. it became a walled city and was noted for its pagodas and silk manufacture. Silk and cotton industries remain important.

Suz·man (sooz-mən), **Helen,** born Helen Gavronsky (1917–). South African politician, for a long time the sole representative of the Progressive Party in the South African Parliament. In 1989 she

was appointed an honorary D.B.E. and retired from parliament, but is on the South African Human Rights Commission (1996–).

Su·zu·ki method (soo-zooki) *n.* A method of teaching the violin to very young children, by imitation and repetition. [After S. *Suzuki* (1898–1998), Japanese music teacher who devised it.]

s.v. 1. sailing vessel. **2.** side valve.

Sval·bard (svál-baard; *Norwegian* sváal-baar). A Norwegian archipelago situated in the Arctic Ocean. It includes the Spitsbergen island group, and is mountainous and mostly covered by ice fields and glaciers. The treaty of Spitsbergen (1920), while recognising Norwegian sovereignty, granted mineral and other rights to all 40 signatories, and both Norway and Russia maintain coal-mining settlements on the island. Svalbard commands the shipping lanes to Murmansk, the only major ice-free port in Russia, and the two countries are in dispute over their common boundary across the Barents Sea, which has potentially valuable oil deposits.

svelte (svelt) *adj.* **svelter, sveltest.** Slender or graceful in figure or outline; slim. [French, from Italian *svelto,* "stretched", slender, from *svellere,* to pull out, stretch out, from Vulgar Latin *exvellere* (unattested), from Latin *evellere* : *ex-,* out + *vellere,* to pull.]

Sven·ga·li (sveng-gaáli, sven-) *n.* A person with an uncanny power to compel another to do his will. [After the villain in *Trilby* (1894), a novel by George Du MAURIER.]

Sverdlovsk. See **Yekaterinburg.**

Sverige. See **Sweden.**

Sve·vo (sváyvō), **Italo,** pen name of Ettore Schmitz (1861–1928). Italian novelist. He is best known for his psychological novel, *La Coscienza di Zeno* (*The Confessions of Zeno,* 1923).

Svizzera. See **Switzerland.**

sw short wave; short-wave.

SW southwest.

Sw. Sweden; Swedish.

swab, swob (swob) *n.* **1.** A small piece of cotton or other absorbent material, usually attached to the end of a stick or wire, and used for cleansing or applying medicine. **2.** A specimen of mucus or other material removed with such an instrument. **3.** A mop for cleaning decks, floors, or other large areas. **4.** A person who uses such a mop, especially on a ship. Also called "swabby". **5.** A lout. —*tr.v.* **swabbed, swabbing, swabs.** To use a swab on; clean or treat with a swab. [Probably from Middle Dutch *swabbe,* mop.]

Swa·bi·a (swáybi-ə). *German* **Schwa·ben** (shvaáabən). A medieval duchy in southwestern Germany, which originally included parts of present-day France and Switzerland. The towns of Swabia formed a series of leagues, starting in 1331, the most important being that of 1488–1534, a powerful association of cities, princes, churchmen, and knights, whose army became a bastion of Habsburg authority under Maximilian I. In the reign of Charles V, its members became divided over the Reformation, and the league collapsed. —**Swa·bi·an** *adj. & n.*

swad·dle (swódd'l) *tr.v.* **-dled, -dling, -dles. 1.** To wrap or bind in bandages; swathe. **2.** To wrap (a baby) in swaddling clothes. **3.** To restrain or restrict; smother. —*n. U.S.* A band or cloth used for swaddling. [Middle English *swadlen, swethelen,* from *swethel,* swaddling clothes, Old English *swæthel,* probably from *swathian,* to SWATHE.]

swaddling clothes *pl.n.* **1.** Formerly, strips of linen or other cloth wound about a newborn infant. **2.** Any restrictions imposed upon the immature. Also called "swaddling bands".

Swa·de·shi (swə-dáy-shi) *n.* In British India, the promotion of Indian-produced goods and the boycott of foreign products, as a policy of the independence movement. [Bengali *svadesi,* from Sanskrit *svadesin* : *sva,* one's own + *desa,* a country.]

swag (swag) *n.* **1.** Goods or property obtained by forcible or illicit means. **1.** Loosely, any goods or valuables, especially when improperly gained. **2. a.** A length of drapery, especially a curtain, bunched and secured at two points so that it hangs in a curve. **b.** An ornamental festoon of flowers or fruit. **c.** A carving or moulding representing this. **3.** *Australian.* The pack of a swagman. —*intr.v.* **swagged, swagging, swags. 1.** *Chiefly British.* To lurch or sway. **2.** *Australian.* To travel around with a pack or swag. [Probably from Scandinavian, akin to Norwegian *swagga,* to sway.]

swage (swayj) *n.* **1.** A tool used in bending or shaping cold metal. **2.** A stamp or die for marking or shaping metal with a hammer. **3.** A swage block. —*tr.v.* **swaged, swaging, swages.** To bend or shape by using a swage. [19th century : from French *s(o)uage*†.]

swage block *n.* A metal block having holes or grooves for shaping metal objects.

swag·ger (swággər) *v.* **-gered, -gering, -gers.** —*intr.* **1.** To walk or conduct oneself with an over-confident or insolent air; strut. **2.** To brag; bluster. —*tr.* To influence or affect by swaggering. —*n.* **1.** A swaggering movement or gait. **2.** Boastful or conceited expression; braggadocio. **3.** A dashing, confident air. [Probably from SWAG.] —**swag·ger·er** *n.* —**swag·ger·ing·ly** *adv.*

swagger stick *n.* A short metal-tipped cane typically carried by military officers.

swag·man (swág-mən, -man) *n., pl.* **-men** (-mən, -men). *Australian.* A man who seeks casual work while travelling about carrying his pack or swag; an itinerant worker.

Swa·hi·li (swə-héeli, swaa-) *n., pl.* **Swahili** or **-lis. 1.** A Bantu language of eastern and central Africa, widely used as a lingua franca. **2.** A member of a Bantu people of Zanzibar and the neighbouring mainland who were original speakers of this language. [Swahili, "(people) belonging to the coasts" : Arabic *sawāḥil,* plural of *sāḥil,* coast + *-īy,* belonging to.] —**Swa·hi·li·an** *adj.*

swain (swayn) *n.* **1.** *Archaic.* A country youth, especially a shepherd. **2.** A lover. Usually used humorously. [Middle English *swein, swayne,* from Old Norse *sveinn,* a boy, herdsman.]

swale *U.S.* **swail** (swayl) *n.* **1.** A low tract of land, especially moist or marshy ground. **2.** Shade. [Middle English, a shade, shady place, perhaps from Scandinavian, akin to Old Norse *svalr,* cool.]

swal·low¹ (swóllō) *v.* **-lowed, -lowing, -lows.** —*tr.* **1.** To cause (food, for example) to pass from the mouth via the throat and the oesophagus into the stomach by muscular action; ingest. **2.** To consume or destroy as if by ingestion; devour. Often used with *up: swallow up smaller businesses.* **3.** To ingest (something unpleasant) reluctantly. Often used with *down.* **4. a.** To bear humbly; tolerate: *swallow an insult.* **b.** To refrain from expressing; suppress: *swallow one's feelings.* **c.** To take back; retract: *swallow one's words.* **5.** To believe without question. **6.** To utter (words) indistinctly. —*intr.* To perform the act of swallowing.

~*n.* **1.** The act of swallowing; a gulp. **2.** The amount that is swallowed at any one time. **3.** *Nautical.* The channel through which a rope runs in a block or a mooring chock. [Middle English *swalowen, swolwen,* Old English *swelgan.*] —**swal·low·er** *n.*

swallow² *n.* **1.** Any of various birds of the family Hirundinidae; especially, *Hirundo rustica,* having long, pointed wings and a usually notched or forked tail. **2.** Broadly, any of various similar birds, such as a swift. [Middle English *swal(o)we, swalu,* Old English *sweal(e)we,* from Germanic *swalwi* (unattested).]

swallow dive *n.* A dive performed with the legs together and straight, the back arched, and the arms at first stretched out from the sides. Also *U.S.* "swan dive".

swallow hole *n.* A **sink hole** (sense 2) *(see).*

swal·low·tail (swóllō-tayl) *n.* **1. a.** The deeply forked tail of a swallow. **b.** Anything resembling such a tail. **2.** *Informal.* A swallow-tailed coat. **3.** Any of various butterflies of the family Papilionidae having a tail-like extension at the end of each hind wing.

swal·low-tailed (swóllō-tayld) *adj.* **1.** Having a deeply forked tail. Said of various birds. **2.** Resembling the tail of a swallow: *a swallow-tailed kite.*

swallow-tailed coat *n.* A **tail coat** *(see).*

swam. Past tense of **swim.**

swa·mi (swaámi) *n., pl.* **-mis. 1.** Lord; master. A Hindu title of respect. **2.** A Hindu religious teacher. **3.** Loosely, a mystic; a yogi. [Hindi *svāmī,* master, from Sanskrit *svāmin,* owner, prince, "one's own master".]

swamp (swomp ‖ *U.S.* also swawmp) *n.* **1.** A lowland region permanently saturated with water. **2.** Loosely, a stretch of marsh ground.

~*v.* **swamped, swamping, swamps.** —*tr.* **1.** To drench in or cover with water or other liquid. **2.** To inundate or burden; overwhelm: *swamped with work.* **3.** To fill or sink (a ship) with water.

~*intr.* To become swamped, as a ship may. [Perhaps of Low German origin, akin to Low German *zwamp,* swamp.] —**swamp·y** *adj.*

swamp boat *n.* A flat-bottomed boat, powered by an aircraft propeller projecting above the stern, and used in swamps or shallow waters. Also called "airboat".

swamp·er (swóm-pər) *n. U.S.* **1.** One who lives in or close to a swamp. **2.** One who clears a swamp or forest. **3. a.** A menial helper, as in a restaurant. **b.** A handyman; an assistant.

swamp fever *n.* **1.** A viral disease in horses, marked by progressive anaemia, a staggering gait, and fever. **2.** *U.S.* Malaria.

swamp·land (swómp-land) *n.* Land of swampy consistency; land having many swamps on it.

swan (swon) *n.* **1.** Any of various large aquatic birds, chiefly of the genus *Cygnus,* having webbed feet, a long slender neck, and usually white plumage. **2.** *Capital* **S.** The constellation, **Cygnus** *(see).* Preceded by *the.* **3.** A poet; a bard.

~*intr.v.* **swanned, swanning, swans. 1.** To pass with an air of blithe superiority: *She swanned by in her new mink coat.* **2. a.** To wander along without apparent worry or care. Used with *around* or *about.* **b.** To deal or proceed with the greatest of ease. Used with *through: swanned through her final exams.* [Middle English *swan(ne), suan,* Old English *swan, suan.*]

Swan (swon), **Sir Joseph Wilson** (1828–1914). British physicist and inventor. He invented the photographic dry plate (1871) and bromide paper (1879). He also devised a carbon-filament electric lamp (1860), which he improved for commercial production (1881).

swan dive *n. U.S.* A **swallow dive** *(see).*

Swanee. See **Suwannee.**

swank (swangk) *intr.v.* **swanked, swanking, swanks.** To act in an ostentatious or pretentious way.

~*n. Informal.* **1.** Ostentatious or pretentious behaviour; swagger. **2.** Showy elegance; style. **3.** *Chiefly British.* A conceited or swaggering person.

~*adj. Informal.* Variant of **swanky.** [19th century (Midlands dialect) : origin obscure.]

swank·y (swángki) *adj. Informal.* **1.** Conceited; showing swank. **2.** Ostentatious; showy. —**swank·i·ly** *adv.* —**swank·i·ness** *n.*

swan neck *n.* A bend in a handrail, tubing, or the like that is double-curved in the shape of a swan's neck.

swan·ner·y (swónnəri) *n., pl.* **-ies.** A place where swans are bred and kept.

Swan River daisy *n.* An Australian plant, *Brachycome iberidifolia,* cultivated for its showy blue or white flower heads.

swan's-down (swónz-down) *n.* **1.** The soft down of a swan. **2.** A

soft woollen fabric used especially for baby clothes.

Swan·sea (swón-zi). *Welsh* **A·ber·ta·we** (ábbər-tów-i). Second largest city in Wales. It is an industrial port situated on Swansea Bay at the mouth of the river Tawe.

swan·skin (swón-skin) *n.* **1.** The skin of a swan with the feathers attached. **2.** Any of several flannel or cotton fabrics with a soft nap.

swan song *n.* **1.** According to legend, the beautiful music uttered only once in a swan's life, just as it is dying. **2.** A farewell appearance, declaration, or work. [Translation of German *Schwanengesang.*]

swan-up·per (swón-úppər) *n. British.* An official employed to catch and mark cygnets.

swan-up·ping (swón-úpping) *n. British.* The practice of catching cygnets and marking their beaks as an indication of ownership; especially, the annual marking of cygnets on the river Thames. [Referring to taking the swans up from the water to be marked.]

swap, swop (swop) *v.* **swapped** or **swopped, swapping** or **swopping, swaps** or **swops.** *Informal.* —*intr.* To exchange one thing for another. —*tr.* To exchange.

~*n. Informal.* An exchange of one thing for another. [Literally, "to strike hands in closing a bargain", Middle English *swappen,* to strike, hit, from Germanic (probably imitative); akin to German *schwappen,* to splash, whack.] —**swap·per** *n.*

SWA·PO, Swa·po (swaápō, swóppō) *n.* Formerly, the *South-West Africa People's Organisation:* a Namibian independence movement.

sward (swawrd) *n.* Land covered with grassy turf; a lawn or meadow. [Old English *sweard, swearth,* skin of the body, rind of bacon; akin to Old Norse *svörthr,* skin.]

swarf (swawrf) *n.* Fine metallic filings or shavings removed by a cutting tool. [Probably from Scandinavian, akin to Old Norse *svarf,* filings.]

swarm¹ (swawrm) *n.* **1.** A large number of insects or other small organisms, especially when in motion. **2.** A group of bees, led by a queen bee, in migration to establish a new colony. **3.** A dense throng of persons or animals, especially when moving in mass.

~*v.* **swarmed, swarming, swarms.** —*intr.* **1. a.** To move or emerge in a swarm. **b.** To leave a hive as a swarm to start a new colony. Used of bees. **2.** To move as a large group or mass of creatures; congregate. **3.** To be overrun or filled. —*tr.* To fill with a crowd; throng. [Old English *swearm.*] —**swarm·er** *n.*

swarm² *v.* **swarmed, swarming, swarms.** —*tr.* To climb quickly by gripping with the arms and legs. —*intr.* To climb something in this way. Usually used with *up.* [16th century : origin obscure.]

swart (swawrt) *adj. Archaic.* Swarthy. [Middle English *swarte, swe(o)rt,* Old English *sweart,* from Germanic *swartaz* (unattested).]

swarth·y (swáwr-thi, -thi) *adj.* **-ier, -iest.** Having a dark or sunburnt complexion. [Earlier *swarty,* from SWART.] —**swarth·i·ly** *adv.* —**swarth·i·ness** *n.*

swash (swosh ‖ *U.S.* also swawsh) *n.* **1.** The splashing of water or other liquid as it hits a solid surface: *the swash of the sea against the rocks.* **2.** The sound of such a splashing.

~*v.* **swashed, swashing, swashes.** —*intr.* **1.** To strike, move, or wash with a splashing sound, as of water. **2.** *Archaic.* To swagger. —*tr.* **1.** To splash (a liquid). **2.** To splash a liquid against. [16th century : imitative.]

swash·buck·ler (swósh-bucklər) *n.* **1.** A flamboyant swordsman or adventurer. **2.** Any sword-wielding bully or ruffian. Also called "swasher". [From the striking of bucklers in fighting.]

swash·buck·ling (swósh-buckling) *adj.* Of or characteristic of a swashbuckler; flamboyant; full of bravado.

swash letter *n.* An ornamental italic letter formed with fancy flourishes and tails. [17th century : *swash†,* oblique, obliquely inclined.]

swas·ti·ka (swóstikə ‖ *U.S.* also swaa-stéeka) *n.* **1.** An ancient cosmic or religious symbol, formed by a Greek cross with the ends of the arms bent at right angles either clockwise or anticlockwise. **2.** The emblem of Nazi Germany, still used as a symbol by fascist groups. [Sanskrit *svastika,* a sign of good luck, from *svasti,* well-being, good luck: *su-,* well + *asti,* "is", being.]

swat, swot (swot) *tr.v.* **swatted** or **swotted, swatting** or **swotting, swats** or **swots.** To deal a sharp blow to, usually with an instrument; slap: *swat flies.*

~*n.* A quick, sharp, or violent blow. [Variant of SQUAT (obsolete sense to "lay flat with a blow").]

swatch (swoch) *n.* **1.** A sample strip cut from a piece of cloth or other material. **2.** A small sample square of knitted or woven work, made in order to gauge tension. [17th century : origin obscure.]

swath (swawth, swoth). *n.* Also **swathe** (swayth ‖ swawth, swoth). **1.** The width of a scythe stroke or a mowing-machine blade. **2. a.** A path of this width made by mowing. **b.** The mown grass or grain lying on such a path. **3.** Something likened to a swath; a strip or belt. **4.** A devastating effect caused as if by a scythe: *cut swaths through her opponents.* —**cut a (wide) swath.** To create a great stir, impression, or display. [Middle English *swathe,* Old English *swæth, swathu,* track, trace, from Germanic *swath-* (unattested).]

swathe¹ (swayth ‖ *U.S.* also swawth, swoth) *tr.v.* **swathed, swathing, swathes. 1.** To wrap or bind with bindings or bandages. **2.** To enfold or envelop: *swathed in furs.*

~*n.* A wrapping, binding, or bandage. [Middle English *swathen,* Old English *swathian†,* to wrap up.] —**swath·er** *n.*

swathe². Variant of **swath.**

swat·ter (swóttər) *n.* **1.** One that swats. **2.** A small meshed or flexible flap attached to a handle, used for killing insects. Also called "fly-swatter".

sway (sway) *v.* **swayed, swaying, sways.** —*intr.* **1.** To move back and forth with a swinging motion; oscillate. **2.** To incline or bend to one side; veer. **3. a.** To incline towards change, as in opinion or feeling; vacillate. **b.** To tend towards in outlook. —*tr.* **1.** To cause to swing from side to side. **2.** To cause to incline or bend towards one side. **3.** *Nautical.* To hoist (a mast or yard) into position. **4. a.** To deter or cause to swerve; dissuade. **b.** To exert influence on or control over. **5.** *Archaic.* **a.** To rule or govern. **b.** To wield as a weapon or sceptre. —See Synonyms at **swing**.
~*n.* **1.** The act of moving from side to side with a swinging motion. **2.** Power; influence. **3.** *Archaic.* Dominion or rule. [Middle English *sweyen, sweghen,* to move, go down, swing, probably from Old Norse *sveigja,* to bend, yield.] —**sway·ing·ly** *adv.*

sway·back (sway-bak) *n.* An excessive inward or downward curvature of the spine, as in horses. —**sway-backed** *adj.*

Swa·zi (swa'azi) *n., pl.* **-zis** or collectively **Swazi. 1.** A member of the Bantu people of Swaziland. **2.** The language of this people, closely related to Zulu. In this sense, also called "siSwati". —**Swa·zi** *adj.*

Swa·zi·land, Kingdom of (swa'azi-land). Small, landlocked African country. In the 1970s, foreign investment made it one of the most prosperous of the small African states, and forestry, mining, and manufacturing are expanding. Even so, about 70 per cent of workers are in farming, and many others work in South Africa. A British protectorate from 1903, Swaziland became independent within the Commonwealth in 1968. In 1973 Sobhuza II (reigned 1921–82) assumed supreme power and abolished the constitution. His successor, Mswati III, has permitted elections to parliament from among nominated leaders, but political parties are still banned. Area, 17 363 square kilometres (6,704 square miles). Capital, Mbabane. Population, 940,000. See map at **South Africa.**

SWbS southwest by south.

SWbW southwest by west.

swear (swair) *v.* **swore** (swor ‖ swôr), **sworn** (sworn ‖ swôrn), **swearing, swears.** —*intr.* **1.** To make a solemn declaration, invoking a deity or some person or thing held sacred, in confirmation of the honesty or truth of such a declaration: *I swear to God I spoke the truth.* **2.** To make a solemn promise; vow. **3.** To use swearwords; blaspheme or curse: *He swears at everyone when he is drunk.* **4.** *Law.* To give evidence or testimony under oath. —*tr.* **1.** To declare solemnly by invoking a sacred personage or thing. **2.** To promise or pledge with a solemn oath; vow. **3.** To utter or bind oneself to (an oath). **4.** To administer a legal oath to. **5.** To say or affirm earnestly and with great conviction. —**swear by. 1.** To name (a sacred personage or thing) as invocation in taking an oath. **2.** To have great reliance upon or confidence in. —**swear in.** To administer a legal or official oath to: *swear in the mayor.* —**swear off.** *Informal.* To pledge to renounce or give up. —**swear out.** *U.S.* To obtain (a warrant for someone's arrest) by making a charge under oath. [Middle English *swer(i)en, swor, swor(n)*, Old English *swerian, swōr* (past singular), *sworen.*] —**swear·er** *n.*

swear·word (swair-wurd) *n.* A word used in an obscene, insulting, or blasphemous way.

sweat (swet) *v.* **sweated** or **sweat, sweating, sweats.** —*intr.* **1.** To excrete the secretion of the sweat glands through the pores in the skin; perspire. **2.** To exude in droplets, as does moisture from certain cheeses or sap from a tree. **3.** To condense atmospheric moisture. **4. a.** To release moisture, as does hay or plants left to dry out. **b.** To ferment, as tobacco does during curing. **5.** *Informal.* To work long and hard. **6.** *Informal.* To suffer much, as for a misdeed. **7.** *Informal.* To fret or worry. —*tr.* **1.** To excrete (moisture) through a porous surface, such as the skin. **2.** To exude (moisture) in droplets on a surface. **3.** To cause to perspire, as by drugs, heat, or strenuous exercise. **4.** To make damp or wet with perspiration. **5.** To cause to work excessively; overwork. **6.** To overwork and underpay (employees). **7.** To heat (metal parts) in order to make a soldered joint. **8.** To cook (vegetables or other food) very slowly with butter in a closed saucepan. —**sweat it out.** *Informal.* **1.** To endure anxiously. **2.** To await (something) anxiously. —**sweat out.** To attempt to cure by sweating: *sweat out a cold.*
~*n.* **1.** The product of the sweat glands of the skin. **2.** Any condensation of moisture in the form of droplets on a surface. **3.** The process of sweating or condition of being sweated. **4.** Strenuous, exhausting labour; drudgery. **5.** An exercise run given to a horse before a race. **6.** *Informal.* An anxious condition; impatience: *in a sweat.* —**no sweat.** *Slang.* Easily done or handled. Often used as an interjection. [Middle English *sweten, swaten,* Old English *swǣtan.*] —**sweat·i·ly** *adv.* —**sweat·i·ness** *n.* —**sweat·y** *adj.*

sweat·band (swet-band) *n.* **1.** A band of fabric or leather sewn inside the crown of a hat as protection against sweat. **2.** A headband tied around the forehead to absorb sweat, worn especially while playing a strenuous game such as tennis.

sweat·box (swet-boks) *n.* A box in which something, such as animal hides or fruit, is fermented by sweating.

sweat·ed (swet tid) *adj.* **1.** Hard and underpaid: *sweated labour.* **2.** Produced by exploited and underpaid workers.

sweat·er (swet tər) *n.* **1.** One that sweats, especially profusely. **2.** That which induces sweating; especially, a sudorific. **3.** A long-sleeved garment made of wool or synthetic yarns and worn on the upper part of the body. Also called "jersey", "jumper".

sweat gland *n.* Any of the numerous small, tubular glands that in humans are found nearly everywhere in the skin and that secrete a watery fluid containing sodium chloride and urea externally through the pores.

sweat·ing sickness (swet ting) *n.* **1.** An acute infectious disease that was epidemic in Europe during the 15th and 16th centuries, characterised by profuse sweating and fever. **2.** A disease of cattle that is transmitted by ticks and is widespread in southern Africa.

sweat·rag (swet-rag) *n. Slang.* **1.** A handkerchief. **2.** A sweatband.

sweat·shirt (swet-shurt) *n.* A long-sleeved cotton jumper worn especially as casual wear or for sport.

sweat·shop (swet-shop) *n.* A workplace or factory where employees work long hours for low wages under bad conditions.

sweat·suit (swet-soot, -sewt) *n. U.S.* A **tracksuit** *(see).*

Swed. Sweden; Swedish.

swede (sweed) *n.* **1.** A plant, *Brassica napobrassica,* cultivated for its root. **2.** The large, fleshy, edible root of this plant, usually white or yellow in colour, which is used as a vegetable and as fodder for livestock. Also *U.S.* "rutabaga", "Swedish turnip", *chiefly Scottish* "turnip". [So named after its introduction into Scotland from Sweden in the 18th century.]

Swe·den (swee'd'n). *Swedish* **Sve·rige** (svair-yě). Kingdom of northern Europe, occupying the east of the mountainous Scandinavian peninsula. It has one of the world's highest living standards, and also one of its most extensive welfare programmes, taxes absorbing more than a third of the national income. Prosperity derives chiefly from manufacturing. The country has large forest and mineral resources, including iron, copper, lead, and uranium. It relies heavily on hydroelectric power, and increasingly on nuclear power, having few fossil fuel deposits. Sweden emerged as a unified nation in the 11th century. It became a great power in the 17th century, but lost its empire early in the next century. Sweden joined the European Union in 1995. Area, 449 964 square kilometres (173,732 square miles). Population, 8,840,000. Capital, Stockholm. —**Swede** (sweed) *n.*

Swe·den·borg (swee'd'n-bawrg), **Emanuel** (1688–1772). Swedish scientist, philosopher, and religious writer. He began having visions (*c.*1743) and afterwards devoted himself to physical and spiritual research. Although he did not preach or found a religious sect, his

writings inspired his followers to set up the New Jerusalem Church.
Swe·den·bor·gi·an·ism (swéed'n-bórji-ən-iz'm, -bórgi-) *n.* Also **Swe·den·borg·ism** (-bawrgiz'm). The theological philosophy of Emanuel Swedenborg that forms the basis for the New Jerusalem Church, claiming direct mystical communication between the world and the spiritual realm and affirming Christ as the true God.
Swed·ish (swéedish) *adj.* Of or pertaining to Sweden, the Swedes, or their culture or language.
~n. **1.** The North Germanic language of Sweden. **2.** *Used with a plural verb.* The people of Sweden. Preceded by *the.*
Swedish massage *n.* A European style of therapeutic massage and exercises for muscles and joints, developed in the 19th century.
Swedish turnip *n. U.S.* A vegetable, the swede.
Swee·ney (swéeni) *n. British Slang.* The **Flying Squad** *(see).* [Rhyming slang, from *Sweeney Todd,* Victorian killer barber.]
sweep (sweep) *v.* **swept** (swept), **sweeping, sweeps.** *—tr.* **1.** To clean or clear the surface or interior of with or as if with a broom or brush: *sweep a chimney.* **2.** To clean or clear away (dust or dirt, for example) with or as if with a broom or brush: *sweep snow from the steps.* **3. a.** To clear (a space) with or as if with a broom. **b.** To clear (objects) away with or as if with a broom: *swept the papers off her desk.* **4.** To touch or brush lightly: *Willow branches swept the ground.* **5. a.** To move, remove, or convey with a flowing motion, as by water: *The wind swept tiles from the roof.* **b.** To move or unbalance emotionally: *Love swept him off his feet.* **6.** To cause to depart; remove or destroy. **7.** To traverse with speed or intensity; range throughout: *Plague swept Europe.* **8.** To traverse, as when searching: *Her gaze swept the horizon.* **9.** To drag the bottom of (a body of water). **10.** To win all the stages of (a game or contest). **11.** To hit (a cricket ball) with a sweep. *—intr.* **1.** To clear or clean a surface with or as if with a broom or brush. **2. a.** To move, surge, or flow with smooth and steady force: *A cool wind swept over the plain.* **b.** To move swiftly or majestically: *She swept by in silence.* **3.** To trail, as a long garment does: *Her veil swept to the floor.* **4.** To extend gracefully or majestically: *The hills sweep down to the sea.*
~n. **1.** The act of sweeping; removal with or as if with a broom or brush. **2.** The motion of sweeping: *a sweep of the arm.* **3.** The range or scope encompassed by sweeping: *the sweep of a machine gun.* **4. a.** A reach or extent: *a sweep of green lawn.* **b.** A curving driveway. **5.** Any curve or contour: *the sweep of his hair.* **6.** One who sweeps; especially, a chimney sweep. **7.** *Usually plural.* Sweepings. **8. a.** The winning of all stages of a game or contest. **b.** A total victory or success. **9.** A long oar used to propel a boat. **10.** A long pole attached to a pivot and with a bucket at one end, used to raise water from a well. **11.** *Informal.* A sweepstake. **12.** *Electronics.* The steady motion of an electron beam across a cathode-ray tube. **13.** A cricketing shot in which the ball is hit near the ground on the leg side with a sweeping movement. **—make a clean sweep.** To get rid of all unwanted objects, people, obligations, or other obstacles. [Middle English *swe(e)pen,* probably from Old English *swēop,* past singular of *swāpan,* to sweep.]
sweep·back (swéep-bak) *n. Aeronautics.* **1.** The backward slant of the leading edge of an aerofoil. **2.** The degree of this slant.
sweep·er (swéepər) *n.* **1.** A person who sweeps. **2.** A **carpet sweeper** *(see).* **3.** In soccer, a player who defends from between the goal and the main defending players. **4.** A **minesweeper** *(see).*
sweep·ing (swéeping) *adj.* **1.** Removing with or as if with a broom or brushing movement. **2.** Influencing or affecting a great area; wide-ranging: *a sweeping definition.* **3.** Very general; without discrimination or reservation: *sweeping generalisations.* **4.** Overwhelming: *a sweeping victory.*
~n. **1.** The action or occupation of one who sweeps. **2.** *Plural.* That which is swept up; debris; litter. **—sweep·ing·ly** *adv.*
sweep-second hand (swéep-seckənd) *n.* A long hand on a clock or watch that measures seconds by moving the space of a minute for each second. Also called "sweep hand".
sweep·stake (swéep-stayk) *n.* Also *chiefly U.S.* **sweep·stakes** (-stayks). **1.** A lottery in which the participants' contributions form a fund to be awarded as a prize to the winner or winners. **2.** Any event or contest, especially a horse race, the result of which determines the winner of such a lottery. **3.** The lottery prize won.
sweet (sweet) *adj.* **sweeter, sweetest.** **1. a.** Having a sugary taste. **b.** Containing or derived from a sugar. **2.** Pleasing to the senses, feelings, or the mind; gratifying: *sweet music; Revenge is sweet.* **3. a.** Adorable; charming; lovable: *a sweet child.* **b.** Good-natured, sweet-tempered. **c.** Kind; nice; pleasant and helpful: *It's sweet of you to give me a lift.* **4. a.** Not saline; fresh: *sweet water.* **b.** *U.S.* Not saline; unsalted: *sweet butter.* **5.** Not spoilt, sour, or decaying; fresh: *This milk is still sweet.* **6.** Free of acid. **7.** *Music.* **a.** Designating jazz characterised by adherence to a melodic line and to a time signature. **b.** Performing jazz in this way. **8.** Designating wine that is not dry or cider or sherry that is neither dry nor medium. **—sweet on.** *Informal.* Fond of (a person); infatuated with.
~n. **1.** The quality of being sweet; sweetness. **2.** Something that is sweet or contains sugar. **3.** *Chiefly British.* A piece of confectionery. **4.** *British.* Anything relatively sweet served as a pudding. **5.** A dear or beloved person. [Middle English *swe(e)te,* Old English *swēte.*] **—sweet·ish** *adj.* **—sweet·ly** *adv.* **—sweet·ness** *n.*
sweet alyssum *n.* A widely cultivated plant, *Lobularia maritima,* native to the Mediterranean region, having clusters of small, fragrant white or purplish flowers.
sweet-and-sour (swéet'n-sówr) *adj.* Made or cooked with vinegar and sugar, as in Chinese cooking: *sweet-and-sour sauce.*
sweet basil *n.* A species of **basil** *(see).*
sweet bay *n.* **1.** A tree, the **bay** *(see).* **2.** A small tree, *Magnolia virginiana,* of the southern United States, having large, fragrant white flowers.
sweet·bread (swéet-bred) *n.* The pancreas or thymus gland of a calf or lamb, used for food. [SWEET + BREAD (euphemism).]
sweet·bri·ar, sweet·bri·er (swéet-brī-ər, -brīr) *n.* A rose, *Rosa rubiginosa* (or *R. eglanteria*), native to Europe, having prickly stems, fragrant leaves, and pink flowers. Also called "eglantine".
sweet cherry *n.* **1.** A widely cultivated tree originating from the wild cherry *Prunus avium,* native to Eurasia, having white flowers and sweet, edible fruit. The sweet cherry group has two subdivisions, the **bigarreau** and the **gean** *(both of which see).* **2.** The fruit of this tree. See **cherry.**
sweet chestnut *n.* See **chestnut** (sense 1).
sweet cicely *n.* **1.** Any of various North American plants of the genus *Osmorhiza,* having aromatic roots, compound leaves, and clusters of small white flowers. **2.** An aromatic European plant, *Myrrhis odorata,* having compound leaves and clusters of small white flowers. In this sense, also called "myrrh".
sweet cider *n.* **1.** Sweet-tasting cider. **2.** *U.S.* Unfermented apple juice. Compare **hard cider.**
sweet clover *n.* A plant, the **melilot** *(see).*
sweet·corn, sweet corn (swéet-kawrn) *n.* A variety of maize, *Zea mays saccharata,* having kernels that are sweet to eat when young; broadly, *British,* maize.
sweet·en (swéet'n) *v.* **-ened, -ening, -ens.** *—tr.* **1.** To make sweet or sweeter by or as if by the addition of sugar. **2.** To make pleasurable or gratifying. **3.** To make bearable; alleviate; lighten. **4.** *U.S. Informal.* To increase the value of (collateral for a loan) by adding more securities. **5.** In poker, to increase the value of (an unwon pot) by adding stakes before reopening. *—intr.* To become sweet.
sweet·en·er (swéet'n-ər) *n.* **1.** That which is added to something to make it sweet; specifically, a sugar substitute such as saccharine. **2.** *Slang.* A bribe.
sweet·en·ing (swéet'n-ing) *n.* **1.** The act or process of making sweet. **2.** Something used to sweeten.
sweet fennel *n.* A variety of fennel, **finochio** *(see).*
sweet fern *n.* An aromatic shrub, *Comptonia peregrina,* of eastern North America, having shallowly lobed, fernlike, aromatic foliage.
sweet flag *n.* A plant, *Acorus calamus,* growing in moist places and having bladelike leaves, minute greenish flowers, and aromatic roots. Also called "calamus".
sweet gale *n.* A plant, the **bog myrtle** *(see).*
sweet gum *n.* **1.** A New World tree, *Liquidambar styraciflua,* having sharply lobed leaves, prickly, ball-like fruit clusters, and wood used to make furniture. Also called "bilsted". **2.** The wood or aromatic resin obtained from this tree.
sweet·heart (swéet-haart) *n.* **1.** One who is loved and is loved by another. Often used as a term of affectionate address. **2.** A lovable, friendly, or generous person.
swee·tie (swéeti) *n.* **1.** *Informal.* A sweetheart; a dear. **2.** *British Informal & Regional.* A sweet (piece of confectionery).
sweet·ie·pie (swéeti-pí) *n. Informal.* A dear; a sweetheart. Used as a term of address.
sweet·ing (swéeting) *n.* **1.** A sweet apple. **2.** *Archaic.* A sweetheart.
sweet marjoram *n.* A species of **marjoram** *(see).*
sweet·meal (swéet-meel) *adj.* Sweetened and made with wholemeal flour. Said of a biscuit.
sweet·meat (swéet-meet) *n.* Any delicacy made with a sweetening agent; specifically, a piece of crystallised fruit. [SWEET + MEAT (food).]
sweet pea *n.* A climbing plant, *Lathyrus odoratus,* native to southern Italy, cultivated for its variously coloured, fragrant flowers.
sweet pepper *n.* **1.** Any of several plants of the genus *Capsicum,* especially *C. frutescens* or *C. annuum,* cultivated for their large, mild-tasting fruits, which are eaten raw in salads or cooked as a vegetable. **2.** The fruit of such a plant. See **green pepper, red pepper.** Also called "capsicum", "pimiento".
sweet potato *n.* **1.** A tropical American vine, *Ipomoea batatas,* cultivated for its thick, orange-coloured, edible root. **2.** The root of this plant, eaten cooked as a vegetable.
sweet-shop (swéet-shop) *n. British.* A small shop selling confectionery, and sometimes tobacco and other items.
sweet·sop (swéet-sop) *n.* **1.** A tropical American tree, *Annona squamosa,* having yellowish-green fruit with sweet, edible pulp. **2.** The fruit of this tree. Also called "sugar apple".
sweet-tempered (swéet-témpərd) *adj.* Docile; by nature gentle and kind. **—sweet-tem·pered·ly** *adv.*
sweet tooth *n.* A fondness for sugar or sweet things.
sweet william *n.* A widely cultivated plant, *Dianthus barbatus,* native to Eurasia, having flat, dense clusters of red or pink flowers.
swell (swel) *v.* **swelled, swollen** (swṓlən) or **swelled, swelling, swells.** *—intr.* **1.** To increase in size or volume as a result of internal pressure; expand. **2. a.** To increase in force, size, number, or degree. **b.** To grow in loudness or intensity: *the sound swelled to a tremendous din.* **3.** To bulge out; protrude, as a sail may. Often used with *out.* **4.** To rise in or like billows above the surrounding level, as waves or clouds may. **5.** To rise up in level or overflow, as a river may. **6.** To be or become filled or puffed up with an emotion, such as pride. *—tr.* To cause to swell: *swelled the chorus of protest.*
~n. **1. a.** The act or process of swelling. **b.** The condition of being swollen. **2.** A swollen part; a bulge or protuberance. **3.** A regular

undulating movement of waves out in the open sea, with no breaking, and considerable distance between successive crests. **4. a.** A rise in the land; a rounded hill. **b.** A long, gently sloping elevation, which rises from the sea bed, but which is far from the surface. **5.** *Informal & Archaic.* One who is fashionably dressed or prominent in fashionable society. **6.** *Music.* **a.** A crescendo followed by a gradual diminuendo. **b.** A sign in a score indicating this. **c.** A device on some instruments, such as the organ or harpsichord, for regulating volume.

~*adj.* **sweller, swellest. 1.** *Archaic.* Fashionably elegant; smart; stylish. **2.** *U.S. Informal* Fine; excellent: *a swell guy.* Often used interjectionally. [Middle English *swellen, swollen,* Old English *swellan, geswollen,* from Germanic *swellan* (unattested).]

Usage: The usual past participial form of this verb is *swollen* (*The river/Her neck/The sail was swollen*), but *swelled* is often used when increases in size or amount are being expressed (*The crowd was swelled by a large number of young people*). A contrast in meaning is sometimes possible, with *swollen* expressing a pejorative sense: compare *Their numbers have swelled to nearly a thousand* (statement of fact) and *Their numbers have swollen to nearly a thousand* (an undesirable development).

swell box *n.* A chamber housing one or more sets of organ pipes and having shutters that can be opened or shut to regulate the volume of tone.

swelled-headed. *U.S.* Variant of **swollen-headed.**

swell·fish (swél-fish) *n., pl.* **-fishes** or **swellfish.** The **puffer** *(see).*

swell·ing (swélling) *n.* **1.** The act of expanding. **2.** The state of being swollen or expanded. **3.** Something that is swollen; especially, an abnormally swollen or protuberant area on the body.

swel·ter (swéltər) *v.* **-tered, -tering, -ters.** —*intr.* To be affected by oppressive heat; sweat or feel faint from heat. —*tr.* **1.** To affect with oppressive heat. **2.** *Archaic.* To exude.

~*n.* Oppressive heat and humidity: *"All the swelter of that urban summer"* (Cyril Connolly). [Middle English *swelt(e)ren,* frequentative of *swelten,* to die, faint from heat, Old English *sweltan,* to die.]

swel·ter·ing (swéltəring) *adj.* Also *rare* **swel·try** (swéltri), **-trier, -triest. 1.** Oppressively hot and humid. **2.** Suffering from oppressive heat. **—swel·ter·ing·ly** *adv.*

swept. Past tense and past participle of **sweep.**

swept·back (swépt-bák) *adj.* Angled rearwards from the points of attachment. Said especially of aircraft wings.

swept·wing (swépt-wing) *adj.* Having sweptback wings.

~*n.* A sweptback wing.

swerve (swerv) *v.* **swerved, swerving, swerves.** —*intr.* To turn aside suddenly and swiftly from a straight or planned course; veer. —*tr.* To cause to swerve; deflect; turn aside.

~*n.* A deflection or deviation; a swerving movement. [Middle English *swerven,* perhaps originally "to make a circular motion in polishing", Old English *sweorfan,* to file away, scour, polish.]

S.W.G. Standard wire gauge.

swift (swift) *adj.* **swifter, swiftest. 1.** Moving or able to move with great speed; fast; fleet. **2.** Coming, occurring, or accomplished quickly; instant: *a swift retort.* **3.** Ready in acting or reacting; prompt: *swift to take steps.* **—**See Synonyms at **fast.**

~*adv.* Quickly; swiftly. Often used in combination: *swift-running.*

~*n.* **1.** A cylinder on a carding machine. **2.** A reel used to hold yarn as it is being wound off. **3.** Any of various dark birds of the family Apodidae, characteristically having long, narrow wings and a relatively short tail. **4.** Any of various small, fast-moving North American lizards of the genera *Sceloporus* and *Uta.* [Middle English *swift(e),* Old English *swift.*] **—swift·ly** *adv.* **—swift·ness** *n.*

Swift (swift), **Jonathan** (1667–1745). Irish-born satirist and poet. His works include *A Tale of a Tub* (1704), which attacked religious extremism, and his masterpiece, *Gulliver's Travels* (1726), a satirical attack on the politics, philosophy, and science of his time.

swift·let (swift-lət, -lit) *n.* Any small cave-dwelling swift of the genus *Collocalia,* of southeast Asia and Australia, whose nests, constructed chiefly of solidified saliva, are used to make birds'-nest soup. [Diminutive of SWIFT. See **-let.**]

swift moth *n.* **1.** The **ghost moth** *(see).* **2.** Any of various moths of the family Hepialidae.

swig (swig) *n. Informal.* A large swallow or drink of liquid; a gulp.

~*v.* **swigged, swigging, swigs.** —*tr. Informal.* To drink eagerly and with great gulps. —*intr. Informal.* To take a large swallow; gulp. Ofted used with *at.* [16th century : origin obscure.]

swill (swil) *v.* **swilled, swilling, swills.** —*tr.* **1.** To drink eagerly, greedily, or to excess. **2.** To flood with water, as for cleaning or washing. Often used with *out.* **3.** To feed (animals) with slops. —*intr.* To drink greedily.

~*n.* **1.** The act or an instance of swilling. **2.** A mixture of liquid and solid food, such as table scraps, fed to animals, especially pigs; slops. **2.** Kitchen waste or rubbish; refuse. [Middle English *swilen,* Old English *swilian,* to wash out.] **—swill·er** *n.*

swim (swim) *v.* **swam** (swam) or *archaic* **swum** (swum), **swum, swimming, swims.** —*intr.* **1.** To propel oneself through water by means of movements of the body or parts of the body such as limbs or fins. **2.** To move as though gliding through water. **3.** To float on water or other liquid. **4.** To be covered or flooded with water or other liquid; be immersed. Usually used with *in* or *with.* **5.** *Informal.* To have a large amount of. Used with *in.* **6.** To experience a floating or dizzy sensation: *Her mind swam on hearing the terrible news.* **7.** To appear to spin or reel lazily: *The nurse's face swam before her eyes as she slowly came to.* —*tr.* **1.** To propel oneself through or across (a body of water) by swimming. **2.** To complete in (a race) by swimming. **3.** To perform (a particular stroke) in swimming. **4.** To cause to swim or float on a body of water.

~*n.* **1.** The act or movements of one that swims. **2.** A period or instance of swimming. **3.** A deep part in a river, containing a lot of fish. **4.** A state of dizziness; a swoon. **—in the swim.** *Informal.* In the current trend of affairs; participating in what is fashionable. [Middle English *swimmen, swam(me), swummen,* Old English *swimman, swamm* (or *swom*), *swummen.*] **—swim·mer** *n.*

swim bladder *n.* An organ in fishes, the **air bladder** *(see).*

swim·mer·et (swímmər-ét) *n.* Any of the paired abdominal appendages of certain aquatic crustaceans, such as shrimps and lobsters, that function primarily as organs of respiration or locomotion. Also called "pleopod". [Diminutive of *swimmer,* from SWIM.]

swim·ming baths (swímming) *pl.n. Sometimes singular.* An indoor, usually public, swimming pool or set of swimming pools.

swimming costume *n.* An item of clothing worn for swimming or sunbathing; typically, trunks for a man, or a woman's one-piece garment that usually leaves the arms, legs, and most of the back bare. Also called "bathing costume", "bathing suit", "swimsuit".

swim·ming·ly (swímming-li) *adv.* With great ease and a high degree of success: *The campaign is proceeding swimmingly.*

swimming pool *n.* A pool built for swimming. Also called "pool".

swim·suit (swím-sōōt, -sewt) *n.* A swimming costume.

Swin·burne (swín-burn, -bərn), **Algernon Charles** (1837–1909). British poet and critic. He is best known for his magnificently rich, often erotic verse, attacking the conventions of Victorian morality.

swin·dle (swínd'l) *v.* **-dled, -dling, -dles.** —*tr.* **1.** To cheat or defraud (a person or group) of money or property. **2.** To obtain (money or property, for example) by fraudulent means. —*intr.* To practise fraud as a habitual means of obtaining money.

~*n.* The act or an instance of swindling; a fraud. [Back-formation from *swindler,* from German *Schwindler,* from *schwindeln,* to be dizzy, swindle, cheat, from Old High German *swintilōn,* frequentative of *swintan,* to vanish, languish, become unconscious, from Germanic *swindan* (unattested).] **—swin·dler** *n.*

Swin·don (swíndən). Town in Wiltshire, southern England. It grew with the opening of workshops of the Great Western Railway (1841), and expanded under the Town Development Act (1952).

swine (swīn) *n., pl.* **swines** (for sense 2) or **swine** (for senses 1 and 2a). **1.** *Usually plural.* A pig. **2. a.** A contemptible, vicious, or coarse person. **b.** An extremely unpleasant or difficult task, problem, or the like. [Middle English *swin(e),* Old English *swīn.*]

swine fever *n.* An infectious, often fatal, viral disease of pigs characterised by fever, lethargy, and distressed breathing. Also *U.S.* "hog cholera".

swine·herd (swīn-herd) *n.* A person who looks after pigs.

swine·pox (swīn-poks) *n.* A disease of domesticated pigs caused by a virus similar to that causing cowpox and smallpox and characterised by skin lesions.

swine vesicular disease *n. Abbr.* **SVD** A highly infectious viral disease of pigs, similar to foot-and-mouth disease, characterised by fever and painful blisters on the feet and snout.

swing (swing) *v.* **swung** (swung), **swung, swinging, swings.** —*intr.* **1. a.** To move rhythmically back and forth, suspended or as if suspended from above; oscillate; sway: *a rope swinging from the mast.* **b.** To move back and forth while attached to a fixed point or thing: *Don't swing on that gate.* **c.** To ride on or propel a swing. **2. a.** To move, walk, run, or the like with a free-swaying motion: *shire horses swinging out of the yard.* **b.** To move from one fixed position to another with a free-swaying motion: *swinging from tree to tree.* **3. a.** To turn in place, as on a hinge or other pivot. **b.** To turn suddenly: *swung round.* **4.** To move in a curve; move from a straight path: *The car swung off the road; The ball swung in towards the wicket.* **5.** To change one's attitudes, emotions, habits, or the like; vacillate. **6.** *Slang.* To be executed by hanging: *You'll swing for this.* **7. a.** To have a compulsive rhythm. Used of popular music. **b.** To play with a compulsive rhythm. Used of popular music performers. **8.** To hit or attempt to hit with a curving, swaying motion of the arm: *She swung at him.* **9.** *Chiefly U.S. Slang.* **a.** To participate actively in youthful fads. **b.** To be a lively success in terms of enjoyment: *the swinging sixties.* **c.** To exchange sexual partners temporarily. —*tr.* **1.** To cause to swing. **2.** To move (a person on a swing) backwards and forwards by pulling or pushing. **3.** To move with a sweeping motion; brandish. **4.** To hang or suspend (something) so that it can sway or move freely. **5.** *Slang.* To manipulate or manage successfully: *Can you swing this deal?* **6.** To arrange or perform (popular music) in the style of swing. **7.** In cricket, to bowl (a ball) in a curving path.

~*n.* **1.** The act or an instance of swinging, especially: **a.** A rhythmic back-and-forth movement. **b.** A single movement or series of movements in one particular direction. **c.** A punch or blow: *took a swing at him.* **d.** A movement from one attitude or opinion to another, such as a change of allegiance or voting: *the swing to Labour.* **2.** The distance traversed while swinging: *The pendulum's swing is 12 inches.* **3.** The manner in which a person or thing swings something, such as a bat or golf club. **4.** Freedom and scope of movement or action. **5. a.** A swaying, graceful motion. **b.** A sweep or swoop: *the swing of a bird across the sky.* **6.** A seat suspended from above for the enjoyment of those who sit on it and make it move back and forth. **7.** Lively or enjoyable activity or pace: *The party went with a swing.* **8.** *Informal.* The normal rhythm or pace of life; the ordinary flow of activities: *back into the swing of things.* **9.** A compulsive rhythm, as found in many types of popular music. **10. a.** An innovation in popular dance music developed about 1935, based on jazz but employing a larger band and simpler harmonic and rhythmic patterns. **b.** The rhythmic quality of this music. **—in full swing.** In action to the maximum speed, capacity, or ability. **—swings and roundabouts.** A situation in which something is gained and lost equally, or in which a gain is balanced by a loss. *~adj.* Pertaining to or performing swing. [Middle English *swingen*, *swang* (past singular), *swungen* (past plural), *swungen*, Old English *swingan*, to whip, strike, fling oneself, *swang*, *swungon*, *geswungen*.]

Synonyms: *swing, oscillate, sway, rock, vibrate, fluctuate, undulate, waver.*

swing bridge *n.* A river or canal bridge that can be pivoted on a vertical central axis to allow ships to pass. Also called "turn bridge".

swing door *n.* Also **swing·ing door** (swĭng-ĭng). A door, often either of a pair, that is hung on double-sided hinges enabling it to be opened in either direction.

swinge (swĭnj) *tr.v.* **swinged, swinges.** *Archaic.* To strike or beat. [Middle English *swengen*, to shake, dash, beat up, Old English *swengan*, to swing, shake.] **—swing·er** (swĭnjər) *n.*

swinge·ing (swĭnjĭng) *adj. British.* **1.** Powerful or brutal: *dealt a swingeing blow.* **2. a.** Harsh; drastic; punitive: *swingeing fines.* **b.** So large as to cause severe damage or distress: *swingeing cuts.*

swing·er (swĭng-ər) *n.* **1.** One that swings. **2.** *Slang.* A person who actively seeks excitement and moves with the latest trends. **3.** *Slang.* A person who is sexually uninhibited; especially, one who engages in swapping sexual partners.

swin·gle·tree (swĭng-g'l-tree) *n.* A pivoted horizontal crossbar to which the harness traces of a draught animal are attached and which is in turn attached to a vehicle or implement. Also called "singletree", "whiffletree", "whippletree". [From *swingle*, wooden instrument for beating hemp, Middle English *swingle*, from Middle Dutch *swinghel*.]

swing·om·e·ter (swĭng-ŏmmĭtər) *n.* An indicator of the swing in voting, used especially on television during general elections.

swing-wing (swĭng-wĭng) *adj.* Being or pertaining to an aircraft with movable wings that can be swept back for fast flight and brought forward for lower speeds, as on takeoff and landing. *~n.* **1.** A swing-wing aircraft. Also called "variable sweep". **2.** Either of the wings of such an aircraft.

swin·ish (swĭnĭsh) *adj.* Resembling or befitting swine; bestial; brutish. **—swin·ish·ly** *adv.* **—swin·ish·ness** *n.*

swipe (swīp) *n.* **1.** A heavy, sweeping blow. **2.** A lever; especially, one that raises the bucket in a well. *~ v.* **swiped, swiping, swipes.** *—tr.* **1. a.** To hit with a sweeping blow. **b.** To pass through a decoding device (a card bearing coded information). **2.** *Slang.* To steal; filch. *—intr.* To make a sweeping blow. [Perhaps variant of SWEEP.]

swipes (swīps) *pl.n. British.* Beer that is weak or inferior. [From SWIPE (verb), in earliest sense, to drink hurriedly, drink a lot.]

swirl (swurl) *v.* **swirled, swirling, swirls.** *—intr.* **1.** To rotate or spin in or as if in a whirlpool or eddy. **2.** To be dizzy or reel; reel. *—tr.* To cause to move with a whirling motion. —See Synonyms at **turn.** *~n.* **1.** The motion or act of whirling or spinning. **2.** Something that swirls; a whirlpool or eddy. **3.** Something that is or has been swirled. **4.** Confusion; turbulence; disorder. [Middle English (Scottish dialect) *swyrl*, eddy, whirlpool, probably of Low German origin, akin to Dutch *zwirrelen*, to whirl.] **—swirl·y** *adj.*

swish (swĭsh) *v.* **swished, swishing, swishes.** *—intr.* **1.** To move or cut with a sibilant whistle or hiss. **2.** To rustle, as certain fabrics do. *—tr.* **1.** To cause to make a swishing movement or sound. **2.** To cut off with a swishing sound. **3.** To whip with a swish or rod. *~n.* **1. a.** A sharp sibilant or rustling sound: *the swish of scythes.* **b.** A movement making such a sound. **2. a.** A rod used for whipping. **b.** A stroke made with such a rod. **3.** *U.S. Slang.* A highly effeminate male. *~adj. Slang.* **1.** *Chiefly British.* Fashionable; posh; luxurious. **2.** *U.S.* Highly effeminate. [Imitative.]

swiss (swĭs) *n. Sometimes capital* **S.** A crisp, sheer cotton cloth used for curtains, light garments, and the like. [From SWISS (because it was first manufactured in Switzerland).]

Swiss (swĭs) *adj.* Of, pertaining to, or characteristic of Switzerland, its inhabitants, its various dialects, or its culture. *~n., pl.* **Swiss. 1.** A native or inhabitant of Switzerland. **2.** One of Swiss descent.

Swiss chard *n.* A vegetable, **chard** (see).

Swiss cheese *n.* A firm white or pale yellow cheese with holes, such as Gruyère.

Swiss cheese plant *n.* See **monstera.**

Swiss Guard *n.* **1.** The group of bodyguards in the Vatican, made up of mercenaries from Switzerland. **2.** Any of these bodyguards.

swiss roll *n.* A cake made of a layer of sponge spread with a filling such as jam or cream and rolled into a cylindrical shape. [SWISS, from Switzerland, where it probably originated.]

switch (swĭch) *n. Abbr.* **sw. 1.** A slender flexible rod, stick, twig, or the like; especially, such a rod used for whipping. **2.** The bushy tip of the tail of certain animals: *a cow's switch.* **3.** A thick bunch of real or synthetic hair used by women as part of a hairstyle. **4.** A flailing or lashing, as with a slender rod. **5.** *Electricity.* A device used to break or open an electrical circuit or to divert current from one conductor to another. **6.** *U.S.* A railway **point** (see). **7.** An exchange or swap, especially one done surreptitiously. **8.** Any sudden transference or shift, as of opinion or attention. *~v.* **switched, switching, switches.** *—tr.* **1.** To whip with or as if with a switch. **2.** To jerk or swish abruptly or sharply. **3.** To shift, transfer, change, or divert: *switch the conversation.* **4.** To exchange: *switch sides.* **5.** To connect, disconnect, or divert (an electric current) by operating a switch. **6.** To cause (an electric current or appliance) to begin or cease operation. Used with *on* or *off*: *switch the radio off.* **7.** *U.S.* To move (rolling stock) from one track to another; shunt. **8.** *Informal.* To provide or produce quickly and effortlessly. Used with *on*: *switch on the charm.* *—intr.* **1.** To shift or change: *switch from coal to oil.* **2.** To be shifted or changed. **—switch off.** *Informal.* To lose interest; cease paying attention: *The lecturer's voice was so dull that I switched off after five minutes.* [Perhaps from Middle Dutch *swijch*, bough, twig.] **—switch·er** *n.*

switch·back (swĭch-bak) *n.* **1.** A road or trail that ascends a steep incline in a winding course. **2.** *Chiefly British.* A roller coaster.

switch·blade (swĭch-blayd) *n. U.S.* A **flick knife** (see).

switch·board (swĭch-bawrd ‖ -bōrd) *n.* **1.** An installation that controls the interconnection of telephone lines, as in a telephone exchange or office. **2.** A panel or set of panels with switches, indicators, and other apparatus for operating electric circuits.

switch-gear (swĭch-geer) *n.* Electrical equipment whose function is to open and close high-current circuits.

switch·man (swĭch-mən) *n., pl.* **-men.** *U.S.* A pointsman (see).

swith·er (swĭthər) *intr.v.* **-ered, -ering, -ers.** *British Regional.* To be undecided or in a state of uncertainty; dither. *~n.* Uncertainty; dither. [16th century : origin obscure.]

Swith·in or **Swith·un** (swĭth-in, -'n, *rarely* swĭth-), **Saint** (died 862). English prelate. He was Bishop of Winchester (852–62). According to tradition, if it rains on St. Swithin's day (July 15) it will rain for 40 days following: on that day in 971 the saint's body was to be transferred from churchyard to cathedral, contrary to his wishes, and heavy rain delayed the proceedings.

Switz. Switzerland.

Swit·zer (swĭtsər) *n. Rare.* **1.** A Swiss. **2.** A member of the Swiss Guard. [Middle High German *Swîzer*, from *Swîz*, SWITZERLAND.]

Swit·zer·land, Confederation of (swĭtsər-lənd). *French* **Suisse** (sweess); *German* **Schweiz** (shvĭts); *Italian* **Sviz·ze·ra** (svĭtsera). Latin name **Hel·ve·tia.** Landlocked country in western Europe. It consists of three regions: the Alps in the south are divided from the Jura mountains of the northwest by the Mitteland plateau. The population includes German, French, and Italian speakers, with a small Romansch minority. Switzerland is a world centre of finance and tourism. Its main exports are watches, clocks, jewellery, instruments, and textiles. It became part of the Holy Roman Empire (10th century), but by 1499 had achieved independence as a loose confederation of cantons. A federal constitution was adopted in 1848. Resolute neutrality kept Switzerland out of both World Wars, and it is not a U.N. member. However, it has become the base of many international groups, including the Red Cross and World Health Organisation. Area, 41 288 square kilometres (15,937 square miles). Population, 7,070,000. Capital, Bern. See map, next page.

swiv·el (swĭvv'l) *n.* **1.** A link, pivot, or other fastening so designed that it permits free turning of attached parts. **2.** A pivoted support that allows an attached object, such as a chair or gun, to turn in a horizontal plane. **3.** A cannon that turns on a pivot. Also called "swivel gun". *~v.* **swivelled** or *U.S.* **swiveled, -elling** or *U.S.* **-eling, -els.** *—tr.* **1.** To turn or rotate on or as if on a swivel. **2.** To secure, fit, or support with a swivel. *—intr.* To turn on or as if on a swivel. —See Synonyms at **turn.** [Middle English *swyvel*, *swevill*, related to or from Old English *swīfan*, to revolve.]

swivel chair *n.* A chair that swivels on its base.

swivel pin *n.* A kingpin (see).

swizz (swĭz) *n.* Also **swizzle.** *British Informal.* **1.** A shame; a disappointment. **2.** A trick; a swindle. [20th century : origin obscure.]

swiz·zle (swĭzz'l) *n.* **1.** Any of various mixed drinks, usually made with rum. **2.** A swizz.

swizzle stick *n.* A rod for stirring mixed drinks or for removing the effervescence from drinks by making them froth up.

swob. Variant of **swab.**

swol·len (swŏlən). Past participle of **swell.** *~adj.* Enlarged; distended.

swol·len-head·ed (swŏlən-hĕddid) *adj.* Also *U.S.* **swelled-head·ed** (swĕld-). Having an excessively high opinion of oneself; conceited.

swoon (swoon) *intr.v.* **swooned, swooning, swoons. 1.** To faint. **2.** To become rapturous or ecstatic. *~n.* A fainting spell. [Middle English *swowenen*, *swounen*, probably back-formation from *swowening*, *swouning*, a gerund formed from *iswowen*, in a swoon, from Old English *geswōgen*, past participle of *swōgan†* (attested only in compounds), to suffocate, choke.]

swoop (swoop) *v.* **swooped, swooping, swoops.** *—intr.* To make a sudden sweeping, pouncing movement, like a bird descending upon its prey. *—tr.* To take or snatch suddenly. Often used with *up.* *~n.* A swift, sudden descent. **—at** or **in one fell swoop.** With one sudden action; all in one go. [Middle English *swopen*, to sweep along, Old English *swāpan*, to swing, sweep, drive.]

swoosh (swoosh, swoosh) *n.* A low, swishing, hissing sound. *~v.* **swooshed, swooshing, swooshes.** *—intr.* To make such a sound, especially by moving. *—tr.* To cause to make or move with such a sound. [Imitative.]

swop. Variant of **swap.**

sword (sord ‖ sōrd) *n.* **1.** A weapon having a handle and a long

SWITZERLAND

blade for cutting or thrusting, often worn ceremonially as a symbol of power or authority. **2.** Any instrument of death, combat, or destruction. **3.** Something that resembles a sword. **4. a.** The use of force, as in war. **b.** Military power or jurisdiction. Preceded by *the*. **—cross swords. 1.** To fight. **2.** To quarrel violently. **—put to the sword.** To kill, especially with a sword. [Middle English *sw(e)ord, swerd*, Old English *sw(e)ord.*]

sword arm *n*. **1.** The arm used to hold a sword. **2.** The right arm.
sword bayonet *n*. A long bayonet resembling and capable of functioning as a sword.
sword·bear·er (sórd-bair-ər ‖ sórd-) *n*. A person who carries the sword of a monarch or dignitary on ceremonial occasions.
sword·bill (sórd-bil ‖ sórd-) *n*. A hummingbird, *Ensifera ensifera,* of tropical South America, having a very long, slender bill.
sword cane *n*. A swordstick.
sword dance *n*. A dance performed with swords, especially one performed around swords laid on the ground.
sword·fish (sórd-fish ‖ sórd-) *n., pl.* **-fishes** or collectively **swordfish.** A large marine game and food fish, *Xiphias gladius,* having a long, swordlike extension of the upper jaw. Also called "broadbill".
sword grass *n*. Any of various grasses or grasslike plants having bladelike, pointed leaves.
sword·knot (sórd-not ‖ sórd-) *n*. A decorative loop or tassel attached to the hilt of a sword.
sword lily *n*. A plant, the **gladiolus** *(see).* [Part translation of Latin *gladiolus,* small sword (referring to the sword-shaped leaves).]
Sword of Damocles *n*. An impending disaster or the permanent threat of it. See **Damocles.**
sword·play (sórd-play ‖ sórd-) *n*. The action or art of using a sword; fencing. **—sword·play·er** *n*.
swords·man (sórdz-mən ‖ sórdz-) *n., pl.* **-men** (-mən). **1.** A person skilled in the use of the sword. **2.** A person armed with a sword. **—swords·man·ship** *n*.
sword·stick (sórd-stik ‖ sórd-) *n*. A cane or light walking stick designed to conceal a sword in its hollow shaft. Also called "sword-cane".
sword·tail (sórd-tayl ‖ sórd-) *n*. A small, brightly coloured freshwater fish, *Xiphophorus helleri,* of Central America, that has a long, tapering extension of the tail fin in the male.
swore. Past tense of **swear.**
sworn. Past participle of **swear.**
swot[1] (swot) *v*. **swotted, swotting, swots.** *British.* **—intr.** To study very hard and diligently; cram. **—tr.** To study (a subject) diligently; work hard at. Usually used with *up*. **~***n*. **1.** A person who studies diligently or too diligently. **2.** A difficult academic subject; a subject that needs hard work. **3.** Diligent study. [Dialect variant of SWEAT.]
swot[2] Variant of **swat.**
swounds, swouns. Variants of **zounds.**
swum. Past participle and *archaic* past tense of **swim.**
swung. Past tense and past participle of **swing.**
swung dash *n*. A curved dash (~) used, for example, to indicate the omission of a word or part of a word, or, in symbolic logic, as the sign for negation. In this dictionary it is used to represent a headword before a second or subsequent part-of-speech label.
Sy. Surrey.
Syb·a·ris (síbbəriss). Ancient Greek colony. It lay near the site of

the modern town of Terranova di Sibari in northern Calabria. In the sixth century Sybaris controlled trade with the Etruscans. Its consequent wealth earned the Sybarites a reputation for pleasure-seeking luxury.
syb·a·rite (síbbə-rīt) *n*. Also capital **S.** A person devoted to pleasure and luxury; a voluptuary. [Latin *Sybarita,* native of Sybaris, from Greek *Subaritēs,* from *Subaris,* SYBARIS.] **—syb·a·rit·ic** (-ríttik), **syb·a·rit·i·cal** *adj*. **—syb·a·rit·i·cal·ly** *adv*.
syc·a·mine (síckə-mīn, -min) *n*. A tree mentioned in the New Testament, thought to be a species of mulberry. Luke 17:6. [Latin *sȳcamīnus,* from Greek *sukaminos,* from Phoenician or Aramaic *shiqmīn* (plural), akin to Hebrew *shiqmīn,* plural of *shiqmāh,* mulberry tree. See also **sycamore.**]
syc·a·more (síckə-mawr ‖ -mōr) *n*. **1.** A Eurasian maple tree, *Acer pseudoplatanus,* having five-lobed leaves and winged fruits. **2.** A plane tree, *Platanus occidentalis,* of eastern North America. **3.** A tree, *Ficus sycomorus,* of northeastern Africa and adjacent Asia, related to the fig. This species is the sycamore of the Bible. [Middle English *sicamour,* from Old French *sicamor,* from Latin *sycomorus,* from Greek *sukamoros* : *suka-,* probably from Hebrew *shiqmāh,* mulberry tree (see **sycamine**) + *moron,* mulberry tree.]
syce, sice (sīss) *n*. A stableman or groom, especially formerly in India. [Hindi *sā'is,* from Arabic *sā'is,* from *sāsa,* to administer.]
sy·cee (sī-sée, -see) *n*. Lumps of pure silver bearing the stamp of a banker or assayer and formerly used in China as money. Also called "sycee silver". [Cantonese *sai si,* "fine silk" (so called because the pure silver can be spun into fine threads), corresponding to Mandarin Chinese *xi sī* : *xi,* thin, fine + *sī,* silk, thread.]
sy·co·ni·um (sī-kóni-əm) *n., pl.* **-nia** (-ə). Also **sy·co·nus** (-kónəss). The fleshy multiple fruit of the fig, consisting primarily of the enlarged floral receptacle. [New Latin, from Greek *sukon,* the fig, probably from the same Mediterranean source as Latin *ficus,* FIG.]
syc·o·phan·cy (síckə-fən-si, *also* síkə-, -fan-) *n., pl.* **-cies.** The act, practice, or behaviour of a sycophant; servile flattery.
syc·o·phant (síckə-fənt, *also* síkə-, -fant) *n*. One who attempts to win favour or advancement by flattering persons of influence; a servile self-seeker. [Latin *sycophanta,* from Greek *sukophantēs,* "fig-shower", "accuser" (from the use of the gesture of the fig in denouncing a criminal), hence an informer, flatterer : *sukon,* fig (see **syconium**) + *-phantēs,* shower, from *phainein,* to show.] **—syc·o·phan·tic** (-fántik), **syc·o·phan·ti·cal** *adj*. **—syc·o·phan·ti·cal·ly** *adv*.
     Synonyms: sycophant, toady, crawler, flatterer.
sy·co·sis (sī-kó-siss) *n*. A chronic inflammation of the hair follicles, especially of the beard and scalp, caused by bacterial infection. [New Latin, from Greek *sukōsis,* eruption resembling a fig : *sukon,* fig (see **syconium**) + -OSIS.]
Syd·ney (síd-ni). The largest city in Australia, and capital of New South Wales. It surrounds Port Jackson or Sydney Harbour, an inlet on the southeast coast. Sydney is the centre of the nation's trade and finance. Its many beaches are popular tourist resorts. Other attractions include the Sydney Harbour Bridge (1932) and Sydney Opera House (1973). Sydney was developed by convict labour, and rapidly expanded in the late 19th century. Today it is one of the leading cultural centres in the southern hemisphere.
Syene. See **Aswan.**
sy·e·nite (sī-ə-nīt) *n*. An igneous rock composed primarily of alkali feldspar together with other minerals, such as hornblende. [Latin

Syēnītēs (lapis), "(stone) of Syene" (where it was first quarried), from *Syēnē,* Syene, from Greek *Suēne.*] —**sy·e·nit·ic** (-níttik) *adj.*

syl., syll. 1. syllable. **2.** syllabus.

syl·la·bar·y (síllə-bəri ‖ -berri) *n., pl.* **-ies.** A list of syllables; especially, a list or set of written characters, each one representing a syllable. [New Latin *syllabārium,* from Latin *syllaba,* SYLLABLE.]

syl·lab·ic (si-lábbik) *adj.* **1.** Of, pertaining to, or consisting of a syllable or syllables. **2.** Designating a consonant that forms a syllable without a vowel, as does the *l* in *riddle* (rídd'l). **3.** Pronouncing every syllable distinctly: *a syllabic reading of a line of poetry.* **4.** Designating a form of verse based on the number of syllables per line rather than on the arrangement of accents or quantities.
~*n.* A syllabic sound. [Medieval Latin *syllabicus,* from Greek *sullabikos,* from *sullabē,* SYLLABLE.] —**syl·lab·i·cal·ly** *adv.*

syl·lab·i·fy (si-lábbi-fī) *tr.v.* **-fied, -fying, -fies.** Also *U.S.* **syl·lab·i·cate** (-kayt), **-cated, -cating, -cates.** To form or divide into syllables. —**syl·lab·i·fi·ca·tion** (-fi-káysh'n), **syl·lab·i·ca·tion** *n.*

syl·la·bise, syl·la·bize (síllə-bīz) *tr.v.* **-bised, -bising, -bises.** To syllabify. [Greek *sullabizein,* from *sullabē,* SYLLABLE.]

syl·la·bism (sílləbiz'm) *n.* **1.** The use of written characters that represent syllables. **2.** Division into syllables. [See **syllabise.**]

syl·la·ble (sílləb'l) *n. Abbr.* **syl., syll. 1.** A unit of spoken language consisting of a vowel or diphthong alone, of a syllabic consonant alone, or of either with one or more consonants. *Of, spoken,* and *consisting* have, respectively, one, two, and three syllables. **2.** One or more letters or phonetic symbols written or printed to approximate a spoken syllable. **3.** The slightest bit or expression.
~*tr.v.* **syllabled, -bling, -bles.** To pronounce (a line of verse, for example) in syllables. [Middle English *sillable,* from Old French *sillabe,* from Latin *syllaba,* from Greek *sullabē,* "a gathering (of letters)", from *sullambanein,* to gather together, spell together : *sun-,* together + *lambanein,* to take, grasp.]

syl·la·bub, sil·la·bub (síllə-bub) *n.* **1.** A cold dessert made with sweetened, thickened cream and wine, spirits, or fruit juice. **2.** A drink consisting of wine or spirits mixed with sweetened milk or cream. [16th century: origin obscure.]

syl·la·bus (síllə-bəss) *n., pl.* **-buses** or **-bi** (-bī). *Abbr.* **syl., syll. 1.** An outline or brief statement of the main points of a text, lecture, or course of study. **2.** *British.* **a.** The topics or subjects to be studied for a particular course, which usually leads to examination. **b.** A list of these, detailing the course requirements. [Medieval Latin, list, from Greek *sullabus,* a misreading (in Cicero's *Letters to Atticus*) of *silluba,* earlier *sittuba†,* book title, label, table of contents.]

syl·lep·sis (si-lép-siss, -lép-) *n., pl.* **-ses** (-seez). *Grammar.* A construction in which one word seems to be in the same semantic relation to two or more other words but in fact is not; a zeugma. An example is: *She lost her coat and her temper.* [Latin, from Greek *sullēpsis,* "a taking together" : *sun-,* together + *lēpsis,* a taking, from *lambanein* (past participle *lēptos*), to take.] —**syl·lep·tic** (-léptik) *adj.*

syl·lo·gise, syl·lo·gize (síllə-jīz) *v.* **-gised, -gising, -gises.** —*intr.* To reason or argue by means of syllogisms. —*tr.* To deduce by syllogism. —**syl·lo·gi·sa·tion** (-jī-záysh'n) *n.* —**syl·lo·gis·er** *n.*

syl·lo·gism (síllə-jíz'm) *n.* **1.** *Logic.* A form of deductive reasoning consisting of a major premise, a minor premise, and a conclusion; for example, *All men are foolish* (major premise); *Smith is a man* (minor premise); *therefore, Smith is foolish* (conclusion). **2.** Reasoning from the general to the specific; deduction. **3.** A subtle or specious piece of reasoning. [Middle English *silogisme,* from Old French, from Latin *syllogismus,* from Greek *sullogismos,* from *sullogizesthai,* to reckon together, infer : *sun-,* together + *logizesthai,* to reckon, reason, from *logos,* word, computation.]

syl·lo·gist (síllə-jist) *n.* A person who uses or is skilled in syllogistic reasoning.

syl·lo·gis·tic (síllə-jístik) *adj.* Also **syl·lo·gis·ti·cal** (-'l). Of, pertaining to, resembling, or consisting of a syllogism or syllogisms.
~*n.* Also **syl·lo·gis·tics** (-jístiks) (*used with a singular verb*). **1.** The branch of logic dealing with syllogisms. **2.** The art of reasoning by syllogism. —**syl·lo·gis·ti·cal·ly** *adv.*

sylph (silf) *n.* **1.** Any of a class of fairy-like beings without souls that were believed to inhabit the air. **2.** A slim, graceful woman or girl. [New Latin *sylphus,* probably coined by Paracelsus by contracting Latin *sylvestris nympha,* nymph of the woods : *sylvestris,* from *sylva,* forest (see **sylvan**) + *nympha,* NYMPH.]

sylph·id (sílfid) *n.* A young or diminutive sylph.
~*adj.* Pertaining to or resembling a sylph. [French *sylphide,* from *sylphe,* sylph, from New Latin *sylphus,* SYLPH.]

syl·va, sil·va (sílvə) *n.* **1.** The trees or forests of a region. **2.** A written work on such trees or forests. [Latin, forest. See **sylvan.**]

syl·van, sil·van (sílvən) *adj.* **1.** Pertaining to or characteristic of woods or forest regions. **2.** Situated in or inhabiting a wood or forest. **3.** Abounding in trees; wooded. —See Synonyms at **rural.**
~*n.* One that lives in or frequents the woods. [Medieval Latin *silvānus,* from Latin *silva, sylva†,* forest.]

syl·van·ite (sílvə-nīt) *n.* A pale brass-yellow to silver-white gold and silver ore, chiefly (Au, Ag)Te₂. [French; found in TRANSYLVANIA.]

syl·va·tic (sil-váttik) *adj.* Growing or occurring in a wood. [Latin *silva,* forest + -ATIC.]

sylviculture. Variant of **silviculture.**

syl·vite (sil-vīt) *n.* Also **syl·vin** (-vin), **syl·vine** (-vīn, -vin), **syl·vin·ite** (-vin-īt) *n.* A colourless vitreous potassium chloride mineral, a major source of potassium compounds. [French, from *sylvine,* from New Latin *(sal digestivus) Sylvii,* "(digestive salt) of Sylvius", probably

after Franz de la Boë *Sylvius* (1614–72), Dutch physician.]

sym-. Variant of **syn-,** used before the letters *b, m,* and *p.*

sym. 1. symbol. **2.** symphony.

sym·bi·ont (sím-bi-ont, -bī-) *n.* Also **sym·bi·ote** (-ōt). Any of the organisms in a symbiotic relationship. [Greek *sumbion,* present participle of *sumbioun,* to live together. See **symbiosis.**]

sym·bi·o·sis (sím-bi-ō-siss, -bī-) *n. Biology.* Any relationship between two or more different organisms in close association, especially one that is of benefit to all the organisms involved. See **mutualism.** [New Latin, from Greek *sumbiōsis,* a living together, from *sumbioun,* to live together : *sun-,* together + *bios,* life.] —**sym·bi·ot·ic** (-óttik), **sym·bi·ot·i·cal** *adj.* —**sym·bi·ot·i·cal·ly** *adv.*

sym·bol (símb'l) *n. Abbr.* **sym. 1.** Something that represents or stands for, or is thought to typify, something else by association, resemblance, or convention; especially, a material object used to represent something invisible such as an idea: *the dove is a symbol of peace.* **2.** A printed or written sign used to represent an operation, element, quantity, quality, or relation, as in mathematics or music: *"Au" is the symbol for gold;* "+" *is the symbol for addition.*
~*tr.v.* **symbolled** or *U.S.* **symboled, -bolling** or *U.S.* **-boling, -bols.** To symbolise. [Latin *symbolum,* sign, token, from Greek *sumbolon,* token for identification (by comparing with its counterpart), from *sumballein,* to compare : *sun-,* together + *ballein,* to throw.]

sym·bol·ic (sim-bóllik) *adj.* Also **sym·bol·i·cal** (-'l). **1.** Of, pertaining to, or expressed by means of a symbol or symbols. **2.** Serving as a symbol. **3.** Characterised by the use of symbolism, as a work of art may be. —**sym·bol·i·cal·ly** *adv.* —**sym·bol·i·cal·ness** *n.*

symbolic logic *n.* A treatment of formal logic in which a calculus or rule-governed system of symbols is used to represent terms, propositions, and relationships. Also called "mathematical logic".

sym·bol·ise, sym·bol·ize (símb'l-īz) *v.* **-ised, ising, ises.** —*tr.* **1.** To be or serve as a symbol of. **2.** To represent or identify by a symbol or symbols. —*intr.* To use symbols. —**sym·bol·i·sa·tion** (-ī-záysh'n ‖ *U.S.* -i-) *n.*

sym·bol·ism (símb'l-iz'm) *n.* **1.** The practice of representing things by means of symbols or of attributing symbolic meanings or significance to objects, events, or relationships. **2.** A system of symbols or representations. **3.** A symbolic meaning or representation. **4.** *Capital* S. The theory or the practice of the Symbolists.

sym·bol·ist (símb'l-ist) *n.* **1.** A person who uses symbols or symbolism. **2. a.** One who interprets or represents conditions or truths by the use of symbolism. **b.** *Capital* S. Any of a group of artists and poets, chiefly French, of the late 19th century who expressed their ideas and emotions indirectly through symbols. —**sym·bo·list, sym·bol·is·tic** (-ístik), **sym·bol·is·ti·cal** *adj.*

sym·bol·o·gy (sím-bólləji) *n.* **1.** The study or interpretation of symbols or symbolism. **2.** The use of symbols. —**sym·bo·log·i·cal** (símbə-lójik'l) *adj.* —**sym·bol·o·gist** (sim-bólləjist) *n.*

sym·met·al·lism (sím-métt'l-iz'm, si-) *n.* Also *chiefly U.S.* **sym·met·al·ism.** A system of coinage in which a unit of currency consists of a combination of two or more metals in fixed proportions. [SYM- + METAL + -ISM.]

sym·met·ri·cal *adj.* **1.** Of, pertaining to, or showing symmetry. **2.** *Botany.* Actinomorphic. **3.** *Logic & Mathematics.* Of, pertaining to, or designating something, such as a function or proposition, that remains unchanged for all permutations of its constituent parts. **4.** *Chemistry.* Having repetitive, similar faces. Said of a crystal. —**sym·met·ri·cal·ly** *adv.* —**sym·met·ri·cal·ness** *n.*

sym·me·trise, sym·me·trize (símmə-trīz, símme-, símmi-) *tr.v.* **-trised, -trising, -trises.** To make symmetrical; impart perfect balance to. —**sym·me·tri·sa·tion** (-trī-záysh'n ‖ *U.S.* -tri-) *n.*

sym·me·try (símmətri, símmitri) *n., pl.* **-tries. 1.** A relationship of characteristic correspondence, equivalence, or identity among constituents of a system or between different systems: *symmetry in political and religious activism.* **2.** Exact correspondence of form and constituent configuration on opposite sides of a dividing line or plane or about a centre or axis. **3.** Structural or functional independence of direction; isotropy. **4.** Beauty as a result of balance or harmonious arrangement. —See Synonyms at **proportion.** [Obsolete French *symmetrie,* from Latin *symmetria,* from Greek *summetria,* from *summetros,* "of like measure".]

sym·pa·thec·to·my (símpə-théktəmi) *n., pl.* **-mies.** The removal of a part of a sympathetic nerve or a number of sympathetic ganglia. [SYMPATH(ETIC) + -ECTOMY.]

sym·pa·thet·ic (símpə-théttik) *adj.* Also **sym·pa·thet·i·cal** (-'l). **1.** Of, expressing, feeling, or resulting from sympathy. **2.** In agreement; favourable; inclined. Used with *to* or *towards.* **3.** Agreeable; congenial: *sympathetic surroundings.* **4.** Pertaining to or acting on the sympathetic nervous system. **5.** Pertaining to or involving oscillation produced by a nearby oscillating system at the same frequency. Said, for example, of vibrations of strings in certain musical instruments. [New Latin *sympatheticus,* from Greek *sumpathētikos,* from *sumpatheia,* SYMPATHY.] —**sym·pa·thet·i·cal·ly** *adv.*

sympathetic ink *n.* Invisible ink *(see).*

sympathetic magic *n.* Magic that seeks to achieve an effect at a distance as by means of an associated or symbolic object, such as a doll that is supposed to represent a person.

sympathetic nervous system *n.* A portion of the **autonomic nervous system** *(see).*

sym·pa·thin (símpəthin) *n.* A substance released at sympathetic nerve endings and involved in the transmission of impulses, now known to be adrenaline or noradrenaline. [SYMPATH(ETHIC) + -IN.]

sym·pa·thise, sym·pa·thize (símpə-thīz) *intr.v.* **-thised, -thising,**

-thises. 1. To feel or express compassion; commiserate. Used with *with.* **2.** To share or understand another's feelings or ideas. Used with *with.* **—sym·pa·this·er** *n.* **—sym·pa·this·ing·ly** *adv.*

sym·pa·tho·lyt·ic (símpə-thō-líttik) *adj.* Of or pertaining to an agent that opposes the activity of the sympathetic nervous system. *~n.* A sympatholytic agent. [SYMPATH(ETIC) + -LYTIC.]

sym·pa·tho·mi·met·ic (símpə-thō-mī-méttik) *adj. Medicine.* Of or pertaining to an agent that stimulates the sympathetic nervous system.
~n. A sympathomimetic agent. [SYMPATH(ETIC) + MIMETIC.]

sym·pa·thy (símpəthi) *n., pl.* **-thies. 1. a.** The act of or capacity for sharing or understanding the feelings of another person. **b.** A feeling or expression of pity or sorrow for the distress of another; commiseration. **2. a.** A relationship or affinity between persons or things in which whatever affects one correspondingly affects the other. **b.** Mutual understanding or affection arising from this. **3.** Favour; agreement; accord: *She is in sympathy with my beliefs.* **4.** A feeling of loyalty; allegiance. **5.** *Physiology.* The mutual influence of different parts of the body on each other. —See Synonyms at **pity.** [Latin *sympathīa,* from Greek *sumpatheia,* from *sumpathēs,* affected by like feelings : *sun-,* like + *pathos,* emotion, feelings.]

sympathy strike *n.* A strike by a body of workers for the purpose of supporting a cause or another group of strikers.

sym·pat·ric (sim-páttrik) *adj. Ecology.* Occupying or occurring in the same or overlapping geographical areas. Said of populations of closely related species. Compare **allopatric.** [SYN- + Greek *patra, patrē,* fatherland, from *patēr,* father.] **—sym·pat·ri·cal·ly** *adv.*

sym·pet·al·ous (sim-pétt'l-əss) *adj. Botany.* **Gamopetalous** *(see).*

sym·phon·ic (sim-fónnik) *adj.* **1.** Pertaining to or having the character or form of a symphony. **2.** Harmonious in sound.

symphonic poem *n.* A musical composition for symphony orchestra, based on an extramusical theme such as a folk tale, usually consisting of a single, extended movement and typical chiefly of the late 19th century. Also called "tone poem".

sym·pho·ni·ous (sim-fṓni-əss) *adj.* In accord; harmonious. **—sym·pho·ni·ous·ly** *adv.*

sym·pho·nist (símfə-nist) *n.* One who composes symphonies.

sym·pho·ny (símfəni) *n., pl.* **-nies. 1.** *Abbr.* **sym.** *Music.* A usually long sonata for orchestra, typically consisting of four related movements. **2. a.** An instrumental passage in a vocal or choral composition. **b.** An instrumental overture or interlude, as in early opera. **3.** Harmony, especially of sound or colour. **4.** Anything characterised by a harmonious combination of elements. [Middle English *symphonie,* harmony of sound, from Old French, from Latin *symphōnia,* from Greek *sumphōnia,* from *sumphōnos,* harmonious : *sun-,* together + *phōnē,* voice, sound.]

symphony orchestra *n.* A large orchestra composed of string, woodwind, brass, and percussion sections, designed for playing symphonic works.

sym·phy·sis (símfi-siss) *n., pl.* **-ses** (-seez). **1.** *Anatomy.* **a.** A type of joint in which the bones are united by fibrocartilage, as between the vertebrae of the backbone. **b.** The line marking such a joint. **2.** The coalescence of similar parts or organs. [New Latin, from Greek *sumphusis,* a growing together (especially of bones), from *sumphuein,* to cause to unite : *sun-,* together + *phuein,* to make grow.] **—sym·phy·se·al, sym·phy·si·al** (-sée-əl, sim-fízzi-əl) *adj.*

sym·po·di·um (sim-pṓdi-əm) *n., pl.* **-dia** (-ə). *Botany.* A primary axis that develops from a series of short lateral branches and has a zigzag or irregular form, as in a cymose inflorescence. Also called "pseudaxis". Compare **monopodium.** [New Latin : SYN- + Greek *podion,* small foot, base, from *pous* (stem *pod-*), foot.] **—sym·po·di·al** *adj.* **—sym·po·di·al·ly** *adv.*

sym·po·si·ac (sim-pṓzi-ak, -pózzi-) *adj.* Of, of the nature of, appropriate to, or occurring at a symposium.
~n. Archaic. A meeting or conference; a symposium.

sym·po·si·arch (sim-pṓzi-aark, -pózzi-) *n.* **1.** The master or director of an ancient Greek symposium. **2.** A toastmaster. [Greek *sumposiarkhos, sumposiarkhēs* : *sumposion,* SYMPOSIUM + -ARCH.]

sym·po·si·um (sim-pṓzi-əm, -pózzi-) *n., pl.* **-siums** or **-sia** (-ə). **1.** A meeting or conference for discussion of some topic. **2.** A collection of writings on a particular topic, as in a magazine or other periodical. **3.** A convivial meeting among the ancient Greeks for drinking, music, and intellectual discussion. [Latin, from Greek *sumposion,* drinking party : *sun-,* together + *posis,* drink.]

symp·tom (símp-təm, sím-) *n.* **1.** Any circumstance or phenomenon regarded as an indication or characteristic of a condition or event. **2.** *Medicine.* Any phenomenon experienced by an individual as a departure from normal function, sensation, or appearance, generally indicating disorder or disease. —See Synonyms at **sign.** [Greek *sumptōma,* occurrence, phenomenon, from *sumpiptein,* to fall together, fall upon, happen : *sun-,* together + *piptein,* to fall.] **—symp·to·mat·ic** (-áttik) *adj.* **—symp·to·mat·i·cal·ly** *adv.*

symp·tom·a·tol·o·gy (símp-təmə-tólləji, sím-) *n.* **1.** The medical science of disease symptoms. Also called "semiology". **2.** The complex of symptoms of a disease. [New Latin *symptomatologia* : Greek *sumptōma* (stem *sumptōmat-*), SYMPTOM + -LOGY.]

syn-, sym- *prefix.* Indicates: **1.** Together or with; for example, **syndactyl, symmetallism. 2.** Same, alike, similar, or at the same time; for example, **sympatric. 3.** Union or fusion; for example, **sympetalous, syncarp.** [Greek *sun-,* from *sun,* together, with. In Greek compounds, *sun-* becomes *sum-* before *b, m, p*; *sul-* before *l*; *su-* before *s* and *z*; borrowed as *sym-, syl-,* and *sy-* respectively.]

syn. synonym; synonymous; synonymy.

syn·ae·re·sis (si-neér-ə-siss, -i- || *U.S. also* -nérrə-) *n., pl.* **-ses** (-seez). Also *U.S.* **syn·er·e·sis** (for sense 1). **1.** The drawing together of two consecutive vowels, ordinarily pronounced separately, into a diphthong or simple vowel, as when *doest* (dóo-ist) contracts to *dost* (dust). Compare **diaeresis, synizesis. 2. Syneresis** *(see).* [Late Latin, from Greek *sunairesis,* a drawing together, from *sunairein* : *sun-,* SYN- + *hairein,* to take.]

syn·aes·the·sia, *U.S.* **syn·es·the·sia** (sín-eess-theéz-yə, -theézh-yə, -theézhə || -iss-) *n.* **1.** The experiencing of a sensation in one part of the body resulting from the stimulation of a different part. **2.** The sensation of a sense other than the sense being stimulated, as when a sound invokes a sensation of colour. [New Latin : SYN- + (AN)AESTHESIA.] **—syn·aes·thet·ic** (-théttik) *adj.*

syn·a·gogue (sínnə-gog) *n.* **1.** A building or place of meeting for Jewish worship and religious instruction. **2.** A congregation of Jews for worship or religious study. **3.** The Jewish religion as organised or typified in such local congregations. Preceded by *the.* [Middle English *synagoge,* from Old French, from Latin *synagōga,* from Greek *sunagōgē,* assembly, from *sunagein,* to bring together : *sun-,* together + *agein,* to lead, drive.] **—syn·a·gog·al** (-gōg'l, -gógg'l), **syn·a·gog·i·cal** (-gójik'l) *adj.*

syn·a·loe·pha, syn·a·le·pha (sínnə-leéfə) *n.* The blending of two adjacent syllables into one syllable, especially of two successive vowels of adjacent syllables; for example, *th' elite* for *the elite.* [New Latin, from Greek *sunal(o)iphē,* from *sunaleiphein,* to smear or melt together, unite two syllables : *sun-,* together + *aleiphein,* to anoint.]

syn·apse (sī́n-aps || *U.S.* sín-, si-náps) *n.* Also **synapsis.** The point at which a nerve impulse passes from an axon of one neurone to the dendrite of another. [New Latin *synapsis,* from Greek *sunapsis,* point of contact, from *sunaptein,* to join together : *sun-,* together + *haptein*†, to fasten, connect.]

syn·ap·sid (sin-ápsid) *n.* A reptile of the subclass Synapsida which existed during the Upper Carboniferous Permian and Triassic periods, having a single pair of lateral temporal openings in the skull.

syn·ap·sis (si-náp-siss) *n., pl.* **-ses** (-seez). **1.** *Biology.* The fusion of homologous chromosome pairs during meiosis. **2.** Variant of **synapse.** [New Latin. See **synapse.**]

syn·ap·tic (sin-áptik) *adj.* Pertaining to a synapse or synapsis.

syn·ar·thro·sis (sínnaar-thrṓ-siss) *n., pl.* **-ses** (-seez). Also **syn·ar·thro·di·a** (-di-ə) *pl.* **-diae** (-di-ee). *Anatomy.* Any of several forms of bone articulation in which the bones are rigidly joined without an intervening cavity. [New Latin, from Greek *sunarthrōsis* : *sun-,* together + *arthrōsis,* articulation, from *arthron,* a joint.]

sync (singk) *n. Informal.* Synchronisation: *The sound is out of sync.* *~v.* **synced** (singkt), **syncing** (síngking), **syncs.** *Informal. —intr.* To synchronise. *—tr.* To synchronise (something) with another.

syn·carp (síng-kaarp || sín-) *n. Botany.* A fleshy fruit composed of the fruits of several flowers or several carpels of a single flower. [SYN- + -CARP.]

syn·car·pous (sin-kárpəss, sing-) *adj. Botany.* Having or consisting of united carpels. [SYN- + -CARPOUS.] **—syn·car·py** (síng-kaarpi, sín-) *n.*

syn·chon·dro·sis (síng-kon-drṓ-siss, sín-) *n.* A slightly movable joint in which the ends of the bones are separated by hyaline cartilage, such as occurs between the ribs and the breastbone in humans. [SYN- + Greek *khondros,* cartilage + -OSIS.]

syn·chro[1] (síng-krō || sín-) *n., pl.* **-chros.** *Machinery.* A **Selsyn** *(see).* [Short for SYNCHRONOUS.]

synchro[2] *n. Informal.* Synchronised swimming.

synchro- *comb. form.* Indicates synchronisation; for example, **synchromesh.** [Shortened from SYNCHRONISE.]

syn·chro·cy·clo·tron (síng-krō-sī́klə-tron || sín-) *n.* A proton and positive ion accelerator, the chief components and configuration of which are similar to those of a **cyclotron** *(see)* and in which the phase of the accelerating potential is synchronised with the frequency of the accelerated particles by frequency modulation to compensate for relativistic increases in particle mass at high speeds.

syn·chro·flash (síng-krō-flash, -krə- || sín-) *n.* A device on a camera that synchronises the peak of a flash created by a flash bulb with the widest opening of the shutter. **—syn·chro·flash** *adj.*

syn·chro·mesh (síng-krō-mesh, -krə- || sín-) *adj.* Designating a gearbox in a motor vehicle in which the gears are synchronised at the same speeds before engaging to effect a smooth change.
~n. A system of gears using this principle.

syn·chron·ic (sing-krónnik, sin-) *adj.* Also **syn·chron·i·cal** (-'l). **1.** Synchronous. **2. a.** Studying the events of a particular time or era without consideration of historical data. **b.** Pertaining to or designating the study of language and linguistic phenomena without reference to any historical perspective. Compare **diachronic. —syn·chron·i·cal·ly** *adv.*

syn·chro·nic·i·ty (síng-krə-níssəti, sín-, -kro-) *n.* Coincidence that is felt to be significant or meaningful; especially, in the philosophy of C.G. Jung, the simultaneous occurrence of two or more events that seem to be linked in a meaningful or significant way without apparently being causally related, for example, the sudden stopping of a clock at the moment of a person's death in the same vicinity.

syn·chro·nise, syn·chro·nize (síng-krə-nīz || sín-) *v.* **-nised, -nising, -nises.** *—intr.* **1.** To occur at the same time; be or become simultaneous. **2.** To operate in unison. *—tr.* **1.** To cause to operate with exact coincidence in time or rate. **2.** To arrange (historical events) so as to indicate parallel existence or occurrence. **3. a.** To cause (sound effects or dialogue) to coincide with an action, in film-making. **b.** To make sounds and actions coincide in (a film).

[From SYNCHRONOUS.] **—syn·chro·ni·sa·tion** (-nī-zāysh'n) *n.*

synchronised swimming *n.* A rhythmic, dancelike form of swimming, synchronised to music. Also informally called "synchro".

syn·chro·nism (síng-krə-niz'm || sín-) *n.* **1.** The condition of being synchronised or synchronous. **2.** A chronological listing of historical personages or events so as to indicate parallel existence or occurrence. **3.** The representation in the same art work of two or more events that occurred at different times. **—syn·chro·nis·tic** (-nístik), **syn·chro·nis·ti·cal** *adj.* **—syn·chro·nis·ti·cal·ly** *adv.*

syn·chro·nous (síng-krənəss || sín-) *adj.* **1.** Occurring at the same time. **2.** Moving or operating at the same rate. **3. a.** Having identical periods. **b.** Having identical period and phase. —See Synonyms at **contemporary.** [Late Latin *synchronos,* from Greek *sunkhronos* : *sun-,* same + *khronos,* time (see **chronic**).] **—syn·chro·nous·ly** *adv.* **—syn·chro·nous·ness** *n.*

synchronous converter *n.* An electrical machine in which a double-wound armature is used to convert alternating current into direct current, or vice versa.

synchronous motor *n.* A motor having a speed directly proportional to the frequency of the electric current that operates it.

synchronous orbit *n.* An orbit having a period the same as the period of axial rotation of the Earth and so oriented that any body in it maintains a position over one point on the Earth's surface. Also called "stationary orbit".

synchronous rotation *n.* **Captured rotation** *(see).*

syn·chro·ny (síng-krəni || sín-) *n., pl.* **-nies.** A synchronous occurrence, movement, or arrangement. [From SYNCHRONOUS.]

syn·chro·scope (síng-krə-skōp) *n.* Also **syn·chron·o·scope** (sing-krónnə-, sin-). An instrument that indicates whether or not two periodic motions are synchronous. [SYNCHRO- + -SCOPE.]

syn·chro·tron (síng-krə-tron || sín-) *n.* An accelerator in which charged particles are accelerated around a fixed circular path by a radio-frequency potential and held to the path by a time-varying magnetic field. [SYNCHRO- + (ELEC)TRON.]

synchrotron radiation *n.* Electromagnetic radiation emitted by high-energy charged particles, such as electrons, spiralling along the lines of force produced by a strong magnetic field. The radiation is emitted at a tangent to the orbit of the particles and occurs in synchrotrons and in some astronomical systems, such as supernova remnants.

syn·clas·tic (sing-klástik, sin-) *adj.* Designating a surface whose curvature at a particular point in a particular direction has the same sign as the curvature, at that point, in a perpendicular direction; that is, it is convex or concave in both directions, as a sphere is. [SYN- (alike) + Greek *klastos,* bent, from *klan,* to bend.]

syn·cli·nal (sing-klīn'l, sin-) *adj.* **1.** Sloping downwards from opposite directions to meet in a common point or line. **2.** *Geology.* Pertaining to, formed by, or forming a syncline.
~*n.* A syncline. [SYN- + Greek *klinein,* to lean.]

syn·cline (síng-klīn || sín-) *n.* A low, troughlike area in bedrock, in which rocks incline together from opposite sides. [Back-formation from SYNCLINAL.]

syn·cli·nor·um (sing-klī-náwrəm) *n.* A large syncline, with minor upfolds and downfolds in its limbs.

syn·com (síng-kom || sín-) *n.* A communications satellite in a synchronous orbit. [*Syn*chronous + *com*munication.]

syn·co·pate (síng-kə-payt) *tr.v.* **-pated, -pating, -pates. 1.** *Grammar.* **a.** To shorten (a word) by means of syncope. **b.** To drop (a letter or sound) from the spelling or pronunciation of a word. **2.** To modify (musical rhythm) by syncopation. [Medieval Latin *syncopāre,* from Late Latin *syncopē,* SYNCOPE.] **—syn·co·pa·tor** (-ər) *n.*

syn·co·pa·tion (sing-kə-páysh'n, -kō- || sín-) *n.* **1.** The act of syncopating or the condition of being syncopated. **2.** Something syncopated. **3.** *Music.* The displacement of an accent or accents in a bar to parts that are not normally accented, as when a normally weak beat is stressed. **4.** *Grammar.* Syncope.

syn·co·pe (síng-kəpi || sín-) *n.* **1.** *Grammar.* The shortening of a word by the omission of a sound, letter, or syllable from the middle of the word; for example, *bo's'n* for *boatswain.* **2.** *Pathology.* A brief loss of consciousness caused by a transient reduction of blood supply to the brain; a faint. [Late Latin, from Greek *sunkopē,* from *sunkoptein,* to chop up : *sun-,* together, thoroughly + *koptein,* to cut off.] **—syn·co·pal** (-kəp'l), **syn·cop·ic** (sing-kóppik, sin-) *adj.*

syn·cre·tise, syn·cre·tize (síng-kri-tīz, -krə- || sín-) *v.* **-tised, -tising, -tises.** —*tr.* To reconcile or attempt to reconcile (differing religious beliefs, for example). —*intr.* To combine differing beliefs. [New Latin *syncretizare,* from Greek *sunkrētizein.* See **syncretism.**]

syn·cre·tism (síng-kri-tiz'm, -krə- || sín-) *n.* **1.** The attempt or tendency to combine or reconcile differing beliefs, as in philosophy or religion. **2.** *Linguistics.* The diachronic fusion of two or more originally different inflectional forms into one. [New Latin *syncretismus,* from Greek *sunkrētismos,* union, from *sunkrētizein,* to unite (in the manner of the Cretan cities) against a common enemy : *sun-,* together + *Krēs* (stem *Krēt-*), CRETAN.] **—syn·cre·tist** *n.* **—syn·cret·ic** (-kréetik, -kréttik), **syn·cre·tis·tic** (-tístik) *adj.*

syn·cy·ti·um (sin-sítti-əm || *U.S.* -síshi-) *n., pl.* **-cytia** (-ə). *Biology.* A mass of protoplasm with many nuclei but no clear cell boundaries. [New Latin : SYN- + CYT(O)- + -IUM.] **—syn·cy·ti·al** *adj.*

syn·dac·tyl, syn·dac·tyle (sin-dák-til, -tīl) *adj.* Also **syn·dac·ty·lous.** *Biology.* Having two or more wholly or partially fused digits.
~*n.* A syndactyl animal. [French *syndactyle* : SYN- + Greek *daktulos,* finger, DACTYL.] **—syn·dac·tyl·ism, syn·dac·ty·ly** (-dáktili) *n.*

syn·des·mo·sis (sín-dez-mō-siss) *n.* The articulation of bones by ligaments. [New Latin, from Greek *sundesmos,* ligament, from *sundein,* to bind. See **syndetic.**] **—syn·des·mot·ic** (-móttik) *adj.*

syn·det·ic (sin-déttik) *adj.* Also **syn·det·i·cal** (-'l). **1.** Serving to connect, as a conjunction does; copulative; conjunctive. **2.** Connected by a conjunction. [Greek *sundetikos,* from *sundetos,* bound together, from *sundein,* to bind together : *sun-,* together + *dein,* to bind.] **—syn·det·i·cal·ly** *adv.*

syn·dic (síndik) *n.* **1.** One appointed to represent a company, university, or other organisation in business transactions; a business agent. **2.** In various European countries, a civil magistrate or similar government official. [French, from Late Latin *syndicus,* from Greek *sundikos,* assistant in a court of justice, public advocate : *sun-,* with + *dikē,* judgment.] **—syn·di·cal** *adj.*

syn·di·cal·ism (síndik'l-iz'm) *n.* A radical political movement that advocates bringing industry and government under the control of trade unions, especially by the use of direct action such as general strikes and sabotage. [French *syndicalisme,* from *(chambre) syndicale,* trade union : *chambre,* chamber + *syndical,* of a trade union, from *syndic,* SYNDIC.] **—syn·di·cal·ist** *adj. & n.*

syn·di·cate (síndi-kət, -kit || -kayt) *n. Abbr.* **synd. 1. a.** An association of people or commercial firms organised to promote some common interest. **b.** An association of people formed to carry out a usually specified enterprise or activity: *a crime syndicate.* **2.** An agency that sells news articles and photographs for publication in a number of newspapers or periodicals simultaneously. **3.** The office, position, or jurisdiction of a syndic or body of syndics.
~*v.* (-kayt) **syndicated, -cating, -cates.** —*tr.* **1.** To organise into a syndicate. **2.** To sell (an article, for example) through a syndicate for publication. —*intr.* To organise a syndicate. [French *syndicat,* from *syndic,* SYNDIC.]

syn·di·o·tac·tic (síndi-ō-táktik, -ə-) *adj.* Designating a stereospecific polymer having alternating stereochemical configurations of the groups on successive carbon atoms in the chain. Compare **isotactic.** [Greek *sunduo,* two together + -TACTIC.]

syn·drome (sín-drōm, -drəm) *n.* **1.** A group of signs and symptoms that collectively indicate or characterise a disease, psychological disorder, or other abnormal condition. **2. a.** A set of signs or symptoms indicating the existence of an undesirable condition, problem, or quality. **b.** Loosely, such a condition, problem, or quality: *"His reclusive side—the withdrawn scholar syndrome, it might be called. . ."* (J. I. M. Stewart). [New Latin, from Greek *sundromē* a running together, concurrence (of symptoms) : *sun-,* together + *dromos,* race, racecourse.] **—syn·drom·ic** (sin-drómmik) *adj.*

syne (sīn) *adv. Scottish.* Since. **—syne** *conj. & prep.*

syn·ec·do·che (si-nék-dəki) *n.* A figure of speech by which a more inclusive term is used for a less inclusive term or vice versa; for example, *eighty sail* for *eighty sailing ships,* or *head* for *cattle.* [Latin, from Greek *sunekdokhē,* from *sunekdekhesthai,* "to take up (or understand) with another" : *sun-,* with + *ekdekhesthai,* to take from, take or understand in a certain sense : *ex,* out of + *dekhesthai,* to take, receive.] **—syn·ec·doch·ic** (sinnek-dóckik) *adj.*

syn·e·col·o·gy (sín-i-kólləji, -ee-) *n.* The study of the environmental interrelationships among communities of organisms. Compare **autecology.** [SYN- + ECOLOGY.] **—syn·e·co·log·ic** (-kə-lojik), **syn·e·co·log·i·cal** *adj.*

syn·er·e·sis (si-neér-ə-siss, -i-) *n., pl.* **-ses** (-seez). Also **syn·aer·e·sis** (for sense 1). **1.** *Chemistry.* Exudation of the liquid component of a gel. **2.** *U.S.* **Synaeresis** *(see).* [Late Latin *synaeresis,* from Greek *sunairesis,* from *sunairein,* to take or draw together, contract : *sun-,* together + *hairein,* to seize, take.]

syn·er·get·ic (sín-ər-jéttik, -er-) *adj.* Also **syn·er·gic** (si-nérjik). Of or pertaining to synergism or synergy.

syn·er·gid cell (si-nérjid) *n.* Either of two haploid cells situated close to the egg cell in the embryo sac of flowering plants. [Greek *sunergos,* working together (see **synergism**) + -ID.]

syn·er·gism (sin-ər-jiz'm, -er-, si-nér-) *n.* **1.** *Biology.* The action of two or more substances, organs, or organisms to achieve an effect greater than the sum of their individual effects. **2.** *Theology.* The doctrine that individual salvation is effected by a combination of human will and divine grace. [New Latin *synergismus,* from Greek *sunergos,* working together : *sun-,* together + *ergon,* work.]

syn·er·gist (sín-ər-jist, -er-, si-nér-) *n.* **1.** *Biology.* A synergetic organ, drug, or substance. **2.** *Theology.* An adherent of synergism. **—syn·er·gis·tic** (-jístik), **syn·er·gis·ti·cal** *adj.*

syn·er·gy (sínərji) *n., pl.* **-gies. 1.** *Biology.* **synergism** *(see).* **2.** Broadly, mutual reinforcement or complementariness. [New Latin *synergia,* from Greek *sunergos,* working together.]

syn·e·sis (sínni-siss) *n. Grammar.* A construction in which a form differs in number but agrees in meaning with the word governing it; for example, *If anyone arrives, tell them to wait.* [New Latin, from Greek *sunesis,* union, quick apprehension, intelligence, from *sunienai,* to bring together, understand : *sun-,* together + *hienai,* to send.]

synesthesia. *U.S.* Variant of **synaesthesia.**

syn·ga·my (síng-gəmi) *n. Biology.* The fusion of two gametes; fertilisation. [SYN- + -GAMY.] **—syn·gam·ic** (sing-gámmik, sin-), **syn·gam·ous** (síng-gəməss) *adj.*

Synge (sing), **J(ohn) M(illington)** (1871–1909). Irish playwright. His plays, which draw on the speech and culture of Irish peasants and fishermen, include *The Playboy of the Western World* (1907).

syn·gen·e·sis (sin-jénnə-siss) *n. Biology.* Sexual reproduction. [New Latin : SYN- + -GENESIS.] **—syn·ge·net·ic** (sínjə-néttik) *adj.*

syn·graft (síng-graaft, sín- || -graft) *n.* An **isograft** *(see).*

syn·i·ze·sis, syn·e·ze·sis (sinni-zeé-siss) *n., pl.* **-ses** (-seez). **1.** The contraction of two syllables into one by joining in pronunciation two adjacent vowels, without forming a recognised diphthong, as when *tower* (tów-ər) is pronounced (táàər). Compare **synaeresis. 2.** *Biology.* The phase of meiosis in which the chromatin contracts into a mass at one side of the nucleus. [Late Latin *synizēsis,* from Greek *sunizēsis,* "collapse", from *sunizein,* to collapse : *sun-,* together + *hizein,* to sit down.]

syn·kar·y·on (sing-kárri-ən, sin-, -on) *n.* The nucleus of a fertilised egg immediately after the male and female nuclei have fused. [New Latin : SYN- + Greek *karuon,* nut.] —**syn·kar·y·on·ic** (-ónnik) *adj.*

syn·od (sínnəd, *also* sín-od) *n.* **1.** A council or assembly of churches or church officials; an ecclesiastical council. **2.** Any council or assembly. [Middle English, from Late Latin *synodus,* from Greek *sunodos,* meeting : *sun-,* together + *hodos,* road, way, journey.] —**syn·od·al** (-'l), **syn·od·i·cal** (si-nóddik'l) *adj.*

sy·nod·ic (si-nóddik) *adj.* **1.** Pertaining to the conjunction of celestial bodies, especially the interval between two successive conjunctions of a planet or the moon with the sun. **2.** Of or pertaining to a synod. —**sy·nod·i·cal·ly** *adv.*

sy·noe·cious, sy·ne·cious (si-néeshəss) *adj.* Botany. Having male and female organs in the same flower or corresponding structure. [SYN- + (MON)OECIOUS.]

syn·o·nym (sínnə-nim, *also* sínno-) *n. Abbr.* **syn. 1.** A word having the same meaning as, or a meaning very similar to, that of another word in the same language; for example, *mix, blend,* and *mingle* are synonyms. Compare **antonym. 2.** A word or expression accepted as a figurative or symbolic substitute for another word or expression; as by word: *Her name has become a synonym for bravery.* **3.** *Biology.* A taxonomic name of an organism that is equivalent to or has been superseded by another designation. [Middle English *sinonyme,* from Latin *synonymum,* from Greek *sunōnumon,* from *sunōnumos,* SYNONYMOUS.] —**syn·o·nym·ic** (-nímmik), **syn·o·nym·i·cal** *adj.* —**syn·o·nym·i·ty** (-nímməti) *n.*

syn·on·y·mise, syn·on·y·mize (si-nónni-mīz) *tr.v.* **-mised, -mising, -mises.** To provide or analyse the synonyms of (a word). —**syn·on·y·mist** (si-nónnimist) *n.*

syn·on·y·mous (si-nónnimǝss) *adj. Abbr.* **syn. 1.** Expressing the same or a similar meaning; being a synonym or synonyms. **2.** Having a particular connotation through association with something specified: *Nazism is synonymous with evil.* [Medieval Latin *synonymus,* from Greek *sunōnumos* : *sun-,* same + *onoma, onuma,* name.] —**syn·on·y·mous·ly** *adv.*

syn·on·y·my (si-nónnəmi) *n., pl.* **-mies.** *Abbr.* **syn. 1.** The quality of being synonymous; equivalence of meaning. **2.** The study and classification of synonyms. **3.** A list, book, or system of synonyms. **4.** The use of synonyms for rhetorical emphasis or effect. **5.** A chronological list or record of the scientific names that have been applied to a species and its subdivisions.

syn·op·sis (si-nóp-siss) *n., pl.* **-ses** (-seez). A brief statement or outline of a subject; a summary; an abstract. [Late Latin, from Greek *sunopsis,* a viewing all together : *sun-,* together + *opsis,* view.]

syn·op·sise, syn·op·size (si-nóp-sīz) *tr.v.* **-sised, -sising, -sises.** To present or write a synopsis of. [Late Greek *sunopsizein,* from Greek *sunopsis,* SYNOPSIS.]

sy·nop·tic (si-nóptik) *adj.* Also **sy·nop·ti·cal** (-'l). **1.** Of or constituting a synopsis or summary. **2.** Presenting an account from the same point of view. **3.** *Often capital* **S.** Of or designating the first three Gospels of the New Testament (Matthew, Mark, and Luke), which correspond closely. **4.** Of or concerning the meteorological conditions at a given time: *a synoptic chart.* —**sy·nop·ti·cal·ly** *adv.*

syn·os·to·sis (sinnoss-tō-siss) *n.* The fusion of two skeletal bones. [New Latin : SYN- + Greek *osteon,* bone + -OSIS.] —**syn·os·tot·ic** (-tóttik) *adj.*

syn·o·vi·a (si-nóvi-ə) *n.* A clear, viscid lubricating fluid secreted by the *synovial membranes* lining joint cavities, sheaths of tendons, and bursae. Also called "synovial fluid". [New Latin *synovia, sinovia* (coined by Paracelsus).] —**syn·o·vi·al** *adj.*

sy·no·vi·tis (sīn-ō-vī-tiss, sín-, -ə-) *n.* Inflammation of the synovial membrane lining a joint cavity, resulting in pain and swelling. [SYNOVIA + -ITIS.]

syn·sep·al·ous (sin-séppəlǝss, sín-) *adj.* Botany. Gamosepalous.

syn·tac·tics (sin-táktiks) *n. Used with a singular or plural verb.* The branch of semiotics that deals with the formal properties of words and expressions, or, more generally, signs and symbols and their interrelations, without reference to their meaning. [From *syntactic,* of syntax, from New Latin *syntacticus,* from Greek *suntaktikos,* putting together, from *suntassein,* to put together. See **syntax.**]

syn·tax (sín-taks) *n.* **1. a.** The way in which words are put together grammatically to form phrases and sentences. **b.** The branch of grammar dealing with this. **c.** The rules for determining grammaticality. **2.** The system of rules governing the construction of well-formed formulas in a system of symbolic logic. **3.** The system of rules in operation in a computer program. [French *syntaxe,* from Late Latin *syntaxis,* from Greek *suntaxis,* from *suntassein,* to put together, arrange in order : *sun-,* together + *tassein,* to arrange.] —**syn·tac·tic** (sin-táktik), **syn·tac·ti·cal** *adj.* —**syn·tac·ti·cal·ly** *adv.*

syn·the·sis (sín-thǝ-siss, -thi-) *n., pl.* **-ses** (-seez). **1.** The combining of separate elements or substances to form a coherent whole. Compare **analysis. 2.** The whole so formed. **3.** *Chemistry.* Formation of a compound from its constituents. **4.** *Philosophy.* **a.** Reasoning from the general to the particular; logical deduction. **b.** In the philosophy of Hegel, the combination of thesis and antithesis in the dialectical process. [Latin, from Greek, a putting together, from

suntithenai, to put together.] —**syn·the·sist** *n.*

syn·the·sise, syn·the·size (sin-thǝ-sīz, -thi-) *v.* **-sised, -sising, -sises.** Also **syn·the·tise** (-tīz). —*tr.* **1.** To combine so as to form a new, complex product, especially by artificial process. **2.** To produce by combining separate elements. —*intr.* To form a synthesis.

syn·the·sis·er (sín-thǝ-sīzǝr, -thi-) *n.* **1.** One that synthesises. **2.** A machine having a keyboard and using solid-state circuitry to produce a wide range of electronic sounds. See **Moog synthesiser.**

syn·thet·ic (sin-théttik) *adj.* Also **syn·thet·i·cal** (-'l). **1.** Pertaining to, involving, or of the nature of a synthesis. **2.** Produced by chemical synthesis; especially, not of natural origin; man-made. **3.** Not genuine; artificial; devised. **4.** *Linguistics.* Designating a language such as Latin or Russian that uses inflectional affixes to express syntactic relationships. In this sense, compare **polysynthetic. 5.** *Philosophy.* Designating a statement or proposition whose truth depends on some fact about the world, rather than depending entirely on the meanings of the words from which it is composed. In this sense compare **analytic.** —See Synonyms at **artificial.** ~ *n.* A synthetic chemical compound or material. [Greek *sunthetikos,* skilled in putting together, component, from *sunthetos,* put together, compounded, composite, from *sunthithenai,* to put together. See **synthesis.**] —**syn·thet·i·cal·ly** *adv.*

synthetic philosophy *n.* **Spencerianism** *(see).*

sy·pher (sífǝr) *tr.v.* **-phered, -phering, -phers.** To overlap and even (chamfered or bevelled plank edges) so that they form a flush surface. [Variant of CIPHER.]

syph·i·lis (sif-ǝ-liss, -i-) *n.* A chronic infectious venereal disease caused by a spirochaete, *Treponema pallidum,* transmitted by direct contact, usually in sexual intercourse, or passed from the mother to the foetus, and progressing through three stages characterised respectively by (*primary syphilis*) local formation of chancres, (*secondary syphilis*) ulcerous skin eruptions, and (*tertiary syphilis*) systemic infection leading to **general paralysis of the insane.** [New Latin, after the supposed first victim of the disease, *Syphilus,* title character of a Latin poem *Syphilis, sive Morbus Gallicus* (1530) by Girolamo Fracastoro, Veronese doctor.] —**syph·i·lit·ic** (-littik) *n. & adj.*

syph·i·loid (sif-ǝ-loyd, -i-) *adj.* Characteristic of syphilis. [SYPHIL(IS) + -OID.]

syph·i·lol·o·gy (sif-ǝ-lóllǝji, -i-) *n.* The sum of knowledge concerning the origin, nature, course, complications, and treatment of syphilis. [SYPHIL(IS) + -LOGY.] —**syph·i·lo·gist** *n.*

syph·i·lo·ma (sif-ǝ-lōmǝ) *n., pl.* **-mas** or **-mata** (-tǝ). A lesion formed in an advanced stage of syphilis; a gumma. [New Latin : SYPHIL(IS) + -OMA.] —**syph·i·lom·a·tous** *adj.*

syphon. Variant of **siphon.**

Syr. Syria; Syriac; Syrian.

Syr·a·cuse (sírǝ-kewz, *U.S.* sírrǝ-). *Italian* **Si·ra·cu·sa** (sirra-kōōza). Seaport on the east coast of Sicily, Italy. It was founded by colonists from Corinth in the eighth century B.C., and became a brilliant centre of Greek culture. However, the city sided with Carthage in the Second Punic War, and fell to the Romans in 212 B.C. Archimedes, a native, directed the city's defence, and was killed during its subsequent sacking.

Syr·dar·ya (seer-daar-yaá). River of Central Asia. Some 2 250 kilometres (1,400 miles) long, it rises in the Kyrgyz Republic, in the Tian Shan range, and flows northwest to the Aral Sea.

Syr·i·a (sírri-ǝ). Official name **Syrian Arab Republic.** Country in the Middle East. Much of it is mountain, steppe, or desert, with fertile lowlands along the coast and in the valleys of the Euphrates and Orontes. Most Syrians are of Arab descent, but there are significant minorities of Kurds, Armenians, and Turkomans. Manufacturing and mining have replaced agriculture as the chief source of national income, though about 30 per cent of workers remain in farming. The main exports are crude oil, cotton, and cotton goods. Tourism is a major industry. Syria was a province of the Ottoman Empire

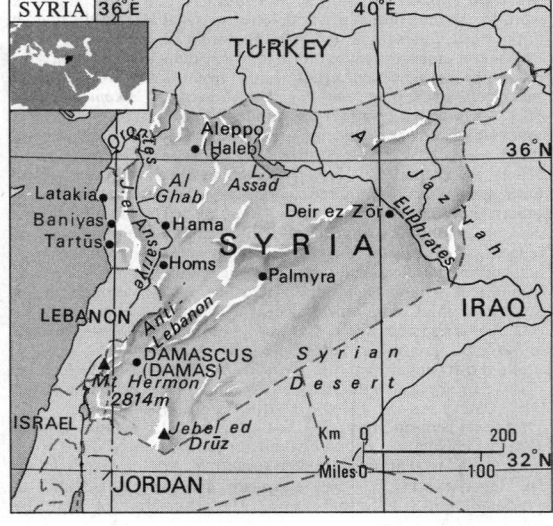

(1516–1918). From 1920 it was a French League of Nations mandate. It became an independent republic (1946) and joined Egypt in the short-lived United Arab Republic (1958–61). The country took part in Arab-Israeli wars after 1948, being firmly aligned against Israel. Syrian troops intervened in the Lebanese civil war (1977, 1983, 1987), and remained in the country. Area, 185 180 square kilometres (71,498 square miles). Population, 14,620,000. Capital, Damascus.

Syr·i·ac (sírri-ak) *n. Abbr.* **Syr.** An ancient Aramaic language spoken in Syria (3rd–13th century A.D.), surviving as the liturgical language of certain eastern Christian churches. —**Syr·i·ac** *adj.*

Syr·i·an (sírri-ən) *adj. Abbr.* **Syr.** Of or pertaining to Syria, its culture, or inhabitants.
~*n.* **1.** A native or inhabitant of Syria. **2.** A member of a Christian church using the Syriac language.

sy·rin·ga (si-ríng-gə) *n.* Either of two shrubs, the **mock orange** or **lilac** (*both of which see*). [New Latin *syringa*, "pipe" (from the use of its hollow stems to make pipes), from Greek *surinx*, SYRINX.]

syr·inge (sírrinj, si-rínj) *n.* **1.** A thin tube with a nozzle and a piston, rubber bulb, or other device that can draw in fluid by suction and expel it by force. **2.** A **hypodermic syringe** (*see*).
~*trv.* **syringed, -inging, -inges.** To clean, spray, or inject with a syringe. [Middle English *syring*, from Medieval Latin *syringa*, from Greek *surinx* (stem *suring-*), SYRINX.]

sy·rin·go·my·e·li·a (si-ríng-gō-mī-éeli-ə) *n.* A chronic disease of the spinal cord characterised by the presence of liquid-filled cavities and leading to spasticity and loss of awareness of pain and temperature. [New Latin : Greek *surinx*, pipe, cavity (see **syrinx**) + *muelos*, marrow, from *mus*, mouse, muscle.]

syr·inx (sírringks) *n., pl.* **syringes** (si-rín-jeez, sírrin-) or **syrinxes**. **1.** A **panpipe** (*see*). **2.** *Zoology.* The vocal organ of a bird, consisting of thin, vibrating muscles at or close to the division of the trachea. [Latin, from Greek *surinx†*, shepherd's pipe, panpipe, pipe.] —**sy·rin·ge·al** (si-rínji-əl) *adj.*

syr·phid (súrfid) *n.* Any fly of the family Syrphidae, many of which have a form or coloration mimicking that of bees or wasps. [New Latin *Syrphidae*, from Greek *surphos†*, gnat.] —**syr·phid** *adj.*

syr·up, *U.S.* **sir·up** (sírrəp ‖ súrrəp) *n.* **1.** A thick, sweet, sticky liquid, consisting of a sugar base, natural or artificial flavouring, and water. **2.** A highly concentrated solution of sugar in water. **3.** The juice of a fruit or plant boiled with sugar until thick and sticky. **4.** A medicine in a sweet-tasting liquid. **5.** Cloying sentimentality. [Middle English *sirop*, from Old French, from Medieval Latin *siropus*, from Arabic *sharāb*, beverage.] —**syr·up·y** *adj.*

sys·sar·co·sis (síssaar-kó-siss) *n.* The union of bones, such as the hyoid bone and lower jaw, by muscle. [New Latin, from Greek *sussarkōsis*, a growing together with flesh, from *sussarkousthai*, to be grown together with flesh : *sun-*, together + *sarkousthai*, passive of *sarkoun*, to grow fleshy, from *sarx*, flesh.]

sys·tal·tic (si-stál-tik, -stáwl- ‖ -stól-) *adj.* Alternately contracting and expanding, as the heart does; pulsating. [Late Latin *systalticus*, from Greek *sustaltikos*, from *sustellein*, to draw together, contract : *sun-*, together + *stellein*, to send, bind, repress, make compact.]

sys·tem (síst-əm, -im) *n.* **1.** A group of interacting, interrelated, or interdependent elements forming or regarded as forming a collective entity. **2.** A functionally related group of elements, as: **a.** The human body regarded as a functional physiological unit. **b.** A group of physiologically complementary organs or parts. **c.** A group of interacting mechanical or electrical components. **d.** A network of structures and channels, as for communications, travel, or distribution. **3.** A structurally or anatomically related group of elements or parts. **4.** A set of interrelated members, as of ideas, principles, rules, procedures, or laws: *metric system.* **5.** A social, economic, or political organisational form. **6.** A naturally occurring group of objects or phenomena. **7.** A set of objects or phenomena

grouped together for classification or analysis, as in: **a.** A **crystal system** (*see*). **b.** *Geology.* The succession of rocks formed during a geological period. **c.** *Astronomy.* A group of associated stars, planets, or other bodies. **8.** A method; an orderly way of doing something. **9.** Orderliness: *bring some system into this chaos.* See Synonyms at **method.** —**get (something) out of (one's) system.** *Informal.* To free oneself from a desire to do or express something by fulfilling it. —**the system.** The established political, social, and economic order or power structure. [Late Latin *systēma*, from Greek *sustēma*, a composite whole, from *sunistanai*, to bring together, combine : *sun-*, together + *histanai*, to cause to stand.]

sys·tem·at·ic (síst-ə-máttik, -i-) *adj.* Also **sys·tem·at·i·cal** (-'l). **1.** Of, characterised by, based upon, or constituting a system. **2.** Carried on in a step-by-step procedure. **3.** Characterised by purposeful regularity; methodical. **4.** Of or pertaining to classification or taxonomy. —See Synonyms at **orderly.** —**sys·tem·at·i·cal·ly** *adv.*

systematic name *n.* A name given to a chemical compound that describes the elements and groups it contains using a set of formal rules. Compare **trivial name.**

sys·tem·at·ics (síst-ə-máttiks, -i-) *n.* Used with a singular verb. *Biology.* The classification of organisms in an ordered system designed to indicate natural relationships.

sys·tem·a·tise, sys·tem·a·tize (síst-ə-mə-tīz, -i-) *tr.v.* **-tised, -tising, -tises.** Also **sys·tem·ise** (-mīz). To formulate as or reduce to a system: *systematising research data.* —**sys·tem·a·ti·sa·tion** (-tī-záysh'n ‖ -ti-) *n.* —**sys·tem·a·tis·er** *n.*

sys·tem·a·tism (síst-ə-mə-tiz'm, -i- ‖ si-stémmə-) *n.* **1.** The practice of classifying or systematising. **2.** Adherence to a system.

sys·tem·a·tist (síst-ə-mə-tist, -i- ‖ si-stémmə-) *n.* **1.** A person who adheres to or formulates a system. **2.** A taxonomist.

Sys·tème in·ter·na·tio·nal d'u·ni·tés (seess-tém án-tair-náss-yonaál dew-nee-táy, dü-) *n. French.* International System of Units. See **SI units.**

sys·tem·ic (si-stémmik, -stéemik) *adj.* **1.** Of or pertaining to a system or systems. **2.** Of, pertaining to, or affecting the entire body.
~*n.* A systemic poison or agent. —**sys·tem·i·cal·ly** *adv.*

systems analysis *n.* An analysis by computer of the methods used in a scientific or technological operation, with a view to making them more efficient. —**systems analyst** *n.*

systems engineering *n.* The branch of engineering concerned with the application of systems analysis, information theory, and ergonomics to practical technological operations.

sys·to·le (sístəli) *n.* The rhythmic contraction of the heart, especially of the ventricles, by which blood is driven through the aorta and pulmonary artery after each dilation or **diastole** (*see*). [Greek *sustolē*, contraction, from *sustellein*, to contract. See **systaltic.**] —**sys·tol·ic** (si-stóllik) *adj.*

syz·y·gy (sízziji) *n., pl.* **-gies. 1.** *Astronomy.* **a.** Either of two points in the orbit of a celestial body at which the body is in opposition to or in conjunction with the Sun. **b.** Either of two points in the orbit of the Moon at which the Moon lies in a straight line with the Sun and the Earth. **c.** The configuration of the Sun, the Moon, and the Earth lying in a straight line. **2.** In classical prosody, the combining of two feet into a single metrical unit. [Late Latin *syzygia*, from Greek *suzugia*, union, coupling, yoke, from *suzugos*, yoked, paired : *sun-*, together + *zugon*, a yoke.] —**sy·zyg·i·al** (si-ziji-əl) *adj.*

Szcze·cin (shchéch-een). *German* **Stet·tin** (shte-téen). Port in northwestern Poland, situated at the mouth of the river Oder on the Baltic Sea. It is a major outlet for Polish coal and has important shipbuilding, chemical, textile and engineering industries.

Szechwan. See **Sichuan.**

Szi·lard (síl-aard), **Leo** (1898–1964). Hungarian-born physicist. He emigrated to the United States in 1937 and during World War II worked on the construction of the atom bomb. He later regretted its construction and urged the abolition of all nuclear weapons.

t, T (tee) *n., pl.* **t's** or *rare* **ts, Ts** or **T's. 1.** The 20th letter of the modern English alphabet. **2.** Any of the speech sounds represented by this letter. **3.** Anything shaped like the letter **T.** —**to a T.** Perfectly; precisely: *She fits the role to a T.* [*To a T*, perhaps from *to a tittle,* to the smallest detail, perfectly. See **tittle.**]

t, T, t., T. Note: As an abbreviation or symbol, *t* may be a small or a capital letter, with or without a full stop. Established forms or those generally preferred precede the definition. When no form is given, all four forms are in general use in that sense. **1.** t. in the time of. [Latin *tempore*.] **2.** T *Physics.* surface tension. **3.** T. tablespoon; tablespoonful. **4.** t. *Commerce.* tare. **5.** t. teaspoon; teaspoonful. **6.** T temperature. **7.** t. tempo. **8.** t., T. *Music.* tenor. **9.** t. *Grammar.* tense. **10.** T *Physics.* tera-. **11.** t., T. territory. **12.** T tesla. **13.** T. Testament. **14.** t., T. time. **15.** T *Mathematics.* time reversal. **16.** t ton; tons. **17.** t tonne; tonnes. **18.** t *Physics.* top. **19.** t. *Grammar.* transitive. **20.** t troy (weights). **21.** T. Tuesday (unofficial). **22.** The 20th in a series; 19th when *J* is omitted.

't (t). **1.** Contraction of *it.* **2.** *Northern English.* Contraction of *the.*

ta (taa) *interj. Chiefly British Informal.* Used to express thanks.

TA Territorial Army (formerly, in Britain).

Taal (taal) *n. South African.* **Afrikaans** (*see*). Preceded by *the.* [Dutch *taal,* language, speech, from Middle Dutch *tāle.*]

tab (tab) *n.* **1.** A projection, flap, or short strip attached to an object to facilitate opening, handling, or identification. **2.** A small, usually decorative, flap or tongue on a garment. **3.** A small auxiliary control surface attached to a larger one to stabilise an aeroplane. **4.** *Military. British.* A coloured insignia worn by a staff officer. **5.** *U.S.* A bill, as for a meal in a restaurant. **6.** A tabulator, as on a typewriter. **7.** A metal ring that is pulled off the top of a can of drink in order to make an opening. Also called "pull-tab", "ring-

pull". 8. *Northern British Slang.* A cigarette. **—keep tabs** or **a tab on.** To keep account of or watch carefully.
~*tr.v.* **tabbed, tabbing, tabs.** To supply with a tab or tabs. [17th century : origin obscure; sense 6, shortening of TABULATOR.]
TAB¹ *n.* A combined vaccine against typhoid, paratyphoid A, and paratyphoid B. [*T*yphoid, paratyphoid *A*, paratyphoid *B*.]
TAB² Totalisator Agency Board (in Australia and New Zealand).
tab. table.
ta·ba·nid (tábbənid || *U.S.* tə-báynid, -bánnid) *n.* Any of various blood-sucking flies of the family Tabanidae, which includes the horseflies. [New Latin *Tabanidae* : Latin *tabānus*†, horsefly + -IDAE.] **—ta·ba·nid** *adj.*
tab·ard (táb-ərd, -aard) *n.* 1. A short tunic or capelike garment worn by a knight over his armour and emblazoned with his coat of arms. 2. A similar garment worn by a herald and bearing his lord's coat of arms. [Middle English, from Old French *tabart*†.]
tab·a·ret (tábbə-rət, -rit) *n.* A strong upholstery fabric having alternating stripes of satin and moiré. [Originally a trademark.]
Ta·bas·co (tə-báskō) *n.* A trademark for a hot, pungent sauce made from the fruit of a species of pepper plant.
tab·by (tábbi) *n., pl.* **-bies.** Also **tab·bis** (tábbiss) (for sense 1). 1. a. A striped or brindled domestic cat. b. A female domestic cat. 2. A rich silk cloth, with a watered or wavy pattern. 3. A plain weave fabric. 4. *Chiefly U.S. Informal.* A prying woman; a gossip.
~*adj.* 1. Striped or brindled. Said of domestic cats. 2. Made of or resembling the cloth, tabby. [(Cloth) from French *tabis,* from Old French *atabis,* from Arabic *'attābī,* originally made at *Al-'attābīya,* a suburb of Baghdad, after Prince *Attāb,* who resided there; (cat) by comparison of coat to cloth; (woman) see **cat.**]
tab·er·na·cle (tábbər-nack'l) *n.* 1. *Often capital* **T.** a. The portable sanctuary in which the Jews carried the Ark of the Covenant through the desert. b. The Jewish temple. c. A temporary or portable dwelling, as used by the Jews during the Exodus. 2. *Often capital* **T.** A case or box on a church altar containing the consecrated host and wine of the Eucharist. 3. A place of worship distinguished from a church; especially, one used by various denominations in Wales or by the Mormon Temple in the United States. 4. A canopied niche used as a shrine. 5. The body considered as the temporary residence of the soul. 6. *Nautical.* A boxlike support in which the heel of a mast is stepped.
~*v.* **tabernacled, -cling, -cles.** —*tr.* To enshrine. —*intr.* To dwell temporarily. [Middle English, from Old French, from Latin *tabernaculum,* tent, diminutive of *taberna,* hut, perhaps from Etruscan. See also **tavern.**] **—tab·er·nac·u·lar** (-náckewlər) *adj.*
ta·bes (táy-beez) *n., pl.* **tabes.** 1. Progressive bodily wasting or emaciation. 2. Tabes dorsalis. [Latin *tābēs,* "a melting".] **—ta·bet·ic** (tə-béttik) *adj.*
tabes dor·sa·lis (dawr-sáy-liss, -saá- || -sá-) *n.* A form of syphilis resulting in a hardening of the dorsal columns of the spinal cord, and in shooting pains, unsteadiness, and loss of ability to coordinate voluntary movements. Also called "locomotor ataxia".
tab·la (túbblə; *also* taáblə) *n.* A pair of small Indian hand drums. [Hindi, from Arabic *ṭablə,* drum.]
tab·la·ture (tábblə-chər, -tewr, -choor) *n.* 1. *Music.* An early system of notation, used especially for lute music, using letters and symbols to indicate playing directions. 2. An engraved tablet or surface. [French, from Medieval Latin *tabulātūra,* from *tabulātus,* tablet, from Latin, boarded, floored, from *tabula,* board. See **table.**]
ta·ble (táyb'l) *n. Abbr.* **tab.** 1. An article of furniture supported by one or more vertical legs and having a flat horizontal surface on which objects can be placed; especially: a. One at which meals are eaten: *a dinner table.* b. One having another specified use: *a bird table.* c. *Often plural.* One used in gambling games. 2. The objects laid out for a meal upon a table: *lay the table.* 3. The food and drink served at meals; fare: *kept an excellent table.* 4. The company of people assembled around a table, as for a meal. 5. The horizontal part of a machine tool where a piece is worked. 6. Either of the leaves of a backgammon board. 7. A plateau or tableland. 8. a. A flat facet cut across the top of a gemstone. b. A stone cut in this fashion. 9. *Music.* The front part of a stringed instrument, the **belly** *(see).* 10. *Architecture.* a. A raised or sunken rectangular panel on a wall. b. A **stringcourse** *(see).* 11. *Geology.* A horizontal rock stratum. 12. In palmistry, a part of the palm framed by four lines. 13. a. An orderly written, typed, or printed display of data, especially a rectangular array exhibiting one or more characteristics of designated entities or categories. b. *Plural.* A set of such tables listing basic arithmetical calculations to be learnt by heart. 14. An abbreviated list, as of the contents of a book. 15. A slab or tablet, as of stone, bearing an inscription or device. 16. *Plural.* A system of laws or decrees; a code: *the tables of Moses.* **—drink (someone) under the table.** *Informal.* To succeed in remaining relatively sober for longer than (someone with whom one is drinking). **—on the table.** 1. *Chiefly British.* Submitted for consideration or acceptance. 2. Postponed or put aside for consideration at a later date. **—turn the tables.** To reverse a situation and gain the upper hand. **—under the table.** *Informal.* 1. Extremely drunk. 2. Secretly or stealthily, especially as a bribe.
~*tr.v.* **tabled, -bling, -bles.** 1. To put or place on a table. 2. *Chiefly British.* To submit (a proposal, for example) for consideration. 3. To postpone consideration of (a piece of legislation, for example); shelve. 4. *Rare.* To tabulate. [Middle English, tablet, board, table, from Old French, from Latin *tabula*†, board, list.]
tab·leau (tábblō || *U.S. also* ta-blṓ) *n., pl.* **-leaux** (-z) or **-leaus.** 1. A vivid or graphic description. 2. A striking incidental scene, as of a picturesque group of people. 3. A moment during a scene of a play when all the actors on stage freeze in position and then resume action as before. 4. A tableau vivant. [French, from Old French *tablel,* diminutive of *table,* TABLE.]
tableau vi·vant (vee-vóN) *n., pl.* **tableaux vivants** (*pronounced as singular*). A scene presented on stage by costumed actors who remain silent and motionless as if in a picture. [French, "living picture".]
ta·ble·cloth (táyb'l-kloth || -klawth) *n., pl.* **-cloths** (-kloths || -klawthz, -klawths, -klothz). A cloth to cover a table, especially in preparation for a meal.
ta·ble-cut (táyb'l-kut) *adj.* Cut with a flat facet across the top. Said of a gemstone.
ta·ble d'hôte (taáb'l dōt) *n., pl.* **tables d'hôte** (*pronounced as singular*). 1. A communal table for all guests at a hotel or restaurant. 2. A meal consisting of several courses and offering a limited number of choices, served at a fixed price in a restaurant or hotel. In this sense, also called "prix fixe". Compare **à la carte.** [French, "table of (the) host".] **—ta·ble d'hôte** *adv.*
ta·ble·land (táyb'l-land) *n.* A flat, elevated region, especially one with steep sides; a plateau; a mesa.
table licence *n.* A licence allowing alcoholic drinks to be served only with meals.
table linen *n.* Tablecloths and napkins.
table money *n.* An allowance made, especially to senior officers in the armed services, for the official entertaining of visitors.
Table Mountain. *Afrikaans* **Ta·fel·berg** (taáf'l-bairkh). The distinctive flat-topped mountain that rises steeply behind Cape Town, South Africa, to a height of 1 087 metres (3,567 feet).
table salt *n.* 1. A refined mixture of salts, chiefly sodium chloride, used in cooking and as a seasoning. Also called "common salt". 2. **Sodium chloride** *(see).*
ta·ble·spoon (táyb'l-spōōn) *n.* 1. A large spoon used for serving food. 2. *Abbr.* **T., tbs., tbsp.** A household cooking measure, equivalent to four teaspoons or 15 millilitres.
ta·ble·spoon·ful (táyb'l-spōōn-fŏŏl) *n., pl.* **-fuls.** *Abbr.* **T., tbs., tbsp.** The amount a tablespoon will hold.
tab·let (táb-lit, -lət) *n.* 1. A small, flat pellet of compressed powdered medication to be taken orally. 2. A slab or plaque, as of stone or ivory, with a surface intended for or bearing an inscription. 3. A thin sheet or leaf, as of clay or ivory, used as a writing surface. 4. A set of such leaves fastened together, as in a book. 5. A pad of writing paper secured along one edge. 6. A small, flat cake of a prepared substance, such as soap. [Middle English *tablette,* from Old French *tablete,* diminutive of *table,* TABLE.]
table talk *n.* Casual mealtime conversation; cultured chat.
table tennis *n.* A game that is like a scaled-down version of lawn tennis, played on a table with a net across it, using wooden bats faced with rubber and a small celluloid ball. See **Ping-Pong. —ta·ble-ten·nis** (táyb'l-tenniss) *adj.*
ta·ble-turn·ing (táyb'l-túrning) *n.* 1. The movement of a table supposedly caused by the spirits of the dead operating through a human medium. 2. Loosely, spiritualism. Often used derogatorily.
ta·ble·ware (táyb'l-wair) *n.* The dishes, glassware, and cutlery used in setting a table for a meal.
table wine *n.* A wine considered suitable to be served with a meal.
tab·loid (tábbloyd) *n.* A newspaper of small format giving the news in condensed form, usually with illustrated, often sensational material. Compare **broadsheet.** [From *Tabloid,* trademark for a tablet of condensed medicine : TABL(ET) + -OID.]
ta·boo, ta·bu (tə-bṓō || ta-) *n., pl.* **-boos, -bus.** 1. A ban or inhibition attached to something by social custom or emotional aversion. 2. A prohibition, especially in Polynesia and other South Pacific Islands, excluding something from use, approach, or mention because of its sacred and inviolable nature. 3. An object, word, or act protected by such a prohibition.
~*adj.* Excluded or forbidden from use, approach, or mention.
~*tr.v.* **tabooed** or **tabued, -booing** or **-buing, -boos** or **-bus.** To exclude from use, approach, or mention; place under taboo. [Tongan *tabu,* perhaps "exceedingly marked", marked as sacred.]
Usage: When this word is used in a specialised discussion (for example, in anthropology), the spelling *tabu* is usual.
ta·bor, ta·bour (táy-bər, -bawr) *n.* A small drum played by a fifer to accompany the fife. [Middle English *tabo(u)r,* from Old French, perhaps from Persian *ṭabīr,* drum. See also **tambour.**]
tab·ou·ret, tab·o·ret (tábbə-rit, -ret || -ray) *n.* 1. A low stool without a back or arms. 2. A low stand or cabinet. 3. An embroidery frame. [French *tabouret,* diminutive of Old French *tabour,* TABOR.]
Ta·briz (ta-bréez). City in northwest Iran. It is a commercial, industrial, and communications centre. Its ancient name was Tauris.
tab·u·lar (tábbewlər) *adj.* 1. Having a plane surface; flat. 2. Organised or arranged in table form. 3. Calculated by means of a table. [Latin *tabulāris,* from *tabula,* TABLE.] **—tab·u·lar·ly** *adv.*
tab·u·la ra·sa (tábbewlə raá-zə, -sə) *n.* 1. A need or opportunity to start from the beginning; a clean slate. 2. The mind before it receives the impressions gained from experience; especially, in the philosophy of Locke, the unformed, featureless mind. [Latin, "erased tablet".]
tab·u·lar·ise, tab·u·lar·ize (tábbewlə-rīz) *tr.v.* **-ised, -ising, -ises.** To tabulate. **—tab·u·lar·i·sa·tion** (-rī-záysh'n || *U.S.* -ri-) *n.*
tab·u·late (tábbew-layt) *tr.v.* **-lated, -lating, -lates.** 1. To arrange, set

out, record, or write in tabular form; condense and list. **2.** To cut or form with a plane surface.
~*adj.* (-lәt, -lit, -layt). Having a plane surface. [Latin *tabula,* TABLE.] **—tab·u·la·tion** (-láysh'n) *n.*
tab·u·la·tor (tábbew-laytәr) *n.* **1.** A person who tabulates. **2.** A machine into which data can be fed for tabulation. **3.** A mechanism on a typewriter for setting automatic stops or margins for columns. Also called "tab". **4.** *Computing.* A device for reading data from punched cards and producing printed lists or totals of the result.
tac·a·ma·hac (táckәmә-hak) *n.* **1.** Any of several aromatic resinous substances used in ointments and incenses. **2.** The **balsam poplar** *(see).* [Spanish *tacamahaca, tacamaca,* from Nahuatl *tecamaca.*]
ta·cet (táy-set, tá-, -ket). *Music.* Be silent. Used as a direction. [Latin, it is silent, from *tacēre,* to be silent.]
tach·e·om·e·ter (tácki-ómmitәr) *n.* Also **ta·chym·e·ter** (ta-kimmitәr, tә-). A theodolite adapted to measure distances, so that distances, elevations, and bearings may be determined rapidly during surveying. [TACHY- + METER.] **—tach·e·o·met·ric** (tácki-ō-méttrik), **tach·e·o·met·ri·cal** *adj.* **—tach·e·o·met·ri·cal·ly** *adv.* **—ta·che·om·e·try** (tacki-ómmәttri) *n.*
tach·i·na fly (táckinә) *n.* Any of several bristly, usually greyish flies of the family Tachinidae, the larvae of which live as parasites within the bodies of other insects. [New Latin *Tachina,* type genus, from Greek *takhinos,* swift, from *takhos,* speed, akin to *takhus,* swift.]
tach·isme (tásh-iz'm, taásh-) *n.* A French school of art, originating in the 1950s and very similar to the American school, **action painting** *(see),* characterised by irregular dabs and splotches of colour thrown haphazardly onto the canvas in a spontaneous fashion. [French, from *tache,* spot, stain.] **—tach·iste** (-ist, -éest) *n. & adj.*
ta·chis·to·scope (tә-kístә-skōp) *n.* An apparatus that projects a series of images onto a screen at rapid speed, used in experiments on visual perception or memory, for example. [Greek *takhistos,* most swift, very swift, from *takhus,* swift + -SCOPE.]
tacho- *comb. form.* Indicates speed; for example, **tachograph.**
tach·o·graph (táckә-graaf, -graf) *n.* A machine that records the measurements of a tachometer, especially one in a vehicle recording its speed and when it was being driven. [TACHO- + -GRAPH.]
ta·chom·e·ter (ta-kómmitәr, tә-) *n.* An instrument used to determine speed, especially the rotational speed of a shaft. [Greek *takhos,* speed, akin to *takhus,* swift + -METER.] **—tach·o·met·ric** (táckә-méttrik) *adj.* **—ta·chom·e·try** (-kómmәtri) *n.*
tachy-, tacheo- *comb. form.* Indicates swift or accelerated; for example, **tachymeter, tachycardia.** [Greek *takhus*†, swift.]
tach·y·car·di·a (tácki-kárdi-ә) *n.* Excessively rapid heartbeat. [New Latin : TACHY- + Greek *kardia,* heart.]
ta·chyg·ra·phy (ta-kíggrәfi) *n.* The art or practice of rapid writing or shorthand; especially, the stenography of the ancient Greeks and Romans. [Greek *takhugraphos,* "swift writer" : TACHY- + -GRAPH.] **—ta·chyg·ra·pher, ta·chyg·ra·phist** *n.* **—tach·y·graph·ic** (tácki-gráffik), **tach·y·graph·i·cal** *adj.* **—tach·y·graph·i·cal·ly** *adv.*
tach·y·lyte, tach·y·lite (tácki-līt) *n.* A black, glassy basaltic rock. [German *Tachylyt,* "that which decomposes quickly (in acids)" : TACHY- + Greek *lutos,* soluble, from *luein,* to dissolve.] **—tach·y·lyt·ic** (-líttik) *adj.*
tachymeter. Variant of **tacheometer.**
tach·y·on (tácki-on) *n. Physics.* A hypothetical elementary particle that travels faster than the speed of light, mathematically equivalent to a normal particle moving backwards in time. [TACHY- + -ON.]
tach·y·pnoe·a, *U.S.* **tach·y·pne·a** (táckip-née-ә) *n.* Abnormally rapid breathing. [New Latin, from TACHY- + Greek *pnoea,* breathing.]
tac·it (tássit) *adj.* **1.** Not spoken; implied or understood: *Her glare was a tacit accusation.* **2. a.** Implied by or inferred from actions or statements. **b.** *Law.* Arising by operation of the law, rather than through direct expression. **3.** *Archaic.* Silent; not speaking. [Latin *tacitus,* silent, from the past participle of *tacēre,* to be silent.] **—tac·it·ly** *adv.* **—tac·it·ness** *n.*
tac·i·turn (tássi-turn) *adj.* Habitually untalkative; laconic; uncommunicative. [French *taciturne,* from Latin *taciturnus,* from *tacitus,* silent, TACIT.] **—tac·i·tur·ni·ty** (-túrnәti) *n.* **—tac·i·turn·ly** *adv.*
tack[1] (tak) *n.* **1.** A short, light nail with a sharp point and a flat head. **2.** *Nautical.* **a.** A rope for holding down the weather clew of a course. **b.** A rope for hauling the outer lower corner of a studdingsail to the boom. **c.** The part of a sail to which a tack is fastened, such as the weather clew of a course. **d.** The lower forward corner of a fore-and-aft sail. **3.** *Nautical.* **a.** The position of a vessel sailing to windward, relative to the trim of its sails. **b.** The act of changing from one tack to another. **c.** The distance or leg sailed between changes of tack. **d.** A sailing course that involves continual changes of tack. **4. a.** A course of action meant to minimise opposition to the attainment of a goal. **b.** An approach, especially one of a series. **5.** A large, loose stitch made as a temporary binding or as a mark. **6.** Stickiness, as of a newly painted surface.
~*v.* **tacked, tacking, tacks.** *—tr.* **1.** To fasten or attach with or as if with a tack or tacks. **2.** To fasten or mark (cloth or a seam, for example) with a loose, temporary stitch. **3.** To put together loosely and arbitrarily: *tacked some stories together.* **4.** To append; add. Used with *on.* **5.** *Nautical.* To bring (a vessel) into the wind in order to change tack. *—intr.* **1.** *Nautical.* **a.** To change the tack of a vessel. **b.** To change tack. Used of a vessel. **2.** To change one's course of action. [Middle English *tak(ke),* from Old North French *taque,* variant of Old French *tache,* nail, fastening, from Germanic.]
tack[2] *n. Informal.* Food; especially inferior food. [Origin unknown.]
tack[3] *n.* The harness for a horse, including the bridle and saddle. Also used adjectivally: *tack room.* [Shortened from TACKLE.]
tack·et (táckit) *n. Chiefly Scottish.* A hobnail. [Middle English, from TACK (nail).]
tack hammer *n.* A light hammer used to drive tacks.
tack·le (táck'l; *also* táyk'l *for noun sense 2*) *n.* **1.** The equipment used in a sport or occupation, especially in fishing. **2. a.** A system of ropes and pulleys for raising and lowering weights. **b.** A rope and its pulley. **3.** *Sports.* In various ball games, an attempt by a player to impede the progress of, or remove the ball from the possession of, an opposing player, by interception or obstruction, or by seizing the player, depending on the rules of the game.
~*v.* **tackled, -ling, -les.** *—tr.* **1.** To take on and wrestle with (an opponent or problem, for example) in order to overcome permanently; come to grips with. **2.** *Sports.* In various ball games, to attempt a tackle on (an opposing player). *—intr. Sports.* To tackle an opponent. [Middle English *takel,* probably from Middle Low German *takel,* from *taken,* to seize.] **—tack·ler** *n.*
tack·y[1], **tack·ey** (tácki) *adj.* **-ier, -iest.** Slightly adhesive or gummy to the touch; sticky. [From TACK (to attach).] **—tack·i·ness** *n.*
tacky[2] *adj.* **-ier, -iest.** *Slang.* **1.** Distasteful or offensive; tasteless. **2.** Shabby; shoddy; cheapskate. [19th century : origin obscure.] **—tack·i·ly** *adv.* **—tack·i·ness** *n.*
tacky[3] *n., pl.* **-ies.** *South African Informal.* A plimsoll. [20th century: origin obscure.]
tac·node (ták-nōd) *n.* In geometry, a point at which two branches of a curve touch and continue without crossing, so as to have a common tangent at this point. Also called "osculation".
ta·co (taákō) *n., pl.* **-cos.** A tortilla folded around a filling, as of minced meat or cheese. [Mexican Spanish, from Spanish, wad, roll, plug, probably from Germanic.]
tac·o·nite (táckә-nīt) *n.* A type of chert, containing magnetite and haematite, mined as a low-grade iron ore. [After the *Taconic* Mountains in New England, United States, where it is found.]
tact (takt) *n.* **1.** The ability to appreciate the delicacy of a situation and to do or say the kindest or most fitting thing; diplomacy. **2.** Skill or ability in dealing with others, especially skill in not giving offence. **3.** *Archaic.* The sense of touch. [French, from Latin *tactus,* sense of touch, from the past participle of *tangere,* to touch.]
Synonyms: *tact, diplomacy, savoir-faire, finesse, subtlety.*
tact·ful (táktf'l) *adj.* Possessing or showing tact; considerate; discreet. **—tact·ful·ly** *adv.* **—tact·ful·ness** *n.*
tac·tic (táktik) *n.* An expedient for achieving a goal; a manoeuvre.
-tactic *adj. comb. form.* Indicates **1.** Pattern, orientation, or position in space; for example, **isotactic, atactic. 2.** Movement; for example, **geotactic, phototactic.**
tac·ti·cal (táktik'l) *adj.* **1.** Of, pertaining to, or using tactics. **2.** Characterised by adroitness, ingenuity, or skill. **3.** *Military.* **a.** Of, pertaining to, used in, or involving operations that are smaller, closer to base, or of less long-term significance than strategic operations: *a tactical unit.* **b.** Carried out in support of military or naval operations: *tactical bombing.*
tactical voting *n.* The practice of voting for a candidate or party one does not positively favour so as to prevent the election of another.
tac·ti·cian (tak-tísh'n, ták-) *n.* **1.** A person skilled in the planning and execution of military tactics. **2.** A clever manoeuvrer.
tac·tics (táktiks) *n.* **1. a.** *Used with a singular verb.* The technique or science of securing the objectives set by strategy; specifically, the art of deploying and directing troops, ships, and aircraft in efficient manoeuvres against the enemy. **b.** The manoeuvres so used. Compare **strategy. 2.** *Used with a plural verb.* Any procedure or set of manoeuvres engaged in to achieve some end or aim. [New Latin *tactica,* from Greek *(ta) taktika,* "(the) matters of arrangement", from the neuter plural of *taktikos,* of order or arrangement, of tactics, from *taktos,* arranged, in order, from *tassein, tattein,* to arrange (in battle formation).]
tac·tile (ták-tīl || *chiefly U.S.* -t'l) *adj.* **1.** Perceptible to the sense of touch; tangible. **2.** Used for feeling: *a tactile organ.* **3.** Of, pertaining to, or proceeding from the sense of touch: *a tactile reflex.* [Latin *tactilis,* from *tactus,* sense of touch.] **—tac·til·i·ty** (-tíllәti) *n.*
tac·tion (táksh'n) *n. Rare.* The act of touching; contact. [Latin *tactiō* (stem *tactiōn-*), from *tangere* (past participle *tactus*), to touch.]
tact·less (tákt-lәss, -liss) *adj.* Lacking in delicacy; bluntly inconsiderate or indiscreet. **—tact·less·ly** *adv.* **—tact·less·ness** *n.*
tac·tu·al (ták-tew-әl, -choo-) *adj.* Of, producing, derived from, or pertaining to the sense of touch; tactile. [Latin *tactus,* sense of touch.] **—tac·tu·al·ly** *adv.*
tad (tad) *n. Chiefly U.S. Informal.* **1.** A small boy. **2.** A little; a bit: *a tad too small.* [Probably from English dialectal *tad,* toad, from Middle English *tadde, tode,* TOAD.]
Tadmor. See **Palmyra.**
tad·pole (tád-pōl) *n.* The aquatic larval stage of a frog or toad, having a tail and external gills that disappear as the limbs develop and the adult stage is reached. [Middle English *taddepol,* "toad head" : *tadde, tode,* TOAD + *pol,* POLL (head).]
Tadzhik. Variant of **Tajik.**
Tadzhikistan. See **Tajikistan.**
tae·di·um vi·tae (téedi-әm vī-tee, tīdi-әm vée-tī) *n.* A feeling of great weariness and boredom with life. [Latin, weariness of life.]
tael (tayl, táy-әl) *n.* **1.** Any of varying units of weight used in eastern Asia, the most common being equivalent to $1^1/_3$ ounces. **2.** A former Chinese monetary unit, equivalent in value to a tael of standard

silver. [Portuguese *tael*, from Malay *tahil, tail,* probably from Hindi *tolā*, a weight, from Sanskrit *tulā*, balance, weight.]

ta'en (tayn). *Archaic & Poetic.* Contraction of **taken.**

tae·ni·a, te·ni·a (teéni-ə) *n., pl.* **-niae** (-ee). **1.** A narrow band or ribbon for the hair worn in ancient Greece. **2.** *Architecture.* The band or fillet separating a Doric frieze from the architrave. **3.** Any ribbon-like anatomical structure. **4.** Any flatworm of the genus *Taenia,* which includes many tapeworms. [Latin, band, ribbon, from Greek *tainia.*]

tae·ni·a·sis (tee-nī-ə-siss) *n.* **1.** Infestation with tapeworms. **2.** The symptoms resulting from tapeworm infestation. [TAENI(A) + -ASIS.]

taf·fe·ta (táffitə) *n.* A glossy, stiff, plain-woven fabric of silk, rayon, or nylon, used especially for women's garments.
~*adj.* **1.** Made of or resembling taffeta. **2.** Reminiscent of shot taffeta in being changeable; inconsistent or fickle. [Middle English *taffeta,* from Old French *taffetas,* from Old Italian *taffettà,* from Turkish *tafta,* from Persian *tāftah,* "woven", from *tāftan,* to weave.]

taffeta weave *n.* **Plain weave** *(see).*

taff·rail (tâf-rayl, -ril, -rəl) *n. Nautical.* **1.** The rail around the stern of a vessel. **2.** The flat upper part of the stern of a vessel, made of wood and often richly carved. [Alteration of earlier *taff(e)rel,* "carved panel", from Dutch *taffereel,* variant of *tafeleel* (unattested), diminutive of *tafel,* panel, table, from Middle Dutch *tāvele,* from Latin *tabula,* TABLE.]

taf·fy (táffi) *n. U.S.* **1.** A chewy sweet of molasses or brown sugar boiled until very thick and then pulled with the hands or by machine until it is glossy and holds its shape. **2.** *Informal.* Wheedling flattery. [Perhaps from TOFFEE OR TAFIA.]

Taf·fy (táffi) *n., pl.* **-fies.** A Welshman. Also used as a term of address. Often considered offensive. [Imitative of the name *Dafydd,* the Welsh version of *David,* patron saint of Wales.]

taf·i·a, taf·fi·a (táffi-ə) *n.* A cheap rum distilled from molasses and refuse sugar in the West Indies. [West Indian Creole, probably alteration of RATAFIA.]

tag[1] (tag) *n.* **1.** A strip of leather, paper, metal, or plastic attached to something or hung from a wearer's neck for the purpose of identification, classification, or labelling: *a price tag.* **2. a.** The plastic or metal tip with which shoelaces and some kinds of string are finished for ease in passing them through eyelets and to prevent them from fraying. **b.** A loop or other attachment by which something may be gripped or hung up. **3.** The contrastingly coloured tip of an animal's tail. **4.** A bright piece of feather, floss, or tinsel surrounding the shank of the hook on a fishing fly. **5. a.** A dirty, matted lock of wool. **b.** A loose lock of hair. **6.** A rag; a tatter. **7.** A small, loose fragment: *tags and snippets.* **8.** An ornamental flourish, as at the end of a signature. **9. a.** A brief quotation, as from the English or Latin classics or the Bible, inserted into a discourse to give it an air of erudition and authority: *Shakespearean tags.* **b.** A cliché, saw, or similar short, conventional idea used to embellish a discourse. **10. a.** The refrain or last lines of a song or poem. **b.** The closing lines of a speech in a play; a cue. **11.** A designation or epithet, especially when unwelcome. **12.** *Computing.* A label assigned to identify data in a computer store.
~*v.* **tagged, tagging, tags.** —*tr.* **1.** To label, identify, or recognise with or as if with a tag. **2.** To fix or attach something else, especially at the end: *tagged an extra paragraph on to the letter.* **3.** To add a literary tag or tags to (a speech, for example). **4.** *Informal.* To follow closely. **5.** To cut the tags from (a sheep). —*intr.* To follow along after; trail after. Usually used with *along.* [Middle English *tagge*†.]

tag[2] *n.* **1.** A children's game in which one player pursues the others until he is able to touch one of them, who then in turn becomes the pursuer. Also called "he", "tig", "tip", "touch". **2.** The act of touching one's partner in tag wrestling.
~*tr.v.* **tagged, tagging, tags. 1.** To touch (another player) in the game of tag. **2. a.** To touch the hand of (one's partner) in tag wrestling. **b.** In baseball, to touch (a runner) with the ball or the glove holding the ball in order to retire him. [Variant of *tig,* perhaps from TICK (tapping sound, originally "a light touch").]

Ta·ga·log (tə-gaá-log, -gá-) *n., pl.* **-logs** or collectively **Tagalog. 1.** A member of a people native to the Philippines and inhabiting Manila and its adjacent provinces. **2.** The Austronesian language spoken by this people. [Tagalog, "(people) from the (Pasig) river" : *taga,* coming from + *ilog,* river.] **—Ta·ga·log** *adj.*

tag·gers (tággərz) *pl.n.* Very thin sheet iron, usually plated with tin.

ta·glia·tel·le (tál-yə-télli || *U.S.* taál-) *n.* A type of pasta cut in flat, narrow strips. [Italian, from *tagliare,* to cut.]

tag·meme (tág-meem) *n.* The smallest syntactic unit that can be shown to have a grammatical function in terms of tagmemics. [Greek *tagma,* order, from *tassein,* to put in order + -EME.]

tag·mem·ics (tag-meémiks) *n. Used with a singular verb. Linguistics.* A theory of grammatical analysis that attempts to show both the formal status of a linguistic unit, such as a noun or morpheme, and its grammatical function in a larger linguistic unit. **—tag·mem·ic** *adj.*

Tagore (tə-gór || -gōr; *Bengali* ta-koór), **Sir (Raban) Rabindranath** (1861–1941). Indian author, poet, and philosopher. He won the Nobel prize for literature in 1913 for his collection of poetry, *Gitanjali,* drawing on traditional Hindu themes.

tag question *n.* A question, such as *isn't it?* or *don't you think?,* appended to the end of a remark.

Ta·gus (táygəss). *Portuguese* **Te·jo** (túzhoo); *Spanish* **Ta·jo** (taákhō). River of Spain and Portugal. It is 940 kilometres (585 miles) long and enters the Atlantic Ocean at Lisbon.

tag wrestling *n.* A wrestling contest between two teams of two wrestlers each, only one member of each team being allowed in the ring at any one time, the other being permitted to enter when he touches his partner on the hand.

ta·hi·na (tə-heé-nə, ta-) *n.* Also **ta·hi·ni** (-ni). A thick paste made from ground sesame seeds. [Arabic.]

Ta·hi·ti (tə-heéti, taa-, ta-). The largest of the Society Islands in French Polynesia. The first European to discover it was the English navigator, Captain Wallis (1767). The chief products are tropical fruits, copra, vanilla, and sugar cane. Papeete, the capital and chief port, is also the capital of French Polynesia.

Ta·hi·tian (tə-heésh'n, taa-, -heéti-ən) *n.* **1.** A native or inhabitant of Tahiti. **2.** The Polynesian language of Tahiti. **—Ta·hi·tian** *adj.*

tahr (tar) *n.* Any of several goatlike mammals of the genus *Hemitragus,* of mountainous regions of Asia. [Nepalese *thar.*]

tah·sil (tə-seél) *n.* An administrative subdivision of a district in India. [Hindi, from Arabic, "collection".]

tah·sil·dar, tah·seel·dar (tə-seél-daar) *n.* An official in India in charge of revenues and taxation in a tahsil. [Urdu *taḥsīldār,* from Persian : Arabic *taḥsīl,* collection + Persian *-dār,* holder.]

Tai (tī) *n.* A family of languages spoken in southeast Asia and south China, including Thai, Lao, and Shan. **—Tai** *adj.*

tai·a·ha (tī-ə-haa) *n.* A long, spearlike Maori weapon. [Maori.]

Tai chi, Tai Chi, Tai Ji (tī jeé || tī cheé) *n.* A Chinese form of callisthenics consisting of a series of movements performed slowly and deliberately, for training both the body and the mind in balance, control, and coordination. Also called "Tai chi chuan". [Chinese *tai jí qúan,* great ultimate boxing.]

tai·ga (tīgə; *also* tī-gaa) *n.* The subarctic coniferous forest of Siberia and of similar regions elsewhere in Eurasia and North America. [Russian *taïga,* from Turkic *taiga,* rocky mountain.]

taiglach. Variant of **teiglach.**

tail[1] (tayl) *n.* **1.** The posterior part of an animal, especially when elongated and extending beyond the trunk or main part of the body. **2.** The bottom, rear, or hindmost part of anything: *the tail of a shirt.* **3.** The rear end of a wagon or other vehicle. **4.** *Aeronautics.* **a.** The rear portion of a fuselage. **b.** An assembly of stabilising planes and control surfaces in this region. Also called "empennage". **5.** The vaned rear portion of any bomb or missile. **6.** Any appendage to the rear or bottom of a thing: *the tail of a kite.* **7.** The long, luminous stream of gas and dust forced from the head of a comet when it is close to the Sun. **8.** Something that follows or takes the last place: *the tail of the journey.* **9.** A retinue or train of followers. **10.** The end of a line or series of persons or things. **11.** The short closing line of certain stanzas of verse. **12.** The refuse or dross remaining from such processes as distilling or milling. **13.** *Printing.* The bottom of a page; the bottom margin. **14.** *Informal.* The trail of a person or animal in flight. **15.** *Informal.* A person assigned to watch and report on someone's movements and actions. **16.** *Slang.* **a.** The buttocks. **b.** The penis. **17.** *Slang.* Women collectively, seen as sexual objects. Considered offensive. **—turn tail.** To run away. **—with (one's) tail between (one's) legs.** In an utterly dejected or defeated state.
~*v.* **tailed, tailing, tails.** —*tr.* **1.** To provide with a tail: *tail a kite.* **2. a.** To deprive of a tail; dock. **b.** To cut the stalks off (fruit). **3.** To wash the bottom of (a baby, for example). Used chiefly in the phrase *top and tail.* **4.** To come towards the end of: *tailing the list.* **5.** To serve as the tail of: *The winning float tailed the parade.* **6.** To connect (objects often dissimilar or incongruous) by or as if by the tail or end: *tail two ideas together.* **7.** *Architecture.* To set one end of (a beam, board, or brick) into a wall. Used with *in* or *on.* **8.** *Informal.* To follow and keep under surveillance. **9.** *Australian.* To tend or herd (sheep or cattle). —*intr.* **1.** *Architecture.* To be inserted at one end, as a floor timber or beam. **2.** *Informal.* To follow. Usually used with *after.* **3.** *Nautical.* **a.** To go aground with the stern foremost. **b.** To be pointed in some direction with the stern when riding at anchor or on a mooring. **—tail off** or **away.** To dwindle.
~*adj.* **1.** Posterior; hindmost. **2.** Coming from behind: *a tail wind.* [Middle English *tayle,* Old English *tæg(e)l.*]

tail[2] *n. Law.* The limitation of the inheritance of an estate to a particular person or his direct descendants.
~*adj. Law.* In tail. Used after the noun and often in combination: *estate tail; fee-tail.* [Middle English *taille, tayle,* from Old French *taille,* cut, division, partition, from *taillier,* to cut, from Vulgar Latin *tāl(l)iāre* (unattested). See **tailor.**]

tail·back (táyl-bak) *n.* A long queue of traffic, especially one stretching back from roadworks or an accident, for example.

tail beam *n. Architecture.* A **tailpiece** *(see).*

tail·board (táyl-bawrd || -bōrd) *n.* A hinged board forming the rear wall of a wagon or truck that can be removed or let down to serve as a ramp in loading or unloading.

tail·coat (táyl-kōt, -kōt) *n.* A man's black coat that is cut away at the front and has a tapering tail at the back which is split into two up to the waist, worn as part of very formal evening dress or as part of a morning suit. Also called "swallow-tailed coat", "tails".

tail end *n.* **1.** The rear or hindmost part of anything. **2.** The very end; the conclusion.

tail·gate (táyl-gayt) *n.* **1.** Either of the pair of gates downstream in a canal lock. Compare **headgate. 2. a.** The tailboard of a vehicle. **b.** The sloping door that forms the back of a hatchback car.
~*v.* **tailgated, -gating, -gates.** *U.S.* —*tr.* To drive so closely behind

(another vehicle) that one cannot stop or swerve in an emergency. —*intr.* To follow another vehicle at too short a distance.

tail·heav·y (táyl-hévvi, -hevvi) *adj.* Having too much weight at the rear either by overloading or from poor design and construction. Said especially of aircraft.

tail·ing (táyling) *n.* **1.** *Plural.* Refuse or dross remaining after such processes as milling, distilling, or mining. **2.** *Architecture.* The part of a tailed beam, brick, or board inside a wall.

taille (tī, táa-yə) *n.* A form of direct royal taxation levied in France before 1789 on nonprivileged subjects and lands, and tending to weigh most heavily on the peasants. [French, a cut, division, from *tailler,* to cut, from Vulgar Latin *tāl(l)iāre* (unattested). See **tailor.**]

tail·light (táyl-līt) *n. Chiefly U.S.* A **rear light** (see). Also called "tail lamp".

tai·lor (táylər) *n.* A person who makes, repairs, and alters garments such as suits, coats, and dresses.
~*v.* **tailored, -loring, -lors.** —*tr.* **1.** To make (a garment), especially to satisfy specific requirements or measurements. **2.** To fit or provide (a person) with clothes made to his measurements. **3.** To make, alter, or adapt for a particular end: *a speech tailored to a special audience.* —*intr.* To pursue the trade of a tailor. [Middle English *taillour,* from Anglo-French, variant of Old French *tailleur,* from Vulgar Latin *tāliātor* (unattested), "cutter", from *tāl(l)iāre* (unattested), to cut, from Latin *tālea*†, twig, cutting.]

tai·lor·bird (táylər-burd) *n.* Any of several Old World tropical birds of the genus *Orthotomus,* characteristically using plant fibres to stitch leaves together in making its nest.

tai·lored (táylərd) *adj.* Simple, trim, or severe in line or design: *a highly tailored suit.*

tai·lor·made (táylər-máyd, -mayd) *adj.* **1.** Made by a tailor. **2.** Perfectly fitted to a condition, preference, or purpose; made or as if made to order: *a job tailor-made for me.*
~*n.* **1.** A garment made by a tailor. **2.** *Informal.* A commercially manufactured cigarette, as opposed to one rolled by hand.

tailor's chalk *n.* A thin piece of hard chalk used in dressmaking for making temporary marks on clothing, as for seams or darts.

tail·piece (táyl-peess) *n.* **1.** Any piece forming an end to something; an appendage. **2.** *Printing.* An engraving or design placed as an ornament at the end of a chapter or at the bottom of a page. **3.** *Architecture.* A beam tailed into a wall. Also called "tail beam". **4.** *Music.* A triangular piece of ebony or other material to which the lower ends of the strings of a violin, cello, or some other stringed instruments are attached.

tail·pipe (táyl-pīp) *n.* The pipe through which exhaust gases from an engine are discharged; the final section of a vehicle's exhaust.

tail·plane (táyl-playn) *n.* A horizontal aerofoil fitted to the tail of an aircraft.

tail·race (táyl-rayss) *n.* **1.** The part of a millrace below the water wheel through which the spent water flows. Compare **headrace.** **2.** A channel for floating away mine tailings and refuse.

tail rotor *n.* A small rotor fitted at the back of a helicopter to produce a sideways thrust, used to counteract the tendency of the body to rotate in the opposite direction to the main rotor.

tails (taylz) *pl.n.* **1.** *Used with a singular verb.* The reverse side of a coin. Compare **heads.** **2. White tie** (see). **3.** A **tailcoat** (see).

tail·skid (táyl-skid) *n.* A skid attached to the rear underside of certain aircraft to act as a runner.

tail·spin (táyl-spin) *n.* **1.** The descent of an aircraft in a **spin** (see), characterised by the rapid spiral movement of the tail section. **2.** *Informal.* A state of emotional collapse; panic.

tail·stock (táyl-stok) *n.* The adjustable stock of a lathe supporting the spindle containing the dead centre.

tail wind *n.* A wind blowing in the same direction as that of the course of a vehicle.

tain (tayn) *n.* **1.** A type of paper-thin tin plate. **2.** Tinfoil used as a backing for mirrors. [French, tinfoil, shortened from *étain,* tin, from Old French *estain,* from Latin *stagnum, stannum,* an alloy of silver and lead.]

Tai·no (tīnṓ) *n., pl.* **-nos** or collectively **Taino. 1.** A member of an extinct aboriginal Arawakan Indian people of the West Indies. **2.** The language of this people. [Spanish, from a native name in the West Indies.] —**Tai·no** *adj.*

taint (taynt) *v.* **tainted, tainting, taints.** —*tr.* **1.** To stain or spoil (a person's honour or reputation). **2.** To make poisonous or rotten; infect or spoil. **3.** To affect with some unpleasant or harmful influence; corrupt. —*intr.* To become tainted or contaminated.
~*n.* **1.** A moral defect considered as a stain or spot. **2.** An infecting touch, influence, or tinge. [Middle English *taynten,* from Anglo-French *teinter,* from Old French *teint,* colour, from Latin *tinctus,* past participle of *tingere,* to dip in liquid, dye.]

tai·pan (tī-pan) *n.* A large venomous Australian snake, *Oxyuranus scutellatus.* [Native Australian name.]

Tai·pei (tī-páy). *Chinese* **Tai·bei** (-báy). Capital city of Taiwan. Situated in the north of the island, it is a major industrial centre.

Tai·ping (tī-píng) *n.* Any of those who took part in the largest uprising in Chinese history (1850–64) against the Manchu dynasty, spreading from southwest China almost to Beijing. The movement was suppressed with the help of British and American troops. [Chinese, "Great Peace" (name of the movement).] —**Tai·ping** *adj.*

Tai·wan (tī-waán, -wán), Official name **Republic of China.** *Portuguese* **For·mo·sa** (fawr-mṓ-sə). Mountainous island off the southeast coast of mainland China. The first Europeans to reach it were the Portuguese (1590) and it became an important centre for trade in the 19th century. China was forced to cede the island to Japan in 1895 but regained it after World War II in 1945. Following defeats by the Communists, the Chinese Nationalists, led by Jiang Jieshi, retreated to Taiwan and its neighbouring islands (1949). Under U.S. sponsorship, rapid industrialisation took place, and trade links between the two countries remain strong. Taiwan lost its United Nations seat to the People's Republic of China (1971), which regards Taiwan as one of its provinces. The United States broke off diplomatic relations and recognised the People's Republic in 1979. Electrical goods, clothing, and textiles are its main exports. Area, 35 989 square kilometres (13,895 square miles). Population, 21,500,000. Capital, Taipei.

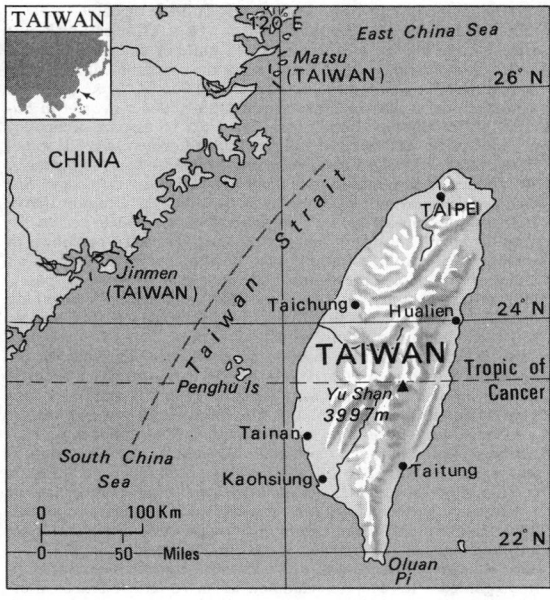

taj (taaj, taazh) *n.* A tall conical cap worn by certain Muslims as a headdress of distinction. [Arabic *tāj,* from Persian *tāj,* "crown".]

Tajik. Variant of **Tadzhik.**

Ta·jik, Ta·dzhik (taá-jik, tá-, taa-jeék). *n., pl.* **Tajik, Tadzhik.** A member of a people of Iranian descent inhabiting Tajikistan and regions of Afghanistan and China. —**Ta·jik, Ta·dzhik** *adj.*

Ta·jik·i·stan, Republic of (ta-jeék-i-stan). Also **Ta·dzhik·i·stan.** Country in central Asia, formerly a constituent republic of the U.S.S.R. It is predominantly mountainous, containing high areas of the Pamir complex. The Amu Darya, Syr Darya, and Zeravshan are the principal rivers. Tajik people make up just over 50 per cent of the population, most of whom are farmers. Area, 143 100 square kilometres (55,252 square miles). Population, 5,587,000. Capital, Dushanbe. See map at **Commonwealth of Independent States.**

Taj Ma·hal (mə-haál, -húl). A mausoleum in Agra, north India. It took almost 20 years (1630–48) to build from white marble carved and inlaid with other stones. It was constructed for Mumtaz-i-Mahal, wife of the Emperor Shah Jahan (who is also buried there).

Tajo. See **Tagus.**

ta·ka (túcka) *n.* The standard monetary unit of Bangladesh, equal to 100 paise. [Bengali.]

ta·ka·he (táa-kaa-hee, -kə-) *n.* An almost extinct flightless bird, *Notornis mantelli,* of New Zealand, having a large bill and brightly coloured plumage. [Maori *takahe* (imitative).]

take (tayk. *Note: the pronunciation* (tek) *is not considered standard*) *v.* **took** (tŏok || tōok), **taken** (táykən), **taking, takes.** —*tr.* **1.** To get into one's possession by force, skill, or artifice, especially: **a.** To capture physically; seize: *take an enemy fortress.* **b.** To kill, snare, or trap (fish or game, for example). **c.** To go away with; remove, often without proper permission: *Someone's taken my pen.* **d.** To capture in the course of a sport or game: *took two wickets; took my queen.* **e.** To obtain as a result of a victory; win: *took the seat at a by-election.* **f.** To seize authoritatively; confiscate. **2.** To grasp with the hands; grip: *take your partner's hand.* **3.** To carry along or cause to go with one to another place: *always takes his umbrella.* **4.** To encounter or catch in a particular situation; come upon; discover: *They'll never take me unawares.* **5.** To aim: *take a shot at.* **6.** To affect favourably; charm; captivate. Usually used in the passive: *completely taken by the puppy.* **7. a.** To put (food or drink, for example) into the body; eat, drink, inhale, or draw in: *take snuff.* **b.** To eat or drink habitually: *Do you take sugar?* **c.** To eat or drink as part of a course of medical treatment: *take tranquillisers.* **8.** To indulge or engage in (healthful or pleasurable treatment, for example): *take a holiday.* **9. a.** To bring or receive into a particular relation, association, or other connection: *take a new partner into the firm.* **b.** To marry: *take a wife.* **10.** To have sexual intercourse with.

Used of a man, as in romantic fiction. **11.** To accept and place under one's care or keeping: *take the children for the weekend.* **12. a.** To appropriate for one's own or another's use or benefit; obtain by purchase; buy. **b.** To buy regularly; especially, to subscribe to: *takes the Times.* **c.** To rent: *take a cottage for the summer.* **13. a.** To assume for or upon oneself: *take the blame.* **b.** To charge or oblige oneself with the fulfilment of (a task or duty, for example); deal with in the appropriate way: *The chaplain took prayers.* **c.** To pledge one's obedience to or adopt as a symbol of one's obedience; impose (a vow or promise) upon oneself: *take the veil.* **d.** To use (time) for a particular end. **e.** To accept or adopt for one's own: *took my side in the argument.* **f.** To require for a correct fitting: *takes size 14.* **g.** To require or have as a fitting or proper accompaniment: *Intransitive verbs take no direct object.* **14.** To obtain through competition: *took the lead.* **15.** To have or come to have: *took the form of a dialogue; taking shape.* **16. a.** To select; pick out; choose: *take any card.* **b.** To follow (a route or course of action): *took a wrong turning.* **c.** To use as a tool or instrument for doing something: *I'm going to tàke scissors to that hair of yours.* **d.** To use as a means of conveyance or transportation: *take a steamer to Europe.* **e.** To obtain or find: *take shelter.* **17.** To assume occupancy of: *take a seat.* **18.** To have as a requirement or necessity for something; require: *This job takes brains; It took three hours to get there.* **19.** To derive through conscious or subconscious influence: *She took her domineering tone from her mother.* **20.** To obtain or derive from a source or sources: *took the figures from an opinion poll.* **b.** To note or record: *took particulars of the case.* **21. a.** To put down in writing; write from dictation: *take a letter.* **b.** To put down an image, likeness, or representation of by or as if by drawing, painting, or photography: *take a photo.* **22. a.** To accept (something owed, offered, or given) either reluctantly or willingly: *took the bait.* **b.** To submit to (something inflicted); endure: *He can't take criticism.* **c.** To withstand or contain successfully: *The dam took the heavy flood waters.* **d.** To accept or believe (something put forth) as true or valid: *I'll take your word for it.* **e.** To follow (advice, a suggestion, or a lead, for example). **f.** To accept, handle, or deal with in a specified way: *takes things in his stride.* **g.** To consider in a particular relation or from a particular viewpoint: *Taken as a whole, it was a success.* **23. a.** To do, perform, or accomplish: *take a bath.* **b.** To perform or execute: *The horse took the jump.* **c.** To engage in or adopt, especially with an end in view: *taking precautions.* **24. a.** To allow to come in; admit; give access or admission to: *takes members only.* **b.** To provide room for; accommodate: *We can't take more than 300 guests.* **c.** To absorb or become saturated or impregnated with (dye, for example). **25. a.** To understand or interpret: *He took my criticism as an insult.* **b.** To consider; assume: *took her to be a policewoman.* Also used with *it*: *I take it you're coming.* **c.** To understand or appreciate: *I take your point.* **d.** To consider as a case in point: *Take children, for example.* **e.** To perceive or feel; experience: *took pride in her work; Don't take offence.* **26. a.** To convey or transport to a place: *This bus takes you to the station.* **b.** To conduct or lead: *That road takes us past the museum.* **c.** To cause to reach (a condition or state): *Her dedication took her to the top of her profession.* **27.** To go with, especially as a chaperone or as the person who pays: *take the children home; took him to the theatre.* **28.** To remove; do away with: *takes all the joy out of life.* **29.** To cause to die; kill; destroy: *The war took both our sons.* **30.** To subtract: *Two take one is one.* **31.** To commit oneself to the study of; enrol in: *take a course in physics.* **32.** *Slang.* To swindle; defraud; cheat: *taken for 40 quid.* —*intr.* **1.** To acquire possession. **2.** To engage or mesh; catch, as gears or other mechanical parts do. **3.** To start growing; root; germinate: *Have the seeds taken?* **4.** To have the intended effect; operate; work: *Glue won't take on that surface.* **5.** To become. Used especially in the phrase *take ill.* **—take aback.** To bewilder; astonish; nonplus. **—take after. 1.** To follow as an example. **2.** To resemble in appearance, temperament, or character: *He takes after his father.* **—take amiss.** To be offended by through misunderstanding. **—take apart. 1.** To divide or analyse (an object or theory, for example) into component parts; disassemble. **2.** *Informal.* To criticise or scold harshly or severely. **3.** *Slang.* **a.** To beat up; thrash. **b.** To defeat overwhelmingly, as in an argument; crush. **—take back. 1.** To retract something stated or written. **2.** To return (an article), especially for an exchange or refund. **3.** To cause to recollect an earlier time: *takes you back.* **4.** To regain. **5.** *Printing.* To move (a part of a printed line) to the preceding line. **—take five** or **ten.** *Chiefly U.S. Informal.* To take a short rest or break, as of five to ten minutes. **—take for. 1.** To consider or suppose to be; regard as: *I take him for a fool.* **2.** To consider mistakenly: *We took you for dead.* **—take it.** *Informal.* To endure abuse, criticism, or other harsh treatment: *You've got to learn to take it in the army.* **—take it lying down.** *Informal.* To submit to unfair or harsh or unjust treatment with no resistance. **—take it out on.** *Informal.* To abuse (another person or thing) in venting one's own anger or frustration. **—take on. 1.** To begin to employ. **2.** To undertake or begin to handle (a task, for example). **3.** To oppose in competition. **4.** To begin to have or acquire: *take on a new image.* **5.** *Informal.* To display emotion; fuss: *Don't take on so!* **—take (someone) out of (himself).** To make less withdrawn or introverted. **—take that.** Used to accompany the delivering of a blow or insult. **—take to. 1.** To have recourse to; go to, as for safety: *took to the woods.* **2.** To set out on: *take to the open road.* **3.** To develop as a habit or steady practice: *take to drink.* **4.** To become adept at: *took to it like a duck to water.* **5.** To become fond of or attracted to: *They took to each other.* **—take upon (oneself). 1.** To accept or assume the responsibility or trouble of. **2.** To assume the right of doing. **—take up with.** *Informal.* To develop a friendship or association with. —See Usage note at **have.**

∼*n.* **1.** The act or process of taking. **2.** The number of fish, game birds, or other animals killed or captured at one time. **3.** *Informal.* **a.** A quantity of anything collected at one time; especially, the amount of money stolen by a thief, profit or receipts taken by a business, or tickets sold by a theatre or cinema. **b.** A share of money stolen or profits or receipts taken. **4. a.** The uninterrupted running of a film or television camera or set of recording equipment in making a film or television programme or cutting a record. **b.** Any of a series of films or recordings of the same scene or sound, the best of which will be picked for final use. **5.** A scene filmed or televised without interrupting the run of the camera. **6. a.** Any physical reaction, such as a rash, indicating a successful vaccination. **b.** A successful skin graft. **7.** An amount of copy set in type at one time. **—on the take.** *Slang.* Receiving or appropriating money illegally. [Middle English *taken, took, taken,* Old English *tacan, tōc, tacen* (unattested), from Old Norse *taka, tōk, tekinn.*]

take·a·way (táyk-ə-way) *adj. Chiefly British.* **1.** Selling cooked food to be eaten off the premises: *a takeaway Chinese restaurant.* **2.** Designating a portion of cooked food taken away from the place of sale to be eaten: *a takeaway meal.*

∼*n.* **1.** A shop or restaurant selling takeaway food. **2.** A takeaway meal.

take down *tr.v.* **1.** To bring to a lower position from a higher. **2.** To dismantle; take apart: *take down the scaffolding.* **3.** To lower the arrogance or self-esteem of (a person). **4.** To put down in writing.

take·down (táyk-down) *adj.* Capable of being taken down or apart. Said chiefly of certain rifles.

take-home pay (táyk-hōm) *n.* The amount of one's salary remaining after income tax has been paid and various other deductions have been made.

take in *tr.v.* **1.** To grant admittance to; receive as a guest or lodger. **2.** To reduce in size; make smaller or shorter: *take in a skirt.* **3.** To include or comprise. **4.** To understand; absorb mentally. **5.** *Informal.* To deceive; swindle. **6.** To look at thoroughly; survey: *take in the sight.*

take-in (táyk-in) *n. Informal.* A deception or swindle.

take off *tr.v.* **1.** To remove (clothing). **2.** To carry off or away. **3.** *Informal.* To imitate or copy, especially in a mocking or humorous manner. **4.** To leave off working for (a period of time): *take the afternoon off.* —*intr.v.* **1.** *Informal.* To go off; start. **2.** To rise up in flight. Used of an aircraft or rocket.

take·off (táyk-off, -awf) *n.* **1.** The act of rising in flight as an aircraft or rocket might do. **2.** *Informal.* An amusing or mocking imitation or caricature of another person. —See Synonyms at **caricature.**

take out *tr.v.* **1.** To extract; remove. **2.** To secure (a licence, for example) by application to an authority. **3.** *Informal.* To escort, as on a date. **4.** In bridge, to cancel (a partner's bid) by bidding a different suit. **5.** *Slang.* **a.** To destroy or eliminate (enemy aircraft, for example). **b.** To kill. **c.** *Sports Informal.* To render (an opponent) ineffective, as by close marking or harsh tackling. **—take-out** (táyk-owt) *adj. & n.*

take over *tr.v.* **1.** To undertake (a responsibility or task, for example) in succession to another. **2.** To assume control or management of; especially, to buy the majority of the shares of (a company). **3.** To move (part of a printed line) to the following line. —*intr.v.* To assume the management of or responsibility for something.

take·o·ver, take-o·ver (táyk-ōvər) *n.* The act or an instance of assuming control or management of or responsibility for something; especially: **1.** The forcible seizure of power, as in a state or political organisation. **2.** The acquisition of the majority of the shares of a company. **—take·o·ver** *adj.*

tak·er (táykər) *n.* A person who takes or takes up something, such as a wager or purchase.

take up *tr.v.* **1.** To raise up; lift. **2.** To reduce in size or length; shorten or tighten: *take up the slack.* **3.** To accept the offer, challenge, or bet of. Used with *on*: *I might take you up on that offer.* **4.** To accept (an offer, option, bet, challenge, or other proposal). **5.** To challenge or question. Used with *on*: *I'd like to take you up on that.* **6.** To use up or occupy (space or time, for example). **7.** To develop an interest in or devotion to: *take up astronomy.* **8.** To become the patron of. **9.** To pursue or raise (a matter). Used with *with*: *better take this up with the boss himself.* **10.** To absorb (a liquid or gas). —*intr.v.* To begin again; resume.

take-up (táyk-up) *n.* **1.** A device for reducing slack or taking up lost motion, as in a loom. **2.** The act of taking or tightening up. **3.** Acceptance, as of an offer.

ta·kin (taá-keen) *n.* A large buffalo-like ruminant, *Budorcas taxicolor,* of the mountains of central Asia, having backward-pointing horns and a shaggy coat. [Tibeto-Burman (Mishmi).]

tak·ing (táyking) *adj.* **1.** Captivating; winning: *a taking smile.* **2.** *Informal.* Contagious; catching. Said of an infectious disease.

∼*n.* **1.** The act of a person or thing that takes. **2.** That which is taken, as a catch of fish. **3.** *Plural.* Receipts, especially of money. **—tak·ing·ly** *adv.* **—tak·ing·ness** *n.*

tal·a·poin (tál-ə-poyn) *n.* A small African monkey, *Miopithecus talapoin* (or *Cercopithecus talapoin*), having a long tail and greenish fur. [French, "Buddhist monk" (from a fancied resemblance), from Portuguese *talapões,* plural of *talapão,* monk, from Mon *tala pōi,* "our lord" (polite address to a monk).]

tal·bot (táwl-bət || tól-, tál-) *n.* A large, white hunting dog of a breed now extinct.

talc (tal-k) *n.* **1.** A fine-grained white, greenish, or grey mineral, essentially $Mg_3Si_4O_{10}(OH)_2$, having a soft, soapy texture and used in talcum and face powder, as a paper coating, and as a filler for paint and plastics. Also called "talcum". **2.** Talcum powder.
~*tr.v.* **talcked** or **talced, talcking** or **talcing, talcs.** To apply talc to (a photographic plate, for example). [French *talc,* from Medieval Latin *talcum,* from Arabic *ṭalq,* from Persian *talk*†.]

tal·cum (tál-kəm) *n.* **1.** Soapstone or talc. **2.** Talcum powder. [Medieval Latin, TALC.]

talcum powder *n.* A fine, often perfumed powder made from purified talc, for use on the skin.

tale (tayl) *n.* **1.** A report or revelation; a recital of facts or happenings: *told her tale of woe.* **2.** A malicious story, piece of gossip, or petty complaint. **3.** A deliberate lie; a falsehood. **4.** A diverting or edifying narrative of real or imaginary events; a story. **5.** *Usually plural.* Anything, whether true or false, told or revealed in breach of confidence, especially to one in authority: *tell tales.* **6.** *Archaic.* A reckoning; a total: *the earthquake's tale of thousands dead.* [Middle English *tale,* Old English *talu,* discourse, narrative.]

tale·bear·er (táyl-bair-ər) *n.* One who spreads malicious stories or gossip; a telltale. —**tale·bear·ing** *adj. & n.*

tal·ent (tál-ənt) *n.* **1.** Natural endowment or ability of a superior quality. **2.** A specific mental or physical aptitude; an innate ability to perform successfully in a particular field. **3.** Gifted people collectively: *local talent.* **4.** *Informal.* Sexually attractive people: *not a lot of talent at this party.* **5.** A variable unit of weight and money used in ancient Greece, Rome, and the Middle East. —See Synonyms at **ability.** [Middle English *talent(e),* from Old English *talente,* unit of weight or money, and Old French *talent,* aptitude, both from Latin *talentum,* unit of weight or money (in Medieval Latin, also "mental aptitude", extended sense from the parable of the talents in Matthew 25:14–30), from Greek *talanton.*]

talent scout *n.* An agent who goes in search of talented people for entertaining, sports, business, or the like.

ta·ler, tha·ler (ta̋alər) *n., pl.* **taler** or **-lers.** Any of numerous silver coins serving as a unit of currency in certain Germanic countries from the 15th to 19th centuries. [German *Taler.* See **dollar.**]

ta·les (táy-leez) *n., pl.* **tales.** *Law.* **1.** A group of persons summoned to fill vacancies on a jury that has become deficient in number. **2.** The writ allowing for such a summons of jurors. [Middle English, from the Medieval Latin phrase *tales de circumstantibus,* "such (persons) from those standing about" (used in the writ), from Latin *tālēs,* plural of *tālis,* such.]

ta·les·man (táy-leez-mən, táylz-, -man) *n., pl.* **-men** (-mən, -men). *Law.* A person summoned under a writ of tales.

tale·tell·er (táyl-tellər) *n.* **1.** An oral narrator. **2.** A person who tells tales; a talebearer. —**tale·tell·ing** *adj. & n.*

ta·li. Plural of **talus.**

Ta·lien. See **Lü-da.**

Talin. See **Tallinn.**

tal·i·on (táli-ən) *n.* **1.** A punishment identical to the offence, such as the death penalty for murder. **2.** The principle of exacting compensation in this way. [Middle English *talioun,* from Old French *talion,* from Latin *tāliō* (stem *tāliōn-*), reciprocal punishment in kind.]

tal·i·ped (tál-i-ped) *adj.* Afflicted with talipes; clubfooted.
~*n.* A person with a clubfoot. [See **talipes.**]

tal·i·pes (tál-i-peez) *n.* A deformity of the human foot; especially, **clubfoot** *(see).* [New Latin *talipes* (stem *taliped-*), "walking on the ankles" : Latin *tālus,* ankle, TALUS + -PED.]

tal·i·pot (tál-i-pot) *n.* A tall palm tree, *Corypha umbraculifera,* of tropical Asia. [Bengali *tālipōt,* palm leaf : Sanskrit *tālī,* fan palm, probably akin to *tāla* (see **toddy**) + *pattra,* feather, leaf.]

tal·is·man (tál-iz-mən, -iss-) *n., pl.* **-mans.** **1.** A small object, such as a stone or amulet, usually marked with magical signs, that is believed to confer on its bearer supernatural powers or protection. **2.** Anything having apparently magical power. [French and Spanish *talisman,* from Arabic *ṭilsām* (plural *ṭilsamān*), from Late Greek *telesma,* completion, consecrated object, from *telein,* to fulfil, consecrate, from *telos,* aim, result.] —**tal·is·man·ic** (-mánnik) *adj.*

talk (tawk) *v.* **talked, talking, talks.** —*tr.* **1.** To articulate (something, such as thoughts and emotions) in words; express by means of speech: *talk treason.* **2.** To speak of or discuss (something): *talk music.* **3.** To speak or know how to speak in (an idiom or language). **4.** To gain, influence, or bring into a specified state by talking: *talked her into coming; talk his way out of trouble.* **5.** To spend (a period of time) by or as if by talking. Used with *away*: *talk the evening away.* —*intr.* **1. a.** To converse by means of spoken language. Often used with *to* or *with*: *talked to each other for hours.* **b.** To express thoughts, desires, hopes, or the like in words. Used with *about* or *of.* **2.** To articulate words: *The baby can talk.* **3.** To imitate the sounds of human speech: *The parrot talks.* **4.** To communicate one's thoughts in a way other than by spoken words: *talk with the hands.* **5.** To express one's thoughts in writing: *Voltaire talks about London in this text.* **6.** To parley or negotiate with someone: *Let's talk before fighting.* **7.** To gossip; spread rumours: *People will talk.* **8.** To allude to something: *What are you talking about?* **9.** To consult or confer with someone: *I'll have to talk to the others first.* **10.** To reveal information concerning oneself or others, especially under pressure: *Has the prisoner talked?* **11.** To be efficacious: *Nothing talks to them but money.* —See Synonyms at **speak.** —**talk about.** *Informal.* **1.** Used to express the opinion that the word or words immediately following are an understatement of the actual case: *Talk about stupid, he's a total idiot.* **2.** To imply as a result of what one is saying or doing: *If we decide to buy, we're talking about six years' savings gone.* —**talk at.** To address (someone) without regard to a response: *She talks at people, never to them.* —**talk big.** *Informal.* To brag. —**talk down. 1.** To address someone patronisingly or as if one were very superior. Used with *to.* **2.** To silence (a person), especially by speaking in a loud and domineering manner. **3.** To assist (an aircraft) to land by giving radio instructions. —**talk out. 1.** To discuss (a matter) exhaustively. **2.** To resolve or settle by discussion. **3.** *British.* To block (proposed legislation) by making prolonged speeches, introducing irrelevant material, or the like. —**talk over.** To consider thoroughly in conversation; discuss: *Let's talk it over.* —**talk round. 1.** To persuade: *I talked her round to my position.* **2.** To speak indirectly about (something): *talked round the subject without coming to the point.* —**talk through.** To show (someone) how to do something by going through it giving step-by-step instructions or explanations. —**talk to.** To give a reprimand to; confer with in an attempt to reform.
~*n.* **1.** An exchange of ideas or opinions; a conversation. **2.** A speech or lecture. **3.** Any hearsay, rumour, or speculation concerning something: *talk of war.* **4.** Any subject of conversation: *the talk of the town.* **5.** *Usually plural.* A conference or negotiation: *peace talks.* **6. a.** A particular manner of speech: *baby talk.* **b.** Any jargon or slang: *street talk.* **7.** Any empty speech or unnecessary discussion: *too much talk and not enough action.* [Middle English *talkien, talken,* probably frequentative formation (with *k*) from Old English *talian,* to reckon, tell, relate.]

Usage: In British English, one talks *to* someone; in American English one often talks *with* someone (*I talked with her briefly yesterday*) though *to* is also possible. *Talk with* in British English can be used only in the sense of "consult": *We talked with the senior officer.*

talk·a·tive (táwkətiv) *adj.* Liking to talk a lot; loquacious. —**talk·a·tive·ly** *adv.* —**talk·a·tive·ness** *n.*

Synonyms: *talkative, loquacious, wordy, garrulous, voluble, effusive, verbose.*

talk back *intr.v.* **1.** To make an impertinent reply: *His father slaps him when he talks back.* **2.** To make a belligerent response: *Our guns will talk back.*

talk·back (táwk-bak) *n.* A system of communication links in a television or radio studio enabling directions to be given while a programme is actually being produced.

talk·er (táwkər) *n.* A person who talks, especially a loquacious or garrulous person.

talk·ie (táwki) *n. Informal.* A cinema film with a sound track.

talk·ing book (táwking) *n.* A tape recording or record of a reading of a book, designed for use by the blind.

talking head *n.* The image of a person on a television documentary or interview who talks at length directly to the camera and is usually seated, with only the head and upper part of the body visible.

talking picture *n.* A talkie. Used especially when such films were first introduced.

talking shop *n. British Informal.* **1.** A meeting or discussion in which views are aired and policy is discussed. **2.** Any place, such as a legislative assembly, where there is much argument and discussion but little positive action.

talk·ing-to (táwking-to͞o, -to͝o) *n., pl.* **-tos.** *Informal.* A scolding, especially one given by a person in authority to a subordinate.

talk show *n. U.S.* A **chat show** *(see).*

talk·y (táwki) *adj.* **-ier, -iest.** Talkative or full of talk.

tall (tawl) *adj.* **taller, tallest. 1. a.** Having greater than average height: *a tall woman.* **b.** Having considerable height, especially in relation to width; lofty: *tall trees.* **2.** Having a specified height: *three feet tall.* **3.** *Informal.* Fanciful or exaggerated: *tall tales.* **4.** *Informal.* Exorbitant or difficult to fulfil or accomplish: *a tall order.* **5. a.** *Archaic.* Brave; courageous. **b.** *Obsolete.* Excellent; comely; fine. —See Synonyms at **high.**
~*adv.* Straight; with proud bearing: *stand tall.* [Middle English *tall,* seemly, handsome, valiant, probably from Old English *getæl,* swift, ready.]

tal·lage (tál-ij) *n.* **1.** An occasional tax levied by the Anglo-Norman kings on crown lands and royal towns. **2.** A tax levied by a feudal lord on his dependants.
~*tr.v.* **tallaged, -laging, -lages.** To levy a tax on. [Middle English *ta(i)llage,* from Old French *taillage,* "a cutting", from *taillier,* to cut, from Vulgar Latin *tāl(l)iāre* (unattested). See **tailor.**]

tall·boy (táwl-boy) *n. British.* A tall chest of drawers, often constructed in separate sections that are mounted vertically together. Compare **highboy.** [TALL + BOY; for this use of *boy,* compare **jack** (fellow, chap) in names of various tools and so on.]

Tal·linn (tál-in). *Russian* **Ta·lin.** *Formerly* **Re·vel, Re·val** (ráy-vəl). Baltic seaport, capital of Estonia. Lying on the Gulf of Finland, it was once a Hanseatic town. It remains a commercial port and a naval and military base.

tal·lith (tál-ith || ta̋al-; *Hebrew* taa-léet) *n., pl.* **tallithim** (-im || ta̋al-i-théem) or **talliths.** A fringed prayer shawl with bands of black or blue, worn especially by Orthodox Jewish men at prayer and on certain solemn occasions. [Hebrew (Mishnaic) *ṭallīth,* "cover", from Hebrew *ṭillēl,* he covered.]

tall oil (taal, tawl) *n.* An oily resinous liquid composed of a mixture of rosin acids and fatty acids obtained as a by-product in the treatment of pine pulp and used in soaps, emulsions, and lubricants. [Partial translation of German *Tallöl,* from Swedish *tallolja* : *tall,* pine, from Old Norse *thöll*†, young pine tree + *Öl,* oil.]

tal·low (tál-ō) *n.* **1.** A mixture of the whitish, tasteless, solid or hard fat obtained from parts of the bodies of cattle, sheep, or horses, and used in foodstuffs or to make candles, leather dressing, soap, and lubricants. **2.** Any of various similar fats, as from plants.
~*tr.v.* **tallowed, -lowing, -lows.** To smear or cover with tallow. [Middle English *talg, talgh, talow,* from Middle Low German *talg, talch.*] **—tal·low, tal·low·y** *adj.*

tal·low-drop (tál-ō-drop) *n.* A style of cutting a gemstone so that it is smooth and convex on one or both sides.

tal·low-wood (tál-ō-wo͝od) *n.* **1.** A large Australian eucalyptus tree, *Eucalyptus microcorys.* **2.** The hard, greasy wood of this tree.

tal·ly (tál-i) *n., pl.* **-lies. 1.** A stick on which notches are made, used, especially formerly, to keep a count or record, as of amounts paid or owing. **2. a.** The reckoning or score kept on such a stick. **b.** Any reckoning or score kept of a game, account, or the like. **3.** A mark or number of marks used in recording a number of acts or objects. **4.** A label, ticket, piece of metal, or the like used for identification or classification. **5.** Anything that is very similar or corresponds to something else; a double or counterpart. **6.** A metal plate attached to a ship's machinery and bearing instructions for its use.
~*v.* **tallied, -lying, -lies.** —*tr.* **1.** To record on a tally. **2.** To reckon or count. **3.** To label with a tally. **4.** To cause to correspond or agree. —*intr.* **1.** To be alike; agree; correspond. **2.** To keep the score or reckoning of a thing. [Middle English *taly, talye,* from Norman French *tallie,* from Medieval Latin *tal(l)ia,* from Latin *tālea,* twig, cutting, stick. See **tailor.**]

tal·ly·ho (tál-i-hō) *interj.* Used to urge hounds in fox hunting.
~*v.* **tallyhoed, -hoing, -hos.** —*tr.* To urge on (hounds) or indicate the sighting of (a fox) by shouting "tallyho". —*intr.* To shout "tallyho".
~*n., pl.* **tallyhos. 1.** The cry of "tallyho". **2.** A kind of fast coach drawn by four horses. [Probably from French *taïaut,* from Old French *thialau, taho,* cry used to urge on hounds.]

tal·ly·man (tál-i-mən) *n., pl.* **-men** (-mən, -men). **1.** A recorder or scorekeeper. **2.** *British.* A travelling salesman who sells goods on credit and collects weekly or monthly payments for them.

Tal·mi gold (tál-mi, taál-) *n.* An alloy of gold and brass, used in making jewellery. [German *Talmigold,* partial translation of French *Talmi-or,* contraction of *Tallois-demi-or,* "half gold (made by) Tallois (a Parisian)".]

Tal·mud (tál-mo͝od, -mud || taál-) *n.* The collection of ancient Rabbinic writings consisting of the Mishnah and the Gemara, constituting the basis of religious authority for traditional Judaism. It exists in two versions, the *Palestinian Talmud* and the longer *Babylonian Talmud.* [Hebrew (Mishnaic) *talmūd,* learning, instruction, from *lāmadh,* he learnt.] **—Tal·mu·dic** (tal-mo͝od-ik, -múd-, -méwd- || taal-), **Tal·mu·di·cal** *adj.* **—Tal·mud·ist** (-mo͝od-ist, -mud-) *n.*

tal·on (tál-ən) *n.* **1. a.** The claw of a bird of prey. **b.** The similar claw of a predatory animal. **2.** Anything similar to or suggestive of a claw. **3.** The part of a lock which the key presses in order to shoot the bolt. **4.** The part of the pack of cards in certain card games left on the table after the deal. **5.** *Architecture.* An ogee moulding. [Middle English, originally "heel", "hinder claw", from Old French, heel, spur, from (unattested) Vulgar Latin *tālō* (stem *tālōn-*), variant of Latin *tālus,* ankle, TALUS.]

ta·luk (taá-lo͝ok, taa-lo͝ok) *n.* In India: **1.** A subdivision of a tax district, consisting of several villages. **2.** Formerly, the hereditary estate of a family. [Urdu, estate, from Arabic.]

ta·lus¹ (táy-ləss) *n., pl.* **-li** (-lī). **1.** A tarsal bone that articulates with the tibia and fibula to form the anklebone. Also called "anklebone", "astragalus". **2.** The ankle. [New Latin, from Latin *tālus,* ankle, probably from Celtic, akin to Irish *sal*†, talon.]

talus² *n., pl.* **-luses. 1. a.** A sloping mass of debris at the base of a cliff. **b.** A **scree** *(see).* **2.** A sloping side of a rampart, fortification, or the like. [French, from Old French, probably from Latin *talūtium,* a technical term in mining in Spain, "outcrop indicating the presence of gold-bearing topsoil", from Celtic.]

tam (tam) *n.* **1.** A hat, the **tam-o'-shanter** *(see).* **2.** Variant of **tom** (a Rastafarian's hat).

TAM television audience measurement.

ta·ma·le (tə-maáli) *n.* A Mexican dish made of fried chopped meat and crushed peppers, highly seasoned, wrapped in maize husks, and steamed. [Mexican Spanish *tamal,* from Nahuatl *tamalli.*]

tam·an·du·a (támmən-do͞o-ə, -déw-, tə-mándoo-aá) *n.* A chiefly arboreal anteater, *Tamandua tetradactyla,* of tropical America, having a dense, furry coat and a prehensile tail. [Portuguese *tamanduá,* from Tupi, "ant-catcher" : *tacy,* ant + *monduar,* to catch.]

tam·a·rack (támmə-rak) *n.* A North American larch tree, *Larix laricina,* having very small cones. [Algonquian.]

tam·a·rau, ta·ma·rao (támmə-rów, -row) *n.* A small, short-horned buffalo, *Anoa mindorensis,* of the island of Mindoro in the Philippines. [Tagalog *tamaráw, timaraw.*]

tam·a·rin (támmə-rin, -raN) *n.* Any of various small, long-tailed monkeys of the family Callithricidae of tropical South America. [French, from Galibi.]

tam·a·rind (támmə-rind) *n.* **1.** A tropical Old World tree, *Tamarindus indica,* with compound leaves and red-striped yellow flowers. **2.** The fruit of this tree, consisting of a long pod with seeds embedded in an edible pulp. [Medieval Latin *tamarindus,* from Arabic *tamr hindī,* "date of India" : *tamr,* date + *hindī,* of India, from Persian *Hind,* India.] **—tam·a·rind** *adj.*

tam·a·risk (támmə-risk) *n.* Any of numerous shrubs or small trees of the genus *Tamarix,* native to Eurasia, having small, scalelike leaves and spikelike clusters of flowers; especially *T. tetrandra,* which is often grown as an ornamental for its feathery foliage. [Middle English *tamarisc, thamarike,* from Late Latin *tamariscus,* variant of Latin *tamarīx*†.]

ta·ma·sha (tə-maáshə) *n.* In India, a public display or entertainment. [Urdu, from Arabic, "a stroll".]

tam·ba·la (támbələ) *n.* A monetary unit of Malawi equal to $^{1}/_{100}$ of a kwacha. [Bantu, "cockerel".]

Tam·bo (támbō), **Oliver** (1917–93). South African politician. An exile from South Africa 1960–90, he was president of the African National Congress from 1977 and chairman from 1991.

tam·bour (tám-boor, -bawr, -bər) *n.* **1.** A drum. **2. a.** A small wooden embroidery frame consisting of two concentric hoops over which the fabric is stretched. **b.** Embroidery made on such a frame. **3.** A rolling front or top for a desk, consisting of narrow strips of wood glued side by side onto canvas. **4.** *Architecture.* Any of various types of circular structure, especially: **a.** The wall of a circular building that is surrounded with columns. **b.** The vertical part of a cupola. **5.** The sloping buttress or projection on the side of a court designed for playing real tennis or fives.
~*v.* **tamboured, -bouring, -bours.** —*tr.* To do (embroidery) on a tambour. —*intr.* To use a tambour in doing embroidery. [Middle English, from Old French, from Arabic *ṭanbūr,* alteration (by confusion with *ṭanbūr,* lute, TAMBOURA) of Persian *ṭabīr,* drum, TABOR.]

tam·bou·ra, tam·bu·ra (tum-bo͝or-ə, tam-) *n.* An unfretted, four-stringed Indian musical instrument resembling a lute, used to provide a harmonic drone. [Hindi, from Persian *ṭanbūr,* from Arabic. See also **tambour.**]

tam·bou·rin (tám-bo͞o-rin, -ráN) *n.* **1.** A long, narrow drum used in Provence. **2.** A Provençal dance in lively two-beat rhythm, accompanied by the tambourin. **3.** A piece of music composed for such a dance. [Provençal *tamborin,* diminutive of *tambor,* TAMBOUR.]

tam·bou·rine (támbə-re͞en) *n.* A musical instrument consisting of a small drumhead with jingling discs fitted into the rim, carried and shaken with one hand and struck with the other. [French *tambourin,* diminutive of TAMBOUR.]

tame (taym) *adj.* **tamer, tamest. 1.** Brought from natural wildness into a domesticated, tractable, or cultivated state. **2.** Naturally unafraid; not timid. Said of animals. **3.** Submissive; servile: *tame obedience.* **4.** Without spirit or excitement; insipid; flat: *a tame Christmas party.* **5.** Sluggish; languid; inactive: *a tame river.*
~*tr.v.* **tamed, taming, tames. 1.** To make tractable; domesticate. **2.** To subdue or curb. **3.** To soften; tone down. [Middle English *tame,* Old English *tam.*] **—tam·a·ble, tame·a·ble** *adj.* **—tame·ly** *adv.* **—tame·ness** *n.* **—tam·er** *n.*

Tam·er·lane (támmər-layn) (1336–1405). Also **Tam·bur·laine** (támbər-layn) or **Ti·mur** (ti-mo͝or). Mongol conqueror. He led his nomadic hordes from his capital at Samarkand in Central Asia to overrun vast areas of Persia, Turkey, Russia, and India.

Tam·il (tám-il, -'l) *n., pl.* **-ils** or collectively **Tamil. 1.** A member of a Dravidian people of south India and Sri Lanka. **2.** The language spoken by this people. **—Tam·il** *adj.*

Tamil Na·du (naa-do͞o). *Formerly* **Ma·dras.** State in southeast India. After Indian independence the area of the Madras Presidency was divided into new Indian states (1953–56). The Tamil-speaking area became Tamil Nadu with its capital at Madras. It is one of the most highly urbanised and industrial areas of India.

Tam·ma·ny (támməni) *n.* An organisation of the U.S. Democratic Party in New York City, founded as a fraternal society in 1789 and notorious in the 19th century for its political corruption. Also called "Tammany Hall". [From *Tammany* Hall, its meeting place, after *Tamanend,* "the affable", 17th-century Delaware chief noted for his friendliness to whites.] **—Tam·ma·ny·ism** *n.* **—Tam·ma·ny·ite** *n.*

Tammerfors. See **Tampere.**

Tam·muz, Tham·muz (tám-o͞oz, -o͞oz, taa-mo͞oz) *n.* The tenth month in the Hebrew calendar, corresponding to part of June and part of July. [Hebrew *Tammūz,* from Babylonian *Du'uzu, Duzu* (name of a god), contractions of *Dumu-zi,* "the son who rises".]

tam·my¹ (támmi) *n.* A fine, glazed, woollen cloth formerly used for linings or undergarments. [17th century : origin obscure.]

tammy² *n., pl.* **-mies.** A tam-o'-shanter.

tam-o'-shan·ter (támmə-shántər) *n.* A brimless Scottish cap, usually woollen, often having a pompom in the centre, and usually pulled down to one side. Also called "tam", "tammy". [After the hero of Robert Burns's poem *Tam o'Shanter.*]

tamp (tamp) *tr.v.* **tamped, tamping, tamps. 1.** To pack down tightly by a succession of blows. **2.** To pack clay, sand, or dirt into (a drill hole) above an explosive. [Back-formation from TAMPION.]

Tam·pax (tám-paks) *n.* A trademark for a menstrual tampon having a cardboard applicator tube.

tam·per¹ (támpər) *intr.v.* **-pered, -pering, -pers. 1.** To interfere in a harmful manner. Used with *with*: *tampering with a mechanism.* **2.** To meddle rashly or foolishly. Used with *with*: *tamper with her feelings.* **3.** To interfere or exert influence surreptitiously so as to bring about an improper state of affairs. Used with *with*: *tamper with a contract.* —See Synonyms at **interfere.** [Originally "to prepare (clay) by mixing", variant of TEMPER.] **—tam·per·er** *n.*

tamper² *n.* **1.** One that tamps; especially, a small instrument for packing down tobacco into a pipe bowl. **2.** A neutron reflector in a nuclear bomb that also delays the expansion of the exploding material, making possible a longer-lasting, more energetic, and more destructive explosion.

Tam·pe·re (támpəri; *Finnish* támpe·re). *Swedish* **Tam·mer·fors** (támmər-fawrss). The second largest city in Finland. It is a major industrial centre and has a cathedral and university.

tam·pi·on (tám-pi-ən) *n.* Also **tom·pi·on** (tóm-). A plug or cover for the muzzle of a cannon or gun to keep out dust and moisture. [Middle English *tamp(y)on,* from Old French *tampon,* cotton plug, TAMPON.]

tam·pon (tám-pon, -pən) *n.* **1.** A plug of absorbent material inserted into the vagina to absorb menstrual blood. **2.** *Medicine.* An absorbent wad inserted into a bodily cavity or wound to check a flow of blood or absorb secretions.
~*tr.v.* **tamponed, -poning, -pons.** To plug or fill with a tampon. [French, from Old French, nasalised variant of *tapon,* from Frankish *tappo* (unattested), plug.]

tam-tam (tám-tam, túm-tum) *n.* Any of a set of musical instruments resembling the gong but made of thinner metal and having a shallower rim. [Hindi *ţamţam* (imitative).]

tan (tan) *v.* **tanned, tanning, tans.** —*tr.* **1.** To convert (hide) into leather, by treating it with a tanning agent, especially one containing tannin. **2.** To make brown by exposure to ultraviolet rays, especially those of the sun. **3.** *Informal.* To thrash; beat. —*intr.* To become brown from exposure to ultraviolet rays.
~*n.* **1.** Light or moderate yellowish brown to brownish orange. **2.** The brown colour imparted to the skin by ultraviolet rays, especially those of the sun. **3. Tanbark** *(see).* **4. Tannin** *(see),* or a solution derived from it.
~*adj.* **1.** Of the colour tan. **2.** Used in or pertaining to tanning. [Middle English *tannen,* from Old English *tannian* and Old French *tanner,* both from Medieval Latin *tannāre,* from *tannum,* oak bark (used in tanning), probably from Gaulish *tanno-,* oak, from Common Celtic *tann-* (unattested).]

tan tangent.

Ta·na (ta̒anə). Also **Tsa·na** (tsa̒anə). Lake in Ethiopia. It has a surface area of approximately 3 100 square kilometres (1,197 square miles) and is 1 830 metres (6,000 feet) above sea level. It is the source of the Blue Nile.

tan·a·ger (tánnijər) *n.* Any of various small New World birds of the family Thraupidae, often having brightly coloured plumage. [New Latin *tanagra,* from Portuguese *tangará,* from Tupi : *atá,* to walk + *carâ,* around.]

Tananarive. See Antavavarivo.

tan·bark (tán-baark) *n.* **1.** The bark of various trees, especially the oak and hemlock, used as a source of tannin. **2.** Shredded bark from which the tannin has been extracted, used to cover circus arenas, racetracks, and other surfaces. Also called "tan".

tan·dem (tándəm) *n.* **1.** A two-wheeled carriage drawn by two horses harnessed one behind the other. **2.** A team of carriage horses harnessed in single file. **3.** A bicycle with two or more saddles, for two or more riders seated one behind the other. **4.** Any arrangement in which two or more persons or objects are placed one behind the other or operate in conjunction with one another: *working in tandem.*
~*adv.* One behind the other.
~*adj.* **1.** Positioned one behind the other. **2.** Working in conjunction with another or one another; cooperative. **3.** *British.* Designating, using, or pertaining to an intermediate automatic telephone exchange: *tandem dialling.* [Latin *tandem,* "exactly then", at length, finally (but jocularly taken to mean "lengthways", "one after another") : *tam,* so, so much + *-dem,* demonstrative suffix.]

Tan·doo·ri (tán-dóor-i, tun-) *n.* A north Indian method of cooking in a charcoal-fired clay oven (a *tandoor*). [Urdu *tandoor,* oven.] —**Tan·doo·ri** *adj.*

tang¹ (tang) *n.* **1.** A sharp, often acrid taste, flavour, or smell, such as that of lemon juice or onions or sea air. **2.** A distinctive quality that adds piquancy. **3.** A trace, hint, or suggestion of something. **4. a.** A sharp point, shank, tongue, or prong. **b.** A projection by which a tool, such as a chisel, sword blade, or knife, is attached to its handle or stock. In this sense, also called "shank".
~*tr.v.* **tanged, tanging, tangs.** To furnish with a tang or give a tang to. [Middle English *tange,* serpent's tongue, insect's sting, probably from Old Norse *tangi,* a sting, point.] —**tang·y** *adj.*

tang² *n.* A loud ringing or vibrating sound; a twang.
~*v.* **tanged, tanging, tangs.** —*tr.* To cause to twang or clang. —*intr.* To twang or clang. [Imitative.]

Tang (tang) *n.* Chinese dynasty (618–906 A.D.). A high cultural period, it is regarded as the golden age of Chinese poetry. Buddhism and its art forms flourished. Expansionist policies and increased trade made the capital Changan (now Xi'an) a famous cosmopolitan centre. —**Tang** *adj.*

Tan·ga·nyi·ka (táng-gən-yéekə, -gan-). Lake in east central Africa. It is situated in the Great Rift Valley, on the borders of Congo (Dem. Rep.), Burundi, Tanzania, and Zambia. Its surface area is about 33 000 square kilometres (12,738 square miles).

Tanganyika. See Tanzania, United Republic of.

tan·ge·lo (tánjə-lō) *n., pl.* **-los. 1.** A hybrid citrus tree that is a cross between certain varieties of grapefruit and tangerine. **2.** The fruit of this tree, having an acid, orange pulp. [*Tangerine* + *pomelo.*]

tan·gen·cy (tán-jən-si) *n.* Also **tan·gence** (-jənss). The condition of being tangent.

tan·gent (tánjənt) *adj.* **1.** Making contact at a single point or along a line; touching but not intersecting. **2.** Diverging from the main point; irrelevant.
~*n.* **1.** A line, curve, or surface touching but not intersecting another line, curve, or surface. **2.** *Abbr.* **tan a.** The ratio of the ordinate to the abscissa of the endpoint of an arc of a unit circle centred at the origin of a Cartesian coordinate system, the arc being of length x and measured anticlockwise from the point (1,0) if x is positive or clockwise if x is negative. **b.** The function of an acute angle in a right-angled triangle that is the ratio of the length of the side opposite the angle to the length of the side adjacent to the angle. **3.** A sudden change of course, as in thought or speech; a digression. Used chiefly in the phrase *at a tangent.* **4.** In a clavichord, a small upright brass pin at the back of a key, that strikes the string when the key is depressed and produces the sound. [New Latin *linea tangēns,* "touching line", from Latin *tangēns* (stem *tangent-*), present participle of *tangere,* to touch.]

tangent galvanometer *n. Physics.* A simple galvanometer having a small magnetic needle free to rotate in a horizontal plane and mounted at the centre on a flat vertical coil through which the current is passed.

tan·gen·tial (tan-jénsh'l) *adj.* Also **tan·gen·tal** (-jent'l). **1.** Of, pertaining to, or moving along or in the direction of a tangent. **2.** Only slightly connected; peripheral. **3.** Going off at a tangent; divergent.
—**tan·gen·ti·al·i·ty** (tan-jénshi-ál-əti) *n.* —**tan·gen·tial·ly** *adv.*

tangent plane *n.* The plane containing all the lines tangent to a specified point on a surface.

Tan·ger (toN-zháy). *English* **Tan·gier** (tan-jéer, tán-, tán-jeer) or **Tan·giers** (-z). Port on the Moroccan side of the Strait of Gibraltar. An ancient Phoenician city, it was held by the Portuguese (1471–1662) and British (1662–84). From 1923–24 it was administered as the International Zone by Britain, France, and Spain, and from 1928 also by Italy. The international status was restored after World War II, but the city was returned to Morocco in 1956.

tan·ger·ine (tánjə-réen) *n.* **1.** A variety of the widely cultivated citrus tree, *Citrus reticulata,* bearing edible fruit having an easily peeled deep-orange skin and sweet, juicy pulp. **2.** The fruit of this tree. **3.** Strong reddish orange to strong or vivid orange. [Short for *tangerine orange,* "orange of Tangier", from TANGER (from where such oranges were first imported).] —**tan·ger·ine** *adj.*

tan·gi·ble (tán-jə-b'l, -ji-) *adj.* **1. a.** Discernible by the touch; capable of being touched; palpable. **b.** Visible and capable of being valued; material; corporeal: *tangible property.* **2.** Capable of being clearly and exactly comprehended; having real substance; concrete: *tangible evidence.* —See Synonyms at **real.**
~*n.* **1.** Something palpable or concrete. **2.** *Plural. Chiefly U.S.* Material assets. [Old French *tangible,* from Late Latin *tangibilis,* from Latin *tangere,* to touch.] —**tan·gi·bil·i·ty** (-bílləti), **tan·gi·ble·ness** *n.* —**tan·gi·bly** *adv.*

tan·gle¹ (táng-g'l) *v.* **-gled, -gling, -gles.** —*tr.* **1.** To mix together or intertwine in a confused mass; snarl. **2.** To involve in hampering or awkward complications; entangle. **3.** To trap; ensnare. —*intr.* **1.** To be or become entangled. **2.** To enter into argument, dispute, or conflict. Used with *with: tangled with the law.*
~*n.* **1.** A confused, intertwined mass. **2.** A jumbled or confused state or condition. **3.** A state of bewilderment. **4.** *Informal.* An argument; an altercation. [Middle English *tangilen,* nasalised variant of *tagilen,* probably from Scandinavian, akin to Swedish dialectal *taggla†,* to entangle.] —**tang·ly** *adj.*

tangle² *n. Chiefly Scottish.* **1.** A large brown seaweed, *Laminaria digitata,* found on the lower areas of a shore. **2.** Any large brown seaweed; oarweed. [Scottish, probably from Old Norse *thöngull.*]

tan·gled (táng-g'ld) *adj.* Complicated in a random or confused way.

tan·go (táng-gō) *n., pl.* **-gos. 1.** A Latin-American ballroom dance in duple time, characterised by long gliding steps and sudden dramatic poses. **2.** The music for this dance.
~*intr.v.* **tangoed, -going, -gos.** To dance the tango. [American Spanish, originally an Afro-American drum dance, possibly of Niger-Congo origin.]

tan·gram (táng-gram ‖ tán-, -grəm) *n.* A Chinese puzzle consisting of a square cut into five triangles, a square, and a rhomboid, to be reassembled into different figures. [Possibly Chinese *táng,* TANG (Chinese dynasty, hence "the Chinese") + -GRAM.]

tanh (than, tansh). hyperbolic tangent.

tan·ist (tán-ist, tháwn-) *n.* Among the ancient Celts, the heir apparent to the chief, elected during the chief's lifetime. [Irish Gaelic *tānaiste,* "second person", from Old Irish *tānaise†,* second, next.]

tan·ist·ry (tán-istri, tháwn-) *n.* The system of electing a tanist.

tank (tangk) *n.* **1.** A large, often metallic container for liquids or gases. **2.** A large, usually manmade, reservoir or cistern, as for drinking water or irrigation; especially, any of a kind common in India. **3.** *Military.* A powerful, turreted, heavily armoured combat vehicle that is mounted with cannon and guns and has caterpillar treads to traverse rough terrain. **4.** *U.S. Slang.* A jail or jail cell.
~*tr.v.* **tanked, tanking, tanks.** To place, store, or process in a tank.
—**tank up.** *Informal.* **1.** To fill up a vehicle with petrol. **2.** *Slang.* **a.** To drink to the point of drunkenness. **b.** To cause to tank up. [Perhaps from Gujarati *tānkh,* pond, cistern, from Sanskrit *taḍāga,* pond, from Dravidian. *Tank* (military vehicle) was originally a British code name, from its resemblance to a benzene tank.]

tan·ka¹, thang·ka (táng-kə, taʹangkə) *n.* A Tibetan religious painting, usually on silk, mounted on a piece of rich material in the form of a hanging scroll. [Tibetan *thaṅka.*]

tanka² *n.* A Japanese verse form in five lines, the first and third composed of five syllables and the rest of seven. [Japanese, "short poem", from Chinese : *duǎn,* short + *ge,* song, poem.]

Tan·ka (tángkə, taʹangkə) *n., pl.* **-kas** or collectively **Tanka.** *Often* *small* t. A member of a people in southern China who live on small boats, clustered in colonies. [Cantonese *tan ka* : *tan*, tribal name represented by the character *dan*, "egg" + *ka*, variant of Mandarin Chinese *jia*, family, people.]

tank·age (tángkij) *n.* **1.** The capacity or contents of a tank or tanks. **2.** The act or process of putting or storing in a tank. **3.** The fee for such storage. **4.** Animal residues left after rendering fat in a slaughterhouse and used for fertiliser or feed.

tank·ard (tángkərd) *n.* **1.** A large drinking cup having a single handle and often a hinged cover; especially, a tall pewter or silver mug. **2.** The amount of liquid contained in a tankard. [Middle English *tankard*, probably related to Middle Dutch *tanckaert†*.]

tank destroyer *n.* A high-speed armoured vehicle equipped with antitank guns.

tanked (tangkt) *adj.* Also **tanked up**. *Slang.* Drunk.

tank engine *n.* A steam locomotive in which the water is carried in tanks mounted on the boiler. It has two rectangular tanks mounted each side (*side tank*) or a single tank around the boiler (*saddle tank*). Also called "tanker", "tank locomotive".

tank·er (tángkər) *n.* **1.** A ship, aeroplane, goods vehicle, railway wagon or other means of transport used to carry liquids, such as oil, in bulk. **2.** A tank engine.

tank farming *n.* The cultivation of plants in tanks of water without soil.

tank top *n.* A sleeveless, tightfitting, usually knitted upper garment with a low neck, worn by women or men over a blouse or shirt.

tank wagon *n.* A railway wagon with a tank for carrying liquids in bulk. Also called "tanker".

tan·nage (tánnij) *n.* **1.** The act, process, or skill of tanning. **2.** Something tanned.

tan·ner¹ (tánnər) *n.* A person who tans hides.

tanner² *n.* British Slang. A sixpenny piece (half a shilling). Not in current usage. [19th century : origin obscure.]

tan·ner·y (tánnəri) *n., pl.* **-ies**. A place where hides are tanned.

Tann·häu·ser (tán-hoyzər). In German legend, a minstrel knight who after having spent a time of revelry with Venus, the goddess of love, sought absolution from the Pope but was refused.

tan·nic (tánnik) *adj.* Pertaining to or obtained from tannin.

tannic acid *n.* A lustrous yellowish to light brown amorphous, powdered, flaked, or spongy mass having the approximate composition $C_{76}H_{52}O_{46}$, derived from the bark and fruit of many plants and used in tanning, as a mordant to fix dyes, to clarify wine and beer, and as an astringent and styptic. Also called "tannin".

tan·nin (tánnin) *n.* **1.** Tannic acid. **2.** Any of various chemically different substances capable of promoting tanning. Also called "tan". [French *tanin*, from *tanner*, to TAN.]

Tan·noy (tánnoy) *n.* A trademark for a public-address system.

Ta·no·an (taánō-ən) *n.* A language family of several American Indian peoples of New Mexico and Arizona. —**Ta·no·an** *adj.*

tanrec. Variant of **tenrec**.

tan·sy (tánzi) *n., pl.* **-sies**. Any of several plants of the genus *Tanacetum*; especially, *T. vulgare*, native to the Old World, having clusters of button-like yellow flowers and pungent, aromatic juice sometimes used medicinally and as a flavouring. [Middle English, from Old French *tanesie*, perhaps from Medieval Latin *athanasia*, an elixir of life, from Greek *athanasia*, immortality : *a-*, not, without + *thanatos*, death.]

tan·tal·ic (tan-tál-ik) *adj.* Of, pertaining to, or containing the element tantalum.

tan·ta·lise, tan·ta·lize (tántə-līz) *tr.v.* **-lised, -lising, -lises**. To tease or torment by or as if by exposing to view but keeping out of reach something that is much desired. [From TANTALUS.] —**tan·ta·li·sa·tion** (-lī-záysh'n) *n.* —**tan·ta·lis·er** *n.* —**tan·ta·lis·ing·ly** *adv.*

tan·ta·lite (tántə-līt) *n.* A black to red-brown mineral, essentially $(Fe,Mn)(Ta,Nb)_2O_6$, distinguished from columbite by the predominance of tantalum over niobium and used as an ore of both elements. [Swedish *tantalit*, from New Latin TANTALUM.]

tan·ta·lous (tántə-ləss) *adj. Chemistry.* Of or containing trivalent tantalum. [TANTAL(UM) + -OUS.]

tan·ta·lum (tántələm) *n. Symbol* **Ta** A very hard, heavy grey metallic element that is exceptionally resistant to chemical attack below 150°C. It is used to make light-bulb filaments, electrolytic capacitors, lightning conductors, nuclear reactor parts, and some surgical instruments. Atomic number 73, atomic weight 180.948, melting point 2 996°C, boiling point 5 425°C, relative density 16.6, valencies 2, 3, 4, 5. [New Latin, after TANTALUS; when immersed in acid it is unaltered, like Tantalus standing in the water.]

tan·ta·lus (tántələss) *n.* A stand in which decanters are displayed locked up. [After TANTALUS.]

Tan·ta·lus (tántələss). *Greek Mythology.* A king who for his crimes was condemned in Hades to stand in water that receded when he tried to drink it, and with fruit hanging above him that receded when he reached for it. [Greek *Tantalos*, "bearer", "sufferer".]

tan·ta·mount (tántə-mownt ‖ *West Indies also* -múngt) *adj.* Equivalent in effect or value. Used after the noun with *to*. [Originally a verb, to "be equal to", from Anglo-French *tant amunter*, to amount to so much : Old French *tant*, so much, from Latin *tantus*, from *tam*, so + *amo(u)nter*, to AMOUNT.]

tan·ta·ra (tántə-rə, -ráə, tan·ta´arə ‖ *U.S. also* -tárrə) *n.* **1.** A fanfare of a trumpet or horn. **2.** A sound resembling such a fanfare. [Latin *taratantara* (imitative).]

tan·tiv·y (tan-tívvi) *adv.* At full gallop or at top speed. —*n., pl.* **tantivies. 1.** A blast on a horn. **2.** A fast and furious gallop; top speed. [Perhaps imitative of galloping horses.]

tant mieux (tón m-yér, -yó) *adv.* French. So much the better.

tan·to (tán-tō ‖ taán-) *adv. Music.* Too much; to an excess. Used as part of a direction: *allegro non tanto*. [Italian.]

tant pis (tón pée) *adv.* French. So much the worse.

tan·tra (tán-trə, tún-) *n. Sometimes capital* **T**. Any of a comparatively recent class of Hindu or Buddhist religious writings, in Sanskrit, concerned with mysticism and magic. [Sanskrit, loom, warp, hence principle, doctrine, from *tanōti*, he stretches or weaves.]

tan·trum (tántrəm) *n.* A fit of bad temper, especially when childish or petulant. [18th century : origin obscure.]

tan·yard (tán-yaard) *n.* A tannery.

Tan·za·ni·a, United Republic of (tánzə-neér, -neé-ə). Commonwealth country in East Africa formed by the union of Tanganyika and Zanzibar in 1964. The mainland formed part of German East Africa until World War I, after which it was administered by the British until its independence in 1961. The sultanate of Zanzibar (and Pemba), a British protectorate from 1890, gained its independence in 1963. Tanzania is mostly plateau, broken by the Great Rift Valley, and mountain areas, including Mount Kilimanjaro. More than 85 per cent of the people living as subsistence cultivators or herders of cattle. Cotton, coffee, cloves, sisal, and diamonds dominate its exports. However, under Dr. Julius Nyerere, president 1962-85, off-shore natural gas was found, manufacturing and tourism were expanded, and the TanZam railway (opened 1975) to Dar es Salaam, opened up the south's coal and iron deposits. Area, 945 087 square kilometres (364,804 square miles). Population, 27,829,000. Capital, Dodoma.

tan·zan·ite (tánzə-nīt) *n.* A hydrated calcium aluminium silicate mineral, exhibiting blue, violet, or greenish coloration, used as a gem. [TANZAN(IA) + -ITE.]

Tao, Dao (tow, dow, taá-ō, daá-ō) *n.* In the philosophy of Taoism: **1.** The universal force that produces harmony in nature. **2.** The way or course in all aspects of life that is the most effective and least conspicuous, and is in harmony with the spirit of nature and the universe. [Chinese *dào*, way.]

Taoi·seach (tée-shə, thée-, -shək, -shəkh) *n.* The prime minister of the Republic of Ireland. [Irish, leader.]

Tao·ism, Dao·ism (tów-iz'm, dów-, *also* taá-ō-, daá-ō-) *n.* **1.** A principal philosophy and system of religion of China founded upon the teachings of Lao-tse, thought to have lived in the sixth century B.C., and based upon the concept of Tao, seeking to achieve practical and spiritual harmony with the universe. **2.** A more recent, popular version of Taoism, incorporating the use of charms and magic. —**Tao·ist** *adj. & n.* —**Tao·is·tic** (-istik) *adj.*

tap¹ (tap) *v.* **tapped, tapping, taps.** —*tr.* **1.** To strike gently but audibly, and usually repeatedly. **2.** To give a light rap with: *tap a pencil.* **3.** To produce with a succession of light blows. **4.** *Chiefly U.S.* To reinforce or repair (shoe heels or toes) by attaching metal taps or a layer of leather or rubber. —*intr.* **1.** To deliver a gentle, light blow or blows. **2.** To walk making light clicks. —*n.* **1. a.** A gentle but audible blow. **b.** The sound made by it. **2.** A metal plate attached to the toe or heel of a shoe, as for tapdancing. [Middle English, from Old French *taper*, from Germanic.]

tap² *n.* **1.** A device consisting of a valve and spout used to regulate delivery of a fluid at the end of a pipe. **2.** A plug for a bunghole, as in a cask; a spigot. **3. a.** Alcoholic drink drawn from a tap. **b.** Alcoholic drink of a particular brew, cask, or quality. **4.** *Surgery.* The removal of bodily fluid: *a spinal tap.* **5.** A tool for cutting an internal screw thread. Compare **die. 6.** A connection made between two points of an electric circuit, used, for example, to provide an intermediate potential. **7.** A concealed listening or recording device fitted to a telephone line or other communications system. Also called "wiretap". **8.** *British.* A **taproom** *(see).* **—on tap. 1.** On draught; tapped from the cask or keg. Said especially of beer. **2.** *Informal.* Available for immediate use; ready.

~tr.v. **tapped, tapping, taps. 1.** To furnish (a cask, for example) with a spigot or tap. **2.** To pierce in order to draw off liquid: *tap a rubber tree.* **3. a.** To draw off (liquid) by tapping. **b.** To extract or exploit as if by tapping: *tapped every possible source of energy.* **4.** *Surgery.* To withdraw fluid from (a bodily cavity). **5.** To make a connection with or open outlets from: *tap a water main.* **6. a.** To fit an electronic tap to (a telephone line, for example). **b.** To listen to or record (a telephone conversation, for example) by means of a tap. **7.** To make a connection in (an electric circuit) so as to draw off an intermediate potential or current. **8.** To cut screw threads in (a collar, socket, or other fitting). **9.** *Slang.* To ask (a person) for money. [Middle English *tappe,* Old English *tæppa.*] **—tap·per** *n.*

ta·pa (taápə) *n.* **1.** The inner bark of the **paper mulberry** *(see).* **2.** A paper-like cloth made in the Pacific islands by pounding this or similar bark. [Marquesan and Tahitian.]

ta·pas (tápəs, taá-paas) *pl. n.* Spanish hot or cold savoury snacks, typically served with drinks. Also used adjectivally: *a tapas bar.* [Spanish, "lids", "covers", from the early custom of presenting the drinks in glasses with their tops covered by such *tapas.*]

tap dance *n.* A dance in which the rhythm is tapped out by the heels and toes in rapid, often intricate steps, the sound emphasised by taps on the dancer's shoes. **—tap-dance** (táp-daanss ‖ -danss) *intr.v.* **—tap dancer** *n.*

tape (tayp) *n.* **1.** A narrow strip of strong woven fabric, such as that used in sewing or bookbinding. **2.** Any continuous narrow, flexible strip of cloth, metal, paper, or plastic, such as adhesive tape, magnetic tape, or ticker tape. **3.** A string stretched across the finishing line of a racetrack to be broken by the winner. **4.** A tape recording. **5.** A tape cartridge.

~v. **taped, taping, tapes.** *—tr.* **1. a.** To fasten, secure, strengthen, or wrap with tape. **b.** To bind together (the sections of a book) by applying strips of tape to. **2.** To measure with a tape measure. **3.** To record (sounds or pictures) on magnetic tape. **—get** or **have (someone** or **something) taped.** *Chiefly British Informal.* To understand thoroughly the mind or workings of; have fully summed up. *—intr.* To make a recording on magnetic tape. [Middle English *tap(p)e,* Old English *tæppa, tæppe.*]

tape cartridge *n.* **1.** A cartridge containing an endless loop of magnetic tape and designed for automatic use on insertion into a compatible sound or video recorder, or a computer system. Also called "tape". **2.** A similar but usually smaller cartridge containing unlooped tape. Also called "cassette", "tape".

tape deck *n.* **1.** A tape recorder and player having no built-in amplifiers or speakers, used as a component in a high-fidelity sound system. **2.** A system of spools, magnetic tape, and a read-write head, used as a computer storage system.

tape grass *n.* An aquatic plant, *Vallisneria spiralis,* having long, grasslike, submerged leaves. Also called "eelgrass".

tape-loop (táyp-lo͝op) *n.* A magnetic tape recording joined in an endless loop so that it constantly replays itself. Also called "loop".

tape machine *n. Chiefly British.* A telegraphic instrument that receives and records stock-market quotations on a paper tape. Also *U.S.* "ticker".

tape measure *n.* A tape of cloth, paper, or steel marked off in a linear scale, as inches or centimetres, used for taking measurements. Also *U.S.* "tapeline".

ta·per (táypər) *n.* **1.** A small or very slender candle. **2.** A long wax-coated wick used to light candles or gas lamps. **3.** Something that gives off a feeble light. **4.** A gradual decrease in thickness or width of an elongated object.

~v. **tapered, -pering, -pers.** *—intr.* **1.** To become gradually narrower or thinner towards one end. **2.** To lessen gradually, as in intensity or significance; diminish; slacken and finally stop. Used with *off.* *—tr.* To cause to taper.

~adj. Gradually decreasing in size towards a point; tapering. [Middle English, from Old English *tapor, tapur,* probably altered from *papur* (unattested), from Latin *papȳrus,* papyrus, wick made of papyrus.] **—ta·per·ing·ly** *adv.*

tape-re·cord (táyp-ri-kawrd, -rə-) *tr.v.* **-corded, -cording, -cords.** To record on magnetic tape.

tape recorder *n.* An apparatus used to record sound on magnetic tape and, usually, to play back sound so recorded.

tape recording *n.* **1. a.** Magnetised tape on which sound has been recorded. **b.** The sound recorded on a magnetic tape. Also called "tape". **2.** The act of recording on magnetic tape.

tap·es·try (táppistri) *n., pl.* **-tries. 1.** A heavy textile fabric having a varicoloured, often pictorial, design woven across the warp, used for wall hangings or furniture coverings, for example. **2.** A textile imitating this. **3.** Anything suggestive of tapestry in its complexity, richness, or variety: *"the fair tapestry of human life"* (Thomas Carlyle). [Middle English *tapstery,* altered from *tapissery, tapecery,* from Old French *tapisserie,* from *tapisser,* to cover with carpet, from *tapis, tapiz,* carpet, from Medieval Greek *tapition,* variant of Greek *tapētion,* diminutive of *tapēs,* carpet.] **—tap·es·tried** *adj.*

ta·pe·tum (tə-peé-təm) *n., pl.* **-ta** (-tə). **1.** *Botany.* A layer of nutritive cells within the sporangium of ferns and related plants or within the anther of flowering plants. **2.** *Anatomy.* A membranous reflecting layer or region in the choroid coat of the eye of certain, notably nocturnal, animals. **3.** A stratum of fibres of the corpus callosum. [New Latin, from Medieval Latin, carpet, from Latin *tapēte,* from Greek *tapēs.* See **tapestry.**] **—ta·pe·tal** *adj.*

tape·worm (táyp-wurm) *n.* Any of various ribbon-like, often very long, segmented flatworms of the class Cestoda, that are parasitic in the intestines of vertebrates, including humans.

tap·i·o·ca (táppi-ṓkə) *n.* A beady starch obtained from the root of the cassava, used for puddings and as a thickening agent in cooking. [Portuguese and Spanish, from Tupi *tipioca,* "residue".]

ta·pir (táy-pər, -peer ‖ tə-peér) *n.* Any ungulate mammal of the genus *Tapirus,* of tropical America or southern Asia, having a heavy body, short legs, and a fleshy proboscis. [Guarani *tapiira.*]

tap·is (táp-ee, -i) *n. Archaic.* A tapestry or similar cloth used as a wall hanging, table cover, or rug. **—on the tapis.** Being discussed or considered. [Middle English, a type of cloth, from Old French *tapiz,* from Vulgar Latin *tappetium* (unattested), from Late Latin, from Greek *tapētion,* diminutive of *tapēs* (stem *tapēt-*), tapestry.]

tap·pet (táppit) *n.* A lever or projecting arm that moves or is moved by contact with another part, usually to communicate a certain motion, as between a driving mechanism and a valve. [From TAP (to strike lightly).]

tap·pit-hen (táppit-hen) *n. Scottish.* **1.** A crested hen. **2.** A large mug with a knobbed lid. [Scottish *tappit,* tufted, crested, from *tap,* dialectal variant of TOP.]

tap·room (táp-ro͞om, -ro͝om) *n.* A bar, as in a hotel or pub.

tap·root (táp-ro͞ot ‖ -ro͝ot) *n. Botany.* The main root of certain plants, usually stouter than the lateral roots and growing straight downwards from the stem.

taps (taps) *n. Used with a singular verb.* In the U.S. armed forces, a bugle call or a drum signal sounded at night as an order to put out lights, and also sounded at military funerals and memorial services. [From TAP (light blow, drumbeat).]

ta·pu (taá-po͞o) *adj. N.Z.* Taboo. [Maori.] **—ta·pu** *n.*

Ta·pu·yan (tə-po͞o-yən, taa-) *n.* A South American Indian family of languages, now spoken only in remote regions of Brazil.

~adj. Of or pertaining to this family of languages or its speakers.

tap water *n.* Water containing dissolved salts as obtained from the normal domestic supply, as distinguished from distilled or deionised water.

tar¹ (tar) *n.* **1.** A dark, oily, viscid mixture, consisting mainly of hydrocarbons, produced by the destructive distillation of organic substances such as wood, coal, or peat. **2. Coal tar** *(see).*

~tr.v. **tarred, tarring, tars.** To coat with tar. **—tar and feather.** To punish a person by covering first with tar and then with feathers. [Middle English *taar, terr,* Old English *te(o)ru.*] **—tar·ry** (taári) *adj.*

tar² *n. Informal.* A sailor. [Short for TARPAULIN.]

Tarabalus al-Gharb. See **Tripoli.**

Tar·a·ca·hi·tian (tárrəkə-heésh'n) *adj.* Of or pertaining to a language family of the Uto-Aztecan group. [From *Tarahumara* and *Cahita,* names of two peoples in Mexico.]

taradiddle. Variant of **tarradiddle.**

ta·ra·ma·sa·la·ta (tə-raáma-sə-laátə, -rámmə-, tárrəmə-) *n.* A pale creamy paste made from the dried, salted, and pressed roe of mullet or cod, seasoned with lemon juice, and served as an hors-d'oeuvre. [Modern Greek : *taramas,* cod's roe + *salata,* SALAD.]

tar·an·tel·la (tárrən-téllə) *n.* **1.** A lively, whirling southern Italian dance once thought to be a remedy for tarantism. **2.** The music for this dance, in $^6/_8$ time. [Italian, diminutive formed from *Taranto,* seaport in south Italy, where tarantism was common.]

tar·an·tism (tárrənt-iz'm) *n.* A malady characterised by an uncontrollable urge to dance, epidemic in southern Italy from the 15th to the 17th century and believed to result from the bite of the tarantula. [New Latin *tarantismus,* after *Taranto.* See **tarantella.**]

ta·ran·tu·la (tə-rántew-lə) *n., pl.* **-las** or **-lae** (-lee). **1.** Any of various large, hairy, chiefly tropical spiders of the family Theraphosidae, capable of inflicting a painful but not seriously poisonous bite. **2.** A wolf spider, *Lycosa tarentula,* of southern Europe, once thought to cause tarantism. [Medieval Latin *tarantula,* from Italian *tarantola,* from *Taranto* (see **tarantella**), where it is common.]

ta·rax·a·cum (tə-ráksəkəm) *n.* **1.** Any plant of the genus *Taraxacum,* which includes the common dandelion, *T. officinale.* **2.** The root of any of these plants, the latex of which is used as a tonic and mild laxative. [Medieval Latin, from Arabic *tarakhshaqūq,* from Persian *talkh,* bitter + *chaqūq,* purslane.]

tar·boosh, tar·bush (taar-bo͞osh) *n.* A brimless, usually red, felt cap with a silk tassel, worn by Muslim men, either by itself or as the base of a turban. [Egyptian Arabic *ṭarbush,* "sweating cap" : Turkish *ter,* sweat + Persian *pūshidān*†, to cover.]

Tar·de·noi·si·an (tárdə-nóyzi-ən) *adj.* Of, pertaining to, or designating a mesolithic culture characterised by the use of small flint tools. [After *Tardenois,* France, where the tools were found.]

tar·di·grade (tárdi-grayd) *n.* Any of various minute, slow-moving arthropods of the class Tardigrada, having eight legs and living in water or damp moss. Also called "water bear".

~adj. **1.** Of or belonging to the Tardigrada. **2.** Slow in thought or action; sluggish. [New Latin *Tardigrada,* from Latin *tardigradus,* slow-moving : *tardus,* slow (see **tardy**) + -GRADE.]

tar·dy (tárdi) *adj.* **-dier, -diest. 1. a.** Occurring or arriving later than expected or scheduled; late. **b.** Acting more slowly than expected, as through reluctance; dilatory. **2.** Moving or progressing slowly; sluggish. [Middle English *tardif, tardive,* slow, from Old French, from Common Romance *tardīvus* (unattested), from Latin *tardus*†, slow.] **—tar·di·ly** *adv.* **—tar·di·ness** *n.*

tar·dy·on (tárdi-on) *n.* An elementary particle that travels more slowly than the speed of light; a normal particle, as opposed to a tachyon. [Latin *tardus,* slow + -ON, after TACHYON.]

tare[1] (tair) *n.* **1.** Any of various small vetches of the genus *Vicia,* such as *V. hirsuta.* **2.** Any of several other weedy plants that grow in cornfields. **3.** The seed of any of these weeds. **4.** *Plural.* Noxious elements, likened to weeds growing among wheat. By allusion to Matthew 13:25: *"his enemy came and sowed tares among the wheat."* [Middle English *tare*†, seed of the vetch.]

tare[2] *n.* **1.** *Abbr.* **t.** The weight of a container or wrapper that is deducted from the gross weight to obtain net weight. **2.** A deduction from gross weight made to allow for the weight of a container. **3.** *Chemistry.* A counterbalance, especially an empty vessel used to counterbalance the weight of a similar container. **4.** The weight of a motor vehicle, especially a lorry, without a load, passengers, or fuel. ~*tr.v.* **tared, taring, tares.** To determine, allow for, or indicate the tare of (a container). [Middle English, from Old French, waste, deficiency, from Medieval Latin *tara,* from Arabic *ṭarḥah,* thing thrown away, from *ṭaraḥa,* to reject, throw.]

targe (tarj) *n. Archaic.* A light shield or buckler. [Middle English, from Old French. See **target.**]

tar·get (tárgit) *n.* **1.** An object with a marked surface that is shot at to test accuracy, such as a padded disc with coloured concentric circles for use in rifle or archery practice. Also used adjectivally: *target practice.* **2.** Anything aimed or fired at. **3. a.** An object of criticism or attack. **b.** Something viewed as an object to be acted on with the aim of transforming it. **4.** A desired end; a goal: *a target of £50.* Also used adjectivally: *a target figure.* **5.** A joint consisting of the neck and breast of a lamb. **6.** The sliding sight on a surveyor's levelling rod. **7.** A small, round shield, especially one worn on the arm in medieval times. **8. a.** A structure in a camera tube with a storage surface that is scanned by an electron beam to generate a signal output current similar to the charge-density pattern stored on the surface. **b.** A usually metal part in an X-ray tube on which a beam of electrons is focused and from which X rays are emitted. ~*tr.v.* **targeted, -geting, -gets. 1.** To have as a target. **2.** To make a target of. [Middle English, from Old French *targette,* diminutive of *targe,* light shield, from Frankish *targa* (unattested).]

target language *n.* The language into which something such as a text or document is translated. Also called "object language". Compare **source language.**

Tar·gum (tár-gəm, -gŏŏm, -gōōm, taar-gŏŏm) *n., pl.* **-gums** or **Tar·gumim** (tár-gōō-mēem). Any of several Aramaic translations or paraphrasings of the Old Testament. [Mishnaic Hebrew *targūm,* translation, interpretation, from Hebrew *tirgēm,* he interpreted.] —**Tar·gum·ic** (-gŏŏmik), **Tar·gum·i·cal** *adj.* —**Tar·gum·ist** *n.*

tar·iff (tárrif) *n.* **1.** A list or system of duties or taxes imposed by a government on imported, or sometimes exported, goods, levied in order to raise revenue and, often, to protect indigenous producers. **2.** A duty or tax in such a system. **3.** Any schedule of prices, fares, or fees, especially in a bar, hotel or restaurant. **4.** *British.* **a.** A schedule of prison sentences for various offences. **b.** A prison sentence taken from a tariff.
~*tr.v.* **tariffed, -iffing, -iffs. 1.** To fix a duty or price on, according to a tariff. **2.** To fix a tariff on or draw up a tariff for. [French *tarif,* from Italian *tariffa* and Spanish *tarifa,* from Turkish *ta'rifa,* from Arabic *ta'rīf,* "information", "notification", from *'arafa,* to notify.]

tar·la·tan (tárlətən) *n.* A thin, stiffly starched open-weave muslin. [French *tarlatane,* perhaps from Portuguese *tarlatana,* irregular variant of *tiritana,* from French *tiretaine,* linsey-woolsey, TARTAN.]

tar·mac (tár-mak) *n.* **1.** *Capital* **T.** A trademark for a bituminous substance used as a binder in paving. **2.** An area paved with this substance, especially the area of an airport where the aircraft land and take off. **3.** A tarmacadam road or pavement. [Shortening of TARMACADAM.] —**tar·mac** *adj.*

tar·mac·ad·am (tármə-káddəm) *n.* A hard flat surface, as for a road or pavement, consisting of layers of crushed stone with a tar binder that is rolled until smooth. [TAR + MACADAM.]

tarn (tarn) *n.* A small mountain lake, especially one in a cirque. [Middle English *terne, tarne,* from Old Norse *tjörn, tjarn*†.]

tar·na·tion (taar-náysh'n) *interj. U.S.* Damnation. Used euphemistically.

tar·nish (tárnish) *v.* **-nished, -nishing, -nishes.** —*tr.* **1.** To dull the lustre of; discolour, especially by exposure to air or dirt. **2.** To detract from or spoil; taint. —*intr.* **1.** To lose lustre; become dull or discoloured. **2.** To become spoiled or tainted.
~*n.* **1.** The condition of being tarnished or tainted. **2.** Something that tarnishes; a stain or film that dulls or discolours. [French *ternir* (present stem *terniss-*), from Germanic *tarnjan* (unattested).] —**tar·nish·a·ble** *adj.*

ta·ro (taárō || *U.S. also* tárrō) *n., pl.* **-ros. 1.** A widely cultivated tropical plant, *Colocasia esculenta,* having broad leaves and a large, starchy, edible rootstock. **2.** The rootstock of this plant. Also called "cocoyam", "dasheen", "eddoe". [Tahitian and Maori.]

tar·ok, tar·oc (tárrək) *n.* A card game developed in Italy in the 14th century, originally played with the full pack of 78 tarot cards. Also called "tarot", "tarots". [Italian *tarocchi,* plural of *tarocco,* TAROT.]

tar·ot (tárrō) *n.* **1.** Any of a set of 78 playing cards consisting of the major and the minor **arcana** (*see*), the former consisting of a joker plus 21 cards depicting vices, virtues, and elemental forces, and the latter consisting of 56 ordinary cards split into 4 suits. The major arcana is used as trumps in the game of tarok and by itself or with some or all of the minor arcana in fortunetelling. **2.** *Usually plural.* Tarok. [French, from Italian *tarocco*†.]

tar·pan (tár-pan) *n.* An extinct wild horse, *Equus caballus,* once common in Europe. [Kirghiz.]

tar·pa·per (tár-paypər) *n.* Heavy paper impregnated or coated with tar, used as a waterproof protective material in building.

tar·pau·lin (tár-páwlin, taar- || *chiefly U.S.* tárpəlin) *n.* **1.** Waterproof canvas used to cover and protect things from moisture. **2.** A sheet of this material. **3. a.** A sailor's hat made of this fabric. **b.** *Archaic.* A sailor. [Earlier *tarpawling* : perhaps TAR + *-pawling,* covering, from PALL (cover).]

tar·pon (tárpən) *n., pl.* **tarpon** or **-pons.** Either of two fish of the genus *Megalops,* especially, a large, silvery game fish, *Megalops atlantica,* of Atlantic coastal waters. [Dutch *tarpoen*†.]

tar·ra·did·dle, tar·a·did·dle (tárrə-didd'l || -dídd'l) *n. Informal.* **1.** A petty falsehood; a fib. **2.** Absurd or pretentious twaddle; nonsense. [18th century: perhaps akin to DIDDLE.]

tar·ra·gon (tárrə-gən || *chiefly U.S.* -gon) *n.* **1.** An aromatic herb, *Artemisia dracunculus,* native to Eurasia. **2.** The leaves of this plant, used as seasoning. [Medieval Latin *tragonia, tarchon,* from Medieval Greek *tarkhōn,* from Arabic *ṭarkhūn,* perhaps "dragon wort", from Greek *drakontion,* adderwort, from *drakōn,* DRAGON.]

tar·ry (tárri) *v.* **-ried, -rying, -ries.** —*intr.* **1.** To delay or be late in going, coming, or acting. **2.** To wait; linger. **3.** To remain or stay temporarily; sojourn. —*tr. Archaic.* To await. —See Synonyms at **stay.** [Middle English *tarien*†.] —**tar·ri·ance** *n. Archaic.* —**tar·ri·er** *n.*

tar·sal (társs'l) *adj.* **1.** Of, pertaining to, or situated near the tarsus of the foot. **2.** Of or pertaining to the tarsus of the eyelid.
~*n.* Any of the seven small bones forming the posterior part of the skeleton of the foot. Also called "tarsale". [New Latin *tarsālis,* from TARSUS.]

tarsal gland *n.* Any of the small sebaceous glands situated below the conjunctiva of the eyelids.

tar·seal (tár-seel) *tr.v.* **-sealed, -sealing, -seals.** *Australian & N.Z.* To surface (a road) with asphalt.
~*n. N.Z.* The surface of a tarsealed road. [TAR + SEAL.]

tar·si·er (tár-si-ər, -ay) *n.* Any of several small nocturnal primates of the genus *Tarsius,* of the Philippines and Indonesia, having large, round eyes and a long tail. [French, from *tarse,* ankle (from its elongated ankles), from New Latin *tarsus,* TARSUS.]

tar·so·met·a·tar·sus (tár-sō-méttə-tár-səss) *n., pl.* **-si** (-sī). A compound bone between the tibia and the toes of a bird's leg, formed by fusion of the tarsal and metatarsal bones. Also called "tarsus". [TARS(US) + METATARSUS.]

tar·sus (tár-səss) *n., pl.* **-si** (-sī). **1. a.** The section of the vertebrate foot between the leg and the metatarsus. **b.** The seven bones making up this section. **2.** A fibrous plate that supports and shapes the edge of the eyelid. **3.** *Zoology.* **a.** The tarsometatarsus. **b.** The distal segmented structure on the leg of an insect or an arachnid. [New Latin, from Greek *tarsos,* frame of wickerwork, (hence) flat surface, sole of the foot, ankle.]

tart[1] (tart) *adj.* **tarter, tartest. 1.** Having a sharp, pungent taste; sour. **2.** Sharp or bitter in tone or meaning; cutting. [Middle English *tart,* Old English *teart,* sharp, severe.] —**tart·ly** *adv.* —**tart·ness** *n.*

tart[2] *n.* **1.** *Chiefly British.* **a.** A pastry case having no top crust, with a usually sweet filling, such as fruit, jam, or custard. **b.** A covered pastry case with a fruit filling; a fruit pie. **2.** *Chiefly U.S.* A small pie for an individual serving, usually without a top crust, having a sweet filling. **3.** *Informal.* A promiscuous woman or prostitute, especially one dressed in a flashy, gaudy, or provocative manner. —**tart up. 1.** To improve the appearance of or redecorate, especially in a cheap, flashy, or gaudy manner. **2.** To dress (oneself) up and put on make-up, especially so as to look sexy and provocative. [Middle English *tarte,* from Old French, variant (influenced by Medieval Latin *tartarum,* TARTAR) of *torte,* from Latin *torta,* round bread, "twisted", from *torquēre,* to turn, twist.]

tar·tan[1] (tárt'n) *n.* **1.** Any of numerous textile patterns consisting of stripes of varying widths and colours crossing at right angles against a solid background, each forming a distinctive design worn by the members of a particular Scottish clan. **2.** A twilled woollen fabric or garment having such a pattern. **3.** Any fabric having a similar pattern. [Probably from Old French *tertaine, tiretaine,* linsey-woolsey, from Old Spanish *tiritaña,* a thin silk stuff, from *tiritar,* to rustle (imitative).] —**tar·tan** *adj.*

tartan[2] *n.* A small, single-masted Mediterranean ship with a large lateen sail. [French *tartane,* from Italian *tartana,* probably from Old Provençal *tartana*†, buzzard.]

tar·tan·ry (tártn'n-ri) *n.* A tendency to overemphasise supposedly typical Scottish mannerisms, dress, or idiom, when writing about or otherwise representing Scotland or the Scottish.

tar·tar[1] (tártər) *n.* **1.** A reddish acid compound, chiefly potassium bitartrate, found in the juice of grapes and deposited on the sides of casks during wine-making. **2.** A hard, yellowish deposit on the teeth, consisting of organic secretions and food particles deposited in various salts, such as calcium carbonate. [Middle English *tartre, tartar,* from Old French *tartre,* from Medieval Latin *tartarum,* from Medieval Greek *tartaron*†.]

tartar[2] *n.* *Sometimes capital* **T.** A ferocious, formidable, or violent-tempered person. [*Tartar,* variant of TATAR.]

Tartar. Variant of **Tatar.**

Tar·tar·e·an (taar-táir-i-ən, -taár-) *adj.* Of or pertaining to Tartarus.

tartar emetic *n.* A poisonous crystalline salt, potassium antimony

tartrate, $K(SbO)C_4H_4O_6$, used as a mordant and formerly as an emetic.

tar·tar·ic (taar-tárrik) *adj.* Of, pertaining to, or derived from tartar or tartaric acid.

tartaric acid *n.* Any of four isomeric crystalline organic compounds, $C_4H_6O_6$, used to make cream of tartar, as a sequestrant, in tanning, and in effervescent drinks, baking powders, and photographic chemicals.

tar·tar·ise, tar·tar·ize (tártə-rīz) *tr.v.* **-ised, -ising, -ises.** To treat, impregnate, or combine with tartar, tartar emetic, or cream of tartar. **—tar·tar·i·sa·tion** (-rī-záysh'n ‖ *U.S.* -ri-) *n.*

tar·tar·ous (tártərəss) *adj.* Consisting of, derived from, or containing tartar.

tartar sauce (taar-tár) *n.* Mayonnaise mixed with chopped onion, olives, pickles, and capers, and served as a sauce with fish. Also called "tartare sauce".

tartar steak *n.* Steak tartare *(see)*.

Tar·ta·rus (tártərəss) *n.* **1.** *Greek Mythology.* **a.** The abysmal regions below Hades where the Titans were confined. **b.** A region of Hades reserved for the most wicked sinners. **2.** Any infernal or hellish region. [Latin, from Greek *Tartaros*†.]

Tar·ta·ry (tártəri). Also **Ta·ta·ry** (táatəri). A historical region comprising the areas of eastern Europe and Asia overrun by Tatars in the 13th and 14th centuries and extending as far east as the Pacific under Genghis Khan.

tart·let (tárt-lət, -lit) *n.* A small tart for an individual serving, with a sweet or savoury filling, such as fruit or cheese.

tar·trate (tártrayt) *n.* A salt or ester of tartaric acid.

tar·trat·ed (taar-tráytid) *adj.* Containing, combined with, or derived from tartaric acid.

tar·tra·zine (tártrə-zeen, -zin) *n.* A yellowish-orange powder that is an azo dye, $C_{16}H_9N_4Na_3O_9S_2$, used to colour textiles, cosmetics, drugs and food. As a food additive it is E102, and is allegedly implicated in hyperactivity in children. [Origin obscure.]

Tar·tu (tártoo). *Swedish & German* **Dor·pat** (dór-pat). City in Estonia, lying on the river Ema. It is an important industrial and commercial centre.

Tar·tuffe (taar-toof, -toof) *n.* A hypocrite; especially, one who affects religious piety. [After *Tartuffe*, title character and hypocrite in the comedy by the French playwright Molière. (1664).] **—Tar·tuff·i·an** *adj.* **—Tar·tuff·ism** *n.*

tart·y (tárti) *adj.* Designating clothes, appearance, or behaviour, especially of women, that are sexually provocative in an obvious and vulgar way.

Tar·zan (tár-z'n, -zan) *n. Sometimes small* **t.** *Informal.* A man with a muscular physique, who possesses great physical strength and virility. Often used humorously. [After *Tarzan,* the hero of a number of stories by E. R. BURROUGHS.]

Tash·kent (tásh-ként) or **Tosh·kent** (tosh-ként). Capital of Uzbekistan, in central Asia, lying in the foothills of the Tian Shan mountains. The city lies in a broad oasis along the river Chirchik, and is one of the largest producers of finished textile goods in Asia.

ta·sim·e·ter (tə-símmitər, ta-) *n.* A device for measuring small temperature changes by the expansion or contraction of a solid. [Greek *tasis,* tension + -METER.]

task (taask ‖ task) *n.* **1.** A specific piece of work assigned by a superior or done as part of one's duties. **2.** Anything that has to be done, especially when difficult or unpleasant. **3.** The function, duty, or purpose of a working person, unit, or thing: *My task is to see fair play.* **—take to task.** To reprimand or censure. **~tr.v. tasked, tasking, tasks. 1.** To assign a task to or impose a task upon. **2.** To overburden with labour; tax. [Middle English *taske, tasque,* tax, work imposed, task, from Anglo-French *tasque,* variant of Old French *tasche,* from Medieval Latin *tasca, taxa,* from *taxāre,* to TAX.]

Synonyms: task, job, chore, assignment.

task force *n.* A temporary grouping of forces and resources for the accomplishment of a specific objective.

task·mas·ter (táask-maastər ‖ tásk-mastər) *n.* One who imposes work, especially heavy or exacting work.

Tas·ma·ni·a (taz-máyni-ə). Island and state of Australia, lying off the southeast of Australia, separated from the mainland by Bass Strait. The state also includes a number of small off-shore islands. The capital is Hobart. The island was discovered by the Dutch explorer, Abel Tasman, in 1642 and named Van Diemen's Land. It was taken by Britain (1803), and its name changed to Tasmania (1853). In 1901 the island became a state of the Commonwealth of Australia. It is mountainous and much forested, and there are several large hydroelectric schemes. Its exports include iron, copper, zinc, tungsten, metal products, timber and wood products, textiles, and wool.

Tasmanian devil *n.* A burrowing carnivorous marsupial, *Sarcophilus harrisii,* of Tasmania, having a predominantly blackish coat, powerful jaws, and a long tail.

Tasmanian wolf *n.* A marsupial, the **thylacine** *(see)*.

Tas·man Sea (tázmən). Arm of the southern Pacific Ocean, lying between Australia and New Zealand.

tass (tass) *n. Chiefly Scottish.* **1.** A small cup or goblet. **2.** A small draught, especially of spirits. [Middle English, from Old French *tasse,* cup, from Arabic *tassah,* basin, from Persian *tast.*]

Tass (tass ‖ *U.S. also* taass) *n.* Formerly, the chief news agency of the Soviet Union. [Russian, from *T(elegrafnoe A(gentstvo) S(ovetskovo) S(oyuza),* Telegraphic Agency of the Soviet Union.]

tasse (tass) *n.* Also **tas·set** (tássit). Any of a series of jointed overlapping metal plates hanging from the corselet, used as armour for the lower trunk and thighs. [Perhaps from Old French *tasse,* pouch, purse, from Middle High German *tasche,* from Old High German *tasca,* from Medieval Latin *tasca,* task, payment. See **task.**]

tas·sel (táss'l) *n.* **1.** An ornament consisting of a bunch of loose threads or cords bound at one end, hung from curtains, clothing, cushions, or the like. **2.** Something that resembles a tassel, such as the pollen-bearing inflorescence of a maize plant. **~v. tasselled** or *U.S.* **-seled, -selling** or *U.S.* **-seling, -sels.** *—tr.* To fringe or decorate with tassels. *—intr.* To put forth a tassel-like inflorescence. Used especially of corn. [Middle English, clasp, fibula, tassel, from Old French *tassel*†.]

taste (tayst) *v.* **tasted, tasting, tastes.** *—tr.* **1.** To distinguish, experience, or judge the flavour or quality of by taking into the mouth. **2.** To eat or drink a small quantity of. **3.** To experience or partake of, especially for the first time: *tasted power.* **4.** *Archaic.* To like or appreciate. **5.** *Obsolete.* To test by touching. *—intr.* **1.** To distinguish, experience, or judge flavours or qualities in the mouth. **2.** To eat or drink a small amount. **3.** To have an experience; partake. Often used with *of.* **4.** To have a distinctive flavour, as specified. Often used with *of: The stew tastes salty; tastes of garlic.* **~n. 1. a.** The sense that distinguishes the sweet, sour, salty, and bitter qualities of dissolved substances in contact with the taste buds on the tongue. **b.** This sense in combination with the senses of smell and touch, which together receive a sensation of a substance in the mouth. **2. a.** The sensation of sweet, sour, salty, or bitter qualities produced by a substance in solution in the mouth. **b.** The sensation produced by any of these qualities together with a distinct smell and texture; a flavour. **3.** A small quantity eaten or tasted. **4.** A brief spell of participating in or experiencing something, often for the first time; a sample: *a taste of fear.* **5.** A distinctive impression left by an event or experience. **6.** A personal preference or liking for something; an inclination. **7. a.** The faculty of discerning what is aesthetically excellent, pleasing, or appropriate; discrimination. **b.** A manner indicative of the quality of such discernment: *dressed with taste.* **8. a.** The sense of what is proper, seemly, or least likely to give offence in a given social situation; discretion. **b.** A manner indicative of the quality of this sense: *a remark in poor taste.* **9.** *Obsolete.* The act of testing; a trial. **—See Synonyms at culture.** [Middle English *tasten,* to examine by touch, taste, from Old French *taster,* from Vulgar Latin *tastāre, taxitāre* (unattested), frequentative of Latin *taxāre,* to touch, frequentative of *tangere.*] **—tast·a·ble** *adj.*

taste bud *n.* Any of numerous spherical or ovoid nests of cells distributed over the tongue. The cells are embedded in the epithelium, consist of gustatory cells and supporting cells, and constitute the organs of taste.

taste·ful (táyst-f'l) *adj.* **1.** Exhibiting good taste. **2.** *Archaic.* Tasty. **—taste·ful·ly** *adv.* **—taste·ful·ness** *n.*

taste·less (táyst-ləss, -liss) *adj.* **1.** Lacking flavour; insipid. **2.** Exhibiting poor taste. **3.** *Archaic.* Unable to taste. **—taste·less·ly** *adv.* **—taste·less·ness** *n.*

tast·er (táystər) *n.* **1.** One who tastes, specifically: **a.** One who samples a food or drink for quality. **b.** One employed to sample food and drink prepared for a master, as a precaution against poisoning. **2.** Any of several devices or implements used in tasting.

tast·y (táysti) *adj.* **-ier, -iest. 1.** Having a pleasing flavour; savoury. **2.** *Slang.* Sexually attractive or appealing. **3.** *Archaic.* Having good taste; tasteful. **—tast·i·ly** *adv.* **—tast·i·ness** *n.*

tat[1] (tat) *v.* **tatted, tatting, tats.** *—intr.* To make tatting. *—tr.* To produce by tatting. [Probably back-formation from TATTING.] **—tat·ter** *n.*

tat[2] *n. Chiefly British Informal.* Worthless or shabby goods. [Back-formation from TATTY.]

tat[3] *n.* See **tit for tat.**

ta-ta (tá-táa, tə-) *interj. British Informal.* Goodbye.

ta·ta·mi (tə-táami, -támmi) *n., pl* **-mis** or **-mi.** A straw mat used as a floor covering in Japan. [Japanese.]

Ta·tar (táatər) *n.* Also **Tar·tar** (tártər). **1. a.** A member of one of the Turkic-speaking tribes that originated in east central Asia or Siberia, and which, with the Mongolian peoples led by Genghis Khan, overran much of central and western Asia and eastern Europe in the 13th century. **b.** After the death of Genghis Khan (1227), a member of any of these groups, Tatar or Mongol. **2.** A descendant of these peoples, now living chiefly in parts of Russia and central Asia. **3.** Any of the Turkic languages of the Tatars. [Middle English *Tartre, Tatar,* from Old French *Tartare,* from Medieval Latin *Tartarus* (probably influenced by Latin (TARTARUS), from Persian *Tātār,* from *Tata,* Turkic ethnic name.] **—Ta·tar, Tar·tar** *adj.*

Tatar Autonomous Soviet Socialist Republic. Former constituent republic of the U.S.S.R. occupying the valleys of the middle Volga and lower Kama rivers. It was a leading producer of natural gas and petroleum in the U.S.S.R. It is now the Tatarstan Republic in the Russian Federation.

ta·ter (táytər) *n. Regional.* A potato.

ta·ters (táytərz) *adj. British Slang.* Cold. Short for *taters in the mould,* rhyming slang for *cold.*

Ta·tra Mountains (táatrə, táttrə). Highest chain of mountains in the Carpathian range of east central Europe, lying in Poland and Czechoslovakia. The highest peak is Mount Gerlachovka, which rises to 2 655 metres (8,710 feet).

tat·ter (táttər) *n.* **1.** A torn and hanging piece of cloth; a shred.

2. *Plural.* **a.** Torn and ragged clothing; rags. **b.** A condition of being reduced as if to shreds or rags: *left her nerves in tatters.*
~*tr.v.* **tattered, -tering, -ters.** To make ragged; reduce to shreds. [Middle English *tatter, tatar,* from Old Norse *taturr* (unattested), *tǫturr,* from Germanic *tath-* (unattested).]

tat·ter·de·mal·ion (táttər-də-máyli-ən, -di- ‖ -mál-i-) *n. Rare.* A person wearing ragged or tattered clothing; a ragamuffin.
~*adj.* Ragged; tattered. [TATTER + obscure second element.]

tat·tered (táttərd) *adj.* **1.** Torn into shreds or tatters; ragged. **2.** Having ragged clothes; dressed in tatters.

tat·ter·sall (táttər-sawl, -s'l) *n. Sometimes capital* **T. 1.** A pattern of variously coloured lines forming squares on a plain, usually light background. **2.** Cloth woven with this pattern. Also used adjectivally: *tattersall check.* [Originally the pattern on blankets used at *Tattersall's* horse market in London, founded by Richard Tattersall (1724–95), British horseman.]

tat·ting (tátting) *n.* **1.** Handmade lace fashioned by looping and knotting a single strand of strong thread on a small hand shuttle. **2.** The act or art of making tatting. [Perhaps related to Scottish *tate†,* tuft.]

tat·tle (tátt'l) *v.* **-tled, -tling, -tles.** —*intr.* **1.** To reveal the plans or activities of another by chattering; blab; gossip. **2.** To chatter aimlessly; prate. —*tr.* To reveal through gossiping.
~*n.* **1.** Aimless chatter; prattle. **2.** Gossip. [Middle Flemish *tatelen,* to babble (imitative).] —**tat·tling·ly** *adv.*

tat·tler (táttlər) *n.* **1.** A person who tattles. **2.** Any of several shore birds related to and resembling the sandpipers, and characteristically having a loud call.

tat·tle·tale (tátt'l-tayl) *n.* A person who tattles on others; a telltale.

tat·too¹ (tə-tóo, ta-) *n., pl.* **-toos. 1.** A signal sounded on a drum or bugle to summon soldiers to quarters at night. **2.** A display of military exercises performed as entertainment especially in the evening: *the Edinburgh tattoo.* **3.** A continuous even drumming or rapping.
~*v.* **tattooed, -tooing, -toos.** —*intr.* To beat out an even rhythm, as with the fingers. —*tr.* To beat or tap rhythmically on; rap or drum on. [Originally *tap-too, tap-tow,* from Dutch *taptoe,* "the shutting off of the taps (at taverns at the end of the day)" : *tap,* tap + *toe,* short for *doe toe,* "do to", shut.]

tattoo² *n., pl.* **-toos.** A permanent mark or design made on the skin by a process of pricking and ingraining an indelible pigment or by raising scars.
~*tr.v.* **tattooed, -tooing, -toos. 1.** To mark (the skin) with a tattoo or tattoos. **2.** To form (a mark or design) on the skin by this process. [Of Polynesian origin, akin to Tahitian *tatau,* Marquesan *tatu.*] —**tat·too·er, tat·too·ist** *n.*

tat·ty¹ (tátti) *adj.* Shabby, untidy, or ragged, especially in dress or appearance. [16th century (Scottish) : ultimately akin to Old English *tættec,* TATTER.] —**tat·ti·ly** *adv.* —**tat·ti·ness** *n.*

tatty² *n., pl.* **-ties.** *Scottish Informal.* A potato.

tau (taw, tow) *n.* The 19th letter of the Greek alphabet, written T, τ. Transliterated in English as *T, t.* [Greek, from Semitic, akin to Hebrew *tāw,* TAV.]

tau cross *n.* A **Saint Anthony's cross** *(see).*

taught. Past tense and past participle of **teach.**

taunt¹ (tawnt) *tr.v.* **taunted, taunting, taunts. 1.** To deride or reproach with contempt; mock; jeer at. **2.** To provoke or incite by taunting: *taunted into action.* —See Synonyms at **ridicule.**
~*n.* A scornful remark or jibe; a jeer. [Perhaps from Old French *tanter, tenter,* to test, tempt, from Latin *temptāre,* TEMPT.] —**taunt·er** *n.* —**taunt·ing·ly** *adv.*

taunt² *adj. Nautical.* Unusually tall. Said of a mast. [Probably from *ataunt,* as much as possible, fully rigged, from Old French *autant,* as much : *al,* other, one more + *tant,* so much, from Latin *tantum,* from *tam,* so.]

Taun·ton (táwn-tən; *locally* ta'an-). Town in Somerset, England, lying on the river Tone. It is the county town of Somerset.

tau particle *n.* A short-lived elementary particle which, together with its associated neutrino, is a member of the lepton family.

taupe (tōp) *n.* Brownish grey to dark yellowish brown. [French, "mole", from Latin *talpa†.*] —**taupe** *adj.*

Tau·po (tówpō). Largest lake in New Zealand, in the centre of North Island, in the district known as Hot Springs. Set among volcanic mountains, the lake is the centre of a holiday resort area.

tau·rine¹ (táw-rīn ‖ -rin) *adj.* Of or resembling a bull. [Latin *taurīnus,* from *taurus,* bull.]

tau·rine² (táw-reen, -rin) *n.* A derivative of the amino acid cysteine, 2-aminoethane sulphonic acid, $C_2H_7NO_3S,$ found in bile. [TAUR(O)- + -INE (so called because first obtained from ox bile).]

tauro-, taur- *comb. form.* Indicates bull or bovine; for example, **taurocholic, taurine.** [Latin *taurus* and Greek *tauros,* bull.]

tau·ro·cho·lic acid (táwr-ŏ-kŏl-ik, -ə-, -kól-) *n.* A crystalline acid, $C_{26}H_{45}NO_7S,$ occurring as a constituent of bile. [TAURO- + CHOLIC ACID (because first obtained from ox bile).]

tau·rom·a·chy (taw-rómməki) *n., pl.* **-chies.** Bullfighting or a bullfight. [Spanish *tauromaquia,* from Greek *tauromakhia* : TAURO- + *makhē,* battle, from *makhesthai,* to fight.]

Tau·rus (táwrəss) *n.* **1.** A constellation in the Northern Hemisphere near Orion and Aries. **2. a.** The second sign of the **zodiac** *(see).* Also called the "Bull". **b.** One born under this sign. [Middle English, from Latin, bull.] —**tau·re·an** (táwri-ən, taw-rée-ən) *n. & adj.*

taut (tawt) *adj.* **tauter, tautest. 1.** Pulled or drawn tight; not slack. **2.** Strained; tense. **3.** Kept in good order and condition neat; tidy;

a taut ship. **4.** Strict in form; polished and well-organised: *a taut piece of writing.* —See Synonyms at **stiff.** [Earlier *taught, tought,* Middle English *toght, toht,* probably variant past participle of *togen, towen,* to pull, Old English *togian.*] —**taut·ly** *adv.* —**taut·ness** *n.*

taut·en (táwt'n) *v.* **-ened, -ening, -ens.** —*tr.* To make taut; stretch tight. —*intr.* To become taut.

tauto-, taut- *comb. form.* Indicates same or identical; for example, **tautomerism, tautonym.** [Greek *tautos,* identical, from *to auto,* the same (neuter) : *to,* the + *autos,* same.]

tau·tol·o·gise, tau·tol·o·gize (taw-tólla-jīz) *intr.v.* **-gised, -gising, -gises.** To use tautology. —**tau·tol·o·gist** *n.*

tau·tol·o·gy (taw-tólləji) *n., pl.* **-gies. 1. a.** Needless repetition of the same sense in different words; redundancy; for example, the statement *Pair off in twos* shows tautology. **b.** An instance of such repetition. **2.** *Logic.* A statement composed of simpler statements in a fashion that makes it true whether the simpler statements are true or false; for example, *Either it will rain tomorrow or it will not rain tomorrow.* [Late Latin *tautologia,* from Greek, from *tautologos,* repeating the same ideas : TAUTO- + *logos,* saying, word (see -LOGY).] —**tau·to·log·i·cal** (táwtə-lójik'l), **tau·to·log·ic, tau·tol·og·ous** (taw-tólla-gəss, *also* -jəss) *adj.* —**tau·to·log·i·cal·ly** *adv.*

tau·tom·er·ism (taw-tómmə-riz'm) *n.* Chemical isomerism characterised by relatively easy interconversion of isomeric forms in equilibrium. [TAUTO- + (ISO)MERISM.] —**tau·to·mer** (táwtəmər) *n.* —**tau·to·mer·ic** (táwtə-mérrik) *adj.*

tau·to·nym (táwtə-nim) *n.* A taxonomic designation, such as *Gorilla gorilla,* in which the genus and species names are the same. Now only used in zoology. [TAUT(O)- + -ONYM.] —**tau·to·nym·ic** (-nímmik), **tau·ton·y·mous** (taw-tónniməss) *adj.* —**tau·ton·y·my** *n.*

tav, taw (taav, taaf) *n.* The 23rd letter of the Hebrew alphabet, corresponding phonetically to *t* or *th* in English. [Hebrew *tāw,* probably "mark", "cross".]

tav·ern (távvərn) *n.* **1.** *Literary.* A pub or inn. **2.** Broadly, an establishment licensed to sell alcoholic drinks to be drunk on the premises; a bar. [Middle English *taverne,* from Old French, from Latin *taberna,* hut, inn, perhaps from Etruscan (see also **tabernacle.**]

ta·ver·na (tə-vérnə) *n.* A restaurant in Greece that sometimes also provides accommodation and live entertainment.

TAVR Territorial and Army Volunteer Reserve (in Britain).

taw¹ (taw) *tr.v.* **tawed, tawing, taws.** To convert (hide) into white leather by mineral tanning, as by soaking in alum and salt. [Middle English *tawen,* Old English *tawian.*] —**taw·er** *n.*

taw² *n.* **1.** A large, often fancy marble used for shooting. **2.** The line from which a player shoots in marbles. **3.** A game played with taws. [18th century : origin obscure.]

taw³. Variant of **tav.**

taw·dry (táwdri) *adj.* **-drier, -driest.** Gaudy and cheap-looking; vulgarly ornamental. [From *tawdry lace,* short for *Seynt Audries lace,* cheap and gaudy lace sold at fairs in honour of St. Audrey or Etheldrida (died A.D. 679), queen of Northumbria and patron saint of Ely who died of a throat tumour regarded as punishment for her fondness for laces.] —**taw·dri·ly** *adv.* —**taw·dri·ness** *n.*

taw·ny (táwni) *n.* Light brown to brownish orange, as is the colour of a lion's body. [Middle English *taune, tawny,* from Anglo-French *taune,* variant of Old French *tane,* tanned, from *taner, tanner,* to TAN.] —**taw·ny** *adj.*

tawny owl *n.* A large common European owl, *Strix aluco,* ranging in colour from tawny chestnut brown to greyish white.

tawse (tawz) *n.* Also **taws.** *Scottish.* A leather strap divided at one end into thin strips, used as an instrument of punishment in schools. [Probably originally the plural of obsolete *taw,* leather strip. See **taw** (verb).]

tax (taks) *n.* **1.** A compulsory financial contribution levied by a government to raise revenue, on the income, profits, or property of persons, groups, or businesses, or on the cost of goods and services. **2.** A burdensome or excessive demand; a strain: *a tax on his patience.*
~*tr.v.* **taxed, taxing, taxes. 1.** To place a tax on (income, property, or goods). **2.** To exact a tax from (a person or organisation). **3.** *Law.* To examine and assess (court costs, for example). **4.** To make exacting or excessive demands upon. **5.** To make a charge against; accuse: *He was taxed with hypocrisy.* [Middle English *taxen,* to assess, tax, from Old French *taxer,* from Medieval Latin *taxāre,* from Latin, frequentative of *tangere,* to touch.] —**tax·a·ble** *adj.* —**tax·a·bil·i·ty, tax·a·ble·ness** *n.* —**tax·er** *n.*

tax·a·tion (tak-sáysh'n) *n.* **1. a.** The act or practice of imposing taxes. **b.** The fact of being taxed. **2.** An amount of money levied by a tax.

tax avoidance *n.* The taking of legal measures to reduce one's tax liability. Also called "avoidance". Compare **tax evasion.**

tax-de·duct·i·ble (táks-də-dúktəb'l) *adj.* That may be set against one's income so that one's tax liability is reduced. Said especially of an expense incurred in the course of one's business.

tax·eme (táks-eem) *n.* A minimal linguistic feature of grammatical arrangement, such as the order or stress of words in a compound or phrase. [TAX(O)- + (PHON)EME.]

tax evasion *n.* The taking of illegal measures to reduce one's tax liability. Also called "evasion". Compare **tax avoidance.**

tax exile *n.* A person who settles in a country other than his own in order to avoid paying high rates of income tax.

tax-free (táks-frée) *adj.* Not subject to taxation. —**tax-free** *adv.*

tax haven *n.* A place that is attractive to companies or individuals because of its relatively low rates of taxation.

tax·i (táksi) *n., pl.* **-is** or **-ies**. A car that carries passengers for a fare, usually calculated by a taximeter. Also called "taxicab", "cab". ~*v.* **taxied, taxiing** or **taxying, taxies** or **taxis**. **1.** To be transported by taxi. **2.** To move slowly on the ground or on the surface of the water before takeoff or after landing. Used of an aircraft. —*tr.* **1.** To transport or convey in a taxi. **2.** To cause (an aircraft) to taxi. [Short for *taximeter cab.*]

taxi dancer *n.* A person, usually a woman, employed by a dance hall or nightclub to dance with the patrons for a fee.

tax·i·der·mist (táksi-dermist, -dérmist, tak-síddərmist) *n.* One whose profession is taxidermy.

tax·i·der·my (táksi-dermi) *n.* The art or operation of preparing, stuffing, and mounting the skins of dead animals for exhibition in a lifelike state. [*Taxi-*, variant of TAXO- + -DERM + -Y.] —**tax·i·der·mal** (-dérm'l), **tax·i·der·mic** (-dérmik) *adj.*

tax·i·me·ter (táksi-meetər) *n.* An instrument installed in a taxi to calculate and show the fare for a particular journey. [French *taximètre : taxe*, tax, charge, from Old French *taxer*, to TAX + -METER.]

tax·ing (táksing) *adj.* Burdensome; wearing. —**tax·ing·ly** *adv.*

tax·i·plane (táksi-playn) *n.* An aeroplane commercially available for short charter flights.

taxi rank *n. British.* An area reserved for taxis waiting for customers. Also called "taxistand".

tax·is (ták-siss) *n., pl.* **taxes** (-seez). **1.** *Biology.* The responsive movement of an entire organism towards or away from an external stimulus. It is not a growth movement. **2.** The moving of an organ, as in a dislocation or hernia, into the normal position by manipulation. [Greek, arrangement, order, from *tattein*, to arrange.]

–taxis, –taxy *comb. form.* Indicates: **1.** Order or arrangement; for example, **phyllotaxy. 2.** Movement towards or away from a specified stimulus; for example, **phototaxis.** [New Latin, from Greek *taxis*, arrangement, order.]

taxo–, tax–, taxi– *comb. form.* Indicates arrangement or order; for example, **taxonomy.** [Greek *taxis*, arrangement, order. See **taxis.**]

tax·on (ták-son) *n., pl.* **taxa** (-sə). *Biology.* A category or formal unit in taxonomic classification, such as a phylum, order, family, genus, or species, characterised by common characteristics in varying degrees of distinction. [Back-formation from TAXONOMY.]

tax·on·o·my (tak-sónnəmi) *n. Abbr.* **taxon. 1.** The science, laws, or principles of classification. **2.** *Biology.* The theory, principles, and process of classifying organisms in established categories according to observed similarities or supposed evolutionary relationships. [French *taxonomie :* TAXO- + -NOMY.] —**tax·o·nom·ic** (táksə-nómmik), **tax·o·nom·i·cal** *adj.* —**tax·o·nom·i·cal·ly** *adv.* —**tax·on·o·mist** (tak-sónnəmist) *n.*

tax·pay·er (táks-pay-ər) *n.* A person who pays or is legally liable to pay taxes.

tax return *n.* A declaration to the tax officials of one's personal income during a given period, so that the appropriate rate of taxation can be calculated.

tax shelter *n.* Any financial operation, such as the acquisition of loss-making assets or the use of special depreciation allowances, used as a means to reduce taxes on current earnings.

tax year *n.* A specific annual period used by a government in calculating taxes, running in Britain from April 6 to April 5 of the following year.

Tay (tay). Longest river in Scotland, rising on Ben Lui in the Grampian mountains and flowing for about 190 kilometres (118 miles) through lochs Dochart and Tay, and into the North Sea through the Firth of Tay. Before entering Loch Dochart it is known as the Fillan, and from there to Loch Tay as the Dochart.

Ta·yg·e·ta¹ (tay-íjitə). *Greek Mythology.* One of the **Pleiades** *(see).*

Tay-Sachs disease (táy-sáks) *n.* An inherited disorder in which excessive amounts of lipid accumulate in the brain, leading to mental subnormality, blindness, and early death. [After Warren *Tay* (1843–1927), British physician, and B.P. *Sachs* (1858–1944), U.S. neurologist.]

Tay·side (táy-sīd). Region of eastern Scotland (1975–96). It included the former counties of Angus, Perthshire, and Kinross. It is now administratively subdivided.

taz·za (tátsə) *n.* A shallow vessel, such as a bowl or vase, shaped like a saucer and often mounted on a pedestal. [Italian, probably from Arabic *tassah*, basin. See **tass.**]

Tb The symbol for the element terbium.

TB tuberculosis.

Tb. tubercle bacillus.

T.B. 1. torpedo-boat. **2.** tuberculosis.

T-bar lift (tée-baar) *n.* A ski lift consisting of a bar suspended like an inverted T against which skiers lean while being towed uphill.

T'bi·li·si (t-bi-lée-si, d-) or **Tif·lis** (tiffliss). Capital of the Republic of Georgia, and formerly the capital of the Georgian S.S.R., lying in the basin of the river Kura. It was a Muslim stronghold in the early Middle Ages, and after the 13th century was ruled by Mongols, Iranians, and the Ottoman Turks until it passed under Russian control in 1800. It is now by far the most important commercial, administrative, and cultural centre in Transcaucasia.

T-bone (tée-bōn) *n.* A tender steak taken from the thin end of the loin and containing a T-shaped bone. Also called "T-bone steak".

tbs., tbsp. tablespoon; tablespoonful.

Tc The symbol for the element technetium.

TCA cycle *n.* The **Krebs cycle** *(see).*

TCDD *n.* Tetrachlorobenzo-p-dioxin; **dioxin** *(see).*

Tchad. See **Chad.**

Tchai·kov·ski (chī-kóffski), **Piotr Ilyich** (1840–94). Russian composer. His music, marked by romantic melodies and its freedom of form, includes many orchestral and stage works, such as the *Pathétique* symphony (1893) and the opera *Eugene Onegin* (1879).

Tchekhov. See **Chekhov.**

TD. Territorial Decoration.

te (tee) *n.* Also **ti.** In tonic sol-fa, a syllable representing the seventh note of a diatonic scale. [Alteration of earlier *si*, from French, from Italian, probably representing Latin *Sancte Iohannes;* see **gamut.**]

Te The symbol for the element tellurium.

tea (tee) *n.* **1.** A shrub, *Camellia sinensis*, of eastern Asia, having fragrant white flowers and evergreen leaves. **2.** The dried leaves of this plant, prepared by various processes and in various stages of growth. **3. a.** An aromatic, slightly bitter drink made by steeping tea leaves in boiling water, often served with milk or lemon, and sugar. **b.** A cup of this drink. **4.** Any of various beverages made by steeping the leaves of certain other plants, or made from beef or other extracts. **5.** Any of various plants having leaves used to make a tealike infusion. **6. a.** *Chiefly British.* An afternoon refreshment usually of biscuits, sandwiches, or light cakes served with tea. **b.** A social occasion, such as a tea party, at which tea is served. **7.** *Chiefly British.* An evening meal; high tea. **8.** *Slang.* Cannabis. [Earlier *tay, tee* (probably via Dutch *thee* and Malay *teh*), from Chinese (Amoy) *te*, equivalent of Mandarin *chá*.]

tea bag *n.* A small porous bag holding tea leaves, dipped into a cup or teapot full of boiling water to make tea.

tea ball *n. Chiefly U.S.* A small perforated metal ball used for immersing tea leaves in hot water. Also called "tea infuser".

tea biscuit *n.* Any of various plain biscuits often served with tea.

tea cake *n. British.* A light, flat, bunlike cake, often with currants, usually toasted and served with butter.

teach (teech) *v.* **taught** (tawt), **teaching, teaches.** —*tr.* **1.** To impart knowledge or skill to; give instruction to: *taught foreign students on Saturdays.* **2.** To provide knowledge of or instruction in, as by giving formal lessons: *taught Latin at a local school.* **3. a.** To cause to learn by example or experience. **b.** To cause to appreciate the inadvisability of a particular course of action: *I'll teach him to go against my orders!* **4.** To advocate; preach: *a religion that teaches forgiveness.* —*intr.* To give instruction, especially as an occupation. [Teach, taught; Middle English *techen, tahte,* Old English *tæcan, tæhte* (past tense), *getǣht* (unattested past participle).]

Synonyms: teach, instruct, educate, tutor, coach, train, school, discipline, drill.

teach·a·ble (téech-əb'l) *adj.* Capable of or receptive to being taught. —**teach·a·bil·i·ty** (-ə-bílləti), **teach·a·ble·ness** *n.* —**teach·a·bly** *adv.*

teach·er (téechər) *n.* One that teaches; especially, a person who is employed to teach.

tea chest *n.* A large, lined box made of a light wood, used for transporting tea.

teach-in (téech-in) *n.* An extended critical discussion of an important topical issue, typically one held in a college or university with the participation of students, lecturers, and guest speakers.

teach·ing (téeching) *n.* **1.** The work or occupation of teachers. **2.** A precept or doctrine.

teaching aid *n.* Something, such as a film strip, tape recorder, or wall chart, that helps a teacher to convey information.

teaching fellow *n.* A postgraduate student who holds a fellowship that provides financial aid, in exchange for some teaching duties. —**teaching fellowship** *n.*

teaching hospital *n.* A hospital associated with a medical school and providing medical students with practical experience.

teaching machine *n.* Any of various devices designed to teach by presenting the student with a planned sequence of statements and questions and providing an immediate response to the answers.

tea cloth *n.* **1.** A small, usually white tablecloth. **2.** A **tea towel** *(see).*

tea cosy *n.* A **cosy** *(see).*

tea·cup (tée-kup) *n.* **1.** A small cup, typically for serving tea or other hot beverages. **2.** The amount that a teacup will hold. In this sense, also called "teacupful".

tea dance *n.* A **thé dansant** *(see).*

tea garden *n.* **1.** An outdoor area, such as a garden adjoining a restaurant or café, in which tea may be served to customers. **2.** A large area where tea is grown; a tea plantation.

teague (tayg) *n.* **1.** *Northern Irish Slang.* A Catholic. Used derogatorily by non-Catholics. **2.** *Archaic.* An Irishman. [Anglicised spelling of the Irish name *Tadhg*.]

tea·house (tée-howss) *n.* A public establishment, especially in the Far East, serving tea and other refreshments.

teak (teek) *n.* **1.** A tall evergreen tree, *Tectona grandis*, of southeastern Asia, having hard, heavy, durable wood. **2.** The yellowish-brown hard wood of this tree, used for furniture and in shipbuilding. **3.** Yellowish brown or greyish to moderate brown. [Portuguese *teca*, from Malayalam *tēkka*.] —**teak** *adj.*

tea·ket·tle (tée-kett'l) *n.* See **kettle.**

teal (teel) *n., pl.* **teals** or collectively **teal. 1.** Any of several small, widely distributed ducks of the genus *Anas*, many of which have brightly marked plumage; especially *A. crecca*, the male of which has a chestnut-coloured head with a distinctive green eye-stripe. **2.** Moderate or dark bluish green to greenish blue. In this sense, also called "teal blue". [Middle English *tele*, akin to Middle Dutch *talinc*, Middle Low German *telink*†.] —**teal** *adj.*

tea leaf *n.* **1.** Any leaf of the tea shrub. **2.** *Plural.* **a.** The small, shredded pieces of this leaf that remain at the bottom of a teapot or teacup after the tea has been drunk. **b. Tea** (sense 2). **3.** *British Slang.* A thief. [Sense 3, rhyming slang.]

team (teem) *n.* **1.** A group of players making up one of the sides in a game or contest. **2.** Any group organised to work together: *a team of medical experts.* **3.** Two or more draught animals harnessed to a vehicle or farm implement. **b.** The vehicle along with the animal or animals harnessed to it. **4.** *Regional.* A brood or flock. **5.** *Obsolete.* Offspring; lineage.
~*v.* **teamed, teaming, teams.** —*tr.* **1.** To harness or join together (horses, for example) so as to form a team. **2.** To bring together with another so as to form a team. Often used with *up: Bill was teamed up with Ben.* **3.** *U.S.* To transport or haul with a draught team. —*intr.* To form a team. Often used with *up.* [Middle English *tem(e),* Old English *tēam,* offspring, brood, team of animals.]

team·mate (teém-mayt) *n.* A fellow member of a team.

team spirit *n.* The morale of a team of people as engendered by a willingness for mutual cooperation.

team·ster (teém-stər) *n.* **1.** A person who drives a team. **2.** *U.S.* A lorry driver.

team·work (teém-wurk) *n.* Cooperative effort by the members of a team to achieve a common goal.

tea party *n.* An informal social gathering, usually in the afternoon, at which tea is served.

tea·pot (teé-pot) *n.* A covered pot with a spout in which tea infuses and from which it is served.

tea·poy (teé-poy) *n.* A small, usually three-legged, table, especially one on which tea is served. [Alteration (influenced by TEA) of Hindi *tipāī* : Hindi *tīn,* three, from Sanskrit *tri* + Middle Persian *pāī,* foot.]

tear[1] (tair) *v.* **tore** (tor || tōr), **torn** (torn || tōrn), **tearing, tears.** —*tr.* **1.** To pull apart or into pieces, especially so as to leave jagged or irregular edges; rend. **2.** To make (an opening) by ripping. **3.** To lacerate (one's skin, for example). **4.** To extract or separate forcefully; wrench. Usually used with *away* or *from.* —*intr.* **1.** To become torn. **2.** To move with heedless speed; rush headlong. Often used with *off* or *along.* **—tear down.** To demolish or destroy: *tear down slums.* **—tear into.** To attack with great violence or vigour: *tore into his arguments.* **—tear off.** *Chiefly British.* To produce hurriedly and casually. **—tear up. 1.** To rip or tear into tiny pieces. **2.** To cancel or annul by or as if by tearing: *tore up an agreement.*
~*n.* **1.** An act of tearing. **2.** The result of tearing; a rip or rent. **3.** *Chiefly British.* A great rush; a hurry. [Tear, tore, torn; Middle English *teren, tore* (earlier *taar*), *toren,* Old English *teran, tær, toren.*]
Synonyms: *tear, rip, rend, split, cleave, sever, slit, slash.*

tear[2] (teer) *n.* **1.** A drop of the clear saline liquid that is secreted by the lachrymal gland of the eye, often as a result of some strong emotion such as grief or joy, and that lubricates the surface between the eyeball and the eyelid. **2.** A drop of any liquid or hardened fluid. **3.** *Plural.* The act of weeping. Often used with *in, into,* or *to: bored to tears; The farewell party left her in tears.* **—without tears.** Presented so as to be easily absorbed or learned: *French without tears.* [Middle English *tere, tear,* Old English *tēar, tehher.*]

tear away (tair) *tr.v.* To bring (especially oneself) to leave, despite reluctance: *could hardly tear myself away.*

tear·a·way (taír-ə-way) *n.* *British.* A rash, impetuous, youth; a hooligan.
~*adj. British.* Of the nature of a tearaway; reckless; impetuous.

tear·drop (teér-drop) *n.* **1.** A single tear. **2.** Something in the shape of a tear.

tear duct (teer) *n.* The **lachrymal duct** *(see).*

tear fault (tair) *n.* A **strike-slip fault** *(see).*

tear·ful (teérf'l) *adj.* **1.** Inclined to or about to cry. **2.** Accompanied by tears: *gave us a tearful account of her marriage.* **3.** Causing tears; pathetic; sad. **—tear·ful·ly** *adv.* **—tear·ful·ness** *n.*

tear gas (teer) *n.* Any of various vapours that on dispersal, usually from grenades or projectiles, irritate the eyes and cause blinding tears. Also called "lachrymator".

tear·ing (taír-ing) *adj. Chiefly British.* Reckless, rash, or impetuous in movement or action: *in a tearing hurry.*

tear-jerk·er (teér-jerkər) *n. Informal.* A grossly pathetic story, drama, performance or song liable to provoke sentimental tears. **—tear-jerk·ing** *adj.*

tear-out (taír-owt) *adj.* Designed to be detached by pulling or tearing, as from a folder: *tear-out matches.*

tea·rooms (teé-rōōmz, -rŏŏmz) *pl.n.* **1.** A restaurant or shop serving tea and other refreshments. Also called "teashop". **2.** *South African.* A small grocery or confectionery store, often open outside normal shopping hours.

tea rose *n.* **1.** Any of several cultivated roses derived from *Rosa odorata,* having fragrant, tea-scented yellowish or pink flowers. **2.** Pale to strong yellowish pink. **—tea-rose** *adj.*

tear sheet (tair) *n.* A page, often perforated, that is designed to be detached easily from a newspaper or periodical.

tease (teez) *v.* **teased, teasing, teases.** —*tr.* **1.** To annoy; pester; bother. **2.** To make fun of; playfully mock. **3.** To arouse hope, curiosity, or desire, especially sexual desire, in without affording satisfaction: *teased him with her sultry looks and skimpy dress.* **4.** To pull apart or loosen (body tissue, for example) for examination. **5.** To disentangle and dress the fibres of (wool, for example). **6.** To raise the nap of (cloth) by dressing, as with a fuller's teasel. **7.** *U.S.* To coax; importune. **8.** *Chiefly U.S.* To backcomb (the hair). —*intr.* To annoy or make fun of someone persistently.
~*n.* **1.** The act of teasing. **2.** A person or thing that teases; especially, one given to playful mocking. [Middle English *tesen, teesen,* to card (wool), tear apart, Old English *tǣsan,* from West Germanic *taisjan* (unattested).] **—teas·ing·ly** *adv.*

tea·sel, tea·zel, tea·zle (teéz'l) *n.* **1.** Any of several plants of the genus *Dipsacus,* native to the Old World, having thistle-like flowers surrounded by prickly bracts. **2. a.** The bristly flower head of *D. fullonum,* used to produce a napped surface on fabrics. **b.** A similar object used for the same purpose.
~*tr.v.* **teaselled** or *U.S.* **-eled, -elling** or *U.S.* **-eling, -els.** To produce a napped surface on (a piece of cloth). [Middle English *tesel, tasel,* Old English *tǣsel,* from West Germanic *taisilā* (unattested), from *taisjan* (unattested), to card, TEASE.] **—tea·sel·ler** *n.*

teas·er (teézər) *n.* **1.** A person who teases. **2.** *Informal.* A problem or puzzle: *a brain teaser.*

tea service *n.* A set of articles, such as matching cups, saucers, and teapot, used in serving tea. Also called "tea set".

Teas·made (teéz-mayd) *n.* A trademark for an automatic tea-making apparatus that can be preset to boil and pour water into a teapot and sound an alarm at a fixed time.

tea·spoon (teéspōōn) *n.* **1.** A small, usually metal, spoon used especially with tea, coffee, and desserts. **2.** *Abbr.* **t., tsp. a.** The amount a teaspoon will hold. Also called "teaspoonful". **b.** A household cooking measure, $^1/_4$ or $^1/_3$ tablespoon (1 or 1 $^1/_3$ drams).

teat (teet) *n.* **1.** A mammary gland or nipple. **2.** Anything resembling a teat, especially a rubber device on a bottle enabling a liquid to be sucked out. [Middle English *tet(t)e,* from Old French, from West Germanic *titta* (unattested), TIT.]

tea towel *n.* A light, absorbent cloth, usually of linen or cotton, used to dry washed dishes and cutlery. Also called "tea cloth", *U.S.* "dish towel".

tea tree *n. Australian.* Any of various trees of the genus *Leptospermum,* the leaves of which were used as a tea substitute.

tea trolley *n. British.* A small table on wheels for serving tea or holding dishes. Also *U.S.* "tea wagon".

Tebet, Tebeth. Variants of **Tevet.**

Tebriz. See **Tabriz.**

tech (tek) *n. British Informal.* A technical college.

tech. **1.** technical. **2.** technology.

tech·ne·ti·um (tek-neé-ti-əm, -shi- || -shəm) *n. Symbol* **Tc** A silvery-grey metal, the first synthetically produced element, having 14 isotopes with masses ranging from 92 to 105 and half-lives up to 2.6×10^6 years. It is used as a tracer and to eliminate corrosion in steel. Atomic number 43, melting point 2,200°C, relative density 11.50, valencies 3, 4, 6, 7. [New Latin, from Greek *tekhnētos,* artificial, from *tekhnē,* art, skill. See **technical.**]

tech·nic (ték-nik) *n.* **1.** *Plural.* The theory, principles, or study of an art or process, especially an industrial or mechanical one. **2.** *Plural.* Technical details, rules, methods, or the like. **3.** *Rare.* Variant of **technique.**
~*adj.* Technical.

tech·ni·cal (ték-nik'l) *adj. Abbr.* **tech. 1. a.** Of or pertaining to that aspect of an art or science requiring practical, applied, mechanical, or scientific skills or knowledge. **b.** Qualified or skilled in the practical mechanical, or applied aspect of an art or science: *a technical expert.* **2. a.** Of, pertaining to, or characteristic of any specialised field or activity: *technical vocabulary.* **b.** Loosely, complicated: *Don't get technical.* **3.** Of, pertaining to, or providing knowledge of any of various subjects that involve practical, applied, mechanical, or industrial skills or knowledge: *a technical college.* **4.** Of, pertaining to, or derived from technique: *showed technical mastery but no feel or imagination.* **5.** Characterised by or based on a rigorously strict interpretation of the appropriate rules: *a technical victory.* **6.** *Finance.* Of or designating a market condition in which prices are determined or affected by internal manipulation and speculation, rather than by any external factors. [Latin *technicus,* from Greek *tekhnikos,* of art or skill, from *tekhnē,* art, skill.] **—tech·ni·cal·ly** *adv.* **—tech·ni·cal·ness** *n.*

technical college *n.* A state educational establishment, especially designed for school leavers and mature students, providing courses in any of various arts and science subjects.

tech·ni·cal·i·ty (ték-ni-kál-əti) *n., pl.* **-ties. 1.** Something meaningful or relevant only according to a strict point of view or ruling. **2.** The condition or quality of being technical.

technical knockout *n. Abbr.* **TKO** In boxing, a victory, with immediate termination of the match, awarded by the referee when it appears that one fighter is in too bad a condition to continue.

tech·ni·cian (tek-nísh'n, ték-) *n.* An expert in a particular skill or technique, as: **1.** A person whose occupation requires training in specific technical skills and processes: *a lighting technician in a television studio.* **2.** One considered from the point of view of his technical skill as opposed to his originality or imagination: *a boring poet although a fine technician.* [TECHN(IC) + -ICIAN.]

tech·ni·col·our (ték-ni-kullər) *adj.* In many vivid, bright colours. [From *Technicolor* (trademark), from TECHNI(CAL) + COLOR.]

technicolour yawn *n. Australian Slang.* An act of vomiting.

tech·nique (tek-neék, ték-) *n.* Also *rare* **tech·nic** (ték-nik) (for sense 2). **1.** The systematic procedure by which a complex or specialised task is accomplished. **2.** The degree of skill or command of fundamentals exhibited, especially in artistic or sporting pursuits. [French, "technical", from Greek *tekhnikos.* See **technical.**]

techno- *comb. form.* Indicates: **1.** Technology; for example, *technophobia.* **2.** Use of state-of-the-art technology; for example, *technopop.*

tech·noc·ra·cy (tek-nókkrə-si) *n., pl.* **-cies. 1.** A system of organisation in which government and industry are controlled by scientific experts or technicians. **2.** A state or country under such a system. [Greek *tekhnē*, art, skill (see **technology**) + -CRACY.] —**tech·no·crat** (ték-nə-krat, -nō-) *n.* —**tech·no·crat·ic** (-kráttik) *adj.*

technol. technology.

tech·no·log·i·cal (ték-nə-lójik'l) *adj.* **1.** Pertaining to or involving technology, especially scientific technology. **2.** Resulting from scientific and industrial progress. —**tech·no·log·i·cal·ly** *adv.*

tech·nol·o·gy (tek-nólləji) *n., pl.* **-gies.** *Abbr.* **tech., technol. 1. a.** The application of science, especially to industrial or commercial objectives. **b.** The entire body of methods and materials used to achieve such objectives. **2.** Broadly, the body of knowledge available to a civilisation that is of use in fashioning implements, practising manual arts and skills, and extracting or collecting materials: *Iron Age technology.* [Greek *tekhnē*, skill, art + -LOGY.] —**tech·nol·o·gist, tech·no·lo·gi·an** (ték-nə-lōj-i-ən, -lój'n) *n.*

techy. Variant of **tetchy.**

tec·ton·ic (tek-tónnik, ték-) *adj.* **1. a.** Pertaining to construction or building. **b.** Architectural. **2.** *Geology.* Pertaining to, causing, or resulting from structural deformation in the earth's crust. [Late Latin *tectonicus*, from Greek *tektonikos*, from *tektōn*, carpenter, builder.]

tec·ton·ics (tek-tónniks, ték-) *n. Used with a singular verb.* **1.** The art or science of construction, especially of large buildings. **2.** The geology of the earth's structural deformation. See **plate tectonics.**

tec·tor·i·al membrane (tek-táw-ri-əl ‖ -tō-) *n.* The membrane covering the organ of Corti in the inner ear.

tec·trix (ték-triks) *n., pl.* **-trices** (-tri-seez). Any of the coverts of a bird's wing. [New Latin, feminine of Latin *tector*, coverer, from *tegere* (past participle *tectus*), to cover.]

tec·tum (téktəm) *n.* The roof of the midbrain.

ted¹ (ted) *tr.v.* **tedded, tedding, teds.** To strew or spread (newly mown grass, for example) for drying. [Middle English *tedden* (attested only in the gerund *teddyng*), from Old Norse *tedhja*, to spread dung, from *tadh*, spread dung.] —**ted·der** *n.*

ted² *n.* A Teddy boy.

teddy bear (téddi-bair) *n.* A child's toy bear, usually stuffed with soft material and covered with a soft, furlike material. Also called "teddy". [After President *Theodore* Roosevelt, once depicted in a cartoon as having spared the life of a bear cub on a hunting trip.]

Teddy boy *n.* In Britain, especially during the 1950s, one of a group of youths affecting a modified style of Edwardian dress and appearance, such as swept-back hair, long sideboards, and straight, tight trousers. Also informally called "ted".

Te De·um (tée dée-əm, táy dáy-əm, -ōōm) *n.* **1.** A Latin hymn, probably written in the early fifth century A.D., beginning with the words *Te Deum laudamus*, "We praise Thee, O God", sung especially at matins or on special occasions, as at a thanksgiving service. **2.** A musical setting of this text.

te·di·ous (téédi-əss) *adj.* Tiresome or uninteresting, especially by reason of extreme length or slowness; wearisome; boring; monotonous: *a tedious music lesson.* —See Synonyms at **boring.** [Middle English, from Old French *tedieus*, from Late Latin *taediōsus*, from Latin *taedium*, TEDIUM.] —**te·di·ous·ly** *adv.* —**te·di·ous·ness** *n.*

te·di·um (téédi-əm) *n.* **1.** The quality of being wearisome or monotonous; tediousness. **2.** The state of being bored; boredom; ennui. [Latin *taedium*, from *taedēret*, to bore, weary.]

tee¹ (tee) *n.* Something shaped like a letter T, as: **1.** A T-shaped pipe connection. **2.** A joint or girder with a T-shaped cross section.

tee² *n.* **1.** A small mound, or a small peg with a concave top, on which a golf ball is placed for an initial drive. **2.** The area at the beginning of each hole from which a golfer makes his first stroke. ~*tr.v.* **teed, teeing, tees.** To place (a golf ball) on a tee. —**tee off. 1.** To drive a golf ball from the tee. **2.** To start; begin: *They teed off the sponsored walk with a toast.* —**tee up.** To place or set up a golf ball for driving. [Earlier *teaz†*.]

tee³ *n.* A mark aimed at in certain games, such as curling or quoits. —**to a tee.** Perfectly; exactly. [Perhaps such marks were originally T-shaped.]

teehee. Variant of **tehee.**

teem¹ (teem) *v.* **teemed, teeming, teems.** —*intr.* **1. a.** To be full and, usually, in motion; abound or swarm. Used with *with: A drop of water teems with microorganisms; a mind teeming with ideas.* **b.** To exist in great quantity; be abundant: *teeming multitudes.* **2.** *Obsolete.* To produce young. —*tr. Archaic.* To give birth to; bear; produce. [Middle English *temen, teamen*, to give birth to, breed, Old English *tīeman, tȳman.*] —**teem·er** *n.*

teem² *v.* **teemed, teeming, teems.** —*intr.* To flow or pour in great quantity. Used chiefly of rain. —*tr. Archaic.* To pour out or empty. [Middle English *temen*, from Old Norse *tōma*, to empty, from Germanic *tōm-*, empty (unattested).]

teen¹ (teen) *adj. Chiefly U.S.* Teenage. —**teen** *n.*

teen² *n. Obsolete.* Injury; grief. [Middle English *tene, teone*, Old English *tēona.*]

–teen *n. suffix.* Used in the names of cardinal numbers **thirteen** to **nineteen.** [Middle English *-tene*, Old English *-tēne, -tȳne.*]

teen·age (téen-ayj) *adj.* Also **teen·aged** (-ayjd). Of, pertaining to, or designating a teenager or teenagers.

teen·ag·er (téen-ayjər) *n.* A person between the ages of thirteen and nineteen inclusive. See Synonyms at **young.**

teens (teenz) *pl.n.* **1.** The numbers that end in *-teen.* **2.** The years of one's age between thirteen and nineteen inclusive.

tee·ny (tééni) *adj.* **-nier, -niest.** Also **teen·sy** (téenzi), **-sier, -siest.** Tiny. [Alteration of TINY.]

teen·sy-ween·sy (téenzi-wéenzi) *adj.* Also **teeny-weeny** (tééni-wéeni). *Informal.* Tiny.

teen·y-bop·per (tééni-boppər) *n. Informal.* A girl in early adolescence who is an avid follower of contemporary fashions and tastes, especially in matters of pop music and clothes. Also called "bopper". [TEEN(-AGE) + BOP (music).]

tee·pee. Variant of **tepee.**

tee shirt. Variant of **T-shirt.**

Tees (teez). River in northeastern England, rising in the northern Pennines and flowing for about 110 kilometres (70 miles) into the North Sea. Its estuary lies near Middlesbrough. Teesside, a former county borough, included the industrial complex of which Middlesbrough, Stockton-on-Tees, and Redcar formed part.

tee·ter (téétər) *intr.v.* **-tered, -tering, -ters. 1.** To walk or move unsteadily or unsurely; totter. **2.** To be in a precarious position or condition: *teetering on the brink of disaster.* **3.** *U.S.* To vacillate. ~*n. U.S.* A seesaw (*see*). [Earlier *titter*, from Middle English *titeren*, probably from Old Norse *titra*, to tremble.]

tee·ter-tot·ter (téétər-tottər) *n. U.S.* A seesaw (*see*).

teeth (teeth) *pl.n.* **1.** Plural of **tooth. 2.** Power; force: *the law lacks teeth.* —**cut (one's) teeth.** To gain one's first experience; practise for the first time. Usually used with *in* or *on.* —**get (one's) teeth into.** To become actively involved in or get a firm grasp of. —**in the teeth of. 1.** Directly and forcefully against. **2.** In defiance of. —**kick in the teeth.** To treat with utter disrespect and callousness. —**lie in (one's) teeth.** To lie directly to or as if to someone's face. —**set (someone's) teeth on edge.** To grate or jar against the sensibilities of; produce an acutely unpleasant sensation in. —**show (one's) teeth.** To show a readiness to fight; threaten defiantly. —**to the teeth.** Completely; lacking nothing: *armed to the teeth.*

teethe (teeth) *intr.v.* **teethed, teething, teethes.** To grow teeth; cut one's teeth in infancy. [Middle English *tethen*, from *tethe*. See **tooth.**]

teeth·ing ring (téething) *n.* A ring of hard rubber or plastic upon which a baby can bite while teething.

teething troubles *pl.n.* Difficulties arising in the initial stages of of a new enterprise, or faults occurring in a newly developed product or system.

tee·to·tal (tee-tốt'l, tée-) *adj.* **1.** Of, practising, or advocating total abstinence from alcoholic drinks. **2.** *U.S. Informal.* Complete; entire.

tee·to·tal·ler, *U.S.* **tee·to·tal·er** (tee-tốt'l-ər, tée-) *n.* A person who abstains completely from alcoholic drink. [*Tee*, first letter in TOTAL + TOTAL (ABSTINENCE).]

tee·to·tum (tée-tốtəm, -tō-túm) *n.* **1.** A kind of top spun with the fingers, usually having four lettered sides and used in games of chance. **2.** Broadly, any type of top spun with the fingers. [Earlier *T-totum*, from the letter *T* inscribed on one of the four sides, standing for Latin *tōtum*, all, and signifying "take all".]

teff, tef, t'ef (tef) *n.* A cereal, *Eragrostis abyssinica,* widely grown in Ethiopia for grain and in certain other countries for fodder. [Amharic *tếf.*]

TEFL (teff'l). Teaching English as a foreign language.

Tef·lon (téf-lon) *n.* A trademark for a waxy, opaque material, polytetrafluoroethylene, used as a coating on cooking utensils and in industrial applications to prevent sticking.

teg (teg) *n.* A sheep in its second year.

teg·men (tég-mən, -men) *n., pl.* **-mina** (-minə). *Biology.* A covering or integument, such as the tough, leathery forewing of certain insects or the inner coat of a seed. [New Latin, from Latin, covering, from *tegere*, to cover.]

Te·gu·ci·gal·pa (te-gōō-si-gál-pə). Capital and largest city of Honduras, lying in the mountain region of southern central Honduras on the river Choluteca.

teg·u·lar (téggew-lər) *adj.* Also **teg·u·lat·ed** (-laytid). **1.** Pertaining to, arranged like, or resembling a tile or tiles. **2.** Overlapping; imbricate: *tegular scales.* [From Latin *tēgula*, tile, from *tegere*, to cover.] —**teg·u·lar·ly** *adv.*

teg·u·ment (téggew-mənt) *n.* An outer covering; an integument. [Middle English, from Latin *tegumentum*, from *tegere*, to cover.] —**teg·u·men·ta·ry** (-méntəri), **teg·u·men·tal** (-mént'l) *adj.*

te·hee, tee·hee (tée-hée) *interj.* Used to express giggling, often mocking, laughter. ~*intr.v.* **teheed, -heeing, -hees.** To utter a giggling, often mocking, laugh.

Teh·ran or **Te·he·ran** (taír-raʹan, té-hə-, -rán). Capital city of Iran, lying in the northern part of the country near Mount Damavand. It is Iran's largest city and most important industrial and commercial centre. It became the capital of Persia in 1788.

Teil·hard de Char·din (tay-yár də shaar-dán), **Pierre** (1881–1955). French Jesuit theologian. He maintained that the universe and mankind are in constant evolution towards a perfect state. He also made valuable contributions in the field of palaeontology.

Te Ka·na·wa (tə kaʹanəwə), **Dame Kiri (Jeanette)** (1944–). New Zealand soprano. Since her debut at the Royal Opera House, Covent Garden, in 1971, she has sung throughout the world.

tek·tite (ték-tīt) *n.* A dark brown to green glassy mass, about 20 millimetres (3/4 inch) in diameter and composed largely of silica, found in various parts of the world and on the Moon, and thought to have formed when a meteorite hit the ground.

tel. 1. telegram; telegraph; telegraphic. **2.** telephone.

te·la (tée-lə) *n., pl.* **-lae** (-lee). A weblike membrane that covers some portion of a bodily organ. [New Latin, from Latin *tēla*, web.]

tel·aes·the·sia, *U.S.* **tel·es·the·sia** (tél-eess-thée-zi-ə, -iss-, -zhi- ‖ -ess-, -zhə) *n.* Perception of or response to distant objects or stimuli without using normal sensory contact, that is, by extrasensory means. [New Latin : TELE- + Greek *aisthēsis*, perception + -IA.] —**tel·aes·thet·ic** (-théttik) *adj.*

tel·a·mon (téllə-mən, -mon) *n., pl.* **telamons**, **telamones** (-mó-neez). *Architecture.* A figure of a man used as a supporting pillar. Compare **caryatid.** [Latin, from Greek *telamōn*, bearer.]

tel·an·gi·ec·ta·sia (tel-ánji-ek-táy-zi-ə, til-, -zhi- ‖ -zhə) *n.* Also **tel·an·gi·ec·ta·sis** (-éktə-siss). A chronic dilation of groups of capillaries of the blood vascular system causing dark-red blotches on the skin. [New Latin : TEL(O)- (end) + Greek *angos*, vessel (see **angiology**) + *ectasis*, dilation, from Greek *ektasis*, expansion, stretching, from *ekteinein*, to stretch out : *ek-*, from *ex*, out + *teinein*, to stretch.] —**tel·an·gi·ec·tat·ic** (-táttik) *adj.*

Tel A·viv–Jaf·fa (tél ə-véev; jáffə). Largest city in Israel, lying in the central part of the country on the Mediterranean coast. It is both a leading resort and the most important industrial and commercial city in the country. Jaffa is an ancient Phoenician city; Tel Aviv was founded in 1909 by Jews who wished to escape from Arab-dominated Jaffa. The two cities were merged in 1950.

tele-, **tel-** *comb. form.* Indicates: **1.** Distance; for example **telaesthesia**, **telecommunication. 2.** Television; for example, **telecast. 3.** Telecommunications; for example, **telecommuter.** [Greek *tēle*, at a distance, far off.]

tel·e·cast (télli-kaast ‖ -kast) *v.* **-cast** or **-casted**, **-casting**, **-casts.** —*intr.* To broadcast by television. —*tr.* To broadcast (a programme) by television.
~*n.* A television broadcast. [TELE (television) + (BROAD)CAST.] —**tel·e·cast·er** *n.*

tel·e·com·mu·ni·ca·tions (télli-kə-méwni-káysh'nz) *n.* **1.** *Used with a singular verb.* The science and technology of communication by electronic transmission of impulses, as by telegraphy, cable, telephony, radio, television, fax, or e-mail. **2.** *Singular.* Communication over long distances.

tel·e·com·mut·er (télli-kə-méwtər) *n.* One who works at home and uses telecommunications to keep in touch with his employer.

tel·e·du (télli-dóo) *n.* A brownish-black carnivorous mammal, *Mydaus javanensis*, of southeast Asia, that is capable of emitting an offensive odour. Also called "stinking badger". [Malay *tēledu*.]

teleg. telegram; telegraph; telegraphic; telegraphy.

tel·e·ge·nic (télli-jénnik, -jéenik) *adj.* Presenting a pleasing appearance on television. [TELE- + (PHOTO)GENIC.]

te·leg·o·ny (ti-léggəni, te-, tə-) *n.* The supposed influence of one sire on offspring sired by subsequent males, of the same female. [TELE- (distance) + -GONY.] —**tel·e·gon·ic** (télli-gónnik), **te·leg·o·nous** (-léggənəss) *adj.*

tel·e·gram (télli-gram) *n. Abbr.* **tel.**, **teleg. 1.** A communication transmitted by telegraph. **2.** The piece of paper that bears the message of a telegram. [TELE- + -GRAM.]

tel·e·graph (télli-graaf, -graf) *n. Abbr.* **tel.**, **teleg. 1.** Any communications system that transmits and receives simple unmodulated electric impulses, especially one in which the transmission and reception stations are directly connected by wires. **2.** A message transmitted by such a system. **3.** *Capital* T. Used as part of the title of certain newspapers: *the Belfast Telegraph.*
~*v.* **telegraphed**, **-graphing**, **-graphs.** —*tr.* **1. a.** To transmit (a message) by telegraph. **b.** To send by means of a telegraphic message: *asked his bank to telegraph some money.* **2.** To send or convey a message to (a person) by telegraph. **3.** To make known unintentionally, as by a sign; especially, in sports, to make (an intended action, such as a pass) obvious to an opponent. —*intr.* To send or transmit a telegram or telegrams. [TELE- + -GRAPH.] —**te·leg·ra·pher** (ti-léggrəfər, te-, tə-), **te·leg·ra·phist** (-léggrəfist) *n.*

tel·e·graph·ese (télli-graaf-éez, -graf-) *n. Informal.* A style of writing that excludes all but the essential words to convey its meaning.

tel·e·graph·ic (télli-gráffik) *adj.* **1.** *Abbr.* **tel.**, **teleg.** Pertaining to or transmitted by telegraph. **2.** Brief or concise, as the wording of a telegram typically is. —**tel·e·graph·i·cal·ly** *adv.*

telegraph plant *n.* A tropical Asiatic plant, *Desmodium gyrans*, having trifoliolate compound leaves, of which the lateral leaflets move or rotate.

telegraph pole *n.* A tall, sturdy pole used to support telegraph or telephone wires.

te·leg·ra·phy (ti-léggrəfi, te-, tə-) *n. Abbr.* **teleg.** The process or act of operating or making telegraphs.

Telegu. Variant of **Telugu.**

tel·e·ki·ne·sis (télli-kī-née-siss, -ki-) *n.* **1.** The movement of objects by scientifically unknown or inexplicable means, as by the exercise of mystical powers. **2.** The ability to produce such movement. [New Latin : TELE- + -KINESIS.] —**tel·e·ki·net·ic** (-néttik) *adj.*

Te·lem·a·chus (ti-lémməkəss, te-, tə-). In Homer, the son of Odysseus and Penelope who helped his father kill Penelope's suitors.

tel·e·mark (télli-maark, télló-) *n. Often capital* T. A turn or stop in skiing executed by shifting the weight forward on the ski that will be on the outside of the turn and pulling its tip gradually inward. [Norwegian, after *Telemark*, region in southern Norway.]

te·lem·e·ter (télli-meetər, ti-lémmitər) *n.* Any of various devices used in telemetry.
~*tr.v.* **telemetered**, **-tering**, **-ters.** To measure and transmit (data) automatically from a distant source, as from a spacecraft or electric power grid, to a receiving station for recording or display. [TELE- + -METER.] —**tel·e·met·ric** (-méttrik), **tel·e·met·ri·cal** *adj.* —**tel·e·met·ri·cal·ly** *adv.*

te·lem·e·try (ti-lémmətri) *n.* The science and technology of automatic measurement and transmission of data by wire, radio, or other means from remote sources, as from space vehicles, to a receiving station for recording and analysis. [TELE- + -METRY.]

tel·en·ceph·a·lon (tél-en-kéffə-lon, -séffə-, -lən) *n.* The anterior portion of the forebrain, including the cerebral cortex, olfactory lobes, and related parts. Also called "endbrain". [TEL(O)- + ENCEPHALON.] —**tel·en·ce·phal·ic** (-si-fál-ik, -sə-, -se-) *adj.*

tel·e·ol·o·gy (télli-ólləji, téeli-) *n., pl.* **-gies. 1.** The philosophical study of manifestations of design or purpose in natural processes or occurrences. **2.** Such overall purpose or design as exhibited in natural phenomena. **3.** The doctrine that such overall purpose or design underlies and determines natural processes. [New Latin *teleologia* : Greek *teleos*, complete, from *telos*, completion, end + -LOGY.] —**tel·e·o·log·i·cal** (-ə-lójik'l), **tel·e·o·log·ic** *adj.* —**tel·e·o·log·i·cal·ly** *adv.* —**tel·e·ol·o·gist** (-ólləjist) *n.*

tel·e·ost (télli-ost, téeli-) *n.* Also **tel·e·os·te·an** (-ósti-ən). A member of the Teleostei (or Teleostomi), a group consisting of fishes having bony skeletons and including the majority of living species. [New Latin *Teleostei*, "ones having complete bony skeletons", and *Teleostomi*, "ones having complete mouths" : Greek *teleos*, complete (see **teleology**) + Greek *osteon*, bone and *stoma*, mouth (see **stomach**).] —**tel·e·ost**, **tel·e·os·te·an** *adj.*

te·lep·a·thy (ti-léppəthi, te-, tə-) *n.* **1.** Transference of thoughts between people by scientifically unknown or inexplicable means. **2.** The ability to produce or engage in such communication. Also called "thought transference". [TELE- + -PATHY.] —**tel·e·path·ic** (télli-páthik) *adj.* —**tel·e·path·i·cal·ly** *adv.* —**te·lep·a·thise**, **te·lep·a·thize** (ti-léppə-thīz, te-, tə-) *intr.v.* —**te·lep·a·thist** (-thist) *n.*

tel·e·phone (télli-fōn) *n. Abbr.* **tel. 1.** An instrument that directly modulates carrier waves with voice or other acoustic source signals to be transmitted to distant locations and that directly reconverts received waves into audible signals; especially, such an instrument connected to others by wire. **2.** A system of such instruments together with connecting and supporting equipment.
~*v.* **telephoned**, **-phoning**, **-phones.** —*tr.* **1.** To call or communicate with (a person) by telephone. **2.** To transmit (a recorded message, television picture, or document) by telephone, using special receiving and sending equipment. —*intr.* To communicate by telephone. [TELE- + -PHONE.] —**tel·e·phon·er** *n.* —**tel·e·phon·ic** (télli-fónnik) *adj.* —**tel·e·phon·i·cal·ly** *adv.*

telephone book *n.* **1.** A book in which one writes useful telephone numbers. **2.** A telephone directory.

telephone box *n.* A small enclosure containing a public telephone. Also called "telephone booth", "call box".

telephone directory *n.* An alphabetical or classified list of all the telephone subscribers in an area, together with their addresses and telephone numbers. Also "telephone book".

telephone exchange *n.* Any of numerous central systems of switches and other equipment that establish connections between individual telephones. Also called "exchange".

telephone number *n.* A set of digits used to identify and call individual subscribers to a telephone system.

telephone receiver *n.* The part of a telephone in which incoming electrical impulses are converted into sound.

te·leph·o·nist (ti-léffənist, te-, tə-) *n.* One who works as an operator at a telephone switchboard.

te·leph·o·ny (ti-léffəni, te-, tə-) *n.* The electrical transmission of sound between distant points, especially by radio or telephone.

tel·e·pho·to (télli-fő-tō, -fő-) *adj.* Of, pertaining to, or designating a photographic lens or lens system used to produce a large image of a distant object.

tel·e·pho·tog·ra·phy (télli-fə-tóggrəfi) *n.* **1.** The process or technique of photographing distant objects, using a telephoto lens or telescope on a camera. **2.** The technique or process of transmitting charts, pictures, and photographs over a distance. —**tel·e·pho·to·graph·ic** (-főtə-gráffik) *adj.*

tel·e·play (télli-play) *n. Chiefly U.S.* A play written or adapted for television.

tel·e·print·er (télli-printər) *n.* An electromechanical typewriter that transmits and receives messages coded in electrical signals by telegraph or telephone. Also *U.S.* "teletypewriter". See **telex.**

Tel·e·promp·ter (télli-promptər) *n.* A trademark for a type of **autocue** (*see*).

Tel·e·ran (télli-ran) *n.* A trademark for a system used in air traffic control in which the image of a ground-based radar unit is televised to aircraft in the vicinity so that a pilot may see his position in relation to other aircraft.

tel·e·scope (télli-skōp) *n.* An instrument for collecting and examining electromagnetic radiation, especially: **1.** An arrangement of lenses or mirrors or both that gathers visible light, permitting direct observation or photographic recording of distant objects. **2.** Any of various devices, such as a radio telescope, used to detect and observe distant objects by their emission, transmission, reflection, or other interaction with invisible radiation.
~*v.* **telescoped**, **-scoping**, **-scopes.** —*tr.* **1.** To cause to slide inwards or outwards in overlapping sections, as the cylindrical sections of a small hand telescope. **2.** To crush or compress inwards or together, especially as the result of a collision. **3.** To make shorter or more precise; condense: *He telescoped his speech into a few dramatic phrases.* —*intr.* To slide inwards or outwards in or as if in

overlapping cylindrical sections; become telescoped. [New Latin *telescopium* or Italian *telescopio,* from Greek *teleskopos,* farseeing : TELE- + *skopos,* watcher.]

tel·e·scop·ic (télli-skóppik) *adj.* **1.** Of or pertaining to a telescope. **2.** Seen through or obtained by means of a telescope. **3.** Visible only by means of a telescope. **4.** Incorporating a telescope: *a telescopic sight.* **5.** Able to discern distant objects; farseeing. **6.** Extensible or compressible by or as if by the successive sliding of overlapping concentric tubular sections: *a telescopic umbrella.* **—tel·e·scop·i·cal·ly** *adv.*

Tel·e·sco·pi·um (télli-skṓpi-əm) *n.* A constellation in the Southern Hemisphere near Scorpius and Sagittarius. [New Latin, from *telescopium,* TELESCOPE.]

te·les·co·py (ti-léskəpi, te-, tə-) *n.* The art or study of making and operating telescopes. **—te·les·co·pist** *n.*

tel·e·spec·tro·scope (télli-spéktrə-skōp) *n.* A spectroscope used in conjunction with an astronomical telescope to enable a spectroscopic analysis to be made of radiation from distant stars.

tel·e·ster·e·o·scope (télli-stérri-ə-skōp, -stéer-i-) *n.* A binocular telescope for stereoscopic viewing of distant objects.

tel·e·tex (télli-teks) *n.* A system enabling typescript messages, especially those produced by word processors, to be electronically transmitted directly over the telephone system. [TELE- + TEX(T).]

tel·e·text (télli-tekst) *n.* **1.** Any of various one-way systems for broadcasting information in the form of text that uses television channels and a specially adapted television set as a receiver. **2.** Information broadcast by this method. Compare **viewdata.**

tel·e·ther·mo·scope (télli-thérmə-skōp) *n.* An apparatus for indicating or recording the temperatures of remote locations.

tel·e·thon (télli-thon) *n.* A long, continuous television programme, usually to raise funds for charity. [TELE- + (MARA)THON.]

Tel·e·type (télli-tīp) *n.* A trademark for a brand of teleprinter. ~*v.* **Teletyped, -typing, -types.** —*intr.* To operate a Teletype. —*tr.* To send a message by Teletype.

tel·e·type·writ·er (télli-tīp-rītər) *n. U.S.* A **teleprinter** *(see).*

te·leu·to·so·rus (ti-lōō-tə-sáw-rəss, te-, tə-, -léw- || -sō-) *n.* A telium. [Greek *teleutē,* end (see **teleutospore**) + SORUS.]

te·leu·to·spore (ti-lōō-tə-spawr, tə-, -léw-, -tō- || -spōr) *n.* A teliospore. [Greek *teleutē,* end, from *telos,* end, completion + SPORE.] **—te·leu·to·spor·ic** (-spórrik, -spáwrik) *adj.*

tel·e·vise (télli-vīz) *v.* **-vised, -vising, -vises.** —*tr.* **1.** To broadcast (a programme) by television. **2.** To film (an event) for a television broadcast. —*intr.* To broadcast by television. [Back-formation from TELEVISION.]

tel·e·vi·sion (télli-vizh'n, téllə-, -vízh'n) *n. Abbr.* **TV 1.** The transmission of visual images of moving and stationary objects, generally with accompanying sound, as electromagnetic waves and the reconversion of received waves into visual images. **2.** An electronic apparatus that receives such waves and displays the reconverted images on a screen. **3.** The integrated audible and visible content of the electromagnetic waves received and converted by such an apparatus; that which is shown by means of television. **4.** The industry of broadcasting television programmes. [French *télévision* : TELE- + VISION.] **—tel·e·vi·sion·al, tel·e·vi·sion·a·ry** (-əri || -erri) *adj.*

television tube *n.* A form of cathode-ray tube designed for use in a television receiver. Also called "picture tube", "tube".

tel·ex (tél-eks) *n.* **1.** A communication system consisting of teleprinters connected to a telephonic network to send and receive signals. **2.** A message sent or received by such a system. **3.** A teleprinter used in such a system. ~*tr.v.* **telexed, -exing, -exes.** To send (a message) or communicate with (a person) by telex. [TEL(ETYPEWRITER) + EX(CHANGE).]

telfer. Variant of **telpher.**

tel·ic (téllik, téelik) *adj.* Directed or tending towards a definite goal or purpose; purposeful. [Greek *telikos,* final, from *telos,* end.]

te·li·o·spore (téeli-ə-spawr, -ō- || -spōr) *n.* A dark, thick-walled spore produced at the end of the summer by rust fungi. It remains dormant through the winter and germinates in the spring to quit the basidium. Also called "telentospore". [TELIUM + SPORE.]

te·li·um (téeli-əm) *n., pl.* **-lia** (-ə). A dark, pustule-like structure formed on plant tissue infected by a rust fungus, and giving rise to teliospores. [New Latin, from Greek *teleios,* complete (formed in the final stage of the cycle of rust fungi), from *telos,* end, completion.] **—te·li·al** *adj.*

tell[1] (tel) *v.* **told** (tōld), **telling, tells.** —*tr.* **1.** To give a detailed account of; narrate; recount: *tell a story.* **2.** To communicate by speech or writing; express with words: *tell a lie; told us the news.* **3.** To make something known to; notify; inform: *told the authorities.* **4.** To show, explain, or make clear: *His face told us he wasn't joking; Will you tell me how to work the copier?* **5.** To make known; reveal; disclose: *tell a secret.* **6. a.** To command; order: *Do what I tell you.* **b.** To warn; advise: *I told you that would happen.* **7.** *Informal.* To assure: *I tell you, he's an honest man.* Often used for emphasis. **8.** To know or come to know, as through observation or experience; discern: *I can always tell when he's lying.* **9.** To distinguish or recognise; discriminate: *can't tell the difference between margarine and butter.* **10.** *Informal.* To make clear one's low or contemptuous opinion of (someone): *Well, that's certainly telling him!* —*intr.* **1.** To give an account, enumeration, or description. **2.** To give evidence or indication: *Silence told of their unease.* **3. a.** To have an effect or impact: *In this game every move tells.* **b.** To have an exhausting or detrimental effect: *Pressure began to tell on her.* **4.** To reveal the secrets of another: *Promise not to tell!* **—tell off. 1.** To count and set apart, especially aloud. **2.** *Informal.* To rebuke severely; scold. **—tell on.** *Informal.* To inform against; tattle on. **—tell (someone) where to get off.** *Slang.* To rebuff or correct in an aggressive manner. **—you're telling me** or **tell me about it.** I know that only too well. Used for emphasis. [Tell, told (past tense), told (past participle); Middle English *tellen, told* (or *tald*), *ytold* (or *ytald*), Old English *tellan, tealde, geteald.*] **—tell·a·ble** *adj.*

tell[2] or **tel** *n.* An artificial hillock, found especially in the Middle East, formed from the accumulation of debris, earth, or other material, on the site of an ancient settlement. [Arabic *tall,* hillock.]

Tell (tel), **William.** Swiss hero. According to legend he was sentenced to shoot an apple off his son's head with a crossbow for an act of disrespect to the Austrian bailiff Gessler. He did so, then shot Gessler. The events supposedly took place *c.*1300.

tell·er (téllər) *n.* **1.** One who tells. **2.** A person appointed to count votes in a legislative assembly, such as the House of Commons. **3.** *Chiefly U.S. & Scottish.* A bank employee who deals directly with the public, receiving and paying out money. **—tell·er·ship** *n.*

tell·ing (télling) *adj.* **1.** Having force or effect; striking. **2.** Full of underlying meaning; revealing: *gave a short, telling cough.* —See Synonyms at **valid. —tell·ing·ly** *adv.*

tell·tale (tél-tayl) *n.* **1.** One who informs on another person; a tattler; a talebearer. **2.** Anything that provides evidence of something secret or hidden, as of a person's feelings or conduct; a revealing sign. Also used adjectivally: *a telltale blush; the telltale pile of empty wine bottles.* **3.** Any of various devices that indicate or register information, especially: **a.** A time clock for recording an employee's attendance. **b.** A device indicating the position of a ship's rudder. **c.** A compass used by the captain of a ship to check the course.

tel·lu·rate (téllewr-ayt) *n.* A salt or ester of telluric acid.

tel·lu·ri·an (te-léwr-i-ən, -lóor-) *adj.* Of, pertaining to, or inhabiting the Earth. ~*n.* **1.** An inhabitant of the Earth; a terrestrial. **2.** Variant of **tellurion.** [Latin *tellūs* (stem *tellūr-*), Earth.]

tel·lu·ric (te-léwr-ik, -tóor-) *adj.* **1.** Of, or relating to the Earth; earthly; terrestrial. **2.** Derived from or containing tellurium, especially with valency 6. [From Latin *tellūs* (stem *tellūr-*), Earth.]

telluric acid *n.* A white, crystalline inorganic acid, H_6TeO_6, that is used as a chemical reagent.

tel·lu·ride (téllewr-īd) *n.* A binary compound of tellurium. [TELLUR(IUM) + -IDE.]

tel·lu·ri·on (te-léwr-i-ən, -lóor-, -on) *n.* Also **tel·lu·ri·an** (-ən). An instrument that shows how the movement of the Earth on its axis and around the Sun causes day and night and the seasons. [Latin *tellūs* (stem *tellūr-*), Earth + -ION.]

tel·lu·ri·um (te-léwr-i-əm, -lóor-) *n. Symbol* **Te** A brittle, silvery-white metallic element, occurring naturally combined with gold and other metals, produced commercially as a by-product of the electrolytic refining of copper, and used to alloy stainless steel and lead, in ceramics, and, in the form of bismuth telluride, in thermoelectric devices. Atomic number 52, atomic weight 127.60, melting point 449.8°C, boiling point 989.8°C, relative density range 6.11-6.27, valencies 2, 4, 6. [New Latin, from Latin *tellūs* (stem *tellūr-*), Earth (by analogy with URANIUM, after the planet *Uranus*).]

tel·lu·ro·me·ter (téllewr-ómmitər) *n.* An electronic surveying device used to measure distances of up to 64 kilometres (40 miles) by the transmission of radio waves between two stations set up at the ends of the unknown distance, and measurement of the time the waves take to travel between the stations. [Latin *tellūs* (stem *tellūr-*), Earth + -METER.]

tel·lu·rous (téllewr-əss, te-léwr-əss, -lóor-) *adj.* Of, relating to, or derived from tellurium, especially with valency 4. [TELLURIUM + -OUS.]

tel·ly (télli) *n., pl.* **-lies.** *Chiefly British Informal.* Television.

telo-, tel- *comb. form.* Indicates: **1.** Completion, perfection, or finality; for example, **telophase. 2.** End or situated at the end; for example, **telencephalon.** [From Greek *telos,* end, completion.]

te·lom·er·i·sa·tion, te·lom·er·i·za·tion (tee-lómmər-ī-záysh'n, ti-, te- || *U.S.* -i-) *n.* The polymerisation of a chemical substance in the presence of a chain transfer agent to give products of relatively low molecular weight. [TELO- + (POLY)MERISATION.]

te·lo·phase (téel-ō-fayz, tél-, -ə-) *n.* The last phase of mitosis and meiosis, in which the daughter chromosomes are grouped either in two diploid daughter cells (mitosis) or four haploid gametes (meiosis). [TELO- + PHASE.]

tel·pher, tel·fer (télfər) *n.* Also **tel·pher·age** (-ij) (for sense 2). **1.** A device for transporting loads consisting of a light car suspended from overhead wire cables and usually driven by electricity. **2.** A transport system using these cars. ~*tr.v.* **telphered, -phering, -phers.** To transport by telpher. [From TEL(E)- + Greek *pherein,* to carry.]

tel·son (télss'n) *n.* A terminal structure of the posterior section of certain arthropods, such as the sting of a scorpion. [New Latin, from Greek, headland, limit, from *telos,* end.]

Tel·u·gu, Tel·e·gu (tél-ə-gōō, -ōō-, -gōō) *n., pl.* **-gus** or collectively **Telugu. 1.** A Dravidian language spoken chiefly in Andhra Pradesh, India. **2.** A member of a Dravidian people who speak this language. **—Tel·u·gu** *adj.*

tem·er·ar·i·ous (témmə-ráir-i-əss) *adj. Formal.* Presumptuously or recklessly daring; rash. [Latin *temerārius,* rash, from *temere,* rashly. See **temerity.**] **—tem·er·ar·i·ous·ly** *adv.* **—tem·er·ar·i·ous·ness** *n.*

te·mer·i·ty (ti-mérrəti, te-, tə-) *n.* Foolhardy or heedless disregard of danger; foolish boldness; recklessness; rashness. [Middle English *temeryte,* from Latin *temeritās,* from *temere,* blindly, rashly.]

Synonyms: *temerity, audacity, impetuosity, effrontery, nerve, cheek, gall.*

temp (temp) *n. Informal.* A person, such as a typist or secretary, who is employed or usually works on a temporary basis.

~*intr.v.* **temped, temping, temps.** *Informal.* To work as a temp.

temp. **1.** in the time of. [Latin *tempore*]. **2.** temperature.

tem·per (témpər) *v.* **-pered, -pering, -pers.** —*tr.* **1.** To modify by the addition of some moderating agent or quality; moderate: *tempered severity with kindness.* **2.** To bring to a suitable or desired consistency, texture, hardness, or other physical condition by or as by blending, admixture, kneading, or a similar process. **3.** To harden, strengthen, or toughen (a metal) by application of heat or by alternate heating and cooling. **4.** *Music.* To adjust or tune (a keyboard instrument) by temperament. —*intr.* To be or become tempered; especially, to reach a suitable degree of hardness or strength. Used of a metal.

~*n.* **1. a.** A person's habitual cast of mind or emotions; a disposition; a temperament: *a sweet temper.* **b.** A temporary state of mind or emotions having a particular character; a mood; a humour: *in a foul temper.* **2.** Calmness of mind or emotions; equanimity; composure: *lost my temper; keep one's temper.* **3. a.** A tendency to become easily angry or irritable: *Control your temper.* **b.** An outburst of rage: *a fit of temper.* **4. a.** The condition of being tempered. **b.** The degree of hardness and elasticity of a metal, usually steel, as a result of tempering. **5.** A substance or agent added to something to alter or modify it. **6.** *Archaic.* A middle course; a compromise between extremes. —See Synonyms at **mood.** [Middle English *temp(e)ren,* Old English *temprian,* to mingle, moderate, from Latin *temperāre,* "to mingle in due proportion", probably from *tempus* (stem *tempor-*), time, due season.] **—tem·per·a·bil·i·ty** (-ə-bílləti) *n.* **—tem·per·a·ble** *adj.* **—tem·per·er** *n.*

tem·per·a (témpərə) *n.* **1.** A painting medium in which pigment is mixed with water-soluble glutinous materials such as egg yolk or white. **2.** Painting done with this medium. [Italian, from *temperare,* to mingle, temper, from Latin *temperāre.* See **temper.**]

tem·per·a·ment (tém-prə-mənt, -pərə-) *n.* **1. a.** The manner of thinking, behaving, or reacting characteristic of a particular individual; a disposition: *a nervous temperament.* **b.** The distinguishing mental and physical characteristics that established the constitution of a person according to medieval physiology, caused by the dominance of one of the four humours. See **humour. 2.** A tendency to become irritable or to be too sensitive; a temper. **3.** *Music.* A method of selecting the intervals between the notes of a scale, such as **equal temperament** *(see),* the system used on modern keyboard instruments. —See Synonyms at **disposition.** [Middle English *temperament,* from Latin *temperāmentum,* "a mixing (of the humours)", from *temperāre,* to mingle, TEMPER.]

tem·per·a·men·tal (tém-prə-mént'l, -pərə-) *adj.* **1.** Of, pertaining to, or arising from temperament or temper. **2.** Excessively sensitive or irritable; easily excited or angered; moody. **3.** *Informal.* Tending to behave or perform in an erratic or unpredictable manner: *a temperamental old car.* **—tem·per·a·men·tal·ly** *adv.*

tem·per·ance (témpərənss, témprənss) *n.* **1.** The condition or quality of being temperate; moderation or self-restraint. **2. a.** Moderation in the consumption of alcoholic drinks. **b.** Total abstinence from alcoholic drinks. —See Synonyms at **abstinence.**

tem·per·ate (témpə-rət, témp-, -rit) *adj.* **1.** Exercising moderation and self-restraint, especially with regard to bodily and emotional indulgence: *a temperate drinker.* **2.** Moderate in degree or quality; tempered. **3. a.** Neither hot nor cold in climate; free from climatic extremes; mild. **b.** Occurring in or characteristic of the temperate zone: *temperate vegetation.* [Middle English, from Latin *temperātus,* from the past participle of *temperāre,* to moderate, TEMPER.]

temperate zone *n. Often capital* **T,** *capital* **Z.** Either of two middle latitude zones of the Earth, the *North Temperate Zone* and the *South Temperate Zone,* lying between about 23°30′ and 66°30′ north and south.

tem·per·a·ture (tém-pri-chər, -pəri-, -rə-, -pərə-) *n. Abbr.* **temp.** *Symbol* **T 1. a.** The degree of hotness or coldness of a body or environment. **b.** A specific degree of hotness or coldness as indicated on or referred to a standard scale; a scalar quantity that is independent of the size of the system and that determines the direction of heat flow between any two systems in thermal contact. **2.** A temperature above normal body temperature, caused by illness. [Originally "a tempering", moderate condition (of weather), from Latin *temperātūra,* from *temperāre,* to mix, TEMPER.]

temperature gradient *n.* The rate of change of temperature with displacement in a given direction from a given reference point.

tem·pered (témpərd) *adj.* **1.** Having a specified type of temper or disposition. Used in combination: *sweet-tempered.* **2.** *Music.* Tuned to temperament; specifically, tuned to equal temperament. Said of a scale, interval, semitone, or intonation. **3.** Having the requisite degree of hardness or elasticity. Said of a metal.

tem·pest (témpist) *n. Literary.* **1.** A violent onrush or storm of wind, frequently accompanied by rain, snow, or hail. **2.** An agitated or tumultuous condition: *battered by the political tempest.*

~*tr.v.* **tempested, -pesting, -pests.** *Poetic.* To disturb or agitate violently. [Middle English *tempeste,* from Old French, from Vulgar Latin *tempesta* (unattested), variant of Latin *tempestās,* storm, weather, season, from *tempus,* time, season. See **temporal.**]

tem·pes·tu·ous (tem-péstew-əss, təm-) *adj.* **1.** Pertaining to, characterised by, or resembling a tempest: *tempestuous weather.* **2.** Tumultuous; stormy; turbulent: *years of tempestuous marriage.* **—tem·pes·tu·ous·ly** *adv.* **—tem·pes·tu·ous·ness** *n.*

Tem·plar (témplər) *n.* **1.** A **Knight Templar** *(see).* **2.** *Small* **t.** *British.* A barrister having chambers in the Middle or Lower Temple in London. [Middle English *templer,* from Anglo-French, variant of Old French *templier,* from Medieval Latin *(mīles) templāri(u)s,* "(soldier) of the temple", from Latin *templum,* TEMPLE.]

tem·plate (tém-plət, -plit, *also* -playt) *n.* Also **tem·plet. 1.** A pattern or gauge, such as a thin metal plate with a cut pattern, used as a guide in making something accurately, as in woodworking, or in replication of a standard object. **2.** A piece of stone or timber used to distribute weight or pressure, as over a door frame. **3.** A macromolecule, such as DNA, RNA, or messenger RNA, the structure of which serves as a guide for the assembly of nucleic acids and polypeptides. [Earlier *templet* (influenced by PLATE), from French, diminutive of Old French *temple,* TEMPLE (device in a loom).]

tem·ple¹ (témp'l) *n.* **1.** A building or place dedicated to religious worship or the presence of a deity. Used chiefly with reference to the sacred buildings of the ancient world, and to those of eastern religions such as Hinduism, Buddhism, or Shintoism. **2.** *Capital* **T.** Any of three successive buildings in ancient Jerusalem dedicated to the worship of God. **3.** A Christian church; especially, a Mormon or French Protestant church. **4.** Anything considered to contain a divine presence: *The body is the temple of the soul.* **5.** Any place or building serving as the focus of a special activity or of something especially valued: *a temple of learning.* **6.** *Capital* **T.** Either of two Inns of Court in London, the **Inner Temple** and **Middle Temple** *(both of which see),* on the site formerly occupied by the Knights Templar. **7.** *U.S.* A synagogue. [Middle English *temple,* from Old English *tempel* and Old French *temple,* from Latin *templum,* sanctuary, space marked for observation by an augur.]

temple² *n.* The flat region on either side of the forehead above the cheek bone. [Middle English, from Old French, from Vulgar Latin *tempula* (unattested), variant of Latin *tempora,* plural of *tempus,* temple of the head.]

temple³ *n.* A device in a loom that keeps the cloth stretched to the correct width during weaving. [Middle English *tempylle,* from Old French *temple,* from Latin *templum,* small piece of wood.]

tem·po (tém-pō) *n., pl.* **-pos** or **-pi** (-pee). **1.** *Abbr.* **t.** *Music.* The relative speed at which a composition is to be played, as indicated by a descriptive or metronomic direction to the performer. **2.** A characteristic rate or rhythm of activity; pace: *the quick tempo of modern life.* [Italian, "time", from Latin *tempus.* See **temporal.**]

tem·po·ral¹ (témp-ərəl, -rəl) *adj.* **1.** Pertaining to, concerned with, or limited by time. **2.** Pertaining to or concerned with earthly life or existence. **3.** Civil, secular, or lay, as distinguished from ecclesiastical: *the Lords temporal.* **4. a.** *Grammar.* Expressing time: *a temporal conjunction.* **b.** Of or pertaining to a verbal tense. [Middle English *temporal,* from Latin *temporālis,* from *tempus*† (stem *tempor-*), time.] **—tem·po·ral·ly** *adv.*

temporal² *adj.* Of, pertaining to, or near the temples of the skull. [Late Latin *temporālis,* from Latin *tempus* (stem *tempor-*), TEMPLE (of the head).]

temporal bone *n.* Either of two complex bones forming the sides and base of the skull and housing the middle and inner ear. Also called "temporal fossa".

tem·po·ral·i·ty (témpə-rál-əti) *n., pl.* **-ties. 1.** The condition of being temporal or temporary. **2. a.** Something that is temporal. **b.** *Usually plural.* Temporal possessions, especially of the church or clergy.

temporal lobe *n.* The part of each cerebral hemisphere associated with the perception and interpretation of sound and possibly with memory.

tem·po·rar·y (témpə-rəri, témp-, *also* -ri || -rerri) *adj.* Lasting, used, or enjoyed for a limited time; impermanent; transient: *a temporary job; temporary relief.* —See Synonyms at **transient.**

~*n.* One that is employed only for a limited time. [Latin *temporārius,* from *tempus* (stem *tempor-*), time. See **temporal.**] **—tem·po·rar·i·ly** (-rərəli, *also* -rəli, -rérrəli) *adv.* **—tem·po·rar·i·ness** *n.*

tem·po·rise, tem·po·rize (témpə-rīz) *intr.v.* **-rised, -rising, -rises. 1.** To compromise or act evasively in order to gain time, avoid argument, or postpone a decision. **2. a.** To act or behave in a way appropriate to particular circumstances. **b.** To yield ostensibly or temporarily to what current conditions demand. [French *temporiser,* from Medieval Latin *temporizāre,* to wait one's time, from Latin *tempus* (stem *tempor-*), time. See **temporal.**] **—tem·po·ri·sa·tion** (-rī-záysh'n || *U.S.* -ri-) *n.*

tempt (tempt) *tr.v.* **tempted, tempting, tempts. 1.** To entice (a person) to commit a usually unwise or immoral act, especially by a promise of reward. **2.** To attract or invite: *I must say I'm tempted by the offer.* **3.** To provoke or to risk provoking: *They tempted fate rashly.* **4.** To incline or dispose strongly: *I was tempted just to give the whole thing up.* **5.** *Archaic.* To put to the test: *God tempted Abraham.* —See Synonyms at **lure.** [Middle English *tempten,* from Old French *tempter,* from Latin *temptāre*†, to try, test, tempt.] **—tempt·a·ble** *adj.* **—tempt·er** *n.*

temp·ta·tion (témp-táysh'n, tem-) *n.* **1.** The act of tempting or the condition of being tempted. **2.** Something that tempts or entices.

tempt·ing (témpting) *adj.* Alluring, enticing, or seductive. **—tempt·ing·ly** *adv.* **—tempt·ing·ness** *n.*

temp·tress (témp-trəss, -triss) *n.* A woman who seeks to seduce a man.

tem·pu·ra (tem-pŏŏr-ə, témpə-rə, -raa) *n.* A Japanese dish of vegetables and seafood dipped in batter and fried in deep fat. [Japanese, "fried food".]

ten (ten) *n.* **1. a.** The cardinal number that is one more than nine. **b.** A symbol representing this, such as 10, X, or x. **2.** A set made up of ten persons or things. **3. a.** The tenth in a series. **b.** A playing card marked with ten pips. **4.** Ten parts: *cut in ten.* **5.** A size, as in clothing, designated as ten. **6.** A bank note or coin having a denomination of ten: *I'll have the money in tens.* **7.** Ten hours after midnight or midday. [Middle English *ten,* Old English *tīen, tēne, tȳn.*] **—ten** *adj.* **—ten•fold** (-fōld, -fōld) *adj. & adv.*

ten. *Music.* **1.** tenor. **2.** tenuto.

ten•a•ble (ténnəb'l) *adj.* Capable of being defended or sustained, as against critical argument or military attack: *a tenable position.* [French *tenable,* from *tenir,* to hold, from Latin *tenēre.*] **—ten•a•bil•i•ty** (ténnə-bílləti), **ten•a•ble•ness** *n.* **—ten•a•bly** *adv.*

ten•ace (tén-ayss, -əss, -iss, te-náyss) *n.* In card games such as bridge and whist, the holding of a combination of two nonconsecutive high cards of a suit, such as the king and the jack. [French, TENACIOUS.]

te•na•cious (ti-náyshəss, te-, tə-) *adj.* **1. a.** Holding or tending to hold or maintain firmly. **b.** Persistent; resolute; stubborn. **2.** Holding together firmly; cohesive. **3.** Clinging to another object or surface; adhesive. **4.** Tending to retain; retentive. —See Synonyms at **strong.** [Latin *tenāx* (stem *tenāc-*), from *tenēre,* to hold.] **—te•na•cious•ly** *adv.* **—te•na•cious•ness** *n.*

te•nac•i•ty (ti-nássəti, te-, tə-) *n.* The condition or quality of being tenacious. See Synonyms at **courage, perseverance.**

te•nac•u•lum (ti-náckew-ləm, te-, tə-) *n., pl.* **-la** (-lə). A long-handled, slender, hooked instrument for lifting and holding parts, such as blood vessels, during surgery. [New Latin, from Late Latin, holder, from Latin *tenēre,* to hold.]

ten•an•cy (ténnən-si) *n., pl.* **-cies. 1.** The possession or occupancy of lands or buildings by title, under a lease, or on payment of rent. **2.** The period of a tenant's occupancy or possession. **3.** The occupation or period of occupation of an office or position; tenure.

ten•ant (ténnənt) *n.* **1.** One who temporarily holds or occupies land, a building, or other property owned by another. **2.** *Law.* One who holds or possesses lands, tenements, and sometimes personal property by any kind of title. **3.** An occupant, inhabitant, or dweller in any place.
~tr.v. **tenanted, -anting, -ants.** To hold as a tenant; occupy; inhabit. [Middle English *tena(u)nt,* from Old French *tenant,* from the present participle of *tenir,* to hold, from Latin *tenēre,* to hold.]

tenant farmer *n.* One who farms land owned by another and pays rent in cash or as a proportion of his produce.

ten•ant•ry (ténnəntri) *n., pl.* **-ries. 1.** Tenants collectively, especially tenant farmers. **2.** The state or condition of being a tenant; tenancy.

tench (tench) *n., pl.* **tenches** or collectively **tench.** An edible Eurasian freshwater fish, *Tinca tinca,* having small scales and two barbels near the mouth. [Middle English *tenche,* from Old French, from Late Latin *tinca,* perhaps from Gaulish.]

Ten Commandments *pl.n.* The ten injunctions given by God to Moses on Mount Sinai, the basis of Mosaic Law. Exodus 20:1–17. Preceded by *the.* Also called "Decalogue".

tend¹ (tend) *intr.v.* **tended, tending, tends. 1.** To move or extend in a particular direction: *Our course tended towards the north.* **2.** To show a natural likelihood or inclination to act in a particular way or produce a particular effect; be apt: *War tends to defeat its purposes.* **3.** To be disposed or inclined: *He tends towards sarcasm.* [Middle English *tenden,* from Old French *tendre,* from Latin *tendere,* to stretch, direct one's course, be inclined.]

tend² *v.* **tended, tending, tends.** *—tr.* **1.** To minister to the needs of; look after: *tend a child.* **2.** To be in charge of; mind: *tend a shop.* *—intr.* **1.** To serve or wait. Used with *on* or *upon.* **2.** *Chiefly U.S. Informal.* To apply one's attention. Used with *to.* [Middle English *tenden,* short for *attenden,* ATTEND.]

Usage: *Tend* and *attend* are distinguished in formal English: one may *tend the sick people of the town* or *attend to the sick people of the town.* The use of *to* with *tend,* in the sense of "apply one's attention", is not standard, especially in British English.

ten•den•cy (téndən-si) *n., pl.* **-cies.** A demonstrated inclination to think, act, develop, or behave in a certain way; a propensity: *a tendency to panic; a tendency to lie.* [Medieval Latin *tendentia,* from Latin *tendēns,* present participle of *tendere,* to stretch, TEND.]

Synonyms: *tendency, trend, current, drift, inclination.*

ten•den•tious, ten•den•cious (ten-dénshəss) *adj.* Written or said with the aim of promoting a particular point of view; not impartial; biased. Used derogatorily. [From TENDENCY.] **—ten•den•tious•ly** *adv.* **—ten•den•tious•ness** *n.*

ten•der¹ (téndər) *adj.* **-derer, -derest. 1. a.** Easily damaged, bruised, or broken; delicate; fragile: *tender skin.* **b.** Easily chewed or cut: *tender beef.* **2.** Young and vulnerable: *of tender age.* **3.** Needing to be handled with tact and sensitivity: *a tender subject.* **4.** Sensitive to frost or severe cold; not hardy. Said of a plant. **5. a.** Easily hurt; sensitive: *a tender conscience.* **b.** Painful; sore. **6. a.** Gentle and solicitous: *a tender mother.* **b.** Expressing gentle emotions; loving: *a tender glance.* **c.** Given to sympathy or kindness; soft: *a tender heart.* **7.** Considerate and protective; careful to ward off harmful influences or avoid harmful action. Often used with *of: tender of her reputation.* **8.** *Nautical.* Apt to lean under sail; crank.
~tr.v. **tendered, -dering, -ders.** *Archaic.* **1.** To make tender. **2.** To treat with tender regard. [Middle English *tender, tendre,* from Old French *tendre,* from Latin *tener,* tender, delicate. **—ten•der•ly** *adv.* **—ten•der•ness** *n.*

tender² *n.* **1.** The act of tendering. **2.** A formal offer, as: **a.** *Law.* An offer of money or goods in payment of an obligation. **b.** A written offer to supply goods or perform work at a stated cost or rate; a bid. **3.** Anything that may be tendered as payment, especially money: *legal tender.*
~v. **tendered, -dering, -ders.** *—tr.* **1.** To offer formally; present: *tendered my resignation.* **2.** To offer (money or goods) in payment: *tendered the correct fare.* *—intr.* To make a tender; bid: *tender for a contract.* —See Synonyms at **offer.** [From Old French *tendre,* to offer, stretch out: see **tend** (move towards).] **—ten•der•er** *n.*

tender³ *n.* **1.** One who tends something. **2.** *Nautical.* A vessel attendant on another vessel or vessels, especially one that ferries supplies between ship and shore. **3.** A railway wagon attached to the rear of a steam locomotive and designed to carry fuel and water.

ten•der•foot (téndər-fŏŏt) *n., pl.* **-foots** or **-feet** (-feet). **1.** An inexperienced person or novice, especially one unaccustomed to rough conditions. **2.** A beginner in the ranks of the Scouts.

ten•der•heart•ed (téndər-hártid) *adj.* Easily moved by another's distress; compassionate. **—ten•der•heart•ed•ly** *adv.* **—ten•der•heart•ed•ness** *n.*

ten•der•ise, ten•der•ize (téndə-rīz) *tr.v.* **-ised, -ising, -ises.** To make (meat) tender, as by marinating, pounding, or applying a tenderiser. **—ten•der•i•sa•tion** (-rī-záysh'n || *U.S.* -ri-) *n.*

ten•der•is•er (téndə-rīzər) *n.* Any substance that tenderises meat by breaking down the meat fibres.

ten•der•loin (téndər-loyn) *n.* A cut of meat from under the short ribs that is the tenderest part of a loin of beef, pork, or the like.

ten•di•ni•tis (téndi-nītiss) *n.* Inflammation of a tendon and its muscle attachments. [New Latin *tendo* (stem *tendin-*), TENDON + -ITIS.]

ten•di•nous (téndinəss) *adj.* **1.** Of, having, or resembling a tendon or tendons. **2.** Sinewy. [New Latin *tendinosus,* from *tendo* (stem *tendin-*), from Medieval Latin *tendō,* TENDON.]

ten•don (téndən) *n.* A band of tough, inelastic fibrous tissue that connects a muscle with its bony attachment; a sinew. [From Medieval Latin *tendō* (stem *tendin-*), from Latin *tendere,* to stretch.]

ten•dril (tén-dril, -drəl) *n.* **1.** A long, slender, coiling extension, as of a stem, serving as an organ of attachment for certain climbing plants, such as the grape. **2.** Something resembling this: *wispy tendrils of hair.* [Probably from obsolete French *tendrillon,* diminutive of Old French *tendron,* cartilage, young shoot, from Vulgar Latin *tenerūmen* (unattested), from Latin *tener,* tender, delicate.]

Ten•e•brae (ténni-bree, -bray) *n. Used with a singular or plural verb. Roman Catholic Church.* The office of matins and lauds sung on the last three days of Holy Week, with a ceremony of candles. [Medieval Latin, from Latin, darkness.]

ten•e•brif•ic (ténni-briffik) *adj. Archaic & Literary.* Serving to obscure or darken. [Latin *tenebrae,* darkness (see **Tenebrae**) + -FIC.]

ten•e•brous (ténnibrəss) *adj.* Also **te•neb•ri•ous** (tə-nébbri-əss, te-). *Literary.* Dark and gloomy. [From Latin *tenebrae,* darkness. See **Tenebrae.**] **—ten•e•bros•i•ty** (ténni-bróssəti) *n.*

ten•e•ment (tén-i-mənt, -ə-) *n.* **1.** A building to live in; a dwelling-house; a residence. **2.** A large building divided into separate flats for rent, typically meeting only minimal standards of facilities and maintenance and usually found in deprived urban areas. Also called "tenement house". **3.** *Chiefly British.* A room or set of rooms leased to a tenant, especially one that is part of a large house or building. **4.** *Law.* Any kind of real property held by one person from another; a holding. [Middle English *tenement,* from Old French, from Medieval Latin *tenementum,* feudal holding, house, from Latin *tenēre,* to hold.] **—ten•e•men•tal** (-mént'l), **ten•e•men•ta•ry** (-méntəri) *adj.*

Te•ne•ri•fe or **Ten•e•riffe** (ténnə-réef; *Spanish* -réefay). Largest and most populated of the Canary Islands, the site of the capital city of Santa Cruz. It is admired for its scenic beauty.

te•nes•mus (ti-néz-məss, ti-, tə-, -néss-) *n.* **1.** A painful attempt to urinate or defaecate. **2.** Pain associated with urination or defaecation. [Medieval Latin, variant of Latin *tenesmos,* from Greek *teinesmos,* "a straining", from *teinein,* to stretch, strain.]

ten•et (tée-net, té-, -nit) *n.* A belief, doctrine, or principle, especially one held by a group of people. [Latin, he holds, from *tenēre,* to hold.]

Ten-Four (tén-fór || -fōr) *interj. Slang.* Yes. Used by users of Citizens' Band Radio.

ten-gal•lon hat (tén-gal-ən) *n.* A felt hat having an exceptionally tall crown and wide brim, popular in the American West.

tenia. Variant of **taenia.**

ten•ner (ténnər) *n. Informal.* A ten-pound note or a ten-dollar note.

Ten•nes•see¹ (ténnə-sée, ténni-). State in the south central United States on the east bank of the Mississippi. The capital is Nashville; the largest city is Memphis. It is an agricultural state, a leading producer of the plantation crops, tobacco and cotton. Tennessee is the nation's leading producer of zinc, and its industries are expanding. It entered the Union in 1796.

Tennessee². River in the south central United States, formed by the confluence of the rivers Holston and French Broad near Knoxville, in Tennessee. It flows for about 1 050 kilometres (650 miles) into the river Ohio at Paducah, in Kentucky. The Tennessee Valley Authority (TVA), formed in 1933, implemented a development plan for the river basin by constructing dams, providing navigable waterways, flood and erosion control, and hydroelectric power.

ten•nis (ténniss) *n.* **1.** A game played with rackets and a light ball by two players (singles) or two pairs of players (doubles) on a court divided by a net. Also used adjectivally: *a tennis shoe; a tennis ball.* **2. Lawn tennis** (see). **3. Real tennis** (see). [Middle English *tenetz, tennys,* probably from Old French *tenez,* imperative of *tenir,* to hold (probably from the call of the server to his opponent in the game), from Latin *tenēre,* to hold.]

tennis elbow *n.* A painful inflammation of the outer elbow resulting from excessive use of the muscles of the forearm.

Ten·ny·son (ténniss'n), **Alfred, 1st Baron** (1809–92). British poet. His first publication, *Poems, Chiefly Lyrical,* appeared in 1830. In 1850, "In Memoriam," written after the death of a close friend, Arthur Hallam, attracted the attention of both Queen Victoria and the Prime Minister, W. E. Gladstone. In the same year Tennyson was made Poet Laureate. "Idylls of the King" (1859) and later poems were inspired by ancient and medieval mythology. Poems like "The Charge of the Light Brigade" (1855) are the best known, but his best work lies in poems such as "Ulysses" (1859). —**Ten·ny·so·ni·an** (-sŏn-yən, -i-ən) *adj. & n.*

teno– *comb. form.* Indicates tendon; for example, **tenotomy.** [From Greek *tenōn,* tendon.]

Te·noch·ti·tlán (ti-nóchti-tlán, -tla'an). The ancient capital of the Aztec empire, on the site now occupied by Mexico City.

ten·on (ténnən) *n.* A projection on the end of a piece of wood shaped for insertion into a mortise.

~*tr.v.* **tenoned, -oning, -ons. 1.** To provide with a tenon. **2.** To join with a tenon. [Middle English, from Old French, from *tenir,* to hold, from Latin *tenēre.*]

tenon saw *n.* A short saw with fine teeth and a reinforced blade back, used for cutting tenons.

ten·or (ténnər) *n.* **1. a.** The general sense, meaning, or drift apparent in something written or spoken. **b.** A steady prevailing course or direction: *couldn't change the dramatic tenor of his life.* **2. a.** *Law.* The exact meaning or actual wording of a document as distinct from its effect. **b.** An exact copy or transcript of a document. **3.** *Abbr.* **ten., T., t.** *Music.* **a.** The highest natural adult male voice. **b.** A part for this voice. **c.** One who sings this part. **d.** The largest and lowest-pitched bell of a set. Also called "tenor bell".

~*adj.* Of, pertaining to, or having the range of a tenor: *a tenor sax.* [Middle English, general meaning, from Old French, from Latin *tenor,* uninterrupted course, a holding on, from *tenēre,* to hold.]

ten·o·rite (ténnə-rīt) *n.* A black copper ore consisting predominantly of copper oxide, CuO, occurring in the oxidised zone of weathered copper lodes.

te·nor·rha·phy (ti-nórrə-fi, te- ‖ -náwrə-) *n., pl.* **-phies.** The surgical uniting of divided tendons with sutures. [TENO- + Greek *-rrhaphia,* from *rhaptein,* to sew.]

te·no·sy·no·vi·tis (téenŏ-sī-nə-vítiss, ténnŏ-, -nŏ-) *n.* Inflammation of a tendon sheath. [TENO- + SYNOV(IA) + -ITIS.]

te·not·o·my (ti-nóttəmi, te-) *n., pl.* **-mies.** The surgical cutting of a tendon for the relief of deformities caused by shortening of a muscle. [TENO- + -TOMY.]

ten·pin bowling (tén-pin) *n.* A game played by rolling a ball down a wooden alley to knock down a triangular group of ten pins. Also called "bowling".

ten·rec (tén-rek) *n.* Also **tan·rec** (tán-, tón-). Any of various insectivorous, often hedgehog-like mammals of the family Tenrecidae, of Madagascar and adjacent islands. [French, from Malagasy *tàndraka.*]

tense¹ (tenss) *adj.* **tenser, tensest. 1.** Tightly stretched; taut; strained: *tense muscles.* **2.** In a state of mental or nervous tension. **3.** Nerve-racking; full of suspense: *a tense situation.* **4.** *Phonetics.* Enunciated with taut vocal muscles, as the consonant *t.* Compare **lax.** —See Synonyms at **stiff.**

~*v.* **tensed, tensing, tenses.** —*tr.* To make tense. —*intr.* To become tense. Often used with *up.* [Latin *tensus,* past participle of *tendere,* to stretch out.] —**tense·ly** *adv.* —**tense·ness, tensity** *n.*

tense² *n. Abbr.* **t. 1.** Any of the inflected forms in the conjugation of a verb that indicate the time (past, present, or future) as well as the continuance (imperfect) or completion (perfect) of the action or state. **2.** A set of such forms indicating a particular time: *the future tense.* [Middle English *tens,* tense, time, from Old French, from Latin *tempus,* time. See **temporal.**]

ten·sile (tén-sīl ‖ *chiefly U.S.* -s'l) *adj.* **1.** Of or pertaining to tension. **2.** Capable of being stretched or extended; ductile. [New Latin *tensilis,* from Latin *tensus,* "stretched", TENSE.] —**ten·sil·i·ty** (tensílləti) *n.*

tensile strength *n.* The resistance of a material to a force tending to tear it apart, expressed as the maximum longitudinal stress it can withstand.

ten·sim·e·ter (ten-símmitər) *n.* An apparatus used to measure differences in vapour pressure. [TENSI(ON) + -METER.]

ten·si·om·e·ter (tén-si-ómmitər) *n.* **1.** An instrument for measuring tensile strength. **2.** A torsion-balance apparatus used to measure the surface tension of a liquid. **3.** An instrument used to measure the moisture content of soil. [TENSIO(N) + -METER.]

ten·sion (ténsh'n) *n.* **1.** The act of stretching or the condition of being stretched. **2.** A force tending to produce elongation or extension. **3. a.** Mental, emotional, or nervous strain. **b.** An uneasy and potentially explosive condition of latent hostility and mistrust between persons or groups: *tension in the Middle East.* **c.** An atmosphere of suspense or suppressed excitement: *Tension mounts as the big match approaches.* **4.** The density of knitted fabrics determined by the size of needles and thickness of yarn, or the number of rows

and stitches needed to complete a given sample of fabric. Also *U.S.* "gauge". **5.** A device for regulating tautness; especially, a device regulating the tautness of thread on a sewing machine. **6.** *Electricity.* Voltage or potential; electromotive force.

~*tr.v.* **tensioned, -sioning, -sions.** To subject to tension; make taut. [Old French, from Latin *tensiō* (stem *tensiōn-*), from *tensus,* TENSE.] —**ten·sion·al** *adj.*

ten·sive (tén-siv) *adj.* Of or causing tension.

ten·sor (tén-sər, -sawr) *n.* **1.** *Anatomy.* Any muscle that tenses a part, making it firm. **2.** *Mathematics.* A set of components of a system in *n* dimensions, used to denote position determined within the context of more than one coordinate system, that may be linearly transformed between coordinate systems. —**ten·so·ri·al** (ten-sáw-ri-əl ‖ -sŏ-) *adj.*

tent¹ (tent) *n.* **1.** A portable shelter of canvas or other waterproof material stretched over a supporting framework of poles, ropes, and pegs. **2.** Something resembling this in construction or outline; especially, a medical tent placed over a patient's head so that his air supply may be regulated.

~*v.* **tented, tenting, tents.** —*intr.* To encamp in a tent. —*tr.* **1.** To form a tent over. **2.** To accomodate in tents. [Middle English *tente,* from Old French, from Vulgar Latin *tenta* (unattested), from the feminine past participle of *tendere,* to stretch.]

tent² *n.* In surgery, a small roll or plug, usually of lint or gauze, for placing in a wound or orifice to keep it open or for probing.

~*tr.v.* **tented, tenting, tents.** To keep (a wound or cut) open with a tent. [Middle English, a probe, from Old French *tente,* from *tenter,* to probe, test, from Latin *tentāre,* variant of *temptāre,* to feel, try, TEMPT.]

tent³ *n. Scottish.* Attention; heed. Used chiefly in the phrase *take tent.* [Middle English *tenten,* from *tent,* attention, short for *attent,* from Old French *attente,* from Latin *attenta,* feminine past participle of *attendere,* ATTEND.]

ten·ta·cle (téntək'l) *n.* **1.** *Zoology.* An elongated, flexible, unsegmented protrusion, such as one of those surrounding the mouth or oral cavity of the hydra, sea anemone, or squid. **2.** *Botany.* One of the hairs on the leaves of insectivorous plants, such as the sundew. **3.** Something resembling a tentacle, especially in ability to grasp or hold. [New Latin *tentaculum,* from Latin *tentāre,* variant of *temptāre,* to touch, feel, TEMPT.] —**ten·tac·u·lar** (ten-táckew-lər), **ten·tac·u·late** (-lət, -lit, -layt), **ten·ta·cled** *adj.*

tent·age (téntij) *n.* A supply of tents or tent equipment.

ten·ta·tive (téntətiv) *adj.* **1.** Of an experimental nature; provisional. **2.** Uncertain; hesitant: *a tentative smile.*

~*n.* Something tentative, such as a plan or proposal. [Medieval Latin *tentātīvus,* from Latin *tentātus,* past participle of *tentāre,* variant of *temptāre,* to feel, try, TEMPT.] —**ten·ta·tive·ly** *adv.* —**ten·ta·tive·ness** *n.*

tent caterpillar *n.* Any of several widely distributed destructive caterpillars of the genus *Malacosoma* that live in colonies in tentlike webs constructed in deciduous trees.

tent dress *n.* A full dress that flares out towards the bottom and is not taken in at the waist.

tent·ed (téntid) *adj.* **1.** Covered with tents: *a tented shoreline.* **2.** Sheltered in tents. **3.** Resembling a tent in shape.

ten·ter (téntər) *n.* **1.** A framework upon which milled cloth is stretched for drying without shrinkage. **2.** *Archaic.* A tenterhook. [Middle English *teyntur,* from Anglo-French *tentur* (unattested), from Medieval Latin *tentōrium,* from Latin *tentus,* past participle of *tendere,* to stretch.]

ten·ter·hook (téntər-hŏŏk ‖ -hŏŏk) *n.* A hooked nail for securing cloth on a tenter. —**on tenterhooks.** In a state of uneasiness, suspense, or anxiety.

tenth (tenth) *n.* **1.** The ordinal number ten in a series. **2.** One of ten equal parts. [Middle English *tenthe,* variant of earlier *tethe,* Old English *tēotha, teogetha.*] —**tenth** *adj. & adv.*

tent stitch *n.* A short diagonal embroidery stitch that forms close even, parallel rows to fill in a pattern or a background.

ten·u·is (ténnew-iss) *n., pl.* **-ues** (-eez). *Phonetics.* A voiceless stop; for example, the English consonants *p, t* and *k* are tenues. [New Latin (translation of Greek *psilos,* plain), from Latin, TENUOUS.]

ten·u·ous (ténnew-əss) *adj.* **1.** Lacking substance and strength; weak; flimsy: *a tenuous argument.* **2.** Having a thin consistency; diluted; rarefied. **3.** Having a thin or slender form. [Earlier *tenuious,* from Latin *tenuis,* thin, rare, fine. —**ten·u·ous·ly** *adv.* —**ten·u·ous·ness** *n.*

ten·ure (tén-yər, -yoor) *n.* **1. a.** The holding of something; especially, the holding or occupying of property for services rendered, the holding of an office. **b.** The terms or condition for such a holding. **c.** The period or duration of such a holding. **2.** *Chiefly U.S.* Permanence of position, as granted to employees in certain fields after a fixed number of years. [Middle English, from Old French, earlier *tenēure,* from *tenir,* to hold, from Latin *tenēre,* to hold.] —**ten·u·ri·al** (te-néwr-i-əl ‖ -nóor-) *adj.* —**ten·u·ri·al·ly** *adv.*

te·nu·to (ti-néw-tŏ, te-, -nŏŏ-) *adj. Abbr.* **ten.** *Music.* Held for the full time value; sustained. Said of a chord or note. —**te·nu·to** *adv.* [Italian, past participle of *tenere,* to hold, from Latin *tenēre.*]

te·o·cal·li (tée-ŏ-kál-i, -ə-; *Spanish* táy-ŏ-ka'a-yee) *n., pl.* **-lis.** Also **te·o·pan** (-pan, -paan). **1.** A temple of ancient Mexico and Central America, usually built upon a mound of a truncated pyramidal shape. **2.** The mound itself. [Nahuatl : *teotl,* god + *calli,* house.]

te·o·sin·te (tée-ŏ-sín-ti, táy-, -ə-, -tay) *n.* A tall Central American grass, *Euchlaena mexicana* (or *Zea mexicana*), closely related to maize and sometimes cultivated for fodder. [Mexican Spanish, from Nahuatl *teocentli* : *teotl,* god + *centli,* dried ear of corn.]

Te·o·ti·hua·cán (táy-ō-tée-wə-kán, -waa-, -kaán). Ancient city of Mexico, one of the oldest urban settlements in ancient America.

te·pal (téep'l, tépp'l) *n. Botany.* A division of the perianth of a flower having petals and sepals that are indistinguishable. [French *tépale,* perhaps a blend of PETAL and SEPAL.]

te·pee, tee·pee, ti·pi (tée-pee) *n.* A cone-shaped tent of skins or bark, supported by poles, used by North American Indians. Compare **wigwam.** [Dakota *tipi,* dwelling.]

tep·id (téppid) *adj.* **1.** Moderately warm; lukewarm. **2.** Lacking wholehearted interest, support, or enthusiasm: *a tepid reception.* [Latin *tepidus,* from *tepēre,* to be lukewarm.] **—te·pid·i·ty** (te-píddəti), **tep·id·ness** *n.* **—tep·id·ly** *adv.*

te·qui·la (ti-kéelə, te-, tə-) *n.* **1.** An alcoholic liquor distilled from a Central American plant, *Agave tequilana.* **2.** The plant itself. [Mexican Spanish, from *Tequila,* district in Mexico.]

ter- *comb. form.* Indicates three, third, or threefold; for example, **tercentenary.** [Latin *ter,* thrice.]

tera- *comb. form.* Symbol **T** Indicates a million million (10^{12}); for example, **terahertz.** [Greek *teras,* monster. See **teratoid.**]

ter·a·hertz (térrə-herts) *n. Abbr.* **THz** One million million (10^{12}) hertz.

Te·rai (tə-rī́) *n.* A belt of marshy, jungly land between the foothills of the Himalayas and the plains of northern India.

ter·aph (térrəf) *n., pl.* **-aphim** (-im). A small domestic image or idol revered by ancient Semitic peoples. [Hebrew *tərāphīm,* a pejorative appellation of these idols, perhaps from *rəpha'im,* "shades".]

terato- *comb. form.* Indicates: **1.** Abnormality; for example, **teratoma.** **2.** A monstrous beast; for example, **teratoid.** [Greek *teras,* (stem *terat-*), monster, marvel.]

ter·a·to·gen (térrə-tō-jen, -tə-, te-ráttə-, te-) *n.* Any agent, such as the drug thalidomide or X-radiation, that induces abnormalities in a developing foetus. [TERATO- + -GEN.] **—ter·a·to·gen·ic** (-jénnik) *adj.* **—ter·a·tog·e·ny** (-tójəni) *n.*

ter·a·tol·o·gy (térrə-tólləji) *n.* **1.** The biological study of the development, anatomy, or abnormalities of monsters. **2.** A story or stories about mythical creatures or beasts. [TERATO- + -LOGY.] **—ter·a·to·log·i·cal** (-tə-lójik'l) *adj.*

ter·a·to·ma (térrə-tṓmə) *n., pl.* **-mas** or **-mata** (-tə). A tumour consisting of different types of tissue, occurring frequently in the testes or ovaries. [TERATO- + -OMA.] **—ter·a·tom·a·tous** (-təss) *adj.*

ter·a·torn·is (terra-tórniss) *n.* A prehistoric bird as tall as a man, with a wing span of 5 metres, believed to have been the world's largest flying bird. [TERATO- + Greek *ornis,* bird.]

ter·bi·um (térbi-əm) *n. Symbol* **Tb** A soft, silvery-grey metallic rare-earth element, used as a solid-state dopant and as a laser material. Atomic number 65, atomic weight 158.924, melting point 1,356°C, boiling point 2,800°C, relative density 8.272, valencies 3, 4. [Discovered in *Ytterby,* a village in Sweden.]

terbium metal *n.* Any of several rare-earth metals separable from other metals as a group and including europium, terbium, and gadolinium.

terbium oxide *n.* An insoluble dark brown powder Tb_2O_3. Also called "terbia".

terce (terss) *n.* Also **tierce** (teerss). **1.** The third of the seven **canonical hours** *(see).* **2.** The time of day set aside for this prayer, usually the third after sunrise. [Middle English *tierce,* from Old French, from Latin *tertia* (noun), from *tertius,* third.]

ter·cel, tier·cel (térss'l) *n.* A male hawk, especially one used in falconry. [Middle English, from Old French, from Vulgar Latin *tertiōlus* (unattested), from Latin *tertius,* third (from the belief that the third egg of a brood was a male).]

ter·cen·te·nar·y (tér-sen-tée-nəri, -tén-, ter-séntin- || -erri) *n., pl.* **-ies.** A 300th anniversary or its celebration. Also called "tricentenary", "tricentennial". **—ter·cen·te·nar·y** *adj.*

ter·cen·ten·ni·al (tér-sen-ténni-əl) *adj.* **1.** Of or lasting for 300 years. **2.** Occurring or happening every 300 years.
~n. A tercentenary.

ter·cet (tér-sit, -set) *n.* In prosody, a unit of three lines, often rhyming with each other or with other tercets. Also called "triplet". [Italian *terzetto,* diminutive of *terzo,* third, from Latin *tertius.*]

ter·e·bene (térrə-been) *n.* A mixture of terpenes prepared from oil of turpentine, used as an expectorant and antiseptic. [French *térébène,* from *térébinthe,* from Old French *terebinte,* TEREBINTH.]

te·reb·ic acid (tə-rébbik, tə-, -réebik) *n.* A white crystalline compound, $C_7H_{10}O_4$, resulting from the action of nitric acid on turpentine. [*Terebic,* from TEREBINTH.]

ter·e·binth (térrə-binth) *n.* A small tree, *Pistacia terebinthus,* of the Mediterranean region, that yields turpentine. [Middle English *therebinthe,* from Old French *t(h)erebinte,* from Latin *terebinthus,* from Greek *terebinthos, terminthos,* of Aegean origin.]

ter·e·bin·thine (térrə-bín-thīn || -thin) *adj.* Also **ter·e·bin·thic** (-thik). **1.** Of or pertaining to the terebinth. **2.** Pertaining to, consisting of, or resembling turpentine.

te·re·do (tə-rée-dō, te-, -ráy-) *n., pl.* **-dos.** Any marine mollusc of the genus *Teredo,* such as the shipworm. [New Latin *Teredo,* from Latin *terēdō,* a kind of worm, from Greek *terēdōn.*]

ter·e·phthal·ic acid (térref-thál-ik) *n.* A white insoluble carboxylic acid, $C_6H_4(COOH)_2$, used to manufacture such polyester resins as Terylene; 1,4-benzenedicarboxylic acid.

ter·ete (térreet, tə-réet, te-) *adj.* Nearly cylindrical in cross-section, as are certain plant stems. [Latin *teres* (stem *teret-*), rounded.]

ter·gi·ver·sate (térji-ver-sayt) *intr.v.* **-sated, -sating, -sates.** *Formal.* **1.** To use evasions or ambiguities; equivocate. **2.** To change sides; defect; apostatise. [Latin *tergiversārī,* "to turn the back", shift : *tergum,* back, TERGUM + *versus,* past participle of *vertere,* to turn.] **—ter·gi·ver·sa·tion** (-sáysh'n) *n.* **—ter·gi·ver·sa·tor** (-saytər) *n.*

ter·gum (tér-gəm) *n., pl.* **-ga** (-gə). *Zoology.* The upper or dorsal surface, especially of a body segment of an insect or other arthropod. [Latin *tergum*†, the back.] **—ter·gal** *adj.*

ter·i·ya·ki (térri-yaáki) *n.* A Japanese dish consisting of skewered and grilled slices of marinated meat or shellfish. [Japanese : *teri,* sunshine, "flame" + *yaki,* to broil.]

term (term) *n.* **1.** A period of time, usually having clearly defined limits, for which something lasts or is intended to last, especially: **a.** A limited period of time that a person serves: *a term of office; a 15-year prison term.* **b.** A period when an educational institution or court of law is in session. **c.** An approximately specified period with regard to which plans or predictions are made: *in the short term.* **2.** A point of time marking the end of a period, as: **a.** A fixed time by which a payment must be made. **b.** The end of a normal period of pregnancy. **3.** *Law.* **a.** A fixed period of time during which an estate may be held. **b.** The estate to be granted for a term. **c.** A period of time allowed a debtor to meet an obligation. **4. a.** A word or phrase that expresses a particular idea or has a particular function: *a term of abuse.* **b.** A word or expression that is part of the jargon of a particular group or activity. **c.** *Plural.* Language or manner of expression employed: *told us in no uncertain terms.* **5.** *Plural.* **a.** Conditions or stipulations that define the nature and limits of an agreement: *peace terms.* **b.** Conditions of payment, as for a service or purchase: *easy credit terms.* **c.** The relation between two persons or groups; footing. Preceded by *on*: *on speaking terms.* **6.** *Mathematics.* **a.** Each of the quantities composing a ratio or a fraction or forming a series. **b.** Each of the quantities connected by addition or subtraction signs in an equation. **7.** *Logic.* **a.** The word or phrase constituting the subject or the predicate of a proposition. **b.** Any of the three parts of a syllogism. **8.** *Archaic.* A limit or boundary. **9.** A statue of a human head, or head and torso, rising from a square tapering pillar, originally marking a boundary. In this sense also called "terminus". **—bring to terms.** To force (a person) to submit or agree. **—come to terms. 1.** To reach an agreement. **2.** To face up to or accept a fact or condition. Used with *with.* **—in terms of.** With regard to; in relation to.
~tr.v. **termed, terming, terms.** To designate; call. [Middle English *terme,* from Old French, from Latin *terminus,* boundary line, boundary, limit.] **—term·less** *adj.* **—term·ly** *adv.*

term. **1.** terminal. **2.** termination.

ter·ma·gant (térməgənt) *n.* A quarrelsome, brawling, or scolding woman; a shrew.
~adj. Overbearing, abusive, or shrewish. [Middle English *Termagaunt, Tervagaunt,* vicious Muslim deity in medieval mystery plays, from Old French *Tervagan(t),* from Italian *Trivigante*†.]

term·er (térmər) *n. Informal.* A person holding a position or confined to a place for a specified time. Usually used in combination: *These patients are long-termers.*

ter·mi·na·ble (términ-əb'l) *adj.* **1.** Capable of being terminated. **2.** Terminating after a designated date: *a terminable annuity.* **—ter·mi·na·bil·i·ty** (-ə-bílləti), **ter·mi·na·ble·ness** *n.* **—ter·mi·na·bly** *adv.*

ter·mi·nal (términ'l) *adj. Abbr.* **term.** **1.** Pertaining to, situated at, or forming the end or boundary of something: *a terminal post.* **2.** *Botany.* Growing or appearing at the end of a stem, branch, stalk, or similar part. **3.** Pertaining to or occurring at the end of a section or series; final. **4.** Pertaining to or occurring in or at the end of a term or each term: *terminal exams.* **5.** Ending in death; fatal. **6.** Very serious; especially, resulting in ruin or collapse. Often used humorously: *terminal laziness.* —See Synonyms at **last.**
~n. Abbr. **term.** **1.** A terminating point, limit, or part; an end; an extremity. **2.** Any ornamental figure or object situated at the end of something. **3.** *Electricity.* **a.** A position in an electric circuit or device at which an electric connection is normally established or broken. **b.** A passive conductor at such a position used to facilitate the connection. **4. a.** A terminus on a railway or bus line. **b.** A building providing services for departing or incoming air travellers, either at an airport or in the city which the airport serves. **5.** An important input/output device forming part of a computer system, especially one that is remote from the computer itself. [Latin *terminālis,* from *terminus,* boundary, TERMINUS.] **—ter·mi·nal·ly** *adv.*

terminal velocity *n.* **1.** The maximum velocity attained by a body falling through a fluid in the Earth's gravitational field. **2.** The maximum velocity attained by a projectile during its parabolic flight. **3.** The velocity of a projectile at the end of its flight. **4.** The maximum velocity that an aircraft can attain, as determined by its drag.

ter·mi·nate (términayt) *v.* **-nated, -nating, -nates.** *—tr.* **1.** To bring to an end or halt: *Terrorist action terminated the truce.* **2.** To occur at or form the end of; conclude; finish. **3.** To end (a pregnancy) prematurely by inducing an abortion. *—intr.* **1.** To come to an end: *Negotiations terminated yesterday.* **2.** To have as an end or result. Often used with *in*: *The war terminated in victory for the Allies.* **3.** To induce an abortion. —See Synonyms at **complete.** [Latin *termināre,* to limit, to terminate, from *terminus,* TERMINUS.] **—ter·mi·na·tive** (-nətiv, -naytiv) *adj.* **—ter·mi·na·tive·ly** *adv.*

ter·mi·na·tion (térmi-náysh'n) *n. Abbr.* **term.** **1.** The act of terminating or the condition of being terminated. **2.** The spatial or temporal end of something; a limit or boundary; conclusion or cessation.

3. A result or outcome of something. 4. The end of a word, as an inflectional ending, suffix, or final morpheme. 5. An abortion. **—ter·mi·na·tion·al** *adj.*

ter·mi·na·tor (térmi-naytər) *n.* **1.** One that terminates. **2.** The dividing line between the bright and shaded regions of the disc of the moon or an inner planet.

ter·mi·nol·o·gy (térmi-nólləji) *n., pl.* **-gies. 1.** The vocabulary of technical terms and usages appropriate to a particular trade, science, or art; nomenclature. **2.** The study of nomenclature. [Medieval Latin *terminus,* expression, from Latin, limit, TERMINUS + -LOGY.] **—ter·mi·no·log·i·cal** (-nə-lójik'l) *adj.* **—ter·mi·no·log·i·cal·ly** *adv.* **—ter·mi·nol·o·gist** (-nólləjist) *n.*

term insurance *n.* A type of life insurance contract for a fixed period, whereby the insured sum is payable only if the insured dies within that period.

ter·mi·nus (térmi-nəss) *n., pl.* **-nuses** or **-ni** (-nī). **1.** The end of something; a final point, extremity, or goal. **2.** A point, station, or town at either end of a railway line or bus route. **3. a.** A boundary or border. **b.** A stone or post marking such a border; especially, a **term** *(see).* [Latin, boundary line, boundary, limit.]

ter·mi·tar·i·um (térmi-táir-i-əm) *n., pl.* **-ria** (-i-ə). The moundlike nest of a termite colony. [TERMITE + -ARIUM.]

ter·mite (tér-mīt) *n.* Any of numerous superficially antlike social insects of the order Isoptera, many species of which feed on wood and are highly destructive to living trees and wooden structures. Also called "white ant". [Latin *termes* (stem *termit-*), variant of *tarmes*†, wood-eating worm.]

term·or (térmər) *n. Law.* A person who holds an estate for a certain term or for life. [Middle English, from Anglo-French *termer,* from TERM.]

terms of reference *pl.n.* **1.** The points an individual or committee is charged to decide or report on. **2.** The factors defining the scope of an inquiry.

tern[1] (tern) *n.* Any of various sea birds of the family Sterninae, related to and resembling the gulls but characteristically smaller, and having black and white plumage and a forked tail. [Scandinavian, akin to Old Norse *therna*†.]

tern[2] *n.* A set of three; especially, a combination of three numbers that wins a lottery prize. [Latin *ternī,* three each, from *ter,* thrice.]

ter·na·ry (térnəri) *adj.* **1.** Composed of three or arranged in threes. **2.** *Mathematics.* **a.** Of, pertaining, or designating a number system that has three as its base. **b.** Involving three variables. **3.** *Chemistry.* Containing three different components or elements. *~n., pl.* **ternaries.** A set or group of three. [Middle English, from Latin *ternārius,* from *ternī,* three each. See **tern.**]

ternary form *n.* A musical structure in three parts, in which the first section is followed by a contrasting section and then repeated.

ter·nate (tér-nayt, -nət, -nit) *adj.* Consisting of three parts, or arranged in groups of three, as, for example, a compound leaf. [New Latin *ternatus,* from Medieval Latin *ternātus,* past participle of *ternāre,* multiply by three, from *ternī,* three each.] **—ter·nate·ly** *adv.*

terne (tern) *n.* **1.** An alloy of three or four parts lead to one part tin, with a tiny percentage of antimony. **2.** Terneplate. [French *terne,* dull, from Old French, from *ternir,* to tarnish + PLATE.]

terne·plate (térn-playt) *n.* Sheet iron or steel plated with terne, used as a roofing material. Also called "terne".

te·ro·tech·nol·o·gy (teér-ō-tek-nólləji) *n.* The management and maintenance of the plant of a business or industry; maintenance engineering. [Greek *terein,* to take care of + TECHNOLOGY.]

ter·pene (tér-peen) *n.* Any of various unsaturated hydrocarbons, $C_{10}H_{16}$, found in essential oils and oleoresins of plants, such as conifers, and used in organic syntheses. [*Terp(entine),* obsolete form of TURPENTINE + -ENE.] **—ter·pe·nic** (ter-peénik), **ter·pe·noid** (térpi-noyd, ter-peé-) *adj.*

ter·pin·e·ol (tər-pínni-ol || -ōl) *n.* Any of three isomeric alcohols, $C_{10}H_{17}OH$, occurring naturally in the essential oils of certain plants and used as a solvent, in perfumes, soaps, and medicine. [TERP(ENE) + -INE + -OL.]

Terp·sich·o·re (terp-síckəri). *Greek mythology.* The Muse of dancing and choral singing. [Greek *Terpsikhorē* : *terpein,* to delight, cheer + *khoros,* dance.]

terp·si·cho·re·an (térpsi-kə-reé-ən, -ko- || -káw-ri-ən, -kō-) *adj.* Of or pertaining to dancing. [From TERPSICHORE.]

ter·ra al·ba (térrə ál-bə || áwl-) *n.* **1.** Finely pulverised gypsum used in making paper, paints, and plastics. **2.** A clay, **kaolin** *(see).* [New Latin, "white earth".]

ter·race (térrəss, térriss) *n.* **1. a.** An open, level, often paved area adjacent to a house, serving as an outdoor living area; a patio. **b.** The flat roof of a house serving a similar purpose, as in warmer climates. **2.** A relatively narrow horizontal shelf of land on the side of a slope, typically one of a landscaped series, having vertical or sloping sides and used for cultivation. **3.** *Geology.* A horizontal or gently inclined shelf or bench, as along the side of a river valley. **4.** *Usually plural.* The unroofed tiers around a football pitch where spectators stand. **5. a.** A row of houses, usually identical in design, built with connecting walls. **b.** A row of houses built on raised ground or on a sloping site. **6.** *Abbr.* **Terr, Trce.** A street, especially one having terraced houses. Used in street names: *Eaton Terrace.* *~tr.v.* **terraced, -racing, -races.** To make into or supply with a terrace: *a terraced hillside.* [Old French *terrasse,* terrace, pile of earth, from Old Provençal *terrassa,* from *terra,* earth, from Latin.]

terraced house *n.* A house that forms one of a row of usually identical buildings linked by connecting walls.

ter·ra·cot·ta, ter·ra-cot·ta (térrə-kóttə) *n.* **1.** A hard, brownish red to yellow material composed of clay, fine sand, and sometimes pulverised pottery waste, usually unglazed, used in pottery and building construction. **2.** Ceramic ware made of this material. **3.** Brownish orange. [Italian, "baked earth".] **—ter·ra·cot·ta** *adj.*

ter·ra fir·ma (térrə fúrmə) *n.* Solid ground; dry land. [Latin.]

ter·ra·form·ing (térrə-forming) *n.* The hypothetical transforming of a heavenly body (such as a planet) and/or its atmosphere to produce conditions more like those of Earth, and thus permit human habitation. [Latin *terra,* earth + *forming.*]

ter·rain (térrayn, te-ráyn, tə-) *n.* **1.** The relief or physical character of an area; its configuration. **2.** *U.S.* A particular geographical area. [French, from Latin *terrēnum,* from *terrēnus,* TERRENE.]

ter·ra in·cog·ni·ta (térrə in-kóg-ni-tə) *n., pl.* **terrae incognitae** (tér-ree-tee). Unknown or unmapped territory. [Latin.]

ter·ra·pin (térrə-pin) *n.* Any chelonian reptile of the family Enrydidae that is equally at home on land and in fresh water, such as the European pond tortoise, *Emys orbicularis.* [Algonquian (Virginia), from Eastern Algonquian *toolepeiwa* (unattested).]

ter·ra·que·ous (te-ráykwi-əss, ti-, tə-, -rákwi-) *adj.* Composed of both land and water. [Medieval Latin *terraqueus* : *terra,* earth, from Latin + *aqueus,* AQUEOUS.]

ter·rar·i·um (te-ráir-i-əm, ti-, tə-) *n., pl.* **-ums** or **-ria** (-i-ə). A small enclosure or closed container in which small plants are grown or small animals, such as turtles or lizards, are kept. [New Latin : Latin *terra,* earth + -ARIUM.]

ter·raz·zo (te-rát-sō, ti-, tə- || -raát-) *n.* A flooring material of marble or other stone chips set in concrete and polished smooth when dry. [Italian, TERRACE.]

ter·rene (térreen, te-reén, ti-, tə-) *adj.* Of or pertaining to the earth; earthly. [Middle English, from Latin *terrēnus,* from *terra,* earth.]

terre·plein (táir-playn, térrə-) *n.* The level ground on an embankment or the platform behind a parapet where heavy guns are mounted. [French *terre-plein,* from Italian *terrapieno,* from *terrapienare,* to fill with earth, terrace : *terra,* earth + *pieno,* full.]

ter·res·tri·al (ti-réstri-əl, te-, tə-) *adj.* **1.** Of or pertaining to the Earth, especially as distinct from the Moon, the stars, and the planets. **2.** Having a worldly, mundane character or quality. **3.** Of, pertaining to, or composed of land as distinct from water or air. **4.** *Biology.* Living or growing on land; not aquatic. *~n.* An inhabitant of the earth, especially, a human being. [Middle English, from Latin *terrestris,* from *terra,* earth.] **—ter·res·tri·al·ly** *adv.* **—ter·res·tri·al·ness** *n.*

terrestrial planet *n.* Any of the four planets nearest the sun, resembling Earth in density and composition: Mercury, Venus, Earth, or Mars.

terrestrial space *n.* The region of space surrounding the earth (up to about 2 500 kilometres; 4,000 miles).

terrestrial telescope *n.* An optical telescope, usually containing a separate lens or prism to give an erect image, that is used to view objects on land or water rather than for making astronomical observations. Compare **astronomical telescope.**

ter·ret, ter·rit (térrit) *n.* **1.** Either of the metal rings on a horse's harness through which the reins pass. **2.** A similar ring on an animal's collar, used for attaching a leash. [Middle English *tyret, toret,* from Old French *to(u)ret,* diminutive of *tour,* "circular movement", from *tourner,* to TURN.]

terre-verte (táir-váirt, tér-vért) *n.* An olive-green pigment used by artists and commonly made from **glauconite** *(see).* [French, "green earth".] **—terre-verte** *adj.*

ter·ri·ble (térrəb'l, térrib'l) *adj.* **1.** Causing terror or fear; dreadful. **2.** Eliciting awe. **3.** Extreme in extent or degree; intense; severe: *a terrible storm.* **4.** Unpleasant; disagreeable: *a terrible time.* **5.** Extremely bad: *a terrible actor.* [Middle English, from Old French, from Latin *terribilis,* from *terrēre,* to frighten.] **—ter·ri·ble·ness** *n.*

ter·ri·bly (térrəbli, térribli) *adv.* **1.** In a terrible manner: *terribly wounded.* **2.** To a great extent; very much: *Would you mind terribly if I opened the window?* **3.** Very. Used as an intensive: *terribly nice.*

ter·ric·o·lous (te-ríckələss, ti-) *adj. Biology.* Living on or in the ground. [Latin *terricola,* land dweller : *terra,* earth + -COLOUS.]

ter·ri·er[1] (térri-ər) *n.* Any of various usually small, active dogs originally bred for hunting animals that live in burrows. [French *(chien) terrier,* from *terrier,* burrow, from *terre,* earth, from Latin *terra.*]

terrier[2] *n. Law.* A document or book enumerating boundaries, acreage, and the conditions of their tenure. [Old French *terrier,* from *terre,* land. See **terrier** (dog).]

Ter·ri·er (térri-ər) *n. British Informal.* A member of the Territorial and Army Volunteer Reserve.

ter·rif·ic (tə-ríffik, ti-) *adj.* **1.** Very good or fine; splendid; magnificent: *a terrific chef.* **4.** Awesome; astounding: *a terrific speed.* **3.** Causing terror or great fear; dreadful; terrifying: *a terrific wail.* **4.** Very bad or unpleasant; frightful: *a terrific headache.* [Latin *terrificus* : *terrēre,* to frighten + -FIC.] **—ter·rif·i·cal·ly** *adv.*

ter·ri·fy (térri-fī) *tr.v.* **-fied, -fying, -fies. 1.** To fill with terror; make deeply afraid. **2.** To force or drive by causing terror; scare; intimidate: *terrified him into signing the contract.* —See Synonyms at **frighten.** [Latin *terrificāre,* from *terrificus,* TERRIFIC.]

ter·rig·e·nous (te-ríjənəss, ti-) *adj.* Derived from the land, especially by erosive action. Said chiefly of sediments. [From Latin *terrigena,* born of the earth : *terra,* earth + -GENOUS.]

ter·rine (te-reén) *n.* **1.** A small earthenware dish with a tightly fitting lid used for cooking and serving patés or other delicacies. **2.** Food cooked in a terrine, especially a type of paté. [French.]

ter·ri·to·ri·al (térri-táw-ri-əl || -tṓ-) *adj. Abbr.* **terr.** **1.** Of or pertaining to a territory or to its powers of jurisdiction. **2.** Pertaining or restricted to a particular territory; regional; local. **3.** Marked by or exhibiting a tendency to guard one's territory: *territorial instincts.* **4.** *Often capital* **T.** Of or designating a volunteer force maintained to provide a reserve.
~*n. Often capital* **T.** A member of a territorial army; especially, a member of the Territorial and Army Volunteer Reserve. **—ter·ri·to·ri·al·ly** *adv.*
Territorial and Army Volunteer Reserve *n. Abbr.* **TAVR.** In Britain, a standing volunteer reserve army originally formed in 1908. Also called "Territorial Army".
Territorial Collectivity. *n.* A term applied by France to some of its overseas dependencies such as Mayotte and St Pierre and Miquelon. [Translation of French *Collectivité territoriale.*]
ter·ri·to·ri·al·ise, ter·ri·to·ri·al·ize (térri-táw-ri-əl-īz || -tṓ-) *tr.v.* **-ised, -ising, -ises. 1.** To make territorial, especially: **a.** To reduce to the status of a territory. **b.** To extend or restrict to a particular territory or territories. **2.** To make one's own territory. **—ter·ri·to·ri·al·i·sa·tion** (-ī-záysh'n || *U.S.* -i-) *n.*
ter·ri·to·ri·al·ism (térri-táw-ri-əl-iz'm || -tṓ-) *n.* **1.** A social system that gives authority and influence in a state to the landowners; landlordism. **2.** A former system of Protestant church government based on the primacy of civil power. In this sense, also called "territorial system". **—ter·ri·to·ri·al·ist** *n.*
ter·ri·to·ri·al·i·ty (térri-táw-ri-ál-əti || -tṓ-) *n.* **1.** The status of a territory. **2.** The behaviour of one who stays close to or jealously guards his territory.
territorial waters *pl.n.* Inland and coastal waters under the jurisdiction of a state; especially, the ocean waters within three miles of the shoreline.
ter·ri·to·ry (térri-tri, -təri) *n., pl.* **-ries.** *Abbr.* **t., T., terr. 1.** An area of land; a district; a region. **2.** The land and waters under the jurisdiction of a state, nation, or sovereign. **3.** *Capital* **T. a.** A part of Canada or Australia not accorded statehood or provincial status. **b.** A part of the United States not admitted as a state, which has a governor and other officers appointed by the president, and its own legislature. **4. a.** An area inhabited by an individual animal, a mating pair, or a group of animals and often vigorously defended against intruders. **b.** A comparable concrete or psychological area regarded by a person as his own inviolable domain. **5.** The area for which a person is responsible as representative or agent: *a salesman's territory.* **6.** The area of a sports field defended by a team. **7.** Any sphere of action or interest; a province. [Middle English, from Latin *territōrium,* from *terra,* land.]
ter·ror (térrər) *n.* **1.** Intense, overpowering fear. **2.** Anything that instils such fear; a terrifying person, thing, or occurrence. **3.** The ability to instil such fear; terribleness: *the terror of the haunted house.* **4.** Systematic violence carried out against private citizens, public property, and political enemies with the aim of enforcing demands or maintaining supremacy: *a reign of terror.* **5.** *Informal.* An annoying or intolerable pest; a nuisance. [Middle English *terrour,* from Old French, from Latin *terror,* from *terrēre,* to frighten.]
ter·ror·ise, ter·ror·ize (térrər-īz) *tr.v.* **-ised, -ising, -ises. 1.** To fill or overpower with terror; terrify. **2.** To coerce or maintain control over by intimidation or fear: *The vandals terrorised their neighbourhood.* **—ter·ror·i·sa·tion** (-ī-záysh'n || *U.S.* -i-) *n.* **—ter·ror·is·er** *n.*
ter·ror·ism (térrər-iz'm) *n.* The use of terror, violence, and intimidation, usually by an underground or revolutionary group but sometimes to achieve a political end. **—ter·ror·ist** *adj. & n.* **—ter·ror·is·tic** (-ístik) *adj.*
terror stricken *adj.* Also **terror struck.** Overcome by terror.
ter·ry (térri) *n., pl.* **-ries. 1.** Any of the uncut loops that form the pile of a fabric. **2.** A pile fabric, usually woven of cotton, with uncut loops on both sides, used for such articles as bath towels and nappies. In this sense, also called "terry cloth". [18th century : origin obscure.]
terse (terss) *adj.* **terser, tersest. 1.** Effectively concise; free of superfluity. **2.** Curt; brusque. —See Synonyms at **concise.** [Originally "polished", "refined", from Latin *tersus,* past participle of *tergēre,* to wipe off, polish. See **deterge.**] **—terse·ly** *adv.* **—terse·ness** *n.*
tertian fever *n.* A form of malaria caused by the invasion of *Plasmodium vivax* into new red blood cells, characterised by a 48-hour life cycle in the human body with a recurrence of fever paroxysms at the end of each such period. Also called "tertian malaria". [*Tertian,* from Latin *tertiānus,* of the third, from *tertius,* third.]
ter·ti·ar·y (tér-shəri, -shi-əri || -shi-erri) *adj.* **1.** Third in place, order, degree, or rank. **2.** Of, designating, or providing education above the secondary level, as in a college or university: *an examination at tertiary level; a tertiary course.* **3.** *Chemistry.* **a.** Pertaining to salts of acids containing three replaceable hydrogen atoms. **b.** Pertaining to organic compounds in which a group, such as an alcohol or amine, is bound to three non-elementary radicals. **4.** Of or pertaining to a **Third Order** *(see)* in a Roman Catholic monastic system. **5.** Involving the provision of services rather than the extraction or production of goods: *tertiary industry; tertiary occupation.* **6.** Of, pertaining to, or designating the short flight feathers nearest the body on the inner edge of a bird's wing.
~*n., pl.* **tertiaries. 1.** A tertiary feather. **2.** A member of a Roman Catholic tertiary order. [Latin *tertiārius,* from *tertius,* third.]
Ter·ti·a·ry (tér-shəri, -shi-əri, || -shi-erri) *adj.* Of, belonging to, or designating the geological time, and system of rocks of the first period of the Cenozoic era, extending from the Cretaceous period of the Mesozoic era to the Quarternary period of the Cenozoic era, characterised by the appearance of modern flora and fauna.
~*n.* The Tertiary period or system of deposits. Preceded by *the.*
tertiary accent *n. Linguistics.* A stress weaker than primary and secondary stress in phonetic systems recognising three or more degrees of stress. Also called "tertiary stress". Compare **primary accent, secondary accent.**
tertiary colour *n.* A colour resulting from the mixture of two secondary colours.
ter·ti·um quid (tér-shi-əm kwíd, -ti-) *n.* Something that cannot be classified into either of two groups, themselves considered to be exhaustive; an intermediate thing or factor. [Late Latin, "third something" (translation of Greek *triton ti*).]
tervalent. Variant of **trivalent.**
Ter·y·lene (térrə-leen, térri-) *n.* A trademark for a synthetic polyester fibre based on terephthalic acid that is used in making crease-resistant clothing, sheets, and the like.
ter·za ri·ma (taírt-sə reé-mə, térts-) *n., pl.* **terze rime** (-say, -may). A verse form consisting of a series of tercets having 10- or 11-syllable lines of which the middle line of one tercet rhymes with the first and third lines of the following tercet. [Italian, "third rhyme".]
TESL (téss'l). Teaching English as a second language.
tes·la (tésslə) *n. Abbr.* **T** The unit of magnetic flux density in SI units, equal to one weber per square metre. [After Nikola TESLA.]
tesla coil *n.* A transformer with an air-core primary and a capacitor-tuned secondary, used as a source of high-frequency high voltage, as for X-ray tubes.
TESOL (teé-sol). Teaching English to speakers of other languages.
tes·sel·late (téssi-i-layt, -ə-) *tr.v.* **-lated, -lating, -lates.** To form into or inlay with a mosaic pattern, as by using small squares of stone or glass. [Latin *tessellātus,* from *tessella,* a small cube, diminutive of *tessera,* TESSERA.] **—tes·sel·la·tion** (-láysh'n) *n.*
tes·ser·a (téssə-rə) *n., pl.* **-serae** (-ree). Any of the small squares of stone or glass used in making mosaic patterns. [Latin, "a square", from Greek *tesseres, tessares,* four.] **—tes·ser·al** *adj.*
tes·se·ract (téssə-rakt) *n. Mathematics.* The four-dimensional extension of a cube. [Greek *tesseres,* four + *aktis,* ray.]
tes·si·tu·ra (téssi-tóor-ə, -téwr-ə) *n. Music.* The range within which most notes of a voice-part fall. [Italian, TEXTURE.]
test¹ (test) *n.* **1.** Any of various procedures by which a person or thing may be examined for certain properties or qualities as: **a.** A series of questions or problems designed to assess knowledge, skill, or aptitude. **b.** A series of operations or functions designed to assess effectiveness or conformity to an appropriate standard: *nuclear weapons tests; an MOT test.* **c.** A diagnostic medical examination: *a pregnancy test.* Also used adjectivally: *test conditions; a test drive.* **2.** Any means or circumstance by which something is examined or evaluated: *put his theories to the test.* **3.** A criterion; a standard. **4. a.** A physical or chemical reaction by which a substance may be detected or its properties ascertained. **b.** The reagent used in such determination. **c.** A positive result obtained. **5.** A cupel.
~*v.* **tested, testing, tests.** —*tr.* **1.** To subject to a test; examine. **2. a.** To determine the presence or properties of (a substance). **b.** To assay (metal) in a cupel. **3.** To try; tax: *tested his patience.* —*intr.* **1.** To exhibit certain properties under test conditions. **2.** To administer a test in order to analyse or diagnose. Used with *for*: *test for acid content.* [Middle English, cupel for treating ores, from Old French, pot, from Latin *testum*†, earthen vessel.]
test² *n.* A hard external covering, such as that of certain insects and other invertebrates. [Latin *testa,* shell. See **testa.**]
tes·ta (téss-tə) *n., pl.* **-tae** (-tee). The often thick or hard outer coat of a seed. [Latin *testa*†, clay, brick, tile, shell.]
tes·ta·ceous (tess-táyshəss) *adj.* **1.** *Biology.* Of, pertaining to, or having a shell or shell-like outer covering. **2.** Having the characteristic reddish-brown or brownish-yellow colour of bricks. [Latin *testāceus,* from *testa,* shell. See **test** (shell).]
tes·ta·cy (téstə-si) *n. Law.* The condition of being testate.
tes·ta·ment (téstə-mənt) *n.* **1.** *Law.* A written document providing for the disposition of one's personal property after death; a will. Used chiefly in the phrase *last will and testament.* **2. a.** Any proof or tribute that testifies to or serves as evidence of something. **b.** A statement of belief or conviction; a credo. **3. a.** *Archaic.* A covenant between humanity and God. **b.** *Capital* **T.** Either of the two main divisions of the Bible, the Old Testament and the New Testament. **c.** *Capital* **T.** The New Testament. [Middle English, from Late Latin *testāmentum* (translation of Greek *diathēkē,* scripture), from Latin, will, from *testārī,* to be a witness, assert, make a will, from *testis,* witness.] **—tes·ta·men·ta·ry** (-méntəri) *adj.*
tes·tate (téss-tayt, -tət, -tit) *adj.* Having made a legally valid will before death. [Middle English, from Latin *testātus,* past participle of *testārī,* to make a will. See **testament.**]
tes·ta·tor (tess-táytər || téss-taytər) *n.* A person who has made a legally valid will before death. [Middle English *testatour,* from Anglo-French, from Latin *testātor,* from *testārī,* to make a will. See **testament.**]
tes·ta·trix (tess-táytriks) *n.* A female testator. [Latin *testātrix,* feminine of *testātor,* TESTATOR.]
test ban *n.* An agreement between nations to forgo tests on certain types of nuclear weaponry.
test bed *n.* An arrangement of measuring instruments used to test engines and other pieces of machinery under load.
test case *n.* **1.** A legal action whose outcome is likely to set a prec-

edent. **2.** Any issue whose outcome is likely to be treated as a precedent.

test cross *n. Genetics.* The crossing of a hybrid exhibiting the dominant phenotype of a particular gene back to a parent homozygous for the recessive allele of this gene, to determine whether the hybrid is homozygous or heterozygous.

test·ed (téstid) *adj.* Having been subjected to a test; certified through testing. Also used in combination to indicate: **1.** Tested by the specified means: *tuberculin-tested; heat-tested.* **2.** Tested for the specified quality or substance: *toxin-tested.*

tes·ter[1] (téstər) *n.* A canopy over a bed, cot, or the like. [Middle English, from Medieval Latin *testerium,* headpiece, from Late Latin *testa,* skull, head, from Latin, shell. See **testa.**]

tes·ter[2] *n.* A former English coin, the **teston** *(see).*

test·er[3] *n.* One that tests.

tes·tes. Plural of **testis.**

tes·ti·cle (téstik'l) *n.* Either of the male reproductive organs, situated in an external scrotum behind the penis in humans and most mammals, that produce spermatozoa and secrete androgens. Also called "testis". [Middle English *testicule,* from Latin *testiculus,* diminutive of *testis,* TESTIS.]

tes·tic·u·late (tess-tíckew-lət, -lit, -layt) *adj.* Also **tes·tic·u·lar** (-lər). **1.** Having the shape of a testicle; ovoid. **2.** Having testicles.

tes·ti·fy (tésti-fī) *v.* **-fied, -fying, -fies.** —*intr.* **1.** To make a declaration of truth or fact under oath; submit testimony. **2.** To make a serious or solemn statement in support of an argument, position, or asserted fact; affirm. **3.** To serve as witness or evidence. Used with *to.* **4.** To make an open profession of religious faith. —*tr.* **1.** To bear witness to; provide evidence for; prove. **2.** To state or affirm under oath. **3.** To declare publicly; make known. [Middle English *testifien,* from Latin *testificārī* : *testis,* witness + *facere,* to make.] **—tes·ti·fi·ca·tion** (-fi-káysh'n) *n.* **—tes·ti·fi·er** *n.*

tes·ti·mo·ni·al (tésti-mṓni-əl) *n.* **1.** A written statement providing evidence of a person's character or ability; a letter of recommendation. **2.** Something given as a tribute for a person's service or achievement.
~*adj.* Relating to or constituting a testimony or testimonial. [Middle English, noun and adjective, from Old French, from Late Latin *testimōniālis,* from Latin *testimōnium,* TESTIMONY.]

tes·ti·mo·ny (tésti-məni || *U.S.* -mōni) *n., pl.* **-nies.** *Abbr.* **test. 1.** A declaration or affirmation of fact or truth, such as that given before a court of law. **2.** Any evidence in support of a fact or assertion; a demonstration or proof. **3.** The collective written and spoken testimony offered in a legal case. **4.** A public declaration regarding a religious experience. **5. a.** The law of Moses, inscribed on the tablets of stone. Exodus 25:16. **b.** *Often capital* **T.** The ark containing these tablets. Exodus 16:34. [Middle English, from Latin *testimōnium,* from *testis,* witness.]

test·ing ground (tésting) *n.* An area or environment where something is subjected to a critical trial: *a nuclear testing ground.*

tes·tis (téss-tiss) *n., pl.* **-tes** (-teez). A testicle. [Latin, "witness" (to masculinity).]

test match *n.* Any of a series of international sports matches, especially in cricket or Rugby football. Also called "test".

tes·ton (téss-tən || -ton) *n.* Also **tes·toon** (tess-tóōn). Any of various coins with the image of a head on one side, specifically: **1.** A 16th-century silver coin of France. **2.** An English coin stamped with the head of Henry VIII, originally worth a shilling and later sixpence. In this sense, also called "tester". [Middle English, from Old French *teste* and Italian *testa,* head, both from Late Latin *testa,* skull, from Latin, shell. See **testa.**]

tes·tos·ter·one (tess-tóstə-rōn) *n.* A male sex hormone, $C_{19}H_{28}O_2$, produced in the testicles and functioning to control secondary sexual characteristics. [TEST(IS) + STER(OL) + -ONE.]

test paper *n.* **1.** A paper saturated with a reagent, such as litmus, used in making chemical tests. **2. a.** A paper or booklet bearing examination questions. **b.** A paper or booklet bearing a student's work for an examination.

test pilot *n.* A pilot who flies aircraft of new or experimental design to test them for conformity to planned standards.

test tube *n.* A cylindrical clear glass tube usually open at one end and rounded at the other, used in laboratory experiments.

test-tube baby *n.* A baby conceived by fertilisation of an ovum outside the body and implanted in the womb at the blastocyst stage.

tes·tu·di·nal (tess-téwdin'l) *adj.* Also **tes·tu·di·nar·y** (-téwdi-nəri || -nerri). **1.** Of, resembling, or relating to a tortoise or turtle. **2.** Of or pertaining to the shell of either of these.

tes·tu·do (tess-téw-dō || -tóō-) *n., pl.* **-dines** (-di-neez). An ancient Roman siege device consisting either of a movable arched screen or of shields held up to interlock over their bearers' heads, protecting the besiegers' approach to a wall. Also called "tortoise". [Latin *testūdo,* "tortoise", a covering, from *testa,* shell. See **testa.**]

tes·ty (tésti) *adj.* **-tier, -tiest. 1.** Irritable; touchy; peevish: *a testy old codger.* **2.** Characterised by irritability, impatience, or exasperation: *a testy remark.* [Middle English *testif,* headstrong, from Anglo-French, from Old French *teste,* head. See **teston.**] **—tes·ti·ly** *adv.* **—tes·ti·ness** *n.*

Tet (tet) *n.* The lunar New Year as celebrated during January or February in Southeast Asia. [Vietnamese *têt,* from Ancient Chinese *tsiet,* "festival" (Mandarin Chinese *jíe).*]

te·tan·ic (tə-tánnik, ti-, tə-) *adj.* Of or pertaining to tetanus.
~*n.* Any poison producing symptoms similar to those of tetanus. **—te·tan·i·cal·ly** *adv.*

tet·a·nise (tétt'n-īz) *tr.v.* **-nised, -nising, -nises.** To affect with tetanic convulsions; produce or induce tetanus in. **—tet·a·ni·sa·tion** (-ī-záysh'n || *U.S.* -i-) *n.*

tet·a·nus (tétt'n-əss) *n.* **1.** An acute, often fatal infectious disease caused by a bacillus, *Clostridium tetani,* that generally enters the body through wounds, and is characterised by rigidity and spasmodic contraction of the voluntary muscles. Also called "lockjaw". **2.** A state of continuous muscular contraction caused by reaction to rapidly repeated stimuli, such as electric shocks. [Learned respelling of Middle English *tetane,* from Latin *tetanus,* from Greek *tetanos,* from adjective, "stretched", from *teinein,* to stretch.] **—tet·a·nal** (-'l), **tet·a·noid** (-oyd) *adj.*

tet·a·ny (tétt'n-i) *n.* An abnormal condition, occurring chiefly in young people, characterised by periodic painful muscular spasms caused by faulty calcium metabolism. [From TETANUS.]

tetch·y, tech·y (téchi) *adj.* **-ier, -iest.** Peevish; irritable. [Probably from obsolete *tecche, tache,* blemish, fault (of character), from Old French *tache, teche,* blemish, from Late Latin *tacca* (unattested), from Gothic *taikns,* sign.] **—tetch·i·ly** *adv.* **—tetch·i·ness** *n.*

tête-à-tête (tét-aa-tét, táyt-aa-táyt, -ə-) *adv.* Together without the intrusion of others; in intimate privacy: *talk tête-à-tête.*
~*adj.* For or between two only; private; intimate.
~*n.* **1.** A private conversation between two people. **2.** A sofa for two, especially an S-shaped one allowing the occupants to face each other. [French, "head to head".]

tête-bêche (tét-bésh) *adj.* Of, pertaining to, or designating a pair of postage stamps printed upside-down in relation to one another. [French : *tête,* head + *bechevet,* "double-headed" : *bes,* twice, from Latin *bis* (see **bi-**) + *chevet,* head (of a bed), from Latin *capitium,* head covering, from *caput,* head.]

teth (teth, tess, tet) *n.* The ninth letter in the Hebrew alphabet. [Hebrew *ṭēth.*]

teth·er (téthər) *n.* **1.** A rope, chain, or halter for an animal, tied fast at one end to allow only a limited range of movement. **2.** The range of one's resources; especially, the limits of one's endurance.
~*tr.v.* **tethered, -ering, -ers.** To restrict or bind with or as if with a tether. [Middle English *tethir,* from Old Norse *tjōthr*†.]

Te·thys (téth-iss, téeth-). **1.** *Greek Mythology.* A Titaness and sea goddess who was both sister and consort of Oceanus. **2.** The sea which lay between the ancient continents of Laurasia and Gondwanaland. **3.** One of the satellites of Saturn.

tet·ra (téttrə) *n., pl.* **-ras** or collectively **-ra.** Any of various small, colourful tropical freshwater fishes of the family Characidae, popular in home aquariums. [Short for New Latin *Tetragonopterus* (former classification of tetras) : TETRAGON (from their squared-off dorsal fins) + -PTER.]

tetra-, tetr- *comb. form.* Indicates four; for example, **tetrachloride, tetracid.** [Greek.]

tet·ra·ba·sic (téttrə-báy-sik) *adj.* **1.** Containing four replaceable hydrogen atoms in a molecule. Said of an acid. **2.** Containing four univalent basic atoms or radicals. Said of a base or salt. **—tet·ra·ba·sic·i·ty** (-bay-síssəti) *n.*

tet·ra·chlo·ride (téttrə-kláw-rīd || -klṓ-) *n.* A chemical compound containing four chlorine atoms per molecule.

tet·ra·chord (téttrə-kawrd) *n.* Especially in ancient music, a series of four diatonic notes encompassing the interval of a perfect fourth. [Greek *tetrakhordon,* from *tetrakhordos* : TETRA- + *khordē,* string.] **—tet·ra·chor·dal** (-kórd'l) *adj.*

te·trac·id (te-trássid) *adj.* **1.** Able to react with four molecules of a monobasic acid. Said of a base. **2.** Containing four replaceable hydrogen atoms. Said of an acid or acid salt.
~*n.* An acid containing four replaceable hydrogen atoms.

tet·ra·cy·clic (téttrə-sīklik, *rarely* -sícklik) *adj.* Designating a molecule containing four rings in its structure.

tet·ra·cy·cline (téttrə-sī-klin, -klīn, -kleen) *n.* A yellow crystalline compound, $C_{22}H_{24}N_2O_8$, synthesised from chlortetracycline or derived from bacteria of the genus *Streptomyces* and used as an antibiotic. [TETRA- + CYCL(IC) + -INE.]

tet·rad (tét-rad, -rəd) *n.* **1.** A group or series of four. **2.** A tetravalent atom, radical, or element. **3. a.** A group of four chromatids formed during meiosis by the pairing of two homologous chromosomes that have each divided into two chromatids. **b.** A body formed of four cells, as, for example, pollen grains from one mother cell. [Greek *tetras* (stem *tetrad-*).] **—te·trad·ic** (te-tráddik) *adj.*

te·trad·y·mite (te-tráddi-mīt) *n.* A steel-grey bismuth ore, chiefly bismuth telluride. [Late Greek *tetradumos,* fourfold (since it occurs in compound twin crystals) : TETRA- + Greek *didumos,* double.]

tet·ra·dy·na·mous (téttrə-dīnə-mass, -dínnə-) *adj. Botany.* Having six stamens, of which two are shorter than the others. [TETRA- + Greek *dynamis,* power (see **dynamic**) + -OUS.]

tet·ra·eth·yl lead (téttrə-ée-thīl || -éth'l) *n.* A colourless, poisonous, oily liquid, $Pb(C_2H_5)_4$, used in petrol for internal-combustion engines as an antiknock agent. Also called "lead tetraethyl".

tet·ra·gon (téttrə-gən || *chiefly U.S.* -gon) *n.* A polygon having four sides and four angles; a quadrilateral. [Late Latin *tetragōnum,* from Greek *tetragōnon* : TETRA- + -GON.]

te·trag·o·nal (te-trággən'l) *n.* **1.** Pertaining to or shaped like a quadrilateral. **2.** In crystallography, having a crystal system in which there are three axes at right angles of which only two are equal.

Tet·ra·gram·ma·ton (téttrə-grámmə-t'n, -ton) *n.* The four Hebrew letters usually transliterated as YHWH or JHVH (Yahweh or Jehovah) and used as a symbol or substitute for the ineffable name of God. [Middle English *Tetragramaton,* from Greek *tetragrammaton,* four-letter word : TETRA- + *gramma* (stem *grammat*-), letter.]

tet·ra·he·dral (téttra-héedral) *adj.* **1.** Having four plane faces. **2.** Of, pertaining to, or formed in tetrahedrons. **—tet·ra·he·dral·ly** *adv.*

tet·ra·he·drite (tettra-hée-drīt) *n.* A greyish-black copper ore, essentially (CuFe)₁₂Sb₄S₁₃, often containing other elements. [German *Tetraëdrit*, from Greek *tetraedros*, four-faced (it occurs in tetrahedral crystals). See **tetrahedron**.]

tet·ra·he·dron (téttra-hée-dran, -hé-) *n., pl.* **-drons** or **-dra** (-dra). A polyhedron with four plane faces. [New Latin, from Late Greek *tetraedron*, from Greek *tetraedros*, four-faced : TETRA- + *hedra*, face.]

tet·ra·hy·dro·can·nab·i·nol (tettra-hī-drō-ka-nábbi-nol, -dra- ‖ -nōl) *n.* A crystalline compound, the active principle of cannabis.

te·tral·o·gy (te-trál-aji) *n., pl.* **-gies.** **1.** In ancient Athens, a series of four dramas, three tragedies and one satyr play, performed at the festivals dedicated to Dionysus. **2.** Any series of four related theatrical or literary works. [Greek *tetralogia* : TETRA- + -LOGY.]

tetralogy of Fal·lot (fálō) *n.* A congenital deformity, giving rise to a "blue baby", involving four particular defects of the heart. [After E.-L. A. *Fallot* (1850–1911), French physician.]

te·tram·er·ous (te-trámmarass) *adj.* **1.** Having or consisting of four similar parts. **2.** *Botany.* Having flower parts, such as sepals, petals, and stamens, in sets of four. [New Latin *tetramerus*, from Greek *tetramerēs* : TETRA- + -MEROUS.] **—te·tram·er·ism** *n.*

te·tram·e·ter (te-trámmitar) *n.* A line of verse consisting of four metrical feet. [Late Latin *tetrametrus*, from Greek *tetrametros*, having four measures : TETRA- + -METER.] **—te·tram·e·ter** *adj.*

tet·ra·ple·gi·a (téttra-plée-ji-a, -ja) *n.* **Quadriplegia** *(see).* [New Latin : *tetra-*, *-plegia*, "stroke". Greek *plēssein*, to strike.] **—tet·ra·ple·gic** *n. & adj.*

tet·ra·ploid (téttra-ployd) *adj.* *Genetics.* Having four times the haploid number of chromosomes.

~*n.* *Genetics.* A tetraploid individual, cell or nucleus. [TETRA- + -PLOID.]

tet·ra·pod (téttra-pod) *adj.* Having four feet, legs, or leglike appendages. [Greek *tetrapous* (stem *tetrapod*-) : TETRA- + -POD.] **—tet·ra·pod** *n.*

te·trap·ter·ous (te-tráptarass) *adj.* Having four wings. Said of certain insects. [Greek *tetrapteros* : TETRA- + -PTEROUS.]

tet·rarch (tét-raark, téet-) *n.* **1.** The ruler of any of the four divisions of a country or province. **2.** Any of four joint rulers. **3. a.** A subordinate ruler. **b.** In the Roman Empire, especially in Syria, a petty prince enjoying limited power under Roman hegemony. [Middle English, from Late Latin *tetrarcha*, from Latin *tetrarchēs*, from Greek *tetrarkhēs* : TETRA- + -ARCH.] **—tet·rarch·y, tet·rarch·ate** (-ayt, -at, -it) *n.* **—te·trar·chic** (te-trárkik, tee-) *adj.*

tet·ra·spore (téttra-spawr ‖ -spōr) *n.* *Botany.* Any of four spores produced in a group from a sporangium, as in certain algae. **—tet·ra·spor·ic, tet·ra·spor·ous** (-spáw-rass ‖ -spō-) *adj.*

tet·ra·stich (téttra-stik) *n.* A poem or stanza that consists of four lines. **—tet·ra·stich·al** (-stick'l), **tet·ra·stich·ic** (-stíckik) *adj.*

te·tras·ti·chous (te-trástikass) *adj.* *Botany.* Arranged in four vertical rows. Said of leaves or flowers on a stalk. [Late Latin *tetrastichus*, having four lines, from Greek *tetrastikhos* : TETRA- + -STICHOUS.]

tet·ra·va·lent (téttra-váylant) *adj.* Having a valency of 4.

tet·rode (téttrōd) *n.* **1.** An electronic vacuum tube with four electrodes, a cathode, a control grid, a screen grid, and an anode. **2.** A transistor with two connections to the base or gate to improve high-frequency performance. [TETR(A)- + -ODE (path).]

te·trox·ide (te-tróksīd) *n.* A chemical compound containing four oxygen atoms per molecule. [TETR(A)- + OXIDE.]

tet·ryl (téttrīl, téttril) *n.* A yellow crystalline explosive consisting of (NO₂)₃C₆H₂N(NO₂)CH₃, used chiefly as a primer or detonator. Also called "nitramine". [TETR(A)- + -YL.]

tet·ter (téttar) *n.* *Archaic.* **1.** Any of various skin diseases such as psoriasis, herpes, and, especially, eczema, characterised by eruptions and itching. **2.** A pimple, blister, or pustule. [Middle English *teter*, Old English *tet(e)r*.]

teuch·ter (téwkhtar) *n.* *Scottish.* **1.** A person from northwest Scotland. **2.** An unsophisticated, rustic person. [Perhaps from Scots Gaelic, "north-country man".]

Teu·ton (téwt'n ‖ tóot'n) *n.* **1.** A member of an ancient people, probably of Germanic or Celtic origin, who lived in Jutland until the late second century B.C., when they migrated southwards. **2.** A member of a people speaking a Germanic language; especially, a German. [Latin *Teutonī.*]

Teu·ton·ic (tew-tónnik ‖ tew-) *adj.* **1.** Of, relating to, or characteristic of the Germanic people or the Teutons. **2.** Of or relating to the Germanic languages.

~*n.* The subfamily of Germanic languages.

Teutonic Knights. German military religious order founded (1190–91) at Acre. In 1211 they moved from Palestine to eastern Europe and after 50 years of campaigning subdued Prussia and many of the East Baltic States. The Order went into decline in the 15th century.

Teu·ton·ism (téwt'n-iz'm ‖ tóot'n-) *n.* **1.** A German practice or idiom. **2.** The German character or civilisation.

Tevere. See **Tiber.**

Te·vet (táy-vet, -váyt) *n.* Also **Te·bet, Te·beth.** The fourth month of the Hebrew year. [Hebrew *ṭēbhēth*, from Akkadian *ṭebētu*, perhaps "month of sinking in", "muddy month", from *ṭebū*, to sink in.]

Tex·as (ték-sass ‖ *locally also* -siz). State in the south central United States, bordering on Mexico. The capital is Austin; the largest cities

are Houston, Dallas, and San Antonio. It is the second-largest state in the Union, after Alaska. Its chief agricultural products are cotton, rice, and cattle, and the chief industry is the manufacture of chemicals. However, the great wealth of Texas is its vast oil resources. Texas was owned by Spain until it gained independence in 1836. It was annexed to the United States in 1845 and admitted as a state of the Union.

Texas fever *n.* An infectious disease of cattle and related animals, caused by a parasitic microorganism, *Babesia bigemina,* and transmitted by ticks.

text (tekst) *n.* **1. a.** The exact and original wording or words of something written or printed. **b.** The words of anything delivered orally, such as a speech or song, appearing in print. **2. a.** The body of a printed work as distinct from a preface, footnote, or appendix; the formal content. **b.** The words in a book as distinct from pictures or illustrations. **3.** A Scriptural passage to be read and expounded in a sermon. **4. a.** A reference used as the starting point of a discussion. **b.** The subject matter of a discourse. **5.** A textbook. **6.** *Printing.* Any of several styles of letters or types. [Middle English *texte*, from Old French, from Medieval Latin *textus*, (Scriptural) text, from Latin, literary composition, "woven thing", from the past participle of *texere*, to weave.]

text·book (tékst-book ‖ -boŏk) *n.* A book used as a standard reference work for the formal study of a particular subject.

~*adj.* Typical; conforming to a stereotype: *a textbook example.*

tex·tile (téks-tīl ‖ *U.S. also* -t'l) *n.* **1.** Cloth; a fabric, especially one that is woven or knitted. **2.** Fibre or yarn for weaving or making into fabric. Also used adjectivally: *the textile industry.* [French, from Latin *textilis*, from *textus*, "woven thing". See **text**.]

tex·tu·al (tékstew-al) *adj.* **1.** Of, pertaining to, or contained in a text. **2.** Based on or conforming to a text. [Middle English, from Old French *textuel*. See **text**, *-al*.] **—tex·tu·al·ly** *adv.*

textual criticism *n.* **1.** Study of a written work that seeks to establish the original text. **2.** Literary criticism stressing scholarly study and analysis of the text. In this sense, also called "criticism".

tex·tu·al·ism (tékstew-al-iz'm) *n.* **1.** Strict adherence to a text, especially of the Scriptures. **2.** Textual criticism, especially of the Scriptures. **—tex·tu·al·ist** *n.*

tex·tu·ar·y (tékstew-ari ‖ -erri) *adj.* Textual.

~*n., pl.* **textuaries.** A specialist in the study of the Scriptures.

tex·ture (téks-char, -tewr) *n.* **1.** The degree of roughness or smoothness of a surface; its feel: *the smooth texture of ivory.* **2. a.** The appearance of a fabric resulting from the woven arrangement of its yarns or fibres. **b.** A surface appearance suggesting the weave of a fabric. **c.** Consistency, as of a liquid. **3.** A grainy, fibrous, woven, or dimensional quality as opposed to a uniformly flat, smooth aspect; surface interest: *Brick walls give a room texture.* **4.** Distinctive or identifying qualities: *the texture of suburban life.* **5.** The representation of the structure of a surface as distinct from colour or form. **6.** In New Criticism, the particular aspect of a poem as distinct from its abstract or universal aspect. **7.** *Music.* A sound pattern created by melody, harmony, and rhythm.

~*tr.v.* **textured, -turing, -tures.** To give a distinctive texture to. [Originally, "weaving", from Latin *textūra*, from *textus*, woven thing. See **text**.] **—tex·tur·al** *adj.* **—tex·tur·al·ly** *adv.*

tex·tured (téks-chard, *pedantically* -tewrd) *adj.* **1.** Having a specified kind of texture. Used in combination: *a rough-textured tweed.* **2.** Having marked texture: *a textured wall of stucco.*

textured vegetable protein *n. Abbr.* **TVP** A type of protein derived from soya beans. It is processed so as to have a meatlike texture, sometimes flavoured, and used chiefly as a meat substitute. Also called "textured soya protein", "spun protein".

tex·tus re·cep·tus (tékstass ri-séptass) *n.* Received text; specifically, the received text of the Greek New Testament. [Latin.]

tfr. transfer.

T.G. transformational (generative) grammar.

T.G.W.U. Transport and General Workers' Union.

–th¹ *n. suffix.* Indicates: **1.** The act or result of the act expressed in the verb root; for example, **spilth**. **2.** The quality suggested by the adjective root; for example, **width**. [Middle English -*th(e)*, Old English -*thu*, -*tho*, from Common Germanic -*ithō* (unattested).]

–th², **-eth** *adj. & n. suffix.* Indicates ordinal numbers; for example, **millionth, fortieth.** [Middle English -*the*, -*te*, Old English -*(o)tha*, -*(o)the*.]

–th³. See **-eth.**

Th *Chemistry.* The symbol for the element thorium.

Th. Thursday.

Tha·ba·na Ntlen·ya·na (taa-baåna ntláyn-yana). Mountain in the Drakensberg range of eastern Lesotho, at 3 482 metres (11,424 feet) the highest peak in southern Africa.

Thai (tī) *n., pl.* **Thais** or collectively **Thai. 1. a.** A native or inhabitant of Thailand. **b.** A member of the predominant ethnic group of Thailand, a people with characteristics of both Mongoloids and Indonesians. **2.** The official language of Thailand, a member of the Tai family. Also called "Siamese". **—Thai** *adj.*

Thai·land (tī-land, -land). Formerly **Si·am** (sī-ám). Kingdom in Southeast Asia. Its heartland is the great plain of the Chao Phraya, a major rice-growing area. Nearly 75 per cent of the workforce are in farming, but manufacturing is expanding rapidly, and fishing and tourism are also important. The present dynasty, founded in 1782, kept Thailand the only Southeast Asian country that was never occupied by a European power (except in war). Absolute monarchy was abandoned in 1932. Area, 514 000 square kilometres

THAILAND

(198,250 square miles). Population, 60,000,000. Capital, Krung Thep (Bangkok).

thal·a·men·ceph·a·lon (thál-əm-en-kéffə-lon, -séffə-) *n. Anatomy.* **1.** The hindmost part of the forebrain. **2.** The **diencephalon** *(see).* [THALAM(US) + ENCEPHALON.] —**thal·a·men·ceph·a·lic** (-si-fál-ik, -ki-, -se-, -ke-) *adj.*

thal·a·mus (thál-ə-məss) *n., pl.* **-mi** (-mī). **1.** *Anatomy.* Either of two large ovoid masses of grey matter that relay sensory stimuli to the cerebral cortex. **2.** *Botany.* The receptacle of a flower. [New Latin, from Greek *thalamos*, inner chamber; perhaps akin to THOLOS.] —**tha·lam·ic** (thə-lámmik) *adj.* —**tha·lam·i·cal·ly** *adv.*

thal·as·saem·i·a, U.S. **thal·as·sem·i·a** (thál-ə-séemi-ə) *n.* An inherited blood disease in which there is an abnormality in the protein portion of the haemoglobin molecule, leading to severe anaemia. Also called "Cooley's anaemia". [Greek *thalassa†*, sea (that is, the Mediterranean) + -AEMIA.]

tha·las·sic (thə-lássik) *adj.* **1.** Of or pertaining to seas or oceans; pelagic. **2.** Of or pertaining to seas and gulfs as distinguished from the oceans. [French *thalassique*, from Greek *thalassa†*, sea.]

thal·as·soc·ra·cy (thál-ə-sóckrə-si) *n., pl.* **-cies.** Supremacy on the seas. [From Greek *thalassokratia : thalassa†*, sea + -o- + -CRACY.] —**thal·as·so·crat** (thə-lássə-krat) *n.*

tha·las·so·ther·a·py (thə-lássō-thérrəpi) *n.* Hydrotherapy using salt water; specifically, thalassotherapy using sea water. [Greek *thalassa†*, sea + -o- + THERAPY.) —**tha·las·so·ther·a·pist** *n.*

thaler. Variant of **taler.**

Tha·li·a (thə-lí-ə, *also* tháyli-ə). *Greek Mythology.* **1.** The Muse of comedy and pastoral poetry. **2.** One of the three **Graces** *(see).* [Greek *Thaleia*, "the blooming one", from *thallein*, to flourish.]

tha·lid·o·mide (thə-líddə-mīd) *n.* A sedative and hypnotic drug, $C_{13}H_{10}N_2O_4$, withdrawn from sale in 1961 following the discovery that its use during early pregnancy could lead to foetal abnormalities, most notably the malformation of limbs. [(PH)THAL(IC ACID) + (IM)ID(E) + (I)MIDE.]

thal·lic (thál-ik) *adj.* Of, pertaining to, or containing thallium, especially with valency 3. [THALL(IUM) + -IC.]

thal·li·um (thál-i-əm) *n.* Symbol **Tl** A soft, malleable, highly toxic metallic element, used in rodent and ant poisons, in photocells, infrared detectors, and low-melting glass. Atomic number 81, atomic weight 204.37, melting point 303.5°C, boiling point 1,457°C, relative density 11.85, valencies 1, 3. [New Latin : Latin *thallus*, green shoot, THALLUS (from its green spectral line) + -IUM.]

thal·loid (thál-oyd) *adj.* Also **thal·loi·dal** (tha-lóyd'l, thə-). Of, resembling, or constituting a thallus. [THALL(US) + -OID.]

thal·lo·phyte (thál-ə-fīt) *n.* Any plant or plantlike organism of the now obsolete division Thallophyta, which included the algae, fungi, and bacteria. These are all now considered to be separate divisions. [New Latin *Thallophyta* : THALL(US) + -PHYTE.] —**thal·lo·phy·tic** (-fíttik) *adj.*

thal·lous (thál-əss) *adj.* Also **thal·li·ous** (-i-əss). Of, pertaining to, or containing thallium, especially with valency 1. [THALL(IUM) + -OUS.]

thal·lus (thál-əss) *n., pl.* **thalli** (-ī, -ee) *or* **-luses.** *Botany.* An undifferentiated stemless, rootless, leafless plant body. [New Latin, from Latin, young shoot, from Greek *thallos*, from *thallein*, to sprout.]

Thames (temz). River in southeast England. It rises in the Cots-

wolds, Gloucestershire, and flows some 340 kilometres (210 miles) generally eastwards to the North Sea via a great estuary. In Oxford it is also known as the Isis. London is protected against its storm surges by a gated flood barrier, completed in 1982.

than (than, *weak form* thən) *conj.* **1.** Used in comparative statements to introduce the second element or clause of a comparison of inequality: *Gateau is richer than cake.* **2.** Used in statements of preference to introduce the less acceptable alternative: *I would rather dance than eat.* **3.** Used in statements expressing difference, especially after *else, other,* and compounds in which they appear: *elsewhere than in Britain; turned out to be none other than Mick Jagger.* ~*prep.* **1.** In comparison with: *She is much cleverer than me.* **2.** Used with expressions of degree or quantity: *more than twice the speed of sound; fewer than 100 people.* —**other than.** Apart from; except for. [Middle English *than(ne),* Old English *thanne, thænne.*]

Usage: In formal usage, sentences such as *She is bigger than I* are preferred to *She is bigger than me,* on the grounds that the sentence is short for *She is bigger than I am.* Similarly, *They liked him more than her* is said to be short for *They liked him more than they liked her,* and therefore different from *They liked him more than she,* which is short for *They liked him more than she liked him.* In informal usage, the objective form of pronouns *(me)* is generally used, and with third-person forms *(him, her),* this usage will often be encountered in relatively formal contexts: *John is much taller than him,* where *John is much taller than he* is felt to be stilted. The use of *what* (more characteristic of British than of American usage) is generally considered to be very informal, and many people avoid it altogether: *He looks much happier today than (what) he did yesterday.* See also **different.**

than·age (tháynij) *n.* **1.** The rank, jurisdiction, or office of a thane; thaneship. **2.** The land held by a thane. [Middle English, from Anglo-French : THANE + -AGE.]

Than·a·tos (thánnə-toss) *n.* **1.** Death as a personification or as a philosophical notion. **2.** *Psychology.* An alleged instinct to self-destruction; the death wish. Compare **Eros.** [Greek, "death".] —**than·a·tot·ic** (-tóttik) *adj.*

thane (thayn) *n.* Also **thegn** (for sense 1). **1.** In Anglo-Saxon England: **a.** A freeman granted land by the king in return for military service. **b.** A man ranking above an ordinary freeman and below a nobleman or ealdorman. **2.** In medieval Scotland, a feudal lord holding land granted by the king, and having the same rank as an earl's son. [Middle English *thayn, theyn,* Old English *theg(e)n,* from Germanic *thegnaz* (unattested); akin to Greek *teknon,* child.]

thane·ship (tháyn-ship) *n.* The position or office of a thane, especially in Scotland.

Than·et, Isle of (thánnit). Northeastern extremity of the county of Kent in southeastern England, formerly an island, now joined to the mainland by silting and the reclamation of land.

thank (thangk) *tr.v.* **thanked, thanking, thanks. 1.** To express gratitude to; give thanks to: *thanked him for his help.* Often used in interjections: *thank God! thank goodness.* **2.** To hold responsible; blame. —**I'll thank you to.** Please. Used to intensify an indignant request. [Middle English *thanken,* Old English *thancian.*]

thank·ful (thángk'l) *adj.* **1.** Grateful. **2.** Expressive of thanks. —**thank·ful·ness** *n.*

thank·ful·ly (thángkf'l-i) *adv.* **1.** In a thankful manner. **2.** *Informal.* Fortunately; *Thankfully, her injuries were only minor.*

thank·less (thángk-ləss, -liss) *adj.* **1.** Not feeling or showing gratitude; ungrateful. **2.** Unappreciated; unlikely to be appreciated: *a thankless task.* —**thank·less·ly** *adv.* —**thank·less·ness** *n.*

thanks (thangks) *pl.n.* **1.** An acknowledgement of a favour, gift, or benefit; gratitude. **2.** An expression of gratitude: *to give thanks.* —**no thanks to.** Without any help from; despite. —**thanks to.** On account of; because of.

~*interj.* Used to express thanks. —**thanks for nothing** or **thanks a bunch.** Used ironically in response to ill-treatment or disappointment. [Plural of obsolete *thank,* Old English *thanc,* from Germanic *thankaz* (unattested).]

thanks·giv·ing (thángks-givving, -gívving) *n.* An act of giving thanks; an expression of gratitude, especially to God.

Thanksgiving Day *n.* A national holiday for giving thanks to God, which in the United States is the fourth Thursday of November and in Canada the second Monday of October. Also "Thanksgiving".

thank you *interj.* **1.** Used to express gratitude. **2.** Used in reply to an offer, typically accepting it, but in some varieties of English (such as South African) declining it. [Short for *I thank you.*]

thank-you (thángkew) *n.* An act or expression of thanks.

~*adj.* Expressing thanks: *a thankyou letter.*

Thá·sos (thássoss). Greek island, lying in the Aegean Sea off the northeast coast of Greece. In ancient times the Phoenicians worked its gold mines, now exhausted; lead-zinc ores are still exploited.

that (that; *weak form for relative pronoun and conjunction* thət) *adj., pl.* **those** (thōz). **1.** Being the one indicated, mentioned, implied, or understood. **2.** Being the one further removed or less obvious: *this card or that card.*

~*pron., pl.* **those. 1.** Used as a demonstrative pronoun with the sense of: **a.** The one indicated, mentioned, implied, or understood. **b.** The further or less immediate one. **c.** The one belonging to the kind or category specified: *The best whisky is that from Scotland.* **2.** Used as a demonstrative pronoun to indicate: **a.** The period, point of time, or incident already mentioned or implied: *felt for my key, and that was when I noticed it was missing; tore up the contract and with that left the room; joined the army after that.* **b.** The place already mentioned or implied: *spent years in the Greek Islands, and that was where he learned to paint.* **c.** The manner, means, or process indicated or already mentioned or implied: *did a computing course, and that's how she got her present job; You open it like that; Don't look at me like that!* **3.** Used as a relative pronoun: **a.** To introduce a restrictive clause: *never got the letter that I sent him.* **b.** To indicate at, in, to, or on which: *the day that we met; every time that I tried; everywhere that we went.* **4. a.** Something: *There is that about him which mystifies me.* **b.** *Plural.* Some people: *There are those who feel it is already too late.* **—and all that.** Also *British informal* **and that.** And so on; and everything related to that. **—at that.** Furthermore; as well: *scored a goal and a good one at that.* **—like that. 1.** Without effort or delay: *solved the problem just like that.* **2.** Of such a kind or character: *She just did what he told her—she's like that.* **—that's that.** That is final; there is an end to it.

~adv. **1.** To such an extent or degree; to that extent; so: *If it cost that much it ought to be good.* **2.** *Informal.* To a great extent; very. Used chiefly in negative statements, except in nonstandard usage: *I wasn't that worried. She was that narked!*

~conj. **1.** Used to introduce a subordinate clause stating a fact, wish, consequence, purpose, or reason: *We supposed that you were lost; she wishes that you would come; so tired that he fell asleep in his chair.* **2.** Used to introduce an elliptical exclamation of desire: *Oh, that I were rich!* [Middle English *that,* Old English *thæt.*]

that·a·way (thát-ə-way) *adv. Informal.* That way; in that direction.

thatch (thach) *n.* **1.** Plant stalks or foliage, such as reeds or palm fronds, used for roofing. **2.** A roof made of this material. **3.** Something resembling a thatched roof, especially the hair of the head.

~tr.v. **thatched, thatching, thatches.** To cover with or as if with thatch. [Middle English *thacche,* from *thacchen,* to thatch, cover, Old English *theccan.*] **—thatch·er** *n.* **—thatch·y** *adj.*

Thatch·er (tháchər), **Margaret (Hilda), Baroness,** born Roberts (1925–). British Tory politician. MP for Finchley 1959–92, she became Leader of the Opposition (1975–9), and was Britain's first woman prime minister (1979–90). Memoirs: *The Downing Street Years: 1979–90* (1993); *The Path to Power* (1995).

that's. Contraction of *that has* or *that is.*

thau·ma·trope (tháwmə-trōp) *n.* A device, such as a card, with partial pictures on each side, which appear to merge when it is swung round. [Greek *thauma,* wonder, marvel + *-tropos,* turning.]

thau·ma·turge (tháwmə-turj) *n.* Also **thau·ma·tur·gist** (-ist). A performer of miracles or magic feats. [Medieval Latin *thaumaturgus,* from Greek *thaumatourgos* : *thauma* (stem *thaumat-*), wonder + *-ergos,* "working", from *ergon,* work.]

thau·ma·tur·gy (tháwmə-turji) *n.* The working of miracles or wonders; magic. **—thau·ma·tur·gic** (-túrjik), **thau·ma·tur·gi·cal** *adj.*

thaw (thaw) *v.* **thawed, thawing, thaws.** *—intr.* **1.** To change from a frozen solid to a liquid by gradual warming. **2.** To lose stiffness, numbness, or impermeability by being warmed. **3.** To become warm enough for snow and ice to melt. Used with *it.* **4.** To become less restrained or tense; relax. *—tr.* To melt or soften (a frozen solid) by gradual warming. **—See Synonyms at melt.**

~n. **1.** The process of thawing. **2.** A period of relatively warm weather during which ice and snow melt. **3.** A relaxation of reserve, restraints, hostilities, or tensions: *a thaw in East-West relations.* [Middle English *thawen,* Old English *thāwian,* from Germanic *thawōjan*† (unattested).]

the¹ (thee; *weak forms* thə *before a consonant sound,* thi *or* thee *before a vowel sound* || *The weak forms* thi *or* thee *before a consonant and* thə *before a vowel are also to be heard*). The definite article, functioning as an adjective. It is used: **1.** Before singular or plural nouns and noun phrases that denote particular or previously specified persons or things. **2.** Before a singular noun, making it generic: *the human arm; plays the violin.* **3. a.** Before a noun, and generally stressed, emphasising its uniqueness or prominence: *That's* THE *show to see this year; Is she really* THE *Elizabeth Taylor?* **b.** Before a noun denoting one that is the best, most notable, or most desirable of its kind: *gave the performance of his life as Othello; This is the place to be!* **4. a.** Before a proper noun denoting something that is the only one of its kind: *the British Museum; the Bible; the Old Kent Road.* **b.** Before a noun denoting any of various natural phenomena that are, or are considered as being, unique: *flew through the air; the wind and the rain; always snows in the winter.* **5. a.** Before a title of rank or office, designating its holder: *the Queen; the prime minister.* **b.** Before a qualifying adjective or noun in certain epithets or titles: *Ivan the Terrible; Edward the Confessor.* **c.** Before the name of certain Scottish or Irish clans, designating the chieftain: *the O'Donoghue.* **6.** Before certain nouns referring to familiar features or adjuncts of daily life, typically indicating the most accessible individual example: *ought to see the doctor; listening to the radio; has gone to the lavatory.* **7. a.** Before nouns denoting parts of the body, instead of the possessive pronoun: *slapped him in the face.* **b.** Before nouns denoting personal possessions or pets, instead of the possessive pronoun: *I've got the car with me; took the dog for a walk.* This use may be considered offensive in phrases such as *the wife.* **8.** Before a noun, indicating the degree or amount of it required for a stated purpose or operation: *haven't the time to see her.* **9. a.** Before an adjective or participle, extending it to signify a class or group and giving it the function of a noun: *the British; a school for the blind; the sick, the wounded, and the dying.* **b.** Before certain passive past participles, indicating an individual in the specified condition: *The accused took the stand.* **c.** Before certain adjectives, indicating an abstract concept: *a taste for the bizarre.* **10.** Before an adjective used absolutely: *the finest we have to offer.* **11.** Before a present participle, signifying the action in the abstract: *the weaving of rugs.* **12.** Before a noun, with the force of *per*: *at a pound the box.* [Middle English *the,* Old English *thē* (originally a demonstrative adjective, later superseding *sē,* masculine singular).]

the² (thee, *weak forms as at* **the¹**) *adv.* To that extent; by that much: *the sooner the better.* [middle English *the, thi,* Old English *thȳ, thē,* instrumental case of *thē,* THE, and *thæt,* THAT.]

the·an·thro·pism (thee-ánthrə-piz'm) *n. Theology.* The doctrine of the union of human and divine natures in Christ. [Late Greek *theanthrōpos,* god-man (*theos,* god + *anthrōpos,* man) + -IC.] **—the·an·throp·ic** (thée-an-thróppik) *adj.* **—the·an·thro·pist** (thee-ánthrəpist) *n.*

the·ar·chy (thée-aarki) *n., pl.* **-chies. 1.** Government or rule by God or a god; theocracy. **2.** A hierarchy or order of gods. [Late Greek *thearkhia* : THE(O)- + -ARCHY.]

the·a·tre, *U.S.* **the·a·ter** (théertər || thée-ətər, *South of England also* thee-éttər) *n.* **1.** A building, room, or, formerly, an outdoor structure such as an amphitheatre for the presentation of plays, films, or other dramatic performances. **2.** Any room with tiers of seats used for lectures or demonstrations; an auditorium. **3.** A room in a hospital or clinic in which surgical operations are performed. Also called "operating theatre". **4. a.** Dramatic literature or performance considered as a branch of art; drama. **b.** A school of dramatic theory. **c.** The milieu or world of actors and playwrights. Preceded by *the.* **d.** The quality or effectiveness of a theatrical production: *This play is good theatre.* **4.** The audience in a theatre. **5.** A place that is the setting for remarkable events; a scene: *a theatre of war.* **6.** *Australian.* A cinema.

~adj. **1.** Of or pertaining to the theatre: *theatre tickets.* **2.** Intended for use in a theatre of war: *theatre nuclear weapons.* [Middle English *theatre,* from Old French, from Latin *theātrum,* from Greek *theatron,* from *theasthai,* to watch, look at, from *thea*†, a viewing.]

the·a·tre·go·er (théertər-gō-ər || thée-ətər-, thee-éttər-) *n.* A person who goes to the theatre, especially habitually.

the·a·tre-in-the-round (théertər-in-thə-równd || thée-ətər-, thee-éttər-) *n., pl.* **theatres-in-the-round 1.** A theatre in which the stage is at the centre of the auditorium, surrounded by seats, and without a proscenium. **2.** Drama written or designed for such a theatre. Also called "arena theatre".

Theatre of Cruelty *n.* A form of theatre, initiated in the 1930s by Antonin Artaud, which aims to depict pain, suffering, and the presence of evil, especially by nonverbal means.

Theatre of the Absurd *n.* A form of theatre which rejects naturalism in order to present the absurdity of the human condition. It is considered to have been founded by Alfred Jarry, but is more readily associated with the work of writers such as Eugène Ionesco.

the·at·ri·cal (thi-áttrik'l) *adj.* **1.** Of, relating to, or suitable for the theatre or dramatic performance. **2.** Marked by the self-display or the exaggerated manner associated with actors; histrionic.

~n. **1.** *Informal.* An actor. **2.** *Usually plural.* A dramatic performance, especially by amateurs. **—the·at·ri·cal·ly** *adv.* **—the·at·ri·cal·ism** (-izm), **the·at·ri·cal·i·ty** (thi-áttri-kál-əti), **the·at·ri·cal·ness** *n.*

the·at·rics (thi-áttriks) *pl.n.* **1.** *Used with a singular verb.* The art of the theatre. **2.** Theatrical effects or mannerisms; histrionics.

the·ba·ine (thée-bi-een, -bay-, thi-báy- || -bə-) *n.* A poisonous alkaloid, $C_{19}H_{21}NO_3$, obtained from opium and having a slight narcotic action. [New Latin *thebaia,* (herb of) Thebes + -INE.]

Thebes¹ (theebz). City of ancient Egypt, occupying the site now partially occupied by Al Uqsur and Karnak, on both sides of the river Nile. It flourished from the mid-22nd to the 18th century B.C., both as a royal residence and as the centre of the worship of the god Amen. Excavations have unearthed ruins of great archaeological and historical importance, among them the nearby Valley of the Tombs of the Kings, and the temples of Karnak and Luxor.

Thebes². City of ancient Greece, lying in eastern Boeotia northwest of Athens, on the site of present-day Thebes, or Thívai. Settlement of the site dates from the early Bronze Age, and it is the scene of the legends of Oedipus and Antigone. Following the Peloponnesian War, Thebes gained military ascendancy in Greece by twice defeating Sparta (375 B.C. and 371 B.C.). Its heyday was short-lived. In 336 B.C. the city was almost completely destroyed by Alexander.

the·ca (thée-kə) *n., pl.* **-cae** (-see, -kee). *Biology.* A case, covering, or sheath, such as the spore case of a moss capsule. [New Latin, from Latin *thēca,* a case, sheath, from Greek *thēkē.*] **—the·cal** (-k'l) *adj.*

the·cate (thée-kayt) *adj.* Also **the·cal** (-k'l). Having a theca; encased or sheathed. [THEC(A) + -ATE.]

thé dan·sant (táy doN-sóN) *n., pl.* **thés dansants** (*pronounced as singular, or* táyz). A dance held while afternoon tea is served. Also called "tea dance". [French.]

thee (thee) *pron. Archaic, Poetic, & Regional.* **1.** The objective case of the second person singular pronoun *thou,* used as the direct or indirect object of a verb, as the object of a preposition, or after *than* or *as* in comparisons in which the first term is in the objective case. **2.** *Nonstandard.* Used in the nominative as well as the objective case in certain religious communities, especially in the Society of Friends in the 19th century. [Middle English, Old English, accusative and dative of *thū,* THOU.]

thee·lin (théelin) *n.* **Oestrone** *(see).* [Irregularly from Greek *thēlus,* female + -IN.]

theft (theft) *n.* **1.** The act or an instance of stealing; the dishonest taking and removing of another's personal property with the intent of permanently depriving the owner. **2.** *Archaic.* That which is stolen. [Middle English *theft(he),* Old English *thēofth,* from Common Germanic *thiufith* (unattested), from *thiuf* (unattested), THIEF.]

the·ine (theé-een, -in) *n.* **Caffeine** *(see).* [New Latin *thea,* tea + -INE; originally believed to be peculiar to tea.]

their (thair || tháy-ər). The possessive form of the pronoun *they.* Used attributively to indicate possession, agency, or reception of an action by the speaker: *their house; suffered their first defeat.* [Middle English, from Old Norse *their(r)a* (genitive plural).]

theirs (thairz || tháy-ərz) *pron.* Absolute form of *their. Used with a singular or plural verb.* Belonging to them; the one or ones belonging to them: *The blue boots are theirs. Mine is here, and theirs is the one on the stairs.* **—of theirs.** Belonging or pertaining to them: *a friend of theirs.* [Middle English, from THEIR.]

the·ism (theé-iz'm) *n.* Belief in the existence of a god or gods; especially, belief in a personal God as creator and ruler of the world, known to humankind through supernatural revelation. Compare **deism, pantheism.** [THE(O)- + -ISM.] **—the·ist** *n.* **—the·is·tic** (thee-ístik), **the·is·ti·cal** *adj.* **—the·is·ti·cal·ly** *adv.*

them (them, *weak form* thəm) *pron.* The objective case of the third person plural pronoun *they.* It is used: **1.** As the direct object of a verb: *She assisted them.* **2.** As the indirect object of a verb: *He offered them a new contract.* **3.** As the object of a preposition: *This letter is addressed to them.* **4.** After *than* or *as* in comparisons in which the first term is in the objective case: *The judges praised us more than them.* **5.** *Chiefly U.S. Informal.* In place of the reflexive pronoun *themselves,* as the indirect object of a verb: *They went to buy them a car.* **6.** In various elliptical, absolute, or interjectional phrases in which it is neither subject nor object: *Them and their big ideas!* **7.** *Nonstandard.* Those. [Middle English *the(i)m,* partly from Old Norse *theim,* partly from Old English *thǣm.*]

the·mat·ic (thi-máttik, thee-) *adj.* **1.** Of, based on, constituting, or relating to a theme or themes. **2.** *Linguistics.* Constituting part of the theme or stem of a word.
~*n.* A thematic vowel or sound sequence. [Greek *thematikos,* from *thema* (stem *themat-*), proposition, THEME.] **—the·mat·i·cal·ly** *adv.*

theme (theem) *n.* **1.** A topic of discourse, discussion, contemplation, or composition, often expressible as a phrase, proposition, or question. **2.** An idea, point of view, or perception embodied and expanded upon in a work of art; an underlying or essential subject of artistic representation; a motif: *the theme of the noble savage in literature.* **3.** *Chiefly U.S.* A short composition assigned to a student as a writing exercise. **4.** *Music.* A melody forming the basis of variations or other development in a composition. Also called "subject". **5.** *Linguistics.* **a.** A stem. **b.** A root. [Middle English *t(h)eme,* theme (of a discussion), from Old French *teme,* from Latin *thema,* from Greek, "thing placed", proposition.]

theme park *n.* An amusement park constructed to evoke a central theme: *"an Elizabethan theme park with . . . Disneyesque paraphernalia" (BBC Radio 4).*

theme song *n.* **1.** A melody or song recurring throughout a dramatic performance and often intended to convey a mood. **2.** *U.S.* A **signature tune** *(see).*

them·selves (thəm-sélvz || them-) *pron.* A specialised form of the third person plural pronoun. It is used: **1.** As a reflexive pronoun forming the direct or indirect object of a verb or the object of a preposition: *hurt themselves; give themselves time; talk to themselves.* **2.** For emphasis, after *they*: *They themselves weren't certain.* **3.** As an emphasising substitute: *Themselves in debt, they couldn't help us.* Sometimes nonstandard: *The Smiths and themselves are in trouble.* **4.** As an indication of (their) real, normal, or healthy condition or identity: *They haven't been themselves lately.*

then (then) *adv.* **1.** At that time: *I was a lot fitter then; If you're still in London then, come and visit us.* **2.** Next in time, space, or order; immediately afterwards. **3.** In that case; accordingly: *If you want to do it, then tell him; all right then—I agree.* **4.** In consequence; with the result that: *Leave by the back door, then nobody will notice.* **5.** In addition; moreover; besides. **6. a.** So it appears; so it may be deduced from what has gone before: *I take it, then, that you're interested.* **b.** By way of summing up or concluding what has gone before: *The allies, then, had suffered badly.* **7. a.** By way of qualifying what has just been stated: *didn't get the job, but then he never really wanted it.* **b.** In contrast; on the other hand: *Then again, we could go to the pub.*
~*pron.* A particular time or moment: *Until then let's stay here.*
~*adj.* Being so at that time: *the then headmistress.* [Middle English *thenne, thann,* Old English *thanne, thænne.*]

Usage: Careful speakers sometimes object to the use of *then* as an adjective, as in *the then prime minister,* preferring such phrases as *the prime minister of the time,* but it is widely used.

the·nar (theé-naar) *n.* **1.** The fleshy mound on the palm of the hand at the base of the thumb. **2.** The sole of the foot. [New Latin, from Greek *thenar,* palm of the hand.] **—the·nar** *adj.*

thence (thenss || *Scottish and U.S. also* thenss) *adv.* **1.** From that place; from there. **2.** From that time; thenceforth. **3.** From that circumstance or source; therefrom. [Middle English *thannes,* from *thanne,* from there, Old English *thanon.*]

thence·forth (thénss-fórth || thénss-, -fōrth) *adv.* From that time forwards; thereafter.

thence·for·wards (thénss-fór-wərdz || thénss-, -fōr-) *adv.* Also **thence·for·ward** (-wərd). From that time or place onwards.

theo-, the- *comb. form.* Indicates a god or gods; for example, **theism, theobromine.** [From Greek *theos,* god.]

the·o·bro·mine (theé-ō-brṓ-meen, -min) *n.* A bitter, colourless alkaloid, $C_7H_8N_4O_2$, derived principally from the cocoa bean, and used as a diuretic and a cardiac stimulant. [New Latin *Theobroma,* "food of the gods", genus including the cacao tree : THEO- + Greek *brōma,* food + -INE.]

the·o·cen·tric (theér-séntrik, theé-ō-, -ə-) *adj.* Centring on God as the prime concern: *a theocentric cosmology.* [THEO- + CENTR(E) + -IC.] **—the·o·cen·tric·i·ty** (-sen-tríssəti), **the·o·cen·trism** *n.*

the·oc·ra·cy (thi-ókrə-si) *n., pl.* **-cies. 1.** A form of government in which a god is regarded as the supreme ruler, and temporal power is in the hands of a priestly order claiming divine sanction. **2.** A state so governed. [Greek *theokratia* : THEO- + -CRACY.]

the·o·crat (theér-krat, theé-ō-, -ə-) *n.* **1.** One who rules in a theocracy. **2.** A believer in theocracy. [THEO- + -CRAT.] **—the·o·crat·ic** (-kráttik), **the·o·crat·i·cal** *adj.* **—the·o·crat·i·cal·ly** *adv.*

the·od·i·cy (thi-óddə-si, -óddi-) *n., pl.* **-cies.** A vindication of divine justice in the face of the paradox that God is both omnipotent and benevolent, and yet permits evil to exist among men. [French *Théodicée,* title of a work (1710) by Leibniz : THEO- + Greek *dykē,* judgment.]

the·od·o·lite (thi-óddə-līt) *n.* A surveying instrument used to measure horizontal and vertical angles with a small telescope that can move in horizontal and vertical planes. [New Latin *theodelitus*†.]

The·od·o·ric (thi-óddorik) known as Theodoric the Great (A.D. *c.*454–526). King of the Ostrogoths, who established the Ostrogothic Kingdom that dominated Italy from the late fifth to the sixth century.

the·og·o·ny (thi-óggəni) *n., pl.* **-nies.** The origin and genealogy of the gods, especially as recounted in ancient epic poetry. [Greek *theogonia* : THEO- + -GONY.] **—the·o·gon·ic** (theer-gónnik, theé-ə-) *adj.* **—the·og·o·nist** (thi-óggənist) *n.*

the·o·lo·gi·an (theer-lṓ-ji-ən, theé-ə-, -jən) *n.* One versed in or studying theology.

the·o·log·i·cal (theer-lójik'l, theé-ə-) *adj.* Of or pertaining to a theology or religious philosophy. **—the·o·log·i·cal·ly** *adv.*

theological virtues *pl.n.* The virtues bestowed on man by a special grace of God; faith, hope, and charity.

the·ol·o·gise (thi-óllə-jīz) *v.* **-gised, -gising, -gises.** —*tr.* To make theological in form or significance. —*intr.* To speculate about theology. **—the·ol·o·gis·er** *n.*

the·ol·o·gy (thi-óllәji) *n., pl.* **-gies. 1.** The study of the nature of God and religious truth; rational inquiry into religious questions, especially those posed by Christianity. **2.** An organised, often formalised body of opinions concerning divinity and humanity's relationship to God. **3.** Loosely, any body of opinions considered, often humorously or disparagingly, as having a religious character: *monetarist theology.* [Middle English *theologie,* from Old French, from Latin *theologia,* from Greek : THEO- + -LOGY.]

the·o·ma·ni·a (theé-ō-máyni-ə, -ə-) *n.* Religious insanity; especially, a belief that one is God.

the·o·mor·phism (theer-mórf-iz'm, theé-ə-, -ō-) *n.* The depiction or conception of man as having the form of a god or of God. [THEO- + MORPH(O)- + -ISM.] **—the·o·mor·phic** *adj.*

the·oph·a·ny (thi-óffəni) *n., pl.* **-nies.** An appearance of God or of a god to a human being; a divine manifestation. [Medieval Latin *theophania,* from Late Greek *theophaneia* : THEO- + Greek *phainein,* to show.]

the·o·phyl·line (theer-fíl-een, theé-ə-, -in, *also* thi-óffil-) *n.* A colourless crystalline alkaloid, $C_7H_8N_4O_2$, derived from tea leaves and also made synthetically. It is an isomer of and has effects similar to theobromine. [THEO(BROMINE) + PHYLL(O)- + -INE.]

the·or·bo (thi-órbō) *n., pl.* **-bos.** A 17th-century lute having two necks and two sets of strings and pegs, one set above and somewhat to the side of the other. [Italian *tiorba*†.]

the·o·rem (theér-əm, -em, -im || theé-ər-) *n.* **1.** *Mathematics & Logic.* A statement or proposition that can be or has been proved on the basis of reasoning from explicit assumptions. **2.** A rule or statement of relations, usually expressed as a formula or equation: *binomial theorem.* [Late Latin *theōrēma,* from Greek, spectacle, intuition, theorem, from *theōrein,* to observe, look at, from *theōros,* spectator, from *thea,* a looking at.]

the·o·ret·i·cal (theer-réttik'l, theér- || theé-ə-) *adj.* Also **the·o·ret·ic** (-réttik). **1.** Pertaining to or based on theory. **2.** Restricted to theory, as: **a.** Lacking verification from experience or experiment. **b.** Lacking practical application. Compare **applied. 3.** Existing only in theory; hypothetical or speculative. [Late Latin *theōrēticus,* from Greek *theōrētikos,* able to perceive, from *theōrein,* to observe. See **theorem.**] **—the·o·ret·i·cal·ly** *adv.*

the·o·re·ti·cian (theér-ə-tísh'n, -e- || theé-ər-) *n.* A student of theory in a science or other field of study.

the·o·ret·ics (theer-réttiks, theér- || theé-ə-) *n. Used with a singular verb.* The theoretical part of a science or other subject; principles.

the·o·rise, the·o·rize (theér-īz || theé-ər-) *intr.v.* **-rised, -rising, -rises. 1.** To develop or formulate a theory or theories. **2.** To think in terms of theory; speculate. **—the·o·ri·sa·tion** (-ī-záysh'n || *U.S.* -i-) *n.* **—the·o·ris·er** *n.*

the·o·rist (theér-ist || theé-ər-) *n.* One skilled in the theoretical rather than practical aspects of a subject.

the·o·ry (theér-i || theé-əri) *n., pl.* **-ries. 1. a.** Systematically organised knowledge applicable in a relatively wide variety of circumstances; especially, a system of assumptions, accepted principles, and rules of procedure devised to analyse, predict, or otherwise explain the nature or behaviour of a given set of phenomena: *the theory of evolution; Marxist economic theory.* **b.** Broadly, any set of beliefs or suppositions serving as a basis for action. **2. a.** That part of a subject dealing with its underlying rules and principles; abstract principles as distinct from practice or experiment: *musical theory*. **b.** The realm of abstract speculation or ideal circumstances: *In theory it should only take a week*. **3.** Broadly, a hypothesis or supposition; an opinion. [Late Latin *theōria*, from Greek, contemplation, theory, from *theōros*, spectator, from *theasthai*, to observe, from *thea*, a viewing.]

theory of games *n.* Mathematics. **Game theory** *(see)*.

the·os·o·phy (thi-óssəfi) *n., pl.* **-phies. 1.** Any of various philosophical or religious systems concerned with a direct intuitive or mystical apprehension of God. **2.** *Capital* **T.** The doctrines and beliefs of a modern religious sect, the Theosophical Society, incorporating aspects of Buddhism and Brahmanism. [Medieval Latin *theosophia*, from Late Greek *theosophia* : THEO- + -SOPHY.] —**the·o·soph·ic** (thi-óssəfist) *n.*

ther·a·peu·tic (thèrrə-péwtik) *adj.* **1.** Having healing or curative powers. **2.** Performed or serving to maintain health. **3.** Of or pertaining to therapeutics. [Greek *therapeutikos*, from *therapeutēs*, one who administers, from *therapeuein*, to administer to (medically). See **therapy**.] —**ther·a·peu·ti·cal·ly** *adv.*

ther·a·peu·tics (thèrrə-péwtiks) *n. Usually used with a singular verb.* The branch of medicine concerned with the treatment of disease or disorders by remedial means. —**ther·a·peu·tist** *n.*

ther·a·pist (thérrəpist) *n.* A specialist in practising a certain form of therapy, such as physiotherapy or psychotherapy.

the·rap·sid (thə-rápsid, thi-, the-) *n.* Any of the large, extinct reptiles of the order *Therapsida*, widespread in Permian and Triassic times, and thought to be the ancestors of the mammals. [New Latin *Therapsida*, from Greek *theraps*, attendant.]

ther·a·py (thérrəpi) *n., pl.* **-pies. 1. a.** The remedial treatment of illness or disability. **b.** A course of such treatment. Often used in combination: *hydrotherapy; speech therapy*. **2. Psychotherapy** *(see)*. [New Latin *therapīa*, from Greek *therapeia*, service, from *therapeuein*, to be an attendant, from *theraps*, attendant.]

Ther·a·va·da (thèrrə-vaádə) *n.* A branch of Buddhism, predominating in Sri Lanka and Southeast Asia, based on a somewhat literal interpretation of the Pali scriptures, and emphasising monastic life. Also called "Hinayana". [Pali *theravāda*, "doctrine of the elders" : *thera*, old, elder, from Sanskrit *sthavira*, thick, stout, old + *vāda*, speech, doctrine, from Sanskrit, sound, statement.]

there (thàir) *adv.* **1.** At or in that place. **2.** To, into, or towards that place; thither: *run there*. **3.** At that point or position: *Hold it right there*. **4.** In that matter or respect: *There we must agree to differ*. **5.** Used to draw attention to someone or something: *There goes the bus!* —**there and then**. Immediately; right at that point. —**there it is**. That is the situation, whether one likes it or not.
~*pron.* (*weak form* thər). **1.** Used, especially with the verb *be*, to introduce a sentence or clause whose real subject follows the verb: *There is someone at the door. There appears to be some disagreement*. **2.** That place: *There is where I should like to live*.
~*adj.* **1.** *Informal*. Existing in that place. Used for emphasis after a noun or demonstrative pronoun: *Take that one there. John there will help you*. **2.** *Nonstandard*. Used for emphasis between a demonstrative pronoun and a noun: *that there dog*.
~*interj*. Used to express emotion, such as relief, satisfaction, or consolation: *There, now I can have some peace!* [Middle English *ther(e)*, Old English *thēr, thǣr*.]

Usage: When *there* appears before a linking verb, such as *be* or *seem*, the verb agrees in number with the following noun: *There is a man; There are several men*. When more than one noun follows the verb, the verb is usually singular if the first noun is singular (*There is a man and three girls in the car*), and plural if the first noun is plural (*There are three girls and a man in the car*). However, a quantity or circumstance perceived as singular or unified may take a singular verb: *There is only £4 in my account; There was laughter and dancing at the party*. Informally, there is a strong tendency to use the contraction *there's* even in sentences where the following noun is plural: *There's three men in the garden*.

there·a·bouts (thàir-ə-bówts) *adv.* Also *chiefly U.S.* **there·a·bout** (-bowt). Near that place, time, quantity, or degree; approximately.

there·af·ter (thàir-aáftər || -áftər) *adv. Formal*. From then on; after that: *an apprentice for three years, an assistant thereafter*.

there·at (thàir-át) *adv. Archaic*. **1.** At that place or point. **2.** By reason of that; as a result of that.

there·by (thàir-bí, -bī) *adv.* **1.** By that means; as a result. **2.** In connection with that: *and thereby hangs a tale*.

there·for (thàir-fór) *adv. Archaic*. For that, this, or it.

there·fore (thàir-fawr || -fōr) *adv.* For that reason; consequently; hence: *The rumour's false and your judgment therefore wrong*. Also used to indicate a logical connection with a preceding clause: *I lost my money; therefore, I could not buy a ticket*.

there·from (thàir-fróm || -frúm) *adv. Archaic*. From that time, place, circumstance, or thing.

there·in (thàir-ín, -in) *adv.* **1.** *Law*. In that place or context. **2.** In that matter or particular.

there·in·af·ter (thàir-in-aáftər || -áftər) *adv. Law*. In a later or subsequent portion, as of a statute or book.

there·of (thàir-óv || -úv) *adv. Formal & Law*. **1.** Of or concerning this, that, or it. **2.** From that cause or origin; therefrom.

there·on (thàir-ón || -áwn) *adv. Formal & Archaic*. **1.** On or upon

this, that, or it. **2.** Following that immediately; thereupon.

there·to (thàir-tōō) *adv.* **1.** *Formal*. To that, this, or it; thereunto. **2.** *Archaic*. In addition.

there·to·fore (thàir-tōō-fór, -tōō-, -tə- || -fōr) *adv. Formal & Law*. Until or prior to that time; before that.

there·un·der (thàir-úndər) *adv. Formal & Law*. Under this or that.

there·up·on (thàir-ə-pón, -pon || -páwn, -pawn) *adv.* **1.** Directly following that. **2.** *Archaic*. **a.** On this or that. **b.** On that account. **c.** On that matter.

there·with (thàir-with, -with) *adv.* Also **there·with·al** (-with-áwl). *Archaic*. **1.** With that, this, or it. **2.** Immediately thereafter.

the·ri·an·throp·ic (thèer-i-an-thróppik) *adj.* Partly human, partly animal. Said of such mythological creatures as the Minotaur. [Greek *thērion*, wild beast + ANTHROPO- + -IC.]

the·ri·o·mor·phic (thèer-i-ō-mórfik, -ə-) *adj.* Having the form of a beast: *theriomorphic gods*. [Greek *thērion*, wild beast + -MORPHIC.]

therm (therm) *n.* A unit of heat equal to one hundred thousand British thermal units or $1.055\,056 \times 10^8$ joules. [From Greek *thermē*, heat, from *thermos*, hot.]

therm-. Variant of **thermo-**.

–therm *n. comb. form*. Indicates heat; for example, **poikilotherm**. [From Greek *thermē*, heat. See **therm**.]

ther·mae (thérmee) *pl.n.* Public baths in the ancient Greek or Roman world. [Latin, from Greek *thermai*, from *thermē*, heat.]

ther·mal (thérm'l) *adj.* Also **ther·mic** (thérmik) (for sense 1). **1.** Of, pertaining to, using, producing, or caused by heat. **2.** Naturally hot or warm: *thermal springs*. **3.** Specially designed to minimise loss of body heat: *thermal underwear*.
~*n.* A rising current of warm air. [French, from Greek *thermē*, heat. See **therm**.] —**ther·mal·ly** *adv.*

thermal barrier *n.* A barrier to flight above a certain speed as a result of the heat produced by air friction. Also "heat barrier".

thermal conductivity *n.* A measure of a substance's ability to transfer heat, expressed as the rate of conduction of heat between opposite faces of a hypothetical unit cube of the substance when there is unit temperature difference between the faces. It is measured in joules per second per metre per kelvin.

thermal efficiency *n.* The **efficiency** *(see)* of a machine.

thermal equator *n.* An imaginary line round the earth that links the point on each meridian that has the highest average temperatures.

thermal equilibrium *n.* A state of a system in which there is no net flow of heat among its components.

thermal spring *n.* A **hot spring** *(see)*.

ther·mal·ise, ther·mal·ize (thérm'l-īz) *v.* **-ised, -sing, -ises.** —*tr.* To cause (neutrons) in a moderator to become thermal neutrons. —*intr.* To become thermal neutrons. —**ther·mal·is·a·tion** (-ī-záysh'n || *U.S.* -i-) *n.*

thermal neutron *n.* A neutron that is approximately in thermal equilibrium with the surrounding medium; especially, one produced by fission, slowed by a moderator, and having a mean velocity of about 2200 metres per second. Also called "slow neutron".

thermal reactor *n.* A nuclear reactor in which most of the fissions are caused by thermal neutrons.

thermal shock *n.* Stress in a material caused by a sharp change of temperature.

thermal unit *n.* See **British thermal unit**.

therm·i·on (thér-mi-ən, -mī- || -on) *n.* An electrically charged particle or ion emitted by a conducting material at high temperatures. [THERM(O)- + ION.] —**therm·i·on·ic** (-ónnik) *adj.*

thermionic current *n.* A flow of thermions.

thermionic emission *n.* The emission of thermions from a conducting material at high temperatures.

therm·i·on·ics (thér-mi-ónniks, -mī-) *n. Used with a singular verb*. The physics of thermionic phenomena; especially, the study and design of thermionic valves.

thermionic valve *n.* An electronic vacuum tube in which the source of electrons is a heated electrode. Also *U.S.* "thermionic tube".

therm·is·tor (ther-místər) *n.* A resistor made of semiconductors having resistance that varies rapidly and predictably with temperature. [THERM(AL) + (RES)ISTOR.]

Ther·mit (thér-mit, -mīt). Also **Thermite** (-mīt). *n.* A trademark for a welding and incendiary mixture of fine aluminium powder with a metallic oxide which when ignited produces an intense heat.

thermo-, therm- *comb. form*. **1.** Indicates heat; for example, **thermogram**. **2.** Indicates thermoelectricity; for example, **thermionics**. [From Greek *thermē*, heat, from *thermos*, hot.]

ther·mo·bar·o·graph (thérmō-bárrə-graaf, -graf) *n.* A device that records both the pressure and temperature of a gas. [THERMO- + BARO- + -GRAPH.]

ther·mo·chem·is·try (thérmō-kémmistri) *n.* The branch of chemistry concerned with the heat produced or absorbed during reactions and other heat-associated chemical phenomena. —**ther·mo·chem·i·cal** (-kémmik'l) *adj.* —**ther·mo·chem·ist** *n.*

ther·mo·cline (thérm-ō-klīn, -ə-) *n.* A temperature gradient in a body of water, such as a lake, in which there is a marked variation of temperature with depth. [THERMO- + -CLINE.]

ther·mo·cou·ple (thérm-ō-kupp'l, -ə-) *n.* **1.** A pair of wires of different metals joined at one end, used to measure temperature by the voltage produced at the junction. **2.** A circuit formed by two different wires joined at both ends, with one junction kept at a constant low temperature and the other at the temperature to be measured. The temperature is proportional to the current in the circuit.

ther·mo·dy·nam·ics (thérm-ō-dī-námmiks, -ə-) *n. Used with a singu-*

lar verb. The physics of the relationships between heat and other forms of energy, especially when used to study the properties of matter. **—ther·mo·dy·nam·ic** *adj.*

thermodynamic scale *n.* A temperature scale based on thermodynamic properties, such that zero on the scale is absolute zero.

thermodynamic temperature *n.* A physical quantity based on the average thermal energy of the random motion of the particles of a system in thermal equilibrium. The unit of thermodynamic temperature is the kelvin.

ther·mo·e·lec·tric·i·ty (thérmō-él-ek-tríssəti, -ilék- ‖ -trízzəti) *n.* **1.** Electricity generated by a flow of heat, as in a thermocouple. **2.** The branch of physics concerned with such electricity and related phenomena. **—ther·mo·e·lec·tric** *adj.* **—ther·mo·e·lec·tri·cal·ly** *adv.*

ther·mo·e·lec·tron (thérmō-i-lék-tron, -lek-) *n.* An electron produced as a result of thermionic emission.

ther·mo·gen·e·sis (thérm-ō-jénnə-siss, -ə-) *n.* The production of heat by physiological processes in the body.

ther·mo·gram (thérm-ō-gram, -ə-) *n.* A record made by a thermograph. [THERMO- + -GRAM.]

ther·mo·graph (thérm-ō-graaf, -ə-, -graf) *n.* A thermometer that records temperatures automatically. [THERMO- + -GRAPH.]

ther·mog·ra·phy (ther-móggrəfi) *n.* Any printing or writing process involving heat; especially, a letterpress technique that produces a raised effect by heating printed matter that has been dusted with special powder. [THERMO- + -GRAPHY.]

ther·mo·junc·tion (thérmō-júngksh'n) *n.* A point of contact between two dissimilar metals at which a thermoelectric current is produced.

ther·mo·la·bile (thérmō-láy-bīl ‖ -bil, -b'l) *adj.* Subject to destruction, decomposition, or great change by moderate heating. Said especially of certain biochemical compounds. Compare **thermostable.** [THERMO- + LABILE.]

ther·mo·lu·mi·nes·cence (thérmō-lóō-mi-néss'nss, -léw-) *n.* Phosphorescence produced by gentle heating of some minerals which have previously absorbed radiation. **—ther·mo·lu·mi·nes·cent** *adj.*

ther·mol·y·sis (ther-móllə-siss) *n.* **1.** *Physiology.* The loss of heat from the body. **2.** *Chemistry.* The dissociation or decomposition of compounds by heat. [THERMO- + -LYSIS.] **—ther·mo·lyt·ic** (thérm-ō-líttik, -ə-) *adj.*

ther·mo·mag·net·ic (thérm-ō-mag-néttik, -ə-) *adj.* Of or pertaining to a change in the temperature of a body as a result of magnetisation or demagnetisation.

ther·mom·e·ter (thər-mómmitər) *n.* An instrument for measuring temperature; especially, one consisting of a graduated, sealed, glass tube with a bulb containing a liquid, typically mercury, that expands and rises in the tube as the temperature increases. [French *thermomètre* : THERMO- + -METER.] **—ther·mo·met·ric** (thérm-əméttrik, -ō-) *adj.* **—ther·mo·met·ri·cal·ly** *adv.*

ther·mom·e·try (thər-mómmətri, ther-) *n.* **1.** The measurement of temperature. **2.** The science and technology of temperature measurement. [THERMO- + -METRY.]

ther·mo·mo·tor (thérm-ō-mōtər, -ə-, -mōtər) *n.* An engine operated by heat, especially by the expansion of heated air.

ther·mo·nu·cle·ar (thérmō-néw-kli-ər ‖ -nōō-) *adj.* **1.** Of, pertaining to, or derived from the fusion of atomic nuclei at high temperatures. **2.** Involving or designating nuclear weapons based on fusion, especially as distinguished from those based on fission.

ther·mo·pe·ri·od·ism (thérmō-péer-i-ədiz'm) *n.* Also **ther·mo·pe·ri·o·dic·i·ty** (-ə-díssəti). The response of certain plants to alternating low and high temperatures over a period, as of days and nights or successive seasons.

ther·mo·phil·ic (thérm-ō-fíllik, -ə-) *n. Biology.* Requiring high temperatures for normal development, as certain bacteria do. Compare **mesophilic, psychrophilic.** [THERMO- + -PHIL(E) + -IC.] **—ther·mo·phile** (-fīl), **ther·mo·phil** (-fil) *n.*

ther·mo·pile (thérm-ō-pīl, -ə-) *n.* A device to measure temperature or generate current, consisting of a number of thermocouples connected in series. [THERMO- + PILE (a heap, "series").]

ther·mo·plas·tic (thérm-ō-plástik, -ə-, -plaastik) *adj.* Becoming soft when heated and hardening when cooled, without change in inherent qualities.
~*n.* A thermoplastic resin, such as polystyrene.

Ther·mop·y·lae (thər-móppi-li, ther-, -lee). A locality in eastern Greece, south of Lamia. A pass between the sea and Mount Oeta to the south, it is the site of a heroic but unsuccessful defence by the Spartans against the Persians (480 B.C.).

ther·mo·set·ting (thérmō-setting) *adj.* Permanently hardening or solidifying on being heated. Said of certain synthetic resins.

Ther·mos flask (thér-moss) *n.* A trademark for a type of vacuum flask. Also called "Thermos".

ther·mo·si·phon (thérmō-sīf-n, -sīf'n) *n.* A cooling system in which the circulation of the coolant relies on differences in density between hot and cold parts of the fluid.

ther·mo·sphere (thérm-ō-sfeer, -ə-) *n.* The innermost shell of the upper atmosphere, between the mesosphere and the exosphere, within which temperatures increase steadily with altitude.

ther·mo·sta·ble (thérmō-stáy-b'l) *adj.* Unaffected by relatively high temperatures. Said especially of biochemical compounds. Compare **thermolabile.** **—ther·mo·sta·bil·i·ty** (-stə-bílləti) *n.*

ther·mo·stat (thérm-ə-stat, -ō-) *n.* A device that automatically responds to temperature changes to maintain a fixed temperature or activate control switches, as in refrigerators and air conditioners.

[THERMO- + -STAT.] **—ther·mo·stat·ic** (-státtik) *adj.*

ther·mo·tax·is (thérm-ō-táksiss, -ə-) *n.* **1.** The directional movement of an entire cell or organism in response to heat. **2.** The normal regulation or adjustment of body temperature. [New Latin THERMO- + -TAXIS.] **—ther·mo·tac·tic** (-táktik), **ther·mo·tax·ic** *adj.*

ther·mo·ther·a·py (thérmō-thérrəpi) *n.* Therapy by application of heat.

ther·mo·tro·pism (thérm-ō-trōp-iz'm, -ə-, ther-móttrəp-) *n. Biology.* Directional growth of plants in response to heat. [THERMO- + -TROPISM.] **—ther·mo·trop·ic** (-trōpik, -tróppik) *adj.*

–thermy *n. comb. form.* Indicates heat; for example, **diathermy.** [New Latin *-thermia,* from Greek *thermē,* heat, from *thermos,* hot.]

the·ro·phyte (théer-ə-fīt, -ō-) *n.* A plant that overwinters as a seed; an annual. [Greek *theros,* summer + -PHYTE.]

the·ro·pod (théer-ə-pod, -ō-) *n.* Any of various bipedal carnivorous dinosaurs of the suborder Theropoda, of the Jurassic and Cretaceous periods, characteristically having small, grasping forelimbs. [New Latin *Theropoda* : Greek *thēr,* beast + -POD.] **—the·rop·o·dan** (theer-róppəd'n, thi-) *adj.* & *n.*

the·sau·rus (thi-sáw-rəss, thee-, thə-) *n., pl.* **-sauri** (-rī) or **-ruses. 1.** A book of selected words or concepts, such as a specialised vocabulary for music, medicine, or the like. **2.** A book of systematically classified synonyms and antonyms. [Latin *thēsaurus,* TREASURE.]

these. Plural of **this.**

The·seus (thée-sewss, *also* -si-əss). *Greek Mythology.* A hero of Athens, who united Attica, slew the Minotaur, and married Phaedra.

the·sis (thée-siss; *for sense 5 also* thé-) *n., pl.* **-ses** (-seez). **1.** A dissertation advancing an original point of view as a result of research, especially as a requirement for an academic degree. **2.** Any proposition or theory that is maintained by argument. **3.** A hypothetical proposition, especially one put forth for the sake of argument; a premise. **4.** The first stage of **dialectic** *(see).* **5. a.** The unstressed part of a foot in verse. **b.** The accented section of a musical measure. Compare **arsis.** [Late Latin, from Greek, a placing, a laying down, position, affirmation, from *tithenai,* to put, place.]

thes·pi·an (théspi-ən) *adj.* Of or pertaining to drama; dramatic. ~*n.* An actor or actress.

Thess. Thessalonians (New Testament).

Thes·sa·lo·ni·an (théssə-lōni-ən) *n.* A native or inhabitant of ancient Thessalonica. **—Thes·sa·lo·ni·an** *adj.*

Thes·sa·lo·ni·ans (théssə-lōni-ənz) *n.* Used with a singular verb. *Abbr.* **Thess.** Either of two books of the New Testament consisting of Epistles from the Apostle Paul to the Christians of Thessalonica.

Thes·sa·lo·ni·ki (Greek théssa-lo-néekee) English **Sa·lon·i·ka** (sə-lónnikə). Port and second-largest city of Greece, situated in the northeast of the country. It was founded in *c.*315 B.C. and later became the capital of the ancient Roman province of Macedonia, where it was known as Thessalonica. It was there that Paul delivered his two epistles to the Thessalonians.

Thes·sa·ly (théssəli). *Greek* **Thes·sa·lía** (théssa-lée-ə). Region of central Greece, consisting of a flat, fertile plain between upland Epirus and the Aegean Sea.

the·ta (théetə ‖ *chiefly U.S.* tháytə). The eighth letter in the Greek alphabet, written Θ, θ. Transliterated in English as *th.* [Greek *thēta,* from a Phoenician cognate of Hebrew *tēth,* TETH.]

The·tis (théttiss, théetiss). *Greek Mythology.* One of the Nereids, the wife of Peleus and mother of Achilles.

the·ur·gy (thée-urji) *n., pl.* **-gies. 1.** Divine or supernatural intervention in human affairs. **2.** Magic performed supposedly with aid of beneficent spirits, as practised by Neo-Platonists. [Late Latin *theurgia,* from Greek *theourgia,* sacramental rite, "mystery" : THEO- + -URGY.] **—the·ur·gic** (thee-úrjik) *adj.* **—the·ur·gist** (thée-urjist) *n.*

thew (thew ‖ thōō) *n. Usually plural.* Muscular power or strength; vigour. [Middle English, habit, characteristic, good physical quality, Old English *thēaw,* usage, custom, characteristic.] **—thew·y** *adj.*

they (thay) *pron.* The third person plural pronoun in the nominative case. **1.** Used to represent the persons or things last mentioned or implied: *There are three parts and they fit perfectly.* **2. a.** Used to represent unspecified persons or people in general: *They say he's having an affair. He's as tough as they come.* **b.** Used to represent those in positions of power; the authorities: *They're pulling down the old town hall.* **3.** *Archaic.* Used of persons as a demonstrative pronoun in the sense of *those:* "*Blessed are they which are persecuted*" (Matthew 5:10). **4.** *Nonstandard.* Used in referring to an indefinite singular antecedent: *If anyone wants a drink, they can get it themselves.* **—See** Usage note at **me.** [Middle English *thei,* partly from Old Norse *their,* partly from Old English *thā.*]

they'd (thayd). Contraction of *they had* or *they would.*

they'll (thayl). Contraction of *they will* or *they shall.*

they're (thair). Contraction of *they are.*

they've (thayv). Contraction of *they have.*

thi–. Variant of **thio–.**

thi·a·mine (thí-ə-meen, -min) *n.* Also **thi·a·min** (-min). A B-complex vitamin, $C_{12}H_{17}ClN_4OS$, produced synthetically and occurring naturally in the bran coat of grains, in yeast, and in meat, that is necessary for carbohydrate metabolism, maintenance of normal neural activity, and the prevention of beriberi. Also called "vitamin B_1". [THI(O)- + (VIT)AMIN.]

thi·a·zine (thí-ə-zeen, -zīn) *n.* Any of a class of organic chemical compounds containing a ring composed of one sulphur atom, one nitrogen atom, and four carbon atoms. [THI(O)- + AZINE.]

thi·a·zole (thī́-ə-zōl) *n.* **1.** A colourless or pale-yellow liquid, C_3H_3NS, containing a five-member ring composed of a nitrogen atom, a sulphur atom, and three carbon atoms, used in making dyes and fungicides. **2.** Any of various derivatives of this compound. [THI(O)- + AZOLE.]
thick (thik) *adj.* **thicker, thickest.** **1. a.** Relatively great in depth or in extent from one surface to the opposite; not thin: *a thick board.* **b.** Relatively great in diameter or cross-section; wide in relation to length: *a piece of thick string.* **2.** Having a specified extent from one surface to the opposite; in thickness: *two inches thick.* **3.** Having constituent parts in a close, compact arrangement; dense; concentrated: *a thick forest.* **4.** Having a viscous consistency; not watery or fluid: *thick treacle.* **5. a.** Existing in great numbers; numerous. Often used in the phrase *thick on the ground.* **b.** Having a great amount or number; abounding: *The area was thick with security men.* **6.** Impenetrable by the eyes; deep: *a thick, gloomy blackness.* **7.** Not easy to hear or understand; indistinct; inarticulate: *the thick slurrings of a drunkard.* **8.** Very noticeable; pronounced: *a thick Birmingham accent.* **9.** Foggy, misty, or hazy: *thick weather.* **10.** *Informal.* Lacking mental agility; stupid: *Get that through your thick head!* **11.** *Informal.* Very friendly; intimate. **12.** *Informal.* Going beyond what is tolerable; excessive. Used chiefly in the phrase *a bit thick.*
~*adv.* So as to be thick; thickly: *Slice it thick.* **—lay it on thick.** *Informal.* **1.** To overstate or give an exaggerated account of something. **2.** To flatter excessively. **—thick and fast.** In rapid succession and great profusion.
~*n.* **1.** The thickest part of something. **2.** The most active, intense, or dense part: *in the thick of the fighting.* **—through thick and thin.** In both good and bad times; faithfully; unwaveringly. [Middle English *thikke,* Old English *thicce.*] **—thick·ish** *adj.* **—thick·ly** *adv.*
thick ear *n. British Informal.* A heavy blow to the ear, given in a fight or as a punishment.
thick·en (thíckən) *v.* **-ened, -ening, -ens.** —*tr.* To make thick or thicker. —*intr.* **1.** To become thickened. **2.** To become more intense, intricate, or complex: *the plot thickens.* **—thick·en·er** *n.*
thick·en·ing (thík-əning, -ning) *n.* **1.** Any material used to thicken a liquid. **2.** A thickened part of something.
thick·et (thíckit) *n.* **1.** A dense growth of shrubs or underbrush; a copse. **2.** Something suggestive of a thicket in impenetrability or thickness: *a thicket of unreality.* [Middle English *thikket* (unattested), Old English *thiccet,* from *thicce,* THICK.]
thick·head (thík-hed) *n.* A stupid person; a blockhead; a numbskull. **—thick·head·ed** (-héddid) *adj.*
thick-knee (thík-nee) *n.* A **stone curlew** *(see).* [From the bird's enlarged tibio-tarsal joint.]
thick·ness (thínk-nəss, -niss) *n.* **1.** The state or condition of being thick. **2.** The dimension between two of an object's surfaces, usually taken to be the dimension of least measure. **3.** A layer, sheet, stratum, or ply. **4.** The thick part or main body of something.
thick·set (thík-sét) *adj.* **1.** Heavily or stockily built; stout and compact. **2.** Positioned or placed closely together: *thickset rose bushes.*
thick-skinned (thík-skínd) *adj.* **1.** Having a thick skin. **2. a.** Insensitive. **b.** Not easily offended.
thick-wit·ted (thík-wíttid) *adj.* Stupid; dull.
thief (theef) *n., pl.* **thieves** (theevz). One who commits theft; especially, a person who steals using surreptitious rather than violent means. [Middle English *thefe,* Old English *thīof, thēof,* from Germanic *theubhaz* (unattested).]
thieve (theev) *v.* **thieved, thieving, thieves.** —*tr.* To take by theft; steal. —*intr.* To act as or be a thief; commit theft. —See Synonyms at **rob.** [Old English *thēofian,* from *thēof,* THIEF.]
thiev·er·y (theévəri) *n., pl.* **-ies.** The act or an instance of thieving.
thiev·ish (theévish) *adj.* **1.** Given to thieving or stealing. **2.** Of, similar to, or characteristic of a thief; stealthy; furtive. **—thiev·ish·ly** *adv.* **—thiev·ish·ness** *n.*
thigh (thī) *n.* **1.** The portion of the human leg between the hip and the knee. **2.** A corresponding structure in other animals. [Middle English *thih,* Old English *thēoh.*]
thigh·bone (thī́-bōn) *n.* The **femur** *(see).*
thig·mo·tax·is (thíg-mō-ták-siss, -mə-) *n.* Movement of an entire cell or organism in response to a direct tactile stimulus. Also called "stereotaxis". [New Latin : Greek *thigma,* touch, from *thinganein,* to touch + -TAXIS.] **—thig·mo·tac·tic** (-tik) *adj.* **—thig·mo·tac·ti·cal·ly** *adv.*
thig·mot·ro·pism (thíg-mō-trŏp-iz'm, -mə-, thig-móttrəp-) *n.* Directional growth of plants in response to contact with a surface or object. Also called "haptotropism". [Greek *thigma,* touch (see **thigmotaxis**) + -TROPISM.] **—thig·mo·tro·pic** (-trŏpik, -tróppik) *adj.*
thill (thil) *n.* Either of the two long shafts between which an animal is fastened when pulling a vehicle. [Middle English *thille*†.]
thim·ble (thímb'l) *n.* **1. a.** A small metal or plastic cup worn to protect the finger that pushes the needle in sewing. **b.** A thimbleful. **2.** Any of various tubular sockets or sleeves in machinery. **3.** *Nautical.* **a.** A metal ring fitted in an eye of a sail to prevent chafing. **b.** A metal ring around which a rope splice is passed. [Middle English *thymbyl,* Old English *thȳmel,* from *thūma,* THUMB.]
thim·ble·ful (thímb'l-fŏŏl) *n.* A very small quantity, as of a liquid.
thim·ble·rig (thímb'l-rig) *n.* **1.** A gambling game, usually a swindle, in which the operator shuffles three inverted thimble-shaped caps, under one of which he has placed a marker, such as a pea, and spectators bet on the location of the marker. **2.** A person who operates such a game.
~*tr.v.* **thimblerigged, -rigging, -rigs.** To swindle with or as if with the thimblerig. **—thim·ble·rig·ger** *n.*
Thim·phu (thím-foo). Also **Thim·bu** (thím-boo). Capital of Bhutan, lying high in the Chinchu valley in the west of the country.
thin (thin) *adj.* **thinner, thinnest.** **1. a.** Relatively small in depth or in extent from one surface to the opposite; not thick. **b.** Not great in diameter or cross-section; narrow in relation to length; fine: *a thin strand.* **2.** Lean or slender; not fat. **3.** Having constituent parts widely separated; sparse; not dense or closely packed: *a thin rain; The crowd grew thinner.* **4.** Lacking force, substance, or body: *a thin brew.* **5.** Unconvincing, feeble, or flimsy: *That excuse is wearing a bit thin.* **6.** Difficult, uncomfortable, or disappointing: *having rather a thin time.* **7.** Lacking resonance or fullness; tinny. Said of sound or tone. **8.** Lacking radiance or intensity. Said of light or colour. **9.** *Photography.* Not having enough contrast to make satisfactory prints. Said of a negative.
~*adv.* So as to be thin; thinly.
~*v.* **thinned, thinning, thins.** —*intr.* **1.** To become thin or thinner. **2.** To become less dense. Often used with *out: The crowd began to thin out.* —*tr.* **1.** To make thin or thinner. **2. a.** To make less dense or crowded: *Plague thinned the enemy's ranks.* **b.** To remove so as to make less dense: *thin out seedlings.* [Middle English *thinne,* Old English *thynne.*] **—thin·ly** *adv.* **—thin·ness** *n.*
thin air *n.* A state of being invisible: *vanished into thin air.*
thine (thīn) *pron.* Absolute form of *thy. Archaic & Poetic.* **1.** Belonging to thee; the one or ones belonging to thee: *Thine is the kingdom.* **2.** Used instead of *thy* before an initial vowel or *h: thine enemy.* [Middle English *thin,* Old English *thīn.*]
thin-film *adj.* Designating or pertaining to an electronic device based on thin layers of metal or semiconductor deposited on a substrate.
thing (thing) *n.* **1.** Anything that can be perceived, known, or thought to have a separate existence; an entity. **2.** The real substance of that which is indicated as distinguished from its appearances or from the name, word, or symbol denoting it. **3.** An entity actually existing in space or time, in constrast to one merely postulated; an object or fact. **4.** An inanimate object as distinct from a living being: *seems more interested in things than in people.* **5.** A living being. Used to emphasise an attitude of pity, affection, contempt, or reproach: *the poor thing.* **6. a.** *Law.* That which can be possessed or owned as distinguished from a person. **b.** *Plural.* Possessions; belongings. **7.** An article of clothing; garment. **8.** *Plural.* The equipment needed for an activity or purpose: *Where are my sewing things?* **9.** An object or entity that cannot or need not be named specifically: *What's this thing for?* **10. a.** An act, deed, or achievement: *expects great things of us; I hope I've done the right thing.* **b.** A product of work: *likes making things with his hands.* **11.** A thought, notion, or statement: *What a funny thing to say!* **12.** A piece of information. **13.** An example or representative of a class: *the latest thing in home computers.* **14. a.** A matter to be dealt with; a concern: *a lot of things on her mind.* **b.** A point, factor, or reason: *and for another thing, it's far too expensive.* **15.** *Plural.* **a.** The general state of affairs; conditions: *How are things?* **b.** A particular or prevailing situation: *helped me to see things differently.* **16.** A characteristic; a particular feature: *one of the things I like about her.* **17.** A turn of events; a circumstance: *the nicest thing that's happened all day.* **18. a.** An illogical feeling or preoccupation; an obsession: *has a thing about cats.* **b.** Something to which undue importance is given: *no need to make such a thing of it.* **19.** *Slang.* An activity uniquely suitable and satisfying to one: *doing his thing.* **—be on to a good thing.** *Informal.* To be in a favourable position to exploit an opportunity. **—know a thing or two.** To have considerable knowledge or skill, especially as a result of long experience. **—see** or **hear things.** To have hallucinations. **—the thing.** **1.** What is conventionally regarded as proper or correct: *His behaviour wasn't quite the thing.* **2.** What is most important or most necessary: *The great thing is to keep on trying.* **3.** What is most fashionable; the rage: *streaked hair was the thing last year.* **4.** The point at issue: *The thing is, do you think he'll believe it?* [Middle English *thing,* Old English *thing,* creature, thing, deed, assembly, from Germanic *thingam* (unattested).]
thing·a·ma·bob, thing·um·a·bob (thíng-ə-mi-bob, -mə-) *n. Informal.* Something for which the exact name has been forgotten or is not known. Also called "thingamajig", "thingumajig", "thingummy". [Whimsical formation from THING.]
thing-in-it·self (thíng-in-it-sélf) *n., pl.* **things-in-themselves** (thíngz-in-thəm-sélvz). An ultimate metaphysical reality conceived by Kant as beyond the perception of human senses and thought; a noumenon.
think (thingk) *v.* **thought** (thawt), **thinking, thinks.** —*tr.* **1.** To have as a thought; formulate in the mind: *think great thoughts.* **2. a.** To reason about or reflect on; ponder: *Think how complex language is.* Often used with *through* or *over: Think the matter through.* **b.** To consider carefully: *Think what you need to bring.* Often used with *out.* **3.** To judge or regard; look upon: *I think it only fair.* **4.** To believe; suppose: *I think it is true.* **5. a.** To have in mind; plan or intend: *I think I'll go to bed. We thought to arrive early but couldn't.* **b.** To expect; anticipate: *I don't think you'll have any trouble.* **6.** To remember; call to mind: *I can't think now what his name was.* **7. a.** To visualise; imagine: *Think what a difference it would make.* **b.** To fathom; understand: *can't think why he did it.* **8.** To bring into a specified condition by mental activity: *She thought herself into a terror of going.* **9.** To be sufficiently thoughtful or attentive: *didn't*

think to say goodbye. **10.** To have one's thoughts centred on; think largely or exclusively in terms of. *—intr.* **1. a.** To exercise the power of reason; conceive of ideas, draw inferences, and use judgment. **b.** To turn over ideas; ponder; reflect. **2.** To weigh the idea; consider the matter: *Think before you answer.* Often used with *about* or *of: They are thinking of moving.* **3.** To recall a thought or image to mind: *can't think of his name; think back to last summer.* **4.** To believe; suppose: *Do you think so?* **5.** To dispose the mind in a specified way: *Think rich.* **—think aloud.** To say what one is thinking. **—think better of.** To decide against after reconsidering. **—think nothing of.** To regard as routine or usual. **—think of. 1.** To regard in the specified way; have as one's opinion of: *always thought of him as reasonable; What do you think of the latest offer?* **2.** To value or approve to the specified extent: *don't think much of that idea.* **3.** To have care or consideration for; be mindful of: *Think of your future.* **4.** To hit on the idea: *never thought of phoning the police.* **—think twice.** To weigh something carefully. **—think up.** To devise or invent.
~n. An act of thinking. [Think, thought, thought; Middle English *thenken, thoughte, thought,* Old English *thencan, thōhte, gethōht.*]
think·a·ble (thíngkəb'l) *adj.* Fit to be considered; conceivable; possible. **—think·a·bly** *adv.*
think·er (thíngkər) *n.* **1.** A person who devotes his time to thinking or is especially capable at thinking. **2.** A person who thinks or reasons in a specified way: *a careful thinker.*
think·ing (thíngking) *n.* **1.** Mental activity; thought. **2.** A way of reasoning or regarding a subject; judgment: *not to my thinking a good idea; the government's thinking on inflation.*
~adj. Characterised by thoughtfulness; rational: *a thinking animal.*
think tank, think-tank (thíngk-tangk) *n.* An institution or group of people established by a government, business, or other organisation to undertake detailed study of particular issues or problems.
thin·ner (thínnər) *n.* A liquid, such as turpentine, mixed with paint to reduce viscosity for ease in application.
thin-skinned (thín-skínd) *adj.* **1.** Having a thin rind or skin. **2.** Oversensitive, especially to reproach or insult.
thio-, thi- *comb. form. Chemistry.* Indicates a compound containing a divalent sulphur atom, especially one in which sulphur has replaced oxygen; for example, **thiophene, thiol.** [From Greek *theion,* sulphur.]
thi·o·car·bam·ide (thí-ō-kárbə-mīd) *n.* Thiourea (see).
thi·o·cy·an·ic acid (thí-ō-sī-ánnik) *n.* An unstable weak acid, HSCN, existing as a colourless gas or white solid.
thi·o·e·ther (thí-ō-éethər) *n.* Any of various organic compounds containing sulphur and having the general formula RSR', where R and R' are organic groups. [THIO- + ETHER.]
Thi·o·kol (thí-ō-kol, -ə- ‖ -kōl) *n.* A trademark for any of various polysulphide polymers in the form of liquids, water dispersions, and rubbers used in seals and sealants.
thi·ol (thí-ol ‖ -ōl) *n.* Any of various organic compounds containing sulphur and having the general formula RSH, where R is an organic group. Also called "mercaptan". [THIO(O)- + -OL.]
thion- *comb. form.* Indicates sulphur; for example, **thionine.** [From Greek *theion,* sulphur.]
thi·o·nine (thí-ə-nīn, -ō-) *n.* Also **thi·o·nin** (-nin). A crystalline derivative used as a violet dye in microscopy. [THION- + -INE.]
thi·o·nyl (thí-ənil) *adj.* Of, pertaining to, or containing the divalent group SO. [THION- + -YL.]
thi·o·pen·tone sodium (thí-ō-pén-tōn) *n.* Also **thi·o·pen·tal sodium** (-pent'l). A hygroscopic powder, $C_{11}H_{17}N_2O_2SNa$, injected intravenously as a general anaesthetic. Also called "sodium pentothal", and "Pentothal Sodium", a trademark. [From THIO- + PENTA-.]
thi·o·phen (thí-ō-fen, -ə-) *n.* Also **thi·o·phene** (-feen). A colourless liquid, C_4H_4S, used as a solvent. [THIO- + PHEN(O)- + -ENE.]
thi·o·sin·a·mine (thí-ō-sínnə-meen, -ə-, -sin-ámmin) *n.* A white crystalline substance occurring in mustard oil, CH_2:$CHCH_2NH$ $CSNH_2$, used in organic synthesis. Also called "1-allyl-2-thiourea". [THIO- + *sin-,* from Latin *sinapis,* mustard + AMINE.]
thi·o·sul·phate (thí-ō-súlfayt, -ə-) *n.* A salt of thiosulphuric acid.
thi·o·sul·phu·ric acid (thí-ō-sul-féwr-ik, -ə-) *n.* An acid, $H_2S_2O_3$, formed by the replacement of an oxygen atom by a sulphur atom in sulphuric acid, known only in solution or by its salts and esters.
thi·o·u·ra·cil (thí-ō-yóor-ə-sil) *n.* A white crystalline substance, $C_4H_4N_2OS$, used in the treatment of hyperthyroidism. [THIO- + URACIL.]
thi·o·u·re·a (thí-ō-yóor-i-ə, -yōō-réer, -rée-ə) *n.* A white, lustrous crystalline compound, $(NH_2)_2CS$, used in photography, photocopying paper, and various organic syntheses. Also called "thiocarbamide". [THIO- + UREA.]
Thí·ra (théerə). Also **San·to·ri·ni** (sántə-réeni). Southernmost of the Cyclades islands in the Aegean Sea, Greece. It is the remains of an ancient volcano. Excavations in the 1960s revealed remains of Théra, a rich Minoan settlement.
third (thurd) *n.* **1.** The ordinal number three in a series. Also written 3rd. **2.** One of three equal parts. **3.** *Music.* **a.** In a diatonic scale, a note three degrees above or below any given note; especially, the third note of a scale. **b.** The interval between two such notes. **c.** The harmonic combination of these notes. **4.** *British.* An honours degree of the third and usually lowest class. **5.** The gear immediately above second in a motor vehicle transmission.
~adv. Also **third·ly** (thúrdli) (for sense 2). **1.** In the third place, rank, or order. **2.** Used to precede the third topic in a list. [Middle English *thride, thirde,* Old English *third(d)a, thridda.*] **—third** *adj.*

third class *n.* **1.** The group or class that is next below the second in quality, value, or the like. **2.** The class of accommodation on a train or other means of transport ranking next below second class and usually of the lowest level of luxury and price. **3.** A class of mail in Canada and the United States comprising unsealed printed matter other than newspapers and magazines. **—third-class** (thúrd-kláass ‖ -kláss) *adj. & adv.*
third degree *n.* Rough treatment or torture of a prisoner, to obtain information or a confession.
third-de·gree burn (thúrd-di-grée) *n.* A severe burn in which the epidermis and dermis are destroyed and the tissues below are also damaged. No longer in technical usage.
third dimension *n.* The dimension of depth or thickness distinguishing an object or representation from an object or representation that exists just in one plane.
Third Estate *n. Sometimes small* t, *small* e. The third-highest social order in a country; specifically, the commons in contrast to the nobility and clergy. See **estate** (sense 7). Compare **fourth estate, Third World.**
third eyelid *n.* The nictitating membrane (see).
third man *n.* In cricket: **1.** A deep fielding position behind and to the off side of the batsman's wicket. **2.** A player in this position.
Third Order *n.* A confraternity of lay people associated with any of various religious orders of the Roman Catholic Church.
third party *n.* **1.** *Law.* A person or party other than the two principals in a transaction, agreement, or case. **2.** A political party organised as opposition to the existing parties in a two-party system.
third-par·ty (thúrd-párti) *adj.* Providing insurance cover against liability arising from accident to other persons or their property.
third person *n. Grammar.* The form of a pronoun or verb used in referring to a person or thing other than the speaker or the one spoken to.
third rail *n.* An extra rail through which the current runs to power the train on some electric railways. **—third-rail** *adj.*
third-rate (thúrd-ráyt, -rayt) *adj.* Of very poor quality; distinctly inferior.
third reading *n.* In passing a law in a legislative body: **1.** In Britain, the final stage of discussion of a bill, following the report stage, during its passage through either House of Parliament. **2.** In the United States, the final reading of a bill before voting.
Third Reich. See **Reich.**
Third Republic *n.* **1.** The French republic and government from the fall of the Commune (1871) until the German occupation (1940). **2.** The period of this republic's existence.
third sex *n.* Homosexuals collectively. Preceded by *the.*
Third World *n.* **1.** The economically underdeveloped or developing countries of Africa, Asia, and Latin America. **2.** These countries when considered as politically non-aligned with the Communist or non-Communist blocs. Preceded by *the.*
thirst (thurst) *n.* **1. a.** The sensation of dryness in the mouth related to a need or desire to drink. **b.** A need or desire to drink. **c.** The physical condition of dehydration produced by a lack of water: *died of thirst.* **2.** An insistent desire; a craving.
~intr.v. **thirsted, thirsting, thirsts. 1.** To feel a need to drink. **2.** To have a strong craving; yearn. Used with *for.* —See Synonyms at **yearn.** [Middle English *thurst, thirst,* Old English *thurst.*]
thirst·y (thúrsti) *adj.* **-ier, -iest. 1.** Desiring or needing to drink. **2.** Arid; parched. **3.** Craving; feeling a strong desire: *thirsty for news.* **4.** Causing thirst: *thirsty work.* **5.** *Informal.* Using or needing a lot of petrol: *a thirsty engine.* **—thirst·i·ly** *adv.* **—thirst·i·ness** *n.*
thir·teen (thúr-téen) *n.* **1. a.** The cardinal number that is one more than twelve. **b.** A symbol representing this, such as 13 or XIII. **2.** A set made up of thirteen persons or things. **3.** The thirteenth in a series. **4.** A size, as in clothing, designated as thirteen. [Middle English *thrittene,* Old English *thrēotīne* : THREE + -TEEN.] **—thir·teen** *adj. & pron.*
thir·teenth (thúr-téenth) *n.* **1.** The ordinal number 13 in a series. Also written 13th. **2.** One of 13 equal parts. **—thir·teenth** *adj. & adv.*
thir·ti·eth (thúrti-əth, -ith) *n.* **1.** The ordinal number 30 in a series. Also written 30th. **2.** One of 30 equal parts. **—thir·ti·eth** *adj. & adv.*
thir·ty (thúrti) *n., pl.* **-ties. 1. a.** The cardinal number that is 10 more than 20. **b.** A symbol representing this, such as 30 or XXX. **2.** A set made up of 30 persons or things. **3.** The thirtieth in a series. **4.** A size, as in clothing, designated as 30. **5.** *Plural.* **a.** The range of numbers from 30 to 39, considered as a range of age, price, temperature, or the like. **b.** The years numbered 30 to 39 in a century. Also used adjectively: *a thirties film.* [Middle English *thritty,* Old English *thrītig* : THREE + -TY.] **—thir·ty** *adj. & pron.*
Thir·ty-nine Articles (thúrti-nín) *pl.n.* A set of points representing the traditional doctrinal position of the Church of England, to which all clergymen formally subscribe.
thir·ty-two-mo (thúrti-tóo-mō) *n., pl.* **-mos. 1.** The page size ($3^1/_2$ by $5^1/_2$ inches) that results when a printers' sheet is folded into 32 equal sections. **2.** A book composed of pages of this size. Also written 32mo.
Thirty Years' War *n.* A series of wars fought mainly in central and western Europe (1618–48), originally for religious reasons but increasingly involving political issues.
this (thiss; *weak form in certain fixed phrases* thəss) *adj., pl.* **these** (theez). **1.** Being the one just mentioned or present in space, time, or thought. **2.** Being the one nearer or more obvious than another, or compared with another. **3.** Being about to be stated or de-

scribed: *began with these words.* **4.** *Informal.* A certain. Used for emphasis or vividness in describing one not previously mentioned: *This old tramp came up and asked me for some money.*
~pron., pl. **these** (theez). **1.** The person or thing present or nearby in space, time, or thought. **2.** The person, thing, or idea just mentioned or understood. **3.** What is about to be stated. **4.** The one that is nearer than another or the one compared with the other: *this one and that.* **5.** This period, point of time, or incident: *died soon after this; with this, he stormed out.*
~adv. Informal. To this extent; so: *a book about this thick.* [This, these; Middle English *this, thes,* Old English *thes* or *thēs, thēos, this* (masculine, feminine, neuter singular).] **—this·ness** *n.*

Usage: Some people argue that *this* should be used only when the reference is forwards (*I would like to say this*), and *that* should be used when the reference is backwards (*That was the reason I was late*); but while there is a genuine restriction on the use of *that,* which has backward reference only (you cannot say *I would like to ask that,* referring to something which is about to be asked), there is no basis in usage or a restriction on *this,* which is frequently used for reference backwards as well as forwards.

this·tle (thíss'l) *n.* **1.** Any of numerous weedy plants, chiefly of the genera *Cirsium, Carduus,* or *Onopordum,* having prickly leaves and usually purplish flowers surrounded by prickly bracts. **2.** Any of various similar or related plants. [Middle English *thistel,* Old English *thistel,* from Germanic *thistilaz* (unattested).]

this·tle·down (thíss'l-down) *n.* The silky down attached to the seeds of a thistle.

thith·er (thíthər || *Scottish and U.S.* thíthər) *adv. Archaic & Literary.* To or towards that place; in that direction; there: *hither and thither.* [Middle English *thither, thider,* Old English *thider, thæder.*]

thith·er·wards (thíthər-wərdz || thíthər-, -wawrdz) *adv.* Also **thith·er·ward** (-wərd). *Archaic & Literary.* In that direction; thither.

thix·o·tro·py (thíks-ə-trōpi, -ō-, thik-sóttrəpi) *n.* The property exhibited by certain gels, such as emulsion paints, of liquefying when stirred or shaken and returning to the semisolid state upon standing. [Greek *thixis,* "touching", from *thinganein,* to touch + -TROPY.] **—thix·o·trop·ic** (-tróppik, -trṓpik) *adj.*

tho, tho' (thō) *conj. Chiefly U.S.* Though.

thole[1] (thōl) *tr.v.* **tholed, tholing, tholes.** *Scottish & Archaic.* To endure; bear. [Middle English *tholen,* Old English *tholian,* to endure.]

thole[2] *n.* Also **thole·pin** (thṓl-pin). **1.** Either of a pair of wooden pegs set in the gunwale of a boat to serve as an oarlock. **2.** A peg or pin used to hold something in place. [Middle English *tholle,* Old English *thol(l).*]

thol·os (thól-oss, thṓl-) *n., pl.* **tholoi** (-oy). A dome-shaped tomb of the type associated with the Mycenaean culture of ancient Greece. [Greek *tholos*†.]

Tho·mism (tṓm-iz'm) *n.* The theological and philosophical system of St. Thomas Aquinas, which became the basis of scholasticism. **—Tho·mist** (-ist) *n. & adj.* **—Tho·mis·tic** (tō-místik) *adj.*

Thomp·son (tómps'n), **(Francis Morgan) "Daley"** (1958–). British athlete. He won a gold medal in the decathlon at the 1980 and 1984 Olympic Games, setting up a fourth world record in 1984.

Thompson submachine gun (tomps'n) *n.* A type of .45-calibre submachine gun. Also informally called "Tommy gun". [After its co-inventor, John *Thompson* (1860–1940), U.S. army officer.]

Thom·son effect (tóm-s'n) *n.* A thermoelectric effect in which a temperature gradient within a solid material is caused by an electrical potential gradient. [After W. *Thomson,* Lord KELVIN.]

thong (thong || *U.S. also* thawng) *n.* **1.** A narrow strip of leather or other material used for binding or lashing. **2.** *U.S. & Australian.* A **flip-flop** *(see).* [Middle English *thong,* Old English *thwong, thwang.*]

Thor (thor). *Norse Mythology.* The god of thunder. [Old Norse *thōrr,* thunder.]

tho·rac·ic (thaw-rássik, tho-, thə- || thō-) *adj.* Of, relating to, or situated in or near the thorax. [Medieval Latin *thoracicus,* from Greek. See **thorax, -ic.**]

thoracic duct *n.* The main duct of the lymphatic system, ascending along the spinal cord and discharging into veins in the neck.

tho·ra·cot·o·my (tháw-rə-kóttəmi || thō-) *n., pl.* **-mies.** Surgical incision of the chest wall. [Latin *thōrāx* (stem *thōrāc-*), THORAX + -TOMY.]

tho·rax (tháw-raks || thṓ-) *n., pl.* **thoraces** (-rə-seez, -ráy-) or **-raxes.** **1.** *Anatomy.* The part of the human body between the neck and the diaphragm, partially encased by the ribs; the chest. **2.** A corresponding part in other animals. **3.** The second or middle region of the body of an arthropod, in insects bearing the legs and wings. [Latin *thōrāx,* from Greek *thōrax*† (stem *thōrak-*), breastplate, coat of mail, chest covering.]

tho·rite (tháw-rīt || thṓ-) *n.* A vitreous brownish-yellow or black thorium ore, essentially $ThSiO_4$. [THOR(IUM) + -ITE.]

tho·ri·um (tháw-ri-əm || thṓ-) *n. Symbol* **Th** A silvery-white metallic element with 13 radioactive isotopes only one of which, thorium 232, occurs naturally. It is used in magnesium alloys and isotope 232 is a potential source of nuclear energy. Atomic number 90, atomic weight 232.038, approximate melting point 1,700°C, approximate boiling point 4,000°C, approximate relative density 11.66, valency 4. [New Latin, after THOR.]

thorium dioxide *n.* A heavy white powder, ThO_2, used mainly in ceramics, gas mantles, and nuclear fuels. Also called "thoria".

thorium series *n. Physics.* A radioactive series by which thorium-232 decays through intermediate nuclides to lead-208.

thorn (thorn) *n.* **1.** *Botany.* A modified branch in the form of a sharp, woody structure. **2.** Any of various shrubs, trees, or woody plants bearing such structures, such as the hawthorn. **3.** Loosely, any of various sharp, spiny protuberances; a prickle or spine. **4.** A source of continual annoyance or distress: *a thorn in one's flesh.* **5.** A runic letter þ originally representing the sounds (th) and (th) and used in writing early Germanic languages, including Old English. It now survives only in Icelandic, representing the sound (th). [Middle English *thorn,* Old English *thorn,* thorn, thornbush.]

thorn apple *n.* Any of various plants of the genus *Datura,* especially, *D. stramonium,* having white flowers and spiny fruits.

thorn·back (thórn-bak) *n.* Either of two rays, *Raja clavata,* of European waters, or *Platyrhinoidis triseriata,* of Pacific waters, having spines along the back.

thorn·bill (thórn-bil) *n.* **1.** Any of various South American hummingbirds of the genus *Chalcostigma* and related genera, having a thornlike bill. **2.** Any of various Australian songbirds of the genus *Acanthiza* and related genera, having short sharp bills.

thorn·y (thórni) *adj.* **-ier, -iest.** **1.** Full of or covered with thorns or thorny plants. **2.** Thornlike; spiny. **3.** Painfully controversial or difficult to resolve; vexatious: *a thorny problem.* **—thorn·i·ness** *n.*

tho·ron (tháw-ron || thṓ-) *n.* A radioactive isotope of radon having a half-life of 54.5 seconds and produced by the disintegration of thorium. [THOR(IUM) + -ON.]

thor·ough (thúrrə || *U.S.* thúrrō) *adj.* **1.** Fully done; completed in every respect or detail: *a thorough search.* **2.** Completely as described; absolute; utter: *a thorough rogue.* **3.** Painstakingly accurate or careful: *a thorough worker.* [Middle English *thorow,* from *thorugh* (adverb), through, Old English *thuruh,* from *thurh,* THROUGH.] **—thor·ough·ly** *adv.* **—thor·ough·ness** *n.*

thor·ough·bred (thúrrə-bred || *U.S.* thúrrō-) *adj.* **1.** Bred of pure stock; purebred; unmixed. **2.** *Capital* **T.** Pertaining or belonging to the Thoroughbred breed of horses. **3.** Thoroughly trained, accomplished, or educated; well-bred. **4.** Marked by characteristics associated with a thoroughbred animal; especially, elegant, high-spirited, or distinguished: *a thoroughbred sports car.*
~n. **1.** A purebred or pedigree animal. **2.** *Capital* **T.** A horse of a breed originating from a cross of Arab stallions with English mares and used widely in horseracing. **3.** A well-bred person.

thor·ough·fare (thúrrə-fair || *U.S.* thúrrō-) *n.* **1.** A public way or path from one place to another. **2.** Right of access or passage; public right of way: *no thoroughfare.* **3.** *Chiefly U.S.* A passage between two bodies of water, such as a canal or strait. [Middle English *thurghfare* : *thurgh,* THROUGH + FARE (passage).]

thor·ough·go·ing (thúrrə-gṓ-ing, -gō- || *U.S.* thúrrō-) *adj.* **1.** Very thorough; complete. **2.** Unmitigated; unqualified; out-and-out.

thor·ough·paced (thúrrə-payst || *U.S.* thúrrō-) *adj.* **1. a.** Trained in all paces or gaits. Said of a horse. **b.** Thoroughly trained. **2.** Thoroughgoing.

thor·ough·pin (thúrrə-pin || *U.S.* thúrrō-) *n.* An abnormal swelling on either side of the hock joint of horses and related animals. [From THOROUGH (passing through); it appears as if a pin were piercing the joint.]

thorp (thorp) *n. Archaic.* A hamlet or village. [Middle English *thorp,* Old English *throp, thorp.*]

Thors·havn (tórs-ha-wən). Capital and chief town of the Faeroes, situated on the island of Streymoy.

those. Plural of **that.**

Thoth (thōth, tōt). *Egyptian Mythology.* The god of the Moon and of wisdom and learning, whose sacred bird was the ibis. He is represented with the head and neck of an ibis, or as a baboon.

thou[1] (thow || *regional weak form* thə) *pron. Archaic, Poetic, & Regional.* The second person singular pronoun in the nominative case. **1.** Used to represent the person or personal being who is spoken to: *"Thou wilt never get thee a husband"* (Shakespeare). **2.** Used in apposition before a noun to indicate address: *"Thou drone, thou snail, thou slug, thou sot!"* (Shakespeare). [Thou, thee, thy or thine; Middle English *thu, the(e), thi* (before a consonant) and *thin* (before a vowel), Old English *thu* (or *thū*), *the* (or *thē*), *thīn.*]

thou[2] (thow) *n., pl.* **thous** or **thou.** **1.** *Slang.* A thousand. **2.** One thousand of an inch (0.0254 millimetre).

though (thō || *Scottish* thō) *conj.* **1.** Despite the fact that; while; although: *Though I failed, I'm glad I tried.* **2.** Conceding or supposing that; even if: *Though I may fail, I will still try.* **3.** However; and yet: *He's the director, though you'd never think so to look at him.*
~adv. Informal. However; nevertheless. **—as though.** As if. [Middle English *thoh, though,* from Old Norse *thō.*]

Usage: The use of *though* as an adverb at the end of a sentence is very common in informal speech (*He did, though*); but formal speech and writing prefer the use of such words as *however* or *nevertheless.* See also **although.**

thought (thawt). Past tense and past participle of **think.**
~n. **1. a.** The act or process of thinking; cogitation. **b.** The faculty or power of reasoning. **2. a.** An object of thinking; what one is thinking about: *lofty thoughts.* **b.** A product of thinking; an idea, opinion, or judgment. **3.** The intellectual activity or output of a particular time, place, or group. **4.** Serious consideration: *give the matter some thought.* **5.** Heed; regard: *with no thought for his life.* **6.** Intention; purpose. **7.** Expectation; hope; anticipation. **8.** A trifle; a bit: *a thought more considerate.* —See Synonyms at **idea.** [Middle English *thought,* a thought, Old English *(ge)thōht.*]

thought·ful (tháwtf'l) *adj.* **1.** Given to thought; contemplative; reflective. **2.** Well thought-out: *a thoughtful essay.* **3.** Careful; heedful. **4.** Showing regard for others; considerate. **—thought·ful·ly** *adv.* **—thought·ful·ness** *n.*

Synonyms: *thoughtful, considerate, indulgent, solicitous.*

thought·less (tháwt-ləss, -liss) *adj.* **1.** Showing lack of thought, as: **a.** Careless; unthinking. **b.** Reckless; rash. **c.** Inconsiderate; inattentive. **2.** Unable to think. —See Synonyms at **careless.** **—thought·less·ly** *adv.* **—thought·less·ness** *n.*

thought-out (tháwt-ówt) *adj.* Produced or developed through the application of thought: *a well thought-out plan.*

thought-pro·vok·ing (tháwt-prə-vōking) *adj.* Stimulating serious or deep thinking: *a thought-provoking lecture.*

thought reading *n.* **Mind reading** *(see).*

thought transference *n.* **Telepathy** *(see).*

thou·sand (thówz'nd) *n., pl.* **thousand** (for senses 1, 2) or **-sands** (for sense 3). **1.** The cardinal number written 1,000, 1000, 10^3, or in Roman numerals M. **2. a.** A thousand monetary units, as of pounds: *He won a thousand at the races.* **b.** A banknote or coin having a denomination of a thousand. **3.** *Often plural.* An indefinitely large number: *thousands of people.* [Middle English *thousande,* Old English *thūsend.*] **—thou·sand** *adj. & pron.*

Thousand and One Nights *pl.n.* The **Arabian Nights** *(see).*

thousand island dressing *n.* A salad dressing made of mayonnaise with chilli sauce or ketchup and various seasonings. [Probably after THOUSAND ISLANDS.]

Thousand Islands. A group of more than 1,800 islands and 3,000 shoals in the St. Lawrence river, stretching for about 80 kilometres (50 miles) east of Lake Ontario. The largest is Wolfe Island.

thou·sandth (thówz'nth) *n.* **1.** The ordinal number thousand in a series. Also written 1,000th. **2.** One of a thousand equal parts. **—thou·sandth** *adj. & adv.*

thp thrust horsepower.

Thrace (thrayss). Region of southeastern Europe, now mostly in northeastern Greece, but also occupying parts of southern Bulgaria and European Turkey. It was colonised by Greeks in the seventh century B.C., and later passed successively to the Roman, Byzantine, and Ottoman Empires.

Thra·cian (thráy-sh'n, -shi-ən) *n.* **1.** A native or inhabitant of Thrace. **2.** The extinct Indo-European language related to Phrygian spoken by the ancient inhabitants of Thrace. **—Thra·cian** *adj.*

Thrale (thrayl), **Hester Lynch,** also known as Mrs. Piozzi (1741–1821). British literary figure, known for her *British Synonymy* (1794) and her friendship with Samuel Johnson which she recounted in her *Anecdotes of the Late Samuel Johnson* (1786).

thrall (thrawl) *n.* Also **thral·dom** (-dəm), *U.S.* **thrall·dom** (for sense 3). **1.** One who is in bondage or servitude; a slave or serf. **2.** One who is a slave to some craving or other powerful influence. **3.** Servitude; bondage. **4.** A state of being enthralled or transfixed. [Middle English *thral(l),* Old English *thrǣl,* from Old Norse *thrǣll,* from Germanic *thrah-* (unattested), to run.]

thrash (thrash) *v.* **thrashed, thrashing, thrashes.** *—tr.* **1.** To beat or flog with or as with a whip. **2.** To swing or strike wildly in a manner suggestive of the action of a flail: *thrashing her arms about.* **3.** To defeat utterly; vanquish. **4.** To thresh. **5.** *Nautical.* To sail (a boat) against opposing winds or tides. *—intr.* **1.** To move the body or a bodily part wildly or violently; lash out. Usually used with *about.* **2.** To strike or flail; strike out. **3.** To thresh. **4.** *Nautical.* To make one's way against opposing tides or winds. **—thrash out. 1.** To discuss fully and bring to a conclusion. **2.** To produce (a plan or agreement, for example) by thorough discussion.

~n. **1.** The act of thrashing. **2.** *Informal.* An occasion of thrashing something out; a meeting. [Originally a variant of THRESH.] **—thrash·er** *n.*

thrash·er[1] (thráshər) *n.* Any of various New World thrushlike songbirds of the genus *Toxostoma,* having a long tail, a long, curved beak, and, in several species, a spotted breast. [Perhaps a variant of dialectal *thrusher,* from THRUSH (songbird).]

thrasher[2]. Variant of **thresher** (shark).

thrash·ing (thráshing) *n.* A severe beating; a whipping.

thra·son·i·cal (thrə-sónnik'l, thray-) *adj.* Boastful. [Latin *Thrasō* (stem *Thrasōn-*), a bragging character in Terence's comedy *Eunuchus,* from Greek *Thrasōn,* from *thrasus,* bold, brave.] **—thra·son·i·cal·ly** *adv.*

thrawn (thrawn) *adj. Northern British.* **1.** Crooked; twisted; out of true. **2.** Cross; bad-tempered; perverse. [Middle English *thrawin,* twisted, from past participle of *thrawen,* to twist, turn, form Old English *thrāwan;* akin to THWART.]

thread (thred) *n.* **1. a.** A fine cord of a fibrous material, such as cotton or flax, made of two or more filaments twisted together, and used in needlework and the weaving of cloth. **b.** A piece of this material. **2.** A strand, or long thin piece of natural or manufactured material. **3.** Anything suggestive of the fineness or thinness of thread. **4.** Anything suggestive of the continuousness and sequence of thread: *the thread of an argument.* **5.** A helical or spiral ridge on a screw, nut, or bolt. **6.** *Plural. U.S. Slang.* Clothes.

~v. **threaded, threading, threads.** *—tr.* **1.** To pass one end of a thread through the eye of (a needle or similar device). **2.** To string (beads or similar objects) onto a thread. **3. a.** To pass or feed (thread or tape, for example) through or into something. **b.** To pass or feed tape, film, or similar material through or into (a machine or camera, for example). **4. a.** to pass cautiously through. **b.** To make (one's way) cautiously, as through a crowded or narrow place. **5.** To occur throughout; pervade. **6.** To machine a thread on (a screw, nut, or bolt). *—intr.* **1.** To wind cautiously through obstacles or along a narrow path. **2.** To proceed by a winding course. **3.** To form a thread when dropped from a spoon, as boiling sugar syrup. [Middle English *thre(e)d,* Old English *thrǣd.*] **—thread·er** *n.* **—thread·like** *adj.*

thread·bare (thréd-bair) *adj.* **1.** Having the nap worn down so that the filling or warp threads show through; frayed or shabby. Said of cloth. **2.** Wearing old, shabby clothing. **3.** Hackneyed; stale. —See Synonyms at **trite.** **—thread·bare·ness** *n.*

thread·fin (thréd-fin) *n.* Any of various chiefly tropical marine fishes of the subfamily Polynemidae, having threadlike rays extending from the lower part of the pectoral fin.

thread mark *n.* A marking made in paper currency by a threading of coloured silk fibres to make counterfeiting difficult.

thread·worm (thréd-wurm) *n.* Any of various threadlike nematode worms, especially the **pinworm** *(see).*

thread·y (thréddi) *adj.* **-ier, -iest. 1.** Consisting of or resembling thread; fibrous. **2.** Tending to form threads, as a syrupy liquid does; viscid. **3.** *Medicine.* Weak and shallow. Said especially of a pulse. **4.** Lacking fullness of tone; thin; weak. **—thread·i·ness** *n.*

threat (thret) *n.* **1.** An expression of an intention to inflict pain, injury, evil, or punishment on a person or thing. **2.** An indication of the impending arrival or occurrence of something harmful or undesirable: *the threat of rain.* **3.** A person, thing, or idea regarded as a possible danger; a menace.

~tr.v. **threated, threating, threats.** *Archaic.* To threaten. [Middle English *thret,* Old English *thrēat,* oppression, use of force, threat.]

threat·en (thrétt'n) *v.* **-ened, -ening, -ens.** *—tr.* **1.** To express a threat against: *threatened him with dismissal.* **2.** To serve as a threat to; endanger; menace. **3.** To give signs or warning of; portend. **4.** To express as a threat. *—intr.* **1.** To express or use threats. **2.** To indicate danger or other harm. [Middle English, Old English *thrēatnian.*] **—threat·en·er** *n.* **—threat·en·ing·ly** *adv.*

Synonyms: *threaten, menace, intimidate.*

three (three) *n.* **1. a.** The cardinal number that is one more than two. **b.** A symbol representing this, such as 3, III, or iii. **2.** A set made up of three persons or things. **3. a.** The third in a series. **b.** A playing card marked with three pips. **4.** Three parts: *cut in three:* **5.** A size, as in clothing, designated as three. **6.** Three hours after midnight or midday. [Middle English *three,* Old English *thrī(e), thrēo.*] **—three** *adj & pron.* **—three·fold** (-fōld) *adj. & adv.*

three-card trick (threé-kárd) *n.* A trick or game in which participants try to guess which of three cards lying face downwards is the queen.

three-col·our (threé-kúllər) *adj.* Designating a colour printing or photographic process in which three primary colours are transferred by three different plates or filters to a surface, reproducing all the colours of the subject matter.

three-cor·nered (threé-kórnərd) *adj.* **1.** Triangular; tricorne: *a three-cornered hat.* **2.** Involving three contestants or parties. Said especially of an election: *a three-cornered fight.*

three-D (threé-deé) *adj.* Three-dimensional. Also written *3-D.*

~n. A three-dimensional medium, display, or performance, especially a cinematic or graphic display. Also written *3-D.*

three-day event (threé-dáy) *n.* An equestrian competition lasting three days, in which riders do a dressage test, ride over a cross-country course, and do a showjumping round.

three-day measles *n. Informal.* German measles.

three-deck·er (threé-déckər) *n.* **1.** A ship having three decks; especially, one of a class of sail-powered warships with guns on three decks. **2.** Anything with three layers; especially, a sandwich having three slices of bread.

three-decker pulpit *n.* A form of pulpit found in English parish churches consisting of the pulpit proper surmounting a reading desk and the clerk's stall.

three-di·men·sion·al (threé-dī-ménsh'n'l, -di-) *adj.* **1.** Of, pertaining to, having, or existing in three dimensions. **2.** Having or appearing to have extension in depth; three-D.

Three Graces *pl.n.* The **Graces** *(see).*

three-lane road (threé-láyn) *n.* A road with three carriageways, one for vehicles going in each direction and one for overtaking vehicles going in either direction.

three-leafed (threé-leéft) *adj.* Also **three-leaved** (-leévd). *Botany.* Divided into three leaflets: *a three-leafed clover.*

three-leg·ged race (threé-légd, -léggid) *n.* A race in which pairs of people run side by side with their adjacent legs tied together.

three-line whip (threé-līn) *n.* In the British Parliament, the strongest form of notice issued by the leaders of a political party, requiring its M.P.s to vote on a forthcoming issue. [From the three underlinings on the written notice, indicating the greatest urgency.]

three-mast·er (threé-maástər || -mástər) *n.* A ship, usually a schooner, with three masts.

three-mile limit (threé-mīl) *n. International Law.* The outer limit of the area extending three miles out to sea from the coast of a country that constitutes that country's **territorial waters** *(see).*

three·pence (threppənss, thrippənss, thrúppənss; *for sense 2* threpénss) *n., pl.* **threepence** or **-pences. 1.** A pre-decimal British coin worth three pennies. **2.** The sum of three pence.

three·pen·ny bit (thrép-ni, thrip-, thrúp-, -əni) *n.* A pre-decimal British coin, a threepence.

three-phase (threé-fáyz) *adj. Electricity.* Designating or pertaining to an electrical supply with three different equal voltages that have the same frequency and differ in phase by 120°.

three-piece (threé-peéss) *adj.* Made in or consisting of three parts or pieces: *a three-piece suit.*

three-ply (thrée-plî, -plî) *adj.* **1.** Consisting of three layers. **2.** Having three strands. Said of knitting wool.

three-point landing (thrée-poynt) *n.* An aeroplane landing in which the tailskid or tail wheel and the two forward wheels all touch the ground simultaneously; a perfect landing.

three-point turn *n.* A way of turning a vehicle in a confined space so that by moving first forwards then backwards then forwards, the vehicle ends up facing in the opposite direction.

three-quar·ter[1] (thrée-kwór-tər, kwáw-, -kór-, -káw-) *adj.* Pertaining to, consisting of, or showing three-fourths of something or extending to three-quarters of the full or normal length.

three-quarter[2] *n.* **1.** In Rugby football, any of four players who play in the three-quarter line. **2.** The position of such a player.

three-quarter binding *n.* A type of bookbinding in which the leather or fabric covering the spine extends onto the covers for one third of their width.

three-quarter line *n.* In Rugby football: **1.** The positions of right wing, left wing, inside centre, and outside centre. **2.** The players occupying these positions.

three-ring circus (thrée-ring) *n. Chiefly U.S.* **1.** A circus having simultaneous performances in three separate rings. **2.** A situation characterised by bewildering and varied activity.

three Rs *pl.n.* Reading, writing, and arithmetic, considered as the fundamentals of elementary education. [From the facetious spelling *reading, 'riting, and 'rithmetic.*]

three·score (thrée-skór ‖ -skŏr) *adj.* Sixty; three times twenty. **—three·score** *n.*

three·some (thréess'm) *adj.* Consisting of or performed by three. ~*n.* **1.** A group of three persons. **2.** Any activity involving three persons; especially, a golf match in which one player competes against two others who alternate their play.

three-square (thrée-skwaír) *adj.* Having an equilateral triangular cross-section: *a three-square file.*

three-wheel·er (thrée-wéel-ər, -hwéel-) *n.* A vehicle such as a motor car or a tricycle, with three wheels.

threm·ma·tol·o·gy (thrémmə-tólləji) *n.* The scientific breeding of domestic plants and animals. [Greek *thremma* (stem *thremmat-*), creature, nursling + -LOGY.]

thren·o·dy (thrénnədi) *n., pl.* **-dies.** A song of mourning or lamentation. [Greek *thrēnōidia*, dirge, lament + *ōidē*, song, ODE.] **—thre·no·di·al** (thri-nŏdi-əl, thre-), **thre·nod·ic** (-nóddik) *adj.* **—thren·o·dist** (thrénnədist) *n.*

thre·o·nine (thrée-ə-nîn, -ŏ-, -nin) *n.* A colourless crystalline amino acid, $C_4H_9NO_3$, derived from the hydrolysis of protein, and an essential component of the human diet. [Irregularly from *threo-*, probably an anagram of ERYTHRO- + -INE.]

thresh (thresh) *v.* **threshed, threshing, threshes.** —*tr.* **1. a.** To beat the stems and husks of (grain or cereal plants) with a machine or flail to separate the grain or seeds from the straw. **b.** To separate (grain or seed) in this manner. **2.** *Rare.* To beat severely; thrash. —*intr.* **1.** To thresh grain. **2.** To thrash about; toss. [Middle English *thresshen,* Old English *therscan.*]

thresh·er (thréshər) *n.* Also **thrash·er** (thráshər) (for sense 3). **1.** One who threshes. **2.** A threshing machine. **3.** Any of various large sharks of the genus *Alopias,* especially *A. vulpinus,* having a tail with a long, whiplike upper lobe.

thresh·ing machine (thréshing) *n.* A farm machine used in threshing grain or seed plants. Also called "thresher".

thresh·old (thrésh-hŏld, -ŏld) *n.* **1.** The piece of wood or stone placed beneath a door; a doorsill. **2.** An entrance or doorway. **3.** The outset; the verge; the beginning: *on the threshold of his career.* **4.** A point or level above which a specified phenomenon occurs and below which it does not: *a tax threshold.* **5.** The intensity below which a mental or physical stimulus cannot be perceived and can produce no response: *a low threshold of pain.* **6.** The value or intensity of a physical quantity that produces a specific effect in some system or device, and below which no effect occurs. Used adjectivally: *a threshold voltage.* ~*adj.* Of, pertaining to, or designating an agreement according to which wage increases are tied to the cost of living. [Middle English *thresshold,* Old English *therscold, threscold.*]

threw. Past tense of **throw.**

thrice (thrîss) *adv.* **1.** Three times. **2.** In a threefold quantity or degree. **3.** *Archaic.* Extremely; greatly. [Middle English *thries,* adverbial genitive of *thrie,* Old English *thriga, thriwa.*]

thrift (thrift) *n.* **1.** Wise economy in the management of money and other resources; frugality. **2.** Any of several densely tufted, chiefly European plants of the genus *Armeria;* especially, *A. maritima,* having rounded clusters of pink flowers. In this sense, also called "sea pink". [Middle English, prosperity, a flourishing, savings, from Old Norse, prosperity, from *thrífask,* to THRIVE.]

thrift·y (thrifti) *adj.* **-ier, -iest. 1.** Wisely economical; frugal. **2.** Industrious and thriving; prosperous. **3.** *Archaic.* Growing vigorously. —See Synonyms at *sparing.* **—thrift·i·ly** *adv.* **—thrift·i·ness** *n.* **—thrift·less** *adj.*

thrill (thril) *v.* **thrilled, thrilling, thrills.** —*tr.* **1.** To cause to feel a sudden intense sensation; excite greatly. **2.** To give great pleasure to; delight. **3.** To cause to quiver or vibrate. —*intr.* **1.** To feel a sudden tingle of emotion. **2.** To quiver, tremble, or vibrate. ~*n.* **1.** A sensation of great excitement. **2.** A tingling or trembling passing through the body as a result of sudden emotion. **3.** An exciting quality or situation. **4.** *Pathology.* A slight vibration that accompanies a heart or vascular murmur, felt when the hand is placed on the chest wall. [Middle English *thrillen,* variant of *thirlen,* to pierce, Old English *thyrlian,* from *thyr(e)l,* hole.]

thrill·er (thrillər) *n.* **1.** One that thrills. **2.** A book, film, or play that is full of mystery and suspense.

thrill·ing (thrilling) *adj.* **1.** Extremely exciting. **2.** Vibrating or pulsating.

thrips (thrips) *n., pl.* **thrips.** Any of various small, often wingless insects of the order Thysanoptera, many of which are destructive to plants. [Latin, woodworm, from Greek *thrips†.*]

thrive (thrîv) *intr.v.* **thrived, throve** (thrŏv) or **thriven** (thrivv'n), **thriving, thrives. 1.** To grow vigorously; flourish. **2.** To improve steadily, as in wealth or position; prosper. [Thrive, throve, thriven; Middle English *thríven, throfe, thriven,* to increase, flourish, from Old Norse *thrífask,* "to grasp for oneself", reflexive of *thrífa†,* to seize.] **—thriv·er** *n.* **—thriv·ing·ly** *adv.*

thro', thro. Variant of **through.**

throat (thrŏt) *n.* **1.** *Anatomy.* **a.** The part of the digestive tract that lies between the rear of the mouth and the oesophagus and includes the pharynx. **b.** The front part of the neck. **2.** *Botany.* The outer, expanded part of a tubular corolla. **3.** Any narrow passage or part shaped like the human throat: *the throat of a tennis racket.* **—jump down (someone's) throat.** To speak sharply and critically to. **—stick in (one's) throat.** *Informal.* To be difficult to express or accept. [Middle English *throte,* Old English *throte, throtu,* from Germanic *thrut-* (unattested).]

throat·lash (thrŏt-lash) *n.* Also **throat·latch** (-lach). A strap passing under the neck of a horse or other animal for holding a bridle or halter in place.

throat microphone *n.* A small microphone that when held or fastened close to the throat is activated by vibrations of the larynx.

throat·y (thrŏti) *adj.* **-ier, -iest.** Uttered or sounding as if uttered deep in the throat; guttural, hoarse, or husky. **—throat·i·ly** *adv.* **—throat·i·ness** *n.*

throb (throb) *intr.v.* **throbbed, throbbing, throbs. 1.** To beat rapidly or violently; pound. **2.** To vibrate, pulsate, or sound with a steady, pronounced rhythm. —See Synonyms at **pulsate.** ~*n.* The act of throbbing; a beat, palpitation, or vibration. [Middle English *throbben* (attested only in the present participle); imitative.] **—throb·bing·ly** *adv.*

throes (thrŏz) *pl.n. Singular* **throe. 1.** Physical pain or anguish, as at the approach of death. **2.** A condition of agonising struggle or effort. **3.** *Singular.* A violent pang or spasm of pain. [Middle English *throwe,* Old English *thrawe†,* paroxysm.]

throm·bin (thrómbin) *n.* An enzyme in blood that helps clotting by reacting with fibrinogen to form fibrin. [THROMB(O)- + -IN.]

thrombo-, thromb- *comb. form.* Indicates a blood clot; for example, thromboplastin, thrombin. [From Greek *thrombos,* THROMBUS.]

throm·bo·cyte (thróm-bŏ-sît, -bə-) *n.* A blood **platelet** (*see*).

throm·bo·cy·to·pe·ni·a (thrómbō-sîtō-péeni-ə) *n.* A decrease in the number of platelets in the blood, resulting in reduced ability of the blood to clot. [THROMBOCYTE + Greek *penia,* poverty, want.]

throm·bo·em·bo·lism (thrómbō-émbəliz'm) *n.* The blocking of a blood vessel by a thrombus dislodged from the vein in which it originated.

throm·bo·phle·bi·tis (thrómbō-fle-bítiss, -flĭ-) *n.* Inflammation of a vein associated with the formation of a blood clot in it.

throm·bo·plas·tic (thróm-bŏ-plástik, -bə-, -pláastik) *adj.* **1.** Causing or promoting blood clotting. **2.** Of or pertaining to thromboplastin.

throm·bo·plas·tin (thróm-bŏ-plástin, -bə-) *n.* A protein complex essential for thrombin formation and blood clotting. Also called "thrombokinase". [THROMB(O)- + -PLAST + -IN.]

throm·bose (thróm-bŏz, throm-bŏz') *v.* **-bosed, -bosing, -boses.** —*tr.* To affect with thrombosis. —*intr.* To become affected with thrombosis. [Back-formation from THROMBOSIS.]

throm·bo·sis (throm-bŏ-siss) *n., pl.* **-ses** (-seez). The formation, presence, or development of a thrombus. See **coronary thrombosis.** [New Latin, from Greek *thrombōsis,* a clotting, from *thrombousthai,* to clot, from *thrombos,* THROMBUS.] **—throm·bot·ic** (-bóttik) *adj.*

throm·bus (thróm-bəss) *n., pl.* **-bi** (-bî). A blood clot that forms in and blocks a blood vessel or that is formed in a heart cavity. [New Latin, from Greek *thrombos†,* lump, clot.]

throne (thrŏn) *n.* **1.** The chair occupied by a sovereign, bishop, or other exalted personage on state or ceremonial occasions. **2.** The power, dignity, or rank of one who occupies a throne: *come to the throne.* **3.** *Plural. Theology.* One of the nine orders of angels. See **angel. 4.** *British Slang.* A lavatory. Used humorously. ~*v.* **throned, throning, thrones.** —*tr.* To enthrone. —*intr.* To occupy a throne; reign. [Middle English, learned respelling of earlier *trone,* from Old French *trone,* from Latin *thronus,* from Greek *thronos.*]

throng (throng) *n.* **1.** A large group of people gathered or crowded closely together. **2.** Any large group of things; a host. ~*v.* **thronged, thronging, throngs.** —*tr.* **1.** To crowd into; fill completely. **2.** To press in upon; surround in large numbers. —*intr.* To gather, press, or move in a throng. [Middle English *throng, thrang,* Old English *thrang,* probably from Germanic *thring-* (unattested), to press, crowd.]

thros·tle (thróss'l) *n.* **1.** *Poetic.* Any of various Old World thrushes; especially, the **song thrush** (*see*). **2.** A machine formerly used for spinning cotton, wool, or other fibre. [Middle English *throstle,* Old English *throstle.*]

throt·tle (thrótt'l) *n.* **1. a.** A valve in an internal-combustion engine that regulates the amount of vaporised fuel entering the cylinders. **b.** A similar valve in a steam engine regulating the amount of steam. Also called "throttle valve". **2.** A lever or pedal controlling this valve. **3.** *Regional.* The throat or windpipe.

~tr.v. **throttled, -tling, -tles. 1. a.** To regulate the flow of (fuel) in an engine. **b.** To regulate the speed of (an engine) with a throttle. **2.** To strangle; choke. **3.** To suppress. [Noun sense 1, perhaps diminutive of THROAT; verb senses 2 and 3, Middle English *throtelen,* to throttle, perhaps from *throte,* THROAT.] **—throt·tler** *n.*

through (thrōō) *prep.* Also *rare* **thro, thro',** *chiefly U.S.* **thru. 1.** In at one side and out at the opposite or another side of. **2.** Among or between; in the midst of: *a walk through the flowers.* **3.** By reason of. **4.** By the means or agency of. **5.** Here and there in; visiting various parts of: *a tour through France.* **6. a.** From the beginning to the end of: *stayed up through the night.* **b.** *Chiefly U.S.* Up to and including: *Monday through Friday.* **7.** At or to the end of; done or finished with, especially successfully: *We are through the initial testing period.* **8.** Without stopping for: *drove through a red light.* **9.** Because of: *He got the job through his father.*

~adv. Also *rare* **thro, thro',** *chiefly U.S.* **thru. 1.** From one end or side to another or opposite end or side. **2.** From beginning to end: *the whole night through.* **3.** Completely; thoroughly: *soaked through.* **4.** To a conclusion or accomplishment: *see the matter through.* **5.** Out into the open: *The sun broke through.* **—through and through. 1.** Throughout. **2.** In every respect; completely.

~adj. Also *chiefly U.S.* **thru. 1.** Passing or extending from one end, side, or surface to another: *a through lounge.* **2.** Allowing continuous passage; unobstructed: *a through road.* **3.** Conveying passengers directly to a destination without changes. Said of a train. **4.** *Informal.* Finished; done. **5.** *Informal.* At the end of one's effectiveness or resources: *He's through financially.* **6.** Connected to the person one wishes to speak to on a telephone line. **7.** *Informal.* No longer involved in an emotional relationship. [Middle English *thru(g)h, thurh,* Old English *thurh, thuruh.*]

Usage: The use of *through* as a preposition in the sense "up to and including" is American English *(Monday through Saturday).* The ambiguity of *to* or *till* in British English *(I shall stay from Monday to Saturday*– does this mean I shall leave on Saturday or Sunday?), and the awkwardness of the phrases *from Monday up to and including Saturday, Monday to Saturday inclusive,* has led to an increased use of the American construction in British in recent years, though not without attracting strong criticism from those who wish to keep British English as free as possible from American influence. A frequent compromise in British English is *through to (Monday through to Saturday).*

through·ly (thrōōli) *adv. Archaic.* Thoroughly.

through·out (throo-ówt) *prep.* In, to, through, or during every part of; all through.

~adv. **1.** In or through all parts; everywhere. **2.** During the entire time or extent.

through·put (thrōō-pōōt) *n.* **1.** *Computing.* The amount of material processed by a computer in a given period. **2.** Loosely, output.

through·way. Variant of **thruway.**

throve. Alternative past tense of **thrive.**

throw (thrō) *v.* **threw** (thrōō || threw), **thrown** (thrōn || thrṓ-ən), **throwing, throws.** *—tr.* **1.** To propel through the air with a swift motion of the arm; hurl. **2.** To discharge into the air by any means. **3.** To hurl with great force, suddenness, or carelessness: *She threw her clothes into a cupboard; He threw himself at his opponent.* **4.** To apply (oneself, for example) with energy: *threw herself into her new job.* **5.** To surrender (oneself) to something: *threw himself on the mercy of the court.* **6. a.** To put on or off hastily or carelessly: *throw on a cape.* **b.** To put quickly into use or place: *throw in extra troops.* **7.** To put abruptly or forcibly into a specified condition or place: *threw him into total confusion; threw the prisoner into jail.* **8.** To form on a potter's wheel: *throw a vase.* **9.** To twist (fibres) into thread. **10. a.** To roll (dice). **b.** To roll (a particular combination) with dice. **11.** To discard or play (a card). **12. a.** To cast (a shadow). **b.** To direct; send: *threw an anxious glance at him.* **13.** To bear (young). Used of cows or horses. Not in current usage. **14.** To deliver (a blow or punch). **15.** To move (a controlling lever or switch). **16.** To send (an opponent in wrestling) to the ground. **17.** To cause (a rider) to leave the saddle and fall to the ground. Used of a horse. **18. a.** To project (the voice). **b.** To cause (one's voice) to appear to be coming from elsewhere than one's mouth. **19.** To give way to (an emotional outburst): *throw a fit.* **20.** *Informal.* To disconcert; nonplus: *The news really threw her.* **21.** *Informal.* To arrange or give (a party, for example). *—intr.* To cast, fling, or hurl something. **—throw off. 1.** To cast out; reject. **2.** To give off; emit. **3.** To rid oneself of: *can't seem to throw off this cold.* **4.** To escape; evade: *managed to throw off his pursuers.* **—throw in the towel** or **sponge.** To give up; accept defeat. [Originally in boxing, a contestant acknowledged defeat by throwing his towel or sponge into the ring.] **—throw out. 1.** To give off; emit. **2.** To reject or discard. **3.** To dismiss or expel. **4.** To offer, as a suggestion or plan. —See Synonyms at **eject. —throw over. 1.** To overturn. **2.** To abandon (a lover, for example). **—throw up. 1.** To abandon; relinquish: *throw up a job.* **2.** To construct hurriedly. **3.** *Informal.* To vomit.

~n. **1.** An act of throwing; a cast; a fling. **2.** The distance, height, or direction of something thrown: *a low throw.* **3. a.** A roll or cast of dice. **b.** The combination of numbers so obtained. **4.** *Informal.* A chance; an attempt. **5.** The technique used to throw an opponent in wrestling. **6.** In dances such as jitterbug or rock'n'roll, a leaping movement in which one partner is apparently thrown into the air and supported by the other. **7.** *U.S.* **a.** A light coverlet. **b.** A scarf or shawl. **8.** *Machinery.* **a.** The length of the radius of a circle described by a crank, cam, or similar part. **b.** The maximum displacement of a part moved by a crank, cam, or the like. **9.** *Geology.* The vertical distance between a rock on one side of a fault and its continuation on the other side. **10.** *Physics.* A single movement of the indicator of a measuring instrument, as in a ballistic galvanometer. [Middle English *throwen, thrawen,* to turn, twist, hence to hurl, cast (presumably "to turn the body in the act of throwing"), Old English *thrāwan,* to turn, twist.] **—throw·er** *n.*

Synonyms: *throw, cast, hurl, fling, toss, sling, heave.*

throw away *tr.v.* **1.** To discard as useless. **2.** To fail to use (an opportunity, for example).

throw·a·way (thrṓ-ə-way) *adj.* **1.** Designed or intended to be discarded after use. **2.** Written or delivered in a low-key or offhand manner: *throwaway lines.*

~n. **1.** Anything designed to be discarded after use. **2.** *Chiefly U.S.* A handbill distributed on the street.

throw back *intr.v.* To revert to a type or stage in one's ancestral past. *—tr.v.* To cause or compel to be dependent: *Her husband's death threw her back on her own resources.*

throw·back (thrṓ-bak) *n.* **1.** A reversion to a former type or ancestral characteristic. **2.** Loosely, an **atavism** *(see).* **3.** Something that refers back to or results from a previous incident, period, or the like: *Her tidiness is a throwback to her days at boarding school.*

thrown. Past participle of **throw.**

throw in *tr.v.* **1.** To add (something extra) with no additional charge. **2.** To add or contribute (a remark) to a conversation.

throw-in (thrṓ-in) *n.* In soccer, a two-handed throw from behind the touchline, used to bring the ball back into play.

throw pillow *n. U.S.* A **scatter cushion** *(see).*

throw rug *n.* A **scatter rug** *(see).*

thru (thrōō). *Chiefly U.S.* Variant of **through.**

thrum¹ (thrum) *v.* **thrummed, thrumming, thrums.** *—tr.* **1.** To play (a stringed instrument) idly or monotonously. **2.** To repeat or recite in a monotonous tone of voice. *—intr.* To strum idly on a stringed instrument.

~n. A thrumming sound. [Imitative.] **—thrum·mer** *n.*

thrum² *n.* **1. a.** The fringe of warp threads left on a loom after the cloth has been cut off. **b.** Any of these threads. **2.** Any loose end, fringe, or tuft of thread. **3.** *Plural. Nautical.* Short bits of rope yarn inserted into canvas to roughen the surface so that it can be used to prevent chafing.

~tr.v. **thrummed, thrumming, thrums. 1.** To cover or trim with thrums; fringe. **2.** *Nautical.* To sew thrums into (canvas). [Middle English *thrum,* Old English *thrum.*]

thrush¹ (thrush) *n.* **1.** Any of various songbirds of the family Turdidae, characteristically having brownish upper plumage and a spotted breast. **2.** Any of various similar or related birds. [Middle English *thrusch(e),* Old English *thrysce.*]

thrush² *n.* **1.** An infection of the mouth or vagina with a fungus, *Candida albicans,* characterised by white eruptions. See **candidiasis. 2.** A suppurative infection of a horse's foot caused by standing in a wet, unhygienic stall. [17th century : origin obscure.]

thrust (thrust) *v.* **thrust, thrusting, thrusts.** *—tr.* **1. a.** To push or drive quickly and forcibly. **b.** To cause to pierce or stab. **2.** To force (oneself or another) into a specified condition or situation. *—intr.* **1.** To shove against something; push. **2.** To pierce or stab at something with a pointed weapon. **3.** To force one's way. **4.** To push or project upwards.

~n. **1.** A forceful shove or push; a lunge. **2. a.** A driving force or pressure. **b.** The forward-directed force developed in a jet or rocket engine as a reaction to the backward ejection of fuel gases at high velocities. **3.** A stab. **4.** The general direction or tendency: *the thrust of an argument.* **5.** *Architecture.* Outward or lateral stress in a structure, such as an arch. **6.** *Geology.* A force of compression in the earth's crust producing folding. [Middle English *thrusten,* from Old Norse *thrȳsta,* to thrust, compress.]

thrust bearing *n. Machinery.* A type of bearing designed to transmit a force along a shaft as well as at right angles to it.

thrust·er (thrústər) *n.* A small rocket motor used to control a spacecraft.

thrust fault *n. Geology.* A reverse fault with a dip so low that the upthrow has moved far forward over the downthrow.

thrust·ing (thrúst-ing) *n.* **1.** Forceful. **2.** Aggressively ambitious. See Synonyms at **ambitious. —thrus·ting·ly** *adv.*

thru·way, through·way (thrōō-way) *n. U.S.* An urban motorway.

Thu·cyd·i·des (thew-siddi-deez || thōō-). Greek historian of the fifth century B.C.; author of *History of the Peloponnesian War.*

thud (thud) *n.* **1.** A dull sound, as that of a heavy object striking a solid surface. **2.** A blow or fall causing such a sound.

~intr.v. **thudded, thudding, thuds.** To make such a sound. [Middle English *thudden,* Old English *thyddan* (imitative).] **—thud** *adv.*

thug (thug) *n.* **1.** A brutal lout; a violent and criminally disposed man. **2.** Any of a former band of professional assassins in India. [Hindi *ṭhag,* cheat, thief, from Sanskrit *sthaga,* robber, from *sthagati,* to cover, hide.] **—thug·ger·y** *n.* **—thug·gish** *adj.*

thug·gee (thúggee, thu-gée) *n.* Formerly, the practices or methods of the thugs in India. [Hindi *ṭhagī,* robbery, from *ṭhag,* THUG.]

thu·ja, thu·ya (thōō-yə) *n.* Any coniferous tree of the genus *Thuja,* having scalelike leaves and small, scaly cones. Also called "arbor vitae". [New Latin, from Greek *thu(i)a†,* name of an African tree.]

Thu·le (théw-lee, -li, thewl ‖ thōo-lee, -li, thōol). The most northerly region of the ancient habitable world, conceived as an island north of Britain by ancient geographers. See **Ultima Thule**.

thu·li·um (théw-li-əm ‖ thōo-) n. Symbol **Tm** A bright silvery rare-earth element having 18 known isotopes with mass numbers ranging from 153 to 176. The X-ray emitting isotope Tm 170 is used in small portable medical X-ray units. Atomic number 69, atomic weight 168.934, melting point 1,545°C, boiling point 1,727°C, relative density 9.332, valency 3. [From THULE.]

thumb (thum) n. **1.** The short first digit of the human hand, opposable to each of the other four digits. **2.** A corresponding digit in other animals, especially primates. **3.** The part of a glove or mitten that covers the thumb. **4.** Architecture. An ovolo (see). **—all thumbs.** Clumsy; awkward. **—hold thumbs.** South African. To cross (one's) fingers, by way of wishing someone well. **—twiddle (one's) thumbs.** To be underoccupied; be bored from having nothing to do. **—under the thumb of.** Under the influence, authority, or power of. ~v. **thumbed, thumbing, thumbs.** —tr. **1.** To handle or soil with the thumb. **2.** Informal. To solicit (a lift) from a passing vehicle by pointing one's thumb in the direction one is travelling. —intr. To hitchhike. **—thumb (one's) nose.** To express scorn or derision by or as if by placing the thumb on the nose and wiggling the fingers. **—thumb through.** To browse rapidly through (the pages of a book or magazine). [Middle English thom(b)e, Old English thūma.]

thumb·hole (thúm-hōl) n. The hole on a wind instrument that is opened or closed with the thumb.

thumb index n. A series of rounded indentations cut into the front edge of a reference book, each labelled, as with a letter, to indicate a section of the book. **—thumb-in·dexed** (thúm-índext) adj.

thumb·nail (thúm-nayl) n. The nail of the thumb. ~adj. **1.** Of the size of a thumbnail. **2.** Brief: a thumbnail sketch.

thumb piano n. Any of various small African musical instruments played with the thumbs.

thumb·print (thúm-print) n. An impression of the ball of the thumb, especially when used as a means of identification. See **fingerprint**.

thumb·screw (thúm-skrōo ‖ -skrew) n. **1.** A screw so designed that it can be turned with the thumb and fingers. **2.** An instrument of torture formerly used to compress the thumb.

thumbs down n. A mark of rejection, disapproval, or prohibition.

thumb·stall (thúm-stawl) n. A sheath or cap worn on the thumb in certain manual tasks or to protect it when injured.

thumbs up n. A mark of approval, acceptance, or encouragement.

thumb·tack (thúm-tak) n. U.S. A drawing pin (see). ~tr.v. **thumbtacked, -tacking, -tacks.** U.S. To affix with a thumbtack.

Thummim. See **Urim and Thummim**.

thump (thump) n. **1.** A blow with a blunt instrument or closed hand. **2.** The muffled sound produced by such a blow or a similarly muted noise; a thud. ~v. **thumped, thumping, thumps.** —tr. **1.** To beat with a blunt or dull instrument, or with the hand or foot, so as to produce a muffled sound or thud. **2.** Informal. To thrash soundly or thoroughly; drub. —intr. **1.** To hit or fall in such a way as to produce a thump. **2.** To walk with heavy steps; stomp. **3.** To throb audibly; pound. [16th century : imitative.] **—thump** adv. **—thump·er** n.

thump·ing (thúmping) adj. **1.** Informal. Large; enormous. **2.** Thoroughly enjoyable. **—thump·ing·ly** adv.

thun·ber·gi·a (thún-bérji-ə, -bérjə) n. Any climbing plant of the genus Thunbergia, native to Old World tropical regions. See **black-eyed Susan**. [After Carl Thunberg (1743–1828), Swedish botanist.]

thun·der (thúndər) n. **1.** The rumbling or crashing sound emitted by rapidly expanding gases after the electrical discharge of lightning. **2.** Any similar sound. **—steal (someone's) thunder. 1.** To anticipate or adopt someone's idea or practice and get the credit oneself. **2.** To divert attention, praise, or recognition from another to oneself. [Phrase attributed to John Dennis (1657–1734), English dramatist, who had introduced a machine to simulate thunder in a play. After learning that a similar device had later been used in another play, he said that the playwright was stealing his thunder.] ~v. **thundered, -dering, -ders.** —intr. **1.** To produce thunder. **2.** To produce sounds like thunder. **3.** To utter loud, vociferous remarks or threats. —tr. To express violently, commandingly, or angrily; roar. [Middle English thunder, thon(d)re, Old English thunor.]

thun·der·bird (thúndər-burd) n. In the mythology of some North American Indians, thunder, lightning, and rain personified as a huge bird.

thun·der·bolt (thúndər-bōlt) n. **1.** The discharge of lightning that accompanies thunder. **2.** A flash of lightning imagined as a bolt or dart hurled from the heavens. **3.** Someone or something resembling a thunderbolt in suddenness, violence, destructive effect, or the like.

thun·der·box (thúndər-boks) n. British Slang. A lavatory, especially a portable one. [Referring to breaking wind.]

thun·der·clap (thúndər-klap) n. **1.** A single sharp crash of thunder. **2.** Anything of similar violence, loudness, or suddenness.

thun·der·cloud (thúndər-klowd) n. **1.** A large, dark cloud charged with electricity and producing lightning and thunder; a cumulonimbus cloud. **2.** Anything of dread or menacing aspect.

thun·der·er (thúndər-ər) n. One that thunders. **—The Thunderer.** A former nickname for The Times newspaper.

thun·der·head (thúndər-hed) n. Chiefly U.S. The swollen upper portion of a thundercloud, often associated with a thunderstorm.

thun·der·ing (thún-dring, -dəring) adj. British Informal. Used as an intensive: a thundering bore. ~adv. Used as an intensive: a thundering good show. **—thun·der·ing·ly** adv.

thun·der·ous (thúnd-rəss, -ərəss) adj. **1.** Of or pertaining to thunder or to a similar sound. **2.** Loud and unrestrained: thunderous applause. **—thun·der·ous·ly** adv.

thun·der·show·er (thúndər-showr, -show-ər) n. A brief rainstorm accompanied by thunder and lightning.

thun·der·stick (thúndər-stik) n. A **bullroarer** (see).

thun·der·stone (thúndər-stōn) n. **1.** Any of various mineral concretions formerly supposed to be thunderbolts, such as a **belemnite** (see). **2.** Archaic. A flash of lightning conceived as a stone.

thun·der·storm (thúndər-stawrm) n. A storm in which intense heating induces air to rise rapidly and form vast cumulonimbus clouds, with heavy rain, lightning, thunder, and sometimes hail.

thun·der·struck (thúndər-struk) adj. Also **thun·der·strick·en** (-strickən). Struck with sudden astonishment or amazement.

thun·der·y (thúndəri) adj. **1.** Indicating or characterised by thunder: thundery weather. **2.** Resembling thunder.

Thur., Thurs. Thursday.

Thur·ber (thúrbər), **James (Grover)** (1894–1961). U.S. humorist and cartoonist. His drawings and writings are collected in My Life and Hard Times (1933) and The Thurber Carnival (1945).

thu·ri·ble (théwr-ib'l ‖ thōor-) n. An incense vessel, a censer (see). [Middle English thoryble, from Old French thurible, from Latin t(h)ūribulum, from t(h)ūs (stem t(h)ūr-), incense, from Greek thuos, (sacrificial) incense, (burnt) offering.]

thu·ri·fer (théwr-ifər ‖ thōor-) n. An altar server or minister who carries a thurible. [New Latin, from Latin thūrifer, "incense bearing" : thūs (stem thūr-), incense (see **thurible**) + -FER.]

Thu·rin·gi·a (thewr-rínji-ə, -rínjə ‖ thoor-). German **Thü·ring·en** (tür-ing-ən). State of Germany, lying south of the Harz Mountains. It was created in 1920 from a number of former duchies and principalities. It became an East German state between 1946 and 1952, and was re-established after the reunification of Germany in 1990. **—Thu·rin·gi·an** adj. & n.

Thurs·day (thúrz-di, -day) n. Abbr. **Thur., Thurs.** The day following Wednesday; the fourth day of the working week. [Middle English thur(e)sday, Old English thūr(e)s dæg (influenced by Old Norse thórsdagr, from earlier thunresdæg, "Thor's day") (translation of Late Latin Jovis diēs, "Jupiter's day") : thunres, genitive of thunor, THUNDER + dæg, DAY.]

thus (thuss) adv. Also nonstandard **thus·ly** (thússli) (for sense 1). **1.** In a manner previously stated or to be stated; in this manner. **2.** To a stated degree or extent; so: thus far. **3.** Therefore; consequently. [Middle English, Old English thus.]

thuya. Variant of **thuja**.

thwack (thwak) tr.v. **thwacked, thwacking, thwacks.** To strike or hit with something flat; whack. ~n. A hard blow with something flat; a whack. [Imitative.] **—thwack** adv. **—thwack·er** n.

thwart (thwort) tr.v. **thwarted, thwarting, thwarts. 1.** To prevent from taking place or being realised; frustrate; block. **2.** To challenge, oppose, or cross. **—See Synonyms at frustrate.** ~n. (also thort). A seat across a boat, on which the oarsman sits. ~adj. **1.** Extending, lying, or passing across something; transverse. **2.** Archaic. Perverse; stubborn. **3.** Adverse, unfavourable. Said of winds and currents. ~adv. Archaic. Athwart; across. ~prep. Archaic. Athwart; across. [Middle English thwert, athwart, across, perverse, from Old Norse thvert, neuter of thverr, transverse.] **—thwart·ed·ly** adv. **—thwart·er** n.

thy (thī). The possessive form of the pronoun thou. Archaic, Regional, & Poetic. Used attributively to indicate possession, agency, or reception of an action by the one addressed by the speaker: "He sees his brood about thy knee." (Tennyson). [Middle English thy, thin, Old English thīn, thine.]

thy·la·cine (thīlə-sīn, -seen) n. A wolflike marsupial, Thylacinus cynocephalus, of forest areas of Tasmania, having dark transverse bands across its back. Also called "Tasmanian wolf". [New Latin thylacinus, from Greek thulakos†, a sack.]

thyme (tīm) n. **1.** Any of several aromatic herbs or low shrubs of the genus Thymus; especially, T. vulgaris, of southern Europe, having small purplish flowers. **2.** The leaves of this plant, used as seasoning. [Middle English t(h)yme, from Old French thym, from Latin thymum, from Greek thumon.]

–thymia n. comb. form. Indicates state of mind or temperament; for example, **schizothymia**. [New Latin, from Greek thumos, soul, spirit, mind, temper.]

thy·mic (thímik) adj. Of or pertaining to the thymus.

thy·mi·dine (thími-deen) n. Biochemistry. A nucleoside consisting of thymine and the sugar ribose. [THYM(INE) + -ID(E) + -INE.]

thy·mine (thí-meen) n. Biochemistry. A pyrimidine base, $C_5H_6N_2O_2$, occurring in DNA. [THYM(IC) + -INE.]

thy·mol (thí-mol) n. A white, crystalline, aromatic compound, $(CH_3)_2CHC_6H_3(CH_3)OH$ derived from thyme oil and other oils and used as an antiseptic, in perfumery, and as a preservative. [THYM(E) + -OL.]

thy·mus (thí-məss) n., pl. **-muses** or **mi** (-mī). **1.** A ductless gland-like structure, situated just behind the top of the breastbone, that during early childhood plays some part in building resistance to disease by producing lymphocytes but in adults is usually vestigial. **2.** The corresponding structure in nonhuman vertebrates. [New Latin, from Greek *thumos†.*]

thy·ra·tron (thǐr-ə-tron) *n. Electronics.* A gas-filled tube having three electrodes, such that an electrical discharge and consequent current flow between the anode and cathode is initiated (but not controlled) by a potential applied to a grid. The device is used as a relay and particle counter. [Originally a trademark, from Greek *thura,* door, valve + -TRON.]

thy·ris·tor (thǐr-rístər) *n. Electronics.* A semiconductor rectifier, such as a silicon-controlled rectifier, in which passage of current is initiated by a voltage applied to a third electrode. It is the solid-state equivalent of a thyratron. [*thyratron* + transistor.]

thy·ro·cal·ci·to·nin (thǐr-ō-kǎl-si-tōnǐn) *n.* A hormone, **calcitonin** *(see).* [THYRO(ID) + CALCITONIN.]

thy·roid (thǐr-oyd) *adj.* Of or relating to the thyroid gland or the thyroid cartilage.
~*n.* **1.** The thyroid gland. **2.** The thyroid cartilage. **3.** A dried and powdered preparation of the thyroid gland of certain domestic animals, used in the treatment of hypothyroid conditions, such as cretinism. [Obsolete French *thyroide,* from Greek *thuroidēs, thureoeidēs,* shaped like a door or oblong shield, from *thureos,* door-shaped : *thura,* door + -OID.]

thyroid cartilage *n.* The largest cartilage of the larynx, having two broad processes that join in front to form the Adam's apple. Also called "thyroid".

thyroid colloid *n. Physiology.* **Colloid** *(see).*

thy·roid·ec·to·my (thǐr-oyd-ěktəmi) *n., pl.* **-mies.** The surgical removal of all or part of the thyroid gland.

thyroid gland *n.* A two-lobed endocrine gland found in all vertebrates, located in front of and on either side of the trachea in humans, and producing the hormone thyroxine. Also called "thyroid".

thy·roid·i·tis (thǐr-oyd-ítiss) *n.* Inflammation of the thyroid gland.

thy·roid-stim·u·lat·ing hormone (thǐr-oyd-stímmew-layting) *n.* Thyrotrophin.

thy·ro·tox·i·co·sis (thǐr-ō-tóksi-kō-siss, -ə-) *n.* The condition resulting from excessive production of thyroid hormone, characterised by weight loss, increased appetite, tremor, palpitations, anxiety, and intolerance of heat. [New Latin : THYRO(ID) + TOXICOSIS.]

thy·ro·tro·phin (thǐr-ə-trō-fin, -ō-, thǐr-róttrə-) *n.* Also **thy·rot·ro·pin** (-pin). A hormone secreted by the anterior pituitary that stimulates and regulates the development and secretion of the thyroid gland hormone. Also called "thyroid-stimulating hormone". [THYRO(ID) + -TROP(E) + -IN.]

thy·rox·ine (thǐr-rók-seen, -sin) *n.* Also **thy·rox·in** (-sin). An iodine-containing hormone, $C_{15}H_{11}I_4NO_4$, produced by the thyroid gland to regulate metabolism and made synthetically for treatment of underactivity of the thyroid gland. [THYR(OID) + OX(Y)- + -IN.]

thyrse (thurss) *n. Botany.* A branched flower cluster, as of the lilac, whose main axis does not terminate in a flower. Also called "thyrsus". [New Latin *thyrsus,* THYRSUS.] —**thyr·soid** (thúr-soyd) *adj.*

thyr·sus (thúr-səss) *n., pl.* **-si** (-sī). **1.** A staff tipped with a pine cone and twined with ivy, represented as carried by Dionysus, and his devotees. **2.** *Botany.* A thyrse. [New Latin, from Latin, from Greek *thursos†.*]

thy·self (thī-sélf || *regional also* thǐ-, thə-, tha-) *pron. Archaic, Regional, & Poetic.* Yourself. Used as the reflexive or emphatic form of *thee* or *thou.*

THz terahertz.

ti[1]. *Music.* Variant of **te.**

ti[2] (tee) *n, pl.* **tis.** Any of several trees or shrubs of the genus *Cordyline,* of tropical Asia and adjacent Pacific regions; especially, *C. australis,* of New Zealand, having a terminal tuft of long, palm-like narrow leaves. [Tahitian and Maori.]

Ti·a·hua·na·co (tée-ə-wə-na'akō) *n.* Ruins near the southeast end of Lake Titicaca, western Bolivia. The Tiahuanaco culture preceded that of the Incas, flourishing *c.* A.D. 1000 to 1300, and spread through Bolivia, northern Chile, and Peru.

Tian·jin or **Tien·tsin** (tyén-jín). Port in Hebei province, northeastern China, lying at the confluence of the Hai river and Grand Canal. It is an important industrial centre.

Tian Shan or **Tien Shan** (tyán shán). Mountain chain of central Asia, extending from the Pamirs in Tajikistan, through northwestern China to the China-Mongolia border. The name means "heavenly mountains".

ti·ar·a (ti-aárə) *n.* **1.** An ornamental semicircular headpiece, made from a precious metal and jewels, worn by women on formal occasions. **2.** The triple crown formerly worn by the pope. [Latin *tiāra,* from Greek *tiara(s)†.*]

Ti·ber (tíbər). *Italian* **Te·ve·re.** River of central Italy. It rises in the Tuscan Apennines, and flows some 406 kilometres (252 miles) through Rome to the Tyrrhenian Sea at Ostia.

Tiberias, Sea of. See **Sea of Galilee.**

Ti·bet (ti-bét). *Chinese* **Xi·zang** or **Si·tsang.** Autonomous region of China, occupying a high plateau in the southwestern extremity of the country to the north and west of the Himalayas. Apart from the fertile valley of the Tsangpo, in southern Tibet, most of the land is suitable only for grazing. Tibet has rich reserves of salt, gold, radioactive ores, and copper. Tibet rose to prominence as an independent kingdom in the 7th century; from the 13th to the 18th century it was under the sway of the Mongols, and in 1720 the Manchu dynasty of China took control of the region, and thereafter China exercised more or less effective suzerainty over it until 1964, when Tibet was formerly made an autonomous region of China. It is a centre of Lamaist Buddhism, but the Dalai Lama and thousands of followers fled the country in 1954. Since 1987, there have been outbreaks of pro-independence rioting. Capital, Lhasa.

Ti·bet·an (ti-bétt'n) *adj.* Of or pertaining to Tibet, its people, or their language or culture.
~*n.* **1.** A member of the Mongoloid people of Tibet. **2.** The Tibeto-Burman language of Tibet.

Ti·bet·o-Bur·man (ti-béttō-búrmən) *n.* Also **Ti·bet·o-Bur·mese** (-búr-méez || -méess). A language family including principally Tibetan, Burmese, Lolo, and Balti, sometimes classed as a subgroup of Sino-Tibetan. —**Ti·bet·o-Bur·man, Ti·bet·o-Bur·mese** *adj.*

tib·i·a (tíbbi-ə) *n., pl.* **-iae** (-ee) or **-ias.** **1.** The inner and larger of the two bones of the lower human leg from the knee to the ankle. Also called "shin", "shinbone". **2.** A homologous bone in animals. **3.** The fourth division of an insect's leg, between the femur and the tarsi. **4.** A kind of ancient flute originally made from an animal's leg bone. [Latin *tībia†,* shinbone, pipe.] —**tib·i·al** *adj.*

tic (tik) *n.* **1.** A habitual spasmodic muscular contraction, usually in the face or extremities, and often of neurotic origin. **2.** Tic douloureux. [French, originally a veterinary term (perhaps imitative).]

tic dou·lou·reux (dōolə-rúr, -rǒ || -rōō) *n.* **Trigeminal neuralgia** *(see).* [French, "painful tic".]

tick[1] (tik) *n.* **1.** The recurring sharp, clicking sound made by a machine, especially by a clock. **2.** *British Informal.* A moment. **3.** A mark used to indicate that an item has been approved, dealt with, or noted.
~*v.* **ticked, ticking, ticks.** —*intr.* **1.** To emit recurring clicking sounds, as a clock does. **2.** To function in a characteristic way, as if by means of a motivating mechanism: *What makes him tick?* —*tr.* **1.** To count or record by means of ticks: *The taximeter ticked off the fare; a clock ticking away the hours.* **2.** To mark (a sum, for example) with a tick. [Middle English *tek* (noun; perhaps imitative); verb, 16th century, of Germanic origin].

tick[2] *n.* **1.** Any of numerous bloodsucking parasitic arachnids of the families Ixodidae and Argasidae within the order Acarina, many of which transmit infectious diseases. **2.** Any of various usually wingless, louselike insects of the family Hippoboscidae, that are parasitic on sheep, goats, and other animals. [Middle English *tyke, teke,* Old English *ticca* (unattested).]

tick[3] *n.* **1.** The cloth case of a mattress or pillow. **2.** Ticking. [Middle English *tikke,* perhaps from Middle Dutch *tēke,* from West Germanic *tēka* (unattested), from Latin *thēca,* cover, case, from Greek *thēkē.*]

tick[4] *n. British Informal.* Credit; trust: *on tick.* [Short for TICKET.]

tick[5] *n.* A children's game, **tag** *(see).* [From TICK (to mark, touch).]

tick bird *n.* The oxpecker *(see).*

tick-borne (tík-bawrn || -bórn) *adj.* Transmitted by ticks. Said of diseases such as typhus.

tick·er (tíckər) *n.* **1.** A **tape machine** *(see).* **2.** *Slang.* A watch. **3.** *Slang.* The heart.

ticker tape *n.* The paper strip on which a tape machine prints.

tick·er-tape parade (tickər-tayp) *n.* A traditional hero's welcome, especially in New York City, in which ticker-tape or ribbons of paper are thrown from buildings as the celebrity parades by.

tick·et (tíckit) *n.* **1.** A paper slip or card indicating that its holder has paid for or is entitled to a service, right, or consideration, such as: **a.** One entitling its holder to use public transport: *a bus ticket.* **b.** One entitling its holder to admission to a place of entertainment, a lecture, or the like: *a theatre ticket.* **c.** One certifying its holder's discharge from the armed forces. **2.** A piece of card or paper enabling property, especially articles of clothing, to be identified and reclaimed by the owner: *a dry-cleaning ticket; a cloakroom ticket.* **3.** A certifying document; especially, a captain's or pilot's licence. **4.** A tag or label attached to goods for sale to indicate their price. **5.** *Chiefly U.S.* A list of candidates proposed or endorsed by a political party. **6.** A **parking ticket** *(see).* **7.** *Informal.* The proper thing: *A change of scene would be just the ticket for her.* **8.** *Plural. South African Informal.* Ruin; the end.
~*tr.v.* **ticketed, -eting, -ets.** **1.** To attach a tag to; label. **2.** To designate for a specified use or end; destine. [Obsolete French *etiquet,* ticket, label, from Old French *estiquet(te),* from *estiquier,* to stick, from Middle Dutch *steken.*]

ticket agency *n.* An office that sells tickets for theatrical and other performances and usually charges a commission. —**ticket agent** *n.*

ticket office *n.* An office, as in a railway station, where transport tickets can be bought.

ticket tout *n. British Informal.* Someone who buys up tickets for popular events, such as Cup Finals, and sells them at inflated prices, typically outside the ground or venue.

tick·et·y-boo (tíckəti-bōo) *adj. British Slang.* Fine; perfect; just right. Not in current usage. [Perhaps from TICKET (the proper thing) + -Y (adjective suffix) + BOO.]

tick·ey (tícki) *n.* The former South African threepenny piece. [Afrikaans, possibly from Malay, *tiga,* three.]

tick fever *n.* Any febrile infectious disease transmitted by ticks.

tick·ing (ticking) *n.* A strong, tightly woven fabric of cotton or linen used to cover a mattress or pillow. Also called "tick".

tick·ing-off (ticking-off, -awf) *n. Chiefly British Informal.* A rebuke; a scolding.

tick·le (tíck'l) *v.* **-led, -ling, -les.** —*tr.* **1.** To touch (the body) lightly with a tingling sensation causing laughter or twitching movements. **2. a.** To tease or excite pleasurably; titillate. **b.** To fill with mirth or

pleasure; delight. —*intr.* To feel or cause a tingling sensation on the skin. **—tickle pink.** *Informal.* To please; delight. Usually used in the passive: *She was tickled pink by the gift.*
~*n.* **1.** The act of tickling. **2.** A tickling sensation. [Middle English *tikelen,* probably from *tiken, ticken*†, to touch lightly.]

tick·ler (tícklər) *n.* **1.** One that tickles. **2.** *Chiefly British Informal.* A difficult problem. **3.** *U.S.* A memorandum book or file to aid the memory.

tick·lish (tíck'l-ish, tícklish) *adj.* **1.** Sensitive to tickling. **2.** Requiring skilful or tactful handling; delicate. **3.** Easily offended or upset; touchy. **—tick·lish·ly** *adv.* **—tick·lish·ness** *n.*

tick off *tr.v.* **1.** *Chiefly British Informal.* To scold or rebuke. **2.** *U.S. Informal.* To make angry; annoy.

tick over *intr.v.* **1.** To run at low speed with the clutch disengaged; idle. Used of an engine. **2.** To operate smoothly but uneventfully, at a normal or relatively low level of productivity. Used of companies, projects, and the like.

tick·o·ver (tík-ōvər) *n.* The speed of an engine while it is idling or ticking over. **—tick·o·ver** *adj.*

tick·seed (tík-seed) *n.* A plant, the **coreopsis** *(see).* [So called from its shape.]

tick·tack, tic-tac (tík-tak) *n.* **1.** *British.* A system of sign language by which bookmakers communicate odds to each other at race meetings. **2.** A steady ticking sound, as of a clock. [Imitative.]

tick·tack·toe, tick-tack-toe (tík-tak-tṓ) *n. U.S.* **Noughts and crosses** *(see).* [Probably TICKTACK (from the sounds made on slates on which the earlier form of the game was played) + TOE.]

tick·tock (tík-tok, -tók) *n.* The ticking sound made by a clock, especially a pendulum clock. [Imitative.] **—tick·tock** *intr.v.*

tick trefoil *n.* Any of various plants of the genus *Desmodium,* having compound leaves with three leaflets, clusters of small purplish or white flowers. [Its sticky seed pods adhere like ticks to animals.]

tick·y-tack·y (tícki-tácki) *n. Chiefly U.S. Informal.* Cheap, shoddy material. [Reduplication of TACKY (cheap, etc).]

t.i.d. *Medicine.* three times a day [Latin *ter in die.*]

tid·al (tī́d'l) *adj.* **1.** Pertaining to, affected by, or having tides: *a tidal river.* **2.** Dependent upon the state or times of the tide: *a tidal ship.* [TIDE + -AL.]

tidal basin *n.* A dock that is filled with water only at high tide.

tidal power *n.* Electricity generated by using the rise and fall of the tides to drive turbines.

tidal wave *n.* **1.** A **storm surge** *(see).* **2.** Loosely, a **tsunami** *(see).* **3.** Something resembling either of these in form or volume.

tidbit *n. U.S.* Variant of **titbit.**

tid·dler (tíddlər, tídd'l-ər) *n. British Informal.* **1.** A very small fish; especially, a stickleback. **2.** A young child, especially one small for its age. **3.** Any relatively small or unimportant object, organisation, or the like. [From TIDDLY (small).]

tid·dly[1] (tíddli, tídd'l-i) *adj. Chiefly British Slang.* Drunk. [19th century (meaning "a drink") : origin obscure.]

tiddly[2] *adj. British Informal.* Small; tiny. [From childish pronunciation of LITTLE.]

tid·dly·winks (tíddli-wingks, tídd'l-i-) *n.* Also **tid·dle·dy·winks** (tídd'l-di-). *Used with a singular verb.* A game in which players try to snap small counters into a cup by pressing them on the edge with a larger counter. [19th century : *tiddlywink*†.]

tide[1] (tīd) *n.* **1. a.** The twice-daily rise and fall in the surface level of the oceans, seas, and lower courses of rivers caused by the gravitational attraction of the Moon and, to a lesser extent, the Sun. **b.** A specific occurrence of such a variation. **c.** The waters in such a variation. See **flood tide, ebb tide, neap tide, spring tide. 2.** Any stress exerted on a body or part of a body by the gravitational attraction of another: *atmospheric tide; solar tide.* **3.** A tendency or movement regarded as alternating and inexorable: *The tide of public opinion has turned.* **4.** A time or season. Now archaic except in combination: *springtide; Christmastide.* **5.** *Archaic.* A favourable occasion; an opportunity. **6.** *Northern British.* A holiday or fair, usually occurring on a saint's day. **—swim with (or against) the tide.** To submit to (or oppose) majority views or trends.
~*v.* **tided, tiding, tides.** —*intr.* **1.** To rise and fall like the tide. **2.** To drift or ride with the tide. —*tr.* To carry along with or as if with the tide. **—tide over.** To support through a difficult period: *The five pounds tided him over until payday.* [Middle English *tid(e),* season, time, tide, Old English *tīd,* season, time.] **—tide·less** *adj.*

tide[2] *intr.v.* **tided, tiding, tides.** *Archaic.* To betide; befall. [Middle English *tiden,* Old English *tīdan,* "to fall as one's lot".]

tide·mark (tī́d-maark) *n.* **1.** A line or artificial indicator marking the high-water or low-water limit of the tides. **2.** *Chiefly British.* A mark showing the level a liquid has reached, such as that left when a bath has been emptied. **3.** *Chiefly British Informal.* A dirty mark on the skin showing the area which has been left unwashed.

tide rip *n.* A rip tide *(see).*

tide table *n.* A list of the times of high and low tides on each day.

tide·wait·er (tī́d-waytər) *n.* Formerly, a customs officer who boarded incoming ships at a harbour.

tide·wa·ter (tī́d-wawtər || *U.S. also* -wottər) *n.* **1.** Water that inundates land at high tide. **2.** Water affected by the tides; especially, tidal streams. **3.** *U.S.* Low coastal land drained by tidal streams.

tide·way (tī́d-way) *n.* **1.** A channel in which a tidal current runs. **2.** The current itself.

tid·ings (tī́dingz) *pl.n.* Information; news: *tidings of great joy.* [Plural of *tiding,* an event, Middle English *tiding,* Old English *tīdung,* perhaps from Old Norse *tidhendi,* events, from *tidhr,* occurring.]

ti·dy (tī́di) *adj.* **-dier, -diest. 1.** Orderly and neat in appearance or procedure. **2.** Orderly in habits; methodical. **3.** Substantial; considerable: *a tidy nest egg.* **4.** *U.S.* Adequate; satisfactory.
~*v.* **tidied, -dying, -dies.** —*tr.* To make tidy; put in order. —*intr.* To put things in order. Often used with *up.*
~*n., pl.* **tidies.** *n.* **1.** *British.* A small container for miscellaneous objects: *a desk tidy.* **2.** *U.S.* A fancy protective covering for the arms or headrest of a chair. [Middle English, timely, seasonable, fair, excellent, from *tid,* season, TIDE.] **—ti·di·ly** *adv.* **—ti·di·ness** *n.*

tie (tī) *v.* **tied, tying, ties.** —*tr.* **1.** To fasten or secure with a cord, rope, strap, or similar means. **2.** To fasten by drawing together the parts or sides with strings or laces and knotting them: *tie one's shoes.* **3. a.** To make (a knot or bow). **b.** To put a knot or bow in: *tie a ribbon.* **4.** To confine or restrict as if with cord. **5.** To bring together closely; unite. **6.** To end (a match or contest) with an equal score. **7.** To bind; commit. **8.** To restrict the freedom of action of. Often used with *down.* **9.** *Music.* To join (notes) by a tie. —*intr.* **1.** To be fastened with strings. **2.** To achieve equal scores in a contest.
~*n.* **1.** A cord, string, or other means by which something is tied. **2. a.** That which unites; a bond: *marital ties.* **b.** That which restricts one's freedom of action: *Pets can be a real tie.* **3.** A long, narrow band of fabric worn usually round the collar of a garment and tied in a knot or bow close to the throat, usually with the ends left hanging down the garment front. Also *U.S.* "necktie". **4.** A beam or rod that joins parts and gives support. **5.** *U.S.* A railway **sleeper** *(see).* **6. a.** A state of equality of scores, votes, or performance in a contest. **b.** A contest resulting in this; a draw. **7.** A match played between two teams; especially, one round in a knockout contest. **8.** *Music.* A curved line put either above or below two notes of the same pitch, indicating that the note is to be sustained for their combined duration. [Middle English *t(e)yen,* Old English *tīgan.*]

tie·back (tī́-bak) *n. U.S.* **1.** A decorative loop of fabric, cord, or metal for parting and draping curtains to the sides. **2.** *Plural.* A pair of curtains meant to be tied back at about midlength.

tie beam *n.* A horizontal beam that connects the rafters in a roof.

tie-break (tī́-brayk) *n.* Also **tie-break·er** (-ər). In tennis, a means of deciding the winner of a set when neither competitor has won after a given number of games by playing a deciding number of points.

tie clip *n.* An ornamental clip that slides sideways onto the ends of a tie and into the shirtfront, thus holding the tie in place.

tied house (tīd) *n.* In Britain: **1.** A pub that is owned by a brewery and sells only the beers made by the brewery. Compare **free house. 2.** A house or cottage that is owned by an employer and is assigned to the holder of a specific job. In this sense, also called "tied cottage".

tie-dye (tī́-dī) *n.* **1.** A method of dyeing fabric in which parts of the fabric are tied so that they will not take the dye, giving the fabric a streaked or mottled look. **2.** A fabric dyed by this method.
~*tr.v.* **tie-dyed, -dyeing, -dyes.** To dye (fabric) by such a method.

tie in *tr.v.* **1.** To bring into conformity; coordinate. **2.** To use as a tie-in. —*intr.v.* To be in conformity; correspond or fit in.

tie-in (tī́-in) *n.* **1.** A connection or relation. **2.** A book, record, souvenir, or other item designed to be sold after demand has been created by a film, television series, or the like. **3.** *U.S.* **a.** The sale of two (occasionally more) products or services so that a minor item is expected to be purchased with the major one. **b.** One of the products or services so offered, usually the minor one.

Tien Shan. See **Tian Shan.**

Tientsin. See **Tianjin.**

tie·pin (tī́-pin) *n.* A kind of brooch or ornamental pin designed to keep the long end of a tie attached to a shirt front. Also *U.S.* "stickpin".

tier[1] (teer) *n.* **1.** Any of a series of rows placed one above another, as in a theatre balcony. **2.** A level; a stratum: *tiers of local government.*
~*v.* **tiered, tiering, tiers.** —*tr.* To arrange in tiers. —*intr.* To rise in tiers. [Earlier *tire,* from French, sequence, rank, from *tirer,* to draw out, from Vulgar Latin *tīrāre*† (unattested).]

ti·er[2] (tī́-ər) *n.* One that ties.

tierce (teers; *for sense 3, also* terss) *n.* **1.** Variant of **terce. 2.** A former measure of liquid capacity, equal to a third of a pipe, or 42 wine gallons. **3.** In card games, a sequence of three cards of the same suit. **4.** The third position in fencing from which a parry or thrust can be made. **5.** *Music.* An interval of a third. [Middle English, one third, the third canonical hour, from Old French, from Latin *tertia* (noun), from Latin *tertius,* third.]

tiercel. Variant of **tercel.**

Ti·er·ra del Fue·go (ti-érrə del fwáy-gō, -áir-ə). Archipelago of islands off the extreme southeastern tip of South America, separated from the mainland by the Strait of Magellan. The eastern half belongs to Argentina, the western to Chile.

tier table (teer) *n.* A small table with two or more usually round tops.

tie up *tr.v.* **1. a.** To invest (money) in such a way that it is not available to be withdrawn and used: *Her money is all tied up in stocks and shares.* **b.** To subject (assets, for example) to such restrictions that they cannot be realised. **2.** To hinder, delay, or stop: *The strike tied up traffic for hours.* **3.** To connect; associate. Used with *with*: *The police tied up the murder with the robbery.* **4.** *Informal.* To bring to completion successfully: *tie up a contract.* **5.** *Informal.* **a.** To be busy or very occupied: *I'm a bit tied up tonight.* **b.** To monopolise or pre-empt the use of: *He ties up the phone for hours.* —*intr.v.* To moor. Used of a ship.

tie-up (tī'-up) *n.* **1.** *Informal.* **a.** A link or connection. **b.** An association or partnership; especially, a merger. **2.** *U.S.* A congested or immobilised condition, such as a traffic jam, work stoppage, or mechanical breakdown.

tiff (tif) *n.* **1.** A petty quarrel. **2.** A fit of irritation.
~*intr.v.* **tiffed, tiffing, tiffs.** To quarrel. [18th century : origin obscure.]

tif·fa·ny (tiffəni) *n., pl.* **-nies.** A thin, transparent gauze of silk or cotton muslin. [Originally, dress for wearing on Twelfth Night (Epiphany), from Old French *tifanie*, Epiphany, from Medieval Latin *theophania*, THEOPHANY.]

Tiffany glass *n.* **Favrile glass** *(see).* [After Louis *Tiffany* (1848 – 1933), U.S. artist.]

tif·fin (tiffin) *n.* In India, a light lunch or snack.
~*intr.v.* **tiffined, -fining, -fins.** To eat tiffin. [Short for obsolete *tiffing*, gerund of *tiff†*, to sip.]

Tiflis. See **Tbilisi.**

tig (tig) *n.* A children's game, **tag** *(see).* [Variant of TICK (ticking).]

ti·ger (tī'gər) *n.* **1. a.** A large carnivorous feline mammal, *Panthera tigris*, of Asia, having a tawny coat with transverse black stripes. **b.** Broadly, any of various other similar felines. **2.** A fierce, aggressive, or audacious person, society, or the like. Also used adjectivally: *the tiger economies of Asia.* [Middle English *tigre*, from Old French, from Latin *tigris*, from Greek.] —**ti·ger·ish** *adj.*

Tiger balm *n.* A trademark for a mentholated ointment used as a decongestant inhalant and as a general panacea.

tiger beetle *n.* Any of numerous active, long-legged, predatory beetles of the family Cicindelidae, chiefly of warm, sandy regions.

tiger cat *n.* Broadly, any of various small felines resembling the tiger in either appearance or behaviour.

tiger lily *n.* A widely cultivated plant, *Lilium lancifolium*, native to Asia, having large, black-spotted reddish-orange flowers.

tiger moth *n.* Any of numerous moths of the family Arctiidae, characteristically having wings marked with spots or lines.

ti·ger's-eye (tī'gərz-ī) *n.* Also **ti·ger-eye** (tī'gər-ī). A yellow-brown semiprecious gemstone of quartz coloured by iron oxide. [From a fancied resemblance.]

tiger shark *n.* A large, chiefly tropical shark, *Galeocerdo cuvieri*, having a greyish-brown body marked with darker stripes.

tiger's milk *n.* A cold drink made from milk powder, orange juice, vegetable oil, and dried yeast.

tiger snake *n.* A venomous snake of the genus *Notechis*, of Australia and Tasmania, marked with brown and yellow stripes.

tight (tīt) *adj.* **tighter, tightest. 1.** Of such close construction, texture, or organisation as to be impermeable, especially by water or air. Often used in combination: *airtight; watertight.* **2.** Fastened, held, or closed securely. **3. a.** Compressed, leaving few or no intervening spaces; compact. **b.** Very full; leaving no spare time or room: *a tight schedule.* **4.** Drawn out to the fullest extent; taut. **5.** Cramped; constrained; rigid. **6.** Close-fitting, often uncomfortably so: *a tight fit.* **7.** Constricted: *a tight feeling in the chest.* **8.** *Informal.* Close-fisted; stingy. **9. a.** Difficult to obtain: *Money is tight.* **b.** Affected by scarcity: *a tight market.* **10.** Difficult to deal with or get out of: *a tight spot.* **11. a.** Strict in discipline or control. **b.** Characterised by such strict control: *runs a tight ship.* **12.** Closely contested: *a tight match.* **13.** *Regional.* Neat and trim. **14.** *Informal.* Drunk.
~*adv.* **1.** Firmly; securely. **2.** Soundly: *sleep tight.* [Middle English, probably variant of *thyght*, thickset, dense, from Old Norse *thēttr*, watertight, dense.] —**tight·ly** *adv.* —**tight·ness** *n.*

tight·en (tīt'n) *v.* **-ened, -ening, -ens.** —*tr.* To make tight or tighter. —*intr.* To become tight or tighter. —**tighten up.** To apply restrictions or constraints. Used with **on:** *The banks intend to tighten up on interest rates.* —**tight·en·er** *n.*

tight·fist·ed (tīt'-fĭstĭd) *adj.* Stingy; mean. See Synonyms at **stingy.**

tight·knit (tīt'-nĭt) *adj.* **1.** Closely connected or integrated: *a tight-knit community.* **2.** Carefully and closely organised.

tight·lipped (tīt'-lĭpt) *adj.* **1.** Having the lips pressed together, as when tense or angry. **2.** Reticent.

tight·rope (tīt'-rōp) *n.* **1.** A tightly stretched rope, usually of wire, on which acrobats perform high above the ground. **2.** A difficult or dangerous situation requiring a careful approach: *on a tightrope.*

tightrope walker *n.* An acrobat who performs on a tightrope.

tights (tīts) *pl.n.* **1.** A close-fitting, stretchable garment, elasticated at the waist and covering each leg and foot, worn by women and girls instead of stockings. Also *U.S.* "pantihose". **2.** Such a garment made from thicker fabric, worn by dancers, gymnasts, and the like of both sexes.

tight·wad (tīt'-wŏd) *n. U.S. Slang.* One who hates to spend money; a miser. [TIGHT + WAD (money).]

tig·lic acid (tĭg'lĭk) *n.* A thick, syrupy poisonous liquid, CH₃CH:C(CH₃)CO₂H, derived from croton oil, having a spicy odour and used in making perfumes and flavouring agents. [From New Latin *(Croton) tiglium*, a seed of the (Croton) species, perhaps from Greek *tilos†*, liquid faeces (from the use of the seeds as a purgative).]

ti·gon (tī'-gən, -gŏn) *n.* Also **ti·gion** (tĭg'-lən, tĭg'-, -lŏn). The offspring of a male tiger and a female lion. [Blend of TIGER and LION.]

Ti·gré (tē'-grey ‖ *U.S.* tee-gráy) *n.* A Semitic language of northern Ethiopia.

ti·gress (tī'-grĭss, -grĕss) *n.* **1.** A female tiger. **2.** A fiercely passionate woman.

Ti·gri·nya (tĭ-gréen-yə, tee-) *n.* A Semitic language of northern Ethiopia.

Ti·gris (tī'-grĭss). River in southwestern Asia, rising in the Taurus Mountains of eastern Turkey and flowing for about 1 850 kilometres (1,150 miles) through Iraq to join the Euphrates and form the Shatt al Arab waterway, which passes through a delta and into the northern end of the Persian Gulf. Its flood-banks, along with those of the Euphrates, supported the agriculture on which the ancient civilisation of Mesopotamia was based.

tike. Variant of **tyke.**

ti·ki (tée'ki) *n.* **1.** *Capital* T. A male figure in Polynesian mythology, sometimes identified as the first man. **2.** A wood or stone image of a Polynesian god. **3.** A Maori figurine representing an ancestor, often intricately carved from greenstone and worn about the neck as a talisman. [Maori.]

til (til, teel) *n.* The sesame plant, especially as used in India as a source of food and oil. [Hindi *til*, from Sanskrit *tila†*.]

ti·lap·i·a (ti-lápp-i-ə, -láypi-) *n.* Any African cichlid fish of the genus *Tilapia*, which broods eggs and young in the mouth and is used as a food fish. [New Latin, probably from an African name.]

til·bur·y (tĭl'-bri, -bəri ‖ -berri) *n., pl.* **-ies.** A light open gig seating two persons, popular in the early 19th century. [Invented by *Tilbury*, a 19th-century London coach maker.]

Til·bur·y (tĭl'-bri, -bəri ‖ -berri). Dockyard district in Essex on the north bank of the river Thames, opposite Gravesend, southeastern England. Tilbury serves as the chief container port of London. It was there in 1588 that Queen Elizabeth I spoke to the English navy on the eve of its engagement with the Spanish Armada.

til·de (tĭld, -ĭ, -ə) *n.* The diacritical mark (˜) placed over the letter *n* in Spanish to indicate the palatal nasal sound (ny) as in *cañon*, or over a vowel in Portuguese to indicate nasalisation as in *lã, pão*. [Spanish, from Latin *titulus*, superscription, TITLE.]

tile (tīl) *n.* **1.** A thin, flat, or convex slab of baked clay, plastic, concrete, cork, or other material, laid in rows to cover walls, floors, and roofs. **2.** A short length of pipe made of clay or concrete, used in sewers and drains. **3.** A hollow fired clay or concrete block used for building walls. **4.** Tiles collectively. **5.** Any of the marked playing pieces in games such as mah-jong. —**on the tiles.** *Informal.* Given over to debauchery: *a night on the tiles.*
~*tr.v.* **tiled, tiling, tiles.** To cover or provide with tiles. [Middle English *til(e), teyele*, Old English *tigele*, from West Germanic *tegala* (unattested), from Latin *tēgula*, from *tegere*, to cover.] —**til·er** *n.*

til·ing (tī'ling) *n.* **1.** Tiles collectively. **2.** A tiled surface.

till¹ (til) *tr.v.* **tilled, tilling, tills.** To prepare (land) for the growing of crops by ploughing, harrowing, and fertilising. [Middle English *tilien, til(l)en*, Old English *tilian*, to work at, labour, cultivate, from Germanic *tilōjan* (unattested), from *tilam* (unattested), aim, fixed point.] —**till·a·ble** *adj.*

till² *prep.* Until.
~*conj.* Until. [Middle English *till*, Old English *til*, probably from Germanic *tilam* (unattested), fixed point. See **till** (cultivate).]
Usage: Till and until are generally interchangeable, the choice between them being largely concerned with considerations of rhythm and balance. *Until* is the more commonly found at the beginning of a sentence. It also tends to stress the duration of time involved more than does *till*, which tends to be used more with reference to a point of time: *We shall have to stay here until he's finished working; Let's stay till ten o'clock and then we'll go.* Many people also find *till* less formal than *until*, as is reflected in the nonstandard use of an apostrophe with this word ('*till* or '*til*).

till³ *n.* A drawer, small box, or compartment for money, especially in a shop; for example, a **cash register** *(see).* [Middle English *tylle†*.]

till⁴ *n.* Geology. **Boulder clay** *(see).* [17th century (Scottish) : origin obscure.]

till·age (tĭl'lij) *n.* **1.** The cultivation of land. **2.** The state of being tilled. **3.** Land that is tilled for crops.

til·land·si·a (ti-lándzi-ə) *n.* Any of various usually epiphytic plants of the genus *Tillandsia*, such as Spanish moss, of tropical and subtropical America. [New Latin, after Elias *Tillands* (died 1693), Swedish botanist.]

till·er¹ (tĭl'lər) *n.* One that tills land.

till·er² *n.* A lever used to turn a rudder and steer a boat. [Middle English *tiler, telor*, beam of a crossbow, from Anglo-French *telier*, weaver's beam, from Medieval Latin *tēlārium*, from Latin *tēla*, web, warp of a fabric, weaver's beam.]

till·er³ *n.* **1.** A shoot, especially one that sprouts from the base of a grass. **2.** A sapling.
~*intr.v.* **tillered, -ering, -ers.** To send forth tillers. [Middle English *tiller* (unattested), Old English *telgor, telgra*.]

Til·ley lamp (tĭl'li) *n.* A trademark for a portable lamp burning vaporised paraffin and having a special type of mantle designed to make it safe in the open air.

til·sit (tĭl'-sit; *German* -zit) *n.* A type of pale, firm, slightly pungent cheese with holes in it. [Originally made in TILSIT (Sovetsk).]

Tilsit. See **Sovetsk.**

tilt¹ (tilt) *v.* **tilted, tilting, tilts.** —*tr.* **1.** To cause to slope, as by raising one end; incline; tip. **2. a.** To aim or thrust (a lance) in a joust. **b.** To charge (an opponent). **3.** To forge with a tilt hammer. —*intr.* **1.** To slope; tilt. **2.** To joust. Used with *at*. **3.** To quarrel. Used with *at*. **4.** To incline towards a specified view or position.
~*n.* **1. a.** An inclination from the horizontal or vertical; a slant. **b.** A sloping surface, as of the ground. **2.** The act of tilting. **3. a.** A medieval sport in which two mounted knights with lances charged together and attempted to unhorse one another. **b.** A thrust or

blow with a lance. **4.** A dispute or other encounter between opponents. **5.** A tilt hammer. **6.** An inclination or bias towards a particular view or position. **—at full tilt.** At full speed. [Middle English *tylten, tilten,* perhaps from Old English *tyltan* (unattested; akin to *tealt,* unsteady), from Germanic.]

tilt² *n.* A canopy or awning for a boat, booth, or wagon.
~tr.v. **tilted, tilting, tilts.** To cover with a tilt. [Middle English *tild, teld,* Old English *teld,* a tent.]

tilth (tilth) *n.* **1.** The cultivation of land; tillage. **2.** The condition of land or soil with respect to encouraging plant growth. **3.** Tilled earth. [Middle English *tilth,* Old English *tilth,* from *tilian,* to TILL (cultivate).]

tilt hammer *n.* A heavy forge hammer having a pivoted lever by which it is tilted up and then allowed to drop.

tilt·yard (tílt-yaard) *n.* An enclosed area for tilting contests.

Tim. Timothy (New Testament).

Tim (tim) *n.* The **speaking clock** *(see).*

tim·bal, tym·bal (tímb'l) *n.* **1.** A kettledrum. **2.** A small cylindrical drum similar to a bongo or conga and used in Latin American music. [French *timbale,* variant (influenced by *cymbale,* cymbal) of obsolete *tamballe,* variant (influenced by *tambour,* tambour) of Spanish *atabal,* a kettledrum, from Arabic *aṭ-ṭabl,* the drum.]

tim·bale (tam-baál, tímb'l) *n.* **1.** A dish, usually of meat, fish, or vegetables in a sauce, or fruit with Chantilly, served in a bowl-shaped mould of pastry, rice, or pasta. **2.** A fireproof porcelain mould used for this dish. [French, "kettledrum", TIMBAL.]

tim·ber (tímbər) *n.* **1.** Trees or wooded land considered as a source of wood. **2. a.** Wood as a building material. **b.** A prepared piece of wood; especially, a beam in a structure. **c.** A rib in a ship's frame. **3.** Suitable or potential material: *He's executive timber.*
~tr.v. **timbered, -bering, -bers.** To support or shore up with timbers.
~interj. Used to warn of a falling tree. [Middle English *timber,* building, building material, Old English *timber.*]

tim·bered (tímbərd) *adj.* **1. a.** Constructed of or covered with timber. **b.** Built with exposed timbers. **2.** Wooded.

tim·ber-fram·ing (tímbər-fráyming) *n.* A method of building in which a frame of timber is erected and then filled in with plaster or bricks. **—tim·ber-frame** *adj.*

tim·ber·head (tímbər-hed) *n. Nautical.* A timber end that projects above the deck and is used as a bollard.

timber hitch *n. Nautical.* A knot used for fastening a rope around a spar or log to be hoisted or towed.

tim·ber·ing (tímbəring) *n.* Timber or work made of it.

tim·ber·land (tímbər-land) *n. U.S.* Forested land considered commercially.

timber line *n.* The limit of altitude or latitude limit beyond which trees do not grow. Also called "tree line".

timber wolf *n.* A greyish wolf, *Canis lupus,* of forested northern regions, especially of North America. Also called "grey wolf".

tim·ber·work (tímbər-wurk) *n.* The part of a structure made with timbers, such as the framework of a boat or house.

tim·bre (támbər, taɴbr, *also* tímbər) *n.* The quality of a sound that distinguishes it from other sounds of the same pitch and volume; especially, the distinctive tone of a musical instrument, a voice, or a voiced speech sound; tone colour. [French, from Old French, a bell struck with a hammer, timbrel, timbre, from Vulgar Latin *timbano* (unattested), a drum, from Medieval Greek *timbanon,* from Greek *tumpanon.* See **tympanum.**]

tim·brel (tímbrəl) *n.* An ancient percussion instrument similar to a tambourine. [Diminutive of Middle English *timbre,* from Old French, a drum, TIMBRE.]

Tim·buk·tu (tím-buk-to͞o). *French* **Tom·bouc·tou** (toɴ-bo͝ok-to͞o). City in central Mali, lying near the river Niger, to which it is connected by a series of canals. It was founded in the 11th century and rose to become one of the great trading centres (especially for gold) and a leading intellectual centre of Islam. It was sacked by Moroccans in 1593 and never regained its economic or cultural status.

time (tīm) *n.* **1. a.** A nonspatial continuum in which events occur in apparently irreversible succession from the past through the present to the future. **b.** Any point or period on this continuum, such as a day, month, or year. **2.** A quantity measuring duration by comparison with some periodic process, such as the Earth's rotation or the vibration of electromagnetic radiation, regarded in relativity theory as a fourth coordinate required to completely specify an event. See **space-time. 3.** An indefinite but finite period on this continuum: *Time will tell; You'll recover in time.* **4.** A specific point on the continuum reckoned in hours and minutes: *Can you tell me the time?* **5.** A system by which such intervals are measured or such numbers are reckoned; solar time: *Greenwich mean time.* **6. a.** *Often plural.* An interval marked by similar events, conditions, or phenomena; especially, a span of years; an era: *Edwardian times; a time of troubles.* **b.** *Plural.* The present with respect to prevailing conditions and trends: *move with the times.* **7. a.** One's lifetime. **b.** One's heyday. **8.** A suitable or opportune moment or season. **9. a.** A moment or period designated, as by custom, for a specified activity: *harvest time; bedtime.* **b.** A moment or period designated for something to happen: *got to work on time.* **c.** A period allotted or given over to a specific activity: *Your time is up; I need time to think.* **d.** A period at one's disposal: *free time; Have you time for a chat?* **10.** An appointed or fated moment, especially of death or giving birth: *died before his time; Her time is near.* **11. a.** One of several instances: *We called on you twice but both times you were out.* **b.** *Plural.* Used to indicate the number of instances by which a quantity is or is to be multiplied: *It's at least three times as big.* **12.** An occasion or experience of a specified kind: *had a marvellous time; showed us a good time.* **13.** *Informal.* A prison sentence: *do time.* **14. a.** The customary period of work: *work full time.* **b.** The period spent working. **c.** A period of apprenticeship: *serve one's time.* **d.** The hourly pay rate: *earned double time on Sundays.* **15.** The rate of speed of a measured activity: *marching in double time.* **16.** The characteristic beat of musical rhythm: *three-four time.* **17.** *British.* The hour at which a bar in a pub closes; closing time: *Time, gentlemen, please!* **18.** *Plural. Capital T.* Used as the title of a newspaper: *The Oxford Times.* **—against time.** With a quickly approaching time limit. **—at one time. 1.** Simultaneously. **2.** At a period or moment in the past. **—at the same time.** However; nonetheless. **—at times.** On occasion; sometimes. **—behind the times.** Out-of-date; old-fashioned. **—bide (one's) time.** To wait for an opportune moment. **—for the time being.** Temporarily. **—from time to time.** Once in a while; at intervals. **—have no time for.** To dislike; be intolerant of: *I've no time for clock-watchers.* **—high time.** Past the time for; fully time. **—in good time. 1.** In a reasonable length of time. **2.** At or before the proper time. **—in no time.** Almost instantly; immediately. **—in time. 1.** Before the time limit expires. **2.** Within an indefinite amount of passing time. **3.** In tempo; keeping the rhythm. **—keep time. 1.** To indicate the correct time. **2.** To maintain the tempo or rhythm. **—kill time.** To occupy oneself in a desultory way while waiting for time to pass. **—make up time.** To compensate for lost time. **—mark time. 1.** To move the feet as though marching but without moving forward. **2.** To act or function in an unproductive or purposeless fashion. **3.** To stop doing something temporarily, usually with a view to restarting when conditions permit. **—once upon a time.** Long ago; once. Used especially to introduce fairy tales. **—on time. 1.** Promptly; according to schedule. **2.** *U.S.* By paying in instalments. **—pass the time of day.** To chat about general topics such as the weather. **—play for time.** To use delaying tactics in order to gain extra time. **—take (one's) time.** To do something in a careful or leisurely fashion. **—time after time.** Repeatedly. **—time and (time) again.** Often; frequently. **—the time of (one's) life.** A highly pleasurable experience. **—time of the month.** One's menstrual period. Used euphemistically. **—time out of mind.** Before recorded time.
~adj. **1.** Of or relating to time. **2.** Constructed so as to be able to be operated at or indicating a particular moment: *a time bomb.* **3.** Payable on a future date or dates: *a time loan.*
~tr.v. **timed, timing, times. 1.** To set the time for (an event or occasion). **2.** To adjust to keep accurate time. **3.** To regulate for the most appropiate sequence of movements or events. **4.** To record the speed or duration of. **5.** To set or maintain the tempo, speed, or duration of. [Middle English *time,* Old English *tīma.*]

time and a half *n.* A rate of pay that is one and a half times the regular rate, as for overtime work.

time and motion study *n.* An analysis of the working methods involved in an industrial operation with a view to improving efficiency. Also called "motion study".

time base *n. Electronics.* An electronic circuit that repeatedly produces a voltage increasing to a given value and falling abruptly to zero or a minimum value, used to deflect the electron beam horizontally in an oscilloscope or television.

time bill *n.* A bill of exchange payable at an indicated future time.

time bomb *n.* **1.** A bomb with a detonating mechanism that can be set for a particular time. **2.** A potentially dramatic or disastrous situation.

time capsule *n.* A sealed container preserving articles and records of contemporary culture for study in the distant future.

time·card (tīm-kaard) *n.* A card, either maintained by the employee or stamped by a time clock, recording an employee's arrival and departure time each day.

time clock *n.* A clock that records the arrival and departure times of employees, usually by punching timecards.

time constant *n. Physics.* A measure of the amount of damping in an oscillating system, such as a vibrating structure or a circuit carrying an alternating signal, measured by the time taken for the amplitude to fall to a value $1/e$ (about 0.368) of its initial value or to increase to $(1 - 1/e)$ (0.632) of its final steady value.

time-con·sum·ing (tīm-kən-sew-ming, -so͞o- || -kon-, -sho͞o-) *adj.* Taking up a great deal of time or too much time.

time deposit *n.* A bank deposit that cannot be withdrawn before a date decided at the time of deposit.

time dilation *n.* Also **time dilatation.** The relativistic slowing of a clock that moves with respect to a stationary observer.

time exposure *n.* **1.** A photographic exposure made for a relatively long period of time. **2.** An image made by such an exposure.

time fuse *n.* A fuse designed to set off an explosive charge after a preset period of time, or to burn for a preset period.

time-hon·oured (tīm-onnərd) *adj.* Honoured because of age or age-old observance.

time immemorial *n.* **1.** Time long past, beyond memory or record. **2.** *Law.* Time antedating legal records.

time·keep·er (tīm-keepər) *n.* **1.** A timepiece. **2.** The person who keeps track of time, as in a sports event or in a place of employment. **—time·keep·ing** *n.*

time-lag, time lag (tīm-lag) *n.* The interval of time between two events, the second of which is usually a result of the first.

time-lapse (tīm-laps) *adj.* Of or using a cinematic technique for filming a naturally slow process, such as the unfolding of a leaf, by photographing it at intervals so that the continuous projection of the frames gives an accelerated view of it.

time·less (tīm-ləss, -liss) *adj.* **1.** Independent of time; unending; eternal. **2.** Unaffected by time; ageless. **—time·less·ly** *adv.* **—time·less·ness** *n.*

time lock *n.* A lock set to open at a specific time.

time·ly (tīm-li) *adj.* **-lier, -liest. 1.** Occurring at a suitable or opportune time; well-timed. **2.** *Archaic.* Early; premature.

~*adv.* **1.** Opportunely; in time. **2.** *Archaic.* Early; soon. [Middle English : TIME + -LY.] **—time·li·ness** *n.*

time machine *n.* An imaginary vehicle supposed to be capable of transporting people backwards and forwards in time.

time off *n.* A period of absence or rest from work as a result of illness, holidays, or the like.

time on *n. Sports. Australian.* Extra time.

time·ous (tīm-əss) *adj. Scottish.* Timely. [TIME + -OUS.] **—time·ous·ly** *adv.*

time-out (tīm-owt) *n.* Also **time out.** *Chiefly U.S.* **1.** A brief cessation of play at the request of a sports team for rest or consultation. **2.** Any short break from work or play.

time·piece (tīm-peess) *n.* An instrument, such as a clock or chronometer, that measures, registers, or records time.

tim·er (tīmər) *n.* **1.** A switch or regulator that controls or activates another mechanism at preset intervals. **2.** A timepiece, especially one used for measuring intervals of time. **3.** A person who keeps track of time; a timekeeper.

time reversal *n. Symbol* **T** A mathematical operation representing a transformation from a given physical system undergoing a given sequence of events (states) to a system in which the exact reverse sequence of states is undergone.

times (tīmz) *prep.* Multiplied by: *Five times two is ten.*

time's arrow *n. Physics.* The existence of a single direction for the passage of time such that time reversal does not occur in physical systems, as indicated by such phenomena as spontaneous increase in entropy, the spreading of waves from a source, or the expansion of the universe.

time·sav·ing (tīm-sayving) *adj.* Saving time through an efficient method or a shorter route. **—time·sav·er** *n.*

time scale *n.* A sequence of events used as a measure of duration or the passing of time.

time·serv·er (tīm-servər) *n.* A person who conforms to the prevailing ways and opinions of his time or condition for personal advantage; an opportunist. **—time·serv·ing** *adj. & n.*

time sharing *n.* **1.** *Computing.* A system in which two or more users communicate with a computer at the same time, data being processed successively for short periods in a way controlled by the computer so that each terminal appears to have sole use of the machine. Compare **batch processing. 2.** A system whereby a number of people each buy a share in a flat, villa, or other holiday accommodation, enabling them each to spend a given period there every year.

time sheet *n.* A sheet of paper recording the hours worked by an employee.

time signal *n.* An announcement, usually on the radio, of the correct time.

time signature *n. Music.* A symbol in the form of a numerical fraction, written at the beginning of a piece of music to indicate the number and length of notes in each bar. Thus ³/₄ means there are three crotchets in each bar; ⁶/₈ means six quavers. The lower number of the two indicates the time value of each note, regarded as a fraction of a semibreve. Also called "signature".

time span *n.* The length of time occupied by or allocated for a particular event or purpose: *the time span of a man's life.*

time-switch (tīm-swich) *n.* A switch whereby a mechanism can be preset to start or finish operating automatically.

time·ta·ble (tīm-tayb'l) *n.* **1.** A list of the times at which certain events, such as arrivals and departures at an airport or railway station, are expected to take place. **2.** A plan giving the times when classes or lectures will take place, as in a school or college. **3.** A schedule for any planned sequence of events. **—time·ta·ble** *tr.v.*

time-test·ed (tīm-testid) *adj.* Having been proved effective by prolonged testing.

time trial *n.* A competitive event, as in sports, that must be completed within a given time.

time value *n.* The length of a musical note in relation to the other notes in the score or in relation to the tempo.

time warp *n.* An imaginary distortion or interruption in the flow of time from past to future, featured typically in science fiction.

time-work (tīm-wurk) *n.* Work paid for in specific time units, as by the hour. Compare **piecework. —time·work·er** *n.*

time-worn (tīm-wawrn || -wŏrn) *adj.* **1.** Showing the effects of long use or wear. **2.** Used too often; trite.

time zone *n.* Any of the 24 equal longitudinal divisions of the Earth's surface in which a standard time, the mean time of a meridian near the centre, is kept, the primary division being that bisected by the Greenwich meridian. Each zone is 15 degrees of longitude in width, with local variations, and observes a clock time one hour earlier than the zone immediately to the east. Also called "international time zone".

tim·id (timmid) *adj.* **-ider, -idest. 1.** Shrinking from dangerous or difficult circumstances; hesitant or fearful. **2.** Shrinking from public attention; shy. **3.** Characterised by hesitancy or lack of courage.

—See Synonyms at **shy.** [Latin *timidus,* from *timēre†,* to fear.] **—ti·mid·i·ty** (ti-middəti), **tim·id·ness** *n.* **—tim·id·ly** *adv.*

tim·ing (tīming) *n.* **1.** The art or operation of regulating occurrence, pace, or coordination to achieve the most desirable effects, as in music, the theatre, athletics, or a machine. **2.** The way in which the distribution of electricity to the plugs of an internal-combustion engine is synchronised with the speed of the engine.

ti·moc·ra·cy (tī-móckrə-si) *n., pl.* **-cies. 1.** A state described by Plato in which love of honour is the guiding principle. **2.** An Aristotelian state in which political power is proportional to property owned. [Old French *tymocracie,* from Medieval Latin *tīmocratia,* from Greek *timokratia* : *timē,* honour, worth + -CRACY.] **—ti·mo·crat·ic** (tĭm-ə-kráttik, -ō-) *adj.*

Ti·mor (tée-mawr, -'-). Mountainous Indonesian island, the largest and easternmost of the Lesser Sunda Islands. The western half of the island, formerly Netherlands Timor, became part of Indonesia in 1949. The eastern half was formerly Portuguese Timor, an overseas province of Portugal from 1914 until 1975.

tim·or·ous (timmərəss) *adj.* Full of apprehensiveness; timid. [Middle English, from Old French *timoureus,* from Medieval Latin *timorōsus,* from Latin *timor,* fear, from *timēre†,* to fear.] **—tim·or·ous·ly** *adv.* **—tim·or·ous·ness** *n.*

Tim·o·thy (timməthi) *n. Abbr.* **Tim.** Either of two books of the New Testament, each an epistle to St. Timothy attributed to St. Paul.

Timothy, Saint. Also **Ti·moth·e·us** (ti-mŏthi-əss, tī- || -mŏthi-). Christian leader of the first century A.D.; convert and companion of St. Paul; legendary martyr.

tim·o·thy grass (timməthi) *n.* A grass, *Phleum pratense,* native to Eurasia, having narrow, cylindrical flower spikes, and widely cultivated for hay. Also called "timothy". [After *Timothy* Hanson, American farmer, who introduced it in the Carolinas about 1720.]

tim·pa·ni, tym·pa·ni (timpəni) *pl.n.* A set of kettledrums. [Italian, plural of *timpano,* kettledrum, from Latin *tympanum,* TYMPANUM.] **—tim·pa·nist** *n.*

timpanum. Variant of **tympanum.**

tin (tin) *n.* **1.** *Symbol* **Sn** A malleable, silvery metallic element obtained chiefly from cassiterite. It is used to coat other metals to prevent corrosion, and forms part of numerous alloys, such as soft solder, pewter, type metal, and bronze. Atomic number 50, atomic weight 118.69, melting point 231.89°C, boiling point 2,507°C, relative density 7.31, valencies 2, 4. **2.** Tin plate. **3.** A tin container or box. **4. a.** An airtight container, usually made of tin-coated iron, in which meat, vegetables, or other foods are preserved; a can. **b.** The contents of such a container; a tinful. **5.** *British.* A type of loaf of bread baked in a long rectangular tin. **6.** *Slang.* Money.

~*tr.v.* **tinned, tinning, tins. 1.** To plate or coat with tin. **2.** To preserve by sealing in airtight tins; can. [Middle English *tin,* Old English *tin,* from Germanic *tinam* (unattested).]

tin·a·mou (tínnə-mōō) *n.* Any of various chicken-like or quail-like birds of the family Tinamidae, of Central and South America. [French, from Galibi *tinamu.*]

tin·cal (tíngk'l) *n.* Crude borax. [Malay *tingkal,* from Sanskrit *ṭankaṇat.*]

tin can *n.* A container of tin-plated metal used especially for preserving food.

tinct (tingkt) *n. Archaic.* A colour or tint.

~*adj. Poetic.* Tinged or tinted. [Latin *tinctus,* past participle of *tingere,* to TINGE.]

tinct. tincture.

tinc·to·ri·al (tingk-táw-ri-əl || -tō-) *adj.* Pertaining to the processes of dyeing or colouring. [Latin *tinctōrius,* from *tinctus,* past participle of *tingere,* to TINGE.]

tinc·ture (tíngkchər) *n. Abbr.* **tinct. 1.** *Archaic.* A dyeing substance; a pigment. **2.** An imparted colour; a tinge; a tint. **3.** A trace or hint. **4.** *Pharmacology.* An alcohol solution of a nonvolatile medicine: *tincture of iodine.* **5.** A particular heraldic metal, colour, or fur. **6.** *Informal.* An alcoholic drink. Used humorously.

~*tr.v.* **tinctured, -turing, -tures. 1.** To stain or tint with a colour. **2.** To infuse, as with a quality; impregnate. [Middle English, from Latin *tinctūra,* a dyeing, from *tinctus,* past participle of *tingere,* TINGE.]

tin·der (tíndər) *n.* Readily combustible material, such as dry twigs, used to kindle fires. [Middle English *tinder,* Old English *tynder,* from Germanic *tund-* (unattested), past participle form of *tend-* (unattested), to burn, kindle.]

tin·der·box (tíndər-boks) *n.* **1.** A metal box for holding tinder, and usually flint and steel. **2.** A potentially explosive place, person or situation.

tine (tīn) *n.* **1.** A branch of a deer's antlers. **2.** A prong on a fork, pitchfork, or similar implement. [Middle English *tind, tene,* Old English *tind,* from Germanic *tind-* (unattested), point.]

tin·e·a (tínni-ə) *n.* Any of several fungous skin diseases. Also called "ringworm". [Latin *tinea†,* a gnawing worm, moth.]

tin ear *n. Informal.* An inability to reproduce accurately, or distinguish between, different sounds, especially different musical notes.

tin·foil (tín-foyl) *n.* **1.** A thin, pliable sheet of tin or of tin-lead alloy, formerly used as a protective wrapping. **2.** Any thin metal foil, such as aluminium foil.

ting (ting) *n.* A single high-pitched metallic sound, as of a small bell. **~***intr.v.* **tinged** (tingd), **tinging, tings.** To give forth such a sound. [Middle English *tyngen* (imitative).]

ting-a-ling (tíng-ə-líng) *n.* The high-pitched sound made by a small bell. [Imitative.] **—ting·a·ling** *adv.*

tinge (tinj) *tr.v.* **tinged** (tinjd), **tingeing** or **tinging**, **tinges**. **1.** To impart a trace of colour to; tint. **2.** To modify, as by the admixture of a contrasting quality: *comedy tinged with tragedy.*
~n. **1.** A faint trace of a colour incorporated or added. **2.** A slight admixture of any modifying quality or property. [Middle English *tyngen*, from Latin *tingere*, to moisten, plunge, dye.]

tin-gle (tíng-g'l) *v.* **-gled**, **-gling**, **-gles.** *—intr.* **1.** To have a prickling, stinging sensation as from the cold, a sharp slap, or excitement: *tingle all over with joy.* **2.** To cause such a sensation or feeling. *—tr.* To cause to tingle.
~n. A tingling sensation. [Middle English *tinglen*, originally, to be affected with a ringing sound in the ears, perhaps variant of TINKLE.] **—tin-gler** *n.* **—tin-gly** *adj.*

tin god *n.* **1.** A person who is unjustifiably or mistakenly revered. **2.** A self-important person in a position of some authority.

tin hat *n. Informal.* A soldier's protective steel helmet.

tink-er (tíngkər) *n.* **1.** A travelling mender of metal household utensils. **2.** *Scottish & Irish.* A Gypsy. **3.** One who is clumsy at his work; a bungler. **4.** An act of tinkering with something.
~v. **tinkered**, **-ering**, **-ers.** *—intr.* **1.** To work as a tinker. **2.** To work at or fiddle with something, often clumsily or ineffectually, with the aim of effecting repairs or improvements. *—tr.* To mend, patch up, or experiment with. —See Synonyms at **interfere.** [Middle English *tyn(e)kere*, perhaps from *tynken*, to TINKLE (perhaps from the sounds made by a tinker at work).]

tinker's damn *n. Slang.* The slightest amount: *not worth a tinker's damn.* Also called "tinker's cuss". [From the tinker's reputed habit of cursing.]

tin-kle (tíngk'l) *v.* **-kled**, **-kling**, **-kles.** *—intr.* To make a series of light metallic sounds, such as those of a small bell. *—tr.* To cause to tinkle.
~n. **1.** A light, clear metallic sound or a sound suggestive of it. **2.** *British Informal.* A telephone call; a ring. **3.** *British Informal.* An act of urinating. [Middle English *tynclen*, frequentative of *tynken* (imitative).] **—tin-kly** *adj.*

tin liz-zie (lízzi) *n. Slang.* A dilapidated or cheap car. [TIN (by analogy with the common food tin) + *Lizzie*, pet form of *Elizabeth.*]

tin-ner (tínnər) *n.* **1.** A tin miner. **2.** A tinsmith. **3.** One who tins things; a canner.

tin-ni-tus (tínnitəss, ti-nítəss) *n.* A sound in the ears, such as buzzing, ringing, or whistling, caused by disease of the inner ear, certain drugs, or by a defect in the auditory nerve. [Latin *tinnītus*, from the past participle of *tinnīre*, to ring, tinkle (imitative).]

tin-ny (tínni) *adj.* **-nier**, **-niest.** **1.** Of, containing, or yielding tin. **2.** Cheaply and badly made. **3.** Having a thin metallic sound. **4.** Tasting or smelling of tin, as food from a tin can.
~n., *pl.* **tinnies.** *Australian Slang.* A can of beer. **—tin-ni-ly** *adv.* **—tin-ni-ness** *n.*

tin-o-pen-er (tín-ōp-nər, -ə̄nər) *n.* An instrument for piercing and opening tin cans.

Tin Pan Alley *n.* **1.** A district associated with players, composers, and publishers of popular music. **2.** The publishers, players, and composers of popular music considered as a group; the world of commercial popular music. [From slang *tin-pan*, noisy, tinny.]

tin plate *n.* Thin sheet iron or steel coated with tin.

tin-plate (tín-playt) *tr.v.* **-plated**, **-plating**, **-plates.** To coat with tin. **—tin-plat-er** *n.*

tin-pot (tín-pot) *adj.* Worthless; contemptible: *a tinpot dictator.*

tin pyrites *n.* A mineral, **stannite** *(see).*

tin-sel (tínss'l) *n.* **1.** Very thin sheets, strips, or threads of a glittering material used as a decoration. **2.** Anything superficially fine or attractive but basically valueless.
~adj. **1.** Made of or decorated or covered with tinsel. **2.** Gaudy and showy but basically valueless.
~tr.v. **tinselled** or *U.S.* **tinseled**, **-selling** or *U.S.* **-seling**, **-sels.** **1.** To decorate with or as if with tinsel. **2.** To give a superficially fine or showy appearance to. [Earlier *tinsele*, adorned with metallic threads, probably from Old French *estincelle*, a spark, from Vulgar Latin *stincilla* (unattested), variant of Latin *scintilla*, spark.] **—tin-sel-ly** *adj.*

tin-smith (tín-smith) *n.* One who makes and repairs things made of light metal, such as tin.

tin-snips (tín-snips) *pl.n.* **Snips** *(see).*

tin-stone (tín-stōn) *n.* A mineral, **cassiterite** *(see).*

tint (tint) *n.* **1.** A shade of a colour, especially a pale or delicate variation; a tinge. **2.** A gradation of a colour made by adding white to it to lessen its saturation. **3.** A slight coloration; a hue. **4.** A barely detectable modifying quality; a trace. **5.** In engraving, a shaded effect produced by a series of fine parallel lines. **6.** *Printing.* A panel of usually pale colour on which matter in another colour, as an illustration, may be printed. **7.** A dye for the hair.
~tr.v. **tinted**, **tinting**, **tints.** To imbue with a tint; colour. [Variant (probably influenced by Italian *tinto*, tint) of earlier *tinct*, from Latin *tinctus*, a dipping or dyeing, from the past participle of *tingere*, to wet, dip]

tin-tack (tín-tak) *n.* A small, tin-covered nail with a broad flat head, usually made of iron.

Tin-tag-el (tin-táj'l). Village on the northern coast of Cornwall, southwestern England. It is the site of a ruined 12th-century castle, reputed to have been the birthplace of King Arthur.

tin-tin-nab-u-la-tion (tínti-nábbew-láysh'n) *n.* The ringing or tinkling of bells. [From TINTINNABULUM.]

tin-tin-nab-u-lum (tínti-nábbew-ləm) *n., pl.* **-la** (-lə). A small, tinkling bell or set of bells. [Latin, from *tintinnāre*, *tintinnīre*, to jingle, reduplication of *tinnīre*, to ring. See **tinnitus.**] **—tin-tin-nab-u-lar** (-lər), **tin-tin-nab-u-lar-y** (-ləri) *adj.*

tint-om-e-ter (tin-tómmitər) *n.* A **colorimeter** *(see)* for measuring concentration. [TINT + -METER.]

Tin-to-ret-to (tíntə-réttō) (1518–94). Venetian painter. Called "Il Tintoretto" because his father had been a dyer, he was a versatile painter, handling religious, mythological, and historical subjects, as well as portraits. Among his many surviving works are *St. George and the Dragon (c.* 1550), and the series of paintings illustrating the life of Christ and the Virgin in the Scuola di San Rocco, in Venice (1576–88).

tin-type (tín-tīp) *n.* A **ferrotype** *(see).*

tin whistle *n.* A **penny whistle** *(see).*

tin-works (tín-wurk) *pl.n. Used with a singular or plural verb.* A place where tin is smelted and rolled.

ti-ny (tíni) *adj.* **-nier**, **-niest.** Extremely small; minute. See Synonyms at **small.** [From Middle English *tine†* (adjective and noun, "a little") + -Y.]

–tion *n. suffix.* Indicates action, process, condition or result; for example, **adsorption.** [Middle English *-cioun*, from Old French *-tion*, from Latin *-tiō* (stem *-tiōn-*) : *-t-*, of the past participial stem + *-iōn-*, -ION.]

tip¹ (tip) *n.* **1.** The end or extremity of something, especially of something pointed or tapering. **2.** A piece or attachment fitted to the end of something, such as a ferrule, the end of a billiard cue, or the filter on a cigarette. **3.** The bud of a leaf on a tea plant. **—the tip of the iceberg.** A small perceptible part of something, such as a problem or task, that hides its true dimensions.
~tr.v. **tipped**, **tipping**, **tips.** **1.** To furnish with a tip. **2.** To cover, decorate, or remove the tip of. **3.** To attach (an insert) in a book by gluing along the binding edge. Often used with *in.* [Middle English *tip(pe)*, probably from Old Norse *typpi* (noun), *typpa* (verb), from Germanic *tupp-* (unattested), TOP.]

tip² *v.* **tipped**, **tipping**, **tips.** *—tr.* **1.** To knock over or upset. Usually used with *over.* **2.** To bring to a slanting position; tilt. **3.** *British.* **a.** To empty (the contents of a container), as by tilting it. **b.** To dump (rubbish). **4.** To touch or raise (one's hat) in greeting. *—intr.* **1.** To topple; overturn. Usually used with *over.* **2.** To become tilted; slant.
~n. **1.** An act of tipping; a tilt or slant. **2.** *British.* **a.** A place for dumping rubbish. **b.** *Informal.* A very dirty or untidy place. [Middle English *typen*, *tipen†.*]

tip³ (tip) *tr.v.* **tipped**, **tipping**, **tips.** **1.** To strike gently; tap. **2.** To hit (a ball), as in cricket or baseball, with a light glancing blow.
~n. **1.** A light blow; a tap. **2.** A game, **tag** *(see).* [Middle English *tippen*, perhaps from Low German.]

tip⁴ *n.* **1.** A small sum of money given as an acknowledgment of services rendered; a gratuity. **2. a.** A piece of advance or inside information given as a guide, as to speculation on the stock market or betting on a race. **b.** Any piece of useful or helpful information.
~v. **tipped**, **tipping**, **tips.** **1.** To give a tip or gratuity to. **2.** To give advance or inside information to. **3.** To mention or regard as a likely winner: *widely tipped to get the top job. —intr.* To give a tip or tips. [Originally a slang word meaning "to give", "to pass to", from TIP (to tap).] **—tip-per** *n.*

tip-and-run (típ-ən-rún) *n.* A version of cricket in which the batsman must attempt a run if the ball hits his bat.

tipi. Variant of **tepee.**

tip off *tr.v.* To provide with a tip-off; warn.

tip-off (típ-off, -awf) *n.* An item of advance or inside information; a hint or warning.

Tip-pe-ra-ry (típpə-raír-i). *Irish.* **Contae Tiobraid Árann.** County in south central Republic of Ireland. It includes the Golden Vale, one of Ireland's most fertile agricultural regions. The county town, Tipperary, has the ruins of a 13th-century Augustinian abbey.

tip-per truck (típpər) *n.* A type of lorry whose rear section can be tilted mechanically so that its load can be discharged. Also called "tipper lorry".

tip-pet (típpit) *n.* **1.** A covering for the shoulders, as of fur, with long ends that hang in front. **2.** A long stole worn by clergymen of the Anglican Church. **3.** A long, hanging part, as of a sleeve, hood, or cape. [Middle English *tipet*, probably a diminutive of TIP (end).]

Tip-pett, Sir Michael (Kemp) (tippit), (1905–97). British composer. His works include the oratorio *A Child of Our Time* (1941), his first opera *The Midsummer Marriage* (1955), the cantata *The Vision of St. Augustine* (1966), and *Caliban's Song* (1995).

Tipp-Ex (típ-eks) *n.* A trademark for a quick-drying correction fluid used to obliterate marks made by writing or typing. **—Tipp-Ex** *tr.v.*

tip-ple (típp'l) *v.* **-pled**, **-pling**, **-ples.** *—intr.* To drink alcoholic liquor, especially habitually or intemperately. *—tr.* To drink (alcoholic liquor), especially habitually.
~n. An alcoholic drink, especially one taken habitually. [Backformation from *tippler*, a tapster, bartender, from Middle English *tipler†.*] **—tip-pler** *n.*

tip-staff (típ-staaf ‖ -staf) *n., pl.* **-staves** (-stayvz ‖ -stavz) or **-staffs.** *Archaic.* A sheriff's officer or court official. [Short for *tipped staff,* a metal-tipped staff carried as a badge of the sheriff's office.]

tip-ster (típstər) *n. Informal.* A person who gives or sells tips to betters or speculators.

tip-sy (típsi) *adj.* **-sier**, **-siest.** **1.** Slightly drunk. **2.** Likely to tip over; unsteady; crooked. [From TIP (to tilt, be unsteady).] —**tip·si·ly** adv. —**tip·si·ness** n.

tipsy cake n. British. Cake soaked with wine or sherry, decorated with almonds and served with custard.

tip·toe (típ-tō) intr.v. **-toed, -toeing, -toes. 1.** To walk or move with one's heels raised and only one's toes and the ball of the foot touching the ground. **2.** To walk stealthily or quietly. ~n. The tip up of a toe. —**on tiptoe. 1.** Standing or walking with one's heels raised. **2.** Full of anticipation; eager. **3.** Silently; stealthily. ~adj. **1.** Standing or walking on tiptoe. **2.** Stealthy; wary. ~adv. On tiptoe.

tip·top (típ-tóp, -top) n. The highest point or degree. ~adj. Excellent; first-rate. ~adv. At the highest point of excellence.

tip-up (típ-up) adj. Having a horizontal part that may be tilted into an upright position, as in a cinema or theatre seat.

TIR International Road Transport [French Transport International Routier].

ti·rade (tīr-ráyd, ti-, -ráad || tír-ayd) n. A long vehement or blustering speech, especially of denunciation or censure; a diatribe. [French, "a stretching" (as in tout d'une tirade, all at one stretch), from Italian tirata, a volley, act of drawing, from tirare, to draw, from Vulgar Latin tīrāre (unattested). See **tier** (layer).]

ti·ra·mi·sù (tírrəmi-soō) n. An Italian dessert that is sponge cake filled with soft sweet cheese and soaked in spirits or liqueur. [Italian, "pull me up" : tira, pull + mi, me + sù, above, up.]

Ti·ra·na or **Ti·ra·në** (ti-ráanə). Capital city of Albania, lying on the river Ishm in Albania's central plain. It is the largest and industrially most important city in the country.

tire¹ (tīr) v. **tired, tiring, tires.** —intr. **1.** To become weak or fatigued as a result of exertion. **2.** To lose interest or grow impatient; weary. Often used with of: He tired of reading. —tr. **1.** To diminish the strength or energy of; weary; fatigue. Often used with out. **2.** To exhaust the interest or patience of; bore. [Middle English tyren, to stop, tire, Old English tēorian†.]

tire² U.S. Variant of **tyre.**

tire³ tr.v. **tired, tiring, tires.** Archaic. To adorn or attire. ~n. Archaic. **1.** Attire. **2.** A covering or ornament for the head or hair. [Middle English tiren, short for attiren, to ATTIRE.]

tired (tīrd) adj. **1. a.** Worn-out; fatigued. **b.** Impatient, fed up, or no longer interested. **2.** Overused; hackneyed.

Synonyms: tired, weary, exhausted, fatigued, jaded.

tire·less (tīr-ləss, -liss) adj. Untiring; indefatigable. —**tire·less·ly** adv. —**tire·less·ness** n.

Ti·re·si·as (tīr-rée-si-əss, -rə-, -ré-, -ass || -zi-). A blind prophet of Thebes prominent in many Greek myths and tragedies.

tire·some (tīr-səm) adj. Causing boredom or annoyance; tedious or irritating. See Synonyms at **boring.** —**tire·some·ly** adv. —**tire·some·ness** n.

tire·wom·an (tīrˈwŏomən) n., pl. **-women** (-wimmin). Archaic. A lady's maid. [From TIRE (attire).]

Ti·rich Mir (téer-ich méer). Mountain peak in the Hindu Kush range, in northern Pakistan. It is the highest peak in the range and rises to 7 692 metres (25,236 feet).

tiro. Variant of **tyro.**

Ti·rol or **Ty·rol** (ti-rŏl, tírrəl). Province in western Austria. The capital is Innsbruck. The province is almost entirely occupied by the Tirolean Alps and is a famous skiing centre. —**Ti·rol·ese** (-éez || éess), **Ti·rol·e·an** (-ee-ən) n. & adj.

Ti·ru·chi·ra·pal·li (tírra-chírra-púlli) or **Trich·i·nop·o·ly** (tríchi-nóppəli). City in southeastern India, lying on the river Cauvery. It is famous both for its gold and silver filigree crafts, and for the shrine of Srirangam, a monument to the god Vishnu, carved into the base of a huge rock.

'tis (tiz). Archaic & Poetic. Contraction of it is.

ti·sane, pti·san (ti-zán, tee- || -záan) n. A herbal infusion or similar preparation, drunk as a beverage or for its mildly medicinal effect. [French, from Latin ptisana, barley, PTISAN.]

Tish·ri (tishri) n. The first month of the civil year in the Hebrew calendar. [Hebrew Tishrī, from Akkadian Tashrītu, from shurrū, to begin.]

Ti·siph·o·ne (tī-síffəni || ti-). One of the three **Furies** (see).

tis·sue (tíshoō, tíssew) n. **1.** Biology. **a.** An aggregation of cells that are specialised to perform a certain function: nervous tissue. **b.** Cellular matter regarded as a collective entity. **2.** A soft, very absorbent piece of paper, generally made up of two thin layers, and used as a disposable handkerchief or towel. **3.** Unsized thin, translucent paper used for packing, wrapping, or protecting delicate articles. Also called "tissue paper". **4.** A woven fabric, usually of a fine, delicate texture. **5.** An interwoven or interrelated series; a web; a network: His evidence was nothing but a tissue of lies. [Middle English tissu, a rich cloth, fine gauze, from Old French, from the past participle of tistre, to weave, from Latin texere.]

tissue culture n. **1.** The growth in a suitable medium of specimens of tissue removed from a living organism. **2.** Tissue grown thus.

tit¹ (tit) n. **1.** Any of various small Old World birds of the family Paridae, such as the **bluetit** (see), typically feeding on insects and seeds. Sometimes called "titmouse". **2.** Any of various similar or related birds. [Probably from Scandinavian, from a word referring to small objects; compare Icelandic titlingr, sparrow.]

tit² n. **1.** Slang. A woman's breast. **2.** A teat or nipple. **3.** Vulgar Slang. A stupid or contemptible person. [Middle English titte, Old

English titt, from West Germanic titta (unattested).]

ti·tan (tīt'n) n. A person of colossal size, strength, ability, or achievement; a giant. [From TITAN.]

Ti·tan¹ (tīt'n). Greek Mythology. One of a family of primordial gods, the children of Uranus and Gaea, overthrown and succeeded by the Olympian gods. [Middle English, from Latin, from Greek Titan, from titō†, day, sun.] —**Ti·tan·ess** n.

Titan² n. Astronomy. The largest satellite of Saturn and probably the largest in the Solar System.

ti·tan·ate (tīt'n-ayt) n. A salt of titanic acid. [TITAN(IUM) + -ATE (salt).]

Ti·ta·ni·a¹ (ti-taán-yə, tī-, -táyn-, -i-ə). In medieval folklore, the queen of the fairies, wife of Oberon.

Titania² n. One of the satellites of the planet Uranus.

ti·tan·ic¹ (tī-tánnik) adj. **1. a.** Having great stature or enormous strength; huge; colossal. **b.** Of enormous scope, power, or influence. **2.** Capital T. Of or pertaining to the Titans. [After TITAN.] —**ti·tan·i·cal·ly** adv.

ti·tan·ic² (tī-tánnik, ti-, -táynik) adj. Pertaining to or containing titanium. Said especially of compounds containing titanium with a valency of 4. [TITAN(IUM) + -IC.]

titanic acid n. **1.** A white, powdered inorganic acid, H_2TiO_3, derived from an acid solution of titanates and used as a mordant. **2.** Titanium dioxide.

ti·tan·if·er·ous (tīt'n-íffərəss) adj. Containing or yielding titanium. [TITANI(UM) + -FEROUS.]

Ti·tan·ism (tīt'n-iz'm) n. The spirit of rebellion; defiance of and revolt against authority, convention, or the established order. [After TITAN.]

ti·tan·ite (tīt'n-īt) n. A mineral, **sphene** (see). [German Titanit : TITAN(IUM) + -ITE.]

ti·ta·ni·um (tī-táyni-əm, ti- || -tánni-) n. Symbol **Ti** A strong, low-density, highly corrosion-resistant, lustrous white metallic element that occurs widely in igneous rocks and is used to alloy aircraft metals for low weight, strength, and high-temperature stability. Atomic number 22, atomic weight 47.90, melting point 1,677°C, boiling point 3,277°C, relative density 4.54, valencies 2, 3, 4. [New Latin, from TITAN. So named by Martin Klaproth who had also named uranium after the planet Uranus. Uranus, in Greek mythology, is the father of the Titans.]

titanium dioxide n. A white powder, TiO_2, used as an opaque white pigment. Also called "titanic acid".

titanium white n. Titanium dioxide used as a paint pigment with great covering power and durability.

ti·tan·o·there (tī-tánnə-theer, -tánnō-) n. Any of various extinct herbivorous mammals of the genus Brontotherium and related genera, of the Eocene and Oligocene epochs, resembling the rhinoceros. [New Latin Titanotherium, "gigantic beast" : TITAN + -THERE.]

ti·tan·ous (tī-tánnəss, ti-, -táynəss) adj. Pertaining to or containing titanium. Said especially of compounds containing titanium with a valency of 3. [TITAN(IUM) + -OUS.]

tit·bit (tit-bit) n. Also U.S. **tid·bit** (tid-). A choice morsel, as of food or gossip.

titch, tich (tich) n. British Informal. A tiny person or thing. [After Little Tich, stage name used by Harry Relph (1867–1928), small English comedian.] —**titch·y** adj.

tit·fer (títfər) n. British Slang. A hat. [Rhyming slang, from tit for tat.]

tit for tat n. Repayment in kind, as for an injury; retaliation. [Variant of earlier tip for tap.]

tithe (tīth) n. **1.** A tenth part of one's annual income or produce, either in kind or money, contributed voluntarily for charitable purposes or due as a tax for the support of the clergy or church. **2.** Any tax or levy of one tenth. **3. a.** The tenth part of something. **b.** A very small part; a fraction. ~tr.v. **tithed, tithing, tithes. 1.** To contribute or pay a tenth part of (one's annual income). **2.** To levy a tithe upon. [Middle English tithe, Old English tēotha, teogetha, TENTH.] —**tith·a·ble** (tĭthəb'l) adj. —**tith·er** (tĭthər) n.

tith·ing (tĭthing) n. **1.** A tithe. **2.** In English history: **a.** A unit consisting of ten householders in the system of **frankpledge** (see). **b.** A rural administrative division originally corresponding to the area occupied by such a unit.

ti·ti (tée-tee || U.S. tee-tée). Any of various small, long-tailed South American monkeys of the genus Callicebus, having long, soft, often brightly coloured fur. [Spanish, perhaps of Tupian origin.]

ti·tian (tísh'n) n. Golden red or auburn. Said of hair. [Often used as a hair colour in paintings by TITIAN.] —**ti·tian** adj.

Ti·tian (tísh'n), born Tiziano Vecellio (téetsi-aánō) (c. 1488–1576). Venetian painter. His greatest works include the altarpiece, The Assumption of the Virgin (1518), the Pesaro Madonna (c. 1520), and Paul III and his Nephews (1546). Titian's brilliant use of colour, and his use of backgrounds, landscapes, and sunsets as part of the composition, made him one of the greatest Renaissance artists.

Ti·ti·ca·ca (títti-kaá-kaa). Lake of South America, lying high in the Andes mountains on the Peru-Bolivia border. It covers some 9 065 square kilometres (3,500 square miles) and is the largest freshwater lake in South America. It is plied by steamboats, and at 3 810 metres (12,500 feet) above sea level, is the world's highest large lake.

tit·il·late (títti-layt) tr.v. **-lated, -lating, -lates. 1.** To stimulate by tickling or touching lightly. **2.** To arouse or excite agreeably. [Latin tītillāre, perhaps akin to titta, TEAT.] —**tit·il·lat·ing·ly** adv. —**tit·il·la·tion** (-láysh'n) n. —**tit·il·la·tive** (-laytiv) adj.

tit·i·vate, tit·ti·vate (títti-vayt) *tr.v.* **-vated, -vating, -vates.** To enhance the appearance of by means of decorative additions; smarten up. [Earlier *tidivate* : perhaps TIDY + (CULTI)VATE.] **—tit·i·va·tion** (-váysh'n) *n.*

tit·lark (tít-laark) *n.* A small bird, the **pipit** *(see).* [TIT(MOUSE) + LARK.]

ti·tle (tī́t'l) *n.* **1.** An identifying name given to a book, play, film, musical composition, work of art, or the like. **2. a.** All the material that appears on the title page of a book. **b.** A general or descriptive heading, as of a book chapter. **c.** A particular book or other publication, rather than any one copy of it: *They publish mainly historical titles.* **3. a.** *Plural.* Written matter included in a film or television programme to give credits. **b.** A subtitle in a cinema film. **4. a.** The heading that names a legal document or statute. **b.** The heading given to any legal action or proceding, showing the name of the court, the name of the parties involved, and other relevant information. **5.** A division of a law book, declaration, or statute, generally larger than a section or article. **6.** *Law.* **a.** The sum of all the factors or events that constitute or justify a person's legal right to control and dispose of property or a claim. **b.** The legal instrument, such as a title deed, that provides evidence of such a right. **7. a.** Anything that provides ground for or justifies a claim. **b.** An acknowledged or alleged right. **8. a.** A formal appellation, such as *Mrs., Dr., Sir,* or *Professor,* prefixed to or substituted for a person's name, and used as a respectful term of address indicating office, rank, or attainment. **b.** Such an appellation as an indication of nobility. **9.** A descriptive appellation; an epithet. **10.** *Sports.* A championship. **11.** Proof that one has a source of income or area of work, as a prerequisite for ordination in the Church of England. **12.** *Roman Catholic Church.* A titular church. —See Synonyms at **right.**
~tr.v. **titled, -tling, -tles.** To give a title to; confer a name upon. [Middle English, from Old French, from Latin *titulus,* superscription, label, title.]

ti·tled (tī́t'ld) *adj.* Having a title, especially of nobility.

title deed *n.* A deed that shows or provides evidence for a person's title to real property.

ti·tle·hold·er (tī́t'l-hōldər) *n.* The unbeaten champion in a particular sporting competition.

title page *n. Abbr.* **t.p.** A page at the front of a book giving the complete title, the names of the author and publisher, and the place of publication.

title role *n.* The part of the character after whom a play or film is named. Also called "name part".

tit·mouse (tít-mowss) *n., pl.* **-mice** (-mīss). A small bird, the **tit** *(see).* [Middle English *titmose*: TIT (bird) + Old English *māse,* titmouse, from West Germanic *maisō* (unattested); assimilated to MOUSE.]

Ti·to (téetō), **Marshal,** born Josip Broz (1892–1980). Communist leader of Yugoslavia. He led the Yugoslav resistance to Nazi occupation from 1941–45. After the war, the Yugoslav monarchy was abolished and Tito became prime minister (1945) and president (1953). In 1948 he broke with the U.S.S.R. and developed Yugoslavia's own brand of national communism, preserving a neutral position in foreign affairs and accepting aid from East and West.

Titograd. See **Podgorica.**

Ti·to·ism (téetō-iz'm) *n.* The Communist policies and practices associated with Marshal Tito of Yugoslavia; especially, the assertion by a Communist state of its national interests independently of and often in opposition to Soviet policy. **—Ti·to·ist** *n. & adj.*

ti·trant (tī́trənt) *n. Chemistry.* The solution added in regulated amounts in a titration. [TITR(E) + -ANT.]

ti·trate (tī-tráyt || *chiefly U.S.* tī́-trayt) *v.* **-trated, -trating, -trates.** *—tr.* To determine the concentration of (a solution) by titration. *—intr.* To perform the operation of titration. [From French *titrer,* from *titre,* TITRE.]

ti·tra·tion (tī-tráysh'n) *n.* **1.** The process or method of determining the concentration of a substance in solution by adding to it a standard reagent of known concentration in carefully measured amounts until a reaction of definite and known proportion is completed, as shown by a colour change or by electrical measurement. **2.** An analogous technique applied to mixtures of gases.

ti·tre, *U.S.* **ti·ter** (tī́tər) *n.* **1.** The concentration of a substance in solution or the strength of such a substance determined by titration. **2.** The minimum volume needed to cause a particular result in titration. **3.** A measure of the amount of antibody present in blood serum. [French, qualification, TITLE (referring to the proportion of gold or silver in an alloy).]

tit·ter (títtər) *intr.v.* **-tered, -tering, -ters.** To utter a nervous, stifled giggle, as in ridicule or childish amusement. [Imitative.] **—tit·ter** *n.* **—tit·ter·er** *n.* **—tit·ter·ing·ly** *adv.*

tittivate. Variant of **titivate.**

tit·tle (títt'l) *n.* **1.** A small diacritical mark, such as an accent, vowel point, or dot over an *i.* **2.** The tiniest bit; an iota. [Middle English *titel,* a diacritical mark, from Medieval Latin *titulus,* from Latin, TITLE.]

tit·tle-tat·tle (títt'l-tatt'l) *n.* Petty gossip; trivial talk.
~intr.v. **tittle-tattled, -tling, -tles.** To engage in idle talk or gossip; prattle. [Reduplication of TATTLE.]

tit·tup (títtəp) *intr.v.* **-tupped** or *U.S.* **-tuped, -tupping** or *U.S.* **-tuping, -tups.** To move in an affected, lively manner; prance.
~n. A lively, affected manner of moving or walking; a prance or caper. [Imitative of the sounds of a horse's hoofs.]

tit·u·ba·tion (títtew-báysh'n) *n.* A staggering or stumbling gait associated with a nodding movement of the head, characteristic of certain nervous disorders. [Latin *titubātiō* (stem *titubātiōn-*), from *titubātus,* past participle of *titubāre*†, to reel, stagger.]

tit·u·lar (títtew-lər) *adj.* **1.** Pertaining to, having the nature of, or constituting a title. **2.** Existing as such in name only; nominal: *the titular head of the company.* **3.** Bearing a title. **4.** Of or designating one of the ancient churches in or near Rome from which a cardinal takes his title.
~n. Also **tit·u·lar·y** (-ləri || -lerri) *pl.* **-ies.** A person who holds a title. [From Latin *titulus,* TITLE.] **—tit·u·lar·ly** *adv.*

titular bishop *n. Roman Catholic Church.* A bishop normally acting as an auxiliary bishop in a diocese, who is nominally appointed to a diocese in a remote part of the world.

Ti·tus (tī́təss) *n. Abbr.* **Tit.** An epistle in the New Testament attributed to Saint Paul and addressed to Titus, his disciple.

Ti·u (tée-ōō). *Germanic Mythology.* The god of war and the sky, identified with the Norse god Tyr. [Old English *Tīw,* from Germanic *Tīwaz* (unattested), akin to Latin *deus,* god. See **Tuesday.**]

Ti·vo·li (tívvə-li; *Italian* téevo-). City in central Italy. It is the site of the Villa d'Este, with its famous Renaissance gardens, built in 1550, and it also has several Roman ruins, including the villa of Emperor Hadrian.

tiz·zy (tízzi) *n., pl.* **-zies.** *Slang.* A state of nervous confusion; a dither. [20th century : origin obscure.]

T-junction (tée-jungksh'n) *n.* A right-angled junction, as of two roads or pipes, forming a shape like the letter T.

TKO technical knockout.

Tl The symbol for the element thallium.

Tlax·ca·la (tlass-kaálə). State in east central Mexico, formerly the territory of the Tlaxcaltec Indians. The state capital, also called Tlaxcala, is the site of the oldest Christian church in the New World, founded by Cortés in 1521.

TLC (tée-el-sée) *n. Informal.* Tender loving care.

Tlin·git (tlíng-git, -kit) *n., pl.* **-gits** or collectively **Tlingit. 1.** A member of any of a group of North American Indian seafaring peoples inhabiting the coastal areas of southern Alaska and northern British Columbia. **2.** A linguistic family of the Na-Dene phylum constituting only the language of the Tlingit.

Tm The symbol for the element thulium.

TM transcendental meditation.

tme·sis (tmée-siss, mée-) *n.* The separation of the parts of a compound word by one or more intervening words; for example, *where I go ever* instead of *wherever I go.* [Late Latin *tmēsis,* "a cutting", from Greek, from *temnein,* to cut.]

TMV tobacco mosaic virus.

TNT *n.* An explosive compound, **trinitrotoluene** *(see).*

to (tōō; *weak forms* tə *before a consonant sound,* tōō *or* tōō *before a vowel sound* || *The weak form* tə *is also to be heard before a vowel, particularly in U.S. speech; also* ti *in Scottish English.*) *prep.* **1.** In a direction towards; so as to approach or come near: *the road to Paris; bear to the right.* **2.** So as to reach or terminate in: *a trip to Paris.* **3.** Altogether and including: *drunk to the last man.* **4.** Through an intervening space or time; right up until: *a nine-to-five job; rotten to the core.* **5.** Through a standard intervening series or arrangement and terminating in: *from A to Z; strong to gale force winds.* **6.** To the extent of: *starved to death.* **7.** In contact with: *dancing cheek to cheek; apply polish to the shoes.* **8.** In front of: *face to face.* **9.** For the attention, benefit, or possession of: *Tell it to me.* **10.** For the purpose of; for: *She worked to that end.* **11.** For, of, or associated with: *the belt to this dress; secretary to the director.* **12.** Concerning or regarding; in response to: *deaf to her pleas.* **13.** In relation with: *parallel to the road.* **14.** Together with or as an accompaniment or addition for: *Sing to the music.* **15.** With regard to: *the way to his heart.* **16.** Composing or constituting; in: *two pints to the quart.* **17.** In correspondence or accordance with: *not to my liking; add sugar to taste.* **18.** So as to reach a specified total or result: *The bill came to £18; all adds up to a remarkable victory.* **19.** Before: *ten to five; only three weeks to Christmas.* **20.** In honour of: *a toast to his success.* **21.** Used in expressions of comparison or contrast: *bears no resemblance to the original plan; won by four goals to two; odds of 20 to 1.* **22.** Used to indicate: **a.** A progression towards a specified condition: *her rise to power.* **b.** An action resulting in a specified condition: *The flag was torn to shreds; To my amazement, he agreed.* **c.** A process of change resulting in a specified condition: *Their laughter soon turned to tears.*
~adv. **1.** Into a position or condition, especially shut or closed: *He slammed the door to.* **2.** Into consciousness: *He came to.* **3.** Into a state of application to the matter, action, or work at hand: *We sat down for lunch and fell to.* **4.** In proximity: *have never seen him close to.* **5.** *Nautical.* Turned into the wind. Used of a sailing vessel. [Middle English *to,* Old English *tō, te.*]

Usage: The use of *to* in place of an infinitive form of the verb is common at the ends of sentences in informal English: *You can go if you want to; Sing if you have to.* Formal English would either drop the *to* or use an alternative form *(Sing if you must).* Of course, the *to* must be retained in such constructions as *They work harder than they seem to* or *I'll go if you want me to.* See also Usage note at **try.**

toad (tōd) *n.* **1.** Any of numerous tailless amphibians chiefly of the family Bufonidae, related to and resembling the frogs but characteristically more terrestrial and having rougher, drier skin. Compare **horned toad** *(see).* **2.** A repulsive person. [Middle English *tadde, tode,* Old English *tādi(g)e*†.]

toad·eat·er (tōd-eetər) *n.* A toady. [Originally, a charlatan's attendant who was hired to pretend to eat toads (thought to be poisonous) to prove that the charlatan could easily expel the poison.]

toad·fish (tŏd-fish) *n., pl.* **toadfish** or **-fishes.** Any of various bottom-dwelling, chiefly marine fishes of the family Batrachoididae, having a broad, flattened head and a wide mouth.

toad·flax (tŏd-flaks) *n.* Any of various plants of the genus *Linaria,* having narrow leaves and spurred, two-lipped flowers; especially, *L. vulgaris.* Also *chiefly U.S.* "butter and eggs". [TOAD + FLAX (from the flaxlike appearance of its foliage).]

toad-in-the-hole (tŏd-in-thə-hŏl) *n. British.* A dish consisting of sausages baked in a batter.

toad spit *n.* An insect secretion, **cuckoo spit** *(see).*

toad·stone (tŏd-stōn) *n.* Dark coloured basaltic or glassy volcanic rock. It is often associated with mineral veins, but contains no ore. [Probably from German, *Tödestein,* dead or worthless stone.]

toad·stool (tŏd-stōol) *n.* An inedible fungus with an umbrella-shaped fruiting body, as distinguished from an edible mushroom. [Middle English *todestool* : *tode,* TOAD + STOOL (from its stool-like shape and the popular association of it with toads, which were thought to be poisonous).]

toad·y (tŏdi) *n., pl.* **-ies.** A servile flatterer; a sycophant. See Synonyms at **sycophant.**
~*v.* **toadied, -ying, -ies.** —*tr.* To be a toady to. —*intr.* To be a toady; fawn. [From TOADEATER.]

to and fro *adv.* In one direction and then the opposite; back and forth. [TO (adverb) + *fro,* Middle English, from Old Norse *frā,* FROM.] —**to-and-fro** (tōō-ən-frŏ) *adv.*

toast¹ (tōst) *v.* **toasted, toasting, toasts.** —*tr.* **1.** To heat and brown (bread, for example) by placing close to a fire, under a grill, or in a toaster. **2.** To warm thoroughly, as before a fire: *toast one's feet.* —*intr.* To become toasted.
~*n.* Sliced bread heated and browned. [Middle English *tosten,* from Old French *toster,* from Vulgar Latin *tostāre* (unattested), from Latin *torrēre* (past participle *tostus*), to dry, parch.]

toast² *n.* **1.** A person, institution, sentiment, or the like to whose health or in whose honour a group of people drink. **2.** The act of proposing to toast the health or honour of a person or thing. **3.** One receiving much acclaim. **4.** *Archaic.* A lady to whose beauty or charms toasts are frequently proposed.
~*v.* **toasted, toasting, toasts.** —*tr.* To drink to the health or honour of. —*intr.* To propose or drink a toast. [From TOAST¹ (from the notion that the name of the lady (sense 4) could flavour the drink like a piece of spiced toast).]

toast·er (tōstər) *n.* A device used to toast bread by exposure to electrically heated wire coils.

toast·ing fork (tōsting) *n.* A long-handled fork, on the prongs of which slices of bread, crumpets, or the like, may be placed and toasted in front of a fire.

toast·mas·ter (tōst-maastər ‖ -mastər) *n.* One who proposes the toasts and introduces the guests or speakers at a banquet.

to·bac·co (tə-băckŏ) *n., pl.* **-cos** or **-coes.** **1.** Any of various plants of the genus *Nicotiana;* especially, *N. tabacum,* native to tropical America, widely cultivated for its leaves, which are used primarily for smoking. **2.** The leaves of cultivated tobacco, dried and processed chiefly for use in cigarettes, snuff, or cigars, or for smoking in pipes. **3.** Products made from tobacco. [Earlier *tabac(c)o,* from Spanish *tabaco,* perhaps from a Taino word referring to leaves rolled for smoking (taken by the Spanish as referring to the plant itself).]

tobacco mosaic virus *n. Abbr.* **TMV** The virus that causes mosaic disease in tobacco plants and the first virus to be discovered (1892).

to·bac·co·nist (tə-băcknist) *n.* **1.** *Chiefly British.* A shopkeeper who sells tobacco, cigarettes, pipes, matches, and other equipment used by smokers. **2.** A dealer in tobacco. [Irregularly from TOBACCO + -IST.]

Tobago Island. See **Trinidad and Tobago.**

to-be (tə-bée, tōō-) *adj.* That is to be; future. Usually used in combination: *bride-to-be.*

To·bit (tŏbit) *n.* A book of the Old Testament Apocrypha, named after its hero, a Hebrew captive in Nineveh. Also called "Tobias".

to·bog·gan (tə-bŏggən) *n.* **1.** A long, light, runnerless vehicle made of thin boards curved upwards at the front, originally used by Canadian Indians and used for transporting goods over snow and ice. **2.** A similar vehicle, often equipped with runners used for coasting down slopes. In this sense, also called "sledge".
~*intr.v.* **tobogganed, -ganing, -gans.** To coast, ride, or travel on a toboggan. [Canadian French *tobagan,* from Algonquian; compare Micmac *tobākan.*] —**to·bog·gan·er, to·bog·gan·ist** *n.*

Toby jug (tŏbi) *n.* A drinking mug usually in the shape of a stout man wearing a large three-cornered hat. Also called "Toby". [From *Toby,* pet form of *Tobias.*]

toc·ca·ta (tə-kaátə, tŏ-) *n.* A composition, for organ or other keyboard instrument, in a free style intended to show off the technical virtuosity of the performer. [Italian, "a touching" (originally a piece intended to show touch technique), from the feminine past participle of *toccare,* to touch, from Vulgar Latin *toccāre* (unattested), to strike, TOUCH.]

Toc H (tŏk āych) *n.* A Christian fellowship founded in 1915 and devoted to social service. [From obsolete telegraphic code for initials *T.H.,* for *Talbot House,* original headquarters of the fellowship in Poperinge, Belgium.]

To·char·i·an, To·khar·i·an (to-kaári-ən, tə-, -kaír-i-) *n.* **1.** A member of a people of possible European origin, with an advanced culture, living in Asia until about the tenth century A.D. **2.** An Indo-European language with eastern and western dialects, *Tocharian A* and *Tocharian B* respectively, known chiefly from Buddhist scriptures written in the Brahmi script of Northern India. [French *Tocharien,* from Latin *Tochari,* from Greek *Tokharoi*†.]

to·col·o·gy, to·kol·o·gy (to-kólləji, tə- ‖ tō-) *n.* Obstetrics. [Greek *tokos,* childbirth, from *tiktein,* to beget + -LOGY.]

to·coph·er·ol (to-kóffə-rol, tə- ‖ tō-, -ōl) *n.* Any of a group of four chemically related compounds, differing slightly in structure, that together constitute **vitamin E** *(see).* Deficiency leads to sterility in rodents, and the vitamin is thought to be necessary for fertility in other vertebrates. [Greek *tokos,* childbirth (see **tocology**) + Greek *pherein,* to carry, bear + -OL.]

toc·sin (tóksin) *n.* **1.** An alarm sounded on a bell, or the bell on which it is sounded. **2.** Any warning sign; an omen. [French, from Old French *toquesain,* from Old Provençal *tocasenh* : *tocar,* to strike (a bell), touch, from Vulgar Latin *toccāre* (unattested), to ring a bell, TOUCH + *senh,* bell, from Latin *signum,* token, SIGN.]

tod¹ (tod) *n.* **1.** A unit of weight used in the wool trade, usually equivalent to 28 pounds. **2.** *British.* A bushy clump, especially of ivy. [Middle English *todd(e),* a unit of weight, probably from Low Dutch; akin to Middle Low German *toddelen,* to fall apart into bunches, and Old High German *zot(t)a,* a tuft, from Germanic *toddōn* (unattested).]

tod² *n. Northern British.* A fox. [Middle English : origin obscure.]

tod³ *n.* **—on (one's) tod.** *British Slang.* Alone; on one's own. [Probably rhyming slang, from *Tod Sloan* (the name of a jockey), *alone.*]

to-day (tə-dáy, tōō-) *adv.* **1.** During or on this present day. **2.** During or at the present time.
~*n.* The present day, time, or age. [Middle English *to day,* Old English *tōdǣg(e),* on this day : TO + *dǣge,* dative of *dǣg,* DAY.]

tod·dle (tódd'l) *intr.v.* **-dled, -dling, -dles. 1.** To walk with short, unsteady steps, as a small child does. **2.** *Informal.* **a.** To go; walk: *toddle down to the pub.* **b.** To depart: *must toddle off.* [16th century (Scottish and northern English) : origin obscure.] —**tod·dle** *n.*

tod·dler (tóddlər) *n.* A child who has learned to walk but not yet perfectly.

tod·dy (tódi) *n., pl.* **-dies. 1.** A drink consisting of whisky or other spirits combined with hot water, sugar, spices, and lemon. Also called "hot toddy". **2. a.** The sweet sap of several tropical Asian palm trees, especially *Caryota urens,* used as a drink and as a leavening agent. **b.** An alcoholic drink fermented from this sap. [Earlier also *tarry,* from Hindi *tārī,* sap of a palm, from *tār,* palm yielding toddy, from Sanskrit *tāla, tāra,* probably from Dravidian; akin to Kannada *taṛ,* Telegu *tāḍu.*]

to-do (tə-dōō, tōō-) *n., pl.* **-dos** (-z). *Informal.* A commotion or fuss. [From the infinitive *to do* (as in phrases *much to do, more to do*), but in sense influenced by ADO.]

to·dy (tódi) *n., pl.* **-dies.** Any of various small, colourful birds of the family Todidae, of the West Indies. [French *todier,* from Latin *todus*†, name of a small bird.]

toe (tō) *n.* **1. a.** Any of the digits of the human foot. **b.** The corresponding digit in other vertebrate animals. **2.** The part of a shoe, sock, or the like that covers the toes. **3. a.** The base or lower tip of something, such as the end of the head on a golf club. **b.** Anything suggestive of a toe in form, function, or location. **—on (one's) toes.** Alert; ready to act. **—tread on (someone's) toes.** To offend or annoy someone, often accidentally, especially by interfering in his sphere of action or responsibility.
~*v.* **toed, toeing, toes.** —*tr.* **1.** To touch, kick, or trace with the toe. **2.** To drive (a golf ball) with the toe of the club. **3. a.** To drive (a nail or spike, for example) obliquely. **b.** To secure (beams, for example) with nails driven obliquely. —*intr.* To walk or move with the toes pointed in a specified direction: *He toes out.* [Middle English *ta, to,* Old English *tā.*]

to·e·a (tó-i-ə) *n.* A monetary unit of Papua, New Guinea, 1/100 of a kina. [From a Papuan language.]

toe·cap (tó-kap) *n.* A reinforced covering of leather or metal for the toe of a shoe or boot.

toe clip *n.* An attachment to a bicycle pedal that fits over the foot to prevent it from slipping.

toed (tōd) *adj.* Having a toe or toes, especially of the specified kind or number. Usually used in combination: *a two-toed sloth.*

toe·hold (tó-hōld) *n.* **1.** A small indentation or ledge on which the toe can find support in climbing; a small foothold. **2.** Any slight or initial advantage or means of access providing a basis for future progress: *Family connections gave him a toehold in politics.* **3.** A wrestling hold in which one competitor wrenches the other's foot.

toe-in (tó-in) *n.* The adjustment of the front wheels of a motor vehicle so that they turn slightly inwards, done to improve steering and minimise tyre wear.

toe·nail (tó-nayl) *n.* **1.** The nail on a toe. **2.** A nail driven obliquely, as to join vertical and horizontal beams.
~*tr.v.* **toenailed, -nailing, -nails.** To secure (beams) with obliquely driven nails.

toe rag *n. British Slang.* A person considered beneath contempt.

toff (tof) *n. British Slang.* **1.** A dandy; a swell. **2.** Any member of the upper classes. [Probably variant of TUFT, a titled undergraduate (from the gold tassel formerly worn on caps by titled students.]

tof·fee (tóffi ‖ táwfi) *n., pl.* **-fies. 1.** A hard or chewy sweet substance made of sugar and butter boiled together. **2.** A small piece of this. **—for toffee.** In any way to any degree. Used to indicate a person's complete lack of competence in a specified field: *can't draw for toffee.* [Variant of TAFFY.]

tof·fee-ap·ple (tóffi-ápp'l) *n.* An apple coated with brittle toffee, usually fixed on the end of a thin stick.

tof·fee-nosed (tóffi-nōzd) *adj. Chiefly British Slang.* Snobbish; stuck-up.

toft (toft ‖ tawft) *n. British Archaic.* **1.** A homestead. **2.** A hillock. [Middle English *toft,* Old English *toft,* site of a building, homestead, from Old Norse *topt.*]

to·fu (tō-fōō) *n.* Bean curd *(see).* [Japanese, from Chinese.]

tog¹ (tog) *n. Informal.* **1.** A coat or cloak. **2.** *Plural.* Clothes. ~*tr.v.* **togged, togging, togs.** *Informal.* To dress or clothe. Often used with *up* or *out.* [Short for 16th-century cant *togeman(s), togman :* probably obsolete *toge,* cloak, from Middle English, from Old French *tog(u)e,* from Latin *toga,* TOGA + *-mans†,* a cant noun suffix.]

tog², TOG *n.* A unit of thermal resistance or insulation used in assessing the warmth of fabrics, continental quilts, and the like: *"I have a duvet ... and it's 13 tog!"* (*Radio Times*). [Probably from *togs* (clothes). See **tog¹.**]

to·ga (tō-gə) *n., pl.* **-gas. 1.** A draped one-piece outer garment worn in public by citizens of ancient Rome. **2.** Any robe or gown characteristic of a particular office or profession. [Latin, from *tegere,* to cover.] —**to·gaed** (tō-gəd) *adj.*

to·geth·er (tə-géthər, tōō-) *adv.* **1.** In or into a single group, body, mass, or place: *We gather together; stick it together with glue.* **2.** Against or in contact with one another: *He rubbed his hands together.* **3.** One with another; mutually or reciprocally: *The shirt and tie go well together.* **4.** Regarded collectively; in total: *She is worth more than all of us together.* **5.** Simultaneously: *All the bells rang out together.* **6.** In uninterrupted succession; at a stretch: *drunk for days together.* **7.** In harmony or accord: *We stand together on this issue.* **8.** *Informal.* **a.** In or into a coherent, compact, well-ordered aggregation: *Try to get your ideas together; got all my bits and pieces together.* **b.** In or into a state of self-possession or effective operation: *Pull yourself together; to get a show together at short notice.* —**get it together.** *Informal.* To manage to act effectively. —**together with.** As well as; and in addition. ~*adj. Slang.* **1.** Stable and well-organised; self-possessed. **2.** Unified and performing effectively. [Middle English *togeder(e),* Old English *tōgædere :* TO + *gad-* (unattested), as in *gæd,* fellowship; akin to GATHER.]

Usage: When *together with* is used following the subject of a sentence, it does not in formal English alter the relationship between the subject and the verb. Thus, in the sentence *The king, together with the two princes, is expected to arrive tonight,* the verb remains in the singular, agreeing with *king,* despite the plural noun following. A similar rule applies to such other phrases as *in addition to, as well as,* and *along with.* In informal speech, however, the proximity of the plural noun to the verb in such cases often prompts the use of a plural form of the verb.

to·geth·er·ness (tə-géthər-nəss, tōō-, -niss) *n.* The quality of being in close relationship or harmony; comradeship or intimacy.

tog·ger·y (tóggəri) *n., pl.* **-ies.** *Informal.* Clothing; togs.

tog·gle (tógg'l) *n.* **1.** A device used to secure or hold something, especially: **a.** A pin inserted in a nautical knot to keep it from slipping. **b.** A bar-shaped crosspiece, such as a button on a duffel coat, attached to the end of or inserted in a loop in a rope, chain, or strap to prevent slipping, to tighten, or to fasten. **2.** An apparatus having a toggle joint. ~*tr.v.* **toggled, -gling, -gles.** To furnish or fasten with a toggle or toggles. [18th century (nautical use) : origin obscure.]

toggle bolt *n.* A fastener consisting of a threaded bolt and a mated toggle.

toggle joint *n.* An elbow-like joint composed of two arms pivoted so that a force applied to their hinge to straighten them produces an outward force at the ends.

toggle switch *n.* A switch in which a projecting lever employing a toggle joint with a spring is used to open or close an electric circuit.

To·go, Republic of (tō-gō) *French.* **République Togolaise** (-layz, -lez). State of West Africa on the Gulf of Guinea. Coffee and cocoa are exported, but the economy is dominated by minerals, with phosphates accounting for 40 per cent of exports. Formerly the German protectorate of Togoland (1894–1914), the area was then divided between Britain and France. In 1956 the west voted to join Ghana on its independence (1957). French Togo became independent as the Republic of Togo in 1960. From 1967 to 1993 the country was a one-party state under General Eyadema, who returned to power in subsequent elections. Area, 56 785 square kilometres (21,919 square miles). Population, 4,200,000. Capital, Lomé. See map at **West African States.** —**To·go·lese** (-leez) *n. & adj.*

to·he·ro·a (tō-ə-rṓ-ə) *n.* **1.** A New Zealand bivalve mollusc, *Amphidesma ventricosum.* **2.** A soup made from this mollusc.

toil¹ (toyl) *intr.v.* **toiled, toiling, toils. 1.** To labour continuously and untiringly; work strenuously. **2.** To proceed or make one's way with difficulty, pain, or strenuous effort: *toiling over the mountains.* ~*n.* **1.** Exhausting labour or effort. **2.** *Archaic.* Strife; contention. —See Synonyms at **work.** [Middle English *toilen,* to struggle, to battle, from Anglo-French *toiler,* Old French *tooilier,* to stir, agitate, from Latin *tudiculāre,* to stir about, from *tudicula,* a mill for crushing olives, diminutive of *tudes,* a hammer.]

toil² *n.* **1.** *Archaic.* A long net or a series of nets for trapping game. **2.** *Usually plural.* Anything in which one is trapped or caught up.

[Old French *toile,* a net, from Latin *tēla;* akin to *texere,* to weave.]

toile (twaal) *n.* **1.** A sheer linen fabric. **2.** A copy of a garment made up using inexpensive material, so that alterations can be made to the design. [French, cloth, net. See **toil** (net).]

toi·let (tóy-lət, -lit) *n.* Also **toi·lette** (twaa-lét) (for senses 2, 4) **1.** A lavatory *(see).* **2.** The act or process of grooming and dressing oneself. **3. a.** The articles used in making one's toilet. **b.** A dressing table. **4.** *Archaic.* A person's style of dress. **5.** The cleansing of a bodily part, as after an operation. [French *toilette,* lavatory, dressing table, from Old French, cloth cover for a dressing table, a dressing table, diminutive of TOILE.]

toilet paper *n.* Thin, absorbent paper, usually in rolls, used for cleansing oneself after defecation or urination. Also called "toilet tissue"; "lavatory paper".

toilet roll *n.* **1.** A length of toilet paper rolled round a cylindrical cardboard tube. **2.** The cardboard tube.

toi·let·ry (tóylətri) *n., pl.* **-ries.** Any article or cosmetic used in dressing or grooming oneself.

toilet set *n.* A matching set of implements used in dressing and grooming, typically consisting of a hand mirror, a hairbrush, a comb, and a clothes brush.

toilet training *n.* The process of training a small child the voluntary control of bladder and bowel movements. —**toi·let-train** (tóy-lət-trayn, -lit-) *tr.v.*

toilet water *n.* Cologne or mild perfume.

toil·some (tóyl-s'm) *adj.* Characterised by or requiring toil; done with difficulty. —**toil·some·ly** *adv.* —**toil·some·ness** *n.*

to-ing and fro-ing (tōō-ing ən frṓ-ing) *n., pl.* **to-ings and fro-ings.** Busy movement back and forth.

to·kay (tō-kay) *n.* A tropical Asian lizard, *Gekko gecko.* See **gecko.** [From Malay *toke* (imitative of its cry).]

To·kay (tō-kī́, tō-, -káy) *n.* **1.** A variety of grape originally grown near Tokay, Hungary. **2.** A sweet wine made from these grapes.

toke (tōk) *n. Slang.* A puff on a cigarette or, especially, a joint (a cannabis cigarette). [20th century : origin obscure.]

To·ke·lau Islands (tókəlow). Group of three atolls in the south central Pacific Ocean, formerly belonging to the Gilbert and Ellice Islands Colony, but since 1948 part of New Zealand. The islands' only product is copra.

to·ken (tókən) *n.* **1.** Something that serves as an indication or representation, as of some fact, event, or emotion; a sign; a symbol. **2.** Something that tangibly signifies something, such as authority, validity, or identity: *The sceptre is a token of kingship.* **3.** A keepsake or souvenir. **4.** A piece of stamped metal or plastic used as a substitute for a coin, as in a public telephone, slot machine, or the like. **5.** A voucher exchangeable for a specified commodity of a stated value: *a record token.* —See Synonyms at **sign.** —**by the same token.** In the same manner; likewise. ~*tr.v.* **tokened, -kening, -kens.** To signify, betoken, or symbolise. ~*adj.* **1.** Done, made, or undertaken as a token, as of good faith or strength of feeling: *a token payment; a token strike.* **2. a.** Purely for the sake of form; nominal; perfunctory: *token resistance.* **b.** Indicative of minimal effort to comply with a statutory requirement or fulfil a moral obligation: *a token woman on the board.* [Middle English *taken, token,* Old English *tāc(e)n.*]

to·ken·ism (tókən-iz'm) *n.* The practice or policy of making only a superficial effort or symbolic gesture towards the accomplishment of a goal, such as racial integration.

Tokharian. Variant of **Tocharian.**

tokology. Variant of **tocology.**

To·kyo (tóki-ō, tōk-yō). Capital of Japan, and one of the world's largest cities, situated in east central Honshu at the head of Tokyo Bay. It has extensive industrial complexes, and is the financial, administrative, educational, and cultural centre of Japan. Founded on the 12th-century village of Edo, it has been extensively rebuilt since World War II, and is now one of the most modern cities. Its seaport is Yokohama.

to·la (tólə) *n.* A unit of weight used in India, equal to the weight of one silver rupee, or 180 troy grains. [Hindi *tolā,* from Sanskrit *tulā,* balance, weight.]

tol·booth, toll·booth (tól-bōōth, -bōōth ‖ tól-, -bəth) *n.* **1.** *Scottish.* A town hall. **2.** *Scottish.* A prison. **3.** *U.S.* A booth at a tollgate where the toll is collected. [Middle English *tolbothe,* toll station, tax-collection booth, town hall (beneath which there were prison cells) : TOLL + BOOTH.]

tol·bu·ta·mide (tol-béwtə-mīd ‖ tōl-) *n.* A white powder, $C_{12}H_{18}N_2O_3S$, administered by mouth in the treatment of diabetes. [TOL(U) + BUT(YRIC ACID) + AMIDE.]

told. Past tense and past participle of **tell.**

tole, tôle (tōl) *n.* Lacquered or enamelled metalware, usually gilded, popular in the 18th century. [French *tôle,* sheet metal, sheet iron, from French dialect, a slab, table, variant of *table,* from Latin *tabula,* a board. See **table.**]

To·le·do (to-láydō, tə-). Capital of Toledo province, central Spain, situated on the river Tagus. It was an important Roman city, the capital of the Visigoth kingdom (534–712), and a Moorish provincial capital (712–1031), when it became famous as a centre of Arab and Hebrew learning. It was reconquered by El Cid and Alfonso VI of León and Castile (1085).

tol·er·a·ble (tól-rəb'l) *adj.* **1.** Able to be tolerated; endurable. **2.** Fair or adequate; passable. —See Synonyms at **average.** [Middle English, from Old French, from Latin *tolerābilis.* See **tolerate.**] —**tol·er·a·bil·i·ty** (-rə-bílləti), **tol·er·a·ble·ness** *n.* —**tol·er·a·bly** *adv.*

tol·er·ance (tóllərənss) *n.* **1.** A disposition towards or capacity for allowing or respecting the beliefs or behaviour of others when these differ from one's own. **2. a.** Leeway for variation from a standard. **b.** The permissible deviation from a specified value of a structural dimension. **3.** The capacity to endure hardship or pain; endurance. **4. a.** Physiological resistance to poison. **b.** The capacity to absorb a drug continuously or in large doses without experiencing its pharmacological effects. [Middle English, from Old French, from Latin *tolerantia.* See **tolerate.**]

tol·er·ant (tóllərənt) *adj.* **1.** Inclined to tolerate the beliefs or behaviour of others; forbearing. **2.** Able to withstand or endure an adverse environmental condition. [From French *tolérant,* present participle of *tolérer,* to tolerate.] **—tol·er·ant·ly** *adv.*

tol·er·ate (tóllə-rayt) *tr.v.* **-ated, -ating, -ates. 1.** To show tolerance towards; especially, to allow (beliefs or practises that differ from one's own) to exist without interference or prohibition. **2.** To put up with; endure or countenance: *would not tolerate laziness.* **3.** *Medicine.* To have tolerance for (a drug or poison). **—See** Synonyms at **bear.** [From Latin *tolerāre,* to bear, tolerate.] **—tol·er·a·tive** (-rətiv, -raytiv) *adj.* **—tol·er·a·tor** (-raytər) *n.*

tol·er·a·tion (tóllə-ráysh'n) *n.* **1.** The act of tolerating or inclination to tolerate. **2.** Official recognition of the rights of individuals and groups to hold dissenting opinions, especially on religion. [From French, from Latin *tolerātio* (stem *tolerātiōn-*). See **tolerate.**]

tol·i·dine (tólli-deen) *n.* Any of several isomeric bases, (H₂NC₆H₃CH₃)₂, derived from toluene, used in the manufacture of dyes and synthetic resins. [TOL(UENE) + -ID(E) + -INE.]

toll¹ (tōl ‖ tol) *n.* **1.** A fixed charge or tax for an access or privilege, especially for passage across a bridge or along a road. **2.** An amount or loss, as of lives, property, or health, incurred as a result of war, disaster, or other adverse condition: *took a heavy toll in lives.* **3.** *U.S.* A charge for a long-distance telephone call. *~tr.v.* **tolled, tolling, tolls.** *Rare.* To exact as a toll. [Middle English *tol(le),* Old English *toll,* from Late Latin *tolonium, telōnium,* a tolbooth, customhouse, from Greek *telōnion,* from *telos,* tax.]

toll² *v.* **tolled, tolling, tolls.** *—tr.* **1.** To sound (a large bell) slowly at regular intervals. **2.** To announce or summon by tolling. *—intr.* To ring with slow and regular strokes. Used of a bell. *~n.* **1.** The act of tolling. **2.** The sound of a tolling bell. [Middle English *tollen,* probably special use of *tollen, tullen,* to entice, lure, perhaps Old English *tollian* (unattested), perhaps from Germanic *tull* (unattested).]

tollbooth. Variant of **tolbooth.**

toll·bridge (tōl-brij ‖ tól-) *n.* A bridge at which a toll is charged before crossing.

toll·gate (tōl-gayt ‖ tól-) *n.* A gate barring passage to a road, tunnel, or bridge until a toll is collected.

toll·house (tōl-howss ‖ tól-) *n.* A house occupied by the toll collector adjoining a tollgate.

Tol·stoy (tól-stoy), **Count Leo Nikolayevich** (1828–1910). Russian writer. He served in the Crimean War, and travelled extensively, before settling down on his family estate as a reforming landlord, religious philosopher, and novelist. At least two of his novels, *War and Peace* (1869) and *Anna Karenina* (1876) are widely thought to be among the greatest ever written.

Tol·tec (tól-tek ‖ tōl-) *n., pl.* **-tecs** or collectively **Toltec.** A member of an ancient Nahuatl people of central and southern Mexico whose culture flourished in about A.D. 1000. **—Tol·tec, Tol·tec·an** (tol-téckən ‖ tōl-) *adj.*

to·lu (tō-lōō, tə-, -léw) *n.* An aromatic resin, obtained from the tree *Myroxylon balsamum,* of South America. [Spanish *tolú,* from Santiago de *Tolú,* Colombia, its place of origin.]

tol·u·ene (tóllew-een) *n.* A colourless flammable liquid, CH₃C₆H₅, obtained from coal tar or petroleum and used in aviation and other high-octane fuels, in dyestuffs, explosives, and as a solvent for gums and lacquers. Also called "methylbenzene", "toluol". [TOLU (from which it was originally obtained) + -ENE.]

to·lu·i·dine (tō-léw-i-deen, tə-, -lōō-) *n.* Any of three isomeric compounds, H₂NC₆H₄CH₃, used to make dyes. [TOLU(ENE) + -ID(E) + -INE.]

tol·u·ol (tóllew-ol ‖ -ōl) *n.* Toluene. [TOLU + -OL.]

tol·yl (tóllil) *n.* The univalent organic radical CH₃C₆H₄. [TOL(U) + -YL.]

tom¹ (tom) *n.* The male of various animals; especially, a male cat that has not been neutered. *~adj.* Male. [From the name *Tom.*]

tom² *n.* Also **tam** (tam). A hat, typically worn by Rastafarians to cover dreadlocks, with a large, baglike crown. [From TAM.]

tom·a·hawk (tómmə-hawk) *n.* **1.** A light axe used as a tool or weapon by North American Indians. **2.** Any similar implement or weapon. **3.** *Australian.* A hatchet. *~tr.v.* **tomahawked, -hawking, -hawks. 1.** To attack or kill with or as if with a tomahawk. **2.** *Australian.* To shear (a sheep) roughly, as if using a hatchet. [Virginia Algonquian *tamahaac, tamohake :* Proto-Algonquian *temah-* (unattested), to cut off by tool + *-aakan* (unattested), noun suffix.]

tom·al·ley (tóm-al-i, tə-mál-i) *n., pl.* **-leys.** The liver of a lobster, esteemed as a culinary delicacy. [Of Cariban origin, akin to Carib *tumali,* sauce of lobster or crab liver.]

to·ma·to (tə-maátō ‖ chiefly *U.S.* -máytō) *n., pl.* **-toes. 1.** A plant, *Lycopersicon esculentum,* native to South America, widely cultivated for its edible, fleshy, usually red fruit. **2.** The fruit of this plant. [Variant of earlier *tomate,* from Spanish, from Nahuatl *tomatl.*]

tomb (tōōm) *n.* **1.** A vault or chamber serving as a repository for a dead body. **2.** Any grave or place of burial. **3.** A monument commemorating the dead. [Middle English *t(o)umbe,* from Anglo-French *tumbe,* Old French *tombe,* from Late Latin *tumba,* sepulchral mound, from Greek *tumbos.*]

tom·bac (tóm-bak) *n.* Any one of several alloys of copper and zinc, used in making inexpensive jewellery. [French, from Dutch *tombak,* from Malay *tambāga,* copper.]

tom·bo·la (tom-bōlə, tómbələ) *n. Chiefly British.* **1.** A lottery game in which winning tickets are drawn out of a revolving container. **2.** A simple form of the game of **bingo** *(see).* [Probably from Italian, from *tombolare,* to tumble.]

Tombouctou. See **Timbuktu.**

tom·boy (tóm-boy) *n.* A high-spirited girl who prefers boys' games to those conventionally played by girls. [TOM (male) + BOY.] **—tom·boy·ish** *adj.*

tomb·stone (tōōm-stōn) *n.* A stone or monument, usually inscribed, marking a grave; a gravestone.

tom·cat (tóm-kat, -kát) *n.* A male cat, especially one that has not been neutered. [After *Tom,* hero of the anonymous work *The Life and Adventures of a Cat* (1760).]

Tom Col·lins (kóllinz) *n.* A cocktail of gin, lemon or lime juice, soda water, and sugar. [Said to be the name of the barman who invented it.]

Tom, Dick, and Harry *n.* Anyone at all; any man taken at random: *Every Tom, Dick, and Harry came to the party.*

tome (tōm) *n.* **1.** A book; especially, a weighty or scholarly book. Often used humorously. **2.** *Archaic.* One of the books in a work of several volumes. [French, from Latin *tomus,* cut, tome, roll of paper, from Greek *tomos,* from *temnein,* to cut, slice.]

-tome *n. comb. form.* Indicates a cutting instrument; for example, **microtome.** [From New Latin *-tomus,* from Greek *-tomos,* a cutting, from *temnein,* to cut.]

to·men·tose (tə-mént-ōz, tō-, -ōss, also tómənt-) *adj. Biology.* Covered with dense, short, matted hairs. [New Latin *tomentosus,* from Latin *tōmentum,* cushion stuffing, TOMENTUM.]

to·men·tum (tə-mén-təm, tō-) *n., pl.* **-ta** (-tə). **1.** *Anatomy.* A network of extremely small blood vessels in the brain passing between the pia mater and cerebral cortex. **2.** *Biology.* A covering of closely matted woolly hairs. [New Latin, from Latin *tōmentum†,* cushion stuffing.]

tom·fool (tóm-fōōl) *n.* A stupid or foolish person; a blockhead. *~adj.* Extremely foolish. [Middle English : *Tom* (name) + FOOL.]

tom·fool·er·y (tóm-fōōləri) *n., pl.* **-ies. 1.** Foolish behaviour. **2.** Something trivial or foolish; nonsense.

tom·my (tómmi) *n., pl.* **-mies.** *British Informal.* **1.** A British soldier, especially a private; a Tommy Atkins. **2.** *Archaic.* A workman's provisions. [From *Tommy,* pet form of *Tom* (name).]

Tommy At·kins (átkinz) *n.* A private of the regular British army. Also called "Tommy", "tommy". [Originally a name used in sample forms for privates in the British army.]

tommy bar *n.* A short metal bar used as a lever to turn a socket spanner or similar tool.

Tommy gun *n.* A **Thompson submachine gun** *(see).*

tom·my·rot (tómmi-rot) *n. Informal.* Utter foolishness; nonsense. [*Tommy,* pet form of *Tom* + ROT.]

to·mog·ra·phy (tə-móggrəfi, to-, tō-) *n.* Any of several techniques for making X-ray pictures of a predetermined plane section of a solid object by blurring out the images of other planes. [Greek *tomos,* a cut, section (see **tome**) + -GRAPHY.]

to·mor·row (tə-mórrō, tōō- ‖ -máwrō) *n.* **1.** The day following today. **2.** The future, especially the near future. *~adv.* On the day following today. [Middle English *to morġe, to mor(o)we,* Old English *tō morgen(ne)* : TO (at, on) + *morgenne,* dative of *morgen,* MORROW.]

tompion. Variant of **tampion.**

Tom Thumb *n.* **1.** A diminutive hero of English folklore. **2.** A tiny person; a midget.

tom·tit (tóm-tit, -tít) *n. British.* A tit or other small bird, especially a bluetit. [*Tom* (name) + TIT(MOUSE).]

tom-tom (tóm-tom) *n.* **1.** A small-headed, usually long and narrow, drum that is beaten with the hands. **2.** A monotonous rhythmical drumbeat or similar sound. [Hindi *ṭamṭam* See **tam-tam.**]

-tomy *n. comb. form.* Indicates a cutting of (a specified part or tissue); for example, **craniotomy.** [From New Latin *-tomia,* from Greek *-tomos,* -TOME.]

ton¹ (tun) *n.* **1.** *Abbr.* **t. a.** An avoirdupois unit of weight used in Britain equal to 2,240 pounds (1016.046909 kilograms). Also called "long ton". **b.** An avoirdupois unit of weight used in the United States equal to 2,000 pounds (907.18 kilograms). Also called "short ton", "net ton". **2.** Any of various units of weight or capacity used in shipping: **a.** A unit of weight or volume used for measuring freight, and varying according to the material being shipped. Its most usual value is a weight of 1000 kilograms or a volume of either 40 cubic feet or 1 cubic metre. Also called "freight ton". **b.** A unit of volume for freight equal to 40 cubic feet. Also called "freight ton", "shipping ton", "measurement ton". **c.** A unit of capacity of ships equal to 100 cubic feet. Also called "register ton". **d.** A unit of displacement of ships equal to a displacement of 35 cubic feet of sea water. Also called "displacement ton". **3.** A **metric ton** *(see).* **4.** *Informal.* **a.** A very heavy weight: *It weighs a ton.* **b.** Often plural. A very large quantity of anything. **5.** *Chiefly British Slang.* An amount or score of a hundred, as for example in pounds, runs, or miles per hour. [Specialised (from 17th century) use of TUN.]

ton² (toN) *n.* Fashionable distinction; elegant style. [French, TONE.]

to·nal (tṓn'l) *adj.* Of or pertaining to a tone, tones, or tonality. [Medieval Latin *tonālis,* from *tonus,* TONE.] **—to·nal·ly** *adv.*

to·nal·i·ty (tō-nál-əti, tə-) *n., pl.* **-ties.** 1. *Music.* **a.** A system or arrangement of seven notes built upon a tonic key. **b.** The arrangement of all the notes and chords of a musical composition in relation to a tonic. 2. The scheme or interrelation of the tones in a painting.

ton·do (tón-dō) *n., pl.* **-di** (-dee) or **-dos.** A circular painting or sculpted relief. [Italian, from *rotondo,* from Latin *rotundus,* round.]

tone (tōn) *n.* 1. **a.** A sound considered with reference to its quality in terms of volume, pitch, duration, or the like. **b.** A musical sound of distinct pitch, a **note** *(see).* 2. *Music.* **a.** The interval of a major second; a whole tone as distinguished from a semitone. **b.** The characteristic quality or timbre of a particular instrument or voice. 3. The pitch of a word used to determine its meaning, as in Chinese. 4. The particular or relative pitch of a word, phrase, or sentence. 5. Manner of expression in speech or writing: *an angry tone of voice.* 6. A general or prevailing character or atmosphere: *The tone of the debate was antagonistic.* 7. **a.** A colour or shade of colour. **b.** The general effect produced, as in a picture, by light and colour. 8. *Physiology.* **a.** The tension in resting muscles. Also called "tonus". **b.** Normal firmness of tissue. 9. *Informal.* High quality; distinction; class: *A duke added tone to the occasion.* ~*v.* **toned, toning, tones.** —*tr.* 1. To give a particular tone or inflection to. 2. To soften or change the colour of (a photographic negative, for example). 3. *Archaic.* To utter with a musical tone; intone. —*intr.* 1. To assume a particular colour quality. 2. To harmonise in colour. **—tone down.** 1. To lessen or soften in tone. 2. To make or become less pronounced or emphatic; moderate. **—tone up.** 1. To increase the tone of. 2. To improve the tone of; strengthen. [Middle English *ton,* from Old French, from Latin *tonus,* a stretching, tone, sound, from Greek *tonos.*]

tone colour *n.* The timbre of a singing voice or instrument. [Translation of German *Klangfarbe.*]

tone-deaf (tōn-déf) *adj.* Incapable of perceiving subtle distinctions of musical pitch.

tone language *n.* A language that distinguishes meanings among words of similar form by variations in pitch and tone.

tone·less (tōn-ləss, -liss) *adj.* 1. Lacking tone. 2. Lacking vitality; listless. **—tone·less·ly** *adv.* **—tone·less·ness** *n.*

to·neme (tōn-eem) *n. Phonetics.* A phoneme in a tone language distinguished from another only by its tone. [TON(E) + -EME.]

tone poem *n.* A **symphonic poem** *(see).*

tone row *n.* A fixed sequence of notes, typically consisting of the 12 notes of the chromatic scale, used as a basis for musical composition. Also called "note row".

tong (tong ‖ *U.S. also* tawng) *n.* A secret society or fraternity of Chinese, especially one allegedly involved in organised crime. [Cantonese *tong,* a hall, auditorium, assembly hall, Mandarin Chinese, equivalent of *táng.*]

ton·ga (tóng-gə) *n.* A light two-wheeled horse-drawn cart or carriage used in India. [Hindi *tāngā.*]

Tong·a, Kingdom of (tóng-ə; *also,* -gə). Also **Friendly Islands.** State in the south Pacific, comprising some 169 tropical islands, 38 of which are inhabited. Most of the people live by growing fruit and vegetables, and fishing. Coconut products and bananas are the chief exports, and tourism is important. Offshore oil has been discovered. A British Protected State from 1900, Tonga became an independent member of the Commonwealth in 1970. Area, 748 square kilometres (289 square miles). Population, 100,000. Capital, Nuku'alofa on Tongatapu island. See map at **Pacific Ocean.**

Ton·gan (tóng-ən, *also* -gən) *n.* 1. A Polynesian language spoken in Tonga. 2. A native or inhabitant of Tonga.

Tongking. See **Tonkin.**

tongs (tongz ‖ *U.S. also* tawngz) *pl.n.* A grasping device consisting of two arms joined at one end by a pivot or hinge. [Middle English *tang(e)s,* Old English *tangan,* plural of *tang(e).*]

tongue (tung ‖ *Northern English also* tong) *n.* 1. The fleshy muscular organ, attached in most vertebrates to the floor of the mouth, that is the principal organ of taste, an important organ of speech in humans, and moves to aid chewing and swallowing. 2. A homologous invertebrate structure, as in insects or certain molluscs. 3. The tongue of an animal, such as a cow, used as food. 4. **a.** The faculty of speech. **b.** A particular spoken language or dialect. 5. Style of utterance or manner of expression: *her sharp tongue.* 6. Anything resembling a tongue in shape, especially in being long, often tapering, and attached at one end, such as: **a.** The flap of material under the laces or buckles of a shoe. **b.** A narrow spit of land; a promontory. **c.** A jet of flame. **d.** A bell clapper. **e.** The harnessing pole attached to the front axle of a horse-drawn vehicle. 7. A protruding strip along the edge of a board that fits into a matching groove on the edge of another board. **—give tongue.** 1. To bay, as hounds do when pursuing their quarry. 2. To voice; utter. **—hold (one's) tongue.** To keep silent. **—on the tip of (one's) tongue.** On the verge of being remembered or expressed. ~*v.* **tongued, tonguing, tongues.** —*tr.* 1. To separate or articulate (musical notes) by the technique of tonguing. 2. To touch or lick with the tongue. 3. **a.** To provide (a board) with a tongue. **b.** To join (boards) by means of a tongue and groove. 4. *Archaic.* To scold. —*intr.* 1. To separate notes on a wind instrument. 2. To

project, as a promontory. [Middle English *t(o)unge,* Old English *tunge;* akin to Latin *lingua.*]

tongue and groove *n.* A joint made by fitting a tongue on the edge of a board into a matching groove on another board.

tongue-in-cheek (túng-in-cheék ‖ tóng-) *adj.* Meant or expressed ironically or facetiously. **—tongue in cheek** *adv.*

tongue-lash·ing (túng-lashing ‖ tóng-) *n. Informal.* A severe scolding.

tongue-tie (túng-tī ‖ tóng-) *n.* Restricted mobility of the tongue resulting from abnormal shortness of the fold of tissue connecting the tongue to the floor of the mouth. ~*tr.v.* **tongue-tied, -tying, -ties.** To make tongue-tied.

tongue-tied (túng-tīd ‖ tóng-) *adj.* 1. Speechless or confused in expression, as from shyness, embarrassment, or astonishment. 2. Affected with tongue-tie.

tongue twister *n.* 1. A word or phrase difficult to articulate rapidly, usually because of a succession of similar consonant sounds; for example, *She sells seashells by the sea shore.* 2. Anything difficult to pronounce.

tongu·ing (túng-ing ‖ tóng-) *n. Music.* An interruption of the wind stream through an instrument by a movement of the tongue.

–tonia *n. comb. form.* Indicates tonicity; for example, **myotonia.** [New Latin, from *tonos.*]

ton·ic (tónnik) *n.* 1. Anything that invigorates, refreshes, or restores. 2. A medicine or other agent that restores or increases bodily well-being. 3. *Music.* The primary note of a diatonic scale; a keynote. 4. *Linguistics.* **a.** A tonic accent. **b.** A voiced sound. ~*adj.* 1. Producing or stimulating physical, mental, or emotional vigour. 2. *Music.* Pertaining to or based on the tonic. 3. *Linguistics.* Carrying the principal stress; accented. Said of a syllable. 4. *Physiology.* **a.** Of or pertaining to normal muscular tension. **b.** Characterised by continuous muscular contraction: *a tonic spasm.* [From New Latin *tonicus,* of tension or tone, from Greek *tonikos,* from *tonos,* a stretching, TONE.]

tonic accent *n.* A stress produced by rising pitch as distinguished from increased volume. Also called "pitch accent", "tonic".

to·nic·i·ty (tō-níssəti, tə-, to-) *n.* 1. The property of having mental or physical tone, or of being tonic. 2. **Tonus** *(see).*

tonic sol-fa (sól-faá) *n. Music.* A system of teaching sight singing and ear-training in which notes of every major or minor scale, regardless of pitch, are identified in the same way by the use of the syllables *doh, ray, me, fah, soh, la,* and *te, doh* being the keynote or tonic of every major scale.

tonic water *n.* A non-alcoholic carbonated drink containing quinine, often used as a mixer with spirits. Also called "tonic".

to·night (tə-nīt, tōō-) *adv.* In or during the present or coming night. ~*n.* This night or the night of this day. [Middle English *to night,* Old English *tōniht :* TO (at, on) + *niht,* NIGHT.]

ton·ka bean (tóngkə) *n.* 1. Any of several South American trees of the genus *Dipteryx,* having seeds that yield coumarin. 2. The seed of any of these trees. [Perhaps from Galibi *tonka.*]

Ton·kin (tón-kín) or **Tong·king** (tóng-). Region of northern Vietnam on the Gulf of Tonkin. It was part of French Indochina (1887-1946), and after the expulsion of the French, it formed the nucleus of North Vietnam (1954–75). Its chief city, Hanoi, is now the capital of the Socialist Republic of Vietnam.

Tonkin, Gulf of. Chinese **Beibu Wan** or **Pei-pu Wan.** Arm of the South China Sea lying between Vietnam and southern China, and bounded in the east by the island of Hainan.

ton·nage (túnnij) *n. Abbr.* **tonn.** 1. The number of tons of water a ship displaces afloat. See **displacement ton.** 2. The capacity of a merchant ship in units of 100 cubic feet. 3. A duty or charge per ton on cargo, as at a port or canal. 4. The total shipping of a country or port, expressed in tons, with reference to carrying capacity. 5. Weight, measured in tons. [TON + -AGE.]

tonne (tun, *also* ton) *n. Abbr.* **t** A metric ton *(see).*

ton·neau (tón-ō, tún- ‖ tun-ó) *n., pl.* **-neaus** or **tonneaux** (-z). 1. The rear seating compartment of an early type of motor car. 2. A detachable waterproof cover used to protect the passenger seats of an open car. In this sense, also called "tonneau cover". [French, "barrel", "cask", from Old French *tonnel.* See **tunnel.**]

to·nom·e·ter (tō-nómmitər) *n.* 1. Any of various instruments for measuring fluid or vapour pressure; especially, one for measuring fluid pressure within the eye. 2. *Music.* An instrument or device, such as a graduated set of tuning forks, used to determine the pitch of a sound. [Greek *tonos,* tension, TONE + -METER.] **—to·no·met·ric** (tōnə-méttrik) *adj.* **—to·nom·e·try** (tō-nómmətri) *n.*

to·no·plast (tó-nō-plast, -nə-, -plaast) *n.* The membrane surrounding the large central vacuole in plant cells. [From Greek *tonos,* a stretching, tension (referring to its regulation of the pressure exerted by cell sap) + -PLAST.]

ton·sil (tón-sil, -s'l) *n.* A mass of lymphoid tissue; especially, either of two such masses embedded in the lateral walls of the aperture between the mouth and the pharynx. See **adenoids.** [Latin *tonsillae* (plural), probably from *tōlēs†,* goitre.] **—ton·sil·ar** (-ər) *adj.*

ton·sil·lec·to·my (tón-sil-éktəmi, -s'l-) *n., pl.* **-mies.** The surgical removal of a tonsil. [Latin *tonsillae,* TONSIL(S) + -ECTOMY.]

ton·sil·li·tis (tón-sil-ítiss, -s'l-) *n.* Tonsil inflammation. [New Latin : Latin *tonsillae,* TONSIL(S) + -ITIS.] **—ton·sil·lit·ic** (-ittik) *adj.*

ton·sil·lot·o·my (tón-sil-óttəmi, -s'l-) *n., pl.* **-mies.** 1. The surgical incision of a tonsil. 2. The surgical removal of part of a tonsil. [Latin *tonsillae,* TONSIL(S) + -OTOMY.]

ton·so·ri·al (ton-sáw-ri-əl ‖ -sṓ-) *adj.* Of or pertaining to hairdressing. Often used humorously. [From Latin *tonsōrius,* from *tonsor,* a barber, from *tonsus,* past participle of *tondēre,* to shear.]

ton·sure (tón-shər, -shoor, -sewr) *n.* **1.** The act of shaving the head or the top or crown of the head, especially as a preliminary to becoming a priest or a member of a monastic order. **2.** The part of a monk's or priest's head so shaven.
~*tr.v.* **tonsured, -suring, -sures.** To shave the head of. [Middle English, from Old French, from Medieval Latin *tonsūra,* from Latin, a shearing, from *tonsus,* past participle of *tondēre,* to shear, shave.]

ton·tine (tón-tīn, -teen, ton-teén) *n.* **1.** An insurance plan whereby a group of participants share an annuity, each share becoming larger as each participant dies, the final survivor receiving the whole. **2.** Each member's share of this. **3.** The subscriptions collectively; the total fund. **4.** The subscribers to such a plan, considered collectively. [French, after Lorenzo *Tonti* (1620–90), Neapolitan banker, who introduced this scheme in France in about 1653.]

Ton·ton Ma·coute (tón-ton-mə-ko͞ot) *n.* A member of a notorious personal police force set up by the Haitian dictator, François Duvalier *(see).* [Haitian Creole, bogeyman.]

ton-up (tún-úp) *adj. British Informal.* Travelling or liking to travel at speeds of more than 100 miles per hour. Said especially of motorcyclists: *ton-up boys.*

to·nus (tṓnəss) *n.* The normal condition of slight tension that occurs in a muscle even when at rest. Also called "tonicity". [New Latin, from Latin, tension, TONE.]

To·ny (tṓni) *n., pl.* **-nies.** Any of several annual awards presented in the United States for outstanding achievement in the theatre. [After *Tony* (Antoinette) Perry, American actress (1888–1946).]

too (to͞o) *adv.* **1.** In addition; also; as well: *He's coming too.* **2.** To a greater degree than is necessary or desirable; excessively: *working too hard.* **3.** Very; extremely; immensely: *only too willing to be of service.* **4.** *Informal.* Indeed; so. Used for emphasis: *said she'd leave him, and she did too.* **—**See Synonyms at **also.** [Emphatic form of Middle English *to,* in addition to, TO.]
Usage: When preceded by *not, too* is often used as a form of understatement in such sentences as *She wasn't too pleased*; but the usage tends to be restricted to informal speech (more formal contexts preferring *none too* or *not very*). The use of the same construction to mean "not very" *(Her re-election is not now considered too likely)* is also mainly informal.

too·dle-oo (to͞od'l-o͞o) *interj.* Also **too·dle-pip** (-píp). *British Informal.* Goodbye. [Imitative, perhaps of a car horn.]

took. Past tense of **take.**

tool (to͞ol) *n.* **1.** An instrument, such as a hammer or rake, used or worked by hand. **2. a.** A machine, such as a lathe, used to cut and shape machinery parts; a machine tool. **b.** The cutting part of such a machine. **3.** Anything used in the performance of an operation; an instrument: *the economic and intellectual tools to restore prosperity.* **4.** Anything regarded as necessary to the carrying out of one's occupation or profession: *Words are the tools of his trade.* **5.** A person used to carry out the designs of another; a dupe. **6. a.** A bookbinder's hand stamp. **b.** A design impressed on a book cover by this means. **7.** *British Slang.* A gun. **8.** *Vulgar Slang.* A penis. **—down tools.** To stop work or go on strike suddenly.
~*v.* **tooled, tooling, tools.** *—tr.* **1.** To form, work, or decorate with a tool or tools. **2.** To provide (a factory, industry, or shop) with the necessary tools, machinery, or equipment. Often used with *up.* **3.** To ornament (a book cover) with a bookbinder's tool. *—intr.* **1.** To work with a tool or tools. **2.** *Informal.* To travel in a vehicle. Often used with *along*: *tooling along the road.* [Middle English *to(o)l,* Old English *tōl.*] **—tool·er** *n.*
Synonyms: *tool, instrument, implement, utensil, appliance, gadget.*

tool·box (to͞ol-boks) *n.* A case for carrying or storing hand tools.

tool·ing (to͞ol-ing) *n.* Work or ornamentation done with tools; especially, stamped or gilded designs on books or leather.

tool·ma·ker (to͞ol-maykər) *n.* A master machinist skilled in making tools and parts. **—tool·mak·ing** *n.*

tool pusher *n. Slang.* A person in charge of the entire drilling operation on an oil platform or at an oil well.

tool·shed (to͞ol-shed) *n.* A small building in which tools are kept; especially, a shed or outhouse containing gardening tools.

toon (to͞on) *n.* **1.** A tall tree, *Cedrela toona* (or *Toona ciliata*), of tropical Asia and Australia, closely related to the mahoganies and having reddish, aromatic wood. **2.** The wood of this tree. [Hindi *tūn,* from Sanskrit *tunna†.*]

toot (to͞ot) *v.* **tooted, tooting, toots.** *—intr.* **1.** To sound a horn, hooter, or whistle in short blasts. **2.** To make this sound. *—tr.* To blow or sound (a horn, hooter, or whistle).
~*n.* **1.** The act or sound of tooting. **2.** *Chiefly U.S. Slang.* A lively time; a spree, especially a drinking spree. Used chiefly in the phrase *go on the toot.* [Probably from Middle Low German *tūten* (imitative).] **—toot·er** *n.*

tooth (to͞oth || to͝oth) *n., pl.* **teeth** (teeth). **1.** In most vertebrates, any of a set of hard, bonelike structures rooted in sockets in the jaws, typically composed of a core of soft pulp surrounded by a layer of hard dentine that is coated with cement or enamel at the crown, and used to seize, hold, or masticate. **2.** A similar structure in invertebrates, such as any of the pointed denticles or ridges on the exoskeleton of an arthropod or the shell of a mollusc. **3.** Any usually small projection resembling a tooth in shape or function, as on a comb, gear, or saw. **4.** A small, notched projection along a margin, especially of a leaf. See also **teeth. —long in the tooth.** Old or elderly. **—tooth and nail.** With great ferocity; as hard as possible.
~*v.* (to͞oth, to͞o*th*) **toothed, toothing, tooths.** *—tr.* **1.** To furnish (a tool, for example) with teeth. **2.** To make a jagged edge on. *—intr.* To mesh; become interlocked. [Tooth, teeth; Middle English *to(o)th, te(e)th,* Old English *tōth, tēth.*]

tooth·ache (to͞oth-ayk || to͝oth-) *n.* An aching pain in or near a tooth.

tooth·brush (to͞oth-brush || to͝oth-) *n.* A small, long-handled brush used for cleaning teeth.

toothed (to͞otht, *rarely* to͞o*th*d || to͝otht) *adj.* **1.** Having teeth. **2.** Having a specified number or type of teeth. Used in combination: *saw-toothed.*

toothed whale *n.* Any whale of the suborder Odontoceti, characterised by having rudimentary teeth. Compare **whalebone whale.**

tooth·less (to͞oth-ləss, -liss || to͝oth-) *adj.* **1.** Lacking teeth. **2.** Lacking force; ineffectual. **—tooth·less·ly** *adv.* **—tooth·less·ness** *n.*

tooth·mug (to͞oth-mug || to͝oth-) *n.* A small mug, typically without a handle, often kept in a bathroom and used to hold water for rinsing the mouth out after brushing the teeth.

tooth·paste (to͞oth-payst || to͝oth-) *n.* A paste used for cleaning the teeth, usually brushed on with a toothbrush.

tooth·pick (to͞oth-pik || to͝oth-) *n.* A small piece of wood or other material, for removing food particles from between the teeth.

tooth·pow·der (to͞oth-powdər || to͝oth-) *n.* A powder used for cleaning the teeth; a powdered dentifrice.

tooth shell *n.* A **tusk shell** *(see).*

tooth·some (to͞oth-s'm || to͝oth-) *adj.* **1.** Delicious; savoury: *a toothsome morsel of pie.* **2.** Pleasant; attractive; tempting: *a toothsome offer.* **—tooth·some·ly** *adv.* **—tooth·some·ness** *n.*

tooth·wort (to͞oth-wurt || to͝oth-, -wawrt) *n.* Any of various parasitic European plants of the genus *Lathraea;* especially *L. squamaria,* having pinkish flowers and a scaly rhizome resembling dentures.

tooth·y (to͞othi || to͝othi) *adj.* **-ier, -iest.** Having or showing prominent teeth. **—tooth·i·ly** *adv.*

too·tle (to͞ot'l) *v.* **-tled, -tling, -tles.** *—tr.* To toot softly on (a flute, for example). *—intr.* **1.** To toot softly and repeatedly, as on a flute. **2.** To move or travel gently or pleasurably. Often used with *along.* [Frequentative of TOOT.] **—too·tle** *n.* **—too·tler** *n.*

toots (to͝ots) *n.* Also **toot·sy, toot·sie** (to͝otsi). *Chiefly U.S. Slang.* Dear; sweetheart. Used affectionately or humorously. [20th century : origin obscure.]

toot·sy, toot·sie (to͝otsi) *n., pl.* **-sies. 1.** A person's foot. Used humorously, especially by or to children. **2.** Variant of **toots.** [Variant of *footsy,* from FOOT.]

top¹ (top) *n.* **1.** The uppermost part, point, surface, or end of anything. **2.** The crown of the head. **3.** The part of a plant, such as a turnip or beetroot, that is above the ground. **4.** Something that covers or forms the uppermost part of something, such as a lid or cap. **5.** *Nautical.* **a.** A platform enclosing the head of each mast of a sailing ship, to which the topmast rigging is attached. **b.** A similar platform, used as a gunsight or for observation, in a warship. **6. a.** In various sports and games, a stroke that lands above the centre of the ball, giving it topspin. **b. Topspin** *(see).* **7.** The highest degree, pitch, or point; a peak; an acme; a zenith. **8. a.** The highest, most important, or most successful position or rank. **b.** A person in this position. **9.** In various card games, the highest card or cards in a suit or a hand. **10.** The best part; the pick; the cream. **11.** A garment such as a blouse or T-shirt, that covers the upper part of the body. **12.** The upper part of something, especially when differentiated in some way, as by being of a different material, colour, or consistency: *stocking tops; top of the milk.* **13.** A drink consisting of a small amount of lemonade added to a specified alcoholic drink: *a beer top; a lager top.* **14.** *Chemistry.* The most volatile component of a distilled mixture; the component that distils first. **15.** *Abbr.* **t.** A quantum number, a property of certain postulated elementary particles. Also called "truth". **—blow (one's) top.** *Slang.* To lose one's temper. **—from top to toe. 1.** From head to foot. **2.** Completely. **—off the top of (one's) head.** Extemporaneously; impromptu. **—on top.** In a dominant, controlling, or successful position. **—on top of. 1.** *Informal.* **a.** In control of. **b.** Fully informed about. **2.** Besides; in addition to. **3.** In close proximity to. **4.** Following closely upon; coming immediately after. **—over the top. 1.** Over the front of a fortification, as an attack in trench warfare. **2.** Going beyond the acceptable; excessive. **—up top.** In terms of mental ability: *He hasn't got much up top.*
~*adj.* **1.** Of, pertaining to, situated on, or forming the top; uppermost. **2.** Utmost; highest. Often used in combination: *top-priority; top-quality; top-rank.* **3.** *Physics.* **a.** Designating a quark flavour required in certain models of elementary particle theory to complement bottom. **b.** *Abbr.* **t.** Designating a particle that contains the top quark.
~*v.* **topped, topping, tops.** *—tr.* **1. a.** To remove the top from. **b.** To prune the upper branches from. **2.** To furnish, form, or serve as a top of. **3.** To reach the top of. **4.** To go over the top of. **5.** To exceed or surpass. **6.** To be at the head or top of; lead: *He topped the list of this season's goal-scorers.* **7.** In various sports and games, to strike the upper part of (a ball), giving it forward spin. **8.** *Slang.* To kill, especially to execute by beheading or hanging. **9.** *Informal.* To wash the face of (a child or patient, for example). Used especially in the phrase *to top and tail.* **10.** *Chemistry.* To remove (the most volatile component) by distillation. *—intr.* To top a ball. **—top off.** To finish, usually in a satisfying way; complete. **—top**

out. 1. To put the framework for the top storey on (a building). 2. a. To lay the last or highest brick or stone of a building. b. To celebrate this event in a ceremony. [Middle English *top(pe)*, Old English *topp*, from Germanic *toppaz* (unattested).]

top² n. A toy consisting of a symmetrical rigid body spun on a pointed end about the axis of symmetry. [Middle English *to(o)p*, Old English *toppt*.]

top-. Variant of **topo-**.

to·paz (tō-paz) n. 1. A colourless, blue, yellow, brown, or pink aluminium silicate mineral, often found in association with granitic rocks and valued as a gemstone, especially in the brown and pink varieties. 2. Any of various yellow gemstones, especially a yellow variety of sapphire. 3. A light-yellow variety of quartz. 4. Either of two colourful South American hummingbirds, *Topaza pyra* or *T. pella*. [Middle English *topace*, from Old French *topace, topaze*, from Latin *topazus*, from Greek *topazost*.]

top boot n. A high boot usually having its upper part trimmed with a contrasting colour or texture of leather.

top brass n. *Used with a singular or plural verb.* The most important people in a business, government, army, or the like.

top·coat (tŏp-kōt) n. 1. A lightweight overcoat. 2. A final covering of paint.

top dog n. *Informal.* A person or group considered to have the highest status or authority, especially as a result of victory in some struggle or competition. —**top-dog** *adj.*

top-drawer (tŏp-drór) *adj.* Of the highest social rank.

top·dress (tŏp-dress, -dréss) *tr.v.* **-dressed, -dressing, -dresses.** To cover (land or a road surface) with loose material that is not worked in; especially, to cover (land that is to be cultivated) with fertiliser.

top dressing n. 1. A covering of fertiliser spread on soil without being ploughed under. 2. A covering of loose gravel on a road.

tope¹ (tōp) v. **toped, toping, topes.** *Archaic.* —*tr.* To drink (alcoholic drinks) habitually and excessively. —*intr.* To drink to excess habitually. [Perhaps from obsolete *top*, drink, influenced by *tope*, an interjection used in proposing a toast, perhaps from French *tope!* agreed! from *toper*, to accept a bet, agree, from Spanish *topar* (perhaps imitative of the striking of hands of two adversaries as a sign of agreement to a bet).]

tope² n. Any of several small sharks, especially *Galeorhinus galeus*. [17th century : perhaps from Cornish.]

tope³ n. A Buddhist shrine, a **stupa** *(see).* [Hindi *tōp*, probably from Prakrit *thūpo*, from Sanskrit *stūpa*, tuft of hair, crown.]

topee. Variant of **topi.**

To·pe·ka (tə-péekə). State capital of Kansas, central United States. It is a major commercial centre for the state's livestock, wheat, and other farm products.

top·er (tōpər) n. A chronic drinker; a drunkard. [From TOPE (to drink).]

top·flight (tŏp-flīt) *adj.* First-rate; superior.

top fruit *pl.n.* Fruit, such as apples, peaches, and cherries, that is grown on trees rather than bushes.

top·full (tŏp-fŏŏl) *adj.* Full to the brim.

top·gal·lant (tŏp-gál-ənt; nautical tə-) *adj. Nautical.* Designating the mast above the topmast, its sails, or rigging. [Alluding to its superior position and to its making a gallant show.]

top-ham·per, top hamper (tŏp-hámpər) n. 1. *Nautical.* Any rigging, cables, spars, or other materials or weight not immediately necessary and stored either aloft or on the upper decks. 2. Cumbersome and unnecessary or meaningless matter.

top hat n. A man's hat having a narrow brim and a tall cylindrical crown, usually made of silk and worn only on formal occasions.

top-heav·y (tŏp-hévvi ‖ *U.S.* -hevvi) *adj.* **-ier, -iest.** 1. Likely to topple because overloaded at the top. 2. Having too many executives in senior positions, and not enough actual workers. Said of a business enterprise. 3. *Finance.* Overcapitalised. —**top-heav·i·ness** n.

To·phet (tō-fet, -fit) n. 1. A place near Gehenna where human sacrifices were made. Jeremiah 19:4. 2. Hell or a hellish place. [Middle English *Tophet(h)*, from Hebrew *tōpheth*, (probably) "altar", place where children were burned, from the root *t-ph-th*, to burn.]

top-hole (tŏp-hōl) *adj. British Informal.* Very good; excellent.

to·phus (tō-fəss) n., *pl.* **-phi** (-fī). *Physiology.* A urate deposit found in tissue, such as cartilage, around the joints of people suffering from gout. Also called "chalkstone". [Latin *tōphus*, TUFA.] —**to·pha·ceous** (tō-fáyshəss) *adj.*

to·pi¹, to·pee (tō-pi, -pee ‖ *U.S. also* tō-pée) n., *pl.* **-pis.** A pith helmet worn for protection against sun and heat. [Hindi *topīt*, hat.]

to·pi² (tō-pi, tóppi) n. An African antelope, *Damaliscus Korrigum*, having a long muzzle and angular curved horns.

to·pi·ar·y (tōpi-əri ‖ -erri) *adj.* Of, designating, or characterised by the clipping or trimming of shrubs or trees into decorative shapes, such as those of animals, birds, or geometric forms.
—*n., pl.* **topiaries.** 1. Topiary work or art. 2. A topiary garden. [French *topiaire*, from Latin *topiārius*, of gardening, from *topia*, landscape gardening, from Greek *topia*, plural of *topion*, a field, small place, diminutive of *topos*, a place. See **topic**.] —**to·pi·a·rist** n.

top·ic (tóppik) n. 1. A subject treated in a speech, essay, thesis, or portion of a discourse; a theme. 2. A subject of discussion or conversation. 3. A subdivision of a theme, thesis, or outline. [Originally from Aristotle's *Topics*, which contains commonplace arguments, from Latin *Topica*, from Greek *(Ta) Topika*, from *topikos*, of a place, commonplace, from *topos†*, a place.]

top·i·cal (tóppik'l) *adj.* 1. Pertaining or belonging to a particular location or place; local. 2. *Medicine.* Applied or pertaining to a local part of the body. 3. Contemporary in reference or allusion; of current interest. 4. Of or pertaining to a particular topic or topics. [Greek *topikos*, of a place. See **topic**.] —**top·i·cal·i·ty** (tóppi-kál-əti) n. —**top·i·cal·ly** *adv.*

topic sentence n. The sentence within a paragraph that states the main thought, and is usually placed at the beginning.

top-knot (tŏp-not) n. 1. A crest or knot of hair or feathers on the crown of the head. 2. Any decorative ribbon, bow, or the like, worn as a headdress. 3. Any of various spiny-scaled flatfish of the genera *Zeugopterus* and *Phrynorhombus;* especially *Z. punctatus.*

top·less (tŏp-ləss, -liss) *adj.* 1. a. Having no top. b. Having no part covering the breasts: *a topless bathing suit.* c. Not wearing a top: *a topless waitress.* 2. *Archaic.* So high as to appear to extend out of sight: *the topless Alps.* —**top·less** *adv.*

top-lev·el (tŏp-levv'l) *adj.* Occurring at the highest level of authority, management, diplomacy, or the like: *top-level negotiations.*

top·loft·y (tŏp-lófti, -lofti ‖ -láwfti, -lawfti) *adj.* **-ier, -iest.** *Informal.* Haughty; pretentious. [Perhaps originally U.S., from TOP + LOFTY, or from *top loft*, topmost storey or gallery.] —**top·loft·i·ness** n.

top·mast (tŏp-maast, -məst ‖ -mast) n. *Nautical.* The mast that is below the topgallant mast in a square-rigged ship and just above the lower mast in a fore-and-aft-rigged ship.

top·most (tŏp-mōst) *adj.* Highest; uppermost.

top·notch (tŏp-nóch) *adj. Informal.* First-rate; excellent.

topo-, top- *comb. form.* Indicates place or region; for example, topology, toponymy. [Greek *topos*, a place.]

to·pog·ra·phy (tə-póggrə-fi, tə-) n., *pl.* **-phies.** *Abbr.* **topog.** 1. The detailed and accurate description of a place or region. 2. The art of graphically representing on a map the exact physical configuration of a place or region. 3. The features of a place or region. 4. The surveying of the features of a place or region. [Middle English *topographie*, from Late Latin *topographia*, from Greek, from *topographein*, to describe a place : TOPO- + *graphein*, to write (see -graphy).] —**to·pog·ra·pher** (-fər) n. —**top·o·graph·ic** (tóppə-gráf-fik), **top·o·graph·i·cal** *adj.* —**top·o·graph·i·cal·ly** *adv.*

to·pol·o·gy (tə-póllə-ji, tə-) n. 1. The topographical study of a given place in relation to its history. 2. The anatomy of specific areas of the body. 3. The study of the properties of geometric configurations invariant under transformation by continuous mappings, that is, those properties of a figure or solid that are unaffected by continuous distortion, such as stretching without tearing or breaking. In this sense, also formerly called "analysis situs". [TOPO- + -LOGY.] —**top·o·log·i·cal** *adj.* —**to·pol·o·gist** (-pólləjist) n.

top·o·nym (tóppə-nim) n. 1. Any name derived from a place or region. 2. The name of a place; a place name. [Back-formation from TOPONYMY.] —**top·o·nym·ic** (-nímmik), **top·o·nym·i·cal** *adj.*

to·pon·y·my (tə-pónnimi, tə-) n., *pl.* **-mies.** 1. The study of place names. 2. *Anatomy.* Nomenclature with respect to a region of the body rather than to organs or structures. Not in current technical usage. [TOP(O)- + -ONYMY.]

top·os (tŏp-oss) n., *pl.* **topoi** (-oy). A basic or stereotypical theme, idea, or the like, especially in literature. [Greek, stock topic, commonplace.]

top·o·type (tóppə-tīp) n. *Biology.* A specimen of an organism taken from the area typical for that species. [TOPO- + -TYPE.]

top·per (tóppər) n. 1. One that takes off tops: *a carrot topper.* 2. *Informal.* A top hat. 3. *British Informal.* A good fellow; an excellent chap. 4. *Informal.* Something that outdoes or caps what has gone before, especially a bantering remark.

top·ping (tópping) n. A sauce, icing, or garnish for food.
—*adj. Chiefly British Informal.* First-rate; excellent.

top·ple (tópp'l) v. **-pled, -pling, -ples.** —*tr.* 1. To push over; overturn. 2. To overthrow, as from an elevated or powerful position. —*intr.* 1. To totter and fall. 2. To lean over as if about to fall. [Frequentative of TOP (to remove the top of).]

tops (tops) *adj. Informal.* First-rate; excellent. —**the tops.** *Informal.* A first-rate or excellent thing or person.

top·sail (tŏp-s'l, -sayl) n. 1. A square sail set above the lowest sail on the mast of a square-rigged ship. 2. A triangular or square sail set above the gaff of a lower sail on a fore-and-aft-rigged ship.

top-se·cret (tŏp-séek-rət, -rit) *adj.* Designating materials or information of the highest level of security classification.

top shell n. Any primitive, winkle-like, marine mollusc of the family Trochidae.

top·side (tŏp-sīd) n. 1. A lean, boneless cut of beef from the top of the leg. 2. *Often plural.* The upper parts of a ship that are above the main deck.
—*adv.* On or to the upper parts of a ship; on deck.

top·soil (tŏp-soyl) n. The surface layer of soil.
—*tr.v.* **topsoiled, -soiling, -soils.** 1. To remove the topsoil from (land). 2. To cover or spread with topsoil.

top·spin (tŏp-spin) n. *Sports.* A forward spin given to a ball by hitting with a sharp, slightly forward-curved stroke.

top·stitch (tŏp-stich) *tr.v.* **-stitched, -stitching, -stitches.** To sew a line of decorative stitching close to the seam or edge of (a garment) on the right side of the fabric.

top·sy-tur·vy (tópsi-túrvi) *adv.* 1. Upside-down. 2. In a confused manner or a state of utter disorder.
—*adj.* In a confused or disordered condition.
—*n.* Confusion; chaos. [Earlier *topsy-tervy, topsy-tirvy* : probably TOP + obsolete *tervy*, to overturn, Middle English *turven*, to wallow, probably from Old English *tierfan* (unattested), to roll.] —**top·sy-tur·vi·ly** *adv.* —**top·sy-tur·vi·ness** n.

top up *tr.v.* **1.** To fill (a container that already contains some liquid) to the top with liquid: *top the car up with petrol; top your drink up.* **2.** *Informal.* To fill up the glass of: *Can I top you up?*

top-up (tóp-up) *n. Informal.* A refill; especially, a replenishment of a glass that is not quite empty: *Can I give you a top-up?*

toque (tōk) *n.* **1.** A small brimless, close-fitting woman's hat. **2.** A plumed velvet cap with a full crown and small rolled brim, especially as worn by men and women in 16th-century France. [French, from Spanish *toca*†.]

tor (tor) *n.* **1.** A high rock or pile of rocks on the top of a hill. **2.** A rocky peak or hill. [Middle English *torre*, Old English *torr*, probably from Old Welsh *twrr*, bulge.]

to·rah (táw-rə, tō-, -raa; *Hebrew* taw-ráa) *n.* **1.** The body of Jewish literature and oral tradition as a whole, containing the laws and teachings of the religion. **2.** *Capital* **T. a.** The Pentateuch. **b.** The scroll of parchment or leather on which the Pentateuch is written, used in a synagogue during services. [Hebrew *tōrāh*, a law, instruction, from *yārāh*, to teach, instruct.]

Tor·bay (tór-báy). Coastal district of Devon, southwest England. It includes Torquay, Paignton, and Brixham, all lying on Tor Bay, and is one of Britain's major tourist areas.

tor·bern·ite (tórbər-nīt) *n.* A green hydrous crystalline phosphate of uranium and copper. [German *Torbernit*, after *Torbern* O. Bergman (1735–84), Swedish chemist.]

torch (torch) *n.* **1.** A small, portable light or lamp consisting of a bulb and dry batteries, encased usually in a metal or plastic cylinder. Also *U.S.* "flashlight". **2.** A portable light produced by the flame of an inflammable material wound about the end of a stick of wood and ignited; a flambeau. **3.** A portable apparatus that produces a very hot flame by the combustion of gases, used in welding and brazing. **4.** *U.S. Slang.* An arsonist. **5.** Anything that serves to illuminate, enlighten, or guide. —**carry a torch for.** To love (someone who does not reciprocate). —**hand on the torch.** To keep a tradition or skill alive by teaching it to others. [Middle English *torche*, from Old French, a torch originally made of twisted straw dipped in wax, from Vulgar Latin *torca* (unattested), from *torquēre*, to twist.]

torch·bear·er (tórch-bair-ər) *n.* **1.** A person who carries a torch. **2.** A person who imparts knowledge, truth, or inspiration to others, as a leader of a movement.

tor·chère (tawr-shaír) *n.* A tall narrow table or stand, especially for supporting candlesticks. [French, from *torche*, TORCH.]

tor·chon lace (tór-sh'n, -shon) *n.* A lace made of coarse linen or cotton thread twisted in simple geometric patterns. [French *torchon*, duster, dishcloth, from Old French, twisted straw, from *torche*, TORCH.]

torch song *n.* A sentimental, often highly emotional popular song about unrequited love. [From the phrase *to carry a torch for.*]

tore¹. Past tense of **tear**.

tore² (tor ‖ tōr) *n. Mathematics & Architecture.* A **torus** (see). [French, from Latin TORUS.]

tor·e·a·dor (tórri-ə-dawr ‖ táwri-) *n.* A bullfighter, especially one mounted on a horse. [Spanish, from *torear* (past participle *toreado*), to fight bulls, from *toro*, a bull, from Latin *taurus*.]

to·re·ro (tə-raír-ō, tō-) *n., pl.* **-ros.** A matador or one of his team. [Spanish, from Late Latin *taurārius*, from Latin *taurus*, a bull.]

to·reu·tics (to-rōō-tiks, tə-, -rēw-) *n. Used with a singular verb.* The art of working metal or other materials by the use of embossing and chasing to form minute detailed reliefs. [From *toreutic*, from Greek *toreutikos*, from *toreutos*, worked in relief, from *toreuein*, to bore through, from *toreus*, a boring tool.] —**to·reu·tic** *adj.*

tor·goch (táwr-gōkh) *n.* A subspecies of the red-bellied char, *Salvelinus alpinus*, found in certain lakes in North Wales. [Welsh, "red belly" : *tor*, belly + *coch*, red.]

to·ri. Plural of **torus**.

tor·ic (tórrik ‖ táw-rik, tō-) *adj.* Of, pertaining to, or shaped like a torus or a part of a torus.

toric lens *n.* A spectacle lens used to correct astigmatism that has one torus-shaped surface with different focal lengths in different directions.

to·ri·i (táw-ri-ee ‖ tō-) *n., pl.* **torii.** The gateway of a Shinto temple, consisting of two uprights with a straight crosspiece at the top and a concave lintel above the crosspiece. [Japanese, "bird residence" : *tori*, bird + *i-*, from *iru*, to dwell.]

Torino. See **Turin**.

tor·ment (tór-ment) *n.* **1.** Great physical pain or mental anguish. **2.** A source of harassment, annoyance, or pain.
~*tr.v.* (tawr-mént ‖ *U.S. also* tór-ment) **tormented, -menting, -ments.** **1.** To cause to undergo great physical pain or mental anguish. **2.** To agitate or upset greatly. **3.** To annoy, pester, or harass. —See Synonyms at **harass**. [Middle English, instrument of torture, torment, from Old French, from Latin *tormentum, torquementum* (unattested), a twisted rope, (instrument of) torture, from *torquēre*, to twist.] —**tor·ment·ing·ly** *adv.*

tor·men·til (táwr-məntil) *n.* A Eurasian plant, *Potentilla erecta* (or *P. tormentilla*), having yellow flowers and leaves divided into five leaflets. [Middle English *tormentille*, from Medieval Latin *tormentilla*†.]

tor·men·tor, tor·ment·er (tawr-méntər ‖ tór-mentər) *n.* **1.** One that torments. **2.** A hanging used at each side of the stage in a theatre directly behind the proscenium, to block the wing area and sidelights from the audience. **3.** A sound-absorbent screen used on a film set or in a film studio to prevent echo.

torn (torn ‖ tōrn). Past participle of **tear**. —**that's torn it.** *British*

Slang. Used to express alarm or distress when some unexpected complication ruins one's plans.
~*adj.* Undecided; struggling to make a choice.

tor·na·do (tawr-náydō) *n., pl.* **-does** or **-dos.** **1.** A rotating column of air usually accompanied by a funnel-shaped downward extension of a cumulonimbus cloud and having a vortex several hundred yards in diameter whirling destructively at speeds of up to 480 kilometres (300 miles) per hour. Also called "cyclone". Compare **waterspout.** **2.** A violent thunderstorm in West Africa and nearby Atlantic waters. **3.** Any whirlwind or hurricane. **4.** Anything resembling a tornado in vigour or destructiveness. —See Synonyms at **wind.** [Variant (influenced by Spanish *tornado*, turned) of Spanish *tronada*, thunderstorm, from the past participle of *tronar*, to thunder, from Latin *tonāre*.] —**tor·na·dic** (-náydik, -náddik) *adj.*

to·roid (táw-royd ‖ tō-) *n.* **1.** In geometry: **a.** A surface generated by a closed curve rotating about, but not intersecting or containing, an axis in its own plane. **b.** A solid having such a shape. **2.** An object having the shape of such a figure. [TOR(US) + -OID.] —**to·roi·dal** (taw-róyd'l, to- ‖ tō-) *adj.*

To·ron·to (tə-róntō). Capital of Ontario, eastern Canada, lying on Lake Ontario. It is the cultural centre of English-speaking Canada, a major port, financial and industrial centre, and an important transport nexus. It was founded in about 1787 and, as York, it became the capital of Upper Canada (1793), but was incorporated as the city of Toronto in 1834.

to·rose (táw-rōz, -rōss ‖ tō-) *adj. Biology.* Cylindrical and having ridges or swellings. [Latin *torōsus*, from *torus*, a TORUS.]

tor·pe·do (tawr-péedō) *n., pl.* **-does.** **1.** A cigar-shaped, self-propelled underwater projectile launched from an aircraft, ship, or submarine, and designed to detonate on contact with or in the vicinity of a target. **2.** Any of various submarine explosive devices, especially a submarine mine. **3.** An explosive fired in an oil or gas well to begin or increase the flow. **4.** Any of several cartilaginous fishes of the genus *Torpedo*, related to the skates and rays. See **electric ray.**
~*tr.v.* **torpedoed, -doing, -does.** **1.** To attack, explode, or destroy with or as if with a torpedo or torpedoes. **2.** To immobilise or render ineffective (a scheme, policy, or the like). [New Latin *Torpedo*, genus of fish that give electric shocks, from Latin *torpēdō*, stiffness, numbness, the torpedo (fish), from *torpēre*, to be stiff.]

torpedo boat *n.* A fast, thinly plated boat equipped with heavy machine guns and torpedoes.

tor·pe·do-boat destroyer (tawr-pée-dō-bōt) *n.* A fast vessel, larger and more heavily armed than a torpedo boat, designed to destroy the latter, but often serving the same purpose.

tor·pe·fy (tórpi-fī) *tr.v.* **-fied, -fying, -fies.** To make torpid. [Latin *torpefacere* : *torpēre*, to be sluggish + *-facere*, -FY.]

tor·pid (tórpid) *adj.* **1.** Deprived of the power of motion or feeling; benumbed. **2.** Dormant; hibernating. **3.** Lethargic; apathetic. —See Synonyms at **inactive.** [Latin *torpidus*, from *torpēre*, to be stiff. See **torpedo.**] —**tor·pid·i·ty** (tawr-píddəti), **tor·pid·ness** *n.* —**tor·pid·ly** *adv.*

tor·por (tórpər) *n.* **1.** A condition of mental or physical inactivity or insensibility. **2.** Lethargy; apathy. —See Synonyms at **lethargy.** [Latin, from *torpēre*, to be stiff. See **torpedo.**]

torque¹ (tork) *n.* **1.** The moment of a force, a measure of its tendency to produce torsion and rotation about an axis, equal to the vector product of the radius vector from the axis of rotation to the point of application of the force by the force applied. **2.** Broadly, a turning or twisting force. [Latin *torquēre*, to twist.]

torque² *n.* A collar, necklace, or armband made of a strip of twisted metal, worn by the ancient Gauls, Germans, and Britons. [French, from Latin *torquēs*, twisted necklace, from *torquēre*, to twist.]

torque converter *n.* A mechanical or hydraulic device for changing the ratio of torque to speed between the input and output shafts of a mechanism.

tor·ques (tór-kweez) *n. Zoology.* A distinctive band of feathers, hair, skin, or coloration around the neck. [Latin *torquēs*, TORQUE².]

torque wrench *n.* A wrench or spanner with a torque gauge built into it to enable nuts and bolts to be tightened to a given torque.

torr (tor) *n.* A unit of pressure equal to one millimetre of mercury (133.32 pascals). [After Evangelista *Torricelli;* see **Torricellian vacuum.**]

tor·re·fy, tor·ri·fy (tórri-fī ‖ táwri-) *tr.v.* **-fied, -fying, -fies.** To scorch, roast, or dry (metallic ores or drugs, for example) by exposing to intense heat. [French *torréfier*, from Latin *torrefacere* : *torrēre*, to parch + *-facere*, -FY.] —**tor·re·fac·tion** (-fáksh'n), **tor·ri·fac·tion** *n.*

Tor·rens, Lake (tórrənz). Salt lake of South Australia. It has an area of 5 776 square kilometres (2,230 square miles) and is the continent's second largest lake. It partly dries out in summer.

tor·rent (tórrənt ‖ táwrənt) *n.* **1.** A turbulent, swift-flowing stream. **2.** A raging flood; a deluge. **3.** Any turbulent or overwhelming flow: *a torrent of abuse.* [French, from Italian *torrente*, from Latin *torrēns* (stem *torrent-*), a burning, a torrent, from the present participle of *torrēre*, to dry, burn.]

tor·ren·tial (tə-rénsh'l, to- ‖ taw-) *adj.* **1.** Of, pertaining to, or having the character of a torrent. **2.** Resembling a torrent; turbulent or unrestrained: *torrential applause.* **3.** Resulting from the action of a torrent or torrents: *torrential erosion.* —**tor·ren·tial·ly** *adv.*

Tor·res Strait (tórriss, tórriz, táwriz). Channel between New Guinea and Cape York, Australia, linking the Arafura and Coral seas. It is notorious for its reefs and shoals. The Spanish explorer

Luis Torres discovered the strait in 1606.

Tor·ri·cel·li·an vacuum (tórri-sélli-ən, -chélli- || táwri-) *n.* The vacuum formed at the top of a vertical glass tube *(Torricellian tube)* with one sealed end, which has been evacuated, filled with mercury, and inverted into a mercury reservoir so that its open end is submerged beneath the mercury. It functions as an indicator of atmospheric pressure. [After Evangelista *Torricelli* (1608–47), Italian physicist and mathematician.]

tor·rid (tórrid || táwrid) *adj.* **1.** Parched with the heat of the sun. **2.** Intensely hot; scorching; burning. **3.** Passionate; ardent. [Latin *torridus,* from *torrēre,* to dry, parch.] **—tor·rid·i·ty** (to-ríddəti, tə- || taw-), **tor·rid·ness** *n.* **—tor·rid·ly** *adv.*

Torrid Zone *n.* The region of the Earth's surface between the Tropics of Cancer and Capricorn.

tor·sade (tawr-sáyd, -saád) *n.* A decorative trimming for hats, consisting of twisted ribbon or cord. [French, from (obsolete) *tors,* twisted, from Late Latin *torsus,* from the past participle of Latin *torquēre,* to twist.]

tor·sion (tórsh'n) *n.* **1. a.** The act of twisting or turning. **b.** The condition of being twisted or turned. **2.** The stress caused when one end of an object is twisted in one direction and the other end is held motionless or twisted in the opposite direction. [Middle English, from Old French, from Late Latin *torsiō* (stem *torsiōn-*), from *torsus,* "twisted". See **torsade.**] **—tor·sion·al** *adj.* **—tor·sion·al·ly** *adv.*

torsion balance *n.* An instrument with which small forces, such as those of gravity, electricity, or magnetism, are measured by means of the torsion they produce in a wire or slender rod.

torsion bar *n.* A part of a motor vehicle's suspension consisting of a bar that twists to maintain stability.

torsk (torsk) *n., pl.* **torsks** or collectively **torsk.** A marine fish, *Brosme brosme,* of the family Gadidae found mainly in the north Atlantic. Also called "tusk", *U.S.* "cusk". [Norwegian, from Old Norse *thorskr.*]

tor·so (tór-sō) *n., pl.* **-sos** or **-si** (-see). **1.** The trunk of the human body. **2.** A statue of the trunk of the human body, especially with the head and limbs missing or truncated. [Italian, a stalk, trunk (of a statue), from Latin *thyrsus,* THYRSUS.]

tort (tort) *n. Law.* Any wrongful act, damage, or injury done wilfully, negligently, or in circumstances involving strict liability, but not involving breach of contract, for which a civil lawsuit for damages can be brought. [Middle English, from Old French, from Medieval Latin *tortum,* from Latin, twisted, distorted, from the neuter past participle of *torquēre,* to twist.] **—tor·tious** (tórshəss) *adj.* **—tor·tious·ly** *adv.*

tor·te (tórtə, tort) *n.* A rich layer cake made with many eggs and little flour and usually containing chopped nuts, cream, fruit, or jam. [German *Torte,* perhaps from Italian *torta,* from Late Latin *tōrta*†, a kind of bread.]

tor·tel·li·ni (tórtə-leéni) *pl.n.* Small, round pieces of pasta folded over a filling. [Italian, diminutive of *tortelli,* another type of pasta, ultimately from Late Latin *torta.* See **tart** (pie).]

tort·fea·sor (tórt-feézər) *n. Law.* One who is guilty of tort. [French *tortfaiseur* : TORT + *faiseur,* doer, from *faire,* to do.]

tor·ti·col·lis (tórti-kólliss) *n.* A contracted state of the neck muscles producing an unnatural position of the head. Also called "wryneck". [New Latin : Latin *tortus,* past participle of *torquēre,* to twist (see **tort**) + *collum,* the neck.] **—tor·ti·col·lar** *adj.*

tor·til·la (tawr-teé-ə, -yə) *n.* A thin unleavened pancake made of corn meal, characteristic of Mexican cookery, usually served hot with various fillings. [American Spanish, diminutive of Spanish *torta,* a round cake, from Late Latin *torta,* TORTE.]

tor·toise (tór-təss; *also sometimes* -toyz) *n.* **1. a.** Any of various terrestrial reptiles of the order Chelonia, characteristically having thick, scaly limbs and a high, rounded shell. **b.** *Chiefly British.* A pond or water tortoise; a **terrapin** *(see).* **2.** One that moves slowly. **3.** A **testudo** *(see).* [Middle English *tortuce, tortu,* from Old French *tortue,* probably from Medieval Latin *tortūca*†.]

tor·toise·shell (tór-tə-shel, -təsh-, -təss-) *n.* **1.** The mottled, translucent brownish covering of the carapace of certain of the sea turtles, especially the hawksbill, used to make combs, jewellery, and other articles. **2.** Any of various similar synthetic substances used for the same purposes. **3.** A domestic cat having fur with brown, black, and yellowish markings. **4.** Any of several butterflies, chiefly of the family Nymphalidae, especially *Nymphalis polychloros,* the large tortoiseshell, and *Aglais urticae,* the small tortoiseshell, having wings with orange, black, and brown markings. **5.** Mottled yellowish-brown. **—tor·toise·shell** *adj.*

tor·tu·os·i·ty (tórtew-óssəti) *n., pl.* **-ties. 1.** The state of being tortuous; twistedness; crookedness. **2.** A bent or twisted part, passage, or thing; a twist; a turn; a winding.

tor·tu·ous (tórtew-əss, tórchoo-) *adj.* **1.** Having or marked by repeated turns or bends; winding; twisting. **2.** Not straightforward; deceitful; devious. **3.** Highly involved; circuitous; complex. [Middle English, from Old French, from Latin *tortuōsus,* from *tortus,* a twist, from the past participle of *torquēre,* to twist.] **—tor·tu·ous·ly** *adv.* **—tor·tu·ous·ness** *n.*

tor·ture (tórchər) *n.* **1.** The infliction of severe physical pain, especially as a means of punishment or coercion. **2.** The undergoing of such pain. **3.** Mental anguish. **4.** A cause of such pain or anguish.
~*tr.v.* **tortured, -turing, -tures. 1.** To subject (a person or animal) to torture. **2.** To afflict with great physical or mental pain. **3.** To twist or turn abnormally; distort. [French, from Late Latin *tortūra,* a twisting, torment, from Latin *tortus,* "twisted". See **tortuous.**] **—tor·tur·er** *n.*

tor·tur·ous (tórchərəss) *adj.* **1.** Of or pertaining to torture. **2.** Causing or inflicting torture. **3.** Excruciatingly painful.

to·rus (táw-rəss || tō-) *n., pl.* **tori** (-rī). **1.** *Architecture.* A large moulding of convex semicircular cross-section, usually found just above the plinth of the base of a classical column. Also called "tore". **2.** *Anatomy.* A bulging or rounded projection or swelling. **3.** *Biology.* A moundlike or rounded structure, such as the receptacle of a flower. **4.** In geometry, a toroid generated by a circle; a surface having the shape of a ring doughnut. In this sense, also called "anchor ring", "tore". **5.** A ring-shaped tube, as in a nuclear reactor. [New Latin, from Latin *torus*†, a protuberance, round swelling.]

To·ry (táw-ri || tō-) *n., pl.* **-ries. 1.** A member or supporter of the British Conservative Party. **2. a.** One who supported James II of England and opposed the Glorious Revolution of 1689. **b.** A member of a British political party, founded in 1689, that was the opposition party to the Whigs, became identified with conservative interests, and has been known as the Conservative Party since about 1832. **3.** Any American who during the War of American Independence favoured the English side. **4.** *Sometimes small* **t. a.** A member or supporter of any Conservative Party, as in Canada. **b.** A conservative or right-wing person. [Probably from Irish *tōraighe* (unattested), runaway, from Old Irish *tōir,* pursue. The name originally denoted an Irishman who, dispossessed by the English in the mid-17th century, became a bandit; it then became a term for any marauder, and was subsequently applied abusively to Irish Catholic royalists, then to supporters of James II, and after 1689 to the English party that initially opposed the Glorious Revolution.] **—To·ry** *adj.* **—To·ry·ism** *n.*

Tos·ca·ni·ni (tóskə-neé-ni) **Arturo** (1867–1957). Italian conductor renowned for his interpretations of Beethoven, Wagner, and Verdi.

tosh (tosh) *n. British Informal.* Nonsense; rubbish; balderdash.

Toshkent. See **Tashkent.**

toss (toss || tawss) *v.* **tossed, tossing, tosses.** *—tr.* **1.** To throw casually or lightly. Often used with *out, aside, down,* or other adverbs. **2.** To throw, fling, or heave continuously about; pitch to and fro. **3. a.** To throw lightly with or as if with the hand or hands; pitch gently or with a sudden slight jerk. **b.** To throw upwards. **4.** *Informal.* To discuss informally; bandy about. **5.** To move or lift (the head) with rapidity: *" 'Idiot!' said the Queen, tossing her head impatiently"* (Lewis Carroll). **6.** To disturb or agitate; upset. **7. a.** To throw (a rider) to the ground. Used of a horse. **b.** To throw (a matador, for example) into the air, using the head or horns. Used of a bull. **8. a.** To throw up (a coin) in order to make a decision according to the side facing upwards when it lands. **b.** To throw up a coin in this way with (someone) in order to decide something. **9.** To mix (a salad) lightly so as to cover with dressing, oil, or the like. **10.** To throw (a pancake) up in the air and catch it again in the pan with the reverse side upwards. *—intr.* **1.** To be thrown here and there; be flung to and fro: *The boat tossed in the turbulent water.* **2.** To move oneself about vigorously; throw oneself from side to side: *toss in one's sleep.* **3.** To throw a coin to decide something. —See Synonyms at **throw. —toss off. 1.** To drink up in one swallow. **2.** To do, finish, accomplish, or perform in a casual, easy manner: *toss off a few jokes.* **3.** *British Vulgar Slang.* To masturbate.
~*n.* **1.** The act of tossing or the condition of being tossed. **2.** The distance something can be tossed. **3.** A rapid movement or lift, as of the head. **4.** A fall from or the experience of being thrown from a horse. **—argue the toss.** To dispute an issue that has already been decided. **—not give a toss.** *Informal.* To not care at all about something. [16th century : origin obscure.]

toss·er (tóssər) *n.* **1.** One that tosses. **2.** *British Vulgar Slang.* A **wanker** *(see).*

toss up *intr.v.* To toss a coin to settle an issue. *—tr.v.* To prepare (food or a meal) quickly or at short notice.

toss-up (tóss-up || táwss-) *n. Informal.* **1.** The tossing of a coin to settle an issue. **2.** An even chance or choice.

tot[1] (tot) *n.* **1.** A small child. **2.** A small amount of something. **3.** A small measure of spirits. [18th century (dialect) : origin obscure.]

tot[2] *tr.v.* **totted, totting, tots.** *Informal.* To total or add. Usually used with *up.* [Shortening of TOTAL.]

tot[3] *n. British Slang.* Rags and bones; rubbish collected by a rag-and-bone man. [19th century : origin obscure.]

to·tal (tōt'l) *n.* **1.** The amount or quantity obtained by addition; a sum. **2.** A whole quantity; an entirety.
~*adj.* **1.** Constituting or pertaining to the whole; entire. **2.** Complete; utter; absolute.
~*v.* **totalled** or *U.S.* **totalled, -talling** or *U.S.* **-taling, -tals.** *—tr.* **1.** To determine the sum or total of. **2.** To equal a total of; amount to. **3.** *Chiefly U.S. Slang.* To demolish (a vehicle) completely in a road accident. *—intr.* To add up; amount. Often used with *to: It totals to three pounds.* [Middle English, of the whole, from Old French, from Medieval Latin *tōtālis,* from Latin *tōtus,* whole.]

total eclipse *n.* An eclipse in which the eclipsed body as seen from the earth is totally hidden. Compare **partial eclipse.**

to·tal·ise, to·tal·ize (tōt'l-īz) *tr.v.* **-ised, -ising, -ises.** To make or combine into a total. **—to·tal·i·sa·tion** (-ī-záysh'n || *U.S.* -i-) *n.*

to·tal·i·sa·tor (tōt'l-ī-zaytər) *n.* Also **to·tal·is·er** (for sense 1). **1.** A system of betting on races whereby the winners receive a share of the total amount bet, in proportion to the sums they have wagered individually, after management expenses and taxes have been deducted. Also informally called "tote", *chiefly U.S.* "pari-mutuel". **2.** The machine that records bets placed under this system.

to·tal·i·tar·i·an (tō-tál-i-táir-i-ən, tṓ-tal-, tə-) *adj.* Of or designating a government or political regime whose main characteristic is considered to be the imposition of monolithic unity in every sphere of the life of its subjects, upheld by authoritarian means. [TOTAL + (AUTHOR)ITARIAN.] **—to·tal·i·tar·i·an·ism** *n.*

to·tal·i·ty (tō-tál-əti, tə-) *n., pl.* **-ties.** **1.** The state or condition of being total. **2.** The whole amount. **3.** The aggregate amount; a sum. **4. a.** The state of an eclipse when it is total. **b.** The length of time during which an eclipse is total.

to·tal·ly (tṓt'l-i) *adv.* Entirely; wholly; completely.

to·ta·ra (tó-tərə) *n.* A conifer, *Podocarpus totara,* of New Zealand having hard reddish wood used in building and furniture-making.

tote[1] (tōt) *tr.v.* **toted, toting, totes.** *Informal.* **1.** To haul; lug. **2.** To have on one's person; pack: *toting guns.*
~*n. Informal.* A load; a burden. [18th century (U.S.) : of obscure (dialectal) origin.] **—tot·er** *n.*

tote[2] *n. Informal.* A totalisator. [Short for TOTALISATOR.]

tote bag *n. Informal.* A very large handbag or shopping bag.

to·tem (tṓtəm) *n.* **1.** An animal, plant, or natural object serving among certain primitive peoples as the emblem of a clan or family by virtue of an asserted ancestral relationship. **2.** A representation of this being. **3.** A social group having a common totemic affiliation. **4.** Any venerated emblem or symbol. [Algonquian; compare Ojibwa *nintōtēm,* "my family mark", from a stem *ōtē-* (unattested), "to be from a local group".] **—to·tem·ic** (tō-témmik) *adj.*

to·tem·ism (tṓtəm-iz'm) *n.* **1.** The belief in kinship through common totemic affiliation or the identification of an individual or group with a totem. **2.** The primitive kinship system of which this is a reflection. **—to·tem·ist** *n.* **—to·tem·is·tic** (-istik) *adj.*

totem pole *n.* **1.** A post carved and painted with a series of totemic symbols and erected before a dwelling, as by certain Indian peoples of the northwestern coast of North America. **2.** *Chiefly U.S. Slang.* A hierarchy: *a low man on the totem pole.*

toth·er, t'oth·er (túthər) *pron. Archaic & Regional.* The other. [Middle English *the tother,* mistaken division of *thet other* : *thet,* the, Old English *thæt,* THAT + OTHER.]

to·ti·pal·mate (tṓti-pál-mayt, -mət, -mit) *adj.* Having webbing that connects each of the four toes, as water birds, such as pelicans and gannets, have. [Latin *tōtus,* whole (see **total**) + PALMATE.]

to·tip·o·ten·cy (tō-tippətən-si, tōti-pṓtən-si) *n.* Also **to·tip·o·tence** (tō-tĭp'ə-təns, tō'tĭ-pōt'əns). **1.** The capacity of a blastomere to develop into a fully formed embryo. **2.** The ability of meristematic cells to specialise in response to hormones from growth centres. [Latin *tōtus,* whole (see **total**) + POTENCY.] **—to·tip·o·tent** *adj.*

tot·ter[1] (tóttər) *intr.v.* **-tered, -tering, -ters. 1. a.** To sway as if about to fall. **b.** To appear about to collapse: *a tottering empire.* **2.** To walk unsteadily or feebly. **3.** To waver; vacillate.
~*n.* The act or condition of tottering. [Middle English *tot(e)ren,* from Middle Dutch *touteren,* to stagger, from Old Saxon *taltron* (unattested).] **—tot·ter·er** *n.* **—tot·ter·y** *adj.*

tot·ter[2] *n. British Slang.* A rag-and-bone man. [TOT (rubbish) + -ER.] **—tot·ting** *n.*

tou·can (tṓō-kən, -kan, -kaan) *n.* Any of various tropical American birds of the family Ramphastidae, having an extremely large, brightly coloured bill and variously coloured plumage. [French, from Portuguese *tucano,* from Tupi *tucana.*]

touch (tuch) *v.* **touched, touching, touches.** *—tr.* **1. a.** To cause or permit a part of the body to come into contact with. **b.** To cause or permit a part of the body, especially the hand, to come into contact with so as to feel. **2.** To bring something into contact with: *touch the plate with a spoon.* **3.** To bring (something) into contact with something else: *touch the match to the paper.* **4.** To tap or nudge very lightly. **5.** To strike or lay hands on in violence. Usually used in the negative: *Don't you dare touch her!* **6.** To use or partake of. Usually used in the negative: *She didn't touch her food.* **7.** To disturb or move by handling. **8. a.** To meet; adjoin; border. **b.** In geometry, to be tangential to. **9. a.** To reach; get to: *touched 90°.* **b.** To come up to; equal in quality: *His work couldn't touch his master's.* **10. a.** To handle or be involved in. Usually used in the negative: *I wouldn't touch that business.* **b.** To treat of; deal with as a subject. **11.** To be pertinent to; concern. **12.** To have an effect upon; act on; change. **13.** To injure or spoil slightly. **14.** To colour slightly; tinge. **15.** To affect the emotions of; move to tender response. **16.** To draw, mark, or shade with light strokes. Often used with *in.* **17.** *Rare.* To strike or pluck the keys or strings of (a musical instrument). **18.** *Rare.* To play (a musical piece). **19.** *Archaic.* To set fire to or kindle. **20.** *Archaic.* To stamp (tested metal). **21.** *Informal.* To borrow from; beg a loan from. Usually used with *for*: *I touched him for £50.* *—intr.* **1.** To touch someone or something. **2.** To be or come into contact. —See Synonyms at **affect.** **—touch at.** To stop briefly at (a port, for example). **—touch off. 1.** To cause to explode; fire. **2.** To initiate (a chain of events, for example); trigger. **3.** To make a portrait of in a sketchy or hasty manner. **—touch on** or **upon. 1.** To deal with (a topic) in passing. **2.** To pertain to; concern. **3.** To approach being; verge on.
~*n.* **1.** The act or an instance of touching. **2.** The physiological sense by which external objects or forces are perceived through contact with the body. **3.** A sensation experienced in touching something with a characteristic texture. **4.** A mild tap or shove. **5.** A discernible mark or effect left by contact with something. **6.** A subtle effect wrought by a small change or addition. **7.** A suggestion; a hint; a tinge. **8.** A mild attack: *a touch of flu.* **9.** A small amount; a trace; a dash: *a touch of paprika.* **10. a.** A manner or technique of striking the keys of a keyboard instrument, such as a piano or typewriter. **b.** The resistance to being struck by the fingers, characteristic of a keyboard. **11. a.** A person's characteristic manner or style of doing something. **b.** A characteristic manner in one's personal relationships. **12.** A facility; a knack: *lose one's touch.* **13.** The state of being in contact with a person or people, or a specified or unspecified reality: *getting out of touch.* **14.** *Rare.* A test or trial, as to establish quality. Used chiefly in the phrase *put to the touch.* **15.** *Archaic.* The official stamp indicating the quality of a metal product; the hallmark. **16.** *Slang.* **a.** The act of approaching someone to borrow or beg a loan. **b.** A sum of money borrowed. **c.** A person liable to be the victim of an approach for a loan. Often used in the phrases *soft touch, easy touch.* **17. a.** In soccer the area just outside the sidelines. **b.** In Rugby football, the area outside and including the sidelines. **18.** In fencing, a scoring hit. **19.** A children's game, **tag** *(see).* [Middle English *to(u)chen,* from Old French *tochier,* from Vulgar Latin *toccāre* (unattested), to strike, ring a bell, touch (probably imitative).] **—touch·a·ble** *adj.* **—touch·a·ble·ness** *n.* **—touch·er** *n.*

touch-and-go, touch and go (túch-ən-gṓ) *adj.* Of unclear outcome; critical; risky.

touch down *intr.v.* **1.** To land, especially briefly, as for repairs. Used of aircraft or spacecraft. **2.** In Rugby football, to touch the ground with the ball behind the goal line, as when scoring a try.

touch·down (túch-down) *n. Abbr.* **TD, td., td 1.** The contact, or moment of contact, of a landing aircraft or spacecraft with the landing surface. **2.** In Rugby football, an act or instance of touching down. **3.** In American football, a play worth six points, accomplished by being in possession of the ball when it is declared dead on or behind the opponent's goal line.

tou·ché (tṓō-shay, tōō-sháy) *interj.* **1.** Used in fencing to acknowledge that one has been touched by one's opponent's foil. **2.** Used to express concession to an opponent for a point well made, as in an argument. [French, "touched".]

touched (tucht) *adj.* **1.** Emotionally affected or moved. **2.** Slightly demented or mentally unbalanced.

touch·hole (túch-hōl) *n.* The opening in early firearms and cannons through which the powder was ignited.

touch·ing (túching) *adj.* Eliciting a tender reaction; moving. See Synonyms at **moving.**
~*prep.* Concerning; about. **—touch·ing·ly** *adv.*

touch judge *n.* In Rugby football, either of the two linesmen who judge whether a ball has gone into touch and whether, in an attempted goal, the ball has passed between the two uprights, and who may inform the referee of instances of foul play.

touch·line (túch-līn) *n.* In various field sports such as soccer and Rugby football, either of the sidelines bordering the playing field.

touch-me-not (túch-mi-not, -mee-, -nót) *n.* Any of several plants of the genus *Impatiens.* See **balsam.** [Its seed pods burst open at the slightest touch when ripe.]

touch paper *n.* A type of paper impregnated with saltpetre so that it burns slowly and without a flame. [From TOUCH (archaic sense "to kindle").]

touch·stone (túch-stōn) *n.* **1.** A hard black stone, such as jasper or basalt, formerly used to test the quality of gold or silver by comparing the streak left on the stone by one of these metals with that of a standard alloy. **2.** A criterion; a standard.

touch-type (túch-tīp) *intr.v.* **-typed, -typing, -types.** To type without having to look at the keyboard, the fingers being trained to locate the keys by position. **—touch-typ·ist** *n.*

touch up *tr.v.* **1.** To make minor changes, additions, or improvements in (a work, photograph, or the like). **2.** *Informal.* To fondle or caress in a sexually stimulating manner.

touch-up (túch-up) *n.* The act or process of finishing or improving by small alterations and additions.

touch·wood (túch-wōōd) *n.* Decayed wood or similar material used as tinder; punk. [From TOUCH (archaic sense "to kindle").]

touch·y (túchi) *adj.* **-ier, -iest. 1.** Apt to take offence with very slight cause; oversensitive. **2.** Requiring tact or skill; precarious; risky: *a touchy situation.* **—touch·i·ly** *adv.* **—touch·i·ness** *n.*

touch·y-feel·y (túchi-féeli) *adj. Informal.* Affectionate in a way that involves touching and the expression of feelings and that may be excessive or premature.

tough (tuf) *adj.* **tougher, toughest. 1.** Strong and resilient; able to withstand great strain without tearing or breaking. **2.** Hard to cut or chew. **3.** Physically hardy; rugged. **4.** Severe; harsh. **5.** Aggressive; pugnacious. **6.** Demanding or troubling; difficult. **7.** Strong-minded; resolute. **8.** *Chiefly U.S.* Vicious; rough. **9.** *Informal.* Unfortunate; too bad. —See Synonyms at **strong.**
~*n. Chiefly U.S.* A hoodlum; a thug. [Middle English *togh,* Old English *tōh.*] **—tough·ly** *adv.* **—tough·ness** *n.*

tough·en (túff'n) *v.* **-ened, -ening, -ens.** *—tr.* To make tough or tougher. *—intr.* To become tough or tougher. **—tough·en·er** *n.*

toughened glass *n.* See **safety glass.**

tough·ie (túffi) *n. Informal.* **1.** A tough person or thing. **2.** A tough or tricky problem.

tough love *n. Informal.* An unsentimental combination of love, firmness, and fairness that is held to be appropriate for dealing with a troubled person whose problems may be of his own making.

tough-mind·ed (túf-mīndid) *adj.* Not sentimental or timorous. **—tough-mind·ed·ly** *adv.* **—tough-mind·ed·ness** *n.*

Tou·lon (tōō-lóN). City of Var département, southeast France.

Tou·louse (tōō-lṓōz). Capital of the Haute-Garonne département, southern France. A major market, cultural centre, and canal port, it is also the centre of the French aviation industry.

Toulouse-Lautrec, Henri (Marie Raymond) de (1864–1901). French artist. He settled in Paris in 1881 and painted an unconventional side of life among the music halls and cafes of Montmartre.

tou·pee (to͞o-pay || *chiefly U.S.* to͞o-páy) *n.* **1.** A partial wig or hairpiece worn, usually by men, to cover a bald spot. **2.** A curl or lock of hair worn during the 18th century as a topknot on a periwig. [French *toupet,* a tuft of hair, forelock, diminutive of Old French *toup,* tuft; see **top** (summit).]

tour (toor, tor) *n.* **1.** A comprehensive trip or journey, usually taken for pleasure or education, with visits to places of interest. **2.** A group organised for such a trip or for a shorter sightseeing excursion. **3.** A brief trip to or through a place for the purpose of seeing it: *a tour of the house.* **4.** A journey to fulfil a round of engagements in several places: *a concert tour.* **5.** A period of duty at a single place or job. **—on tour.** Giving theatrical or concert performances, or the like, while touring.

~v. **toured, touring, tours.** *—intr.* To go on a tour. *—tr.* **1.** To make a tour of. **2.** To present (a theatrical performance) on a tour. [Middle English, one's turn, a turning, from Old French *tour, to(u)rn,* turn, circuit, from Latin *tornus,* lathe. See **turn.**]

tou·ra·co, tu·ra·co (to͝or-ə-kō) *n., pl.* **-cos.** Any of various African birds of the family Musophagidae, many of which have brightly coloured plumage. [French, from a West African name.]

Tou·raine (to͞o-ráyn; *French* to͞o-rén). Former province of west central France. A rich agricultural area famous for its grain, fruit and wines, it is sometimes called the "Garden of France". It is also a major tourist area noted for its châteaus. Tours is the chief city.

tour·bil·lion (toor-bíl-yən, tur-, to͝orbilən) *n.* **1.** A whirlwind. **2.** A firework rocket that has a spiral flight. [French *tourbillon,* ultimately from Latin *turbō* (stem *turbin-*), whirlwind. See **turbine.**]

tour de force (to͝or də fórss, tór || fṓrss) *n., pl.* **tours de force.** A feat of strength or virtuosity; a masterly achievement. [French.]

tour·er (to͝or-ər, tór-) *n.* A large open car for five or more persons, popular in the 1920s. Also called "touring car".

tour·ism (to͝or-iz'm, tór-) *n.* Also **tour·is·try** (-istri) (for sense 1). **1.** The practice of travelling for pleasure. **2.** The business of providing tours and services for tourists.

tour·ist (to͝or-ist, tór-) *n.* A person who is travelling for pleasure. *~adj.* Also **tour·is·tic** (toor-ístik, tawr-). Of or for tourists.

tourist class *n.* A grade of travel accommodation for passengers that is less luxurious than first class or cabin class.

tourist trap *n. Informal.* A place or event to which large numbers of tourists are attracted, and at which visitors are often exploited, as by overcharging.

tour·ist·y (to͝or-isti, tór-) *adj. Informal.* Like, suitable for, full of, or spoilt by tourists. Used derogatorily.

tour·ma·line (to͝or-mə-lin, túr-, -leen) *n.* A complex crystalline silicate containing aluminium, boron, and other elements, used in electronic instrumentation and as a gemstone. [French, from Sinhalese *toramalli,* cornelian.]

Tour·nai (toor-náy). Also **Tournay.** *Flemish* **Door·nik** or **Door·nijk** (dór-nik, do͝or-). Also **Tournay.** City of Hainaut province, western Belgium, on the river Scheldt. A market and textile centre.

tour·na·ment (to͝or-nəmənt, tór-, túr-) *n.* **1.** A contest involving a number of contestants who compete in a series of elimination games or trials. **2. a.** A medieval sport in which mounted contestants endeavoured to unseat one another with lances or swords; a jousting match. **b.** A meeting or festivity at which such matches and other chivalric displays took place. [Middle English *tornement,* from Old French *torneiement,* from *torneier,* to TOURNEY.]

tour·ne·dos (to͝or-nə-dō, túr-) *n., pl.* **-dos.** A small beef steak cut from the centre of the fillet, often bound in bacon or suet for cooking. [French : *tourner,* to TURN + *dos,* back.]

tour·ney (to͝or-ni, tór-, túr-) *intr.v.* **-neyed, -neying, -neys.** To compete in a medieval tournament.

~n., pl. **tourneys.** A medieval tournament. [Middle English *torneyen,* from Old French *torneier,* "to turn around" (from the combatants' turning around for each attack), from Vulgar Latin *tornidiāre* (unattested), to wheel, turn, from Latin *tornus,* a lathe, TURN.]

tour·ni·quet (tóor-ni-kay, tór-, túr- || *chiefly U.S.* -kit) *n.* Any device used to stop temporarily the flow of blood through a large artery in a limb; especially, a cloth band tightened around a limb, often over a pad placed to focus pressure on the artery. [French, "a turning instrument", swivel.]

Tours (toor). Capital of the Indre-et-Loire département, west central France. It is a tourist centre for the Loire valley, and a market and manufacturing centre.

tou·sle (tówz'l) *tr.v.* **-sled, -sling, -sles. 1.** To disarrange or rumple; dishevel. **2.** To handle roughly; mistreat.

~n. **1.** A dishevelled mass, as of hair. **2.** A dishevelled state. [Middle English *touselen,* frequentative of *-tusen†,* to pull about.]

tous-les-mois (to͞o-lay-mwáa) *n.* **1.** A West Indian plant, *Canna edulis,* with red flowers and purple stems, widely cultivated for its edible starchy rhizomes. **2.** The rhizome or starch obtained from this plant. [French, "every month", probably a phonetic approximation of West Indian *tolomane* (native name).]

Tous·saint l'Ou·ver·ture (toosáN lo͞ovairtúr), **Pierre Dominique** (*c.*1743–1803). Haitian revolutionary. With the help of the French he led a force which expelled the British and Spanish (1798). The French later seized him (1802) and he died in a French prison.

tout (towt) *v.* **touted, touting, touts.** *Informal. —intr.* **1.** To solicit customers, votes, or patronage, especially in a brazen way. **2. a.** To obtain horseracing information for use in betting, as by spying on the training of racehorses. **b.** To deal in such information. **3.** To buy sought-after tickets at the normal price and sell at inflated prices. *—tr.* **1.** To solicit or importune. **2.** To obtain or sell information on (a racing horse or stable) for the guidance of betters. **3.** To publicise as being of great worth; praise excessively: *highly touted by the press.* **4.** To sell (tickets that are hard to obtain), usually outside the relevant venue and at high prices.

~n. Informal. **1.** A person who obtains information on racehorses and their prospects and sells it to betters. **2.** A person who solicits customers persistently or brazenly. **3.** A person who touts tickets. [Middle English *tuten,* to peep, watch, Old English *tūtian* (unattested), from Germanic *tūt-* (unattested), to stick out, protrude.] **—tout·er** *n.*

tout court (to͞o ko͝or) *French.* Plainly and simply: *They're not Eurocommunists—they're Communists tout court.*

to·va·risch, to·va·rish, to·va·rich (tə-vaárish, to-) *n. Russian.* Comrade. Used as a term of address.

tow¹ (tō) *tr.v.* **towed, towing, tows.** To draw, drag, or pull along usually by a chain or rope, or the like.

~n. **1.** An act of towing. **2.** The condition of being towed. Used chiefly in the phrases *on tow* or *in tow.* **3.** Something being towed, such as a barge or car. **4.** Something that tows, such as a tugboat. **5.** A rope or cable used in towing. **—in tow. 1.** Following or accompanying. **2.** Under one's sway or control; in one's charge. [Middle English *togen, towen,* Old English *togian;* akin to TUG.]

tow² *n.* **1.** Coarse broken flax or hemp fibre, either prepared for spinning or to be discarded. **2.** A bunch of synthetic fibres. [Middle English *towe,* probably Old English *tow-,* "spinning".]

tow·age (tṓ-ij) *n.* **1.** The act or service of towing. **2.** A charge for towing.

to·ward (tə-wáwrd, to͞o-, tord || tōrd) *prep. Chiefly U.S.* Towards. *~adj.* (tṓ-ərd || tord, tōrd). **1.** *Rare.* Favourable. **2. a.** *Archaic.* In progress. **b.** *Obsolete.* Imminent. [Middle English *toward,* Old English *tōweard,* coming, favourable, future : TO + -WARD.]

to·ward·ly (tṓ-ərd-li || tórd, tṓrd-) *adj. Archaic.* **1.** Promising. **2.** Advantageous; favourable. **—to·ward·li·ness** *n.*

to·wards (tə-wáwrdz, to͞o-, tordz || tōrdz) *prep.* Also *chiefly U.S.* **toward. 1.** In the direction of. **2.** In a position facing: *The back of the chair was towards me.* **3.** Just before in time; approaching: *It began to rain towards morning.* **4.** With regard to; in relation to: *I can't understand his attitude towards us.* **5. a.** In furtherance of or partial fulfilment of: *£10 a month towards a new car.* **b.** By way of achieving; with a view to: *efforts towards peace.*

tow·bar (tṓ-baar) *n.* A rigid metal bar fixed to a vehicle, with suitable fittings enabling it to be attached to another vehicle, caravan, boat, or the like and used in towing.

tow·boat (tṓ-bōt) *n.* A **tugboat** *(see).*

tow·el (tów-əl, towl) *n.* A piece of absorbent cloth or paper used for wiping or drying. **—throw in the towel.** *Informal.* To give up; quit in defeat.

~v. **towelled** or *U.S.* **toweled, -elling** or *U.S.* **-eling, -els.** *—tr.* **1.** To wipe or rub dry with a towel. **2.** *Chiefly Australian Informal.* To beat or thrash. *—intr.* To dry oneself with a towel. [Middle English *towelle,* from Old French *toail(l)e,* from Frankish *thwahljō* (unattested), from Germanic *thwahan* (unattested), to bathe.]

tow·el·ling (tów-əl-ing, tówl-) *n.* **1.** Any of various absorbent fabrics, usually of cotton or linen, and having a nap, used for making towels, flannels, and the like. **2.** *Chiefly Australian Informal.* A beating or thrashing.

tow·er (tów-ər, towr) *n.* **1. a.** An exceptionally tall, usually equilateral, square or circular building. **b.** An exceptionally tall part of a building, usually having a particular function: *a church tower.* **2.** A tall framework or structure, the elevation of which is functional, as for observation, signalling, or pumping. **3.** A fortress or prison, often consisting of or incorporating a tower. **4.** A tall mobile wooden framework used in medieval warfare to help soldiers scale the walls of an enemy castle.

~intr.v. **towered, -ering, -ers. 1.** To rise to a conspicuous height; loom: *towering above our heads.* **2.** To be pre-eminent: *He towers above all others.* **3.** To soar or to fly directly upwards before swooping or falling. Used of certain birds. [Middle English *to(u)r,* from Old English *torr* and Old French *tor, tur,* both from Latin *turris,* from Greek, probably of Mediterranean origin.] **—tow·ered** *adj.*

tower block *n.* A high block of flats or offices with a large number of floors, occupying a relatively small ground area.

tower crane *n.* A crane consisting of a cantilever beam pivoted so that it can rotate at the top of a framework tower.

Tower Hamlets. Borough of Greater London created in 1965 from the boroughs of Stepney, Bethnal Green, and Poplar.

tow·er·ing (tów-ər-ing, tówr-) *adj.* **1.** Of imposing height. **2.** Outstanding; pre-eminent. **3.** Awesomely intense; furious: *a towering rage.* —See Synonyms at **high.**

tower of strength *n.* An extremely supportive or dependable person. [Popularised by use in Shakespeare's *Richard III* (1594); ". . .the King's name is a tower of strength" (Act V, scene 3).]

tow·head (tṓ-hed) *n.* **1.** A head of blonde hair. **2.** One having such hair. [From TOW (hemp).] **—tow·head·ed** (-hédded) *adj.*

tow·line (tṓ-līn) *n.* A **towrope** *(see).*

town (town || *West Indies also* tung) *n.* **1.** A large group of buildings and roads within a fixed boundary, where people live and work, larger than a village and, typically, smaller than most cities. **2.** The commercial district or centre of a town. **3.** The nearest town: *going to town.* **4.** Towns in general or urban life: *I prefer the country to the town.* **5.** The residents of a town. **6.** The ordinary, permanent inhabitants of a university town, as opposed to the academic community. Compare **gown.** **7.** The dominant city or town of an area. **—go to town.** *Informal.* To do something energetically with no inhibitions or restrictions; go all out. **—on the town.** *Informal.* On a spree. **—paint the town red.** *Informal.* To go on an elaborate or wild spree. [Middle English *t(o)un, town,* Old English *tūn,* an enclosed place, homestead, village.]

town clerk *n.* **1.** Until 1974, the chief administrative officer, secretary, and legal adviser of a British town. **2.** *Chiefly U.S.* A public official in charge of keeping the records of a town.

town crier *n.* A person formerly employed by a town to walk the streets proclaiming announcements. Also called "bellman".

town·ee (tówn-eé) *n.* Also **town·ie, town·y** (tówni) *pl.* **-ies.** *Informal.* **1.** A town-dweller as opposed to a country-dweller. **2.** A resident of a university town as opposed to a student. Used derogatorily.

town gas *n.* Coal gas supplied for domestic or industrial use.

town hall *n.* The building where many of the local government officials of a town are based, where municipal business is conducted, and where public meetings may be held.

town house *n.* **1.** A person's house or other residence in the city as distinguished from one in the country. **2.** A terraced house, especially a fashionable one. **3.** A town hall.

town meeting *n.* A legislative assembly of townspeople.

town planning *n.* The designing of a town or urban area such that houses, roads, and public amenities are planned as an integrated whole. **—town planner** *n.*

town·ship (tówn-ship || *West Indies also* túng-) **1.** In South Africa, an urban area specifically set aside for coloured or black people to live in. **2.** In Canada and the United States, a subdivision of a province or county having local government powers. **3.** In Australia and New Zealand, a small town. **4.** Formerly in England, a unit of local government such as a parish, part of a town, or a small town. **5.** The residents of a township.

towns·man (tównz-mən || *West Indies also* túngz-) *n., pl.* **-men** (-mən). **1.** A resident of a town. **2.** A fellow-resident of a town.

towns·peo·ple (tównz-peep'l || *West Indies also* túngz-) *pl.n.* The inhabitants or citizens of a town or city. Also called "townsfolk".

towns·wom·an (tównz-wŏŏmən || *West Indies also* túngz-) *n., pl.* **-women** (-wimmin). **1.** A woman resident of a town. **2.** A woman residing in the same town as oneself.

tow·path (tō-paath || -path) *n., pl.* **-paths** (-paathz || -paths, -pathz). A path along a canal or river, still sometimes used by animals towing boats.

tow·rope (tō-rōp) *n.* A strong rope or cord used in towing a vehicle, especially a car. Also called "towline".

tox-, toxo-, toxico- *comb. form.* Indicates poison; for example, **toxaemia.** [From Latin *toxicum,* poison. See **toxic.**]

tox·ae·mi·a (tok-seémi-ə) *n.* **1.** A condition in which bacterial toxins produced at a local source of infection are contained in the blood. Also called "blood poisoning". **2.** The condition of pre-eclampsia or eclampsia in the later stages of pregnancy. [New Latin : TOX- + -AEMIA.] **—tox·ae·mic** *adj.*

tox·al·bu·min (tóks-ál-bew-min, -al-béw-) *n.* Any of various toxic albumin proteins.

tox·ic (tóksik) *adj.* **1.** Of or pertaining to a toxin. **2.** Harmful, destructive, or deadly; poisonous. [Late Latin *toxicus,* from Latin *toxicum,* poison for arrows, from Greek *toxikon,* from *toxikos,* of or for a bow, from *toxon,* a bow.] **—tox·i·cal·ly** *adv.*

tox·i·cant (tóksikənt) *n.* A poison or poisonous agent.
~*adj.* Poisonous; toxic. [Medieval Latin *toxicāns* (stem *toxicant-*), present participle of *toxicāre,* to poison, from Latin *toxicum,* poison. See **toxic.**]

tox·ic·i·ty (tok-síssəti) *n., pl.* **-ties.** **1.** The quality or condition of being toxic. **2.** The degree to which a poison is toxic.

tox·i·co·gen·ic (tóksi-kō-jénnik) *adj.* Also **tox·i·gen·ic.** **1.** Producing poison or toxic substances. **2.** Derived from toxic matter. [From TOXIC + -GENIC.]

tox·i·col·o·gy (tóksi-kólləji) *n.* The study of the nature, effects, and detection of poisons and the treatment of poisoning. [TOXIC + -LOGY.] **—tox·i·co·log·i·cal** (-kə-lójik'l) *adj.* **—tox·i·co·log·i·cal·ly** *adv.* **—tox·i·col·o·gist** (-kólləjist) *n.*

tox·i·co·sis (tóksi-kō-siss) *n., pl.* **-ses** (-seez). Any pathological condition resulting from poisoning. [New Latin : TOXIC + -OSIS.]

toxic shock syndrome *n.* A rare infection that is characterised by vomiting, fever, a rash, and a sharp drop in blood pressure. Most known cases have occurred in women using vaginal tampons.

tox·in (tók-sin) *n.* Also **tox·ine** (-seen). A poisonous substance, secreted by certain organisms and capable of causing toxicosis when introduced into the body tissues but also capable of inducing a counteragent or an antitoxin. [TOX- + -IN.]

tox·in·an·ti·tox·in (tóksin-ánti-toksin) *n.* A mixture of a toxin, as from diphtheria, and its antitoxin with a slight excess of toxin, formerly used as an active (live) vaccine in the United States.

tox·oid (tóks-oyd) *n.* A toxin that has lost toxicity but has retained the capacity to stimulate the production of or combine with antitoxins, used in immunisation. [TOX- + -OID.]

tox·oph·i·lite (tok-sóffi-līt) *n. Formal.* A lover of archery; an archer.
~*adj.* Also **tox·o·phil·ic** (tóksə-fíllik). *Formal.* Of, pertaining to, or loving archery. [From *Toxophilus* (1545), a book by Roger Ascham, from Greek *toxon,* bow + *-philos,* -PHILE + -ITE.]

tox·o·plas·mo·sis (tóksō-plaz-mō-siss) *n.* A disease caused by infection with a microorganism, *Toxoplasma gondii,* usually producing only mild symptoms except if contracted by a pregnant woman, when it can cause blindness and mental retardation in the foetus. [New Latin : *toxoplasma,* from : Latin *toxicum,* poison (see **toxic**) + PLASMA + -OSIS.] **—tox·o·plas·mic** (-plázmik) *adj.*

toy (toy) *n.* **1.** An object designed to be played with, especially by children. Also used adjectivally: *toy soldiers.* **2.** Something of little importance; a trifle. **3.** A small ornament; a bauble; a trinket. **4.** A diminutive thing or person. **5.** A dog of a very small breed or one much smaller than is characteristic of its breed, usually kept as a pet. Also used adjectivally: *a toy poodle.*
~*intr.v.* **toyed, toying, toys.** To amuse oneself idly; trifle. Used with *with.* [Middle English *toye*†, dallying, amorous sport.]

toy boy *n. Informal.* A young man or boy viewed as a sex object. [From the notion that they are viewed as mere toys.]

tr. **1.** *Grammar.* transitive. **2.** translated; translation; translator. **3.** transpose; transposition. **4.** treasurer. **5.** *Law.* trust; trustee.

tra·be·at·ed (tráybi-aytid) *adj.* Also **tra·be·ate** (-ət, -it, -ayt). *Architecture.* Having horizontal beams or lintels rather than arches. [Latin *trabs,* a beam, timber.] **—tra·be·a·tion** (-áysh'n) *n.*

tra·bec·u·la (trə-béckew-lə) *n., pl.* **-lae** (-lee). **1.** A small supporting beam or bar. **2.** *Anatomy.* Any of the supporting strands of connective tissue projecting into an organ and constituting part of the framework of that organ. **3.** *Botany.* A transverse rodlike or platelike structure, often extending across a cavity. [New Latin, from Latin, diminutive of *trabs,* a beam.] **—tra·bec·u·lar** (-lər) *adj.*

trace[1] (trayss) *n.* **1.** A visible mark or sign of the former presence or passage of some person, thing, or event. **2.** A barely perceptible indication of something; a touch. **3. a.** A minute quantity. **b.** A quantity of rainfall or other precipitation too small to be measured. **c.** A constituent, such as a chemical compound or element, present in quantities less than a standard limit. **4. a.** A footprint or track left by an animal or person. **b.** *U.S.* A path or trail through a wilderness that has been beaten out by the passage of animals or people. **5.** *Archaic.* A way or route followed. **6.** A line drawn by a recording instrument, such as a cardiograph.
~*v.* **traced, tracing, traces.** *—tr.* **1.** To follow the course or trail of. **2.** To ascertain the successive stages in the development or progress of. **3. a.** To search back in time to find the origin of. Often used with *back.* **b.** To locate or discover (a cause, for example) by searching or researching evidence. **4. a.** To delineate or sketch (a figure). **b.** To give an outline or rough idea of (a plan). Often used with *out.* **5.** To imprint (a design) on something. **6.** To form (letters) with special concentration or care. **7.** To copy by following lines seen through a sheet of transparent paper. **8.** To make a design or series of markings on (a surface). **9.** To cover or decorate with tracery. **10.** To record (a variable), as on a graph. *—intr.* **1.** To make one's way; follow a path. Used with *along* or *through.* **2.** To have origins; be traceable. Used with *back.* [Middle English, a path, a course, from Old French, from *tracier,* to make one's way, from Vulgar Latin *tractiāre* (unattested), to drag, from Latin *tractus,* a dragging. See **tract** (expanse).] **—trace·a·bil·i·ty** (-ə-bílləti), **trace·a·ble·ness** *n.* **—trace·a·ble** *adj.* **—trace·a·bly** *adv.* **—trace·less** *adj.* **—trace·less·ly** *adv.*

Synonyms: *trace, vestige, track, trail, spoor.*

trace[2] *n.* **1.** Either of two side straps or chains connecting a harnessed draught animal to the vehicle it is pulling. **2.** In fishing, a short connecting piece of line between the hook and the main line. **3.** A bar or rod, hinged at either end to another part, that transfers movement from one part of a machine to another. **—kick over the traces.** To free oneself from constraints; become unruly. [Middle English *trais,* a pair of traces, from Old French, plural of *trait,* a pulling, a strap, from Latin *tractus,* a dragging. See **tract** (expanse).]

trace element *n.* An element required in minute amounts by an organism to maintain certain essential physiological processes.

trac·er (tráyssər) *n.* **1.** One that traces. **2.** A person employed to locate missing goods or persons. **3.** An investigation or inquiry organised to trace missing goods or persons. **4.** Any of several instruments used in making tracings or other drawings. **5.** *Military.* A tracer bullet. **6.** An identifiable substance, such as a dye or radioactive isotope, that can be followed through the course of a mechanical or biological process, providing information on the process or on the redistribution of the parts or elements involved.

tracer bullet *n.* A bullet that leaves a luminous or smoky trail, and whose path can therefore be observed. Also called "tracer".

trac·er·y (tráyssəri) *n., pl.* **-ies.** Ornamental work or a pattern of interlaced and ramified lines; specifically, the lacy openwork in a Gothic window. [From TRACE (draw).] **—trac·er·ied** *adj.*

tra·che·a (trə-kée-ə || *U.S.* tráyki-ə) *n., pl.* **-as** or **-cheae** (-ee, -ī). **1.** *Anatomy.* A thin-walled tube of cartilaginous and membranous tissue descending from the larynx to the bronchi and carrying air to the lungs. Also called "windpipe". **2.** *Zoology.* Any of the internal respiratory tubes of insects and some other terrestrial arthropods. **3.** *Botany.* A **vessel** *(see).* [Middle English *trache,* from Medieval Latin *trāchēa,* from Late Latin *trāchīa,* from Greek (*artēria*) *trakheia,* "rough (artery)", from the feminine of *trakhus,* rough.] **—tra·che·al, tra·che·ate** *adj.*

tra·che·id (tráyki-id) *n.* Any of the elongated, tapering, supporting and conductive cells in woody tissue. [TRACHE(O)- + -ID.]

tra·che·i·tis (tráyki-ítiss) *n.* Inflammation of the trachea. [New Latin : TRACHE(O)- + -ITIS.]

tracheo-, trache- *comb. form.* Indicates the trachea; for example,

tracheotomy, tracheitis. [New Latin, from Medieval Latin *trāchēa,* TRACHEA.]

tra·che·o·phyte (tráyki-ō-fīt, -ə-) *n.* Any plant with xylem- and phloem-conducting tissues; a vascular plant.

tra·che·ot·o·my (tráyki-óttəmi) *n., pl.* **-mies.** The act or procedure of cutting into the trachea through the neck, usually designed to facilitate breathing when the upper air passage is obstructed. Also called "tracheostomy". [TRACHEO- + -TOMY.]

tra·cho·ma (trə-kṓmə, tra-) *n.* A contagious viral disease of the conjunctiva of the eye characterised by inflammation, and scarring of the cornea, which may lead to blindness. [New Latin, from Greek *trakhōma* : *trakhus,* rough + -OMA.] **—tra·cho·ma·tous** *adj.*

tra·chyte (tráy-kīt, trá-) *n.* A light-coloured, fine-grained, igneous rock consisting essentially of alkali feldspar. [French, "rough stone" : Greek *trakhus,* rough (see **trachea**) + -ITE.] **—tra·chyt·ic** (trə-kíttik), **trach·y·toid** (-ki-toyd) *adj.*

trac·ing (tráyssing) *n.* **1.** A reproduction made by placing a transparent sheet on top of the original and copying the lines seen through it. **2.** A graphic record made by a recording instrument, such as a cardiograph.

track¹ (trak) *n.* **1. a.** A mark, such as a footprint, left by the passage of a person, animal, or thing; a trace. **b.** The path, route, or course indicated by such marks; a trail. **2.** A path or course travelled, such as a line of flight. **3.** A course of action; a method of inquiry or proceeding: *on the right track.* **4.** A rough path or road. **5.** A specially prepared road or course laid out for horse- or dog-racing or running events. **6.** *U.S.* Track events. **7.** A rail or set of parallel rails, such as those on which a train runs. **8.** An endless segmented band of metal plates driven by the wheels of certain tractors and tanks to enable them to move across rough ground. **9.** The distance between each of a pair of wheels, such as the front wheels of a motor vehicle or the paired wheels of an aircraft undercarriage. **10.** The path of a particle as observed in a cloud chamber, bubble chamber, or photographic emulsion. **11.** A separate path on a magnetic recording tape: *nine-track tape.* **12.** A separate section of a gramophone record on which a particular composition, song, or movement is recorded. —See Synonyms at **trace.** **—cover (one's) tracks.** To keep what one has done secret or hidden. **—in (one's) tracks.** Exactly where one is at a given moment. **—keep track of.** To follow the course or progress of. **—lose track of.** To fail to follow the course or progress of. **—make tracks.** *Informal.* To move or go hurriedly. **—off the beaten track.** In a little-known or secluded place. **—on the track of. 1.** Following in pursuit. **2.** Coming near to an understanding of the character or intentions of.
~*v.* **tracked, tracking, tracks.** —*tr.* **1.** To follow the footprints or traces of; trail. **2.** To pursue successfully; seek and find. Often used with *down*: *tracked down the culprit.* **3.** To move over or along; traverse. **4.** To observe or monitor the course of (aircraft, for example), as by radar. **5.** To focus on and film (a moving person or object) by swivelling or changing position. Used of a camera or camera operator. —*intr.* **1.** To keep a constant distance apart. Used of a pair of wheels. **2.** To be in alignment. **3.** To pursue a track; trail. **4.** To move around, often in a set path, while focusing on and filming an object. Used of a camera. **5.** To move in the groove of a gramophone record. Used of a stylus or pickup. [Middle English *trak,* trace, trail, footprints, from Old French *trac,* perhaps Middle Dutch *trek,* a drawing, from *trekken,* to draw, pull. See **trek.**] **—track·a·ble** *adj.* **—track·er** *n.* **—track·less** *adj.*

track² *v.* **tracked, tracking, tracks.** —*tr.* To tow, or pull; especially, to tow (a boat) from a tow path. —*intr.* To be pulled along; travel by towing. [Probably from Dutch *trekken,* to pull, assimilated to TRACK (course, path, etc).] **—track·er** *n.*

track and field *n. U.S.* **Athletics** *(see).* **—track-and-field** *adj.*

track events *pl.n.* The running and racing events at an athletics meeting as distinguished from the field events.

tracking station *n.* An observing station for maintaining radar or radio contact with an object in the atmosphere or in space.

track-lay·ing vehicle (trák-lay-ing) *n.* A motor vehicle, such as a tank and certain tractors and excavators, in which the wheels drive an endless track to enable it to move across rough ground.

track record *n.* **1.** *Informal.* The past achievements and failures of an individual, group, or thing. **2.** The fastest run, highest jump, or the like achieved at a particular sports ground or racing track.

track rod *n.* A rod joining the front wheels of a motor vehicle to ensure that they can be steered together.

track shoe *n.* Either of a pair of light shoes worn by runners, often having steel spikes attached to the soles to give them a firm grip.

track suit *n.* A warm jacket and trousers that are tight-fitting around the ankles, wrists, and waist, and loose elsewhere, worn to keep warm, as during training or exercise.

tract¹ (trakt) *n.* **1.** An expanse of land; a region. **2.** *Anatomy.* **a.** A system of organs and tissues that together perform one specialised function: *the alimentary tract.* **b.** A bundle of nerve fibres having a common origin, termination, and function. **3.** *Archaic.* A stretch or lapse of time. [Latin *tractus,* "a drawing", course, tract, region, from *trahere* (past participle *tractus*), to draw.]

tract² *n.* A distributed paper or pamphlet containing a declaration or appeal, especially one put out by a religious or political group. [Middle English *tracte,* shortened from Latin *tractātus,* a discussion, treatise, from the past participle of *tractāre,* to pull violently, discuss. See **tractable.**]

tract³ *n.* The verses from Scripture sung during Lent or on Ember days after the gradual in the Tridentine Mass. [Middle English *tracte,* from Medieval Latin *tractus,* from Latin, "a drawing out" (the verses are sung without a break by one voice). See **tract** (area).]

trac·ta·ble (trák-təb'l) *adj.* **1.** Easily managed or controlled; governable. **2. a.** Easily handled or worked; malleable. **b.** Treatable by data processing: *computer-tractable data.* —See Synonyms at **obedient.** [Latin, *tractābilis,* from *tractāre,* to pull violently, to manage, frequentative of *trahere* (past part. *tractus*), to draw, pull.] **—trac·ta·bil·i·ty** (-tə-bílləti), **trac·ta·ble·ness** *n.* **—trac·ta·bly** *adv.*

Trac·tar·i·an·ism (trak-táir-i-ən-iz'm) *n.* The religious opinions and principles of the founders of the Oxford movement, put forth in a series of 90 pamphlets entitled *Tracts for the Times,* published in Oxford (1833–41). **—Trac·tar·i·an** *adj.* & *n.*

trac·tate (trák-tayt) *n.* A treatise; an essay. [Latin *tractātus,* TRACT.]

trac·tile (trák-tīl ‖ *U.S. also* -t'l) *adj.* Capable of being drawn out in length, as certain metals; ductile. **—trac·til·i·ty** (trak-tílləti) *n.*

trac·tion (tráksh'n) *n.* **1.** The act of drawing or pulling a load, for example, especially by motive power. **2.** The condition of being drawn or pulled. **3.** Adhesive friction, as of a wheel on a road surface or rail. **4.** The pulling power of a locomotive. **5.** *Medicine.* The use of weights, straps, and the like to exert a continuous pull on a part of the body to assist the healing of injuries. [Medieval Latin *tractiō* (stem *tractiōn-*), from Latin *tractus,* past participle of *trahere,* to draw, pull.] **—trac·tion·al, trac·tive** *adj.*

traction engine *n.* A steam-powered vehicle formerly used on roads or over rough ground to pull heavy loads.

trac·tor (tráktər) *n.* **1.** A small vehicle, powered by an internal combustion engine, having large, heavily treaded tyres, or sometimes tracks, and used in farming for pulling machinery. **2.** A short, powerful motor vehicle having a cab and no body, used for pulling large trailers or transporting heavy containers, as in articulated lorries. **3.** An aircraft having a propeller mounted in front of the supporting surfaces. In this sense, also called "tractor aircraft". [New Latin, from Latin *tractus.* See **traction.**]

trade (trayd) *n.* **1.** An occupation, especially one requiring skilled labour; a craft. **2.** The business of buying and selling; commerce. **3. a.** A particular business, industry, or market. **b.** The persons working in or associated with a specific business or industry. **4. a.** The customers, collectively, of a specific business or industry. **b.** The amount of custom of a business or industry at a particular time or place: *the holiday trade.* **5.** An instance of buying or selling; a transaction. **6.** An exchange of one thing for another. **7.** *Plural.* The trade winds. —See Synonyms at **business.**
~*v.* **traded, trading, trades.** —*intr.* **1. a.** To engage in buying and selling for profit. **b.** To have business relations. Often used with *with*: *prepared to trade with Cuba.* **2.** To make an exchange of one thing for another. **3.** To shop or buy regularly at a given shop. —*tr.* **1.** To give in exchange for something else. **2.** To buy and sell (shares, for example). **3.** To pass back and forth: *We traded anecdotes.* **—trade on.** To put to advantage; exploit: *He traded on his war-wounds for sympathy.* [Middle English *tra(i)d, trade,* a course, way, track, from Middle Low German *trade,* a track, path.]

trade cycle *n.* A regular fluctuation in the trade or economic conditions of most capitalist countries consisting of a movement from a state of high activity (prosperity or boom) to a state of low activity (depression) and back again.

trade discount *n.* A discount on the list price granted by a manufacturer or wholesaler to buyers in the same trade.

trade gap *n. Economics.* **1.** An excess of a country's visible imports over its visible exports. **2.** The amount of this excess.

trade in *tr.v.* To give (an old item) to a dealer in part exchange or as partial payment for a new purchase.

trade-in (tráyd-in) *n.* **1.** A piece of merchandise accepted as partial payment for a new purchase. **2.** A transaction involving such an item. **3.** The amount allowed for such an item. Also used adjectivally: *trade-in value.*

trade·mark (tráyd-maark) *n.* **1.** A name, symbol, or other device identifying a product, officially registered and legally restricted to the use of the owner or manufacturer. **2.** A distinctive sign by which a person or thing comes to be known.
~*tr.v.* **trademarked, -marking, -marks. 1.** To label (a product) with a trademark. **2.** To register as a trademark.

trade name *n.* **1.** The name by which a commodity, service, process, or the like is known to the trade. **2.** A trademark consisting solely of a name. **3.** The name under which a business enterprise operates.

trade-off, trade-off (tráyd-off, -awf) *n.* An exchange of one thing in return for another; especially, a giving up of something desirable for something else regarded as more desirable. **—trade·off** *adj.*

trade paper *n.* A newspaper or periodical published regularly by or for a particular business or industry to give pertinent news and developments. Also called "trade journal", "trade magazine".

trade plate *n.* Either of a pair of number plates attached to a motor vehicle temporarily by a motor dealer or manufacturer before registration, after the road-fund licence has expired, or to transfer insurance liability, from the insured to a third party, usually to a garage.

trade price *n.* The price charged by a wholesaler to a retailer.

trad·er (tráydər) *n.* **1.** A person who trades; a dealer. **2.** A ship employed in foreign trade.

trade route *n.* A sea lane used by trading ships.

trad·es·can·tia (trád-iss-kánti-ə, -ess-) *n.* Any plant of the genus *Tradescantia,* characteristically having a jointed succulent stem and three-petalled flowers, such as the house plant, wandering Jew. [New Latin, after John *Tradescant* (1608–62), English botanist.]

trade secret *n.* **1.** A secret formula, method, or device that gives a manufacturer an advantage over competitors. **2.** A scheme, trick, or the like to which a person attributes his success and which he keeps secret.

trades·man (tráydz-mən) *n., pl.* **-men** (-mən). **1.** A person engaged in the retail trade, especially a shopkeeper. **2.** A skilled worker; a craftsman. **—trades·wom·an** *n.*

trades·peo·ple (tráydz-peep'l) *pl.n. British.* People engaged in the retail trade, especially shopkeepers.

Trades Union Congress *n.* The umbrella organisation to which most British trade unions belong. Also called "T.U.C."

trade union *n.* Also *British* **trades union.** *Abbr.* **T.U.** An association of workers in a particular trade or occupation or group of trades, formed to further and protect their common interests by concerted action, such as collective bargaining for improved wages, hours, and conditions. **—trade u·nion·ism** *n.* **—trade u·nion·ist** *n.*

trade wind *n.* An extremely consistent system of winds occupying most of the tropics, constituting the major component of the general circulation of the atmosphere, blowing northeasterly in the Northern Hemisphere and southeasterly in the Southern Hemisphere. [From the phrase *to blow trade,* to blow in a regular course, from TRADE (in the obsolete sense of a course).]

trad·ing estate (tráyding) *n. British.* An area in which numerous factories and business premises are situated, especially an area deliberately built or set aside for such a purpose.

trading post *n.* A station or general shop in a sparsely settled area established by traders to barter supplies for local products.

trading stamp *n.* A stamp given by a retailer to a buyer for each purchase of a specified amount and able to be redeemed in quantity, by the buyer, for merchandise.

tra·di·tion (trə-dísh'n) *n.* **1.** The passing down of elements of a culture from generation to generation, especially by oral communication. **2. a.** A mode of thought or behaviour followed by a people continuously from generation to generation; a cultural custom or usage. **b.** A set of such customs and usages viewed as a coherent body of precedents influencing the present. **c.** A set of such customs followed in a particular art. **3.** A body of unwritten religious precepts. **4.** Any time-honoured practice or a set of such practices. **5.** *Law.* The transfer of property to another. [Middle English *tradicion,* a handing down, a surrender, from Old French, from Latin *trāditiō* (stem *trāditiōn-),* from *trādere,* to hand over : *trāns-,* over + *dare,* to give.]

tra·di·tion·al (trə-dísh'n-'l) *adj.* Also **tra·di·tion·ar·y** (-əri || -erri). **1.** Pertaining to or in accord with tradition. **2.** Of or pertaining to trad jazz. **—tra·di·tion·al·ise** *tr.v.* **—tra·di·tion·al·ly** *adv.*

tra·di·tion·al·ism (trə-dísh'n'l-iz'm) *n.* **1.** Adherence to tradition; especially, excessive reverence for religious tradition. **2.** A religious doctrine holding that all knowledge is derived from original divine revelation and is transmitted by tradition. **—tra·di·tion·al·ist** *n.* & *adj.* **—tra·di·tion·al·is·tic** (-ístik) *adj.*

tra·di·tion-di·rect·ed (trə-dísh'n-dīr-rektid, -də-, -dī-) *adj.* Guided by tradition and the values of one's forebears, rather than by independent personal principles: *a tradition-directed personality.* Compare **inner-directed, other-directed.**

trad·i·tor (tráddi-tər) *n., pl.* **-tors** or **-tores** (-táw-reez || -tṓ-). Any of the early Christians who surrendered sacred objects or betrayed fellow Christians during the Roman persecutions. [Middle English *traditour,* from Latin *trāditor,* traitor, from *trādere,* to hand over, betray. See **tradition.**]

trad jazz (trad) *n.* Jazz of a traditional style based on the early jazz of New Orleans and Chicago in the 1920s. [*Trad*itional *jazz.*]

tra·duce (trə-déwss || -dṓōss) *tr.v.* **-duced, -ducing, -duces.** To speak falsely or maliciously of; slander; defame. See Synonyms at **malign.** [Latin *trādūcere,* to lead across, make public, expose to ridicule : *trāns-,* across + *dūcere,* to lead.] **—tra·duce·ment** *n.* **—tra·duc·er** *n.* **—tra·duc·i·ble** *adj.* **—tra·duc·ing·ly** *adv.*

tra·du·cian·ism (trə-déw-si-ən-iz'm, -shi-, -shən- || -dṓō-) *n. Theology.* The belief that the soul is inherited from the parents along with the body. Compare **creationism.** [Medieval Latin *trāduciānus,* believer in this doctrine, from *trādux,* inheritance, from Latin *trādūcere,* to lead across, TRADUCE.] **—tra·du·cian·ist** *n.* **—tra·du·cian·is·tic** (-ístik) *adj.*

Tra·fal·gar, Cape (trə-fál-gər; *Spanish* tra-fal-gár). Headland of southwest Spain, lying between the Strait of Gibraltar and Gulf of Cádiz. It gave its name to the naval battle of 1805, when the British, under Nelson, destroyed Napoleon's battlefleet.

traf·fic (tráffik) *n.* **1. a.** The commercial exchange of goods; trade. **b.** Illicit or blackmarket trade: *traffic in drugs.* **2. a.** The business of moving passengers and cargo by means of a system of transportation. **b.** The amount of cargo or number of passengers conveyed. **3. a.** The passage of persons, vehicles, or messages through routes of transportation or communication. **b.** The vehicles using a particular road or route: *heavy traffic.* **c.** The volume of messages passing through a system of communication. **4.** Connections; dealings: *have traffic with the devil.* —See Synonyms at **business.** *~intr.v.* **trafficked, -ficking, -fics. 1.** To carry on trade, especially illegal trade. **2.** To have dealings. Usually used with *with.* [French *traffique,* from Old Italian *traffico,* from *trafficare*†, to trade.] **—traf·fick·er** *n.*

traf·fi·ca·tor (tráffi-kaytər) *n.* A metal and plastic illuminated arm formerly on motor vehicles that could be raised to indicate a left or right turn. Compare **indicator.** [*Traffic* + (indic)*ator.*]

traffic circle *n. U.S.* A **roundabout** *(see).*

traffic island *n.* A raised area over which cars may not pass, placed at a junction of thoroughfares or between opposing traffic lanes. Also called "island", "refuge".

traffic jam *n.* A situation in which a large number of motor vehicles on the road are brought to a standstill or can move only very slowly, caused by heavy traffic or an accident, for example.

traffic light *n.* A road signal that beams a red or green light or an amber warning light to direct traffic to stop or proceed. Also called "traffic signal".

traffic warden *n.* A person who is empowered to enforce parking rules and who assists the police in controlling road traffic.

trag·a·canth (trággə-kanth || *U.S. also* trájə-, -santh) *n.* **1.** Any of various thorny shrubs of the genus *Astragalus* of northern temperate regions, yielding a gum used in pharmacy, adhesives, and textile printing. **2.** The gum of such a shrub. [French, from Latin *tragacantha,* from Greek *tragakantha,* "goat's thorn" : *tragos,* goat (see **tragedy**) + *akantha,* thorn.]

tra·ge·di·an (trə-jéedi-ən) *n.* **1.** A writer of tragedies. **2.** An actor of tragic roles. [Middle English *tragedien,* from Old French, from *tragedie,* TRAGEDY.]

tra·ge·di·enne (trə-jéedi-én) *n.* A woman who plays tragic roles in the theatre. [French *tragédienne.*]

trag·e·dy (trájədi) *n., pl.* **-dies. 1.** A dramatic or literary work in which the principal character engages in a morally significant struggle ending in ruin or profound disappointment; specifically: **a.** A classical verse drama in which a noble principal character is brought to ruin essentially as a consequence of some extreme quality which is both his greatness and his downfall. **b.** A Renaissance or modern drama resembling the classical model in representing terrible struggle and calamity, but freer in style and choice of principal character. **c.** Any serious play or narrative that deals with sad or calamitous events and has an unhappy and usually morally significant ending. **2.** The branch of drama dealing with such plays. **3.** Any dramatic, disastrous event, especially one of some moral significance. **4.** The tragic aspect or element of something. [Middle English *tragedie,* from Old French, from Latin *tragoedia,* from Greek *tragōidia,* "goat-song" (probably the name of a form of choric ceremony associated with (goat-)satyr plays) : *tragos*†, goat + *ōidē,* song, from *aeidein,* to sing.]

trag·ic (trájik) *adj.* Also *rare* **trag·i·cal** (-'l). **1.** Pertaining to, in the style of, or having the character of tragedy. **2.** Writing or performing in tragedy: *a tragic poet.* **3.** Having the elements of tragedy; involving death, grief, or destruction: *a tragic accident.* **4.** Mournful or grave: *Don't look so tragic!* [French *tragique,* from Latin *tragicus,* from Greek *tragikos,* from *tragos,* goat. See **tragedy.**] **—trag·i·cal·ly** *adv.* **—trag·i·cal·ness** *n.*

trag·i·com·e·dy (tráji-kómmədi) *n., pl.* **-dies. 1.** A drama that combines elements of both tragedy and comedy. **2.** The branch of drama dealing with such plays. **3.** An incident or situation having both comic and tragic elements. [French *tragicomédie,* from Late Latin *tragicōmoedia,* from Latin *tragicocōmoedia* : TRAGIC + COMEDY.] **—trag·i·com·ic** *adj.* **—trag·i·com·i·cal·ly** *adv.*

trag·o·pan (trággə-pan) *n.* Any of several Asian pheasants of the genus *Tragopan,* of which the male has brightly coloured plumage and two hornlike appendages on the head. [Latin *tragopān,* fabulous bird in Ethiopia, from Greek *tragopan,* "goat of Pan" : *tragos,* goat (see **tragedy**) + *Pan,* PAN.]

tra·gus (tráy-gəss) *n., pl.* **-gi** (-jī, -gī). **1.** The projection of skin-covered cartilage in front of the opening of the external ear. **2.** Any of the hairs growing at the entrance of the external ear. [New Latin, from Greek *tragos,* goat (the hair resembles a goat's beard).]

tra·hi·son des clercs (trī-i-ZON day klair) *n.* A betrayal of a cause or of their proper standards by intellectuals. [French, "treason of the intellectuals", from the title of a book (1927) by Julien Benda (1867–1956).]

trail (trayl) *v.* **trailed, trailing, trails.** *—tr.* **1.** To allow to drag or stream behind, as along the ground. **2.** To drag, pull, or tow. **3. a.** To form (a course, path, or track). **b.** To make a path or track through. **4.** To follow the traces or scent of, as in hunting; track. **5. a.** To follow slowly or wearily. **b.** To lag behind (an opponent). **6.** To advertise or pre-publicise (a film or television programme) by means of a trailer. **7.** To hint at the possibility of (a scheme or venture), as a subtle means of ascertaining other's attitudes to such a course. **8.** *Military.* To carry (a rifle) horizontally in the right hand with the arm extended straight downwards. *—intr.* **1.** To drag or be dragged along, brushing the ground. **2.** To extend, grow, or droop along the ground or over a surface, as a vine or plant might. **3.** To drift in a tenuous stream, as smoke from a cigarette. **4.** To become gradually fainter. Usually used with *away* or *off: Her voice trailed off sadly.* **5. a.** To walk slowly or wearily. **b.** To walk with dragging steps; trudge. **6.** To fall behind in competition; lag. *~n.* **1.** Something that hangs down loosely or drags along the ground: *trails of ribbons.* **2.** That which is drawn along or follows behind; a train. **3.** The part of a gun carriage that rests or slides on the ground. **4. a.** A mark, trace, course, or path left by a moving body. **b.** The scent of a person or animal. **c.** A blazed path or beaten track, as through woods or wilderness. **5.** A **trailer** (sense 4). **6.** The act or an instance of trailing. —See Synonyms at **trace, way.** [Middle English *trailen,* probably from Old French *trailler* and Middle Low German *treilen,* to tow, both from Vulgar Latin *tragulāre* (unattested), to drag, from Latin *trāgula,* dragnet, from *trahere,* to pull.]

trail bike *n.* A light, strong motor bike with special suspension and ridged tyres, used for riding over rough ground.

trail·blaz·er (tráyl-blayzər) *n.* **1.** One who blazes a trail. **2.** A leader in any field; a pioneer. **—trail·blaz·ing** *n. & adj.*
trail boss *n. U.S.* The man in charge of a cattle drive in the West.
trail·er (tráylər) *n.* **1.** One that trails. **2.** A large transport vehicle designed to be hauled by a tractor, as in an articulated lorry. **3.** A two- or four-wheeled road vehicle used to carry a boat or other load to be towed behind a car. **4.** A short filmed advertisement for a film or television programme, containing extracts from the film or programme. **5.** *U.S.* A **caravan** *(see).*
trailer trash *pl.n. Chiefly U.S. Informal.* Dysfunctional no-hopers of the sort that are held to live in caravans rather than proper houses and don't mind revealing their problems in public, or even on T.V. [From *trailer,* caravan + *trash,* as in *white trash.*]
trailing edge *n.* The rearmost edge of a structure, especially of an aerofoil.
trail rope *n.* A rope for guiding or dragging, as on a dirigible or gun carriage.
train (trayn) *n.* **1. a.** A string of connected railway carriages or goods wagons drawn by a locomotive. **b.** Transport or travel by railway. **2.** An orderly succession of related events or thoughts; a sequence. **3.** A set of linked mechanical parts: *a train of gears.* **4.** Something that follows or is drawn along behind, such as part of a dress or robe that trails behind the wearer. **5.** A body of persons following behind in attendance; a retinue: *a train of admirers.* **6.** A service unit of men, vehicles, and equipment following and attending an army. **7.** A long line of moving persons, animals, or vehicles. **8.** A string of gunpowder that acts as a fuse for exploding a charge. **—in train.** In preparation or under way. —See Synonyms at **series.**
~v. **trained, training, trains.** *—tr.* **1.** To coach in or accustom to some mode of behaviour or performance. **2.** To make proficient with specialised instruction and practice. **3.** To prepare physically, as with exercise or a regimen; make fit: *train a long-distance runner.* **4.** To cause (a plant, for example) to take a desired course or shape, as by manipulating. **5.** To focus or direct; aim. Usually used with *on* or *upon*: *Train your sights on the hilltop.* **6.** *Rare.* To draw, drag, or trail. *—intr.* To give or undergo a course of instruction, coaching, or exercises. —See Synonyms at **teach.** [Middle English *trayne,* from Old French *train,* from *tra(h)iner,* to drag, from Vulgar Latin *tragināre* (unattested), from *tragere* (unattested), variant of Latin *trahere.*] **—train·a·ble** *adj.*
train·band (tráyn-band) *n.* A militia trained as a supplement to the army in England from the 16th to the 18th century. [Originally *trained band.*]
train·bear·er (tráyn-bair-ər) *n.* An attendant who holds up the train of a robe or dress, as in a procession.
train·ee (tráy-née) *n.* A person who is being trained. Also used adjectivally: *a trainee salesman.* **—train·ee·ship** *n.*
train·er (tráynər) *n.* **1.** One who trains, especially one who coaches athletes, racehorses, or show animals. **2.** A contrivance or apparatus used in training. **3.** A type of running shoe.
train·ing (tráyning) *n.* **1.** The act, process, or routine of one who trains. **2.** The state of being trained. **3.** Good physical condition: *I'm out of training.*
train·load (tráyn-lōd) *n.* The full capacity of a railway train.
train spotter *n.* A person who engages in the pastime of collecting the numbers of railway locomotives. **—train spotting** *adj. & n.*
traipse (trayps) *intr.v.* **traipsed, traipsing, traipses.** *Informal.* **1.** To walk about casually. **2.** To walk wearily or slowly; trudge.
~n. A tiring walk. [16th century : origin obscure.]
trait (tray, trayt) *n.* **1.** A distinguishing feature, as of a person's character. **2.** *Rare.* A stroke; a touch. —See Synonyms at **quality.** [French, from Old French, pencil mark, stroke, from Latin *tractus,* a pulling, a drawing, from the past participle of *trahere,* to pull, drag.]
trai·tor (tráytər) *n.* A person who betrays his country, a cause, or a trust; especially, one who has committed treason. [Middle English *traitour,* from Old French, from Latin *trāditor.* See **traditor.**]
trai·tor·ous (tráytərəss) *adj.* **1.** Having the character of a traitor; disloyal. **2.** Constituting treason: *a traitorous act.* —See Synonyms at **faithless. —trai·tor·ous·ly** *adv.* **—trai·tor·ous·ness** *n.*
trai·tress (tráy-triss, -tress, -trəss) *n.* A female traitor.
tra·jec·to·ry (trájik-tri, -təri, trə-jéktəri) *n., pl.* **-ries. 1.** The path of a moving particle or body, especially such a path in three dimensions. **2.** In geometry, a curve that cuts all of a given family of curves or surfaces at the same angle. [Originally an adjective, from Medieval Latin *trājectōrius,* from Latin *trājectus.* See **traject.**]
tram[1] (tram) *n.* **1.** A vehicle used for public transport on the roads. It runs on rails and is electrically powered, usually by overhead wires. Also called "tramcar". *U.S.* "streetcar", "trolley (car)". **2.** A four-wheeled, open box-shaped wagon or iron car run on tracks in a mine. Also called "tram car". [Originally "shaft or frame of a truck", from Middle Low German, Middle Dutch *trame,* beam.]
tram[2] *n.* **1.** A machine gauge; a trammel. **2.** Accurate mechanical adjustment: *The device is in tram.*
~tr.v. **trammed, tramming, trams.** To adjust or align (mechanical parts) with a trammel. [Shortened from TRAMMEL.]
tram[3] *n.* A heavy silk thread used for the weft, or cross threads, in fine velvet or silk. [French *trame,* from Old French *traime,* woof, from Latin *trāma*†.]
tram·lines (trám-līnz) *pl.n.* **1.** The rails on which a tram runs. Also called "tramway". **2. a.** In tennis, either of the pairs of parallel lines that run down the sides of the court, or in badminton, any of the pairs that surround the court. **b.** The space between any of these pairs of lines. In this sense, also *U.S.* "alley".
tram·mel (trámm'l) *n.* **1.** *Often plural.* Something that restricts activity or free movement; a hindrance. **2.** *Chiefly U.S.* A shackle used to teach a horse to amble. **3.** A vertically set fishing net of three layers, consisting of a finely meshed net between two nets of coarse mesh. Also called "trammel net". **4. a.** An instrument for describing ellipses. **b.** A **beam compass** *(see).* **c.** The pivoted beam of a beam compass. **5.** An instrument for gauging and adjusting parts of a machine. **6.** *Chiefly U.S.* An arrangement of links and a hook in a fireplace for raising or lowering a kettle.
~tr.v. **trammelled** or *U.S.* **trammeled, -melling** or *U.S.* **-meling, -mels. 1.** To confine or hinder. **2.** To entrap. Sometimes used with *up.* **3.** To adjust (a machine) with a trammel. [Middle English, *tramale,* trammel net, from Old French *tramail,* from Late Latin *tremaculum* : *trēs,* three + *macula,* mesh, spot.] **—tram·mel·ler** *n.*
tra·mon·ta·na (tramən-taánə) *n.* A cold north wind sweeping down from the mountains in Italy and the Mediterranean.
tra·mon·tane (trə-món-tayn, trámmən-) *adj.* **1. a.** Dwelling beyond or coming from the far side of the mountains, especially the Alps as viewed from Italy. **b.** Foreign. **c.** Barbarous. **2.** Sweeping down from the mountains. Said of a wind.
~n. **1.** A person who lives beyond the mountains; an outsider; a foreigner. **2.** In Italy, a north or cold wind. [Middle English, from Italian *tramontano,* from Latin *trānsmontānus* : *trāns-,* beyond + *montānus,* mountainous (see **mountain**).]
tramp (tramp) *v.* **tramped, tramping, tramps.** *—intr.* **1.** To walk with a firm, heavy step; trudge. **2. a.** To go on foot; hike. **b.** To wander about aimlessly, as a tramp. *—tr.* **1.** To traverse on foot: *tramp the fields.* **2.** To tread down; trample: *tramp the snow down.*
~n. **1. a.** A heavy footfall; a stamp. **b.** A heavy rhythmic tread, as of a marching army. **c.** The sound produced by heavy walking or marching. **2. a.** A walking trip; a hike. **b.** An arduous walk. **3.** A person who travels aimlessly about on foot, doing odd jobs or begging for a living; a vagrant. **4.** *Chiefly U.S. Slang.* **a.** A prostitute. **b.** A promiscuous girl or woman. **5.** A cargo vessel that has no regular schedule but takes on freight wherever it may be found and discharges it wherever required. Also called "tramp steamer". **6. a.** A metal plate attached to the sole of a shoe for protection, as when using a spade to dig ground. **b.** The part of the spade on which the foot rests. [Middle English *trampen,* probably from Middle Low German.] **—tramp·er** *n.*
tram·ple (trámp'l) *v.* **-pled, -pling, -ples.** *—tr.* **1.** To beat down with the feet so as to crush, bruise, violate, or destroy; stamp upon. **2.** To treat harshly or ruthlessly, as if stepping or stamping upon. *—intr.* **1.** To tread heavily. **2.** To treat contemptuously or insensitively. Used with on: *He trampled on her feelings.*
~n. The action or sound of treading underfoot. [Middle English *tramp(e)len,* frequentative of *trampen,* to TRAMP.] **—tram·pler** *n.*
tram·po·line (trámpə-leen, -lin) *n.* A sheet of strong, taut canvas attached with springs to a metal frame and used for jumping on and performing acrobatic feats on.
~intr.v. **trampolined, -lining, -lines.** To compete, perform, or exercise on a trampoline. [From Italian *trampolino,* "performance on stilts", from *trampoli,* stilts, from Germanic.] **—tram·po·lin·er, tram·po·lin·ist** *n.*
tram·way (trám-way) *n. British.* A set of tramlines.
trance (traanss || transs) *n.* **1.** A hypnotic, cataleptic, or ecstatic state. **2.** A state of detachment from one's physical surroundings, as in contemplation or daydreaming. **3.** A dazed state, as between sleeping and waking; a stupor.
~tr.v. **tranced, trancing, trances.** To put into a trance. [Middle English *traunce,* from Old French *transe,* from *transir,* "to pass (from life to death)", depart, from Latin *transīre,* to go across. See **transit.**]
tranche (traansh, traanch || tranch) *n.* Any of the parts of a financial transaction, each of which is typically subject to different conditions (as of payment). [French, portion, slice; block (as of shares).]
trank (trangk) *n. Informal.* A tranquilliser.
tran·ny, tran·nie (tránni) *n., pl.* **-nies.** *Chiefly British Informal.* **1.** A transistor radio. **2.** In photography or graphics, a transparency; a slide. [*Tran-,* abstracted from *transistor,* + -Y.]
tran·quil (tránkwil) *adj.* **1.** Free from agitation or other disturbance; calm; unruffled; serene: *a tranquil rural life.* **2.** Steady; even: *a tranquil flame.* —See Synonyms at **calm, still.** [Latin *tranquillus.*] **—tran·quil·li·ty** (trang-kwílləti) *n.* **—tran·quil·ly** *adv.* **—tran·quil·ness** *n.*
tran·quil·lise, tran·quil·lize, *U.S.* **tran·quil·ize** (trángkwil-īz) *v.* **-ised, -ising, -ises.** *—tr.* To make tranquil; quiet. *—intr.* To become tranquil. **—tran·quil·li·sa·tion** (-ī-záysh'n || *U.S.*-i-) *n.*
tran·quil·lis·er (trángkwil-īzər) *n.* **1.** Something that tranquillises, such as music. **2.** Any of various drugs used to calm or pacify.
trans- *comb. form.* Indicates: **1.** Across or over; for example, **transpolar. 2.** Beyond or above; for example, **transcend, transpontine. 3.** From one place to another; for example, **translocate. 4.** Moving, transferring, or transporting; for example, **transship. 5.** Changing; for example, **transliterate. 6.** Having a greater atomic number; for example, **transuranic. 7.** A chemical compound in which two identical atoms or groups are on opposite sides of the plane of a double bond; for example, **trans-butadiene.** Compare **cis-.** ***Note:*** Many compounds other than those entered here may be formed with *trans-.* In forming compounds, *trans-* is normally joined with the following element without space or hyphen: *transculturation.* If the second element begins with a capital letter, it is usually separated with a hyphen: *trans-Canadian.* Note, however, that certain com-

pounds have become one word: *transatlantic, Transcaucasia.* [Latin *trāns,* across, over, beyond, through, through and through.]
trans. **1.** transaction. **2.** *Grammar.* transitive. **3.** translated; translation; translator. **4.** transpose; transposition. **5.** transverse.
trans·act (tran-zákt, traan-, trən-, -sákt) *v.* **-acted, -acting, -acts.** *—tr.* To do, carry out, perform, manage, or conduct (business or affairs, for example). *—intr.* To do business; negotiate. [Latin *transigere* (past participle *transactus*), to drive or carry through, complete : *trāns-,* through + *agere,* to drive.] **—trans·ac·tor** *n.*
trans·ac·ti·nide (tránz-ákti-nīd, traánz- || tránss-) *n.* Any of the artificially produced chemical elements with an atomic number in excess of 103. [TRANS- + ACTINIDE.]
trans·ac·tion (tran-záksh'n, traan-, trən-, -sáksh'n) *n. Abbr.* **trans.** **1.** The act of transacting or the fact of being transacted. **2.** Something transacted; especially, a piece of business. **3.** *Plural.* Published papers, discussions, or other proceedings, as of a conference, academic meeting, or the like. **—trans·ac·tion·al** *adj.*
transactional analysis *n.* A method of psychoanalysis concentrating on an individual's social exchanges or transactions in his relationships with others. Such exchanges are analysed in terms of roles (child, parent, or adult), goals, games, and the like.
trans·al·pine (tránz-ál-pīn, traánz-, tranz-, traanz- || transs-) *adj.* Pertaining to, living on, or coming from the other side of the Alps, especially as seen from Italy.
∼n. One who lives beyond the Alps.
Transalpine Gaul. The section of Gaul northwest of the Alps.
trans·at·lan·tic (tránz-ət-lántik, traánz-, -at- || tránss-) *adj.* **1.** On or from the other side of the Atlantic. **2.** Spanning or crossing the Atlantic.
Trans·cau·ca·si·a (tránz-kaw-káyzi-ə, traánz-, -káyzhə || tránss-). Region south of the Caucasus Mountains, lying between the Black and Caspian seas. After the Russian Revolution, this oil-rich region was a short-lived Soviet republic (1917–23). It was then divided into three Soviet republics, that in 1991 became independent as Georgia, Armenia, and Azerbaijan.
trans·ceiv·er (tran-seévər, traan-) *n.* A device consisting of a radio receiver and transmitter. [TRANS(MITTER) + (RE)CEIVER.]
tran·scend (tran-sénd, traan-) *v.* **-scended, -scending, -scends.** *—tr.* **1. a.** To pass beyond (a limit that humans can grasp): *an emotion that transcends understanding.* **b.** To exist above and independently of (material experience or the universe): *God transcends the world of phenomena.* **2.** To rise above or across; surpass; exceed: *Try to transcend your selfish desires* *—intr.* To be outstanding; excel. —See Synonyms at **excel.** [Middle English *transcenden,* from Old French *transcendre,* from Latin *transcendere,* "to climb over" : *trāns-,* over + *scandere,* to climb.]
tran·scen·dent (tran-séndənt, traan-) *adj.* **1.** Surpassing others of the same kind; pre-eminent. **2.** *Philosophy.* **a.** Transcending the Aristotelian categories. **b.** Especially in Kant's theory of knowledge, designating knowledge that is beyond the limits of experience. **3.** Above and independent of the material universe. Said of God. In this sense, compare **immanent.** **—tran·scen·dence, tran·scen·den·cy, tran·scen·dent·ness** *n.* **—tran·scen·dent·ly** *adv.*
tran·scen·den·tal (trán-sen-dént'l, traán-, -s'n-) *adj.* **1.** *Philosophy.* **a.** Concerned with the a priori or intuitive basis of knowledge. **b.** Asserting a fundamental irrationality or supernatural element in experience. **2.** Rising above common thought or ideas; exalted; mystical. **3.** *Mathematics.* **a.** Not capable of being determined by any combination of a finite number of equations with rational number coefficients. **b.** Not expressible as an integer or quotient of integers. Said of numbers, especially nonrepeating infinite decimals. **—tran·scen·den·tal·ly** *adv.*
tran·scen·den·tal·ism (trán-sen-dént'l-iz'm, traán-, -s'n-) *n.* **1.** *Philosophy.* **a.** The belief that knowledge of reality is dependent on a priori or intuitive knowledge rather than on objective experience. **b.** Any doctrine based on this belief, such as the philosophies of Kant and Emerson. **2.** The quality or condition of being transcendental. **3. a.** Any unrigorous philosophising or casual speculation. **b.** Exalted or irrational language. **—tran·scen·den·tal·ist** *n.*
transcendental meditation *n. Abbr.* **T.M.** A simple form of meditation derived from Hindu traditions and practised mainly in western countries, in which mental relaxation is promoted by the repeated silent utterance of a mantra.
trans·con·ti·nen·tal (tránz-kónti-nént'l, traánz- || tránss-) *adj.* Spanning or crossing a continent.
tran·scribe (tran-skrīb, traan-) *tr.v.* **-scribed, -scribing, -scribes.** **1.** To write or type a copy of; write out fully, as from shorthand notes: *transcribe a letter.* **2.** *Computing.* To transfer (information) from one recording and storing system to another. **3.** To adapt or arrange (a musical composition) for a voice or instrument other than the original. **4.** To record, usually on tape, for broadcasting at a later date. **5.** To represent (speech sounds) by phonetic symbols. **6.** To represent in a different alphabet; transliterate. **7.** *Genetics.* To cause transcription of (DNA). [Latin *transcrībere,* to copy, "write over" : *trāns-,* from one place to another, across + *scrībere,* to write.] **—tran·scrib·a·ble** *adj.* **—tran·scrib·er** *n.*
tran·script (trán-skript, traán-) *n.* Something transcribed; especially, a written, typed, or printed copy, as of a legal record. [Middle English *transcri(p)t,* from Old French *transcrit,* from Latin *transcriptum,* from the past participle of *transcrībere,* TRANSCRIBE.]
tran·scrip·tion (tran-skrípsh'n, traan-) *n.* **1. a.** The act or process or an instance of transcribing. **b.** The state of being transcribed. **2.** Something that has been transcribed, especially: **a.** A representation of speech sounds in phonetic symbols. **b.** An adaptation of a musical composition. **c.** A recorded radio or television programme. **3.** *Genetics.* The transfer of genetic information in DNA to RNA, usually by the synthesis of messenger RNA in which DNA acts as a template. **—tran·scrip·tion·al, tran·scrip·tive** *adj.* **—tran·scrip·tion·al·ly, tran·scrip·tive·ly** *adv.*
trans·cul·tu·ra·tion (tránz-kúlchə-ráysh'n, traánz- || tránss-) *n.* Cultural change induced by the introduction of elements of a foreign culture. [TRANS- + CULTURE + -ATION.]
trans·cur·rent (transs-kúrrənt, traanss-) *adj.* Extending, passing, or running transversely.
transcurrent fault *n.* A **strike-slip fault** *(see).*
trans·duc·er (tranz-déw-sər, traanz-, transs-, traanss- || -dōō) *n.* *Physics.* Any of various substances or devices, such as a piezoelectric crystal or a photoelectric cell, that convert input energy of one form into output energy of another. [Latin *transdūcere,* to lead across, transfer : *trāns-,* across + *dūcere,* to lead.]
trans·duc·tion (tranz-dúksh'n, traanz-, transs-, traanss-) *n.* **1.** The transfer of genetic material from one bacterial cell to another by a bacteriophage. **2.** *Physics.* The process of converting energy from one form into another. [Latin *transductiō* (stem *transductiōn-*), a transfer, from *transdūcere,* to transfer. See **transducer.**]
tran·sect (tran-sékt, traan-) *tr.v.* **-sected, -secting, -sects.** To divide by cutting transversely. [TRANS- + Latin *secāre* (past participle *sectus*), to cut.] **—tran·sec·tion** *n.*
tran·sept (trán-sept, traán-) *n. Architecture.* **1.** The shorter portion of a cross-shaped church, consisting of two arms that run across and at right-angles to the main body of the church. **2.** Either of the two arms. [New Latin *transeptum* : TRANS- + SEPTUM (partition).]
trans·e·unt (trán-zi-ənt, traán-, -si-) *adj. Philosophy.* Productive of effects outside of the mind. Compare **immanent.** [Latin *transiēns* (oblique stem *transeunt-*), going over, TRANSIENT.]
trans·fer (transs-fér, traanss- || tránss-fer, traánss-) *v.* **-ferred, -ferring, -fers.** *—tr.* **1.** To convey or shift from one person, thing, or place to another: *transferred to a new job.* **2.** To change or shift (the meaning of a word, phrase, or the like), especially by figurative use. **3.** To make over the possession or legal title of to another. **4.** To convey (a drawing, pattern, mural, or design) from one surface to another. **5.** To sell or move (a professional sportsman) from one club to another. *—intr.* **1.** To move oneself, as from one location, job, or school to another. **2.** To change from one train, aeroplane, or the like to another. —See Synonyms at **convey.**
∼n. (tránss-fer, traánss- || -fər). Also **trans·fer·al** (transs-fér-əl, traanss-), **trans·fer·ral** (for senses 1, 2). *Abbr.* **tfr., transf.** **1. a.** The act or process of transferring. **b.** The state of being transferred. **2.** Any person or object that has or has been transferred, especially: **a.** A sports player, especially a footballer, who has moved from one club to another. Also used adjectivally: *transfer list.* **b.** A design conveyed or to be conveyed from one surface, usually paper, to another. **3.** *Chiefly U.S.* A ticket entitling a passenger to change from one train, bus, or the like to another. **4.** *Law.* **a.** The conveyance of title, property, or shares from one owner to another. **b.** The document effecting such conveyance. [Middle English *transferren,* from Old French *transferer,* from Latin *trānsferre,* to bear across : *trāns-,* across + *ferre,* to bear.] **—trans·fer·a·bil·i·ty** (-ə-bílləti) *n.* **—trans·fer·a·ble** (transs-fér-əb'l, traanss-, tránss-fər-, traánss-, -frəb'l) *adj.* **—trans·fer·rer** *n.*
transferable vote *n.* **1.** A vote that, although cast for one particular candidate, may be transferred to another candidate specified by the voter, if for example, the voter's first choice is eliminated. **2.** The vote cast or indication made in favour of this second candidate. **3.** The system providing for such voting.
trans·fer·ase (tránss-fər-ayz, traánss-, -ayss) *n.* Any of various enzymes that catalyse the transfer of radicals from one molecule to another.
transfer charge call *n.* A **reverse-charge call** *(see).*
trans·fer·ee (tránss-fer-eé, traánss-) *n.* **1.** *Law.* One to whom a transfer of title or property is made. **2.** One who is transferred.
trans·fer·ence (tránss-fərənss, traánss-, -frənss, transs-fér-ənss, traanss-) *n.* **1. a.** An act or process or an instance of transferring. **b.** The condition of being transferred. **2.** *Psychology.* The process in and by which an individual's feelings, thoughts, and wishes shift from one person to another; especially, this process in psychoanalysis where the analyst is made the object of the shift. **—trans·fer·en·tial** (tránss-fə-rénsh'l, traánss-) *adj.*
transfer fee *n.* A sum of money paid for a transfer; especially, a fee paid for a footballer by one football club to another.
transfer income *n.* Income regarded as a simple transfer of funds from one part of the community to another, rather than as a return for goods and services. It includes government subsidies, unemployment benefits, pensions, and the like, and is not calculated as part of the national income. Also called "transfer payment".
trans·fer·or (transs-fér-ər, traanss-, tránss-fer-, traánss-) *n. Law.* A person who makes a transfer of title or property.
transfer paper *n.* Any of various types of specially coated paper used for transferring designs from one surface to another.
trans·fer·rin (transs-férrin) *n.* A blood globulin that can combine reversibly with and transport iron ions in the body. [TRANS- + FERR(O)- + -IN.]
transfer RNA *n.* Any of various small RNA molecules, each specific for a particular amino acid, that during synthesis carry amino acids to the ribosomes and arrange them along the messenger RNA molecule, where they are joined by peptide bonds to form a protein.

Also called "s RNA", "soluble RNA", "t RNA".

trans•fig•u•ra•tion (tránss-figgewr-áysh'n, traánss-, -figgər-, tránss-fíggewr-, traanss-, -fíggər-) *n.* **1.** A radical transformation of figure or appearance; a metamorphosis. **2.** *Capital* **T. a.** The sudden emanation of radiance from Jesus's person that occurred on the mountain. Matthew 17:2; Mark 9:2. **b.** The Christian commemoration of this, observed on August 6. **3.** The act or an instance of transfiguring, or the state of being transfigured.

trans•fig•ure (transs-fíggər, traánss- || *chiefly U.S.* -fíggewr) *tr.v.* **-ured, -uring, -ures. 1.** To transform the figure or appearance of; alter radically, especially so as to improve. **2.** To exalt; glorify. [Middle English, from Latin *trānsfigūrāre* : *trāns-*, change + *figūra,* FIGURE.] **—trans•fig•ure•ment** *n.*

trans•fi•nite (tránss-fī-nīt, traánss-) *adj.* Beyond the finite.

transfinite number *n.* Any cardinal or ordinal number representing the size of a set of numbers too large to be counted.

trans•fix (transs-fíks, traanss-) *tr.v.* **-fixed, -fixing, -fixes. 1.** To pierce through with or as if with a pointed weapon. **2.** To fix fast; impale. **3.** To render motionless, as with terror, amazement, or awe. [Latin *transfīgere* (past participle *transfīxus*) : *trans-,* through + *fīgere,* to pierce, fix.] **—trans•fix•ion** (-fíksh'n) *adj.*

trans•form (transs-fórm, traanss-) *v.* **-formed, -forming, -forms.** *—tr.* **1.** To change markedly the form, character, or appearance of, especially for the better: *His new wife has transformed him!* **2.** To change the nature, function, or condition of; convert. **3.** *Mathematics.* To subject to a mathematical transformation. **4.** *Electricity.* To subject to the action of a transformer. *—intr.* To undergo a transformation. —See Synonyms at **change.**

∼n. (tránss-fawrm, traánss-). The result, especially a mathematical quantity or linguistic construction, of a transformation. [Middle English, from Old French, from Latin *transformāre* : TRANS- + FORM.] **—trans•form•a•ble** (-fórməb'l) *adj.*

trans•for•ma•tion (tránss-fər-máysh'n, traánss-, -fawr-) *n.* **1. a.** The act of transforming. **b.** The state or an instance of being transformed. **c.** Something that has been transformed. **2.** Any extreme or radical change, especially for the better. **3.** *Mathematics.* **a.** The replacement of the variables in an algebraic expression by their values in terms of another set of variables. **b.** A mapping of one space onto another or onto itself. **4.** *Physics.* A change of one nuclide into another as a result of an alpha decay or a beta decay. **5.** *Linguistics.* **a.** The process of converting a syntactic construction into a semantically equivalent construction according to the rules shown to generate the syntax of the language. **b.** A construction derived by such transformation. **5.** *Rare.* A woman's wig. [Middle English, from Late Latin *transformātio* (stem *transformātiōn-*). See **transform.**] **—trans•for•ma•tive** (transs-fórmətiv, traanss-) *adj.*

trans•for•ma•tion•al•gen•e•ra•tive grammar (transs-fər-máysh'n'l-jén-rətiv, traánss-, -fawr-, -jénnə-) *n. Linguistics.* A grammar that accounts for the constructions of a language by linguistic transformations and phrase structures, on the assumption that languages have a **deep structure** and a **surface structure** *(both of which see).* Also called "transformational grammar".

trans•form•er (transs-fórmər, traanss-) *n.* **1.** One that transforms. **2.** A device used to transfer electric energy, usually that of an alternating current, from one circuit to another; especially, a pair of multiply wound, inductively coupled wire coils that effect such a transfer with a change in voltage, current, phase, or other electric characteristic. See **step-down transformer, step-up transformer.**

trans•fuse (trans-féwz, traanss-) *tr.v.* **-fused, -fusing, -fuses. 1.** To transfer (liquid) by pouring from one vessel into another. **2.** To permeate; infuse. **3.** *Medicine.* To administer a transfusion of or to. [Middle English *transfusen,* from Latin *trānsfundere* (past participle *trānsfūsus*) : *trāns-*, from one place to another + *fundere,* to pour.] **—trans•fus•er** *n.* **—trans•fus•i•ble** *adj.* **—trans•fu•sive** (-féw-siv, -ziv) *adj.*

trans•fu•sion (transs-féwzh'n, traanss-) *n.* **1.** The act or process or an instance of transfusing. **2.** *Medicine.* The injection of whole blood, plasma, or another solution into the bloodstream of a person.

trans•gress (transs-gréss, traanss-, tranz-, traanz-) *v.* **-gressed, -gressing, -gresses.** *—tr.* **1.** To go beyond or over (a limit or boundary). **2.** To act in violation of (the law, for example). *—intr.* To trespass; sin. [Latin *trānsgredī* (past participle *trānsgressus*), to step across : *trāns-*, across + *gradī,* to step.] **—trans•gress•i•ble** *adj.* **—trans•gres•sive** *adj.* **—trans•gres•sive•ly** *adv.* **—trans•gres•sor** (-ər) *n.*

trans•gres•sion (transs-grésh'n, traanss-, tranz-, traanz-) *n.* **1.** The violation of a law, command, or duty; a crime or sin. **2.** The exceeding or overstepping of due bounds or limits. —See Synonyms at **breach.**

tran•ship. Variant of **transship.**

trans•hu•mance (transs-héwmənss, traanss-) *n.* The movement of livestock and herders to different grazing grounds with the changing of the seasons. [French, from *transhumer,* to make seasonal movement of livestock, from Spanish *transhumar* : Latin *trāns-*, from one place to another + *humus,* earth, ground.] **—trans•hu•mant** *adj.* & *n.*

tran•si•ent (trán-zi-ənt, traán-, -si-, -zh-, -shi- || *chiefly U.S.* -shənt, -zhənt) *adj.* **1.** Passing away with time; transitory; fleeting. **2.** Passing through from one place to another; stopping only briefly: *transient labourers.* **3.** *Physics.* Decaying with time, especially as a simple exponential function of time. **4.** *Music.* Adopted only in passing, as a link; not essential to the harmony: *a transient chord.*

∼n. **1.** One that is transient. **2.** *Physics.* A transient phenomenon or property, especially a transient electric current. [Latin *transiēns* (stem *transient-*), present participle of *transīre,* to go over : *trāns-*, over, across + *īre,* to go.] **—tran•si•ence** (-ənss), **tran•si•en•cy** (-ən-si), **tran•si•ent•ness** *n.* **—tran•si•ent•ly** *adv.*

Synonyms: *transient, transitory, ephemeral, fleeting, fugitive, momentary, evanescent, temporary, provisional.*

trans•il•lu•mi•nate (tránz-i-lóomi-nayt, traánz-, -léwmi- || tránss-) *tr.v.* **-nated, -nating, -nates.** *Medicine.* To place a strong light behind (a translucent body part) to show up fluid, lesions, cavities, or the like. **—trans•il•lu•mi•na•tion** (-náysh'n) *n.*

tran•sis•tor (tran-zístər, traan-, -sístər) *n.* **1.** A semiconductor device used for amplification, switching, and detection, typically containing two rectifying junctions, and usually having three terminals and characteristically operating so that the current between one pair of terminals controls the current between the other pair, one terminal being common to input and output. **2.** A radio equipped with transistors. In this sense, also called "transistor radio". [Originally a trademark : *trans*fer + *resistor.*]

tran•sis•tor•ise, tran•sis•tor•ize (tran-zístər-īz, traan-, -sístər-) *tr.v.* **-ised, -ising, -ises. 1.** To equip (an electronic circuit or device) with transistors. **2.** To design or refit (a machine, factory, or the like) to use transistors.

tran•sit (trán-zit, traán-, -sit) *n.* **1. a.** The act of passing over, across, or through; passage. **b.** The movement or conveyance of goods or persons from one place to another. **2.** A transition or change, especially from one life to another at death. **3.** *Astronomy.* **a.** The apparent passage of a celestial body across the observer's meridian. **b.** The passage of a smaller celestial body across the disc of a larger celestial body. **4.** A way, passage, or route. **—in transit. 1.** While being moved or conveyed. **2.** Only stopping temporarily; continuing one's journey. Said especially of airline passengers.

∼v. **transited, -siting, -sits.** *—tr.* **1.** To pass over, across, or through. **2.** To revolve (the telescope of a surveying transit) about its horizontal transverse axis in order to reverse its direction. *—intr. Astronomy.* To make a transit. [Latin *transitus,* from the past participle of *transīre,* to go across. See **transient.**]

transit camp *n.* A temporary camp for the accommodation of people in transit such as emigrants, refugees, or soldiers.

transit instrument *n.* A telescope mounted on a horizontal east-west axis used to observe the passage of stars across the meridian.

tran•si•tion (tran-zísh'n, traan-, -sízh'n || -sísh'n) *n.* **1. a.** The act or process or an instance of changing from one form, state, activity, or place to another. **b.** The length of time involved in such a change. **2.** Passage from one subject to another, as in discourse. **3.** *Music.* **a.** A modulation, especially a brief one. **b.** A passage connecting two themes. **4.** *Physics.* **a.** In quantum mechanics, the change of a system from one energy state to another. **b.** A change in a nuclide involving either a transformation to another nuclide or a change in energy level as a result of gamma-ray emission. **5.** In various arts, a change from one tradition or style to another, or a combination of elements of an older style and a newer style as in transitional architecture. **—tran•si•tion•al, tran•si•tion•ar•y** (-əri || -erri) *adj.* **—tran•si•tion•al•ly** *adv.*

transitional architecture *n.* Architecture of the period, around the year 1100, of transition from the Romanesque to the Gothic. In Britain it is marked by a combination of the Norman and early English styles.

transition element *n.* **1.** Any of the elements that serve as transitional links between the most and the least electropositive in a series of elements, and that are characterised by high melting points, densities, magnetic moments, multiple valencies, and the ability to form stable complex ions. **2.** Any of the elements in which an inner electron shell rather than an outer shell is only partially filled, generally taken to include elements 21–30, 39–48, and 57–80. Also called "transition metal".

transition temperature *n.* The temperature at which there is a sudden change in a particular physical property of a substance, such as its crystalline structure, conductivity, or magnetism. Also called "transition point".

tran•si•tive (trán-zə-tiv, traán-, -sə-, -zi-, -si-) *adj.* **1.** *Abbr.* **t., tr., trans.** *Grammar.* **a.** Expressing an action that is carried from the subject to the object. **b.** Designating a verb or verb construction that requires a direct object to complete its meaning; for example, the verb *vanquish* is always transitive, and the verb *win* is sometimes transitive. **2.** Characterised by or effecting transition. **3.** *Mathematics & Logic.* Designating a relationship such that if A and B have a particular relation, and B and C have the same relation, then so do A and C; for example, if A is a number which has a value less than that of B, and the value of B is less that that of C, then the value of A is less than that of C: therefore "is less than" is a transitive relationship.

∼n. Abbr. **t., tr., trans.** *Grammar.* A transitive verb. [Late Latin *transitīvus,* passing over (as from the subject to the object), from Latin *transitus,* TRANSIT.] **—tran•si•tive•ly** *adv.* **—tran•si•tive•ness, tran•si•tiv•i•ty** (-tívvəti) *n.*

tran•si•to•ry (trán-zi-tri, traán-, -si-, -zə-, -sə-, -təri) *adj.* Existing or occurring only briefly; short-lived; passing. See Synonyms at **transient.** [Middle English *transitorie,* from Anglo-French, from Late Latin *transitōrius,* from Latin, adapted for passing through, from *transitus,* TRANSIT.] **—tran•si•to•ri•ly** *adv.* **—tran•si•to•ri•ness** *n.*

transitory action *n.* A legal action or case that may be brought in any country, and not merely in the one in which it originated.

Transjordan. See **Jordan, Hashemite Kingdom of.**

Trans·kei (tránss-kī, traánss-, tránz-, traánz-). Former autonomous region of South Africa established as the homelands of the Xhosa people, and incorporated into Kwazulu-Natal province. Area, 43 077 square kilometres (16,632 square miles). Population (Xhosa), 2,300,000 (plus 1,000,000 in South Africa). Capital, Umtata. —**Trans·kei·an** *n. & adj.*

transl. translated; translation.

trans·late (tranz-láyt, traanz-, transs-, traanss-, trənz- || *U.S. also* tránss-layt, tránz-) *v.* **-lated, -lating, -lates.** —*tr.* **1.** To express in another language, systematically retaining the original sense. **2. a.** To put in simpler terms; explain. **b.** To see the significance of; infer; interpret. **3.** To convey from one form or style to another; convert. **4.** To transfer (a bishop) to another see. **5.** To move or transfer. **6. a.** *Theology.* To convey to heaven without natural death. **b.** To move or promote to a higher or more exalted position. Often used humorously: *He's been translated to the peerage.* **7.** *Physics.* To subject (a body) to translation. **8.** *Genetics.* To cause translation of (messenger RNA). **9.** *Archaic.* To transport; enrapture. —*intr.* **1. a.** To make a translation. **b.** To work as a translator. **2.** To admit of or be capable of translation. **3.** *Aerospace.* To move from one place to another in space by means of reaction power. [Middle English *translaten,* to transport, to translate, from Latin *translātus* (past participle of *transferre,* to carry across, transfer, translate) : *trāns-,* across + *-lātus,* "carried".] —**trans·lat·a·bil·i·ty** (-ə-bílləti), **trans·lat·a·ble·ness** *n.* —**trans·lat·a·ble** *adj.*

trans·la·tion (tranz-láysh'n, traanz-, transs-, traanss-, trənz-, trənss-) *n. Abbr.* **transl., trans., tr. 1. a.** The act or process or an instance of translating, especially from one language to another. **b.** The condition of being translated. **2.** A translated version of a text. **3.** *Physics.* Motion of a body in which every point of the body moves parallel to, and the same distance as, every other point of the body; nonrotational displacement. **4.** *Biochemistry.* The decoding of the genetic information in a messenger RNA molecule so that it may be used to synthesise protein molecules. —**trans·la·tion·al** *adj.*

trans·la·tor (tranz-láytər, traanz-, transs-, traanss-, trənz-, trənss- || *U.S. also* tránss-laytər, tránz-) *n. Abbr.* **tr., trans. 1.** One who translates; especially, one professionally employed to translate written works. **2.** An interpreter. —**trans·la·to·ri·al** (tráz-lay-táw-ri-əl, traanz-, tránss-, traánss- || -tō-) *adj.*

trans·lit·er·ate (tranz-líttə-rayt, traanz-, transs-, traanss-) *tr.v.* **-ated, -ating, -ates.** To represent (letters or words) in the corresponding characters of another alphabet. [TRANS- + Latin *littera,* LETTER + -ATE.] —**trans·lit·er·a·tion** (-ráysh'n) *n.*

trans·lo·cate (tránz-lō-káyt, traánz-, tránss-, -lə- || *U.S. also* -lō-kayt) *tr.v.* **-cated, -cating, -cates.** To cause to change from one position to another; displace; move.

trans·lo·ca·tion (tránz-lō-káysh'n, traánz- tránss-, traánss-, -lə-) *n.* **1.** A change in location. **2.** *Genetics.* A chromosomal aberration in which sections from different chromosomes are interchanged. **3.** The movement of mineral nutrients, food materials, and the like in plants.

trans·lu·cent (tranz-lóō-s'nt, traanz-, transs-, traanss-, -léw-) *adj.* Transmitting light but causing sufficient diffusion to eliminate perception of distinct images. Compare **transparent, opaque.** [Latin *translūcēns* (stem *translūcent-*), present participle of *translūcēre,* to shine through : *trāns-,* through + *lūcēre,* to shine.] —**trans·lu·cence, trans·lu·cen·cy** *n.* —**trans·lu·cent·ly** *adv.*

trans·lun·ar (tránz-lóō-nər, traánz-, tránss-, traánss-, -léw-) *adj.* Lying beyond the moon. Compare **cislunar.**

trans·lu·na·ry (tranz-lóō-nəri, traanz-, transs-, traanss-, -léw-) *adj.* **1.** Translunar. **2.** Unearthly; visionary. [TRANS- + *-lunary.*]

trans·ma·rine (tránz-mə-réen, traánz-, tránss-, traánss-) *adj.* **1.** Crossing the sea. **2.** Being beyond or coming from across the sea. [Latin *transmarīnus* : *trāns-,* across, beyond + *mare,* sea.]

trans·mi·grant (tranz-mīgrənt, traanz-, transs-, traanss-) *n.* **1.** One who transmigrates; an immigrant. **2.** An immigrant in transit through a country to the country in which he intends to settle.

trans·mi·grate (tránz-mī-gráyt, traánz-, tránss-, traánss- || *U.S.* -mī-grayt, -mī-grayt) *intr.v.* **-grated, -grating, -grates. 1.** To migrate. **2.** To pass into another body after death. Used of the soul. —**trans·mi·gra·tor** (-ər) *n.* —**trans·mi·gra·to·ry** (-mī-grə-tri, -təri, -mī-gráytəri) *adj.*

trans·mi·gra·tion (tránz-mī-gráysh'n, traánz-, tránss-, traánss-) *n.* **1.** The act or process of transmigrating. **2.** The passing of a soul into another body after death; metempsychosis. Also called "transmigration of souls". —**trans·mi·gra·tion·ism** *n.*

trans·mis·si·ble (tranz-míssə-b'l, traanz-, transs-, traanss-) *adj.* Capable of being transmitted. —**trans·mis·si·bil·i·ty** (-bílləti) *n.*

trans·mis·sion (tranz-mísh'n, traanz-, transs-, traanss-) *n.* **1. a.** The act or process of transmitting. **b.** The state of being transmitted. **2.** Something transmitted, such as a message. **3. a.** An assembly of gears and associated parts by which power is transmitted from the engine of a motor vehicle to a driving axle. **b.** A system of gears. **4.** The sending of modulated carrier waves from a transmitter; a broadcast. [Latin *transmissiō* (stem *transmissiōn-*), from *transmissus,* past participle of *transmittere,* TRANSMIT.] —**trans·mis·sive** (-míssiv) *adj.*

transmission line *n.* A coaxial cable, waveguide, or other system of conductors used to transfer information from one place to another.

trans·mis·siv·i·ty (tránz-mi-sívvəti, traánz-, tránss-, traánss-) *n. Physics.* A measure of the ability of a medium to transmit radiation given by the internal transmittance of unit length of a material.

trans·mit (tranz-mít, traanz-, transs-, traanss-) *v.* **-mitted, -mitting, -mits.** —*tr.* **1.** To send from one person, thing, or place to another; convey. **2.** To cause to spread; pass on: *transmit an infection.* **3.** To impart or convey to others by heredity; hand down. **4.** *Electronics.* **a.** To send (a signal), as by wire or radio. **b.** To broadcast (a television or radio programme). **5.** *Physics.* To cause (a disturbance) to propagate through a medium. **6.** To convey (force or energy) from one part of a mechanism to another. —*intr.* To send out a signal. —See Synonyms at **convey.** [Middle English *transmitten,* from Latin *transmittere,* to send across : *trāns-,* across + *mittere,* to send.] —**trans·mit·ta·ble, trans·mit·ti·ble** *adj.* —**trans·mit·tal** *n.*

trans·mit·tance (tranz-mítt'nss, traanz-, transs-, traanss-) *n.* **1.** The act or process of transmitting; a transmission. **2.** *Physics.* The ratio of the radiant energy transmitted to the total radiant energy incident on a given body. Compare **absorptance, reflectance.**

trans·mit·tan·cy (tranz-mítt'n-si, traanz-, transs-, traanss-) *n. Physics.* The transmittance of a solution divided by the transmittance of a pure solvent of identical dimensions.

trans·mit·ter (tranz-míttər, traanz-, transs-, traanss-) *n.* **1.** One that transmits. **2.** A telegraphic sending instrument. **3.** The portion of a telephone that converts the incident sounds into electrical impulses that are conveyed to a remote receiver. **4.** Electronic equipment that generates and amplifies a carrier wave, modulates it with a signal derived from speech or other sources, and radiates the resulting signal from an aerial. **5.** In physiology, a **neurotransmitter** *(see).*

trans·mog·ri·fy (tranz-móggri-fī, traanz-, transs-, traanss-) *tr.v.* **-fied, -fying, -fies.** To change into a different shape or form, especially one that is fantastic or bizarre. Often used humorously. [17th century : origin obscure.] —**trans·mog·ri·fi·ca·tion** (-fi-káysh'n) *n.*

trans·mon·tane (tranz-món-tayn, traanz-, transs-, traanss- || -montáyn) *adj.* Located beyond a mountain or mountain range; tramontane. [Latin *trānsmontānus,* TRAMONTANE.]

trans·mu·ta·tion (tránz-mew-táysh'n, traánz-, tránss-, traánss-) *n.* **1.** The act of transmuting. **2.** The state of being transmuted. **3.** In alchemy, the alleged conversion of base metals into gold or silver. **4.** *Physics.* The transformation of one element into another by one or a series of nuclear reactions. [Middle English, from Old French, from Late Latin *transmūtātiō* (stem *transmūtātiōn-*). See **transmute.**] —**trans·mu·ta·tion·al, trans·mut·a·tive** (-méwtətiv, -mew-táytiv) *adj.*

trans·mute (tranz-méwt, traanz-, transs-, traanss-) *tr.v.* **-muted, -muting, -mutes.** To change from one form, nature, substance, or state into another; transform. See Synonyms at **change.** [Middle English *transmuten,* from Latin *transmūtāre* : *trāns-,* from one to another + *mūtāre,* to change.] —**trans·mut·a·bil·i·ty** (-ə-bílləti), **trans·mut·a·ble·ness** *n.* —**trans·mut·a·ble** *adj.* —**trans·mut·a·bly** *adv.* —**trans·mut·er** *n.*

trans·na·tion·al (tránz-násh'n'l, traánz-, -náshn'l) *adj.* Not confined to a single nation; extending across national frontiers; multinational; international.
∼*n.* A transnational company; a multinational.

trans·o·ce·an·ic (tránz-ōshi-ánnik, traánz-, -ō-si- || tránss-) *adj.* **1.** Situated beyond or on the other side of the ocean. **2.** Spanning or crossing the ocean.

tran·som (tránss'm) *n.* **1.** A horizontal bar that is situated between a door and a window above it. **2.** A horizontal dividing bar of wood or stone in a window. **3.** A window that has been divided with a transom. **4.** *Chiefly U.S.* A **fanlight** *(see).* **5.** *Nautical.* Any of several transverse beams affixed to the sternpost of a wooden ship and forming part of the stern. **6.** The horizontal beam on a cross or gallows, or the top piece of a trilith. [Middle English *traunson,* crossbeam, lintel, perhaps from Latin *transtrum* : *trāns-,* across + *-trum,* suffix denoting an instrument.] —**tran·somed** *adj.*

tran·son·ic (tran-sónnik, traan-) *adj.* Of or pertaining to aerodynamic flow or flight conditions at speeds close to the speed of sound. [TRANS- + (SUPER)SONIC.]

transp. transport; transportation.

trans·pa·cif·ic (tránss-pə-síffik, traánss-) *adj.* **1.** Crossing the Pacific Ocean. **2.** Situated across or beyond the Pacific Ocean.

trans·par·en·cy (transs-párrən-si, traanss-, tranz-, traanz-, trənss-, trənz-, -páir-ən-) *n., pl.* **-cies.** Also **trans·par·ence** (-párrənss, -páir-ənss) (for sense 1). **1.** The quality or state of being transparent. **2.** A transparent object; especially, a photographic slide whose image is made visible by light shining through from behind.

trans·par·ent (transs-párrənt, traanss-, tranz-, traanz-, trənss-, trənz-, -páir-ənt) *adj.* **1.** Capable of transmitting light so that objects or images can be seen clearly. Compare **translucent, opaque. 2.** Permeable to electromagnetic radiation of specified frequencies, as to visible light or radio waves. **3.** Of such fine or open texture that objects may be easily seen on the other side; diaphanous; sheer. **4.** Easily understood or detected; flimsy or obvious: *transparent lies.* **5.** Guileless; candid; open. [Middle English, from Old French, from Medieval Latin *trānspārēns* (stem *transpārent-*), present participle of *trānspārēre,* to be seen through : Latin *trāns-,* through + *pārēre,* to show (see **appear**).] —**trans·par·ent·ly** *adv.* —**trans·par·ent·ness** *n.*

tran·spi·ra·tion (trán-spi-ráysh'n, traán-, -spə-) *n.* The act or process of transpiring, especially through the stomata of plant tissue or the pores of the skin.

tran·spire (tran-spír, traan-) *v.* **-spired, -spiring, -spires.** —*tr.* **1.** To secrete (water containing waste products) through the pores of the skin; perspire. **2.** To lose (water vapour) from the surface of a plant, mainly through open stomata. **3.** To become known; come to light. Used impersonally with a clause. **4.** *Informal.* **a.** To happen; occur. **b.** To come to pass; turn out. Used impersonally with a clause. —*intr.* **1.** To secrete water containing waste products through animal pores. **2.** To lose water vapour from a plant surface. **3.** To become known; come to light. **4.** *Informal.* **a.** To happen; occur. **b.** To come to pass; turn out. [French *transpirer,* from Old French : Latin *trāns-,* out + *spīrāre,* to breathe.]

Usage: *Transpire* is frequently used in the general sense of "happen, occur": *The accident transpired when the lights changed,* or "come to pass, turn out": *It transpired that the weather was awful,* but these uses attract purist criticism, which holds that the figurative sense of the word should be restricted to "come to light": *It transpired that he had been in prison once before.*

trans·plant (transs-plaant, traanss- || -plánt) *v.* **-planted, -planting, -plants.** —*tr.* **1.** To uproot and replant (a growing plant). **2.** To transfer from one place or residence to another; resettle; relocate. **3.** In surgery, to transfer (tissue or an organ) from one body, or body part, to another. —*intr.* **1.** To admit or be capable of being transplanted. **2.** To survive transplanting.

~*n.* (tránss-plaant, tráanss- || -plant). **1.** Something transplanted. **2.** The act or process of transplanting: *a heart transplant.* [Middle English *transplaunten,* from Late Latin *transplantāre* : Latin *trans-,* across + *plantāre,* to plant (see **plant**).] **—trans·plan·ta·tion** (tránssplaan-táysh'n, tráanss-, -plan-) *n.* **—trans·plant·er** *n.*

trans·po·lar (tránz-pṓlər, tráanz- || tránss-) *adj.* Extending across or crossing over either of the geographic polar regions.

tran·spond·er (tran-spóndər, traan-) *n.* A radio or radar receiver-transmitter activated for transmission by reception of a predetermined signal. [*trans*mitter + res*ponder.*]

trans·pon·tine (tránz-pón-tīn, tráanz- || tránss-) *adj.* **1.** Situated across or beyond a bridge. **2.** Of or pertaining to the part of London on the south side of the Thames or the melodramatic plays performed there in the 19th century. [TRANS- + Latin *pōns* (stem *pont-*), bridge + -INE.]

trans·port (tránss-pórt, tráanss- || -pṓrt, tránss-pawrt, tráanss-, -pōrt) *tr.v.* **-ported, -porting, -ports.** **1.** To carry from one place to another; convey. **2.** To move to strong emotion; enrapture; carry away: *transported by the scene.* **3.** Especially formerly, to send abroad to a penal colony; deport. —See Synonyms at **convey.**

~*n.* (tránss-pawrt, tráanss-, -pōrt). *Abbr.* **transp. 1.** The act of transporting; conveyance. **2.** The state or condition of being transported by emotion; rapture. **3.** A ship used to transport troops or military equipment. **4.** A vehicle, such as an aircraft, used to transport passengers, mail, or freight. **5. a.** The system of transporting passengers or goods in a particular country or area: *public transport.* **b.** The vehicles, such as buses and trains, used in such a system. **6.** Especially formerly, a deported convict. —See Synonyms at **ecstasy.** [Middle English *transporten,* from Old French *transporter,* from Latin *trānsportāre* : *trāns-,* from one place to another + *portāre,* to carry.] **—trans·port·a·bil·i·ty** (-ə-billəti) *n.* **—trans·port·a·ble** (-pórt-əb'l || -pṓrt-) *adj.* **—trans·port·er** *n.* **—trans·port·ive** *adj.*

trans·por·ta·tion (tránss-pawr-táysh'n, tráanss- || -pōr-, -pər-) *n.* *Abbr.* **transp. 1.** The act of transporting. **2.** The state of being transported. **3.** *Chiefly U.S.* **Transport** (senses 5a,b). **4.** *U.S.* A charge for transporting; a fare.

transport café *n.* In Britain, a café serving cheap, simple food and situated on or near a main road, especially for the use of lorry drivers and other motorists.

transporter bridge *n.* A bridge that has a large moving platform supported by cables, used especially for carrying vehicles.

trans·pose (transs-pṓz, traanss-) *tr.v.* **-posed, -posing, -poses.** **1.** To reverse or transfer the order or place of; interchange. **2.** To put into a different place or order: *transposed the words of a sentence.* **3.** *Mathematics.* To move (a term) from one side of an algebraic equation to the other side, reversing its sign to maintain equality. **4.** *Music.* To write or perform (a composition) in a key other than the original or given key. **5.** *Obsolete.* To transform.

~*n.* *Mathematics.* A matrix that is generated by interchanging the rows and columns of the original matrix. [Middle English *transposen,* from Old French *transposer* : Latin *trāns-,* from one place to another + French *poser,* to place, POSE.] **—trans·pos·a·ble** *adj.* **—trans·pos·er** *n.*

trans·po·si·tion (tránss-pə-zísh'n, tráanss-) *n.* Also **trans·pos·al** (transs-pṓz'l, traanss-). *Abbr.* **tr. 1.** The act of transposing. **2.** The state of being transposed. **3.** Something that has been transposed. [French. See **trans-, position.**] **—trans·po·si·tion·al** *adj.*

trans·put·er (transs-péwtər) *n.* Trade name for an ultra-small computer on a single silicon chip. [*trans*istor + com*puter.*]

trans·sex·u·al (tránz-sék-sew-əl, tráanz-, trán-, tráan-, -shoo-, -shŏŏl) *n.* A person who is born belonging anatomically to one sex but who feels him- or herself to be, or desires to become, a member of the opposite sex; especially, one who has undergone a sex change, usually through surgery and hormone therapy. **—trans·sex·u·al** *adj.* **—trans·sex·u·al·ism** *n.*

trans·ship (transs-shíp, traanss-, tranz-, traanz-, tran-, traan-) *v.* **-shipped, -shipping, -ships.** Also **tran·ship.** —*tr.* To transfer from one vessel or vehicle to another for reshipment. —*intr.* To transfer cargo from one vessel or vehicle to another. **—trans·ship·ment** *n.*

tran·sub·stan·ti·ate (trán-səb-stán-shi-ayt, tráan-, -si- || -sub-) *tr.v.* **-ated, -ating, -ates. 1.** To change (one substance) into another; transmute; transform. **2.** *Theology.* To change the substance of (the Eucharistic bread and wine) into the body and blood of Christ. [Medieval Latin *transubstantiāre* : Latin *trāns-,* change + *substantia,* SUBSTANCE.]

tran·sub·stan·ti·a·tion (trán-səb-stán-shi-áysh'n, tráan-, -si- || -sub-) *n.* **1.** *Theology.* The doctrine that the bread and wine of the Eucharist are transformed into the body and blood of Christ, although their appearance remains the same. Compare **consubstantiation. 2.** The conversion of one substance into another; a transformation. **—tran·sub·stan·ti·a·tion·al·ist** *n.*

tran·su·date (trán-sew-dayt, tráan-, -zew-, tran-séw-, traan-, -zéw- || -sŏŏ-, -zŏŏ-) *n.* A substance that has undergone transudation.

tran·sude (tran-séwd, traan-, -zéwd || -sŏŏd, -zŏŏd) *intr.v.* **-suded, -suding, -sudes.** To exude or pass through a membrane or skin, in the manner of perspiration. [New Latin *transudare* : Latin *trāns-,* through + *sūdāre,* to sweat.] **—trans·u·da·tion** (-dáysh'n) *n.* **—tran·su·da·to·ry** (-ə-tri, -təri, trán-sew-dáytəri, tráan-, -zew-) *adj.*

trans·u·ran·ic (tránz-yoor-ánnik, tráanz- || tránss-) *adj.* Also **trans·u·ra·ni·an** (-ayni-ən), **trans·u·ra·ni·um** (-ayni-əm). Having an atomic number greater than 92. [TRANS- + URAN(IUM) + -IC.]

Trans·vaal (tránz-vaál, tráanz-, tránss-, tráanss-, -vaal || *locally also* -faál). Former province of northeast South Africa, lying between the Vaal and Limpopo rivers, now divided into four provinces : North, North West, Mpumalang, and Gauteng. It was the Republic's richest province, having enormous mineral wealth, especially gold and diamonds, and fertile veldt for crops and grazing. Pretoria was the capital and Johannesburg the largest city. Boer settlers set up the South African Republic (1857), which was annexed by Britain (1877). After enormous gold finds on the Witwatersrand (1886) settlers, particularly Britons, flocked in. Tensions led to war between Britain and the Boers (1899), and as a result, Transvaal was made a crown colony (1902). It joined the Union of South Africa in 1910.

trans·val·ue (tranz-vál-yŏŏ, traanz- || transs-) *tr.v.* **-ued, -uing, -ues.** To evaluate by a new standard or principle, especially one that varies from conventional standards. **—trans·val·u·a·tion** *n.*

trans·ver·sal (tranz-vérss'l, traanz- || transs-) *adj.* Transverse.

~*n.* In geometry, a line that intersects a system of lines. Also called "traverse".

trans·verse (tránz-verss, tráanz-, tranz-vérss, traanz- || tránss-, transs-) *adj.* *Abbr.* **trans. 1.** Situated or lying across; athwart; crosswise. **2.** Designating a flute whose mouthpiece is on its side and is thus held horizontally and parallel to the players lips. Said of the modern flute as distinguished from the recorder.

~*n.* *Abbr.* **trans.** Something transverse, such as a part or beam. [Latin *trānsversus,* from the past participle of *trānsvertere,* to turn or direct across : *trāns-,* across + *vertere,* to turn.] **—trans·verse·ly** *adv.* **—trans·verse·ness** *n.*

transverse colon *n.* The part of the colon that lies across the upper part of the abdominal cavity.

transverse process *n.* A lateral projection from a vertebra.

transverse wave *n.* A wave in which the displacement of the transmitting field or medium is at right angles to the direction of propagation. Compare **longitudinal wave.**

trans·vest·ism (tranz-vést-iz'm, traanz- || transs-) Also **trans·ves·tit·ism** (-véstīt-) *n.* The practice or condition of being a transvestite. Also called "Eonism".

trans·ves·tite (tranz-vést-īt, traanz- || transs-) *n.* A person who wears clothes normally worn by the opposite sex, for sexual stimulation. Also called "cross-dresser". [From *transvest* : TRANS- + Latin *vestīre,* to dress, clothe.] **—trans·ves·tite** *adj.*

Tran·syl·va·ni·a (trán-sil-váyni-ə, tráan-). *Romanian* **Ar·deal** (aard-yál) or **Transilvania;** *Hungarian* **Er·dély** (áir-day); *German* **Sie·ben·bürg·en** (zéeb'n-bűrgən). Plateau region of central Romania, lying between the Carpathians and Transylvanian Alps, with rich mineral, agricultural and forest resources.

Transylvanian Alps. Also **the Southern Carpathians.** Mountain range of central Romania. It extends 360 kilometres (225 miles) eastwards from the Iron Gate gorge on the Danube. Mount Moldoveanu is its highest peak (2 543 metres; 8,343 feet).

trap¹ (trap) *n.* **1.** A device for catching and holding animals, such as a net, a concealed pit, or a sensitive clamplike apparatus that springs shut suddenly. **2. a.** Any stratagem or device for betraying, tricking, or exposing an unwary or unsuspecting person. **b.** Anything that serves to catch, catch out, or ensnare an unwary or unsuspecting person: *fell into the trap of underestimating amateur opposition.* **c.** Anything that attracts, catches, and holds. Also used in combination: *Our garden is a real suntrap.* **3.** A device for sealing a passage against the escape of gases; especially, a U-shaped or S-shaped bend in a drainpipe that prevents the return flow of gases by holding a quantity of water as a barrier. **4.** A device that hurls clay pigeons or discs into the air to be shot at. **5.** In golf, a **bunker** *(see).* **6.** A light two-wheeled vehicle with springs. **7.** A trap door. **8.** Any of the stall-like compartments in which a greyhound is held and which springs open to release the dog at the start of a race. **9.** *Usually plural. Informal.* In jazz, percussion instruments, such as snare drums, cymbals, or bells. **10.** *Slang.* The mouth.

~*v.* **trapped, trapping, traps.** —*tr.* **1.** To catch in or as if in a trap; ensnare. **2.** To seal off (gases) by a trap. **3.** To furnish or provide with a trap or traps. —*intr.* **1.** To set traps for game. **2.** To trap fur-bearing animals, especially as an occupation. [Middle English *trappe,* Old English *træppe*†.]

trap² *n.* *Usually plural.* **1.** *Obsolete.* Trappings; a caparison. **2.** *British.* Belongings; personal gear.

~*tr.v.* **trapped, trapping, traps.** To furnish with trappings. Often used with *out.* [Middle English *trappe,* probably from Old French *drap,* cloth, from Late Latin *drappus,* from Celtic.]

trap³ *n. Geology.* **1.** A fine-grained igneous rock with a characteristically steplike configuration. **2.** A structure in which oil or gas may collect. Also called "traprock". [Swedish *trapp,* from *trappa,* step, stair, from Middle Low German *trappe.*] **—trap·pe·an** (tráppi-ən), **trap·pous** (tráp-əss) *adj.*

trapan. Variant of **trepan** (to trick).

trap cut *n.* A method of cutting a gem so that it has a flat crown and an intricately shaped pavilion. [Probably from Dutch *trap,* stairs, flight of steps; akin to TRAP (steplike configuration).]

trap door *n.* **1.** A hinged or sliding door in a floor, roof, or ceiling. **2.** The opening covered by a trap door.

trap-door spider (tráp-dór || -dōr) *n.* Any of various spiders of the family Ctenizidae, that construct a silk-lined burrow concealed by a hinged lid.

tra·peze (trə-péez) *n.* A short horizontal bar suspended from the ends of two parallel ropes, used for exercises or for acrobatic stunts. [French *trapèze,* from Late Latin *trapezium,* TRAPEZIUM.]

tra·pe·zi·form (trə-péezi-fawrm) *adj.* Formed in the shape of a trapezium. [TRAPEZI(UM) + -FORM.]

tra·pe·zi·um (trə-péezi-əm) *n., pl.* **-ums** or **-zia** (-ə). **1. a.** A quadrilateral having two parallel sides. **b.** *U.S.* A trapezoid. **2.** A bone in the wrist at the base of the thumb. [Late Latin, from Greek *trapezion,* small table, diminutive of *trapeza,* table, "four-footed" : *tra-,* four + *peza,* foot.]

tra·pe·zi·us (trə-péezi-əss) *n., pl.* **-uses.** Either of two large, flat, triangular muscles running from the base of the back of the head to the middle of the back and across to the shoulder blade. They support, and make it possible to raise, the head and shoulders. [New Latin *(musculus) trapezius,* "trapezium-shaped (muscle)".]

tra·pe·zo·he·dron (trə-péezō-hée-drən, tráppizō-, -hé-) *n., pl.* **-drons** or **-dra** (-drə). Any of several forms of crystal with trapeziums as faces. Also called "trisoctahedron". [TRAPEZ(IUM) + -HEDRON.]

trap·e·zoid (tráppi-zoyd) *n.* **1. a.** A quadrilateral having no parallel sides. **b.** *U.S.* A trapezium. **2.** A small bone in the wrist. [New Latin *trapezoides,* from Greek *trapezoeidēs,* trapezium-shaped : *trapeza,* table (see **trapezium**) + -OID.] **—trap·e·zoid, trap·e·zoi·dal** (-zóyd'l) *adj.*

trap·per (tráppər) *n.* One whose occupation is trapping animals for their furs.

trap·pings (tráppingz) *pl.n.* **1.** An ornamental covering or harness for a horse; a caparison. **2.** Articles of dress or adornment, especially those that are characteristic of or symbolise something, such as a particular position or office: *the trappings of a judge.* **3.** Objects, marks, or appearances that are characteristic of or symbolise something: *the trappings of power.*

Trap·pist (tráppist) *n.* A member of a branch of the Cistercian order of monks, known for austerity and absolute silence, established in 1664 in La Trappe, Normandy. **—Trap·pist** *adj.*

traprock *n.* A configuration in igneous rocks, **trap** *(see).*

trap·shoot·ing (tráp-shōōting) *n.* The sport of shooting at clay pigeons or other objects hurled into the air from spring traps. **—trap·shoot·er** *n.*

tra·pun·to (trə-pōōntō) *n., pl.* **-tos.** Quilting having a raised effect made by outlining the design with running stitches and then filling it with padding such as cotton. [Italian, from the past participle of *trapungere,* to embroider : Latin *trans-,* through + *pungere,* to prick, pierce.]

trash (trash) *n.* **1. a.** Cheap or empty language, talk, or ideas. **b.** Worthless literary or artistic material. **2.** Something broken off or removed to be discarded; especially, plant trimmings. **3.** *Chiefly U.S.* Worthless or discarded material or objects; refuse. **4.** The bits of sugar cane that remain after the extraction of its juice. **5.** *Chiefly U.S.* A person or group of persons that is held in disdain.

~*tr.v.* **trashed, trashing, trashes.** **1.** To cut off leaves or branches from; especially, to lop off the outer leaves from (growing sugar cane). **2.** *Slang.* **a.** To disprove or discredit (an argument). **b.** To beat (someone) up. **c.** *U.S.* To virtually destroy; reduce to trash. [16th century : origin obscure.] **—trash·i·ly** *adv.* **—trash·i·ness** *n.* **—trashy** *adj.*

trash can *n. U.S.* A **dustbin** *(see).*

trass (trass) *n.* A volcanic earth used in hydraulic cement. [Dutch *terras,* from French *terrasse,* pile of earth, from Old French *terrasse, terrace,* TERRACE.]

trat·to·ri·a (trát-ə-rée-ə; *Italian* -taw-; *also* tra-táwri-ə) *n.* An Italian restaurant. [Italian, from *trattore,* innkeeper, restaurateur, from French *traiteur,* from *traiter,* to entertain, TREAT.]

trau·ma (tráw-mə, trów-) *n., pl.* **-mas** or **-mata** (-tə). **1.** *Pathology.* A wound, especially one produced by sudden physical injury. **2.** *Psychiatry.* An emotional shock that creates substantial and lasting damage to the psychological development of the individual, generally leading to neurosis. [Greek, wound, hurt.]

trau·mat·ic (traw-máttik, trow-) *adj.* **1.** Of or causing a trauma: *a traumatic shock.* **2.** *Informal.* Awful; unpleasant. [Late Latin *traumáticus,* from Greek, from TRAUMA.] **—trau·mat·i·cal·ly** *adv.*

traumatise, trau·ma·tize (tráw-mə-tīz, trów-) *tr.v.* **-tised, -tising, -tises.** **1.** To wound or injure. **2.** To cause (someone) to undergo a psychological trauma.

trau·ma·tism (tráw-mə-tiz'm, trów-) *n.* **1.** A trauma. **2.** Any condition arising from a trauma.

tra·vail (tráv-ayl || trə-váyl) *n.* **1.** *Literary.* **a.** Strenuous mental or physical exertion; labour; toil. **b.** Tribulation or agony; anguish. **2.** *Archaic.* The labour of childbirth.

~*intr.v.* **travailed, -vailing, -vails.** **1.** *Literary.* To labour strenuously; toil. **2.** *Archaic.* To be in the labour of childbirth. [Middle English, from Old French, from *travailler,* to work hard, from Vulgar Latin *tripāliāre* (unattested), to torture, from *tripālium* (unattested), torture instrument (made of three stakes), from Latin *tripālis,* having three stakes : *tri-,* three + *pālus,* stake.]

trave (trayv) *n.* **1.** A wooden frame for confining a lively horse so that it can be shod. **2.** *Architecture.* **a.** A crossbeam. **b.** A section, as of a ceiling, formed by crossbeams. [Middle English, from Old French, stake, beam, from Latin *trabs.*]

trav·el (trávv'l) *v.* **-elled** or *U.S.* **-eled, -elling** or *U.S.* **-eling, -els.** *—intr.* **1.** To go from one place to another; journey: *travelled all over Europe.* **2.** To be transmitted; move, as sound or light moves. **3.** To move, advance, or proceed, especially in a specified way: *travelling faster than the speed of sound.* **4. a.** To be a travelling salesman: *He travels for a record company.* **b.** To be a travelling salesman selling specified merchandise. Used with *in*: *travels in cosmetics.* **5.** To admit of being transported without damage or loss of quality: *Some wines travel poorly.* **6.** *Informal.* To move swiftly. *—tr.* To pass or journey over or through; traverse.

~*n.* **1.** The act or process of travelling. **2.** The distance moved by a mechanical part. **3.** *Plural.* **a.** A series of journeys. **b.** *Chiefly U.S.* A written account of these. [Middle English *travailen,* to toil, make a (toilsome) journey, from Old French *travailler,* to TRAVAIL.]

travel agency *n.* A business that makes travel arrangements for customers, as by booking tickets for flights and other journeys, booking accommodation, arranging tours, or the like. **—travel agent** *n.*

trav·e·la·tor (trávv'l-aytər) *n.* A **moving pavement** *(see).*

trav·elled (trávv'ld) *adj.* **1.** Having travelled widely; experienced in travel. **2.** Much frequented by travellers. Usually used in combination: *a well-travelled route.*

trav·ell·er (tráv-lər, -'l-ər) *n.* **1. a.** A person who is travelling. **b.** One who has travelled or who customarily travels. **c.** *Chiefly British.* A gypsy. **2.** *Chiefly British.* A travelling salesman. **3.** *Nautical.* **a.** A metal ring that moves freely back and forth on a rope, rod, or spar. **b.** The rope, rod, or spar on which such a ring moves. **4.** A part of a mechanism that can move only in a fixed direction.

traveller's cheque *n.* A cheque purchasable, especially from a bank, in various denominations, which can be exchanged for money in banks or hotels of many countries, but only with the holder's own endorsement against his original signature.

trav·el·ler's-joy (tráv-lərz-jóy, -'l-ərz-) *n.* Any of several climbing vines of the genus *Clematis*; especially, *C. vitalba,* of the Old World, having clusters of greenish flowers and pale grey feathery fruit in dense clusters. Also called "old man's beard".

trav·el·ling salesman (tráv'ling) *n.* A salesman who solicits business orders or sells merchandise through personal dealings with potential customers met by travelling round a given territory. Also *British* "commercial traveller", *chiefly British* "traveller".

travelling wave *n.* A wave in which the peaks and troughs move continuously away from the source.

trav·e·logue, *U.S.* **trav·e·log** (trávv'l-og, *rarely* -ōg || -awg) *n.* **1.** A lecture illustrated by travel slides or films. **2.** A narrated film about travels. [TRAVEL + -LOGUE.]

trav·el-sick·ness (trávv'l-sik-nəss, -niss) *n.* Nausea resulting from travelling in a moving vehicle. Also called "motion sickness". **—trav·el-sick** *adj.*

trav·erse (trávvərss, trávverss, trə-vérss) *v.* **-ersed, -ersing, -erses.** *—tr.* **1.** To travel across, over, or through. **2.** To move to and fro over; cross and recross. **3. a.** To go up or down (a slope) diagonally, as when climbing or skiing. **b.** To go across (a slope) rather than down, as when skiing. **4.** To move (a gun, for example) laterally; cause to swivel. **5.** To extend across; cross. **6.** To look over carefully; examine. **7.** To go counter to; thwart. **8.** *Law.* To deny formally (an allegation of fact by the opposition) in a suit. **9.** *Nautical.* To brace (a yard) fore and aft. *—intr.* **1.** To move or go along, across, or back and forth. **2.** To turn laterally; swivel. **3.** To traverse a slope. **4.** In fencing, to slide one's blade down towards the hilt of an opponent's weapon, while exerting pressure against his blade.

~*n.* **1. a.** The act of traversing; a passing across, over, or through. **b.** A route or path across a slope or precipice, for example. **2.** Something lying across something else, especially: **a.** An intersecting line, a **transversal** *(see).* **b.** *Architecture.* A structural crosspiece; a transom. **c.** *Architecture.* A gallery, deck, or loft crossing from one side of a building, such as a church, to the other. **d.** A railing, curtain, screen, or other barrier. **e.** A defensive barrier across a rampart or trench, such as a bank of earth thrown up for protection from enfilade fire. **3.** Something that obstructs and thwarts; a hindrance; an obstacle. **4. a.** *Nautical.* The zigzag route of a vessel forced by contrary winds to sail on different courses. **b.** A diagonal or horizontal course made by a skier across a slope. **5.** The horizontal swivel of a mounted gun. **6. a.** A lateral movement, as of a lathe tool across a piece of work. **b.** A part of a mechanism that moves in this manner. **7.** In surveying, a line established by sighting in the measurement of a tract of land. **8.** *Law.* The formal denial of an allegation of fact in a suit.

~*adj.* Lying or extending across; transverse. [Middle English *traversen,* from Old French *traverser,* from Late Latin *trā(ns)versāre,* from Latin *transversus,* TRANSVERSE.] **—trav·ers·a·ble** *adj.* **—tra·**

vers·al (trə-vérss'l) *n.* **—trav·ers·er** *n.*

trav·er·tine (trávvər-tin, -teen) *n.* **1.** A light-coloured, porous calcite, $CaCO_3$, deposited from solution in ground or surface waters. **2.** A compact type of calcium carbonate, used as a facing material in construction. [Italian *travertino,* earlier *tivertino,* from Latin *(lapis) Tīburtīnus,* "(stone) of Tibur".]

trav·es·ty (tráv-ə-sti, -i-) *n., pl.* **-ties. 1.** An exaggerated or grotesque imitation intended to ridicule; especially, a farcical and grotesque parody of a serious literary work or theme. **2.** Broadly, any event or situation that has become or been turned into a parody of itself: *The debate became a travesty.*
~*tr.v.* **travestied, -tying, -ties.** To make a travesty of; ridicule. [French *travesti,* past participle of *travestir,* to ridicule, from Italian *travestire,* "to disguise" : *tra-,* across, from Latin *trāns-,* indicates change + *vestire,* to dress, from Latin *vestīre,* from *vestis,* garment.]

tra·vois (trə-vóy, trávvoy) *n., pl.* **travois** (-z) or **travoises** (-ziz). Also **tra·voise** (-z). A primitive sledge formerly used by the Plains Indians of North America, consisting of a platform or netting supported by two long trailing poles, the forward ends of which are fastened to a dog or horse. [Canadian French, variant of French *travail,* perhaps same as TRAVAIL.]

trawl (trawl) *n.* **1.** A large, tapered fishing net of flattened conical shape, towed along the sea bottom. Also called "trawl net". **2.** *U.S.* A multiple fishing line, a **setline** *(see).* Also called "trawl line".
~ *v.* **trawled, trawling, trawls.** —*tr.* **1.** To catch (fish) with a trawl. **2.** To search painstakingly; examine: *trawl the files.* —*intr.* **1. a.** To fish with a trawl net or line. **b.** To search painstakingly: *trawl through the files.* **2.** To troll. [Perhaps from Dutch *tragel,* dragnet, from Middle Dutch *traghel,* from Latin *trāgula,* from *trahere,* to pull, draw.]

trawl·er (tráwlər) *n.* **1.** A vessel used for trawling. **2.** One who trawls.

tray (tray) *n.* **1.** A flat, shallow receptacle of wood, metal, or the like, with a raised edge or rim, used for carrying, holding, or displaying articles. **2.** A tray with food on it: *brought her up a tray.* **3.** A shallow, open, boxlike receptacle, often made of wire, and used to hold papers, letters, or the like. [Middle English *tray,* Old English *trīg, trēg,* from Germanic *traujam* (unattested); akin to TREE.]

treach·er·ous (tréchərəss) *adj.* **1.** Betraying a trust; traitorous; disloyal. **2. a.** Not to be relied upon; not dependable. **b.** Not to be trusted; deceptive; dangerous: *treacherous waters.* **—treach·er·ous·ly** *adv.* **—treach·er·ous·ness** *n.*

treach·er·y (tréchəri) *n., pl.* **-ies. 1.** Wilful betrayal of fidelity, confidence, or trust; perfidy; treason. **2.** An act or instance of this. [Middle English *trecherie, tricherie,* from Old French, from *trichier,* to TRICK.]

trea·cle (tréek'l) *n.* **1.** *British.* **a. Golden syrup** *(see).* **b.** A type of thick dark syrup obtained in refining sugar. Also *U.S.* **molasses. 2.** A medicinal compound formerly used as an antidote for poison. **3.** Cloying speech or sentiment. [Middle English *triacle,* antidote for poison, from Old French, from Latin *thēriaca,* from Greek *(antidotos) thēriakē,* from *thērion,* poisonous beast, diminutive of *thēr,* beast.] **—trea·cly** (tréekli) *adj.*

tread (tred) *v.* **trod** (trod), or *archaic* **trode** (trōd), **trodden** (trŏd'n) or **trod, treading, treads.** —*tr.* **1.** To walk on, over, or along. **2.** To press down with the foot; trample: *treading grapes.* **3.** To make (a path, for example) by walking or trampling. **4.** To perform or execute by walking or dancing. Used chiefly in the phrase *tread a measure.* **5.** To deposit by walking or trampling: *Don't tread dirt onto my clean floor.* **6.** To copulate with. Used of male birds. —*intr.* **1.** To go on foot; walk; step. **2. a.** To tread so as to press, crush, or injure someone or something. Used with *on* or *upon.* **b.** To subdue or hurt. Used with *on* or *upon* : *trod on her feelings.* **—tread lightly.** To act or proceed tactfully and sensitively.
~*n.* **1. a.** The act, manner, or sound of treading. **b.** An instance of treading; a step. **2.** The horizontal part of a step in a staircase. Also called "treadboard". **3.** The part of a wheel that makes contact with the ground or rails. **4. a.** The grooved face of a motor-vehicle tyre. **b.** The thickness of the grooves and ridges on a tyre: *not much tread left.* **5.** The part of a sole of a shoe that touches the ground. [Tread, trod (or trode), trodden; Middle English *treden, trode, troden,* Old English *tredan, træd* (plural *trǣdon*), *treden.*] **—tread·er** *n.*

tread·le (trédd'l) *n.* A pedal or lever operated by the foot for circular drive, as in a potter's wheel or sewing machine.
~*intr.v.* **treadled, -ling, -les.** To work a treadle. [Middle English *tredel,* Old English *tredel,* step of a stair, from *tredan,* TREAD.] **—tread·ler** (tréddlər) *n.*

tread·mill (tréd-mil) *n.* **1.** A mechanism used to produce rotary motion, operated by one or more persons or animals walking on moving steps inside or outside a wheel, or treading an endless sloping belt, especially one used formerly as a prisoner's punishment. **2.** Any monotonous task or routine.

treas. treasurer; treasury.

trea·son (tréez'n) *n.* **1.** Violation of allegiance towards one's sovereign or country; especially, the betrayal of one's own country by waging war against it or by consciously and purposely acting to aid its enemies. **2.** Any betrayal of trust or confidence; treachery. [Middle English *treison,* from Anglo-French *tre(i)soun,* from Medieval Latin *trāditiō* (stem *trāditiōn-),* from Latin, a handing over. See **tradition.**] **—trea·son·ous** *adj.* **—trea·son·ous·ly** *adv.*

trea·son·a·ble (tréez'n-əb'l) *adj.* Pertaining to or involving treason. **—trea·son·a·ble·ness** *n.* **—trea·son·a·bly** *adv.*

treas·ure (trézhər) *n.* **1.** Accumulated, stored, or cached wealth in the form of valuables, such as money or jewels. **2.** A person or thing considered especially precious or valuable.
~*tr.v.* **treasured, -uring, -ures. 1.** To accumulate and save for future use; hoard. **2.** To value or prize highly: *treasured fond memories.* —See Synonyms at **appreciate.** [Middle English *tresor,* from Old French, from Vulgar Latin *tresaurus* (unattested), variant of Latin *thēsaurus,* from Greek *thēsauros*†.] **—treas·ure·a·ble** *adj.*

treasure house *n.* Any place that contains treasure or something considered to be treasure: *a treasure house of humour.*

treasure hunt *n.* A game in which players seek to be the first to find a hidden prize using a series of clues.

treas·ur·er (trézhərər) *n. Abbr.* **tr., treas. 1.** A person having charge of funds or revenues for a corporation, club, society, or the like. **2.** A financial officer or recorder of public funds for a government. [Middle English *tresourer,* from Old French *tresorier,* from *tresor,* TREASURE.] **—treas·ur·er·ship** *n.*

treasure trove (trōv) *n.* **1.** *Law.* Any treasure found hidden or buried whose owner is unknown. In English law, treasure trove is money, bullion, or objects made of precious metal, and it belongs to the Crown. **2.** Any discovery of great value. [Anglo-French *tresor trove,* "discovered treasure" : Old French *tresor,* TREASURE + *trove,* past participle of *trover,* to find, compose (see **trouvère**).]

treas·ur·y (trézhəri) *n., pl.* **-ies.** *Abbr.* **treas. 1.** A place where treasure is kept or stored. **2.** A place where private or public funds are received, kept, managed, and disbursed. **3.** Such funds or revenues. **4. a.** Any collection of valuables or things considered to be valuable. **b.** A source of something valuable, such as wisdom. **5.** *Capital* **T.** The executive department of a government in charge of the collection, management, and expenditure of the public revenue. [Middle English *tresorie,* from Old French, from *tresor,* TREASURE.]

treasury bill *n.* In Britain, a bill similar to a bill of exchange, issued by the Bank of England, that bears no interest (but is purchased at a discount) and promises to pay the bearer a sum of money on a certain date, usually soon after purchase.

treasury note *n.* **1.** In Britain, a note that was issued as money during World War I. **2.** A note or bill issued by the U.S. Treasury as legal tender for all debts.

treat (treet) *v.* **treated, treating, treats.** —*tr.* **1.** To act or behave in a specified manner towards: *treated her horse well.* **2.** To regard or consider in a certain way. Usually used with *as: treated the affair as a joke.* **3. a.** To consider and deal with in a specified manner: *You haven't treated his case fairly.* **b.** To deal with in writing or speech, usually in a specified manner or style: *The book treats certain philosophical questions in detail.* **4.** To deal with or represent in a specified manner or style, as in art or literature: *treat a subject poetically.* **5. a.** To entertain or provide with a gift at one's own expense: *treated her to dinner and dancing.* **b.** To give (someone or oneself) something as a treat: *treated myself to a bottle of wine.* **6.** To subject to some process, action, or change, especially: **a.** To give medical aid to. **b.** To subject to a chemical or physical process or application. —*intr.* **1.** To deal with a subject or topic in writing, speaking, or thought. Usually used with *of: The essay treats of courtly love.* **2.** To pay for another's entertainment, food, or the like. **3.** *Rare.* To negotiate; bargain. Used with *with.*
~*n.* **1.** Something, such as food or entertainment, paid for by someone other than for whom the treat is primarily intended. **2.** The act of treating. **3.** Anything considered a special delight or pleasure. [Middle English *treten,* from Old French *traitier,* from Latin *tractāre,* to drag, handle, treat, frequentative of *trahere* (past participle *tractus*), to draw, drag.] **—treat·a·ble** *adj.* **—treat·er** *n.*

trea·tise (trée-tiz, -tiss) *n.* A formal account in writing treating systematically of some subject. [Middle English *tretis,* from Norman French, from Old French *traitier,* TREAT.]

treat·ment (treet-mənt) *n.* **1.** The act or manner of treating something, such as a person or a literary subject: *sensitive treatment of characters.* **2. a.** The application of remedies with the object of effecting a cure; therapy. **b.** The substance or remedy applied. **3.** A more detailed and full version of a film or television script. **—the (full) treatment. 1.** *Informal.* All that goes with or is usual to a particular person, thing, or event; especially, an elaborate way of treating something: *I want a haircut, shave, and the full treatment.* **2.** *Slang.* Aggressive, rough, or bad handling; brutal treatment: *gave the opposing team the treatment.*

trea·ty (tréeti) *n., pl.* **-ties. 1. a.** A formal agreement between two or more states containing terms of trade, peace, alliance, or the like; a pact. **b.** A document embodying this. **2.** Any contract or agreement; especially, one between two persons concerning the buying of property. **3.** Negotiation for the purpose of reaching an agreement. [Middle English *tretee,* from Old French *traite,* from Medieval Latin *tractātus,* from Latin, past participle of *tractāre,* TREAT.]

treaty port *n.* A port kept open for trade according to the terms of a treaty; especially, formerly in the Far East, any of several such ports open to foreign commerce.

treb·le (trébb'l) *adj.* **1.** Triple; threefold. **2.** *Music.* Of, having, or performing the highest part, voice, or range. **3.** High-pitched; shrill.
~*n.* **1.** *Music.* **a.** The highest part, voice, instrument, or range; soprano. **b.** A player who performs the highest instrumental part. **c.** A singer who performs the highest voice part, especially a boy singer as opposed to a female soprano. **2.** A high, shrill sound or voice. **3.** A number or amount three times as much or as many as another. **4. a.** In darts, the narrow ring between the double and the bull's eye. **b.** A score obtained by hitting this ring.
~*v.* **trebled, -ling, -les.** —*tr.* To make triple. —*intr.* To become triple. [Middle English, from Old French, from Latin *triplus,* TRI-

PLE.] **—treb·le·ness** n. **—treb·ly** (trébbli) adv.

treble chance n. In Britain, a method of betting on the football pools in which points are awarded to correct guesses as to which matches will result in draws, home wins, or away wins. A guess that correctly predicts a draw is awarded more points than one guessing either of the other two types of result.

treble clef n. Music. A symbol, 𝄞, centred on the second line of a staff (the treble staff) to indicate the position of G above middle C. Also called "G clef".

treb·u·chet (trébbew-shet, -chét, -shét) n. Also **treb·uc·ket** (-ket, -két). A medieval catapult for hurling heavy stones. [Middle English, from Old French, pitfall, from trebucher, to stumble.]

tre·cen·to (tray-chéntō) n. The 14th century, with reference especially to Italian art and literature. [Italian, "three hundred", short for (mil) trecento, (one thousand) three hundred : tre, three, from Latin trēs + cento, hundred, from Latin centum.]

tree (tree) n. **1.** A usually tall woody plant, distinguished from a shrub by having comparatively greater height and, characteristically, a single trunk with branches arising at an appreciable distance from the ground, rather than several stems. **2.** Broadly, a plant or shrub resembling a tree but without a woody trunk, such as a palm. **3.** A wooden beam, post, stake, or bar used as a part of a framework or structure. **4.** Archaic. A gallows; a gibbet. **5.** Often capital T. Archaic & Poetic. The cross on which Jesus was crucified. **6.** A saddletree (see). **7.** Something suggestive of a tree: a clothes tree. **8.** A diagram showing a family lineage; a family tree. **9.** See Christmas tree. **—bark up the wrong tree.** Informal. To misdirect one's energies wastefully. **—grow on trees.** To be in abundant, free supply: Money doesn't grow on trees. **—up a tree.** Informal. In a situation of hopeless confusion or embarrassment.

~tr.v. **treed, treeing, trees. 1.** To force to climb a tree in evasion of pursuit. **2.** Informal. To force into a difficult position; corner. **3.** To stretch (shoes) on a shoetree. [Middle English tree, Old English treo(w).]

tree-creep·er (trée-kreepar) n. A small, brown-speckled bird, Certhia familiaris, having a downward-curved beak and habitually found creeping around tree trunks in search of food.

tree diagram n. A branching diagram especially suited to represent the analysis of a structure, such as a sentence, by subdividing it into component parts.

tree fern n. Any of various treelike tropical ferns, especially of the family Cyatheaceae, having a woody, trunklike stem and a terminal crown of large, divided fronds.

tree frog n. Any of various small, arboreal frogs of the family Polypedatidae, having long toes terminating in adhesive discs. Also called "tree toad".

tree heath n. A shrub or tree, the briar (see).

tree-hop·per (trée-hoppar) n. Any insect of the family Membracidae, that damages trees by sucking sap.

tree line n. The timber line (see).

tree mallow n. A tall biennial mallow plant, Lavatera arborea, of coastal regions and having purple-veined, dark pink flowers.

treen (treen) pl.n. Wooden dishes and utensils.

~adj. Made of wood: treen ware.

tree-nail (trée-nayl, trénn'l) n. Also **tre-nail** (trénn'l), **trun-nel** (trúnn'l). A wooden peg which swells when wet, used to fasten timbers, especially in shipbuilding.

tree of heaven n. A tree, the ailanthus (see).

tree of knowledge n. The tree in the Garden of Eden whose forbidden fruit was eaten by Adam and Eve, causing loss of innocence (the Fall). Genesis 2:9, 17; 3:6. Also called "tree of knowledge of good and evil".

tree of life n. **1.** A tree, the arborvitae (see). **2.** A tree in the Garden of Eden whose fruit, if eaten, gave man immortality. Genesis 3:22. **3.** The tree in the new Jerusalem whose leaves were for the healing of the nations. Revelation 22:2.

tree-run·ner (trée-runnar) n. Any of various Australian birds. See sittella.

tree-shrew (trée-shrōō ‖ -shrew) n. Any squirrel-like, primitive primate of the family Tupaiidae, which retain many characteristics typical of the insectivores.

tree sparrow n. A woodland bird, Passer montanus, similar to the house sparrow but having a chestnut crown and white head markings.

tree surgery n. The treatment of diseased or damaged trees by filling cavities, pruning, and bracing branches. **—tree surgeon** n.

tree toad n. A tree frog (see).

tref (trayf) adj. Unclean and unfit for consumption according to Jewish dietary law, as pork, lobster, or horse meat are. Compare kosher. [Yiddish treyf, from Hebrew terēphāh, "torn", flesh of an animal torn by wild beasts, from tāraf, to tear.]

tre·foil (tréf-oyl, rarely trée-, tri-fóyl) n. **1.** Any of various plants of the genera Trifolium and Lotus, having compound leaves with three leaflets. **2.** Any ornament, symbol, or architectural form having the appearance of a trifoliate leaf. See bird's-foot trefoil. [Middle English, from Anglo-French trifoil, from Latin trifolium, three-leaved grass : tri-, three + folium, leaf.] **—tre-foiled** adj.

tre·ha·la (tri-há·alə) n. A sugar-like, edible substance obtained from the pupal case of an Old World beetle, Larinus maculatus. [New Latin, from Turkish tīgāla, from Persian tīghāl†.]

tre·ha·lose (tri-há·al-ōz, -ōss) n. A sweet-tasting, crystalline disaccharide, $C_{12}H_{22}O_{11} \cdot 2H_2O$, found in trehala and in many fungi that store it instead of starch. [TREHAL(A) + -OSE.]

treil·lage (tráylij, tray-yáazh) n. Latticework; especially, a trellis for vines. [French, from Old French, from treille, arbour, from Latin trichila†, bower, arbour.]

trek (trek) intr.v. **trekked, trekking, treks. 1.** To make a slow or arduous journey. **2.** Especially in South Africa: **a.** To draw or pull a wagon. Used of an ox. **b.** To travel by ox wagon.

~n. **1.** A journey or a part of a journey, especially when slow or difficult. **2.** A migration; especially, one involving a slow journey with wagons, such as the migration of the Boers from 1835 to 1837. [Afrikaans, from Middle Dutch trekken, to pull, draw, travel, akin to Old High German trechan†.] **—trek·ker** n.

trel·lis (trélliss) n. **1.** A structure of open latticework; especially, one used for supporting vines and other creeping plants. **2.** An arbour or arch made with such a structure.

~tr.v. **trellised, -lising, -lises. 1.** To provide with a trellis; especially, to support (a creeping plant) on a trellis. **2.** To make into or in the form of a trellis. [Middle English trelis, from Old French treliz, a coarse fabric, later (influenced by treillage, TREILLAGE) trellis, from Vulgar Latin trilīcius (unattested), from Latin trilīx, triple-twilled : tri-, three + līcium†, thread.]

trel·lis·work (trélliss-wurk) n. Latticework.

trem·a·tode (trémma-tōd) n. Any of numerous parasitic flatworms of the class Trematoda, having a thick outer cuticle, and one or more suckers for attaching to host tissue. Also called "fluke".

~adj. Of or belonging to the Trematoda. [New Latin Trematoda, from Greek trēmatodēs, having a vent to the intestinal canal (taken to mean "having holes", perhaps from the cavity of the suckers) : trēma, perforation + -ODE (like).]

trem·ble (trémb'l) intr.v. **-bled, -bling, -bles. 1.** To shake involuntarily, as from fear, cold, or sickness; quake or shiver; shake. **2.** To feel or express fear or anxiety: I tremble at the thought. **3.** To vibrate; quiver: leaves trembling in the wind. **—See Synonyms at shake.**

~n. **1.** The act or state of trembling. **2.** Sometimes plural. A convulsive fit of trembling, especially as a result of a disease. [Middle English trem(b)len, from Old French trembler, from Vulgar Latin tremulāre (unattested), from Latin tremulus, TREMULOUS.] **—trem·bler** n. **—trem·bling·ly** adv. **—trem·bly** adj.

trem·bles (trémb'lz) n. Usually used with a singular verb. In veterinary medicine, louping ill (see).

trembling disease n. A disease, kuru (see).

tre·men·dous (tri-mén-dəss, -dəs ‖ chiefly Irish English -jəss) adj. **1.** Capable of making one tremble; terrible: the tremendous tragedy of war. **2. a.** Extremely large in amount, extent, or degree; enormous: a tremendous task. **b.** Informal. Marvellous; wonderful; excellent: We had a tremendous time. **—See Synonyms at enormous.** [Latin tremendus, gerundive of tremere, to tremble.] **—tre·men·dous·ly** adv. **—tre·men·dous·ness** n.

trem·o·lite (trémmə-līt) n. A white to dark-grey calcium magnesium amphibole, $Ca_2Mg_5Si_8O_{22}(OH)_2$, usually occurring in aggregates, used as a substitute for asbestos. [French trémolite, first found in Tremola, valley in southern Switzerland.]

trem·o·lo (trémmə-lō) n., pl. **-los.** Music. **1. a.** A tremulous effect produced by the rapid repetition of a single note, especially when playing a bowed instrument. **b.** A similar effect produced by the rapid alternation of two notes, usually a third or greater interval apart. Compare trill. **2.** A device on an organ for producing this effect. Also called "tremolant", "tremulant". **3.** A vibrato in singing, used for emotional effect or resulting from poor vocal control. Compare vibrato. [Italian, "tremulous".]

trem·or (trémmər; in sense 2 also tréemər) n. **1.** A shaking or vibrating movement or short series of movements of the earth; a small earthquake: an earth tremor. **2. a.** An involuntary trembling motion of the body, as from a state of nervous agitation or illness. **b.** A mental or emotional state characterised by such trembling. **3.** A nervous quiver or shiver; a thrill. **4.** Any trembling, shaking, or vibrating movement: a tremor of aspen leaves. **5.** A tremulous sound; a quaver. [Middle English tremour, from Old French, from Latin tremor, from tremere, to tremble.]

trem·u·lous (trémmew-ləss) adj. Also **trem·u·lant** (-lənt). **1. a.** Vibrating or quivering; trembling. **b.** Produced by or suggestive of someone tremulous: tremulous handwriting. **2.** Timid; fearful; timorous. [Latin tremulus, from tremere, to tremble.] **—trem·u·lous·ly** adv. **—trem·u·lous·ness** n.

trenail. Variant of treenail.

trench (trench) n. **1.** A deep furrow. **2.** A ditch. **3. a.** A long, narrow ditch embanked with its own soil and used for concealment and protection in warfare. **b.** Plural. A system of such ditches, used especially as a defensive position. **4.** A long, deep, narrow depression in the sea bed.

~v. **trenched, trenching, trenches. —tr. 1.** To cut or dig a trench or trenches in. **2.** To fortify with a trench or trenches. **3.** To carve or make a cut in. **—intr. 1.** To dig a trench or ditch. **2.** To verge or encroach. Used with on or upon. [Middle English trenche, long narrow ditch, path cut through, from Old French, from trenchier, to cut, dig, probably from Vulgar Latin trincāre (unattested), from Latin truncāre, to mutilate, from truncus, torso.]

trench·ant (trénchənt) adj. **1.** Keen; incisive; penetrating: a trenchant comment. **2.** Forceful; effective; vigorous: a trenchant argument. **3.** Distinct; sharply defined; clear-cut. **4.** Archaic & Poetic. Sharp-edged. Said of a sword. **—See Synonyms at incisive.** [Middle English, cutting, from Old French, present participle of trenchier, to cut. See trench.] **—trench·an·cy** n. **—trench·ant·ly** adv.

trench coat *n.* A loose-fitting, belted, military style raincoat with pockets and straps on the shoulders.

trench·er[1] (trénchər) *n.* **1.** A wooden board or plate, used especially in former times, for cutting or serving food on. **2.** A stiff academic cap, a **mortarboard** *(see).* Also called "trencher cap". [Middle English *trenchour,* cutting board, from Anglo-French, from Old French *trenchier,* to cut. See **trench.**]

trencher[2] *n.* One that digs trenches.

trench·er·man (trénchər-mən) *n., pl.* **-men** (-mən). **1.** A hearty, big eater. **2.** *Archaic.* A sponger; a parasite; hanger-on.

trench fever *n.* An acute infectious relapsing fever caused by a microorganism, *Rickettsia quintana,* and transmitted by a louse, *Pediculus humanus.*

trench foot *n.* A form of frostbite of the feet, often afflicting soldiers obliged to stand in cold water for long periods of time.

trench knife *n.* A knife, used in warfare, having a long, double-edged blade.

trench mortar *n. Military.* A **mortar** *(see).*

trench mouth *n.* A form of gingivitis characterised by pain, foul odour, and the formation of a grey film over the diseased area. Also called "Vincent's disease".

trench warfare *n.* Warfare conducted between two armies who are facing each other in trenches.

trend (trend) *n.* **1.** A direction of movement; a course; a flow: *a trend of thought.* **2.** A general inclination or tendency: *a trend away from smoking.* **3.** A fashion; a style. —Synonyms at **tendency.**
~intr.v. **trended, trending, trends. 1.** To extend, bend, turn, or move in a specified direction: *The prevailing wind trends northeast.* **2.** To have a general tendency; tend: *mood trending towards gloom.* [Middle English *trenden,* to turn, roll, revolve, Old English *trendan,* from Germanic *trand-* (unattested).]

trend·setter (trénd-sétting) *n.* One who initiates or popularises a fashion or trend. **—trend-set·ting** *adj.*

trend·y (tréndi) *adj.* **-ier, -iest.** *Informal.* **1.** Of, in accordance with or consciously following the latest fad or fashion. Usually used derogatorily: *Fortunately, it is now considered trendy to be open-minded.* **2.** Of or involving trendy people: *a trendy party.*
~n., pl. **trendies.** *Informal.* A trendy person. Usually used derogatorily. **—trend·i·ly** *adv.* **—trend·i·ness** *n.*

Trent (trent). River of central England. Rising on Staffordshire's Biddulph Moor, it flows 270 kilometres (170 miles) to join the Ouse, forming the Humber estuary.

Trent, Council of *n.* A council of the Roman Catholic Church held periodically in Trento, Italy, between 1545 and 1563, which attempted to find a political solution to the Reformation, clarified Catholic doctrine, and initiated reform within the Church.

trente et qua·rante (trónt ay ka-rónt). **Rouge et noir** *(see).*

Tren·ti·no-Al·to A·di·ge (tren-teénō-ál-tō-áadi-jay). Formally **Ve·ne·zi·a Tri·den·ti·na** (ve-nétsi-ətree-den-teénə) (1919–47) Autonomous Alpine region of northeast Italy. Agriculture, forestry, and tourism are the principal industries. Trento is the capital.

tre·pan[1] (tri-pán, trə-) *n.* **1.** A rock-boring tool used in mining for sinking shafts. **2.** An early type of trephine used in surgery. **3.** A tool for making large circular holes or grooves.
~tr.v. **trepanned, -panning, -pans. 1.** To bore (a shaft) with a trepan. **2.** To cut a disc from with a trepan. **3.** In surgery, to trephine. [Middle English *trepane,* from Medieval Latin *trepanum,* from Greek *trupanon,* auger, borer, from *trupan,* to pierce, from *trupē,* hole.] **—trep·a·na·tion** (tréppə-náysh'n) *n.*

trepan[2] *tr.v.* **-panned, -panning, -pans.** Also **tra·pan** (trə-). *Archaic.* To trap; ensnare; trick.
~n. Archaic. **1.** A prankster; a trickster. **2.** A trick; a stratagem. [17th century : originally *trapan,* probably thieves' slang for TRAP.]

tre·pang (tri-páng) *n.* **1.** Any of several sea cucumbers of the genus *Holothuria,* of the southern Pacific and Indian oceans. **2.** The eviscerated and dried or smoked body of any of these animals, used as food in the East. Also called "bêche-de-mer". [Malay *tĕripang.*]

tre·phine (tri-feén, tre-, trə-, -fīn) *n.* A surgical instrument having circular, sawlike edges, used to cut out discs of tissue, usually bone from the skull.
~tr.v. **trephined, -phining, -phines.** In surgery, to operate on with a trephine; trepan. [Earlier *trafine,* from Latin *trēs fīnes,* three ends; perhaps formed after TREPAN.] **—treph·i·na·tion** (tréffi-náysh'n) *n.*

trep·i·da·tion (tréppi-dáysh'n) *n.* **1.** A state of alarm or dread; nervous apprehension. **2.** Quivering or trembling, especially as a result of disease or illness. —See Synonyms at **fear.** [Latin *trepidātiō* (stem *trepidātiōn-*), from *trepidāre,* to hurry with alarm, tremble at, from *trepidus,* alarmed.]

trep·o·neme (tréppə-neem) *n.* Also **trep·o·ne·ma** (-neémə). Any of a group of spirochaetes of the genus *Treponema,* including those that cause syphilis and yaws. [New Latin *Treponema,* "twisted thread" (from its shape) : Greek *trepein,* to turn + *nēma,* thread.]

tres·pass (trés-pəss || -paass, -pass) *intr.v.* **-passed, -passing, -passes. 1.** *Archaic.* To commit an offence or sin; err; transgress. **2.** To infringe upon the privacy, time, or attention of another. Used with *on* or *upon: "I must . . . not trespass too far on the patience of a good-natured critic"* (Henry Fielding). **3.** *Law.* To invade the property, rights, or person of another without his consent and with the intention, actual or implied, of committing violence; especially, to commit the tort of entering onto another's land without permission and causing damage.
~n. **1.** The transgression of a moral or social law, code, or duty. **2.** An intrusion or infringement upon another. **3.** *Law.* **a.** The tort of trespassing. **b.** A legal suit brought for this. —See Synonyms at **breach.** [Middle English *trespassen,* from Old French *trespasser,* from Medieval Latin *transpassāre* : Latin *trāns-,* across + Medieval Latin *passāre* to PASS.] **—tres·pass·er** *n.*

tress (tress) *n.* **1.** A lock, plait, or braid of hair, especially of a woman's hair. **2.** *Plural.* The long flowing hair or a woman. [Middle English *tresse,* from Old French *tresse, trece*†.]

tres·tle (tréss'l) *n.* **1.** A horizontal beam or bar held up by two pairs of divergent legs and used as a support. **2.** A framework consisting of vertical, slanted supports and horizontal crosspieces supporting a bridge. [Middle English *trestel,* from Old French, from Vulgar Latin *transtellum* (unattested), diminutive of Latin *transtrum,* crossbeam. See **transom.**]

trestle table *n.* A table consisting of a board or boards supported by a trestle.

tres·tle·tree (tréss'l-tree) *n. Nautical.* Either of two horizontal beams set into a masthead to support the crosstrees.

tres·tle·work (tréss'l-wurk) *n.* A trestle or system of trestles, such as that supporting a bridge.

tret (tret) *n.* Formerly, an allowance made to purchasers of goods sold by weight, so as to account for waste occurring during transport. [Middle English, from Anglo-French, Old French, a drawing, draught, variant of TRAIT; sense development obscure.]

Tretch·i·koff (tréchikof), **Vladimir** (1913–). Russian-born South African painter with immense popular appeal. He specialises in softly-lit, romanticised paintings of human figures and faces.

tre·val·ly (trə-váli) *n.* Any Australian food fish of the genus *Caranx.* [Probably alteration of CAVALLY.]

trews (trōōz || trewz) *pl.n.* Close-fitting, usually tartan trousers. [Irish *trius,* Gaelic *triubhas.*]

trey (tray) *n.* A card or dice, with three pips. [Middle English *treis, treye,* from Old French *treis,* from Latin *trēs,* three.]

tri- *comb. form.* Indicates: **1.** Three, as in number of parts or elements; for example, **trioxide. 2. a.** Appearance or occurrence in intervals of three; for example, **tricentennial. b.** Appearance or occurrence three times during; for example, **triweekly.** [Latin and Greek, three.]

tri·a·ble (trī-əb'l) *adj.* **1.** Capable of being tried. **2.** *Law.* Subject to judicial examination. **—tri·a·ble·ness** *n.*

tri·ac·id (trī-ássid, trī-) *adj.* Also **tri·a·cid·ic** (trī-a-síddik, -ə-). **1.** Able to react with three molecules of a monobasic acid. Said of a base. **2.** Containing three replaceable hydrogen atoms. Said of an acid or an acid salt.
~n. An acid containing three replaceable hydrogen atoms.

tri·ad (trī-əd, -ad) *n.* **1.** A group of three persons or things; a trio; a trinity. **2.** *Music.* A chord of three notes; especially, one built on a given root note plus a major or minor third and a perfect fifth. **3.** A literary form used in medieval Welsh and Irish literature, consisting of aphorisms grouped in threes. [Late Latin *trias* (stem *triad-*), the number three, from Greek.] **—tri·ad·ic** (trī-áddik) *adj.*

Tri·ad (trī-əd) *n.* **1.** A member of a Chinese secret society notorious as an international crime syndicate trafficking especially in narcotics. **2.** Such a society itself. [Influenced by the Chinese name of such a society, *San He Hui,* "three unite society", held to suggest the union of Heaven, Earth, and Man.]

tri·age (trī-ij, treé-aazh || tree-áazh) *n.* **1.** The act of sorting according to quality. **2.** The act or process of assigning or allocating limited resources so as to achieve the greatest possible benefit; especially, the allocating of limited treatment facilities for battlefield casualties so as to maximise the number of survivors. [French, sorting : *trier,* pick out, sift (see **try**) + -AGE.]

tri·al (trī-əl) *n.* **1.** *Law.* The examination of evidence and applicable law by a competent tribunal, such as a judge and jury, to decide on a charge or claim: *a murder trial.* **2. a.** The act or process of testing, trying, or putting to the proof by actual or simulated use and experience: *a trial of one's faith.* **b.** A single complete instance of such testing, especially as part of a series of tests or experiments: *The new aircraft crashed during its third trial.* **3.** *Rare.* An effort or attempt: *He succeeded on his fourth trial.* **4.** A trouble, problem, or difficulty: *Life is full of little trials.* **5.** A test of patience or endurance: *He was a trial to his parents.* **6.** *Usually plural.* A series of competitions or tests designed to establish the individual ability and skill of the participants: *horse trials; held trials to pick the team.* **—on trial. 1.** In the state or process of being tried, as before a court of law. **2.** In the state or process of being tested or tried out.
~adj. **1.** Of or pertaining to a trial or trials. **2.** Made, done, used, or performed during the course of a trial or trials: *gave his car a trial run.* [Anglo-French *trial, triel,* from Old French *trier,* TRY.]

trial and error *n.* **1.** An empirical method of attempting to solve a problem or achieve a certain result, consisting of repeating experiments until error is eliminated or the desired result is achieved. **2.** A method of acquiring a skill by trying out various actions or processes until success is achieved. **—tri·al-and-er·ror** *adj.*

trial balance *n. Abbr.* **t.b.** In bookkeeping, a statement of all the open debit and credit items in a double-entry ledger made to make sure they are equal.

trial balloon *n. Chiefly U.S.* A preliminary statement or campaign tried out on a small scale to test public reaction. [Originally applied to a balloon for testing weather conditions.]

trial court *n. Law.* The court in which a case is first heard and where issues of fact are decided.

trial jury *n.* A **petit jury** *(see).*

trial marriage *n.* The living together of a couple for a trial period in order to ascertain their compatability with regard to marriage.

tri·am·cin·o·lone (trī́-am-sínnə-lōn) *n.* A synthetic corticosteroid hormone applied as a cream or lotion to reduce inflammation. [*Tri-* + *amyl* + *cinene* (a terpine) + *prednisolone.*]

tri·an·gle (trī́-ang-g'l) *n.* **1.** The plane figure formed by connecting three points not in a straight line by straight-line segments; a three-sided polygon. **2.** Something having the shape of this figure, such as the wooden frame in which snooker balls are placed at the start of a game. **3.** Any of various flat, three-sided drawing and drafting guides, used especially to draw straight lines at specific angles. **4.** *Music.* A percussion instrument consisting of a piece of metal in the shape of a triangle, open at one angle. **5.** See **eternal triangle.** [Middle English, from Old French, from Latin *triangulum,* from *triangulus,* three-angled : *tri-,* three + *angulus,* ANGLE.]

triangle of vectors *n. Mathematics.* A triangle formed by three lines representing the magnitudes and directions of three vectors, such as forces or velocities that are in equilibrium.

tri·an·gu·lar (trī-áng-gew-lər; *rarely* tri-) *adj.* **1.** Of, pertaining to, or shaped like a triangle; three-cornered; three-sided. **2.** Having a triangle for a base: *a triangular pyramid.* **3.** Pertaining to, involving, or consisting of three interrelated entities, such as three persons, objects, or ideas: *a triangular athletics match between Eire, Iran, and Spain.* **—tri·an·gu·lar·i·ty** (-lárrəti, trī́-) *n.* **—tri·an·gu·lar·ly** *adv.*

tri·an·gu·late (trī-áng-gew-layt, *rarely* tri-) *tr.v.* **-lated, -lating, -lates.** **1.** To divide into triangles. **2.** To survey by triangulation. **3.** To make triangular. **4.** To measure by using trigonometry.
~*adj.* (*also* -lət, -lit). **1.** Of or pertaining to triangles; triangular. **2.** Made up of or marked with triangles.

tri·an·gu·la·tion (trī́-áng-gew-láysh'n, trī́-, *rarely* tri-) *n.* **1.** A surveying technique in which a region is divided into a series of triangular elements based on a line of known length so that accurate measurements of distances and directions may be made by the application of trigonometry. **2.** The network of triangles so laid out. **3.** The location of an unknown point, as in navigation, by forming a triangle having the unknown point and two known points as the vertices.

Tri·an·gu·lum (trī-áng-gew-ləm) *n.* A constellation in the northern sky near Aries and Andromeda. [Latin, TRIANGLE.]

Triangulum Aus·tra·le (aw-stráyli, o-). A constellation in the southern sky near Apus and Norma. [Latin, "southern triangle".]

tri·ar·chy (trī́-aarki) *n., pl.* **-chies.** **1.** Government by three persons; a triumvirate. **2.** A country governed by three rulers. [Greek *triarkhia* : *tri-,* three + -ARCHY.]

Tri·as·sic (trī-ássik) *adj.* Of, belonging to, or designating the geological period, system of rocks, and sedimentary deposits of the first period of the Mesozoic era, after the Permian period of the Paleozoic era and before the Jurassic period of the Mesozoic era.
~*n. Geology.* The Triassic period or system of deposits. Preceded by *the.* [Late Latin *trias,* TRIAD (from the subdivision of the strata of this period into three groups in Germany).]

tri·a·tom·ic (trī́-ə-tómmik) *adj. Chemistry.* Containing three atoms per molecule.

tri·ax·i·al (trī-áksi-əl) *adj.* Having three axes.

tri·a·zine (trī́-əz-een, trī-áz-, -in) *n.* **1.** Any of three isomeric compounds, $C_3H_3N_3$, each having three carbon and three nitrogen atoms in a six-membered ring. **2.** Any compound derived from these isomers.

tri·a·zole (trī́-əz-ōl, trī-áz-, -ol) *n.* **1.** Any of several compounds with composition $C_2H_3N_3$ having a five-membered ring of two carbon atoms and three nitrogen atoms. **2.** Any compound derived from one of these isomers.

trib·ade (tríbbəd) *n. Rare.* A lesbian. [French, from Latin *tribas,* from Greek, "she who rubs", from *tribein,* to rub.] **—trib·a·dism** (-iz'm) *n.*

trib·al (trī́b'l) *adj.* Pertaining to or of the nature of a tribe or tribes.
~*n.* A member of one of the indigenous tribal peoples of India. **—trib·al·ly** *adv.*

trib·al·ism (trī́b'l-iz'm) *n.* **1.** The condition of being made up of or organised into tribes. **2.** The organisation, culture, or beliefs of a tribe. **3.** The sense of belonging to a tribe; tribal loyalty. **—trib·al·ist** *n.* **—trib·al·is·tic** (-ístik) *adj.*

tri·ba·sic (trī-báysik, trī́-) *adj.* **1.** Having three replaceable hydrogen atoms per molecule. Said of an acid. **2.** Having three univalent basic atoms or radicals per molecule. Said of a base or salt.

tribe (trīb) *n.* **1.** A unit of social organisation, especially among primitive peoples but also surviving in some modern societies, consisting of a group of people claiming a common ancestry, usually sharing a common culture, and originally living together under a chief or headman. **2.** A political, ethnic, or ancestral division of ancient states and cultures, especially: **a.** Any of the three divisions of the ancient Romans, namely, the Latin, Sabine, and Etruscan. **b.** Any of the 12 divisions of ancient Israel. **c.** A phyle of ancient Greece. **3. a.** A group of persons with a common occupation, interest, or habit. Often used derogatorily: *a whole tribe of public school boys invaded the restaurant.* **b.** *Informal.* A large family. **4.** *Biology.* A taxonomic category sometimes placed between a family and a genus. [Middle English *tribu, tribe,* from Old French *tribu,* from Latin *tribus,* division of the Roman people, perhaps from *tri-* (unattested), three (referring to Latin, Sabine, and Etruscan).]

tribes·man (trībz-mən) *n., pl.* **-men** (-mən). A member of a tribe.

tribes·wom·an (trībz-wŏŏmən) *n., pl.* **-women** (-wimmin). A female member of a tribe.

tribo- *comb. form.* Indicates friction; for example, **triboelectricity, triboluminescence.** [From Greek *tribos,* rubbing.]

tri·bo·e·lec·tric·i·ty (trī́bō-éllek-trissəti, -i-lék- || -trízzəti) *n. Physics.* Electricity that is produced by friction. **—tri·bo·e·lec·tric** (-i-léktrik) *adj.*

tri·bol·o·gy (trī-bólləji) *n.* The study of friction and lubrication.

tri·bo·lu·mi·nes·cence (trī́bō-lŏŏ-mi-néss'nss, -léw-) *n. Physics.* Luminescence produced by certain crystals as a result of friction or crushing. **—tri·bo·lu·mi·nes·cent** *adj.*

tri·brach (tríb-rak, trī́b-) *n.* A metrical foot of three short or unstressed syllables. [Latin *tribrachys,* from Greek *tribrakhus* : *tri-,* three + *brakhus,* short.] **—tri·brach·ic** (tri-bráckik, trī-) *adj.*

tri·bro·mo·eth·a·nol (trī-brōmō-éthə-nol || -nōl) *n.* Also **tri·brom·eth·a·nol** (-brōm-). A white crystalline compound, CBr_3CH_2OH, having a slight aromatic odour and taste, and used to produce complete unconsciousness.

trib·u·la·tion (tríbbew-láysh'n) *n.* **1.** *Often plural.* Great affliction, trial, or distress; suffering: *the tribulations of the persecuted.* **2.** An experience or condition that causes such distress. [Middle English *tribulacioun,* from Old French *tribulation,* from Late Latin *trībulātiō* (stem *trībulātiōn-*), from *trībulāre,* to oppress, from Latin, to press, from *trībulum,* threshing sledge.]

tri·bu·nal (trī-béwn'l, tri-) *n.* **1.** A seat or court of justice. **2.** The platform or seat upon which a judge or other presiding officer sits in court. **3.** A committee or board set up to adjudicate or investigate a particular matter or dispute: *a rent tribunal.* **4.** Anything having the power of determining or judging: *the tribunal of public opinion.* [Latin *tribūnāl(e),* court of the tribunes, tribunal, from *tribūnālis,* of a tribune, from *tribūnus,* TRIBUNE (official).]

trib·une[1] (tríbbewn || *U.S. also* tri-béwn) *n.* **1.** In ancient Rome, an official chosen by the plebs to protect their rights against the patricians. **2.** Any protector or champion of the common people. [Middle English, from Latin *tribūnus,* "head of the tribe", tribune, from *tribus,* TRIBE.] **—trib·u·nar·y** (-əri || -erri) *adj.* **—trib·u·nate, trib·une·ship** *n.*

tribune[2] *n.* **1.** A raised platform or dais from which a speaker addresses an assembly. **2.** In a church: **a.** An apse. **b.** A bishop's throne within an apse. **c.** A raised area or gallery. [French, from Italian *tribuna,* from Medieval Latin *tribūna,* variant of Latin *tribūnāl(e),* TRIBUNAL.]

trib·u·tar·y (tríbbew-tri, -təri || -terri) *adj.* **1.** Making additions or offering supplies; contributory; subsidiary. **2.** Having the nature of a tribute: *a tributary payment.* **3.** Paying or required to pay tribute. **4.** Flowing into a larger body of water. Said of a river or stream.
~*n., pl.* **tributaries.** **1.** One that pays tribute. **2.** *Abbr.* **trib.** A stream or river flowing into a larger stream or river. In this sense, compare **distributary.** **—trib·u·tar·i·ly** *adv.* **—trib·u·tar·i·ness** *n.*

trib·ute (tríbbewt) *n.* **1. a.** A gift, payment, declaration, or other acknowledgment of gratitude, respect, or admiration: *"To love and grief tribute of verse belongs"* (John Donne). **b.** That which is a worthy or creditable reflection of the person or thing mentioned: *The new church was a tribute to their faith.* **2. a.** A sum of money or other valuables paid by one ruler or nation to another as acknowledgment of submission or as the price for protection by that nation. **b.** Any payment made for protection. **3. a.** In feudal times, any payment or tax given by a vassal to his overlord. **b.** The obligation to make such a payment. [Middle English *tribut,* from Latin *tribūtum,* from the neuter past participle of *tribuere,* to give, distribute (as among the Roman tribes), from *tribus,* TRIBE.]

tri·car·box·y·lic acid cycle (trī-kárb-ok-síllik) *n.* The **Krebs cycle** *(see).*

trice (trīss) *tr.v.* **triced, tricing, trices.** To hoist and secure (a sail, for example); lash. Usually used with *up.*
~*n.* A very short period of time; a moment; an instant. Used chiefly in the phrase *in a trice.* See Synonyms at **moment.** [Middle English *trisen,* from Middle Dutch, akin to Middle Dutch *trise*†, pulley; noun sense, Middle English *at a tryse,* "at a pull".]

tri·cen·ten·ni·al (trī́-sen-ténni-əl) *adj.* Also **tri·cen·te·nar·y** (-téenəri, -ténnəri). Tercentenary.
~*n.* Also **tri·cen·te·nar·y.** A tercentenary event or celebration.

tri·ceps (trī́-seps) *n., pl.* **triceps** or **-cepses** (-sepsiz). Any three-headed muscle, especially the large muscle running along the back of the upper arm and serving to extend the forearm. [Latin, three-headed : *tri-,* three + *caput,* head.]

tri·cer·a·tops (trī-sérrə-tops) *n.* A three-horned herbivorous dinosaur of the genus *Triceratops,* of the Cretaceous period, having a bony plate covering the neck. [New Latin *Triceratops* : TRI- + Greek *keras* (stem *kerat-*), horn + *ōps,* eye, face.]

trich-. Variant of **tricho-.**

tri·chi·a·sis (tri-kī́-ə-siss) *n.* **1.** A condition of ingrowing hairs about an orifice, especially of ingrowing eyelashes. **2.** The presence of hairlike bodies in the urine. [Late Latin, from Greek *trikhiasis* : TRICH(O)- + -IASIS.]

tri·chi·na (tri-kī́-nə) *n., pl.* **-nae** (-nee) or **-nas.** A parasitic nematode worm, *Trichinella spiralis,* infesting the intestines of various mammals, and having larvae that move through the blood vessels and become encysted in the muscles. [New Latin, from Greek *trikhinos,* hairy, from *thrix,* hair.]

trich·i·nise, trich·i·nize (trícki-nīz') *tr.v.* **-nised, -nising, -nises.** To infect with trichinae. **—trich·i·ni·sa·tion** (-nī-záysh'n || *U.S.* -ni-) *n.*

trich·i·no·sis (trícki-nṓ-siss) *n.* Also **trich·i·ni·a·sis** (-nī́-ə-siss). A disease caused by eating inadequately cooked meat containing trichinae, and characterised by intestinal disorders, fever, muscular swelling, pain, and delirium. [New Latin : TRICHIN(A) + -OSIS.]

tri·chi·nous (trícki-nəss, tri-kī́-) *adj.* **1.** Containing trichinae: *trichi-*

nous pork. **2.** Of or relating to trichinae or trichinosis.

trich·ite (trík-īt) *n.* A small needle-shaped filament or crystal. [German *Trichit* : TRICH(O)- + -ITE.] —**tri·chit·ic** (trī-kíttik) *adj.*

tri·chlo·ride (trī-kláw-rīd ‖ -klō-) *n.* A compound containing three chlorine atoms per molecule.

tri·chlo·ro·a·ce·tic acid (trī-kláw-rō-ə-séetik, -séttik ‖ -klō-) *n.* A colourless, deliquescent, corrosive, crystalline compound, CCl₃COOH, used as a herbicide and applied locally as an astringent and antiseptic.

tri·chlo·ro·eth·yl·ene (trī-kláw-rō-éth'l-een ‖ -klō-) *n.* Also **tri·chlor·eth·yl·ene** (-kláwr- ‖ -klōr-), **tri·chlo·ro·eth·ene** (trī-kláw-rō-éeth-een). A colourless, toxic liquid, CHCl:CCl₂, used to degrease metals, as an extraction solvent for oils and waxes, as a refrigerant, in dry cleaning, and as a fumigant.

tri·chlo·ro·phe·nox·y·a·ce·tic acid (trī-kláw-rō-fen-óksi-ə-séetik, -séttik ‖ -klō-) *n.* A synthetic auxin, 2,4,5-trichlorophenoxyacetic acid, C₈H₅Cl₃O₃, that is used as a herbicide. Also called "2, 4, 5-T".

tricho-, trich- *comb. form.* Indicates hair or hairlike part; for example, **trichogyne**, **trichogyne**. [Greek *trikho-*, from *thrix* (stem *trikh-*), hair.]

trich·o·cyst (tríckə-sist) *n.* One of the minute capsule-like bodies in the outer cytoplasm of certain protozoans, capable of ejecting a threadlike or bristle-like extension. [TRICHO- + -CYST.] —**trich·o·cys·tic** (-sístik) *adj.*

trich·oid (trík-oyd, trík-) *adj.* Resembling hair; hairlike. [Greek *trikhoeidēs* : TRICH(O)- + -OID.]

tri·chol·o·gy (tri-kóllə-ji) *n.* The study of hair and its diseases.

trich·ome (trík-ōm, trík-) *n.* A hairlike or bristle-like outgrowth, as from the epidermis of a plant. [German *Trichom*, from Greek *trikhōma*, hair growth, from *trikhoun*, to furnish with hair, from *thrix* (stem *trikh-*), hair.] —**tri·chom·ic** (tri-kŏmik, trī-, -kómmik) *adj.*

trich·o·mo·nad (trík-ō-món-ad, -ə-, -mōn-) *n.* Any of various flagellate protozoans of the genus *Trichomonas*, occurring in the digestive and urogenital tracts of vertebrates. [New Latin *Trichomonas* (stem *Trichomonad-*) : TRICHO- + -MONAD.]

trich·o·mo·ni·a·sis (trík-ō-mə-nī-ə-siss, -ə-, -mo-, -mō-) *n.* **1.** A vaginal infection caused by a protozoan, *Trichomonas vaginalis*, and resulting in inflammation and discomfort. **2.** Any infection caused by trichomonads. [New Latin : *Trichomonas*, TRICHOMON(AD) + -IASIS.]

tri·chop·ter·an (trī-kóptərən, tri-) *n.* Any insect of the order Trichoptera, which comprises the caddis flies. [New Latin *Trichoptera*, "hairy winged" : TRICHO- + -PTER.]

tri·cho·sis (tri-kó-siss) *n.* Disease of the hair. [New Latin, from Greek *trikhōsis*, growth of hair, from *trikhoun*, to furnish with hair. See **trichome**.]

tri·chot·o·my (trī-kóttəmi, tri-) *n., pl.* **-mies.** A dividing into three parts. [Greek *trikha*, in three parts + -TOMY.] —**trich·o·tom·ic** (tríkə-tómmik, tríckə-), **tri·chot·o·mous** (-kóttəməss) *adj.* —**tri·chot·o·mous·ly** *adv.*

-trichous *adj. comb. form.* Indicates specified kinds of hair; for example, **amphitrichous**. [Greek *-trikhos*, from *thrix* (stem *trikh-*), hair.]

tri·chro·ism (trí-krō-iz'm) *n.* The property possessed by certain minerals of exhibiting three different colours when illuminated by white light and viewed from three different directions. [Greek *trikhroos*, "tricoloured" : TRI- + -CHRO(OUS) + -ISM.] —**tri·chro·ic** (trī-krō-í) *adj.*

tri·chro·mat·ic (trí-krō-máttik, -krə-) *adj.* Also **tri·chrome** (-krōm), **tri·chro·mic** (-krōmik). **1.** Of, relating to, or having three colours, as in photography or printing. **2.** Having visual perception of the three primary colours, as in normal vision. —**tri·chro·ma·tism** (-krōmətiz'm) *n.*

trick (trik) *n.* **1.** A device or action designed to achieve an end by deceptive or fraudulent means; a stratagem; a ruse. **2.** A mischievous action; a practical joke; a prank. **3.** A deceptive or delusive appearance; an illusion: *a trick of the sunlight.* **4.** A peculiar trait or characteristic, such as a mannerism: *had the trick of blinking as she spoke.* **5.** The best quality or method needed to accomplish something; a knack: *Patience is the trick here.* **6.** A feat of magic or legerdemain. **7.** A difficult, dexterous, or clever act, designed to amuse or entertain. **8.** In card games: **a.** All the cards played in a single round, one from each player. **b.** One such round. **9.** A period or turn of duty, as at the helm or a ship. **10.** *U.S. Slang.* **a.** A prostitute's client. **b.** A session with any one client, as carried out by a prostitute. —See Synonyms at **artifice.** —**do the trick.** *Informal.* To bring about the desired result. —**how's tricks.** *Informal.* Used to enquire how a person is or how things are going.
~*v.* **tricked, tricking, tricks.** —*tr.* **1.** To swindle or cheat; deceive; delude. **2.** To ornament, dress, or adorn. Used with *up* or *out.* —*intr.* To practise deception or trickery.
~*adj.* **1.** Of, pertaining to, or involving tricks. **2.** Designed or made for doing a trick or tricks: *a trick flower.* [Middle English *trik*, from Old French (dialect) *trique*, Old French *triche*, from *trichier*, to deceive, perhaps from Vulgar Latin *triccāre* (unattested), from Latin *trīcārī*, to start difficulties, dally, play tricks, from *trīcae†*, trifles, tricks. See also **intricate, extricate.**] —**trick·er** *n.*

trick·er·y (tríckəri) *n., pl.* **-ies.** The practice or use of tricks; deception by stratagem; artifice.

trick·le (trík'l) *v.* **-led, -ling, -les.** —*intr.* **1.** To flow or fall in drops or in a thin, intermittent stream; drip gently but steadily. **2.** To move or proceed slowly or bit by bit: *The audience trickled in.* —*tr.* To cause to trickle: *trickle oil into the mayonnaise.*

~*n.* **1.** The act or condition of trickling. **2.** Any slow, small, or irregular quantity of something that moves, proceeds, or occurs intermittently. [Middle English *triklen* (perhaps imitative).]

trickle charger *n.* A mains-operated device for charging accumulators by passing a low current over a long period.

trickle-down·theory *n.* The notion that whatever directly benefits those at the top economically or socially will eventually work its way down to benefit indirectly those lower down, without the need for anything to be done directly on their behalf. Often derogatory. —**trickle-down** *adj.*

trick or treat *n.* The custom practised, especially in the United States, by children on Hallowe'en, of going from door to door dressed in costume and saying "trick or treat", as a demand for sweets, cakes, or the like.

trick·ster (tríkstər) *n.* One who plays tricks or deceives.

trick·sy (tríksi) *adj.* **1.** Playful; prankish; mischievous. **2.** Crafty or sly. **3.** *Archaic.* Smart; spruce; dapper. [From TRICK.]

trick·y (tríki) *adj.* **-ier, -iest. 1.** Given to or characterised by deception or trickery; crafty; sly; wily: *a tricky politician.* **2.** Requiring caution or skill; difficult: *a tricky question; a tricky situation.* —See Synonyms at **dishonest, sly.** —**trick·i·ly** *adv.* —**trick·i·ness** *n.*

tri·clin·ic (trī-klínnik) *adj.* Having three unequal axes intersecting at oblique angles. Said of certain crystals. [TRI- + -CLINIC.]

tri·clin·i·um (trī-klín-i-əm, trī-) *n., pl.* **-nia** (-ni-ə). **1.** A couch or set of couches surrounding three sides of a table, used by the ancient Romans for reclining at meals. **2.** A room containing such a couch or couches. [Latin *triclīnium*, from Greek *triklinion*, diminutive of *triklinos*, room with three couches : *tri-*, three + *klinē* couch.]

tri·col·our (trí-kullər) *adj.* Also **tri·col·oured** (-d). Having three colours.
~*n.* (trík'l-ər) **1.** A tricolour flag. **2.** *Sometimes capital* **T.** The French or Irish flag. Preceded by *the.*

tri·corn, tri·corne (trí-kawrn) *n.* A hat having the brim turned up on three sides.
~*adj.* Having three projections, horns, or corners. [French *tri·corne*, from Latin *tricornis*, three-horned : *tri-*, three + *cornū*, horn.]

tri·cos·tate (trī-kóstayt) *adj.* Having three costae or riblike ridges.

tri·cot (tréek-ō, trík-) *n.* **1.** A plain, warp-knitted cloth of any of various yarns. **2.** A soft ribbed cloth of wool or a wool blend, usually used for dresses. [French, from *tricoter†*, to knit.]

tric·o·tine (tríckə-téen, tréekə-) *n.* A sturdy worsted fabric with a double twill, used for dresses and suits. [French, from TRICOT.]

tri·crot·ic (trī-króttik) *adj. Medicine.* Having three waves or elevations to one beat of the pulse. [From Greek *trikrotos*, having a triple beat : *tri-*, three + *krotein*, to beat.] —**tri·cro·tism** (-krot-iz'm, trī-, -krət-) *n.*

tri·cus·pid (trī-kúspid, trí-) *adj.* Also **tri·cus·pi·dal** (-'l), **tri·cus·pi·date** (-ayt). **1.** Having three points or cusps, as a molar tooth. **2.** *Anatomy.* Pertaining to the tricuspid valve of the heart.
~*n. Anatomy.* A tricuspid organ or part, especially a tooth. [Latin *tricuspis* (stem *tricuspid-*) : *tri-*, three + *cuspis*, point, CUSP.]

tricuspid valve *n.* The three-segmented valve of the heart that keeps the blood from flowing back from the right ventricle into the right atrium.

tri·cy·cle (trí-sik'l) *n.* A vehicle, used especially by small children that has three wheels, normally two at the back and one at the front and is usually propelled by pedals. Also informally called "trike". —**tri·cy·cle** *intr.v.*

tri·cy·clic (trī-sicklik, -síklik) *adj. Chemistry.* Having or pertaining to a molecular structure with three rings.
~*n.* A tricyclic antidepressant.

tri·dac·tyl (trī-dáktil, trí-) *adj.* Also **tri·dac·ty·lous** (-əss). Having three toes, claws, or similar parts on each limb. [Greek *tridaktulos*, three-fingered : *tri-*, three + *daktulos*, finger (see **dactyl**).]

tri·dent (trí·d'nt) *n.* A long, three-pronged fork or weapon as used by one hunting fish or formerly by gladiators; especially, the three-pronged spear carried by Neptune or Poseidon.
~*adj.* Also **tri·den·tate** (trī-déntayt, trí-). Having three teeth, prongs, or similar protrusions. [Latin *tridēns* (stem *trident-*), three-toothed : *tri-*, three + *dēns*, tooth.]

Trident II missile *n.* A U.S. submarine-launched ballistic missile armed with eight nuclear warheads.

Tri·den·tine (tri-dén-tīn, trī-, -teen, -tin) *adj.* Of or relating to the Council of Trent or to the results or decrees of that Council.
~*n.* A Roman Catholic who conforms rigorously to the Tridentine Creed formulated at the Council of Trent. [Medieval Latin *Tridentīnus*, from *Tridentum*, ancient form of TRENT.]

Tridentine Mass *n.* The Mass in the rite laid down by Pius V in 1570 following the reforms of the Council of Trent, used throughout the Roman Catholic Church until replaced by the various revisions which followed the Second Vatican Council.

tried. Past tense and past participle of **try.**

tri·en·ni·al (trī-énni-əl, trí-) *adj.* **1.** Occurring every third year. **2.** Lasting three years.
~*n.* **1.** A third anniversary. **2.** A triennial thing, event, or celebration. [From TRIENNIUM.] —**tri·en·ni·al·ly** *adv.*

tri·en·ni·um (trī-énni-əm, trí-) *n., pl.* **-ums** or **-nia** (-ə). A period of three years. [Latin *triennium* : *tri-*, three + Latin *annus*, year.]

tri·er (trí-ər) *n.* One that tries; especially, a person who continues to make repeated attempts at something, despite failure.

tri·er·arch (trí-ə-raark) *n.* In ancient Greece: **1.** The captain of a trireme. **2.** An Athenian who had the responsibility of outfitting and maintaining a trireme as a part of his civic duties. [Latin *triēr-*

archus, from Greek *triērarkhos* : *triērēs,* trireme + -ARCH.]

tri·er·ar·chy (trī-ə-raarki) *n., pl.* **-chies.** In ancient Greece: **1.** The authority or office of the commander of a trierarch. **2.** The ancient Athenian system whereby individual citizens furnished and maintained triremes as a part of their public duty.

Tri·es·te (tree-ést; *Italian* -éstay). *Serbo-Croat* **Trst.** Seaport and capital of Friuli-Venezia Giulia region, northeast Italy. It is an important industrial and tourist centre. It was held by Austria from 1382 until 1919 and was the subject of a dispute with Yugoslavia after World War II.

tri·fa·cial (trī-fáysh'l) *adj. Anatomy.* Trigeminal.

tri·fid (trī́-fid) *adj.* Divided or cleft into three narrow parts or lobes. [Latin *trifidus* : *tri-,* three + -FID.]

tri·fle (trī́f'l) *n.* **1.** Something of slight importance or very little value. **2.** A small amount of something; a little: *The book only cost a trifle.* **3.** A dessert typically consisting of a layer of sponge cake covered with jam or fruit, soaked in wine, sprinkled with almonds, and topped with custard and whipped cream. **4. a.** A moderately hard variety of pewter. **b.** *Plural.* Utensils made from this. **—a trifle.** Slightly; somewhat: *a trifle stingy.*

~v. **trifled, -fling, -fles.** *—intr.* **1.** To deal with something as if it were of little significance or value. Usually used with *with*: *not a person to be trifled with.* **2.** To act, perform, or speak with little seriousness or purpose; jest. **3.** To play or toy with something; handle things idly. *—tr.* To waste (time or money, for example). Often used with *away.* [Middle English *trifle, truf(f)le,* from Old French *truf(f)le,* variant of *tru(f)fe*†, trickery, deceit.] **—tri·fler** *n.*

tri·fling (trī́fling) *adj.* **1.** Of slight importance; insignificant. **2.** Characterised by frivolity or idleness. —See Synonyms at **trivial.** **—tri·fling·ly** *adv.*

tri·fo·cal (trī-fṓk'l, trī́-) *adj.* Having three focal lengths.

~n. Plural. Glasses having trifocal lenses.

tri·fold (trī́-fōld) *adj.* Triple; having three parts. [TRI- + -FOLD.]

tri·fo·li·ate (trī-fṓli-ət, -it, -ayt) *adj.* Also **tri·fo·li·at·ed** (-aytid). Having three leaves, leaflets, or leaflike parts: *a trifoliate compound leaf.*

tri·fo·li·o·late (trī-fṓli-əl-ət, -it, -ayt) *adj.* Having three leaflets.

tri·fo·ri·um (trī-fáw-ri-əm ‖ -fṓ-) *n., pl.* **-foria** (-ə). *Architecture.* A gallery of arches set in the wall above the arches of the nave choir, and sometimes the transept of a church. [Medieval Latin *triforium*†, special name (in Gervase of Canterbury, *c.* 1185) applied to the gallery in Canterbury Cathedral, but subsequently taken to mean "structure with three openings" (Latin *tri-,* three + *fores,* doors) and thus applied to the elevated gallery characteristic of Gothic architecture, sometimes having three arches or openings.]

tri·form (trī́-fawrm) *adj.* Having three different forms or parts.

tri·fur·cate (trī́-fur-kət, -fúr-, -kit, -kayt) *adj.* Also **tri·fur·cat·ed** (-kaytid). Having three forks or branches. **—tri·fur·ca·tion** (-káysh'n) *n.*

trig[1] (trig) *adj. Archaic & Regional & U.S.* **1.** Trim; neat; tidy. **2.** In good condition; firm; strong.

~tr.v. **trigged, trigging, trigs.** *Archaic & Regional.* To make trim or neat, especially in dress. Often used with *up* or *out.* [Middle English, true, active, from Old Norse *tryggr;* akin to TRUE.] **—trig·ly** *adv.* **—trig·ness** *n.*

trig[2] *tr.v.* **trigged, trigging, trigs. 1.** To stop (a wheel) from rolling, as with a trig. **2.** To prop up; support.

~n. A wedge or other braking device. [Perhaps from Scandinavian, akin to Old Norse *tryggr,* true, firm. See **trig** (trim).]

trig. trigonometric; trigonometry.

tri·gem·i·nal (trī-jémmin'l) *adj. Anatomy.* Pertaining to the trigeminal nerve; trifacial.

trigeminal nerve *n.* Either of the fifth pair of cranial nerves that divides into the ophthalmic, maxillary, and mandibular nerves. [New Latin, from Latin, three born at a birth, threefold (probably from its three branches) : *tri-,* three + *geminus,* twin-born, twin.]

trigeminal neuralgia *n.* Intensely painful paroxysms of the facial area around the trigeminal nerve. Also called "tic douloureux".

trig·ger (triggər) *n.* **1.** The lever pressed by the finger to discharge a firearm. **2.** Any similar device used to release or activate a mechanism. **3.** Anything that activates or sets off an action or series of events: *Murder was the trigger for the uprising.* **4.** *Electronics.* A pulse or a circuit that initiates the action of another component.

~tr.v. **triggered, -gering, -gers. 1.** To initiate; activate; set off. Often used with *off*: *triggered off public outcry.* **2.** To fire or explode (a weapon). [Earlier *tricker,* from Dutch *trekker,* something pulled, from Middle Dutch *trecker,* from *trecken,* to pull, travel. See **trek.**]

trig·ger·fish (tríggər-fish) *n., pl.* **-fishes** or collectively **triggerfish.** Any of various brightly coloured fishes of the family Balistidae, of warm coastal seas, characteristically having sharp, erectile dorsal spines.

trigger flower *n.* Any of numerous plants of the genus *Stylidium,* confined mainly to Australia, that have a column of fused stamens which dusts the backs of insects with pollen.

trig·ger-hap·py (tríggər-happi) *adj. Informal.* Inclined to react in a violent, rash manner at the slightest provocation, as by firing a gun.

tri·glyc·er·ide (trī-glíssə-rīd, trī́-) *n.* A natural fat or oil formed by combination of one molecule of glycerol with three molecules of fatty acids.

tri·glyph (trigglif, trī́-glif) *adj. Architecture.* An ornament in a Doric frieze, consisting of a projecting block having three parallel vertical channels on its face. [Latin *trīglyphus,* from Greek *trigluphos* : *tri-,* three + *gluphē,* carving, GLYPH.] **—tri·glyph·ic** (tri-glíffik, trī-) *adj.*

tri·gon (trī́-gən, -gon) *n.* **1.** A triangular lyre or harp of Roman and Greek antiquity. **2.** In astrology, a **triplicity** *(see).* **3.** *Archaic.* A triangle. [Latin *trigonum,* triangle, from Greek *trigōnon,* from *trigōnos,* triangular : *tri-,* three + -GON.]

trig·o·nal (tríggən'l) *adj.* **1.** Triangular. **2.** In crystallography, pertaining to or belonging to the crystal system with three unequal axes that are equally inclined to each other at an angle other than 90°.

trigonometric function *n.* **1.** A function of an angle expressed as the ratio of two of the sides of a right-angled triangle that contains the angle, named sine, cosine, tangent, or the like. In general, for any angle formed in a coordinate plane by the intersection of the abscissal axis with the radius vector from the origin to a point in the plane, the ratio of any two of the values abscissa, ordinate, and radius vector of that point. Also called "circular function". **2.** A function composed of a combination of trigonometric functions.

trig·o·nom·e·try (triggə-nómmətri) *n. Abbr.* **trig.** The study of the properties and applications of trigonometric functions. [New Latin *trigonometria* : Greek *trigōnon,* triangle, TRIGON + -METRY.] **—trig·o·no·met·ric** (-nə-méttrik), **trig·o·no·met·ri·cal** *adj.* **—trig·o·no·met·ri·cal·ly** *adv.*

trig·o·nous (trígganəss, *also* trī́-gōnəss) *adj.* Three-sided, especially in cross section: *a trigonous stem.* Compare **triquetrous.** [From Greek *trigōnos,* three-cornered. See **tri-, -gon.**]

tri·graph (trī́-graaf, -graf) *n.* A conjunction of three letters representing a single speech sound; for example the letters *e, a,* and *u* in the word *beau* form a trigraph. Also called "triphthong". [TRI- + -GRAPH, after *digraph.*]

tri·he·dron (trī-heéd-rən, -héd-) *n., pl.* **-drons** or **-dra** (-rə). A figure formed by the intersection of three noncoplanar lines. Also "trihedral". [New Latin : TRI- + -HEDRON.] **—tri·he·dral** *adj. & n.*

tri·hy·drate (trī́-hī́-drayt) *n.* A compound containing three molecules of water of crystallisation per molecule in the compound.

tri·hy·dric (trī-hī́drik) *adj.* Also **tri·hy·drox·y** (trī́-hī-dróksi). Containing three hydroxide groups per molecule. Said especially of alcohols.

trike (trīk) *n. Informal.* A **tricycle** *(see).*

tri·lat·er·al (trī-láttrəl, trī́-, -láttərəl) *adj.* Having three sides. [Latin *trilaterus* : *tri-,* three + *latus* (stem *later-*), side (see **lateral**).] **—tri·lat·er·al·ly** *adv.*

tri·lat·er·al·ism (trī́-láttrəl-iz'm, -láttərəl-) *n.* The political policy of encouraging friendly relations between three nations or regions, especially between North America, Japan, and Europe. **—tri·lat·er·al·ist** *n.*

tril·by (trílbi) *n., pl.* **-bies.** *British.* **1.** A felt hat with an indented crown and narrow brim, worn by a man. **2.** *Plural. Slang.* Feet. [19th century : after the heroine of *Trilby,* a novel by George du Maurier. The hat was popularised in the stage version.]

tri·lin·e·ar (trī-línni-ər, trī́-) *adj.* Pertaining to, having, or bounded by three lines.

tri·lin·gual (trī-líng-gwəl) *adj.* Having or expressed in three languages.

tri·lit·er·al (trī-líttrəl, trī́-, -líttərəl) *adj.* Consisting of three letters. Used chiefly of consonantal roots in Semitic languages.

~n. A three-letter word or word element.

tri·lith (trī́-lith) *n.* A group of three large stones usually with two standing upright and supporting a third, often found in prehistoric henge monuments. [Greek *trilithon* : TRI- + -LITH.]

trill (tril) *n.* **1.** A fluttering or tremulous sound, such as that made by certain birds; a warble. **2.** *Music.* The rapid alternation of two notes either a whole tone or a semi-tone apart. Compare **tremolo.** **3.** *Phonetics.* **a.** A rapid vibration of one speech organ against another, as of the tongue against the alveolar ridge in Spanish *rr.* **b.** A speech sound pronounced with such a vibration.

~v. **trilled, trilling, trills.** *—tr.* **1.** To sound, sing, or play with a trill. **2.** *Phonetics.* To articulate with a trill. *—intr.* To produce or give forth a trill. [Italian *trillo,* (from *trillare*†, to trill.]

tril·lion (tríl-yən) *n., pl.* **trillion** (for senses 1, 2). **1.** *British.* The cardinal number represented by 1 followed by 18 zeros, usually written 10^{18}. **2.** A **billion** (sense 1). **3.** *Plural.* An indefinitely large number; a great many. [French : TRI- + (M)ILLION, by analogy with *billion.*] **—tril·lion** *adj.*

tril·lionth (tríl-yənth) *n.* **1.** The ordinal number one trillion in a series. **2.** One of a trillion equal parts. **—tril·lionth** *adj. & adv.*

tril·li·um (trílli-əm) *n.* Any of various plants of the genus *Trillium,* of North America and eastern Asia, usually having a single whorl of three leaves, and a variously coloured, three-petalled flower. [New Latin : TRI- + *(vertic)illium* : Latin *(vertic)illus,* whorl, VERTICIL + -IUM.]

tri·lo·bate (trī́-lōb-ayt, -lōb-, -ləb-) *adj.* Also **tri·lo·bal** (-lṓb'l), **tri·lo·bat·ed** (-lō-baytid, -lṓ-), **tri·lobed** (-lōbd). Having three lobes, as certain leaves have.

tri·lo·bite (trī́-lō-bīt, -lə-) *n.* Any of numerous extinct marine arthropods of the class Trilobita, of the Palaeozoic era, having a segmented exoskeleton divided by furrows into three longitudinal lobes. [New Latin *Trilobites* (division), from Greek *trilobos,* "three-lobed" : *tri-,* three + *lobos,* LOBE.] **—tri·lo·bit·ic** (-bíttik) *adj.*

tri·loc·u·lar (trī-lóckew-lər) *adj.* Having three chamber-like divisions or cavities. Said especially of plant reproductive structures.

tril·o·gy (trílləji) *n., pl.* **-gies.** A group of three dramatic or literary works by the same author that are related in subject or theme, such as three ancient Greek tragedies written to be performed in immediate succession. [Greek *trilogia* : TRI- + -LOGY.]

trim (trim) *v.* **trimmed, trimming, trims.** *—tr.* **1. a.** To make neat or

tidy by clipping, smoothing, or pruning: *trimmed his beard.* **b.** To make tidy or put into order, especially in appearance. Often used with *up*: *trimmed himself up.* **2.** To remove (excess) by or as if by cutting: *trim off the rotten bark; trimmed the budget.* **3.** To ornament; decorate: *trim the dress with a band of lace.* **4.** *Informal.* **a.** To thrash. **b.** To defeat soundly. **c.** To cheat. **d.** To rebuke or scold. **5.** *Nautical.* **a.** To adjust (the sails and yards of a ship) so that they receive the wind properly. **b.** To balance (a ship) by shifting its cargo or contents. **6.** To balance (an aircraft) in flight by regulating the control surfaces and tabs. —*intr.* **1.** *Nautical.* **a.** To be in or retain equilibrium. Used of a ship. **b.** To make the sails and yards of a ship ready for sailing. **2. a.** To affect cautious neutrality between conflicting interests. **b.** To fashion one's views for momentary popularity or advantage.
~*n.* **1. a.** Order, arrangement, or appearance; condition: *in good trim.* **b.** A condition of good health, fitness or order: *got himself in trim.* **2. a.** Mouldings, framework, or other exterior ornamentation. **b.** Adornment or decoration, as for clothing. **3.** Dress or equipment. **4.** Excised or rejected material, such as film that has been cut in editing. **5.** A clipping or trimming to make neat: *The verge needs a trim; My fringe needs a trim.* **6.** *U.S.* A commercial window display. **7.** *Nautical.* **a.** The readiness of a vessel for sailing, with regard to ballast, sails, and yards. **b.** The balance of a ship. **c.** The difference between the draught at the bow and at the stern. **8.** The position of an aircraft relative to its horizontal axis.
~*adj.* **trimmer, trimmest. 1.** In good or neat order or condition. **2.** In good shape; slim. [Perhaps from Middle English *trimmen* (unattested), Old English *trymman, trymian,* to strengthen, arrange.] —**trim·ly** *adv.* —**trim·ness** *n.*
tri·ma·ran (trĭmə-răn, -răn) *n.* A sailing vessel with three hulls set side by side. [TRI- + (CATA)MARAN.]
Trim·ble (trĭmb'l) **(William) David** (1944–). Northern Irish politician. He was called to the Bar of Northern Ireland in 1969 and elected Ulster Unionist M.P. for Upper Ban in 1990. He has been leader of the Ulster Unionist party since 1995.
tri·mer (trĭmər) *n. Chemistry.* An oligomeric compound consisting of three identical monomeric molecules or groups. [TRI- + -MER.]
trim·er·ous (trĭmmərəss) *adj.* **1.** Having three similar segments or parts. **2.** *Botany.* Having flower parts, such as petals, sepals, and stamens, in sets of three. Also written *3-merous.* [New Latin *trimerus,* from Greek *trimerēs* : TRI- + -MEROUS.] —**trim·er·ism** *n.*
tri·mes·ter (trĭ-mĕstər, trĭ-) *n.* **1.** A period or term of three months. **2.** *U.S.* In some universities, any of three equal academic terms into which the year is divided. Compare **semester.**
~*adj.* Also **tri·mes·tral** (-mĕstrəl), **tri·mes·tri·al** (-mĕstri-əl). Of or pertaining to periods of three months. [French *trimestre,* from Latin *trimestris,* "of three months" : *tri-,* three + *mēnsis,* month.]
trim·e·ter (trĭmmĭtər) *n.* A line of verse consisting of three metrical feet. [Latin *trimetrus,* from Greek *trimetros* : TRI- + METER.] —**tri·met·ric** (trĭ-mĕttrĭk), **tri·met·ri·cal** *adj.*
tri·meth·a·di·one (trĭ-mĕthə-dī-ōn) *n.* A granular, crystalline substance, $C_6H_9NO_3$, used in treating petit mal epilepsy. Also called "troxidone".
trimetric projection *n.* A method of projection, used especially for mechanical drawings, in which the representation involves three axes with arbitrary angles and scales.
tri·met·ro·gon (trĭ-mĕttrə-gən, -gŏn) *n.* A system of aerial photography in which one vertical and two oblique photographs are simultaneously taken for use in topographic mapping. [TRI- + Greek *metron,* measure, METER + -GON.]
trim·mer (trĭmmər) *n.* **1.** A person or machine that trims, especially any of various devices used for trimming, such as a hedge trimmer. **2.** A person who changes his opinions to suit the needs of the moment; a timeserver. **3.** *Electronics.* A variable component used to make fine adjustments to capacity, resistance, or the like. **4.** *Architecture.* A beam across an opening, such as a hearth, into which the ends of joists can be fitted.
trim·ming (trĭmmĭng) *n.* **1.** That which is added as decoration; especially, a band of lace, embroidery, or the like used to decorate clothing. **2.** *Plural.* Accessories; extras: *roast turkey with all the trimmings.* **3.** *Plural.* That which is removed when something is trimmed; excess. **4.** *Informal.* A sound defeat, beating, or punishment.
tri·mo·lec·u·lar (trĭ-mə-lĕckew-lər, -mo-, -mō-) *adj.* Pertaining to or formed from three molecules.
tri·month·ly (trĭ-mŭnthli) *adj.* Done, occurring, or appearing every three months. —**tri·month·ly** *adv.*
tri·morph (trĭ-mawrf) *n.* **1.** A substance that occurs in three distinct forms. **2.** One of the forms in which such a substance occurs. [Back-formation from TRIMORPHIC.]
tri·mor·phic (trĭ-mór-fĭk) *adj.* Also **tri·mor·phous** (-fəss). **1.** *Biology.* Having or occurring in three differing forms. **2.** *Chemistry.* Crystallising in three distinct forms. [TRI- + -MORPH(OUS) + -IC.] —**tri·mor·phi·cal·ly** *adv.* —**tri·mor·phism** *n.*
Tri·mur·ti (tri-mŏorti) *n. Hinduism.* The Vedic triad of Brahma, Vishnu, and Shiva. [Sanskrit *trimūrti* : *tri,* three + *mūrti†,* form.]
tri·nal (trĭn'l) *adj.* Having three parts; threefold; triple. [Latin *trīnālis,* from Latin *trīnus,* TRINE.]
tri·na·ry (trĭnəri) *adj.* Consisting of three parts or proceeding by threes; ternary. [From Late Latin *trīnārius,* from Latin *trīnus,* TRINE.]
trine (trīn) *adj.* **1.** Threefold; triple. **2.** In astrology, of or designating the trine aspect of two plants.

~*n.* **1.** A group of three. **2.** In astrology, the aspect of two planets when 120 degrees apart. [Middle English, from Old French, from Latin *trīnus,* from *trīnī,* three each.]
Trin·i·dad and To·ba·go, Republic of (trĭnni-dad, -dăd; tə-báygō, tō-). A state of the southeastern Caribbean, an independent republic within the Commonwealth. Both islands are woody and hilly; oil and asphalt are the chief products. Area, 5 128 square kilometres (1,980 square miles). Population 1,265,000. Capital, Port of Spain.

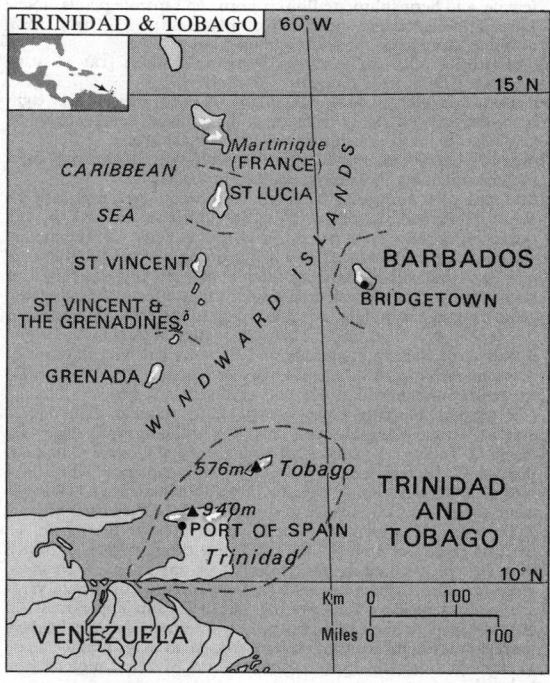

Tri·nil man (treenil) *n.* **Java man** *(see).* [After *Trinil,* village in Java, where remains were found.]
Trin·i·tar·i·an (trĭnni-taĭr-i-ən) *adj.* **1.** Describing or relating to the Trinity. **2.** Believing or professing belief in the Trinity or the doctrine of the Trinity. Compare **Unitarian. 3.** Pertaining to the Order of the Holy Trinity.
~*n.* **1.** A person who believes in the doctrine of the Trinity. **2.** A member of the Order of the Holy Trinity, founded in 1198 for the ransoming of Christian captives from the Muslims. —**Trin·i·tar·i·an·ism** *n.*
tri·ni·tro·ben·zene (trĭ-nĭtrō-bén-zeen, -ben-zéen) *n.* A yellow crystalline compound, $C_6H_3(NO_2)_3$, derived from trinitrotoluene and used as an explosive.
tri·ni·tro·cre·sol (trĭ-nĭtrō-krée-sol ‖ -sōl) *n.* A yellow crystalline compound, $CH_3C_6H(NO_2)_3OH$, used in high explosives.
tri·ni·tro·glyc·er·in (trĭ-nĭtrō-glíssə-reen, -rĭn) *n. Chemistry.* **Nitroglycerin** *(see).*
tri·ni·tro·phe·nol (trĭ-nĭtrō-fée-nol ‖ -nōl) *n.* **Picric acid** *(see).*
tri·ni·tro·tol·u·ene (trĭ-nĭtrō-tóllew-een) *n.* A yellow crystalline compound, $CH_3C_6H_2(NO_2)_3$, used mainly as a high explosive. Also called "TNT", "trinitrotoluol".
trin·i·ty (trĭnnəti, trĭnniti) *n., pl.* **-ties. 1.** The state or condition of being three. **2.** A group of three; a triad. Also called "triunity". [Middle English *trinite,* from Old French, from Latin *trīnitās,* from *trīnus,* TRINE.]
Trinity *n.* **1.** *Theology.* The union of three divine figures, the Father, Son, and Holy Ghost, in one Godhead. **2.** Trinity Sunday.
Trinity Brethren *pl.n.* The members of Trinity House.
Trinity House *n.* A British association that takes measures to safeguard shipping around the coastline, as by providing and maintaining lighthouses and buoys.
Trinity Sunday *n.* The first Sunday after Pentecost, or Whitsunday, dedicated to the Trinity. Also called "Trinity".
Trinity term *n.* In some British universities and colleges, the summer term. [After TRINITY SUNDAY.]
trin·ket (trĭngkit) *n.* **1.** Any small ornament, such as a piece of jewellery. **2.** A trivial thing; a trifle. [16th century : origin obscure.]
tri·noc·u·lar (trĭ-nóckew-lər) *adj.* Pertaining to or having a binocular eyepiece with an additional lens system for photographic recording. Said especially of microscopes. [TRI- + (BI)NOCULAR.]
tri·no·mi·al (trĭ-nómi-əl, trĭ-) *adj.* **1.** Consisting of three names or terms, as a taxonomic designation may. **2.** *Mathematics.* Having three algebraic terms connected by plus or minus signs.
~*n.* **1.** A three-part taxonomic designation indicating genus, species, and subspecies or variety, such as *Brassica oleracea botrytis,* the cauliflower. **2.** *Mathematics.* A trinomial algebraic expression. [TRI- + (BI)NOMIAL.]

tri·o (trée-ō) *n., pl.* **-os.** **1.** Any three people or things joined or associated. **2.** *Music.* **a.** A composition for three performers. **b.** The people (collectively) who perform a trio or trios. **c.** The middle section of a minuet or scherzo, a march, or of various dance forms. [Italian, variant (influenced by *duo*) of Latin *tria,* neuter of *trēs,* three.]

tri·ode (trī-ōd) *n.* A type of thermionic valve containing an anode, a cathode, and a control grid. [TRI- + -ODE (path).]

tri·oe·cious, tri·e·cious (trī-éeshəss, trī-) *adj. Botany.* Having male, female, and hermaphrodite flowers borne on separate plants. [New Latin *Trioecia,* former order of such plants : TRI- + Greek *oikia,* dwelling, from *oikos,* house.] **—tri·oe·cious·ly** *adv.*

tri·ol (trī-ol || -ōl) *n. Chemistry.* Trihydric alcohol. [TRI- + -OL.]

tri·o·le·in (trī-óli-in) *n. Chemistry.* Olein (see).

tri·o·let (trée-ō-let, trī-, -ə-, -lət, -lit) *n.* A poem or stanza of eight lines constructed on two rhymes, the scheme being *abaaaab.* [French, diminutive of *trio,* from Italian, TRIO.]

tri·ox·ide (trī-ók-sīd, trī-) *n.* Also **tri·ox·id** (-sid). A chemical compound containing three oxygen atoms per molecule.

trip (trip) *n.* **1. a.** A going from one place to another, especially by ship or aeroplane; a voyage; a journey: *a trip to America.* **b.** Any excursion or journey: *a trip to the shops.* **2.** *Slang.* **a.** The mental state or experience induced by a hallucinogen, such as LSD: *an acid trip.* **b.** A hallucinogenic drug: *drop a trip.* **c.** Any experience or state of mind that is considered similar to the effects of a hallucinogenic drug in being stimulating, exciting, or extremely subjective: *a power trip.* **3.** A light or nimble tread or step. **4.** A stumble or fall. **5.** A way of causing a stumble or fall, as by catching the foot of someone walking. **6.** A mistake, slip, or blunder. **7. a.** A catch for tripping a mechanism. **b.** The action of such a catch. **~***v.* **tripped, tripping, trips.** *—intr.* **1.** To stumble; fall: *tripped over.* **2.** To move nimbly with or as if with light, rapid steps: *trip along.* **3.** To make a mistake; go wrong: *tripped up on the last question.* **4.** To be released, as a tooth on an escapement wheel in a watch. **5.** *Rare.* To take a trip. **6.** *Slang.* To experience a hallucinogenic drug. *—tr.* **1.** To cause to stumble or fall. Often used with *up.* **2.** To trap or catch in an error or inconsistency. **3.** *Archaic.* To perform (a dance) nimbly. **4.** To release a catch, trigger, or switch that sets (a mechanism, for example) in operation. **5.** *Nautical.* **a.** To raise (an anchor) from the bottom. **b.** To tip or turn (a yardarm) into a position for lowering. **c.** To lift (an upper mast) in order to remove the pin or fid before lowering. [Middle English, short journey, light movement, from *trippen,* to walk lightly, cause to stumble, from Old French *trip(p)er,* from Middle Dutch *trippen,* to hop.]

tri·pal·mi·tin (trī-pál-mətin, trī-) *n. Chemistry.* Palmitin *(see).*

tri·par·tite (trī-pár-tīt, trī-) *adj.* **1.** Composed of or divided into three parts. **2.** Pertaining to or executed by three parties. **3.** *Botany.* Divided into three parts. Said especially of leaves.

tri·par·ti·tion (trī-paar-tish'n) *n.* Division into three parts or among three parties: *the tripartition of a defeated nation.*

tripe (trīp) *n.* **1.** The pale, rubbery lining of the stomach of cattle or other ruminants, used as food. **2.** *Informal.* Anything with no meaning or value; rubbish or nonsense. [Middle English, from Old French *tripe†.*]

tri·ped·al (trī-pédd'l) *adj.* Having three feet or legs; tripodal. [Latin *tripedālis :* *tri-,* three + *pēs* (stem *ped-*), foot.]

tri·pet·al·ous (trī-pétt'l-əss) *adj. Botany.* Having three petals.

trip·ham·mer (trip-hammər) *n.* Also **trip hammer.** A heavy, power-operated hammer that is lifted by a cam or lever and then dropped.

tri·phen·yl·me·thane (trī-féen-īl-mée-thayn, -fén-) *n.* A colourless, crystalline hydrocarbon, $(C_6H_5)_3CH$, from which a large number of synthetic dyes are derived by substitution.

tri·phib·i·ous (trī-fíbbi-əss, trī-) *adj.* Taking place on land, at sea, and in the air. Said of military operations. [TRI- + (AM)PHIBIOUS.]

triph·thong (trif-thong, *also* trip- || *U.S. also* -thawng) *n.* **1.** A compound vowel sound resulting from the combination of three simple ones and functioning as a unit. **2.** A trigraph *(see).* [TRI- + (DI)PHTHONG.] **—triph·thon·gal** (-thóng-g'l || -tháwng-) *adj.*

triph·y·lite (tríffi-līt) *n.* Also **triph·y·line** (-leen). A vitreous bluish-grey mineral $LiFePO_4$. [TRI- + Greek *phulon,* tribe (see **phyletic**) + -ITE (from its three bases).]

tri·pin·nate (trī-pínnayt, trī-) *adj. Botany.* Divided into leaflets that are subdivided into smaller, further subdivided leaflets or lobes, as are the fronds of some ferns. **—tri·pin·nate·ly** *adv.*

tri·plane (trī-playn) *n.* An aeroplane with wings on three levels.

tri·ple (tripp'l) *adj.* **1.** Consisting of three parts; threefold. **2.** Three times as many or as much. **~***n.* **1.** A number or quantity three times as great as another. **2.** A group or set of three; a triad. **~***v.* **tripled, -ling, -les.** *—tr.* To make three times as great in number or amount. *—intr.* To be or become three times as great in number or amount. [Middle English, from Old French, from Latin *triplus :* *tri-,* three + *-plus,* "-fold".] **—tri·ply** *adv.*

Tri·ple Alliance (tripp'l) *n.* An alliance between three countries, especially: **1.** The alliance of England, Sweden, and the Netherlands against France in 1668. **2.** The alliance of England, France, and the Netherlands against Spain in 1717, called the Quadruple Alliance when joined by Austria in 1718. **3.** The Dreibund formed by Germany, Austria-Hungary, and Italy in 1882.

Triple Entente *n.* The military alliance of Great Britain, France, and Russia before World War I to counterbalance the Dreibund.

triple jump *n.* An athletics field event in which the competitor, after a run-up, must cover in a continuous movement the greatest distance possible with a hop, a step, and a jump.

triple point *n. Physics.* The point at which the solid, liquid, and gas phases of a given substance are all in equilibrium with each other.

trip·let (tríp-lət, -lit) *n.* **1.** A group or set of three of one kind. **2.** Any of three children born at one birth. **3.** In prosody, a tercet *(see).* **4.** A group of three musical notes having the time value of two notes of the same kind. **5.** *Physics.* A multiplet *(see)* with three components. [*Triple* + doublet.]

tri·ple-tail (tripp'l-tayl) *n.* Any of several chiefly marine fishes of the genus *Labotes;* especially, the North American *L. surinamensis,* having prominent dorsal and anal fins that resemble extra tails.

triple time *n.* A musical time or rhythm having three beats in each bar, with the accent on the first beat. Also called "triple measure". **—tri·ple-time** (tripp'l-tīm, -tīm) *adj.*

tri·ple-tongu·ing (tripp'l-túng-ing || *Northern England also* -tóng-) *n.* The playing of a wind instrument in a fast tempo, moving the tongue as if to pronounce repeatedly t, k, and t. Compare **double-tonguing, single-tonguing. —tri·ple-tongue** *v.*

tri·plex (trí-pleks || tríp-) *adj.* Composed of three parts; threefold; triple. [Latin, threefold, triple.] **—tri·plex** *n.*

Tri·plex (trí-pleks) *n.* In Britain, a trademark for a type of safety glass consisting of two glass sheets sandwiching a transparent sheet of plastic, used especially in car windows.

trip·li·cate (tríppli-kət, -kit, -kayt) *adj.* Threefold; especially, made with three identical copies. **~***n.* **1.** Any of a set of three identical objects or copies. **2.** The state of being in three copies: *The contract was in triplicate.* **~***tr.v.* (-kayt) **triplicated, -cating, -cates.** **1.** To increase threefold; triple. **2.** To make three identical copies of. [Latin *triplicātus,* past participle of *triplicāre,* to triple, from *triplex* (stem *triplic-*), TRIPLEX.] **—trip·li·cate·ly** *adv.* **—trip·li·ca·tion** (-káysh'n) *n.*

trip·lic·i·ty (tri-plíssəti, trī-) *n., pl.* **-ties.** **1.** The condition or quality of being triple. **2.** A group or set of three. **3.** In astrology, any of four groups of the zodiac, each consisting of three signs. In this sense, also called "trigon". [Middle English *triplicite,* a trigon, from Late Latin *triplicitās,* quality of being triple, from TRIPLEX.]

trip·lo·blas·tic (tripplō-blástik) *adj.* Having a body made up from three embryonic germ layers. Said of all animals except protozoans, sponges, and coelenterates. Compare **diploblastic.** [*Triplo-,* threefold, from Greek *triploos* + -BLAST + -IC.]

trip·loid (trípployd) *adj.* Having three times the haploid number of chromosomes in each nucleus. **~***n.* An organism having such sets of chromosomes. [Greek *triploos,* triple + (HAPL)OID.]

tri·pod (trī-pod) *n.* **1.** A three-legged stool, table, or the like. **2.** An adjustable three-legged stand, as for supporting a camera. [Latin *tripūs* (stem *tripod-*), from Greek *tripous,* three-footed : *tri-,* three + *-pous,* -POD.] **—trip·o·dal** (-'l, tríppəd'l) *adj.*

trip·o·li (tríppəli) *n.* A porous, lightweight, siliceous rock of various colours, used as an abrasive. [Found in TRIPOLI, Libya.]

Trip·o·li (tríppəli). Ancient name *Oea.* Capital and chief port of Libya. Founded by the Phoenicians, probably in the 7th century B.C., it was held in turn by the Romans, Vandals, Byzantines, and Arabs. It fell to the Ottoman Turks (1551) and was a stronghold of the Barbary Pirates (16th–19th centuries). The city was taken by the Italians (1910) and British (1943).

tri·pos (trī-poss) *n., pl.* **-poses.** At Cambridge University, any of the courses or examinations for the B.A. degree with honours. [Variant of Latin *tripūs,* TRIPOD, referring to a stool on which formerly an appointed bachelor of arts sat at a graduation ceremony to deliver a humorous address; later, to verses written for this occasion, to a list of students qualified for honours in mathematics written on the back of the verses, and later to honours examinations in mathematics and in other subjects.]

trip·per (tríppər) *n.* **1.** *Chiefly British Informal.* A short-term holidaymaker. **2.** A tripping device on a mechanism.

trip·pet (tríppit) *n.* A cam or projection in a mechanism designed to strike another part at regular intervals. [Middle English *tripet,* piece of wood used in a game, from *trippen,* to TRIP.]

trip·ping (trípping) *adj.* Moving or stepping lightly and briskly; easy; nimble: *a tripping tongue.* **—trip·ping·ly** *adv.*

trip·tane (tríp-tayn) *n.* A liquid hydrocarbon, C_7H_{16}, used as an antiknock additive in aviation fuels. [Short for *trimethylbutane.*]

trip·tych (trip-tik, *also* -tich) *n.* **1.** A tableau of three hinged or folding panels bearing a religious story in painting or carving, used as an altarpiece. **2.** A hinged writing tablet consisting of three leaves, used in ancient times. [Greek *triptukhos,* threefold : *tri-,* three + *ptukhē,* fold (see **diptych**).]

trip·tyque (trip-téek) *n.* A customs permit for the passage of a motor vehicle. [French, TRIPTYCH (referring to its three sections).]

trip·wire (trip-wīr) *n.* A wire that activates an alarm, trap, or the like when brushed in passing.

tri·que·trous (trī-kwée-trəss, -kwe-) *adj.* Triangular and acutely angled, especially in cross section: *a triquetrous stem.* Compare **trigonous.** [Latin *triquetrus,* three-cornered.]

tri·reme (trī-reem, trī-) *n.* An ancient Greek or Roman galley or warship, having three tiers of oars on each side. [Latin *trirēmis,* having three tiers of oars : *tri-,* three + *rēmus,* oar.]

tri·sac·cha·ride (trī-sácka-rīd, trī-) *n. Chemistry.* A carbohydrate that upon hydrolysis yields three monosaccharides.

tri·sect (trī-sékt, trī-) *tr.v.* **-sected, -secting, -sects.** To divide into

three, usually equal, parts. [TRI- + -SECT.] —**tri·sec·tion** (-séksh'n) *n.* —**tri·sec·tor** (-séktər) *n.*
tri·sep·al·ous (trī-sépp'l-əss) *adj.* Having three sepals.
tri·shaw (trī-shaw) *n.* A light, pedalled rickshaw with three wheels. [TRI- + (RICK)SHAW.]
tri·skel·i·on (trī-skélli-ən, tri-, -on) *n., pl.* **-ia** (-ə). Also **tri·skele, tri·scele** (trīss-keel, triss-). A figure consisting of three curved lines or branches, or three stylised human arms or legs, radiating from a common centre. [New Latin, from Greek *triskelēs,* three-legged : *tri-,* three + *skelos,* leg.]
tris·mus (trizməss) *n. Pathology.* **Lockjaw** *(see).* [Greek *trismos, trigmos,* a scream, a grating (of the teeth).] —**tris·mic** *adj.*
tris·oc·ta·he·dron (triss-óktə-heéd-rən, -héd-) *n., pl.* **-drons** or **-dra** (-rə). **1.** In geometry, a solid figure having 24 congruent triangular faces and an octahedron as a base. **2.** In crystallography, a **trapezohedron** *(see).* [Greek *tris,* thrice + OCTAHEDRON.] —**tris·oc·ta·he·dral** *adj.*
tri·so·mic (trī-sṓmik, trī-) *adj. Genetics.* Having one chromosome represented three times in an otherwise diploid set. [TRI- + (CHROMO)SOM(E) + -IC.] —**tri·some** (trī-sōm) *n.*
Tris·tan (tristən). Also **Tris·tram** (triss-trəm). A hero of medieval legend who fell in love with Iseult, the bride of King Mark of Cornwall, after they accidentally drank a love potion.
Tris·tan da Cu·nha (tristən də kōōn-ə, -yə). Group of volcanic islands in the South Atlantic. Only one of the four, Tristan, is inhabited, by fewer than 300 people, descendants of a British garrison placed there in 1816 when Napoleon was exiled to St. Helena, of which the group is a dependency. Edinburgh is the capital.
tri·ste·a·rin (trī-steér-in, -steé-ər-) *n. Chemistry.* **Stearin** *(see).*
trist·ful (tristf'l) *adj.* Also **triste** (trist, treest). *Archaic.* Sorrowful; gloomy. [Middle English *trist,* from Old French *triste,* from Latin *trīstis*†, gloomy.] —**trist·ful·ly** *adv.* —**trist·ful·ness** *n.*
tris·tich (tristik) *n.* A stanza or strophic unit of three lines. [TRI- + (DI)STICH.] —**tri·stich·ic** (tri-stickik) *adj.*
tri·stim·u·lus (trī-stímmew-ləss) *adj.* Of or pertaining to the values of the three primary colours that when combined additively produce a colour to match the colour of an unknown sample.
tri·sul·phide (trī-súl-fīd, trī-) *n.* A sulphide containing three sulphur atoms per molecule.
tri·syl·la·ble (trī-silləb'l, trí-, -silləb'l) *n.* A word consisting of three syllables. —**tri·syl·lab·ic** (-si-lábbik) *adj.* —**tri·syl·lab·i·cal·ly** *adv.*
tri·tan·o·pi·a (trītə-nṓpi-ə, trittə-) *n.* A rare visual defect involving an inability to distinguish the colour blue. [New Latin, "ability to see only one third (of the colours of the spectrum)" : Greek *tritos,* a third + *anopia,* blindness : AN- (not) + -OPIA.] —**tri·tan·op·ic** *adj.*
trite (trīt) *adj.* **triter, tritest. 1.** Overused and commonplace; lacking interest or originality. **2.** *Archaic.* Frayed or worn by use. [Latin *trītus,* past participle of *terere,* to rub (away), wear out.] —**trite·ly** *adv.* —**trite·ness** *n.*
Synonyms: *trite, hackneyed, shopsoiled, stereotyped, commonplace, threadbare, stale, banal.*
tri·the·ism (trī-thee-iz'm) *n.* A belief in three gods; specifically, the belief that the Father, Son, and Holy Ghost are three separate and distinct gods. —**tri·the·ist** *n.* —**tri·the·is·tic** (-istik) *adj.*
trit·i·ate (tritti-ayt ‖ trishi-) *tr.v.* **-ated, -ating, -ates.** To treat with tritium; especially, to replace the hydrogen atoms in (a molecule) by tritium atoms for labelling. [TRITIUM + -ATE.] —**trit·i·a·tion** *n.*
trit·i·ca·le (tritti-kaáli, -káyli) *n.* A fertile, hybrid cereal obtained by crossing wheat and rye. [Latin *triticum,* wheat + *secale,* rye.]
trit·i·um (tritti-əm ‖ *U.S. also* trishi-) *n.* A rare radioactive hydrogen isotope with atomic mass 3 and half-life 12.5 years, prepared artificially for use as a tracer and as a constituent of hydrogen bombs. [New Latin, from Greek *tritos,* third.]
tri·ton¹ (trīt'n) *n.* Any of various chiefly tropical marine gastropod molluscs of the genus *Cymatium* and related genera, having a pointed, spirally twisted, often colourfully marked shell. [After TRITON, whose trumpet is a shell.]
tri·ton² (trī-ton) *n.* The nucleus of a tritium atom consisting of two neutrons and one proton. [TRIT(IUM) + -ON.]
Tri·ton¹ (trīt'n). *Greek Mythology.* **1.** A god of the sea, son of Poseidon and Amphitrite, portrayed as having the head and trunk of a man and the tail of a fish. **2.** Any of a race of lesser sea deities.
Triton² *n.* The larger satellite of the planet Neptune.
tri·tone (trī-tōn) *n. Music.* An interval composed of three whole tones. [Greek *tritonos,* having three tones : TRI- + TONE.]
trit·u·rate (trittewr-ayt, trichər-) *tr.v.* **-rated, -rating, -rates.** To crush, grind, or pound into fine particles or a powder; pulverise.
~*n.* (-ət, -it, -ayt). A triturated substance, especially a powdered drug. Also called "trituration". [Late Latin *trītūrāre,* to pulverise corn, from Latin *trītūra,* a rubbing or chafing, from *trītus,* past participle of *terere,* to rub.] —**trit·u·ra·ble** (-əb'l) *adj.*
trit·u·ra·tion (trittewr-áysh'n, trichər-) *n.* **1.** The act or process of triturating something. **2.** A triturate. **3.** The composing of a dental amalgam by mortar and pestle.
tri·umph (trī-əmf, -umf) *intr.v.* **-umphed, -umphing, -umphs. 1.** To be victorious or successful; win; prevail. **2.** To rejoice over a success or victory; exult. **3.** In ancient Rome, to receive honours upon return from a victory.
~*n.* **1.** The instance or fact of being victorious; success. **2.** A remarkable achievement or feat. **3.** Exultation or merriment derived from victory or success. **4.** A public celebration in ancient Rome to welcome a returning victorious commander and his army. [Middle English, from Old French *triumphe(r),* from Latin *triumphāre,* from *triumphus,* a triumph, variant of Old Latin *triumpus,* probably from Greek *thriambos,* hymn to Bacchus.] —**tri·umph·er** *n.*
tri·um·phal (trī-úmf'l) *adj.* **1.** Pertaining to or having the nature of a triumph. **2.** Celebrating or commemorating a victory: *a triumphal procession; a triumphal arch.* —See Usage note at **triumphant.**
tri·um·phal·ism (trī-úmf'l-iz'm) *n.* Crowing over the triumphs of one's own side, viewpoint, etc. —**tri·um·phal·ist** *n. & adj.*
tri·um·phant (trī-úmfənt) *adj.* **1.** Exulting in success or victory. **2.** Victorious; conquering; successful. —**tri·um·phant·ly** *adv.*
Usage: *Triumphant* and *triumphal* are not usually interchangeable. *Triumphant* now generally means exulting in success or victory: *The football team returned home triumphant. Triumphal* is a more specific term, describing the formal celebration of a triumph: *There was a triumphal procession to mark the navy's return.*
tri·um·vir (trī-úm-vər, tri-, trī-əm-, -vur) *n., pl.* **-virs** or **-viri** (-vi-ree, -və-, -rī). Any of three men sharing public administration or civil authority, as in ancient Rome. [Latin, singular of *triumvirī,* from *trium virōrum,* "(one) of three men", genitive of *trēs virī,* three men.] —**tri·um·vi·ral** *adj.*
tri·um·vi·rate (trī-úmvər-ət, tri-, -it, -ayt) *n.* **1.** A group of three men jointly governing a realm. **2. a.** The office or term of a triumvir. **b.** Government by triumvirs. **3.** Any association or group of three. [Latin *triumvirātus,* from *triumvir,* TRIUMVIR.]
tri·une (trī-yōōn) *adj.* Being three in one. Said especially of the single Godhead of the Trinity.
~*n. Rare.* **1.** A trinity. **2.** *Capital* **T.** The holy Trinity. [TRI- + Latin *ūnus,* one.]
tri·u·ni·ty (trī-yōōnəti) *n., pl.* **-ties.** A **trinity** *(see).*
tri·va·lent (trī-váylənt, trī-) *adj.* Also **ter·va·lent** (ter-, tér-). *Chemistry.* **1.** Having a valency of 3. **2.** Having three valencies. —**tri·va·lence, tri·va·len·cy** *n.*
tri·valve (trī-valv) *adj.* Having three valves. —**tri·valve** *n.*
triv·et (trivvit) *n.* **1.** A three-legged stand made of iron or a similar metal, used for supporting cooking vessels in a fireplace. **2.** A metal stand with short feet, used under a hot dish on a table. [Middle English *trevet,* probably Old English *trefet,* from Latin *tripēs,* "three-footed" : *tri-,* three + *pēs,* foot.]
triv·i·a¹ (trivvi-ə). Plural of **trivium.**
~*pl.n.* Insignificant or inessential matters; trivialities; trifles. [New Latin, plural of TRIVIUM (sense influenced by TRIVIAL).]
triv·i·al (trivvi-əl) *adj.* **1.** Of little importance or significance; trifling. **2.** Ordinary; commonplace. **3.** Concerned with or involving trivia. **4.** *Mathematics.* Having or pertaining to solutions with zero values. **5.** Of or pertaining to the trivium. [Latin *triviālis,* pertaining to the TRIVIUM (hence, commonplace, of little account; sense development perhaps influenced by later scorn for medieval learning).] —**triv·i·al·ly** *adv.*
Synonyms: *trivial, trifling, paltry, petty.*
triv·i·al·ise (trivvi-ə-līz) *tr.v.* **-ised, -ising, -ises.** To make trivial; devalue. —**triv·i·al·i·sa·tion** (-lī-záysh'n ‖ *U.S.* -li-) *n.*
triv·i·al·i·ty (trivvi-álǝti) *n., pl.* **-ties. 1.** The condition or quality of being trivial. **2.** A trivial matter, idea, or occurrence.
trivial name *n.* **1.** In taxonomic nomenclature, the term following the genus name and designating the species, as *troglodytes* in *Pan troglodytes,* the chimpanzee. **2.** A vernacular name as distinguished from a taxonomic designation. **3.** *Chemistry.* A name for a compound that is not systematic and gives no indication of the compound's molecular structure, such as *toluene* for *methylbenzene.*
triv·i·um (trivvi-əm) *n., pl.* **-ia** (-ə). The first division of the seven liberal arts in medieval schools, consisting of grammar, logic, and rhetoric. Compare **quadrivium.** [Medieval Latin, from Latin, place where three roads meet : *tri-,* three + *via,* road, way.]
tri·week·ly (trī-weékli, trī-) *adj.* Happening, done, or appearing: **1.** Three times a week. **2.** Every three weeks.
~*adv.* **1.** Three times a week. **2.** Every three weeks.
~*n., pl.* **triweeklies.** A periodical published triweekly.
-trix *n. suffix, pl.* **-trices** or **-trixes.** Indicates: **1.** Feminine agency, corresponding to masculine or common nouns in *-tor;* for example, **testatrix. 2.** A geometric line, point, or surface; for example, **directrix.** [Latin *-trix* (stem *-tric-*).]
t RNA *n.* **Transfer RNA** *(see).*
Tro·bri·and Islands (trṓbri-and, -ənd). Archipelago lying off Papua New Guinea, by which the islands are administered. The chief island is Kirwana (or Trobriand).
tro·car (trṓ-kaar) *n.* A sharp-pointed surgical instrument within a cannula, used to puncture a body cavity and remove fluid. [French *trocart,* "three-sided instrument" (referring to its triangular shape) : *trois,* three, + *carre,* side.]
tro·cha·ic (trə-káy-ik, trō-) *adj.* Of, pertaining to, or consisting of trochees.
~*n.* A trochaic metrical foot, line of verse, or poem. [French *trochaïque,* from Latin *trochaicus,* from Greek *trokhaikos,* from *trokhaios.* See **trochee.**]
tro·chal (trṓk'l) *adj.* Shaped like a wheel: *the trochal disc of a rotifer.* [Greek *trokhos,* wheel, from *trekhein,* to run.]
tro·chan·ter (trō-kántər) *n.* **1.** Any of several bony processes on the upper part of the femur of many vertebrates. **2.** The second proximal segment of the leg of an insect. [Greek *trokhantēr,* from *trekhein,* to run. See **trochal.**]
troche (trōsh, *rarely* trōk, -i) *n.* A small circular medicinal lozenge; a pastille. [Earlier *trochies* (plural), from Middle English *trociske* (singular), from Late Latin *trochiscus,* from Greek *trokhiskos,* diminutive of *trokhos,* wheel. See **trochal.**]

tro·chee (trṓ-kee, -ki) *n.* A metrical foot consisting of a long syllable followed by a short (in quantitative verse), or a stressed syllable followed by an unstressed (in accentual verse). There are four trochees in the following line: *Peter, Peter, pumpkin eater.* Also called "trochaic". Compare **iamb.** [Latin, from Greek *trokhaios (pous),* running (foot), from *trekhein,* to run.]
troch·le·a (tróckli-ə) *n., pl.* **-leae** (-ee). An anatomical structure that resembles a pulley, such as the part of the distal end of the humerus that articulates with the ulna. [Latin, system of pulleys, from Greek *trokhileia.*]
troch·le·ar (tróckli-ər) *adj.* **1.** Of, resembling, or situated near a trochlea. **2.** Of or pertaining to the trochlear nerve. **3.** *Botany.* Shaped like a pulley.
∼*n.* The trochlear nerve.
trochlear nerve *n.* Either of the fourth pair of cranial nerves, which supplies the superior oblique muscle of the eyeball.
tro·choid (trṓk-oyd, trók-) *adj.* Also **tro·choi·dal** (trō-kóyd'l, tro-). **1.** Capable of or exhibiting rotation about a central axis. **2.** Permitting rotation, as does a pulley or pivot.
∼*n.* In geometry, a plane curve formed by the locus of a point on the radius or on an extension of the radius of a circle, as the circle rolls along a fixed straight line. [Greek *trokhoeidēs,* resembling a wheel, wheel-like, circular : *trokhos,* wheel (see **troche**) + -OID.] **—tro·choi·dal·ly** *adv.*
troch·o·phore (trók-ō-fawr, -ə- || -fōr) *n.* The small aquatic larva of various invertebrates, including certain molluscs and annelids. [Greek *trokhos,* wheel (see **troche**) + -PHORE (from its spheroidal body and ring of cilia).]
trod. Past tense and alternative past participle of **tread.**
trod·den. Past participle of **tread.**
trode. *Archaic.* Past tense of **tread.**
trof·fer (tróffər) *n.* An inverted, usually metal trough suspended from a ceiling as a fixture for fluorescent lighting tubes. [From *troff-,* variant of TROUGH.]
trog (trog) *intr.v.* **trogged, trogging, trogs.** *British Informal.* To trudge; plod wearily. Often used with *along.* [TRUDGE + SLOG.]
trog·lo·dyte (trόg-lə-dīt, -lō-) *n.* **1.** A prehistoric cave dweller. **2.** A person likened to a caveman, as in reclusiveness or brutishness. **3.** An anthropoid ape, such as the gorilla. [Latin *Trōglodyta,* from Greek *Trōglodutēs,* singular of *Trōglodutai,* variant (influenced by *trōglos,* cave, and *-dutai,* those who enter) of *Trōgodutai*†, name of an Ethiopian people.] **—trog·lo·dyt·ic** (-díttik), **trog·lo·dyt·i·cal** *adj.*
tro·gon (trṓ-gon) *n.* Any of various colourful tropical birds of the family Trogonidae, which includes the quetzal. [New Latin, "gnawer", from Greek *trōgōn,* present participle of *trōgein,* gnaw.]
troi·ka (tróykə) *n.* **1. a.** A kind of small Russian carriage drawn by a team of three horses abreast. **b.** A team of three horses abreast. **2.** A triumvirate. [Russian *troyka,* from *troye,* three (collectively).]
troil·ism (tróyl-iz'm) *n.* Sexual intercourse engaged in by three people, usually two women and one man. [Probably from French *trois,* three (as in *ménage à trois*) + *-l-,* as in *dualism.*]
Troi·lus (trṓ-i-ləss, tróy-). *Greek Mythology.* A son of Priam of Troy, killed by Achilles. Cressida's lover in medieval romance.
Tro·jan (trṓjən) *n.* **1.** A native or inhabitant of ancient Troy. **2.** A person of courageous determination or energy.
∼*adj.* Of or pertaining to ancient Troy or its residents. [Middle English, from Latin *Trōjānus,* from *Trōjā,* TROY.]
Trojan horse *n.* **1.** *Greek Mythology.* The hollow wooden horse in which the Greeks hid and gained entrance to Troy, later opening the gates to their army. In this sense, also called "Wooden Horse". **2.** Any subversive group or device insinuated within enemy ranks.
Trojan War *n. Greek Mythology.* The prehistoric ten-year war waged against Troy by the confederated Greeks, ending in the burning of Troy. Homeric legend gives the cause as the abduction of the Spartan queen, Helen, by Paris, a Trojan prince.
troll[1] (trōl; *also, especially for senses 5, 6,* trol) *v.* **trolled, trolling, trolls.** *—tr.* **1.** To fish for by trailing a baited line from behind a slowly moving boat. **2.** To trail (a baited line) in fishing. **3.** To sing in succession the parts of (a round, for example). **4.** To sing heartily: *troll a carol.* **5.** To roll or revolve. *—intr.* **1.** To fish by trailing a line, as from a moving boat. **2.** To sing heartily or gaily. **3.** To be sung or uttered in a rolling, hearty manner: *The tune trolled on.* **4.** To roll or spin round. **5.** *British Informal.* To wander; stroll. Often used with *along.* **6.** *Chiefly British Slang.* To cruise looking for sexual partners. Used of a man.
∼*n.* **1.** The act of trolling for fish. **2.** A lure used for trolling, such as a spoon or spinner. [Middle English *trollen*†, to ramble, roll.]
troll[2] (trōl, trol) *n.* **1.** A supernatural creature of Scandinavian folklore variously portrayed as a friendly or mischievous dwarf, or sometimes a dangerous giant, that lives in caves, in the hills, or under bridges. **2.** A tiny, hairy plastic monster, often put as decoration on the end of a pencil. [Old Norse *troll*†, monster, demon.]
trol·ley (trólli) *n., pl.* **-leys. 1.** *Chiefly British.* Any of various low two- or four-wheeled carts, especially: **a.** A small, sometimes tiered, table on casters used for carrying food, dishes, and other household objects from room to room. **b.** A shopping cart used in supermarkets. **c.** A luggage cart used in stations, airports, or the like. **2. a.** *British.* A trolley bus. **b.** *U.S.* A trolley car. **3.** A wheeled carriage, cage, or basket that is suspended from and travels on an overhead track. **4.** A device that collects electric current from an underground conductor, an overhead wire, or a third rail, and transmits it to the motor of an electric vehicle. **5.** *Chiefly British.* A small truck or car operating on a track and used in a mine, quarry, or factory for conveying materials.
∼*v.* **trolleyed, -leying, -leys.** *—tr.* To convey by trolley. *—intr.* To travel by trolley. [Originally dialect, from TROLL (to move about).]
trolley bus *n.* An electric bus that does not run on tracks and is powered by electricity from an overhead wire. Also *British* "trolley".
trolley car *n. U.S.* A **tram.** Also *U.S.* "trolley", "streetcar".
trol·lop (tróllәp) *n.* **1.** A slovenly, untidy woman. **2.** A loose woman; a strumpet. [17th century : perhaps akin to TRULL.]
Trol·lope (tróllәp), **Anthony** (1815–82). British novelist. His ecclesiastical novels set in the imaginary county of Barsetshire include *The Warden* (1885), *Barchester Towers* (1857), and *The Last Chronicle of Barset* (1867). Among his novels dealing with political life are *Phineas Finn* (1869) and *The Eustace Diamonds* (1873).
trom·bic·u·li·a·sis (trom-bíckew-lī́-ә-siss) *n.* Also **trom·bic·u·lo·sis** (-lṓ-siss), **trom·bi·di·a·sis** (trómbi-dī́-ә-siss). *Pathology.* Infestation with mites of the genus *Trombicula,* which if untreated results in severe dermatitis. [New Latin : *Trombicula,* genus of mites, diminutive of *Trombidium*† + -IASIS.]
trom·bone (trom-bṓn || trәm-, tróm-bōn) *n.* **1.** A brass musical instrument consisting of a long cylindrical tube bent upon itself twice, ending in a bell-shaped mouth, and varied in length to produce different notes by means of a U-shaped slide. **2.** The member of an orchestra who plays the trombone. [French from Italian, augmentative of *tromba,* trumpet, from Old High German *trumpa,* TRUMP.] **—trom·bon·ist** *n.*
trom·mel (trómm'l) *n.* A revolving cylindrical sieve used for sizing rock and ore. [German *Trommel,* barrel, drum, from Middle High German *trummel,* from *trumme,* drum, akin to Middle Dutch *tromme,* DRUM.]
tromp (tromp) *v.* **tromped, tromping, tromps.** *Informal. —intr.* To walk heavily and noisily; tramp. *—tr.* **1.** To trample underfoot. **2.** *U.S. Informal.* To defeat soundly; trounce. **—tromp on.** *U.S. Informal.* To abuse verbally. [Blend of TRAMP and STOMP.]
trompe (tromp) *n.* An apparatus in which water falling through a perforated pipe entrains air into and down the pipe to produce an air blast for a furnace or forge. [French, "trumpet", from Old French. See **trump** (trumpet).]
trompe l'oeil (tróɴp lṓ-i) *n.* **1.** A technique of depicting objects so realistically that the viewer is tricked into believing they really exist in three dimensions. **2.** A trick painting in this style, such as a window frame on a sheer brick wall. [French, "deceive the eye".]
tron (tron) *n. Scottish.* Also **trone** (trōn). A bulk-weighing machine for merchandise. [Middle English, from Old French *trone,* from Latin *trutina,* from Greek *trutanē,* balance, pair of scales.]
-tron *n. comb. form.* Indicates: **1.** A vacuum tube; for example, **dynatron. 2.** A device for manipulating subatomic particles; for example, **cyclotron.** [Greek, suffix denoting instrument.]
tro·na (trṓnә) *n.* A natural vitreous grey or white mineral, $Na_2CO_3 \cdot NaHCO_3 \cdot 2H_2O$, used as a source of sodium compounds. [Swedish, probably from Arabic *trōn,* short for *naṭrūn,* natron.]
Trond·heim (trónd-hīm; *Norwegian* trón-yem). Formerly **Ni·da·ros** (née̍də-rŏŏss). Seaport of central Norway. Founded (997) on the south side of Trondheim Fjord, it is an important fishing centre.
troop (trōōp) *n. Abbr.* **trp. 1.** A group or company of people, animals, or things. **2.** *Military.* **a.** A division of a cavalry unit, commanded by a captain. **b.** A group of soldiers. **c.** *Informal.* A soldier: *40 troops died.* **3.** *Plural.* Military units; soldiers. **4.** A unit of two or more patrols of Scouts or Girl Guides. **5.** *Informal.* A great many; a lot. **—**See Synonyms at **flock.**
∼*v.* **trooped, trooping, troops.** *—intr.* **1.** To move or go as a throng. **2.** To proceed; move along: *children trooping home.* **3.** *Archaic.* To consort; associate. Used with *with. —tr. Chiefly British Military.* To parade (a flag) ceremonially. Used chiefly in the phrases *troop the colour, trooping the colour.* [French *troupe,* back-formation from *troupeau,* herd, from Medieval Latin *troppus*†.]
troop carrier *n.* A vehicle, aircraft, or ship built to carry troops.
troop·er (trṓōpәr) *n.* **1. a.** A cavalryman. **b.** A cavalry horse. **2.** *Australian & U.S.* A policeman mounted on a horse or motor cycle. **3.** *Chiefly British Informal.* A troopship. **—swear like a trooper.** To swear frequently and obscenely.
troop·ship (trōōp-ship) *n.* A ship, usually one that has been modified or converted, designed for carrying troops.
troost·ite (trōōst-īt) *n.* A reddish mineral, a variety of **willemite** *(see),* in which the zinc is partly replaced by manganese. [After Gerald *Troost* (1776–1850), U.S. geologist.]
trop. tropic; tropical.
tro·pae·o·lum (tro-pée-ә-lәm, trō-) *n., pl.* **-lums** or **-la** (-lә). Any trailing or climbing succulent plant of the South American genus *Tropaeolum;* especially, the garden nasturtium, *T. majus,* which has orange, yellow, or red spurred flowers and smooth leaves. [New Latin, from Latin *tropaeum,* TROPHY (referring to the leaves and flowers, which resemble shields and helmets).]
trope (trōp) *n.* **1.** The figurative use of a word or expression; a figure of speech. **2.** A word or phrase interpolated as an embellishment in the sung parts of certain medieval liturgies. [Latin *tropus,* from Greek *tropos,* a turn, way, manner, from *trepein,* to turn.]
-trope *n. comb. form.* Indicates: **1.** Orientation or development towards; for example, **heliotrope. 2.** A version; for example, **allotrope.** [Greek *tropos,* turn, turning, from *trepein,* to turn.]
troph·al·lax·is (tróffә-láksiss || trōfә-) *n.* The mutual exchange of food between adults and larvae that occurs among certain social insects such as ants and wasps. [New Latin, from TROPHO- +

Greek *allaxis,* exchange, from *allassein,* to change.]

troph·ic (trófik || *chiefly U.S.* trōfik) *adj.* Of or pertaining to nutrition or to the nutritive processes. [Greek *trophikos,* nursing, from *trophē,* food, from *trephein,* to nourish.] **—troph·i·cal·ly** *adv.*

trophic level *n. Ecology.* A group of organisms that occupy the same position on a food chain in that they obtain their food, ultimately from plants, by the same number of steps.

tropho– *comb. form.* Indicates nutrition; for example, **trophoblast.** [Greek *trophē,* food, from *trephein,* to nourish.]

troph·o·blast (tróf-ə-blast, -ō-, -blaast || trōf-) *n.* The outermost layer of cells of the morula that attaches the fertilised ovum to the wall of the mammalian uterus and acts as a nutritive pathway. Also called "trophoderm". [TROPHO- + -BLAST.] **—troph·o·blas·tic** (-blástik) *adj.*

troph·o·zo·ite (tróf-ə-zō-īt, -ō- || trōf-) *n.* A protozoan of the class Sporozoa in the active feeding stage. [TROPHO- + ZO(O)- + -ITE.]

tro·phy (trōfi) *n., pl.* **-phies. 1.** A prize or memento, such as a cup or plaque, received as a symbol of victory, especially in sports. **2.** An accumulation of captured arms or other spoils kept as a memorial of victory. **3.** A specimen or part, such as a lion's head, preserved as a token of a successful hunt. **4.** In ancient Greece and Rome, the captured arms and spoils of a defeated enemy set up as a memorial, often on the field of battle. **5.** *Architecture.* A marble carving or bronze cast depicting a group of weapons, armour, or the like placed upon a four-sided or circular base as an ornament. **6.** Any memento, as of one's personal achievements. [French *trophee,* from Latin *trophaeum,* from Greek *tropaion,* "monument of the enemy's defeat", from *tropaios,* of turning, of defeat, from *tropē,* a turn, repulse of the enemy. See **trope.**] **—tro·phied** *adj.*

–trophy *n. comb. form.* Indicates a specified type of nutrition or growth; for example, **hypertrophy.** [New Latin *-trophia,* from Greek, from *trophē,* food. See **tropho-.**]

trophy wife *n. Informal.* A wife regarded as her husband's trophy or status symbol; specifically, a bimbo married as a trophy wife.

trop·ic (tróppik) *n. Abbr.* **trop. 1.** *Astronomy.* Either of two circles on the celestial sphere parallel to and at an angular distance of 23° 27′ from the equator and forming the limits of the apparent northern and southern passages of the Sun. **2.** *Geography.* Either of the two corresponding parallels of latitude on the earth that constitute the boundaries of the Torrid Zone. See **tropic of Cancer, tropic of Capricorn. 3.** *Plural.* The region of the earth's surface lying between these latitudes; the Torrid Zone. Usually preceded by *the.*

~adj. Of or pertaining to the tropics; tropical. [Middle English *tropik,* solstice point at which the Sun "turns" back and moves towards the Earth, from Late Latin *tropicus,* from Greek *tropikos,* of turning, from *tropē,* a turn. See **trope.**]

–tropic *adj. comb. form.* Indicates turning in response to a specified stimulus; for example, **phototropic.** [Greek *tropos,* a turn, TROPE.]

trop·i·cal[1] (tróppik'l) *adj. Abbr.* **trop. 1.** Of, indigenous to, or characteristic of the tropics. **2.** Hot and humid; sultry; torrid. **—trop·i·cal·ly** *adv.*

trop·i·cal[2] (tróppik'l; *also* trōpik'l) *adj.* Of or pertaining to a rhetorical trope.

tropical cyclone *n.* A very low pressure area 80 to 160 kilometres (50 to 100 miles) in radius that originates in tropical regions and is frequently marked by winds of hurricane strength circulating around the calm eye in the centre of the region.

trop·i·cal·ise (tróppik'l-īz) *tr.v.* **-ised, -ising, -ises. 1.** To make tropical. **2.** To make suitable for a tropical climate, as by adapting to tropical temperatures.

tropical storm *n.* A tropical cyclone having winds ranging from 48 kilometres (30 miles) to 160 kilometres (75 miles) per hour.

tropical year *n.* The time interval between two successive passages of the Sun through the vernal equinox; the calendar year, or 365.2422 mean solar days. Also called "solar year". See **year.**

trop·ic·bird (tróppik-burd) *n.* Any of several predominantly white sea birds of the genus *Phaëthon,* of warm regions, having a pair of long, slender, projecting tail feathers.

tropic of Cancer *n.* The parallel of latitude 23° 30′ north of the equator, the northern boundary of the Torrid Zone, and the most northerly latitude at which the Sun reaches an altitude of 90°.

tropic of Capricorn *n.* The parallel of latitude 23° 30′ south of the equator, the southern boundary of the Torrid Zone, and the most southerly latitude at which the Sun reaches an altitude of 90°.

tro·pine (trō-peen, -pin) *n.* Also *U.S.* **tro·pin** (-pin). A white, crystalline, poisonous alkaloid, $C_8H_{15}NO$, having an odour like that of tobacco and used to treat spasms. [Short for ATROPINE.]

tro·pism (trōp-iz'm) *n. Biology.* The directional growth movement of a plant part in response to an external stimulus. Also called "tropic movement". [Greek *tropos,* turn (see **-trope**) + -ISM.] **—tro·pis·mat·ic** (-iz-máttik), **tro·pis·tic** (-ístik) *adj.*

–tropism *n. comb. form.* Indicates the growth of a plant part in response to a specified stimulus; for example, **phototropism.** [Greek *tropos,* turn. See **tropo-.**]

tropo– *comb. form.* Indicates turning or change, especially change of temperature or condition; for example, **troposphere.** [Greek *tropos,* a turn, change.]

tro·pol·o·gy (tro-pólləji, trō-) *n., pl.* **-gies. 1.** The use of tropes in speech or writing. **2.** A mode of Biblical scholarship insisting on the morally edifying interpretation of tropes in Scripture. [Late Latin *tropologia,* from Late Greek : Greek *tropos,* TROPE + -LOGY.] **—tro·po·log·ic** (tróppə-lójik, trōpə-), **tro·po·log·i·cal** *adj.* **—tro·po·log·i·cal·ly** *adv.*

tro·po·pause (tróppə-pawz, trōpə-) *n.* The boundary between the upper troposphere and the lower stratosphere that varies in altitude from 8 kilometres (5 miles) at the poles to 16 kilometres (10 miles) at the equator.

tro·po·phyte (tróppə-fīt, trōpə-) *n.* A plant adapted to changeable climatic conditions. **—tro·po·phyt·ic** (-fíttik) *adj.*

tro·po·sphere (tróppə-sfeer, trōpə-) *n.* The lowest region of the atmosphere between the earth's surface and the tropopause, characterised by decreasing temperature with increasing altitude. **—tro·po·sphe·ric** *adj.*

–tropous *adj. comb. form.* Indicates a turning away; for example, **amphitropous, anatropous.** [Greek *-tropos,* of turning, from *trepein,* to turn.]

trop·po (tróppō) *adv. Music.* Too much. Usually used with the negative in the cautionary phrase *ma non troppo,* as a direction: *allegro ma non troppo.* [Italian.]

–tropy *n. comb. form.* Indicates the condition of turning; for example, **allotropy, thixotropy.** [Greek *-tropia,* from *-tropos,* -TROPOUS.]

trot (trot) *n.* **1.** The gait of a horse or other four-footed animal, between a walk and a canter in speed, in which diagonal pairs of legs move forwards together. **2.** A ride on a horse at this pace. **3.** A human gait, faster than a walk; a brisk step. **4.** A race for trotters. **5.** An old woman; a crone. **6.** *Chiefly British Rare.* A toddler. **7.** *Australian Slang.* A run of luck. **8.** *U.S. Informal.* A translation used by a student; a crib. **—on the trot. 1.** In succession. **2.** Busy, bustling about. **—the trots.** *Slang.* Diarrhoea.

~v. **trotted, trotting, trots.** *—intr.* **1.** To go or move at a trot. **2. a.** To proceed rapidly; hurry. **b.** To go; move. Often used with *along.* **3.** To fish in a fast-moving current using a weighted line. *—tr.* To cause to move at a trot. **—trot out.** *Informal.* To bring out and show for or as if for inspection or admiration. [Middle English, from Old French, from *troter,* to trot, from Vulgar Latin *trottāre* (unattested), from Frankish *trottōn* (unattested).]

Trot (trot) *n. British Slang.* **1.** A Trotskyist. **2.** Loosely, any Communist. In both senses, used derogatorily.

troth (trōth; *rarely* troth || trawth) *n. Archaic.* **1.** Good faith; fidelity. **2.** One's pledged fidelity; especially, a betrothal: *plight one's troth.*

~tr.v. **trothed, trothing, troths.** *Archaic.* To pledge or betroth. [Middle English *trouth(e),* Old English *trēowth,* TRUTH.]

troth·plight (trōth-plīt, tróth- || tráwth-) *n. Archaic.* A betrothal.

~tr.v. **trothplighted, -plighting, -plights.** *Archaic.* To betroth. [Middle English *trouth plight* : TROTH + PLIGHT (pledge).]

Trot·sky (trótski), **Leon,** born Lev Davidovich Bronstein (1879–1940). Russian revolutionary. He was one of the leaders of the Bolshevik Revolution (1917). His policy for permanent revolution led to dismissal from the Politburo by Stalin (1926) and eventual exile from Russia (1929). He moved to Mexico (1937), where he was assassinated three years later. In 1989 the Soviet authorities revealed that he had been killed by the secret police.

Trot·sky·ism (trótski-iz'm) *n.* The theories of Communism advocated by Leon Trotsky and his followers, who argued for the permanent worldwide revolution of the proletariat and bitterly opposed the leadership of Stalin. **—Trot·sky·ist** *adj. & n.*

Trot·sky·ite (trótski-īt) *n.* A Trot. **—Trot·sky·ite** *adj.*

trot·ter (tróttər) *n.* **1.** A horse that trots; especially, one trained for harness racing. **2.** *Informal.* A foot; especially, the foot of a pig prepared as food.

trou·ba·dour (trōōbə-door, -dawr || -dōr) *n.* **1.** Any of a class of lyric poets of the 12th and 13th centuries attached to the courts of Provence and northern Italy, who composed songs in complex metrical forms. Compare **trouvère. 2.** A strolling minstrel. [French, Old French, from Old Provençal *trobador,* from *trobar,* to invent, compose poetry, variant of Old French *trover.* See **trouvère.**]

troub·le (trúbb'l) *n.* **1.** A state of distress, affliction, danger, or need. **2.** Something that contributes to such a state; a difficulty or problem: *One trouble after another delayed the job.* **3.** Exertion; effort; pains: *went to a lot of trouble.* **4.** A condition of pain, disease, or malfunction: *heart trouble.* **5.** *Plural.* Political unrest or war. Usually used euphemistically: *the troubles in Cyprus.* **—in trouble.** *Informal.* **1.** At a disadvantage. **2.** Due to be admonished or punished: *in big trouble with the boss.* **3.** *Chiefly British.* Pregnant. Said euphemistically of an unmarried woman.

~v. **troubled, -ling, -les.** *—tr.* **1.** To agitate; stir up: *troubled waters.* **2.** To afflict with pain or discomfort. **3.** To cause distress or confusion in; vex; perturb. **4.** To inconvenience; bother: *May I trouble you to close the window?; Please don't trouble yourself.* **5.** *West Indian.* To interfere with. *—intr.* To take pains: *to trouble over every detail.* [Middle English, from Old French, from *troubler,* to trouble, from Vulgar Latin *turbulāre,* from *turbulus,* confused, from Latin *turbidus,* TURBID.] **—troub·ler** *n.* **—troub·ling·ly** *adv.*

troub·le·mak·er (trúbb'l-maykər) *n.* A person who habitually stirs up trouble or strife. **—troub·le·mak·ing** *adj. & n.*

troub·le-shoot·er (trúbb'l-shōōtər) *n. Chiefly U.S.* A person who locates and eliminates sources of trouble, as in mechanical operations or diplomatic affairs. **—troub·le·shoot·ing** *adj. & n.*

troub·le·some (trúbb'l-s'm) *adj.* **1.** Causing trouble, especially repeatedly; worrisome. **2.** Difficult; trying. —See Synonyms at **hard. —troub·le·some·ly** *adv.* **—troub·le·some·ness** *n.*

trouble spot *n.* A place of recurring trouble or unrest, especially political unrest.

troub·lous (trúbbləss) *adj. Archaic & Poetic.* Attended with trouble; uneasy; troubled. **—troub·lous·ly** *adv.* **—troub·lous·ness** *n.*

trou-de-loup (trōō-də-lōō) *n., pl.* **trous-de-loup** (*pronounced as sin-*

gular). *Military.* Any of a series of conical pits having pointed stakes set upright in their centres, formerly used to provide an obstacle to enemy cavalry. [French, "wolf's pit".]

trough (trof || trawf; *some bakers say* trow) *n.* **1.** A long, narrow, generally shallow receptacle, especially one for holding water or feed for animals. **2.** A gutter under the eaves of a roof. **3.** A long, narrow depression, as between waves or ridges. **4.** A low point in a business cycle or on a statistical graph. **5.** *Meteorology.* An elongated region of low atmospheric pressure, often associated with a front. **6.** *Physics.* A minimum point in a wave or alternating signal. [Middle English *trough,* Old English *trog.*]

trounce (trownss) *tr.v.* **trounced, trouncing, trounces. 1.** To thrash; beat. **2.** To defeat decisively. [16th century (meaning "harass, afflict") : origin obscure.]

troupe (trōōp) *n.* A company or group, especially of touring actors, singers, or dancers.
~*intr.v.* **trouped, trouping, troupes.** To tour with a theatrical company. [French, TROOP.]

troup·er (trōōpər) *n.* **1.** A member of a theatrical company. **2.** A veteran actor or performer. **3.** *Informal.* A plucky and staunch colleague or worker.

troup·i·al (trōōpi-əl) *n.* Any of several tropical American birds of the genus *Icterus,* related to the orioles and New World blackbirds; especially, *I. icterus,* having orange and black plumage. [French *troupiale,* from *troupe,* flock, TROOP (from its living in flocks).]

trou·ser (trówzər) *adj.* Of, for, or being a part of, trousers: *a trouser pocket.* [Back-formation from TROUSERS.]

trou·sers (trówzərz) *pl.n.* An outer garment for covering the body from the waist to the ankles, divided into two tubelike sections to fit each leg separately. **—wear the trousers.** *Chiefly British.* To be the dominant party: *Who wears the trousers in this house?* [Variant (influenced by DRAWERS) of earlier *trouse,* from Gaelic *triubhas* (singular), TREWS.]

trou·ser-suit (trówzər-sōōt, -sewt) *n. Chiefly British.* A woman's two-piece outfit consisting of trousers and a matching jacket or top.

trous·seau (trōō-sō || trōō-sṓ) *n., pl.* **-seaux** (-z) or **-seaus.** The special wardrobe assembled by a bride before her wedding, especially in former times. [French, from Old French, diminutive of *trusse,* a bundle. See **truss.**]

trout (trowt) *n., pl.* **trouts** (for all senses) or **trout** (for senses 1, 2). **1.** Any of various freshwater or anadromous food and game fishes of the genera *Salmo* and *Salvelinus,* usually having a speckled body. **2.** Broadly, any of various similar fishes. **3.** *British Slang.* A silly old person. [Old English *trūht,* from Late Latin *tructa*†.]

trou·vère (trōō-váir) *n.* Also **trou·veur** (-vúr, -vṓr). Any of a school of poets flourishing in northern France from the 11th to the 13th centuries, who chiefly wrote narrative works, such as the chansons de geste. Compare **troubadour.** [French, from Old French *trovere,* from *trover,* to invent, find, compose poetry, from Vulgar Latin *tropāre* (unattested), to use tropes, from Latin *tropus,* TROPE.]

tro·ver (trṓvər) *n. Law.* A common-law action to recover damages for personal property illegally withheld or wrongfully converted to use by another. [Anglo-French, from Old French. See **trouvère.**]

trow (trō) *intr.v.* **trowed, trowing, trows.** *Archaic.* To think; suppose; trust. [Middle English *trowen, trewen,* Old English *trēowian.*]

trow·el (trów-əl) *n.* **1.** A flat-bladed hand tool for levelling, spreading, or shaping substances such as cement or mortar. **2.** A small implement with a pointed, scoop-shaped blade used in gardening for digging or lifting plants, and similar tasks.
~*tr.v.* **trowelled** or *U.S.* **troweled, -elling** or *U.S.* **-eling, -els.** To spread, smooth, dig, or scoop with or as if with a trowel. [Middle English *trowell,* from Old French *truelle,* from Late Latin *truella,* variant of Latin *trulla,* diminutive of *trua*†, stirring spoon, ladle.]

trox·i·done (tróksi-dōn) *n.* **Trimethadione** *(see).*

troy (troy) *adj. Abbr.* **t** Of or expressed in troy weight. [Middle English *troye,* from Anglo-French, probably first used at a fair in *Troyes,* France.]

Troy (troy). Ancient city in northwestern Asia Minor near the Dardanelles, also called Ilion (Latin Ilium). Its remains were first excavated (1870–90) by Heinrich Schliemann. The site revealed ten major periods of occupation since the Early Bronze Age. The Troy of Homer's *Iliad* and *Odyssey* was probably a city destroyed by fire in the middle of the 13th century B.C. after a long siege.

Troyes (*French* trwaa). Capital of the Aube département, and formerly of the Champagne, northeastern France, on the river Seine.

troy weight *n. Abbr.* **t** A system of units used in weighing precious metals and gems, in which the grain is the same as in the avoirdupois system and the pound contains 12 ounces, 240 pennyweights, or 5,760 grains. [See **troy.**]

trp. troop.

trs. transpose.

Trst. See **Trieste.**

tru·an·cy (trōō-ən-si || tréw-) *n., pl.* **-cies.** Also **tru·ant·ry** (-tri). **1.** An act or instance of playing truant. **2.** The condition of being truant.

tru·ant (trōō-ənt || tréw-) *n.* **1.** One who is absent without permission, especially from school. **2.** A person who shirks work or duty.
~*adj.* **1.** Absent without permission, especially from school. **2.** Idle, lazy, or neglectful. **—play truant.** To absent oneself from school, especially habitually, without authorisation.
~*intr.v.* **truanted, -anting, -ants.** To play truant. [Middle English, beggar, idle rogue, from Old French, from Gaulish *trugant-.*]

truce (trōōss || trewss) *n.* A temporary cessation or suspension of hostilities by agreement of the contending forces; an armistice. [Middle English *trewes,* plural of *trewe,* truce, peace, Old English *trēow,* faith, pledge.]

Trucial States. See **United Arab Emirates.**

truck[1] (truk) *n.* **1. a.** *Chiefly British.* A sturdy motor vehicle with an open back designed for transporting loads. **b.** *Chiefly U.S.* A **lorry** *(see).* **2.** A two-wheeled barrow for moving heavy objects by hand. **3.** A wheeled platform, sometimes equipped with a motor, for conveying loads in a warehouse or freight yard. **4.** *British.* A railway freight wagon without a top. **5.** One of the swivelling frames of wheels under each end of a railway carriage, tram, or the like. **6.** The swivelling frame of wheels under a skateboard. **7.** *Nautical.* A disc-shaped block at the head of a mast with holes used for hoisting or lowering flags or sails.
~*v.* **trucked, trucking, trucks.** —*tr.* To transport by truck. —*intr.* **1.** To carry goods by truck. **2.** *Chiefly U.S.* To drive a truck. **3.** *Chiefly U.S. Slang.* To make one's way; saunter: *trucking on down the avenue.* [Perhaps short for TRUCKLE ("pulley").]

truck[2] *v.* **trucked, trucking, trucks.** —*tr.* **1.** To exchange; barter. **2.** *Rare.* To peddle. —*intr.* To have dealings or commerce; traffic.
~*n.* **1.** Trade goods; articles of commerce. **2.** Barter; exchange. **3.** The payment of wages in goods or kind rather than money. **4.** *U.S.* Garden produce grown for the market. **5.** *Informal.* Dealings; business: *I'll have no truck with them.* **6.** *Informal.* Worthless articles; rubbish. [Middle English *trukken,* from an Anglo-French, akin to Medieval Latin *trocāre,* to exchange, barter.]

truck·age (trúckij) *n. U.S.* **1.** The transportation of goods by truck. **2.** A charge for this.

truck·er (trúckər) *n. U.S.* **1.** A truck driver. **2.** A person or company engaged in trucking goods.

truck farm *n. U.S.* A **market garden** *(see).* Also called "truck garden". **—truck farmer** *n.* **—truck farming** *n.*

truck·le (trúck'l) *n.* A small wheel or roller; a caster.
~*intr.v.* **truckled, -ling, -les.** To be servile or submissive; yield weakly. Used with *to.* [Middle English *trocle,* pulley, from Anglo-French, from Latin *trochlea,* system of pulleys. See **trochlea.**]

truckle bed *n.* A low bed on casters that can be rolled under another bed when not in use. Also called "trundle bed".

truck·load (trúk-lōd) *n.* The quantity or weight that a truck carries.

truck·man (trúk-mən) *n., pl.* **-men** (-mən). *U.S.* **1.** A truck driver. **2.** A person engaged in the trucking business; a trucker.

truck system *n.* The system of paying wages in goods instead of money, especially as practised during the Industrial Revolution.

truc·u·lence (trúckew-lənss) *n.* Also **truc·u·len·cy** (-i). **1.** Pugnacity; belligerence. **2.** Savagery.

truc·u·lent (trúckew-lənt) *adj.* **1.** Disposed to fight; defiant; recalcitrant. **2.** Savage and cruel; fierce. **3.** Vitriolic; scathing. [Latin *truculentus,* from *trux* (stem *truc-*), fierce.] **—truc·u·lent·ly** *adv.*

Tru·deau (trōō-dō || -dṓ; *French* trü-), **Pierre (Elliott)** (1919–). Canadian statesman. As Liberal P.M. (1968–79) he opposed French separatism and introduced (1970) a brief spell of martial law to counteract agitation in Quebec. P.M. again 1980–84.

trudge (truj) *intr.v.* **trudged, trudging, trudges.** To walk in a laborious or weary way; plod.
~*n.* A long, tedious walk. [16th century : origin obscure.]

trudg·en, trudg·eon (trújən) *n.* A swimming stroke in which a double overarm movement is combined with a scissors kick. Also called "trudgen stroke". [Introduced from Argentina by John *Trudgen,* 19th-century British swimmer.]

true (trōō || trew) *adj.* **truer, truest. 1.** Consistent with fact or reality; not false or erroneous. **2. a.** Exactly conforming to a rule, standard, or pattern: *true to form.* **b.** Proper: *a true soufflé.* **3.** Reliable; accurate: *a true prophecy.* **4.** Real; genuine: *true suede.* **5.** Faithful, as to a friend, vow, or cause; steadfast; loyal: *a true socialist.* **6.** *Archaic.* Honourable; upright. **7.** Sincerely felt or expressed; unfeigned: *true sorrow.* **8.** Fundamental; essential: *her true motives.* **9.** Rightful; legitimate: *the true heir.* **10.** Accurately shaped or fitted. **11.** Accurately placed, delivered, or thrown. **12.** Determined with reference to the earth's axis, not the magnetic poles: *true north.* **13.** Conforming to the requirements of the definiton; properly or accurately so called: *The horseshoe crab is not a true crab.* **14.** Flat and horizontal: *a true level.* **15.** *Physics.* Not apparent or relative. Said of a physical property. —See Synonyms at **real, faithful. —come true.** To become fact; conform to expectation or prediction. **—too true.** Correct; right. Often used as a rueful interjection.
~*adv.* **1.** Rightly; truthfully. **2.** Unswervingly; exactly: *aimed true.* **3.** So as to conform to the ancestral type or stock: *breed true.*
~*tr.v.* **trued, truing** or **trueing, trues.** To adjust or fit so as to conform with a standard. Often used with *up.*
~*n.* **1.** Truth. **2.** Proper alignment or adjustment: *in or out of true.* [Middle English *trewe,* Old English *trēowe,* loyal, trustworthy.] **—true·ness** *n.*

true bearing *n.* The angular distance clockwise from a meridian of longitude.

true bill *n.* **1.** *Law.* In the United States and formerly in Britain, a bill of indictment endorsed by a grand jury. **2.** A true assertion.

true-blue, true blue (trōō-blōō || tréw-, -blew) *n.* **1.** *Chiefly British.* A staunch conservative. **2.** A person of unswerving loyalty. [Originally a 17th-century Scottish Presbyterian or Covenanter, from the colour blue adopted in opposition to the Royalists' red.] **—true-blue** *adj.*

true·born (trōō-bawrn || tréw-) *adj.* Being authentically or genuinely as specified, by or as if by birth.

true-life (trōō-līf ‖ trēw-) *adj.* Based on fact; having happened in reality. Said of reports, stories, and works of literature.

true-love (trōō-luv ‖ trēw-) *n.* 1. One's beloved; a sweetheart. 2. A plant, **herb Paris** (*see*).

true lovers' knot *n.* A love knot (*see*).

true-pen-ny (trōō-penni ‖ trēw-) *n., pl.* **-nies.** *Archaic.* An honest fellow; a trusty person. [By association with a genuine coin.]

true rhyme *n.* Perfect rhyme (*see*).

true rib *n.* Any of the ribs, in humans any of the upper seven, that are attached to the sternum by a costal cartilage.

Truf-faut (trōō-fō ‖ trōō-fō; *French* trü-), **François** (1932–84). French film director. His films include *Les Quatre cents Coups* (a prize-winner at Cannes Film Festival, 1959), *Jules et Jim* (1961), *Day for Night* (1973, Oscar), and *Le Dernier Métro* (1980).

truf-fle (trŭff'l) *n.* 1. Any of various fleshy subterranean fungi, chiefly of the genus *Tuber,* often valued as food. 2. A small, round, rich sweet made from chocolate, egg, and butter, and usually flavoured with a liqueur. [Obsolete French, variant of Old French *truffe,* from Old Provençal *trufa,* from Vulgar Latin *tūfera* (unattested), from Latin *tūber,* tuber, truffle.]

trug (trŭg) *n. British.* A shallow, usually oval, basket made from strips of wood and used for carrying flowers, vegetables, or fruit. Also called "Sussex trug". [16th century : dialect variant of TROUGH.]

tru-ism (trōō-iz'm ‖ trēw-) *n.* A statement of an obvious or self-evident truth. See Synonyms at **cliché.** —**tru-is-tic** (trōō-ĭstik) *adj.*

Tru-jil-lo Mo-li-na (trōō-khēe-yō mo-léenə ‖ mō-), **Rafael Leonidas** (1891–1961). Dominican dictator, president (1930–38, 1942–52) of the Dominican Republic. His policies brought some social and economic progress, but his tyranny led to his assassination.

trull (trŭl) *n. Archaic.* A strumpet; a harlot. [Perhaps from German *Trulle,* from Middle High German *trolle,* clumsy person, akin to Old Norse *troll,* creature, TROLL.]

tru-ly (trōō-li ‖ trēw-) *adv.* 1. Sincerely; genuinely. 2. Truthfully; accurately. 3. Indeed; really: *truly ugly.*

Tru-man (trōōmən), **Harry S** (1884–1972). U.S. statesman. He was the 33rd president (1945–53) of the United States, succeeding to office on the death of F.D. Roosevelt. He authorised (1945) the use of the nuclear bomb on Japan, which ended World War II. He initiated (1949) the establishment of NATO.

tru-meau (trōōmō, trōō-mō) *n., pl.* **trumeaux** (-z). *Architecture.* A piece of wall, pillar, or other divider between two openings, such as a pair of windows or a twin archway. [French, panel between two windows, from Old French *trumel,* from Frankish *thrum* (unattested), from *thrum,* bit.]

trump¹ (trŭmp) *n.* 1. In card games: **a.** *Often plural.* A suit whose cards are declared to outrank all other cards for the duration of a hand or game. **b.** Any card of such a suit. 2. A key resource to be used at the opportune moment. 3. *Informal.* A reliable or admirable person. —**come up trumps.** 1. To turn out well; end satisfactorily. 2. To be successful.

~*v.* **trumped, trumping, trumps.** —*tr.* 1. To take (a card or trick) with a trump. 2. To outdo (an opponent) with or as if with a trump. —*intr.* To play a trump card. —**trump up.** To devise fraudulently; concoct; counterfeit. [Variant of TRIUMPH.]

trump² *n. Archaic.* A trumpet or trumpet call: *the last trump.* [Middle English *trompe,* from Old French, from Old High German *trumpa,* akin to Old Norse *trumba*†.]

trump card *n.* 1. A playing card cut or turned up to determine which suit shall be trumps. 2. Any card of the agreed trump suit. 3. A powerful resource or gambit used when all else has failed.

trumped-up (trŭmpt-ŭp) *adj.* Devised in order to deceive; concocted: *trumped-up charges.*

trump-er-y (trŭmpəri) *n., pl.* **-ies.** 1. Showy but worthless finery; bric-a-brac. 2. Nonsense; rubbish.

~*adj.* Showy but valueless. [Middle English *trompery,* from Old French *tromperie,* from *tromper*†, to cheat.]

trum-pet (trŭmpit) *n.* 1. **a.** A soprano brass wind instrument consisting of a long metal tube looped once and ending in a flared bell, the modern type being equipped with three valves for producing variations in pitch. **b.** The member of an orchestra who plays the trumpet. 2. Something shaped like or sounding like a trumpet. 3. An organ stop that produces a tone like that of the trumpet. 4. **a.** Music produced by a trumpet. **b.** A resounding call, such as that of the elephant. 5. An ear trumpet. —**blow (one's) own trumpet.** *British.* To boast; show off.

~*v.* **trumpeted, -peting, -pets.** —*intr.* 1. To play a trumpet. 2. To give forth a resounding call. Used especially of an elephant. —*tr.* To sound or proclaim loudly. [Middle English *trompette,* from Old French, diminutive of *trompe,* TRUMP (trumpet).]

trum-pet-er (trŭmpitər) *n.* 1. A trumpet-player, especially one in a cavalry regiment. 2. A person who announces something, as on a trumpet; a herald. 3. Any of several large birds of the genus *Psophia,* of tropical South America, having a loud, resonant call. 4. The trumpeter swan. 5. Any of several large Australian and New Zealand food fishes; especially, the species *Latris lineata,* which is silvery with yellow stripes. 6. A breed of domestic pigeon.

trumpeter swan *n.* A large white swan, *Cygnus buccinator,* of western North America, having a black bill and a loud, bugle-like call. Also called "trumpeter".

trum-pet-ma-jor (trŭmpit-máyjər) *n.* Formerly, the head trumpeter of a cavalry regiment.

trun-cal (trŭngk'l) *adj.* Of or pertaining to a trunk, as of a body or tree. [Alteration of TRUNK + -AL.]

trun-cate (trung-káyt, trúng-kayt) *tr.v.* **-cated, -cating, -cates.** 1. **a.** To shorten by or as if by cutting off the end or top; lop. **b.** To cut short; abbreviate (a quoted passage, for example). 2. To replace (the edge of a crystal) with a plane face.

~*adj.* (trúng-kayt). 1. Appearing to terminate abruptly, as a leaf or a coiled gastropod shell that lacks a spire. 2. Truncated. [Latin *truncāre,* to maim, from *truncus,* torso, TRUNK.] —**trun-cate-ly** *adv.* —**trun-ca-tion** (-káysh'n) *n.*

trun-ca-ted (trung-káytid ‖ trúng-kaytid) *adj.* 1. Having the apex cut off and replaced by a plane, especially one parallel to the base. Said of a solid geometric figure such as a cone or pyramid. 2. Cut short or abbreviated, as a quoted passage may be. 3. Truncate.

trun-cheon (trúnchən) *n.* 1. A short cudgel carried by policemen. 2. A staff carried as a symbol of office or authority; a baton. 3. A thick cutting from a plant, as for grafting.

~*tr.v.* **truncheoned, -cheoning, -cheons.** 1. To beat with a truncheon. Used especially of a policeman. 2. *Archaic.* To bludgeon. [Middle English *tronchon,* fragment, club, from Old French, from Vulgar Latin *truncio,* from Latin *truncus,* torso, TRUNK.]

trun-dle (trúnd'l) *n.* 1. The motion or noise of rolling. 2. A small wheel or roller. 3. **a.** The pinion of a lantern. **b.** Any of the bars on a lantern pinion.

~*v.* **trundled, -dling, -dles.** —*tr.* 1. To push or propel on wheels or rollers. 2. *Archaic.* To spin; twirl. —*intr.* To move along in a slow and cumbersome manner by or as if by rolling. [Variant of dialectal *trendle,* wheel, from Middle English *trendil,* Old English *trendel,* circle, from Germanic *trand-;* akin to TREND.] —**trun-dler** *n.*

trundle bed *n.* A truckle bed (*see*).

trunk (trungk) *n.* 1. The main woody axis of a tree. 2. **a.** The human body excluding the head and limbs; the torso. **b.** An analogous part of other organisms, such as the thorax of an insect. 3. A main body, apart from tributaries or appendages. 4. *Architecture.* The shaft of a column. 5. A proboscis; specifically, the long, prehensile proboscis of an elephant. 6. See **trunk line.** 7. A large packing case or box that is fastened with clasps, used as luggage or for storage. 8. *U.S.* The **boot** (*see*) of a car. 9. A chute or conduit. 10. *Nautical.* **a.** A shaft connecting two or more decks. **b.** The housing for the centreboard of a vessel. **c.** A structure projecting above part of a main deck, such as a covering over a ship's hatches or a cabin. 11. *Plural.* Men's shorts worn for swimming or athletics.

~*adj.* Of or designating the main body or line of a system: *a trunk road.* [Middle English *trunke,* from Old French *tronc,* a tree trunk, from Latin *truncus.*]

trunk call *n. Chiefly British.* A telephone call made on a trunk line.

trunk-fish (trúngk-fish) *n., pl.* **-fishes** or collectively **trunkfish.** Any of various tropical marine fishes of the family Ostraciidae, having boxlike armour enclosing the body. Also called "boxfish".

trunk hose *pl.n.* Short, ballooning breeches, extending from the waist to midthigh, worn by men in the 16th and 17th centuries. Also called "trunk breeches". [Probably from obsolete *trunk,* to cut short, from Latin *truncāre,* to TRUNCATE.]

trunk line *n.* 1. A direct line between two distant telephone switchboards. 2. The main line of a transport system, such as a railway or canal system.

trunnel. Variant of **treenail.**

trun-nion (trún-yən, -i-ən) *n.* A pin or gudgeon; especially, either of two small cylindrical projections on a cannon or movable container forming an axis on which it pivots. [French *trognon,* core of fruit, tree trunk, from Old French, perhaps from *estrongner,* to cut off the branches, variant of *estronchier* : *es-,* from Latin *ex-,* off + *tronchier,* to cut, from Latin *truncāre,* to TRUNCATE.] —**trun-nioned** *adj.*

Tru-ro (trōōr-ō ‖ trēwr-ō). Administrative centre of Cornwall, southwest England. Lying at the confluence of the rivers Kenwyn and Allen, it is a small port and tourist centre.

truss (trŭss) *n.* 1. *Medicine.* A supportive device or belt worn to prevent the protrusion of a hernia. 2. *Engineering.* A framework of wooden beams or metal bars, often arranged in triangles, to support a roof, bridge, or similar structure. 3. *Architecture.* A bracket; a corbel. 4. Something gathered into a bundle; a pack. 5. *British.* A bundle of a set weight of straw or hay, generally 60 pounds (27 kilograms) of new hay, 56 pounds (25 kilograms) of old hay, or 36 pounds (16 kilograms) of straw. 6. *Nautical.* An iron fitting by which a lower yard is secured to a mast. 7. A compact cluster of flowers or fruit at the end of a stalk.

~*tr.v.* **trussed, trussing, trusses.** 1. To tie up or bind. Often used with *up.* 2. To bind or skewer the wings or legs of (a fowl) before cooking. 3. To enclose or confine (the body) in tight-fitting clothes. Often used with *up.* 4. To support or brace with a truss. [Middle English *trusse,* a bundle, from Old French *tr(o)usse,* from *tr(o)usser,* to tie in a bundle, perhaps from Vulgar Latin *torsāre* (unattested), from *torsus* (unattested), past participle of Latin *torquēre,* to twist.]

truss bridge *n.* A bridge supported by trusses.

truss-ing (trússing) *n.* 1. The parts forming a truss. 2. A system of trusses supporting a structure.

trust (trŭst) *n.* 1. Firm reliance on the integrity, ability, or character of a person or thing; confident belief; faith. 2. The person or thing in which confidence is placed. 3. Custody; care. 4. Something committed into the care of another; a charge. 5. The condition and resulting obligation of having confidence placed in one: *a position of public trust.* 6. Reliance on something in the future; hope. 7. Reliance on the intention and ability of a purchaser to pay in the future; credit. 8. *Abbr.* **tr.** *Law.* **a.** A legal title to property held by one party (the trustee) for the benefit of another (the beneficiary). **b.** The confidence reposed in a trustee when giving him legal title to property to administer for another, and his obligation with respect to the property and the beneficiary. **c.** The property so held. **d.** The right of the beneficiary to the property. **9.** A group of companies organised for the purpose of reducing competition and controlling prices throughout a business or industry. **10.** A trust territory (*see*). **—in trust.** In the charge of a trustee.

~*v.* **trusted, trusting, trusts.** *—intr.* **1.** To rely; depend. Used with *in* or *to.* **2.** To be confident; hope. **3.** To sell on credit. *—tr.* **1.** To have confidence in; feel sure of. **2.** To expect with assurance; assume. **3.** To believe. **4.** To place in the care of another; entrust. **5.** To grant discretion to confidently: *Shall I trust her with the boat?* **6.** To extend credit to. —See Synonyms at **rely.**

~*adj.* Maintained in trust. [Middle English *truste,* probably from Old Norse *traust,* confidence, firmness.] **—trust·a·bil·i·ty** (-ə-bílləti) *n.* **—trust·a·ble** *adj.* **—trust·er** *n.*

Synonyms: trust, faith, confidence, reliance, dependence.

trust account *n.* **1.** A savings account deposited in the name of a trustee, after whose death the balance is payable to a specified beneficiary. Also called "trustee account". **2.** Property under trustee control.

trust·bust·er (trúst-bustər) *n. U.S. Informal.* A government official who works to dissolve illegal business combinations (trusts).

trust company *n.* A commercial bank or other company that manages trusts.

trus·tee (trúss-tée, truss-) *n. Abbr.* **tr.** **1.** A person or agent, such as a bank, holding legal title to property in order to administer it for a beneficiary. **2.** A member of a board elected or appointed to direct the funds and policy of an institution. **3.** A garnishee.

~*tr.v.* **trusteed, -teeing, -tees.** **1.** To place (property) in the care of a trustee. **2.** To garnishee (property).

trustee process *n. Garnishment (see).*

trus·tee·ship (trúss-tée-ship, truss-) *n.* **1.** The position or function of a trustee. **2. a.** The administration of a territory by a country or countries, supervised by the United Nations. **b.** *Often capital* **T.** A region so administered; a trust territory. Compare **mandate.**

trust·ful (trústf'l) *adj.* Trusting. **—trust·ful·ly** *adv.*

trust fund *n.* An estate, especially money and securities, held or settled in trust.

trust·ing (trústing) *adj.* Inclined to believe or confide readily; full of trust. **—trust·ing·ly** *adv.* **—trust·ing·ness** *n.*

trust territory *n.* A colony or territory placed under the administration of a country or countries by commission of the United Nations. Also called "trust". Compare **mandate.**

Trust Territory of the Pacific Islands, U.N. See **Pacific Islands, UN Trust Territory of.**

trust·wor·thy (trúst-wurthi) *adj.* Warranting trust; dependable; reliable. **—trust·wor·thi·ly** *adv.* **—trust·wor·thi·ness** *n.*

trust·y (trústi) *adj.* **-ier, -iest.** Dependable; faithful; reliable.

~*n., pl.* **trusties.** A trusted person; specifically, a convict granted privileges for good behaviour. **—trust·i·ly** *adv.* **—trust·i·ness** *n.*

truth (trōōth ‖ trewth) *n., pl.* **truths** (trōōthz, trōōths ‖ trewthz, trewths). **1.** Conformity to knowledge, fact, or logic. **2.** Fidelity to an original or standard. **3. a.** Reality; actuality. **b.** *Often capital* **T.** That which is considered to be the supreme reality and to have the ultimate meaning and value of existence. **4.** A statement proven to be or accepted as true; the opposite of a falsehood. **5.** Sincerity; integrity; honesty. **6.** *Physics.* **Top** (*see*). **—truth to tell.** To tell the truth; speaking frankly. [Middle English *trewthe, treothe,* Old English *trēowth, trīewth.*]

Synonyms: truth, veracity, verity, verisimilitude, authenticity.

truth drug *n. Informal.* Any drug that reduces inhibitions and promotes relaxation, as used by certain authorities during interrogation. Also called "truth serum".

truth·ful (trōōth-f'l ‖ trewth-) *adj.* **1.** Consistently telling the truth; honest. **2.** Corresponding to reality; true. **—truth·ful·ly** *adv.* **—truth·ful·ness** *n.*

truth-function (trōōth-fungksh'n ‖ trewth-) *n.* A compound proposition in logic, such as a conjunction or negation, the truth-value of which is always determined by the truth-values of the components.

truth set *n. Mathematics & Logic.* A set of values that satisfy a given equation or statement. Also called "solution set".

truth table *n. Logic.* A table listing the truth-values of a proposition that result from all the possible combinations of the truth-values of its components.

truth-val·ue (trōōth-val-yōō ‖ trewth-) *n. Logic.* Either the truth or the falsity of a proposition.

try (trī) *v.* **tried, trying, tries.** *—tr.* **1.** To taste, sample, or otherwise test in order to determine strength, effect, worth, or desirability. **2. a.** To examine or hear (evidence or a case) by judicial process. **b.** To put (an accused person) on trial. **3.** To subject to strain or hardship; tax: *The last steep ascent tried her every muscle.* **4.** To melt (lard, for example) in order to separate out impurities; render down. Often used with *out.* **5.** To make an effort (to do or accomplish something); attempt. Used chiefly with an infinitive or *and: Try to do it; try and find out.* **6.** To smooth, fit, or align accurately. *—intr.* To make an effort; strive.

~*n., pl.* **tries. 1.** An attempt; an effort. **2.** A test; a trial. **3. a.** In Rugby football, the act of touching the ball down behind the opposing team's goal line, giving the team the right to kick for goal. In Rugby Union a try scores four points and in Rugby League three points. **b.** The score so gained. [Middle English *trien,* to separate,

pick out, sift, from Old French *trier*†.]

Usage: Try and is widely encountered in informal speech, especially in such established phrases as *try and stop, try and get* (*Try and get some rest*), *try and make* (*You try and make me do it!*). Formal usage prefers the use of *to* at all times: *tried to buy a car.*

try·ing (trī-ing) *adj.* Causing annoyance, strain, or distress. **—try·ing·ly** *adv.* **—try·ing·ness** *n.*

trying plane *n.* A long plane used to produce level surfaces on planks.

try·ma (trī-mə) *n., pl.* **-mata** (-mətə). A drupe, such as a walnut, having a tough epicarp that separates from the shell of the fruit. [New Latin, from Greek *truma, trumē,* a hole (from the hollow drupe).]

try on *tr.v.* **1.** To put on (an article of clothing) to see whether it fits or suits one. **2.** *Chiefly British Informal.* To attempt to fool or deceive somebody with (tricks or games): *Don't try on your tricks with me.* **—try it on.** *British Informal.* **1.** To attempt to fool or deceive somebody. **2.** To make sexual advances: *He tried it on with me, so I told him just where he could get off.*

try-on (trī-on) *n. Informal.* **1.** The act of trying on clothes. **2.** *British.* An attempt to fool or deceive.

try out *tr.v.* To put to experimental use in order to test. *—intr.v. Chiefly U.S.* To undergo a competitive qualifying test, as for a job. Used with *for.*

try-out (trī-owt) *n. Informal.* **1.** An experimental test or trial. **2.** *Chiefly U.S.* A test to ascertain the qualifications of applicants, as for an athletics team or for a theatrical part.

try·pan·o·some (tríppənə-sōm, tri-pánnə-) *n.* Any of various parasitic protozoans of the genus *Trypanosoma,* transmitted to the vertebrate bloodstream by certain insects, and often causing diseases such as sleeping sickness. [New Latin *Trypanosoma,* "auger-bodied" (from its shape) : Greek *trupanon,* an auger, borer, from *trupan,* to bore, from *trupa, trupē,* a hole + -SOME (body).] **—try·pan·o·som·ic** (-sŏmik) *adj.*

try·pan·o·so·mi·a·sis (tríppən-ə-sō-mī-ə-siss, tri-pán-, -ō-, -sə-) *n.* Any disease caused by a trypanosome. [New Latin : TRYPANO-SOM(E) + -IASIS.]

try·pars·am·ide (tri-pársə-mīd) *n.* A white crystalline powder, $C_8H_{10}AsN_2O_4Na·1/2H_2O$, used in the treatment of spirochaetal and trypanosomic diseases. [Originally a trade name : *tryp*anosome + *arsenic* + *amide.*]

tryp·sin (trípsin) *n.* One of the proteolytic enzymes of the pancreatic juice, important in the digestive processes. [Greek *tripsis,* a rubbing (first obtained by rubbing the pancreas with glycerin), from *tribein,* to rub + -IN.] **—tryp·tic** (tríptik) *adj.*

tryp·sin·o·gen (trip-sínnə-jən, -jen) *n.* The substance produced by the pancreas that is converted into trypsin when acted upon by certain enzymes. [From TRYPSIN + -GEN.]

tryp·to·phan (tríptə-fan) *n.* **tryp·to·phane** (-fayn). An amino acid, $C_{11}H_{12}N_2O_2$, found in certain pulses, that is an essential element in human nutrition and a precursor of serotonin. [TRYP(SIN) + (PEP)T(IC) + -PHAN(E).]

try·sail (trī-s'l, -sayl) *n. Nautical.* A small fore-and-aft sail hoisted abaft the foremast and mainmast in a storm to keep a ship's bow to the wind. Also called "spencer". [From TRY (noun, in the obsolete nautical sense of "lying to in a storm").]

try square *n.* A carpenter's tool consisting of a ruled metal straightedge set at right angles to a wooden straight piece, used for measuring and marking square work. Also called "square".

tryst (trist, *rarely* trīst) *n. Archaic & Poetic.* **1.** An agreement between lovers to meet at a certain time and place. **2.** The meeting or meeting place so arranged.

~*intr.v.* **trysted, trysting, trysts.** *Archaic & Poetic or Scottish.* To arrange or keep a tryst. [Middle English, from Old French *triste,* an appointed station in hunting, perhaps from Scandinavian, akin to Old Norse *treysta,* to trust, make firm.] **—tryst·er** *n.*

tsade. Variant of **sade.**

Tsana. See **Tana, Lake.**

Tsangpo. See **Brahmaputra.**

tsar, tzar (zar, tsar) *n.* Also *chiefly U.S.* **czar. 1.** A king or emperor; specifically, one of the former monarchs of the Russian empire. **2.** Formerly, any of several south Slavonic monarchs, such as the kings of Bulgaria. **3.** See **czar.** [Russian *tsar',* from Gothic *kaisar,* emperor, ultimately from Latin *Caesar.*] **—tsar·dom** *n.*

Usage: The spelling of *tsar* and its derivatives with the Latin transliteration *cz* dates from a German commentary of the 16th century; *ts,* as the more accurate phonetic transcription, is now the preferred spelling in British English. However, the older *czar* is still the accepted form in American English, and this is the usual spelling for the extended sense of "petty tyrant" or "supremo".

tsar·e·vitch (záar'ə-vich, tsa'ərə-; *Russian* tsaryáyveech) *n.* The eldest son of a tsar. [Russian : TSAR + -*evich,* male patronymic suffix.]

tsa·rev·na (zaa-révnə, tsaa-; *Russian* tsaryénə) *n.* **1.** The daughter of a tsar. **2.** The wife of a tsarevitch. [Russian : TSAR + -*evna,* feminine patronymic suffix.]

tsar·ism (záar-iz'm, tsáar-) *n.* The system of government in Russia under the tsars; autocracy. **—tsar·ist** *n. & adj.*

tsa·rit·sa (zaa-rítsə, tsaa-) *n.* **1.** An empress of Russia. **2.** The wife of a tsar. Also called "tsarina". [Russian : TSAR + -*itsa,* feminine suffix.]

Usage: The Russian word for "empress" is correctly *tsaritsa,* with the Slavonic feminine suffix. The form *tsarina* is a borrowing from German, with the Teutonic suffix *-in* influenced by Romance words such as *signorina.*

tsessebe. Variant of **sassaby.**

tset·se fly, tzet·ze fly (tsétsi, tétsi) *n.* Any of several bloodsucking African flies of the genus *Glossina,* often carrying and transmitting pathogenic trypanosomes to human beings and livestock. [Afrikaans, from Tswana.]

TSH. thyroid stimulating hormone.

Tshi. Variant of **Twi.**

Tshi·lu·ba (chi-lōōbə) *n.* The language of the Luba people, used as a trade language in Zaire. See **Luba.** —**Tshi·lu·ba** *adj.*

T-shirt, tee shirt (tée-shurt) *n.* A short-sleeved, collarless casual shirt worn by both sexes. [So called from its shape.]

Tshom·be (chómbi), **Moïse (Kapenda)** (1919–69). Congolese statesman. He was president (1960–63) of the breakaway province of Katanga, and prime minister of the Congo (1964–65) until dismissed by President Kasavubu, and condemned to death in absentia in 1967.

Tsinan. See **Jinan.**

Tsinghai. See **Qinghai.**

tsk tsk *interj. Informal.* Used to express disapproval, especially ironically.

tsp. teaspoon; teaspoonful.

T-square (tée-skwair) *n.* A T-shaped ruler with a short, sometimes sliding, perpendicular crosspiece at one end, used by draughtsmen for establishing and drawing parallel lines.

tsu·na·mi (tsōō-naami, soo-) *n.* A very large ocean wave caused by an underwater earthquake or volcanic eruption. Also (erroneously) "tidal wave". [Japanese : *tsu,* port + *nami,* wave.]

tsu·tsu·ga·mu·shi disease (tsōōt-sōō-gə-mōōshi, sōōt-, -sə-) *n.* **Scrub typhus** *(see).* [Japanese : *tsutsuga,* illness + *mushi,* an insect.]

Tsve·ta·ye·va (tsvi-tī-ivə), **Marina Ivanovna** (1892–1941). Russian poet. Her highly original verse is distinguished by its staccato rhythms and its directness.

Tswa·na (tswaanə, swaanə) *n.* **1.** A member of a Bantu people of southern Africa, living mainly in Botswana. **2.** The Sotho language of the Tswana people. —**Tswa·na** *adj.*

T.T. 1. teetotal; teetotaller. **2.** Tourist Trophy. **2.** tuberculin-tested.

TTL 1. through the lens; used to designate a type of camera light meter. **2.** transistor-transistor logic.

T.U. trade union.

Tu·a·mo·tu Archipelago (tōōə-mō̄-too). *French* **Tou·a·mo·tou** (too-amō-tōō). Group of 80 small islands in the southern Pacific Ocean, part of French Polynesia.

Tuan (tōō-aán, twaán) *n.* A Malayan form of respectful address, equivalent to the English *Sir* or *Mr.* [Malay : master, lord.]

Tua·reg (twaáreg) *n., pl.* **-regs** or collectively **Tuareg.** A member of one of the tall, nomadic, Hamitic-speaking or Berber-speaking peoples who occupy the western and central Sahara and an area along the Niger and have adopted the Muslim religion. [Arabic *Tawāriq.*] —**Tau·reg** *adj.*

tu·a·ta·ra (tōō-ə-taárə) *n.* A lizard-like reptile, *Sphenodon punctatum,* of New Zealand, the only surviving representative of the order Rhynchocephalia that flourished during the Mesozoic era. [Maori.]

tub (tub) *n.* **1. a.** A large round, flat-bottomed vessel, usually wider than it is tall, originally made of wooden staves held together with hoops, and used for packing, storing, or washing. **b.** A small container resembling such a vessel in shape and used for packaging ice cream or margarine, for example. **c.** The contents of a tub or the amount that a tub will hold. Also called "tubful". **2.** *Informal.* A bath or the act of taking a bath. **3.** *Informal.* **a.** A wide, clumsy, slow-moving boat. **b.** A strong broad boat used for rowing practice. **4. a.** A bucket used for conveying ore or coal up a mine shaft. **b.** A coal wagon used in a mine.

~*v.* **tubbed, tubbing, tubs.** —*tr.* **1.** To pack or store in a tub. **2.** *Informal.* To wash or bathe in a tub. —*intr. Informal.* To take a bath. [Middle English *tubbe, tobbe,* from Middle Dutch and Middle Low German *tubbe†.*] —**tub·ba·ble** *adj.* —**tub·ber†** *n.*

tu·ba (téw-bə || tōō-) *n., pl.* **-bas** or **-bae** (-bee) (for sense 3). **1.** A large, valved, brass musical wind instrument with a bass pitch. **2.** A reed stop in an organ, having eight-foot pitch. **3.** An ancient Roman war trumpet. [Italian, from Latin, a trumpet, akin to Latin *tubus,* TUBE.]

tu·bal (téwb'l || tōōb'l) *adj.* Of, pertaining to, or occurring in a tube, especially the Fallopian tube.

tu·bate (téw-bayt || tōō-) *adj.* Forming or having a tube.

tub·by (túbbi) *adj.* **-bier, -biest. 1.** *Informal.* Short and fat. **2.** Having a dull sound; lacking resonance. —**tub·bi·ness** *n.*

tube (tewb || tōōb) *n.* **1. a.** A hollow cylinder that conveys a fluid or functions as a passage. **b.** An organic structure so shaped or so functioning; a duct. **2.** A small, flexible cylindrical container sealed at one end and having a cap at the other, for pigments, toothpaste, or other pastelike substances. **3.** The cylindrical part of a wind instrument. **4. a.** A **vacuum tube** *(see).* **b.** A **cathode-ray tube** *(see),* especially in a television set. **c.** Any electronic **valve** *(see).* **5.** *Botany.* The lower, joined part of a gamopetalous corolla or a gamosepalous calyx. **6.** *British.* An underground railway system, especially the one in London. Preceded by *the.* Also used adjectivally: *a tube train.* **7.** *Australian Informal.* A can of beer. **8.** *Chiefly U.S. Informal.* Television. Preceded by *the.* **9.** *Plural. Informal.* The Fallopian tubes.

~*tr.v.* **tubed, tubing, tubes. 1.** To provide with a tube or tubes; insert a tube in: *tube a tyre.* **2.** To place in or enclose in a tube. [French, from Latin *tubus†.* See also **tuba.**]

tube foot *n.* Any of the numerous external, fluid-filled muscular tubes of echinoderms, such as the starfish, serving primarily as organs of locomotion.

tube·less tyre (téwb-ləss, -liss || tōōb-) *n.* A pneumatic vehicular tyre in which the air is held in the assembly of casing and rim without an inner tube.

tu·ber (téw-bər || tōō-) *n.* **1.** *Botany.* A swollen, usually underground stem or root, such as the potato or dahlia, bearing buds from which new plant shoots arise. **2.** *Anatomy.* A swelling; a tubercle. [Latin *tūber,* a lump, swelling, tumour.]

tu·ber·cle (téw-bər-k'l, -ber- || tōō-) *n.* **1.** A small, rounded prominence or growth, such as a wartlike excrescence on the roots of some leguminous plants or a knoblike projection in the skin or on a bone. **2.** *Pathology.* **a.** A nodule or swelling. **b.** The characteristic lesion of tuberculosis. [Latin *tūberculum,* diminutive of *tūber,* TUBER.]

tubercle bacillus *n. Abbr.* **Tb.** A rod-shaped bacterium, *Mycobacterium tuberculosis,* that causes tuberculosis.

tu·ber·cu·lar (tew-bérkew-lər || tōō-, tōō-) *adj.* **1.** Of, pertaining to, or covered with tubercles; tuberculate. **2.** Of, pertaining to, or suffering from tuberculosis. **3.** Possessing or characterised by the presence of tubercles.

~*n.* A person suffering from tuberculosis.

tu·ber·cu·late (tew-bérkew-lət, -lit || tōō-, tōō-) *adj.* Also **tu·ber·cu·la·ted** (-láytid). **1.** Having tubercles. **2.** Tubercular. —**tu·ber·cu·late·ly** *adv.* —**tu·ber·cu·la·tion** (-láysh'n) *n.*

tu·ber·cu·lin (tew-bérkew-lin || tōō-, tōō-) *n.* A sterile liquid derived from cultures of tubercle bacilli, used in the diagnosis and treatment of tuberculosis. [Latin *tūberculum,* TUBERCLE + -IN.]

tuberculin test *n.* The **Mantoux test** *(see).* —**tu·ber·cu·lin-test·ed** (tew-bérkew-lin-téstid) *adj.*

tu·ber·cu·loid (tew-bérkew-loyd || tōō-) *adj.* **1.** Resembling tuberculosis. **2.** Resembling a tubercle.

tu·ber·cu·lo·sis (tew-bérkew-lō̄-siss || tōō-, tōō-) *n. Abbr.* **TB, T.B. 1.** An infectious disease of humans and animals, caused by a micro-organism, *Mycobacterium tuberculosis,* and manifesting itself in lesions of the lung, bone, and other parts of the body. **2.** Tuberculosis of the lungs. Also called "consumption", "phthisis". [New Latin : Latin *tūberculum,* TUBERCLE + -OSIS.]

tu·ber·cu·lous (tew-bérkew-ləss || tōō-, tōō-) *adj.* **1.** Of, pertaining to, or having tuberculosis. **2.** Of, affected with, or caused by tubercles. [New Latin *tuberculosus,* from Latin *tūberculum,* TUBERCLE.]

tube·rose (téwbə-rōz || téwb-, tōōbə-, tōōb-, -rōss, -rōz) *n.* A tuberous plant, *Polianthes tuberosa,* native to Mexico, cultivated for its fragrant white flowers, which yield an expensive perfume, *tuberose obsolute.* [New Latin *(Polianthes) tuberosa,* from the feminine of Latin *tūberōsus,* TUBEROUS.]

tu·ber·os·i·ty (téwbə-róssəti || tōōbə-) *n., pl.* **-ties.** A projection or protuberance, especially one at the end of a bone for the attachment of a muscle or tendon.

tu·ber·ous (téwbə-rəss || tōō-) *adj.* Also **tu·ber·ose** (-róz, -róss). **1.** *Botany.* **a.** Producing or bearing tubers. **b.** Resembling a tuber: *a tuberous root.* **2.** *Rare.* Covered with small, rounded projections; knobby. [Latin *tūberōsus,* full of lumps, from *tūber,* TUBER.]

tube worm *n.* Any sedentary, tube-dwelling bristle worm, such as the lugworm or the ragworm.

tu·bi·fex (téwbi-feks || tōōbi-) *n., pl.* **-fexes** or collectively **tubifex.** Any of various small, slender, reddish freshwater worms of the genus *Tubifex,* often used as food for tropical aquarium fish. [New Latin *Tubifex,* from Latin *tubus,* TUBE (each one is partially enclosed in a tube) + *-fex,* "maker".]

tub·ing (téwb-ing || tōōb-) *n.* **1.** A length of tube or material in the form of a tube. **2.** Tubes collectively. **3.** A system of tubes.

tub thumper *n. Informal.* A soapbox orator; a vehement public speaker. —**tub-thump·ing** (túb-thumping) *n. & adj.*

Tu·bua·i Islands (toobwá-ee). Formerly **Austral Islands.** Group of small volcanic islands in the southern Pacific Ocean, part of French Polynesia.

tu·bu·lar (téw-bewlər || tōō-) *adj.* **1.** Having the form of a tube. **2.** Made or consisting of a tube or tubes. —**tu·bu·lar·i·ty** (-bew-lárrəti) *n.*

tubular bells *pl.n.* A musical instrument consisting of a set of long metal tubes that are tuned to the musical scale and struck with a mallet to simulate the sound of bells. Compare **chimes.**

tu·bu·late (téw-bew-lət, -lit, -layt || tōō-) *adj.* Also **tu·bu·lat·ed** (-laytid). **1.** Formed into or resembling a tube; tubular. **2.** Provided with a tube.

~*tr.v.* (-layt) **tubulated, -lating, -lates.** To provide with or form into a tube. [Latin *tubulātus,* from *tubulus,* diminutive of *tubus,* TUBE.] —**tu·bu·la·tion** (-láysh'n) *n.* —**tu·bu·la·tor** (-laytər) *n.*

tu·bule (téw-bewl || tōō-) *n.* A very small tube or tubular structure. [Latin *tubulus,* diminutive of *tubus,* TUBE.]

tu·bu·lif·er·ous (téw-bew-lifferəss || tōō-) *adj.* Having or consisting of tubules. [TUBULE + -FEROUS.]

tu·bu·li·flo·rous (téw-bewli-fláw-rəss || tōō-, flō̄-) *adj.* Having flowers or florets with tubular corollas. [From TUBUL(E) + -FLOROUS.]

tu·bu·lous (téw-bewləss || tōō-) *adj.* **1.** Tubular. **2.** Composed of tubes or having tubular parts. [New Latin *tubulosus,* from Latin *tubulus,* TUBULE.] —**tu·bu·lous·ly** *adv.*

T.U.C. The **Trades Union Congress** *(see).*

Tu·ca·na (tew-káy-nə, tōō-, -káa-) *n.* A constellation in the polar region of the Southern Hemisphere near Indus and Hydrus, containing the smaller **Magellanic cloud** *(see).* [Tupi *tucana,* TOUCAN.]

tu·chun (tŏŏ-chŏŏn, dŏŏ-jŏŏn, -jŭn) n., pl. **-chuns** or **tuchun**. Formerly, a Chinese military governor of a province. [Chinese dū jūn : dū, to supervise + jūn, army.] —**tu·chun·ate** n. —**tu·chun·ism** n.

tuck[1] (tŭk) v. **tucked, tucking, tucks.** —tr. **1.** To make one or more folds in. **2.** To gather up the ends of (a garment, for example) and thrust into a space between two surfaces so as to secure or confine: tuck one's shirt into one's trousers. **3. a.** To put (something) into a place or space where it will be concealed, confined, or snug: tuck the letter into your bag; a cabin tucked away in the woods. **b.** To store in a safe spot; save. Used with away: He's millions tucked away. **4.** To cover (a child, for example) snugly in bed. Used with in or up. **5.** To draw in; contract. —intr. To make tucks. —**tuck in** or **away.** Chiefly British Informal. To eat (food) heartily or greedily.
~n. **1.** A flattened pleat or fold in a garment, especially a very narrow one stitched in place. **2.** An act of tucking something in. **3.** Nautical. The part of a ship's hull under the stern where the ends of the bottom planks come together. **4.** British Informal. Food, especially sweets and cakes. [Middle English tukken, tucken, to pull or put up, put away (hence, consume), from Middle Low German and Middle Dutch tucken; akin to TUG.]

tuck[2] n. British Regional. A beat or tap, especially on a drum. [From obsolete t(o)uk, to beat the drum, sound the trumpet, from Middle English tukken, from Old North French toquer, to strike, touch, from Vulgar Latin toccāre (unattested), to TOUCH.]

tuck[3] n. Archaic. A slender sword; a rapier. [Earlier to(c)ke, from French (Normandy dialect) étoc, from Old French estoc, "a tree trunk", sword, sword point, from Frankish stok (unattested).]

tuck·er[1] (tŭckər) n. **1.** One that tucks. **2.** A piece of linen or frill of lace formerly worn by women around the neck and shoulders. **3.** Australian Informal. Food. [TUCK (fold, food) + -ER.]

tucker[2] tr.v. **-ered, -ering, -ers.** Australian & U.S. Informal. To weary; exhaust. Usually used in the passive with out: I'm all tuckered out. [Frequentative of TUCK (to pull under).]

tuck·et (tŭckit) n. A trumpet fanfare. [From obsolete t(o)uk, to sound the trumpet. See **tuck** (drumbeat).]

tuck shop (tŭck-shŏp) n. British. A shop that sells sweets and cakes, especially one in a school. [From TUCK (food).]

-tude n. suffix. Indicates a condition or state of being; for example, **exactitude.** [Old French, from Latin -tūdō.]

Tu·dor (tĕw-dər ‖ tŏŏ-). The family name of the English royal family from Henry VII (1485) to Elizabeth I (1603).
~n. A member of this family, especially when a monarch: the Tudors and Stuarts.
~adj. **1.** Of or pertaining to the Tudors. **2. a.** Of, pertaining to, or characteristic of the period of Tudors (1485–1603). **b.** Of, designating, or characteristic of the architectural style of the Tudor period, with exposed beams as a typical feature.

Tues·day (tĕwz-di, -day ‖ tŏŏz-) n. Abbr. **Tues.** The day of the week following Monday; the second day of the working week. [Middle English tiwesday, tuesdai, Old English tīwesdæg, "day of Tiu" : Tīw, TIU + dæg, DAY.]

tu·fa (tĕw-fə ‖ tŏŏ-) n. **1.** The porous, spongy calcium carbonate deposited round a spring. **2.** U.S. Tuff (see). [Obsolete Italian tufa, tufo, from Latin tōphus, tōfus†.] —**tu·fa·ceous** (tew-fáyshəss) adj.

tuff (tŭf) n. A rock composed of cemented or fused fragments less than 2 millimetres (¹/₁₂ inch) in diameter which have been ejected from a volcano. Also U.S. "tuffa". [French tuf, tuffe, from obsolete Italian tufo, TUFA.] —**tuff·a·ceous** (tuf-áyshəss) adj.

tuf·fet (tŭffit) n. **1.** A clump or tuft of grass. **2.** A small mound or hillock. [Perhaps variant of TUFT.]

tuft (tŭft) n. **1.** A short cluster of hair, feathers, grass, or the like, attached at the base or growing close together. **2.** A dense clump of trees or bushes.
~v. **tufted, tufting, tufts.** —tr. **1.** To provide or ornament with a tuft or tufts. **2.** To pass threads through the layers of (a quilt, mattress, or upholstery), securing the thread ends with a knot or button in the depressions thus created. —intr. To separate or form into tufts; grow in a tuft. [Middle English tuft, toft, from Old French tof(f)e, from Germanic.] —**tuft·er** n. —**tuft·y** adj.

tuft·ed duck (tŭftid) n. A diving duck, Aythya fuligula, with a drooping purple-black crest in the male.

tug (tŭg) v. **tugged, tugging, tugs.** —tr. **1.** To pull at vigorously; strain at. **2.** To move by pulling with great effort or exertion; haul; drag: tugged her out of bed. **3.** To tow by tugboat. —intr. **1.** To pull hard: She tugged at my boots. **2.** To toil or struggle; strain. **3.** Archaic. To vie; contend.
~n. **1.** A strong pull or pulling force: the tug of the sea. **2.** A hard struggle between opposing parties or parties: a tug between duty and desire. **3.** A tugboat. **4.** A rope, chain, or strap used in hauling; especially, a harness trace. [Middle English tuggen, toggen, intensive form akin to Old English tēon, to draw, pull, tow.] —**tug·ger** n.

tug·boat (tŭg-bōt) n. A powerful small boat designed for towing larger vessels. Also called "towboat", "tug".

tug of love n. Informal. A struggle between a divorced or separated couple for the custody of their child or children.

tug of war n. **1.** A contest of strength and skill in which two teams tug on opposite ends of a rope, each trying to pull the other across a line marked out between them. **2.** A struggle for supremacy.

tug·rik (tŏŏg-reek, -rik) n. The basic monetary unit of the Mongolian People's Republic, equal to 100 möngö. Also called "tögrög". [Mongolian dughurik, "round object", wheel.]

tu·i (tŏŏ-i) n. A New Zealand honeyeater, Prosthemadera novaeseelandiae, having greenish-brown plumage and two patches of curly white feathers at the throat. Also called "parson bird". [Maori.]

tu·i·tion (tew-ísh'n ‖ tŏŏ-) n. **1.** Teaching or instruction, especially of individuals or small groups, and often on a commercial basis. **2.** A fee for instruction. **3.** Archaic. Guardianship. [Middle English, protection, tutelage, from Old French, from Latin tuitiō (stem tuitiōn-), protection, a watching, from tuērī, to look at, watch, protect.] —**tu·i·tion·al, tu·i·tion·ar·y** (-ĕri ‖ -erri) adj.

tu·la·rae·mi·a (tŏŏ-lə-réemi-ə, tĕw-) n. An infectious disease caused by the bacterium Pasteurella tularensis, transmitted from infected rodents to humans by insect vectors or by handling infected animals, and characterised by fever and swelling of the lymph nodes. Also called "rabbit fever". [New Latin : Tulare, a county in California where it was discovered + -AEMIA.]

tu·lip (tĕw-lip ‖ tŏŏ-) n. **1.** Any of several bulbous plants of the genus Tulipa, native to Asia, widely cultivated for their showy, bell-shaped, variously coloured flowers. **2.** The flower or bulb of this plant. [New Latin Tulipa, from Turkish tül(i)bend, TURBAN (from its turban-shaped flower).]

tulip tree n. Either of two trees of the genus Liriodendron; L. tulipifera of North America and L. chinensis of China, both having tulip-shaped yellow flowers and soft, easily worked wood. Also called "tulip poplar".

tu·lip·wood (tĕw-lip-wŏŏd ‖ tŏŏ-) n. **1.** The wood of the tulip tree. **2.** The irregularly striped, ornamental wood of any of several other trees. —**tu·lip·wood** adj.

tulle (tewl ‖ tŏŏl; French tül) n. A fine starched net of silk, rayon, or nylon, used for veils, tutus, or evening dresses, for example. [French, originally produced in Tulle, southwestern France.]

tum (tŭm) n. Informal. The stomach. [See **tummy**.]

tum·ble (tŭmb'l) v. **-bled, -bling, -bles.** —intr. **1. a.** To fall or roll end over end: kittens tumbling over each other. **b.** To fall helplessly or precipitately; pitch headlong. **c.** To move in confusion or disorder; proceed haphazardly: Children tumbled out of the bus. **2.** To perform acrobatic feats, such as somersaults or twists. **3. a.** To fall or be toppled, as from a position of power or eminence. **b.** To collapse: and the walls came tumbling down. **c.** To drop suddenly and rapidly: Prices tumbled. **4.** To come accidentally; stumble. Used with on or upon. **5.** Informal. To come to a sudden understanding; catch on: tumbled to what she was saying. —tr. **1.** To cause to fall suddenly or violently; overturn or overthrow. **2.** To spill, throw, or mix together haphazardly. **3.** To disturb the order of; disarrange; rumple. **4.** To toss or whirl in a drum or tumbler, especially: **a.** To treat in a tumbling box. **b.** To dry in a tumble drier.
~n. **1.** An act of tumbling; a fall. **2.** A condition of confusion or disorder. **3.** A disorderly heap or mass. [Middle English tumblen, from Middle Low German tummelen, Old High German tumalōn, frequentative of tāmōn; akin to Old English tumbian, to dance, and French tomber, to fall.]

tum·ble·bug (tŭmb'l-bug) n. Any of various beetles of the family Scarabaeidae, that roll up balls of dung to protect their eggs and serve as food for the newly hatched larvae.

tum·ble·down (tŭmb'l-down) adj. Informal. Dilapidated; rickety.

tumble drier n. A machine that dries clothes by tumbling them in a heated rotating drum. Also called "tumbler drier".

tum·ble·home (tŭmb'l-hōm) n. The inward curve of a ship's or boat's topsides above the point of greatest breadth.

tum·bler (tŭmblər) n. **1.** One that tumbles; specifically, an acrobat or gymnast. **2. a.** A drinking glass, originally with a rounded bottom. **b.** A flat-bottomed glass having no handle or stem. **c.** The contents of or the amount held by a drinking glass; a tumblerful. **3.** A toy made with a weighted, rounded base so that it can rock over and then right itself. **4.** Any of a breed of domestic pigeons characteristically tumbling or somersaulting in flight. **5.** A piece in a gunlock that forces the hammer forward by action of the mainspring. **6.** The part in a lock that releases the bolt when moved by a key. **7. a.** The drum of a tumble drier. **b.** A tumbling box. **8. a.** A projecting piece on a revolving or rocking part in a mechanism that transmits motion to the part it engages. **b.** The rocking frame that moves a gear into place in a selective transmission, as in a motor vehicle.

tumbler gear n. Machinery. A set of gears operated by a tumbler.

tum·ble·weed (tŭmb'l-weed) n. Any of various densely branched New World plants, chiefly of the genus Amaranthus, that when withered break off and are rolled about by the wind.

tumbling box n. A revolving drum in which objects, such as gemstones, are reduced in size, polished, or cleaned by tumbling with abrasives. Also called "rumble", "tumbler", "tumbling barrel".

tum·brel, tum·bril (tŭm-brəl, -bril) n. **1.** A two-wheeled covered cart formerly used to transport tools and ammunition. **2.** A farm cart that can be tilted to dump a load, as of dung. **3.** A crude cart used to carry condemned prisoners, as to the stake or to the guillotine during the French Revolution. [Middle English tomberel, from Old French, from tomber, fall, to leap, overturn, from Frankish tūmon, perhaps from Germanic tumōjan- (unattested), to leap. See **tumble**.]

tu·me·fa·cient (tĕwmi-fáy-si-ənt, -shi-, -shənt ‖ tŏŏmi-) adj. Producing or tending to produce swelling or tumefaction. [Latin tumefaciēns (stem tumefacient-), present participle of tumefacere, to cause to swell : tumēre, to swell + facere, to make.]

tu·me·fac·tion (tĕwmi-fáksh'n ‖ tŏŏmi-) n. **1. a.** The action or process of puffing or swelling. **b.** A swollen condition. **2.** A puffy or

swollen part. [French, from Latin *tumefactus,* past participle of *tumefacere,* to cause to swell. See **tumefacient.**] **—tu·me·fac·tive** *adj.*
tu·me·fy (téwmi-fī || tōōmi-) *v.* **-fied, -fying, -fies.** *—tr.* To cause to swell. *—intr.* To swell; become tumid. [Old French *tumefier* : Latin *tumēre,* to swell + -FY.]
tu·mes·cent (tew-méss'nt || tōō-) *adj.* Swelling; somewhat tumid. [Latin *tumēscēns* (stem *tumēscent-*), present participle of *tumēscere,* to begin to swell, from *tumēre,* to swell.] **—tu·mes·cence** *n.*
tu·mid (téw-mid || tōō-) *adj.* **1.** Swollen; distended. Said of a bodily part or organ. **2.** Of a bulging shape; protuberant. **3.** Overblown; bombastic: *tumid prose.* [Latin *tumidus,* from *tumēre,* to swell.] **—tu·mid·i·ty** (tew-míddəti || tōō-), **tu·mid·ness** *n.* **—tu·mid·ly** *adv.*
tum·my (túmmi) *n., pl.* **-mies.** *Informal.* The stomach. [Baby-talk variant of STOMACH.]
tu·mour, *U.S.* **tu·mor** (téw-mər || tōō-) *n.* **1.** A noninflammatory abnormal growth arising from existing tissue but growing independently of the normal rate or structural development of such tissue and serving no physiological function. **2.** Any swollen part. [Latin *tumour,* from *tumēre,* to swell.]
tu·mult (téw-mult, -m'lt || tōō-) *n.* **1.** The din and commotion of a great crowd: *the tumult of the marketplace.* **2.** A disorderly commotion or disturbance; especially, a riot or insurrection. **3.** Agitation of the mind or emotions. [Middle English *tumulte,* from Old French, from Latin *tumultus.*]
tu·mul·tu·ar·y (tew-múltew-əri || tōō-) *adj.* Marked by haste, disorder, or confusion. [Latin *tumultuārius,* from *tumultus,* TUMULT.]
tu·mul·tu·ous (tew-múltew-əss || tōō-, tə-) *adj.* **1.** Full of tumult and commotion; noisy; clamorous: *tumultuous applause.* **2.** Making a tumult; turbulent; riotous: *a tumultuous crowd.* **3.** Confusedly or violently agitated: *a tumultuous heart.* **—tu·mul·tu·ous·ly** *adv.* **—tu·mul·tu·ous·ness** *n.*
tu·mu·lus (téw-mew-ləss || tōō-) *n., pl.* **-li** (-lī). An ancient artificial mound; especially, a burial mound or a barrow. [Latin, a raised heap of earth, hillock, tumulus.] **—tu·mu·lar** (-mewlər) *adj.*
tun (tun) *n.* **1.** A large cask for liquids, especially beer or wine. **2.** A measure of capacity for wine and other liquids, usually equivalent to 252 wine gallons. [Middle English *tunne, tonne,* a measure of wine, Old English *tunne,* cask, vat, from Medieval Latin *tunna.*]
tu·na[1] (téw-nə, tōō-) *n., pl.* **-nas** or collectively **tuna. 1. a.** Any of various, often large marine food fishes of the genus *Thunnus* and related genera, many of which, including *T. thynnus* and the albacore, are commercially important sources of tinned fish. Also called "tunny". **b.** Any of several related fishes, such as the bonito. **2.** The tinned or commercially processed flesh of any of these fishes. In this sense, also called "tuna fish". [American Spanish, ultimately from Latin *thunnus.* See **tunny.**]
tu·na[2] (tōō-nə, téw-) *n.* **1.** Any of several tropical American cacti of the genus *Opuntia,* which includes the prickly pears; especially, *O. tuna,* bearing edible red fruit. **2.** The fruit of such a plant. [Spanish, from Taino.]
tu·na[3] (téw-nə || tōō-) *n. N.Z.* A freshwater eel. [Maori.]
tun·a·ble, tune·a·ble (téwn-əb'l || tōōn-) *adj.* **1.** *Archaic.* Tuneful or melodious. **2.** *Rare.* Able to be tuned. **—tun·a·ble·ness** *n.*
tun·dra (túndrə) *n.* An area between the perpetual snow and ice of Arctic regions and the tree line, having a permanently frozen subsoil and supporting low-growing vegetation such as lichens, mosses, dwarf shrubs, and stunted trees. [Russian, from Lapp *tundar*; akin to Finnish *tunturi,* an Arctic hill, a bare hill.]
tune (tewn || tōōn) *n.* **1.** A succession of musical notes forming a melody, especially one of simple and easily remembered character. **2. a.** Correct musical pitch. **b.** The state of being properly adjusted for pitch: *a piano out of tune.* **3. a.** Agreement in pitch: *play in tune with the piano.* **b.** Concord or agreement; harmony: *in tune with the times.* **c.** *Archaic.* Frame of mind; disposition. **4.** *Electronics.* The adjustment of a receiver or circuit for maximum response to a given signal or frequency. **5.** *Archaic.* A musical sound or note. **—call the tune.** To be in a position to control events. **—change (one's) tune.** To change one's approach or attitude. **—to the tune of.** To the sum or amount of.
~v. **tuned, tuning, tunes.** *—tr.* **1.** To put (a musical instrument) in the desired pitch with mechanical adjustments. **2.** To adjust so as to bring into harmony or accord; adapt; attune: *tune oneself to life in the tropics.* **3.** To adjust (an engine) for maximum performance. **4.** To adjust (a radio or television receiver) to receive signals at a particular frequency. **5.** *Archaic.* To utter musically; sing. *—intr.* To become attuned. **—tune in.** To tune a radio or television to receive a particular programme. [Middle English, variant of TONE.]
tune·ful (téwn-f'l || tōōn-) *adj.* **1.** Full of tune; melodious; musical. **2.** Producing musical sounds. **—tune·ful·ly** *adv.* **—tune·ful·ness** *n.*
tune·less (téwn-ləss, -liss || tōōn-) *adj.* **1.** Not melodious or tuneful; unmusical. **2.** Giving no music; silent. **—tune·less·ly** *adv.* **—tune·less·ness** *n.*
tun·er (téwn-ər || tōōn-) *n.* **1.** One that tunes: *a piano tuner.* **2.** A device for tuning; especially, an electronic circuit or device used to select signals at a specific radio frequency for amplification and conversion to sound.
tune up *tr.v.* **1.** To bring (a musical instrument) into proper pitch. **2.** To adjust (a motor or engine) to efficient working order. *—intr.v.* To bring an instrument or set of instruments, as in an orchestra, into proper pitch before a performance.
tune-up (téwn-up || tōōn-) *n.* An adjustment of a motor or engine to put it in the most efficient working order.
tung oil (tung) *n.* A yellow oil extracted from the seeds of the tung tree and used as a drying agent in varnishes and paints and for waterproofing. Also called "Chinese wood oil".
tung·state (túng-stayt) *n.* A chemical compound derived from tungstic acid and containing tungsten with a valency of 6. [TUNGST(EN) + -ATE.]
tung·sten (túng-stən, *rarely* -sten, -stin) *n. Symbol* **W** A hard, brittle, corrosion-resistant, grey to white metallic element extracted from wolframite, scheelite, and other minerals, having the highest melting point and lowest vapour pressure of any metal. Tungsten and its alloys are used in high-temperature structural materials, electrical elements, notably lamp filaments, and instruments requiring thermally compatible glass-to-metal seals. Atomic number 74, atomic weight 183.85, melting point 3 410°C, boiling point 5 927°C, relative density 19.3 (20°C), valencies 2, 3, 4, 5, 6. Also *rare* "wolfram". [Swedish, "heavy stone" : *tung,* heavy, from Old Norse *thungr* + *sten,* from Old Norse *steinn.*] **—tung·sten·ic** (tung-sténnik) *adj.*
tungsten carbide *n.* An extremely hard, fine grey powder with composition WC, used in tools, wear-resistant machine parts, and abrasives.
tungsten lamp *n.* An incandescent electric lamp with a tungsten filament.
tungsten steel *n.* A hard, heat-resistant steel containing tungsten.
tung·stic (túng-stik) *adj.* Of, pertaining to, or containing tungsten, especially with a valency of 6. [From TUNGSTEN.]
tungstic acid *n.* Any of various acids containing tungstites; especially, a powder, H_2WO_4, used in making textiles and plastics.
tung·stite (túng-stīt) *n.* A yellow or yellowish-green mineral, essentially WO_3, resulting from the alteration of tungsten ores. [TUNGST(EN) + -ITE.]
tung tree *n.* Any of several Asian trees of the genus *Aleurites*; especially, *A. cordata,* cultivated for its seeds that yield a commercially valuable drying oil. Also called "tung-oil tree". [Mandarin Chinese *tóng* + TREE.]
Tun·gus (tōōng-gōōss, túng-, -gōōz) *n., pl.* **-guses** or collectively **Tungus. 1.** A member of a Mongoloid people inhabiting eastern Siberia. **2.** The Tungusic language of this people. [Russian *Tunguz,* a Tungus, from Yakut *tungus,* from Turkic *tungus,* pig (probably because many Tungus were pig breeders).] **—Tun·gus** *adj.*
Tun·gus·ic (tōōng-gōōss-ik, tung-, -gōōz-) *n.* A subfamily of the Altaic family of languages, including the Tungus and Manchu languages, spoken in eastern Siberia and northern Manchuria.
~adj. Of or pertaining to the Tungus people or to Tungusic.
tu·nic (téw-nik || tōō-) *n.* **1. a.** A loose-fitting garment, sleeved or sleeveless, extending to the knees and worn by women and men especially in ancient Greece and Rome. **b.** A medieval surcoat. **2. a.** A long plain close-fitting jacket, usually with a high stiff collar, forming part of a military or police uniform. **b.** A long plain sleeved or sleeveless blouse worn over a skirt by women. **c.** A **gymslip** *(see).* **3.** *Anatomy.* A coat or layer enveloping an organ or part. **4.** *Botany.* A membranous outer covering, as of a seed. **5.** A tunicle. [Latin *tunica,* a sheath, tunic, from a Phoenician source, from Aramaic *kittūnā,* akin to Hebrew *kəthōnet.* See also **chiton.**]
tu·ni·ca (téw-ni-kə || tōō-) *n., pl.* **-cae** (-kee, -see, -kī). *Anatomy.* An integument; a tunic. [New Latin, from Latin, TUNIC.]
tu·ni·cate (téwni-kət, -kit, -kayt || tōōni-) *n.* Any of various chordate marine animals of the subphylum Urochordata (or Tunicata), having a cylindrical or globular body enclosed in a tough outer covering, or tunic, and including the sea squirts and salps.
~adj. **1.** Of or pertaining to the tunicates. **2.** *Anatomy.* Having a tunic. **3.** *Botany.* Having concentric layers, as does the bulb of an onion. [Latin *tunicātus,* past participle of *tunicāre,* to clothe with a tunic, from *tunica,* TUNIC.]
tu·ni·cle (téw-nik'l || tōō-) *n.* A short vestment worn over the alb by a subdeacon or with the dalmatic by a bishop or cardinal. Also called "tunic". [Middle English, from Latin *tunicula,* diminutive of *tunica,* TUNIC.]
tuning fork *n.* A small two-pronged instrument that when struck produces a sound of fixed pitch.
Tu·nis (téw-niss || tōō-). Capital of Tunisia. Lying in the northeast of the country on a lagoon inland from the Gulf of Tunis, it is southwest of the site of Carthage.
Tu·nis·i·a, Republic of (tew-nízzi-ə, -níssi- || tōō-). Largely desert country of North Africa. The economy is dominated by oil, which accounts for more than a third of the country's exports. Despite little farmland, 40 per cent of workers are in agriculture, and olive oil is a major export. A French protectorate from 1881, Tunisia became independent in 1956. A year later, the Bey was deposed, and an Arab republic declared. Area, 163 610 square kilometres (63,170 square miles). Population, 9,090,000. Capital, Tunis. **—Tu·ni·si·an** *n. & adj.* See map, next page.
tun·nel (túnn'l) *n.* **1.** A passage excavated underground, through a hill or mountain, or under a river or sea, especially one for a road or railway. **2.** An underground gallery in a mine. **3.** An animal's burrow. **4.** *Archaic.* The flue of a chimney.
~v. **tunnelled** or *U.S.* **tunneled, -nelling** or *U.S.* **-neling, -nels.** *—tr.* **1.** To make a tunnel under or through. **2.** To make by or as if by excavating: *tunnel a passage; tunnel one's way out.* *—intr.* **1.** To make a tunnel. **2.** *Physics.* To pass through a barrier by the tunnel effect. Used of a particle. [Middle English *tonel,* a pipelike net for catching birds, from Old French *ton(n)el,* a cask, from *tonne,* a tun, from Medieval Latin *tunna, tonna,* TUN.] **—tun·nel·ler** *n.*
tunnel diode *n. Electronics.* A semiconductor diode with a very

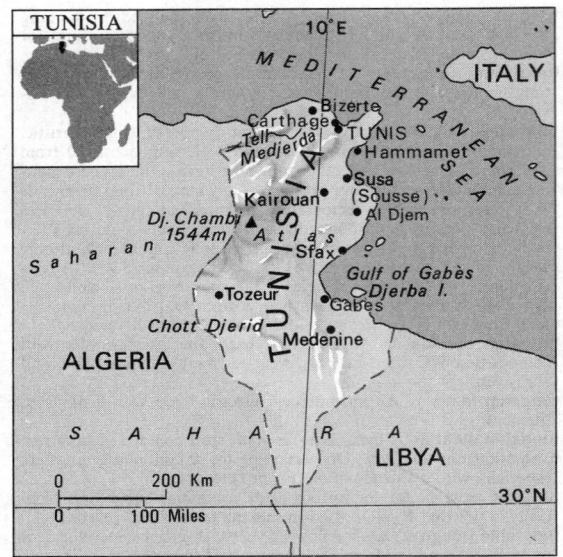

TUNISIA

narrow, heavily doped, p-n junction across which electrons travel by the tunnel effect. Also called "Esaki diode".

tunnel disease *n. Medicine.* **Decompression sickness** (see).

tunnel effect *n. Physics.* An effect, explained by quantum mechanics, by which a particle can pass through a barrier even though it does not have enough energy to overcome the barrier according to classical mechanics.

tunnel vision *n.* 1. A defect or restriction of lateral vision. 2. *Informal.* An inability to take a broad or long-term view of a situation because of obsessive concentration on a single one of its problems or aspects.

tun·ny (túnni) *n., pl.* **-nies** or collectively **tunny.** A fish, the tuna (*see*). [French *thon*, from Provençal *ton*, from Latin *thunnus*, from Greek *thunnos*, akin to Hebrew *tannîn*, "great sea monster".]

tup (tup) *n.* 1. *Chiefly British.* A male sheep; a ram. 2. A heavy metal body; especially, the head of a power hammer.
~*tr.v.* **tupped, tupping, tups.** To copulate with (a ewe). Used of a ram. [Middle English *toupe, tup(pe)†*, a ram.]

Tu·pa·ma·ro (tŏopa-maárŏ) *n., pl.* **-ros.** A member of an extreme left-wing urban guerrilla organisation in Uruguay. [After *Tupac Amaru,* 18th-century Peruvian Indian leader of a rebellion against the Spanish.] —**Tu·pa·ma·ro** *adj.*

tu·pe·lo (téw-pi-lŏ, -pa- ‖ tŏo-) *n., pl.* **-los.** 1. Any of several trees of the genus *Nyssa;* especially, *N. aquatica,* of the southeastern United States, having soft, light wood. 2. The wood of any of these trees. [Creek *ito opilwa,* "swamp tree" : *ito,* tree + *opilwa,* swamp.]

Tu·pi (tŏo-pée, tŏopi) *n., pl.* **-pis** or collectively **Tupi.** 1. A member of a group of South American Indian peoples living along the coast of Brazil, in the Amazon valley, and in Paraguay. 2. The language of these peoples, a branch of Tupi-Guarani. —**Tu·pi, Tu·pi·an** (-ən) *adj.*

Tu·pi-Gua·ra·ni (tŏo-pée-gwáəra-née, tŏopi-) *n.* A family of languages spoken throughout large areas of coastal Brazil, the Amazon valley, and northeastern South America. —**Tu·pi-Gua·ra·ni, Tu·pi-Gua·ra·ni·an** *adj.*

tuppence. *British Informal.* Variant of **twopence.**

tuppenny. *Chiefly British Informal.* Variant of **twopenny.**

tup·pen·ny ha'pen·ny (túp-ni háyp-ni, túppəni) *adj. Informal.* Of poor quality or of little value.

Tupperware (túppər-wair) *n.* A trademark for a range of polythene containers used especially in the home for storing food.

tu quo·que (téw kwŏkwi, tŏo, kwŏkwi) *n. Latin.* A retort accusing an accuser of a similar fault or offence. [Latin, "you also".]

turaco. Variant of **touraco.**

Tu·ra·ni·an (tewr-ráyni-ən, -raáni- ‖ tŏo-) *adj.* 1. A language group, **Ural-Altaic** (*see*). 2. A member of any of the peoples who speak languages of this group. [Persian *Tūrān,* region north of the Oxus River.] —**Tu·ra·ni·an** *adj.*

tur·ban (túrbən) *n.* 1. A man's headdress of Muslim origin but also worn by Sikhs and some Hindus, consisting of a long scarf of linen, cotton, or silk wound round the head or a cap. 2. Any hat or headdress resembling a turban; especially, a type of brimless hat worn by women. [French *turbant, tolliban,* from Italian *turbante, tolipante,* from Turkish *tül(i)bend,* Persian *dulband†*.] —**tur·baned** *adj.*

tur·ba·ry (túrbəri) *n., pl.* **-ries.** 1. A place where peat can be dug; a peat bog. 2. *Law.* In England, the right to dig peat or turf on common land or someone else's ground. [Middle English *turbary(e),* turf land, peat bog, from Anglo-French, from Old French *t(o)urberie,* Medieval Latin *turbāria,* from *turba,* turf, from Germanic.]

tur·bel·la·ri·an (túr-bi-láiri-ən, -bə-) *n.* Any of various chiefly aquatic ciliate flatworms of the class Turbellaria. [New Latin *Turbellaria,* from Latin *turbellae* (plural), bustle, stir (their cilia vibrate and produce little whirls in the water), from *turba,* turmoil, uproar.

See **turbid.**] —**tur·bel·la·ri·an** *adj.*

tur·bid (túrbid) *adj.* 1. Containing sediment or foreign particles stirred up or suspended; muddy; cloudy: *turbid water.* 2. Heavy, dark, or dense, as smoke or fog. 3. In turmoil; muddled: *the turbid life of Bombay.* [Latin *turbidus,* wild, confused, muddy, from *turba,* turmoil, uproar, probably from Greek *turbē,* disorder.] —**tur·bid·i·ty** (tur-bíddəti), **tur·bid·ness** *n.* —**tur·bid·ly** *adv.*

tur·bi·nal (túrbin'l) *adj.* Also **tur·bi·nate** (túrbi-nət, -nit, -nayt). 1. Having the shape of a cone resting on its apex. 2. Having the shape of a scroll.
~*n. Anatomy.* A turbinate bone. [Latin *turbō* (stem *turbin-*), a spinning thing, top. See **turbine.**]

tur·bi·nate (túrbi-nət, -nit, -nayt) *adj.* Also **tur·bi·nat·ed** (-naytid). 1. Variant of **turbinal.** 2. *Zoology.* Spiral and decreasing sharply in diameter from base to apex. Said of a shell. 3. *Anatomy.* Designating a small scroll-like bone that extends horizontally along the lateral wall of the nasal passage. [Latin *turbinātus,* from *turbō* (stem *turbin-*), a top. See **turbine.**]

tur·bine (túr-bĭn, -bìn) *n.* Any of various machines in which the kinetic energy of a moving fluid is converted to rotational energy by the impulse or reaction of the fluid with a series of buckets or blades arrayed about the circumference of a wheel or cylinder. See **gas turbine, impulse turbine, reaction turbine.** [French, from Latin *turbō* (stem *turbin-*), a spinning thing, top, whirlwind, perhaps from Greek *turbē,* disorder.]

tur·bit (túrbit) *n.* Any of a breed of domestic pigeons having a small crested head and a ruffled breast. [Perhaps from Latin *turbō,* top (see **turbine**), referring to its shape.]

tur·bo (túrbō) *n., pl.* **-os.** A car or other vehicle with an engine fitted with a turbocharger.

turbo– *comb. form.* Indicates turbine, or pertaining to or driven by a turbine; for example, **turbojet.** [From TURBINE.]

tur·bo·charg·er (túrbō-chaarjər) *n.* A device that uses the exhaust gas of an internal-combustion engine to drive a turbine that in turn drives a supercharger attached to the engine.

tur·bo·elec·tric (túrbō-i-léktrik, -ə-) *adj.* Designating, pertaining to, or using electricity produced by a turbine.

tur·bo·fan (túrbō-fǎn, -fan) *n.* 1. A turbojet engine in which a fan supplements the total thrust by forcing air diverted from the main engine directly into the hot turbine exhaust. 2. An aircraft in which such an engine is used.

tur·bo·gen·er·ator (túrbō-jénnə-raytər) *n.* A large electric generator in a power station driven by a turbine.

tur·bo·jet (túrbō-jét, -jet) *n.* 1. A jet engine having a turbine-driven compressor and developing thrust from the exhaust of hot gases. 2. An aircraft in which such an engine is used.

tur·bo·prop (túrbō-próp, -prop) *n.* 1. A turbojet engine used to drive an external propeller. Also called "prop-jet". 2. An aircraft in which such an engine is used. [Short for *turbopropeller.*]

tur·bo·ram·jet (túrbō-rám-jet) *n.* 1. A turbojet engine that at high speeds compresses air taken in as a ramjet and increases exhaust velocities with an afterburner. 2. An aircraft in which such an engine is used.

tur·bo·su·per·charg·er (túrbō-sŏo-pər-chaarjər, -séw-) *n.* A supercharger that uses an exhaust-driven turbine to maintain air-intake pressure in high-altitude aircraft.

tur·bot (túrbət) *n., pl.* **-bots** or collectively **turbot.** 1. A European flatfish, *Scophthalmus maximus,* prized as food. 2. Any of various similar or related flatfishes. [Middle English, from Old French, probably from Old Swedish *törnbut,* turbot, "thorn-flatfish" (presumably referring to its shape), from *törn,* thorn + *but,* flat fish.]

tur·bu·la·tor (túrbew-laytər) *n.* Any device designed to cause turbulence in fluids. [From TURBULENT.]

tur·bu·lence (túrbewlənss) *n.* 1. The state or quality of being agitated, violently disturbed, or in commotion. 2. Turbulent flow. 3. Disturbances in the atmosphere, such as air pockets and currents.

tur·bu·lent (túrbewlənt) *adj.* 1. Violently agitated or disturbed: *turbulent rapids.* 2. Having a restless, uncertain, or chaotic character; stormy: *a turbulent period of history.* 3. Inclined to unrest or disorder; unruly; tumultuous. [Latin *turbulentus,* from *turba,* confusion. See **turbid.**] —**tur·bu·lent·ly** *adv.*

turbulent flow *n.* The motion of a fluid having local velocities and pressures that fluctuate randomly. Also called "turbulence". Compare **laminar flow, streamline flow.**

Turcoman. Variant of **Turkoman.**

turd (turd) *n.* 1. *Vulgar.* A piece of excrement. 2. *Vulgar Slang.* A worthless or contemptible person. [Old English *tord.*]

tu·reen (tə-réen, tewr-, tŏo-) *n.* A broad, deep, often oval, dish with a lid used for serving soups, stews, or the like. [Earlier *ter(r)ene,* from French *terrine,* "earthen vessel", from Old French, feminine of *terrin,* from Vulgar Latin *terrīnus,* from Latin *terra,* earth.]

turf (turf) *n., pl.* **turfs** or archaic **turves** (turvz). 1. A surface layer of earth containing a dense growth of grass and its matted roots; sod. 2. A piece cut from such a layer of earth or sod. 3. A piece of peat that is burned for use as fuel. 4. *Slang.* A bailiwick; a manor. —**the turf.** 1. A racecourse. 2. The sport or business of racing horses; the world of racing. —**turf out.** *British Informal.* To throw out; expel; eject. [Middle English *turf,* Old English *turf.*] —**turf·y** *adj.*

turf accountant *n. British.* A bookmaker (*see*).

Tur·ge·nev (toor-gyáyn-yef, tur-, -gáyn-, -yev), **Ivan Sergeyevich** (1818–83). Russian writer. His collection of stories, *A Sportsman's Sketches* (1852), contributed towards the emancipation of the serfs. His novels, such as *Fathers and Children* (1862), are eloquent portrayals of the ineffectual Russian gentry.

tur·ges·cence (tur-jéss'nss) *n.* **1.** The process of swelling up, or the condition of being swollen. **2.** Pomposity; self-importance. [Latin *turgēscens* (stem *turgēscent-*), present participle of *turgēscere*, inceptive of *turgēre*, to be swollen. See turgid.] —**tur·ges·cent** *adj.*

tur·gid (túrjid) *adj.* **1.** Distended; swollen; bloated. **2.** Excessively ornate in style or language; grandiloquent. **3.** Fully expanded from water intake. Said of plants. [Latin *turgidus*, from *turgēre†*, to be swollen, swell.] —**tur·gid·i·ty** (tur-jíddati), **tur·gid·ness** *n.* —**tur·gid·ly** *adv.*

tur·gor (túr-gər, -gawr) *n. Biology.* The normal fullness or tension produced by the fluid content of blood vessels, capillaries, and plant or animal cells. The maintenance of turgor is the primary method of support in herbaceous plants. [Late Latin, from Latin *turgēre*, to be swollen. See turgid.]

Tu·rin (tëwr-rín, tew- ‖ tōō-). *Italian* **Tor·i·no** (to-réenō). City of northwestern Italy. The capital of Piedmont and of Turin province, it was founded by the Romans at the confluence of the Po and Dora Riparia rivers. It is the former capital of the Kingdom of Sardinia (1720), and of Italy (1861–65). The 15th century cathedral has a chapel containing the "Shroud of Turin", considered by some to be the cloth in which the body of Christ was wrapped after the Crucifixion.

tur·i·on (tëwr-i-ən, tóor-) *n.* A bud produced by many aquatic plants that is shed from the parent plant and remains dormant until the spring. [French, from Latin *turiō* (stem *turiōn-*), shoot.]

Turk (turk) *n.* **1.** A native or inhabitant of Turkey. **2.** A member of any of the Turkic-speaking peoples who originated in Turkestan. **3.** *Informal.* A brutal or tyrannical person.

Turk. Turkey; Turkish.

Tur·ka·na, Lake (toor-káana, tur-). Formerly **Lake Rudolf.** Lake of east Africa. The continent's fifth largest lake, approximately 250 kilometres (185 miles) long and up to 55 kilometres (34 miles) wide, it lies in the Great Rift Valley on the borders of Kenya, Ethiopia, and Sudan.

Turkestan, Chinese. See Xinjiang Uigur Zizhiqu.

tur·key (túrki) *n., pl.* **-keys** or collectively **turkey.** **1. a.** A large North American bird, *Meleagris gallopavo*, that has brownish plumage and a bare, wattled head and neck and is widely domesticated for food. **b.** A related bird, *Agriocharis ocellata*, of Mexico and Central America. **2.** *U.S. Slang.* **a.** A film, play, or other production that fails; a flop. **b.** An inept or undesirable person; a misfit. —**talk turkey.** *Chiefly U.S. Informal.* To discuss in a straightforward and direct manner. [Short for TURKEY COCK.]

Tur·key, Republic of (túrki). State in southeastern Europe and western Asia, mostly covering the Anatolian plateau (Asia Minor). Farming is the main occupation, cotton, tobacco, and textile yarns and fabrics providing 66 per cent of exports. Turkey has reserves of coal, lignite, oil, and iron, and chrome is exported. Tourism and expatriate workers are important sources of foreign exchange. The country was the centre of the Ottoman Empire for almost 700 years, but became a republic in 1923. There were several military governments from 1946, but parliamentary democracy has ruled since 1983. Turkey is now developing relations with the Turkic former constituent republics of the U.S.S.R. Relations with Greece are uneasy because of Cyprus and the disputed border. Istanbul is the largest city and chief port. Area, 779 452 square kilometres (300,948 square miles). Population, 62,690,000. Capital, Ankara.

turkey buzzard *n.* A New World vulture, *Cathartes aura*, having dark plumage and bare red head and neck similar to that of the turkey. Also called "turkey vulture".

turkey cock *n.* **1.** A male turkey. **2.** *Informal.* A strutting, conceited man. [Originally applied to the guinea fowl (with which the American bird was later mistakenly identified), first imported by the Portuguese from Africa by way of Turkey.]

Turkey red *n.* A brilliant red. [The colour was often used in cotton cloth manufactured in Turkey.] —**Tur·key-red** (túrki-réd, -red) *adj.*

turkey trot *n.* A ragtime dance of the early 20th century, characterised by a springy walk with the feet well apart and a swinging up-and-down movement of the shoulders.

Tur·ki (túr-kee) *adj.* **1.** Of or pertaining to Turkic. **2.** Of or pertaining to the Turkic-speaking peoples, especially those speaking an Eastern Turkic language.
~*n.* Any Turkic language or Turkic speaker.

Tur·kic (túrkik) *n.* A subdivision of the Altaic family of languages, including Turkish, Turkoman, Azerbaidzhani, Tatar, Uzbek, Uigur, Kirgiz, Karakalpak, Chuvash, Chagatai, and Yakut.
~*adj.* **1.** Of or pertaining to the language or people of Turkey. **2.** Of or pertaining to Turkic.

Turk·ish (túrkish) *adj.* *Abbr.* **Turk.** **1.** Of or pertaining to Turkey or the Turks. **2.** Of or pertaining to the Turkic language of Turkey.
~*n.* The Turkic language of Turkey. When written in the Arabic script, as it was until 1930, it is generally referred to as "Ottoman Turkish" or "Osmanli".

Turkish bath *n.* **1.** A steam bath inducing heavy perspiration, usually followed by a shower and often a massage. **2.** *Often plural.* An establishment where such bathing facilities are available.

Turkish coffee *n.* Strong, sweet black coffee made from very finely ground beans and served in tiny cups.

Turkish delight *n.* A gelatinous sweet of Turkish origin, cut into cubes and dredged in icing sugar.

Turkish Empire. See Ottoman Empire.

Turkish Republic of North Cyprus. The northern part of Cyprus, occupied by Turkey in 1974. It is recognised by no nation other than Turkey.

Turkish towel *n.* A thick rough terry towel.

Tur·ki·stan or **Tur·ke·stan** (túrki-staán, -stán). Region of central Asia. A crossroads for trade and conquest, it is now divided between China, Afghanistan, Kazakhstan, Uzbekistan, Turkmenistan, the Kyrgyz Republic, and Tajikistan.

Turk·men·i·stan (túrk-ménni-staán, -stán). Also **Turk·me·ni·a** (-méeni-ə). Former constituent republic of the U.S.S.R., lying east of the Caspian Sea, and established as a republic in 1925. Largely consisting of the desert of the Kara Kum, it has a population concentrated around oases, where subsistence farming is the chief occupation. Area, 488 100 square kilometres (188,457 square miles). Population, 4,570,000. Capital, Ashgabat. See map at **Commonwealth of Independent States.** —**Turk·me·ni·an** *n. & adj.*

Tur·ko·man, Tur·co·man (túrkə-mən, -man, -maan) *n., pl.* **-mans.** Also **Turk·man** (túrk-) (for sense 1), **Turk·men** (-men) (for sense 2). **1.** Any of a formerly nomadic people inhabiting Turkmenistan, Uzbekistan, and Kazakhstan. **2.** The Turkic language of this people. —**Tur·ko·man, Tur·co·man** *adj.*

Turks and Cai·cos Islands (káy-koss). Two groups of islands in the Bahamas, western Atlantic Ocean, forming a self-governing British Overseas Territory. Grand Turk is the seat of government.

Turk's-cap lily (túrks-káp) *n.* Any of various cultivated lilies having colourful, turban-shaped flowers, such as the **martagon** (*see*).

Turk's-head (túrks-héd) *n. Nautical.* A turban-shaped knot made by winding a smaller rope around a larger one.

Tur·ku (tóor-kōō). *Swedish* **Å·bo** (áw-bōō). Provincial capital of southwest Finland, the country's capital until 1812. An ice-free Baltic port, it exports timber and dairy products.

Turkut. See **Old Turkic.**
tur·mer·ic (túrmərik) *n.* **1.** A plant, *Curcuma longa,* of India, having yellow flowers and an aromatic rootstock. **2.** The powdered rootstock of this plant, used to flavour or colour food and as a yellow dye. **3.** Any of several other plants having similar roots. [Earlier *tarmaret,* from Old French *terre mérite,* from Medieval Latin *terra merita,* "meritorious earth", alteration of a native name.]
turmeric paper *n.* Paper saturated with turmeric and used as an indicator for the presence of alkalis, which turn the paper brown, or for boric acid, which turns it red-brown.
tur·moil (túr-moyl) *n.* A state of violent agitation or utter confusion; tumult. [16th century : origin obscure.]
turn (turn) *v.* **turned, turning, turns.** *—tr.* **1.** To cause to move around a central point; cause to rotate or revolve: *The wind turns the sails of the windmill.* **2.** To cause to move around in order to achieve a desired result: *turn the handle to open.* **3.** To alter or control the functioning of (a mechanical device, for example), especially by means of a rotating or similar movement: *turn the radio down.* **4.** To perform or accomplish by rotating or revolving: *turn a somersault.* **5. a.** To change the position of so that the underside becomes the upperside: *turn the steak.* **b.** To dig or plough (soil) to bring the undersoil to the surface. **c.** To reverse the material of (a collar or cuff, for example) so that the inner side becomes the outer. **d.** To reverse or fundamentally disturb the order, disposition, or character of: *turned the room upside down in her search; turned the argument completely on its head.* **6. a.** To produce a rounded shape in (wood or metal, for example) by applying a cutting tool while rotating on a lathe. **b.** To produce a rounded form in by any means: *turn a heel in knitting a sock.* **c.** To give shape or form to by rotating: *turn a vase on a potter's wheel.* **d.** To give distinctive, artistic, or elegant form to: *turn a phrase.* **7.** To weigh in the mind; think over; ponder. Often used with *over*: *turn an idea over.* **8. a.** To change the position of by moving through an arc of a circle: *turned her chair to face me.* **b.** To change the position of by folding, twisting, or bending: *turn the blankets down.* **c.** To change the position of so as to show another side: *turn the page.* **d.** To injure by twisting: *turn an ankle.* **e.** To upset or make nauseated: *That turns my stomach.* **9. a.** To change the direction or course of: *turn the car round.* **b.** To cause (a cricket ball) to change direction on pitching; spin. **10.** To divert or deflect: *turn aside a blow.* **11.** To reverse the course of; cause to retreat: *turn the enemy.* **12.** To make a course around or about: *turn the corner.* **13.** To change, affect, or influence the character or tendency of: *a speech that turned the election.* **14.** To disturb the emotional or mental balance of; unsettle: *"Sudden prosperity had turned Garrick's head."* (Lord Macaulay). **15.** To set or point in a specified way or direction: *turned her back on them.* **16.** To set going in a specified direction; direct: *turned our steps back home.* **17.** To aim or focus; train: *turn a spotlight on the intruders.* **18.** To direct (the attention, interest, or mind, for example) towards or away from something: *turn a deaf ear.* **19.** To devote or apply (oneself or one's efforts, for example) to something: *turned my hand to a bit of decorating.* **20.** To reach or surpass (a specified age, time, or amount): *only just turned thirty.* **21.** To cause to act or go against; make antagonistic. **22.** To send, drive, or let go: *threatened to turn us out; turn the dog loose.* **23.** To pour, let fall, or otherwise release (contents) from a receptacle: *turn the dough onto a floured board.* **24.** To make sour; curdle: *The milk has turned.* **25.** To affect or change the colour of: *Autumn turns the leaves.* **26.** To change or convert; transform. Often used with *into*: *turned the cinema into a bingo hall.* **27.** To cause to take on a specified character, nature, or appearance: *Worry turned her hair grey.* **28. a.** To make a bend or curve in: *turn a bar of steel.* **b.** To blunt or dull (the edge of a cutting instrument). **29.** To earn: *turn an honest penny.* *—intr.* **1.** To move round an axis or centre; rotate; revolve. **2.** To appear to revolve or whirl, as in dizziness or giddiness: *My head keeps turning.* **3.** To roll from side to side or back and forth: *tossed and turned all night.* **4.** To operate a lathe. **5.** To change one's position so as to face in a different or opposite direction: *turned away at the sight; Everyone turned round as I entered.* **6. a.** To move so as to follow a different or opposite course; take a new direction: *turned and ran; turned into a side street.* **b.** To change direction on pitching. Used of a cricket ball. **7.** To change in behaviour or attitude so as to become hostile or antagonistic: *turned against her former colleagues.* **8.** To attack suddenly and violently with no apparent motive: *The dog turned on me.* **9.** To direct one's attention, interest, or thought towards or away from something. **10.** To adopt a new religion; become converted. **11.** To switch one's loyalty from one side or party to another. **12.** To have recourse for help, support, or information: *didn't know who to turn to; turned to drugs.* **13.** To devote or apply oneself to something, as to a field of study. **14. a.** To depend for its outcome; rely: *Success turns on the effectiveness of our advertising.* **b.** To have a particular focal point or central feature; hinge: *The debate turned on the issue of subsidies.* **15. a.** To undergo a change: *Our luck finally turned.* **b.** To change by passing from one state into another; become transformed: *Our surprise turned to horror.* **c.** To change so as to assume the specified nature, role, or characteristics; become: *turned traitor; It suddenly turned cold; turn into a pumpkin.* **16.** To become sour; curdle or ferment. **17.** To change colour. **18.** To become dull or blunt after bending back. Used of the edge of a cutting instrument. **—turn down. 1.** To reduce the speed, volume, intensity, or flow of. **2.** *Informal.* To reject or refuse (an offer or proposal, for example). **—turn in. 1. a.** To deliver over, as to the police: *turned herself in.* **b.** *Chiefly U.S.* To hand in; give in: *turn in an income-tax return.* **2.** To register or produce: *turned in a creditable performance.* **3.** *Informal.* To go to bed. **—turn to.** To begin work; apply oneself to a task.
~n. **1.** An act of turning or being turned around an axis or centre; a rotation or revolution. **2.** The act or an action of turning to face or move in a different or opposite direction: *a right turn.* **3.** A point at which something turns or turns off; a bend or junction; a turning: *take the first turn on the left.* **4.** A point of change in time: *the turn of the century.* **5.** A deviation from an existing course or trend; a new departure or development: *took a turn for the worse.* **6.** A right, duty, or opportunity to do something allotted to an individual according to some roster or implicitly agreed order of succession: *My turn to do the washing up.* **7.** A period of participation in something: *a turn at creative writing.* **8.** A characteristic mood, style, or habit; a natural inclination: *a speculative turn of mind.* **9.** A propensity or adeptness: *a turn for carpentry.* **10.** A deed or action having a specified effect on another: *One good turn deserves another.* **11.** Advantage or purpose: *It served her turn.* **12.** A short walk or excursion: *a turn in the park.* **13.** A twist or other distortion in shape. **14.** The condition of being twisted or wound. **15. a.** A winding of one thing about another. **b.** A single wind or convolution, as of wire upon a spool. **16.** *Music.* A figure or ornament consisting of four notes in rapid succession, the second and fourth of which are identical, with the first a degree above, and the third a degree below. **17.** A distinctive form of style or expression: *a nice turn of phrase.* **18.** An attack of illness or severe nervousness; a fit; a spell. **19.** *Informal.* A momentary shock or scare: *I had quite a turn when I heard the news.* **20. a.** A brief performance, as in the theatre or circus; an act: *a music-hall turn.* **b.** A performer in such an act. **21. a.** A transaction on the stock market involving both a sale and a purchase. **b.** The profit made by a jobber on such a transaction, being the difference between the buying and selling prices of a stock or commodity. **22.** *Australian.* A party. **—at every turn.** At every point or moment; continually. **—by turns.** Alternately; one after another. **—in turn.** In the proper order or sequence. **—out of turn. 1.** Not in the proper order or sequence. **2.** At an inappropriate time or in an inappropriate manner. **—take turns.** To take part or do something in order, one after another. **—to a turn.** To a precise degree; perfectly: *The roast was done to a turn.* [Middle English *turnen, tornen,* from Old English *tyrnan, turnian* and Old French *to(u)rner,* both from Latin *tornāre,* to turn in a lathe, round off, from *tornus,* a lathe, from Greek *tornos,* tool for drawing a circle, circle, lathe.]
Synonyms: *turn, rotate, revolve, gyrate, spin, whirl, circle, eddy, swirl, swivel, roll.*
turn·a·bout (túrn-ə-bowt) *n.* **1.** The act of turning round and facing or moving in the opposite direction. **2.** A shift or reversal in opinion, policy, or allegiance.
turn·a·round (túrn-ə-rownd) *n. Chiefly U.S.* **Turnround** *(see).*
turn bridge *n.* A **swing bridge** *(see).*
turn·buck·le (túrn-buck'l) *n.* A metal coupling device consisting of an oblong piece internally threaded at both ends, into each end of which a threaded rod is screwed. It is used for tightening a rod or wire rope.
turn·coat (túrn-kōt) *n.* One who traitorously switches allegiance.
turn·er (túrnər) *n.* One who or that which turns; specifically, a person who works a lathe.
Tur·ner (túrnər), **J(oseph) M(allord) W(illiam)** (1775–1851). British painter. Perhaps the most original of English painters, his abstract treatment of light, colour, and space was taken up by the French impressionists. His works include *The Fighting Téméraire* (1839), and *Rain, Steam and Speed* (1844).
turn·er·y (túrnəri) *n., pl.* **-ies. 1.** The work or workshop of a lathe operator. **2.** Objects made on a lathe.
turn·ing (túrning) *n.* **1. a.** A deviation or change of course. **b.** A point at which a road or path turns off from another: *missed our turning and got lost.* **2.** The shaping of metal or wood on a lathe.
turning circle *n.* The circle with the smallest circumference within which a motor vehicle can turn.
turning point *n.* **1.** A point at which significant changes occur or crucial decision must be made; a decisive moment. **2.** *Mathematics.* A maximum or minimum point on a curve.
tur·nip (túrnip) *n.* **1.** A widely cultivated plant, *Brassica rapa,* native to the Old World, having a large, edible yellow or white root. **2.** The root of this plant, eaten as a vegetable. **3.** Any of several similar or related plants. **4.** *Scottish & Northern English.* A **swede** *(see).* [Earlier *turnepe* : *tur-* (origin and meaning unknown) + *nepe,* turnip, from Middle English *nepe,* Old English *nǣp,* from Latin *nāpus* (see **napiform**).]
turnip cabbage *n.* A vegetable, **kohlrabi** *(see).*
turn·key (túrn-kee) *n., pl.* **-keys.** The keeper of the keys in a prison; a jailer.
~adj. Chiefly U.S. Supplied, or requiring the supply of something, in a fully equipped or operational state: *a turnkey apartment.*
turn off *tr.v.* **1.** To stop the operation, activity, or flow of; shut off or switch off. **2.** *British.* To discharge (an employee). **3.** *Informal.* **a.** To fail to interest sexually. **b.** To annoy, bore, or repel: *This continuous chatter turns me off.* *—intr.v.* To leave a path or road at a particular point and take another: *turn off at junction 14.*
turn·off (túrn-off, -awf) *n.* **1.** The point where a road or path branches off from the main thoroughfare. **2.** *Slang.* Something that is irritating or repellent, especially sexually.

turn on *tr.v.* **1. a.** To cause to operate or flow by turning a switch or control: *turn on the television.* **b.** *Informal.* To produce as if by turning a switch: *turn on the charm.* **2.** *Informal.* **a.** To excite sexually. **b.** To produce a pleasurable response in; delight or stimulate. *—intr.v. Slang.* To take a hallucinogenic or narcotic drug.

turn·on (túrn-on || -awn) *n. Slang.* Someone or something that excites, stimulates, or interests, especially sexually.

turn out *tr.v.* **1.** To switch off (a light, for example). **2.** To produce or manufacture. **3.** To empty the contents of: *turn out the attic.* **4.** To dress or equip. **5.** To put (a horse) out to pasture for rest or retirement. *—intr.v.* **1.** To come out or assemble, as for a public event or entertainment. **2. a.** To be found or proved, as after experience or trial: *It turned out that she had been lying all along.* **b.** To come to be in the end; end up: *turned out to be a fine day.* **3.** *Informal.* To get out of bed.

turn·out (túrn-owt) *n.* **1.** The number of people at a gathering; attendance. **2.** The proportion of registered voters actually voting in a given election. **3.** The amount of goods produced; output. **4.** The way in which a person or group is dressed or equipped. **5.** An outfit of a carriage with its horse or horses; an equipage.

turn over *tr.v.* **1.** To transfer or hand over, especially to the police. **2.** To cause (an internal-combustion engine) to go through at least one cycle. **3. a.** To buy and resell (stock) or invest and get back (capital) in the course of trade. **b.** To do business to the extent or amount of: *turn over millions every year.* *—intr.v.* To go through at least one cycle. Used of an internal-combustion engine.

turn·o·ver (túrn-ōvər) *n.* **1.** The act of turning over; an upset or overthrow. **2.** A small pastry made by covering one half of a circular piece of dough with fruit, preserves, or other filling, and sealing the other half over on top. **3. a.** The number of times a particular stock of goods is sold and restocked during a given period of time. **b.** The rate at which a stock of goods is turned over. **4. a.** The total amount or value of business transacted during a given period of time. **b.** The ratio of this amount to the value of a company's issued shares, showing the number of times the company's share-capital has been turned over in the given period. Also called "capital turnover". **5. a.** The number of workers taken on by an employer to replace those who have left. **b.** The ratio of this number to the number of employed workers.
~adj. Capable of being folded down or over: *a turnover collar.*

turn·pike (túrn-pīk) *n. Abbr.* **tpk. 1.** Formerly in Britain: **a.** A tollgate. **b.** A road whose upkeep was paid for by tolls levied on its users. **2.** In the United States, a motorway whose users pay a toll. [Middle English *turnepike,* a revolving barrier furnished with spikes used to block a road : *turnen,* to TURN + PIKE.]

turn·round (túrn-rownd || *West Indies also* -rungd) *n.* Also *U.S.* **turnaround. 1.** A reversal or major change of direction: *a turnround in the economy.* **2. a.** The time needed to complete the process whereby a ship, aircraft, train, or the like arrives, unloads, takes on fuel, passengers, and cargo, and is ready to leave again. **6.** The time needed to complete any manufacturing or industrial process.

turn·sole (túrn-sōl) *n.* Any plant, such as the heliotrope, that moves or is believed to move in response to the Sun. [Middle English *turnesole,* from Old French *tournesol,* Italian *tornasole* : *tornare,* from Latin *tornāre,* to TURN + *sole,* the Sun, from Latin *sōl.*]

turn·spit (túrn-spit) *n.* One that turns a roasting spit; especially, a small dog formerly used in a treadmill to turn a roasting spit.

turn·stile (túrn-stīl) *n.* **1.** A mechanical device used to control passage from one public area to another, typically consisting of several horizontal arms supported by and radially projecting from a central vertical post. **2.** A similar structure that permits the passage of persons, but not of horses or cattle.

turn·stone (túrn-stōn) *n.* A wading bird, *Arenaria interpres,* having tortoiseshell-coloured plumage in summer, and dull brown in winter. [From its habit of turning over stones in search of food.]

turn·ta·ble (túrn-tayb'l) *n.* **1.** A circular horizontal rotating platform equipped with a railway track, used for turning locomotives. **2.** A similar device for turning road vehicles. **3. a.** The circular horizontal rotating platform of a record player on which the record is placed. **b.** The mechanical path of a record player excluding the amplifying circuitry and speakers. **4.** Any similar rotating platform or disc, as on a microscope.

turntable ladder *n.* A ladder, usually mounted on a fire engine, that can be mechanically rotated and extended.

turn up *tr.v.* **1.** To find; unearth. **2.** *British Informal.* To cause to vomit; nauseate. *—intr.v.* **1.** To be found; come to light: *turned up at last.* **2.** To make an appearance; arrive. **3.** *Informal.* To happen, especially unexpectedly.

turn·up (túrn-up) *n.* **1.** Something that is turned up or turns up; specifically, the turned-up fold at the bottom of a trouser leg. **2.** *British Informal.* An unexpected occurrence or turn of events. Often used in the phrase *a turnup for the books.*

tur·pen·tine (túrpən-tīn) *n. Abbr.* **turp. 1.** A thin volatile essential oil, consisting of a mixture of terpenes, obtained by steam distillation or other means from the wood or the exudate of certain pine trees, and used as a paint thinner, solvent, and medicinally as a liniment. Also called "oil of turpentine", "spirits of turpentine", "turps". **2.** The sticky mixture of resin and volatile oil from which this oil is distilled. **3.** A similar resinous liquid obtained from the terebinth. **4.** Any of several similar liquids obtained from petroleum and used as thinners for paints and varnishes. Also called "turpentine substitute", "white spirit".
~tr.v. **turpentined, -tining, -tines. 1.** To apply turpentine to or mix turpentine with. **2.** To extract turpentine from (a tree). [Middle English *turpentyne,* resin of the terebinth, from Old French *ter(e)bentine,* from Latin *terebinthina,* from *terebinthus,* TEREBINTH.]

tur·peth (túrpith) *n.* **1.** A vine of the genus *Ipomoea,* of tropical Asia and Australia, having roots that yield a resinous substance used medicinally as a purgative. **2.** The root of this plant. [Middle English *turbit,* from Old French, from Medieval Latin *turbit(h)um, turpetum,* from Arabic *turbid, turbed.*]

Tur·pin (túrpin), **Dick** (1706–39). British highwayman who was hanged on what is now York Racecourse.

tur·pi·tude (túrpi-tewd || -to͞od) *n.* **1.** Baseness; depravity. **2.** A base, immoral act. [Latin *turpitūdō,* from *turpis*†, ugly, vile.]

turps (turps) *n. Used with a singular verb. Informal.* Turpentine. [Colloquial shortening of TURPENTINE.]

tur·quoise (túr-kwoyz, -kwaaz, -kwawz, -koyz) *n.* **1.** A blue to blue-green mineral, a basic hydrous phosphate of aluminium and copper, mainly $CuAl_6(PO_4)_4(OH)_8{\cdot}4H_2O$. It is prized as a gemstone in its polished blue form. **2.** Light to brilliant bluish green. [Middle English *turkeis,* from Old French *(pierre) turqueise,* "Turkish (stone)", from *turqueis,* Turkish (it was first found in Turkestan), from *Turc,* TURK.] **—tur·quoise** *adj.*

tur·ret (túrrit, túrrət) *n.* **1.** A small ornamented tower or tower-shaped projection on a building. **2.** *Military.* A low, heavily armoured structure, usually rotating horizontally, containing mounted guns and their crew, as on a warship or tank. **3.** A domelike gunner's enclosure projecting from the fuselage of a military aircraft. **4.** A tall wooden structure mounted on wheels, used in ancient warfare by besiegers to scale the walls of a fortress. **5.** An attachment for a lathe consisting of a rotating, cylindrical block holding various cutting tools. [Middle English *t(o)uret,* from Old French *t(o)urete,* diminutive of *t(o)ur,* a TOWER.]

tur·ret·ed (túrrit-id, túrrət-) *adj.* **1.** Furnished with a turret or turrets. **2.** Having the shape or form of a turret, as do certain long-spired gastropod shells.

tur·tle[1] (túrt'l) *n.* **1.** Any of various marine reptiles of the order Chelonia, having horny, toothless jaws and the body enclosed in a bony or leathery shell into which the head, limbs, and tail can be withdrawn in most species. **2.** *U.S.* Any chelonian reptile; a turtle, tortoise, or terrapin. **—turn turtle.** To turn upside-down; capsize.
~intr.v. **turtled, -tling, -tles.** To hunt for turtles, especially as an occupation. [Perhaps variant of French *tortue,* TORTOISE.]

turtle[2] *n. Archaic.* A turtledove: *"the voice of the turtle is heard in our land"* (Song of Solomon 2:12). [Middle English *turtle,* Old English *turtla, turtle,* from Latin *turtur*†.]

tur·tle·back (túrt'l-bak) *n.* A projection built so as to arch over the deck of a ship at the bow and sometimes also at the stern, as a protection against high seas.

tur·tle·dove (túrt'l-duv) *n.* A slender European dove, *Streptopelia turtur,* having a white-edged tail and a soft, cooing voice. [TURTLE (dove) + DOVE.]

tur·tle·neck (túrt'l-nek) *n.* **1.** A relatively high, round collar on a sweater, that fits closely about the neck. **2.** A sweater having such a collar.

turves. *Archaic.* Plural of **turf.**

Tus·can (túskən) *adj.* **1.** Of or pertaining to Tuscany, its people, or their dialect of Italian. **2.** Of or pertaining to the Tuscan order.
~n. **1.** A native or inhabitant of Tuscany. **2.** Any of the Italian dialects spoken in Tuscany, especially the dialect of Florence.

Tuscan order *n. Architecture.* A classical order similar to Roman Doric, but having an unfluted shaft with a simplified base, capital, and entablature.

Tus·ca·ny (túskəni). *Italian* **Tos·ca·na** (toskáanə). Region of western central Italy. It was inhabited in pre-Roman times by the Etruscans, and became, with the rise of the Medicis of Florence, a Grand Duchy (1569–1860). Its dialect was selected as textbook Italian on the country's unification. The chief cities are Florence (the capital), Livorno, and Pisa.

tu·sche (to͞osh || *U.S.* to͞oshə) *n.* A substance used for drawing in lithography and as a resist in etching and silk-screen printing. [German *Tusche,* from *tuschen,* to ink up, from French *toucher,* to TOUCH.]

tush[1] (tush) *interj.* Used to express mild reproof, disapproval, or admonition: *Tush, tush, my dear, it's nothing to fuss about.*

tush[2] *n. Rare.* A tusk. [Middle English *tusche,* Old English *tūsc.*]

tusk[1] (tusk) *n.* **1.** An elongated, pointed tooth, usually one of a pair, extending outside the mouth in certain animals, such as the walrus, elephant, or wild boar. **2.** Any long, projecting tooth or toothlike part.
~tr.v. **tusked, tusking, tusks.** To dig or gore with the tusks or a tusk. [Middle English *tux, tuske,* Old English *tūx, tūsc.*]

tusk[2] *n.* A fish, the **torsk** *(see).*

tusk·er (túskər) *n.* An animal bearing tusks, such as a wild boar.

tusk shell *n.* Any marine mollusc of the class Scaphopoda, having a tusk-shaped shell. Also called "tooth shell".

tus·sah (túss-ə, -aw) *n.* Also **tus·ser** (-ər), **tus·sore** (-ər, -awr, *also* to͞o-sór || -ōr). **1.** An Asian silkworm, *Antheraea paphia,* that produces a coarse brownish or yellowish silk. **2.** The silk itself, or a fabric woven from it. [Hindi *tasar,* from Sanskrit *tasara,* a shuttle (probably from the shape of its cocoon).]

Tus·saud (to͞o-sáwd, tə-, -sṓ), **Madame,** born Marie Gresholtz (1760–1850). Swiss-born wax modeller. She was imprisoned during the French Revolution and modelled heads of the guillotined victims. She moved to England (1802) and eventually opened a museum which is still a tourist attraction in London.

tus·sis (tússiss) n. Medicine. A cough. [Latin.] —**tus·sal, tus·sive** adj.

tus·sle (túss'l) intr.v. -**sled, -sling, -sles.** To fight or struggle roughly.

~n. 1. A rough-and-tumble struggle; a scuffle. 2. Any disorderly struggle or conflict: a tussle for power. [Middle English tussillen, probably from -t(o)usen, to TOUSLE.]

tus·sock, tuss·uck (tússək) n. 1. A clump or tuft of growing grass or a similar plant. 2. A tuft, as of hair or feathers. [Probably variant of dialectal tusk†, a tuft of hair, rushes.] —**tus·sock·y** adj.

tussock grass n. Any of various grasses or sedges that typically grow in tussocks; especially, species in the genus Poa.

tussock moth n. Any of various moths of the family Lymantriidae, having hairy caterpillars that are often destructive to trees.

Tu·tan·kha·mun (tŏō-tang-kaa-mŏōn, -mŏōn) or **Tu·tan·kha·men** (-kaá-men, -tang-, -mən) (c. 1358–c. 1340 B.C.). Egyptian pharaoh of the 18th dynasty. His tomb and its magnificent contents was discovered almost intact (1922) by the British archaeologists Howard Carter and the Earl of Carnarvon.

tu·te·lage (téw-ti-lij, -tə- ‖ tŏō-) n. 1. The function or capacity of a guardian; guardianship. 2. The act or capacity of a tutor; instruction; teaching. 3. The state of being under a guardian or tutor. [Latin tūtēla, a watching, from tūtor, TUTOR.]

tu·te·lar·y (téw-ti-ləri, -tə- ‖ tŏō-, -lerri) adj. Also **tu·te·lar** (-lər). 1. Of or pertaining to a guardian or guardianship. 2. Acting as a guardian or protector, especially over a particular place or person; protective.

~n. A tutelary saint, deity, or spirit. [Late Latin tūtēlāris, from Latin tūtēla, TUTELAGE.]

tu·tor (téw-tər ‖ tŏō-) n. 1. a. A private teacher, often employed by a household. b. One who gives additional, special, or remedial instruction. 2. In most British universities and colleges, a member of staff who is responsible for the welfare of a number of students and usually for supervising their studies. 3. In Roman and Scottish law, the guardian of a minor and of the minor's property. 4. British. A practical instruction book: a guitar tutor.

~v. **tutored, -toring, -tors.** —tr. 1. To act as a tutor to; especially, to instruct or teach privately. 2. To discipline or treat sternly, as a tutor might. 3. To act as the guardian to; have the care of. —intr. To function as a tutor or private instructor. —See Synonyms at **teach.** [Middle English tutour, from Old French, from Latin tūtor, a guardian, from tūtus, past participle of tuērī, to watch, protect.]

tu·to·ri·al (tew-táw-ri-əl ‖ tŏō-, -tŏ-) n. A period of intensive tuition given, especially in a university, to an individual student or a small number of students.

~adj. Of or pertaining to a tutor. [Latin tūtōrius. See tutor, -al.]

tutorial system n. An instructional system in which college or university tutors are responsible for the special supervision of students individually or in small groups.

tu·tor·ship (téw-tər-ship ‖ tŏō-) n. 1. The office or functions of a tutor. 2. Tutelage.

tut·san (túts'n) n. 1. A yellow-flowered evergreen undershrub, Hypericum androsaemum, having berries that turn purplish black when ripe. 2. Either of two related plants, H. hircinum or H. inodorum. See **Saint John's wort.** [Middle English, from Anglo-French tutsaine (French, toute-saine), "all healthy" (the plants were believed to have various healing properties).]

tut·ti (tŏōt-ee, -i ‖ tŏōt-) adv. Music. All together. Used as a direction to indicate that all performers are to take part.

~n., pl. **tuttis.** 1. A passage of ensemble music intended to be executed by all the performers simultaneously. 2. The tonal effect thus produced. [Italian, all, from Latin tōtus.] —**tut·ti** adj.

tut·ti-frut·ti (tŏōtti-frŏōtti, tŏōti-, -frŏōti) n. 1. A confection, especially ice cream, containing a variety of chopped candied fruits. 2. A flavouring simulating the flavour of many fruits. 3. A preserve of chopped, mixed fruits.

~adj. Having a combination of fruit flavours. [Italian, "all fruits".]

tut-tut (tút-tút; as an interjection, usually a single or repeated voiceless alveolar click) interj. Also **tut.** Used to express annoyance, impatience, or mild reproof.

~intr.v. **tut-tutted, -tutting, -tuts.** Also **tut.** To say tut-tut in annoyance, impatience or mild reproof.

~n. An exclamation of tut-tut.

tut·ty (tútti) n. An impure zinc oxide obtained as a sublimate from the flues of zinc-smelting furnaces and used as a polishing powder. [Middle English tutie, from Old French, from Arabic tūtiyā.]

tu·tu (tŏō-tŏō) n. A skirt worn for classical ballet consisting of many layers of gathered sheer fabric, which is either brief and encircles the waist or extends to below the knee. [French.]

Tu·tu (tŏō-tŏō), **Desmond (Mpilo), Archbishop** (1931–). South African theologian, and winner of 1984 Nobel peace prize. Anglican Archbishop of Cape Town (1986–95, emeritus 1995–). Chairman, Truth and Reconciliation Commission (1995–98).

Tu·va·lu (tŏōvə-lŏō). Formerly **Ellice Islands.** Country of the southwestern Pacific, consisting of nine islands. Established as a British protectorate in 1892, it became part of the Gilbert and Ellice Islands Colony in 1915, from which it broke away in 1975. Independence was granted in 1978. Area, 26 square kilometres (10 square miles). Population, 10,000. Capital, Funafuti. See map at **Pacific Ocean.**

tu-whit tu-whoo (tŏō-wit tŏō-wŏō, tə-, -hwit, -hwŏō) n. A conventional rendering of the call of an owl.

tux·e·do (tuk-séedō) n., pl. -**dos.** Chiefly U.S. Sometimes capital T. 1. A dinner jacket (see). 2. U.S. Black tie (see). [From the name of a club in Tuxedo Park, New York, where it became popular.]

tu·yère (twee-yáir) n. The pipe, nozzle, or other opening through which air is forced into a blast furnace or forge to facilitate combustion. [French, from Old French tuyere, from tuyau, a pipe, probably from Frankish thūta (unattested), imitative.]

TV n. Informal. Television. —**TV** adj.

TV dinner n. A packaged ready-to-serve meal, usually frozen in an aluminium tray, that can be heated in an oven.

TVP textured vegetable protein.

Twad·dell scale (twódd'l, two-dél) n. A scale for measuring relative density, especially of acids. [After William Twaddell (died c. 1840), Scottish inventor.]

twad·dle (twódd'l) intr.v. -**dled, -dling, -dles.** Also **twat·tle** (twótt'l). To talk foolishly.

~n. Also **twat·tle.** 1. Foolish, trivial, or idle talk or chatter. 2. Silly pretentious speech or writing. [From earlier twattle, alteration of TATTLE.] —**twad·dler** n.

twain (twayn) adj. Archaic. Two.

~n. Poetic. A set of two: "Oh, East is East, and West is West, and never the twain shall meet" (Rudyard Kipling). [Middle English tweien, tweyen, Old English twēgen (nominative and accusative masculine), two.]

Twain (twayn), **Mark** Pen name of Samuel Langhorne Clemens (1835–1910). U.S. novelist. He is best known for his two masterpieces, Tom Sawyer (1876), and Huckleberry Finn (1884), based on his boyhood experiences.

twang (twang) v. **twanged, twanging, twangs.** —intr. 1. To emit a sharp, vibrating sound, as the string of a musical instrument sounds when plucked. 2. To be released or to resound with a sharp, vibrating sound. Used especially of an arrow. —tr. 1. To cause to make a sharp, vibrating sound. 2. To utter with a twang.

~n. 1. A sharp, vibrating sound, such as that made by a plucked string. 2. A notably nasal tone of voice, especially as a peculiarity of certain regional accents. 3. Any sound resembling either of these. [Imitative.] —**twang·y** adj.

'twas (twoz, weak form twəz ‖ twuz). Regional & Poetic. Contraction of it was.

twat (twot, twat) n. Vulgar Slang. 1. The female genitalia. 2. A woman or girl considered as a sexual object. This term is considered to be extremely offensive. 3. A worthless or vile person. Used derogatorily. [17th century : origin obscure.]

tway·blade (twáy-blayd) n. 1. Any of various small terrestrial orchids of the genus Listera, having two basal, unstalked leaves and a terminal cluster of greenish or reddish flowers. 2. Any other orchid with only two leaves. [Translation of Medieval Latin bifolium, "two-leaved" : obsolete English tway, two, Middle English twei, Old English twēge, short for twēgen, TWAIN + BLADE.]

tweak (tweek) tr.v. **tweaked, tweaking, tweaks.** 1. To pinch, pluck, or twist sharply. 2. Slang. In motor racing, to tune (a car or engine) finely for peak performance, as before a race.

~n. A sharp, twisting pinch. [Probably variant of dialectal twick, Middle English twikken; akin to TWITCH.] —**tweak·y** adj.

twee (twee) adj. British Informal. 1. Excessively or affectedly pretty, sentimental or quaint. 2. Rare. Sweet; cute. [From tweet, childish or affected pronunciation of SWEET.]

tweed (tweed) n. 1. A coarse, rugged, often knobbly woollen cloth made in any of various twill weaves, and used chiefly for suits and coats. Also used adjectivally: a tweed suit. 2. Plural. Clothing made of this cloth. [Originally a trademark, misspelling (influenced by the river TWEED) of tweel, tweeled, Scottish variants of TWILL.]

Tweed (tweed). River of northern Great Britain. Rising in the Tweedsmuir Hills in the Borders of Scotland, it flows some 156 kilometres (97 miles) to the North Sea at Berwick.

Tweeddale. See Peeblesshire.

twee·dle·dum and twee·dle·dee (tweéd'l-dúm; tweéd'l-deé) n. Two persons or groups resembling each other so closely that they are practically indistinguishable. [After Tweedledum and Tweedledee, proverbial rival violinists supposedly representative of Handel and G.B. Bononcini, who had a musical rivalry.]

tweed·y (tweédi) adj. **tweedier, tweediest.** 1. Of, made of, or resembling tweed. 2. Chiefly British Informal. Given to the healthy, outdoor, country life, especially that led by members of the British gentry (who are reputed to wear a lot of tweed). —**tweed·i·ness** n.

'tween (tween) Poetic. Contraction of between.

tween-decks (tweén-deks) n. The space between two decks of a ship. —**tween-deck** (-dek) adj.

tween·y (tweéni) n., pl. **tweenies.** British Informal. A between maid, as one who helps two others, such as the cook and housemaid.

tweet (tweet) intr.v. **tweeted, tweeting, tweets.** To utter a weak, chirping sound, as a young or small bird does.

~n. A weak, chirping sound.

~interj. Also **tweet tweet.** Used to imitate the sound of a bird. [Imitative.]

tweet·er (tweétər) n. A loudspeaker designed to reproduce high-pitched sounds in a high-fidelity audiofrequency system. Compare **woofer.** [From TWEET.]

tweeze (tweez) tr.v. **tweezed, tweezing, tweezes.** Chiefly U.S. To handle or extract with tweezers. [Back-formation from TWEEZERS.]

tweez·ers (tweézərz) pl.n. Any small, usually metal, pincer-like tool used for plucking or handling small objects. [Originally "a set or

case of small instruments", from obsolete *tweezes,* plural of *tweeze, etweese,* from the plural of *etwee,* from French *étui,* ÉTUI.]
twelfth (twelth, twelfth) *n.* **1.** The ordinal number 12 in a series. **2.** Any of 12 equal parts. **3.** *Music.* **a.** A 12-degree interval in a diatonic scale; an octave plus a fifth. **b.** A note 12 degrees below or above a given note. [Middle English *twelfthe,* Old English *twelfta.*] **—twelfth** *adj. & adv.*
Twelfth-day (twélth-day, twélfth-) *n.* The day of Epiphany, January 6, 12 days after Christmas and traditionally marking the end of the Christmas season.
twelfth man *n.* A reserve player for a cricket team.
Twelfth-night (twélth-nīt, twélfth-, -nīt) *n.* The evening of January 5, before Twelfth-day, formerly celebrated with various festivities. **—Twelfth-night** *adj.*
Twelfth·tide (twélth-tīd, twélfth-) *n.* The season of Epiphany.
twelve (twelv) *n.* **1. a.** The cardinal number that is one more than 11; a dozen. **b.** A symbol representing this, such as 12 or XII. **2.** A set made up of twelve persons or things. **3.** The twelfth in a series. **4.** A size, as in clothing, designated as 12. **5.** Midnight or midday. Also called "twelve o'clock". [Middle English *twelfe, twelve,* Old English *twelf.*] **—twelve** *adj.*
Twelve Apostles *pl.n.* The 12 disciples chosen by Jesus. Preceded by *the.* Also called the "Twelve".
twelve·mo (twélv-mō) *n., pl.* **-mos. Duodecimo** *(see).*
twelve·month (twélv-munth) *n.* A year or period of twelve months.
Twelve Tables *n.* The earliest code of Roman laws, written down 451–450 B.C. Preceded by *the.* [Translation of Latin *Duodecim Tabulae,* referring to the 12 original compilations (fifth century B.C.) which, when complete, were incised on bronze plates and hung in the Forum.]
twelve-note (twélv-nōt) *adj. Music.* Pertaining to, consisting of, or based on an atonal arrangement of the traditional 12 chromatic notes, as invented and used by Arnold Schoenberg. Also *chiefly U.S.* "twelve-tone".
twen·ti·eth (twénti-əth, -ith) *n.* **1.** The ordinal number 20 in a series. **2.** Any of 20 equal parts. **—twen·ti·eth** *adj. & adv.*
twen·ty (twénti) *n. pl.* **-ties. 1. a.** The cardinal number that is 10 more than 10; a score. **b.** A symbol representing this such as 20 or XX. **2.** A set made up of 20 persons or things. **3.** The twentieth in a series. **4.** A size, as in clothing, designated as 20. **5.** A bank note or coin having a denomination of 20. **6.** *Plural.* **a.** The range of numbers from 20 to 29, considered as a range of age, price, or temperature, for example. **b.** *Capital* **T.** The years numbered 20 to 29 in a century. Also used adjectivally: *a Twenties hairstyle.* [Middle English *twenty,* Old English *twēntig.*] **—twen·ty** *adj.*
twen·ty-one (twénti-wún) *n. U.S.* **pontoon** *(see).*
twen·ty-twen·ty (twénti-twénti) *adj.* Having perfect vision. Usually written *20/20.*
'twere (twer, twair, *weak form* twər). *Poetic.* Contraction of *it were.*
twerp, twirp (twerp) *n. Slang.* A weak, stupid, or contemptible person; a fool. [20th century : origin obscure.]
Twi, Tshi (twee, chwee) *n.* A dialect of Akan spoken in western Africa, especially by the Ashanti. **—Twi, Tshi** *adj.*
twi·bil, twi·bill (twī-bil) *n.* **1.** A battle-axe with two cutting edges. **2.** A mattock with one arm like an axe and the other like an adze. [Middle English, Old English *twibil(l)* : *twi-,* two + BILL (instrument).]
twice (twīss) *adv.* **1.** In two cases or on two occasions; two times. **2.** In doubled degree or amount: *twice as many.* [Middle English *twice, twiges,* Old English *twiges,* from *twige, twiga,* twice.]
twice-laid (twīss-layd) *adj.* Made from strands of old or used rope.
Twick·en·ham (twíckənəm). District of west London. Situated in the borough of Richmond on the north bank of the Thames, it is a mainly residential area.
twid·dle (twídd'l) *v.* **-dled, -dling, -dles.** *—tr.* To turn over or around, especially idly or lightly; fiddle with: *twiddle the knobs on the radio.* *—intr.* **1.** To turn something over or around idly or lightly; fiddle. Used with *with.* **2.** To twirl or rotate aimlessly.
~n. The act of twiddling; an idle, twirling motion. [Probably a blend of TWIRL and FIDDLE.] **—twid·dler** *n.*
twig[1] (twig) *n.* A small branch or slender shoot, as of a tree or shrub. [Middle English *twig(ge),* Old English *twigge.*]
twig[2] *v.* **twigged, twigging, twigs.** *British Informal.* *—intr.* To suddenly comprehend a situation; catch on. *—tr.* **1.** To understand. **2.** *Rare.* To observe or watch; to notice. [18th century : origin obscure.]
twig·gy (twíggi) *adj.* **-gier, -giest. 1.** Resembling a twig or twigs; slender; fragile. **2.** Abounding in twigs.
twi·light (twī-līt) *n.* **1.** The state of fading illumination of the atmosphere by the Sun as or after it sets. **2.** The time interval during which the Sun's centre is below the horizon at an angle less than 6° (*civil twilight*), 12° (*nautical twilight*), or 18° (*astronomical twilight*). **3.** Any dim or faint illumination. **4.** Any period or condition of decline, as after growth, glory, or success; a waning: *in the twilight of her life.*
~adj. Pertaining to or characteristic of twilight. [Middle English *twilight,* "light between (night and day)", half-light : *twi-,* half, two, Old English *twi-* + LIGHT.]
Twilight of the Gods *n.* **Götterdämmerung** *(see).*
twilight sleep *n.* An analgesic and amnesiac condition induced by an injection of morphine and scopolamine, characterised by the absence of sensibility to pain without loss of consciousness, and administered during labour in childbirth.
twilight zone *n.* **1.** An area or state that is not clearly defined or limited. **2.** A dilapidated or run-down area of a city.
twill (twil) *n.* **1.** A cloth with diagonal parallel ribs produced by passing the weft yarn alternately over one warp yarn and then under two or more. **2.** The weave used to produce such cloth.
~tr.v. **twilled, twilling, twills.** To weave (cloth) so as to produce the pattern of twill. [Middle English *twyl(l), twyle,* Old English *twilic,* "two-threaded" : *twi-,* two (see **twilight**) + Latin *(bi)līx,* "two-threaded" : BI- + *līcium,* a thread (see **trellis**).] **—twill** *adj.*
'twill (twil). *Regional and Poetic.* Contraction of *it will.*
twilled (twild) *adj.* Woven so as to have diagonal parallel ribs.
twin (twin) *n.* **1.** Either of two offspring born at the same birth. **2.** Either of two identical or similar persons, animals, or things; a counterpart. **3.** *Capital* **T.** *Plural.* The constellation and sign of the zodiac, **Gemini** *(see).* Preceded by *the.* **4.** A crystal composed of two parts which are orientated differently, but joined together so that a crystallographic direction or plane is common to both. Also called "macle".
~adj. **1.** Being two or either of two offspring born at the same birth. **2.** Being either of two identical or similar persons, animals, or things: *a twin bed.* **3.** Consisting of two identical or similar related or connected parts.
~v. **twinned, twinning, twins.** *—intr.* **1.** To give birth to twins. **2.** *Archaic.* To be either of twin offspring. **3.** To be paired or coupled. *—tr.* **1.** To give birth to, as twins. **2.** To provide a match or counterpart to; pair. [Middle English *twin, twyn* (adjective and noun), Old English *twinn* (adjective only), *getwinn.*]
twin·ber·ry (twín-bəri, -bri, -berri) *n., pl.* **-ries.** The **partridgeberry** *(see).* [From the single berry formed from a pair of flowers.]
twine (twīn) *v.* **twined, twining, twines.** *—tr.* **1.** To twist (threads, for example) together; intertwine. **2.** To form by twisting, intertwining, or interlacing. **3.** To encircle or coil about: *A vine twined the fence.* **4.** To wind, coil, or wrap around (something): *twined a rope around the post.* *—intr.* **1.** To become twisted, interlaced, or interwoven. **2.** To wind or coil. Usually used with *around.* **3.** To go in a winding course; twist about: *a stream twining through the forest.*
~n. **1.** A strong string or cord formed from two or more threads of hemp, cotton, or the like twisted together. **2.** Any thing or part formed by twining: *a twine of dough.* **3.** A tangle; a knot. **4.** The act or process of twining. [Middle English *twinen,* from *twin,* a rope of two strands, Old English *twīn,* from *twī-,* two.] **—twin·er** *n.*
twin·flow·er (twín-flow-ər, -flowr) *n.* A creeping evergreen plant, *Linnaea borealis,* of northern regions, having roundish leaves and paired, bell-shaped, pinkish flowers.
twinge (twinj) *n.* **1.** A sharp, sudden physical pain. **2.** A mental or emotional pang: *a twinge of conscience.*
~v. **twinged, twinging, twinges.** *—tr.* **1.** To cause to feel a sharp pain. **2.** *Obsolete.* To tweak; pinch. *—intr.* To feel a twinge or twinges. [Middle English *twengen, twynchen,* to pinch, wring, Old English *twengan.*]
twin·kle (twíngk'l) *v.* **-kled, -kling, -kles.** *—intr.* **1.** To shine with slight, intermittent gleams, as distant lights or stars do; flicker or glimmer. **2.** To be bright or sparkling, as with delight. Used of the eyes. **3.** *Archaic.* To blink or wink. *—tr.* To cause to twinkle. —See Synonyms at **flash.**
~n. **1.** A slight, intermittent gleam of light; a glimmer; a sparkle. **2.** A sparkle of merriment or delight in the eye. **3.** A brief interval; a twinkling. [Middle English *twynklen,* Old English *twinclian,* frequentative of *twincan* (unattested), to wink, from West Germanic *twink-* (unattested).] **—twin·kler** *n.*
twin·kling (twíngkling) *n.* The time it takes to blink once; an instant. Also called "twinkling of an eye".
twinned (twind) *adj.* **1.** Born at a single birth. **2.** Paired or coupled with something identical or similar. **3.** Formed from crystals by the process of twinning.
twin·ning (twínning) *n.* **1.** The bearing of twins. **2.** A pairing or union of two similar or identical things. **3.** The formation of twin crystals.
twin-screw (twín-skrōō ‖ -skrew) *adj.* Having two propellers, one on either side of the keel, that usually revolve in opposite directions. Said of a ship.
twin-set (twín-set) *n. Chiefly British.* A matching cardigan and sweater worn by a woman.
twin town *n.* **1.** *British.* Either of two towns in different countries usually similar in some way, such as size or industrial make-up, that are formally associated, especially by having reciprocal cultural visits. **2.** Either of two towns facing each other across a river.
twirl (twurl) *v.* **twirled, twirling, twirls.** *—tr.* **1.** To rotate or revolve briskly; swing in a circle; spin. **2.** To twist or wind around: *twirl thread on a spindle.* *—intr.* **1.** To move or spin around rapidly, suddenly, or repeatedly. **2.** To whirl or turn suddenly; make an about-face. Usually used with *about* or *around.*
~n. **1.** A twirling or being twirled; a quick spinning or twisting. **2.** Something twirled; a curl or twist. [Perhaps alteration (influenced by WHIRL) of obsolete *tirl,* TRILL.]
twirp. Variant of **twerp.**
twist (twist) *v.* **twisted, twisting, twists.** *—tr.* **1. a.** To entwine (two or more threads) so as to produce a single strand. **b.** To form in this manner: *twist a length of rope.* **2.** To wind or coil (vines or rope, for example) around something. **3.** To interweave: *twist flowers in one's hair.* **4. a.** To impart a coiling or spiral shape to. **b.** To turn repeatedly while holding one end firm. **5. a.** To turn or open by turning. **b.** To pull, break, or snap by turning. Used with *off*: *twist off a dead*

branch. **6.** To wrench or sprain: *twist one's wrist.* **7.** To alter the normal aspect of; contort: *twist one's mouth into a wry smile.* **8.** To alter or distort the intended meaning of. *—intr.* **1.** To be or become twisted. **2.** To move or progress in a winding course; meander. **3.** To squirm; writhe: *twist with pain.* **4. a.** To turn round, especially in an uneasy way. **b.** To rotate or revolve. **5.** To dance the twist. —See Synonyms at **distort.**
~n. **1.** Something twisted or formed by winding, especially: **a.** A length of yarn, cord, or thread, especially a strong silk thread used mainly to bind the edges of buttonholes. **b.** Tobacco leaves processed into the form of a rope or roll. **c.** *British.* A simple packet made by rolling a piece of paper round something and twisting the ends. **d.** Bread or other bakery products for which the dough was twisted before baking. **e.** A sliver of citrus peel twisted over or dropped into a drink to impart flavour. **2. a.** The act of twisting or the condition of being twisted; a spin or twirl; a rotation. **b.** A sharp bend or turn. **3.** A vigorous wrench or turn. **4. a.** The state of being twisted into a spiral; torsional stress or strain. **b.** The degree or angle of such stress. **5.** A sprain or wrench, as of a muscle. **6. a.** A sudden or unexpected change in a course of events or a surprising revelation, as in a novel, play, or the like: *Saki's stories always have a twist in the tail.* **b.** A sudden change or departure from a pattern, usually for the worse: *a twist of fate.* **7.** A contortion or distortion, as of the face. **8.** A personal inclination or eccentricity; a penchant or flaw: *a twist in her character.* **9.** A dance, popular especially in the 1960s, characterised by vigorous twisting of the waist from side to side with the knees bent. Preceded by *the.* **10.** *British Informal.* A trick or swindle. [Middle English *twysten,* from Old English *-twist,* a rope.] **—twist·a·bil·i·ty** (-ə-bílləti) *n.* **—twist·a·ble** *adj.* **—twist·ing·ly** *adv.*

twist drill *n.* A drill having deep helical grooves along the shank from the point.

twist·ed (twístid) *adj.* Perverted; weird and evil: *a twisted mind.*

twist·er (twístər) *n.* **1.** One that twists; specifically, a mechanical device for spinning or twisting yarn or rope. **2.** *British Informal.* A dishonest person; a swindler. **3.** *U.S. Informal.* A cyclone or a tornado.

twist grip *n.* A ratchet-controlled, rotating device attached to the ends of some handlebars. On some bicycles and motorcycles it is used as a gear-changing control and on most motorcycles it is used as an accelerator.

twit[1] (twit) *tr.v.* **twitted, twitting, twits.** To taunt, ridicule, or tease, especially for embarrassing mistakes or faults. See Synonyms at **ridicule.**
~n. **1.** The act of twitting. **2.** A reproach, gibe, or taunt. [Earlier *(a)twite,* Middle English *atwiten,* Old English *ætwītan,* to reproach with : *æt-* (indicating opposition), from *æt,* from, AT + *witan,* to reproach, ascribe to.]

twit[2] *n. British Informal.* A stupid person; an idiot: *an upper-class twit.* [19th century (originally dialect) : perhaps from TWIT (a person who taunts).]

twitch (twich) *v.* **twitched, twitching, twitches.** *—tr.* To draw, pull, or move suddenly and sharply; jerk: *The fisherman twitched his line.* *—intr.* **1.** To move jerkily or spasmodically. **2.** To ache sharply from time to time; twinge.
~n. **1.** A sudden involuntary or spasmodic muscular movement: *a nervous twitch.* **2.** A sudden pulling; a jerk or tug. **3.** A looped cord used to restrain a horse by tightening it around the animal's upper lip. **—in a twitch.** *Informal.* In a state of nervousness or agitation. [Middle English *twicchen,* perhaps of Low German origin, akin to Low German *twikken.*] **—twitch·ing·ly** *adv.*

twitch grass *n.* **Couch grass** *(see).*

twitch·er (twíchər) *n. Informal.* A birdwatcher who relentlessly pursues the aim of spotting a particular bird, disregarding the sanctuary and well-being of the birds.

twitch·y (twíchi) *adj. Informal.* Agitated or nervous.

twite (twīt) *n.* A Eurasian finch, *Acanthis flavirostris,* resembling the linnet, but having no red plumage on the crown, and found in moorland regions. [Imitative of its call.]

twit·ter (twíttər) *v.* **-tered, -tering, -ters.** *—intr.* **1.** To utter a succession of light chirping or tremulous sounds, as a bird does; chirrup. **2.** To titter; giggle. **3.** To tremble or talk nervously, as with excitement. *—tr.* To utter or say with a twitter: *twittered his greeting.*
~n. **1.** The light chirping sounds made by certain birds. **2.** Light, tremulous speech or laughter. **3.** A state of agitation or excitement; a flutter. Used especially in the phrase *in a twitter.* [Middle English *twiteren,* akin to Old High German *zwizzirōn,* from West Germanic *twittwīrōjan* (imitative).] **—twit·ter·er** *n.* **—twit·ter·y** *adj.*

twixt, 'twixt (twikst) *prep. Archaic & Poetic.* Betwixt.

two (to͞o) *n.* **1. a.** The cardinal number that is one more than one. **b.** A symbol representing this, such as 2, II, or ii. **2.** A set made up of two persons or things. **3. a.** The second in a series. **b.** A playing card marked with two pips. **4.** A size, as in clothing, designated as two. **5.** Two hours after midnight or midday. **—in two. 1.** So as to be in two separate units: *split in two.* **2.** So as to have two thicknesses or layer: *fold in two.* **—put two and two together.** To reach a correct, usually obvious conclusion after considering a given set of circumstances. **—that makes two of us.** That is true of or applies to myself as well. [Middle English *two,* Old English *twā, tū.*] **—two** *adj.*

two-bit (to͞o-bit) *adj. U.S. Slang.* **1.** Worth very little; insignificant. **2.** Cheap; shoddy. [From TWO BITS.]

two bits *n. U.S. Informal.* **1.** Twenty-five cents. **2.** A petty sum.

two-by-four (to͞o-bī-fór, -bi- || -fōr) *adj.* Measuring two by four inches, or in the same ratio in other units.
~n. Any length of timber measuring about 2 by 4 inches or trimmed to $1^5/_8$ inches in thickness and $3^3/_8$ inches in width.

two-di·men·sion·al (to͞o-dī-ménsh'n'l, -di-) *adj.* **1.** Having only two dimensions, usually length and width; planar; flat. **2.** *Informal.* Lacking dimension or completion; limited in range or depth.

two-edged (to͞o-éjd) *adj.* **1.** Having a cutting edge on both sides. Said of a razor or sword blade, for example. **2.** Having two contrasting effects, meanings, or interpretations.

two-faced (to͞o-fáyst) *adj.* **1.** *Informal.* Hypocritical or double-dealing; deceitful. **2.** Having two faces or surfaces. **—two-fac·ed·ly** (-fáyssid-li, -fáyst-) *adv.* **—two-fac·ed·ness** *n.*

two·fold (to͞o-fōld, -fōld) *adj.* **1.** Having two components. **2.** Having twice as much or twice as many; double.
~adv. Two times as much or as many; doubly.

2,4,5-T (to͞o-fór-fīv-teé) *n.* **Trichlorophenoxyacetic acid** *(see).*

two-hand·ed (to͞o-hándid) *adj.* **1.** Requiring the use of two hands at once: *a two-handed sledgehammer.* **2.** Made to be operated or engaged in by two people. **3.** Able to use both hands with equal facility; ambidextrous. **4.** Having two hands.

two-mast·er (to͞o-maast-ər || -mást-) *n.* A sailing vessel rigged with two masts.

two-name (to͞o-náym) *adj. Finance. U.S.* Pertaining to or designating a promissory note bearing the signatures of two persons liable to the obligation.

two-party system (to͞o-párti) *n.* A political system, such as currently prevails in the United States and traditionally in Great Britain, in which two major political parties dominate.

two·pence (túppənss; *in sense 1 also* to͞o-pénss, -penss) *n.* Also *informal* **tup·pence.** *British.* **1.** Two pennies regarded as a monetary unit. **2.** A silver coin worth two pennies, since 1662 minted only for distribution on Maundy Thursday. **3.** A copper coin of this value minted during the reign of George III. **4.** A very small amount; a whit: *didn't care twopence about politics.*

two·pen·ny (túppəni, túp-ni; *in sense 1 also* to͞o-penni) *adj.* Also *British Informal.* **tup·pen·ny** **1.** Worth or costing twopence. **2.** Cheap; worthless; tuppenny-ha'penny.

two-phase (to͞o-fáyz) *adj.* Pertaining to two alternating electrical currents with phases at 90°; quarter-phase.

two-piece (to͞o-peess) *adj.* Made in or consisting of two parts or pieces: *a two-piece suit.*
~n. A two-piece suit or swimming costume.

two-ply (to͞o-plī, -plī) *adj.* **1.** Made of two interwoven layers. **2.** Consisting of two thicknesses or strands: *two-ply knitting yarn.*
~n., pl. **-plies.** Any two-ply material, such as wool or yarn.

two-seat·er (to͞o-seétər) *n.* A motor vehicle, especially a sports car, or an aeroplane that has seating for two people.

Two Sic·i·lies, the (síss'l-iz || -eez). The former kingdoms of Sicily and Naples, ruled jointly (1443–58; 1504–1713; 1759–1815), and united (1815–60).

two-sid·ed (to͞o-sīdid) *adj.* Having two sides or involving two positions: *a two-sided dispute.*

two·some (to͞o-səm) *n.* **1.** Two people together; a pair or couple; a duo. **2.** A game played by two people, in golf.

two-step (to͞o-step) *n.* **1.** A ballroom dance in 2/4 time and characterised by long, sliding steps. **2.** The music composed for such a dance. **—two-step** *adj.*

two-stroke (to͞o-strōk) *adj.* Designating an internal-combustion engine in which the piston or pistons make two strokes for each explosion. Compare **four-stroke.**

two-time (to͞o-tīm) *tr.v.* **-timed, -timing, -times.** *Informal.* **1.** To deceive or betray. **2.** To be unfaithful to (a spouse or lover). **—two-tim·er** (-tīmər) *n.* **—two-tim·ing** (-tīming) *adj.*

two-tone (to͞o-tōn) *adj.* Of two shades or colours: *two-tone shoes.*

'twould (two͝od, *weak form* twəd). *Regional and Poetic.* Contraction of *it would.*

two-up (to͞o-up) *n.* A gambling game, played especially in Australia, in which bets are made on whether two coins tossed up will both land with heads or tails facing upwards.

two-way (to͞o-wáy) *adj.* **1.** Affording passage to vehicular traffic in two directions: *a two-way street.* **2.** Permitting communication in two directions: *two-way radio.* **3. a.** Expressive of or involving mutual action or responsibility. **b.** Involving two participants on a reciprocal basis. **4.** Permitting the flow in either of two directions: *a two-way valve.* **5.** Controlling an electric current at two places.

-ty[1] *n. suffix.* Indicates a condition or quality; for example, **royalty.** [Middle English *-te(e), -tie,* from Old French *-te, -tet,* from Latin *-tās* (stem *-tāt-*), akin to Greek *-tēs,* Sanskrit *-tat, -tati.*]

-ty[2] *suffix.* Indicates a multiple of ten; for example, **forty, fifty, sixty.** [Middle English *-ty, -ti,* Old English *-tig.*]

ty·coon (tī-ko͞on, tī-) *n.* **1.** *Informal.* A wealthy and powerful businessman or industrialist; a magnate. **2.** A title formerly applied to the Japanese shogun. [Japanese *taikun,* title of a shogun, from Ancient Chinese *t'ai kiuən,* emperor : *tài,* great (Mandarin *dà*) + *kiuən,* prince, sovereign (Mandarin *jūn*).]

tyke, tike (tīk) *n.* **1.** *Informal.* A small child, especially a mischievous one. **2.** *Chiefly Scottish.* A mongrel or cur. **3.** *Chiefly Scottish.* A mean or uncouth fellow; a boor. **4.** A **Yorkshire tyke** *(see).* [Middle English, from Old Norse *tīk,* a bitch.]

Ty·ler (tīlər), **Wat** (died 1381). English rebel. He led the peasants' revolt (1381) against Richard II's poll tax. He was killed by the Lord Mayor of London, Sir William Walworth, after making fresh demands of the King, who had already made concessions.

ty·lo·sis (tī-lṓ-siss) *n., pl.* **-loses** (-seez). Also **ty·lose** (tī-lōz, -lōss). *Botany.* An ingrowth from an adjoining cell into a water-conducting vessel, often found in old, damaged, or diseased wood, that may wholly block the vessel. [Greek *tulōsis* : *tulē,* callus + -osis.]

tymbal. Variant of **timbal.**

tym·pan (tímpən) *n.* **1.** *Printing.* A padding of paper or cloth placed over the platen of a printing press to provide support for the sheet being printed. **2.** *Architecture.* A tympanum. **3.** A tightly stretched sheet or membrane, as on the head of a drum. [Middle English *tympan, timpan,* a drum, Old English *timpana,* from Latin *tympanum.* See **tympanum.**]

tympani. Variant of **timpani.**

tym·pan·ic (tim-pánnik) *adj.* Also **tym·pa·nal** (tímpən'l) (for sense 2). **1.** Pertaining to or resembling a drum. **2.** *Anatomy.* Of or pertaining to the tympanum. [From TYMPANUM.]

tympanic bone *n.* The part of the temporal bone of the skull that partially encloses the auditory canal and supports the tympanic membrane.

tympanic cavity *n.* The **middle ear** *(see).*

tympanic membrane *n.* The thin, semitransparent, oval-shaped membrane separating the middle ear from the external ear. Also called "eardrum", "tympanum".

tym·pa·nist (tímpənist) *n.* The member of an orchestra who plays the kettledrums and other percussion instruments. [Latin *tympanista,* from Greek *tumpanistēs,* from *tumpanizein,* to beat a drum, from *tumpanon,* a drum. See **tympanum.**]

tym·pa·ni·tes (tìmpə-nī-teez) *n.* A distension of the abdomen resulting from the accumulation of gas or air in the abdomen. [Middle English, from Late Latin *tympanītēs,* from Greek *tumpanītēs,* from *tumpanon,* a drum. See **tympanum.**]

tym·pa·ni·tis (tìmpə-nītiss) *n.* Inflammation of the middle ear. [TYMPANUM + -ITIS.]

tym·pa·num, tim·pa·num (tímpə-nəm) *n., pl.* **-na** (-nə) or **-nums. 1. a.** The **middle ear** *(see).* **b.** The tympanic membrane; the eardrum. **c.** The middle ear and the tympanic membrane combined. **2.** *Zoology.* A membranous external auditory structure, as in certain insects. **3.** *Architecture.* **a.** The recessed, ornamental space or panel enclosed by the cornices of a triangular pediment. **b.** A similar space between an arch and the lintel of a portal. Also called "tympan". **4.** The diaphragm of a telephone. **5.** The tympan on a drum; a drumhead. [Medieval Latin, the eardrum, from Latin, a drum, from Greek *tumpanon.*]

tym·pa·ny (tímpəni) *n., pl.* **-nies. 1.** Tympanites. **2.** *Archaic.* An inflated manner or style; bombast. [Medieval Latin *tympanias,* "a drumlike swelling", from Greek *tumpanias,* from *tumpanon,* a drum. See **tympanum.**]

Tyn·dale (tínd'l), **William** (*c.* 1494–1536). English Protestant reformer and biblical translator. His highly literary translation of the New Testament (begun at Cologne 1525) became the basis of the Authorised, or King James, Version of the Bible. He was strangled at the stake as a heretic, and his body afterwards burned.

Tyn·dall effect (tínd'l) *n.* The **Rayleigh scattering** of light by very small particles. [After John *Tyndall* (1820–93), Irish physicist.]

Tyne (tīn) *n.* River of northeastern England. Formed by the confluence of the North and South Tynes at Hexham, it flows 48 kilometres (30 miles) east to the North Sea.

Tyne and Wear (weer). From 1974 to 1997 a metropolitan county of northeast England that was created from parts of Northumberland and Durham. It is now subdivided into Unitary Authority areas.

Tyn·wald (tínwəld) *n.* The parliament of the Isle of Man.

typ·al (típ'l) *adj. Rare.* Pertaining to or serving as a type; typical.

type (tīp) *n.* **1. a.** A group of persons or things sharing common traits or characteristics that distinguish them as an identifiable group or class; a kind; a category. **b.** A subdivision of a kind or category: *three main types of error.* **2.** A person or thing having the features of a group or class; a standard example: *a type of the red-haired Celt.* **3.** An example or model; an embodiment: *"He was the perfect type of a military dandy"* (Joyce Cary). **4.** *Informal.* **a.** A person regarded as being typical of a specified class, such a profession, rank, or social group: *a bar full of rugby types.* **b.** One embodying the features or characteristics associated with a specified group or class: *She's not the ballet type.* **5.** A figure, representation, or symbol of something to come, such as an event in the Old Testament that foreshadows another in the New Testament. **6. a.** A taxonomic designation, such as the name of a species or genus, used as the basis of ascription to or characterisation of the next highest taxonomic category. **b.** A specimen or sample used as the basis of description of a species; a holotype. **7.** *Printing.* **a.** A small block of metal or wood bearing a raised letter or character on the upper end, that, when inked and pressed upon paper, leaves a printed impression. **b.** Such pieces collectively. **c.** Letters or characters photographically exposed onto light-sensitive material, such as film or bromide paper, subsequently used to prepare a printing image in photocomposition. **d.** A typeface: *in heavy type.* **e.** Letters and characters produced by traditional printing methods or by photocomposition; printing matter. **8.** A pattern, design, or image impressed or stamped upon the face of a coin. **—true to type.** Appearing or behaving in a characteristic way.

~*adj.* **1.** Standard; typical: *type examples.* **2.** Of or pertaining to printing or typesetting: *type size.*

~*v.* **typed, typing, types. —tr. 1.** To write (something) with a type-writer; typewrite. **2.** To determine the type of (a blood sample or tissue). **3.** To classify according to a particular type: *typed her a heroine.* **4.** To represent or typify. **5.** To prefigure; foreshadow. *—intr.* To work at a typewriter; typewrite. [Middle English, from Late Latin *typus,* a form, type, from Latin, figure, image, from Greek *tupos,* a blow, impression, from *tuptein,* to strike.]

Synonyms: *type, kind, sort, nature, character, ilk.*

Usage: In standard English, *type* is followed by *of* in constructions such as *that type of leather,* though the *of* is sometimes omitted in regional speech. Many people prefer to restrict their use of *type* to those contexts where a specific, clearly definable category is involved, and to use *kind* or *sort* where the reference is more general *(that sort of thing; the kind of person I would trust).*

–type *n. comb. form.* Indicates: **1.** Type or representative form; for example, **monotype. 2.** Stamping or printing type, or photographic process; for example, **collotype. 3. a.** Belonging to a specified type or class: *reference-type works.* **b.** Resembling or related to something specified: *a Chablis-type wine.* [French, from Latin *-typus,* from Greek *-tupos,* from *tupos,* TYPE.]

type-bar (típ-baar) *n.* Any of the movable bars in a typewriter carrying letters or characters.

type-case (típ-kayss) *n.* A case divided into compartments for holding printing type.

type-cast (típ-kaast ‖ -kast) *tr.v.* **-cast, -casting, -casts. 1.** To cast in an acting role akin or suited to one's own personality, background, or physical appearance. **2.** To assign repeatedly to the same kind of part or role: *typecast as a scarlet woman.*

type·face (típ-fayss) *n. Printing.* **1.** The surface of a body of type that makes the impression. **2.** The impression itself. **3.** The size, design, or style of the letter or character on the type. **4.** The full range of type of the same design. Also called "face".

type foundry *n.* A factory where metal printing type is cast. **—type founder** *n.* **—type founding** *n.*

type genus *n.* The name of a taxonomic genus that is designated as representative of the family to which it belongs; for example, the genus *Canis,* which includes dogs and wolves, is the type genus of the family Canidae.

type-high (típ-hī) *adj.* As high as the standard height of type, 0.9175 of an inch in Britain, and 0.9186 of an inch in the United States.

type metal *n. Printing.* An alloy used for making metal types, consisting mainly of tin, lead, and antimony.

type·script (típ-skript) *n.* **1.** A typewritten copy, as of a book or document. **2.** Typewritten matter.

type-set (típ-set) *tr.v.* **-set, -setting, -sets.** To set (type) for printing.

type·set·ter (típ-settər) *n.* **1.** A person who sets type; a compositor. **2.** A machine used for setting type.

type species *n.* The name of a taxonomic species designated as representative of the genus to which it belongs; for example, *Panthera pardus,* the leopard, is the type species of the genus *Panthera.*

type specimen *n.* A **holotype** *(see).*

type·write (típ-rīt) *v.* **-wrote** (-rōt), **-written** (-ritt'n), **-writing, -writes.** *—tr.* To write (a letter, for example) with a typewriter; type. *—intr.* To write with a typewriter; type. [Back-formation from TYPEWRITER.]

type·writ·er (típ-rītər) *n. Abbr.* **typw. 1.** A keyboard machine, sometimes electrically powered, that prints characters and numerals, traditionally by means of a set of metal hammers bearing raised type that strike the paper through an inked ribbon or carbon tape, or using various other devices, such as a **daisywheel** or **golfball** *(both of which see),* when actuated by pressed keys. **2.** *Archaic.* A typist. **3.** *Printing.* A style of type that resembles typewritten copy.

type·writ·ing (típ-rīting) *n.* **1.** The act, process, or skill of using a typewriter. **2.** Copy produced by typewriting; typescript.

typh·li·tis (tif-lītiss) *n.* Inflammation of the caecum. [New Latin, from Greek *tuphlon,* caecum (from *tuphlos,* blind) + -ITIS.] **—typh·li·tic** (-líttik) *adj.*

ty·phoid (tí-foyd) *n.* An acute, highly infectious disease caused by the typhoid bacillus, *Salmonella typhi,* transmitted by contaminated food or water and characterised by red rashes, high fever, and, in severe cases, intestinal haemorrhaging. Also called "enteric fever", "typhoid fever".

~*adj.* Also **ty·phoi·dal** (tī-fóyd'l). Of, pertaining to, or resembling typhoid. [TYPH(US) + -OID.]

Ty·phon (tí-f'n, -fon). *Greek Mythology.* A monster called by Hesiod the son of Typhoeus.

ty·phoon (tí-fóon, tī-) *n.* A small, intense tropical cyclone occurring in the western Pacific or the China Sea. See Synonyms at **wind.** [Cantonese *daai fung,* "great wind", corresponding to Chinese (Mandarin) *dàfēng¹* : *dà,* great + *fēng,* wind (but in form influenced by Greek *Tuphōn,* TYPHON).] **—ty·phon·ic** (tī-fónnik) *adj.*

ty·phus (tí-fəss) *n.* Any of several forms of an infectious disease caused by microorganisms of the genus *Rickettsia,* especially when flea-borne as in *endemic typhus,* louse-borne as in *epidemic typhus,* or mite-borne as in *scrub typhus,* and characterised generally by severe headache, sustained high fever, depression, delirium, and widespread rashes. Also called "ship fever", "typhus fever". [New Latin, from Greek *tuphos,* (fever causing) delusion, from *tuphein,* to make smoke.] **—ty·phous** (-fəss) *adj.*

typ·i·cal (típpik'l) *adj.* Also **typ·ic** (típpik). **1.** Exhibiting the traits or characteristics peculiar to a kind, class, group, or the like; representative of a whole group: *a typical suburban community.* **2. a.** Of or pertaining to a representative specimen; characteristic; distinctive. **b.** Characteristic of a particular individual: *That sort of behav-*

iour is typical of her. **3. a.** Conforming to a type. **b.** *Biology.* Having the characteristics of a particular taxonomic. **4.** Of the nature of, constituting, or serving as a type; emblematic. —See Synonyms at **characteristic, usual.** [Late Latin *typicālis,* from *typicus,* typical, from Greek *tupikos,* impressionable, from *tupos,* impression, TYPE.] —**typ·i·cal·i·ty** (típpi-kál-əti), **typ·i·cal·ness** *n.*

typ·i·cal·ly (típpi-kli, -k'l-i) *adj.* **1.** In the respects usually associated with the specified category: *She is typically English.* **2.** In normal or typical circumstances; usually: *Roads are typically used by cars.*

typ·i·fy (típpi-fī) *tr.v.* **-fied, -fying, -fies. 1.** To serve as a typical example of; embody the essential characteristics of. **2.** To represent by an image, form, or model; symbolise. [From TYP(E) + -FY.] —**typ·i·fi·ca·tion** (-fi-káysh'n) *n.* —**typ·i·fi·er** *n.*

typ·ist (típist) *n.* One who operates a typewriter, especially as a form of employment.

ty·po (típō) *n., pl.* **-os.** *Informal.* A typographical error.

ty·pog·ra·pher (tī-póggrəfər) *n.* **1.** A printer or compositor. **2.** One skilled in the design or layout of printed matter.

typographical error *n.* A mistake in printing, typing, or writing.

ty·pog·ra·phy (tī-póggrəfi) *n., pl.* **-phies. 1. a.** The process of printing material using type. **b.** The art and technique of this. **2.** The arrangement or appearance of printing matter. [Medieval Latin *typographia* : Greek *tupos,* impression, TYPE + -GRAPHY.] —**ty·po·graph·ic** (típ-ə-gráffik, -ō-), **ty·po·graph·i·cal** *adj.* —**ty·po·graph·i·cal·ly** *adv.*

ty·pol·o·gy (tī-pólləji) *n., pl.* **-gies. 1.** The study of types, especially according to a systematic classification. **2.** A theory or doctrine of types, as in scriptural studies. [Greek *tupos,* impression, TYPE + -LOGY.] —**ty·po·log·i·cal** (típə-lójik'l) *adj.* —**ty·po·log·i·cal·ly** *adv.* —**ty·pol·o·gist** (tī-pólləjist) *n.*

typw. typewriter; typewritten.

Tyr, Tyrr (teer, tewr, tür). *Norse Mythology.* A god of war, son of Odin. [Old Norse *Tȳr.*]

ty·ra·mine (tír-ə-meen, tírrə-) *n.* A colourless, crystalline amine, $C_8H_{11}NO$, found in mistletoe, putrefied animal tissue, certain cheeses, and ergot, and also produced synthetically, used in medicine. [TYR(OSINE) + AMINE.]

ty·ran·ni·cal (ti-ránnik'l, tī-, tīr-) *adj.* Also **ty·ran·nic** (-ránnik). **1.** Of, pertaining to, or characteristic of a tyrant. **2.** Despotic; arbitrary; oppressive. —**ty·ran·ni·cal·ly** *adv.* —**ty·ran·ni·cal·ness** *n.*

ty·ran·ni·cide (tī-ránni-sīd, tī-, tīr-) *n.* **1.** The killing of a tyrant. **2.** One who kills a tyrant. —**ty·ran·ni·ci·dal** (-sīd'l) *adj.*

tyr·an·nise, tyr·an·nize (tírrə-nīz) *v.* **-nised, -nising, -nises.** —*intr.* **1.** To exercise absolute power, especially arbitrarily. **2.** To rule as a tyrant. —*tr.* To treat tyrannically; crush; oppress. [French *tyranniser,* from Late Latin *tyrannizāre,* from Latin *tyrannus,* TYRANT.] —**tyr·an·nis·er** *n.* —**tyr·an·nis·ing·ly** *adv.*

ty·ran·no·saur (ti-ránna-sawr, tī-, tīr-) *n.* Also **ty·ran·no·saur·us** (-sáwrəss). Any large carnivorous dinosaur of the genus *Tyrannosaurus,* of the Cretaceous period; especially *T. rex,* which had small forelimbs and a large head. [New Latin : Greek *turannos,* TYRANT + -SAUR.]

tyr·an·nous (tírrənəss) *adj.* Characterised by tyranny; despotic; tyrannical. —**tyr·an·nous·ly** *adv.*

tyr·an·ny (tírrəni) *n., pl.* **-nies. 1.** A government in which a single ruler exercises absolute power, especially in an unjust, cruel, or arbitrary manner. **2.** The office, authority, or jurisdiction of such a ruler. **3.** Absolute power, especially when exercised unjustly or cruelly. **4.** The arbitrary use of such power; a tyrannical act. **5.** Excessively rigorous control: *the tyranny of etiquette.* [Middle English *tyrannye,* from Old French *tyrannie,* from Late Latin *tyrannia,* from Greek *turannia,* from *turannos,* TYRANT.]

ty·rant (tír-ənt) *n.* **1.** An absolute ruler who governs arbitrarily without constitutional or other restrictions, especially one in ancient Greece. **2.** A ruler who exercises power in a harsh, cruel manner; an oppressor. **3.** Any tyrannical or despotic person. [Middle English *tyra(u)nt,* from Old French *tyran(t),* from Latin *tyrannus,* from Greek *turannos,* probably from a source in Asia Minor.]

tyrant flycatcher *n.* A bird of the family Tyrannidae, the **flycatcher** *(see).* [Referring to its habit of repelling all birds from its territory.]

tyre, *U.S.* **tire** (tīr) *n.* **1.** A solid or air-filled covering for a wheel, typically of rubber or a similar elastic synthetic material, fitted round the wheel's rim to absorb shock and provide traction. **2.** A hoop of iron or heavy rubber fitted about the rim of a wheel. ~*tr.v.* **tyred, tyring, tyres.** To fit with a tyre or tyres.

Tyre (tīr). Port of northwestern Lebanon, present-day Sur. Founded by the Phoenicians, it became one of the great trade centres of the ancient world. Taken by the Crusaders in 1124, it was destroyed by Muslims in 1291, and was never completely rebuilt.

tyre chain *n.* A snow chain *(see).*

Tyr·i·an pur·ple (tírri-ən) *n.* A reddish dyestuff obtained from the bodies of certain molluscs of the genus *Murex,* and highly prized in ancient times. [After *Tyre,* source of the dye.]

ty·ro, ti·ro (tír-ō) *n., pl.* **-ros.** An inexperienced person; a beginner; a neophyte. [Medieval Latin *tȳrō,* from Latin *tīrō†,* a young soldier, recruit.]

ty·ro·li·enne (ti-róli-én) *n.* **1.** A Tyrol peasant dance in ¾ time. **2.** A song composed for this dance, featuring the yodel. [French, *(danse) tyrolienne,* Tyrolean (dance).]

Tyrol. See **Tirol.**

Ty·rone (ti-rón). County of west Northern Ireland. It is a hilly, predominantly agricultural county, and its traditional flax and brewing industries have declined. Omagh is the county town.

ty·ro·sin·ase (tír-ə-sin-ayz, -ō-, tirrō-, ti-róssin-, -ayss) *n.* A copper-containing enzyme of plant and animal tissues that catalyses the production of melanin from tyrosine. [TYROSIN(E) + -ASE.]

ty·ro·sine (tír-ə-seen, tírrə-, -sin) *n.* A white crystalline non-essential amino acid, $C_9H_{11}NO_3$, derived from the hydrolysis of protein, that is a precursor of adrenaline, thyroxine, and melanin. [Greek *turos,* cheese + -INE.]

ty·ro·thri·cin (tír-ō-thrí-sin) *n.* A greyish to brown mixture of antibiotics obtained from cultures of the soil bacteria *Bacillus brevis,* and applied locally for the treatment of infections caused by Gram-positive bacteria. [New Latin *Tyrothrix* (stem *Tyrothric-*), generic name for certain spore-forming bacteria, "cheese-haired" : Greek *turos,* cheese + *thrix,* hair + -IN.]

Ty·son (tí-sən), **Michael (Gerard),** known as Mike (1966–). U.S. boxer. He became the youngest ever world heavyweight champion in 1986. He lost his title in 1989 to James "Buster" Douglas, was in prison (1992–95), beat Frank Bruno to regain his title (1996), but lost it the same year.

tzar, tzarevitch, tzarevna, tzaritsa. Variants of **tsar, tsarevitch, tsarevna, tsaritsa.**

Tzi·gane (tsi-gaan, si-, tsee-, see-) *n.* A gypsy, especially a Hungarian gypsy. ~*adj.* Of or pertaining to Tziganes or their music. [French, from Hungarian *czigány.*]

U

u, U (yoo) *n., pl.* **u's** or *rare* **us, Us** or **U's. 1.** The 21st letter of the modern English alphabet. **2.** Any of the speech sounds represented by this letter. **3.** Anything shaped like the letter **U.** Often used in combination: *a U-turn.*

u, U, u., U. *Note:* As an abbreviation or symbol, *u* may be a capital or a small letter, with or without a full stop. Established forms or those generally preferred precede the definition. When no form is given, all four forms are in general use in that sense. **1. u., U.** uncle. **2. U** *Mathematics.* union. **3. u.** unit. **4. U.** university. **5. u., U.** upper. **6. U** The symbol for the element uranium. **7.** The 21st in a series; 20th when *J* is omitted.

U¹ (yoo) *adj. British Informal.* Considered to be typical of or appropriate to the upper class, especially in language usage. Compare **non-U.** [Abbreviation of *upper class.*]

U² (yoo) *n., pl.* **Us** or **U's.** In Britain, a film designated as being suitable for a person of any age. Also used adjectivally: *a U film.* [Abbreviation of *universal.*]

U³ (yoo) *n.* A Burmese title of respect used before the name of a man.

Uabh Failghe. See **Offaly.**

UAM underwater-to-air missile.

UAR, U.A.R. United Arab Republic.

UART *n.* Universal asynchronous receiver transmitter; a type of radio set.

UB40 *n.* An unemployed person claiming unemployment benefit. [From the number of the form filled in by claimants of unemployment benefit.]

Ubangi-Shari. See **Central African Republic.**

Ü·ber·mensch (yoo-bər-mensh; *German* ü-) *n., pl.* **-menschen** (-'n). *German.* A superman, as in the philosophy of Nietzsche. [German, "over-man".]

u·bi·e·ty (yoo-bí-əti) *n.* The condition of being located in a particular place. [Medieval Latin *ubietās,* from *ubi,* where.]

u·biq·ui·tous (yoo-bíkwitəss) *adj.* Being or seeming to be everywhere at the same time; omnipresent: *their ubiquitous influence.* [From UBIQUITY.] —**u·biq·ui·tous·ly** *adv.* —**u·biq·ui·tous·ness** *n.*

u·biq·ui·ty (yoo-bíkwəti) *n.* Existence everywhere at the same time; omnipresence. [New Latin *ubiquitas,* from Latin *ubíque,* everywhere : *ubī,* where + *-que,* generalising particle.]

U-boat (yoo-bōt) *n.* A German submarine. [German *U-boot,* short for *Unterseeboot,* "undersea boat".]

U-bolt (yoo-bōlt ‖ -bolt) *n.* A bolt shaped like the letter U, fitted with a thread and nut at each end.

u.c. *Printing.* upper case.

UCCA (úckə). Universities Central Council on Admissions.

Uc·cel·lo (ōō-chéllō), **Paolo**, born Paolo di Dono (1397–1475). Florentine painter and craftsman, best known for his experiments with perspective and foreshortening. Among his works are three paintings of *The Rout of San Romano* (1456–60).

U.D.A., UDA Ulster Defence Association.

u·dal (yōō'd'l) *n.* A system of freehold possession of land that preceded the feudal system and is still used in Orkney and Shetland. [Orkney and Shetland dialect, from Old Norse *ōthal*, from Germanic *ōth-* (unattested); akin to ATHELING.] **—u·dal** *adj.*

ud·der (uddər) *n.* The baglike mammary organ characteristic of cows, sheep, and goats, having two or four teats. [Middle English *udder,* Old English *ūder.*]

UDI Unilateral Declaration of Independence.

u·do (ōō-dō) *n.* A Japanese plant, *Aralia cordata,* of which the young shoots are cooked and eaten as a vegetable. [Japanese.]

u·dom·e·ter (yōō-dómmitər) *n.* A **rain gauge** *(see).* [French *udomè-tre,* from Latin *ūdus,* damp + -METER.]

U.D.R., UDR Ulster Defence Regiment.

UFO, u·fo (*sometimes* yōōfō) *n., pl.* **-FOs, -fos.** An **unidentified flying object** *(see).*

u·fol·o·gy (yōō-fólləji) *n.* The study of UFOs or the practice of trying to spot them. [UFO + -LOGY.] **—u·fo·log·i·cal** (yōōfə-lójik'l) *adj.* **—u·fol·o·gist** (yōō-fóllǝjist) *n.*

U·gan·da (yōō-gándə ‖ *U.S. also* -gáandə). Land-locked republic in east central Africa. Most of the country lies on a high plateau, more than 1 070 metres (3,500 feet) above sea level. Some 90 per cent of Ugandans live by subsistence farming, and coffee accounts for over 75 per cent of exports. There are reserves of copper and tin, and the Owen Falls hydroelectric scheme satisfies most energy needs. A British protectorate from 1894, Uganda became independent within the Commonwealth in 1962, with the kabaka (king) of Buganda as president. He was succeeded by Milton Obote (1966), who returned Amin (1971–78). Obote himself was ousted by a military coup in 1985. After 18 months of warfare, the leader of the National Resistance Army, Yoweri Museveni, took over. Area, 241 139 square kilometres (93,104 square miles). Population, 20,260,000. Capital, Kampala.

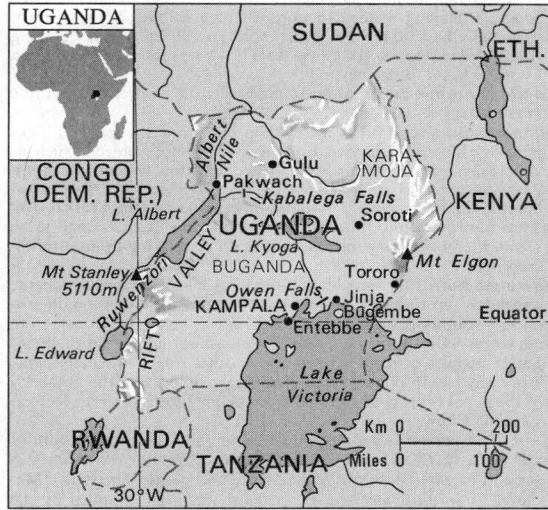

U·ga·rit·ic (ōōgə-ríttik) *n.* The Semitic language of the ancient city-state of Ugarit (on the site of Ras Shamra in present-day Syria). **—U·ga·rit·ic** *adj.*

U.G.C. University Grants Committee.

ugh (ōōkh, ukh, *and various back unrounded vowel-sounds*) *interj.* Used to express horror, disgust, or repugnance.

Ug·li (úggli) *n., pl.* **-lis** or **-lies.** Trade name of a citrus fruit indigenous to Jamaica: a cross between a grapefruit and a tangerine. Also called "Ugli fruit". [Perhaps from UGLY (from its ugly wrinkled rind).]

ug·li·fy (úggli-fī) *tr.v.* **-fied, -fying, -fies.** To make ugly; disfigure. [UGLY + -FY.] **—ug·li·fi·ca·tion** (-fi-káysh'n) *n.*

ug·ly (úggli) *adj.* **-lier, -liest. 1.** Displeasing to the eye; unsightly. **2.** Repulsive or offensive in any way; objectionable. **3.** Morally reprehensible. **4.** Threatening; ominous: *ugly weather.* **5.** Marked by or inclined towards anger or bad feelings: *An ugly scene developed.* [Middle English *ugli(c),* frightful, repulsive, from Old Norse *uggligr,* from *uggr†,* fear.] **—ug·li·ly** *adv.* **—ug·li·ness** *n.*

ugly duckling *n.* One considered ugly or unpromising at first but having the potential of becoming beautiful or admirable in maturity. [After the cygnet in the story by Hans Christian Andersen.]

U·gri·an (ōō-gri-ən, yōō-) *n.* **1.** A member of a group of Finno-Ugric peoples of western Siberia and Hungary, including the Magyars. **2.** Ugric. [Old Russian *Ugrin'* (plural *Ugre*), from Common Sla-

vonic *Og'rin'* (unattested), from Turkic *Onogouroi.* See also **Hungary.**] **—U·gri·an** *adj.*

U·gric (ōō-grik, yōō-) *n.* A branch of the Finno-Ugric subfamily of languages consisting of Magyar (Hungarian), Ostyak, and Vogul. **—U·gric** *adj.*

uhf, UHF ultrahigh frequency.

uh-huh (ú-hu, ə-hə, *often nasalised, also* m̓-hm) *interj. Informal.* Yes.

uh·lan, u·lan (ōō-laan, yōō-, -lən, ōō-láan) *n.* A member of a body of cavalry armed with lances that formed part of the former Polish army, and later, the former German army. [German *u(h)lan,* from Polish *ulan,* from Turkish *oğlan,* "youth", from *oğul,* son.]

UHT *Ultra Heat-Treated:* refers to homogenised milk heated rapidly and then cooled, so as to stay usable longer in an unopened container.

uh-uh (ú'ú, ə'ə) *interj. Informal.* **1.** No. **2.** Used to express the realisation that trouble is near.

u·hu·ru (ōō-hoor-ōō, -hóorrōō) *n. East African.* Liberty; freedom. Used chiefly as a slogan by African independence movements. [Swahili.]

Ui·gur, Ui·ghur (wée-goor, yóo-i-) *n.* **1.** A member of a Turkic people dominant in Mongolia and eastern Turkestan from the 8th to the 12th centuries, now inhabiting northwestern China. **2.** The East Turkic language of this people. **—Ui·gu·ri·an** (-góor-i-ən) *adj.*

u·in·ta·there (yoo-intə-theer) *n.* Any of a number of extinct mammals resembling the rhinoceros, fossils of which have been found in North America. Also called "dinoceras". [After the *Uinta* Mountains, Utah, where fossil remains were discovered + -*there,* from Greek *thērion,* wild beast.]

u·in·ta·ite (yōō-intə-īt) *n.* A bitumen, **gilsonite** *(see).* [After the *Uinta* basin (Utah and Wyoming), where it was discovered.]

U·ist (yōō-ist). Name of two islands in the Outer Hebrides, off the northwestern coast of Scotland, North Uist and South Uist. Most of the population are crofters.

uit·land·er (áyt-landər) *n. South African.* **1.** A foreigner. **2.** *Capital U.* A native of Great Britain who resided in either of the former republics of the Orange Free State and Transvaal. [Afrikaans, from Dutch.]

u·ja·maa (ōōjə-máa) *n.* **1.** A plan for developing cooperation and communal ideals amongst different peoples in Tanzania. Also used adjectivally: *a ujamaa village.* **2.** A village practising this. [Swahili, family, brother : *u-,* prefix indicating state or condition + *jamaa,* family, from Arabic *jamā"a,* community.]

Ujiji. See **Kigoma-Ujiji.**

Uj·jain (ōō-jīn, ōōj-, -jayn). City in the state of Madhya Pradesh, in central India, on the river Siprā. It is one of the seven sacred Hindu cities in India.

U.K., UK United Kingdom.

u·kase (yōō-káyz, -káyss ‖ yōō-kayss, ōō-káaz) *n.* **1.** A proclamation of the tsar having the force of law in imperial Russia. **2.** Any authoritative order or decree; an edict. [French, from Russian *ukaz,* decree, from *ukazat',* to order, direct : *u-,* intensive prefix, "away" + -*kazat',* to show.]

u·ki·yo·e (ōō-kée-yō-áy, -yáy) *n.* A Japanese style of art in painting and printmaking, characterised by the simple depiction of scenes or objects from ordinary life. [Japanese : *ukiyo,* life + *e,* picture.]

Ukraine (yōō-kráyn). Formerly **Little Russia.** Republic in eastern Europe, formerly a constituent republic of the U.S.S.R. After Russia, the Ukraine is the most heavily populated and economically important of the former Soviet republics. Its steppe lands are one of the great wheat-producing regions of Europe and the republic as a whole provided nearly a quarter of the U.S.S.R.'s food supply. It is also a major producer of coal and iron ore. Area, 603 700 square kilometres (233,090 square miles). Population, 51,090,000. Capital, Kiev. See map at **Commonwealth of Independent States.**

U·krain·i·an (yōō-kráyni-ən, *rarely* -krīni-) *n.* **1.** An inhabitant or native of the Ukraine. **2.** A Slavonic language, similar to but distinct from Russian, that is spoken by most natives of the Ukraine. Also formerly called "Little Russian". [Ukrainian *Ukrayina,* from Old Russian *Ukraina,* "borderland" : *u-,* away from, at + *kraï,* edge, brink, end.] **—U·krain·i·an** *adj.*

u·ku·le·le (yōōkə-láyli ‖ ōōkə-) *n.* A small four-stringed guitar originally from Hawaii. [Hawaiian *'ukulele,* "jumping little flea" (said to be nickname of Edward Putvis, 19th-century British officer, who popularised the instrument) : *'uku,* flea + *lele,* jumping.]

ulan. Variant of **uhlan.**

U·lan Ba·tor (ōō-laan baa-tawr). Capital of the Republic of Mongolia, lying on the river Tola. It is the chief commercial and industrial city of the country and, lying on the Trans-Siberian railway, is also the main transport junction.

U·la·no·va (ōō-lán-əvə, -laán-), **Galina Sergeyevna** (1910–98). Russian prima ballerina noted for her roles in *Swan Lake* and *Giselle.* From 1962 until her death she was ballet mistress to the Bolshoi.

–ular *adj. suffix.* Indicates a relationship or resemblance; for example, **tubular.** [Latin -*ulāris,* from -*ulus,* -ULE.]

Ul·bricht (ōōl-brikht), **Walter** (1893–1973). East German statesman. He was general secretary of the Socialist Unity Party from 1950, and became chairman (1960) of the newly-established council of state. He erected the Berlin Wall (1961).

ul·cer (úl-sər) *n.* **1. a.** An inflammatory, often suppurating lesion on the skin or an internal mucous surface of the body, resulting in necrosis of the tissue and taking a long time to heal. **b.** A necrotic lesion of the stomach or duodenum. **2.** Any corrupting condition or influence. [Middle English, from Old French *ulcere,* from Lati-

ulcus (stem *ulcer-*), a sore, ulcer.]

ul·cer·ate (úl-sə-rayt) *v.* **-ated, -ating, -ates.** —*intr.* To become affected with or as if with an ulcer. —*tr.* To affect with ulcers. —**ul·cer·a·tive** (-rətiv, -raytiv) *adj.*

ul·cer·a·tion (úl-sə-ráysh'n) *n.* **1.** The development of an ulcer. **2.** An ulcer or ulcerous condition.

ul·cer·ous (úl-sərəss) *adj.* **1.** Pertaining to or exhibiting ulcers. **2.** Corrupting; having a bad influence. —**ul·cer·ous·ly** *adv.*

-ule *n. suffix.* Indicates smallness; for example, **granule, valvule.** [French *-ule,* from Latin *-ulus* (masculine), *-ula* (feminine), *-ulum* (neuter), diminutive suffixes.]

u·le·ma, u·la·ma (ōōl-i-mə, -ə-, -maa) *n., pl.* **-mas** or **ulema. 1.** The body of scholars or priests trained in traditional Muslim religion and law. **2.** A Muslim scholar or religious leader. [Turkish *'ulemā,* from Arabic *'ulamā',* "wise men", plural of *'ālim,* wise, learned, from *'alimā,* to know.]

-ulent *adj. suffix.* Indicates abundance or fullness; for example, **flatulent.** [Old French, from Latin *-ulentus.*] —**ulence** *n. suffix.*

u·lex·ite (yōō-leks-īt, -liks-, yōō-léks-) *n.* A white mineral, $NaCa-B_5O_9.8H_2O$, that forms round masses of very fine acicular crystals. [After George *Ulex* (died 1883), German chemist + -ITE.]

ul·lage (úllij) *n.* **1.** The amount of liquid, grain, or the like within a container that is lost during shipment or storage, as through leakage. **2.** The amount by which a container, such as a cask or bottle, falls short of being full. [Middle English, from Anglo-French *ulliage,* Old French *ouillage,* from *ouiller,* to fill up a cask to the bunghole, from *oeil,* eye, bunghole, from Latin *oculus.*]

Ulls·wa·ter (úlz-wawtər). Second-largest lake in England, lying in the Lake District, and about 12 kilometres (7.5 miles) long.

Ulm (ōōlm). Industrial city in southern Germany, lying on the river Danube. Mentioned in records as early as the mid-9th century, it was a leading commercial centre during the Middle Ages.

ul·na (úl-nə) *n., pl.* **-nas** or **-nae** (-nee). *Anatomy.* **1.** The bone extending from the elbow to the wrist on the side opposite to the thumb. **2.** The corresponding bone in the forelimb of other vertebrates. [New Latin, from Latin, elbow, arm.] —**ul·nar** (-nər) *adj.*

u·lot·ri·chous (yōō-lóttri-kəss) *adj.* Having wiry or woolly hair. Said especially of negroid peoples. [New Latin, "woolly-haired", from Greek *oulothrix* (stem *oulotrikh-*) : *oulos,* woolly, curly + *thrix,* hair.] —**u·lot·ri·chy** (-ki) *n.*

ul·ster (úl-stər) *n.* A loose, long overcoat made of a heavy cloth and often belted. [After ULSTER (the coat was first made in Belfast).]

Ul·ster (úl-stər). Northernmost of the four ancient provinces of Ireland, no longer of political or administrative meaning. It consisted of nine counties, six of which (Antrim, Armagh, Down, Fermanagh, Londonderry, and Tyrone) now constitute Northern Ireland, itself still popularly known as Ulster. The three other counties (Cavan, Donegal, and Monaghan) are in the Republic of Ireland.

Ulster Defence Association *n. Abbr.* **U.D.A., UDA** A Protestant paramilitary organisation in Northern Ireland.

Ul·ster·man (úl-stər-mən, -man) *n., pl.* **-men** (-mən, -men). A native or inhabitant of Ulster. —**Ul·ster·wo·man** *n.*

ult. 1. ultimate; ultimately. **2.** ultimo. —See Usage note at **inst.**

ul·te·ri·or (ul-téer-i-ər) *adj.* **1.** Lying beyond what is evident, revealed, or avowed; especially, concealed intentionally so as to deceive: *an ulterior motive.* **2.** Lying beyond or outside the area of immediate interest. **3.** Occurring later; subsequent. [Latin, farther, comparative of *ulter* (unattested), on the other side.]

ul·ti·ma (últimə) *n.* The last syllable of a word. [Latin, feminine of *ultimus,* farthest, last. See **ultimate.**]

ul·ti·mate (últi-mət, -mit) *adj. Abbr.* **ult. 1.** Completing a series or process; final; conclusive. **2.** Representing the farthest possible extent of analysis or division into parts: *ultimate constituent.* **3.** Fundamental; elemental. **4.** Of the greatest possible size or significance; maximum. **5.** Farthest; most remote. **6.** Representing the greatest possible sophistication or development of something: *the ultimate bicycle.* —See Synonyms at **last.**
~*n.* **1.** The basic or fundamental element or principle. **2.** The final point; the conclusive result. **3.** The maximum; the greatest extreme. [Medieval Latin *ultimātus,* past participle of *ultimāre,* to come to an end, from Latin *ultimus,* farthest, last, superlative degree of *ulter* (unattested), on the other side.] —**ul·ti·mate·ness** *n.*

ul·ti·mate·ly (últi-mət-li, -mit-) *adv.* At last; in the end; eventually.

Ultima Thu·le (thēw-li, thōō-) *n.* **1.** The northernmost region of the habitable world as thought of by ancient geographers. **2.** Any distant territory or destination. **3.** A remote goal or ideal. [Latin, "farthest Thule".]

ul·ti·ma·tum (últi-máy-təm ‖ -maá-) *n., pl.* **-tums** or **-ta** (-tə). A final statement of terms made by one party to another; especially, in diplomatic negotiations, a statement that expresses or implies the threat of serious penalties if the terms are not accepted. [New Latin, from Medieval Latin, neuter of *ultimātus,* last, ULTIMATE.]

ul·ti·mo (últi-mō) *adv. Abbr.* **ult.** In or of the month before the present one. Compare **proximo.** [Latin *ultimo (mense),* in last (month), from *ultimus,* last, ULTIMATE.]

ul·ti·mo·gen·i·ture (últi-mō-jénni-chər, -choor, -tewr) *n. Law.* A principle by which the youngest child inherits the estate of one or both of his parents. Compare **primogeniture.** [Latin *ultimus* + *-geniture,* as in PRIMOGENITURE.]

ul·tra (últrə) *adj.* Immoderately adhering to a belief, fashion, or course of action; extreme.
~*n.* An extremist. [Originally shortened from French *ultra-royaliste.* See **ultra-.**]

ultra– *prefix.* Indicates: **1.** Surpassing or beyond a specified limit, range, or scope; for example, **ultramicroscopic, ultrasonic. 2.** Exceeding what is usual, moderate, or proper to an extreme degree; for example, **ultraconservative.** *Note:* Many compounds other than those entered here may be formed with *ultra-.* In forming compounds, *ultra-* is normally joined with the following element without a space or hyphen: *ultramodern; ultrafashionable.* However, if the second element begins with a capital letter or with the letter *a,* it is separated with a hyphen: *ultra-British, ultra-atomic.* [Latin, from *ultrā,* beyond, from *ulter* (unattested), on the other side.]

ul·tra·cen·tri·fuge (últrə-séntri-fewj) *n.* A convection-free high-velocity centrifuge used in the separation of colloidal or submicroscopic particles. —**ul·tra·cen·trif·u·gal** (-sen-tríffewg'l, -séntri-féwg'l) *adj.* —**ul·tra·cen·trif·u·ga·tion** (-few-gáysh'n) *n.*

ul·tra·con·ser·va·tive (últrə-kən-sérvətiv ‖ -kon-) *adj.* Conservative to an extreme, especially in political beliefs; reactionary.
~*n.* One who is extremely conservative.

ul·tra·crep·i·da·ri·an (últrə-kréppi-daír-i-ən) *adj.* Acting or speaking outside one's experience, knowledge, or ability.
~*n.* One who acts or speaks beyond the sphere of his experience or knowledge; especially, an ignorant critic. [Latin *ultrā crepidam,* "beyond the sole", alluding to a story about the Greek painter Apelles and a cobbler, who pointed out to Apelles that he had painted a slipper with the wrong number of ties. Having made this successful criticism, the cobbler criticised on the following day the leg of the figure in the painting, to which Apelles replied that he should confine himself to remarks about slippers and not judge "beyond the sole".]

ul·tra·fiche (últrə-feesh) *n.* A microfiche in which the reduction factor is 100 or more. [ULTRA- + (MICRO)FICHE.]

ul·tra·fil·tra·tion (últrə-fil-tráysh'n) *n.* Filtration of colloidal solution through a semipermeable membrane. —**ul·tra·fil·ter** (-filtər) *n.*

ul·tra·high frequency (últrə-hī) *n. Abbr.* **uhf, UHF** A band of radio frequencies from 300 to 3,000 megahertz.

ul·tra·ism (últrə-iz'm) *n.* Extremism, especially in politics; radicalism. [ULTRA + -ISM.] —**ul·tra·ist** *adj. & n.* —**ul·tra·is·tic** (-ístik) *adj.*

ul·tra·ma·rine (últrə-mə-réen) *n.* **1.** A blue pigment made from powdered lapis lazuli. **2.** Any similar pigment made synthetically by heating clay, sodium carbonate, and sulphur together. **3.** Vivid or strong blue to purplish blue.
~*adj.* **1.** Having a deep to purplish blue colour. **2.** Of or from some place beyond the sea. [Medieval Latin *ultrāmarīnus,* "(coming from) beyond the sea" (because lapis lazuli was imported from Asia by sea) : Latin *ultrā-,* beyond + *mare,* sea.]

ul·tra·mi·crom·e·ter (últrə-mī-krómmitər) *n.* An extremely accurate micrometer.

ul·tra·mi·cro·scope (últrə-mī́krə-skōp) *n.* A microscope with high-intensity illumination used to study very minute objects, such as colloidal particles, by means of their diffraction system, which appears as a bright spot against a black background. Also called "dark-field microscope". —**ul·tra·mi·cros·co·py** (-mī-króskəpi) *n.*

ul·tra·mi·cro·scop·ic (últrə-mī́krə-skóppik) *adj.* **1.** Too small to be seen with an ordinary microscope. **2.** Of or relating to an ultramicroscope.

ul·tra·mod·ern (últrə-móddərn, -módd'n) *adj.* Extremely modern; absolutely up-to-date. —**ul·tra·mod·ern·ism** *n.* —**ul·tra·mod·ern·ist** *n.* —**ul·tra·mod·ern·is·tic** (-ístik) *adj.*

ul·tra·mon·tane (últrə-món-tayn ‖ -mon-táyn) *adj.* **1.** Of or designating peoples or regions lying on the other side of the mountains, especially, south of the Alps. **2.** Strongly supporting the authority of the papal court over national or diocesan authority in the Roman Catholic Church.
~*n.* **1.** A person living beyond the mountains, especially, south of the Alps. **2.** *Often capital* **U.** A Roman Catholic who advocates support of papal policy in ecclesiastical and political matters. [Medieval Latin *ultrāmontānus,* beyond the mountain (applied by the French to the papal court at Rome) : Latin *ultrā-,* beyond + *mōns* (stem *mont-*), mountain.]

Ul·tra·mon·ta·nism (últrə-món-ti-niz'm, -tə-, -tay-) *n.* The policy that absolute authority in the Roman Catholic Church should be vested in the pope. Compare **Gallicanism.** —**Ul·tra·mon·ta·nist** *n.*

ul·tra·mun·dane (últrə-mun-dáyn, -mún-dayn) *adj.* Extending or being beyond the world or the limits of the universe. [Latin *ultrā-mundānus* : *ultrā-,* beyond + *mundus,* the world.]

ul·tra·na·tion·al·ism (últrə-násh-n'l-iz'm, -násh'n-'l-) *n.* Extreme nationalism, especially when opposed to international cooperation. —**ul·tra·na·tion·al** *adj.* —**ul·tra·na·tion·al·ist** *n. & adj.* —**ul·tra·na·tion·al·is·tic** (-ístik) *adj.*

ul·tra·short (últrə-shórt) *adj.* Designating or pertaining to radio waves with a wavelength less than 10 metres.

ul·tra·son·ic (últrə-sónnik) *adj.* Pertaining to or designating acoustic frequencies above the range audible to the human ear, or above approximately 20 kilohertz.

ul·tra·son·ics (últrə-sónniks) *n. Used with a singular verb.* **1.** The acoustics of ultrasonic sound. **2.** A technology using ultrasonic sound, as for medical therapy.

ul·tra·sound (últrə-sownd) *n.* Ultrasonic sound.

ul·tra·struc·ture (últrə-strúkchər) *n.* The detailed structure of a cell, tissue, or organ that can be seen by electron microscopy but not by light microscopy. Also called "fine structure". —**ul·tra·struc·tur·al** (-strúkchərəl) *adj.*

ul·tra·vi·o·let (últrə-vī́-ə-lət, -lit) *adj. Abbr.* **UV, U.V. 1.** Of, belong-

ing, or designating the range of radiation wavelengths from about 0.4 micrometres, just beyond the violet in the visible spectrum, to about 4.0 nanometres, on the border of the X-ray region. **2.** Generating, using, or sensitive to such radiation.
~n. Ultraviolet radiation or the ultraviolet region of the electromagnetic spectrum.

ultraviolet lamp n. A mercury-vapour lamp that produces ultraviolet light.

ul·tra vi·res (últra vír-eez, ōoltraa véer-ayz) adv. Law. Beyond one's legal authority or rights. [Latin.] **—ul·tra vi·res** adj.

ul·tra·vi·rus (últra-vīr-əss) n. A virus small enough to pass through the finest filter.

ul·u·late (yōolew-layt ‖ chiefly U.S. úllew-) intr.v. **-lated, -lating, -lates.** To howl, hoot, wail, or lament loudly. [Latin ululāre, to howl (imitative).] **—ul·u·la·tion** (-láysh'n) n.

um (um, 'm, erm) interj. Used when hesitating in speech, or to express doubt or uncertainty.

u·man·gite (yōo-máng-gīt) n. A rare ore of selenium, Cu₃Se₂. [German Umangit, after Sierra de Umango, province in northwestern Argentina + -ITE.]

Ulysses. The Latin name for **Odysseus.**

U·may·yad (ōo-mí-ad, ōo-, -yad). Also **Om·mi·ad** (ə-, o-). A dynasty of rulers of the Muslim Empire (A.D. 661–750) and Muslim Spain (A.D. 756–1031). [After Ummayah, its founder.]

um·bel (úmb'l, úm-bel) n. Botany. A flat-topped or rounded flower cluster in which the individual flower stalks arise from about the same point as in the carrot and related plants. [New Latin umbella, from Latin, an umbrella, diminutive of umbra, shadow.]

um·bel·late (úm-bəl-ət, -bel-, -bil-, -it, -ayt, um-bél-) adj. Having, forming, or of the nature of an umbel.

um·bel·lif·er (um-béllifər) n. Any umbelliferous plant.

um·bel·lif·er·ous (úm-bə-líffərəss, -be-, -bi-) adj. Botany. **1.** Bearing umbels. **2.** Belonging to the plant family Umbelliferae. [New Latin umbellifer : umbella, UMBEL + -FEROUS.]

um·bel·lule (um-béllewl, úm-bə-lewl, -be-, -bi-) n. Also **um·bel·let** (úm-bə-lit, -be-, -bi-, -lét). Botany. Any of the smaller secondary umbels forming a compound umbel. [New Latin umbellula, diminutive of umbella, UMBEL.]

um·ber (úmbər) n. **1.** A natural brown earth composed of ferric oxide, silica, alumina, lime, and manganese oxides and used as pigment. **2.** Any of the shades of brown produced by umber in its various states.
~tr.v. **umbered, -bering, -bers.** To coat or colour with or as with umber. [Old French umbre, short for terre d'Umbre, "earth of Umbria".] **—um·ber** adj.

Um·ber·to I (ōom-baírtō) (1844–1900). King of Italy. He succeeded his father, Victor Emmanuel II, in 1878, and led Italy into the Triple Alliance with Austria-Hungary and Germany (1882). He was assassinated by an anarchist at Monza.

Umberto II (1904–83). Last King of Italy. He became king (May 1946) on the abdication of his father, Victor Emmanuel III, but was forced to abdicate a month later when a national referendum voted for a republic.

um·bil·i·cal (um-bíllik'l, úmbi-lík'l) adj. **1.** Of, pertaining to, or resembling an umbilicus. **2.** Pertaining to or located near the central area of the abdomen.
~n. Aerospace. An umbilical cord.

umbilical cord n. **1.** Anatomy. The flexible, cordlike structure connecting the foetus at the navel with the placenta and containing two umbilical arteries and one vein that nourish the foetus and remove its wastes. **2.** Aerospace. **a.** Any of various external electrical lines or fluid tubes supplying a rocket before launch. **b.** The line that supplies an astronaut with oxygen and in some cases with communications while he is outside the spacecraft. In this sense, also called "umbilical".

um·bil·i·cate (um-bílli-kət, -kit, -kayt) adj. Also **um·bil·i·cat·ed** (-kaytid) **1.** Having a central mark or depression resembling a navel. **2.** Having an umbilicus. **—um·bil·i·ca·tion** (-káysh'n) n.

um·bil·i·cus (um-bílli-kəss, úmbi-lí-kəss) n., pl. **-ci** (-sī). **1.** The navel. **2.** Biology. Any similar small opening or depression, such as the hollow at the base of the shell of some gastropod molluscs or an opening in the shaft of a feather. [Latin umbilīcus; akin to Greek omphalos, navel, and UMBO.]

um·ble pie (úmb'l) n. A humble pie (see).

um·bles (úmb'lz) Archaic. Entrails, **numbles** (see).

um·bo (úmbō) n., pl. **umbones** (um-bó-neez). **1.** A boss or knob at the centre of a shield. **2.** Biology. A similar knoblike protuberance, such as the central hump on a mushroom cap. **3.** Anatomy. A small projection at the centre of the outer surface of the tympanic membrane of the ear. [Latin umbō (stem umbōn-); akin to NAVEL.]

um·bo·nate (úmbə-nət, -nit, -nayt) adj. Also **um·bo·nal** (um-bốn'l), **um·bon·ic** (um-bónnik). Having or resembling a knob or knoblike protuberance. [Latin umbō (stem umbōn-), knob + -ATE.]

um·bra (úm-brə) n., pl. **-bras** or **-brae** (-brée). **1.** A dark area; specifically, the blackest part of a shadow from which all light is cut off. **2.** Astronomy. **a.** The shadow region over an area of the Earth where a solar eclipse is total. **b.** The darkest region of a sunspot. [Latin umbra, shadow.]

um·brage (úmbrij) n. **1.** Offence; resentment: took umbrage at their rudeness. **2.** Archaic & Poetic. **a.** Something that affords shade. **b.** Shadow or shade. **3.** Archaic. A shadowy or indistinct indication; a hint. [Middle English, shade, from Old French, from Vulgar Latin umbrāticum (unattested), neuter of Latin umbrāticus, of a

shadow, from umbra, shadow, UMBRA.]

um·bra·geous (um-bráyjəss) adj. **1.** Affording or forming shade; shady or shading. **2.** Inclined to take umbrage; touchy. **—um·bra·geous·ly** adv. **—um·bra·geous·ness** n.

um·brel·la (um-brélla) n. **1.** A device for protection from the weather consisting of a collapsible canopy mounted on a central rod. **2.** Anything that covers or protects. **3.** Military. An **air cover** (see). **4.** An all-encompassing category, organisation, or authority by means of which many different things or groups are linked. **5.** Zoology. The contractile gelatinous, rounded mass constituting the major part of the body of most jellyfishes.
~adj. Covering or encompassing a wide variety of things: an umbrella term. [Italian ombrella, diminutive of ombra, shade, from Latin umbra.]

umbrella bird n. Any of several tropical American birds of the genus Cephalopterus; especially, C. ornatus, having a retractile black crest and a long, feathered wattle.

umbrella tree n. **1.** Any of several trees of the genus Magnolia, of the southeastern United States; especially, M. tripetala, having large leaves clustered in an umbrella-like form at the ends of the branches. **2.** Any of several other trees having leaves growing in an umbrella-like cluster.

Um·bri·a (úm-bri-ə; Italian ōōm-). Largely mountainous region of central Italy, comprising the provinces of Perugia and Terni. The principal town is Perugia. It gets its name from the tribe called the Umbri, who settled in the region in the 7th century B.C.

Um·bri·an (úmbri-ən) adj. **1.** Of or pertaining to Umbria or its people, culture, dialect, or ancient language. **2.** Designating a Renaissance school of painting which included Perugino and Raphael.
~n. **1.** An inhabitant or native of ancient or modern Umbria. **2.** The extinct Italic language of ancient Umbria.

u·mi·ak, oo·mi·ak (ōomi-ak) n. A large open Eskimo boat made of skins stretched on a wooden frame, usually propelled by paddles. Compare **kayak**. [Eskimo.]

um·laut (ōom-lowt) n. Linguistics. **1.** A change in a vowel sound caused by partial assimilation to a vowel or semivowel, originally occurring in the following syllable, now usually lost. An example is English bed, produced by umlaut from the earlier Germanic form in Gothic badi. Also called "vowel mutation". Compare **ablaut**. **2.** A vowel sound changed in this manner, such as the German ä, ö, or ü. **3.** The diacritical mark (¨) placed over a vowel to indicate an umlaut, especially in German. **—See diaeresis.**
~tr.v. **umlauted, -lauting, -lauts. 1.** To modify (a vowel sound) by umlaut. **2.** To write or print (a vowel) with an umlaut. [German Umlaut : um-, prefix indicating alteration, "around", from Middle High German um(b)-, from umbe, from Old High German umbi + Laut, sound, from Middle High German lūt, from Old High German hlūt.]

um·pire (úm-pīr) n. **1.** A person appointed to make rulings and control the progress of the game in various sports, especially tennis, cricket, and baseball. Compare **referee**. **2.** A person selected or empowered to settle a dispute between other persons or groups. **3.** A judge; an arbiter. **—See Synonyms at judge.**
~v. **umpired, -piring, -pires.** —tr. To act as umpire in or of; referee; arbitrate. —intr. To be or act as an umpire. [Middle English (an) oumpere, originally (a) noumpere, (an) umpire, from Old French nomper, nonper, "non-peer" (that is, not a contestant but a third person called in to arbitrate) : non-, not + per, match, equal, PEER.] **—um·pir·age** (-ij), **um·pire·ship** (-ship) n.

ump·teen (úmp-téen, úm-) adj. Informal. Large but indefinite in number: umpteen reasons; umpteen guests. [Humorous term based on -TEEN; umpty, Morse code signaller's term for dash, also meaning a great number (through association with numerals in -TY.] **—ump·teen** pron. **—ump·teenth** adj.

Um·ta·li (ōom-taáli). City in eastern Zimbabwe, near the border with Mozambique. Its scenic mountain setting makes it a popular tourist town.

un–¹ prefix. Indicates not or contrary to; for example, **unhappy.** Note: Many compounds other than those entered here may be formed with un-. In forming compounds, un- is normally joined with the following element without space or a hyphen: unnamed. However, if the second element begins with a capital letter, it is separated with a hyphen: un-American. [Middle English un-, Old English un-.]

un–² prefix. Indicates: **1.** Reversal of an action; for example, **unlock, unmake. 2.** Deprivation; for example, **unman, unsex, unfrock. 3.** Release or removal from; for example, **unearth, unyoke, unhorse. 4.** Intensified action; for example, **unloose.** [Middle English un-, Old English un-, variant of ond-, and-, against.]

Usage: The prefixes non-, un-, and in- are all used in combination to indicate negation. It often happens that two of these prefixes can be applied to the same adjective, with a resulting difference of emphasis in each case. Non- tends to suggest simply the absence or irrelevance of the quality conveyed by the original adjective, and is therefore fairly neutral and literal in force. Un- and in- (including its assimilated forms il-, im-, and ir-) tend to suggest the contrary of the desired or expected qualities conveyed by the original adjective and has a more strongly negative and derogatory force. Thus nonscientific and nonhuman apply to matters unrelated to the realm of the scientific or the human, whereas unscientific and inhuman suggest the contrary of normal standards of scientific or human conduct. However, this distinction applies only when both negative forms of an adjective are in current usage.

'un, un (ən, 'n) *pron. Informal & Regional.* One; a person, animal, or thing of a specified kind: *She's a good 'un.* [Weak form of **one**.]

UN, U.N. United Nations.

UNA United Nations Association (in the United Kingdom).

un·a·bashed (ún-ə-básht) *adj.* Not disconcerted or embarrassed; poised. —**un·a·bash·ed·ly** (-báshid-li, -básht-) *adv.*

un·a·bat·ed (ún-ə-báytid) *adj.* With no loss of force or intensity: *They fought with unabated violence.* —**un·a·bat·ed·ly** *adv.*

un·a·ble (un-áyb'l, ún-) *adj.* **1.** Lacking the necessary power, authority, or means; not able. **2.** Lacking mental or physical capability or efficiency: *unable to walk.*

un·a·bridged (ún-ə-bríjd) *adj.* Having the original content; not condensed or shortened. Said of books, documents, or the like.

un·ac·cent·ed (ún-ak-séntid, -ək- || -ák-sentid) *adj.* **1.** Having no diacritical mark. Said of a word, syllable, or letter. **2.** Having weak stress or no stress, or lacking some other specific phonological feature. Said of a speech segment or syllable.

un·ac·com·pa·nied (ún-ə-kúmpə-nid, -kúmp- || -need) *adj.* **1.** Not accompanied: *unaccompanied luggage.* **2.** *Music.* Solo; without accompaniment.

un·ac·com·plished (ún-ə-kúm-plisht, -kóm-) *adj.* **1.** Not completed or done; unfinished. **2.** Lacking accomplishments.

un·ac·count·a·ble (ún-ə-kównt-əb'l) *adj.* **1.** Not able to be accounted for; inexplicable; mysterious. **2.** Not liable to be held to account; not accountable. —**un·ac·count·a·bil·i·ty** (-ə-bílləti), —**un·ac·count·a·ble·ness** *n.* —**un·ac·count·a·bly** *adv.*

un·ac·count·ed-for (ún-ə-kównt-id-fawr) *adj.* **1.** Not explained, understood, or taken into account; inexplicable or unexpected. **2.** Missing or absent without explanation, as from a roll call or after a military operation.

un·ac·cus·tomed (ún-ə-kústəmd) *adj.* **1.** Not used to; not accustomed. Used with *to.* **2.** Unfamiliar: *unaccustomed surroundings.*

u·na cor·da (ṓnə kórdə) *adv. Music.* With the soft pedal depressed. Used as a direction to a pianist. [Italian, "one string" (the action of the pedal causes one piano string to be struck instead of three.)]

un·a·dop·ted (ún-ə-dóptid) *adj.* **1.** Not adopted. Said of a child. **2.** *British.* Not maintained by a local authority. Said of a road.

un·a·dorned (ún-ə-dórnd) *adj.* Without embellishment or artificiality; simple; natural.

un·a·dul·ter·at·ed (ún-ə-dúltə-raytid) *adj.* **1.** Not mingled or diluted with extraneous matter; pure. **2.** Out-and-out; utter.

un·ad·vised (ún-əd-vízd || -ad-) *adj.* **1.** Having received no advice; not informed. **2.** Ill-advised; rash; imprudent. —**un·ad·vis·ed·ly** (-vízid-li) *adv.* —**un·ad·vis·ed·ness** *n.*

un·af·fect·ed¹ (ún-ə-féktid) *adj.* Not changed, modified, or affected.

unaffected² *adj.* Without pretension; sincere; genuine. —See Synonyms at **naive, sincere.** —**un·af·fect·ed·ly** *adv.* —**un·af·fect·ed·ness** *n.*

un·al·loyed (ún-ə-lóyd) *adj.* **1.** Not in mixture with other metals; pure. **2.** Complete; unqualified: *an unalloyed success.*

un·a·neled (ún-ə-néeld) *adj. Archaic.* Not having received extreme unction.

u·nan·i·mous (yōō-nánnimməss) *adj.* **1.** Sharing the same opinions or views; being in complete harmony or accord. **2.** Based on or characterised by complete assent or agreement. [Latin *ūnanimus,* "of one mind" : *ūnus,* one + *animus,* soul, mind.] —**u·na·nim·i·ty** (yōō-nə-nímməti, -na-), **u·nan·i·mous·ness** *n.* —**u·nan·i·mous·ly** *adv.*

un·an·swer·a·ble (un-áan-sər-əb'l, ún- || -án-) *adj.* **1.** Impossible to answer. Said of a question. **2.** Irrefutable; incontrovertible.

un·ap·peal·a·ble (ún-ə-péeləb'l) *adj. Law.* Not subject to appeal.

un·ap·proach·a·ble (ún-ə-prṓch-əb'l) *adj.* **1.** Not friendly; aloof; distant. **2.** Not accessible; inapproachable. —**un·ap·proach·a·bil·i·ty** (-ə-bílləti), **un·ap·proach·a·ble·ness** *n.* —**un·ap·proach·a·bly** *adv.*

un·apt (ún-ápt) *adj.* **1.** Not suitable or appropriate; inapt. Often used with *for.* **2.** Not likely; not liable. Used with *to.* **3.** Slow-witted; stupid. —**un·apt·ly** *adv.* —**un·apt·ness** *n.*

un·arm (un-árm) *tr.v.* **-armed, -arming, -arms.** *Archaic.* To divest of armour or arms; especially, to assist in taking off armour.

un·armed (un-ármd) *adj.* **1.** Lacking weapons or armour; defenceless. **2.** *Biology.* Having no thorns or spines. **3.** Not fitted with a detonator. Said of a bomb, missile, or other explosive device.

un·a·shamed (ún-ə-sháymd) *adj.* **1.** Open and without restraint or embarrassment: *unashamed luxury.* **2.** Not feeling or revealing any remorse, shame, or need for apology. —**un·a·sham·ed·ly** (-sháymid-li) *adv.* —**un·a·sham·ed·ness** *n.*

un·asked (ún-áaskt || -áskt) *adj.* **1.** Uninvited. **2.** Not requested or demanded.

un·as·sail·a·ble (ún-ə-sáyl-əb'l) *adj.* **1.** Not capable of being disputed or disproven; undeniable; unquestionable. **2.** Not capable of being attacked or seized successfully; impregnable. —**un·as·sail·a·bil·i·ty** (-ə-bílləti), **un·as·sail·a·ble·ness** *n.* —**un·as·sail·a·bly** *adv.*

un·as·sum·ing (ún-ə-séwm-ing, -sōōm- || -shōōm-) *adj.* Not pretentious, boastful, or ostentatious; modest. —**un·as·sum·ing·ly** *adv.* —**un·as·sum·ing·ness** *n.*

un·at·tached (ún-ə-tácht) *adj.* **1.** Not attached or joined, especially to surrounding tissue. **2. a.** Not committed to or dependent upon a person, group, or organisation. **b.** Not engaged, married, or involved in a serious sexual or romantic relationship. **3.** *Law.* Not possessed or seized as security.

un·at·tend·ed (ún-ə-téndid) *adj.* **1.** Not being attended to, looked after, or watched. **2.** Without attendants; not in company; alone.

3. Not being paid attention to or listened to.

un·at·test·ed (ún-ə-téstid) *adj.* Not attested. Used in linguistic descriptions, as in the etymologies of this dictionary, to designate a form whose existence is not established by documentary evidence but is reliably inferred from comparative evidence.

u·nau (yōō-now, ṓō-, -naw) *n.* A two-toed **sloth** *(see).*

un·a·vail·ing (ún-ə-váyling) *adj.* Having no effect; achieving nothing; futile. —**un·a·vail·ing·ly** *adv.*

u·na vo·ce (yōōnə vṓsi, ṓō-naa vṓ-chay) *adv. Latin.* With one voice; unanimously.

un·a·void·a·ble (ún-ə-vóyd-əb'l) *adj.* **1.** Not able to be avoided; inevitable. **2.** *Law.* Not able to be voided or nullified. —**un·a·void·a·bil·i·ty** (-bílləti-ə), **un·a·void·a·ble·ness** *n.* —**un·a·void·a·bly** *adv.*

un·a·ware (ún-ə-waír) *adj.* Not aware or cognisant. ~*adv.* Unawares.

un·a·wares (ún-ə-waírz) *adv.* **1.** By surprise; unexpectedly. **2.** Without knowledge or plan: *We came upon it unawares.* [Middle English *unwares,* variant of *unware* (adverb), Old English *unwær* : UN- + AWARE + -s (adverbial suffix).]

un·backed (ún-bákt) *adj.* **1.** Lacking backing or support. **2.** Designating a candidate, horse, or the like on which no bets are placed. **3.** Not having a back, as a bench. **4.** Never ridden. Said of a horse.

un·bal·ance (ún-bál-ənss, un-) *tr.v.* **-anced, -ancing, -ances. 1.** To upset the balance, stability, or equilibrium of. **2.** To derange. ~*n.* The condition of being unbalanced; lack of balance.

un·bal·anced (ún-bál-ənst, un-) *adj.* **1.** Not balanced. **2. a.** Mentally deranged. **b.** Not of sound judgment; erratic; irrational. **3.** Not satisfactorily adjusted, so that debit and credit do not correspond. Said of an account.

un·bar (ún-bár) *tr.v.* **-barred, -barring, -bars.** To remove the bar or bars from; unlock; open.

un·bat·ed (ún-báytid) *adj.* **1.** Unabated. **2.** *Archaic.* Not blunted by a guard on the tip. Said of a fencing foil, sword, or the like.

un·bear·a·ble (un-baír-əb'l, ún-) *adj.* Not able to be endured; intolerable. —**un·bear·a·bly** *adv.*

un·beat·a·ble (un-béet-əb'l, ún-) *adj.* **1.** Unable to be surpassed or defeated. **2.** First-rate; excellent. —**un·beat·a·bly** *adv.*

un·beat·en (ún-béet'n, ún-) *adj.* **1. a.** Undefeated. **b.** Not broken. Said of a record, as in sports. **2.** Untrodden.

un·be·com·ing (ún-bi-kúmming, -bə-) *adj.* **1.** Not appropriate, attractive, or flattering: *an unbecoming dress.* **2.** Not seemly; indecorous; improper: *an unbecoming remark.* —See Synonyms at **improper.** —**un·be·com·ing·ly** *adv.* —**un·be·com·ing·ness** *n.*

un·be·got·ten (ún-bi-gótt'n, -bə-) *adj.* **1.** Not yet begotten; as yet unborn. **2.** Self-existent; eternal.

un·be·known (ún-bi-nṓn, -bə-) *adv.* Also **un·be·knownst** (-nṓnst). Without the knowledge of. Usually used with *to.* ~*adj.* Not known. Usually used with *to.* [UN- + obsolete *beknown,* known, Middle English *beknowen,* past participle of *beknowen,* to get to know, Old English *becnāwan* : BE- + *cnāwan,* KNOW.]

un·be·lief (ún-bi-léef, -bə-) *n.* Lack of belief or faith, especially in religious matters.

un·be·liev·a·ble (ún-bi-léev-əb'l, -bə-) *adj.* Incapable of being believed; incredible. —**un·be·liev·a·bil·i·ty** (-ə-bílləti), **un·be·liev·a·ble·ness** *n.* —**un·be·liev·a·bly** *adv.*

un·be·liev·er (ún-bi-léevər) *n.* One who lacks belief or faith, especially in a particular religion.

un·be·liev·ing (ún-bi-léeving, -bə-) *adj.* Lacking belief; sceptical, especially in religious matters. —**un·be·liev·ing·ly** *adv.*

un·bend (ún-bénd) *v.* **-bent** (-bént), **-bending, -bends.** —*tr.* **1.** To relax; release from mental tension, strain, or formality. **2.** To release (a bow, for example) from flexure or tension. **3.** *Nautical.* To untie or loosen (a rope or sail). **4.** To straighten (something crooked or bent). —*intr.* **1.** To become less tense; relax. **2.** To become less strict or less formal. **3.** To become straight.

un·bend·ing (ún-bénding) *adj.* **1.** Unyielding or uncompromising. **2.** Stern or severe. —**un·bend·ing·ly** *adv.* —**un·bend·ing·ness** *n.*

un·bi·ased (ún-bí-əst) *adj.* Without bias or prejudice; impartial. See Synonyms at **fair.** —**un·bi·ased·ly** *adv.* —**un·bi·ased·ness** *n.*

un·bid·den (ún-bídd'n) *adj.* **1.** Not commanded; voluntary. **2.** Not invited; unasked: *unbidden company.*

un·bind (ún-bínd) *tr.v.* **-bound** (-bównd), **-binding, -binds. 1.** To untie or unfasten (wrappings or bindings, for example). **2.** To release from restraints or bonds; free.

un·birth·day (ún-búrth-di, -day) *n. Informal.* Any day that is not one's birthday. Also used adjectively: *an unbirthday party.*

un·blessed (ún-blést) *adj.* **1.** Deprived of a blessing. **2.** Unholy; evil. —**un·bless·ed·ness** (-bléssid-) *n.*

un·blink·ing (ún-blíngking, un-) *adj.* **1.** Without blinking. **2.** Without visible emotion. **3.** Fearless in facing reality. —**un·blink·ing·ly** *adv.*

un·blown (ún-blṓn) *adj.* Unopened. Said of a flower.

un·blush·ing (ún-blúshing, un-) *adj.* **1.** Without shame or embarrassment. **2.** Not blushing. —See Synonyms at **shameless.** —**un·blush·ing·ly** *adv.*

un·bolt (ún-bṓlt || -bólt) *tr.v.* **-bolted, -bolting, -bolts.** To release the bolts of (a door or gate); unlock.

un·bolt·ed (ún-bṓlt-id || -bólt-) *adj.* Not sifted. Said of flour, grain, or the like.

un·born (ún-bórn) *adj.* Not yet in existence; not yet born.

un·bos·om (ún-bṓoz'm, un- || -bṓoz'm) *v.* **-omed, -oming, -oms.** —*tr.* **1.** To confide (one's thoughts or feelings). **2.** To relieve (oneself) of troublesome thoughts or feelings. —*intr.* To reveal one's thoughts or feelings.

un·bound (ún-bównd, un-) Past tense and past participle of **unbind.**

~*adj.* **1.** Not bound. Said of a book. **2.** Free from bonds or shackles; unconfined. **2.** *Linguistics.* Designating a morpheme that is or can be a full and independent word when standing alone.

un·bound·ed (ún-bównd-id, un-) *adj.* **1.** Having no boundaries or limits. **2.** Not kept within bounds; unrestrained: *unbounded enthusiasm.* —**un·bound·ed·ly** *adv.* —**un·bound·ed·ness** *n.*

un·bowed (ún-bówd, un-) *adj.* **1.** Not bowed; not bent. **2.** Not subdued; unyielding: *The warriors returned bloody but unbowed.*

un·brace (ún-bráyss) *tr.v.* **-braced, -bracing, -braces.** **1.** To set free by removing bands or braces. **2.** To release from tension; relax. **3.** To weaken; make slack.

un·bred (ún-bréd) *adj.* **1.** Not taught or instructed; untaught. **2.** *Archaic.* Ill-bred; impolite.

un·bri·dle (ún-bríd'l, un-) *tr.v.* **-dled, -dling, -dles.** **1.** To take the bridle off (a horse). **2.** To remove restraints from; free.

un·bri·dled (ún-bríd'ld, un-) *adj.* **1.** Not wearing or fitted with a bridle. **2.** Unrestrained; uncontrolled. —**un·bri·dled·ly** *adv.*

un·bro·ken (ún-brókən, un-) *adj.* **1.** Not broken or tampered with; intact. **2.** Not violated or breached. **3.** Uninterrupted; continuous; even. **4.** Not tamed; not trained to accept a harness. Said of a horse. **5.** Not disordered or disturbed. **6.** Not surpassed. Said of a record, as in sports. —**un·bro·ken·ly** *adv.* —**un·bro·ken·ness** *n.*

un·buck·le (ún-búck'l, un-) *tr.v.* **-led, -ling, -les.** **1.** To loosen or undo the buckle or buckles of. **2.** To remove by unbuckling.

un·bur·den (ún-búrd'n, un-) *tr.v.* **-dened, -dening, -dens.** To free from or relieve of a burden or trouble: *unburden one's mind.*

un·but·ton (ún-bútt'n, un-) *v.* **-toned, -toning, -tons.** —*tr.* **1.** To unfasten the button or buttons of. **2.** To free or remove (a button) from a buttonhole. **3.** To make informal or relaxed. —*intr.* **1.** To undo a button or buttons. **2.** To relax.

un·called-for (ún-káwld-fawr, un-) *adj.* **1.** Unwarranted; impertinent; unnecessary. **2.** Not required or requested.

un·can·ny (un-kánni, ún-) *adj.* **-nier, -niest.** **1.** So unexpected as to seem preternatural: *She bore an uncanny resemblance to my sister.* **2.** Exciting wonder and fear; strange: *an uncanny laugh.* —See Synonyms at **weird.** —**un·can·ni·ly** *adv.* —**un·can·ni·ness** *n.*

un·cap (ún-káp, un-) *v.* **-capped, -capping, -caps.** —*tr.* To remove the cap or covering of (a container). —*intr.* To remove one's head covering as a sign of deference.

un·cared-for (ún-káird-fawr, un-) *adj.* Not looked after; neglected.

un·car·ing (ún-káiring, un-) *adj.* Devoid of concern or sympathy.

un·ceas·ing (ún-séessing, un-) *adj.* Not ceasing or letting up; continuous. —**un·ceas·ing·ly** *adv.* —**un·ceas·ing·ness** *n.*

un·cer·e·mo·ni·ous (ún-sérri-mốni-əss) *adj.* **1.** Without the due formalities; abrupt; rude. **2.** Not ceremonious; informal. —**un·cer·e·mo·ni·ous·ly** *adv.* —**un·cer·e·mo·ni·ous·ness** *n.*

un·cer·tain (un-sér-t'n, ún-, -tin) *adj.* **1.** Not known or established; questionable; doubtful: *an uncertain outcome.* **2.** Not determined; vague; undecided: *uncertain plans.* **3.** Not having sure knowledge. **4.** Subject to change; variable: *uncertain weather.* **5.** Unsteady; fitful: *uncertain light.* —**un·cer·tain·ly** *adv.*

un·cer·tain·ty (un-sér-t'n-ti, ún-, -tin-) *n., pl.* **-ties.** Also **un·cer·tain·ness** (for sense 1). **1.** The condition of being in doubt; lack of certainty. **2.** Something that is uncertain.

    Synonyms: uncertainty, doubt, dubiety, scepticism.

uncertainty principle *n.* The principle in quantum mechanics that the product of the uncertainties in the values of certain related variables, as of the position and momentum of a particle, is greater than or equal to Planck's constant divided by 4π. Also called "Heisenberg uncertainty principle"

un·chain (ún-cháyn) *tr.v.* **-chained, -chaining, -chains.** To release from or as if from a chain or bond; set free.

un·chan·cy (un-cháan-si, ún- ‖ -chán-) *adj. Scottish.* **1.** Unlucky; ill-fated. **2.** Threatening; dangerous. [UN- (not) + CHANCY (in obsolete sense, "lucky").]

un·charged (ún-chárjd) *adj.* **1.** Not loaded. Said of a weapon. **2.** *Law.* **a.** Not subject to a charge. Said of land. **b.** Not formally accused. **3.** Lacking electric charge.

un·char·i·ta·ble (ún-chárritəb'l, un-) *adj.* Not charitable or generous; unkind; judging harshly. —**un·char·i·ta·ble·ness** *n.* —**un·char·i·ta·bly** *adv.*

un·chart·ed (ún-chártid, un-) *adj.* Not charted or recorded on or as if on a map or plan; unexplored; unknown.

un·chaste (ún-cháyst, un-) *adj.* Not chaste or modest. —**un·chaste·ly** *adv.* —**un·chaste·ness, un·chas·ti·ty** (-chástəti) *n.*

un·chris·tian (ún-kríst-yən, un-, -kríss-chən) *adj.* **1.** Not in accordance with the spirit or principles of Christianity; especially, lacking any consideration for one's fellow human beings. **2.** Not Christian; heathen. **3.** *Informal.* Uncivilised; barbarous.

un·church (ún-chúrch) *tr.v.* **-churched, -churching, -churches.** **1.** To expel from a church or from church membership; excommunicate. **2.** To deprive (a congregation, sect, or building) of the status of a church.

un·cial (ún-si-əl, -shi-, -sh'l) *adj. Sometimes capital* **U.** Of, pertaining to, or designating a style of writing characterised by fairly rounded capital letters and found especially in Greek and Latin manuscripts of the fourth to the ninth century A.D. It provided the model from which most of the capital letters in the modern Roman alphabet are derived.

~*n. Sometimes capital* **U.** **1.** The uncial style or hand. **2.** An uncial letter or manuscript. [Late Latin *unciāles (litterae),* "letters of an inch long" (applied loosely by St. Jerome to uncial letters), plural of Latin *unciālis,* of an inch, from *uncia,* a twelfth part, ounce, inch, from *ūnus,* one.]

un·ci·form (ún-si-fawrm) *adj.* Hook-shaped.

~*n.* Any hook-shaped part or structure; especially, the **hamate bone** (see). In this sense, also called "unciform bone". [New Latin *unciformis* : Latin *uncus,* hook + -FORM.]

un·ci·nate (ún-si-nət, -nit, -nayt) *adj.* **1.** Hooked at the tip. **2.** Of or possessing uncini. [Latin *uncīnātus,* from *uncīnus,* hook, UNCINUS.]

un·ci·nus (un-sí-nəss) *n., pl.* **-ni** (-nī). A small hooklike structure, such as any of the setae of certain annelid worms. [New Latin, from Latin, hook, barb, from *uncus,* hook.]

un·cir·cum·cised (ún-súrkəm-sīzd) *adj.* **1.** Not circumcised. **2.** Not Jewish; Gentile. **3.** Heathen. **4.** Spiritually impure. —**un·cir·cum·ci·sion** (-sízh'n) *n.*

un·civ·il (ún-sívv'l, un-, -sívvil) *adj.* **1.** Impolite; discourteous; rude. **2.** *Archaic.* Uncivilised; barbarous. —**un·civ·il·ly** *adv.*

un·civ·i·lised (ún-sívv'l-īzd, un-, -sívvil) *adj.* **1.** Not civilised; barbarous. **2.** Lacking education, manners, culture, or sophistication.

un·clad (ún-klád) *adj.* Not wearing clothes; naked.

un·clasp (ún-kláasp ‖ -klásp) *v.* **-clasped, -clasping, -clasps.** —*tr.* **1.** To release or loosen the clasp of. **2.** To release or loosen from a grasp or embrace. —*intr.* To release or relax a clasp or grasp.

un·class·i·fied (ún-klássi-fīd, un-) *adj.* **1.** Not placed or included in order or in a class or category. **2.** Not classified for security purposes. Said of information.

un·cle (úngk'l) *n.* **1.** *Abbr.* **u., U. a.** The brother of one's mother or father. **b.** The husband of one's aunt. **c.** Any close adult male friend of one's parents. In both senses often used with a Christian name as a title or term of address. —**my uncle.** *Slang.* The pawnbroker. [Middle English *uncle,* from Old French *oncle,* from Late Latin *aunculus,* variant of Latin *avunculus,* maternal uncle, diminutive of *avus,* grandfather.]

un·clean (ún-kléen, un-) *adj.* **-cleaner, -cleanest.** **1.** Not clean; foul or dirty. **2.** Morally defiled; unchaste. **3.** Ceremonially impure. —**un·clean·ly** *adv.* —**un·clean·ness** *n.*

un·clear (ún-kléar) *adj.* **-clearer, -clearest.** Not clearly defined; confused or ambiguous.

un·clench (ún-klénch) *v.* **-clenched, -clenching, -clenches.** —*tr.* To loosen from a clenched position; relax; open: *unclench one's fists.* —*intr.* To become unclenched.

Uncle Sam *n. Abbr.* **U.S.** A personification of the U.S. Government, represented as a tall, thin man with a white beard and wearing a blue tailcoat, red-and-white-striped trousers, and a tall hat with a band of stars. [Extension from *U.S.* (for *United States*); said to be a jocular interpretation of this abbreviation (stamped on U.S. Army supply packages during the War of 1812).]

Uncle Tom *n. Chiefly U.S.* **1.** A black person who is held to be humiliatingly subservient or deferential to whites. **2.** Any person regarded as a traitor to his own group by excessive tolerance of or cooperation with the oppressors of that group. [After the black slave in *Uncle Tom's Cabin* (1852), novel by Harriet Beecher Stowe.]

un·clog (ún-klóg) *tr.v.* **-clogged, -clogging, -clogs.** To clear a blockage from (a drain, for example).

un·close (ún-klóz) *v.* **-closed, -closing, -closes.** —*tr.* To open or disclose. —*intr.* To become opened or disclosed.

un·clothe (ún-klóth) *tr.v.* **-clothed** or **-clad** (-klád), **-clothing, -clothes.** To remove the clothing or cover from; strip.

un·co (úngkō) *adj. Scottish.* **1.** Unusual; odd; striking. **2.** Mysterious; uncanny.

~*n., pl.* **uncos.** *Scottish.* **1.** An unusual or amazing person. **2.** A stranger. **3.** *Plural.* News.

~*adv. Scottish.* To an excessive degree; remarkably. [Middle English (Scottish) *unkow,* variant of UNCOUTH.]

un·coil (ún-kóyl) *v.* **-coiled, -coiling, -coils.** —*tr.* To unwind; untwist. —*intr.* To become unwound or untwisted.

un·com·fort·a·ble (un-kúmf-təb'l, -kúmfər-) *adj.* **1.** Experiencing physical discomfort. **2.** Uneasy; ill-at-ease. **3.** Causing anxiety; disquieting. —**un·com·fort·a·ble·ness** *n.* —**un·com·fort·a·bly** *adv.*

un·com·mer·cial (ún-kə-mérsh'l) *adj.* **1.** Not engaged in or involving trade or commerce. **2.** Not in accordance with the spirit or methods of commerce; not businesslike. **3.** Not commercially viable; uneconomical.

un·com·mit·ted (ún-kə-míttid) *adj.* Not pledged to a specific cause or course of action.

un·com·mon (un-kómmən, ún-) *adj.* **-moner, -monest.** **1.** Not common; unusual; rare. **2.** Wonderful; remarkable. **3.** Unusually large or intense.

~*adv. Archaic & Regional.* Uncommonly. —**un·com·mon·ness** *n.*

un·com·mon·ly (un-kómmənli) *adv.* **1.** In a manner or to a degree that is not common or usual. **2.** Used as an intensive: *That chap was uncommonly polite.*

un·com·mu·ni·ca·tive (ún-kə-méwni-kətiv, -kaytiv) *adj.* Not disposed to be communicative; taciturn; reserved. —**un·com·mu·ni·ca·tive·ly** *adv.* —**un·com·mu·ni·ca·tive·ness** *n.*

un·com·pro·mis·ing (un-kómprə-mīzing, ún-) *adj.* Not making concessions; inflexible; rigid. —**un·com·pro·mis·ing·ly** *adv.*

un·con·cern (ún-kən-sérn ‖ -kon-) *n.* **1.** Lack of interest; indifference; apathy. **2.** Lack of concern or apprehensiveness.

un·con·cerned (ún-kən-sérnd ‖ -kon-) *adj.* **1.** Not interested; indifferent. **2.** Not anxious or apprehensive; unworried. —See Synonyms at **indifferent.** —**un·con·cern·ed·ly** (-sérnid-li) *adv.* —**un·con·cern·ed·ness** *n.*

un·con·di·tion·al (ún-kən-dísh'n'l || -kon-) *adj.* Without conditions or limitations; absolute. —**un·con·di·tion·al·ly** *adv.*

un·con·di·tioned (ún-kən-dísh'nd || -kon-) *adj.* **1.** Unconditional; absolute; unrestricted. **2.** *Psychology.* Not resulting from conditioning or learning; reflex or instinctive.

unconditioned response *n.* A response evoked by a stimulus independently of any learning or conditioning process. Formerly called "unconditioned reflex".

un·con·form·a·ble (ún-kən-fórm-əb'l || -kon-) *adj.* **1.** Not conforming or capable of conforming. **2.** *Geology.* Showing unconformity. —**un·con·form·a·bil·i·ty** (-ə-bílləti), **un·con·form·a·ble·ness** *n.* —**un·con·form·a·bly** *adv.*

un·con·for·mi·ty (ún-kən-fórməti || -kon-) *n., pl.* **-ties. 1.** Lack of conformity; nonconformity. **2.** *Geology.* An eroded space or space caused by lack of deposit, that separates younger strata from older rocks. Compare **disconformity.**

un·con·nect·ed (ún-kə-néktid) *adj.* **1.** Not joined or connected. **2.** Not coherent; disconnected. —**un·con·nect·ed·ly** *adv.* —**un·con·nect·ed·ness** *n.*

un·con·quer·a·ble (ún-kóngkərəb'l) *adj.* Incapable of being overcome or defeated.

un·con·scion·a·ble (ún-kónsh'n-əb'l) *adj.* **1.** Not restrained by conscience; unscrupulous. **2.** Beyond prudence or reason; immoderate; excessive. —**un·con·scion·a·ble·ness** *n.* —**un·con·scion·a·bly** *adv.*

un·con·scious (un-kónshəss, ún-) *adj.* **1.** Completely lacking in awareness, as in a coma or deep sleep. **2.** Without conscious awareness. **3.** *Psychology.* Pertaining to or originating in the unconscious; unavailable for direct conscious scrutiny: *unconscious resentment.* **4.** Not consciously intended; involuntary.
~*n. Psychology.* The division of the psyche not subject to direct conscious observation but inferred from its effects on conscious processes and behaviour. Preceded by *the.* —See Usage note at **conscious.** —**un·con·scious·ly** *adv.* —**un·con·scious·ness** *n.*

un·con·sid·ered (ún-kən-síddərd || -kon-) *adj.* **1.** Not reasoned or considered; rash: *an unconsidered remark.* **2.** Not taken into account; disregarded.

un·con·sti·tu·tion·al (ún-kón-sti-téwsh'n-'l || -tōōsh'n-) *adj.* Not in accord with or not permitted by the principles in a constitution. —**un·con·sti·tu·tion·al·i·ty** (-ál-ə̄ti) *n.* —**un·con·sti·tu·tion·al·ly** *adv.*

un·con·trol·la·ble (ún-kən-trṓl-əb'l || -kon-) *adj.* Not able to be controlled or governed. —**un·con·trol·la·bil·i·ty** (-ə-bílləti), **un·con·trol·la·ble·ness** *n.* —**un·con·trol·la·bly** *adv.*

un·con·ven·tion·al (ún-kən-vénsh'n-'l || -kon-) *adj.* Not adhering to or in accord with conventional standards, manners, or styles. —**un·con·ven·tion·al·i·ty** (-ál-ə̄ti) *n.* —**un·con·ven·tion·al·ly** *adv.*

un·co·or·di·na·ted (ún-kō-órdi-naytid) *adj.* **1.** Lacking planning, method, or organisation. **2.** Lacking physical or mental coordination. —**un·co·or·di·na·ted·ly** *adv.*

un·cork (ún-kórk) *tr.v.* **-corked, -corking, -corks. 1.** To draw the cork from. **2.** To free from a sealed or constrained state: *uncork feelings of anger; uncork a punch.*

un·count·a·ble (ún-kównt-əb'l) *adj.* Not able to be counted; innumerable.

un·count·ed (ún-kównt-id) *adj.* **1.** Not counted. **2.** Unable to be counted; innumerable: *uncounted hosts of angels.*

un·cou·ple (ún-kúpp'l, un-) *tr.v.* **-pled, -pling, -ples. 1.** To disconnect (something coupled). **2.** To release; unleash.

un·couth (un-kōōth, ún-) *adj.* **1.** Crude; unrefined; rude. **2.** Awkward or clumsy; ungraceful: *an uncouth gait.* **3.** *Archaic.* Foreign; unfamiliar. [Middle English *unc(o)uth,* unknown, strange, Old English *uncūth* : *un-,* not + *cūth,* known, past participle of *cunnan.*] —**un·couth·ly** *adv.* —**un·couth·ness** *n.*

un·cov·e·nant·ed (ún-kúvvənəntid) *adj.* **1.** Not bound by a covenant. **2.** Not promised or guaranteed by a covenant. **3.** Not approved or permitted by a covenant.

un·cov·er (ún-kúvvər, ún-) *v.* **-ered, -ering, -ers.** —*tr.* **1.** To remove the cover from; unveil or uncap. **2.** To bring to light or disclose; reveal. **3.** To remove the hat from (one's head) in respect or reverence. —*intr.* **1.** To remove a cover. **2.** To bare the head in respect or reverence.

un·cov·ered (ún-kúvvərd, un-) *adj.* **1.** Having no cover or protection. **2.** Lacking insurance cover. **3.** Bareheaded.

un·cross (ún-króss || -kráwss) *tr.v.* **-crossed, -crossing, -crosses.** To move (one's legs, for example) from a crossed position.

un·crowned (ún-krównd) *adj.* **1.** Not having yet been crowned. **2.** Having the power or influence of a monarch or other prominent figure but not the title.

UNC·TAD (úngk-tad) *n.* United Nations Conference on Trade and Development.

unc·tion (úngksh'n) *n.* **1.** The act of anointing as part of a religious, ceremonial, or healing ritual. See **Sacrament of the Sick. 2.** An ointment or oil; a salve. **3.** Something that serves to soothe or restore; a balm. **4.** Affected, insincere; or exaggerated charm or earnestness; unctuousness. [Middle English, from Latin *unctiō* (stem *unctiōn-*), from *unguere* (past participle *unctus*), to anoint.]

unc·tu·ous (úngk-tew-əss, -choo-) *adj.* **1.** Having the quality or characteristics of oil or ointment; greasy; slippery. **2.** Containing or composed of oil or fat. **3.** Characterised by affected, exaggerated, or insincere charm or earnestness. **4.** Abundant in organic materials; soft and rich: *unctuous soil.* [Middle English, from Medieval

Latin *unctuōsus,* from Latin *unctum,* ointment, from *unctus,* past participle of *unguere,* to anoint.] —**unc·tu·os·i·ty** (-óssəti), **unc·tu·ous·ness** *n.* —**unc·tu·ous·ly** *adv.*

un·cus (úngkəss) *n., pl.* **unci** (ún-sī). *Biology.* A hook-shaped part or process; especially, the projection from the lower surface of the cerebrum. [New Latin, from Latin, hook.]

un·cut (ún-kút) *adj.* **1.** Not cut. **2.** Having the page edge not slit or trimmed. Said of a book. **3.** Not ground to a specific shape. Said of a gemstone. **4.** Not condensed, abridged, or shortened, as by editing for the purposes of censorship.

un·damped (ún-dámpt) *adj.* **1.** *Physics.* Not tending towards a state of rest; not damped. Said of oscillations. **2.** Not stifled or discouraged; unchecked: *His ardour was undamped.*

un·daunt·ed (ún-dáwnt-id, un- || -daánt-) *adj.* Not discouraged or disheartened; resolute; fearless. See Synonyms at **brave.** —**un·daunt·ed·ly** *adv.* —**un·daunt·ed·ness** *n.*

un·dead (ún-déd) *adj.* Being, as a zombie or a vampire is, not dead without being fully alive either.

un·dec·a·gon (un-déckə-gən, -gon) *n.* A polygon having eleven angles and eleven sides. [Latin *undecim,* eleven, after *decagon.*]

un·de·ceive (ún-di-séev) *tr.v.* **-ceived, -ceiving, -ceives.** To free from illusion or deception. —**un·de·ceiv·able** *adj.* —**un·de·ceiv·er** *n.*

un·de·cid·ed (ún-di-sídid) *adj.* **1.** Not yet determined or settled; open. **2.** Not having reached a decision; uncommitted. —**un·de·cid·ed·ly** *adv.* —**un·de·cid·ed·ness** *n.*

un·de·fend·ed (ún-di-féndid) *adj.* **1.** Not defended. **2.** Without having a defence entered. Said of a lawsuit.

un·de·mon·stra·tive (ún-di-mónstrətiv) *adj.* Not tending to outward expressions of feeling; reserved. —**un·de·mon·stra·tive·ly** *adv.* —**un·de·mon·stra·tive·ness** *n.*

un·de·ni·a·ble (ún-di-nī-əb'l) *adj.* **1.** Not able to be denied; irrefutable; certain. **2.** Unquestionably good; outstanding; excellent. —**un·de·ni·a·bly** *adv.*

un·der (úndər) *prep.* **1.** In or to a lower position or place than: *a signature under a painting.* **2.** Beneath the surface of: *under the ground.* **3.** Beneath the assumed surface or guise of: *under a false name.* **4.** Less than; smaller than. **5.** Less than the required amount or degree of; less than the standard of: *under voting age.* **6.** Inferior to in quality, status, or rank. **7. a.** Subject to the authority, rule, instruction, or influence of: *under a dictatorship; under the impression that it was already finished.* **b.** During the reign, regime, or government of: *Under Stalin there was little free discussion.* **8.** During the time conventionally assigned to a specified sign of the zodiac: *born under Virgo.* **9.** Undergoing or receiving the effects of: *under intensive care.* **10.** Subject to the restraint or obligation of: *under contract.* **11.** Within the group or classification of: *listed under biology; under the heading of.* **12.** In the process of: *under discussion.* **13.** In view of; because of: *under these conditions.* **14.** With the authorisation of; attested by; by virtue of: *under the king's seal.* **15.** Sowed or planted with: *an acre under oats.* **16.** Powered or propelled by: *under steam.* —See Usage Note at **below.**
~*adv.* **1.** In or into a place below or beneath something. **2.** In or into a subordinate or inferior condition or position. **3.** So as to be submerged or enveloped by something. **4.** *Informal.* In or into a state of unconsciousness. **5.** So as to be less than the required amount or degree. —**go under. 1.** To sink or drown. **2.** To yield or surrender, as to an anaesthetic, for example. **3.** To fail or fall through. Used of a business.
~*adj.* **1.** Located or moving beneath or on the lower surface. **2.** Lower in rank, power, or authority; subordinate; inferior. **3.** Less than is required or customary; substandard. **4.** Lower in amount or degree. [Middle English *under,* Old English *under.*]

under- *prefix.* Indicates: **1.** Location below or under; for example, **underground, underclothes. 2.** Inferiority in rank or importance; for example, **undersecretary. 3.** Degree, rate, or quantity that is lower or less than normal, proper, or sufficient; for example, **underestimate, undernourished. 4.** Secrecy or treachery; for example, **undermine, underhand. Note:** Many compounds other than those entered here may be formed with *under-.* In forming compounds, *under-* is joined with the following element without space or a hyphen: *underrate; undergrow.* [Middle English *under-,* Old English *under-,* from UNDER.]

un·der·a·chieve (úndər-ə-chéev) *intr.v.* **-chieved, -chieving, -chieves.** To perform below an expected level, especially in schoolwork. —**un·der·a·chiev·er** *n.*

un·der·act (úndər-ákt) *v.* **-acted, -acting, -acts.** —*tr.* **1.** To perform (a dramatic role) weakly or feebly. **2.** To understate (a dramatic role) intentionally. —*intr.* To perform a dramatic role weakly or with intentional restraint.

un·der·age (úndər-áyj) *adj.* Below the customary or required age; especially, below the legal age, as for drinking or voting.

un·der·arm[1] (úndər-aarm) *adj.* **1.** Located, placed, or used under the arm. **2.** In or of the armpit.
~*n.* The armpit.

underarm[2] *adj. & adv. Sports.* With the hand kept below the level of the shoulder, as when bowling in cricket, or serving in tennis.

un·der·bel·ly (úndər-belli) *n., pl.* **-lies. 1.** The lowest part of an animal's body. **2.** Any vulnerable or weak part or aspect. Used chiefly in the phrase *soft underbelly.*

un·der·bid (úndər-bíd) *v.* **-bid, -bidding, -bids.** —*tr.* **1.** To bid lower than (a competitor). **2.** In bridge, to bid less than the full value of (one's hand). —*intr.* To make too low a bid. —**un·der·bid·der** *n.*

un·der·bod·y (úndər-boddi) *n.* The underside or lower part, as of an animal's body or a vehicle.

un·der·bred (úndər-bréd) *adj.* **1.** Not of pure stock; of mixed breeding. Said of an animal. **2.** Ill-bred; vulgar. Said of a person.

un·der·buy (úndər-bī) *tr.v.* **-bought** (-báwt), **-buying, -buys. 1.** To buy something at a lower price than (someone else). **2.** To buy for less than the actual value. **3.** To buy an insufficient quantity of.

un·der·cap·i·tal·ise, un·der·cap·i·tal·ize (úndər-káppit'l-īz) *tr.v.* **-ised, -ising, -ises.** To provide (a commercial enterprise or other venture) with insufficient capital for efficiency or viability.

un·der·car·riage (úndər-karrij) *n.* **1.** The landing gear of an aircraft. **2.** The supporting framework of a carriage or other vehicle.

un·der·cart (úndər-kaart) *n. Informal.* The undercarriage of an aircraft.

un·der·charge (úndər-chárj) *v.* **-charged, -charging, -charges.** *—tr.* **1.** To charge (someone) less than is customary or required. **2.** To load (a firearm) with an insufficient charge. *—intr.* To make or levy charges lower than is customary or required.
~*n.* (also -chaarj). An insufficient or improper charge.

un·der·class, un·der·class (úndər-klaass) *n.* Those in a society, regarded as a possibly threatening social class, who are poor, have low self-esteem, feel social alienation, do not strive for upward mobility, and typically have no permanent or regular employment. Compare **lumpenproletariat.**

un·der·clay (úndər-klay) *n.* A grey clay, **fireclay** *(see),* occurring beneath coal seams.

un·der·clothes (úndər-klōthz, -klōz) *pl.n.* Also **un·der·cloth·ing** (-klōthing). **Underwear** *(see).*

un·der·coat (úndər-kōt) *n.* Also **un·der·coat·ing** (-ing) (for senses 3, 4). **1.** A coat worn beneath another coat. **2.** A covering of short hairs or fur concealed by the longer outer hairs of an animal's coat. **3. a.** A coat of paint or sealing material applied to a surface before the topcoat is applied. **b.** The paint or sealing material used for this. **4.** *U.S.* An **underseal** *(see).*
~*tr.v.* **undercoated, -coating, -coats.** To apply an undercoat to.

un·der·cov·er (úndər-kúvvər, -kuvvər) *adj.* Performed or acting in secret; especially, concerned with or engaged in espionage or secret inquiries: *an undercover investigation.*

un·der·croft (úndər-kroft || -krawft) *n.* An underground chamber or vault; especially, a crypt. [Middle English *under croft*: UNDER + *croft(e),* vault, from Medieval Latin *crupta,* variant of Latin *crypta,* CRYPT.]

un·der·cur·rent (úndər-kurrənt) *n.* **1.** A current, as of air or water, below another current or beneath a surface. **2.** An underlying feeling, tendency, force, or influence often contrary to what is superficially evident: *quietly but with an undercurrent of passion.*

un·der·cut (úndər-kút) *v.* **-cut, -cutting, -cuts.** *—tr.* **1.** To make a cut under or below. **2.** To cut material away from, as in carving, in order to create an overhang. **3.** To charge less than (a competitor) for goods or services. **4.** To undermine or outmanoeuvre (a rival), as by swift or unexpected action. **5.** To strike (a ball) with backspin by hitting downwards as well as forwards, as in golf and tennis. *—intr.* To undercut someone or something.
~*n.* (-kut). **1.** A cut made in the under part to remove material. **2.** A part so removed. **3.** *Chiefly British.* The tender under part of a sirloin of beef. **4.** *Sports.* **a.** A spin given to a ball, a **backspin** *(see).* **b.** A cut or slice imparting such a spin. **5.** *Chiefly U.S.* A notch cut in a tree to direct its fall and ensure a clean break.

un·der·de·vel·oped (úndər-di-vélləpt) *adj.* **1.** Not adequately or normally developed; immature; deficient: *an underdeveloped mind in an underdeveloped body.* **2.** In photography, processed in too weak a developing solution, or for too short a time, or at too low a temperature to produce a normal degree of contrast. **3.** Poor and economically primitive, usually because of insufficient capital and an inadequate social infrastructure. **—un·der·de·vel·op·ment** *n.*

un·der·dog (úndər-dog || -dawg) *n.* **1.** One who loses or is expected to lose a contest or struggle, as in sport or politics. **2.** One who is at a disadvantage or is being oppressed.

un·der·done (úndər-dún) *adj.* Cooked lightly or insufficiently.

un·der·dressed (úndər-drést) *adj.* Dressed too informally for a given situation.

un·der·drive (úndər-drīv) *n.* A gearing device causing the output drive shaft to rotate at a slower rate than the engine input shaft.

un·der·em·ployed (úndər-im-plóyd) *adj.* Not fully employed.

un·der·es·ti·mate (úndər-ésti-mayt) *v.* **-mated, -mating, -mates.** *—tr.* **1.** To estimate at too low a quantity, degree, or size. **2.** To have too low a regard for the worth, strength, or character of. *—intr.* To make too low an estimate of a quantity, degree, or size.
~*n.* (-mət, -mit, -mayt). An estimate that is too low. **—un·der·es·ti·ma·tion** (-máysh'n) *n.*

un·der·ex·pose (úndər-ik-spóz, -ek-) *tr.v.* **-posed, -posing, -poses.** To expose insufficiently; especially, to expose (film, for example) for too short a time or to insufficient light or radiation to produce normal image contrast. **—un·der·ex·po·sure** (-spózhər) *n.*

un·der·feed (úndər-féed) *tr.v.* **-fed** (-féd), **-feeding, -feeds. 1.** To feed insufficiently. **2.** To supply with fuel from below.

un·der·felt (úndər-felt) *n.* **1.** A thick felt fabric used for laying under carpets to increase their resilience or to give extra insulation. **2.** A piece of such felt laid under a carpet.

un·der·floor (úndər-flór || -flór) *adj.* Located beneath the floor: *underfloor heating.*

un·der·foot (úndər-fŏt) *adv.* **1.** Under the foot or feet, and often on the ground: *trampled the flowers underfoot.* **2.** Below one's feet; di-

rectly below. **3.** In the way. **4.** In a state of subjection.

un·der·fur (úndər-fur) *n.* The dense, soft, fine fur beneath the coarse outer hairs of certain mammals.

un·der·gar·ment (úndər-gaarmənt) *n.* A garment that is worn under outer garments; especially, one worn next to the skin.

un·der·gird (úndər-gúrd) *tr.v.* **-girded** or **-girt, -girding, -girds.** To gird, support, or strengthen from beneath, by or as if by passing a rope underneath.

un·der·glaze (úndər-gláyz) *adj.* Applied to pottery before it is glazed. Said of a pigment or decoration.
~*n.* (-glayz). A pigment or decoration so applied.

un·der·go (úndər-gō) *tr.v.* **-went** (-wént), **-gone** (-gón || -gáwn, -ga'an), **-going, -goes** (-gōz). **1.** To experience; be subjected to. **2.** To endure; suffer; sustain. [Middle English *undergon,* to submit to, go through : *under,* UNDER + *gon,* to GO.]

un·der·grad·u·ate (úndər-gráddew-ət, -grájoo-, -it) *n.* A university student who has not yet received a first degree. Also informally called "undergrad". **—un·der·grad·u·ate** *adj.*

un·der·ground (úndər-grownd) *adj.* **1.** Occurring, operating, or situated below the surface of the Earth. **2.** Hidden or concealed; clandestine. **3.** Of, pertaining to, or designating an organisation involved in secret or illegal activity, such as the subversion of an established political or social order. **4.** Of, pertaining to, or describing an avant-garde movement or its music, publications, and art, usually privately produced and often concerned with social or artistic experiment.
~*n.* **1.** A clandestine, often nationalist, organisation engaged in or encouraging the usually violent overthrow of a government in power, such as an occupying military government. **2.** An underground railway; especially, the underground railway system in London. Usually preceded by *the.*
~*adv.* (also -grównd). **1.** Below the surface of the Earth. **2.** In or into secrecy or hiding: *They went underground.*

underground railway *n.* An urban railway system usually running in tunnels below the ground. Also *chiefly U.S.* "subway".

un·der·grown (úndər-grōn, -grōn) *adj.* Not fully grown; puny.

un·der·growth (úndər-grōth) *n.* Low-growing plants, saplings, and shrubs beneath taller trees. Also *chiefly U.S.* "underbrush", "underbush".

un·der·hand (úndər-hánd, -hand) *adj.* **1.** Secret and deceitful; treacherous; sneaky; underhanded. **2.** *Sports.* Underarm. **—See** Synonyms at **dishonest, secret.**
~*adv.* **1.** With an underhand movement. **2.** Slyly and secretly.

un·der·hand·ed (úndər-hándid) *adj.* **1.** Secret and deceitful. **2.** Lacking the required number of workers or players; shorthanded. **—un·der·hand·ed·ly** *adv.* **—un·der·hand·ed·ness** *n.*

un·der·hung (úndər-húng) *adj.* **1. a.** Protruding beyond the upper jaw. Said of a lower jaw. **b.** Having such a lower jaw. **2.** Resting on or mounted along a supporting track. Said of a sliding door.

un·der·in·sure (úndər-in-shóor, -shór || -shéwr) *tr.v.* **-sured, -suring, -sures. 1.** To insure (possessions) below their full value. **2.** To fail to protect (oneself) with adequate insurance.

un·der·laid (úndər-láyd) *adj.* **1.** Placed or laid underneath. **2.** Supported or raised by something from beneath; having an underlay.

un·der·lay (úndər-láy) *v.* **-laid, -laying, -lays. 1.** To put (one thing) under another. **2.** To provide with a base or sublining. **3.** *Printing.* To raise or support by underlays.
~*n.* (-lay). **1.** Something laid underneath; especially, felt or foam rubber placed under a carpet for added insulation and resilience. **2.** *Printing.* A piece of paper or other material used under type to raise the level of a printing bed.

un·der·let (úndər-lét) *tr.v.* **-let, -letting, -lets. 1.** To let (property) at less than the proper value. **2.** To sublet.

un·der·lie (úndər-lī) *tr.v.* **-lay** (-láy), **-lain** (-láyn), **-lying, -lies. 1.** To lie or be located under or below. **2.** To be the support or basis of; account for: *Many facts underlie my decision.* **3.** *Finance.* To take precedence over (another claim, security, liability, or the like).

un·der·line (úndər-līn || -līn) *tr.v.* **-lined, -lining, -lines. 1.** To draw a line under, especially to distinguish or emphasise (a written word or passage). **2.** To emphasise or stress.
~*n.* (-līn, -līn). A line drawn under writing to indicate emphasis or italic type.

un·der·ling (úndərling) *n.* A subordinate or lackey.

un·der·ly·ing (úndər-lī-ing) *adj.* **1.** Basic; fundamental. **2.** Implicit; hidden: *an underlying meaning.* **3.** *Finance.* Taking precedence; prior: *an underlying claim.*

un·der·manned (úndər-mánd) *adj.* Without sufficient workers or troops; shorthanded.

un·der·men·tioned (úndər-ménsh'nd) *adj.* Mentioned or referred to later or below, in a written work.

un·der·mine (úndər-mīn) *tr.v.* **-mined, -mining, -mines. 1.** To dig a mine or tunnel beneath. **2.** To weaken by wearing away a base or foundation: *Water undermined the foundations.* **3. a.** To weaken or impair by degrees or imperceptibly; sap: *Late hours undermine one's health.* **b.** To weaken, injure, or ruin insidiously or secretly: *His campaign undermined the chairman's authority.*

un·der·most (úndər-mōst) *adj.* Lowest in position, rank, or place.
~*adv.* In or to the lowest place.

un·der·neath (úndər-néeth) *adv.* In or to a place beneath; below.
~*prep.* Under; below; beneath. See Usage note at **below.**
~*adj.* Lower; under.
~*n.* The lower part or side. [Middle English *undernethe,* from Old English *underneothan* : UNDER + *neothan,* below.]

un·der·nour·ish (úndər-núrrish) *tr.v.* **-ished, -ishing, -ishes.** To provide with insufficient quantity or quality of nourishment to sustain proper health and growth. **—un·der·nour·ish·ment** *n.*

un·der·paint·ing (úndər-paynting) *n.* A sketch of a painting, revealing the design, shading, and often colouring, over which the final painting is executed.

un·der·pants (úndər-pants) *pl.n.* An undergarment, chiefly for boys and men, worn over the lower abdomen, buttocks, hips, and sometimes thighs.

un·der·part (úndər-paart) *n.* 1. A part on the lower surface, especially of an animal or plant. 2. A subordinate role, as in a play.

un·der·pass (úndər-paass ‖ -pass) *n.* 1. A passage underneath something; especially, a section of road that passes under another road or a railway line. 2. An intersection formed in this way.

un·der·pay (úndər-páy) *tr.v.* **-paid, -paying, -pays.** To pay insufficiently or less than deserved. **—un·der·pay·ment** *n.*

un·der·pin (úndər-pín) *tr.v.* **-pinned, -pinning, -pins.** 1. To support from below, as with props, girders, masonry, or the like. 2. To corroborate or substantiate.

un·der·play (úndər-pláy, -play) *v.* **-played, -playing, -plays.** *—tr.* 1. To act (a role) subtly or with restraint. 2. To act (a role) weakly or sketchily. 3. To present or deal with subtly or with restraint; play down. *—intr.* 1. To underplay a role. 2. In card games, to play a low card while holding a higher card of the same suit.

un·der·plot (úndər-plot) *n.* A subsidiary plot, as in a play or novel.

un·der·price (úndər-príss) *tr.v.* **-priced, -pricing, -prices.** To price below normal or appropriate value.

un·der·priv·i·leged (úndər-prívvə-lijd, -prívvi-) *adj.* Lacking the rights, opportunities, and economic or educational advantages enjoyed by other members of one's community; deprived.

un·der·pro·duc·tion (úndər-prə-dúksh'n ‖ -prō-) *n.* Production below full capacity or below demand.

un·der·proof (úndər-próof ‖ -prōof) *adj.* Having a smaller proportion of alcohol than **proof spirit** *(see)*.

un·der·prop (úndər-próp) *tr.v.* **-propped, -propping, -props.** 1. To prop (something) from below. 2. To support or sustain.

un·der·quote (úndər-kwōt) *tr.v.* **-quoted, -quoting, -quotes.** 1. To offer (goods or services) for sale at a price lower than the official list or market price; undersell. 2. To quote a lower price than that quoted by (another).

un·der·rate (úndər-ráyt) *tr.v.* **-rated, -rating, -rates.** To regard (someone's abilities, for example) as having less value or quality than is due; undervalue; underestimate.

un·der·run (úndər-rún) *tr.v.* **-ran** (-rán), **-run, -running, -runs.** 1. To run or pass beneath. 2. *Nautical.* To haul (a line or cable) onto a boat for inspection or repair.

un·der·score (úndər-skór, -skawr ‖ -skōr, -skōr) *tr.v.* **-scored, -scoring, -scores.** 1. To draw a line under. 2. To emphasise or stress. *~n.* A line drawn under writing to indicate emphasis or italic type.

un·der·sea (úndər-see) *adj.* Pertaining to, existing, occurring, or designed for use beneath the surface of the sea. *~adv.* (-sée). Beneath the surface of the sea.

un·der·seal (úndər-seel, -séél) *tr.v.* **-sealed, -sealing, -seals.** To place a protective coating on the underside of; especially, to apply a heavy tar or rubber-like substance on the underneath of a motor vehicle to prevent corrosion. Also *U.S.* "undercoat".

Underseal *n.* A trademark for a preparation used to protect the underside of vehicles.

Under Secretary *n.* 1. An officer in the British government service of a grade above that of Assistant Secretary. Also called "Permanent Under Secretary". 2. In Britain, any of various junior ministers in certain government departments. Also called "Parliamentary Under Secretary".

un·der·sell (úndər-sél) *tr.v.* **-sold** (-sōld), **-selling, -sells.** 1. To sell goods at a lower price than (another seller). 2. To sell (goods) for less than the full or normal price. 3. To advertise or publicise moderately or inadequately. 4. To present or regard (oneself) as having less ability or worth than one actually has. **—un·der·sell·er** *n.*

un·der·set (úndər-set) *n.* An ocean undercurrent.

un·der·sexed (úndər-sékst) *adj.* Having less sexual potency or desire than normal.

un·der·shirt (úndər-shurt) *n. U.S.* A **vest** *(see).*

un·der·shoot (úndər-shōōt) *v.* **-shot** (-shót), **-shooting, -shoots.** *—tr.* 1. To shoot a projectile below or short of (a target). 2. *Aeronautics.* **a.** To start one's final approach to (a landing area) too low or too soon. **b.** To land an aircraft short of (a landing area). *—intr.* To shoot or land short of a target or a landing area.

un·der·shot (úndər-shot) *adj.* 1. Driven by water passing from below. Said of a waterwheel. 2. Projecting beyond the upper jaw. Said of a lower jaw.

un·der·shrub (úndər-shrub) *n.* A low-growing shrub.

un·der·side (úndər-sīd, sīd) *n.* The side or surface that is underneath; the bottom side.

un·der·signed (úndər-sínd, -sīnd) *adj.* 1. Having placed one's signature at the bottom of a document. 2. Having a signature at the bottom or the end. Said of documents. 3. Signed at the bottom of a document: *the undersigned names.* *~n., pl.* **undersigned.** The person who has signed at the bottom of a document. Preceded by *the.*

un·der·sized (úndər-sízd) *adj.* Also **un·der·size** (-síz) Being of less than normal or sufficient size.

un·der·skirt (úndər-skurt) *n.* 1. A petticoat. 2. One skirt of a layered dress or skirt gown over which outer skirts are draped.

un·der·sleeve (úndər-sleev) *n.* A sleeve worn under an outer sleeve; especially, an ornamental sleeve designed to extend below or show through slashes in the outer sleeve.

un·der·slung (úndər-slúng) *adj.* 1. Having springs attached to the axles from below. Said of a vehicle. 2. Supported from above. 3. Having a low centre of gravity.

un·der·soil (úndər-soyl) *n.* Soil below the ground surface.

un·der·staffed (úndər-staáft ‖ -stáft) *adj.* Having too small a staff or fewer staff than usual: *an understaffed hospital.*

un·der·stand (úndər-stánd) *v.* **-stood** (-stóōd), **-standing, -stands.** *—tr.* 1. To perceive and comprehend the nature and significance of: *"I don't pretend to understand the Universe—it's a great deal bigger than I am"* (Thomas Carlyle). 2. To know thoroughly by close contact with or long experience of: *understood the customs of the Far East.* 3. **a.** To grasp or comprehend the meaning intended or expressed by (another): *understand Shakespeare.* **b.** To comprehend the meaning, language, sounds, form, or symbols of: *Do you understand French?* 4. To know and be tolerant or sympathetic towards (the needs, feelings, or views of another): *My wife doesn't understand me.* 5. To learn indirectly, as by hearsay; gather; assume. 6. To take something as meaning; conclude; infer: *Am I to understand that you are staying the night?* 7. To accept as an agreed fact or condition; regard as definite: *It is understood that the fee will be five pounds.* 8. To supply or add (a meaning or words, for example) mentally. *—intr.* 1. To have understanding, knowledge, sympathy, or comprehension: *"Hear and understand"* (Matthew 15:10). 2. To learn indirectly or at second-hand; gather: *They were just married, or so I understand.* 3. To draw an inference. **—give (someone) to understand.** *Formal.* To cause (someone) to believe or think. **—make (oneself) understood.** To communicate (one's) meaning clearly. **—See Synonyms at apprehend.** [Middle English *understanden,* Old English *understandan* : UNDER- + STAND.] **—un·der·stand·a·ble** *adj.* **—un·der·stand·a·bly** *adv.*

un·der·stand·ing (úndər-stánding) *n.* 1. The quality or condition of one who understands; comprehension. 2. The faculty by which one understands; intelligence. 3. Individual or specified judgment or outlook in a matter; opinion; interpretation. 4. An agreement between two or more persons or groups, especially when informal and implicit. 5. A reconciliation of differences; an agreement: *They finally reached an understanding.* 6. A usually harmonious relationship between people. **—on the understanding that.** On condition that; provided that. **—See Synonyms at reason.** *~adj.* 1. Having or characterised by comprehension, good sense, or discernment. 2. Intelligently sympathetic and compassionate. **—un·der·stand·ing·ly** *adv.*

un·der·state (úndər-stáyt) *v.* **-stated, -stating, -states.** *—tr.* 1. To express with undue restraint and cause to seem less important than is the case. 2. To express with restraint or lack of emphasis, especially ironically or for dramatic impact or elegance: *dress with quietly understated elegance.* 3. To state (a number, quantity, or the like) lower than is warranted: *understate one's age.* *—intr.* To understate something. **—un·der·state·ment** (-stáyt-mənt, -stayt-) *n.*

un·der·steer (úndər-stéér, -steer) *intr.v.* **-steered, -steering, -steers.** To turn or tend to turn less sharply than the driver intends. Used of a motor vehicle. *~n.* (-steer). A tendency towards or instance of understeering.

un·der·stood (úndər-stōōd) *adj.* 1. Agreed upon; assumed. 2. Not expressed; implied.

un·der·strap·per (úndər-strappər) *n.* A subordinate; an underling.

un·der·stra·tum (úndər-straá-təm, -stráy-, -straa-, -stray- ‖ -strá-, -stra-) *n., pl.* **-tums** or **-ta** (-tə). A substratum.

un·der·stud·y (úndər-studdi) *v.* **-ied, -ying, -ies.** *—tr.* 1. To study or know (a role) so as to be able to replace the regular actor or actress when required. 2. To act as an understudy to. *—intr.* To act as an understudy. *~n., pl.* **understudies.** 1. An actor or actress who studies a role so as to be able to replace the regular actor or actress when required. 2. Any person trained to do the work of another.

un·der·take (úndər-táyk) *v.* **-took** (-tōōk ‖ -tōōk), **-taken, -taking, -takes.** *—tr.* 1. **a.** To decide or agree to do: *undertake a task.* **b.** To set about; begin. 2. To take upon oneself; commit oneself to: *He undertook to pay all the costs.* 3. To promise; guarantee. *—intr.* *Archaic.* To make oneself responsible. Used with *for.* [Middle English *undertaken,* to accept, take in hand : UNDER- + TAKE.]

un·der·tak·er (úndər-taykər) *n.* One whose business it is to arrange for the burial or cremation of the dead and to assist at funeral rites.

un·der·tak·ing (úndər-táyking; -tayking *for sense 3*) *n.* 1. **a.** A task or assignment undertaken. **b.** An enterprise or venture. 2. A guarantee, engagement, or promise. 3. The profession or duties of an undertaker.

un·der-the-count·er (úndər-thə-kówntər) *adj.* Transacted or sold illicitly. **—under the counter** *adv.* Compare **over-the-counter.**

un·der-the-ta·ble (úndər-thə-táyb'l) *adj.* Not straightforward; secret or underhand.

un·der·things (úndər-thingz) *pl.n.* Underwear.

un·der·thrust (úndər-thrust) *n. Geology.* A reverse geological fault in which the rocks on the under surface of a fault plane move below the static rocks on the upper surface.

un·der·tint (úndər-tint) *n.* A slight or subtle tint.

un·der·tone (úndər-tōn) *n.* 1. A tone of low pitch or volume, especially of spoken sound. 2. **a.** A pale or subdued colour. **b.** A colour applied under or seen through another colour. 3. An underlying or implied tendency or meaning; an undercurrent.

un·der·tow (úndər-tō) *n.* **1.** The seaward pull of waves receding after they have broken on a shore. **2.** Any strong undercurrent moving in a direction other than that of the surface current.

un·der·trick (úndər-trik) *n.* A trick, especially in bridge, the loss of which prevents a declarer from making his contract.

un·der·trump (úndər-trúmp) *intr.v.* **-trumped, -trumping, -trumps.** In card games, to play a trump lower than one already played when a trump has not been led.

un·der·val·ue (úndər-vál-yōō) *tr.v.* **-ued, -uing, -ues. 1.** To assign too low a value to; underestimate. **2.** To have too little regard or esteem for. **—un·der·val·u·a·tion** (-áysh'n) *n.*

un·der·vest (úndər-vest) *n.* A vest.

un·der·wa·ter (úndər-wáter) *adj.* Being, occurring, used, or performed beneath the surface of the water. **—un·der·wa·ter** *adv.*

un·der·way (úndər-wáy) *adj.* Occurring or employed while in motion: *underway refuelling.*

un·der·wear (úndər-wair) *n.* Clothing worn under the outer clothes and next to the skin. Also called "underclothes", "underclothing".

un·der·weight (úndər-wáyt) *adj.* Weighing less than is normal, healthy, or required.
~*n.* Insufficiency of weight.

un·der·went. Past tense of **undergo.**

un·der·whelm (úndər-wélm, -hwélm) *tr.v.* **-whelmed, -whelming, -whelms.** To fail to excite or make enthusiastic. Often used humorously. [UNDER- + *-whelm,* as in OVERWHELM.]

un·der·wing (úndər-wing) *n.* **1.** Either of a pair of hind wings partially or wholly covered by the forewings, as in certain moths. **2.** Any of various moths of the genus *Calocala,* having brightly coloured underwings.

un·der·wood (úndər-wŏŏd) *n.* Shrubs and small trees growing beneath taller trees; underbrush; undergrowth.

un·der·world (úndər-wurld) *n.* **1.** Any region, realm, or dwelling place conceived to be below the surface of the earth; especially, the world of the dead in classical mythology; Hades. **2.** Those engaged in usually organised crime and vice, considered collectively. **3.** *Rare.* The opposite side of the earth; the antipodes. **4.** *Archaic.* The world beneath the heavens; the earth.

un·der·write (úndər-rīt, -rīt) *v.* **-wrote** (-rōt, -rōt), **-written** (-rítt'n, -ritt'n), **-writing, -writes. 1. a.** To write (one's signature, for example) at the bottom; subscribe. **b.** To sign or endorse (a document). **2.** To assume financial responsibility for; guarantee (an enterprise) against failure: *underwrite a theatrical production.* **3. a.** To sign (an insurance policy), thus assuming liability in case of certain losses. **b.** To insure. **c.** To insure against losses totalling (a given amount). **4.** *Finance.* To guarantee the purchase of (a full issue of shares or bonds); specifically, to agree to buy the unsold part of (a share issue) at a fixed time and price. **5.** To support or agree to (a decision, for example). *—intr.* To act as an underwriter; especially, to issue an insurance policy. [Middle English, translation of Latin *subscrībere.*]

un·der·writ·er (úndər-rītər) *n. Abbr.* **U/w 1.** A person or firm engaged in an insurance business; specifically, an insurance agent who assesses the risk of enrolling an applicant for coverage or a policy. **2.** A person or company that guarantees the purchase of a full issue of shares or bonds.

un·de·scend·ed testicle (ún-di-séndid) *n.* A testicle that has remained within the inguinal canal and has not descended to the scrotum.

un·de·serv·ed (ún-di-zérved) *adj.* Not merited; unjustifiable; unfair. **—un·de·serv·ed·ly** (-zérvid-li) *adv.*

un·de·sir·a·ble (ún-di-zīr-əb'l) *adj.* **1.** Not desirable; unwanted. **2.** Unpleasant; objectionable.
~*n.* An undesirable person. **—un·de·sir·a·bil·i·ty** (-ə-billəti) *n.* **—un·de·sir·a·bly** *adv.*

un·de·vel·oped (ún-di-vélləpt) *adj.* **1.** Not developed or fully grown; immature. **2.** Not put to full use or not having reached full potential: *undeveloped talent.* **3.** Not yet economically exploited to the full.

un·dies (ún-diz ‖ -deez) *pl.n. Informal.* Underwear; especially, women's underwear.

un·dine (ún-deen, -dīn, un-déen, ŏŏn-) *n.* A female water spirit who, according to Paracelsus, could earn a soul by marrying a mortal and bearing his child. [New Latin *Undina,* from Latin *unda,* wave.]

un·di·rect·ed (ún-di-réktid, -dī-, -dīr-) *adj.* **1.** Without object or purpose. **2.** Having no prescribed destination. Said of mail.

un·dis·charged (ún-diss-chárjd) *adj.* **1.** Not unloaded. Said of a ship's cargo. **2. a.** Not fulfilled: *an undischarged obligation.* **b.** Not paid: *an undischarged debt.* **3.** Not released or freed from obligation: *an undischarged bankrupt.*

un·dis·tin·guished (úndi-stíng-gwisht) *adj.* **1.** Not set apart; without any distinction: *His appearance was undistinguished.* **2.** Having no particularly good features; mediocre.

un·dis·trib·u·ted (ún-di-stríbbewtid ‖ -dístri-bewtid) *adj. Logic.* Not referring or applying to all members of a class. Said of a term or proposition.

un·do (ún-dŏŏ, un-) *v.* **-did** (-díd), **-done** (-dún), **-doing, -does** (-dúz). *—tr.* **1.** To reverse or erase; cancel; annul. **2.** To untie, disassemble, or loosen: *undo a shoelace.* **3.** To open (a parcel, for example); unwrap. **4. a.** To ruin the reputation or prospects of. **b.** To throw into confusion; unsettle. *—intr.* To come open or undone. [Middle English *undon,* from Old English *undōn,* to unfasten, untie, annul, destroy : UN- + *dōn,* to DO.] **—un·do·er** *n.*

un·do·ing (ún-dŏŏ-ing, un-) *n.* **1.** The act of reversing or annulling

something accomplished; cancellation. **2.** The act of unfastening or loosening. **3. a.** Ruin; destruction. **b.** The act of bringing to ruin. **c.** The cause of ruin; downfall.

un·do·mes·ti·cat·ed (ún-də-mésti-kaytid, -dō-) *adj.* **1 a.** Not tame. Said of an animal. **b.** Not being a type of animal typically kept and put to work by human beings. **2.** Uninterested in or unaccustomed to family life or basic household chores.

un·doubt·ed (un-dówtid) *adj.* Accepted as beyond question.

un·doubt·ed·ly (un-dówtid-li) *adv.* It is not to be doubted that. See Usage note at **doubtless.**

un·dreamt-of (un-drémt-ov, ún-, -drémpt- ‖ -uv) *adj.* Also **un·dreamed-of** (-drémt-, -drémpt-, -dréemd-). Barely or not entertained even in wishful fantasy: *undreamt-of success.*

un·dress (ún-dréss, un-) *v.* **-dressed, -dressing, -dresses.** *—tr.* **1.** To remove the clothing of; strip. **2.** To remove the bandages from (a wound or burn, for example). *—intr.* To take off one's clothing; strip.
~*n.* **1.** Informal as distinguished from formal dress or uniform. **2.** Nakedness or near nakedness.

un·dressed (ún-drést, un-) *adj.* **1. a.** Naked. **b.** Not fully dressed. **2.** Not specially prepared or processed: *undressed leather.* **3. a.** Not prepared for cooking or eating. Said of certain meats. **b.** Without dressing or sauce. Said of a salad. **4.** Not treated or bandaged: *an undressed wound.*

un·due (ún-déw, un- ‖ -dŏŏ) *adj.* **1.** Exceeding what is appropriate or normal; excessive. **2.** Not just, proper, or legal: *undue use of power.* **3.** Not yet payable or due.

un·du·lant (úndewlənt ‖ úndələnt) *adj.* Resembling waves in occurrence, appearance, or motion. [UNDUL(ATE) + -ANT.]

undulant fever *n.* **Brucellosis** (see).

un·du·late (úndew-layt ‖ úndə-) *v.* **-lated, -lating, -lates.** *—tr.* **1.** To cause to move in a smooth wavelike motion. **2.** To give a wavelike appearance or form to. *—intr.* **1.** To move in waves or in a smooth wavelike motion; ripple. **2.** To have a wavelike appearance or form. —See Synonyms at **swing.**
~*adj.* (-lət, -lit, -layt). Also **un·du·la·ted** (-laytid). Having a wavy outline or appearance: *leaves with undulate margins.* [Late Latin *undulāre,* from *undula,* diminutive of Latin *unda,* wave.]

un·du·la·tion (úndew-láysh'n ‖ úndə-) *n.* **1.** A regular rising and falling or movement to alternating sides; a movement in waves. **2.** A wavelike form, outline, or appearance. **3.** Any of a series of waves or wavelike segments; a pulsation.

un·du·la·to·ry (úndew-lətri, -lətəri, -laytəri, -láytəri) *adj.* Of, pertaining to, or caused by undulation; undulating.

un·du·ly (ún-déw-li, un- ‖ -dŏŏ-) *adv.* **1.** Excessively; immoderately. **2.** In disregard of a legal or moral precept.

un·du·ti·ful (ún-déwti-f'l, un- ‖ -dŏŏti-) *adj.* **1.** Lacking a sense of duty. **2.** Unreliable or disobedient.

un·dy·ing (ún-dí-ing, ún-) *adj.* Endless; everlasting; immortal.

un·earned (ún-érnd) *adj.* **1.** Not gained by work or service. **2.** Not deserved. **3.** Not yet earned: *unearned interest.*

unearned income *n.* An income coming from property, interests, or other investments as opposed to from wages and salaries.

unearned increment *n.* An increase in the value of a property independent of the owner's efforts, as from a general rise in demand for land or the improvement of nearby land.

un·earth (ún-érth, un-) *tr.v.* **-earthed, -earthing, -earths. 1.** To bring up out of the earth; dig up; uproot. **2.** To bring to light; discover.

un·earth·ly (un-érthli) *adj.* **-lier, -liest. 1.** Not of the earth; ideal or spiritual; supernatural. **2.** Ghostly; weird and unaccountable; unnatural. **3.** Ridiculously unreasonable or uncustomary; absurd: *out of bed at an unearthly hour.* —See Synonyms at **weird. —un·earth·li·ness** *n.*

un·ease (un-éez, ún-) *n.* A sense of discomfort, dissatisfaction, or apprehension.

un·eas·y (un-éezi, ún-) *adj.* **-ier, -iest. 1.** Lacking a sense of security; anxious or apprehensive: *The farmers were uneasy until the crop was in.* **2.** Causing constraint or awkwardness: *an uneasy silence.* **3.** Awkward or unsure in manner; constrained: *uneasy with strangers.* **4.** Not conducive to or causing rest: *an uneasy sleep.* **—un·eas·i·ly** *adv.* **—un·eas·i·ness** *n.*

un·em·ploy·a·ble (ún-im-plóy-əb'l, -em-) *adj.* Not able to find or keep a job.
~*n.* One who cannot be employed.

un·em·ployed (ún-im-plóyd, -em-) *adj.* **1.** Out of work; jobless. **2.** Not being used; idle.

un·em·ploy·ment (ún-im-plóymənt, -em-) *n.* **1.** The state of being out of work. **2.** The number or percentage of people in a community who are out of work.

unemployment benefit *n.* In Britain, regular payment made by the state to an unemployed person who has contributed to a state fund. See **supplementary benefit.**

un·en·light·ened (ún-in-lít'nd, -en-) *adj.* **1.** Not educated; ignorant. **2.** Not informed of something. **3.** Prejudiced, superstitious, and unreasoning.

un·e·qual (ún-éekwəl, un-) *adj.* **1.** Not the same in extent, quantity, rank, or social position. **2.** Consisting of or having ill-matched opponents: *an unequal running race.* **3.** Having unbalanced sides or parts; asymmetric. **4.** Not even or consistent; variable; irregular. **5.** Not having the required abilities; inadequate. Used with *to:* "*It was maddening to be unequal to many enterprises*" (D.H. Lawrence).
~*n.* One that is unequal. **—un·e·qual·ly** *adv.*

un·e·qualled (ún-éekwəld, un-) *adj.* Not matched or parallelled by others of its kind; unrivalled.

un·e·quiv·o·cal (ún-i-kwívvək'l) *adj.* Admitting of no doubt or misunderstanding; unambiguous; clear: *an unequivocal rejection.* —**un·e·quiv·o·cal·ly** *adv.*

un·err·ing (ún-ér-ing, un- ‖ -érring) *adj.* Committing no mistakes; consistently accurate. —**un·err·ing·ly** *adv.*

U·NES·CO (yōō-néskō) *n.* United Nations Educational, Scientific, and Cultural Organisation: an independent agency of the United Nations, established to promote international cooperation in science, art, and education.

un·es·sen·tial (ún-i-sénsh'l) *adj.* Not necessary; not of importance. ~*n.* A non-essential.

un·e·ven (ún-éev'n, un-) *adj.* -**vener**, -**venest**. 1. a. Not equal, as in size, length, or quality. b. Having ill-matched opponents. 2. a. Not consistent or uniform: *an uneven colour.* b. Not consistent in quality: *an uneven performance.* 3. Not smooth or level: *the very uneven surface of a cobblestone road.* 4. Not straight or parallel: *slightly uneven margins.* 5. *Archaic.* Not fair or equitable. 6. Designating an odd number. —See Synonyms at **rough**. —**un·e·ven·ly** *adv.* —**un·e·ven·ness** *n.*

un·e·vent·ful (ún-i-véntf'l) *adj.* Lacking in significant or disrupting incidents: *an uneventful tour of duty.* —**un·e·vent·ful·ly** *adv.* —**un·e·vent·ful·ness** *n.*

un·ex·am·pled (ún-ig-záamp'ld, -eg- ‖ -ik-, -zámp'ld) *adj.* Without precedent; unparalleled: *a display of unexampled aggression.*

un·ex·cep·tion·a·ble (ún-ik-sépsh'n-əb'l, -ek-) *adj.* Beyond any reasonable objection; quite satisfactory. —**un·ex·cep·tion·a·ble·ness** *n.* —**un·ex·cep·tion·a·bly** *adv.*

un·ex·cep·tion·al (ún-ik-sépsh'n'l, -ek-) *adj.* 1. Not varying from the normal; usual; ordinary. 2. Not subject to exceptions; absolute. —**un·ex·cep·tion·al·ly** *adv.*

Usage: Unexceptional and unexceptionable are not interchangeable. Unexceptional means "usual, ordinary"; *unexceptionable* means "not open to objection", "to which one cannot take exception". Compare: *Her argument was unexceptional* (it was familiar), *Her argument was unexceptionable* (it was quite acceptable).

un·ex·pect·ed (ún-ik-spéktid, -ek-) *adj.* Coming without warning; unforeseen: *an unexpected proposal.* —**un·ex·pect·ed·ly** *adv.* —**un·ex·pect·ed·ness** *n.*

un·ex·pe·ri·enced (un-ik-speér-i-ənst ‖ -ek-) *adj.* 1. Not having been experienced; not directly known: *a hitherto unexperienced sensation.* 2. *Rare.* Inexperienced; unpractised or inexpert.

un·ex·pressed (un-ik-sprést, -ek-) *adj.* 1. Not expressed, unsaid: *filled with unexpressed resentment.* 2. Understood, implicit, without needing to be expressed: *the unexpressed premise in her argument.*

un·fail·ing (ún-fáyling) *adj.* 1. Constant; unflagging: *unfailing patience.* 2. Inexhaustible; endless: *an unfailing supply.* 3. Incapable of error; infallible. —**un·fail·ing·ly** *adv.*

un·fair (ún-fáir, un-) *adj.* -**fairer**, -**fairest**. 1. Not just or even-handed; biased: *an unfair decision.* 2. Contrary to laws or conventions; unethical: *powerless to prevent unfair trading.* —**un·fair·ly** *adv.* —**un·fair·ness** *n.*

un·faith·ful (ún-fáythf'l, un-) *adj.* 1. Not adhering to a pledge or contract; disloyal. 2. Having sexual relations with someone who is not one's spouse or long-term sexual partner; specifically, guilty of adultery. 3. Not justly representing or reflecting the original; inaccurate: *an unfaithful translation.* 4. *Archaic.* Without or deficient in religious faith; unbelieving. —See Synonyms at **faithless**. —**un·faith·ful·ly** *adv.* —**un·faith·ful·ness** *n.*

un·fal·ter·ing (un-fáwl-təring, ún- ‖ -fól-) *adj.* Not hesitating; steady; unwavering.

un·fa·mil·iar (ún-fə-míl-yər) *adj.* 1. Not within one's knowledge; strange: *unfamiliar faces.* 2. Not being acquainted; not conversant: *unfamiliar with flying.* —**un·fa·mil·i·ar·i·ty** (-i-árrəti) *n.* —**un·fa·mil·iar·ly** *adv.*

un·fas·ten (ún-fáass'n, un- ‖ -fáss'n) *v.* -**tened**, -**tening**, -**tens**. —*tr.* To separate the connecting parts of; unloosen or open. —*intr.* To become loosened or separated.

un·fa·thered (ún-fáathərd, un-) *adj.* 1. a. Having no father; fatherless. b. Having no known father; illegitimate; bastard. 2. Of uncertain or unknown origin or authenticity: *unfathered rumours.*

un·fath·om·a·ble (un-fáth'm-əb'l) *adj.* 1. Too deep to be measured. 2. Incomprehensible; inscrutable. —**un·fath·om·a·ble·ness** *n.* —**un·fath·om·a·bly** *adv.*

un·fa·vour·a·ble, *U.S.* **un·fa·vor·a·ble** (un-fáyv-rəb'l, un-, -ərəb'l) *adj.* 1. Unpromising; not propitious. 2. Adverse; opposed. 3. Harmful. 4. Unpleasing. —**un·fa·vour·a·ble·ness** *n.* —**un·fa·vour·a·bly** *adv.*

un·feed (ún-féed) *adj.* Not paid a fee.

un·feel·ing (un-féeling) *adj.* 1. Not sensitive to others' feelings; unsympathetic; callous. 2. Having no physical feeling or sensation; insentient. —**un·feel·ing·ly** *adv.* —**un·feel·ing·ness** *n.*

un·feigned (ún-fáynd, ún-) *adj.* Not simulated; genuine. See Synonyms at **sincere**. —**un·feign·ed·ly** (un-fáynid-li) *adv.*

un·fet·tered (ún-féttərd, un-) *adj.* Unrestrained; free: *her joy was unfettered.*

un·fin·ished (ún-fínnisht, un-) *adj.* 1. Not brought to an end; incomplete: *unfinished business.* 2. Not having received special processing; natural: *unfinished wood.*

un·fit (ún-fít, un-) *adj.* 1. Not meant or adapted for some usually specified purpose; inappropriate. Usually used with *for.* 2. Below the required standard; inadequate. Usually used with *for.* 3. Not in

good health; in bad physical condition. —*tr.v.* **unfitted**, -**fitting**, -**fits**. To cause to be unsuited or unqualified; disqualify. —**un·fit·ly** *adv.* —**un·fit·ness** *n.*

un·fix (ún-fíks) *tr.v.* -**fixed**, -**fixing**, -**fixes**. To unfasten.

un·flag·ging (ún-flágging, un-) *adj.* Not weakening or stopping; untiring.

un·flap·pa·ble (ún-fláp-əb'l) *adj.* *Informal.* Not easily upset, disconcerted or excited, even in a crisis; calm. —**un·flap·pa·bil·i·ty** (-ə-billəti) *n.*

un·fledged (ún-fléjd, un-) *adj.* 1. Not yet sufficiently developed to fly. Said of a young bird lacking flight feathers. 2. Inexperienced, immature, or untried.

un·flinch·ing (un-flínching, ún-) *adj.* Without fear or indecision; unshrinking; resolute. —**un·flinch·ing·ly** *adv.*

un·fold (ún-fṓld, un- *Note:* un- *especially for senses tr. 3 and intr. 2, 3*) *v.* -**folded**, -**folding**, -**folds**. —*tr.* 1. To open and spread out; extend (something folded). 2. To remove the coverings from; disclose to view. 3. To reveal gradually by written or spoken explanation; make known. —*intr.* 1. To become spread out; open out. 2. To be revealed gradually to the understanding: *as the plot unfolds.* 3. To develop.

un·for·get·ta·ble (ún-fər-géttəb'l ‖ -fawr-) *adj.* Earning a permanent place in the memory; memorable: *an unforgettable sunset.* —**un·for·get·ta·bly** *adv.*

un·formed (ún-fórmd) *adj.* 1. Having no definite shape or structure; shapeless and unorganised. 2. Not yet developed to maturity. 3. Not yet given a physical existence; uncreated.

un·for·tu·nate (un-fórch-nət, ún-, -nit, -ənət, -ənit) *adj.* 1. Characterised by undeserved lack of good fortune; unlucky. 2. Causing misfortune; disastrous. 3. Regrettable; deplorable: *an unfortunate lack of good manners.* ~*n.* A victim of bad luck, disaster, poverty, or other misfortune. —**un·for·tu·nate·ly** *adv.* —**un·for·tu·nate·ness** *n.*

un·found·ed (ún-fówndid, un-) *adj.* 1. Not yet established. 2. Not based on fact or sound evidence; groundless: *unfounded accusations.* —**un·found·ed·ly** *adv.* —**un·found·ed·ness** *n.*

un·freeze (ún-fréez) *v.* -**froze** (-frṓz), -**frozen** (-frṓz'n), -**freezing**, -**freezes**. —*tr.* 1. To thaw out. 2. To ease or eliminate restrictions on (wages, prices, credit, manufactured goods, and the like). —*intr.* To thaw.

un·fre·quent·ed (ún-fri-kwéntid ‖ -fréekwəntid) *adj.* Receiving few or no visitors.

un·friend·ly (ún-fréndli, un-) *adj.* -**lier**, -**liest**. 1. Not disposed to friendship; hostile; disagreeable. 2. Indicating a bad prospect; unfavourable. —**un·friend·li·ness** *n.*

un·frock (ún-frók, un-) *tr.v.* -**frocked**, -**frocking**, -**frocks**. To strip of priestly privileges and functions.

un·fruit·ful (ún-frṓot-f'l, un- ‖ -fréwt-) *adj.* 1. Not bearing fruit or offspring; barren. 2. Unprofitable or unsuccessful: *an unfruitful attempt to woo investors.* —See Synonyms at **sterile**. —**un·fruit·ful·ly** *adv.* —**un·fruit·ful·ness** *n.*

un·furl (ún-fúrl) *v.* -**furled**, -**furling**, -**furls**. —*tr.* To spread or open out; unroll: *unfurled the Jolly Roger in defiance.* —*intr.* To become spread or opened out.

un·gain·ly (un-gáynli, ún-) *adj.* -**lier**, -**liest**. 1. Without grace or ease of movement; clumsy. 2. Difficult to move or use; unwieldy. —See Synonyms at **awkward**. ~*adv.* In a clumsy manner. —**un·gain·li·ness** *n.*

un·gen·er·ous (ún-jénnərəss, un-) *adj.* 1. Not generous; stingy. 2. Harsh in judgment; unkind: *a rather ungenerous review.* —**un·gen·er·ous·ly** *adv.*

un·get·at·a·ble (ún-get-áttəb'l) *adj.* *Informal.* Inaccessible: *the washing machine trap door was unget-at-able.*

un·girt (ún-gúrt) *adj.* *Archaic.* 1. Having the belt, girdle, or other restraining or supporting garment removed or loosened. 2. Loose or free; slack.

un·god·ly (ún-gódli, un-) *adj.* -**lier**, -**liest**. 1. Not revering God; impious. 2. Sinful; wicked. 3. *Informal.* a. Outrageous; unreasonable: *He called at an ungodly hour.* b. Very unpleasant or annoying: *an ungodly din.* —**un·god·li·ness** *n.*

un·gov·ern·a·ble (ún-gúvvərnəb'l, un-, -gúv-nəb'l) *adj.* Not able to be controlled; an *ungovernable temper.* See Synonyms at **unruly**. —**un·gov·ern·a·ble·ness** *n.* —**un·gov·ern·a·bly** *adv.*

un·gra·cious (ún-gráyshəss, un-) *adj.* 1. Lacking social manners; rude. 2. Not welcome or acceptable; unattractive: *an ungracious task.* —**un·gra·cious·ly** *adv.* —**un·gra·cious·ness** *n.*

un·gram·mat·i·cal (ún-grə-máttik'l) *adj.* 1. Not in accord with the rules of a prescriptive grammar. 2. Not in accord with a language as used by a native speaker. —**un·gram·mat·i·cal·i·ty** (-kál-əti) *n.* —**un·gram·mat·i·cal·ly** *adv.*

un·grate·ful (un-gráytf'l, ún-) *adj.* 1. Without due feeling or expression of gratitude, thanks, or appreciation. 2. Not agreeable or pleasant; repellent: *an ungrateful task.* 3. Not increasing yield when cultivated. Said of land. —**un·grate·ful·ly** *adv.* —**un·grate·ful·ness** *n.*

un·grudg·ing (ún-grújing, un-) *adj.* Generous; willing or freely given: *ungrudging praise.* —**un·grudg·ing·ly** *adv.*

un·gual (úng-gwəl ‖ -l) *adj.* 1. Of or pertaining to the fingernails or toenails. 2. Of, resembling, or bearing a hoof, nail, or claw. [Latin *unguis*, UNGUIS.]

un·guard·ed (ún-gárdid, un-) *adj.* 1. Without guard or protection; vulnerable. 2. Unprepared or imprudent; incautious: *caught in an unguarded moment.* 3. Free from guile; open. —**un·guard·ed·ly**

adv. **—un·guard·ed·ness** *n.*

un·guent (úng-gwənt; *rarely* -gew-ənt || ún-, -jənt) *n.* A salve for soothing or healing; an ointment. [Middle English, from Latin *unguentum*, from *unguere*, to anoint.]

un·guic·u·late (ung-gwíckew-lət, un-, -lit, -layt) *adj.* **1.** *Zoology.* Having nails or claws. Said of a mammal. **2.** *Botany.* Having a claw-shaped base: *unguiculate petals.*
~*n.* A mammal having nails or claws. [New Latin *unguiculatus*, from Latin *unguiculus*, fingernail, diminutive of *unguis*, UNGUIS.]

un·guis (úng-gwiss || ún-) *n., pl.* **-gues** (-gweez). **1.** A nail, claw, hoof, or clawlike structure. **2.** The clawlike base of some petals. [Latin *unguis*, claw, nail.]

un·gu·la (úng-gew-lə) *n., pl.* **-lae** (-lee). *Mathematics.* **1.** A cone or cylinder truncated by a plane not parallel to its base. **2.** *Rare.* A hoof. [Latin, "hoof" (from its shape), diminutive of UNGUIS.] **—un·gu·lar** (-lər) *adj.*

un·gu·late (úng-gew-lət, -lit, -layt || ún-) *adj.* **1. a.** Having hoofs. **b.** Hooflike. **2.** Of or belonging to the former order Ungulata, now divided into the orders Perissodactyla and Artiodactyla, and including hoofed mammals such as horses, cattle, deer, and pigs.
~*n.* An ungulate mammal. [Late Latin *ungulātus*, from Latin *ungula*, diminutive of *unguis*, UNGUIS.]

un·gu·li·grade (úng-gewli-grayd) *adj.* Walking on hooves. Said of horses and similar animals. [Latin *ungula*, hoof (see **ungula**) + -GRADE.]

un·hal·low (ún-hál-ō, un-) *tr.v.* **-lowed, -lowing, -lows.** *Archaic.* To profane; desecrate.

un·hal·lowed (ún-hál-ōd, un-) *adj.* **1.** Not hallowed or consecrated. **2.** *Literary.* Immoral; wicked.

un·hand (ún-hánd) *tr.v.* **-handed, -handing, -hands.** To remove one's hand or hands from; let go: *"Unhand me, you villain!"*

un·hand·y (ún-hándi) *adj.* **-ier, -iest. 1.** Difficult to handle or manage; unwieldy; cumbersome: *an unhandy desk.* **2.** Lacking manual skill or dexterity: *an unhandy child.* **—un·hand·i·ly** *adv.* **—un·hand·i·ness** *n.*

un·hap·py (un-háppi, ún-) *adj.* **-pier, -piest. 1.** Not happy or joyful; sad. **2.** Not bringing or enjoying good fortune; unlucky. **3.** Not suitable or tactful; inappropriate. **—un·hap·pi·ly** (*often* -háppəli) *adv.* **—un·hap·pi·ness** *n.*

un·har·ness (ún-hárniss) *tr.v.* **-nessed, -nessing, -nesses. 1.** To remove the harness from. **2.** To release or liberate (energy or emotions, for example). **3.** To take armour off (someone).

un·health·y (un-hélthi, ún-) *adj.* **-ier, -iest. 1.** In a state of ill health; sick. **2.** Characterising or symptomatic of ill health: *an unhealthy pallor.* **3.** Causing or conducive to poor health; unwholesome. **4. a.** Harmful to character or moral health; corrupting. **b.** Indicating a morbid or disturbed mental state: *an unhealthy interest in violence.* **5.** *Informal.* Of a risky nature; dangerous. **—un·health·i·ly** (*often* -hélthəli) *adv.* **—un·health·i·ness** *n.*

un·heard (ún-hérd) *adj.* **1.** Not sensed by the ear. **2.** Not given a hearing; not listened to: *his protests went unheard.* **3.** *Archaic.* Obscure; unknown.

un·heard-of (ún-hérd-ov, un- || -uv) *adj.* **1.** Not previously known; unknown. **2.** Without precedent: *unheard-of riches.* **3.** Highly offensive or outrageous.

un·hes·i·tat·ing (un-hézzi-tayting, ún-) *adj.* **1.** Prompt; ready. **2.** Unfaltering; steadfast. **—un·hes·i·tat·ing·ly** *adv.*

un·hinge (un-hínj, un-) *tr.v.* **-hinged, -hinging, -hinges. 1.** To remove (a door) from the hinges. **2.** To confuse; disrupt. **3.** To derange; unbalance: *He was unhinged by a traumatic shock.*

un·ho·ly (un-hóli, un-) *adj.* **-lier, -liest. 1.** Not hallowed or consecrated. **2.** Wicked; immoral. **3.** *Informal.* Outrageous; unreasonable. **—un·ho·li·ly** *adv.* **—un·ho·li·ness** *n.*

un·hook (ún-hŏok, un- || -hŏok) *tr.v.* **-hooked, -hooking, -hooks. 1.** To release or remove from a hook or hooks. **2.** To unfasten the hook or hooks of.

un·hoped-for (un-hópt-fawr, ún-) *adj.* Not expected but pleasant; beyond what was anticipated.

un·horse (ún-hórss, un-) *tr.v.* **-horsed, -horsing, -horses. 1.** To cause to fall from a horse. Usually used in the passive. **2.** To overthrow or dislodge; upset.

un·hur·ried (un-húrrid || -húrreed) *adj.* **1.** Moving or acting at a leisurely or moderate pace. **2.** Done in a slow, deliberate way, or at a casual pace: *an unhurried inspection at the barracks.* **—un·hur·ried·ness** *n.* **—un·hur·ried·ly** *adj.*

u·ni (yŏoni) *n. Informal.* A university.

uni– *comb. form.* Indicates the state of being single or of having or consisting of only one; for example, **unicameral, unicostate.** [Latin, from *ūnus,* one.]

U·ni·at (yŏoni-at) *n.* Also **U·ni·ate** (-ayt, -ət, -it). A member of a Uniat Church.
~*adj.* Of or pertaining to a Uniat Church or its members, practices, or doctrines. [Russian *uniyat,* from Polish *uniat,* from *unja,* "church-union" (of the Greek and the Roman Catholic Churches), from Late Latin *ūniō,* UNION.]

Uniat Church *n.* Also **Uniate Church.** Any Eastern Church that acknowledges the supremacy of the pope but retains its own distinctive liturgy.

u·ni·ax·i·al (yŏoni-áksi-əl) *adj.* **1.** Having only one axis; monaxial. Said especially of plants having a single main stem. **2.** Having one direction along which double refraction of light does not take place. Said of a crystal.

u·ni·cam·er·al (yŏoni-kám-rəl, kámmə-) *adj.* Having or consisting

of a single legislative chamber. [UNI- + CAMERA (chamber).]

UNICEF (yŏoni-sef) *n.* United Nations Children's Fund (formerly, *United Nations International Children's Emergency Fund*). An agency of the United Nations that coordinates aid programmes in developing countries for improving the education and welfare of children and the health of pregnant women or mothers of young children.

u·ni·cel·lu·lar (yŏoni-séllewlər) *adj. Biology.* Consisting of one cell; one-celled: *unicellular organisms.*

u·ni·col·our (yŏoni-kullər) *adj.* Of a single colour; monochromatic.

u·ni·corn (yŏoni-kawrn) *n.* **1.** An imaginary creature usually represented as a white horse with a spiral horn projecting from its forehead. **2.** A representation of this creature, often used in heraldry. **3.** A two-horned animal, possibly the wild ox or rhinoceros, mentioned in the Old Testament. [Middle English, from Old French, from Latin *ūnicornis* : UNI- + *cornū,* horn.]

u·ni·cos·tate (yŏoni-kóss-tayt || -káwss-) *adj.* Having a single main costa, rib, or riblike part: *a unicostate leaf.* [UNI- + COSTA.]

u·ni·cy·cle (yŏoni-sīk'l) *n.* A vehicle consisting of a frame mounted over a single wheel and usually propelled by pedals. Also called "monocycle". **—u·ni·cy·clist** (-sīklist) *n.*

un·i·den·ti·fied flying object (ún-ī-dénti-fīd) *n.* **1.** *Abbr.* **UFO** A flying or apparently flying object of an unknown nature. **2.** A **flying saucer** (see).

u·ni·di·men·sion·al (yŏoni-dī-ménsh'n'l, -di-) *adj.* **1.** Existing in one dimension only. **2.** Lacking depth; superficial.

u·ni·di·rec·tion·al (yŏoni-di-réksh'n'l, -dī-, -dīr-) *adj.* Having, operating, or moving in one direction only.

u·ni·fi·ca·tion (yŏoni-fi-káysh'n) *n.* **1.** An act or instance of uniting or unifying. **2.** The condition of being unified.

U·ni·fi·ca·tion Church (yŏoni-fi-káysh'n) *n.* The church of the Moonies (see).

u·ni·fied field theory (yŏoni-fīd) *n.* A physical theory that combines the treatment of two or more types of fields in order to deduce previously unrecognised interrelationships; especially, such a theory, as yet unidentified, unifying the theories of nuclear, electromagnetic, and gravitational forces.

unified tax *n.* A graduated income tax as operated in Britain.

u·ni·fi·lar (yŏoni-filər) *adj.* Having or utilising only one thread, wire, fibre, or the like.

u·ni·fo·li·ate (yŏoni-fóli-ət, -it, -ayt) *adj.* Having a single leaf.

u·ni·fo·li·o·late (yŏoni-fóli-ə-layt, -lət, -lit) *adj.* Compound in structure, but having a single leaflet.

u·ni·form (yŏoni-fawrm) *adj.* **1. a.** Always the same; unchanging; unvarying: *a uniform gait.* **b.** Without fluctuation or variation; consistent; regular: *a uniform flow.* **2.** Being the same as another or others; identical; consonant: *a uniform size.* **3.** Consistent in appearance; having an unvaried texture, colour, or design. **4.** Conforming to the same standard; consistent in application, judgment, or the like. —See Synonyms at **steady.**
~*n.* **1.** Distinctive dress intended to identify those who wear it as members of a specific group: *soldiers in uniform.* **2.** A single outfit of such dress.
~*tr.v.* **uniformed, -forming, -forms. 1.** To make uniform. **2.** To provide with or dress in a uniform. [Old French *uniforme,* from Latin *ūniformis,* of one form : UNI- + -FORM.] **—u·ni·form·ness** *n.* **—u·ni·form·ly** *adv.*

u·ni·for·mi·tar·i·an·ism (yŏoni-fórmi-taír-i-ən-iz'm) *n. Geology.* The theory that all geological phenomena may be explained as the result of existing forces having operated in the past. **—u·ni·for·mi·tar·i·an** *adj. & n.*

u·ni·for·mi·ty (yŏoni-fórməti) *n., pl.* **-ties. 1.** The state or condition in which everything is uniform, regular and unvaried. **2.** Consistency, conformity, or lack of variety, often to an extreme degree, to the point of monotony; sameness.

u·ni·fy (yŏoni-fī) *v.* **-fied, -fying, -fies.** —*tr.* **1.** To make into a unit; consolidate. **2.** To make uniform. —*intr.* To be made into a unit. [French *unifier,* from Late Latin *ūnificāre* : UNI- + Latin *facere,* to make.] **—uni·fi·er** *n.*

u·ni·lat·er·al (yŏoni-láttrəl, -láttərəl) *adj.* **1. a.** Of, on, pertaining to, involving, or affecting only one side. **b.** Performed or undertaken by only one side: *unilateral disarmament.* **2.** Obligating only one of two or more parties, nations, or persons: *a unilateral contract.* **3.** Emphasising or recognising only one side of a subject. **4.** Having only one side. **5.** Tracing the lineage of one parent only: *a unilateral genealogy.* Compare **bilateral. 6.** *Botany.* Having leaves or other parts on one side of an axis only. **—u·ni·lat·er·al·ly** *adv.* **—u·ni·lat·er·al·ism** *n.* **—u·ni·lat·er·al·ist** *n. & adj.*

unilateral declaration of independence. *n. Abbr.* **UDI.** A declaration of independence made by a colony or other dependent state contrary to the wishes and without the agreement of the protecting state, especially that made by the minority government of Rhodesia in 1965 in defiance of Britain.

u·ni·lat·er·al·ist (yŏoni-láttrəlist) *n.* One who favours unilateral action, especially unilateral disarmament. Compare **multilateralist.** **—u·ni·lat·er·al·ist** *adj.*

u·ni·lin·gual (yŏoni-líng-gwal||gew-əl) *adj.* Speaking, knowing, using, or expressed in only one language; monolingual.

u·ni·loc·u·lar (yŏoni-lóckewlər) *adj. Botany.* Having a single compartment or chamber: *a unilocular ovary.* [UNI- + LOCULUS.]

un·i·mag·in·a·ble (ún-i-májinəb'l) *adj.* Beyond one's comprehension; inconceivable: *the consequences of his action were unimaginable.* **—un·i·mag·in·a·bly** *adv.*

un·im·peach·a·ble (ún-im-péechəb'l) *adj.* **1.** Beyond doubt; unquestionable. **2.** Blameless; beyond reproach. **—un·im·peach·a·bil·i·ty** (-bílliti) *n.* **—un·im·peach·a·bly** *adv.*
un·im·proved (ún-im-próovd) *adj.* **1.** Not improved; not bettered. **2.** Not made use of or put to advantage. **3.** Not built upon or cultivated so as to increase in value. Said of land.
un·in·cor·po·rat·ed (ún-in-kórpə-raytid) *adj. Law.* Not required to be registered. Said of a company.
un·in·hab·it·a·ble (ún-in-hábbitəb'l) *adj.* Not fit for habitation, especially human habitation.
un·in·hib·i·ted (ún-in-híbbitid) *adj.* **1.** Not inhibited; open: *uninhibited laughter.* **2.** Free from normal social or moral constraints. **—un·in·hib·i·ted·ly** *adv.* **—un·in·hib·it·ed·ness** *n.*
un·in·spired (ún-in-spírd) *adj.* Not stimulating to the mind or imagination; mediocre; dull.
un·in·tel·li·gent (ún-in-téllijənt) *adj.* **1.** Not intelligent; stupid. **2.** Not endowed with intelligence. Said of nonsentient beings. **—un·in·tel·li·gence** *n.* **—un·in·tel·li·gent·ly** *adv.*
un·in·ten·tion·al (ún-in-ténsh'n'l) *adj.* Not deliberate or intended. **—un·in·ten·tion·al·ly** *adv.*
un·in·ter·est·ed (ún-ín-trəst-id, un-, -trist-, -tərest-, -trest-) *adj.* **1.** Not paying attention; not interested; indifferent; unconcerned. See Usage note at **disinterested. 2.** Not having a financial interest. **—un·in·ter·est·ed·ly** *adv.* **—un·int·er·est·ed·ness** *n.*
un·in·ter·rup·ted (ún-íntər-rúptid, -intər-) *adj.* Without interruption; continuous. **—un·in·ter·rup·ted·ly** *adv.*
u·ni·nu·cle·ate (yóoni-néw-kli-ət, -it, -ayt || -nóo-) *adj.* Having a single nucleus. Said of a cell.
un·ion (yóon-yən, -i-ən) *n.* **1.** The act of uniting or the state of being united. **2.** A combination so formed; especially, an alliance or confederation of persons, parties, or political entities for mutual interest or benefit. **3.** *Symbol* **U** *Mathematics.* A set consisting of all members of two or more given sets. Compare **intersection. 4.** Agreement, especially resulting from an alliance; concord; harmony. **5. a.** The state of matrimony. **b.** A marriage. **c.** Sexual intercourse. **6.** Formerly in Britain: **a.** A combination of parishes for joint administration of relief for the poor. **b.** A workhouse maintained by such a union. **7.** A **trade union** *(see).* **8.** A coupling device for connecting parts, as pipes or rods. **9.** A device on a flag or ensign, occupying the upper inner corner or the entire field, that signifies the union of two or more sovereignties. **10.** *Capital* **U. a.** An organisation or society at a college or university that deals with student administration and provides facilities for recreation. **b.** A building housing such facilities. **11.** A piece of fabric made from two different kinds of yarn. **—the Union. 1. a.** The union of the English and Scottish thrones (1603–1707) or parliaments (from 1707). **b.** The union of Great Britain and Ireland (1801–1920) or of Great Britain and Northern Ireland (since 1920). **2.** The United States of America, especially during the Civil War. **3.** The former Union of South Africa.
~adj. Of or pertaining to a trade union. [Middle English, from Late Latin *ūniō* (stem *ūniōn-*), unity, from Latin *ūnus,* one.]
union card *n.* A membership card in a trade union.
union catalogue *n.* A library catalogue combining the contents of a number of catalogues or listing the contents of more than one library.
un·ion·ise, un·ion·ize (yóon-yən-īz, -i-ən-) *v.* **-ised, -ising, -ises.** *—tr.* **1.** To organise (a work force) into a trade union. **2.** To recruit (workers or members) into a trade union. *—intr.* **1.** To organise or form a trade union. **2.** To join a trade union. **—un·ion·i·sa·tion** (-ī-záysh'n || *U.S.* -i-) *n.*
un·ion·ism (yóon-yən-iz'm, -i-ən-) *n.* **1.** The principle or theory of forming a union. **2.** The principles, theory, or system of unions, especially trade unions. **3.** Loyalty to a union, especially to a trade union. **4.** *Capital* **U.** Loyalty to the United Kingdom of Great Britain and Ireland or Northern Ireland. **—un·ion·ist, Unionist** *n.*
Unionist Party *n.* Formerly, the dominant political party of Northern Ireland, supported by the Protestant majority and identified with the Union with Britain.
Union Jack *n.* **1.** The flag of the United Kingdom. Also officially called the "Union Flag". **2.** *Usually small* **u**, *small* **j**. *Chiefly U.S.* Any flag consisting entirely of a union. [UNION (device on a flag, specifically the combined crosses of St. George, St. Andrew, and St. Patrick) + JACK (flag).]
Union of South Africa. See **South Africa.**
Union of Soviet Socialist Republics. *Abbr.* **U.S.S.R.** Also **Soviet Union.** Formerly **Russia.** Former federation of 15 national republics lying in eastern Europe and northern Asia, in extent the largest, and in population the third largest, country in the world. The largely industrial economy was centrally planned, and society was tightly controlled. A unified Russian state emerged when several principalities united under Moscow (15th century), and gradually expanded into Asia. The Russian empire became a great power in the 18th century, and by 1914, its boundaries were roughly those of 1991. The Revolution (1917) brought Lenin and the Communists to power, and the U.S.S.R. was set up (1922). From 1985, policies of economic restructuring (*perestroika*) and openness (*glasnost*) failed to improve the standard of living, but led to democratic reform, and to the growth of nationalism in the republics. In 1991 the U.S.S.R. broke up into 15 separate independent countries, 12 of them still loosely linked within the Commonwealth of Independent States. The capital of the U.S.S.R., Moscow, became the capital of the largest of these states, the Russian Federation (Russia). The others are Ukraine, Belarus, Moldova, Georgia, Armenia, Azerbaijan, Turkmenistan, Uzbekistan, Kazakhstan, Tajikistan and the Kyrgyz Republic. Estonia, Latvia, and Lithuania remained outside the Commonwealth. See map at **Commonwealth of Independent States.**
union shop *n.* A business or other place of employment whose employees are required to join an often named trade union within a stated period of time after being hired. Compare **closed shop, open shop.**
u·nip·a·rous (yoo-níppərəss) *adj.* **1.** Producing only one offspring at a time. **2.** Having produced only one offspring. Said of a woman. **3.** *Botany.* Forming a single axis at each branching. Said of some flower clusters. [UNI- + -PAROUS.]
u·ni·per·son·al (yóoni-pérss'n'l) *adj.* **1.** Being manifested as or existing in the form of only one person: *a unipersonal spirit.* **2.** *Grammar.* Used only in one person; specifically, used only in the third person singular. Said of certain verbs, for example *snows.*
u·ni·pla·nar (yóoni-pláy-nər || -naar) *adj.* Situated or occurring in one plane.
u·ni·po·lar (yóoni-pólər) *n.* **1.** *Physics.* Having, acting by means of, or produced by a single pole. **2.** *Anatomy.* Of or designating a nerve cell having a single process extending from the cell body.
u·nique (yoo-néek || yoo-) *adj.* **1.** Being the only one of its kind; solitary; sole. **2.** Being without an equal or equivalent; unparalleled. **3.** *Informal.* Outstanding; remarkable. **4.** *Mathematics.* Giving, having, or designating a single solution: *a unique solution to an equation.* —See Synonyms at **single.** [French, from Latin *ūnicus,* only, sole.] **—u·nique·ly** *adv.* **—u·nique·ness** *n.*
Usage: The absolute sense of the word *unique* precludes its being used in any comparative way. In careful usage, intensifying adverbs (such as *most, almost, rather, very,* or *somewhat*) are avoided. On the other hand, phrases such as *the most unique,* in the sense of "most unusual", will often be encountered in casual speech, and suggest that a less absolute sense has emerged in modern English, although this readily attracts criticism. *Almost* and *nearly* are not usually criticised when used with *unique* in informal contexts on the grounds that no sense of degree is involved. The intensifying use of *quite* (*It's quite unique!*) is also widely used in modern informal English.
u·ni·sex (yóoni-seks) *adj.* **1.** Designed to be worn or used by people of either sex: *a unisex sauna.* **2.** Selling or using unisex goods: *a unisex boutique.*
u·ni·sex·u·al (yóoni-sék-sew-əl, -shoo-, -shool, -sh'l) *adj.* **1.** Of or pertaining to only one sex. **2.** *Biology.* Having either male or female sexual organs but not both. **—u·ni·sex·u·al·i·ty** (-álәti) *n.* **—u·ni·sex·u·al·ly** *adv.*
u·ni·son (yóo-ni-s'n, -z'n) *n.* **1. a.** Identity of musical pitch; the interval of a perfect prime. **b.** The agreement or coincidence in pitch of musical parts. **c.** The performance or combination of musical parts at the same pitch or in octaves. **2.** Any speaking of the same words simultaneously by two or more speakers. **3.** Any instance of agreement; concord; harmony. **—in unison. 1.** In harmony or agreement: *whistling in unison; almost in unison on methods of treatment.* **2.** Simultaneously. [Old French, from Late Latin *ūnisonus,* of the same sound : UNI- + Latin *sonus,* sound.]
u·nis·o·nous (yoo-níss'n-əss) *adj.* Also **u·nis·o·nal** (-'l), **u·nis·o·nant** (-ənt). Sounding or composed to sound in unison.
u·nit (yóonit) *n. Abbr.* **u. 1. a.** A single individual or entity. **b.** An individual, group, structure, or other entity regarded as an elementary structural or functional constituent of a whole. **2.** A group regarded as a distinct entity within a larger group. **3. a.** A mechanical part or module. **b.** An entire apparatus or the equipment that performs a specific function. **c.** A group of people performing a usually specified function: *an editorial unit.* **4.** A precise quantity in terms of which the magnitudes of other quantities of the same kind can be stated. **5. a.** The number immediately to the left of the decimal point in the Arabic numeral system. **b.** The least positive integer; one. **6.** A single share in a unit trust. **7.** A place in a building or complex set aside for a specified activity: *an intensive care unit.* **8.** A piece of furniture to be fitted and used with complementary pieces: *a kitchen unit.* **9.** *Military.* **a.** An organised tactical or administrative group that is a subdivision of a larger group. **b.** A large piece of equipment, such as a tank or ship. **10.** An amount of a drug required to produce a specific result.
~adj. Designating or having a value of one in some unitary system: *a line of unit length.* [16th century : from Latin *ūnus,* one, probably by analogy with *digit* (used to replace *unity* as a translation of Greek *monas,* MONAD, in Euclid).]
Unit. Unitarian; Unitarianism.
U·ni·tar·i·an (yóoni-táir-i-ən) *n.* **1.** A monotheist who rejects the doctrine of the Trinity. Compare **Trinitarian. 2.** *Abbr.* **Unit.** A member of a Christian denomination that rejects the doctrine of the Trinity and emphasises freedom and tolerance in religious belief and the autonomy of each congregation. See **Universalist. 3.** *Small* **u.** An advocate of unity or centralisation, especially in government.
~adj. Abbr. **Unit. 1.** Of, pertaining to, or supporting the Unitarians or their beliefs. **2.** *Small* **u.** Pertaining to or advocating unity or centralisation, especially in government. [New Latin *unitarius,* from Latin *ūnitās,* UNITY.] **—U·ni·tar·i·an·ism** *n.*
u·ni·tar·y (yóoni-tri, -təri || -terri) *adj.* **1.** Of, pertaining to, or characteristic of a unit. **2.** Having the nature of a unit; whole. **3.** Based on or characterised by unity. **4.** Serving or used as a unit, especially of measurement. **5.** Pertaining to or designating a political system in which all governing power rests with a central government.

Unitary Authority area *n.* In the United Kingdom, a single-tier local-government administration area of a type that came into being in or after 1996.

unitary symmetry *n.* An approximate symmetry law in which all hadrons comprise combinations, allowed by group theory, of any two or three quarks.

unit cell *n.* The smallest group of atoms, ions, or molecules having a spatial configuration that is characteristic of a particular crystal lattice.

unit character *n. Genetics.* A character inherited as a single unit and determined by a single gene.

unit cost *n.* The cost of producing one article, calculated by averaging from the total production cost of such articles.

u·nite (yŏŏ-nīt, yŏŏ- ‖ yŏŏ-) *v.* **united, uniting, unites.** —*tr.* **1.** To bring together into a whole. **2.** To bring together or combine (people) in interest, purpose, or action, as in an association. **3.** To join (a couple) in marriage. **4.** To cause to adhere; bond. **5.** To have or demonstrate in combination: *He unites common sense with vision.* —*intr.* **1.** To become or seem to become joined, formed, or combined into a unit. **2.** To join and act together in a common purpose or endeavour. **3.** To be or become bound together by adhesion. —See Synonyms at **join.** [Middle English *uniten,* from Late Latin *ūnīre* (past participle *ūnītus*), from Latin *ūnus,* one.]

u·nit·ed (yŏŏ-nītĕd, yŏŏ- ‖ yŏŏ-) *adj.* **1.** Joined; combined. **2.** Produced by two or more people acting jointly. **3.** Being in agreement. —**u·nit·ed·ly** *adv.*

United Arab Emirates. Formerly **Tru·cial States** (trŏŏsh'l). Federation of seven sheikdoms (Abū Dhabi, Ajman, Dubai, Fujairah, Rās al Khaimah, Sharjah, and Umm al Qaiwain) on the southern coast of The Gulf. Most of the land is flat, sandy desert. The mainstay of the economy is petroleum production. The seven emirates, once known as the "Pirate Coast", concluded a treaty with Britain (1853), and from 1892, Britain looked after their foreign affairs and defence. The present federation (formed 1971) has a friendship treaty with Britain. A single council of ministers replaced the emirate ministries in 1974. Area, 77 700 square kilometres (30,000 square miles). Population, 2,260,000. Capital, Abū Dhabi. See map at **Gulf States.**

United Arab Republic. The union of the Arab Republic of Egypt and the Syrian Arab Republic (1958–61).

United Kingdom. Official name **United Kingdom of Great Britain and Northern Ireland.** Constitutional monarchy of northwest Europe, comprising England, Wales, Scotland, and Northern Ireland. Manufacturing is the largest sector of its economy, with some 30 per cent of the workforce, and the main exports are industrial plant, chemicals, crude oil (extracted from the North Sea since the mid-1970s), and motor vehicles. The country is self-sufficient in energy, fossil fuels catering for 95 per cent of its needs. Agriculture employs only 2 per cent of workers, yet provides 50 per cent of the nation's food. Some 30 per cent of workers are in the public sector. Wales became an English principality in 1284. Scotland and England were officially joined as Great Britain in 1707. The United Kingdom was formed by the union of Great Britain and Ireland in 1801, but southern Ireland broke away in 1921. Area, 241 752 square kilometres (93,341 square miles). Population, 58,780,000. Capital, London. See map, next page.

United Nations *n. Abbr.* **UN.** Used with a singular or plural verb. An international organisation of independent countries, with its headquarters in New York, formed in 1945 to promote international security and cooperation.

United Nations Trust Territory *n.* A **trust territory** *(see).*

United Party *n.* A former South African political party (1934–77), founded in 1934 by Jan Smuts, the official Opposition for most of the period after World War II.

United Provinces *n.* **1.** The Dutch republic that existed from the revolt of the Netherlands against Spain to its conquest by Republican France (1579–1795). **2.** Former name of Uttar Pradesh State, India

United Reformed Church *n.* A Protestant church formed by the merger of the Presbyterian Church of England and some Congregational Churches in England and Wales in 1972.

United States of America. Federal republic of 50 constituent states and the District of Columbia, smaller than Canada in extent, but in population the fourth largest country in the world. It is both the world's leading industrial nation and one of the world's major food suppliers. It is the world's leading producer of coal, natural gas, beef, maize, cheese, soya beans, copper, aluminium, and synthetic rubber. The country is largely self-sufficient, enjoying one of the world's highest living standards. However, crude oil accounts for nearly 25 per cent of its imports. Machinery, chemicals, motor vehicles, and cereals (maize and wheat) are the chief exports. The industrial centres of New York, Chicago, Los Angeles, Philadelphia, Houston, and Detroit are the largest cities. The region was colonised in the 17th century, mainly by the British and French, and the indigenous American Indians were increasingly displaced. Following the Declaration of Independence in 1776 and the subsequent war against the British, the union was formed in 1787, the original 13 states being the Thirteen Colonies along the Atlantic seaboard. In the Civil War (1861–65), the northern states defeated those of the South. The last two states to be admitted to the Union were Alaska and Hawaii. Area 9 809 155 square kilometres (3,787,319 square miles). Population, 266,560,000. Capital, Washington (District of Columbia). See map, page 1643.

unit factor n_2 A gene that determines a unit character.

u·ni·tive (yŏŏnitiv ‖ yŏŏ-nītiv) *adj.* Tending to promote unity.

u·nit-linked policy (yŏŏnit-linkt) *n.* A life assurance policy whose investment benefits are in proportion to the number of units held by the policyholder.

unit magnetic pole *n.* The strength of a magnetic pole that will repel a similar magnetic pole with a force of one dyne when the poles are one centimetre apart.

unit of account *n.* **1.** A unit of money used for accounting purposes rather than as a means of payment, and not necessarily corresponding to actual currency denomination. Also *chiefly U.S.* "money of account". **2.** The standard currency unit of a country. **3.** An artificial currency unit used, for example, by the European Community for fixing farm prices.

unit price *n.* A price of goods calculated for each unit, such as a kilogram or litre.

unit process *n.* Any of several standard chemical engineering processes, such as distillation, used in industry.

unit trust *n. British.* An investment company purchasing shares in numerous enterprises and issuing equal units for public sale from the combined portfolio. Also *U.S.* "mutual fund". Compare **investment trust.**

u·ni·ty (yŏŏnəti) *n., pl.* **-ties. 1.** The state of being one; singleness. **2.** The state, quality, or condition of harmony or agreement; concord. **3.** The state of being combined into a whole; unification. **4.** A combination or union of parts into a whole. **5. a.** An ordering of all elements in a work of art or literature so that each contributes to a unified aesthetic effect. **b.** The effect thus produced. **6.** Singleness or constancy of purpose or action; continuity. **7.** *Mathematics.* **a.** The number l. **b.** An element I in a groupoid satisfying $x·I = x = I·x$ for each x in the groupoid. Also called "identity". **8.** *Plural.* Three principles of dramatic composition, derived from Aristotle's *Poetics.* They require that a drama should have only one plot, the action of which should be contained within one day and confined to one locality. [Middle English *unite,* from Old French, from Latin *ūnitās* (stem *ūnitāt-*) from *ūnus,* one.]

univ. 1. universal. **2.** university.

Univ. 1. Universalist. **2.** University.

u·ni·va·lent (yŏŏni-váylənt) *adj. Chemistry.* Monovalent. —*n. Genetics.* A chromosome that is not paired with its homologue during meiosis.

u·ni·valve (yŏŏni-valv) *n.* **1.** A mollusc, especially a gastropod such as a limpet, having a shell consisting of single piece. **2.** The shell of such a mollusc. ~*adj.* Pertaining to or having such a shell.

u·ni·ver·sal (yŏŏni-vérss'l) *adj. Abbr.* **univ. 1.** Of, pertaining to, extending to, or affecting the entire world or all within the world; worldwide. **2.** Including, pertaining to, or affecting all members of the class or group under consideration: *the universal scepticism of philosophers.* **3.** Applicable or common to all purposes, conditions, or situations. **4.** Of or pertaining to the universe or cosmos; cosmic. **5.** Comprising all or many subjects; comprehensively broad: *universal interests.* **6.** *Mechanics.* Adapted or adjustable to many sizes, fittings or uses. **7.** *Logic.* Predicable of all the members of a class or genus denoted by the subject. Said of a proposition. ~*n.* **1.** *Philosophy.* **a.** A universal logical proposition. **b.** A general or abstract concept or term considered absolute or axiomatic, such as a Platonic idea. **2.** Any general or widely held principle, concept, or notion. **3.** A trait or pattern of behaviour characteristic of all the members of a particular culture or of all human beings. **4.** *Linguistics.* **a.** Any feature posited as an obligatory characteristic of all languages and therefore innate in every child before language is even acquired. **b.** A formal rule posited as essential for the analysis of any language. —**u·ni·ver·sal·ness** *n.*

universal constant *n.* A **fundamental constant** *(see).*

universal donor *n.* A person of blood type O, whose blood is compatible with most other blood types and can therefore be safely used for most transfusions.

universal gas constant *n. Physics.* The **gas constant** *(see).*

u·ni·ver·sal·ise, u·ni·ver·sal·ize (yŏŏni-vérss'l-īz) *tr.v.* **-ised, -ising, -ises.** To make universal; generalise. —**u·ni·ver·sal·i·sa·tion** (-ī-záysh'n ‖ *U.S.* -i-) *n.*

u·ni·ver·sal·ism (yŏŏni-vérss'l-iz'm) *n.* **1.** *Capital* **U.** *Theology.* The doctrine of universal salvation. Also called "apocatastasis". **2.** Universality. —**u·ni·ver·sal·is·tic** (-ístik) *adj.*

U·ni·ver·sal·ist (yŏŏni-vérss'l-ist) *n. Abbr.* **Univ.** One who believes that salvation is extended to all humankind; especially, a member of a Christian denomination that adheres to this doctrine. ~*adj.* Of or pertaining to Universalism or Universalists.

u·ni·ver·sal·i·ty (yŏŏni-ver-sál-əti) *n., pl.* **-ties. 1.** The quality, fact, or condition of being universal. **2.** Intellectual versatility.

universal joint *n.* A joint or coupling that allows parts of a machine not collinear with each other limited freedom of movement in any direction while transmitting rotary motion. Also called "universal coupling".

universal language *n.* An artificial language, such as Esperanto, designed for use by all nationalities.

u·ni·ver·sal·ly (yŏŏni-vérss'l-i) *adv.* Without exception; everywhere and in all circumstances: *These restrictions apply universally.*

universal motor *n.* An electric motor capable of running on either a direct-current or an alternating-current supply.

universal set *n.* A mathematical set containing all elements of the variety under consideration.

UNITED KINGDOM

ORKNEY
ISLANDS

Fair Isle

O R K N E Y

Westray   Sanday

Mainland   Kirkwall
Stromness
Hoy   South
Ronaldsay

ORKNEY
ISLANDS

Cape Wrath   Thurso   Wick

2°W   0°

Yell   Unst

Mainland   Fetlar

Foula   SHETLAND
ISLANDS
Lerwick

60°N

SHETLAND
ISLANDS

Fair Isle

Flannan   Lewis
Isles   Stornoway

58°N

St Kilda

WESTERN   Ullapool

Harris   H I G H L A N D   Elgin

ISLES   MORAY   Peterhead

North   Moray Firth

Uist   Portree   Inverness   ABERDEENSHIRE

South   Isle of   Loch   Aberdeen

Uist   Skye   Lochalsh   Ness   Dee

Lochboisdale   GRAMPIAN Mts

Barra   Rùm   Mallaig   Ben Nevis   1344m

Fort William   PERTH &   ANGUS

Coll   KINROSS   Arbroath

Tobermory   Tiree   Perth   Dundee

Mull   OBAN   STIRLING   FIFE   St Andrews

Loch   Stirling 7   Dunfermline   Firth of Forth

Jura   Lomond   Falkirk   EDINBURGH   Dunbar

Islay   Greenock 4   6 9   Berwick upon Tweed

Paisley   5 8 10

NORTH   Motherwell   Galashiels

AYRSHIRE   EAST   SOUTH   BORDERS   Tweed

Arran   AYRSHIRE   LANARKSHIRE   Cheviot Hills

Ayr   Kilmarnock

SOUTH   DUMFRIES   NORTHUMBERLAND

AYRSHIRE   AND   Tyne   1-5

Stranraer   GALLOWAY   Dumfries   Newcastle upon Tyne

Castle   Sunderland

Douglas   Solway Firth   Carlisle

Whitehaven   Workington   CUMBRIA   893m   DURHAM   HARTLEPOOL

Lake   950m   Wear   Durham

District   Scafell Pikes   Tees 6   Middlesbrough

977m   Darlington

Barrow-in-Furness   NORTH   YORKSHIRE   Scarborough

Lancaster   Vale of

ISLE OF MAN   York   York

DOUGLAS   EAST RIDING

OF YORKSHIRE

Blackpool   LANCASHIRE   Bradford   Leeds   Kingston upon Hull

Preston   Blackburn   8-13

Bolton   Huddersfield   Scunthorpe   30

14-18   Wigan   19-27   Oldham Barnsley   Doncaster   31

St Helens   Manchester   Sheffield   Lincoln

Liverpool   Salford   LINCOLNSHIRE

28   29

Holyhead   Anglesey   Chester   CHES.   The

Colwyn   DERBY   NOTTS   Wash

Caernarfon   Bay   1   2   Dee   Stoke-on-Trent   Lincoln

CONWY   Nottingham   King's Lynn   Cromer

GWYNEDD   Snowdon   STAFFS   Derby   Vale of   NORFOLK   Great

1085m   E N G L A N D   Belvoir   Norwich   Yarmouth

Shrewsbury   32   LEICS.   33   The   Breckland   Lowestoft

POWYS   SHROPS.   34-40 W.   Leicester   Fens

Aberystwyth   Wolverhampton   Birmingham   CAMBS.

CEREDIGION   WARKS.   NORTHANTS   Cambridge   SUFFOLK

W A L E S   WORCS.   Coventry   Northampton   Bedford   Ipswich

Cardigan   HEREFS.   Stratford   Worcester   BEDS.   Harwich

Bay   Wye   Hereford   Vale of   Banbury   Luton   HERTS.   Colchester

Fishguard   Evesham   Cheltenham   Chiltern   50   ESSEX

PEMBROKESHIRE   CARMARTHEN-   Severn   GLOS.   OXON.   Hills   Southend-on-Sea

SHIRE   Brecon   886m   10   Gloucester   Oxford   Reading   Windsor 48   LONDON

Milford Haven   Carmarthen   Beacons   8   Cotswold   Vale of   45   46 47 49   Canterbury

Swansea   3   5   6 7   9   Newport   42   Bristol   White Horse   North   Downs   KENT

4   11   CARDIFF   43   Bath   WILTS.   Medway   Dover

41   Thames   Folkestone

Bristol Channel   Stonehenge   SURREY   The Weald   Dungeness

Lundy   Exmoor   White Horse   HANTS   South Downs   Hastings

Barnstaple   SOMERSET   Salisbury   W.   E.

Taunton   Southampton   SUSSEX   SUSSEX   Brighton

D E V O N   DORSET   Portsmouth

Exeter   Bournemouth   Isle of Wight

Poole   ISLE OF

Bodmin   Weymouth   WIGHT

Moor   Dartmoor   Torbay

CORNWALL   Torquay

Penzance   Plymouth

Land's End   E N G L I S H   C H A N N E L   50°N

Isles of Scilly   FRANCE

N O R T H   S E A

A T L A N T I C
O C E A N

S C O T L A N D

U N I T E D

K I N G D O M

NORTHERN   LOND.   ANTRIM

IRELAND   Giant's Causeway   Larne

Londonderry   BELFAST

Sperrin   683m   Lisburn

TYRONE   Mts

Lower   Lough   DOWN

Lough Erne   Neagh   Armagh   Mourne

Enniskillen   FERM.   ARMAGH   Newry   852m   Mts

I R E L A N D

I R I S H

S E A

Outer Hebrides

Inner Hebrides

The Minch

CAMPSIAN Mts

Firth of Clyde

North Channel

S T   G E O R G E ' S   C H A N N E L

UNITARY AREA NAMES IN SCOTLAND:

1 Inverclyde
2 W. Dunbartonshire
3 E. Dunbartonshire
4 Renfrewshire
5 E. Renfrewshire
6 N. Lanarkshire
7 Clackmannan
8 Falkirk
9 W. Lothian
10 Midlothian
11 E. Lothian

UNITARY AREA NAMES IN ENGLAND:

1-5 N. Tyneside, S. Tyneside, Newcastle upon Tyne, Gateshead, Sunderland
6 Stockton-on-Tees
7 Redcar & Cleveland
8-13 Calderdale, Bradford, Leeds, Kirklees, Barnsley, Wakefield
14-18 Liverpool, Sefton, Knowsley, St Helens, Wirral
19-27 Manchester, Bury, Bolton, Salford, Trafford, Wigan, Tameside, Stockport
28 Warrington
29 Halton
30 North Lincolnshire
31 N.E. Lincolnshire
32 Telford & Wrekin
33 Rutland
34-40 Birmingham, Walsall, Sandwell, Dudley, Solihull, Coventry, Wolverhampton
41 N. Somerset
42 S. Gloucestershire
43 Bath & N.E. Somerset
44 Swindon
45 W. Berkshire
46 Wokingham
47 Windsor & Maidenhead
48 Bracknell Forest
49 Slough
50 Thurrock
51 Medway Towns

UNITARY AREA NAMES IN WALES:

1 Denbighshire
2 Flintshire
3 Neath Port Talbot
4 Bridgend
5 Rhondda Cynon Taff
6 Merthyr Tydfil
7 Blaenau Gwent
8 Caerphilly
9 Torfaen
10 Monmouthshire
11 Vale of Glamorgan

Km   0   50   100
Miles   0   50

UNITED STATES OF AMERICA

Universal Soul *n.* The Hindu concept of Brahman as the sacred syllable Om. Also called "Universal Spirit".

universal suffrage *n.* National suffrage extended to all adults above a certain age regardless of sex or race unless they are judged criminal or insane.

universal time *n.* *Abbr.* **U.T.** Greenwich Mean Time *(see).*

u·ni·verse (yōōni-verss) *n.* **1.** *Sometimes capital* **U.** All observed or postulated physical phenomena; the cosmos. **2. a.** The earth together with all its inhabitants and created things. **b.** All humankind. **3.** In science fiction: **a.** Another system of time, space, and matter coexisting with or corresponding to our own in an as yet undiscovered dimension, as, for example, in antimatter. **b.** Loosely, a vast and undiscovered star system or galaxy. **4.** The sphere or realm in which something exists or takes place. **5.** *Logic.* The universe of discourse. **6.** *Statistics.* A **population** *(see).* [Middle English, from Old French *univers,* from Latin *ūniversum,* the whole world (translation of Greek *to holon,* "the whole"), neuter of *ūniversus,* whole, entire, "turned into one" : UNI- + *versus,* past participle of *vertere,* to turn.]

universe of discourse *n.* *Logic.* A field containing all the entities referred to in a discourse or argument. Also called "universe".

u·ni·ver·si·ty (yōōni-vérssəti, -vérsti) *n., pl.* **-ties.** *Abbr.* **U., uni., univ., Univ.** **1.** An institution for higher learning with teaching and research facilities that awards undergraduate and postgraduate degrees. **2.** The buildings and grounds of a university. **3.** The students, teaching staff, and governing body of a university, regarded collectively. [Middle English *universite,* from Old French, from Medieval Latin *ūniversitās (magistrorum et scholarium),* "society (of masters and students)", from Late Latin *ūniversitās* (stem *ūniversitāt-*), a society, guild, from Latin, the whole, from *ūniversus,* whole. See **universe.**]

u·niv·o·cal (yōō-nívvək'l) *adj.* Having only one meaning.
~*n.* A word or term having only one meaning. [Late Latin *ūnivocus* : UNI- + Latin *vōx* (stem *vōc-*), voice.] —**u·niv·o·cal·ly** *adv.*

un·just (un-júst, un-) *adj.* **1.** Violating principles of justice; unfair. **2.** *Archaic.* Faithless; dishonest. —**un·just·ly** *adv.* —**un·just·ness** *n.*

un·kempt (ún-kémpt, un-) *adj.* **1. a.** Uncombed; dishevelled: *unkempt hair.* **b.** Lacking a neat or cared-for appearance; untidy: *an unkempt lawn.* **2.** *Archaic.* Unpolished; rude; rough. —See Synonyms at **sloppy.** [UN- (not) + *kempt,* past participle of archaic *kemb,* to comb, Middle English *kemben,* Old English *cemban.*] —**un·kempt·ly** *adv.* —**un·kempt·ness** *n.*

un·kind (un-kīnd, ún-) *adj.* **-kinder, -kindest.** **1.** Unfeeling; unsympathetic. **2.** Cruel; harsh: *an unkind wind.* —**un·kind·ness** *n.*

un·kind·ly (un-kīndli, ún-) *adv.* In an unkind manner.
~*adj.* **-lier, -liest.** Unkind. —**un·kind·li·ness** *n.*

un·knit (ún-nít) *v.* **-knit** or **-knitted, -knitting, -knits.** —*tr.* **1.** To unravel or undo (something knitted or tied). **2.** To smooth out (something wrinkled, especially the brow). —*intr.* To become unknit or undone.

un·know·a·ble (ún-nō-əb'l, un-) *adj.* Impossible to know or comprehend; beyond the range of human experience or understanding.
~*n.* Something that cannot be known. —**the Unknowable.** The ultimate reality underlying all phenomena that is beyond human comprehension. —**un·know·a·ble·ness** *n.* —**un·know·a·bly** *adv.*

un·know·ing (ún-nō-ing, un-) *adj.* Not knowing; uninformed; unaware. —**un·know·ing·ly** *adv.*

un·known (ún-nōn) *adj.* **1.** Not known; unfamiliar; strange. **2. a.** Not identified, discovered, or ascertained: *an unknown factor.* **b.** Not established or verified. **3.** Not famous: *an unknown author.* —**unknown to.** Without the knowledge of.
~*n.* **1.** One that is unknown. **2.** The world postulated as existing beyond sensory perception; the supernatural. Preceded by *the.* **3.** *Mathematics.* **a.** A quantity of unknown numerical value. **b.** The symbol for this quantity. —**unknown·ness** *n.*

unknown quantity *n.* A person, thing, or event whose outcome, behaviour, or effects cannot be predicted.

Unknown Soldier *n.* An anonymous soldier whose tomb is set up in public as a tribute to all the unidentified casualties of a national war. Preceded by *the.*

un·lace (ún-láyss) *tr.v.* **-laced, -lacing, -laces.** **1. a.** To loosen or undo the lace or laces of. **b.** To remove or loosen the clothing of. **2.** *Obsolete.* To disgrace.

un·lade (ún-láyd) *v.* **-laded, -lading, -lades.** —*tr.* **1.** To unload (a cargo). **2.** To unload (a ship). —*intr.* To discharge a cargo.

un·lash (ún-lásh) *tr.v.* **-lashed, -lashing, -lashes.** To untie the lashing of; loosen.

un·latch (ún-lách) *v.* **-latched, -latching, -latches.** —*tr.* To unfasten or open by releasing the latch. —*intr.* To become or admit of being unfastened or opened.

un·law·ful (ún-láwf'l, un-) *adj.* **1.** Not lawful; in violation of law; illicit. **2.** *Archaic.* Illegitimate. Said of offspring. —**un·law·ful·ly** *adv.* —**un·law·ful·ness** *n.*

unlawful assembly *n.* An assembly of three or more people collaborating for any unlawful purpose.

un·lay (ún-láy) *v.* **-laid** (-láyd) **-laying, -lays.** *Nautical.* —*tr.* To untwist the strands of (a cable or rope). —*intr.* To untwist.

un·lead·ed (ún-léddid) *adj.* **1.** Not surfaced or weighted with lead. **2.** Not mixed with lead. Said of fuels. **3.** *Printing.* Not spaced or separated with lead; set solid. Said of typeset matter.

un·learn (ún-lérn) *tr.v.* **-learnt** (-lérnt) or *U.S.* **-learned, -learning, -learns.** To put (something learnt) out of the mind; forget.

un·learn·ed (ún-lérnid *for senses 1, 2;* -lérnd, -lérnt *for sense 3*) *adj.* **1.** Not educated; ignorant or illiterate. **2.** Not skilled or versed in a specified discipline. **3.** *Chiefly U.S.* Unlearnt. —See Synonyms at **ignorant.** —**un·learn·ed·ly** (-lérnidli) *adv.*

un·learnt (ún-lérnt) *adj.* Also *chiefly U.S.* **unlearned.** Not acquired by training or studying: *an unlearnt response.*

un·leash (ún-léesh, un-) *tr.v.* **-leashed, -leashing, -leashes.** To release or loose from or as if from a leash: *unleash one's fury.*

un·leav·ened (ún-lévv'nd) *adj.* **1.** Made without leavening. Said especially of the bread of the Passover. **2.** Not lightened or alleviated: *A week of drudgery unleavened by amusement.*

un·less (ən-léss, un-, ún-) *conj.* Except on the condition that; except under the circumstances that.
~*prep. Rare.* Except; except for. [Middle English *unlesse,* alteration of *onlesse (than* or *that),* originally *(up)on less than,* "on a less condition than," hence except, if . . . not : ON + LESS.]

Usage: The expressions *unless and until* and *unless or until* are sometimes heard in emphatic speech and writing, but they attract criticism on the grounds that the senses of the two words overlap, and that one of the words is sufficient to express the meaning: *You will receive no further credit unless/until this sum is paid.*

un·let·tered (ún-léttərd) *adj.* **1. a.** Not educated. **b.** Illiterate. **2.** Without lettering. —See Synonyms at **ignorant.**

un·li·censed (ún-líss'nst, ún-) *adj.* **1.** Having no licence. **2.** Unauthorised. **3.** Unrestrained.

un·like (ún-lík) *adj.* **1.** Not alike; different; dissimilar. **2.** Not equal. ~*prep.* **1.** Different from; not like. **2.** Not typical of: *It's unlike Emily to lose her cool that way.* —**un·like·ness** *n.*

un·like·li·hood (un-líkli-hŏŏd, ún-) *n.* The state of being unlikely or improbable; improbability.

un·like·ly (un-líkli, ún-) *adj.* **-lier, -liest. 1.** Not likely; improbable. **2.** Likely to fail: *a most unlikely candidate.* —**un·like·li·ness** *n.*

un·lim·ber (ún-límbər) *v.* **-bered, -bering, -bers.** —*tr.* **1.** To detach (a gun or caisson) from its limber. **2.** To make ready for action. —*intr.* To prepare for action.

un·lim·it·ed (un-límmitid, ún-) *adj.* **1.** Having no limits, bounds, or qualifications. **2.** *Finance. British.* Unlimited in liability should business fail. —**un·lim·it·ed·ly** *adv.* —**un·lim·it·ed·ness** *n.*

un·lined (ún-línd) *adj.* **1.** Not marked with lines. **2.** Not wrinkled: *an unlined brow.* **3.** Not backed with a lining: *an unlined coat.*

un·link (ún-língk) *tr.v.* **-linked, -linking, -links.** To disconnect the links of; unfasten.

un·list·ed (un-lístid, ún-) *adj.* **1.** Not appearing on a list. **2.** Designating stock or securities not listed on a stock exchange. **3.** *U.S.* Ex-directory.

un·live (un-lív) *tr.v.* **-lived, -living, -lives.** To live in such a manner as to undo or annul (earlier years or their consequences); reverse.

un·load (ún-lód, un-) *v.* **-loaded, -loading, -loads.** —*tr.* **1. a.** To remove the load or cargo from. **b.** To discharge (a cargo or load). **2. a.** To relieve (oneself, for example) of something oppressive; unburden. **b.** To relieve oneself of (a duty, for example) by giving it to another. **c.** To pour forth (one's troubles). **3.** To remove the charge from (a firearm). **4.** To dispose of, especially by selling in great quantity; dump. —*intr.* To discharge a cargo or other burden. —**un·load·er** *n.*

un·lock (ún-lók, un-) *v.* **-locked, -locking, -locks.** —*tr.* **1. a.** To undo (a lock) by turning a key or a corresponding part. **b.** To undo the lock of. **2. a.** To cause to open; unfasten. **b.** To give access to: *unlocked her heart.* **3.** To set free; release. **4.** To provide a solution to: *unlock a mystery.* —*intr.* To become or admit of being unlocked.

un·looked-for (un-lŏŏkt-fawr, ún- ‖ -lŏŏkt-) *adj.* Not looked for or expected; unforeseen.

un·loose (ún-lŏŏss, un-) *tr.v.* **-loosed, -loosing, -looses. 1.** To let loose or unfasten; release; set free. **2.** To relax; ease (one's grip, for example). [Middle English *unlo(o)sen* : UN- (intensive) + *lo(o)sen,* to loosen, from *lo(o)s,* LOOSE.]

un·loos·en (un-lŏŏss'n, ún-) *tr.v.* **-ened, -ening, -ens.** To make less tight or firmly secured; unloose.

un·love·ly (ún-lúvli) *adj.* **-lier, -liest.** Not beautiful or pleasant; disagreeable; repugnant. —**un·love·li·ness** *n.*

un·luck·y (un-lúcki, ún-) *adj.* **-ier, -iest. 1.** Subjected to or marked by misfortune. **2.** Forecasting bad luck; inauspicious. **3.** Not producing the desired outcome; disappointing; regrettable. —**un·luck·i·ly** *adv.* —**un·luck·i·ness** *n.*

un·made (ún-máyd) *adj.* Not made up tidily for sleeping in. Said of a bed.

un·make (ún-máyk) *tr.v.* **-made** (-máyd) **-making, -makes. 1.** To deprive of position, rank, or authority; depose. **2.** To ruin; destroy. **3.** To alter the characteristics of. —**un·mak·er** *n.*

un·man (ún-mán) *tr.v.* **-manned, -manning, -mans. 1.** To cause to lose courage. **2.** To deprive of virility; emasculate. **3.** To remove the men from.

un·man·age·able (un-mánnijə'b'l, ún-) *adj.* Difficult to control.

un·man·ly (ún-mánli, un-) *adj.* **-lier, -liest. 1.** Not showing or marked by qualities conventionally associated with men, such as strength or self-control. Said typically of a man. **2. a.** Dishonourable; degrading. **b.** Cowardly. —**un·man·li·ness** *n.*

un·manned (ún-mánd) *adj.* **1.** Without a crew: *an unmanned ship.* **2.** *Obsolete.* Untrained. Said of a hawk.

un·man·nered (un-mánnərd, ún-) *adj.* **1.** Without manners; rude. **2.** Without mannerisms.

un·man·ner·ly (un-mánnərli, ún-) *adj.* Rude; ill-mannered. —**un·man·ner·li·ness** *n.*

un·marked (ún-márkt) *adj.* **1.** Not bearing a mark. **2.** Not observed or noticed. **3.** Not marked with corrections, a price, or the like. **4.** *Linguistics.* Of or pertaining to that one of a connected pair of words or linguistic units which is the more general or neutral; for example, in the pairs *dog* and *dogs* and *dog* and *bitch, dog* is the unmarked form.

un·mask (ún-máask ‖ -másk) *v.* **-masked, -masking, -masks.** —*tr.* **1.** To remove a mask from. **2.** To disclose the true character of; expose. **3.** *Military.* To expose the presence of (weapons), as by removing camouflage. —*intr.* To remove one's mask.

un·mean·ing (un-méening) *adj.* **1.** Meaningless. **2.** Expressionless; vacant. —**un·mean·ing·ly** *adv.* —**un·mean·ing·ness** *n.*

un·meas·ured (un-mézhərd) *adj.* **1.** Not yet measured. **2.** Measureless. **3.** *Music.* Without a fixed beat or bars.

un·men·tion·a·ble (un-ménsh'n-əb'l, ún-) *adj.* **1.** Not fit to be mentioned. **2.** Unspeakable. —**un·men·tion·a·ble·ness** *n.* —**un·men·tion·a·bly** *adv.*

un·men·tion·a·bles (un-ménsh'n-əb'lz) *pl.n.* Underwear. Now only in humorous usage.

un·mer·ci·ful (un-mérssif'l, ún-) *adj.* **1.** Having no mercy; merciless. **2.** Excessive: *unmerciful heat.* —**un·mer·ci·ful·ly** *adv.* —**un·mer·ci·ful·ness** *n.*

un·mind·ful (un-míndf'l, ún-) *adj.* Careless; forgetful; oblivious. Used with *of: unmindful of the time.* See Synonyms at **forgetful.** —**un·mind·ful·ly** *adv.* —**un·mind·ful·ness** *n.*

un·mis·tak·a·ble, un·mis·take·a·ble (ún-mi-stáykəb'l) *adj.* Obvious; evident; easily identifiable. —**un·mis·tak·a·ble·ness** *n.* —**un·mis·tak·a·bly** *adv.*

un·mit·i·gat·ed (un-mítti-gaytid) *adj.* **1.** Not diminished or moderated in intensity or severity; unrelieved. **2.** Absolute; unqualified. Used as an intensive: *an unmitigated lie.* —**un·mit·i·gat·ed·ly** *adv.*

un·moor (ún-mŏŏr, -mór) *v.* **-moored, -mooring, -moors.** —*tr.* **1.** To release from or as if from moorings. **2.** To release (a ship) from all but one anchor. —*intr.* To cast off moorings.

un·mor·al (ún-mórrəl ‖ -máwrəl) *adj.* Having no moral quality or sense; amoral. —**un·mo·ral·i·ty** (-mə-rál-əti, -mo- ‖ -maw-) *n.* —**un·mor·al·ly** *adv.*

un·mur·mur·ing (ún-múrmər-ing) *adj.* Not quibbling or complaining. —**un·mur·mur·ing·ly** *adv.*

un·muz·zle (un-múzz'l) *tr.v.* **-zled, -zling, -zles. 1.** To remove the muzzle from. **2.** To free from censorship; allow to speak or write freely.

un·my·e·lin·a·ted (ún-mí-əlin-aytid) *adj.* Lacking a myelin sheath. Said of certain nerve fibres.

un·named (ún-náymd) *adj.* **1.** Having no name. **2.** Not referred to by name.

un·nat·u·ral (un-nách-rəl, ún-, -ərəl) *adj.* **1.** Violating natural law. **2.** Inconsistent with an individual pattern or custom. **3.** Deemed to deviate from a behavioural, ethical, or social norm: *unnatural practices.* **4.** Contrived or constrained; artificial: *an unnatural manner.* **5.** Outrageously violating natural or proper feelings; inhuman. —**un·nat·u·ral·ly** *adv.* —**un·nat·u·ral·ness** *n.*

un·nec·es·sar·y (un-néss-ə-sri, ún-, -i-, -səri, -serri) *adj.* Not necessary; needless or superfluous. —**un·nec·es·sar·i·ly** (-srəli, -sərəli, -serrəli, -sérrəli) *adv.* —**un·nec·es·sar·i·ness** *n.*

un·nerve (ún-nérv) *tr.v.* **-nerved, -nerving, -nerves.** To deprive of composure, confidence, or firmness of resolve.

unnil-. *comb. form.* Indicates a chemical element with an atomic number between 101 and 109.

un·nil·bi·um (oon-ílbi-əm) *n.* The chemical element **nobelium** (see).

un·nil·hex·i·um (ŏŏnnil-héksi-əm) *n.* Symbol **Unh** A synthetic radioactive chemical element with an atomic number of 106.

un·nil·pent·i·um (ŏŏnnil-pénti-əm) *n.* Symbol **Unp** A synthetic radioactive chemical element with an atomic number of 105.

un·nil·quad·i·um (ŏŏnnil-kwóddi-əm) *n.* Symbol **Unq** A synthetic radioactive chemical element with an atomic number of 104. Formerly called "kurchatovium", "rutherfordium".

un·nil·sept·i·um (ŏŏnnil-sépti-əm) *n.* Symbol **Uns** A synthetic radioactive chemical element with an atomic number of 107.

un·nil·tri·um (ŏŏnnil-trí-əm, un-íltri-əm) *n.* The chemical element **lawrencium** (see).

un·nil·un·i·um (ŏŏnnil-yŏŏni-əm) *n.* The chemical element **mendelevium** (see).

un·num·bered (ún-númbərd) *adj.* **1.** Not numbered; countless. **2.** Not marked with an identifying number.

U.N.O. (*sometimes* yŏŏ-nŏ). United Nations Organisation.

un·ob·tru·sive (ún-əb-trŏŏ-siv ‖ -ob-, tréw-, -ziv) *adj.* **1.** Not readily noticeable. **2.** Discreet. —**un·ob·tru·sive·ly** *adv.* —**un·ob·tru·sive·ness** *n.*

un·oc·cu·pied (ún-óckew-pīd, un-) *adj.* **1.** Not inhabited; vacant. **2.** Not occupied by foreign troops. **3.** Unemployed; idle.

un·of·fi·cial (ún-ə-fish'l ‖ -ŏ-) *adj.* **1.** Not official. **2.** Not acting officially. **3.** Not ratified by official trade union representatives: *unofficial strike action.* —**un·of·fi·cial·ly** *adv.*

un·or·gan·ised (ún-órgə-nīzd, un-) *adj.* **1.** Lacking order, system, or unity. **2.** Having no organic properties. **3.** Not unionised.

un·or·tho·dox (ún-órtho-doks, un-) *adj.* Not orthodox. —**un·or·tho·dox·ly** *adv.* —**un·or·tho·dox·y** (-i) *n.*

Unp The symbol for the element unnilpentium.

un·pack (ún-pák) *v.* **-packed, -packing, -packs.** —*tr.* **1.** To remove the contents of (a suitcase, for example). **2.** To remove from a container or from packaging. **3. a.** To remove a pack from (a pack animal). **b.** To unload the contents of (a motor vehicle). —*intr.* To unpack goods, a trunk, or the like. —**un·pack·er** *n.*

un·paid (ún-páyd) *adj.* **1.** Not yet paid: *an unpaid bill.* **2.** Serving without pay; unsalaried. **3.** Awaiting wages due.

un·pal·at·a·ble (un-pál-ətəb'l, ún-) *adj.* **1.** Unpleasant to the taste. **2.** Disagreeable; unpleasant: *unpalatable truths.*

un·par·al·leled (un-párrə-leld, ún-) *adj.* Without parallel; unmatched; unequalled.

un·par·lia·men·ta·ry (ún-párl-i-méntri, un-, -ə-, -méntəri, -yə-) *adj.* Not in accordance with parliamentary procedure.

un·peg (ún-pég) *tr.v.* **-pegged, -pegging, -pegs. 1.** To remove the peg or pegs from. **2.** To allow (wages, prices, and the like) to fluctuate without restriction.

un·peo·ple (ún-péep'l) *tr.v.* **-pled, -pling, -ples.** To depopulate.

un·per·fo·rat·ed (ún-pérfə-raytid, un-) *adj.* **1.** Lacking perforations. **2.** *Philately.* Imperforate.

un·per·son (ún-perss'n) *n., pl.* **unpersons. 1.** A person whose existence is denied or ignored by the authorities, especially in a totalitarian state. **2.** An insipid or unimpressive person. In both senses, also called "nonperson".

un·pick (ún-pík) *tr.v.* **-picked, -picking, -picks.** To undo (sewing) by removing stitches: *unpick a seam.*

un·pin (ún-pín) *tr.v.* **-pinned, -pinning, -pins. 1.** To remove a pin or pins from. **2.** In chess, to free (a piece).

un·pleas·ant (un-plézz'nt) *adj.* **-anter, -antest.** Not pleasing; offensive; disagreeable. **—un·pleas·ant·ly** *adv.*

un·pleas·ant·ness (un-plézz'nt-nəss, -niss) *n.* **1.** The condition or quality of being unpleasant. **2. a.** An unpleasant experience or situation. **b.** An argument or quarrel.

un·plug (ún-plúg, un-) *tr.v.* **-plugged, -plugging, -plugs. 1.** To remove a plug, stopper, or obstruction from. **2. a.** To remove (an electric plug) from a socket. **b.** To disconnect (an electric appliance) by removing its plug from a socket.

un·plumbed (ún-plúmd) *adj.* **1.** Not explored as to depth or meaning; not fathomed: *unplumbed waters; an unplumbed theory.* **2.** Having no plumbing. Said of a building, for example.

un·pop·u·lar (ún-póppew-lər, un-) *adj.* **1.** Lacking public approval or acceptance. **2.** Not approved of; out of favour: *You're unpopular with her these days.* **—un·pop·u·lar·i·ty** (-lárrəti) *n.*

un·prec·e·dent·ed (un-préssi-dentid, ún-, -prée-si-, -d'nt-id) *adj.* Without precedent; unheard of. **—un·prec·e·dent·ed·ly** *adv.*

un·pre·dict·a·ble (ún-pri-díkt-əb'l, -prə-) *adj.* Not predictable. **—un·pre·dict·a·bil·i·ty** (-ə-bílləti), **un·pre·dict·a·ble·ness** *n.* **—un·pre·dict·a·bly** *adv.*

un·prej·u·diced (ún-préjŏŏdist, un-) *adj.* Free from prejudice; impartial. See Synonyms at **fair.**

un·pre·med·i·tat·ed (ún-pri-méddi-taytid, -pree-) *adj.* Spontaneous; not planned: *"His one act of rebellion was quite unpremeditated"* (R. Prawer Jhabvala). See Synonyms at **extemporaneous.**

un·pre·pared (ún-pri-páird, -prə-) *adj.* **1.** Having made few or no preparations. **2.** Not equipped to meet a contingency. **3.** Not steeled, as to face a shock. **4.** Impromptu. **—un·pre·par·ed·ly** (-páir-id-li, -páird-) *adv.* **—un·pre·par·ed·ness** *n.*

un·pre·pos·sess·ing (ún-préepə-zéssing, -zessing) *adj.* Failing to impress favourably; unattractive; nondescript. **—un·pre·pos·sess·ing·ly** *adv.*

un·pre·ten·tious (ún-pri-ténshəss, -prə-) *adj.* Lacking affectation or pretention; unostentatious; modest. **—un·pre·ten·tious·ness** *adv.*

un·priced (ún-príst) *adj.* **1.** Having no fixed or attached price. **2.** *Archaic & Poetic.* Priceless.

un·prin·ci·pled (ún-prín-si-p'ld, un-, -sə-) *adj.* Lacking principles or moral scruples; unscrupulous: *unprincipled behaviour.*

un·print·a·ble (ún-príntəb'l, un-) *adj.* Not fit for publication, especially on grounds of infringing public taste or morality, libel laws, or the like.

un·pro·duc·tive (ún-prə-dúktiv ‖ -prō-) *adj.* **1.** Producing or yielding little or nothing. **2.** *Economics.* Adding nothing to exchangeable value. **—un·pro·duc·tive·ly** *adv.* **—un·pro·duc·tive·ness** *n.*

un·pro·fes·sion·al (ún-prə-fésh'n'l ‖ -prō-) *adj.* **1.** Not conforming to the standards of a profession. **2.** Amateurish. **3. a.** Not in a profession. **b.** Not a qualified member of a professional group. **—un·pro·fes·sion·al·ly** *adv.*

un·prof·it·a·ble (ún-próffit-əb'l, un-) *adj.* **1.** Not making a profit. **2.** Not profitable; serving no purpose; useless. **—un·prof·it·a·bil·i·ty** (-ə-bílləti) *n.* **—un·prof·it·a·bly** *adv.*

un·prompt·ed (ún-prómptid, un-) *adj.* Spontaneous; not asked for or suggested.

un·pro·nounce·a·ble (ún-prə-nówn-səb'l ‖ -prō-) *adj.* **1.** Difficult to pronounce correctly. **2.** Not fit to be mentioned. Said of obscenities.

un·pro·vid·ed (ún-prə-vídid ‖ -prō-) *adj.* Not supplied, furnished, or equipped. Used with *with.* **—unprovided for.** Not provided with an adequate means of support: *He left his children unprovided for.*

un·put·down·a·ble (ún-pŏŏt-dównəb'l, -pŏŏt-, un-) *adj. Informal.* So interesting that the reader cannot put it aside. Said of a book.

Unq The symbol for the element unnilquadium.

un·qual·i·fied (ún-kwólli-fīd, un-). *Note: usually* ún- *for sense 1, un- for sense 2) adj.* **1.** Lacking the required qualifications. **2.** Without reservations; unconditional: *unqualified admiration.* Often used as an intensive: *an unqualified disaster.*

un·ques·tion·a·ble (un-kwéss-chən-əb'l, ún-, -kwésh-) *adj.* Beyond question or doubt; indisputable; certain. **—un·ques·tion·a·bil·i·ty** (-ə-bílləti), **un·ques·tion·a·ble·ness** *n.* **—un·ques·tion·a·bly** *adv.*

un·ques·tioned (un-kwéss-chənd, ún-, -kwésh-) *adj.* **1.** Not subjected to questioning. **2. a.** Unquestionable. **b.** Not called into question or examination; not doubted.

un·ques·tion·ing (un-kwéss-chən-ing, ún-, -kwésh-) *adj.* Asking no questions; not doubting or hesitating. **—un·ques·tion·ing·ly** *adv.*

un·qui·et (ún-kwī-ət, un-) *adj.* **-eter, -etest. 1.** Emotionally or mentally uneasy; agitated; disturbed. **2.** Characterised by unrest or uncertainty; turbulent: *unquiet times.* **—un·qui·et·ly** *adv.* **—un·qui·et·ness** *n.*

un·quote (ún-kwót, un-) *interj.* Used in speaking to indicate the end of a quotation.

un·rav·el (un-rávv'l, ún-) *v.* **-elled** or *U.S.* **-eled, -elling** or *U.S.* **-eling, -els.** —*tr.* **1. a.** To undo or unpick the knitted or woven fabric of. **b.** To separate (entangled threads). **2.** To separate and clarify the elements of (something mysterious or baffling); solve. —*intr.* To become unravelled.

un·read (un-réd) *adj.* **1.** Not read, studied, or perused. **2.** Having read little; ignorant: *unread in the classics.*

un·read·a·ble (ún-réed-əb'l, un-) *adj.* **1.** Illegible. **2.** Not interesting to read; dull. **3.** Incomprehensible; obscure. **—un·read·a·bil·i·ty** (-ə-bílləti), **un·read·a·ble·ness** *n.* **—un·read·a·bly** *adv.*

un·read·y¹ (ún-réddi, un-) *adj.* **-ier, -iest. 1.** Not ready or prepared. **2.** Slow in grasp or response; not prompt. **—un·read·i·ly** *adv.* **—un·read·i·ness** *n.*

unready² *adj. Archaic.* Unadvised; rash. Now used only in the title *Ethelred the Unready.* [UN- (lacking) + REDE + -Y, assimilated to *unready* (not ready).]

un·re·al (ún-réerl, un-, -rée-əl ‖ -réel) *adj.* **1.** Not real or substantial; imaginary; artificial. **2.** *Slang.* Amazing; out of this world: *Unreal, man!* **—un·re·al·i·ty** (-ri-ál-əti, -ree-) *n.*

un·re·al·is·tic (ún-reer-lístik, -réer-, -rée-ə- ‖ -reel-ístik, -réel-) *adj.* **1.** Lacking verisimilitude. **2.** Unlikely. **3. a.** Deluded; irrational. **b.** Not feasible or practicable. **—un·re·al·is·ti·cal·ly** *adv.*

un·rea·son (ún-réez'n) *n.* **1.** Absence or lack of reason; irrationality. **2.** Nonsense; absurdity.

un·rea·son·a·ble (un-réez'n-əb'l, ún-, -réeznəb'l) *adj.* **1.** Not governed by or based upon reason. **2.** Exceeding reasonable limits; exorbitant; immoderate. —See Synonyms at **excessive.** **—un·rea·son·a·ble·ness** *n.* **—un·rea·son·a·bly** *adv.*

unreasonable behaviour *n. Law.* Misconduct by a spouse given as grounds for divorce, especially when this demonstrates emotional or sexual incompatibility.

un·rea·son·ing (un-réez'n-ing, ún-, -réezning) *adj.* Not governed by reason; irrational. **—un·rea·son·ing·ly** *adv.*

un·re·con·struct·ed (ún-rée-kən-strúktid, -ree- ‖ -kon-) *adj.* **1.** Left unrepaired: *unreconstructed ruins.* **2.** Unreconciled to social and economic change: *an unreconstructed male chauvinist.*

un·reeve (ún-réev) *v.* **-reeved** or **-rove** (-rŏv), **-reeved** or **-roven** (-rŏv'n), **-reeving, -reeves.** *Nautical.* —*tr.* To withdraw (a rope, cable, or line) from a block, thimble, or other opening. —*intr.* **1.** To become unreeved. **2.** To unreeve a rope.

UNREF. United Nations Refugee Emergency Fund.

un·re·fined (ún-ri-fínd, -rə-) *adj.* **1.** Not processed. Said of natural products such as oil or sugar. **2.** Coarse or brutish.

un·re·gen·er·ate (ún-ri-jénnə-rət, -rə-, -rit) *adj.* **1.** Not reformed or repentant. **2.** Obstinately prejudiced. **—un·re·gen·er·a·cy** (-rə-si) *n.* **—un·re·gen·er·ate·ly** *adv.*

un·re·hearsed (ún-ri-hérst, -rə-) *adj.* Not rehearsed. See Synonyms at **extemporaneous.**

un·re·lent·ing (ún-ri-lénting, -rə-) *adj.* **1.** Inexorable; merciless: *unrelenting fate.* **2.** Not diminishing in intensity, speed, or effort. **—un·re·lent·ing·ly** *adv.* **—un·re·lent·ing·ness** *n.*

un·re·li·a·ble (ún-ri-lī-əb'l, -rə-) *adj.* Not reliable. **—un·re·li·a·bil·i·ty** (-ə-bílləti), **un·re·li·a·ble·ness** *n.* **—un·re·li·a·bly** *adv.*

un·re·lieved (ún-ri-léevd, -rə-) *adj.* Not varied in any way; uniform: *unrelieved boredom.* **—un·re·liev·ed·ly** (-léevid-li) *adv.*

un·re·li·gious (ún-ri-líjəss, -rə-) *adj.* **1.** Irreligious. **2.** Having no connection with religion. **—un·re·li·gious·ly** *adv.*

un·re·mit·ting (ún-ri-mítting, -rə-) *adj.* Never slackening; incessant; persistent. **—un·re·mit·ting·ly** *adv.* **—un·re·mit·ting·ness** *n.*

un·re·quit·ed (ún-ri-kwítid, -rə-) *adj.* Not reciprocated. Said of feelings: *He pined away from unrequited love.*

un·re·served (ún-ri-zérvd, -rə-) *adj.* **1.** Not reserved for a particular use or person: *an unreserved seat.* **2.** Given without reservation; unqualified: *unreserved praise.* **3.** Not reserved in manner; frank. **—un·re·serv·ed·ly** (-zérvid-li) *adv.* **—un·re·serv·ed·ness** *n.*

un·re·spon·sive (ún-ri-spón-siv, -rə-) *adj.* Not responsive. **—un·re·spon·sive·ly** *adv.* **—un·re·spon·sive·ness** *n.*

un·rest (ún-rést, un-) *n.* **1.** Uneasiness; disquiet. **2.** Agitation; rebellion: *social unrest.*

un·re·strained (ún-ri-stráynd, -rə-) *adj.* **1. a.** Unchecked. **b.** Not given to restraint. **2.** Not constrained; natural. **—un·re·strain·ed·ly** (-stráynid-li) *adv.*

un·rid·dle (ún-rídd'l) *tr.v.* **-dled, -dling, -dles.** To solve or explain (a riddle or mystery).

un·ri·fled (ún-rīf'ld) *adj.* Having a smooth bore. Said of a gun.

un·rig (un-ríg) *tr.v.* **-rigged, -rigging, -rigs.** *Nautical.* To strip (a vessel) of rigging.

un·right·eous (un-ríchəss, ún-, -rít-yəss) *adj.* **1.** Not righteous; wicked: *an unrighteous man.* **2.** Not right or fair; unjust: *unrighteous laws.* **—un·right·eous·ly** *adv.* **—un·right·eous·ness** *n.*

un·rip (ún-ríp) *tr.v.* **-ripped, -ripping, -rips.** To open, separate, or detach by ripping. [UN- (intensive) + RIP.]

un·ripe (ún-ríp) *adj.* **-riper, -ripest.** Also **un·rip·ened** (-rípənd) **1.** Not matured or ripe. **2.** Not fully developed; immature. **3.** Not ready or prepared. **—un·ripe·ness** *n.*

un·ri·valled (un-rív'ld, ún-) *adj.* Unequalled; supreme.

un·roll (ún-rŏl, un-) *v.* **-rolled, -rolling, -rolls.** —*tr.* **1.** To unwind and open out (something rolled up). **2.** To unfold; reveal. —*intr.* To become unrolled.

un·root (ún-rŏŏt ‖ -rŏŏt) *tr.v.* **-rooted, -rooting, -roots.** *Archaic.* To uproot.

un·round (ún-równd, un- ‖ *West Indies also* -rúngd) *tr.v.* **-rounded, -rounding, -rounds.** *Phonetics.* To pronounce (a vowel sound) with the lips in a flattened or neutral position.

UNRRA United Nations Relief and Rehabilitation Administration.

un·ruf·fled (ún-rúff'ld, un-) *adj.* Not ruffled or agitated; calm. See Synonyms at **cool.**

un·ru·ly (ún-rŏŏli ‖ -réwli) *adj.* **-lier, -liest.** Difficult or impossible to govern; not amenable to control or discipline: *unruly locks of hair; the unruly mob.* [Middle English *unruly* : UN- + *ruly,* easy to govern, from *rule*, RULE.] **—un·rul·i·ness** *n.*

Synonyms: unruly, ungovernable, intractable, refractory, recalcitrant, wilful, headstrong, wayward.

UNRWA United Nations Relief and Works Agency.

un·sad·dle (ún-sádd'l, un-) *v.* **-dled, -dling, -dles.** **—tr.** 1. To remove the saddle from. 2. To throw from the saddle; unhorse. **—intr.** To remove the saddle from a horse.

Uns The symbol for the element unnilseptium.

un·said (ún-séd, un-) *adj.* Not mentioned: *best left unsaid.*

un·sat·u·rate (un-sáchər-ət, ún-, -sáttewr-, -it, -ayt) *n.* An unsaturated chemical compound.

un·sat·u·rat·ed (ún-sáchər-aytid, un-, -sáttewr-) *adj.* 1. Of or designating a compound, especially of carbon, containing atoms that share more than one valency bond. 2. Capable of dissolving more of a solute at a given temperature. **—un·sat·u·ra·tion** (-áysh'n) *n.*

un·sa·vour·y (ún-sáyvəri, un-) *adj.* 1. Distasteful or disagreeable. 2. Morally offensive: *an unsavoury old lecher.* **—un·sa·vour·i·ly** *adv.* **—un·sa·vour·i·ness** *n.*

un·say (ún-sáy, -say) *tr.v.* **-said** (-séd, -sed), **-saying, -says** (-séz, -sez ‖ -sáyz, -sayz). To retract (something said).

un·scathed (ún-skáythd, un-) *adj.* Unharmed; uninjured.

un·schooled (ún-skóold) *adj.* 1. Not schooled; uninstructed. 2. Not the result of training; natural.

un·sci·en·tif·ic (ún-sī-ən-tíffik, -sī-) *adj.* 1. Not in accordance with the principles of science; especially, deemed lacking in objectivity. 2. Not familiar with science. **—un·sci·en·tif·i·cal·ly** *adv.*

un·scram·ble (ún-skrámb'l, un-) *tr.v.* **-bled, -bling, -bles.** 1. To disentangle; straighten out; resolve. 2. To restore (a scrambled message) to intelligible form. **—un·scram·bler** *n.*

un·screw (ún-skróo, un- ‖ -skréw) *v.* **-screwed, -screwing, -screws.** **—tr.** 1. To take out the screw or screws from. 2. To loosen, adjust, or detach by rotating. **—intr.** To become or admit of being unscrewed.

un·scru·pu·lous (un-skróo-pewləss, ún- ‖ -skréw-) *adj.* Without scruples; contemptuous of what is right or honourable. **—un·scru·pu·lous·ly** *adv.* **—un·scru·pu·lous·ness** *n.*

un·seam (ún-séem) *tr.v.* **-seamed, -seaming, -seams.** To undo the seam or seams of.

un·search·a·ble (ún-sérchəb'l, un-) *adj.* Beyond research; inscrutable; imponderable.

un·sea·son·a·ble (un-séez'n-əb'l, ún-, -séeznəb'l) *adj.* 1. Not suitable to or appropriate for the season. 2. Not characteristic of the time of year. 3. Poorly timed; inopportune. **—un·sea·son·a·ble·ness** *n.* **—un·sea·son·a·bly** *adv.*

un·sea·soned (ún-séez'nd) *adj.* 1. Not made savoury with seasoning. 2. Inadequately aged or seasoned; not ripe or mature: *unseasoned wood.* 3. Inexperienced. **—un·sea·soned·ness** *n.*

un·seat (ún-séet) *tr.v.* **-seated, -seating, -seats.** 1. To remove from a seat, especially from a saddle. 2. To dislodge from a position or office.

un·seem·ly (un-séemli) *adj.* **-lier, -liest.** Not in good taste; indecorous; unbecoming. See Synonyms at **improper.** **~adv.** In an unseemly manner. **—un·seem·li·ness** *n.*

un·seen (ún-séen) *adj.* 1. Not directly evident; invisible. 2. Not previously read or studied: *We were set an unseen translation.* **~n.** Chiefly British. An exercise involving translation of an unseen text, usually one that is to be translated into one's own language.

un·sel·fish (ún-sélfish, un-) *adj.* Not selfish; generous. **—un·sel·fish·ly** *adv.* **—un·sel·fish·ness** *n.*

un·set (ún-sét) *adj.* 1. Not yet firm, stiff, or solidified, as jelly or concrete. 2. Unmounted. Said especially of a precious stone. 3. *Printing.* Not yet typeset.

un·set·tle (ún-sétt'l, un-) *v.* **-tled, -tling, -tles.** **—tr.** 1. To displace from a settled condition; disrupt. 2. To agitate mentally; make uneasy; disturb. **—intr.** To become unsettled.

un·set·tled (ún-sétt'ld, un-) *adj.* 1. a. Disordered; disturbed: *unsettled times.* b. Worried; restless. 2. Variable; uncertain: *unsettled weather.* 3. Not determined or resolved: *an unsettled issue.* 4. Not paid or adjusted: *an unsettled bill.* 5. Not disposed of according to law: *an unsettled estate.* 6. Unpopulated. 7. Not fixed or established, as in a residence or routine. **—un·set·tled·ness** *n.*

un·sex (ún-séks, un-) *tr.v.* **-sexed, -sexing, -sexes.** To deprive of sexual capacity or sexual attributes.

un·shak·a·ble, un·shake·a·ble (ún-sháykəb'l, ún-) *adj.* Incapable of being shaken or weakened; rigid; entrenched: *unshakeable convictions.* **—un·shak·a·bly** *adv.*

un·shap·en (ún-sháypən, un-) *adj.* Also **un·shaped** (-sháypt) (for sense 1). 1. Not shaped or formed. 2. Misshapen.

un·sheathe (ún-shéeth, un-) *tr.v.* **-sheathed, -sheathing, -sheathes.** To draw from or as if from a sheath or scabbard.

un·ship (ún-shíp) *v.* **-shipped, -shipping, -ships.** **—tr.** 1. To unload from a ship; discharge. 2. To remove (a tiller or other piece of nautical gear) from its proper place. **—intr.** To be removable or detachable.

un·sight·ed (ún-síitid) *adj.* 1. Not sighted or examined. 2. Not equipped with or assisted by a sight for aiming. 3. Blind. 4. Not having a clear view. **—un·sight·ed·ly** *adv.*

un·sight·ly (un-sít-li) *adj.* **-lier, -liest.** Unpleasant or offensive to look at; unattractive. **—un·sight·li·ness** *n.*

un·sized (ún-sízd) *adj.* Not coated or treated with size.

un·skil·ful (un-skilf'l) *adj.* Without skill or proficiency; not adroit; clumsy. **—un·skil·ful·ly** *adv.* **—un·skil·ful·ness** *n.*

un·skilled (ún-skíld) *adj.* 1. Lacking skill or technical training.

2. Requiring no training or skill. 3. Showing no skill; crude.

un·slaked lime (ún-sláykt) *n.* Calcium oxide (see).

un·sling (ún-slíng) *tr.v.* **-slung** (-slúng), **-slinging, -slings.** 1. To remove from a sling or a slung position. 2. *Nautical.* To remove the slings of (a yard, for example).

un·snap (ún-snáp) *tr.v.* **-snapped, -snapping, -snaps.** To undo the snaps of; unfasten.

un·snarl (ún-snárl) *tr.v.* **-snarled, -snarling, -snarls.** To free of snarls; disentangle.

un·so·cia·ble (un-sósh-əb'l, un-) *adj.* 1. Not disposed to seek the company of others; not companionable; reserved. 2. Not conducive to social exchange: *an unsociable atmosphere.* **—un·so·cia·bil·i·ty** (-ə-bílləti), **un·so·cia·ble·ness** *n.* **—un·so·cia·bly** *adv.*

un·so·cial (ún-sósh'l) *adj.* Chiefly British. 1. Not compatible with or conducive to a full social life: *Because of the night shift duty she has to keep unsocial hours.* 2. Unsociable. **—un·so·cial·ly** *adv.*

un·so·lic·it·ed (ún-sə-líssitid ‖ -sō-) *adj.* Not solicited or asked for.

un·so·phis·ti·cat·ed (ún-sə-físti-kaytid ‖ -sō-) *adj.* Not sophisticated. See Synonyms at **naive.** **—un·so·phis·ti·cat·ed·ly** *adv.*

un·sound (ún-sównd ‖ *West Indies also* -súngd) *adj.* **-sounder, -soundest.** 1. Not in strong or healthy condition; not sound or stable. 2. Not soundly based in logic or fact; invalid. 3. Not based on sound commercial or economic principles; not viable. 4. Failing to conform to a given set of principles or dogmas: *an ideologically unsound policy.* **—un·sound·ly** *adv.* **—un·sound·ness** *n.*

un·spar·ing (un-spáir-ing) *adj.* 1. Not frugal. 2. Unmerciful; severe. **—un·spar·ing·ly** *adv.* **—un·spar·ing·ness** *n.*

un·speak·a·ble (un-spéekəb'l) *adj.* 1. Beyond description; inexpressible: *unspeakable happiness.* 2. Inexpressibly bad or objectionable. **—un·speak·a·ble·ness** *n.* **—un·speak·a·bly** *adv.*

un·sphere (un-sféer) *tr.v.* **-sphered, -sphering, -spheres.** *Archaic.* To remove (a star, for example) from its sphere.

un·spoilt (ún-spóylt) *adj.* Also **un·spoiled** (-spóylt, -spóyld). Not marred in beauty or character by modernisation, industrialisation, or the like: *an unspoilt fishing village.*

un·spo·ken (ún-spókən, un-) *adj.* 1. Not uttered or expressed: *She bristled with unspoken resentment.* 2. Understood without the need for words: *an unspoken pact between them.* **—un·spo·ken·ly** *adv.*

un·spot·ted (ún-spóttid) *adj.* 1. Unnoticed; unseen. 2. Not spotted or stained. 3. Morally unblemished. **—un·spot·ted·ness** *n.*

un·sta·ble (ún-stáyb'l, un-) *adj.* **-bler, -blest.** 1. a. Tending strongly to change. b. Not constant; fluctuating. 2. a. Of fickle temperament; irresponsible. b. Psychologically maladjusted. 3. Not firmly placed; unsteady. 4. *Chemistry.* a. Decomposing readily. b. Highly or violently reactive. 5. *Physics.* a. Decaying with relatively short lifetime. Said of subatomic particles. b. Radioactive. **—un·sta·ble·ness** *n.* **—un·sta·bly** *adv.*

un·stead·y (ún-stéddi, un-) *adj.* **-ier, -iest.** 1. Not securely in place; unstable. 2. Fluctuating; inconstant. 3. Wavering; uneven: *an unsteady voice.* 4. Unsure; precarious: *unsteady legs.* **~tr.v.** **unsteadied, -ying, -ies.** To cause to become unsteady. **—un·stead·i·ly** *adv.* **—un·stead·i·ness** *n.*

un·step (ún-stép) *tr.v.* **-stepped, -stepping, -steps.** *Nautical.* To remove (a mast) from a step.

un·stick (ún-stík) *tr.v.* **-stuck** (-stúk), **-sticking, -sticks.** To free from being stuck.

un·stop (ún-stóp) *tr.v.* **-stopped, -stopping, -stops.** 1. To remove a stopper or stop from. 2. To remove an obstruction from; open.

un·stopped (ún-stópt) *adj.* 1. Not stopped. 2. *Phonetics.* Capable of being prolonged. Said of vowels, nasals, and fricative or liquid consonants. Not in current technical usage. 3. Subject to enjambment. Said of line of poetry.

un·strat·i·fied (ún-strátti-fīd) *adj.* Lacking definite layers. Said of rocks.

un·streamed (ún-stréemd) *adj.* In British schools, not segregated or divided into streams according to ability.

un·stressed (ún-strést) *adj.* 1. Not stressed or having the weakest stress. Said of a segment of speech. 2. Not emphasised.

un·stri·at·ed (ún-strī-áytid ‖ *chiefly U.S.* -strī-aytid) *adj.* 1. Lacking striations; smooth-textured. 2. Composed of spindle-shaped cells that lack striations; unstriped. Said of involuntary muscle.

un·string (ún-stríng) *tr.v.* **-strung** (-strúng), **-stringing, -strings.** 1. To remove from a string. 2. To unfasten the strings of. 3. To weaken the nerves or resolve of; unnerve.

un·striped (ún-strípt) *adj.* 1. Not striped. 2. Unstriated. Said of involuntary muscle.

un·struc·tured (ún-strúkchərd, un-) *adj.* 1. Lacking a clear or formal structure or organisation. 2. *Psychology.* Having no intrinsic or objective meaning; meaningful by subjective interpretation only. Said of items, such as inkblots or incomplete sentences, on projective tests. Compare **structured.**

un·strung (ún-strúng) *adj.* 1. Having a string or strings loosened or removed. 2. Emotionally upset; unnerved.

un·stuck (ún-stúk) *adj.* 1. Freed from being stuck. 2. Mentally unhinged. **—come unstuck.** *Informal.* To fail to achieve an intended result; go wrong: *All her plans came unstuck.*

un·stud·ied (ún-stúddid, un-) *adj.* 1. Not contrived for effect; natural. 2. Not having been instructed; unversed. Used with *in.*

un·sub·stan·tial (ún-səb-stánsh'l, -staánsh'l ‖ -sub-) *adj.* 1. Lacking material substance; insubstantial. 2. Lacking firmness or strength; flimsy. 3. Lacking basis in fact; insubstantial. **—un·sub·stan·ti·al·i·ty** (-stánshi-ál-əti) *n.* **—un·sub·stan·tial·ly** *adv.*

un·suc·cess·ful (ún-sək-sésf'l ‖ -suk-) *adj.* Not succeeding; without success. —**un·suc·cess·ful·ly** adv. —**un·suc·cess·ful·ness** n.

un·suit·a·ble (ún-soot-əb'l, un-, -séwt-) adj. Not suitable; inappropriate. —**un·suit·a·bil·i·ty** (-ə-bílləti), **un·suit·a·ble·ness** n. —**un·suit·a·bly** adv.

un·sung (ún-súng) adj. 1. Not sung. 2. Not honoured or praised in song; uncelebrated: unsung heroes.

un·sure (ún-shoor, un-, -shor || -shéwr) adj. 1. Lacking confidence. 2. Uncertain of the facts. 3. Precarious; unstable; unreliable. —**un·sure·ly** adv. —**un·sure·ness** n.

un·sus·pect·ed (ún-sə-spéktid) adj. 1. Not under suspicion. 2. Not known to exist. —**un·sus·pect·ed·ly** adv.

un·sus·pect·ing (ún-sə-spékting) adj. Not suspicious; trusting. —**un·sus·pect·ing·ly** adv.

un·swathe (ún-swáyth || -swáwth, -swaáth) tr.v. -swathed, -swathing, -swathes. Archaic. To remove the swathings from; unbind.

un·swear (un-swaír) v. -swore (-swór || -swór), -sworn (-swórn || -sworn), -swearing, -swears. —tr. To retract (an oath). —intr. To recant or retract something sworn.

un·swerv·ing (un-swérving) adj. Unwavering; constant: unswerving loyalty. —**un·swerv·ing·ly** adv.

un·tan·gle (ún-táng-g'l, un-) tr.v. -gled, -gling, -gles. 1. To free from a tangle; disentangle. 2. To clarify; resolve.

un·taught (ún-táwt) adj. 1. Not instructed; ignorant. 2. Not acquired by instruction; natural; untutored. —See Synonyms at **ignorant**.

un·teach (ún-téech) tr.v. -taught (-táwt), -teaching, -teaches. 1. To cause to forget or unlearn something. 2. To negate (what has been taught) with contradictory information.

un·ten·a·ble (ún-tén-əb'l, un-, -téen-) adj. 1. Incapable of being maintained, defended, or vindicated: an untenable proposition. 2. Not suitable for occupation. —**un·ten·a·bil·i·ty** (-ə-bílləti) n.

un·think (ún-thíngk) tr.v. -thought (-tháwt), -thinking, -thinks. To dismiss from the mind; disregard.

un·think·a·ble (un-thíngkəb'l) adj. 1. Not thinkable; inconceivable. 2. Not to be thought of or considered; out of the question. 3. Contrary to what is reasonable or probable. —**un·think·a·ble·ness** n. —**un·think·a·bly** adv.

un·think·ing (ún-thíngking, un-) adj. 1. Not thinking or mindful; inattentive; heedless. 2. Not deliberate; inadvertent. —**un·think·ing·ly** adv. —**un·think·ing·ness** n.

un·thought-of (ún-tháwt-ov, ún- || -uv) adj. Inconceivable; not imagined or considered.

un·thread (ún-thréd) tr.v. -threaded, -threading, -threads. 1. To draw out the thread from (a needle, for example). 2. To unravel. 3. To find one's way out of (a labyrinth, for example).

un·ti·dy (un-tídi, ún-) adj. -dier, -diest. 1. Not neat and tidy; slovenly. 2. Lacking orderliness or organisation. —See Synonyms at **sloppy**.
~tr.v. **untided**, -dying, -dies. To make untidy. —**un·ti·di·ly** adv. —**un·ti·di·ness** n.

un·tie (ún-tí) v. -tied, -tying, -ties. —tr. 1. To undo or loosen (a knot or something knotted). 2. To free from something that binds or restrains. 3. To straighten out (difficulties or perplexities). —intr. To become untied.

un·til (ən-tíl, un-, ún-; weak form ən-til, -t'l) prep. 1. a. Up to the time of: We danced until dawn. b. As far as: Keep going straight until the third set of traffic lights. 2. Before a specific time. Used with a negative: not until Friday. 3. Chiefly Scottish. To; unto.
~conj. 1. Up to the time that. 2. Before. Used with a negative: You can't have your pudding until you eat your greens. 3. To the point or extent that. See Usage note at **till**. [Middle English until(l), to, towards, up to, till : un-, from Old Norse und, unto + til, TILL.]

un·time·ly (un-tímli, ún-) adj. -lier, -liest. 1. Occurring or done at an inappropriate time; inopportune. 2. Occurring too soon; premature: untimely death.
~adv. 1. Inopportunely. 2. Prematurely. —**un·time·li·ness** n.

un·tir·ing (un-tír-ing, ún-) adj. 1. Not tiring. 2. Not ceasing despite fatigue or difficulties; persistent. —**un·tir·ing·ly** adv.

un·ti·tled (un-tít'ld) adj. 1. Having no right or claim. 2. Having no title: an untitled novel; untitled nobility.

un·to (ún-too, -too; also, before consonant sounds only, úntə) prep. Poetic & Archaic. To: Unto us a child is born. [Middle English un-, to (see **until**) + TO.]

un·told (ún-tóld) adj. 1. Not told or revealed: untold secrets. 2. Beyond description or enumeration: untold suffering.

un·touch·a·ble (un-túch-əb'l, ún-) adj. 1. Not to be touched. 2. Out of reach; unobtainable. 3. Beyond the reach of criticism, impeachment, or attack. 4. Loathsome, unpleasant, or defiling to the touch.
~n. A harijan (see). —**un·touch·a·bil·i·ty** (-ə-bílləti) n.

un·touched (un-túcht, ún-) adj. 1. Not used or touched: untouched by human hand. 2. Not discussed or referred to. 3. Not moved emotionally. 4. Not harmed or damaged: killed her, but left the child untouched. 5. Not modified or changed: untouched photographs.

un·to·ward (ún·to-wáwrd, -too-, -to-ərd || -tórd, -tórd) adj. 1. Unfavourable; unpropitious. 2. Characterised by disaster or misfortune. 3. Inappropriate; offensive: untoward advances. 4. Archaic. Hard to control; refractory. —**un·to·ward·ly** adv. —**un·to·ward·ness** n.

un·tram·melled (un-trámm'ld, ún-) adj. Unrestrained; not confined to rigid boundaries.

un·trav·elled (un-trávv'ld, un-) adj. 1. Not traversed, as a road. 2. Not having travelled widely or far.

un·tread (ún-tréd) tr.v. -trod (-tród), -trodden (-tródd'n) or -trod, -treading, -treads. Archaic. To retrace (one's course).

un·tried (ún-tríd) adj. 1. Not attempted, tested, or proved. 2. Not tried in court.

un·true (ún-troo, un- || -tréw) adj. -truer, -truest. 1. Contrary to fact; false. 2. Deviating from a standard; not straight, even, or exact. 3. Disloyal; unfaithful. —**un·tru·ly** adv.

un·truss (ún-trúss) v. -trussed, -trussing, -trusses. —tr. 1. To unfasten; undo. 2. Archaic. To undress. —intr. Archaic. To remove one's clothes, especially one's breeches.

un·truth (ún-trooth, un- || -tréwth) n. 1. A lie. 2. The state or quality of being untrue; falsity.

un·truth·ful (ún-trooth-f'l, un- || -tréwth-) adj. 1. Given to falsehood; mendacious. 2. Contrary to truth. —See Synonyms at **dishonest**. —**un·truth·ful·ly** adv. —**un·truth·ful·ness** n.

un·tuck (ún-túk) tr.v. -tucked, -tucking, -tucks. To cause to hang out or not be tucked in: Your shirt has become untucked.

un·tu·tored (ún-tóotərd || -tóotərd) adj. 1. Having had no formal education or instruction: an untutored genius. 2. Unsophisticated; unrefined: an untutored palate. —See Synonyms at **ignorant**.

un·twine (ún-twín) v. -twined, -twining, -twines. —tr. 1. To loosen or separate (strands of twisted fibre, for example). 2. To disentangle. —intr. To become untwined.

un·twist (ún-twíst, un-) v. -twisted, -twisting, -twists. —tr. To loosen or separate (that which is twisted together) by turning in the opposite direction; unwind. —intr. To become untwisted.

un·used (ún-yoozd, un- for senses 1, 2; -yoost for sense 3) adj. 1. Not in use or put to use. 2. Never having been used. 3. Not accustomed. Used with to: unused to city traffic.

un·u·su·al (un-yoozh-oo-əl, ún-, -yoozh-wəl, -'l, -yoo-əl) adj. Not usual or common. —**un·u·su·al·ly** adv. —**un·u·su·al·ness** n.

un·ut·ter·a·ble (un-úttrəb'l, -úttərəb'l) adj. 1. Not capable of being uttered or expressed; too profound to be expressed in words. 2. Not capable of being pronounced. 3. Utter; complete: an unutterable idiot. —**un·ut·ter·a·ble·ness** n. —**un·ut·ter·a·bly** adv.

un·var·nished (ún-várnisht, un-) adj. 1. Not varnished. 2. Stated or otherwise presented without any effort to soften, disguise, or obfuscate: The unvarnished truth.

un·veil (ún-váyl, un-) v. -veiled, -veiling, -veils. —tr. 1. To remove a veil or other covering from. 2. To disclose; reveal. —intr. To take off one's veil; reveal oneself.

un·veil·ing (un-váyling, ún-) n. A ceremony at which a portrait, monument, or other work of art is disclosed for the first time to public view.

un·voice (ún-vóyss) tr.v. -voiced, -voicing, -voices. Phonetics. To utter without vibrating the vocal cords; devoice.

un·voiced (ún-vóyst) adj. 1. Not expressed or uttered. 2. Phonetics. Voiceless.

un·waged (ún-wáyjd) adj. Not receiving a salary or wage. Said especially of a student or unemployed person.

un·war·rant·a·ble (un-wórrənt-əb'l || -wáwrənt-) adj. Not justifiable; inexcusable. —**un·war·rant·a·bly** adv.

un·war·rant·ed (un-wórrənt-id || -wáwrənt-) adj. Having no justification; groundless.

un·war·y (un-waír-i, ún-) adj. -ier, -iest. Not alert to danger or deception; unguarded. —**un·war·i·ly** adv. —**un·war·i·ness** n.

un·washed (ún-wósht || -wáwsht) adj. Not washed; unclean.
~n. The lower classes or the masses. Used derogatorily in the phrase the great unwashed.

un·watched (ún-wócht || U.S. also -wáwcht) adj. Not manned. Said of an automatic device.

un·wa·ver·ing (un-wáyvəring) adv. Not wavering; constant: unwavering accuracy; unwavering honesty. —**un·wa·ver·ing·ly** adv.

un·wea·ried (un-weér-id, ún- || -eed) adj. 1. Not tired; fresh. 2. Never wearying; tireless. —**un·wea·ried·ly** adv.

un·well (un-wél, un-) adj. Not well; ailing; ill. —See Synonyms at **sick**.

un·wept (ún-wépt) adj. 1. Not mourned or wept for: the unwept dead. 2. Not shed. Said of tears.

un·whole·some (ún-hól-s'm, un-) adj. 1. Injurious to physical, mental, or moral health. 2. Suggestive of disease or degeneracy. 3. Offensive or loathsome. —**un·whole·some·ly** adv. —**un·whole·some·ness** n.

un·wield·y (un-weéldi) adj. -ier, -iest. 1. Difficult to carry or manage because of bulk or shape. 2. Cumbersomely large or unmanageable: an unwieldy bureaucracy. 3. Clumsy; ungainly. —See Synonyms at **heavy**. —**un·wield·i·ly** adv. —**un·wield·i·ness** n.

un·willed (ún-wíld) adj. Involuntary; spontaneous.

un·will·ing (un-wílling, ún-) adj. 1. Hesitant; loath. 2. Done, given, or said reluctantly: unwilling consent. —**un·will·ing·ly** adv. —**un·will·ing·ness** n.

un·wind (ún-wínd, un-) v. -wound (-wównd), -winding, -winds. —tr. 1. To reverse the winding or twisting direction of; unroll; uncoil. 2. To separate the tangled parts of; disentangle. —intr. 1. To become unwound. 2. Informal. To become less tense; relax. —**un·wind·a·ble** adj.

un·wink·ing (ún-wíngking, un-) adj. Vigilant; careful. —**un·wink·ing·ly** adv. —**un·wink·ing·ness** n.

un·wis·dom (ún-wízdəm) n. Lack of wisdom; foolishness.

un·wise (ún-wíz) adj. -wiser, -wisest. Lacking wisdom; foolish or imprudent. —**un·wise·ly** adv. —**un·wise·ness** n.

un·wish (ún-wísh) tr.v. -wished, -wishing, -wishes. 1. To cease to wish for. 2. To wish out of existence.

un·wished-for (un-wísht-fawr, ún-) adj. Not wished for or desired: unwished-for criticism.

un·wit·ting (un-wítting) *adj.* **1.** Not knowing; unaware: *an unwitting victim of fraud.* **2.** Not intended; unintentional. [Middle English *un-*, not + *witting*, present participle of *wit(t)en*, to know, Old English *witan.*] **—un·wit·ting·ly** *adv.* **—un·wit·ting·ness** *n.*

un·wont·ed (un-wṓnt-id || -wónt-, *chiefly U.S.* -wáwnt-, -wúnt-) *adj.* Not habitual or ordinary; unusual. **—un·wont·ed·ly** *adv.* **—un·wont·ed·ness** *n.*

un·world·ly (ún-wúrldli, un-) *adj.* **-lier, -liest. 1.** Not of this world; extraterrestrial. **2.** Concerned with matters of the spirit or soul. **3.** Not worldly-wise; naive. **—un·world·li·ness** *n.*

un·wor·thy (un-wúrthi, ún-) *adj.* **-thier, -thiest. 1.** Insufficient in worth; undeserving. Usually used with *of.* **2.** Not suiting or befitting. Usually used with *of.* **3.** Lacking value or merit; worthless. **4.** Vile; despicable. **—un·wor·thi·ly** *adv.* **—un·wor·thi·ness** *n.*

un·wrap (ún-ráp, un-) *v.* **-wrapped, -wrapping, -wraps.** *—tr.* To remove the wrappings from; open. *—intr.* To become or admit of being unwrapped.

un·writ·ten (ún-rítt'n, un-) *adj.* **1.** Not written or recorded. **2.** Forceful or effective through custom or tradition; not codified: *an unwritten rule.*

unwritten law *n.* A code, rule, or law of morality, conduct, procedure, or the like whose authority comes from custom, tradition, or general usage rather than formal legislation or regulation.

un·yield·ing (ún-yéelding, un-) *adj.* Inflexible; unwilling to move from a given position. — See Synonyms at **inflexible.**

un·yoke (ún-yṓk, un-) *v.* **-yoked, -yoking, -yokes.** *—tr.* **1.** To release (a draught animal) from a yoke. **2.** To separate or disjoin. **3.** To liberate. *—intr.* **1.** To remove a yoke. **2.** *Archaic.* To stop working.

un·zip (ún-zíp, un-) *v.* **-zipped, -zipping, -zips.** *—tr.* To open or unfasten (a zip or something held by a zip). *—intr.* To become unzipped.

up (up) *adv.* **1.** From a lower towards a higher position. **2.** In or at a higher position. **3. a.** From a reclining to an upright position: *setting up the deckchairs.* **b.** Out of bed: *It's time you got up.* **4. a.** Above a surface: *coming up for air.* **b.** From or off a surface: *pick it up.* **c.** Above the horizon: *The sun came up.* **5. a.** Into view or consideration: *brought up the problem of redundancy pay.* **b.** Into existence or operation: *set up a committee.* **6.** In or towards a position conventionally regarded as higher, as on a scale, chart, or map. **7.** Towards the speaker or the place or person referred to: *She went right up to the policeman.* **8. a.** In or towards a better position: *going up in the world.* **b.** *British.* In or towards a capital city or university, especially Oxford or Cambridge: *I'm going up to London; She's going up to Oxford to read maths.* **9.** Before a court, magistrate, or an official board: *Your case is coming up for consideration.* **10.** To or at a higher price. **11.** So as to advance, increase, or improve: *Sales have gone up again.* **12. a.** With or to a greater volume: *turn the music up.* **b.** To a higher pitch. **13.** Into a state of excitement or turbulence: *He's quite wound up.* **14. a.** So as to detach or unearth: *pull up weeds.* **b.** As an ejection from inside the body: *threw his meal up.* **15.** To a stop: *She drew up at the kerb.* **16.** Apart; into pieces: *tore it up.* **17.** *Nautical.* To windward. **18.** Completely; entirely: *Eat your meal up.* **19.** Used as an intensive to suggest thoroughness or conclusiveness of an action: *cleaning up; typing up a list.* **20. a.** All together: *add up; collect up.* **b.** From nothing: *cook up a plot; dreamed up from thin air.* **21.** *U.S.* Each; apiece: *The score was eight up.* **—up** or **up with.** Used interjectionally as a cry of support: *Up United!*

~adj. **1.** High or relatively high. **2. a.** Standing; erect. **b.** Out of bed. **3. a.** Moving or directed upwards: *an up escalator.* **b.** *British.* Towards a big city, especially London. Said of a train, railway line, platform, or the like. **4.** Actively functioning; healthy: *up and about.* **5.** Rising towards the flood level. **6. a.** Marked by agitation or acceleration: *The winds are up.* **b.** Prepared to fight: *up in arms.* **7.** *Informal.* Taking place; going on: *What's up?* **8.** Being considered; under study: *a contract up for renewal.* **9.** Charged; on trial. **10.** Finished; over: *His time was up.* **11.** Failed or lost hopelessly: *It's all up with me.* **12.** *Informal.* Well-informed: *not up on sports.* **13.** Being ahead of an opponent: *up two holes in a golf match.* **14. a.** In tennis and similar games, not having bounced twice. Said of the ball. **b.** In the saddle. Said of a jockey. **c.** At bat. Said of a baseball player. **15.** *Nautical.* Bound for a specified place. **16.** In the process of being repaired. Said of a road. **17.** *Physics.* Designating a quark with two-thirds the charge on the proton, and no strangeness, charm, or bottom. **—up against.** Confronted with; facing. **—up for. 1.** Free for: *up for sale; up for grabs.* **2.** Running as a candidate for: *up for re-election.* **—up to. 1.** Occupied with; especially, devising or scheming: *idlers up to no good.* **2.** Primed or prepared for: *Are you up to the challenge?* **3.** Dependent upon: *It's up to us.* **4.** As far as and including: *up to five of them.*

~prep. **1.** From a lower to or towards a higher point on. **2.** Towards or at a point farther along: *up the road.* **3.** In a direction towards the source of: *up river.* **4.** Against: *up the wind.* **—up yours.** *Slang.* Used interjectionally as an insult to express contempt or refusal.

~n. **1.** An upward slope; a rise or ascent (of a ball, for example). **2.** An upward movement or trend. **—on the up and up.** *Informal.* **1.** *British.* Rising rapidly in status, achievement, or mood. **2.** *U.S.* Open and honest.

~v. **upped, upping, ups.** *—tr.* **1.** To increase or improve. **2.** To raise. *—intr.* **1.** To get up; rise. **2.** *Informal.* To act suddenly or unexpectedly. Usually used with *and*: *upped and left.* [Middle English *up*, upward, and *uppe*, on high, Old English *ūp* and *uppe.*]

up– *prefix.* Indicates: **1.** Up; for example, **uplift. 2.** Upper or better; for example, **upmost. 3.** Upwards; for example, **upsweep. 4.** Upside-down; for example. **upend, upturn. 5.** Resulting; for example, **upshot.** ***Note:*** Many compounds other than those entered here may be formed with *up-*. In this dictionary in forming compounds, *up-* is normally joined with the following element without space or hyphen: **upend.** However, the separate word **up** appears in a few phrases that are hyphenated. Among those entered here are: **up-and-coming, up-and-down, up-bow, up-market,** and **up-to-the-minute.** —See Usage note at **down.** [Middle English *up-*, Old English *ūp-*, *upp-*, upwards, on high.]

up-and-com·ing (úp-ən-kúmming) *adj.* Likely to achieve success or improved status; promising or enterprising: *an up-and-coming young actress; an up-and-coming suburb.* **—up-and-com·er** *n.*

up and down *adv.* Backwards and forwards or in all directions: *pacing up and down.* **—up and down** *prep.*

up-and-down (úp-ən-dówn || *West Indies also* -dúng) *adj.* **1.** Characterised by alternating upward and downward movement; fluctuating. **2.** *Chiefly U.S.* Vertical; perpendicular.

up-and-o·ver (úp-ən-ṓvər, -ənd-) *adj.* Opened by being raised and slipped over into a horizontal position: *an up-and-over door.*

U·pan·i·shad (ōō-púnni-shəd, yōō-, -pánni-, -shad, -shaad) *n.* Any of a group of philosophical treatises contributing to the theology of Hinduism, elaborating upon the earlier Vedas. [Sanskrit *upaniṣad*, "a sitting down near to" : *úpa*, near to + *ni*, down + *ṣad-*, to sit.] **—U·pan·i·shad·ic** (-shúddik, -sháddik, -sháadik) *adj.*

u·pas (yōō-pəss || -pass) *n.* **1.** A tree, *Antiaris toxicaria*, of tropical Asia, once thought to be fatal to anyone who came near to or touched it, that yields a juice used as an arrow poison. Also called "upas-tree". **2.** The poison obtained from this tree or similar trees or plants. [Javanese, poison, dart poison.]

up·beat (úp-beet) *n.* **1.** *Music.* An unaccented beat, upon which the conductor's hand is raised; especially, the last beat of a bar. Compare **downbeat. 2.** An upward trend, as in one's fortune or career. Used chiefly in the phrase *on the upbeat.*

~adj. Informal. Optimistic; happy; cheerful.

up·bow (úp-bō) *n.* A stroke executed towards the heel of the bow on a violin or similar stringed instrument. Compare **down-bow.**

up·braid (up-bráyd, úp-) *tr.v.* **-braided, -braiding, -braids.** To reprove sharply; scold or chide vehemently; censure. See Synonyms at **scold.** [Middle English *upbreyden*, Old English *ūpbrēdan*, "to throw up against", reproach : *ūp-*, up + *bregdan*, to move quickly, throw, weave.] **—up·braid·er** *n.* **—up·braid·ing·ly** *adv.*

up·bring·ing (úp-bring-ing) *n.* The rearing and training received during childhood.

up·build (úp-bíld, up-) *tr.v.* **-built** (-bílt), **-building, -builds.** To build up; enlarge or enhance. **—up·build·er** *n.*

up·cast (úp-kaast || -kast) *adj.* Directed or thrown upwards.

~n. **1.** Something cast upwards. **2.** A ventilating shaft, as in a mine.

up·com·ing (úp-kumming) *adj. U.S.* Anticipated; forthcoming.

up·coun·try (úp-kúntri || *U.S.* -kuntri) *n.* The inland or interior region of a country.

~adj. (-kúntri). **1.** Located in, originating from, or characteristic of the upcountry. **2.** Countrified; unsophisticated.

~adv. (up-kúntri). In, to, or towards the upcountry.

up·date (úp-dáyt) *tr.v.* **-dated, -dating, -dates. 1.** To bring up to date: *update a textbook.* **2.** *Computing.* To amend (data or programs, for example) so as to produce a new version, with a new address number.

~n. (úp-dayt). Current or updated information. **2.** The act of updating something.

up·draught (úp-draaft || -draft) *n.* An upward current of air.

~adj. Designating a carburettor in which the mixture is drawn upwards against gravity.

up·end (up-énd) *v.* **-ended, -ending, -ends.** *—tr.* **1.** To stand, set, or turn on one end. **2.** To overturn or overthrow; upset. *—intr.* To be upended.

up-front, up front (úp-frúnt) *adj. Informal.* **1.** Frank; direct; forthright. **2.** Advance: *up-front payments.* **—up-front** *adv.*

up·grade (up-gráyd || *chiefly U.S.* úp-grayd) *tr.v.* **-graded, -grading, -grades. 1.** To raise to a higher grade, standard, or position. **2.** To improve the quality of (a manufactured product, for example).

~n. (úp-grayd). *U.S.* An incline leading uphill.

~adj. U.S. Uphill.

~adv. U.S. Uphill.

up·growth (úp-grōth) *n.* **1.** Upward growth or development. **2.** Something that has grown up.

up·heav·al (up-héev'l) *n.* **1.** A sudden and violent disruption or upset. **2.** *Geology.* A lifting up of the Earth's crust by the movement of stratified or other rocks. [UP- + HEAVE + -AL.]

up·hill (úp-híl) *adj.* **1.** Going up a hill or slope. **2.** Prolonged and laborious.

~n. (úp-hil). An upward slope or incline.

~adv. (-híl). **1.** To or towards higher ground; upwards. **2.** Against adversity; with difficulty.

up·hold (up-hṓld) *v.* **-held** (-héld), **-holding, -holds.** *—tr.* **1. a.** To maintain or affirm in the face of a challenge. **b.** To support or stand by (a person or cause, for example). **2.** To prevent from falling or sinking; support. **3.** To hold aloft; raise. *—intr. Northern British.* To declare; maintain. —See Synonyms at **support.** [Middle English *upholden* : UP- + HOLD.] **—up·hold·er** *n.*

up·hol·ster (up-hṓl-stər, əp- ‖ -hól-) *tr.v.* **-stered, -stering, -sters.** **1.** To provide (chairs, sofas, or similar soft furniture) with stuffing, springs, cushions, and covering fabric. **2.** To furnish (rooms) with curtains, carpets, and similar accessories. [Back-formation from UPHOLSTERER.]

up·hol·ster·er (up-hṓl-stərər, əp- ‖ -hól-) *n.* A person who upholsters furniture as an occupation. [Obsolete *upholster*, a dealer in or repairer of small wares, Middle English *upholdester*, one who upholds or repairs, from *upholden*, to UPHOLD.]

up·hol·ster·y (up-hṓl-stəri, əp-, -stri ‖ -hól-) *n., pl.* **-ies.** **1.** The fabrics and other materials used in upholstering. **2.** The act, craft, or business of upholstering.

UPI, U.P.I. United Press International.

up·keep (úp-keep) *n.* **1.** The act or process of maintaining something in good condition. **2.** The cost of such maintenance.

up·land (úp-lənd ‖ -land) *n. Often plural.* The higher parts of a region, country, or tract of land. —**up·land** *adj.*

upland cotton *n.* **1.** A cotton plant, *Gossypium hirsutum*, native to tropical America and widely cultivated for its fibre. **2.** The fibre of this plant.

up·lift (up-lift) *tr.v.* **-lifted, -lifting, -lifts.** **1.** To lift up or raise aloft. **2.** To raise to a high spiritual, intellectual, or social level; exalt. ~*adj.* (úp-lift). Uplifting: *an uplift bra.* ~*n.* (úp-lift). **1.** The act, process, or result of raising or lifting up. **2.** Any agent or influence causing upward movement or lifting. **3.** A movement to improve social, moral, or intellectual standards. **4.** *Geology.* An upheaval.

up·load (úp-lōd) *tr.v.* **-loaded, -loading, -loads.** *Computing.* To transfer (data or programs) from a small computer to a main computer. Compare **download**. [*upline* + *load*.]

up·mar·ket (úp-márkit) *adj. Chiefly British.* **1.** Of, designating, or intended for consumers belong to the higher socioeconomic groups. **2.** Superior in quality or style. Compare **down-market**.

upmost. Variant of **uppermost**.

up·on (ə-pón ‖ up-ón, ə-páwn, -pún) *prep.* On. [Middle English (formed after Old Norse *upp ā*) : UP + ON.]

Usage: Upon is basically interchangeable with *on*, although it is slightly more formal. It is always used however, in fixed phrases such as the following: *Once upon a time; upon my word; (winter) is almost upon us; (row) upon (row) of (seats).* See Usage note at **on**.

up·per (úppər) *adj. Abbr.* **up, u., U. 1.** Higher in place, power, position, or rank. **2. a.** Situated on higher ground. **b.** Lying farther inland. **c.** Northern. **3.** *Capital* **U.** *Geology & Archaeology.* Being a later division of the period named. **4.** *Mathematics.* Designating or pertaining to the highest value in a set. ~*n.* **1.** That part of a shoe or boot above the sole. **2.** *Informal.* An upper berth. **3.** *Plural. Informal.* The upper teeth or a set of upper dentures. **4.** *Slang.* A drug, often an amphetamine, used as a stimulant. Compare **downer**. —**on (one's) uppers.** *Informal.* Impoverished. [Referring to someone whose shoe soles have worn away].

upper atmosphere *n.* That part of the atmosphere above 30 kilometres high and inaccessible to direct observation by balloon.

upper bound *n.* A number that is not exceeded by any number in a given set.

upper case *n. Abbr.* **u.c. 1.** Capital letters. **2.** The case of printing type containing the capital letters and special characters.

up·per-case (úppər-káyss) *adj. Abbr.* **u.c.** *Printing.* Pertaining to or designating capital letters; capital. ~*tr.v.* **upper-cased, -casing, -cases.** To print in upper-case letters.

upper class *n. Often plural.* The usually small class in a society considered to rank highest, socially or economically; especially, the aristocracy. —**up·per-class** (úppər-kláass ‖ -kláss) *adj.*

upper crust *n. Informal.* The upper class.

up·per-cut (úppər-kut) *n. Boxing.* A short swinging blow directed upwards, as to the opponent's chin. —**up·per-cut** *v.*

upper hand *n.* A position of control or advantage. Preceded by *the.*

Upper House *n.* The branch of a bicameral legislature such as the House of Lords in the British Parliament. Also called "Upper Chamber". Compare **Lower House**.

up·per·most (úppər-mōst) *adj.* Also **up·most** (úp-mōst). Highest in position, place, rank, or influence; topmost; foremost. ~*adv.* In the highest or most prominent rank, position, or place; first: *whatever idea is uppermost in your mind.*

Upper Vol·ta (vól-tə ‖ vōl-). *French* **Haute-Volta**. See **Burkina**.

up·pish (úppish) *adj.* **1.** *British Informal.* Tending to be snobbish or arrogant. **2.** Designating a stroke in cricket which sends the ball too high, so that it is liable to be easily caught. [UP + -ISH.] —**up·pish·ly** *adv.* —**up·pish·ness** *n.*

up·pi·ty (úppəti, úppiti) *adj. Informal.* **1.** Petulant or recalcitrant. **2.** Snobbish; uppish. [From UP.]

Upp·sa·la or **Up·sa·la** (úp-saalə, ōōp-, up-sáalə, ōōp-; *Swedish* ōōp-saalə). City in eastern Sweden, lying on the river Fyrisân, just northwest of Stockholm. Its 13th century cathedral has traditionally been used for the coronation of Swedish monarchs.

up·raise (up-ráyz, úp-) *tr.v.* **-raised, -raising, -raises.** *Archaic & Poetic.* To raise or lift up; elevate.

up·rear (up-réer, úp-) *v.* **-reared, -rearing, -rears.** —*tr.* To raise or lift up. —*intr.* To be raised up; rise.

up·right (úp-rīt) *adj.* **1. a.** In a vertical position, direction, or stance. **b.** Erect in posture or carriage. **2.** Morally respectable; honourable; righteous. —See Synonyms at **vertical**. ~*adv.* In a vertical or erect position: *walk upright.* ~*n.* **1.** A perpendicular position; verticality. **2.** Something stand-

ing upright, such as a beam. **3.** An upright piano. [Middle English *upright*, Old English *ūpriht* : UP- + RIGHT.] —**up·right·ly** *adv.* —**up·right·ness** *n.*

upright piano *n.* A piano having the strings mounted vertically in a rectangular case with the keyboard at a right angle to the case. Also called "upright". Compare **grand piano**.

up·rise (úp-rīz, úp-) *intr.v.* **-rose** (-rṓz), **-risen** (-rízz'n), **-rising, -rises. 1.** To get up or stand up; rise. **2.** To go, move, or incline upwards; ascend. **3.** To rise into view, especially from below the horizon. ~*n.* (úp-rīz). **1.** The act or process of rising up. **2.** Something that rises or slopes up.

up·ris·ing (úp-rīzing, -rīzing) *n.* **1.** A revolt; an insurrection. **2.** *Archaic.* An upward slope. —See Synonyms at **rebellion**.

up·riv·er (úp-rívvər) *adv.* Towards or near the source of a river; in the direction opposite to that of the flow of water. ~*n.* A region lying upriver. —**up·riv·er** *adj.*

up·roar (úp-rawr ‖ -rōr) *n.* **1.** A condition of noisy excitement and confusion; a tumult. **2.** A heated controversy. —See Synonyms at **noise**. [Alteration (influenced by ROAR) of Dutch *oproer*, from Middle Dutch : *op*, up + *roer*, confusion.]

up·roar·i·ous (up-ráw-ri-əss, úp- ‖ -rṓ-) *adj.* **1.** Causing or accompanied by an uproar. **2.** Loud and full, as laughter; boisterous. **3.** Causing hearty laughter; hilarious. [UPROAR + -IOUS.] —**up·roar·i·ous·ly** *adv.* —**up·roar·i·ous·ness** *n.*

up·root (up-rṓōt ‖ -rṓot) *tr.v.* **-rooted, -rooting, -roots. 1.** To tear or remove (a plant and its roots) from the ground. **2.** To destroy or remove completely; eradicate. **3.** To force to leave an accustomed or native location. —**up·root·ed·ness** *n.* —**up·root·er** *n.*

up·rush (úp-rush) *n.* An upward rush, as of blood to the face or an emotion from the subconscious.

ups and downs *pl.n.* Alternating periods of good and bad fortune or high and low spirits.

up·set (up-sét) *v.* **-set, -setting, -sets.** —*tr.* **1.** To overturn or capsize; tip over. **2.** To disturb in usual or normal functioning, order, or course. **3.** To distress or perturb mentally or emotionally. **4.** To defeat unexpectedly. **5.** To cause illness or indigestion in (the stomach). **6.** To make shorter and thicker by hammering on the end; swage. —*intr.* **1.** To become overturned; tip over; capsize. **2.** To become disturbed. ~*n.* (úp-set). **1. a.** An act of upsetting. **b.** The condition of being upset. **2.** A disturbance, disorder, or agitation. **3.** A bodily disorder: *a stomach upset.* **4.** A game or contest in which the favourite is defeated. **5. a.** A tool used for upsetting; a swage. **b.** An upset part or piece. ~*adj.* (úp-sét). **1.** Overturned; capsized. **2.** Disordered; disturbed. **3.** Suffering from indigestion, nausea, or a similar condition: *an upset stomach.* **4.** Agitated; distraught. **5.** Overthrown; defeated. [Originally "to set up", "erect", later "to overset", Middle English *upsetten* : UP- + *setten*, to SET.] —**up·set·ter** *n.* —**up·set·ting·ly** *adv.*

upset price *n. U.S. & Scottish.* The reserve price at an auction.

up·shot (úp-shot) *n.* The final result; the outcome. See Synonyms at **effect**. [Originally the last shot at an archery contest, hence an outcome or decision.]

up·side-down (úp-sīd-dówn ‖ *West Indies also* -dúng) *adj.* **1.** Overturned completely so that the upper side is down. **2.** In great disorder or confusion; topsy-turvy. ~*adv.* Also **upside down. 1.** With the upper side down. **2.** Topsy-turvy. —**turn upside-down.** To ransack. [Alteration (influenced by obsolete *upside*) of earlier *upsedown*, Middle English *up so doun*, "up as if down" : UP + SO + DOWN.] —**up·side-down·ness** *n.*

upside-down cake *n.* A single-layer cake or sponge pudding baked with sliced fruit at the bottom, then served with the fruit side up.

up·sides (úp-sīdz) *adv. British.* Equal, as by retaliation or revenge. Used with *with*.

up·si·lon (yōōp-sī́-lən, ōō-, -lon, *also* yōōpsi-‖ upsi-) *n.* The 20th letter in the Greek alphabet, written Υ, υ. Transliterated in English as *U, u,* or *y,* and as *v* or *f* when it follows a vowel in Modern Greek. [Medieval Greek *u psilon*, "simple upsilon" (name adopted for graphic *u* as distinguished from graphic *oi*, both of which were pronounced identically as (ee) in Late Greek) : Greek *u,* upsilon + *psilon,* neuter of *psilos,* bare, simple, mere.]

up·spring (úp-spring) *intr.v.* **-sprang** (-spráng) or **-sprung** (-sprúng), **-sprung, -springing, -springs.** *Archaic & Poetic.* **1.** To spring up, as from the soil. **2.** To come into being; arise.

up·stage (úp-stáyj, up-) *adj.* **1.** At, pertaining to or involving the rear of a stage. **2.** *Informal.* Haughty; aloof. ~*adv.* Towards, to, on, or at the back part of the stage. ~*tr.v.* **upstaged, -staging, -stages. 1.** To distract the audience's attention from (another actor), as by standing behind him or forcing him to face upstage. **2.** *Informal.* To steal the show from; force out of the spotlight. **3.** *Informal.* To treat haughtily.

up·stairs (úp-stáirz) *adv.* **1.** In, on, or to an upper floor or storey; up the stairs. **2.** *Informal.* In or to a higher rank. **3.** *Informal.* Mentally: *not all there upstairs.* —**kick upstairs.** *Informal.* To dispose of by promoting to an ineffectual position. ~*adj.* Of or on an upper floor or floors: *an upstairs bathroom.* ~*n. Used with a singular or plural verb.* **1.** A floor or the floors above ground level or a given level. **2.** *British Informal.* Formerly, the masters of a house as opposed to their servants. Compare **downstairs**.

up·stand·ing (up-stánding, úp-) *adj.* **1.** Standing erect or upright. **2.** Morally upright; honest. —**be upstanding.** To stand up. Used in the imperative in courts of law when the judge enters or leaves **—up·stand·ing·ness** n.

up·start (úp-staart) n. **1.** One that springs up suddenly; specifically, a person of humble origin who attains sudden wealth or consequence; a parvenu. **2.** A person having an exaggerated sense of his own importance or ability: *cocky little upstart.*

~*adj.* **1.** Suddenly raised to a position of consequence. **2.** Characteristic of an upstart; self-important; presumptuous.

~*intr.v.* (-stárt) **upstarted, -starting, -starts.** *Archaic.* To spring or start up suddenly.

up·state (úp-stayt) *adj.* *U.S.* Pertaining to or designating that part of a state lying inland or farther north of a large city.

~*n.* The upstate region. **—up·state** (-stáyt) *adv.* **—up·stat·er** n.

up·stream (úp-stréem, -streem) *adv.* In, at, or towards the source of a stream or current.

~*adj.* *Finance.* Closer to the point of production or manufacture than to the point of sale.

up·stroke (úp-strōk) n. **1.** An upward stroke, as of a brush. **2.** The upward movement of a piston in a reciprocating engine or pump in which the cylinder is cleared of fluid.

up·surge (úp-surj) n. A rapid upward swell or rise.

up·sweep (úp-sweep) n. **1.** A curve or sweep upwards. **2.** *U.S.* A hairstyle that is smoothed upwards at the back and piled on top of the head.

~*tr.v.* (-sweep, -sweep) **upswept** (-swépt, -swept), **-sweeping, -sweeps.** To brush, curve, or sweep upwards.

up·swing (úp-swing) n. An upward swing or trend; an increase, as in movement or activity: *an upswing on the stock market.*

up·sy-dai·sy (úpsi-dáyzi, úpsə-) *interj.* Used when swinging a child into the air or expressing concern over its fall. [From earlier *up-a-daisy;* irregularly from UP; compare LACKADAISICAL.]

up·take (úp-tayk) n. **1.** Understanding; comprehension: *very quick on the uptake.* **2.** A passage for drawing up smoke or air; a flue or ventilating shaft. **3.** An act of taking in or absorbing, especially into a living organism.

up·throw (úp-thrō) n. **1.** A throwing upwards. **2.** *Geology.* An upward displacement of rock on one side of a fault.

up·thrust (úp-thrust) n. **1.** A thrusting or pushing upwards. **2.** *Geology.* An upheaval of the earth's surface.

up·tight (úp-tít) *adj.* *Slang.* **1.** Tense; nervous; repressed. **2.** Angry. **—up·tight·ness** n.

up-to-date, up to date (úp-tə-dáyt) *adj.* Informed of or reflecting the latest improvements, facts, or style; modern. **—up-to-date·ly** *adv.* **—up-to-date·ness** n.

up-to-the-min·ute, up to the minute (úp-tə-thə-mínnit) *adj.* Being or having the most recent information, style, or fashion. **—up-to-the-min·ute·ness** n.

up·town (úp-tówn) *adv.* *Chiefly U.S.* In or towards the upper part of a town or city, or away from its business centre. Compare **downtown.** **—up·town** *adj.*

~*n.* (-town). *Chiefly U.S.* The upper part of a town or city; the part away from its business centre. Compare **downtown.** **—up·town** *adj.*

up·turn (up-túrn, úp-turn) v. **-turned, -turning, -turns.** —*tr.* **1.** To turn (soil, for example) up or over. **2.** To upset; overturn. **3.** To direct upwards. —*intr.* To turn over or up.

~*n.* (úp-turn). An upward movement, curve, or trend.

UPU Universal Postal Union.

up·ward (úp-wərd) *adj.* Directed or moving towards a higher place or position.

~*adv.* *Chiefly U.S.* Variant of **upwards. —up·ward·ly** *adv.* **—up·ward·ness** n.

up·wards (úp-wərdz) *adv.* Also *chiefly U.S.* **upward. 1.** In, to, or towards a higher place, level, or position. **2.** To or towards the source, origin, or interior. **3.** Towards the head or upper parts. **4.** Towards a higher amount, degree, or rank: *Prices soared upwards.* **5.** Towards a later time or greater age. **6.** Towards something greater or better. **—upwards of.** More than; in excess of. [Middle English *upward,* Old English *ūpweard* : UP- + -WARD.]

up·wind (úp-wínd) *adv.* In or towards the direction from which the wind blows.

~*adj.* **1.** Going against the wind. **2.** On the windward side.

Ur (ur, oor). Ancient city of Sumer, southern Mesopotamia, whose site was discovered in the 19th century. The great ziggurat of Ur, which still stands in crumbling condition, was built by King Ur-Nammu, who established the third dynasty of Ur in *c.* 2060 B.C.

ur-¹. Variant of **uro-¹, uro-².**

ur-² n. *prefix. Sometimes capital* **U.** Indicates: **1.** Primitive, basic; for example, *ur-legend.* **2.** The original version of; for example, *urtext.* [German.]

u·ra·cil (yóor-ə-sil, yór-) n. A pyrimidine, $C_4H_4N_2O_2$, a constituent of RNA. [UR(O)- + AC(ETIC) + -IL(E).]

u·rae·mi·a, *U.S.* **u·re·mi·a** (yoor-réemi-ə, yoo-) n. The presence of excess urea and other waste products in the blood, which occurs in kidney disease and is characterised by headache, nausea, vomiting, and lethargy. Also called "azotaemia". [New Latin : UR(O)- + -AEMIA.] **—u·rae·mic** *adj.*

u·rae·us (yoor-rée-əss, yoo-) n., *pl.* **uraei** (-ī) or **uraeuses.** The figure of the sacred serpent, depicted on the headdress of ancient Egyptian rulers and deities as an emblem of sovereignty. [New Latin, from Late Greek *ouraios,* from Egyptian for "cobra".]

U·ral (yóor-əl, oor-). River in Russia and Kazakhstan, rising in the south Ural mountains and flowing south and west for about 2 540 kilometres (1,580 miles) until it empties into the Caspian Sea at Gurjev.

U·ral-Al·ta·ic (yoor-əl-al-táy-ik, yór-) n. A hypothetical group of languages including the Uralic and Altaic families, characterised by agglutination and vowel harmony. Also called "Turanian". **—U·ral-Al·ta·ic** *adj.*

U·ral·ic (yoor-rál-ik, yoo-) n. Also **U·ra·li·an** (-rávli-ən). A family of languages including the Finno-Ugric and Samoyed subfamilies.

~*adj.* Of or designating this language family.

u·ral·ite (yóor-əl-īt, yór-) n. An amphibole mineral that replaces pyroxene in some igneous and metamorphic rocks. [German *Uralit,* after the URAL MOUNTAINS + -ITE.]

Ural Mountains. Also **Urals.** Mountain range in Russia and Kazakhstan, extending for about 2 400 kilometres (1,500 miles) southwards from the Arctic coast. It is generally considered to form, with the river Ural, part of the boundary between Europe and Asia.

u·ra·ni·a (yoor-rávni-ə, yóo-) n. **Uranium dioxide** (see). [New Latin : URANIUM + -a (oxide).]

U·ra·ni·a (yoor-rávni-ə, -yóo- ‖ yew-). *Greek Mythology.* The Muse of astronomy. [Latin, from Greek *Ourania,* "the heavenly one", from *ouranos,* heaven. See **Uranus.**]

U·ra·ni·an (yoor-rávni-ən, yóo-) *adj.* **1.** Of or pertaining to the planet Uranus. **2.** Celestial. **3.** Of or pertaining to astronomy or to the Muse Urania. **4.** Of or pertaining to homosexuality.

~*n.* **1.** A fictional inhabitant of the planet Uranus. **2.** *Rare.* A homosexual.

u·ran·ic (yóor-ránnik, yóo-) *adj.* **1.** *Archaic.* Of or relating to the heavens; celestial. **2.** *Chemistry.* Of, pertaining to, or derived from uranium, especially with a valency higher than in comparable uranous compounds. [Sense 1, from Latin *ūranus,* heaven, from Greek *ouranos.* See **Uranus.** Sense 2, from uranium.]

u·ran·ide (yóor-ən-īd, yór-) n. Any element having an atomic number in excess of 91. [URAN(IUM) + -IDE.]

u·ra·ni·nite (yoor-rávni-nīt, yóo-, -ránni-) n. A complex brownish-black mineral, chiefly UO_2 partially oxidised to U_3O_8 and containing variable amounts of radium, lead, thorium, rare-earth metals, helium, argon, and nitrogen. Also called "pitchblende". [German *Uranin,* uraninite : URAN(IUM) + -IN.]

u·ran·ism (yóor-ən-iz'm, yór-) n. *Rare.* Homosexuality, especially of males. [19th century : from German *Uranismus,* from Greek *ouranios,* heavenly (taken as meaning "spiritual"), from *ouranos†,* sky, heaven.]

u·ran·ite (yóor-ən-īt, yór-) n. Either of two uranium-bearing minerals, **torbernite** (copper uranite) or **autunite** (lime uranite). [URAN(IUM) + -ITE.]

u·ra·ni·um (yoor-rávni-əm, yóo-) n. *Symbol* **U** A heavy silvery-white metallic element, radioactive, easily oxidised, and having 14 known isotopes of which uranium-238 is the most abundant in nature. The element occurs in several minerals, including uraninite and carnotite, from which it is extracted and processed for use in research, nuclear fuels, and nuclear weapons. Atomic number 92, atomic weight 238.03, melting point 1,132°C, boiling point 3,818°C, relative density 18.95, valencies 3, 4, 5, 6. [New Latin, after the planet URANUS (to contrast with the recently named TELLURIUM).]

uranium-235 n. The uranium isotope with mass number 235 and half-life 7.13 × 10^8 years, fissionable with slow neutrons and capable in a critical mass of sustaining a chain reaction that can proceed explosively with appropriate mechanical arrangements.

uranium-238 n. The most common isotope of uranium, having mass number 238 and half-life 4.51 × 10^9 years, nonfissionable but producing when irradiated with neutrons fissionable plutonium-239.

uranium dioxide n. A black toxic crystalline powder, UO_2, formerly used in ceramic glazes, now used to pack nuclear fuel rods. Also called "urania".

uranium series n. A radioactive series of elements that starts with uranium-238 and ends with the stable element lead-206.

uranium trioxide n. A radioactive orange powder, UO_3, used in uranium refining and as a colouring agent in ceramics.

urano-, uran-. *comb. form.* Indicates: **1.** The heavens; for example, **uranography. 2.** Uranium; for example, **uranyl.** [Greek *ouranos†,* sky, heaven.]

u·ra·nog·ra·phy (yóor-ə-nóggrə-fi, yór-) n. The branch of astronomy concerned with mapping the stars, galaxies, or other heavenly bodies. [URANO- + -GRAPHY.] **—u·ra·nog·ra·pher** (-fər), **u·ra·nog·ra·phist** n. **—u·ra·no·graph·ic, u·ra·no·graph·i·cal** *adj.*

u·ra·nous (yóor-ənəss, yór-, *also* yoor-rávnəss, yóo-) *adj.* *Chemistry.* Of or pertaining to uranium, especially with a valency lower than in comparable uranic compounds.

U·ra·nus¹ (yóor-ənəss, yór-; yoor-rávnəss, yóo-). *Greek Mythology.* The earliest supreme god, a personification of the sky, who was the son and consort of Gaea and the father of the Cyclopes and Titans. [Latin *Ūranus,* from Greek *Ouranos,* personification of *ouranos†,* heaven.]

Uranus² n. The seventh planet from the Sun, revolving about it every 84.02 years at a distance of approximately 2 870 million kilometres (1,790,000,000 miles). It has an equatorial diameter of 51 800 kilometres (32,200 miles), a mass 14.6 times that of Earth, and 15 satellites. [After the god URANUS.]

u·ra·nyl (yóor-ə-nil, yór-) n. The divalent radical UO_2. [URAN(IUM) + -YL.]

urase. Variant of **urease.**

u·rate (yóor-ayt, yór-) n. A salt or ester of uric acid. [UR(IC ACID) + -ATE.] **—u·rat·ic** (yoor-ráttik, yóo-) *adj.*

ur·ban (úrbən) *adj.* **1.** Pertaining to, located in, or constituting a town or city. **2.** Characteristic of the geography, life, or functions of a town or city. Compare **rural**. [Latin *urbānus,* from *urbs†,* city.]

urban district *n.* **1.** A former administrative district of England, Wales, and Northern Ireland, resembling a borough but lacking a borough charter. **2.** Any of 49 medium-sized towns in the Republic of Ireland possessing elected councils.

ur·bane (ur-báyn, úr-) *adj.* Having or showing the refined manners of polite society; elegant. See Synonyms at **suave**. [French *urbain, urbaine,* from Latin *urbānus,* characteristic of city life, URBAN.] **—ur·bane·ly** *adv.* **—ur·bane·ness** *n.*

ur·ban·ise, ur·ban·ize (úrbən-īz) *tr.v.* **-ised, -ising, -ises. 1.** To make urban in nature or character. **2.** To cause or increase the migration of (country people) into cities. **—ur·ban·i·sa·tion** (-ī-záysh'n ‖ *U.S.* -i-) *n.*

ur·ban·ism (úrbən-iz'm) *n.* **1.** The culture or lifestyle of city dwellers. **2.** *Chiefly U.S.* The study of this. **3.** *Chiefly U.S.* Urbanisation.

ur·ban·ite (úrbən-īt) *n.* A city dweller.

ur·ban·i·ty (ur-bánnəti, úr-) *n., pl.* **-ties. 1.** Refinement and elegance of manner; polished courtesy. **2.** *Plural.* Courtesies; civilities.

urban renewal *n.* The government-sponsored destruction of slum areas with a view to the construction of new housing.

urban sprawl *n.* The spread of urban areas into the countryside.

ur·bi et or·bi (úr-bee et ór-bee, óor-, -bi) *Latin.* To the city (of Rome) and to the world. Said of a solemn blessing by the pope.

U.R.C. United Reformed Church.

ur·ce·o·late (úr-si-ə-lət, ur-sée-, -lit, -layt) *adj.* Urn-shaped: *an urceolate corolla.* [New Latin *urceolatus,* from Latin *urceolus,* diminutive of *urceus,* jug, akin to *urna,* URN.]

ur·chin (úrchin) *n.* **1.** A poor, dirty, ragged child; a ragamuffin. **2.** A small, mischievous child; a scamp. **3. A sea urchin** (*see*). **4.** *Archaic & Regional.* A hedgehog. [Middle English variant of *(h)irchon,* hedgehog, from Old North French *herichon,* from Latin *(h)ērīcius,* from *(h)ēr,* hedgehog.]

ur·dé, ur·dee (úr-di, -day, -dee) *adj. Heraldry.* Having points; pointed. [16th century : probably a misreading of French *videe* in the phrase *crois aiquisseé et videé,* cross sharply pointed and reduced.]

Ur·du (óor-dŏo, úr-, -dŏo) *n.* A Hindustani language spoken in Pakistan, where it is the principal language, in Afghanistan, and by Muslims in India. [Hindi *urdū,* short for *zabān-i-urdū,* "language of the camp" : Persian *zabān,* language + *urdū,* army, camp, from Turkish *ordū,* HORDE.]

–ure *n. suffix.* Indicates: **1.** An act or process; for example, **era·sure. 2.** A resulting condition; for example, **composure. 3.** A function or office or a body performing a function; for example, **legislature.** [Middle English, from Old French, from Latin *-ūra.*]

u·re·a (yŏor-i-ə, yór-; yoor-rée-ə, yŏo-, -réer) *n.* A white crystalline or powdery compound, CO(NH₂)₂, found as an excretion product of protein metabolism in mammalian urine and other body fluids. A synthesised form is used as fertiliser, in animal feed, and in resins. [New Latin, from Latin *urée,* formed from *urine,* URINE.] **—u·re·al, u·re·ic** (yoor-rée-ik, yŏo-) *adj.*

u·re·a-for·mal·de·hyde resin (-fawr-mál-di-hīd) *n.* Any of various thermosetting resins made by combining urea and formaldehyde and widely used to make moulded household and mechanical objects and in cavity wall insulation.

u·re·ase (yŏor-i-ayz, yór-, -ayss) *n.* Also **u·rase** (yŏor-ayz, yór-, -ayss). An enzyme occurring in urine, various plants, and as a secretion of certain microorganisms that catalyses the hydrolysis of urea to ammonia and carbon dioxide and is used to determine the urea content of blood and urine. [URE(A) + -ASE.]

u·re·di·um (yoor-rée-di-əm, yŏo-) *n., pl.* **-dia** (-di-ə). Also **u·re·din·i·um** (yoor-i-dínni-əm, yór-) *pl.* **-ia** (-ə). A reddish, pustule-like structure formed on the tissue of a plant infected by a rust fungus and having hyphae that produce uredospores. Also called "uredosorus". [New Latin, from Latin *ūrēdo* (stem *ūrēdin-*), blight, burning itch, UREDO.] **—u·re·di·al** *adj.*

u·re·do (yoor-réedŏo, yŏo-) *n., pl.* **uredines** (-réedi-neez) *Pathology.* **Urticaria** (*see*). [Latin *ūrēdo,* blight, burning itch, from *ūrere,* to burn.]

u·re·do·spore (yoor-réed-ō-spawr, yŏo-, ə- ‖ -spŏr) *n.* A reddish spore that is produced in the uredium of a rust fungus and that spreads to and infects other plants.

u·re·ide (yŏor-i-īd, yór-) *n. Chemistry.* Any of various derivatives of urea. [URE(A) + -IDE.]

uremia. *U.S.* Variant of **uraemia.**

u·re·o·te·lic (yŏor-i-ō-téelik, yór-; yoor-rée-, yŏo-; -téllik) *adj.* Excreting most excess nitrogen in the form of urea. Said of such animals as amphibians and mammals. [UREA + Greek *telos,* end + -IC (referring to urea as the end-product).]

u·re·ter (yoor-réetər, yŏo-) *n.* The long, narrow duct that conveys urine from the kidney to the urinary bladder. [New Latin, from Greek *ourētēr,* from *ourein,* to urinate, from *ouron,* urine.] **—u·re·ter·al, u·re·ter·ic** (yŏor-i-térrik, yór-) *adj.*

u·re·thane (yŏor-i-thayn, yór-) *n.* **1.** A colourless crystalline or white granular compound, C₃H₇NO₂, used as a treatment for leukaemia and as a solvent. Also called "ethyl carbamate". **2.** Any of several esters, other than the ethyl ester, of carbamic acid. **3. Polyurethane** (*see*). [French *uréthane* : UR(O)- (urine) + ETH(YL) + -AN(E).]

u·re·thra (yŏor-rée-thrə, yŏo-) *n., pl.* **-thras** or **-thrae** (-three). The canal through which urine is discharged in most mammals and which serves as the male genital duct. [Late Latin *ūrēthra,* from

Greek *ourēthra,* from *ourein,* to urinate, from *ouron,* urine.] **—u·re·thral** *adj.*

u·re·thri·tis (yŏor-i-thrí-tiss, yór-) *n.* Inflammation of the urethra. [New Latin : URETHR(A) + -ITIS.] **—u·re·thrit·ic** (-thríttik) *adj.*

u·re·thro·scope (yoor-réethrə-skōp, yŏo-) *n.* An instrument for examining the interior of the urethra. [URETHR(A) + -SCOPE.] **—u·re·thros·co·py** (yŏor-i-thróskəpi, yór-) *n.*

u·ret·ic (yoor-réttik, yŏo-) *adj.* Of or relating to urine; urinary. [Late Latin *ūrēticus,* from Greek *ourētikos,* from *ourein,* to urinate, from *ouron,* urine.]

U·rey (yŏor-i), **Harold Clayton** (1893–1981). U.S. physicist. He is known chiefly for his discovery (1931) of deuterium, and his work on the separation of isotopes and the structure of atoms and molecules. He won (1934) the Nobel prize for chemistry.

urge (urj) *v.* **urged, urging, urges.** **—tr. 1.** To drive forwards or onwards forcefully; impel; spur. **2.** To entreat earnestly and repeatedly; plead with; exhort: *The board was urged to approve the budget.* **3.** To advocate persistently; recommended emphatically: *urge passage of the bill.* **4.** To persuade, force, or otherwise move to some course of action. **5.** *Archaic & Literary.* To stimulate; excite. **—intr. 1.** To present a forceful argument, claim, or case. **2.** To exert an impelling force; push vigorously.

—n. 1. The act of urging. **2.** An irresistible or impelling force, influence, or instinct. [Latin *urgēre,* to push, press.] **—urg·ing·ly** *adv.*

> **Synonyms:** urge, press, exhort, encourage, coax.

ur·gen·cy (úrjən-si) *n., pl.* **-cies. 1.** The quality or condition of being urgent; imperativeness; pressing importance: *the urgency of their appeal.* **2.** A pressing necessity.

ur·gent (úrjənt) *adj.* **1.** Compelling immediate action; imperative; pressing: *She's away on urgent business.* **2.** Insistent or importunate; earnest: *urgent pleas.* **3.** Conveying or relating a sense of urgency: *an urgent tone.* [Middle English, from Old French, from Latin *urgēns* (stem *urgent-*), present participle of *urgēre,* to push, press, URGE.] **—ur·gent·ly** *adv.*

> **Synonyms:** urgent, pressing, imperative.

–urgy *n. comb. form.* Indicates a technique or technology; for example, **metallurgy, theurgy.** [New Latin *-urgia,* from Greek *-ourgos,* "worker", from *ergon,* work.]

–uria *n. comb. form. Pathology.* Indicates: **1.** A diseased condition of the urine; for example, **pyuria. 2.** A substance in the urine; for example, **albuminuria.** [New Latin, from Greek *-ouria,* from *ouron,* urine.]

u·ric (yŏor-ik, yór-) *adj.* Pertaining to, contained in, or obtained from urine. [UR(O)- + -IC.]

uric acid *n.* A white crystalline compound, C₅H₄N₄O₃, the end product of purine metabolism in man and other primates, birds, terrestrial reptiles, and most insects.

u·ri·co·su·ric (yŏor-i-kō-séwr-ik, yór-, -kə-, -sóor- ‖ -shóor-) *adj.* Promoting the excretion of uric acid in the urine. Said of certain drugs used to treat gout. [*Urico-,* combining form of URIC ACID + -s- (connective) + URIC.]

u·ri·co·te·lic (yŏor-i-kō-téelik, yór-, -kə-, -téllik) *adj.* Exreting most excess nitrogen in the form of uric acid. Said of birds. [*Urico-,* combining form of URIC ACID + Greek *telos,* end + -IC (referring to uric acid as the end-product).]

u·ri·dine (yŏor-i-deen, yór-) *n.* A white, odourless powder, C₉H₁₂N₂O₆, that is the nucleoside of uracil, important in carbohydrate metabolism and used in biochemical experiments. [UR(O)- + -ID(E) + -INE.]

U·ri·el (yŏor-i-əl, yór-). One of the four archangels in Hebrew tradition. [Hebrew *ūrī'ēl,* probably "God is my light".]

U·rim and Thum·mim (yŏor-im, yór-, óor-; thúmmim) *pl.n.* Objects carried by the chief priests of ancient Israel and probably used to divine the will of God. Exodus 28:30; Leviticus 8:8.

urin– Variant of **urino-.**

u·ri·nal (yoor-rín'l, yŏor-i-nl', yór-) *n.* **1. a.** An upright wall fixture used by men for urinating. **b.** A room or other place containing such a fixture or fixtures. **2.** A receptacle for urine, such as one used by a bedridden patient. Also called "urinary". [Middle English, chamber pot, from Old French *urinal,* from Late Latin *ūrīnal,* from *ūrīna,* URINE.]

u·ri·nal·y·sis (yŏor-i-nál-ə-siss, yór-) *n., pl.* **-ses** (-seez). The chemical analysis of urine. [New Latin : URIN(O)- + (AN)ALYSIS.]

u·ri·nant (yŏor-i-nənt, yór-) *adj. Heraldry.* With the head downwards. [Latin *ūrīnāns* (stem *ūrīnant-*), diving, present participle of *ūrīnāri,* to dive.]

u·ri·nar·y (yŏor-i-nəri, yór- ‖ -nerri) *adj.* Of or relating to urine, its production, function, or excretion.

—n., pl. urinaries. A urinal.

urinary bladder *n.* A muscular membrane-lined sac situated in the anterior part of the pelvic cavity and used as a urine reservoir prior to excretion.

urinary calculus *n.* A solid concretion of mineral and organic substances in the urinary system. Also called "urolith".

u·ri·nate (yŏor-i-nayt, yór-) *intr.v.* **-nated, -nating, -nates.** To excrete urine. [Medieval Latin *ūrīnāre,* from Latin *ūrīna,* URINE.] **—u·ri·na·tion** (-náysh'n) *n.* **—u·ri·na·tive** (-nətiv, -naytiv) *adj.*

u·rine (yŏor-in, yór- ‖ -īn) *n.* The fluid and dissolved substances, including urea, secreted by the kidneys, stored in the bladder, and excreted from the body through the urethra. [Middle English, from Old French, from Latin *ūrīna.*]

u·ri·nif·er·ous (yŏor-i-níffərəss, yór-) *adj.* Conveying urine.

urino–, urin– *comb. form.* Indicates urine; for example, **urinalysis, urinogenital.** [Latin *ūrīna,* URINE.]

urinogenital. Variant of **urogenital.**

u·ri·nous (yŏor-i-nəss, yór-) *adj.* Also **u·ri·nose** (-nōz, -nōss). Of, resembling, or containing urine.

urn (urn) *n.* **1.** A vase of varying size and shape, usually large with a pedestal, and used especially as a receptacle for the ashes of the cremated dead. **2.** A large vaselike vessel, often made of stone and planted with flowers, used as a garden ornament. **3.** A large closed metal vessel with a tap used for warming or serving tea or coffee; a samovar. **4.** *Botany.* The spore-bearing part of a moss capsule. [Middle English *urne,* a vessel containing the ashes of the dead, burial urn, from Latin *urna.*]

uro-¹, ur- *comb. form.* Indicates urine or the urinary tract; for example, **urogenital, uridine.** [New Latin, from Greek *ouro-,* from *ouron,* urine.]

uro-², ur- *comb. form.* Indicates a tail; for example, **uropod.** [New Latin, from Greek *oura,* tail.]

u·ro·chord (yŏor-ō-kawrd, yór-, -ə-) *n. Zoology.* A notochord limited to the caudal region, as in larval tunicates. [URO- (tail) + CHORD.] —**u·ro·chor·dal** (-kórd'l) *adj.*

u·ro·chrome (yŏor-ō-krōm, yór-, -ə-) *n.* The pigment responsible for the normal yellow colour of urine. [URO- + -CHROME.]

u·ro·dele (yŏor-ō-deel, yór-, -ə-) *n.* Any amphibian of the order Urodela, characterised by a long body and tail and including the newts and salamanders. [French *urodèle* : URO- (tail) + Greek *dēlos,* evident.] —**u·ro·dele** *adj.*

u·ro·gen·i·tal (yŏor-ō-jénnit'l, yór-, -ə-) *adj.* Also **u·ri·no·gen·i·tal** (-inō-). Of, pertaining to, or involving both the urinary and genital functions.

u·ro·lith (yŏor-ō-lith, yór-, -ə-) *n. Pathology.* A **urinary calculus** *(see).* [URO- + -LITH.] —**u·ro·lith·ic** (-lithik) *adj.*

u·rol·o·gy (yŏor-róllǝji, yŏo-) *n.* The medical study of the physiology and pathology of the urogenital tract. [URO- + -LOGY.] —**u·ro·log·i·cal** (yŏor-ə-lójik'l, yór-, -ō-) *adj.* —**u·rol·o·gist** (-róllǝjist) *n.*

–uronic *adj. comb. form.* Indicates a connection with urine; for example, **hyaluronic.** [Greek *ouron,* urine.]

u·ro·pod (yŏor-ə-pod, yór-, -ō-) *n.* Either of a pair of posterior abdominal appendages of certain crustaceans, such as the lobster or shrimp. [URO- (tail) + -POD.] —**u·rop·o·dal** (yoor-róppəd'l, yŏo-), **u·rop·o·dous** (-róppədəss) *adj.*

uropygial gland *n.* An oil-secreting gland at the base of a bird's tail. Also called "oil gland".

u·ro·pyg·i·um (yŏor-ə-píji-əm, yór-, -ō-) *n.* The posterior part of a bird's body, from which the tail feathers grow; the rump. [New Latin, from Greek *ouropugion* : URO- (tail) + *pugē,* rump.] —**u·ro·pyg·i·al** *adj.*

u·ros·co·py (yoor-róskəpi, yŏo-) *n., pl.* **-pies.** *Medicine.* The examination of urine with a microscope. [URO- + -SCOPY.]

u·ro·style (yŏor-ō-stīl, yór-, -ə-) *n.* A rod-shaped bone forming the terminal section of the backbone in frogs and toads. [URO- (tail) + Greek *stulos,* column.]

–urous *adj. comb. form.* Indicates a tail or type of tail; for example, **anurous.** [New Latin *-urus,* from Greek *-ouros,* from *oura,* tail.]

Ur·sa Major (úr-sə) *n.* A constellation in the region of the north celestial pole, near Draco and Leo, containing the seven stars that form the Plough. Also called the "Great Bear". [Latin *ursa,* feminine of *ursus,* bear. See **ursine.**]

Ursa Minor *n.* A ladle-shaped constellation with **Polaris** *(see)* at the tip of its handle. Also *U.S.* "Little Bear", "Little Dipper".

ur·sine (úr-sīn) *adj.* Of or characteristic of a bear. [Latin *ursīnus,* from *ursus,* bear.]

Ur·spra·che (óor-shpraakhə) *n.* A reconstructed language set up as the parent of groups of related languages, as, for example, Indo-European, the hypothetical ancestor of Latin, Greek, Slavic, Celtic, and Germanic. Compare **protolanguage.** [German, "protolanguage."]

Ur·su·line (úrss-yŏo-līn, úrsh-, -lin ‖ -ə-, -leen) *n.* A member of an order of nuns of the Roman Catholic Church, founded in about 1537 and devoted to the education of girls. [After Saint *Ursula,* legendary British princess supposedly martyred with 11,000 handmaidens by Huns at Cologne in the 5th century.] —**Ur·su·line** *adj.*

Ur·text (óor-tekst) *n.* **1.** A reconstructed proto-text set up as the basis of variants in extant later texts. **2.** *Small* **u.** The original text of a work of art, especially of musical composition. [German, "proto-text".]

ur·ti·cant (úrtik-ənt) *adj.* Causing itching or stinging.
—*n.* A substance that causes itching or stinging.

ur·ti·car·i·a (úrti-káiri-ə) *n.* A skin condition characterised by intensely itching red, raised patches and usually caused by allergic reactions to internal or external agents. Also called "hives", "nettle rash", "uredo". [New Latin, from Latin *urtīca,* nettle. See **urticate.**]

ur·ti·cate (úrti-kayt) —*intr.v.* **-cated, -cating, -cates.** To produce urticaria or a stinging sensation. —*tr.* To practise urtication on. [Medieval Latin *urtīcāre,* from Latin *urtīca†,* nettle.]

ur·ti·ca·tion (úrti-káysh'n) *n.* **1.** The sensation of having been stung by nettles. **2.** *Medicine.* Formerly, a lashing with nettles as treatment of a paralysed part of the body. **3.** Urticaria.

U·ru·guay (yŏor-ə-gwī, óorrə-, -ōō-, -gwī ‖ -gway). State on the east coast of South America. Its economy rests on cattle and sheep, with meat, hides, and wool accounting for 70 per cent of its exports. Disputed by Spain and Portugal from the 17th century, and by Brazil and Argentina in the 19th century, Uruguay emerged as an

independent nation in 1828. Area, 176 215 square kilometres (68,019 square miles). Population, 3,200,000. Capital, Montevideo. —**U·ru·guay·an** (-gwī-ən) *n. & adj.*

Uruguay. River in South America. It flows for about 1 610 kilometres (1,000 miles) from southern Brazil into the Rio de la Plata.

Urum·qi or **Urum·ch'i** (ōō-rōŏm-chi). Also **Wu·lu·mu·ch'i.** Capital of Xinjiang Uigur Zizhiqu, northwest China, known as Tihwa before 1954. It is a major agricultural and industrial centre.

Urundi. See **Burundi.**

u·rus (yŏor-əss, yór-) *n.* An extinct bovine mammal, the **aurochs** *(see).* [Latin *ūrus,* from Germanic.]

u·ru·shi·ol (yoor-rōōshi-ol, yŏo-, ə-, ōō- ‖ -ōl) *n.* A toxic substance present in the resin of plants of the genus *Rhus,* which includes poison ivy and the lacquer tree, *R. verniciflua,* from which a black Japanese lacquer is obtained. [Japanese *urushi,* lacquer + -OL.]

us (uss, *weak form* əss ‖ *North of England* uz, əz) *pron.* The objective case of the first person plural pronoun *we.* It is used: **1.** As the direct object of a verb: *He assisted us.* **2.** As the indirect object of a verb: *They offered us a ride.* **3.** As the object of a preposition: *They came to us first.* **4.** After *than* or *as* in comparisons in which the first term is in the objective case: *They gave you more than us.* **5.** *Chiefly British Informal.* Me: *Go on, give us a smile.* **6.** *Chiefly U.S. Informal.* In place of the reflexive pronoun *ourselves,* as the indirect object of a verb: *We'll get us some dinner.* **7.** In various elliptical, absolute, or interjectional phrases in which it is neither subject nor object: *Who, us? Lucky us!* See Usage notes at **me, we.** [Middle English *us,* Old English *ūs.*]

US, U.S. 1. United States. **2.** unserviceable. **3.** useless.

u.s. ubi supra.

USA, U.S.A. 1. Union of South Africa. **2.** United States Army. **3.** United States of America.

us·a·ble, use·a·ble (yōoz-əb'l) *adj.* **1.** Capable of being used. **2.** In a fit condition for use; intact or operative. —**us·a·bil·i·ty** (-ə-bílləti), **us·a·ble·ness** *n.* —**us·a·bly** *adv.*

USAF, U.S.A.F. United States Air Force.

us·age (yōo-sij, -zij) *n.* **1. a.** The act or manner of using or treating; use or employment. **b.** The act of using. **2.** Customary practice; habitual use. **3.** The actual or expressed way in which a language or its elements are used, interrelated, or pronounced in expression: *contemporary English usage.* **4.** An instance of this; a particular expression in speech or writing: *a nonce usage.* —See Synonyms at **habit.** [Middle English, from Old French, from *user,* to USE.]

Usage: Usage is a more specialised term than *use. Use* is preferable when the sense relates broadly to employment or usefulness: *Those materials have a wide use these days. Usage* is preferred when the sense relates to "customary use", as in the "Usage notes" throughout this dictionary.

us·ance (yōoz'nss) *n.* **1.** *Commerce.* The length of time, established by custom and varying between countries, that is allowed for payment of a foreign bill of exchange. **2.** *Archaic.* Interest accruing on a loan. [Middle English *usaunce,* custom, usage, from Old French *usance,* from Vulgar Latin *ūsantia* (unattested), from *ūsāre* (unattested), to USE.]

U.S.D.A.W. (úss-daw, úz-). Union of Shop, Distributive and Allied Trades.

use (yōoz) *v.* **used** (yōozd), **yoost** *for intr. sense*), **using, uses.** —*tr.* **1.** To bring or put into service; employ, as for some purpose: *use soap for washing; use our telephone.* **2. a.** To make a practice or a habit of employing: *uses margarine in her sandwiches; doesn't use his wits.* **b.** To employ or utter (words or phrases): *uses clichés all the time.* **3.** To conduct oneself towards in a specified manner: *used you unkindly.* **4.** To consume or expend the whole of; deplete or exhaust. Often used with *up.* **5.** *Informal.* To exploit for one's own advantage or gain: *He gave nothing to his friends; he merely used them.* **6.** To take (a habit-forming drug), especially habitually. **7.** To make a practice of calling or designating oneself by (a title, name, or the like): *He doesn't use "Sir" in his private life.* —*intr.* To do or be habitually. Now used only in the past tense to show a former habitual action or state: *This bathroom used to be a stable; I used to play football every Saturday.* —See Usage note at **utilise.**

—n. (yōōss). **1. a.** The act of using; the application or employment of something, as for some purpose: *the use of a pencil for writing.* **b.** The condition or fact of being used or occupied: *This toilet is no longer in use.* **c.** The fact of having been used: *This car has had a lot of use.* **2.** The manner of using; usage: *the proper use of power tools.* **3. a.** The permission, privilege, or benefit of using something: *have use of the car.* **b.** The power or ability to use something: *lose the use of one arm.* **4.** The need or occasion to use or employ: *Do you still have any use for this book?* **5.** The quality of being suitable or adaptable to an end; usefulness: *There's no use (in) discussing it.* **6.** The goal, object, or purpose for which something is used. **7.** *Archaic.* Accustomed or usual procedure; habitual practice; custom. **8.** *Law.* **a.** The enjoyment of property, as by occupying or exercising it. **b.** The benefit or profit of lands and tenements of which the legal title and possession are vested in another who holds them in trust for the beneficiary. **c.** The arrangement establishing the equitable right to such benefits and profits. **9.** The special or distinctive form of ritual, ceremony, or public worship practised in a particular church, ecclesiastical district, or community. **—have no use for.** To have no tolerance for or patience with; dislike. **—make use of. 1.** To find occasion to use. **2.** To exploit. [Middle English *usen,* from Old French *user,* from Vulgar Latin *ūsāre* (unattested), frequentative of Latin *ūtī*† (past participle *ūsus*), to use.]

Usage: As an auxiliary verb, *use* always occurs in the past tense, followed by *to*: *He used to play football.* In interrogative sentences, there is some variation in usage. *Used he to (play football)?* is an older construction, found especially in British English, and still sometimes used in formal speech; the more modern and widely used form in both British and American informal English is *did he use(d) to.* A similar set of distinctions applies to the negative forms: *He usedn't to go/used not to go* is the older construction, found especially in British English, and preferred by conservative speakers; the alternative form, *didn't use(d) to,* is the more common form nowadays. In all of these constructions the pronunciation is usually yōōst, yōōss; compare yōōzd, yōōz for other senses.

used (yōōzd) *adj.* Not new; secondhand: *a used car.* **—used to** (yōōst). Accustomed to: *I'm not used to all this rich food.*

use·ful (yōōss-f'l) *adj.* **1.** Capable of being used advantageously or beneficially; serviceable. **2.** Commendably productive: *doing some useful work at school.* **—use·ful·ly** *adv.* **—use·ful·ness** *n.*

use·less (yōōss-ləss, -liss) *adj.* **1.** Having no beneficial purpose or use; of little or no worth; meaningless. **2.** Futile; pointless; to no avail. **—use·less·ly** *adv.* **—use·less·ness** *n.*

us·er (yōōzər) *n.* **1.** One that uses. **2.** *Law.* The exercise or enjoyment of any right or property. **3.** *Slang.* A drug addict.

us·er-friend·ly (yōōzər-fréndli) *adj.* Easy to use: *user-friendly computer programs.* [Possibly from German *benutzerfreundlich: Benutzer,* user + *freundlich,* friendly.] **—us·er-friend·li·ness** *n.*

ush·er (úshər) *n.* **1.** One who serves as official doorkeeper and usually keeps order, as in a law court or legislative chamber. See **serjeant at arms. 2.** A person employed to escort people to their seats, as in a cinema, theatre, or stadium. **3.** A male attendant at a wedding. **4.** An official who precedes persons of rank in a procession. *—tr.v.* **ushered, -ering, -ers. 1.** To serve as an usher to; escort. **2.** To lead or conduct; cause to enter. Used with *through* or *into*: *ushered her through the door.* **3.** To precede and introduce; serve as the beginning of. Usually used with *in.* [Middle English, from Anglo-French *usser,* variant of Old French *ussier,* from Medieval Latin *ūstiārius,* variant of Latin *ōstiārius,* doorkeeper, from *ōstium,* entrance, river mouth, from *ōs,* mouth, orifice.]

ush·er·ette (úshə-rét) *n.* A woman who takes tickets and shows people to their seats in a cinema.

Üs·kü·dar (üskü-daar). Urban district of Turkey, incorporated in Istanbul and formerly known as Scutari. During the Crimean War (1854–56), it was a British base.

us·que·baugh (úskwi-baw ‖ -baa) *n. Irish & Scottish.* Whisky. [Irish and Scots Gaelic *uisge beatha,* "water of life".]

U.S.S. 1. United States Senate. **2.** United States Ship.

U.S.S.R. Union of Soviet Socialist Republics.

Us·ti·nov (yōōsti-nof, -nov), **Sir Peter (Alexander)** (1921–). British actor, director, and playwright. His films include *Spartacus* (1960) and *Murder on the Nile* (1978). He was president of the World Federalist Movement (1992–96).

u·su·al (yōōzh-oo-əl, yōōzh-wəl, -'l, -yoo-əl) *adj. Abbr.* **usu. 1.** Such as is commonly or frequently encountered, experienced, observed, or used; ordinary; normal. **2.** Habitual or customary; particular. **—the usual.** One's customary meal, drink, or the like. [Middle English, from Old French, from Late Latin *ūsuālis,* ordinary, from Latin *ūsus,* use, custom, from the past participle of *ūtī,* to USE.] **—u·su·al·ly** *adv.* **—u·su·al·ness** *n.*

Synonyms: *usual, typical, habitual, customary, accustomed.*

u·su·cap·tion (yōōss-yoo-kápsh'n, yōōz- ‖ -ə-) *n. Law.* Formerly, ownership resulting from prolonged possession.

u·su·fruct (yōōss-yoo-frukt, yōōz- ‖ -ə-) *n. Law.* The right to make use of and enjoy the profits and advantages of something belonging to another so long as the property is not damaged or altered in any way. [Latin *ūsusfrūctus,* "use (and) enjoyment" : *ūsus,* use (see **usual**) + *frūctus,* enjoyment, FRUIT.]

u·su·fruc·tu·ar·y (yōōss-yoo-frúk-tew-əri, yōōz-, -choo- ‖ -ə-, -erri) *n., pl.* **-ies.** A person who holds property by usufruct. *—adj.* Of or of the nature of a usufruct.

u·su·rer (yōōzh-ərər,-rər) *n.* **1.** A person who lends money at an exorbitant or unlawful rate of interest. **2.** *Obsolete.* A moneylender. [Middle English, from Anglo-French, from Medieval Latin *ūsūrārius,* from Latin *ūsūra,* interest, USURY.]

u·su·ri·ous (yoo-zéwr-i-əss, yoo-, -zóor-, -zhóor-) *adj.* **1.** Practising usury. **2.** Of, pertaining to, or constituting usury: *a usurious rate of interest.* **—u·su·ri·ous·ly** *adv.* **—u·su·ri·ous·ness** *n.*

u·surp (yoo-zúrp, yoo- ‖ *chiefly U.S.* -súrp) *v.* **-surped, -surping, -surps.** *—tr.* **1.** To seize and hold (the power, position, or rights of another) by force and without legal right or authority. **2.** To take over or occupy physically and wrongfully (territory or possessions for example); appropriate. *—intr.* To commit such illegal seizure; encroach. [Middle English *usurpen,* from Old French *usurper,* from Latin *ūsūrpāre,* to take forcibly into use.] **—u·surp·er** *n.* **—u·sur·pa·tion** (yoo-zur-páysh'n) *n.*

u·su·ry (yōō-zhōō-ri, -zhə-, -zhri, -zhoor-i) *n., pl.* **-ries. 1.** The act or practice of lending money at an exorbitant or illegal rate of interest. **2.** Such an excessive rate of interest. **3.** *Archaic.* The act or practice of lending money at any rate of interest. [Middle English, from Anglo-French *usurie* (unattested), from Medieval Latin *ūsūria,* from Latin *ūsūra,* use of money lent, interest, from *ūsus,* use. See **usual.**]

ut (ut, ōōt) *n. Music.* A syllable representing the note *C,* otherwise represented by *do,* in the French system of tonic sol-fa. See **gamut.** [Latin *ut,* that (first word of a hymn to St. John the Baptist).]

U.T. universal time.

U·tah (yōō-taa ‖ *locally & U.S.* -taw). State in the western United States, one of the so-called Rocky Mountain states. The capital and largest city is Salt Lake City. It is an important mining state, and has valuable deposits of petroleum. The region was first settled permanently in 1847 by Mormons seeking refuge from persecution, and the state has ever since been the home of the American Mormons. It was admitted to the Union in 1896.

Ute (yōōt) *n., pl.* **Ute** or **Utes. 1.** A member of a Uto-Aztecan-speaking North American Indian people formerly inhabiting Utah, Colorado, and New Mexico and now living on reservations in Utah and Colorado. **2.** The language of this people.

u·ten·sil (yoo-tén-s'l, -sil) *n.* **1.** An instrument or container, especially one used domestically, as in a kitchen. **2.** Any instrument or tool; an implement. —See Synonyms at **tool.** [Middle English *utensele,* from Old French *utensile,* from Latin *ūtēnsilia,* "things for use", from the neuter plural of *ūtēnsilis,* fit for use, from *ūtī,* to USE.]

u·ter·ine (yōōtə-rīn ‖ -rin) *adj.* **1.** Of or pertaining to the uterus. **2.** Having the same mother but different fathers. [Late Latin *uterīnus,* from *uterus,* UTERUS.]

u·ter·us (yōōtərəss) *n.* **1.** A pear-shaped muscular organ located in the pelvic cavity of female mammals that receives and holds the fertilised ovum during the development of the foetus and is the principal agent in its expulsion at birth. Also called "womb". **2.** A similar part of the female reproductive tract in many invertebrates, serving as a repository for the storage or development of eggs or embryos. [Latin *uterus.*]

Ut·gard (ōōt-gaard, ōōt-). *Norse Mythology.* The home of Utgard-Loki. Also called "Jotunheim".

Ut·gard-Lo·ki (ōōt-gaard-lōki). *Norse Mythology.* An invincible giant.

U·ther Pen·drag·on (yōōthər). A legendary king of Britain and father of King Arthur.

u·tile (yōō-tīl ‖ -til) *adj. Rare.* Useful. [Middle English *utyle,* from Old French *utile,* from Latin *ūtilis.* See **utility.**]

u·til·ise, u·til·ize (yōōti-līz, yōōtə-) *tr.v.* **-ised, -ising, -ises. 1.** To put to use for a certain purpose. **2.** To make productive use of or to find a use for. [French *utiliser,* from Italian *utilizzare,* from *utile,* useful, from Latin *ūtilis.* See **utility.**] **—u·til·is·a·ble** *adj.* **—u·til·i·sa·tion** (-lī-záysh'n ‖ *U.S.* -li-) *n.* **—u·til·is·er** *n.*

Usage: The tendency for *utilise* to replace *use* in business and official English is open to criticism as an example of needless jargon. Careful usage maintains a distinction between these verbs, *use* having a general sense of "put into service" (*The machinery should be used as little as possible*), *utilise* having a narrower sense of "make useful or productive" (*We shall utilise the spare parts to save money*).

u·til·i·tar·i·an (yoo-tílli-táir-i-ən, yōōtili-) *adj.* **1.** Of or pertaining to utilitarianism. **2.** Useful and practical rather than decorative. *—n.* An advocate of utilitarianism. [UTILIT(Y) + -ARIAN.]

u·til·i·tar·i·an·ism (yoo-tílli-táir-i-ən-iz'm, yōōtili-) *n.* **1.** The ethical theory, originally proposed by Jeremy Bentham and John Stuart Mill, that all moral, social, or political action should be directed towards achieving the greatest good for the greatest number of people, where "good" is taken to be "happiness". **2.** The belief that what is useful is good.

u·til·i·ty (yoo-tílləti) *n., pl.* **-ties. 1.** The condition or quality of being useful; usefulness. **2.** A useful article or device. **3.** A public service, such as gas, electricity, water, or transport. **4.** In utilitarianism, the principle that the greatest good is the greatest happiness for the greatest number. *—adj.* Useful or practical and, especially in wartime, standardised. [Middle English *utilite,* usefulness, from Old French, from Latin *ūtilitās* (stem *ūtilitāt-*), from *ūtilis,* useful, from *ūtī,* to USE.]

utility room *n.* A room in a house usually containing a boiler, washing-machine, dryer, or other domestic appliances, and often also used for storage.

ut in·fra (ōōt ín-fraa, ut, -frə). *Abbr.* **ut inf.** *Latin.* As below.

u·ti pos·si·de·tis (yōōtī póssi-déetiss) *n.* A principle of international law providing that a belligerent state is entitled to absolute possession and control of the territory occupied by it at the end of a war. [Latin, as you possess.]

ut·most (út-mōst, -məst) *adj.* **1.** Being or situated at the farthest limit or point; most extreme. **2.** Of the highest or greatest degree, amount, intensity, or the like: *a matter of the utmost secrecy.* —*n.* The greatest possible amount, degree, or extent; the maximum. [Middle English *utmost, ut(te)mast,* Old English *ūt(e)mest,* outermost : *ūt(e),* out + *-mest,* -MOST.]

U·to·Az·tec·an (yōōtō-áz-teckən) *n.* **1.** A large language family of North and Central American Indians, including Ute, Pima, Hopi, Shoshone, Nahuatl, and other languages. **2.** A member of a people speaking a Uto-Aztecan language. [UT(E) + -O- + AZTEC.] —**U·to·Az·tec·an** *adj.*

u·to·pi·a (yōō-tōpi-ə) *n. Sometimes capital* **U. 1.** A condition, place, or situation of social or political perfection. **2.** Any idealistic goal or concept for social and political reform. Compare **dystopia.** [After *Utopia,* an imaginary island and ideal commonwealth, the subject of Sir Thomas More's book of this title (1516) : New Latin, "no-place" : Greek *ou†,* not, no + *topos,* place (see **topic**).]

u·to·pi·an (yōō-tōpi-ən) *adj.* Excellent or ideal but existing only in visionary or impractical thought or theory. —*n.* A zealous but impractical reformer of human society.

u·to·pi·an·ism (yōō-tōpi-ən-iz'm) *n.* The ideals or principles of a utopian; idealistic and impractical social theory.

U·trecht (yōō-trekt, -trékt; *Dutch* ū-trekht). City in the central Netherlands, lying on a branch of the lower Rhine. It was a leading commercial town in the Middle Ages and is now an industrial and financial centre. The Peace of Utrecht brought the War of the Spanish Succession to an end in 1713–14.

u·tri·cle (yōōtrik'l) *n.* Also **u·tric·u·lus** (yōō-trickew-ləss), *pl.* **-li** (-lī). **1.** A small, delicate membranous sac connecting with the semicircular canals of the inner ear and functioning in the maintenance of bodily equilibrium and coordination. **2.** *Botany.* A small, bladder-like one-seeded fruit. [French *utricule,* from Latin *ūtriculus,* diminutive of *ūter,* leather bag or bottle, perhaps from Greek *hudria,* water pot, pitcher, from *hudōr,* water.] —**u·tric·u·lar** (-lər) *adj.*

U·tril·lo (yōō-tríllō; *French* ū-tree-yō), **Maurice** (1883–1955). French painter, best known for his paintings of Paris street scenes.

ut su·pra (ōot sōō-praa, ut séw-, -prə). *Abbr.* **ut sup.** *Latin.* As above.

Ut·tar Pra·desh (ōōttər prə-désh, -dáysh). Formerly **United Provinces.** State in north central India. With more than 88 million people, it is the country's most populous state. The capital is Lucknow. Agriculture and food processing are the chief economic activities.

ut·ter[1] (úttər) *tr.v.* **-tered, -tering, -ters. 1.** To express audibly; emit (a sound): *uttered a sign of relief.* **2.** To express in words; say or write: *uttered his name; uttered the truth.* **3.** To put (counterfeit money, for example) into circulation. —See Synonyms at **vent.** [Middle English *utt(e)ren, outren,* from Middle Dutch *ūteren,* to drive away, announce, speak.] —**ut·ter·a·ble** *adj.* —**ut·ter·er** *n.*

ut·ter[2] *adj.* Complete; absolute; entire. [Middle English *utter,* Old English *ūtera, ūttra,* outer, external, comparative of *ūt,* OUT.]

ut·ter·ance[1] (úttrənss, úttərənss) *n.* **1. a.** The act of uttering or expressing vocally. **b.** The power of speaking. **2.** Something that is uttered or expressed.

ut·ter·ance[2] (úttərənss) *n. Archaic.* The uttermost end or extremity; bitter end; death: *fight to the utterance.* [Middle English *utt(e)raunce,* from Old French *outrance,* from *outrer,* to go beyond limits, from Vulgar Latin *ultrāre* (unattested), from Latin *ultrā,* beyond, from *uls,* beyond.]

ut·ter·ly (úttərli) *adv.* Completely; absolutely; entirely.

ut·ter·most (úttər-mōst, -məst) *adj.* **1.** Utmost. **2.** Farthest. —*n.* Utmost. [Middle English *uttermost, uttermest* : UTTER (outer, complete) + -MOST.]

U-turn (yōō-turn) *n.* **1.** A turn, as by a vehicle, completely reversing the direction of travel. **2.** Any complete change or reversal, as of mind or policy: *Will the government make a U-turn on wages?*

UV, U.V. Ultraviolet.

u·va·rov·ite (yōō-vaárə-vīt, ōō-) *n.* An emerald-green garnet, $Ca_3Cr_2(SiO_4)_3$, found in chromium deposits. [German *Uvarovit;* discovered by Count Sergei *Uvarov* (1785–1855), Russian statesman.]

u·ve·a (yōōvi-ə) *n.* The pigmented vascular layer of the eye including the iris, ciliary body, and choroid. [Medieval Latin *ūvea,* from Latin *ūva,* grape (from its round shape).] —**u·ve·al** *adj.*

u·ve·i·tis (yōōvi-ítiss) *n.* Inflammation of the uvea. [New Latin : UVE(A) + -ITIS.]

u·vu·la (yōōvew-lə) *n.* The small, conical, fleshy mass of tissue suspended from the centre of the soft palate above the back of the tongue. [Middle English, from Late Latin, "small grape" (from the shape of the uvula), diminutive of Latin *ūva,* a grape.]

u·vu·lar (yōōvew-lər) *adj.* **1.** Pertaining to or associated with the uvula. **2.** *Phonetics.* Articulated by vibration of the uvula or with the back of the tongue near or touching the uvula.

u·vu·li·tis (yōōvew-lítiss) *n.* Inflammation of the uvula. [New Latin: UVUL(A) + -ITIS.]

ux·o·ri·al (uk-sáw-ri-əl ‖ ug-, -záw-, -sō-, -zō-) *adj. Formal & Literary.* Pertaining to, characteristic of, or befitting a wife. [From Latin *uxōrius,* of a wife, UXORIOUS.]

ux·o·ri·cide (uk-sáw-ri-sīd ‖ ug-, -záw-, -sō-, -zō-) *n. Formal & Literary.* **1.** The killing of a wife by her husband. **2.** A man who kills his wife. [Medieval Latin *uxōricīdium,* the murder of one's wife : Latin *uxor,* wife + -CIDE.] —**ux·o·ri·cid·al** (-sīd'l) *adj.*

ux·o·ri·ous (uk-sáw-ri-əss ‖ ug-, -záw-, -sō-, -zō-) *adj. Formal & Literary.* **1.** Excessively or irrationally devoted to one's wife. **2.** Indicative of or revealing such devotion. [Latin *uxōrius,* from *uxor,* wife.] —**ux·o·ri·ous·ly** *adv.* —**ux·o·ri·ous·ness** *n.*

Uz·bek (ōōz-bek, úz-) *n.* Also **Uz·beg** (-beg), **Us·bek** (ōōss-, úss-), **Us·beg 1.** A member of a group of Turkic people inhabiting Uzbekistan. **2.** The Turkic language spoken by the Uzbeks.

Uz·bek·i·stan (ōōz-becki-staán), **Republic of.** Former constituent republic of the U.S.S.R., lying in central Asia. It is the chief supplier of cotton and rice to the rest of the former U.S.S.R. and it has also valuable reserves of petroleum and natural gas. Area, 447 400 square kilometres (172,742 square miles). Population, 22,910,000. Capital, Tashkent. See map at **Commonwealth of Independent States.**

V

v, V (vee) *n., pl.* **v's** or *rare* **vs, Vs** or **V's. 1.** The 22nd letter of the modern English alphabet. **2.** Any of the speech sounds represented by this letter. **3.** Anything shaped like the letter **V.**

v, V, v., V. *Note:* As an abbreviation or symbol, *v* may be a small or a capital letter, with or without a full stop. Established forms or those generally preferred precede the definition. When no form is given, all four forms are in general use in that sense. **1. V** The symbol for the element vanadium. **2. V** *Physics.* velocity. **3. V.** venerable (in titles). **4. v.** verb. **5. v.** verse. **6. v.** version. **7. v.** verso. **8. v.** versus. **9. v., V.** very. **10. v., V.** vice (in titles). **11. V** victory (used by the Allies in World War II). **12. v.** vide. **13. v., V.** village. **14. v.** violin. **15. V.** viscount; viscountess. **16. v.** vocative. **17. v.** voice. **18. V** *Electricity.* volt. **19. V** volume. **20. v.** volume (book). **21. v.** von. **22. v.** vowel. **23. v, V** The Roman numeral for five. **24.** The 22nd in a series; 21st when *J* is omitted.

V-1 (vée-wún ‖ -wón) *n.* A **flying bomb** *(see).* [German *Vergeltungswaffe eins,* "retaliation weapon (number) one".]

V-2 (vée-tōō) *n.* A long-range liquid-fuelled rocket used by the Germans as a ballistic missile in World War II. [German *Vergeltungswaffe zwei,* "retaliation weapon (number) two".]

V.A. 1. vice admiral. **2.** vicar apostolic. **3.** *U.S.* Veterans' Administration. **4.** Royal Order of Victoria and Albert.

Vaal (vaal ‖ *locally* faal). River in northeastern South Africa, rising in Mpumalanga province and flowing for about 1 200 kilometres (750 miles) into the Orange river.

vac (vak) *n. Chiefly British Informal.* A **vacation** *(see).*

vac. vacuum.

va·can·cy (váykən-si) *n., pl.* **-cies. 1.** The state or condition of being vacant or unoccupied; emptiness. **2.** An empty or unoccupied space; a gap. **3.** A position, office, or place of accommodation that is unfilled or unoccupied. **4.** Emptiness of mind; inanity. **5.** A crystal defect caused by the absence of an atom, ion, or molecule in a crystal lattice. **6.** *Archaic.* A period of leisure; idleness. [VAC(ANT) + -ANCY or from Medieval and Late Latin *vacāntia.*]

va·cant (váykənt) *adj.* **1.** Containing nothing; empty; unfilled. **2.** Without an incumbent or occupant: *a vacant professorship.* **3.** Not occupied or put to use: *a vacant property.* **4.** *Law.* Not claimed, as by an heir: *a vacant estate.* **5. a.** Lacking intelligence or knowledge: *"Then gay ideas crowd the vacant brain"* (Alexander Pope). **b.** Expressionless; blank; unresponsive: *a vacant stare.* **6.** Unfilled by any activity: *vacant hours.* —See Synonyms at **empty.** [Middle English *vaca(u)nt,* from Old French *vacant,* from Latin *vacāns* (stem *vacānt-*), present participle of *vacāre,* to be empty.] —**va·cant·ly** *adv.* —**va·cant·ness** *n.*

vacant possession *n. Law.* Ownership of an unoccupied house or dwelling, and hence the right of immediate occupation.

va·cate (və-káyt, *rarely* vay- ‖ *U.S.* váy-kayt) *v.* **-cated, -cating, -cates.** —*tr.* **1. a.** To cease to occupy or hold; give up; leave. **b.** To empty of occupants or incumbents. **2.** *Law.* To make void; countermand; annul. —*intr.* To leave a job, office, lodging, or the like. [Latin *vacāre,* to be empty.]

va·ca·tion (və-káysh'n ‖ *U.S.* vay-) *n.* **1.** A fixed period of holidays; especially, one during which the law courts and universities suspend activities. **2.** *Chiefly U.S.* A holiday. **3.** *Archaic.* An act or instance of vacating. —*intr.v.* **vacationed, -tioning, -tions.** *U.S.* To take or spend a holiday. [Middle English *vacacioun*, from Old French *vacation*, from Latin *vacātiō* (stem *vacātiōn*-), freedom, release from occupation, from *vacāre*, to be empty, be free. See **vacate**.] —**va·ca·tion·er**, **va·ca·tion·ist** *n.*

vac·ci·nal (váksin'l) *adj.* Caused by or pertaining to vaccine or vaccination.

vac·ci·nate (váksi-nayt) *v.* **-nated, -nating, -nates.** *Medicine.* —*tr.* To inoculate with a vaccine in order to produce immunity against smallpox, diphtheria, typhoid fever, poliomyelitis, cholera, typhus, and other infectious diseases. —*intr.* To perform a vaccination. [From VACCINE.] —**vac·ci·na·tor** (-naytər) *n.*

vac·ci·na·tion (váksi-náysh'n) *n.* **1.** Inoculation with a vaccine in order to protect against a given disease. **2.** A scar left on the skin by such an inoculation.

vac·cine (vák-seen, -sin ‖ *U.S. also* vak-séen) *n.* **1.** A suspension of attenuated or killed disease-causing microorganisms, as of viruses or bacteria, incapable of inducing severe infection but capable, when inoculated, of stimulating the production of antibodies (and therefore conferring immunity) against the virulent microorganisms. **2.** Such a suspension prepared from the cowpox virus and inoculated against smallpox. ~*adj.* **1.** Of or derived from cows, especially from cows infected with cowpox. **2.** Of or pertaining to cowpox. **3.** Of or pertaining to vaccination. [French *(virus) vaccine*, (virus) of cowpox, from Latin *vaccīnus*, pertaining to cows, from *vacca*, cow.]

vac·cin·i·a (vak-sínni-ə) *n.* Cowpox *(see).* [New Latin, from Latin *vaccīnus*, of cows. See **vaccine**.]

vache·rin (vásha-ráɴ, vásh-) *n.* A French dessert consisting of a meringue shell filled with cream, fruit, or ice cream.

vac·il·late (vássi-layt) *intr.v.* **-lated, -lating, -lates. 1.** To swing indecisively from one course of action or opinion to another; be irresolute; waver. **2.** To sway from one side to the other; fluctuate; oscillate. —See Synonyms at **hesitate**. [Latin *vacillāre†*, to waver.] —**vac·il·la·tion** (-láysh'n) *n.* —**vac·il·la·tor** (-laytər) *n.*

vac·il·lat·ing (vássi-layting) *adj.* Also *rare* **vac·il·lant** (vássilənt), **vac·il·la·to·ry** (-lə-tri, -təri, -laytəri, -láytəri). Inclined to waver; irresolute. —**va·cil·lat·ing·ly** *adv.*

va·cu·i·ty (va-kéw-əti, və-) *n., pl.* **-ties. 1.** Total absence of matter; emptiness. **2.** An empty space; a vacuum. **3.** Lack of thought or intelligence; emptiness of mind. **4.** Absence of meaningful occupation; idleness: *"the crew, being patient people, much given to slumber and vacuity"* (Washington Irving). **5.** The quality or fact of being devoid of something specified: *a vacuity of taste.* **6.** Something, especially a remark, utterly without substance or point; an inanity. [Old French *vacuite*, from Latin *vacuitās* (stem *vacuitāt*-), from *vacuus*, empty. See **vacuum**.]

vac·u·o·lat·ed (váckew-ə-laytid, -ō-) *adj.* Also **vac·u·o·late** (-lət, -lit, -layt). Containing a vacuole or vacuoles.

vac·u·ole (váckew-ōl) *n.* Any small cavity in the cytoplasm of a cell, plant, or animal, that contains air, water, sap, partially digested food or other materials. [French, "little vacuum", from Latin *vacuum*, VACUUM.] —**vac·u·o·lar** (-ōlər) *adj.* —**vac·u·o·la·tion** (-ə-láysh'n, -ō-) *n.*

vac·u·ous (váckew-əss) *adj.* **1.** Devoid of matter; empty. **2. a.** Stupid; dull. **b.** Expressionless. **3.** Devoid of substance or meaning; inane. **4.** Purposeless; unoccupied; idle. —See Synonyms at **empty**. [Latin *vacuus*, empty. See **vacuum**.] —**vac·u·ous·ly** *adv.* —**vac·u·ous·ness** *n.*

vac·u·um (váckew-əm, vák-yōōm, -yōōm) *n., pl.* **-ums** or **vacua** (váckew-ə) (except for sense 4). *Abbr.* **vac. 1. a.** The absence of matter. **b.** A space empty of matter. **c.** A space in which the pressure is significantly lower than atmospheric pressure. **d.** A space relatively empty of matter. **2.** A state or feeling of emptiness; a void. **3.** A state of being sealed off from external or environmental influences; isolation. **4.** A vacuum cleaner. ~*adj.* **1.** Pertaining to or used to create a vacuum. **2.** Containing air or other gas at a reduced pressure. **3.** Working by means of suction or by maintaining of a partial vacuum. ~*v.* **vacuumed, -uming, -ums.** —*tr.* To clean with a vacuum cleaner. —*intr.* To use a vacuum cleaner. [Latin, neuter of *vacuus*, empty, from *vacāre*, to be empty.]

vacuum aspiration *n. Medicine.* A therapeutic method of abortion carried out under anaesthetic, before the twelfth week of pregnancy.

vacuum cleaner *n.* An electrical appliance that draws light dirt from surfaces by suction. —**vacuum-clean** *v.*

vacuum distillation *n.* A form of distillation in which the liquid to be distilled is maintained at a reduced pressure in order to lower its boiling point.

vacuum extractor *n. Medicine.* A suction cap that can be attached to the head of a foetus in order to aid delivery.

vacuum flask *n.* A bottle or flask having a partial vacuum between its inner and outer walls, designed to maintain the desired temperature of the contents. Also called "flask", "Thermos flask", "Dewar flask", *U.S.* "vacuum bottle".

vacuum gauge *n.* A device for determining the pressure in a partial vacuum.

vac·u·um-packed (váckew-əm-pákt, vák-yōōm, -yōōm-, -pakt) *adj.* **1.** Packed in an airtight container with little or no air. **2.** Sealed under low pressure or a partial vacuum.

vacuum pump *n.* A pump used to evacuate air from an enclosed space.

vacuum tube *n.* An electronic **valve** *(see).*

V.A.D. *n.* A member of Voluntary Aid Detachment, serving as nursing assistants during World War I.

va·de me·cum (vấa-di-máy-kōōm, váy-, -mée-, -kum, -kəm) *n.,pl.* **vade mecums. 1.** A useful thing that a person constantly carries with him. **2.** A guidebook or other ready reference book. [Latin, "go with me".]

va·dose (váy-dōz, -dōss) *adj.* Of, pertaining to, or designating water that occurs below the Earth's surface and above the water table. [Latin *vadōsus*, full of shallows, from *vadum*, ford.]

Va·duz (va-dŏots, -dŏots; *German* fa-). Capital of Liechtenstein. It is a tourist centre and the site of a castle, built in 16th-century style.

vag·a·bond (vágga-bond) *n.* **1.** A person without a fixed home who moves from place to place and has no apparent means of support. **2.** A vagrant; a tramp. **3.** A wandering rogue; a rascal. ~*adj.* **1.** Of, pertaining to, or characteristic of a wanderer; nomadic. **2.** Aimless; drifting; straying. **3.** Irregular in course or behaviour; unpredictable. ~*intr.v.* **vagabonded, -bonding, -bonds.** To lead a vagabond's life; roam about. [Middle English *vagabound*, from Old French *vagabond*, from Latin *vagābundus*, wandering, from *vagārī*, to wander, from *vagus*, wandering, undecided, VAGUE.] —**vag·a·bond·age** *n.* —**vag·a·bond·ism** *n.*

va·gar·y (váygəri, və-gáír-i) *n., pl.* **-ies.** An extravagant or erratic notion or action; a flight of fancy. —See Synonyms at **caprice**. [Originally "a roaming tour", a ramble, from Latin *vagārī*, to wander, from *vagus*, wandering, undecided, VAGUE.]

va·gi·na (və-jī-nə) *n., pl.* **-nas** or **-nae** (-nee) **1.** *Anatomy.* **a.** The passage leading from the external genital orifice to the uterus in female mammals. **b.** A similar structure in some invertebrates. **2.** *Biology.* A sheathlike structure or part, such as that formed by the base of a leaf enclosing a stem. [Latin *vāgīna*, sheath.] —**vag·i·nal** (-n'l, *also* vájin'l) *adj.*

vag·i·nate (váji-nayt, -nət, -nit) *adj.* Also **vag·i·nat·ed** (-naytid). Forming or enclosed in a sheath.

vag·i·nec·to·my (váji-nέktəmi) *n., pl.* **-mies. 1.** Surgical excision of all or part of the vagina. **2.** Surgical excision of the serous membrane covering the testis and epididymis. [VAGIN(O)- + -ECTOMY.]

vag·i·nis·mus (váji-níz-məss, -níss-) *n.* Sudden and painful contraction of the muscles surrounding the vagina. [New Latin : VAGIN(O)- + -ISM.]

vag·i·ni·tis (váji-nítiss) *n.* Inflammation of the vagina. Also called "colpitis". [New Latin : VAGIN(O)- + -ITIS.]

vagino–, vagin– *comb. form.* Indicates the vagina; for example, **vaginectomy.** [From Latin *vāgīna*, sheath.]

va·got·o·my (vay-góttəmi, va-) *n., pl.* **-mies.** Surgical cutting of any of the branches of the vagus nerve, used to diminish the secretion of acid and pepsin by the stomach and to control a peptic ulcer. [VAG(US) + -TOMY.]

va·go·to·ni·a (váyg-ə-tōni-ə, -ō-) *n.* Pathological overactivity of the vagus nerve. [New Latin : VAG(US) + -TONIA.]

va·go·trop·ic (váyg-ə-tróppik, -ō-, -trōpik) *adj.* Affecting or acting on the vagus nerve. Said chiefly of drugs. [VAG(US) + -TROPIC.]

va·gran·cy (váygrən-si) *n., pl.* **-cies. 1.** The state of being a vagrant. **2.** The conduct or mode of existence of a vagrant. **3.** *Rare.* A wandering in mind or thought.

va·grant (váygrənt) *n.* **1.** A person who wanders from place to place without a fixed home or livelihood and ekes out a living by begging or stealing; a tramp; a vagabond. **2.** A wanderer; a rover. ~*adj.* **1.** Wandering from place to place; homeless and without work; roving. **2.** Wayward; unrestrained. **3.** Moving in a random fashion; not fixed in place. [Middle English *vag(a)raunt*, from Anglo-French, probably from Latin *vagārī*, to wander, from *vagus*, wandering, undecided, VAGUE.] —**va·grant·ly** *adv.*

vague (vayg) *adj.* **vaguer, vaguest. 1.** Not clearly expressed or outlined; inexplicit; indefinite: *vague instructions.* **2. a.** Uncertain or indefinite in thought or expression: *She was vague about her future.* **b.** Mildly confused or muddled, as in one's thinking. **3.** Lacking definite shape, form, or character; not clearly defined: *vague plans.* **4.** Ambiguous in meaning or application: *"Right" and "wrong" seem vague to too many people.* **5.** Indistinctly felt, perceived, understood, or recalled; hazy: *a vague uneasiness.* —See Synonyms at **ambiguous**. [Old French, from Latin *vagus†*, wandering, undecided, vague. See also **extravagant**.] —**vague·ly** *adv.* —**vague·ness** *n.*

va·gus (váy-gəss) *n., pl.* **-gi** (-jī, -gī). Either of the tenth and longest pair of cranial nerves, passing through the neck and thorax into the abdomen and supplying sensation to part of the ear, the larynx, and the pharynx, motor impulses to the vocal-cord muscles, and motor and secretory impulses to the abdominal and thoracic viscera. Also called "vagus nerve", "pneumogastric nerve". [New Latin *vagus (nervus)*, "wandering (nerve)", from Latin *vagus*, wandering, VAGUE.] —**va·gal** (váyg'l) *adj.*

va·hi·ne (vaa-héeni) *n.* In Tahiti, a woman, especially one who is married. [Maori.]

vail (vayl) *v.* **vailed, vailing, vails.** *Archaic.* —*tr.* **1.** To lower (a banner, for example). **2.** To doff (a hat or headpiece) as a token of respect or submission. —*intr.* **1.** To descend; to lower. **2.** To doff one's hat. [Middle English *valen*, short for *avalen*, to let fall, from Old French *avaler*, to lower, from Vulgar Latin *advallāre* (unattested), from Latin *ad vallem*, "to the valley" : *ad*, to + *vallis, vallēs*, valley.]

vain (vayn) *adj.* **vainer, vainest. 1.** Not yielding the desired outcome; unsuccessful; futile; fruitless: *a vain attempt.* **2.** Lacking substance or worth; hollow; idle: *vain talk.* **3.** Showing undue preoccupation with or pride in one's appearance or accomplish-

ments; conceited: *He wasn't just immodest, he was shamelessly vain.*
4. *Archaic.* Foolish. **—in vain. 1.** Without effect or avail; to no use
or purpose: *Our labour was in vain.* **2.** Without due respect or piety;
profanely. Used chiefly in the phrase *take the name of God in vain.*
[Middle English, from Old French, from Latin *vānus,* empty.]
—vain·ly *adv.* **—vain·ness** *n.*

vain·glo·ri·ous (váyn-gláw-ri-əss ‖ -glō-) *adj.* **1.** Showing excessive
vanity; boastful. **2.** Characterised by or proceeding from vainglory.
—vain·glo·ri·ous·ly *adv.* **—vain·glo·ri·ous·ness** *n.*

vain·glo·ry (váyn-gláw-ri ‖ -glō-, -glaw-, -glō-) *n., pl.* **-ries. 1.** Boastful and unwarranted pride in one's accomplishments or qualities.
2. Vain and ostentatious display. [Middle English *vein glory, wayn-
glori,* from Old French *vaine glorie,* from Latin *vānus glōria,* empty
pride : *vānus,* vain + *glōria,* pride, GLORY.]

vair (vair) *n.* **1.** A fur, probably squirrel, much used in medieval
times to line and trim robes. **2.** *Heraldry.* A heraldic representation
of squirrel fur. [Middle English *veir, vaire,* variegated fur, from Old
French *vair,* from Latin *varius,* variegated, VARIOUS.]

Vaish·na·va (vǐshnəvə) *n.* A Hindu sect that worships Vishnu.
[Sanskrit *viṣṇava,* of Vishnu, from *Viṣṇu,* VISHNU.] **—Vaish·na·
vism** *n.*

Vais·ya (vǐsh-yə, víss-) *n.* **1.** The Hindu merchant and business
caste, originally composed of farmers and herders. **2.** A member of
this caste. See **caste.** [Sanskrit *vaisya,* "settler".]

val. valuation; value.

val·ance (vál-ənss) *n.* **1.** A short ornamental curtain or piece of
drapery hung across the top of a window or along a shelf, canopy,
or the like, or from the frame or mattress of a bed to the floor, often
to conceal structural detail. **2.** A decorative board or metal strip
similar to this.
~tr.v. **valanced, -ancing, -ances.** To supply with a valance. [Mid-
dle English *valaunce,* perhaps from Anglo-French *valance* (unattested), equivalent to Old French *avaler,* to lower (see **vail**) +
-ANCE.]

vale[1] (vayl) *n. Archaic & Poetic.* **1.** A valley; a dale. **2.** The world as
a scene of sorrow: *this vale of dross and tears.* [Middle English *vale,
vaal,* from Old French *val,* from Latin *vallēs, vallis.*]

va·le[2] (váy-li, vá-, vá́a-, -lay) *interj. Archaic.* Used to express leave-
taking or farewell.
~n. Archaic. A farewell. [Latin *valē,* imperative of *valēre,* to be
strong or well.]

val·e·dic·tion (vál-i-díksh'n) *n.* **1.** An act or instance of saying good-
bye; a farewell; a leave-taking. **2.** A speech or statement made at a
time of leaving. [From Latin *valedīcere,* to say farewell : *valē,* VALE
(farewell) + *dīcere,* to say (by analogy with *benediction*).]

val·e·dic·to·ry (vál-i-díktəri) *adj.* Pertaining to or by way of a farewell.
~n., pl. **valedictories.** A farewell address.

Va·len·cia[1] (və-lén-shi-ə, -si-; *Spanish* ba-lénth-ya). Region of eastern Spain, lying on the Mediterranean coast and comprising the
provinces of Alicante, Castellón de la Plana, and Valencia. Its fertile coastal plain has won it the name of the "garden of Spain".

Valencia[2]. City in eastern Spain, with a port on the Mediterranean
lying on the river Turia. It is the capital of the province of the same
name and the third-largest city in Spain. It dates from at least the
second century B.C. and was the headquarters of the Loyalist government (1936–37) during the Spanish Civil War.

Va·len·ci·ennes (vál-ən-si-én, -ON-, -énz) *n.* A fine type of lace with
a floral pattern originally manufactured at Valenciennes, Nord département, France. Also called "Valenciennes lace".

va·lency (váylən-si) *n., pl.* **-cies.** Also *chiefly U.S.* **va·len·ce**
(váylənss). **1.** *Chemistry.* **a.** The capacity of an atom or group of
atoms to combine in specific proportions with other atoms or
groups of atoms. **b.** An integer, often one of several for any given
element, used to represent this capacity in terms of an arbitrary
assignment of 1 to an atom or group capable of forming a single
bond with chlorine and of –1 to an atom or group capable of forming a single bond with hydrogen. **2.** Broadly, the capacity of something to unite, react, or interact with something else. [Late Latin
valentia, strength, capacity, from Latin *valēns* (stem *valent-*), present
participle of *valēre,* to be strong.]

valency bond *n.* A covalent bond between atoms.

valency electron *n.* An electron in an outer or next to the outer
shell of an atom that can participate in forming chemical bonds
with other atoms.

valency shell *n.* A shell of an atom that contains the valency electrons.

val·en·tine (vál-ən-tīn) *n.* **1. a.** A greetings card of a sentimental or
humorous nature sent, usually, to one of the opposite sex on Saint
Valentine's Day (February 14). **b.** A card or gift sent as a token of
love to one's sweetheart on Saint Valentine's Day. **2.** A person
singled out as one's sweetheart on Saint Valentine's Day.

Valentine's Day, Valentines Day. Saint Valentine's Day *(see).*

Val·en·ti·no (vál-ən-téenō), **Rudolph** born Rodolpho Gugliemi di Va-
lentina d'Antonguolla (1895–1926). Italian film actor. His roles in
The Sheik (1921), *Blood and Sand* (1922), and other romantic films
of the silent cinema made him the leading idol of the 1920s.

Valéra, Eamon de. See **De Valéra, Eamon.**

va·le·ri·an (və-léer-i-ən) *n.* **1.** Any of various plants of the genera
Valeriana or *Centranthus,* having dense clusters of small white or
pinkish flowers; especially, *V. officinalis,* native to Eurasia and
widely cultivated. **2.** The dried roots of *V. officinalis,* used medicinally as a sedative. [Middle English, from Old French *valeriane,*

from Medieval Latin *valeriāna (herba),* apparently from Latin
Valeriānus, of Valeria, Roman province, from *Valerius,* name of a
Roman gens.]

va·le·ric acid (və-léer-ik, -lérrik) *n.* **Pentanoic acid** *(see).* [Obtained
from the root of VALERIAN.]

Va·lé·ry (va-le-rée), **Paul (Ambroise)** (1871–1945). French poet, essayist, and critic. He is best remembered for his philosophic poem
La jeune Parque (1917) and the collection *Charmes* (1922), which
included "Le Cimetière marin".

val·et (vál-it, -i, -ay ‖ *U.S. also* va-láy) *n.* **1.** A man's male servant,
who looks after his clothes and performs other personal services.
2. An employee in a hotel or on a ship, for example, who performs
personal services for guests or passengers.
~v. **valeted, -eting, -ets.** *—tr.* To act as a personal servant to;
attend. *—intr.* To work as a valet. [French, from Old French *vaslet,* originally "young nobleman", "squire", from Medieval Latin
vassellitus (unattested), diminutive of *vassus* (unattested), VASSAL.]

va·let de cham·bre (vál-ay də- shónbr, va-láy, shónbrə) *n., pl.* **va·
lets de chambre** *(pronounced as singular). French.* A man's valet.

Valetta. See **Valletta.**

val·e·tu·di·nar·i·an (vál-i-téw-di-naír-i-ən ‖ -tōō-) *n.* A chronic
invalid; especially, one excessively concerned with his health.
~adj. **1.** Chronically ailing; sickly; infirm. **2.** Endeavouring to recover health. **3.** Constantly and morbidly concerned with one's
health. [Latin *valētūdinārius,* in poor health, from *valētūdō* (stem
valētūdin-), state of health, from *valēre,* to be strong.] **—val·e·tu·di·
nar·i·an·ism** *n.*

val·e·tu·di·nar·y (vál-i-téw-din-ri, -əri ‖ -tōō-, -erri) *adj.* Valetudinarian.
~n. A valetudinarian.

val·gus (vál-gəss) *adj. Pathology.* Displaced outwards from the central line of the body.
~n., pl. **valguses. 1.** A deformity of the foot causing the sufferer to
walk on the outer side of the foot. **2.** Any of various other deformities involving a turning or twisting from the midline of the body.
[Latin *valgus†,* bowlegged.]

Val·hal·la (val-hál-ə) *n.* Also **Wal·hal·la** (val-, wal-, wol-). *Norse Mythology.* The great hall of immortality in which the souls of warriors
slain heroically were received by Odin and enshrined. [Old Norse
Valhöll : *valr,* those slain in battle + *höll,* hall.]

val·iant (vál-yənt) *adj.* Possessing, acting with, or showing valour;
brave; courageous. See Synonyms at **brave.** [Middle English *vali-
aunt,* from Anglo-French, from Vulgar Latin *valiente* (unattested),
from Latin *valēns,* present participle of *valēre,* to be strong.] **—val·
ian·cy, val·iance, val·iant·ness** *n.* **—val·iant·ly** *adv.*

val·id (vál-id) *adj.* **1.** Well-grounded; sound; supportable: *a valid
objection.* **2.** Producing the desired results; efficacious: *valid methods.* **3. a.** Legally sound and effective; incontestable; binding: *a
valid title.* **b.** Current; in effect: *valid till the end of the month.*
4. *Logic.* **a.** Containing premises from which the conclusion may
logically be derived: *a valid argument.* **b.** Correctly inferred or deduced from a premise: *a valid conclusion.* **5.** *Archaic.* Of sound
health; robust. [French *valide,* from Old French, from Latin *validus,* strong, effective, from *valēre,* to be strong.] **—va·lid·ly** *adv.*
—va·lid·i·ty (və-líddəti, va-), **va·lid·ness** *n.*
Synonyms: *valid, sound, convincing, telling, conclusive.*

val·i·date (vál-i-dayt) *tr.v.* **-dated, -dating, -dates. 1.** To declare or
make legally valid. **2.** To substantiate; verify. **—See** Synonyms at
confirm. —val·i·da·tion (-dáysh'n) *n.*

va·line (váyl-een, vál-) *n.* A crystalline amino acid, $C_5H_{11}NO_2$, essential for normal growth and health. [VAL(ERIC ACID) + -INE.]

va·lise (və-léez, va-, -léess) *n. Chiefly U.S.* A piece of hand luggage
such as a small suitcase or bag. [French, from Italian *valigia,* akin
to Medieval Latin *valisia†.*]

Val·i·um (vál-i-əm) *n.* **1.** A trademark for a tranquilliser or sedative
used to relieve tension and anxiety. Also called "diazepam". **2.** A
dose (e.g. a tablet) of Valium.

Val·ky·rie (val-kéer-i, -kírri, vál-kirri ‖ *U.S. also* -kír-i) *n.* Also **Wal·
ky·rie** (val-). *Norse Mythology.* Any of Odin's handmaidens who
hover over battlefields, choosing warriors to be victorious and conducting the souls of slain heroes to Valhalla. [Old Norse *valkyrja,*
"chooser of the slain".]

Va·lla·do·lid (vál-ə-dō-líd, -do-, -də-; *Spanish* bál-ya-do-léeth, -lée).
City in northern Spain, the capital of the province of the same
name, lying at the confluence of the rivers Pisuerga and Esgueva.

val·la·tion (va-láysh'n, və-) *n. Archaic.* An earthwork wall used for
military defence; a rampart. [Late Latin *vallātiō* (stem *vallātiōn-*),
from Latin *vallāre,* to surround with a rampart, from *vallum,* palisade, rampart, from *vallus,* stake.] **—val·la·to·ry** (-láytəri) *adj.*

val·lec·u·la (va-léckew-lə, və-) *n., pl.* **-lae** (-lee). *Biology.* A shallow
groove, depression, or furrow. [Late Latin, variant of Latin *valli-
cula,* diminutive of *vallēs,* VALLEY.] **—val·lec·u·lar** (-lər), **val·lec·u·
late** (-lət, -lit, -layt) *adj.*

Val·le d'A·os·ta (vál-lay da-óstə). Region of northwestern Italy, occupying the upper basin of the river Dora Baltea. It has a distinct
French linguistic and cultural heritage and was made an autonomous region in 1945. Aosta is the capital.

Val·let·ta or **Va·let·ta** (və-léttə). Capital city of Malta, lying on a
high promontory between two deep harbours on the northeastern
coast. It contains numerous relics of the Knights of Malta as well as
the 16th-century cathedral and governor's palace.

val·ley (vál-i) *n., pl.* **-leys. 1.** An elongated lowland between ranges
of mountains or hills, or other uplands, often having a river or

stream running along the bottom. **2.** An extensive land area drained or irrigated by a river system: *the Indus valley.* **3.** Any depression or hollow resembling or suggesting a valley, as where two slopes of a roof meet. [Middle English *valey,* from Anglo-French, from Vulgar Latin *vallāta* (unattested), from Latin *vallis, vallēs.*]

Valley of the Kings. Long, narrow valley in Egypt, the site of ancient Thebes and now occupied by Luxor and Karnak. It is the site of at least 60 tombs of Egyptian pharaohs of the 18th, 19th, and 20th dynasties, including the tomb of Tutankhamun.

Valley of the Ten Thousand Smokes. Valley in the Katmai National Monument, a national park in southern Alaska. Since the massive volcanic eruption of Mount Novarupta in 1912, the valley has emitted hot gases through its countless cracks.

val·lum (vál-əm) *n.* A large rampart erected as a means of defence, especially one built by the ancient Romans. [Latin, collective noun from *vallus,* stake.]

Va·lois[1] (vál-waa, val-wáa). French royal dynasty, from 1328–1589. They succeeded the Capetian line when Philip, Count of Valois, became Philip VI (1328–50). They were succeeded by the Bourbons.

Valois[2]. A historic region and former duchy of northern France.

Valois, Dame Ninette de. See **de Valois, Dame Ninette.**

va·lo·ni·a (və-lṓni-ə) *n.* An extract from the dried acorn cups of an oak tree, *Quercus aegilops,* of eastern Europe and Asia Minor, used chiefly in tanning and dyeing. [Italian *vallonia,* from Modern Greek *balania,* plural of *balani,* acorn, from Greek *balanos.*]

val·or·ise, val·or·ize (vál-ə-rīz) *tr.v.* **-ised, -ising, -ises.** To establish and maintain the price of (a commodity) artificially, especially by government action. [Back-formation from French *valorisation,* from *valour,* VALOUR.] **—val·or·i·sa·tion** (-rī-záysh'n || *U.S.* -ri-) *n.*

val·or·ous (vál-ərəss) *adj.* Having or showing great personal bravery; valiant. See Synonyms at **brave.** **—val·or·ous·ly** *adv.* **—val·or·ous·ness** *n.*

val·our, *U.S.* **val·or** (vál-ər) *n.* Courage and boldness, especially as shown in battle; bravery in the face of great danger. See Synonyms at **courage.** [Middle English *valour,* value, worth, from Old French, from Latin *valour,* from *valēre,* to be strong, be of value.]

Val·pa·rai·so (vál-pə-rī-zō || -ráy-; *Spanish* bal-pa-ra-ée-sō). City in central Chile, lying on the Pacific coast just to the northwest of Santiago. It is Chile's chief port and second largest city. The city is built on a natural amphitheatre, and funicular railways connect the industrial docklands with the higher residential districts.

valse (vaalss, valss) *n.* A waltz. Used especially in titles of pieces of music. [French.]

val·u·a·ble (vál-yoo-əb'l, -yŏŏb'l || -yəb'l) *adj.* **1.** Having considerable monetary or material value for use or exchange: *a few moments of your valuable time.* **2.** Highly useful or serviceable for a particular purpose: *valuable advice.* **3.** Having admirable or esteemed qualities or characteristics. —See Synonyms at **costly.**
—n. Plural. Valuable personal possessions, such as jewellery. **—val·u·a·ble·ness** *n.* **—val·u·a·bly** *adv.*

val·u·a·tion (vál-yoo-áysh'n) *n. Abbr.* **val.** **1.** The act or process of assessing the value or price of something; an appraisal. **2.** The assessed value or price of something. **3.** An estimation or appreciation of the worth, merit, or character of something: *set a high valuation on friendship.* **—val·u·a·tion·al** *adj.*

val·u·a·tor (vál-yoo-aytər) *n.* One who makes valuations; a valuer.

val·ue (vál-yōō, -yŏŏ) *n. Abbr.* **val.** **1.** An amount, as of goods, services, or money, considered to be a fair and suitable equivalent for something else; a fair price or return: *The meal was expensive, but good value.* **2. a.** The amount of money for which something can be exchanged on the open market; monetary or material worth. **b.** Power to buy or exchange: *The value of the pound has fallen.* **3. a.** Relative worth in terms of utility, quality, desirability, or importance: *the value of a good education; a novel of little value.* **b.** The usefulness of something in producing a particular effect or furthering a particular end: *The gesture cost them nothing, but had great propaganda value.* **4.** *Plural.* Those qualities regarded by a person or group as important and desirable; a set of standards and principles: *rejected the materialistic values of western society.* **5.** Precise meaning or import, as of a carefully considered word. **6.** *Mathematics.* An assigned or calculated numerical quantity. **7.** *Music.* The relative duration of a note or rest. **8.** The relative darkness or lightness of a colour in a picture. **9.** *Phonetics.* The sound quality of a letter or diphthong. **—good value.** *Informal.* Interesting and entertaining company: *She's very good value.* **—value for money.** Well worth the money paid; fair exchange.
~tr.v. **valued, -uing, -ues.** **1.** To determine or estimate the worth or value of; appraise. **2.** To regard highly; prize; esteem. **3.** To rate according to relative estimate of worth or desirability; evaluate. **4.** To assign a value to (a unit of currency, for example). —See Synonyms at **appreciate.** [Middle English, from Old French, from the feminine past participle of *valoir,* to be worth, from Latin *valēre,* to be strong, be of value.]

val·ue-ad·ded tax (vál-yoo-áddid) *n. Abbr.* **VAT, V.A.T.** A tax on the estimated market value added to any product or service at each stage of its manufacture or distribution, ultimately passed on to the consumer.

val·ued (vál-yōōd, -yŏŏd) *adj.* Highly regarded; much esteemed.

valued policy *n.* An **agreed-value policy** *(see).*

value judgment *n.* A judgment based upon or reflecting one's personal moral and aesthetic values; a subjective evaluation.

val·ue·less (vál-yoo-ləss, -liss) *adj.* Having no value; worthless.

val·u·er (vál-yoo-ər) *n.* A person whose job is to assess the monetary value of real property, such as land, buildings, or works of art.

val·vate (vál-vayt) *adj.* **1.** Having valvelike parts. **2.** *Botany.* Meeting at the edges without overlapping, as petals may.

valve (valv) *n.* **1. a.** Any of various devices that regulate the flow of gases, liquids, or loose materials through structures, such as piping, or through apertures by opening, closing, or obstructing ports or passageways. **b.** The movable control element of such a device. **c.** *Music.* A device in a brass wind instrument that permits change in pitch by allowing a rapid varying of the length of the tube. **2.** *Anatomy.* A membranous structure in a hollow organ or passage, as in an artery or vein, that retards or prevents the return flow of a bodily fluid. **3.** *Biology.* **a.** Any of the paired, hinged shells of many molluscs and of brachiopods. **b.** A similar paired part, as of the cell wall of a diatom. **4.** *Botany.* **a.** Any of the sections into which a seed pod or other dehiscent fruit splits. **b.** A lidlike covering of an anther. **5.** A partially evacuated sealed glass tube containing a cathode and anode, usually with one or more intervening electrodes (grids) between which a current can be maintained. The device is used for rectification and, when there are one or more grids, for amplification and as the main component of an oscillator. Also called "electronic valve", *U.S.* "vacuum tube". **6.** *Archaic.* Any of the leaves of a double or folding door.
~tr.v. **valved, valving, valves.** To provide with or control by means of a valve or valves. [Middle English, leaf of a door, from Latin *valva.*]

valve gear *n. Machinery.* The system of rocker arms, pushrods, and the like operating the valves in an engine.

valve-in-head engine *n. U.S.* An **overhead-valve engine** *(see).*

val·vu·lar (vál-vew-lər) *adj.* Pertaining to, having, or operating by means of valves or valvelike parts.

val·vule (vál-vewl) *n.* Also **val·vu·la** (-vew-lə) *pl.* **-lae** (-lee). A small valve or valvelike structure. [New Latin *valvula,* diminutive of Latin *valva,* leaf of a door, VALVE.]

val·vu·li·tis (vál-vew-lītiss) *n.* Inflammation of a valve, especially of a cardiac valve. [New Latin : *valvula,* VALVUL(E) + -ITIS.]

vam·brace (vám-brayss) *n.* Armour used to protect the forearm. [Middle English *va(u)mbras,* from Anglo-French *vauntbras,* short for Old French *avauntbras,* "forearm" : *avant,* before (see **vanguard**) + *bras,* arm, from Latin *bracchium.*] **—vam·braced** *adj.*

va·moose (və-mōōss, va-) *intr.v.* **-moosed, -moosing, -mooses.** *Chiefly U.S. Slang.* To leave hurriedly. [Spanish *vamos,* "let's go", from Latin *vādāmus,* from *vādere,* to go.]

vamp[1] (vamp) *n.* **1.** The upper part of a boot or shoe covering the instep and extending over the toe. **2. a.** Something patched up or refurbished. **b.** Something rehashed, such as a book based on old material. **3.** An improvised musical accompaniment.
~v. **vamped, vamping, vamps.** *—tr.* **1.** To provide (a shoe) with a new vamp. **2.** To patch up; refurbish. **3.** To put together; fabricate; or improvise. Usually used with *up.* **4.** *Music.* To improvise (a simple accompaniment or tune). *—intr.* To improvise simple accompaniments, variations of tunes, or the like. [Middle English *vampe,* from Anglo-French *vaumpé* (unattested), Old French *avantpie* : *avant,* before + *pie(d),* foot, from Latin *pēs.*] **—vamp·er** *n.*

vamp[2] *n. Informal.* An unscrupulously seductive woman who uses her sex appeal to entrap and exploit men.
~v. **vamped, vamping, vamps.** *Informal. —tr.* To seduce or exploit (a man) in the manner of a vamp. *—intr.* To play the part of a vamp. [Shortening of VAMPIRE.]

vam·pire (vám-pīr) *n.* **1.** In folklore, a reanimated corpse that rises from the grave at night to bite and then suck the blood of sleeping persons. **2.** One who preys upon others, such as an extortionist or a vamp. **3. a.** Any of various tropical American bats of the family Desmodontidae, that feed on the blood of living mammals. **b.** Any of various other bats, such as those of the family Megadermatidae, erroneously believed to feed on blood. In senses 3a and 3b, also called "vampire bat". [French, from German *Vampir,* from Magyar *vampir,* probably from Russian *upyr',* from Kazan Tatar *ubyr,* witch.] **—vam·pir·ic** (vam-pírrik) *adj.*

vam·pir·ism (vám-pīr-iz'm) *n.* **1.** Belief in the vampires of folklore. **2.** The practice of a vampire; bloodsucking.

van[1] (van) *n.* **1.** A covered motor vehicle for transporting goods and, sometimes, people. **2.** *Chiefly British.* A covered railway carriage for carrying goods, mail, or luggage, especially a **guard's van** *(see).* **3.** *British.* A gypsy **caravan** *(see).* [Short for CARAVAN.]

van[2] *n.* The vanguard; the forefront. [Short for VANGUARD.]

van[3] *n.* **1.** *Archaic.* Any winnowing device, such as a fan. **2.** *Poetic.* A wing. [Middle English *van(ne),* variant (western and southern) of FAN and partly from Old French *van,* both from Latin *vannus.*]

van[4] *n. British Informal.* An **advantage** *(see)* in tennis. **—van in.** Advantage to the server. **—van out.** Advantage to the receiver.

van·a·date (vánnə-dayt) *n. n.* Any of three anions, VO_3, VO_4, or V_2O_7. [From VANADIUM.]

va·nad·ic (və-náddik, -náydik) *adj.* Of or containing trivalent or pentavalent vanadium. [VANADIUM + -IC.]

va·nad·ic acid *n.* **1.** An acid containing a vanadate group, especially HVO_3, H_3VO_4, or $H_4V_2O_7$, not existing in a pure state. **2.** Vanadium pentoxide. [VANADATE + -IC.]

va·nad·i·nite (və-náddi-nīt) *n.* A deep ruby-red or yellow to brown mineral of vanadium and lead sometimes with impurities of arsenic and phosphorus, essentially $(PbCl)Pb_4(VO_4)_3$. [VANAD(IUM) + -IN + -ITE.]

va·na·di·um (və-náydi-əm) *n. Symbol* **V** A bright white soft ductile metallic element found in several minerals, notably vanadinite and carnotite, having good structural strength and used in rust-resistant high-speed tools, as a carbon stabiliser in some steels, as a titanium-steel bonding agent, and as a catalyst. Atomic number 23, atomic weight 50.942, melting point 1,917°C, boiling point 3,000°C, relative density 6.11, valencies 2, 3, 4, 5. [New Latin, after Old Norse *Vanadīs*, name of the goddess Freya : *vana-*, akin to *Vanr*, fertility god + *dīs*†, woman, goddess.]

vanadium pentoxide *n.* A yellow to red crystalline powder, V_2O_5, used as a catalyst in various organic reactions and as a starting material for other vanadium salts. Also called "vanadic acid".

vanadium steel *n.* Steel alloyed with vanadium for added strength, hardness, and high-temperature stability.

van·ad·ous (vánnə-dəss, və-náy-) *adj.* Of or containing divalent vanadium. [VANAD(IUM) + -OUS.]

Van Allen belt *n.* Either of two zones of electrically charged particles, trapped by the Earth's magnetic field, which form two belts above the atmosphere over the equatorial regions. They lie at about 3 200 kilometres (2,000 miles) and 17 700 kilometres (11,000 miles) from the Earth. [After J.A. *Van Allen* (born 1914), U.S. physicist.]

va·nas·pa·ti (və-núspə-ti, -náspə-) *n.* A hydrogenated vegetable fat used in India as a cooking oil in place of ghee. [Hindi, from Sanskrit, name of a plant : *vana*, forest + *pati*, lord.]

Van·brugh (vánbrə, *sometimes* van-brōō), **Sir John** (1664–1726). English architect and playwright. He designed Castle Howard and Blenheim Palace. His plays include *The Provok'd Wife* (1697), and *The Relapse* (1696).

Vance (vanss), **Cyrus** (1917–). U.S. statesman. He represented President Johnson in Korea (1968), and was U.S. negotiator at the Paris peace talks on Vietnam (1968–69). He was secretary of state (1977–80), U.N. special envoy in former Yugoslavia (1991), and co-chairman of the Yugoslavia Peace Conference (1992–93).

Van·cou·ver (van-kōōvər). City in southwestern British Columbia, Canada, lying across the Strait of Georgia from Vancouver Island. It is Canada's chief Pacific port, and third-largest city.

Vancouver Island. Island off British Columbia, Canada. It is the largest offshore island on the west coast of North America, occupying 32 137 square kilometres (12,408 square miles).

V & A., V and A. Victoria and Albert Museum.

van·dal (vánd'l) *n.* **1.** A person who wilfully or maliciously defaces or destroys public or private property. **2.** One who spoils or destroys artistic or cultural achievement. [From VANDAL.]

Van·dal (vánd'l) *n.* A member of a Germanic people that overran Gaul, Spain, and northern Africa in the fourth and fifth centuries A.D. and sacked Rome in A.D. 455. [Latin *Vandalus*, "wanderer" from Germanic.] **—Van·dal·ic** (van-dál-ik) *adj.*

van·dal·ise, van·dal·ize (vándə-līz) *tr.v.* **-ised, -ising, -ises.** To commit an act of vandalism on. [From VANDAL.]

van·dal·ism (vándə-liz'm) *n.* **1.** The wilful or malicious destruction of public or private property, especially of anything beautiful or artistic. **2.** The spoiling or destruction of artistic or cultural achievement.

Van de Graaff generator (ván də graaf, graf) *n.* An electrostatic generator in which electric charge is either removed from or transferred to a large hollow spherical electrode by a rapidly moving belt, in some configurations producing potentials over a million volts, and used with an acceleration tube as an electron or ion accelerator. [After Robert *Van de Graaff* (1901–67), U.S. physicist.]

Van·der·bilt (vándər-bilt), **Cornelius** (1794–1877). American businessman. He was founder of the family fortune which he built up on railway and shipping interests.

Van der Post (van dər pōst, fan), **Sir Laurens (Jan)** (1906–96). South African author. Among his best-known works are *The Lost World of the Kalahari* (1958) and *A Story like the Wind* (1972).

van der Rohe, Ludwig Mies. See **Mies van der Rohe.**

van der Waals force (ván dər waalz || wawlz) *n.* A weak interatomic or intermolecular attraction arising from the interaction of dipoles induced in neighbouring atoms or molecules. [After Johannes D. *van der Waals* (1837–1923), Dutch physicist.]

Van Diemen's Land. See **Tasmania.**

Van Dyck or **Vandyke** (ván dīk, van), **Sir Anthony** (1599–1641). Flemish painter. He was painter to Charles I, and is famous for his portraits of the English court. His style greatly influenced the development of British portraiture. His works include *Charles I on Horseback*, and *Thomas Killigrew and Lord Croft.*

Van·dyke (ván-dīk, van-) *n.* **1.** A painting by Sir Anthony Van Dyck. **2.** A Vandyke beard or collar.
—*tr.v.* **vandyked, -dyking, -dykes.** To cut or shape (cloth) with deeply indented or scalloped edges, as on a Vandyke collar.

Vandyke beard *n.* A short, pointed beard. Also called "Vandyke". [A style worn by subjects in many Van Dyck portraits.]

Vandyke brown *n.* Moderate to dark brown. [From its frequent use by VAN DYCK.] **—Van·dyke-brown** *adj.*

Vandyke collar *n.* A large collar of linen or lace having a deeply indented or scalloped edge. Also called "Vandyke". [A type of collar depicted in many Van Dyck portraits.]

vane (vayn) *n.* **1.** A thin plate of wood or metal, often shaped like a cock or an arrow, that pivots on an elevated vertical spindle to indicate the direction of the wind; a weather vane; a weathercock. **2.** Any of several usually relatively thin, rigid, flat, or sometimes curved surfaces radially mounted along an axis, that is turned by or used to turn a fluid, such as a blade in a turbine or a sail on a windmill. **3.** The flattened part of a feather, consisting of a series of barbs on either side of the shaft. **4. a.** The movable target on a levelling rod. **b.** A sight on a quadrant or compass. **5.** Any of the metal guidance or stabilising fins attached to the tail of a bomb or other missile. [Middle English *vane, fane*, Old English *fana*, banner, from Germanic *fanon* (unattested).]

Vä·nern (vénnərn, vaírnərn). Lake in southwestern Sweden, drained by the river Götaälv into the Kattegatt. It is the largest lake in Sweden and the third largest in Europe.

va·nes·sa (və-néssə) *n.* Any butterfly of the genus *Vanessa*, such as the painted lady and red admiral. Also called "vanessid butterfly". [New Latin (reason for name obscure).]

van Eyck (ván īk, van), **Jan** (*c.* 1390–1441). Flemish painter. He is noted for his realistic paintings, brilliant colouring, and minute detail. His works include *The Arnolfini Marriage, Man in a Red Turban*, and *The Adoration of the Lamb*, begun by his brother Hubert.

vang (vang) *n. Nautical.* A guy rope running from the peak of a gaff or derrick to the deck. [Earlier *fang*, a device for gripping, Old English, from Old Norse *fang*, catch, grasp; akin to Dutch *vang*, from *vangen*, to catch, seize.]

Van Gogh (ván gókh, van, góf || gō; *Dutch* khókh), **Vincent** (1853–90). Dutch painter. His early work portrayed Dutch peasant life in sombre, dark colours; his later work in Provence (1888) was painted in bold brilliant colours. His life was filled with suffering and despair, culminating in insanity and his suicide.

van·guard (ván-gaard) *n.* **1. a.** The foremost position in an army or fleet advancing into battle. **b.** The foremost or leading position, as in an artistic or intellectual trend or movement. **2.** Those occupying any such position. Also called "van". [Middle English *vantgard*, short for *avaunt garde*, from Old French. See **avant-garde.**]

va·nil·la (və-níllə) *n.* **1.** Any of various tropical American orchids of the genus *Vanilla;* especially, *V. planifolia*, cultivated for its long, narrow seed pods from which a flavouring agent is obtained. **2.** The aromatic seed pod of this plant. Also called "vanilla pod", *chiefly U.S.*, "vanilla bean". **3.** A flavouring extract prepared from these seed pods or produced synthetically. Also used adjectivally: *vanilla ice cream.* [Spanish *vainilla*, "little sheath" (from its elongated fruit), from *vaina*, sheath, pod, from Latin *vāgīna*.]

va·nil·lic (və-níllik) *adj.* Of, pertaining to, or derived from vanilla or vanillin.

va·nil·lin (və-níllin, vánnilin) *n.* A white or yellowish crystalline compound, $C_8H_8O_3$, found in vanilla pods and certain balsams and resins and used in perfumes, flavourings, and pharmaceuticals.

Va·nir (vaá-neer) *pl.n. Norse Mythology.* An early race of gods who dwelt with the Aesir in Asgard. [Old Norse *Vanr*, fertility god.]

van·ish (vánnish) *v.* **-ished, -ishing, -ishes.** —*intr.* **1.** To disappear or become invisible, especially quickly or in an unexplained or magical manner. **2.** To fade or decay to nothing; pass out of perceived existence: *The choir's last notes vanished.* **3.** *Mathematics.* To become zero. Used of a function or variable. —*tr.* To cause to disappear. [Middle English *vanisshen*, from Old French *esvanir* (present stem *esvaniss-*), from Vulgar Latin *exvānīre* (unattested), variant of Latin *ēvānēscere* : *ex-*, away from + *vānēscere*, to disappear, "become empty", from *vānus*, empty.] **—van·ish·er** *n.*

vanishing cream *n.* A cosmetic face cream containing less oil than cold cream, which becomes colourless when applied and is used as a powder base or skin cleanser.

vanishing point *n.* **1.** A point in a drawing at which parallel lines drawn in perspective converge or seem to converge. **2.** A point at which a thing disappears or ceases to exist.

van·i·ty (vánnəti) *n., pl.* **-ties. 1.** The quality or condition of being vain; preoccupation with or excessive pride in one's appearance or accomplishments; conceit. **2.** Lack of usefulness, worth, or effect; hollowness; futility; worthlessness. **3. a.** Something that is vain, futile, or worthless. **b.** Something about which one is vain or conceited. **4.** *U.S.* A dressing table. [Middle English *vanite*, from Old French, from Latin *vānitās* stem *vānitāt-*), from *vānus*, empty, vain.]

vanity case *n.* A small handbag or case used by women for carrying cosmetics or toiletries.

Vanity Fair *n. Sometimes small* **v**, *small* **f.** Any place or scene of empty, idle amusement and ostentation, especially the social world. [From the fair in Bunyan's *Pilgrim's Progress.*]

vanity unit *n.* A type of dressing-table for a bathroom or bedroom consisting of a small basin with a flat surround built into a free-standing cupboard unit.

van·quish (váng-kwish || ván-) *tr.v.* **-quished, -quishing, -quishes. 1. a.** To defeat or conquer in battle; subjugate. **b.** To defeat in any contest, conflict, or competition. **2.** To overcome or subdue (an emotion, for example); suppress: *His success vanquished his fears.* —See Synonyms at **defeat.** [Middle English *vencusen, vaynquysshen*, from Old French *vainquir* (present stem *vanquiss-*), variant of *vaintre*, from Latin *vincere.*] **—van·quish·a·ble** *adj.* **—van·quish·er** *n.* **—van·quish·ment** *n.*

Van Rie·beeck (van reé-bek, fan), **Jan (Anthonisz)** (1619–77). Dutch commander of the first settlement at the Cape of Good Hope, established in 1652.

van·tage (vaán-tij || ván-) *n.* **1. a.** An advantage in a competition or conflict; superiority. **b.** A position, condition, or opportunity likely to provide superiority or advantage. Often used in the phrase *vantage ground.* **2.** A position that affords a broad overall view or perspective as of a place or situation. Often used in the phrase *vantage point.* **3.** In tennis, an **advantage** *(see).* [Middle English, from Anglo-French, short for Old French *avantage*, ADVANTAGE.]

Van't Hoff (vont háwf, font, hóff), **Jacobus Henricus** (1852–1911).

Dutch chemist, a pioneer in the field of stereochemistry. In 1901 he was awarded the first Nobel prize for chemistry.

Va·nu·a·tu (vaánōō-aátōō). Formerly **New Hebrides.** Group of 12 small islands and numerous islets in the southwest Pacific Ocean. The largest island is Espiritu Santo. The islands are largely volcanic and forested. The chief exports are copra, fish, and beef. From 1897 the islands were administered as a condominium by France and Great Britain, until 1980 when they became the 44th member of the Commonwealth. Area, 12 190 square kilometres (4,707 square miles). Population, 170,000. Capital, Vila, on Efate. See map at **Pacific Ocean.**

van·ward (ván-wərd) *adj. Rare.* Located in the van or front; advanced.

vap·id (váppid) *adj.* **1.** Lacking life, spirit, or animation; dull; insipid: *vapid conversation.* **2.** Lacking taste, zest, or flavour; flat; stale: *vapid beer.* [Latin *vapidus.*] —**va·pid·i·ty** (va-píddəti, və-), **vap·id·ness** *n.* —**vap·id·ly** *adv.*

va·por·es·cence (váypə-réss'nss) *n.* The formation of vapour.

va·po·ret·to (váppə-rét-o, váypə-) *n., pl.* **-ti** (-tee) or **tos.** A steamboat carrying passengers along a regular route, especially one that operates like a bus along the canals of Venice. [Italian, diminutive of *vapore,* steamboat, ultimately from Latin *vapor,* steam.]

va·por·if·ic (váypə-ríffik) *adj.* **1.** Producing or turning to vapour. **2.** Having the nature of vapour; vaporous. [VAPOUR + -FIC.]

va·por·ise, va·por·ize (váypə-rīz) *v.* **-ised, -ising, -ises.** —*tr.* To convert (a solid or liquid) to vapour, especially by heating. —*intr.* To be converted into vapour. —**va·por·is·a·ble** *adj.* —**va·por·i·sa·tion** *n.*

va·por·is·er (váypə-rīzər) *n.* One that vaporises; especially, a device used to vaporise medicine for inhalation.

va·por·ous (váypərəss) *adj.* **1.** Pertaining to or resembling vapour. **2. a.** Producing vapours; volatile. **b.** Giving off or full of vapours. **3.** Insubstantial, vague, or ethereal: *"the imponderable mysterious and vaporous illusions of twilight"* (John Cowper Powys). **4.** Extravagantly fanciful; high-flown: *vaporous conjecture.* —**va·por·os·i·ty** (váypə-róssəti), **va·por·ous·ness** *n.* —**va·por·ous·ly** *adv.*

va·pour, *U.S.* **va·por** (váypər) *n.* **1.** Any barely visible or cloudy diffused matter, such as mist, fumes, or smoke, suspended in the air. **2. a.** The state of a substance that exists below its critical temperature and that may be liquefied by application of sufficient pressure. **b.** Broadly, the gaseous state of any substance that is liquid or solid under ordinary conditions. **3. a.** The vaporised form of a substance for use in industrial, military, or medical processes. **b.** A mixture of a vapour and air, such as the explosive petrol-air mixture burnt in an internal-combustion engine. **4.** *Archaic.* **a.** Something unsubstantial, worthless, or fleeting. **b.** A fantastic or foolish idea. **5.** *Plural. Archaic.* **a.** Exhalations within a body organ, especially the stomach, supposed to affect the mental or physical condition. **b.** A nervous disorder such as depression or hysteria. Preceded by *the.*
~*v.* **vapoured, -pouring, -pours.** —*tr.* To vaporise. —*intr.* **1.** To be emitted or dispersed as vapour. **2.** To engage in idle, boastful talk. **3.** *Archaic.* To rise as vapour. [Middle English *vapour,* from Old French *vapeur, vapour,* from Latin *vapor,* steam.]

vapour bath *n.* **1.** A closed compartment or bath with an apparatus for applying steam to the body. **2.** A bath taken in such a place.

vapour density *n.* The density of a gas or vapour divided by the density of hydrogen both at standard temperature and pressure.

va·pour·er moth (váypərər) *n.* A common moth, *Orgyia antiqua,* the tufted caterpillars of which are a serious pest of trees. [From VAPOUR (verb, in archaic sense, "to rise as vapour"), referring to the rapid flight of the male.]

va·pour·ing (váypəring) *adj.* Foolishly bombastic; boastful.
~*n.* Boastful or bombastic talk or behaviour. —**va·pour·ing·ly** *adv.*

va·pour·ish (váypərish) *adj.* **1.** Suggestive of or like vapour. **2.** *Archaic.* Affected by the vapours; inclined towards low spirits.

vapour lock *n.* A pocket of vaporised petrol in the fuel line of an internal-combustion engine that obstructs normal flow of fuel.

vapour pressure *n.* The pressure exerted by a vapour in equilibrium with its solid or liquid phase.

vapour trail *n.* A visible condensation trail in the sky caused by a high-flying aircraft passing through a region of supercooled air. Also called "condensation trail", "contrail".

va·que·ro (va-káir-ō || vaa-) *n., pl.* **-ros.** *U.S.* A cowboy; a herdsman. [Spanish, from *vaca,* cow, from Latin *vacca.*]

var. **1.** variable. **2.** variant. **3.** variation. **4.** variety. **5.** various.

va·ra (vaárə) *n.* A Spanish, Portuguese, and Latin American unit of linear measure, varying from 80 to 110 centimetres (32 to 43 inches). [Spanish and Portuguese, "rod", "yardstick", from Latin *vāra,* forked pole, from *vārus,* bent inward.]

va·rac·tor (vaír-áktər, -aktər) *n.* A semiconductor device with a capacitance that varies with the voltage applied to it. [*Var*ying re*actor.*]

Va·ra·na·si (və-raánə-si). City in the state of Uttar Pradesh, in north central India, lying on the river Ganges. It was formerly called Benares. It is the holiest Hindu city, called Kasi by Hindus, and has more than 1,500 temples, shrines, and palaces.

Va·ran·gi·an (və-ránji-ən) *n.* Any of a group of Scandinavian seafarers who established a dynasty in Russia in the 9th century, and from whom Byzantine emperors in the 10th and 11th centuries recruited their bodyguards (the *Varangian Guard*). [Medieval Latin *Varangus,* from Medieval Greek *Barangos,* from Old Norse *Væringi,* probably "confederate", from *vār,* agreement, pledge.]

var·ec (várrek) *n.* The ash of **kelp** *(see).* [French, from Old Norse *wrek* (unattested), something driven ashore, WRECK.]

Va·rèse (va-ráyz), **Edgard** (1883–1965). French-born composer. He emigrated to the United States (1916). His compositions, characterised by dissonance, unpitched sounds, and complex rhythms, include *Ionisation* (1931), and *Poème Electronique* (1958).

Var·gas (vár-gəss), **Getúlio (Dornelles)** (1883–1954). Brazilian politician. He seized power (1930) and won an election in 1934. From 1937 he governed as dictator after forming a fascist New State, modelled on Portugal. He was ousted in 1945 and re-elected in 1950. A political crisis (1954) led to his resignation and suicide.

va·ri·a (vaír-i-ə) *n.* A miscellany, especially of literary works. [Latin, neuter plural of *varius,* VARIOUS.]

va·ri·a·ble (vaír-i-əb'l) *adj. Abbr.* **var.** **1. a.** Liable, likely, or able to change or vary; subject to variation; changeable. **b.** Inconstant; fickle. **c.** Of uneven quality. **2.** *Mathematics.* Having no fixed quantitative value. **3.** Changing, as in direction or intensity: *variable winds.* **4.** Designating an electrical component, the value of which can be varied: *a variable resistor.*
~*n. Abbr.* **var.** **1.** Anything that varies or is liable to variation. **2.** A variable star. **3.** *Mathematics.* **a.** A quantity capable of assuming any of a set of values. **b.** A symbol representing such a quantity. **4.** *Logic.* **a.** A symbol often *p, q,* or *r,* representing a proposition. **b.** A symbol, often *x, y,* or *z,* representing a class of objects or the name of an individual object in a function or a sentence. —**va·ri·a·bil·i·ty** (-ə-bílləti), **va·ri·a·ble·ness** *n.* —**va·ri·a·bly** *adv.*

variable cost *n.* Cost that fluctuates directly with output changes.

variable star *n.* A star whose brightness varies because of internal changes or periodic eclipsing of component stars.

va·ri·ance (vaír-i-ənss) *n.* **1. a.** The act of varying; alteration or modification. **b.** The state or quality of being variant or variable; variation; difference. **c.** A difference between what is expected and what actually occurs. **2.** A difference of opinion; dissension; a dispute. **3.** *Law.* **a.** A discrepancy between two statements or documents in a legal proceeding. **b.** *U.S.* A licence to engage in an act contrary to a usual rule. **4.** *Statistics.* The dispersion of a set of data as measured by taking the mean of the squares of the variations from the mean of the frequency distribution. **5.** *Chemistry.* The number of thermodynamic variables required to specify a state of equilibrium of a system, given by the phase rule. —See Synonyms at **discord.** —**at variance.** **1.** In a state of discrepancy; differing; conflicting. Said of things: *The facts are at variance.* **2.** In a state of dispute or dissension; quarrelling: *The factions are at variance.*

va·ri·ant (vaír-i-ənt) *adj.* **1.** Having or exhibiting variation; differing. **2.** Tending or liable to vary; variable; changeable. **3. a.** Deviating from a standard or norm. **b.** Exhibiting slight difference.
~*n. Abbr.* **var.** Something that differs, usually only slightly, from another in form, such as a different spelling or pronunciation of the same word. [Middle English, from Old French, from Latin *variāns* (stem *variant-*), present participle of *variāre,* VARY.]

va·ri·ate (vaír-i-ət, -it, -ayt) *n.* **1.** *Statistics.* A random variable with a numerical value that is defined on a given sample space. **2.** *Rare.* A variable. [Latin *variāre,* VARY.]

va·ri·a·tion (vaír-i-áysh'n) *n. Abbr.* **var.** **1. a.** The act, process, or result of varying; change or deviation. **b.** The state or fact of being varied. **2.** The extent or degree of such varying or deviation: *a variation of ten kilograms in weight.* **3.** A natural compass error, **magnetic declination** *(see).* **4.** Something that is slightly different from another of the same type. **5.** *Biology.* **a.** Marked difference or deviation from characteristic form, function, or structure. **b.** An organism or plant exhibiting such difference or deviation. **6.** *Mathematics.* A function that relates the values of one variable to those of other variables. **7.** A musical form that is an altered version of some given theme, diverging from it by melodic ornamentation and by changes in harmony, rhythm, or key. **b.** Any of a series of such forms based on a single theme. **8.** In classical ballet, a solo dance. —See Synonyms at **difference.** [Middle English, from Old French, from Latin *variātiō* (stem *variātiōn-*), from *variāre,* VARY.] —**var·i·a·tion·al** *adj.*

var·i·cel·la (várri-séllə) *n.* **Chickenpox** *(see).* [New Latin, irregular diminutive of VARIOLA.] —**var·i·cel·loid** *adj.*

var·i·ces. Plural of **varix.**

varico–, varic– *comb. form.* Indicates varix or varicose veins; for example, **varicocele, varicosis.** [Latin *varix* (stem *varic-*), VARIX.]

var·i·co·cele (várri-kō-seel, -kə-) *n.* **1.** A varicose condition of the veins of the testicle, producing a swelling of the scrotum. **2.** Any of various other varicose conditions. [VARICO- + -CELE (tumour).]

va·ri·col·oured (vaír-i-kullərd) *adj.* Having a variety of colours; variegated; motley.

var·i·cose (várri-kōz, -kōss) *adj.* **1.** Designating blood or lymph vessels that are abnormally dilated, knotted, and tortuous, as in the legs or less commonly in the rectum or testes. **2.** Causing unusual swelling. [Latin *varicōsus,* from VARIX.]

var·i·co·sis (várri-kṓ-siss) *n.* The state of being varicose. [VARIC(O)- + -OSIS.]

var·i·cos·i·ty (várri-kóssəti) *n., pl.* **-ties.** **1.** Varicosis. **2. a.** A varicose distension or swelling. **b.** The state of having varicose veins.

var·i·cot·o·my (várri-kóttəmi) *n., pl.* **-mies.** Subcutaneous incision to remove varicose veins. [VARICO- + -TOMY.]

va·ried (vaír-id || -eed) *adj.* **1.** Having various kinds or forms; marked by variety. **2.** Modified or altered. **3.** Varicoloured; variegated. —See Synonyms at **miscellaneous.** —**var·ied·ly** *adv.*

va·rie·gate (vaír-i-gayt, -i-ə-) *tr.v.* **-gated, -gating, -gates.** **1.** To change the appearance of, especially by marking with different colours; streak. **2.** To give variety to; make varied. [Late Latin *variēgāre,* from Latin *varius,* VARIOUS.]

va·rie·gat·ed (váir-i-gaytid, -i-ə-) *adj.* **1.** Having streaks, marks, or patches of a different colour or colours. **2.** Having lighter or white areas due to mutation or infection, for example. Said of leaves and petals. **3.** Distinguished or characterised by variety; diversified.

va·rie·ga·tion (váir-i-gáysh'n, -i-ə-) *n.* The state of being variegated; diversified coloration.

va·ri·e·tal (və-rí-ət'l) *adj.* Of, indicating, or named after a biological variety. [From VARIETY.] **—va·ri·e·tal·ly** *adv.*

va·ri·e·ty (və-rí-əti) *n., pl.* **-ties.** *Abbr.* **var. 1. a.** The condition or quality of being various or varied; diversity. **b.** A lack of monotony or sameness that keeps something interesting. **2.** A number or collection of varied things, especially of a particular group; an assortment: *a great variety of races living in London.* **3. a.** A different kind, sort, or form of something of the same general classification. **b.** Something belonging to such a kind, form, or sort. **4.** *Biology.* **a.** A taxonomic group below the species. Used by specialists in different fields as a substitute for various taxonomic categories such as race, stock, strain, and breed. **b.** An organism, especially a plant, belonging to such a group. **5.** The type of theatrical entertainment or branch of the theatre consisting of variety shows. Also used adjectively: *a variety act.* See Synonyms at **musical comedy.** [French *variete,* from Latin *varietās* (stem *varietāt-*), from *varius,* VARIOUS.]

variety meat *n. U.S.* Offal.

variety show *n.* A theatrical entertainment consisting of successive diverse acts, such as songs, dances, and comedy sketches.

variety store *n. U.S.* A retail store carrying a large variety of cheap goods. Also called "variety shop".

va·ri·form (váir-i-fawrm) *adj.* Having a variety of forms; diversiform. [VARI(O)- + -FORM.]

vario-, vari- *comb. form.* Indicates variety or difference; for example, **variometer, variform.** [Latin *varius,* VARIOUS.]

va·ri·o·la (və-rí-ələ, váir-i-ólə) *n.* **Smallpox** *(see).* [New Latin, from Medieval Latin, pustule, from Latin *varius,* speckled, VARIOUS.]

va·ri·o·late (váir-i-ə-layt, -lət, -lit) *adj.* Having pustules or scars like those of smallpox.
—tr.v. **-lated, -lating, -lates.** To inoculate with smallpox. **—va·ri·o·la·tion** (-láysh'n) *n.*

va·ri·o·lite (váir-ə-līt) *n.* A basic rock, originally glassy, which has developed a variolitic texture. [Medieval Latin *variola,* smallpox, VARIOL(A) + -ITE.]

var·i·o·lit·ic (váir-i-ō-líttik) *adj.* Of or designating a structure or texture consisting of spherules of minute radiating fibres, generally of plagioclase, and having a pock-marked appearance.

va·ri·o·loid (váir-i-ə-loyd) *n.* A mild form of smallpox in persons who have previously been vaccinated or who have previously had the disease.
—adj. Resembling smallpox. [VARIOL(A) + -OID.]

va·ri·o·lous (váir-i-ōləss, və-rí-ə-ləss) *adj.* Pertaining to, characteristic of, or resembling smallpox. [VARIOL(A) + -OUS.]

va·ri·om·e·ter (váir-i-ómmitər) *n.* **1.** A variable inductor used to measure variations in terrestrial magnetism. **2.** A form of variable inductor. **3.** An indicator in a glider or other aircraft showing the rate of climb or descent. [VARIO- + -METER.]

va·ri·o·rum (váir-i-áwrəm, várri- ‖ -ó-) *n.* **1.** An edition particularly of the complete works of a classical author, with notes by scholars or editors. **2.** An edition containing various versions of a text.
—adj. Designating or pertaining to a variorum. [Short for Latin *editiō cum notīs variōrum,* edition with the notes of various (commentators), from *variōrum,* genitive plural of *varius,* VARIOUS.]

va·ri·ous (váir-i-əss) *adj. Abbr.* **var. 1. a.** Of diverse kinds. **b.** Unlike; different. **2.** More than one; numerous; several. **3.** Many-sided; varying; versatile. **4.** Having a variegated nature or appearance. **5.** Being one of a class or group but individual and separate: *The various reports all agreed.* **6.** *Archaic.* Changeable; variable.
—pron. Nonstandard. Some; a certain amount: *spoke to various of the demonstrators.* [Latin *varius,* speckled, variegated, changeable.] **—var·i·ous·ly** *adv.* **—var·i·ous·ness** *n.*

Var·is·can (vərískən) *adj.* Hercynian.

var·is·cite (várri-sīt) *n.* A green mineral, a hydrated phosphate of aluminium, essentially AlPO$_4$.2H$_2$O, that occurs as modular masses. [German *Variscit,* from Medieval Latin *Variscia,* ancient name of the Vogtland district of Saxony + -ITE.]

va·ris·tor (váir-ístər) *n.* A semiconductor device with a variable, voltage-dependent resistance; especially, one with a negative voltage characteristic. [From *varying* trans*istor.*]

va·ri·type (váir-i-tīp) *v.* **-typed, -typing, -typing.** *—tr.* To prepare and set (copy) on a Varityper. *—intr.* To use a Varityper. **—var·i·typ·ist** *n.*

Va·ri·typ·er (váir-i-tīpər) *n.* A trademark for a type of typewriter that can be used to prepare copy in a variety of typefaces.

va·rix (váir-iks) *n., pl.* **-ices** (várri-seez, váir-i-). **1.** A vein that is abnormally dilated and twisted. **2.** Any of the longitudinal ridges marking a resting stage in the development of the lip of a gastropod shell. [Latin, swollen vein.]

var·let (várlit) *n. Archaic.* **1.** An attendant or servant. **2.** A knight's page. **3.** A rascal; a knave. [Middle English, from Old French, variant of *vaslet, valet,* VALET.]

var·let·ry (várlitri) *n. Archaic.* **1.** A crowd of attendants or menials. **2.** A disorderly crowd; a rabble.

var·mint (vármint) *n. Regional.* A person or animal considered un-

desirable, obnoxious, or troublesome. [Variant of VERMIN.]

Var·na (várnə). City in eastern Bulgaria, lying on the Black Sea. It is the country's chief port and naval base, and a major industrial centre. It was called Stalin (1949–57).

var·nish (várnish) *n.* **1. a.** An oil-based preparation containing a solvent and an oxidising or an evaporating binder, used to coat a surface with a hard, glossy, thin film. Also called "oil varnish". **b.** A similar preparation consisting of shellac or a synthetic resin, which is dissolved in a solvent, such as alcohol. The solvent evaporates leaving a hard glossy film. Also called "spirit varnish". **c.** A naturally produced substance, such as the sap of certain trees, that dries forming a hard glossy surface. **2. a.** The smooth coating or gloss resulting from the application of varnish. **b.** Something resembling or likened to varnish. **3.** Any deceptively attractive external appearance; an outward show.
—tr.v. **varnished, -nishing, -nishes. 1.** To cover with varnish. **2.** To give a smooth and glossy finish to. **3.** To give a deceptively nice appearance to; gloss over. **4.** To cover (nails) with nail polish. [Middle English *vernisch,* from Old French *vernis,* from Medieval Latin *veronix,* sandarac, from Medieval Greek *berenikē,* perhaps from Greek *Berenikē,* Berenice, city in Cyrenaica, Libya, where varnishes were first used.] **—var·nish·er** *n.*

varnish tree *n.* Any of several trees having milky juice used to make varnish; especially, the **lacquer tree** *(see).*

var·si·ty (várssəti) *n., pl.* **-ties. 1.** *British Informal.* A university; especially, formerly, Oxford or Cambridge. Now chiefly used adjectivally to designate a sporting event between Oxford and Cambridge: *the varsity match.* **2.** *Australian, South African, & N.Z. Informal.* Any university. **3.** *U.S.* The principal team representing a university, college, or school in sports or other competitions. [Shortened and altered from UNIVERSITY.] **—var·si·ty** *adj.*

Var·u·na (vúrrōō-nə, várrōō-). *Hinduism.* The Vedic god of the skies and seas. [Sanskrit *Varuṇa.*]

va·rus (váir-əss) *n. pl.* **-uses. 1.** A deformity of the legs causing them to bend inwards; knock-knee. **2.** A deformity of the foot causing the person to walk on the inner edge of the sole. [Latin, "knock-kneed".]

varve (varv) *n. Geology.* **1.** A layer of sediment deposited in one year. **2.** A pair of distinct layers of sediment, indicating seasonal deposits. [Swedish *varv,* layer, turn, from *varva,* to bend, turn, from Old Norse *hverfa.*]

va·ry (váir-i) *v.* **-ied, -ying, -ies.** *—tr.* **1.** To make or cause changes in the characteristics or attributes of; modify or alter. **2.** To make diverse; give variety to: *vary one's diet.* **3.** To introduce under new aspects; express in a different manner. *—intr.* **1. a.** To undergo or show change: *a varying society.* **b.** To vary in direct relation to a specified variable. Used with *with: Her temper varies with the number of children at home.* **2.** To be different; deviate or depart. Used with *from.* **3.** To undergo successive or alternate changes in attributes or qualities. —See Synonyms at **change.** [Middle English *varien,* from Old French *varier,* from Latin *variāre,* from *varius,* speckled, changeable.] **—var·i·er** *n.*

vas (vass, vaass) *n., pl.* **vasa** (váy-zə, vaá- ‖ -sə). An organic vessel or duct. [Latin *vās†,* vessel.]

Va·se·ré·ly (va-za-re-leé; *Hungarian* vósho-ray), **Victor** (1908–97). Hungarian-born painter. He moved to Paris (1930) where his abstract works showed the influence of constructivism. By the 1960s he was regarded as one of the leading exponents of op art.

Va·sa·ri (və-saá-ri, *Italian* va-zaá-), **Giorgio** (1511–74). Italian painter, architect, and art historian. His *Lives of the Most Eminent Italian Architects, Painters and Sculptors,* traces the history of Renaissance art from Giotto to Michelangelo.

vas·cu·lar (váskew-lər) *adj. Biology.* Of, characterised by, or containing vessels for the transmission or circulation of plant or animal fluids such as blood, lymph, or sap. [Latin *vāsculum,* diminutive of *vās,* vessel, VAS.]

vascular bundle *n.* A strand of supportive and conductive plant tissue consisting essentially of xylem and phloem.

vas·cu·lar·i·sa·tion, vas·cu·lar·i·za·tion (váskewlə-rī-záysh'n ‖ *U.S.* -ri-) *n.* The development of vessels, especially new blood capillaries, in an organ or part.

vascular plant *n.* Any plant of the division Tracheophyta, which includes the ferns and seed-bearing plants characterised by a system of specialised conductive and supportive tissue.

vascular tissue *n.* Plant tissue consisting of vascular bundles.

vas·cu·lum (váskew-ləm) *n., pl.* **-la** (-lə). A small box or case used for carrying newly collected plant specimens. [Latin *vāsculum,* small vessel. See **vascular.**]

vas def·er·ens (déffə-renz ‖ -rənz) *n., pl.* **vasa deferentia** (-rénshi-ə). Either of a pair of vertebrate ducts that carry sperm from the epididymal duct to the ejaculatory duct. [New Latin, "carrying-off vessel".]

vase (vaaz, *old-fashioned* vawz ‖ vayz, *chiefly U.S.* vayss) *n.* An open vessel, usually tall and often shaped like a cylinder, made of glass, crystal, earthenware, or the like, and used chiefly for holding flowers or as an ornament. [French, from Latin *vās,* vessel, VAS.]

va·sec·to·my (və-séktəmi, va-) *n., pl.* **-mies.** Surgical cutting of the vas deferens, used, when both are cut, as a means of male sterilisation. [VAS (DEFERENS) + -ECTOMY.]

Vas·e·line (vássə-leen, -léen, -lin) *n.* A trademark for a petroleum jelly used primarily as a vehicle for external applications of medicinal agents, as a soothing or lubricating covering for the skins, and as a protective coating for metal surfaces.

vaso–, vas– *comb. form.* Indicates a blood vessel; for example, **vasomotor**. [Latin *vās*, vessel, VAS.]

va·so·ac·tive (váy-zō-áktiv, -sō– ‖ vá-) *adj.* Causing dilation or constriction of the blood vessels, especially the arteries.

va·so·con·stric·tion (váy-zō-kən-stríksh'n, -sō– ‖ vá-, -kon-) *n.* Constriction of a blood vessel.

va·so·con·stric·tor (váy-zō-kən-stríktər, -sō– ‖ vá-, -kon-) *n.* An agent, such as a nerve or a drug, that causes vasoconstriction. **—va·so·con·stric·tive** *adj.*

va·so·dil·a·ta·tion (váy-zō-dĭ-lay-táysh'n, -sō-, -lə- ‖ vá-, -dí-) *n.* Also **va·so·dil·a·tion** (-láysh'n). Dilation of a blood vessel.

va·so·di·la·tor (váy-zō-dī-láytər, -sō– ‖ vá-, -di-) *n.* An agent, such as a nerve or drug, that causes vasodilatation. **—va·so·di·la·tive** *adj.*

va·so·mo·tor (váy-zō-mótər, -sō– ‖ vá-) *adj.* Causing or regulating vasoconstriction or vasodilatation.

va·so·pres·sin (váy-zō-préssin, -sō– ‖ vá-) *n.* A hormone secreted by the pituitary gland that increases the reabsorption of water by the kidneys and constricts the blood vessels. Also called "antidiuretic hormone". [From *Vasopressin* (a trademark).]

vas·sal (váss'l) *n.* **1.** A person who held land from a feudal lord and received protection in return for homage and allegiance. **2.** One that is subject or subservient to another; a subordinate or dependent. Also used adjectivally: *a vassal state.* **3.** Loosely, a minion or slave. [Middle English, from Old French, from Medieval Latin *vassallus*, from Vulgar Latin *vassus* (unattested), servant, valet, from Celtic *wasso-* (unattested), young man, squire.]

vas·sal·age (vássəlij) *n.* **1.** The condition of being a vassal. **2.** The service, homage, and fealty required of a vassal. **3.** *Literary.* A position of subordination or subjection; servitude. **4.** The land held by a vassal; a fief. **5.** Vassals collectively or the vassals of a particular lord.

vast (vaast ‖ vast) *adj.* **vaster, vastest. 1.** Very great in size, number, amount, or quantity. **2.** Very great in area or extent; immense. **3.** Very great in degree or intensity: *made a vast difference.* —See Synonyms at **enormous.** ~*n.* **1.** *Archaic & Poetic.* An immense space. **2.** *Regional.* A great number, amount, or quantity. [Latin *vastus*, immense, vast.] **—vast·ly** *adv.* **—vast·ness** *n.*

vas·ti·tude (vaáss-ti-tewd, váss- ‖ -tōōd) *n.* Rare. Also **vas·ti·ty** (-təti). Immensity; vastness. [Latin *vastitās*, from *vastus*, VAST.]

vast·y (vaásti ‖ vásti) *adj.* -**ier, -iest.** *Archaic.* Vast.

vat (vat) *n.* A large vessel, such as a tub, cistern, or barrel, used to store or hold liquids. ~*tr.v.* **vatted, vatting, vats.** To place into or treat in a vat. [Middle English *vat, fat*, Old English *fæt*, from Germanic *fatam* (unattested), vessel.]

VAT, V.A.T. (*often* vat). Value-added tax.

vat dye *n.* Any of a series of dyes that produce a fast colour by impregnating the fibre with a reduced soluble form that is then oxidised to an insoluble form.

vat·ic (váttik) *adj.* Also **vat·i·cal** (-'l). Of or characteristic of a prophet; oracular. [Latin *vātēs*, prophet.]

Vat·i·can (váttikən) *n. Abbr.* **Vat. 1.** The official residence of the pope in Vatican City, within the city of Rome, Italy. Preceded by *the.* **2.** The papal government; the papacy. Also used adjectivally: *a Vatican decree.* [French, from Latin *Vāticānus (mōns)*, the Vatican (Hill), of Etruscan origin.]

Vatican City. *Italian* **Città del Vaticano.** Independent state, the smallest in the world, lying within Rome, in central Italy. Its independence was established by the Lateran Treaty (1929) between Pius XI and King Victor Emmanuel III. The state is ruled by the pope, and administered by a lay governor and council appointed by him. It is the supreme government of the Roman Catholic Church, which with tourism and sale of its postage stamps provides the state's income. St. Peter's basilica lies within the Vatican City, sometimes known as the Holy See. Area, 44 hectares (0.17 square miles). Population, 1,000.

Vatican Council *n.* Either of two Roman Catholic ecumenical councils: **1.** *First Vatican Council* (1869–70), which accepted the definition of papal infallibility. **2.** *Second Vatican Council* (1962–65), convened to discuss the position of the Church in the modern world and which led to wide-ranging reforms, in particular the replacement of Latin by vernacular languages in public worship.

Vat·i·can·ism (váttikən-iz'm) *n.* The policies and authority of the Vatican, especially with regard to papal infallibility. Often used derogatorily.

va·tic·i·nal (va-tíssin'l, və-) *adj.* Rare. Prophetic.

va·tic·i·nate (va-tíssi-nayt, və-) *v.* -**nated, -nating, -nates.** *Rare.* —*tr.* To prophesy; foretell. —*intr.* To be a prophet. [Latin *vāticinārī*, from *vātēs*, prophet. See vatic.] **—va·tic·i·na·tor** (-naytər) *n.*

va·tic·i·na·tion (va-tíssi-náysh'n, və-) *n.* Rare. **1.** The act of prophesying. **2.** A prediction or prophecy.

vau. Variant of **vav.**

vau·de·ville (vŏ-də-vil, váw-, -veel ‖ *U.S. also* vŏd-vil, váwd-, vód-) *n.* **1.** *U.S. Music hall (see).* **2.** A light comic play that often includes songs, pantomime, and dances. **3.** A popular, often satirical, song. [French, from Old French *vaudevire*, short for *chanson du Vau de Vire*, type of satirical song, especially those of O. Basselin, 15th-century poet born in *Vau de Vire*, in the Valley of Vire, a region in Normandy, from *vau, val*, VALE.]

vau·de·vil·li·an (vŏ-də-vílli-ən, váw-, -víl-yən, -véel- ‖ vŏd-, váwd-, vód-) *n.* One who works in vaudeville, especially as a performer.

~*adj.* Of or pertaining to vaudeville.

Vau·dois (vŏ-dwaa, -dwaaz, vŏ-dwaá, -dwaáz) *pl.n.* The **Waldenses** *(see).*

Vaughan Wil·liams (váwn wíl-yəmz), **Ralph** (1872–1958). British composer. He was greatly influenced by folk tunes and Tudor music, as is evident in his *Fantasia on a Theme by Thomas Tallis* (1910). His works include nine symphonies, the ballet *Job* (1931), and the opera *The Pilgrim's Progress* (1948–49).

vault¹ (vawlt ‖ volt) *n.* **1. a.** An arch, usually of stone, brick, or concrete, forming the supporting structure of a ceiling or roof. **b.** Any arched overhead covering resembling or thought to resemble a vault, such as the sky. **2.** A room or space with arched walls and ceiling, especially when underground, such as a cellar or storeroom. **3.** A room or compartment, often built of steel, for the safekeeping of valuables: *a bank vault.* **4.** A burial chamber, especially when underground. **5.** *Anatomy.* An arched cavity.

~*tr.v.* **vaulted, vaulting, vaults. 1.** To construct or supply with an arched ceiling; cover with a vault. **2.** To build or make in the shape of a vault; arch. [Middle English *vaute, voute,* from Old French, from Vulgar Latin *vol(vi)ta* (unattested), a turn, vault, variant of Latin *volūta,* feminine past participle of *volvere,* to turn.]

vault² *v.* **vaulted, vaulting, vaults.** —*tr.* To jump or leap over, especially with the aid of a support, such as the hands or a pole. —*intr.* **1.** To jump or leap, especially with the use of the hands or a pole. **2.** To achieve or surmount something, as if by bounding vigorously: *vault into a position of wealth.*

~*n.* The act of vaulting; a jump. [Old French *volter,* from Italian *voltare,* to turn (a horse), leap, gambol, from Vulgar Latin *volvitāre* (unattested), frequentative of Latin *volvere,* to turn.] **—vault·er** *n.*

vault·ing¹ (váwlt-ing ‖ vólt-) *n.* **1.** The practice or craft of building vaults. **2.** Vaults collectively. **3.** A vault or vaulted construction.

vaulting² *adj.* **1.** Leaping upwards or over. **2.** Reaching too far; exaggerated: *vaulting ambition.* **3.** Used for leaping over: *a vaulting horse.*

vaunt (vawnt ‖ vaant) *v.* **vaunted, vaunting, vaunts.** —*tr.* To describe in boastful terms; brag about. —*intr.* To boast; brag. —See Synonyms at **boast.**

~*n.* A boastful remark or speech of extravagant self-praise. [Middle English *va(u)nten,* from Old French *vanter,* from Late Latin *vānitāre* (attested only in the present participle *vānitāns*), to be vain, from Latin *vānus,* empty, vain.] **—vaunt·er** *n.* **—vaunt·ing·ly** *adv.*

vaunt-cour·i·er (váwnt-kŏŏri-ər, -kúrri- ‖ vaánt-) *n. Archaic.* One sent in advance, especially a herald. [Old French *avant-cour(r)ier :* *avant,* in front of + COURIER.]

vav (vawv, vaav) *n.* Also **vau** (vow), **waw** (wow). The sixth letter of the Hebrew alphabet. [Hebrew.]

vav·a·sour, vav·a·sor, vav·as·sor (vávvə-soor, -sawr ‖ -sōr) *n.* In the feudal system, a vassal who ranked directly below a baron or peer, with other vassals under him. [Middle English *vavasour,* from Old French, from Medieval Latin *vavassor,* perhaps contraction of *vassus vassōrum,* "vassal of vassals". See **vassal.**]

vb. verb; verbal.

V.C. 1. vice chairman. **2.** vice chancellor. **3.** vice consul. **4.** Victoria Cross. **5.** Vietcong.

VCR video cassette recorder.

VD, V.D. venereal disease.

v.d. 1. vapour density. **2.** various dates.

VDU *n., pl.* **VDUs** or **VDU's.** A **visual display unit** *(see).*

Ve·a·dar, Ve·a·dar (váy-ə-daar, vée-) *n.* An extra month of the Hebrew year, having 29 days, added in leap years after the regular month of Adar. Also called "Adar Sheni". [Hebrew *va'adhar,* "and Adar".]

veal (veel) *n.* The meat of a calf. [Middle English *veel,* from Old French, from Latin *vitellus,* diminutive of *vitulus,* calf, "yearling".]

veal·y (véeli) *adj.* -**ier, -iest. 1.** Of or like veal. **2.** Not fully developed; immature.

vec·tor (véktər) *n.* **1.** *Mathematics.* A quantity completely specified by a magnitude and a direction. Compare **scalar.** **2.** *Pathology.* An organism that carries pathogens from one host to another. **3.** Broadly, any force or influence.

~*tr.v.* **vectored, -toring, -tors.** To guide (a pilot, aircraft, or the like) by means of radio communication, according to vectors. [Latin *vector,* carrier, from *vehere* (past participle *vectus*), to carry.] **—vec·to·ri·al** (vek-táw-ri-əl ‖ -tó-) *adj.*

vector field *n.* A region of space in which a vector quantity exerts a field, at any point of which the field strength can be represented by a vector.

vector product *n.* A vector, **C**, that has magnitude equal to the product of the magnitudes of two vectors, **A** and **B**, and the sine of the angle between **A** and **B**, and having a direction perpendicular to the plane containing **A** and **B** and in a right-handed coordinate system directed so that a right-handed rotation about **C** carries **A** into **B** through an angle not greater than 180 degrees. It is usually written **A** × **B**. Also called "cross product". Compare **scalar product.**

vector sum *n.* A vector that is the resultant of two other vectors, as determined by the parallelogram rule.

Ve·da (váy-də, vée-) *n.* Any of the oldest sacred writings of Hinduism, including the psalms, incantations, hymns, and formulas of worship incorporated in four collections called the Rig-Veda, the Yajur-Veda, the Sama-Veda, and the Atharva-Veda. [Sanskrit *veda,* "knowledge".] **—Ve·dic** (-dik) *adj.*

ve·da·li·a (vi-dáyli-ə, və-) *n.* An Australian beetle, *Rodolia cardina-*

lis, that is used in all citrus-growing regions to control the scale insect *Icerya purchasi.* [New Latin : origin obscure.]

Ve·dan·ta (vi-dántə, ve-, və-, -daántə) *n.* The system of Hindu philosophy that further develops the implications in the Upanishads that all reality is a single principle, Brahman, and teaches that the believer's goal is to transcend the limitations of individual consciousness and realise his unity with Brahman. [Sanskrit *vedanta,* "complete knowledge of the Veda" : *veda,* VEDA + *anta,* end.] **—Ve·dan·tic** *adj.* **—Ve·dan·tism** *n.* **—Ve·dan·tist** *n.*

V-E Day (veé-eé) *n.* The day of victory for the Allied forces in Europe during World War II; officially, May 8, 1945. [Short for *Victory in Europe Day.*]

Ved·da, Ved·dah (véddə) *n.* Any of a small, dark-skinned, wavy-haired aboriginal people of Sri Lanka [Sinhalese, "hunter", from Dravidian, akin to Tamil *vēttam,* hunting.]

ve·dette, vi·dette (vi-dét, və-) *n.* **1.** A mounted sentry stationed in advance of an outpost. **2.** A small scouting boat used to observe and report on an opposing naval force. In this sense, also called "vedette boat". [French, from Italian *vedetta,* variant (influenced by *vedere,* to see) of *veletta,* from Spanish *vela,* a watch, from *velar,* to watch, from Latin *vigilāre,* from *vigil,* awake.]

Ve·dic (váy-dik, veé-) *adj.* Of or pertaining to the Veda or Vedas or to the Hindu culture that produced them.
~n. The early Sanskrit in which the Vedas are written.

veep (veep) *n. U.S. Slang.* **1.** A vice president. **2.** *Capital* **V.** The Vice President of the United States. [From the abbreviation V.P.]

veer¹ (veer) *v.* **veered, veering, veers.** *—intr.* **1.** To turn aside from a course, direction, or purpose; swerve; shift. **2.** To shift in direction by a clockwise motion. Used of the wind. Compare **back.** **3.** *Nautical.* To change the direction of a ship by turning the head away from the direction of the wind; wear ship. *—tr.* **1.** To alter the direction of; turn. **2.** *Nautical.* To change the course of (a ship) by turning away from the direction of the wind.
~n. A change in direction; a swerve. [French *virer,* from Vulgar Latin *vīrāre* (unattested), perhaps variant (influenced by Latin *vibrāre,* VIBRATE) of Latin *gȳrāre,* GYRATE.]

veer² *tr.v.* **veered, veering, veers.** *Nautical.* To let out or release (an anchor chain or line, for example). [Middle English *veren,* from Middle Dutch *vieren.*]

veg (vej) *n., pl.* **veg.** *British Informal.* A vegetable: *meat and two veg.*

Ve·ga (veégə || váygə) *n.* The brightest star in the constellation Lyra. [Medieval Latin, from Arabic *(al nasr) al wāqi',* the constellation Lyra, "the falling (vulture)".]

Ve·ga (Carpio) (váygə), **Lope (Félix) de** (1562–1635). Spanish poet and his country's first great dramatist. Most of his themes were drawn from history, and of almost 2,000 plays 500 still survive.

ve·gan (veégən) *n.* A strict vegetarian; one who consumes no animal products at all. [Shortened from VEGETARIAN.] **—ve·gan** *adj.*

veg·e·ta·ble (véj-təb'l, véjə-, véji-) *n.* **1. a.** A plant cultivated for an edible part or parts, such as its roots, stems, leaves, or flowers. **b.** The edible part of such a plant. **2.** An organism classified as a plant; a member of the plant kingdom. **3.** A person who leads a monotonous, passive, or merely physical (that is, without a normal mental life) existence.
~adj. **1.** Of, pertaining to, or derived from a plant or plants. **2.** Suggesting or like a vegetable, as in passivity or dullness of existence; monotonous; inactive. [Middle English, living, growing, from Old French, from Medieval Latin *vegetābilis,* from Late Latin, enlivening, from Latin *vegetāre,* to enliven, from *vegetus,* lively, from *vegēre,* to be lively.]

vegetable butter *n.* Any of various edible fatty substances resembling butter and of plant origin.

vegetable ivory *n.* A hard, ivory-like material obtained from the **ivory nut** *(see)* and used in making small objects such as buttons.

vegetable marrow *n.* A **marrow** *(see).*

vegetable oil *n.* Any of various oils obtained from plants, used in food products and industrially.

vegetable oyster *n.* A plant, **salsify** *(see).*

vegetable silk *n.* Any of several silky fibres from the seed pods of certain plants.

vegetable sponge *n.* A **dishcloth gourd** *(see).*

vegetable tallow *n.* Any of various waxy fats obtained from certain plants used in making soap and candles.

vegetable wax *n.* A waxy substance of plant origin, usually secreted in thin flakes by the epidermal cells.

veg·e·tal (véjit'l) *adj.* **1.** Of, pertaining to, or characteristic of a plant or plants. **2.** Pertaining to growth rather than to sexual reproduction; vegetative. [French, from Old French *vegeter,* to grow, from Late Latin *vegetāre,* from Latin, to enliven. See **vegetable.**]

veg·e·ta·ri·an (véji-taír-i-ən) *n.* **1.** One who eats no meat or fish. **2.** One who practises or advocates vegetarianism.
~adj. **1.** Eating no meat or fish. **2.** Pertaining to, practising, or advocating vegetarianism. **3.** Consisting of vegetables or nonflesh foods: *a vegetarian diet.* **4.** Serving, presenting, or advocating no meat or fish: *a vegetarian cookbook; a vegetarian café.* [From VEGETABLE (coined in 1847 by the Vegetarian Society at Ramsgate).]

veg·e·ta·ri·an·ism (véji-taír-i-ən-iz'm) *n.* The practice of or belief in avoiding eating meat or fish or, more strictly, eating only vegetables and plant products, usually for health or moral reasons.

veg·e·tate (véji-tayt) *intr.v.* **-tated, -tating, -tates.** **1.** To grow or sprout as a plant does. **2.** *Pathology.* To grow or spread abnormally. **3.** To lead an existence that is monotonous, passive, or lacks mental stimulation. [Late Latin *vegetāre,* to grow, from Latin, to enliven. See **vegetable.**]

veg·e·ta·tion (véji-táysh'n) *n.* **1.** The plants of an area or region; plant life collectively. **2.** The act or process of vegetating. **3.** *Pathology.* Any abnormal growth on the body.

veg·e·ta·tive (véji-tətiv, -taytiv) *adj.* Also **veg·e·tive** (-tiv). **1.** Of, pertaining to, or characteristic of plants or plant growth. **2.** *Biology.* **a.** Of, pertaining to, or capable of growth. **b.** Of, pertaining to, or functioning in processes such as growth or nutrition, rather than sexual reproduction. **c.** Of or pertaining to asexual reproduction, such as fission or budding. **3.** Monotonous, passive, or lacking mental stimulation.

ve·he·ment (veé-ə-mənt, -i- || -hə-, -hi-) *adj.* **1.** Characterised by forcefulness of expression or intensity of emotion, passion, or conviction; ardent; emphatic: *vehement denial.* **2.** Marked by or full of vigour or energy; strong; violent. [Old French, from Latin *vehemēns*† (stem *vehement-*).] **—ve·he·mence, ve·he·men·cy** *n.* **—ve·he·ment·ly** *adv.*

ve·hi·cle (veé-ik'l, -ək'l || -hick'l) *n.* **1.** Any conveyance for carrying passengers, goods, or equipment, moving along the ground or in the air or space, often one moving on wheels such as a car. **2.** Anything through or by which something, such as thought, power or information is conveyed, transmitted, expressed, or achieved: *the play was a vehicle for her political views.* **3.** A play, role, or piece of music used to display the special talents of one performer or company. **4.** In pharmacology, a substance of no therapeutic value used as the medium in which active medicines are administered. **5.** A substance, such as oil, in which paint pigments are mixed for application. [French *véhicule,* from Latin *vehiculum,* from *vehere,* to carry.] **—ve·hic·u·lar** (vi-híckew-lər, və- || vee-) *adj.*

veil (vayl) *n.* **1.** A piece of cloth, often wide-meshed and semi-transparent, worn by women over the head, shoulders, and often part of the face for concealment, protection, or as a token of modesty. **2.** A length of netting attached to a woman's hat or headdress for decoration, hanging before all or part of the face. **3.** The part of a nun's headdress that frames the face and falls over the shoulders. **4.** A piece of light fabric hung to separate or conceal what is behind it; a curtain. **5.** Anything that conceals, separates, or screens like a curtain: *a veil of secrecy.* **6.** *Biology.* A membranous covering, such as that partially or completely enveloping the developing fruiting body of certain mushrooms; a velum. **—beyond the veil.** In the afterlife; after death. **—draw a veil over.** To refrain from discussing or describing. **—take the veil.** To become a nun.
~v. **veiled, veiling, veils.** *—tr.* **1.** To cover with a veil. **2.** To conceal, mask, or disguise with or as if with a veil: *veiling kindness under apparent severity.* *—intr.* To wear a veil. [Middle English *veile,* from Anglo-French, from Latin *vēla,* neuter plural of *vēlum,* covering, veil.]

veiled (vayld) *adj.* **1.** Covered with a veil. **2.** Partially concealed, masked, or disguised: *veiled threats; veiled promises.*

veil·ing (váyling) *n.* **1.** A veil. **2.** Gauzy material used for veils.

vein (vayn) *n.* **1.** *Anatomy.* A vessel that transports blood towards the heart. **2.** Loosely, any blood vessel. **3.** *Botany.* Any of the vascular bundles that form the branching framework and support of a leaf. **4.** *Zoology.* Any of the chitinous, usually longitudinal ribs that stiffen and support the wing of an insect. **5.** *Geology.* A sheet of rock or mineral which infills a fissure or crevice in a pre-existing rock and is an economic source of ore; a lode. Compare **bed, mass.** **6.** A long, wavy strip with a colour different from its surround, as in wood or marble, or as mould in cheese. **7.** Any fissure, crack, or cleft. **8.** A distinctive character, quality, or tendency; a strain or streak: *a vein of pessimism.* **9.** A transient or temporary attitude or mood; turn of mind: *a talk in a serious vein.*
~tr.v. **veined, veining, veins.** **1.** To supply or fill in streaked patterns with or as if with veins. **2.** To mark or decorate with veins. [Middle English *veine,* from Old French, from Latin *vēna*†, vein.] **—vein·al, vein·y** *adj.*

veined (vaynd) *adj.* Exhibiting veins; having veinlike features or markings.

vein·let (váyn-lət, -lit) *n.* A small or secondary vein, as of an insect's wing.

vein·stone (váyn-stōn) *n.* Mineral matter in a vein exclusive of the ore; gangue.

Ve·la (veélə) *n.* A constellation of the Southern Hemisphere in the Milky Way, near Antlia and Carina. [Latin *vēla,* sail, VEIL (from the sail-like shape of the constellation).]

ve·la·men (vi-láy-mən, və-, -mən) *n., pl.* **velamina** (-lámminə). **1.** *Anatomy.* Any membranous covering or integument; a velum. **2.** *Botany.* The spongy outer covering of the aerial roots of epiphytic orchids and certain other plants, capable of absorbing atmospheric moisture. [Latin *vēlamen,* covering, from *vēlāre,* to cover, from *vēlum,* covering. See **velum.**]

ve·lar (veélər) *adj.* **1. a.** Of or pertaining to a velum. **b.** Concerning or using the soft palate. **2.** *Phonetics.* Formed with the back of the tongue on or near the soft palate, as (g) in *good* and (k) in *cup.*
~n. A velar sound. Also called "guttural". [New Latin *velaris,* from Latin *vēlum,* VELUM.]

ve·lar·ise, ve·lar·ize (veélə-rīz) *tr.v.* **-ised, -ising, ises.** *Phonetics.* To articulate (a sound) by retracting the back of the tongue towards the soft palate. **—ve·lar·is·a·tion** (-rī-záysh'n || *U.S.* -ri-) *n.*

ve·late (veél-ayt, -ət, -it) *adj. Biology.* Having or covered by a velum or veil. [Latin *vēlātus,* past participle of *vēlāre,* to cover, from *vēlum,* veil, covering. See **velum.**]

Ve·láz·quez (vi-láss-kwiz, ve-, -kiz, -kez, -kwith; *Spanish* be-láth-keth), **Diego Rodriguez de Silva y** (1599–1660). Spanish painter. He was appointed (1623) court painter to Philip IV, and worked on many portraits of the royal family. Among his other works are *Pope Innocent X* and the *Rokeby Venus*.

Vel·cro (vél-krō) *n.* A trademark for a material used as a fastener, usually consisting of a backing with a surface of minute nylon hooks and loops that fasten tightly with another piece of Velcro when pressed together. The two surfaces can be separated with a strong tug or abrupt pulling action.

veld, veldt (felt, velt) *n.* **1. a.** The open grassland area of South Africa; open country. **b.** Grazing or farming land. **2.** A particular tract of such land. [Afrikaans *veld,* from Middle Dutch *velt, veld,* field, open country.]

veld·skoen (félt-skŏŏn) *n.* A **velskoen** *(see).* [Afrikaans, "field shoe", alteration of VELSKOEN.]

vel·i·ger (véllijər) *n.* The free-swimming larva of certain marine gastropods. [New Latin : *vel(um),* sail + *-ger,* -GEROUS.]

vel·le·i·ty (ve-lée-əti, və-, -láy-) *n., pl.* **-ties.** *Rare.* **1.** The lowest level of volition. **2.** A mere wish not accompanied by action or effort to obtain it. [Medieval Latin *velleitās,* from Latin *velle,* to wish.]

vel·lum (véllәm) *n.* **1.** A fine parchment made from the skins of calf, lamb, or kid and used for the pages and binding of fine books. **2.** A work written or printed on vellum. **3.** A heavy off-white fine-quality paper resembling vellum. [Middle English *velim,* from Old French *velin,* from *veel,* calf, VEAL.] **—vel·lum** *adj.*

ve·lo·ce (vi-lóchi, ve-, və-) *adv. Music.* Rapidly. Used as a direction. [Italian, from Latin *vēlōx* (stem *vēlōc-*), fast. See **velocity.**]

vel·o·cim·e·ter (vél-ō-símmitər, véel-) *n.* A device for measuring velocity or speed. [Latin *vēlōx* (stem *vēlōc-*) + -METER.]

ve·loc·i·pede (vi-lóssi-peed, və-) *n.* **1.** An early bicycle propelled by pushing the feet along the ground while straddling the vehicle. **2.** Any of several early bicycles having pedals attached to the front wheel. [French *vélocipède,* "swift-footed" : Latin *vēlōx,* fast (see **velocity**) + -PED.]

ve·loc·i·ty (vi-lóssəti, və-) *n., pl.* **-ties.** **1.** Broadly, rapidity or speed. **2.** *Abbr.* **v** *Physics.* A vector quantity, the rate of change of position in a given direction. **3.** Distance travelled in a given amount of time. [French *vélocité,* from Latin *vēlōcitās* (stem *vēlōcitāt-*), from *vēlōx* (stem *vēlōc-*), fast.]

velocity modulation *n.* The modulation of an electron beam by alternately accelerating and decelerating them by means of a radio-frequency field in a cavity resonator.

ve·lo·drome (véel-ə-drōm, vél-, -ō-) *n.* A sports arena specially built with a banked track for cycle and, often, motorcycle racing. [French *vélodrome,* from Latin *vēlōx,* swift + -DROME.]

ve·lours, ve·lour (və-lóor) *n., pl.* **-lours** (-lóor). **1.** Any of various closely napped, velvet-like fabrics, used chiefly for clothing and upholstery. **2.** A felt resembling velvet, used in making hats. [French, from Old French *velo(u)s,* from Latin *villōsus,* hairy, from *villus,* shaggy hair, wool.]

ve·lou·té (vi-lŏŏ-tay, ve-, və- || *U.S.* véllŏŏ-táy) *n.* A white sauce made with flour, butter, and a chicken or veal stock. [French, "velvety".]

vel·skoen (fél-skŏŏn, vél-) *n. South African.* A shoe or ankle boot of rough suede. Also called "veldskoen". [Afrikaans, "hide shoe".]

ve·lum (vée-ləm) *n., pl.* **-la** (-lə). **1.** *Biology.* A covering or partition of thin membranous tissue, such as the veil of a mushroom. **2.** *Anatomy.* Any of various veil-like structures, such as the soft palate. [New Latin, from Latin *vēlum,* veil, covering, sail.]

ve·lure (və-léwr, -lóor) *n.* **1.** *Archaic.* Velvet or a velvet-like fabric. **2.** A soft pad used for smoothing silk hats. [Variant of French *velours,* VELOURS.]

ve·lu·ti·nous (vi-lŏŏ-tinəss, və-, -léw-) *adj.* Covered with dense, soft, silky hairs; velvety. [New Latin *velutinus,* from Medieval Latin *velūtum,* velvet, from *villūtus,* velvety, shaggy. See **velvet.**]

vel·vet (vélvit) *n.* **1. a.** A fabric made usually of silk or a synthetic fibre such as rayon or nylon, and having a smooth, dense pile and a plain back. **b.** Anything likened to the surface of this fabric. **2.** Smoothness; softness. **3.** The soft covering on the newly developing antlers of deer and related animals. **—on velvet.** A position of prosperity or advantage.

~adj. **1.** Made of or covered with velvet. **2.** Resembling velvet. **3.** Soft and rich: *velvet tones.* [Middle English *veluet,* from Old French *veluotte,* from *velu,* shaggy, from Medieval Latin *villūtus,* from Latin *villus,* shaggy hair, wool.] **—vel·vet·y** *adj.*

vel·vet·een (vélvi-téen) *n.* A velvet-like fabric made of cotton.

Ven. venerable.

ve·na (vée-nə, váy-) *n., pl.* **-nae** (-nee, -nī). *n. Anatomy.* A vein. [Latin *vēna,* VEIN.]

ve·na ca·va (káy-və, kaá-) *pl.* **venae cavae** (-vee, -vī). Either of the two large veins in air-breathing vertebrates that enter and return blood to the right atrium of the heart. [Latin, "hollow vein".]

ve·nal (véen'l) *adj.* **1. a.** Open or susceptible to bribery. **b.** Capable of betraying one's honour, duty, or scruples for a price; corruptible. **2.** Marked by corrupt or morally reprehensible dealings: *a venal era.* **3.** Obtainable by purchase or bribery rather than by merit. [Latin *vēnālis,* for sale, from *vēnum,* sale.] **—ve·nal·ly** *adv.*

ve·nal·i·ty (vee-nál-əti, vi-) *n., pl.* **-ties.** **1.** The quality of being open to bribery or corruption. **2.** The use of a position of trust for dishonest gain.

ve·nat·ic (vee-náttik, vi-) *adj.* Also **ve·nat·i·cal** (-'l). **1.** Pertaining to or used in hunting. **2.** Devoted to or engaged in hunting for sport or livelihood. [Latin *vēnāticus,* from *vēnārī,* to hunt.]

ve·na·tion (vee-náysh'n, ve-) *n.* The distribution or arrangement of veins in a leaf or insect's wing. [From VENA.] **—ve·na·tion·al** *adj.*

vend (vend) *v.* **vended, vending, vends.** *—tr.* **1.** *Law.* To sell. **2.** To sell small goods, especially in the street; peddle. **3.** *Rare.* To offer (an idea, for example) for public consideration. *—intr.* **1.** To sell goods; be a vendor. **2.** To have a market. [French *vendre,* from Latin *vēndere* : *vēnum,* sale + *dare,* to give.]

Ven·da[1] (vén-də) *n., pl.* **-das** or collectively **Venda.** **1.** A member of a black South African people living chiefly in the northeast of the country. **2.** Their Bantu language. **—Ven·da** *adj.*

Venda[2]**.** One of the former Bantu homelands in South Africa, intended for the Venda and lying in what is now Northern Province. Only South Africa recognised it officially. Area, 6 500 square kilometres (2,509 square miles). Population (Venda), 350,000 (plus 112,000 in South Africa). Capital, Thohoyandou.

ven·dace (vén-dayss) *n., pl.* **-daces** or collectively **vendace.** A small whitefish, *Coregonus albula,* found in certain lakes in northern Europe. [New Latin *vandesius,* from Old French *vendese, vendoise,* from Gaulish *vindesia* (unattested); akin to Gaulish *vindos* (unattested), white.]

vend·ee (vén-dée) *n.* A buyer.

Ven·dée (VON-dáy). Département in western France, lying on the Bay of Biscay. It is largely an agricultural region, with some forest land and fishing ports. The administrative centre is La Roche-sur-Yon. The Vendée Wars were a series of peasant revolts (1793–96).

ven·det·ta (ven-déttə, vén-) *n.* **1.** A hereditary blood feud between two families, perpetuated by retaliatory acts of revenge. **2.** A hostile and malicious campaign. **3.** Any act or attitude motivated by vengeance. [Italian, revenge, from Latin *vindicta,* from the feminine past participle of *vindicāre,* to revenge, VINDICATE.]

vend·i·ble (véndəb'l) *adj.* Capable of being sold; suitable for sale. *~n.* Something that can be sold.

vending machine *n.* A machine that dispenses goods such as cigarettes or confectionery when money is inserted. Also called "automat", "vendor".

ven·dor, ven·der (vén-dər, *for sense 2 also* -dór) *n.* **1.** A person who sells or vends; a pedlar. **2.** *Law.* The party to a contract who sells something, especially a piece of property. **3.** A vending machine.

ven·due (vén-dew || -dŏŏ, *U.S. also* -dŏŏ) *n. U.S.* A public sale; an auction. [Dutch *vendu,* from Old French *vendue,* from *vendre,* VEND.]

ve·neer (və-néer) *n.* **1.** A thin finishing or surface layer, as of fine wood or laminated plastic, bonded to an inferior substratum, such as an inexpensive wood. **2.** Any of the thin layers glued together in making plywood. **3.** An outward show that enhances but misrepresents what lies beneath; a superficially impressive appearance: *a veneer of politeness.*

~tr.v. **veneered, -neering, -neers.** **1.** To overlay (a surface) with a decorative or fine material. **2.** To glue together (layers of wood) in making plywood. **3.** To conceal (something common or crude) with an attractive but superficial appearance; gloss over. [Earlier *fineer,* from German *Furnier,* from *furniren,* to furnish, veneer, from French *fournir,* to FURNISH.] **—ve·neer·er** *n.*

ve·neer·ing (və-néer-ing) *n.* **1.** Material used as a veneer. **2.** A surface of veneer.

venepuncture. Variant of **venipuncture.**

ven·er·a·ble (vénnə-rəb'l) *adj.* **1.** Worthy of reverence or respect by virtue of dignity, character, position, or age. **2.** Commanding respect or reverence by association: *venerable relics.* **3.** *Abbr.* **V., Ven.** Honoured above others. Used as: **a.** A title of respect for an Anglican archdeacon. **b.** A title given to a Roman Catholic who has attained the first degree of sanctity. —See Synonyms at **old.** [Middle English, from Old French, from Latin *venerābilis,* from *venerārī,* VENERATE.] **—ven·er·a·ble·ness, ven·er·a·bil·i·ty** (-rə-bílləti) *n.* **—ven·er·a·bly** *adv.*

ven·er·ate (vénnə-rayt) *tr.v.* **-ated, -ating, -ates.** To regard with respect, reverence, or heartfelt deference. See Synonyms at **revere.** [Latin *venerārī,* from *venus* (stem *vener-*), love.] **—ven·er·a·tor** *n.*

ven·er·a·tion (vénnə-ráysh'n) *n.* **1.** The act of venerating. **2.** Profound respect or reverence. **3.** The condition or status of one who is venerated. —See Synonyms at **honour.**

ve·ne·re·al (vi-néer-i-əl, və-) *adj.* **1.** Of or pertaining to sexual intercourse. **2. a.** Transmitted by sexual intercourse. **b.** Of or pertaining to venereal disease. **3.** Of or pertaining to the genitals. [Middle English *venereall*e, from Latin *venereus,* from *venus* (stem *vener-*), love, lust.]

venereal disease *n. Abbr.* **VD** Any of several contagious diseases, such as syphilis and gonorrhoea, contracted through sexual intercourse.

ve·ne·re·ol·o·gy (vi-néer-i-óllәji, və-) *n.* The medical study of venereal disease. [VENERE(AL) + -LOGY.] **—ve·ne·re·ol·o·gist** *n.*

ven·er·y[1] (vénnəri) *n. Archaic.* Indulgence in or the pursuit of sexual activity. [Middle English *venerie,* from Medieval Latin *veneria,* from Latin *venus* (stem *vener-*), love.]

venery[2] *n. Archaic.* The art, act, or sport of hunting; the chase. [Middle English *venerie,* from Old French, from *vener,* to hunt, from Latin *vēnārī.*]

ven·e·sec·tion (vénni-séksh'n, véeni-, -seksh'n) *n. Surgery.* **Phlebotomy** *(see).* [Medieval Latin *vēnae sectiō,* cutting of a vein : Latin *vēnae,* genitive of *vēna,* vein, VENA + *sectiō,* SECTION.]

Ve·ne·tia (vi-née-shə, və-, ve-, -shi-ə). *Italian* **Veneto.** Region of northeastern Italy, on the Adriatic Sea. Venice is the capital.

Ve·ne·tian (vi-néesh'n, və-, -néeshi-ən) *adj.* Of or pertaining to Venice, its culture, or its inhabitants.
~n. 1. A native or inhabitant of Venice. **2.** *Usually small* **v.** A venetian blind. [Middle English *Venecien,* from Old French, from Medieval Latin *Venetiānus,* from Latin *Venetia,* VENICE.]
venetian blind *n. Sometimes capital* **V.** *Often plural.* A window screen consisting of a number of thin horizontal slats that may be raised and lowered by means of one cord and all set at a desired angle by means of another cord, thus regulating the amount of light admitted.
venetian blue *n.* Strong blue to greenish blue.
Venetian glass *n.* Fine, delicate glassware originally made near Venice.
venetian red *n.* **1.** Deep to strong reddish brown. **2.** A pigment of this colour made from ferric oxide.
Venetian school *n.* A school of painting originating in Venice in the 15th century and flourishing in the 16th century, notable for its mastery of colour and perspective.
Venezia. See Venice.
Venezia Tridentina. See Trentino-Alto Adige.
Ven·e·zue·la (vénni-zwáylə, vénne-, vénnə- ‖ -zwéelə; *Spanish* bénne-swélla), **Republic of.** Country on the north coast of South America. It is a major oil producer, and one of Latin America's richest countries. Oil and oil products account for 90 per cent of its exports, iron ore another 5 per cent. The economy is being restructured and new industries developed. Ruled by Spain from 1500, Venezuela was liberated by Simón Bolívar (1821), forming part of Gran Colombia until 1830. A series of dictators ended with the overthrow of Pérez Jiménez (1958). Venezuela claims the Esseqibo territory, some 73 per cent of neighbouring Guyana. Area, 912 050 square kilometres (352,145 square miles). Population, 22,310,000. Capital, Caracas. —**Ven·e·zue·lan** *n. & adj.*

venge (venj) *tr.v.* **venged, venging, venges.** *Archaic.* To avenge. [Middle English *vengen,* from Old French *venger.* See **vengeance.**]
venge·ance (vénjənss) *n.* The act or motive of punishing another in payment for a wrong or injury he has committed; retribution: *He had been betrayed, and now wanted vengeance.* —**with a vengeance. 1.** With great violence or fury. **2.** To a greater extent; excessively. Used as an intensive: *The weather has turned cold with a vengeance.* [Middle English, from Old French, from *venger,* to revenge, from Latin *vindicāre,* to revenge, VINDICATE.]
venge·ful (vénjf'l) *adj.* **1.** Desiring vengeance; vindictive: *a vengeful old man.* **2.** Indicating or proceeding from a desire for revenge: *a vengeful frown.* **3.** Inflicting or serving to inflict vengeance: *a vengeful blow.* —See Synonyms at **vindictive.**
ve·ni·al (véen-i-əl) *adj.* Easily excused or forgiven; pardonable: *a venial offence.* [Middle English, from Old French, from Late Latin *veniālis,* forgiveness.] —**ve·ni·al·i·ty** (-ál-əti), **ve·ni·al·ness** *n.* —**ve·ni·al·ly** *adv.*
venial sin *n. Theology.* A sin which, though evil, does not totally estrange the soul from God's grace. Compare **mortal sin.**
Ven·ice (vénniss). *Italian.* **Ve·ne·zia** (ve-néts-ya). Port in northeast Italy. The capital of Venetia, and of Venezia province, it lies in its lagoon, on 118 alluvial islands, mostly separated by narrow canals crossed by some 400 bridges. It was subject to sinking and flood damage, but this has been checked by major engineering works. A road and rail causeway link it to the mainland. Founded in the fifth century A.D., Venice built a wealthy maritime empire around the northeast Mediterranean by the 13th century. As the Venetian Republic it gained extensive lands in north Italy (15th century); however, from 1600 eastern territories were lost to the Turks, and the republic fell to Austria (1797), and was ceded to Italy (1866). Venice is world famous for its art and architecture, including the Byzantine cathedral of St. Mark (begun 830). Tourism, textiles, and glass are its main industries.
ven·i·punc·ture, ven·e·punc·ture (vénni-punkchər, véeni-) *n.* Puncture of a vein, as for drawing blood, intravenous feeding, or administration of medicine. [VENA + PUNCTURE.]

ve·ni·re (və-nír-i) *n. Chiefly U.S. Law.* **1.** A writ issued by a judge to a sheriff, ordering him to summon prospective jurors. Also called "venire facias". **2.** The panel of prospective jurors from which a jury is selected. [Medieval Latin *venīre (facias),* "(you are to cause) to come" (words used in the writ), from Latin *venīre,* to come.]
ve·ni·re·man (və-nír-i-mən) *n., pl.* **-men** (-mən). *Chiefly U.S.* A person summoned to jury duty under a venire.
ven·i·son (vénz'n, vénni-z'n, -s'n) *n.* **1.** The flesh of a deer, used for food. **2.** *Archaic.* The flesh of any game animal thus used. [Middle English *veneso(u)n,* from Old French, from Latin *vēnātiō* (stem *vēnā-tiōn-*), hunting, game, from *vēnārī,* to hunt.]
Venn diagram (ven) *n.* A diagram in which mathematical sets or the terms of a logical argument or syllogism are represented by circles, the position and overlap of which indicate the way in which the different sets or terms are related. [After John *Venn* (1834-1923), British logician.]
ven·o·gram (vénnə-gram, véenə-) *n.* An X-ray picture of a vein or veins. [Latin *vēna,* VEIN + -GRAM.]
ve·nog·ra·phy (ve-nóggrəfi, vi-) *n.* The study using X-rays of a vein or veins following the injection of a radio-opaque substance. [Latin *vēna,* VEIN + -GRAPHY.]
ven·om (vénnəm) *n.* **1.** A poisonous secretion of some animals, such as certain snakes, spiders, scorpions, or insects, usually transmitted by a bite or sting. **2.** *Rare.* Any poison. **3.** Malice; evil; spite. [Middle English *venim,* from Old French, from Vulgar Latin *venī-men* (unattested), variant of Latin *venēnum,* poison.]
ven·om·ous (vénnəməss) *adj.* **1.** Secreting and transmitting venom: *a venomous snake.* **2.** Full of or containing venom. **3.** Malicious; malignant; spiteful: *a venomous utterance.* —**ven·om·ous·ly** *adv.* —**ven·om·ous·ness** *n.*
ve·nose (vée-nōz, -nōss) *adj.* **1.** Having noticeable veins or veinlike markings. **2.** Venous. [Latin *vēnōsus,* VENOUS.]
ve·nos·i·ty (vi-nóssəti) *n.* **1.** The condition or quality of being venous or venose. **2.** An accumulation of blood in the venous system.
ve·nous (véenəss) *adj.* **1.** Of or pertaining to a vein or veins. **2.** Designating or pertaining to blood carried in the veins. [Latin *vēnōsus,* from *vēna,* vein.] —**ve·nous·ly** *adv.* —**ve·nous·ness** *n.*
vent¹ (vent) *n.* **1.** An opening permitting the passage or escape of liquids, gases, fumes, steam, or the like: *a vent above the kitchen stove.* **2.** A means of escaping or leaving a confined space; an exit. **3.** The small hole at the breech of an ancient gun through which the charge is ignited. **4.** *Geology.* A volcano shaft or an aperture in the Earth's crust through which lava and gases can escape. **5.** *Zoology.* The cloacal or anal excretory opening in animals such as birds, reptiles, amphibians, and fish. —**give vent to.** To give utterance to; express or release: *gave vent to their indignation.*
~v. vented, venting, vents. —*tr.* **1.** To give utterance to; express: *venting his sorrows.* **2.** To relieve through the expression of emotion. **3.** To discharge through a vent. **4.** To provide with a vent. —*intr.* To come to the surface to breathe. Used of an otter or beaver. [Middle English *venten,* to provide with an outlet, Old French *esventer,* to let out air, from Vulgar Latin *exventāre* (unattested) : Latin *ex-,* out + *ventus,* wind.] —**vent·less** *adj.*
Synonyms: vent, express, utter, voice, air, broach.
vent² *n.* A narrow opening, often forming a flap, at the side or back of a garment such as a jacket. [Middle English *vent, fent,* from Old French *fente,* slip, from Vulgar Latin *findita* (unattested), from past participle of Latin *findere,* to cleave.]
vent·age (véntij) *n.* **1.** A small opening; a vent. **2.** Any of the small finger-holes in the tube of a wind instrument such as a recorder.
ven·tail (vén-tayl) *n.* The lower front part of a medieval helmet, fitting over the neck. [Middle English, from Old French *vantail,* leaf of a window, from *vent,* wind, air, from Latin *ventus.*]
vent·er¹ (véntər) *n.* One that vents.
venter² *n.* **1. a.** *Biology.* The abdomen or belly. **b.** The wide swelling portion of a muscle. **2.** *Botany.* The swollen base of an archegonium containing the developing egg cell. **3.** *Law.* The womb as the source of offspring. [Anglo-French, from Latin, belly, womb.]
ven·ti·late (vénti-layt) *tr.v.* **-lated, -lating, -lates. 1.** To admit fresh air into a room in order to replace stale air. **2.** To circulate within (a room or mine, for example) in order to freshen. Used of air. **3.** To provide with a vent or a similar means of airing. **4.** To expose (a substance) to the circulation of fresh air, as for the purpose of retarding spoilage. **5.** To expose to public discussion or examination: *The workers ventilated their grievances.* **6.** To aerate or oxygenate (blood). [Middle English *ventilaten,* to blow away, from Latin *ventilāre,* to fan, from *ventus,* wind.] —**ven·ti·la·tion** *n.*
ven·ti·la·tor (vénti-laytər) *n.* **1.** One that ventilates; especially, a device, such as an exhaust fan, that expels stale air and circulates fresh air. **2.** *Medicine.* A device used to ensure the passage of air into and out of the lungs in patients who cannot breathe normally. —**ven·ti·la·to·ry** (-lətri, -laytəri, -láytəri) *adj.*
ven·tral (véntrəl) *adj.* **1.** *Anatomy.* **a.** Pertaining to or situated on or close to the belly; abdominal. **b.** Pertaining to the anterior aspect or front of the human body or the lower surface of the body of an animal. **2.** *Botany.* Of or on the upper or inner surface of an organ such as a leaf facing the main axis; adaxial. [French, from Latin *ventrālis,* from *venter,* VENTER.] —**ven·tral·ly** *adv.*
ventral fin *n. Zoology.* A pelvic fin *(see).*
ven·tri·cle (véntrik'l) *n.* A small anatomical cavity or chamber, as of the brain or heart, especially: **1.** The chamber on the left side of the heart that receives arterial blood from the left atrium and contracts

to drive it into the aorta. **2.** The chamber on the right side of the heart that receives venous blood from the vena cava and drives it via the right atrium into the pulmonary artery. **3.** Any of the four fluid-filled cavities of the brain. Also called "ventriculus". [Middle English, from Old French, from Latin *ventriculus,* diminutive of *venter,* VENTER.] **—ven·tric·u·lar** (ven-tríckewlər) *adj.*

ven·tri·cose (véntri-kōz, -kōss) *adj.* Also **ven·tri·cous** (-kəss). *Biology.* Inflated or swollen, especially on one side. [New Latin *ventricosus,* from Latin *venter,* VENTER.] **—ven·tri·cos·i·ty** (-kóssəti) *n.*

ven·tric·u·lus (ven-tríckew-ləss) *n., pl.* **-li** (-lī). **1.** A hollow digestive organ; especially, the stomach of an insect or the gizzard of a bird. **2.** A ventricle. [Latin, VENTRICLE.]

ven·tril·o·quise, ven·tril·o·quize (ven-tríllə-kwīz) *intr.v.* **-quised, -quising, -quises.** To engage in ventriloquism.

ven·tril·o·quism (ven-tríllə-kwiz'm) *n.* Also **ven·tril·o·quy** (-kwi). A method of producing vocal sounds so that they seem to originate in a source other than the speaker, as from a mechanical dummy. [Late Latin *ventriloquus,* "speaking from the belly" : Latin *venter,* VENTER + *loquī,* to speak.] **—ven·tri·lo·qui·al** (véntri-lṓkwi-əl) *adj.* **—ven·tri·lo·qui·al·ly** *adv.* **—ven·tril·o·quist** (ven-tríllə-kwist) *n.* **—ven·tril·o·quis·tic** (-kwístik) *adj.*

Ven·tris (véntriss), **Michael (George Francis)** (1922–56). British architect and scholar. He deciphered Linear B, a hieroglyphic script of late Minoan Crete.

ven·ture (vénchər) *n.* **1.** An undertaking that is dangerous, daring, or of doubtful outcome. **2.** Something at hazard in such an undertaking; a stake. **—at a venture.** By mere chance or fortune; at hazard; at random.

~v. **ventured, -turing, -tures.** *—tr.* **1.** To expose to danger or risk; stake: *ventured his entire fortune on the enterprise.* **2.** To brave the dangers of: *ventured the high seas in a light boat.* **3.** To express at the risk of denial, criticism, or censure; dare: *ventured a mild cough of protest.* *—intr.* **1.** To take a risk or dare; make a venture. **2.** To go somewhere by or as if by taking a risk: *ventured into the forest.* [Middle English *venturen, venteren,* short for *aventuren,* from *aventure,* ADVENTURE.] **—ven·tur·er** *n.*

Venture Scout *n.* A Scout, aged about 16 or more, who belongs to a senior branch of the Scouts.

ven·ture·some (vénchər-s'm) *adj.* **1.** Disposed to venture or to take risks; daring; bold. **2.** Involving risk or danger; hazardous. **—ven·ture·some·ly** *adv.* **—ven·ture·some·ness** *n.*

ven·tu·ri (ven-téwr-i, -tŏŏr-) *n.* **1.** A short tube with a constricted throat that is used to determine fluid pressures and velocities by measurement of differential pressures generated at the throat as a fluid traverses the tube. Also called "venturi tube". **2.** A constricted throat in the air passage of a carburettor, causing a reduction in pressure by means of which fuel vapour is drawn out of the carburettor bowl. [After G.B. *Venturi* (1746–1822), Italian physicist, whose study inspired its invention.]

ven·tur·ous (vénchərəss) *adj.* **1.** Courageous and daring; adventurous; bold. **2.** Hazardous, dangerous, or risky. **—ven·tur·ous·ly** *adv.* **—ven·tur·ous·ness** *n.*

ven·ue (vénnew) *n.* **1.** A location designated for an event, such as a meeting, concert, or sports match. **2.** *Law.* **a.** The locality where a crime is committed or a cause of action occurs. **b.** Formerly, the locality or political division from which a jury must be called and in which a trial must be held. **c.** Formerly, the clause within a declaration naming the locality in which the trial is occurring or will occur. **3.** Formerly, the clause in an affidavit naming the locality where it was made and sworn to. [Middle English, arrival, assault, from Old French, from the feminine past participle of *venir,* to come, from Latin *venīre.*]

ven·ule (vénnewl) *n.* A minute vein, such as one joining with a capillary or branching from a vein in an insect's wing. [Latin *vēnula,* diminutive of *vēna,* VEIN.] **—ven·u·lar** (-ər) *adj.*

Ve·nus[1] (veénəss) *Roman Mythology.* The goddess of love and beauty, identified with the Greek Aphrodite. [Middle English *Venus,* Old English *Venus,* from Latin, personification of *venus,* love.]

Venus[2] *n.* The second planet from the sun, having an average radius of 6 100 kilometres (3,800 miles), a mass 0.815 times that of the earth, and a sidereal period of revolution about the sun of 224.7 days at a mean distance of approximately 108 million kilometres (67.2 million miles). [After the goddess VENUS.]

Ve·nu·sian (vi-néw-zi-ən, və-, -si- || -nŏŏ-, -zh'n) *adj.* Pertaining to or characteristic of the planet Venus.

~n. A hypothetical inhabitant of the planet Venus.

Venus's comb *n.* **Shepherd's needle** *(see).*

Venus's flower basket *n.* A sponge of the genus *Euplectella,* of deep marine waters, having a delicate, white, lattice-like, cylindrical skeleton.

Venus's-flytrap *n.* Also **Venus flytrap.** An insectivorous plant, *Dionaea muscipula,* of boggy areas of the southeastern United States, having hinged leaf blades that close and entrap insects.

Venus's girdle *n.* A ribbon-shaped marine animal, *Cestum veneris,* having a jelly-like iridescent body up to 1.5 metres (5 feet) in length.

Ve·nus's-hair (veénə-siz-hair) *n.* A maidenhair fern, *Adiantum capillus-veneris,* of subtropical and temperate areas.

Ve·nus's-look·ing-glass (veénə-siz-lŏŏk-ing-glaass || -lŏŏk-, -glass) *n.* Any of various annual weedy plants of the genus *Legousia* (or *Specularia*); especially *L. hybrida,* which has purple flowers.

ver. **1.** verse. **2.** version.

ve·ra·cious (və-ráyshəss, vi-, ve-) *adj.* **1.** Honest; truthful. **2.** Accurate; precise. [Latin *vērāx* (stem *vērāc-*), truth.] **—ve·ra·cious·ly** *adv.* **—ve·ra·cious·ness** *n.*

ve·rac·i·ty (və-rássəti, vi-, ve-) *n., pl.* **-ties.** **1.** Habitual adherence to the truth. **2.** Conformity to truth or fact; accuracy; precision. **3.** Something that is true. —See Synonyms at **honesty, truth.** [Medieval Latin *vērācitās,* from Latin *vērāx,* truth. See **veracious.**]

Ve·ra·cruz (veér-ə krŏŏz, vair-; *Spanish* bérra krŏŏss). City and port in Veracruz state, Mexico, lying on the Gulf of Mexico. It is the industrial centre of one of Mexico's richest oil-producing regions.

ve·ran·dah, ve·ran·da (və-rándə) *n.* A porch or balcony, usually roofed and often partly enclosed, extending along the outside of a building; a gallery. [Hindi, from Portuguese, from *varare* (unattested), to surround with poles, from *vara,* pole, from Latin *vāra,* forked pole, from *vārus,* bent inward.] **—ver·ran·dahed** *adj.*

ve·rat·ri·dine (və-ráttri-deen, vi-, ve-, -din) *n.* A yellowish-white, amorphous powdered alkaloid, $C_{36}H_{51}NO_{11}$, obtained from sabadilla seeds. [VERATR(INE) + -ID + -INE.]

ver·a·trine (vérrə-treen, -trin) *n.* A poisonous mixture of colourless crystalline alkaloids extracted from sabadilla seeds and formerly used medicinally as a counterirritant. [French *vératrine,* from New Latin *Veratrum,* genus name of a hellebore, from Latin *vērātrum,* hellebore, perhaps from *veru,* spit.]

verb (verb) *n. Abbr.* **v., vb.** **1.** In most languages, that part of speech that expresses existence, action, or occurrence. **2.** Any of the words exemplifying this part of speech; for example, *be, run,* or *conceive.* **3.** Any phrase or other construction used as a verb.

~adj. Grammar. Verbal: *a verb phrase.* [Middle English *verbe,* from Old French, from Latin *verbum,* word.]

ver·bal (vérb'l) *adj. Abbr.* **vb.** **1.** Of, pertaining to, or associated with words: *a verbal symbol.* **2.** Concerned with words rather than with the facts or ideas they represent: *a merely verbal ceasefire.* **3.** Expressed or transmitted in speech; unwritten: *a verbal contract.* **4.** Literal; word for word: *a verbal translation.* **5.** *Grammar.* **a.** Pertaining to, having the nature or function of, or derived from a verb. **b.** Used to form verbs: *a verbal suffix.*

~n. Grammar. **1.** A verbal noun, adjective, or other word based on a verb and preserving some of the verb's characteristics. **2.** *British Slang.* **a.** A spoken, as opposed to written, confession made by a suspect during police questioning and introduced as evidence at his trial. **b.** Verbal, rather than physical, abuse. [Old French, from Late Latin *verbālis,* from Latin *verbum,* word, VERB.] **—ver·bal·ly** *adv.*

Usage: *Verbal* is used as well as *oral* to express the notion of "by word of mouth", but it can also refer to what is written *(He sent me a verbal account of what was said at the meeting). Oral* can refer only to what is spoken, and is thus often preferred when there is a possibility of ambiguity (in such phrases as *verbal agreement*).

ver·bal·ise, ver·bal·ize (vérb'l-īz) *v.* **-ised, -ising, -ises.** *—tr.* **1.** To express in words: *He couldn't verbalise what he was feeling.* **2.** To convert (a noun, for example) to verbal use. *—intr.* **1.** To express oneself in words. **2.** To be verbose. **—ver·bal·i·sa·tion** (-ī-záysh'n || *U.S.* -i-) *n.* **—ver·bal·i·ser** *n.*

ver·bal·ism (vérb'l-iz'm) *n.* **1.** An expression in words; a word or phrase. **2.** A meaningless or clichéd phrase or sentence, especially one resulting from an emphasis on words over content or idea. **3.** A disposition towards or the habitual use of such merely declamatory, ornate, or empty constructions.

ver·bal·ist (vérb'l-ist) *n.* **1.** One skilled at using words. **2.** One who favours words over ideas or facts. **—ver·bal·is·tic** *adj.*

verbal noun *n.* A noun derived from a verb; in English, either a gerund or an infinitive; for example, the word *smoking* and the phrases *to think* and *to be* in the sentences *Smoking causes cancer* and *To think is to be.*

ver·ba·tim (ver-báy-tim, vər-, *also* -baa-) *adj.* Using exactly the same words; word for word. [Middle English, from Medieval Latin, from Latin *verbum,* word, VERB.] **—ver·ba·tim** *adv.*

ver·be·na (vər-beénə, ver-) *n.* **1.** Any of various chiefly New World plants of the genus *Verbena;* especially, any of several species cultivated for their showy, variously coloured flowers. See **vervain.** **2.** Any of several similar or related plants, such as the **lemon verbena** *(see).* [New Latin *Verbena,* from Latin *verbēna,* usually in plural *verbēnae,* sacred boughs of olive or myrtle. See **vervain.**]

ver·bi·age (vérbi-ij) *n.* **1.** Words in excess of those needed for clarity or precision; wordiness. **2.** The favouring or use of such an excess of words. **3.** *Rare.* The manner in which one expresses oneself in words; diction. [French, from Latin *verbum,* word, VERB.]

verb·i·fy (vérbi-fī) *v.* **-fied, -fying, -fies.** *—tr.* To use (a noun, for example) as a verb; form into a verb. *—intr.* To be verbose.

ver·bose (vər-bṓss) *adj.* Using or containing an excessive number of words; wordy; prolix. See Synonyms at **talkative.** [Latin *verbōsus,* from *verbum,* word, VERB.] **—ver·bose·ly** *adv.* **—ver·bose·ness, ver·bos·i·ty** (-bóssəti) *n.*

ver·bo·ten (fər-bṓt'n, fair-, vər-) *adj. Informal.* Rigorously forbidden. [German, from Old High German *farboten,* past participle of *farbiotan,* to forbid.]

verb. sap. (verb sáp) *Latin.* Used to conclude a remark or clinch an argument by suggesting that no further explanation is needed. [Abbreviation of Latin phrase *verbum sapienti (sat est),* a word to the wise (suffices).]

ver·dant (vérd'nt) *adj.* **1.** Green with vegetation; covered with a green growth: *verdant, fertile land.* **2.** Green in colour. **3.** Inexperienced or unsophisticated. [Perhaps from Old French *verdeant,* present participle of *verdoier, verdier,* to become green, from *verd, vert,* green, from Latin *viridis*, from *virēre*, to be green.] **—ver·dan·cy** *n.* **—ver·dant·ly** *adv.*

verd antique, verde antique (verd) *n.* **1.** A dull-green mottled or veined serpentine marble used in interior decoration. **2.** Verdigris on ancient bronze, copper, and brass. **3.** A green porphyry. [French, "ancient green".]

Verde, Cape. Peninsula of Senegal, jutting into the Atlantic ocean. Its tip, Cape Almadies, is the westernmost extremity of Africa.

ver·der·er (vérdərər) *n.* Formerly, the official in charge of the royal forests of England. [Anglo-French, from Old French *verdier*, from *verde*, *verte*, green, "forest." See **verdant**.]

Ver·di (vaír-di, -dee), **Giuseppe** (1813–1901). Italian composer. Among his works are the operas *Rigoletto* (1851), *Il Trovatore* (1853), *La Traviata* (1853), and *Aida* (1871). His work introduced the new idea of music drama to Italian opera.

ver·dict (vérdikt) *n.* **1.** The decision reached by a jury at the conclusion of a legal proceeding: *a verdict of not guilty.* **2.** An expressed conclusion; a judgment: *the verdict of history.* [Middle English *verdit*, from Anglo-French, variant of Old French *veirdit*, *voirdit*, "true saying" : *veir*, true, from Latin *vērus* + *dit*, saying, from Latin *dictum*, from the neuter past participle of *dīcere*, to speak, say.]

ver·di·gris (vérdi-griss, -greess, -gree) *n.* **1.** A blue or green basic copper acetate, used as a paint pigment, fungicide, and insecticide. **2.** A green patina or crust of copper carbonate formed on copper, brass, and bronze exposed to air or sea water for long periods of time. In this sense, also called "aerugo", "verd antique". Compare **patina**. [Middle English *vertegres*, from Old French *vertegrez*, *vert-de-Grice*, "green of Greece".]

ver·di·ter (vérditər) *n.* Either of two basic carbonates of copper, azirite and malachite, used as a blue or green pigment. [Old French *verd de terre*, "green of earth".]

Ver·dun (ver-dún; *French* vair-dáɴ, -dṓɴ). Town in northeastern France, lying on the river Meuse, in the Meuse département. In 1916 the battle of Verdun, which lasted from February to December was one of the longest and fiercest battles of World War I.

ver·dure (vér-jər, -dewr) *n.* **1.** The fresh, vibrant greenness of flourishing vegetation. **2.** Such vegetation itself: *lush verdure.* **3.** Any fresh or flourishing condition: *the verdure of childhood.* [Middle English, from Old French, from *verd*, green. See **verdant**.] **—ver·dur·ous** *adj.* **—ver·dur·ous·ness** *n.*

Ver·ee·nig·ing (fə-réeniking; *Afrikaans* -ráynə<u>kh</u>əng). City in northeastern South Africa, lying on the river Vaal in Gauteng province. It was founded as the centre of the surrounding coal-mining area in 1892 and has now become one of the chief manufacturing centres in South Africa.

verge¹ (verj) *n.* **1.** The extreme edge, rim, or margin of something; the brink: *the verge of a stream.* **2. a.** An enclosing boundary. **b.** The space enclosed by such a boundary. **3.** *British.* The stretch of grass bordering a road. **4.** The point beyond which an action, state, or condition is likely to begin or occur: *the verge of a nervous breakdown.* **5.** *Architecture.* **a.** The edge of the tiling that projects over a roof gable. **b.** The body of a classical column; a pillar. **6.** A rod, wand, or staff carried as an emblem of authority or office. **7.** In feudal times, the rod held by a tenant swearing fealty to his lord. **8.** Formerly, the area of jurisdiction of the Lord High Steward, especially the surroundings of the royal court. **9.** The spindle of a balance wheel in an early clock or watch; especially, such a spindle in a clock with vertical escapement. **10.** The male reproductive organ of an invertebrate. —See Synonyms at **border**.

~*intr.v.* **verged, verging, verges. 1.** To approach the verge or limit; come near. Usually used with *on* or *upon*: *Her idea verged on genius.* **2.** To constitute a verge or limit; be a border. Used with *on* or *upon*: *a housing estate verging on the slum area.* [Middle English, margin, from Old French, from Latin *virga*†, rod, strip.]

verge² *intr.v.* **verged, verging, verges.** To slope or incline. Used with *to* or *towards.* [Latin *vergere*, to tend towards.]

verg·er (vérjər) *n.* **1.** A person who takes care of the interior of a church and acts as an attendant during ceremonies. **2.** A person who carries the verge before a scholastic, legal, or religious dignitary in a procession.

Vergil. See **Virgil**.

ver·glas (vaír-glaa) *n.* A thin coating of ice or sleet, as on a rock. [French, from Old French *verre-glaz*, "glass-ice" : *verre*, from Latin *vitrum*, glass + *glaz*, ultimately from Latin *glaciēs*, ice.]

ve·rid·i·cal (ve-ríddik'l, vi-, və-) *adj.* Also **ve·rid·ic** (-ríddik). **1.** Expressing the truth; accurate; veracious. **2.** *Psychology.* Designating dreams, visions; hallucinations, or the like that coincide accurately with future events or apparently unknowable present realities. [Latin *vēridicus* : *vērus*, true + *dīcere*, to say.] **—ve·rid·i·cal·i·ty** (-ríddi-kál-əti) *n.* **—ve·rid·i·cal·ly** *adv.*

ver·i·est (vérri-ist) *adj. Archaic.* Used as an intensive: *the veriest fop and fool.* [Superlative of VERY.]

ver·i·fi·ca·tion (vérrifi-káysh'n) *n.* **1.** The act of verifying or condition of being verified. **2. a.** A confirmation of the truth of a theory or fact. **b.** The evidence for such a confirmation. **c.** A formal statement of such a confirmation. **3.** *Law.* **a.** Formerly, a short formulaic oath concluding a pleading and affirming that the pleader is ready to prove his allegations. **b.** The evidence used in trying to prove such allegations. **—ver·i·fi·ca·tive** (-kaytiv) *adj.*

ver·i·fy (vérri-fī) *tr.v.* **-fied, -fying, -fies. 1.** To prove the truth of by the presentation of evidence or testimony; substantiate. **2.** To determine or test the truth or accuracy of, as by comparison, investigation, or reference: *Scientific claims are not accepted until verified.* **3.** *Law.* **a.** To affirm formally or under oath. **b.** To append a verification to (a pleading); conclude with a verification. —See Synonyms at **confirm**. [Middle English *verifien*, from Old French *verifier*, from Medieval Latin *vērificāre* : Latin *vērus*, true + *facere*, to make.] **—ver·i·fi·a·ble** (-fī-əb'l || -fī-əb'l) *adj.* **—ver·i·fi·er** *n.*

ver·i·ly (vérrəli, vérrili) *adv. Archaic.* **1.** In truth; in fact; of a certainty. **2.** With confidence; assuredly. [Middle English *verraily*, from *verray*, true, VERY.]

ver·i·sim·i·lar (vérri-símmilər) *adj.* Appearing to be true or real; probable; likely. [Latin *vērisimilis* : *vēri*, of truth, from *vērum*, truth, from *vērus*, true + *similis*, SIMILAR.] **—ver·i·sim·i·lar·ly** *adv.*

ver·i·si·mil·i·tude (vérri-si-mílli-tewd || -tōōd) *n.* **1.** The quality of appearing to be true or real; likelihood. **2.** Something that has the appearance of being true or real. —See Synonyms at **truth**. [Latin *vērisimilitūdō*, from *vērisimilis*, VERISIMILAR.]

ve·rism (véer-iz'm || vérriz'm) *n.* Realistic portrayal in art and literature. [Italian *verismo*, from *vero*, true, from Latin *vērus*.] **—ver·ist** *n.* & *adj.* **—ve·ris·tic** (vi-rístik, və-, ve-) *adj.*

ve·ris·mo (ve-ríz-mō, *Italian* -réez-) *n.* A late 19th-century artistic movement, originating in Italy and influential particularly in opera, which concentrated on realistic, everyday themes, and tended to treat them in a melodramatic way. [Italian, from *vero*, true.]

ver·i·ta·ble (vérritəb'l) *adj.* **1.** Unquestionably true; actual. **2.** Having the qualities of. Used as an intensive: *He's a veritable wolf.* —See Synonyms at **real**. [Middle English, from Old French, from *verite*, VERITY.] **—ver·i·ta·ble·ness** *n.* **—ver·i·ta·bly** *adv.*

ver·i·ty (vérrəti) *n., pl.* **-ties. 1.** The condition or quality of being real, accurate, or correct. **2.** A statement, principle, or belief considered to be of established and permanent truth. —See Synonyms at **truth**. [Middle English *verite*, from Old French, from Latin *vēritās* (stem *vēritāt-*), from *vērus*, true.]

ver·juice (vér-jōōss || -jewss) *n.* **1.** The acidic juice of sour or unripe fruit, such as grapes or crab apples. **2.** Bitterness or sourness, as of temper. [Middle English *verjus*, from Old French *vertjus* : *vert*, green (see **verdant**) + *jus*, JUICE.]

ver·kramp·te (fər-krámp-tə, -krúmp-) *n.* **1.** In South Africa, a person of very conservative political views who opposes liberalisation of government policy, especially in respect of the race laws. **2.** *South African.* Any extremely conservative, bigoted, or narrow-minded person. Compare **verligte**. [Afrikaans, "restricted".] **—ver·kramp** (-krámp, -krúmp), **ver·kramp·te** *adj.*

Ver·laine (vair-láyn, vər-), **Paul** (1844–96). French poet. After associating with the Parnassian poets, whose influence is evident in his early poetry, he became a leader of the symbolists. His works include *Fêtes galantes* (1869), *Sagesse* (1881), and the critical studies *Les Poètes maudits* (1884).

ver·lig·te (fər-lí<u>kh</u>-tə) *n.* **1.** In South Africa, any of the more progressive National Party supporters who favoured a slight liberalisation of government and party policy, especially in respect of the race laws. **2.** *South African.* Any relatively progressive and broad-minded person. Compare **verkrampte**. [Afrikaans, "enlightened".] **—ver·lig** (-lí<u>kh</u>), **ver·lig·te** *adj.*

Ver·meer (vər-méer, ver-, vair-), **Jan** (1632–75). Dutch painter. He painted mostly interior scenes where he used to great effect his mastery of highlighting and colour. About 40 of his paintings are known, including *The Lady standing at the Virginals.*

ver·meil (vér-mayl, -mil) *n.* **1.** *Poetic.* Vermilion or bright-red. **2.** Gilded metal, such as silver, bronze, or copper.

~*adj.* Bright red in colour. [Middle English *vermayl*, from Old French *vermeil*, from Late Latin *vermiculus*, from Latin, small worm, cochineal (which yields a red dye), from *vermis*, worm.]

vermi- *comb. form.* Indicates a worm or worms; for example, **vermicide**. [Latin *vermis*, worm.]

ver·mi·cel·li (vérmi-chélli, -sélli) *n.* **1.** A food consisting of wheat flour paste made into long threads, thinner than spaghetti. **2.** An edible decoration for cakes or desserts, consisting of tiny strands of chocolate or chocolate-coloured sugar. [Italian, plural of *vermicello*, diminutive of *verme*, worm, from Latin *vermis*.]

ver·mi·cide (vérmi-sīd) *n.* A substance used to kill worms. [VERMI- + -CIDE.] **—ver·mi·cid·al** (-sīd'l) *adj.*

ver·mic·u·lar (ver-míckewlər, vər-) *adj.* **1.** Having the shape or motion of a worm. **2.** Having wormlike markings; vermiculate. **3.** Caused by or pertaining to worms. [Medieval Latin *vermiculāris*, from Latin *vermiculus*, diminutive of *vermis*, worm.] **—ver·mic·u·lar·ly** *adv.*

ver·mic·u·late (ver-míckew-layt, vər-) *tr.v.* **-lated, -lating, -lates.** To adorn or decorate with wavy or winding lines: *vermiculate a jar.*

~*adj.* (-lət, -lit, -layt). **1.** Bearing wormlike wavy lines. **2.** Having a wormlike motion; twisting or wriggling. **3.** Sinuous; tortuous; devious. **4.** Infested with worms; worm-eaten. [Latin *vermiculārī*, to be full of worms, from *vermiculus*, small worm. See **vermeil**.]

ver·mic·u·la·tion (ver-mickew-láysh'n, vər-, vér-mickew-) *n.* **1.** Motion resembling that of a worm; especially, the wavelike contractions of the intestine; peristalsis. **2.** Wormlike marks or carvings, as in a mosaic or masonry. **3.** The condition of being worm-eaten.

ver·mic·u·lite (ver-míckew-līt, vər-) *n.* Any of a group of micaceous hydrated silicates of varying composition, related to the chlorites and used as heat insulation and as a planting medium for starting plant seeds and cuttings. [Latin *vermiculus*, small worm (see **vermeil**) + -ITE (from the wormlike projections it forms when subjected to the blowpipe).]

ver·mi·form (vérmi-fawrm) *adj.* Resembling or having the shape of a worm. [New Latin *vermiformis* : VERMI- + -FORM.]

vermiform appendix *n.* The wormlike, closed, projection of the caecum found in certain mammals including humans, in whom it is vestigial. Also called "appendix," "vermiform process".

ver·mi·fuge (vérmi-fewj) *n.* Any agent that expels or destroys intestinal worms. Also called "anthelminthic". [VERMI- + -FUGE.] —**ver·mi·fug·al** (-féwg'l) *adj.*

ver·mil·ion, ver·mil·lion (vər-míl-yən, ver-) *n.* 1. A bright red **mercuric sulphide** *(see),* used as a pigment. 2. Vivid red to reddish orange. Also called "Chinese red", "cinnabar". ~*adj.* **ver·mil·lion.** Vivid red to reddish orange in colour. ~*tr.v.* **vermilioned, -ioning, -ions.** Also **ver·mil·lion.** To colour or dye vermilion. [Middle English *vermelyon,* from Old French *vermeillon,* from *vermeil,* VERMEIL.]

ver·min (vérmin) *n., pl.* **vermin.** 1. *Plural.* Collectively, various small animals or insects that are destructive, annoying, or injurious to health, such as cockroaches or rats. 2. *Plural.* Collectively, various animals that prey on game, such as foxes or weasels. 3. **a.** *Rare.* A vile, destructive, or worthless person. **b.** Such persons collectively: *"the most pernicious race of little odious vermin that nature ever suffered to crawl upon the surface of the earth"* (Jonathan Swift). [Middle English, from Old French, from Vulgar Latin *vermīnum* (unattested), from Latin *vermis* (stem *vermin-*), worm.]

ver·mi·na·tion (vérmi-náysh'n) *n.* 1. Infestation with vermin or worms. 2. The breeding of worms, larvae, or vermin.

ver·min·ous (vérminəss) *adj.* 1. Of, pertaining to, or infested with vermin. 2. Of the nature of vermin; repulsive; noxious. —**ver·mi·nous·ly** *adv.*

ver·miv·o·rous (ver-mívvərəss) *adj.* Feeding on worms. [VERMI- + -VOROUS.]

Ver·mont (vər-mónt, ver-). State in the northeastern United States, one of the New England states, to the east of upper New York state with a northern boundary with Canada. The capital is Montpelier; the largest city is Burlington. It entered the Union in 1791.

ver·mouth (vér-məth, -mōōth, *chiefly U.S.* vər-mōōth, ver-) *n.* Any of several white wines, either sweet or dry, flavoured with aromatic herbs and spices, and often used chiefly as an ingredient in cocktails. [French *vermout,* from German *Wermut,* WORMWOOD.]

ver·nac·u·lar (vər-náckewlər) *n.* 1. The standard native language of a country or locality. 2. The informal everyday speech of a country or locality. 3. The idiom of a particular trade or profession: *in the legal vernacular.* 4. An idiomatic word, phrase, or expression. 5. The commonly used name of a plant or animal as distinguished from the taxonomic designation. ~*adj.* 1. Native to or commonly spoken by the members of a particular country or locality. Said of a language or dialect. 2. Using the native language of a locality as distinct from literary language. Said of a writer. 3. Pertaining to, spoken in, or written in the native language or dialect. 4. Pertaining to the style of architecture and decoration peculiar to a specific culture or locality. 5. *Rare.* Occurring or existing in a particular locality; endemic: *a vernacular disease.* 6. Designating or pertaining to the commonly used nonscientific name of a plant or animal. [Latin *vernāculus,* domestic, from *verna,* native slave, probably from Etruscan.] —**ver·nac·u·lar·ly** *adv.*

ver·nac·u·lar·ism (vər-náckewlər-iz'm) *n.* 1. The use of, or the doctrine favouring the use of, the vernacular. 2. A vernacular word, phrase, or expression.

ver·nal (vérn'l) *adj.* 1. Of, pertaining to, or occurring in the spring. 2. Characteristic of or resembling spring. 3. Fresh and young; youthful. [Latin *vernālis,* from *vernus,* of spring, from *vēr,* spring.] —**ver·nal·ly** *adv.*

vernal equinox *n.* 1. *Astronomy.* The point in Aries at which the ecliptic intersects the celestial equator, the sun having a northerly motion. 2. The time when the sun passes through this point, about March 21, when day and night are approximately equal all over the earth. Compare **autumnal equinox.**

vernal grass *n.* Any of various Eurasian grasses of the genus *Anthoxanthum,* such as the sweet-scented *A. odoratum.*

ver·nal·i·sa·tion, ver·nal·i·za·tion (vérn'l-ī-záysh'n || *U.S.* -i-) *n.* The exposure of certain plants or their seeds to a period of low temperature which is necessary for them to flower or flower earlier than usual. Used especially of winter varieties of cereals.

ver·na·tion (ver-náysh'n) *n. Botany.* The arrangement of the folded leaves in a bud. [New Latin *vernatio,* from Latin *vernāre,* to flourish, from *vernus,* VERNAL.]

Verne (vairn), **Jules** (1828–1905). French writer. The founder of modern science fiction, he foresaw submarines and space travel. The best known of his adventure stories are *Journey to the Centre of the Earth* (1864) and *Around the World in 80 Days* (1873).

Ver·ner's Law (vér-nərz, vaír-). *Linguistics.* A law stating essentially that Proto-Germanic non-initial voiceless fricatives in voiced environments became voiced when the previous syllable was unstressed in Proto-Indo-European. [After Karl Adolf *Verner* (1846–96), Danish philologist.]

ver·ni·er (vérni-ər) *n.* 1. A small, movable auxiliary graduated scale attached parallel to a main graduated scale, calibrated to indicate fractional parts of the subdivisions of the larger scale, and used on certain precision instruments to increase accuracy in measurement. 2. Any auxiliary device designed to facilitate fine adjustments or measurements on precision instruments. Also called "vernier scale". ~*adj.* Of or pertaining to a vernier. [After Pierre *Vernier* (1580–1637), French mathematician.]

vernier calliper *n.* A measuring instrument consisting of an L-shaped frame with a linear scale along its longer arm and an L-shaped sliding attachment with a vernier scale, used to read directly the dimension of an object represented by the separation between the inner or outer edges of the two shorter arms.

vernier rocket *n.* A small rocket engine used primarily to make fine adjustments in velocity and trajectory. Also called "thruster", "vernier engine".

Ve·ro·na (və-rŏ́nə, vi-, ve-). City in northeastern Italy, lying on the river Adige in the Venetia region. A strategic pre-Roman city, it is now a major industrial and agricultural centre.

Ver·o·nal (vérrə-n'l || -nawl) *n.* A trademark for **barbitone** *(see).*

Ve·ro·ne·se (vérrō-náy-zay, *Italian* -say), **Paolo.** born Paolo Caliari. (1528–1588). Italian painter of the Venetian school. He is known particularly as a decorative artist. His works include *Marriage at Cana,* and the *Feast in the House of Levi.*

ve·ron·i·ca¹ (və-rónnikə) *n.* Any of various plants of the genus *Veronica,* which includes the speedwells. [Perhaps from the name *Veronica.*]

veronica² *n.* 1. The representation or image of the face of Jesus, which, according to legend, was impressed upon the handkerchief offered to him by Saint Veronica on the road to Calvary. 2. The handkerchief itself. 3. Any similar representation of Jesus' face on a textile fabric. [Medieval Latin, from Late Latin *Veraiconica,* (Saint) Veronica : *vēra, vērus,* true + *iconica, iconicus,* pertaining to an image, from *icon,* image, ICON.]

veronica³ *n.* In bullfighting, a manoeuvre in which the matador stands immobile and passes the cape slowly before the charging bull. [Spanish, from the name *Veronica.*]

Ver·roc·chio (və-rócki-ō, ve-, -rŏ́ki-), **Andrea del.** born Andrea di Michele de Francesco di Cioni. (1435–1488). Florentine sculptor, painter, and craftsman. He is best known for his magnificent equestrian statue of *Colleoni* at Venice.

ver·ru·ca (və-rōō-kə, vi-, ve-) *n., pl.* **-cas** or **-cae** (-see). 1. *Medicine.* A wart especially one on the sole of the foot. 2. *Biology.* A wartlike projection, as on some leaves. [Latin *verrūca.*]

ver·ru·cose (vérroo-kŏz, -kōss, və-rōō-) *adj.* Also **ver·ru·cous** (-kəss). Covered with warts or wartlike projections. [Latin *verrucōsus,* from *verrūca,* VERRUCA.]

vers versed sine.

Ver·sailles (vair-sī́, ver-). City in north central France, lying on the southwestern outskirts of Paris. It was a village until Louis XIV built his palace and transferred his court to it (1682). Both the German Empire and the Third French Republic were proclaimed at Versailles (1871) and the negotiations which ended World War I by the Treaty of Versailles (1919) were conducted there.

Versailles, Treaty of *n.* 1. The treaty (1919) imposed on Germany after the end of World War I. 2. The treaty (1783) ending the War of American Independence. See **Paris, Treaty of.**

ver·sant (vérss'nt) *n.* 1. The slope of a side of a mountain or mountain range. 2. The general slope of any region. [French, from Latin *versāns* (stem *versant-*), present participle of *versārī,* to turn frequently. See **versatile.**]

ver·sa·tile (vérssə-tīl || *chiefly U.S.* -t'l) *adj.* 1. Capable of turning competently from one task, subject, or occupation to another; having a generalized aptitude. 2. Having varied uses or serving many functions: *The potato is a most versatile vegetable.* 3. Inconstant or variable; changeable. 4. *Biology.* Capable of moving freely in all directions, as the antenna of an insect or the loosely attached anther of a flower may be. [French, from Latin *versātilis,* from *versārī,* frequentative of *vertere,* to turn.] —**ver·sa·tile·ly** *adv.* —**ver·sa·til·i·ty** (-tílləti) *adv.* —**ver·sa·tile·ness** *n.*

verse (verss) *n. Abbr.* **v., ver.** 1. **a.** A line of words arranged in accordance with the principles of prosody; one line of poetry. **b.** A subdivision of any metrical composition, such as a stanza of a hymn or of a long poem. 2. Metrical or rhymed composition; poetry as distinct from prose. 3. Light metrical composition as distinct from serious poetry. 4. An instance of such composition; a light poem. 5. A specified type of metrical composition, such as *elegiac verse, blank verse,* or *free verse.* 6. A specified type of metrical structure: *iambic verse.* 7. Any of the numbered subdivisions of a chapter in the Bible. ~*v.* **versed, versing, verses.** *Rare.* —*tr.* To versify (prose, for example). —*intr.* To versify; write poetry. [Middle English *vers,* from Old English *fers* and Old French *vers,* from Latin *versus,* "a turning of the plough," furrow, line, verse, from the past participle of *vertere,* to turn.]

versed (verst) *adj.* Knowledgeable, skilled, or trained. Used with *in: versed in canon law.* [French *versé* or Latin *versātus,* past participle of *versārī,* to be engaged in, frequentative of *vertere,* to turn.]

versed cosine *n. Abbr.* **covers** *Mathematics.* A trigonometric function of an angle equal to one minus the sine of that angle. Also called "coversine".

versed sine *n. Abbr.* **vers** *Mathematics.* A trigonometric function of an angle equal to one minus the cosine of that angle. Also called "versine". [New Latin *sinus versus,* "inverse-order sine", from Latin *versus,* turned. See **verse** (poetry).]

ver·si·cle (vérssik'l) *n.* 1. A short verse. 2. A short sentence spoken or chanted by a priest and followed by a response from the congregation. [Middle English, from Old French *versicule,* from Latin *versiculus,* diminutive of *versus,* VERSE.] —**ver·si·cu·lar** (ver-sickewlər) *adj.*

ver·si·col·our (vérssi-kullər) *adj.* Also **ver·si·col·oured** (-kullərd). 1. Having a variety of colours; variegated. 2. Changing in colour;

iridescent. [Latin : *versus,* turned, changed (see **verse**) + COLOUR.]
ver·si·fi·er (vérssi-fī-ər) *n.* One who versifies. See Synonyms at **poet**.
ver·si·fy (vérssi-fī) *v.* **-fied, -fying, -fies.** —*tr.* **1.** To change from prose into metrical form. **2.** To treat or tell in verse; write a poem about: *versify Bible stories.* —*intr.* To write verses; especially, to write light or worthless poetry. [Middle English *versifien,* from Old French *versifier,* from Latin *versificāre* : *versus,* VERSE + -FY.] —**ver·si·fi·ca·tion** (-fi-káysh'n) *n.*
ver·sine (vér-sīn) *n. Mathematics.* A versed sine.
ver·sion (vérsh'n, vérzh'n) *n. Abbr.* **v., ver. 1.** A description, narration, or account related from the specific or subjective viewpoint of the narrator: *Her version of the accident differed from his.* **2. a.** A translation. **b.** *Usually capital* **V.** A translation of the entire Bible or of a part of it: *the King James Version.* **3.** A variation of any prototype; a variant: *"At home we played soccer . . . and sometimes a version of hurling"* (Brendan Behan). **4.** An adaptation of a work of art or literature into another medium or style: *Lamb's version of Shakespeare; the film version.* **5.** *Medicine.* **a.** Manipulation of a foetus in the uterus to bring it into a favourable position for delivery. **b.** A deflection of an organ, such as the uterus, from its normal position. [From Medieval Latin *versiō* (stem *versiōn-*), conversion, translation, from Latin *vertere,* to turn, change.] —**ver·sion·al** *adj.*
vers li·bre (vaír léebr) *n. French.* **Free verse** *(see).*
ver·so (vér-sō) *n., pl.* **-sos.** *Abbr.* **v., vo. 1.** *Printing.* The left-hand page of a book or the reverse side of a sheet of paper as opposed to the **recto** *(see).* **2.** The back of a coin or medal. Compare **obverse.** [Latin *versō (folio),* "(the page) being turned", the page one sees when the leaf is turned over, ablative of *versus,* turned. See **versus.**]
verst (verst) *n.* A Russian measure of linear distance, equivalent to just over a kilometre (about two-thirds of a mile). [French *verste,* from Russian *versta,* "line".]
ver·sus (vér-səss || -səz) *prep. Abbr.* **v., vs. 1.** Against. Used in law and in sports: *the plaintiff versus the defendant; Spurs versus QPR at Wembley.* **2.** As an alternative to; in contrast with: *death versus dishonour.* [Medieval Latin, from Latin, turned towards, from the past participle of *vertere,* to turn.]
vert (vert) *n.* **1.** In former English forest law: **a.** Any green vegetation that can serve as cover for deer. **b.** The right to cut such vegetation. **2.** *Heraldy.* The colour green. [Middle English *verte,* from Old French *vert,* green. See **verdant.**]
vert. vertical.
ver·te·bra (vérti-brə) *n., pl.* **-brae** (-bree) or **-bras.** Any of the bones or cartilaginous segments forming the spinal column. [Latin, joint, vertebra, "something to turn on", from *vertere,* to turn.]
ver·te·bral (vértibrəl) *adj.* **1.** Relating to or of the nature of a vertebra. **2.** Having or consisting of vertebrae.
vertebral canal *n. Anatomy.* The **spinal canal** *(see).*
vertebral column *n. Anatomy.* The **spinal column** *(see).*
ver·te·brate (vérti-brət, -brit, -brayt) *n.* Any member of the subphylum Vertebrata, a primary division of the phylum Chordata that includes the fishes, amphibians, reptiles, birds, and mammals, all of which are characterised by a segmented bony or cartilaginous spinal column.
~*adj.* **1.** Having a backbone or spinal column. **2.** Of or characteric of a vertebrate or vertebrates. [Latin *vertebrātus,* from *vertebra,* VERTEBRA.]
ver·te·bra·tion (vérti-bráysh'n) *n.* The process or result of division into vertebrae or similar segments.
ver·tex (vér-teks) *n., pl.* **-texes** or **-tices** (-ti-seez). **1.** The highest point of anything; the apex; the summit. **2.** *Anatomy.* **a.** The highest point of the skull. **b.** The top of the head. **3.** *Astronomy.* The highest point reached in the apparent motion of a celestial body. **4.** In geometry: **a.** The point at which two or more lines or edges intersect. **b.** The fixed point that is one of the three generating characteristics of a conic section. [Latin, whirl, crown of the head, highest point, from *vertere,* to turn.]
ver·ti·cal (vértik'l) *adj. Abbr.* **vert. 1.** At right angles to the horizon; extending perpendicularly from a plane; upright. Compare **horizontal. 2.** Pertaining to or situated at the vertex or highest point; directly overhead. **3.** *Anatomy.* Of or pertaining to the vertex of the head. **4.** *Economics.* Pertaining to, composed of, or controlling all the grades, stages, or levels in the manufacture and sale of a product: *vertical integration through takeovers.* Compare **horizontal. 5.** Moving straight up or down or up and down.
~*n. Abbr.* **vert. 1.** A vertical line, plane, circle, or the like. **2.** A vertical position. **3.** A vertical pillar, pole, or the like. [French, from Late Latin *verticālis,* from Latin *vertex* (stem *vertic-*), VERTEX.] —**ver·ti·cal·i·ty** (vérti-kál-əti), **ver·ti·cal·ness** *n.* —**ver·ti·cal·ly** *adv.*
Synonyms: *vertical, upright, perpendicular, plumb.*
vertical circle *n. Astronomy.* Any great circle on the celestial sphere, passing through the zenith and the nadir, and thus perpendicular to the horizon.
vertical file *n.* A collection of ephemera, such as pamphlets, sheets of paper, and mounted photographs, arranged for ready reference.
vertically opposite angles *pl.n.* Either pair of the two pairs of equal angles formed opposite each other by two intersecting lines.
vertical take-off *n.* The take-off of an aircraft in a perpendicularly upward direction.
vertical union *n. U.S.* An **industrial union** *(see).*
ver·ti·ces. Alternative plural of **vertex.**
ver·ti·cil (vérti-sil) *n. Biology.* A circular arrangement, as of flowers or leaves, about a point on an axis; a whorl. [Latin *verticillus,* the whirl of a spindle, diminutive of *vertex,* whirl, VERTEX.]
ver·ti·cil·las·ter (vérti-si-láss-tər) *n. Botany.* An inflorescence, such as that of the white dead-nettle, resembling a whorl but actually arising in axils of opposite leaves. [VERTICIL + -ASTER.] —**ver·ti·cil·las·trate** (-trət, -trit, -trayt) *adj.*
ver·ti·cil·late (ver-tíssil-ət, vérti-síl-ət, -it, -ayt) *adj.* Also **ver·ti·cil·lat·ed** (-aytid). Arranged in or forming a whorl or whorls. —**ver·ti·cil·late·ly** *adv.* —**ver·ti·cil·la·tion** (-áysh'n) *n.*
ver·tig·i·nous (ver-tíjinəss) *adj.* **1.** Revolving; whirling; rotary. **2.** Affected by vertigo; dizzy. **3.** Tending to produce vertigo: *vertiginous speed.* **4.** Liable to quick change; unstable; inconstant. [Latin *vertīginōsus,* from *vertīgō* (stem *vertīgin-*), VERTIGO.] —**ver·tig·i·nous·ly** *adv.* —**ver·tig·i·nous·ness** *n.*
ver·ti·go (vérti-gō, *rarely* ver-tī-) *n., pl.* **-goes** or **vertigines** (ver-tíji-neez). **1.** The sensation of dizziness and the feeling that oneself or one's environment is whirling about. **2.** A confused, disorientated state of mind. [Latin *vertīgō,* "a whirling", from *vertere,* to turn.]
ver·tu. Variant of **virtu.**
Verulamium. See **St. Albans.**
ver·vain (vér-vayn) *n.* A perennial plant, *Verbena officinalis,* native to Europe having clusters of tiny, purplish-blue flowers. [Middle English *verveine,* from Old French, from Latin *verbēna,* often in plural *verbēnae,* sacred leaves or twigs of olive, myrtle, or laurel.]
verve (verv) *n.* **1.** Energy and enthusiasm in the expression of ideas and especially in artistic endeavour: *The play lacks verve.* **2.** Vitality; liveliness; vigour. [French, from Old French, fancy, fanciful expression, from Latin *verba,* plural of *verbum,* word.]
ver·vet (vérvit) *n.* A small, long-tailed African monkey, *Cercopithecus aethiops,* having a yellowish-brown or greenish coat. [French, short for *vert grivet* : *vert,* green (see **verdant**) + GRIVET.]
Ver·woerd (fər-vóort), **Hendrik Frensch** (1901–1966). South African statesman. While prime minister (1958–66), he pursued a policy of apartheid, and took South Africa out of the Commonwealth (1961). He was assassinated in Cape Town.
ver·y (vérri || vúrri) *adv. Abbr.* **v., V. 1.** In a high degree; extremely; exceedingly: *very happy.* **2.** Truly. Used as an intensive with superlatives: *the very best way to proceed.* **3.** Precisely: *the very same one.* —**not very. 1.** Not at all: *not very satisfied with the service.* **2.** Only a little: *He's not very much better.*
~*adj.* **verier, -iest. 1.** Complete; absolute; utter: *at the very end of his career.* **2.** Identical; selfsame: *There goes the very man I met.* **3.** Used as an intensive to emphasise the importance of the thing described: *The very mountains crumbled.* **4.** Particular; precise: *the very centre of town.* **5.** Mere: *The very mention of the name was frightening.* **6.** Actual: *caught in the very act.* **7.** As if actual. Used to reinforce a metaphor: *His fists are very rocks.* **8.** *Archaic.* Genuine; real; true: *"Like very sanctity she did approach"* (Shakespeare). [Middle English *verray,* from Old French *ver(r)ai,* true, real, from Vulgar Latin *vērāius* (unattested), from Latin *vērus,* true.]
Usage: *Very* may be used to modify a past participle, as in *She was very tired; She seems very interested,* where the past participle clearly has an adjectival function. However, in such sentences as *she was delayed/disliked/inconvenienced,* where the participle still seems partly verbal in function, more formal usage prefers *much, very much,* or *greatly,* and *very* has often been criticised in this kind of context.
very high frequency *n. Abbr.* **VHF, vhf** A band of radio frequencies falling between 30 and 300 megahertz.
Ve·ry light (véér-i, vérri) *n.* A coloured flare fired from a pistol (a *Very pistol*) as a signal or for temporary illumination. [After Edward W. *Very* (died 1910), U.S. naval officer.]
very low frequency *n. Abbr.* **VLF, vlf** A band of radio frequencies falling between 3 and 30 kilohertz.
ve·si·ca (véssi-kə, vée-si-, vi-sī-) *n., pl.* **-cae** (-see, -kee, -kī). **1.** A bladder; especially, the urinary bladder or the gallbladder. **2.** A vesica piscis. [Latin *vēsīca,* bladder, blister.] —**ves·i·cal** (véssik'l) *adj.*
vesica pis·cis (véssikə píssiss) *n.* A pointed oval shape formed by or as if by the intersection of two circles and used in medieval art, often as an aureole, to surround a sacred figure. Also called "vesica". [Latin, "fish's bladder".]
ves·i·cant (véssikənt) *n.* A blistering agent; especially, such an agent, as mustard gas, used in chemical warfare. —**ves·i·cant** *adj.*
ves·i·cate (véssi-kayt) *v.* **-cated, -cating, -cates.** —*tr.* To blister. —*intr.* To be or become blistered. [Late Latin *vēsīcāre,* from Latin *vēsīca,* bladder, blister, VESICA.] —**ves·i·ca·tion** (-káysh'n) *n.*
ves·i·ca·to·ry (véssi-kətri, -kaytəri, -káytəri) *adj.* Vesicant.
~*n., pl.* **vesicatories.** A vesicant.
ves·i·cle (véssik'l) *n.* **1.** A small bladder-like vacuole, cell, or cavity. **2.** *Anatomy.* A small bladder or sac, especially one containing fluid. **3.** *Pathology.* A serum-filled blister formed in or beneath the skin. **4.** An air-filled cavity found in certain aquatic plants. **5.** A small cavity formed in volcanic rock during solidification. [French *vésicule,* from Latin *vēsīcula,* diminutive of *vēsīca,* VESICA.]
ve·sic·u·lar (vi-síckewlər) *adj.* **1.** Of or pertaining to vesicles. **2.** Composed of or containing vesicles. **3.** Having the form of a vesicle. —**ve·sic·u·lar·ly** *adv.*
ve·sic·u·late (vi-síckew-layt) *v.* **-lated, -lating, -lates.** —*tr.* To make vesicular; blister. —*intr.* To become blistered or vesicular.
~*adj.* (-lət, -lit, -layt) **1.** Of, pertaining to, or resembling vesicles. **2.** Full of or bearing vesicles; vesicular. —**ve·sic·u·la·tion** (-láysh'n) *n.*
Ves·pa·sian (ve-spáyzh-'n, -yən, -spáyzi-ən), Latin name Titus Flavius Vespasianus (A.D. 9–79). Roman emperor (69–79). He restored

the empire's finances, reformed the army, patronised the arts, and began the building of the Coliseum.

ves·per (véspər) *n.* **1.** A bell used to summon persons to vespers. Also called "vesper bell". **2.** *Archaic.* Evening.
—*adj.* **1.** Of or pertaining to vespers. **2.** Pertaining to, appearing in, or appropriate to evening: *a vesper serenade.* [From VESPER.]

Vesper *n.* Formerly, the **evening star** *(see).* [Middle English, from Latin, evening, the evening star.]

ves·per·al (véspərəl) *n.* **1.** A book containing the words and hymns to be used at vespers. **2.** A covering used to protect the altar cloth between services.

ves·pers (véspərz) *pl.n. often capital* **V. 1. a.** The sixth of the seven **canonical hours** *(see).* **b.** The time of day set aside for this prayer, in the late afternoon or evening. **2.** Any service of worship held in the late afternoon or evening. **3.** *Roman Catholic Church.* A service held on Sundays or holy days which includes the office of vespers.

ves·per·tine (véss-pər-tīn, -per-) *adj.* Also **ves·per·ti·nal** (-tīn'l). **1.** Pertaining to or appearing in the evening. **2.** *Botany.* Opening or blooming in the evening. **3.** *Zoology.* Becoming active in the evening; crepuscular. **4.** *Astronomy.* Moving towards the horizon in the evening. [Latin *vespertīnus*, from *vesper*, evening, VESPER.]

ves·pi·ar·y (véspi-əri ‖ -erri) *n., pl.* **-ies.** A nest or colony of wasps or hornets. [Latin *vespa*, wasp + (AP)IARY.]

ves·pid (véspid) *n.* Any of various insects of the family Vespidae, which includes the common wasp and hornet. [New Latin *Vespidae*, from Latin *vespa*, wasp. See **vespiary**.] —**ves·pid** *adj.*

ves·pine (véss-pīn) *adj.* Of, pertaining to, or resembling a wasp or wasps. [From Latin *vespa*, wasp. See **vespiary**.]

Ves·puc·ci (ve-spōōchi), **Amerigo** (1454–1512). Italian navigator. He made several voyages to the New World and discovered (1499) the mouths of the Amazon, and (1501) the mouth of the Rio de la Plata. America is named after him.

ves·sel (véss'l) *n.* **1.** A hollow utensil used as a container, especially for liquids. **2.** A boat, ship, barge, or the like designed to transport passengers or freight on water. **3.** An airship. **4.** *Anatomy.* A duct, canal, or other tube for containing or circulating a bodily fluid: *a blood vessel.* **5.** *Botany.* Any of the tubular conductive structures of plant vascular tissue, consisting of cylindrical cells that are attached end to end. **6.** A person considered as a receptacle or agent of some specified quality: *a vessel of mercy.* [Middle English, from Old French *vaissel, vessel*, from Late Latin *vascellum*, diminutive of Latin *vās*, vessel, VAS.]

vest (vest) *n.* **1.** A simple undergarment covering the upper part of the body. **2.** *Chiefly U.S. & Australian.* A waistcoat. **3.** *Rare.* A fabric trimming or decoration worn by women to cover the bosom. **4.** *Archaic.* Clothing; dress. **5.** *Archaic.* An ecclesiastical vestment.
—*v.* **vested, vesting, vests.** —*tr.* **1.** To clothe or dress, as with ecclesiastical vestments. **2.** To place (authority, property, or rights, for example) in the control of someone. Used with *in: He vested his estate in his son.* **3.** To place authority, power, or the like, in the control of. Used with *with: The council was vested with enormous power.* —*intr.* **1.** To dress oneself, especially in ecclesiastical vestments. **2.** To be or become legally vested in a person or persons; come into the possession of someone. [French *veste*, from Italian, from Latin *vestis*, garment.]

ves·ta (véstə) *n. Archaic.* A short friction match made of wax or wood. [After the goddess VESTA.]

Vesta[1]. *Roman Mythology.* The goddess of the hearth, identified with the Greek goddess Hestia and worshipped in a temple containing the sacred fire tended by the vestal virgins. [Latin.]

Vesta[2] *n.* The third-largest asteroid in the solar system, having a diameter of approximately 380 kilometres (240 miles). [After the goddess VESTA.]

ves·tal (vést'l) *adj.* **1.** Pertaining to or sacred to Vesta. **2.** Pertaining to or characteristic of the vestal virgins; chaste; pure.
—*n.* **1.** A vestal virgin. **2.** A virgin woman. **3.** *Rare.* A nun.

vestal virgin *n.* Any of the four or six virgin priestesses who tended the sacred fire in the temple of Vesta in ancient Rome.

vest·ed (véstid) *adj.* **1.** *Law.* **a.** Settled, complete, or absolute; without contingency. Said of property or a right. **b.** Having unqualified present or future possession of a property or right. Said of a person, persons, or an organisation. **2.** Dressed or clothed, especially in ecclesiastical vestments.

vested interest *n.* **1.** *Law.* A right or title to ownership of property that can be conveyed to another. **2.** A strong concern for something, such as a state of affairs or an institution, from which one expects private benefit. **3.** *Usually plural.* A group that has a vested interest.

ves·ti·ar·y (vésti-əri ‖ -erri) *adj.* Of or pertaining to clothes.
—*n., pl.* **vestiaries.** A dressing room, cloakroom, or vestry. [Middle English *vestiarie*, from Old French, from Medieval Latin *vestiārium*, from Latin, wardrobe, from *vestiārius*, of clothes, from *vestis*, garment.]

vestibular nerve *n.* A division of the **acoustic nerve** *(see).*

ves·ti·bule (vésti-bewl) *n.* **1.** A small entrance hall or antechamber between two doors of a house or building. **2.** *Chiefly U.S.* An enclosed area at the end of a passenger car on a railway train. **3.** *Anatomy.* Any cavity, chamber, or channel that serves as an approach or entrance to another cavity or canal. [French, from Latin *vestibulum*†.] —**ves·tib·u·lar** (ve-stíbbew-lar) *adj.*

ves·tib·u·lo·coch·le·ar nerve (ve-stíbbew-lō-kóckli-ər) *n.* The **acoustic nerve** *(see).*

ves·tige (véstij) *n.* **1.** A visible trace, evidence, or sign of something

that has once existed but now no longer exists or appears. **2.** A very small quantity; a hint: *a vestige of garlic; not a vestige of truth in his claim.* **3.** *Biology.* A small, degenerate, or rudimentary organ or part existing in an organism as a usually nonfunctioning remnant of an organ or part fully developed and functional in a preceding generation or earlier developmental stage. —See Synonyms at **trace**. [French, from Latin *vestīgium*†, footprint, trace.]

ves·tig·i·al (ve-stíji-əl, -stíjəl) *adj.* **1.** Of, pertaining to, or constituting a vestige. **2.** *Biology.* Occurring or persisting as a rudimentary or degenerate structure. —**ves·tig·i·al·ly** *adv.*

vest·ment (véss-mənt, vést-) *n.* **1.** A garment; especially, a robe or gown worn as an indication of office or state. **2.** *Ecclesiastical.* Any of the ritual robes worn by clergymen, altar boys, or other assistants at services or rites; especially, a garment worn at the celebration of the Eucharist. [Middle English *vestiment*, from Old French *vestimentum*, from *vestīre*, to dress, from *vestis*, garment. See **vest**.] —**vest·ment·al** (vest-mént'l) *adj.*

vest-pock·et (vést-pockit) *adj. Chiefly U.S.* **1.** Designed to fit into a waistcoat pocket. **2.** Relatively small; diminutive.

ves·try (véstri) *n., pl.* **-tries. 1.** A room in or adjoining a church where the clergy put on their vestments and where these robes and other sacred objects are stored; a sacristy. **2.** A meeting room in a church. **3.** In the Anglican and Episcopal churches, a committee of members of the parish or congregation that administers the affairs of the parish or congregation. **4.** In the Anglican Church, a meeting of this group or of the entire congregation or the place in which the meeting is held. [Middle English *vestrie*, variant of *vestiarie*, VESTIARY.]

ves·try·man (véstri-mən) *n., pl.* **-men** (-mən). A member of a vestry.

ves·ture (véss-chər, -tewr) *n. Archaic.* **1.** Clothing; apparel. **2.** Anything that covers or cloaks: *hills in a vesture of mist.*
—*tr.v.* **vestured, -turing, -tures.** *Archaic.* To cover with vesture; clothe. [Middle English, clothes, from Old French, from Late Latin *vestītūra*, from Latin *vestīre*, to clothe. See **vestment**.]

ve·su·vi·an (vi-séw-vi-ən, və-, -sōō-) *n.* A match formerly used for lighting cigars; a fusee. [From VESUVIUS.]

ve·su·vi·an·ite (vi-séw-vi-ə-nīt, və-, -sōō-) *n.* A mineral, **idocrase** *(see).* [*Vesuvian*, of VESUVIUS (because first found in the lava of the volcano) + -ITE.]

Ve·su·vi·us (vi-séw-vi-əss, və-, -sōō-). Active volcano in southern Italy. Rising some 1 280 metres (4,200 feet) from the Bay of Naples, it has a seismological station on its west slope. In A.D. 79 the first recorded eruption destroyed Pompeii, Stabiae, and Herculaneum.

vet[1] (vet) *n.* A person trained and authorised to treat animals medically. Also called "veterinary", formally "veterinary surgeon", *U.S.* "veterinarian".
—*tr.v.* **vetted, vetting, vets. 1.** *Informal.* To give medical treatment to (an animal). **2.** To examine or investigate and appraise for acceptability: *vet a manuscript; carefully vetted for the job.* [Shortening of VETERINARY.]

vet[2] (vet) *n. U.S. Informal.* An ex-serviceman; a military veteran.

vet. **1.** veteran. **2.** veterinary. **3.** veterinary surgeon.

vetch (vech) *n.* **1.** Any of various climbing or twining plants of the genus *Vicia*, having pinnate leaves and small, usually purplish flowers. **2.** Any of various similar related plants such as the milk vetches and the kidney vetch. [Middle English *fecche*, from Old North French *veche*, from Latin *vicia*.]

vetch·ling (véchling) *n.* Any of several plants of the genus *Lathyrus*, having pinnate leaves, slender tendrils, winged or angled stems, and variously coloured pealike flowers. [VETCH + -LING.]

veter. veterinary.

vet·er·an (véttrən, véttərən) *n. Abbr.* **vet. 1.** One who has a long record of service in a given activity or capacity or long experience, especially one who has seen much active service as a member of the armed forces. **2.** *U.S.* An ex-serviceman.
—*adj.* **1.** Experienced because of long service: *a veteran politician.* **2.** Pertaining to or suggestive of a veteran or veterans. [French *vétéran*, from Latin *veterānus*, from *vetus* (stem *veter*-), old.]

veteran car *n.* A motor car made before 1919. Compare **vintage car**.

Veterans Day *n.* November 11, observed as a national holiday in the United States, the U.S. equivalent of **Armistice Day** *(see).*

vet·er·i·nar·i·an (véttrə-naír-i-ən, véttərə-) *n. U.S.* A vet.

vet·er·i·nar·y (vétt'n-ri, véttrin-, véttərin-, -əri ‖ -erri) *adj. Abbr.* **vet., veter.** Of, pertaining to, or designating the science of the diagnosis and treatment of diseases and injuries of animals, especially domestic animals.
—*n., pl.* **veterinaries.** A vet. [Latin *veterīnārius*, from *veterīnae*, cattle.]

veterinary medicine *n.* The medical science of the prevention, diagnosis, and treatment of animal diseases and injuries. Also called "veterinary science".

veterinary surgeon *n. Abbr.* **vet. V.S.** *Formal.* A vet.

vet·i·ver (véttivər) *n.* **1.** A grass, *Vetiveria zizanioides*, of tropical Asia, cultivated for its aromatic roots that yield an oil used in perfumery. **2.** The root of this plant. [French *vetiver, vetyver*, from Tamil *veṭṭivēru : veṭṭi*, worthlessness + *vēru*, useless.]

ve·to (vée-tō) *n., pl.* **-toes. 1.** The vested power or constitutional right of a sovereign or a branch or department of government, especially the right of a chief executive or an upper legislative body, to reject a bill passed by a (lower) legislative body and thus prevent or delay its enactment into law. **2.** The exercise of this right. **3.** *U.S.* The official document communicating the rejection and the reasons

for it. Also called "veto message". **4.** The right of any full or permanent member of various other policy-making bodies, such as the United Nations Security Council, to prevent the passage of a resolution. **5.** Any authoritative prohibition or rejection of a proposed or intended act.
—tr.v. **vetoed, -toing, -toes. 1.** To prevent (a legislative bill) from becoming law by exercising the power of veto. **2.** To forbid or prevent authoritatively; prohibit. [Latin *vetō,* I forbid, from *vetāre*†, to forbid.] **—ve·to·er** *n.*

vex (veks) *tr.v.* **vexed, vexing, vexes. 1.** To irritate or annoy, as with petty matters; bother; pester. **2.** To cause serious suffering to; plague or afflict. **3.** To confuse; baffle; puzzle. **4.** *Formal.* To debate (a problem) at length; bring up repeatedly for discussion. **5.** *Archaic.* To toss about or stir up; agitate. —See Synonyms at **annoy.** [Middle English *vexen,* from Old French *vexer,* from Latin *vexāre,* to shake, annoy.] **—vex·er** *n.* **—vex·ing·ly** *adv.*

vex·a·tion (vek-sáysh'n) *n.* **1.** The act of vexing. **2.** The state or condition of being vexed; annoyance. **3.** One that vexes; a source of irritation or annoyance.

vex·a·tious (vek-sáyshəss) *adj.* **1.** Causing or creating vexation; annoying; irksome. **2.** Full of vexation; disturbed; annoyed. **3.** *Law.* Instituted without sufficient grounds, to serve solely as an annoyance to a defendant. Said of legal actions. **—vex·a·tious·ly** *adv.* **—vex·a·tious·ness** *n.*

vexed (vekst) *adj.* **1.** Irritated; annoyed; troubled. **2.** Much debated; subject to controversy. Used chiefly in the phrase *a vexed question.* **—vex·ed·ly** (véksid-li) *adv.* **—vex·ed·ness** *n.*

vex·il·lar·y (vek-sílləri || *U.S.* véksə-lerri) *n., pl.* **-ies. 1.** A member of the oldest class of army veterans who served under a special standard in ancient Rome. **2.** A standard-bearer.
—adj. Also **vex·il·lar** (vek-síllər, véksilər). Of or pertaining to a banner or standard. [Latin *vexillārius,* from *vexillum,* flag. See **vexillum.**]

vex·il·late (vek-síll-ayt, véksil-, -ət, -it) *adj.* Having a vexillum.

vex·il·lol·o·gy (véksi-lóllәji) *n.* The study of flags. [Latin *vexillum,* flag + -LOGY.] **—vex·il·lol·o·gist** *n.*

vex·il·lum (vek-síl-əm) *n., pl.* **vexilla** (-ə). **1.** *Botany.* A usually enlarged upper petal of certain flowers; a standard. **2.** *Zoology.* The weblike part of a feather; a vane. **3.** In ancient Rome, a military flag or standard. **4.** The small division of troops serving under such a standard. **5.** A ceremonial flag of a bishop, used especially in processions. [Latin, flag, diminutive of *vēlum,* cloth, veil, sail.]

V.F. 1. vicar forane. **2.** video frequency. **3.** visual field.

v.g. very good.

V.G. vicar general.

vhf, VHF very high frequency.

v.i. vide infra.

V.I. 1. Virgin Islands. **2.** volume indicator.

vi·a (ví-ə, vír || veé-ə) *prep.* **1. a.** By way of; through: *the route to Cardiff via Reading and Oxford.* **b.** By way of and stopping at: *We can go home via the shops.* **2.** By means of: *I'll get the parcel to you via a friend of mine.* [Latin *viā,* ablative of *via,* road, way.]

vi·a·ble (ví-əb'l) *adj.* **1.** Capable of living. Said of a newborn infant, or a foetus that has reached the stage of development that will permit it to survive and develop under normal conditions. **2.** Capable of living, developing, or germinating under favourable conditions. Said of seeds, spores, or eggs. **3.** Capable of actualisation, as a project might be; practicable: *a viable method of reducing costs.* —See Synonyms at **possible.** [French, from Old French, from *vie,* life, from Latin *vīta.*] **—vi·a·bil·i·ty** (ví-ə-bílləti) *n.*

Vi·a Do·lo·ro·sa (veé-ə dóllə-rṓ-sə || dṓlə-) *n.* **1.** Jesus' route from Pilate's judgment hall to Calvary. **2.** A difficult or painful course or experience. [Latin, "sad road".]

vi·a·duct (ví-ə-dukt) *n.* A series of spans or arches used to carry a road or railway over a wide valley or over other roads or railways. [Latin *via,* road, way (see **via**) + (AQUA)DUCT.]

Vi·a·gra (vī-ággrə, vee-) *n.* **1.** A trademark for an anti-impotence drug to inhibit the action of an enzyme that normally breaks down a chemical necessary for getting and keeping an erection. Also called sildenafil citrate. **2.** A dose (e.g. a tablet) of Viagra.

vi·al (ví-əl) *n.* A small container, usually glass, for liquids. Also called "phial".
—tr.v. **vialled** or *U.S.* **vialed, -alling** or *U.S.* **-aling, -als.** To put or keep in or as if in a vial. [Middle English *viole,* variant of *fiole,* PHIAL.]

vi·a me·di·a (ví-ə meé-di-ə, veé-ə máy-) *n.* A middle route, policy, or course avoiding extremes. [Latin.]

vi·and (ví-ənd) *n.* **1.** An article of food. **2.** *Plural.* Provisions; victuals. [Middle English *viaunde,* from Old French *viande,* from Vulgar Latin *vī(v)anda* (unattested), variant of Latin *vīvenda,* gerundive of *vīvere,* to live.]

Viang·chan, Vien·tiane (vyén-tyán, -tyaán). Capital and largest city of Laos. It lies on the north bank of the Mekong (the border with Thailand), and has many canals. It is the country's main trade outlet (via Bangkok), and has been its capital since 1899. Nearby is the ruined capital of a Lao kingdom (1707–1827).

vi·at·ic (vī-áttik) *adj.* Also **vi·at·i·cal** (-'l). *Formal.* Of or pertaining to travelling, a road, or a way. [Latin *viāticus.* See **viaticum.**]

vi·at·i·cum (vī-átti-kəm, vi-) *n., pl.* **-ca** (-kə) or **-cums. 1.** Holy communion as given to a dying person or one in danger of death. **2.** *Rare.* Supplies for a journey. [Latin *viāticum,* travelling provisions, from *viāticus,* of a road or journey, from *via,* way, road. See **via.**]

vibes (vībz) *pl.n.* **1.** *Slang.* An unspoken and often unconscious message given by one person or group to another, or the resulting emotional reaction; vibrations: *bad vibes.* **2.** *Informal.* A vibraphone. [Shortened from VIBRATIONS.] **—vib·ist** *n.*

vi·brac·u·lum (vī-bráckew-ləm) *n., pl.* **-la** (-lə). *Zoology.* Any of the long, whiplike filaments on the surface of certain bryozoan colonies. [New Latin, diminutive formation from Latin *vibrāre,* to shake, brandish, VIBRATE.] **—vi·brac·u·lar** (-lər) *adj.* **—vi·brac·u·loid** (-loyd) *adj.*

vi·brant (víbrənt) *adj.* **1.** Exhibiting, characterised by, or resulting from vibration; vibrating. **2.** Pulsing or throbbing with energy or activity: *vibrant verse.* [Latin *vibrāre* (see **vibrate**) + -ANT.] **—vi·bran·cy** *n.* **—vi·brant·ly** *adv.*

vi·bra·phone (víbrə-fōn) *n.* An electronic percussion instrument similar to a marimba but having metal bars and rotating discs in the resonators to produce a vibrato. Also called "vibra-harp", informally "vibes". [VIBRA(TE) + -PHONE.] **—vi·bra·phon·ist** (-fōnist) *n.*

vi·brate (vī-bráyt || *U.S.* ví-brayt) *v.* **-brated, -brating, -brates.**
—intr. **1.** To move back and forth rapidly; oscillate. **2.** To produce a sound; resonate. **3.** To be moved emotionally; thrill: *vibrate with excitement.* **4.** To fluctuate or waver in making choices; vacillate.
—tr. **1.** To cause to tremble or quiver. **2.** To cause to move back and forth rapidly. **3.** To produce (sound) by vibration. —See Synonyms at **swing.** [Latin *vibrāre.*]

vi·bra·tile (víbrə-tīl || *U.S. also* -t'l) *adj.* **1.** Characterised by vibration. **2.** Capable of or adapted to vibratory motion. [French, from Latin *vibrāre,* VIBRATE.] **—vi·bra·til·i·ty** (-tílləti) *n.*

vi·bra·tion (vī-bráysh'n) *n.* **1.** The act or an instance of vibrating. **2.** The condition of being vibrated. **3.** *Physics.* **a.** A rapid linear motion of a particle or of an elastic solid about an equilibrium position. **b.** Any periodic process. **4.** A single complete vibrating motion; a quiver; a tremor. **5.** *Usually plural. Slang.* **a.** A distinctive emotional reaction by a person to another person or thing, instinctively sensed or experienced. **b.** The atmosphere or subtle message producing such a reaction. **—vi·bra·tion·al** *adj.*

vi·bra·to (vi-braátō || vee-) *n., pl.* **-tos.** *Music.* A tremulous or pulsating effect produced in an instrumental or vocal tone by barely perceptible minute and rapid variations in pitch. Compare **tremolo.** [Italian, from Latin *vibrātus,* past participle of *vibrāre,* VIBRATE.]

vi·bra·tor (vī-bráytər || *U.S.* ví-braytər) *n.* **1.** Something that vibrates. **2.** An electrically or battery operated device used for massage. **3.** A dildo with a vibrating tip, used for sexual stimulation. **4.** An electrical device consisting basically of a vibrating conductor interrupting a current.

vi·bra·to·ry (víbrə-tri, -təri, vī-bráytəri) *adj.* Also **vi·bra·tive** (vībráytiv || víbrətiv). **1.** Of, characterised by, or consisting of vibration. **2.** Causing vibration. **3.** Vibrating or capable of vibration.

vib·ri·o (vibbri-ō) *n., pl.* **-os.** Any of various S-shaped or comma-shaped microorganisms of the genus *Vibrio,* especially *V. cholerae,* which causes cholera. [New Latin, arbitrarily from Latin *vibrāre,* VIBRATE (from their vibratory motion).] **—vib·ri·oid** (-oyd) *adj.*

vi·bris·sa (vī-bríss-ə) *n., pl.* **-brissae** (-brissee). A stiff hair or hair-like projection, such as a nostril hair, any of the whiskers of a cat, or any of the modified feathers near the beak of an insectivorous bird. [Latin *vibrissae* (plural), from *vibrāre,* VIBRATE.]

vi·bur·num (vī-búrnəm) *n.* **1.** Any of various shrubs or trees of the genus *Viburnum,* characteristically having clusters of small white flowers and berry-like red or black fruit. **2.** The bark of certain of these trees containing substances used medicinally. [New Latin *Viburnum,* from Latin *vīburnum*†, wayfaring tree.]

vic. 1. vicar. **2.** vicinity.

vic·ar (víckər) *n. Abbr.* **vic. 1.** In the Church of England, the appointed priest of a parish. **2.** In the Episcopal Church of the United States, a clergyman in charge of a chapel. **3.** In the Anglican Communion generally, a clergyman acting in the place of a rector or bishop. **4.** *Roman Catholic Church.* A deputy or representative for an ecclesiastic. See **Vicar of Christ. 5.** One who fulfils the duties of another; a substitute; a deputy. [Middle English, from Old French *vicaire,* from Latin *vicārius,* a substitute, from *vicārius,* substituting, acting for, from *vicis,* change, turn, office.]

vic·ar·age (víckərij) *n.* **1.** The residence of a vicar. **2.** *Rare.* The benefice of a vicar.

vicar apostolic *n., pl.* **vicars apostolic.** *Abbr.* **V.A.** *Roman Catholic Church.* **1. a.** A titular bishop who, as a representative of the Holy See, administers a region that is not yet a diocese. **b.** A titular bishop appointed to administer to a vacant see in which the succession of bishops has been interrupted. **2.** Formerly, a bishop delegated by the pope to act in his stead in a particular region.

vicar fo·rane (fo-ráyn || faw-, fō-) *n., pl.* **vicars forane.** *Abbr.* **V.F.** *Roman Catholic Church.* A priest who by a bishop's appointment exercises limited jurisdiction over the clergy in a distant district of a diocese. [From Late Latin *forānus,* FOREIGN.]

vicar general *n., pl.* **vicars general.** *Abbr.* **V.G. 1.** *Roman Catholic Church.* A priest acting as deputy to a bishop to assist him in the administration of his diocese. **2.** An ecclesiastical official, usually a layman, who assists an Anglican archbishop or bishop in administrative and judicial duties.

vi·car·i·al (vi-káir-i-əl, vī-) *adj.* **1.** Of or pertaining to a vicar or vicars. **2.** Acting as or having the position of a vicar. **3.** Vicarious or delegated, as powers of an ecclesiastical office might be.

vi·car·i·ate (vi-káir-i-ət, vī-, -it, -ayt) *n.* Also **vic·ar·ate** (víckər-). **1.** The office rank, or authority of a vicar. **2.** The district under a vicar's jurisdiction. [Medieval Latin *vicāriātus,* from Late Latin *vi-*

cārius, vicar, VICARIOUS.]

vi·car·i·ous (vi-kaír-i-əss, vī-) *adj.* **1.** Performed or endured by one person substituting for another; fulfilled by the substitution of the actual offender with some other person or thing: *vicarious punishment.* **2.** Acting in place of someone or something else; delegated; substituted: *a vicarious power of authority.* **3.** Experienced or enjoyed through sympathetic or imaginative participation in the experiences of another: *a vicarious thrill.* **4.** *Physiology.* Occurring in or performed by a part of the body not normally associated with a certain function. [Latin *vicārius,* substituting, from *vicis,* change, turn, office.] **—vi·car·i·ous·ly** *adv.* **—vi·car·i·ous·ness** *n.*

Vicar of Christ *n. Roman Catholic Church.* The pope considered as the earthly deputy of Christ.

vic·ar·ship (vickər-ship) *n.* The office or tenure of a vicar.

vice¹ (vīss) *n.* **1.** An evil, degrading, or immoral practice or habit; a serious moral failing. **2.** Wicked or evil conduct or habits; indulgence in degrading practices; depravity; corruption. **3. a.** Sexual immorality; especially, prostitution. **b.** Sexual perversion. **4.** A slight personal failing; a foible: *His only vice is partiality for practical jokes.* **5.** A flaw or imperfection; a defect; a fault: *the vices in his theory.* **6.** *Archaic.* A physical defect or weakness. **7.** An item of abnormal or perverse behaviour in a domestic animal such as a tendency in a horse to bite. **8.** *Capital* **V.** A character representing a particular or generalised vice, often represented in English morality plays as a or jester or buffoon. —See Synonyms at **fault.** [Middle English, from Old French, from Latin *vitium,* blemish, offence, vice.]

vice², *U.S.* **vise** *n.* A clamping device, especially one with a pair of adjustable jaws, used for holding a workpiece while it is hammered, filed, sawn, or the like.

~tr.v. **viced, vicing, vices.** To secure with or as if with a vice.

vice³ (vīss) *n. Abbr.* **v., V.** One who acts in the place of another; a deputy.

~prep. (vī-si) In place of; replacing. [Latin *vice,* ablative of *vicis,* change.]

vice– *prefix.* Indicates one representing or substituting or able to act or deputise for another; for example, **vice-chairman, vice-chamberlain, viceregal.** [Middle English *vis-,* from Old French, from Late Latin *vice-,* from Latin *vice,* in place of, VICE.]

vice-ad·mir·al (vīss-ádmərəl, vīss-) *n. Abbr.* **V.A., V. Adm.** A naval officer ranking between an admiral and a rear admiral, equivalent in rank to a lieutenant-general in the Army or an air marshall in the Air Force. **—vice-ad·mir·al·ty** (-ti) *n.*

vice-chan·cel·lor (vīss-chaán-slər, vīss-, -sələr || -chán-) *n. Abbr.* **V.C. 1.** In many universities, the principal or chief administrator, especially where the chancellorship is a purely honorary post. **2.** *U.S. Law.* A judge in equity courts ranking below a chancellor. **3.** *British Law.* Formerly, a judge in the court of chancery who assisted the Lord Chancellor. **4.** A deputy or substitute for a chancellor. **—vice-chan·cel·lor·ship** *n.*

vice-consul (vīss-kónss'l) *n. Abbr.* **V.C.** A consular officer who is subordinate to and a deputy of a consul or consul general. **—vice-con·su·lar** (-kón-sew-lər) *adj.* **—vice-con·su·late** (-kón-sew-lət, -lit, -layt) *n.* **—vice-con·sul·ship** *n.*

vice·ge·ren·cy (vīss-jérrən-si, -jeérən-) *n., pl.* **-cies. 1.** The position, function, or authority of a vicegerent. **2.** A district under a vicegerent's jurisdiction.

vice·ge·rent (vīss-jérrənt, -jeér-ənt) *n.* **1.** A person appointed by a ruler or head of state to act as an administrative deputy. **2.** *Roman Catholic Church.* **a.** The pope. **b.** Any other bishop or priest considered as the earthly deputy of God or Christ. [Medieval Latin *vicegerēns* : VICE- + GERENT.] **—vice·ge·ral, vice·ge·rent** *adj.*

vic·e·nar·y (víssi-nri, -nəri || -nerri) *adj.* **1.** Consisting of or pertaining to 20. **2.** Designating a notation system based on 20. [Latin *vīcēnārius,* from *vīcēnī,* 20 each, from *vīgintī,* 20.]

vi·cen·ni·al (vī-sénni-əl, vi-) *adj.* **1.** Happening once every 20 years. **2.** Existing or lasting for 20 years. [Late Latin *vīcennium,* period of 20 years : Latin *vīciēs,* 20 times, from *vīgintī,* 20 + *annus,* year.]

Vi·cen·za (vee-chéntsə). City in Venetia, northeastern Italy. Capital of Vicenza province and a powerful medieval city, it has a Gothic cathedral and some fine Palladian architecture.

vice-president (vīss-prézzi-d'nt, vīss- || -dent) *Abbr.* **V.P., V. Pres. 1.** An officer ranking immediately below a president, usually empowered to assume the president's duties under such conditions as absence, illness, or death. **2.** *U.S.* A deputy of a president, especially in a large business enterprise, in charge of a separate department or location: *vice-president in charge of marketing.* **—vice-pres·i·den·cy** *n.* **—vice-pres·i·den·tial** (-dénsh'l) *adj.*

vice·re·gal (vīss-reég'l) *adj.* **1.** Of or pertaining to a viceroy. **2.** *Chiefly Australian.* Of or pertaining to a governor-general. [VICE- + REGAL.] **—vice·re·gal·ly** *adv.*

vice-regent (vīss-reéjənt) *n.* One who acts as a regent's deputy. **—vice-re·gen·cy** *n.* **—vice-re·gent** *adj.*

vice·reine (vīss-ráyn, -rayn) *n.* **1.** The wife of a viceroy. **2.** *Rare.* A female viceroy. [French : VICE- + *reine,* queen, from Latin *rēgīna,* feminine of *rēx,* king.]

vice·roy (vīss-roy) *n., pl.* **-roys.** A governor of a country, province, or colony, ruling as the representative of a sovereign or king. [French : *vice-* + *roi,* king, from Latin *rēx.*]

vice·roy·al·ty (vīss-róy-əlti || -roy-) *n., pl.* **-ties. 1.** The office, rank, or authority of a viceroy. **2.** The term of service of a viceroy. **3.** A district or province governed by a viceroy. Also called "viceroyship".

vice squad *n.* A police division charged with the control of vice, especially prostitution and gambling.

vi·ce ver·sa (vī-si vér-sə || vīss) *Abbr.* **v.v.** The order or meaning being reversed; with principal items transposed; conversely. Said of a preceding statement: *He betrayed her, or vice versa.* [Latin, "the position being changed" : *vice,* ablative singular of *vicis,* change, office, position + *versā,* ablative feminine singular of *versus,* past participle of *vertere,* to turn, change.]

Vi·chy (veéshi, víshi; *French* vee-sheé). A health resort of central France. Situated on the Allier river in the Allier département, it is world famous for its mineral springs. During World War II, it was the seat of the collaboratist Pétain government.

vi·chy·ssoise (veéshi-swaáz, víshi-) *n.* A thick, creamy leek and potato soup, usually served cold. [French, "of Vichy".]

Vichy water *n.* **1.** A naturally effervescent mineral water from the springs at Vichy, France, reputed to have medicinal benefits. **2.** Any sparkling mineral water resembling this. Also called "Vichy", "vichy".

vic·i·nage (víssinij) *n.* **1. a.** A limited region around a particular area; a neighbourhood; a vicinity. **b.** A number of places collectively that are situated near one another. **2.** The residents of a particular neighbourhood. **3.** The state of living in a neighbourhood; proximity; nearness. [Middle English *vesinage,* from Old French *visenage,* from Vulgar Latin *vīcīnāticum* (unattested), from *vīcīnus,* neighbour. See **vicinity.**]

vic·i·nal (víssin'l) *adj.* **1.** Of, belonging to, or restricted to a limited area or neighbourhood; nearby; adjacent. **2.** Designating a local road as opposed to a main road or highway. **3.** *Chemistry.* Approximating, resembling, or taking the place of a fundamental crystal form or face. **4.** *Chemistry.* Designating or pertaining to substituted atoms or groups on adjacent atoms in a molecule. Compare **gem.** [Latin *vīcīnālis,* from *vīcīnus,* neighbour. See **vicinity.**]

vi·cin·i·ty (vi-sínnəti, vī-) *n., pl.* **-ties.** *Abbr.* **vic. 1.** The state of being near in space or relationship; proximity; propinquity: *two restaurants in close vicinity.* **2.** A nearby, surrounding, or adjoining region; a neighbourhood; a locality. [Latin *vīcīnitās* (stem *vīcīnitāt-*), from *vīcīnus,* neighbour, from *vīcus,* village.]

vi·cious (víshəss) *adj.* **1.** Having the nature of vice, evil, or immorality; depraved; debased. **2.** Addicted to vice, immorality, or depravity; malicious; reprobate; evil. **3.** Characterised by spite or malice: *vicious gossip.* **4.** Failing to meet a standard or criterion; having a fault, flaw, or defect: *a vicious syllogism.* **5.** *Archaic.* Impure; foul; diseased. **6.** Disposed to or characterised by violence or destructive behaviour. **7.** Behaving in an unruly or potentially dangerous manner: *a vicious animal.* **8.** Being of an extreme or intense degree: *a vicious hurricane.* —See Synonyms at **cruel.** [Middle English, from Old French, from Latin *vitiōsus,* from *vitium,* VICE.] **—vi·cious·ly** *adv.* **—vi·cious·ness** *n.*

vicious circle *n.* **1.** A situation in which the solution of one problem in a chain of circumstances creates a new problem that leads back to the original problem and increases the difficulty of solving it. **2.** A condition in which a disorder or disease gives rise to another which subsequently affects the first. **3.** *Logic.* A **circle** *(see).*

vi·cis·si·tude (vī-síssi-tewd, vi- || -tōōd) *n.* **1.** *Usually plural.* Any change or variation in something; mutability. **2.** Natural change or variation; alterations manifested in nature and human affairs. **3.** An alteration or variation in fortune. **4.** An alternating change; a succession. [From French, from Latin *vicissitūdō,* from *vicissim,* in turn, from *vicis,* change, turn.]

vi·cis·si·tu·di·nar·y (vī-síssi-téw-din-əri, vi-, -d'n- || -tōō-, -erri) *adj.* Also **vi·cis·si·tu·di·nous** (-əss). Having or showing vicissitudes.

Vick·ers (víckərz), **Jon** (1926–). Canadian tenor. He is acclaimed for his performances in operas by Wagner and Verdi.

Vicks·burg (víks-burg). A river port of the southeastern United States. Situated on the Mississippi at its confluence with the Yazoo river, it was the site of a siege in the American Civil War that culminated in the Confederate surrender (1863).

Vick·y (vícki), pen name of Victor Weisz (1913–66). German-born Hungarian cartoonist. He made his name as a political cartoonist with various London newspapers.

Vi·co (veékō), **Giambattista,** also called Giovanni Battista Vico (1668–1744). Italian historical philosopher. He was the first philosopher to see history in terms of the rise and fall of human societies, and to make use of myths and legends as historical evidence.

vi·comte (vee-kónt) *n. Feminine* **vi·com·tesse** (-kon-téss). A French nobleman, equal in rank to a British viscount. [French, VISCOUNT.]

vic·tim (víktim) *n.* **1.** Someone who is put to death or subjected to torture or suffering by another. **2.** A living creature slain and offered as a sacrifice to a deity or as part of a religious rite. **3.** One who is harmed by or made to suffer from an act, circumstance, agency, or condition: *victims of war.* **4.** A person who suffers injury, loss, or death as a result of a voluntary undertaking: *a victim of his own scheming.* **5.** A person who is tricked, swindled, or taken advantage of; a dupe. [Latin *victima.*]

vic·tim·ise, vic·tim·ize (víkti-mīz) *tr.v.* **-ised, -ising, -ises. 1.** To single out unfairly for punishment, or abuse; discriminate against and bully. **2.** To subject to a swindle or fraud. **3.** To make a victim of by or as if by slaying. **—vic·tim·i·sa·tion** (-mī-záysh'n || *U.S.* -mi-) *n.* **—vic·tim·is·er** *n.*

vic·tim·less (víktim-ləss, -liss) *adj.* Designating a legal offence, such as possession of drugs, in which there is no victim involved, except perhaps the offender himself.

vic·tor (víktər) *n.* **1.** One who defeats or vanquishes an adversary;

the winner in a fight, battle, or war. **2.** A winner of a contest or struggle. [Middle English, from Latin, from *vincere* (past participle *victus*), to conquer.]

Victor Emmanuel II (1820–78). The last king of Sardinia and first king of Italy. He became king of Sardinia (1849–61) on the abdication of his father, Charles Albert. After becoming king of Italy (1861) he completed its unification by acquiring Venice (1866), and Rome (which he made his capital) (1871).

vic·to·ri·a (vik-táw-ri-ə ‖ -tṓ-) *n.* **1.** A low, light, four-wheeled carriage for two with a folding top and an elevated driver's seat in front. **2.** A touring car with a folding top usually covering only the rear seat. **3.** A **victoria plum** *(see).* **4.** Any of various water lilies of the South American genus *Victoria,* having large, round, floating leaves. [After Queen Victoria.]

Victoria[1] (vik-táw-ri-ə ‖ -tṓ). State of southeastern Australia. The second smallest and most densely populated of the Australian states, it is, with irrigation, a leading farming state, producing cereals, fruit and vegetables, dairy produce, wine, meat and wool. It supplies some 70 per cent of Australia's petroleum, its other minerals including natural gas, brown coal, and gold. Victoria's industries, concentrated around the capital, Melbourne, include metals and machinery, textiles, clothing, footwear, and vehicles.

Victoria[2]. The capital of British Columbia, Canada. Situated on the southeast tip of Vancouver Island, it was founded (1843) by the Hudson Bay Company.

Victoria[3] Former capital of Hong Kong. Lying on the northeast shore of Hong Kong Island, it is the territory's biggest city, and chief port, and is also known as Hong Kong or Xianggang.

Victoria, Lake. Also **Victoria Ny·an·za.** Africa's largest lake and the world's second-largest freshwater body. It covers 69 452 square kilometres (26,815 square miles), and lies in a shallow depression between the two arms of the Great Rift Valley.

Victoria, Queen (1819–1901). Queen of Great Britain and Empress of India. She was the daughter of George III's fourth son, Edward, Duke of Kent, and became Queen (1837) on the death of her uncle, William IV. In 1876 she was proclaimed Empress of India by Disraeli. Her great sense of duty and strict moral code set the pattern for 19th-century Britain. During her reign, constitutional government was fully developed, and the crown's prestige restored.

Victoria Cross *n. Abbr.* **V.C.** An award in the shape of a bronze Maltese cross, the highest military decoration awarded in the British and Commonwealth armed forces for conspicuous valour.

Victoria Falls. Falls on the Zambezi river, on the border between Zambia and Zimbabwe. Forming the world's third-largest falls, their total width can span over a kilometre (just over half a mile). They were discovered (1855) by David Livingstone, and named in honour of Queen Victoria.

Vic·to·ri·an (vik-táw-ri-ən ‖ -tṓ-) *adj.* **1.** Of or pertaining to Queen Victoria or the period of her reign: *a Victorian novel.* **2.** Exhibiting qualities usually associated with the time of Queen Victoria, such as moral severity or hypocrisy, middle-class stuffiness, and pompous conservatism. **3.** Pertaining to, designating, or constructed in the highly ornamented, massive style of architecture, decor, and furnishings popular in 19th-century England. **4.** Of or pertaining to any of the various geographical units named Victoria.
~*n.* A person belonging to or exhibiting characteristics typical of the period of Queen Victoria.

Vic·to·ri·a·na (vik-táw-ri-áanə ‖ -tṓ-, -ánnə, -áynə) *n. Used with a singular verb.* Assorted objects such as books, photographs, and ornaments, of the Victorian period. [Victoria + -ana.]

Vic·to·ri·an·ism (vik-táw-ri-ən-iz'm ‖ -tṓ-) *n.* **1.** The state of having Victorian characteristics, as in attitude, style, or taste. **2.** Something exhibiting Victorian characteristics.

victoria plum *n.* A plum of a variety having large, red, sweet fruits. Also called "victoria". [After Queen Victoria.]

vic·to·ri·ous (vik-táw-ri-əss ‖ -tṓ-) *adj.* **1.** Having overcome an opponent or enemy; triumphant; conquering. **2.** Characteristic of or expressing a sense of victory or fulfilment: *a victorious smile.* [Middle English, from Latin *victōriōsus,* from *victōria,* VICTORY.] —**vic·to·ri·ous·ly** *adv.* —**vic·to·ri·ous·ness** *n.*

vic·to·ry (vík-tri, -təri) *n., pl.* **-ries.** *Abbr.* **V 1.** Final and complete defeat of the enemy in a military engagement. **2.** Any successful struggle against an opponent or obstacle. **3.** The state of having triumphed. [Middle English, from Old French *victorie,* from Latin *victōria,* from *victor,* VICTOR.]

vic·tress (vík-triss, -tress) *n.* A female victor.

vict·ual (vítt'l) *n.* Also *nonstandard* **vit·tle.** *Usually plural.* **1.** Food fit for human consumption. **2.** Provisions; food supplies.
~*v.* **victualled** or *U.S.* **victualed, -ualling** or *U.S.* **-ualing, -uals.** Also *nonstandard* **vit·tle, -tled, -tling, -tles.** —*tr.* To provide with food. —*intr.* **1.** To lay in food supplies. **2.** *Rare.* To eat. [Middle English *vitaille,* from Old French, from Late Latin *victūālia,* plural of *victūālis,* provision, from Latin *victus,* sustenance, from the past participle of *vīvere,* to live.]

vict·ual·ler (vítt'l-ər) *n.* Also *U.S.* **vict·ual·er.** **1.** A supplier of victuals; a sutler. **2.** A supply ship. **3.** *Chiefly British.* One who is allowed to sell alcohol, such as an innkeeper or publican; a licensed victualler.

vi·cu·ña (vi-kéwn-ə, vī-, -kṓ-, -kṓn-yə) *n.* Also **vi·cu·na.** **1.** A llama-like ruminant mammal, *Vicugna vicugna,* of the central Andes, having fine, silky fleece. **1. a.** The fleece of this animal. **b.** Fabric made from this fleece. [Spanish, from Quechua *wikúña.*]

Vi·dal (vi-dál, -dáal), **Gore** (1925–). U.S. novelist and essayist. His

works include the historical novels *Burr* (1974) and *Lincoln* (1984), the satirical novel *Myra Breckinridge* (1968), and the memoirs *Palimpsest* (1995).

vi·de (vī-dee, -di, vidday) *Latin. Abbr.* **v., vid.** See. Used to direct a reader's attention: *vide page 64.* [Imperative of *vidēre,* to see.]

vide an·te (ánti ‖ *U.S.* áanti) *Latin.* See before.

vide in·fra (ínfrə) *Abbr.* **v.i.** *Latin.* See below.

vi·de·li·cet (vi-déeli-set, vī-, -dáyli-ket) *adv. Abbr.* **viz.** (see note at **viz**). That is; namely. Used to introduce examples, lists, or items. [Latin *vidēlicet,* it is easy (literally, permissible) to see, plainly, namely : *vidēre,* to see (see **vide**) + *licet,* it is permitted, from *licēre,* to be permitted. See **leisure**.]

vid·e·o (víddi-ō) *adj.* Of or pertaining to television, especially to systems for recording and playing back television sound and images.
~*n., pl.* **-os. 1.** A video cassette recorder or video player. **2.** A recording made for playing back on a television set. **3.** A short video film made as promotional material or, especially, to accompany the playing of a pop music record: *nice video, shame about the song.* **4.** The visual portion of a televised broadcast, as distinguished from **audio** *(see).* **5.** *Chiefly U.S.* Television: *a star of stage, screen, and video.* [From Latin *vidēre,* to see. See **vide**.]

video camera *n.* A small hand-held camera similar to a cine camera but recording on video cassettes for subsequent playback through a television set.

video cassette *n.* A video tape contained in a cassette.

video cassette recorder *n. Abbr.* **VCR** A device for receiving broadcast television signals and for recording and playing back television pictures and sound by means of magnetic tape cassettes. Also called "video".

video disc *n.* A flat disc on which moving pictures and sound are recorded for playing through a television set. A laser beam is used to sense variations in height on the surface of the disc, and convert them into electronic pulses for playback.

video frequency *n.* A frequency suitable for use in producing television images, lying in the range 50 hertz to 5 megahertz.

video game *n.* Any of various games, played either between two persons or between one person and the machine, in which electronic controls are manipulated to manoeuvre small images on a display screen such as a television screen.

video nasty *n.* A video film characterised by its sensational subject matter and typically containing scenes of violence, sadism, and explicit sex.

vid·e·o·phone (víddi-ō-fōn) *n.* A communication device that incorporates both telephone and television, allowing two people to talk to and see each other at the same time. [VIDEO + (TELE)PHONE.]

video player *n.* A device for playing video discs or tapes through a television set. Also called "video".

video recorder *n.* A device for recording and playing back television signals using magnetic tape, cassettes, or other media.

vid·e·o·scan (víddi-ō-skan) *n.* A technique of machine character recognition in which a video camera records the shapes of the characters and matches the signals with data held in machine storage.

vid·e·o·tape (víddi-ō-tayp) *n.* A relatively wide **magnetic tape** *(see)* used to record television images, usually with the associated sound, for subsequent playback or broadcasting. —**vid·e·o·tape** *v.*

video terminal *n.* A visual display unit *(see).*

vid·e·o·tex (víddi-ō-teks) *n.* Any system for transmitting a wide variety of computer-stored information in teletext or viewdata form.

vide post (pōst) *Latin.* See below; see after.

vide su·pra (sṓo-prə, séw-) *Abbr.* **v.s.** *Latin.* See above.

vid·i·con (víddi-kon) *n.* A small television camera tube that forms a charge-density image on a photoconductive surface for subsequent electron-beam scanning, used especially for hand-held cameras and closed-circuit systems. [VID(EO) + ICON(OSCOPE).]

vie (vī) *v.* **vied, vying, vies.** —*intr.* To strive for victory or superiority; contend; compete, as in an athletic contest. Used with *for* or *with.* —*tr. Archaic.* **1.** To offer or display for the sake of competition; match. **2.** To wager; bet. —See Synonyms at **rival.** [Shortened from Middle English *envien,* from Old French *envier,* to challenge, bid, from Latin *invītāre,* INVITE.]

Vi·en·na (vi-énnə). *German* **Wien** (veen). The capital of Austria, situated on the river Danube. In 1918, with the collapse of the Austro-Hungarian empire, Vienna was reduced from being the capital of one of the world's largest empires to the capital of a small country. Hitler's march into Vienna (1938) temporarily united Austria and Germany, but at the end of World War II the Allies divided the city into occupied sectors; it was not until 1955 that it was again a free city. An important cultural centre, Vienna was the home of Haydn, Mozart, Beethoven, Schubert, Brahms, Mahler, and Strauss. —**Vi·en·nese** (-ə-néez, veer- ‖ néess) *n. & adj.*

Vientiane. See **Viangchan.**

Vierwaldstättersee. See **Lucerne, Lake.**

Vi·et·cong (vi-ét-kóng, vée-et-) *n., pl.* **Vietcong.** Also **Vi·et Cong.** *Abbr.* **V.C. 1.** In the Vietnam war, the National Liberation Front of South Vietnam, a communist revolutionary movement. **2.** The guerrilla and armed forces of this movement. **3.** A member of this movement or these forces. [Short for Vietnamese *Viet Nam Cong Sam,* Vietnamese Communist.] —**Vi·et·cong** *adj.*

Vi·et·minh (vi-ét-mín, vée-et-) *n., pl.* **Vietminh.** Also **Vi·et Minh. 1.** The Vietnamese league for national independence formed by an alliance of patriotic and revolutionary forces under the leadership of Ho Chi Minh that defeated the Japanese and the French between

1941 and 1954. **2.** A member of this front, especially of its armed forces. [Vietnamese, short for *Viet Nam Doc Lap Dong Minh Hoi*, Vietnam Federation of Independence.] —**Vi·et·minh** *adj.*

Vi·et·nam, Socialist Republic of (vi-ét-nám, vée-et-, -naám) Also **Vi·et Nam.** State of southeast Asia. It has two fertile rice-growing areas, the Mekong and Red-Black river deltas, separated by the Annamese range. The Kinh (Han Chinese people) founded the province of Tonkin in North Vietnam (*c.* 100 B.C.). Independent (939), it expanded to control all Vietnam by 1802, but was incorporated into French Indochina in the late 19th century. Liberation movements arose, and the Vietminh, active during the Japanese occupation of World War II, defeated the French at Dien Bien (1954). The country was then divided at the 17th parallel into North Vietnam, a Soviet client state led by Ho Chi Minh, and South Vietnam. The French withdrew from the south (1956), and from 1960, there was civil war. This brought U.S. intervention to aid the south, which ended in 1973. The south fell to the communists (1975), and the present state was set up (1976). Ethnic Chinese began fleeing the country (1978), and Vietnamese "boat people" became an international refugee problem. Vietnam occupied Cambodia in late 1978, but withdrew 11 years later. Some 70 per cent of Vietnamese are farmers. The north's considerable mineral resources, including coal, lignite, iron ore, chrome, bauxite, oil and gas, have been used in rapid industrialisation. Area, 331 114 square kilometres (127,884 square miles). Population, 75,180,000. Capital, Hanoi.

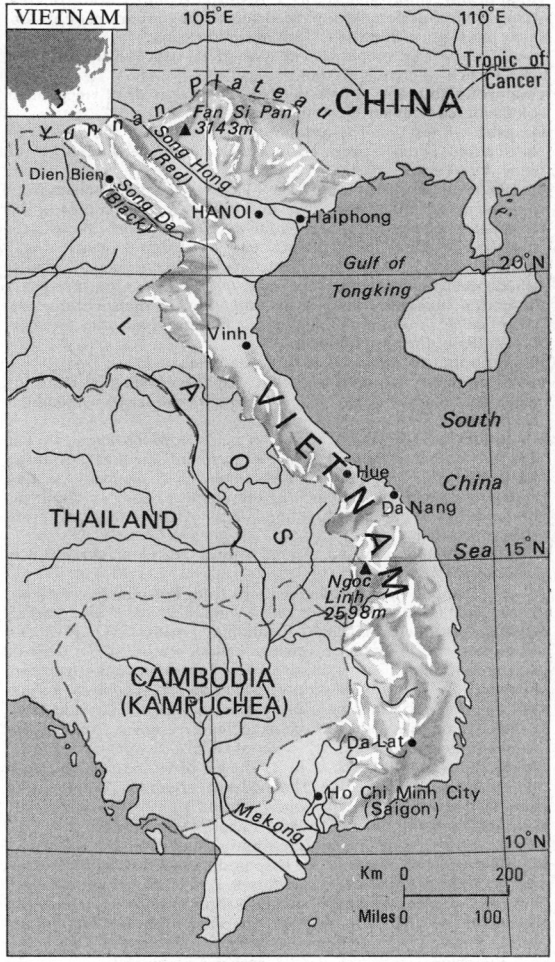

Vi·et·nam·ese (vi-ét-nə-méez, vée-et-, -na- ‖ -méess) *n., pl.* **Vietnamese. 1.** A native or inhabitant of Vietnam. **2.** The language of Vietnam, commonly considered as belonging to the Mon-Khmer subfamily of Austro-Asiatic languages. Formerly called "Annamese". —**Vi·et·nam·ese** *adj.*

view (vew) *n.* **1.** An examination or inspection. **2.** A systematic survey; coverage: *a wide-ranging view of trends in philosophy.* **3.** *Often plural.* A specific perception, observation, or interpretation; a thought: *her views on the situation.* **4.** *Often plural.* A personal opinion. **5.** The field of vision: *The ship came into view.* **6. a.** A prospect or vista: *From here you get a fine view of the town.* **b.** Visual access or vantage: *a room with a view.* **c.** A picture of a landscape. **d.** An aspect, as of something seen from a given vantage point. **7.** Consideration: *have a plan in view.* **8.** Expectation; chance: *has no view of success.* **9.** In hunting, especially fox-hunting, a sighting of the quarry. **10.** *Law.* A formal inspection by a judge or jury of a corpse, a disputed property, or the scene of an alleged crime. —See Synonyms at **opinion.** —**in view of.** Taking into account; in consideration of. —**on view.** Being exhibited; placed so as to be seen. —**take a dim** or **poor view of.** To regard disapprovingly or unfavourably. —**with a view to.** With the intention or hope of.
~*v.* **viewed, viewing, views.** —*tr.* **1.** To see; behold; be present at a showing of: *view the exhibition.* **2.** To examine; inspect: *view the figures.* **3.** To survey or study mentally; consider: *We view the recent developments with alarm.* **4.** In hunting, especially fox-hunting, to sight (the quarry). **5.** To watch (television). **6.** To visit and inspect (a house, for example) when considering a purchase. **7.** *Law.* To inspect formally (a corpse, a disputed property, or the scene of an alleged crime). —*intr.* To watch television. —See Synonyms at **see.** [Middle English *vewe*, from Old French *veue*, from the feminine past participle of *veoir*, to see, from Latin *vidēre.*]

view·da·ta (véw-day-tə, -daa-, -da-) *n.* **1.** A two-way system for transmitting information to subscribers by telephone or cable television to an adapted television set or computer terminal. **2.** Information transmitted by this method. Compare **teletext.**

Viewdata *n.* The former name for **Prestel** (*see*).

view·er (véw-ər) *n.* **1.** One who views; especially, one who views television. **2.** Any optical device used to facilitate the viewing of photographic transparencies by illuminating or magnifying them.

view·find·er (véw-findər) *n.* A system of lenses in a camera enabling the operator to see the scene that is to be photographed. Also called "finder".

view hal·loo, view hal·loa (hə-lóo, ha- ‖ hóllər) *n.* **1.** A strident call given during a fox hunt by a servant or a follower to inform the huntsman that a fox has been sighted. **2.** A loud cry or clarion call announcing a sudden appearance or advent.
~*interj.* Used in fox-hunting to announce the sighting of a fox.

view·ing (véw-ing) *n.* **1.** The act or habit of watching television. **2.** Television programmes collectively: *peak-hour viewing.*

view·less (véw-ləss, -liss) *adj.* **1.** Lacking a view. **2.** *Poetic.* Invisible.

view·point (véw-poynt) *n.* A point of view.

vi·ges·i·mal (vi-jéssim'l) *adj.* **1.** Twentieth. **2.** Proceeding or occurring in intervals of 20. **3.** Based on or pertaining to 20. [From Latin *vīgēsimus, vīcēsimus,* twentieth, from *vīcēnī,* twenty each, from *vīgintī,* twenty.]

vig·il (víjil) *n.* **1. a.** A watch kept during normal sleeping hours. **b.** The duration of such a watch. **2.** The eve of a religious festival as observed by devotional watching. **3.** *Usually plural.* Ritual devotions observed on the eve of a holy day. [Middle English *vigile,* from Old French, from Latin *vigilia,* from *vigil,* alert.]

vig·i·lance (víjilənss) *n.* **1.** The state or quality of being vigilant; watchfulness. **2.** A chronic inability to sleep.

vigilance committee *n.* **1.** In inadequately policed communities, especially in North America, an informal council exercising police power for the capture, speedy trial, and summary punishment of criminal offenders. **2.** Any similar body of citizens organised to protect members of the community.

vig·i·lant (víjilənt) *adj.* On the alert; watchful. [Middle English, from Old French, from Latin *vigilāns* (stem *vigilant-*), present participle of *vigilāre,* to be alert, from *vigil,* alert.] —**vig·i·lant·ly** *adv.*

vig·i·lan·te (víji-lánti)' *n.* One belonging to a vigilance committee. [Spanish, from Latin *vigilāns,* VIGILANT.]

vigil light *n.* **1.** A small candle kept burning in the chancel of some Christian churches to symbolize the presence of the Blessed Sacrament; an altar light. **2.** A candle lit by a worshipper for a special devotional purpose.

vi·gnette (vin-yét, veen-, *rarely* -ét) *n.* **1. a.** An unenclosed decorative design placed at the beginning or end of a book or a chapter of a book. **b.** Decorative tracery along the border of a page. **2.** An unbordered portrait that shades off into the surrounding colour at the edges. **3.** A literary, dramatic, or cinematic sketch having the intimate charm and subtlety attributed to vignette portraits: *The film was just a series of vignettes of medieval life.*
~*tr.v.* **vignetted, -gnetting, -gnettes. 1.** To soften the edges of (a picture) in the style of a vignette. **2.** To illustrate or embellish with vignettes. **3.** To portray in a vignette. [French, from Old French, "young vine", diminutive of *vigne,* VINE.]

vi·gnet·ter (vin-yét-ər, veen-, *rarely* -ét-) *n.* Also **vi·gnet·tist** (-ist) (for sense 2). **1.** A device used to print borderless illustrations and photographs. **2.** A person who makes or specialises in vignettes.

Vi·gny (veen-yée), **Alfred (Victor, comte) de** (1797–1863). French poet, novelist, and dramatist. He was one of the leaders of the French Romantic movement. His works include the play *Chatterton* (1835), *Cinq Mars* (1826), a historical novel, and *Les Destinées* (1864), a collection of poems which reveal his stoical pessimism.

vi·go·ro·so (víggə-rő-sō, véegə-, -zō) *adv. Music.* Vigorous; with emphasis and spirit. Used as a direction. [Italian, from Medieval Latin *vigōrōsus,* from Latin *vigour,* VIGOUR.] —**vi·go·ro·so** *adj.*

vig·or·ous (víggərəss) *adj.* **1.** Strong and healthy; robust; hardy. **2.** Energetic; lively. —See Synonyms at **active, healthy.** —**vig·or·ous·ly** *adv.* —**vig·or·ous·ness** *n.*

vig·our, *U.S.* **vig·or** (víggər) *n.* **1.** Active physical or mental strength. **2.** The capacity for natural growth and survival, as of plants or animals. **3.** Expressive power or forcefulness, as of language. **4.** The most flourishing or active stage; the prime; the high point: *in the vigour of manhood.* **5.** *Chiefly U.S.* Legal effectiveness or validity. **6.** Energetic and rigorous exercise of power: *effected* with *vigour and resolution.* [Middle English *vigour,* from Old French, from Latin *vigor,* from *vigēre,* to be lively or vigorous.]

Vi·king (vī́king) *n. Sometimes small* **v.** Any of the Scandinavian mariners whose pirate bands attacked and pillaged coastal settlements of northern and western Europe from the eighth to the eleventh centuries. [Old Norse *vīkingr†.*] —**Vi·king** *adj.*

vil. village.

vi·la·yet (vi-lä́-yet, vée-laa-yét) *n.* An administrative division of Turkey. [Turkish *vilâyet,* from Arabic *wilāyah,* province, from *wāli,* governor.]

vile (vīl) *adj.* **viler, vilest.** 1. Loathsome to the mind or senses; disgusting: *vile language; a vile smell.* 2. Unpleasant or objectionable: *a vile play.* 3. Miserably poor; wretched: *a vile existence.* 4. Depraved; ignoble. 5. Degrading; menial. [Middle English *vyle,* from Old French *vil,* from Latin *vīlis†.*] —**vile·ly** *adv.* —**vile·ness** *n.*

vil·i·fy (villi-fī) *tr.v.* **-fied, -fying, -fies.** To defame; denigrate. See Synonyms at **malign.** [Middle English *vilifien,* from Late Latin *vīlificāre* : Latin *vīlis,* VILE + *facere,* to make.] —**vil·i·fi·ca·tion** (-fi-káysh'n) *n.* —**vil·i·fi·er** *n.*

vil·i·pend (villi-pend) *tr.v.* **-pended, -pending, -pends.** *Rare.* 1. To view or treat with contempt; despise. 2. To disparage or abuse. [Middle English *vilipenden,* from Old French *vilipender,* from Latin *vīlipendere* : *vīlis,* VILE + *pendere,* to weigh, consider.]

vil·la (villə) *n.* 1. A large, luxurious country residence. 2. In ancient Rome, a country estate with a substantial house. 3. *Chiefly Scottish.* A detached or semi-detached middle-class house in the suburbs. 4. *Chiefly British.* A holiday home, as at a seaside resort or holiday camp. [Italian, from Latin *vīlla,* country house.]

Vi·lla (vée-ə; *Spanish* béel-ya), **Pancho,** born Doroteo Arango, also known as Francisco Villa (1877–1923). Mexican bandit and revolutionary. He was active in successive revolts against Mexican governments (1910–15). After coming to terms with the Mexican Government (1920) he disbanded his army. He was assassinated.

vil·lage (villij) *n. Abbr.* **v., V., vil.** 1. A small group of dwellings in a rural area, usually ranking in size between a hamlet and a town. 2. In some North American states, an incorporated community smaller in population than a town. 3. An old and distinctive urban district having its own particular character, usually quainter and better preserved than its surroundings, and in some cases actually being a former rural village now absorbed into a metropolitan or suburban area. 4. The inhabitants of a village; villagers. —*adj.* 1. Of or pertaining to a village. 2. Characteristic of villages; rustic. [Middle English, from Old French, from *ville,* village, farm, from Latin *vīlla,* VILLA.]

vil·lag·er (villijər) *n.* An inhabitant of a village.

vil·lain (villən; *for senses 3 and 4 also* vil-in, -ayn) *n.* 1. A depraved, base-minded person; a scoundrel. 2. A dramatic or fictional character who is typically at odds with the hero. 3. *British Slang.* A criminal. 4. *Obsolete.* A vile, brutish peasant. 5. Variant of **villein.** [Middle English *vilain,* from Old French, originally "feudal serf", from Medieval Latin *vīllānus,* from Latin *vīlla,* country house.]

vil·lain·ess (villə-niss, -ness, -néss) *n.* A female villain.

vil·lain·ous (villənəss) *adj.* 1. Viciously wicked or criminal. 2. Extremely unpleasant; obnoxious. —**vil·lain·ous·ly** *adv.* —**vil·lain·ous·ness** *n.*

vil·lain·y (villəni) *n., pl.* **-ies.** 1. Viciousness of conduct or action. 2. Baseness of mind or character. 3. A treacherous or vicious act.

Vil·la-Lo·bos (villə ló-boss, vée-lə, -laa; *Portuguese* véela ló-bóoss), **Heitor** (1887–1959). Brazilian composer. He was mainly self-taught, and his many works are influenced by Brazilian folksong.

vil·la·nelle (villə-nél) *n.* A 19-line poem of fixed form consisting of five tercets and a final quatrain based on two rhymes, with the first and third lines of the first tercet repeated alternately as a refrain closing the succeeding stanzas and joined as the final couplet of the quatrain. [French, from Italian *villanella,* an old rustic Italian song, from *villanello,* rustic, from *villano,* peasant, from Medieval Latin *vīllānus.* See **villain.**]

vil·lat·ic (vi-láttik) *adj. Rare.* Rustic; rural. [Latin *vīllāticus,* from *vīlla,* VILLA.]

–ville (vil) *n. comb. form. Chiefly U.S. Slang.* Indicates a place of a specified kind; for example, *Redneckville.* —*n. & adj. comb. form.* Indicates a condition or state of a specified kind; for example, *dullsville; thrillsville.* [Abstracted from town names common in the United States (for example, *Charlottesville*), from French *ville,* town, ultimately from Latin *vīlla.*]

vil·lein (vil-ən, -in, -ayn) *n.* Also **vil·lain.** In feudal times, a member of a class of serfs who held the legal status of freemen in their dealings with all persons except their lord, to whom they owed certain services or rents in return for their land. [Middle English *villein,* variant of *vilain,* VILLAIN.]

vil·lein·age (víl-ən-ij, -in-, -ayn-) *n.* 1. The legal status or condition of a villein. 2. The legal tenure by which a villein held his land. Also called "bondage".

vil·li·form (villi-fawrm) *adj.* Having the form of a villus or the appearance of villi.

Vil·lon (vee-yón), **François,** born François de Montcorbier (*c.* 1430–?). French poet. He led a life of vagrancy after studying at the University of Paris. A sentence to hang was commuted to banishment in 1463 and nothing is known of him after that date. His only surviving works are the satirical *Lais* (1456) and *Testament* (*c.* 1461), and a few other poems.

vil·los·i·ty (vi-lóssəti) *n., pl.* **-ties.** 1. The condition of being villous. 2. A villous surface or coating. 3. A villus or set of villi.

vil·lous (vil-əss) *adj.* Also **vil·lose** (-ōz, -ōss). 1. Of, pertaining to, resembling, or covered with villi. 2. *Botany.* Covered with fine, unmatted hairs. [Middle English, from Latin *villōsus,* from *villus,* shaggy hair, VILLUS.] —**vil·lous·ly** *adv.*

vil·lus (vil-əss) *n., pl.* **villi** (-ī). 1. *Biology.* Any minute projection arising from a mucous membrane. 2. *Botany.* A fine, hairlike epidermal outgrowth. [Latin, shaggy hair.]

Vil·ni·us (vílni-əss, -ōoss). Capital of Lithuania. Founded in the tenth century on the river Vilija, it became the capital of the grand duchy of Lithuania in 1323. In 1569 it was severely damaged in the wars following the union between Poland and Lithuania, and became part of Russia on the partition of Poland (1795). Between 1920 and 1939 it again reverted to Poland.

vim (vim) *n. Informal.* Ebullient vitality and energy. [Latin *vim,* accusative of *vīs,* power.]

Vim·i·nal (vímmin'l) *n.* One of the seven hills of Rome. [Latin *Vīminālis (collis),* "(hill) of osiers" (from the willow copse on the hill), from *vīmen,* osier.]

vi·min·e·ous (vi-mínni-əss) *adj. Botany.* Having or pertaining to long, flexible shoots. [Latin *vimineus,* from *vīmen,* osier.]

vin–. Variant of **vini–.**

vi·na (véenə) *n.* A stringed musical instrument of India that has a long, fretted fingerboard with resonating gourds at each end. [Hindi *vīṇā,* from Sanskrit *vīṇāh†.*]

vi·na·ceous (vī-náyshəss) *adj.* Having the colour of red wine; wine-red. [Latin *vīnāceus,* of wine, from *vīnum,* wine.]

vin·ai·grette (vin-ay-grét, -i-) *n.* 1. A small decorative bottle or container with a perforated top, used for holding an aromatic restorative, such as smelling salts. 2. Vinaigrette sauce. —*adj.* Served or prepared with vinaigrette sauce. [French, from Old French *vinaigre,* VINEGAR.]

vinaigrette sauce *n.* A cold sauce or dressing made of vinegar and oil flavoured with herbs or other seasonings.

vi·nasse (vi-náss) *n.* The residue left in a still after the process of distillation. [French, from Latin *vīnācea,* feminine of *vīnāceus,* of wine, VINACEOUS.]

vin·blas·tine (vin-bláss-teen, -blaass-) *n.* An alkaloid obtained from a periwinkle plant, *Vinca rosea,* that is used to treat cancer of the lymphatic system. [Shortened from *vincaleucoblastine* : New Latin *vinca,* periwinkle + *leucoblast* (LEUCO- + -BLAST) + -INE.]

vin·ca (víngkə) *n.* Any plant of the genus *Vinca;* especially, a **periwinkle** (see). [New Latin, from Latin *(per)vinca,* PERIWINKLE.]

Vin·cent's disease (vínss'nts) *n. Pathology.* **Trench mouth** (see). Also called "Vincent's angina". [After Hyacinthe *Vincent* (1862–1950), French physician.]

Vinci, Leonardo da. See **Leonardo da Vinci.**

vin·ci·ble (vínss-əb'l, -ib'l) *adj. Rare.* Capable of being overcome or defeated. [Latin *vincibilis,* from *vincere,* to conquer.] —**vin·ci·bil·i·ty** (-ə-billəti, -i-) *n.*

vin·cu·lum (víngkew-ləm) *n., pl.* **-la** (-lə). 1. *Mathematics.* A bar drawn over two or more algebraic terms to indicate that they are to be treated as a single term. 2. *Anatomy.* **a.** A ligament. **b.** Any connecting band or fold, such as the umbilical cord or the membranes below the tongue. 3. A bond or tie. [Latin, band, cord, from *vincīre†,* to tie.]

Vin·da·loo (víndə-lóo) *adj.* Served with a hot, sour curry sauce: *chicken Vindaloo.* —*n.* A vindaloo dish. [Indic, perhaps from Portuguese *vin d'alho,* garlic wine (as a sauce), from *vinho,* wine + *d',* of + *alho,* garlic.]

vin·di·ca·ble (víndikəb'l) *adj.* Justifiable. [VINDIC(ATE) + -ABLE.]

vin·di·cate (víndi-kayt) *tr.v.* **-cated, -cating, -cates.** 1. To clear of accusation, blame, suspicion, or doubt with supporting arguments or proof. 2. To justify or support: *vindicate one's claim.* 3. To justify or prove the worth of, especially in the light of later developments. [Latin *vindicāre,* to claim, defend, revenge, from *vindex,* claimant, defender, avenger.] —**vin·di·ca·tor** (-kaytər) *n.*

vin·di·ca·tion (víndi-káysh'n) *n.* 1. The act of vindicating or condition of being vindicated. 2. The evidence, argument, event, or the like, that serves to justify a claim or deed.

vin·di·ca·to·ry (víndi-kə-tri, -təri, -kaytəri, -káytəri) *adj.* 1. Vindicating; justifying. 2. Exacting retribution; punitive.

vin·dic·tive (vin-díktiv) *adj.* 1. Disposed to seek revenge; revengeful. 2. Unforgiving; bitter; spiteful. 3. *Law.* Designating damages awarded in excess of simple compensation in order to punish the defendant. [From Latin *vindicta,* vengeance, from *vindicāre,* to revenge, VINDICATE.] —**vin·dic·tive·ly** *adv.* —**vin·dic·tive·ness** *n.*

Synonyms: vindictive, spiteful, vengeful, revengeful.

vine (vīn) *n.* 1. Any plant having a flexible stem supported by climbing, twining, or creeping along a surface. 2. The stem of such a plant. 3. **a.** A grapevine. **b.** Grapevines collectively: *products of the vine.* [Middle English, from Old French *vine, vigne,* from Latin *vīnea,* from the feminine of *vīneus,* of wine, from *vīnum,* wine.] —**vin·y** *adj.*

vine-dress·er (vīn-dressər) *n.* A person who cultivates and tends grapevines.

vin·e·gar (vínnigər) *n.* 1. A sour, impure dilute solution of acetic acid obtained by fermentation beyond the alcohol stage and used as a condiment and preservative. 2. *Informal.* Sourness; ill temper. [Middle English *vinegre,* from Old French *vinaigre, vyn egre* : *vin,* wine, from Latin *vīnum* + *aigre,* sour, from Latin *acer,* sharp.]

vinegar eel *n.* A small nematode worm, *Turbatrix aceti,* that feeds on the organisms that cause fermentation in vinegar. Also called "eelworm", "vinegar worm".

vinegar fly *n.* Any of various flies of the genus *Drosophila* that often become pests by breeding in poorly sealed preserves and pickles.
vin·e·gar·roon (vínnigə-ro͞on) *n.* Also **vin·e·ga·rone** (-rṓn). A large, nonvenomous scorpion-like arachnid, *Mastigoproctus giganteus,* of the southern United States and Mexico, that emits a strong odour of vinegar when disturbed. [Mexican Spanish *vinagrón,* from Spanish *vinagre,* vinegar, from Old French *vinaigre.* See **vinegar.**]
vin·e·gar·y (vínnigər-i) *adj.* Also **vin·e·gar·ish** (-ish). **1.** Having the nature of vinegar; sour; acid: *a vinegary taste.* **2.** Sour in disposition or speech; ill-tempered.
vine maple *n.* A maple, *Acer circinatum,* of western North America, having red fruits and white and purple flowers.
vin·er·y (vī́nəri) *n., pl.* **-ies.** An area or greenhouse for growing vines.
vine·yard (vín-yərd; *also spelling pronunciations* vī́n-, -yaard) *n.* **1.** A plot of ground planted with cultivated grapevines. **2.** *Informal.* A sphere of spiritual, mental, or physical endeavour.
vingt-et-un (vánt-ay-úrn, vánt-, -o͞on, -ṓn) *n.* A card game, **pontoon** *(see).* [French, twenty-one (the maximum score of a hand).]
vini–, vino–, vin– *comb. form.* Indicates wine; for example, **viniculture, vinometer, vinyl.** [From Latin *vīnum,* wine.]
vi·nic (vī́nik) *adj.* Of, contained in, or derived from wine. [From Latin *vīnum,* wine. See **vine.**]
vin·i·cul·ture (vínni-kulchər, -kúlchər || vī́ni-) *n.* The cultivation of grapes and making of wine; viticulture. **—vin·i·cul·tur·al** *adj.* **—vin·i·cul·tur·ist** *n.*
Vin·land (vín-lənd, -land). Also **Vine·land** (vī́n-). An area of Newfoundland. Situated around the Hudson Straits and the Gulf of St. Lawrence according to the Vinland Map (1440), the area was supposedly explored by Leif Ericsson in the 11th century.
vi·no (véenō) *n., pl.* **-nos.** *Informal.* Wine. [Italian and Spanish, from Latin *vīnum,* wine. See **vine.**]
vi·nom·e·ter (vī-nómmitər, vi-) *n.* A hydrometer used to determine the percentage of alcohol in a wine.
vin or·di·naire (váN órdi-naír) *n., pl.* **vins ordinaires** (*pronounced as singular*). *French.* An ordinary inexpensive wine; a table wine.
vi·nous (vī́nəss) *adj.* **1.** Of or pertaining to wine or its consumption: *a vinous party.* **2.** Affected or caused by the consumption of wine: *a vinous nose; vinous laughter.* **3.** Having the colour of wine. [Latin *vinōsus,* from *vīnum,* wine. See **vine.**] **—vi·nos·i·ty** (vī-nóssəti) *n.*
vin·tage (víntij) *n.* **1.** The yield of wine or grapes from a particular vineyard or district during one season. **2.** Wine, usually of high quality, identified as to year and vineyard or district of origin. Also called "vintage wine". **3.** The year in which or place where a particular wine was bottled. **4.** The harvesting of a grape crop or the initial stages of winemaking. **5.** The season for such harvesting or winemaking. **6.** *Informal.* Any group or collection of persons or things sharing certain characteristics. **7.** *Informal.* A year or period of origin: *a dress of 1942 vintage.*
~adj. **1.** Designating wine of an outstandingly good year. **2.** Characterised by excellence, maturity, and enduring appeal; venerable; classic. **3.** Typical of the best work of a specified author or other artist: *vintage Coward.* **4.** Old or outmoded. [Middle English *vyntage,* variant (influenced by *vineter,* VINTNER) of *vendage,* from Old French, from Latin *vindēmia,* grape gathering : *vīnum,* wine (see **vine**) + *dēmere,* to take off : *dē-,* off + *emere,* to take.]
vintage car *n.* A motor car made between 1919 and 1930. Compare **veteran car.**
vin·tag·er (víntijər) *n.* A harvester of wine grapes.
vintage year *n.* **1.** The year in which a vintage wine is produced. **2.** Any year of outstanding achievement or success.
vint·ner (víntnər) *n.* A wine merchant. [Middle English *vineter,* from Old French *vinetier,* from Medieval Latin *vīnātārius,* from Latin *vīnētum,* vineyard, from *vīnum,* wine. See **vine.**]
vi·nyl (vī́n'l, vī́nil) *n.* **1.** The univalent chemical radical CH_2:CH-, derived from ethene. **2.** Any of various compounds containing this group, typically highly reactive, easily polymerised, and used as basic materials for plastics. **3.** Any of various synthetic resins, typically tough, flexible, and shiny, used, for example, in coverings, clothing, and paints. **4.** *Informal.* LPs and forty-fives contrasted with CDs. Compare **shellac. —on vinyl.** Commercially recorded as an LP. [VIN(I)- + -YL.] **—vi·nyl** *adj.*
vinyl chloride *n.* A flammable gas, CH_2:CHCl, used as a monomer for polyvinyl chloride (PVC). Also called "chloroethene".
Vi·ny·lite *n.* A trademark for a type of vinyl plastic.
vi·ol (vī́-əl) *n.* **1.** Any of a family of stringed instruments, chiefly of the 16th and 17th centuries, having a fretted fingerboard, usually six strings, a flat back, and played with a curved bow. **2.** A viola da gamba. [Old French *viole,* from Old Provençal *viola,* VIOLA (instrument).]
vi·o·la[1] (vi-ṓlə, vée-ə-lə) *n.* **1.** A four-stringed musical instrument of the violin family, slightly larger than a violin, tuned a fifth lower, and having a deeper, more sonorous tone; the alto or tenor violin. **2.** An organ stop usually of eight-foot or four-foot pitch yielding stringlike tones. [Italian, from Old Provençal *viola, viula,* perhaps from *violar,* to play the viola (imitative).]
vi·o·la[2] (vī́-ə-lə, vée-, -ō-, vī-ṓlə, vi-) *n.* Any plant of the genus *Viola,* which includes the violets and pansies. [New Latin *Viola,* from Latin *viola,* VIOLET.]
vi·o·la·ble (vī́-ə-ləb'l) *adj.* Capable of being violated or easily broken. **—vi·o·la·bil·i·ty** (-lə-bílləti), **vi·o·la·ble·ness** *n.* **—vi·o·la·bly** *adv.*
vi·o·la·ceous (vī́-ə-láyshəss, vée-) *adj.* **1.** Of or belonging to the family Violaceae, which comprises the violets and pansies. **2.** Having a violet colour. [Latin *violāceus* : *viola,* VIOLET + -ACEOUS.]
vi·o·la da brac·cio (vi-ṓlə də braáchō) *n.* A stringed instrument of the viol family with approximately the range of the viola. [Italian, "viola of the arm".]
vi·o·la da gam·ba (vi-ṓlə də gámbə || *U.S.* gaámbə). **1.** A stringed instrument, the bass of the viol family, with approximately the range of the cello. Also called "viol", "bass viol", "gamba". **2.** An organ stop of eight-foot pitch yielding tones similar to those of the viola da gamba. [Italian, "viola of the leg".]
vi·o·la d'a·mo·re (vi-ṓlə da-máw-ray || daa-, -mṓ-) *n.* A stringed instrument, the tenor of the viol family, having 7 stopped strings and 7 or 14 sympathetic strings that produce a characteristic silvery tone. [Italian, "viola of love".]
vi·o·late (vī́-ə-layt || -ō-) *tr.v.* **-lated, -lating, -lates. 1.** To break (a law or regulation, for example) intentionally or unintentionally; fail to keep; transgress. **2.** To injure the person or property of; especially, to rape. **3.** To do harm to (property or qualities considered sacred); profane; desecrate. **4.** To disturb rudely or improperly; break in upon without right: *violate the peace.* [Middle English *violaten,* from Latin *violāre,* from *vīs,* force.] **—vi·o·la·tive** (-lətiv, -laytiv) *adj.* **—vi·o·la·tor** (-laytər) *n.*
vi·o·la·tion (vī-ə-láysh'n || -ō-) *n.* **1.** The act of violating or the condition of being violated. **2.** An instance of violation; a transgression: *violations of the ceasefire.* —See Synonyms at **breach.**
vi·o·lence (vī́-ə-lənss || -ō-, vī́lənss) *n.* **1.** Physical force exerted for the purpose of violating, damaging, or abusing: *"The essence of war is violence"* (T.B. Macaulay). **2.** An act or instance of violent action or behaviour. **3.** Intensity or severity, as in natural phenomena; untamed force: *the violence of a hurricane.* **4.** The abusive or unjust exercise of power; an outrage; a wrong. **5.** Abuse or injury to meaning, content, or intent: *do violence to a text.* **6.** Vehemence of feeling or expression; fervour.
vi·o·lent (vī́ə-lənt || -ō-, vī́lənt) *adj.* **1.** Displaying or proceeding from extreme or uncontrolled physical force or rough action. **2.** Exhibiting intense force or effect; extreme: *violent contrast.* **3.** Caused by or displaying undue mental or emotional force: *a violent antipathy.* **4.** Characterised by the immoderate use of force; severe; harsh. **5.** Caused by unexpected force or injury rather than by natural causes: *a violent death.* [Middle English, from Old French, from Latin *violentus.*] **—vi·o·lent·ly** *adv.*
violent storm *n.* A wind whose speed is 28.5 to 32.6 metres per second (56 to 63 knots), force 11 on the Beaufort scale.
vi·o·let (vī́-ə-lət, -lit || -ō-, vī́-lət) *n.* **1.** Any of various low-growing plants of the genus *Viola,* having spurred, irregular flowers that are characteristically purplish-blue but sometimes yellow or white. **2.** Any of several similar but unrelated plants, such as the **African violet** *(see).* **3.** Any of a group of colours, reddish blue in hue, that may vary in lightness and saturation; the hue of that portion of the spectrum that may be evoked in the normal observer by radiant energy of wavelengths approximately 420 nanometres. **4.** A dye or pigment of this colour. **5. a.** Any object of this colour. **b.** Clothing of this colour. [Middle English, from Old French *violete,* diminutive of *viole,* from Latin *viola,* from the same Mediterranean origin as Greek *ion,* violet. See **iodine.**] **—vi·o·let** *adj.*
vi·o·lin (vī-ə-lín || -ō-, -lin) *n. Abbr.* **v. 1.** A stringed instrument played with a bow, having four strings tuned at intervals of a fifth, an unfretted fingerboard, and a shallower body than the viol, and capable of great flexibility in range, tone, and dynamics. Also informally called "fiddle". **2.** A violinist. [Italian *violino,* diminutive of *viola,* VIOLA (instrument).] **—vi·o·lin·ist** (vī-ə-línnist, -linnist) *n.*
vi·o·list (*For sense 1* vi-ṓlist, *for sense 2* vī́-əlist) *n.* **1.** *U.S.* A person who plays the viola. **2.** A person who plays a viol.
Viol·let-le-Duc (vi-ō-láy-lə-dū́k, *French* -lel-), **Eugène Emmanuel** (1814–79). French architect and author. He was a leader of the Gothic revival in France and designed the restoration of many medieval buildings including Notre Dame in Paris, and the city of Carcassonne.
vi·o·lon·cel·list (vī́-ə-lən-chéllist, vée-, -lin-) *n.* A **cellist** *(see).*
vi·o·lon·cel·lo (vī́-ə-lən-chéllō, vée-, -lin-) *n., pl.* **-los.** A **cello** *(see).* [Italian, diminutive of *violone,* VIOLONE.]
vi·o·lone (vī́-ə-lōn, vée-ə-lṓ-nay) *n.* **1.** A stringed instrument, the double bass of the viol family, with approximately the range of a modern double bass. **2.** A 16-foot organ stop yielding stringlike tones similar to a cello. [Italian, augmentative of *viola,* VIOLA (instrument).]
vi·o·my·cin (vī́-ō-mī́-sin, -ə-) *n.* An antibiotic obtained from various species of the bacterium *Streptomyces,* used to treat tuberculosis. [VIO(LET) (referring to the colour of the soil mould) + -MYCIN.]
VIP (vée-ī-pée) *n., pl.* **VIPs** or **VIP's.** A person regarded as being very important, and therefore accorded specially courteous or luxurious treatment; a dignitary or celebrity. [*V*ery *I*mportant *P*erson.]
vi·per (vī́pər) *n.* **1.** Any of various venomous Old World snakes of the family Viperidae; especially, a common Eurasian species, *Vipera berus,* which is also called "adder". **2.** A **pit viper** *(see).* **3.** Broadly, any venomous or supposedly venomous snake. **4.** A treacherous or malicious person. [Old French *vipere,* from Latin *vīpera,* snake, contracted from *vivipara* (unattested), "that which produces living young" (from the ancient belief that vipers were viviparous) : *vīvus,* alive + *parere,* to produce.]
vi·per·ine (vī́pə-rīn || -rin) *adj.* Of, resembling, or characteristic of a viper.
vi·per·ous (vī́pər-əss) *adj.* Also **vi·per·ish** (-ish). **1.** Suggestive of a

viper or venomous snake. **2.** Venomous; spiteful; malicious.

viper's bugloss *n.* A bristly plant, *Echium vulgare,* native to Eurasia, having bright blue flowers. Also *U.S.* "blueweed".

vir·a·gin·i·ty (virrə-jinnəti) *n.* Masculine mentality and psychology in a woman. [From Latin *virāgō* (stem *virāgin-*), manlike woman, VIRAGO.] —**vir·a·gin·ous** (vi-rájinəss) *adj.*

vi·ra·go (vi-ra´a-gō, -ráy-) *n., pl.* **-goes** or **-gos.** **1.** A noisy, domineering woman; a scold. **2.** *Archaic.* A large, strong, or courageous woman; an Amazon. [Latin *virāgō,* from *vir,* man.]

vi·ral (vīr-əl) *adj.* Of, pertaining to, or caused by a virus. [From VIRUS.]

vir·e·lay (vírri-lay) *n.* Also *French* **vi·re·lai** (veer-láy). Any of several medieval French verse and song forms, especially one in which each stanza has two rhymes, the end rhyme recurring as the first rhyme of the following stanza. [Middle English *virelai,* from Old French, variant (influenced by *lai,* LAY) of *vireli,* perhaps originally a meaningless refrain.]

vir·e·o (vírri-ō) *n., pl.* **-os.** Any of various small New World birds of the genus *Vireo,* having greyish or greenish plumage. [Latin *vireo,* greenfinch, from *virēre,* to be green.]

vi·res·cence (vi-réss'nss) *n.* The state or process of becoming green; specifically, the abnormal development of green coloration in plant parts normally not green.

vi·res·cent (vi-réss'nt) *adj.* Becoming green; greenish. [Latin *virēscēns* (stem *virēscent-*), present participle of *virēscere,* to become green, from *virēre,* to be green.]

vir·ga (vúrgə) *n.* Wisps of precipitation streaming from a cloud but evaporating before reaching the earth. [Latin, twig, stripe.]

vir·gate¹ (vúr-gət, -git, -gayt) *adj.* Shaped like a wand or rod; straight, long, and slender. [Latin *virgātus,* made of twigs, from *virga,* twig. See **virga.**]

virgate² *n.* An early English measure of land area of varying extent but most often equivalent to about 30 acres. [Medieval Latin *virgāta,* from *virga,* a measure, yard, from Latin, twig. See **virga.**]

Vir·gil or **Ver·gil** (vérjil), born Publius Vergilius Maro (70-19 B.C.). Roman poet. His greatest work is his epic poem *Aeneid,* which tells of the wanderings of Aeneas after the sack of Troy. Among his other works are his *Ecologues,* and the *Georgics.*

vir·gin (vúrjin) *n.* **1.** A person who has not experienced sexual intercourse. **2.** A chaste or unmarried woman; a maiden. **3.** An unmarried woman who has taken religious vows of chastity. **4.** *Capital* **V.** Mary, the mother of Jesus. Preceded by *the.* Also called "Blessed Virgin". **5.** Any female animal that has not mated. **6.** *Capital* **V.** The constellation and the sign of the zodiac, **Virgo** *(see).*
—*adj.* **1.** Characteristic of or appropriate to a virgin; chaste; maidenly. **2.** In a pure or natural state; untouched; unsullied: *virgin snow.* **3.** Unused, uncultivated, or unexplored: *the virgin west of 19th-century America.* **4.** Existing in native or raw form; not processed or refined. **5.** Happening for the first time; initial: *"guiding my virgin steps on the hard road of letters"* (Somerset Maugham). **6.** Obtained directly from the first pressing. Said of vegetable oils. **7.** Unprocessed. Said of wool. **8.** Obtained by smelting ore, rather than recycling scrap. Said of metals. **9.** *Physics.* Not having experienced any collisions. Said of neutrons. [Middle English, from Old French *virgine,* from Latin *virgō†* (stem *virgin-*).]

vir·gin·al¹ (vúrjin'l) *adj.* **1.** Pertaining to, characteristic of, or befitting a virgin; chaste; pure. **2.** Remaining in a state of virginity. **3.** Untouched or unsullied; fresh.

virginal² *n.* Often *plural.* A small, legless rectangular harpsichord popular in the 16th and 17th centuries. [From VIRGIN (because it was played by young girls).]

virgin birth *n.* Sometimes *capital* **V,** *Capital* **B.** *Theology.* The doctrine that Jesus was miraculously begotten by God and born of Mary, who was a virgin.

Vir·gin·ia¹ (vər-jínni-ə). State of the United States. Bordering the Mid-Atlantic, it has land borders with Maryland, West Virginia, Kentucky, Tennessee, and North Carolina. First settled by the English (1607), it was named after Queen Elizabeth, "the Virgin Queen". One of the original 13 states, it was re-admitted to the Union in 1870, following the American Civil War, during which it was part of the Confederacy. Richmond is the state capital.

Virginia² *n.* Cured tobacco of a kind originally grown in Virginia.

Virginia creeper *n.* **1.** A North American climbing vine, *Parthenocissus quinquefolia,* having compound leaves with five leaflets and bluish-black, berry-like fruit. Also called "woodbine". **2.** A similar vine from China and Japan, *P. tricuspidata* (or *Ampelopsis veitchii*). Also called "Japanese ivy".

Virginia fence *n. U.S.* A **worm fence** *(see).* Also *U.S.* "Virginia rail fence".

Virginia reel *n.* **1.** A country dance in which couples, initially facing each other from two parallel lines, perform various figures to the instructions of a caller. **2.** A piece of music for this dance.

virginia stock *n.* Sometimes *capital* **V.** An annual plant, *Malcolmia maritima,* from southern Europe, having four-petalled lilac, red, or white flowers and often grown in gardens. [After *Virginia,* where it was cultivated.]

Virgin Islands. An archipelago in the Caribbean of about one hundred islands east of Puerto Rico. About one-third are owned by Britain, two-thirds by the United States.

vir·gin·i·ty (vər-jínnəti) *n., pl.* **-ties. 1.** The condition of being a virgin; virginal chastity. **2.** The state of being pure, unsullied, or untouched.

Virgin Mary *n.* The mother of Jesus, **Mary** *(see).* Usually preceded by *the.*

Virgin Queen *n.* See **Elizabeth I of England.** Usually preceded by *the.*

Vir·go (vúrgō) *n.* **1.** A constellation in the region of the celestial equator near Leo and Libra. **2. a.** The sixth sign of the **zodiac. b.** One born under this sign. Also the "Virgin". [Latin *virgō,* VIRGIN.]

virgo in·tac·ta (in-táktə, ín-) *n., pl.* **virgines intactae** (vúr-ji-neez in-ták-tee, -gi-nayz -tī). A virgin girl or woman with an intact hymen. [Latin, "untouched virgin".]

vir·gu·late (vúrgew-lət, -lit, -layt) *adj.* Shaped like a small rod. [From Latin *virgula,* small rod. See **virgule.**]

vir·gule (vúrgewl) *n.* A punctuation mark, a **solidus** *(see).* [French, comma, from Latin *virgula,* small rod, from rod, twig.]

vir·id (vírrid) *adj.* Green with or as if with vegetation; verdant. [Latin *viridis,* green, from *virēre,* to be green.] —**vi·rid·i·ty** (vi-riddəti) *n.*

vir·i·des·cent (vírri-déss'nt) *adj.* **1.** Green or slightly green. **2.** Turning green. [Latin *viridis,* green, VIRID + -ESCENT.] —**vir·i·des·cence** *n.*

vi·rid·i·an (vi-riddi-ən) *n.* A durable bluish-green pigment. [From Latin *viridis,* green, VIRID.]

vir·ile (virrīl ‖ *U.S. also* vírrəl) *adj.* **1.** Of or having the characteristics of an adult male. **2.** Having qualities traditionally associated with men, such as strength, vigour, or force. **3.** Of or pertaining to male sexual functions. [Middle English, from Old French *viril,* from Latin *virīlis,* from *vir,* man.]

vir·i·lism (vírriliz'm) *n.* The abnormal development of male characteristics in a woman. [VIRILE + -ISM.]

vi·ril·i·ty (vi-ríllati, və-) *n., pl.* **-ties. 1. a.** Masculine vigour; potency. **b.** Manhood. **2.** Qualities of strength or for forcefulness traditionally ascribed to men.

vi·ri·on (vīr-i-on, virri-) *n.* The complete inert form of a virus as found outside a host cell, consisting of a protein coat surrounding a strand or strands of nucleic acid. [From *viri-,* combining form of VIRUS + -ON (particle).]

vi·rol·o·gy (vīr-óllǝji) *n.* The study of viruses and viral diseases. [VIR(US) + -LOGY.] —**vi·ro·log·i·cal** (vīr-ǝ-lójik'l) —**vi·rolo·gist** (vīr-óllǝjist) *n.*

vir·tu (vur-toō, veer-) *n.* Also **ver·tu** (ver-). **1.** A knowledge of or taste for the fine arts. **2.** The quality of being beautiful, rare, or otherwise interesting to a collector. Used in the phrases *articles of virtu* and *objects of virtu.* **3.** Such articles or objects collectively. [Italian *virtu,* taste, virtue, from Latin *virtūs,* VIRTUE.]

vir·tu·al (vúr-choo-əl, -tew-, -chōol) *adj.* **1.** Being as specified in essence or effect though not in actual fact, form, or name: *He resigned from his job, but it was a virtual dismissal.* **2.** Of or pertaining to virtual reality: *a virtual battleground.* [Middle English *virtuall,* effective, powerful, from Medieval Latin, *virtuālis,* from Latin *virtūs,* capacity, VIRTUE.] —**vir·tu·al·i·ty** (-ál-ǝti) *n.*

virtual focus *n.* The point from which divergent rays of reflected or refracted light seem to have emanated, as from the image of a point in a plane mirror.

virtual image *n.* An image from which rays of reflected or refracted light appear to diverge, as from an image seen in a plane mirror.

vir·tu·al·ly (vúr-choo-ǝli, -chǝli, -tew-) *adv.* In essence or in effect though not in actual fact; for all practical purposes; essentially; nearly but not absolutely.

virtual particle *n. Physics.* A particle that is not detected but is considered to exist for a very brief period of time, during which it is emitted by one real particle and absorbed by another, thereby transmitting a force between the two. Electromagnetic interaction, for example, is considered to result from exchange of *virtual photons* between charged particles.

virtual reality *n.* A realistic impression of a given setting, such as a battleground or building, created through a three-dimensional visual display that is generated by a computer but regulated by the user, often by means of special goggles, gloves, or other equipment.

virtual storage *n. Computing.* Memory in which the effective capacity is increased by the linking of the main memory to an external memory, such as a magnetic disk, so that they function together.

vir·tue (vúr-tew, -choō) *n.* **1.** The quality of moral excellence, righteousness, and responsibility; probity; goodness. **2.** Conformity to standard morality or mores, as by abstention from vices; rectitude. **3. a.** A specific type of moral excellence or other exemplary quality considered meritorious; a worthy practice or ideal: *the virtue of integrity.* **b.** Any of the particular moral excellences considered exemplary in philosophy and theology. See **cardinal virtues. 4.** Chastity or virginity, especially that of a woman: *lost her virtue.* **5. a.** A particular efficacious or beneficial quality. **b.** A preferable quality; an advantage: *The plane has the virtue of speed.* **6.** Effective force or power; efficacy. **7.** *Plural. Theology.* One of the orders of angels. See **angel.** —**by** or **in virtue of.** On the grounds or basis of; by reason of. —**make a virtue of necessity.** To appear to do freely or by inclination what one is forced to do anyway. [Middle English *vertu,* from Old French, from Latin *virtūs,* manliness, strength, capacity, from *vir,* man.]

vir·tu·os·i·ty (vúr-tew-óssǝti, -choo-) *n., pl.* **-ties.** The technical skill, fluency, or style exhibited by a virtuoso.

vir·tu·o·so (vúr-tew-ṓ-sō, -choo-, -zō) *n., pl.* **-sos** or **-si** (-see, -zee). **1.** A musician with masterly skill, technique, or personal style; a brilliant performer. **2.** One with masterly skill or technique in any field, especially in the arts. **3.** A connoisseur or dilettante.

~adj. Showing or requiring virtuosity: *a virtuoso performance.* [Italian, from Late Latin *virtuōsus,* virtuous, skilful, from Latin *virtūs,* VIRTUE.] **—vir·tu·os·ic** (-óssik) *adj.*

vir·tu·ous (vúr-choo-əss, -tew-) *adj.* **1.** Exhibiting virtue; righteous: *virtuous conduct.* **2.** Possessing or characterised by chastity; pure: *a virtuous woman.* —See Synonyms at **moral.** **—vir·tu·ous·ly** *adv.* **—vir·tu·ous·ness** *n.*

vir·u·lent (vírrew-lənt, vírrōō- || vírrə-) *adj.* **1.** Extremely harmful or pathogenic and taking rapid effect. Said of a disease, toxin, or microorganism. **2.** Bitterly hostile or antagonistic; venomously spiteful; full of hate. **3.** Intensely irritating, obnoxious, or harsh: *virulent prejudice.* [Middle English, from Latin *vīrulentus,* from *vīrus,* VIRUS.] **—vir·u·lence** (-lənss) *n.* **—vir·u·lent·ly** *adv.*

vi·rus (vīr-əss) *n., pl.* **-ruses. 1.** Any of various submicroscopic pathogens consisting essentially of a core of a single nucleic acid surrounded by a protein coat, having the ability to replicate only inside a living cell. **2.** Any disease believed to be caused by a virus. **3. a.** Any malevolent and corrupting force: *the virus of racism.* **b.** A defect introduced deliberately into computer software; especially, a virus whose effects spread when the software is run, so as to impair the program increasingly. —See Usage note at **germ.** [Latin *vīrus,* poison, slime.]

vi·sa (veé-zə || *U.S. also* -sə) *n.* **1.** An official authorisation appended to a passport or similar document, permitting entry into and travel within a particular country or region. **2.** Any authorisation or mark of authorisation.

~tr.v. **visaed** (-zəd), **-saing** (*often* -zəring), **-sas. 1.** To make a visa in (a passport). **2.** To give a visa to. [French, from Latin *vīsa,* "things seen", neuter plural of *vīsus,* past participle of *vidēre,* to see.]

vis·age (vízzij) *n. Literary.* **1.** The face or facial expression of a person; a countenance. **2.** Appearance; aspect: *the visage of winter.* [Middle English, from Old French, from *vis,* face, from Latin *vīsus,* from the past participle of *vidēre,* to see.]

vis·aged (vízzijd) *adj. Literary* Having a specified kind of visage. Used in combination: *square-visaged.*

vis-à-vis (veéz-aa-veé, víz-, -ə-, -a-, -vee) *n., pl.* **vis-à-vis.** Either of two persons or things opposite, each other, such as partners in various dances. **2.** Either of two persons corresponding to each other in status, ability or position; a counterpart. **3.** A carriage carrying two passengers sitting opposite each other.

~adv. Face to face.

~prep. **1.** Compared with; in relation to. **2.** Opposite to; face to face with. [French, "face to face".] **—vis-·à-vis** *adj.*

Vi·sa·yan (vee-sī-ən, -saá-yən) *n., pl.* **-yans** or collectively **Visayan.** Also **Bi·sa·yan** (bee-). **1.** A member of the largest group of native people of the Philippines, found in the Visayan Islands. **2.** The Austronesian language spoken by these people. **—Vi·sa·yan** *adj.*

vis·ca·cha, viz·ca·cha (vi-skaáchə, -skáchə) *n.* Any of several gregarious, burrowing South American rodents of the genera *Lagostomus* and *Lagidium,* related to and resembling the chinchilla. [Spanish, from Quechua *wiscacha.*]

vis·cer·a (víssərə) *pl.n. Singular* **viscus** (vískəss). **1.** The internal organs of the body, especially those contained within the abdominal and thoracic cavities. **2.** Loosely, the intestines. [Latin *vīscera,* plural of *vīscus*†, body organ.]

vis·cer·al (víssərəl) *adj.* **1.** Pertaining to, situated in, or affecting the viscera. **2.** Pertaining to or derived from emotions and intuition rather than the intellect: *a visceral sense of disaster.*

visceral leishmaniasis *n.* A tropical disease, **leishmaniasis** *(see).*

vis·cer·o·mo·tor (víssə-rō-mōtər) *adj. Physiology.* Producing or related to movements of the viscera. [VISCER(A) + MOTOR.]

vis·cid (víssid) *adj.* **1.** Thick and adhesive. Said of a fluid. **2.** Covered with a sticky or clammy coating, as certain leaves are. [Late Latin *viscidus,* from Latin *viscum,* mistletoe, birdlime. See **viscous.**] **—vis·cid·i·ty** (vi-síddəti), **vis·cid·ness** *n.* **—vis·cid·ly** *adv.*

vis·com·e·ter (vi-skómmitər) *n.* Also **vis·co·sim·e·ter** (viskə-símmitər). Any of various instruments or pieces of apparatus used to measure viscosity. Also called "viscosimeter". [VISCO(SITY) + -METER.] **—vis·co·met·ric** (vísk-ō-méttrik, -ə-) *adj.*

Vis·con·ti (veess-kón-tee, viss-), **Gian Galeazzo** (1351–1402). Duke of Milan (1378–1402). By conquest, intrigue, and purchase he united Milan with neighbouring cities into one powerful state.

Visconti, Luchino, born Luchino Visconti de Modrone (1906–76). Italian film director. His films, noted for their visual composition, include *The Leopard* (1963) and *Death in Venice* (1971).

vis·cose (vísk-ōss, -ōz) *n.* **1.** A thick, golden-brown viscous solution of cellulose xanthate, used in the manufacture of rayon and cellophane. **2.** Viscose rayon.

~adj. **1.** *Rare.* Viscous. **2.** Of, relating to, or made from viscose. [Middle English, sticky, viscid, from Late Latin *viscōsus,* VISCOUS.]

viscose rayon *n.* A rayon made by reconverting cellulose from a soluble xanthate form to tough fibres by washing in acid.

vis·cos·i·ty (vi-skóssəti) *n., pl.* **-ties. 1.** The condition or property of being viscous. **2.** *Physics. Symbol* **η.** The degree to which a fluid resists flow under an applied force, measured by the tangential stress on the fluid divided by the resulting velocity gradient under conditions of streamline flow. [Middle English, from Medieval Latin *viscōsitās* (stem *viscōsitāt-*), from *viscōsus,* VISCOUS.]

vis·count (vī-kownt) *n. Abbr.* **V., Visc., Visct.** A peer ranking below an earl and above a baron. [Middle English, from Old French *visconte,* from Medieval Latin *vicecomes* : VICE (substitute) + *comes,* COUNT.] **—vis·count·cy** (-si), **vis·count·y** (-i) *n.*

vis·count·ess (vī-kownt-iss ||-ess, -éss) *n. Abbr.* **V., Vis., Visc., Visct.** **1.** The wife or widow of a viscount. **2.** A female viscount.

vis·cous (vískəss) *adj.* **1.** Having relatively high resistance to flow. **2.** Viscid; sticky. [Middle English *viscouse,* from Anglo-French *viscous,* from Late Latin *viscōsus,* from Latin *viscum,* mistletoe, birdlime (made from mistletoe berries).] **—vis·cous·ly** *adv.* **—vis·cous·ness** *n.*

vis·cus. Singular of **viscera.**

vise. *U.S.* Variant of **vice** (tool).

Vish·nu (vísh-nōō) *n.* The Hindu deity worshipped as the preserver and second member of the trinity with Brahma and Shiva, and as the chief deity by the Vaishnava. [Sanskrit *Viṣṇu*†.]

vis·i·bil·i·ty (vízzi-bílləti) *n., pl.* **-ties. 1.** The fact, state, or degree of being visible. **2.** *Abbr.* **vis.** The greatest distance under given weather conditions to which it is possible to see without the aid of instruments. [French *visibilité,* from Latin *vīsibilis,* VISIBLE.]

vis·i·ble (vízzəb'l, vízzib'l) *adj.* **1.** Capable of being seen; perceptible to the eye: *a visible object.* **2.** Obvious to the eye: *a visible change of expression.* **3.** Manifest; apparent: *no visible solution.* **4.** Available; on hand: *the visible supply.* **5.** Publicly conspicuous; in the public eye: *a highly visible politician.* **6.** Prepared to receive visitors. **7.** Constructed or designed to keep important parts in easily accessible view: *a visible file.* **8.** Represented visually, as by symbols. **9.** *Economics.* Designating items of international trade consisting of goods rather than services. Compare **invisible.**

~n. Plural. Economics. Imports and exports of goods as opposed to those of services. Compare **invisible.** [Middle English, from Old French, from Latin *vīsibilis,* from *vīsus,* sight, VISION.] **—vis·i·ble·ness** *n.* **—vis·i·bly** *adv.*

visible balance *n. Economics.* The **balance of trade** *(see).*

visible radiation *n.* Electromagnetic radiation that can be detected by the normal human eye; light.

visible speech *n.* A system of phonetic notation used as an aid for teaching speech to the deaf and consisting of diagrams of the organs of speech in the positions required to articulate sounds.

Vis·i·goth (vízzi-goth) *n.* A member of the western group of Goths that invaded the Roman Empire in the fourth century A.D. and settled in France and Spain, establishing a monarchy that lasted until the early eighth century A.D. Compare **Ostrogoth.** [From Late Latin *Visigothi* (plural), probably "West Goths".] **—Vis·i·goth·ic** (-góthik) *adj.*

vi·sion (vízh'n) *n.* **1. a.** The faculty of sight: *poor vision.* **b.** That which can be, is, or has been seen. **2.** Unusual competence in discernment or perception; intelligent foresight: *a woman of vision.* **3.** The manner in which one sees or conceives of something. **4.** A mental image produced by the imagination: *He has visions of himself as a hero.* **5. a.** The mystical experience of seeing as if with the eyes the supernatural or a supernatural being. **b.** That which is thus experienced or seen. **6.** A person or thing of extraordinary beauty. **7.** The image on a television screen.

~tr.v. **visioned, -sioning, -sions.** To see in or as if in a vision. [Middle English, from Old French, from Latin *vīsiō* (stem *vīsiōn-*), from *vīsus,* sight, from the past participle of *vidēre,* to see.] **—vi·sion·al** *adj.* **—vi·sion·al·ly** *adv.*

vi·sion·ar·y (vízh'n-əri || -erri) *adj.* **1.** Characterised by vision or foresight: *a visionary statesman.* **2.** Having the nature of or seen in fantasies or dreams. **3** Characterised by or given to mystical visions, prophecies, or revelations. **4.** Characterised by or given to impractical ideas; unrealistic: *a visionary fool* **5.** Not practicable at present; idealistic; utopian: *a visionary scheme.*

~n., pl. **visionaries. 1.** One who has visions; a seer; a prophet. **2.** One who is given to impractical or speculative ideas; a dreamer. **3.** One with great imagination or foresight.

vis·it (vízzit) *v.* **-ited, -iting, -its.** *—tr.* **1.** To go or come to see (a person), as by way of friendship or duty; call on: *visiting his sister.* **2.** To go or come to see (a place), as on a tour: *visit a museum.* **3.** To stay with as a guest. **4. a.** To go or come to see in a professional capacity: *The priest visited the condemned man.* **b.** To go or come to (an institution, for example) in an official capacity, as to inspect or examine. **5.** To go or come to for a particular purpose: *I visit the bank on Fridays.* **6.** To go or come to for medical or other treatment: *visit the dentist.* **7.** To afflict; assail: *A plague visited the village.* **8. a.** To inflict punishment upon or for: *"I shall visit their sin upon them".* (Exodus 32:34). **b.** To inflict (anger or retribution, for example) upon someone or something. **9.** *Archaic.* To come to in order to comfort or bless. Said of the Deity. *—intr.* **1.** To pay a call or calls. **2.** To inflict punishment; take revenge. **3.** *U.S. Informal.* To converse or chat: *Stay and visit with me for a while.*

~n. **1.** An act or instance of visiting a person, place, or thing. **2.** A stay or sojourn as a guest. **3. a.** An act of visiting in a professional capacity: *The doctor's visit was very brief.* **b.** An act of visiting in an official capacity, as for an inspection or examination. **4.** *Law.* The boarding of a foreign ship during wartime to establish its nationality, purpose, and cargo. Used especially in the phrase *right of visit and search.* [Middle English *visiten,* from Old French *visiter,* from Latin *visitāre,* to go to see, from *vīsāre,* to view, from *vīsus,* sight, VISION.] **—vis·it·a·ble** *adj.*

vis·i·tant (vízzitənt) *n.* **1.** A supernatural being; a ghost or spectre. **2.** A visitor; especially, a pilgrim or tourist. **3.** A migratory animal or bird that stops in a particular place for a limited period of time.

~adj. Archaic. Visiting. [Latin *visitāns* (stem *visitānt-*), present participle of *visitāre,* to VISIT.]

vis·i·ta·tion (vízzi-táysh'n) *n.* **1.** A visit for the purpose of makin official inspection or examination, such as one made by a bi a church in his diocese. **2. a.** A visit or social call. **b.** A visit or social call that is unwelcome or unduly long. Used humorously. **3.** *U.S.* A divorced or separated parent's right of access to the children of the marriage. **4. a.** A visit of punishment or affliction or of comfort and blessing, regarded as being ordained by God. **b.** A calamitous event or experience; a grave misfortune. **5.** The appearance or arrival of a supernatural being. **6.** *Capital* **V. a.** The visit of the Virgin Mary to her cousin Elizabeth. Luke 1:39–56. **b.** The Church festival held on July 2 in commemoration of this visit. **—vis·i·ta·tion·al** *adj.*

vis·i·ta·to·ri·al (vízzitə-táw-ri-əl || -tō-) *adj.* Also **vis·i·to·ri·al** (vízzi-). **1.** Of or pertaining to an official visitor or visit. **2.** Having the right or power of visitation.

visiting card *n.* A small card printed with one's name and address presented as an introduction or left when the person one wishes to see is absent. Also called "card", *U.S.* "calling card".

visiting fireman *n. U.S. Informal.* **1.** An influential visitor who is entertained impressively. **2.** A visitor to a city who is welcomed because he is thought to be a free spender.

visiting professor *n.* A person, especially a lecturer or professor on sabbatical leave, holding a professorship at the invitation of a university or other institution, often in another country for an academic year.

vis·i·tor (vízzitər) *n.* **1.** One who pays a visit; a guest; a caller. **2.** A sightseer or tourist. **3.** A migratory animal, especially a bird, pausing in transit at a place; a visitant. **4.** An official, especially at a college, holding nominal powers of inspection or supervision.

vis ma·jor (víss máyjər) *n., pl.* **vires majores** (vī́r-eez mə-jáw-reez || -jṓ-) *Law.* An overwhelming force of circumstance or nature having unavoidable consequences that can exempt one from the obligations of a contract; force majeure. [Latin, "greater force".]

vi·sor, vi·zor (vī́zər) *n.* **1.** A fixed or movable shield fitted at the top of a car windscreen to protect against glare. **2.** A protective shield held or worn in front of the face, used when welding or doing other dangerous tasks. **3.** *Chiefly U.S.* A peak on a cap. **4.** The front piece of the helmet of a suit of armour, capable of being raised and lowered and designed to protect the eyes, nose, and forehead. **5.** *Archaic.* Any means of concealment or disguise; a mask.
~tr.v. **visored** (vī́zərd) **-soring, -sors.** Also **vi·zor.** To mask or protect with a visor. [Middle English *viser,* from Anglo-French, from Old French *vis,* face, from Latin *vīsus,* sight, VISION.]

vis·ta (vístə) *n.* **1.** A distant view seen through a passage, as between buildings or rows of trees; a scene; a prospect. **2.** The passage framing the approach to such a scene; an avenue. **3.** A comprehensive awareness of a series of remembered, present, or anticipated events: *"He opened a vista into a mean life."* (Rebecca West). [Italian, from *visto,* past participle of *vedere,* to see, from Latin *vidēre.*]

Vis·tu·la (vístewlə). *Polish* **Wis·ła** (veéss-waa). River in Poland. Rising in the Beskid mountains, it flows 1 094 kilometres (680 miles) north and northwest to enter the Baltic at Gdansk.

vis·u·al (vízzew-əl, ví<u>zh</u>ew-, ví<u>zh</u>oo- || ví<u>zh</u>'l) *adj. Abbr.* **vis. 1.** Serving, resulting from, or pertaining to the sense of sight. **2.** Capable of being seen by the eye; visible. **3.** *Physics.* Optical. **4.** Done, maintained, or executed by the sight only: *visual navigation.* **5.** Having the nature of or producing an image in the mind. **6.** Involving sight: *visual instruction; visual humour.*
~n. Usually plural. Any form of graphic material, such as a film, display, or photograph, used for educational or publicity purposes. [Middle English, from Late Latin *vīsuālis,* from Latin *vīsus,* VISION.] **—vis·u·al·ly** *adv.*

visual aids *pl.n.* Graphic material and the devices for presenting it, such as posters and display boards, used in education to impart instruction by visual means.

visual arts *pl.n.* Arts such as painting and sculpture whose works exist in permanent and static form rather than requiring performance, as ballet does, and whose aesthetic appeal is primarily to the visual sense, as opposed to such arts as music and poetry.

visual display unit *n.* An electronic device for displaying computer-prompted words and diagrams on a cathode-ray screen. Also called "VDU", "video terminal".

visual field *n. Abbr.* **V.F.** The entire area visible to the immobile eye or eyes at a given moment; the field of vision.

vis·u·al·ise, vis·u·al·ize (vízzew-ə-līz, ví<u>zh</u>ew-, ví<u>zh</u>oo- || ví<u>zh</u>-) *v.* **-ised, -ising, -ises.** *—tr.* To form a mental image or vision of; envisage. *—intr.* To form a mental image or images. **—vis·u·al·i·sa·tion** (-lī-záysh'n || *U.S.* -li-) *n.* **—vis·u·al·is·er** *n.*

visual purple *n.* A pigment of the retina, **rhodopsin** *(see).*

vi·tal (vī́t'l) *adj.* **1.** Of, affecting, or characteristic of life: *vital processes.* **2.** Necessary to the continuation of life; life-sustaining: *vital functions.* **3.** Full of life; energetic; vigorous; animated: *Her dancing is vital yet controlled.* **4.** *Poetic.* Imparting life or animation; invigorating. **5. a.** Having immediate importance; essential; indispensable: *vital to our success.* **b.** Crucial; decisive: *a vital innings.* **6.** Concerned with or recording data pertinent to lives. **7.** *Archaic.* Destructive to life; fatal; deadly: *a vital wound.* —See Synonyms at **necessary.** [Middle English, from Old French, from Latin *vītālis,* from *vīta,* life.] **—vi·tal·ly** *adv.* **—vi·tal·ness** *n.*

vital capacity *n. Physiology.* The maximum amount of air that can be expelled from the lungs after breathing in as deeply as possible.

vital force *n.* A hypothetical life force suggested by early biologists as the driving force behind the evolution and development of organisms. [Translation of French *élan vital.*]

vi·tal·ise, vi·tal·ize (vī́t'l-īz) *tr.v.* **-ised, -ising, -ises. 1.** To endow with life. **2.** To invigorate or animate. **—vi·tal·i·sa·tion** (-ī-záysh'n || *U.S.* -i-) *n.* **—vi·tal·is·er** *n.*

vi·tal·ism (vī́t'l-iz'm) *n.* The philosophical doctrine that life processes possess a unique character radically different from physiochemical phenomena and therefore cannot be explained in empirical terms. **—vi·tal·ist** *n.* **—vi·tal·is·tic** (-ístik) *adj.*

vi·tal·i·ty (vī-tál-əti) *n., pl.* **-ties. 1.** Vigour; energy; exuberance. **2.** The power to survive or evolve: *impaired the firm's vitality.* **3.** That which distinguishes the living from the nonliving; an energy, force, or principle characteristic of life; vital force. **4.** The capacity to live, grow, or develop.

vi·tals (vī́t'lz) *pl.n.* **1.** Any bodily parts or organs regarded as the centre or source of life: *sensed disaster in his vitals.* **2.** Those bodily organs whose continued functioning is essential for life. **3.** The reproductive organs, especially those of the male. **4.** Those elements essential to continued functioning, as in a system.

vital stain *n.* Any biological stain that can be used to colour living material, as for examination under a microscope.

vital statistics *pl.n.* **1.** Data that record significant events and dates in human life, as the rate of births, deaths, and marriages. **2.** *Informal.* The measurements of a woman's bust, waist, and hips.

vi·ta·min (víttə-min, vī́tə-) *n.* Also *rare* **vi·ta·mine** (-min, -meen). Any of various relatively complex organic substances occurring naturally in plant and some animal tissue, and essential in small amounts for the control of metabolic processes. [German *Vitamine*: Latin *vīta,* life + AMINE (so called because it was once thought to contain an amino acid).] **—vi·ta·min·ic** (mínnik) *adj.*

vitamin A *n.* Vitamin A_1 or a mixture of vitamins A_1 and A_2, occurring principally in fish-liver oils and some yellow and dark-green vegetables, functioning in normal cell growth and development. A deficiency causes hardening and roughening of the skin, night blindness, and degeneration of mucous membranes. Also called "retinol".

vitamin A_1 *n.* A yellow crystalline compound, $C_{20}H_{30}O$, extracted from fish-liver oils. See **vitamin A.**

vitamin A_2 *n.* A golden-yellow oil, $C_{20}H_{28}O$, occurring in pike-liver oils and having approximately 40 per cent of the biological activity of vitamin A_1. See **vitamin A.**

vitamin B *n.* **1.** Vitamin B complex. **2.** A member of the vitamin B complex, especially thiamine.

vitamin B_1. Thiamine *(see).*

vitamin B_2 *n.* **Riboflavin** *(see).*

vitamin B_6 *n.* **Pyridoxine** *(see).*

vitamin B_{12}. A complex, cobalt-containing coordination compound produced in the normal growth of certain microorganisms, found in liver, and widely used to treat pernicious anaemia. Also called "cyanocobalamin".

vitamin B_c *n.* **Folic acid** *(see).*

vitamin B complex *n.* A group of vitamins originally thought to be a single substance, generally regarded as including thiamine, riboflavin, niacin, pantothenic acid, biotin, pyridoxine, folic acid, lipoic acid, inositol, and vitamin B_{12}, and occurring chiefly in yeast, liver, eggs, and some vegetables.

vitamin C *n.* **Ascorbic acid** *(see).*

vitamin D *n., pl.* **D vitamins.** Any of several chemically similar compounds produced in general by ultraviolet irradiation of sterols, obtained from milk, fish, and eggs, required for normal bone growth, and used to treat rickets in children and osteomalacia in adults. Also called "calciferol".

vitamin E *n.* Any of several chemically related viscous oils, especially $C_{29}H_{50}O_2$, found chiefly in grains and vegetable oils. A deficiency causes sterility in certain mammals, but the effects in humans are uncertain. Also called "tocopherol".

vitamin G *n. Chiefly U.S.* **Riboflavin** *(see).*

vitamin K *n., pl.* **K vitamins.** Any of several natural and synthetic substances essential for the promotion of blood clotting and prevention of haemorrhage; especially menaquinone *(vitamin K_2)* and phylloquinone *(vitamin K_1).*

vitamin P *n.* **Bioflavonoid** *(see).*

vi·tel·lin (vi-téllin, vī-) *n.* A protein found in egg yolk. [VITELL(US) + -IN.]

vi·tel·line (vi-tél-īn, vī-, -in) *adj.* **1.** Pertaining to or associated with the yolk of an egg: *the vitelline membrane.* **2.** Having the yellow colour of an egg yolk; dull yellow. [VITELL(US) + -INE.]

vitelline membrane *n. Zoology.* A membrane that forms around a fertilised egg to prevent other sperm from entering.

vi·tel·lus (vi-télləss, vī-) *n., pl.* **-luses** or **-li** (-téllī). *Rare.* The yolk of an egg. [Latin.]

vi·ti·ate (víshi-ayt) *tr.v.* **-ated, -ating, -ates. 1.** To impair the value or quality of; make faulty or impure; spoil. **2.** To corrupt morally; pervert. **3.** To invalidate or render (a contract, for example) legally ineffective. [Latin *vitiāre,* from *vitium,* defect, fault.] **—vi·ti·a·ble** (-əb'l) *adj.* **—vi·ti·a·tion** (-áysh'n) *n.* **—vi·ti·a·tor** (-aytər) *n.*

vit·i·cul·ture (vítti-kulchər, vī́ti-) *n.* The cultivation of grapes, especially for wine-making. [Latin *vītis,* vine + CULTURE.] **—vit·i·cul·tur·al** (-kúlchərəl) *adj.* **—vit·i·cul·tur·ist** *n.*

vit·i·li·go (vítti-lī́gō) *n.* A skin disease, **leucoderma** *(see).* [Latin *vitilīgō,* cutaneous eruption.]

Vi·to·ria (vee-táwri-ə). A city in northern Spain. The capital of Álava province, it was founded (sixth century) by the Visigoths. Wellington defeated the French there in the Peninsular War (1813).

vit·re·ous (víttri-əss) *adj.* **1.** Pertaining to, resembling, or having the nature of glass; glassy. **2.** Obtained or made from glass. **3.** Of or pertaining to the vitreous body or vitreous humour. [Latin *vitreus,* from *vitrum†,* glass.] —**vit·re·os·i·ty** (-óssəti) **vit·re·ous·ness** *n.*

vitreous body *n.* A gelatinous body of matter composed mainly of vitreous humour that fills the part of the eyeball between the retina and the lens.

vitreous enamel *n.* **Porcelain enamel** *(see).*

vitreous humour *n.* A watery fluid that is a major component of the vitreous body.

vitreous silica *n.* Silica that has been fused to form a hard transparent heat-resistant glass, used especially for making scientific apparatus.

vi·tres·cence (vi-tréss'nss) *n.* **1.** Transformation into glass. **2.** The state of becoming vitreous or like glass.

vi·tres·cent (vi-tréss'nt) *adj.* **1.** Tending to become glass or like glass. **2.** Capable of being turned into glass. [Latin *vitrum,* glass (see **vitreous**) + -ESCENT.]

vit·ri·fi·ca·tion (vittrifi-káysh'n) *n.* **1.** The act or process of vitrifying or the state of being vitrified. **2.** Something vitrified.

vit·ri·form (vitri-fawrm) *adj.* Resembling glass in form or appearance. [Latin *vitrum,* glass + -FORM.]

vit·ri·fy (vittri-fī) *v.* **-fied, -fying, -fies.** —*tr.* To change or make into glass or a similar substance, especially through melting. —*intr.* To become vitreous. [French *vitrifier,* from Old French : Latin *vitrum,* glass (see **vitreous**) + -FY.] —**vit·ri·fi·a·bil·i·ty** (-fī-ə-billəti) *n.* —**vit·ri·fi·a·ble** (-fī-əb'l, -fī-) *adj.*

vit·ri·ol (vittri-əl, -ol ‖ -ōl) *n.* **1.** *Chemistry.* **a.** Sulphuric acid. **b.** Any of various sulphates of metals, such as ferrous sulphate (green vitriol), zinc sulphate (white vitriol), or copper sulphate (blue vitriol). **2.** Vituperative statements or feelings.

~*tr.v.* **vitrioled** or **-olled, -oling** or **-olling, -ols.** **1.** To expose or subject to vitriol. **2.** To attack or injure with vitriol. [Middle English, from Old French, from Medieval Latin *vitriolum,* from Latin *vitrum,* glass (from the appearance of its sulphates). See **vitreous.**]

vit·ri·ol·ic (vittri-óllik) *adj.* **1.** Of, similar to, or derived from a vitriol. **2.** Bitterly scathing; caustic: *a vitriolic review.*

vit·ri·ol·ise, vit·ri·ol·ize (vittri-əl-īz) *tr.v.* **-ised, -ising, -ises.** **1.** To expose or subject to vitriol. **2.** To convert into vitriol. **3.** To attack or injure with vitriol. —**vit·ri·ol·i·sa·tion** (-ī-záysh'n ‖ U.S. -i-) *n.*

Vi·tru·vi·us (vi-trŏŏvi-əss), (late 1st c. B.C. and early 1st c. A.D.). Roman architect and engineer. His treatise, *De architectura,* the only complete Roman architectural work to survive, influenced architects of the Classical revival, such as Palladio and Alberti, and others through to the 18th century.

vit·ta (vít-ə) *n., pl.* **-tae** (-ee). **1.** *Biology.* A streak or band of colour. **2.** *Botany.* An oil tube in the fruit of certain plants, such as the carrot or parsley. [Latin, headband.] —**vit·tate** (-ayt) *adj.*

vi·tu·per·ate (vī-téw-pə-rayt, vi- ‖ -tŏŏ-) *tr.v.* **-ated, -ating, -ates.** To rail against severely or abusively; revile; berate. See Synonyms at **malign.** [Latin *vituperāre.*] —**vi·tu·per·a·tor** (-raytər) *n.*

vi·tu·per·a·tion (vī-téw-pə-ráysh'n, vi- ‖ -tŏŏ-) *n.* **1.** Abusive censure or blame. **2.** Invective; railing. **3.** The act of vituperating.

vi·tu·per·a·tive (vī-téw-pə-rətiv, vi-, -raytiv ‖ -tŏŏ-) *adj.* Harshly abusive; acrimonious: *a vituperative note.* —**vi·tu·per·a·tive·ly** *adv.*

vi·va¹ (véevə) *interj.* Used to express acclamation, salute, or applause.

~*n.* A shout of "viva". [Italian, from *vivere,* to live, from Latin *vīvere.*]

vi·va² (vívə) *n. British.* An examination consisting of an interview rather than of written papers; a viva voce examination.

~*v.* **vivaed** or **-va'd** (vívəd), **-vaing** (*often* vívəring), **-vas** or **va's.** —*tr.* To examine by means of a viva. —*intr.* To undergo a viva. [Shortened from VIVA VOCE.]

vi·va·ce (vi-váa-chi, -chay ‖ vee-) *adv. Music.* Lively; vivaciously; briskly. Used as a direction. [Italian, from Latin *vīvāx,* VIVACIOUS.]

vi·va·cious (vi-váyshəss, vī-) *adj.* Animated; sprightly; spirited. [Latin *vīvāx* (stem *vīvāci-*), lively, from *vīvere,* to live.] —**vi·va·cious·ly** *adv.* —**vi·va·cious·ness** *n.*

vi·vac·i·ty (vi-vássəti, vī-) *n.* The condition or quality of being vivacious; liveliness.

Vi·val·di (vi-vál-di), **Antonio** (1678–1741). Italian composer and violinist. He is chiefly remembered for his concertos, particularly *The Four Seasons,* a set of four violin concertos.

vi·van·dière (vée-voNd-yáir) *n.* Formerly, especially in France, a woman who accompanied troops to sell them extra food, supplies, and drink. [French, feminine of *vivandier,* provisioner, from Old French, from *viande,* VIAND.]

vi·var·i·um (vi-vaír-i-əm, vī-) *n., pl.* **-ums** or **-varia** (-ə). A place or enclosure for keeping and breeding living animals for observation or research. [Latin : *vīvus,* alive (see **vivify**) + -ARIUM.]

vi·va vo·ce (vívə vō̌-si, -chi) *adj.* By word of mouth; spoken; oral. ~*n.* A viva voce examination. [Middle Latin, "with the living voice".] —**vi·va vo·ce** *adv.*

vive (veev) *interj. French.* Used to acclaim, salute, or applaud a person or personification specified: *Vive la France!*

vi·ver·rine (vī-vérrīn, vi- ‖ -vérrin) *n.* A member of the family Viverridae, which includes carnivorous mammals such as the civets and mongooses. [From Latin *viverra,* ferret.] —**vi·ver·rine** *adj.*

viv·id (vívvid) *adj.* **1.** Perceived as bright and distinct; brilliant: *the vivid evening star.* **2. a.** Having intensely bright colours: *a vivid tapestry.* **b.** Very bright or strong. Said of colour. **3.** Full of the vigour and freshness of immediate experience: *vivid emotions.* **4. a.** Evoking lifelike images within the mind; heard, seen, or felt as if real: *a*

vivid description. **b.** Active in forming or retaining lifelike images: *a vivid imagination.* [Latin *vīvidus,* full of life, lifelike, from *vīvere,* to live.] —**viv·id·ly** *adv.* —**viv·id·ness** *n.*

viv·i·fy (vívvi-fī) *tr.v.* **-fied, -fying, -fies.** **1.** To give or bring life to; animate. **2.** To make more lively, intense, or striking; enliven. [French *vivifier,* from Late Latin *vīvificāre* : Latin *vīvus,* alive + *facere,* to do.] —**viv·i·fi·ca·tion** (-fi-káysh'n) *n.* —**viv·i·fi·er** *n.*

vi·vip·a·rous (vi-víppərəss, vī-) *adj.* **1.** *Zoology.* Giving birth to living offspring that develop within the mother's body. Said of most mammals. Compare **oviparous, ovoviviparous.** **2.** *Botany.* **a.** Germinating or producing seeds that germinate before becoming detached from the parent plant. **b.** Producing bulbils or new plants rather than seed. [Latin *vīviparus* : *vīvus,* alive (see **vivify**) + -PAROUS.] —**viv·i·par·i·ty** (vívvi-párrəti) *n.* —**vi·vip·a·rous·ly** *adv.*

viv·i·sect (vívvi-sékt, -sekt) *v.* **-sected, -secting, -sects.** —*tr.* To perform vivisection on (a live animal). —*intr.* To carry out vivisection. [Back-formation from VIVISECTION.] —**viv·i·sec·tor** (-ər) *n.*

viv·i·sec·tion (vívvi-séksh'n) *n.* **1.** The act of cutting into or dissecting the body of a living animal, especially for scientific research. **2.** Extremely detailed and often destructive criticism or analysis, as of a film or book. [Latin *vīvus,* alive (see **vivify**) + -SECTION.] —**viv·i·sec·tion·al** *adj.*

viv·i·sec·tion·ist (vívvi-séksh'n-ist) *n.* **1.** A person who performs a vivisection. **2.** A person who favours the continued use of vivisection for scientific research, and opposes movements to modify or abolish it.

vix·en (víks'n) *n.* **1.** A female fox. **2.** A quarrelsome, shrewish, or malicious woman. [Middle English *fixene,* Old English *fyxe,* she-fox.] —**vix·en·ish** *adj.* —**vix·en·ly** *adj. & adv.*

Vi·yel·la (vī-éllə) *n.* A trademark for a soft fabric made of a mixture of wool and cotton, used especially for clothing. —**Vi·yel·la** *adj.*

viz. videlicet. *Note: Viz.* is never pronounced (viz) when formally reading something aloud: it is replaced by its gloss, "namely". In informal speech, however, it is often pronounced (viz). Though *viz* is an abbreviation of *videlicet,* it is rarely read out as "videlicet"—except in humorous or highly formal contexts.

viz·ard (vízzərd) *n.* Also **vis·ard.** *Archaic.* **1.** A visor on a helmet. **2.** A mask. [Earlier *vizar, viser,* variants of VISOR.]

viz·ca·cha. Variant of **viscacha.**

vi·zier (vi-zéer, víz-eer ‖ -yər) *n.* Also **vi·zir.** A high officer, such as a provincial governor or chief adviser, in various Muslim governments, especially in the Ottoman Empire. [French *vizir,* from Turkish *vezīr,* from Arabic *wazīr,* porter, from *wazara,* to bear, carry.] —**vi·zier·i·al** (vi-zéer-i-əl) *adj.*

vi·zier·ate (vi-zéer-ət, víz-eer-, -it, -ayt ‖ -yər-) *n.* The office, authority, or term of office of a vizier. Also called "vizieralty", "viziership".

vi·zor. Variant of **visor.**

vizs·la (vízhlə) *n.* A hunting dog of a Hungarian breed, having a smooth golden-red coat. [After *Vizsla,* Hungary, where the breed originated.]

V-J Day (vée-jáy) *n.* The day of victory for the Allied forces over Japan in World War II; in Britain, August 15, 1945, and in the United States, September 2, 1945. [Short for *Victory in Japan Day.*]

Vlaanderen. See **Flanders.**

Vlach (vlaakh) *n.* A member of a widely scattered people, speaking a Romanian dialect, living in southeastern Europe in early medieval times.

~*adj.* Of, pertaining to, or designating this people, their culture, or their Romanian dialect.

Vla·di·mir I, (vláddi-meer, *Russian* vla-dée-), **St.** also known as Vladimir the Great (c. 965–1015). The first Christian ruler of Russia. He extended Russia's dominions from the Ukraine to the Baltic Sea, making Kiev his capital.

Vla·di·vos·tok (vláddi-vóstok, *Russian* -vuss-tók). A Pacific seaport of Russia. The capital of the Primorye Territory, between Amur Bay and the Golden Horn, it is a major naval base.

Vla·minck (vla-máNk), **Maurice de** (1876–1958). French painter. With André Derain and Henri Matisse he was one of the leading exponents of fauvism. He is noted for his stormy, aggressive landscapes.

vlei (flay) *n. South African.* A low-lying stretch of soggy ground; a marsh. [Afrikaans, from Dutch *vallei,* akin to VALLEY.]

vlf, VLF very low frequency.

V neck (vée-nek) *n.* **1.** A neck or collar of a garment that has a V-shaped front, tapering to a point rather than being rounded. **2.** A garment, especially a sweater, having such a neck. —**V-neck, V-necked** (-nekt) *adj.*

vo. verso.

voc. vocative.

vocab. vocabulary.

vo·ca·ble (vōkəb'l) *n.* **1.** A word considered only as a sequence of sounds or letters rather than as a unit of meaning. **2.** A sound that can be voiced; a vowel.

~*adj.* Capable of being voiced or spoken. [French, from Old French, from Latin *vocābulum,* an appellation, from *vocāre,* to call.]

vo·cab·u·lar·y (və-kábbew-ləri, vō- ‖ -lerri) *n., pl.* **-ies.** *Abbr.* **vocab.** (*sometimes* vō-kab). **1.** A list of words and often phrases, usually arranged alphabetically and defined or translated; a lexicon or glossary. **2.** All the words of a language. **3.** The sum of words used by, understood by, or at the command of a particular person or group. **4.** A command or reserve of expressive techniques; repertoire: *a dancer's vocabulary of movement.* [Medieval Latin *vōcabulārium,* from *vocābulārius,* of words, from Latin *vocābulum,* an appellation, name. See **vocable.**]

vo·cal (vṓk'l) *adj.* **1. a.** Of or pertaining to the voice. **b.** For or rendered by the voice rather than an instrument: *a vocal line.* **2.** Uttered or produced by the voice: *a vocal prayer.* **3.** Having a voice; capable of emitting sound or speech. **4.** Full of voices; resounding with speech: *a vocal gathering.* **5.** Quick to speak or criticise; outspoken: *vocal dissidents.* **6.** *Phonetics.* **a.** Vocalic. **b.** Voiced.
~n. **1.** *Phonetics.* A vocal sound. **2.** *Plural.* The music sung by a vocalist, rather than the instrumental accompaniment. [Middle English, from Latin *vōcālis,* speaking, talking, from *vōx,* voice.] **—vo·cal·ly** *adv.* **—vo·cal·ness** *n.*

vocal cords *pl.n.* The lower of two pairs of bands or folds in the larynx that vibrate when pulled together and when air passes over them from the lungs, thereby producing vocal sounds. Also called "vocal folds".
Usage: Association of the voice with music and therefore with musical chords sometimes leads to the nonstandard spelling *vocal chords.* The form *vocal folds* is preferred by specialists.

vo·cal·ic (vō-kál-ik, və-) *adj.* **1.** Containing many vowel sounds. **2.** Pertaining to or having the nature of a vowel or vowels.

vo·cal·ise¹, vo·cal·ize (vṓk'l-īz) *v.* **-ised, -ising, -ises.** *—tr.* **1.** To make vocal; produce with the voice. **2.** To give voice to; articulate. **3.** To mark (a vowelless Hebrew text, for example) with diacritical vowel points. **4.** *Phonetics.* **a.** To change (a consonant) into a vowel. **b.** To voice. *—intr.* **1.** To use the voice; especially, to sing. **2.** *Phonetics.* To be changed into a vowel. **—vo·cal·i·sa·tion** (-ī-záysh'n || *U.S.* -i-) *n.* **—vo·cal·is·er** *n.*

vo·cal·ise² (vō-kə-léez, -ka-) *n.* A wordless musical composition, especially for the voice. [French.]

vo·cal·ism (vṓk'l-iz'm) *n.* **1.** The use of the voice in speaking or singing. **2.** The act, technique, or art of singing. **3.** A vowel or vocalic sound. **4.** A system of vowels, as within a specific language.

vo·cal·ist (vṓk'l-ist) *n.* A singer, especially in a jazz or pop group.

vocal score *n.* A musical score transcribing the voice parts in full and the orchestral parts reduced to a piano accompaniment.

vo·ca·tion (və-káysh'n, vō-) *n.* **1.** A regular occupation or profession; especially, one for which one is specially suited or qualified. **2.** An urge or predisposition to undertake a certain kind of work, especially a religious career; a calling. [Middle English *vocacioun,* divine call to a religious life, from Old French *vocation,* from Latin *vōcātiō* (stem *vōcātiōn-*), a calling, summoning, from *vōcāre,* to call.]

vo·ca·tion·al (və-káysh'n'l, vō-) *adj.* **1.** Of or pertaining to vocations or one's vocation. **2.** Pertaining to, providing, or undergoing training in a special skill to be pursued as a trade or profession. **—vo·ca·tion·al·ly** *adv.*

voc·a·tive (vóckətiv) *adj.* **1.** Pertaining to, characteristic of, or used in calling. **2.** *Abbr.* **v., voc.** Designating, pertaining to, or inflected in the grammatical case used in certain languages, such as Latin or Polish, to denote the person or thing being addressed.
~n. Abbr. **v., voc. 1.** The vocative case. **2.** A form or construction in this case. [Middle English *vocatif,* from Old French, from Latin *vocātīvus,* from *vōcāre,* to call. See **vocation.**] **—voc·a·tive·ly** *adv.*

vo·cif·er·ate (vō-síffə-rayt, və-) *v.* **-ated, -ating, -ates.** *—intr.* To cry out vehemently, especially in protest; exclaim. *—tr.* To utter (a protest, for example) loudly and insistently. [Latin *vōciferārī* : *vōx* (stem *vōci-*), voice (see **vocal**) + *ferre,* to bear] **—vo·cif·er·a·tion** (-ráysh'n) *n.* **—vo·cif·er·a·tor** (-raytər) *n.*

vo·cif·er·ous (vō-síffərəss, və-) *adj.* **1.** Making an outcry, as in protest. **2.** Characterised by loudness and vehemence. [From VOCIFERATE.] **—vo·cif·er·ous·ly** *adv.* **—vo·cif·er·ous·ness** *n.*

vo·coid (vṓ-koyd) *n.* A speech sound articulated with air from the lungs flowing through the mouth over the centre of the tongue without friction; a vowel or semivowel. [Latin *vōx* (stem *vōc-*), voice (see **vowel**) + -OID.] **—vo·coid** *adj.*

vod·ka (vódkə) *n.* An alcoholic drink of Russian origin, formerly distilled from fermented wheat mash, now also made from a mash of rye, wheat, or potatoes. [Russian, diminutive of *voda,* water.]

voet·sek (fŏŏt-sek, -sak) *interj. South African Slang.* Used as a rough command to scare or chase away an animal or person. [Afrikaans, from Dutch *voort seg ik,* "away say I".]

voet·stoots (fŏŏt-stoorts) *adj. Law. South African.* Designating a sale of an item, especially a house, in which its condition, good or bad, is accepted by the buyer who cannot then claim redress if it proves unsatisfactory. [Afrikaans, from Dutch, from phrase *met de voet te stoten,* "to push (aside) with the foot", hence figuratively, (to sell) without assuming responsibility.] **—voet·stoots** *adv.*

vogue (vōg) *n.* **1.** The prevailing fashion, practice, or style: *in vogue.* **2.** Popular acceptance or favour; popularity.
~adj. Fashionable; in widespread current use; popular: *vogue words.* —See Synonyms at **fashion.** [French, fashion, "rowing", from *voguer,* to row, go along smoothly, from Old French, from Old Low German *wogon* (unattested).] **—vog·uish** *adj.*

Vo·gul (vṓg'l) *n.* **1.** A member of a people living in western Siberia. **2.** The language of this people, of the Finno-Ugric family of languages. [Russian, from Ostyak *Uogal', Uogat'.*]

voice (vóyss) *n. Abbr.* **v. 1. a.** The sound or sounds produced by the vocal organs of a vertebrate, especially by those of a human being. **b.** The natural and characteristic manner of speaking or sound of the speech of a specified person: *recognised your voice.* **2.** The ability to produce such sounds: *lost her voice.* **3.** Any sound resembling or reminiscent of vocal utterance: *the voice of the bugles.* **4.** The specified quality, condition, or timbre of vocal sound: *A hoarse voice.* **5. a.** Oral or verbal expression: *give voice to one's anger.* **b.** Any means of making something known: *the voice of the nation; the voice of experience.* **c.** The right or opportunity to express a choice or opinion: *had no voice in their own future.* **6.** *Obsolete.* **a.** Rumour or report. **b.** Reputation or fame. **7.** *Grammar.* A verb form indicating the relation between the subject and the action expressed by the verb. See **active, passive. 8.** *Phonetics.* The expiration of air through vibrating vocal folds, used in the production of the vowels and voiced consonants. Compare **breath. 9. a.** Musical tone produced by the vibration of vocal folds and resonated within the throat and head cavities. **b.** The quality or condition of a person's singing: *a bass voice; in excellent voice.* **c.** A singer: *a choir of fine voices.* **10.** Any of the melodic parts for a musical composition. In this sense, also called "voice part". **—throw (one's) voice.** To make one's voice seem to come from elsewhere, as a ventriloquist does. **—with one voice.** In unison; unanimously.
~tr.v. **voiced, voicing, voices. 1.** To express or utter; give voice to: *voice an objection.* **2.** *Phonetics.* To utter with voice. **3.** *Music.* To regulate the tone of (the pipes of an organ, for example). —See Synonyms at **vent.** [Middle English, from Old French *vois, voix,* from Latin *vōx.*]

voice box *n.* The larynx.

voiced (voyst) *adj.* **1.** Having a voice or having a specified kind of voice. Often used in combination: *harsh-voiced.* **2.** *Phonetics.* Uttered with vibration of the vocal folds, as the consonants *d* and *b* are in English. Compare **voiceless.**

voice·ful (vóyssf'l) *adj. Poetic.* Having a voice; especially, having a loud voice; resounding. **—voice·ful·ness** *n.*

voice·less (vóyss-ləss, -liss) *adj.* **1. a.** Having no voice; mute; silent. **b.** Not expressed by means of the voice. **2.** *Phonetics.* Uttered without vibration of the vocal cords, as the consonants *t* and *p* are in English. Compare **voiced. 3.** Unable to sing. **4.** Not having the right to speak or vote. —See Synonyms at **dumb. —voice·less·ly** *adv.* **—voice·less·ness** *n.*

voice-o·ver (vóyss-ōvər, -ōvər) *n.* **1.** In cinematic films and television, the voice of a narrator or commentator who does not appear on camera. **2.** The script read by such a narrator.

voice part *n. Music.* A voice.

voice·print (vóyss-print) *n.* An electronically recorded graphic representation of voice, typically with time plotted on the horizontal axis, frequency on the vertical, and amplitude exhibited in a series of contour lines.

voice vote *n.* A vote that is decided on the relative volume of noise of those shouting "aye" and "no".

void (voyd) *adj.* **1.** Containing no matter; empty. **2.** Unoccupied; unfilled. Said of an office or position. **3.** Devoid; lacking. Used with *of: void of understanding.* **4.** Ineffective; useless. **5.** Having no legal force or validity; null. **6.** Having no cards in a suit: *Her hand was void in diamonds.* —See Synonyms at **empty.**
~n. **1.** Something that is void; an empty space; a vacuum. **2.** An open space or break in continuity; a gap. **3.** A feeling or state of emptiness, loneliness, or loss. **4.** In card games, the state of not having any cards in a particular suit. **5.** An empty space or gap, as in a wall for a window.
~v. **voided, voiding, voids.** *—tr.* **1.** To make void or of no effect; invalidate. **2. a.** To empty or take out (the contents of something). **b.** To evacuate (body wastes). **3.** *Archaic.* To leave; vacate. *—intr.* To evacuate body wastes. —See Synonyms at **nullify.** [Middle English, from Old French *voide, vuide,* from Vulgar Latin *vocitus* (unattested), from *vocāre,* to be empty.] **—void·er** *n.*

void·a·ble (vóydəb'l) *adj.* Capable of being voided; especially, capable of being annulled. **—void·a·ble·ness** *n.*

void·ance (vóydənss) *n.* **1. a.** The act of voiding, emptying, or evacuating. **b.** The act of making legally void; annulment. **2.** The condition of being vacant; emptiness.

void·ed (vóydid) *adj. Heraldry.* Having the central area cut out or left vacant, leaving a narrow border or outline.

voile (voyl; *French* vwaal) *n.* A light sheer fabric of cotton, rayon, silk, or wool used in dressmaking or for furnishings. [French, from Latin *vēla,* neuter of *vēlum,* cloth, veil.]

voir dire (vwár déer) *n. Law.* **1.** A preliminary examination concerning the competence of a prospective witness or juror. **2.** The oath administered in such an examination. [Old French, "to speak the truth" : *voir,* truth, from Latin *vērus* + *dire,* to say, from Latin *dīcere.*]

voix cé·leste (vwaá si-lést, say-) *n.* An organ stop that produces a gentle tremolo effect. Also called "vox angelica". [French, "celestial voice".]

vol. 1. volcano. **2.** volume. **3.** volunteer.

vo·lant (vṓlənt) *adj.* **1.** Flying or capable of flying. **2.** *Poetic.* Moving quickly or nimbly; agile. **3.** *Heraldry.* Depicted with the wings extended as in flying. [Latin *volāns* (stem *volānt-*), present participle of *volāre,* to fly.]

Vo·la·pük (vóllə-pŏŏk, vṓlə-, -pŏŏk, -pük) *n.* An international language invented in 1879, based mainly on English, Latin, and German, and other European languages. [*Vol,* from English WORLD + *pük,* from English SPEECH: coined by its inventor Johann Schleyer (1831–1912), German linguist.] **—Vo·la·pük·ist** *n.*

vo·lar (vṓlər) *adj.* Of or pertaining to the sole of the foot or the palm of the hand. [From Latin *vola,* palm, sole.]

vol·a·tile (vóllə-tīl || *U.S.* -t'l) *adj.* **1.** Evaporating readily at normal temperatures and pressures. **2.** Capable of being readily vaporised. **3.** Changeable, as: **a.** Inconstant; fickle. **b.** Tending to violence;

explosive. **c.** Lighthearted; flighty. **d.** Unstable; unpredictable. **e.** Ephemeral; fleeting. **4.** Designating a computer memory which loses stored information when power is cut off. **5.** *Obsolete.* Flying or capable of flying; volant.
~*n.* A volatile substance. [Middle English *volatil*, flying, fleeting, from Old French, from Latin *volātilis*, from *volāre*, to fly.]

volatile oil *n.* A rapidly evaporating oil, especially an essential oil, that does not leave a stain.

vol·a·til·ise, vol·a·til·ize (vo-látti-līz, vō-, və-, vólləti-) *v.* **-ised, -ising, -ises.** —*intr.* **1.** To become volatile. **2.** To pass off in vapour; evaporate. —*tr.* **1.** To make volatile. **2.** To cause to evaporate. —**vol·a·til·is·a·ble** *adj.* —**vol·a·til·i·sa·tion** (-lī-záysh'n || *U.S.* -li-) *n.* —**vol·a·til·is·er** *n.*

vol·a·til·i·ty (vóllə-tílləti) *n.* The quality or state of being volatile.

vol·au·vent (vól-ə-von, -ō-, -vong, -von, -vón) *n.* A light pastry shell filled with a savoury mixture such as meat or fish in a sauce. [French, "flight in the wind".]

vol·can·ic (vol-kánnik) *adj.* **1.** Of or resembling an erupting volcano. **2.** Produced by or discharged from a volcano. **3.** Powerfully explosive: *a volcanic temper.*

volcanic glass *n.* A volcanic igneous rock of vitreous or glassy texture, such as obsidian or pitchstone.

vol·can·ise, vol·can·ize (vólkə-nīz) *tr.v.* **-ised, -ising, -ises.** To subject to or change by the effects of volcanic heat. —**vol·can·i·sa·tion** (-nī-záysh'n || *U.S.* -ni-) *n.*

vol·can·ism (vólkən-iz'm) *n.* Also **vul·can·ism** (vúlkən-). Volcanic force or activity. [VOLCANO + -ISM.]

vol·ca·no (vol-káynō) *n., pl.* **-noes** or **-nos.** *Abbr.* **vol. 1.** A vent in the Earth's crust through which molten lava and gases are ejected. **2.** A mountain formed by the materials so ejected. [Italian, from Latin *Volcānus*, VULCAN.]

vol·can·ol·o·gy (vól-kə-nólləji) *n.* Also **vul·can·ol·o·gy** (vúl-). The branch of Earth science concerned with volcanic phenomena. —**vol·can·o·log·i·cal** (-nə-lójik'l) *adj.* —**vol·can·ol·o·gist** *n.*

vole[1] (vōl) *n.* Any of various rodents of the genus *Microtus* and related genera, resembling rats or mice but having a relatively short tail. [Earlier *volemouse*, "field mouse", from Norwegian *voll*, field, from Old Norse *völlr*.]

vole[2] (vōl) *n.* The winning of all the tricks in a card game; a grand slam. [French, from *voler*, to fly, from Old French, from Latin *volāre*.]

Vol·ga (vólgə) *n.* River of European Russia. Europe's longest river, and Russia's most important, it rises in the Valdai Hills and flows 3 690 kilometres (2,293 miles) east into the Caspian Sea at Astrakhan. Almost entirely navigable, it provides hydro-electric power and irrigation.

Vol·go·grad (vól-gə-grad, -gō-; *Russian* vəlgə-grát). Formerly **Sta·lin·grad** (staálin-grad). City in southern Russia on the river Volga. It is an important river port and trading centre. The Battle of Stalingrad (1942–43), in which the city was almost destroyed, was a turning point in World War II.

vol·i·tant (vóllitənt) *adj.* **1.** Flying or capable of flying. **2.** Moving about rapidly. [Latin *volitāns* (stem *volitānt*-), present participle of *volitāre*, frequentative of *volāre*, to fly.]

vol·i·ta·tion (vólli-táysh'n) *n.* The act of flying or the ability to fly; flight. —**vol·i·ta·tion·al** *adj.*

vo·li·tion (və-lísh'n, vō-) *n.* **1.** An act of willing, choosing, or deciding. **2.** A conscious choice; a decision. **3.** The power or capability of choosing; the will. [French, from Medieval Latin *volitiō* (stem *volitiōn*-), from Latin *velle* (present stem *vol*-), to wish.] —**vo·li·tion·al** *adj.* —**vo·li·tion·al·ly** *adv.*

vol·i·tive (vóllitiv) *adj.* **1.** Pertaining to or originating in the will. **2.** Expressing a wish or permission.

volk (folk) *n. South African. Often capital* **V.** The Afrikaner people. Preceded by *the.* [Afrikaans, from Dutch, people.]

Völk·er·wan·der·ung (föelkər-van-dər-ŏŏng, -vaan-) *n.* German. The migration from the 2nd to the 11th century of Germanic and Slavic peoples into Southern and Western Europe.

vol·ley (vólli) *n., pl.* **-leys. 1. a.** The simultaneous discharge of a number of missiles. **b.** The missiles thus discharged. **2.** A bursting forth of a number of things simultaneously: *a volley of oaths.* **3.** *Sports.* A shot, stroke, hit, or kick made at a moving ball before it touches the ground. **4.** In cricket: **a.** A ball bowled so as to reach the batsman before bouncing. **b.** The flight of such a ball.
~*v.* **volleyed, -leying, -leys.** —*tr.* **1.** To discharge (missiles or abuse, for example) in or as if in a volley. **2.** *Sports.* To strike, hit, or kick (a moving ball) before it touches the ground. —*intr.* **1.** To be discharged in or as if in a volley. **2.** To sound loudly and continuously, as guns may. **3.** *Sports.* To make a volley. [French *volée*, from Vulgar Latin *volāta* (unattested), flight, from Latin *volātus*, past participle of *volāre*, to fly.] —**vol·ley·er** *n.*

vol·ley·ball (vólli-bawl) *n.* **1.** A court game in which two teams volley a ball by hand over a high net, each team attempting to ground it on the opposing team's side. **2.** The ball used in this game.

vo·lost (vól-ost, vōl-) *n.* **1.** In the former Soviet Union, a local unit of the government; a rural soviet. **2.** In tsarist Russia, an administrative division consisting of several villages. [Russian.]

vol·plane (vól-playn) *intr.v.* **-planed, -planing, -planes.** To glide towards the ground with the engine cut off. Used of an aircraft or winged missile.
~*n.* The glide of an aircraft. [French *vol plané* : *vol*, flight, from *voler*, to fly, from Latin *volāre* (see **volant**) + *plané*, past participle of *planer*, to PLANE (to soar).]

Vol·sci (vól-skee, -sī) *pl.n.* A people of ancient Latium in South-

western Italy whose territory was conquered by the Romans in the fourth century B.C.

Vol·scian (vól-ski-ən, -shi-, -si-) *n.* **1.** The Italic language of the Volsci, related to Umbrian. **2.** A member of the Volsci. —**Vol·scian** *adj.*

Vol·sun·ga Saga (vól-sŏŏng-gə) *n.* An Icelandic saga, recorded in the 13th century, dealing with the exploits of a family of warriors, in particular Sigurd, descended from the great heroic king Volsung. The saga is related to the German **Nibelungenlied** *(see).* [Old Norse, "Saga of the Volsungs".]

volt[1] (vōlt || volt) *n. Abbr.* **V** The SI unit of electric potential and electromotive force, equal to the difference of electric potential between two points on a conducting wire carrying a constant current of one ampere when the power dissipated between the points is one watt. [After Count VOLTA.]

volt[2], **volte** (volt || vōlt) *n.* **1.** A circular movement executed by a horse in dressage. **2.** In fencing, a sudden movement made in order to avoid a thrust. [French *volte*, a turn, from Italian *volta*, from Vulgar Latin *volvita* (unattested), from *volvitāre* (unattested), frequentative of Latin *volvere*, to turn.]

vol·ta (vól-tə) *n., pl.* **-te** (-tay). **1.** A brisk dance, in triple time, that was popular in the 16th century. **2.** A piece of music for such a dance. **3.** *Music.* A time, turn, or occasion of a specified ordinal number. Used as a direction: *prima volta.* [Italian, turn, from feminine past participle of *volgere*, to turn, from Latin *volvere*, to roll.]

Vol·ta (vól-tə, vól-), **Alessandro (Giuseppe Antonio Anastasio), Count** (1745–1827). Italian physicist. A pioneer in the sphere of electricity, he invented the *electrophorus* (1775), a device to accumulate electricity, and the voltaic pile (1800).

Vol·ta (vól-tə || vōl-). River of Ghana. West Africa's chief river, it is formed by the union of the Black Volta and the White Volta 64 kilometres (40 miles) northwest of Jenji. Its course carries it 1,125 kilometres (700 miles) southeast and south to the Gulf of Guinea. It has been dammed to produce hydro-electricity.

volt·age (vōl-tij || vól-) *n.* Electromotive force or potential difference, usually expressed in volts.

voltage divider *n.* A resistor or series of resistors provided with taps at certain points to make available a fixed or variable fraction of the applied voltage.

vol·ta·ic (vol-táy-ik || vōl-) *adj.* **1.** Pertaining to or designating electricity or electric current produced by chemical action; galvanic. **2.** Producing electricity by chemical action. [After Count VOLTA.]

voltaic battery *n.* An electric battery composed of a primary cell or cells.

voltaic cell *n. Electricity.* A primary cell *(see).*

voltaic couple *n.* A pair of dissimilar conductors in contact or in the same electrolytic solution, resulting in a difference of potential between them. Also called "galvanic couple"

voltaic pile *n.* A source of direct current consisting of a number of alternating discs of two different metals separated by acid-moistened pads, forming primary cells connected in series. Also called "pile".

Vol·taire (vol-taír), pen-name of François-Marie Arouet (1694–1778). French philosopher and writer. His writings epitomise the Age of Enlightenment, often attacking injustice and intolerance. His best-known works include *Candide* (1759) and the *Dictionnaire philosophique* (1764).

vol·ta·ism (vóltə-iz'm, *often* vóltər-) *n. Electricity.* Galvanism *(see).* [VOLTA(IC) + -ISM.]

vol·tam·e·ter (vol-támmitər || vōl-) *n.* An instrument for measuring the quantity of an electric current, using the gas generated by or the amount of metal deposited by electrolysis.

volt·am·me·ter (vōlt-ám-meetər, -eetər) *n.* An instrument designed to measure current or potential. [VOLT-AM(PERE) + -METER.]

volt-am·pere (vōlt-ám-pair || vólt-, -peer) *n.* A unit of electric power equal to the product of one volt and one ampere, equivalent to one watt.

volte. Variant of **volt** (movement).

volte-face (vólt-fáass, -fáss || vōlt-) *n., pl.* **-faces** (pronounced as *singular*) or **volte-face.** An about-face; a reversal, as in policy.

volt·me·ter (vōlt-meetər) *n.* An instrument, such as a galvanometer, for measuring potential differences in volts.

vol·u·ble (vóllew-b'l) *adj.* **1.** Characterised by a ready flow of words in speaking; fluent; loquacious. **2.** *Archaic.* Turning easily on an axis; rotating. **3.** Twining or twisting, as a plant. —See Synonyms at **talkative.** [French, from Latin *volūbilis*, from *volvere* (past participle *volūtus*), to turn.] —**vol·u·bil·i·ty** (-bílləti), **vol·u·ble·ness** *n.* —**vol·u·bly** *adv.*

vol·ume (vóllewm) *n.* **1.** *Abbr.* **v., vol.** A collection of written or printed sheets bound together; a book. **2.** *Abbr.* **v., vol.** A book that forms part of a series or set of books. Also used adjectivally and in combination: *a two-volume edition.* **3.** Any written material that has been assembled as an individual unit, such as a set of issues of a magazine in a library. **4.** A roll of parchment; a scroll. **5.** *Abbr.* **V a.** The size or extent of a three-dimensional object or region of space. **b.** Broadly, the capacity of such a region or of a specified container. **6.** *Often plural.* A large amount: *volumes of praise.* **7. a.** The amplitude or loudness of a sound. **b.** A control, as on a radio, for adjusting loudness. **8.** A quantity or total: *The volume of sales has increased.* —**speak volumes.** To be informative or deeply significant. [Middle English, roll of parchment, from Old French, from Latin *volūmen*, from *volvere*, to roll, turn.]

vol·umed (vóllewmd) *adj. Poetic.* Forming a rounded or dense mass: *volumed smoke.*

vo·lu·me·ter (vo-léw-mitər, və-, -lōō-) *n.* Any of several instruments for measuring the volume of liquids, solids, and gases.

vol·u·met·ric (vólle-méttrik) *adj.* Of or pertaining to measurement of volume. Compare **gravimetric.** —**vol·u·met·ri·cal·ly** *adv.*

volumetric analysis *n.* 1. Quantitative analysis using accurately measured, especially titrated, volumes of standard chemical solutions. 2. The analysis of a gas by volume.

vo·lu·mi·nous (və-léw-minəss, vo-, -lōō-) *adj.* 1. Having great volume, fullness, size, or number. 2. a. Filling or capable of filling volumes. Said of writing. b. Prolific in speech or writing. 3. *Archaic.* Having many coils; winding: *the voluminous labyrinth.* [Late Latin *volūminōsus,* having many folds, from Latin *volūmen,* roll of writing, VOLUME.] —**vo·lu·mi·nos·i·ty** (-mi-nóssəti), **vo·lu·mi·nous·ness** *n.* —**vo·lu·mi·nous·ly** *adv.*

vol·un·ta·rism (vólləntəriz'm) *n.* 1. *Philosophy.* The doctrine that the will is primary or dominant over the intellect. 2. The view that a project or course of action should be based on voluntary participation. 3. Voluntaryism. —**vol·un·ta·rist** *n.* —**vol·un·ta·ris·tic** (-ístik) *adj.*

vol·un·tar·y (vóllən-tri, -təri ‖ -terri) *adj.* 1. Arising from one's own free will; acting on one's own initiative: *"Ignorance, when it is voluntary, is criminal"* (Samuel Johnson). 2. Acting or serving in a specified capacity willingly and without constraint or guarantee of reward. 3. Controlled by, consisting of, supported by, or done with the aid of contributions or volunteers: *voluntary organisations.* 4. Capable of exercising will; volitional. 5. Proceeding from impulse; spontaneous. 6. *Law.* a. Acting or performed without external persuasion or compulsion. b. Without legal obligation. c. Without payment: *a voluntary conveyance.* 7. Normally controlled by or subject to individual volition: *voluntary responses.*

~*n., pl.* **voluntaries.** 1. Any act or work not imposed or demanded by another. 2. The section of a competitor's performance whose contents are chosen by the competitor himself, as in a music or skating competition. 3. *Music.* a. A piece of solo organ music, occasionally improvised, that is played usually before and sometimes during or after a church service. b. A composition based on or intended for such a performance. 4. *Obsolete.* A volunteer. [Middle English, from Latin *voluntārius,* from *voluntās,* will, free will, from *velle* (present stem *vol-*), to wish.] —**vol·un·tar·i·ly** (‖ *also* -térrəli) *adv.* —**vol·un·tar·i·ness** *n.*

Synonyms: voluntary, intentional, deliberate, wilful, willing, spontaneous.

vol·un·tar·y·ism (vóllən-tri-iz'm, -təri- ‖ -terri-) *n.* The principle of reliance on voluntary donations rather than state funds, as for churches or schools. Also called "voluntarism". —**vol·un·tar·y·ist** *n.*

voluntary muscle *n.* Muscle normally controlled by individual volition. See **striated muscle.**

vol·un·teer (vóllən-téer) *n. Abbr.* **vol.** 1. A person who performs or gives his services of his own free will. 2. *Law.* a. A person who renders aid, performs a service, or assumes an obligation voluntarily. b. A person who holds property under a deed made without requiring anything in return, such as the heir in a will. 3. A person who voluntarily does military service, especially when temporary. 4. A cultivated plant growing from self-sown or accidentally dropped seed.

~*adj.* 1. Pertaining to or consisting of volunteers: *a volunteer militia.* 2. Enlisted or serving as a volunteer. 3. Growing from self-sown or accidentally dropped seed. Said of a plant or crop.

~*v.* **volunteered, -teering, -teers.** —*tr.* To give or offer to give on one's own initiative. —*intr.* To enter into or offer to enter into any undertaking of one's own free will. [French *volontaire,* from Latin *voluntārius,* VOLUNTARY.]

vo·lup·tu·ar·y (və-lúp-tew-əri, -choo-, -chəri ‖ -erri) *n., pl.* **-ies.** A person whose life is given over to luxury and sensual pleasures; a sensualist. [Latin *voluptuārius,* from *voluptārius,* from *voluptās,* pleasure. See **voluptuous.**] —**vo·lup·tu·ar·y** *adj.*

vo·lup·tu·ous (və-lúp-tew-əss, -choo-) *adj.* 1. Consisting of or characterised by strong visual and tactile delights: *voluptuous forms.* 2. Devoted to or frequently indulging in sensual gratifications. 3. a. Full and appealing in form, especially in a sexually appealing way: *a voluptuous mouth.* b. Directed towards or anticipating sensuous gratification: *voluptuous thoughts.* c. Arising from the satisfying of luxurious or sensual desires. [Middle English, from Old French *voluptueux,* from Latin *voluptuōsus,* from *voluptās,* pleasure.] —**vo·lup·tu·ous·ly** *adv.* —**vo·lup·tu·ous·ness** *n.*

vo·lute (və-léwt, vo-, vō-, -lōōt) *n.* 1. A spiral, scroll-like ornament such as that used on an Ionic capital. 2. A twisted or spiral formation, such as any of the whorls of a gastropod shell. 3. Any of various marine gastropod molluscs of the family Volutidae, having a spiral, often colourfully marked shell.

~*adj.* Also **vo·lut·ed** (-id). Having a spiral form; spirally twisted or rolled. [French, from Latin *volūta,* scroll, from the feminine past participle of *volvere,* to turn.]

vo·lu·tion (və-léwsh'n, vo-, vō-, -lōōsh'n) *n.* 1. A turn or twist about a centre; a spiral. 2. *Zoology.* Any of the whorls of a spiral shell. [From Latin *volvere* (past participle *volūtus*), to turn. See **volute.**]

vol·va (vól-və) *n., pl.* **-vae** (vee). A cuplike structure around the base of the stalk of certain fungi, a remnant of the veil. [Latin *volva, vulva,* covering.] —**vol·vate** (-vayt) *adj.*

vol·vox (vól-voks) *n.* Any of various flagellate green algae of the genus *Volvox,* that form hollow, spherical multicellular colonies.

[New Latin, from Latin *volvere,* to turn, roll. See **volute.**]

vol·vu·lus (vólvewləss) *n., pl.* **-luses.** A partial or complete obstruction of the intestine caused by abnormal twisting. [New Latin, from Latin *volvere,* to turn. See **volute.**]

vo·mer (vṓmər) *n.* A flat thin bone that forms part of the nasal septum. [Latin *vōmer,* ploughshare.] —**vo·mer·ine** (-īn, vómmər-, -in) *adj.*

vom·i·ca (vómmi-kə) *n., pl.* **-cae** (-see). 1. The profuse expectoration of putrid matter. 2. a. An abnormal pus-containing cavity in a lung, caused by the deterioration of tissue. b. The purulent matter contained in such a cavity. [Latin, boil, ulcer, from *vomere,* to VOMIT.]

vom·it (vómmit) *v.* **-ited, -iting, -its.** —*intr.* 1. To eject part or all of the contents of the stomach through the mouth, usually in a series of involuntary spasmodic movements. 2. To be discharged forcefully and abundantly; spew forth. —*tr.* 1. To eject from the stomach through the mouth. 2. To eject or discharge in a gush; spew out.

~*n.* 1. The act of ejecting matter from the stomach. 2. Matter ejected from the stomach. 3. An emetic. [Middle English *vomiten,* from Latin *vomere* (past participle *vomitus*).] —**vom·it·er** *n.*

vomiting gas *n. Chemistry.* **Chloropicrin** (see).

vom·i·tive (vómmitiv) *adj.* Pertaining to or causing vomiting.
~*n.* An emetic.

vom·i·to·ry (vómmi-tri, -təri) *adj.* Inducing vomiting; vomitive.
~*n., pl.* **vomitories.** 1. Something that induces vomiting. 2. An aperture through which matter is discharged. 3. Any of the passageways of a Roman amphitheatre leading from the outside wall to the foot of the banked seats.

vom·i·tu·ri·tion (vómmi-tewr-ish'n) *n.* Forceful but ineffectual attempts at vomiting; retching. [VOMIT + (MICT)URITION.]

vom·i·tus (vómmitəss) *n.* 1. Vomited matter. 2. Vomiting. [Latin, past participle of *vomere,* to VOMIT.]

von Braun, Wernher. See **Braun.**

von Neumann, John. See **von Neumann.**

von Richthofen, Baron Manfred. See **von Richthofen.**

von Sternberg, Josef. See **Sternberg.**

von Stroheim, Erich. See **von Stroheim.**

voo·doo (vōōdō) *n., pl.* **-doos.** 1. A religious cult of African origin practised in the Western Hemisphere mainly by the blacks of Haiti and characterised by a belief in sorcery and fetishes and by rituals in which participants communicate by trance with ancestors, saints, or animistic deities. 2. A charm, fetish, spell, or curse believed by adherents of this cult to hold magic power. 3. A person who practises voodoo. —See Synonyms at **magic.**

~*tr.v.* **voodooed, -dooing, -doos.** To place under the influence of a voodoo spell. [Dahomey *vodu.*] —**voo·doo** *adj.*

voo·doo·ism (vōōdō-iz'm) *n.* 1. The view of life and death embodied in the voodoo cult. 2. The practice of voodoo. —**voo·doo·ist** *n.* —**voo·doo·is·tic** (-ístik) *adj.*

Voor·trek·ker (fōōr-treckər, vóor-) *n. Often small* **v.** 1. Any of the original Boer pioneers who migrated from the Cape of Good Hope in the 1830s; a participant in the **Great Trek** *(see).* 2. In South Africa, a member of an Afrikaner youth organisation similar to the Scouts and Girl Guides. [Dutch : *voor,* forward, advance + TREK + -ER.]

vo·ra·cious (və-ráyshəss, vo-, vaw-) *adj.* 1. Consuming or eager to consume great amounts of food; ravenous. 2. Having an insatiable appetite for some activity or pursuit: *a voracious reader.* [Latin *vorax* (stem *vorāci-*), from *vorāre,* to devour.] —**vo·ra·cious·ly** *adv.* —**vo·ra·cious·ness** *n.*

vor·la·ge (fór-laagə ‖ -fōr-) *n.* A posture assumed in skiing in which the skier leans forwards from the ankles, usually without lifting the heels. [German *Vorlage* : *vor,* before, from Old High German *fora* + *Lage,* stance, from Old High German *lāga.*]

-vorous *adj. comb. form.* Indicates eating or feeding on; for example, **herbivorous.** [Latin *-vorus,* from *vorāre,* to devour.]

Vor·ster (fórstər), **Balthazar Johannes** (1915-83). Known as John. South African politician, leader of the National Party and prime minister of South Africa (1966-78) and subsequently president of South Africa (1978-79). He was a leading advocate of apartheid.

vor·tex (vór-teks) *n., pl.* **-texes** or **-tices** (-ti-seez). 1. Fluid flow involving rotation about an axis; a whirlwind; a whirlpool. 2. Any activity or situation that is regarded as drawing into its centre and engulfing all that surrounds it: *swept up in the vortex of hippie culture.* [Latin *vortex, vertex,* from *vertere,* to turn.]

vor·ti·cal (vórti-k'l) *adj.* Also **vor·ti·cose** (-kōz, -kōss). Pertaining to or resembling a vortex; whirling. [From Latin *vortex* (stem *vortic-*), VORTEX.] —**vor·ti·cal·ly** *adv.*

vor·ti·cel·la (vórti-sél-ə) *n., pl.* **-lae** (-ee). Any of various bell-shaped, ciliated, stalked protozoans of the genus *Vorticella.* [New Latin *Vorticella,* from Latin *vortex* (stem *vortic-*), VORTEX.]

vor·ti·cism (vórti-siz'm) *n.* A short-lived English art movement that arose in 1914 as a result of the impact of futurist ideas on a small group of artists and writers led by Wyndam Lewis. —**vor·ti·cist** *n.*

vor·tig·i·nous (vawr-tíjinəss) *adj.* Whirling; vortical. [From Latin *vortīgō* (stem *vortīgin-*), variant of *vertīgō,* a whirling, from *vertere,* to turn. See **vertex.**]

Vosges Mountains (vōzh). Mountain range of eastern France. Extending 240 kilometres (150 miles) south-southwest to north-northeast, it is separated from Germany's Black Forest by the Rhine's rift valley. Before World War I, the mountains formed the border between Germany and France.

vo·tar·ess (vŏtə-riss, -ress). *n.* Also **vo·tress** (vŏt-). A female votary.

vo·ta·ry (vŏtə-ri) *n., pl.* **-ries.** Also **vo·ta·rist** (-rist). **1.** A person bound by vows to live the religious life; a monk or nun. **2.** Any person fervently devoted, as to a religion, leader, or ideal. —*adj. Archaic.* **1.** Consecrated by a vow. **2.** Resembling or pertaining to a vow. [From Latin *vŏtus,* past participle of *vovēre,* to vow.]

vote (vŏt) *n.* **1.** A formal expression of preference, opinion, or will, as in favour of a candidate for office or a proposed resolution of an issue. **2.** That by which such a preference is made known, such as a raised hand or a ballot. **3.** The number of votes cast in an election or to resolve an issue: *a heavy vote in his favour.* **4.** A group of voters: *the Labour vote.* **5.** The result of an election, referendum, or the like. **6. a.** The right to participate as a voter; suffrage. **b.** A person who has such a right. **7.** Something that is to be or has been decided, expressed, or granted by voting. —**cast (one's) vote.** To make known, deposit, or give in one's vote. —*v.* **voted, voting, votes.** —*intr.* **1.** To express one's preference, will, or opinion by a vote; cast one's vote. **2.** To cast one's vote in a specified manner: *vote Liberal.* —*tr.* **1.** To express one's preference for; endorse by a vote. **2.** To bring into existence or make available by vote: *vote new funds for a programme.* **3.** To bring to a specified condition by voting: *voted her out; voted the Tories into office.* **4.** To declare or pronounce by general consent: *voted the play a success.* **5.** *Informal.* To suggest; advocate: *I vote that we forget all about it.* —**vote down.** To defeat by casting a negative vote. [Latin *vŏtum,* vow, from *vŏtus,* past participle of *vovēre,* to vow.] —**vot·a·ble, vote·a·ble** *adj.* —**vote·less** *adj.* —**vot·er** *n.*

voting machine *n.* An apparatus used at a polling station that mechanically records and counts votes.

vo·tive (vŏtiv) *adj.* **1.** Given or dedicated in fulfilment of a vow or pledge: *a votive offering.* **2.** Expressing a wish, desire, or vow: *a votive prayer.* [Latin *vŏtīvus,* from *vŏtum,* vow, VOTE.]

votive mass *n. Roman Catholic Church.* A mass that may be celebrated at the priest's discretion, as for a special intention or in honour of a given saint, instead of the mass appointed for the day.

vouch (vowch) *v.* **vouched, vouching, vouches.** —*tr.* **1.** To substantiate by supplying evidence; verify. **2.** *Law.* Formerly, to summon (a landowner) as a witness to give proof of ownership. **3.** *Archaic.* To cite (an authority, doctrine, or principle, for example) as supporting evidence for one's statements, opinions, or actions. **4.** *Obsolete.* To assert; declare. —*intr.* **1.** To furnish a guarantee; give personal assurance. Used with *for.* **2.** To function or serve as a guarantee; furnish supporting evidence. Used with *for: a deed that vouched for his courage.* —*n. Obsolete.* A declaration of opinion; an assertion. [Middle English *vouchen,* to summon (as a witness), from Old French *voucher,* from Latin *vŏcāre,* to call.]

vouch·er (vówchər) *n.* **1.** A person who vouches; a supporter, sponsor, or witness. **2.** A signed or stamped document that serves as proof that the terms of a transaction have been met. **3.** *Chiefly British.* A document or card that can be exchanged for goods or services: *a gift voucher.*

vouch·safe (vówch-sáyf, vowch-) *tr.v.* **-safed, -safing, -safes.** *Literary.* To condescend to grant or bestow (a reply, favour, or privilege, for example); deign: *vouchsafed us no explanation.* [Middle English *vouchen sauf,* "to warrant as safe" : VOUCH (obsolete sense "to warrant") + SAFE.] —**vouch·safe·ment** *n.*

vous·soir (vōō-swár) *n.* Any of the wedge-shaped stones that form the curved parts of an arch or vaulted ceiling. [French, from Old French *vossoir,* from Vulgar Latin *volsōrium* (unattested), from *volsus* (unattested), variant of Latin *volutus.* See **volution.**]

vow (vow) *n.* **1.** An earnest promise or pledge that binds one to perform a specified act or behave in a certain manner; especially, a solemn promise to live and act in accordance with the prescriptions of a religious body: *a nun's vows.* **2.** A formal declaration or assertion. —**take vows.** To enter a religious order. —*v.* **vowed, vowing, vows.** —*tr.* **1.** To promise or pledge solemnly. **2.** To make a pledge or threat to undertake: *vowing revenge on their persecutors.* **3.** To declare or assert emphatically or formally: *"Well, I vow it is as fine a boy as ever was seen!"* (Henry Fielding). —*intr.* To express a promise or pledge; make a vow. [Middle English *vowe,* from Old French, from Latin *vŏtum.* See **vote.**] —**vow·er** *n.*

vow·el (vów-əl, vowl) *n. Abbr.* **v. 1.** *Phonetics.* A speech sound created by the relatively free passage of breath through the larynx and oral cavity, usually forming the most prominent and central sound of a syllable. Compare **consonant. 2.** A letter that represents such a sound, as, in the English alphabet, *a, e, i, o, u,* and sometimes *y.* —*adj.* Of or constituting a vowel or vowels. [Middle English *vowelle,* from Old French *vouel,* from Latin *(littera) vōcālis,* "sounding (letter)", from *vōx* (stem *vōc-*), voice.] —**vowelless** *adj.*

vowel fracture *n. Linguistics.* **Breaking** *(see).*

vowel gradation *n. Linguistics.* **Ablaut** *(see).*

vow·el·ise, vow·el·ize (vów-ə-līz) *tr.v.* **-ised, -ising, -ises.** To provide with vowel points. —**vow·el·i·sa·tion** (-lī-záysh'n ‖ *U.S.* -li-) *n.*

vowel mutation *n. Linguistics.* **Umlaut** *(see).*

vowel point *n.* Any of a number of diacritical marks written above or below consonants to indicate a preceding or following vowel, as in languages such as Hebrew and Arabic that are usually written without vowel letters.

vox an·gel·i·ca (vóks an-jéllikə) *n.* An organ stop, the **voix céleste** *(see).* [Latin, "angelic voice".]

vox hu·ma·na (vóks hew-maánə) *n.* An organ reed stop that pro-

duces tones supposedly imitative of the human voice. [Latin, "human voice".]

vox pop (vóks póp) *n., pl.* **vox pops.** *British Informal.* The opinion of a person who is interviewed informally in a public place by a radio or television reporter. **2.** The act of canvassing for such opinions, as by television reporters. [Abbreviation of VOX POPULI.]

vox po·pu·li (vóks póppew-lī, -lee) *n.* Popular opinion or sentiment. [Latin, "voice of the people".]

voy·age (vóy-ij) *n.* **1.** A long journey, usually to a foreign or distant land; especially, a journey across an open sea or ocean. **2.** A record or account of a journey of exploration or discovery. **3.** *Obsolete.* An ambitious project or undertaking. —*v.* **voyaged, -aging, -ages.** —*intr.* To make a voyage. —*tr.* To travel or sail over in a journey. [Middle English, from Old French *veiyage,* from Latin *viāticum.* See **viaticum.**] —**voy·ag·er** *n.*

vo·ya·geur (vwĭ-aa-zhúr, vóy-ə-, zhŏr) *n., pl.* **-geurs** *(pronounced as singular).* A woodsman, boatman, or guide, especially one employed by fur companies to transport furs and supplies between remote stations. [French, "voyager".]

voy·eur (vwĭ-úr, vwĭ-, vwaa-yúr) *n.* One who derives sexual pleasure from watching other people undress or engage in sexual activity. [French, "watcher", from *voir,* to see.] —**voy·eur·ism** *n.* —**voy·eur·is·tic** (vwĭ-ur-ístik) *adj.* —**voy·eur·ist·i·cal·ly** *adv.*

V.P. vice president.

V-par·ti·cle (vee-paartik'l) *n.* Any of several neutral elementary particles with half-lives in the range of 10^{-10} to 10^{-6} second. [From the V-shaped tracks left by their decay products in a cloud chamber.]

V. Pres. vice president.

V.R. **1.** Queen Victoria (Latin *Victoria Regina).* **2.** variant reading. **3.** Volunteer Reserve.

vrai·sem·blance (vráy-som-blónss, -son-blónss) *n.* The outward appearance of being true or true to life, especially in literature; verisimilitude. [French : *vrai,* true + SEMBLANCE.]

V. Rev. Very Reverend.

V.R.I. Victoria, Queen and Empress (Latin *Victoria Regina et Imperatrix).*

vroom (vrōōm) *interj.* Used to imitate the sound of a fast-moving motor vehicle.

vrot (frot) *adj South African Slang.* **1.** Rotten; putrid. **2.** Disappointing; unsuccessful: *a vrot performance.* [Afrikaans, from Dutch *verrotten,* to rot.]

vs. versus.

v.s. vide supra.

V.S. veterinary surgeon.

V-shaped (vée-shaypt) *adj.* Having the shape of the letter *V: geese flying in a V-shaped formation.*

V sign *n.* **1.** A symbol of victory formed by holding the raised index and middle fingers in the shape of a V, with the palm facing outwards. **2.** The same sign but with the palm facing inwards, used as an indication of hate, contempt, or defiance.

V.S.O. **1.** very special (old) (applied to cognac, Armagnac or port). **2.** Voluntary Service Overseas; a British organisation that arranges for young people to do voluntary work and teaching in developing countries.

V.S.O.P. very superior old pale (usually applied to cognac or Armagnac that is at least four years old).

VT fuse *n. Military.* A **proximity fuse** *(see).* [V(ARIABLE) T(IME) FUSE.]

VTOL vertical takeoff and landing.

VTR video tape recorder.

vug, vugh (vug) *n. Geology.* A small cavity in a rock or vein, especially one lined with crystals. [Cornish *vooga,* cave.]

Vul·can (vúlkən). *Roman Mythology.* The god of fire and craftsmanship, especially metalworking, identified with the Greek god Hephaestus. [Latin *Vulcānus, Volcānus,* perhaps obscurely related to Cretan *Welkhanoc,* from Hittite *Valhannasses†.*]

vul·ca·ni·an (vul-káyni-ən) *adj.* Also **Vul·ca·ni·an, Vul·can·ic** (-kánnik) (for sense 2). **1.** *Geology.* Pertaining to or coming from a volcano or volcanic eruption. **2. a.** Pertaining to the god Vulcan. **b.** Pertaining to craftsmanship or metalworking.

vul·can·ise, vul·can·ize (vúlkə-nīz) *tr.v.* **-ised, -ising, -ises. 1.** To improve the strength, resiliency, and freedom from stickiness and odour of (rubber) by combining with sulphur or other additives in the presence of heat and pressure. **2.** To treat (other substances) similarly. [From VULCAN.] —**vul·can·is·a·ble** *adj.* —**vul·can·i·sa·tion** (-nī-záysh'n ‖ *U.S.* -ni-) *n.* —**vul·can·iz·er** *n.*

vulcanism. Variant of **volcanism.**

vul·can·ite (vúlkən-īt) *n.* A hard material made by heavy vulcanisation of rubber, used for insulators and containers. Also called "ebonite". [VULCAN + -ITE.]

vul·can·ol·o·gy (vúlkə-nólləji) *n.* **Volcanology** *(see).*

vulg. vulgar.

Vulg. Vulgate.

vul·gar (vúlgər) *adj.* **1. a.** Deficient in taste, delicacy, or refinement. **b.** Ill-bred; boorish; crude. **c.** Tasteless in appearance or quality; garish: *a vulgar display of wealth.* **2.** *Abbr.* **vulg.** Obscene or indecent; offensive; coarse or bawdy: *a vulgar joke.* **3.** Of or associated with the masses as distinguished from the educated or cultivated classes; common. **4.** *Abbr.* **vulg.** Spoken by or expressed in a form of a language spoken by the common people; vernacular: *the vulgar tongue.* —See Synonyms at **coarse.** —*n.* **1.** *Archaic.* The common people; especially, the ignorant and uncultivated: *"The vulgar thus through imitation err."* (Alexander

Pope). **2.** *Obsolete.* The vernacular. [Middle English, from Latin *vulgāris,* from *vulgus†,* the common people.] —**vul·gar·ly** *adv.* —**vul·gar·ness** *n.*

vulgar fraction *n.* A simple fraction *(see).*

vul·gar·i·an (vul-gâir-i-ən) *n.* A vulgar person; especially, one who makes a conspicuous display of his money.

vulgarise, vul·gar·ize (vúlgə-rīz) *tr.v.* **-ised, -ising, -ises. 1.** To render vulgar; debase; cheapen. **2.** To popularise. —**vul·gar·i·sa·tion** (-rī-záysh'n ‖ *U.S.* -ri-) *n.* —**vul·gar·is·er** *n.*

vul·gar·ism (vúlgəriz'm) *n.* **1.** Vulgarity. **2.** A word, phrase, or manner of expression common in ordinary speech but considered incorrect. **3.** An obscene, indecent, or crude word or phrase.

vul·gar·i·ty (vul-gárrəti) *n., pl.* **-ties. 1.** The condition or quality of being vulgar; tastelessness; coarseness. **2.** Something, such as an act or expression, that offends good taste or propriety.

Vulgar Latin *n.* The common speech of ancient Rome, differing from the literary or standard Latin used by the educated classes and forming the basis for the development of the Romance languages. Compare **Classical Latin.**

vul·gate (vúl-gayt, -gət, -git) *n.* **1.** The common speech of a people; the vernacular. **2.** A widely accepted text or version of a work. ~*adj.* Widely distributed and accepted; popular. [From Latin *vulgātus,* common, popular. See **Vulgate.**]

Vulgate *n. Abbr.* **Vulg.** The Latin translation of the Bible made by Saint Jerome at the end of the fourth century A.D., now used in a revised form as the Roman Catholic authorised version. See **Bible.** [Late Latin *vulgāta (ēditiō),* "the popular (edition)", from Latin *vulgātus,* common, popular, from *vulgāre,* to make commonly known, from *vulgus,* common people. See **vulgar.**] —**Vul·gate** *adj.*

vul·ner·a·ble (vúln-ərəb'l, -rəb'l, *also* vún-) *adj.* **1.** Susceptible to injury, either physical or emotional; unprotected from danger. **2.** Susceptible to physical attack; insufficiently defended. **3. a.** Liable to censure or criticism; assailable. **b.** Suffering from emotional or psychological insecurity. **c.** Liable to succumb to persuasion or temptation. **4.** *Bridge.* In a position to receive greater penalties or bonuses. Said of a team that has won one game of a rubber. [Late Latin *vulnerābilis,* from Latin *vulnerāre,* to wound, from *vulnus* (stem *vulner-*), wound.] —**vul·ner·a·bil·i·ty** (-ərə-billəti), —**vul·ner·a·ble·ness.** —**vul·ner·a·bly** *adv.*

vul·ner·ar·y (vúlnə-rəri ‖ -rerri) *adj. Rare.* Used in the healing or treating of wounds. ~*n. Rare.* A remedy so used. [Latin *vulnerārius,* from *vulnus* (stem *vulner-*), wound. See **vulnerable.**]

Vul·pec·u·la (vul-péckewlə) *n.* A constellation in the Northern Hemisphere near Cygnus and Sagitta. [Latin *vulpēcula,* diminutive of *vulpēs,* fox. See **vulpine.**]

vul·pine (vúl-pīn ‖ -pin) *adj.* Also **vul·pec·u·lar** (-péckewlər). **1.** Of, resembling, or characteristic of a fox. **2.** Clever; devious; cunning. [Latin *vulpīnus,* from *vulpēs,* fox.]

vul·ture (vúlchər) *n.* **1.** Any of various large birds of the family Accipitridae, of the Old World, or the family Cathartidae, of the New World, characteristically having dark plumage, a naked head and neck, and feeding on carrion. **2.** A person of a rapacious or predatory nature. [Middle English, from Old French *voltour,* from Latin *vultur.*]

vul·tur·ine (vúl-chər-īn, -chŏŏr-, -tewr-) *adj.* Also **vul·tur·ous** (-əss). **1.** Pertaining to or characteristic of a vulture. **2.** Suggestive of a vulture; rapacious; predatory.

vul·va (vúl-və) *n., pl.* **-vae** (-vee). The external female genitalia including the labia majora, labia minora, clitoris, and vestibule of the vagina. [Latin *vulva, volva,* womb, covering.] —**vul·val, vul·var, vul·vate** (-vayt) *adj.* —**vul·vi·form** (-vi-fawrm) *adj.*

vul·vi·tis (vul-vítiss) *n. Pathology.* Inflammation of the vulva. [New Latin : VULV(A) + -ITIS.]

vul·vo·vag·i·ni·tis (vúlvō-váji-nítiss) *n. Pathology.* Inflammation of the vulva and vagina. [*Vulvo-,* combining form of VULVA + VAGIN(A) + -ITIS.]

vv. verses.

v.v. vice versa.

vy·ing (ví-ing) *adj.* Competing; contending. —**vy·ing·ly** *adv.*

w, W (dúbb'l-yōō, -yōō) *n., pl.* **w's** or *rare* **ws, W's** or **Ws. 1.** The 23rd letter of the modern English alphabet. **2.** Any of the speech sounds represented by this letter.

w, W, w., W. *Note:* As an abbreviation or symbol, *w* may be a small or a capital letter, with or without a full stop. Established forms or those generally preferred precede the definition. When no form is given, all four forms are in general use in that sense. **1. W** The symbol for the element tungsten. [Formerly called WOLFRAM]. **2. W** *Electricity.* watt. **3. W** Wednesday. **4. w.** week. **5. w.** weight. **6. W** Welsh. **7. w.** west; western. **8. w.** wicket. **9. w.** wide (in cricket). **10. w.** width. **11. w.** wife. **12. w.** with. **13. W** women's (size in clothing). **14. w, W** *Physics.* work. **15.** The 23rd in a series.

W.A. Western Australia.

W.A.A.A.F. Women's Auxiliary Australian Air Force.

Waac (wak) *n.* A member of the Women's Army Auxiliary Corps.

WAAC Women's Army Auxiliary Corps (formerly in Britain and the United States).

Waaf (waf) *n.* A member of the Women's Auxiliary Air Force.

WAAF Women's Auxiliary Air Force (formerly in Britain).

wabble. Variant of **wobble.**

Wac (wak) *n. U.S.* A member of the Women's Army Corps.

WAC, W.A.C. Women's Army Corps (in the United States).

wack (wak) *n.* A friend. Usually used in direct address to a male Liverpudlian.

wack·er (wáckər) *n.* Also **whacker.** *Northern English Informal.* A Liverpudlian.

wack·y (wácki) *adj.* **-ier, -iest.** Also **whack·y** (wácki, hwácki). *Informal.* Highly irrational or erratic; crazy; silly. [Probably variant of dialectal *whacky,* a fool, from *whack-head,* "one stunned by a heavy blow on the head", from WHACK.]

wad (wod) *n.* **1.** A small mass of soft material, often folded or rolled, used especially for padding, stuffing, packing, or stopping holes. **2.** A compressed ball, roll, or lump of something, as of tobacco. **3. a.** A plug, as of cloth or paper, used to hold in a powder charge in a muzzle-loading gun or cannon. **b.** A disc of felt or paper, to keep the powder and shot in place in a shotgun cartridge. **4.** *Informal.* A large bundle of something rolled up tightly; especially, a bundle of bank notes. **5.** *Often plural. Informal.* A large amount, especially of money. **6.** *Geology.* Hydrated manganese oxides, usually in a soft, black, earthy form, probably resulting from the decomposition of other manganese minerals. ~*v.* **wadded, wadding, wads.** —*tr.* **1.** To compress into a wad. **2.** To pad, pack, line, or plug with wadding. **3. a.** To hold (shot or powder) in place with a wad. **b.** To insert a wad in (a gun). —*intr.* To form into a wad. [Perhaps akin to Dutch *watten,* padding.]

wad·ding (wódding) *n.* **1.** A wad or wads collectively. **2.** A soft or fibrous substance used for padding or stuffing, especially layers of carded cotton or wool. **3.** Material for gun wads.

wad·dle (wódd'l) *intr.v.* **-dled, -dling, -dles. 1.** To walk with short steps that tilt the body from side to side, as a duck does. **2.** To walk heavily and clumsily with a pronounced sway. ~*n.* A waddling gait. [Probably frequentative of WADE.]

wad·dy (wóddi) *n., pl.* **-dies.** *Australian.* A heavy straight stick used as a club or thrown as a missile by Australian Aborigines. ~*tr.v.* **waddied, -dying, -dies.** To strike with a waddy. [An Australian native name, perhaps from English WOOD.]

wade (wayd) *v.* **waded, wading, wades.** —*intr.* **1.** To walk in or through water or something that similarly impedes normal movement. **2.** To make one's way arduously. Often used with *through: wade through a boring report.* **3.** To make a vigorous and determined start or attack. Used with *in* or *into.* —*tr.* To cross or pass through by wading. ~*n.* The act of wading. [Middle English *waden,* to go, walk through (water), Old English *wadan,* to go, wade.]

Wade, (Sarah) Virginia (1945–). British tennis player. She won the Wimbledon women's singles championship (1977). She also won the United States (1968), Italian (1971) and Australian (1972) titles.

wad·er (wáydər) *n.* **1.** One that wades. **2.** Any of numerous long-legged birds of the order Charadriiformes, such as cranes, that frequent shallow water. Also called "wading bird". **3.** *Plural.* Waterproof high boots or a waterproof garment that covers the legs and extends as far as the waist, worn especially by anglers.

wadge (woj) *n.* Also **wodge.** *British Informal.* A thick bundle; a wad. [Alteration of WEDGE (probably influenced by WAD).]

wa·di (wóddi, *rarely* wáddi, wáadi) *n., pl.* **-dis.** Also **wa·dy** *pl.* **-dies.** In north Africa and southwest Asia, a valley, gully, or riverbed that remains dry except after heavy rain. [Arabic *wādī.*]

wad·mal (wódm'l) *n.* A rough, thick, woollen cloth, formerly used for outer garments by country people in Northern Europe. [Middle English, from Old Norse *vathmal* : *vath,* cloth + *mal,* measure.]

wad·set (wód-set) *n.* An obsolete Scottish form of mortgage. [Middle English : *wad,* Scottish variant of obsolete *wed* ("covenant", "pledge") + SET; probably from Old English phrase *tō wedde settan* (unattested), to put to pledge.]

WAF, W.A.F. Women in the Air Force (in the United States).

wa·fer (wáyfər) *n.* **1.** A small, thin, crisp, sweetened biscuit, eaten especially with ice cream. **2.** A small, thin disc of unleavened bread used in the Eucharist. **3.** In pharmacology, a flat tablet of rice paper or dried flour paste encasing a powdered drug. **4.** A small disc of adhesive material used as a seal for papers. **5.** *Electronics.* A

small, thin, flat circular disc of a semiconducting material, such as pure silicon, that is masked, oxide-coated, doped, and otherwise processed for ultimate separation into numerous individual electronic devices or for packaging as an integrated circuit.
—*tr.v.* **wafered, -fering, -fers.** To seal or fasten together with a wafer. [Middle English *wafre*, from Anglo-French, from Old North French *waufre*, from Middle Low German *wāfel.* Compare **wafer**.]

waff (waf, waaf) *v.* **waffed, waffing, waffs.** *Northern British.* —*intr.* To wave; flutter. —*tr.* To cause to wave or flutter.
—*n. Northern British.* **1.** A waving motion. **2.** A waft; a gust of air. **3.** A glimpse. [Middle English (northern) *waffen,* variant of *waven,* to WAVE.]

waf·fle[1] (wóf'l) *n.* A light, crisp batter cake baked in a waffle iron. [Dutch *wafel,* from earlier *waefel,* from Middle Low German *wāfel.* Compare **wafer**.]

waffle[2] *intr.v.* **-fled, -fling, -fles.** *Chiefly British Informal.* To speak or write in a verbose but aimless or meaningless manner.
—*n. Chiefly British Informal.* Evasive, vague, or verbose speech or writing. [Of dialect origin, frequentative of *waff,* to yelp.]

waffle iron *n.* An appliance having hinged, indented metal plates that impress a grid pattern into waffle batter as it bakes.

waft (woft, waaft ‖ wawft, waft) *v.* **wafted, wafting, wafts.** —*tr.* To carry, cause to go, or send floating gently through the air or over water: *a breeze wafting the odour of roses.* —*intr.* To float easily and gently on or as if on the air or water; drift.
—*n.* **1.** Something, such as a scent, carried through the air. **2.** A light breeze; a rush of air. **3.** The act of wafting or waving. **4.** *Nautical.* **a.** A flag used for signalling or indicating wind direction. **b.** A signal with such a flag. [Originally "to convoy (ships)", from obsolete *wafter,* a convoy, Middle English *waughter,* from Middle Dutch *wachter,* a guard, from *wachten,* to watch, guard.]

waft·age (wóft-ij, waaft- ‖ wáwft-, wáft-) *n.* Conveyance over water or passage through the air.

waf·ture (wóf-chər, waaf- ‖ wáwf-, wáf-) *n. Archaic.* **1.** The act or action of waving; a waving movement. **2.** The action of wafting.

wag[1] (wag) *v.* **wagged, wagging, wags.** —*tr.* **1.** To move briskly and repeatedly from side to side, to and fro, or up and down. **2.** To move rapidly in talking, especially in gossiping. Used of the tongue. —*tr.* To wag (a part of the body) as in playfulness, agreement, admonition, or chatter: *wagged his tail.*
—*n.* An act or motion of wagging. [Middle English *waggen,* ultimately from Old English *wagian,* to totter.] —**wag·ger** *n.*

wag[2] *n.* A humorous or facetious person.
—*tr.v.* **wagged, wagging, wags.** *Chiefly Australian & N.Z.* To play truant from (school). [Perhaps from obsolete *waghalter,* someone likely to be hanged : WAG (verb) + HALTER (hangman's noose).]

wage (wayj) *n.* **1.** *Sometimes plural.* Payment to a worker for labour or services; especially, remuneration on an hourly, daily, or weekly basis or by the piece. Also used adjectively: *wage packet.* Compare **salary**. **2.** *Plural. Economics.* The portion of the national product that represents the aggregate paid for all contributing labour and services as distinguished from the portion retained by management or reinvested in capital goods.
—*tr.v.* **waged, waging, wages.** To engage in or carry on (something aggressive and sustained, such as a war or campaign). [Middle English, a pledge, wage, soldier's pay, from Old North French, from Germanic *wadhjam* (unattested).]

wage earner *n.* **1.** A person who works for wages. **2.** One whose earnings support a household.

wa·ger (wáyjər) *n.* **1.** An agreement under which each better pledges a certain amount to the other depending upon the outcome of an unsettled matter. **2.** The matter bet on; a gamble. **3.** Something staked on an uncertain outcome; a bet.
—*v.* **wagered, -gering, -gers.** —*tr.* To risk or stake (an amount or possession) on an uncertain outcome; bet. —*intr.* To make a wager; bet. [Middle English, a pledge, prize at a contest, from Anglo-French *wageure,* from Old North French *wagier,* to pledge, from *wage,* a pledge, WAGE.] —**wa·ger·er** *n.*

wager of battle *n.* A former method of trial in Britain, first introduced in Norman times, whereby a defendant's innocence was put to the test in single combat.

wager of law *n.* A former method of trying an accused person in Britain, in which the accused swore his innocence under oath and 11 people who knew him had to do likewise.

wa·ges (wájiz) *n.* Used with a singular or plural verb. *Literary.* A fitting return or recompense; a requital: *"For the wages of sin is death"* (Romans 6:23).

wage scale *n.* The scale of wages paid to employees for the various jobs within an industry or organisation.

wage-work·er (wáyj-wurkər) *n. U.S.* A wage earner.

wag·ga (wógga) *n. Australian.* A blanket made from from sacks or hessian bags. [After WAGGA WAGGA.]

Wag·ga Wag·ga (wógga wógga). Town of New South Wales, southeastern Australia. Situated on the river Murrumbidgee, it is a trade and service centre for the Riverina and Western Slopes regions.

wag·ger·y (wággəri) *n., pl.* **-ies. 1.** Waggish behaviour or spirit; drollery. **2.** A droll remark or act. [From WAG (joker).]

wag·gish (wággish) *adj.* Characteristic of a wag; playfully humorous. See Synonyms at **playful**. —**wag·gish·ly** *adv.* —**wag·gish·ness** *n.*

wag·gle (wágg'l) *v.* **-gled, -gling, -gles.** —*tr.* To move (an attached part) with short, quick motions: *She waggled her foot impatiently.* —*intr.* To move shakily; wobble.
—*n.* A waggling motion. [Frequentative of WAG.] —**wag·gly** *adj.*

Wag·ner (vaág-nər), **(Wilhelm) Richard** (1813–83). German composer. He developed the use of leitmotifs to pioneer opera as music drama. His most famous work is his operatic cycle, *Der Ring des Nibelungen,* an epic treatment of German mythology.

Wag·ne·ri·an (vaag-néer-i-ən) *adj.* **1.** Of or pertaining to Richard Wagner, his music, or his theories. **2.** Characteristic or suggestive of the music dramas of Wagner, especially their grandness and emphasis on drama as well as music.
—*n.* Also **Wag·ner·ite** (vág-nər-īt). An admirer or disciple of Richard Wagner.

wag·on (wággən) *n.* Also *chiefly British* **wag·gon. 1.** A four-wheeled, usually horse-drawn vehicle having a large rectangular body for transporting loads and often a detachable cover. **2.** *British.* A railway goods vehicle, especially an open goods car. **3.** *Chiefly U.S.* **a.** A light transport or delivery vehicle, such as a milk float. **b.** A station wagon (*see*). **c.** A police van used for transporting prisoners. **d.** A child's low four-wheeled cart. **e.** A trolley used when serving drinks or food. **4.** *Obsolete.* A chariot. —**off the wagon.** *Slang.* No longer abstaining from alcoholic drinks. —**on the wagon.** *Slang.* Abstaining from alcoholic drinks.
—*tr.v.* **wagoned, -oning, -ons.** Also *chiefly British* **wag·gon.** To transport by wagon. [Earlier *wagen, waghen,* from Dutch, from Middle Dutch; akin to Old English *wægn,* WAIN.]

wag·on·er (wággənər) *n.* **1.** A wagon driver. **2.** *Obsolete.* A driver of a chariot.

wag·on·ette (wággə-nét) *n.* A light horse-drawn wagon with two seats, facing lengthways, placed behind the driver's seat.

wa·gon-lit (vág-ON-lé, vaág-, -on-, -lee) *n., pl.* **wagons-lits** or **wagon-lits** (-z, *or pronounced as singular*). A sleeping car on a European railway train. [French : *wagon,* railway car + *lit,* bed.]

wag·on·load (wággən-lōd) *n.* The load held by one wagon.

wagon train *n.* A line or train of wagons travelling cross-country.

wag·tail (wág-tayl) *n.* Any of various birds of the genus *Motacilla* and related genera, having a long, wagging tail.

Wah·ha·bi, Wa·ha·bi (waa-haáa-bi, wə-) *n.* Also **Wah·ha·bite** (-bīt). A member of a Muslim sect founded by Abd-al Wahhab in the 18th century, known for its strict observance of the original words of the Koran and flourishing mainly in Saudi Arabia. —**Wah·ha·bism, Wa·ha·bism** (-biz'm) *n.*

wa·hi·ne (waa-hée-ni, -nay) *n.* A woman or wife, especially a Polynesian or Maori woman. [Hawaiian and Maori.]

wah-wah, wa·wa (waá-waa) *n.* **1.** A wavering sound produced by alternately covering and uncovering the bell of a trumpet or trombone with a mute. **2.** A similar sound produced by an electric guitar by means of an electronic attachment (a *wah-wah pedal*).

waif[1] (wayf) *n.* **1. a.** A stray homeless person, especially a forsaken or orphaned child. **b.** An abandoned young animal. **2.** Something found and unclaimed, such as an object cast up by the sea. [Middle English *waife, wayf,* ownerless property, from Anglo-French *waif, weif,* variant of Old North French *gaif,* from Scandinavian.]

waif[2] *n.* A small flag for signalling; a waft. [Probably from Scandinavian, akin to Old Norse *veif,* a waving thing.]

Wai·ka·to (wī-káttō). Longest river of New Zealand. Rising in Lake Taupo on North Island it flows 425 kilometres (260 miles) through dairylands to enter the Tasman Sea south of Auckland.

wail (wayl) *v.* **wailed, wailing, wails.** —*intr.* **1.** To grieve or protest loudly and bitterly; lament. **2.** To make a prolonged, high-pitched sound suggestive of a cry: *wailing winds.* —*tr.* **1.** *Poetic.* To lament over; bewail. **2.** To express plaintively. —See Synonyms at **cry.**
—*n.* **1.** A long, loud, high-pitched cry as of grief or pain. **2.** Any similar sound. [Middle English *wailen, weilen,* probably from Old Norse *veila* (unattested), to moan, lament; akin to *vei,* WOE.] —**wail·er** *n.* —**wail·ing·ly** *adv.*

wail·ful (wáylf'l) *adj.* **1.** Resembling a wail; mournful; plaintive. **2.** Issuing a sound like a wail.

Wail·ing Wall (wáyling) *n.* A wall in the old city of Jerusalem believed to be a remnant of the Temple of Herod (the second temple of Jerusalem) and revered by Jews as a place of pilgrimage, lamentation, and prayer. Also called the "Western Wall".

wain (wayn) *n. Poetic & Regional.* A large, open farm wagon. [Middle English, Old English *wæg(e)n, wæn.*]

wain·scot (wáyn-skət, wén-, -skot ‖ -skōt) *n.* **1.** A facing or panelling, usually of wood, applied to the walls of a room. **2.** The lower part of an interior wall when finished in a material different from that of the upper part.
—*tr.v.* **wainscoted** or **-scotted, -scoting** or **-scotting, -scots.** To line or panel (a room or wall) with wainscot. [Middle English *waynscot(te), weynshet,* from Middle Low German *wagenschot,* perhaps "timber for wagons" : *wagen,* WAGON + *schot,* planking.]

wain·scot·ing (wáyn-skət-ing, wén-, -skot- ‖ -skōt-) *n.* Also **wain·scot·ting. 1.** A wainscoted surface of a wall or walls; panelling. **2.** Wood or other material for such panelling.

wain·wright (wáyn-rīt) *n.* A builder and repairer of wagons.

waist (wayst) *n.* **1.** The part of the human trunk between the bottom of the rib cage and the pelvis. **2. a.** The part of a garment that encircles the waist of the body. **b.** Formerly, the upper part of a garment, extending from the shoulders to the waistline; especially, the bodice of a woman's dress. **3.** The middle section or part of an object, especially when narrower than the rest, as on a violin or hourglass. **4.** *Nautical.* The middle part of the deck of a ship between the forecastle and the quarter-deck. **5.** The centre portion of an aircraft; the fuselage. [Middle English *wa(a)st,* Old English *wæst* (unattested), growth, size of body; akin to WAX (to grow).]

waist·band (wáyst-band ‖ -bənd) n. A band of material encircling and fitting the waist, as on a pair of trousers or a skirt.

waist·cloth (wáyst-kloth ‖ -klawth) n., pl. **-cloths** (-kloths ‖ -klawthz, klawths, -klothz). Archaic. A loincloth.

waist·coat (wáyss-kōt, wáyst-, old-fashioned wéss-kət, -kit) n. 1. Chiefly British. A waistlength, close-fitting, sleeveless garment, usually buttoning up the front and typically worn by men over a shirt and under a suit jacket. Also U.S. "vest". 2. A garment formerly worn by men under a doublet.

waist·ed (wáystid) adj. 1. Having a waist or a part like a waist. 2. Having a waist of a specified kind. Used in combination: low-waisted.

waist·line (wáyst-līn) n. 1. a. The natural indentation of the body at the waist; the place at which the circumference of the waist is smallest. b. The measurement of this circumference. 2. The point or line at which the skirt and bodice of a dress join.

wait (wayt) v. **waited, waiting, waits.** —intr. 1. a. To remain inactive, defer action, or stay in one spot until something anticipated occurs or until a specified time: Wait until I get home! b. To tarry until another catches up: Wait for me! 2. To be in a state of readiness or expectancy: waiting for our results. 3. To be temporarily neglected, unattended to, or postponed: The trip had to wait. 4. To work as a waiter or waitress. —tr. 1. To remain or stay in expectation of; await: wait one's turn. 2. Informal. To delay (a meal or event); postpone. —See Synonyms at **stay. —wait for it.** Chiefly British Informal. Used as an exclamation before saying something that is surprising, important, or newsworthy. —**wait on.** Also (for senses 1, 2, 3) **wait upon. 1. a.** To serve the needs of; be in attendance upon. b. To take orders from and serve food and drink to (customers in a restaurant). c. To be the waiter in attendance on (a table in a restaurant). 2. To make a formal call upon; visit. 3. Literary. To follow as a result. 4. Regional. To wait for. —**wait out.** To wait until the termination of: wait out a war. —**wait up.** To postpone going to bed in anticipation of something or someone. ~n. 1. The act of waiting or the time spent waiting. 2. Plural. British. a. Formerly, a group of musicians employed by a town or city to play in parades, public ceremonies, or the like. b. A group of musicians who perform carols in the streets at Christmas time. —**lie in wait.** To be on the watch; especially, to wait in ambush. [Middle English waiten, wayten, to watch, lie in wait, wait, from Germanic wahtan (unattested), to watch.]

Usage: Wait is generally used intransitively (I'll wait); await is generally transitive (A car awaits her at the station). When used with reference to persons and physical objects, wait for is normal (We were waiting for a train), await being extremely formal (We were awaiting the train). When used with reference to intangible things or abstract notions, await is much less restricted (We're awaiting the announcement), and is only a little more formal than wait for.

wait·a·bit (wáytəbit) n. Any of several plants having sharp, often hooked thorns. [Translation of South African Dutch wacht-en-bitje (because the thorns catch hold of passers-by).]

wait·er (wáytər) n. 1. A man who serves at a table, as in a restaurant. 2. A tray or salver.

wait·ing (wáyting) n. The act of remaining stationary or inactive; especially, the act of parking a car by the roadside: No waiting. —**in waiting.** In attendance, especially at a royal court.

waiting game n. The stratagem of allowing time to pass before acting, in order to gain an advantage.

waiting list n. A list of persons waiting, as for an appointment, vacancy, or the like.

waiting room n. A room, as at a railway station or doctor's surgery, for the use of persons waiting.

wait·ress (wáy-triss, -trəss) n. A woman or girl who serves at a table, as in a restaurant.

waive (wayv) tr.v. **waived, waiving, waives. 1.** To relinquish or give up (a claim or right) voluntarily. **2.** To refrain from insisting upon or enforcing (a rule or penalty, for example); dispense with. **3.** To put aside temporarily; defer. —See Synonyms at **relinquish.** [Middle English weiven, to outlaw, abandon, relinquish, from Anglo-French weyver, variant of Old North French gaiver, from gaif, ownerless property. See **waif.**]

waiv·er (wáyvər) n. **1.** The intentional relinquishment of a right, claim, or privilege. **2.** A document that evidences such an act. [Anglo-French weyver, from weyver, to WAIVE.]

Waj·da (vī-də, -daa), **Andrzej** (1926–). Polish film director. His trilogy, A Generation (1954), Kanal (1956), and Ashes and Diamonds (1958), depicts wartime and postwar Poland. Later films include The Wedding (1972) and Man of Iron (1981).

wake[1] (wayk) v. **woke** (wōk) or rare **waked** (waykt), **woken** (wōkən) or chiefly British & regional **woke** or archaic **waked, waking, wakes.** —intr. **1. a.** To cease to sleep; become awake; awaken. Often used with up. **b.** To be brought into a state of awareness, attention, or alertness. Often used with to, up, or up to: woke to the facts; wake up and listen. **2.** Archaic & Irish. To keep watch or guard, especially over a corpse. **3.** To be or remain awake. Now used chiefly in the present participle: during all his waking hours. —tr. **1.** To rouse from sleep; awaken. Often used with up. **2.** To stir, as from a dormant or inactive condition; rouse: wake old animosities. **3.** To make aware; alert: It woke him to the facts. **4. a.** Archaic. To keep a vigil over. **b.** Archaic & Irish. To hold a wake over. ~n. **1. a.** Archaic. A watch; a vigil. **b.** A watch over the body of a deceased person before burial, sometimes accompanied by festivity.

2. a. In Britain, a parish festival held annually, often in honour of the patron saint. **b.** Usually plural. In northern England, an annual holiday during which many factories close for a week or more. **3.** The condition of being awake: between wake and sleep. [Middle English wakien and waken, Old English wacian, to be awake and wacan (unattested), to rouse.]

Usage: The verbs wake, waken, awake, and awaken each have transitive and intransitive uses. Awake is largely used intransitively (I awoke at six), and waken transitively (I wakened her at six). In passive constructions, the verbs awaken and waken are more widely used than the verbs awake or wake (I was awakened/wakened by the phone). Wake is especially common with up, is the most frequently used of all these verbs, and may be transitive or intransitive. Awake and awaken are the more prevalent verbs in figurative usage: She awoke to the danger; Her suspicions were awakened.

wake[2] n. **1.** The visible track of turbulence left by something moving through water: the wake of a ship. **2.** The track or course left behind anything that has passed: The war left nothing but destruction in its wake. —**in the wake of. 1.** Following directly upon. **2.** In the aftermath of; as a consequence of. [Probably Middle Low German wake, from Old Norse vök, a hole or crack in ice.]

Wake·field (wáyk-feeld). City and administrative centre of west Yorkshire, northern England. Situated on the river Calder.

wake·ful (wáykfʼl) adj. **1. a.** Not sleeping or not able to sleep. **b.** Without sleep; sleepless. **2.** Watchful; alert; vigilant. —**wakeful·ly** adv. —**wake·ful·ness** n.

wake·less (wáyk-ləss, -liss) adj. Unbroken. Said of sleep.

wak·en (wáykən) v. **-ened, -ening, -ens.** —tr. **1.** To rouse from sleep; awake. **2.** To rouse from a quiescent or inactive state; stir. —intr. To become awake; wake up. See Usage note at **wake.** [Middle English wak(e)nen, Old English wæcn(i)an.] —**wak·en·er** n.

wake·rife (wáyk-rīf) adj. Chiefly Scottish. Wakeful; alert; vigilant. [Middle English : WAKE (noun) + RIFE.]

wake·rob·in (wáyk-robbin) n. Any of various plants of the family Araceae, especially the cuckoopint. [WAKE (rouse) + Robin (man's name).]

Waks·man (wáksmən), **Selman Abraham** (1888–1973). Russian-born U.S. biologist. He discovered the antibiotics actinomycin (1940), and streptomycin (1943). He won the Nobel prize for physiology or medicine (1952).

Wa·la·chi·a (wo-láyki-ə, wə-). Region of south Romania, southeast Europe. Situated between the Transylvanian Alps and the river Danube, it was founded as a principality (1290) and was ruled by Turkey from 1387 until united with Moldavia (1859) to form Romania. Its chief town is Bucharest.

Wal·den·ses (wawl-dén-seez, wol-) pl.n. A Christian sect of dissenters originating in southern France in the late 12th century under the leadership of Peter Waldo, a Lyons merchant. Also called "Vaudois". —**Wal·den·si·an** (-si-ən, -shʼn) adj & n.

wald·grave (wáwl-grayv, wáwld- ‖ wól-, wóld-) n. In medieval Germany, a king's officer in charge of a royal forest. [German Waldgraf : Wald, forest + Graf, count, ruler.]

Wald·heim (vált-hīm), **Kurt** (1918–). Austrian statesman. He was secretary general of the United Nations (1972–81), and was elected president of Austria (1986–92).

Wal·dorf salad (wáwl-dawrf ‖ wól-) n. A salad of diced raw apples, celery, and walnuts mixed with mayonnaise. [Originally served in the Waldorf-Astoria Hotel, New York City.]

wale[1] (wayl) n. **1.** A mark raised on the flesh, as by a whip; a weal. **2. a.** Any of the parallel ribs or ridges in the surface of a fabric such as corduroy. **b.** The texture or weave of such a fabric: a wide wale. **3.** A ridge woven round a basket to strengthen it. **4.** Nautical. **a.** The gunwale. **b.** Any of the heavy planks or strakes extending along the sides of a wooden ship. [Middle English wale, a ridge, gunwale, Old English walu, a ridge of earth or stone, weal.]

wale[2] (wayl) n. Northern British. **1.** A choice. **2.** Something that is chosen or picked out as the best. ~tr.v. **waled, waling, wales.** To choose; select. [Middle English, from Old Norse val, choice.]

Wa·ler (wáylər) n. A horse exported from Australia, especially from New South Wales. [New South] Wal(es) + -ER.]

Wales (waylz). Welsh **Cym·ru** (kŏomri). Principality of Great Britain. Bounded by the Irish channel to the north and west, the Bristol Channel to the south, and England to the east, it forms the western peninsula of Great Britain. It is crossed by many mountains, including the Cambrians which rise to 1 085 metres (3,560 feet) at Mount Snowdon, and is drained by the rivers Usk, Severn, Dee, and Wye. The north is an agricultural region where livestock are bred and cereals and vegetables are grown, while the extensive coalfield of the south has fuelled many industries including iron and steel, tinplate, and copper manufacture. Decreased demand during the 1970s and 1980s, however, has led to the closure of many plants and diversification into light industry. Incorporated with England since the Act of Union (1536) it has a distinctive culture and a language still widely spoken. Its capital is Cardiff.

Wa·le·sa (va-wén-sə), **Lech** (1943–). President of Poland (1990–95). He was an electrician at the Lenin shipyard in Gdansk, and was an active trade union leader, becoming a founder and chairman of Solidarity, an independent trade union banned from 1981 to 1989. He won the Nobel peace prize (1983).

Walhalla. Variant of **Valhalla.**

walk (wawk) v. **walked, walking, walks.** —intr. **1.** To advance at a walk; move by steps. **2.** To roam about in visible form; appear.

Used of a ghost or other spirit. **3.** To travel or go on foot, especially for pleasure or exercise. **4.** To conduct oneself or behave in a particular manner; live. **5.** In cricket, to leave one's crease in acknowledgment that one is out. **6.** In basketball, to move illegally while holding the ball; travel. **7.** To disappear as a result of theft; be stolen: *My calculator's walked!* **8.** *Chiefly U.S. Slang.* To be acquitted; walk free of guilt. —*tr.* **1.** To go or pass over, on, or through by walking: *walk the streets.* **2.** To bring to a specified condition or state by walking: *walk someone to exhaustion.* **3.** To cause to walk or proceed at a walk: *walk a horse uphill.* **4.** To accompany in walking; escort on foot: *walk her home.* **5.** To assist or force to walk. **6.** To traverse on foot in order to survey or measure; pace off. **7.** To move (a heavy or cumbersome object) in a manner suggestive of walking. **—walk all over.** To treat contemptuously or inconsiderately. **—walk away from.** *Chiefly U.S. Informal.* **1.** To outdo, outrun, or defeat with little difficulty. **2.** To survive (an accident) with very little injury. **—walk away with.** *Informal.* To win very easily. **—walk into. 1.** To obtain (a job, for example) easily. **2.** To encounter or be caught by (a trap, for example), inadvertently or through carelessness. **—walk off. 1.** To leave abruptly or rudely. **2.** To purge or rid oneself of by walking: *walked off his anger.* **—walk off with.** *Informal.* **1.** To walk away with. **2.** To steal. **—walk out on.** *Informal.* To desert; abandon.

∼*n.* **1. a.** The gait of a human being or other biped in which the feet are lifted alternately with one part of a foot always on the ground. **b.** The gait of a quadruped, slower than a trot, in which at least two feet are always touching the ground. **c.** The gait of a horse in which the feet touch the ground in the four-beat sequence of near hind foot, off forefoot, off hind foot, near forefoot. **d.** The self-controlled movement in space of an astronaut. **2.** The act or an instance of walking; especially, a stroll for pleasure or exercise. **3. a.** The rate at which one walks; a walking pace. **b.** The characteristic way in which one walks. **4.** The distance covered or to be covered by walking. **5.** A place designed for walking on or along, such as a pavement or promenade. **6.** A route or circuit particularly suitable for walking: *one of the prettiest walks in the area.* **7.** A race in which contestants must walk. **8.** An enclosed area for the exercise or pasture of livestock. **9. a.** An arrangement of trees or shrubs planted in widely spaced rows. **b.** The space between such rows. **10.** *Chiefly British.* The round of a postman, trader, or the like. [Middle English *walken* and *walkien,* respectively from Old English *wealcan,* to roll, toss, and *wealcian,* to roll up, muffle up.]

walk·a·bout (wáwk-ə-bowt) *n.* **1.** A period spent by an Australian Aborigine wandering in the bush. Often used in the phrase *go walkabout.* **2.** A stroll made by an important person, such as a monarch or foreign dignitary, among a crowd.

walk·a·way (wáwk-ə-way) *n. U.S.* A **walkover** *(see).*

walk·er (wáwkər) *n.* **1.** One that walks. **2.** A light, wheeled framework with a seat in the middle, used to support a baby learning to walk. **3.** A light framework with bars that can be leant on, used by a disabled person for support and balance when walking.

walk·ie-talk·ie (wáwki-táwki, -tawki) *n.* Also **walk·y-talk·y** *pl.* **-ies.** A battery-powered, portable sending and receiving radio set.

walk-in (wáwk-ín, -in) *adj.* **1.** Large enough to admit entrance: *a walk-in wardrobe.* **2.** *U.S.* Located so as to be entered directly from the street: *a walk-in apartment.* **—walk-in** (-in) *n.*

walk·ing (wáwking) *adj.* Regarded as having the capabilities or qualities of a specified inanimate object: *He's a walking bomb.*

walking bass *n.* In jazz, an accompaniment played on a bass instrument, especially a double bass, one note to each beat of the bar.

walking papers *pl.n. Chiefly U.S. Informal.* **Marching orders** (2).

walking stick *n.* **1.** A cane or staff used as an aid in walking. **2.** *U.S.* A **stick insect** *(see).*

walk of life *n.* An occupation, profession, or social class: *People from all walks of life supported the cause.*

walk-on (wáwk-on || -awn) *n.* A minor role, usually non-speaking, in a theatrical production. Also called "walk-on part".

walk out *intr.v.* **1.** To go on strike. **2.** To leave or resign, especially abruptly, as a sign of disagreement or anger. **3.** *British Archaic.* To go out together as a courting couple.

walk·out (wáwk-owt) *n.* **1.** A strike by workers. **2.** The act of leaving a meeting, company, or organisation, especially as a sign of protest.

walk over *tr.v.* **1.** *Informal.* To treat inconsiderately or contemptuously. **2.** To gain an easy or uncontested victory over.

walk·o·ver (wáwk-ōvər) *n.* **1.** A horse race with only one horse entered, won by the formality of walking the course. **2.** A victory secured as a formality in a contest through the failure of one party to compete. **3.** *Informal.* An easily won contest or an easy achievement.

walk through *tr.v.* To perform (a play, acting role, or dance, for example) in a rudimentary fashion, as at a first rehearsal.

walk-through (wáwk-thrōō) *n.* A rehearsal at which the performers walk through their parts or steps.

walk·up, walk-up (wáwk-up) *n. U.S.* **1.** A block of flats or offices with no lift. **2.** A flat or office in such a building. **—walk·up** *adj.*

walk·way (wáwk-way) *n.* **1.** A passage or path for walking, such as one that connects parts of a building. **2.** A **moving pavement** *(see).*

Walkyrie. Variant of **Valkyrie.**

walky-talky. Variant of **walkie-talkie.**

wall (wawl) *n.* **1.** An upright structure of masonry, wood, plaster, or other building material serving to enclose, divide, or protect an area; specifically, a vertical construction forming an inner partition or exterior side of a building. Also used adjectivally and in combination: *wall hangings; wallpaper.* **2.** *Usually plural.* A continuous structure of masonry or other material forming a rampart and built for defensive purposes. **3.** A structure of stonework, cement, or other material built to retain a flow of water; a dam, levee, or dyke. **4.** Something resembling a wall in appearance, function, or construction, such as a very steep or vertical rock face on a mountain. **5.** *Anatomy.* The internal surface of a body cavity: *the abdominal wall.* **6.** In surfing, the vertical surface of a wave. **7.** Something resembling a wall in impenetrability or strength: *a wall of silence.* **8.** An extreme or desperate condition or position, such as defeat or ruin. Used in such phrases as *drive to the wall* and *go to the wall.* **9.** In soccer, a group of players forming a line in order to try to prevent the opposition from taking a direct shot at the goal. **10.** The physical and psychological barrier allegedly encountered by marathon runners, usually after about 20 miles (32 kilometres). Preceded by *the.* **—up the wall.** *Informal.* **1.** Crazy; mad. **2.** Very angry; furious.

∼*tr.v.* **walled, walling, walls. 1.** To enclose, surround, or fortify with or as if with a wall. **2.** To divide or separate with or as if with a wall: *wall off half a room.* **3.** To enclose within a wall; immure. **4.** To block or close (an opening or passage, for example) with or as if with a wall. [Middle English *wal(le),* Old English *weall,* from Latin *vallum,* palisade, wall, from *vallus,* stake.]

wal·la·by (wóllәbi) *n., pl.* **-bies** or collectively **wallaby. 1.** Any of various marsupials of the genus *Wallabia* and related genera, of Australia and adjacent islands, related to and resembling the kangaroos but smaller. **2.** *Capital* **W.** A member of Australia's international Rugby Union team. [Australian native name *wolabā.*]

wallaby grass *n.* Any of various tussock grasses of the genus *Danthonia,* abundant in Australasia and used as winter fodder.

Wallace (wólliss, wólləss), **Edgar,** born Horatio E.W. Richard (1875–1932). British novelist. His books include *The Four Just Men* (1905), and *Sanders of the River* (1911).

Wallace, Sir William (*c.* 1270–1305). Scottish patriot. He led the resistance to Edward I, and captured Stirling Castle (1297). He was proclaimed warden of Scotland, but was later routed at Falkirk (1298) and eventually captured and hanged.

Wallace's line *n.* The hypothetical dividing line between the Oriental and Australasian zoogeographical regions, running between the Indonesian islands Bali and Lombok. [After Alfred Russel *Wallace* (1823–1913), British naturalist.]

wal·lah, wal·la (wóllə) *n. British Informal.* **1.** One employed in a specified occupation or activity. Used in combination: *a kitchen wallah.* **2.** A man; a chap. [Hindi *-wālā,* adjectival suffix, mistaken by Europeans for a suffix indicating a man.]

wal·la·roo (wóllə-rōō) *n., pl.* **-roos.** A kangaroo, *Macropus robustus,* of hilly regions of Australia. [Australian native name *wolárū.*]

wall bars *pl.n.* A framework of horizontal bars attached to a wall, used for gymnastic exercises.

wall·board (wáwl-bawrd || -bōrd) *n.* Any of several structural boards or sheets of various materials, such as gypsum plaster encased in paper or compressed wood fibres and chips, used in construction as a substitute for plaster or wood panels.

wall creeper *n.* A long-billed crimson and greyish bird, *Tichodroma muraria,* of alpine regions of the Old World, characteristically seeking food on rocky cliffs or walls.

walled plain *n.* A very large, flat-bottomed, crater-like feature on the moon's surface, having a diameter up to about 240 kilometres (150 miles).

Wal·ler (wóllər), **Edmund** (1606–87). British poet. He is known chiefly for his harmonious love lyrics, which include *On a Girdle* and *Go, Lovely Rose* (from his *Poems* of 1645).

Waller, Thomas Wright known as Fats, (1904–43). U.S. jazz musician and songwriter. His many compositions include *Honeysuckle Rose* and *Ain't Misbehavin'.*

wal·let (wóllit) *n.* **1.** A small, flat folding case, usually made of leather or vinyl material, for holding paper money, cards, photographs, or other articles. **2.** *Archaic & Regional.* A small bag for carrying personal necessities on a journey, especially as formerly used by a pilgrim. [Middle English *walet,* a pilgrim's knapsack or provisions bag, probably from Anglo-French *walet* (unattested), from Germanic.]

wall·eye (wáwl-ī) *n.* **1.** *Pathology.* **a.** An eye in which the cornea is white or opaque, as in leucoma of the eye. **b.** An eye in which the iris is white, partly coloured, or a different colour from the other eye. **c.** A squint in which the lines of sight of the eyes diverge. **2.** A freshwater food and game fish, *Stizostedion vitreum,* of North America, having large, conspicuous eyes. Also called "walleyed pike" or "pike perch". [Back-formation from WALLEYED.]

wall·eyed (wáwl-īd, -īd) *adj.* **1.** Having or affected by walleye. **2.** *U.S.* Having large bulging or staring eyes, as some fish do. [Variant (influenced by WALL) of Middle English *wawil-eghed,* from Old Norse *vagleygr* : *vagl* (unattested), perhaps film over the eye + *-eygr,* -eyed, from *auga,* an eye.]

wall fern *n.* A fern, the common **polypody** *(see).*

wall·flow·er (wáwl-flowr) *n.* **1.** A widely cultivated plant, *Cheiranthus cheiri,* native to Europe, having fragrant, variously coloured flowers and common on rocks and old walls. **2.** Any of various similar, related plants. **3.** *Informal.* A person who does not participate in the activity at a social event, especially a dance, because of shyness or unpopularity.

wal·lies (wálliz) *pl.n. Scottish.* False teeth. [From WALLY (made of china).]

Wal·lis (wólliss), **Sir Barnes (Neville)** (1887–1979). British aeronautical engineer. Among his many contributions to aircraft design were the airship R100 (first flew 1930), the Wellesley (1935) and the Wellington (1939) and the bouncing bombs (1943) which were used to destroy the Ruhr dams in Germany in World War II. He also designed (1945–71) swept wing supersonic aircraft.

wall knot *n. Nautical.* A knot made at the end of a rope by undoing the strands and weaving them together, to prevent unravelling. [18th century: probably from Scandinavian and akin to Norwegian and Swedish *valknut,* Danish *valknude,* double knot, secure knot.]

wall mustard *n.* A plant, **stinkweed** (*see*).

Wal·loon (wo-lóon, wə-) *n.* **1.** A member of a French-speaking people of Celtic descent inhabiting southern and southeastern Belgium and adjacent regions of France. Compare **Fleming. 2.** The French dialect of this people. [Old French *Wallon,* from Medieval Latin *Wallō* (stem *Wallōn-*), a foreigner, Welshman, from Germanic.] —**Wal·loon** *adj.*

wal·lop (wóllap) *v.* **-loped, -loping, -lops.** *Informal.* —*tr.* **1.** To beat soundly; thrash. **2.** To defeat thoroughly. —*intr.* **1.** *Informal.* To move in a rolling, clumsy manner; lumber. **2.** To boil noisily and vigorously.
~*n. Informal.* **1.** A hard or severe blow. **2. a.** The capacity or effect of striking such a blow: *a punch that packs a wallop.* **b.** The capacity to create a forceful effect; impact. **3.** *British Slang.* Beer. [Earlier "to make violent, heavy motions", from Middle English *walopen,* to gallop, from Old North French *waloper,* from Frankish *walahlaupan* (unattested), "to jump well" : *wala* (unattested), well + *hlaupan* (unattested), to jump, run.]

wal·lop·er (wóllapər) *n.* **1.** One that wallops. **2.** *Australian Slang.* A policeman.

wal·lop·ing (wólləping) *adj. Informal.* Very large; huge; strapping: *a walloping fish.*
~*adv. Informal.* Used as an intensifier: *a walloping great fish.*
~*n. Informal.* A sound thrashing or defeat.

wal·low (wóllō) *intr.v.* **-lowed, -lowing, -lows. 1.** To roll the body about indolently or clumsily in water, snow, mud, or the like. **2.** To luxuriate or indulge oneself unrestrainedly, as in sensual pleasure or emotions: *wallow in self-pity.* **3.** To move with difficulty in a clumsy or rolling manner; flounder. **4.** To swell or surge forth; billow.
~*n.* **1.** An act of wallowing. **2.** A pool of water, mud, or the like where animals go to wallow. **3.** The depression, pool, or pit produced by wallowing animals. [Middle English *walowen,* Old English *wealwian.*] —**wal·low·er** *n.*

wall·pa·per (wáwl-paypər) *n.* Paper, usually coloured and printed with designs, pasted to the wall as a decorative covering.
~*v.* **wallpapered, -pering, -pers.** —*tr.* To cover with wallpaper. —*intr.* To decorate a wall or room with wallpaper.

wall plate *n.* **1.** A horizontal timber situated along the top of a wall at eaves level for bearing the ends of joists or rafters. **2.** A plate used to attach a bracket or similar device to a wall.

wall rock *n.* The rock that forms the walls of a vein or lode.

wall rocket *n.* Any of various yellow-flowered plants of the genus *Diplotaxis* found growing on lime rocks and walls, especially *D. muralis.*

Wall Street *n.* The controlling financial interests of the United States. [From the name of the main street of the financial district of New York City.]

wall-to-wall (wáwl-tə-wáwl, -toō-) *adj.* **1.** Covering a floor completely: *wall-to-wall carpeting.* **2.** Ubiquitous; pervasive: *wall-to-wall muzak.*

wal·ly[1] (wóli) *adj. Scottish.* **1.** Made of china. Said of an ornament. **2.** Fine; excellent.
~*n. Scottish.* An ornament; a trinket. [16th century (adjective, "excellent"), 18th century (noun, "toy, trinket") : origin obscure.]

wal·ly[2] *n., pl.* **-lies.** *British Slang.* An inept and foolish person. [From *Wally,* diminutive of *Walter.* Compare **charlie.**]

wal·nut (wáwl-nut, -nət ‖ wól-) *n.* **1.** Any of several trees of the genus *Juglans,* having round fruit enclosing an edible nut. **2.** The ridged or corrugated two-lobed nut of such a tree. **3.** The hard, dark-brown wood of such a tree, used for gunstocks and in cabinetwork. **4.** Moderate yellowish-brown.
~*adj.* **1.** Made of the wood of the walnut. **2.** Having the colour walnut. [Middle English *walnot,* Old English *walh-hnutu* (translation of Latin *nux gallia,* "Gaulish or foreign nut").]

Wal·pole (wáwl-pōl, wól-), **Horace,** 4th Earl of Orford (1717–97). British writer and wit, son of Sir Robert Walpole. His novel, *Castle of Otranto* (1765), set the fashion for gothic literature.

Walpole, Sir Robert, 1st Earl of Orford (1676–1745). British statesman. As First Lord of the Treasury and Chancellor of the Exchequer (1715–17, 1721–42) he led the Whig administration and was regarded as Britain's first prime minister (although the office was not officially recognised until 1905).

Wal·pur·gis Night (val-poór-giss, vaal-, -púr-). The eve of May Day which according to German legend was the occasion of a witches' Sabbath on the Brocken peak in the Harz mountains. [Partial translation of German *Walpurgisnacht* : *Walpurgis,* St. Walburga, seventh-century English nun and missionary, whose feast day falls on May Day + NIGHT.]

wal·rus (wáwl-rəss, -russ ‖ wól-) *n., pl.* **-ruses** or collectively **walrus.** A large marine mammal, *Odobenus rosmarus,* of Arctic regions, having tough, wrinkled skin and large tusks. [Probably from Dutch,

perhaps a metathetic formation influenced by *walvisch,* "whale fish", from a Germanic source akin to Old English *horschwæl,* Old Norse *hrosshvalr,* "horse-whale".]

walrus moustache *n.* A bushy, drooping moustache. [From the resemblance to the tusks of a walrus.]

Wal·ter (vaáltər), **Bruno,** born B.W. Schlesinger (1876–1962). German conductor. His repertory was wide, but he is remembered especially for his interpretations of Mozart and Mahler.

Wal·ter Mit·ty (wáwl-tər mitti ‖ wól-) *n.* An ordinary, often inadequate, person who indulges in fantastic daydreams about his own triumphs. [After the hero of *The Secret Life of Walter Mitty,* a story by James Thurber.]

Wal·ton (wáwl-tən, wól-), **Ernest Thomas Sinton** (1903–95). Irish physicist. With Sir John Cockcroft he was the first to succeed (1931) in splitting the atom. He shared the Nobel prize (1951) with Cockcroft for this work in nuclear physics.

Walton, Izaak (1593–1683). English author. He wrote biographies of John Donne and other churchmen, but is best known for the fishing classic *The Compleat Angler* (1653, enlarged frequently).

Walton, Sir William (Turner) (1902–83). British composer. He established his reputation (1923) with *Façade,* an extravaganza accompanying poems by Edith Sitwell, but his later work, such as the oratorio *Belshazzar's Feast* (1931), *Symphony No. 1* (1935), and his film music, is neo-Romantic in style.

waltz (wawlss, wawlts ‖ wolss, wolts) *n.* **1.** A smooth, flowing ballroom dance in which couples rotate and progress at the same time. **2.** A piece of music for this dance in triple time with a strong accent on the first beat.
~*v.* **waltzed, waltzing, waltzes.** —*intr.* **1.** To dance the waltz. **2.** To move effortlessly, confidently, or casually. **3.** To accomplish a task, chore, or assignment with little effort. Often used with *through: waltzed through her exams.* —*tr.* **1.** To dance the waltz with. **2.** To lead or force to move briskly and purposefully; march: *waltzed him into the headmaster's office.* [German *Walzer,* from Middle High German *walzen,* to roll, turn, dance, from Old High German *walzan,* to roll.] —**waltz·er** *n.*

Wal·vis Bay (wáwl-viss, -fish). Atlantic port of Namibia, formerly an exclave of Cape Province, Republic of South Africa, with which it is connected by railway, it exports minerals, including uranium. Fishing is also important.

waly. *Scottish.* Variant of **wally.**

wam·ble (wómb'l) *intr.v.* **-bled, -bling, -bles.** *Chiefly British Regional.* **1.** To move in a weaving, wobbling, or rolling manner. **2.** To turn or roll. Used of the stomach.
~*n. Chiefly British Regional.* **1.** A wobble or roll. **2.** A feeling of nausea. [Middle English *wam(e)len,* to feel nausea, probably from Scandinavian; akin to Old Norse *vamla.*] —**wam·bling·ly** *adv.* —**wam·bly** *adj.*

Wam·pa·no·ag (wámpə-nō-ag) *n., pl.* **-ags** or collectively **Wampanoag. 1.** A member of an Algonquian-speaking North American Indian people, formerly inhabiting eastern Rhode Island and adjacent parts of Massachusetts. **2.** The language of this people. —**Wam·pa·no·ag** *adj.*

wam·pum (wómpəm) *n.* **1.** Small cylindrical beads made from polished shells, formerly used by North American Indians as currency and as jewellery. Also called "peag". **2.** *U.S. Informal.* Money. [Short for WAMPUMPEAG.]

wam·pum·peag (wómpəm-peeg) *n.* Wampum made from white shell beads. [From Algonquian (Southeastern New England) *wampumpeage,* "white strings".]

wan (won) *adj.* **wanner, wannest. 1.** Unnaturally pale, as from physical or emotional distress. **2.** Suggestive of or indicating weariness, illness, or unhappiness; melancholy: *a wan expression.*
~*intr.v.* **wanned, wanning, wans.** *Poetic.* To become pale. [Middle English *wan,* gloomy, wan, Old English *wann*†, dusky, dark, livid.] —**wan·ly** *adv.* —**wan·ness** *n.*

wand (wond) *n.* **1.** A supple, thin twig or stick. **2.** A stick or baton used by a magician, conjurer, or diviner. **3.** A slender rod carried as a symbol of office. **4.** A conductor's baton. [Middle English *wand(e), wond(e),* from Old Norse *vöndr.*]

wan·der (wóndər) *v.* **-dered, -dering, -ders.** —*intr.* **1.** To move about with no destination or purpose; roam aimlessly. **2.** To make one's way by an indirect route in a leisurely fashion; amble; stroll: *wander towards town.* **3.** To proceed in an irregular course; meander: *This path wanders over hill and dale.* **4.** To go astray: *wander from the path of righteousness.* **5.** To think or express oneself unclearly or incoherently: *His mind is beginning to wander.* **6.** To stray from a subject or issue; digress; become sidetracked: *wandering off the point.* —*tr.* To wander across or through: *wander the forests.*
~*n.* The act or an instance of wandering; a stroll; an amble. [Middle English *wand(e)ren,* Old English *wandrian.*] —**wan·der·er** *n.* —**wan·der·ing·ly** *adv.*

Synonyms: *wander, ramble, roam, rove, range, meander, stray.*

wandering albatross. The largest of the albatrosses, *Diomedea exulans,* having a wingspan of over three metres (ten feet).

wandering Jew *n.* Either of two trailing plants, *Tradescantia fluminensis* or *Zebrina pendula,* native to tropical America, having usually striped variegated foliage and popular as house plants. [Fancifully named after the WANDERING JEW.]

Wandering Jew *n.* The subject of a medieval legend, condemned to wander until the Day of Judgment for having mocked Christ on the day of Crucifixion.

wan·der·lust (wóndər-lust, va'andər-loōst) *n.* A strong or irresistible impulse to travel. [German *Wanderlust* : *wandern,* to wander + *Lust,* desire, delight.]

wan·der·oo (wóndə-roō) *n.* A monkey, *Macaca silenus,* of south-central Asia, having a glossy black coat and a ruff of grey hair about the face. [Sinhalese *vanduru,* plural of *vandurā,* "forest-dweller", monkey, from Sanskrit *vānara,* from *vana,* a forest.]

wan·doo (won-doō) *n.* A white-barked eucalyptus tree, *Eucalyptus wandoo* (or *E. redunca*), having durable, reddish-brown wood. [From a native Australian language.]

wane (wayn) *intr.v.* **waned, waning, wanes. 1.** To decrease gradually in extent, intensity, or degree; dwindle; decline: *Their influence was waning.* **2.** To show a decreasing illuminated area from full moon to new moon. Used of the moon. Compare **wax. 3.** To approach an end.

~n. **1.** The act or process of waning; a gradual declining or diminishing. **2.** A period or phase of waning; specifically, the period of the decrease of the moon's visible surface. **3.** A defective edge of a plank where it has been imperfectly sawn. **—on the wane.** In a period of decline; waning. [Middle English *wan(i)en,* Old English *wanian,* to lessen. In the sense "defective edge of a log", from Middle English *wane,* defect, shortage, Old English *wana.*]

wan·gle (wáng-g'l) *v.* **-gled, -gling, -gles.** *Informal.* —*tr.* **1.** To make, achieve, or get by contrivance: *tried to wangle his way into the top job.* **2.** To manipulate or juggle (accounts, for example), especially fraudulently. **3.** To extricate (oneself) from difficulty. —*intr.* **1.** To use indirect, devious, or fraudulent methods. **2.** To extricate oneself by subtle or indirect means, as from difficulty.

~n. Informal. An act of wangling. [Originally a printer's term, "to manipulate or devise a substitute for", perhaps blend of WAGGLE and dialectal *wankle,* unsteady, wavering, Middle English *wankel,* Old English *wancol.*] **—wang·ler** *n.*

wan·i·gan, wan·ni·gan (wónnigən) *n. U.S.* **1.** A supply chest in a logging camp. **2.** A hut in a logging camp, either mounted on wheels or on a raft or boat. [Ojibwa *wanikkan,* "man-made hole".]

wank (wangk) —*intr.v.* **wanked, wanking, wanks.** *Chiefly British.* **1.** *Vulgar Slang.* To masturbate. **2.** *Vulgar Slang.* To behave or speak in a pretentious, silly, or ostentatious manner.

~n. Chiefly British. **1.** *Vulgar Slang.* An instance of masturbating. **2.** *Slang.* Pretentious, silly, or showy behaviour. [20th century : origin obscure.]

Wankel engine (vángk'l; *also* wángk'l || *U.S.* vaángk'l, waángk'l) *n.* A rotary internal-combustion engine in which a triangular rotor turning in a specially shaped housing performs the functions allotted to the pistons of a conventional engine, thereby allowing great savings in weight and moving parts. [After Felix *Wankel* (1902–88), German engineer.]

wank·er (wángkər) *n. Chiefly British. Slang.* A person who behaves in a silly, pretentious, or ostentatious manner. Used derogatorily. [WANK + -ER.] **—wank·y** *adj.*

Wan·li Chang·cheng. See **Great Wall of China.**

wan·na (wónnə || wáwnə, wúnnə). *Informal.* Contraction of *want to.*

wan·na·be (wónnə-bee, -bi || wáwnə-, wúnnə-) *n. Slang.* Someone who wants or tries to be someone else (such as a celebrity).

~ adj. Slang. Would-be: *Wannabe Spice Girls.*

want (wont || wawnt, wunt) *v.* **wanted, wanting, wants. 1.** To desire; wish for. Often used with the infinitive: *He wants to leave; always wants the biggest piece.* **2.** To need or require: "*'Your hair wants cutting,' said the Hatter.*" (Lewis Carroll). **3. a.** To desire the presence or assistance of: *You're wanted by the boss.* **b.** To seek with intent to capture: *The fugitive is wanted by the police.* **4. a.** To lack or fall short in (something, especially a desirable quality): *She wants tact.* **b.** To fall short by (a specified amount): "*Wants a few minutes of five o'clock.*" (Charles Dickens). **5.** *Informal.* Should or ought. Used with the infinitive: *You want to get your head examined.* —*intr.* **1.** To have need; be lacking. Used with *for*: *wants for nothing.* **2.** To be destitute or needy. **3.** To be disposed; like; wish: *Call her if you want.* **—want in** (or **out**). *Informal.* **1.** *Chiefly Scottish & U.S.* To wish to enter (or leave): *The dog wants out.* **2.** To wish to join (or leave) a project, business, or other undertaking.

~n. **1.** The condition or quality of lacking something usual or necessary; lack; absence: *stayed at home, for want of anything better to do.* **2.** Pressing need; destitution: *live in want.* **3.** Something needed or desired: *moderate wants.* [Middle English *wanten,* from Old Norse *vanta,* to be lacking.]

Usage: *Want,* in the sense of "need", is found chiefly in British English: *The car wants washing.* (*The car wants washed* is nonstandard British English). The use of *want* with *for* in the general sense of "wish, desire" is nonstandard American English (*She wants for you to travel by train*), though it is acceptable everywhere to say *what she wants is for you to travel by train.* Likewise, *She wants you should travel by train* is nonstandard American English.

want·ing (wónt-ing || wáwnt-, wúnt-) *adj.* **1.** Absent, lacking, or deficient. **2.** Not up to standards or expectations.

~prep. **1.** Without. **2.** Minus; less: *an hour wanting fifteen minutes.*

wan·ton (wón-tən || wáwn-) *adj.* **1.** Immoral or unchaste; lewd. **2.** Marked by or influenced by unprovoked, gratuitous maliciousness; capricious; arbitrary: *wanton destruction.* **3.** Pointlessly and unrestrainedly excessive: *wanton extravagance.* **4.** *Poetic.* Luxuriant; overabundant: *wanton tresses.* **5.** *Archaic & Poetic.* Frolicsome; playful. **6.** *Obsolete.* Rebellious; refractory.

~v. **wantoned, -toning, -tons.** —*intr.* To act, grow, or move in a wanton manner; be wanton. —*tr.* To waste or squander wantonly.

~n. An immoral, lewd, or licentious person, especially a woman. [Middle English *wantowen,* lacking discipline, lewd : *wan-, un-,* lacking, Old English *wan-* + *towen,* Old English *togen,* past participle of *tēon,* to draw, bring up.] **—wan·ton·ly** *adv.* **—wan·ton·ness** *n.*

wap·en·take (wáppən-tayk, wóppən-) *n.* A historical division of some northern counties in England, corresponding roughly to the hundred in other shires. [Middle English *wapentake,* subdivision, court of each division, Old English *wǣpengetæc,* from Old Norse *vāpnatak,* "taking of weapons" (vote by an assembly by brandishing of weapons, hence assembly) : *vāpna,* genitive plural of *vāpn,* a weapon + *tak,* a taking, from *taka,* to take.]

wap·i·ti (wóppiti) *n., pl.* **-tis** or **wapiti.** A large North American deer, *Cervus canadensis.* Also called "elk". [Shawnee *wapiti,* "white rump" : Proto-Algonquian *wap-* (unattested), white + *-itwiy-* (unattested), rump.]

wap·pen·shaw, wap·pen·schaw (wáppən-shaw, wóppən-) *n.* Also **wappenshawing** (-ing). Formerly, in Scotland, a periodical muster of the fighting men of a district, for inspection purposes. [16th century (later revived by Sir Walter Scott) : northern and Scottish dialect *wapen,* from Old Norse *vapn,* WEAPON + *s(c)haw,* SHOW.]

war (wawr) *n.* **1. a.** A state of open, armed, often prolonged conflict carried on between nations, states, or parties. **b.** *Often capital* **W.** A particular instance of such conflict: *the Trojan War.* **c.** The period of such conflict. **d.** A formally declared state of war in which certain internationally recognised conventions are supposed to apply. **2. a.** Any condition of active antagonism or contention: *an advertising war.* **b.** A concerted effort or campaign to combat or put an end to something: *the continuing war against disease.* **3.** The techniques or procedures of war; military science; strategy. **—at war.** In an active state of conflict or contention: *"Life and death are at war within us"* (Thomas Merton). **—have been in the wars.** *Informal.* To be damaged or injured, as from fighting or rough treatment.

~intr.v. **warred, warring, wars. 1.** To wage or carry on war. **2.** To be in a state of antagonism or rivalry; contend.

~adj. Of, resulting from, or used in war: *a war wound; a war cry.* [Middle English *werre, warre,* from Old North French *werre;* akin to Old High German *werra,* confusion, strife.]

War Warwickshire.

war. warrant.

war·a·tah (wórrə-taá, -taa) *n. Australian.* Any shrub of the genus *Telopea;* especially *T. speciosissima,* which has bright red flowers borne in terminal clusters. [From a native Australian language.]

war baby *n.* A child born during wartime.

War·beck (wáwr-bek), **Perkin** (*c.* 1474–99). Flemish-born impostor, and pretender to the English throne. In the Yorkist plot against Henry VII he claimed to be Richard, Duke of York (presumed murdered with his brother, Edward). After unsuccessful sieges he was captured by Henry's troops, tried, and executed.

war·ble[1] (wáwrb'l) *v.* **-bled, -bling, -bles.** —*tr.* To sing with trills, runs, or other melodic embellishments. —*intr.* **1.** To sing with trills, runs, or quavers. **2.** To produce a warbling sound.

~n. The act or an instance of warbling. [Middle English, from Old North French *werbler,* from *werble,* a warbling, melody, from Frankish *hwirbilōn* (unattested), to whirl, trill.]

war·ble[2] *n.* **1.** An abscessed swelling under the hide of the back of cattle or other animals, caused by the larva of a warble fly. **2.** The warble fly, especially in its larval stage. **3.** A hard lump of tissue on a horse's back caused by rubbing of the saddle. [16th century : perhaps from a Scandinavian compound corresponding to obsolete Swedish *varbulde.*] **—war·bled** *adj.*

warble fly *n.* Any of several flies of the family Oestridae, especially of the genus *Hypoderma,* whose larvae form warbles within the bodies of cattle and other animals.

war·bler (wáwrblər) *n.* **1.** Any of various small, brownish or greyish Old World birds of the family Sylviidae. **2.** Any of various small New World birds of the family Parulidae, many of which have yellowish plumage or markings. **3.** One that warbles.

war bonnet *n.* A ceremonial headdress used by some North American Plains Indians consisting of a cap or band and a trailing extension decorated with erect feathers.

war bride *n.* A woman who marries a serviceman during wartime, especially when she and her husband are of different nationalities.

war club *n.* A weapon consisting of a weight of iron or stone fixed to a handle, formerly used by American Indians.

war correspondent *n.* A journalist, reporter, or commentator assigned to report directly from a war or combat area.

war crime *n.* Any of various crimes committed during a war and considered to be in violation of the conventions of warfare, such as mistreatment of prisoners of war or genocide. **—war criminal** *n.*

war cry *n.* **1.** A cry uttered by combatants as they attack; a battle cry. **2.** A phrase or slogan used to rally people to a cause.

ward (wawrd) *n.* **1.** A division of a city or town for administrative and representative purposes; especially, an electoral district. **2.** A historical division of some northern English and Scottish counties corresponding roughly to the hundred or wapentake. **3.** A large room in a hospital, especially one set aside for the care of a particular group of patients. **4.** One of the divisions of a prison or other penal institution. **5.** An open court or area of a castle or fortification enclosed by walls. **6. a.** *Law.* A child or incompetent person placed under the care or protection of a guardian or court. Also called "ward of court". **b.** Any person under the protection or care of another. **7.** The state of being under guard; custody. **8.** The act of guarding or protecting; especially, guardianship of a minor or incompetent. **9.** A means of protection; a defence. **10.** A defensive

movement or attitude, especially in fencing; a guard. **11. a.** The projecting ridge of a lock or keyhole that prevents the turning of any key other than the proper one. **b.** The notch cut into a key that corresponds to such a ridge.
~*tr.v.* **warded, warding, wards. 1.** To turn aside; parry; avert; deflect. Usually used with *off: ward off a blow.* **2.** *Archaic.* To guard, watch over, or protect. [Middle English *ward(e)*, a guarding, place for guarding, person or thing in one's care, Old English *weard*, a watching over.]
-ward *adj. suffix.* Indicates direction towards; for example, **skyward, westward.**
~*adv. suffix. Chiefly U.S.* Variant of -wards. [Middle English *-ward*, Old English *-weard.*]
　　Usage: The suffixes *-ward* and *wards* are both used to express direction of movement: *backward(s), eastward(s), homeward(s).* As adverbs, the forms without *-s* are predominant in American English, while those with *-s* prevail in British English. Only the forms without *-s* are regularly used as adjectives: *a backward glance.*
Ward, Barbara, Baroness Jackson (1914–81). British economist and conservationist. Her books on ecology and political economy include *Spaceship Earth* (1966) and *Only One Earth* (1972).
Ward, Mrs Humphry, born Mary Augusta Arnold (1851–1920). Tasmanian-born novelist. Her books are concerned with religious and social issues, the best known being *Robert Elsmere* (1888).
Ward, Sir Joseph George (1856–1930). New Zealand statesman. He was Prime Minister (1906–12, 1928–30).
war dance *n.* A tribal dance performed before a battle or as a celebration after a victory.
ward·ed (wáwrdid) *adj.* Having notches or wards. Said of a key or lock.
war·den (wáwrd'n) *n.* **1.** A person who is in charge of or takes care of someone or something. **2.** An official charged with the enforcement of certain laws and regulations, such as an air-raid warden or traffic warden. **3.** *British.* The principal or governor of certain colleges, universities, schools, or hospitals. **4.** *British Archaic.* **a.** The chief executive official in charge of a port or market. **b.** Any of various crown officers having administrative duties. **5.** A church-warden. **6.** *U.S.* The governor of a prison. [Middle English *wardein*, from Old North French, variant of Old French *guarden*, GUARDIAN.] **—war·den·ship** *n.*
ward·er¹ (wáwrdər) *n.* **1.** A prison guard. **2.** A guard, porter, or watchman of a gate or tower. [Middle English, from Anglo-French *wardere*, from Old North French *warder*, variant of Old French *garder*, to keep, GUARD.] **—war·der·ship** *n.*
warder² *n.* A baton formerly carried as a symbol of authority and used by a ruler or commander to signal orders. [Short for Middle English *warderer*, perhaps a jocular use of obsolete *warderere*, "look out behind" : Anglo-French *ware*, beware, from Germanic + *derere*, behind, from Vulgar Latin *dē retrō* (unattested) : Latin *dē*, from + *retrō*, behind.]
ward heeler *U.S. Slang.* A local worker for a professional politician. Usually used derogatorily.
ward·i·an case (wáwrdi-ən) *n.* A case with glass sides, designed for growing or transporting delicate ferns or similar plants. [After N. B. *Ward* (died 1868), British botanist.]
ward·mote (wáwrd-mōt) *n.* Formerly, a meeting of the citizens of a ward; especially, a meeting of the liverymen and the alderman of a ward in the City of London. [Middle English. See **ward, moot.**]
ward·ress (wáwrd-riss, -ress) *n.* A female prison guard.
ward·robe (wáwr-drōb) *n.* **1.** A tall cabinet or cupboard with a rail, hooks, or shelves, in which clothes are kept. **2.** Garments collectively; especially, all the articles of clothing belonging to one person. **3. a.** The costumes belonging to a theatre or theatrical company. **b.** The place in which they are kept. **4.** The department in charge of clothes, jewellery, and the like in a royal or noble household. [Middle English *warderobe*, from Old North French : *warder*, to guard, keep, from Germanic + *robe*, ROBE.]
wardrobe trunk *n.* A large trunk with drawers and a hanging rail, designed to stand on end and serve as a wardrobe.
ward·room (wáwrd-rōōm, -rŏŏm) *n.* **1.** The living area and dining room for the commissioned officers, excepting the captain, on a warship. **2.** These officers collectively.
-wards *adv. suffix. Also chiefly U.S.* **-ward.** Indicates in the direction towards; for example, **backwards, windwards.**
ward·ship (wáwrd-ship) *n.* **1.** The state of being a ward or in the charge of a guardian. **2.** Guardianship; custody.
ware¹ (wair) *n.* **1.** Manufactured articles of the same general kind. Often used in combination to indicate: **a.** Articles made of the specified material: *glassware.* **b.** Articles of the specified type: *ovenware; computer software.* **c.** Pottery or ceramics of a specified type or make: *earthenware; Delft ware.* **2.** *Plural.* **a.** Articles of commerce; goods. **b.** Any immaterial asset or benefit, such as a service or personal accomplishment, that is regarded as an article of commerce. [Middle English *ware*, Old English *waru.*]
ware² *tr.v.* **wared, waring, wares.** *Archaic.* To beware of. Used chiefly in the imperative: *Ware hounds!.*
~*adj. Archaic & Poetic.* **1.** Watchful; wary. **2.** Aware. [Middle English *waren*, Old English *warian.*]
ware³ *tr.v.* **wared, waring, wares.** *Chiefly Scottish.* To spend, waste, or squander (money, goods or time, for example). [Middle English, from Old Norse *verja*, to invest, spend money, literally, to clothe; akin to Old English *werian*, to clothe, WEAR.]
ware·house (waír-howss) *n.* **1.** A place in which goods or merchan-

dise are stored; a storehouse. **2.** *British.* A large shop, usually selling goods wholesale.
~*tr.v.* **warehoused, -housing, -houses.** To place or store in a warehouse, especially in a bonded or government warehouse.
ware·house·man (waír-howss-mən) *n., pl.* **-men** (-mən). A person who owns, manages, or works in a warehouse.
war·fare (wáwr-fair) *n.* **1.** The waging of war; especially, military operations marked by a specified characteristic: *guerrilla warfare; chemical warfare.* **2.** Conflict of any kind; struggle; strife: *psychological warfare.* [Middle English *werrefare*, a going to war : *warre, werre*, WAR + *fare*, a journey, Old English *faru* and *fær.*]
War·fa·rin (wáwrfərin) *n.* A trademark for a colourless crystalline compound, $C_{19}H_{16}O_4$, used to kill rodents and medicinally as an anticoagulant. [Patented by *Wisconsin Alumni Research Foundation* + (COUM)ARIN.]
war game *n.* **1.** *Sometimes plural.* A simulated battle in military training manoeuvres. **2.** A board game using models or blocks to represent troops and weapons, used to test tactical knowledge.
war·head (wáwr-hed) *n.* A part of the armament system in the forward part of a projectile, such as a guided missile, torpedo, or bomb, containing the explosive charge.
War·hol (wáwr-hol, -hōl), **Andy** born Andrew von Warhol (1931–87). U.S. pop artist and film producer. He became known in the 1960s with outsize paintings of everyday objects, such as soup tins, and silk-screen portraits of film stars. His films, often erotic and controversial, include *The Chelsea Girls* (1968).
warhorse (wáwr-hawrss) *n.* **1.** A horse used in combat; a charger. **2.** *Informal.* A person who has been through many battles, struggles, or fights; an old campaigner.
war·i·son (wórri-s'n, wárri-) *n.* A bugle call giving the command to attack; a war cry. [Middle English, wealth, reward, from Old Northern French, variant of Old French *garison*, provision, store, defence, GARRISON; sense derives from misuse by Sir Walter Scott.]
war·like (wáwr-līk) *adj.* **1.** Belligerent; hostile. **2.** Of or pertaining to war; martial. **3.** Threatening or indicative of war.
war·lock (wáwr-lok) *n.* A male witch, sorcerer, or wizard. [Middle English *warloghe*, Old English *wǣloga*, "oath-breaker" : *wǣr*, faith, pledge + *-loga*, liar, from *lēogan*, to lie.]
war·lord (wáwr-lawrd) *n.* A military commander exercising civil power in a given region, whether in nominal allegiance to the national government or in defiance of it.
warm (wawrm) *adj.* **warmer, warmest. 1.** Somewhat hotter than temperate; having or producing a comfortable and agreeable degree of heat; moderately hot: *a warm climate.* **2.** Having the natural heat of living beings. **3.** Preserving or imparting heat: *a warm overcoat.* **4.** Having or causing a sensation of unusually high bodily heat, as from exercise or hard work. **5.** Marked by enthusiasm; fervent; ardent: *warm support.* **6.** Characterised by liveliness, excitement or disagreement; heated; animated: *a warm debate.* **7.** Marked by or revealing friendliness or sincerity; sympathetic; cordial: *a warm reception.* **8.** Loving; passionate; amorous: *a warm embrace.* **9.** Excitable, impetuous, or quick to be aroused: *a warm temper.* **10.** Predominantly red or yellow in tone; suggesting heat: *a warm brownish colour.* **11.** Recently made; fresh: *a warm trail.* **12.** Close to discovering, guessing, or finding something, as in certain games. **13.** *Informal.* Uncomfortable because of danger or annoyance.
~*v.* **warmed, warming, warms.** —*tr.* **1.** To make warm or warmer. Often used with *up.* **2.** To make zealous or ardent; inspire with life, zest, or colour; enliven. **3.** To fill with pleasant emotions: *warmed by the thought of her return.* —*intr.* **1.** To become warm or warmer. Often used with *up.* **2.** To become ardent, enthusiastic, or animated. Usually used with *to: began to warm to his subject.* **3.** To become kindly disposed or friendly. Usually used with *to* or *towards: felt the audience warming to her.*
~*n. Informal.* A warming or heating. **2.** A warm place. Preceded by *the.* [Middle English *warm*, Old English *wearm.*] **—warm·er** *n.* **—warm·ish** *adj.* **—warm·ly** *adv.* **—warm·ness** *n.*
warm-blood·ed (wáwrm-blúddid) *adj. Zoology.* Homoiothermic.
warmed-o·ver (wáwrmd-ōvər) *adj. U.S. Informal.* **1.** Reheated; warmed up. Said of food. **2.** Not new, fresh, or spontaneous; stale.
warm-heart·ed (wáwrm-hártid) *adj.* Kind; friendly; sympathetic. **—warm·heart·ed·ly** *adv.* **—warm·heart·ed·ness** *n.*
warming pan *n.* A metal pan with a cover and a long handle, designed to hold hot liquids or coals and formerly used to warm a bed. Also called "bedpan".
war·mon·ger (wáwr-mung-gər ‖ -mong-) *n.* One who advocates or attempts to stir up war. **—war·mon·ger·ing** *adj. & n.*
warm sector *n.* A wedge of warm air between the warm front and the cold front of a depression.
warmth (wawrmth) *n.* **1.** The state, sensation, or quality of producing, having or preserving a moderate degree of heat. **2.** Excitement or intensity, as of love or passion; ardour; zeal. **3.** Friendliness, sincerity, or affection. **4.** The glowing effect produced by using predominantly red or yellow colours. [Middle English *warmth*, Old English *wiermthu* (unattested).]
warm up *intr.v.* **1.** To exercise or practise, as in preparation for an athletic event. **2.** To become ready for operation. Used of an engine, for example. **3.** To become more enthusiastic, exciting, or animated. —*tr.v.* **1.** To reheat (food). **2.** To make (a car, for example) ready for operation by raising to efficient working temperature. **3.** To exercise (a horse, for example), immediately prior to a competition. **4.** To make more enthusiastic, exciting, or animated: *warm up the conversation with some juicy gossip.*

warm-up (wáwrm-up) *n.* An act, process, or period of warming up.
warn (wawrn) *v.* **warned, warning, warns.** *—tr.* **1.** To make aware of potential or probable harm, danger, or evil; caution. **2.** To admonish as to action or behaviour. **3.** To notify (a person) to go or stay away. Usually used with *off* or *away.* **4.** To notify or apprise in advance: *He warned us that he might be late.* *—intr. & tr.* To give a warning. [Middle English *warnen,* Old English *w(e)arnian,* to take heed, warn.] **—warn·er** *n.*
Synonyms: *warn, admonish, caution, forewarn.*
warn·ing (wáwrning) *n.* **1.** An intimation, threat, or sign of impending danger or evil. **2. a.** Advice to beware, as of a person or thing. **b.** Counsel to desist from an undesirable course of action. **3.** A cautionary or deterrent example.
~adj. Acting or serving as a warning. **—warn·ing·ly** *adv.*
warning coloration *n.* The conspicuous markings by which a poisonous or distasteful animal can be recognised by potential predators. Also called "aposematic coloration."
War of American Independence *n.* The war fought between Great Britain and her colonies in North America (1775–83) by which the colonies won independence. Also called "American Revolution", "Revolutionary War".
War of 1812 *n.* A war between the United States and Great Britain (1812–14), fought over the rights of neutrals on the high seas and issues related to American westward expansion.
war of nerves *n.* A conflict in which attempts are made to wear down or destroy the morale of one's opponent by psychological means, such as progaganda, delaying tactics, and intimidation.
War of Secession *n.* The **Civil War** *(see)* of the United States.
War of the Spanish Succession *n.* A war fought by Great Britain, the Netherlands, and the Holy Roman Empire against France and Spain (1701–14), over the succession in Spain after the death of Charles II. The Treaty of Utrecht placed Louis XIV's grandson Philip V on the Spanish throne.
warp (wawrp) *v.* **warped, warping, warps.** *—tr.* **1.** To turn or twist out of shape, especially lastingly. **2.** To turn from a correct, healthy, or true course; pervert; corrupt. **3.** In weaving, to arrange (yarn or thread) so as to form a warp. **4.** *Nautical.* To move (a vessel) by hauling on a line that is fastened to or around a piling, anchor, or pier. **5.** To flood (land) so as to deposit alluvial sediment for agriculture. *—intr.* **1.** To become warped, as through the action of heat or damp. **2.** To turn aside from a true, correct, or natural course; go astray; deviate. **3.** *Nautical.* To warp a vessel. **—**See Synonyms at **distort.**
~n. **1.** The state of being warped. **2.** A distortion or twist, especially in a piece of wood. **3.** A warped condition of the mind; a perversion or deviation. **4.** The threads that run lengthways in a fabric, crossed at right angles by the weft. **5.** *Nautical.* A towline used in warping a vessel. [Middle English *werpen,* to warp, throw, Old English *weorpan,* to throw (away).] **—warp·er** *n.*
war paint *n.* **1.** Pigments applied to the face or body by certain tribes, such as the Indians of North America, preparatory to going to war. **2.** *Informal.* Cosmetics such as lipstick, rouge, or mascara. **3.** *Informal.* Official dress; regalia.
war·path (wáwr-paath || -path) *n., pl.* **-paths** (-paa<u>th</u>z || -paths, -pa<u>th</u>z). **1.** The route taken by a party of North American Indians on the attack. **2.** A hostile course or mood. Used in the phrase *on the warpath.*
war·plane (wáwr-playn) *n.* A combat aircraft.
war·rant (wórrənt || wáwrənt) *n. Abbr.* **war., wrnt. 1.** Authorisation or certification; sanction, as given by a superior. **2.** Justification, as for an action or belief; grounds. **3.** Something that provides assurance or confirmation. **4.** A writing, writ, or other order that serves as authorisation for something, specifically: **a.** A voucher authorising payment or receipt of money. **b.** A warehouse receipt for goods received for storage. **c.** *Law.* A judicial writ authorising an officer to make a search, seizure, or arrest or to carry out a judicial sentence. **d.** *Military.* A warrant officer's certificate of appointment.
~tr.v. **warranted, -ranting, -rants. 1. a.** To guarantee the truth of (a statement); assert confidently. **b.** To assure (a person) of a fact. **2.** To attest to or make oneself answerable for the quality or authenticity of; especially, to guarantee (a product) to be as represented in terms of type, quality, or quantity. **3.** To guarantee the immunity or security of. **4.** To provide adequate grounds for; justify. **5.** To grant authorisation or sanction to; authorise or empower. **6.** *Law.* To guarantee clear title to (real property, for example). [Middle English *war(r)ant,* protector, protection, authorisation, from Old North French *warant,* probably from Medieval Latin *warantus,* from Old High German *werenti,* "the one protecting", present participle of *werren,* to protect, guarantee.] **—war·rant·a·ble** *adj.* **—war·rant·a·ble·ness** *n.* **—war·rant·a·bly** *adv.* **—war·rant·er** *n.*
war·ran·tee (wórrən-teé || wáwrən-) *n. Law.* A person to whom a warranty is made.
warrant officer *n. Abbr.* **WO, W.O.** *Military.* An officer intermediate in rank between a noncommissioned officer and a commissioned officer, having authority by virtue of a warrant.
war·ran·tor (wórrən-tər, -tór || wáwrən-) *n. Law.* A person who makes a warrant or gives a warranty to another.
war·ran·ty (wórrən-ti || wáwrən-) *n., pl.* **-ties. 1.** Official authorisation, sanction, or warrant. **2.** Justification or valid grounds for an act or course of action. **3.** *Law.* **a.** An assurance by the seller of property that the goods or property are as represented or will be as promised; especially, such as assurance accompanied by an explicit acceptance of responsibility for any repairs that become necessary during a stated period. **b.** A guarantee by the party being insured that the facts are as stated in reference to an insurance risk or that conditions will be fulfilled to keep the contract effective. **c.** A covenant by which the seller of land binds himself and his heirs to defend the security of the estate conveyed. **d.** A judicial writ; a warrant. [Middle English *warantie,* from Old North French, from the feminine past participle of *warantir,* to guarantee, from *warant,* protection, WARRANT.]
war·ren (wórrən || wáwrən) *n.* **1. a.** An area where rabbits live in burrows. **b.** A colony of rabbits. **2.** Formerly, an enclosure for small game animals or birds. **3.** Any mazelike place in which one may easily get lost. [Middle English *warenne,* from Old North French, from Germanic.]
war·ren·er (wórrənər || wáwrənər) *n.* One who keeps a warren.
war·ri·gal (wórrəg'l) *n. Australian.* A dingo.
~adj. Untamed; wild. [From a native Australian language.]
war·ri·or (wórri-ər || wáwri-) *n.* One engaged or experienced in battle. Also used adjectivally: *a warrior race.* [Middle English *werreour,* from Old North French *werreieor,* from *werreier,* to make war, from *werre,* WAR.]
War·rum·bun·gle Range (wórrəm-búng-g'l). Volcanic range of New South Wales, Australia. A national park since 1953, it rises to 1 228 metres (4,028 feet) at Mount Exmouth.
War·saw (wáwr-saw). *Polish* **War·sza·wa** (vaar-shaávə). Capital of Poland. Situated on the river Vistula, it was founded in the 13th century, first became the capital in 1596, and was ruled by Russia as an independent kingdom (1815–1917), becoming the capital again in 1918. It was badly damaged during World War II and its Jewish ghetto was destroyed. Some 400,000 of the Jewish population were moved to concentration camps and the remaining 60,000 or so were massacred after an attempted uprising (1943). Rebuilt according to its previous plan, it is a major cultural commercial, industrial, and educational centre.
Warsaw Pact *n.* A treaty of mutual military alliance signed in Warsaw in 1955 by most Communist countries of the Eastern bloc: Albania, Bulgaria, Czechoslovakia, East Germany, Hungary, Poland, Romania, and the U.S.S.R. By 1991 it was effectively disbanded. Also called "Eastern European Mutual Assistance Treaty".
war·ship (wáwr-ship) *n.* Any ship constructed or equipped for use in battle.
war·sle (wáwrss'l) *v.* **-sled, -sling, -sles.** *Northern British.* *—intr.* To wrestle or struggle. *—tr.* To wrestle with. [Middle English, metathetic variant of WRESTLE.] **—war·sler** *n.*
Wars of the Roses. *See* **Roses, Wars of the.**
wart (wawrt) *n.* **1.** A limited area of enlarged skin cells caused by a virus, covered with a keratinous layer, and occurring typically on the hands or feet. Also called "verruca". **2.** Any similar protuberance, as on a plant. **—warts and all.** Without attempting to disguise defects. [Middle English *werte, wart,* Old English *wearte.*]
wart hog *n.* A wild African pig, *Phacochoerus aethiopicus,* having tusks and wartlike protuberances on the face.
war·time (wáwr-tīm) *n.* A period in which a war is in progress. Often used adjectivally: *wartime austerities.*
wart·y (wáwrti) *adj.* **-ier, -iest. 1.** Having or covered with warts or wartlike protuberances. **2.** Of or resembling a wart or warts.
war whoop *n.* A war cry, especially of North American Indians.
War·wick (wórrik), **Richard Neville, Earl of** (1428–1471). English statesman, known as The Kingmaker. During the Wars of the Roses he fought for the Yorkists and secured the throne (1461) for Edward IV. He then changed sides and restored (1470) the Lancastrian Henry VI. He was killed at the battle of Barnet.
War·wick·shire (wórrik-shər, -sheer). County of central England. Having lost its industrial region around Coventry and Birmingham to the West Midlands (1974–97), its economy is now mainly agricultural, including market gardening, wheat growing, and dairy farming.
war·y (waír-i) *adj.* **-ier, -iest. 1.** On one's guard; alert to possible danger or deception; watchful. **2.** Characterised by caution: *a wary glance.* [From obsolete *ware,* wary, from Middle English *ware,* Old English *wær.*] **—war·i·ly** *adv.* **—war·i·ness** *n.*
was (woz, *weak form* wəz || wuz). First and third person singular past indicative mood of **be.**
wash (wosh || wawsh) *v.* **washed, washing, washes.** *—tr.* **1.** To cleanse, using water or other liquid, and often a cleansing agent such as soap or bleach, by immersing, flushing, rubbing, or scrubbing. **2.** To remove by, or as if by, washing: *wash a stain from one's hands.* Often used with *off, out,* or *away*: *wash away one's guilt; wash out a dirty mark.* **3.** To clean (itself) by licking. Used of an animal. **4.** To make moist or wet; dampen; drench: *Tears washed her cheeks.* **5.** To flow over, against, or past: *shores washed by ocean tides.* **6.** To carry along or sweep away through the action of flowing or moving water. Often used with *off, out,* or *away*: *His body was washed out to sea.* **7.** To erode, remove, damage, or destroy by moving water. Used with *out* or *away: The roads were washed out.* **8.** To serve as an effective cleaning agent for: *This soap washes wool.* **9.** To cover or coat with a watery layer of paint or other colouring substance. **10.** *Chemistry.* **a.** To purify (a gas) by passing through or over a liquid, as to remove soluble matter. **b.** To pass a solvent, such as distilled water, through (a precipitate). **11.** *Mining.* To remove particulate constituents from (an ore) by immersion in or agitation with water. *—intr.* **1.** To wash oneself: *wash for dinner.* **2.** To wash clothes, dishes, or the like in or by means of water or other liquid. **3.** To undergo washing without fading, shrinkage, or other damage: *This*

fabric will wash. **4.** *British Informal.* To hold up under examination; be convincing: *Your excuse won't wash!* **5.** To be cleaned or removed by washing. Usually used with *out*: *The colours washed out.* **6.** To be carried away, removed, or drawn along by the action of flowing or moving water: *Bits of wreckage washed up on the shore.* Often used with *out* or *away*: *Some of the topsoil washed away in the storm.* **7.** To flow, sweep, or beat. Often used with *against, along,* or *over*: *The waves washed over the pilings.* **—wash down. 1.** To clean (a car, for example) by washing with water from top to bottom. **2.** To follow the ingestion of (food, for example) with a drink. **—wash (one's) hands of. 1.** To refuse to accept responsibility for. **2.** To abandon or renounce. **—wash up. 1.** *British.* To wash crockery, cutlery, and the like after use. **2.** *U.S.* To wash one's dirty face and hands.

~*n.* **1.** The act or process of washing or being washed. **2.** A quantity of articles, especially clothing, washed or intended for washing. **3.** Kitchen refuse fed to pigs; swill. **4.** Malt or similar substances undergoing fermentation prior to distillation. **5.** Any preparation or product used in washing or coating, especially: **a.** A cosmetic or medicinal liquid, such as a mouthwash. **b.** A thin water-based paint or distemper. **6. a.** A thin layer of watercolour or Indian ink spread on a surface. **b.** Any light tint or hue: *a wash of red sunset.* **7. a.** The rush or surge of water or waves. **b.** The sound of this. **8. a.** The removal or erosion of soil, subsoil, or the like by the action of moving water. **b.** A deposit of recently eroded debris. **9. a.** An area of low or marshy ground washed by tidal waters. **b.** A stretch of shallow water. **10.** A turbulence in air or water caused by the motion or action of an oar, propeller, jet, or aerofoil. **11.** *Western U.S.* The dry bed of a stream. **—come out in the wash. 1.** To turn out well in the end. **2.** To come inevitably to light. Used of scandal.

~*adj. U.S. Informal.* **1.** Used for washing. **2.** Capable of being washed; washable. [Middle English *waschen, wasshen,* Old English *wæscan, wacsan,* from Germanic *wa(t)skan* (unattested).]

wash·a·ble (wósh-əb'l || wáwsh-) *adj.* Capable of being washed without fading or other damage. **—wash·a·bil·i·ty** (-ə-bílləti) *n.*

wash-and-wear (wósh-ən-wair, -ənd- || wáwsh-) *adj.* Treated so as to be easily or quickly washed or rinsed clean and to require little or no ironing: *a wash-and-wear shirt.*

wash·ba·sin (wósh-bayss'n || wáwsh-) *n.* **1.** A basin that can be filled with water for washing the face and hands. Also *British* "wash-hand basin", *U.S.* "washbowl". **2.** *British.* A sink (as in a bathroom) that is a washbasin. Also *British* "wash-hand basin".

wash·board (wósh-bawrd || wáwsh-, -bōrd) *n.* **1. a.** A board having a corrugated surface of metal, wood, or the like, upon which clothes can be rubbed in the process of laundering. **b.** Such a board used as a percussion instrument. **2.** *U.S.* A **skirting board** *(see).* **3.** *Nautical.* A thin plank fastened to the side of a boat or to the sill of a port to keep out the sea and the spray.

wash·bowl (wósh-bōl || wáwsh-) *n. U.S.* A washbasin (sense 1).

wash·cloth (wósh-kloth || wáwsh-, -klawth) *n., pl.* **-cloths** (-kloths || -klawthz, -klawths, -klothz). *U.S.* A **facecloth** *(see).*

wash·day (wósh-day || wáwsh-) *n.* A day, often the same day of every week, set aside for doing the household washing.

wash drawing *n.* **1.** The technique of producing drawings or paintings using washes of colour. **2.** A drawing or painting so produced.

washed-out (wósht-ówt || wáwsht-) *adj.* **1.** Lacking colour or intensity; pale; faded. **2.** *Informal.* Exhausted; tired-looking.

washed-up (wósht-úp || wáwsht-) *adj.* **1.** No longer successful or needed; finished. **2.** *Chiefly U.S.* Ready to give up; wearied.

wash·er (wósh-ər || wáwsh-) *n.* **1.** One that washes. **2.** *Machinery.* A small perforated disc, as of metal, rubber, leather, or plastic, placed beneath a nut or at an axle bearing or joint to relieve friction, prevent leakage, or distribute pressure. **3.** A machine or apparatus for washing; especially, a washing machine, a dishwasher, or an industrial plant for washing gases. **4.** *Australian.* A facecloth.

washer-up (wósh-ər-úp || wáwsh-) *n. British Informal.* A person who does the washing-up.

wash·er·wom·an (wósh-ər-wŏŏmən || wáwsh-) *n., pl.* **-women** (-wimmin) A woman who washes clothes for a living; a laundress.

wash·ing (wósh-ing || wáwsh-) *n.* **1.** The act or process of one that washes. **2.** A quantity of articles washed or intended to be washed at one time: *the week's washing.* **3.** The residue after an ore or other material has been washed. **4.** *Sometimes Plural.* The liquid that is used to wash something. **5.** A thin coat of paint or other liquid.

washing machine *n.* A domestic apparatus, usually powered by electricity and often plumbed into the domestic water supply and drains, used to wash clothes, household linen, and the like.

washing powder *n.* Detergent in the form of powder for washing clothes and other textiles.

washing soda *n.* A hydrated **sodium carbonate** *(see),* used as a general cleanser. Also called "sal soda".

Wash·ing·ton (wósh-ing-tən || wáwsh-). Coastal state of the northwest United States. Bordering Canada and the Pacific Ocean which indents the state at Puget sound, it is chiefly mountainous except for the basin of the river Columbia in the east. It is crossed by the Cascade and Coast mountain ranges. The capital is Olympia.

Washington, George (1732–1799). American statesman and general. He commanded the American forces during the War of Independence (1775–83), and became (1789) first U.S. president.

Washington D.C. Capital of the United States. Situated in the east of the country on the river Potomac, it is coterminous with the District of Columbia, and was built as a planned city (1790–1800) by a Frenchman, Pierre L'Enfant. The federal capital since 1800, it was burnt by the British (1814). Its many famous buildings include the White House, the Capitol, and the Lincoln Memorial.

washing-up (wósh-ing-úp || wáwsh-) *n.* **1.** The act of washing plates, dishes, glass, silver, saucepans, and the like, after a meal. **2.** The plates and dishes waiting to be washed.

wash leather *n.* **1.** Soft leather, such as chamois or split sheepskin. **2.** A piece of such leather, typically used for cleaning cars and windows or polishing metal.

wash out *tr.v.* **1.** To clean the inside of: *wash out a jam jar.* **2.** To cause the postponement or abandonment of (an outdoor event): *The match was washed out by a freak storm.*

wash·out (wósh-owt || wáwsh-) *n.* **1. a.** The erosion of a relatively soft geological surface by a transient stream of water. **b.** A channel produced by this. **2.** *Informal.* A total failure or disappointment.

wash·room (wósh-rōōm, -rŏŏm || wáwsh-) *n.* **1.** *British.* A room having communal washing facilities. **2.** *U.S.* A lavatory.

wash sale *n. U.S.* The illegal buying of stock by a seller's agents to give the impression of an active market.

wash·stand (wósh-stand || wáwsh-) *n.* A stand designed to hold a basin and jug of water for washing.

wash·tub (wósh-tub || wáwsh-) *n.* A tub or similar container used for washing clothes.

wash·y (wóshi || wáwshi) *adj.* **-ier, -iest. 1.** Watery; diluted: *washy tea.* **2.** Lacking intensity or vigour; wishy-washy. **—wash·i·ness** *n.*

was·n't (wózz'nt || wúzz'nt). Contraction of *was not.*

wasp (wosp || wasp, wawsp) *n.* Any of numerous social or solitary insects, chiefly of the superfamilies Vespoidea and Sphecoidea, commonly having a slender black and yellow striped abdomen, membranous wings, and in the females an ovipositor often modified as a sting. [Middle English *waspe,* Old English *wæsp, wæps.*]

Wasp, WASP, wasp (wosp || wasp, wawsp) *n.* In the United States, a person of Caucasoid, northern European, largely Protestant stock whose members are held by some to constitute the most privileged and influential group in American society. [*W*hite *A*nglo-*S*axon *P*rotestant.] **—Wasp, Wasp·ish, Wasp·y** *adj.*

wasp·ish (wósp-ish || wásp-, wáwsp-) *adj.* **1.** Pertaining to or suggestive of a wasp. **2.** Easily irritated or annoyed; irascible; snappish. **—wasp·ish·ly** *adv.* **—wasp·ish·ness** *n.*

wasp waist *n.* A very slender or tightly corseted waist. **—wasp·waist·ed** *adj.*

wasp·y (wóspi || wáspi, wáwspi) *adj.* **-ier, -iest.** Characteristic of a wasp; wasplike.

was·sail (wóss-ayl, wáss-, -'l || wáwss-) *n.* **1.** A salutation or toast formerly given in drinking someone's health or as an expression of good will at a festivity. **2.** The drink used in such toasting, commonly ale or wine spiced with roasted apples and sugar. **3.** A riotous festivity characterised by much drinking.

~*intr.v.* **wassailed, -sailing, -sails.** To engage in or drink a wassail. [Middle English *wassayl,* contraction of *wæs hæil,* from Old Norse *ves heill,* be in good health : *ves,* imperative singular of *vesa, vera,* to be + *heill,* hale, healthy.] **—was·sail·er** *n.*

Was·ser·mann reaction (wássər-mən, wóssə-; *German* vássər-man) *n.* A diagnostic test for syphillis involving the fixation of inactivation of a complement by antibodies to the causative organism, *Treponema pallidum,* in a blood serum sample. Also called "Wassermann test". See **complement fixation.** [After August von *Wassermann* (1866–1925), German bacteriologist.]

wast. *Archaic.* Second person singular past tense of **be.**

wast·age (wáystij) *n.* **1.** Loss by deterioration, wear, destruction, or the like. **2.** The gradual process of wasting. **3.** An amount that is wasted or lost by wear. **4.** See **natural wastage.**

waste (wayst) *v.* **wasted, wasting, wastes.** *—tr.* **1.** To use, consume, or expend thoughtlessly or carelessly; use to no avail; squander. **2.** To cause to lose energy, strength, or vigour; exhaust, tire, or enfeeble. **3.** To fail to take advantage or make profitable use of lose: *waste an opportunity.* **4. a.** To lay waste; devastate. **5.** *U.S. Slang.* To kill. *—intr.* **1.** To lose energy, strength, or vigour; become weak or enfeebled. Often used with *away.* **2.** To become wasted or consumed. **3.** *Archaic.* To pass: *Time is wasting.*

~*n.* **1.** The act of wasting or the condition of being wasted; thoughtless or careless expenditure, consumption, or use: *a waste of talent; gone to waste.* **2.** A place, region, or land that is uninhabited or uncultivated; a desert or wilderness. **3. a.** Any useless or worthless by-product of a manufacturing process; useless excess material. **b.** Something that escapes without being used, such as steam. **4.** Rubbish, refuse. **5. a.** The undigested residue of food eliminated from the body. **b.** The useless by-products of metabolism.

~*adj.* **1.** Regarded or discarded as worthless or useless: *waste paper.* **2.** Used as a conveyance or container for refuse: *a waste bin.* **3.** Not cultivated or inhabited. **4.** Excreted from the body as useless. [Middle English *wasten,* from Old North French *waster,* from Vulgar Latin *wāstāre* (unattested), from Latin *vāstāre,* to make empty, from *vāstus,* empty.]

wast·ed (wáystid) *adj.* **1.** Needless or superfluous: *wasted words; a wasted journey.* **2.** Physically haggard, as from disease or dissipation. —See Synonyms at **haggard.**

waste·ful (wáystf'l) *adj.* **1.** Characterised by heedless wasting; extravagant. **2.** *Archaic.* Causing waste or devastation; destructive. **—waste·ful·ly** *adv.* **—waste·ful·ness** *n.*

waste·land (wáyst-land) *n.* **1.** An uncultivated or desolate area; a barren or ravaged land. **2.** Any place, era, or aspect of life considered as lacking in spiritual, aesthetic, or other humanising qualities; a vacuum: *a cultural wasteland.*

waste·pap·er basket (wáyst-páypər) *n.* An open-topped container for paper and other dry rubbish, usually made of wickerwork. Also *U.S.* "wastebasket".

wastepaper bin *n.* An open-topped container for dry rubbish, usually made of metal.

waste pipe *n.* A pipe carrying off liquid waste from baths, washbasins, sinks, and the like. Compare **soil pipe.**

waste product *n.* **1.** Useless or worthless debris produced during or as a result of a manufacturing or other process. **2.** Organic waste matter such as urine, faeces, or dead cells.

wast·er (wáystər) *n.* A person who wastes; a spendthrift or ne'er-do-well; a wastrel.

wast·ing (wáysting) *adj.* **1.** Gradually deteriorating or being convinced. **2.** Sapping the strength, energy, or substance of the body; emaciating: *a wasting disease.*

wasting asset *n.* A fixed asset, such as a mine or oil well, or a property on a lease, that diminishes in value over the years.

wast·rel (wáystrəl) *n.* A profligate or loafer; a good-for-nothing. [WASTE + -*rel*, diminutive suffix (often derogatory), from Old French -*erel(le)*.]

watch (woch ‖ *U.S. also* wawch) *v.* **watched, watching, watches.** —*intr.* **1.** To look or observe attentively or carefully. **2.** To look and wait expectantly or in anticipation. Used with *for: watch for an opportunity.* **3.** To be on the lookout or alert; be constantly observant or vigilant. **4.** To stay awake at night while serving as a guard, sentinel, or watchman. **5.** To stay awake at night as a religious exercise; keep vigil. —*tr.* **1.** To look at steadily; observe carefully or continuously. **2.** To guard; keep a watchful eye on. **3.** To observe the course of mentally; keep informed about: *watching the opinion polls.* —**watch it.** *Informal.* To be careful. Usually used in the imperative. —**watch out.** To be careful or on the alert; take care. ~*n.* **1.** The act or process of keeping awake or mentally alert, especially for the purpose of guarding. **2.** Any of the periods into which the night was formerly divided; a part of the night. **3.** A period of close observation, often in order to discover something: *a watch during the child's illness.* Also in combinations: *Crimewatch UK.* **4.** A person or group of persons serving, especially at night, to guard or protect: *a Neighbourhood Watch scheme.* **5.** The post or period of duty of a guard, sentinel, or watchman. **6.** A small, portable timepiece, driven by springs or powered by batteries; especially one worn on the wrist or carried in the pocket. **7. a.** A period of wakefulness, especially one observed as a religious vigil. **b.** A wake. **8.** *Nautical.* **a.** Any of the periods of time into which the day aboard ship is divided and during which a part of the crew is assigned to duty. **b.** The members of a ship's crew on duty during a specific watch. **c.** A chronometer on a ship. —**keep watch.** To be alert, looking or waiting (for someone). —**on the watch.** On the lookout; waiting for something or someone expectantly. [Middle English *wa(c)chen, wecchen,* Old English *wæccan,* to be or stay awake, keep *vigil.*]

watch·case (wóch-kayss) *n.* The casing for the mechanism of a watch.

watch·dog (wóch-dog) *n.* **1.** A dog trained to guard property. **2.** A person who serves as a guardian or protector against waste, loss, or illegal practices. Often used adjectivally: *a watchdog committee.*

watch·er (wóchər) *n.* **1.** One that watches or observes. **2.** One who observes the progress or development of something. Used in combination: *a China-watcher.* **3.** A person keeping vigil, as at a sick person's bedside.

watch·ful (wóchf'l) *adj.* **1.** Closely observant or alert; vigilant. **2.** *Archaic.* Awake; not sleeping. —See Synonyms at **aware.** —**watch·ful·ly** *adv.* —**watch·ful·ness** *n.*

watch glass *n.* **1.** A concavo-convex glass disc used to cover the face of a watch. **2.** A similarly shaped shallow glass dish used as a beaker cover or evaporating surface.

watch·mak·er (wóch-maykər) *n.* One whose occupation is making or repairing watches. —**watch·mak·ing** *n.*

watch·man (wóch-mən) *n., pl.* -**men** (-mən, -men). A man employed to stand guard or keep watch.

watch night *n.* A religious service held on New Year's Eve, especially by Methodists.

watch pocket *n.* A small pocket in a waistcoat, originally intended for holding a pocket watch.

watch·tow·er (wóch-towr, -tow-ər) *n.* An observation tower upon which a guard or lookout is stationed to keep watch, as for enemies or forest fires or over prisoners.

watch·word (wóch-wurd) *n.* **1.** A prearranged reply to a challenge, as from a guard or sentry; a password. **2.** A rallying cry; a slogan embodying the essential principles of a group.

wa·ter (wáwtər ‖ *U.S. also* wóttər, *so also in compounds*) *n.* **1.** A clear, colourless, nearly odourless and tasteless liquid, H_2O, essential for most plant and animal life and the most widely used of all solvents. Melting point 0°C (32°F), boiling point 100°C (212°F), relative density (4°C) 1.0000. **2. a.** Any of various forms of water: *salt water; holy water.* **b.** *Usually plural.* Naturally occurring mineral water, as at a spa: *taking the waters at Bath.* **3. a.** Any body of water, such as a sea, lake, river, or stream. **b.** *Plural.* A particular stretch of sea or ocean; especially, the territorial waters of a state: *escorted out of British waters.* **4.** Water as supplied to consumers; the water supply: *turning off the water for repairs.* **5. a.** Depth of water considered in terms of its suitability for navigation. **b.** The level of the tide: *high water.* **6.** Any one of the liquids passed out of the body, such as urine, perspiration, or tears. **7.** *Often plural.* The fluid surrounding the foetus in the uterus; amniotic fluid. **8.** An aqueous solution of any substance, especially a gas: *ammonia water.* **9.** A wavy finish or sheen, as of a fabric. **10.** *Finance.* Shares in a company that has watered its share capital. Also called "watered stock". **11. a.** The transparency and lustre of a gem. **b.** Degree; quality: *of the first water.* **12.** In ancient thought, one of the four **elements** *(see).* —**above water.** Out of trouble. —**back water.** To cause a boat to slow, stop, or reverse its motion by placing the blade of an oar or paddle in the water and pushing it towards the boat. —**break water.** To release fluid when the amniotic sac is ruptured in childbirth. Used of a woman in labour. —**by water.** By boat. —**hold water.** To be logical or consistent: *His story holds water.* —**make** (or **pass**) **water.** To urinate. —**pour** or **throw cold water on.** *Informal.* To make discouraging remarks about (a plan, for example). —**water under the bridge.** Something that happened in the past and should be forgotten. ~*v.* **watered, -tering, -ters.** —*tr.* **1.** To pour or sprinkle water upon; make wet. **2. a.** To give drinking water to. **b.** To lead (an animal) to drinking water. **3.** To dilute or weaken by or as if by adding water. Often used with *down.* **4.** To give a sheen to the surface of (silk, linen, or metal). **5.** To increase (the share capital of a company) without any corresponding increase in the true value of the company's assets. **6.** To irrigate (land). —*intr.* **1.** To produce or discharge fluid; *eyes watering from the smoke.* **2.** To produce saliva in anticipation of food. Used of the mouth. **3.** To take on a supply of water. Used of a ship. **4.** To drink water. Used of an animal. —**make (one's) mouth water.** To cause to anticipate with relish. [Middle English *water,* Old English *wæter.*] —**wa·ter** *adj.* —**wa·ter·er** *n.* —**wa·ter·ish** *adj.*

wa·ter·age (wáwtər-ij) *n. British.* **1.** The movement of goods or merchandise by water. **2.** The fee paid for this.

water bailiff *n. British.* An official responsible for enforcing laws on fishing or shipping.

water ballet *n.* **1.** The art of dancelike movement in water; synchronised swimming. **2.** Any performance of this kind.

water bear *n.* A **tardigrade** *(see).*

wa·ter·bed (wáwtər-bed) *n.* An inflatable mattress designed to be filled with water and used as a bed.

water beetle *n.* Any of various aquatic beetles, especially of the family Dytiscidae, characteristically having a smooth, oval body and flattened hind legs specially adapted for swimming.

water bird *n.* Any swimming or wading bird.

water biscuit *n.* A plain unsweetened biscuit.

water blister *n.* A blister having a nonpurulent watery content.

water boatman *n.* Any of various aquatic insects of the families Corixidae and Notonectidae, having long, oarlike hind legs adapted for swimming.

wa·ter·borne (wáwtər-born ‖ -bōrn) *adj.* **1.** Floating on or supported by water; afloat. **2.** Transported by water, as freight may be. **3.** Transmitted in water, as a disease germ may be.

wa·ter·brain (wáwtər-brayn) A disease of sheep, **gid** *(see).*

water brash *n.* Regurgitation of watery acid from the stomach; heartburn.

wa·ter·buck (wáwtər-buk) *n.* Any of several African antelopes of the genus *Kobus,* having curved, ridged horns and frequenting swamps or bodies of water.

water buffalo *n.* A large buffalo, *Bubalus bubalis,* of southern Eurasia having spreading backward-curving horns and often domesticated, especially as a draught animal. Also called "carabao".

water bug *n.* Any of various insects of wet places; especially, a large aquatic insect of the family Belostomatidae.

wa·ter·bus (wáwtər-buss) *n.* A large motorboat used for carrying fare-paying passengers on rivers or canals, as in Venice.

water cannon *n.* An apparatus capable of firing water at high pressure, used especially to disperse crowds or control riots.

Water Carrier. The constellation and sign of the zodiac **Aquarius** *(see).* [Translation of Latin *aquarius.*]

water chestnut *n.* **1.** A Chinese sedge, *Eleocharis tuberosa,* having an edible corm. **2.** The succulent corm of this plant, used in Oriental cookery. **3.** A floating aquatic plant, *Trapa natans,* native to Asia, bearing nutlike fruit. Also called "water caltrop".

water clock *n.* Any of various time-keeping or time-measuring devices, such as a **clepsydra** *(see),* based on the motion of running water. Also called "water glass".

water closet *n. Abbr.* **w.c.** A room or booth containing a lavatory.

wa·ter·col·our (wáwtər-kullər) *n.* **1.** A paint composed of a water-soluble pigment. **2.** A work done in watercolours. **3.** The art of using watercolours. —**wa·ter·col·our** *adj.* —**wa·ter·col·our·ist.**

wa·ter·cool (wáwtər-kōōl) *tr.v.* -**cooled, -cooling, -cools.** To cool (an engine) with water, especially with circulating water.

water cooler *n.* A vessel, device, or apparatus for cooling, storing, and dispensing drinking water.

wa·ter·course (wáwtər-kawrss ‖ -kōrss) *n.* **1.** A **waterway** *(see).* **2.** The bed or channel of a waterway.

wa·ter·cress (wáwtər-kress) *n.* **1.** A plant, *Nasturtium officinale,* native to Eurasia, growing in freshwater ponds and streams and having pungent leaves used in salads, soups, and as a garnish. **2.** Any of several similar, related plants.

water cure *n. Medicine.* Hydropathy or hydrotherapy.

water cycle *n.* The cycle of evaporation and condensation that controls the distribution of the earth's water as it evaporates from the seas, rivers, and lakes into the atmosphere, condenses into a precipitated form as rain, sleet, or snow and flows back into the sea by way of rivers. Also called "hydrological cycle", "hydrologic cycle".

water diviner *n.* A person able to detect the existence of water under the ground by using a divining rod.

water dog *n.* **1.** A dog accustomed to water, especially one trained to retrieve waterfowl. **2.** One who is at home in or on the water.

watered-down (wáwtərd-dówn ‖ *U.S. also* wóttərd-) *adj.* Reduced in effectiveness or impact.

watered stock *n. Finance.* **Water** (*see*).

wa·ter·fall (wáwtər-fawl) *n.* A steep descent of water from a height; a cascade.

water flea *n.* Any of various small aquatic crustaceans of the order Cladocera, characteristically swimming with a jerking motions.

Wa·ter·ford (wáwtər-fərd ‖ wóttər). *Irish* **Contae Port Lairge.** County of Munster province, south Republic of Ireland. Bordering the Atlantic Ocean, it has the Comeragh and Monavullagh mountain ranges, and is crossed by the rivers Suir and Blackwater. Its chief industries are the raising of cattle, fishing, brewing, and distilling. Waterford is the county town.

Waterford glass *n.* A fine kind of bluish-tinted domestic glassware made in the town of Waterford in the Republic of Ireland.

wa·ter·fowl (wáwtər-fowl) *n.*, *pl.* **-fowls** or collectively **waterfowl.** A swimming bird, such as a duck or goose.

wa·ter·front (wáwtər-frunt) *n.* An area of land, especially built-up land in a town, abutting on a body of water, such as a lake or harbour. Also used adjectivally: *A waterfront café.*

water gap *n.* A transverse cleft in a mountain ridge through which a stream flows.

water gas *n.* A fuel gas containing about 40 per cent carbon monoxide, 50 per cent hydrogen, and small amounts of carbon dioxide and nitrogen, made by passing steam and air over heated coke.

water gate *n.* **1.** A **floodgate** (*see*). **2.** A gate that provides access to a body of water.

water gauge *n.* An instrument indicating the level of water, as in a boiler, tank, reservoir, or stream. Also called "water glass".

water glass *n.* **1.** A drinking glass or goblet. **2.** A tube or similar structure having a glass bottom for making observations below the surface of the water. **3. Sodium silicate** (*see*). **4.** A water gauge. **5.** A **water clock** (*see*).

water hammer *n.* **1.** A banging noise heard in a water pipe following an abrupt alteration of the flow with resulting pressure surges. **2.** A similar noise in steam pipes, caused by steam bubbles entering a cold pipe partially filled with water.

water hen *n.* Any of various birds of the family Rallidae, especially the gallinule.

water hole *n.* A small natural depression in which water collects; especially, a pool used by animals as a watering place.

water hyacinth *n.* A floating aquatic plant, *Eichhornia crassipes,* native to tropical America, having bluish-purple flowers and often forming dense masses in ponds and streams.

water ice *n.* A dessert made from frozen puréed fruit or flavoured syrup. Also called "sorbet".

wa·ter·ing can (wáwtər-ing ‖ *U.S. also* wóttər-) *n.* A vessel with a long spout and sometimes a perforated nozzle, used to water plants. Also *U.S.* "watering pot".

watering hole *n. Informal.* A place serving alcoholic drinks to the public. Used humorously. [After the watering places where wild animals congregate to drink.]

watering place *n.* **1.** A place where animals find water. **2.** A health resort with mineral springs; a spa.

water jacket *n.* A casing containing water circulated by a pump, used around a part to be cooled, especially in water-cooled internal-combustion engines.

water jump *n.* An obstacle consisting of a pond or ditch, usually preceded by a fence, over which riders or athletes must jump in a steeplechase or show jumping competition.

wa·ter·less (wáwtər-ləss, -liss ‖ *U.S. also* wóttər-) *adj.* **1.** Without water; dry. **2.** Not requiring water. Said especially of a cooling system.

water level *n.* **1.** The height of the surface of a body of water. **2.** *Geology.* A **water table** (*see*). **3.** The water line of a ship.

water lily *n.*, *pl.* **water lilies. 1.** Any of various aquatic plants of the genus *Nymphaea,* having floating leaves and showy, variously coloured flowers; especially, the common white water lily *N. alba.* **2.** Any of various similar or related plants.

water line *n.* **1.** *Nautical.* **a.** The line on the hull of a ship to which the water surface rises. **b.** Any of several lines parallel to this marked on the hull of a ship, indicating the depth to which the ship sinks under various loads. **2.** A line or stain, as that left on a sea wall, indicating the height to which water has risen or may rise.

wa·ter·logged (wáwtər-logd ‖ *U.S. also* wóttər-, -lawgd) *adj.* **1.** Heavy and sluggish in the water because of flooding in the hold. Said of a ship. **2.** Soaked or saturated with water: *waterlogged fields.* [WATER + *-logged,* probably "made (unmanageable) like a log in water", from LOG.]

Wa·ter·loo (wáwter-lóo ‖ *U.S. also* wótter-) *n.* A disastrous or crushing defeat. Usually used in the phrase *meet one's Waterloo.* [After *Waterloo* in Belgium, where Napoleon met his defeat (1815).]

water main *n.* A principal pipe in a system of pipes for conveying water, especially one installed underground.

wa·ter·man (wáwtər-mən) *n.*, *pl.* **-men** (-mən, -men). **1.** A boatman. **2.** A skilled oarsman. **—wa·ter·man·ship** *n.*

wa·ter·mark (wáwtər-maark) *n.* **1.** A mark showing the height to

which water has risen; especially, a line indicating the levels of high and low tide. **2.** A translucent design impressed on paper during manufacture and visible when the finished paper is held to the light. **3.** The metal pattern that produces this design.

~*tr.v.* **watermarked, -marking, -marks. 1.** To mark (paper) with a watermark. **2.** To impress (a pattern or design) as a watermark.

water meadow *n.* A meadow irrigated and fertilised by the periodic flooding of a nearby river.

wa·ter·mel·on (wáwtər-mellən) *n.* **1.** A vine, *Citrullus vulgaris,* native to Africa, cultivated for its large, edible fruit. **2.** The fruit of this plant, having a hard green rind and sweet, watery, pink or reddish flesh.

water milfoil *n.* Any of various aquatic plants of the genus *Myriophyllum,* having feathery, finely dissected leaves.

water mill *n.* A mill with water-driven machinery.

water moccasin *n.* A venomous snake, *Agkistrodon piscivorus,* of the southern United States. Also called "cottonmouth".

water mole *n. Australian.* The **duck-billed platypus** (*see*).

water nymph *n.* A nymph living in or near water, such as a **naiad,** a **nereid,** or an **oceanid,** (*all of which see*).

water of crystallisation *n.* Water in chemical combination with a crystal and necessary for the maintenance of crystalline properties but capable of being removed by sufficient heat.

water of hydration *n.* Water chemically combined with a substance so that it can be removed, as by heating, without substantially changing the chemical composition of the substance.

water ouzel *n.* A bird, the **dipper** (*see*).

water pepper *n.* **1.** A marsh plant, *Polygonum hydropiper* having reddish stems, greenish flowers, and acrid-tasting leaves. **2.** Any of various similar and related plants. Also called "smartweed".

water pimpernel *n.* A plant, the **brookweed** (*see*).

water pipe *n.* **1.** A pipe that carries water. **2.** A **hookah** (*see*).

water pistol *n.* A toy gun that squirts water.

water plantain *n.* Any of various aquatic plants of the family Alismataceae, having branching clusters of small white or pinkish flowers; especially, *Alisma plantago-aquatica.*

water polo *n.* A water sport with two teams of swimmers, each of which tries to pass a ball into the other's goal.

wa·ter·pow·er (wáwtər-powər) *n.* **1.** The power of running or falling water as used for driving machinery, especially for generating electricity. **2.** A source of such power, such as a waterfall. **3.** A water right owned by a mill.

wa·ter·proof (wáwtər-próof ‖ -próof) *adj.* **1.** Impenetrable to or unaffected by water. **2.** Made of or treated with rubber, plastic, or a sealing agent to resist water penetration.

~*n.* A waterproof material or garment.

~*tr.v.* **waterproofed, -proofing, -proofs.** To make waterproof. [WATER + -PROOF.]

water purslane *n.* A trailing weed, **purslane** (*see*).

water-rail (wáwtər-rayl) *n.* A shy, marsh-dwelling bird of northern Europe, *Rallus aquaticus,* having a long, red bill.

water rat *n.* **1.** Any of various semiaquatic rodents, such as the water vole or muskrat. **2.** *Slang.* One who frequents a waterfront area, especially a loafer or petty thief.

water rate *n.* A charge levied on consumers for the use of a public water supply.

wa·ter·re·pel·lent (wáwtər-ri-péllənt, -rə-) *adj.* Resisting penetration by but not entirely impervious to water.

wa·ter·re·sis·tant (wáwtər-ri-zístənt, -rə-) *adj.* Resistant to wetting but not waterproof.

water right *n.* The right to draw or otherwise make use of water from a particular source, such as a lake, irrigation canal, or stream.

water sapphire *n.* A deep-blue cordierite from Sri Lanka often used as a gemstone.

wa·ter·scape (wáwtər-skayp) *n.* A seascape.

water scorpion *n.* Any of various aquatic insects of the family Nepidae, having a respiratory tube that resembles a scorpion's tail.

wa·ter·shed (wáwtər-shed) *n.* **1.** A ridge of high land dividing two areas that are drained by different river systems. **2.** The region draining into a river, river system, or body of water. **3.** A crucially important time or event; a turning point. [Probably translation of German *Wasserscheide.*]

wa·ter·side (wáwtər-sīd) *n.* Land bordering any body of water; a bank; a shore. **—wa·ter·side** *adj.*

wa·ter·ski (wáwtər-skee) *intr.v.* **-skied, -skiing, -skis.** To ski on water while being towed by a speedboat.

~*n.* A broad ski used in water-skiing. **—wa·ter·ski·er** *n.*

water snake *n.* Any of various aquatic or semiaquatic snakes of the genus *Natrix.*

water softener *n.* **1.** Any substance that reduces the temporary or permanent hardness of water. **2.** Any device or apparatus used to treat water in order to reduce its hardness.

water soldier *n.* A perennial aquatic plant, *Stratiotes aloides,* that remains submerged except at flowering time, when rosettes of long, narrow, serrated leaves, surrounding three-petalled white flowers, break the surface.

water spaniel *n.* A spaniel of a breed characterised by a curly, water-resistant coat, often used for retrieving waterfowl.

water spider *n.* A spider, *Argyroneta aquatica,* that constructs and lives in an underwater chamber, which it fills with air bubbles trapped in the hairs of its body.

wa·ter·spout (wáwtər-spowt) *n.* **1.** A funnel-shaped tornado or lesser whirlwind occurring over water and resulting in a whirling column of spray and mist. Compare **tornado**. **2.** A hole or pipe from which water is discharged.

water sprite *n.* A sprite or nymph living in or near the water.

water strider *n.* A **pondskater** *(see)*.

water supply *n.* **1.** The water available for a community or region. **2.** The sources and delivery system of such water.

water table *n.* **1.** The level under the ground in permeable or porous rock below which the ground is saturated with water. Also called "water level". **2.** A projecting ledge, moulding, or stringcourse on a building, designed to throw off rainwater.

water tiger *n.* The predacious larva of a **diving beetle** *(see)*.

wa·ter·tight (wáwtər-tīt) *adj.* **1.** So assembled or constructed that water cannot enter or escape; waterproof. **2.** Having no flaws or loopholes; incapable of being faulted or misconstrued: *a watertight argument; a watertight contract.*

water tower *n.* **1.** A standpipe or tank mounted on a tower used as a reservoir or for maintaining equal pressure on a water system.

water vapour *n.* Water diffused as a vapour in the atmosphere, especially at a temperature below the boiling point.

water vole *n.* A large aquatic vole, *Arvicola terrestris*. Also called "water rat".

water wagtail *n.* The **pied wagtail** *(see)*.

wa·ter·way (wáwtər-way) *n.* **1.** A river, channel, canal, or other navigable body of water used for travel or transport. Also called "watercourse". **2.** A channel at the edge of a ship's deck to drain away water.

wa·ter·weed (wáwtər-weed) *n.* **1.** Any of various aquatic plants. **2.** Pondweed.

water wheel *n.* **1.** A wheel propelled by falling or running water, used as a source of power. **2.** A wheel, with buckets attached to its rim, used for raising water.

water wings *pl.n.* A device consisting of a pair of joined inflatable waterproof bags placed under the arms of a person, especially a child, learning to swim.

wa·ter·works (wáwtər-wurks) *pl.n.* **1. a.** The reservoirs, tanks, buildings, pumps, pipes, and other apparatus that constitute a public water supply system. **b.** A single unit, such as a pumping station, within such a system. Often used with a singular verb. **2.** An exhibition of moving water, such as a fountain or waterfall. **3.** *Informal.* **a.** Tears: *turned on the waterworks.* **b.** The urinary system.

wa·ter·y (wáwtəri ‖ *U.S. also* wóttəri) *adj.* **-ier, -iest. 1.** Filled with, consisting of, or containing water; moist; wet: *watery soil.* **2.** Resembling or suggestive of water; liquid. **3. a.** Containing too much water; diluted: *watery soup.* **b.** Sodden, as from overcooking in water. **4.** Without force; insipid: *watery prose.* **5.** Secreting or discharging water or watery fluid, especially as a symptom of disease. —**wa·ter·i·ness** *n.*

watery grave *n.* Death by drowning.

Wat·ling Street (wót-ling). Roman road in England. It ran from London via St. Albans and Leicester to Wroxeter near Shrewsbury.

Wat·son-Crick model (wóts'n-krík) *n.* The molecular model constructed by J.D. Watson and F.H.C. Crick to show the structure of DNA. See **double helix.**

Wat·son (wóts'n), **James Dewey** (1928–). U.S. biologist. With Francis Crick he worked out the detailed structure of DNA (deoxyribonucleic acid), which led to the unravelling of the genetic code. He shared the Nobel prize for medicine (1962).

Watson, John Christian (1867–1941). Australian statesman. He was leader of the Labor Party (1901–1907), and became (1904) Australia's first Labor prime minister.

watt (wot) *n. Abbr.* **W** An SI unit of power equal to one joule per second. [After James WATT.]

Watt (wot), **James** (1736–1819). British engineer. He made fundamental improvements to the Newcomen steam engine, which eventually resulted in the modern high-pressure steam engine.

wat·tage (wóttij) *n.* **1.** An amount of power, especially electric power, expressed in watts. **2.** The electric power required by an appliance or device.

Wat·teau (wótō, *French* va-tó), **(Jean) Antoine** (1684–1721). French painter, the originator of the *fêtes galantes* (scenes of gallantry). Among his masterpieces is the *Embarcation for Cythera* (1717).

watt-hour (wót-ówr) *n. Abbr.* **W-hr, whr.** A unit of energy, especially electrical energy, equal to the energy of one watt acting for one hour and equivalent to 3,600 joules.

wat·tle (wótt'l) *n.* **1.** Poles intertwined with twigs, reeds, or branches for use in construction, as of walls or fences. **2.** Materials thus used. **3.** A fleshy, often brightly coloured fold of skin hanging from the neck or throat, characteristic of certain birds and some lizards. **4.** Any of various Australian trees or shrubs of the genus *Acacia.* ~*tr.v.* **wattled, -tling, -tles. 1.** To construct from wattle. **2.** To weave into wattle. **3.** To bind together by intertwining twigs or other material. [Middle English *wattel,* Old English *watel, watul*†.] —**wat·tle** *adj.* —**wat·tled** *adj.*

wattle and daub *n.* Wattle plastered with clay or mud, formerly used as a building material. —**wattle-and-daub** *adj.*

wat·tle·bird (wótt'l-burd) *n.* **1.** Any of several birds of the genus *Anthochaera*, of Australia and adjacent regions, having wattles on each side of the head. **2.** Any of various New Zealand birds of the family Callaeidae, having wattles on either side of the bill.

watt·me·ter (wót-meetər) *n.* An instrument for measuring in watts the power flowing in a circuit.

Wa·tu·si (wə-tóo-zi, waa-, -si) *n., pl.* **-sis** or collectively **Watusi.** A

member of a pastoral people of Rwanda and Burundi in central equatorial Africa, distinguished by their tall stature.

Waugh, Evelyn (Arthur St. John) (1903–1966). British novelist. His satirical novels, such as *Decline and Fall* (1928) and *Vile Bodies* (1930), lampooned fashionable society. His later works, notably *Brideshead Revisited* (1945), revealed his interest in Roman Catholicism, to which he converted (1930).

wave (wayv) *v.* **waved, waving, waves.** —*intr.* **1.** To be moved back and forth or up and down by or as by a current of air; shake, sway, flutter, or undulate: *branches waving in the wind.* **2.** To make a signal with an up-and-down or back-and-forth movement with the hand or with an object in the hand: *waved at us from across the street.* **3.** To have an undulating, wavelike form or appearance; curve or curl: *Her hair waves naturally.* —*tr.* **1.** To move or sweep back and forth or up and down through the air, either once or repeatedly: *waved her fan; waved his magic wand.* **2. a.** To signal or express by waving the hand or something held in the hand: *He waved goodbye.* **b.** To signal to (a person) to move in a specified direction: *waved us on; waved him aside.* **3.** To arrange into curves, curls, or undulations: *wave one's hair.*

~*n.* **1. a.** A ridge or swell moving along the surface of a large body of water and generated by the action of gravity or the wind. **b.** A small ridge or swell moving across the interface of two fluids and dependent on the surface tension. **2.** *Often plural.* The sea or the surface of the sea: *vanished beneath the waves.* **3.** Something resembling a wave or waves, as **a.** A moving curve or a succession of curves in or upon a surface; an undulation: *waves of wheat in the wind.* **b.** A curve or a succession of curves, as in the hair. **c.** Any curved shape, outline, or pattern. **4.** A movement up and down or back and forth: *a wave of the hand.* **5.** A sudden surge or rise, as of an emotion or pattern of behaviour, sweeping irresistibly over an individual or through a group; a surge: *a wave of indignation; a wave of panic selling.* **6.** A widespread, persistent meteorological condition, especially of temperature: *a cold wave.* **7.** A group of people, animals, or instances that act, move, or exist together, especially one of a series or succession: *came with the first wave of settlers.* **8.** *Physics.* **a.** A disturbance or oscillation propagated from point to point in a medium or in space and described, in general, by mathematical specification of its amplitude, velocity, frequency, and phase. **b.** A graphic representation of the variation of such a disturbance with time. **9.** *Plural. Chiefly U.S. Slang.* A disturbance or upset. Used in the phrase *make waves.* [As verb, Middle English *waven,* Old English *wafian,* to move back and forth (especially with the hands). As a noun, perhaps variant (influenced by the verb WAVE) of Middle English *wawe, waghe,* probably Old English *wǣg,* motion, wave.] —**wavelike** *adj.* —**wav·er** *n.*

wave·band (wáyv-band) *n.* A range of frequencies, especially any of those assigned to radio transmissions.

wave equation *n.* **1.** A partial differential equation in one, two, or three dimensions, the solution of which represents the propagation of a wave with constant velocity. **2.** The fundamental equation of wave mechanics, the **Schrödinger wave equation** *(see).*

wave·form (wáyv-fawrm) *n.* The mathematical representation of a wave, especially a graph of amplitude at a fixed point against time.

wave front *n.* A surface of a propagating wave that is the locus of all points having identical phase, the surface being usually, but not always, perpendicular to the direction of propagation.

wave function *n.* A mathematical function used in wave mechanics to describe a given state of a quantum system, the square of the amplitude of the function at a given point being representative of the probability of the system in that state being found at that point.

wave-guide (wáyv-gīd) *n. Electronics.* A system of material boundaries in the form of a solid dielectric rod or dielectric-filled tubular conductor, usually of rectangular cross-section, capable of guiding high-frequency electromagnetic waves.

wave·length (wáyv-length, -lengkth ‖ -lenth) *n.* **1.** *Physics.* In a periodic wave, the distance between two points of corresponding phase in consecutive cycles. **2.** *Informal.* A person's characteristic way of thinking and feeling: *We're not on the same wavelength.*

wave·let (wáyv-lit, -lət) *n.* A small wave or ripple.

wa·vell·ite (wáyvə-līt) *n.* A white, yellowish, or brownish hydrated aluminium phosphate, $Al_5(PO_4)_4(OH)_6 \cdot 9H_2O$, that occurs usually as small spheres with radiating internal structure. [After William *Wavell* (died 1829), British physician.]

wave mechanics *n.* The formulation of quantum mechanics, based on the wave equation of Schrödinger.

wave-me·ter (wáyv-meetər) *n.* A device for determining the wavelength or frequency of radio waves.

wave number *n.* The frequency of a wave divided by its velocity of propagation; the reciprocal of the wavelength.

wave-par·ti·cle duality (wáyv-pártik'l) *n. Physics.* The exhibition of both wavelike and particle-like properties by a single entity, such as a photon or an electron. See **quantum theory.**

wave power *n.* Energy obtained by using the momentum of waves to generate electricity. —**wave-pow·ered** *adj.*

wa·ver (wáyvər) *intr.v.* **-vered, -vering, -vers. 1.** To swing or move back and forth; sway. **2.** To show irresolution or indecision; vacillate. **3.** To become uncertain or unsure; falter: *Her confidence never wavered.* **4.** To tremble, quaver, or shake. Used of a sound, such as a voice or a musical note. **5.** To flicker, flash, or glimmer. Used of light. —See Synonyms at **hesitate, swing.**

~*n.* An act of wavering. [Middle English *waveren,* to wander, stray, fluctuate, from Old Norse *vafra,* to move unsteadily, hover.]

—wa·ver·er n. **—wa·ver·ing·ly** adv.

wave theory n. A theory put forward by Christian Huygens (1629–95) that light is transmitted in the form of waves. Compare **corpuscular theory.**

wave train n. Physics. A succession of similar wave pulses.

wave trap n. An electronic filtering device designed to exclude unwanted signals or interference from a receiver.

wa·vy (wáyvi) adj. **-vier, -viest. 1.** Moving or proceeding in a wavelike form or motion; sinuous. **2.** Having curls, curves, or undulations: wavy hair. **3.** Characteristic of, resembling, or suggestive of waves. **4.** Abounding in, having, or rising in waves: a wavy sea. **—wav·i·ly** adv. **—wav·i·ness** n.

waw. Variant of **vav.**

wax¹ (waks) n. **1. a.** Any of various natural or synthetic, viscous or solid heat-sensitive substances, consisting essentially of high molecular weight hydrocarbons or esters of fatty acids, characteristically insoluble in water but soluble in most organic solvents. **b.** A substance secreted by bees; beeswax. **c.** A waxy substance found in the ears; cerumen. **2.** A solid plastic or pliable liquid substance of mineral origin, primarily petroleum, such as ozocerite or paraffin, used in paper coating, as insulation, in crayons, and often in medicinal preparations. **3.** A resinous mixture used by shoemakers to wax their thread. **4.** Any person or thing resembling or suggestive of wax, especially in being readily moulded and impressionable. ~tr.v. **waxed, waxing, waxes.** To coat or treat with wax. ~adj. Made of or resembling to wax. [Middle English wax, wexe, Old English weax, wæx, beeswax.]

wax² intr.v. **waxed, waxing, waxes. 1.** To increase gradually in size, number, strength, or intensity. **2.** To show an increasing illuminated area; increase in illumination or progress towards being full. Used of the moon. Compare **wane. 3.** To grow or become as specified: wax angry. [Middle English wexen, Old English weaxan.]

wax³ n. British Informal. A temper; a rage. Not in current usage.

wax bean n. The **butter bean** (see).

wax·ber·ry (wáks-bəri, -bri) n., pl. **-ries.** The waxy fruit of the wax myrtle or the snowberry.

wax·bill (wáks-bil) n. Any of various tropical Old World birds of the genus Estrilda and related genera, having a short, often brightly coloured waxy beak.

wax·en (wáks'n) adj. **1.** Consisting of or covered with wax. **2.** Suggestive of wax, as: **a.** Pale. **b.** Smooth and shiny. **c.** Pliable or impressionable.

wax insect n. Any insect that secretes wax, especially the Oriental species Ericerus pe-la, bred on a small scale for its wax.

wax myrtle n. A shrub, Myrica cerifera, of the southeastern United States, having evergreen leaves and small, berry-like fruit with a waxy coating. Also called "candleberry".

wax palm n. Any of several palm trees that yield wax, such as Copernica cerifera, the source of carnauba wax, or Ceroxylon andicola, of South America.

wax paper n. Also **waxed paper.** Paper that has been made moistureproof by treatment with wax.

wax·plant (wáks-plaant ‖ -plant) n. A tropical Old World vine, Hoya carnosa, having waxy white or pinkish flowers.

wax·wing (wáks-wing) n. Any of several birds of the genus Bombycilla, having crested heads, predominantly brown plumage, and waxy red tips on the secondary wing feathers.

wax·work (wáks-wurk) n. **1.** The art of modelling in wax. **2. a.** Figures or ornaments made of wax; especially, life-size wax representations of famous persons. **b.** A single such representation. **3.** Plural. An exhibition of waxwork in a museum. **—wax·work·er** n.

wax·y¹ (wáksi) adj. **-ier, -iest. 1.** Resembling wax in colour or consistency, especially: **a.** Pale, smooth, and lustrous. **b.** Pliable or impressionable. **2.** Consisting of, abounding in, or covered with wax. **—wax·i·ness** n.

waxy² adj. British Informal. Bad-tempered; annoyed. Not in current usage.

way (way) n. Also regional **ways** (wayz) (for sense 9). **1. a.** A road, path, or track providing a route from one place to another. **b.** Such a road considered as a place where people live: She lives over the way. **c.** A specific street: Landsdowne Way. **d.** A right of way in law. **2. a.** Room or space free of obstacles and allowing forward movement: clear the way for a parade; get out of the way. **b.** An absence of factors impeding progress or action; opportunity for advance or activity: an agreement that has opened the way for a lasting peace. **3.** A course that is or may be used in going from one place to another: Show me the way to go home. **4. a.** Progress or travel along a particular route, in a particular direction, or towards a particular end: on my way to work; leading the way in the fight against cancer. **b.** Forward movement or progress towards a desired end, effected as specified: elbowed his way to the front; fought her way to the top in a competitive business. **c.** Forward motion or rate of progress of a vessel through water: The ship gathered way. **5.** A path or course of experience, life, or conduct: went our separate ways after the war. **6. a.** A method or manner of performing an action or achieving an end: There must be some way of mending it; Should I do it this way? **b.** A means or expedient that may be employed to effect a result: had no way of contacting you. **7. a.** Often plural. A characteristic or habitual mode of living, behaving, or happening: the American way of life; mend one's ways; these little debts have a way of mounting up. **b.** A particularly effective or persuasive manner: a way with words; has a way with women. **8.** Free-

dom or scope to do as one wishes: if I had my way; always gets her own way. **9.** Distance in general, whether spatial, temporal, or conceptual: a good way off; have come some way towards an agreement. **10. a.** Direction of motion or aspect: come this way; glanced my way. **b.** A district or region considered as lying in a specified direction: call by if you're ever over our way; down Mexico way. **11.** An aspect, particular, or feature: I agree with you in some ways. The situation is in no way comparable. **12.** The range or scope of one's observation or experience: Wealth never came his way. **13.** Informal. A state or condition, especially with regard to health or prosperity: in a bad way financially. **14.** Type, category, or description: not much in the way of a plot. **15.** Plural. A set of parallel longitudinal strips on a surface that serves to guide a moving part in a machine. **16.** Plural. Nautical. The timbered structure from which a ship slides when launched. **—See Synonyms at method. —by the way** or **by.** Incidentally; in passing. **—by way of. 1.** Through; by route of. **2.** As a means of; in order to serve as: He made no comment by way of apology. **—give way. 1.** To yield, submit, or agree. **2.** To fall or break down under pressure. **—go out of (one's** or **the) way.** To inconvenience oneself in doing something beyond that which is required. **—have** or **want it both ways.** To have or want the benefit or enjoyment of two states of affairs that are mutually incompatible. **—in a way.** To some extent. **—put (someone) in the way of.** To provide with (an opportunity of gaining an advantage). **—see (one's) way (clear) to.** To be willing or find it possible to do something. **—under way. 1.** In motion or operation; already initiated or started. **2.** Making progress or headway. **3.** Nautical. Not anchored and not moored to a fixed object. ~adv. Informal. **1.** At a great distance; far: way off yonder. **2.** By a great distance or to a great degree: way over budget. [Middle English wey(e), wei(e), way, Old English weg, a road, path. Adverbial use, from AWAY.]

Synonyms: way, path, route, course, passage, pass, trail.

-way adj. comb. form. Indicates composition from a specified number of elements: a two-way mirror; a three-way partnership.

way·bill (wáy-bil) n. A document containing a list of goods and shipping instructions relative to a shipment.

way·far·er (wáy-fair-ər) n. One who travels; especially, one who travels by foot. [Middle English weyfarere : wey, WAY + fare, a journey, travelling, Old English faru.] **—way·far·ing** adj.

wayfaring tree n. A shrub, Viburnum lantana, having clusters of white flowers and berries that turn from red to black. [It frequently grows along roadsides.]

way·lay (way-láy ‖ wáy-lay) tr.v. **-laid, -laying, -lays. 1.** To lie in wait for and ambush. **2.** To stop and accost unexpectedly. **—way·lay·er** n.

way·leave (wáy-leev) n. A right of way over or through land, as for the transport of goods or the running of a pipeline that differs from an ordinary right of way in being granted to an applicant for a specific purpose. [WAY + LEAVE (permission).]

Wayne (wayn), **John,** born Marion Michael Morrison (1907–79). U.S. film actor. He is noted for his tough hero roles in classic westerns such as Stagecoach (1939), Red River (1948), and True Grit (1969), for which he won an Academy Award.

way-out (wáy-ówt) adj. Informal. Strange or unconventional.

-ways adj. & adv. comb. form. Indicates manner, direction, or position; for example, **sideways.** [Middle English -ways, -weys, from way(e)s, wey(e)s, in (such) a way, Old English weges, adverbial genitive of weg, WAY.]

ways and means pl.n. **1.** Methods or resources that may be used to achieve a particular end. **2.** The methods of raising the revenue needed to meet the expenditure of a state.

way·side (wáy-sīd) n. The side or edge of a road. **—fall by the wayside.** To fail to continue; give up. ~adj. Near or at the edge of a road: a wayside inn.

way·ward (wáy-wərd) adj. **1.** Wanting one's own way in spite of the advice or wishes of another; wilful; headstrong. **2.** Swayed by caprice; erratic; unpredictable. **—See Synonyms at contrary, unruly.** [Middle English, short for awayward, turned away : AWAY + -WARD.] **—way·ward·ly** adv. **—way·ward·ness** n.

way·worn (wáy-wawrn ‖ -wōrn) adj. Wearied from travelling.

Wb Physics. weber.

WbN west by north.

WbS west by south.

W.C. water closet.

W.C.C. World Council of Churches.

W/Cdr. Wing Commander.

we (wee; weak form wi) pron. The first person plural pronoun in the nominative case. **1.** Used to represent the speaker or writer and one or more others that share in the action of a verb. **2.** Sometimes used instead of I by a monarch, or by an editor who purports to speak for a publication. **3.** Informal. Used in place of you in playful intimacy, especially with children, or in a patronising manner: Are we going to eat our cereal? **4.** Often used to represent people in general: We cannot see beyond the grave. **—See Usage note at me.** [Middle English we, Old English wē.]

W.E.A. Workers' Educational Association.

weak (week) adj. **weaker, weakest. 1.** Lacking physical strength, energy, or vigour; feeble: He was weak after his illness. **2.** Liable to fail under pressure, stress, or strain; lacking resistance: a weak link in a chain. **3.** Lacking firmness of character, strength of will, or force of conviction. **4. a.** Lacking effectiveness or force; inadequate: a weak defence. **b.** Not easily defended or sustained: in a weak bargaining position. **5. a.** Lacking strength or intensity: a weak voice. **b.** Having a low concentration of an active or essential ingredient: weak tea; a weak gin and tonic. **6.** Lacking the capacity to function well or in a normal manner; unsound or easily upset: a weak stomach; a weak heart. **7.** Having or showing less than average ability, talent, or resources in a specified field: a weak student; a weak batting line-up. **8.** Based on or showing faulty logic, lack of coherence, or poor presentation; not persuasive or convincing: a weak argument; a weak plot. **9.** Incapable of the effective exercise of authority; lacking the power or political will to rule: a weak government; weak leadership. **10.** Lacking or deficient in a specified thing, as a quality or component. **11.** Linguistics. Of or designating those verbs in English or other Germanic languages that form a past tense by means of a dental suffix; for example, start, started; have, had; bring, brought. Compare **strong. 12.** Phonetics. Unstressed or unaccented. **13.** Prosody. Designating a verse ending having a final unstressed syllable. **14.** Finance. Marked by or showing lack of firmness and a falling tendency in prices or value: a weak pound. [Middle English waike, we(i)ke, from Old Norse veikr, pliant, flexible.] —**weak·ly** adv.

Synonyms: weak, feeble, frail, infirm, decrepit, debilitated.

weak·en (wéekən) v. **-ened, -ening, -ens.** —tr. To make weak or weaker. —intr. To become weak or weaker. —**weak·en·er** n.

weaker sex n. The female sex. Usually used facetiously, preceded by the.

weak·fish (wéek-fish) n., pl. **-fishes** or collectively **weakfish.** Any of several marine food and game fishes of the genus Cynoscion; especially, C. regalis, of North American Atlantic waters. [Obsolete Dutch weekvische, weekvis : week, soft, WEAK (probably from its soft, fleshy mouth, which pulls very weakly on a line when caught) + Middle Dutch visch, vis, FISH.]

weak interaction n. An interaction between elementary particles that is some 10^{12} times weaker than the strong interaction and is responsible for some particle decays, the beta decay of a radioactive nucleus, and for the emission and absorption of neutrino. Also called "weak force". Compare **electromagnetic interaction, gravitational interaction, strong interaction.**

weak-kneed (wéek-néed) adj. Irresolute; timid.

weak·ling (wéekling) n. A person of weak constitution or character.

weak·ly (wéekli) adj. **-lier, -liest.** Sickly; delicate in health.

weak-mind·ed (wéek-míndid) adj. **1.** Irresolute; indecisive. **2.** Feeble-minded; foolish. —**weak-mind·ed·ness** n.

weak·ness (wéek-nəss, -niss) n. **1. a.** The state or quality of being weak. **b.** An instance or display of this. **2.** A defect or failing. **3. a.** A special fondness; a foible: a weakness for chocolates. **b.** Something for which one has an irresistible desire. —See Synonyms at **fault.**

weak sister n. U.S. Informal. A member of a group who is considered a weakling or an incompetent.

weal¹ (weel) n. Archaic. **1.** Prosperity; happiness: in weal and woe. **2.** The welfare of the community; the general good: the public weal. [Middle English we(o)le, Old English we(o)la, wealth, well-being.]

weal² n. **1.** A ridge on the flesh raised by a blow; a welt. **2.** A hard, raised, white patch on the skin caused by acute irritation, as from an insect bite or nettle sting. Also called "wheal". [Variant (influenced by WHEAL) of WALE (ridge).]

weald (weeld) n. British. Archaic. **1.** A woodland. **2.** An area of open rolling upland. [Middle English weld(e), weeld, Old English weald, variant of wald, WOLD.]

wealth (welth) n. **1.** A great quantity of valuable material possessions or resources; riches. **2.** The state of being rich; affluence. **3.** A profusion or abundance: a wealth of advice. **4.** Economics. All goods and resources having economic value. [Middle English welthe, well-being, riches, from wele, WEAL (welfare).]

wealth·y (wélthi) adj. **-ier, -iest. 1.** Prosperous; affluent. **2.** Possessing in abundance. —**wealth·i·ly** adv. —**wealth·i·ness** n.

wean¹ (ween) tr.v. **weaned, weaning, weans. 1.** To accustom (the young of a mammal) to solid food after a diet of mother's milk. **2.** To detach (a person) from that to which he is accustomed or devoted. [Middle English wenen, wa(i)nen, Old English wenian, to accustom, train, wean.]

wean² (ween ‖ wayn) Northern British n. A child. [Contraction of Scottish wee ane, wee one.]

wean·ling (wéenling) n. A recently weaned child or animal. —adj. Recently weaned.

weap·on (wéppən) n. **1.** Any instrument or bodily part used as a means of attack or defence in combat. **2.** Any means employed to get the better of another. —tr.v. **weaponed, -oning, -ons.** To supply with a weapon; arm. [Middle English wepen, wepne, Old English wæp(e)n, from Germanic wæpnam† (unattested).]

weap·on·eer (wéppə-néer) n. **1.** An individual who arms and otherwise prepares a nuclear weapon for release onto a target. **2.** An individual who designs or devises nuclear or other weapons. —**weap·on·eer·ing** n.

weap·on·ry (wéppənri) n. Weapons collectively.

wear¹ (wair) v. **wore** (wawr ‖ wōr), **worn** (wawrn ‖ wōrn), **wearing, wears.** —tr. **1.** To be dressed in or have on or about the body, as for clothing, adornment, or protection: wearing a hat; must wear your seat belt; wore a delightful perfume. **2.** To have or carry habitually on one's person: wears glasses. **3.** To affect or exhibit: wear a smile. **4.** To bear, carry, or maintain in a specified manner: wears her hair long. **5.** To fly or display (colours), as does a ship, jockey,

or knight. **6.** To impair, consume, waste, efface, or erode by or as if by long or hard use, friction, or exposure to the elements: worn by repeated child-bearing. Often used with away, down, or off: shoes worn down at the heels. **7. a.** To produce by constant use, rubbing, or exposure: They eventually wore hollows in the steps. **b.** To bring to the specified condition through attrition or prolonged use: pebbles worn smooth. **8. a.** To fatigue; weary: worn by the effort. **b.** To diminish; exhaust: His incessant criticism wore her patience. **9.** British Informal. To accept or agree to; find acceptable: asked for a day off, but her boss wouldn't wear it. —intr. **1. a.** To withstand the effects of use or activity in the specified way: That suit will wear badly. **b.** To withstand the effects of time and experience in the specified way: Those friendships wear best that are based on mutual understanding. **2.** To be brought to the specified condition through attrition or prolonged use: This jersey has worn through; His excuses wore thinner over the years. **3.** To pass gradually or tediously: The hours wore on endlessly. —**wear down.** To break down the resistance of by relentless pressure. —**wear off. 1.** To diminish gradually and vanish: The pain wore off. **2.** To become effaced; rub off: The gilt soon wore off. —**wear out. 1.** To make or become unusable through heavy use. **2.** To use up; consume: She is wearing out her welcome. **3.** To exhaust; tire completely.

~n. **1.** The act of wearing or state of being worn; use: The coat has had heavy wear. **2.** Clothing, especially of a specified kind or for a specified use. Often used in combination: footwear; rainwear; menswear. **3.** Gradual impairment, waste, or diminution from use or attrition: signs of wear. **4.** The capacity to withstand use; durability: The tyre has plenty of wear left. [Middle English wer(i)en, Old English werian, wear, carry.] —**wear·a·bil·i·ty** n. —**wear·a·ble** adj. —**wear·er** n.

wear² v. **wore, worn, wearing, wears.** Nautical. —tr. To make (a sailing ship) come about with the wind aft: wear ship. —intr. To come about with the stern to windward. [Earlier weare†.]

wear and tear n. Loss, damage, or depreciation resulting from ordinary use or exposure.

wea·ri·ful (wéer-i-f′l) adj. Rare. **1.** Wearisome; tedious. **2.** Full of weariness. —**wea·ri·ful·ly** adv. —**wea·ri·ful·ness** n.

wea·ri·less (wéer-i-ləss, -liss) adj. Tireless. —**wea·ri·less·ly** adv.

wear·ing (waír-ing) adj. Tiring; exhausting. —**wear·ing·ly** adv.

wea·ri·some (wéer-i-səm) adj. Causing exasperation or fatigue; tedious. —**wea·ri·some·ly** adv. —**wea·ri·some·ness** n.

wea·ry (wéer-i) adj. **-rier, -riest. 1.** Exhausted, especially from prolonged exertion; fatigued. **2.** Expressive of or prompted by fatigue or resignation: a weary smile. **3.** Exhausted in patience, tolerance, spirit, or interest: weary of his jibes. **4. a.** Causing fatigue; exhausting. **b.** Irksome; tedious; wearisome. —See Synonyms at **tired.**

~v. **wearied, -rying, -ries.** —tr. To make weary; fatigue. —intr. To become weary; grow tired or exasperated. [Middle English wery, weri(e), Old English wērig, from Germanic wōriga (unattested).] —**wear·i·ly** adv. —**wear·i·ness** n.

wea·sand (wéez'nd, wizz'nd) n. Archaic. The gullet or throat. [Middle English wesa(u)nt, wesand, wosen, Old English wāsend, wǣsend (unattested), gullet, from West Germanic wāsand- (unattested).]

wea·sel (wéez'l) n. **1.** Any of various small carnivorous mammals of the genus Mustela, having a slender body, long tail, short legs, and brownish fur; especially, M. nivalis. **2.** Chiefly U.S. A treacherous or sneaky person.

~intr.v. U.S. Informal. **weaseled, -seling, -sels.** To be evasive; equivocate. —**weasel out.** U.S. Informal. To back out of a situation or commitment in a sneaky or cowardly manner. [Middle English wesele, wesill, Old English we(o)sule, wesle, from West Germanic wisulōn† (unattested).] —**wea·sel·ly** adv.

weasel word n. A word of an equivocal nature used to deprive a statement of its force or to evade a direct commitment. [Alluding to the weasel's supposed ability to suck up the contents of an egg without doing obvious damage to the shell.]

weath·er (wéthər) n. **1.** The state of the atmosphere at a given time and place, described by specification of variables such as temperature, moisture, wind velocity, and pressure. **2.** The unpleasant or destructive effects of atmospheric conditions: We must protect the houses from the weather. **b.** Violent conditions, such as high winds and heavy rain, at sea and in the air: We flew into weather over the Azores. —**make heavy weather of.** To exaggerate the difficulty of something to be done. —**under the weather.** Informal. **1.** Slightly indisposed; unwell. **2. a.** Drunk. **b.** Suffering from a hangover.

~v. **weathered, -ering, -ers.** —tr. **1.** To expose to the action of the weather, as for drying, seasoning, or colouring. **2.** To discolour, disintegrate, wear, or otherwise affect by exposure. **3.** To pass through safely; survive: weather a crisis. **4.** To cause (a roof, for example) to slope so as to shed water. **5.** Nautical. To pass to windward of, despite bad weather. —intr. **1.** To become discoloured, disintegrate, or otherwise show the effects of exposure to the weather: The cottage walls had weathered and mellowed. **2.** To resist or withstand the effects of weather or adverse conditions.

~adj. **1.** Of, pertaining to, or designating the side of a ship towards the wind; windward. **2.** Of, pertaining to, or used in weather forecasting. [Middle English weder, wethyr, Old English weder.]

weather balloon n. A balloon used to carry instruments aloft to gather meteorological data in the atmosphere.

weath·er·beat·en (wéthər-beet'n) adj. **1.** Worn by exposure to the weather. **2.** Tanned or coarsened from being outdoors.

weath·er·board (wéthər-bawrd ‖ -bôrd) n. Any of a series of boards having one edge thicker than the other, overlapped to clad the outer walls of buildings. Also *U.S.* "clapboard".

weath·er·board·ing (wéthər-bawrding ‖ -bórding) *n.* **1.** Weatherboards collectively. **2.** A wall or other area made of weatherboards.

weath·er·bound (wéthər-bownd) *adj.* Delayed, halted, or kept indoors by bad weather.

weath·er·cock (wéthər-kok) *n.* **1.** A weather vane in the form of a cock. **2.** One that is fickle.
~*intr.v.* **weathercocked, -cocking, -cocks.** To have a tendency to veer in the direction of the wind. Used of an aircraft or a missile.

weather deck *n.* The deck of a ship that is open to the sky.

weather eye *n.* An eye trained to recognise indications of weather changes. **—keep (one's) weather eye open.** To stay alert; keep on the lookout.

weather forecast *n.* A description of prevailing and expected weather conditions, as in a newspaper or a television broadcast. **—weather forecaster** *n.*

weath·er·glass (wéthər-glaass ‖ -glass) *n.* A barometer or similar instrument used to indicate atmospheric conditions.

weath·er·ing (wéthəring) *n.* Any of the chemical or mechanical processes by which rocks exposed to the weather decay to soil.

weath·er·ly (wéthərli) *adj. Nautical.* Capable of sailing close to the wind with little drift to leeward. **—weath·er·li·ness** *n.*

weath·er·man (wéthər-man) *n., pl.* **-men** (-men). **1.** A person who makes weather forecasts, especially on radio or television. **2.** *Capital* **W.** A member of a U.S. anarchist group active in the late 1960s.

weather map *n.* A map or chart depicting the meteorological conditions over a specific geographical area at a specific time.

weath·er·proof (wéthər-proof ‖ -proof) *adj.* Able to withstand exposure to weather without damage.
~*tr.v.* **weatherproofed, -proofing, -proofs.** To make weatherproof.

weather ship *n.* An oceangoing vessel equipped to make meteorological observations.

weather station *n.* A station at which meteorological observations are gathered, recorded, and released.

weath·er·strip (wéthər-strip) *tr.v.* **-stripped, -stripping, -strips.** To fit or equip with weather stripping.

weather stripping *n.* **1.** A narrow piece of material, such as rubber, felt, or metal, installed around doors and windows to protect an interior from external extremes of temperature. Also called "weather strip". **2.** Such pieces collectively.

weather vane *n.* A vane for indicating wind direction.

weath·er·wise (wéthər-wīz) *adj.* Skilled in predicting shifts in the weather, public opinion, or the like.

weath·er·worn (wéthər-wawrn ‖ -wórn) *adj.* Weather-beaten.

weave (weev) *v.* **wove** (wōv) or **weaved** (only form for transitive sense 6), **woven** (wōv'n) or *rare* **wove, weaving, weaves.** —*tr.* **1. a.** To make (cloth) by interlacing the threads of the weft and the warp on a loom. **b.** To interlace (threads) into cloth. **2.** To construct by interlacing or interweaving strips or strands of material: *weave a basket.* **3. a.** To interweave or combine (elements) into a whole: *He wove the incidents into a story.* **b.** To fashion or contrive (something complex or elaborate) in this way. **4.** To introduce (something new or contrasting) into some material or composition: *wove folk tunes into the symphony.* **5.** To spin (a web or cocoon, for example). Used of a spider or insect. **6.** To make (a path or way) by winding in and out or from side to side: *weave one's way through traffic.* —*intr.* **1. a.** To engage in weaving an article. **b.** To work at a loom. **2.** To move in and out or from side to side: *The dancers wove in and out of the trees; He was so drunk that he wove from side to side.* **—get weaving.** *British Informal.* **1.** To get started; begin some activity. **2.** To hurry up.
~*n.* The pattern, method of weaving, or construction of a fabric: *a twill weave; a loose weave.* [Weave, wove, woven; Middle English *weven, wo(o)f,* woven or *weven,* Old English *wefan, wæf, wefen.*]

weav·er (wéevər) *n.* **1.** One who weaves, especially as an occupation. **2.** A weaverbird.

weav·er·bird (wéevər-burd) *n.* Any of various chiefly tropical Old World birds of the family Ploceidae, many of which build complex communal nests of intricately woven vegetation. Also called "weaver", "weaver finch".

weaver's hitch *n. Nautical.* A knot, the **sheet bend** *(see).* Also called "weaver's knot".

web (web) *n.* **1. a.** A textile fabric, especially one being woven on a loom or in the process of being removed from it. **b.** The structural part of cloth as distinguished from its pile or pattern. **2.** A latticed or woven structure; an interlacing of materials. **3.** A structure of threadlike filaments characteristically spun by spiders or certain insect larvae. **4.** Anything intricately constructed; a complex or elaborate network, especially one designed to ensnare or deceive: *a web of deceit.* **5.** A fold of skin or membranous tissue; especially, the membrane connecting the toes of certain water birds and mammals. **6.** The vane of a feather. **7.** *Architecture.* The surface between the ribs of a ribbed vault. **8.** A metal sheet or plate connecting the heavier sections, ribs, or flanges of any structural element. **9.** A thin metal plate or strip, as the bit of a key, the blade of a saw, or the like. **10.** A continuous roll of paper, such as newsprint, especially of the kind used in web printing presses. **11.** *Capital* **W.** The **World Wide Web** *(see).* Also used adjectivally: *Web sites; Websites.*
~*tr.v.* **webbed, webbing, webs. 1.** To provide with a web. **2.** To cover or envelop with a web. **3.** To ensnare in a web. [Middle English *web(be),* Old English *web(b).*] **—webbed** *adj.* **—web·by** *adj.*

Webb (web), **Beatrice,** born Beatrice Potter (1858–1943). British socialist. See **Webb, Sidney James.**

Webb, Mary (Meredith) (1881–1927). British novelist. She wrote

tragic novels, the best-known being *Precious Bane* (1924).

Webb, Sidney (James), 1st Baron Passfield (1859–1947). British economist and socialist. He was one of the founders of the London School of Economics (1895). He and his wife, Beatrice Webb, helped to found (1884) the Fabian Society. Together they wrote *History of Trade Unionism* (1894) and *English Local Government* (1906–29).

web·bing (wébbing) *n.* **1.** Sturdy cotton or nylon fabric woven in widths generally of from one to six inches, for use where strength is required, as for seat belts, brake lining, or upholstering. **2.** Anything forming a web.

we·ber (váybər, wébbər) *n. Abbr.* **Wb** The SI unit of magnetic flux equal to the magnetic flux that in linking a circuit of one turn produces in it an electromotive force of one volt as it is uniformly reduced to zero within one second. [After Wilhelm E. *Weber* (1804–91), German physicist.]

Web·er (váybər), **Carl Maria von** (1786–1826). German composer. He is best known for his opera, *Der Freischütz* (1821), which was among the first in the German romantic tradition.

Weber, Max (1864–1920). German social scientist. He was one of the founders of the modern analytical method of sociology. His works include *The Protestant Ethic and the Spirit of Capitalism* (1904) and *Methodology of the Social Sciences* (1904).

Webern (váybərn), **Anton von** (1883–1945). Austrian composer. His works, which are characterised by brevity and tonal dissonance, include two symphonies and a concerto for nine instruments (1934).

web-foot·ed (wéb-footid) *adj.* Having feet with webbed toes.

web member *n.* Any of the structural elements connecting the top and bottom flanges of a lattice girder or the outside members of a truss.

web offset *n.* An offset method of printing using a web press.

web press *n.* A rotary printing press that prints on a continuous roll of paper.

web·ster (wéb-stər) *n. Archaic.* A weaver. [Middle English *web(e)-ster,* Old English *webbestre,* feminine of *webba,* a weaver, from *webb,* a **WEB.**]

Webster, John (*c.* 1580–*c.* 1634). English dramatist. His works include *The White Devil* (1612), and *The Duchess of Malfi* (1623).

Webster, Noah (1758–1843). U.S. lexicographer and author. He is best known for his *American Dictionary of the English Language* (1828), which did much to standardise American spelling.

web·wheel (wéb-weel, -hweel) *n.* **1.** Any wheel in which the rim, spokes, and hub are cast or formed from one piece of metal. **2.** A spokeless wheel.

wed (wed) *v.* **wedded, wed** or **wedded, wedding, weds.** —*tr.* **1.** To take as husband or wife; marry. **2.** To perform the marriage ceremony for; join in matrimony. **3. a.** To join, unite, or associate. **b.** To cause to be indissolubly attached or devoted. Used chiefly in the passive: *wedded to socialism.* —*intr.* To take a husband or wife; marry. [Middle English *wedden,* Old English *weddian,* to engage (to do something), marry.]

we'd (weed, wid). Contraction of *we had, we should,* or *we would.*

Wed. Wednesday.

wed·ding (wédding) *n.* **1.** The act of marrying; the ceremony or celebration of a marriage. Also used adjectively: *wedding guests.* **2.** The anniversary of a marriage: *a silver wedding.* **3.** A close association or union. **—See Synonyms at marriage.**

wedding breakfast *n.* A celebratory meal taken by the bride and groom and guests after a wedding.

wedding cake *n.* A large decorated cake, often arranged in tiers, pieces of which are given to wedding guests and kept for absent friends and relations.

wedding ring *n.* A ring, often a plain gold band, given by one spouse to the other during the wedding ceremony and typically worn throughout married life.

wedge (wej) *n.* **1.** A piece of metal or wood tapered into a solid V-shape for insertion in a narrow crevice and used for splitting, tightening, securing, or levering. **2. a.** Anything in the shape of a wedge: *a wedge of cheese.* **b.** A wedge-shaped formation, as in ground warfare. **3.** A wedge heel. **4.** Any tactic, event, policy, or idea that tends to divide or split associations of people. **5.** *Meteorology.* A region of relatively high atmospheric pressure in which the isobars are V-shaped. **6.** *Golf.* An iron with a very slanted face, used to lift the ball from sand, for example. **7.** Any of the triangular characters of cuneiform writing. **—the thin end of the wedge.** An apparently unimportant occurrence that seems likely to lead to more or more serious occurrences of a similar nature.
~*v.* **wedged, wedging, wedges.** —*tr.* **1.** To split or force apart with or as if with a wedge. **2.** To tighten or fix in place with a wedge. **3.** To crowd, push, or force into a limited space. —*intr.* To become lodged or jammed like a wedge. [Middle English *wegge,* Old English *wecg,* a wedge, ingot of metal.]

wedge heel *n.* **1.** A solid heel on a woman's shoe that forms a continuous wedge shape tapering from the back of the shoe to the front. **2.** A shoe with a wedge heel. Also called "wedge", *U.S.* "wedgie".

Wedg·wood (wéj-wood) *n.* A type of pottery or china made by Josiah Wedgwood (1730–95) and his successors; especially, jasperware, a fine ware with classical figures in white cameo relief on an unglazed blue or otherwise coloured background.

Wedgwood blue *n.* A clear, pale or greyish blue, characteristically found as an unglazed background on Wedgwood pottery.

Wedgwood, Dame C(icely) V(eronica) (1910–). British historian.

Among her works are *The Thirty Years' War* (1938), *Oliver Cromwell* (1939), and *The Political Career of Rubens* (1975).

wed·lock (wĕd-lok) *n.* The state of being married; matrimony. See Synonyms at **marriage.** —**out of wedlock.** Of, to, or by parents not married to one another: *born out of wedlock.* [Middle English *wedlo(c)ke,* Old English *wedlāc,* "pledge-giving", marriage vow : *wedd,* a pledge + *-lāc,* suffix denoting activity.]

Wednes·day (wĕnz-di, wĕdd'nz-, -day) *n. Abbr.* **Wed.** The day of the week following Tuesday; the third day of the working week. [Middle English *Wodnesday,* Old English *Wōdnesdæg,* "Woden's day" (translation of Latin *Mercurii diēs,* "day of Mercury").]

wee¹ (wee) *adj.* **weer** (wee-ər), **weest** (wee-ist). **1.** Very small; tiny. **2.** Very early: *the wee small hours.*
~*n. Scottish.* A short time; a little bit: *bide a wee.* [Middle English *we,* from *we(i),* a little, a small amount, Old English *wæge,* a weight.]

wee² (wee) *n.* Also **wee-wee** (wee-wee). *British Informal.* **1.** Urine. **2.** An act of urinating. Used by and to children.
~*intr.v.* **weed, weeing, wees.** Also **wee-wee.** *British Informal.* To urinate. Used by and to children. [20th century : shortened from *wee-wee†.*]

weed (weed) *n.* **1.** A plant considered undesirable, unattractive, or troublesome; especially, one growing where it is not wanted in cultivated ground. **2.** Any of various usually common or abundantly growing plants. Usually used in combination: *seaweed; chickweed.* **3.** The leaves or stems of a plant as distinguished from the seeds: *dill weed.* **4. a.** *Informal.* Tobacco. Often preceded by *the.* **b.** *Informal.* A cigarette. **c.** *Chiefly U.S. Slang.* Marijuana. **5.** Something useless, detrimental, or worthless; especially, an animal unfit for breeding. **6.** *Informal.* A weak, slightly built, or cowardly person.
~*v.* **weeded, weeding, weeds.** —*tr.* **1.** To remove weeds from; clear of weeds: *weed a flowerbed.* **2. a.** To remove (weeds). Usually used with *out: weed out dandelions.* **b.** To eliminate as unsuitable or unwanted. Usually used with *out: weed out unqualified applicants.* —*intr.* To remove weeds from a plot. [Middle English *weed,* Old English *wēod†.*] —**weed·er** *n.*

weed·kill·er (weed-killər) *n.* Any substance, such as a synthetic plant hormone, used to kill weeds.

weeds (weedz) *pl.n.* **1.** *Plural.* Mourning clothes: *widow's weeds.* **2.** *Singular. Archaic.* A token of mourning, as a black band worn usually on the sleeve. [Middle English *wede,* a garment, Old English *wǣd* and *wǣde,* a garment, from Germanic *wǣdhiz* (unattested).]

weed·y (wee-di) *adj.* **-ier, -iest. 1.** Full of or consisting of weeds. **2.** Resembling or characteristic of a weed. **3.** *Informal.* Timid; unassertive: *Don't be so weedy.* **4.** *Informal.* Of a thin, slight build. —**weed·i·ly** *adv.* —**weed·i·ness** *n.*

wee folk *pl.n.* Fairies; elves. Preceded by *the.*

week (week) *n. Abbr.* **w., wk. 1. a.** A period of seven days: *a week of rain.* **b.** A seven-day calendar period, especially one starting with Sunday and continuing to the next Saturday: *this week.* **2. a.** A week designated by an event or holiday occurring within it: *Christmas week.* **b.** A week set aside for the honouring of some specified cause or institution: *Gay Pride Week.* **3. a.** The part of a calendar week devoted to work; the working week: *doing a three-day week.* **4. a.** One week from a specified day: *I'll see you Friday week.* **b.** One week ago from a specified day: *It was Friday week that we last met.* [Middle English *wike, weke,* Old English *wice, wicu.*]

week·day (week-day) *n.* Any day of the week except Sunday and, usually, Saturday.

week·end (week-ĕnd, -end) *n.* The end of the week; usually, Saturday and Sunday, and often the period from Friday evening to the end of Sunday evening.
~*adj.* **1.** Occurring or done at the weekend: *a weekend job.* **2.** For use at weekends: *a weekend cottage.*
~*intr.v.* **weekended, -ending, -ends.** To spend the weekend.

week·end·er (week-ĕndər ‖ -endər) *n.* **1.** A person who takes a holiday or pays a visit, especially habitually, at weekends. **2.** *Australian.* A weekend or holiday cottage.

week·ly (week-li) *adv.* **1.** Once a week. **2.** Every week. **3.** By the week.
~*adj.* **1.** Occurring or done once a week or each week. **2.** Computed by the week.
~*n., pl.* **weeklies.** A publication issued once a week.

week·night (week-nīt) *n.* The night or evening of a weekday.

ween (ween) *tr.v.* **weened, weening, weens.** *Archaic.* To think; suppose. [Middle English *wenen,* Old English *wēnan,* from Germanic *wǣniz* (unattested), opinion.]

wee·ny (wee-ni) *adj.* **-nier, -niest.** *Informal.* Very small; tiny; wee. [Blend of WEE and TINY or TEENY.]

weep (weep) *v.* **wept** (wept), **weeping, weeps.** —*tr.* **1.** To mourn; lament or cry over. **2.** To shed (tears). **3.** To bring to a specified condition by weeping: *She wept herself into a state of exhaustion.* **4.** To ooze, exude, or let fall (drops of liquid), as a wound or sore might. —*intr.* **1.** To express intense, usually painful, emotion by shedding tears; shed tears. **2.** To mourn or grieve. Used with *for.* **3.** To emit or run with drops of moisture. —See Synonyms at **cry.**
~*n.* Often *plural. Informal.* A period or fit of weeping. [Middle English *we(o)pen,* Old English *wēpan.*]

weep·er (wee-pər) *n.* **1.** One that weeps. **2.** A hired mourner. **3.** A token of mourning, such as a black hatband or veil.

weep·ing (wee-ping) *adj.* Having slender, drooping branches: *a weeping fig.*

weeping willow *n.* A widely cultivated tree, *Salix babylonica,* native to China, having long, drooping branches and narrow leaves.

weep·y (wee-pi) *adj.* **-ier, -iest.** Tearful; prone to crying.
~*n., pl.* **weepies.** *Informal.* A sentimental work of fiction, especially a film.

wee·ver (wee-vər) *n.* Any of several marine fishes of the family Trachinidae, having venomous spines. [Perhaps from Old French *wivre,* a serpent, viper, from Latin *vīpera,* VIPER.]

wee·vil (wee-vil, wee-v'l) *n. Zoology.* Any of numerous beetles, chiefly of the family Curculionidae and characteristically having a downward-curving snout, that are destructive to plants and stored plant products. [Middle English *wevel,* Old English *wifel,* a beetle.] —**wee·vil·y, wee·vil·ly** *adj.*

wee-wee. Variant of **wee.**

w.e.f. with effect from.

weft (weft) *n.* **1. a.** The horizontal threads interlaced through the warp in a woven fabric; filling; woof. **b.** Yarn to be used for the weft. **2.** Woven fabric. [Middle English *wefte, weft,* Old English *wefta, weft,* from Germanic *weft-* (unattested), from *webh-* (unattested), WEAVE.]

wei·ge·la (wī-gee-lə, wi-, -jee-, wīgilə, *often* wi-jee-li-ə) *n.* Any of various shrubs of the genus *Weigela;* especially, *W. florida,* widely cultivated for its pink, white, or red flowers. [New Latin, after Christian E. *Weigel* (1748–1831), German physician.]

weigh¹ (way) *v.* **weighed, weighing, weighs.** —*tr.* **1.** To determine the weight of by or as if by using scales or a balance. **2.** To measure off, especially by using scales, an amount equal in weight to. Usually used with *out: weigh out a pound of cheese.* **3. a.** To balance in one's mind to determine the worth of; evaluate; consider or compare. Often used with *up: weighed up the pros and cons.* **b.** To choose carefully; deliberate over: *weigh one's words.* **4.** To cause to sag by the addition of weights or burdens; oppress; force down. Used with *down.* **5.** *Nautical.* To raise (anchor). —*intr.* **1.** To have or be of a specified weight. **2.** To carry weight; be considered important; have influence; especially, to have the specified degree of importance or influence: *a fact that weighed heavily in his favour.* **3.** To be a burden or weight; bear down. Used with *on* or *upon: His troubles weighed down on him.* —**weigh into.** To attack. [Middle English *weghen, weien,* Old English *wegan,* to carry, balance in the scale, weigh.] —**weigh·er** *n.*

weigh² *n. Nautical.* Way. Used only in the phrase *under weigh.* [Variant (erroneously from the phrase *to weigh anchor*) of WAY.]

weigh·bridge (way-brij) *n.* A weighing machine having a metal platform at ground level, used for weighing heavy loads such as vehicles.

weigh in *intr.v.* **1.** To be weighed before or after a sporting contest. **2.** To have a specified weight measured at a weigh-in: *weighed in at 15 stone.* **3.** To have one's luggage weighed and checked before boarding an aeroplane. **4.** *Informal.* To enter an argument, discussion, or the like, especially to contribute a telling point: *She weighed in with a few pertinent facts.*

weigh-in (way-in) *n.* The act or occasion of checking the weight of a sports contestant, especially of a boxer before a fight or a jockey after a race.

weight (wayt) *n. Abbr.* **wt. 1.** A measure of the heaviness or mass of an object. **2.** The gravitational force exerted by the Earth or another celestial body on an object, equal to the product of the object's mass and the local value of the acceleration of free fall. **3. a.** A unit measure of this force. **b.** A system of such measures. **4.** The measured heaviness of a specific object. **5.** Any object used principally to exert a force by virtue of its gravitational attraction to the Earth, especially: **a.** A metallic solid used as a standard of comparison in weighing. **b.** An object used to hold something down. **c.** A counterbalance in a machine. **d.** A dumbbell or a solid metal disc balanced on a crossbar, lifted for exercise or in athletic competition. **6.** *Mathematics.* One of a set of numbers assigned as multipliers to quantities to be averaged to indicate the relative importance of each quantity's contribution to the average. **7. a.** Anything heavy; a load. **b.** Burden; oppressiveness; pressure: *the weight of responsibilities.* **8.** The greatest part or stress; preponderance: *the weight of evidence.* **9. a.** Influence; importance; authority: *His opinions carried little weight with her.* **b.** Ponderous quality; significance: *the weight of his words.* **10.** A classification according to comparative lightness or heaviness: *the best boxer in Britain at this weight.* Usually used in combination: *a heavyweight boxer; a lightweight suit.* —See Synonyms at **importance.** —**by weight.** According to weight rather than volume or other measure. —**pull (one's) weight.** To do one's fair share. —**throw (one's) weight about** or **around.** To make an aggressive show of one's importance.
~*tr.v.* **weighted, weighting, weights. 1.** To add heaviness to, by or as if by attaching a weight; make heavy or heavier. **2.** To load down; burden. **3.** To treat (fabric) with chemical substances in order to give it body or extra weight. **4.** *Mathematics.* To assign a weight or weights to. **5.** To cause to have a particular bias or confer a particular advantage: *The entry procedure tends to be weighted in favour of Oxbridge graduates.* **6.** To assign to (a horse) the weight it must carry as a handicap in a race. [Middle English *wighte, weit(e),* Old English *wiht, gewiht.*]

weighting (way-ting) *n.* A special consideration or allowance; especially, an extra payment added to an employee's salary to compensate for high living costs in a particular area: *London weighting.*

weight·less (wayt-ləss, -liss) *adj.* **1.** Having little or no weight. **2.** Experiencing little or no gravitational force. —**weight·less·ly** *adv.* —**weight·less·ness** *n.*

weight·lift·ing (wayt-lifting) *n.* The lifting of heavy weights in a prescribed manner as an exercise or in athletic competition. **—weight·lift·er** *n.*

weight training *n.* Working out with weights for physical fitness.

weight·watch·er (wáyt-wochər) *n.* One who takes care to keep his body weight within certain limits, as by diet and exercise. **—weight·watching** *n.*

weight·y (wáyti) *adj.* **-ier, -iest. 1.** Heavy; ponderous. **2.** Burdensome; oppressive. **3.** Of great consequence; momentous: *weighty decisions.* **4.** Carrying weight, as: **a.** Forceful; efficacious: *a weighty argument.* **b.** Authoritative; influential. —See Synonyms at **heavy.** **—weight·i·ly** *adv.* **—weight·i·ness** *n.*

Weil (vīl) **Simone** (1909–43). French mystic and religious philosopher. Her writings include *Waiting on God* (1951), and *The Need for Roots* (1952).

Weill (vīl), **Kurt** (1900-1950). German composer. He collaborated with Brecht on *The Threepenny Opera* (1928) and *The Rise and Fall of the City of Mahagonny* (1927).

Wei·mar (vī-maar). City in central Germany. Situated on the river Ilm, it was a cultural centre during the 18th and 19th centuries. It was the capital of Saxe-Weimar-Eisenach (1815–1918) and was where the constitution of the Weimar Republic (1918 – 1933), the name of the German Republic, was drawn up. It was overthrown by Hitler.

Wei·mar·an·er (vī-mə-raanər, wī-, -raánər) *n.* A large dog of a breed originating in Germany, having a smooth greyish coat.

weir (weer) *n.* **1.** A dam placed across a river or canal to raise or divert the water, as for a millrace, or to regulate the flow. **2.** A fence or wattle placed in a stream to catch or retain fish. [Middle English *wer(r)e,* Old English *wer.*]

weird (weerd) *adj.* **weirder, weirdest. 1.** Suggestive of or concerned with the supernatural; unearthly; eerie; uncanny. **2.** Of an odd and inexplicable character; unusual; bizarre; fantastic. **3.** *Archaic.* Of or pertaining to fate or the Fates.
~n. Scottish & Archaic. **1.** Fate; destiny. **2.** One's assigned lot or fortune; kismet. **—dree (one's) weird.** To endure or submit to one's fate. [Middle English *werde, wirde,* having power to control fate, from *wird, werd,* fate, destiny, Old English *wyrd.*] **—weird·ly** *adv.* **—weird·ness** *n.*
Synonyms: *weird, eerie, uncanny, unearthly.*

weird·o (weérd-ō) *n., pl.* **-oes.** Also **weird·ie** (weérdi). *Slang.* An unusually strange or eccentric person.

Weiss (vīss), **Peter** (1916–82). Swedish author, born in Germany. His works include *The Persecution and Assassination of Marat* (1964) and *The Investigation* (1965).

Weiz·mann (vīts-man), **Chaim (Azriel)** (1874–1952). Israeli statesman and chemist. He was the first president of Israel (1949–1952).

we·ka (wéckə) *n.* A flightless bird, *Gallirallus australis,* of New Zealand, having brown, mottled plumage. [Maori.]

welch. Variant of **welsh.**

Welch. *Archaic.* Variant of **Welsh.**

wel·come (wélkəm) *adj.* **1.** Received with pleasure and hospitality into one's company or home: *a welcome guest.* **2.** Agreeable or gratifying: *a welcome respite.* **3.** Cordially permitted or invited: *You're welcome to join us.* **4.** Used as a polite acknowledgment of an expression of gratitude: *"Thank you!" "You're welcome!".* —**make (someone) welcome.** To receive someone hospitably.
~n. **1.** A cordial greeting to or reception of an arriving person. **2.** The state of being welcome: *to outstay one's welcome.* **3.** A greeting or reception of the specified kind: *an unfriendly welcome.*
~tr.v. **welcomed, -coming, -comes. 1.** To greet, receive, or entertain cordially or hospitably. **2.** To receive or accept gladly: *welcome a little privacy.* **3.** To greet or receive in a particular, usually unpleasant, way: *was welcomed with a hail of bullets.*
~interj. Used to greet cordially a visitor or recent arrival. [Middle English *welcume,* alteration (by influence of WELL and of Old French *bien venu*) of Old English *wilcuma,* a welcome guest, and *wilcume,* the greeting of welcome : *wil-,* pleasure + *cuma,* corner.] **—wel·come·ly** *adv.* **—wel·come·ness** *n.* **—wel·com·er** *n.*

weld[1] (weld) *v.* **welded, welding, welds.** *—tr.* **1. a.** To join (metals) by applying heat, sometimes with pressure and sometimes with an intermediate or filler metal having a high melting point. **b.** To produce by welding. **2.** To bring into close association; bring together as a unit. *—intr.* To be or become capable of being welded.
~n. **1.** The union of two metal parts by welding. **2.** The joint so formed. [Variant (influenced by past tense and past participle *welled*) of WELL (to pour forth, in the obsolete sense of to weld).] **—weld·able** *adj.* **—weld·a·bil·i·ty** **—weld·er** *n.* **—weld·less** *adj.*

weld[2] (weld) *n.* **1.** A plant, the **dyer's rocket** *(see).* **2.** The yellow dye obtained from this plant. [Middle English *welde, wold,* Old English *wealde, walde* (unattested).]

wel·fare (wél-fair) *n.* **1. a.** Health, happiness, and general well-being. **b.** Prosperity. **2.** Welfare work. **3.** *U.S.* Social assistance. [Middle English *welfare,* well-being, from the phrase *wel faren,* to fare well, Old English *wel faran* : *wel,* WELL + *faran,* to go, FARE.]

welfare state *n.* **1.** A social system whereby the state assumes primary responsibility for the welfare of its citizens, as by means of government-run health and social security schemes. **2.** A nation characterised by its adoption of this system.

welfare work *n.* Organised work, especially done by government or charitable agencies, designed to improve the social and economic conditions of the poor and other disadvantaged members of society.

wel·far·ism (wélfair-iz'm) *n. U.S.* The set of policies, practices, and social attitudes associated with the welfare state. Used derogatorily.

wel·kin (wélkin) *n. Archaic.* **1.** The vault of heaven; the sky: *make the welkin ring.* **2.** The upper air. [Middle English *w(e)olcne, welken,* a cloud, the sky, firmament, Old English *wolc(e)n.*]

we'll (weel). Contraction of *we will* and *we shall.*

well[1] (wel) *n.* **1.** A deep hole or shaft dug or drilled to obtain water, oil, gas, or the like. **2.** A cavity or space resembling this in shape or function, such as an inkwell. **3.** An open space extending vertically through the floors of a building, as for stairs or ventilation. **4.** An enclosure in a ship's hold for the pumps. **5.** A cistern with a perforated bottom in the hold of a fishing vessel for keeping fish alive. **6.** *British.* The central space in a law court, directly in front of the judge's bench where the counsel or solicitor sits. **7. a.** A spring or fountain. **b.** A mineral spring. **c.** *Plural.* A watering place; a spa. **8.** A source to be drawn upon: *a well of information.*
~v. **welled, welling, wells.** *—intr.* **1.** To rise to the surface, ready to flow. **2.** To rise or surge from some inner source: *She felt anger welling up in her mind.* *—tr.* To pour forth. [Middle English *well(e), walle,* Old English *wœlla, well, wiella.*]

well[2] *adv.* **better** (béttər), **best** (best). **1.** Satisfactorily: *The interview went quite well.* **2. a.** In a good or proper manner; with skill: *sing well.* **b.** With care or attention. **3.** In a comfortable or affluent manner: *live well.* **4.** Advantageously: *married well.* **5. a.** With reason or propriety; properly; reasonably: *I can't very well say no.* **b.** Probably; indeed: *You may well need your umbrella.* **6.** Prudently: *You would do well to say nothing.* **7.** Closely or familiarly; intimately: *I know him well.* **8.** In a kindly or approving manner; graciously; favourably: *speak well of him.* **9.** Thoroughly; completely: *well cooked.* **10.** Entirely; fully: *well worth seeing.* **11. a.** To a considerable or suitable extent or degree: *I'm well pleased.* **b.** *Slang.* Very: *I'm well happy!* **12.** Far: *well in advance.* **Note:** The adverb *well* combines with many adjectives, usually derived from the participles of verbs, to form attributive modifiers before nouns: *a well-regulated life; a well-read woman.* In such use the elements are joined with a hyphen, and are so entered below (e.g. **well-read**). However, when *well* modifies an adjective used predicatively, the two words are usually written separately: *His life was well regulated. The woman is well read.* **—as well. 1.** In addition; also. **2.** With equal or better effect: *I might as well go.* **—as well as.** In addition to; moreover. **—pretty well.** Nearly. **—well and truly.** Completely; absolutely. **—well away. 1.** Having made considerable progress. **2.** *Informal.* Drunk. **—well in with.** In a position to influence or be favoured by: *well in with the management.*
~adj. **1.** In a satisfactory state or circumstances; right; proper. Usually used predicatively: *All is well.* **2. a.** In good health; not ailing or diseased. **b.** Cured or healed. Said chiefly of a wound. **3. a.** Advisable; prudent: *It would be well not to ask.* **b.** Fortunate; gratifying: *It is well that you stayed.* —See Synonyms at **healthy.** **—(just) as well. 1.** Advisable; prudent. **2.** Fortunate; good. **—leave well (enough) alone.** To refrain from meddling with what is satisfactory.
~interj. **1.** Used to express surprise. **2.** Used to introduce a remark, resume a narrative, or simply to gain time to collect one's thoughts. [Middle English *wel(e), well,* Old English *wel.*]
Usage: *As well as,* in the sense of "in addition to", does not have the force of *and,* and therefore a singular noun preceding *as well as* continues to govern a singular verb: *The London firm, as well as its Scottish subsidiary, is short of capital.* A plural verb is sometimes casually used, but is not generally acceptable.

well-advised (wél-əd-vīzd || -ad-) *adj.* **1.** Sensible; prudent: *You'd be well advised to stay.* **2.** Considered; showing careful thought: *a well-advised action.*

well-appointed (wél-ə-póyntid) *adj.* Properly furnished and equipped: *a well-appointed flat.*

well·a·way (wéllə-wáy) *interj.* Also **well·a·day** (-dáy). *Archaic.* Alas! Woe is me!
~n., pl. **wellaways.** Also **well·a·day.** A lamentation. [Middle English *weilawey, wellaway,* Old English *wei lā wei,* variant (influenced by Old Norse *vei,* woe) of *wā lā wā* : *wā,* woe + *lā,* LO + *wā,* woe.]

well-bal·anced (wél-bál-ənst) *adj.* **1.** Evenly proportioned, balanced, or regulated. **2.** Mentally stable; sensible; sane.

well-be·ing (wél-beé-ing, -bee-) *n.* The state of being healthy, happy, or prosperous; welfare.

well-born (wél-bórn) *adj.* Coming of good stock; especially, born of a noble family.

well-bred (wél-bréd) *adj.* **1.** Of good upbringing; well-mannered; refined. **2.** Of good breed or pedigree. Said of an animal.

well-built (wél-bílt) *adj.* **1.** Soundly built. **2.** Tall and muscular.

well-chosen (wél-chōz'n) *n.* Carefully chosen for a deliberate effect: *well-chosen words.*

well-connected (wél-kə-néktid) *adj.* Related to or otherwise connected with upper-class or influential people.

well-dis·posed (wél-diss-pōzd) *adj.* Disposed to be kindly, friendly, or sympathetic.

well-done (wél-dún) *adj.* **1.** Cooked all the way through: *a well-done steak.* **2.** Satisfactorily or properly accomplished.

well-earned (wél-érnd) *adj.* Fully deserved.

Welles (welz), **(George) Orson** (1915–85). American actor and film director. He starred in and directed *Citizen Kane* (1940). His other films include *The Magnificent Ambersons* (1942), *The Third Man* (1949), *The Trial* (1962), and *Catch-22* (1970).

well-fa·voured (wél-fáyvərd) *adj.* Attractive; comely; handsome.

well-formed (wél-fórmd) *adj.* **1.** Having a good shape or attractive form. **2.** Properly constituted according to a set of logical or grammatical rules: *a well-formed formula; a well-formed sentence.*

well-found (wĕl-fównd) *adj.* Properly furnished or equipped; well-appointed: *well-found premises.*

well-found·ed (wĕl-fówndid) *adj.* Well-substantiated; based on sound judgment, reasoning, or evidence.

well-groomed (wĕl-gro͞omd ‖ -gro͝omd) *adj.* 1. Showing attentive care to personal appearance; neat. 2. Carefully tended or curried: *a well-groomed horse.* 3. Trim and tidy: *well-groomed hair.*

well-ground·ed (wĕl-grówndid) *adj.* 1. Adequately versed in a subject; having a sound basic knowledge. 2. Having a sound basis; well-founded.

well-head (wĕl-hĕd) *n.* 1. The source of a well or stream. 2. The top or head of a well, especially an oil well. 3. A principal source or fountainhead.

well-heeled (wĕl-hḗeld) *adj. Slang.* Having plenty of money.

well-hung (wĕl-húng) *adj. Vulgar Slang.* Having a large penis or large genitalia. Said of a man. [WELL + *hung,* in obsolete sense, said especially of animals, "having pendent organs", past participle of HANG.]

wel·lies (wĕllíz) *pl.n. Informal.* Wellington boots.

Wel·ling·ton (wĕlling-tən). Capital of New Zealand, situated on Cook Strait on the south coast of North Island. It was founded in 1840 and has been the seat of government since 1865. Surrounded by mountains, it is a port and industrial centre.

Wellington, Arthur Wellesley, 1st Duke of, also known as The Iron Duke (1769–1852). British soldier and statesman. He commanded the British army during the Peninsular War, defeating the Napoleonic forces in Spain in 1813, and invading France in 1814. He defeated Napoleon at the Battle of Waterloo (1815), which finally ended the Napoleonic wars. He became prime minister (1828–30). He passed the Catholic Relief Bill (1829), but opposed the Reform Bill (1831–32).

Wellington boot *n. Sometimes small w.* 1. A calf- or knee-length, waterproof, rubber, or rubberised boot. Also called "gumboot". 2. A leather boot extending to the top of the knee in front but cut lower at the back. Also called "Wellington". [After the 1st Duke of WELLINGTON.]

wel·ling·ton·i·a (wĕlling-tṓni-ə) *n.* A redwood tree, the **giant sequoia** *(see).* [After the 1st Duke of WELLINGTON.]

well-in·ten·tioned (wĕl-in-ténshənd) *adj.* 1. Well-meant. 2. Well-meaning.

well-knit (wĕl-nít) *n.* 1. Well-built but compact. 2. Tightly constructed or properly put together: *a well-knit story.*

well-known (wĕl-nṓn) *adj.* 1. Widely known; familiar or famous. 2. Fully known.

well-man·nered (wĕl-mánnərd) *adj.* Polite; courteous.

well-mean·ing (wĕl-mḗening) *adj.* Having or prompted by good intentions, though often with unhappy consequences.

well-meant (wĕl-mént) *adj.* Kindly or honestly intended.

well-nigh (wĕl-nī́) *adv.* Nearly; almost.

well-off (wĕl-óff, -áwf) *adj.* 1. In fortunate circumstances. 2. Wealthy; prosperous. 3. Adequately provided.

well-oiled (wĕl-óyld) *adj. Informal.* Drunk.

well-preserved (wĕl-pri-zérvd) *adj.* Not seeming or looking old.

well-read (wĕl-réd) *adj.* Knowledgeable through having read extensively: *clever, but not well read.*

well-rounded (wĕl-równdid) *adj.* 1. Apt and complete: *a well-rounded speech.* 2. Plump and pleasantly curving; shapely: *a well-rounded figure.* 3. a. Marked by breadth, fullness, and variety: *a well-rounded education.* b. Having a broad, full, and varied background and education.

Wells (wĕlz). City of Somerset, southwest England, at the foot of the Mendips. It is known for its cathedral (12th–13th century) with its carved west front, and for its medieval city walls.

Wells (wĕlz), **H(erbert) G(eorge)** (1866–1946). British novelist. He won success with science-fiction works such as *The Time Machine* (1895). His concern for social and political issues was expressed in comic novels such as *The History of Mr. Polly* (1910), and in later theoretical works such as *The Outline of History* (1920).

well-spo·ken (wĕl-spṓkən) *adj.* 1. a. Having an educated, socially acceptable way of speaking. b. Speaking well; articulate. 2. Chosen or expressed with aptness or propriety.

well-spring (wĕl-spring) *n.* 1. The source of a stream or spring; a fountainhead. 2. An abundant source or supply: *a wellspring of ideas.*

well-stacked (wĕl-stákt) *adj. Informal.* Having a full and shapely figure; especially, having large breasts. Said of a woman and often considered offensive.

well-tem·pered (wĕl-témpərd) *adj. Music.* Adjusted to or conforming to the system of equal temperament. Said of a musical instrument or a scale.

well-thought-of (wĕl-tháwt-ov ‖ -uv) *adj.* Respected; esteemed.

well-thought-out (wĕl-thawt-ówt) *adj.* Carefully considered or devised.

well-thumbed (wĕl-thúmd) *adj.* Showing signs of frequent use. Said of a book.

well-timed (wĕl-tímd) *adj.* Occurring or done at an opportune time.

well-to-do (wĕl-tə-do͞o) *adj.* Prosperous; affluent; well-off. [From the phrase *to do well.*]

well-tried (wĕl-tríd) *adj.* Thoroughly tested; of proven value.

well-turned (wĕl-túrnd) *adj.* 1. Shapely: *a well-turned ankle.* 2. Concisely or aptly expressed: *a well-turned phrase.*

well-up·hol·stered (wĕl-up-hṓl-stərd, -əp- ‖ -hól) *adj. Informal.* Fat; corpulent. Used humorously.

well-wish·er (wĕl-wishər) *n.* A person who wishes another well; one who extends good wishes. —**well-wish·ing** *adj. & n.*

well-worn (wĕl-wáwrn ‖ -wórn) *adj.* 1. Showing signs of much wear or use. 2. Repeated too often; trite; hackneyed.

Wels·bach burner (wĕlz-bak; *German* vélss-bakh) *n.* A trademark for a gauze mantle impregnated with cerium and thorium compounds and used with a gas burner that becomes incandescent when heated, producing light. Also called "gas mantle". [After Baron Carl Auer von Welsbach (1858–1929), Austrian chemist.]

welsh, welch (welsh) *intr.v.* **welshed** or **welched, welshing** or **welching, welshes** or **welches.** *Slang.* 1. To swindle a person by not paying a debt or wager. 2. To fail to fulfil an obligation: *welsh on a promise.* [19th century : origin obscure.] —**welsh·er** *n.*

Welsh (welsh) *adj.* Also *archaic* **Welch.** *Abbr.* **W.** Of or pertaining to Wales, its people, its language, or its culture.
~*n.* 1. *Used with a plural verb.* The people of Wales. Preceded by *the.* 2. The Celtic language of Wales. [Middle English *Wal(i)sche,* Old English *Wælisc, Wel(i)sc,* from *W(e)alh,* a Welshman, from Germanic *walhaz* (unattested), foreign, from Latin *Volcae,* name of a Celtic people.]

Welsh corgi *n.* A corgi *(see).*

Welsh dresser *n.* A dresser consisting of a set of open shelves on top of a sideboard or set of cupboards. [Originally made and used in Wales.]

Welsh·man (wĕlsh-mən) *n., pl.* **-men** (-mən, -men). A male native of Wales. —**Welsh·wom·an** *n.*

Welsh onion *n.* A perennial plant, *Allium fistulosum,* originally from Siberia, bearing globose clusters of yellowish-white flowers on a swollen hollow stem.

Welsh poppy *n.* A poppy, *Meconopsis cambrica,* with large yellow flowers.

Welsh rabbit *n.* A dish made of melted or toasted cheese, and sometimes milk, seasonings, and beer, served hot on toast. Also called "Welsh rarebit". [A fanciful culinary term.]

Welsh springer spaniel *n.* See **springer spaniel.**

Welsh terrier *n.* A terrier of a breed originating in Wales, having a wiry black-and-tan coat and resembling a small Airedale.

welt (welt) *n.* 1. A strip of leather or other material stitched into a shoe between the sole and the upper. 2. A strip of material, such as tape or covered cord, sewn into a seam as reinforcement or trimming; welting. 3. a. A ridge or bump raised on the skin by a lash or blow or sometimes by an allergic disorder; a weal. b. *Informal.* A lash or blow producing such a mark.
~*tr.v.* **welted, welting, welts.** 1. To reinforce or trim with a welt or welting. 2. To beat severely; flog. 3. To raise a welt or welts on. [Middle English *welte, walt,* perhaps Old English *wealt†, waelt* (both unattested).]

Welt·an·schau·ung (vĕl-tan-shṓw-o͞ong) *n., pl.* **-ungs** or **-ungen** (-o͞ongən). A comprehensive world view or philosophy of life, especially from a particular standpoint. [German, "world view".]

wel·ter (wĕltər) *intr.v.* **-tered, -tering, -ters.** 1. To writhe, roll, or wallow. 2. To lie soaked in blood. 3. To be deeply immersed or involved in something. 4. To roll and surge, as the sea does.
~*n.* 1. Turbulence; tossing: *"bright welter of wave-cords"* (Ezra Pound). 2. a. A state of upheaval or turmoil. b. A confused mass; a jumble: *a welter of papers and magazines.* [Middle English *welteren,* perhaps from Middle Dutch.]

wel·ter·weight (wĕltər-wayt) *n.* 1. a. An amateur boxer weighing between 63.5 and 67 kilograms (10 stone and 10 stone 8 pounds). b. A professional boxer weighing between 10 stone and 10 stone 7 pounds (63.5 and 66.5 kilograms). 2. A wrestler weighing between 68 and 74 kilograms (10 stone 10 pounds and 11 stone 9 pounds). [19th century *welter†,* heavy-weight horseman or boxer + WEIGHT.]

welt·ing (wĕlting) *n.* Material, such as a cord or strip, used to welt a seam.

Welt·schmerz (vĕlt-shmairts) *n.* Sadness over the evils of the world, especially as an expression of romantic pessimism. [German, "world pain".]

wel·witsch·i·a (wel-wíchi-ə) *n.* A gymnosperm plant, *Welwitschia mirabilis,* found in desert regions of southwest Africa, having a short, upright, mainly underground stem, two straplike leaves, and conelike arrangements of its flowers. [After F.M.J. *Welwitsch* (1807–72), Austrian-born Portuguese botanist.]

Wem·bley (wĕmbli). Area of the Borough of Brent, Greater London. Its stadium is the scene of the annual Football Association Cup Final and similar sporting events.

wen[1] (wen) *n.* A cyst containing sebaceous matter, especially one on the scalp. —**the Great Wen.** London. [Middle English *wenne, wen,* Old English *wen(n).*]

wen[2] *n.* An Old English runic letter represented by the Modern English *w.* [Old English *wen,* variant of *wyn(n),* pleasure, joy (a word beginning with the letter chosen to represent the letter).]

wench (wench) *n.* 1. A young woman or girl; especially, a peasant girl. Now used familiarly or humorously. 2. *Archaic.* A female servant. 3. *Archaic.* A wanton woman; a prostitute.
~*intr.v.* **wenched, wenching, wenches.** *Archaic.* To be promiscuous or consort with prostitutes. Used of a man. [Middle English *wenche,* short for *wenchel,* a girl, maid, Old English *wencel,* a child of either sex, maid.] —**wench·er** *n.*

wend (wend) *v.* **wended** or *archaic* **went** (went), **wending, wends.** —*tr.* To proceed on or along (one's) way; go. —*intr. Archaic.* To go one's way; proceed. [Middle English *wenden,* Old English *wendan,* to turn around or away, direct, happen.]

Wend (wend) *n.* A member of a Slavonic people inhabiting Saxony and Brandenburg. Also called "Sorb", "Sorbian".

Wend·ish (wéndish) *adj.* Of or pertaining to the Wends or their language.
~*n.* The West Slavonic language of the Wends. Also called "Lusatian", "Sorbian".

Wendy house (wéndi) *n. British.* A small model house for children to play in. [After the house built for *Wendy,* a girl in J.M. Barrie's play *Peter Pan* (1904).]

Wens·ley·dale (wénzli-dayl) *n.* 1. A long-haired breed of sheep. 2. A type of white, or sometimes blue, cheese with a crumbly texture. [After *Wensleydale,* North Yorkshire.]

went. 1. Past tense of **go.** 2. *Archaic.* Past tense and past participle of **wend.**

wen·tle·trap (went'l-trap) *n.* Also **wen·del·trap** (wénd'l-). Any of various marine snails of the family Epitoniidae, having a tapering spiral shell with raised longitudinal ridges. [Dutch *wenteltrap,* from Middle Dutch *wendeltrappe,* "winding stair", spiral shell : *wendel,* winding, from *wenden,* to wind + *trappe,* a step, stairs.]

wept. Past tense and past participle of **weep.**

were (wer, wair; *weak form* wər). 1. Plural and second person singular of the past indicative of **be.** 2. Past subjunctive of **be.**

Usage: In clauses expressing clearly hypothetical conditions, *were* is the standard form of the verb *be: if I were you; she spoke as if she were ill. Was* is often heard in such sentences, but generally only in informal speech. When the clause expresses a condition that is not purely hypothetical or contrary to fact, *was* is standard: *I looked to see if/whether the way was clear.* This is also the case in indirect speech: *She asked whether I was happy with the car.* There are, however, several occasions when the hypothetical status of the expression is unclear, and in such cases, usage is mixed *(she spoke as though everything were/was settled);* but *were* continues to be the predominant form in formal contexts, especially in American English. In formal conditional sentences *were* may be inverted: *Were she to study, she would learn* (= *If she were to study she would learn*).

we're (weer). Contraction of *we are.*

weren't (wernt). Contraction of *were not.*

were·wolf (wéer-wulf, waír-) *n., pl.* **-wolves** (-woolvz). In legend and folklore, a person transformed into a wolf or capable of assuming the form of a wolf; a lycanthrope. [Middle English *wer(e)wolf,* Old English *wer(e)wulf :* probably *wer,* a man + *wulf,* a WOLF.]

wer·geld (wúr-geld, waír-) *n.* Also **wer·gild** (-gild). In Anglo-Saxon and Germanic law, a price set upon a man's life on the basis of his rank and paid as compensation by the family of a slayer to the kindred or lord of a slain man to free the culprit of further punishment or obligation. [Middle English (Scottish) *weregehelde,* Old English *wergeld,* "man-payment" : *wer,* a man + *geld,* payment.]

wer·ner·ite (wúrnə-rīt) *n. Mineralogy.* **Scapolite** *(see).* [French, after A.G. Werner (1750–1817), German mineralogist.]

wert (wert). *Archaic.* Second person singular past indicative and past subjunctive of **be.**

Wes·ker (wéskər), **Arnold** (1932–). British playwright. His works include the *Roots* trilogy (1958–60), *Chips with Everything* (1962), and *Said the Old Man to the Young Man* (1978).

wes·kit (wéskit) *n. Informal.* A waistcoat. [Variant of WAISTCOAT.]

Wes·ley (wéss-li, wéz), **John** (1703–91). English religious leader and founder of Methodism. He and his brother Charles (1707–88), a writer of hymns, were ordained into the Church of England, but came under the influence of the more austere evangelical Christianity of the Moravians. Wesley travelled throughout the country preaching at open-air meetings, often to large working-class audiences. Although Methodism encountered the opposition of the Anglican Church, it was only formally founded after Wesley's death.

Wes·ley·an (wéz-li-ən, wéss-) *adj.* Of or pertaining to John or Charles Wesley or to Methodism.
~*n.* A Methodist, especially one belonging to the Wesleyan Methodist denomination based on the teachings of John and Charles Wesley. —**Wes·ley·an·ism** *n.*

Wes·sex (wéssiks). Former kingdom of the West Saxons, England. With varying boundaries it extended from the English Channel to the Thames and beyond, and from Devon to Sussex.

west (west) *n. Abbr.* **w, W, w., W.** 1. a. The direction opposite that of the earth's axial rotation; the general direction of the sunset. b. The cardinal point on the mariner's compass 270° clockwise from north and directly opposite east. 2. Any area or region lying in this direction. 3. *Often capital* **W.** a. The part of the earth west of Asia and Asia Minor, especially Europe and North America; the Occident. b. The Western Hemisphere. c. The western part of any country or region. 3. a. One of four positions arranged like the four compass points. b. In card games such as bridge, a player considered to occupy this position. —**the West.** 1. The developed countries of the non-Communist world, especially Europe and North America. 2. In the United States, the region west of the Mississippi.
~*adj.* 1. To, towards, of, facing, or in the west. 2. Coming from or originating in the west. Said of a wind. 3. *Capital* **W.** Officially or conventionally designating the western part of a country, continent, or other geographical area: *West Bengal; West Germany.*
~*adv.* In, from, or towards the west. —**go west.** *Informal.* 1. To die. 2. To founder; collapse; end in disaster. [Middle English *west,* Old English *west.*]

West, Mae. (1892–1980). U.S. actress. She is remembered as the sex symbol of the 1930s in comedies such as *I'm No Angel* (1933), and *My Little Chickadee* (1939).

West, Dame Rebecca, born Cicely Isabel Fairfield (1892–1983). British novelist, journalist, and critic. Among her books are *The Thinking Reed* (1936) and *The Birds Fall Down* (1966).

West African States. Region of Africa lying between the Sahara and the Gulf of Guinea. With the exception of Liberia, all eleven states are former colonies of European countries which gained their independence after World War II.

West Asia. See **Middle East, The.** —**West Asian** *adj. & n.*

West Atlantic *n.* A branch of the Niger-Congo language family, including Fulani and Wolof.

West Bank. Territory on the west bank of the river Jordan. It was

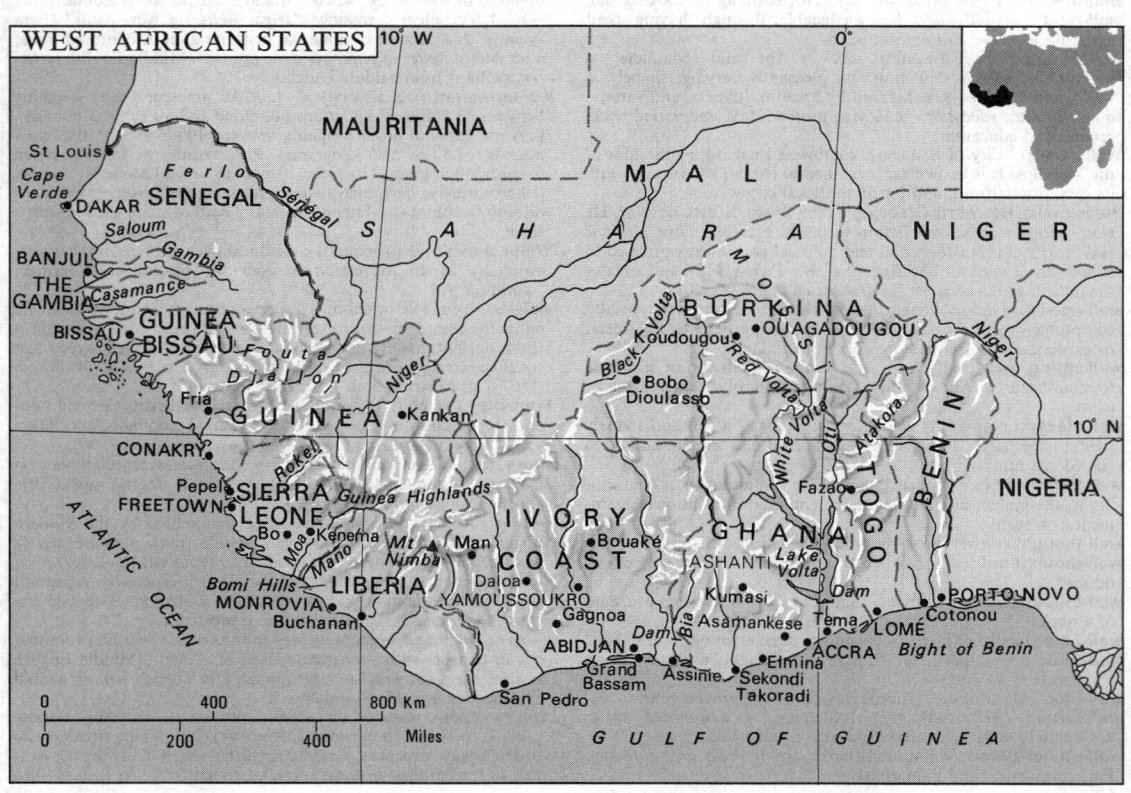

WEST AFRICAN STATES

part of Palestine before passing to Jordan in 1949, and was captured by the Israelis (1967). Including part of Jerusalem, Nablus, Hebron, and the hills of Judaea and Samaria, it is considered to be strategically important by the Israelis, and to be the natural homeland for the Palestinians by the Palestine Liberation Organisation. Since 1987 Israeli-Arab unrest has escalated.

West Bengal. State of northeast India. Situated on the Bay of Bengal and bordered by Bangladesh in the east, it was part of the former province of Bengal partitioned in 1947 between India and Pakistan. It includes part of the Ganges delta and extends to the Himalayas in the far north. Its capital is Calcutta.

West Berlin. See **Berlin.**

west-bound (wést-bownd) *adj. Abbr.* **w.b.** Going towards the west.

west by north *n. Abbr.* **WbN** The direction or point on the mariner's compass halfway between due west and west-northwest; 78° 45′ west of due north. **—west by north** *adv. & adj.*

west by south *n. Abbr.* **WbS** The direction or point on the mariner's compass halfway between due west and west-southwest; 101° 15′ west of due north. **—west by south** *adv. & adj.*

West Country *n.* The southwestern counties of England, especially Somerset, Devon, and Cornwall.

West End *n.* The western part of central London, well-known for its fashionable shops and places of entertainment, and including Mayfair, Piccadilly Circus, Oxford Street, and Hyde Park.

west-er (wéstər) *intr.v.* **-ered, -ering, -ers. 1.** To move westwards. Used of the Sun, the Moon, or a star. **2.** To shift to the west. Used of the wind.
~*n.* A westerly. [Middle English *west(e)ren,* from WEST.]

west-er-ly (wéstərli) *adj.* **1.** Situated in or towards the west. **2.** Coming from the west. Said of a wind.
~*n., pl.* **westerlies.** A storm or wind from the west. [From obsolete *wester,* western, from Middle English *wester,* Old English *westra.*] **—west-er-ly** *adv.*

west-ern (wéstərn) *adj. Abbr.* **w, W, w., W. 1.** Situated towards, in, or facing the west. **2.** Coming from the west. Said of a wind. **3.** Growing in the west. **4.** *Often capital* **W.** Of, pertaining to, or characteristic of western regions or the West. **5.** *Capital* **W.** Of, pertaining to, or characteristic of the developed countries of the non-Communist world, especially Europe and North America: *Western technology.* **6.** *Often capital* **W.** Of, pertaining to, or characteristic of the American West. **7.** *Capital* **W.** Of or pertaining to the Western Church.
~*n. Often capital* **W.** A novel or film dealing with frontier or cowboy life in the American West. [Middle English *west(e)ren,* Old English *westerne.*]

Western Australia. Largest state of Australia. Covering approximately a third of the country, it is bounded by the Indian Ocean on the north, west, and south and is mainly desert in the interior. Its mineral reserves include gold, iron, coal, oil, and bauxite. Its population is densest in the fertile southwest where wheat and fruit are grown and livestock are raised, while industries, chiefly situated around the capital, Perth, include oil refining and iron and steel.

Western Cape. Province in South Africa created in 1994 out of the southwest of the former Cape Province. Capital, Cape Town.

Western Church *n.* **1.** The church of the Western Roman Empire, acknowledging the primacy of the see of Rome. **2.** Any of the churches that have developed from this, especially the Roman Catholic Church.

west-ern-er (wéstərnər) *n. Sometimes capital* **W. 1.** A native or inhabitant of the west, particularly Europe and North America. **2.** A native or inhabitant of the western United States.

Western Europe. Political region of Europe. During the Cold War period most of the 24 independent states of Western Europe looked to the United States for military alliance, to counter Soviet influence in Eastern Europe. Switzerland and Austria maintained strict neutrality. Since the relaxing of Soviet control in the Eastern Bloc, however, the distinction between Western and Eastern Europe has been blurred. See map, next page.

Western Hemisphere *n.* The half of the earth that includes all of North and South America, the surrounding waters, and all neighbouring islands.

western hemlock *n.* A sprucelike tree, *Tsuga heterophylla,* from North America, characteristically having drooping leaf shoots and branches in irregular whorls.

west-ern-ise, west-ern-ize (wéstər-nīz) *v.* **-ised, -ising, -ises.** To influence with, adopt, or cause to adopt, customs and styles of living characteristic of the industrially developed countries of the West. **—west-ern-i-sa-tion** (-nī-záysh'n ‖ *U.S.* -ni-) *n.*

Western Isles. See **Hebrides.**

west-ern-most (wéstərn-mōst) *adj.* Farthest west.

western roll *n.* A method of performing the high jump in athletics, in which the whole body is flung upwards and rolls over the bar in a position parallel to it. [Apparently so called to contrast this method with a different one, the *eastern roll.*]

Western Roman Empire *n.* The western part of the Roman Empire, especially after the division established by the emperor Theodosius in A.D. 395, and lasting until A.D. 475. Also called "Western Empire". See **Byzantine Empire.**

Western Sahara. Territory of northwest Africa. Bordering the Atlantic Ocean it is extremely arid and has reserves of phosphates. Formerly Spanish Sahara, it was divided (1976) between Morocco and Mauritania, although Mauritania later withdrew (1979). The Polisario Front, a guerrilla movement resisting Moroccan rule, pro-

claimed (1976) the Saharan Arab Democratic Republic, which was recognised by many Arab and other states.

Western Samoa. See **Samoa.**

Western Wall *n.* The **Wailing Wall** *(see).*

West Frisians. See **Frisian Islands.**

West Germanic *n.* A subdivision of the Germanic languages that includes High German, Low German, Dutch, Afrikaans, Flemish, Frisian, English, and Yiddish.

West Germany. The unofficial name for the former German Federal Republic. See **Germany.**

West Gla-mor-gan (glə-mórgən). County of south Wales (1974–96), now subdivided into Unitary Authority areas. It was formed from the former county of Glamorganshire, and the county borough of Swansea.

West Greek *n.* A principal dialectal division of Ancient Greek, comprising Doric and Northwest Greek.

West Highland terrier *n.* A dog of a small breed of terrier having short legs and tail and a white coat. Also called "West Highland white terrier".

West Indies. Archipelago of Central America. Extending between Florida and Venezuela, it separates the Atlantic Ocean from the Caribbean Sea and the Gulf of Mexico. It includes the Greater Antilles (Cuba, Hispaniola, Jamaica and Puerto Rico), the Lesser Antilles (Barbados, Trinidad, Tobago, and the Leeward and Windward Isles) and The Bahamas.

west-ing (wésting) *n.* **1.** *Nautical.* **a.** The distance sailed by a ship on a westerly course. **b.** The longitudinal distance from a given meridian on a westward course. **2.** A westward direction or movement. [From WEST.]

West I-ri-an (irri-ən). *Indonesian* **Ir-i-an Ja-ya** (írrən, ée-i-, jí-ə). Province of Indonesia, Southeast Asia, the western half of New Guinea. Before its transfer to Indonesia (1963) it was known as Netherlands New Guinea. It is largely swampland.

West Lo-thian (lóthi-ən). Unitary Authority area, eastern central Scotland, bordering the Firth of Forth. Absorbed (1975–96) into Lothian Region, it has now regained its administrative status.

West-meath (wést-meéth). *Irish* **Contae Na Hiarmhidhe.** Inland county of Leinster province, north central Republic of Ireland. It has many lakes, including loughs Ree and Ennell.

West Midlands. Former metropolitan county of west central England (1974–97). Covering most of the Black Country, it was created from northeast Worcestershire, southeast Staffordshire, and northwest Warwickshire. Now administratively subdivided.

West-min-ster (wést-min-stər, west-mín-. *Note: the pronunciation* -minni-, -mínni- *is nonstandard.*), **City of.** Borough of Greater London, southeast England. Situated on the north bank of the river Thames, it contains many famous buildings, including the Houses of Parliament, Westminster Abbey, and Buckingham Palace, as well as Hyde Park.

West-mor-land (wést-mər-lənd, wéss-). Former county of northwestern England. Incorporated (1974) into Cumbria, it included much of the Lake District. The county town was Appleby.

west-north-west (wést-north-wést *Nautical* -nor-) *n. Abbr.* **WNW** The direction or point on the mariner's compass halfway between west and northwest; 67° 30′ west of due north.
~*adj.* Situated towards, facing, or in this direction.
~*adv.* In, from, or towards this direction.

Wes-ton standard cell (wéstən) *n.* A standard cadmium primary cell that produces an electromotive force of 1.018,636 volts at 20°C. It consists of a mercury anode and a cadmium amalgam cathode immersed in an electrolyte of saturated cadmium sulphate. Also called "cadmium cell". [From a trademark.]

West Pakistan. See **Pakistan.**

West-phal-i-a (wést-fáyli-ə, west-). *German* **West-fa-len** (véstfaalən). Former province of Prussia, part of North Rhine-Westphalia in western Germany since 1946. It was created as a duchy (12th century), passing to Prussia through the Congress of Vienna (1815). Chiefly low-lying, it includes the industrial Ruhr valley in the west.

West Saxon *n.* **1.** An Old English dialect spoken in Wessex, the chief literary dialect of England before the Norman Conquest. **2.** A member of a Saxon people inhabiting Wessex during the centuries before the Norman Conquest.

West Slavonic *n.* The western division of the Slavonic languages, consisting of Czech, Polish, and Slovak.

west-south-west (wést-sowth-wést; *nautical* -sow-) *n. Abbr.* **WSW** The direction or point on the mariner's compass halfway between west and southwest; 112° 30′ west of due north.
~*adj.* Situated towards, facing, or in this direction.
~*adv.* In, from, or towards this direction.

West Sussex. County of southern England. Extending northwards from the English Channel across the South Downs to the western end of the Weald, it is mainly agricultural in character, producing dairy goods, barley, and vegetables. The administrative centre is Chichester.

West Virginia. Mountain state of eastern central United States. Divided by the Allegheny mountains, 80 per cent of the state lies to the west on the hilly Appalachian plateau, while to the east lies the Great Appalachian Valley. The capital is Charleston.

west-ward (wéstwərd) *adj.* Also **west-ward-ly** (-li). Towards, facing or in the west.
~*n.* A westward direction, point, or region.
~*adv. Chiefly U.S.* Variant of **westwards.**

west·wards (wĕst-wərdz) *adv.* Also *chiefly U.S.* **westward** (-wərd). Towards the west; in a westerly direction.

West Yorkshire. County of northern central England (1974–97), created from part of the former West Riding of Yorkshire, and the industrial county boroughs of Bradford, Dewsbury, Halifax, Huddersfield, Leeds, and Wakefield. It has textile industries and coal fields. It is now administratively subdivided.

wet (wet) *adj.* **wetter, wettest. 1.** Covered or saturated with a liquid, especially water; moistened; damp. **2.** Not yet dry or firm: *wet plaster.* **3.** Stored or preserved in liquid. **4.** Used or prepared with water or other liquids. **5. a.** Rainy or humid: *wet weather.* **b.** Characterised by frequent or heavy rainfall or snowfall: *a wet climate.* **6.** Designating a process, system, or device in which liquids play a prominent part: *a wet photocopier.* **7.** *British Informal.* Feeble; faint-hearted. [Perhaps shortened from *wet behind the ears* (immature, inexperienced).] **8.** *British Informal.* Characteristic of, pertaining to, or composed of the liberal members of a group, especially of the liberal wing of the British Conservative party: *a wet rebellion in the Cabinet.* **9.** *Informal.* **a.** Allowing the production and sale of alcoholic drinks: *a wet state.* **b.** *British.* Allowing the sale of alcoholic drinks on Sundays: *a wet county.* **—wet through.** Completely wet, soaking wet; drenched, sodden

~*n.* **1.** That which makes wet; moisture. **2.** Rainy or snowy weather: *go out into the wet.* **3.** *British Informal.* A feeble, timid, or stupid person. **4.** *British Informal.* A relatively liberal member of a group; especially, a member of the British Conservative party typically opposing hard-line economic policies: *Tory wets.* **5.** *British Slang.* A drink. **6.** *U.S. Informal.* One who supports the legal production and sale of alcoholic drinks.

~*v.* **wetted** or **wet, wetting, wets. —***tr.* **1.** To make wet; moisten or dampen: *wet a sponge.* **2.** To make (a bed, one's clothes, or oneself) wet by urinating. *—intr.* To become wet. [Middle English *wet,* Old English *wĕt, wĕt.*]

Synonyms: *wet, damp, moist, dank, humid.*

Usage: The past tense and past participle forms of this verb are *wet* in American English, and in British English when the action takes place without deliberation (*We got wet through; The baby wet the bed*). In other circumstances, *wetted* is used in British English (*They wetted the wall before applying the paste*), and this form has some use also in American English. See also **fit** and **quit.**

wet-and-dry-bulb **thermometer** (wĕt-and-drī-bulb) *n.* A **psychrometer** *(see).*

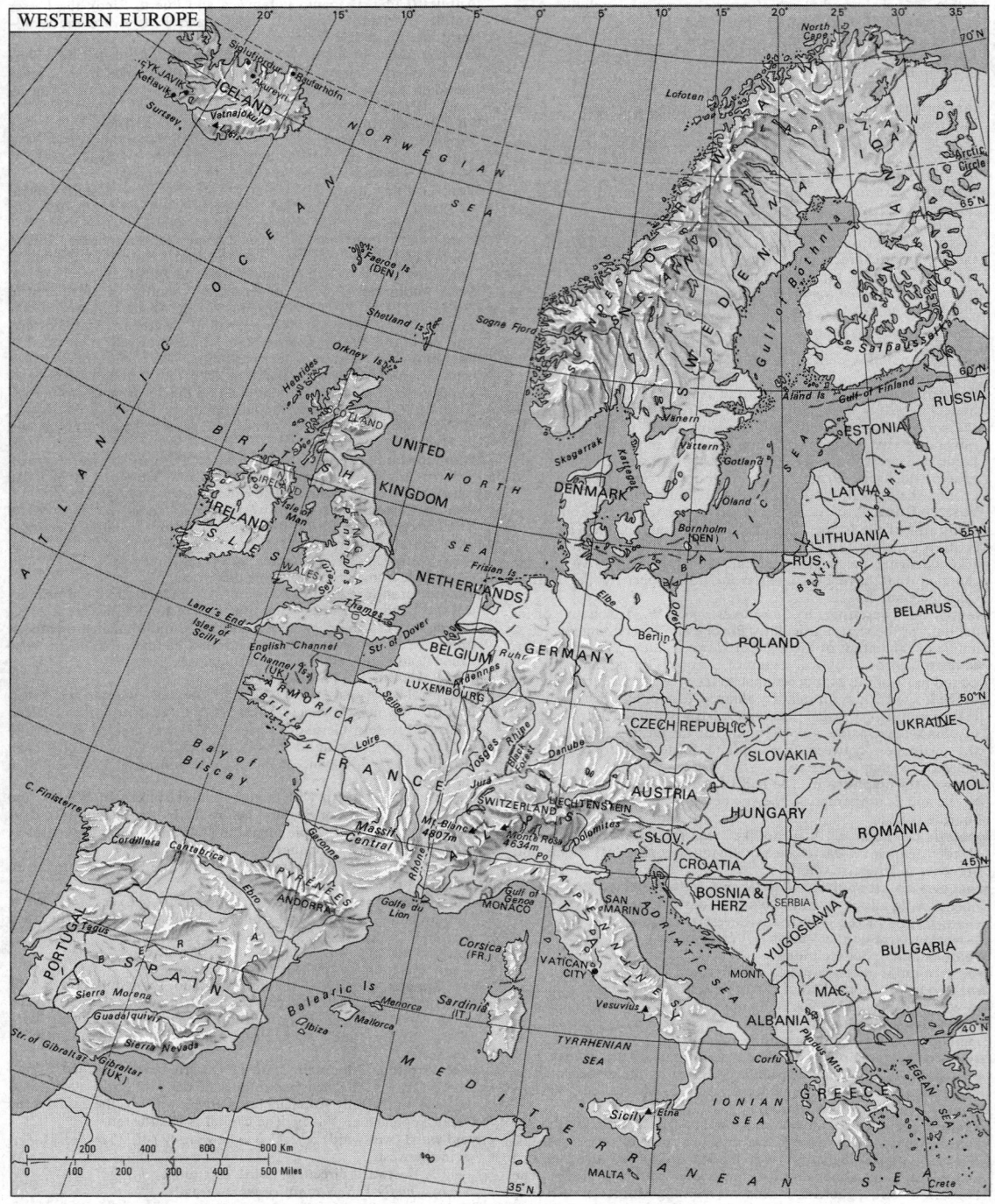

WESTERN EUROPE

wet·back (wĕt-bak) *n.* A Mexican immigrant who crosses the U.S. border illegally, as by swimming or wading across the Rio Grande.

wet blanket *n. Informal.* One who discourages enjoyment, enthusiasm, or the like. [Originally a soaked blanket used in putting out fires.]

wet cell *n.* A primary cell having an electrolyte in the form of a liquid bath. Compare **dry cell.**

wet dream *n.* An erotic dream had by a man or boy accompanied by sexual climax and emission of semen.

wet fish *n. British.* Uncooked fish, usually fresh, smoked, or frozen, as sold in a fishmonger's shop as opposed to a fish-and-chip shop. Also used adjectivally: *a wet-fish merchant.*

wet fly *n.* An artificial fishing fly designed to be used under water. Compare **dry fly.**

weth·er (wĕthər) *n.* A gelded male sheep. [Middle English *wether,* wether, a ram, Old English *wether.*]

wet·lands (wĕt-landz) *pl.n. Sometimes singular.* A lowland area, such as a marsh or swamp, that is saturated with moisture, especially when considered as the natural habitat of wildlife.

wet look *n.* A very shiny finish given to the surface of fabrics used to make clothes, shoes, and accessories. Also used adjectivally: *A wet-look handbag.*

wet monsoon *n. Meteorology.* A monsoon *(see).*

wet nurse *n.* A woman who breastfeeds another woman's child.

wet-nurse (wĕt-nŭrss) *tr.v.* **-nursed, -nursing, -nurses. 1.** To serve as a wet nurse for. **2.** To treat with excessive care or solicitude.

wet pack *n.* The usual form of a therapeutic **pack** *(see),* having been immersed in hot or cold water and then wrung out.

wet rot *n.* **1.** A disease of timber caused by various fungi of the genus *Coniophora.* **2.** Any fungus causing wet rot.

wet suit *n.* A tight-fitting rubber suit worn for warmth by divers, wind-surfers, and the like.

wetting agent *n.* Any compound that causes a liquid to spread more easily across or penetrate into the surface of a solid by reducing the surface tension of the liquid.

we've (weev, wiv). Contraction of *we have.*

Wex·ford (wĕks-fərd). County of Leinster province, southeast Republic of Ireland. Bordering the Irish sea, it was the first county colonised by the English (1169). The county town is Wexford.

Wey·den (vīd'n), **Rogier van der,** also known as Roger de la Pasture (*c.*1400–64). Flemish painter. He is best known for his altarpiece, the *Deposition* (*c.*1435).

wf *Printing.* Wrong fount.

WFTU World Federation of Trade Unions.

wh. white.

whack (wak, hwak) *v.* **whacked, whacking, whacks.** *—tr.* **1.** To strike with a sharp blow; slap. **2.** To score or get by hitting. Usually used with *up: whacked up a huge number of runs. —intr.* To deal a sharp, resounding blow.

~n. **1. a.** A sharp, swift blow. **b.** The sound made by such a blow. **2.** *Informal.* A fair share: *Give me my whack.* **3.** *Informal.* An attempt; a try: *have a whack at it.* **—out of whack.** *U.S. Informal.* Improperly ordered or balanced; not functioning correctly. [Perhaps variant of THWACK.]

whacked (wakt, hwakt) *adj. British Informal.* Tired out; exhausted.

whack·er. Variant of **wacker.**

whack·ing (wăcking, hwăcking) *adj. Chiefly British Informal.* Superlative; very great.

~adv. Chiefly British Informal. Used as an intensive: *whacking great tusks.*

whack·y. *U.S.* Variant of **wacky.**

whale¹ (wayl, hwayl) *n., pl.* **whales** or collectively **whale. 1.** Any of various marine mammals of the order Cetacea, having a generally fishlike form with forelimbs modified to form flippers and a tail with horizontal flukes; especially, one of the very large species as distinguished from the smaller dolphins, porpoises, and others. **2.** *Informal.* A superlative example of the thing specified. Used with *of: a whale of a time.*

~intr.v. **whaled, whaling, whales.** To engage in the hunting of whales. [Middle English *whale,* Old English *hwæl.*]

whale² *v.* **whaled, whaling, whales.** *Chiefly U.S.* *—tr.* To strike repeatedly with a whip, stick, or the like; flog. *—intr.* To attack vehemently. Often used with *away.* [Variant of WALE.]

whale·back (wáyl-bak, hwáyl-) *n.* A steamship with the bow and upper deck rounded so as to shed water.

whale·boat (wáyl-bōt) *n.* **1.** A long rowing boat, pointed at both ends and designed to move and turn swiftly, formerly used in the pursuit and harpooning of whales. **2.** Any boat of similar size and shape. Also called "whaler".

whale·bone (wáyl-bōn, hwáyl-) *n.* **1.** The durable, elastic, hornlike material forming plates or strips in the upper jaw of whalebone whales. Also called "baleen". **2.** An object made of this material, such as a corset stay.

whalebone whale *n.* Any of various whales of the suborder Mysticeti, lacking teeth and characteristically filtering plankton through plates of whalebone. Also called "mysticete". Compare **toothed whale.**

whale oil *n.* A yellowish oil obtained from whale blubber, used in making soap and candles and as a lubricating oil.

whal·er (wáyl-ər, hwáyl-) *n.* **1.** One who hunts or processes whales. **2.** A whaling ship. **3.** A whaleboat.

whale shark *n.* A large shark, *Rhincodon typus,* of warm marine waters, having a spotted body and feeding chiefly on plankton.

whal·ing (wáyl-ing, hwáyl-) *n.* The business or practice of hunting, killing, and processing whales.

wham (wam, hwam) *n.* **1.** A forceful, resounding crash or blow. **2.** The sound of such a crack or blow; a thud.

~v. **whammed, whamming, whams.** *Informal.* *—tr.* To strike or smash into with resounding impact. *—intr.* To smash with great force. [Imitative.]

whang¹ (wang, hwang) *n. Informal.* **1.** A thong or whip of hide or leather. **2. a.** A lashing blow, as by a whip. **b.** The sound of such a blow.

~tr.v. **whanged, whanging, whangs.** *Informal.* **1.** To beat or whip with a thong. **2.** To beat with a sharp blow or blows. [Variant of Middle English *thwang,* THONG.]

whang² *v.* **whanged, whanging, whangs.** *Informal.* *—tr.* To strike so as to produce a loud, reverberant noise. *—intr.* To produce a loud, reverberant noise.

~n. Informal. A loud, reverberant noise. [Imitative.]

whang·ee (wang-ée, hwang-, -gée) *n.* **1.** Any of several bamboo-like Asian grasses of the genus *Phyllostachys.* **2.** A walking stick made from the woody stem of such a plant. [Chinese *huáng,* a type of bamboo, probably *Phyllostachys aurea.*]

wha·re (wórri) *n. N.Z.* **1.** A Maori hut. **2.** Any hut or simple dwelling, as at the beach or out in the country. [Maori.]

wharf (wawrf, hwawrf) *n., pl.* **wharves** (wawrvz, hwawrvz) or **wharfs. 1.** A specially made landing place, such as a concrete platform, at which vessels may tie up and load or unload. **2.** *Obsolete.* A shore or river bank.

~v. **wharfed, wharfing, wharfs.** *—tr.* **1.** To moor (a vessel) at a wharf. **2.** To take to or store on a wharf. **3.** To furnish, equip, or protect with a wharf or wharves. *—intr.* To berth at a wharf. [Middle English *wharfe, wherf,* Old English *hwearf.*]

wharf·age (wáwr-fij, hwáwr-) *n.* **1.** The use of a wharf or wharves. **2.** The charges for this. **3.** Wharves collectively.

wharf·ie (wáwrfi) *n. Australian and N.Z. Informal.* A wharf labourer; a docker or dockhand.

wharf·in·ger (wáwr-finjər, hwáwr-) *n.* The owner or manager of a wharf. [WHARF + -*inger,* as in words like HARBINGER.]

Whar·ton (wáwrt'n, hwáwrt'n), **Edith** (**Newbold Jones**) (1862–1937). U.S. novelist. Her novels include *The House of Mirth* (1905) and *The Age of Innocence* (1920).

what (wot, hwot ‖ *regional weak forms* wət, hwət) *pron.* **1.** Used as an interrogative pronoun in various types of question: **a.** Used in questions asking for a specification or identification: *What is your name? What does she do for a living? What are these papers on my desk?* **b.** Used in requests for repetition, clarification, or explanation: *He said what? What are these papers doing on my desk? What do you think she meant by that? What did you do that for?* **c.** Used when questioning the value or significance of a person or thing: *What are possessions to a dying man?* **d.** Used in rhetorical questions as the equivalent of a negative statement: *What's the point in arguing?* **2.** That or those which. Used as a relative pronoun: **a.** The thing or things that: *What I like about him is his honesty. Listen to what I tell you.* **b.** Anything or everything that; whichever thing that: *come what may; did what they could to save him.* **3. a.** *Nonstandard.* Which, who, or that: *It's the poor what gets the blame.* **b.** *Informal.* Something: *I'll tell you what.* **—and what not.** And other less prominent or unspecified things; and so on. **—what about. 1.** What information is there on? **2.** What do you think about? have you considered? **—what have you.** That which remains and need not be mentioned; all the rest. **—what if.** What would occur if? Suppose that? **—what of it.** How is it important? what does it matter? **—what's what.** *Informal.* The fundamentals and details of a situation or process; the true state or condition. **—what with.** Taking into consideration; in view of: *What with the heat and humidity, we really suffered.*

~adj. **1.** Which particular one or ones of many: *What university are you attending? What sort of car is that? You should know what musical that song is from.* **2.** Of what kind or nature: *What news is there of the Test Match?* **3.** Whatever; all that; as much or many as: *They soon repaired what damage had been done.* **4.** How astonishing or exceptional in good or bad qualities: *What weather! What a bore! I'd forgotten what a fool he was.* **5.** *Archaic.* How much; which degree of: *What love do you bear for her?*

~adv. **1.** How; how much; in what respect: *What does it matter?* **2.** To what an astonishing or exceptional degree: *What lovely weather!*

~interj. **1.** Used to express surprise, incredulity, or other strong emotion and sudden excitement. **2.** *British Informal.* Used to request agreement: *A fine evening, what?* Now chiefly with humorously. [Middle English *what,* Old English *hwæt.*]

what·ev·er (wot-évvər, hwot- ‖ wət-, hwət-) *pron.* Also *poetic* **what·e'er** (-áir), **what ever** (for sense 4). **1.** Everything or anything that: *Do whatever you please.* **2.** What amount that; the whole of what: *Whatever is left over is yours.* **3.** No matter what; regardless of what: *Whatever happens, we'll meet here tonight.* **4.** *Informal.* What. Used as an intensive: *Whatever does he mean?* **5.** An unspecified but similar thing: *write with pencils, pens, or whatever.*

~adj. **1.** Of any number or kind; any: *Whatever requests you make will be granted.* **2.** All of; the whole of: *He applied whatever strength he had left to the task.* **3.** No matter what: *I'll stand by her, whatever she's done.* **4.** Of any kind at all. Used for emphasis following the noun modified: *No campers whatever are allowed.*

what for *n. Informal.* Punishment; sharp retribution: *I'll give him* *what for if he ever tries a stunt like that again!*

what-not (wŏt-not, hwŏt-) *n.* **1.** A minor or unspecified object or article; a trivial item. **2.** A set of light, open shelves for ornaments.

what's (wots, hwots) **1.** Contraction of *what is.* **2.** Contraction of *what has.*

what-so-ev-er (wŏt-sō-ĕv́vər, hwŏt-) *pron.* Also *poetic* **what-so-e'er** (-air). Whatever.
~*adj.* Whatever. Used for emphasis: *no power whatsoever.*

wheal (weel, hweel) *n.* Variant of **weal** (a welt). [Variant influenced by obsolete *wheal,* to suppurate) of WALE (ridge).]

wheat (weet, hweet) *n.* **1.** Any of various cereal grasses of the genus *Triticum;* especially, *T. aestivum,* widely cultivated in many varieties for its edible grain. **2.** The grain of such a plant, ground to produce flour used in cooking, especially for bread, cakes, and pasta products. [Middle English *whet(e),* Old English *hwǣte.*]

wheat-ear (weet-eer, hweet-) *n.* A brown, black, and white bird, *Oenanthe oenanthe,* of northern regions. [Back-formation from *wheatears* (taken as plural), "white-rumped (bird)" : probably WHITE + Middle English *ers,* ARSE.]

wheat-en (weet'n, hweet'n) *adj.* Of, pertaining to, or derived from wheat.

wheat germ *n.* The vitamin-rich embryo of the wheat kernel, separated before milling for use as a cereal or food supplement.

wheat-meal (weet-meel, hweet-) *n.* Brown wheat flour.
~*adj.* Designating flour, or bread made from such flour, from which a proportion of the wheat kernel has been extracted.

Wheat-stone bridge (weet-stōn, hweet-) *n.* An instrument or circuit consisting of four resistors, or their equivalent, connected in a loop, with a galvanometer linking the junction between one pair and the other, used to determine the value of an unknown resistance when the other three resistances are known. [After Sir Charles *Wheatstone* (1802–75), British physicist.]

wheat-worm (weet-wurm, hweet-) *n.* A nematode worm, *Anguina tritici,* that is parasitic on and destructive to wheat.

whee-dle (weed'l, hweed'l) *v.* **-dled, -dling, -dles.** —*tr.* **1.** To persuade or attempt to persuade by flattery or guile; cajole: *wheedled us into agreeing.* **2.** To obtain through the use of flattery or guile. —*intr.* To use flattery or cajolery to achieve one's ends. [Perhaps from German *wedeln,* "to wag the tail", fawn, from Middle High German *wadelen,* from Old High German *wadal,* tail.] —**whee-dler** *n.* —**whee-dling-ly** *adv.*

wheel (weel, hweel) *n.* **1.** A solid disc or a rigid circular ring connected by spokes to a hub, designed to turn round an axle passed through the centre. **2.** Anything resembling such a device in appearance or movement or having such a device as its principal part or characteristic, as: **a.** In the Middle Ages, an instrument to which a victim was bound for torture. **b.** A type of firework that rotates while burning. **c.** A device for directing the course of a ship. **d.** The steering device on a vehicle. **e.** *U.S. Informal.* A bicycle. **f.** A spinning wheel. **g.** A water wheel. **h.** A potter's wheel. **i.** A device used in roulette and other games of chance. **3.** *Plural.* The procedures and processes involved in an enterprise: *the wheels of commerce.* **4. a.** The act or process of turning; a revolution or rotation. **b.** Circular motion. **5.** *Military.* A manoeuvre to change the direction of movement of a formation, as of troops or ships, in which the formation is maintained while the outer unit describes an arc and the inner unit remains in the same place as a pivot. **6.** *Plural. Slang.* A motor vehicle or access thereto. **7.** *Chiefly U.S. Slang.* One with a great deal of power or influence. Usually used in the phrase *a big wheel.* —**at** or **behind the wheel.** **1.** Operating the steering mechanism of a vehicle; driving. **2.** In charge; directing or controlling. —**oil the wheels.** To make things go smoothly. —**wheels within wheels.** A complex series of actions and interactions.
~*v.* **wheeled, wheeling, wheels.** —*tr.* **1.** To roll, move, or transport on a wheel or wheels, especially: **a.** To push (a container or vehicle equipped with wheels). **b.** To transport (a person or object) in or on such a container or vehicle. **c.** To propel (oneself) in a wheelchair. **2.** To cause to turn round or as if round a central axis; revolve; rotate. —*intr.* **1.** To turn round or as if round a central axis; revolve; rotate. **2.** To roll, move, or transport oneself on or as if on a wheel or wheels. **3.** To fly or move in a curving or circular course. **4.** To turn or whirl round in place; pivot. Often used with *round.* **5.** To reverse one's opinion or practice. Often used with *about.* —**wheel and deal.** *Informal.* To conduct one's business in a complex, scheming way. [Middle English *wheel(e),* Old English *hwēol, hweogol.*]

wheel animalcule *n.* A microorganism, a **rotifer** *(see).*

wheel-back chair (weel-bak, hweel-) *n.* An upright wooden chair, having a back whose frame is made from a single strip of wood that is bent to fit into the seat at either side.

wheel balancing *n.* The process of checking that the wheels of a motor vehicle are perfectly balanced when rotating, in order to avoid unwanted vibrations at high speed.

wheel-bar-row (weel-barrō, hweel-) *n.* A one- or two-wheeled vehicle with handles, used to convey small, heavy, or unwieldy loads by hand, as in a garden or on a building site.

wheel-base (weel-bayss, hweel-) *n.* The distance from front to rear axle in a motor vehicle.

wheel-chair (weel-chair, hweel-) *n.* A chair mounted on large wheels for the use of the sick or disabled.

wheeled (weeld, hweeld) *adj.* Having a wheel or wheels. Often used in combination: *four-wheeled.*

wheel-er (weel-ər, hweel-) *n.* **1.** One that wheels. **2.** A thing that

moves on or is equipped with a wheel or wheels. Often used in combination: *a three-wheeler.* **3.** A wheel horse.

wheel-er-deal-er (weel-ər-deelər, hweel-) *n. Informal.* A person who wheels and deals; a sharp operator.

wheel horse *n.* In a team, the horse that follows the leader and is harnessed nearest to the front wheels.

wheel-house (weel-howss, hweel-) *n.* An enclosed area on the deck or bridge of a vessel from which the vessel is controlled when under way. Also called "pilothouse".

wheel-ie (weel-i, hweel-) *n. Informal.* An act of riding a bicycle with the front wheel lifted off the ground: *do a wheelie.* [Diminutive of WHEEL.]

wheel lock *n.* **1.** A firing mechanism in certain obsolete small arms, in which a small wheel produces sparks by revolving against a flint. **2.** A locking mechanism attached to one wheelnut of the wheel of a car, preventing its removal.

wheel-man (weel-mən, hweel-, -man) *n., pl.* **-men** (-mən, -men). Also **wheels-man** (weelz-, hweelz-) (for sense 2). **1.** A bicyclist. **2.** *U.S.* One who steers a ship; a helmsman.

wheel-wright (weel-rīt, hweel-) *n.* One whose trade is the building and repairing of wheels.

wheen (ween, hween) *n. Scottish.* A number; a few: *a wheen o'bairns.* [Middle English, Old English *hwēne,* instrumental of *hwōn,* (a) few.]

wheeze (weez, hweez) *v.* **wheezed, wheezing, wheezes.** —*intr.* **1.** To breathe with difficulty, producing a hoarse whistling sound. **2.** To make a sound suggestive of laborious breathing. —*tr.* To produce or utter with a hoarse whistling sound.
~*n.* **1.** A wheezing sound. **2.** *Informal.* A clever idea or trick. **3.** *Informal.* An old joke. [Middle English *whesen,* probably from Old Norse *hvæsa,* to hiss.] —**wheez-er** *n.* —**wheez-ing-ly** *adv.*

wheez-y (weezi, hweezi) *adj.* **-ier, -iest.** **1.** Given to wheezing. **2.** Marking a wheezing sound. —**wheez-i-ly** *adv.* —**wheez-i-ness** *n.*

whelk[1] (welk || *rarely* hwelk) *n.* **1.** Any of various large, sometimes edible marine snails of the family Buccinidae, having pointed, turreted shells. **2.** The flesh of an edible whelk, eaten as food. [Middle English *w(h)elke,* Old English *weoloc, wioloc*†.]

whelk[2] *n. Pathology.* A swelling, protuberance, or pustule. [Middle English *whelke,* Old English *hwylca*†.] —**whelk-y** *adj.*

whelm (welm, hwelm) *tr.v.* **whelmed, whelming, whelms.** *Archaic.* **1.** To overwhelm. **2.** To cover with water; submerge. [Middle English *whelmen,* to turn over, Old English *hwelman* (unattested).]

whelp (welp, hwelp) *n.* **1.** A young offspring of a dog, wolf, or similar animal. **2. a.** A mere child or youth. **b.** An impudent boy or young man. **3.** Any of the ridges on the barrel of a windlass or capstan.
~*v.* **whelped, whelping, whelps.** —*intr.* To give birth to a whelp or whelps. —*tr.* To give birth to (a whelp or whelps). [Middle English *w(h)elpe,* Old English *hwelp,* from Germanic.]

when (wen, hwen || *regional weak forms* wən, hwən) *adv.* **1.** At what time: *When does the show start? I'll tell you when you can leave.* **2.** During which time: *When was he at Oxford?* **3.** At, on, or during which. Used with expressions of time: *on the day when war was declared; one of those weeks when everything goes wrong.*
~*conj.* **1.** At the time that: *in the spring, when the snow melts.* **2.** At the moment at which; as soon as: *Switch off the pump when the pressure reaches 30 pounds.* **3.** At the times at which; whenever: *When the wind blows, the doors rattle.* **4.** During the time at which; while: *when I was younger.* **5.** Despite the fact that: *carried on talking when he knew we were bored.* **6.** Considering that; since; if: *Why bother when you know he'll refuse?* **7.** Whereupon; and then: *We were in a strong position, when suddenly rain stopped play.*
~*pron.* What or which time: *Since when has this been going on?*
~*n.* The time or date: *Have they decided the where and when?* [Middle English *when, wane,* Old English *hwanne, hwenne.*]

when-as (wen-áz, hwen-) *conj. Archaic.* **1.** When or whenever. **2.** Whereas. **3.** Considering that; inasmuch as.

whence (wenss, hwenss) *adv. Formal & Archaic.* **1.** From where; from what place, source, or cause. **2.** From or out of which: *returned to the land whence he came.*
~*conj. Formal & Archaic.* **1.** And from here; and thence: *The path led to a sundial, whence it continued to the gate.* **2.** By reason of which; and from this: *He was not dead, whence we took comfort.* [Middle English *whennes,* from *whenne,* whence, Old English *hwanon.*]

whence-so-ev-er (wĕnss-sō-ĕv́vər, hwĕnss-) *adv. Archaic.* From whatever place or source.
~*conj.* From any place or source that.

when-ev-er (wen-ĕv́vər, hwen-) *adv.* Also **when ever** (for sense 2), *poetic* **when-e'er** (-air). **1.** At whatever time: *Whenever you feel like leaving, just let me know.* **2.** When. Used as an intensive: *Whenever did you hear that?* **3.** *Informal.* At any unspecified time: *next Tuesday, Wednesday, or whenever.*
~*conj.* Also *poetic* **when-e'er.** **1.** At any time that: *Come whenever it suits you.* **2.** Every time that: *He smiles whenever he sees her.* —See Usage note at **ever.**

when-so-ev-er (wĕn-sō-ĕv́vər, hwĕn-) *adv.* At whatever time at all; whenever.
~*conj.* Whenever.

where (wair, hwair) *adv.* **1.** At or in what place: *Where is the telephone?* **2.** In what situation or position: *Where would we be without your help?* **3.** From what place or source: *Where did you get this idea?* **4.** To what place; towards what end: *Where is this argument leading?* **5.** At or in which. Used with expressions of place: *the house where I live; the point where his argument is least convincing.*

~*conj.* **1.** In the place in which: *Where she works, they have a staff canteen.* **2.** In or to a place in which: *lives where the weather is warm; We should go where it's quieter.* **3.** In or to any place in which; wherever: *has to go where the work is.* **4.** In a situation in which: *Where anyone else would have been furious, she just laughed.* **5.** In which place; and there: *walked outside, where I was waiting.* ~*pron.* Which place: *Where did they come from?* ~*n.* The place or occasion: *We know the when but not the where of it.* [Middle English *wher(e)*, Old English *hwǣr.*]

where·a·bouts (waír-ə-bówts–, hwaír-ə–) *adv.* About where; in, at, or near what place: *Whereabouts do you live?* ~*n.* (-bowtss). *Used with a singular or plural verb.* The approximate location of someone or something.

where·as (wair-áz, hwair-) *conj.* **1.** It being the fact that; inasmuch as. Often used to introduce a formal document. **2. a.** While on the one hand. **b.** On the other hand; by contrast with that.

where·at (wair-át, hwair-) *conj. Archaic.* **1.** At which place. **2.** At which point or event; whereupon.

where·by (wair-bí, hwair- ‖ *U.S.* hwar-, hwer-, war-, wer-) *adv.* **1.** *Formal.* In or by means of which. **2.** *Archaic.* By what means; how: *"Whereby shall I know this?"* (Luke 1:18).

where·fore (waír-fawr, hwair- ‖ ōr) *adv. Archaic.* **1.** For what purpose or reason; why. **2.** On account of which. ~*conj. Archaic.* Why: *Wherefore did he come?* ~*n.* A purpose or cause. Now used chiefly in the phrase *whys and wherefores.* [Middle English *wherfor* : WHERE + FOR.]

where·from (wair-fróm, hwair-) *adv. Archaic.* From what or where; whence.

where·in (wair-ín, hwair-) *adv.* **1.** In what; how: *Wherein did I sin?* **2.** In which thing, place, or situation: *the bed wherein I lay.*

where·in·to (wair-ín-tŏŏ, hwair-, -tŏŏ) *adv. Archaic.* Into what or which.

where·of (wair-óv, hwair- ‖ -úv) *adv. Archaic.* **1.** Of what or which. **2.** Of whom.

where·on (wair-ón, hwair- ‖ -awn) *adv. Archaic.* On which or what.

where·so·ev·er (waír-sō-évvər, hwaír-) *conj.* Also *poetic* **where·so·e'er** (-aír). In, to, or from whatever place at all; wherever.

where·through (wair-thrŏŏ, hwair-) *adv.* Through, because of, or during which.

where·to (wair-tŏŏ, hwair-) *adj.* Also *archaic* **where·un·to** (-ún-tŏŏ, -tŏŏ). **1.** To what place; towards what end. **2.** To which.

where·up·on (waír-əp-ón, hwaír-, -áwn) *adv. Archaic.* On which or what: *a table whereupon a lavish feast was spread.* ~*conj.* **1.** At which point; after which. **2.** As a consequence of which.

wher·ev·er (wair-évvər, hwair-, wər-, hwər-) *adv.* Also **where ever** (for sense 2), *poetic* **where·er'e** (-aír). **1.** In or to whatever place: *Wherever she goes, he goes too.* **2.** Where. Used as an intensive: *Wherever did you hear that?* **3.** *Informal.* At or in any unspecified place: *can be used in the home, the office, or wherever.* ~*conj.* Also *poetic* **where·e'er.** **1.** In or to whichever place or situation that: *sit wherever you like.* **2.** In every place or situation that: *followed wherever she went.* [Middle English *wherever* : WHERE + EVER.] —See Usage note at **ever.**

where·with (wair-wíth, hwair-, -wíth) *adv.* With what or which: *the pen wherewith I write.* ~*pron. Archaic.* The thing or things with which: *"Make ready wherewith I may sup"* (Luke 17:8).

where·with·al (waír-with-awl, hwaír-, with-, -áwl) *adv. Archaic.* Wherewith. ~*pron. Archaic.* Wherewith. ~*n.* The necessary means, especially financial means: *to have the wherewithal for war.*

wher·ry (wérri, hwérri) *n., pl.* **-ries.** **1.** A light, swift rowing boat built for one person and often used in racing. **2.** A kind of sailing barge used in East Anglia. [Middle English *whery†.*]

whet (wet, hwet) *tr.v.* **whetted, whetting, whets.** **1.** To sharpen (a knife or other tool); hone. **2.** To make more keen; stimulate; heighten: *The noise whetted his curiosity.* ~*n.* **1.** Something that sharpens or stimulates. **2.** *Informal.* An appetiser or aperitif. [Middle English *whetten*, Old English *hwettan.*]

wheth·er (wéthər, hwéthər) *conj.* **1.** If it is so that; if the case is that. Used in indirect questions to introduce one alternative: *Ask whether the museum is open.* **2.** If it happens that; in case. Used to introduce the first of a set of possibilities and sometimes one or more other possibilities: *Whether he wins or (whether he) loses, this is his last fight; I'm seeing her, whether in Rome, London, or Paris.* ~*pron. Archaic.* Which of the two. Use in direct or indirect questions. **—whether or no.** Regardless of circumstances. [Middle English *whether*, Old English *hwæther, hwether.*]

whet·stone (wét-stōn, hwét-) *n.* A stone for honing tools.

whew (hwew, hwŏŏ) *interj.* Used to express relief or amazement. Usually partially unvoiced in imitation of a whistle. [Middle English *whewe* (imitative).]

whey (way, hway) *n.* The watery part of milk that separates from the curds, as in the process of making cheese. Also called "serum". [Middle English *whey*, Old English *hwæg*, from Germanic *khwuja-* (unattested).] **—whey·ey** *adj.*

whey-face (wáy-fayss, hwáy-) *n.* A person with a pallid face. **—whey-faced** *adj.*

which (wich, hwich) *pron.* **1.** What particular one or ones: *Which of these is yours? One of these is yours, I'm not sure which.* **2.** The thing, animal, group of people, or event previously designated or implied, specifically: **a.** Used as a relative pronoun in a clause that provides additional information about the antecedent: *my house, which is small and old.* **b.** Used as a relative pronoun preceded by *that* or *those*, or by a preposition in a clause that defines or restricts the antecedent: *the subject on which he spoke; took those which belonged to him.* **c.** Used instead of *that* as a relative pronoun in a clause that defines or restricts the antecedent: *The film which was shown later was better.* **3.** *Archaic.* The person designated or implied. Used as a relative pronoun: *Our Father, which art in Heaven.* **4.** Any of the things, events, or persons designated or implied; whichever: *Choose which you like best.* **6.** A thing or circumstance that: *He left early, which was wise.* ~*adj.* **1.** What particular one or ones of a number of things or persons: *Which part of town? He asked me which colour I preferred.* **2.** Any one or any number of; whichever: *Use which door you please.* **3.** Being the one or ones previously designated: *It started to rain, at which point we ran.* Sometimes used to refer to a clause: *told us he was married, which surprised me.* [Middle English *which, wilke*, Old English *hwilc, hwelc.*]

which·ev·er (wich-évvər, hwich-) *pron.* **1.** Any one or ones. **2.** No matter which; regardless of what one or ones. ~*adj.* **1.** Any one or any number of a group of things or persons: *Read whichever books you please.* **2.** No matter what; regardless of which: *It's a long trip whichever road you take.*

which·so·ev·er (wích-sō-évvər, hwích-) *pron.* Whichever. ~*adj.* Whichever. Used for emphasis.

whick·er (wíck-ər, hwíck-) *intr.v.* **-ered, -ering, -ers.** To whinny or snigger. ~*n.* A whinny or snigger. [Imitative.]

whidah. Variant of **whydah.**

whiff (wif, hwif) *n.* **1.** A slight, gentle gust or breath of air; a waft: *a whiff of cool air.* **2.** A brief, passing odour carried in the air; a momentary smell: *"a whiff of lilac drifted across the room"* (Elizabeth Bowen). **3.** A slight trace or suggestion: *a whiff of scandal.* **4.** An inhalation, as of air, perfume or tobacco smoke: *Take a whiff of this pipe.* **5.** *British.* A small cigar. ~*v.* **whiffed, whiffing, whiffs.** —*intr.* **1.** To be carried in brief gusts; waft. **2.** To draw in or breathe out air, smoke, or some other vapour. **3.** *British Informal.* To have an unpleasant smell. —*tr.* **1.** To blow or convey in whiffs. **2.** To inhale through the nose; smell; sniff. **3.** To draw in or breathe out (air or tobacco smoke, for example). [Imitative.] **—whiff·er** *n.*

whif·fle (wiff'l, hwiff'l) *v.* **-fled, -fling, -fles.** —*intr.* **1.** To move or think erratically; vacillate. **2.** To blow in fitful gusts; puff. Used of the wind. **3.** To produce a light whistling sound, as of wind. **4.** To move as if blown by wind; flutter. —*tr.* To blow, displace, or scatter with gusts of air. [From WHIFF (to blow).]

whif·fle·tree (wiff'l-tree, hwiff'l-) *n. U.S.* A **swingletree** (see).

Whig (wig, hwig) *n.* **1.** In the 17th century, a supporter of the Presbyterian cause in Scotland. **2.** From the late 17th to the mid-19th century, a member or supporter of one of the two major British political parties, opposed to the Tories and eventually succeeded by the Liberals. Early Whigs chiefly represented the aristocracy and sought the limitation of the power of the monarchy, while in the late 18th and early 19th centuries the Whigs came increasingly to represent the new industrial interests and to become a party of reform. **3.** In modern politics, one who identifies strongly with the Whig tradition, typically (in Britain) a member of the Liberal party. **4.** In the United States, a member of a political party (1834–55) formed to oppose the Democratic Party, succeeded by the Republican Party, and favouring high tariffs and a loose interpretation of the Constitution. [Probably short for *Whiggamore*, one of a body of 17th-century Scottish insurgents : perhaps *whig†*, to drive + Middle English *mere*, horse, MARE.] **—Whig, Whig·gish** *adj.*

Whig·ger·y (wíg-əri, hwig-) *n., pl.* **-ies.** Also **Whig·gism** (-iz'm). The principles or practices of Whigs.

while (wīl, hwīl) *n.* **1.** A period of time. Usually used in adverbial phrases: *stay for a while; sang (all) the while.* **2.** The time, effort, or trouble taken in doing something: *It is not worth my while to go yet.* **—once in a while.** Now and then; very occasionally. ~*conj.* **1.** As long as; during the time that: *It was lovely while it lasted.* **2.** Although: *While I respect your opinion, I can't agree with you.* **3.** Whereas: *While some of us are rushed off our feet, John never does a stroke of work.* **4.** And similarly; what is more: *Postal charges are rising by 20 per cent, while telephone charges may go up even more.* **5.** *Northern British.* Until: *had to wait while he finished.* ~*prep. Northern British.* Until: *while next week.* ~*tr.v.* **whiled, whiling, whiles.** Also **wile, wiled, wiling, wiles.** To spend (time) idly or pleasantly. Usually used with *away*: *whiled the hours away.* [Middle English *while, qwile*, Old English *hwīl.*]

Usage: The use of *while* in sentences like *Jean is French, John is English, while Jan is Polish* tends to attract criticism from purists, who find it inelegant. Indeed, all senses of *while* other than the strictly temporal have received criticism, usually on the grounds of a potential ambiguity: *She spent her youth in Wales, while her mother grew up in England.* See also **whilst.**

whiles (wīlz, hwīlz) *conj. Archaic.* While. [Middle English, adverbial genitive of WHILE.]

whi·lom (wí-lom, hwí-) *adj. Archaic.* Former; erstwhile. ~*adv. Archaic.* Formerly. [Middle English *whilom*, Old English *hwīlum*, dative plural of *hwīl*, WHILE.]

whilst (wīlst, hwīlst) *conj. Chiefly British.* While. [Middle English *whylst,* from WHILES.]

> **Usage:** *Whilst* has now been generally replaced by *while* in standard English. It is still used in certain literary contexts, and may still be heard among older British speakers.

whim (wim, hwim) *n.* **1.** A sudden or capricious idea; a passing fancy. **2.** Arbitrary thought or impulse; caprice: *governed by whim.* **3.** *Mining.* A vertical horse-powered drum used as a hoist. —See Synonyms at **caprice.** [Short for earlier *whim-wham†.*]

whim·brel (wim-brəl, hwim-) *n.* A greyish-brown wading bird, *Numenius phaeopus,* having long legs and a long, downward-curving bill. [Imitative of its cry.]

whim·per (wim-pər, hwim-) *v.* **-pered, -pering, -pers.** —*intr.* **1.** To cry or sob with soft intermittent sounds; whine. To complain whiningly. —*tr.* To utter in a whimper. —See Synonyms at **cry.** ~*n.* A low, broken, whining sound; a whine. [Dialectal *whimp* (imitative).] —**whim·per·er** *n.* —**whim·per·ing·ly** *adv.*

whim·si·cal (wim-zik'l, hwim-) *adj.* **1.** Capricious; playful; arbitrary. **2.** Unusual; fantastic; odd. [From WHIMSY.] —**whim·si·cal·i·ty** (-zi-káləti) *n.* —**whim·si·cal·ly** *adv.*

whim·sy, whim·sey (wim-zi, hwim-) *n., pl.* **-sies, -seys. 1.** A tendency to have or show a fanciful, often humorous approach to life; whimsicality: *loved whimsy and nonsense verse.* **2.** An odd or capricious idea; an idle fancy. **3.** Anything quaint, fanciful, or odd. [Probably from WHIM.]

whin[1] (win, hwin) *n.* A spiny shrub, **gorse** *(see).* [Middle English *whynne†.*]

whin[2] *n.* Whinstone. [Middle English *quint†.*]

whin·chat (win-chat, hwin-) *n.* A brownish Old World bird, *Saxicola rubetra,* frequenting open country. [From WHIN (gorse) (the bird is often found around gorse bushes).]

whine (wīn, hwīn) *v.* **whined, whining, whines.** —*intr.* **1.** To utter a plaintive, high-pitched, protracted sound, as in pain, fear, supplication, or complaint. **2.** To complain or protest in a peevish, protracted fashion. **3.** To produce a sustained noise of relatively high pitch. Used of a machine. —*tr.* To utter with a whine. ~*n.* **1.** A whining sound. **2.** A peevish complaint. [Middle English *whinen,* Old English *hwīnan.*] —**whin·er** *n.* —**whin·ing·ly** *adv.* —**whin·y** *adj.*

whinge (winj, hwinj) —*intr.v.* **whinged, whinging, whinges.** *Informal.* To whine or complain. ~*n. Informal* A whine; a complaint. [Northern English dialect, from Late Old English *hwinsian* (imitative); akin to German *winseln,* to WHINE.]

whin·ny (wínni, hwínni) *v.* **-nied, -nying, -nies.** —*intr.* To neigh, especially in a gentle tone. Used chiefly of a horse. —*tr.* To express in a whinny. ~*n., pl.* **whinnies.** The sound made in whinnying; a neigh. [Probably from WHINE (imitative).]

whin·stone (win-stōn, hwin-) *n.* Any of various hard, dark-coloured rocks, especially basalt and chert. Also called "whin".

whip (wip, hwip) *v.* **whipped, whipping, whips.** —*tr.* **1.** To strike with repeated strokes, as of a lash, strap, or rod; beat. **2. a.** To punish or chastise in this manner; flog; thrash. **b.** To afflict, castigate, or reprove severely. **3.** To drive, urge, force, or bring by or as if by means of a whip: *whipped his horse on; tried to whip the team into shape.* **4.** To strike or affect in a manner similar to whipping or lashing: *Icy winds whipped his face.* **5.** To beat (cream or eggs, for example) into a froth or foam. **6.** To move (something) with a sudden, rapid motion; take, put, or remove quickly: *whipped out a revolver; whipped off his cap.* **7.** To sew with a loose overcast or overhand stitch; whipstitch. **8.** To wrap or bind (a rope, for example) with twine to prevent unravelling or fraying. **9.** *Nautical.* To hoist by means of a rope passing through an overhead pulley. **10.** To fish (a stream or pool) by casting the line onto the water with a whipping motion. **11.** *Informal.* To defeat; outdo: *well and truly whipped by a superior team.* —*intr.* **1.** To move or proceed briskly: *just going to whip down to the shops; whipped through the report in 10 minutes.* **2.** To move in a manner similar to a whip; thrash or snap about: *Branches whipped against the windows.* ~*n.* **1.** An instrument, either a flexible rod or a flexible thong or lash attached to a handle, used for driving animals or administering corporal punishment. **2.** A whipping or lashing motion or stroke. **3.** Flexibility, as in the shaft of a golf club. **4.** A whipper-in. **5.** In the British Parliament and other legislative bodies: **a.** A member of a party responsible for enforcing party discipline, and especially for ensuring the attendance and supervising the voting behaviour of members at an important division. **b.** A written notice requiring party members to attend a particular session and vote according to the party line. See **three-line whip. c.** The condition of being subject to the discipline of a particular party: *resigned the Labour whip.* **6.** A sweet dish made with beaten egg whites or cream, often with fruit or fruit flavouring: *prune whip.* **7.** A windmill arm. **8.** *Nautical.* A hoist consisting of a single rope passing through an overhead pulley. **9.** A fairground ride, consisting of small cars that move in a rapid, whipping motion. —**whip in.** To keep (a pack of hounds) together by using a whip; act as a whipper-in. —**whip up. 1.** To arouse; excite: *whip up a crowd; whip up enthusiasm.* **2.** *Informal.* To prepare (a meal, for example) quickly. [Middle English *wippen,* perhaps from Middle Low German or Middle Dutch, to vacillate, swing.] —**whip·per** *n.*

whip bird *n.* Any of various Australian birds having a cry resembling the crack of a whip, such as *Psophodes olivaceus.*

whip·cord (wíp-kawrd, hwip-) *n.* **1.** A worsted fabric with a distinct diagonal rib. **2.** A strong twisted or braided cord sometimes used in making whiplashes.

whip graft *n.* A horticultural graft in which a tongue cut on the sloping base of the scion is inserted into a slit made on the sloping top of the stock.

whip hand *n.* A dominating position; the upper hand. Preceded by *the.*

whip·lash (wíp-lash, hwip-) *n.* **1.** The lash or thong of a whip. **2.** An injury to the spine in the neck region caused by an abrupt jerking motion of the head, either backwards or forwards. In this sense, also called "whiplash injury". —**whip·lash** *adj.*

whip·per-in (wíppər-ín, hwippər-) *n., pl.* **whippers-in. 1.** In foxhunting, one who assists the huntsman in handling a pack of hounds. Also called "whip". **2.** *Archaic.* A parliamentary whip.

whip·per·snap·per (wíppər-snappər, hwippər-) *n.* An impertinent but insignificant person. [Perhaps from *whipsnapper,* suggesting noisy but insignificant activity.]

whip·pet (wíppit, hwippit) *n.* A short-haired, swift-running dog of a breed developed in England, resembling the greyhound but smaller. [Perhaps from obsolete *whippet,* to move quickly, from *whip it.*]

whip·ping (wíping, hwipping) *n.* **1.** A thrashing administered especially as punishment. **2.** Material, such as cord or thread, used to lash or bind parts.

whipping boy *n.* **1.** One who gets the blame for the faults of others, especially of his superiors; a scapegoat. **2.** A boy formerly educated with a prince or other young nobleman and whipped for the latter's misdeeds.

whip·ple·tree (wipp'l-tree, hwipp'l-) *n.* A **swingletree** *(see).*

whip·poor·will (wíppər-wil, hwippər- ‖ *U.S. also* -wil) *n.* A brownish nocturnal North American bird, *Caprimulgus vociferus,* having a distinctive call of which its name is imitative.

whip·saw (wíp-saw, hwip-) *n.* A narrow two-man crosscut saw. ~*tr.v.* **whipsawed** or **-sawn** (-sawn), **-sawing, -saws. 1.** To cut with a whipsaw. **2.** To defeat or get the better of in two ways at once or by the joint action of two parties.

whip scorpion *n.* Any of various nonvenomous scorpionlike arachnids of the order Pedipalpi, such as the vinegarroon.

whip snake *n.* Any of various slender nonvenomous snakes, such as *Coluber gemonensis* of Eurasia and any of the genus *Masticophis,* of the New World.

whip·stall (wip-stawl, hwip-) *n.* A usually intentional stall in which a small aircraft enters a vertical climb, pauses, slips backwards momentarily, then drops nose downwards.

whip·stitch (wíp-stich, hwip-) *tr.v.* **-stitched, -stitching, -stitches.** To sew with overcast stitches, as in finishing a fabric edge or binding two pieces of fabric together. ~*n.* A stitch or stitches made in this manner.

whip·stock (wíp-stok, hwip) *n.* The handle of a whip.

whip·worm (wíp-wurm, hwip-) *n.* A slender, parasitic roundworm, *Trichuris trichiura,* that infests the large intestine in humans.

whirl (wurl, hwurl) *v.* **whirled, whirling, whirls.** —*intr.* **1.** To revolve rapidly about a centre or axis. **2.** To rotate or spin rapidly. **3.** To turn aside or away rapidly; wheel. **4.** To have the sensation of spinning; reel. **5.** To move along rapidly in or as if in a wheeled vehicle. —*tr.* **1.** To cause to rotate or turn rapidly. **2.** To drive or carry along at great speed, in a circular or curving course. **3.** To hurl. —See Synonyms at **turn.** ~*n.* **1.** The act of rotating or revolving rapidly. **2.** Something that whirls or is whirled, as a cloud of dust. **3.** A state of confusion; a tumult; a turmoil. **4.** A hurried succession or round of events: *the social whirl.* **5.** A state of mental confusion or giddiness; dizziness: *My head is in a whirl.* **6.** *Informal.* A short trip; a spin. **7.** *Informal.* A brief try. Usually used in the phrase *give it a whirl.* [Middle English *whirlen,* from Old Norse *hvirfla.*] —**whirl·er** *n.*

whirl·i·gig (wúr-li-gig, hwúr-) *n.* **1.** Any of various spinning toys. **2.** A roundabout or merry-go-round. **3.** Something that is continuously whirling or in a state of constant movement or change. **4.** The whirligig beetle. [Middle English *whirlegigge* : *whirlen,* WHIRL + *gigg(e),* spinning top.]

whirligig beetle *n.* Any of various beetles of the family Gyrinidae that circle about rapidly on the surface of quiet water.

whirl·pool (wúrl-pool, hwúrl-) *n.* **1.** Water in rapid rotating movement, as from the converging of two tides, tending to draw any floating object into the centre and down; an eddy or vortex. **2.** Anything suggesting the rapid turbulence of whirling water.

whirl·wind (wúrl-wind, hwúrl-) *n.* **1.** A column of air centred on an area of low atmospheric pressure, rotating violently around a more or less vertical axis and moving forward; a tornado. **2.** A small, momentary current of such whirling air over dusty flat land; a dust devil. **3.** Anything rushing or whirling impetuously, confusedly, or destructively. —See Synonyms at **wind.** ~*adj.* Very rapid or impetuous: *a whirlwind courtship.*

whirl·y·bird (wúr-li-burd, hwúr-) *n. Chiefly U.S. Informal.* A helicopter. [From WHIRL + BIRD.]

whirr (wur, hwur) —*intr.v.* **whirred, whirring, whirrs.** Also chiefly *U.S.* **whir.** To move so as to produce a continuous vibrating or buzzing sound, as some machines or the wings of certain birds do. ~*n.* A sound of buzzing or vibration. [Middle English *whirren,* from Scandinavian, akin to Danish *hvirre.*]

whisht (wisht, hwisht) *interj. Scottish & Irish.* Hush. ~ *tr.v. Scottish & Irish.* **whishted, whishting, whishts.** To hush; silence. [Middle English (imitative).]

whisk (wisk, hwisk) *v.* **whisked, whisking, whisks.** —*tr.* **1.** To move or remove with quick light sweeping motions: *whisking away the flies with its tail.* **2.** To carry or convey quickly and unobtrusively: *was whisked off to the Palace in an official car.* **3.** To whip (eggs or cream). —*intr.* To move lightly, nimbly, and rapidly.
∼*n.* **1.** A quick light sweeping motion. **2.** A small bundle, as of twigs or feathers, especially one used for brushing away dust or flies. **3.** A kitchen utensil, typically made of looped wire, for beating or whipping foodstuffs. [Middle English (Scottish) *quhisken,* from Scandinavian, akin to Swedish *viska*†.]
whisk·er (wísk-ər, hwísk-) *n.* **1.** *Plural.* **a.** The unshaven hair on a man's face; the beard, especially that part of it growing on the sides of the face. **b.** A moustache. **2.** A hair from the beard. **3.** Any of the long stiff bristles or hairs growing near the mouth of certain animals. **4.** *Informal.* A narrow margin; a hair's-breadth: *He lost by a whisker.* **5.** *Nautical.* One of two spars or booms projecting from the side of a bowsprit for spreading the jib or flying-jib guys. Also called "whisker boom". **6.** *Chemistry.* Any of the extremely fine filamentary crystals that can be grown from supersaturated solutions of certain minerals and metals and that possess extraordinary shear strength and unusual electrical or surface properties. [From WHISK.] **—whisk·ered, whisk·er·y** *adj.*
whis·key (wíski, hwíski) *n., pl.* **-keys. 1.** Whisky distilled in Ireland or in the United States. **2.** A drink of whiskey.
Usage: When made in Scotland (or Canada), the spelling is *whisky*; this is the dominant British form. *Whiskey* is the usual American English spelling, and it is also used of Irish whiskey.
whiskey sour *n. U.S.* A cocktail made with whiskey, lemon juice, and sugar.
whisky (wíski, hwíski) *n., pl.* **-kies. 1.** An alcoholic spirit distilled from fermented grain, typically from malted barley in Scotland and Ireland, and from maize or rye in the United States and Canada, and containing approximately 40 to 50 per cent ethanol by volume. **2.** A drink of whisky. —See Usage note at **whiskey.** [Shortened from obsolete *Whiskybae,* variant of USQUEBAUGH.]
whis·per (wíss-pər, hwíss-) *n.* **1.** Soft speech produced without vibration of the vocal cords. **2.** Something uttered in this manner. **3.** A secretly or surreptitiously expressed belief, rumour, or hint. **4.** A low rustling sound.
∼*v.* **whispered, -pering, -pers.** —*intr.* **1.** To speak softly, without the resonance produced by vibration of the vocal cords. **2.** To speak quietly or secretively, as by way of gossip, slander, or intrigue. **3.** To make a soft rustling sound, as surf or leaves do. —*tr.* **1.** To utter very softly. **2.** To say or suggest secretly or confidentially. [Middle English *whisperen,* Old English *hwisprian* (imitative).] **—whis·per·er** *n.*
whispering campaign *n.* A concerted effort to discredit a person or group by disseminating unfavourable allegations and rumours by word of mouth.
whist (wist, hwist) *n.* A card game for two pairs of players, in which each pair tries to win as many as possible of the 13 available tricks. [Perhaps variant of WHISK, from the whisking up of the tricks.]
whis·tle (wíss'l, hwíss'l) *v.* **-tled, -tling, -tles.** —*intr.* **1.** To produce a clear musical sound or series of sounds by forcing air through an aperture formed by pursing the lips. **2.** To produce a clear, shrill, sharp musical sound or series of sounds by some other method, as by blowing on or through a device. **3.** To produce a high-pitched sound when moving swiftly through the air: *Bullets whistled past.* **4.** To emit a sharp, high-pitched, often shrill note or cry, as some birds and animals do. **5.** To summon or signal by whistling: *whistled to his dog to follow him.* **6.** *Informal.* To request or expect something with no chance of success: *wants his money back, but he can whistle for it.* —*tr.* **1.** To produce by whistling: *whistle a tune.* **2.** To summon, signal, or direct by whistling.
∼*n.* **1.** A device or instrument for making whistling sounds by means of the breath, air, or steam. **2.** A sound produced by such a device or by whistling through the lips. **3.** Any whistling sound, as of an animal, a projectile, or the wind. **4.** The act of whistling. **5.** A whistling sound used to summon or command, or to give a signal. **6.** *Informal.* The mouth and throat. Used chiefly in the phrase *wet one's whistle.* **—blow the whistle on.** *Informal.* To expose and so put a stop to (any shady or undesirable activity or those involved in it). [Middle English *whist(e)len,* Old English *hwistlian* (imitative).]
whis·tler (wíss-lər, hwíss-) *n.* **1.** One that whistles. **2.** Any of various birds that produce a whistling sound, such as certain Australian flycatchers and the goldeneye duck. **3.** A marmot, *Marmota caligata,* of the mountains of northwestern North America, having a greyish coat and a shrill, whistling cry. **4.** *Physics.* An electromagnetic wave of audio frequency produced by atmospheric disturbances such as lightning, having a characteristically decreasing frequency responsible for a whistling sound of descending pitch in detection equipment. **5.** A horse having a respiratory disease characterised by wheezing.
Whis·tler (wíss-lər, hwíss-), **James (Abbott) McNeill** (1834–1903). U.S. painter. His works concentrate more on tone and colour than draughtsmanship. They include a portrait of his mother (*Arrangement in Grey and Black,* 1872), and *Old Battersea Bridge* (*c.*1875).
whistle stop *n.* **1.** One of a series of brief visits or appearances, especially by a candidate in an election. **2.** *U.S.* A small town at which a train stops only if signalled.
whis·tle-stop (wíss'l-stop, hwíss'l-) *intr.v.* **-stopped, -stopping, -stops.** *Chiefly U.S.* To conduct a political campaign by making brief appearances or speeches in a series of small towns.
∼*adj.* Conducted in this way: *a whistle-stop tour.*
whistling swan *n.* A North American swan, *Cygnus columbianus,* having a black beak marked with yellow at the base.
whit (wit, hwit) *n.* A particle; the least bit. Usually used with a negative. [Variant of Middle English *wi(g)ht,* creature, WIGHT.]
Whit (wit, hwit) *n.* **1. Pentecost** *(see).* **2. Whitsuntide** *(see).*
Whit·bread (wít-bred, hwít-), **Fatima** (1961–). British athlete. In 1986 she threw the javelin a women's world record distance of 77.44 metres (254 feet 1 inch).
white (wīt, hwīt) *n. Abbr.* **wh. 1.** An achromatic colour of maximum lightness, the complement of black, the other extreme of the neutral grey series. Although typically a response to maximum stimulation, white appears always to depend upon contrast. **2.** The white or nearly white part of something, as: **a.** The albumen of an egg. **b.** The white part of an eyeball. **c.** A blank area on a printed surface. **3.** Something white or nearly white, as: **a.** White clothes: *dressed all in white.* **b.** *Plural.* A white or cream outfit or item of clothing, as worn for some sports: *cricket whites.* **c.** A white wine. **d.** A white pigment: *titanium white.* **e.** A white breed of animal. **f.** The white ball in billiards or snooker. **g.** The white or light-coloured pieces in draughts or chess, or the player using them. **h.** The outermost ring of a target. **i.** A hit in this ring. **4.** *Sometimes capital* **W. a.** A person belonging to a race or group characterised by relatively light complexion. **b.** In South Africa, a member of the classified race group comprising such persons, usually of European descent. **5.** Any of various butterflies of the family Pieridae having white wings with some black markings, such as the **cabbage white** *(see).* **7.** *Plural. Medicine.* Leucorrhoea. **8.** A member of any of several reactionary or counterrevolutionary political groups active in Europe from the 18th to the early 20th centuries.
∼*adj.* **whiter, whitest. 1.** Being of the colour white; devoid of hue, as new snow is. **2.** Approaching this colour, as: **a.** Translucent and having a pale yellow colour: *white wine.* **b.** Pale green. Said of certain grapes. **c.** Pale grey; silvery and lustrous, as silver or tin or objects made of such metals. **d.** Silvery or light grey with age: *white hair.* **e.** Bloodless as from illness or fear; blanched. **3.** Light or whitish in colour or having light or whitish parts. Used with animal and plant names: *white whale; white clover.* **4. a.** Having the comparatively pale complexion typical of Caucasoids. **b.** Of, pertaining to, characteristic of, or consisting of white people: *white opinion; a predominantly white neighbourhood.* **c.** Reserved for white people, as in a system of racial segregation: *a white beach.* **5.** Not written or printed upon; blank. **6. a.** Pure; untainted; innocent. **b.** *Informal.* Fair; decent; honourable. **7. a.** Wearing a white habit: *white nuns.* **b.** Marked by the wearing of white by the bride: *a white wedding.* **8.** Accompanied by or mantled with snow: *a white Christmas.* **9. a.** Incandescent: *white heat.* **b.** Intensely heated; impassioned: *white with fury.* **10.** Reactionary or counterrevolutionary. **11.** Whitish in colour as a result of some degree of processing. Said of some foodstuffs: *white bread; white rice.* Compare **brown. 12.** With milk or cream added. Said of coffee.
∼*tr.v.* **whited, whiting, whites. 1. a.** *Printing.* To create or leave blank spaces in (printed or illustrated matter). **b.** To efface with correction fluid. In both senses, often used with *out*: *white out a line.* **2. a.** *Archaic.* To whiten; whitewash. **b.** *Obsolete.* To blanch. [Middle English *white,* Old English *hwīt,* white, white of an egg.] **—whit·ish** *adj.*
White, Patrick (1912–90). Australian novelist. His works include *The Happy Valley* (1939), *Voss* (1957), and *A Fringe of Leaves* (1976). He was awarded the Nobel prize (1973).
white admiral *n.* A Eurasian butterfly, *Limenitis camilla,* having brown wings marked with white.
white alkali *n.* **1.** Any of several mineral salts, such as sodium sulphate or sodium chloride, that appear as a white deposit on certain alkaline soils. **2.** Refined sodium carbonate.
white ant *n.* A **termite** *(see).*
white asbestos, *n.* A variety of asbestos, **chrysotile** *(see).*
white·bait (wīt-bayt, hwīt-) *n.* **1.** The young of various fishes, such as the herring, considered a delicacy when fried. **2.** Any of various other small edible fishes.
white·beam (wīt-beem, hwīt-) *n.* A European tree, *Sorbus aria,* the leaves of which have a whitish down on the undersurface.
white bear *n.* The **polar bear** *(see).*
white blood cell *n.* A **leucocyte** *(see).*
white bryony *n.* A climbing European vine, *Bryonia dioica,* having lobed leaves, greenish-white flowers, and scarlet berries.
white·cap (wīt-kap, hwīt-) *n.* A wave with a crest of foam.
white cedar *n.* **1.** Any of several North American coniferous trees having light-coloured wood, such as *Thuja occidentalis,* both having scalelike leaves. **2.** The wood of any of these trees.
white cell *n.* A **leucocyte** *(see).*
white cloud *n.* A small, brightly coloured freshwater fish, *Tanichthys albonubes,* native to China and popular in home aquariums.
white clover *n.* A common clover, *Trifolium repens,* native to Eurasia, having rounded white flower heads.
white coal *n.* Water regarded as a source of power.
white-col·lar (wīt-kóllər, hwīt-) *adj.* Of, pertaining to, or designating those workers, usually salaried, whose work usually does not involve manual labour and who maybe expected to dress with some degree of formality. Compare **blue-collar.**
white corpuscle *n.* A **leucocyte** *(see).*
white currant *n.* **1.** A shrub, *Ribes sativum,* cultivated for its edible berries. **2.** The small, round, white berry of this shrub.

white damp *n.* A poisonous gas, consisting primarily of carbon monoxide, that occurs in coal mines.

whited sepulchre *n.* A hypocrite; an evil person who pretends to be holy or good. Matthew 23:27.

white dwarf *n.* A faint highly dense star that is believed to represent the final stage in the evolution of a star of about the mass of the Sun.

white elephant *n.* **1.** A rare whitish or light-grey form of the Asian elephant, often regarded with special veneration in regions of south-eastern Asia. **2.** Something that is large, costly, and perhaps impressive, but expensive to maintain, unproductive, and consequently unwanted. **3.** An expensive project or venture which comes to nothing or turns out to be a failure. **4.** Any possession no longer wanted by its owner. [Referring to custom of the kings of Siam, who would express displeasure with a courtier by the gift of a white elephant, the upkeep of which was ruinously expensive.]

white-eye (wīt-ī, hwīt-) *n.* Any of various small greenish birds of the genus *Zosterops,* of Africa, southern Asia, and the Pacific islands, having a narrow ring of white feathers around each eye. Also *Australian* "silver-eye".

white-face (wīt-fayss, hwīt-) *n.* Completely white make-up, as worn by clowns.

white-faced (wīt-fāyst, hwīt-) *adj.* **1.** Pale; pallid. **2.** Having a white patch extending from the muzzle to the forehead.

white feather *n.* A sign of cowardice. [A gamecock with a white feather is regarded as a poor fighter.]

white-fish (wīt-fish, hwīt-) *n., pl.* **-fishes** or collectively **whitefish.** **1.** Any of various freshwater food fishes of the genus *Coregonus,* occurring in the Northern Hemisphere and having a generally silvery colour. **2.** Any of various similar or related fishes.

white flag *n.* A white cloth or flag signalling surrender or truce.

white-fly (wīt-flī, hwīt-) *n., pl.* **-flies.** Any of various small whitish insects of the family Aleyrodidae, often injurious to plants.

white-foot-ed mouse (wīt-fŏŏtid, hwīt-) *n.* The **deer mouse** *(see).*

white fox *n.* The **arctic fox** *(see)* in its winter colour phase.

White Friar *n.* A **Carmelite** *(see).* [After the colour of his habit.]

white frost *n.* **Hoarfrost** *(see).*

white gold *n.* An alloy of gold and nickel or palladium, and sometimes containing small amounts of silver, copper or zinc, having the colour of platinum.

white goods *pl.n.* Electrical household appliances such as refrigerators and washing machines, typically having a white exterior.

white gum *n.* Any of various Australian eucalyptus trees having pale-coloured bark.

White-hall (wīt-hawl, hwīt-, -hawl). The British government; especially, the government departments as distinguished from Parliament. [From *Whitehall,* a street in London where many departments of the government are located.]

White-head (wīt-hed, hwīt-), **A(lfred) N(orth)** (1861 – 1947). British philosopher and mathematician. One of the founders of mathematical logic, his *Principia Mathematica* (1910-13) was written in collaboration with Bertrand Russell.

white-head-ed (wīt-héddid, hwīt-) *adj.* **1.** Having white hair or plumage on the head. Said of a bird or animal. **2. a.** White-haired, as from old age. **b.** Fair-haired. **3.** *Chiefly Irish.* Favourite; darling: *the white-headed boy.*

white heat *n.* **1. a.** The temperature of a white-hot substance. **b.** The physical condition of a white-hot substance. **2.** A state of intense emotion or excitement.

white hole *n.* A hypothetical astrophysical object formed by the emergence of matter and energy from a space-time singularity through the event horizon.

white hope *n.* See **great white hope.**

white horehound *n.* A plant, the **horehound** *(see).*

white horses *pl.n.* Waves capped with foam; whitecaps.

white-hot (wīt-hót, hwīt-) *adj.* So hot as to glow with a bright white light; broadly, hotter than red-hot.

White House *n.* **1.** The official residence of the president of the United States in Washington, D.C. **2.** The supreme executive authority of the U.S. government.

white iron pyrites *n.* A mineral, **marcasite** *(see).*

white knight *n.* A person or group that mounts a rescue operation to save a company threatened by takeover or closure. [20th century: perhaps from the association of *knights* with rescuing those in distress and of *white* with purity and virtue.]

white lead *n.* **1.** A heavy white poisonous compound of basic lead carbonate, lead silicate, or lead sulphate, used in paint pigments. Also called "ceruse". **2.** A form of putty consisting of white lead in boiled linseed oil.

white leather *n.* Also **whit-leath-er** (wīt-lethər, hwīt-). Leather that has been specially treated so as to make it white.

white leg *n.* A disease, **milk leg** *(see).*

white lie *n.* A diplomatic or well-intentioned untruth.

white light *n.* Light, such as sunlight, that contains the whole spectrum of visible radiation in approximately equal proportions.

white line *n.* A solid or broken line of white paint marked on a road surface to indicate traffic lanes.

white magic *n.* Magic used for good purposes or against evil.

white man's burden *n.* The gratuitously assumed duty of the white peoples to govern and bring white civilisation to the nonwhite peoples of the world. [From "The White Man's Burden" (1899), a poem by Rudyard Kipling.]

white matter *n.* White brain and spinal-cord tissue, consisting mostly of myelinated nerve fibres. Compare **grey matter.**

white meat *n.* Light-coloured meat, especially of poultry. Compare **red meat.**

white metal *n.* Any of various whitish alloys, having relatively low melting points, such as pewter, and containing high percentages of tin, lead or antimony.

white mica *n.* A mineral, **muscovite** *(see).*

white mulberry *n.* A tree, *Morus alba,* native to China, having whitish or purplish fruit. Its leaves provide food for silkworms.

white mustard *n.* A Eurasian plant, *Brassica hirta* (or *Sinapis alba*), from whose seeds the condiment mustard is prepared.

whit-en (wīt'n, hwīt'n) *v.* **-ened, -ening, -ens.** —*tr.* To make white, as by bleaching or the application of whitewash. —*intr.* To become white. **—whit-en-er** *n.*

white-ness (wīt-nəss, hwīt-, -niss) *n.* **1.** The condition or quality of being white. **2.** Paleness or pallor. **3.** Moral purity; innocence. **4.** A white substance or area.

white noise *n.* Acoustical or electrical noise in which the intensity is the same at all frequencies within a given band.

white oak *n.* A large oak, *Quercus alba,* of eastern North America, having heavy, hard, light-coloured wood.

white-out (wīt-owt, hwīt-) *n.* **1.** A polar weather condition caused by a heavy cloud cover over the snow, in which the light coming from above is approximately equal to the light reflected from below, and which is characterised by the absence of shadow, the invisibility of the horizon, and the discernibility of only very dark objects. **2.** *Australian.* **Correction fluid** *(see).*

white paper *n.* *Often capital* **W,** *capital* **P.** An official statement or report published by a government, providing information on a particular issue and presenting the government's own policy.

white pepper *n.* See **pepper.**

white pine *n.* **1.** A timber tree, *Pinus strobus,* of eastern North America, having needles in clusters of five and durable, easily worked wood. **2.** The wood of any of these trees.

white plague *n.* *Informal.* Tuberculosis of the lungs.

white pointer *n.* A white shark.

white poplar *n.* A tree, *Populus alba,* native to Eurasia, having leaves with whitish undersides. Also called "abele".

white rat *n.* A white variety of rat used in scientific research.

White Russian *adj.* **Belorussian** *(see).*

white sapphire *n.* A pure form of corundum, used as a gem.

white sauce *n.* A sauce made with butter, flour, and milk, cream, or stock, sometimes used as a basis for other sauces.

White Sea. *Russian* **Be-lo-ye Mo-re.** Gulf of the Barents Sea, northwestern Russia. Part of the Arctic Ocean, it lies between the Kola and Kanin peninsulas, and has the port of Arkhangelsk on its shore. It is linked by canal with the Baltic Sea.

white shark *n.* A large, whitish, man-eating shark, *Carcharodon carcharias.* Also called "great white shark", "white pointer".

white slave *n.* A woman held unwillingly for purposes of prostitution. **—white-slave** *adj.* **—white slavery** *n.*

white slaver *n.* A procurer of white slaves.

white spirit *n.* A distillate of petroleum, **turpentine** *(see).*

white squall *n.* A sudden squall occurring in tropical or subtropical waters, characterised by the absence of a dark cloud and the presence of white-capped waves or broken water.

white supremacy *n.* The theory that the white race is inherently superior to and therefore entitled to rule over all other races. **—white supremacist** *n.*

white-thorn (wīt-thorn, hwīt-) *n.* The **hawthorn** *(see).*

white-throat (wīt-thrōt, hwīt-) *n.* Either of two Old World songbirds, *Sylvia communis* or *S. curruca,* having brownish plumage and a white throat.

white tie *n.* **1.** A white bow tie worn as a part of men's formal evening dress. **2.** The most formal type of men's evening dress, which includes a tailcoat. Also called "tails". Compare **black tie.**

white trash *n.* *Southern U.S.* A **poor white** *(see)* or poor whites as a class. Used derogatorily.

white vitriol *n.* *Chemistry.* **Zinc sulphate** *(see).*

white-wall tyre (wīt-wawl, hwīt-) *n.* A tyre on a motor vehicle having a white band on the visible side. Also called "whitewall".

white-wash (wīt-wosh, hwīt- ‖ -wawsh) *n.* **1.** A mixture of lime and water, often with whiting, size, or glue added, that is used to whiten walls, concrete, or the like. **2.** An attempt to conceal or gloss over mistakes or failures, especially so as to free those responsible from possible blame. **3.** *Informal.* A defeat in a game in which the loser scores no points.
~*tr.v.* **whitewashed, -washing, -washes. 1.** To paint or coat with or as if with whitewash. **2.** To gloss over (a mistake, for example). **3.** *Informal.* To prevent (an opponent) from scoring any points in a game. **—white-wash-er** *n.*

white water *n.* Turbulent or frothy water, as in rapids.

white whale *n.* A small whale, *Delphinapterus leucas,* white when full-grown, chiefly of northern waters. Also called "beluga".

white witch *n.* A person who practises **white magic** *(see).*

white-wood (wīt-wŏŏd, hwīt-) *n.* The soft, light-coloured wood of any of various trees such as the tulip tree, basswood, or cottonwood. **—white-wood** *adj.*

whit-ey (wīt-i, hwīt-) *n., pl.* **-eys.** *Chiefly U.S. Slang.* A white man or white people collectively. Used derogatorily, especially by blacks.

whith-er (wither-ər, hwith-) *adv.* **1.** To what place, result, or condition: *Whither are we wandering?* **2.** To which: *the shores whither the storm tossed them.*

~*conj.* **1.** To whatever place, result, or condition: *"whither thou goest, I will go"* (Ruth 1:16). **2.** To the place in or to which. [Middle English *whider, whither,* Old English *hwider.*]

whith·er·so·ev·er (wĭth-ər-sō-ĕ́vvər, hwĭth-) *conj.* To whatever place; to any place whatsoever.

whit·ing¹ (wĭt-ing, hwĭt-) *n.* A pure white grade of chalk that has been ground and washed for use in paints, ink, and putty. [Middle English *whityng,* from *whiten,* to white, from WHITE.]

whiting² *n.* **1.** A food fish, *Gadus merlangus,* of European Atlantic waters, related to the cod. **2.** Any of various Australian marine food fishes of the genus *Sillago.* **3.** Any of several marine fishes of the genera *Menticirrhus* and *Merluccius,* of North American coastal waters. [Middle English *whitynge,* from Middle Dutch *wijting* : apparently WHIT(E) + -ING (one having the quality of).]

whit·ish (wĭt-ish, hwĭt-) *adj.* Somewhat or almost white.

Whit·lam (wĭt-ləm, hwĭt-) **(Edward) Gough** (1916–). Australian politician. He was prime minister (1972–75).

whitleather. Variant of **white leather.**

whit·low (wĭt-lō, hwĭt-) *n.* An abscess of the area of a finger or toe around the nail. [Middle English *whitflawe, whit(f)lowe* : WHITE + *flawe,* fissure, FLAW.]

Whit·man (wĭt-mən, hwĭt-), **Walt(er)** (1819–92). U.S. poet. His *Leaves of Grass* (1855), which he later expanded, was written without regard to conventional metre and rhyme, and examines ideas which include freedom and comradeship.

Whit Monday *n.* The Monday following Whit Sunday.

Whit·sun (wĭts'n, hwĭts'n) *adj.* Of, pertaining to, or observed on Whit Sunday or at Whitsuntide.
~*n.* Whitsuntide. [Middle English *whitsone,* short for *whitsonday,* WHIT SUNDAY.]

Whit Sunday *n.* **Pentecost** (*see*). [Middle English *whitsonday,* Old English *hwīta sunnandæg,* "white Sunday" (from a tradition of clothing the newly baptised in white robes on Whitsunday).]

Whit·sun·tide (wĭts'n-tīd, hwĭt-s'n) *n.* The week beginning with Pentecost, especially the first three days of this week. Also called "Whit".

whit·tle (wĭtt'l, hwĭtt'l) *v.* **-tled, -tling, -tles.** —*tr.* **1.** To cut small bits or pare shavings from (a piece of wood). **2.** To fashion or shape in this way. **3.** To reduce, wear down, or destroy gradually as if by whittling with a knife. Usually used with *down, away,* or *off: He whittled down his expenses by 60 pounds.* —*intr.* To whittle wood with a knife. [Middle English *whyttel,* variant of *thwitel,* from *thwiten,* to whittle down, Old English *thwītan.*] —**whit·tler** *n.*

Whit·tle (wĭtt'l, hwĭtt'l), **Sir Frank** (1907–96). British aeronautical inventor. While in the R.A.F. he designed and developed the jet engine for aircraft which first flew in 1941.

whit·tlings (wĭttlĭngz, hwĭttlĭngz) *pl.n.* The chips and shavings from a piece of wood being whittled.

whiz, whizz (wĭz, hwĭz) *v.* **whizzed, whizzing, whizzes.** —*intr.* **1.** To make a whirring, buzzing, or hissing sound, as of something rushing through the air. **2.** *Informal.* To move or fly at a high speed. —*tr.* *Informal.* To move or take rapidly: *whizzed him off to hospital.* ~*n., pl.* **whizzes. 1.** A whizzing sound or a swift movement producing such a sound. **2.** *Slang.* One who has remarkable skill in a specified field: *a whiz at tennis.* [Imitative.]

whiz kid *n.* *Informal.* A person who achieves great success, especially in business, at an early age, usually as a result of exceptional talent or acumen; wunderkind. Sometimes used derogatorily.

whizz-bang (wĭz-bang, hwĭz-) *n.* A small-calibre high-speed shell used during World War I. It was fired in a flat trajectory and so was heard only an instant before landing and exploding.

who (hōō; *weak forms* hōō, *sometimes* ōō, ŏō) *pron.* **1.** What or which person or persons. Used as the nominative case of the interrogative pronoun in direct or indirect questions: *Who left? Do you know who won?* **2.** That. Used as a relative pronoun when the antecedent is human. **a.** In a clause that defines or restricts the antecedent: *The boy who came yesterday.* **b.** In a clause that provides additional information about the antecedent: *My brother, who is a doctor, advised me to diet.* **3.** And he, she, or they in turn. Used as a relative pronoun: *I got the story from Iain, who had heard it from his friend Terry.* **4.** *Archaic.* Any person or persons that; whoever: *Who dares, wins.* [Who, whose, whom; Middle English *who* or *qwa, whoos, whom(e),* Old English *hwā, hwæs, hwǣm.*]

Usage: Who (and *whoever*) are the appropriate forms to use when the pronoun is subject of a clause, or follows the verb *to be* (*Who arrived?, That is the man who arrived*). Whom (and *whomever*) are the recommended forms when the pronoun is object of a verb or governed by a preposition (*That is the man whom I saw; To whom did you speak?*). However, constructions with *whom* are generally felt to be formal, or appropriate to writing, and they are often avoided in general conversation (*Who did you speak to?*), though *whom* has to be used when governed by a preposition. Confusion sometimes occurs when the relative clause contains a parenthetic verb phrase, as in *He saw a man who he says was at the party: who* is appropriate to this construction, according to the above rules, because it is the subject of the verb *was,* the *he says* being parenthetic, but many people, doubtless aware of the strict grammatical rule concerning the use of *whom,* and sensing the use of a subject pronoun immediately following, in this example, opt mistakenly for the use of the object form (*He saw a man whom he says . . .*).

W.H.O. World Health Organization.

whoa (wō ‖ hō, hwō) *interj.* Used in commanding a horse to stop. [Middle English *whoo,* variant of HO (halt).]

who·dun·it, who·dun·nit (hōō-dúnnit) *n.* *Informal.* A mystery story, typically one based on a search for the perpetrator of a crime, usually a murder. [WHO + DONE + IT.]

who·ev·er (hōō-ĕ́vvər) *pron.* Also **who ever** (for sense 3). **1.** Anyone that; any person who. **2.** No matter who: *The culprit will be punished, whoever he is.* **3.** What person ever; who. Used as an intensive: *Whoever told you that?* —See Usage note at **who.**

whole (hōl) *adj.* **1.** Containing all the appropriate component parts; complete: *The archaeologists found a whole 12th-century chess set.* **2.** Not divided or disjoined; in one unit: *bake the apples whole.* **3. a.** Sound; healthy or intact: *a whole organism.* **b.** *Archaic.* Restored; healed. **4.** Constituting the full amount, extent, or duration; entire: *He cried the whole trip home.* **5.** Having the same parents: *a whole sister.* **6.** *Mathematics.* Integral; not fractional.
~*adv.* Completely; wholly: *gave us a whole new perspective.*
~*n.* **1.** All of the component parts or elements of a thing. **2.** A complete entity or system. —**as a whole.** Altogether; all things considered. —**on the whole.** Considering everything; in general. [Middle English *hool, (w)holle,* sound, unharmed, Old English *hāl.*]

whole blood *n.* Blood drawn from a living human being for use in transfusion, from which no constituent has been removed.

wholefood (hōl-fōōd) *n.* Food that is refined and processed as little as possible from its natural state, such as brown rice. Also used adjectively *a wholefood shop.*

whole gale *n.* A wind of 24.5 to 28.4 metres per second (55 to 63 miles per hour), force 10 on the Beaufort Wind Scale.

whole-heart·ed (hōl-hártid) *adj.* Marked by or undertaken with sincerity, enthusiasm, or complete commitment. See Synonyms at **sincere.** —**whole-heart·ed·ly** *adv.* —**whole-heart·ed·ness** *n.*

whole hog *n.* *Slang.* The whole way or the fullest extent. Used chiefly in the phrase *go the whole hog.* [Perhaps referring to buying a whole pig's carcass rather than individual joints.]

whole life insurance *n.* A type of life insurance policy whereby the insured pays premiums throughout his lifetime, and the sum insured is payable on his death, whenever it may be.

whole-meal (hōl-meel) *adj.* **1.** Made from the entire grain of wheat, including the bran: *wholemeal flour.* **2.** Made with wholemeal flour: *wholemeal bread.*

whole milk *n.* Milk from which no constituent has been removed.

whole·ness (hōl-nəss, -niss) *n.* The state or quality of being whole.

whole note *n.* *Music. U.S.* A **semibreve** (*see*).

whole number *n.* **1.** An integer. **2.** A natural number.

whole·sale (hōl-sayl) *n. Abbr.* **whsle.** The sale of goods in large quantities, as for resale by a retailer.
~*adj.* **1.** Pertaining to or engaged in the sale of goods in this way. **2.** Sold in large bulk or quantity, usually at a lower cost. **3.** Made or accomplished extensively and indiscriminately; blanket: *the wholesale elimination of life by nuclear weapons.*
~*adv.* **1.** In large bulk or quantity; on wholesale terms. **2.** Extensively and indiscriminately.
~*v.* **wholesaled, -saling, -sales.** —*tr.* To sell wholesale. —*intr.* **1.** To engage in wholesale selling. **2.** To sell wholesale. [From the phrase *by (the) whole sale.*] —**whole·sal·er** *n.*

whole·some (hōls'm) *adj.* **1.** Conducive to sound health or well-being; salubrious. **2.** Conducive to moral or social well-being; salubrious. **3.** Physically, mentally, or morally sound; healthy. —See Synonyms at **healthy.** [Middle English *holsom,* Old English *hālsum* (unattested).] —**whole·some·ly** *adv.* —**whole·some·ness** *n.*

whole tone *n.* A musical interval equal to two semitones. Also *U.S.* "whole step".

whole-wheat (hōl-weet, -hweet) *adj.* Wholemeal.

who'll (hōōl, hōōl, ōōl, ŏōl). Contraction of *who will* or *who shall.*

whol·ly (hōli, hōl-li) *adv.* **1.** Entirely; totally: *wholly irrelevant.* **2.** Exclusively; without reservation or exception: *a life wholly devoted to the cause.*

whom (hōōm, *occasional weak form* hōōm) *pron.* The objective case of **who.** See Usage note at **who.**

whom·ev·er (hōōm-ĕ́vvər) *pron.* The objective case of **whoever.**

whom·so·ev·er (hōōm-sō-ĕ́vvər) *pron. Formal.* The objective case of **whosoever.**

whoop (hōōp, wōōp ‖ hōōp) *n.* **1.** A cry of exultation or excitement. **2.** A hooting cry, as of a bird. **3.** The paroxysmal gasp characteristic of whooping cough.
~*v.* **whooped, whooping, whoops.** —*intr.* **1.** To utter a loud shout or cry expressing exultation or excitement. **2.** To utter a hooting cry. **3.** To make the paroxysmal gasp characteristic of whooping cough. —*tr.* **1.** To utter with a whoop. **2.** To chase, call, urge on, or drive with a whoop or whoops: *whooping the horses on down the road.* —**whoop it up.** *Slang.* **1.** To have a wild, noisy celebration. **2.** To arouse interest or enthusiasm. [Middle English (imitative).]

whoop·ee (wōō-pée, wōōppee, wōō-, *or with* h-) *interj. Slang.* Used to express excitement and exuberance. —**make whoopee** (wōōp-pee). To celebrate riotously. [From WHOOP.]

whoop·er (hōōp-ər, wōōp-) *n.* **1.** One that whoops. **2.** An Old World swan, *Cygnus cygnus* (or *Olor cygnus*), having a loud cry. Also called "whooper swan".

whoop·ing cough (hōōp-ing ‖ wōōp-) *n.* An infectious disease caused by the bacterium *Haemophilus pertussis,* involving catarrh of the respiratory passages and characterised by spasms of coughing interspersed with deep, noisy inspiration. Also called "pertussis".

whooping crane *n.* A large, long-legged North American bird, *Grus americana,* now very rare, having black and white plumage and a shrill, trumpeting cry.

whoops (wo͞ops, hwo͞ops, wŏŏps, hwŏŏps) *interj.* Used to express mild surprise or apology, as in reaction to a fall or mistake.

whoosh (wo͞osh, wŏŏsh, hwo͞osh, hwŏŏsh) *intr.v.* **whooshed, whooshing, whooshes.** To hurtle or gush with a low hissing sound suggestive of great speed.
~*n.* A whooshing sound. [Imitative.]

whop (wop, hwop) *tr.v.* **whopped, whopping, whops. 1.** To beat; thrash. **2.** To defeat utterly.
~*n.* A heavy blow or thud. [Middle English *whappen,* variant of dialect *wappen†.*]

whop·per (wŏppər, hwŏppər) *n.* **1.** Something exceptionally big or remarkable. **2.** A gross untruth. [WHOP + -ER.]

whop·ping (wŏp-ing, hwŏp-) *adj.* Exceptionally big or remarkable.
~*adv.* Thoroughly; resoundingly: *a whopping great lie.*

whore (hor ‖ hôr) *n.* **1.** A prostitute. **2.** A promiscuous woman. Used derogatorily.
~*intr.v.* **whored, whoring, whores. 1.** To have sexual intercourse or consort with whores. **2.** To be or act as a whore. [Middle English *ho(o)re,* Old English *hōre.*]

whore·dom (hór-dəm ‖ hôr-) *n.* **1.** Fornication or prostitution. **2.** In Biblical use, idolatry. [Middle English *hordom,* from Old Norse *hōrdōmr.*]

whore·house (hór-howss ‖ hôr-) *n.* A brothel.

whore·mas·ter (hór-maastər ‖ hôr-, -mastər) *n. Archaic.* One who consorts with whores; a fornicator.

whore·mong·er (hór-mung-gər ‖ hôr-, -múng-) *n.* A whoremaster.

whore·son (hór-s'n ‖ hôr-) *n. Archaic.* A bastard. Used derogatorily, sometimes in direct address.
~*adj. Archaic.* Abominable; bastardly.

whor·ish (hór-ish ‖ hôr-) *adj.* Characteristic of a whore; lewd.
—**whor·ish·ly** *adv.* —**whor·ish·ness** *n.*

whorl (wurl, hwurl ‖ wawrl, hwawrl) *n.* **1.** A small flywheel that regulates the speed of the spindle of a spinning wheel. **2.** *Botany.* An arrangement of three or more parts, such as leaves or petals, radiating from a single organ or node. **3.** *Zoology.* A single turn or volution of a spiral shell. **4.** One of the three basic patterns by which fingerprints are classified, characterised by ridges forming complete circles. Compare **arch, loop. 5.** *Architecture.* An ornamental device consisting of stylised vine leaves and tendrils. **6.** A coil, curl, or convolution: *whorls of golden hair.* [Middle English *whorle,* perhaps variant of *whirle,* a whirl, from *whirlen,* to WHIRL.]

whorled (wurld, hwurld ‖ wawrld, hwawrld) *adj.* Having, forming or arranged in a whorl or whorls.

whor·tle·ber·ry (wúrt'l-berri, hwúrt'l-, -bəri, -bri) *n., pl.* **-ries.** *Botany.* **1.** A small European shrub, *Vaccinium myrtillus,* having edible blackish berries. **2.** The fruit of this shrub. Also called "bilberry", "huckleberry", "blaeberry". [Dialect variant of Middle English *hurtleberry : hurt†,* + BERRY.]

whose (ho͞oz, *for sense 2 occasional weak form* o͞oz) *pron.* **1.** The one belonging to which person or persons. Used as the possessive form of *who* in direct or indirect questions: *Whose is that bike?* **2.** Of or belonging to which person or thing. Used as a relative pronoun: *a law whose provisions are not yet clear.*
~*adj.* Of or belonging to which person. Used in direct or indirect questions: *Whose bike is that?* [Middle English *whos, whas, hwas,* Old English *hwæs.*]
Usage: *Whose* can refer to both animate and inanimate entities — that is, it relates to nouns which in other circumstances would be referred to as *which.* There is an alternative possessive form, *of which,* but it is usually very cumbersome – though found in this dictionary.

whose·so·ev·er (ho͞oz-sō-évvər) *pron. & adj. Formal.* Whosoever.

whos·ev·er (ho͞oz-évvər) *pron. & adj.* Of or belonging to whomever.

who·so (ho͞o-sō) *pron. Formal.* Who; whoever; whatever person.

who·so·ev·er (ho͞o-sō-évvər) *pron. Formal.* Whoever.

why (wī, hwī) *adv.* **1.** For what purpose, reason, or cause; with what intention, justification, or motive: *Why were you absent?.* **2.** On account of which: *the reason why he was so annoyed.*
~*conj.* The reason for which: *That's why I arrived so late; why I mention it is that I thought you'd be interested.*
~*n., pl.* **whys. 1.** The cause or intention underlying a given action or situation. **2.** A difficult problem or question; a mystery.
~*interj.* Used to express indignation, surprise, or impatience. [Middle English *why,* Old English *hwȳ.*]
Usage: In the construction *the reason why,* the repetition of the notion of "reason", which is part of the sense of *why,* often leads to criticism. Critics would prefer using *why* or *the reason* alone.

whyd·ah, whid·ah (widdə, hwiddə) *n.* Any of several African weaverbirds of the genus *Vidua,* the breeding plumage of the male being predominantly black with long tail feathers. Also called "widow bird". [Variant of WIDOW (BIRD), altered by association with *Whidah* (Ouidah), Dahomey.]

W.I. 1. West Indian; West Indies. **2.** Women's Institute (in Britain).

Wich·i·ta (wíchi-taw) *n., pl.* **-tas** *or collectively* **Wichita. 1.** A member of a confederacy of Caddoan-speaking North American Indians, formerly living between the Arkansas river and central Texas. **2.** The language of these people.

wick¹ (wik) *n.* **1.** A cord or strand of loosely woven, twisted fibres, as on a candle or oil lamp, that draws up fuel to the flame by capillary action. **2.** Any similar device that conveys liquid by capillary action. —**get on (someone's) wick.** *British Informal.* To annoy intensely. [Middle English *wike,* Old English *wēoce,* akin to Middle Low German *wēke* and Old High German *wiohha†.*]

wick² *n. Obsolete.* A village or town. Now surviving only in place names such as *Warwick.* [Middle English *wik(e),* Old English *wīc,* from West Germanic *wīka* (unattested), from Latin *vīcus.*]

wick·ed (wickid) *adj.* **-eder, -edest. 1. a.** Evil; depraved; bad; sinful: *wicked habits.* **b.** Vicious; savage: *a wicked murder.* **2.** Mischievous or playfully malicious: *a wicked joke.* **3.** Harmful; pernicious: *a wicked cough.* **4.** Obnoxious; offensive: *a wicked stench.* **5.** *Informal.* Formidable; excellent: *had a wicked, spinning tennis serve.* [Middle English, from *wicke,* wicked, Old English *wicca,* wizard.]
—**wick·ed·ly** *adv.* —**wick·ed·ness** *n.*

wick·er (wickər) *n.* **1.** A flexible shoot, as of a willow, used in weaving baskets or certain articles of furniture. **2.** Wickerwork.
~*adj.* Constructed, consisting of, or covered with wicker. [Middle English *wiker,* from Scandinavian, akin to Swedish *viker.*]

wick·er·work (wickər-wurk) *n.* **1.** Woven wicker. **2.** Objects or articles made of this.

wick·et (wickit) *n.* **1.** A small door or gate, especially one built into or near a larger one. **2.** A sluice gate for regulating the amount of water in a millrace or a canal or for emptying a lock **3.** *U.S.* A small window or opening, often fitted with glass or a grating. **4.** In cricket: **a.** Either of the two sets of three stumps, topped by bails, that forms the target of the bowler and is defended by the batsman. **b.** The area between these two sets of stumps, the **pitch** (*see*). **c.** The turn of a batsman or the termination of his innings: *India scored five runs for two wickets.* **d.** The period during which two batsmen are in together. **5.** *U.S.* In croquet, a **hoop** (*see*). —**keep wicket.** To play as a wicketkeeper. —**on a good wicket.** In a favourable situation. —**on a sticky wicket. 1.** On a soft, damp wicket, as in cricket. **2.** In an unfavourable situation. [Middle English, from Old North French *wiket,* from Germanic.]

wick·et·keep·er (wickit-keepər) *n.* In cricket, the player positioned immediately behind the wicket guarded by the batsman who is facing the bowling.

wick·i·up, wik·i·up (wicki-up) *n.* A frame hut covered with matting, bark, brush, or similar materials, used by the nomadic Indians of North America. [Fox *wikiyapi,* "house", from Proto-Algonquian *wikiwahmi* (unattested), WIGWAM.]

Wick·low (wík-lō). Coastal county of Leinster province, Republic of Ireland. Bordering the Irish Sea, it is largely pastureland with the Wicklow mountains at its centre, rising to 926 metres (3,039 feet) at Lugnaquilla. The county town and port is Wicklow.

Wi·dal reaction (vi-dál, vee-) *n.* A test for typhoid fever in which the presence or absence of antibodies against the causative bacteria is determined by agglutination techniques. [After Fernand *Widal* (1862–1929), French physician.]

widdershins. Variant of **withershins.**

wide (wīd) *adj.* **wider, widest. 1.** Extending over a relatively large area from side to side; broad. **2.** Having a specified extent from side to side; in width: *a ribbon two inches wide.* **3.** Having great range or scope: *a wide selection; wide reading.* **b.** Including or extending to many different things: *a wide observation.* **4.** Full or ample, as clothing might be. **5.** Fully open or extended: *look with wide eyes.* **6.** Located or located away from or missing a given goal or point: *wide of the target.* **7.** Failing to realise or deal with a relevant point or issue: *wide of the mark.* **8.** *Phonetics.* Lax. —See Usage note at **broad.**
~*adv.* **1.** Over a large area; extensively: *journey far and wide.* **2.** To the full extent; completely: *the door was open wide.* **3.** So as to miss the target; astray. **4.** *Sports.* At or towards the sides of a pitch or court: *kept playing the ball wide to stretch the Italian defence.*
~*n.* A ball bowled outside of the batsman's reach in cricket, counting as a run for the batting team. [Middle English *wide,* Old English *wīd.*] —**wide·ly** *adv.* —**wide·ness** *n.*

wide-an·gle lens (wīd-ang-g'l) *n.* A lens that has a relatively short focal length and permits an angle of view wider than about 70°.

wide-a·wake (wīd-ə-wáyk) *adj.* **1.** Completely awake. **2.** Alert.
~*n.* A soft felt hat with a wide brim.

wide-bod·ied (wīd-bóddid) *adj.* Designating an aircraft with a wide fuselage to accommodate a large number of passengers.

wide boy *n. British Informal.* A man who makes his living by underhand or shady means.

wide-eyed (wīd-īd) *adj.* **1.** With the eyes completely opened, as in wonder. **2.** Innocent; credulous.

wid·en (wīd'n) *v.* **-ened, -ening, -ens.** —*tr.* To make wider. —*intr.* To be or become wide or wider. —**wid·en·er** *n.*

wide-o·pen (wīd-ópən) *adj.* **1.** Opened completely: *a wide-open door.* **2.** Vulnerable, as to attack: *left himself wide-open.* **3.** With the outcome uncertain: *a wide-open match.* **4.** Without laws or law enforcement: *a wide-open town.*

wide-screen (wīd-skréen) *adj.* Pertaining to or involving a screen whose width is greater than its height.

wide-spread (wīd-spréd, -spred) *adj.* **1.** Spread or scattered over a considerable extent. **2.** Occurring or accepted widely.

widgeon. Variant of **wigeon.**

widg·et (wij-it) *n. Informal.* Something which is hypothetical, or for which the exact name has been forgotten, or is unknown; especially, a small mechanical or electronic device. [Probably a variant of GADGET.]

wid·ow (widdō) *n.* **1.** A woman whose husband has died and who has not remarried. **2.** In card games, an additional hand dealt to the table. **3.** An incomplete line of type, especially one ending a paragraph, carried over to the top of the next page or column.
~*tr.v.* **widowed, -owing, -ows. 1.** To make a widow of. Used

chiefly in the past participle. [Middle English *wid(e)we*, Old English *widuwe*.] —**wid·ow·hood** *n.*

widow bird. The **whydah** *(see).* [From its black plumage.]

wid·ow·er (wĭddō-ər) *n.* A man whose wife has died and who has not remarried. [Middle English *widewer*, from *widewe*, WIDOW.]

widow's cruse *n.* An unfailing or inexhaustible supply. [Biblical allusion (I Kings 17:10-16).]

widow's mite *n.* A small but relatively generous contribution made by one who has little. [Biblical allusion (Mark 12:42).]

widow's peak *n.* A hairline having a V-shaped point at the middle of the forehead. Also called "peak". [From the superstition that it is a sign of early widowhood.]

widow's walk *n.* *U.S.* A railed, rooftop gallery on a dwelling, designed to observe vessels at sea.

width (width, wĭt-th ‖ with) *n. Abbr.* **w.** 1. The state, quality, or fact of being wide. 2. The measurement of the extent of something from side to side; the size of something in terms of its wideness. 3. Something that has a particular width; especially, in sewing, a piece of fabric measured from selvage to selvage: *a skirt having four widths.* 4. The distance extending parallel with the shortest sides of a rectangular swimming pool. [From WIDE.]

width·wise (width-wīz, wĭt-th- ‖ with-) *adv.* From side to side; in terms of width.

wield (weeld) *tr.v.* **wielded, wielding, wields.** 1. To handle (a weapon or tool, for example). 2. To exercise or exert (power or influence). —See Synonyms at **handle.** [Middle English *welden*, Old English *wealdan* and *wieldan.*] —**wield·a·ble** *adj.* —**wield·er** *n.*

wield·y (weeldi) *adj.* **-ier, -iest.** Easily wielded or managed.

Wien. See **Vienna.**

wie·ner (weenər) *n.* A wienerwurst. [German, short for WIENER-WURST.]

Wie·ner schnit·zel (veenər shnĭts'l). A breaded veal cutlet. [German, "Vienna cutlet".]

wie·ner·wurst (weenər-wurst, -woorst, -wōōsht) *n. U.S.* A type of smoked pork or beef sausage, similar to a frankfurter. Also called "wiener". [German, "Vienna sausage".]

wife (wīf) *n., pl.* **wives** (wīvz). *Abbr.* **w.** 1. A woman married to a man. 2. *Archaic.* A woman, especially one of peasant stock. Now used chiefly in certain phrases: *old wives' tales.* —**take to wife.** *Archaic.* To marry. [Middle English *wif(e)*, Old English *wīf*, from Germanic *wīf* (unattested), woman.] —**wife·hood, wife·dom** *n.* —**wife·less** *adj.* —**wife·ly** *adj.*

wife-swapping (wīf-swopping) *n.* The act or practice of couples exchanging their wives or partners, usually for a night or short period of time, for sexual activity.

wig (wig) *n.* A headpiece of artificial or human hair worn as personal adornment, part of a costume, or to conceal baldness. —*tr.v.* **wigged, wigging, wigs.** *British Informal.* To scold or censure. [Shortened from PERIWIG.] —**wigged** *adj.* —**wig·less** *adj.*

wig·an (wĭggən) *n.* A stiff fabric used for stiffening. [First made in *Wigan*, northwest England.]

wi·geon, wid·geon (wĭjən) *n. pl.* **-geons** or collectively **wigeon.** Any of various ducks, such as the Eurasian species *Anas penelope,* having a brown and whitish plumage.

wig·ger·y (wĭggəri) *n., pl.* **-ies.** 1. A wig or wigs collectively. 2. The practice of wearing wigs.

wig·ging (wĭgging) *n. British Informal.* A telling off or scolding. [19th century : slang use of WIG (false hair).]

wig·gle (wĭgg'l) *v.* **-gled, -gling, -gles.** —*intr.* To move, twist, or proceed with short irregular movements from side to side or up and down. —*tr.* To cause to move in such a fashion: *wiggle one's toes.* —*n.* The act of wiggling; a wiggling movement or course. —**get a wiggle on.** *U.S. Slang.* To hurry or hurry up. [Middle English *wiglen,* from Middle Dutch or Middle Low German *wiggelen.*] —**wig·gler** *n.* —**wig·gly** *adj.*

wight¹ (wīt) *n. Archaic.* A human being; a person. [Middle English *wight,* Old English *wiht.*]

wight² *adj. Archaic.* Courageous; brave. [Middle English *wiht,* from Old Norse *vīgt,* neuter of *vīgr,* able in battle.]

Wight (wīt), **Isle of.** Unitary Authority area and island off the south of England. Separated from the mainland by the Solent and Spithead channels, it is a popular holiday centre and agricultural area.

Wig·ner (wĭg-nər), **Eugene Paul** (1902–95). U.S. physicist. Born in Hungary, he worked on the first atomic reactor, as well as on the atomic bomb. He shared the Nobel prize for physics (1963).

Wig·town (wĭg-town). Former county of southwest Scotland. Merged (1975) with Dumfries and Galloway, it includes the Rhinns of Galloway double peninsula and the port of Stranraer.

wig·wag (wĭg-wag) *v.* **-wagged, -wagging, -wags.** —*tr.* 1. To move (a flag, for example) back and forth, especially as a means of signalling. 2. To signal (a message) by such motions. —*intr.* 1. To move back and forth; to wag. 2. To signal by waving the hand or a device, such as a flag. —*n.* 1. The act or practice of giving signals by wigwagging. 2. A message so relayed. [Dialectal *wig,* perhaps from WIGGLE + WAG.] —**wig·wag·ger** *n.*

wig·wam (wĭg-wam ‖ chiefly *U.S.* -waam) *n.* **1. a.** A North American Indian dwelling, commonly having an arched or domed framework overlaid with bark, hides, or mats. Compare **tepee. b.** Loosely, any tent used by North American Indians. 2. A play tent used by children. [Eastern Abnaki *wikəwam,* from Proto-Algonquian *wikiwahmi* (unattested), perhaps from root *wik-* (unattested), to dwell.]

wikiup. Variant of **wickiup.**

Wil·ber·force (wĭlbər-fawrss ‖ -fōrss), **William** (1759–1833). British politician and social reformer. He served as an M.P. (1780–1825) and campaigned for the abolition of the slave trade, achieved in 1807, and for the abolition of slavery, achieved in 1833.

wil·co (wĭlkō) *interj.* Used, especially in radio communications, to indicate that one will carry out an instruction. [Abbreviation of *I will comply.*]

wild (wīld) *adj.* **wilder, wildest.** 1. Occurring, growing, or living in a natural state; not domesticated, cultivated, or tamed: *wild strawberries.* 2. Not inhabited; desolate: *wild country.* 3. Uncivilised or barbarous; savage: *wild natives.* 4. **a.** Lacking discipline, restraint, or control; unruly. **b.** Excessive in noise and behaviour; lively and loud: *a wild party; the conference became wild.* 5. Disorderly; disarranged: *Her hair was wild.* 6. Boisterous; ungoverned; frenzied: *wild laughter.* 7. Full of intense, irrepressible emotion: *wild with jealousy.* 8. **a.** *Chiefly U.S.* Eccentric; notoriously odd or amusing: *a wild character.* **b.** Extravagant; fantastic: *a wild idea.* 9. Furiously disturbed or turbulent; tempestuous: *a wild night at sea.* 10. Reckless; risky: *a wild gamble.* 11. Random or spontaneous; whimsical: *make a wild guess.* 12. Deviating widely; erratic: *a wild shot.* 13. In card games, having an arbitrary equivalence or value determined by the holder's needs or choice: *playing poker with jokers wild.* —**wild about.** *Informal.* Attracted to or excited by: *wild about her new boyfriend; not wild about rice pudding.*

~*adv.* In a wild manner. —**run wild.** To live, behave, or grow in an unrestrained manner.

~*n.* Often plural. An uninhabited or uncultivated region: *the wilds of Greenland.* —**the wild.** A natural, unrestrained life or state; nature. [Middle English *wilde,* Old English *wilde.*] —**wild·ly** *adv.* —**wild·ness** *n.*

wild and woolly *adj. Informal.* Marked by or characteristic of the rough, lawless atmosphere of former frontier America.

wild basil *n.* See **basil.**

wild boar *n.* A wild Eurasian pig, *Sus scrofa,* having a grey or black coat and prominent tusks. Also called "boar".

wild carrot *n.* A plant, **Queen Anne's lace** *(see).*

wild·cat (wīld-kat) *n.* 1. A Eurasian wild cat, *Felis sylvestris,* with a thick coat and a bushy tail. 2. Any of various wild felines of small to medium size; especially, one of the genus *Lynx.* 3. A quick-tempered or fierce person, especially a woman. 4. An oil well drilled in an area not known to yield oil.

~*adj.* 1. Risky or unsound, especially financially. 2. Accomplished or operating without official sanction or authority.

~*v.* **wildcatted, -catting, -cats.** —*tr.* To prospect for (oil, for example) in an area not known to be productive. —*intr.* To wildcat in an area not known to be productive. —**wild·cat·ter** *n.*

wildcat strike *n.* A strike not authorised by the appropriate union.

wild celery *n.* An aromatic plant, *Apium graveolens,* that is the ancestor of cultivated celery.

wild cherry *n.* A Eurasian cherry tree, *Prunus avium,* having white flowers and red round fruits. It is the ancestor of the cultivated sweet cherry. Also called "gean".

wild dog *n.* The **dingo** *(see).*

Wilde (wīld), **Oscar (Fingal O'Flahertie Wills)** (1854–1900). Irish-born dramatist, poet, and humorist. Renowed as a wit in London literary circles, he achieved recognition with the novel *The Picture of Dorian Grey* (1891); other works include *Poems* (1881) and the plays *Lady Windermere's Fan* (1892) and *The Importance of Being Earnest* (1895). Convicted and sentenced (1895) to two years' imprisonment for a homosexual relationship with Lord Alfred Douglas (1870–1945), on his release he went into exile in France, where he wrote his most famous poem, *The Ballad of Reading Gaol* (1898).

wil·de·beest (wil-di-beest, vil-, -də-) *n., pl.* **-beests** or collectively **wilde beest.** A mammal, the **gnu** *(see).* [Obsolete Afrikaans : Dutch *wild,* wild, from Middle Dutch *wilt, wilde* + *beest,* beast, from Middle Dutch *beeste,* from Old French *beste,* BEAST.]

wil·der (wĭldər) *v.* **-dered, -dering, -ders.** *Archaic.* —*tr.* 1. To lead astray; mislead. 2. To bewilder; confuse; perplex. —*intr.* 1. To lose one's way. 2. To become bewildered. [Perhaps a back-formation from WILDERNESS.] —**wil·der·ment** *n.*

Wil·der (wĭldər), **Billy (Samuel)** (1906–). Austrian-born U.S. film director. His films include *Double Indemnity* (1944), *Some Like It Hot* (1959), and *Fedora* (1978).

Wilder, Thornton (Niven) (1897–1975). U.S. playwright and novelist. His work includes the novel the *Bridge of San Luis Rey* (1927) and the plays *Our Town* (1938) and *The Skin of Our Teeth* (1942).

wil·der·ness (wĭldər-nəss, -niss) *n.* 1. Any unsettled, uncultivated region left in its natural condition, especially: **a.** A large wild tract of land covered with dense vegetation or forests. **b.** An extensive area that is barren or empty, such as a desert or ocean; a waste. **c.** A piece of land set aside to grow wild. 2. Something likened to a wild region in bewildering vastness, confusion, or unchecked profusion: *a wilderness of industrial estates.* 3. A period of being removed from a usually specified activity: *has come out of the political wilderness.* [Middle English *wildernesse,* Old English *wildēornes,* from *wildēor,* wild beast.]

wild-eyed (wīld-īd) *adj.* Glaring in or as if in anger, terror, stupor, or madness.

wild·fire (wīld-fīr) *n.* 1. A highly flammable material formerly used in warfare. 2. A raging fire that travels and spreads rapidly. 3. Lightning occurring without thunder being heard. 4. A luminosity that appears at night hovering over marshland; ignis fatuus.

wild flower *n.* **1.** A flowering plant that grows in a natural, uncultivated state. **2.** The flower of such a plant.

wild-fowl (wīld-foul) *n., pl.* **-fowls** or collectively **wildfowl.** A wild bird, such as a duck, goose, or quail, hunted as game.

~*intr.v.* **wildfowled, -fowling, -fowls.** To hunt wildfowl. —**wildfowl·er** *n.*

wild ginger *n.* A North American plant, *Asarum canadense,* having broad leaves, a single brownish flower, and an aromatic root.

wild-goose chase (wīld-goōss). A hopeless or foolish pursuit of an unattainable or imaginary object. [Originally a race similar to the flight of geese, where the object was to follow accurately and at a definite interval.]

wild hyacinth *n.* Any of various wildflowers superficially resembling a hyacinth, such as the bluebell.

wild·ing (wīlding) *n.* **1.** A plant that grows wild or has escaped from cultivation; especially, a wild apple tree or its fruit. **2.** A wild animal. [From WILD.]

wild-life (wīld-līf) *n.* Wild animals and vegetation; especially, animals living in a natural, undomesticated state.

wild-ling (wīldling) *n.* A wild plant or animal; especially, a wild plant transplanted to a cultivated spot.

wild marjoram *n.* See **marjoram.**

wild mustard *n.* **Charlock** (*see*).

wild oat *n.* **1.** *Usually plural.* A grass, *Avena fatua,* native to Eurasia, related to the cultivated oat. **2.** *Plural.* The indiscretions of youth, especially sexually promiscuous behaviour. Used in the phrase *sow one's wild oats.*

wild olive *n.* Any of various trees resembling the olive; especially, the **oleaster** (*see*).

wild pansy *n.* Any of several pansy-like plants of the genus *Viola.*

wild rice *n.* **1.** A tall aquatic grass, *Zizania aquatica,* of northern North America, bearing edible grain. **2.** The grain of this plant.

wild rose *n.* Any of various uncultivated roses, having a single whorl of petals and including the dogrose.

wild rubber *n.* Rubber extracted from uncultivated rubber trees.

wild rye *n.* Any of various grasses of the genus *Elymus,* resembling cultivated rye in having bristly spikes.

wild type *n.* The typical form of an organism as it occurs in nature, as distinguished from mutant specimens that may result from selective breeding.

Wild West *n.* The western United States during the period of its settlement, especially with reference to its lawlessness.

wild-wood (wīld-woōd) *n.* A forest or wooded area in its natural state.

wile¹ (wīl) *n.* **1.** *Usually plural.* **a.** A deceitful stratagem or trick. **b.** A disarming or seductive manner, device, or procedure. **2.** Trickery; cunning; deceit. —See Synonyms at **artifice.**

~*tr.v.* **wiled, wiling, wiles.** To influence or lead by means of wiles; entice; lure. [Middle English *wil,* perhaps from Old Norse *wihl-* (unattested).]

wile². Variant of **while** (verb).

wil-ful, *U.S.* **will-ful** (wil-fʹl). **1.** Said or done in accordance with one's will; intended; deliberate. **2.** Inclined to impose one's will; obstinate; headstrong. —See Synonyms at **contrary, voluntary, unruly.** —**wil-fully** *adv.* —**wil-full-ness** *n.*

Wilkes (wilks), **John** (1727–97). British politician and journalist. He worked for parliamentary reform, American independence, and religious toleration.

Wil-kins (wilkinz), **Maurice Hugh Frederick** (1916–). British biophysicist. Born in New Zealand, he worked, during World War II, on the atomic bomb in California. He shared the Nobel prize with Crick and Watson (1962) for work on the structure of DNA.

will¹ (wil) *n.* **1.** The mental faculty by which one deliberately chooses or decides upon a course of action. **2.** A disposition to exercise this faculty; determination: *a will to win.* **3.** That which is desired or decided upon, especially by a person in authority. **4.** Deliberate intention or wish: *against his will.* **5.** Free discretion; pleasure; inclination: *wandered about at will.* **6.** Bearing or attitude towards others; disposition: *full of good will.* **7.** The power to exert control over conflicting mental and emotional tendencies and arrive at one's own decision: *He's got enough will to resist temptation.* **8. a.** A legal declaration of how a person wishes his possessions to be disposed of after his death. **b.** The document containing this declaration. —**a will of (one's) own.** A tendency to behave in an erratic or unpredictable way. Used humorously. —**with a will.** With eagerness and energy.

~*v.* **willed, willing, wills.** —*tr.* **1.** To decide upon; choose: *Tell me what you have willed.* **2.** To desire; yearn for: *will one's own destruction.* **3.** To decree; dictate; order: *The queen willed that he should be exiled.* **4.** To resolve with a forceful will; determine: *God willed that we would question our existence.* **5.** To influence or induce by sheer force of will or by supernatural power: *We tried to will the sun to come out.* **6.** To bequeath; grant in a legal will. —*intr.* **1.** To exercise the will; use the power of the will. **2.** To decree or make a firm choice. [Middle English *will(e),* Old English *will, willa.*] —**will-a-ble** *adj.*

will² (wil; *weak forms* ʹl, wəl) *v.* past **would** (woōd; *weak forms* d, əd, wəd) also *archaic* **wouldest** (woōddist) or **wouldst** (woōdst) for second person singular, present **will** (also *archaic* **wilt** (wilt) for second person singular). Used as an auxiliary followed by an infinitive without *to* or, in reply to a question or suggestion, with the infinitive understood. It can indicate: **1.** Simple futurity: *They will appear later.* **2. a.** Likelihood or certainty: *You will regret this.*

b. Inevitability: *Everyone will die.* **3.** Willingness: *Will you help me with this package?* **4.** Requirement or command: *You will report to me afterwards.* **5.** Customary or habitual action: *She would spend hours in the library.* **6.** Capacity or ability: *This metal will not crack under heavy pressure.* **7.** Probability or expectation: *That will be the postman ringing.* **8.** Determination; resolution: *I will do it if I have to burst a blood vessel!* —See Usage note at **shall.** —*intr.* To have a desire: *Sit here, if you will.* —*tr.* To desire; wish: *Do what you will.* [Will, would, wouldest; Middle English *willen, wolde, woldest,* Old English *wyllan, wolde, woldest.*]

willed (wild) *adj.* Having a will of a specified kind. Usually used in combination: *weak-willed.*

wil-lem-ite (wilə-mīt) *n.* A vitreous to resinous silicate of zinc, Zn_2SiO_4, a minor ore of zinc. [Dutch *willemit,* from *Willem,* William, after *William* I (died 1843), king of the Netherlands.]

wil-let (willit) *n.* A long-billed American shore bird, *Catoptrophorus semipalmatus.* [Imitative of its cry.]

Wil-liam I¹ (wil-yəm), known as **William the Conqueror** (*c.* 1027–87). The first Norman king of England (1066–87) and Duke of Normandy (1035–87). He invaded England (1066) on the grounds that succession to the English throne had been promised to him by his cousin Edward the Confessor. He defeated Harold at Hastings and as king adopted a feudal constitution.

William I², Known as **William the Silent** (1533–84). Prince of Orange. Inheriting the principality in 1544, he was made governor of Holland, Zeeland, and Utrecht (1559) by Philip II of Spain, whom he opposed for his persecution of Protestants. He led the revolt against Spanish rule (1568) but succeeded only briefly in unifying the Protestant north with the Catholic south.

William II¹ (1859–1941). German emperor (1888–1918). The grandson of Queen Victoria, he pursued aggressive policies, supporting the Afrikaners in South Africa, and Austria's demands on Serbia (1914) although when war became apparent, he strove for peace. He was forced to abdicate after Germany's defeat in World War I.

William II², known as **William Rufus** (*c.* 1056–1100). King of England (1087–1100). He was the second son of William the Conqueror, on whose death he succeeded to the throne.

William III, known as **William of Orange** (1650–1702). King of England (1689–1702). Married to Mary, daughter of James II (1677), he was asked by the opposition to James to invade England, and landed at Torbay (1688). He was proclaimed joint monarch with Mary (1689) after James fled, and defeated him at the Boyne (1690).

William IV (1765–1837). King of Great Britain and Ireland (1830–37). The third son of George III and brother of George IV, he was known as the sailor king because of his naval career, rising to the office of Lord High Admiral (1827–28). He left no surviving legitimate children and was succeeded by his niece Victoria.

Williams, Shirley (Vivien Teresa Brittain), Baroness (1930–). British politician. She held office in two Labour governments (1974–9), but became a founder of the SDP (1981) and was an SDP M.P. (1981–3). Autobiography: *Snakes and Ladders* (1996).

Williams, Tennessee, born Thomas Lanier Williams (1911–83). U.S. playwright. His works examine family tensions and feelings of frustration, particularly in women. Frequently set in the Deep South, his plays include *The Glass Menagerie* (1944), *A Streetcar Named Desire* (1947), and *Cat on a Hot Tin Roof* (1955).

Williams, William Carlos (1883–1963). U.S. imagist poet. It was not until the 1940s that he established his reputation with the work in 5 volumes, *Paterson* (1946–58). His poetry is noted for its clarity, naturalism, and concern with American themes.

Williamson, Malcolm (Benjamin Graham Christopher) (1931–). Australian composer, a British resident since 1953. His works include symphonies, the opera *Our Man in Havana* (1963), and the *Mass of Christ the King* (1977). A pianist and organist, he was appointed Master of the Queen's Music (1975).

William Tell. See **Tell, William.**

William the Lion (1143–1214). King of Scotland (1165–1214). The brother of Malcolm IV and grandson of David I, he invaded Northumberland and was captured and taken to France. He was forced to perform homage for his kingdom as the price of freedom, but in 1189 Richard I of England abandoned all claims on payment of 10,000 marks.

wil-lies (williz) *pl.n. Slang.* Feelings of uneasiness. Preceded by *the*: *This place gives me the willies.* [19th century : origin obscure.]

will-ing (willing) *adj.* **1.** Disposed to accept or tolerate; prepared: *willing to overlook your mistakes.* **2.** Acting or ready to act gladly; eagerly compliant: *very willing to help; willing helpers.* **3.** Done, given, accepted, or offered freely and heartily. —See Synonyms at **voluntary.** —**will-ing-ly** *adv.* —**will-ing-ness** *n.*

will-o'-the-wisp (wil-əthə-wisp, -əth-) *n.* **1. Ignis fatuus** (*see*). **2.** One that is alluring, delusive, or misleading. [Originally *Will with the wisp,* from *Will,* pet form of *William* + WISP, in obsolete sense handful of hay (used as torch).]

wil-low (willō) *n.* **1.** Any of various deciduous trees or shrubs of the genus *Salix,* having usually narrow leaves, flowers borne in catkins, and strong, lightweight wood. **2.** The wood of any of these trees. **3.** Something made from willow, especially a cricket bat. **4.** A textile machine consisting of a spiked drum revolving inside a chamber fitted internally with spikes, used to open and clean unprocessed cotton or wool.

~*tr.v.* **willowed, -lowing, -lows.** To open and clean (textile fibres) with a willow. [Middle English *wilowe,* Old English *welig.*]

wil-low-herb (willō-herb) *n.* Any of various plants of the genus *Epi-*

lobium, such as *E. angustifolium,* rosebay willowherb, that have narrow leaves and terminal clusters of pink, purplish, or white flowers.

willow pattern *n.* A traditional, Chinese-style, blue-on-white design typically consisting of a willow tree, bridge, river, and figures, used on household china.

willow warbler *n.* A Eurasian warbler, *Phylloscopus trochilis,* having a yellowish-brown plumage with pale underparts.

wil·low·y (wíllō-i) *adj.* **-ier, -iest. 1.** Planted with or abounding in willows. **2.** Resembling or suggestive of a willow tree, especially: **a.** Flexible; pliant. **b.** Slender and graceful.

will-pow·er (wíl-pow-ər, -powr) *n.* The ability to exercise control over one's actions and bring them into line with one's decisions or wishes; strength of mind and purpose.

wil·ly (willi) *n., pl.* **-lies.** *Chiefly British Informal.* A penis. [From *willy,* pet form of *William.*]

wil·ly-nil·ly (wíli-nílli) *adv.* Whether desired or not.
~*adj.* Being or occurring whether desired or not. [Variant of *will I nill I,* "be I willing, be I unwilling".]

Wil·ming·ton (wilmingtən). Industrial city in Delaware, eastern United States. Situated on the Delaware river, it was founded by Swedish colonists in 1638 and is an important port with extensive shipyards.

Wil·son (wil-s'n) **, Sir Angus (Frank Johnstone)** (1913-91). British novelist and short-story writer. His satirical works include *Anglo-Saxon Attitudes* (1956), *The Old Men at the Zoo* (1961), *As If by Magic* (1973), and *Setting the World on Fire* (1980).

Wilson, Charles Thomson Rees (1869-1959). British physicist. He invented the Wilson cloud chamber, which permitted the observation and photography of the movement of charged particles (1911). He won the Nobel prize in physics (1927).

Wilson, Colin (Henry) (1931-). British author. His works cover a wide spectrum, including thrillers such as *Necessary Doubt* (1964), and studies of the paranormal, such as *The Occult* (1971).

Wilson, Edmund (1895-1972). U.S. author and critic. His works include *Axel's Castle* (1931), a study of the symbolists, *To The Finland Station* (1940), *The Scrolls from the Dead Sea* (1955), and *The American Earthquake* (1958).

Wilson, (James) Harold, Baron Wilson of Rievaulx (1916-95). British Labour prime minister (1964-70; 1974-76). He succeeded Hugh Gaitskell as party leader (1963), became prime minister with the Labour victory of 1964, and faced many problems, which included those of Rhodesia and Northern Ireland, and resistance amongst his supporters to the introduction of a prices and incomes policy. He resigned without warning in 1976.

Wilson, (Thomas) Woodrow (1856-1924). Twenty-eighth President of the United States (1913-21). His presidency saw the introduction of prohibition and resistance to U.S. involvement in World War I, although he reversed the latter policy after the German U-boat campaign (1917). He laid the basis for a peace settlement and at the Paris Peace Conference achieved the acceptance of the League of Nations in the Treaty of Versailles (1919). He was awarded the Nobel peace prize (1919), but the treaty was rejected by the U.S. Senate, and he suffered a physical breakdown.

Wilson cloud chamber (wíl-sən). See **cloud chamber.** [After C.T.R. WILSON.]

Wilson's disease *n.* A hereditary disorder of copper metabolism in which excess copper is deposited in tissues and organs, such as the liver (causing jaundice and cirrhosis) and brain (causing mental deterioration). [After S. Wilson (1878-1937), British neurologist.]

wilt¹ (wilt) *v.* **wilted, wilting, wilts.** —*intr.* **1.** To become limp or flaccid; droop: *Plants wilted in the heat.* **2.** To become less active, energetic, or spirited; weaken. —*tr.* To cause to wilt.
~*n.* **1.** The act of wilting or the state of being wilted. **2.** Any of various plant diseases characterised by slow or rapid collapse of terminal shoots, branches, or entire plants. [Variant of dialectal *wilk, welk,* from Middle English *welken,* from Middle Dutch.]

wilt². *Archaic.* Second person singular present tense of **will.**

Wil·ton (wiltən) *n.* A kind of carpet having a velvety surface formed by the cut loops of a pile. [From *Wilton,* Wiltshire, England.]

Wilts. Wiltshire.

Wilt·shire¹ (wilt-sher, -sheer). County of south central England. With the Marlborough Downs in the north and Salisbury Plain in the south, it is chiefly agricultural with the growing of wheat and barley and the raising of pigs, sheep, and dairy cattle. Large areas of Salisbury Plain are used for military training. The town of Wilton is famous for its carpets. Inhabited since ancient times, the area has prehistoric remains at Stonehenge, Avebury, and Silbury Hill. The county town is Trowbridge.

Wilt·shire² *n.* A sheep of a horned breed with very short fleece, reared for meat.

wi·ly (wíli) *adj.* **-lier, -liest.** Full of wiles; guileful; calculating. See Synonyms at **sly.** [WILE + -LY.] **—wil·i·ly** *adv.* **—wil·i·ness** *n.*

wim·ble (wimb'l) *n.* Any of numerous hand tools for the boring of holes, as a brace and bit or a gimlet.
~*tr.v.* **wimbled, -bling, -bles.** To bore with or as if with a wimble. [Middle English, from Anglo-French, perhaps from Middle Dutch *wimmel.*]

Wim·ble·don (wimb'ldən). District in the Greater London Borough of Merton. It is the location of the All-England Lawn Tennis Club, where international championships have been held since 1877.

wimp (wimp) *n. British Informal.* One who lacks strength of charac-

ter or resolution; an insipidly ineffectual person. [Back-formation from W(H)IMPER.]

wim·ple (wimp'l) *n.* **1.** A cloth wound round the head, framing the face, and drawn into folds beneath the chin, worn by women in medieval times and as part of the habit of certain orders of nuns. **2.** *Archaic.* **a.** A fold or pleat in cloth. **b.** A ripple, as on the surface of water. **c.** A curve or bend. **d.** *Scottish.* A cunning twist.
~*v.* **wimpled, -pling, -ples.** —*tr.* **1.** To cover or furnish with a wimple. **2.** *Archaic.* **a.** To cause to form ripples. **b.** To cause to form or lie in folds. —*intr.* **1.** *Archaic.* To form or lie in folds. **2. a.** To ripple. **b.** To meander. [Middle English *wimpel,* Old English *wimpel.*]

Wim·py (wimpi) *n.* A trademark for a type of hamburger.

Wims·hurst machine (wimz-hurst) *n.* An electrostatic generator having mica or glass discs rotating in opposite directions with metal carriers on which charges are produced by induction, used chiefly as a demonstration apparatus. [After James *Wimshurst* (1832-1903), British engineer.]

win (win) *v.* **won** (wun ‖ won)**, winning, wins.** —*intr.* **1.** To achieve victory over others in any kind of contest. **2.** To achieve success in an effort or venture. **3.** To struggle through to a desired place or condition: *We won through; She won home.* **4.** To finish first in a race: *won by a length.* —*tr.* **1.** To achieve victory in: *win a race; win an argument.* **2.** To be the successful party in predicting or guessing (an outcome, such as the result of a bet): *Willis won the toss for England.* **3.** To receive or gain through victory in a contest: *won the World Cup; won the seat from Labour at the last election.* **4.** To get as a reward: *won a medal in the Falklands conflict; my poem won (me) a prize.* **5.** To achieve through effort or merit: *win an advantage; won recognition.* **6.** To take in battle; capture. **7.** To succeed in gaining the favour or support of; prevail upon. Sometimes used with *over* or *round*: *His eloquence won us over.* **8. a.** To gain the affection or loyalty of: *won a friend for life.* **b.** To appeal successfully to (someone's loyalty, sympathy, or other emotion). **c.** To persuade (a person) to marry one. **9.** In mining: **a.** To discover and open (a vein or deposit); render fit for mining. **b.** To extract from a mine. **10.** *Archaic.* To reach with effort or difficulty: *The ship won a safe port.*
—win out. *Informal.* To succeed or prevail.
~*n.* **1.** A victory or success, especially in a competition. **2.** An amount won or earned: *a pools win.* [Win, won, won; Middle English *winnen,* to win, strive, Old English *winnan,* to strive.]

wince¹ (winss) *intr.v.* **winced, wincing, winces.** To shrink or start involuntarily, as in pain or distress; flinch.
~*n.* A wincing movement or gesture. [Middle English *wincen,* to kick, wince, from Anglo-French *wencir* (unattested), from Germanic.] **—winc·er** *n.*

wince² *n.* A roller on which cloth may be moved and lowered into a vat of dye. [Variant of WINCH.]

win·cey·ette (wín-si-ét) *n.* A fairly light cotton fabric with a soft nap, used especially in making nightclothes.

winch (winch) *n.* **1.** A stationary motor-driven or hand-powered hoisting machine having a drum round which a rope or chain winds as the load is lifted. **2.** The crank used to give motion to a grindstone or similar device.
~*tr.v.* **winched, winching, winches.** To hoist or move with or as if with a winch. [Middle English *winche,* a pulley, Old English *wince.*] **—winch·er** *n.*

Win·ches·ter¹ (win-chistər ‖ -chestər). County town of Hampshire, southern England. Situated on the river Itchen, it was once the capital of Wessex and after the Norman Conquest and the rise of London, remained England's chief seat of learning. Its Norman cathedral, built on a Saxon church, is the longest in Britain and the burial place of many Saxon monarchs.

Winchester² *n.* A trademark for a breechloading repeating rifle with lever action and a magazine attached horizontally under the barrel. [After Oliver *Winchester* (1810-80), U.S. manufacturer.]

wind¹ (wind) *n.* **1.** A current of air moving at any speed; especially, a natural and perceptible movement of air parallel to or along the ground. **2. a.** A movement or current of air blowing from one of the four cardinal points of the compass: *the four winds.* **b.** The direction from which a strong or prevailing current of air comes: *The wind is northeast.* **3.** Moving air carrying an odour, scent, or sound. **4.** A current or stream of air generated by a fan, bellows, or other artificial means. **5. a.** A wind instrument, such as a flute or clarinet. **b.** *Plural.* The section of an orchestra or band that plays these instruments. **6.** Gas produced in the body during digestion; flatulence. **7.** Respiration; breath; especially, normal or adequate breathing. **8.** A pervasive or irresistible force or influence: *a wind of change.* **9.** Utterance empty of meaning; verbiage. **—before the wind.** Moving forward with the wind behind. **—between wind and water. 1.** The part of a ship near its waterline exposed to buffeting by waves. **2.** At or in a vulnerable point. **—break wind.** To eject intestinal gas from the anus or mouth. **—get wind of.** *Informal.* To receive a hint or intimation of. **—get the wind up.** *Informal.* To become frightened. **—how the wind blows** or **lies.** What developments arise or what the current trends are. **—in the wind.** Likely to occur; in the offing. **—put the wind up.** *Informal.* To frighten. **—raise the wind.** *Informal.* To obtain the requisite funds. **—sail close to the wind. 1.** To sail or travel as directly against the wind as possible. **2.** To live or manage frugally and economically. **3.** To approach near to the limits of what is acceptable; verge on impropriety, dishonesty, or danger. **—take the wind out of (someone's) sails.** To rob of an advantage; deflate.

~*tr.v.* **winded, winding, winds. 1.** To expose to the free movement of air; ventilate or dry. **2. a.** To catch a scent or trace of. **b.** To pursue by following a scent. **3.** To cause to be out of or short of breath, especially by a blow to the stomach. **4.** To afford a recovery of breath: *winded their horses after a gallop.* [Middle English *wind*, Old English *wind*.]

  Synonyms: *wind, breeze, zephyr, blast, gust, gale, whirlwind, tornado, hurricane, typhoon.*

wind² (wīnd) *v.* **wound** (wownd) or *rare* **winded, winding, winds.** ~*tr.* **1.** To wrap (something) round an object or centre once or repeatedly: *wound thread round a reel; wound a scarf round his neck.* **2.** To wrap or encircle in a series of coils; entwine. **3.** To unwind or remove by unwinding. Used with *off.* **4.** To proceed on (one's way) with a curving or twisting course. **5.** To present or introduce in a disguised or devious manner: *He wound a plea for money into his letter.* **6.** To turn (a crank of handle, for example) in a series of circular motions. **7.** To coil the spring of (a clock or other mechanism) by turning a stem, cord, or the like. Often used with *up.* **8.** To lift or haul by means of a windlass or winch. —*intr.* **1.** To move in or as if in a bending or coiling course: *The road winds round up to the monastery.* **2. a.** To move in or have a spiral or circular course. **b.** To be or become coiled or spiralled about something. **3.** To be twisted or warped. Used of a board, for example. **4.** To proceed misleadingly or insidiously in speech or conduct. **5.** To become wound. —**wind down.** To decrease or diminish in activity, energy, intensity, or scope, especially so as to stop gradually: *winds down after work; winding down our South African operations.* ~*n.* **1.** The act of winding. **2.** A single turn, twist, or curve. [Wind, wound, wound; Middle English *winden, wond, wonden,* Old English *windan, wond, wunden.*]

wind³ (wīnd) *tr.v.* **winded** (wīndid) or **wound** (wownd), **winding, winds. 1.** To blow (a wind instrument). **2.** To sound by blowing. [From WIND (air).] —**wind·er** *n.*

wind·age (windij) *n.* **1. a.** The effect of wind on the course of a projectile. **b.** The point or degree at which the wind gauge or sight of a rifle or gun must be set to compensate for the effect of the wind. **2.** In ballistics, the difference, in a given firearm, between the diameter of the projectile fired and the diameter of the bore of the firearm. **3.** The disturbance of air caused by the passage of a fast-moving object, such as a railway train or missile. **4.** *Nautical.* The part of the surface of a ship that is left exposed to the wind.

wind·bag (wind-bag) *n.* **1.** *Informal.* A talkative person who communicates nothing of substance or interest. **2.** A flexible air-holder, as in bellows or bagpipes.

wind·blast (wind-blaast ‖ -blast) *n.* **1.** A very strong gust of wind. **2.** Injury caused by air friction to the pilot of a high-speed aircraft who has used his ejection seat.

wind·blown (wind-blōn) *adj.* **1.** Blown or dispersed by the wind. **2.** Growing or shaped in a manner governed by the prevailing winds. **3.** Windswept. Said of a woman's hair style.

wind·borne (wind-born ‖ -bōrn) *adj.* Carried by the wind. Said especially of plant seeds and pollen.

wind·bound (wind-bownd) *adj.* Unable to sail because of high or contrary winds. Said of a sailing ship.

wind·break (wind-brayk) *n.* A hedge, row of trees, or fence serving to lessen or break the force of the wind.

wind·bro·ken (wind-brōkən) *adj.* Suffering from the heaves or some other impairment of respiration. Said of a horse.

wind·burn (wind-burn) *n.* Reddening and irritation of the skin caused by prolonged exposure to strong winds. —**wind·burnt** (wind-burnt) *adj.*

wind·cheat·er (wind-cheetər) *n.* A close-fitting jacket, often with elasticated cuffs and waistband, worn especially as protection from the cold and the wind. Also called "windjammer", *U.S.* "windbreaker".

wind-chill factor (wind-chil) *n. Meteorology.* A measure of the cooling power of the air in relation to wind speed and air temperature.

wind cone (wind) *n.* A wind indicator, a **windsock** (*see*).

wind·er (wīndər) *n.* **1.** A person, thing, or mechanism that winds, especially: **a.** A key or other device for winding up a spring-driven mechanism. **b.** An engine for raising and lowering cages in a mine shaft. **2.** A spool, barrel, or other object round which material is wound. **3.** Any of the steps of a winding staircase.

Win·der·mere (windər-meer) **, Lake.** Lake in Cumbria, northwest England. Situated in the Lake District, it is the largest lake in England, being 17 kilometres (10.5 miles) long and 1.6 kilometres (1 mile) wide, and is drained by the river Leven into Morecambe Bay.

wind·fall (wind-fawl) *n.* **1.** Something that has been blown down by the wind, such as a ripened fruit. **2.** A sudden and unexpected piece of good fortune or financial gain.

wind·flow·er (wind-flowr) *n.* The **wood anemone** (*see*).

wind·gall (wind-gawl) *n.* A soft tumour on a horse's leg just above the fetlock.

wind gauge *n.* **1.** An **anemometer** (*see*). **2.** A device attached to the sights of a gun, enabling allowance to be made for the effect of wind on the projectile.

wind gap (wind) *n.* A shallow gap or ravine on the side of a deep mountain ridge.

wind harp (wind) *n.* An **Aeolian harp** (*see*).

Wind·hoek (wind-hŏŏk, wint-, vint-). Capital of Namibia. Situated on a plateau in the centre of the country, it was capital of German South West Africa (1892) until taken by South African troops during World War I.

wind·hover (wind-hovvər ‖ -huvvər) *n. British Regional.* A **kestrel** (*see*). [WIND + HOVER, from its habit of hovering in one spot.]

wind·ing (wīnding) *n.* **1. a.** The act of one that winds. **b.** One complete turn of something wound. **2. a.** A thing in a wound condition; a spiral. **b.** A curve or bend, as in a road. **3.** *Electricity.* **a.** Wire wound into a coil. **b.** The manner in which such a coil is wound. **c.** A single loop of such a coil. —*adj.* **1.** Twisting or turning; sinuous. **2.** Spiral: *a winding staircase.* —**wind·ing·ly** *adv.*

winding sheet (wīnding) *n.* A sheet for wrapping a dead body; a shroud.

wind instrument (wind) *n.* Any musical instrument sounded by wind, especially by the player's breath, such as a clarinet, trumpet, or harmonica.

wind·jam·mer (wind-jammər) *n.* **1.** A large sailing ship. **2.** A crew member of a windjammer. **3.** A windcheater. [From WIND + JAM (verb).]

wind·lass (windləss) *n.* Any of numerous hauling or lifting machines consisting essentially of a drum or cylinder wound with rope and turned by a crank. ~*tr.v.* **windlassed, -lassing, -lasses.** To raise with a windlass. [Middle English *wyndlas,* variant of *windas,* from Anglo-French, from Old Norse *vindáss* : *vinda,* to wind + *áss†,* pole.]

win·dle·straw (wind'l-straw) *n. British Regional.* A thin dried grass stalk. [Middle English *windlestraw* (unattested), Old English *windelstrēaw* : *windel,* basket, from WIND + *strēaw,* STRAW.]

wind·mill (wind-mil) *n.* **1.** A mill or other machine that runs on the energy generated by a wheel of adjustable blades, slats, or sails rotated by the wind. **2.** Anything similar to a windmill in appearance or operation. **3.** A toy consisting of vanes of coloured paper or plastic pinned to the end of a stick in such a way that they turn when blown on. Also *U.S.* "pinwheel". **4.** A person or thing imagined to be threatening or evil. Used chiefly in the phrase *tilting at windmills.* [Sense 4 is a reference to Cervantes' Don Quixote, who imagined windmills were evil giants.]

win·dow (windō) *n.* **1.** An opening constructed in a wall or roof, as of a building or vehicle, that functions to admit light or air to an enclosure and is usually framed and spanned with glass mounted to permit opening and closing. **2. a.** A framework enclosing a pane of glass; a sash. **b.** A pane of glass, clear plastic, or the like; a windowpane. **3.** Any opening that resembles a window in function or appearance, such as the transparent space on an envelope that reveals the address printed on the enclosure. **4.** A code name for strips of foil dropped from aircraft as a radar countermeasure; chaff. **5.** The area or space immediately behind a window, especially at the front of a shop. **6.** A part of the electromagnetic spectrum in which radiation passes through a specified medium; for example, the radio window in the ionosphere lies between 50 gigahertz and 15 megahertz. **7.** A brief period during which a specified event can take place: *a launch window.* ~*tr.v.* **windowed, -dowing, -dows.** To provide with or as if with a window. [Middle English *window(e),* from Old Norse *vindauga* : *vindr,* wind, air + *auga,* eye.]

window box *n.* **1.** A usually long and narrow box for growing plants typically placed outdoors on a windowsill or ledge. **2.** Either of the vertical grooves on the inner sides of a window frame for the weights that counterbalance a sliding sash.

win·dow-dress·ing (windō-dressing) *n.* **1. a.** A decorative display of retail merchandise in shop windows. **b.** Goods and trimmings used in such displays. **2.** A superficially attractive presentation, as of statistics, ideas, or policies, intended to highlight what is favourable and to conceal what is unpalatable. —**win·dow-dress·er** *n.*

win·dow·pane (windō-payn) *n.* A plate of glass in a window.

window seat *n.* Any place for sitting next to a window, as in the recess of a bay window or on a public transport vehicle.

window shade *n. U.S.* A **blind** (*see*).

win·dow-shop (windō-shop) *intr.v.* **-shopped, -shopping, -shops.** To look at goods in shop windows without making purchases. —**win·dow-shop·per** *n.*

win·dow·sill (windō-sil) *n.* The horizontal ledge at the base of a window opening.

wind·pipe (wind-pīp) *n. Anatomy.* The **trachea** (*see*).

wind·pol·li·nat·ed (wind-pólli-naytid) *adj.* Pollinated by windborne pollen. Said of certain plants.

wind rose (wind) *n.* Any of a class of meteorological diagrams depicting the distribution of wind direction over a period of time. [German *Windrose,* "a rose of winds", compass card.]

wind·row (wind-rō) *n.* **1.** A long row of cut hay or grain left to dry in a field before being bundled. **2.** A row, as of leaves or snow, heaped up by the wind. ~*tr.v.* **windrowed, -rowing, -rows.** To shape or arrange into a windrow.

wind scale *n.* Any scale, such as the Beaufort scale, that gives a numerical value to the force or speed of wind.

wind·screen (wind-skreen, win-) *n.* A sheet of curved or flat toughened glass that forms the front window of a motor vehicle. Also called "screen", *U.S.* "windshield".

windscreen wiper *n.* An electrically operated rubber blade, usually one of a pair, that clears the windscreen of a motor vehicle of rain, snow, or dirt.

wind·shake (wind-shayk) *n.* A crack or separation between growth rings in timber, attributed to the straining of tree trunks in high winds.

wind·shield (wind-sheeld) *n.* **1.** Something placed to protect a person or object from the wind. **2.** *U.S.* A windscreen.

wind·sock (wind-sok) *n.* A large, tapered, open-ended sleeve, pivotally attached to a standard, that indicates the direction of the wind blowing through it. Also called "air sock", "drogue", "wind cone", "wind sleeve".

Wind·sor[1] (winzər). The family name of the British royal family since 1917.

Windsor[2]. Town west of London, southern central England. Windsor Castle has been a royal residence since the time of William the Conqueror (11th century).

Windsor, Duke of. See Edward VIII.

Windsor chair *n.* A type of comfortable wooden chair typically having a high, curving, spoked back with arms, and outward-slanting legs connected by a crossbar.

Windsor knot *n.* A wide, triangular, tie knot.

wind·storm (wind-stawrm) *n.* A storm with high winds or violent gusts but little or no rain.

wind·suck·er (wind-suckər) *n.* A horse given to noisily swallowing quantities of air. —**wind·suck·ing** *adj. & n.*

wind·surf·ing (wind-surfing) *n.* The sport of sailing over water on a small, open vessel consisting of a large surfboard equipped with a sail. —**wind·surf** *intr.v.* —**wind·surf·er** *n.*

wind·swept (wind-swept) *adj.* **1.** Exposed to or moved by the force of the wind. **2.** Dishevelled by or as if by exposure to the wind: *a windswept appearance.*

wind tee (wind) *n.* A large weather vane with a horizontal T-shaped wind indicator, commonly found at airfields.

wind tunnel (wind) *n.* A chamber through which air is forced at controllable velocities in order to study the aerodynamic flow around and effects on aerofoils, scale models, or other objects mounted within.

wind up (wind). **1.** To bring to an end; conclude; settle. **2.** To make anxious, tense, or excited: *The children are getting wound up about their holidays.* **3.** To arrange for liquidation of (a company). ~*intr.v.* **1.** *Informal.* **a.** To bring something to a conclusion: *wound up by proposing a toast.* **b.** To come finally to a specified condition or situation: *wound up on the wrong side of the law.* **2.** To go into liquidation. Used of a company.

wind-up (wind-up) *n. Chiefly U.S. Informal.* **1.** The act of bringing something to a conclusion. **2.** The concluding part, as of an action, presentation, or speech.

wind·ward (windwərd) *n.* **1.** The direction from which the wind blows. **2.** The side exposed to the wind. —**to (the) windward of.** Favourably situated with respect to. ~*adj.* **1.** Of or moving towards the quarter from which the wind blows. **2.** Of or on the side exposed to the wind or to prevailing winds. ~*adv.* In a direction from which the wind blows; against the wind. Compare **leeward.**

Windward Islands. Archipelago of volcanic origin, southeast West Indies. The southern part of the Lesser Antilles, it extends southwards from the Leeward Islands, and includes Dominica, Grenada, St. Lucia, St. Vincent, and Martinique.

wind·y (windi) *adj.* **-i·er, -i·est.** **1.** Characterised by the prevalence of strong winds: *a windy day.* **2.** Exposed to or swept by the wind. **3. a.** Characterised by lack of substance; empty; airy. **b.** Characterised by long-windedness, self-importance, or verbosity; full of talk. **4.** Affected by or causing flatulence. **5.** *Informal.* Nervous; frightened; shaky. —**wind·i·ly** *adv.* —**wind·i·ness** *n.*

wine (win) *n.* **1.** The fermented juice of any of various kinds of grapes making an alcoholic drink. **2.** The fermented juice of any of various other fruits or plants: *pear wine.* **3.** Something that intoxicates or exhilarates. **4.** The dark purplish colour of red wine. —**new wine in old bottles.** New thought or principles that cannot be integrated with old traditional ways. ~*v.* **wined, wining, wines.** —*tr.* To provide or entertain with wines: *The guests were wined and dined.* —*intr.* To drink wine. [Middle English win(e), Old English wīn, from West Germanic wīna- (unattested), from Latin vīnum.]

wine·bib·ber (win-bibbər) *n.* One who drinks excessive amounts of wine. [WINE + BIB, in archaic verbal sense, to drink.] —**wine·bib·bing** *adj. & n.*

wine cellar *n.* **1.** A place, especially a cellar, for storing wine. **2.** A stock of wines.

wine gallon *n.* A former unit of liquid measure used for wine, equivalent to the modern U.S. gallon (231 cubic inches or 3.79 litres).

wine·glass (win-glaass ‖ -glass) *n.* **1.** A glass from which wine is drunk; especially, a stemmed glass of a standard size having a capacity of approximately one sixth of a standard bottle of wine. **2.** The amount a wineglass will hold. In this sense, also called a "wineglassful".

wine·grow·er (win-grō-ər) *n.* One who owns a vineyard and produces wine. —**wine·grow·ing** *adj. & n.*

wine lake *n.* A large surplus of wine occurring as a result of overproduction by EU growers. Compare **butter mountain.**

wine palm *n.* Any of various palm trees having sap or juice from which wine is prepared.

wine·press (win-press) *n.* A vat in which the juice is pressed from grapes.

win·er·y (winəri) *n., pl.* **-ies.** A winemaking establishment.

wine·skin (win-skin) *n.* A bag for holding and dispensing wine,

made from goatskin or other animal skin.

wine-tast·ing (win-taysting) *n.* The act or occasion of evaluating the quality of wine by tasting it. —**wine-tast·er** *n.*

wing (wing) *n.* **1.** Either of a pair of specialised organs of flight, as: **a.** The feather-covered modified forelimb of a bird. **b.** The membranous tissue supported by the elongated digits of the forelimb of a bat. **c.** A veined, membranous structure extending from the thorax of an insect. **d.** The enlarged pectoral fin of a flying fish. **2.** Any organ or structure homologous to or resembling a wing. **3.** *Botany.* **a.** A thin or membranous extension, as of the fruit of the sycamore or ash or along a twig or stem. **b.** Any of the lateral petals of the flower of a pea or related plant. **4.** Either of two winglike appendages believed to be part of the bodies of supernatural or fabulous creatures, such as angels, demons, or dragons. **5.** *Aeronautics.* An aerofoil whose principal function is providing lift; especially, either of two such aerofoils symmetrically positioned on each side of the fuselage of an aircraft. **6.** Anything that resembles a wing in appearance, function, or position relative to a main body: *water wings.* **7.** *Literary.* A means of flight or of rapid movement: *Fear lent wings to his feet.* **8.** Something that is moved by or moves against the air, as a weather vane. **9.** The part of the body of a motor vehicle around the wheels. Also *U.S.* "fender". **10.** An aerofoil fitted to a racing car to improve road holding. **11.** A folding section, as of a double door or of a movable partition. **12.** In the theatre: **a.** A flat of scenery projecting onto the stage from the side. **b.** The unseen backstage area on either side of the stage. **13.** A section of a building or structure projecting from the main or central part. **14.** Either of the two side projections on the back of a wing chair. **15.** A group affiliated with or subordinate to an older or larger organisation: *the political wing of the I.R.A.* **16.** A section of a party or other group holding distinct, especially radical, political views: *the right wing; the left wing.* **17.** *Military.* Either the left or right flank of an army or a naval fleet lined up for battle. **18.** *Sports.* **a.** Either of the forward positions played near the sideline, as in soccer or hockey. **b.** One playing in such a position. **19. a.** In the Royal Air Force and some other air forces, a tactical unit usually consisting of three to five squadrons. **b.** In the U.S. air force, a unit larger than a group but smaller than a division. **20.** *Plural.* Emblematic wings worn on the jacket by one who has qualified as an air pilot. —**clip (someone's) wings.** To restrict the movement, activity, or freedom of. —**in the wings.** Ready to come forward when required. —**on the wing. 1.** In flight; flying. **2.** Moving; travelling. —**spread** or **stretch (one's) wings.** To develop or exploit one's talents to the full. —**take wing. 1.** To fly off; soar away. **2.** To leave in a rush. —**under (one's) wing.** Under one's protection; in one's care. ~*v.* **winged, winging, wings.** —*intr.* To move on or as if on wings; fly. —*tr.* **1.** To furnish with wings. **2.** To feather (an arrow). **3. a.** To send (an arrow, for example) in flight. **b.** To cause or enable to move quickly; speed. **4.** To make (one's way) swiftly by or as if by flying. **5.** To wound superficially, as in the wing or arm. **5.** To furnish (a building, for example) with wing or subordinate extensions. —**wing it.** *Slang.* To improvise or ad-lib in a theatrical performance. [Middle English wenge(n), from Old Norse vængi, accusative plural of vængr, bird's wing.]

wing and wing *adv. Nautical.* With sails extended on both sides.

Win·gate (win-gayt), **Orde (Charles)** (1903–1944). British general. He worked with Jewish guerrillas in Palestine (1935–39), and during World War II defeated the Italians in Ethiopia (1941). In Burma he organised the specially trained Chindit forces.

wing-bow (wing-bō) *n.* A mark of colour on the bend of the wing in a domestic fowl.

wing-case (wing-kayss) *n.* Either of the two hard, leathery, modified forewings that cover and protect the delicate hindwings of certain insects at rest, especially beetles.

wing chair *n.* An armchair with a high back from which project large, enclosing sidepieces or wings.

wing collar *n.* A stiff, stand-up, shirt collar with the corners turned down, that is worn by men especially on formal occasions.

wing commander *n. Abbr.* **W/Cdr.** An officer of the Royal Air Force and certain other air forces, ranking between a group captain and a squadron leader.

wing-ding (wing-ding) *n. Chiefly Australian & N.Z. Slang.* A lavish or lively party or celebration. [20th century : origin obscure.]

winged (wingd; *also poetic* wing-id) *adj.* **1.** Having wings or wing-like appendages. **2.** Moving on or as if on wings; flying. **3.** Soaring; elevated; sublime. **4.** Swift; fleet.

wing·er (wing-ər) *n.* **1.** *British.* A forward playing on the wing, as in soccer or hockey. **2.** One who belongs to the specified political wing of a party or other group. Used in combination: *left-wingers.*

wing·less (wing-lass, -liss) *adj.* Having no wings or having only rudimentary wings. Said especially of primitive insects of the subclass Apterygota, which includes the springtails and bristletails.

wing·let (wing-lət, -lit) *n.* A small or rudimentary wing.

wing loading *n.* The gross weight of an aircraft divided by the wing area. Used in stress analysis.

wing nut *n.* A nut with winglike projections for thumb and forefinger leverage in turning. Also called "butterfly nut".

wing-o·ver (wing-ōvər) *n.* A flight manoeuvre or stunt in which an aircraft enters a climbing turn until almost stalled and is allowed to fall while the turn is continued until normal flight is attained in a direction opposite the original heading.

wing·span (wing-span) *n.* The linear distance from wing tip to wing tip of an aircraft, bird, or insect. Also called "wingspread".

wing tip *n.* The extreme edge of a wing, as of a bird or aircraft.

wink[1] (wingk) *v.* **winked, winking, winks.** —*intr.* **1.** To close and open the eyelid of one eye deliberately, as to convey a message, signal, or suggestion. **2.** To close and open the eyelids of both eyes; blink. **3. a.** To shine fitfully; twinkle: *winking stars.* **b.** To flash intermittently, as the direction indicator on a car does. —*tr.* **1.** To close and open (an eye or the eyes) rapidly. **2.** To signal or express as by the winking of an eye or by flashing a light. **—wink at.** To pretend not to see: *winked at corruption in his ministry.*
~*n.* **1.** An act of winking. **2.** The extremely brief time required for a wink. **3.** A signal or hint conveyed by winking. **4.** A gleam; a twinkle. **5.** *Informal.* A brief moment of sleep. **—tip (someone) the wink.** *British Informal.* To give a hint to. [Middle English *winken,* Old English *wincian,* to close one's eyes.]

wink[2] *n.* Any of the small, round discs used in the game of tiddlywinks. [Shortened from TIDDLYWINKS.]

wink·er (wingkər) *n.* **1.** One that winks. **2.** A **blinker** *(see).*

win·kle (wíngk'l) *n.* Any of various snail-like marine gastropod molluscs of the genus *Littorina,* such as *L. littorea,* the flesh of which is edible. Also called "periwinkle".
~*tr.v.* **winkled, -kling, -kles.** *Informal.* To prise out; extract. Usually used with *out.* [Shortened from PERIWINKLE.]

winkle-pickers (wíngk'l-pickərz) *pl.n. Informal.* Men's and women's shoes with very pointed toes, originally fashionable in the 1950s and 1960s.

win·ner (wínnər) *n.* **1.** One that wins, especially in a sporting contest. **2.** *Informal.* One that is assured of success: *His latest film is a winner.*

win·ning (wínning) *adj.* **1.** Successful; victorious. **2.** Charming; engaging: *a winning personality.*
~*n.* **1.** The act of one that wins; victory. **2.** *Plural.* That which has been won; especially, money won by gambling. **3.** A section of a mine that has been recently prepared or opened for working. **—win·ning·ly** *adv.* **—win·ning·ness** *n.*

winning gallery *n.* In real tennis, an opening below the side penthouse. A ball played into this opening is counted as a win.

winning post *n.* The post at the end of a racecourse.

Win·ni·peg (winni-peg). Capital of Manitoba province, south central Canada. It is situated at the confluence of the Red and Assiniboine rivers, and is south of Lake Winnipeg.

win·now (winnō) *v.* **-nowed, -nowing, -nows.** —*tr.* **1.** To separate the chaff from (grain) by means of a current of air. **2.** To blow (chaff) off or away. **3.** To scatter or disperse by blowing. **4.** To blow upon; cause to flutter or fly: *hair winnowed by the breeze.* **5.** To examine closely in order to separate the good from the bad; analyse; sift. **6.** To separate (a desirable or undesirable part); eliminate by sorting. Often used with *out.* **7.** *Archaic.* To beat or fan (the air) as with wings. —*intr.* **1.** To separate grain from chaff. **2.** To separate the good from the bad.
~*n.* **1.** A device for winnowing grain. **2.** An act of winnowing. [Middle English *windowen, wynwen,* Old English *windwian,* from *wind,* WIND.] **—win·now·er** *n.*

win·o (wīnō) *n., pl.* **winos.** *Slang.* A person, especially a tramp or vagrant, who is habitually drunk on wine.

win·some (win-səm) *adj.* Winning; charming; engaging. [Middle English *winsum,* Old English *wynsum* : *wyn,* joy + *-sum,* -SOME.] **—win·some·ly** *adv.* **—win·some·ness** *n.*

win·ter (wíntər) *n.* **1.** The usually coldest season of the year, occurring between autumn and spring. In the Northern Hemisphere it extends from the winter solstice to the vernal (or spring) equinox and is popularly considered to comprise December, January, and February; in the Southern Hemisphere it falls between the summer solstice and the autumnal equinox, or, popularly, June, July, and August. **2.** *Poetic.* A year as expressed through the recurrence of this season. **3.** Any period characterised by coldness, misery, barrenness, or death.
~*v.* **wintered, -tering, -ters.** —*intr.* To pass or spend the winter. —*tr.* To lodge, keep, or care for during the winter: *wintering the sheep in the stable.*
~*adj.* **1.** Pertaining to, characteristic of, suitable for, or occurring in winter: *a winter coat; winter weather.* **2. a.** Capable of being stored for use during the winter. Said of fruits or vegetables. **b.** Planted in the autumn and harvested in the spring or summer: *winter wheat.* [Middle English, Old English *winter,* from Germanic *wentrus* (unattested), probably akin to WET.] **—win·ter·er** *n.* **—win·ter·less** *adj.* **—win·ter·ly** *adj.*

winter aconite *n.* A frequently cultivated European plant, *Eranthis hyemalis,* having a solitary yellow flower that blooms in winter or early spring.

winter cherry *n.* The **Chinese lantern plant** *(see).*

win·ter-feed (wíntər-feed) *tr.v.* **-fed** (-fed), **-feeding, -feeds.** To feed (livestock) when grazing is not possible, as in the winter.

win·ter·green (wíntər-green) *n.* **1. a.** A low-growing plant, *Gaultheria procumbens,* of eastern North America, having white or pinkish flowers, aromatic evergreen leaves, and spicy, edible red berries. Also called "checkerberry". **b.** A medicinal oil or flavouring obtained from this plant. **2.** Any of several similar or related plants, such as: **a.** Any plant of the genus *Pyrola,* such as *P. minor,* having round pink flowers. [Translation of Dutch *wintergroen.*]

win·ter·ise, win·ter·ize (wíntə-rīz) *tr.v.* **-ised, -ising, -ises.** To prepare or equip (a house or car, for example) for winter weather.

winter jasmine *n.* A shrub, *Jasminum nudiflorum,* native to China but widely cultivated for its yellow, winter-blooming flowers.

win·ter·kill (wíntər-kil) *v.* **-killed, -killing, -kills.** *Chiefly U.S.* —*tr.* To kill (plants, for example) by exposing to extremely cold winter weather. —*intr.* To die from exposure to cold winter weather. Used especially of plants. **—win·ter·kill** *n.*

Winter Olympic Games *pl.n.* An international sporting event in which representatives of different countries compete in winter sports, formerly held in the same year as the **Olympic Games** *(see).* Also called "Winter Olympics".

winter rose *n.* A plant, the **Christmas rose** *(see).*

winter savory *n.* See **savory** (plant).

winter solstice *n. Astronomy.* A **solstice** *(see).*

winter sports *n.* Sports, such as skiing or bobsleighing, that take place on snow and ice.

win·ter·time (wíntər-tīm) *n.* The winter season.

win·try (wíntri) *adj.* **-trier, -triest.** Also **win·ter·y** (wín-təri, -tri) **-ier, -iest. 1.** Characteristic of winter; cold. **2.** Suggestive of winter; cheerless. [Old English *wintrig.*] **—win·tri·ly** *adv.* **—win·tri·ness** *n.*

win·y (wīni) *adj.* **-ier, -iest.** Having the qualities or taste of wine; intoxicating; heady.

winze (winz) *n.* In mining, an inclined or vertical shaft or passage between levels. [Variant of earlier *winds,* probably from Middle English *wynde,* windlass, perhaps from Middle Dutch or Middle Low German *winde.*]

wipe (wīp) *tr.v.* **wiped, wiping, wipes. 1.** To subject to light rubbing or friction, as with a cloth or paper, in order to clean or dry: *wipe the dishes; wipe the table.* **2.** To remove or get rid of by or as if by wiping. Usually used with *off* or *away*: *wiped away her tears; Wipe that smile off your face.* **3.** To rub, move, or spread over something: *wiped his shoes on the rug.* **4.** In plumbing, to form (a joint) by spreading solder with a piece of cloth or leather.
~*n.* **1.** The act of wiping. **2.** Something used for wiping, as: **a.** A commercially produced treated tissue: *a box of baby wipes.* **b.** *Slang.* A handkerchief. **3.** *Informal.* **a.** A blow; a swipe. **b.** A sideswipe; a gibe. [Middle English *wipen,* Old English *wīpian.*]

wipe out *tr.v.* **1.** To destroy; annihilate: *wiped out a tribe.* **2.** To remove; eradicate: *wipe out a memory.* —*intr.v. Slang.* In surfing, to lose balance and fall or jump off a surfboard.

wipe-out (wīp-owt) *n.* **1.** The act or an instance of wiping out. **2.** *Slang.* A fall or jump off a surfboard. **3.** Total loss of radio reception as a result of interference by another signal.

wip·er (wīpər) *n.* **1.** One that wipes. **2.** A device designed for wiping, such as a windscreen wiper. **3.** In a machine, a cam that projects from a rotating horizontal shaft to activate another part. **4.** *Electricity.* A movable electrical contact, as in a rheostat.

wire (wīr) *n.* **1. a.** A usually pliable metallic strand or rod made in many lengths and diameters, sometimes clad and often electrically insulated, used chiefly for structural support or to conduct electricity. **b.** Such strands collectively, used as a fencing material, for example. **2.** A group of such strands bundled or twisted together as a functional unit; a cable. **3.** Something resembling a wire, as in slenderness or stiffness. **4.** *Chiefly U.S. Informal.* The telegraph service: *sent it by wire.* **5.** *Informal.* A telegram. **6.** The screen on which sheets of paper are formed in a papermaking machine. **7.** A metal snare, as for catching rabbits. **8.** *U.S.* The finishing line of a racetrack. **9.** *Slang.* A recording device concealed on one's person: *wear a wire.* **—get (one's) wires crossed.** *Informal.* To get confused or mixed up. **—pull wires** *Chiefly U.S.* To use secret or underhand means to accomplish something; pull strings.
~*adj.* Made of or resembling a wire or wires: *a wire brush.*
~*v.* **wired, wiring, wires.** —*tr.* **1.** To bind, connect, or attach with a wire or wires. **2. a.** To equip with a system of electrical wires. **b.** *Slang.* To equip with a concealed recording device. **3.** *Informal.* **a.** To send by telegraph: *wire congratulations.* **b.** To send a telegram to. **4.** To snare with a wire. **5.** In croquet, to hit (a ball) behind a hoop and block an opponent's shot. —*intr.* To send a telegram; telegraph. [Middle English *wir(e),* Old English *wīr.*]

wire cloth *n.* A mesh woven of fine wire.

wire-draw (wīr-draw) *tr.v.* **-drew** (-drōō || -drew), **-drawn** (-drawn), **-drawing, -draws. 1.** To draw (metal) into wire. **2.** To protract (a subject, for example) inordinately; spin out. **—wire·draw·er** *n.*

wire gauge *n.* **1.** A gauge for measuring the diameter of wire, usually in the form of a disc having variously sized slots in its periphery or a long graduated plate with similar slots along its edge. **2.** A standardised system of wire sizes.

wire gauze *n.* A material woven of very fine wires.

wire glass *n.* Sheet glass reinforced with wire-netting.

wire·grass (wīr-graass || -grass) *n.* Any of various grasses having tough, wiry roots or rootstocks, such as **Bermuda grass** *(see).*

wire-haired (wīr-haird) *adj.* Having a coat of stiff, wiry hair. Said of breeds of dogs: *a wire-haired terrier.*

wire·less (wīr-ləss, -liss) *adj.* **1.** Without wires. **2.** Radio.
~*n.* **1.** Radio. **2.** A radio set.
~*v.* **wirelessed, -lessing, -lesses.** —*tr.* To communicate with by wireless telegraphy or radiotelephone. —*intr.* To communicate in this way; radio.

wireless telegraphy *n.* Telegraphy by radio rather than by long-distance transmission lines. Also called "radio telegraphy".

wireless telephone *n.* **Radiotelephone** *(see).*

wire-net·ting (wīr-nétting) *n.* Netting made of woven wire, as for fences.

wire recorder *n.* A forerunner of the tape recorder that recorded sound on a spool of wire rather than on magnetic tape.

wire·tap (wīr-tap) **wiretapped, -tapping, -taps.** *tr.v.* To tap (a telephone line). **—wire·tap** *n.* **—wire·tap·per** *n.*

wire wheel *n.* **1.** A wheel with wire spokes, especially one on a sports car. **2.** A rotary wire brush, especially one that is power operated.

wire wool *n.* A tangled mass of fine wire used to rub metal surfaces to remove dirt or rust. Also called "steel wool".

wire·work (wīr-wurk) *n.* **1.** Wire fabric. **2.** Articles made of wire or wire fabric.

wire·worm (wīr-wurm) *n.* The wirelike larva of various click beetles, that cause severe damage by boring into the roots of many plants.

wire-wove (wīr-wōv) *adj.* **1.** Designating a high-grade writing paper with a smooth finish. **2.** Made of woven wire.

wir·ing (wīr-ing) *n.* **1.** The act of attaching, connecting, or installing wires. **2.** A system of electric wires, as in a building.

wir·ra (wírrə) *interj. Irish.* Used to express sorrow or perplexity. [Short for Irish Gaelic *a Muire,* "Oh, Mary".]

Wir·ral (wírrəl), **The.** Peninsula in northwest England. Situated between the Mersey and Dee estuaries, it includes Wallasey, Birkenhead, Ellesmere Port, and Port Sunlight.

wir·y (wīr-i) *adj.* **-ier, -iest. 1.** Made of or consisting of wire. **2.** Resembling wire, as in fineness and stiffness: *wiry hair.* **3.** Sinewy and lean; slender but tough. Said of people and animals. **—wir·i·ly** *adv.* **—wir·i·ness** *n.*

Wis·con·sin (wiss-kón-sin). State in the northern central United States. Extending from the Mississippi river to lakes Superior and Michigan, it has over 8,500 lakes and is mainly low-lying with extensive forests. The capital is Madison.

wis·dom (wízdəm) *n.* **1.** Enlightened understanding of what is true or right, usually acquired through long experience, as distinguished from a partial or specialised knowledge: *"The only wisdom we can hope to acquire/ Is the wisdom of humility"* (T.S. Eliot). **2.** Common sense; sagacity; good judgment. **3.** Accumulated learning; erudition. **4.** Wise sayings or teaching: *the wisdom of the ancients.* —See Synonyms at **knowledge.** [Middle English *wisedom,* Old English *wīsdōm* : *wīs,* WISE + -DOM.]

Wisdom of Jesus, the Son of Si·rach (sīr-ak) *n.* A book of the Apocrypha, **Ecclesiasticus** *(see).*

Wisdom of Solomon *n.* A book of the Apocrypha.

wisdom tooth *n.* Any of four molars, the last on each side of both jaws, usually erupting much later than the others. [Translation of New Latin *dentes sapientiae* (plural).]

wise[1] (wīz) *adj.* **wiser, wisest. 1.** Imbued with, based on, or suggestive of wisdom or discernment for what is true or right: *a wise decision.* **2.** Possessed of or showing common sense; prudent; sensible: *It would be wise not to mention this to anyone.* **3.** Shrewd; crafty: *a wise move.* **4.** *Informal.* Having knowledge or information; informed; aware: *came away none the wiser; soon got wise to his plan.* **5.** *Archaic.* Archaic. Having magical or occult powers. **6.** *Chiefly U.S.* Offensively self-assured; arrogant. **—wise up.** *Chiefly U.S. Slang.* To become aware or sophisticated. Often used with *to.* [Middle English *wis(e),* Old English *wīs.*] **—wise·ly** *adv.*

wise[2] *n. Archaic.* **1.** Method or manner of doing; fashion; way. **2.** Degree or respect: Used chiefly in the phrases *in no wise* and *in any wise.* [Middle English *wise,* Old English *wīse, wīs,* manner.]

-wise *adj. or adv. suffix.* Indicates: **1.** Manner, direction, or position; for example, **clockwise. 2.** *Informal.* With reference to; for example, **taxwise.** [Middle English *-wise,* in a certain manner, Old English *-wīsan,* from *wīse,* WISE (manner).]

Usage: The indiscriminate use of *-wise,* as in *taxwise, timewise, moneywise,* is associated by many people with an unpleasant business jargon. In careful speech it is preferable to use a longer phrase instead, for example, *as far as tax is concerned.*

wise·a·cre (wīz-aykər) *n. Informal.* An offensively self-assured person who affects to be wise. [Middle Dutch *wijsseggher,* soothsayer, variant (influenced by *segghen,* to say) of Old High German *wīssago, wīzago,* seer.]

wise·crack (wīz-krak) *n. Informal.* A flippant, cleverly sardonic remark or retort; a joke or gibe. See Synonyms at **joke.**
~*intr.v.* **wisecracked, -cracking, -cracks.** *Informal.* To make a wisecrack. **—wise·crack·er** *n.*

wise guy *n. Informal.* A self-assured person who affects an air of superior knowledge; a know-all.

Wise·man (wīzmən), **Nicholas Patrick Stephen** (1802–65). British cardinal. He was the first Roman Catholic Archbishop of Westminster (1850), after the controversial restoration of the English Catholic hierarchy.

wi·sent (wéez'nt, véez'nt) *n.* The European bison, *Bison bonasus.* See **bison.** [German *Wisent,* from Old High German *wisunt.*]

wish (wish) *n.* **1.** A feeling of longing or desire for something. **2. a.** An expression, often unspoken, or confession of such a desire: *make a wish.* **b.** A known or expressed aspiration or request: *went against my wishes.* **3.** An object of desire; something wished for: *You've got your wish.* **4.** *Usually plural.* An expressed desire for the welfare, happiness, or health of someone: *Send her my best wishes.*
~*v.* **wished, wishing, wishes.** —*tr.* **1.** To have as a wish, as: **a.** To want: *I wish to leave now.* **b.** To desire (something unattainable): *I wish I'd never been born.* **c.** To desire or request (someone) to do something: *I wish you'd come to the point.* **d.** To desire or long for (someone or something) to be in a specified state: *wished him a thousand miles away; I wish this job were finished.* **2.** To entertain or express a hope that a specified state or quality will befall or be enjoyed by (someone): *wish you all a Happy New Year; wished him no harm.* **3.** To confer or impose; foist. Used with *on: wouldn't wish him on my worst enemy.* —*intr.* **1.** To have or feel a desire. Usually used with *for: wish for the moon.* **2.** To express a wish. [Middle English *wisshen,* Old English *wȳscan.*] **—wish·er** *n.*

wish·bone (wísh-bōn) *n.* **1.** The forked bone, or furcula, anterior to the breastbone of most birds, formed by the fusion of the clavicles. **2.** Anything of a similar shape; especially, a V-shaped member of the suspension of a motor vehicle. [So called from its use as a wish token. When it is snapped apart by two people, the person getting the longer piece will supposedly have his wish fulfilled.]

wish·ful (wíshf'l) *adj.* Having or expressing a wish or longing. **—wish·ful·ly** *adv.* **—wish·ful·ness** *n.*

wish fulfilment *n.* **1.** The gratification of a desire. **2.** In psychoanalysis, the mind's enactment of a suppressed or frustrated desire, as in dreaming or fantasy.

wishful thinking *n.* Belief based on what one wishes to be true, rather than on what is actually true. **—wishful thinker** *n.*

wish-wash (wísh-wosh ‖ -wawsh) *n. Informal.* **1.** A thin, watery drink. **2.** Insipid talk or writing. [Reduplication of WASH.]

wish·y-wash·y (wíshi-woshi ‖ -wawshi) *adj.* **-ier, -iest.** *Informal.* **1.** Watery; thin; weak. **2.** Lacking in substance, quality, or force; feeble; insipid. [Reduplication of *washy,* from WASH.]

wisp (wisp) *n.* **1.** A small bunch or bundle, as of straw, hair, or grass. **2. a.** Someone or something thin, frail, slight, or brief: *a wisp of a smile; a wisp of a girl.* **b.** A thin or faint streak or fragment, as of smoke or clouds. **3.** A flock of birds, especially of snipe.
~*v.* **wisped, wisping, wisps.** —*tr.* **1.** To twist into a wisp. **2.** To rub down (a horse) with a wisp of straw. —*intr.* To move or drift in the manner of a wisp of smoke. [Middle English *wisp, wips*†.] **—wisp·y** *adj.*

wist. *Archaic.* Past tense and past participle of **wit** (to know).

wis·ter·i·a (wi-stéer-i-ə) *n.* Any of several climbing woody vines of the genus *Wisteria,* having compound leaves and drooping clusters of showy purplish or white flowers. [New Latin *Wisteria,* after Caspar *Wistar* (1761–1818), U.S. anatomist.]

wist·ful (wístf'l) *adj.* Full of a melancholy yearning; longing pensively. [Originally "attentive", from obsolete *wistly*† (influenced by *wishful*).] **—wist·ful·ly** *adv.* **—wist·ful·ness** *n.*

wit[1] (wit) *n.* **1.** The natural ability to perceive or know; understanding; intelligence; good sense: *had the wit to wrap up in the cold weather.* **2.** *Usually plural.* **a.** Ingenuity; resourcefulness: *using one's wits; live by one's wits.* **b.** Sound mental faculties; mind; sanity: *scared out of one's wits.* **3. a.** The ability to perceive and express in an ingeniously humorous manner the relationship or similarity between seemingly incongruous or disparate things: *Shavian wit.* **b.** One noted for this ability; especially, one skilled in repartee. **c.** This quality of wit as manifested in speech or writing. —See Synonyms at **mind. —at (one's) wits' end.** At the limit of one's mental resources; utterly at a loss. **—have** or **keep (one's) wits about (one).** To remain alert or calm, especially in a crisis. [Middle English, Old English.]

Synonyms: *wit, humour, repartee, sarcasm, irony.*

wit[2] *v.* **wist** (wist), **witting,** present indicative **I wot** (wot), **thou wost** (wost), **he wot, we, you, they wite** (wīt) or **witen** (wīt'n). *Archaic.* —*tr.* To be or become aware of; know; learn. —*intr.* To know. **—to wit.** That is to say; namely. [Middle English *witen,* Old English *witan.*]

wit·an (witt'n, wittan) *pl.n.* In Anglo-Saxon England, the **witenagemot** *(see).* [Old English *witan,* plural of *wita,* councillor.]

witch (wich) *n.* **1.** A person who practises magic and sorcery or is believed to have dealings with the devil. **2.** An ugly or vicious old woman; a hag. **3.** *Informal.* A bewitching young woman or girl.
~*tr.v.* **witched, witching, witches. 1.** To work or cast a spell upon; bewitch. **2.** To cause, bring, or effect by witchcraft. [Middle English *wicche,* Old English *wicce* (feminine), *wicca* (masculine).]

witch·craft (wích-kraaft ‖ -kraft) *n.* **1.** The practices of a witch; black magic; sorcery. **2.** A fascinating or irresistible influence, attraction, or charm. —See Synonyms at **magic.**

witch doctor *n.* A medicine man or shaman, especially among African peoples, reputedly having powers both to heal and to harm through sorcery and herbalism.

witch elm. Variant of **wych elm.**

witch·er·y (wíchəri) *n., pl.* **-ies. 1.** Sorcery; witchcraft. **2.** Power to charm or fascinate.

witch·es'-broom (wíchiz-brōōm, -brŏŏm) *n.* An abnormal, brushlike growth of weak, closely clustered shoots or branches on a tree or woody plant, caused by fungi or viruses.

witches' Sabbath *n.* A midnight meeting of demons, witches, and sorcerers, supposely presided over by Satan and marked by orgies and demonic rites. Also called "sabbat".

witch·et·ty grub (wíchiti) *n.* Any of various long, edible, wood-boring grubs that are the larvae of certain Australian moths and beetles. [*Witcheety,* from an Aboriginal name.]

witch hazel, wych hazel *n.* **1.** Any of several shrubs of the genus *Hamamelis;* especially, *H. virginiana,* of eastern North America, having yellow flowers that bloom in late autumn or winter. **2.** An alcoholic solution containing an extract of the bark and leaves of this shrub, applied externally as a mild astringent. [Middle English *wyche,* WYCH (ELM) + HAZEL.]

witch hunt *n.* **1.** A rigorous search to detect witches, especially in the Middle Ages. **2.** A campaign launched on the pretext of investigating subversive or dishonest activities but aimed at exposing and harassing political opponents or holders of dissenting views.

—witch·hunt·er *n.* **—witch·hunt·ing** *adj. & n.*

witch·ing (wíching) *adj.* **1.** Pertaining to or appropriate for witchcraft: *the witching hour.* **2.** Having power to charm or enchant; bewitching.
~n. Witchcraft. **—witch·ing·ly** *adv.*

witch of Ag·ne·si (an-yáyzi || *chiefly U.S.* aan-) *n.* A plane mathematical curve with the equation $x^2y = 4a^2(2a\text{-}y)$. [After Maria Gaetana *Agnesi* (1718–99), Italian mathematician; probably referring to the resemblance of the curve to a witch's hat.]

wite[1] (wīt) *n. British Regional.* Blame; fault. [Middle English *wite,* Old English *wīte,* fine, penalty.]

wite[2]. *Archaic.* Also **wit·en.** First, second, and third person plural present indicative of **wit** (to know).

wit·e·na·ge·mot (wít'n-ə-gi-mṓt) *n.* **1.** An Anglo-Saxon advisory council to the king, composed of about 100 nobles, prelates, and other officials, convened at intervals to discuss administrative and judicial affairs. **2.** The members of this council. In both senses, also called "witan". [Old English *witena gemōt* : *witena,* genitive plural of *wita,* councillor + *gemōt,* meeting, assembly; see **moot.**]

with (with || with) *prep. Abbr.* **w. 1. a.** As a companion of; accompanying: *Who went with him?* **b.** In the partnership of: *painted the house with a friend.* **2.** In the company or house of: *spent the weekend with a friend.* **3.** Having as a possession, attribute, or characteristic: *a man with a moustache; the girl with the stutter.* **4.** In a manner characterised by: *perform with skill; spoke with confidence.* **5.** In the charge or keeping of: *She left the letter with the doorman.* **6.** In the opinion or estimation of: *if it's all right with you.* **7. a.** In support of; on the side of: *voted with the opposition.* **b.** Of the same opinion or belief as: *He is with us on that.* **8.** In the same way as; like: *He believes, with Orwell, that some animals are more equal than others.* **9.** In the same group or mixture as; among: *Mix the flour with the eggs. Go and stand with the others.* **10.** In the membership or employment of: *He is with a publishing company.* **11. a.** Having or using as a means or agency: *spattered with mud; threatened him with the sack; eat with a fork.* **b.** Using as a material or ingredient: *filled his glass with beer; made it with fruit from the garden.* **12. a.** In spite of; notwithstanding: *With all his talent, he could not get a job.* **b.** Taking into account; in view of: *With all his talent, he ought to get a job. With our luck, it'll probably rain.* **13.** In the same direction as: *bend with the wind.* **14.** At the same time as: *rise with the sun.* **15.** In the matter of or in regard to: *satisfied with her progress.* **16.** In comparison or contrast to: *a dress identical with the one she has just bought.* **17.** In a harmonious relationship to: *The curtains don't really go with the carpet.* **18.** Having received: *With her permission, he left.* **19. a.** And; plus; added to: *beans with chips.* **b.** Inclusive of; counting: *That makes ten of us, with the children.* **20.** In opposition or antagonism to; against: *wrestling with an opponent; quarrelled with his neighbour.* **21.** To; onto: *Couple the first car with the second.* **22.** So as to be free of or separated from: *part with a friend.* **23.** In the course of: *We grow older with the hours.* **24.** In proportion to: *wines that improve with age.* **25.** *Informal.* Understanding; following the line of thought of: *Are you still with me?* **26.** As well as; in favourable comparison to: *She sings with the best of them.* **27. a.** Under the influence of; because of: *trembling with fear.* **b.** As a result of; thanks to: *With improved medical facilities, many of these patients now live longer.* **c.** Immediately following or attendant upon: *With the death of his brother, he inherited the title. He tore up the contract and, with that, stormed out.* **28.** In a situation in which there is or are: *He scored the winning goal with only seconds to go. With their best batting already gone, England are in trouble.* **29.** In the case of; as far as concerns: *With most people, voting is determined by economic factors.* **30.** In the care of: *leave it with me and I'll see to it.* **31.** Used to indicate the other party in any type of transaction or relationship: *chatting with his neighbour; works with handicapped children.* **32.** Used without a verb in expressions having the force of a wish or command: *On with the show! To hell with your stupid ideas!* **—in with.** In league or association with: *He is in with the wrong crowd.* **—with it.** *Informal.* **1.** Aware of modern trends; up-to-date. **2.** Alert and understanding: *I'm not with it this morning.* [Middle English *with,* with, against, by means of, Old English *with,* against or in opposition to, together with.]

Usage: When *with* introduces a phrase following a singular subject, it does not affect the relationship between that subject and the verb: *The king, with his two sons, has arrived.* In casual speech, the plural meaning of the whole sometimes causes speakers to make the verb plural, but this is better avoided. See also **together, well.**

with·al (with-áwl || with-) *adv.* **1.** *Literary.* Besides; in addition. **2.** *Literary.* Despite that; nevertheless. **3.** *Archaic.* Therewith: *a maid for him to marry withal.*
~prep. Archaic. With. [Middle English *with al(le)* : WITH + ALL.]

with·draw (with-dráw, with-) *v.* **-drew** (-dróo || -dréw), **-drawn** (-dráwn), **-drawing, -draws.** *—tr.* **1.** To take back or away; remove: *withdrew fifty pounds from his account.* **2.** To recall; retract: *withdrew the charges.* *—intr.* **1.** To move or draw back; retreat; retire. **2. a.** To remove oneself from activity or a social environment. **b.** To remove the centre of one's concern away from external activity; become detached. [Middle English *withdrawen* : *with,* away from, WITH + *drawen,* to pull, DRAW.]

with·draw·al (with-dráw-əl, with-, -dráwl, *often* -dráwrəl) *n.* Also **with·draw·ment** (-dráwmənt). **1.** The act or an instance of withdrawing, especially: **a.** A retreat, retirement, or disengagement. **b.** A detachment, as from emotional involvement. **c.** A removal of something that has been deposited: *made a large withdrawal from her account.* **2.** Termination of the administration of a habit-forming substance, which usually precipitates specific mental and physical *withdrawal symptoms.* **3.** The act of **coitus interruptus** *(see).*

withdrawn. Past participle of **withdraw.**
~adj. **1.** Remote; isolated. **2.** Socially retiring; introverted; shy. **3.** Detached; preoccupied.

withe (with, with, wīth) *n.* A tough, supple twig, especially a willow twig, used for binding things together; a withy.
~tr.v. **withed, withing, withes.** To bind with withes. [Middle English *witthe, withe,* Old English *withthe.*]

with·er (wíthər) *v.* **-ered, -ering, -ers.** *—intr.* **1.** To dry up or shrivel from or as if from loss of moisture: *The flowers withered in the sun.* **2.** To lose freshness, vitality, or strength; fade: *Hope withered away; withered under his sarcasm.* *—tr.* **1.** To cause to shrivel or fade. **2.** To cause to feel belittled; cut down; abash: *withered her with a glance.* [Middle English *widderen,* perhaps variant of *wederen,* to weather, from *weder,* WEATHER.]

with·er·ite (wíthə-rīt) *n.* A white, yellow, or grey vitreous mineral, barium carbonate, $BaCO_3$. [After William *Withering* (1741–99), English physician.]

with·ers (wíthərz) *pl.n.* The high point of the back of a horse, or of a similar or related animal, at the base of the neck and between the shoulder blades. [Perhaps from obsolete *wither-,* denoting opposition (the withers resist or "oppose" a load), from Middle English *wither-,* Old English *wither-,* from *wither,* against.]

with·er·shins (wíthər-shin) *adv.* Also **wid·der·shins** (wíddər-). *Chiefly Scottish.* In a direction opposite to the course of the sun; anticlockwise. [Middle Low German *weddersin(ne)s,* from Middle High German *widersinnes,* "countercourse" : *wider,* against + *sinnes,* genitive of *sin,* journey, direction.]

with·hold (with-hṓld, with-) *v.* **-held** (-héld), **-holding, -holds.** *—tr.* **1.** To keep in check; restrain. **2.** To refrain from giving, granting, or permitting: *withhold permission.* *—intr.* To refrain; forbear. **—**See Synonyms at **keep.** [Middle English *withholden* : *with,* back, away from, WITH + *holden,* to HOLD.] **—with·hold·er** *n.*

with·hold·ing tax (with-hṓlding, with-) *n.* In the United States, a portion of an employee's pay withheld by his employer, who then pays it to the government as partial payment of the employee's income tax.

with·in (with-in || with-) *adv. Formal.* **1.** In or into the inner part; inside. **2.** In or belonging to a community or group: *the enemy within.* **3.** Inside the body, mind, heart, or soul; inwardly: *Purify me within.*
~prep. **1.** In the inner part or parts of; inside: *The kingdom of heaven is within you.* **2.** Inside the limits or extent of in time, degree or distance: *within ten miles of home; separated within a year of their marriage.* **3.** Inside the fixed limits of; not exceeding or transgressing: *within the laws of the land.* **4.** In the scope, sphere, or range of: *within the medical profession; within sight but not within reach.*

with·in·doors (with-ín-dórz || with-, -dṓrz) *adv. Archaic.* Indoors.

with-it (wíth-it || wíth-) *adj. Informal.* Up-to-date; trendy.

with·out (with-ówt, with-) *adv.* **1.** *Formal.* In or on the outside. **2.** *Formal.* Externally; outwardly. **3.** With something lacking or missing: *We can get along without.*
~prep. **1.** Not having; lacking: *a family without a car.* **2. a.** With no or none of; in the absence of: *without help.* **b.** Not accompanied by: *no smoke without fire.* **3.** *Archaic.* At, on, to, or towards the outside or exterior of: *without the walls.* **4.** With neglect or avoidance of: *went by without speaking to us.*
~conj. Archaic & Regional. Unless. [Middle English *withouten,* Old English *withūtan* : *with,* not together with, separated, WITH + *ūtan,* outside of, from *ūt,* OUT.]

with·out·doors (with-ówt-dórz || with-, -dṓrz) *adv. Archaic.* Outside a house or shelter; out of doors.

with·stand (with-stánd, with-) *v.* **-stood, -standing, -stands.** *—tr.* **1.** To oppose with effort or force; resist. **2.** To resist or endure successfully; stand up to: *withstood years of hard wear.* *—intr.* To offer resistance. **—**See Synonyms at **oppose.** [Middle English *withstanden,* Old English *withstandan* : *with,* against, WITH + *standan,* to STAND.] **—with·stand·er** *n.*

with·y (wíthi || wíthi) *adj.* Resembling a withe in wiriness or toughness: *a withy young boxer.*
~n., pl. **withies. 1.** A rope or band made of withes. **2.** A long, flexible twig, such as that of an osier. **3.** A tree or shrub having such twigs. [Middle English *wythy,* flexible twig, willow wand, Old English *wīthig.*]

wit·less (wít-ləss, -liss) *adj.* Lacking intelligence or wit; stupid. **—wit·less·ly** *adv.* **—wit·less·ness** *n.*

wit·ling (wít-ling) *n. Archaic.* One who thinks himself a wit.

wit·ness (wít-nəss, -niss) *n.* **1.** One who has perceived something and who can give evidence for its occurrence: *Were there any witnesses to the accident?* **2.** Anything that serves as evidence; a testimony. **3.** *Law.* **a.** One who is called upon to testify before a court. **b.** One who is called upon to be present at a transaction in order to attest to what took place. **c.** One who signs his name to a document for the purpose of attesting to its authenticity. **4.** An attestation to a fact, statement, or event.
~v. **witnessed, -nessing, -nesses.** *—tr.* **1.** To be present at or have direct personal knowledge of (an event, for example). **2.** To provide or serve as evidence of. **3.** To be the setting or site of: *This auditorium witnesses many ceremonies.* **4.** To attest to the legality or authenticity of (a document) by signing one's name. **5.** To consider

as evidence or proof. Used parenthetically in the imperative: *The C.B.I. (witness its recent report) is clearly losing patience with the government.* —*intr.* To furnish or serve as evidence; testify. [Middle English *witnes(se),* Old English *witnes,* witness, knowledge, from *wit,* knowledge, WIT.] —**wit·ness·er** *n.*

witness box *n.* The place in a courtroom from which a witness presents testimony. Also *U.S.* "witness stand", "stand".

wit·ted (wíttid) *adj.* Having wits or understanding as specified. Used in combination: *dim-witted; half-witted.*

Wit·ten·berg (vít'n-berg; *German* vítt'n-bairk). Town in eastern Germany. Situated on the river Elbe, it is where Martin Luther nailed his 95 theses to the door of the Schlosskirche (1517), so initiating the Protestant Reformation.

wit·ter (wíttər) *intr. v. British Informal.* To chatter trivially, tediously, or complainingly: *always wittering on about their problems.* [From Scottish and regional *whitter* or *quitter,* to twitter, probably akin to Swedish *quittra* and Danish *kvidre.*]

Witt·gen·stein (vít-gən-shtīn, -stīn), **Ludwig (Johann Josef)** (1889–1951). Austrian philosopher. A follower of Frege and Russell, he worked on theories of language and in his *Tractatus Logico-Philosophicus* (1921) he helped to develop logical positivism. His other important work, *Philosophical Investigations,* published (1953) after his death, examined linguistic ambiguities in philosophical statements.

wit·ti·cism (wítti-siz'm) *n.* A witty remark or saying. See Synonyms at **joke.** [From WITTY (influenced by CRITICISM).]

wit·ting (wítting). *Archaic.* Present participle of **wit** (to know). ~*adj.* **1.** Aware or conscious. **2.** Done intentionally or with premeditation; deliberate. —**wit·ting·ly** *adv.*

wit·tol (wítt'l) *n. Archaic.* A man who tolerates his wife's infidelity. [Middle English *wetewold : weten, witen,* to WIT (know) + *(coke)-wold,* CUCKOLD.]

wit·ty (wítti) *adj.* **-tier, -tiest. 1.** Possessing, characterised by, or demonstrating wit in speech or writing; ingenious and humorous. **2.** *Archaic.* Intelligent. —**wit·ti·ly** *adv.* —**wit·ti·ness** *n.*

Wit·wa·ters·rand (wit-wáwtərz-rand, witt-wawtərz-; *locally* vit-vaatərz-, -raánd, -rónt, -raánt). Region in the Republic of South Africa, also informally known as the Rand or the Reef. Dominated by ridges forming the watershed of the Vaal and Olifants rivers, its gold reserves, exploited since 1886, account for almost one third of world output.

wive (wīv) *v.* **wived, wiving, wives.** *Archaic.* —*tr.* **1.** To marry (a woman); take as a wife. **2.** To provide a wife for. —*intr.* To marry a woman. [Middle English *wiven,* Old English *wīfian,* from *wīf,* WIFE.]

wivern. Variant of **wyvern.**

wives. Plural of **wife.**

wiz (wiz) *n. Informal.* A person considered exceptionally gifted or skilled; a wizard. [Short for WIZARD.]

wiz·ard (wízzərd) *n.* **1.** A male witch; a sorcerer or magician. **2.** A person who is skilful or clever at a particular activity: *a wizard at cooking.* **3.** *Archaic.* A wise man or sage. ~*adj.* **1.** Of or pertaining to wizards or wizardry. **2.** *Chiefly British Informal.* Excellent; wonderful. [Middle English *wysard : wys, wis,* WISE + -ARD.]

wiz·ard·ry (wízzədri) *n.* The art, skill, or practice of a wizard; witchcraft; sorcery.

wiz·en¹ (wízz'n) *v.* **-ened, -ening, -ens.** —*intr.* To wither or sear; dry up; shrivel. —*tr.* To cause to wither or dry up. ~*adj.* Variant of **wizened.** [Middle English *wisenen,* Old English *wisnian.*]

wiz·ened (wízz'nd) *adj.* Also **wizen.** Shrivelled or dried up, as through age; withered.

wk. **1.** weak. **2.** week.

WL, w.l. waterline.

WLM Women's Liberation Movement.

W.M.O World Meteorological Organisation.

WNW west-northwest.

WO, W.O. **1.** warrant officer. **2.** wireless operator.

woad (wōd) *n.* **1.** An Old World plant, *Isatis tinctoria,* formerly cultivated for its leaves than yield a blue dye. **2.** The dye obtained from this plant. [Middle English *wod(e),* Old English *wād†.*]

woad·wax·en (wōd-waks'n) *n.* A shrub, **dyer's greenweed** (*see*). [Variant (influenced by WOAD) of WOODWAXEN.]

wob·be·gong (wóbbi-gong) *n.* Any of various Australian sharks of the family Orectolobidae, having brown and white markings. [From a native Australian language.]

wob·ble, wab·ble (wóbb'l) *v.* **-bled, -bling, -bles.** —*intr.* **1.** To move or sway unsteadily from side to side. **2.** To tremble or quaver; shake: *Her voice wobbled with emotion.* **3.** To waver or vacillate in one's opinions, feelings, or the like. —*tr.* To cause to wobble. ~*n.* The act or an instance of wobbling, as in a movement or sound. [Perhaps from Low German *wabbeln.*] —**wob·bler** *n.*

wobble board *n.* In Australia, a flexible, rectangular sheet, as of masonite, used as a musical instrument, that produces a low booming sound when bent back and forwards.

wob·bly (wóbbli) *adj.* **-blier, -bliest.** Tending to wobble; unsteady; shaky.

Wob·bly (wóbbli) *n., pl.* **-blies.** A member of the Industrial Workers of the World (I.W.W.). [20th century : origin obscure.]

Wode·house (wōd-howss), **Sir P(elham) G(renville)** (1881–1975). British comic novelist. He introduced his most famous characters, the aristocratic Bertie Wooster and his manservant

Jeeves, in the stories in *The Man with Two Left Feet* (1917).

Wo·den, Wo·dan (wōd'n). The chief god in Anglo-Saxon mythology, often identified with the Norse god Odin. [Old English *Wōden.*]

wodge. Variant of **wadge.**

woe (wō) *n.* **1.** Deep sorrow; grief. **2.** *Literary.* Misfortune; calamity: "*Woe unto you that are full!*" (Luke 6:25). **3.** *Usually plural.* A difficulty; a trouble: *Life is full of woes.* —See Synonyms at **regret.** ~*interj. Literary.* Used to express sorrow or dismay: *Woe is me!* [Middle English *wo(e),* Old English *wā* (interjection).]

woe·be·gone (wō-bi-gon ‖ -gaan, -gawn) *adj.* **1.** Mournful, sorrowful, or pathetic in appearance. **2.** *Archaic.* Struck by disaster; afflicted. [Middle English *wo begon : wo(e),* WOE + *begon,* beset, from *begon,* to beset, go about : *be-,* about + *gon,* to GO.]

woe·ful (wōf'l) *adj.* **1.** Afflicted with woe; mournful. **2.** Pitiful, wretched, or deplorable: *a woeful attempt at a poem.* —**woe·ful·ly** *adv.* —**woe·ful·ness** *n.*

wog·gle (wógg'l) *n.* A leather ring used to secure the neckerchief of a Scout or Guide uniform.

wok (wok) *n.* A large bowl-shaped metal pan used, especially in Chinese cooking, for frying, steaming, and the like. [Cantonese.]

woke. Past tense and *chiefly British & Regional* past participle of **wake.**

wok·en. Past participle of **wake.**

wold (wōld) *n.* A stretch of open, unforested, rolling countryside or moorland. [Middle English *wold,* a forest, hill, Old English *weald, wald,* from Germanic *walthus* (unattested).]

wolf (wŏŏlf) *n., pl.* **wolves** (wŏŏlvz). **1. a.** A carnivorous mammal, *Canis lupus,* of the Northern Hemisphere, that hunts in packs and is related to and resembles the dogs. **b.** The fur of such an animal. **2.** Any of various similar or related mammals. **3.** The destructive larva of any of various moths, beetles, or flies. **4. a.** One who is rapacious, predatory, and fierce. **b.** *Informal.* A man given to avid amatory pursuit of women. **5.** *Music.* **a.** A harshness in some notes of a bowed stringed instrument produced by defective vibration. **b.** Dissonance in some intervals of a keyboard instrument tuned to a system of unequal temperament. —**cry wolf.** To raise a false alarm. —**have** or **hold a wolf by the ears.** To be in a dangerous or precarious situation. —**keep the wolf from the door.** To ward off or avert hunger or poverty. —**throw to the wolves.** To abandon to certain destruction. —**wolf in sheep's clothing.** A person who conceals his malicious nature or intentions under a friendly exterior. ~*tr.v.* **wolfed, wolfing, wolfs.** To eat voraciously. Often used with *down.* [Middle English *wolf(e),* Old English *wulf.*] —**wolf·ish** *adj.* —**wolf·ish·ly** *adv.*

Wolf (volf), **Hugo** (1860–1903). Austrian composer. Chiefly a composer of songs, he set the poetry of Goethe and Italian and Spanish writers, and wrote the opera *Der Corregidor* (1895).

Wolf Cub *n. Chiefly British.* Formerly, a Cub Scout.

wolf dog *n.* **1.** A dog trained to hunt or ward off wolves. **2.** The offspring of a dog and a wolf.

Wolfe (wŏŏlf), **James** (1727–59). British army officer. He led the successful assault on the French stronghold of Louisbourg in Nova Scotia. He was killed at the battle of the Plains of Abraham (1759), which won the city of Quebec for Britain and led to the conquest of Canada.

Wolfe, Thomas (Clayton) (1900–38). U.S. novelist. His works include *Look Homeward Angel* (1929) and the posthumously published *You Can't Go Home Again* (1940).

Wolff·i·an body (wŏŏlfi-ən) *n.* The **mesonephros** (*see*). [After Kasper Friedrich *Wolff* (1733–94), German embryologist.]

wolf fish *n.* Any of several northern slender marine fishes of the genus *Anarhichas,* having sharp, powerful teeth and no pelvic fins.

wolf·hound (wŏŏlf-hownd) *n.* Any of various large dogs that have been trained to hunt wolves or other large game. See **borzoi, Irish wolfhound.**

wolf pack *n.* Submarines or aircraft that attack as a group.

wolf·ram (wŏŏlfrəm) *n.* The element **tungsten** (*see*). [German *Wolfram* : perhaps Middle High German *wolf,* wolf, + *rām,* dirt, black, probably akin to Sanskrit *Rāma,* RAMA.]

wolf·ram·ite (wŏŏlfrə-mīt) *n.* Any of several red-brown to black minerals with the general formula $(Fe,Mn)WO_4$, a major source of tungsten. [German *Wolframit,* from WOLFRAM.]

wolfs·bane (wŏŏlfs-bayn) *n.* A plant, the **monkshood** (*see*).

wolf spider *n.* Any spider of the family Lycosidae, having long stout legs and hunting their prey. Also called "hunting spider".

wolf whistle *n.* A short, distinctive whistle rising to a high note and then diminishing again to a low note, used vulgarly by a man to express sexual admiration for a woman. —**wolf-whistle** (wŏŏlf-wiss'l) *v.*

wol·las·ton·ite (wŏŏllstə-nīt) *n.* A mineral, calcium silicate, $CaSiO_3$, found in metamorphic rocks and used in various ceramics, paints, plastics, and cements. [After William *Wollaston* (1766–1828), British physicist.]

Wol·las·ton prism (wŏŏllstən) *n.* A prism cut from quartz that separates the ordinary and extraordinary components of unpolarised light. [After W. H. *Wollaston;* see **wollastonite.**]

Woll·stone·craft (wŏŏl-stən-kraaft ‖ -kraft), **Mary** (1759–97). British radical and feminist. As a publisher's adviser, she met various radicals including Tom Paine and her husband William Godwin. Her works include *A Vindication of the Rights of Women* (1792), and a reply to Burke in *View of the French Revolution* (1794). She died giving birth to her daughter, who became Mary Shelley.

Wo·lof (wóllof ‖ *U.S.* wṓ-lawf) *n.* A West Atlantic language of Senegal. —**Wo·lof** *adj.*

Wolse·ley (wǒolzli), **Garnet Joseph, 1st Viscount** (1833-1913). British field-marshal. He won the battle of Tall al Kabir (1882), led the expedition to relieve General Gordon at Khartoum (1884–85), and became commander-in-chief of the Army (1895-1899).

Wolsey, Thomas (*c.* 1475-1530). English cardinal. He rose to become the Bishop of Lincoln and Archbishop of York (1514) and a cardinal and Lord Chancellor of England (1515). He controlled foreign policy and worked for the increase of England's power. He was indecisive over Henry VIII's wish to divorce Catherine of Aragon, was prosecuted (1529), and arrested for high treason (1530).

Wol·ver·hamp·ton (wǒolvǝr-hámptǝn). Town near Birmingham, west central England. It has long been a centre for metal-working, particularly locks and keys. Other industries include motor vehicles, bicycles, chemicals, and aircraft.

wol·ver·ine (wǒolvǝ-reen) *n.* A carnivorous mammal, *Gulo gulo* (or *G. luscus*), of northern regions, having dark fur and a bushy tail. Also called "glutton", "carcajou". [Earlier *wolvering*, irregularly from WOLF.]

wolves. Plural of **wolf.**

wom·an (wǒommǝn) *n., pl.* **women** (wímmin). **1. a.** An adult female human being, as distinguished from a man or a girl. **b.** A woman of a specified status or occupation, or concerned with a specified sphere of activity. Used in combination: *a noblewoman; a policewoman.* **2.** Women collectively; womankind: *Woman is more resistant than man.* **3.** Feminine quality or aspect; womanliness. Usually preceded by *the: brought out the woman in him.* **4.** A female employed to do household duties. **5.** *Informal.* A wife or female lover. —See Usage note at **lady.**
~*adj.* Female as opposed to male. [Middle English *wumman, wimman,* Old English *wīfmann : wīf,* WIFE + *man(n),* person, MAN.]

wom·an·hood (wǒommǝn-hǒod) *n.* **1.** The state of being a woman. **2.** Feminine nature or qualities. **3.** Womankind.

wom·an·ise, wom·an·ize (wǒommǝ-nīz) *v.* **-ised, -ising, -ises.** —*tr.* To give feminine characteristics to. —*intr.* To indulge in casual affairs with women habitually or excessively. Used of a man. —**wom·an·is·er** *n.*

wom·an·ish (wǒommǝnish) *adj.* **1.** Characteristic of a woman; womanly. **2.** Considered more typical of or appropriate to the nature of a woman than of a man; effeminate; weak. —**wom·an·ish·ly** *adv.* —**wom·an·ish·ness** *n.*

wom·an·kind (wǒommǝn-kīnd) *n.* Female human beings collectively; women.

wom·an·ly (wǒommǝnli) *adj.* **-lier, -liest.** Having the qualities, such as warmth and compassion, thought of as being typical of or appropriate to a woman. —**wom·an·li·ness** *n.*

womb (wǒom) *n.* **1.** The **uterus** *(see).* **2. a.** A place where something is generated or developed. **b.** Any protective and confining organ, receptacle, or place. **3.** *Obsolete.* The belly. [Middle English *womb(e),* Old English *wamb,* from Germanic *wambō* (unattested).]

wom·bat (wǒm-bat) *n.* Either of two Australian marsupials, *Phascolomis ursinus* or *Lasiorhinus latifrons,* somewhat resembling small bears. [Native Australian name.]

womb leas·ing (lée-sing) *n.* The practice whereby a **surrogate mother** *(see)* bears a child for another woman, usually in return for financial reward. Also called "surrogacy".

wom·en·folk (wimmin-fōk) *pl.n.* **1.** Women collectively. **2.** A particular group of women, as those belonging to one family.

Women's Institute *n.* In Britain and some Commonwealth countries, an organisation, especially in rural areas, that holds meetings and talks for women interested in social and domestic matters.

women's lib·ber (líbbǝr) *n.* *Informal.* An adherent of the Women's Movement. Usually used derogatorily.

Women's Liberation Movement *n. Abbr.* **WLM** The social and political movement that originated in Europe and the United States in the 19th century seeking to bring into effect the principles of **feminism** *(see).* Among the early exponents of the movement were emancipated black slaves in the United States and suffragettes in Britain. Also called "Women's movement", informally "Women's Lib". —**women's liberationist** *n.*

won[1] (wun, won) *intr.v.* **wonned, wonning, wons.** *Archaic.* To dwell or abide. [Middle English *won(i)en,* Old English *wunian.*]

won[2] (won) *n., pl.* **won. 1.** The basic monetary unit of South Korea, equal to 100 jeon, jon or chon. **2.** The basic monetary unit of North Korea, equal to 100 jeon, jon or chon. [Korean.]

won[3]. Past tense and past participle of **win.**

won·der (wúndǝr) *n.* **1.** That which arouses awe, astonishment, or admiration; a marvel. Also used adjectively: *a wonder cure; a wonder horse.* **2.** The feeling or emotion aroused by a wonder, characterised by admiration, awe, and sometimes bewilderment. **3.** A matter for surprise: *It's a wonder you weren't killed. No wonder it's not working —you haven't plugged it in.* **4.** *Plural. Informal.* Something miraculous or impressively successful in effect: *The advert did wonders for sales.* **5.** See **Seven Wonders of the World.** —**for a wonder.** Surprisingly. —**small wonder.** It is hardly surprising.
~*v.* **wondered, -dering, -ders.** —*intr.* **1. a.** To ponder with curiosity; speculate. **b.** To entertain doubts: *I often wonder about his honesty.* **2.** To have a feeling of awe or admiration; marvel. —*tr.* **1.** To feel curiosity about. **2.** *Chiefly British.* To feel surprise at: *I wonder that you're still awake.* **3.** Used to express a polite inquiry or request: *I wonder whether you would mind shutting the door.* [Middle English *wonder,* Old English *wundor.*] —**won·der·er** *n.*

Usage: The use of a double negative construction with this verb is commonly found in informal English, though it should be avoided in more formal contexts: *I shouldn't wonder if she doesn't arrive by ten* (in the sense "I expect her to arrive by ten").

won·der·ful (wúndǝrf'l) *adj.* **1.** Capable of exciting wonder; astonishing: *amazed at the scheme's wonderful simplicity.* **2.** Fine; excellent. —**won·der·ful·ly** *adv.* —**won·der·ful·ness** *n.*

won·der·land (wúndǝr-land) *n.* **1.** A marvellous imaginary realm. **2.** A marvellous place or scene that is real and not imaginary.

won·der·ment (wúndǝrmǝnt) *n.* **1.** Astonishment, awe, or surprise. **2.** Puzzlement or curiosity. **3.** Something that produces wonder.

Wonders of the Ancient World. The **Seven Wonders of the World** *(see).*

won·der·worker (wúndǝr-wurkǝr) *n.* One who performs miracles or achieves exceptional success.

won·drous (wúndrǝss) *adj. Literary.* Wonderful.
~*adv. Archaic.* To a wonderful or remarkable extent. —**won·drous·ly** *adv.*

won·ga-won·ga (wóngǝ-wóngǝ) *n.* **1.** A large pigeon, *Leucosarcia melanoleuca,* of Australia. **2.** Any of several Australian vines of the genus *Pandorea.* [From a native Australian language.]

won·ky (wóngki) *adj.* **-kier, -kiest.** *British Informal.* **1.** Shaky; unsteady. **2.** Not straight; askew. **3.** Wrong; faulty. [20th century : origin obscure.]

Won·san (wón-sán). Capital of Kangwon province, southeastern North Korea. Situated on the Sea of Japan, it is an industrial and communications centre, port, and naval base.

wont (wōnt ‖ wont, *U.S. also* wawnt, wunt) *adj. Formal.* Accustomed or used to. Usually used with an infinitive: *He was wont to drink port after dinner.*
~*n. Formal.* Usage or custom: *rose early, as was her wont.*
~*v.* **wont, wont** or **wonted, wonting, wonts.** *Archaic.* —*tr.* To accustom. —*intr.* To be in the habit of doing something. [Middle English *wont,* from the past participle of *wonen,* to be accustomed, dwell, to WON.]

won't (wōnt). Contraction of *will not.*

wont·ed (wōnt-id ‖ wónt-, *U.S. also* wáwnt-, wúnt-) *adj. Formal.* Accustomed; usual. Used before the noun: *at the wonted hour.*

woo (wǒo) *v.* **wooed, wooing, woos.** —*tr.* **1.** To seek the affection of with intent to marry. **2. a.** To seek to achieve; try to gain; court: *wooed the favour of the public with tax cuts.* **b.** To make efforts to gain the favour or compliance of; tempt: *wooing the electorate.* **3.** To entreat, solicit, or importune. —*intr.* To court a woman. [Middle English *wowen,* Old English *wōgian†.*] —**woo·er** *n.*

wood[1] (wǒod) *n.* **1. a.** The tough, fibrous cellular substance constituting the xylem of trees and shrubs, lying beneath the bark and consisting largely of cellulose and lignin. **b.** Such a substance used for any of a wide variety of purposes, as for building material or fuel. **2.** *Often plural.* A dense growth of trees; a small forest. **3.** An object or part made of wood, especially: **a.** *Music.* A woodwind instrument. **b.** A golf club having a wooden head. **c.** A cask or barrel for storing wine or other alcoholic drinks: *a pint of beer from the wood.* **d.** The frame of a tennis racket, as opposed to its strings. **e.** A wooden ball used in the game of bowls. —**not see the wood for the trees.** To be unable to get an overall or general view because of a confusing mass of details. —**out of the wood** or **woods.** Free of difficulties or dangers. —**touch wood. 1.** To place the hand against a wooden object in an act of superstition to avert bad luck or misfortune, especially after having made a positive statement about someone or something. **2.** Used as an interjection in place of or as well as the act of touching wood.
~*adj.* **1.** Made of or consisting of wood; wooden. **2.** Associated with, used on, or containing wood: *a wood screw; a wood box.* **3.** Growing or living in woods or forests.
~*v.* **wooded, wooding, woods.** —*tr.* **1.** To supply or fuel with wood. **2.** To cover with trees; forest. —*intr.* To gather or be supplied with wood. [Middle English *wode,* Old English *wudu.*]

wood[2] *adj. Archaic.* Violently insane. [Middle English *wo(o)d,* Old English *wōd.*]

Wood, Sir Henry (Joseph), born Paul Klenovsky (1869-1944). British conductor and organist. He introduced the Promenade Concerts in London at the Queen's Hall (1895), which he conducted until his death, and championed many contemporary composers.

Wood, John (1704-54). English architect. Known as Wood of Bath, from the 1720s he designed many of its buildings and streets in the Palladian style. His son John Wood (1728-81) designed the Assembly Rooms and the Royal Crescent.

wood alcohol *n.* **Methanol** *(see).*

wood anemone *n.* Either of two plants, *Anemone nemorosa,* of Europe, or *A. quinquefolia,* of eastern North America, having deeply divided leaves and a solitary white or pink flower. Also called "windflower".

wood ant *n.* A reddish European ant, *Formica rufa,* whose anthills are found in woodlands.

wood avens *n.* A plant, **herb bennet** *(see).*

wood·bine (wǒodbīn) *n.* Any of various climbing vines, especially: **1.** An Old World honeysuckle, *Lonicera periclymenum,* having yellowish flowers. **2.** *U.S.* The **Virginia creeper** *(see).* [Middle English *wodebinde,* Old English *wudubinde : wudu,* WOOD + *bindan,* to BIND.]

wood·block (wǒod-blok) *n.* **1.** A woodcut. **2.** *Music.* A partially hollowed out block of hard wood struck with a drumstick, used as a percussion instrument.

wood·bor·er (wŏŏd-bawrər ‖ -bōrər) *n.* Any of various insects, insect larvae, or molluscs that bore into wood.

wood·carv·ing (wŏŏd-kaarving) *n.* **1.** The art of carving in wood. **2.** An object carved from wood. **—wood·carv·er** *n.*

wood·chat (wŏŏd-chat) *n.* An Old World bird, *Lanius senator,* having black and white plumage with a reddish crown.

wood·chuck (wŏŏd-chuk) *n.* A common rodent, *Marmota monax,* of northern and eastern North America, having a short-legged, heavy-set body and grizzled brownish fur. Also called "ground hog". [Variant (by folk etymology) of Cree *oček,* from Proto-Algonquian *wečyeka* (unattested), "fisher".]

wood coal *n.* **1.** Charcoal. **2.** Lignite.

wood·cock (wŏŏd-kok) *n., pl.* **-cocks** or collectively **woodcock.** Either of two related game birds, *Scolopax rusticola,* of the Old World, or *Philohela minor,* of North America, having brownish plumage, short legs, and a long bill. [Middle English *wodecok,* Old English *wuducocc : wudu,* WOOD + *cocc,* COCK.]

wood·craft (wŏŏd-kraaft ‖ -kraft) *n.* **1.** The act, process, or art of working with wood. **2.** Skill and experience in matters pertaining to the woods, such as hunting, fishing, or camping.

wood·cut (wŏŏd-kut) *n.* **1.** A piece of wood upon which a design for printing is engraved, especially along the grain. Also called "wood block". **2.** A print made from such a piece of wood. Also called "woodblock", "woodprint".

wood·cut·ter (wŏŏd-kuttər) *n.* A person who cuts wood or trees. **—wood·cut·ting** *n.*

wood·ed (wŏŏdid) *adj.* Having or covered with trees or woods.

wood·en (wŏŏdd'n) *adj.* **1.** Made or consisting of wood. **2.** Stiff; inflexible. **3.** Lifeless; expressionless. **—wood·en·ly** *adv.* **—wood·en·ness** *n.*

wood engraving *n.* **1.** A piece of wood upon which a design for printing is engraved, usually across the grain. **2.** The art or process of making wood engravings. **3.** A print made from such a piece of wood.

wood·en·head (wŏŏdd'n-hed) *n. Informal.* A stupid person; a blockhead. **—wood·en·head·ed** (-héddid) *adj.*

Wooden Horse *n.* The **Trojan horse** (*see*).

wooden spoon *n.* A booby prize, especially awarded to one who comes last in a sports competition. [After the former custom at Cambridge of presenting a wooden spoon to the lowest-ranking of the students taking honours in the mathematical tripos.]

wood grouse *n.* A bird, the **capercaillie** (*see*).

wood ibis *n.* Any of several large wading birds of the family Ciconiiformes, related to and resembling the storks; especially, *Mycteria americana* of the New World.

wood·land (wŏŏdlənd) *n.* Land having a cover of trees and shrubs. *~adj.* Of or indigenous to such a wooded area. **—wood·land·er** *n.*

wood·lark (wŏŏd-laark) *n.* An Old World songbird, *Lullula arborea,* resembling but smaller than the skylark.

wood louse *n.* Any of various small terrestrial crustaceans having a flattened segmented body and found in damp, shady places, especially under logs and stones. Also called "slater", "pill bug".

wood·man (wŏŏd-mən) *n., pl.* **-men** (-mən). A woodcutter or woodsman.

wood·note (wŏŏd-nōt) *n.* **1.** A song or call characteristic of a woodland bird. **2.** A piece of music or poetry resembling a bird's song in its spontaneity.

wood nymph *n.* A nymph of the forest; a dryad.

wood·peck·er (wŏŏd-peckər) *n.* Any of various birds of the family Picidae, having strong claws and a stiff tail adapted for clinging to and climbing trees, and a chisel-like bill for drilling through bark and wood.

wood pigeon *n.* A large Eurasian pigeon, *Columba palumbus,* having a white band on each wing. Also called "ringdove".

wood·pile (wŏŏd-pīl) *n.* A pile of wood, especially when stacked for use as fuel.

wood·print (wŏŏd-print) *n.* A **woodcut** (*see*).

wood pulp *n.* Any of various cellulose pulps ground from wood, chemically processed, and used to make paper.

wood·ruff (wŏŏd-ruf) *n.* Any of various plants of the genera *Galium* and *Asperula* in the bedstraw family; especially, *G. odoratum,* which has fragrant white flowers and whorls of narrow leaves, formerly used, when dried, as bedding and stuffing. [Middle English *woderofe,* Old English *wudurofe : wudu,* WOOD *-rofe,* of uncertain origin; perhaps akin to Middle Low German *röve,* turnip.]

wood·rush (wŏŏd-rush) *n.* Any of various plants of the genus *Luzula,* resembling rushes but having long white hairs on the leaves and stems and generally found in drier habitats.

wood·screw (wŏŏd-skrōō ‖ -skrew) *n.* A tapered metal screw that is driven into wood, plaster, and the like with a screwdriver.

wood·shed (wŏŏd-shed) *n.* A shed in which firewood is stored.

woods·man (wŏŏdz-mən) *n., pl.* **-men** (-mən). One who works or lives in the woods or is versed in woodcraft; a forester.

wood sorrel *n.* Any of various plants of the genus *Oxalis,* having compound leaves with three leaflets; especially, *O. acetosella,* which has mauve-veined white flowers.

wood spirit *n.* **Methanol** (*see*).

Wood·stock[1] (wŏŏd-stok). Town of Oxfordshire, south central England. Situated north of Oxford, it was the site of a royal palace, where Elizabeth I was imprisoned by Mary I (1554). The nearby Blenheim palace (1724) was designed by Sir John Vanbrugh.

Woodstock[2]. Town in southeastern New York, United States. It was the site (1969) of a huge rock music festival.

wood sugar *n.* **Xylose** (*see*).

woods·y (wŏŏdzi) *adj.* **-ier, -iest.** *U.S. Informal.* Of, relating to, or suggestive of the woods.

wood tar *n.* A black, syrup-like viscous fluid that is a by-product of the destructive distillation of wood and is used in pitch, wood preserving oils, preservatives, and medicines.

wood·turn·ing (wŏŏd-turning) *n.* The art or process of shaping wood into various forms on a lathe. **—wood·turn·er** *n.*

wood vinegar *n. Chemistry.* **Pyroligneous acid** (*see*).

wood warbler *n.* A woodland bird, *Phylloscopus sibilatrix,* having a yellow breast and distinct yellow eyestripe.

Wood·ward (wŏŏd-wərd), **Robert Burns** (1917–79). U.S. chemist. The first scientist to synthesise various organic compounds including quinine, cortisone, and chlorophyll, he was awarded the Nobel prize in chemistry (1965).

wood·wax·en (wŏŏd-waks'n) *n.* A shrub, the **dyer's greenweed** (*see*). [Middle English *wodewexen,* Old English *wudu weaxe : wudu,* WOOD + probably *weaxan,* to grow, WAX.]

wood·wind (wŏŏd-wind) *n.* **1.** A group of musical wind instruments formerly made of wood but nowadays often of metal or plastic, that includes the bassoons, clarinets, flutes, oboes, and sometimes the saxophones. **2.** *Plural.* The section of an orchestra composed of woodwind instruments. **—wood·wind** *n.*

wood·work (wŏŏd-wurk) *n.* **1.** The art or skill of woodcarving or carpentry. **2.** Objects made of or work done in wood; especially, wooden interior fittings in a house, such as doors, staircases, or windowsills. **—wood·work·er** *n.* **—wood·work·ing** *n. & adj.*

wood·worm (wŏŏd-wurm) *n.* **1.** Any of various insect larvae that bore into wood, especially those of the furniture beetle and death-watch beetle. **2.** The riddled effect produced in wood by such larvae.

wood·y (wŏŏddi) *adj.* **-ier, -iest. 1.** Forming or consisting of wood; ligneous: *woody tissue.* **2.** Characterised by the presence of wood or xylem: *woody plants.* **3.** Characteristic or suggestive of wood: *a woody smell.* **4.** Covered with trees; wooded. **—wood·i·ness** *n.*

woody nightshade *n.* **Bittersweet** (*see*).

woof[1] (wŏŏf ‖ wŏŏf) *n.* **1.** The threads that run crosswise in a woven fabric, at right angles to the warp threads; the weft. **2.** The texture of a woven fabric. [Variant (influenced by WARP) of Middle English *oof,* Old English *ōwef : ō-,* from *on,* ON + *wefan,* to weave.]

woof[2] (wŏŏf) *n.* **1.** The deep, gruff bark of a dog. **2.** A sound similar to this.
~intr.v. **woofed, woof·ing, woofs.** To utter a woof. [Imitative.]

woof·er (wŏŏfər ‖ wŏŏffər) *n.* A loudspeaker designed to reproduce bass frequencies. Compare **tweeter.** [From WOOF (sound).]

woof·ter (wŏŏftər) *n. Chiefly British Informal.* A male homosexual, especially if effeminate. Usually used derogatorily. [Variant of POOFTER, with *W-* as in *woman.*]

wool (wŏŏl) *n.* **1.** The dense, soft, often curly hair forming the coat of sheep and certain other mammals. **2. a.** Yarn carded, spun, and processed from this for use in woven, knitted, and embroidered textiles. **b.** Loosely, any yarn used for knitting, even when mixed with synthetic fibres. **3.** Any filamentous or fibrous covering or substance suggestive of the texture or appearance of wool: *steel wool.* **—pull the wool over (someone's) eyes.** To deceive; trick. *~adj.* Of, pertaining to, or consisting of wool or woollen material. [Middle English *wolle, wull,* Old English *wull.*]

wooll·en, *U.S.* **wool·en** (wŏŏlən) *adj.* Of, pertaining to, or consisting of wool. *~n. Plural.* Fabric or clothing made from wool, especially when knitted.

Woolf (wŏŏlf), **Leonard (Sidney)** (1880–1969). British writer, the husband of Virginia Woolf. A member of the Fabians and co-founder with his wife of the Hogarth Press (1917), his works include *After the Deluge* (1931–39) and an autobiography (1960–69).

Woolf, (Adeline) Virginia, born Adeline Virginia Stephen (1882–1941). British novelist and member of the Bloomsbury group. In an experimental stream-of-consciousness style, her novels include *Mrs Dalloway* (1925), *To the Lighthouse* (1927), and *The Waves* (1931). She also wrote essays and critical works, including *A Room of One's Own* (1929). She committed suicide.

wool fat *n.* **Lanolin** (*see*).

wool·gath·er·ing (wŏŏl-gathəring) *n.* Absent-minded indulgence in fanciful daydreams. **—wool·gath·er·er** *n.*

wool·grow·er (wŏŏl-grō-ər) *n.* A person who breeds sheep or other animals for the production of wool. **—wool·grow·ing** *adj.*

wool in the grease *n.* **Grease** (*see*).

wool·ly (wŏŏlli) *adj.* **-lier, -liest. 1. a.** Pertaining to, consisting of, or covered with wool. **b.** Resembling wool. **2.** *Informal.* **a.** Lacking clarity; or definition; hazy; fuzzy: *woolly thinking.* **b.** Lacking decisiveness; resolution, or commitment: *a woolly liberal.* *~n., pl.* **woollies. 1.** *Informal.* A garment made of wool; especially, a cardigan, sweater, or the like. **2.** *Usually plural. Chiefly U.S.* A sheep. **—wool·li·ly** *adv.* **—wool·li·ness** *n.*

woolly aphis *n.* Any aphid, such as those of the genera *Eriosoma* and *Prociphalus,* that secretes white, waxy strands around its body.

woolly bear *n.* **1.** The hairy caterpillar of any of various tiger moths, especially that of *Arctia caja.* **2.** The larva of the carpet beetle (*Anthrensus verbasci*).

woolly mammoth *n.* See **mammoth.**

wool·pack (wŏŏl-pak) *n.* **1.** A large bag used for packing wool or fleeces for shipment. **2.** A cumulus cloud.

wool·sack (wŏŏl-sak) *n.* In Britain: **1.** The official seat of the Lord

Chancellor in the House of Lords. **2.** The Lord Chancellorship. Preceded by *the.*

wool·shed (wŏŏl-shed) *n.* A building or complex of buildings in which sheep are sheared and wool is prepared for market.

wool·skin (wŏŏl-skin) *n.* A sheepskin with the wool still on it.

wool-sort·er's disease (wŏŏl-sawtərz) *n.* A type of pneumonia resulting from infection of the lungs with anthrax bacilli.

wool-sta·pler (wŏŏl-stayplər) *n.* A dealer in wool; especially, one who buys wool from the producer, grades it, and sells it to a manufacturer. **—wool-sta·pling** *adj.* & *n.*

woom·e·ra, wom·e·ra (wŏŏmmərə) *n. Australian.* A notched stick used by Australian Aborigines to hold a spear, giving increased leverage. [From an Australian native name (New South Wales).]

Woom·e·ra Mar·a·lin·ga (wŏŏmmərə márrə-líng-gə). Town in south central South Australia. Situated on an Aboriginal reserve near Lake Torrens, it is the site of the Long Range Weapons Establishment (since 1947), a space and missile rocket test centre.

Woop Woop (wŏŏp-wŏŏp) *n. Australian Informal.* Any remote district or town. Used humorously. [20th century : origin obscure.]

Woot·ton (wŏŏtt'n), **of Ab·in·ger** (ábbinjər), **Barbara Frances, Baroness** (1897–1988). British social scientist. Her books include *Freedom under Planning* (1945), *Social Science and Social Pathology* (1959), and *Crime and Penal Policy* (1978).

woo·zy (wōōzi || wŏŏzzi) *adj.* **-ier, -iest.** *Informal.* **1.** Dazed; stunned; confused. **2.** Dizzy or queasy, as from drink. [Perhaps variant of OOZY.] **—woo·zi·ly** *adv.* **—woo·zi·ness** *n.*

wop-wops (wóp-wops) *n. N.Z. Informal.* A remote district or town: *He lives out in the wop-wops.* [20th century : origin obscure.]

Worces·ter[1] (wŏŏstər). County town of Worcestershire, western central England. Situated on the river Severn, it has a 14th-century cathedral with a Norman crypt, and was the site of Cromwell's defeat of Charles II and the Scots (1651).

Worcester[2] *n.* A fine china or porcelain made in Worcester from 1751. Also called "Worcester porcelain", "Worcester china".

Worces·ter·shire (wŏŏstər-shər, -sheer) County of western central England. It was included in the county of Hereford and Worcester (1974–97). The county town is Worcester.

Worcestershire sauce *n.* A piquant sauce made from soya sauce, vinegar, and spices, originally made in Worcester. Also called "Worcester sauce".

Worcs. Worcestershire.

word (wurd) *n.* **1. a.** A sound or a combination of sounds that symbolises and communicates a meaning and may consist of a single morpheme or of a combination of morphemes. **b.** A written or printed representation of this. **2. a.** Something that is said; a short conversation or discussion: *Could I have a quick word with you?* **3.** *Plural.* The text of a vocal musical composition; the lyrics. **4.** An assurance or promise; a declared intention: *said he'd do it and was as good as his word; I give you my word.* **5. a.** A command or direction; an order: *executed at the general's word.* **b.** A verbal signal; a password or watchword: *Mum's the word.* **6. a.** News or information: *the latest word.* **b.** Rumour: *Word has it he's married.* **7.** A sequence of 32, 36, 48, or 64 bits used to store or operate upon information in a computer system. **8. a.** *Plural.* A dispute or argument; a quarrel. **b.** A quarrelsome remark: *Words were exchanged between umpire and batsman.* **9.** *Capital* **W. a.** The **Logos** *(see).* **b.** The Scriptures or Gospel of the Christian Church: *the Word of God.* **—(upon) my word. 1.** Used to express surprise, shock, or admiration. **2.** *Australian.* Used to express agreement. **—put in a (good) word for.** To recommend; speak favourably of. **—take (someone) at (his) word.** To be convinced of another's sincerity and act in accordance with his statement. **—word for word. 1.** Repeated in the same words; verbatim. **2.** Finding an equivalent translation for each word in turn.

~tr.v. **worded, wording, words. 1.** To express in words. **2.** *Australian Informal.* To advise; inform. Often used with *up.* [Middle English *word,* Old English *word.*]

word·age (wúrdij) *n.* **1.** The use of an excessive number of words; verbiage. **2.** The number of words used, as in a novel or an article. **3.** Wording.

word association *n.* **1.** An early psychoanalytical technique in which the patient says the first word to come into his mind in response to a key word. **2.** A party game in which players in turn say a word connected with the previous one.

word blindness *n.* Either of two disorders causing difficulties with reading and writing, **alexia** or **dyslexia** *(both of which see).* **—word-blind** *adj.*

word·book (wúrd-bŏŏk || -bōōk) *n.* A vocabulary; a dictionary.

word·break (wúrd-brayk) *n. Printing.* The point of division of a word when it is run on from one line to the next.

word class *n. Linguistics.* A part of speech, such as a noun, verb, or adjective.

word deafness *n.* A form of aphasia in which information in the form of speech is incomprehensible. **—word-deaf** *adj.*

word·ing (wúrding) *n.* **1.** The act or style of expressing in words; phraseology; diction. **2.** The words themselves as they are deployed or arranged.

word·less (wúrd-ləss, -liss) *adj.* Without words; unspoken; inarticulate; silent. **—word·less·ly** *adv.* **—word·less·ness** *n.*

word order *n.* The syntactic arrangement of words in a sentence, clause, or phrase.

word-perfect (wúrd-pér-fikt || -fekt) *adj.* **1.** Memorised perfectly: *a word-perfect recitation.* **2.** Remembering or repeating one's words perfectly.

word play *n.* **1.** Verbal wit. **2.** A play on words; a pun.

word processor *n.* An electronic device consisting of a keyboard similar to a typewriter, a microprocessor, and a cathode-ray screen that together enable copy, as for letters or documents, to be stored on magnetic disk, corrected, and printed. **—word processing** *n.*

word square *n.* **1.** A group of words arranged in a square that read the same vertically and horizontally. **2.** A puzzle whose solution is a word square.

Words·worth (wúrds-wərth, -wurth), **William** (1770–1850). British poet. He was influenced by his early life in the Lake District and by the optimism of the immediately post-revolutionary France. Conveying a mystical feeling of unity with nature, his works include *Poems in Two Volumes* (1807), containing "Ode to Immortality" and "The Daffodils", and his verse autobiography, *The Prelude* (written 1805, published 1850). He became Poet Laureate in 1843.

word·y (wúrdi) *adj.* **-ier, -iest. 1.** Expressed in or using more words than are necessary. **2.** Pertaining to, consisting of, or having the nature of words; verbal. —See Synonyms at **talkative. —word·i·ly** *adv.* **—word·i·ness** *n.*

wore. 1. Past tense of **wear** (to be clothed in). **2.** Past tense of **wear** (to turn. Used of a ship).

work (wurk) *n.* **1.** Physical or mental effort or activity directed towards the production or accomplishment of something; toil; labour. **2.** Employment; a job: *look for work; out of work.* **3.** The means by which one earns one's livelihood; a trade, craft, business, or profession. **4. a.** Something that is being, or must be, done, made, or performed, especially as a part of one's occupation; a duty or task: *begin the day's work.* **b.** The amount of this done or required. **5. a.** Something done, made, or performed through the agency, effort, or activity of a person or thing: *said the killings were the work of a vicious maniac; a work of genius.* **b.** A task or action occupying the specified amount of time: *It was the work of a few minutes.* **6. a.** *Often plural.* The output of an artist or artisan considered or collected as a whole: *the works of Verdi.* **b.** A piece of needlework or embroidery. **7.** Any material or piece being processed in a machine during manufacture; a workpiece. **8. a.** A place of employment: *Don't phone me at work.* **b.** The part of a day during which one works: *met her after work; late for work.* **9.** The manner or style of working or the quality of treatment; workmanship: *good work.* **10.** Action producing an intended or expected effect: *waited for the poison to do its work.* **11.** A froth produced during the process of fermentation, as on vinegar, cider, or other liquid. **12.** *Physics. Abbr.* **w, W** The transfer of energy from one physical system to another; especially, the transfer of energy to a body by the application of force, usually calculated as the product of the force and the distance moved by the point of application in the direction of the force. —See **works. —have one's work cut out.** Have a lot to do. **—out of work.** Unemployed. **—make short work of.** *Informal.* **1.** To deal with very quickly or easily. **2.** To overcome (an opponent). **—set to work.** To begin doing something.

~v. **worked** or *archaic* **wrought** (rawt), **working, works.** *—intr.* **1.** To exert one's efforts for the purpose of doing, making, or achieving something; labour or toil. **2. a.** To be employed; have a job. **b.** To have an influence, result, or effect, as on a person, the mind, or the like: *The plea for help worked on their compassion.* **3. a.** To operate; function. **b.** To operate effectively: *Is the phone working?* **c.** To arrive at or be brought to a specified state, especially gradually or by repeated movement: *The stitches worked loose.* **4.** To proceed or progress slowly and laboriously. **5.** To move or contort from emotion or pain: *His mouth worked with fear.* **6.** To behave or respond in a specified way when handled or processed: *Not all metals work easily.* **7.** To ferment. **8.** *Nautical.* **a.** To be under strain in heavy seas so that seams loosen and fastenings become slack. **b.** To sail against the wind. **9.** To undergo small motions that result in friction and wear: *The gears work against each other.* **10.** To attempt to influence or persuade. Used with *on* or *upon.* *—tr.* **1.** To cause or effect; bring about: *I can't work miracles.* **2.** To cause to operate or function; handle or use: *work a power mower.* **3.** To make or force to work or to do work: *Sue works her employees hard.* **4.** To excite, rouse, or provoke: *He worked me into a rage.* **5.** *Informal.* To arrange, especially by somewhat devious means; contrive: *Try to work it so we both get our holiday at the same time.* **6.** *Informal.* To use or employ for one's own ends or purposes; exploit: *You have to learn how to work the system.* **7.** *Informal.* To practise trickery or deception on; cheat. **8.** To carry on one's occupation in; cover: *This postman works our street.* **9.** To cause to ferment. **—work back.** *Australian Informal.* To work overtime. **—work off.** To get rid of by work or effort: *work off extra pounds; work off a debt.* **—work over.** *Slang.* To inflict severe physical damage upon; beat up. **—work up. 1.** To develop or proceed gradually towards a point: *The film works up to a thrilling climax.* **2.** To arouse the emotions of; excite; stir up: *worked up the crowd into a frenzy.* **3.** To produce by working: *work up an appetite.* [Middle English *werke, worke,* Old English *we(o)rc,* act, deed, work.]

Synonyms: *work, labour, toil, drudgery.*

-work *n. comb. form.* Indicates: **1.** Work done using the specified tools or materials; for example, **needlework, pokerwork. 2.** A product of work done in the specified medium; for example, **woodwork, paintwork. 3.** Work performed in a specified way or of a specified type; for example, **nightwork, piecework.**

work·a·ble (wúrkə-b'l) *adj.* **1.** Capable of being worked, dealt with, or handled. **2.** Capable of working effectively or successfully; practicable or feasible. —See Synonyms at **possible**. —**work·a·bil·i·ty** (-bíllǝti), **work·a·ble·ness** *n.* —**work·a·bly** *adv.*

work·a·day (wúrkǝ-day) *adj.* **1.** Pertaining to working days; everyday. **2.** Mundane; commonplace: *the workaday world.* [Middle English *werkeday,* a workday : *werke,* WORK + DAY.]

work·a·hol·ic (wúrkǝ-hóllik) *n.* A person who suffers from a compulsive need to work excessively hard. [WORK + *alcoholic.*] —**work·a·hol·ism** (-hol-iz'm) *n.*

work·bag (wúrk-bag) *n.* A bag to hold material, such as needlework, on which one is working, or implements needed for work.

work·bench (wúrk-bench) *n.* A sturdy table or bench at which a machinist, mechanic, or carpenter works.

work·book (wúrk-bŏŏk ‖ -bŏŏk) *n.* **1.** A booklet containing problems and exercises, typically one that is published in conjunction with a textbook and has spaces in which answers are to be written. **2.** A manual containing operating instructions, as for an appliance or a machine. **3.** A book in which a record is kept of work proposed or accomplished.

work·box (wúrk-boks) *n.* A box or basket for implements or materials used in sewing or other work. Also called "work basket".

work·day (wúrk-day) *n.* A working day.

work·er (wúrkǝr) *n.* **1. a.** One that works. **b.** One who works in a specified way or at a specified occupation: *a fast worker; an office worker.* **2. a.** An employee, as opposed to an employer or manager. **b.** One who does manual or industrial labour. **3.** One who belongs to the working class. **4.** One of the sterile females of certain social insects, such as the ant or bee, that performs specialised work.

work·er-priest (wúrkǝr-préest) *n. Roman Catholic Church.* A priest, especially in France, who spends time in secular employment.

workers' cooperative *n.* An enterprise in which all workers share control over production, distribution and exchange, often with equal profit-sharing, regardless of individual function.

work ethic *n.* A belief in the virtues of dutiful hard work and its moral superiority to leisure, play, or other activities that are considered unproductive.

work·fare (wúrk-fair) *n. Chiefly U.S.* State benefit payment, especially to the unemployed, on condition that the recipient does publicly funded work or enrols for retraining. [*Work* + wel*fare, U.S.,* social assistance.]

work force *n.* **1.** Those workers employed in a specific project; a staff. **2.** All workers potentially available to a nation, project, industry, or the like.

work function *n.* The energy required to remove an electron from a solid; especially, the work exerted against coulomb forces in removing an electron from just inside to just outside the surface of a metal.

work hardening *n.* The increase in strength that sometimes accompanies plastic deformation of a solid, especially a metal. —**work-hard·en** *tr.v.*

work·horse (wúrk-hawrss) *n.* **1.** A horse that is used for labour rather than for racing or riding. **2.** *Informal.* A person who works tirelessly, especially at difficult or arduous tasks.

work·house (wúrk-howss) *n.* **1.** A former public institution in Britain in which the poor were fed and housed in return for labour. **2.** An American prison in which limited sentences are served by manual labour.

work in *tr.v.* To insert by adjustment, ingenious contrivance, or effort. —*intr.* To be thus inserted.

work-in *n.* A method of industrial action where workers prevent the closure of a plant or office by occupying and running it themselves.

work·ing (wúrking) *adj.* **1.** Pertaining to, used for, or spent in working: *a working breakfast; working clothes.* **2.** Adequate or appropriate for performing work or achieving effective results: *in working order; a working majority.* **3.** Capable of being used as the basis of further work: *a working hypothesis.*
~*n.* **1.** *Usually plural.* The way in which something works. **2.** The excavations in a mine or quarry or the part of them being worked.

working capital *n.* **1.** The assets of a business enterprise that can be applied to its operation. **2.** The current assets of an individual or business enterprise as opposed to the current liabilities.

working class *n. Often plural.* The poorest, most underprivileged stratum of a society, whose members earn wages rather than salaries, typically by means of unskilled manual labour; the proletariat. —**working-class** (wúrking-kláass ‖ -kláss) *adj.*

working day *n.* **1.** That part of a day set aside for work: *a six-hour working day.* **2.** A day on which work is usually done, as opposed to a weekend or holiday.

working drawing *n.* An engineering drawing, architect's plan, or the like, that is used by a machinist, builder, or other worker to make or build the subject of the drawing.

working man *n.* A man who works for wages, especially at manual labour. —**working woman** *n.*

working papers *pl.n.* Legal documents necessary in certain countries to guarantee the right of an individual to employment.

working party *n.* **1.** A temporary committee set up to research and investigate a particular matter. **2.** A group of prisoners or soldiers sent out for manual labour.

working storage *n.* The part of a computer's data-storage disk that is reserved for data to be temporarily stored during the running of a program.

working substance *n.* **1.** A substance, especially a fluid, that undergoes changes of pressure, temperature, and volume in a heat engine. Also called "working fluid". **2.** The substance in a thermometer that expands and contracts.

working week *n.* Also *U.S.* **work week.** That part of a week set aside for work: *a three-day working week.*

work·less (wúrk-lǝss, -liss) *adj.* Unemployed.

work·load (wúrk-lōd) *n.* The amount of work assigned to or done by a machine, worker, or unit of workers in a given time period.

work·man (wúrk-mǝn) *n., pl.* **-men** (-mǝn). **1.** A man who performs some form of manual or industrial labour. **2.** A person who works in a specified way: *A bad workman blames his tools.*

work·man·like (wúrkmǝn-līk) *adj.* **1.** Characteristic of or befitting a skilled workman or craftsman: *workmanlike pottery.* **2.** Of satisfactory but not outstanding quality: *a workmanlike performance.*

work·man·ship (wúrkmǝn-ship) *n.* **1.** The art, skill, or technique of a workman. **2.** The quality of such art, skill, or technique: *silver of poor workmanship.* **3.** Something produced or achieved by work or effort; handiwork.

work of art *n.* **1.** A piece of artistic work deemed valuable or superior. **2.** Anything likened to this in beauty or workmanship.

work out *tr.v.* **1.** To find a solution for; solve. **2.** To formulate or develop: *work out a plan.* **3.** To exhaust (a mine, soil, or the like). **4.** To fulfil (an obligation or debt, for example) by working instead of paying money. **5.** To accomplish by work or effort. —*intr.v.* **1.** To come or make its way out: *a nail working out of a board.* **2.** To have a specified result: *work out badly.* **3.** To prove successful, effective, or satisfactory: *Did your job work out?* **4.** To perform a series of exercises or drills.

work·out (wúrk-owt) *n.* **1.** A period of exercise or practice, especially in athletics. **2.** An ordeal that may have a successful outcome.

work·peo·ple (wúrk-peep'l) *pl.n.* Those who work for wages.

work·piece (wúrk-peess) *n.* Any piece or part in the process of manufacture by machine or by hand.

work·place (wúrk-pláyss) *n.* A place where work is done.

work·room (wúrk-rōōm, -rŏŏm) *n.* A room where work is done, especially manual work.

works *n., pl.* **works. 1.** A factory, plant, or similar buildings or complex of buildings where a usually specified type of industry is carried on. Often used in combination: *a gasworks; a steelworks.* **2.** *Plural.* The internal mechanism of an object: *the works of a watch.* **3.** *Plural.* Engineering structures, such as bridges or dams. **4.** A structure for fortification or defence. —**in the works.** *Informal.* Being processed or prepared. —**the works.** *Informal.* **1.** Everything; the whole of a set: *He had the works, from the avocado to the port and cigars.* **2.** Extreme punitive treatment.

work-sharing (wúrk-sháiring) *n.* The practice of **job-sharing** (see).

work·shop (wúrk-shop) *n.* **1.** An area, room, or establishment in which manual or industrial work is done. **2. a.** A group of people who meet for a seminar in some specialised field: *a creative-writing workshop.* **b.** A meeting or seminar held by such a group.

work·shy (wúrk-shī) *adj.* Habitually avoiding work.

work station *n.* An area (as in an office) assigned to one person to work in; specifically, a computerised work station.

work-stud·y (wúrk-studdi) *n.* A management method of evaluating the efficiency of employees.

work·ta·ble (wúrk-tayb'l) *n.* A table designed for a specific task or activity, such as needlework or graphic arts.

work·top (wúrk-top) *n.* A wide flat surface used for working on, especially one in a kitchen. Also called "work surface".

work-to-rule (wúrk-tǝ-rōōl, -tōō- ‖ -réwl) *n. Chiefly British.* A type of industrial action in which employees deliberately follow all working rules, however trivial, so painstakingly that production is drastically cut. —**work to rule** *intr.v.*

work·wom·an (wúrk-wŏŏmǝn) *n., pl.* **-women** (-wimmin). A woman who performs some form of labour.

world (wurld) *n.* **1.** The earth. **2.** The universe. **3.** The earth and its inhabitants collectively. Also used adjectivally: *world champion; world English.* **4.** The human race. **5. a.** Humankind considered as social creatures; human society: *turned her back on the world.* **b.** People as a whole; the public: *The story burst upon the world.* **6.** *Often capital* **W.** A specified part of the earth: *the Western World.* **7.** A particular period in history, including its people, culture, and social order: *the Victorian world.* **8.** Any realm, domain, or kingdom: *the insect world.* **9.** A field or sphere of human activity: *the world of advertising.* **10.** Everything that concerns or contributes to the life of an individual: *felt his whole world collapsing around him.* **11.** A specified way of life or state of being: *the world of the rich.* **12.** Secular life and its morality as distinguished from the religious or spiritual life: *a man of the world.* **13. a.** Human existence; mortal life: *came into the world.* **b.** A supposed state of existence beyond death: *the next world.* **14.** *Often plural.* A large amount; much: *did him a world of good; worlds apart.* **15.** A planet or other celestial body: *the possibility of life on another world.* —**dead to the world.** Fast asleep or unconscious. —**for all the world.** *Informal.* To all intents and purposes; for all practical purposes: *He looked for all the world like a film star.* —**on top of the world.** *Informal.* Elated, exultant, or blissful. —**out of this world.** *Informal.* Excellent; fine. —**world without end.** For ever and ever. [Middle English *w(e)orld,* Old English *world, weorold,* from Germanic, from *weraz* (unattested), man + *aldh-* (unattested), age.] See maps, pages 1726-9.

World Bank *n.* An international bank founded in 1945 to assist the economic development of the Third World by means of loans from richer nations. Also officially called "International Bank for Reconstruction and Development".

THE WORLD (PHYSICAL)

world-class (wúrld-klaass ‖ -klass) *adj*. Being one of or worthy of the best in the world.

World Council of Churches *n. Abbr.* **W.C.C.** An ecumenical grouping of Christian Churches, excluding the Roman Catholics, founded in 1948 to further the aims of Christian unity.

World Court *n*. **1.** The Permanent Court of International Justice, established by the League of Nations (1920). **2.** The **International Court of Justice** *(see)*.

World Cup *n*. **1.** A soccer championship competition. The finals are held every four years, between national teams selected in a qualifying competition. **2.** The World Cup trophy.

World Health Organization *n. Abbr.* **W.H.O.** A United Nations agency, founded in 1948 and based in Geneva, that serves to coordinate and improve health activities worldwide.

world line *n. Physics*. The line representing the path of an object through the four-dimensional space-time continuum.

world-ling (wúrldling) *n*. A person absorbed in or devoted to this world; a worldly person.

world-ly (wúrldli) *adj*. **-lier, -liest. 1.** Of, pertaining to, or devoted to the temporal world; not spiritual or religious; secular. **2.** Sophisticated or cosmopolitan; worldly-wise. **—world-li-ness** *n*.

world-ly-wise (wúrldli-wīz) *adj*. Experienced in the ways of the world; sophisticated and shrewd, often to the point of cynicism.

world power *n*. A political entity whose actions consistently influence or change the course of international events.

world-shak-ing (wúrld-shayking) *adj*. Of great significance.

world soul *n*. A spiritual principle relating to the world as the human soul relates to a human being.

world view *n*. A particular way of viewing and interpreting the world; a philosophy of life.

World War I *n. Abbr.* **W.W.I** A war fought from 1914 to 1918, in which Great Britain, France, Russia, Belgium, Italy, Japan, the United States, and other allies defeated Germany, Austria-Hungary, Turkey, and Bulgaria. Also called "First World War", "Great War".

World War II *n. Abbr.* **W.W.II** A war fought from 1939 to 1945, in which Great Britain, France, the U.S.S.R., the United States, and other allies defeated Germany, Italy, and Japan. Also called "Second World War".

world-wea-ry (wúrld-weer-i) *adj*. **-rier, -riest.** Tired of the world and the pleasures afforded by it. **—world-wea-ri-ness** *n*.

world-wide (wúrld-wíd) *adj*. Reaching or extending throughout the world; universal. **—world-wide** *adv*.

World Wide Fund for Nature *n*. An international organisation, founded in 1961 as "World Wildlife Fund", for the protection and conservation of wildlife and wilderness areas worldwide.

World Wide Web *n. Abbr.* **WWW.** A worldwide system for accessing information on the Internet. Also called "Web".

worm (wurm) *n.* **1.** Any of various invertebrates, such as those of the phyla Annelida, Nematoda, or Platyhelminthes, having a long, flexible rounded or flattened body, often without obvious appendages. **2.** Any of various insect larvae having a soft, elongated body. **3.** Any of various unrelated animals resembling a worm in habit or appearance, as the shipworm or the slow-worm. **4.** An object or device that is like a worm in appearance or action, such as a threaded screw, a spiral-shaped tube in a heat exchanger, or a condenser in a still. **5.** A shaft with a helical groove cut in it so that it can function as part of a worm gear. **6.** An insidiously tormenting or devouring force: *"The worm of conscience still begnaw thy soul"* (Shakespeare). **7.** *Informal.* **a.** A pitiable creature; a poor wretch. **b.** A contemptible despicable person; one of no moral worth. **8.** *Plural. Pathology.* Intestinal infestation with worms or wormlike parasites. In this sense, also called "helminthiasis".
~*v.* wormed, worming, worms. —*tr.* **1.** To make (one's way) with or as if with the sinuous crawling motion of a worm. **2.** To elicit by artful or devious means. Used with *out.* **3.** To cure of intestinal worms. **4.** *Nautical.* To wrap yarn or twine around (rope). —*intr.* **1.** To move in a sinuous manner suggestive of a worm. **2.** To make one's way by artful or devious means towards an objective. Used with *into* or *out of.* [Middle English *worm*, Old English *wyrm*, worm, serpent.]

worm-cast (wúrm-kaast) *n.* A coil of evacuated earth or sand that has passed through the body of an earthworm or lugworm and has been deposited on the surface of the ground, especially along the sea shore.

worm-eat-en (wúrm-eet'n) *adj.* **1.** Bored through or gnawed by worms. **2.** Full of wormholes. **3.** Decayed; worn-out; decrepit.

worm gear *n.* **1.** A gear consisting of a threaded shaft and a wheel with teeth that mesh into it. **2.** A worm wheel.

worm-hole (wúrm-hōl) *n.* A hole made by a burrowing worm. —worm-holed *adj.*

worm screw *n.* The threaded shaft of a worm gear. Also called "worm".

worm-seed (wúrm-seed) *n.* The dried unopened flowers of the sea wormwood (see).

worm's-eye view (wúrmz-ī) *n.* A view from below or from a lowly or grass-roots level. Compare bird's-eye view.

worm wheel *n.* The toothed wheel of a worm gear. Also called "worm gear".

worm-wood (wúrm-wŏŏd) *n.* **1.** Any of several aromatic plants of the genus *Artemisia;* especially, *A. absinthium,* native to Europe, yielding a bitter extract used in making absinthe and in flavouring certain wines. Also called "absinthe". **2.** Something distressing or embittering. [Middle English *wormwode,* variant (influenced by WORM and WOOD) of *wermode,* Old English *wermōd,* from Germanic *wer-mōd-, wor-mōd-* (unattested). See also vermouth.]

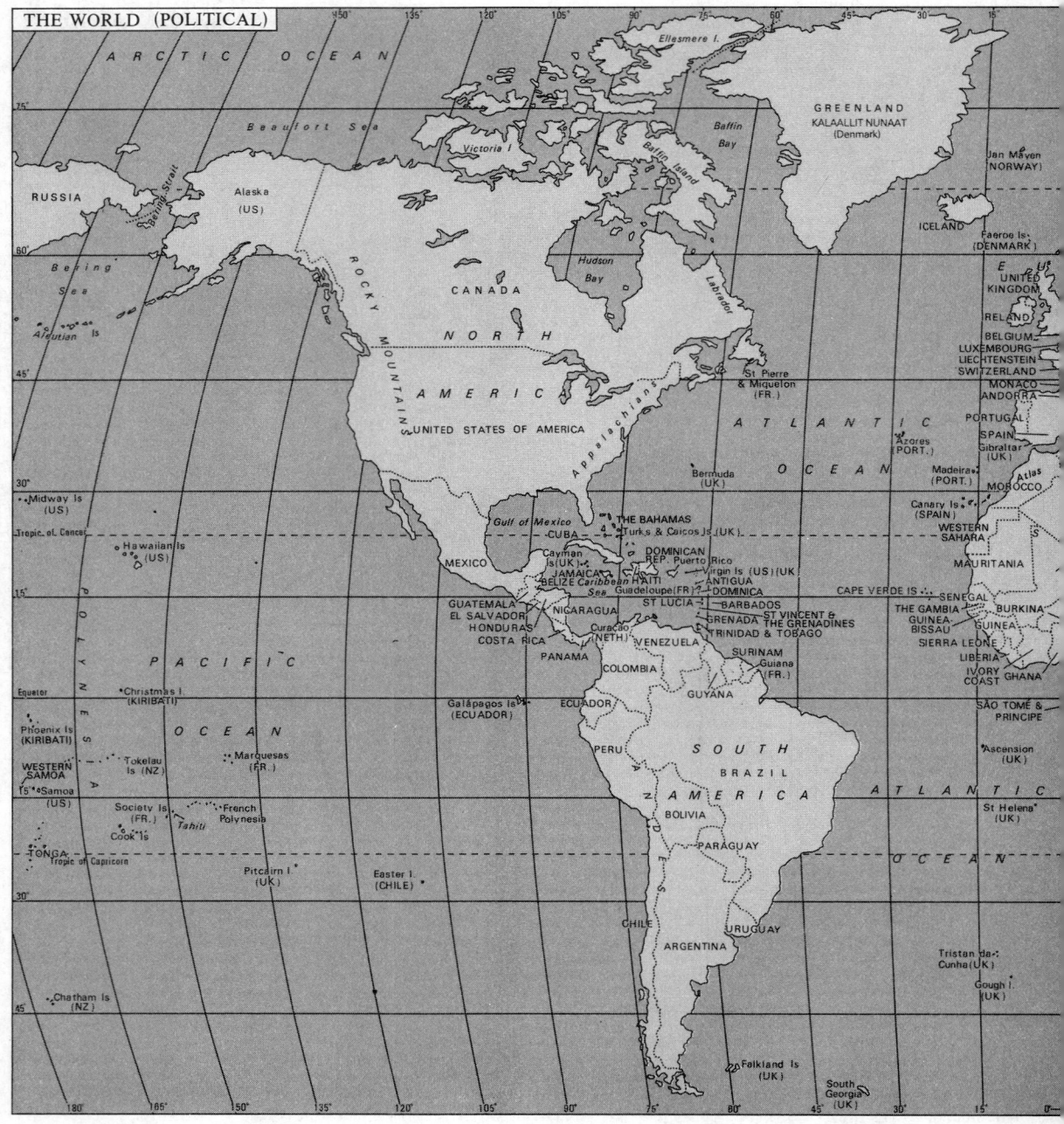

THE WORLD (POLITICAL)

worm·y (wûrmi) *adj.* **-ier, -iest. 1.** Infested with or damaged by worms. **2.** Suggestive of a worm; especially, grovelling or insinuating. **—worm·i·ness** *n.*

worn (wawrn ‖ wôrn). Past participle of **wear**.
~*adj.* **1.** Affected by wear or use. **2.** Impaired or damaged by wear or use: *worn elbows on a coat.* **3. a.** Exhausted; spent. **b.** Showing exhaustion; drawn. **—See Synonyms at haggard.** [Middle English, past participle of *weren,* to WEAR.]

worn-out (wâwrn-ówt ‖ wôrn-) *adj.* **1.** Worn or used until no longer usable: *a worn-out suit.* **2.** Thoroughly exhausted; spent.

wor·ri·ment (wúrrimənt) *n. Chiefly U.S. Informal.* **1.** The act of worrying or state of being worried. **2.** A source of anxiety or concern; a worry.

wor·ri·some (wúrri-səm) *adj.* **1.** Causing worry or anxiety. **2.** Tending to worry; anxious. **—wor·ri·some·ly** *adv.*

wor·rit (wúrrit) *v.* **worrited, -riting, -rits.** *Archaic & Regional.* **—***intr.* To fret; worry. **—***tr.* To pester; annoy. [Probably alteration of WORRY, perhaps influenced by WHERRIT.]

wor·ry (wúrri ‖ wórri) *v.* **-ried, -rying, -ries. —***intr.* **1.** To feel uneasy about some uncertain or threatening matter; be troubled or agitated. **2.** To pull, bite, or tear at something: *The dog worried at the bone.* **3.** To work or proceed doggedly in the face of difficulty or hardship; struggle: *worried away at a problem.* **—***tr.* **1.** To cause to feel anxious, distressed, or troubled. **2.** To bother; annoy: *Don't*

worry me with your complaints. **3. a.** To seize with the teeth and shake or tug at repeatedly: *a dog put down for worrying sheep.* **b.** To attack roughly and repeatedly; harass. **c.** To touch, move, fiddle with, or handle idly; toy with: *worrying the sore tooth with his tongue.*
~*n., pl.* **worries. 1.** The act of worrying or the condition of being worried; mental uneasiness or anxiety. **2.** A source of nagging concern or uneasiness. **—See Synonyms at anxiety.** [Middle English *worien, wirien,* to seize by the throat, harass, Old English *wyrgan,* to strangle.] **—wor·ried·ly** *adv.* **—wor·ri·er** *n.*

worry beads *pl.n.* A bead bracelet kept in the hand and constantly toyed with to relieve boredom or tension, originally used by men in Greece and the Middle East.

worse (wurss). **1.** Comparative of **bad. 2.** Comparative of **ill.**
~*adj.* Also *archaic* **wors·er** (wúrssər). **1.** More inferior, as in quality, condition, or effect. **2.** More severe or unfavourable. **3.** Further from a standard; less desirable or satisfactory. **—worse luck.** *Informal.* Unfortunately. **—the worse for wear.** Shoddy or rundown.
~*adv.* In a worse way.
~*n.* Something that is worse. **—for the worse.** Into a worse state or condition. [Middle English *wors(e),* Old English *wyrsa.*]

wors·en (wúrss'n) *v.* **-ened, -ening, -ens. —***intr.* To be or become worse. **—***tr.* To make worse.

wor·ship (wúrship) *n.* **1.** The reverent love and allegiance accorded

a deity, idol, or sacred object. **2.** A set of ceremonies, prayers, or other religious forms by which this love is expressed. **3.** Ardent devotion; adoration. **4.** *Often capital* **W.** *Chiefly British.* A title or form of address for magistrates, mayors, and certain other dignitaries. Used with *His, Her, Your,* or *Their.*

~*v.* **worshipped** or *U.S.* **worshiped, -shipping** or *U.S.* **-shiping, -ships.** —*tr.* **1.** To honour and love as a deity; venerate. **2.** To regard with great admiration or devotion; idolise. —*intr.* **1.** To participate in religious rites of worship. **2.** To perform any act of worship. —See Synonyms at **revere.** [Middle English *worschipe,* Old English *weorthscipe,* honour, dignity, reverence : *weorth,* WORTH + -SHIP.] —**wor·ship·per** *n.*

wor·ship·ful (wúrshipf'l) *adj.* **1.** Given to or expressive of worship; reverent or adoring. **2.** *Chiefly British.* Worthy of honour and respect; distinguished. Used especially as an honorific title for certain officers and for certain livery companies. —**wor·ship·ful·ly** *adv.* —**wor·ship·ful·ness** *n.*

worst (wurst). **1.** Superlative of **bad. 2.** Superlative of **ill.**

~*adj.* **1.** Most inferior, as in quality, condition, or effect. **2.** Most severe or unfavourable. **3.** Furthest from an ideal or standard; least desirable or satisfactory.

~*n.* Something that is worst: *at one's worst; do one's worst.* —**at worst. 1.** Under the worst foreseeable circumstances; if the worst should happen. **2.** From the least favourable point of view. —**get**

the worst of it. To suffer a defeat or disadvantage. —**if the worst comes to the worst.** If the very worst should happen; at the very worst.

~*adv.* In the worst manner or degree.

~*tr.v.* **worsted, worsting, worsts.** To gain the advantage over; to get the better of; defeat. [Middle English *worste, wurst,* Old English *wyrsta.*]

wor·sted (wo͝oss-tid, -təd ‖ wúrss-) *n.* **1.** Firm-textured, compactly twisted woollen yarn made from long-staple fibres. **2.** Fabric made from such yarn. [Middle English *worsted,* first made in *Worthstede* (now Worstead), a village in Norfolk.] —**wor·sted** *adj.*

wort (wurt ‖ wawrt) *n.* **1.** A plant, especially one formerly used as a medicinal herb. Now used only in combination: *liverwort; milkwort.* **2.** An infusion of malt fermented to make beer. [Middle English *wort, wurt,* Old English *wyrt,* plant, herb.]

worth[1] (wurth) *n.* **1.** The quality of something that renders it desirable, useful, or valuable: *the worth of higher education.* **2.** The material or market value of something: *have a worth of ten million pounds.* **3.** The number or quantity of something that may be purchased for a specified sum: *five pounds' worth of petrol.* **4.** The quality within a person that commands respect; merit.

~*prep.* **1.** Equal in value to something specified: *He's not worth her little finger.* **2.** Deserving of; meriting: *a proposal worth consideration.* **3.** Having wealth or riches amounting to: *He's worth a quar-*

ter of a million. **—for all (one) is worth.** To the utmost of one's powers or ability. **—for what it's worth.** Even though it may not be important. [Middle English *worth,* Old English *weorth.*]

worth² *intr.v.* **worthed, worthing, worths.** *Archaic.* To befall; betide: "*Howl ye, Woe worth the day!*" (Ezekiel 30:2). [Middle English *worthen,* Old English *weorthan.*]

worth·less (wúrth-lǝss, -liss) *adj.* **1.** Without worth, use, or value. **2.** Without moral worth; low and despicable. **—worth·less·ly** *adv.* **—worth·less·ness** *n.*

worth·while, worth-while (wúrth-wíl, -hwíl) *adj.* Sufficiently valuable or important to justify the expenditure of time or effort.
Usage: This is written as a whole, or with a hyphen, when used before a noun (*a worthwhile experience*). Used after a verb, it is usually written as two words (*the experience was worth while*).

wor·thy (wúrthi) *adj.* **-thier, -thiest. 1.** Having worth, merit, or value; useful or valuable. **2.** Honourable; admirable: *a worthy fellow.* **3.** Having sufficient worth; deserving: *worthy to be revered; worthy of acclaim.* **4.** Appropriate; suitable: *a large crowd, worthy of this great occasion.*
~n., pl. **worthies. 1.** A person esteemed for his worth, dignity, or importance. **2.** An eminent or distinguished person. Often used humorously: *local worthies.* **—wor·thi·ly** *adv.* **—wor·thi·ness** *n.*

-worthy *adj. comb. form.* Indicates: **1.** Of sufficient worth or importance for; for example, **newsworthy. 2.** Deserving of; for example, **blameworthy. 3.** Safe or suitable for travel by means of; for example, **roadworthy.**

wost. *Archaic.* Second person singular present tense of **wit** (to know).

wot. *Archaic.* First and third person singular present tense of **wit** (to know).

Wo·tan (vō-taan) A Teutonic god identified with Woden.

wot·cher, wot·cha (wóchǝr) *interj. Slang.* Used as a greeting or to attract attention.

would (wŏŏd; *weak forms* wǝd, ǝd, d). Past tense of **will** (defective verb), often used as an auxiliary verb expressing various shades of attendant meaning indicating: **1.** A custom or habitual action in the past: *In her young days she would go skiing every winter.* **2.** *Chiefly British.* A stubborn action in the past: *Well, you would go and discuss politics with the barber.* **3.** A polite request or command: *Would you step this way, please.* **4.** Attempt or intention: *Those who would disregard the rules must bear the consequences.* **5.** Desire or preference: *Treat others as you would have them treat you.* **6.** *Archaic.* A heartfelt wish: *Would that he were in my arms again.* **7.** *Chiefly British.* Approximation or estimate: *That house would cost about £80,000.* **8. a.** Probability: *He would be a millionaire by now if he had taken my advice.* **b.** Condition; contingency of one condition upon another: *If you would only get home in time, we could have dinner together now and then.* **9.** Doubt, disdain, cynicism, or the like: *It would seem that I am under arrest again.* **10.** Moderation of the directness or bluntness of a request or statement: *My client would like to take issue with you there.*
Usage: Would have is sometimes used in conditional clauses introduced by *if,* but standard English prefers *had,* both in formal speech and in writing; *If John had gone, he would have seen her* (not *If John would have gone...*). Similarly, following the verb *wish, had* is the preferred form: *I wish that she had* (not *would have*) *gone.*

would-be (wŏŏd-bee, -bi) *adj.* Desiring or pretending to be: *a would-be hero.*

would·n't (wŏŏd'nt). Contraction of *would not.*

wouldst (wŏŏdst), **would·est** (wŏŏddist). *Archaic.* Second person singular past tense of **will** (defective verb).

Woulfe bottle (wŏŏlf) *n.* A glass laboratory bottle with two necks or sometimes more, used for bubbling a gas through a liquid. [After Peter *Woulfe* (died 1803), British chemist.]

wound¹ (wŏŏnd) *n.* **1.** An injury to a person or animal in which the skin or other external organic surface is torn, pierced, cut, or otherwise broken, as a result of violence, accident, or surgery. **2.** An injury to the tissue of a plant. **3.** An injury to the feelings. **—lick (one's) wounds.** To recuperate after a defeat.
~v. **wounded, wounding, wounds.** *—tr.* To inflict a wound or wounds upon. *—intr.* To inflict a wound or wounds. **—See** Synonyms at **injure.** [Middle English *wound(e),* Old English *wund.*]

wound² (wownd). **1.** Past tense and past participle of **wind** (to wrap). **2.** Alternative past tense and past participle of **wind** (to sound).

wound·wort (wŏŏnd-wurt ‖ -wawrt) *n.* **1.** Any of several plants of the genus *Stachys,* having downy leaves formerly used to treat wounds. **2.** Any of several similarly used plants.

wove. Past tense and *rare* past participle of **weave.**

woven. Past participle of **weave.**

wove paper (wōv) *n.* Paper made on a closely woven wire roller or mould and having a very faint mesh pattern or none at all. Compare **laid paper.**

wow¹ (wow) *interj. Informal.* Used in expressing wonder, amazement, or the like.
~n. Chiefly U.S. Informal. An outstanding success.
~tr.v. **wowed, wowing, wows.** *Chiefly U.S. Informal.* To have a strong and usually pleasurable impact on.

wow² *n.* A slow variation in the pitch of sound reproduced by a record player or tape recorder, usually the result of irregular movement of a mechanical part. [Imitative.]

wow·ser (wówzǝr) *n. Australian Slang.* An extremely puritanical person; a prude, killjoy, or teetotaller. [20th century : from English

dialect *wow* (imitative), to wail, whine, complain.]

W.P.B., w.p.b. wastepaper basket.

W.P.C. woman police constable.

w.p.m. words per minute.

W.R. 1. *Medicine.* Wassermann reaction. **2.** Western Region.

W.R.A.C. Women's Royal Army Corps.

wrack¹ (rak) *n.* **1.** A remnant or vestige of something destroyed. **2.** Wreckage, especially of a ship cast ashore. **3.** A tangled mass of seaweed or other marine vegetation, cast ashore or floating. **4.** Variant of **rack** (ruin).
~tr.v. **wracked, wracking, wracks.** To cause the ruin of; wreck. [Middle English *wrack,* Old English *wræc,* punishment, vengeance, and Middle Dutch *wrak,* wreckage, wrecked ship.]

wrack². Variant of **rack** (clouds).

W.R.A.F. Women's Royal Air Force.

wraith (rayth) *n.* **1.** An apparition of a living person, supposed to appear just before he dies. **2.** The ghost of a dead person. **3.** Anything pale and insubstantial, such as a tree seen through mist. [16th century Scottish : origin obscure.]

wran·gle (ráng-g'l) *v.* **-gled, -gling, -gles.** *—intr.* **1.** To dispute noisily or angrily; quarrel; bicker. **2.** To engage in debate or controversy. *—tr.* **1. a.** To win or obtain by argument. **b.** To force or persuade (someone) by argument. **2.** *Western U.S.* To herd (horses or other livestock). **—See** Synonyms at **argue.**
~n. **1.** An angry, noisy, or vehement argument or dispute. **2.** The act of wrangling. [Middle English *wranglen,* probably of Low German origin; akin to Low German *wrangeln.*]

wran·gler (ráng-glǝr) *n.* **1.** One who wrangles. **2.** In Britain, a student who gains first-class honours in Part II of the tripos in mathematics at Cambridge University. **3.** *U.S.* A cowboy, especially one who tends saddle horses.

wrap (rap) *v.* **wrapped** or **wrapt, wrapping, wraps.** *—tr.* **1.** To arrange or fold about in order to cover or protect something: *She wrapped her coat about her.* **2.** To cover, envelop, pack, or encase. **3.** To clasp, fold, or coil about something: *She wrapped her arms about his neck.* **4.** To envelop and obscure, often with the effect of concealing or disguising the nature of: *Fog wrapped the countryside.* **5.** To immerse in a specified condition. Usually used in the passive: *wrapped in grief; wrapped in thought.* *—intr.* To coil, wind, or twist about or around something: *The flag wrapped around the pole.*
~n. **1. a.** A garment to be wrapped or folded about a person, especially about the shoulders, such as a cloak or shawl. **b.** *Plural.* Warm outer clothing: *First put on your wraps, and then you can go out to play.* **2.** A blanket. **3.** A wrapping or wrapper. **—keep under wraps.** To keep secret or concealed. **—take the wraps off.** To disclose to the public; reveal. [Middle English *wrappen†.*]

wrap·a·round (ráp-ǝ-rownd) *adj.* Also **wrap·o·ver** (-ōvǝr), **wrapround** (-rownd). **1.** Having ends that curve back or that overlap the sides. **2.** Designating a garment, such as a skirt, that is open to the hem and wrapped round the body before being fastened.
~n. Also **wrap·o·ver** (for sense 1), **wrap·round. 1.** A wraparound garment. **2.** *Printing.* A flexible relief plate wrapped round a cylinder in letterpress printing.

wrap·per (ráppǝr) *n.* **1.** One that wraps. **2.** The paper or other material in which something is wrapped: *a sweet wrapper.* **3.** The paper encircling a magazine or newspaper sent by post. **4.** *Chiefly British.* A book jacket. **5.** The tobacco leaf covering a cigar. **6.** A loose dressing gown or negligee.

wrap·ping (rápping) *n. Sometimes plural.* The material in which something is wrapped.

wrapt. Alternative past tense of **wrap.**

wrap up *tr.v.* **1.** To settle finally or successfully; conclude: *wrap up a business deal.* **2.** *Chiefly U.S.* To encompass in a few words; summarise. *—intr.v.* **1.** To put on warm clothing. **2.** *Informal.* To stop talking; keep quiet. Usually used in the imperative. **—wrapped up.** Immersed or absorbed: *wrapped up in his research.*

wrap-up (ráp-up) *n. U.S.* A brief summary of the news.

wrasse (rass) *n.* Any of numerous chiefly tropical, often brightly coloured marine fishes of the family Labridae. [Cornish and Welsh *gwracht†,* "old woman".]

wrath (roth, rawth, raath ‖ rath) *n.* **1.** Violent, resentful anger; rage; fury. **2.** Divine retribution. **3.** *Archaic.* A fit of violent anger. **—See** Synonyms at **anger.**
~adj. Archaic. Wrathful. [Middle English *wrath(th)e,* Old English *wræththu,* from *wrāth,* angry.]

wrath·ful (róth-f'l, ráwth-, ráath- ‖ ráth-) *adj.* **1.** Full of wrath; fiercely angry. **2.** Proceeding from or expressing wrath: *wrathful vengeance.* **—wrath·ful·ly** *adv.* **—wrath·ful·ness** *n.*

wreak (reek) *tr.v.* **wreaked, wreaking, wreaks. 1.** To inflict (vengeance or punishment) upon a person. **2.** To express or gratify (anger, malevolence, or resentment); vent. **3.** To bring about; cause: *wreak havoc.* **4.** *Archaic.* To take vengeance for; avenge. [Middle English *wreken,* Old English *wrecan,* to drive, expel.] **—wreak·er** *n.*

wreath (reeth) *n., pl.* **wreaths** (reethz, reeths). **1. a.** A ring or circlet of flowers or leaves worn on the head, placed as a memorial, or used as a decoration. **b.** A representation of this, as in woodwork. **2.** A curling shape; a ring: *wreaths of smoke.* [Middle English *wrethe,* Old English *writha,* from weak grade of *wrīthan,* to WRITE.]

wreathe (reeth) *v.* **wreathed, wreathing, wreathes.** *—tr.* **1.** To twist, coil, or entwine into a wreath or a wreathlike shape or contour. **2.** To crown, decorate, or encircle with or as with a wreath. **3.** To coil or curl. **4.** To form a wreath around. *—intr.* **1.** To assume the form of a wreath. **2.** To curl, writhe, or spiral: *The smoke wreathed upwards.* [From WREATH.]

wreck (rek) *n.* **1. a.** The action of wrecking or the condition of being wrecked; destruction. **b.** The accidental destruction of a ship; shipwreck. **2.** The stranded hulk of a ship that has been gravely damaged, as by being driven onto rocks. **3.** The remains of something that has been wrecked or ruined. **4.** Fragments of a ship or its cargo cast ashore by the sea after a shipwreck; wreckage. **5.** A person, animal, or thing in a shattered, dilapidated, or debilitated state: *He's a nervous wreck.*
~*v.* **wrecked, wrecking, wrecks.** —*tr.* **1.** To cause to undergo shipwreck. **2.** To bring to a state of ruin; disable or destroy; undermine. —*intr.* To suffer destruction, ruin, or shipwreck. —See Synonyms at **ruin.** [Middle English *wrek,* from Anglo-French *wrec,* from Scandinavian; akin to Old Norse *(v)rek,* wreckage.]

wreck·age (réckij) *n.* **1.** The act of wrecking or the condition of being wrecked. **2.** The debris of anything wrecked.

wreck·er (réckər) *n.* **1.** One that wrecks or destroys: *a wrecker of dreams.* **2.** *Chiefly U.S.* A person who demolishes buildings or breaks up motor vehicles for a living. **3. a.** *Chiefly U.S.* A person, piece of equipment, or vehicle employed in recovering or removing a wreck; especially, a **breakdown van** *(see).* **b.** One who salvages wrecked cargo or parts. **4. a.** Formerly, one who lured a vessel to destruction, as on a rocky coastline, in order to plunder. **b.** *Archaic.* A plunderer.

wreck·fish (rék-fish) *n., pl.* **-fishes** or collectively **wreckfish.** The **stone bass** *(see).* [From its often being found near wrecks.]

wren (ren) *n.* **1.** Any of various small, brownish birds of the family Troglodytidae. **2.** Any of various similar birds. [Middle English *wrenne,* Old English *wrenna,* from Germanic *wrend(il)a-* (unattested).]

Wren (ren) *n. British Informal.* A member of the Women's Royal Naval Service.

Wren, Sir Christopher (1632–1723). English architect and mathematician. Educated at Oxford, he became professor of astronomy at both London (1657) and Oxford (1661) and helped to form the Royal Society. He designed St. Paul's Cathedral, Greenwich Hospital, and Pembroke College chapel, Cambridge.

wrench (rench) *n.* **1.** A sudden sharp, forcible twist or turn. **2.** An injury produced by twisting or straining. **3.** A sudden tug at one's emotions; a surge of sorrow, anguish, or similar emotion. **4. a.** A break in relations or a parting that causes emotional distress. **b.** The pain this causes. **5.** A deliberate distortion in the original form or meaning of something written or spoken. **6.** *U.S.* A spanner. **b.** *British.* Any of various specialised adjustable spanners, especially a **monkey wrench** and a **torque wrench** *(both of which see).*
~*v.* **wrenched, wrenching, wrenches.** —*tr.* **1. a.** To twist or turn suddenly and forcibly. **b.** To twist and sprain: *wrenched her knee.* **2. a.** To force free by pulling at; yank; wrest. Usually used with *off* or *away.* **b.** To pull with a wrench. **3.** To pull at the feelings or emotions of; distress: *It wrenched her to say good-bye.* **4.** To distort or twist the original character or import of: *wrenched the text to prove her point.* —*intr.* To give a wrench, twist, or turn. [Middle English *wrenchen,* to twist, wrench, Old English *wrencan,* to twist.]

wrest (rest) *tr.v.* **wrested, wresting, wrests.** **1.** To obtain by or as by pulling with violent twisting movements: *wrest a book out of another's hands.* **2.** To usurp forcefully: *wrest power.* **3.** To obtain or extract by extortion, guile, or persistent effort: *wrest the meaning from an obscure poem.* **4. a.** To distort or twist the nature or meaning of: *wrested my words out of context.* **b.** To misapply.
~*n.* **1.** The action or an instance of wresting. **2.** *Archaic.* A small tuning key for the pins of a harp or piano. [Middle English *wresten,* Old English *wrǣstan,* to twist; akin to WRIST.] —**wrest·er** *n.*

wres·tle (réss'l) *v.* **-tled, -tling, -tles.** —*intr.* **1.** To take part in a fight or competition consisting of grappling and attempting to throw or immobilise one's opponent, especially under certain contest rules. **2.** To contend; struggle; grapple. Used with *with* or *against*: *town planners wrestling with budget cuts.* **3.** To strive in an effort to gain mastery: *wrestle with temptation.* —*tr.* **1. a.** To take part in (a wrestling match). **b.** To wrestle with. **2.** To make (one's way, for example) by or as if by wrestling: *wrestled her way through the crowd.*
~*n.* **1.** An act of wrestling; especially, a wrestling match. **2.** A struggle. [Middle English *wrest(e)len,* Old English *wrǣstlian.*] —**wres·tler** *n.*

wres·tling (réssling) *n.* Any of various sporting exercises or contests between two competitors and sometimes teams who attempt to throw or immobilise each other by grappling.

wrest pin *n.* Any of the pins to which the strings, especially of a keyboard stringed instrument, are attached and by which they are tuned.

wretch (rech) *n.* **1.** A miserable, unfortunate, or unhappy person. **2.** A base, mean, or despicable person: *"A stony adversary, an inhuman wretch"* (Shakespeare). [Middle English *wrecche,* Old English *wrecca,* wretch, exile.]

wretch·ed (réchid) *adj.* **1.** Living in degradation and misery; miserable: *wretched beggars huddling on the pavement.* **2.** Attended by misery and woes: *a wretched life.* **3.** Of a poor or mean character; dismal: *a wretched building.* **4.** Contemptible; despicable. **5.** Inferior in performance or quality: *a wretched translation.* **6.** Very unpleasant; deplorable. **7.** Used as an intensive: *a wretched nuisance.* —See Synonyms at **sad.** [Middle English *wrecched,* irregularly from *wrecche,* WRETCH.] —**wretch·ed·ly** *adv.* —**wretch·ed·ness** *n.*

wri·er. Alternative comparative of **wry.**

wri·est. Alternative superlative of **wry.**

wrig·gle (rigg'l) *v.* **-gled, -gling, -gles.** —*intr.* **1.** To turn or twist the body with sinuous writhing motions; squirm. **2.** To proceed with writhing motions. **3.** To worm one's way into or out of a situation; insinuate or extricate oneself by sly or subtle means: *He's always wriggling out of his responsibilities.* —*tr.* **1.** To move with a wriggling motion: *wriggle a toe.* **2.** To make (one's way, for example) by wriggling: *He wriggled his way into favour.*
~*n.* **1.** A wriggling movement. **2.** A sinuous path, line, marking, or the like. [Middle English *wrigglen,* from Middle Low German *wriggeln.*] —**wrig·gler** *n.* —**wrig·gly** *adj.*

wright (rīt) *n.* A person who constructs or repairs something. Now used only in combination: *playwright; shipwright.* [Middle English *wright,* Old English *wryhta, wyrhta.*]

Wright (rīt), **Frank Lloyd** (1867–1959). U.S. architect. He studied civil engineering and adapted its methods to architecture. Famous examples of his work include the Robie House (1909) in Chicago and the Guggenheim Museum (completed 1959).

Wright, Judith (1915–). Australian poet. Examining Australian themes in a frequently introspective style, her works include *Woman to Man* (1950), *Alive* (1972), and *The Double Tree* (1978). Her *Collected Poems: 1942–1985* came out in 1994.

Wright, Orville (1871–1948), and **Wilbur** (1867–1912). U.S. pioneer aviators. The brothers ran a bicycle firm until they made the first successful powered flight in a heavier-than-air machine (1903). They later formed a production company.

wring (ring) *v.* **wrung** (rung) or *rare* **wringed, wringing, wrings.** —*tr.* **1.** To twist, squeeze, or compress, especially so as to extract liquid. Often used with *out.* **2.** To extract (liquid) by twisting or compressing. **3.** To wrench or twist forcibly or painfully: *wring someone's neck.* **4.** To clasp and twist or squeeze (one's hands), as in distress. **5.** To take hold of and shake energetically (someone's hand), as in congratulation. **6.** To cause distress to; affect with painful emotion: *wring someone's heart.* **7.** To obtain or extract by applying force or pressure: *wring the truth out of a person.* —*intr. Archaic.* To writhe or squirm, as in pain.
~*n.* The act or an instance of wringing; a squeeze or twist. [Middle English *wringen,* Old English *wringan.*]

wring·er (ríng-ər) *n.* One that wrings; especially, a device in which laundry is pressed between rollers to extract water.

wring·ing (ríng-ing) *adv.* Used as an intensive: *wringing wet.*

wrin·kle[1] (ríngk'l) *n.* **1.** A small furrow, ridge, or crease on a normally smooth surface, caused by crumpling, folding, or shrinking. **2.** A line or crease in the skin, as from age.
~*v.* **wrinkled, -kling, -kles.** —*tr.* **1.** To make a wrinkle or wrinkles in. **2.** To draw up so as to form wrinkles; pucker: *wrinkle one's nose in disdain.* —*intr.* To acquire or be affected with wrinkles. [Middle English, back-formation from *wrinkled,* wrinkled, probably Old English *gewrinclod,* serrated, winding, participle of *gewrinclian,* to wind.] —**wrin·kly** *adj. & n.*

wrinkle[2] *n. Informal.* An ingenious trick or method; a useful or clever hint; a dodge. [Middle English *wrinkel,* crooked action, trick, specialised use of *wrinkle,* WRINKLE.]

wrist (rist) *n.* **1. a.** The junction between the hand and forearm. **b.** *Anatomy.* The system of bones forming this junction. Also called "carpus". **2.** The part of a sleeve or glove that encircles the wrist. [Middle English *wrist,* Old English *wrist.*]

wrist·band (ríst-band) *n.* A band, as on a long sleeve or on a wristwatch, that encircles the wrist.

wrist·drop (ríst-drop) *n.* Paralysis of the muscles that raise back the hand, caused by compression of the nerve or by damage to the nerve, as in lead poisoning.

wrist·let (ríst-lət, -lit) *n.* **1.** A band of material worn round the wrist for warmth or support. **2.** A bracelet.

wrist·lock (ríst-lok) *n.* A wrestling hold in which an opponent's wrist is gripped and twisted to immobilise him.

wrist pin *n.* **1.** A pin attached to a wheel parallel to its axle, to function as a bearing for a crank. **2.** *Chiefly U.S.* A **gudgeon pin** *(see).*

wrist·watch (ríst-woch) *n.* A watch on a band worn about the wrist.

wris·ty (rísti) *adj.* Using or characterised by flexible movements of the wrist: *a wristy conducting style.*

writ[1] (rit) *n.* **1.** *Law.* A written order issued by a court, in the name of the Crown or of the state commanding the person to whom it is addressed to perform or cease performing some stated act. **2.** *Archaic.* Writings: *holy writ.* [Middle English *writ,* Old English *writ,* from Germanic *wrītan* (unattested), to scratch. See **write.**]

writ[2]. *Archaic.* Past tense and past participle of **write.** —**writ large.** On a magnified scale; in a large or emphasised form: *He treated war just as a childhood game writ large.*

write (rīt) *v.* **wrote** (rōt) or *archaic* **writ** (rit), **written** (rítt'n) or *archaic* **writ, writing, writes.** —*tr.* **1.** To form (letters, symbols, words, or sentences) on a surface such as paper, using a pen, pencil, or other tool. **2.** To spell: *How do you write your name?* **3.** To form (words) in cursive rather than printed script. **4.** To compose, especially as an author or musician: *write a memo; write a symphony; write one's memoirs.* **5.** To draw up in legal form; draft: *write a will.* **6.** To fill in with the required information: *write a cheque.* **7.** To cover with writing: *wrote five pages in an hour.* **8.** To set down; record: *write one's thoughts.* **9.** To relate or communicate by writing: *wrote that he was planning to extend his holiday.* **10.** To underwrite (an insurance policy). **11.** To have sufficient knowledge of (a language or writing system) to be able to compose in it in writing: *able to read German but not write it. She can speak Chinese but can't write it.* **12.** To depict clearly; mark: *"Utter dejection was written on every face."* (Winston Churchill). **13.** To ordain by fate or prophecy: *It is written that the Empire will fall.* **14.** To record (data) in a computer storage device. **15.** *Chiefly U.S.* To send a letter to. —*intr.* **1.** To trace or form letters, words, or symbols on paper or another surface. **2.** To produce articles, books, or other matter to be read. **3.** To compose a letter or letters; communicate by letter: *wrote to say he'd be three days late; I wish you'd write more often.* —**write out. 1.** To set down fully in writing. **2.** To remove (a character) from a long-running radio or television serial: *was written out of "Cross-roads" when her contract expired.* [Middle English *writen,* Old English *wrītan,* from Germanic *wrītan* (unattested), to tear, scratch.]

write down *tr.v.* **1.** To put into writing. **2.** *Accounting.* To reduce the book value of (an asset). **3.** To disparage in writing. **4.** To write in an affectedly simple or condescending style. Often used with *to.*

write-down (rīt-down) *n. Accounting.* A reduction of the book value of an asset.

write in *intr.v.* To communicate or make a request by letter. —*tr. U.S.* **1.** To cast a vote for (one not listed on a ballot), as by inserting his name. **2.** To cast (a vote) in this way.

write-in (rīt-in) *n. U.S.* **1.** A vote for one not listed on a ballot, usually cast by the insertion of his name in a space provided. **2.** A candidate voted for in this way. Also used adjectivally: *a write-in campaign.*

write off *tr.v.* **1.** To reduce to zero the book value of (an asset that has become worthless). **2.** To cancel from accounts as a loss. **3.** To consider with resignation as a loss or failure. **4.** *Informal.* To wreck beyond repair: *wrote off his car on the M.1.*

write-off (rīt-off, -awff) *n.* **1. a.** A cancellation in account books. **b.** The debt or asset thus cancelled. **c.** The amount cancelled or lost. **2.** *Informal.* Something regarded as being beyond repair or redemption; especially, a badly damaged car.

writ·er (rītər) *n.* **1.** One who writes, especially for a living. **2.** One who composes literary works. **3.** A composer of musical works.

writer's cramp *n.* A cramp chiefly affecting the muscles of the thumb and two adjacent fingers after prolonged writing.

Writer to the Signet *n. Abbr.* **W.S.** A member of the oldest and most influential society of solicitors in Scotland.

write up *tr.v.* **1.** To write a report or description of, as for publication. **2.** To bring (a journal, for example) up to date.

write-up (rīt-up) *n.* A published account, review, or notice, especially a favourable one.

writhe (rīth) *v.* **writhed, writhed** or *archaic* **writhen** (rīth'n), **writhing, writhes.** —*intr.* **1.** To twist or squirm, as in pain, struggle, or embarrassment. **2.** To move with a twisting or contorted motion. —*tr.* To cause to twist or squirm; contort: *"He writhed himself quite off his stool in the excitement of his feelings"* (Charles Dickens). ~*n.* An act or instance of writhing; a contortion. [Middle English *writhen,* Old English *wrīthan.*] —**writh·er** *n.*

writ·ing (rīting) *n.* **1.** Written form: *Put it in writing.* **2. a.** Language symbols or characters written or imprinted on a surface. **b.** The art of using such symbols as a means of communication: *the invention of writing.* **3.** Any written work; especially, a literary composition. **4.** The activity, art, or occupation of a writer. **5.** Handwriting or handwritten matter: *couldn't read his writing.* —**the writing on the wall.** An indication of approaching defeat or catastrophe. ~*adj.* Of, pertaining to, or used in writing: *writing paper.*

Writ·ings (rītingz) *pl.n.* **Hagiographa** (see). Preceded by *the.*

writ of execution *n. Law.* A writ ordering the enforcement of a judgment.

writ of summons *n. Law.* A writ directing a person to appear in court to answer a complaint.

writ·ten. Past participle of **write.**

W.R.N.S. Women's Royal Naval Service.

wrnt. warrant.

Wroc·law (vrōts-laaf, -lav; *Polish* -waaf). Capital and port of Wroc-law province, southwest Poland. Situated on the river Oder, it was a Hanseatic city (1368–1474) before passing to the Habsburgs (1526) and Prussia (1742).

wrong (rong ‖ rawng) *adj.* **1.** Not correct; erroneous. **2. a.** Contrary to conscience, morality, or law; wicked; immoral. **b.** Unfair or unjust. **3.** Not required, intended, or wanted: *We took a wrong turn.* **4.** Not fitting or suitable; inappropriate; improper: *the wrong moment.* **5.** Not in accordance with an established usage, method, or procedure. **6.** Not functioning properly; out of order; amiss. **7.** Unacceptable or undesirable according to social convention. ~*adv.* In a wrong manner or direction; mistakenly; erroneously. —**get wrong.** To misunderstand. —**go wrong. 1.** To take a wrong turn or make a wrong move: *Where did we go wrong?* **2.** To happen or turn out badly; go amiss. ~*n.* **1. a.** That which is morally wrong: *to know right from wrong.* **b.** An unjust, injurious, or immoral act or circumstance. **2. a.** An invasion or violation of another's legal rights. **b.** *Law.* An infringement, especially one leading to a civil action; a tort. **3.** The condition of being mistaken or to blame: *in the wrong.* —See Synonyms at **injustice.** ~*tr.v.* **wronged, wronging, wrongs. 1.** To treat unjustly or injuriously. **2.** To discredit unjustly; malign. **3.** To treat dishonourably; especially, to seduce (a woman). [Middle English *wrang, wrong,* probably from Scandinavian; akin to Danish *vrang,* Old Norse

rangr and *vrangr* (unattested), awry; akin to WRING.] —**wrong·er** (róng-ər) *n.* —**wrong·ly** *adv.*

Usage: The adverbs *wrong* and *wrongly* are usually interchangeable, especially in the sense of "erroneously", when used after a verb: *She spelt it wrongly/wrong.* However *wrong* is somewhat informal, and should be avoided in careful writing or speech. Before the verb, or for a verb form used adjectivally, *wrongly* is obligatory: *It was wrongly spelt; a wrongly conceived plan.*

wrong·do·er (róng-dōō-ər ‖ ráwng-) *n.* One who does wrong morally or legally. —**wrong·do·ing** *n.*

wrong fount *n. Abbr.* **wf** *Printing.* The incorrect fount. Used, as in proofreading, to indicate a typeface of the wrong kind.

wrong·foot (róng-foŏt ‖ ráwng-) *tr.v.* **-footed, -footing, -foots. 1.** In tennis and various other sports, to mislead (one's opponent) into balancing on the wrong foot, and thereby pass him on the other side. **2.** To mislead or surprise (a person) into an embarrasing or foolish action: *He wrong-footed me with a surprise question.*

wrong·ful (róng-f'l ‖ ráwng-) *adj.* **1.** Wrong; injurious; marked by injustice or unfairness: *wrongful dismissal.* **2.** Contrary to law; unlawful; illegal. —**wrong·ful·ly** *adv.* —**wrong·ful·ness** *n.*

wrong·head·ed (róng-héddid ‖ ráwng-) *adj.* **1.** Persistently erroneous in judgment. **2.** Wrong in stubborn defiance of the evidence. —**wrong·head·ed·ly** *adv.* —**wrong·head·ed·ness** *n.*

wrote. Past tense of **write.**

wroth (rōth, roth ‖ rawth) *adj. Archaic.* Wrathful; angry. [Middle English *wrath, wroth,* Old English *wrāth.*]

wrought (rawt). *Archaic.* Past tense and past participle of **work.** ~*adj.* **1.** Created or put together with care and deliberation. **2.** Shaped by hammering with tools, rather than by casting. Said of metals or metalwork. **3.** Made or embellished delicately or elaborately: *wrought snuffboxes.* —**wrought up.** Agitated; excited.

wrought iron *n.* An easily welded or forged iron containing approximately 0.2 per cent carbon and total impurities less than approximately 0.5 per cent. —**wrought-i·ron** *adj.*

wrung. Past tense and past participle of **wring.**

W.R.V.S. Women's Royal Voluntary Service.

wry (rī) *adj.* **wrier** or **wryer, wriest** or **wryest. 1.** Temporarily twisted in an expression of distaste or displeasure: *On tasting the wine, she pulled a wry face.* **2.** Drily humorous, often with a touch of irony: *a wry public speaker; a wry joke.* **3.** Abnormally twisted or bent to one side; crooked. Said of the features or the neck. **4.** At variance with what is right, proper, or suitable; perverse. [Middle English *wrien,* to bend, twist, turn aside, Old English *wrīgian,* to proceed, turn.] —**wry·ly** *adv.* —**wry·ness** *n.*

wry·bill (rī-bil) *n.* A plover native to New Zealand, *Anarhynchus frontalis,* having a right-handed twist to its beak.

wry·neck (rī-nek) *n.* **1.** Either of two Old World birds, *Jynx torquilla* or *J. ruficollis,* that are capable of twisting the neck all the way round to look backwards. **2.** *Pathology.* **Torticollis** (see).

W.S. Writer to the Signet.

WSW west-southwest.

wt. weight.

Wu (wōō) *n.* Any Chinese dialect spoken in the valley and delta regions of the Chang Jiang (Yangtze river.) [Mandarin, *wú.*]

Wu·han (wōó-hán, -haán). Capital and port of Hubei province, People's Republic of China. Situated at the confluence of the Chang Jiang and Han Shui rivers, it is formed from the cities of Hanyang, Wuchang, and Hankou Yangtze.

Wuh·sien. See **Suzhou.**

wul·fen·ite (wōolfə-nīt) *n.* A yellow to orange-red or brown mineral, $PbMoO_4$, used as a molybdenum ore. [German *Wulfenit,* after Franz X. von *Wulfen* (1728–1805), Austrian mineralogist.]

Wun·der·kind (wúndər-kind; *German* vōondər-kint) *n., pl.* **-kinds** or **-kinder** (kindər). *Sometimes small* **w. 1.** A person who attains great success or an advanced position in his profession, art, or the like at a relatively early age; whiz kid. **2.** A child prodigy. [German, "wonder child".]

Wup·per·tal (vōopər-taal). Industrial city in North Rhine-Westphalia, Germany. It lies on the river Wupper in the Ruhr valley, and was formed in 1929 from the twin towns of Elberfeld and Barmen, and Vohwinkel and several smaller towns.

wurst (wurst, vurst; *German* voorst ‖ *U.S. also* wōost, wōosht) *n.* A large sausage of seasoned and usually cooked meat, of a type produced in German-speaking countries. [German *Wurst,* from Old High German *wurst.*]

Würt·tem·berg (vúrtəm-berg, wúrtəm-, -bairg; *German* vúrtəm-bairk). Former kingdom of southwestern Germany. A duchy from 1495, it was a kingdom (1806–1918) and joined the German Reich in 1870. It was incorporated (1952) into the newly formed state of Baden-Württemberg.

wuth·er·ing (wúthəring) *adj. Northern British.* **1.** Affected by swirling wind; blustery. **2.** Blowing strongly and noisily. Said of the wind. [Variant of dialect *whithering,* from *whither,* to bluster, from Scandinavian; akin to Old Norse *hvitha,* squall of wind, Old English *hwitha,* breeze.]

Wu·xian. See **Suzhou.**

W.W.I World War I.

W.W.II World War II.

WWW World Wide Web.

Wy·att (wī-ət), **Sir Thomas,** (c. 1503–42). English poet and courtier. In Henry VIII's favour, he was sent on various missions abroad but was twice imprisoned on a charge of being the lover of Anne Boleyn (1536) and for suspected treason (1541). He is credited with the introduction of the Petrarchan sonnet into English poetry.

wych elm, wich elm (wich) *n.* **1.** An Old World elm, *Ulmus glabra,* often planted as a shade tree. **2.** The wood of this tree. [Middle English *wyche,* Old English *wice.*]

wych hazel. Variant of **witch hazel.**

Wyc·liffe (wĭcklif), **John** (*c.* 1329–84). English religious reformer. He spoke out against Church abuses and despite papal censure issued a condemnation of absolution, penances, and indulgences, denied transubstantiation, and issued the first translation of the Bible in English. He sent out itinerant preachers to spread his philosophy, but his followers, called Lollards, were imprisoned, although Wycliffe remained untouched. After his death, his works were again condemned by the Church. —**Wyc·lif·fite, Wyc·lif·ite** *n. & adj.*

Wye (wī). River of Wales and England. Rising in the Plynlimmons, it flows 210 kilometres (130 miles) mainly southeast to enter the estuary of the river Severn near Chepstow.

Wy·eth (wī-əth), **Andrew (Newell)** (1917–). U.S. painter. Working mainly in watercolour and egg tempera, he painted American landscapes and people in a restrained, naturalistic style. His many works include *Christina's World* (1948), *That Gentleman* (1960), *Garret Room* (1962), and *Day of the Fair* (1963).

Wyke·ham·ist (wĭckəmist) *n.* A pupil or former pupil of Winchester College, an English public school. [After William of *Wykeham* (1324–1404), Bishop of Winchester, Chancellor of England, and founder of the school.] —**Wyke·ham·ist** *adj.*

wynd (wīnd) *n. Scottish.* A narrow lane; an alley. [Middle English, probably from *wynden,* to go, Old English *windan,* to WIND.]

Wy·o·ming (wī-ōming). State of the western United States. With the Great Plains in the northeast, and crossed by the Rocky Mountains in the west, it is rich in mineral reserves. Its capital is Cheyenne.

wy·vern, wi·vern (wĭvərn) *n.* A two-legged dragon with wings and a barbed and knotted tail. [17th century : Variant of earlier *wyver,* from Old French, from Latin *vīpera,* VIPER.]

x, X (eks) *n., pl.* **x's** or *rare* **xs, Xs** or **X's. 1.** The 24th letter of the modern English alphabet. **2.** Any of the speech sounds represented by this letter. **3.** Anything shaped like the letter **X. 4.** The mark **X** inscribed to represent the signature of an illiterate person.

x, X, x., X. *Note:* As an abbreviation or symbol, *x* may be a small or a capital letter, with or without a full stop. Established forms or those generally preferred precede the definition. When no form is given, all four forms are in general use in that sense. **1. X** A symbol for Christ or Christian. **2. x.** *Finance.* ex. **3. x** *Printing.* A symbol used, as in proofreading, to indicate a mechanical defect in type. **4. X** The symbol for a kiss. **5. X** A symbol placed on a map or diagram to mark the location or position of a point. **6. X** A symbol placed on a ballot paper, questionnaire, or the like, to indicate one's preference among alternatives. **7. x, X** The Roman numeral for ten. **8. x** A symbol used in marking school exercises, examination papers, or the like, to indicate an error. **9.** *Mathematics.* **x** The symbol for: **a.** An unknown number. **b.** An algebraic variable. **10. X** The symbol for reactance. **11.** Any unknown or unnamed factor, thing, or person. **12.** The 24th in a series; 23rd when *J* is omitted. **13.** The first in a series consisting of *x, y,* and *z.* **14.** *Biology.* Hybrid (cross).

x *tr.v.* **x'd** or **xed** (ekst), **x·ing** or **x'ing** (ĕksing), **x's** or **xes** (ĕksiz). **1.** To mark or sign with an *x.* **2.** To delete, cancel, or obliterate with a series of x's. Usually used with *out.*

X *n., pl.* **Xs** or **X's** (ĕksiz). Formerly, a film not permitted to be shown publicly to persons under a certain age, which in Britain is 18. Also used adjectively: *an X film.* Now indicated in Britain by the symbol 18.

xan·thate (zán-thayt) *n.* A salt or ester of a xanthic acid; especially, a simple xanthic acid salt, as of sodium or potassium, used as a flotation collector for copper, silver, and gold. [XANTH(O)- + -ATE.] —**xan·tha·tion** (zan-tháysh'n) *n.*

xan·thic acid (zánthik) *n.* Any of various unstable acids of the form ROC(S)SH, in which R is usually an alkyl radical. [Greek *xanthos†,* yellow (referring to the colour of its salts).]

xan·thine (zán-theen, -thīn, -thin) *n.* A yellowish-white purine base, $C_5H_4N_4O_2$, found in blood, urine, and some plants. [French *xanthine* : XANTH(O)- + -INE.]

Xan·thip·pe (zan-thĭppi, gzan-, -tĭppi). The wife of Socrates; proverbial as a shrewish and scolding woman.

xantho-, xanth– *comb. form.* Indicates the colour yellow; for example, **xanthochroid, xanthoma.** [New Latin, from Greek *xanthos†,* yellow.]

xan·tho·chroid (zán-thō-kroyd, -thə-) *adj.* Having a light complexion and light hair.
~*n.* A xanthochroid individual. [New Latin *xanthochroi,* light-haired, fair-skinned people : XANTH(O)- + Greek *ōkhros,* pale, wan + -OID.]

xan·tho·ma (zan-thōmə) *n.* A skin disease characterised by nodular yellowish patches, especially on the eyelids. [New Latin : XANTH(O)- + -OMA.]

xan·tho·phyll (zán-thō-fil, -thə-) *n.* Any of a class of yellow carotenoid pigments, the commonest of which is lutein, found with chlorophyll in green plants and in egg yolk. [French *xanthophylle* : XANTHO- + -PHYLL.]

xan·thous (zánthəss) *adj.* **1.** Yellow. **2.** Having light-brown or yellowish skin. Compare **melanous.** [Greek *xanthos†,* yellow.]

Xan·thus (zánthəss). Ancient city of Lycia, west Asia Minor. Situated on the river Xanthus in modern Turkey, it was captured by the Persians (*c.* 546 B.C) and later the Romans (*c.* 42 B.C.).

x-ax·is (ĕks-ak-siss) *n., pl.* **x-axes** (-seez). **1.** The horizontal axis of a two-dimensional Cartesian coordinate system. **2.** One of three axes in a three-dimensional Cartesian coordinate system.

X-chro·mo·some (ĕks-krōmə-sōm) *n.* The larger of the two types of sex chromosome. It is associated with female characteristics in most animals, including humans, and occurs in pairs in such female animals, and paired with the **Y-chromosome** *(see)* in males.

Xe The symbol for the element xenon.

xe·bec, ze·bec, ze·beck (zée-bek) *n.* A small three-masted Mediterranean vessel with both square and triangular sails, once used commonly by Arab corsairs. [Earlier *chebec,* from French, from Italian *sciabecco,* from Arabic *shabbāk.*]

Xe·na·kis (ze-naákiss, *Greek* kse-), **Iannis** (1922–). Romanian-born in France. Greek composer. Applying mathematics to composition and sometimes using a computer, he has written such works as *Poème électronique* (1958), *Duel* (1959), and *Pléiades* (1978).

xe·ni·a (zéeni-ə) *n. Botany.* An effect produced on a structure by the introduction of male genes; for example, a visible change in the endosperm of a seed caused by the pollen nucleus when it fuses with the endosperm nucleus. [New Latin, from Greek, the condition of a guest, from *xenos,* stranger, guest.]

xeno–, xen– *comb. form.* Indicates strange, foreign, or different; for example, **xenolith, xenophobe.** [New Latin, from Greek *xenos,* stranger.]

xen·o·cryst (zén-ə-krist, -ō-) *n.* A crystal foreign to the igneous rock in which it occurs. [XENO- + CRYST(AL).]

xe·nog·a·my (ze-nóggəmi, zee-, zi-) *n. Botany.* The transfer of pollen from one plant to another; cross-pollination. [XENO- + -GAMY.] —**xe·nog·a·mous** *adj.*

xen·o·gen·e·sis (zén-ə-jénni-siss, -ō-) *n. Biology.* **1.** The supposed production of offspring markedly different from and showing no relationship to either of its parents. **2. Alternation of generations** *(see).* [XENO- + -GENESIS.] —**xen·o·ge·net·ic** (-jə-néttik), **xen·o·gen·ic** (-jénnik) *adj.*

xen·o·graft (zén-ō-graaft, zéen-, -ō- ‖ -graft) *n.* A type of tissue graft, a **heterograft** *(see).* [XENO- + GRAFT.]

xen·o·lith (zén-ə-lith, zéen-, -ō-) *n.* A rock fragment foreign to the igneous mass in which it occurs. [XENO- + -LITH.]

xen·o·mor·phic (zén-ə-mórfik, zéen-, -ō-) *adj.* Designating a mineral constituent of an igneous rock that lacks its characteristic crystal form as a result of deformation. [XENO- + -MORPHIC.]

xen·on (zénnon, zée-non) *n. Symbol* **Xe** A colourless, odourless, highly unreactive gaseous element found in minute quantities in the atmosphere, extracted commercially from liquefied air, and used in stroboscopic, bactericidal, and flash lamps and lasers. Atomic number 54, atomic weight 131.30, melting point –111.9°C, boiling point –108.1°C, density (gas) 5.897 grams per cubic metre, relative density (liquid) 3.52 (–109°C). [Greek, neuter of *xenos,* stranger.]

xen·o·phobe (zén-ə-fōb, zéen-, -ō-) *n.* A person unduly fearful or contemptuous of strangers or foreigners, or of foreign ideas and cultures, especially as reflected in his political or cultural views. [XENO- + -PHOBE.] —**xen·o·pho·bi·a** (-fōbi-ə) *n.* —**xen·o·pho·bic** (-fōbik) *adj.*

Xen·o·phon (zénnəf'n) (*c.* 430–*c.* 354 B.C.). Greek soldier, essayist, and historian. A friend and pupil of Socrates, he gave an account of the philosopher's death in the *Apology.* He accompanied the expedition of Cyrus the Younger against King Artaxerxes Mnemon of Persia and on the death of Cyrus (401 B.C.) assumed command of 10,000 Greeks. He led his troops from the centre of the Persian empire to the Black Sea. He recorded their harrowing journey in the *Anabasis.*

xen·o·pus (zénnəpəss) *n.* Any clawed toad of the African genus *Xenopus;* especially *X. laevis,* which has been used in pregnancy testing since it produces eggs when injected with the urine of a pregnant woman. In its native South Africa the species *Xenopus laevis* is called the "platanna". [New Latin : XENO- + -pus, foot (see -pod).]

xe·ric (zéer-ik, zérrik) *adj.* Of, characterised by, or adapted to an extremely dry habitat. [Greek *xēros*, dry.]

xero-, xer- *comb. form.* Indicates dryness; for example, **xerophyte, xerosis.** [New Latin, from Greek *xēros*, dry.]

xe·ro·der·ma (zéer-ŏ-dérmə) *n.* Also **xe·ro·der·mi·a** (-dérmi-ə). 1. Abnormal dryness of the skin. 2. A skin disease, **ichthyosis** *(see).* [New Latin : XERO- + -DERMA.] —**xer·o·der·mat·ic** (-der-máttik), **xer·o·der·ma·tous** (-dérmətəss) *adj.*

xe·rog·ra·phy (zeer-róggrəfi, ze-) *n.* A dry photographic or photocopying process in which a negative image formed by a resinous powder on an electrically charged plate is electrically transferred to and thermally fixed as positive on a paper or other copying surface. [XERO- + -GRAPHY.] —**xer·o·graph·ic** (zéer-ə-gráffik) *adj.*

xe·roph·i·lous (zeer-óffiləss) *adj.* Flourishing in or able to withstand a dry, hot environment. [XERO- + -PHILOUS.]

xe·roph·thal·mi·a (zéer-of-thálmi-ə, -op-) *n.* Extreme dryness of the conjunctiva, thought to result from vitamin A deficiency. [Late Latin *xerophthalmia,* from Greek *xērophthalmia* : XER(O)- + OPHTHALMIA.] —**xer·oph·thal·mic** (-thál-mik) *adj.*

xe·ro·phyte (zéer-ə-fīt, -ō-) *n.* A plant, such as a cactus, that grows in arid and is adapted to an environment deficient in moisture. Compare **hydrophyte, mesophyte.** [XERO- + -PHYTE.] —**xer·o·phyt·ic** (-fíttik) *adj.* —**xer·o·phyt·i·cal·ly** *adv.*

xe·ro·sere (zéer-ə-seer, -ō-) *n.* A sequence of ecological communities beginning in a dry area. [XERO- + SERE (series).]

xe·ro·sis (zeer-rṓ-siss, zi-) *n.* Abnormal dryness, especially of the skin, conjunctiva, or mucous membranes. [New Latin : XER(O)- + -OSIS.] —**xe·rot·ic** (-róttik) *adj.*

Xer·ox (zéer-oks) *n.* 1. A trademark for a photocopying process or machine using xerography. 2. A copy made on a Xerox machine. —*tr.v.* **Xeroxed, -oxing, -oxes.** *Sometimes small* **x.** To reproduce or print by means of a Xerox machine. —**Xer·ox** *adj.*

Xer·xes I (zérkseez) (*c.* 519–465 B.C.). King of Persia (486–465 B.C.). Succeeding to the throne on the death of his father Darius I, he organised a vast army which defeated the Greeks at Thermopylae, and destroyed Athens (480 B.C.), but on the defeat of his navy at Salamis (480 B.C.) and of his army at Plataea (479 B.C.), he retreated to Persia where he was later assassinated.

x-height (éks-hīt) *n. Printing.* The height of a lower-case x. Compare **cap-height.**

Xho·sa (káw-sə, kṓ-, -zə. *Note: the initial* Xh *properly denotes an aspirated voiceless alveolar lateral click). n., pl.* **-sas** *or collectively* **Xhosa.** 1. A member of a southern African Bantu people living mainly in the Cape Province of the Republic of South Africa. 2. The Bantu language akin to Zulu spoken by the Xhosa, of the Niger-Congo family of languages.

xi (sī, ksī, zī; *Greek* ksee) *n., pl.* **xis.** 1. The 14th letter in the Greek alphabet, written Ξ, ξ. Transliterated in English as *X, x,* or *ks.* 2. *Symbol* Ξ *Physics.* Any of four elementary particles in the baryon family.

Xia·men or **Hsia·men** (syá-a-mún). Also **A·moy** (ə-móy). Port of southeast China. Situated in Fujian province on Xiamen island, it stands opposite Taiwan. After its capture by the British during the Opium War (1841), it became a treaty port (1842). Today it is an important industrial city and tourist centre.

Xi'an, Hsi-an, or **Sian** (shée-áan). Formerly **Changan.** Capital of Shaanxi province, northwest China. Situated in the valley of the river Wei, it was the capital of the Ch'in dynasty (255–206 B.C.), and at times of the Han and Tang dynasties. Jiang Jieshi, leader of the Kuomintang, was held hostage here (1936) until he agreed to join with the communists against the Japanese.

Xiang Jiang (shée-áang jyáng). Also **Hsiang Chiang** or **Siang Kiang.** River of south central China. It rises in Guangxi Zhuang, and flows 1 150 kilometres (715 miles) through Hunan to the Dongting Hu (lake). Its valley is an ancient routeway and farming area.

Xi Jiang (sée jyáng). Also **Hsi Chiang** or **Si Kiang;** *English* **West River.** River of south China. Rising in Yunnan province, southwest China, it flows 1 900 kilometres (1,200 miles) eastwards to enter the South China Sea through a delta. Navigable by large ships, it passes Guangzhou (Canton).

Xin·jiang Uigur Zizhiqu. Also **Sin-kiang Uighur Autonomous Region** or **Chinese Turkestan.** Region of western China. It is a high plateau enclosed by the Pamirs, Kunlun Shan, Altun Shan, and Tian Shan, and includes the Takla Makan desert, with the Tarim basin, and many salt lakes. Its many oases produce wheat, maize, and millet. There are considerable reserves of coal, tungsten, molybdenum, and oil. Most of the people are Turkic-speaking Muslims. The region came under Chinese control in the 16th century, but was later contested by Russia. Urumqi is the capital.

xiphi-, xiph- *comb. form.* Indicates sword; for example, **xiphisternum.** [New Latin, from Greek *xiphos,* sword, probably of Oriental origin.]

xiph·i·ster·num (ziffi-stér-nəm) *n., pl.* **-na** (-nə). The lowest or hindmost and smallest of the three divisions of the breastbone. Also called "xiphoid", "xiphoid process".

xiph·oid (zíffoyd, zī-foyd) *adj.* 1. Having the shape of a sword. 2. Of or pertaining to the xiphisternum. —*n.* The xiphisternum. [Greek *xiphoeidēs,* "sword-shaped" : XIPHI- + -OID.]

xiph·o·su·ran (ziffə-séwr-ən, zífə-, -sóor-) *n.* Any arthropod of the order Xiphosura, which includes the horseshoe crab and many extinct forms. —*adj.* Of or belonging to the order Xiphosura. [New Latin *Xiphosura,* "sword-tailed ones" : XIPHI- + -*ura,* plural of -*urus,* -UROUS.]

Xizang. See **Tibet.**

XL extra large.

X·mas (kríss-məss, éks-) *n. Informal.* Christmas. [From the Greek letter *X,* transliterated as *Kh* (see **chi**) and representing Greek *Khristos,* CHRIST.]

Usage: This form occurs mainly in commercial writing, as on Christmas cards, and is not generally used in other contexts, unless there is a concern to save space (as in newspaper headlines).

XP See **chi-rho.**

X-ra·di·a·tion, x-ra·di·a·tion (éks-ráydi-áysh'n) *n.* 1. Treatment with or exposure to X-rays. 2. Radiation composed of X-rays.

X rated *adj. Informal.* **Adult** (sense 2b). [From *X* (film rating).]

X-ray, x-ray (éks-ray, -ráy) *n.* 1. **a.** A relatively high-energy photon with wavelength in the approximate range from 0.4 to 100 nanometres. **b.** *Usually plural.* A stream of such photons, used for their penetrating power in radiography, radiology, radiotherapy, and research. 2. A photograph taken with X-rays. In this sense, also called "X-ray photograph". —*tr.v.* **X-rayed** or **x-rayed, -raying, -rays.** 1. To irradiate with X-rays. 2. To photograph by means of X-rays. [Translation of German *X Strahlen* (plural), so called because their exact nature was not known.] —**X-ray** *adj.*

X-ray astronomy *n.* The study of the X-rays from celestial bodies detected by satellites and rockets above the earth's atmosphere.

X-ray crystallography *n.* The study of crystal structure by means of X-ray diffraction.

X-ray diffraction *n.* The diffraction of X-rays by the atoms or ions of a crystal, according to a characteristic pattern that enables information to be obtained on the structure of the crystal.

X-ray microscope *n.* An instrument used to render a highly magnified image of the atomic structure of a crystalline system by means of the contrasts arising from the differences in such a structure's absorption or emission of X-rays.

X-ray star *n.* A star that emits most of its radiation in the X-ray part of the electromagnetic spectrum.

X-ray therapy *n.* Radiotherapy with X-rays.

X-ray tube *n.* A vacuum tube containing electrodes that accelerate electrons and direct them to a metal anode, where their impacts produce X-rays.

xy·lan (zī-lan) *n.* A yellow, gummy pentosan found in plant cell walls and yielding xylose upon hydrolysis. [XYL(O)- + -AN.]

xy·lem (zī-ləm, -lem) *n. Botany.* The supporting and water-conducting tissue of vascular plants, consisting primarily of tracheids and vessels; woody tissue. Compare **phloem.** [German *Xylem,* from Greek *xulon,* wood.]

xy·lene (zī-leen) *n.* 1. Any of three flammable isomeric hydrocarbons, $C_6H_4(CH_3)_2$, of the benzene series, obtained from wood and coal tar. Also called "xylol". 2. A mixture of these isomers used as a solvent in making lacquers and rubber cement and as an aviation fuel. [XYL(O)- + -ENE.]

xy·li·dine (zīli-deen, zilli-, -dīn, -din) *n.* 1. Any of six toxic isomers, $(CH_3)_2C_6H_3NH_2$, derived from xylene, used chiefly as dye intermediates. 2. Any of various mixtures of these isomers. [XYL(O)- + -ID + -INE.]

xylo-, xyl- *comb. form.* Indicates: 1. Wood; for example, **xylograph; xylophone.** 2. Xylene; for example, **xylidine.** [Greek *xulon†,* wood.]

xy·lo·graph (zílə-graaf, -graf) *n.* 1. An engraving on wood. 2. An impression from a wood block. —*tr.v.* **xylographed, -graphing, -graphs.** To print from a wood engraving. —**xy·log·ra·pher** (zī-lóggrəfər) *n.*

xy·log·ra·phy (zī-lóggrəfi) *n.* 1. Wood engraving, especially of an early period. 2. The art of printing texts or illustrations, sometimes with colour, from wood blocks, as distinct from typography. [French *xylographie* : XYLO- + -GRAPHY.] —**xy·lo·graph·ic** (zílə-gráffik) *adj.* —**xy·lo·graph·i·cal·ly** *adv.*

xy·loid (zī-loyd) *adj.* Of or similar to wood. [XYL(O)- + -OID.]

xy·loph·a·gous (zī-lóffəgəss) *adj.* Feeding on wood. Said especially of certain insects. [Greek *xylophagos* : XYLO- + -PHAGOUS.]

xy·lo·phone (zílə-fōn, zíllə-) *n.* A musical percussion instrument consisting of a mounted row of wooden bars graduated in length to sound a chromatic scale, played with two small mallets. [XYLO- + -PHONE.] —**xy·lo·phon·ic** (-fónnik) *adj.* —**xy·lo·phon·ist** (zī-lóffənist, zílə-fōnist) *n.*

xy·lose (zī-lōss, -lōz) *n.* A white crystalline aldose sugar, $C_5H_{10}O_5$, used in dyeing and tanning, and in diabetic diets. Also called "wood sugar". [XYL(O)- + -OSE.]

xy·lot·o·my (zī-lóttəmi) *n.* The preparation of sections of wood for microscopic study. [XYLO- + -TOMY.]

xyst (zist) *n.* Also **xys·tus** (zístəss). In ancient Greece, a covered portico, used by athletes for exercise. 2. In ancient Rome, a long tree-lined garden walk or terrace. [Latin *xystus,* from Greek *xustos,* "scraped smooth", from *xuein,* to scrape.]

xys·ter (zístər) *n.* A surgical instrument for scraping bones. [New Latin, from Greek *xuster,* scraper, from *xuein,* to scrape.]

Y

y, Y (wī) *n., pl.* **y's** or *rare* **ys, Ys** or **Y's. 1.** The 25th letter of the modern English alphabet. **2.** Any of the speech sounds represented by this letter. **3.** Anything shaped like the letter **Y**.

y, Y, y., Y. *Note:* As an abbreviation or symbol, *y* may be a small or a capital letter, with or without a full stop. Established forms or those generally preferred precede the definition. When no form is given, all four forms are in general use in that sense. **1. Y** hypercharge. **2. y** ordinate. **3. y.** year. **4. Y** yen (currency). **5. Y, Y.** *U.S.* A shortened form of the abbreviations Y.M.C.A., Y.W.C.A. **6. Y** The symbol for the element yttrium. **7.** *Mathematics.* The symbol for an algebraic variable. **8.** The 25th in a series; 24th when *J* is omitted. **9.** The second in a series consisting of *x, y,* and *z*.

y-, i- *prefix. Archaic.* Indicates the past participle; for example, **yclept.** [Middle English *i-, y-,* Old English *ge-,* from Germanic *ga-* (unattested).]

-y¹, -ey *adj. suffix.* Indicates: **1.** The existence, possibility, or possession of something specified; for example, **curly, rainy. 2.** A relationship or resemblance to something specified; for example, **glassy, watery.** [Middle English *-ie, -y, -ey,* Old English *-ig, -æg,* from Common Germanic *-iga, -aga* (unattested).]

-y² *suffix.* Indicates: **1.** A condition, state of being, or quality; for example, **beggary, jealousy. 2.** An instance or result of engaging in a specified activity; for example, **entreaty, delivery.** [Middle English *-ie,* from Old French, from Latin *-ia, -IA.*]

-y³, -ey, -ie *n. suffix.* Indicates: **1.** Smallness or diminutiveness in a person or thing; for example, **kiddy, doggy. 2.** Familiarity or endearment; for example, **sweetie, daddy. 3.** A relationship or resemblance of a person or thing to a quality or thing specified; for example, **bookie, trendy.** [Middle English *-ie.*]

yab·ber (yabbər) *intr.v.* **-bered, -bering, -bers.** *Australian & N.Z. Informal.* To jabber.

yab·by (yábbi) *n., pl.* **-bies.** *Australian & N.Z. Informal.* A crayfish.

yacht (yot) *n.* Any of various sailing or powered vessels, generally with smart, graceful lines, used for pleasure cruises or racing. —*intr.v.* **yachted, yachting, yachts.** To race, sail, or cruise in a yacht. [Earlier *yaught,* from obsolete Dutch *jaghte,* short for *jaght(-schip),* "chasing (ship)", from *jagen,* to chase, hunt, from Germanic *jagojan* (unattested).] —**yacht·ing** *n. & adj.*

yachts·man (yóts-mən) *n., pl.* **-men** (-mən). A person who owns or sails a yacht. —**yachts·man·ship** *n.*

yachts·wom·an (yóts-wōōmən) *n., pl.* **-women** (-wimmin). A woman who owns or sails a yacht.

yaf·fle (yáff'l) *n.* The green woodpecker *(see).* [Imitative of its cry.]

ya·gi (yaági, yággi) *n. Electronics.* A directional radio and television aerial consisting of a horizontal conductor with several insulated dipoles parallel to and in the plane of the conductor. Also called "yagi antenna". [After H. *Yagi* (1888–1976), Japanese engineer.]

yah¹ (yaa) *adv. Informal.* Yes. [Variant of YEA.]

yah² *interj.* Used to express derision, defiance, or disgust.

ya·hoo (yə-hōō, yaa- ‖ *U.S. also* yaá-hōō, yáy-) *n., pl.* **-hoos.** A crude or brutish person. [After the *Yahoos,* a race representing the brutish side of humanity in Jonathan Swift's *Gulliver's Travels.*]

Yahr·zeit (yáwrt-sīt, yaárt-) *n. Judaism.* Any of the anniversary days of the death of a close relative, observed by saying Kaddish, lighting a memorial candle, and sometimes fasting. [Yiddish, from Middle High German *jārzīt,* anniversary : *jār,* YEAR + *zīt,* time, TIDE.]

Yah·weh, Jah·weh (yaá-way). Also **Jah** (yaa), **Yah·veh** (-vay), **Jah·veh.** A name for God assumed by modern scholars to be a rendering of the pronunciation of the **Tetragrammaton** *(see).*

Yah·wist, Jah·wist (yaá-wist) *n.* Also **Yah·vist** (-vist). The author of the earliest sources of the Hexateuch, in which God is called Yahweh. Also called "Jehovist". Compare **Elohist.** —**Yah·wist, Jah·wis·tic** (yaa-wístik) *adj.*

yak¹ (yak) *n.* A long-haired bovine mammal, *Bos grunniens,* of the mountains of central Asia, where it is often domesticated. [Tibetan *gyag.*]

yak², yack (yak) *intr.v.* **yakked** or **yacked, yakking** or **yacking, yaks** or **yacks.** *Slang.* Also **yak·et·y-yak** (yáckiti-yăk). To talk or chatter persistently and meaninglessly. —*n. Slang.* Continuous, meaningless chatter. [Imitative.]

Ya·kut (ya-kōōt, yaa-) *n.* **1.** A member of a people living in northeastern Siberia, in the Russian Federation. **2.** The Turkic language of this people, of the Altaic family of languages.

ya·ku·za (yaákoo-zaa, -zə) *n., pl.* **-zas** or **-za.** A Japanese gangster. [Japanese, "the worst sort", from the name of a card game in which the worst sort of hand consists of the three cards *ya,* eight + *ku,* nine + *-za* (from *san*), three.]

Yale (yayl). See **New Haven** (Conn.).

Yale lock *n.* A trademark for a door lock having a revolving barrel operated by a flat, serrated key. Compare **deadlock, mortice lock.**

Yal·ta (yál-tə ‖ yáwl-). City in southern Ukraine. Situated on the Black Sea in the Crimea, it is a health and holiday resort. It was the site of the Yalta Conference (1945).

yam (yam) *n.* **1.** Any of various chiefly tropical vines of the genus *Dioscorea,* many of which have edible tuberous roots. **2.** The starchy root of such a vine, used in the tropics as food. **3.** *Chiefly U.S.* A sweet potato having reddish flesh. [Portuguese *inhame,* "edible", perhaps from Fulani *nyami,* to eat.]

Ya·ma·ni (yə-maáni), **Sheikh Ahmed Zaki** (1930–). Saudi Arabian Minister of Petroleum and Mineral Resources (1962–86), he was the leading figure in OPEC (Organisation of Petroleum Exporting Countries), and the prime mover in the Arab oil strategy of the 1970s and 1980s.

ya·men (yaá-men, -mən) *n.* The office or residence of any public official in the Chinese Empire. [Mandarin Chinese *yá mén : yá,* office of a magistrate + *mén,* door.]

yam·mer (yámmər) *v.* **-mered, -mering, -mers.** *Informal.* —*intr.* **1.** To complain peevishly or whimperingly. **2.** To talk volubly and loudly. —*tr.* To utter or say in a complaining or clamorous tone. ~*n. Informal.* An act or instance of yammering. [Alteration of earlier *yomer,* Middle English *yomeren,* Old English *geōmrian,* to lament, from *gēomor,* sorrowful, from Common Germanic.] —**yam·mer·er** *n.*

Yan'an, Yen-an, Yen·an (yán-aán, yén-, -án). Industrial city of Shaanxi province, east central China. It was the refuge of the Chinese Communists following the Long March, and was their capital from World War II until they captured Beijing (Peking) in 1949.

yang (yang) *n. Sometimes capital* **Y.** In Chinese dualistic philosophy, the active, male cosmic element, force, or principle that is opposite but complementary to **yin** *(see).* [Mandarin Chinese *yáng,* the sun, masculine element.]

Yang (yang), **Chen Ning** (1922–). Chinese-born American physicist. He was awarded the Nobel prize (1957) with Tsung-Dao Lee for the development of the theory discrediting the parity law.

yan·gon (yáng-gón, yang-). See **Rangoon.**

Yangtze Kiang. See **Chang Jiang.**

yank (yangk) *v.* **yanked, yanking, yanks.** *Informal.* —*tr.* To pull or extract suddenly; jerk: *yanked her out of the chair.* —*intr.* To pull on something suddenly; jerk. ~*n.* A sudden vigorous pull; a jerk. [19th century : origin obscure.]

Yan·kee (yángki) *n.* Also **Yank** (yangk) (sense 1). *Informal.* **1.** A native or inhabitant of the United States; an American. **2.** A native or inhabitant of a Northern state of the United States; especially, a Union soldier during the American Civil War. **3.** A native or inhabitant of New England. Sometimes used derogatorily in all senses. [Perhaps from Dutch *Janke,* diminutive of *Jan,* John (used derisively of the Dutch in the 17th century, applied to inhabitants of New England in the 18th century).] —**Yan·kee** *adj.* —**Yan·kee·dom** *n.*

Yankee Doo·dle (dōōd'l) *n.* A Yankee. [From the title of a song popular during the War of American Independence.]

Yan·kee·ism (yángki-iz'm) *n.* **1.** The quality of being a Yankee, as in one's character or way of thinking. **2.** A Yankee custom, characteristic, or peculiarity, as of language or pronunciation.

Ya·oun·dé (yaá-ōōn-dáy). Capital of the Republic of Cameroon, West Central Africa, founded by German traders (1888).

yap (yap) *n.* **1.** A sharp, shrill bark, as of a small dog; a yelp. **2.** *Slang.* Noisy, stupid, or scolding talk; jabbering. **3.** *U.S. Slang.* A crude, loud, stupid person. **4.** *Chiefly U.S. Slang.* The mouth. ~*v.* **yapped, yapping, yaps.** —*intr.* **1.** To emit a yap or yaps; bark shrilly; yelp. **2.** *Slang.* To talk noisily, stupidly, annoyingly, or at excessive length; jabber. —*tr.* To utter or express by yapping: *The Queen of Hearts yapped her disapproval to Alice.* [Imitative.]

ya·pok, ya·pock (yə-pók) *n.* An aquatic marsupial mammal, *Chironectes minimus,* of tropical America, having dense fur, webbed hind feet, and a long tail. [After *Oyapock,* river in north Brazil.]

Yar·bor·ough (yár-bərə, -brə ‖ *chiefly U.S.* -burrō) *n. Sometimes small* **y.** A full hand of 13 cards in bridge or whist containing no card higher than a nine. [After Charles Anderson Worsley (1809–97), Second Earl of *Yarborough,* who is said to have unsuccessfully bet 1,000 to 1 that such a hand would not occur.]

yard¹ (yard) *n.* **1.** *Abbr.* **yd** A unit of length in the British Imperial System, equal to 0.9144 metre (3 feet). **2.** *Nautical.* A long, tapering spar slung usually at right angles to a mast to support and spread the head of a square sail, lugsail, or lateen. [Middle English *yerde, yarde,* Old English *gerd,* staff, twig, measuring rod, from West Germanic *gazdjō* (unattested).]

yard² *n.* **1.** A tract of ground adjacent to, surrounding, or surrounded by a building or group of buildings. **2.** A tract of ground, often enclosed, used for a specific type of work, business, or other activity. Often used in combination: *shipyard; graveyard.* **3.** An area provided with a system of tracks where railway trains are made up and carriages are shunted, stored, or serviced. **4.** *U.S.* A winter pasture for deer or other grazing animals. **5.** An enclosed tract of ground in which animals, such as chickens or pigs, are kept. **6.** *U.S.* The garden of a house, especially if relatively small. —**the Yard.**

Informal. In Britain, **Scotland Yard** *(see).*

~*v.* **yarded, yarding, yards.** —*tr.* To enclose, collect, or put in or as if in a yard. —*intr.* To gather in or as if in a yard. [Middle English *yarde, yard,* Old English *geard,* enclosure, residence, from Germanic *gardaz* (unattested).]

yard·age¹ (yárdij) *n.* **1.** The amount or length of something measured in yards. **2.** Cloth sold by the yard.

yardage² *n.* **1.** The use of a railway yard for loading and transporting cattle. **2.** The fee paid for such use.

yard·arm (yárd-aarm) *n.* Either end of the yard of a square sail.

yard grass *n.* Any of several weedy grasses of the genus *Eleusine.*

yard·man (yárd-mən, -man) *n., pl.* **-men** (-mən, -men). A man employed in a yard, especially a railway yard.

yard of ale *n.* **1.** An extremely long and narrow drinking glass, about a yard long, and having a volume usually of two or three pints. **2.** The beer or ale held by such a glass, sometimes drained in one draught in competitions in British pubs.

yard·stick (yárd-stik) *n.* **1.** A graduated measuring stick one yard in length. **2.** Any test or standard used in measurement, comparison, or judgment.

yare (yair) *adj. Archaic.* **1.** Responding easily; manageable; manoeuvrable. Said of a sea vessel. **2.** Bright; lively; quick. **3.** Ready; prepared.
~*adv. Obsolete.* Soon; quickly; promptly. [Middle English *yare,* Old English *gearo, gearu,* finished, ready.] —**yare·ly** *adv.*

Yarmouth. See **Great Yarmouth.**

yar·mul·ke (yármǝlkǝ) *n., pl.* **-kes.** A small skullcap worn by male Jews on religious and celebratory occasions and by male Orthodox Jews at all times. [Yiddish, from Polish and Ukrainian *yarmulka,* perhaps from Turkish *yağmurluk,* raincoat, from *yağmur,* rain.]

yarn (yarn) *n.* **1.** A continuous strand of twisted threads of natural or synthetic material, such as wool, cotton, flax, or nylon, used in weaving or knitting. **2.** *Informal.* A long, involved story or a tale of real or fictitious adventures, often elaborated upon by the teller during the telling.
~*intr.v.* **yarned, yarning, yarns.** *Informal.* To tell a long, complicated story; spin a yarn. [Middle English *yarn,* Old English *gearn.*]

yarn·dyed (yárn-dīd) *adj.* Said of material that is woven from yarn already dyed.

yar·row (yárrō) *n.* Any of several plants of the genus *Achillea;* especially, *A. millefolium,* native to Eurasia, having finely dissected foliage and flat clusters of usually white flowers. Also called "milfoil". [Middle English *yar(ro)we,* Old English *gearwe,* from West Germanic *garw-* (unattested).]

yash·mak, yash·mac (yásh-mak) *n.* A veil worn by Muslim women in public to cover their faces. [Arabic *yashmaq, yashmak.*]

Yass-Canberra. See **Australian Capital Territory.**

yat·a·ghan, yat·a·gan (yáttǝ-gǝn, -gan) *n.* Also **at·a·ghan** (áttǝ-). A Turkish single-edged sword or scimitar having a slightly S-shaped blade with a pommel or knob on the end, and lacking a handle guard. [Turkish *yatağan.*]

yau·ti·a (yáwti-ǝ) *n.* Any of various tropical American plants of the genus *Xanthosoma;* especially *X. sagittifolium,* which is cultivated for its starchy tubers. Also called "cocoyam". [American Spanish, from Taino.]

yaw (yaw) *v.* **yawed, yawing, yaws.** —*intr.* **1.** To deviate temporarily from the intended course. Used of a ship. **2.** To turn about the vertical axis. Used of an aircraft or projectile. —*tr.* To cause to yaw.
~*n.* **1.** The action of yawing. **2.** The extent of this movement, measured in degrees. [16th century : origin obscure.]

yawl (yawl) *n.* **1.** A two-masted fore-and-aft-rigged sailing vessel similar to the ketch but having a smaller jigger mast stepped abaft the rudder. Also called "dandy". **2.** A ship's small boat, manned by oarsmen. Compare **ketch.** [Middle Low German *jolle†.*]

yawn (yawn) *v.* **yawned, yawning, yawns.** —*intr.* **1.** To open the mouth wide with a deep intake of air, usually involuntarily, from drowsiness, fatigue, or boredom. **2.** To open wide; gape: *The chasm yawned at our feet.* —*tr.* To utter wearily, as if in yawning.
~*n.* **1.** An act or instance of yawning. **2.** *Informal.* A dull or boring event or person. [Middle English *yonen, yenen,* Old English *geonian, ginian.*] —**yawn·er** *n.* —**yawn·ing·ly** *adv.*

yawp (yawp) *intr.v.* **yawped, yawping, yawps.** *U.S.* **1.** To utter a sharp cry; bark; yelp. **2.** *Slang.* To talk loudly and stupidly.
~*n.* **1.** A bark; a yelp. **2.** *Slang.* Loud, stupid talk. [Middle English *yolpen,* perhaps variant of *yelpen,* YELP.]

yaws (yawz) *n. Used with a singular verb.* An infectious tropical skin disease, caused by a spirochaete, *Treponema pertenue,* and characterised by multiple red pimples. Also called "framboesia". [17th century : perhaps from a Cariban word.]

y-ax·is (wī-ak-siss) *n., pl.* **y-axes** (-seez). **1.** The vertical axis of a two-dimensional Cartesian coordinate system. **2.** One of three axes in a three-dimensional Cartesian coordinate system.

Y-chro·mo·some (wī-krŏmǝ-sōm) *n.* The smaller of the two types of sex chromosome, associated with male characteristics in most animals, including humans, and occurring paired with one **X-chromosome** *(see)* in the body cells of such male animals.

y-clept, y-cleped (i-klépt). *Archaic.* Past participle of **clepe.**

yd yard (measurement).

ye¹ (thee, *also* yee) *adj. Archaic.* The. Still used in names, humorously or for effect, to convey a sense of history: *ye olde taverne.* [Incorrect transcription resulting from the resemblance between the runic letter called thorn (properly transcribed as *th*) and the letter *y* in certain Middle English manuscripts. See **thorn**.]

ye² (yee) *pron.* **1.** *Poetic & Archaic.* You (plural). **2.** *Regional.* You (singular). [Middle English, Old English *gē.*]

yea (yay) *adv.* **1.** Yes; aye. Now archaic except in recording or expressing a vote. **2.** *Archaic.* Indeed; truly.
~*n.* **1.** A statement or vote in favour of a motion. **2.** One who votes in favour of a motion: *The yeas have it.* [Middle English *ye, ya,* Old English *gēa,* yes.]

yeah (yair) *adv. Informal.* Yes. [Informal pronunciation of *yes.*]

yean (yeen) *v.* **yeaned, yeaning, yeans.** —*intr.* To bear young. Used of sheep and goats. —*tr.* To bear; give birth to. [Middle English *yenen,* Old English *geēanian* (unattested) : *ge-,* Y- + *ēanian,* to bear young, to lamb.]

yean·ling (yéen-ling) *n.* The young of a sheep or goat; a lamb or kid. [YEAN + -LING (little).] —**yean·ling** *adj.*

year (yeer) *n. Abbr.* **y., yr.** **1.** The period of time as measured by the Gregorian calendar in which the earth completes a single revolution around the sun. It is divided into 12 months, 52 weeks, or 365 or 366 days, and begins on January 1 and ends on December 31. Also called "calendar year". **2.** See **sidereal year.** **3.** See **tropical year.** **4.** A period of about equal length in other calendars. **5.** Any period of approximately this duration: *We were married a year ago.* **6.** A period equal to the calendar year but beginning on a different date: *a fiscal year.* **7.** A set period of time, usually shorter than 12 months, devoted to some special activity: *the academic year.* **8.** A group of students that form any of a number of distinct levels of academic progress at a school, college, or other educational institution: *Sarah was in the same year as James at Cambridge; She's a third-year student.* **9.** *Plural.* Age; especially, old age: *feeling his years.* **10.** *Plural.* Time; especially, a long time: *It will take years to do it.* —**the year dot.** *Informal.* A very early stage or time. —**year and a day.** *Law.* In various legal matters, a period of time specified to ensure that a full year is completed. —**year in, year out.** Continuously or regularly over a long period of time. [Middle English *year, yere,* Old English *gēar.*]

year·book (yéer-bŏŏk, yér- ‖ -bŏŏk) *n.* A documentary, memorial, or historical book published every year, containing information about the previous year and for the current year.

year·ling (yéer-ling, yér-) *n.* **1.** An animal that is one year old or has not completed its second year. **2.** A thoroughbred racehorse, regarded as a colt or filly one year old dating from January 1 of the year that it was foaled. —**year·ling** *adj.*

year·long (yéer-long, yér- ‖ -lawng) *adj.* Lasting through one year.

year·ly (yéer-li, yér-) *adj.* **1.** Occurring once a year or every year; annual. **2.** Of or lasting for a year.
~*adv.* Once a year; annually.

yearn (yern) *intr.v.* **yearned, yearning, yearns.** **1.** To have a strong or deep desire; be filled with longing. Usually used with *for* or *to: yearns for his native land.* **2.** *Literary.* To feel deep pity, sympathy, or tenderness. [Middle English *yernen,* Old English *gyrnan, giernan,* to strive, desire.] —**yearn·ing·ly** *adv.*
Synonyms: *yearn, long, pine, hanker, hunger, thirst.*

yearn·ing (yérning) *n.* A deep longing.

year·round (yéer-równd, yér-) *adj.* Existing, active, or continuous throughout the year; during all seasons.

yeast (yeest) *n.* **1.** Any of various unicellular fungi of the genus *Saccharomyces* and related genera, reproducing by budding and capable of fermenting carbohydrates. **2.** Froth consisting of yeast cells together with the carbon dioxide they produce in the process of fermentation, present in or added to fruit juices and other substances in the production of alcoholic beverages. **3.** A commercial preparation, either in powdered or compressed form, containing yeast cells and inert material such as meal, and used especially as a leavening agent or as a dietary supplement to treat vitamin B deficiency. **4.** Foam; froth. **5.** An agent of ferment or activity.
~*intr.v.* **yeasted, yeasting, yeasts.** **1.** To ferment. **2.** To froth or foam. [Middle English *yest,* Old English *gist, gyst.*]

yeast·y (yéesti) *adj.* **-ier, -iest.** **1.** Of, similar to, or containing yeast. **2.** Causing or characterised by a ferment. **3.** Restless; turbulent. **4.** Frothy; frivolous. —**yeast·i·ly** *adv.* —**yeast·i·ness** *n.*

Yeats (yayts), **William Butler** (1865–1939). Irish poet and playwright. He helped to found the Irish National Theatre Company at the Abbey Theatre, Dublin; he wrote many short plays, mostly on mythological themes. His poetry varies from early love lyrics to the complex symbolist poems of such later collections as *The Winding Stair* (1929) and *Last Poems* (1939). Nobel prize (1923).

Ye·ka·te·rin·burg (yi-káttǝrin-burg; *Russian* yi-kǝ-tirrin-bŏŏrk). Also **Je·ka·te·rin·burg, Ekaterinburg** (yi-), and from 1924 to 1992 **Sverd·lovsk** (sveerd-lófsk). A city in central Russia, situated in the eastern foothills of the Ural mountains. In 1918, Tsar Nicholas II was executed here with his family. It is an industrial and cultural centre, and a junction on the Trans-Siberian Railway.

yell (yel) *v.* **yelled, yelling, yells.** —*intr.* To cry out loudly, as in pain, fright, surprise, or enthusiasm. —*tr.* To utter loudly; shout.
~*n.* **1.** A loud cry; a shriek; a shout. **2.** *U.S.* A rhythmic cheer uttered or chanted in unison by a group: *a college yell.* [Middle English *yellen,* Old English *giellan,* to sound, shout, from Germanic *gel-, gal-* (unattested).] —**yell·er** *n.*

yel·low (yéllō) *n.* **1.** Any of a group of colours of a hue resembling that of ripe lemons and varying in lightness and saturation; the hue of that portion of the spectrum lying between green and orange; one of the psychological primary hues, evoked in the normal observer by radiant energy of wavelength approximately 580 nano-

metres; also one of the subtractive primaries. **2.** A pigment or dye having this hue. **3.** Something that has this hue, such as: **a.** Yellow clothing. **b.** The yellow ball in snooker. **c.** In the United States, an amber traffic light. **4.** The yolk of an egg. **5.** *Plural.* Any of various plant diseases usually caused by fungi of the genus *Fusarium* or viruses of the genus *Chlorogenus* and characterised by yellow or yellowish discoloration.
~*adj.* **1.** Of the colour yellow. **2.** Designating a person or a people, such as the mongoloid race, having yellowish skin. **3.** *Slang.* Cowardly. **4.** Treating news material in a sensational, exaggerated way. Said of newspapers, especially in the phrase *the yellow press.*
~*v.* **yellowed, -lowing, -lows.** —*tr.* To make or render yellow. —*intr.* To become yellow. [Middle English *yelwa, yelow,* Old English *geolu.*] —**yel·low·ish, yel·low·y** *adj.* —**yel·low·ly** *adv.* —**yel·low·ness** *n.*

yellow archangel *n.* A creeping perennial woodland plant, *Lamiastrum galeobdolon,* resembling the white dead-nettle but having yellow flowers. Also called "yellow dead-nettle".

yel·low·bark (yéllō-baark) *n.* A kind of tree bark, **calisaya** *(see).*

yel·low-bel·lied (yéllō-béllid) *adj.* **1.** Having a belly yellow or yellowish in colour, as certain birds and fish do. **2.** *Slang.* Cowardly.

yel·low·bird (yéllō-burd) *n.* Any of various yellow or predominantly yellow birds.

yellow fever *n.* An acute infectious disease of subtropical and tropical New World areas, caused by a virus transmitted by a mosquito of the genus *Aëdes* and characterised by jaundice and dark-coloured vomit resulting from haemorrhages. Also called "yellow jack".

yellow flag *n.* A common yellow-flowered iris, *Iris pseudacorus,* found by streams and on marshy land.

yel·low-ham·mer (yéllō-hammər) *n.* A Eurasian bird, *Emberiza citrinella,* having brown and yellow plumage. Also called "yellow bunting". [Earlier *yelambre :* perhaps YELLOW + *-ambre,* ultimately from Old English *amore, omer,* an unidentified bird.]

yellow jack *n.* **1.** Yellow fever. **2.** *Nautical.* A yellow flag hoisted to request pratique or to warn of disease on board.

Yel·low·knife (yéllō-nīf). Capital of Northwest Territories, north Canada. Situated on the Great Slave Lake, it was founded (1935) after the discovery of gold and is a mining and commercial centre.

yel·low·legs (yéllō-legz) *n., pl.* **yellowlegs.** Either of two North American wading birds, *Tringa melanoleuca* or *T. flavipes,* having yellow legs and a long, narrow bill, found in Europe as vagrants.

yellow lines *pl.n.* In Britain, yellow stripes painted along the sides of a roadway to indicate parking restrictions. *Double yellow lines* forbid parking at all times; *single yellow lines* forbid parking at certain times.

yellow metal *n.* **1.** A form of brass containing about 60 per cent copper and 40 per cent zinc. **2.** Gold *(see).*

Yellow Pages *pl.n.* Trade name for a telephone directory or section of a directory, printed on yellow pages, that classifies businesses alphabetically according to the service they provide.

yellow peril *n.* The threat or the alleged threat that Oriental races, especially the Chinese, will invade or destroy Europe or Western civilised countries.

yellow pimpernel *n.* See **pimpernel.**

yellow poplar *n.* The **tulip tree** *(see).*

yellow rattle *n.* A semiparasitic annual plant, *Rhinanthus minor,* having two-lipped yellow flowers and an inflated fruit inside which the ripened seeds rattle.

Yellow River. See **Huang He.**

Yellow Sea. *Chinese* **Huang Hai** or **Hwang Hai** (hwáng hí). Inlet of the west Pacific Ocean. Situated between Korea and northeast China, it receives its name from the yellow silt carried into it by the Huang He (Yellow River), Yalü Jiang, and Liao He.

yellow spot *n.* A part of the human retina, the **macula lutea** *(see).*

Yel·low·stone National Park (yéllō-stōn). The oldest and largest national park of the United States. Lying mainly in Wyoming, with small areas in Idaho and Montana, it is chiefly a volcanic plateau in the Rocky mountains. Established in 1872, it has over 3,000 geysers and hot springs, the best-known being Old Faithful.

yellow streak *n.* A proneness to cowardice and disloyalty.

yel·low-tail moth (yéllō-tayl) *n.* A white silky moth, *Euproctis similis,* with a tuft of yellow hairs at the end of the abdomen.

yellow water lily *n.* A yellow-flowered aquatic plant, *Nuphar lutea,* having large floating leaves. Also called "brandy bottle".

yel·low-wood (yéllō-wŏŏd) *n.* **1.** A tree, *Cladrastis lutea,* of the southeast United States, having compound leaves, drooping clusters of white flowers, and yellow wood yielding a yellow dye. Also *U.S.* "gopherwood". **2.** Any of various other trees having yellow wood. **3.** The wood of any of these trees.

yelp (yelp) *v.* **yelped, yelping, yelps.** —*intr.* To utter a sharp, short bark or cry, as in pain or surprise. Used especially of a dog. —*tr.* To utter by yelping.
~*n.* A sharp, short cry or bark. [Middle English *yelpen,* to cry aloud, Old English *gielpan,* to boast, exult (imitative).] —**yelp·er** *n.*

Yel·tsin (yél-tsin), **Boris (Nicolayevich)** (1931–). Russian politician. Head of the Communist Party in Moscow from 1985, he has been a prominent radical since the early days of glasnost. In 1991 he was elected president of the Russian Federation with wide powers, increased under the new constitution of 1993. Re-elected 1996.

Yem·en (yémmən), **Republic of.** Poor, desert country in the southwest Arabian Peninsula, southwest Asia, formed by the unification in 1990 of the former Yemen Arab Republic and South Yemen. Much

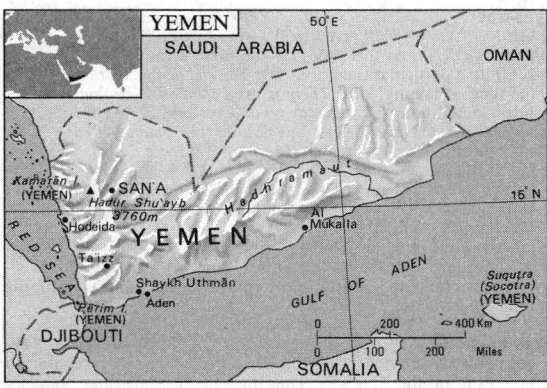

of the country is arid or mountainous, though there are fertile areas in the Hadhramaut valley and the coastal plains. The people live chiefly from the land, producing millet, wheat, cotton, coffee, sheep, and goats. Aden's oil refinery accounts for the bulk of exports, petroleum being the major import. Yemenis working abroad are another important source of foreign exchange. Area, 536 869 square kilometres (207,286 square miles). Population, 15,920,000. Capital, San'a. —**Yem·en·i** *n. & adj.*

Yemen Arab Republic. Former republic in southwest Asia. See **Yemen, Republic of.**

yen[1] (yen) *intr.v.* **yenned, yenning, yens.** *Informal.* To yearn; long. ~*n. Informal.* A yearning; a longing. [Cantonese *yan,* craving, corresponding to Mandarin Chinese *yĭn.*]

yen[2] *n., pl.* **yen. 1.** *Symbol* **Y.** The basic monetary unit of Japan. **2.** A coin or note worth one yen. [Japanese *en,* from Mandarin Chinese *yuán,* "round (piece)", dollar.]

Yenan. See **Yan'an.**

yeo·man (yŏ-mən) *n., pl.* **-men** (-mən). **1.** An independent farmer; especially, formerly in England, a member of a class of small freeholding farmers below the gentry. **2.** A yeoman of the guard. **3.** Formerly, an attendant, servant, or lesser official in a royal or noble household. **4.** A petty officer chiefly concerned with signalling in the Royal Navy or with clerical duties in certain other navies. **5.** *Archaic.* An assistant or other subordinate, as of a sheriff or craftsman. **6.** A member of the British volunteer yeomanry. [Middle English *yoman, yuman,* perhaps contraction of *yongman :* YOUNG + MAN.]

yeo·man·ly (yŏmənli) *adj.* **1.** Pertaining to or ranking as a yeoman. **2.** Characteristic of or befitting a yeoman; sturdy, staunch, or workmanlike. —**yeo·man·ly** *adv.*

yeoman of the guard *n.* A member of a ceremonial guard attending the British sovereign and royal family, consisting of 100 yeomen with their officers.

yeo·man·ry (yŏmənri) *n.* **1.** The class or a body of yeomen. **2.** A British volunteer cavalry force organised in 1761 to serve as a home guard and later incorporated into the Territorial Army (1907).

yep (yep) *adv.* Also **yup** (yup). *Informal.* Yes. [From ·YES (after NOPE).]

yer·ba ma·té (yaír-bə máa-tay, yér-, maa-táy) *n.* A tree, the **maté** *(see).* [Spanish *yerba,* herb, from Latin *herba,* plant, HERB.]

Ye·re·van (yérri-ván, -vaán). Also **Erevan** (érri-). Capital of Armenia. Situated on the river Razdan, it passed several times between Persia and Turkey until ceded to Russia (1828). It is an industrial centre.

yes (yess) *adv.* **1.** It is so; as you say or ask; opposed to "no". Used in expressing affirmation, agreement, positive confirmation, or consent. **2.** Indeed; what is more. Used to introduce a more emphatic phrase: *I could do with a drink, yes, a very strong drink.* **3.** I hear you and am ready to give my attention to you. Used in response to being addressed or summoned.
~*n., pl.* **yeses. 1.** An affirmative or consenting response. **2.** An affirmative vote or voter. [Middle English *yes,* Old English *gese :* probably *gēa,* YEA + *síe,* "may it be", third-person singular present subjunctive of *béon,* to BE.]

ye·shi·va, ye·shi·vah (yə-shée-və) *n., pl.* **-vas** or **-voth** (-vot, -vót). **1.** An Orthodox Jewish school for rabbinical and Talmudic studies. **2.** A Jewish day school for religious and secular studies.

yes-man (yéss-man) *n., pl.* **-men** (-men). *Informal.* A person who slavishly agrees with his superior or any other person with whom he wishes to ingratiate himself; a sycophant.

yester– *comb. form.* Indicates: **1.** The day before the present day; for example, **yestermorning. 2.** A previous and indeterminate period of time; for example, **yesteryear.** [Middle English *yister-,* Old English *geostra(n).*]

yes·ter·day (yéstər-di, -day) *n.* **1.** The day before the present day. **2.** *Sometimes plural.* Time in the immediate or recent past.
~*adv.* **1.** On the day before the present day. **2.** A short while ago. [Middle English *yesterdai,* Old English *geostran dæg :* YESTER- + DAY.]

yes·ter·year (yéstər-yeer, -yer) *n. Literary.* **1.** The year before the current one. **2.** Time past, especially as thought of nostalgically; yore. —**yes·ter·year** *adv.*

yes·treen (ye-strḗen) *n. Scottish.* Yesterday evening. [Middle English : YESTER- + E'EN (evening).] **—yes·treen** *adj.*

yet (yet) *adv.* **1.** At this time; for the present; now: *Don't sing yet.* **2.** Up to a particular time; thus far: *The end had not yet come.* **3.** In the time remaining; still: *There is yet a solution to be found.* **4.** Besides; in addition: *Play the tape yet another time.* **5.** Even; still: *a yet sadder tale.* **6.** Nevertheless; but despite this: *young yet wise.* **7.** At some future time; eventually: *They may yet score a goal.* **—as yet.** Up to the present time; up to now.
~conj. Nevertheless; and despite this: *He said he would be late, yet he arrived on time.* —See Synonyms at **but.** [Middle English *yet, yit,* Old English *gīet(a)*†.]
   Usage: Yet, as an adverb of time in the sense "up to the present", occurs with the perfect tense: *Have they arrived yet?* However, it is often used, mainly in informal American English, with the simple past tense: *Did you eat yet?*

ye·ti (yĕtti) *n.* The **abominable snowman** *(see).* [Tibetan.]

Yev·tu·shen·ko (yĕv-tōō-shḗngkō; *Russian* yiftōō-shḗngkə), **Yev·geny (Alexandrovich)** (1933–). Russian poet. His works contained criticisms of the U.S.S.R. They include *A Precocious Autobiography* (1963) and *Stolen Apples* (1972). In 1995 he published *Premorning* (poetry) and *The Verses of the Century* (anthology of 20th-century Russian poetry).

yew (yōō ‖ yew) *n.* **1.** Any of several evergreen trees or shrubs of the genus *Taxus,* of which the flat, dark-green needles and often the scarlet berries are poisonous. **2.** The wood of a yew; especially, the durable, fine-grained wood of an Old World species, *T. baccata,* used in cabinetmaking and for archery bows. [Middle English *ew,* Old English *ēow, īw.*]

Y-fronts *pl. n.* Tight-fitting underpants for men or boys in which the front opening has seams in the shape of an inverted Y.

Ygg·dra·sil, Yg·dra·sil (ĭgdrə-sil) *n. Norse Mythology.* The great ash tree that holds together earth, heaven, and hell by its roots and branches. [Old Norse, probably "the horse of Yggr" : *Yggr,* Odin, from *yggr,* variant of *uggr,* frightful (see **ugly**) + *drasill*†, horse.]

Y.H.A. Youth Hostels Association (in Britain).

YHWH, YHVH, JHWH, JHVH The Hebrew Tetragrammaton representing the name of God.

Yid·dish (yĭddish) *n.* A language derived from High German dialects with additional vocabulary drawn from Hebrew and from Slavonic languages, written in Hebrew characters and spoken chiefly as a vernacular in eastern European Jewish communities and by emigrants from these communities throughout the world. Also called "Judaeo-German". [Yiddish *Yidish,* from Middle High German *jüdisch,* Jewish, from *Jüde,* Jew, from Old High German *judo,* from Latin *Jūdaeus,* JEW.] **—Yid·dish** *adj.*

Yid·dish·ism (yĭddish-iz'm) *n.* **1.** The advocacy or promotion of Yiddish language and literature. **2.** A word, expression, or usage characteristic of Yiddish.

yield (yeeld) *v.* **yield·ed, yield·ing, yields.** *—tr.* **1.** To give forth by or as if by a natural process, especially by cultivation: *a field that yields much corn.* **2.** To provide or give in return; be productive of: *an investment that yields six per cent.* **3.** To surrender (something) in deference or defeat; relinquish: *yielded the field to a rival.* **4.** To grant or concede: *yield right of way; yield the point in the argument.* *—intr.* **1.** To provide or give a return; be productive. **2.** To give up; surrender; submit. **3.** To give way to pressure, force, or persuasion: *the bolts eventually yielded to our blows.* **4.** To give way or precedence; be overcome. Used with *to: yielded to the logic of her case.* —See Synonyms at **relinquish.**
~n. **1.** The amount yielded or produced; a product. **2.** The profit obtained from investment; a return. **3.** The energy released by an explosion, especially by a nuclear explosion, expressed in units of weight of TNT required to produce an equivalent release: *a 100-megaton yield.* **4.** The amount of a specific product produced by a chemical reaction, often expressed as a percentage of the stoichiometric quantity obtainable. [Middle English *yieldan,* Old English *gieldan,* to yield, pay, from Germanic *geldhan* (unattested), to pay.] **—yield·er** *n.*
   Synonyms: yield, relent, bow, defer, submit, capitulate.

yield·ing (yḗelding) *adj.* Inclined to yield; submissive. **—yield·ing·ly** *adv.* **—yield·ing·ness** *n.*

yield point *n.* The point, beyond the elastic limit of a material, at which a sudden increase in strain occurs with only a small increase in stress.

yin (yin) *n. Often capital* **Y.** The passive, female cosmic element, force, or principle that is opposite but complementary to **yang** *(see)* in Chinese dualistic philosophy. [Mandarin Chinese *yīn,* the moon, shade, femininity.]

yip (yip) *n. U.S.* A sharp, high-pitched bark; a yelp.
~intr.v. **yipped, yipping, yips.** *U.S.* To make such sounds; yelp. [Imitative.]

yip·pee (yíppi, yi-peé) *interj.* Used to express joy, elation, or excitement.

yips (yipss) *pl. n. Informal.* In sports, especially golf, an attack of tension or nervous twitching that affects concentration and performance adversely. Used with *the.* [Origin obscure.]

-yl *n. comb. form. Chemistry.* Indicates a radical; for example, **carbonyl, ethyl.** [French *-yle,* from Greek *hulē,* wood, matter.]

y·lang-y·lang, i·lang-i·lang (éelang-éelang) *n.* **1.** A tropical Asian tree, *Cananga odorata* (or *Canangium odoratum*), having fragrant greenish-yellow flowers that yield an oil used in perfumery. **2.** An oil or perfume obtained from the flowers of this tree. [Tagalog *alang-ilang.*]

y·lem (ī-ləm, -lem) *n.* The hypothetical matter, thought to consist of neutrons, from which the chemical elements may have been derived, in the big-bang theory of the creation of the universe. [Middle English, from Old French, from Latin *hȳlē,* from Greek *hulē,* matter.]

Y.M.C.A. Young Men's Christian Association.

Y.M.H.A. Young Men's Hebrew Association.

-yne *n. comb. form. Chemistry.* Indicates a triple bond in a compound; for example, **alkyne, ethyne.**

yob (yob) *n. Also* **yob·bo** (yóbbō). *British Informal.* A loutish or ill-mannered youth or man. [Back-slang for BOY.]

yod[1]**, yodh** (yod, yōōd) *n.* The tenth letter of the Hebrew alphabet. [Hebrew *yōdh,* from *yādh,* hand.]

yod[2] *n.* The sound (y), especially when considered as a historical phonetic description. [Probably from YOD (Hebrew letter).]

yo·del (yōd'l) *v.* **-delled** *or U.S.* **-deled, -delling** *or U.S.* **-deling, -dels.** *—intr.* To sing so that the voice fluctuates between the normal chest voice and a falsetto. *—tr.* To sing (a melody without words) in this fashion.
~n. A song or cry that is yodelled. [German *jodeln* (imitative).] **—yo·del·ler** *n.*

yo·ga (yōgə) *n.* **1.** *Often capital* **Y.** A Hindu discipline aimed at training the consciousness for a state of perfect spiritual insight and union with the universal spirit. **2.** A system of exercises practised as part of this discipline to promote control of the body and mind. Also called "hatha yoga". [Sanskrit, union, yoking.] **—yo·gic** *adj.* **—yo·gism** *n.*

yogh (yog, yōg, yōk, yōkh) *n.* A Middle English letter ʒ representing a velar or palatal fricative, usually voiced. [Middle English *yogh, yok,* perhaps from *yok,* YOKE (from its shape).]

yog·hurt, yog·urt (yóggərt, yóggoort ‖ *chiefly U.S.* yŏ-gərt, -goort) *n.* A food of a custard-like consistency, prepared from milk curdled by bacteria, especially *Lactobacillus bulgaricus* and *Streptococcus thermophilus,* and often sweetened or flavoured with fruit. [Turkish *yoğurt.*]

yo·gi (yōgi) *n., pl.* **-gis.** *Also* **yo·gin** (yōgin). **1.** One who practises yoga. **2.** One who teaches or is a master of yoga. [Hindi, from Sanskrit *yogin,* from *yoga,* YOGA.]

yo·him·bine (yō-him-been) *n.* A poisonous alkaloid, $C_{21}H_{26}N_2O_3$, derived from the bark of a tree, *Corynanthe yohimbe* used in medicine as an adrenergic blocking agent, and formerly used as an aphrodisiac. [New Latin *yohimbe* (the tree), from Bantu.]

yoicks (yoyks) *interj.* Used as a hunting cry to urge the hounds after the fox.

yoke (yōk) *n., pl.* **yokes** *or* **yoke** (for sense 2). **1.** A crossbar with two U-shaped pieces that encircle the necks of a pair of oxen, mules, or other draught animals working in a team. **2.** A pair of draught animals joined by such a device or trained to work together. **3.** A frame or crossbar designed to be carried across a person's shoulders with equally weighed loads, such as buckets of water, suspended from each end. **4.** A bar used with a double harness to connect the collar of each horse to the tongue of a wagon, coach, or other trailer. **5.** *Nautical.* A crossbar on a ship's rudder to which the steering cables are connected. **6.** A clamp or vice that holds a part in place or controls its movement or that holds two parts together. **7.** A piece of a garment that is closely fitted, either around the neck and shoulders or at the hips, and from which an unfitted or gathered part of the garment falls. **8.** Something that connects or joins together; a bond: *the yoke of marriage.* **9.** A structure made of two upright spears with a third laid across them, under which conquered enemies of ancient Rome were forced to march in subjection. **10.** Any form or symbol of subjugation or bondage: *the yoke of a dictator.* —See Synonyms at **couple.**
~v. **yoked, yoking, yokes.** *—tr.* **1.** To fit or join with a yoke. **2. a.** To harness a draft animal to. **b.** To harness (a draught animal) to something. **3.** To connect, join, or bind together. **4.** *Obsolete.* To force into bondage or servitude; oppress. *—intr.* To become connected, joined, or bound together. [Middle English *yok,* Old English *geoc.*]

yoke·fel·low (yōk-fellō) *n.* A companion or partner, as in work or marriage. Also called "yokemate".

yo·kel (yōk'l) *n.* A country bumpkin or rustic; especially, one who is gullible or naive. [Perhaps from dialectal *yokel,* green woodpecker (probably imitative of its note).]

Yo·ko·ha·ma (yōkō-haámə). Capital and port of Kanagawa prefecture, Honshu island, Japan. Situated on Tokyo Bay, it is the country's third largest city. It was badly damaged by an earthquake (1923) and bombing in World War II.

yolk (yōk) *n.* **1.** The nutritive material of an animal ovum, consisting primarily of protein and fat; especially, the yellow, usually spheroidal mass of the egg of a bird or reptile, surrounded by the albumen. **2.** A greasy substance found in unprocessed sheep's wool. [Middle English *yolke,* Old English *geoloca, geolca,* from *geolu,* YELLOW.] **—yolked** *adv.* **—yolk·y** *adj.*

yolk sac *n. Zoology.* A membranous sac attached to the embryo and providing early nourishment in the form of yolk in bony fishes, sharks, reptiles, birds, and primitive mammals, and functioning as the circulatory system of the human embryo prior to the initiation of internal circulation by the pumping of the heart.

Yom Kip·pur (yóm kíppər, ki-poór) *n.* The holiest Jewish holiday, celebrated on the tenth day of Tishri, on which fasting and prayer for the atonement of sins are prescribed. Also called "Day of Atonement". [Hebrew *yōm kippūr : yōm,* day + *kippūr,* atonement, from *kippēr,* they covered, they made atonement.]

yomp (yomp) *n. Slang.* The act of advancing on foot carrying one's equipment, especially military equipment, at a fast pace. [Perhaps imitative of the sound of rapid marching.] —**yomp** *intr.v.*

yon (yon) *adj.* **1.** *Chiefly Northern British.* That. **2.** *Poetic.* Yonder. ~*pron. Chiefly Northern British.* That. ~*adv. Poetic.* Yonder. [Middle English *yon,* Old English *geon.*]

yon·der (yóndər) *adj.* Being at an indicated distance, usually within sight. ~*adv.* In or at that indicated relatively distant place; over there. [Middle English *yonder,* from *yond,* YOND.]

yo·ni (yṓni) *n.* In Hinduism, a representation of the vulva symbolising the feminine principle. [Sanskrit *yōni†,* abode, womb.]

yonks (yongks) *adv. Informal.* A long time; ages: *left yonks ago.* Probably a slang variant of *years* or *donkey's years.*

yoo·hoo (yṓo-hṓo) *interj.* Used to attract someone's attention.

yore (yor ‖ yōr) *n.* Time long past. Now archaic except ↵ the phrase *days of yore.* [Middle English *yore,* Old English *gēara,* formerly, once, perhaps from the genitive plural of *gēar,* YEAR.]

york (york) *tr. v.* **yorked, yorking, yorks.** *Cricket.* To bowl a yorker or dismiss by bowling a yorker to (a batsman). [Back-formation from YORKER.]

York[1] (york) *n.* The family name of the English royal family from 1461 to 1485.

York[2]. *Latin.* **E·bo·ra·cum** (é-baw-raákəm, áy-). City of north Yorkshire, northeast England. Situated at the confluence of the rivers Ouse and Foss, it was a Roman military post. An important market for the wool trade during the Middle Ages, York is a walled city with many medieval remains and is overlooked by the cathedral, York Minster (13th–15th century).

York, Richard Plantagenet, 3rd Duke of (1411–60). English nobleman. A descendant of the third son of Edward III, he was named by Henry VI as heir to the throne until Henry himself had a son. His claims led to the outbreak of the Wars of the Roses (1455–85) between the Yorkists and Lancastrians, and after Yorkist victories he was reinstated as heir. He was killed in battle at Wakefield.

york·er (yórkər) *n.* In cricket, a ball bowled with speed directly at the feet of the facing batsman. [Probably associated with Yorkshire County Cricket Club.]

York·ist (yórkist) *n.* A member of the Yorkist faction in the Wars of the Roses (1455–85). —**York·ist** *adj.*

York·shire (yórk-shər, -sheer). Former county of northeast England. Bordering the North Sea, in 1974 its area was redistributed between the counties of Humberside, North Yorkshire, West Yorkshire, and South Yorkshire, with more changes in 1997. It was a centre of the woollen industry during the Middle Ages and developed around its western coalfield during the Industrial Revolution.

Yorkshire fog *n.* A common tufted grass, *Holcus lanatus,* having downy stems and leaves. [From the foggy impression made by its leaves and from its prevalence in Yorkshire.]

Yorkshire pudding *n.* A light, puffy, unsweetened baked pudding made from a batter of eggs, flour, and milk, and traditionally served with roast beef.

Yorkshire terrier *n.* A toy terrier of a breed developed in Yorkshire, having a long, bluish-grey and tan coat.

Yorkshire tyke (tīk) *n. Informal.* A native or inhabitant of Yorkshire. Also called "tyke".

Yo·ru·ba (yórrōōbə, yáw-rōōbə) *n., pl.* **-bas** or collectively **Yoruba.** **1.** A member of a West African Negro people living chiefly in southwestern Nigeria. **2.** The Kwa language of this African people. —**Yo·ru·ban** *adj.*

Yo·sem·i·te National Park (yō-sémməti). Park in eastern California, United States. It is a mountainous region with many lakes, rivers, gorges, and falls, including the Yosemite falls, the highest in North America (739 metres; 2,425 feet).

you (yṓo; *weak form* yṓo ‖ yə) *pron.* The second person singular or plural pronoun in the nominative or objective case. **1.** Used to represent the one or ones addressed by the speaker: **a.** As subject: *You are always hounding me.* **b.** As the direct object of a verb: *I'll hit you.* **c.** As the indirect object of verb: *My friend will give you a thrashing.* **d.** As the object of a preposition: *He'll set his dog on you.* **2. a.** Used in apposition before a noun to indicate address: *You fool!* **b.** *Informal.* Used to people of either sex in the friendly *U.S.* phrase *you guys* and the humorously censorious *British* phrase *you lot.* **3.** *Chiefly U.S. Informal.* Used in place of the reflexive pronouns *yourself* or *yourselves,* as the indirect object of a verb: *You went and bought you a new tractor.* **4.** Used in various elliptical, absolute, or interjectional phrases in which it is neither subject nor object: *You and your so-called friends!* **5.** Used to represent unspecified persons or people in general: *You have to be ruthless in a ruthless world.* In more formal contexts, the pronoun *one* is often preferred. —**you know what** or **who.** One that is unspecified but felt by the speaker to be known to the person addressed. ~*n.* The individuality or image of the person being addressed: *to find the real you; That shirt is really you.* —See Usage note at **me.** [Middle English *you, eow,* Old English *ēow,* dative and accusative of *gē,* ye.]

you-all (yṓo-áwl, yawl) *pl.pron. U.S. Regional.* You. Used in addressing informally two or more persons or referring to two or more persons.

you'd (yṓod; *weak form* yṓod ‖ yəd). Contraction of *you had* or *you would.*

you'll (yṓol; *weak form* yṓol ‖ yəl). Contraction of *you will* or *you shall.*

young (yung) *adj.* **younger** (yúng-gər), **youngest** (yúng-gist). **1.** Being in the early or undeveloped period of life or growth; not old. **2. a.** Newly begun or formed; not advanced: *The evening is young.* **b.** Recently introduced; not long established: *a young firm.* **3. a.** Pertaining to or suggestive of youth or early life: *young for her age.* **b.** Vigorous or fresh; youthful. **c.** Lacking experience; immature; green: *Her sophistication made him feel very young.* **4.** Designating the junior of two people having the same name. Usually used in the comparative: *Pitt the younger.* **5.** *Often capital* **Y.** Designating a political group or movement, often adopting progessive ideas or policies, that aims its appeal at the younger members of a population or community. **6.** *Geology.* Being of an early stage in a geological cycle. Said of bodies of water and land formations. ~*n., pl.* **young. 1.** *Plural.* Young persons collectively; youth. Preceded by *the.* **2.** Offspring; brood: *a lioness with her young.* —**with young.** Pregnant. Said of an animal. [Middle English *yong,* Old English *geong.*] —**young·ish** *adj.*

Synonyms (*adj.* & *n.*): *young, youth, juvenile, adolescent, teenager.*

Young (yung), **Brigham** (1801–77). U.S. religious leader. He became president of the Mormon church in 1844, following the death of Joseph Smith. He led the migration of the Mormons to Utah, and founded Salt Lake City in 1847.

Young, Edward (1683–1765). English poet and playwright. He is best known for his book-length didactic blank-verse poem *The Complaint, or Night Thoughts on Life, Death and Immortality* (1742–45).

Young, Thomas (1773–1829). British physicist and physician. He revived the wave theory of light and postulated the three-colour theory of colour vision. Also an Egyptologist, he helped to decipher the hieroglyphics of the Rosetta Stone.

young blood *n.* Young people with energy, enthusiasm, fresh ideas, and similar qualities.

young fogey *n. British.* A young person, usually middle-class or upper-middle-class in background, characterised by a self-conscious conservatism and refinement in literary and other tastes. [After the phrase *old fogey,* by humorous analogy.]

young lady. A female lover or girlfriend.

young·ling (yúng-ling) *n. Archaic.* **1.** A young person. **2.** A young animal. **3.** A young plant. [Middle English *yongling,* Old English *geongling* : YOUNG + -LING (noun suffix).] —**young·ling** *adv.*

young man *n.* A male lover or boyfriend.

Young Pretender. See Charles Edward **Stuart.**

Young's modulus *n.* The ratio of the stress per unit area of cross-section on a wire or rod under tension or compression to the longitudinal strain. Also called "Young's modulus of elasticity". [After Thomas YOUNG.]

young·ster (yúng-stər) *n.* **1.** A young person or child. **2.** A young animal.

Young Turk *n.* A progressive or rebellious member of a political party or other organised group. [Originally a member of a Turkish revolutionary party in the early 20th century.]

young woman *n.* A female lover or girlfriend.

youn·ker (yúngkər) *n. Archaic.* A young man; a youngster. [Dutch *jonker,* from Middle Dutch *jonckher, jonchere,* young nobleman : *jonc,* young + *here,* master, lord.]

your (yor, yoor ‖ yər, yōr). The possessive form of the pronoun *you. Abbr.* **yr. 1.** Used attributively to indicate possession, agency, or reception of an action by the one or ones addressed by the speaker: *your wallet; pursuing your tasks; suffered your first rebuff.* **2.** Used to designate something having special significance to you: *Today is your day.* **3.** *Informal.* Used to suggest a person or thing commonly experienced as being typical of a specified group or set: *not one of your scatterbrained philosophers.* **4.** Used to indicate possession, agency, or reception of an action by any unspecified person or persons: *The house is on your right.* In more formal contexts, the pronoun *one's* is often preferred in this sense. [Middle English *your,* Old English *ēower,* genitive of *gē,* ye. See **you.**]

you're (yoor, yor ‖ yər, yōr). Contraction of *you are.*

yours (yorz, yoorz ‖ yōrz). Possessive pronoun, absolute form of *your.* **1.** Belonging to you; your own. Used predicatively: *The brown boots are yours.* **2.** The one or ones belonging or pertaining to you. Used substantively: *If I can't find my hat, I'll take yours.* **3.** Used as a convention in the closing of letters especially in the phrases *yours sincerely, yours faithfully,* and *yours truly.* **4.** *British Informal.* Your place; your home: *Let's meet at yours.* —**of yours.** Belonging or pertaining to you: *a friend of yours.* —**you and yours.** You and your family. —**What's yours?** *Informal.* What do you want to drink? [Middle English *youres,* genitive of YOUR.]

your·self (yawr-sélf, yoor-, yər-) *pron., pl.* **-selves** (-sélvz). A specialised form of the second person pronoun. It is used: **1.** As a reflexive pronoun, forming the direct or indirect object of a verb or the object of a preposition: *hurt yourself; give yourself time; talk to yourself.* **2.** For emphasis: *Do it yourself; You yourself weren't certain.* **3.** As an emphasising substitute: *He invited only Tom and yourself; Yourself in debt, you couldn't help them.* **4.** As an indication of (your) real, normal, or healthy or condition identity: *You have not been yourself lately.*

Usage: **Yourself** is not acceptable as a substitute for *you* in formal style, though it is commonly so used informally: *She wants to see Joan and yourself; Yourself and the others will be expected later; How's yourself?* It is particularly common in Irish English. It is with *yourself* and *yourselves* that standard English now distinguishes singular from plural in the second person: *You yourself know your duty; You yourselves know your duty.*

yours truly *pron. Informal.* I; myself; me: *Yours truly had to pay for* *dinner as usual.* [From the phrase used to sign off at the close of a formal letter.]

youse (yo͞oz) *pl. pron. Regional.* You (plural).

youth (yo͞oth) *n., pl.* **youths** (yo͞othz || yo͞oths). **1.** The condition or quality of being young. **2.** Any quality such as vigour, enthusiasm, rashness, inexperience, or freshness, typically associated with youth. **3.** An early period of development or existence. **4. a.** The time of life between childhood and maturity. **b.** *Used with a plural verb.* Young people collectively. **c.** A young person; especially, a young man. —See Synonyms at **young.** [Middle English *youthe,* Old English *geoguth.*]

youth club *n.* A place where the young people of a particular area can go and join in leisure activities or social events.

youth custody *n.* In Britain, a sentence of up to 18 months passed on young offenders aged between 15 and 21.

youth custody centre *n.* In Britain, a disciplinary institution, replacing the borstal, where young offenders aged between 15 and 21 may be detained and given work and training.

youth·ful (yo͞othf'l) *adj.* **1.** Possessing youth; still young. **2.** Characteristic of youth; vigorous; fresh; active. **3.** Of or belonging to youth. **4.** In an early stage of development; new. **5.** *Geology.* Young. —**youth·ful·ly** *adv.* —**youth·ful·ness** *n.*

youth hostel *n.* A place offering simple, temporary accommodation and sometimes food to people, especially young people. Also called "hostel".

youth-quake (yo͞oth-kwayk) *n. Informal.* The earthquake-like impact of youth culture on contemporary society. [Blend of *youth* + *(earth)quake.*]

you've (yo͞ov; *weak form* yo͞ov || yəv). Contraction of *you have.*

yowe (yow) *n. Scottish.* A **ewe** *(see).*

yowl (yowl) *v.* **yowled, yowling, yowls.** —*intr.* To utter a loud, long, cry; howl; wail. —*tr.* To say or utter with such a cry. ~*n.* A loud, mournful cry; a wail. [Middle English *youlen* (imitative).]

Yo·yo (yō-yō) *n., pl.* **-yos.** **1.** A trademark for a toy in the shape of a spool, around which a string is wound. The string is attached to the finger, and the Yo-yo is spun up and down by moving the hand. **2.** *U.S. slang.* Small y. A stupid or clumsy person.

Ypres (eepr, ēeprə; *also facetiously* wīpərz). *Flemish* **Ieper** (ēepər). Town of West Flanders, southwestern Belgium. Situated on the river Yperlee, it was a prosperous textile centre during the Middle Ages and was the site of three battles during World War I.

Y-quem (ee-kém) *n.* A variety of Sauterne wine. [After Château d'*Yquem,* an estate in southwest France, where it is produced.]

yr. 1. year. **2.** younger. **3.** your.

yrs. 1. years. **2.** yours.

-yse See Usage note at **-ise.**

Yseult. Variant of **Iseult.**

YTS Youth Training Scheme.

yt·ter·bi·a (i-térbi-ə) *n.* Ytterbium oxide. [New Latin, from YTTERBIUM.]

yt·ter·bite (i-tér-bīt) *n.* A mineral, **gadolinite** *(see).*

yt·ter·bi·um (i-térbi-əm) *n. Symbol* Yb A soft, bright, silvery rare-earth element occurring in two allotropic forms and used as an X-ray source for portable irradiation devices, in some laser materials, and in some special alloys. Atomic number 70, atomic weight 173.04, melting point 824°C, boiling point 1,427 °C, relative density 6.977 or 6.54 depending on allotropic form, valencies 2, 3. [New Latin; discovered at *Ytterby,* Sweden.) —**yt·ter·bic** *adj.*

ytterbium oxide *n.* A colourless hygroscopic compound, Yb_2O_3, used in certain alloys. Also called "ytterbia".

yt·tri·a (ittri-ə) *n.* Yttrium oxide.

yt·tri·um (íttri-əm) *n. Symbol* Y. A silvery, lustrous metallic element, not a rare earth but occurring in nearly all rare-earth minerals and resembling them chemically, used in various metallurgical applications, notably to increase the strength of magnesium and aluminium alloys. Atomic number 39, atomic weight 88.905, melting point 1,509°C, boiling point 3,338 °C, relative density 4.47, valency 3. [New Latin, from YTTR(IA).] —**yt·tric** *adj.*

yttrium oxide *n.* A yellowish powder, Y_2O_3, used in optical glasses, ceramics, and colour-television tubes. Also called "yttria".

yu·an (yo͞o-án) *n., pl.* **yuan. 1. a.** The basic monetary unit of the People's Republic of China, equal to 10 jiao or 100 fen. **b.** The basic monetary unit of Taiwan, equal to 100 cents. **2.** A coin or note worth one yuan. [Mandarin Chinese *yuán,* round (piece), dollar.]

Yu·ca·tán Peninsula (yo͞okə-taàn, -tán). Peninsula of Central America. Separating the Gulf of Mexico from the Caribbean Sea, it is mainly a limestone plateau situated largely in southeast Mexico. It includes Belize and north Guatemala, and was once the centre of the Mayan civilisation of which there remain many archaeological sites. Lumbering and fishing are its chief industries, and tourism is important.

Yuc·a·tec (yo͞okə-tek) *n., pl.* **-tecs** or collectively **Yucatec. 1.** A member of an American Indian people inhabiting the Yucatán Peninsula. **2.** The Mayan language of this people.

yuc·ca (yúckə) *n.* Any of various New World plants of the genus *Yucca,* often tall and stout-stemmed, and having a terminal cluster of white flowers. [Spanish *yuca,* from Cariban.]

yuck, yuk (yuk, yukh) *interj. Slang.* Used to express disgust or distaste. ~*n. Slang.* Something yucky. [Imitative.]

yuck·y, yuk·ky (yúcki) *adj.* **-ier, -iest.** *Slang.* Disgusting; revolting.

Yue, Yüeh (ywe) *n.* **Cantonese** *(see).*

Yu·ga (yo͞ogə) *n.* Also **Yug** (yo͞og). *Hinduism.* One of the four ages constituting the cycle of history. [Sanskrit, yoke, pair, age.]

Yu·go·sla·vi·a (yo͞o-gō-slaávi-ə, -gə-), **Federal Republic of.** Also **Ju·go·sla·vi·a.** Federal republic of southeast Europe. Situated in the Balkan peninsula, it is chiefly mountainous except in the northeast where fertile lowlands are drained by the river Danube. It was formed in 1918 as the Kingdom of the Serbs, Croats, and Slovenes, and gained its present name in 1929. It was occupied by the Germans during World War II, after which Tito, a Communist, became president; he later broke with the U.S.S.R. (1948). In 1991-92 the constituent republics of Slovenia, Croatia, Bosnia and Herzegovina, and Macedonia and the province of Kosovo declared their independence unilaterally, and except in Slovenia and Macedonia armed conflict broke out between ethnic communities, involving federal troops. Most of the breakaway republics obtained international recognition, and in 1992 the formation of a new, smaller Yugoslavia was announced, consisting only of Serbia and Montenegro. Area (1991) 102 173 square kilometres (39,449 square miles). Population, 10,570,000. Capital, Belgrade. —**Yu·go·slav** (-slaav, -slaàv), **Yu·go·sla·vi·an** (-slaávi-ən) *n. & adj.*

yuk (yuk, yukh). Variant of **yuck.**

Yu·ka·wa (yo͞o-kaà-wə), **Hideki** (1907–81). Japanese nuclear physicist. In 1935 he predicted the existence of the group of elementary particles called mesons, later observed by scientists. He received the Nobel prize for physics (1949).

Yu·kon¹ (yo͞o-kon). Territory of northwest Canada on the Beaufort Sea, bordering Alaska. It includes Mount Logan, Canada's highest peak (6 050 metres; 19,850 feet), and is sparsely populated. It was the site of the Klondike gold rush in the 1890s. Its capital is White-horse.

Yukon². River of North America. Formed by the confluence of the rivers Lewes and Pelly in south central Yukon. Canada, it flows 3 220 kilometres (2,000 miles), first northwestwards to Alaska then southwestwards to enter the Bering Sea through a wide shallow delta.

yuk·ky (yúcki). Variant of **yucky.**

yu·lan (yo͞o-lan) *n.* A tree, *Magnolia denudata,* native to China and often cultivated for its large, cup-shaped, fragrant white flowers. [Mandarin Chinese *yù lán,* "jade orchid" : *yù,* jade + *lán²,* orchid.]

Yule (yo͞ol) *n.* Christmas or the season or feast celebrating Christmas. [Middle English *yole, yule,* Old English *gēol(a)†.*]

yule log *n.* A large log traditionally burned in the fireplace at Christmas.

Yule·tide (yo͞ol-tīd) *n.* The Christmas season.

Yu·ma (yo͞omə) *n., pl.* **-mas** or collectively **Yuma. 1.** A member of a Yuman-speaking North American Indian people of southwest Arizona and the adjacent parts of California and Mexico. **2.** The language of this people. [Spanish *Yuma†.*]

Yu·man (yo͞omən) *n.* A language family comprising the languages of the Yuma and Mohave Indians and other North American Indian languages. —**yu·man** *adj.*

yum·my (yúmmi) *adj.* **-mier, -miest.** *Informalo.* Delightful; delicious; enticing. [From YUM YUM.] ~ *interj. Informal.* Used to express eager anticipation or appreciation of something delicious, delightful or enticing.

yum yum (yúm-yúm) *interj. Informal.* Used to express appreciation or eager anticipation of delicious food. [Imitative of the sound made when food is tasted.]

Yun·nan or **Yün·nan** (yŏo-nán, yŏon-, *Chinese* yŭn-). Mountainous province of southwest China, bordering Vietnam, Laos and Burma. It is crossed by the rivers Huang, Lancang (Mekong), and Nu (Salween). Its capital is Kunming.

yup. Variant of **yep.**

yup·pie, yup·py (yúppi) *n. Informal.* A young urban professional or young upwardly mobile professional; especially, one viewed as affluent and trendily chic. —**yup·pie, yup·py** *adj.*

yuppie flu *n. Informal.* **Myalgic encephalomyelitis** (*see*).

yup·pi·fy (yúppi-fī) *tr.v.* To endow a house, flat, neighbourhood or the like with the characteristics favoured by yuppies. [*yupp(ie)* + *-i-* + *-fy*.]

yurt (yoort) *n., pl.* **yurta** (yoórta) or **yurts.** A circular, domed, portable tent used by the nomadic Mongols of Siberia. [Russian *yurta*, from Turkic; akin to Turkish *yurt*, home.]

Y.W.C.A. Young Women's Christian Association.

Y.W.H.A. Young Women's Hebrew Association.

ywis. Variant of **iwis.**

Z

z, Z (zed ‖ *U.S.* zee) *n., pl.* **z's** or *rare* **zs, Zs** or **Z's.** **1.** The 26th letter of the modern English alphabet. **2.** Any of the speech sounds represented by this letter. **3.** Anything shaped like the letter *z*, such as a **z-bend** (*see*).

z, Z, z., Z. *Note:* As an abbreviation or symbol, *z* may be a small or a capital letter, with or without a full stop. Established forms or those generally preferred precede the definition. When no form is given, all four forms are in general use in that sense. **1.** Z atomic number. **2.** Z impedance. **3.** z. zero. **4.** z. zone. **5.** The 26th in a series; 25th when *J* is omitted. **6.** The third in a series consisting of *x*, *y*, and *z*. **7.** The symbol of an algebraic variable, especially the third variable in a tertiary equation.

za·ba·glio·ne (zá-bal-yŏni, zá́a-, -bəl-, -yŏnay; *Italian* tsa-) *n.* A dessert consisting of egg yolks, sugar,. and wine, usually Marsala wine, beaten until thick and frothy and served either hot or cold. [Italian *zaba(gl)ione*.]

Zach·a·ri·as (zácke-rī́-əss). Also **Zach·a·ri·ah** (-ə). The husband of Elizabeth and father of John the Baptist. He underwent a period of muteness because he was lacking in faith. Luke 1:5.

Zad·kine (zád-keen, *French* zat-kéen), **Ossip** (1890–1967). French sculptor. Born in Smolensk, Russia, he studied in London and moved to Paris (1909) where he was heavily influenced by cubism in his representations of the human form. His most famous work is the memorial to the destruction of Rotterdam in World War II, *The Destroyed City* (1954).

zaf·fer, zaf·fre (záffər) *n.* An impure oxide of cobalt, used to produce a blue colour in enamel and in the making of smalt. [Italian *zaffera*, from Old French *safre*, from Arabic *ṣufr*, yellow copper.]

zaf·tig (záf-tik, -tig) *adj. Chiefly U.S. Slang.* **1.** Bosomy. **2.** Having a full, shapely figure; voluptuous. [Yiddish *zaftik*, juicy, from Middle High German *saftec*, from *saft*, juice, from Old High German *saf*.]

zag (zag) *n.* A sharp turn in a different direction. ~ *intr.v.* **zagged, zagging, zags.** To make a sharp turn or change of course. [Shortened from ZIGZAG.]

Za·greb (zaa-greb). Capital of Croatia. Situated on the river Sava, it was a Roman city and became a centre for Slav nationalism in the 19th century.

Zag·re·us (zággri-əss). *Greek Mythology.* A god worshipped in Orphic cults and identified with Dionysus.

zai·bat·su (zī-bat-sŏo) *n., pl.* **zaibatsu.** Any powerful commercial combine of Japan controlled by a few leading families. [Japanese, from Chinese *cái fá*, plutocrat : *cái*, wealth + *fá*, powerful person or family.]

za·ire (zaa-éer, zī-) *n.* The basic monetary unit of the former Zaire, equal to 100 makuta.

Za·ire (zaa-éer, zī-) River of central Africa. See **Congo.**

Zaire, Republic of. *French* **Zaïre.** Formerly **Belgian Congo** (1908–60); **Democratic Republic of Congo** (1960–71). Republic of central Africa. See **Congo, Democratic Republic of the.** —**Za·ir·e·an** (zaa-éer-i-ən), **Za·ir·ese** (-eer-éez ‖ -éess) *n. & adj.*

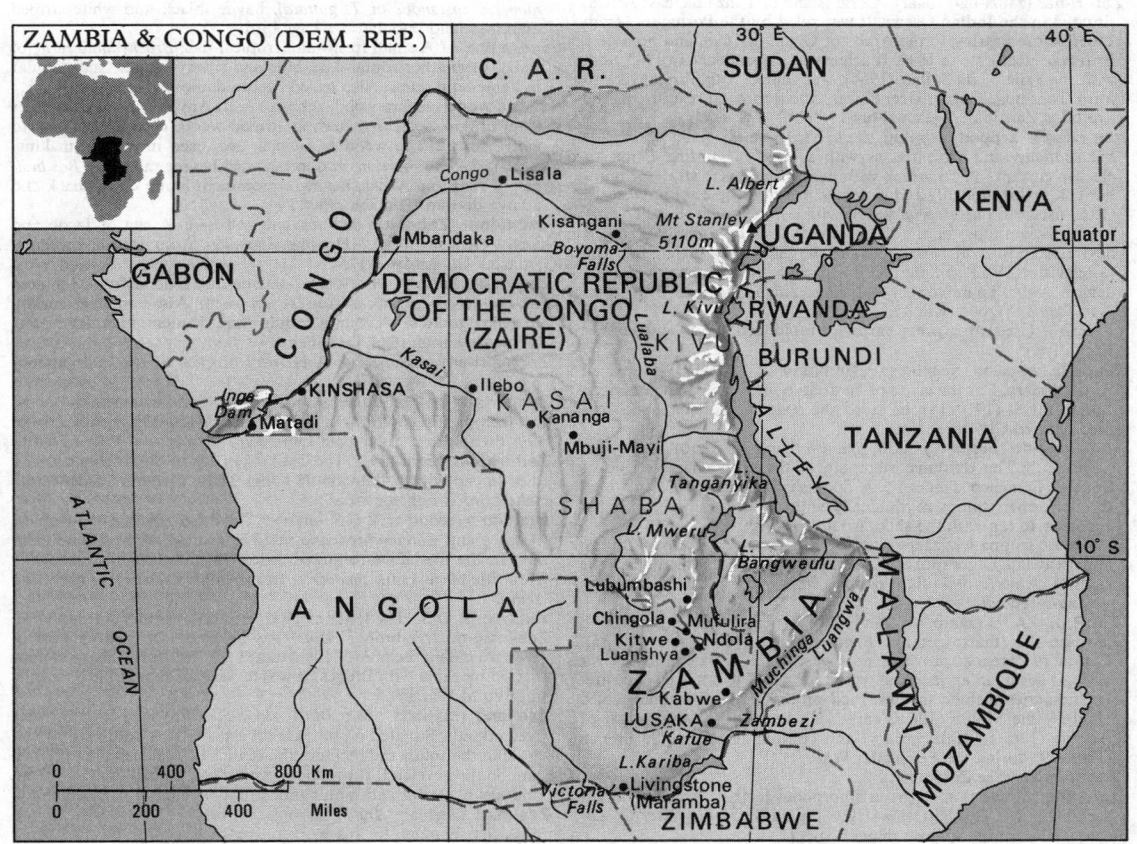

ZAMBIA & CONGO (DEM. REP.)

za·kat (zaá-kat) *n.* A proportion of the income of a devout Muslim set aside to be devoted to the poor. [Arabic.]

Zam·be·zi (zam-beézi). River of southern Africa. Rising in northwest Zambia, it flows 2 735 kilometres (1,700 miles) chiefly eastwards, forming the Zambia-Zimbabwe border, and enters the Indian Ocean through a wide delta near Chinde, Mozambique. Despite the many rapids along its length, it is navigable in stretches; it includes the Victoria Falls and the Kariba and Cabora Bassa dams.

Zam·bi·a (zámbi-ə), **Republic of.** Republic of southern central Africa. It consists chiefly of plateau, with mountains to the north and northeast, and the basins of the Zambezi and Kafue rivers to the west. It produces maize, groundnuts, cotton, tobacco, and sugar, while cattle-rearing is important in the east. Copper, zinc, cobalt, and emeralds are mined, and it has unexplored iron deposits. Explored by Livingstone (1850s to 1870s), it became the British protectorate of Northern Rhodesia (1911), was incorporated into the Federation of Rhodesia and Nyasaland (1953–63), and achieved independence in 1964. Area, 752 614 square kilometres (290,586 square miles). Population, 8,280,000. Capital, Lusaka. —**Zam·bi·an** *n. & adj.* See map at **Congo.**

za·mi·a (záymi-ə) *n.* Any of various chiefly tropical American cycads of the genus *Zamia*, having a thick, usually underground trunk and a crown of palmlike terminal leaves. [New Latin *Zamia*, from a misreading of *(nūces) azāniae*, pine (nuts), probably from Greek *azainein*, to dry, parch.]

za·min·dar, ze·min·dar (zə-mín-daar, -min-dár) *n.* **1.** An official in India during the Mogul empire assigned to collect the land taxes of his district. **2.** A native landholder in British colonial India, responsible for collecting and paying to the government the taxes on the land under his jurisdiction. [Persian *zamīndār* : *zamīn*, earth, land + *-dār*, holder, from Old Persian *dār-*, to hold.]

za·min·da·ri (zámmin-daári, zə-méen-) *n., pl.* **-is.** Also **ze·min·da·ry** (zémmin-, zə-méen-) *pl.* **-ies. 1.** The system of tax collection by zamindars. **2.** The area administered by a zamindar. [Hindi *zamīndāri*, from Persian, from *zamīndār*, ZAMINDAR.]

zanana. Variant of **zenana.**

Z.A.N.U., ZANU (zaá-nōō). Zimbabwe African National Union.

Zanuck (zánuk), **Darryl F(rancis)** (1902–79). U.S. film producer. He was co-founder of Twentieth-Century Pictures (1933) and vice president when it merged with Fox Films (1935) to become Twentieth-Century Fox. Among his many successful films are, the first talkie *The Jazz Singer,* and *The Grapes of Wrath.*

za·ny (záyni) *n., pl.* **-nies. 1.** A ludicrous, buffoonish character in old comedies who attempts feebly to mimic the tricks of the clown. **2.** A comical person given to extravagant or outlandish behaviour. *—adj.* **zanier, -niest. 1.** Inventively and eccentrically humorous; bizarrely funny. **2.** Ludicrously comical; clownish; droll. [Italian *zani, zanni,* buffoon, from *Zanni,* dialectal variant of *Gianni,* pet form for *Giovanni,* John.]

Zan·zi·bar (zánzi-bár, -baar). Coral island of Tanzania, east Africa, situated in the Indian Ocean. It was ruled by the Portuguese from 1503, before passing to the Arabs of Oman in 1698, and became a British protectorate in 1890. It achieved independence in 1963, and, with the exile of its Sultan (1964), was united with Tanganyika to form Tanzania. Cocoa, rice, cloves, and copra are exported. The capital is Zanzibar. —**Zan·zi·bar·i** (-baári) *n. & adj.*

zap (zap) *v.* **zapped, zapping, zaps.** *Slang.* —*tr.* **1.** To destroy or kill suddenly and violently, as with a burst of gunfire, flame, or electric current. **2.** To attack with heavy firepower; strafe or bombard. **3.** To hit suddenly and violently. **4.** To add spice or interest to. Often used with *up: zap up a stew with a fancy sauce.* **5. a.** To surf (channels, stations, or the like), especially with a remote-control device. **b.** To turn off, turn on, or surf the channels or programmes of (a television, VCR, or the like), especially with a remote-control device. —*intr.* To move very fast: *zapped along the road.* *—n. Slang.* Vigour; vitality. *~ interj.* Used to express surprise, rapid action, or suddenness. [Imitative.]

Za·pa·ta (zə-paáta; *Spanish* sa-), **Emiliano** (*c.* 1877–1919). Mexican revolutionary. For the cause of agrarian reform he led an American Indian revolt (1910–15); he ruled the state of Morelos, and occupied Mexico City three times.

za·pa·te·a·do (záppə-tay-aádō; *Spanish* tháppa-, -aáthō) *n., pl.* **-dos.** *Spanish.* **1.** The rhythmic stamping of the heels characteristic of Spanish flamenco dances. **2.** A Spanish flamenco dance in which the performer stamps rhythmically with his heels. [Spanish, from *zapatear,* to tap with the shoe, from *zapáto,* shoe.]

Zap·o·tec (záppə-tek, záapə-, sáapə-) *n.* **1.** Any of a group of Central American languages spoken in southern Mexico. **2.** A member of the Central American Indian people who speak these languages. —**Zap·o·tec** *adj.*

Z.A.P.U., ZAPU (zaá-pōō). Zimbabwe African People's Union.

Za·ra·go·za (thárrə-gốthə). *English* **Sar·a·gos·sa** (sárrə-góssə). Capital of Zaragoza province, northeast Spain. Situated on the river Ebro, it lies in an agricultural region for which it is a market centre. Its industries include textiles, food processing, and leather goods. Held by the Moors (8th to early 12th century), it was capital of Aragon (12th to 15th century) and resisted sieges by the French (1808–09) during the Peninsular War.

Zarathustra. See **Zoroaster.**

zar·a·tite (zárrə-tīt) *n.* A green amorphous form of hydrated nickel carbonate, NiCO$_3$·2Ni(OH)$_2$·4H$_2$O. [Spanish *zaratita,* after G. *Zárate,* 19th-century Spanish mineralogist.]

za·re·ba, za·ri·ba, za·ree·ba (zə-réebə) *n.* **1.** An enclosure of bushes or stakes protecting a campsite or village in northeast Africa. **2.** A campsite or village so protected. [Arabic *zarībah,* pen for cattle, from *zarb,* sheepfold.]

zarf (zaarf) *n.* A chalice-like holder for a hot coffee cup, typically made of ornamented metal, used in the Middle East. [Arabic *ẓarf,* "container".]

zastruga. Variant of **sastruga.**

Za·to·pek (zátto-pek), **Emil** (1922–). Czech athlete. The greatest long-distance runner of his day, he won the 10 000 metres at the London Olympic Games (1948), and at the Helsinki Olympic Games (1952) he won the 5 000 metres, the 10 000 metres, and the marathon.

zax (zakss). Variant of **sax** (tool). [Variant of SAX (tool).]

z-ax·is (zéd-ak-siss || *U.S.* zée-) *n., pl.* **z-axes** (-akseez). **1.** One of the three axes in a three-dimensional Cartesian coordinate system. **2.** The vertical axis of an aircraft.

za·yin (zaá-yin, zīn) *n.* The seventh letter of the Hebrew alphabet. [Hebrew *zayin,* "weapon", from Aramaic.]

z-bend (zéd-bend || *U.S.* zée-) *n.* A pair of successive sharp bends on a road.

zeal (zeel) *n.* Enthusiastic and diligent devotion in pursuit of a cause, ideal, or goal; fervent adherence or service; extreme and ardent commitment: *religious zeal.* See Synonyms at **passion.** [Middle English *zele,* from Late Latin *zēlus,* from Greek *zēlos.*]

Zealand. See **Sjælland.**

zeal·ot (zéllət) *n.* **1.** One who is zealous; a fanatically committed person. See Synonyms at **fanatic. 2.** *Capital* Z. A member of a Jewish sect that resisted Roman rule in Palestine during the first century A.D. [Late Latin *zēlōtes,* from Greek *zēlōtēs,* from *zēlos,* ZEAL.]

zeal·ot·ry (zéllətri) *n.* Excessive zeal; fanaticism.

zeal·ous (zélləss) *adj.* Filled with or motivated by zeal; ardent; enthusiastic; fervent. See Synonyms at **eager.** —**zeal·ous·ly** *adv.* —**zeal·ous·ness** *n.*

ze·a·tin (zée-ə-tin) *n.* *Botany.* A naturally occurring cytokinin (a plant growth substance) found in maize kernels. [New Latin *Zea,* genus name for maize (see **zein**) + *-tin,* as in *kinetin.*]

zebec, zebeck. Variants of **xebec.**

Zeb·e·dee (zébbi-dee). A fisherman whose sons James and John became disciples of Jesus. Matthew 4:21.

ze·bra (zéebrə, zébbrə) *n.* Any of several horselike African mammals of the genus *Equus,* having characteristic overall markings of conspicuous dark and whitish stripes. [Portuguese, from Old Spanish *zebra, zebro†,* wild ass.]

zebra crossing (*usually* zébbrə) *n.* A pedestrian crossing, in which the road is painted with broad white stripes, where pedestrians may cross at any time and have precedence over road-using vehicles. [From the zebra-like painted stripes.]

zebra finch *n.* A small Australian bird, *Poephila castanotis* (or *Taeniopygia castanotis* or *T. guttata*), having black and white striped markings, and popular as a cage bird.

zebra fish *n.* A small freshwater tropical fish, *Brachydanio rerio,* of India, having horizontal dark-blue and silvery stripes, and popular in home aquariums. Also called "zebra danio".

ze·bra·wood (zéebrə-wŏŏd, zébbrə-) *n.* **1.** Any of several African or tropical American trees having striped wood, especially *Connarus guianensis.* **2.** The wood of such a tree, used in cabinet-making.

ze·bu (zée-bōō, -bew) *n.* A domesticated bovine mammal, *Bos indicus,* of Asia and Africa, having a prominent hump on the back and a large dewlap. [French *zébu†.*]

Zeb·u·lon¹, Zeb·u·lun (zébbew-lən, ze-béw-). A son of Jacob and Leah. Genesis 30:20. [Hebrew *Zəbhūlōn,* from *zəbhūl,* dwelling, from *zābhal,* he dwelt.]

Zebulon², Zebulun *n.* A tribe of Israel descended from Zebulon.

zec·chi·no (ze-kée-nō, tse-) *n., pl.* **-ni** (-nee) Also **zec·chin** (zéckin, ze-kéen), **zech·in.** A coin, a sequin (see). [Italian, SEQUIN.]

Zech. Zechariah (Old Testament).

Zech·a·ri·ah¹ (zéckə-rí-ə). A Hebrew prophet of the sixth century B.C.

Zechariah² *n. Abbr.* **Zech.** A book of the Old Testament.

zed (zed) *n. Chiefly British.* The letter z. [Middle English *zed,* from Old French *zede,* from Late Latin *zēta,* ZETA.]

Zed·e·ki·ah (zéddi-kí-ə). The last king of Judah (597–586 B.C.), who died in captivity at Babylon. II Kings 24:17. [Hebrew, *Şidqīyāh(ū),* "the Lord is righteousness".]

zed·o·ar·y (zéddō-əri || *U.S.* -erri) *n.* The dried rhizome of a tropical Asian plant, *Curcuma zedoaria,* used as a stimulant and condiment and in the manufacture of cosmetics. [Middle English *zeodoarye,* from Medieval Latin *zeodoaria,* from Arabic *zadwār,* from Persian *zedwār†.*]

zee (zee) *n. U.S.* The letter z. [Variant (17th-century) of ZED.]

Zee·brug·ge (zée-brŏŏgə; *Dutch* záy-brükhə). Deep-water port of West Flanders, Belgium. It is situated on the North Sea and connected by canal with Bruges. It was a German submarine base during World War I.

Zee·land (záy-lənd, zée-; *Dutch* záy-lant). Province of southwest Netherlands. Situated on the Scheldt estuary, it is bordered by Belgium in the south and includes the islands of Walcheren and North and South Beveland. It produces sugar beet, grains, flax, and fruit, and has chemical and motor industries. Its capital is Middelburg.

Zee·man (zéemən; *Dutch* záy-man), **Pieter** (1865–1943). Dutch physicist. Famous for his work on magneto-optics, he discovered the **Zeeman effect.** In 1902 he shared the Nobel prize for physics with H.A. Lorentz.

Zeeman effect *n.* The splitting of single spectral lines of an emission spectrum into three or more polarised components when the radiation source is in a magnetic field. [After Pieter ZEEMAN.]

Zef·fi·rel·li (zéffi-rélli), **Franco** (1923–). Italian stage and film director. Beginning his career as an actor and stage designer, he achieved recognition for directing a series of operas, including *La Cenerentola* (1953) at La Scala and *I Pagliacci* (1959) at Covent Garden. His films include *The Taming of the Shrew* (1966), *Romeo and Juliet* (1967), and *Hamlet* (1990).

ze·in (zée-in) *n.* A prolamine protein derived from maize and used in the manufacture of various plastics, coatings, and lacquers. [New Latin *Zea,* genus name for maize, from Greek *zea, zeia,* one-seeded wheat + -IN.]

Zeiss (zīss; *German* tsīss), **Carl** (1816–88). German industrialist and optician. After establishing his first workshop at Jena (1846), he joined Ernest Abbe (1866) to produce field glasses, microscopes, and later cameras, using new optical techniques and materials, including heat-resistant glass.

Zeit·geist (tsīt-gīst, zīt-) *n.* The spirit of the time; the taste and outlook characteristic of a period or generation. [German, "time-spirit".]

zemindar. Variant of **zamindar.**

zemindary. Variant of **zamindari.**

zemst·vo (zémst-vō) *n., pl.* **-vos.** An elective council responsible for the local administration of a provincial district in tsarist Russia. [Russian, from *zemlya,* land.]

ze·na·na (ze-náanə, zi-) *n.* Also **za·na·na** (zə-). The part of a house in Asian countries such as India and Pakistan reserved for the women of the household. [Hindi *zenāna,* from Persian, from *zan,* woman.]

Zen Buddhism (zen) *n.* A Chinese and Japanese school of Mahayana Buddhism that asserts that enlightenment can be attained through meditation, self-contemplation, and intuition rather than through the scriptures. Also called "Zen". [Japanese *zen,* meditation, from Chinese *chan;* akin to Sanskrit *dhyāna,* he meditates.] —**Zen Buddhist** *n. & adj.*

Zend (zend) *n.* **1.** The Zend-Avesta. **2.** Formerly, a language, **Aves·tan** (*see*).

Zend-A·ves·ta (zénd-ə-véstə) *n.* The entire body of sacred writings of the Zoroastrian religion. Also called "Zend". [Persian *zandavastā, zendastā,* from *Avesta-va-zend,* Avesta with an interpretation : Middle Persian *apastāk,* AVESTA + *va,* with + *zend†,* interpretation.] —**Zend-A·ves·ta·ic** (-vess-táy-ik) *adj.*

Zener diode *n.* A semiconductor diode used as a voltage regulator, in which at a specific reverse voltage there is a sharp increase in reverse current. [After C.M. *Zener* (1905–), U.S. physicist.]

ze·nith (zénnith, zéenith) *n.* **1.** The point on the celestial sphere that is directly above the observer. **2.** The highest point above the observer's horizon attained by a celestial body. **3.** The highest point of any path or course; a point of culmination; a peak; a summit. —See Synonyms at **summit.** [Middle English, from Old French *cenith,* from Old Spanish *zenit,* from Arabic *samt,* road, in *samt ar-ra's,* road (over) the head.] —**zen·ith·al** *adj.*

zenithal projection *n.* A form of map projection in which a part of the earth's surface is projected onto a plane tangential to it such that all points have their true compass bearings from the central point.

Ze·no·bi·a (zi-nóbi-ə, ze-) (third century A.D.). Queen of Palmyra (part of Syria) from 267 A.D. Acceding to the throne after the death of her husband Odenathus, she acted as regent for her son and extended her empire to include Syria, Egypt, and part of Asia Minor. In 272 she was defeated and captured by the Roman emperor Aurelian.

Ze·no of Citium (sítti-əm, kítti-) (*c.*334–*c.*262 B.C.). Greek philosopher. He founded the Stoic school of philosophy, which taught that virtue is necessarily good, and that most objects of desire, such as material possessions, family, and honours are morally indifferent or at best only relatively good.

ze·o·lite (zée-ə-līt) *n.* Any of a large group of hydrous calcium and aluminium silicate minerals or their corresponding synthetic compounds, used chiefly as molecular filters, water-softeners, and ion-exchange agents. [Swedish *zeolit,* "boiling stone" (because it swells and boils under the blowpipe) : Greek *zeein,* to boil + -LITE.]

Zeph. Zephaniah (Old Testament).

Zeph·a·ni·ah¹ (zéffə-nī-ə). A Hebrew prophet of the seventh century B.C.

Zephaniah² *n. Abbr.* **Zeph.** A book of the Old Testament containing the prophecies of Zephaniah.

zeph·yr (zéffər) *n.* **1. a.** A gentle breeze. **b.** The west wind. **2.** Any of various light, soft fabrics, yarns, or garments. **3.** Any airy, insubstantial, or passing thing. —See Synonyms at **wind.** [Middle English *Zephyrus,* from Latin *zephyrus,* from Greek *zephuros,* akin to *zophos†,* darkness, west.]

Zeph·y·rus (zéffərəss). *Greek Mythology.* A god personifying the gentle west wind. [Latin, from Greek *Zephuros,* from *zephuros,* ZEPHYR.]

Zep·pe·lin (zéppə-lin; *German* tséppə-leen) *n. Sometimes small* z. A rigid airship having a long, cylindrical body. [After its inventor, Ferdinand von ZEPPELIN.]

Zeppelin, Ferdinand, Graf von (1838–1917). German inventor. After retiring from the army (1891), he designed and built the first

Zeppelin, which first flew on 2 July 1900.

Zer·matt (zér-mat; *German* tsair-mát). Resort of Valais canton, south Switzerland. Situated at the foot of the Matterhorn, it is a mountaineering and winter sports centre.

ze·ro (zée-rō) *n., pl.* **-ros** or **-roes.** *Abbr.* **z. 1.** The numeral, or numerical symbol, "0"; a nought. **2.** *Mathematics.* **a.** An element of a set that when added to any other element in the set produces a sum identical with the element to which it is added. **b.** A cardinal number indicating the absence of any or all units under consideration. **c.** An ordinal number indicating an initial point or origin. **d.** An argument at which the value of a function vanishes. **3. a.** The starting point on a scale of measurement. **b.** The position on a scale marking the point between positive and negative values. **4.** The temperature indicated by the numeral 0 on a thermometer. **5.** A sight setting that enables a firearm to shoot on target. **6.** One having no influence or importance; a nonentity; a nobody. **7.** The lowest point: *His prospects were set at zero.* **8.** Nothing; nil. ~*adj.* **1.** Of, pertaining to, or being zero. **2. a.** Having no measurable or otherwise determinable value. **b.** Absent, inoperative, or irrelevant in specified circumstances: *zero energy.* **3. a.** Limited by cloud cover to little or no vertical visibility. **b.** Permitting little or no horizontal visibility. **4.** *Informal.* No; not any: *She showed zero interest in my problems.* ~*tr.v.* **zeroed, -roing, -roes.** To adjust (an instrument or device) to zero value. —**zero in. 1.** To aim or concentrate firepower on an exact target location. **2.** To adjust the aim or sight of by repeated firings. **3.** To converge intently; move near; close in: *The children zeroed in on the toy display.* [French *zéro,* from Italian *zero,* from Medieval Latin *zephirum,* from Arabic *şifr,* zero, CIPHER.]

zero gravity *n.* The state of weightlessness; the condition of not experiencing the effects of gravity.

zero hour *n.* The scheduled time for the start of an operation or action, especially a concerted military attack. Also called "H-hour".

ze·ro-point energy (zéer-ō-poynt) *n.* The irreducible minimum energy possessed by a substance at the temperature of absolute zero.

zero population growth *n. Abbr.* **ZPG** The limiting of population increase to the number of live births needed to maintain the existing population level.

ze·ro-rate (zéer-ō-rayt) *tr.v.* **-rated, -rating, -rates.** To exempt (goods or services) from value-added tax.

zero-sum (zée-rō-súm) *adj.* Of, pertaining to, or designating a situation in which a gain by one person or side must be matched by a loss by another person or side: *a zero-sum game where no one can lose – but no one can win, either.* [From the net change or *sum* of zero produced when gains and losses cancel one another out.]

ze·roth (zéer-ōth) *n.* Anything, such as an element or term, that is considered to come before the first in a series. [ZERO + -TH (suffix of ordinals and fractions).] —**ze·roth** *adj. & adv.*

zest (zest) *n.* **1.** Added flavour or interest; piquancy; charm. **2.** Spirited enjoyment; wholehearted interest; gusto: *"At fifty-three he retains all the heady zest of adolescence"* (Kenneth Tynan). **3.** The outermost part of the rind of an orange or lemon, used as flavouring. ~*tr.v.* **zested, zesting, zests.** To give zest, charm, or spirit to. [French *zest†,* orange or lemon peel.] —**zest·ful** *adj.*

ze·ta (zéetə || *U.S. also* záytə) *n.* The sixth letter in the Greek alphabet, written Z, ζ. Transliterated in English as Z, z. [Late Latin *zēta,* from Greek, probably from Semitic, akin to Hebrew *zayit,* Aramaic *zētā.*]

ZETA (zéetə) *n.* Zero-energy *t*hermonuclear *a*pparatus: a torus-shaped ring in which a plasma is contained by magnetic fields in order that thermonuclear reactions may be examined.

Zet·land (zetlənd). See **Shetland Islands.**

zeug·ma (zéwg-mə || zōōg-) *n.* **1.** The use of a single word, especially a verb or adjective, to apply to two or more nouns, when its sense is appropriate to only one of them; for example, *He held his tongue and his oath; Pedal your bicycle rather than your car.* **2.** Loosely, a syllepsis. Compare **syllepsis.** [Latin, from Greek *zeugma,* a joining, uniting, yoking.]

Zeus (zewss || zée-əss, zōōss). The presiding god of the Greek pantheon, ruler of the heavens and father of other gods and mortal heroes. [Greek.]

Zhan·jiang (ján-jyáng). Formerly **Guangzhon Bay.** Seaport in Guangdong Province, south China, having a large harbour. In 1898 it was made a French foreign concession and its architecture still retains some foreign influence.

Zhe·jiang or **Che-chiang** or **Che-kiang** (jə-jáng). China's smallest, most densely populated province, lying on the East China Sea coast. The north is part of the Chang Jiang valley, and the south, apart from the Fuchun Jiang valley, is mountainous. Zhejiang is a major rice, soya bean, wheat, cotton, and tea producing area. Its capital is the industrial port of Hangzhou.

Zheng·zhou or **Cheng-chou** or **Cheng-chow** (júng-jó). Also **Cheng·hsien.** Capital of Henan province, south central China. An important industrial city and rail centre, situated on the Huang He, it produces heavy machinery and textiles.

Zhi·to·mir (zhi-tómmeer). Capital of Zhitomir oblast, Ukraine. Situated on the river Teterev, it is a market centre for an agricultural region producing wheat and hops. Its industries include textiles and furniture.

Zhou *n.* See **Chou.**

Zhou En-lai or **Chou En-Lai** (jŏ en-lí) (1898–1976). Chinese statesman. After studying in Japan and Europe, he became an increasingly important leader in the Chinese Communist Party. He organised a general strike in Shanghai (1927) and later an insurrection in Nanching. He was the first prime minister (1949–76) and foreign minister (1949–58) of the People's Republic of China.

Zhu·jiang or **Chu-chiang** (jōō-jyáng). *English* **Pearl** or **Canton**. River of southeast China. On its large, fertile delta lie the cities of Guangzhou (Canton) and Macau, and the outlet of Hong Kong.

Zhu·kov (zhōō-kov; *Russian* -kəf), **Georgi Konstantinovich** (1896–1974). Marshal of the U.S.S.R. Entering the Red Army in 1918, he rose to army chief of staff (1941). He directed the counteroffensive at Stalingrad (1943), relieved Leningrad (1943), and captured Berlin (1945). He served under Khrushchev as defence minister (1955–57) but was attacked for "political mistakes" (1957).

Zi·a ul-Haq (zée-ə oʻol-hák). **General Mohammed** (1924–88). President of Pakistan. An army general, he led the military coup which overthrew President Bhutto (1977) and martial law administrator and then president (1978). Under his rule, general elections were postponed, Bhutto was executed, and strict Islamic laws were introduced.

zib·e·line, zib·el·line (zíbbə-līn, -lin, -leen) *n.* 1. A thick, lustrous, soft fabric of wool and other animal hair, such as mohair, having a silky nap. 2. *Rare.* The sable or its fur. [Old French, from Old Italian *zibellino,* from Slavic, akin to Russian *sobol†.*]

zib·et, zib·eth (zíbbit) *n.* A civet cat, *Viverra zibetha,* of southeast Asia. [Italian *zibetto,* from Medieval Latin *zibethum,* from Arabic *zabād,* CIVET.]

Zieg·feld (zéeg-feld, zíg-), **Flo(renz)** (1867–1932). U.S. theatre manager. Adapting the style of the Parisian Folies-Bergère, he became famous for his extravagant revues, known as the Ziegfeld Follies (1907–32). The discoverer of many entertainers, including Eddie Cantor and W.C. Fields, he produced musicals such as *Show Boat* (1927) and *Bitter Sweet* (1929).

Zieg·ler (zéeg-lər; *German* tséeg-), **Karl** (1898–1973). German organic chemist. For his work on long-chain polymers, and the use of catalysts to control polymerisation in plastics production, he shared the Nobel prize with Giulio Natta (1963).

Ziegler catalyst *n. Chemistry.* Any of a class of industrial catalysts that are mixed metal halides and organometallic compounds, used for promoting polymerisation reactions to make stereospecific plastics with improved strength and other properties. The original such catalyst was a mixture of titanium chloride (TiCl₄) and aluminium trimethyl (Al(CH₃)₃), used to make high-density polythene from ethylene. [After Karl ZIEGLER.]

zig·gu·rat (zíggōō-rat, zíggə-) *n.* Also **zik·ku·rat** (zíckōō-, zíckə-). A temple tower of the ancient Assyrians and Babylonians, having the form of a terraced pyramid of successively receding storeys. [Assyrian *ziqquratu,* summit, mountain top, from *zaqaru,* to be high.]

zig·zag (zíg-zag) *n.* 1. A line or course that proceeds by sharp turns in alternating directions. 2. Any of a series of such sharp turns. 3. Something exhibiting one or a series of sharp turns, such as a road or design.
~*adj.* Having or moving in a zigzag.
~*adv.* In a zigzag manner or pattern.
~*v.* **zigzagged, -zagging, -zags.** —*intr.* To move in or form a zigzag. —*tr.* To cause to move in or form a zigzag. [French, from German *Zickzack,* expressive formation.]

zig·zag·ger (zig-zaggər) *n.* 1. A person or thing that zigzags. 2. A sewing-machine attachment for sewing zigzag stitches.

zilch (zilch) *n. U.S. Slang.* 1. Zero; nothing. 2. An insignificant person; a nonentity. [Variant of ZERO.]

zil·lion (zil-yən, zílli-ən) *n. Chiefly U.S. Informal.* An extremely large indefinite number. Used humorously.
~*adj. Informal.* Very many. [z- (perhaps representing an indefinite large number) + (M)ILLION.]

Zim·ba·bwe (zim-baáb-wi, -báb-, -way). Landlocked country of south central Africa. It is made up of highveld and lowveld, including the Limpopo lowlands and forested Zambezi valley. Agriculture, mainly at subsistence level, accounts for only 16 per cent of its gross domestic product, and manufacturing 25 per cent. U.N. sanctions (imposed 1965) led to considerable diversification of manufacturing. The country has major reserves of timber and minerals, including coal. Its chief exports are gold, tobacco, iron and steel, chrome ore, asbestos, cotton, and nickel. Tourism is also important. Cecil Rhodes and his British South Africa Company obtained mineral rights in and claimed what are now Matabeleland and Mashonaland in the 1880s. From 1898 these formed the British colony of Southern Rhodesia, which became self-governing in 1923. The area was part of the Federation of Rhodesia and Nyasaland (1953–63), which broke up largely because of African opposition to the dominance of Southern Rhodesia's white minority. Led by Ian Smith, the minority government failed to arrive at an independence settlement with Britain, largely because it would not accept (black) majority rule, and made an illegal unilateral declaration of independence (1965). A republic was declared (1970), but Rhodesia was increasingly isolated in the world, and the government faced a protracted guerrilla war from the Zimbabwe African People's Union (ZAPU), led by Joshua Nkomo, and the Zimbabwe African National Union (ZANU), led by Robert Mugabe. Eventually, as an outcome of the Commonwealth Conference of 1979, a peace formula involving majority rule was agreed, and under British supervision, elections were held (March, 1980). Mugabe became independent Zimbabwe's first prime minister (April, 1980), and in 1987 he became president. In 1988 ZANU and ZAPU merged,

effectively creating a one-party state. Area 390 580 square kilometres (150,764 square miles). Population, 11,910,000. Capital, Harare (formerly Salisbury).

Zim·mer (zímmər) *n.* A trademark for a lightweight, sturdy, metal frame that has four rubber-tipped feet and a wide, curved crossbar that is easy to hold, used as a support when walking by the elderly or disabled. Also called "Zimmer frame".

zinc (zingk) *n. Symbol* **Zn** A bluish-white, lustrous metallic element that is brittle at room temperatures but malleable when heated. It is used to form a wide variety of alloys including brass, bronze, German silver, various solders, and nickel silver, in galvanising iron and other metals, for electric fuses, anodes, and meter cases, and in roofing, gutters, and various household objects. Atomic number 30, atomic weight 65.37, melting point 419.5°C, boiling point 908°C, relative density 7.14 (25°C), valency 2.
~*tr.v.* **zinced** or **zincked, zincing** or **zincking, zincs.** To coat or treat with zinc; galvanise. [German *Zink,* perhaps from *Zinke,* prong (so named because it becomes jagged in the furnace), from Old High German *zinko.*]

zinc·ate (zíng-kayt) *n.* Any of several chemical compounds derived from the reaction of zinc or zinc oxide with certain alkali solutions.

zinc blende *n.* A mineral, **sphalerite** (*see*).

zinc chloride *n.* A white soluble solid, ZnCl₂, used as a wood preservative, soldering flux, and medical astringent. Also called "butter of zinc".

zinc·if·er·ous (zing-kíffərəss) *adj.* Designating a compound, ore, or mineral that contains zinc.

zinc·ite (zíng-kīt) *n.* A red to -yellow-orange zinc ore, essentially ZnO.

zin·co·graph (zíngkə-graaf, -graf) *n.* 1. A prepared zinc plate used in zincography. 2. A print or picture obtained from such a plate. [ZINC + -GRAPH.]

zin·cog·ra·phy (zing-kóggrəfi) *n.* The process of engraving zinc printing plates. [ZINC + -GRAPHY.] —**zin·cog·ra·pher** *n.* —**zinc·o·graph·ic** (zíngkə-gráffik), **zinc·o·graph·i·cal** *adj.*

zinc ointment *n. Medicine.* A salve consisting of about 20 per cent zinc oxide with beeswax or paraffin and petrolatum, used in the treatment of skin diseases.

zinc oxide *n.* An amorphous white or yellowish powder, ZnO, used as a pigment, in compounding rubber, in the manufacture of plastics, and in pharmaceuticals and cosmetics. Also called "Chinese white", "zinc white".

zinc spinel *n.* A mineral, **gahnite** (*see*).

zinc sulphate *n.* A colourless crystalline compound, ZnSO₄·7H₂O, used medicinally as an emetic and astringent, as a fungicide, and in wood and skin preservatives. Also called "white vitriol".

zinc white *n.* A paint pigment, zinc oxide.

zing (zing) *n.* 1. A brief high-pitched humming or buzzing sound, such as that made by a swiftly passing object or a taut vibrating string. 2. Zest; vigour.
~*intr.v.* **zinged, zinging, zings.** *Informal.* 1. To make or move with such a sound. 2. To move quickly or vigorously. [Imitative.]

zin·ga·ro (zíng-gə-rō, tséeng-, -gaa-) *n., pl.* **-ri** (-ree). *Feminine* **zin·ga·ra** (-rə, -raa) *pl.* **-re** (-ray). A Gypsy. [Italian *zingaro,* probably from Greek *Athinganoi†* (plural), name of an oriental people.]

zin·jan·thro·pus (zin-jánthrə-pəss, zín-jan-thrō-) *n.* Any extinct primate of the genus *Zinjanthropus.* See **australopithecine.** [New Latin : Arabic *Zinj,* East Africa + Greek *anthrōpos,* man.]

zink·en·ite, zinck·en·ite (zíngkə-nīt) *n.* A steel-grey mineral, essentially Pb₆Sb₁₄S₂₇. [German *Zinkenit,* after J.K.L. *Zinken* (1790–1862), German mineralogist.]

zin·ni·a (zínni-ə) *n.* Any of various plants of the genus *Zinnia,* native to tropical America; especially, *Z. elegans,* widely cultivated for its showy, variously coloured flowers. [New Latin *Zinnia,* after Johann Gottfried *Zinn* (1727–59), German botanist and physician.]

Zi·no·viev (zi-nŏv-i-ev; *Russian* -yif), **Gregory Evseyevich** (1883–1936). Soviet politician. Chairman of the Comintern from 1919, he was an influential government member until expelled from the party (1927). He was executed in a Stalinist purge. The publication in Britain of a forged letter allegedly from him contributed to the downfall of the Labour government (1924).

Zi·on (zī'-ən) *n.* Also **Si·on** (sī'-ən). **1. a.** The Jewish people; the Israelites. **b.** The Jewish homeland as a symbol of Judaism. **c.** *Literary.* Ancient Jerusalem. **2. a.** A place or religious community regarded as sacredly devoted to God; a city of God. **b.** Heaven. **3.** An idealised harmonious community; a utopia. **4.** In Rastafarian ideology, the promised land. [Middle English *Sion,* Old English, from Late Latin *Siōn,* from Greek *Seiōn,* from Hebrew *Ṣiyōn.*]

Zion, Mount. **1.** The part of Jerusalem that constituted the City of David. **2.** The hill in Jerusalem on which Solomon's temple was built.

Zi·on·ism (zī'-ə-niz'm) *n.* **1.** A plan or movement of the Jewish people to return from the Diaspora to Palestine. **2.** A movement originally aimed at the re-establishment of a Jewish national homeland and state in Palestine and now concerned with the development of Israel. —**Zi·on·ist** *adj. & n.* —**Zi·on·is·tic** (-nístik) *adj.*

zip (zip) *n.* **1.** A fastening device consisting of parallel rows of metal or nylon teeth on adjacent edges of an opening which are interlocked by a sliding tab. Also called "zip fastener", *U.S.* "zipper". **2.** A brief, sharp, hissing sound, such as that made by a flying arrow. **3.** *Informal.* Energetic activity; zest; vim.
~*v.* **zipped, zipping, zips.** —*intr.* **1. a.** To move or act with a speed that makes or suggests a brief, sharp, hissing sound: *The cars zipped by endlessly.* **b.** To act or proceed swiftly and energetically. **2.** To become fastened by a zip. Often used with *up.* —*tr.* To fasten with a zip. Often used with *up.* [Imitative.]

zip code *n. Sometimes capital* **Z,** *capital* **C.** *U.S.* A post code *(see).* [Zone Improvement Program.]

zip·py (zíppi) *adj.* **-pier, -piest.** *Informal.* Full of energy; brisk; lively; snappy.

zir·con (zúr-kən, -kon) *n.* A brown to colourless mineral, essentially ZrSiO₄, which is heated, cut, and polished to form a brilliant bluewhite gem. [German *Zirkon,* from French *jargon,* from Italian *giargone,* from Arabic *zarqūn,* from Persian *zargūn,* gold-coloured : *zar,* gold + *gūn-*†.]

zir·con·ate (zúrkə-nayt) *n.* Any of several chemical compounds formed by heating zirconium oxide with a metal carbonate or oxide in the presence of an acid. [ZIRCON + -ATE.]

zir·co·ni·um (zur-kŏni-əm) *n. Symbol* **Zr** A lustrous, greyish-white, strong, ductile metallic element obtained primarily from zircon and used chiefly in ceramic and refractory compounds, as an alloying agent, in nuclear reactors, and in medical prosthesis. Atomic number 40, atomic weight 91.22, melting point 1,171°C, boiling point 4,377°C, relative density 6.53 (calculated), principal valency 4. [New Latin, from ZIRCON.]

zirconium oxide *n.* A hard, white, amorphous powder, ZrO₂, derived from zirconium and also found naturally, used chiefly in pigments, refractories, ceramics, and as an abrasive. Also called "zirconia".

zit (zit) *n. Slang.* A pimple. [20th century : imitative of bursting pimple.]

zith·er (zíth-ər, zíth-) *n.* Also **zith·ern** (-ərn). A musical instrument consisting of a flat sounding box with about 30 to 40 strings stretched over it and played horizontally with the fingertips or a plectrum. [German *Zither,* from Old High German *zithera, cithera,* from Latin *cithara,* from Greek *kithara,* CITHARA.] —**zith·er·ist** *n.*

zi·zith (tsítsiss, tsee-tséet) *pl.n.* The tassels or fringes of thread on the four corners of prayer shawls worn by orthodox Jewish males. [Hebrew *ṣīṣīth,* tassel.]

zizz (ziz) *n. British Informal.* A short sleep; a doze. [Probably from ZZZ.]

zlo·ty (zlótti) *n., pl.* **-tys** or **zloty. 1.** The basic monetary unit of Poland, equal to 100 groszy. **2.** A coin worth one zloty. [Polish *złoty,* "golden", from *złoto,* gold.]

Zn The symbol for the element zinc.

zo. Variant of dzo.

zo–. Variant of zoo-.

–zoa *n. comb. form.* Indicates certain animal organisms or taxonomic groups; for example, **entozoa, Protozoa.** [New Latin, from Greek *zōia,* plural of *zōion,* animal.]

–zoan *n. comb. form. Zoology.* Indicates animals within a taxonomic group; for example, **protozoan.** [From -ZOA.]

zo·di·ac (zódi-ak) *n.* **1. a.** *Astronomy.* A band of the celestial sphere, extending about eight degrees to either side of the ecliptic, that represents the path of the principal planets, the Moon, and the Sun. **b.** In astrology, this band divided into 12 equal parts called signs of the zodiac, each 30 degrees wide, bearing the name of a constellation for which it was originally named but with which it no longer coincides owing to the precession of the equinoxes. **2.** A diagram or figure representing the signs of the zodiac. **3.** A complete circuit; a circle. [Middle English, from Old French *zodiaque,* from Latin *zōdiacus,* from Greek *zōidiakos (kuklos),* "(circle) of carved figures", from *zōidion,* carved figure, sign of the zodiac, diminutive of *zōion,* animal.] —**zo·di·a·cal** (zō-dī'-ək'l) *adj.*

zodiacal light *n.* A faint hazy cone of light, often visible in the west just after sunset or in the east just before sunrise, apparently caused

by the reflection of sunlight from meteoric particles surrounding the sun.

zo·e·trope (zṓ-i-trōp) *n.* An optical toy consisting of a case containing a cylinder bearing pictures of figures which appear to move as they are viewed through a slit in the case while the cylinder revolves. [Originally a trademark; from Greek *zōē,* life + *tropos,* a turning, from *trepein,* to turn.]

Zof·fa·ny (zóffəni), **Johann** (*c.* 1733–1810). German painter. Living chiefly in London from 1761, he secured royal patronage and painted many royal portraits, as well as theatrical scenes.

Zog I (zog) (1895–1961). King of Albania (1928–43). Educated in Istanbul, he served as prime minister (1922–24) and president (1925–28) but fled the country after its invasion by Italy (1939). He first settled in England but later moved to Egypt and France. He abdicated in 1943.

–zoic *adj. comb. form.* Indicates: **1.** A specified kind of animal existence; for example, **holozoic. 2.** A specified geological division; for example, **Mesozoic.** [Greek *zōikos,* of animals, from *zōion,* animal.]

zois·ite (zóy-sīt) *n.* A grey or pink mineral, essentially Ca₂Al₃(SiO₄)₃(OH). [German *Zoisit,* named after its discoverer, Baron S. *Zois* von Edelstein (1747–1819), Slovenian nobleman.]

Zo·la (zóla; *French* zō-lá'a), **Émile (Édouard Charles Antoine)** (1840–1902). French novelist. Leader of the naturalist movement, he worked as a clerk and journalist before establishing his reputation with *Thérèse Raquin* (1867). Through the portrayal of a single extended family in *Les Rougon-Macquart,* a series of 20 novels including *L'Assommoir* (1877), *Nana* (1880), and *Germinal* (1885), he provided a detailed account of contemporary social problems. He was obliged to flee France for a year after publishing *J'accuse* (1898), a defence of Alfred Dreyfus.

zoll·ver·ein (zólvər-īn; *German* tsólfər-) *n.* **1.** *Often capital* **Z.** A union of German states during the 19th century that established a uniform tariff on imports from nonmembers and free trade among themselves. **2.** Any customs or tariff union. [German *Zollverein,* "custom union".]

zom·bie, zom·bi (zómbi) *n.* **1.** A snake god of voodoo cults in West Africa, Haiti, and the southern United States. **2. a.** A supernatural power or spell that according to voodoo belief can enter into and reanimate a dead body. **b.** A corpse revived in this way. **3.** *Informal.* One who appears lifeless, apathetic, or stupid. [Of West African origin.]

zo·nal (zṓn'l) *adj.* Also **zo·na·ry** (zṓnəri). **1.** Of or associated with a zone or zones. **2.** Divided into zones. —**zo·nal·ly** *adv.*

zonal soil *n.* A soil with a profile that depends largely on the type of vegetation it supports and the climate to which it is exposed.

zo·nate (zṓ-nayt) *adj.* Also **zo·nat·ed** (zō-náytid, zṓ-naytid). Having zones; belted, striped, or ringed.

zo·na·tion (zō-náysh'n) *n.* **1.** Arrangement or formation in zones; zonate structure. **2.** *Ecology.* The distribution of organisms in biogeographic zones.

zone (zōn) *n. Abbr.* **z.** **1.** An area, region, or division distinguished from adjacent parts by some distinctive feature or character: *a danger zone; an erogenous zone.* **2. a.** *Geography.* Any of the five regions of the surface of the earth that are loosely divided according to prevailing climate and latitude, including the Torrid Zone, the North and South Temperate Zones, and the North and South Frigid Zones. **b.** A similar division on any planet. **3.** In geometry, a portion of a sphere bounded by the intersections of two parallel planes with the sphere. **4.** *Ecology.* An area characterised by distinct physical conditions and populated by communities of certain kinds of organism. **5.** *Geology.* A region or stratum distinguished by composition or content. **6. a.** A section or division of an area or territory established to distinguish it from other similar areas for a specific purpose: *a fare zone.* **b.** A municipal area in a city designated for a particular type of building, enterprise, or activity: *residential zone.* **7.** *Archaic.* A belt or girdle. —See Synonyms at **area.**
~*tr.v.* **zoned, zoning, zones. 1.** To divide into zones. **2.** To designate or mark off into zones. **3.** To surround or encircle with or as if with a belt or girdle. [Latin *zōna,* girdle, zone, from Greek *zōnē.*]

zone refining *n.* A method of redistributing the impurities in a semiconductor material by melting a small section or zone of a bar of the material and causing the molten zone to move along the length of the bar. Purification can be achieved by concentrating the impurities at the end of the bar, which is later removed.

zone-time (zṓn-tīm) *n.* Standard time used at sea according to the time zone in which a ship is located.

zonked (zongkt) *adj. Chiefly U.S. Slang.* **1.** Intoxicated by alcohol or drugs. **2.** Extremely tired, confused, or disorientated. [20th century : origin obscure.]

zoo (zōō) *n., pl.* **zoos.** A public park or institution in which living animals are kept, bred, and exhibited to the public. Also called "zoological garden". [Short for ZOOLOGICAL GARDEN.]

zoo–, zo– *comb. form.* Indicates animals or animal forms; for example, **zoology, zoogeography, zooid.** [Greek *zōio-,* from *zōion, zōon,* living being, animal.]

zo·o·chem·is·try (zṓ-ə-kémmistri, -ō-) *n.* Animal biochemistry.

zo·o·chore (zṓ-ə-kawr, -ō- ‖ -kōr) *n.* A plant dispersed by animals. [ZOO- + -CHORE.]

zoogeog. zoogeography.

zoogeographic region *n.* An extensive region of the earth, such as central and southern Africa, characterised by the dominance of certain kinds of animal life.

zo·o·ge·og·ra·phy (zṓ-ə-jee-óggrəfi, zōō-, -ō-) *n. Abbr.* **zoogeog.**

The biological study of the geographical distribution of animals. —zo·o·ge·og·ra·pher *n.* —zo·o·ge·o·graph·ic (-jée-ə-gráffik, -ō-), zo·o·ge·o·graph·i·cal *adj.* —zo·o·ge·o·graph·i·cal·ly *adv.*

zo·o·gloe·a, zo·o·gle·a (zō-ə-glée-ə) *n., pl.* **-ae** (-ee) or **-as.** Any of various bacteria of the genus *Zoogloea,* forming colonies in a jelly-like secretion. [New Latin : ZOO- + Medieval Greek *glia, gloia,* glue.]

zo·og·ra·phy (zō-óggrəfi) *n.* The biological description of animals. [ZOO- + -GRAPHY.] —zo·og·ra·pher *n.* —zo·o·graph·ic (zō-ə-gráffik), zo·o·graph·i·cal *adj.*

zo·oid (zō-oyd) *n.* **1.** *Biology.* An organic cell or organised body that has independent movement within a living organism; especially, a motile gamete such as a spermatozoon. **2.** *Zoology.* Any of the usually microscopic animals forming an aggregate or colony, as of polyzoans or hydrozoans. [ZO(O)- + -OID.] —zo·o·i·dal (zō-óyd'l) *adj.*

zool. zoological; zoology.

zo·ol·a·try (zō-óllətri) *n., pl.* **-tries.** The worship of animals. [New Latin *zoolatria* : ZOO- + -LATRY.] —zo·ol·a·ter *n.* —zo·ol·a·trous *adj.*

zo·o·log·i·cal (zō-ə-lójik'l, zō-; *sometimes* zōō-lójik'l) *adj.* Also *chiefly U.S.* **zo·o·log·ic** (-ə-lójik). *Abbr.* **zool.** **1.** Of or pertaining to animals or animal life. **2.** Of or pertaining to the science of zoology. —zo·o·log·i·cal·ly *adv.*

zoological garden *n.* A zoo (see).

zo·ol·o·gist (zō-ólləjist, zōō-) *n.* One who specialises in the study of animals.

zo·ol·o·gy (zō-ólləji, zōō-) *n., pl.* **-gies.** *Abbr.* **zool.** **1.** The biological study of animals. **2.** The animal life of a particular area. **3.** The characteristics of an animal group or category: *the zoology of fish.* **4.** A book or scholarly work on animals. [New Latin *zoologia* : ZOO- + -LOGY.]

zoom (zōōm) *v.* **zoomed, zooming, zooms.** —*intr.* **1.** To make a continuous low-pitched buzzing or humming sound. **2.** To move while making such a sound. **3.** To climb suddenly and sharply in an aeroplane. **4.** To move or act very rapidly: *zoom up to town.* **5. a.** To move rapidly towards or away from a photographic subject. Used of a camera. Often used with *in* or *out.* **b.** To simulate such a movement, as by means of a zoom lens. Often used with *in* or *out.* —*tr.* To cause to zoom.
—*n.* The act or sound of zooming. [Imitative.]

zo·om·e·try (zō-ómmətri) *n.* Measurement and comparison of the sizes of animals or animal parts, especially the measurement of bulk. [ZOO- + -METRY.] —zo·o·met·ric (zō-ə-méttrik), zo·o·met·ri·cal *adj.* —zo·o·met·ri·cal·ly *adv.*

zoom lens *n.* A camera lens whose focal length can be rapidly changed, allowing rapid change in the size of an image.

zo·o·mor·phism (zō-ə-mór-fiz'm) *n.* Also **zo·o·mor·phy** (-mórfi). **1.** The attribution of animal characteristics or qualities to a god or gods. **2.** The use of animal forms in symbolism, literature, or art. [ZOO- + -MORPH + -ISM.] —zo·o·mor·phic *adj.*

-zoon *n. comb. form.* Indicates an individual animal or independently moving organic unit; for example, **spermatozoon.** [New Latin, from Greek *zōion, zōon,* living being, animal.]

zo·on·o·sis (zō-ónnə-siss, zō-ə-nō-) *n., pl.* **-ses** (-seez). A disease such as rabies or malaria that can be transmitted from animals to man. [New Latin : ZOO- + Greek *nosos,* illness.]

zo·oph·a·gous (zō-óffəgəss) *adj.* Feeding on animal matter. [ZOO- + -PHAGOUS.]

zo·o·phile (zō-ə-fīl ‖ -fil) *n.* A lover of animals; especially, one opposed to vivisection. [ZOO- + -PHILE.] —zo·o·phil·ic (-fillik) *adj.* —zo·oph·i·lism (zō-óffiliz'm) *n.*

zo·oph·i·lous (zō-óffiləss) *adj.* **1.** *Botany.* Pollinated by animals. **2.** Of, pertaining to, or characterised by zoophilism.

zo·o·pho·bi·a (zō-ə-fóbi-ə) *n.* An irrational fear of animals. [New Latin : ZOO- + -PHOBIA.] —zo·o·pho·bous (zō-óffəbəss) *adj.*

zo·o·phyte (zō-ə-fīt) *n.* An invertebrate animal such as a sea anemone or sponge that remains attached to a surface and superficially resembles a plant. [Greek *zōophuton* : ZOO- + -PHYTE.] —zo·o·phyt·ic (-fittik), zo·o·phyt·i·cal *adj.*

zo·o·plank·ton (zō-ə-plángktən) *n.* Small crustaceans, fish larvae, and other, often microscopic, aquatic animals that make up the animal part of plankton.

zo·o·plas·ty (zō-ə-plasti) *n.* Surgical transfer of tissue from an animal to man. [ZOO- + -PLASTY.] —zo·o·plas·tic (-plástik) *adj.*

zo·o·sperm (zō-ə-sperm) *n.* *Biology.* A spermatozoon (see). [ZOO- + -SPERM.]

zo·o·spo·ran·gi·um (zō-ə-spaw-ránji-əm, -spə- ‖ -spō-) *n., pl.* **-gia** (-ji-ə). *Botany.* A sporangium in which zoospores develop.

zo·o·spore (zō-ə-spawr ‖ -spōr) *n.* A motile, flagellated asexual spore, as of certain algae and fungi. —zo·o·spor·ic (-spáwr-ik ‖ -spōr-), zo·o·spor·ous (zō-óspərəss, zō-ə-spáwr-əss ‖ -spōr-) *adj.*

zo·os·ter·ol (zō-óstə-rol ‖ -rōl) *n.* *Biochemistry.* Any of several animal sterols, such as cholesterol.

zo·o·tech·nics (zō-ə-tékniks) *n.* *Used with a singular or plural verb.* Zootechny. [ZOO- + Greek *tekhnē,* art.]

zo·o·tech·ny (zō-ə-tekni) *n.* The domestication, breeding, and improvement of animals; the technology of animal husbandry. Also called "zootechnics". [ZOO- + *technē,* art.] —zo·o·tech·ni·cal (-téknik'l) *adj.* —zo·o·tech·ni·cian (-tek-nísh'n) *n.*

zo·ot·o·my (zō-óttəmi) *n.* **1.** Dissection of animals other than man. **2.** Comparative anatomy. [ZOO- + -TOMY.] —zo·o·tom·ic

1746

(zō-ə-tómmik), zo·o·tom·i·cal *adj.* —zo·o·tom·i·cal·ly *adv.* —zo·ot·o·mist (zō-óttəmist) *n.*

zoot suit (zōōt) *n.* *Slang.* A man's suit, popular especially in the United States during the early 1940s, characterised by tapering trousers with turn-ups and a long jacket with wide lapels and wide, padded shoulders. [*Zoot,* rhyming formation based on SUIT.]

zor·ille, zor·il (zórril, zə-ríl) *n.* Also **zor·il·la** (zə-rílə). An African mammal, *Ictonyx striatus,* resembling the skunk in appearance and defensive action. [French, from Spanish *zorrillo, zorrilla,* "small fox", from *zorro,* fox, from Old Spanish *zorrar†,* to drag.]

Zor·o·as·ter (zórrō-ástər) (*c.* 628–551 B.C.). Also **Zar·a·thus·tra** (zárrə-thōostrə). Persian prophet. As a priest in northwest Persia, he founded the religion Zoroastrianism after he had a divine vision. He wrote the Gathas, a collection of hymns in honour of the god Ormazd.

Zor·o·as·tri·an·ism (zórrō-ástri-ə-niz'm ‖ zōrō-) *n.* The dualistic religious system founded in Persia by Zoroaster and set forth in the Zend-Avesta, teaching the worship of Ormazd, god of creation, light, and goodness, who is engaged in a continual struggle against Ahriman, spirit of evil and darkness. Also called "Mazdaism". —Zo·ro·as·tri·an *adj.* & *n.*

zos·ter (zóstər) *n.* A belt or girdle worn by men in ancient Greece. [Latin, from Greek *zōstēr,* girdle.]

Zou·ave (zōō-áav, zwáav) *n.* **1.** A member of a French infantry unit, formerly composed of Algerian recruits, characterised by colourful oriental uniforms and precision drilling. **2.** A member of any group modelled on the French Zouaves; especially, a member of such a unit of the Union Army in the American Civil War. [French, from *zwāwa,* Algerian tribal name.]

zounds (zowndz, zōōndz) *interj.* Also **swounds** (zwowndz, zowndz, zōōndz), **swouns** (zwownz, zownz, zōōnz). *Archaic.* Used to express anger, surprise, or indignation. [Euphemism for *God's wounds.*]

zoy·si·a (zóyzi-ə) *n.* Any of several creeping grasses of the genus *Zoysia,* native to Asia and Australia, and widely cultivated as a lawn grass. [New Latin *Zoysia;* after Karl von Zois (died 1800), German botanist.]

ZPG zero population growth.

Z-pro·pyl·pi·per·i·dine (zéd-prō-pil-pi-pérri-deen, -pī-, -din) *n.* Coniine (see).

Zr The symbol for the element zirconium.

zuc·chet·to (zōō-kéttō, tsōō-) *n., pl.* **-tos.** *Roman Catholic Church.* A skullcap worn by clergymen, varying in colour according to the rank of the wearer. It is white, red, or purple for a pope, cardinal, or bishop respectively. [Italian, incorrect diminutive of *zucca,* gourd, head, from Late Latin *cucutia,* gourd, probably from Latin *cucurbita,* GOURD.]

zuc·chi·ni (zōō-kéeni) *n., pl.* **zucchini.** *Chiefly U.S.* A courgette. [Italian, plural of *zuchino,* diminutive of *zucca,* gourd. See **zucchetto.**]

Zuck·er·man (zúckərmən), **Solly, Baron** (1904–93). South African-born British scientist. Trained as an anatomist, he served as chief scientific adviser to the British government (1964–71). His books include *Scientists and War* (1966) and *From Apes to Warlords* (1978).

Zug·spitz·e (tsŏok-shpitsə). Mountain of southern Germany. Situated in the Bavarian Alps near the Austrian border, it is the highest peak in Germany, 2963 metres (9721 feet).

zug·zwang (tsŏok-tsvang) *n.* In chess, a situation in which a player must take his turn, even though it is to his disadvantage.
—*tr.v.* **zugzwanged, -zwanging, -zwangs.** To force (one's opponent) into such a situation. [German : *Zug,* (a) move + *Zwang,* force, compulsion.]

Zui·der Zee (zídər zée; *Dutch* zóydər záy). Former inlet of the North Sea, northeastern Netherlands. A drainage project (begun 1920) separated the inlet from the sea by a dyke (completed 1932), dividing it into the Ijsselmeer and the Waddenzee.

Zuid-Holland, Zuidholland. See **South Holland.**

Zu·lu (zōō-lōō) *n., pl.* **-lus** or collectively **Zulu.** **1.** A member of a tall, Negroid people of southeastern Africa, formerly a powerful warrior nation originally living in northeastern Natal. **2.** The Bantu language spoken by this people. —**Zu·lu** *adj.*

Zu·lu·land (zōōlōō-land). Southern African region, formerly in northeastern Natal province. The historic home of the Zulus, it rose to power during the early 19th century, resisting the Boer settlers until its final defeat by the British (1879). Part of Natal from 1897, it corresponded roughly to the Bantu homeland of Kwa-Zulu, and is now in KwaZulu-Natal province.

zup·pa in·gle·se (tsŏoppə ing-gláy-say) *n.* A pudding resembling a trifle, originally made with a macaroon base. [Italian, "English soup".]

Zü·rich (zéwr-ik, zóor-; *German* tsú-rikh). Capital of Zürich canton, northeastern Switzerland. Situated on the river Limmat on the north shore of Lake Zürich, it is the cultural centre of German-speaking Switzerland, and is best known for its banking and financial facilities.

Zweig (tsvīk), **Stefan** (1881–1942). Austrian Jewish writer. Influenced by Freud, he was a prolific and popular writer of both fiction and non-fiction. His best-known work is the novel *Beware of Pity* (1939).

zwie·back (zwée-bak, -baak ‖ zwī-, swī-, swée-) *n.* A type of bread, usually sweetened, baked first as a loaf and later cut into slices and toasted. [German *Zwieback,* "twice-baked (bread)".]

Zwing·li (zwíng-li, swing-; *German* tsvíng-), **Ulrich** (1484–1531).

Swiss Protestant reformer. Ordained as a Roman Catholic priest (1506), he became a preacher in Zurich (1518) where he spoke out against the selling of indulgences. He became leader of the Reformation in Switzerland but was killed in an attack on Zurich by the Catholic forest cantons. He predated Luther in many of his ideas and greatly influenced Calvin.

Zwing·li·an (zwíng-li-ən, swíng-, tsvíng-, -gli-) *adj.* Of or pertaining to Zwingli or to his theological system, especially his doctrine that the physical body of Christ is not present in the Eucharist and that the ceremony is merely a symbolic commemoration of Christ's death.
~*n.* A follower of Zwingli. —**Zwing·li·an·ism** *n.* —**Zwing·li·an·ist** *n.*

zwit·ter·i·on (zwíttər-ī-ən, tsvíttər-) *n. Physics.* An ion carrying both a positive and a negative charge, thus forming an electrically neutral molecule. [German *Zwitterion,* "mongrel ion" : *Zwitter,* mongrel, hybrid, from Old High German *zwitar(a)n,* from *zwi-,* twice + ION.] —**zwit·ter·i·on·ic** (-ī-ónnik) *adj.*

Zwor·y·kin (zwáwrikin), **Vladimir Kosma** (1889–1982). U.S. physicist. Born in Russia, he took U.S. citizenship in 1924. He invented the iconoscope (1938) and the first practical television camera, and helped to develop the electron microscope (1939).

zyg·a·poph·y·sis (zíggə-póffi-siss, zígə-) *n., pl.* **-ses** (-seez). *Anatomy.* Either of two usually paired processes of a vertebra that articulate with corresponding parts of adjacent vertebrae. [ZYG(O)- + APOPHYSIS.] —**zyg·a·po·phys·e·al** (-sée-əl, -pə-fī-zi-əl) *adj.*

zygo-, zyg– *comb. form.* Indicates: **1.** Yoke or pair; for example, **zygodactyl, zygapophysis. 2.** Union or fusion; for example, **zygospore, zygomorphic.** [New Latin, from Greek *zugon,* yoke.]

zy·go·dac·tyl (zígō-dáktil, zíggə-) *adj.* Also **zy·go·dac·tyl·ous** (-əss). Having two toes projecting forwards and two projecting backwards. Said of certain birds.
~*n.* A zygodactyl bird.

zy·go·ma (zī-gṓ-mə, zi-) *n., pl.* **-mata** (-mətə) or **-mas. 1.** The zygomatic bone. **2.** The zygomatic arch. [New Latin, from Greek *zugṓma,* bolt, bar, yoke, from *zugoun,* to yoke, connect.] —**zy·go·mat·ic** (zí-gō-máttik, -gə-, zi-) *adj.*

zygomatic arch *n.* The bony arch in vertebrates that extends along the side or front of the skull beneath the orbit. Also called "zygoma".

zygomatic bone *n.* A small quadrangular bone in vertebrates on the side of the face below the eye, forming, in mammals, part of the orbit and part of the zygomatic arch. Also called "cheekbone", "jugal", "malar", "zygoma".

zy·go·mor·phic (zígō-mórfik, zíggō-) *adj.* Also **zy·go·mor·phous** (-fəss). Bilaterally symmetrical so as to be capable of being symmetrically divided only along a single longitudinal plane. Said of flowers. Compare **actinomorphic.** [ZYGO- + -MORPHIC.] —**zy·go·mor·phism** *n.*

zy·go·sis (zī-gṓ-siss, zi-) *n., pl.* **-ses** (-seez). The union of gametes to form a zygote; conjugation. [ZYG(O)- + -OSIS.]

zy·go·spore (zígō-spawr, zíggō- ‖ -spōr) *n.* A thick-walled spore formed from the zygote in certain algae or fungi.

zy·gote (zī-gōt, ziggōt) *n.* The cell formed by the union of two gametes. [Greek *zugōtos,* joined, yoked, from *zugoun,* to join, to yoke.] —**zy·got·ic** (zī-góttik, zi-) *adj.* —**zy·got·i·cal·ly** *adv.*

zy·go·tene (zígə-teen, zíggə-) *n.* The second stage of meiotic prophase during which the homologous chromosomes pair to form bivalents. [ZYGO(TE) + -TENE.]

zy·mase (zī-mayz, -mayss) *n.* The enzyme complex, first isolated from yeast, that converts hexose sugars to ethanol and carbon dioxide. [ZYM(O)- + -ASE.]

–zyme *n. comb. form.* Indicates an enzyme; for example, **lysozyme.** [Greek *zumē,* leaven.]

zymo-, zym– *comb. form.* Indicates fermentation; for example, **zymolysis, zymase.** [New Latin, from Greek *zumē,* leaven.]

zy·mo·gen (zī-mō-jen, -mə-, -jən) *n.* The inactive protein precursor of an enzyme. [ZYMO- + -GEN.]

zy·mo·gen·ic (zī-mō-jénnik, -mə-) *adj.* Also **zy·mog·e·nous** (zī-mójinəss, zi-). **1.** Of or pertaining to a zymogen. **2.** Capable of causing fermentation. **3.** Enzyme-producing.

zy·mol·o·gy (zī-mólləji) *n.* The chemistry of fermentation. [New Latin *zymologia* : ZYMO- + -LOGY.] —**zy·mo·log·ic** (-mə-lójik), **zy·mo·log·i·cal** *adj.* —**zy·mol·o·gist** (zī-mólləjist) *n.*

zy·mol·y·sis (zī-mólli-siss) *n.* Fermentation. Also called "zymosis". [ZYMO- + -LYSIS.] —**zy·mo·lyt·ic** (zímə-líttik) *adj.*

zy·mom·e·ter (zī-mómmitər) *n.* An instrument used for determining the degree of fermentation. [ZYMO- + -METER.]

zy·mo·scope (zímə-skōp) *n.* An instrument used to determine fermentation efficiency by measuring the amount of carbon dioxide produced. [ZYMO- + -SCOPE.]

zy·mo·sis (zī-mṓ-siss, zi-) *n.* **1.** Zymolysis. **2.** *Medicine.* The process of infection or an infectious disease. [New Latin, from Greek *zumōsis,* fermentation, from *zumoun,* to leaven, ferment, from *zumē,* leaven.] —**zy·mot·ic** (-móttik) *adj.* —**zy·mot·i·cal·ly** *adv.*

zy·mur·gy (zī-murji) *n.* The branch of chemistry concerned with fermentation processes in brewing. [ZYM(O)- + -URGY.]

zzz, zzzz. A convention used to indicate, as in a cartoon, that a person is asleep.

WEIGHTS AND MEASURES

The system of measurement used for centuries in Britain, the Commonwealth and the USA has been the **Imperial**, or FPS system, based on the **F**oot, **P**ound and **S**econd. A new system was founded in France during the French Revolution and became known as the **Metric**, or CGS system, based on the **C**entimetre, **G**ram and **S**econd.

A modernised form of the metric system was agreed at an international conference in 1960. It is known as the **Système International d'Unités** (SI), or International System of Units. Britain, in common with a large part of the world, is adopting SI as its primary system of measurements.

Metric units

Length

	1 millimetre	0·03937 in
10 mm	1 centimetre	0·39 in
10 cm	1 decimetre	3·94 in
100 cm	1 metre	39·37 in
1,000 m	1 kilometre	0·62 mile

Area

	1 square millimetre	0·0016 sq. in
	1 square centimetre	0·155 sq. in
100 sq. cm	1 square decimetre	15·50 sq. in
10,000 sq. cm	1 square metre	10·76 sq. ft
10,000 sq. m	1 hectare	2·47 acres

Volume

	1 cubic centimetre	0·061 cu. in
1,000 cu. cm	1 cubic decimetre	61·024 cu. in
1,000 cu. dm	1 cubic metre	35·31 cu. ft
(liquid)	1 litre	1·76 pints
100 litres	1 hectolitre	22 gallons

Weight

	1 gram	0·035 oz
1,000 g	1 kilogram	2·2046 lb
1,000 kg	1 tonne	0·9842 ton

Imperial units

Length

	1 inch	2·54 cm
12 in	1 foot	30·48 cm
3 ft	1 yard	0·9144 m
1,760 yd	1 mile	1·6093 km

Area

	1 square inch	6·45 sq. cm
144 sq. in	1 square foot	0·093 m²
9 sq. ft	1 square yard	0·836 m²
4,840 sq. yd	1 acre	0·405 ha
640 acres	1 square mile	259·00 ha

Volume

	1 cubic inch	16·3871 cm³
1,728 cu. in	1 cubic foot	0·028 m³
27 cu. ft	1 cubic yard	0·765 m³
(liquid)	1 pint	0·57 litre
2 pints	1 quart	1·14 litres
4 quarts	1 gallon	4·55 litres

Weight

	1 ounce	28·3495 g
16 oz	1 pound	0·4536 kg
14 lb	1 stone	6·35 kg
8 stones	1 hundredweight	50·8 kg
20 cwt	1 ton	1·016 tonnes

How to convert units of measurement

Metric to Imperial

To convert	*into*	*multiply by*
Length		
millimetres	inches	0·0394
centimetres	inches	0·3937
metres	feet	3·2808
metres	yards	1·0936
kilometres	miles	0·6214
Area		
square centimetres	square inches	0·155
square metres	square feet	10·764
square metres	square yards	1·196
hectares	acres	2·471
square kilometres	square miles	0·386
Volume		
cubic centimetres	cubic inches	0·061
cubic metres	cubic feet	35·315
cubic metres	cubic yards	1·308
litres	pints	1·760
litres	gallons	0·220
Weight		
grams	ounces	0·0352
kilograms	pounds	2·2046
tonnes	tons	0·9842

Imperial to metric

To convert	*into*	*multiply by*
Length		
inches	millimetres	25·4
inches	centimetres	2·54
feet	metres	0·3048
yards	metres	0·9144
miles	kilometres	1·6093
Area		
square inches	square centimetres	6·4516
square feet	square metres	0·0929
square yards	square metres	0·836
acres	hectares	0·405
square miles	square kilometres	2·58999
Volume		
cubic inches	cubic centimetres	16·387
cubic feet	cubic metres	0·0283
cubic yards	cubic metres	0·7646
fluid ounces	millilitres	28·41
pints	litres	0·568
gallons	litres	4·55

Weight

ounces	grams	28·35
pounds	kilograms	0·45359
tons	tonnes	1·016

Conversion tables

The figures in the tinted central column of the tables on the next four pages refer to measurements in either the metric system (left) or imperial system (right).

For example, in the table below, the figure '10' in the centre column, if taken to represent 10 inches, will convert to 254 millimetres, the figure in the left-hand column. If, on the other hand, '10' is taken to represent 10 millimetres, it will convert to 0·39 inches, the figure in the right-hand column.

Length — Millimetres and inches

Exact conversion

1 mm = 0·0394 in   1 in = 25·4 mm

Approximate conversion

1 mm = $\frac{1}{32}$ in   1 in = 25 mm

Millimetres		Inches
3·2	$\frac{1}{8}$	
6·4	$\frac{1}{4}$	
9·5	$\frac{3}{8}$	
12·7	$\frac{1}{2}$	
15·9	$\frac{5}{8}$	
19·0	$\frac{3}{4}$	
22·2	$\frac{7}{8}$	
25·4	1	0·04
50·8	2	0·08
76·2	3	0·12
101·6	4	0·16
127·0	5	0·20
152·4	6	0·24
177·8	7	0·28
203·2	8	0·31
228·6	9	0·35
254·0	10	0·39
279·4	11	0·43
304·8	12	0·47

Length — Centimetres and inches

Exact conversion

1 cm = 0·3937 in   1 in = 2·540 cm

Approximate conversion

1 cm = $\frac{2}{5}$ in   1 in = 2·5 cm

Centimetres		Inches
0·3	$\frac{1}{8}$	
0·6	$\frac{1}{4}$	
1·0	$\frac{3}{8}$	
1·3	$\frac{1}{2}$	
1·6	$\frac{5}{8}$	
1·9	$\frac{3}{4}$	
2·2	$\frac{7}{8}$	
2·5	1	0·39
5·1	2	0·79
7·6	3	1·18
10·2	4	1·57
12·7	5	1·97
15·2	6	2·36
17·8	7	2·76
20·3	8	3·15
22·9	9	3·54
25·4	10	3·94

Length — Metres and feet

Exact conversion

1 m = 3·2808 ft   1 ft = 0·3048 m

Approximate conversion

1 m = 3 ft $3\frac{3}{8}$ in   1 ft = 0·3 m

Metres		Feet
0·3	1	3·3
0·6	2	6·6
0·9	3	9·8
1·2	4	13·1
1·5	5	16·4
1·8	6	19·7
2·1	7	23·0
2·4	8	26·2
2·7	9	29·5
3·0	10	32·8
4·6	15	49·2
6·1	20	65·6
7·6	25	82·0
9·1	30	98·4
10·7	35	114·8
12·2	40	131·2
13·7	45	147·6
15·2	50	164·0
22·9	75	246·1
30·5	100	328·1

Length — Metres and yards

Exact conversion

1 m = 1·0936 yds   1 yd = 0·9144 m

Approximate conversion

1 m = 1 yd 3 in   1 yd = 0·9 m

Metres		Yards
0·9	1	1·1
1·8	2	2·2
2·7	3	3·3
3·7	4	4·4
4·6	5	5·5
5·5	6	6·6
6·4	7	7·7
7·3	8	8·7
8·2	9	9·8

Metres		Yards
9·1	10	10·9
13·7	15	16·4
18·3	20	21·9
22·9	25	27·3
27·4	30	32·8
32·0	35	38·3
36·6	40	43·7
41·1	45	49·2
45·7	50	54·7
68·6	75	82·0
91·4	100	109·4

Length — Kilometres and miles

Exact conversion

1 km = 0·6214 mile   1 mile = 1·6093 km

Approximate conversion

1 km = $\frac{5}{8}$ mile   1 mile = 1·6 km

Kilometres		Miles
1·6	1	0·6
3·2	2	1·2
4·8	3	1·9
6·4	4	2·5
8·0	5	3·1
9·7	6	3·7
11·3	7	4·3
12·9	8	5·0
14·5	9	5·6
16·1	10	6·2
24·1	15	9·3
32·2	20	12·4
40·2	25	15·5
48·3	30	18·6
56·3	35	21·7
64·4	40	24·9
72·4	45	28·0
80·5	50	31·1
88·5	55	34·2
96·6	60	37·3

Area — Square centimetres and square inches

Exact conversion   *Approximate conversion*

1 sq. cm = 0·155 sq. in   1 sq. cm = $\frac{1}{6}$ sq. in
1 sq. in = 6·4516 sq. cm   1 sq. in = 6·5 sq. cm

Sq. centimetre		Sq. inch
6·45	1	0·16
12·90	2	0·31
19·35	3	0·47
25·81	4	0·62
32·26	5	0·78
38·71	6	0·93
45·16	7	1·09
51·61	8	1·24
58·06	9	1·40
64·52	10	1·55
70·97	11	1·71

Sq. centimetre		Sq. inch
77·42	12	1·86
83·87	13	2·02
90·32	14	2·17
96·77	15	2·33
103·23	16	2·48
109·68	17	2·64
116·13	18	2·79
122·58	19	2·95
129·03	20	3·10

Area — Square metres and square feet

Exact conversion   *Approximate conversion*

1 m² = 10·7639 sq. ft   1 m² = $10\frac{3}{4}$ sq. ft
1 sq. ft = 0·0929 m²   1 sq. ft = 0·1 m²

Sq. metres		Sq. feet
0·09	1	10·8
0·19	2	21·5
0·28	3	32·3
0·37	4	43·1
0·46	5	53·8
0·56	6	64·6
0·65	7	75·3
0·74	8	86·1
0·84	9	96·9
0·93	10	107·6
1·02	11	118·4
1·11	12	129·2
1·21	13	139·9
1·30	14	150·7
1·39	15	161·5
1·49	16	172·2
1·58	17	183·0
1·67	18	193·8
1·77	19	204·5
1·86	20	215·3

Area — Hectares and acres

Exact conversion   *Approximate conversion*

1 hectare = 2·471 acres   1 hectare = $2\frac{1}{2}$ acres
1 acre = 0·4047 hectares   1 acre = 0·5 hectares

Hectares		Acres
0·40	1	2·5
0·81	2	4·9
1·21	3	7·4
1·62	4	9·9
2·02	5	12·4
2·43	6	14·8
2·83	7	17·3
3·24	8	19·8
3·64	9	22·2
4·05	10	24·7
4·45	11	27·2
4·86	12	29·7
5·26	13	32·1
5·67	14	34·6
6·07	15	37·1

Hectares		Acres
6·47	16	39·5
6·88	17	42·0
7·28	18	44·5
7·69	19	46·9
8·09	20	49·4

Area — Square kilometres and square miles

Exact conversion

1 km² = 0·3861 sq. mile
1 sq. mile = 2·58999 km²

Approximate conversion

1 km² = 3/8 sq. mile
1 sq. mile = 2·5 km²

Sq. km		Sq. miles
2·6	1	0·39
5·2	2	0·77
7·8	3	1·16
10·4	4	1·54
12·9	5	1·93
15·5	6	2·32
18·1	7	2·70
20·7	8	3·09
23·3	9	3·47
25·9	10	3·86
28·5	11	4·25
31·1	12	4·63
33·7	13	5·02
36·3	14	5·41
38·8	15	5·79
41·4	16	6·18
44·0	17	6·56
46·6	18	6·95
49·2	19	7·34
51·8	20	7·72

Volume — Litres and pints

Exact conversion

1 litre = 1·7598 pints
1 pint = 0·568 litre

Approximate conversion

1 litre = 1¾ pints
1 pint = 0·5 litre

Litres		Pints
0·57	1	1·76
1·14	2	3·52
1·70	3	5·28
2·27	4	7·04
2·84	5	8·80
3·41	6	10·56
3·98	7	12·32
4·55	8	14·08
5·11	9	15·84
5·68	10	17·60

Volume — Litres and gallons

Exact conversion

1 litre = 0·220 gallon
1 gallon = 4·546 litres

Approximate conversion

1 litre = ¼ gallon
1 gallon = 4·5 litres

Litres		Gallons
4·55	1	0·22

Litres		Gallons
9·09	2	0·44
13·64	3	0·66
18·18	4	0·88
22·73	5	1·10
27·28	6	1·32
31·82	7	1·54
36·37	8	1·76
40·91	9	1·98
45·46	10	2·20
68·19	15	3·30
90·92	20	4·40
113·65	25	5·50

Weight — Kilograms and pounds

Exact conversion

1 kg = 2·2046 lb
1 lb = 0·45359 kg

Approximate conversion

1 kg = 2¼ lb
1 lb = 0·5 kg

Kilograms		Pounds
0·45	1	2·2
0·91	2	4·4
1·36	3	6·6
1·81	4	8·8
2·27	5	11·0
2·72	6	13·2
3·18	7	15·4
3·63	8	17·6
4·08	9	19·8
4·54	10	22·0
4·99	11	24·3
5·44	12	26·5
5·90	13	28·7
6·35	14	30·9
6·80	15	33·1
7·26	16	35·3
7·71	17	37·5
8·16	18	39·7
8·62	19	41·9
9·07	20	44·1

Weight — Kilograms and stones

Exact conversion

1 kg = 0·1575 stone
1 stone = 6·350 kg

Approximate conversion

1 kg = ⅛ stone
1 stone = 6·5 kg

Kilograms		Stones
6·35	1	0·16
12·70	2	0·31
19·05	3	0·47
25·40	4	0·63
31·75	5	0·79
38·10	6	0·94
44·45	7	1·10
50·80	8	1·26
57·15	9	1·42
63·50	10	1·57

Weight — Kilograms and hundredweights

Exact conversion

1 kg = 0·0197 cwt   1 cwt = 50·8023 kg

Approximate conversion

1 kg = $\frac{1}{50}$ cwt   1 cwt = 50 kg

Kilograms		Hundredweights	Kilograms		Hundredweights
50·8	1	0·02	152·4	3	0·06
101·6	2	0·04	203·2	4	0·08
			254·0	5	0·10
			304·8	6	0·12
			355·6	7	0·14
			406·4	8	0·16
			457·2	9	0·18
			508·0	10	0·20

Temperature

Exact conversion F° = (C° × 1·8) + 32   C° = (F° − 32) ÷ 1·8

QUICK GUIDE

°C	°F
0	32
+5	41
10	50
15	59
20	68
25	77
30	86
35	95
40	104
45	113
50	122
55	131
60	140
65	149
70	158
75	167
80	176
85	185
90	194
95	203
100	212

Degrees C.	⇄	Degrees F.	Degrees C.	⇄	Degrees F.	Degrees C.	⇄	Degrees F.
−34·4	−30	−22·0	−9·4	+15	+59·0	+15·6	+60	+140·0
−33·9	−29	−20·2	−8·9	+16	+60·8	+16·1	+61	+141·8
−33·3	−28	−18·4	−8·3	+17	+62·6	+16·7	+62	+143·6
−32·8	−27	−16·6	−7·8	+18	+64·4	+17·2	+63	+145·4
−32·2	−26	−14·8	−7·2	+19	+66·2	+17·8	+64	+147·2
−31·7	−25	−13·0	−6·7	+20	+68·0	+18·3	+65	+149·0
−31·1	−24	−11·2	−6·1	+21	+69·8	+18·9	+66	+150·8
−30·6	−23	−9·4	−5·5	+22	+71·6	+19·4	+67	+152·6
−30·0	−22	−7·6	−5·0	+23	+73·4	+20·0	+68	+154·4
−29·4	−21	−5·8	−4·4	+24	+75·2	+20·6	+69	+156·2
−28·9	−20	−4·0	−3·9	+25	+77·0	+21·1	+70	+158·0
−28·3	−19	−2·2	−3·3	+26	+78·8	+21·7	+71	+159·8
−27·8	−18	−0·4	−2·8	+27	+80·6	+22·2	+72	+161·6
−27·2	−17	+1·4	−2·2	+28	+82·4	+22·8	+73	+163·4
−26·7	−16	+3·2	−1·7	+29	+84·2	+23·3	+74	+165·2
−26·1	−15	+5·0	−1·1	+30	+86·0	+23·9	+75	+167·0
−25·6	−14	+6·8	−0·6	+31	+87·8	+24·4	+76	+168·8
−25·0	−13	+8·6	0	+32	+89·6	+25·0	+77	+170·6
−24·4	−12	+10·4	+0·6	+33	+91·4	+25·6	+78	+172·4
−23·9	−11	+12·2	+1·1	+34	+93·2	+26·1	+79	+174·2
−23·3	−10	+14·0	+1·7	+35	+95·0	+26·7	+80	+176·0
−22·8	−9	+15·8	+2·2	+36	+96·8	+27·2	+81	+177·8
−22·2	−8	+17·6	+2·8	+37	+98·6	+27·8	+82	+179·6
−21·7	−7	+19·4	+3·3	+38	+100·4	+28·3	+83	+181·4
−21·1	−6	+21·2	+3·9	+39	+102·2	+28·9	+84	+183·2
−20·6	−5	+23·0	+4·4	+40	+104·0	+29·4	+85	+185·0
−20·0	−4	+24·8	+5·0	+41	+105·8	+30·0	+86	+186·8
−19·4	−3	+26·6	+5·5	+42	+107·6	+30·6	+87	+188·6
−18·9	−2	+28·4	+6·1	+43	+109·4	+31·1	+88	+190·4
−18·3	−1	+30·2	+6·7	+44	+111·2	+31·7	+89	+192·2
−17·8	0	+32·0	+7·2	+45	+113·0	+32·2	+90	+194·0
−17·2	+1	+33·8	+7·8	+46	+114·8	+32·8	+91	+195·8
−16·7	+2	+35·6	+8·3	+47	+116·6	+33·3	+92	+197·6
−16·1	+3	+37·4	+8·9	+48	+118·4	+33·9	+93	+199·4
−15·6	+4	+39·2	+9·4	+49	+120·2	+34·4	+94	+201·2
−15·0	+5	+41·0	+10·0	+50	+122·0	+35·0	+95	+203·0
−14·4	+6	+42·8	+10·6	+51	+123·8	+35·6	+96	+204·8
−13·9	+7	+44·6	+11·1	+52	+125·6	+36·1	+97	+206·6
−13·3	+8	+46·4	+11·7	+53	+127·4	+36·7	+98	+208·4
−12·8	+9	+48·2	+12·2	+54	+129·2	+37·2	+99	+210·2
−12·2	+10	+50·0	+12·8	+55	+131·0	+37·8	+100	+212·0
−11·7	+11	+51·8	+13·3	+56	+132·8	+38·3	+101	+213·8
−11·1	+12	+53·6	+13·9	+57	+134·6	+38·9	+102	+215·6
−10·6	+13	+55·4	+14·4	+58	+136·4	+39·4	+103	+217·4
−10·0	+14	+57·2	+15·0	+59	+138·2	+40·0	+104	+219·2